BOOKS IN PRINT®

1995-96

This edition of
BOOKS IN PRINT 1995-96
was prepared by the R.R. Bowker's
Database Publishing Group in
collaboration with the Publication Systems Department

Database Publishing Group
Leigh Yuster-Freeman, Vice President, Production - Bibliographies

Editorial
Beverley Lamar, Senior Managing Editor
Doret Dixon, Senior Editor
Edward Han, Ila Joseph, George Krubski, Assistant Editors
Dorothy Perry-Gilchrist, Coordinator
Kathleen A. Keiderling, Associate Editor, Enhancements

Subject Guide
Judy Salk, Executive Editor
Angela Barrett and Kate Magrath, Senior Associate Editors
Mark D. MacDonald and Joseph V. Tondi, Assistant Editors

Quality Control
Raymond Padilla, Senior Editor
Daniel Dickholtz, Senior Associate Editor

Production
Doreen Gravesande, Production Director
Myriam Nunez, Managing Editor
Barbara Holton and Frank McDermott, Senior Editors
Megan Roxberry and John D. Smith, Senior Associate Editors
Clarice D. Isaacs, Assistant Editor

Electronic Data Transfer Group
Frank Accurso, Senior Managing Editor
Mary Craig Daley, Managing Editor
William Zavorskas, Senior Associate Editor

Publishers Authority Data
&
International Standard Book Number Agency
Don Riseborough, Senior Managing Editor
William D. McCahery and Lynn Ann Sahner, Senior Editors
Diana Fumando, Coordinator
Janet Weiss, Assistant Editor

Data Collection & Processing Group
Bonnie Walton, Manager
Cheryl Patrick and Rhonda McKendrick, Coordinators
Leslie Fisher and Cynthia Werry, Assistant Coordinators

Editorial Systems Group
John Roney, Vice President, Information Systems
Gary Aiello, Director, Bibliographical and Advertising Systems
Mark Heinzelman and John Nesselt, Project Leaders

Computer Operations Group
Nick Wikowski, Director, Network/Computer Operations
Max Kobrinsky, Manager
Jack Murphy, Supervisor

Robert H. Doran, Jr., Publisher

BOOKS IN PRINT®

1995-96

VOLUME 3

AUTHORS • L-R

R.R. BOWKER

A Reed Reference Publishing Company
New Providence, New Jersey

Published by R.R. Bowker
A Reed Reference Publishing Company
121 Chanlon Rd., New Providence, New Jersey 07974

Andrew W. Meyer, Chief Operating Officer
Peter E. Simon, Vice President, Business Development and Database Publishing
Stanley Walker, Senior Vice President, Corporate Marketing
Edward J. Roycroft, Senior Vice President, Sales

R.R. Bowker has used its best efforts in collecting and preparing material for inclusion in Books in Print 1994-95, but does not warrant that the information herein is complete or accurate, and does not assume, and hereby disclaims, any liability to any persons for any loss or damage caused by errors or omissions in Books In Print 1995-96, whether such errors or omissions result from negligence, accident or any other cause.

International Standard Book Numbers: Set 0-8352-3644-7
Vol. 1 0-8352-3645-5, Vol. 2 0-8352-3646-3
Vol. 3 0-8352-3647-1, Vol. 4 0-8352-3648-X
Vol. 5 0-8352-3649-8, Vol. 6 0-8352-3650-1
Vol. 7 0-8352-3651-X, Vol. 8 0-8352-3652-8
OP-OSI 0-8352-3653-6
Vol. 9 0-8352-3654-4
International Standard Serial Number 0068-0214
Library of Congress Catalog Card Number 4-12648

Printed and bound in the United States of America

ISBN 0-8352-3644-7

BOOKS IN PRINT®
1995-96

Volume 3
AUTHORS
L-R

L

***L. A. Times Staff.** En la Onda: Guia Del Times Para los Condados de Los Angelos & Orange. 1994. pap. 12.00 (*1-883792-05-3*) LA Times.
— Inside Track: The Times Guide to Los Angeles & Orange Counties. 1994. pap. 12.00 (*1-883792-04-5*) LA Times.
L, Brian. Perfectionism. 20p. (Orig.). 1985. pap. 1.55 (*0-89486-259-6*, 1404B) Hazelden.
L. C. W. The Autobiography of a Magdalen. reprint ed. 9.75 (*0-87651-208-2*) Southern U Pr.
L, Elizabeth. Food for Thought. 400p. 1980. 9.00 (*0-89486-090-9*, 1074A) Hazelden.
***L. F. Garlinghouse Corp. Staff.** 300 Best Selling Home Plans. 7th ed. 1995. 7.95 (*0-938708-64-3*) L F Garlinghouse Co.
L. F. Garlinghouse Corp. Staff, ed. Traditional Home Plans. 4th ed. LC 92-75092. 192p. 1993. 4.95 (*0-938708-44-9*) L F Garlinghouse Co.
— Vacation, Retirement, & Leisure. 3rd ed. LC 92-75089. 144p. 1993. 3.95 (*0-938708-46-5*) L F Garlinghouse Co.
L. H. Gray Conference Staff. Fast Processes in Radiation Chemistry & Biology: Proceedings of the Fifth L. H. Gray Conference, University of Sussex, 1973. Adams, G. E., ed. LC 74-23613. 393p. reprint ed. pap. 112.10 (*0-317-09013-5*, 2015694) Bks Demand.
L. J., Lawrence, tr. see Furtwangler, Wilhelm.
***L. Jackson, Becky.** Dieting: A Dry Drunk - The Workbook. 1995. 16.95 (*0-9635972-1-3*) BLJ-Nautilus.
L. L. Research Staff. The Law of One, Bk. II. LC 90-72156. 160p. (Orig.). 1991. pap. 9.95 (*0-924608-09-9*, Whitford Pr) Schiffer.
— The Law of One, Bk. IV. LC 90-72156. 224p. (Orig.). 1991. pap. 12.95 (*0-924608-10-2*, Whitford Pr) Schiffer.
L-L Research Staff, jt. auth. see Hatonn.
L-L Research Staff, jt. auth. see Ra.
L. L. Research Staff
L, Mary, jt. auth. see R, Mark.
L. R. A. Staff. Constitution of the Kingdom of Nepal: 2047 & Electoral Laws. (C). 1991. text ed. 40.00 (*0-7855-0131-2*, Pub. by Ratna Pustak Bhandar) St Mut.
L. Yan Mau, jt. auth. see Liu, F.
L-Z Fang & Li, S. X. Creation of the Universe. 192p. (C). 1989. text ed. 52.00 (*9971-5-0600-9*); pap. text ed. 23.00 (*9971-5-0601-7*) World Scientific Pub.
***La-Anyane, Seth.** Economics of Agricultural Development in Tropical Africa. fac. ed. LC 82-13510. 169p. Date not set. pap. 48.20 (*0-7837-7501-6*, 2047005) Bks Demand.
La Balle, Bella. Bad Taste Celebrity Jokes. 144p. (Orig.). 1993. pap. 4.99 (*1-56171-232-9*, S P I Bks) Sure Sellers.
La Barge, R. L. All the Pieces Will Fit. LC 86-71712. (Illus.). 195p. (Orig.). 1986. pap. 6.95 (*0-9617796-0-8*) Allfit.
La Barr, Ralph & La Barr, Shirley. Gold in the Fire. 196p. (Orig.). 1994. pap. 8.99 (*1-56043-654-9*) Destiny Image.
La Barr, Shirley, jt. auth. see La Barr, Ralph.
La Barre, Harriet. Blackwood's Daughter. large type ed. (Ulverscroft Ser.). 496p. 1994. 21.95 (*0-7089-3060-3*) Ulverscroft.
***La Barre, Weston.** Culture in Context. (C). 1994. text ed. 40.00 (*1-885809-00-X*); pap. text ed. 19.95 (*1-885809-01-8*) Psyche Pr NY.
— Muelos: A Stone Age Superstition About Sexuality. LC 84-14232. 168p. 1984. text ed. 37.00 (*0-231-05960-4*) Col U Pr.
— The Peyote Cult. 5th ed. LC 89-40225. (Illus.). 352p. 1989. pap. 15.95 (*0-8061-2214-5*) U of Okla Pr.
— Shadow of Childhood: Neoteny & the Biology of Religion. LC 90-50691. 192p. 1991. 18.95 (*0-8061-2328-1*) U of Okla Pr.
— They Shall Take up Serpents: Psychology of the Southern Snake-Handling Cult. (Illus.). 208p. (C). 1992. reprint ed. pap. text ed. 9.95 (*0-88133-663-7*) Waveland Pr.
La Bastille, Anne. Woodswoman. 1991. pap. 11.95 (*0-14-015334-9*, Penguin Bks) Viking Penguin.
La Bella, A., jt. ed. see Bianco, Lucio.
La Belle, Jenijoy. The Echoing Wood of Theodore Roethke. LC 76-3265. (Princeton Essays in Literature Ser.). 189p. reprint ed. pap. 53.90 (*0-8357-8865-2*, 2033387) Bks Demand.
— Herself Beheld: The Literature of the Looking Glass. LC 88-47734. 240p. 1988. 33.95 (*0-8014-2202-7*) Cornell U Pr.
— Herself Beheld: The Literature of the Looking Glass. LC 88-47734. 240p. 1990. reprint ed. pap. 12.95 (*0-8014-9704-3*) Cornell U Pr.
La Belle, Thomas J. & Ward, Christopher R. Multiculturalism & Education: Diversity & Its Impact on Schools & Society. LC 93-5712. (SUNY Series, Frontiers in Education). 211p. 1994. 57.50 (*0-7914-1939-8*); pap. 18.95x (*0-7914-1940-1*) State U NY Pr.
La Belle, Thomas J., jt. ed. see Hawkins, John N.
La Berge, Ann F. Mission & Method: The Early Nineteenth-Century French Public Health Movement. (Cambridge History of Medicine Ser.). (Illus.). 330p. (C). 1992. 69.95 (*0-521-40406-1*) Cambridge U Pr.
La Bern, Arthur. Goodbye Piccadilly, Farewell Leicester. 1976. 19.95 (*0-8488-0176-8*) Amereon Ltd.
La Billardiere, J. De. Novae Hollandiae Plantarum Specimen: 1894-06, 2 vols. in 1. 1966. 156.00 (*3-7682-0344-1*) Lubrecht & Cramer.
La Billardiere, J. J. Icones Plantarum Syriae Rariorum: Descriptionibus & Observationibus Illustratar 1791-1812. (Illus.). 1968. 60.00 (*3-7682-0540-1*) Lubrecht & Cramer.
La Blanc. Contemporary Black Biography, Vol. 1. 525p. 1991. 45.00 (*0-8103-5546-9*) Gale.
— Contemporary Black Biography, Vol. 2. 1992. 45.00 (*0-8103-8554-6*, 101344) Gale.
— Contemporary Black Biography, Vol. 3. 1992. 45.00 (*0-8103-8555-4*, 101345) Gale.
— Contemporary Black Biography, Vol. 4. 1993. 45.00 (*0-8103-8556-2*, 101346) Gale.
— Contemporary Black Biography, Vol. 5. 1993. 45.00 (*0-8103-8557-0*, 101347) Gale.
— Contemporary Black Biography, Vol. 6. 1994. 45.00 (*0-8103-8558-9*, 101348) Gale.
— Contemporary Black Biography, Vol. 7. 1994. 45.00 (*0-8103-8559-7*, 101349) Gale.
— Contemporary Black Biography, Vol. 8. 1994. 45.00 (*0-8103-5739-9*, 101733) Gale.
— Contemporary Musicians, Vol. 11. 1994. 65.00 (*0-8103-8552-X*, 004903) Gale.
— Contemporary Musicians, Vol. 12. 1994. 65.00 (*0-8103-8553-8*, 004904) Gale.
***La Bo.** Looking Black. 31p. (Orig.). 1993. pap. 5.95 (*1-56411-123-7*) Untd Bros & Sis.
La Bossiere, Camille R. The Victorian Fol Sage: Comparative Readings on Carlyle, Emerson, Melville & Conrad. LC 87-480005. 136p. 1989. 29.50 (*0-8387-5145-8*) Bucknell U Pr.
La Bossiere, Camille R., ed. Context North America: Canadian - U. S. Literary Relations. 168p. 1994. pap. 22.00 (*0-7766-0360-4*, Pub. by Univ Ottawa Pr CN) Paul & Co Pubs.
La Botz, Dan. The Crisis of Mexican Labor. LC 88-2707. 228p. 1988. text ed. 49.95 (*0-275-92600-1*, C2600, Greenwood Pr) Greenwood.
— Democracy in Mexico. 250p. 1995. 35.00 (*0-89608-508-2*); pap. 15.00 (*0-89608-507-4*) South End Pr.
— Edward L. Doheny: Petroleum, Power, & Politics in the United States & Mexico. LC 90-20670. 224p. 1991. text ed. 55.00 (*0-275-93599-X*, C3599, Praeger Pubs) Greenwood.
— Rank & File Rebellion: Teamsters for a Democratic Union. (Haymarket Ser.). 360p. 1990. 60.00 (*0-86091-289-2*, A4498, Pub. by Verso UK); pap. 18.95 (*0-86091-505-0*, A4502, Pub. by Verso UK) Routledge Chapman & Hall.
— A Troublemaker's Handbook: How to Fight Back Where You Work - & Win! (Illus.). 262p. (Orig.). 1991. pap. text ed. 17.00 (*0-914093-04-5*) Labor Notes.
La Bounty, Blanca, jt. auth. see Rice, Dona.
La Brack, Bruce, ed. The Sikhs of Northern California, 1904-1975. LC 87-45787. (Immigrant Communities & Ethnic Minorities in the U. S. & Canada Ser.: No. 22). 1988. 67.50 (*0-404-19432-X*) AMS Pr.
***La Bree, Ben, ed.** Camp Fires of the Confederacy. (Illus.). 560p. 1994. reprint ed. lib. bdg. 55.00 (*0-8328-4350-4*) Higginson Bk Co.
La Brie, Henry G. The Black Press in America: A Bibliography. 1974. pap. 3.50 (*0-89080-003-0*) Mercer Hse.
La Brie, Henry G., III, intro. A Survey of Black Newspapers in America. LC 80-80551. (Mass Communication & Journalism Ser.). 72p. (Orig.). 1980. 6.00 (*0-89080-034-0*) Mercer Hse.
La Brie, Vicki G. A Learning Disabilities Activity Guide for the Elementary Classroom. 50p. (Orig.). 1975. pap. 3.50 (*0-89080-029-4*) Mercer Hse.
La Brum, Rebecca, ed. see Emal, Janet & Taylor, Elizabeth.
La Bruyere, Jean D. Caracteres. (Folio Ser.: No. 693). (FRE.). 1962. pap. 9.95 (*2-07-036693-6*) Schoenhof.
La Bruyere, Jean de. Maximes et Pensees. 9.95 (*0-686-54264-9*) Fr & Eur.
— Oeuvres Completes. Benda, Julien, ed. 768p. (FRE.). 1978. lib. bdg. 95.00 (*0-7859-3760-9*, 2070102947) Fr & Eur.
La Capra, Dominick. Representing the Holocaust: History, Theory, Trauma. LC 93-33885. 248p. 1994. 29.95 (*0-8014-2997-8*) Cornell U Pr.
La Cavera, Anthony, jt. auth. see Thomas, George.
La Chance, Paul R., ed. Asian Arts in America: Seeds of the Inner Life. (West & the Wider World Ser.: Vol. 5). (Illus.). 380p. (C). 1988. 29.95 (*0-940121-11-5*) Cross Cultural Pubns.
La Chanson de Roland. Chanson de Roland (Medieval & Modern French) (Folio Ser.: No. 1155). (FRE.). pap. 10.95 (*2-07-037150-6*) Schoenhof.
La Charite, Raymond C. Recreation, Reflection & Re-Creation: Perspectives on Rabelais's Pantagruel. LC 79-53402. (French Forum Monographs: No. 19). 137p. (Orig.). 1980. pap. 10.95 (*0-917058-18-6*) French Forum.
La Charite, Raymond C., ed. O un Amy! Essays on Montaigne in Honor of Donald M. Frame. LC 76-47501. (French Forum Monographs: No. 5). 341p. (Orig.). (ENG & FRE.). 1977. pap. 16.95 (*0-917058-04-6*) French Forum.
— Rabelais's Incomparable Book: Essays on His Art. LC 85-80421. (French Forum Monographs: No. 62). 247p. (Orig.). 1986. pap. 17.95 (*0-917058-63-1*) French Forum.
— Writing the Renaissance: Essays on Sixteenth-Century French Literature in Honor of Floyd Gray. LC 91-73985. (French Forum Monographs: No. 77). 266p. (Orig.). 1992. pap. 17.95 (*0-917058-81-X*) French Forum.
La Charite, Virginia A. The Dynamics of Space: Mallarme's Un Coup De Des Jamais N' abolira le Hasard. LC 86-82794. (French Forum Monographs: No. 67). 192p. (Orig.). 1987. pap. 13.95 (*0-917058-68-2*) French Forum.
— Twentieth-Century French Avant-Garde Poetry, 1907-1990. LC 92-71330. (French Forum Monographs: No. 80). 185p. (Orig.). 1992. pap. 17.95 (*0-917058-85-2*) French Forum.
La Cicciolina, intro. Erotic Tales. 1993. 7.98 (*1-55521-868-7*) Bk Sales Inc.
La Clair, Ruth, ed. see Cunningham, John T.
La Claire, John, jt. auth. see Bold, Harold C.
***La Coccinella.** The Complete Party Book: Hundreds of Things to Do & Make. (Illus.). 48p. (J). (ps-3). 1995. 19.95 (*1-56397-488-6*, Wordsong) Boyds Mills Pr.
La Coste, Warren. Holy Rider: The Priest & the Gang. LC 92-60565. 304p. 1992. 22.95 (*0-88282-114-8*) New Horizon NJ.
La Cotardiere, Philippe de. Larousse Dictionnaire de l'Espace. 280p. 1993. 55.00 (*0-7859-5605-0*, 2037490054) Fr & Eur.
La Cour, Donna W., ed. Artists in Quotation: A Dictionary of the Creative Thoughts of Painters, Sculptors, Designers, Writers, Educators, & Others. LC 88-7946. 208p. 1989. lib. bdg. 32.50x (*0-89950-379-9*) McFarland & Co.
La Cour, Marshall & Lathrop, Irvin T. Photo Technology. 320p. 1992. 31.96 (*0-87006-899-7*) Goodheart.
La Croix, Richard R., ed. Augustine on Music: An Interdisciplinary Collection of Essays. LC 87-22012. (Studies in the History & Interpretation of Music: Vol. 6). 120p. 1988. lib. bdg. 59.95 (*0-88946-431-6*) E Mellen.
La Curne De Sainte Palaye, Jean B. Dictionnaire Historique de l'Ancien Langage Francois Ou Glossaire de la Langue Francoise, 10 vols., Set. lxxxvi, 4775p. 1972. reprint ed. write for info. (*3-487-04251-7*, Pub. by Georg Olms GW) Lubrecht & Cramer.
La Dage, John H. Modern Ships: Elements of Their Design, Construction & Operation. 2nd ed. LC 65-21747. (Illus.). 391p. reprint ed. pap. 111.50 (*0-8357-8228-X*, 2033968) Bks Demand.
La Dow, Charles R. Aristotle's Secret. (Illus.). 92p. (Orig.). 1986. pap. 8.95 (*0-9617232-0-3*) C R LaDow.
La Duke, Betty. Companeras: Women, Art & Social Change in Latin America. (Illus.). 176p. (Orig.). 1985. pap. 14.95 (*0-87286-172-4*) City Lights.
La Farge, Ann. Gertrude Stein. (American Women of Achievement Ser.). (Illus.). 112p. (J). (gr. 5 up). 1988. lib. bdg. 17.95 (*1-55546-678-8*) Chelsea Hse.
La Farge, Catherine. Sir Thomas Malory. 1990. 40.00 (*0-7463-0714-4*, Pub. by Northcote UK) St Mut.
La Farge, John. Artist's Letters from Japan. LC 74-130311. (Library of American Art Ser.). (Illus.). 1970. reprint ed. lib. bdg. 45.00 (*0-306-70064-6*) Da Capo.
— Considerations on Painting. LC 70-9611. (Library of American Art Ser.). 1969. reprint ed. lib. bdg. 42.50 (*0-306-71824-3*) Da Capo.
— Great Masters. LC 68-16945. (Essay Index Reprint Ser.). 1977. reprint ed. 30.95 (*0-8369-0604-7*) Ayer.
— Interracial Justice. 1978. 21.95 (*0-405-10839-7*, 11846) Ayer.
La Farge, Mabel, ed. see Adams, Henry.
La Farge, Oliver. All the Young Men. LC 75-41169. reprint ed. 36.00 (*0-404-14566-3*) AMS Pr.
— La Costumbre en Santa Eulalia. Penalosa, Fernando, tr. (Illus.). 242p. (Orig.). (SPA.). 1994. pap. 11.95 (*1-886502-06-4*, Ediciones Yax Te) Yax Te Press.
— Eagle in the Egg. LC 78-169425. (Literature & History of Aviation Ser.). 1972. reprint ed. 33.95 (*0-405-03767-8*) Ayer.

L

— Laughing Boy. 259p. (J). 1981. reprint ed. lib. bdg. 21.95 (*0-89967-041-5*) Harmony Raine.

La Farge, Oliver, jt. auth. see Reichard, Gladys A.

La Farge, Phyllis, jt. ed. see Berman, Sheldon.

La Farge, Phyllis, tr. see Giraudoux, Jean.

La Farge, Tom. The Crimson Bears, Pt. 1. (New American Fiction Ser.: No. 26). 272p. (Orig.). 1993. pap. 12.95 (*1-55713-074-4*) Sun & Moon CA.

— A Hundred Doors Pt. II: The Crimson Bears. (New American Fiction Ser.: No. 31). 228p. (Orig.). 1995. pap. 12.95 (*1-55713-192-9*) Sun & Moon CA.

La Fauci, H. M. & Richter, P. Team Teaching at the College Level. LC 73-88573. 1970. 76.00 (*0-08-006946-0*, Pub. by Pergamon Repr UK) Franklin.

La Fave, Wayne & Israel, Jerold. Criminal Procedure, Vol. 3. 2nd ed. (Criminal Practice Ser.). 912p. Date not set. text ed. write for info. (*0-314-87381-3*) West Pub.

La Fayette, Marie M. Princesse de Cleves. (Folio Ser.: No. 778). (FRE.). 1958. pap. 9.95 (*2-07-036778-9*) Schoenhof.

La Fayette, Marie-Madeleine D. Princesse de Cleves. 1958. write for info. (*0-318-63581-X*) Fr & Eur.

La Fayette, Marie-Madeleine de. Romans et Nouvelles. 468p. 1967. 27.50 (*0-7859-0689-4*) Fr & Eur.

— Romans et Nouvelles: Avec: La Princesse de Cleves, La Comtesse de Tende, La Princesse de Montpensier, Zaide. Magne, Emile, ed. (Illus.). 488p. (FRE.). 1961. pap. 24.95 (*0-7859-1496-X*, 2705001638) Fr & Eur.

***La Ferle, Cynthia G.** Old Houses, Good Neighbors: Reflections & Celebrations of Everyday Life in a Small Town. 112p. (Orig.). 1994. pap. 10.00 (*0-9642404-0-8*) Self Rel Pubng.

***La Ferriere, P. & Burda, Vernon L.** Tipton's Crew. LC 94-37481. 1994. pap. 9.95 (*0-89802-492-7*) Beautiful Am.

***La Flesche, Francis.** Dictionary of the Osage Language. (Bureau of American Ethnology Bulletins Ser.). 406p. 1995. lib. bdg. 109.00 (*0-7812-4109-X*) Rprt Serv.

— A Dictionary of the Osage Language. reprint ed. 69.00 (*0-403-03580-5*) Scholarly.

— Dictionary of the Osage Language. LC 90-43115. 412p. 1990. reprint ed. lib. bdg. 59.00 (*1-878592-20-3*); reprint ed. pap. 39.00 (*1-878592-19-X*) Native Amer Bk Pubs.

— The Middle Five: Indian Schoolboys of the Omaha Tribe. LC 78-17409. (Illus.). xxiv, 156p. 1978. reprint ed. 20.00 (*0-8032-2852-X*); reprint ed. pap. 7.95x (*0-8032-7901-9*) U of Nebr Pr.

— War Ceremony & Peace Ceremony of the Osage Indians. (Bureau of American Ethnology Bulletins Ser.). 280p. 1995. lib. bdg. 89.00 (*0-7812-4101-4*) Rprt Serv.

La Flesche, Francis, jt. auth. see Fletcher, Alice C.

La Follette, Robert M. LaFollette's Autobiography: A Personal Narrative of Political Experiences. 362p. 1960. reprint ed. pap. 14.95 (*0-299-02194-7*) U of Wis Pr.

La Follette, Robert M., ed. The Making of America: Industry & Finance. LC 73-2516. (Big Business; Economic Power in a Free Society Ser.). 1973. reprint ed. 34.95 (*0-405-05096-8*) Ayer.

La Follette, Suzanne. Art in America. 361p. 1993. reprint ed. lib. bdg. 89.00 (*0-7812-5277-6*) Rprt Serv.

— Concerning Women. LC 72-2610. (American Women Ser.: Images & Realities). 320p. 1978. reprint ed. 24.95 (*0-405-04464-X*) Ayer.

La Fond, John Q., jt. auth. see Durham, Mary L.

***La Font, Suzanne.** The Emergence of an Afro-Caribbean Legal Tradition: Gender Relations & Family Court Use in Kingston, Jamaica. LC 94-29005. 250p. (C). 1994. text ed. 64.95x (*1-880921-92-8*) Austin & Winfield.

— The Emergence of an Afro-Caribbean Legal Tradition: Gender Relations & Family Court Use in Kingston, Jamaica. LC 94-29005. 250p. (YA). 1994. pap. text ed. 44.95x (*1-880921-91-X*) Austin & Winfield.

La Fontaine. The Hare & the Tortoise. (Illus.). 32p. (J). 1987. 16.00 (*0-19-279625-9*); pap. 7.50 (*0-19-272126-7*) OUP.

— The Lion & the Rat. (Illus.). 32p. (J). 1987. 16.00 (*0-19-279607-0*); pap. 7.50 (*0-19-272167-4*) OUP.

— The North Wind & the Sun. (Illus.). 32p. (J). 1987. pap. 7.50 (*0-19-272168-2*) OUP.

La Fontaine, Gary. Trout Flies: Proven Patterns. 260p. 1993. 39.95 (*0-9626663-1-9*) Greycliff Pub.

La Fontaine, Jean. Child Sexual Abuse. 240p. 1990. text ed. 54.95 (*0-7456-0560-5*); pap. 21.95 (*0-7456-0561-3*) Blackwell Pubs.

La Fontaine, Jean de. A Hundred Fables of La Fontaine. (Illus.). 208p. (J). (gr. 2-6). 2.98 (*0-517-40206-8*) Random Hse Value.

La Fontaine, Jean De. Mrs. Fox & Mrs. Stork: Chinese Edition. Wang, May S., tr. (Interlingo Ser.). (Illus.). 19p. (Orig.). (CHI.). (J). (gr. k-12). 1993. pap. 2.95 (*0-922852-22-7*) Another Lang Pr.

La Fontaine, Jean de. Oeuvres Completes, Vol. 1. Collinet, Jean-Pierre, ed. 1728p. (FRE.). 1993. lib. bdg. 150.00 (*0-7859-3761-7*, 2070102963) Fr & Eur.

La Fontaine, Jean de & Calder, Alexander. Selected Fables. Clark, Eunice, tr. (Illus.). 86p. pap. 4.50 (*0-486-21878-3*) Dover.

La Fontaine, Mary, jt. auth. see La Fontaine, Ray.

***La Fontaine, Ray & La Fontaine, Mary.** Oswald Talked: The New Evidence in the JFK Assassination. 400p. 1995. 22.95 (*1-56554-029-8*) Pelican.

La Fontaine, Ray, tr. see Martorell, Joanot.

***La Force, Beatrice.** Alpine: History of a Mountain Settlement. 6th ed. (Illus.). 529p. 1994. reprint ed. pap. 25.00 (*0-9643749-0-0*) Sky Mesa Pr.

La Forge, Raymond W., jt. auth. see Hills, Gerald E.

La Forte, Robert A. & Himmel, Richard. Down the Corridor of Years: A Centennial History of the University of North Texas in Photographs, 1890-1990. LC 89-16447. (Illus.). 304p. 1989. 35.00 (*0-929398-05-X*) UNTX Pr.

La Forte, Robert S. & Marcello, Ronald E., eds. Remembering Pearl Harbor: Eyewitness Accounts by U. S. Military Men & Women. LC 90-40179. (Illus.). 320p. 1991. 24.95 (*0-8420-2371-2*) Scholarly Res Inc.

La Franboise, Clifford, jt. ed. see Gordon, John.

La Freniere, Annette, ed. see Jones, Martha T.

La Freniere, Annette, ed. see Seib, Philip.

La Freniere, Annette, ed. see Warren, Betsy.

La Garde, Louis A. Gunshot Injuries: How They Are Inflicted, Their Complications & Treatment. 2nd ed. (Illus.). 480p. 1991. reprint ed. 34.95 (*0-935856-12-9*) Lancer.

La Gorce, Pierre F. Histoire de la Seconde Republique Francaise, 2 Vols, 1. LC 76-171635. reprint ed. write for info. (*0-404-07136-8*) AMS Pr.

— Histoire de la Seconde Republique Francaise, 2 Vols, 2. LC 76-171635. reprint ed. write for info. (*0-404-07137-6*) AMS Pr.

— Histoire de la Seconde Republique Francaise, 2 Vols, Set. LC 76-171635. reprint ed. 155.00 (*0-404-07135-X*) AMS Pr.

— Histoire du Second Empire, 7 Vols, Set. LC 77-90101. (FRE.). reprint ed. 595.00 (*0-404-01960-9*) AMS Pr.

— Histoire Religieuse de la Revolution Francaise, 5 Vols. (FRE.). reprint ed. write for info. (*0-318-50600-9*) AMS Pr.

— Histoire Religieuse de la Revolution Francaise, 5 Vols, 1. LC 71-88239. (FRE.). reprint ed. 76.50 (*0-404-03811-5*) AMS Pr.

— Histoire Religieuse de la Revolution Francaise, 5 Vols, 2. LC 71-88239. (FRE.). reprint ed. 76.50 (*0-404-03812-3*) AMS Pr.

— Histoire Religieuse de la Revolution Francaise, 5 Vols, 3. LC 71-88239. (FRE.). reprint ed. 76.50 (*0-404-03813-1*) AMS Pr.

— Histoire Religieuse de la Revolution Francaise, 5 Vols, 4. LC 71-88239. (FRE.). reprint ed. 76.50 (*0-404-03814-X*) AMS Pr.

— Histoire Religieuse de la Revolution Francaise, 5 Vols, 5. LC 71-88239. (FRE.). reprint ed. 76.50 (*0-404-03815-8*) AMS Pr.

— Histoire Religieuse de la Revolution Francaise, 5 Vols, Set. LC 71-88239. (FRE.). reprint ed. 382.50 (*0-404-03810-7*) AMS Pr.

La Greca, Annette M., et al, eds. Stress & Coping in Child Health. LC 91-38224. (Advances in Pediatric Psychology Ser.). 413p. 1991. lib. bdg. 42.00 (*0-89862-112-7*) Guilford Pr.

La Greca, G., et al, eds. CAPD: A Decade of Experience. (Contributions to Nephrology Ser.: Vol. 89). (Illus.). x, 288p. 1991. 198.50 (*3-8055-5307-2*) S Karger.

La Grille, Robert L. San Diego Dining Directory, 1993. (Illus.). 137p. (Orig.). 1993. spiral bd. 19.95 (*0-9636048-0-5*) Cntywide Dining.

La Guardia, David M. Advance on Chaos: The Sanctifying Imagination of Wallace Stevens. LC 83-40012. 210p. 1983. text ed. 25.00 (*0-87451-269-7*) U Pr of New Eng.

La Guardia, Dolores & Guth, Hans P. American Visions: Multi-Cultural Literature for Writers. LC 94-6444. 768p. (C). 1995. pap. 25.95 (*1-55934-322-2*) Mayfield Pub.

La Guma, A. In the Fog of the Season's End. LC 72-93381. 1973. 8.95 (*0-89388-058-2*) Okpaku Communications.

La Guma, Alex. In the Fog of the Seasons' End. LC 72-93381. 180p. 1973. 6.95 (*0-685-28732-7*, 89388-2) Okpaku Communications.

— Time of the Butcherbird. LC 79-670199. (African Writers Ser.). 119p. 1979. pap. 9.95 (*0-435-90758-1*) Heinemann.

La Guma, Alex, ed. Apartheid: A Collection of Writings on South African Racism. 239p. (Orig.). reprint ed. pap. 68.20 (*0-7837-0584-0*, 2040928) Bks Demand.

La Hausse, Paul. Brewers, Beerhalls, & Boycotts: A History of Liquor in South Africa. (History Workshop Topic Ser.: No. 2). (Illus.). 67p. (C). 1988. pap. 9.95 (*0-86975-332-0*, Pub. by Ravan Pr ZA) Ohio U Pr.

La Lande, Michael. The Hot Tub Cooks. Gilbert, Helen et al, eds. 74p. 1980. 1.95 (*0-9605582-0-9*) HTC Pub.

La Laurencie, Lionel D. Les Createurs De l'Opera Francais. LC 80-2287. reprint ed. 26.00 (*0-404-18854-0*) AMS Pr.

— Lully. 2nd ed. LC 76-43923. (Music & Theatre in France in the 17th & 18th Centuries Ser.). (FRE.). reprint ed. 39.50 (*0-404-60167-7*) AMS Pr.

— Lully. LC 77-3976. (Music Reprint Ser.). (Illus.). (FRE.). 1977. reprint ed. lib. bdg. 32.50 (*0-306-70894-9*) Da Capo.

La Leche League International Staff. Whole Foods for the Whole Family. 2nd ed. LC 93-80166. (Illus.). 306p. 1993. spiral bd. 16.95 (*0-912500-43-3*) La Leche.

— Womanly Art of Breastfeeding. 1991. pap. 9.95 (*0-452-26726-9*, Plume) NAL-Dutton.

— The Womanly Art of Breastfeeding. 4th rev. ed. LC 87-15355. (Illus.). 384p. 1983. pap. 8.95 (*0-452-26000-0*, Plume) NAL-Dutton.

— The Womanly Art of Breastfeeding: Thirty-Fifth Anniversary Edition. (Illus.). 480p. 1991. reprint ed. pap. 12.95 (*0-452-26623-8*, Plume) NAL-Dutton.

***La Loca.** The Mayan. Karol, Pamala, ed. (Illus.). 39p. 1988. pap. 10.00 (*0-9619965-0-1*) Bone Scan Pr.

La Loge, Bobby A. Drugs & Your Child: What Can a Parent Do? 32p. (Orig.). 1987. pap. 8.95 (*0-938147-03-X*) Flying Eagle.

— The Inner Light. (Illus.). 84p. (Orig.). 1985. pap. 4.75 (*0-938147-00-5*) Flying Eagle.

— John Brooks Henderson: No One Knows He Freed the Slaves. (Illus.). 125p. (Orig.). 1987. pap. text ed. 8.95 (*0-938147-05-6*) Flying Eagle.

— The Science of Dreamology: How to Interpret Dreams Correctly & Enjoy Greater Happiness. (Illus.). 84p. (Orig.). 1987. pap. text ed. 10.00 (*0-938147-17-X*) Flying Eagle.

— The Secrets to Winning: You Are a Winner. 44p. (Orig.). 1986. pap. 4.95 (*0-938147-01-3*) Flying Eagle.

La Mance, Lora S., jt. auth. see Stowe, A. A.

La Mann, Angela. Mom Is Going to Stop It. (Cityscapes Ser.). 27p. (J). (gr. k). 1992. pap. text ed. 23.00 (*1-56843-014-0*); pap. text ed. 4.50 (*1-56843-064-7*) BGR Pub.

La Manna, Manfredi, jt. ed. see Norman, George.

La Mantia, F. P., ed. Thermotropic Liquid Crystal Polymer Blends. LC 92-61560. 190p. 1992. pap. text ed. 65.00 (*0-87762-960-9*) Technomic.

***La Mar, Gerd N., ed.** Nuclear Magnetic Resonance of Paramagnetic Macromolecules. LC 94-48061. (NATO ASI Ser.: Series C, Mathematical & Physical Sciences: Vol. 457). 1995. lib. bdg. 185.50 (*0-7923-3348-9*) Kluwer Ac.

La Mar, Virginia A., ed. see Shakespeare, William.

La Mara, jt. auth. see Liszt, Franz.

La Marcha, Maureen, jt. auth. see Bowman, Daria P.

La Meri. Gesture Language of the Hindu Dance. LC 63-23185. (Illus.). 1979. reprint ed. 26.95 (*0-405-08723-3*, Pub. by Blom Pubns UK) Ayer.

La Mettrie, Julien O. Man a Machine. 216p. (ENG & FRE.). 1974. pap. 7.50 (*0-87548-041-1*) Open Court.

La Moille, T. G. & Parsons, Eugene, comps. Favorite Speaker. enl. rev. ed. LC 72-5591. (Granger Index Reprint Ser.). 1977. reprint ed. 17.95 (*0-8369-6373-3*) Ayer.

La Monica, Elaine. Management in Nursing: An Experiential Approach That Makes Theory Work for You. LC 90-9455. 464p. 1990. 47.95 (*0-8261-6580-X*) Springer Pub.

La Monica, Elaine L. The Humanistic Nursing Process. LC 84-23694. 400p. (C). 1985. pap. text ed. 38.75 (*0-534-04428-X*) Jones & Bartlett.

— Nursing Leadership & Management: An Experiential Approach. LC 82-20193. 300p. (C). 1983. reprint ed. pap. 35.20 (*0-86720-377-3*) Jones & Bartlett.

La Mont Johnson, D., et al, eds. Computers in the Special Education Classroom. LC 86-22834. (Computers in the Schools Ser.: Vol. 3, No. 3-4). 194p. 1987. text ed. 39.95 (*0-86656-257-5*) Haworth Pr.

La Monte, John L. & Lewis, Winston B. The Sicilian Campaign, 10 July-17 August 1943. LC 93-23206. (Illus.). 1994. 9.50 (*0-945274-17-3*) Naval Hist Ctr.

La Monte, Robert R. & Mencken, H. L. Men vs. the Man: A Correspondence Between Robert Rives La Monte, Socialist & H. L. Mencken, Individualist. LC 79-172220. (Right Wing Individualist Tradition in America Ser.). 1975. reprint ed. 23.95 (*0-405-00429-X*) Ayer.

La Morte, Michael W. School Law: Cases & Concepts. (Illus.). 448p. (C). 1982. write for info. (*0-13-793695-8*) P-H.

— School Law: Cases & Concepts. 4th ed. LC 92-13674. 1992. text ed. write for info. (*0-205-14157-9*) Allyn.

— School Law: Cases & Concepts. 5th ed. LC 95-7736. 1996. write for info. (*0-205-16568-0*) Allyn.

La Motte, Ellen N. Civilization: Tales of the Orient. LC 76-122727. (Short Story Index Reprint Ser.). 1977. 19.95 (*0-8369-3560-8*) Ayer.

— Snuffs & Butters. LC 74-125226. (Short Story Index Reprint Ser.). 1977. 19.95 (*0-8369-3593-4*) Ayer.

La Motte-Foque, Friedrich H. Undine. Gosse, Edmund, tr. LC 76-48431. (Library of World Literature Ser.). 1985. reprint ed. 22.50 (*0-88355-558-1*) Hyperion Conn.

La Nauze, J. A. Making of the Australian Constitution. 369p. 1974. reprint ed. 39.95 (*0-522-84016-7*) Intl Spec Bk.

La Nauze, J. A. & Nurser, Elizabeth. Walter Murdoch's Alfred Deakin on Books & Men: Letters & Comments, 1900-1918. 1974. 24.95 (*0-522-84056-6*) Intl Spec Bk.

La Nauze, John. Walter Murdoch: A Biographical Memoir. 1977. 24.95 (*0-522-84119-8*) Intl Spec Bk.

La Niece, Susan & Craddock, Paul. Metal Plating & Patination: Cultural, Technical & Historical Developments. LC 93-18065. 305p. 1993. 75.00 (*0-7506-1611-3*) Buttrwrth-Heinemann.

La Nuevo, P. C. From the Roots - The Last Rural Frontier. 1994. 12.95 (*0-8062-4922-6*) Carlton.

La, Opinion Editors, tr. see Los Angeles Children's Museum Staff.

La Parra, Marco. Secret Holy War of Santiago de Chile. Thomas, Charles P., tr. LC 93-19641. (Emerging Voices: New International Fiction Ser.). 1994. 24.95 (*1-56656-127-2*); pap. 12.95 (*1-56656-123-X*) Interlink Pub.

La Patra, Jack, jt. auth. see Dowdle, Walter.

La Pensee, Clive. The Historical Companion to House Brewing. 156p. 1990. pap. 35.00 (*0-9515685-0-7*, Pub. by Montag Pubns UK) St Mut.

— You Should Brew Too! 1992. pap. 35.00 (*0-9515685-2-3*, Pub. by Montag Pubns UK) St Mut.

La Perchia, Alexander. All God's Children. LC 86-91204. 1987. 9.95 (*0-87212-197-6*) Libra.

La Perouse, Comte D. Voyages & Adventures of La Perouse. Gassner, Julius S., tr. (Illus.). 180p. 1969. 14.00 (*0-87022-445-X*) UH Pr.

La Perriere, Guillaume D. Le Theatre Des Bons Engins. LC 63-7783. 1963. reprint ed. 50.00 (*0-8201-1036-1*) Schol Facsimiles.

La Pierre, Dominique, jt. auth. see Collins, Larry.

La Pierre, Keith C. That Strange Little Man, Bk. 1. (Blacksmith Legends Ser.). (Illus.). 32p. (J). (gr. 2 up). 1991. lib. bdg. 14.95 (*0-9631513-0-4*) Lee Pub NY.

— The Wanna Beezzz. LC 93-78057. (Illus.). 34p. (J). (ps-3). 1993. 8.95 (*0-9631513-1-2*); lib. bdg. write for info. (*0-9631513-2-0*) Lee Pub NY.

***La Pierre, Yvette.** Mapping a Changing World. 64p. (YA). (gr. 8 up). 1995. 17.95 (*1-56566-096-X*) Thomasson-Grant.

La Place, Viana. Panini, Bruschetta, Crostini: The Sandwich, Italian Style. LC 93-39917. 1994. 20.00 (*0-688-11325-7*) Hearst Bks.

— Verdura. LC 90-49304. (Illus.). 320p. 1991. 22.95 (*0-688-08764-7*) Morrow.

La Place, Viana & Kleiman, Evan. Cucina Fresca. LC 84-48466. (Illus.). 224p. 1987. pap. 15.00 (*0-06-096211-9*, PL 6211, PL) HarpC.

— Cucina Rustica. LC 89-27853. 320p. 1990. 23.00 (*0-688-07764-1*) Morrow.

— Pasta Fresca: An Exuberant Collection of Fresh, Vivid & Uncomplicated Pasta Recipes from the Authors of Cucina Fresca. Bramson, Ann, ed. LC 88-9294. (Illus.). 224p. 1988. 19.95 (*0-688-07763-3*) Morrow.

La Plante, Lynda. Entwined. 1993. 22.00 (*0-688-09243-8*) Morrow.

— Prime Suspect, 1. 1993. mass mkt. 4.99 (*0-440-21494-7*) Dell.

— Prime Suspect, 2. 1993. mass mkt. 4.99 (*0-440-21495-5*) Dell.

— Prime Suspect 3. large type ed. LC 95-11461. 457p. 1995. pap. 20.95 (*0-7862-0471-0*) Thorndike Pr.

***La Plante, Richard.** Hog Fever. 288p. 1995. 22.95 (*0-312-85884-1*) Forge NYC.

— Leopard. 320p. 1994. 22.95 (*0-312-85532-X*) Forge NYC.

— Leopard. 336p. 1995. mass mkt. 5.99 (*0-8125-3020-9*) Tor Bks.

— Mantis. 352p. 1994. mass mkt. 5.99 (*0-8125-3019-5*) Tor Bks.

— Steroid Blues. 320p. 1995. 22.95 (*0-312-85810-8*) Forge NYC.

— Tegne. 1995. write for info. (*0-615-00544-6*) Tor Bks.

La Plante, Royal. The Myrtlewood Grove. Van Treese, James B., ed. 360p. 1994. pap. 12.95 (*1-56901-073-0*) NW Pub.

***La Plantz, Shereen.** Cover to Cover: Creative Techniques for Making Beautiful Books, Journals & Albums. Dierks, Leslie, ed. LC 94-24439. (Illus.). 144p. 1995. 24.95 (*0-937274-81-X*, Lark Bks) Sterling.

La Point, June L. And How Are We Today? (Illus.). 96p. 1984. pap. 4.95 (*0-930422-32-5*) Dennis-Landman.

La Pointe, P. R. & Hudson, J. A. Characterization & Interpretation of Rock Mass Joint Patterns. (Special Paper Ser.: No. 199). (Illus.). 45p. 1985. pap. 2.00 (*0-8137-2199-7*) Geol Soc.

La Porte, Linda M., jt. auth. see Meitler, Neal D.

La Porte, Todd R., ed. Organized Social Complexity: Challenge to Politics & Policy. 360p. 1975. 60.00 (*0-691-07569-7*) Princeton U Pr.

— Organized Social Complexity: Challenge to Politics & Policy. LC 74-25606. reprint ed. pap. 110.60 (*0-7837-9366-9*, 2060109) Bks Demand.

— Social Responses to Large Technical Systems: Control or Anticipation. (C). 1991. lib. bdg. 94.00 (*0-7923-1192-2*) Kluwer Ac.

La Potin, Armand S. The Minisink Patent. Bruchey, Stuart, ed. LC 78-56697. (Management of Public Lands in the U. S. Ser.). 1979. lib. bdg. 25.95 (*0-405-11340-4*) Ayer.

La Potin, Armand S., ed. Native Ameriacan Voluntary Organizations. LC 86-25764. (Ethnic American Voluntary Organizations Ser.). 204p. 1987. text ed. 42.95 (*0-313-23633-X*, LAN/, Greenwood Pr) Greenwood.

La Puma, John. Ethics Consultation: A Practical Guide. LC 93-28098. 1993. pap. 29.95 (*0-86720-797-3*) Jones & Bartlett.

La Puma, Salvatore. The Boys of Bensonhurst. LC 86-7100. (Flannery O'Connor Award for Short Fiction Ser.). 136p. 1987. 15.95 (*0-8203-0891-9*) U of Ga Pr.

— A Time for Wedding Cake. 1991. 18.95 (*0-393-02890-9*) Norton.

La Ramee, Pierre, see Petrus Ramus, pseud..

La Ramee, Pierre D. The Latine Grammar of P. Ramus. LC 78-26236. (English Experience Ser.: No. 289). 1971. reprint ed. 16.00 (*90-221-0289-0*) Walter J Johnson.

***la Regina, Adriano, ed.** Scripta Latina. (Illus.). 682p. 1993. 125.00 (*88-7097-023-X*, J P Getty Museum) J P Getty Trust.

La Rivers, Ira. Fishes & Fisheries of Nevada. (Illus.). 800p. 1994. 49.95 (*0-87417-256-X*) U of Nev Pr.

La Roche, Jacob. Die Homerische Textkritik im Alterthum. viii, 496p. (GER.). 1992. write for info. (*3-487-09636-6*, Pub. by Georg Olms GW) Lubrecht & Cramer.

La Rochefoucauld, Francois de. Oeuvres Completes. Martin-Chauffier, Robert, ed. 1056p. (FRE.). 1935. lib. bdg. 110.00 (*0-7859-3762-5*, 2070103013) Fr & Eur.

— La Vie en Angleterre au 18e Siecle. 260p. 12.50 (*0-686-54282-7*) Fr & Eur.

La Rochefoucauld, Francois de & Lafond, Jean. Maximes et Reflexions Diverses. (Folio Ser.: No. 728). 286p. (FRE.). 1976. 8.95 (*2-07-036728-2*) Schoenhof.

La Rochelle, David. A Christmas Guest. (Illus.). 32p. (J). (ps-3). 1988. lib. bdg. 18.95 (*0-87614-325-7*, Carolrhoda); pap. 5.95 (*0-87614-506-3*, Carolrhoda) Lerner Group.

La Rochelle, Pierre Drieu. The Comedy of Charleroi & Other Stories. (Illus.). 236p. 1980. 9.95 (*0-903747-03-0*) Writers & Readers.

— Secret Journal & Other Writings. Hamilton, Alastair, tr. 112p. 1980. 9.95 (*0-903747-02-2*) Writers & Readers.

La Rosa, Mathilde, tr. see Boni, Ada.

La Rue, A. Aging & Neuropsychological Assessment. (Critical Issues in Neuropsychology Ser.). (Illus.). 376p. 1991. 45.00 (*0-306-44062-8*, Plenum Pr) Plenum.

La Rue, Andre & Casciani, Clement. Dictionnaire d'Argot et des Principales Locutions Populaires: Histoire de l'Ar. 190p. (FRE.). 1986. pap. 14.95 (*0-8288-1939-4*, F136760) Fr & Eur.

La Russo, Louis, II. Momma's Little Angels. 1979. pap. 4.75 (*0-8222-0769-9*) Dramatists Play.

La Salle, C. W., 2nd, ed. see Taylor, Bayard.

An Asterisk (*) at the beginning of an entry indicates that the title is appearing in BIP for the first time.

La Salle, Joseph P., ed. see Applied Mathematics Symposium Staff.

La, Scuola, Editrice, Brescia, Italy, tr. see Bettoni, Efrem.

La Serna, Ramon G. Dali. 1990. 29.98 (*1-55521-342-1*) Bk Sales Inc.

La Sister, Coy M. Business Training & Technical Assistance Providers in New York City. 41p. 1985. pap. text ed. 4.75 (*0-88156-070-7*) Comm Serv Soc NY.

La Sor, W. S., et al. Old Testament Survey: The Message, Form, & Background of the Old Testament. 698p. (C). 1982. 34.99 (*0-8028-3556-2*) Eerdmans.

La Teef, Nelda. Working Women for the Twenty-First Century: Fifty Women Reveal Their Pathways to Success. Williamson, Susan, ed. 258p. 1992. pap. 13.95 (*0-913589-66-7*) Williamson Pub Co.

La Tempa, Susan, jt. auth. see Kaplan, Mitch.

La Toison, M. Infrared & Its Thermal Applications. 158p. 1970. text ed. 124.00 (*0-677-61170-6*) Gordon & Breach.

La Touche, Denis, jt. auth. see La Touche, Sarah.

La Touche, Marie, jt. auth. see Trask, George G.

La Touche, Sarah & La Touche, Denis. Europe on a Plate: Eating, Drinking & Travelling Around Europe. (Illus.). 256p. (Orig.). 1992. pap. 14.95 (*0-86470-011-3*, Pub. by Benton-Guy Pub NZ) Seven Hills Bk.

La Tour, Kathy. For Those Who Live: Helping Children Cope with the Death of a Brother or Sister. 145p. 1983. 9.95 (*0-9612870-0-4*) K LaTour.

La Tour-Landry, G. Book of the Knight of la Tour-Landry. Wright, T., ed. (EETS, OS Ser.: No. 33). 1972. reprint ed. 36.00 (*0-527-00033-7*) Periodicals Srv.

La Tour-Landry, Geoffroy D. The Book of the Knight of la Tour-Landry. Taylor, G. S., ed. LC 79-8366. reprint ed. 28.00 (*0-404-18350-6*) AMS Pr.

La Tourelle, Maggie & Courtenay, Anthea. Thorsons Introductory Guide to Kinesiology: Touch for Health. 1993. pap. 11.00 (*0-7225-2699-7*) Thorsons SF.

La Tourrette, Jacqueline. The Wild Harp. 576p. (Orig.). 1981. pap. 2.95 (*0-449-14408-9*, GM) Fawcett.

La Tourrette, Joe. Washington Wildlife Viewing Guide. (Illus.). 96p. (Orig.). 1993. pap. 5.95 (*1-56044-150-X*) Falcon Pr MT.

La Valle, John J. Coping When a Parent Is in Jail. LC 94-8245. 1995. 15.95 (*0-8239-1967-6*) Rosen Group.

— Everything You Need to Know about Being a Male Survivor of Rape or Sexual Assault. LC 94-44981. (Need to Know Library). (J). 1995. write for info. (*0-8239-2084-4*) Rosen Group.

La Valle, Maria T., tr. see Grant, Wilson W.

La Vallee Poussin, Louis D. The Way to Nirvana: Six Lectures on Ancient Buddhism As a Discipline of Salvation. LC 77-27154. (Hibbert Lectures: 1916). reprint ed. 39.50 (*0-404-60417-X*) AMS Pr.

La Verdiere, L. Luke. 1989. pap. 21.00 (*0-86217-008-7*, Pub. by Veritas IE) St Mut.

La Verendrye, Pierre G. Journals & Letters of Pierre Gaultier de Varennes de la Verendrye & His Sons, with Correspondence Between the Governors of Canada & the French Court, Touching the Search for the Western Sea, Vol. 16. Burpee, Lawrence J., ed. LC 68-28605. 548p. 1969. reprint ed. text ed. 85.00 (*0-8371-5055-8*, LAJL) Greenwood.

La Verne, Walker & Planadeball, Marta J. Stories Made Easy for Spanish Speakers. LC 86-6913. 75p. 1986. pap. 6.00 (*0-8477-3344-0*) U of PR Pr.

La Vey, Anton S. Satanic Bible. 1976. mass mkt. 6.50 (*0-380-01539-0*) Avon.

La Via, Mariano F., jt. ed. see Hill, Rolla B., Jr.

La Volpe, Giulio. Studies on the Theory of General Dynamic Economic Equilibrium. (Classics in the History & Development of Economics Ser.). 90p. (C). 1993. text ed. 69.95 (*0-312-08104-9*) St Martin.

La Vopa, Anthony J. Grace, Talent, & Merit: Poor Students, Clerical Careers & Professional Ideology in Eighteenth Century Germany. (Illus.). 512p. 1988. 74.95 (*0-521-35041-7*) Cambridge U Pr.

Laabi, Abdellatif. Rue du Retour. Kaye, Jacqueline, tr. LC 88-63241. 250p. (Orig.). 1989. 17.95 (*0-930523-64-4*); pap. 9.95 (*0-930523-65-2*) Readers Intl.

Laabs, Gerald. Big Sister. 412p. 1994. pap. 12.95 (*1-56901-413-2*) NW Pub.

Laacke, R. J., ed. California Forest Soils: A Guide for Professional Foresters & Resource Managers & Planners. LC 79-62985. (Illus.). 184p. (Orig.). 1979. pap. text ed. 5.00 (*0-931876-32-X*, 4094) ANR Pubns CA.

Laak, Jan J., et al, eds. Developmental Tasks: Towards a Cultural Analysis of Human Development. LC 94-12546. 285p. (C). 1994. lib. bdg. 88.50 (*0-7923-2905-8*) Kluwer Ac.

Laak, Rein. Wastewater Engineering Design for Unsewered Areas. 2nd rev. ed. LC 86-50173. 181p. 1986. 39.00 (*0-87762-462-3*) Technomic.

Laakaniemi, Ray. Newswriting in Transition. 1994. pap. text ed. 23.95 (*0-8304-1347-2*) Nelson-Hall.

Laake, Deborah. Secret Ceremonies. 1994. mass mkt. 5.99 (*0-440-21780-6*) Dell.

— Secret Ceremonies. LC 92-40449. 1993. 20.00 (*0-688-09304-3*) Morrow.

Laakmann, G. Psychopharmaco-Endocrinology & Depression Research. (Illus.). xii, 219p. 1990. pap. 64.00 (*0-387-52075-9*) Spr-Verlag.

Laakso, Lila. E. J. Pratt: An Annotated Bibliography. 220p. (C). 1980. pap. text ed. 9.00 (*0-920763-60-X*, Pub. by ECW Press CN) Genl Dist Srvs.

Laakso, Toini P., ed. see Hannula, Reino.

Laaksonen, Oiva. Management in China: During & after Mao in Enterprises, Government & Party. (Studies in Organization: No. 12). 379p. (C). 1988. text ed. 54.95 (*3-11-009958-6*) De Gruyter.

— Management in China: During & after Mao in Enterprises, Government & Party. (Studies in Organization: No. 12). 379p. (C). 1988. text ed. 54.95 (*0-89925-025-4*) De Gruyter.

Laaksonen, Pirjo. Consumer Involvement: Concepts & Research. LC 93-45989. 224p. 1994. 65.00x (*0-415-09760-6*, B3912, Routledge NY) Routledge.

Laaly, Heshmat O. The Science & Technology of Traditional & Modern Roofing Systems: The New Bible of Roofing, 2 Vols. LC 91-90263. (Illus.). 3152p. 1992. 350.00 (*0-9629669-0-8*) Laaly Sci. THE MOST COMPREHENSIVE BOOK EVER WRITTEN ON ALL ASPECTS OF ROOFING materials & systems containing over 3,150 pages, with 80 chapters in 2 hardcover 8 1/2" x 11" volumes, 1,100 illustrated figures & photos & over 500 tables with index. Includes manufacturing, selection, performance, testing, design, economic, statistics, application, management & maintenance, the latest reference & further reading guide for each chapter. Chapters on materials include all major foreign & domestic roofing material manufactured & suppliers' toll-free telephone numbers & addresses. Truly a self-contained reader-friendly encyclopedia of roofing. This "New Bible of Roofing" is INTERNATIONALLY RECOGNIZED & ACCEPTED WORLDWIDE as a major publication & wealth of knowledge written for architects, engineers, spec writers, ROOFING CONSULTANTS, contractors, building superintendents & managers. Suitable for college & university roofing course curricula. 1992 ABI World Lifetime Achievement Award winner. Hardcover (set) $350.00 (USD) ISBN: 0-9629669-0-8. 15lbs. overnight shipping to U.S. add $16.00, Canada add $40.00 (USD). FOR THIS RARE BARGAIN DELIVERED OVERNIGHT, send your check payable to Dr. H. Laaly, 9037 Monte Mar Dr., Los Angeles, CA 90035-4235, or call (800) 559-6090 CODE 45 for brochure & order form. ***Publisher Provided Annotation.***

Laane, C., et al, eds. Biocatalysis in Organic Media. 438p. 1987. 146.25 (*0-444-42785-6*) Elsevier.

Laane, Jaan, ed. Structures & Conformations of Non-Rigid Molecules: Proceedings of the NATO Advanced Research Workshop, Reisenburg, Germany, September 6-10, 1992. (NATO Advanced Science Institutes Series C: Mathematical & Physical Sciences). 656p. (C). 1993. lib. bdg. 241.00 (*0-7923-2415-3*) Kluwer Ac.

Laanpere, H. Finnish-Esthonian-Finnish Dictionary: Suomi-Eesti-s. 499p. (EST & FIN.). 1977. pap. 49.95 (*0-8288-5436-X*, M9641) Fr & Eur.

Laar, Mart. War in the Woods: Estonia's Struggle for Survival, 1944-56. Ets, Tiina, tr. (Illus.). 272p. 1992. 38.00 (*0-929590-08-2*); pap. 18.95 (*0-929590-09-0*) Compass Pr.

Laarhoven, Ruurdje. Triumph of Moro Diplomacy: The Maguindanao Sultanate in the 17th Century. 287p. (Orig.). (C). 1989. pap. 15.00 (*971-10-0390-2*, Pub. by New Day Pub PH) Cellar.

Laarman, Edward J. Nuclear Pacifism: "Just War" Thinking Today. LC 84-47543. (American University Studies: Theology & Religion: Ser. VII, Vol. 4). 210p. 1984. pap. text ed. 20.55 (*0-8204-0121-8*) P Lang Pubs.

Laarman, Jan, et al. Choice of Technology in Forestry: A Philippine Case Study. (Illus.). (C). 1981. pap. 9.50 (*0-686-30446-2*, Pub. by New Day Pub PH) Cellar.

Laarman, Jan G. & Sedjo, Roger A. Global Forestry: Issues for Six Billion People. 1992. text ed. write for info. (*0-07-035702-1*) McGraw.

LaArta, Moulton. Nature's Medicine Chest, Set 4. 96p. 1975. 7.50 (*0-935596-07-0*) Nat Med Chest.

Laas, Virginia J., ed. Wartime Washington: The Civil War Letters of Elizabeth Blair Lee. (Illus.). 588p. 1991. 39.95 (*0-252-01802-8*) U of Ill Pr.

Laasch, Jack & Benton, Scott. Fishing Lake Michigan Illinois - Indiana. (Lake Michigan Ser.). (Illus.). 84p. 1988. pap. 6.95 (*0-939314-19-3*) Fishing Hot.

Laasch, Jack & Brich, Steve. Fishing Lake Michigan Southern Wisconsin. (Lake Michigan Ser.). (Illus.). 80p. 1988. pap. 6.95 (*0-939314-18-5*) Fishing Hot.

Laasch, Jack & Knops, Bob. Fishing Lake Michigan: Central Wisconsin. (Lake Michigan Ser.). (Illus.). 88p. 1988. pap. 6.95 (*0-939314-17-7*) Fishing Hot.

Laasch, Jack, et al. Fishing Northern Illinois' Top 20 Lakes. (Illus.). 112p. 1989. pap. 9.95 (*0-939314-25-8*) Fishing Hot.

Laaser, G. Vergleichende Systematische Studien An Basidiomycetenheften Unter Besonderer Beruecksichtigung der Hefestadien. (Bibliotheca Mycologica Ser.: Vol. 130). (Illus.). 336p. (GER.). 1989. pap. text ed. 84.50 (*3-443-59031-4*, Pub. by Gebruder Borntraeger GW) Lubrecht & Cramer.

Laaser, Mark. The Secret Sin: Healing the Wounds of Sexual Addiction. 208p. 1992. pap. 9.99 (*0-310-54911-6*) Zondervan.

— Seeing Yourself Through Gods Eyes. 1990. pap. 7.99 (*0-310-52841-0*) Zondervan.

***Laaser, Mark & Hopkins, Nancy, eds.** Healing the Soul of a Church. 250p. (Orig.). 1995. pap. text ed. write for info. (*0-8146-2333-6*, Litug Pr Bks) Liturgical Pr.

Laaser, U., et al, eds. Costs & Benefits in Health Care & Prevention: An International Approach to Priorities in Medicine. (Illus.). 180p. 1990. pap. 31.00 (*0-387-52708-7*) Spr-Verlag.

Laato, Antti. Josiah & David Redivivus: The Historical Josiah & the Messianic Expectations of Exilic & Postexilic Times. (Coniectanea Biblica. Old Testament Ser.: No. 33). 416p. (Orig.). 1992. pap. 66.00x (*91-22-01475-6*, Pub. by Almqv & Wiksell SW) Coronet Bks.

— The Servant YHWH & Cyrus: A Reinterpretation of the Exilic Messianic Programme in Isaiah 40-55. (Coniectanea Biblica. Old Testament Ser.: No. 35). 307p. (Orig.). 1992. pap. 52.50x (*91-22-01529-9*, Pub. by Almqv & Wiksell SW) Coronet Bks.

***Laato, Timo.** Paul & Judaism: An Anthological Approach. McElwain, T., tr. LC 95-10342. (South Florida Studies in the History of Judaism: Vol. 115). Orig. Title: Paulus und Judentum. 1995. write for info. (*0-7885-0100-3*) Scholars Pr GA.

Lab, Doug & Lab, Olivia K. My Life in My Hands: Living on with Cystic Fibrosis. Witkin, Robyn, ed. 163p. 1990. pap. 7.50 (*0-9629216-0-2*) LabPro Pr.

Lab, Olivia K., jt. auth. see Lab, Doug.

Lab, Steven P. Crime Prevention: Approaches, Practices & Evaluations. 2nd ed. LC 91-76928. 327p. (C). 1992. pap. 24.95 (*0-87084-401-6*) Anderson Pub Co.

Lab, Steven P., jt. auth. see Whitehead, John T.

Lab, Susan V., jt. ed. see Cunningham, Patricia A.

Lab-Volt Staff. Experiments in Electricity for Use with Lab-Volt EMS Equipment. 23p. 1993. teacher ed 10.00 (*0-8273-5996-9*) Delmar.

Laba. Rheological Properties of Cosmetics & Toiletries. (Cosmetic Science & Technology Ser.: Vol. 13). 440p. 1994. 185.00 (*0-8247-9090-1*) Dekker.

Laba, Roman. The Roots of Solidarity: A Political Sociology of Poland's Working Class Democratization. (Illus.). 267p. 1991. text ed. 29.95 (*0-691-07862-9*) Princeton U Pr.

Labacus, Thelma. A Genuine Antique Person Is. (Illus.). 1993. pap. write for info. (*0-9639812-1-8*) Laid Back Ent.

LaBadie, Horace, Jr. Build Your Own Low-Cost PostScript Printer & Save a Bundle. 2nd ed. 1993. pap. text ed. 19.95 (*0-07-035887-7*, Windcrest) TAB Bks.

***LaBadie, Horace.** Data Security: How to Bulletproof Your Hardware & Software. 1994. pap. 34.95 (*1-55958-750-4*) Prima Pub.

LaBadie, Horace W. Build Your Own PostScript Laser Printer & Save a Bundle. 1991. pap. text ed. 16.95 (*0-07-157701-7*) McGraw.

LaBadie, Horace W., Jr. Build Your Own PostScript Laser Printer & Save a Bundle. (Illus.). 144p. 1991. 24.95 (*0-8306-4738-4*, 3738, Windcrest); pap. 16.95 (*0-8306-3738-9*, Windcrest) TAB Bks.

— Build Your Own PostScript Printer & Save a Bundle. 2nd ed. LC 92-41245. 1993. 19.60 (*0-8306-4306-0*) TAB Bks.

***LaBadie, Horace W.** Create Your Own Graphics Workstation. LC 94-31175. 1995. pap. text ed. 24.95 (*0-07-035955-5*, Windcrest) TAB Bks.

LaBadie, Horace W., Jr. Upgrade Your Computer Printer & Save a Bundle. 1993. text ed. 29.95 (*0-07-035836-2*); pap. text ed. 19.95 (*0-07-035837-0*) McGraw.

— Upgrade Your Computer Printer & Save a Bundle. (Illus.). 288p. 1992. 29.95 (*0-8306-3954-3*, 4144, Windcrest); pap. 19.95 (*0-8306-3955-1*, 4144, Windcrest) TAB Bks.

Labadie, J. W., et al, eds. Computerized Decision Support Systems for Water Managers. 992p. 1989. pap. text ed. 85.00 (*0-87262-717-9*, 717) Am Soc Civil Eng.

Labadie, Joseph A. Anarchism. 1976. 250.00 (*0-87700-231-2*) Revisionist Pr.

— Doggerel for the Underdog. (Men & Movements in the History & Philosophy of Anarchism Ser.). 1979. lib. bdg. 250.00 (*0-87700-308-4*) Revisionist Pr.

— Russian Verses. (Men & Movements in the History & Philosophy of Anarchism Ser.). 1979. lib. bdg. 59.95 (*0-87700-309-2*) Revisionist Pr.

— Sing Songs & Some That Don't. (Men & Movements in the History & Philosophy of Anarchism Ser.). 1979. lib. bdg. 59.95 (*0-87700-310-6*) Revisionist Pr.

— What Is Love? (Men & Movements in the History & Philosophy of Anarchism Ser.). 1979. lib. bdg. 59.95 (*0-87700-311-4*) Revisionist Pr.

— Windows. (Men & Movements in the History & Philosophy of Anarchism Ser.). 1979. lib. bdg. 59.95 (*0-87700-312-2*) Revisionist Pr.

Labadie, Laurance. Do Banks Create Money? (Men & Movements in the History & Philosophy of Anarchism Ser.). 1979. lib. bdg. 250.00 (*0-685-96388-8*) Revisionist Pr.

— Humanism & Morality. (Men & Movements in the History & Philosophy of Anarchism Ser.). 1979. lib. bdg. 250.00 (*0-685-96397-7*) Revisionist Pr.

— Jesus As an Anarchist. (Men & Movements in the History & Philosophy of Anarchism Ser.). 1979. lib. bdg. 59.95 (*0-685-96404-3*) Revisionist Pr.

— Laurance Labadie: Individualist, Anarchist & Mutualist, Vol. 1. (Men & Movements in the History & Philosophy of Anarchism Ser.). 1976. lib. bdg. 59.95 (*0-87700-248-7*) Revisionist Pr.

— The Money Racket. (Men & Movements in the History & Philosophy of Anarchism Ser.). 1979. lib. bdg. 59.95 (*0-685-96406-X*) Revisionist Pr.

— The Process of Social Degeneration. (Men & Movements in the History & Philosophy of Anarchism Ser.). 1979. lib. bdg. 59.95 (*0-685-96409-4*) Revisionist Pr.

— Selected Essays. LC 78-78149. (Libertarian Broadsides Ser.: No. 7). (Illus.). 1978. pap. 1.50 (*0-87926-022-X*) R Myles.

— A Way Out: Anarchist, Mutualist & Individualist Essays. (Men & Movements in the History & Philosophy of Anarchism Ser.). 1980. lib. bdg. 250.00 (*0-686-60065-7*) Revisionist Pr.

Labadie, Pamela, jt. auth. see Altug, Sumru.

LaBahn, Kathleen J. Anna Segher's Exile Literature: The Mexican Years (1941-1947) (American University Studies: Germanic Languages & Literature: Ser. I, Vol. 37). 208p. 1986. text ed. 30.50 (*0-8204-0195-1*) P Lang Pubs.

Labaky, Mansour. The Roads to Nowhere: A Child of Lebanon. Annelyse, Allen, tr. LC 87-32305. 1988. pap. 4.95 (*0-932506-61-5*) St Bedes Pubns.

Laballe, Chip. Jock Joke Book. 1994. pap. 4.99 (*1-56171-312-0*, S P I Bks) Sure Sellers.

Laban, Brian. Classic Mercedes-Benz: The Three-Pointed Star. (Illus.). 160p. 1994. 19.98 (*0-89660-045-9*, Artabras) Abbeville Pr.

— Classic Porches: Generations of Genius. 1993. 19.98 (*0-89660-044-0*, Artabras) Abbeville Pr.

— MGB: The Complete Story. (Crowood Autoclassics "Legend of the Road" Ser.). (Illus.). 192p. 1990. 35.95 (*1-85223-358-3*, Pub. by Crowood UK) Motorbooks Intl.

Laban, Rudolf. A Life for Dance: The Autobiography of Rudolf Laban. Ullman, Lisa, tr. 193p. (C). 1975. 19.95 (*0-7121-1231-6*, Pub. by MacDonald & Evans UK) Princeton Bk Co.

Laban, Rudolf & Lange, Rod. Laban's Principles of Dance & Movement Notation. 2nd ed. 61p. (C). 1975. 14.95 (*0-7121-1648-6*, Pub. by MacDonald & Evans UK) Princeton Bk Co.

Labana, K. S., et al, eds. Breeding Oilseed Brassicas. (Monographs on Theoretical & Applied Genetics: Vol. 19). 296p. 1993. 139.00 (*0-387-55854-3*) Spr-Verlag.

Labana, S. S. & Dickie, R. A., eds. Characterization of Highly Cross-Linked Polymers. LC 83-25733. (ACS Symposium Ser.: No. 243). 321p. 1984. lib. bdg. 54.95 (*0-8412-0824-7*) Am Chemical.

Labana, Sandy, pref. Advanced Coatings Technology. (Illus.). 256p. 1991. 85.00 (*1-56378-001-1*) ESD.

Laband, David N. & Heinbuch, Deborah. Blue Laws: The History, Economics, & Politics of Sunday Closing Laws. LC 85-45930. 240p. 1987. text ed. 37.95 (*0-669-12416-8*) Free Pr.

Laband, David N. & Lentz, Bernard F. The Roots of Success: Why Children Follow in Their Parents' Career Footsteps. LC 84-26309. 192p. 1985. text ed. 45.00 (*0-275-90132-7*, C0132, Praeger Pubs) Greenwood.

Laband, David N., jt. auth. see Lentz, Bernard F.

Laband, J. & Haswell, R., eds. Pietermaritzburg, 1838-1988: A New Portrait of an African City. 1988. 25.00 (*0-86980-639-4*, Pub. by Univ Natal Pr SA) Intl Spec Bk.

Laband, John. Kingdom in Crisis: The Zulu Response to the British Invasion of 1879. Beckett, Ian F., ed. (War, Armed Forces & Society Ser.). 240p. 1992. 59.95 (*0-7190-3582-1*, Pub. by Manchester Univ Pr UK) St Martin.

Labanick, George. Biology 110 Lab Manual. 2nd rev. ed. (Illus.). 110p. (C). 1990. 11.00 (*1-878045-03-2*) Whittier Pubns.

Labanowski, J. K. & Andzelm, J. W., eds. Density Functional Methods in Chemistry. (Illus.). xv, 443p. 1994. 59.00 (*0-387-97512-8*) Spr-Verlag.

Labanyi, Jo. Myth & History in the Contemporary Spanish Novel. 288p. (C). 1989. 69.95 (*0-521-24622-9*) Cambridge U Pr.

Labanyi, Jo, intro. Galdos. LC 92-12957. (Modern Literatures in Perspective Ser.). 280p. (C). 1993. text ed. 53.50 (*0-582-08529-2*, 79633); pap. text ed. 28.50 (*0-582-08530-6*, 79632) Longman.

Labanyi, Jo, jt. ed. see Charnon-Deutsch, Lou.

Labanyi, Jo, tr. see Galdos, Benito P.

Labanyi, Jo, jt. ed. see Graham, Helen.

Labanyi, Jo, tr. see Traba, Marta.

Labanyi, Jo, tr. see Vazquez Rial, Horacio.

Labanyi, Peter, tr. see Negt, Oskar & Kluge, Alexander.

Labarca & Hendrickson. Nuevas Dimensiones. 2nd ed. 1992. pap. 33.95 (*0-8384-2335-3*); Nuevas alturas. student ed, pap. 29.95 (*0-8384-2336-1*) Heinle & Heinle.

— Nuevas Dimensiones. 2nd ed. 1992. student ed, pap. 27.95 (*0-8384-2334-5*) Heinle & Heinle.

Labarca, jt. auth. see Halty-Pfaff.

Labarca, A. & Hendrickson, J. Nuevas Dimensiones, Set. 1988. audio, pap. text ed. 32.95 (*0-8384-1880-5*) Heinle & Heinle.

Labarca, Angela, et al, eds. Issues in L2: Theory as Practice - Practice as Theory. LC 89-37180. (Delaware Symposia on Language Studies: Vol. 7). 296p. (C). 1990. text ed. 55.00 (*0-89391-521-1*) Ablex Pub.

Labarca, Angela & Hendrickson, James M. Our Global Village. 226p. (C). 1984. pap. text ed. 14.75 (*0-15-567730-6*) HB Coll Pubs.

Labarca, Angela, jt. auth. see Galloway, Vicki.

LaBarca, Angela, jt. auth. see Hendrickson, James M.

Labarca, Angela, jt. auth. see Lantolf, James P.

LaBare, Martha. Shooting Star & Other Poems. 64p. (Orig.). 1982. pap. 4.50 (*0-9609090-2-8*) Swollen Magpie.

L

Labaree, Benjamin. Colonial Massachusetts: A History. LC 79-33. (History of the American Colonies Ser.). 349p. 1979. lib. bdg. 35.00 (0-527-18714-3) Kraus Intl.

Labaree, Benjamin W. America's Nation-Time: 1607-1789. 272p. 1976. reprint ed. pap. 9.95 (0-393-00821-5) Norton.

— The Boston Tea Party. LC 79-5423. (Illus.). 360p. 1979. reprint ed. text ed. 37.50 (0-930350-16-2); reprint ed. pap. text ed. 15.95 (0-930350-05-7) NE U Pr.

— Supplement (1971-1986) to Robert G Albion's Naval & Maritime History: An Annotated Bibliography. 232p. 1988. pap. 13.95 (0-913372-46-3) Mystic Seaport.

Labaree, David F. The Making of an American High School: The Credentials Market & Central High School of Philadelphia. LC 87-10595. 272p. (C). 1988. 36.00x (0-300-04091-1) Yale U Pr.

— The Making of an American High School: The Credentials Market & the Central High School of Philadelphia, 1838-1939. 222p. (C). 1992. reprint ed. pap. text ed. 16.00 (0-300-05469-6) Yale U Pr.

Labaree, Leonard W., ed. see Franklin, Benjamin.

Labarge, Margaret W. Simon De Montfort. LC 75-22643. (Illus.). 312p. 1975. reprint ed. text ed. 35.00 (0-8371-8359-6, LASM, Greenwood Pr) Greenwood.

— A Small Sound of the Trumpet: Women in Medieval Life. LC 86-47509. (Illus.). 288p. 1988. reprint ed. pap. 17.00 (0-8070-5627-8, BP 789) Beacon Pr.

LaBarge, S., jt. ed. see Gackenbach, Jayne.

Labarge, William. Desert Voices. 1991. mass mkt. 4.95 (0-06-100354-9, Harp PBks) HarpC.

— Sweetwater Gunslinger 201. 1991. 14.95 (0-8306-8515-4) TAB Bks.

Labarge, William H. Hornet's Nest. 1991. mass mkt. 5.50 (0-515-10608-9) Jove Pubns.

LaBarge, William H. Road to Gold. 1993. mass mkt. 5.50 (0-06-104139-4, Harp PBks) HarpC.

— Sweetwater Gunslinger 201. 1986. text ed. 14.95 (0-07-156064-5) McGraw.

LaBarge, William H. & Holt, Robert L. Sweetwater: Gunslinger 201. Gentle, Ernest J., ed. LC 83-73237. (Illus.). 192p. 1983. 14.60 (0-8168-8515-X, 28515, TAB-Aero) TAB Bks.

— Sweetwater Gunslinger Two Hundred One. (Illus.). 192p. 14.95 (0-685-47251-5, 28515, TAB-Aero) TAB Bks.

LaBarre, George H. Collecting Stocks & Bonds, 3 vols., Set. (Illus.). 368p. 1981. pap. 14.85 (0-941538-00-1) G H LaBarre.

— Collecting Stocks & Bonds, Vol. I. rev. ed. (Illus.). 108p. 1981. pap. 4.95 (0-941538-01-X) G H LaBarre.

— Collecting Stocks & Bonds, Vol. II. (Illus.). 128p. 1981. pap. 4.95 (0-941538-02-8) G H LaBarre.

— Collecting Stocks & Bonds, Vol. III. (Illus.). 132p. 1981. pap. 4.95 (0-941538-03-6) G H LaBarre.

Labarre, Harriet. Blackwood's Daughter. 1992. mass mkt. 3.99 (0-8041-0797-1) Ivy Books.

LaBarre, James, jt. auth. see Mitchell, William.

LaBarre, Weston. The Ghost Dance: The Origins of Religion. 677p. 1990. reprint ed. pap. 19.95x (0-88133-561-4) Waveland Pr.

LaBastida, Aurora. Nine Days to Christmas. (J). (ps-3). 1991. 14.95 (0-670-84165-X) Viking Child Bks.

Labastida, Aurora, jt. auth. see Ets, Marie H.

LaBastille, Anne. Beyond Black Bear Lake: Life at the Edge of the Wilderness. (Illus.). 1988. pap. 10.95 (0-393-30539-2) Norton.

— Birds of the Mayas: Field Guide to Birds of the Maya World. (Illus.). Date not set. 12.00 (0-614-04833-8) W Wind Pubns.

Labastille, Anne. Birds of the Mayas: Field Guide to Birds of the Maya World. (Illus.). 120p. 1994. pap. 12.00 (0-9632846-5-7) W Wind Pubns.

— Mama Poc. 1990. 19.95 (0-393-02830-5) Norton.

LaBastille, Anne. Mama Poc: An Ecologist's Account of the Extinction of a Species. (Illus.). 320p. 1991. pap. 10.95 (0-393-30800-6) Norton.

— The Wilderness World of Anne Labastille. (Illus.). 120p. 1992. pap. 14.95 (0-9632846-0-6) W Wind Pubns.

— Women & Wilderness. LC 80-14369. (Paperback Library). (Illus.). 320p. 1984. reprint ed. 12.00 (0-87156-828-4) Sierra.

— Woodswoman. 1978. pap. 8.95 (0-525-48367-5, Dutton) NAL-Dutton.

Labat, Jean B. Nuevo Viaje a Islas de la America, Vol. 1. Cardenas-Ruiz, Manuel, ed. LC 83-3591. Orig. Title: Nouveau Vouage aux Isles de l'Amerique. (Illus.). 279p. (SPA.). 1984. pap. 6.50 (0-8477-0876-4) U of PR Pr.

***Labat, Joseph.** Des Identites Culturelles et des Paradigmes de l'Occident dans Leur Relativite. (FRE.). 1995. write for info. (0-7734-2914-X) E Mellen.

Labat, Rene. L' Akkadien de Boghaz-Koi. LC 78-72748. (Ancient Mesopotamian Texts & Studies). reprint ed. 37.50 (0-685-91790-8) AMS Pr.

Labate, Lillian, jt. ed. see Chandler, William J.

L'Abate, Luciano. Building Family Competence: Primary & Secondary Prevention Strategies. (Illus.). 240p. (C). 1990. text ed. 38.00 (0-8039-3488-2) Sage.

— Family Evaluation: A Psychological Approach. (C). 1994. text ed. 39.95 (0-8039-4238-9); pap. text ed. 18.95 (0-8039-4239-7) Sage.

— Family Psychology II: Theory, Therapy, Enrichment, & Training. 300p. (Orig.). (C). 1988. pap. text ed. 26.50 (0-8191-6680-4) U Pr of Amer.

— The Handbook of Family Psychology & Therapy, 2 vols., I. LC 84-71293. (Professional Bks.). (C). 1985. text ed. 68.95 (0-534-10443-6) Brooks-Cole.

L'Abate, Luciano, ed. Handbook of Developmental Family Psychology & Psychopathology. (Series on Personality Processes). 496p. 1993. text ed. 55.00 (0-471-53527-3) Wiley.

L'Abate, Luciano & Bagarozzi, Dennis A. Sourcebook of Marriage & Family Evaluation. LC 92-22541. 336p. 1993. 40.95 (0-87630-676-8) Brunner-Mazel.

L'Abate, Luciano & Bryson, Charles H., eds. A Theory of Personality Development. (Personality Processes Ser.). 304p. 1993. text ed. 49.95 (0-471-30303-8) Wiley.

L'Abate, Luciano & Cox, Janet. Programmed Writing: A Self-Administered Approach for Intervention with Individuals, Couples & Families. LC 90-27793. 336p. (C). 1992. text ed. 68.95 (0-534-14484-5) Brooks-Cole.

L'Abate, Luciano & McHenry, Sherry. Handbook of Marital Interventions. 414p. Date not set. pap. 32.00 (1-56821-203-8) Aronson.

L'Abate, Luciano & Young, Linda. Casebook: Structured Enrichment Programs for Couples & Families. LC 86-26880. 402p. 1987. 55.95 (0-87630-451-X) Brunner-Mazel.

L'Abate, Luciano, jt. auth. see Weeks, Gerald R.

L'Abate, Luciano, et al. Handbook of Differential Treatment for Addictions. 380p. (C). 1991. text ed. 53.95 (0-205-13237-5) Allyn.

— Methods of Family Therapy. LC 85-21484. (Illus.). 304p. 1986. text ed. 66.00 (0-13-579376-9) P-H.

Labatt, Lori, jt. ed. see Littlejohn, Bruce.

Labatut, Jean & Lane, Wheaton J., eds. Highways in Our National Life: A Symposium. LC 72-5058. (Technology & Society Ser.). (Illus.). 554p. 1972. reprint ed. 35.95 (0-405-04710-X) Ayer.

LaBau, Vernon J., ed. see IUFRO Staff.

LaBauve, Sandy & Kehoe, George. Shave Ten Strokes in Twelve Days: A Woman Golfer's Guide to a More Successful Game. (Illus.). 128p. (Orig.). 1994. pap. 9.95 (0-399-51860-6, Perigree Bks) Berkley Pub.

LaBaw, Jeanine L. & Lepley, Mary M. The Mother's Guide to a Healthier Pregnancy & Easier Birth. (Illus.). 1991. audio 24.95 (0-9627583-0-2) Lifesounds.

***Labbance, Bob.** The Centennial History of the Woodstock Country Club. 26p. 1995. 40.00 (0-9622354-2-3); pap. text ed. 12.00 (0-9622354-3-1) NEGS.

— Golf Courses of New Hampshire: From the Mountains to the Sea. (Illus.). 184p. (Orig.). 1989. pap. 13.95 (0-9622354-0-7) NEGS.

Labbance, Bob & Cornwell, David. The Golf Courses of New Hampshire: From the Mountains to the Sea. Levitan, Jeanie, ed. (Illus.). 186p. (Orig.). 1989. pap. write for info. (0-318-64855-5) NEGS.

— Vermont Golf Courses: A Player's Guide. LC 87-61132. (Illus.). 144p. (Orig.). 1987. pap. 14.95 (0-933050-47-X) New Eng Pr VT.

Labbance, Bob, jt. auth. see Cornwell, David.

L'Abbate, Antonia, ed. The Role of Oxygen Radicals in Cardiovascular Disease. (C). 1988. lib. bdg. 114.50 (0-89838-407-9) Kluwer Ac.

L'Abbate, Antonio. Frontiers in Cardiology for the Eighties. Donato, Luigi A., ed. 1984. text ed. 109.00 (0-12-220680-0) Acad Pr.

***Labbe, Armand J.** Guardians of the Life Stream: Shamans, Art & Power in Prehispanic Central Panama. Rodriguez, Aleida, ed. (Illus.). 168p. (C). 1995. 39.95 (0-9633959-3-9) Bowers Mus.

— Leigh Wiener: Portraits. (Illus.). 114p. 1987. pap. 29.95 (0-9619146-0-2) Seven Four One.

***Labbe, Armand J., ed.** Tribute to the Gods: Treasures of the Museo del Oro. Inga, Maria & De Rhodes, Hanka, trs. (Illus.). 92p. 1992. pap. 25.00 (0-9633959-1-2) Bowers Mus.

***Labbe, Armand J. & Apodaca, Paul.** Images of Power: Masterworks of the Bowers Museum of Cultural Art. Bryant, J. et al, eds. (Illus.). 176p. 1992. 35.00 (0-9633959-0-4) Bowers Mus.

Labbe, Dolores E. Jim Crow Comes to Church: The Establishment of Segregated Catholic Parishes in South Louisiana. 1978. 17.95 (0-405-10838-9, 11845) Ayer.

Labbe, John. Fares Please! Those Portland Trolley Years. LC 79-50502. (Illus.). 160p. (Orig.). 1980. 17.95 (0-87004-287-4); pap. 12.95 (0-87004-278-5) Caxton.

Labbe, John, jt. auth. see Carranco, Lynwood.

Labbe, John T. & Replinger, Peter J. Logging to the Salt Chuck: Over 100 Years of Railroad Logging in Mason County Washington. Martin, F. Raoul, ed. (Logging Railroads of Washington State Ser.). (Illus.). 186p. (Orig.). 1989. pap. 36.95 (0-915370-09-3) NW Short Line.

Labe, Louise. Oeuvres Poetiques; Rymes de Pernette du Guille; Blasons du Corps Feminin. (Poesie Ser.). 188p. (FRE.). 1983. pap. 11.95 (2-07-032238-6) Schoenhof.

Labedz, Leopold. The Use & Abuse of Sovietology. 372p. 1988. 44.95 (0-88738-252-5) Transaction Pubs.

Labedz, Leopold, ed. Revisionism: Essays on the History of Marxist Ideas. (Essay Index Reprint Ser.). 1977. reprint ed. 26.95 (0-518-10166-5) Ayer.

Labedz, Leopold & Urban, George, eds. Sino-Soviet Conflict. LC 65-18351. 1965. 16.95 (0-8023-1070-2) Dufour.

Labedz, Leopold, jt. ed. see Hayward, Max.

LaBeff, Emily E., jt. auth. see Chalfant, H. Paul.

Labella, Vincenzo. Season of Giants 1492-1508: Michelangelo, Leonardo, Raphael. (Illus.). 1990. 45.00 (0-316-85646-0) Little.

LaBelle, Anne. The Best of Conejo: The Community Resource Guide. 200p. (Orig.). 1992. pap. 9.95 (0-9634949-0-2) Labelle.

LaBelle, Charlene G. A Guide to Backpacking with Your Dog. LC 92-33143. (Illus.). 96p. (Orig.). 1992. pap. 9.95 (0-931866-59-6) Alpine Pubns.

LaBelle, Dave. Lessons in Death & Life. Judd, Alan & Perry, Rex, eds. (Illus.). 112p. (C). 1994. text ed. 24.95 (0-9630770-0-7) D LaBelle.

Labelle, G. & Leroux, Pierre, eds. Combinatoire Enumerative: Proceedings of the "Colloque de Combinatoire Enumerative" Held at Universite du Quebec a Montreal, May 28-June 1, 1985. (Lecture Notes in Mathematics Ser.: Vol. 1234). xiv, 387p. 1987. pap. 54.50 (0-387-17207-6) Spr-Verlag.

***Labelle, Jacques & LeClere, Christian, eds.** Lexiques-Grammaires Compares en Francais: Actes Du Colloque International De Montreal (3-5 Juin 1992) LC 95-15436. (Lingvisticae Investigationes Supplementa Ser.: No. 17). 250p. 1995. lib. bdg. 45.00x (1-55619-257-6) Benjamins North Am.

Labelle, Micheline. Ideologie De Couleur et Classes Sociales En Haiti. LC 80-477747. (Collection Recherches Caraibes). (Illus.). 393p. (FRE.). reprint ed. pap. 112.10 (0-7837-6941-5, 2046770) Bks Demand.

Labelle, Nicole. Les Differents Styles de la Musique En France: le Psaume: Vol. 1, Commentaire. (Wissenschaftliche Abhandlungen-Musicological Studies: Vol. 31). 268p. (FRE.). 1981. lib. bdg. 6.00 (0-912024-97-6) Inst Mediaeval Mus.

— Les Differents Styles De la Musique En France: le Psaume: Vol. 2, Transcriptions A. (Wissenschaftliche Abhandlungen-Musicological Studies: Vol. 31). 168p. (FRE.). 1981. lib. bdg. 6.00 (0-912024-98-4) Inst Mediaeval Mus.

— Les Differents Styles De la Musique En France: le Psaume: Vol. 3, Music. (Wissenschaftliche Abhandlungen-Musicological Studies: Vol. 32). 168p. (FRE.). 1981. lib. bdg. 6.00 (0-912024-99-2) Inst Mediaeval Mus.

LaBelle, Susan. Flopsy, Mopsy & Cottontail: A Little Book of Paper Dolls in Full Color. (Illus.). 48p. (J). (gr. 1 up). 1983. pap. 2.95 (0-486-24376-1) Dover.

Labelle, Susan W. Bunny Rabbit Birthday Stickers. (Illus.). (J). (gr. k-3). 1992. pap. 1.00 (0-486-27326-1) Dover.

— Country Rabbit Easter Stickers. (Illus.). (J). (gr. k-3). 1993. pap. 1.00 (0-486-27815-8) Dover.

LaBelle, Susan W. Little Peter Rabbit Paper Dolls in Full Color. (J). (gr. 3 up). 1985. pap. 2.95 (0-486-24813-5) Dover.

LaBelle, Susan W., illus. Peter Rabbit Postcards in Full Color. 12p. 1984. pap. 3.50 (0-486-24617-5) Dover.

LaBelle, Thomas J. Nonformal Education & the Poor in Latin America & the Caribbean: Stability, Reform, or Revolution. LC 85-25783. 384p. 1986. text ed. 36.95 (0-275-92078-X, C2078, Praeger Pubs) Greenwood.

LaBello, Susan, tr. see Derossi, Flavia.

Labensky, Sarah R. & Hause, Alan M. On Cooking: Techniques from Expert Chefs. LC 94-15232. 1994. 49.95 (0-13-195449-0) P-H.

***Laber-Laird, Kathy, et al, eds.** Handbook of Rabbit & Rodent Medicine. LC 94-45569. (Pergamon Veterinary Handbook Ser.). 1995. text ed. 105.00 (0-08-042505-4, Pergamon Pr); pap. text ed. 49.00 (0-08-042504-6, Pergamon Pr) Elsevier.

Laberge, C. M., jt. ed. see Knoppers, B. M.

LaBerge, Charles. Four & Forty. Kammeier, Cy, ed. LC 88-71684. (Illus.). 204p. 1988. text ed. 12.95 (0-9621764-0-0) CBG Enterprises.

***LaBerge, David.** Attentional Processing: The Brain's Art of Mindfulness. LC 94-38071. (Illus.). 256p. 1995. text ed. 35.00 (0-674-05268-4, LABATT) HUP.

LaBerge, Gene. Geology of the Lake Superior Region. LC 93-80796. (Illus.). 288p. (Orig.). 1994. pap. 20.00 (0-945005-15-6) Geoscience Pr.

LaBerge, Stephen. Lucid Dreaming. 304p. 1986. mass mkt. 4.95 (0-345-33355-1) Ballantine.

Laberge, Stephen & Rheingold, Howard. Exploring the World of Lucid Dreaming. 1991. mass mkt. 5.99 (0-345-37410-X) Ballantine.

Laberthonniere, Lucien. Etudes sur Descartes, 2 tomes, Set. 836p. (FRE.). 1935. pap. 59.95 (0-7859-1539-7, 2711640809) Fr & Eur.

Labes, M. M., jt. auth. see Brown, G. H.

Labes, M. M., jt. ed. see Brown, Glen H.

Labesse, J. P., et al, eds. Cohomology of Arithmetic Groups & Automorphic Forms: Proceedings of a Conference Held in Luminy-Marseille, May 22-27, 1989. (Lecture Notes in Mathematics Ser.: Vol. 1447). v, 358p. 1990. pap. 47.00 (0-387-53422-9) Spr-Verlag.

Labetoulle, J., ed. see Fourteenth International Teletraffic Congress-ITC 14 Staff.

Labeyrie, L. D., jt. ed. see Berger, W. H.

Labeyrie, V., ed. The Ecology of Bruchids Attacking Legumes: Proceedings of the International Symposium Held at Tours, 1980. (Series Entomologica: No. 19). 1981. lib. bdg. 121.50 (90-6193-883-X) Kluwer Ac.

Labeyrie, V., et al, eds. Insects - Plants. (Series Entomologica). (C). 1987. lib. bdg. 184.00 (90-6193-642-X) Kluwer Ac.

Labh, Baidyanath. Panna in Early Buddhism: Philosophy Analysis with Special Reference to the Visuddhimagga. (C). 1991. text ed. 17.50 (0-8364-2654-1, Pub. by Manohar II) S Asia.

— Panna in Early Buddhism: With Special Reference to Visuddhimagga. xii, 163p. Date not set. 14.00 (0-685-62638-5, Estrn Bk Linkers) Nataraj Bks.

Labhart, A. Clinical Endocrinology: Theory & Practice. LC 75-11535. 1976. 60.00 (0-387-90175-2) Spr-Verlag.

LaBianca, Alice. No More Tomorrows. LC 90-61382. (Illus.). 426p. 1991. 24.95 (0-9626453-0-3) MCM Entertainment.

LaBianca, Oystein & Lucelle, Larry, eds. Hesban 2: Environmental Foundations: Studies of Climatical, Geological, Hydrological, & Phytological Conditions in Hesban & Vicinity. LC 86-72952. (Heshbon Ser.: Vol. 2). 184p. (C). 1986. text ed. 45.99 (0-943872-15-4) Andrews Univ Pr.

LaBianca, Oystein S. Hesban 1: Sedentarization & Nomadization: Food System Cycles at Hesban & Vicinity in Transjordan. Geraty, Lawrence T., ed. LC 89-82543. (Heshbon Excavations Final Reports: Vol. 1). (Illus.). 380p. (C). 1990. text ed. 45.99 (0-943872-00-6) Andrews Univ Pr.

LaBiance, Oystein S., ed. see Ibach, Robert D., Jr.

Labib, Muhammad. The Seven Martyrs of Hurmuzak. Momen, Moojan, tr. & frwd. by. (Illus.). 80p. 1981. 11.50 (0-85398-105-1); pap. 5.50 (0-85398-104-3) G Ronald Pub.

Labica, G. & Bensussan, G. Critical Dictionary of Marxism: Dictionnaire Critique de Marxisme. 1256p. (FRE.). 1985. 150.00 (0-8288-2252-2, F70761) Fr & Eur.

Labiche, Eugene. L' Affaire de la Rue de Lourcine. 64p. (FRE.). 1989. pap. 13.95 (0-7859-1551-6, 2851812416) Fr & Eur.

— Le Baron de Fourchevif. (FRE.). pap. 10.95 (0-7859-5349-3) Fr & Eur.

— La Cagnotte. 182p. (FRE.). 1990. pap. 9.95 (0-7859-1257-6, 2038712123) Fr & Eur.

— Celimare le Bien Aime. (FRE.). 1978. pap. 14.95 (0-7859-5350-7) Fr & Eur.

— Un Chapeau de Paille d'Italie. 160p. (FRE.). 1987. pap. 9.95 (0-7859-5351-5) Fr & Eur.

— La Cigale Chez les Fourmis. (FRE.). pap. 10.95 (0-7859-5352-3) Fr & Eur.

— La Commode de Victorine. (FRE.). pap. 12.95 (0-7859-5353-1) Fr & Eur.

— La Fille Bien Gardee. 92p. (FRE.). 1986. pap. 8.95 (0-7859-4651-9) Fr & Eur.

— Grammaire. 74p. (FRE.). 1986. pap. 12.95 (0-7859-4581-4) Fr & Eur.

— Un Jeune Homme Presse. 9.95 (0-686-54228-2) Fr & Eur.

— J'Invite le Colonel. 9.95 (0-686-54229-0) Fr & Eur.

— La Main Teste. 9.95 (0-686-54230-4) Fr & Eur.

— Maman Sabouleux. 9.95 (0-686-54231-2) Fr & Eur.

— Mon Ismenie. 9.95 (0-686-54232-0) Fr & Eur.

— Un Monsieur Qui a Brule une Dame. 9.95 (0-686-54233-9) Fr & Eur.

— Un Monsieur Qui Prend la Mouche. 9.95 (0-686-54234-7) Fr & Eur.

— Nouveau Theatre Choisi. 9.95 (0-686-54235-5) Fr & Eur.

— L' Omelette a la Follembuche. Marc, Michel, ed. 50p. (FRE.). 1947. pap. 9.95 (0-7859-5360-4) Fr & Eur.

— La Perle de la Canebiere. 9.95 (0-686-54245-2) Fr & Eur.

— Permettez, Madame. 9.95 (0-686-54246-0) Fr & Eur.

— Les Petits Oiseaux. 9.95 (0-686-54247-9) Fr & Eur.

— La Piece de Chambertin. 9.95 (0-686-54248-7) Fr & Eur.

— Un Pied dans le Crime. 9.95 (0-686-54249-5) Fr & Eur.

— La Poudre Aux Yeux. 9.95 (0-686-54250-9) Fr & Eur.

— A Slap in the Farce & A Matter of Wife & Death. (Farce Ser.: Vol. 2). 1987. pap. 7.95 (0-936839-82-1) Applause Theatre Bk Pubs.

— La Station Champbaudet. 9.95 (0-686-54251-7); pap. 4.95 (0-686-54252-5) Fr & Eur.

— Les Suites d'un Premier Lit. 9.95 (0-686-54253-3) Fr & Eur.

— Theatre, Vol. 1. (FRE.). 1990. pap. 16.95 (0-7859-3002-7) Fr & Eur.

— Theatre, Vol. 2. (FRE.). 1991. pap. 14.95 (0-7859-3003-5) Fr & Eur.

— Theatre, Vol. 3. 509p. (FRE.). 1964. 10.95 (0-8288-9835-9, F108552) Fr & Eur.

— Les Trente-Sept Sous de Monsieur Montaudouin. 9.95 (0-686-54256-8) Fr & Eur.

— Two Plays by Eugene Labiche: Ninety in the Shade, & Dust in Your Eyes. 1962. pap. 4.75 (0-8222-0343-X) Dramatists Play.

— Vingt-Neuf Degres a l'Ombre. 9.95 (0-686-54257-6) Fr & Eur.

— Les Vivacites du Capitaine Tic. 9.95 (0-686-54258-4) Fr & Eur.

— Voyage Autour de Ma Marmite. 9.95 (0-686-54259-2) Fr & Eur.

— Le Voyage de M. Perrichon. Barsacq, Andre, ed. (FRE.). 1954. 7.95 (0-7859-0011-X, F65490); pap. 5.95 (0-686-54261-4) Fr & Eur.

— Le Voyage de Monsieur Perrichon. (Coll. Mises en Scene). pap. 9.50 (0-685-34925-X) Fr & Eur.

Labiche, Eugene & Sigaux, Gilbert. Oeuvres Completes: Deux Profonds Scelerats, Un Mari qui Prende du Ventre, Espagnolas et Boyardinos, Vol. 4. (Illus.). (FRE.). 1967. 85.00 (0-7859-5356-6) Fr & Eur.

— Oeuvres Completes: Il Est de la Police, La Memoir d'Hortense, Doit-on le Dire?, Vol. 8. (Illus.). (FRE.). 1968. 85.00 (0-7859-5359-0) Fr & Eur.

— Oeuvres Completes: J'ai Compromis ma Femme, Le Vivacite du Capitaine Tic, L'Amour En Sabot, Vol. 6. (Illus.). (FRE.). 1968. 85.00 (0-7859-5557-7) Fr & Eur.

— Oeuvres Completes: Je Croque ma Tante, Le Clou aux Maris, L'Avare aux gants Jaunes, Vol. 5. (Illus.). 1968. 55.00 (0-7859-5357-4) Fr & Eur.

— Oeuvres Completes: Monsieur de Coylin, L'Avocat Loubet, L'Article, Vol. 1. (Illus.). 960p. (FRE.). 1966. 85.00 (0-7859-5354-X) Fr & Eur.

— Oeuvres Completes: Premier Prix de Piano, L'Homme qui manque le Coche, Le Bergere de la Rue Monthabar, Vol. 7. (Illus.). (FRE.). 1968. 85.00 (0-7859-5358-2) Fr & Eur.

— Oeuvres Completes: Un Jeune Homme Tomorrow Presse, Le Club Champenois, Oscar XXVIII, Vol. 2. (Illus.). (FRE.). 1967. 85.00 (0-7859-5355-8) Fr & Eur.

— Oeuvres Completes: Une Clarinette qui Passe, La Femme qui perd ses Jarretiers, on Demande Deux Culottieres, Vol. 3. (Illus.). (FRE.). 1967. 85.00 (0-7859-5556-9) Fr & Eur.

LaBier, Douglas. Modern Madness. 1986. 16.30 (0-201-11775-4) Addison-Wesley.

An Asterisk (*) at the beginning of an entry indicates that the title is appearing in BIP for the first time.

*__Labig, Charles E.__ Preventing Violence in the Workplace. LC 95-117. 224p. 1995. 24.95 (*0-8144-0287-9*) AMACOM.

Labignan, Italo, jt. auth. see Waszczuk, Henry.

Labije, J. Ten & Balner, H., eds. Coping with Cancer & Beyond: Cancer Treatment & Mental Health. (Publications of the Helen Dowling Institute for Biopsychosocial Medicine: Vol. 5). 240p. 1992. pap. 39.00 (*90-265-1223-6*, Pub. by Swets Pub Serv NE) Taylor & Francis.

Labine, Clem & Flaherty, Carolyn, eds. The Old-House Journal Compendium. LC 78-4360. (Illus.). 400p. 1983. 35.00 (*0-87951-080-3*); pap. 22.95 (*0-87951-186-9*) Overlook Pr.

Labine, Clem & Poore, Patricia, eds. Old-House Journal 1981 Yearbook: A One-Volume Compilation of All the Editorial Pages Printed in the Old-House Journal in 1981. (Yearbook Ser.). (Illus.). 304p. (Orig.). 1981. pap. 18.00 (*0-942202-05-8*) Old Hse Journ Corp.

— Old-House Journal 1983 Yearbook: A One-Volume Compilation of All the Editorial Pages Printed in the Old-House Journal in 1983. (Yearbook Ser.). (Illus.). 256p. (Orig.). 1983. pap. 18.00 (*0-942202-08-2*) Old Hse Journ Corp.

Labine, Clem, ed. see Old-House Journal Editors.

Labine, P., jt. ed. see Raman, A.

Labine, Paul, jt. ed. see Moran, George C.

Labinger, Harvey. The Libel: A Contradiction of True Belief. Davick, Pamela, ed. LC 87-60209. 272p. (Orig.). 1987. pap. write for info. (*0-942415-01-9*) One Eighty Pr.

Labinger, Maddie. Introduction to Word Processing. (C). 1983. pap. text ed. 50.00 (*0-273-01960-0*, Pub. by Pitman Pubng UK) St Mut.

Labinger, Maddie, ed. Pocket Guide: Wang System 5. (C). 1984. pap. text ed. 50.00 (*0-273-01962-7*, Pub. by Pitman Pubng UK) St Mut.

Labinger, Maddie, et al. Computer Handbook: Wordstar. (C). 1985. pap. text ed. 50.00 (*0-273-02496-5*, Pub. by Pitman Pubng UK) St Mut.

Labini, Paolo S. Economic Growth & Business Cycles: Prices & the Process of Cyclical Development. (Economists of the Twentieth Century Ser.). 304p. 1993. 69.95 (*1-85278-833-X*, Pub. by E Elgar Pub UK) Ashgate Pub Co.

Labiosa-Cassone, Libyan. Team Language Learning for French, Spanish & German. Rose, Diana, ed. (Illus.). (Orig.). 1991. pap. 199.00 (*0-685-54740-X*, Pub. by Accel Lrn Sys UK) Acclrtd Learn.

Labistour, Leon. Making Ships in Bottles: Beginners to Advanced. 1994. pap. 17.95 (*0-8128-8558-9*, Scrbrough Hse) Madison Bks UPA.

Labit, C., jt. auth. see Tziritas, G.

Lablanc, Michael. Professional Sports Team Histories, 4 Vols., Vol. 1. 1994. 149.00 (*0-8103-8858-8*, 101502) Gale.

— Professional Sports Team Histories: Major League Baseball, Vol. 2. 1994. 49.00 (*0-8103-8860-X*, 101504) Gale.

— Professional Sports Team Histories: National Basketball Association, Vol. 1. 1994. 49.00 (*0-8103-8859-6*, 101503) Gale.

— Professional Sports Team Histories: National Football League, Vol. 3. 1994. 49.00 (*0-8103-8861-8*, 101505) Gale.

— Professional Sports Team Histories: National Hockey League, Vol. 4. 1994. 49.00 (*0-8103-8862-6*, 101506) Gale.

LaBlanc, Michael L. Contemporary Musicians, Vol. 1. 1989. 65.00 (*0-8103-2211-0*) Gale.

— Contemporary Musicians, Vol. 2: Profiles of the People in Music, Vol. 2. 350p. 1989. 65.00 (*0-8103-2212-9*) Gale.

LaBlanc, Michael L., ed. Contemporary Musicians, Vol. 3. 300p. 1990. 65.00 (*0-8103-2213-7*) Gale.

LaBlang, Bonnie T., jt. auth. see Hayes, Joanne L.

*__LaBlaude, Pierre A.__ The Gardens of Versailles. (Illus.). 160p. 1994. 35.00 (*1-85759-043-0*, Pub. by P Wilson Pubs) Sothebys Pubns.

LaBo. Looking Black. 31p. (Orig.). 1993. pap. text ed. 3.95 (*1-56411-055-9*) Untd Bros & Sis.

Labo, James A. A Practical Introduction to Borehole Geophysics. Mentemeier, Samuel H. & Gardner, Gerald H., eds. LC 87-60425. (Geophysical References Ser.: No. 2). (Illus.). 336p. 1987. text ed. 62.00 (*0-931830-39-7*) Soc Expl Geophys.

Laboda, Gene. A Peek at Life from Another Planet. LC 83-62346. 96p. (Orig.). 1983. pap. 4.95 (*0-914279-00-9*) Pyramid Pub Co.

Laboda, Lawrence R. From Selma to Appomattox: The History of the Jeff Davis Artillery. (Illus.). 392p. (C). 1995. text ed. 30.00 (*0-942597-80-X*) White Mane Pub.

LaBombard, Joan. Calendar. (Illus.). 32p. 1985. 40.00 (*0-938364-02-2*) Orirana Pr.

— The Counting of Grains. Iddings, Kathleen, ed. LC 90-60172. (American Book Ser.). 99p. (Orig.). 1983. per., pap. text ed. 10.00 (*0-931289-03-3*) San Diego Poet Pr.

— The Winter Watch of the Leaves. Iddings, Kathleen, ed. LC 92-60839. (American Book Ser.). 98p. (Orig.). 1993. per. 10.00 (*0-931289-10-6*) San Diego Poet Pr.

LaBombarde. Nondiscrimination Requirements for Qualified Pension & Profit-Sharing Plans: A Guide To. 392p. 1991. pap. 35.00 (*0-685-67156-9*, 4842) Commerce.

LaBonte, Gail. The Arctic Fox. LC 88-18967. (Remarkable Animals Ser.). (Illus.). 60p. (J). (gr. 3 up). 1988. lib. bdg. 13.95 (*0-87518-390-5*, Dillon Silver Burdett) Silver Burdett Pr.

— Leeches, Lampreys, & Other Cold-Blooded Bloodsuckers. LC 91-12620. (First Bks.). (Illus.). 64p. (J). (gr. 5-8). 1991. lib. bdg. 13.93 (*0-531-20027-2*) Watts.

— The Llama. LC 88-16407. (Remarkable Animals Ser.). (Illus.). 60p. (J). (gr. 3 up). 1988. text ed. 13.95 (*0-87518-393-X*, Dillon Silver Burdett) Silver Burdett Pr.

— The Miniature Horse. LC 89-26046. (Remarkable Animals Ser.). (Illus.). 60p. (J). (gr. 3 up). 1990. text ed. 13.95 (*0-87518-424-3*, Dillon Silver Burdett) Silver Burdett Pr.

— The Tarantula. (Remarkable Animals Ser.). (Illus.). 60p. (J). (gr. 3 up). 1991. lib. bdg. 13.95 (*0-87518-452-9*, Dillon Silver Burdett) Silver Burdett Pr.

*__LaBonte, George.__ Fishing for Sailfish. Barrett, Linda, ed. (Illus.). 232p. (Orig.). 1994. pap. write for info. (*0-923155-21-X*) Fisherman Lib.

***LaBonte, Larry. In the Beginning. (Illus.). 160p. 1995. 50.00 (*1-887390-00-6*) Kiki Coll.**

These 73 exquisite tritone reproductions covering the genesis of Relationship represent a 10 year photographic study by internationally acclaimed photographer, Larry LaBonte. The work is presented in three sections: Waiting, The Child & Relationship. Waiting is a view of pregnancy when nature shows us her intrinsic beauty. They are metaphors of the time when women learn to adapt for someone yet unknown. It is a time of questioning. The Child is a series of striking images showing the beautiful form of infants' bodies. There is something akin to seeing an old soul when locking gaze with a newborn. For the child, the intensity & love he or she finds in a parent's gaze ignites its feelings of belonging, security & curiosity. Relationship is a series of very moving images giving the viewer a focused glimpse at the special moments when the genesis of a relationship begins to unfold between a parent & a new human being. While these situations are universal for every parent, it is LaBonte's unique focus on the act of paying attention that stimulates the observer to think on many different levels. This shows the positive side of parenting -- great gift for any new parent! ***Publisher Provided Annotation.***

LaBonte, Richard, jt. ed. see Barnett, Lisa.

LaBonty, Jan, jt. auth. see Danielson, Kathy E.

Labonville, J., jt. auth. see Block, J.

Labor Center Reporter Editorial Board Staff. Labor & the Economy: A Guide for Trade Unionists. (Orig.). 1989. pap. 7.50 (*0-937817-06-6*) CLRE UCAL Berk.

Labor, Earl & Reesman, Jeanne C. Jack London. rev. ed. LC 93-49825. (Twayne's United States Author Ser.: No. 230). 208p. 1994. text ed. 21.95x (*0-8057-4033-3*, Twayne) Macmillan.

Labor, Earle, ed. The Portable Jack London. LC 93-38740. 1994. 13.95 (*0-14-017969-0*, Penguin Bks) Viking Penguin.

Labor, Earle G. Jack London. (Twayne's United States Authors Ser.: No. 230). 1977. text ed. 20.95 (*0-8057-0455-8*, 96, Twayne) Macmillan.

Labor, Earle G., ed. see London, Jack.

Labor, Earle G., et al, eds. The Complete Short Stories of Jack London, 3 vols., Set. LC 92-44856. (Illus.). 2700p. (C). 1993. 180.00 (*0-8047-2058-4*) Stanford U Pr.

— The Short Stories of Jack London. 784p. 1992. pap. 14.95 (*0-02-022371-4*, Pub. by Gebrueder Borntraeger GW) Macmillan.

Labor Institute Staff. Hazardous Materials Workbook. 6th ed. (Illus.). 374p. (Orig.). 1992. 22.50 (*0-945257-50-3*) Apex Pr.

Labor Institute Staff, jt. auth. see Public Health Institute Staff.

Labor, John, tr. see Von Jhering, Rudolf.

Labor Publishing Company Staff. Labor: Its Rights & Wrongs. LC 75-334. (Radical Tradition in America Ser.). 321p. 1975. reprint ed. 25.85 (*0-88355-237-X*) Hyperion Conn.

Labor Staff. Diccionario Enciclopedica Labor, 10 vols., Set. 3758p. (SPA.). 1990. 1,795.00 (*0-7859-5911-4*, 8433503901) Fr & Eur.

— Diccionario Enciclopedica Labor, Vol. 1. 374p. 1990. 195.00 (*0-7859-6462-2*) Fr & Eur.

— Diccionario Enciclopedica Labor, Vol. 2. 374p. (SPA.). 1990. 195.00 (*0-7859-5912-2*, 8433503928) Fr & Eur.

— Diccionario Enciclopedica Labor, Vol. 3. 374p. (SPA.). 1990. 195.00 (*0-7859-5913-0*, 8433503936) Fr & Eur.

— Diccionario Enciclopedica Labor, Vol. 4. 374p. (SPA.). 1990. 195.00 (*0-7859-5914-9*, 8433503944) Fr & Eur.

— Diccionario Enciclopedica Labor, Vol. 5. 374p. (SPA.). 1990. 195.00 (*0-7859-5915-7*, 8433503952) Fr & Eur.

— Diccionario Enciclopedica Labor, Vol. 6. 374p. (SPA.). 1990. 195.00 (*0-7859-5916-5*, 8433503960) Fr & Eur.

— Diccionario Enciclopedica Labor, Vol. 7. 374p. (SPA.). 1990. 195.00 (*0-7859-5917-3*, 8433503979) Fr & Eur.

— Diccionario Enciclopedica Labor, Vol. 8. 374p. (SPA.). 1990. 195.00 (*0-7859-5918-1*, 8433503987) Fr & Eur.

— Diccionario Enciclopedica Labor, Vol. 9. 374p. (SPA.). 1990. 195.00 (*0-7859-5919-X*, 8433503995) Fr & Eur.

— Diccionario Enciclopedica Labor, Vol. 10. (SPA.). 1990. 195.00 (*0-7859-5920-3*, 8433504002) Fr & Eur.

— Enciclopedia Labor: La Enciclopedia Organica de Nuestro Tiempo, 12 vols., Set. 3rd ed. 10000p. (SPA.). 1976. 1,795.00 (*0-8288-5668-0*, S12295) Fr & Eur.

— Enciclopedia Labor de la Mujer y del Hogar: La Mujer, los Hijos, la Casa y la Alimentacion, 4 vols., Set. 2nd ed. 1280p. (SPA.). 1976. 250.00 (*0-8288-5669-9*, S50457) Fr & Eur.

— Enciclopedia Labor 3, 3 vols., Set. 2nd ed. 1193p. (SPA.). 1972. 195.00 (*0-8288-6384-9*, S-12294) Fr & Eur.

— Lexicolabor: Diccionario Enciclopedico Ilustrado, 4 vols., Set. 2216p. (SPA.). 1977. 395.00 (*0-8288-5484-X*, S50443) Fr & Eur.

Laboratory Manual for Medical Microbiology Staff. Laboratory Manual for Medical Microbiology. Schools of Medicine & Dentistry, State University of New York at Buffalo, Department of Microbiology Staff, ed. (Microbiology Ser.: No. 11). (Illus.). 195p. reprint ed. pap. 55.60 (*0-7837-0617-0*, 2040962) Bks Demand.

*__Laboratory Network Program Staff.__ Facilitating Systemic Change in Science & Mathematics Education: A Toolkit for Professional Developers. 800p. (C). 1995. text ed. write for info. (*1-878234-08-0*) Reg Lab Educ IOT NE Isls.

Laboratory Quality Assurance Committee of the American Association for Clinical Chemistry, Inc. Staff. Guidelines for Providing Quality Stat Laboratory Services. 26p. 1987. 5.00 (*0-915274-46-9*) Am Assn Clinical Chem.

Laborde, A. M. Le Marquis et la Marquise de Sade. (American University Studies: Romance Languages & Literature: Ser. II, Vol. 108). 216p. (C). 1989. text ed. 41.95 (*0-8204-0899-9*) P Lang Pubs.

Laborde, Alice M. Diderot et l'Amour. (Stanford French & Italian Studies: No. 17). vi, 114p. 1979. pap. 46.50 (*0-915838-22-2*) Anma Libri.

— Diderot et Mme. de Puisieux. (Stanford French & Italian Studies: Vol. 36). 1985. pap. 46.50 (*0-915838-54-0*) Anma Libri.

LaBorde, Allyson, ed. Corporate Image: Communicating Visions & Values. (Report Ser.: No. 1038). 57p. (Orig.). 1993. pap. text ed. 100.00 (*0-8237-0510-2*) Conference Bd.

*__Laborde, Claude.__ Dictionnaire des Histoires Droles Super Erotiques. (FRE.). 1993. pap. 45.00 (*0-7859-8051-2*, 2840690543) Fr & Eur.

Laborde, E. D., tr. see Robequain, Charles.

*__Laborde, Errol.__ The Buzzard Wore a Tutu: Chronicles of Life & Adventures in New Orleans. (Illus.). 112p. (Orig.). 1994. pap. 8.95 (*0-9643874-0-9*) Urban Press.

— Mardi Gras! A Celebration. Rogers, Mary A., ed. (Illus.). 200p. 1981. 29.95 (*0-937430-03-X*); pap. 15.95 (*0-937430-02-1*) Picayune Pr.

Laborde, Gene Z. Fine Tune Your Brain: Skills to Sell Your Idea to Someone Else. (Communication Ser.). (Illus.). 240p. 1987. 19.95 (*0-9613172-8-0*) Syntony Inc Pub.

Laborde, Genie Z. Fine Tune Your Brain: When Everything's Going Right & What to Do When It Isn't. 1988. 24.95 (*0-933347-30-8*); pap. 13.95 (*0-933347-20-0*) Syntony Inc Pub.

— Influencing with Integrity: Management Skills for Communication & Negotiation. LC 83-51129. (Illus.). 235p. 1988. 24.95 (*0-9613172-0-5*); pap. 12.95 (*0-933347-10-3*) Syntony Inc Pub.

— Ninety Days to Communication Excellence. (Communication Ser.). 100p. 1985. 9.95 (*0-317-53169-7*) Syntony Inc Pub.

Laborde, J-M. Intelligent Learning Environments: the Case of Geometry. (NATO ASI Series F: Computer & Systems Sciences, Special Programme AET: Vol. 117). 255p. 1993. 69.00 (*0-387-56807-7*) Spr-Verlag.

Laborde, Jean B. Essai sur la Musique Ancienne et Moderne, 4 vols., Set. LC 76-43922. (Music & Theatre in France in the 17th & 18th Centuries Ser.). reprint ed. 355.00 (*0-404-60180-4*) AMS Pr.

LaBorde, Michael, jt. auth. see Ritter, Beverly L.

Laborde Printers Staff, ed. see Alfonso, Betty A.

LaBoskey, Vicki K. Development of Reflective Practice: A Study of Preservice Teachers. LC 93-46110. 192p. (C). 1994. text ed. 38.00 (*0-8077-3335-0*); pap. 18.95 (*0-8077-3334-2*) Tchrs Coll.

LaBossiere, Mike, jt. auth. see Pass, Geoff.

LaBotz, Dan. Mask of Democracy: Labor Suppression in Mexico Today. 270p. (Orig.). 1992. 35.00 (*0-89608-438-8*); pap. 14.00 (*0-89608-437-X*) South End Pr.

Labouchere, Rachel. Abiah Darby 1716-1794: Wife of Abraham Darby Second of Coalbrookdale. (C). 1989. 36.00 (*1-85072-018-5*, Pub. by W Sessions UK); 21.00 (*1-85072-017-7*, Pub. by W Sessions UK) St Mut.

— Deborah Darby of Coalbrookdale, 1754-1810. (Illus.). 468p. (C). 1993. 21.00 (*1-85072-100-9*, Pub. by W Sessions UK) St Mut.

Laboul, Andre. Insurance & Other Financial Services: Structural Trends. 156p. (Orig.). 1992. pap. 28.00 (*92-64-13653-3*) OECD.

*__LaBouliere, Raymond H.__ Book of Electrical Formulas Solving Unknown Values: Solving Unknown Values. 140p. (Orig.). 1995. pap. text ed. write for info. (*0-9644626-0-5*) R H LaBouliere.

*__LaBounty, Char.__ How to Establish & Maintain Service Level Agreements. Etchison, Jim et al, eds. (Illus.). (Orig.). Date not set. pap. text ed. write for info. (*1-57125-009-3*) Help Desk Inst.

*__LaBounty, William P., comp.__ Index to the Map of McLean County, Illinois. LC 94-44406. 1994. write for info. (*0-943788-06-4*) McLean County.

Labour Canada Staff. Employment Standards Legislation in Canada 1993-1994. 121p. (Orig.). 1992. pap. 26.00 (*0-660-14937-0*, Pub. by Canada Commun Grp CN) Accents Pubns.

— Industrial Relations Legislation in Canada - 1993-1994. 64p. (Orig.). 1993. pap. 19.50 (*0-660-14938-9*, Pub. by Canada Commun Grp CN) Accents Pubns.

Labour Housing Group Staff. Right to a Home. Griffiths, David, ed. 194p. 1984. 42.50 (*0-85124-399-1*, Pub. by Spokesman Bks UK) Coronet Bks.

— The Roof over Your Head: A Housing Programme for Labour. Darke, Jane, ed. 128p. (Orig.). 1992. pap. 33.50 (*0-85124-531-5*, Pub. by Spokesman Bks UK) Coronet Bks.

Laboureur, Sylvain. Laboureur's Graphic Work: Catalogue Raisonne. (Illus.). 828p. (FRE.). 1989. 150.00 (*1-55660-056-9*) A Wofsy Fine Arts.

— Laboureur's Illustrated Books. 664p. (FRE.). 1990. 150.00 (*1-55660-139-5*) A Wofsy Fine Arts.

Labouvie-Vief, Gisela. Psyche & Eros: Mind & Gender in the Life Course. LC 93-21292. 336p. (C). 1994. 59.95 (*0-521-43340-1*); pap. 18.95 (*0-521-46824-8*) Cambridge U Pr.

Labov, William. The Social Stratification of English in New York City. LC 66-24073. 513p. reprint ed. pap. 146.30 (*0-8357-3348-3*, 2039581) Bks Demand.

— Sociolinguistic Patterns. (Conduct & Communication Ser.). 362p. 1973. pap. 20.95 (*0-8122-1052-2*) U of Pa Pr.

Labovitz, Annette & Labovitz, Eugene. Time for My Soul: A Treasury of Jewish Stories for Our Holy Days. LC 86-32243. 448p. 1987. 30.00 (*0-87668-954-3*) Aronson.

Labovitz, Annette & Labovitz, Eugene, eds. A Touch of Heaven: Eternal Stories for Jewish Living. LC 90-166. 304p. 1990. 30.00 (*0-87668-886-5*) Aronson.

Labovitz, Annette, jt. auth. see Labovitz, Eugene.

Labovitz, Arthur & Pearson, Anthony. Transesophageal Echocardiography: Basic Principles & Clinical Applications. (Illus.). 135p. 1992. pap. text ed. 42.00 (*0-8121-1578-3*) Williams & Wilkins.

Labovitz, Arthur J. & Williams, George A. Doppler Echocardiography: The Quantitative Approach. 3rd ed. 1992. text ed. 33.00 (*0-8121-1429-9*) Williams & Wilkins.

Labovitz, Esther K. The Myth of the Heroine: The Female Bildungsroman in the Twentieth-Century. 2nd ed. (American University Studies: General Literature: Ser. XIX, Vol. 4). 272p. 1987. text ed. 49.95 (*0-8204-0360-1*) P Lang Pubs.

*__Labovitz, Eugene & Labovitz, Annette.__ A Sacred Trust Vol. 1: Talmudic Age, Medieval Age, & Sephardic Age, Vol. 1. LC 94-68316. 303p. 1995. pap. 18.00 (*0-914615-12-2*) I Nathan Pub Co.

— A Sacred Trust Vol. 2: Silver Age of Poland, Vol. 2. 200p. 1995. pap. 12.00 (*0-914615-13-0*) I Nathan Pub Co.

— A Sacred Trust Vol. 3: America-Jewish Experience, Return to Israel Period, Vol. 3. 240p. 1995. pap. 12.00 (*0-914615-14-9*) I Nathan Pub Co.

Labovitz, Eugene, jt. auth. see Labovitz, Annette.

Labovitz, Eugene, jt. ed. see Labovitz, Annette.

Labovitz, George, et al. Making Quality Work: A Leadership Guide for the Results-Driven Manager. LC 93-61340. 200p. (C). 1993. pap. 16.00 (*0-939246-54-6*) Oliver Wight.

Labovitz, John R. Presidential Impeachment. LC 77-76300. 1978. 40.00 (*0-300-02213-1*) Yale U Pr.

Labovitz, Sanford I. & Hagedorn, Robert B. Introduction to Social Research. 3rd ed. 1981. text ed. write for info. (*0-07-035777-3*) McGraw.

Laboy, Roberto G. Puerto Rico: Tema y Motivo en la Poesia Hispanica. LC 80-53520. (Senda Antologica Ser.). (Orig.). (SPA.). (C). 1980. pap. 8.50 (*0-918454-21-2*) Senda Nueva.

Labra, Carilda O. Dust Disappears. Barkan, Stanley H., ed. Gioseffi, Daniela & Garcia, Enildo, trs. (Review Latin-American Writers (Cuban) Chapbook Ser.: No. 1). (Illus.). 48p. (ENG & SPA.). 1991. 15.00 (*0-89304-150-5*); 15.00 (*0-89304-152-1*); pap. 5.00 (*0-89304-151-3*) Cross-Cultrl NY.

— Dust Disappears. Barkan, Stanley H., ed. Gioseffi, Daniela & Garcia, Enildo, trs. (Review Latin-American Writers (Cuban) Chapbook Ser.: No. 1). (Illus.). 48p. (ENG & SPA.). 1991. 5.00 (*0-89304-153-X*); Audio cassette 60 mins. audio 10.00 (*0-89304-154-8*) Cross-Cultrl NY.

LaBrake, Lynn, ed. Directory of Agencies Collecting Statistical Data from College & University Libraries. 46p. 1986. 15.00 (*0-8389-7033-8*) Library Admin.

LaBrake, Mary L. Test for Differences. LC 92-16719. 1992. write for info. (*0-201-63411-2*) Addison-Wesley.

LaBranche, Bud. Woodcarving the Female Head. (Illus.). 60p. (YA). (gr. 8 up). 1986. pap. 8.95 (*0-88625-137-0*) Durkin Hayes Pub.

Labrash & McKay. Easy As ABC. 1985. pap. 10.95 (*0-934986-15-0*) New Harbinger.

Labre, R. M., ed. Accidents in the Year 2000. (C). 1989. lib. bdg. 45.00 (*0-685-44900-9*); pap. text ed. 60.00 (*0-7923-0475-6*) Kluwer Ac.

LaBrecque, John L., ed. Ocean Margin Drilling Program Atlases, Vol. 13. (Regional Atlas Ser.). 1986. pap. 195.00 (*0-86720-263-7*) Jones & Bartlett.

*__Labrecque, Lisa, ed.__ Unity: A Celebration of Gay Games IV & Stonewall. 168p. (Orig.). 1994. pap. 29.95 (*0-9643182-0-2*) Labrecque Pub.

LaBrecque, Ron, jt. auth. see Markman, Ronald.

LaBrecque, S. V., jt. auth. see Nies, J. I.

Labrie. Androgens & Prostate Cancer. Date not set. write for info. (*0-8493-5824-8*) CRC Pr.

L

Labrie, F., ed. Seventh International Congress of Endocrinology Abstracts: Proceedings of Congress Held 1-7 July, 1984, in Quebec City, Canada. (International Congress Ser.: No. 652). 1708p. 1984. 166.75 (*0-444-80587-7*, Excerpta Medica) Elsevier.

Labrie, F. & Proulx, L. Endocrinology. (International Congress Ser.: Vol. 655). 1985. 321.00 (*0-444-80637-7*) Elsevier.

Labrie, F., jt. auth. see Mauvais-Jarvis, P.

Labrie, F., et al. LHRH & Its Analogues: Basic & Clinical Aspects. (International Congress Ser.: Vol. 656). 1985. 183.75 (*0-444-80642-3*) Elsevier.

Labrie, Roger P., jt. ed. see Pranger, Robert J.

Labrie, Roger P., et al. United States Arms Sales Policy: Background & Issues. LC 87-72491. (AEI Studies: No. 359). 96p. reprint ed. pap. 27.40 (*0-8357-4539-2*, 2037430) Bks Demand.

Labrie, Ross. The Art of Thomas Merton. LC 79-1341. 188p. 1979. pap. 9.95 (*0-912646-55-1*) Tex Christian.

— The Writings of Daniel Berrigan. (Illus.). 284p. (C). 1989. lib. bdg. 50.00 (*0-8191-7495-5*) U Pr of Amer.

Labriola, A. Essais sur la Conception Materialiste de L'Historie. (Reimpressions G & B Ser.). 320p. 1971. pap. text ed. 77.00 (*0-677-50415-2*) Gordon & Breach.

***Labriola, Albert C., ed.** Milton Studies. 272p. (C). 1996. 49.95x (*0-8229-3914-2*) U of Pittsburgh Pr.

— Milton Studies, Vol. XXIX. LC 69-12335. 208p. (C). 1993. text ed. 49.95 (*0-8229-3732-8*) U of Pittsburgh Pr.

— Milton Studies, Vol. XXX. (Illus.). 232p. 1994. text ed. 49.95 (*0-8229-3772-7*) U of Pittsburgh Pr.

— Milton Studies, Vol. XXXI. 256p. (C). 1995. 49.95 (*0-8229-3861-8*) U of Pittsburgh Pr.

Labriola, Albert C. & Sichi, Edward, Jr., eds. Milton's Legacy in the Arts. LC 86-43037. (Illus.). 239p. 1988. 30.00 (*0-271-00497-5*) Pa St U Pr.

Labriola, Albert C. & Smeltz, John W. The Bible of the Poor: A Facsimile & Edition of the British Library Blockbook C.9 d.2. LC 90-38474. (Illus.). 200p. 1990. text ed. 38.00 (*0-8207-0229-3*); pap. text ed. 22.50 (*0-8207-0230-7*) Duquesne.

Labriola, Antonio. Socialism & Philosophy. LC 79-90007. 223p. (C). 1980. 25.00 (*0-914386-21-2*); pap. 15.00 (*0-914386-22-0*) Telos Pr.

Labriolle, Pierre C. Les Sources de l'Histoire du Montanisme. LC 80-13175. (Heresies of the Early Christian & Medieval Era Ser.: Second Ser.). reprint ed. 57.50 (*0-404-16184-7*) AMS Pr.

Labrique, F., jt. auth. see Seguier, G.

Labro, Philippe. Des Bateaux Dans la Nuit. (Folio Ser.: No. 1645). (FRE.). pap. 10.95 (*2-07-037645-1*) Schoenhof.

— Ete dans l'Ouest. (Folio Ser.: No. 2169). 297p. (FRE.). 1988. pap. 9.95 (*2-07-038258-3*) Schoenhof.

— Etudiant Etranger. (Folio Ser.: No. 1961). 302p. (Orig.). (FRE.). 1988. pap. 10.95 (*2-07-038043-2*) Schoenhof.

— Des Feux Mal Eteints. (Folio Ser.: No. 1162). (FRE.). pap. 9.95 (*2-07-037162-X*) Schoenhof.

— The Foreign Student. Byron, William R., tr. 288p. 1988. pap. 10.00 (*0-345-34696-3*, Ballantine Trade) Ballantine.

— Le Petit Garcon. Coverdale, Linda, tr. 320p. 1992. 23.00 (*0-374-18448-8*) FS&G.

— Petit Garcon. (Folio Ser.: No. 2389). (FRE.). pap. 9.95 (*2-07-038526-4*) Schoenhof.

Labrosse, Darcia. Greg's My Egg! (Illus.). 32p. (J). (ps-1). 1994. 15.95 (*0-86264-411-9*, Pub. by Andersen Pr UK) Trafalgar.

Labrosse, Jean J. Micro Controller OS. 320p. 1992. pap. text ed. 30.00 (*0-13-031352-1*) P-H.

Labrousse, E. Esquisse du Mouvement de Prix et Des Revenus Sur France Au XVIIIe Siecle, 2 vols. 695p. 1984. write for info. (*2-903928-11-8*) Gordon & Breach.

Labrousse, Henri L., jt. auth. see Koburger, Charles W., Jr.

LaBrucherie, Roger A. Barbados, a World Apart. (Illus.). 132p. 1993. 29.95 (*0-939302-28-4*) Imagenes.

— A Barbados Journey. (Illus.). 112p. 1982. 24.95 (*0-939302-07-1*) Imagenes.

— Hawaiian World, Hawaiian Heart. (Illus.). 228p. 1989. 44.95 (*0-939302-16-0*); 55.00 (*0-939302-17-9*) Imagenes.

— Imagenes de Puerto Rico. Zayas, Carmen D. et al, trs. (Illus.). 144p. (SPA.). 1985. 30.00 (*0-685-08566-X*) Imagenes.

— Imagenes de Puerto Rico. limited ed. Zayas, Carmen D. et al, trs. (Illus.). 144p. (SPA.). 1985. 45.00 (*0-685-08567-8*) Imagenes.

— Imagenes De Santo Domingo: A Reminiscence of the Dominican Republic. Espinosa, Mayra C., tr. (Illus.). 112p. (Orig.). 1978. pap. 12.00 (*0-939302-00-4*) Imagenes.

— Images of Barbados. 2nd ed. (Illus.). 112p. 1979. pap. 12.00 (*0-939302-01-2*) Imagenes.

— Images of Bermuda. (Illus.). 112p. 1981. 19.95 (*0-939302-04-7*) Imagenes.

— Images of Bermuda. rev. ed. (Illus.). 144p. 1989. 29.95 (*0-939302-21-7*); 32.95 (*0-939302-22-5*) Imagenes.

— Images of Puerto Rico. (Illus.). 144p. 1985. 32.95 (*0-939302-23-3*); 29.95 (*0-939302-10-1*); pap. 19.95 (*0-939302-24-1*) Imagenes.

— Puerto Rico, Borinquen Querida: A Loving Portrait of an Island. (Illus.). 156p. 1991. 34.95 (*0-939302-26-8*); 44.95 (*0-939302-27-6*) Imagenes.

Labrum, E. A., ed. Civil Engineering Heritage: Eastern & Central England. 288p. 1994. 24.00 (*0-685-75139-2*, 1970-X) Am Soc Civil Eng.

Labrun, N. R. Solar Radiophysics. McLean, Donald J., ed. (Illus.). 550p. 1985. 89.95 (*0-521-25409-4*) Cambridge U Pr.

Labrut, Michele. The New Key to Panama. Henriques, Leslie, ed. (New Key Ser.). (Illus.). 288p. (Orig.). 1995. pap. 13.95 (*1-56975-015-7*) Ulysses Pr.

***LaBruzza, Anthony & Mendez-Villarrubia, Jose M.** Using DSM-IV: A Clinician's Guide to Psychiatric Diagnosis. LC 94-28534. 472p. 1995. 47.50 (*1-56821-333-6*) Aronson.

Labuda, Michael. Creative Reading for Gifted Learners: A Design for Excellence. 2nd ed. LC 85-10789. 178p. reprint ed. pap. 50.80 (*0-8357-2640-1*, 2040128) Bks Demand.

LaBudde, K. Programming Concepts. 384p. 1987. pap. text ed. write for info. (*0-07-035778-1*) McGraw.

Labunka, Miroslav & Rudnytzky, Leonid, eds. The Ukrainian Catholic Church: 1945-1975. LC 76-26753. 1976. 7.50 (*0-686-28475-5*) St Sophia Religious.

Labunski, Richard. Libel & the First Amendment: Legal History & Practice in Print & Broadcasting. LC 85-24656. 327p. (Orig.). 1989. pap. 19.95 (*0-88738-790-X*) Transaction Pubs.

Labunski, Richard E. The First Amendment Under Siege: The Politics of Broadcast Regulation. LC 80-39675. (Contributions in Political Science Ser.: No. 62). x, 184p. 1981. text ed. 49.95 (*0-313-22756-X*, LFA/, Greenwood Pr) Greenwood.

***Laburna.** Optical Spanish Manual. 1999. pap. write for info. (*0-7506-9674-5*, Focal) Buttrwrth-Heinemann.

Labus, James B. The Physician Assistant Medical Handbook. LC 94-17891. (Illus.). 752p. 1995. pap. text ed. 35.00 (*0-7216-5169-0*) Saunders.

Labuszewski, John W. & Nyhoff, John E. Trading Financial Futures: Markets, Methods, Strategies, & Tactics. LC 87-28570. 1988. text ed. 45.00 (*0-471-60675-8*) Wiley.

— Trading Options on Futures: Markets, Methods, Strategies, & Tactics. LC 87-29656. 1988. text ed. 39.95 (*0-471-60676-6*) Wiley.

Labuszwski, John W. Trading Options on Futures: Markets, Methods, Strategies & Tactics. 2nd ed. 1994. 45.00 (*0-471-30393-3*) Wiley.

Labuta, Joseph A. Basic Conducting Techniques. 2nd ed. 272p. (C). 1989. pap. text ed. write for info. (*0-13-058322-7*) P-H.

— Basic Conducting Techniques. 3rd ed. LC 94-26505. 336p. 1994. pap. text ed. write for info. (*0-13-307257-6*) P-H.

Labute, J., jt. auth. see Kisilevsky, H.

Labuz, Ronald. The Computer in Graphic Design: From Technology to Style. LC 92-9981. 1993. text ed. 49.95 (*0-442-00971-2*) Van Nos Reinhold.

— Contemporary Graphic Design. 1991. text ed. 39.95 (*0-442-31887-1*) Van Nos Reinhold.

LaBuz, Ronald. Typography & Typesetting. (Illus.). 375p. 1988. text ed. 39.95 (*0-442-25966-2*) Van Nos Reinhold.

Labuz, Ronald A. How to Typeset from a Wordprocessor: An Interfacing Guide. 219p. 1984. pap. 39.95 (*0-8352-1899-6*) Bowker.

Labuza, T. P. Shelf-Life Dating of Foods. 500p. 1982. 77.00 (*0-917678-14-1*) Food & Nut Pr.

Labuza, Theodore P. & Erdman, John. Food Science & Nutritional Health: An Introduction. (Illus.). 558p. 1984. pap. text ed. 42.50 (*0-314-69660-1*); teacher ed, pap. text ed. write for info. (*0-314-78015-7*) West Pub.

Labuza, Theodore P., jt. ed. see Harlander, Susan K.

***Labuza, Theodore P., et al, eds.** Maillard Reactions in Chemistry, Food, & Health: Proceedings of the Fifth International Symposium on the Maillard Reaction, Held at the University of Minnesota, 1993. 458p. 1994. 149.95 (*0-85186-802-9*, R6802) CRC Pr.

Laby, Lorraine J., et al. Step by Step: WiordPerfect 6.0, Lotus 1-2-3, dBASE IV, DOS 6.0. LC 94-17416. (Increasing Your Productivity Ser.). 1994. 27.00 (*0-02-800958-4*) Glencoe.

Laby, T. H., jt. auth. see Kaye, G. W.

Labys, W. C., et al, eds. International Commodity Market Modelling: Advanced Methodology & Applications. (International Studies in Economic Modelling). 352p. 1990. 125.00 (*0-412-35690-2*, A5102) Chapman & Hall.

— Quantitative Methods for Market Oriented Economic Analysis over Space & Time. (Contemporary Studies in Energy Analysis & Policy: Vol. 9). 1988. 73.25 (*0-89232-607-7*) Jai Pr.

Labys, Walter C. Primary Commodity Markets & Models: An International Bibliography. 298p. 1987. text ed. 95.00 (*0-566-05324-1*, Pub. by Avebury Pub UK) Ashgate Pub Co.

Labys, Walter C., ed. Quantitative Methods for Market-Oriented Economic Analysis over Space & Time. (Illus.). 337p. 1989. text ed. 76.95 (*0-566-07024-3*) Ashgate Pub Co.

Labys, Walter C. & Nadiri, M. Ishaq, eds. Commodity Markets & Latin American Development: A Modeling Approach; Conference on Commodity Models in Latin America. LC 79-16533. 296p. reprint ed. pap. 84.40 (*0-317-10232-X*, 2051974) Bks Demand.

Labys, Walter C., jt. auth. see Cromwell, Jeff B.

Labzowsky, L., et al. Relativistic Effects in the Spectra of Atomic Systems. (Illus.). 352p. 1993. 116.00 (*0-7503-0223-2*) IOP Pub.

***Lac, Leo D.** Fireproof Homebuilding. LC 95-56. 1995. text ed. 40.00 (*0-07-018091-1*) McGraw.

Lacaj, Henrik & Fishta, Filip. Latin-Albanian Dictionary: Fjalor Latinisht-Shqip. 556p. (ALB & LAT.). 1980. 24.95 (*0-8288-1089-3*, F89900) Fr & Eur.

Lacal. Ras Superfamily of GTPases. 1993. 210.00 (*0-8493-5214-2*, RC268) CRC Pr.

***LaCalamita.** The Ultimate Espresso Machine Cookbook. 1995. 27.50 (*0-684-81336-X*) S&S Trade.

Lacalamita, M. & Di Gammateo, F., eds. Filmlexicon Degli Autori e Delle Opere, 7 vols., 1. (Illus.). (ITA.). 1972. 36.95 (*0-405-08506-0*) Ayer.

— Filmlexicon Degli Autori e Delle Opere, 7 vols., 2. (Illus.). (ITA.). 1972. 33.95 (*0-405-08507-9*) Ayer.

— Filmlexicon Degli Autori e Delle Opere, 7 vols., 3. (Illus.). (ITA.). 1972. 33.95 (*0-405-08508-7*) Ayer.

— Filmlexicon Degli Autori e Delle Opere, 7 vols., 4. (Illus.). (ITA.). 1972. 33.95 (*0-405-08509-5*) Ayer.

— Filmlexicon Degli Autori e Delle Opere, 7 vols., 5. (Illus.). (ITA.). 1972. 33.95 (*0-405-08510-9*) Ayer.

— Filmlexicon Degli Autori e Delle Opere, 7 vols., 6. (Illus.). (ITA.). 1972. 33.95 (*0-405-08511-7*) Ayer.

— Filmlexicon Degli Autori e Delle Opere, 7 vols., 7. (Illus.). (ITA.). 1972. 33.95 (*0-405-08512-5*) Ayer.

— Filmlexicon Degli Autori e Delle Opere, 7 vols., Set. (Illus.). (ITA.). 1968. 210.00 (*0-405-08505-2*) Ayer.

Lacalamita, Tom. The Ultimate Bread Machine Cookbook: An Insider's Guide to Automatic Bread Making. LC 93-1513. 1993. 25.00 (*0-671-88023-3*) S&S Trade.

LaCalamita, Tom. Ultimate Pasta Machine Cookbook. 1994. 25.00 (*0-671-50102-X*) S&S Trade.

Lacam, Guy. La Fin de l'Empire Romain et le Monnayage or en Italie, 2 vols., Set. 1983. 215.00 (*0-318-19613-1*) Numismatic Fine Arts.

Lacambra-Ayala, Tita. Pieces of String & Other Stories. 138p. (Orig.). 1984. pap. 9.50 (*971-10-0186-1*, Pub. by New Day Pub PH) Cellar.

Lacambre, G., et al. Paintings at the Orsay Museum. (Illus.). 160p. 1987. text ed. 29.95 (*0-935748-72-5*) Scala Books.

Lacan, Ernest. Esquisses Photographiques a Propos de L'Exposition Universelle et de la Guerre D'Orient. Bunnell, Peter C. & Sobieszek, Robert A., eds. LC 76-24665. (Sources of Modern Photography Ser.). (FRE.). 1979. reprint ed. lib. bdg. 15.95 (*0-405-09642-9*) Ayer.

Lacan, Jacques. Ecrits, Vol. 1. (FRE.). 1970. pap. 16.95 (*0-7859-2669-0*) Fr & Eur.

— Ecrits, Vol. 2. (FRE.). 1971. pap. 14.95 (*0-7859-2671-2*) Fr & Eur.

— Ecrits: A Selection. Sheridan, Alan, tr. 352p. 1982. pap. 12.95 (*0-393-30047-1*) Norton.

— The Four Fundamental Concepts of Psycho-Analysis. 1995. 23.00 (*0-8446-6852-4*) Peter Smith.

— The Four Fundamental Concepts of Psycho-Analysis. Sheridan, Alan, tr. 304p. 1981. pap. 14.95 (*0-393-00079-6*) Norton.

— Le Seminaire, Vol. 11: Les Quatre Concepts Fodaementaux de la Psychanalyse. (FRE.). 1990. pap. 19.95 (*0-7859-2719-0*) Fr & Eur.

— The Seminar of Jacques Lacan: The Psychoses 1955-1956, Bk. 3. Miller, Jacques-Alain, ed. Grigg, Russell, tr. LC 92-28360. 352p. 1993. 35.00 (*0-393-03467-4*) Norton.

— The Seminars of Jacques Lacan: Freud's Writings on Technique 1953-1954. Miller, Jacques-Alain, ed. Forrester, John & Tomaselli, Sylvana, trs. (Lacan's Series of Seminars: Bk. 1). 1988. 24.95 (*0-393-01895-4*) Norton.

— Speech & Language in Psychoanalysis. Wilden, Anthony, tr. LC 68-15446. 368p. (C). 1981. pap. 14.95 (*0-8018-2617-9*) Johns Hopkins.

— Television: A Challenge to the Psychoanalytic Establishment. 1990. 24.95 (*0-393-02496-2*) Norton.

Lacapa, Kathleen & Lacapa, Michael. Less than Half, More than Whole. LC 94-13132. (Illus.). 40p. (J). (gr. k up). 1994. 14.95 (*0-87358-592-5*) Northland AZ.

Lacapa, Michael. Antelope Woman: An Apache Folktale. LC 92-4198. (Illus.). 48p. (J). (gr. 3 up). 1992. 14.95 (*0-87358-543-7*) Northland AZ.

— Antelope Woman: An Apache Folktale. LC 92-4198. (Illus.). 48p. (J). (gr. 3 up). 1995. reprint ed. pap. 7.95 (*0-87358-647-6*) Northland AZ.

— The Flute Player: An Apache Folktale. LC 89-63749. (Illus.). 48p. (J). (gr. 2 up). 1990. 14.95 (*0-87358-500-3*) Northland AZ.

Lacapa, Michael, jt. auth. see Lacapa, Kathleen.

***Lacapa, Michale.** The Flute Player: An Apache Folktale. LC 89-63749. (Illus.). 48p. (J). (gr. 2 up). 1995. 7.95 (*0-87358-627-1*) Northland AZ.

LaCapra, Dominick. History & Criticism. LC 84-16990. 152p. (C). 1987. pap. 10.95 (*0-8014-9324-2*) Cornell U Pr.

— History, Politics, & the Novel. LC 87-6686. 240p. (C). 1987. 34.50 (*0-8014-2033-4*); pap. 12.95 (*0-8014-9577-6*) Cornell U Pr.

— Madame Bovary on Trial. LC 81-70714. 224p. 1982. 32.50 (*0-8014-1477-6*); pap. 11.95 (*0-8014-9361-7*) Cornell U Pr.

— A Preface to Sartre. LC 78-58022. 256p. 1978. 33.50 (*0-8014-1175-0*); pap. 12.95 (*0-8014-9448-6*) Cornell U Pr.

— Rethinking Intellectual History: Texts, Contexts, Language. LC 83-7218. 352p. 1983. pap. 17.95x (*0-8014-9886-4*) Cornell U Pr.

— Soundings in Critical Theory. LC 89-30080. 248p. 1989. 34.95 (*0-8014-2322-8*); pap. 12.95 (*0-8014-9572-5*) Cornell U Pr.

LaCapra, Dominick, ed. The Bounds of Race: Perspectives on Hegemony & Resistance. LC 91-11896. 360p. 1991. 44.50 (*0-8014-2553-0*); pap. 16.95 (*0-8014-9789-2*) Cornell U Pr.

LaCapra, Dominick & Kaplan, Steven L., eds. Modern European Intellectual History: Reappraisals & New Perspectives. LC 82-7418. 318p. 1982. pap. 16.95 (*0-8014-9881-3*) Cornell U Pr.

Lacar, Luis Q. Muslim-Christian Marriages in the Philippines: Studies Made in North Cotabato. (Humanities Publications Ser., Silliman University: No. 2). (Illus.). 100p. (C). 1981. lib. bdg. 5.00 (*0-686-31074-8*, Pub. by New Day Pub PH) Cellar.

Lacarra, J. M., ed. see Menendez Pidal, Ramon.

Lacarra, Marcel. Le Temps des Verbes. 2nd ed. 96p. (FRE.). 1984. pap. 19.95 (*0-8288-3355-9*, 2801105260) Fr & Eur.

Lacarra, Maria J., ed. see Juan Manuel, Don.

Lacarriere, Jacques. The Gnostics. Rootes, Nina, tr. 138p. (Orig.). (FRE.). 1989. pap. 8.95 (*0-87286-243-7*) City Lights.

LaCarrubba, Joseph & Zimmer, Louis. How to Buy, Install, & Maintain Your Own Telephone Equipment. 4th rev. ed. LC 81-8047. (Illus.). 52p. (Orig.). (C). 1981. pap. 5.00 (*0-930256-09-3*) Almar.

Lacasa, Jaime, jt. auth. see Noble, Judith.

Lacasa, R. & Bustamante, I. D. Spanish-English, English-Spanish Political, Legal & Economics Dictionary: Diccionario de Derecho, Economia y Politica Espanol-Ingles-Espanol. 4th ed. 763p. (ENG & SPA.). 1991. 125.00 (*0-8288-0404-4*, S39842) Fr & Eur.

Lacasas, J., jt. auth. see Noble, J.

Lacassagne, Jean Pierre, ed. see Sand, George, et al.

LaCasse, Maurice A. Nostradamus: The Voice That Echoes Through Time. (Illus.). 208p. (Orig.). 1992. 19.95 (*1-56167-088-X*) Noble Hse MD.

Lacava, Ann, ed. Guide to the Preparation of Theses & Dissertations. 7th rev. ed. 80p. (C). 1991. pap. text ed. 5.95 (*0-9625933-1-1*) Univ TN Grad Schl.

— Guide to the Preparation of Theses & Dissertations. 8th ed. 144p. (C). 1994. pap. text ed. 7.95 (*0-9625933-2-X*) Univ TN Grad Schl.

Laccetti, Silvio R., ed. New Jersey Profiles in Public Policy. 1990. 22.00 (*0-940390-05-1*) Comwealth Bks NJ.

***Lace, William W.** The Battle of Hastings. LC 95-11711. (Battles of the Middle Ages Ser.). (J). 1996. lib. bdg. write for info. (*1-56006-416-1*) Lucent Bks.

— The Hundred Years' War. LC 93-22871. (World History Ser.). (J). (gr. 6-9). 1994. 16.95 (*1-56006-233-9*) Lucent Bks.

— Michelangelo. LC 92-46996. (Importance of Ser.). (Illus.). 111p. (J). (gr. 5-8). 1993. lib. bdg. 16.95 (*1-56006-038-7*) Lucent Bks.

— Sports Great Nolan Ryan. LC 92-41693. (Sports Great Books Ser.). (Illus.). 64p. (J). (gr. 4-10). 1993. lib. bdg. 15.95 (*0-89490-394-2*) Enslow Pubs.

— Top Ten Football Quarterbacks. LC 93-40469. (Sports Top Ten Ser.). (Illus.). 48p. (J). (gr. 4-10). 1994. lib. bdg. 15.95 (*0-89490-518-X*) Enslow Pubs.

— Top Ten Football Rushers. LC 93-40470. (Sports Top Ten Ser.). (Illus.). 48p. (J). (gr. 4-10). 1994. lib. bdg. 15.95 (*0-89490-519-8*) Enslow Pubs.

— The Wars of the Roses. LC 95-14367. (World History Ser.). (J). 1995. lib. bdg. write for info. (*1-56006-419-6*) Lucent Bks.

Lace, Wm. W. Elizabethan England. (World History Ser.). (Illus.). 128p. (J). (gr. 5-9). 1995. lib. bdg 16.95 (*1-56006-278-9*, 2789) Lucent Bks.

— The Importance of Winston Churchill. (Importance of... Ser.). (Illus.). 128p. (J). (gr. 5-9). 1995. lib. bdg. 16.95 (*1-56006-067-0*, 0670) Lucent Bks.

LaCelle-Peterson, Mark W., jt. ed. see Finkelstein, Martin J.

LaCentra, Walter. The Authentic Self: Toward a Philosophy of Personality. (American University Studies: Philosophy: Ser. V, Vol. 36). 211p. (C). 1987. text ed. 35.95 (*0-8204-0460-8*) P Lang Pubs.

LaCerra, Charles, jt. auth. see Krase, Jerome.

Lacerte, Michael, jt. ed. see Shrey, Donald E.

LaCerva, V. A. Medical Examination Review: Pediatrics. 7th ed. (Clinical Sciences Ser.: Vol. 11, No. 7). 250p. 1986. pap. 18.00 (*0-444-01036-X*) Elsevier.

— Medical Examination Review: Pediatrics. 8th ed. 225p. 1990. pap. 19.95 (*0-8385-5773-2*, A5773-5, Medical Exam) Appleton & Lange.

Lacey, ed. see Cicero.

Lacey, A. A., jt. ed. see Brown, K. J.

Lacey, A. A., jt. ed. see Knops, R. J.

Lacey, A. J. Light Microscopy in Biology: A Practical Approach. (Practical Approach Ser.). (Illus.). 348p. 1989. 70.00 (*0-19-963036-4*, IRL Pr) OUP.

Lacey, A. R. Bergson. 240p. 1989. 39.95 (*0-415-03007-2*, A3519) Routledge.

— Bergson. LC 93-15348. (Arguments of the Philosophers Ser.). 256p. 1993. pap. 17.95 (*0-415-08763-5*, B2453) Routledge.

— A Dictionary of Philosophy. 266p. 1990. pap. 15.95 (*0-415-05872-4*, A4927) Routledge.

— Modern Philosophy: An Introduction. 296p. 1982. pap. 10.95 (*0-7100-0974-7*, RKP) Routledge.

Lacey, A. R., tr. see Philoponus.

Lacey, Christina K., et al. South Dakota's American Mother: The Life Story of Christina K. Lacey - South Dakota State Mother - 1946. LC 89-8452. (Illus.). 160p. (Orig.). 1989. 12.95 (*0-9622491-0-6*); pap. 9.95 (*0-9622491-1-4*) Pheasant Pr.

Lacey, Douglas. The Latin Plus. 1986. I. student ed 12.50 (*0-89894-020-6*); II. student ed 12.50 (*0-685-11183-0*); III. student ed 12.95 (*0-89894-021-4*); pap. text ed. 12.50 (*0-89894-018-4*) Advocate Pub Group.

Lacey, E. A., tr. & intro. The Delight of Hearts: Or, What You Will Not Find in Any Book. (Illus.). 240p. (Orig.). 1988. lib. bdg. 25.00 (*0-940567-08-3*); pap. 14.95 (*0-940567-09-1*) Gay Sunshine.

Lacey, E. A., tr. see Caminha, Adolfo.

Lacey, E. A., tr. see Leyland, Winston, ed.

Lacey, E. A., tr. see Zapata, Luis.

Lacey, Elizabeth A. The Complete Frog: A Guide for the Very Young Naturalist. LC 88-9343. (Illus.). 72p. (J). (gr. k-4). 1989. 12.95 (*0-688-08017-0*); lib. bdg. 12.88 (*0-688-08018-9*) Lothrop.

— What's the Difference? A Guide to Some Familiar Animal Look-Alikes. (Illus.). 80p. (J). (gr. 4-7). 1993. 14.95 (*0-395-56182-5*, Clarion Bks) HM.

Lacey, Frederick B. Resolving Modern Evidence Problems. 1985. 10.00 (*1-55681-023-7*) Natl Inst Trial Ad.

Lacey, Geraldine. Creating Topiary. (Illus.). 148p. 1987. 39.50 (*1-870673-00-X*, Pub. by Garden Art Pr UK) Antique Collect.

Lacey, H. E. The Isometric Theory of Classical Banach Spaces. LC 74-394. (Grundlehren der Mathematischen Wissenschaften Ser.: Vol. 208). 270p. 1974. 89.00 (0-387-06562-8) Spr-Verlag.

Lacey, Henry C. To Raise, Destroy, & Create. LC 80-50078. 220p. 1981. 15.00 (0-87875-185-8) Whitston Pub.

Lacey, Hugh, ed. see Ellacuria, Ignacio, et al.

Lacey, Hugh, jt. auth. see Schwartz, Barry.

Lacey, James, jt. auth. see Carothers, Gibson.

Lacey, Jerome. Financial Instruments Markets: An Advanced Study of Cash-Futures Relationships. 1986. 5.00 (0-317-65341-5) Chicago Bd Trade.

Lacey, Jim & Keough, Allen H. Radiation Curing: A Discussion of Advantages, Features & Applications. LC 80-52815. 97p. pap. 27.70 (0-317-10943-X, 2019120) Bks Demand.

— Radiation Curing: A Discussion of Advantages, Features & Applications. (Illus.). 98p. 1983. 38.00 (0-938648-15-2, 2004) T-C Pubns CA.

***Lacey, Joel.** Essential Camera Skills: The Complete Introductory Guide to SLR Photography. (Illus.). 128p. 1995. pap. 12.95 (0-240-80230-6, Focal); pap. 12.95 (0-240-82030-4, Focal) Buttrwrth-Heinemann.

Lacey, John, ed. Trichothecenes & Other Mycotoxins: Proceedings of the International Mycotoxin Symposium, Sydney, Australia, August 1984, Vol. 198. LC 85-16907. (Progress in Mycotoxins Research Ser.). 1986. text ed. 389.00 (0-471-90751-0) Wiley.

Lacey, John M., jt. auth. see Flamholtz, Eric G.

Lacey, John R. The Law & Policy of International Business: Selected Issues: A Featschrift for William Sprague Barnes. 300p. (C). 1991. lib. bdg. 44.00 (0-8191-8232-X) U Pr of Amer.

Lacey, Julia S., et al. How to Survive Your Computer Workstation: Fifteen Easy Steps to Workstation Comfort. 2nd ed. (Illus.). 208p. 1992. pap. 14.95 (0-9623656-0-2) CRT Servs.

Lacey, Kenneth. Profit Measurement & Price Changes. LC 82-48370. (Accountancy in Transition Ser.). 148p. 1982. lib. bdg. 15.00 (0-8240-5323-0) Garland.

Lacey, Laurie. Micmac Medicines: Remedies & Recollections. (Illus.). 128p. 1993. pap. 10.95 (1-55109-041-4, Pub. by Nimbus Publishing Ltd CN) Chelsea Green Pub.

Lacey, Malcolm, jt. auth. see Ward, David.

Lacey, Margaret. Silent Friends: A Quaker Quilt. LC 91-66321. 108p. 1995. 14.95 (0-935153-15-2) Stormline Pr.

Lacey, Michael J., ed. Government & Environmental Politics: Essays on Historical Developments since World War II. LC 89-22761. 336p. 1991. reprint ed. pap. text ed. 16.95 (0-943875-15-3) Johns Hopkins.

— Religion & Twentieth-Century American Intellectual Life. (Woodrow Wilson Center Ser.). (C). 1989. 47.95 (0-521-37560-6) Cambridge U Pr.

— Religion & Twentieth-Century American Intellectual Life. (Woodrow Wilson Center Ser.). 224p. (C). 1991. pap. 14.95 (0-521-40775-3) Cambridge U Pr.

— The Truman Presidency. (Woodrow Wilson Center Ser.). (C). 1989. 64.95 (0-521-37559-2) Cambridge U Pr.

— The Truman Presidency. (Woodrow Wilson Center Ser.). 480p. (C). 1991. pap. 19.95 (0-521-40773-7) Cambridge U Pr.

Lacey, Michael J. & Furner, Mary O., eds. The State & Social Investigation in Britain & the United States. (Woodrow Wilson Center Ser.). 500p. (C). 1993. 54.95 (0-521-41638-8) Cambridge U Pr.

Lacey, Michael J. & Haakonssen, Knud, eds. A Culture of Rights: The Bill of Rights in Philosophy, Politics & Law, 1791 & 1991. (Woodrow Wilson Center Ser.). (Illus.). 512p. (C). 1991. 64.95 (0-521-41637-X) Cambridge U Pr.

— A Culture of Rights: The Bill of Rights in Philosophy, Politics & Law, 1791 & 1991. (Woodrow Wilson Center Ser.). 496p. (C). 1992. pap. 19.95 (0-521-44653-8) Cambridge U Pr.

Lacey, Nelson J., jt. auth. see Chambers, Donald R.

Lacey, Nicola. State Punishment: Political Principles & Community Values. (International Library of Philosophy). 256p. 1988. text ed. 49.95 (0-415-00171-4) Routledge.

— State Punishment: Political Principles & Community Values. LC 94-17878. (International Library of Philosophy Ser.). 256p. 1994. pap. 17.95 (0-415-10938-8, B4695) Routledge.

***Lacey, Nicola, ed.** A Reader on Criminal Justice. (Oxford Readings in Socio-Legal Studies). 288p. 1995. pap. 17.95 (0-19-876361-1) OUP.

— A Reader on Criminal Justice. (Oxford Readings in Socio-Legal Studies). 288p. 1995. 59.00 (0-19-876362-X) OUP.

Lacey, Nicola, jt. auth. see Frazer, Elizabeth.

***Lacey, Nicola, et al.** Reconstructing Criminal Law: Text & Materials. (Law in Context Ser.). 568p. (C). 1994. text ed. 70.00 (0-297-82027-3); pap. text ed. 39.95 (0-297-82028-1, Trans) Northwestern U Pr.

Lacey, Pat. Rosemary Cottage. large type ed. 1990. pap. 12. 95 (0-7089-6930-5, Trailtree Bookshop) Ulverscroft.

— Summer at Saint Pierre. large type ed. 1991. pap. 13.95 (0-7089-6979-8, Trailtree Bookshop) Ulverscroft.

— The Vintage Year. large type ed. (Linford Romance Library). 288p. 1992. pap. 14.95 (0-7089-7282-9, Trailtree Bookshop) Ulverscroft.

Lacey, Paul. Quakers & the Use of Power. LC 81-85558. 32p. (Orig.). 1982. pap. 3.00 (0-87574-241-6) Pendle Hill.

Lacey, Paul A. Education & the Inward Teacher. LC 88-60795. (Orig.). 1988. pap. 3.00 (0-87574-278-5) Pendle Hill.

— The Inner War Forms & Themes in Recent American Poetry. LC 78-171500. 142p. reprint ed. pap. 40.50 (0-685-16127-7, 2026954) Bks Demand.

— Leading & Being Led. LC 85-63379. (Orig.). 1985. pap. 3.00 (0-87574-264-5) Pendle Hill.

Lacey, Penny & Lomas, Jeanette. Support Services & the Curriculum: A Practical Guide to Collaboration. 224p. 1993. pap. 29.00 (1-85346-222-5, Pub. by D Fulton UK) Taylor & Francis.

Lacey, Richard W. Hard to Swallow: A Brief History of Food. LC 93-20808. (Illus.). 256p. (C). 1994. 22.95 (0-521-44001-7) Cambridge U Pr.

***Lacey, Rick.** Cat Fever. LC 94-36091. 1994. 24.95 (0-9642466-0-0) Karson Pubng.

Lacey, Robert. Ford: The Men & the Machine. 832p. 1987. mass mkt. 5.95 (0-345-34312-3) Ballantine.

— Grace. 416p. 1994. 24.95 (0-399-13872-2) Putnam Pub Group.

— Grace. large type ed. LC 94-42978. 613p. 1995. 25.95 (0-7838-1199-3, Large Print Bks) Hall.

— The Kingdom. 656p. 1983. mass mkt. 5.95 (0-380-61762-5) Avon.

— The Life & Times of Henry VIII. 224p. 1992. 24.95 (1-55859-451-5) Abbeville Pr.

— Little Man: Meyer Lansky & the Gangster Life. 1991. 24. 95 (0-316-51168-4) Little.

— Little Man: Meyer Lansky & the Gangster Life. (Illus.). 704p. 1992. mass mkt. 5.99 (0-316-51163-3) Little.

Lacey, Robert E., ed. see Membrane Processes for Industry Symposium Staff.

Lacey, Sarah. File under: Deceased. LC 93-25498. 192p. 1993. 17.95 (0-312-09807-3, Pub. by Thomas Dunne Bks) St Martin.

— File under: Deceased. large type ed. 321p. 1994. pap. 16. 95 (1-85389-475-3) Ulverscroft.

— File under: Missing. 224p. 1994. 19.95 (0-312-10982-2, Pub. by Thomas Dunne Bks) St Martin.

***Lacey, Stephen.** British Realist Theatre: The New Wave in Its Context, 1956-1965. LC 94-44677. 1995. write for info. (0-415-07782-6); pap. write for info. (0-415-12311-9) Routledge.

— Scent in Your Garden. 1991. 40.00 (0-316-51169-2) Little.

— The Startling Jungle: Colour & Scent in the Romantic Garden. LC 88-46166. (Illus.). 253p. 1989. reprint ed. 19.95 (0-87923-712-0) Godine.

Lacey, Stephen & Hobhouse, Penelope. Lawns & Ground Cover: The National Trust Guide. (Illus.). 112p. 1993. pap. 19.95 (1-85145-874-3, Pub. by Pavilion UK) Trafalgar.

Lacey, Steve. Tales of Old - Alaska. 1993. 13.95 (0-533-10619-2) Vantage.

Lacey, Sylvia, jt. auth. see Esser, Aristide H.

***Lacey, Theresa J.** The Blackfeet. Porter, Frank W., 3rd, ed. LC 94-38594. (Indians of North America Ser.). (Illus.). 144p. (YA). (gr. 5 up). 1995. 18.95 (0-7910-1681-1); pap. 7.95 (0-7910-2491-1) Chelsea Hse.

Lacey, Thomas A. The Reformation & the People. LC 83-45583. reprint ed. 22.00 (0-404-19901-1) AMS Pr.

Lacey, Vincent A., jt. ed. see Allen, Howard W.

Lacey, Vincent A., jt. auth. see Katsinas, Stephen G.

Lacey, W. & Wilson, B. Res Publica: Roman Politics & Society According to Cicero (Scources in Translation) 346p. 1978. reprint ed. 22.95 (0-906515-09-2, Pub. by Brstl Class Pr UK) Focus Info Gr.

Lacey, W. G., ed. Census of India, 1931, Bihar & Orissa. 1987. reprint ed. 145.00 (0-8364-2070-5, Pub. by Usha I) S Asia.

Lach, Donald. Asia in the Making of Europe, Vol. I: The Century of Discovery, Book 1. 568p. 1994. pap. text ed. 29.95 (0-226-46731-7) U Ch Pr.

Lach, Donald F. Asia in the Eyes of Europe: Sixteenth Through Eighteenth Centuries. LC 90-26873. 1991. 6.00 (0-943056-14-4) Univ Chi Lib.

— Asia in the Making of Europe, Vol. I: The Century of Discovery, Book 2. 504p. 1994. pap. text ed. 27.50 (0-226-46732-5) U Ch Pr.

— Asia in the Making of Europe, Vol. II: A Century of Wonder, Book 1: The Visual Arts. 1994. pap. text ed. 24.95 (0-226-46730-9) U Ch Pr.

— Asia in the Making of Europe, Vol. II: A Century of Wonder, Book 2: The Literary Arts. xxiv, 408p. 1994. pap. text ed. 24.95 (0-226-46733-3) U Ch Pr.

— Asia in the Making of Europe, Vol II: A Century of Wonder, Book 3: The Scholarly Disciplines. 440p. 1994. pap. text ed. 24.95 (0-226-46734-1) U Ch Pr.

Lach, Donald F. & Van Kley, Edwin J. Asia in the Making of Europe Vol. III: A Century of Advance, 4 bks., Bk. 1. (Illus.). 674p. 1993. 85.00 (0-226-46753-8) U Ch Pr.

— Asia in the Making of Europe Vol. III: A Century of Advance, 4 bks., Bk. 2. (Illus.). 544p. 1993. 75.00 (0-226-46754-6) U Ch Pr.

— Asia in the Making of Europe Vol. III: A Century of Advance, 4 bks., Bk. 3. (Illus.). 488p. 1993. 65.00 (0-226-46755-4) U Ch Pr.

— Asia in the Making of Europe Vol. III: A Century of Advance, 4 bks., Bk. 4. (Illus.). 560p. 1993. 85.00 (0-226-46756-2) U Ch Pr.

— Asia in the Making of Europe Vol. III: A Century of Advance, 4 bks., Set. (Illus.). 1993. 300.00 (0-226-46757-0) U Ch Pr.

Lach, Donald F., jt. auth. see Gottschalk, Louis.

Lach, Donald F., tr. see Leibniz, Gottfried W.

Lach, E. M. New York Practice Guide: Business & Commercial, 3 vols. (New York Practice Guides Ser.). 1987. Updates. ring bd. write for info. (0-8205-1517-5) Bender.

LaChance, Albert. Greenspirit: Twelve Steps in Ecological Spirituality. 208p. 1991. pap. 13.95 (1-85230-263-1) Element MA.

Lachance, Albert J., jt. ed. see Carroll, John E.

LaChance, Carol W. The Way of the Mother: The Lost Journey of the Feminine. 160p. 1992. pap. 12.95 (1-85230-267-4) Element MA.

Lachance, Denis, jt. ed. see Manion, Paul D.

***Lachance, Gerald R., et al.** Quantitative X-Ray Fluorescence Analysis: Theory & Application. 1995. text ed. 98.00 (0-471-95167-6) Wiley.

Lachance, Paul, tr. see Angela of Foligno.

LaChance, Paul, tr. see Flood, David & Matura, Thadee.

Lachance, Paul, tr. see Leclerc, Eloi.

Lachance, Paul, tr. see Matura, Thaddbee.

Lachance, Paul, tr. see Vorreux, Damien.

Lachance, Paul A., jt. ed. see Bauernfeind, J. Christopher.

Lachant, Neil A., jt. ed. see Skeel, Roland T.

Lachapell, jt. auth. see Duquet.

LaChapelle, Dolores. Deep Powder Snow: Forty-Years of Ecstatic Skiing, Avalanches, & Earth Wisdom. (Illus.). 112p. (Orig.). 1993. pap. text ed. 6.95 (1-882308-21-2) Kivaki Pr.

— Sacred Land, Sacred Sex - Rapture of the Deep: Concerning Deep Ecology & Celebrating Life. 384p. (C). 1992. reprint ed. pap. 24.95 (1-882308-11-5) Kivaki Pr.

LaChapelle, E. R. The ABC of Avalanche Safety. 2nd ed. LC 85-21393. (Illus.). 112p. 1985. pap. 6.95 (0-89886-103-9) Mountaineers.

Lachapelle, G., jt. ed. see Schwarz, K. P.

Lachapelle, Guy, et al. The Quebec Democracy: Structures, Processes & Policies. 1993. pap. text ed. write for info. (0-07-551394-3) McGraw.

LaCharite, Christopher L., jt. auth. see Meisenhelder, Janice B.

LaCharite, Raymond C. & Brooks, Richard A., eds. A Critical Bibliography of French Literature: The Sixteenth Century, Vol. 2. rev. ed. (Critical Bibliography of French Literature Ser.). 872p. 1985. text ed. 115.00x (0-8156-2308-9) Syracuse U Pr.

***LaCharity, Ralph.** Kaddish. (Illus.). 45p. (Orig.). 1995. pap. write for info. (1-878888-21-8) Nine Muses.

LaChat, Michael R., jt. ed. see Myers, Max A.

Lachatnere, Diana. Preliminary Listing of the San Francisco Manuscript Collections in the Library of the California Historical Society. 64p. 1980. 4.50 (0-910312-51-6) Calif Hist.

Lachecki, Marina & Kasperson, James. More Teaching Kids to Love the Earth. (Illus.). 192p. (Orig.). (YA). 1994. pap. 14.95 (1-57025-040-5) Pfeifer-Hamilton.

Lachelin, Gillian, jt. auth. see Liu, David.

Lachelin, Gillian C. Introduction to Clinical Reproductive Endocrinology. 216p. 1991. pap. text ed. 70.00 (0-7506-1171-5) Buttrwrth-Heinemann.

Lacheman, E. R., jt. ed. see Owen, David I.

Lacheman, Ernest R. & Maidman, Maynard P. Joint Expedition with the Iraq Museum at Nuzi VII: Miscellaneous Texts. LC 89-1382. (Studies on the Civilization & Culture of Nuzi & the Hurrians: Vol. 3). (Illus.). xii, 307p. 1989. text ed. 47.50 (0-931464-45-5) Eisenbrauns.

Lacheman, Ernest R., et al, eds. The Eastern Archives of Nuzi & Excavations at Nuzi, Vol. 9, Pt. 2. LC 93-20366. (Studies on the Civilization & Culture of Nuzi & the Hurrians: Bk. 4). (Illus.). xii, 450p. 1993. 65.00 (0-931464-64-1) Eisenbrauns.

Lachenmayr, Bernhard & Vivell, Patrick M. Perimetry & Its Clinical Correlations. 320p. 1993. 99.00 (0-86577-480-3) Thieme Med Pubs.

Lachenmayr, Bernhard j. & Vivell, Patric M. Perimetry & Its Clinical Correlations. Blodi, Frederick C., tr. LC 93-11758. 1993. write for info. (3-13-117201-0) Thieme Med Pubs.

Lachenmeyer, Charles. Democracy As a Planning System. (Analysis Ser.). 33p. (Orig.). 1981. pap. text ed. 18.00 (0-938526-03-0) Inst Analysis.

— Productive Performance. (Analysis Ser.). 51p. (Orig.). 1980. pap. text ed. 18.00 (0-938526-01-4) Inst Analysis.

Lachenmeyer, Charles W. The Language of Sociology. LC 72-164501. 125p. 1974. pap. text ed. 16.00 (0-231-08338-6) Col U Pr.

— Thought Control in America: A New Technology Analysis. 140p. 1982. pap. 10.00 (0-938526-04-9) Inst Analysis.

Lacher, Mortimer J. & Redman, John, eds. Hodgkin's Disease: The Consequences of Survival. LC 89-2735. (Illus.). 447p. 1989. text ed. 89.50 (0-8121-1204-0) Williams & Wilkins.

Lacher, R. C., ed. Math - Chem - Comp 1987: Proceedings of an International Conference on the Interfaces between Mathematics, Chemistry & Computer Science, Dubrovnik, Yugoslavia, 22-26 June 1987. (Studies in Physical & Theoretical Chemistry: Vol. 54). 378p. 1988. 141.00 (0-444-42930-1) Elsevier.

Lachiama, Jim, ed. Pittsburgh Pirates Yearbook. (Illus.). 160p. (Orig.). 1989. pap. write for info. (0-318-64831-8) Sherman Media.

Lachica, Eduardo, et al. Asian Issues (Nineteen Eighty-Five) (Asian Agenda Report Ser.: No. 3). (Illus.). 86p. (Orig.). (C). 1986. lib. bdg. 28.00 (0-8191-5342-7); pap. 10.50 (0-8191-5343-5) U Pr of Amer.

***Lachieze-Rey, Marc.** Cosmology: A First Course. (Illus.). 140p. (C). 1995. write for info. (0-521-47441-8); pap. write for info. (0-521-47966-5) Cambridge U Pr.

Lachinov, B., tr. see Darkov, A. & Kuznetsov, V.

Lachkar, Joan. The Narcissistic - Borderline Couple: A Psychoanalytic Perspective on Marital Treatment. LC 91-28228. 224p. 1992. 29.95 (0-87630-634-2) Brunner-Mazel.

Lachlan, Angus, jt. auth. see Alhric, Candace.

Lachman, jt. auth. see Taybi, Hooshang.

***Lachman, Barbara.** The Journal of Hildegard of Bingen. 1995. 12.00 (0-517-88390-2, Bell Tower) Crown Pub Group.

— The Journal of Hildegard of Bingen. braille ed. 395p. 1994. text ed., vinyl bd. 31.60 (1-56956-550-3, BR9516) W A T Braille.

— The Journal of Hildegard of Bingen, Advent 1151-Epiphany 1153: A Novel. LC 92-40768. 1993. 20.00 (0-517-59169-3, Bell Tower) Crown Pub Group.

Lachman, Beth E., jt. auth. see Camm, Frank.

***Lachman-Chapin, Mildred, ed. & illus.** Reverberations: Mothers & Daughters. 44p. (Orig.). 1995. pap. 19.95 (1-879260-32-8) Evanston Pub.

Lachman, Charles, ed. & tr. Evaluations of Sung Dynasty Painters of Renown: Liu Tao-Chiun's Sung-Ch'ao Ming-Hua P'ing. (T'oung Pao Monographies: No. XVI). (Illus.). xiii, 115p. 1990. pap. 54.50 (90-04-08966-7) E J Brill.

***Lachman, David C.** The Marrow Controversy, 1718-1723. 517p. Date not set. 55.00 (0-946068-33-X) Attic Pr.

— The Marrow Controversy, 1718-1723: An Historical & Theological Analysis. LC 92-5154. (Rutherford Studies in Historical Theology). 516p. 1992. reprint ed. lib. bdg. 119.95 (0-7734-1649-8) E Mellen.

Lachman, Elizabeth, tr. see Hoffmann, Nicolas, ed.

Lachman, Ernest & Faulkner, Kenneth K. Case Studies in Anatomy. 3rd ed. (Illus.). (C). 1981. pap. text ed. 16.95 (0-19-502813-9) OUP.

Lachman, Frank M., jt. auth. see Stolorow, Robert D.

***Lachman, Gary.** Two Essays on Colin Wilson: World Rejection & Criminal Romantics; From Outsider to Post-Tragic Man. (Colin Wilson Studies: No. 6). 64p. 1994. 25.00x (0-8095-6776-8); pap. 15.00x (0-946650-52-7) Borgo Pr.

Lachman, Herbert M., jt. ed. see Papolos, Demitri F.

Lachman, Leon, et al, eds. The Theory & Practice of Industrial Pharmacy. 3rd ed. LC 84-27806. (Illus.). 902p. 1986. text ed. 105.00 (0-8121-0977-5) Williams & Wilkins.

Lachman, Ludwig M. MarktprozeB und Erwartungen: Studien zur Theorie der Marktwirtschaft. Walentik, Leonhard & Grinder, W., trs. 336p. 1984. 105.00 (3-88405-035-4) Philosophia Pr.

Lachman, Marvin. A Reader's Guide to the American Novel of Detection. (G. K. Hall Reference Ser.). 200p. 1993. text ed. 45.00 (0-8161-1803-5, Hall Reference) Macmillan.

Lachman, Roy, ed. see Kasschau, Richard A.

Lachman, Roy, et al. Cognitive Psychology & Information Processing: An Introduction. 592p. (C). 1979. text ed. 69.95 (0-89859-131-7) L Erlbaum Assocs.

Lachman, Seymour & Kosmin, Barry A. One Nation Under God: Religion in Contemporary American Society. LC 93-1339. 1993. 25.00 (0-517-58789-0, Harmony) Crown Pub Group.

Lachman, Sheldon J. The Foundations of Science. 15.50 (0-911586-97-0); pap. 10.50 (0-911586-95-4) Wahr.

Lachman, Vicki D. Stress Management: A Manual for Nurses. 227p. 1983. pap. 19.50 (0-685-06533-2, 792424, Grune) Saunders.

***Lachman, Yael.** 101 Crafty Creatures in Your House. LC 95-2177. (J). 1995. 14.95 (1-56261-226-3) John Muir.

Lachmann, G. Boundary Layer & Flow Control: Its Principles & Application, 2 vols., Set. LC 60-9645. 1961. 552.00 (0-08-009346-9, Pub. by Pergamon Repr UK) Franklin.

Lachmann, H., jt. ed. see Polster, J.

Lachmann, Karl, ed. Nibelunge Noth und die Klage: Nach den Aeltesten Ueberlieferungen mit Bezeichnung des Unechten und mit den Abweichungen der gemeinen Lesart. 6th ed. (C). 1960. 10.00 (3-11-000177-2); pap. 21.55 (3-11-000178-0) De Gruyter.

Lachmann, Karl, ed. see Lessing, Gotthold E.

Lachmann, Karl, ed. see Wolfram Von Eschenbach.

***Lachmann-Miller, Lyn & Taylor, Lorraine S.** Schools for All: Educating Children in a Diverse Society. LC 94-26265. (Illus.). 416p. 1995. pap. 36.95 (0-8273-5957-8) Delmar.

Lachmann, P. J., et al, eds. Clinical Aspects of Immunology. 5th ed. LC 92-48808. 1993. 295.00 (0-86542-297-4) Blackwell Sci.

— Fourteenth International Complement Workshop, Cambridge, U. K., September 1991 Abstracts: Complement & Inflammation Journal, Vol. 8, Nos. 3-4. (Journal: Complement & Inflammation). 136p. 1991. pap. 75.25 (3-8055-5472-9) S Karger.

Lachmann, Richard. From Manor to Market: Structural Change in England, 1536-1640. LC 87-40146. (Illus.). 184p. (C). 1987. text ed. 35.00 (0-299-11420-1); pap. text ed. 17.75 (0-299-11424-4) U of Wis Pr.

Lachmann, Richard, ed. Encyclopedic Dictionary of Sociology. 4th ed. LC 85-72122. (Illus.). 336p. (C). 1991. pap. text ed. 14.95 (0-87967-886-0) Dushkin Pub.

***Lachmund, Carl.** Living with Liszt: From the Diary of Carl Lachmund, an American Pupil of Liszt, 1882-1884. Walker, Alan, ed. & anno. by. LC 94-36461. (Franz Liszt Studies Ser.: Vol. 4). 1995. 48.00 (0-945193-56-4) Pendragon NY.

Lachmund, Jens & Stollberg, Gunnar, eds. The Social Construction of Illness: Historical, Sociological & Anthropological Perspectives. 240p. (Orig.). 1992. pap. 68.50 (3-515-05839-7) Coronet Bks.

Lachmund, Margarethe. With Thine Adversary in the Way: A Quaker Witness for Reconciliation. Kite, Florence, tr. LC 79-91957. (Orig.). 1979. pap. 3.00 (0-87574-228-9) Pendle Hill.

***Lachner, Dorothea.** Andrew's Angry Words. (Illus.). 32p. (J). (gr. k-3). 1995. 14.95 (1-55858-435-8); lib. bdg. 14. 88 (1-55858-436-6) North-South Bks NYC.

— The Gift from Saint Nicholas. James, J. Alison, tr. LC 95-953. (Illus.). 1995. 14.95 (1-55858-456-0); lib. bdg. write for info. (1-55858-457-9) North-South Bks NYC.

Lachner, Ernest A., jt. auth. see Fraser, Thomas H.

***Lachnit, Carroll.** Murder in Brief. 272p. (Orig.). 1995. pap. text ed. 4.99 (0-425-14790-8) Blvd Books.

Lacho, Lubomir & Biros, Florence W. Reason for Treason. (Illus.). 256p. 8.95 (0-936369-41-8) Son-Rise Pubns.

L

L

— Reason for Treason: A True Story of Intrigue & Romance. (Illus.). 250p. 1994. pap. 8.95 (0-936369-07-8) Son-Rise Pubns.

Lachs, John. George Santayana. (United States Authors Ser.: No. 536). 152p. 1988. text ed. 22.95 (0-8057-7517-X, Pub. by Royal Botanic Garden UK) Macmillan.

— Intermediate Man. LC 81-4806. 152p. (C). 1981. 27.50 (0-915145-12-X); pap. text ed. 9.95 (0-915145-13-8) Hackett Pub.

— Mind & Philosophers. LC 87-2076. 252p. (Orig.). 1987. pap. 17.50 (0-8265-1222-4) Vanderbilt U Pr.

— The Relevance of Philosophy to Life. LC 94-44987. (Vanderbilt Library of American Philosophy). 336p. 1995. 29.95 (0-8265-1262-3) Vanderbilt U Pr.

Lachs, John, ed. Animal Faith & Spiritual Life: Previously Unpublished & Uncollected Writings by George Santayana with Critical Essays on His Thought. LC 67-20665. (Century Philosophy Ser.). 1967. 39.50 (0-89197-607-8) Irvington.

Lachs, John, ed. see Fichte, J. G.

Lachs, John, tr. see Fichte, J. G.

Lachs, John, ed. see Santayana, George.

Lachs, Manfred. The Teacher in International Law. 1982. lib. bdg. 110.00 (90-247-2566-6) Kluwer Ac.

— The Teacher in International Law: Teachings & Teaching. 2nd rev. ed. LC 86-2540. 1986. pap. text ed. 69.50 (90-247-3313-8) Kluwer Ac.

Lachs, Samuel T. Humanism in Talmud & Midrash. LC 91-58956. 152p. 1993. 32.50 (0-8386-3468-0) Fairleigh Dickinson.

— Rabbinic Commentary on the New Testament: The Gospels of Matthew, Mark & Luke. 600p. 1987. 39.50 (0-88125-089-9); pap. 22.95 (0-88125-115-1) Ktav.

Lachs, Shirley, ed. see Santayana, George.

Lachterman, David, tr. see Scheler, Max.

Lachterman, David R. The Ethics of Geometry: A Genealogy of Modernity. 288p. 1989. 49.50 (0-415-90053-0, Routledge NY); pap. 17.95 (0-415-90141-3, Routledge NY) Routledge.

***Lachtman, Ofelia D.** The Girl from Playa Blanca. LC 95-9864. (J). 1995. write for info. (1-55885-148-8, Pinata Bks); pap. write for info. (1-55885-149-6, Pinata Bks) Arte Publico.

— Pepita Talks Twice. LC 95-9869. (J). 1995. pap. write for info. (1-55885-077-5, Pinata Bks) Arte Publico.

— A Shell for Angela. LC 94-36140. 208p. (Orig.). 1995. pap. 9.95 (1-55885-123-2) Arte Publico.

LaChuisa, Michael J. First Lady Suite. Date not set. pap. 4.75 (0-8222-1408-3) Dramatists Play.

— Hello Again. Date not set. pap. 4.75 (0-8222-1407-5) Dramatists Play.

— Lucky Nurse & Other Musical Plays. 1993. 4.75 (0-8222-1354-0) Dramatists Play.

***LaChuk, J.** Frank Pachmayr: The Story of America's Master Gunsmith & His Guns. (Illus.). 1995. 50.00 (0-614-04260-7) Safari Pr.

— Frank Pachmayr: The Story of America's Master Gunsmith & His Guns. limited ed. (Illus.). 254p. 1995. boxed 85.00 (1-57157-031-4) Safari Pr.

— Frank Pachmayr, the Story of America's Master Gunsmith & His Guns. (Illus.). 254p. 1995. 50.00 (1-57157-017-9) Safari Pr.

Lacity, Mary C. & Hirschheim, Rudy A. Information Systems Outsourcing. LC 92-41996. (Series in Information Systems). 250p. 1993. text ed. 43.50 (0-471-93882-3) Wiley.

***Lacity, Mary C. & Hisrchheim, Rudy.** Beyond the Information Systems Outsourcing Bandwagon: Downsizing, Rightsizing, Outsourcing...Insourcing? LC 95-12057. (Information Systems Ser.). 1995. text ed. 55.00 (0-471-95822-0) Wiley.

Lack, David. Ecological Isolation in Birds. LC 70-151286. (Illus.). 416p. 1971. 37.50 (0-674-22442-6) HUP.

Lack, Davie L. Island Biology: Illustrated by the Land Birds of Jamaica. LC 75-7194. (Studies in Ecology: No. 3). (Illus.). 463p. reprint ed. pap. 132.00 (0-7837-4831-0, 2044478) Bks Demand.

Lack, Elizabeth, jt. ed. see Campbell, Bruce.

Lack, Ernest E. Pathology of Adrenal & Extra-Adrenal Paragaglia. LC 93-32870. (Major Problems in Pathology Ser.: Vol. 29). 1994. text ed. 68.50 (0-7216-5263-8) Saunders.

Lack, Ernest E., ed. Pathology of the Adrenal Glands. (Contemporary Issues in Surgical Pathology Ser.: Vol. 14). (Illus.). 388p. 1990. text ed. 102.00 (0-443-08590-0) Churchill.

— Pathology of the Adrenal Glands. LC 89-22177. (Contemporary Issues in Surgical Pathology Ser.: No. 14). (Illus.). 399p. 1990. reprint ed. pap. 113.80 (0-7837-6812-5, 2046644) Bks Demand.

***Lack, John & Templeton, Jacqueline, eds.** Bold Experiment: A Documentary History of Australian Immigration since 945. (Illus.). 304p. 1995. pap. 39.95 (0-19-553548-0) OUP.

Lack, Leon C. Selective Attention & the Control of Binocular Rivalry. (Psychological Studies: No. II). 1978. pap. text ed. 66.15 (90-279-7644-9) Mouton.

Lack, Paul D. The Texas Revolutionary Experience: A Political & Social History, 1835-1836. LC 91-23368. (Southwestern Studies: No. 10). 360p. 1992. 39.50 (0-89096-497-1) Tex A&M Univ Pr.

Lack, Peter. Birds on Lowland Farms. 149p. 1992. pap. 35.00 (0-11-242922-X, HM2922X, Pub. by HMSO UK) UNIPUB.

Lack, Peter, comp. The Atlas of Wintering Birds in Britain & Ireland. (Illus.). 352p. 1990. text ed. 49.95 (0-85661-043-7, 784643, Pub. by Poyser UK) Acad Pr.

Lack, Sylvia A., jt. auth. see Twycross, Robert G.

***Lack, Tony & Gifford, Nigel.** Equipment & Catering. (C). 1992. 24.00x (0-907649-55-6, Pub. by Expedit Advisory Centre UK) St Mut.

Lackawanna School District Staff. Elementary Writing Folder. 1988. 25.00 (0-88047-200-6, 8805) DOK Pubs.

Lackener, Bede K. The Eleventh-Century Background of Citeaux. LC 70-152484. (Cistercian Studies: No. 8). xxii, 305p. 1972. 7.50 (0-87907-808-1) Cistercian Pubns.

Lackey, Alvin, ed. Sociological Practice, Vol. 8: Community. 246p. (C). 1990. pap. 30.00 (0-87013-278-4) Mich St U Pr.

Lackey, Dale, jt. auth. see Sunderland, Bill.

Lackey, Douglas P. The Ethics of War & Peace. 208p. (C). 1988. pap. text ed. write for info. (0-13-290925-1) P-H.

— God, Immortality, Ethics: A Concise Introduction to Philosophy. 118p. (C). 1990. pap. 16.95 (0-534-12042-3) Intl Thomson.

— Moral Principles & Nuclear Weapons. LC 84-11540. (Philosophy & Society Ser.). (Illus.). 284p. (C). 1984. 56.50 (0-8476-7116-X) Rowman.

— Moral Principles & Nuclear Weapons. 288p. 1986. pap. 22.50 (0-8476-7515-7) Rowman.

Lackey, Ellen A., jt. auth. see Armstrong, Thomas J.

Lackey, George H., Jr., jt. auth. see Friedman, Myles I.

Lackey, Larry A., Sr. How to Survive in Today's Economy. 112p. 1994. pap. 29.95 (1-885102-00-3); student ed, audio 207.00 (1-885102-01-1) Busn Mgmt Inst.

Lackey, Louana M. The Pottery of Acatlan: A Changing Mexican Tradition. LC 81-40280. (Illus.). 208p. 1982. 37.50 (0-8061-1811-3) U of Okla Pr.

— The Pottery of Acatlan: A Changing Mexican Tradition. LC 81-40280. (Illus.). 176p. 1991. pap. 19.95 (0-8061-2301-X) U of Okla Pr.

Lackey, Mary. Fifty Years of Recipes from the Ravelled Sleeve. LC 88-82333. 582p. (Orig.). 1988. pap. 12.95 (0-9621301-0-9) Ravelled Sleeve.

Lackey, Mercedes. Arrow's Fall. (Heralds of Valdemar Ser.: Bk. 3). 320p. 1988. reprint ed. pap. 4.99 (0-88677-400-4) DAW Bks.

— Arrow's Flight. (Heralds of Valdemar Ser.: Bk. 2). 320p. 1987. reprint ed. mass mkt. 4.99 (0-88677-377-6) DAW Bks.

— Bardic Voices, Bk. 1: The Lark & the Wren. 496p. 1992. mass mkt. 5.99 (0-671-72099-6) Baen Bks.

— Burning Water. 320p. 1992. mass mkt. 4.99 (0-8125-2485-3) Tor Bks.

— By the Sword. 1991. mass mkt. 6.99 (0-88677-463-2) DAW Bks.

— Children of the Night: A Diana Tregarde Investigation. 320p. 1992. mass mkt. 4.99 (0-8125-2272-9) Tor Bks.

— The Eagle & the Nightingale. LC 94-27320. (Bardil Voices Ser.). 416p. 1995. 22.00 (0-671-87636-8) Baen Bks.

— Heralds, Harpers & Havoc Songbook. Lee, Teri, ed. (Arrows Trilogy - Heralds of Valdemar Ser.). (Illus.). 40p. (Orig.). Date not set. pap. 10.00 (1-879795-01-9) Firebird Arts.

— Jinx High. 320p. (Orig.). 1991. mass mkt. 4.99 (0-8125-2114-5) Tor Bks.

— The Last Herald-Mage, 3 vols. in 1. (Illus.). 912p. 1992. 14.98 (1-56865-019-1, GuildAmerica) Dbldy Bk Music.

— Magic's Pawn. (Last Herald-Mage Ser.: No. 1). 1989. mass mkt. 4.99 (0-88677-352-0) DAW Bks.

— Magic's Price. (Last Herald-Mage Ser.: No. 3). 1990. mass mkt. 5.99 (0-88677-426-8) DAW Bks.

— Magic's Promise. (Last Herald-Mage Ser.: Bk. 2). 1990. mass mkt. 5.99 (0-88677-401-2) DAW Bks.

— The Oathbound. (Vows & Honor Ser.: Bk. 1). 320p. 1988. mass mkt. 4.99 (0-88677-414-4) DAW Bks.

— Oathbreakers. (Vows & Honor Ser.: Bk. 2). 1989. mass mkt. 5.99 (0-88677-454-3) DAW Bks.

— The Robin & the Kestrel. (Bardic Voices Ser.: No. II). 432p. (Orig.). 1994. mass mkt. 5.99 (0-671-87628-7) Baen Bks.

— The Robin & the Kestrel: Bardic Voices, Bk. II. LC 93-11286. (Bardic Voices Ser.). 432p. 1993. 20.00 (0-671-72183-6) Baen Bks.

— Sacred Ground. 384p. 1994. 22.95 (0-312-85281-9) Tor Bks.

— Sacred Ground. 1995. mass mkt. 5.99 (0-8125-1965-5) Tor Bks.

— Storm Rising. 448p. 1995. pap. 21.95 (0-88677-660-0) DAW Bks.

— Storm Warning. (Mage Storms Ser.: Bk. One). 432p. 1994. 21.95 (0-88677-611-2) DAW Bks.

— Storm Warning. 432p. 1995. pap. 5.99 (0-88677-661-9) DAW Bks.

— Vows & Honor, 2 vols. in 1. 480p. 1993. 8.98 (1-56865-083-3, GuildAmerica) Dbldy Bk Music.

— Winds of Change. (Mage Winds Ser.: Bk. 2). 448p. (Orig.). 1992. 20.00 (0-88677-534-5) DAW Bks.

— Winds of Fate. (Mage Winds Ser.: Bk. 1). 464p. 1992. mass mkt. 5.99 (0-88677-516-7) DAW Bks.

— Winds of Fury. 464p. 1993. 20.00 (0-88677-562-0) DAW Bks.

— Winds of Fury. (Mage Winds Ser.: Bk. 3). 448p. 1994. reprint ed. mass mkt. 5.99 (0-88677-612-0) DAW Bks.

Lackey, Mercedes & Dixon, Larry. The Black Gryphon. 464p. 1994. pap. 22.00 (0-88677-577-9) DAW Bks.

— The Black Gryphon. 464p. 1995. 5.99 (0-88677-643-0) DAW Bks.

— Born to Run. 1992. mass mkt. 5.99 (0-671-72110-0) Baen Bks.

— Chrome Circle. (Orig.). 1994. mass mkt. 5.99 (0-671-87615-5) Baen Bks.

— The White Gryphon. 400p. 1995. 21.95 (0-88677-631-7) DAW Bks.

Lackey, Mercedes & Emerson, Ru. Fortress of Frost & Fire. (Bard's Tale Ser.). 448p. 1993. mass mkt. 5.99 (0-671-72162-3) Baen Bks.

Lackey, Mercedes & Guon, Ellen. Freedom Flight. 1992. mass mkt. 4.99 (0-671-72145-3) Baen Bks.

— A Knight of Ghosts & Shadows. (Orig.). 1990. mass mkt. 4.99 (0-671-69885-0) Baen Bks.

— Summoned to Tourney. (Urban Elven Fantasy Ser.). 320p. (Orig.). 1992. mass mkt. 4.99 (0-671-72122-4) Baen Bks.

Lackey, Mercedes & Lisle, Holly. When the Bough Breaks. (Serrated Edge Ser.). 288p. 1993. mass mkt. 5.99 (0-671-72154-2) Baen Bks.

Lackey, Mercedes & Sheperd, Mark. Wheels of Fire. (Serrated Edge Ser.). 400p. 1992. mass mkt. 4.99 (0-671-72138-0) Baen Bks.

Lackey, Mercedes & Shepherd, Mark. Prison of Souls. (Bard's Tale Ser.). 368p. (Orig.). 1993. mass mkt. 5.99 (0-671-72193-3) Baen Bks.

Lackey, Mercedes & Sherman, Josepha. Bardic Choices: A Cast of Corbies. 272p. 1994. mass mkt. 5.99 (0-671-72207-7) Baen Bks.

— Castle of Deception. (Bard's Tale Ser.). 320p. (Orig.). 1992. mass mkt. 5.99 (0-671-72125-9) Baen Bks.

Lackey, Mercedes, jt. auth. see Anthony, Piers.

Lackey, Mercedes, jt. auth. see Bradley, Marion Zimmer.

Lackey, Mercedes, jt. auth. see Cherryh, C. J.

Lackey, Mercedes, jt. auth. see McCaffrey, Anne.

Lackey, Mercedes, jt. auth. see Norton, Andre.

Lackey, Mike. Beavis & Butt-Head: Greatest Hits. 96p. 1994. pap. 12.95 (0-7851-0030-X) Marvel Entmnt.

— Beavis & Butt-Head No. 2: Trashcan Edition. 96p. 1994. pap. 12.95 (0-7851-0048-2) Marvel Entmnt.

Lackey, Misty. Arrows of the Queen. (Heralds of Valdemar Ser.: Bk. 1). 320p. 1987. reprint ed. mass mkt. 4.99 (0-88677-378-4) DAW Bks.

Lackey, Pat N. Invitation to Talcott Parsons' Theory. LC 84-71504. 224p. (C). 1987. text ed. 28.95 (0-88105-052-0) Cap & Gown.

Lackey, Richard S., ed. Cite Your Sources: A Manual for Documenting Family Histories & Genealogical Records. LC 85-20371. 94p. 1985. pap. 9.95 (0-87805-286-0) U Pr of Miss.

Lackey, Richard S., jt. ed. see Barnes, Donald R.

***Lackey, Scott A.** The Rebirth of the Habsburg Army: Friedrich Beck & the Rise of the General Staff. LC 95-7897. (Contributions in Military Studies). 272p. 1995. text ed. 59.95 (0-313-29361-9, Greenwood Pr) Greenwood.

Lackey, Walter F. History of Newton County, Arkansas. (Illus.). 432p. 1994. reprint ed. lib. bdg. 45.00 (0-8328-4000-9) Higginson Bk Co.

Lackie, Ann M., ed. Immune Mechanisms in Invertebrate Vectors. (Symposian of the Zoological of London: No. 56). (Illus.). 300p. 1987. 75.00 (0-19-854004-3) OUP.

Lackie, Gordon L., ed. see De Grott, Anton C.

Lackie, J. M. Cell Movement & Cell Behaviour. (Illus.). 224p. 1986. pap. text ed. 34.95 (0-04-574035-6) Routledge Chapman & Hall.

***Lackie, J. M. & Dow, J. A. T., eds.** The Dictionary of Cell Biology. 2nd ed. (Illus.). 380p. 1995. text ed. 45.00 (0-12-432562-9) Acad Pr.

— The Dictionary of Cell Biology. 2nd ed. (Illus.). 380p. 1995. pap. text ed. write for info. (0-12-432563-7) Acad Pr.

Lackie, J. M., jt. ed. see Armitage, J. P.

Lackie, J. M., jt. ed. see Curtis, A. S.

Lackie, Joe & Tansi, Bill. Converting OCL to AS-400 CL. (Fastpath Bks.). 203p. 1993. pap. text ed. 99.95 (1-884322-04-2) Comp Applicatns.

***Lackie-Tarry, Helen.** Language & Context: A Functional Linguistic Theory of Register. Birch, David, ed. LC 95-3907. 1995. write for info. (1-85567-271-5, Pub. by Pinter Pubs UK) St Martin.

Lackmann, Ron. Let's Make a Movie. (Illus.). 80p. (J). (gr. 5-8). 1994. pap. 12.95 (0-9640925-0-6) Pleasant Mt.

***Lackmann, Ronald W.** Same Time, Same Station: An Encyclopedia of North American Network Radio from the 1920's to the Present. LC 95-5662. 1995. write for info. (0-8160-2862-1) Facts on File.

Lackner, Bede K., ed. Stephen of Sawley: Treatises. O'Sullivan, Jeremiah F., tr. 1984. 24.95 (0-87907-636-4) Cistercian Pubns.

Lackner, Bede K. & Philp, Kenneth R., eds. Essays on Medieval Civilization. LC 77-17068. (Walter Prescott Webb Memorial Lectures: No. 12). 178p. 1978. 12.95 (0-292-72023-8) Tex A&M Univ Pr.

— Essays on Modern European Revolutionary History. LC 76-43976. (Walter Prescott Webb Memorial Lectures: No. 11). 132p. 1977. 10.95 (0-292-72021-1) Tex A&M Univ Pr.

Lackner, Bede K., jt. ed. see Stark, Gary D.

Lackner, Helen. P.D.R. Yemen: Outpost of Socialist Development in Arabia. 219p. 1985. 30.00 (0-685-13333-8, Pub. by Ithaca UK) Evergreen Dist.

Lackner, Karl, et al, eds. Festschrift fuer Wilhelm Gallas zum 70. Geburtstag. 457p. (C). 1973. 126.95 (3-11-004062-X) De Gruyter.

Lackner, Lucas. Internal Exile. 64p. (Orig.). 1984. pap. 6.95 (0-915643-02-2) Santa Barb Pr.

Lackner, Marie & Paterno, Cynthia. Practice RCT Reading Exam, Set. 1982. 11.95 (0-937820-34-2); 11.95 (0-937820-35-0) WestSea Pub.

— RCT Reading. 198p. 1989. teacher ed 3.25 (0-937820-59-8) WestSea Pub.

— RCT Reading. rev. ed. 198p. 1989. pap. 7.95 (0-937820-58-X) WestSea Pub.

Lackner, Stephen. Beckmann. (Masters of Art Ser.). (Illus.). 128p. 1991. 22.95 (0-8109-3109-5) Abrams.

— Max Beckmann. (CAL Art Ser.). 1984. 14.95 (0-517-55000-8, Crown) Crown Pub Group.

***Lackney, Jeffery A., et al.** The Costs of Facility Development: A Comparative Analysis of Public & Private Sector Facility Development Processes & Costs. (Illus.). vi, 175p. (C). 1995. 20.00 (0-938744-90-9, R94-9) U of Wis Ctr Arch-Urban.

***Lackney, Jeffery A.** Educational Facilities: The Impact & Role of the Physical Environment of the School on Teaching, Learning & Educational Outcomes. (Illus.). vi, 118p. (C). 1995. 15.00 (0-938744-85-2, R94-4) U of Wis Ctr Arch-Urban.

Lackney, Jeffery A., jt. auth. see Moore, Gary T.

***LaCkore, Madeleine & Sexton, Christine.** Ladies First. 250p. 1995. pap. 8.95 (1-56901-564-3) NW Pub.

Lackovic, V., jt. ed. see Borecky, L.

Lackritz, James R., jt. auth. see Oltman, Debra O.

Lackritz, Wendy, ed. see Whiddon, Debra.

Lacks, Cissy. Downtown Lady. LC 76-41077. 1976. pap. 2.95 (0-933530-00-5) Beanie Bks.

Lacks, Patricia. Bender Gestalt Screening for Brain Dysfunction. (Personality Processes Ser.: No. 223). 223p. 1984. text ed. 64.95 (0-471-88046-9, Wiley-Interscience) Wiley.

Laclau, Ernesto. The Making of Political Identities. LC 93-50722. (Phronesis Ser.). 1994. 64.95 (0-86091-409-7, Pub. by Verso UK); pap. 18.95 (0-86091-663-4, Pub. by Verso UK) Routledge Chapman & Hall.

— New Reflections on the Revolution of Our Time. 300p. 1988. text ed. 42.50 (0-86091-202-7, Pub. by Verso UK); pap. text ed. 14.95 (0-86091-919-6, Pub. by Verso UK) Routledge Chapman & Hall.

Laclau, Ernesto & Mouffe, Chantal. Hegemony & Socialist Strategy: Towards a Radical Democratic Politics. 197p. 1985. pap. text ed. 15.95 (0-86091-769-X, Pub. by Verso UK) Routledge Chapman & Hall.

LaClaviere, R., jt. auth. see De Maulde, L.

Laclos, Pierre A. Dangerous Acquaintances. Aldington, Richard, tr. LC 83-45443. reprint ed. 37.50 (0-404-20149-0) AMS Pr.

***Laclotte & Ziegler.** The Louvre Antiquities. (Illus.). 296p. 1994. 35.00 (1-85759-042-2) Scala Books.

Laclotte, Michel. Larousse des Grands Peintres, Vol. 2. (FRE.). 1984. pap. 32.95 (0-7859-3945-8) Fr & Eur.

— Treasures of the Louvre. LC 92-38308. (Tiny Folios Ser.). (Illus.). 464p. 1993. pap. 11.95 (1-55859-477-9) Abbeville Pr.

— Treasures of the Louvre. LC 93-2270. 1993. write for info. (0-89660-037-8, Artabras) Abbeville Pr.

Laclotte, Michel, ed. Les Avions, Vol. 1: Des Origines a la Premiere Guerre Mondiale. 480p. (FRE.). 1984. pap. 32.95 (0-7859-4828-7) Fr & Eur.

Laclotte, Michel & Cuzin, Jean P. The Louvre: European Painting. LC 82-61016. (Illus.). 256p. 1983. 35.00 (0-935748-49-0) Scala Books.

Laco, V. I. English - Czech, Czech - English Dictionary. 576p. 1993. 39.95 (0-8288-8454-4) Fr & Eur.

Lacobucci, Ed. OS-2 Programmer's Guide, Vol. 1. 2nd ed. 1990. pap. text ed. 29.95 (0-07-881533-9) McGraw.

***Lacock, Marie-Paule, et al.** New Developments in Myocardial Imaging: Technetium 99m Tc Sestamibi. 1993. 120.00 (1-85317-112-3) Scovill Paterson.

LaCocque, Andre. Daniel in His Time. Crenshaw, James, ed. (Studies on Personalities of the Old Testament). 257p. 1987. text ed. 34.95 (0-87249-481-0) U of SC Pr.

— The Feminine Unconventional: Four Subversive Figures in Israel's Tradition. LC 89-48026. (Overtures to Biblical Theology Ser.). 128p. (Orig.). 1990. pap. 11.00 (0-8006-1559-X, 1-1559) Augsburg Fortress.

LaCocque, Andre & LaCocque, Pierre E. Jonah: A Psycho-Religious Approach to the Prophet. 289p. 1990. 34.95 (0-87249-674-0) U of SC Pr.

LaCocque, Pierre E., jt. auth. see LaCocque, Andre.

Lacoe, Addie. Just Not the Same. LC 91-44041. (Illus.). 32p. (J). (ps-3). 1992. 14.95 (0-395-59347-6) HM.

— One, Two & Three: What Does Each One See? (Illus.). 32p. (J). (gr. k-3). 1995. 15.40 (1-56294-523-8) Millbrook Pr.

Lacoius-Petruccelli, Alberto. Perinatal Asphyxia. 188p. 1987. 55.00 (0-306-42358-8, Plenum Pr) Plenum.

Lacomara, Aelred, ed. The Language of the Cross. 1977. 5.95 (0-8199-0617-4, Frncscn Herld) Franciscan Pr.

Lacomba, E. A. & Llibre, J. Hamilton System & Celestial Mechanics. (Advanced Series in Nonlinear Dynamics). 216p. 1993. text ed. 78.00 (981-02-1370-0) World Scientific Pub.

Lacombat, Michael J. & Wittekoek, Steve, eds. Optical Microlithography & Metrology for Microcircuit Fabrication. 206p. 1990. 62.00 (0-8194-0174-9, VOL. 1138) SPIE.

Lacombe. Physical Chemistry of the Solid State: Applications to Metals & Their Compounds. 1984. 200.00 (0-444-42370-2) Elsevier.

Lacombe, Dany. Blue Politics: Pornography & the Law in the Age of Feminism. 288p. (C). 1994. 50.00 (0-8020-2854-3); pap. 18.95 (0-8020-7352-2) U of Toronto Pr.

***Lacombe de Prezel, Honore.** Dictionnaire Iconologique. 1972. write for info. (0-7859-8042-3, 2-8266-0209-8) Fr & Eur.

Lacombe, J. M., et al. English Style Skill-Builders: A Self-Improvement Program for Information Processors. 4th ed. 308p. 1985. text ed. 17.12 (0-07-011317-3) McGraw.

Lacombe, J. M., jt. auth. see Cleary, J. B.

LaCombe, Joan, jt. auth. see Fruehling, Rosemary T.

LaCombe, Michael A. Medicine Made Clear: House Calls from a Maine Country Doctor. Francis, Edward L., ed. (Illus.). 400p. 1989. 21.95 (0-9623199-0-2) Dirigo Bks.

***LaCombe, Michael A., ed.** On Being A Doctor. 1994. write for info. (0-943126-39-8) Amer Coll Phys.

Lacombe, Michele, jt. ed. see Lennox, John.

Lacombe, P., jt. ed. see Delisle, L.

***Lacome.** Walking Through the Jungle. LC 92-53018. 1995. pap. text ed. 4.99 (1-56402-526-8) Candlewick Pr.

Lacome, Julie. Garden Fingerwiggles. LC 94-10448. (J). 1995. write for info. (1-56402-478-4) Candlewick Pr.

— I'm a Jolly Farmer. LC 92-47374. (Illus.). 32p. (J). (ps up). 1994. 13.95 (1-56402-318-4) Candlewick Pr.

An Asterisk (*) at the beginning of an entry indicates that the title is appearing in BIP for the first time.

— Seaside Fingerwiggles. LC 94-14877. 1995. write for info. (1-56402-479-2) Candlewick Pr.
— Walking Through the Jungle. LC 92-53018. (Illus.). 32p. (J). (ps). 1993. 13.95 (1-56402-137-8) Candlewick Pr.
Lacon Watson, E. H. Lectures to Living Authors. LC 68-54354. (Essay Index Reprint Ser.). 1977. 19.95 (0-8369-0603-9) Ayer.
Laconi, Donald V. Fundamentals of Food Preparation: A Laboratory Text-Workbook. 1995. pap. text ed. 40.95 (0-471-59523-3) Wiley.
***LaConte, Greg.** Well Versed in Business: Straight Talk Can You Relate? (Illus.). 128p. 1994. pap. 10.00 (0-9642872-0-X) LaConte & Assocs.
LaConte, P., et al. Human & Energy Factors: Factors in Urban Planning; A Systems Approach. 1982. 50.00 (90-247-2688-3) Kluwer Ac.
LaConte, P. & Haines, Y. Y. Water Resources & Land-Use Planning: A Systems Approach. 1982. lib. bdg. 126.50 (90-247-2726-X) Kluwer Ac.
Laconte, Pierre & Epstein, G. Environment of Human Settlements: Human Well Being in Cities, Vol. 1. LC 76-5192. 1976. 137.00 (0-08-020978-5, Pub. by Pergamon Repr UK) Franklin.
— Environment of Human Settlements: Human Well Being in Cities, Vol. 2. LC 76-5192. 1976. 162.00 (0-08-021177-1, Pub. by Pergamon Repr UK) Franklin.
Laconte, Pierre, ed. see World Environment & Resources Council (WERC) Staff.
Lacoque, A. & Vasquez, F. R. The Newcomer & the Bible. 24p. 1971. 3.00 (0-685-50456-5) Ctr Migration.
Lacordaire, Henry D. Henri Dominique Lacordaire: Essay on the Re-establishment in France of the Order of Preachers. Tugwell, Simon, ed. (Dominican Sources Ser.). 70p. 1983. pap. 4.00 (0-9511202-1-2, Pub. by Dominican Sources UK) Parable.
Lacoren, Nestor R. The New Woman: A Tribute to Mercedes Sosa. Latin Culture Productions Staff, ed. LC 90-61383. (Illus.). 150p. (Orig.). (ENG & SPA.). 1990. pap. 14.95 (0-9627004-0-1) Latin Cul Prod.
Lacorne, Denis, et al, eds. The Rise & Fall of Anti-Americanism: A Century of French Perception. 280p. 1990. text ed. 45.00 (0-312-04206-X) St Martin.
Lacosta, Francisco C., ed. see Poncela, Enrique J.
Lacoste, Michel C. Kandinsky. (CAL Art Ser.). (Illus.). 1988. 14.95 (0-517-53884-9, Crown) Crown Pub Group.
***Lacoste, Yves.** Dictionnaire de Geopolitique. 1679p. (FRE.). 1993. 185.00 (0-7859-8616-2, 208035101x) Fr & Eur.
— Ibn Khaldun: The Birth of History & the Past of the Third World. Macey, David, tr. 214p. 1985. pap. text ed. 16.95 (0-86091-789-4, Pub. by Verso UK) Routledge Chapman & Hall.
Lacoue-Labarthe, Philippe. Musica Ficta: Figures of Wagner. LC 94-15594. 1995. 35.00 (0-8047-2376-1) Stanford U Pr.
— The Subject of Philosophy. Trezise, Thomas et al, trs. LC 92-29837. (Theory & History of Literature Ser.: Vol. 83). 232p. (ENG & FRE.). (C). 1993. text ed. 49.95 (0-8166-1697-3); pap. text ed. 19.95 (0-8166-1698-1) U of Minn Pr.
Lacoue-Labarthe, Philippe & Nancy, Jean-Luc. The Literary Absolute: The Theory of Literature in German Romanticism. Barnard, Philip & Lester, Cheryl, trs. LC 87-10047. (SUNY Series, Intersections). 169p. 1988. 59.50 (0-88706-660-7); pap. 19.95 (0-88706-661-5) State U NY Pr.
Lacoue-Labarthe, Philippe, jt. auth. see Nancy, Jean-Luc.
Lacoue-Labarthe, Phillipe. Typography: Mimesis, Philosophy, Politics. Fynsk, Christopher, ed. LC 88-36989. 312p. 1989. 42.50 (0-674-91700-6) HUP.
Lacoume, J. L., ed. Higher Order Statistics: Proceedings of the International Signal Processing Workshop on Higher Order Statistics, Chamrousse, France, July 10-12, 1991. LC 92-21711. 1992. write for info. (0-444-89654-6) Elsevier.
Lacoume, J. L., et al, eds. Signal Processing IV: Theories & Applications, 3 vols., Set. 1770p. 1988. 346.25 (0-444-70516-3, North Holland) Elsevier.
Lacoume, J. L. & Stora, R. Signal Processing, Pt. 1. (Les Houches Summer School Processing Ser.: Vol. 45, No. 1). 1987. 115.50 (0-444-87058-X) Elsevier.
— Signal Processing, Pt. 2. (Les Houches Summer School Processing Ser.: Vol. 45, No. 2). 1987. 128.25 (0-444-87059-8) Elsevier.
Lacoume, J. L., et al, eds. Signal Processing. 900p. 1987. 213.00 (0-444-87027-X, North Holland) Elsevier.
Lacour, Barbara B. Called to Action: The Knights of Columbus in Louisiana, 1962-1992. Gomez, Irvon J. et al, eds. LC 94-76030. (Illus.). 480p. 1994. 28.00 (0-9640808-1-8) LA St Council.
***Lacour, Christian.** Dictionnaire des Noms Propres de l'Academie de Nimes. 155p. (FRE.). 1990. pap. 105.00 (0-7859-8168-3, 2869712324) Fr & Eur.
Lacour, Jean-Pierre. Lexique du Marketing. 128p. 1993. pap. 19.95 (0-7859-5641-7, 2735208230) Fr & Eur.
***Lacour, Nicole, et al.** Dictionnaire Francais-Pyreneen, Pyreneen-Francais. 1991. write for info. (0-7859-8170-5, 2-86971-317-7) Fr & Eur.
***LaCourse, Donald E., ed.** The Handbook of Solid Modeling. LC 95-4022. 1995. text ed. 89.50 (0-07-035788-9) McGraw.
LaCourse, Jon, jt. auth. see Haynes, J. H.
Lacoursiere, Roy. The Life Cycle of Groups: Group Developmental Stage Theory. LC 79-27112. 317p. 1980. 42.95 (0-87705-469-X) Human Sci Pr.
Lacous Labarthe, Philippe. Heidegger, Art & Politics: The Fiction of the Political. Turner, Chris, tr. 176p. 1990. pap. 19.95 (0-631-17155-X) Blackwell Pubs.
Lacoutre, Jean, tr. see Friedlander, Saul & Hussein, Mahmoud.
Lacouture, Jean. De Gaulle: The Rebel 1890-1944. O'Brian, Patrick, tr. (Illus.). 640p. 1993. pap. 15.95 (0-393-30999-1) Norton.
— De Gaulle: The Ruler 1945-1970. Sheridan, Alan, tr. (Illus.). 668p. 1993. pap. 15.95 (0-393-31000-0) Norton.
— De Gaulle: The Ruler 1945-1970, Vol. II. Sheridan, Alan, tr. (Illus.). 700p. (C). 1992. 29.95 (0-393-03084-9) Norton.
— De Gaulle, Vol. 1: The Rebel 1890-1944. 1990. 29.95 (0-393-02699-X) Norton.
— Leon Blum. Holoch, George, tr. LC 81-20083. 571p. 1982. 49.95 (0-8419-0775-7); pap. 29.50 (0-8419-0776-5) Holmes & Meier.
— Pierre Mendes France. Holoch, George, tr. LC 84-10912. 494p. (FRE.). 1984. 39.50 (0-8419-0856-7) Holmes & Meier.
Lacovara, Peter. Deir El-Ballas: Preliminary Report on the Deir el-Ballas Expedition, 1980-1986. (American Research Center in Egypt, Reports: Vol. 12). x, 84p. 1990. text ed. 31.50 (0-936770-24-4, Pub. by Amer Res Ctr Egypt UA) Eisenbrauns.
Lacovetta, Franca. Such Hardworking People: Italian Immigrants in Postwar Toronto. (Illus.). 336p. 1992. 44.95 (0-7735-0874-0, Pub. by McGill CN) U of Toronto Pr.
Lacqueur, Walter & Breitman, Richard. Breaking the Silence: The German Who Exposed the Final Solution. LC 93-33566. (Tauber Institute for the Study of European Jewry Ser.: No. 18). (Illus.). 320p. (C). 1994. reprint ed. pap. 17.95 (0-87451-672-2) U Pr of New Eng.
Lacret-Subirat, Fabian. Lacret: Algebra One. (Illus.). 488p. (J). (gr. 9-12). 1982. text ed. 15.00 (0-943144-03-5); text ed. 8.00 (0-685-05744-5) Lacret Pub.
— Lacret Mathematics Basic Skills. (Illus.). 467p. (J). (gr. 7-12). 1986. pap. 15.00 (0-943144-17-5) Lacret Pub.
— Lacret Plane Geometry. (Illus.). 510p. (J). (gr. 7-12). 1983. 15.00 (0-943144-05-1) Lacret Pub.
— Lacret Plane Geometry: Grade 9-12. enl. rev. ed. (Illus.). 510p. 1985. text ed. 15.00 (0-943144-15-9); pap. text ed. 15.00 (0-943144-14-0) Lacret Pub.
— Mastering HSPT-Math Skills. (Illus.). 250p. (J). (gr. 7-12). 1986. write for info. (0-318-61369-7); pap. 15.00 (0-943144-19-1) Lacret Pub.
— Mastering Math Basic Skills Workbook. (Illus.). 251p. (J). (gr. 7). 1987. pap. 8.48 (0-943144-21-3) Lacret Pub.
Lacroix, Arild & Witte, Karl-Heinz. Design Tables for Discrete Time Normalized Low-Pass Filters. 295p. (C). 1986. pap. 19.00 (0-89006-215-3) Artech Hse.
Lacroix, Jean, jt. auth. see Bougerol, Philippe.
LaCroix, Jean, jt. auth. see Carmona, Rene.
Lacroix, Jean-Guy & Levesque, Benoit. Communication in Quebec: The State of the Art. 96p. Date not set. pap. 12.00 (0-88477-026-5) Intl General.
Lacroix, Jean-Michel, jt. ed. see Remie, Cornelius H.
LaCroix, John W. Troggs & Doogles in Thistledom. (J). 1992. 7.95 (0-533-10129-8) Vantage.
Lacroix, M., jt. auth. see Magnien, Victor.
LaCroix, Mary. The Remnant. 535p. 1987. reprint ed. pap. 16.95 (0-87604-201-9, 7610) ARE Pr.
— Sons of Darkness, Sons of Light. 537p. (Orig.). 1987. pap. 9.95 (0-87604-202-7) ARE Pr.
LaCroix, Michael J. MINITEX & ILLINET: Two Library Networks. (Occasional Papers: No. 178). 1987. pap. 5.00 (0-685-34541-6) U of Ill Lib Info Sci.
***LaCroix, Nitya.** Book of Massage & Aromatherapy. 1994. 14.99 (0-517-10256-0) Random Hse Value.
— Erotic Massage: Simple, Sensuous Techniques for Enhancing Sexual Pleasure. LC 93-45576. (Illus.). 128p. 1994. pap. 15.00 (0-06-251070-3) Harper SF.
— Learn Massage in a Weekend. LC 92-53046. 1992. 15.50 (0-679-41675-7) Knopf.
— Massage for Total Stress Relief. 1991. 16.00 (0-679-73511-9, Villard Bks) Random.
— Sensual Massage. LC 90-4101. 128p. (Orig.). 1990. pap. 15.95 (0-8050-1231-1, Owl) H Holt & Co.
Lacroix, Pat, jt. auth. see Fernandes, Kim.
LaCroix, Richard. History of the Membership Campground Industry: Shangrila or Paradise Lost. Stephenson, Maye & Mooney, Gary, eds. (Illus.). 151p. (Orig.). 1991. pap. 9.95 (0-9627738-0-8) Gary Publishing.
***LaCroix, Sumner J., et al, eds.** Emerging Patterns of East Asian Investment in China: From Korea, Taiwan, & Hong Kong. LC 94-44252. 328p. (C). 1995. text ed. 60.00 (1-56324-542-6, East Gate Bk) M E Sharpe.
— Emerging Patterns of East Asian Investment in China: From Korea, Taiwan, & Hong Kong. LC 94-44252. 328p. (C). 1995. pap. text ed. 22.50 (1-56324-543-4, East Gate Bk) M E Sharpe.
LaCroix, W. L. Four Questions on Persons: A Philosophical Dialectic. LC 81-43510. 214p. (Orig.). 1982. pap. text ed. 26.00 (0-8191-2094-4) U Pr of Amer.
— Meaning & Reason in Ethics. rev. ed. LC 79-52963. 1979. pap. text ed. 16.00 (0-8191-0786-7) U Pr of Amer.
— War & International Ethics: Tradition & Today. 316p. (Orig.). (C). 1988. lib. bdg. 51.00 (0-8191-6707-X); pap. text ed. 26.00 (0-8191-6708-8) U Pr of Amer.
LaCrosse, John. Randy. 224p. 1980. 10.95 (0-932282-47-4) Caledonia Pr.
— The Story of Ch'ing. 1979. pap. 3.00 (0-932282-46-6) Caledonia Pr.
LaCrosse, Richard B., Jr. The Frontier Rifleman. 1989. 14.95 (0-913150-57-6) Pioneer Pr.
Lacroux, Jean-Pierre, jt. auth. see Haury, Pierre.
Lactantius. Divine Institutes, Bks. 1-7. LC 64-18669. (Fathers of the Church Ser.: Vol. 49). 495p. 1964. 29.95 (0-8132-0049-0) Cath U Pr.
— Minor Works. LC 64-18669. (Fathers of the Church Ser.: Vol. 54). 241p. 1965. 15.95 (0-8132-0054-7) Cath U Pr.
Lacue, Juan J., tr. see Francisco, C. T.
Lacueva, Francisco. Catolicismo Romano: Roman Catholicism. (SPA.). 6.95 (84-7228-001-2, 220146, Pub. by Edit Clie SP) TSELF.
— Un Dios en Tres Personas: One God in Three Persons. (SPA.). 6.95 (84-7228-121-3, 220234, Pub. by Edit Clie SP) TSELF.
— Doctrinas De la Gracia: The Doctrines of Grace. (SPA.). 5.50 (84-7228-193-0, 220235, Pub. by Edit Clie SP) TSELF.
— Escatologia II: Dispensational Eschatology II. (SPA.). 8.95 (84-7228-781-5, 220374, Pub. by Edit Clie SP) TSELF.
— Espiritualidad Trinitaria: Trinity in the Life of the Believer. (SPA.). 6.95 (84-7228-787-4, 222325, Pub. by Edit Clie SP) TSELF.
— Etica Cristiana: Christian Ethics. (SPA.). 6.50 (84-7228-176-0, 220237, Pub. by Edit Clie SP) TSELF.
— El Hombre: Su Grandeza y Su Miseria: Man: His Greatness & Misery. (SPA.). 5.95 (84-7228-257-0, 220239, Pub. by Edit Clie SP) TSELF.
— La Iglesia: Cuerpo De Cristo: Church: The Body of Christ. (SPA.). 7.95 (84-7228-091-8, 220240, Pub. by Edit Clie SP) TSELF.
— Mensajes de Siempre para los Hombres: Eternal Messages for the Modern Man. (SPA.). 3.95 (84-7228-609-6, 220588, Pub. by Edit Clie SP) TSELF.
— Nuevo Testamento Interlineal Griego: Interlinear Greek-Spanish N.T. (SPA.). 26.95 (84-7228-877-3, 220494, Pub. by Edit Clie SP) TSELF.
— Persona & Obra de Jesucristo: Person & Work of Jesus Christ. (SPA.). 8.95 (84-7228-471-9, 220243, Pub. by Edit Clie SP) TSELF.
LaCugna, Catherine M. God for Us: The Trinity & Christian Life. LC 91-55444. 448p. 1993. reprint ed. pap. 18.00 (0-06-064913-5) Harper SF.
— The Theological Methodology of Hans Kung. LC 81-16654. (American Academy of Religion Academy Ser.). 1982. 19.95 (0-89130-546-7, 01 01 39) Scholars Pr GA.
LaCugna, Catherine M., ed. Freeing Theology: The Essentials of Theology in Feminist Perspective. LC 92-56129. 256p. 1993. pap. 18.00 (0-06-064935-6) Harper SF.
LaCugna, Charles S. An Introduction to Labor Arbitration. LC 88-5810. 292p. 1988. text ed. 57.95 (0-275-93047-5, C3047, Praeger Pubs) Greenwood.
LaCure, Jeffrey R. Adopted Like Me. 24p. (J). (ps-2). 1993. pap. 9.95 (0-9635717-0-2) Adoption Advocate.
Lacuria, Paul F. Les Harmonies De L'etre Exprimees Par les Nombres. LC 75-36848. (Occult Ser.). (FRE.). 1976. reprint ed. 60.95 (0-405-07964-8) Ayer.
Lacy, Al. Beloved Enemy. (Battles of Destiny Ser.: No. 3). 320p. 1994. pap. 4.99 (0-88070-626-0, Multnomah Bks) Questar Pubs.
— Blizzard Bk. 3: Journeys of the Stranger. 1995. pap. 9.99 (0-88070-702-X) Questar Pubs.
— A Heart Divided. 320p. 1993. pap. 9.99 (0-88070-591-4, Multnomah Bks) Questar Pubs.
— Joy from Ashes: Battle of Destiny: Fredericksburg. 1995. pap. 9.99 (0-88070-720-8) Questar Pubs.
— Legacy. (Journeys of the Stranger Ser.: No. 1). 320p. 1994. pap. 4.99 (0-88070-619-8, Multnomah Bks) Questar Pubs.
— A Promise Unbroken. 320p. 1993. pap. 9.99 (0-88070-581-7, Multnomah Bks) Questar Pubs.
— Shadowed Memories. 320p. 1994. pap. 6.99 (0-88070-657-0, Multnomah Bks) Questar Pubs.
— Silent Abduction. (Stranger Ser.: No. 2). 320p. 1994. pap. 6.99 (0-88070-674-0, Multnomah Bks) Questar Pubs.
Lacy, Alan C., jt. auth. see Hastad, Douglas N.
Lacy, Alex B., Jr., ed. Power in American State Legislatures, Vol. 11. LC 74-216. 1966. 11.00 (0-930598-10-5) Tulane Stud Pol.
Lacy, Allen. American Gardener. 1990. pap. 10.95 (0-374-52217-0, Noonday) FS&G.
— Farther Afield: A Gardener's Excursions. 273p. 1986. 17.95 (0-374-15355-8) FS&G.
— Farther Afield: A Gardener's Excursions. 288p. 1988. pap. 8.95 (0-374-52063-1) FS&G.
— The Gardener's Eyes & Other Essays. LC 95-1574. 304p. 1995. pap. 14.95 (0-8050-3952-X) H Holt & Co.
— Gardening with Groundcovers & Vines. LC 92-56201. (Illus.). 256p. 1993. 35.00 (0-06-016913-3, HarpT) HarpC.
— Home Ground: A Gardener's Miscellany. 1992. pap. 10.95 (0-395-60730-2) HM.
— Home Ground: A Gardener's Miscellany. 1995. 21.00 (0-8446-6864-8) Peter Smith.
Lacy, Allen, ed. The American Gardener: A Sampler. LC 87-37965. 324p. 1988. 18.95 (0-374-10404-2) FS&G.
Lacy, Allen, ed. see Lawrence, Elizabeth.
Lacy, Barbara L. Cooking with Beer: In the Spirit of Things. (Illus.). 56p. 1987. pap. 5.95 (0-9617721-0-7) Golightly Pubns.
— From Grandma Lacy's Kitchen. (Illus.). 105p. 1989. spiral bd. 6.95 (0-9617721-1-5) Golightly Pubns.
— The Life & (Cooking) Times of an American Missionary in India: Recipes & Adventures of Rosetta Gempler Bell. (Illus.). 60p. 1993. pap. text ed. 5.95 (0-9617721-2-3) Golightly Pubns.
— Texas Trash: And Other Great Recipes from Good Friends in the Lone Star State. (Illus.). 123p. (Orig.). 1991. spiral bd. write for info. (0-9617721-3-1) Golightly Pubns.
Lacy, Brian. Siege City: The Story of Derry & Londonderry. (Town History Ser.). 288p. (Orig.). 1990. pap. 26.00 (0-85640-443-8, Pub. by Blackstaff Pr IE) Dufour.
Lacy, C. Rosary Novenas. 1974. pap. write for info. (0-02-645810-1) Macmillan.
Lacy, Charles, et al. Drug Information Handbook 1993. (Rapid Drug Finders Ser.). 1081p. 1993. pap. 29.50 (0-916589-05-6) Lexi-Comp.
— Drug Information Handbook, 1994-95. 2nd ed. (Rapid Drug Finders Ser.). 1189p. 1994. pap. 32.50 (0-916589-14-5) Lexi-Comp.
— Drug Information Handbook, 1995-96. 3rd ed. (Clinical Reference Library). 1995. pap. 33.75 (0-916589-31-5) Lexi-Comp.
Lacy, Creighton B. The Word-Carrying Giant: The Growth of the American Bible Society. LC 77-22655. 311p. 1977. pap. 6.95 (0-87808-425-8) William Carey Lib.
Lacy, Dan M. Freedom & Communications. 2nd ed. LC 65-19107. 122p. reprint ed. pap. 34.80 (0-8357-6120-7, 2034450) Bks Demand.
Lacy, Donald C. Healing Echoes: Values for Christian Unity. Sherer, Michael L., ed. (Orig.). 1986. pap. 6.55 (0-89536-826-9, 6835) CSS OH.
— Jewels from John. (Orig.). 1993. pap. 4.95 (1-55673-531-6) CSS OH.
Lacy, E. Readings on Historical Method. 1969. pap. text ed. 7.95 (0-8290-1180-3) Irvington.
Lacy, Edward A. Complete Guide to Understanding Electronic Diagrams. 368p. 1989. text ed. 61.00 (0-13-160920-3) P-H.
Lacy, Edward A. & Hoss, Robert J. Fiber Optics. 2nd ed. LC 92-42130. 1993. text ed. 50.00 (0-13-321241-6) P-H.
Lacy, Eric R. Antebellum Tennessee. 314p. 1980. 10.95 (0-932807-06-2) Overmountain Pr.
Lacy, G. H. Breve Historia Del Cristianismo: A Concise History of the Christian. (SPA.). 5.50 (84-7645-274-8, 223325, Pub. by Edit Clie SP) TSELF.
— Comentario Epistola a los Efesios: Paul's Letter to Ephesians. (SPA.). 5.50 (84-7645-077-X, 223139, Pub. by Edit Clie SP) TSELF.
— Introduccion a la Teologia Sistematica. 417p. (SPA.). 1989. reprint ed. pap. 9.50 (0-311-09032-X) Casa Bautista.
Lacy, George W., jt. auth. see Barzelay, Martin E.
Lacy, Gerald M., ed. see Lawrence, D. H.
***Lacy, Hermagene P.** The Descendants of Frederick & Caroline Palenske of Wabaunsee County, Kansas. (Illus.). vii, 225p. Date not set. text ed. 20.00 (0-938717-50-2) Shumway Family Hist.
***Lacy, Jack.** S.H.O.R.T.S. Some Humorous Opinions Regarding Today's Society. Gilliland, Mary E., ed. (Illus.). 120p. (Orig.). Date not set. pap. 9.95 (0-9643918-0-5) Triple J Pr.
***Lacy, James A.** Systems Engineering Management: Achieving Total Quality. LC 91-21576. (Illus.). 336p. 1995. text ed. 70.00 (0-9644627-0-2) J Lacy Consult.
— Systems Engineering Management: Achieving Total Quality. 1992. text ed. 39.00 (0-07-035789-7) McGraw.
— Systems Engineering Management: Achieving Total Quality. 336p. 1991. 36.95 (0-8306-2304-3) TAB Bks.
Lacy, Jo. Life Is a Gift: My Experience with the Serious Illness of My Child. (Illus.). 60p. (Orig.). 1987. pap. 2.95 (0-936625-11-2, New Hope AL) Womans Mission Union.
Lacy, John. Dramatic Works of John Lacy, Comedian. Maidment, James & Logan, W. H., eds. LC 67-18423. 1972. reprint ed. 24.95 (0-405-08722-5) Ayer.
Lacy, John C., jt. auth. see Miranda, Fausto C.
Lacy, John F. The Remington 700: A History & User's Manual. LC 89-91161. (Illus.). 208p. 1989. 44.95 (0-9622303-0-8) J F Lacy.
Lacy, Linda. Astrology for Dogs. LC 89-29516. (Other Dog Bks.). (Illus.). 1990. 12.95 (0-87714-142-8) Denlingers.
Lacy, M., ed. Understanding Computer Systems Architecture. 400p. (C). 1991. 75.00 (1-870941-81-0) St Mut.
Lacy, Madison S. & Morgan, Don. Hollywood Cheesecake. 288p. 1983. reprint ed. pap. 19.95 (0-8065-0830-2, Citadel Pr) Carol Pub Group.
— Leg Art: Sixty Years of Hollywood Cheesecake. (Illus.). 256p. 1981. 19.95 (0-8065-0734-9, Citadel Pr) Carol Pub Group.
Lacy, Margaret S., tr. see Martinson, Moa.
Lacy, Margriet B., ed. The Low Countries: Multidisciplinary Studies. LC 89-24778. (Publications of the American Association for Netherlandic Studies: Vol. 3). (Illus.). 266p. (C). 1990. lib. bdg. 45.00 (0-8191-7587-0) U Pr of Amer.
Lacy, Marie L. Know Yourself Through Color. rev. ed. 1987. pap. 24.00 (0-85030-825-9, Pub. by Aquarian Pr UK) Thorsons SF.
Lacy, Mary G., et al. Price-Fixing by Governments, Four Twenty-Four B. C. to Nineteen Twenty-Six A. D. 1979. lib. bdg. 69.95 (0-685-96464-7) Revisionist Pr.
Lacy, Maryanne, jt. auth. see McCall, Peter.
***Lacy, Norris, ed.** Lancelot-Grail: The Old French Arthurian Vulgate & Post-Vulgate in Translation, Vol. 3. LC 92-1674. 352p. 1995. 65.00 (0-8153-0747-0, H1878) Garland.
Lacy, Norris, tr. see Grigsby, John, ed.
Lacy, Norris J. Reading Fabliaux. LC 93-8245. 192p. 1993. Alk. paper. 30.00 (0-8153-1510-4, H1805) Garland.
***Lacy, Norris J., ed.** Lancelot-Grail: The Old French Arthurian Vulgate & Post-Vulgate in Translation. LC 92-1674. 296p. 1995. 65.00 (0-8153-0748-9, H1896) Garland.
— Lancelot-Grail: The Old French Arthurian Vulgate & Post-Vulgate in Translation, Vol. I. LC 92-1674. 456p. 1992. 75.00 (0-8240-7733-4, H941) Garland.
— Lancelot-Grail: The Old French Arthurian Vulgate & Post-Vulgate in Translation, Vol. II. LC 92-1674. 342p. 1993. 65.00 (0-8153-0746-2, H1826) Garland.
— Lancelot-Grail: The Old French Arthurian Vulgate & Post-Vulgate Cycles in Translation, 5 vols., Set. 3500p. 375.00 (0-8240-0700-X) Garland.
Lacy, Norris J. & Nash, Jerry C., eds. Essays in Early French Literature, Presented to Barbara M. Craig. 186p. 1982. 16.00 (0-917786-28-9) Summa Pubns.
Lacy, Norris J., jt. auth. see Martin, Mary L.

Lacy, Norris J., et al, eds. The Arthurian Encyclopedia. LC 87-47756. (Illus.). 650p. 1987. 16.95 (*0-87226-164-6*) P Bedrick Bks.

— The New Arthurian Encyclopedia. LC 90-237000. (Illus.). 615p. 1991. 90.00 (*0-8240-4377-4*, H931) Garland.

Lacy, Robert T. Diagnosis: Cataract. LC 82-73668. (Illus.). (Orig.). 1982. pap. 7.95 (*0-9611782-0-5*) Britton Inc.

Lacy, Robin T. A Biographical Dictionary of Scenographers: 500 B. C. to 1900 A. D. LC 90-14004. 784p. 1990. text ed. 99.50 (*0-313-27429-0*, LBD/, Greenwood Pr) Greenwood.

Lacy, Ruby. Searcy County Arkansas Marriages, Vol. III. 53p. (Orig.). 1987. pap. write for info. (*0-942977-25-4*) Lacy Pubs.

Lacy, Sondra & Kenna, Peggy. Passport to China. (Passport to Globalization Ser.). (Orig.). 1993. pap. 4.95 (*0-9635880-7-9*) Kenlay Press.

— Passport to France. (Passport to Globalization Ser.). 48p. (Orig.). 1993. pap. 4.95 (*0-9635880-2-8*) Kenlay Press.

— Passport to Germany. (Passport to Globalization Ser.). 48p. (Orig.). 1993. pap. 4.95 (*0-9635880-3-6*) Kenlay Press.

— Passport to Italy. (Passport to Globalization Ser.). 48p. (Orig.). 1993. pap. 4.95 (*0-9635880-5-2*) Kenlay Press.

— Passport to Japan. (Passport to Globalization Ser.). 48p. (Orig.). 1993. pap. 4.95 (*0-9635880-4-4*) Kenlay Press.

— Passport to Korea. (Passport to Globalization Ser.). 48p. (Orig.). 1993. pap. 4.95 (*0-9635880-6-0*) Kenlay Press.

— Passport to Mexico. (Passport to Globalization Ser.). 48p. (Orig.). 1993. pap. 4.95 (*0-9635880-0-1*) Kenlay Press.

— Passport to Taiwan. (Passport to Globalization Ser.). 48p. (Orig.). 1993. pap. 4.95 (*0-9635880-1-X*) Kenlay Press.

Lacy, Sondra, jt. auth. see Kenna, Peggy.

Lacy, Stanhope, Jr. Mukate & Will Underwood. 300p. 1984. 14.95 (*0-9612362-1-3*) L Stanhope.

Lacy, Stanley. There Are Hungry Hearts. 1992. 7.95 (*0-533-09633-2*) Vantage.

Lacy, Stephen, et al. Media Management: A Casebook Approach. (Communication Textbook Journalism Subseries). 408p. 1993. pap. 32.50 (*0-8058-1308-X*) L Erlbaum Assocs.

— Media Management: A Casebook Approach. (Communication Textbook Journalism Subseries). 408p. 1993. text ed. 79.95 (*0-8058-0659-8*) L Erlbaum Assocs.

Lacy, Stephen & Simon, Todd F. The Economy & Regulation of United States Newspapers. LC 91-36511. (Communication & Information Science Ser.). 296p. 1993. 55.00 (*0-89391-753-2*); pap. 25.00 (*0-89391-820-2*) Ablex Pub.

***Lacy, Stephen, et al.** Media Management: A Casebook Approach. (Communication Textbook Journalism Subseries). 28p. 1993. teacher ed, pap. write for info. (*0-8058-1452-3*) L Erlbaum Assocs.

Lacy, Susana B., ed. see Salazar, William B.

Lacy, Suzanne, ed. Mapping the Terrain: New Genre Public Art. LC 94-35417. (Illus.). 296p. (Orig.). 1995. pap. 18.95 (*0-941920-30-5*) Bay Pr.

Lacy, Thomas F. Kaniksu: Stories of the Northwest. (Illus.). 128p. (Orig.). 1994. pap. 11.95 (*1-879628-06-6*) Keokee ID.

Lacy-Thompson, Tony. Informix-SQL: Tutorial & Reference. 200p. 1991. pap. text ed. 46.00 (*0-13-465121-9*) P-H.

— Informix-SQL 5.0. 250p. (C). 1993. pap. text ed. 28.50 (*0-13-030727-0*) P-H.

Lacy, William J., jt. ed. see Petros, James K., Jr.

Laczko, Frank & Phillipson, Chris. Changing Work & Retirement: Social Policy & the Older Worker. 192p. 1991. 90.00 (*0-335-09931-9*, Open Univ Pr); pap. 32.00 (*0-335-09930-0*, Open Univ Pr) Taylor & Francis.

Laczko, Gina. Iroquois Silverwork: From the Museum of the American Indian - Heye Foundation. (Illus.). 17p. 1980. 7.00 (*0-685-70932-9*) Gal Assn NY.

Laczko, Leslie S. Pluralism & Inequality in Quebec. 288p. 1994. text ed. 49.95 (*0-312-10064-7*) St Martin.

Laczniak, Gene R. & Murphy, Patrick E. Marketing Ethics: Guidelines for Managers. LC 85-40107. 208p. 1985. text ed. 27.95 (*0-669-10833-2*); text ed. 16.95 (*0-669-10832-4*) Free Pr.

Lad, Usha & Lad, Vasant. Ayurvedic Cooking for Self-Healing. (Illus.). 192p. (Orig.). 1993. spiral bd., pap. 15.95 (*1-883725-00-3*) Ayurvedic Pr.

Lad, Vasant. Ayurveda, the Science of Self-Healing: A Practical Guide. LC 83-80620. (Illus.). 176p. (Orig.). 1990. pap. text ed. 9.95 (*0-914955-00-4*) Lotus Light.

Lad, Vasant, jt. auth. see Frawley, David.

Lad, Vasant, jt. auth. see Lad, Usha.

Lada, Charles J., jt. ed. see Kylafis, Nikolaos D.

Lada, D. L., ed. Network Planning in the Nineteen Nineties: Proceedings of the Fourth International Network Planning Symposium, Palam de Mallorca, Spain, 17-22. 400p. 1989. 92.50 (*0-444-88083-6*, North Holland) Elsevier.

Ladak, Alan, tr. see Lawin, P., et al, eds.

Ladak, Mohamed S. Nutty from Nut. 82p. 1986. pap. 15.00 (*0-317-57722-0*, Pub. by A H S Ltd UK) St Mut.

Ladan, A., jt. auth. see Groen-Prakken, Han.

Ladany, L. The Catholic Church in China. LC 87-23. (Perspectives on Freedom Ser.: No. 7). (Orig.). 1987. pap. 16.25 (*0-932088-12-0*) Freedom Hse.

Ladany, Laszlo. The Communist Party of China & Marxism, 1921-1985: A Self Portrait. (Publication Ser.: No. 362). 585p. 1992. pap. text ed. 24.95 (*0-8179-8622-7*) Hoover Inst Pr.

— Law & Legality in China: The Testament of a China-Watcher. Nath, Marie-Luise, ed. 224p. 1992. text ed. 36.00 (*0-8248-1473-8*) UH Pr.

Ladanye, Thomas W. Anatomy of an Affair: or Whatever Happened to "And They Lived Happily Ever After"? Van Treese, James B., ed. 212p. 1993. pap. 7.95 (*1-880416-89-1*) NW Pub.

Ladanyi, Branko, jt. ed. see Andersland, Orlando B.

Ladas, Alice K., et al. The G Spot. 256p. 1983. mass mkt. 5.99 (*0-440-13040-9*) Dell.

Ladas, G., jt. auth. see Finizio, N.

Ladas, G., ed. see Gyori, I.

Ladas, G., jt. auth. see Kocic, V. L.

Ladas, Stephen. Patents, Trademarks, & Related Rights: National & International Protection, 3 vols. LC 73-89709. 1888p. 1975. 175.00 (*0-674-65775-6*) HUP.

Ladas, Stephen P. The Exchange of Minorities: Bulgaria, Greece & Turkey. LC 77-87521. (Illus.). reprint ed. 56.00 (*0-404-16596-6*) AMS Pr.

Ladbrooke, Peter H. MMIC Design: GaAs FETs & HEMTS. (Microwave Library). 365p. 1989. text ed. 75.00 (*0-89006-314-1*) Artech Hse.

Ladbury, Ann. Dressmaking with Basic Patterns. (Illus.). 120p. 1983. pap. 19.95 (*0-7134-3850-9*, Pub. by Batsford UK) Trafalgar.

— Sewing Book. 1990. 14.99 (*0-517-00193-4*) Random Hse Value.

Ladd. Abilene: The Sharpshooter. (Gunsmoke Western Ser.). 12.95 (*0-86220-930-7*, C0722, Gunsmoke) Chivers N Amer.

— Abilene Bk. V: The Half-Breed. (Gunsmoke Western Ser.). 12.95x (*0-86220-935-8*, C0723, Gunsmoke) Chivers N Amer.

— Genetic Algorithms in C++ 1995. pap. write for info. (*1-55851-459-7*) H Holt & Co.

Ladd, jt. auth. see McLaren, Paul.

Ladd, Alex, tr. see Capoeira, Nestor.

***Ladd, Barry.** Reflections of a Country Doctor. 1995. write for info. (*0-944435-37-8*) Glenbridge Pub.

Ladd, Brian. Urban Planning & Civic Order in Germany, 1860-1914. (Historical Studies: Vol. 105). (Illus.). 326p. 1990. 37.50 (*0-674-93115-7*) HUP.

Ladd, D., et al, eds. Protection of Semiconductor Chip Masks in the United States. (IIC Studies: Vol. 8). 99p. 1986. pap. 60.00 (*0-89573-484-2*) VCH Pubs.

Ladd, D. Robert. The Structure of Intonational Meaning: Evidence from English. LC 79-3093. 250p. reprint ed. pap. 71.30 (*0-685-16319-9*, 2056235) Bks Demand.

Ladd, D. Robert, jt. ed. see Docherty, Gerard J.

Ladd, D. Robert, tr. see Pascu, Stefan.

***Ladd, Dean.** Faithful Warriors. rev. ed. Shepherd, Sylvia, ed. (Illus.). 264p. 1994. reprint ed. pap. 15.95 (*0-9638217-0-9*) Ladd Communs.

Ladd, Doris M. The Making of a Strike: Mexico Silver Workers' Struggles in Real del Monte, 1766-1775. LC 87-5897. (Illus.). x, 205p. 1988. 25.00 (*0-8032-2876-7*) U of Nebr Pr.

— Mexican Women in Anahuac & New Spain: Three Study Units: Aztec Roles, Spanish Notary Revelations, Creole Genius. (Latin American Curriculum Units for Junior & Community Colleges Ser.). vii, 87p. (Orig.). (C). 1979. pap. text ed. 4.95 (*0-86728-003-4*) U TX Inst Lat Am Stud.

***Ladd, Doug.** Tallgrass Prairie Wildflowers: A Field Guide. LC 95-6990. (Nature Conservancy Bks.). (Illus.). 1995. 19.95 (*1-56044-299-9*) Falcon Pr MT.

Ladd, Douglas M., jt. auth. see Mohlenbrock, Robert H.

***Ladd, Everett C.** The American Ideology: An Exploration of the Origins, Meaning, & Role of American Political Ideas. (Occasional Papers & Monographs Ser.: No. 1). (Illus.). 90p. (Orig.). (C). 1994. pap. text ed. 9.95 (*1-887415-00-9*) RCPOR.

Ladd, Everett C., Jr. American Polity. 3rd ed. (C). 1989. disk write for info. (*0-318-63777-4*) Norton.

— The American Polity. 3rd ed. (C). 1993. student ed, pap. text ed. 15.95 (*0-393-96352-7*) Norton.

— The American Polity. 5th ed. (C). 1993. pap. text ed. 37.95 (*0-393-96351-9*); teacher ed, pap. text ed. write for info. (*0-393-96353-5*) Norton.

— Ideology in America: Change & Response in a City, a Suburb, & a Small Town. (Illus.). 404p. (C). 1986. reprint ed. pap. text ed. 32.00 (*0-8191-5219-6*) U Pr of Amer.

Ladd, Everett C., Jr. & Hadley, Charles D. Transformations of the American Party System: Political Coalitions from the New Deal to the 1970's. (Illus.). 371p. (C). 1975. pap. text ed. 6.95 (*0-393-09203-8*) Norton.

Ladd, Everett C., Jr., ed. see Ladd, Everett C., et al.

Ladd, Everett C., jt. auth. see Roper Center for Public Opinion Research Staff.

Ladd, Everett C., et al. The American Polity Reader. Shannon, W. Wayne, Jr. & Ladd, Everett C., Jr., eds. (C). 1993. pap. text ed. write for info. (*0-393-96306-3*) Norton.

— The American Polity Reader. 2nd ed. Shannon, W. Wayne, Jr. & Ladd, Everett C., Jr., eds. (C). 1993. pap. text ed. 21.95 (*0-393-96305-5*) Norton.

***Ladd, Everett Carll & Bowman, Karlyn H.** Attitudes toward the Environment: Twenty-Five Years After Earth Day. (AEI Studies in Public Policy Ser.). 55p. (Orig.). 1995. pap. 9.95 (*0-8447-7032-9*) Am Enterprise.

Ladd, Forrest E. You Can Break That Habit. (Christian Living Ser.). 32p. 1988. pap. 2.50 (*0-8341-0056-8*) Beacon Hill.

Ladd-Franklin, Christine. Colour & Colour Theories. LC 73-2971. (Classics in Psychology Ser.). 1977. reprint ed. 23.95 (*0-405-05143-3*) Ayer.

Ladd, Gary. Lake Powell: A Photographic Essay of Glen Canyon National Recreation Area. Schlenz, Mark A., ed. (Illus.). 96p. 1994. 29.95 (*0-944197-30-2*); pap. 16.95 (*0-944197-29-9*) Companion CA.

Ladd, Gary W., jt. ed. see Berndt, Thomas J.

Ladd, Gary W., jt. ed. see Parke, Ross D.

Ladd, George E. El Apocalipsis de Juan: Un Comentario. Canclini, Arnoldo, tr. LC 78-50625. 269p. (Orig.). (SPA.). pap. 7.50 (*0-89922-111-4*) Edit Caribe.

— Blessed Hope. 1956. pap. 9.99 (*0-8028-1111-6*) Eerdmans.

— Commentary on the Book of Revelation of John. 1971. pap. 14.99 (*0-8028-1684-3*) Eerdmans.

— Creo en la Resurreccion de Jesus. Blanch, Miguel, tr. LC 77-79934. (Serie Creo). 204p. (SPA.). 1977. pap. 6.25 (*0-89922-091-6*) Edit Caribe.

— Critica Del Nuevo Testamento (The New Testament & Criticism) Chavez, Moises, tr. 176p. (Orig.). (SPA.). 1991. pap. 5.95 (*0-311-04365-8*) Casa Bautista.

— L' Evangile du Royaume. Cosson, Annie L., ed. Martin, Marie-Therese, tr. 192p. (FRE.). 1985. pap. 3.55 (*0-8297-1012-4*) Life Pubs Intl.

— Gospel of the Kingdom. 1959. pap. 7.99 (*0-8028-1280-5*) Eerdmans.

— New Testament & Criticism. 1966. pap. 11.99 (*0-8028-1680-0*) Eerdmans.

— A Theology of the New Testament. rev. ed. Hagner, Donald A., ed. 740p. (C). 1993. pap. text ed. 34.99 (*0-8028-0680-5*) Eerdmans.

Ladd, George T. Introduction to Philosophy: An Inquiry after a Rational System of Scientific Principles in the Relation to the Ultimate Reality. LC 75-3220. reprint ed. 29.50 (*0-404-59216-3*) AMS Pr.

— Knowledge, Life & Reality: An Essay in Systemic Philosophy. LC 75-3221. reprint ed. 37.50 (*0-404-59217-1*) AMS Pr.

— Philosophy of Conduct: A Treatise of the Facts, Principles, & Ideals of Ethics. LC 75-3222. reprint ed. 46.50 (*0-404-59218-X*) AMS Pr.

— Philosophy of Knowledge: An Inquiry into the Nature, Limits & Validity of Human Cognitive Faculty. LC 75-3223. reprint ed. 57.50 (*0-404-59219-8*) AMS Pr.

— Philosophy of Mind: An Essay in the Metaphysics of Psychology. LC 82-45804. 432p. reprint ed. 55.00 (*0-404-59220-1*) AMS Pr.

— The Philosophy of Religion, 2 vols. LC 75-3225. 1976. reprint ed. 82.50 (*0-404-59221-X*) AMS Pr.

— Psychology, Descriptive & Explanatory: A Treatise of the Phenomena, Laws & Development of Human Mental Life. LC 75-3226. reprint ed. 46.50 (*0-404-59224-4*) AMS Pr.

— The Teacher's Practical Philosophy: A Treatise of Education As a Species of Conduct. LC 75-3228. reprint ed. 22.50 (*0-404-59226-0*) AMS Pr.

Ladd, George T., tr. see Lotze, Hermann.

Ladd, George W. Imagination in Research: An Economist's View. 152p. (C). 1987. pap. text ed. 11.95 (*0-8138-0987-8*) Iowa St U Pr.

Ladd, Gloria. Moose. LC 89-51967. 174p. (Orig.). 1990. pap. 8.95 (*0-916383-97-0*) Aegina Pr.

Ladd, H. S. & Hoffmeister, J. E. Geology of Lau, Fiji. (BMB Ser.: No. 181). 1969. reprint ed. 80.00 (*0-527-02289-6*) Periodicals Srv.

— Geology of Vitilevu Fiji. (BMB Ser.: No. 119). 1969. reprint ed. 40.00 (*0-527-02225-X*) Periodicals Srv.

Ladd, Helen F. & Yinger, John. America's Ailing Cities: Fiscal Health & the Design of Urban Policy. rev. ed. 352p. reprint ed. pap. text ed. 15.95 (*0-8018-4244-1*) Johns Hopkins.

Ladd, James D. Amphibious Techniques. LC 84-10003. (Modern Military Techniques Ser.). (Illus.). 48p. (J). (gr. 5 up). 1985. pap. 4.95 (*0-8225-9505-2*, Lerner Publctns) Lerner Group.

— Amphibious Techniques. LC 84-10003. (Modern Military Techniques Ser.). (Illus.). 48p. (YA). (gr. 5 up). 1985. lib. bdg. 14.95 (*0-8225-1379-X*, Lerner Publctns) Lerner Group.

— Military Helicopters. (Modern Military Techniques Ser.). (Illus.). 48p. (J). (gr. 5 up). 1987. lib. bdg. 14.95 (*0-8225-1382-X*, Lerner Publctns) Lerner Group.

Ladd, Jennifer. Subject India: A Semester Abroad. LC 89-45010. 176p. 1990. pap. 16.95 (*0-933662-79-3*) Intercult Pr.

Ladd, Jerrold. Out of the Madness: From the Projects to a Life of Hope. (Illus.). 208p. 1994. 19.95 (*0-446-51744-5*) Warner Bks.

— Out of the Madness: From the Projects to a Life of Hope. 208p. 1996. pap. 10.99 (*0-446-67105-3*) Warner Bks.

Ladd, Jim. Radio Waves: Life & Revolution on the FM Dial. (Illus.). 320p. 1992. pap. 12.95 (*0-312-07786-6*) St Martin.

***Ladd, John.** Archeological Investigations in the Parita & Santa Maria Zones of Panama. (Bureau of American Ethnology Bulletins Ser.). 291p. 1995. lib. bdg. 89.00 (*0-7812-4193-6*) Rprt Serv.

— The Metaphysical Element of Justice: Kant. 192p. (C). 1965. pap. write for info. (*0-02-367100-9*) Macmillan.

Ladd, John, ed. Ethical Relativism. 152p. 1985. reprint ed. pap. text ed. 16.00 (*0-8191-4567-X*) U Pr of Amer.

Ladd, John W. & Buffler, Richard T. Ocean Margin Drilling Program Atlases, Vol. 7. (Regional Atlas Ser.). 1985. pap. 195.00 (*0-86720-257-2*) Jones & Bartlett.

Ladd, Joseph B. Literary Remains. 1972. reprint ed. lib. bdg. 18.50 (*0-8422-8141-X*) Irvington.

Ladd, Justin. The Barlow Brides. large type ed. LC 92-41190. 1993. 14.95 (*0-8161-5723-5*) G K Hall.

— The Deputy. large type ed. (Nightingale Series Large Print Bks.). 315p. (Orig.). 1992. pap. 14.95 (*0-8161-5324-8*, Nightingale) Hall.

— The Night Riders. large type ed. 322p. 1989. pap. 13.95 (*0-8161-4820-1*) G K Hall.

— The Peacemaker. large type ed. (Abilene Ser.: Bk. 1). 1995. pap. 16.95 (*0-7838-1137-3*) Hall.

***Ladd, Kevin.** Gone to Texas: Genealogical Abstracts from "The Telegraph & Texas Register" 1835-1841. 322p. (Orig.). 1994. pap. text ed. 25.00 (*0-7884-0005-3*) Heritage Bk.

Ladd, Linda. Dragon Fire. 368p. (Orig.). 1992. mass mkt. 4.99 (*0-380-75698-6*) Avon.

— Dreamsong. 320p. (Orig.). 1988. pap. 3.95 (*0-380-75205-0*) Avon.

— Fireglow. 336p. 1986. mass mkt. 4.50 (*0-380-89640-0*) Avon.

— Frostfire. 1990. mass mkt. 4.50 (*0-380-75695-1*) Avon.

— Midnight Fire. 384p. 1991. mass mkt. 4.50 (*0-380-75696-X*) Avon.

— Moonspell. 368p. 1985. pap. 3.95 (*0-380-89639-7*) Avon.

— Silverswept. (Avon Romance Ser.). 368p. 1987. pap. 3.95 (*0-380-75204-2*) Avon.

— White Lily. 384p. (Orig.). 1993. pap. 4.99 (*0-451-40363-0*, Topaz) NAL-Dutton.

— White Orchid. 384p. (Orig.). 1995. mass mkt. 5.50 (*0-451-40555-2*, Topaz) NAL-Dutton.

— White Rose. 384p. (Orig.). 1994. pap. 4.99 (*0-451-40479-3*, Topaz) NAL-Dutton.

— Wildstar. 272p. 1984. pap. 3.95 (*0-380-87171-8*) Avon.

***Ladd, Louise.** The Anywhere Ring: Miracle Island, No. 1. 176p. (Orig.). 1995. pap. text ed. 3.99 (*0-425-14879-3*) Berkley Pub.

Ladd, M. F. & Palmer, R. A. Structure Determination by X-ray Crystallography. LC 94-6538. 1994. pap. write for info. (*0-306-44751-7*) Plenum.

— Structure Determination by X-Ray Crystallography. 3rd ed. (Illus.). 600p. (C). 1993. 59.50 (*0-306-44290-6*, Plenum Pr) Plenum.

Ladd, M. F. & Palmer, R. A., eds. Theory & Practice of Direct Methods in Crystallography. LC 79-10566. (Illus.). 436p. 1980. 85.00 (*0-306-40223-8*, Plenum Pr) Plenum.

Ladd, Mark. Chemical Bonding in Solids & Fluids. 1995. text ed. 55.00 (*0-13-474933-2*) P-H.

Ladd, Mason, et al. Model Code of Evidence. xxiii, 435p. 1942. 63.50 (*0-686-91052-4*, 5070) Am Law Inst.

Ladd, R. E., jt. auth. see Forman, E. N.

Ladd, R. S., ed. see American Society for Testing & Materials Staff.

Ladd, Richard & Girard, Colette. AP French: A Guide for the Language Course. 154p. 1992. 18.45 (*0-8013-0640-X*, 78580); teacher ed 11.95 (*0-8013-0641-8*, 78581) Longman.

— AP French: A Guide for the Language Course, Set. 154p. 1992. audio 39.95 (*0-8013-0642-6*, 78582) Longman.

Ladd, Richard S., ed. Treasure Maps & Charts in the Library of Congress: A Descriptive List by a Reference Librarian. LC 64-60033. 1988. pap. 5.00 (*0-87380-161-X*) Rio Grande.

***Ladd, Rosalind E.** Children's Rights Revisioned: Philosophical Readings. LC 95-3845. 1996. pap. 18.95 (*0-534-23532-8*) Intl Thomson.

Ladd, Rosalind E., jt. auth. see Forman, Edwin N.

***Ladd, Scott.** Win 32 API: A Programmers Reference. 1995. pap. 39.95 (*1-55851-427-9*) M&T Bks.

Ladd, Scott R. Applying Zortech C. 1992. pap. write for info. (*0-201-56302-9*) Addison-Wesley.

— Applying Zortech C Plus Plus with Disks. 1992. pap. write for info. (*0-201-56303-7*) Addison-Wesley.

— C Plus Plus by Example. 1992. pap. 29.95 (*1-55851-261-6*) M&T Bks.

— C Plus Plus Components & Algorithms. 816p. (Orig.). 1992. pap. 29.95 (*1-55851-225-X*) M&T Bks.

— C++ Components & Algorithms. LC 94-26770. 476p. 1994. pap. 39.95 (*1-55851-408-2*) M&T Bks.

— C++ Templates & Tools. LC 95-9703. 428p. 1995. 39.95 (*1-55851-437-6*) M&T Bks.

— Defensive Programming with C Plus Plus: Program Planning, Diagnosis, & Design. 1993. disk, pap. 49.95 (*0-471-30341-0*); pap. text ed. 29.95 (*0-471-30339-9*) Wiley.

— Visual C Plus Plus X Insider. 1994. 26.95 (*0-471-00777-3*) Wiley.

Ladd-Taylor, Molly. Mother-Work: Women, Child Welfare, & the State, 1890-1930. LC 93-9926. (Women in American History Ser.). 232p. 1994. 39.95 (*0-252-02044-8*) U of Ill Pr.

— Mother-Work: Women, Child Welfare, & the State, 1890-1930. 224p. (C). 1995. pap. 14.95 (*0-252-06482-8*) U of Ill Pr.

Ladd, Veronica. The Look of Love. (First Love Ser.). 158p. 1995. pap. 17.00 (*0-671-53408-4*) Silhouette.

Ladd, W. Ladd Family: The Descendants of Daniel of Haverhill, Mass., Joseph of Portsmouth, New Hampshire, John of Burlington, New Jersey, John of Charles City County, Virginia. (Illus.). 425p. reprint ed. lib. bdg. 72.00 (*0-317-92810-4*); reprint ed. pap. 64.00 (*0-8328-0744-3*) Higginson Bk Co.

Ladd, W. H. Auditing Advertising Agencies. Campbell, Lee A., ed. (Briefing Ser.). 44p. 1993. pap. text ed. 20.00 (*0-89413-279-2*) Inst Inter Aud.

Ladd, William. Dissertation on the Subject of a Congress of Nations, for the Adjustment of International Disputes Without Recourse to Arms. 156p. 1994. reprint ed. lib. bdg. 47.50 (*0-8377-2415-5*) Rothman.

— An Essay on a Congress of Nations for the Adjustment of International Disputes Without Resort to Arms. LC 72-137550. (Peace Movement in America Ser.). 162p. 1972. reprint ed. lib. bdg. 22.95 (*0-89198-078-4*) Ozer.

— On the Duty of Females to Promote the Cause of Peace. 1972. lib. bdg. 59.95 (*0-8490-0765-8*) Gordon Pr.

Ladde, et al. Oscillation Theory of Differential Equations with Deviating Arguments. (Pure & Applied Mathematics Ser.: Vol. 110). 328p. 1987. 140.00 (*0-8247-7738-7*) Dekker.

Ladde, G. S. & Sambandham, M., eds. Proceedings of Dynamic Systems & Applications, Vol. 1. (Illus.). 438p. (C). 1994. 100.00 (*0-9640398-4-2*); pap. 75.00 (*0-9640398-5-0*) Dynamic Pubs.

Laddie, Hugh, et al. Modern Law of Copyright. 2nd ed. 916p. 1994. boxed 495.00 (*0-406-61697-3*, UK) Butterworth Legal Pubs.

Ladds, P. W. A Colour Atlas of Lymph Node Pathology in Cattle. (Illus.). 88p. (C). 1986. reprint ed. pap. text ed. 37.95 (*0-8138-0028-5*) Iowa St U Pr.

An Asterisk (*) at the beginning of an entry indicates that the title is appearing in BIP for the first time.

Lade, Arnie. Acupuncture Points: Images & Functions. LC 88-82703. 363p. (C). 1989. text ed. 29.50 (*0-939616-08-4*) Eastland.

Lade, John, ed. see Headington, Christopher.

***Lade, Val.** Eighteenth-Century Decoupage. (Milner Craft Ser.). (Illus.). 117p. 1995. 19.95 (*1-86351-133-4*, Pub. by S Milner AT) Sterling.

Ladefoged, Peter. A Course in Phonetics. 2nd ed. 300p. (Orig.). (C). 1982. pap. text ed. 24.00 (*0-15-515178-9*) HB Coll Pubs.

— A Course in Phonetics. 3rd ed. LC 91-78390. (Illus.). 300p. (Orig.). (C). 1993. pap. text ed. 26.75 (*0-15-500173-6*) HB Coll Pubs.

— Elements of Acoustic Phonetics. LC 62-8349. 1971. pap. text ed. 11.95 (*0-226-46785-6*) U Ch Pr.

— Elements of Acoustic Phonetics. 2nd ed. LC 95-9057. 1996. write for info. (*0-226-46763-5*); pap. write for info. (*0-226-46764-3*) U Ch Pr.

— Preliminaries to Linguistic Phonetics. 1980. pap. text ed. 11.95 (*0-226-46787-2*) U Ch Pr.

***Ladefoged, Peter & Maddieson, Ian.** The Sounds of the World's Languages. (Phonological Theory Ser.). (Illus.). 400p. (C). 1995. write for info. (*0-631-19814-8*); pap. write for info. (*0-631-19815-6*) Blackwell Pubs.

***Ladeira.** Health in the New Communications Age. LC 95-79593. (Studies in Health Technology & Informatics). 1995. 120.00 (*90-5199-224-6*) IOS Press.

Ladeira, E. A., ed. Brazil Gold Ninety-One - the Economics, Geology, Geochemistry & Genesis of Gold Deposits: Proceedings of the Symposium Brazil Gold '91, Belo Horizonte, Minas Gerais, Brazil, 13-17 May, 1991. (Illus.). 844p. (C). 1991. text ed. 120.00 (*90-6191-195-8*, Pub. by A A Balkema NE) Ashgate Pub Co.

Ladejinsky, Wolf. Agrarian Reform As Unfinished Business: The Selected Papers of Wolf Ladejinsky. Walinsky, Louis, ed. (World Bank Research Publications Ser.). 1977. 35.00 (*0-19-920095-5*) OUP.

Ladell, J. L. Needle Density, Pith Size & Tracheid Length in Pine. 1963. 50.00 (*0-686-45538-X*) St Mut.

LaDell, Leo. The Durandrium Find. Amthor, Terry K., ed. (Space Master Ser.). (Illus.). 32p. (Orig.). (YA). (gr. 12). 1989. pap. 6.00 (*1-55806-021-9*, 9105) Iron Crown Ent Inc.

— Legacy of the Ancients. Amthor, Terry K., ed. (Space Master Ser.). (Illus.). 32p. (Orig.). (YA). (gr. 12). 1989. pap. 6.00 (*1-55806-035-9*, 9106) Iron Crown Ent Inc.

LaDell, Leo, ed. see Crowdis, John.

LaDell, Leo, ed. see Foley, Tod.

Lademan, Miriam A., ed. see Hooker, Irene H. & Brindle, Susan A.

Laden & Felger. Antiperspirants & Deodorants. (Cosmetic Science & Technology Ser.: Vol. 7). 440p. 1988. 160.00 (*0-8247-7893-6*) Dekker.

Laden, Caroline S., ed. see Institute for Paralegal Training Staff.

Laden, Hyman N. & Gildersleeve, T. R. System Design for Computer Applications. LC 63-17363. 336p. reprint ed. pap. 95.80 (*0-317-09782-2*, 2007075) Bks Demand.

Laden, Janis. Bewitching Minx. 512p. 1993. mass mkt. 3.99 (*0-8217-4233-7*) Zebra.

— Fires in the Snow. 320p. 1992. mass mkt. 3.99 (*0-8217-3809-7*) Zebra.

— Moonlight Veil. 1991. pap. 3.95 (*0-8217-3495-4*) Zebra.

— Noble Mistress. 1987. pap. 3.95 (*0-8217-2169-0*) Zebra.

— Sapphire Temptation. 320p. 1990. pap. 3.95 (*0-8217-3054-1*) Zebra.

— Scottish Rose. 1989. pap. 3.95 (*0-8217-2750-8*) Zebra.

— A Whisper of Scandal. 448p. 1993. mass mkt. 3.99 (*0-8217-4106-3*) Zebra.

Laden, Marie-Paule. Self-Imitation in the Eighteenth-Century Novel. 196p. 1987. text ed. 32.50 (*0-691-06705-8*) Princeton U Pr.

Laden, Nina. The Night I Followed the Dog. LC 93-31008. (J). 1994. 13.95 (*0-8118-0647-2*) Chronicle Bks.

— Private I. Guana: The Case of the Missing Chameleon. LC 95-2828. (J). 1995. write for info. (*0-8118-0940-4*) Chronicle Bks.

Ladenburg, R. W., et al, eds. Physical Measurements in Gas Dynamics & Combustion. LC 54-13127. 606p. reprint ed. pap. 172.80 (*0-317-09134-4*, 2000097) Bks Demand.

Ladenburg, Thomas. The Causes of the American Revolution. (SSEC American History Ser.). (Illus.). 132p. (Orig.). 1989. pap. 21.95 (*0-89994-326-8*) Soc Sci Ed.

— The Federalist Era. (American History Ser.). (Illus.). 86p. (Orig.). 1989. pap. 18.95 (*0-89994-327-6*) Soc Sci Ed.

— Making the Constitution. (SSEC American History Ser.). (Illus.). 166p. (Orig.). 1988. pap. 21.95 (*0-89994-321-7*) Soc Sci Ed.

Ladenburg, Thomas & Tegnell, Geoffrey. From Hot to Cold War. (SSEC American History Ser.). (Illus.). (Orig.). 1990. pap. 21.95 (*0-89994-354-3*) Soc Sci Ed.

Ladendecker, Dianne. Holidays & Holy Days, Vol. 2. 44p. 1988. pap. text ed. 6.95 (*0-8497-4856-9*, C8811) Kjos.

Ladendorf, Sandra F. Successful Southern Gardening: A Practical Guide for Year-round Beauty. LC 88-20634. (Illus.). x, 294p. (C). 1989. 29.95 (*0-8078-1831-3*); pap. 16.95 (*0-8078-4241-9*) U of NC Pr.

Ladenheim-Gil, Randy, ed. see Machlin, Milt.

Ladenheim, Melissa. The Sauna in Central New York. (Illus.). xiv, 25p. (Orig.). 1986. pap. 2.95 (*0-942690-35-4*) DeWitt Hist.

Ladenheim, Randy, ed. see Feldman, David.

Ladenheim, Randy, ed. see Quinn, James.

Ladenson, Alex. Library Law & Legislation in the United States. LC 81-23176. (Library Administration Ser.: No. 1). 203p. 1982. 20.00 (*0-8108-1513-3*) Scarecrow.

Ladenson, Alex, ed. American Library Laws. LC 83-21543. 2019p. reprint ed. pap. 180.00 (*0-7837-5915-0*, 2045714) Bks Demand.

***Ladenson, Robert F.** Ethics in the American Workplace: Policies & Decisions. 500p. (Orig.). 1995. pap. 34.90 (*0-934753-41-5*) LRP Pubns.

Lader, Curt, jt. auth. see Klose, Nelson.

Lader, Errol. Diagnosis & Treatment of Temporomandibular Joint & Myofascial Pain Dysfunctions. Hogue, Calvin, tr. LC 83-50819. (Illus.). 150p. 1983. pap. text ed. 75.00 (*0-9610782-4-3*) Vadare.

— Handbook of Exercises for Eliminating Headaches. (Illus.). 65p. 1983. pap. 2.95 (*0-9610782-6-X*) Vadare.

— Managing Chronic Orofacial Pain with Transcutaneous Electroneural Stimulation. LC 85-50702. (Illus.). 300p. 1986. pap. text ed. 85.00 (*0-9610782-5-1*) Vadare.

— TMJ: Clinical & Practice Managememt. 116p. ring bd. 85. 00 (*0-9610782-0-0*) Vadare.

— TMJ: Systems Manual of Insurance & Practice Management. 97p. spiral bd. 65.00 (*0-9610782-1-9*) Vadare.

Lader, I. Will. PM & the Art of Not Taking Out the Garbage. 1991. pap. write for info. (*1-878515-41-1*) W S Dawson.

Lader, Lawrence. Abortion. LC 66-18592. 1966. 5.95 (*0-672-50601-7*, Bobbs) Macmillan.

— The Margaret Sanger Story, & the Fight for Birth Control. LC 73-11855. (Illus.). 352p. 1975. reprint ed. text ed. 65.00 (*0-8371-7076-1*, LAMS, Greenwood Pr) Greenwood.

— A Private Matter: RU-486 & the Abortion Crisis. 250p. 1995. 24.95 (*1-57392-012-6*) Prometheus Bks.

— Ru Four Hundred Eighty-Six: The Pill That Could End the Abortion Wars & Why American Women Don't Have It. 1991. 16.30 (*0-201-57069-6*) Addison-Wesley.

— RU486: The Pill That Could End the Abortion Wars & Why American Women Don't Have It. 1992. pap. 9.57 (*0-201-60819-7*) Addison-Wesley.

***Lader, Malcolm.** The Age of Anxiety: A Reassessment. 24p. 1984. pap. 4.00 (*0-904674-09-6*, Pub. by Octagon Pr UK) ISHK Bk Service.

Lader, Malcolm, ed. Priorities in Psychiatric Research. LC 80-40583. 245p. reprint ed. pap. 69.90 (*0-317-26111-8*, 2024280) Bks Demand.

Lader, Malcolm, jt. ed. see Edwards, Griffith.

Lader, Malcolm H., ed. Psychopharmacology of Addiction. (British Association for Psychopharmacology Monographs: No. 10). (Illus.). 194p. 1988. 55.00 (*0-19-261626-9*) OUP.

— Studies of Schizophrenia: Papers Read at the World Psychiatric Association Symposium, "Current Concepts of Schizophrenia", London, November, 1972. LC 76-382728. (British Journal of Psychiatry. Special Publication Ser.: No. 10). 170p. reprint ed. pap. 48.50 (*0-318-34928-0*, 2031465) Bks Demand.

Lader, Malcolm H. & Herrington, Reginald. Biological Treatments in Psychiatry. (Illus.). 416p. 1990. 80.00 (*0-19-261644-7*); pap. 37.50 (*0-19-261939-X*) OUP.

Lader, Malcolm H., jt. ed. see Clare, A. W.

Lader, Malcolm H., jt. auth. see Edwards, J. G.

Lader, Malcolm H., et al. Patterns of Improvement in Depressed In-Patients. (Maudsley Monographs: No. 30). 128p. 1987. 45.00 (*0-19-712154-3*) OUP.

Lader, Malcolm H., et al, eds. The Nature of Alcohol & Drug-Related Problems. (Society for the Study of Addiction Monograph Ser.: No. 2). (Illus.). 232p. 1992. 67.50 (*0-19-262138-6*) OUP.

Lader, Melvin P. Arshile Gorky. LC 84-24268. (Modern Masters Ser.). (Illus.). 128p. 1985. 32.95 (*0-89659-525-0*); pap. 22.95 (*1-55859-249-0*) Abbeville Pr.

Lader, Melvin P., contrib. Arshile Gorky: Three Decades of Drawings. LC 90-62329. (Illus.). 72p. 1990. pap. 20.00 (*0-935037-38-1*) G Peters Gallery.

Laderer, Mandy. Fit-Kids: Getting Kids Hooked on Fitness Fun. LC 93-74028. 200p. 1994. pap. 19.95 (*0-9639178-1-1*) Allure Pubng.

***Laderman.** Business Week's Guide to Mutual Funds. 5th ed. 1995. pap. text ed. 14.94 (*0-07-035216-X*) McGraw.

— Business Week's Guide to Mutual Funds. 5th ed. 1995. 24.95 (*0-07-035215-1*) McGraw.

Laderman, Carol. Taming the Wind of Desire: Psychology, Medicine, & Aesthetics in Malay Shamanistic Performance. LC 90-38031. (Comparative Studies of Health Systems & Medical Care: Vol. 29). (Illus.). 386p. 1991. 40.00 (*0-520-06916-1*); pap. 16.00 (*0-520-08258-3*) U CA Pr.

— Wives & Midwives: Childbirth & Nutrition in Rural Malaysia. LC 83-47664. (Comparative Studies of Health Systems & Medical Care: Vol. 7). (Illus.). 267p. (C). 1984. 48.00 (*0-520-04924-1*); pap. 13.00 (*0-520-06036-9*) U CA Pr.

Laderman, Jeffrey M. Business Week's Guide to Mutual Funds. 4th ed. 1994. pap. text ed. 14.95 (*0-07-035961-X*) McGraw.

— Business Week's Guide to Mutual Funds. 4th ed. 1994. text ed. 24.95 (*0-07-035960-1*) McGraw.

Ladeveze, P., ed. Local Effects in the Analysis of Structures. (Studies in Applied Mechanics: Vol. 12). 342p. 1985. 107.75 (*0-444-42520-9*) Elsevier.

Ladeveze, P. & Zienkiewicz, O. C., eds. New Advances in Computational Structural Mechanics: Proceedings of the European Conference on New Advances in Computational Structural Mechanics, Giens, France, 2-5 April 1991. LC 92-9902. (Studies in Applied Mechanics: Vol. 32). 1992. write for info. (*0-444-89057-2*) Elsevier.

Ladew, Donald P. Stradivarius. 304p. 1995. 21.95 (*0-7867-0136-6*) Carroll & Graf.

Ladewig, D., ed. Drogen & Alkohol. (Illus.). xii, 220p. 1980. pap. 26.50 (*3-8055-1624-X*) S Karger.

— Drogen & Alkohol Series, Vol. 3: Folgestudien und Therapieabbruch. (Illus.). vi, 174p. (GER.). 1984. pap. 46.50 (*3-8055-3874-X*) S Karger.

Ladewig, D., jt. ed. see Pletscher, A.

Ladewig, James. Antonio Mortaro, Primo De Canzoni Da Sonare a Quattra Voci. LC 88-754002. (Italian Instrumental Music of the Sixteenth & Early Seventeenth Centuries Ser.: Vol. 13). 168p. 1989. 76.00 (*0-8240-4512-2*) Garland.

— Giovanni Domenico Rognoni Taeggio: Canzoni a 4. & 8. Voci...Libro Primo (Milan, 1605) LC 92-34416. (Italian Instrumental Music of the Sixteenth & Early Seventeenth Centuries Ser.: Vol. 16). 264p. 1993. 82.00 (*0-8240-4515-7*) Garland.

Ladewig, James, ed. Agostino Soderini: Canzoni a 4. & 8. Voci...Libro Primo (Milan, 1608) LC 91-760648. (Italian Instrumental Music of the Sixteenth & Early Seventeenth Centuries Ser.: Vol. 19). 264p. 1992. 75.00 (*0-8240-4518-1*) Garland.

— Annibale Padovano: Il Primo Libro de Ricercari a Quattro Voci, Venice, 1556. LC 93-48854. (Italian Instrumental Music of the Sixteenth & Early Seventeenth Centuries Ser.: Vol. 4). 208p. 1994. 69.00 (*0-8240-4503-3*) Garland.

— Canzonas & Capricio from the Seconda Aggiunta Alli Concerti Raccolti Dal Molto Reverendo Don Francesco Lucino a Due, Tre e Quattro Voci, di Diversi Eccellenti Autori...Novamente Raccolta, & Data in Luce Da Filippo Lomazzo, (Milan, 1617) & Nicolo Corradini il Primo Libro De Canzoni Francese a 4. & Alcune Suonate (Venice, 1624) LC 94-43627. (Italian Instrumental Music of the Sixteenth & Seventeenth Centuries Ser.: Vol. 29). 224p. 1995. 78.00 (*0-8240-4528-9*) Garland.

— Claudio Merulo: Il Primo Libro de Recercari da Cantare, a Quattro Voci. Venice, 1574. LC 87-750977. (Italian Instrumental Music of the Sixteenth & Early Seventeenth Centuries Ser.). 235p. 1987. lib. bdg. 86.00 (*0-8240-4504-1*) Garland.

— Claudio Merulo: Ricercari da Cantare a Quattro Voci-- Libro Terzo - Venice 1608, Vol. 7. LC 87-754765. (Italian Instrumental Music of the Sixteenth & Early Seventeenth Centuries Ser.). 1988. lib. bdg. 86.00 (*0-8240-4506-8*) Garland.

— Claudio Merulo: Ricercari da Cantare a Quattro Voci... Libro Secondo, Venice, 1607. LC 87-752604. (Italian Instrumental Music of the Sixteenth & Early Seventeenth Centuries Ser.: Vol. 6). 1987. lib. bdg. 92.00 (*0-8240-4505-X*) Garland.

— Francesco Rovigo & Ruggier Trofeo Canzoni da Suonare a Quattro et a otto Milan (1613) LC 88-750072. (Italian Instrumental Music of the Sixteenth & Early Seventeenth Centuries Ser.). 174p. 1988. lib. bdg. 76.00 (*0-8240-4521-1*) Garland.

— Francesco Usper: Ricercari et Arte Francesi a Quattro Voci (Venice, 1595) LC 89-756045. (Italian Instrumental Music of the Sixteenth & Early Seventeenth Centuries Ser.: Vol. 11). 158p. 1990. 76.00 (*0-8240-4510-6*) Garland.

— Giacomo Filippo Biumi: Canzoni Alla Francese a 4. & a 8. Con Alcune Arie de Correnti a 4 (Milan, 1627) LC 89-754694. (Italian Instrumental Music of the Sixteenth & Early Seventeenth Centuries Ser.: Vol. 30). 204p. 1990. 81.00 (*0-8240-4529-7*) Garland.

— Giovanni Antonio Cangiasi: Scherzi Forastieri Per Suonare a Quattro Voci (Milan, 1614) LC 91-751636. (Italian Instrumental Music of the Sixteenth & Early Seventeenth Centuries Ser.: Vol. 24). 181p. 1991. 86.00 (*0-8240-4523-8*) Garland.

— Jacques Buus: Il Secondo Libro di Recercari, da Cantare, & Sonare d'Organo & Altri Stromenti, a Quatro Voci, Venice, 1549. LC 92-43817. (Italian Instrumental Music of the Sixteenth & Early Seventeenth Centuries Ser.: Vol. 3). 192p. 1993. 66.00 (*0-8240-4502-5*) Garland.

— Lodovico Viadana: Sinfonie Musicali a Otto Voci... Commode Per Concertare con Ogni Sorte Di Stromenti.. .Opera XVIII (Venice, 1610), Pt. 1 & 2. LC 93-29317. (Italian Instrumental Music of the Sixteenth & Early Seventeenth Centuries Ser.: Vol. 21). (Illus.). 504p. 1994. 158.00 (*0-8240-4520-3*) Garland.

— Ottavio Bariolla: Caprici, Overo Canzoni a Quattro... Libro Terzo (Milan, 1594) LC 94-47251. (Italian Instrumental Music of the Sixteenth & Seventeenth Centuries Ser.: Vol. 12). 216p. 1995. 80.00 (*0-8240-4511-4*) Garland.

— Pietro Lappi: Canconi da Suonare ... a 4. 5. 6. 7. 8. 9. 10. 11. 12 & 13. Libro Primo (Venice, 1616) LC 90-754170. (Italian Instrumental Music of the Sixteenth & Early Seventeenth Centuries Ser.: Vol. 26). 328p. 1991. 86.00 (*0-8240-4525-4*) Garland.

— Stefano Bernardi: Sonatas & Sinfonias from the "Motetti in Cantilena a Quattro Voci, con Alcune Canzoni per Sonare con Ogni Sorte di Strumenti" (Venice, 1613) & the "Concerti Academici con Varia di Sinfonie a Sei Voci...Libro Primo" (Venice, 1615-1616) LC 91-761355. (Italian Instrumental Music of the Sixteenth & Early Seventeenth Centuries Ser.: Vol. 23). 192p. 1992. 68.00 (*0-8240-4522-X*) Garland.

Ladewig, James, ed. see Grillo, Giovanni B.

Ladewig, Patricia A., et al. Essentials of Maternal-Newborn Nursing. 700p. (C). 1986. text ed. write for info. (*0-201-12680-X*, Health Sci) Addison-Wesley.

— Essentials of Maternal-Newborn Nursing. 2nd ed. Hunter, Debra, ed. 889p. (C). 1990. text ed. 56.95 (*0-201-13238-9*); write for info. (*0-201-53238-7*) Addison-Wesley.

— Essentials of Maternal-Newborn Nursing. 3rd ed. LC 93-36915. 909p. (C). 1994. text ed. 56.95 (*0-8053-5589-8*) Benjamin-Cummings.

Ladewig, Theodor, et al, eds. Vergils Gedichte, Band 1: Bukolika und Georgika. xlii, 292p. (GER.). 1973. write for info. (*3-296-15871-5*, Pub. by Georg Olms GW) Lubrecht & Cramer.

— Vergils Gedichte, Band 2: Buch I-VI der Aneis. vi, 341p. (GER.). write for info. (*3-296-15872-3*, Pub. by Georg Olms GW) Lubrecht & Cramer.

— Vergils Gedichte, Band 3: Buch VII-XII der Aneis. vi, 308p. (GER.). 1973. write for info. (*3-296-15873-1*, Pub. by Georg Olms GW) Lubrecht & Cramer.

Ladewski, G. Lucky, jt. auth. see Szymarek, Gene.

Ladewski, G. Stachowiak & Ladewski, Sally W. Ladies First: Marriage Records of St. Joseph County, Indiana, 1831-1859. xi, 159p. (Orig.). 1988. pap. 12.50 (*1-55613-113-5*) Heritage Bk.

Ladewski, Paul, jt. auth. see Burke, Larry.

Ladewski, Sally W., jt. auth. see Ladewski, G. Stachowiak.

Ladha, J. K., et al, eds. Biological Nitrogen Fixation for Sustainable Agriculture: Extended Version of Papers Presented in the Symposium, Role of Biological Nitrogen Fixation in Sustainable Agriculture, at the 13th Congress of Soil Science, Kyoto, Japan, 1990. LC 92-10783. (Developments in Plant & Soil Sciences Ser.: Vol. 49). (C). 1992. lib. bdg. 106.50 (*0-7923-1774-2*) Kluwer Ac.

Ladies Aid Society Staff. The Kelly Cook Book. 2nd ed. 28p. 1981. pap. 3.00 (*0-9617036-1-X*) Bandar Log.

Ladies Auxiliary Hadar Zion Staff. Plain & Simple Family Cookbook. 189p. 1991. 9.95 (*0-944070-37-X*) Targum Pr.

Ladies Home Journal Editors & Christian Science Monitor Editors. America's Twelve Great Women Leaders During the Past Hundred Years As Chosen by the Women of America. LC 74-90600. (Essay Index Reprint Ser.). 1977. 17.95 (*0-8369-1202-0*) Ayer.

Ladies' Home Journal Staff. Ladies' Home Journal One Hundred Great Dessert Recipes. 1994. 14.95 (*0-696-20032-5*) Meredith Bks.

— Ladies' Home Journal One Hundred Great Soup, Stew & Chili Recipes. 1993. 14.95 (*0-696-20033-3*) Meredith Bks.

— LHJ: 100 Great Cookie Recipes. 144p. 1994. 14.95 (*0-696-20073-2*) Meredith Bks.

— LHJ: 100 Healthy Main Dish. 144p. 1994. 14.95 (*0-696-20072-4*) Meredith Bks.

Ladies' Home Journal Staff, ed. Ladies' Home Journal One Hundred Great Chicken Recipes. (Illus.). 144p. 1994. 14.95 (*0-696-04655-5*) Meredith Bks.

Ladies of the Mission Staff. Old Brewery & the New Mission House at the Five Points. LC 72-112563. (Rise of Urban America Ser.). (Illus.). 1976. reprint ed. 29.95 (*0-405-02461-4*) Ayer.

Ladiges, P. Y. & Martinelli, L. W. Plant Systematics in the Age of Molecular Biology. (Illus.). 172p. 1990. pap. 50. 00 (*0-643-05098-1*, Pub. by CSIRO AT) Intl Spec Bk.

Ladiges, Pauline Y., jt. ed. see Littlejohn, M. J.

***Ladik, Janos & Forner, Wolfgang.** The Beginnings of Cancer in the Cell: An Interdisciplinary Approach. LC 94-21255. 1994. 54.50 (*0-387-57962-1*) Spr-Verlag.

Ladik, Janos J. Quantum Theory of Polymers As Solids. LC 87-29159. (Illus.). 432p. 1987. 89.50 (*0-306-42434-7*, Plenum Pr) Plenum.

Ladik, Janos J. & Andre, Jean-Marie, eds. Quantum Chemistry of Polymers: Solid State Aspects. LC 84-3367. 1984. lib. bdg. 132.00 (*90-277-1741-9*) Kluwer Ac.

Ladik, Katalin. Stories of the Seven-Headed Sewing Machine. limited ed. B'Racz, Emoke, tr. 28p. 1992. pap. 4.50 (*0-685-64797-8*) New Native Pr.

Ladimer, Irving & McCarthy, Jane. Resolving Faculty Disputes. LC 81-67937. 80p. 1981. pap. 8.00 (*0-943001-12-9*) Am Arbitration.

***Lading, L., et al, eds.** Optical Diagnostics for Flow Processes. (Illus.). 406p. 1994. 110.00 (*0-306-44817-3*, Plenum Pr) Plenum.

Ladis, Andrew. The Brancacci Chapel, Florence. LC 93-6995. (Great Fresco Cycles of the Renaissance Ser.). 1993. 23.50 (*0-8076-1311-8*) Braziller.

— Italian Renaissance Maiolica from Southern Collections. Eiland, William U., ed. (Illus.). 118p. 1989. Exhibition catalogue. 25.00 (*0-915977-03-6*) Georgia Museum of Art.

— Taddeo Gaddi: Critical Reappraisal & Catalogue Raisonne. (Illus.). 288p. 1983. 70.00 (*0-8262-0382-5*) U of Mo Pr.

Ladis, Andrew, et al, eds. The Craft of Art: Originality & Industry in the Italian Renaissance & Baroque Workshop. LC 93-40992. (Illus.). 288p. (C). 1995. 40.00 (*0-8203-1648-2*) U of Ga Pr.

Ladisch, Michael R. & Bose, Arindam, eds. Harnessing Biotechnology for the 21st Century: Proceedings of the Ninth International Biotechnology Symposium & Exposition, Crystal City, Virginia, August 19-21, 1992. LC 92-21791. (Conference Proceedings Ser.). (Illus.). 640p. 1992. 149.95 (*0-8412-2477-3*) Am Chemical.

Ladisch, Michael R., et al, eds. Protein Purification: From Molecular Mechanisms to Large-Scale Processes. LC 90-35551. (ACS Symposium Ser.: No. 427). (Illus.). 302p. 1990. 69.95 (*0-8412-1790-4*) Am Chemical.

Ladislas, Robert & Hornebeck, William, eds. Elastin & Elastases, Vol. I. 1989. 216.00 (*0-8493-6428-0*, QP552) CRC Pr.

Ladizinsky, Eric. More Magical Science: Magic Tricks for Young Scientists. (Illus.). 64p. (J). (gr. 3-7). 1994. pap. 4.95 (*1-56565-110-3*) Lowell Hse.

Ladizinsky, Eric, jt. auth. see Amato, Carol.

Ladizinsky, Eric, jt. auth. see Melton, Lisa.

Ladjevardi, Habib. Labor Unions & Autocracy in Iran. 352p. 1985. 39.95x (*0-8156-2343-7*) Syracuse U Pr.

— Reference Guide to the Iranian Oral History Project. (Orig.). 1988. 4.95 (*0-932885-04-7*) Harvard CMES.

Ladley, Anne. Moriah's Magic. large type ed. LC 93-15497. 1993. 13.95 (*1-56054-749-9*) Thorndike Pr.

— Prescription for Love. large type ed. 235p. 1992. reprint ed. lib. bdg. 13.95 (*1-56054-478-3*) Thorndike Pr.

Ladley, Barbara & Wilford, Jane. Money & Finance: Sources of Print & Nonprint Materials. LC 80-13943. (Sourcebook Ser.). 208p. 1980. 35.00 (0-918212-23-5) Neal-Schuman.

Ladman, Jerry R., ed. Mexico: A Country in Crisis. LC 86-50098. 176p. 1987. pap. 13.00 (0-87404-096-5) Tex Western.

Ladman, Jerry R. & Morales, Juan A., eds. Redemocratization in Bolivia: A Political-Economic Analysis of the Siles Zuazo Government, 1982-1985. 150p. Date not set. text ed. write for info. (0-87918-065-X) ASU Lat Am St.

Ladmore, Richard. Civil Litigation. (C). 1992. text ed. 48.00 (1-85431-231-6, Pub. by Blackstone Pr UK) W W Gaunt.

Ladner, Benjamin, ed. The Humanities in Precollegiate Education, 83rd Yearbook of the National Society for the Study of Education, Pt. II. LC 83-62345. x, 210p. 1985. pap. text ed. 8.00 (0-226-60143-9, Natl Soc Stud Educ) U Ch Pr.

***Ladner, Gerhart B.** God, Cosmos, & Humankind: The World Of Early Christian Symbolism. Dunlap, Thomas, tr. (Illus.). 260p. 1995. 45.00 (0-520-08549-3) U CA Pr.

Ladner, Joyce, jt. ed. see Edelman, Peter.

***Ladner, Joyce A.** Tomorrow's Tomorrow: The Black Woman. 332p. (C). 1995. pap. text ed. 12.00 (0-8032-7956-6, Bison Books) U of Nebr Pr.

Ladner, Mildred D. O. C. Seltzer: Painter of the Old West. LC 78-21379. (GOAA Ser.: Vol. 1). (Illus.). 240p. 1979. pap. 29.95 (0-8061-2114-9) U of Okla Pr.

— William de la Montagne Cary: Artist on the Missouri River. LC 83-40329. (Gilcrease-Oklahoma Series on Western Art & Artists: Vol. 3). (Illus.). 264p. 1984. 48.50 (0-8061-1774-5) U of Okla Pr.

Ladner, Saryn J. & Tillman, Hope N. The Internet & Special Librarians: Use, Training, & the Future. LC 93-23789. 194p. 1993. pap. 33.00 (0-87111-413-5) SLA.

Ladner, Sharyn, comp. Networking & Special Libraries. 1990. spiral bd. 20.00 (0-87111-353-8) SLA.

Lado International College Staff & Lado, Robert. Branching Out, No. One. rev. ed. (Illus.). 229p. (C). 1993. pap. text ed. 14.95 (1-879580-55-1) Lado Intl Pr.

— Branching Out, No. Two. rev. ed. (Illus.). 203p. (C). 1993. pap. text ed. 14.95 (1-879580-56-X) Lado Intl Pr.

Lado, Robert. Basic Conversations in English, Bk. 2. (Illus.). 131p. (C). 1993. pap. text ed. 8.95 (1-879580-54-3) Lado Intl Pr.

— Basic Conversations in English: Book I. (Illus.). (Orig.). (C). 1992. pap. text ed. 8.95 (1-879580-50-0) Lado Intl Pr.

— The Big Bad Wolf: Level 2. (Reading Playhouse Ser.). (Illus.). 24p. (J). (ps). 1985. pap. 3.95 (1-879580-53-5); 1.95 (1-879580-52-7) Lado Intl Pr.

— Lado, Bk. 1. 3rd ed. (C). 1989. pap. text ed. 9.00 (0-13-522244-3) P-H.

— Lado, Bk. 2. 3rd ed. (C). 1989. pap. text ed. 9.00 (0-13-522269-9) P-H.

— Lado, Bk. 4. 3rd ed. (C). 1989. pap. text ed. 9.00 (0-13-522301-6) P-H.

— Lado, Bk. 5. 3rd ed. (C). 1990. pap. text ed. 9.00 (0-13-522327-X) P-H.

— Lado, Bk. 6. 3rd ed. (C). 1990. pap. text ed. 9.00 (0-13-522343-1) P-H.

— Lado English Series, Bk. 1. (Illus.). (C). (gr. 7-12). 1987. student ed 4.50 (0-13-522061-0, 18751); teacher ed 11.00 (0-13-522129-3, 18757); pap. text ed. 6.50 (0-13-522004-1, 18745); audio 75.00 (0-13-522186-2, 58763) Prentice ESL.

— Lado English Series, Bk. 2. 1987. teacher ed 11.00 (0-13-522137-4, 18758); student ed 4.50 (0-13-522079-3, 18752); pap. text ed. 7.50 (0-13-522012-2, 18746) Prentice ESL.

— Lado English Series, Bk. 3. 1987. teacher ed 9.00 (0-13-522145-5, 18753); student ed 4.50 (0-13-522087-4, 58765); pap. text ed. write for info. (0-13-522020-3, 18747); audio 75.00 (0-13-522202-8) Prentice ESL.

— Lado English Series, Bk. 4. 1987. teacher ed 11.00 (0-13-522152-8, 18754); student ed 4.50 (0-13-522095-5, 58766); pap. text ed. write for info. (0-13-522038-6, 18748); audio 75.00 (0-13-522210-9) Prentice ESL.

— Lado English Series, Bk. 5. (Illus.). 198p. (gr. 7-12). 1987. teacher ed 11.00 (0-13-522160-9, 18761); student ed 4.50 (0-13-522103-X, 58767); pap. text ed. write for info. (0-13-522046-7, 18749); audio 75.00 (0-13-522228-1) Prentice ESL.

— Lado English Series, Bk. 6. (Illus.). 1987. teacher ed 11.00 (0-13-522178-1, 18762); student ed 4.50 (0-13-522111-0, 18756); pap. text ed. write for info. (0-13-522053-X, 18750); audio 75.00 (0-13-522236-2, 58768) Prentice ESL.

— The Lado Picture Dictionary. 128p. 1992. pap. text ed. 8.00 (0-13-521451-3) P-H.

— Lado Picture Dictionary. rev. ed. LC 92-36959. (Illus.). 1993. pap. text ed. 8.00 (0-13-061680-X) P-H.

— Linguistics Across Cultures: Applied Linguistics for Language Teachers. 1957. pap. 18.95 (0-472-08542-5) U of Mich Pr.

— My First Thirty-Two Words: Level 1. (Reading Playhouse Ser.). (Illus.). 34p. (J). (ps). 1985. 9.95 (1-879580-51-9) Lado Intl Pr.

— Teaching English Across Cultures. 1988. text ed. 14.95 (0-07-035769-2) McGraw.

Lado, Robert, jt. auth. see Lado International College Staff.

Ladoo, Harold S. No Pain Like This Body. (Caribbean Writers Ser.). 141p. 1987. pap. 8.95 (0-435-98874-3) Heinemann.

— Yesterdays. 110p. (Orig.). 1974. pap. 4.95 (0-88784-329-8, Pub. by Hse of Anansi Pr CN) Genl Dist Srvs.

LaDou, Joseph. Occupational Medicine. (Illus.). 608p. (C). 1990. pap. text ed. 38.95 (0-8385-7207-3, A7207-2) Appleton & Lange.

LaDou, Joseph, ed. Occupational Health & Safety. 2nd ed. LC 90-62550. (Illus.). 484p. (C). 1993. 99.95 (0-87912-154-8, 12219-0000) Natl Safety Coun.

Ladouceur, David J. Plutarch Themistocles. (Bryn Mawr Greek Commentaries Ser.). 80p. (Orig.). (C). 1989. pap. text ed. 6.00 (0-929524-60-8) Bryn Mawr Commentaries.

Ladouceur, Paul A. Chiefs & Politicians: The Politics of Regionalism in Northern Ghana. LC 79-670408. (Legon History Ser.). 318p. reprint ed. pap. 90.70 (0-317-27751-0, 2025230) Bks Demand.

Ladousse, Gillian P. Speaking Personally: Quizzes & Questionnaires for Fluency Practice. 113p. 1983. pap. 11.95 (0-521-28869-X) Cambridge U Pr.

LaDoux, Rita C. Georgia. (Hello U. S. A. Ser.). (Illus.). 72p. (J). (gr. 3-6). 1991. lib. bdg. 17.50 (0-8225-2703-0, Lerner Publctns) Lerner Group.

— Iowa. Lerner Geography Department Staff, ed. (Hello U. S. A. Ser.). (Illus.). 72p. (J). (gr. 3-6). 1992. lib. bdg. 17.50 (0-8225-2724-3, Lerner Publctns) Lerner Group.

— Louisiana. LC 92-13365. (Hello U. S. A. Ser.). (J). (gr. 3-6). 1993. lib. bdg. 17.50 (0-8225-2740-5, Lerner Publctns) Lerner Group.

— Missouri. (Hello U. S. A. Ser.). (Illus.). 72p. (J). (gr. 3-6). 1991. lib. bdg. 17.50 (0-8225-2710-3, Lerner Publctns) Lerner Group.

— Montana. Lerner Geography Department Staff, ed. (Hello U. S. A. Ser.). (Illus.). 72p. (J). (gr. 3-6). 1992. 17.50 (0-8225-2714-6, Lerner Publctns) Lerner Group.

— Oklahoma. Lerner Geography Department Staff, ed. (Hello U. S. A. Ser.). (Illus.). 72p. (J). (gr. 3-6). 1992. lib. bdg. 17.50 (0-8225-2717-0, Lerner Publctns) Lerner Group.

Ladovic, Zdravko J. Illegal Love: Love Without Permission. 1993. 10.00 (0-533-12074-8) Vantage.

Ladra, Kathleen M., ed. see Steinbrecher, Thomas P.

Ladson-Billings, Gloria. The Dreamkeepers: Successful Teachers of African American Children. LC 94-10316. (Education Ser.). 208p. 1994. 22.00 (1-55542-668-9) Jossey-Bass.

Ladson, Etta M. Live Long & Prosper. (Illus.). 33p. 1992. Tchr's. ed. teacher ed 11.95 (0-9630574-2-1) Jewelgate.

Ladson, Etta M. Strange Land Songs. (Illus.). 146p. (YA). (gr. 7-12). 1992. text ed. 14.95 (0-9630574-0-5) Jewelgate.

***Ladue Chapel, Missouri Staff.** Celebrating Our Past, Building for the Future: Ladue Chapel, 1943-1993. (Illus.). 128p. (Orig.). 1993. pap. text ed. 9.95 (1-881576-18-3) Providence Hse.

Ladue, Myron. The Newcomers. 389p. (Orig.). 1989. pap. 15.00 (0-9623443-0-3) M Ladue.

LaDuke, Betty. Africa: Through the Eyes of Women Artists. LC 91-72496. (Illus.). 1991. 45.95 (0-685-56372-3); pap. 15.95 (0-86543-199-X) Africa World.

— Africa: Women's Art, Women's Lives. 1995. pap. 18.95 (0-86543-435-2) Africa World.

— Women Artists: Multi-Cultural Visions. LC 91-68511. (Illus.). 205p. 1992. 49.95 (0-932415-77-6); pap. 16.95 (0-932415-78-4) Red Sea Pr.

Ladurie, Emmanuel L. Carnival in Romans. LC 79-52163. 426p. 1979. pap. 8.95 (0-8076-0991-9) Braziller.

— Jasmin's Witch. Pearce, Brian, tr. LC 87-9393. (Illus.). 222p. 1987. 17.95 (0-8076-1181-6) Braziller.

— Love, Death & Money in the Pays D'Oc. Sheridan, Alan, tr. LC 82-9422. 597p. 1982. 30.00 (0-8076-1038-0) Braziller.

— Montaillou: The Promised Land of Error. Bray, Barbara, tr. (Illus.). 1979. pap. 11.96 (0-394-72964-1, Vin) Random.

— The Peasants of Languedoc. Day, John, tr. LC 74-4286. (Illus.). 382p. 1977. reprint ed. pap. 15.95 (0-252-00635-6) U of Ill Pr.

Ladusaw, William A., jt. auth. see Pullum, Geoffrey K.

Ladwai, Z., jt. auth. see Ch Lai.

***Ladwig, Dieter.** Slot Machines. 1994. 12.98 (0-7858-0072-7) Bk Sales Inc.

***Ladwig, James G.** Academic Distinctions: Theory & Methodology in the Sociology of School Knowledge. 192p. 1995. 55.00x (0-415-91187-7, B7167, Routledge NY); pap. 17.95 (0-415-91188-5, B7171, Routledge NY) Routledge.

Ladwig, Lewis R., jt. auth. see Kirkham, Robert M.

Ladwig, T. Industrial Fire Prevention & Protection. 1991. text ed. 54.95 (0-442-23678-6) Van Nos Reinhold.

Ladwig, Tim, illus. Psalm Twenty-Three. LC 93-73111. 56p. 1993. 20.00 (1-56977-025-5) Af Am Family Pr.

Ladwig, Tom. Granny Had a Word for It. LC 88-60751. (Illus.). 58p. 1988. pap. 3.95 (0-914546-75-9) Rose Pub.

Ladwig, Tom, illus. How to Talk Dirty Like Grandad. LC 85-60070. 42p. 1985. pap. 3.95 (0-914546-59-7) Rose Pub.

Lady Allen of Hurtwood. Planning for Play. LC 69-16908. 144p. 1969. pap. 10.95 (0-262-51013-8) MIT Pr.

***Lady Caroline Lamb.** Glenarron. Watson, Frances, ed. 336p. (Orig.). 1995. pap. 7.50 (0-460-87468-3, Everyman's Classic Lib) C E Tuttle.

Lady Dorchester, ed. see Broughton, John C.

Lady Dowding Muriel. Beauty-Not the Beast. (Illus.). 292p. Date not set. 19.95 (0-8464-4206-X) Beekman Pubs.

Lady Durning-Lawrence. Smith: Notes & Illustrations Concerning the Family History of James Smith. (Illus.). 156p. 1991. reprint ed. pap. 24.00 (0-8328-2170-5) Higginson Bk Co.

Lady Easthope, tr. see Ubicini, M. A.

***Lady Evans.** Hair-Dressing of Roman Ladies as Illustrated on Coins. (Illus.). 44p. 1994. reprint ed. pap. 12.50 (0-9644376-0-0) Paaka Enter.

***Lady Green.** The Sexually Dominant Woman: A Workbook for Nervous Beginners. 100p. 1994. pap. 9.95 (0-9639763-0-3) Greenery Pr.

Lady Gregory. Cuchulain of Muirthemne: The Story of the Men of the Red Branch of Ulster. 5th ed. (Coole Edition of the Collected Works of Lady Gregory Ser.: Vol. 2). 1973. pap. 15.95 (0-19-519739-9) OUP.

— Irish Folk-History Plays, 2 vols., Set. 1988. reprint ed. lib. bdg. 99.00 (0-7812-0470-4) Rprt Serv.

— Poets & Dreamers: Studies & Translations from the Irish. LC 73-17133. (Studies in Irish Literature: No. 16). 1974. lib. bdg. 75.00 (0-8383-1725-1) M S G Haskell Hse.

Lady Llanover, ed. see Delany, Mary.

Lady Lugard. A Tropical Dependency: An Outline of the Ancient History of the Western Sudan with an Account of the Modern Settlement of Northern Nigeria. 508p. Date not set. reprint ed. 54.00 (0-933121-72-5) Black Classic.

***Lady McCrady.** The Perfect Ride. LC 94-35193. (Parents Magazine Read Aloud Original Ser.). (Illus.). (J). 1995. write for info. (0-8368-1123-2) Gareth Stevens Inc.

Lady Muck. Magic Muck: The Complete Guide to Compost. (Illus.). 1994. 17.95 (1-85793-261-7, Pub. by Pavilion UK) Trafalgar.

Lady Murasaki. The Tale of Genji. 1993. 22.00 (0-679-42467-9, Modern Lib) Random.

Lady Queenborough. Judaism. 1982. lib. bdg. 55.95 (0-87700-410-2) Revisionist Pr.

Lady Sabrina. Reclaiming the Power: The How & Why of Practical Ritual Magic. LC 92-8696. (Practical Guide to Personal Power Ser.). (Illus.). 256p. 1992. 9.95 (0-87542-166-0) Llewellyn Pubns.

Lady Sandys. The Awakening Letters, Vol. 2. Sandys, Cynthia & Lehmann, Rosamond, eds. 104p. (Orig.). Date not set. pap. 17.95 (0-8464-4211-6) Beekman Pubs.

Lady Sara. Book of Light. 155p. 1989. 12.95 (0-939708-28-0) Magickal Childe.

Ladyman, David, ed. see Addams, Shay.

Ladyman, David, jt. ed. see Addams, Shay.

Ladyman, Heather M., jt. ed. see Ritter, Mary A.

Ladyzenskaja, O. A., ed. see Steklov Institute of Mathematics, Academy of Sciences, U. S. S. R. Staff.

Ladyzenskaja, O. A., et al. Linear & Quasilinear Equations of Parabolic Type. LC 68-19440. (Translations of Mathematical Monographs: Vol. 23). 648p. 1988. reprint ed. pap. 96.00 (0-8218-1573-3, MMONO-23) Am Math.

Ladyzhenskaya, O. Boundary Value Problems of Mathematical Physics XIII. LC 67-6187. (STEKLO Ser.: Vol. 179). 266p. 1989. pap. 139.00 (0-8218-3127-5, STEKLO-179) Am Math.

Ladyzhenskaya, O. A. The Mathematical Theory of Viscous Incompressible Flow. 2nd ed. (Mathematics & Its Applications Ser.). (Illus.). 242p. 1969. text ed. 205.00 (0-677-20760-3) Gordon & Breach.

Ladyzhenskaya, O. A., ed. Boundary Value Problems of Mathematical Physics & Related Aspects of Function Theory. LC 69-12506. (Seminars in Mathematics Ser.: Vol. 14, Pt. 4). (Illus.). 163p. (RUS.). reprint ed. pap. 46.50 (0-8357-7369-8, 2020698) Bks Demand.

— Boundary Value Problems of Mathematical Physics, XIV. LC 67-6187. (Proceedings of the Steklov Institute of Mathematics Ser.: Vol. 188). 239p. 1991. reprint ed. 132.00 (0-8218-3141-0, STEKLO/188C) Am Math.

— St. Petersburg Mathematical Society: Proceedings. (Translation Ser. 2: Vol. 159). 225p. 1994. 115.00 (0-8218-7510-8) Am Math.

Ladyzhenskaya, O. A. & Vershik, A. M., eds. Proceedings of the St. Petersburg Mathematical Society, Vol. I. (Translations - Series Two: Vol. 155). 223p. 1993. 99.00 (0-8218-7505-1, TRANS2/155C) Am Math.

Ladyzhenskaya, Olga A. Attractors for Semi-Groups & Evolution Equations. (Lezioni Lincee Lectures). 100p. (C). 1991. 44.95 (0-521-39030-3); pap. 17.95 (0-521-39922-X) Cambridge U Pr.

— The Boundary Value Problems of Mathematical Physics. Lohwater, J., tr. (Applied Mathematical Sciences Ser.: Vol. 49). 350p. 1985. 87.00 (0-387-90989-3) Spr-Verlag.

Laederach, Jurg. Sixty-Nine Ways to Play the Blues. Wortsmann, Peter, tr. (Foreign Agents Ser.). 192p. (Orig.). (C). 1990. pap. 6.00 (0-936756-62-4) Autonomedia.

Laege, F. K. Secular Inflation. Catty, F. B., tr. 106p. 1961. lib. bdg. 42.50 (90-277-0098-2) Kluwer Ac.

Lael Miller, Linda. Taming Charlotte. Marrow, Linda, ed. 352p. 1993. mass mkt. 5.99 (0-671-73754-6, Pocket Star Bks) PB.

Lael, Richard L. Arrogant Diplomacy: U. S. Policy Toward Colombia, 1903-1922. LC 87-12987. 216p. 1987. 40.00 (0-8420-2287-2) Scholarly Res Inc.

— The Yamashita Precedent: War Crimes & Command Responsibility. LC 82-17024. 177p. 1982. lib. bdg. 40.00 (0-8420-2202-3) Scholarly Res Inc.

***Laemer, Richard.** Native's Guide to New York: 750 Ways to Have the Time of Your Life in the City. 3rd rev. ed. LC 95-1533. 1995. write for info. (0-7615-0020-0) Prima Pub.

Laemmlen, Ann & Owen, Jackie. The Articles of Faith Learning Book. 171p. (J). (gr. 3-6). 1990. student ed, pap. 7.95 (0-87579-400-9) Deseret Bk.

Laendner, Geoffrey C. A Failed Strategy: The Offshore Oil Industry's Development of the Outer Continental Shelf. LC 92-35380. (Government & the Economy Ser.). 216p. 1993. 56.00 (0-8153-1229-6) Garland.

Laennec, Christine M., tr. see Paulhan, Jean.

Laerm, Joshua & Freeman, B. J. Fishes of the Okefenokee Swamp. LC 85-16486. (Illus.). 128p. 1986. 15.00 (0-8203-0820-X); pap. 7.50 (0-8203-0841-2) U of Ga Pr.

Laermer, Richard. Bargain Hunting in Greater New York: Including the Five Boroughs & the Suburban Discount Malls of New Jersey, Connecticut, & Upstate New York. 250p. (Orig.). 1990. pap. 9.95 (1-55958-030-5) Prima Pub.

— The Gay & Lesbian Handbook to New York City. 1994. write for info. (0-318-72470-7, Plume); pap. 10.95 (0-452-27022-7, Plume) NAL-Dutton.

— Native's Guide to New York: Seven Hundred Fifty Ways to Have the Time of Your Life in the City. 2nd rev. ed. (Illus.). 225p. (Orig.). 1991. pap. 12.95 (1-55958-114-X) Prima Pub.

Laertius, Diogenes. De Vitis, Dogmatis et Apophthegmatis Clarorum Philosophorum, 4 vols., Set. xxxii, 2587p. (GER.). 1981. reprint ed. write for info. (3-487-07067-7, Pub. by Georg Olms GW) Lubrecht & Cramer.

— La Vie de Pythagore de Diogene Laerce. (Memoires de l'Academie Royale de Belgique. Classe des Lettres et des Sciences Morales et Politiques Ser. 2). 272p. (GER.). 1988. reprint ed. write for info. (3-487-09032-5, Pub. by Georg Olms GW) Lubrecht & Cramer.

Laerum, Ole D. & Bjerknes, R., eds. Flow Cytometry in Hematology. (Analytical Cytology Ser.). (Illus.). 272p. 1992. text ed. 105.00 (0-12-432940-3) Acad Pr.

***Laes, Ronald G.** Women in Sports Hawaii 1996. 24p. 1994. write for info. (0-9644546-0-2) Goldsmiths.

Laet, Joannes de. The Empire of the Great Mogol. Hoyland, J. S., tr. 266p. reprint ed. text ed. 22.00 (0-685-13403-2) Coronet Bks.

Laetsch, Theodore. Jeremiah. 1987. pap. 19.95 (0-570-03218-0, 15-2003) Concordia.

— Minor Prophets. 1956. 19.95 (0-570-03249-0, 15-1719) Concordia.

Laetsch, Theodore, ed. The Abiding Word, Set. 1974. pap. 49.95 (0-570-07203-4, 12HH2612) Concordia.

Laeufer, Christiane & Morgan, Terrell A., eds. Theoretical Analyses in Romance Linguistics: Selected Papers from the Symposium XIX, Ohio State University, April 21-23, 1989. LC 92-15113. (Current Issues in Linguistic Theory Ser.: No. 74). viii, 515p. 1992. 156.00 (1-55619-130-8) Benjamins North Am.

Laevastu, Taivo. Marine Climate, Weather & Climate Changes in Fisheries & Ocean Resources. LC 92-40470. 204p. 1993. text ed. 57.95 (0-470-22049-X) Halsted Pr.

Laface, P. & De Mori, Renato, eds. Speech Recognition & Understanding: Recent Advances, Trends & Applications. (NATO ASI Series F: Computer & Systems Sciences, Special Programme AET: Vol. 75). 576p. 1992. 144.00 (0-387-54032-6) Spr-Verlag.

Lafaille, Robert & Fulder, Stephen, eds. Towards a New Science of Health. LC 93-3282. 1994. 59.95 (0-415-08171-8) Routledge.

LaFaive, Douglas. How to Settle Your Claim for Auto Damage. rev. ed. (Law Kits Ser.). 180p. (Orig.). 1992. pap. 19.95 (1-879191-06-7) Forms Man.

LaFaive, Douglas L. The Claims Game - How to Play to Win: How to Present, Evaluate & Settle Your Automobile Injury Claim. Urband, Vesta, ed. 80p. (Orig.). 1991. pap. 19.95 (0-9629403-0-5) Puck Pr.

LaFantasie, Glenn W., ed. see Williams, Roger.

Lafar, Uz, jt. ed. see Chaghtai, Mirza S.

LaFarelle, Lorenzo G. Bernardo de Galvez: Hero of the American Revolution. 92p. 1992. 14.95 (0-89015-849-5) Sunbelt Media.

LaFarge, Albert. United States Flea Market Directory. 432p. (Orig.). 1993. pap. 6.00 (0-380-77079-2, Confident Collect) Avon.

LaFarge, Ann. Pearl Buck. (American Women of Achievement Ser.). (Illus.). 112p. (J). (gr. 5 up). 1988. lib. bdg. 17.95 (1-55546-645-1) Chelsea Hse.

LaFarge, Ann, ed. A Bride's Passion. 352p. 1993. mass mkt. 4.50 (0-8217-4198-5) Zebra.

— A Christmas Kiss. 352p. 1992. mass mkt. 4.50 (0-8217-3975-1) Zebra.

— Home for Christmas. 352p. 1992. mass mkt. 3.99 (0-8217-3979-4) Zebra.

— The Joy of Christmas. 512p. 1994. mass mkt. 4.99 (0-8217-4749-5) Zebra.

— Merry Christmas, My Love. 480p. 1993. mass mkt. 4.50 (0-8217-4379-1) Zebra.

— Murder under the Tree. 320p. 1993. mass mkt. 3.99 (0-8217-4376-7) Zebra.

— To Mother with Love. 480p. 1993. mass mkt. 4.50 (0-8217-4138-1) Zebra.

Lafarge, Catherine, ed. Dilemmes du Roman. LC 89-84497. (Stanford French & Italian Studies: Vol. 65). 364p. (FRE.). 1990. pap. 46.50 (0-915838-80-X) Anma Libri.

LaFarge, Oliver. Behind the Mountains. 188p. 1994. reprint ed. pap. 12.00 (0-912880-07-4) Charles Pub.

— Laughing Boy. 192p. (YA). (gr. 10). 1971. pap. 3.50 (0-451-52244-3, Sig Classics) NAL-Dutton.

— Laughing Boy. 245p. (J). 1981. reprint ed. lib. bdg. 24.95 (0-89966-367-2) Buccaneer Bks.

— The Mother Ditch. Ortego, Pedro R., tr. LC 82-10712. (Illus.). 64p. (ENG & SPA.). (J). (gr. 1-12). 1983. pap. 8.95 (0-86534-009-9) Sunstone Pr.

LaFarge, Oliver & Morgan, Arthur N. Santa Fe: The Autobiography of a Southwestern Town. LC 59-7958. 436p. 1985. pap. 19.95 (0-8061-1696-X) U of Okla Pr.

LaFarge, Oliver, et al. Introduction to American Indian Art: Includes Extensive Biblio Entitled Indian Arts North of Mexico, 2 vols. in 1. (Illus.). 217p. 1985. pap. 17.50 (0-87380-151-2) Rio Grande.

Lafarge, Rene. Jean-Paul Sartre: His Philosophy. LC 75-105727. 208p. reprint ed. pap. 59.30 (0-317-26697-7, 2024368) Bks Demand.

LaFargue, Michael. Tao & Method: A Reasoned Approach to the Tao Te Ching. (SUNY Series in Chinese Philosophy & Culture). 642p. (C). 1994. 74.50 (0-7914-1601-1) State U NY Pr.

An Asterisk (*) at the beginning of an entry indicates that the title is appearing in BIP for the first time.

— The Tao of the Tao Te Ching: A Translation & Commentary. LC 91-18284. (SUNY Series in Chinese Philosophy & Culture). 270p. 1992. pap. 12.95 (*0-7914-0986-4*) State U NY Pr.

Lafargue, Paul. Karl Marx, the Man. 4th ed. 1972. pap. 0.50 (*0-935534-36-9*) NY Labor News.

— Religion of Capital. 9th ed. 1967. pap. 0.50 (*0-935534-38-5*) NY Labor News.

— The Right to Be Lazy. 1972. 250.00 (*0-87968-039-3*) Gordon Pr.

— Selected Marxist Writings of Paul Lafargue. Broadhead, Richard, ed. 530p. (C). 1984. pap. 25.00 (*0-916695-05-0*) Ctr Social Hist.

LaFargue, Thomas E. China & the World War. 45.00 (*0-86527-023-6*) Fertig.

— China's First Hundred: Educational Mission Students in the United States, 1872-1881. LC 87-10404. (Washington State University Press Art Ser.). (Illus.). 184p. 1987. reprint ed. pap. 11.25 (*0-87422-035-1*) Wash St U Pr.

Lafary, J. D. & Lecaillon, J. The Political Dimension of Economic Adjustment. Morrisson, Christian, ed. (Political Feasibility of Adjustment Ser.). 139p. (Orig.). 1993. pap. 24.00 (*92-64-13967-2*) OECD.

LaFasto, Frank M., jt. auth. see Larson, Carl E.

Lafaurie, Andre-Jean & Lefevre, Jean-Francois. Golf: Great Courses of the World. (Illus.). 192p. 1991. 19.98 (*0-89660-016-5*, Artabras) Abbeville Pr.

***Lafave.** Criminal Justice & the Supreme Court. 375p. 1990. pap. 12.95 (*0-02-897215-5*) Macmillan.

LaFave, Wayne R. Criminal Law, 1994: Pocket Part. 2nd ed. (Hornbook Ser.). 65p. 1994. pap. text ed. 6.50 (*0-314-04363-2*) West Pub.

— Modern Criminal Law: Cases, Comments, & Questions. 2nd ed. (American Casebook Ser.). 903p. (C). 1989. reprint ed. text ed. 45.00 (*0-314-82177-5*) West Pub.

— Search & Seizure: A Treatise on the Fourth Amendment, 4 vols. 2nd ed. 2400p. 1986. text ed. write for info. (*0-314-30073-2*) West Pub.

LaFave, Wayne R. & Israel, Jerold H. Criminal Procedure. 2nd ed. (Hornbook Ser.). 1309p. (C). 1993. reprint ed. text ed. 41.00 (*0-314-79327-5*) West Pub.

— Criminal Procedure, Vols. 1-5. LC 84-10391. (Criminal Practice Ser.). 2283p. 1993. reprint ed. text ed. write for info. (*0-314-79279-1*) West Pub.

— Criminal Procedure, Pocket Part 1993. 55p. 1993. pap. text ed. 5.00 (*0-314-02929-X*) West Pub.

— Criminal Procedure, 1994: Pocket Part for Use in 1994-1995. 2nd ed. (Hornbook Ser.). 63p. (C). 1994. 6.50 (*0-314-04810-3*) West Pub.

LaFave, Wayne R. & Scott, Austin W., Jr. Criminal Law. 2nd ed. (Hornbook Ser.). 918p. 1991. reprint ed. text ed. 37.00 (*0-314-26045-5*) West Pub.

— Criminal Law, 1993: Pocket Part. 2nd ed. (Hornbook Ser.). 60p. 1993. pap. text ed. 5.00 (*0-314-02242-2*) West Pub.

— Substantive Criminal Law. 2nd ed. LC 86-7795. (Criminal Practice Ser.). 1300p. 1986. text ed. write for info. (*0-314-98403-8*) West Pub.

LaFave, Wayne R., jt. auth. see Israel, Jerold H.

LaFave, Wayne R., jt. auth. see Kamisar, Yale.

LaFavore, Michael, ed. Men's Health Advisor. LC 91-47971. 288p. (Orig.). 1992. pap. 14.95 (*0-87596-125-8*, 05-024-2) Rodale Pr Inc.

LaFay, Bob. Home Owners' Tax Breaks. 2nd ed. Thomason, Greg & Wemple, Michelle, eds. 300p. 1994. pap. 39.95 (*0-9639801-0-6*) Home Owners Tax.

— Home Owners' Tax Breaks. 3rd ed. Thomason, Greg & Wemple, Michelle, eds. 282p. 1994. pap. 39.95 (*0-9639801-1-4*) Home Owners Tax.

Lafaye, Jacques. Quetzalcoatl & Guadalupe: The Formation of Mexican National Consciousness, 1531-1813. Keen, Benjamin, tr. LC 75-20889. xxx, 336p. (C). 1987. pap. text ed. 16.95 (*0-226-46788-0*) U Ch Pr.

Lafayette Junior League Members. Talk about Good II. 9.95 (*0-935032-50-9*) Jr League Lafayette.

Lafayette Junior League Members Staff. Talk about Good. 450p. 1967. 11.95 (*0-935032-00-2*) Jr League Lafayette.

Lafayette, Le Marquis de. Lafayette in the Age of the American Revolution, Selected Letters & Papers, 1776-1790, Vol. I: December 7th, 1776-March 30th, 1778. Idzerda, Stanley J. & Smith, Roger E., eds. LC 76-50268. (Lafayette Papers). (Illus.). 535p. 1977. 57.50 (*0-8014-1031-2*) Cornell U Pr.

— Lafayette in the Age of the American Revolution, Selected Letters & Papers, 1776-1790, Vol. II: April 10th, 1778-March 20th, 1780. Idzerda, Stanley J. et al, eds. LC 76-50268. (Lafayette Papers). (Illus.). 520p. 1979. 57.50 (*0-8014-1246-3*) Cornell U Pr.

— Lafayette in the Age of the American Revolution, Selected Letters & Papers, 1776-1790, Vol. III: April 27th, 1780-March 29th, 1781. Idzerda, Stanley J. et al, eds. LC 76-50268. (Lafayette Papers). (Illus.). 577p. 1980. 57.50 (*0-8014-1335-4*) Cornell U Pr.

— Lafayette in the Age of the American Revolution, Selected Letters & Papers, 1776-1790, Vol. IV: April 1st, 1781-December 23rd, 1781. Idzerda, Stanley J. et al, eds. LC 76-50268. (Lafayette Papers). (Illus.). 600p. 1981. 57.50 (*0-8014-1336-2*) Cornell U Pr.

— Lafayette in the Age of the American Revolution, Selected Letters & Papers, 1776-1790, Vol. V: January 4th, 1782-December 29th, 1785. Idzerda, Stanley J. & Crout, Robert R., eds. LC 76-50268. (Lafayette Papers). (Illus.). 528p. 1983. 57.50 (*0-8014-1576-4*) Cornell U Pr.

***Lafayette, Leslie.** Why Don't You Have Kids? Living a Full Life Without Parenthood. 320p. 1995. 20.00 (*0-8217-4853-X*) Kensington MI.

Lafayette, Marie J. The Princess of Cleves. LC 77-22941. 210p. 1977. reprint ed. text ed. 38.50 (*0-8371-9729-5*, LAFPC, Greenwood Pr) Greenwood.

Lafayette, Marie J., et al. The Letters of Lafayette & Jefferson. LC 78-19274. 1979. 35.95 (*0-405-10593-2*) Ayer.

Lafayette, R., jt. auth. see Deliere, J.

LaFeber, Walter. America, Russia, & the Cold War: 1945-1984. 5th ed. 320p. (C). 1985. pap. text ed. write for info. (*0-318-62574-1*, KnopfC) Knopf.

— America, Russia, & the Cold War, 1945-1992. 7th ed. LC 92-22914. (America in Crisis Ser.). 1992. pap. text ed. write for info. (*0-07-035853-2*) McGraw.

— The American Age: U. S. Foreign Policy at Home & Abroad, from 1750 to the Present. 2nd ed. (Illus.). (C). 1994. One Vol. Ed.: 1750-Present. pap. text ed. 25.95 (*0-393-96474-4*); Vol. 1: 1750-1920. pap. text ed. 21.95 (*0-393-96475-2*); Vol. 2: 1896-Present. pap. text ed. 21.95 (*0-393-96476-0*) Norton.

— The Cambridge History of American Foreign Relations: The American Search for Opportunity, 1865-1913. LC 92-36165. 1993. 27.95 (*0-521-38185-1*) Cambridge U Pr.

— Cambridge History of American Foreign Relations Vol. 2: The American Search for Opportunity, 1865-1913. (Illus.). 272p. (C). 1995. pap. 15.95 (*0-521-48383-2*) Cambridge U Pr.

— Inevitable Revolutions: The United States in Central America. 2nd rev. ed. 448p. 1993. pap. 13.95 (*0-393-30964-9*) Norton.

— Liberty & Power: U. S. Diplomatic History, 1750-1945. (New American History Ser.). 30p. (C). 1991. reprint ed. 5.00 (*0-87229-063-8*) Am Hist Assn.

— The New Empire: An Interpretation of American Expansion, 1860-1898. 457p. 1967. pap. 14.95 (*0-8014-9048-0*) Cornell U Pr.

— The Panama Canal: The Crisis in Historical Perspective. (Illus.). 384p. 1990. reprint ed. pap. 13.95 (*0-19-506192-6*) OUP.

— The Third Cold War. LC 81-80739. (Charles Edmondson Historical Lectures). 42p. (Orig.). 1981. pap. 4.50 (*0-918954-25-8*) Baylor Univ Pr.

LaFeber, Walter & Polenberg, Richard. The American Century: A History of the United States since the 1890's. 2nd ed. 546p. (C). 1979. text ed. write for info. (*0-394-34193-7*) Random.

LaFeber, Walter, jt. ed. see McCormick, Thomas.

LaFeber, Walter, et al. The American Century: A History of the United States since the 1890s, Vol. 1. 4th ed. 1992. text ed. write for info. (*0-07-035772-2*) McGraw.

— The American Century: A History of the United States since 1941, Vol. 2. 4th ed. 1992. text ed. write for info. (*0-07-035829-X*) McGraw.

***LaFemina, Gerry.** 23 Below. 56p. (Orig.). 1994. pap. 6.95 (*0-9642273-2-0*) Back Porch Pr.

Laferriere, Daniel. Sign & Subject: Semiotic & Psychoanalytic Investigations into Poetry. (Studies in Semiotics: No. 14). 103p. (Orig.). 1978. pap. 17.00 (*90-316-0138-1*, Pub. by Gruner NE) Benjamins North Am.

Lafeuer, Carolyn. The Murals of Charles Newcomb: A Story of Hagerstown, Indiana. 105p. 1994. 30.00 (*0-932970-96-6*) Prinit Pr.

Lafeuille, Germaine, ed. see Hippocrates.

Lafever, Minard. Beauties of Modern Architecture. 2nd ed. LC 68-29602. (Architecture & Decorative Art Ser.: Vol. 18). (Illus.). 1968. reprint ed. lib. bdg. 35.00 (*0-306-71040-4*) Da Capo.

LaFevers, Stephen & Marshall, Loren. Prehospital Care for the EMT-Intermediate Assessment & Intervention. (C). 1984. teacher ed write for info. (*0-8359-5603-2*, Reston); pap. text ed. 33.00 (*0-8359-5579-6*, Reston) P-H.

LaFevor, C. S., jt. auth. see Hendrix, T. G.

Lafevre, John L. How You Really Get Hired: The Inside Story from a College Professor. 3rd ed. LC 92-17054. 256p. 1993. pap. 11.00 (*0-13-444159-1*, Arco Test) P-H Gen Ref & Trav.

Laffaille, Maurice. Dufy's Complete Paintings, 4 vols. suppl. ed. 1513p. (FRE.). 1977. Incls. supplement. 2,100.00 (*0-685-30935-5*) A Wofsy Fine Arts.

— Dufy's Complete Paintings, 4 vols., Set. 1513p. (FRE.). 1977. 1,700.00 (*1-55660-112-3*) A Wofsy Fine Arts.

Laffal, Florence. Breads of Many Lands. LC 73-94308. 1975. pap. 12.95 (*0-913622-01-X*) Gallery Pr.

Laffal, Julius. A Concept Dictionary of English with Computer Programs for Content Analysis. LC 89-81593. (Orig.). 1990. disk, pap. 150.00 (*0-913622-06-0*) Gallery Pr.

— A Source Document in Schizophrenia, Whoever Had Most Fish Would Be Lord & Master. LC 74-82625. 340p. (C). 1979. 19.95 (*0-913622-02-8*) Gallery Pr.

Laffal, Ken. Vivolo & His Wooden Children. LC 76-11492. (Illus.). 144p. 1976. 19.95 (*0-913622-04-4*) Gallery Pr.

Laffan, Brigid. Integration & Co-Operation in Europe. (UACES Studies of Contemporary Europe). 192p. 1992. write for info. (*0-415-06338-8*, A7198); pap. write for info. (*0-415-06339-6*, A7202) Routledge.

Laffan, R. G. The Serbs: Guardians of the Gate. (Reprints Ser.). 299p. 1990. 17.95 (*0-88029-413-2*) Dorset Pr.

Laffeaty, Christina. Where the Hills Reply. 359p. 1992. 24.95 (*0-340-54674-3*, Pub. by H & S UK) Trafalgar.

Laffer, Arthur B. Private Short-Term Capital Flows. LC 75-159. (Business Economics & Finance Ser.: No. 5). 160p. reprint ed. pap. 45.60 (*0-7837-0651-0*, 2040990) Bks Demand.

Laffer, Arthur B., jt. ed. see Canto, Victor A.

Laffer, U., ed. Regional Chemotherapy. (Antibiotics & Chemotherapy Ser.: Vol. 40). (Illus.). viii, 100p. 1988. 71.25 (*3-8055-4670-X*) S Karger.

Laffer, U. & Duerig, M., eds. Chirurgische Traumatologie & Rehabiltation. (Basler Beitraege zur Chirurgie Ser.: Vol. 3). (Illus.). vi, 118p. 1990. 65.75 (*3-8055-5164-9*) S Karger.

— Ethik, Technik, Konzepte. (Basler Beitraege zur Chirurgie Ser.: Vol. 1). (Illus.). x, 138p. 1988. pap. 46.50 (*3-8055-4926-1*) S Karger.

Laffer, U., jt. ed. see Duerig, M.

Laffer, U., et al, eds. Implantable Drug Delivery Systems. (Illus.). viii, 68p. 1991. pap. 32.00 (*3-8055-5434-6*) S Karger.

— Modelle Interdisziplinaeren Handelns: 25 Jahre Department Chirurgie Basel. (Basler Beitraege zur Chirurgie Ser.: Vol. 5). (Illus.). viii, 162p. 1993. pap. 78.50 (*3-8055-5708-6*) S Karger.

— Traumatologie und Rehabilitation, No. 2: Organverletzungen. (Basler Beitraege zur Chirurgie Ser.: Vol. 4). (Illus.). vi, 118p. 1992. 71.25 (*3-8055-5459-1*) S Karger.

Lafferty, et al. Wellness: Promoting Positive Lifestyles. 484p. 1988. pap. text ed. 29.95 (*0-88725-101-3*) Hunter Textbks.

Lafferty & Assoc. Staff, ed. see Fife, Lynn H.

Lafferty & Associates Staff, ed. see Fife, Lynn H.

Lafferty, Edward L., et al. Parallel Computing: An Introduction. LC 93-866. (Illus.). 134p. 1993. 45.00 (*0-8155-1329-1*) Noyes.

Lafferty, Eileen. Out of the Nest, into the Frying Pan: A Cookbook for Kids Who Have Left Home & Other Fledgling Gourmets. LC 84-72116. (Illus.). 346p. (Orig.). 1984. pap. 9.95 (*0-9613994-0-6*) Bird Hand Pub.

Lafferty, Elaine. When You Hear Hoof. 1992. pap. 18.95 (*0-13-957440-9*) P-H.

Lafferty, James R., Sr. Ben Messick. LC 89-92682. (Illus.). 96p. 1993. 70.00 (*1-883246-01-6*); pap. 45.00 (*1-883246-02-4*) Eclectic Gal.

— Ben Messick. deluxe limited ed. LC 89-92682. (Illus.). 96p. 1993. boxed 350.00 (*1-883246-00-8*) Eclectic Gal.

Lafferty, Janet, ed. see Fife, Lynn H.

Lafferty, Jerry. Learning Power: A Student's Guide to Success. Moore, Melissa, ed. LC 92-72769. (Illus.). 138p. (Orig.). (YA). (gr. 7-12). 1993. Incl. six audio cass. audio 34.95 (*1-881843-29-7*) Alpha Educ Inst.

Lafferty, Joan M., jt. auth. see Pynes, Joan E.

Lafferty, Kevin J., jt. auth. see Eisenbarth, George S.

Lafferty, Libby. Earthquake Preparedness for Office, Home, Family & Community. (Illus.). 1994. pap. 5.00 (*0-9641072-1-X*) Lafferty & Assocs.

Lafferty, Libby & Lafferty, Tina. Be Ready, Be Safe for Earthquakes: A Child's Guide to Preparedness. (Illus.). 32p. (Orig.). (J). (gr. k-4). 1994. pap. text ed. 3.50 (*0-9641072-0-1*) Lafferty & Assocs.

Lafferty, Lida & Flood, Bo. Born Early: A Premature Baby's Story for Children. LC 94-92186. (Illus.). 40p. (Orig.). (J). (ps-4). 1995. pap. 8.95 (*0-9641413-0-2*) Songbird Pubng.

Lafferty, Perry. The Downing of Flight Six Heavy. 1990. 18.95 (*1-55611-213-0*) D I Fine.

— Downing of Flight Six Heavy. 384p. 1992. mass mkt. 4.99 (*1-55817-622-5*, Pinnacle NY) Windsor NY.

— Jablonski & the Erotomaniac: A Jack Jablonski Thriller. 1992. 19.95 (*1-55611-323-4*) D I Fine.

— Jablonski of L. A. 1991. 18.95 (*1-55611-262-9*) D I Fine.

Lafferty, Peter. Force & Motion. LC 92-6927. (Eyewitness Science Ser.). (Illus.). 64p. (J). (gr. 3-6). 1992. 15.95 (*1-879431-85-8*) Dorling Kindersley.

— Heat & Cold. (Let's Investigate Science Ser.). 64p. (J). (gr. 3-5). 1995. lib. bdg. write for info. (*0-7614-0033-8*, Benchmark NY) Marshall Cavendish.

— The Night Sky. (Let's Investigate Science Ser.). 64p. (J). (gr. 3-5). 1995. lib. bdg. write for info. (*0-7614-0029-X*, Benchmark NY) Marshall Cavendish.

— What's Inside Everyday Things? LC 95-2060. (What's Inside Series). (Illus.). 44p. (YA). (gr. 3 up). 1995. 16.95 (*0-87226-396-7*) P Bedrick Bks.

— The World of Science. LC 94-20019. (One Hundred One Questions & Answers Ser.). (J). 1994. 9.95 (*0-8160-3219-X*) Facts on File.

Lafferty, Peter & Jefferis, David. Pedal Power: The History of Bicycles. LC 89-29307. (Wheels Ser.). (Illus.). 32p. (J). (gr. 5-8). 1990. lib. bdg. 13.23 (*0-531-14084-9*) Watts.

— Superbikes: The History of Motorcycles. (Wheels Ser.). (Illus.). 32p. (J). (gr. 5-8). 1990. lib. bdg. 12.40 (*0-531-14039-3*) Watts.

— To the Rescue: The History of Emergency Vehicles. LC 89-21541. (Wheels Ser.). (Illus.). 32p. (J). (gr. 5-8). 1990. lib. bdg. 13.23 (*0-531-14085-7*) Watts.

Lafferty, Peter & Rowe, Julian. The Inventor Through History. LC 92-43262. (Journey Through History Ser.). (Illus.). 48p. (J). (gr. 5-8). 1993. 15.95 (*1-56847-013-4*) Thomson Lrning.

Lafferty, Peter & Rowe, Julian, eds. The Dictionary of Science. 678p. 1994. 45.00 (*0-13-304718-0*) S&S Trade.

Lafferty, Peter, jt. auth. see Jefferis, David.

Lafferty, R. A. Archipelago. deluxe limited ed. (Lost Manuscript Ser.). 283p. 1979. 100.00 (*0-936414-02-2*) Manuscript Pr.

— The Flame Is Green. deluxe ed. Thornhill, Ira M., ed. (Illus.). 240p. 1985. 35.00 (*0-911169-05-9*) Corroboree Pr.

— The Flame Is Green. Thornhill, Ira M., ed. (Illus.). 240p. 1985. reprint ed. 25.00 (*0-911169-04-0*) Corroboree Pr.

— Golden Gate & Other Stories. Thornhill, Ira M., ed. (Illus.). 240p. 1983. 20.00 (*0-911169-00-8*) Corroboree Pr.

— Half a Sky. Thornhill, Ira M., ed. (Illus.). 240p. 1984. 25.00 (*0-911169-03-2*) Corroboree Pr.

— Half a Sky. deluxe ed. Thornhill, Ira M., ed. (Illus.). 240p. 1984. 35.00 (*0-911169-02-4*) Corroboree Pr.

— Heart of Stone, Dear & Other Stories. (Booklet Ser.: No. 12). 43p. (Orig.). 1983. pap. 2.00 (*0-936055-09-X*) C Drumm Bks.

— It's Down the Slippery Cellar Stairs. (Booklet Ser.: No. 14). 42p. 1984. pap. 2.00 (*0-936055-11-1*) C Drumm Bks.

— It's Down the Slippery Cellar Stairs: Thoughts on Fiction, Writing, & Science Fiction. 2nd expanded rev. ed. LC 95-5201. (I. O. Evans Studies in the Philosophy & Criticism of Literature: No. 17). 104p. 1995. lib. bdg. 25.00x (*0-8095-0901-6*); pap. 15.00x (*0-8095-1901-1*) Borgo Pr.

— Laughing Kelly & Other Verses. (Booklet Ser.: No. 11). 16p. (Orig.). 1983. pap. 1.00 (*0-936055-08-1*) C Drumm Bks.

— The Man Who Made Models & Other Stories. (Booklet Ser.: No. 18). 51p. (Orig.). 1984. pap. 2.50 (*0-936055-16-2*) C Drumm Bks.

— My Heart Leaps Up, Chapters 7 & 8. (Booklet Ser.: No. 29). 49p. (Orig.). 1988. pap. text ed. 2.75 (*0-936055-37-5*) C Drumm Bks.

— My Heart Leaps Up, Chapters 9 & 10. (Booklet Ser.: No. 35). 63p. (Orig.). 1990. pap. text ed. 3.50 (*0-936055-41-3*) C Drumm Bks.

— My Heart Leaps Up, Chapters 9 & 10. deluxe ed. (Booklet Ser.: No. 35). 63p. (Orig.). 1990. pap. 6.00 (*0-936055-42-1*) C Drumm Bks.

— My Heart Leaps Up, Chs. 5 & 6. (Booklet Ser.: No. 28). 53p. (Orig.). 1987. pap. 2.95 (*0-936055-33-2*) C Drumm Bks.

— My Heart Leaps Up: Chapters 3 & 4. (Drumm Booklet Ser.: No. 26). 44p. (Orig.). 1987. pap. 2.75 (*0-936055-30-8*) C Drumm Bks.

— Okla Hannali. LC 91-50692. 240p. 1991. pap. 10.95 (*0-8061-2349-4*) U of Okla Pr.

— Sinbad, the Thirteenth Voyage. 176p. (Orig.). 1989. pap. 9.95 (*0-9623824-1-8*) Broken Mirrors Pr.

— Slippery & Other Stories. (Booklet Ser.: No. 19). 39p. (Orig.). 1985. pap. 2.00 (*0-936055-18-9*) C Drumm Bks.

— Snake in His Bosom & Other Stories. (Booklet Ser.: No. 13). 44p. (Orig.). 1983. pap. 2.00 (*0-936055-10-3*) C Drumm Bks.

— Through Elegant Eyes: Stories of Austro & the Men Who Know Everything. Thornhill, Ira M., ed. LC 83-72190. (Illus.). 240p. 1983. 20.00 (*0-911169-01-6*) Corroboree Pr.

Lafferty, Sarah R. Gary Rieveschi: Projects & Proposals 1973-1987. (Illus.). 1987. 9.95 (*0-917562-49-6*) Contemp Arts.

— Photovisions. (Illus.). 1987. 9.95 (*0-917562-48-8*) Contemp Arts.

Lafferty, Tina, jt. auth. see Lafferty, Libby.

Lafferty, William M. & Rosenstein, Eliezer, eds. The Challenge of New Technology & Macro Political Change. LC 93-9607. (International Handbook of Participation in Organizations Ser.: Vol. 3). 1993. 89.00 (*0-19-828382-2*) OUP.

Laffey, Alice. First & Second Chronicles. (Bible Commentary - Old Testament Ser.: No.10). 96p. 1985. pap. 3.95 (*0-8146-1417-5*) Liturgical Pr.

— The First & Second Kings. (Bible Commentary - Old Testament Ser.: No. 9). 112p. 1985. pap. text ed. 3.95 (*0-8146-1416-7*) Liturgical Pr.

— An Introduction to the Old Testament: A Feminist Perspective. LC 86-46436. 240p. 1988. pap. 15.00 (*0-8006-2078-X*, 1-2078, Fortress Pr) Augsburg Fortress.

Laffey, James L. Methods of Reading Instruction. LC 77-31440. (Reading Research Profiles Ser.). 72p. reprint ed. pap. 25.00 (*0-685-23596-3*, 2026253) Bks Demand.

Laffie, Lesli S., jt. ed. see Youngs, Maralee.

Laffie, Lynn, ed. see Bryant, Gary.

Laffin, John. The Australian Army at War 1899-1975. (Men-at-Arms Ser.: No. 123). (Illus.). 48p. pap. 11.95 (*0-85045-418-2*, 9056, Pub. by Osprey UK) Stackpole.

— Brassey's Battles: Three Thousand Five Hundred Years of Conflict, Campaigns & Wars from A-Z. 484p. 1986. 44.00 (*0-08-031185-7*, Pub. by Brasseys UK) Brasseys Inc.

— Brassey's Battles: 3,500 Years of Conflict, Campaigns & Wars from A-Z. (Illus.). 484p. 1995. pap. 23.95 (*1-85753-176-0*, Pub. by Brasseys UK) Brasseys Inc.

— British Butchers & Bunglers of World War I. LC 92-18632. (Illus.). 224p. (YA). (gr. 9-12). 1992. pap. text ed. 16.00 (*0-7509-0179-9*) A Sutton Pub.

— Damn the Dardanelles! The Agony of Gallipoli. (Illus.). 224p. 1990. 22.00 (*0-86299-590-6*) A Sutton Pub.

— Guide to Australian Battlefields of the Western Front 1916-1918. (Illus.). 192p. (Orig.). 1993. pap. 19.95 (*0-86417-468-3*, Pub. by Kangaroo Pr AT) Seven Hills Bk.

— Hitler Warned Us. (Illus.). 128p. 1995. pap. 24.95 (*1-85753-103-5*, Pub. by Brasseys UK) Brasseys Inc.

— The Israeli Army in the Middle East Wars, 1948-73. (Men-at-Arms Ser.: No. 127). (Illus.). 48p. 1984. pap. 11.95 (*0-85045-450-6*, 9059, Pub. by Osprey UK) Stackpole.

— Panorama of the Western Front. (Illus.). 1993. 30.00 (*0-7509-0352-X*) A Sutton Pub.

— War Annual One (1985-86) 187p. 1986. 35.95 (*0-08-031211-X*, Pub. by Brasseys UK) Brasseys Inc.

— War Annual Two (1986-87) (Illus.). 242p. 1987. 35.95 (*0-08-034751-7*, Pub. by Brasseys UK) Brasseys Inc.

— A Western Front Companion 1914-1918. (Illus.). 224p. 1995. 29.95 (*0-7509-0061-X*) A Sutton Pub.

— The Western Front Illustrated. (Illus.). 224p. 1991. 34.00 (*0-86299-789-5*) A Sutton Pub.

— The World in Conflict War Annual No. 6: Contemporary Warfare Described & Analysed. (War Annual Ser.: No. 6). (Illus.). 500p. 1994. 50.00 (*0-08-041330-7*, Pub. by Brasseys UK) Brasseys Inc.

— The World in Conflict: War Annual Five: Contemporary Warfare Described & Analysed. (War Annual Ser.: No. 5). (Illus.). 240p. 1991. 29.95 (*0-08-040712-9*, Pub. by Brasseys UK) Brasseys Inc.

L

— The World in Conflict 1989: War Annual Three. (Illus.). 234p. 1988. 35.95 (0-08-036265-6, Pub. by Brasseys UK) Brasseys Inc.

— The World in Conflict 1990: War Annual Four. (Illus.). 194p. 1990. text ed. 35.95 (0-08-037334-8) Macmillan.

— World War I in Postcards. LC 89-36281. (Illus.). 256p. 1989. 25.00 (0-86299-370-9); pap. 15.00 (0-86299-612-0) A Sutton Pub.

Laffin, John, jt. ed. see Baynes, John.

Laffin, Richard. The Jewelers' Guide to Creative Pricing. Holmes, George, ed. 64p. (Orig.). 1990. pap. 19.95 (0-931744-15-6, CR-027) Jewelers Bk Club.

Laffin, Richard F. Jeweler's Inventory Manual. rev. ed. 170p. 1988. spiral bd. 49.95 (0-931744-13-X, CR-020) Jewelers Bk Club.

***Laffite, Jean.** The Journal of Jean Laffite: The Privateer-Patriot's Own Story. 153p. Date not set. reprint ed. pap. 12.50 (0-9646846-0-8) Dogwood TX.

Laffling, John. Toward High Precision Machine Translation: Based on Contrastive Textology. LC 91-33903. (Distributed Language Translation Ser.: No. 7). xiv, 178p. (C). 1991. lib. bdg. 75.40 (3-11-013388-1) Mouton.

Laffoley, Paul. Paul Laffoley: The Phenomenology of Revelation. Wasilik, Jeanne M., ed. (Illus.). 112p. 1989. 30.00 (1-878607-06-5) Kent Gallery.

Laffoni, Robert, ed. The Illustrated History of Paris & the Parisians. (Illus.). 292p. 1958. lib. bdg. 35.00 (0-8288-3996-4) Fr & Eur.

Laffont, Bompiani. Dictionnaire des Oeuvres de Tous les Temps et de Tous les Pays. 1981. lib. bdg. 275.00 (0-8288-2600-5) Fr & Eur.

— Dictionnaire des Personnages Litteraires et Dramatiques de Tous les Tempes et de Tous les Pays. (FRE.). 83.95 (0-8288-9900-2, F12885) Fr & Eur.

— Dictionnaires Oeuvres Contemporains: Dictionary of Contemporary Works. (FRE.). 1977. 225.00 (0-8288-5462-9, M6129) Fr & Eur.

Laffont, Jean-Jacques. The Economics of Uncertainty & Information. Bonin, John P. & Bonin, Helene, trs. 312p. 1989. 37.50 (0-262-12136-0) MIT Pr.

— Essays in the Economics of Uncertainty. LC 79-19771. (Economic Studies: No. 149). 150p. 1980. 15.00 (0-674-26555-6) HUP.

— The Fundamentals of Public Economics. Bonin, John P. & Bonin, Helene, trs. (Illus.). 288p. (Orig.). 1988. 35.00 (0-262-12127-1) MIT Pr.

***Laffont, Jean-Jacques, ed.** Advances in Economic Theory Vol. 1: Sixth World Congress. (Econometric Society Monographs: No. 20). 336p. (C). 1995. pap. 19.95 (0-521-48459-6) Cambridge U Pr.

— Advances in Economic Theory Vol. 2: Sixth World Congress. (Econometric Society Monographs: No. 21). 464p. (C). 1995. pap. 19.95 (0-521-48460-X) Cambridge U Pr.

— Advances in Economic Theory, Vol. 1: Sixth World Congress. (Econometric Society Monographs: No. 20). 450p. (C). 1993. 59.95 (0-521-41666-3) Cambridge U Pr.

— Advances in Economic Theory, Vol. 2: Sixth World Congress. (Econometric Society Monographs: No. 21). 400p. (C). 1993. 59.95 (0-521-43019-4) Cambridge U Pr.

Laffont, Jean-Jacques & Moreaux, Michel, eds. Dynamics, Incomplete Information & Industrial Economics. Laisney, Francois, tr. 288p. (C). 1991. text ed. 54.95 (0-631-16967-9) Blackwell Pubs.

Laffont, Jean-Jacques & Tirole, Jean. A Theory of Incentives in Regulation & Procurement. (Illus.). 640p. 1993. 42.50 (0-262-12174-3) MIT Pr.

Laffont, Jean-Jacques, jt. auth. see Green, J.

Laffont, Robert. Dictionnaire des Auteurs, 4 vols., Set. 1980. lib. bdg. 150.00 (0-8288-2614-5, F12570) Fr & Eur.

— Dictionnaire des Auteurs, Vol. 4: Qa-Zw. 759p. (FRE.). 1980. pap. 45.00 (0-7859-4429-X, 2221501756) Fr & Eur.

— Dictionnaire des Oeuvres de Tous les Temps et de Tous les Pays (Dictionary of the Works of All Times & Places) Litterature. 882p. (FRE.). pap. 45.00 (0-7859-4622-5) Fr & Eur.

Laffont, Robert, ed. Dictionnaire des Oeuvres de Tous les Tempes et de Tous les Pays. 1980. pap. 45.00 (0-7859-4426-5) Fr & Eur.

Laffont, Robert & Bompiani, Valentino. Dictionnaire des Personnages. 3rd ed. 776p. (FRE.). 1984. pap. 49.95 (0-7859-5120-2) Fr & Eur.

***Laffont, Robert & Bompiano, Valentino.** Dictionnaire des Oeuvres de Tous les Temps et de Tous les Pays Litterature, Philosophie, Musique, Sciences, 7 vols. (FRE.). 1980. 265.00 (0-7859-8630-8, 222101183x) Fr & Eur.

***Laffont Staff.** Dictionnaire de la Sagesse Orientale Bouddhisme, Hindouisme, Taoisme, Zen. 780p. (FRE.). 1989. pap. 45.00 (0-7859-7805-4, 2221056116) Fr & Eur.

— Dictionnaire du Cinema Vol. 2: Les Actuers. 1128p. (FRE.). 1984. pap. 55.00 (0-7859-7811-9, 2221071638) Fr & Eur.

Laffort, Paul, jt. ed. see Martin, Guy.

***Laffra, C., et al, eds.** Object-Oriented Programming for Graphics. (Focus on Computer Graphics Ser.). 278p. 1994. 61.00 (0-387-58314-9) Spr-Verlag.

Laffrado, Laura. Hawthorne's Literature for Children. LC 91-28002. 176p. 1992. 27.50 (0-8203-1417-X) U of Ga Pr.

Lafili, Louis, jt. ed. see Campbell, Dennis.

Lafili, Louis, et al, eds. Survey of the International Sale of Goods. 375p. 1986. lib. bdg. 81.00 (90-6544-241-3) Kluwer Ac.

Lafitte, Francois. The Internment of Aliens. 260p. 1988. 37. 50 (1-870352-55-6) Denali Press.

Lafkowitz, Natalie. From Process to Product: Writing from Experience for Beginning & Intermediate ESL Students. (Illus.). 256p. (C). 1986. pap. text ed. 17.95 (0-13-331695-5) P-H.

LaFlamme, Alan G. Green Turtle Cay: An Island in the Bahamas. (Illus.). 110p. (Orig.). (C). 1985. pap. text ed. 8.50 (0-88133-186-4) Waveland Pr.

Laflamme, Gilles, et al, eds. Flexibility & Labour Markets in Canada & the United States. (Research Ser.: No. 94). 315p. 1989. pap. 24.00 (92-9014-462-9) Intl Labour Office.

Laflamme, Simon. La Cociete Integree: De la Circulation Des Biens, Des Idees et Des Personnes. LC 91-45433. (Worcester Polytechnic Institute Studies in Science, Technology, & Culture: Vol. 12). 328p. (FRE.). 1993. 54.95 (0-8204-1869-2) P Lang Pubs.

Lafler, Joanne. The Celebrated Mrs. Oldfield: The Life & Art of an Augustan Actress. LC 88-34654. (Illus.). 240p. (C). 1989. 29.95 (0-8093-1485-1) S Ill U Pr.

LaFlesche, Francis, jt. auth. see Fletcher, Alice C.

Lafleur & Brooks. Exploring Medical Language. 3rd ed. 612p. 1993. spiral bd. 27.95 (0-8016-6984-7) Mosby Yr Bk.

— Text & Audiotape Package for Exploring Medical. 612p. 1993. 32.95 (0-8016-7679-7) Mosby Yr Bk.

LaFleur & Starr. Exploring Medical Language. 2nd ed. (Illus.). 640p. 1988. text ed. 28.95 (0-8016-2944-6) Mosby Yr Bk.

Lafleur, jt. auth. see Brooks.

Lafleur, B. Dictionary of Idiomatic French Expressions. 670p. (FRE.). 1991. 65.00 (0-685-62923-6, 2801109479) Fr & Eur.

— Dictionary of Idiomatic French Expressions. 2nd ed. 670p. (FRE.). 1991. lib. bdg. 65.00 (0-8288-3314-1, 2801109479) Fr & Eur.

Lafleur-Brooks, Myrna L. Health Unit Coordinating. 3rd ed. (Illus.). 541p. 1992. pap. text ed. 30.95 (0-7216-4302-7) Saunders.

***LaFleur-Brooks, Myrna W. & Gillingham, Elaine T.** Certification Review Book for Health Unit Coordinators. 2nd ed. 176p. 1994. pap. text ed. 20.00 (0-7216-5669-2) Saunders.

LaFleur, Bruce, jt. auth. see LaFleur, Terri.

***Lafleur, Bruno.** Dictionnaire des Expressions. 672p. (FRE.). 1984. 59.95 (0-7859-7698-1, 2040152679) Fr & Eur.

— Dictionnaire des Locutions Idiomatiques Francaises. 669p. (FRE.). 1980. pap. 105.00 (0-7859-8292-2, 3261048042) Fr & Eur.

Lafleur, J., ed. see Bentham, Jeremy.

Lafleur, Laurence J. Discourse on Method: Descartes. 72p. (C). 1956. pap. write for info. (0-02-367160-2) Macmillan.

— Meditation on First Philosophy: Descartes. 104p. (C). 1960. pap. write for info. (0-02-367170-X) Macmillan.

— Philosophical Essays. Descartes. (Library of Liberal Arts: No. 99). 264p. (C). 1964. pap. write for info. (0-02-367240-4) Macmillan.

Lafleur, Laurence J., tr. see Descartes, Rene.

LaFleur, Myrna W. & Schneider, Patricia. Skills Practice Manual for Health Unit Coordinating. 3rd ed. (Illus.). 272p. 1993. pap. text ed. 18.95 (0-7216-4303-5) Saunders.

LaFleur, Richard A. Latin Poetry. 1987. teacher ed 28.00 (0-8013-0140-8, 75804); pap. text ed. 12.57 (0-8013-0133-5, 75797) Longman.

LaFleur, Robert G., ed. Groundwater As a Geomorphic Agent. (Binghamton Symposia in Geomorphology: International Ser.: No. 13). (Illus.). 384p. (C). 1984. text ed. 80.00 (0-04-551069-5) Routledge Chapman & Hall.

LaFleur, Terri. Compendium of Lottery Statistics 1992. 207p. 1992. pap. 100.00 (1-883567-50-5) TLF Pubns.

— LaFleur's Lottery Interim Report: Fiscal 1992 Sales & Analysis. 54p. 1992. pap. 40.00 (1-883567-57-2) TLF Pubns.

— LaFleur's Ninety One North American Gambling Abstract. 258p. 1991. pap. 139.00 (1-883567-55-6) TLF Pubns.

— The Lottery Book. 167p. 1991. pap. 100.00 (1-883567-52-1) TLF Pubns.

— Nineteen Ninety-Four World Lottery Almanac. 388p. 1994. pap. text ed. 149.00 (1-883567-64-5) TLF Pubns.

LaFleur, Terri & Lafleur, Bruce. LaFleur World Gambling Abstract, 1993. 297p. 1992. pap. 175.00 (1-883567-56-4) TLF Pubns.

LaFleur, Terri & LaFleur, Bruce. LaFleur's European Lottery Abstract. 202p. 1992. pap. 100.00 (1-883567-53-X) TLF Pubns.

— LaFleur's Lottery Interim Report, Vol. Two: Fiscal 1993 Sales & Analysis. 55p. 1993. pap. 45.00 (1-883567-59-9) TLF Pubns.

— LaFleur's Principles of Contemporary Lottery Marketing. 192p. 1992. pap. 100.00 (1-883567-51-3) TLF Pubns.

LaFleur, Terri & Lafleur, Bruce. LaFleur's Video Lottery Terminal & Keno Report. 70p. 1993. pap. 45.00 (1-883567-58-0) TLF Pubns.

LaFleur, Terri & LaFleur, Bruce. LaFleur's Video Lottery Terminal Report. 68p. 1992. pap. 40.00 (1-883567-54-8) TLF Pubns.

— LaFleur's World Gambling Almanac, 1994. 325p. 1993. pap. 185.00 (1-883567-60-2) TLF Pubns.

— World Lottery Almanac, 1993. 394p. 1993. pap. 139.00 (1-883567-61-0) TLF Pubns.

LaFleur, Tom & Brennan, Gale. Bingo the Bear. (Illus.). 16p. (Orig.). (J). (gr. k-6). 1981. pap. 1.25 (0-685-02454-7) Brennan Bks.

— Henry the Hound. (Illus.) 16p. (Orig.). (J). (gr. k-6). 1982. pap. 1.25 (0-685-05556-6) Brennan Bks.

— Isadore the Dinosaur. (Illus.). 16p. (Orig.). (J). (gr. k-6). 1981. pap. 1.25 (0-685-02456-3) Brennan Bks.

— Spunky the Monkey. (Illus.). 16p. (Orig.). (J). (gr. k-6). 1981. pap. 1.25 (0-685-02457-1) Brennan Bks.

— Tuffy the Tiger. (Illus.). 16p. (J). (gr. k-6). 1982. pap. 1.25 (0-685-05557-4) Brennan Bks.

— Woolly the Wolf. (Illus.). 16p. (Orig.). (J). (gr. k-6). 1981. pap. 1.25 (0-685-02459-8) Brennan Bks.

***LaFleur, William.** Liquid Life: Abortion & Buddhism in Japan. 1994. pap. 14.95 (0-691-02965-2) Princeton U Pr.

LaFleur, William, et al, eds. Flowing Traces: Buddhism in the Literary & Visual Arts of Japan. (Illus.). 296p. 1992. text ed. 42.50 (0-691-07365-1) Princeton U Pr.

LaFleur, William R. The Karma of Words: Buddhism & the Literary Arts in Medieval Japan. LC 82-45909. 232p. (C). 1983. pap. 14.00 (0-520-05622-1) U CA Pr.

— Liquid Life: Abortion & Buddhism in Japan. (Illus.). 280p. 1992. text ed. 24.95 (0-691-07405-4) Princeton U Pr.

LaFleur, William R., ed. Dogen Studies. LC 85-16427. (Studies in East Asian Buddhism: No. 2). 288p. 1985. pap. text ed. 19.00 (0-8248-1011-2) UH Pr.

LaFleur, William R., ed. see Abe, Masao.

Laflin, Jack. Serpent in Paradise. 1992. 16.95 (0-533-10084-4) Vantage.

Lafo, Rachel R. Allan Wexler: Table-Building-Landscape & Proposals for a Picnic Area. (Illus.). 8p. (Orig.). 1992. pap. 1.00 (0-945506-10-4) DeCordova Mus.

— Anne Griffith Johnson Paintings: Orleonok Pitkin. (Illus.). 1981. pap. 1.00 (0-914435-05-1) Marylhurst Art.

— Belief in the Underground: The Art of Marcy Hermansader. LC 90-80631. (Orig.). 1990. pap. 12.00 (0-945506-05-8) DeCordova Mus.

— Eight Artists - Eight Visions: 1990. LC 90-82380. (Orig.). 1990. bds. 7.00 (0-945506-06-6) DeCordova Mus.

— The Surrealism of Everyday Life: Paintings by Gerry Bergstein. LC 89-50130. (Illus.). 32p. (Orig.). 1989. pap. write for info. (0-945506-02-3) DeCordova Mus.

— Ten Artists - Ten Visions: 1989. LC 89-51080. (Orig.). 1989. bds. 6.00 (0-945506-03-1) DeCordova Mus.

Lafo, Rachel R. & Capasso, Nicholas. Eleven Artists - Eleven Visions: 1992. 1992. bds. 6.00 (0-945506-08-2) DeCordova Mus.

— Eleven Artists - Eleven Visions: 1993. 1993. bds. 6.00 (0-945506-13-9) DeCordova Mus.

— Nine Artists - Nine Visions: 1991. 1991. bds. 6.00 (0-945506-07-4) DeCordova Mus.

Lafo, Rachel R. & Westfall, Stephen. Gregory Amenoff: Works on Paper, 1975-1992. (Illus.). 40p. (Orig.). 1993. pap. write for info. (0-945506-12-0) DeCordova Mus.

LaFollette, jt. auth. see Hunter.

***LaFollette, Hugh.** Persons & Personal Relationships: Love, Identity & Ethics. 256p. (C). 1995. write for info. (0-631-19684-6); pap. write for info. (0-631-19685-4) Blackwell Pubs.

LaFollette, Hugh, jt. auth. see Aiken, William.

LaFollette, Hugh, jt. ed. see Graham, George.

LaFollette, Karen, jt. auth. see Roberts, Paul C.

LaFollette, Marcel C. Making Science Our Own: Public Images of Science, 1910-1955. LC 89-20555. (Illus.). 312p. 1990. lib. bdg. 45.00 (0-226-46778-3) U Ch Pr.

Lafollette, Marcel C. Stealing into Print: Fraud, Plagiarism, & Misconduct in Scientific Publishing. 1992. 30.00 (0-520-07831-4) U CA Pr.

LaFollette, Marcel C. & Stine, Jeffrey K., eds. Technology & Choice: Readings from Technology & Culture. (Illus.). 336p. 1991. pap. 16.95 (0-226-46777-5) U Ch Pr.

— Technology & Choice: Readings from Technology & Culture. (Illus.). 336p. 1991. lib. bdg. 34.95 (0-226-46776-7) U Ch Pr.

LaFollette, Robert M., ed. The Making of America: Labor. LC 72-89744. (American Labor, from Conspiracy to Collective Bargaining Ser., No. 1). 433p. 1970. reprint ed. 34.95 (0-405-02132-1) Ayer.

Lafon, Jacqueline L., jt. auth. see Volcansek, Mary L.

Lafon, Michel. French-Comorian (Shingazidja) Lexicon. 239p. (FRE.). 1991. 69.95 (0-8288-6922-7, 2738411010) Fr & Eur.

Lafon, Robert. Diccionario de Psicopedagogia y Psiqiatria del Nino: French - Spanish. 5th ed. 1056p. (FRE & SPA.). 1993. lib. bdg. write for info. (0-7859-3677-7, 8428107556) Fr & Eur.

— Vocabulaire de Psychopedagogie et de Psychiatrie de L'enfant: Vocabulary of Child Psychiatry & Educational Psychology. 3rd ed. 868p. (FRE.). 1973. 95.00 (0-8288-6335-0, F-19440) Fr & Eur.

LaFon, Ron, ed. & illus. Euphorbia Journal, Vol. 1. 270p. (C). 1982. 55.00 (0-912647-00-0) Strawberry.

— Euphorbia Journal, Vol. 2. 270p. (C). 1983. 45.00 (0-912647-01-9) Strawberry.

— Euphorbia Journal, Vol. 3. 270p. (C). 1984. 45.00 (0-912647-02-7) Strawberry.

— Euphorbia Journal, Vol. 4. 270p. (C). 1985. 45.00 (0-912647-08-6) Strawberry.

— Euphorbia Journal, Vol. 5. 270p. (C). 1987. 45.00 (0-912647-05-1) Strawberry.

— Euphorbia Journal, Vol. 6. 270p. (C). 1989. 45.00 (0-912647-06-X) Strawberry.

— Euphorbia Journal, Vol. 7. 270p. (C). 1991. 45.00 (0-912647-04-3) Strawberry.

LaFon, Ron, ed. see Rowley, Gorden.

***LaFon, Ruth.** Kelly, the Ventriloquist Ghost. (J). 1995. 8.95 (0-8062-5175-1) Carlton.

Lafond, Jean, jt. auth. see La Rochefoucauld, Francois de.

Lafond, Patrick & Vaughan, Richard. L' Anglais de l'Expert-Comptable. 159p. (FRE.). 1993. pap. 69.95 (0-7859-1661-X, 2906471054) Fr & Eur.

LaFond, Richard E., ed. Cancer: The Outlaw Cell. 2nd ed. LC 88-14517. (Illus.). xxiii, 289p. 1988. 29.95 (0-8412-1419-0); pap. 19.95 (0-8412-1420-4) Am Chemical.

***Lafond, Virginia.** Grieving Mental Illness: A Guide for Patients & Their Caregivers. 96p. 1994. 30.00 (0-8020-0614-0); pap. 12.95 (0-8020-7578-9) U of Toronto Pr.

***Lafont, B. & Yildiz, F.** Tablettes Cuneiformes De Tello Au Musee d'Istambul: Datant De l'Epoque De la IIIe Dynastie d'Ur. 296p. 1989. pap. text ed. 46.50 (90-6258-065-3, Pub. by Netherlands Inst NE) Eisenbrauns.

Lafont, Ghislain. God, Time & Being. Maluf, Leonard, tr. LC 91-27423. 348p. (Orig.). 1992. pap. 34.95 (0-932506-89-5) St Bedes Pubns.

LaFont, Jan. The Mirror on the Town Hall. 150p. (Orig.). 1982. pap. 3.50 (0-9603596-3-X) Fontastic.

LaFontaine, Gary. Caddisflies. (Illus.). 336p. 1989. 35.00 (0-941130-98-3) Lyons & Burford.

— The Dry Fly: New Angles. (Illus.). 308p. 1990. 39.95 (0-9626663-0-0) Greycliff Pub.

LaFontaine, Gary, jt. auth. see Cordes, Ron.

LaFontaine, H. C. Apollonius of Tyana. (Orig.). 1993. pap. 5.95 (1-55818-234-9) Holmes Pub.

Lafontaine, J., et al. Riemannian Geometry. (Universitext Ser.). x, 248p. 1987. pap. 29.00 (0-387-17923-2) Spr-Verlag.

Lafontaine, J. Donald, et al. The Moths of America North of Mexico, Fascicle 25.1: Noctuoidea, Noctuidae (Part), Plusiinae. Hodges, R. W. et al, eds. LC 91-65196. (Illus.). 182p. (C). 1991. pap. text ed. 70.00 (0-933003-06-4) Wedge Entomological.

Lafontaine, J. Donald. The Moths of America North of Mexico, Fascicle 27.2: Noctuoidea, Noctuidae: Noctuinae (Part-Euxoa) Hodges, R. W. et al, eds. LC 87-50657. (Illus.). 235p. (C). 1987. pap. text ed. 75.00 (0-933003-03-X) Wedge Entomological.

Lafontaine, Jacques, jt. ed. see Audin, Michele.

LaFontaine, Jean de, jt. auth. see Wildsmith, Brian.

Lafontaine, Monique, ed. see Lafontaine, Steve.

Lafontaine, Steve. Mazda Wankel Rotary Aviation Conversion Resource Book. Lafontaine, Monique, ed. (Illus.). 32p. (Orig.). 1990. pap. text ed. 10.00 (0-9625685-0-3) Lafontaine Pr.

— Oildrum Cookbook: Fifty-Five Back to Basic, Appropriate Technology Devices You Can Build from a Steel Oildrum. Lafontaine, Monique, ed. (Illus.). 200p. (Orig.). 1990. pap. text ed. 10.00 (0-9625685-1-1) Lafontaine Pr.

Lafora, Nicolbas de & Kinnaird, Lawrence. New York Film Festival Programs, Nineteen Sixty-Three to Nineteen Seventy-Five. 1977. 65.95 (0-405-07619-3, 11479) Ayer.

LaForce, Beatrice. Devil's Cuspidor. 1981. pap. 1.75 (0-686-37157-7) Eldridge Pub.

Lafore, Laurence D. Long Fuse: An Interpretation of the Origins of World War I. 2nd ed. (Critical Periods of History Ser.). (Orig.). (C). 1990. pap. text ed. 21.00 (0-397-47242-0) HarpCollege.

— The Long Fuse: An Interpretation of the Origins of World War I. LC 81-1514. (Critical Periods of History Ser.). 282p. 1981. reprint ed. text ed. 67.50 (0-313-22969-4, LALF, Greenwood Pr) Greenwood.

Lafore, Robert. Lafore's Windows Programming Ridiculously Made Easy: Only What You Keed to Know. (Illus.). 610p. (Orig.). 1993. disk, pap. 29.95 (1-878739-23-9) Waite Group Pr.

— Waite Group's C Programming Using Turbo C Plus Plus. 2nd ed. 1990. pap. 29.95 (0-672-22737-1) Sams.

— Waite Groups C Programming Using Turbo C Plus Plus. 2nd ed. 816p. 1993. pap. 34.95 (0-672-30399-X) Sams.

— Waite Group's Microsoft C Programming for the PC. 2nd ed. 1990. pap. 29.95 (0-672-22738-X) Sams.

— The Waite Group's Turbo C Programming for the PC. rev. ed. (Illus.). 720p. 1989. pap. 29.95 (0-672-22660-X) Sams.

***Lafore, Robert W.** Object-Oriented Programming in C++ 2nd rev. ed. Orig. Title: Object-Oriented Programming in Turbo C++. 850p. 1994. disk, pap. 34.95 (1-878739-73-5) Waite Group Pr.

***Laforest, Guy.** Trudeau & the End of a Canadian Dream. Browne, Paul L. & Weinroth, Michelle, trs. 240p. 1995. 44.95 (0-7735-1300-0); pap. 17.95 (0-7735-1322-1) U of Toronto Pr.

LaForest, Sandra, jt. auth. see MacIvor, Virginia.

Laforest, Thomas & LaRochelle, Jeffrey. Our French Canadian-Ancestors, Vol. II. rev. ed. LC 83-81941. (Illus.). 290p. 1990. pap. 15.00 (0-914163-02-7) L I S I Pr.

Laforest, Thomas J. & LaRochelle, Jeffrey. Our French Canadian Ancestors, Vol. III. rev. ed. LC 83-81941. (Illus.). 296p. 1985. pap. 15.00 (0-914163-03-5) L I S I Pr.

Laforest, Thomas J. & Lebel, Gerard. Our French Canadian Ancestors, Vol. IX. LC 83-81941. (Illus.). 321p. 1989. pap. 15.00 (0-914163-09-4) L I S I Pr.

— Our French Canadian Ancestors, Vol. X. LC 83-81941. (Illus.). 312p. 1990. pap. 15.00 (0-914163-10-8) L I S I Pr.

— Our French Canadian Ancestors, Vol. XI. LC 83-81941. (Illus.). 310p. 1990. pap. 15.00 (0-914163-11-6) L I S I Pr.

— Our French Canadian Ancestors, Vol. XII. LC 83-81941. (Illus.). 300p. 1991. pap. 15.00 (0-914163-12-4) L I S I Pr.

— Our French-Canadian Ancestors, Vol. XIV. LC 83-81941. (Illus.). 310p. 1992. pap. 15.00 (0-914163-14-0) L I S I Pr.

— Our French Canadian Ancestors, Vol. XVI. LC 83-81941. (Illus.). 280p. 1993. pap. 15.00 (0-914163-16-7) L I S I Pr.

— Our French Canadian Ancestors, Vol. XVIII. LC 83-81941. (Illus.). 290p. 1994. pap. 15.00 (0-914163-18-3) L I S I Pr.

L

— Our French Canadian Ancestors, Vol. XV. LC 83-81941. (Illus.). 284p. 1992. pap. 15.00 (*0-914163-15-9*) L I S I Pr.

Laforest, Thomas J. & Rochelle, Jeffrey La. Our French-Canadian Ancestors, Vol. I. rev. ed. LC 83-81941. (Illus.). 300p. 1993. reprint ed. pap. 15.00 (*0-914163-01-9*) L I S I Pr.

Laforest, Thomas J. & Saint-Onge, Jacques. Our French Canadian Ancestors, Vol. XVII. LC 83-81941. (Illus.). 280p. 1993. pap. 15.00 (*0-914163-17-5*) L I S I Pr.

Laforest, Thomas J. & Saintonge, Jacques. Our French-Canadian Ancestors, Vol. IV. LC 83-81941. (Illus.). 296p. 1986. pap. 15.00 (*0-914163-04-3*) L I S I Pr.

— Our French Canadian Ancestors, Vol. V. LC 83-81941. (Illus.). 288p. 1987. pap. 15.00 (*0-914163-05-1*) L I S I Pr.

— Our French-Canadian Ancestors, Vol. VI. LC 83-81941. (Illus.). 312p. 1988. pap. 15.00 (*0-914163-06-X*) L I S I Pr.

— Our French Canadian Ancestors, Vol. VII. LC 83-81914. (Illus.). 298p. 1988. pap. 15.00 (*0-914163-07-8*) L I S I Pr.

— Our French Canadian Ancestors, Vol. VIII. LC 83-81914. (Illus.). 284p. 1989. pap. 15.00 (*0-914163-08-6*) L I S I Pr.

— Our French Canadian Ancestors, Vol. XIII. LC 83-81941. (Illus.). 310p. 1991. pap. 15.00 (*0-914163-13-2*) L I S I Pr.

LaForester, Wilford A., jt. auth. see Lee, Harry O.

***Laforet, Carmen.** Isla y los Demonios. 2nd ed. 312p. 1991. pap. 19.95 (*0-7859-5142-3*) Fr & Eur.

— Nada. Ennis, Glafyra, tr. LC 92-31936. (Catalan Studies: Vol. 8). 243p. (Orig.). (C). 1993. pap. text ed. 29.95 (*0-8204-2064-6*) P Lang Pubs.

Laforet, Claude. La Vie Musicale Au Temps Romantique. LC 77-4153. (Music Reprint Ser.: 1977). 1977. reprint ed. lib. bdg. 29.50 (*0-306-70890-6*) Da Capo.

LaForge, Carol & Morse, Linda. Diabetic Delights. LC 93-70972. 184p. 1993. spiral bd. 16.95 (*0-9637774-0-8*) Diabetic Delghts.

Laforge, Frank & Laforge-Webb, Laura. Among the Pleiades & Other Stars. (Illus.). 200p. 1993. pap. 15.95 (*0-8059-3417-0*) Dorrance.

Laforge, Larry, ed. Boston Rocks. 1987. pap. 9.00 (*0-685-19188-5*) MIT Outing.

LaForge, Ralph, jt. auth. see Somer, Elizabeth.

LaForge, Raymond, jt. auth. see Hills, Gerald E.

LaForge, Raymond, jt. auth. see Ingram, Thomas N.

Laforge-Webb, Laura, jt. auth. see Laforge, Frank.

LaForgia, Gerard M. Local Organizations for Rural Health in Panama: Community Participation, Bureaucratic Reorientation, & Political Will. (Special Series on Rural Local Organization: No. 8). 153p. 1985. 7.50 (*0-86731-035-9*) Cornell CIS RDC.

Laforgue, Jules. Berlin, la Cour et la Ville. LC 77-10273. reprint ed. 26.00 (*0-404-16325-4*) AMS Pr.

— Lettres a un Ami: 1880-1886, avec le Fac-Simile d'Une Lettre Inedite a Stephane Mallarme. LC 77-10274. 240p. reprint ed. 47.50 (*0-404-16326-2*) AMS Pr.

— Moral Tales. Smith, William J., tr. LC 84-25498. (Illus.). 224p. 1985. 17.95 (*0-8112-0942-3*); pap. 8.95 (*0-8112-0943-1*, NDP594) New Directions.

— Moralites Legendaires. (Folio Ser.: No. 855). 243p. (FRE.). 1977. pap. 8.95 (*2-07-036855-6*) Schoenhof.

LaForgue, Jules. Poems of Jules LaForgue. Terry, Patricia, tr. LC 86-4617. 217p. 1986. reprint ed. text ed. 55.00 (*0-313-25210-6*, LFPO, Greenwood Pr) Greenwood.

Laforgue, Jules. Poesies Completes, Tome 1: Les Complaintes. Premiers Poemes. (Poesie Ser.). (FRE.). 1979. pap. 15.95 (*2-07-032181-9*) Schoenhof.

LaForgue, Jules. Poesies Completes, Tome 2: L'Imitation de Notre Dame la Lune. Le Concile Feerique. Etc... (Poesie Ser.). (FRE.). 1979. pap. 11.95 (*2-07-032182-7*) Schoenhof.

Laforgue, Jules. Six Moral Tales from Jules Laforgue. Newman, Frances, ed. LC 77-10275. 296p. reprint ed. 49.50 (*0-404-16327-0*) AMS Pr.

Laforgue, Jules, tr. see Whitman, Walt.

Laforgue, Rene. Clinical Aspects of Psychoanalysis. Hall, Joan, tr. (Psychoanalysis: Examined & Re-Examined Ser.). 300p. 1984. reprint ed. lib. bdg. 35.00 (*0-306-76235-8*) Da Capo.

Laforre, Timmy R. Acidosis--Index of New Information & Medical Research Bible. 150p. 1994. 44.50 (*0-7883-0086-5*); pap. 39.50 (*0-7883-0087-3*) ABBE Pubs Assn.

— Alkalosis--Index of New Information & Medical Bible of Research. 150p. 1994. 44.50 (*0-7883-0088-1*); pap. 39.50 (*0-7883-0089-X*) ABBE Pubs Assn.

Laforse, Martin W. & Drake, James A. Popular Culture & American Life: Selected Topics in the Study of Twentieth Century American Popular Culture. LC 80-27809. 264p. (C). 1981. pap. text ed. 19.95 (*0-88229-778-3*) Nelson-Hall.

LaForte & Odom. Our National Heritage, Vol. 2: Essays in American History Since 1865. 384p. 1993. per. 19.95 (*0-8403-8295-2*) Kendall-Hunt.

LaForte, Robert S., et al, eds. With Only the Will to Live: Accounts of Americans in Japanese Prison Camps, 1941-1945. LC 93-42419. 320p. 1994. 24.95 (*0-8420-2464-6*) Scholarly Res Inc.

LaFortune, Claude. Greeting Jesus: Let's Make the Nativity Scene. (Illus.). 24p. (Orig.). (J). 1988. student ed 5.95 (*0-89622-384-1*) Twenty-Third.

Lafortune, M., tr. see Fruhwald, Franz X. & Blackwell, D. Eric, eds.

LaFosse, Robert & Wentink, Andrew M. Nothing to Hide. 343p. 1987. 18.95 (*1-55611-051-0*) D I Fine.

Lafouge, Jean-Pierre. Etude sur l'Orientalisme d'Eugene Fromentin dans ses "Recits Algeriens" (American University Studies: Romance Languages & Literature: Ser. II, Vol. 100). 252p. (C). 1988. text ed. 36.50 (*0-8204-0820-4*) P Lang Pubs.

Lafountain, James. Van Richten's Guide to Vampires: Ravenloft Accessory. (Advanced Dungeons & Dragons, Second Edition; Al-Qadim Ser.). (Illus.). 1992. pap. 10.95 (*1-56076-151-2*, RR3) TSR Inc.

LaFountain, Julie, jt. ed. see Miller, Allan W.

LaFountain, William. Setting Limits: Parents, Kids & Drugs. 36p. 1982. 2.00 (*0-89486-145-X*, 1418B) Hazelden.

Lafourcade, Bernard, ed. see Lewis, Wyndham.

Lafourcade, Bernard, jt. auth. see Morrow, Bradford.

Lafourcade, G. Arnold Bennett: A Study. LC 74-176494. (English Literature Ser.: No. 33). 1971. reprint ed. lib. bdg. 59.95 (*0-8383-1360-4*) M S G Haskell Hse.

Lafourcade, Georges. Arnold Bennett: A Study. LC 70-148345. reprint ed. 37.50 (*0-404-08859-7*) AMS Pr.

Lafourche Heritage Society. Historical Scenes of Thibodaux: A Sesquicentennial Volume. (Illus.). 200p. 1988. 30.00 (*0-9617559-2-X*) Oubres Bks.

Laframboise, Leon W. History of the Administrative & Technical Services Branch of Service Insignia. (Branch of Service Insignia Ser.). (Illus.). 542p. (C). 1986. text ed. 40.00 (*0-9613855-0-2*) L W Laframboise.

LaFranc, Elsie, jt. ed. see Blustain, Harvey.

LaFrance, Arthur B. & Loewy, Arnold. Criminal Procedure: Trial & Sentencing. LC 93-46987. 1994. write for info. (*0-87084-179-3*) Anderson Pub Co.

LaFrance, David G. The Mexican Revolution in Puebla, 1908-1913: The Maderista Movement & the Failure of Liberal Reform. LC 88-34923. 272p. 1989. 40.00 (*0-8420-2293-7*) Scholarly Res Inc.

LaFrance, David G. & Jones, Errol D., eds. Latin American Military History: An Annotated Bibliography. LC 92-12606. (Military History Bibliographies Ser.: Vol. 12). 752p. 1992. 110.00 (*0-8240-4634-X*, H01024) Garland.

Lafrance, Jean. My Vocation Is Love. 175p. (C). 1990. 39.00 (*0-85439-393-5*, Pub. by St Paul Pubns UK) St Mut.

***LaFrance, Peter.** Beer Basics: A Quick & Easy Guide. LC 94-49717. 1995. pap. text ed. 12.95 (*0-471-11936-9*) Wiley.

LaFrance, Pierre. Fundamental Concepts in Communication. 448p. 1990. boxed 53.00 (*0-13-335738-4*) P-H.

LaFrance, Scott, jt. auth. see Duis, Perry.

LaFray, Joyce. Cuba Cocina! The Tantalizing World of Cuban Cooking--Yesterday, Today, & Tomorrow. LC 94-1594. 1994. 25.00 (*0-688-11067-3*) Hearst Bks.

— Guide to Florida's Best Restaurants. 192p. (Orig.). 1995. pap. 11.95 (*0-89815-727-7*) Ten Speed Pr.

LaFray, Joyce, ed. see Garcia, Clarita.

LaFray, Joyce, ed. see Schoolsky, Robert.

Lafreniere. Low-Back Patient: Treatment by Physical Therapy. 1979. 31.50 (*0-89352-033-0*) Mosby Yr Bk.

LaFreniere, Annette, ed. see Jones, Martha T.

LaFreniere, Barbara B., jt. auth. see LaFreniere, Ed.

***LaFreniere, Ed & LaFreniere, Barbara B.** Complete Guide to Life in Florida. 3rd ed. LC 94-42574. (Illus.). 422p. 1995. pap. 16.95 (*1-56164-066-2*) Pineapple Pr.

Lafreniere, Gyslaine F., jt. auth. see Persinger, Michael A.

Lafreniere, Lori, jt. auth. see Webb, Kenneth.

Lafrentiere. Body Techniques. 1984. 26.50 (*0-89352-205-8*) Mosby Yr Bk.

***LaFromboise, Teresa D.** American Indian Life Skills Development Curriculum. LC 95-6546. 1995. write for info. (*0-299-14920-X*); pap. write for info. (*0-299-14924-2*) U of Wis Pr.

Lafuma, Louis, jt. auth. see Pascal, Blaise.

Lag, Jul, ed. Geomedicine. 256p. 1990. 167.00 (*0-8493-6755-7*, RA792) CRC Pr.

Lagace, Paul A., ed. Composite Materials, Vol. 2: Fatigue & Fracture. (Special Technical Publication Ser.: No. STP 1012). (Illus.). 420p. 1989. text ed. 64.00 (*0-8031-1190-8*, 04-010120-33) ASTM.

Lagache, Daniel. The Works of Daniel Lagache: Selected Papers, 1938-1964. Holder, Elisabeth, tr. 446p. 1993. pap. 54.95 (*0-946439-89-3*, Pub. by Karnac Bks UK) Brunner-Mazel.

Lagadec, Patrick. Major Technological Risk: An Assessment of Industrial Disasters. (Illus.). 536p. 1982. 219.00 (*0-08-028913-4*, Pub. by Pergamon Repr UK) Franklin.

— Preventing Chaos in a Crisis: Strategies for Prevention, Control, & Damage Limitation. LC 92-33415. 1993. text ed. 29.95 (*0-07-707774-1*) McGraw.

— States of Emergency: Technological Failures & Social Destabilization. 283p. 1990. text ed. 42.95 (*0-7506-1124-3*) Buttrwrth-Heinemann.

Lagal, Roy. Find an Ounce of Gold a Day. Dawson, Hal, ed. LC 88-60013. (Guidebook Ser.). (Illus.). 52p. (Orig.). 1988. pap. 3.00 (*0-915920-52-2*) Ram Pub.

— Gold Panning Is Easy. rev. ed. LC 92-61347. (Illus.). 134p. (Orig.). 1992. pap. 9.95 (*0-915920-79-4*) Ram Pub.

— Weekend Prospecting. Dawson, Hal, ed. LC 88-60012. (Illus.). 82p. (Orig.). 1988. pap. 3.95 (*0-915920-48-4*) Ram Pub.

Lagal, Roy, et al. Modern Electronic Prospecting. Dawson, Hal, ed. LC 88-61452. (Illus.). 81p. 1988. pap. 9.95 (*0-915920-58-1*) Ram Pub.

Lagana, Antonio, ed. Supercomputer Algorithms for Reactivity, Dynamics & Kinetics of Small Molecules. (C). 1989. lib. bdg. 147.50 (*0-7923-0226-5*) Kluwer Ac.

Lagane, Rene, jt. auth. see Dubois, Jean.

Lagarce, Jean-Luc. Madame Knipper's Journey to Eastern Prussia. Antal, Paul, tr. (Publications Ser.: No. 9). 92p. (Orig.). 1984. pap. text ed. 8.95 (*0-913745-10-3*) Ubu Repertory.

Lagarde, A. & Michard, L. Collection Litteraire, 6 vols. Incl. Vol. 1. Moyen Age. 23.95 (*2-04-016207-0*); Vol. 2. Seizieme Siecle. 24.95 (*2-04-016209-7*); Vol. 3. Dix-Septieme Siecle. 28.95 (*2-04-016211-9*); Vol. 4. Dix-Huitieme Siecle. 28.95 (*2-04-016213-5*); Vol. 5. Dix-Neuvieme Siecle. 31.95 (*2-04-016216-X*); Vol. 6. Vingtieme Siecle. 39.95 (*2-04-018000-1*); Illus.). (FRE.). write for info. (*0-318-55654-5*) Schoenhof.

***Lagarde, David.** Satellite TV for Dummies: The Common Sense Guide to Home Installation of a Satellite Receiving System. (Illus.). 90p. (Orig.). 1994. pap. 19.95 (*1-885913-00-1*) Sterling Pubng.

***Lagarde, Francois.** Rene Girard ou la Christinaisation des Sciences Humanies. LC 93-23078. (Sociocriticism: Literature, Society & History Ser.: Vol. 7). 212p. (C). 1994. text ed. 45.95 (*0-8204-2289-4*) P Lang Pubs.

Lagarde, Philippe. Practical Dictionary to Understand the Study of Cancer: Dictionnaire Pratique du Cancer: Pour Comprendre le Langage du Cancerologue. (FRE.). 1984. 59.95 (*0-8288-1812-6*, M404) Fr & Eur.

Lagarias, J. & Todd, M. Mathematical Developments Arising from Linear Programming: (Proceedings of the Conference) LC 90-22942. (CONM Ser.: Vol. 114). 341p. 1991. 61.00 (*0-8218-5121-7*, CONM-114) Am Math.

Lagarias, Peter C. Effective Closing Argument. suppl. ed. 817p. 1991. 80.00 (*0-87473-434-7*) Michie Butterworth.

Lagarkov, A. N. & Rutkevich, Igor M. Ionization Waves in Electrical Breakdown of Gases. 240p. 1993. write for info. (*3-540-94075-8*) Spr-Verlag.

Lagasse, Emeril & Tirsch, Jessie. Emeril's New New Orleans Cooking. LC 92-33497. (Illus.). 1993. 23.00 (*0-688-11284-6*) Morrow.

Lagasse, J. Linear Circuit Theory: Study of Electric Circuits. 294p. 1968. text ed. 241.00 (*0-677-61520-5*) Gordon & Breach.

LaGattuta, Margo & Speltus, Carol. The Dream Givers. 88p. 1990. pap. 8.95x (*0-941363-12-0*) Lake Shore Pub.

Lagatutta, Margo. Embracing the Fall. 1994. pap. 11.95 (*0-911051-71-6*) Plain View.

Lage, Dietmar. Martin Luther's Christology & Ethics. LC 89-77128. (Texts & Studies in Religion: Vol. 45). 192p. 1990. lib. bdg. 79.95 (*0-88946-834-6*) E Mellen.

Lage, Gustavo A. & Nathan, Harvey K. Psychotherapy, Adolescents, & Self-Psychology. LC 90-4924. 500p. 1991. 60.00 (*0-8236-5403-6*) Intl Univs Pr.

***Lageira, Jacinto, et al.** Jean-Marc Bustamante. 128p. 1995. pap. 23.50 (*2-906571-44-X*) Dist Art Pubs.

Lageman, August G. The Moral Dimensions of Marriage & Family Therapy. LC 92-33573. 138p. (Orig.). (C). 1993. lib. bdg. 39.50 (*0-8191-8965-0*); pap. text ed. 19.50 (*0-8191-8966-9*) U Pr of Amer.

Lagemann, Ellen. Nursing History: New Perspectives, New Possibilities. (C). 1983. text ed. 18.95 (*0-8077-2730-X*) Tchrs Coll.

Lagemann, Ellen C. A Generation of Women: Education in the Lives of Progressive Reformers. LC 79-13528. (Illus.). 215p. 1979. 25.00 (*0-674-34471-5*) HUP.

— The Politics of Knowledge: The Carnegie Corporation, Philanthropy, & Public Policy. LC 89-16634. 365p. 1989. text ed. 40.00 (*0-8195-5204-6*, Wesleyan Univ Pr) U Pr of New Eng.

— The Politics of Knowledge: The Carnegie Corporation, Philanthropy, & Public Policy. LC 89-16634. xvi, 348p. 1992. pap. text ed. 16.95 (*0-226-46780-5*) U Ch Pr.

— Private Power for the Public Good: A History of the Carnegie Foundation for the Advancement of Teaching. LC 83-168179. (Illus.). 268p. 1988. pap. 15.95 (*0-8195-6127-4*, Wesleyan Univ Pr) U Pr of New Eng.

***Lagemann, Ellen C., ed.** Nursing History: New Perspectives, New Possibilities. LC 82-10320. 229p. 1983. pap. 65.30 (*0-7837-8950-5*, 2049662) Bks Demand.

Lagemann, Robert T. The Garland Collection of Classical Physics Apparatus at Vanderbilt University. LC 84-81830. (Illus.). 317p. (Orig.). 1984. pap. 12.95 (*0-9613702-0-3*) Folio Pubs.

Lagendijk, Arnoud. The Internationalisation of the Spanish Automobile Industry & Its Regional Impact: The Emergence of a Growth-Periphery. (Tinbergen Institute Ser.). 298p. 1994. pap. 26.50 (*90-5170-231-0*, Pub. by Thesis Pubs NE) IBD Ltd.

Lagendijk, Reginald L. & Biemond, Jan. Iterative Identification & Restoration of Images. (International Series in Engineering & Computer Science, VLSI, Computer Architecture, & Digital Screen Processing). 224p. (C). 1990. lib. bdg. 78.00 (*0-7923-9097-0*) Kluwer Ac.

Lagendijk, Reginald L., jt. ed. see Sezan, Ibrahim.

Lager, Carl H., jt. auth. see Snell, Daniel C.

***Lager, Cathy C.** Fingernail Moon: Mama's Journal. Stiefel, Dorothy, ed. 50p. 1995. pap. 8.95 (*0-9646714-0-9*) Taylor Made Pubns.

Lager, Eric & Zwerling, Isreal. Psychotherapy in the Community. Gardner, Alvin F., ed. (Allied Health Professions Monograph). 208p. (C). 1983. 22.50 (*0-87527-315-7*) Green.

Lager, Fred. Ben & Jerry's, The Inside Scoop: How Two Real Guys Built a Business With Social Conscience and a Sense of humour. LC 93-39176. 1994. reprint ed. 22.50 (*0-517-59716-0*) Crown Pub Group.

Lagerborg, Mary B. Incessant Drumbeat. (Illus.). 224p. (Orig.). 1992. pap. 8.95 (*0-87508-968-2*) Chr Lit.

Lagerborg, Mary B., jt. auth. see Wilson, Mary.

Lagerborg, Mary B., jt. auth. see Wilson, Mimi.

Lagercrantz, Hugo, jt. ed. see Von Euler, Curt.

Lagercrantz, Olof. August Strindberg. Hollo, Anselm, tr. LC 84-42803. 400p. 1984. 25.50 (*0-374-10685-1*) FS&G.

Lagercrantz, Rose & Lagercrantz, Samuel. Is It Magic? Norlen, Paul, tr. LC 89-63054. (Illus.). (J). (gr. k-3). 1990. 13.95 (*91-29-59182-1*, Pub. by R & S Bks) FS&G.

Lagercrantz, Samuel, jt. auth. see Lagercrantz, Rose.

Lagerfeld, Karl. Madonna Superstar: Photographs. 1991. pap. 10.95 (*0-393-30766-2*) Norton.

***Lagergren, Paul.** The 12 Tiger Steps Out of Nicotine Addiction: A Step Study Guide for Nicotine Addiction. LC 95-90081. (Illus.). 256p. 1995. pap. 19.95 (*0-9645492-4-7*) Tigerworks Pub.

Lagerkvist, C. I., et al, eds. Asteroids, Comets & Meteors, Vol. 3: Proceedings of a Meeting Held at the Astronomical Observatory of Uppsala University, June 12-16, 1989. (Illus.). 620p. (Orig.). 1990. pap. 375.00x (*91-506-0777-4*, Pub. by Almqv & Wiksell SW) Coronet Bks.

Lagerkvist, Par. Barabbas. 1955. pap. 4.95 (*0-394-70134-8*) Random.

— Barabbas. Blair, Alan, tr. (Vintage International Ser.). 1989. pap. 8.00 (*0-679-72544-X*, Vin) Random.

— The Dwarf. Dick, Alexandra, tr. 228p. (Orig.). 1958. pap. 9.95 (*0-374-52135-2*, Noonday) FS&G.

— Five Early Works. Swanson, Roy A., tr. LC 87-35394. 200p. 1989. lib. bdg. 89.95 (*0-88946-019-1*) E Mellen.

— Modern Theatre: Seven Plays & an Essay. Buckman, Thomas R., tr. & intro. by. LC 64-11582. 329p. reprint ed. pap. 88.90 (*0-7837-6029-9*, 2045841) Bks Demand.

— Sibyl. Walford, Naomi, tr. 1963. pap. 5.95 (*0-394-70240-9*, Vin) Random.

Lagerkvist, Par, jt. auth. see Bekessy, Emery.

Lagerkvist, Par F. Evening Land - Aftonland. Auden, W. H. & Sjoberg, Leif, trs. LC 75-16172. 195p. (ENG & SWE.). reprint ed. pap. 55.60 (*0-7837-3621-5*, 2043487) Bks Demand.

***Lagerlof.** The Changeling. 1994. pap. text ed. 4.99 (*0-517-13542-6*) Random Hse Value.

— The Changeling. pap. 4.99 (*0-517-13541-8*) Random.

Lagerlof, Margaretha. Ideal Landscapes: Carracci, Poussin & Lorrain. 256p. 1991. 45.00 (*0-300-04763-0*) Yale U Pr.

Lagerlof, Selma. The Further Adventures of Nils. rev. ed. Johnson, Nancy, ed. Howard, Velma S., tr. (Travels of Nils Holgersson Ser.: Bk. 2). (Illus.). 262p. (J). (gr. 4-12). 1992. pap. 12.95 (*0-9615394-4-5*) Skandisk.

— The Legend of the Christmas Rose. LC 89-77511. (Illus.). 32p. (J). (ps up). 1990. lib. bdg. 15.95 (*0-8234-0821-3*) Holiday.

— The Wonderful Adventures of Nils. 540p. 1992. reprint ed. lib. bdg. 36.95 (*0-89966-936-0*) Buccaneer Bks.

— The Wonderful Adventures of Nils, Bk. 1. rev. ed. Howard, Velma S., tr. (Travels of Nils Holgersson Ser.). (Illus.). 254p. (J). (gr. 4-12). 1991. pap. 12.95 (*0-9615394-3-7*) Skandisk.

Lagerlof, Selma O. The Changeling. 1992. pap. 15.99 (*0-685-52495-7*) McKay.

— From a Swedish Homestead. Brochner, Jessie, tr. LC 73-116959. (Short Story Index Reprint Ser.). 1977. 24.95 (*0-8369-3463-6*) Ayer.

— Jerusalem. Brochner, Jessie, tr. LC 76-98777. 396p. 1970. reprint ed. text ed. 65.00 (*0-8371-3120-0*, LAJE, Greenwood Pr) Greenwood.

— The Lowenskold Ring. Schenck, Linda, tr. (Norvik Press Series B: No. 8). 117p. 1991. pap. 21.00 (*1-870041-14-3*, Pub. by Norvik Pr UK) Dufour.

***Lagerloff, Selma.** Invisable Links. Anderson, Greta, ed. 1995. pap. 9.95 (*1-57216-023-3*) Penfield.

— The Wonderful Adventures of Nils. Howard, Velma S., ed. & tr. by. LC 94-41647. (Illus.). 256p. (J). 1995. pap. text ed. 6.95 (*0-486-28611-8*) Dover.

— The Wonderful Adventures of Nils, 1907. 1995. pap. 10.95 (*1-57216-005-5*) Penfield.

LaGerould, Terry, jt. auth. see Whiting, Wayne.

Lagerquist, L. DeAne. In America the Men Milk the Cows: Factors of Gender, Ethnicity & Religion in the Americanization of Norwegian-American Women. LC 91-26844. (Chicago Studies in the History of American Religion Ser.: Vol. 12). 190p. 1991. 50.00 (*0-926019-49-X*) Carlson Pub.

Lagerquist, Sally L. Addison-Wesley's Nursing Examination. 2nd ed. 1982. pap. 26.50 (*0-201-14190-6*, Health Sci) Addison-Wesley.

— Addison-Wesley's Nursing Examination Review. 3rd ed. 1987. pap. 23.75 (*0-201-14497-2*) Addison-Wesley.

— Addison Wesley's Nursing Examination Review. 4th ed. 752p. (C). 1991. pap. text ed. 32.25 (*0-8053-4002-5*) Addison-Wesley.

Lagerquist, Syble. Philip Johnston & the Navajo Code Talkers. (Indian Culture Ser.). (J). (gr. 4-12). 1975. 4.95 (*0-89992-038-1*) Coun India Ed.

Lagers, G. H. Design Adjustments of a Jack up for Production or Extended Well Testing. 1989. 125.00 (*90-6314-512-8*, Pub. by Lorne & MacLean Marine) St Mut.

— Design Adjustments of a Jack-up for Production or Extended Well Testings. (C). 1989. 95.00 (*0-89771-728-7*, Pub. by Lorne & MacLean Marine) St Mut.

***Lagerspetz, Eerik.** The Opposite Mirrors: An Essay on the Conventionalist Theory of Institutions. LC 94-42237. (Law & Philosophy Library: Vol. 22). 1995. lib. bdg. 96.00 (*0-7923-3325-X*) Kluwer Ac.

Lagerstam, Catharina. Hedging of Contracts, Anticipated Positions, & Tender Offers: A Study of Corporate Foreign Exchange Rate Risk & - or Price Risk. 202p. (Orig.). 1990. pap. 91.50x (*0-685-41472-8*, Pub. by Almqv & Wiksell SW) Coronet Bks.

Lagerstrom, P. A. Matched Aymptotic Expansions. (Applied Mathematical Sciences Ser.: Vol. 76). (Illus.). xiii, 251p. 1988. 47.00 (*0-387-96811-3*) Spr-Verlag.

Lagerwerff, Ellen. Astrology Can Make Sense. 84p. 1985. 6.00 (*0-86690-260-0*, L2457-014) Am Fed Astrologers.

Lageson, David R. & Spearing, Darwin. Roadside Geology of Wyoming. Alt, David & Hyndman, Donald, eds. LC 88-1650. (Roadside Geology Ser.). (Illus.). 288p. (Orig.). 1988. pap. 14.00 (*0-87842-216-1*) Mountain Pr.

LaGesse & Henkel, eds. Airborne Reconnaissance, No. XI. 1987. 38.00 (*0-89252-868-0*, 833) SPIE.

Laggner, A. N., jt. ed. see Lenz, K.

Laggner, P. & Glatter, O., eds. Trends in Colloid & Interface Science VII. (Progress in Colloid & Polymer Science Ser.: Vol. 93). 412p. 1994. 149.00 (*0-387-91454-4*) Spr-Verlag.

Lagler, Karl F., jt. auth. see Hubbs, Carl L.

Lagler, Karl F., et al. Ichthyology. 2nd ed. LC 76-50114. 506p. 1977. Net. text ed. write for info. (*0-471-51166-8*) Wiley.

Lagnado, Lucette M. & Dekel, Sheila C. Children of the Flames: Dr. Josef Mengele & the Untold Story of the Twins of Auschwitz. (Illus.). 320p. 1992. pap. 12.95 (*0-14-016931-8*, Penguin Bks) Viking Penguin.

Lagnan, Pierre. La Commissaire Dans la Truffiere. 250p. (FRE.). 1991. pap. 11.95 (*0-7859-4348-X*, 2070383245) Fr & Eur.

Lagneborg, Rune, jt. ed. see Pipes, R. Byron.

Lagner, Marshall J., jt. auth. see Rhoades, Rufus V.

Lagnese, J. E. & Lions, J. L. Modelling Analysis & Control of Thin Plates. (Recherches en Mathematiques Appliquees Ser.: Vol. 6). 185p. 1990. pap. 36.00 (*0-387-51550-X*) Spr-Verlag.

Lagnese, J. E., et al. Modeling, Analysis & Control of Dynamic Elastic Multi-Link Structures. LC 94-3096. (Systems & Control Ser.). 388p. 1994. 69.50 (*0-8176-3705-2*) Birkhauser.

Lagnese, John E. Boundary Stabilization of Thin Plates. (Studies in Applied Mathematics: No. 10). viii, 176p. 1989. pap. 38.75 (*0-89871-237-8*) Soc Indus-Appl Math.

***Lagnese, John E., et al, eds.** Control & Optimal Design of Distributed Parameter Systems. LC 95-2606. (IMA Volumes in Mathematics & Its Applications: Vol. 70). (Illus.). 264p. 1995. 59.00 (*0-387-94490-7*) Spr-Verlag.

Lago, Armando M., jt. auth. see Brown, Charles J.

Lago, M. T., jt. ed. see Dupree, A. K.

Lago, Mary. E.M. Forster: A Literary Life. LC 94-9973. (Literary Lives Ser.). 1994. write for info. (*0-312-12178-4*) St Martin.

Lago, Mary, ed. see Burne-Jones, Edward C.

Lago, Mary M. & Beckson, Karl, eds. Max & Will: Max Beerbohm & William Rothenstein, Their Friendship & Letters, 1893-1945. LC 74-30853. (Illus.). 200p. 1976. 26.00 (*0-674-55661-5*) HUP.

Lago, Mary M., ed. see Forster, E. M.

Lago, Mary M., ed. see Rothenstein, William & Tagore, Rabindranath.

***Lagoe, J. Arthur.** First Steps: A New Believer's Survival Guide. LC 94-76861. 111p. (Orig.). 1994. pap. 5.50 (*0-9641761-0-6*) Aletheia WA.

***Lagomarcino, Virgil.** A Window on Main Street: Life above the Corner Drug. (Illus.). 136p. 1995. pap. 10.95 (*0-8138-2949-6*) Iowa St U Pr.

Lagomarsino, David & Wood, Charles T., eds. The Trial of Charles I: A Documentary History. LC 89-40356. (Illus.). 167p. 1989. pap. 14.95 (*0-87451-499-1*) U Pr of New Eng.

Lagomarsino, Nancy. The Secretary Parables. LC 91-16373. 72p. (Orig.). 1991. pap. 9.95 (*0-914086-92-8*) Alicejamesbooks.

— Sleep Handbook. LC 86-72477. 72p. (Orig.). (C). 1987. 15.95 (*0-914086-68-5*); pap. 9.95 (*0-914086-69-3*) Alicejamesbooks.

Lagon, Mark P. The Reagan Doctrine: Sources of American Conduct in the Cold War's Last Chapter. LC 93-23676. 208p. 1994. text ed. 49.95 (*0-275-94798-X*, Praeger Pubs) Greenwood.

Lagoni, Laurel S., et al, eds. The Human-Animal Bond & Grief. (Illus.). 496p. 1994. pap. text ed. 42.00 (*0-7216-4577-1*) Saunders.

Lagoon, Steve, jt. auth. see Devore, Steve.

Lagopoulos, Alexandros P. & Boklund-Lagopoulou, Karin. Meaning & Geography: The Social Conception of the Region in Northern Greece. LC 91-43000. (Approaches to Semiotics Ser.: No. 104). xiv, 453p. (C). 1992. lib. bdg. 183.10 (*3-11-012956-6*) Mouton.

Lagoria, Georgianna, jt. auth. see Malone, Kelly.

Lagorio, Henry J. Earthquakes, an Architect's Guide to Nonstructural Seismic Hazards. 1990. text ed. 74.95 (*0-471-63302-X*) Wiley.

Lagorio, Henry J. & Mader, George G. Earthquake in Campania-Basilicata, Italy, Nov. 23, 1980: Architectural & Planning Aspects. 103p. 1981. 12.00 (*0-318-17285-2*, EP-43) Earthquake Eng.

Lagorio, Irene R. Art History's Innovators. (Illus.). 93p. (Orig.). 1992. pap. 8.95 (*0-9633541-0-8*) Arina Pr.

Lagorio, Jeanne. Life Cycle: Classroom Activities for Helping Children to Live with Daily Change & Loss. LC 92-33575. 128p. 1993. 19.95 (*0-913705-85-3*) Zephyr Pr AZ.

— The Life Cycle Education Manual: A Guide for Teachers & Helping Professionals: To Help Children Cope with Daily & Significant Loss. rev. ed. 216p. 1992. pap. text ed. 29.95 (*0-9633195-9-0*) Empower in Act.

Lagos, Deloris K. The Sun Will Shine. (J). 1993. 7.95 (*0-8062-4786-X*) Carlton.

Lagos, Gustavo & Godoy, Horacio H. Revolution of Being: A Latin American View of the Future. LC 77-3848. (Preferred Worlds for the 1990's Ser.). 1977. 24.95 (*0-02-917840-1*) Free Pr.

Lagos, Maria L. Autonomy & Power: The Dynamics of Class & Culture in Rural Bolivia. LC 93-48809. (Ethnohistory Ser.). 224p. (Orig.). (C). 1994. text ed. 39.95 (*0-8122-3213-5*); pap. text ed. 14.95 (*0-8122-1500-1*) U of Pa Pr.

Lagos-Pope, Maria-Ines, ed. Exile in Literature. LC 87-47726. 144p. 1988. 29.50 (*0-8387-5126-1*) Bucknell U Pr.

Lagos, Ramona. Varia Coleccion: Ensayos sobre Literatura Hispano-Americana. (American University Studies: Ser. XXII, Vol. 5). 320p. (C). 1989. text ed. 44.95 (*0-8204-1059-4*) P Lang Pubs.

Lagoudas, D. C., jt. ed. see Allen, D. H.

Lagoudas, D. C., jt. auth. see Edelen, Dominic G.

Lagouelle, Henri. Essai sur la Conception Juridique De la Propriete Fonciere Dans le Tres Anciendroit Normand: Premiere Partie, la Conception Feodale. LC 80-2020. reprint ed. 34.50 (*0-404-18574-6*) AMS Pr.

Lagowski, Barbara, jt. auth. see Sullivan, George.

Lagowski, Barbara J., jt. auth. see Rabin, Susan.

Lagowski, J. J. Modern Inorganic Chemistry. LC 72-90374. (Undergraduate Chemistry Ser.: No. 6). 824p. reprint ed. pap. 180.00 (*0-7837-3363-1*, 2043321) Bks Demand.

Lagowski, J. J. & Sienko, M. J., eds. Metal-Ammonia Solutions: Proceedings of the International Conference on the Nature of Metal-Ammonia Solution, Ithaca, N.Y., 1969. 522p. 1976. 209.00 (*0-08-020794-4*, Pub. by Pergamon Repr UK) Franklin.

Lagowski, J. J. & Sorum, C. Harvey. Introduction to Semimicro Qualitative Analysis. 7th ed. 368p. (C). 1991. pap. text ed. write for info. (*0-13-496894-8*) P-H.

***Lagowsky.** Macmillan Encyclopedia of Chemistry, 4 vols. 1996. 350.00 (*0-02-897225-2*) Macmillan.

LaGoy, Peter K. Risk Assessment: Principles & Applications for Hazardous Waste & Related Sites. LC 94-2510. (Illus.). 244p. 1994. 48.00 (*0-8155-1349-6*) Noyes.

Lagoy, Stephen P., ed. New Perspectives on Urban Crime. 112p. 1981. pap. 8.95 (*0-932930-44-1*) Pilgrimage Inc.

Lagrakov, Andrei N. & Rutkevich, Igor M. Ionization Waves in Electrical Breakdown of Gases. LC 93-27847. (Illus.). 240p. 1993. 59.00 (*0-387-94075-8*) Spr-Verlag.

LaGrand, James. The Earliest Christian Mission to 'All Nations' LC 93-42357. (USF-Rochester-Saint Louis Studies on Religion & the Social Order: Vol. 5). 1994. write for info. (*1-55540-937-7*) Scholars Pr GA.

***LaGrand, Louis E.** Changing Patterns of Human Existence: Assumptions, Beliefs & Coping with the Stress of Change. 216p. 1988. pap. 25.95 (*0-398-06220-X*) C C Thomas.

— Changing Patterns of Human Existence: Assumptions, Beliefs & Coping with the Stress of Change. 216p. (C). 1988. 42.95x (*0-398-05464-9*) C C Thomas.

LaGrange, Mike. Ballistics in Perspective: A Guide for Weapon Choice in the Hunting of Game in Zimbabwe. rev. ed. Kaytis, Nancy, ed. 1990. reprint ed. 12.95 (*0-9624807-2-X*) PHS Pub Div.

LaGrange, Randy L. Policing American Society. LC 92-28103. 1993. text ed. 36.95 (*0-8304-1267-0*) Nelson-Hall.

LaGravanese, Richard. The Fisher King: The Illustrated Screenplay. (Screenplay Ser.). (Illus.). 204p. (Orig.). 1991. pap. 12.95 (*1-55783-098-3*) Applause Theatre Bk Pubs.

***LaGreca, Annette.** Helping Children Prepare for & Cope with Natural Disasters: A Manual for Professionals Working with Elementary School Children. (Illus.). 100p. (Orig.). (C). 1995. pap. text ed. 30.00x (*0-7881-1624-X*) Diane Pub.

Lagree, Michel, ed. see Mayeur, Jean-Marie & Hilaire, Yves-Marie.

LaGrega, Michael. Hazardous Waste Management. 1994. text ed. 65.32 (*0-07-019552-8*) McGraw.

LaGrone, Leila S. An East Texas Feud: Regulator-Moderator War. LC 93-46916. 1994. 15.95 (*0-89015-960-2*) Sunbelt Media.

LaGrone, Oliver. Dawnfire & Other Poems. LC 88-83008. (Illus.). 133p. (YA). (gr. 9-12). 1989. per., pap. 9.00 (*0-916418-72-3*) Lotus.

***Lagua, Rosalinda T. & Claudio, Virginia S.** Nutrition & Diet Therapy Reference Dictionary. 4th rev. ed. LC 95-14630. Orig. Title: Nutrition & Diet Therapy Dictionary. 1995. text ed. write for info. (*0-412-07051-0*) Chapman & Hall.

***Lagua, Rosalinga T. & Claudio, Virginia S.** Nutrition & Diet Therapy Reference Dictionary. 4th ed. LC 95-14630. Orig. Title: Nutrition & Diet Therapy Dictionary. 1995. pap. write for info. (*0-412-07061-8*) Chapman & Hall.

Laguardia. Red. 1985. 16.95 (*0-02-567230-4*) Macmillan.

LaGuardia, Cheryl. A CD-ROM Primer: The ABCs of CD-ROM. 250p. 1994. pap. 39.95 (*1-55570-167-1*) Neal-Schuman.

***LaGuardia, Cheryl, ed.** The Upside of Downsizing: Using Library Instruction to Cope. LC 95-13157. 1995. write for info. (*1-55570-217-1*) Neal-Schuman.

LaGuardia Community College Staff. Basic Speech Communication. 128p. (C). 1994. spiral bd. 14.36 (*0-8403-8168-9*) Kendall-Hunt.

LaGuardia, Delores & Guth, Hans P. American Voices: Multicultural Literacy & Critical Thinking. LC 92-26825. 693p. 1992. pap. text ed. 24.95 (*1-55934-185-8*); teacher ed, pap. text ed. write for info. (*1-55934-186-6*) Mayfield Pub.

***LaGuardia, Dolores, et al.** Teaching American Visions: Multicultural Literature for Writers. LC 94-6444. 185p. (Orig.). (C). 1994. teacher ed, pap. text ed. write for info. (*1-55934-323-0*) Mayfield Pub.

LaGuardia, Fiorello H. The Making of an Insurgent: An Autobiography, 1882-1919. LC 85-24782. (Illus.). 222p. 1986. reprint ed. text ed. 55.00 (*0-313-22769-1*, LAMI, Greenwood Pr) Greenwood.

Laguardia, G., jt. ed. see Chevigny, B. G.

LaGuardia, Robert. Monty: A Biography. 1988. pap. 8.95 (*1-55611-110-X*, Primus Lib Contemp) D I Fine.

***Lague, Louise.** The Working Mom's Book of Hints, Tips, & Everyday Wisdom. LC 95-5094. 128p. (Orig.). 1995. pap. 7.95 (*1-56079-461-5*, Petersons Pacesetter) Petersons Guides.

Laguerre & Melon. El Jibaro de Puerto Rico. 1968. 14.95 (*0-87751-007-5*) E Torres & Sons.

***Laguerre, Danielle V.** Black Ties. Date not set. pap. 15.00 (*0-9646413-0-5*) Tenaj Pub Hse.

Laguerre, E. Oeuvres, 2 Vols. LC 70-125075. 1971. reprint ed. text ed. 69.50 (*0-8284-0263-9*) Chelsea Pub.

Laguerre, Enrique. Los Amos Benevolos. 2nd ed. LC 76-21797. 258p. 1990. pap. 7.95 (*0-8477-3523-0*) U of PR Pr.

— Complete Works of Enrique Laguerre, 2 vols., Set. (Puerto Rico Ser.). 1975. 250.00 (*0-8490-2890-6*) Gordon Pr.

Laguerre, Enrique & Melon, Esther. The Jibaro in Puerto Rico: Symbol & Figure. (Puerto Rico Ser.). 1979. 59.95 (*0-8490-2951-1*) Gordon Pr.

Laguerre, Michael S. The Informal City. LC 94-16010. 1994. text ed. 40.00 (*0-312-12209-8*) St Martin.

Laguerre, Michel S. American Odyssey: Haitians in New York City. LC 83-21078. (Anthropology of Contemporary Issues Ser.). (Illus.). 200p. 1984. pap. 15.95 (*0-8014-9270-X*) Cornell U Pr.

— The Military & Society in Haiti. LC 92-19919. 240p. (C). 1993. text ed. 29.95 (*0-87049-773-1*) U of Tenn Pr.

— Urban Poverty in the Caribbean: The Martinican Experience. LC 89-77908. 180p. 1990. text ed. 49.95 (*0-312-04495-X*) St Martin.

Laguette, Doris, tr. see Laurentin, Rene.

***Laguette, Ernest.** Via Dolorosa. LC 94-61407. 110p. (Orig.). 1994. pap. 4.00 (*1-877678-29-5*) Riehle Found.

Laguette, Ernesto V., tr. see Laurentin, Rene.

LaGuma, Alex. In the Fog of the Season's End. (African Writers Ser.). 181p. 1972. pap. 9.95 (*0-435-90110-9*, 90110) Heinemann.

— Walk in the Night & Other Stories. 129p. 1967. pap. 9.95 (*0-8101-0139-4*) Northwestern U Pr.

LaGumina, Salvatore J. From Steerage to Suburb: Long Island Italians. LC 87-20842. (CMS Migration & Ethnicity Ser.). 285p. 1989. 19.50 (*0-934733-33-3*); pap. 14.50 (*0-934733-28-7*) Ctr Migration.

Lagumina, Salvatore J. New York at Mid-Century: The Impellitteri Years. LC 92-8844. 272p. 1992. text ed. 49.95 (*0-313-27205-0*, LBC, Greenwood Pr) Greenwood.

Lagumina, Salvatore J., jt. auth. see Cavaioli, Frank J.

Laguna, Theodore De. Introduction to the Science of Ethics. LC 72-4166. (Select Bibliographies Reprint Ser.). 1977. reprint ed. 25.95 (*0-8369-6887-5*) Ayer.

Lagunoff, Susan, jt. auth. see Dempsey, K. Ann.

Lagus, P. L., jt. ed. see Trechsel, H. R.

***Lah, Michael.** Re-engineering at Work. 250p. 1995. 51.95 (*0-566-07642-X*, Pub. by Gower UK) Ashgate Pub Co.

Laha, R. G., jt. auth. see Lukacs, E.

LaHaie, I. J., ed. Ultrawideband Radar. 1992. 62.00 (*0-8194-0777-1*, 1631) SPIE.

Laham, Martha. Marketing: A Contemporary Workbook. 200p. 1993. spiral bd. 17.95 (*0-8403-8726-1*) Kendall-Hunt.

Laham, Nicholas. Why the United States Lacks a National Health Insurance Program. 216p. 1993. pap. text ed. 18.95 (*0-275-94779-3*, Praeger Pubs) Greenwood.

— Why the United States Lacks a National Health Program. LC 93-3167. (Contributions in Political Science Ser.: No. 331). 216p. 1993. Alk. paper. text ed. 59.95 (*0-313-28745-7*, GM8745) Greenwood.

Lahane, Brendan. Wizards & Witches. (Enchanted World Ser.). (Illus.). 144p. 1984. lib. bdg. 25.93 (*0-8094-5205-7*) Time-Life.

Lahav. Thrombospondin. 1993. 169.95 (*0-8493-4929-X*, QP552) CRC Pr.

LaHaye, Berverly & LaHaye, Tim. La Familia Sujeta al Espiritu. 208p. 1980. 4.95 (*0-88113-085-0*) Edit Betania.

LaHaye, Beverly. Como Desarrollar el Temperamento de Su Hijo. 182p. 1979. 4.95 (*0-88113-036-2*) Edit Betania.

— The Desires of a Woman's Heart. 272p. 1994. pap. 9.99 (*0-8423-1372-9*) Tyndale.

— The Desires of a Woman's Heart: Encouragement for Women When Traditional Values Are Challenged. LC 93-12911. 1993. 16.99 (*0-8423-7945-2*) Tyndale.

— How to Develop Your Child's Temperament. LC 77-73633. 1977. pap. 6.99 (*0-89081-034-6*) Harvest Hse.

— La Mujer Sujeta al Espiritu. 208p. 1978. 3.95 (*0-88113-210-1*) Edit Betania.

— The Spirit-Controlled Woman. LC 76-5562. 1976. pap. 6.99 (*0-89081-020-6*) Harvest Hse.

— The Spirit-Controlled Woman. rev. ed. LC 94-29312. 1995. pap. 9.99 (*1-56507-223-5*) Harvest Hse.

***LaHaye, Beverly & LaHaye, Tim.** A Nation Without a Conscience. LC 94-26145. 1994. 16.99 (*0-8423-5018-7*) Tyndale.

LaHaye, Beverly, jt. auth. see LaHaye, Tim.

Lahaye, Jacques & Ehrburger, Pierre, eds. Fundamental Issues in Control of Carbon Gasification Reactivity. (C). 1991. lib. bdg. 193.00 (*0-7923-1080-2*) Kluwer Ac.

Lahaye, Jacques & Prado, G., eds. Fundamentals of the Physical-Chemistry of Pulverized Coal Combustion. (C). 1987. lib. bdg. 166.50 (*90-247-3573-4*) Kluwer Ac.

LaHaye, T. Aumente el Poder de Su Personalidad (Increase Personality Power) (SPA.). Date not set. 2.49 (*0-8423-6516-8*, 498040) Editorial Unilit.

— Manual Del Temperamento-Tela (Your Temperament, Discover-Potential) (SPA.). Date not set. 15.99 (*0-8423-6322-X*, 490214) Editorial Unilit.

Lahaye, Tim. El Acto Matrimonial: The Act of Marriage. (SPA.). 7.95 (*84-7228-269-4*, 220009, Pub. by Edit Clie SP) TSELF.

LaHaye, Tim. Battle for the Mind: You Are Engaged in Battle for the Mind, a Subtle Warfare. LC 82-21453. 1982. student ed, pap. 3.99 (*0-8007-1341-9*) Revell.

— Beginning of the End. rev. ed. 1991. reprint ed. 8.99 (*0-8423-0264-6*) Tyndale.

— Casados pero Felices (How to Be Happy Though Married) (SPA.). 1986. 4.25 (*0-8423-6252-5*, 490210) Editorial Unilit.

— Comienzo Del Fin (The Beginning of the End) (SPA.). 1992. 3.99 (*0-8423-6253-3*, 490211) Editorial Unilit.

— Como Estudiar la Biblia por Si Mismo. 192p. 1977. 4.95 (*0-88113-042-7*) Edit Betania.

— Finding the Will of God in a Crazy, Mixed-up World: From Confusion to Conclusion. 176p. 1989. 12.95 (*0-310-27170-3*) Zondervan.

— How to Be Happy Though Married. 1968. pap. 7.99 (*0-8423-1501-2*) Tyndale.

— How to Be Happy Though Married. (Living Bks.). 1979. 4.99 (*0-8423-1499-7*) Tyndale.

— How to Study Bible Prophecy for Yourself. LC 90-36388. (Illus.). 192p. (Orig.). 1990. pap. 7.99 (*0-89081-817-7*) Harvest Hse.

— How to Study the Bible for Yourself. LC 76-5568. 1976. pap. 7.99 (*0-89081-021-4*) Harvest Hse.

— How to Win over Depression PA. 224p. 1976. pap. 5.99 (*0-310-26982-2*, 18082P) Zondervan.

— I Love You, But Why Are We So Different? 1991. pap. 9.99 (*0-89081-879-7*) Harvest Hse.

— No Fear of the Storm: Why Christians Will Escape All the Tribulation. 252p. (Orig.). 1992. 15.99 (*0-88070-514-0*, Multnomah Bks) Questar Pubs.

— No Temas a la Tormenta (No Fear of the Storm) (SPA.). 1994. 7.99 (*1-56063-708-0*, 498554) Editorial Unilit.

Lahaye, Tim. Revelation-Illustrated & Made Plain. rev. ed. 456p. 1974. pap. 10.99 (*0-310-26991-1*, 18073P) Zondervan.

LaHaye, Tim. Six Keys to a Happy Marriage. 1978. pap. 2.99 (*0-8423-5895-1*) Tyndale.

— Spirit-Controlled Temperament. LC 93-17269. 1993. 8.99 (*0-8423-6220-7*) Tyndale.

Lahaye, Tim. Spirit-Controlled Temperament. large type ed. 1986. 13.95 (*0-8027-2563-5*) Walker & Co.

LaHaye, Tim. Temperamentos Controlados (Spirit Controlled Temperaments) (SPA.). 1990. 3.99 (*0-8423-6254-1*, 490212) Editorial Unilit.

— Temperamentos Transformados (Transformed Temperaments) (SPA.). 1986. 3.99 (*0-8423-6255-X*, 490213) Editorial Unilit.

— Transformed Temperaments. 293p. Date not set. pap. 5.99 (*0-8423-7304-7*) Tyndale.

— Transformed Temperaments. 1971. 5.99 (*0-685-73452-8*); pap. 8.99 (*0-8423-7306-3*) Tyndale.

Lahaye, Tim. Transforming Your Temperament. 1991. 9.98 (*0-88486-040-X*, Inspiratnl Pub) Arrowood Pr.

LaHaye, Tim. Understanding the Male Temperament: What Every Man Would Like to Tell His Wife about Himself.. .but Won't. LC 77-8245. 192p. 1977. pap. 8.99 (*0-8007-0864-4*); pap. 8.99 (*0-8007-5009-8*) Revell.

— El Varon y Su Temperamento. 217p. 1978. 4.95 (*0-88113-340-X*) Edit Betania.

Lahaye, Tim. Vida en el Mas Alla: Life in the Afterlife. (SPA.). 5.50 (*84-7228-611-8*, 220942, Pub. by Edit Clie SP) TSELF.

LaHaye, Tim. What Everyone Should Know about Homosexuality. 1980. pap. 4.99 (*0-8423-7933-9*) Tyndale.

— What Everyone Should Know about Homosexuality: Homosexualidad: Lo que Es, Lo que Hace y Como Superarla. Duffer, Hiram, tr. (Una Respuesta Cristiana Ser.). 144p. (Orig.). (SPA.). 1991. pap. 4.95 (*0-311-46126-3*) Casa Bautista.

— Why You Act the Way You Do. 342p. 1988. pap. 5.99 (*0-8423-8212-7*) Tyndale.

— Your Temperament Can Change. 1978. pap. 2.99 (*0-8423-8750-1*) Tyndale.

LaHaye, Tim & LaHaye, Beverly. The Act of Marriage: The Beauty of Married Love. 1976. pap. 10.99 (*0-310-27061-8*, 18077P) Zondervan.

— The Act of Marriage: The Beauty of Married Love. 1978. pap. 5.99 (*0-310-27062-6*, 18083P) Zondervan.

— Against the Tide. 288p. 1993. 16.99 (*0-88070-578-7*, Multnomah Bks) Questar Pubs.

— The Spirit-Filled Family. expanded rev. ed. 1995. pap. 9.99 (*1-56507-332-0*) Harvest Hse.

— What Lovemaking Means to a Man: Practical Advice to Married Men About Sex. LC 83-18338. 64p. 1984. pap. 4.99 (*0-310-27102-9*, 18338P) Zondervan.

— What Lovemaking Means to a Woman: Practical Advice to Married Women About Sex. LC 83-18339. 64p. 1984. pap. 4.99 (*0-310-27052-9*, 18339P) Zondervan.

LaHaye, Tim & Phillips, Bob. Anger Is a Choice. 160p. (Orig.). 1982. pap. 7.99 (*0-310-27071-5*, 18335P) Zondervan.

LaHaye, Tim, jt. auth. see LaHaye, Berverly

Lande, James A. Planning for Change: A Course of Study in Ecological Planning, Grades 9-12. 1982. text ed. 15.95 (*0-8077-2685-0*) Tchrs Coll.

Lahee, A., tr. see Ibach, Harald & Luth, Hans.

Lahee, F. H., jt. ed. see Wrather, W. E.

Lahee, Henry C. Annals of Music in America. LC 72-107810. (Select Bibliographies Reprint Ser.). 1977. 23.95 (*0-8369-5185-9*) Ayer.

— Annals of Music in America. LC 78-97889. reprint ed. 32.50 (*0-404-03801-8*) AMS Pr.

— Annals of Music in America: A Chronological Record of Significant Musical Events. 298p. 1990. reprint ed. lib. bdg. 69.00 (*0-7812-9031-7*) Rprt Serv.

— Famous Singers of Today & Yesterday. reprint ed. lib. bdg. 59.00 (*0-7812-0765-7*) Rprt Serv.

— Grand Opera in America. LC 72-2050. reprint ed. 36.00 (*0-404-09909-2*) AMS Pr.

— Grand Opera in America. LC 76-154157. (Select Bibliographies Reprint Ser.). 1977. reprint ed. 25.95 (*0-8369-5773-3*) Ayer.

An Asterisk (*) at the beginning of an entry indicates that the title is appearing in BIP for the first time.

Laheta, Bob. The Key Guidelines for Quickly Finding a Professional Position. Tedeschi, Frank, ed. 77p. (Orig.). (C). 1988. pap. text ed. 12.00 (*0-929403-00-2*) T&H Pr.

***Lahey, Benjamin B.** Psychology: An Introduction. 5th ed. 784p. (C). 1995. pap. text ed. write for info. (*0-697-27484-5*) Brown & Benchmark.

— Psychology: An Introduction, Language Enhancement Guide. 5th ed. 112p. (C). 1994. pap. text ed. write for info. (*0-697-26250-2*) Brown & Benchmark.

— Psychology: An Introduction, Study Guide. 5th ed. 400p. (C). 1995. student ed, pap. text ed. write for info. (*0-697-14521-2*) Brown & Benchmark.

— Psychology: An Introduction, Study Guide. 5th ed. (C). 1995. student ed, disk write for info. (*0-697-26753-9*); student ed, disk write for info. (*0-697-26754-7*); student ed, disk write for info. (*0-697-26755-5*) Brown & Benchmark.

— Psychology: An Introduction with Student Practice Test. 272p. 1995. student ed write for info. (*0-614-03036-6*); student ed, audio write for info. (*0-614-03037-4*) Brown & Benchmark.

Lahey, Benjamin B. & Kazdin, Alan E., eds. Advances in Clinical Child Psychology, Vol. 3. LC 77-643411. (Illus.). 494p. 1980. 45.00 (*0-306-40374-9*, Plenum Pr) Plenum.

— Advances in Clinical Child Psychology, Vol. 4. LC 77-643411. 380p. 1981. 65.00 (*0-306-40705-1*, Plenum Pr) Plenum.

— Advances in Clinical Child Psychology, Vol. 5. LC 77-643411. 392p. 1982. 65.00 (*0-306-41043-5*, Plenum Pr) Plenum.

— Advances in Clinical Child Psychology, Vol. 6. LC 77-643411. 344p. 1983. 65.00 (*0-306-41330-2*, Plenum Pr) Plenum.

— Advances in Clinical Child Psychology, Vol. 7. LC 77-643411. 368p. 1984. 65.00 (*0-306-41659-X*, Plenum Pr) Plenum.

— Advances in Clinical Child Psychology, Vol. 8. LC 77-643411. 344p. 1985. 65.00 (*0-306-41963-7*, Plenum Pr) Plenum.

— Advances in Clinical Child Psychology, Vol. 9. LC 77-643411. 420p. 1986. 65.00 (*0-306-42241-7*, Plenum Pr) Plenum.

— Advances in Clinical Child Psychology, Vol. 10. LC 77-643411. 378p. 1987. 65.00 (*0-306-42536-X*, Plenum Pr) Plenum.

— Advances in Clinical Child Psychology, Vol. 11. LC 77-643411. (Illus.). 414p. 1988. 69.50 (*0-306-42892-X*, Plenum Pr) Plenum.

— Advances in Clinical Child Psychology, Vol. 12. (Illus.). 275p. 1989. 69.50 (*0-306-43271-4*, Plenum Pr) Plenum.

— Advances in Clinical Child Psychology, Vol. 13. LC 77-643411. (Illus.). 426p. 1990. 69.50 (*0-306-43479-2*, Plenum Pr) Plenum.

— Advances in Clinical Child Psychology, Vol. 14. (Illus.). 346p. 1991. 69.50 (*0-306-43957-3*, Plenum Pr) Plenum.

Lahey Clinic Staff. Global Outreach Cookbook. LC 93-71223. 1993. write for info. (*0-87197-371-5*) Favorite Recipes.

Lahey, David. Athletic Scholarships: Making Your Sports Pay. 200p. (YA). 1992. pap. 12.95 (*1-895629-06-3*, Pub. by Warwick Pub CN) Firefly Bks Ltd.

Lahey, G. Gerard Manley Hopkins. LC 72-95435. (Studies in Poetry: No. 38). 1969. reprint ed. lib. bdg. 75.00 (*0-8383-0986-0*) M S G Haskell Hse.

Lahey, G. F. Gerard Manley Hopkins. 1973. 250.00 (*0-87968-030-X*) Gordon Pr.

Lahey, Gerald. Gerard Manley Hopkins. (BCL1-PR English Literature Ser.). 172p. 1992. reprint ed. lib. bdg. 69.00 (*0-7812-7565-2*) Rprt Serv.

Lahey, James F., jt. auth. see Wahl, Eberhard W.

Lahey, James F., et al. Atlas of Five-Day Normal Sea-Level Pressure Charts for the Northern Hemisphere. 80p. 1958. spiral bd. 50.00 (*0-299-01663-3*) U of Wis Pr.

— Atlas of Five Hundred Millibar Wind Characteristics for the Northern Hemisphere. 96p. 1958. spiral bd. 50.00 (*0-299-01703-6*) U of Wis Pr.

— Atlas of Three Hundred Millibar Wind Characteristics for the Northern Hemisphere. 128p. 1960. spiral bd. 50.00 (*0-299-01963-2*) U of Wis Pr.

Lahey, Margaret. Language Disorders & Language Development. 560p. (C). 1988. write for info. (*0-02-367130-0*) Macmillan.

Lahey, Miriam P., et al. Recreation, Leisure, & Chronic Illness: Therapeutic Rehabilitation As Intervention in Health Care. LC 93-16983. (Loss, Grief & Care Ser.: Vol. 6, No. 4). (Illus.). 162p. 1993. lib. bdg. 29.95 (*1-56024-418-6*) Haworth Pr.

Lahey, R. T., ed. Boiling Heat Transfer: Modern Developments & Advances. LC 92-24921. 1992. write for info. (*0-444-89499-3*) Elsevier.

Lahey, R. T. & Moody, F. J. The Thermal Hydraulics of a Boiling Water Nuclear Reactor. 2nd ed. LC 93-12785. 1993. 65.00 (*0-89448-037-5*) Am Nuclear Soc.

Lahey, R. T., ed. see Basic Mechanisms in Two-phase Flow & Heat Transfer Symposium Staff.

Lahey, Richard. Gifted Program Evaluation. 1991. 24.95 (*0-88047-287-1*, 9106) DOK Pubs.

— Math Quiz Bowl. 1989. 7.50 (*0-88047-164-6*, 8906) DOK Pubs.

— Quiz Bowl I. (Illus.). 56p. (Orig.). (J). (gr. 4-12). 1982. teacher ed 7.50 (*0-88047-012-7*, 8216) DOK Pubs.

— Quiz Bowl II. (Illus.). 56p. (Orig.). (J). (gr. 4-12). 1984. 7.50 (*0-88047-037-2*, 8408) DOK Pubs.

— Teamwork Counts. 1991. 14.95 (*0-88047-285-5*, D9103) DOK Pubs.

Lahey, Richard T., Jr. & Wallis, Graham B., eds. Non-Equilibrium Two-Phase Flows: Papers Presented at the Winter Annual Meeting of ASME, Houston, TX, November 30-December 5, 1975. LC 75-25192. 67p. reprint ed. pap. 25.00 (*0-317-08087-3*, 2016830) Bks Demand.

Lahiff, James M., jt. auth. see Huseman, Richard C.

***Lahiri, Aloka.** Chaitanya Movement in Eastern India. (C). 1993. 30.00 (*81-85094-67-5*, Pub. by Punthi Pus II) S Asia.

Lahiri, D., jt. auth. see Rao, C.

Lahiri, Kajal. The Econometrics of Inflation Expectations. (Studies in Monetary Economics: Vol. 7). 250p. 1981. 69.25 (*0-444-86208-0*, North Holland) Elsevier.

Lahiri, Kajal & Moore, Geoffrey H., eds. Leading Economic Indicators: New Approaches & Forecasting Records. (Illus.). 400p. (C). 1991. 74.95 (*0-521-37155-4*) Cambridge U Pr.

— Leading Economic Indicators: New Approaches & Forecasting Records. (Illus.). 400p. (C). 1992. pap. 27.95 (*0-521-43858-6*) Cambridge U Pr.

Lahiri, Latika, tr. Chinese Monks in India by I Ching. 160p. 1986. 22.50 (*81-208-0062-1*, Pub. by Motilal Banarsidass II) S Asia.

***Lahiri-Munir, D. & Garcia, C.** Retinal Pigment Epithelial Transplantation. (Medical Intelligence Unit Ser.). 100p. 1995. write for info. (*1-57059-255-1*) R G Landes.

Lahiri, Nayanjot. The Archaeology of Indian Trade Routes up to the Century 200 B. C. Resource Use, Resource Access & Lines of Communication. (Illus.). 475p. 1992. 32.00 (*0-19-562814-4*) OUP.

— Pre-Ahom Assam. (C). 1991. 16.00 (*0-685-50019-5*, Pub. by Munshiram Manoharial II) S Asia.

Lahiri, Pradip K. Bengali Muslim Thought 1818-1947. (C). 1991. 14.00 (*81-7074-067-3*, Pub. by KP Bagchi IA) S Asia.

***Lahiri, R. M.** The Annexation of Assam. (C). 1994. text ed. 16.00 (*81-7102-008-9*, Pub. by Firma KLM) S Asia.

Lahiri, Sukhamay, jt. ed. see West, John B.

Lahiri, Sukhamay, et al, eds. Chemoreceptors & Reflexes in Breathing: Cellular & Molecular Aspects - The Julius H. Comroe Memorial Volume. (Illus.). 408p. 1989. 75.00 (*0-19-505227-7*) OUP.

— Response & Adaptation to Hypoxia: Organ to Organelle. (Clinical Physiology Series - An American Physiological Society Book). (Illus.). 272p. 1991. 65.00 (*0-19-506244-2*) OUP.

Lahiri, Tarapada. Crime & Punishment in Ancient India. xiii, 207p. 1986. text ed. 22.50 (*81-7027-093-6*, Pub. by Radiant Pubs II) S Asia.

Lahita, Robert G. Systemic Lupus Erythematosus. 2nd ed. (Illus.). 1002p. 1992. text ed. 179.00 (*0-443-08785-7*) Churchill.

Lahita, Robert G., ed. Systemic Lupus Erythematosus. LC 86-11007. (Illus.). 1024p. reprint ed. pap. 180.00 (*0-7837-2586-8*, 2042748) Bks Demand.

Lahlou, B. & Vitiello, P., eds. Aquaculture: Fundamental & Applied Research. LC 93-38053. (Coastal & Estuarine Studies: Vol. 43). 1993. 42.00 (*0-87590-257-X*) Am Geophysical.

Lahlou, B., jt. ed. see Kirsch, R.

Lahlou, B., jt. ed. see Truchot, J.

Lahm, Frank P, jt. auth. see Chandler, Charles D.

Lahmani, F., ed. Photophysics & Photochemistry above 6 EV: Proceedings of the International Meeting of the Societe de Chimie Physique, 38th, Bombannes, 21-27 September, 1984. (Studies in Physical & Theoretical Chemistry: Vol. 35). 672p. 1985. 207.75 (*0-444-42463-6*) Elsevier.

Lahodny, Jan. Competitive Drills for Winning Basketball. 225p. 1986. text ed. 21.95 (*0-13-154949-9*, Parker Publishing Co) P-H.

LaHood, Charles G. & Sullivan, Robert C. Reprographic Services in Libraries: Organization & Administration. LC 75-25585. (LTP Publication Ser.: No. 19). 80p. reprint ed. pap. 25.00 (*0-317-26573-3*, 2023954) Bks Demand.

LaHood, Marvin J., ed. Tender Is the Night: Essays in Criticism. LC 77-85091. 222p. reprint ed. pap. 63.30 (*0-8357-9246-3*, 2017625) Bks Demand.

***Lahore, J. & Rothnie, W.** Butterworths Annotated Acts: Copyright Act. Date not set. write for info. (*0-409-31001-8*, Austral) Butterworth Legal Pubs.

Lahore, James. Intellectual Property in Australia - Copyright. 413.00 (*0-409-49350-3*) Butterworth Legal Pubs.

— Intellectual Property in Australia - Patents, Designs & Trade Marks Law. 1981. ring bd. 412.00 (*0-409-30037-3*) Butterworth Legal Pubs.

Lahore, James, ed. Intellectual Property Reports, 25 vols., Set. ring bd. 2,244.00 (*0-409-48872-0*) Butterworth Legal Pubs.

***Lahori, Maulana A.** Commentators of the Holy Quran. 130p. (Orig.). 1995. text ed. 19.95 (*1-56744-506-3*) Kazi Pubns.

Lahoz, Javier V., jt. ed. see Uso, Pasqual M.

Lahr, Georgiana L. Jolly Holiday Plays. LC 81-50753. 181p. 1982. 8.95 (*0-533-05001-4*) Vantage.

— A Symphony of Songs. 1985. 8.95 (*0-533-06179-2*) Vantage.

Lahr, Grace, ed. see Waconia Heritage Association Staff.

Lahr, Jane & Tabori, Lena, eds. Love: A Celebration in Art & Literature. LC 82-5680. (Illus.). 240p. 1982. 45.00 (*0-941434-20-6*) Stewart Tabori & Chang.

Lahr, Jeff. Christmas Carol: A Cradle, Cross & Crown. 48p. (Orig.). 1992. pap. text ed. 2.95 (*0-87227-175-7*) Reg Baptist.

— Time of Miracles. 40p. 1991. pap. 2.95 (*0-87227-170-6*) Reg Baptist.

Lahr, John. Coward the Playwright. 200p. 1983. pap. 3.95 (*0-380-64683-8*, Discus) Avon.

— Coward the Playwright. (Illus.). 176p. 1983. 11.95 (*0-413-48050-X*, A0065) Heinemann.

— Dame Edna Everage & the Rise of Western Civilization: Backstage with Barry Humphries. LC 92-2261. 1992. 22.00 (*0-374-13456-1*) FS&G.

— Diary of a Somebody: Based on the Orton Diaries. LC 88-37726. 79p. (Orig.). 1989. pap. 7.95 (*0-87910-124-5*) Limelight Edns.

— Prick up Your Ears: The Biography of Joe Orton. LC 86-96. (Illus.). 320p. 1986. reprint ed. pap. 14.95 (*0-87910-057-5*) Limelight Edns.

Lahr, Luralyn & Hinkle, Harry, eds. Arts Express Teacher's Guide. (Arts Express TV Ser.). 56p. 1983. pap. 3.50 (*0-910475-93-8*) KET.

Lahr, Michael L., jt. auth. see Stevens, Benjamin H.

Lahrson, Ann. Homeschooling in Oregon: The Handbook. LC 94-65549. 275p. 1994. pap. 14.95 (*0-9640813-7-7*) Out of the Box.

Lahsaeizadeh, Abdolali. Contemporary Rural Iran. 366p. 1993. 68.95 (*1-85628-417-4*, Pub. by Avebury Pub UK) Ashgate Pub Co.

Lahti. Contact Utricaria Syndrome. 1995. write for info. (*0-8493-7352-2*) CRC Pr.

Lahti, Kai, jt. auth. see Hedlund, Laura.

***Lahti, N. E.** Plain Talk about Art: The Language of Art from A to Z. 4th rev. ed. LC 94-90022. 203p. 1994. pap. 11.00 (*0-9620147-1-0*) York Bks.

Lahti, P. J. & Mittelstaedt, P., eds. Foundations of Modern Physics: Proceedings of the Symposium on "The Foundations of Modern Physics: 50 Years of the Einstein-Podolsky-Rosen Gedanken Experiment", Joensuu, Finland, 16-20 June 1985. 718p. 1985. 116.00 (*9971-5-0004-3*); pap. 75.00 (*9971-5-0005-1*) World Scientific Pub.

— The Foundations of Modern Physics, 1990: Symposium. 540p. 1990. pap. 55.00 (*981-02-0417-5*) World Scientific Pub.

Lahti, P. J. & Mittlestaedt, P., eds. Foundations of Modern Physics 87: The Copenhagen Interpretation 60 Years after the Como Lecture. 544p. (C). 1988. pap. 47.00 (*9971-5-0460-X*) World Scientific Pub.

Lahti, Robert E. Innovative College Management. LC 73-10938. (Jossey-Bass Higher Education Ser.). 198p. reprint ed. pap. 56.50 (*0-317-41815-7*, 2025660) Bks Demand.

Lahti-Wagner, Jean, jt. auth. see Schwanke, Dik.

***Lahti, Will & Salmela, David W.** Karhun Otsa: Bear's Forehead. 52p. (Orig.). 1992. pap. text ed. 6.95 (*0-9632975-1-1*) Finnish Amer.

Lahue, Fabian J. Electronic Troubleshooting. LC 93-24452. 1993. 23.16 (*0-02-819904-9*) Glencoe.

Lahue, Kal. Mercury Outboard Shop Manual, 1972-1989: 45-225 HP. (Illus.). 343p. (Orig.). 1989. pap. 32.95 (*0-89287-396-5*, B726) Clymer Pub.

— OMC Stern Drive Shop Manual 1964-1986. (Illus.). 384p. (Orig.). 1988. pap. 32.95 (*0-89287-398-1*, B730) Clymer Pub.

Lahue, Kalton. Mercruiser Stern Drive Shop Manual 1964-1987. (Illus.). 628p. (Orig.). pap. 32.95 (*0-89287-613-1*, B740) Clymer Pub.

***Lahue, Kalton C.** Auto Chassis: Suspension, Steering & Brakes. Conty, ed. 500p. (C). 1995. student ed, spiral bd. write for info. (*0-314-04694-1*) West Pub.

— Automotive Brakes & Antilock Braking Systems. LC 93-46889. (Automotive Ser.). 500p. 1994. pap. text ed. 49.25 (*0-314-02838-2*) West Pub.

— Automotive Chassis: Suspension, Steering, & Brakes. LC 94-42860. (West's Automotive Ser.). 1995. pap. text ed. 52.00 (*0-314-04549-X*) West Pub.

— Automotive Chassis: Suspension, Steering, & Brakes. LC 94-43215. (West's Automotive Ser.). 1995. pap. text ed. 38.25 (*0-314-04551-1*) West Pub.

— Automotive Undercar: Suspension, Steering & Electronic Systems. LC 94-43216. (West's Automotive Ser.). 1995. spiral bd. write for info. (*0-314-04550-3*) West Pub.

— Electronic Automatic Transmissions. LC 93-31296. 1994. write for info. (*0-02-801365-4*) Glencoe.

— Interior Lighting. Smith, Cheryl, ed. LC 90-84632. (Illus.). 112p. (Orig.). 1991. pap. 9.95 (*0-89721-227-4*) Ortho Info.

— Roofs & Sidings. Smith, Cheryl, ed. LC 90-86165. 112p. 1991. pap. 9.95 (*0-89721-237-1*) Ortho Info.

Lahue, Kalton C., ed. see Leigh, Bob, et al.

Lahue, Robert, ed. Methods in Neurobiology, Vol. 1. LC 80-15623. 614p. 1981. 110.00 (*0-306-40517-2*, Plenum Pr) Plenum.

— Methods in Neurobiology, Vol. 2. LC 80-15623. 682p. 1981. 110.00 (*0-306-40518-0*, Plenum Pr) Plenum.

LaHue, Sanford P., Sr., ed. Solutions for Pavement Rehabilitation Problems. 304p. 1986. 29.00 (*0-87262-578-8*) Am Soc Civil Eng.

LaHurd, Jeff. Quintessential Sarasota: Stories & Pictures from the 1920's-1950's. (Illus.). 128p. (Orig.). 1990. pap. 8.95 (*1-879026-00-7*) Clubhouse Pub.

Lahusen, Suzanne, jt. ed. see Preston-Dunlop, Valerie.

Lahusen, Thomas & Kuperman, Gene, eds. Late Soviet Culture: From Perestroika to Novostroika. LC 92-28051. (Post-Contemporary Interventions Ser.). 344p. 1993. lib. bdg. 49.95 (*0-8223-1290-5*); pap. text ed. 18.95 (*0-8223-1291-3*) Duke.

Lai, C., jt. auth. see Hromadka, Theodore V., II.

Lai, C. H., ed. Gauge Theory of Weak & Electromagnetic Interactions. 458p. 1981. text ed. 52.00 (*9971-83-023-X*); pap. text ed. 30.00 (*9971-83-022-1*) World Scientific Pub.

— Ideals & Realities: Selected Essays of Abdus Salem. 2nd ed. 400p. 1987. text ed. 59.00 (*9971-5-0315-8*); pap. text ed. 37.00 (*9971-5-0316-6*) World Scientific Pub.

Lai, C. H., jt. ed. see Hassan, Z.

Lai, C. H., jt. ed. see Mohapatra, R. N.

Lai, C. L., et al, eds. Viral Hepatitis B Infection: Vaccine & Control. 304p. 1984. 85.00 (*9971-950-80-4*) World Scientific Pub.

Lai, David. Amiga Developers Reference Guide, Edition 1.3. 3rd ed. LC 88-92561. 228p. (C). 1988. pap. 19.95 (*0-945119-02-X*) Pacific Pr CA.

— Photoshop Type Magic. (Illus.). 208p. (Orig.). 1995. pap. 25.00 (*1-56830-220-7*) Alpha Bks IN.

Lai, David A. Icons for the Masses: The Complete Guide to Creating, Editing & Customizing Icons. (Illus.). 168p. (Orig.). 1993. pap. 17.95 (*1-56609-081-4*) Peachpit Pr.

Lai, Eric & Birren, Bruce W., eds. Electrophoresis of Large DNA Molecules: Theory & Applications. (Current Communications in Cell & Molecular Biology Ser.: No. 1). (Illus.). 180p. (C). 1991. text ed. 34.00 (*0-87969-360-6*) Cold Spring Harbor.

Lai, Eric, jt. auth. see Birren, Bruce.

***Lai, Francis.** Common Sense Medicine. 200p. 1996. pap. 8.95 (*0-7610-0472-6*) NW Pub.

***Lai, G. Y. & Sorrell, G., eds.** Materials Performance in Waste Incineration Systems. (Illus.). 538p. 1992. 90.00 (*1-877914-31-2*) NACE Intl.

Lai, Him M., et al. Island: Poetry & History of Chinese Immigrants on Angel Island, 1910-40. LC 91-8372. (Illus.). 174p. (CHI & ENG.). 1991. pap. 16.95 (*0-295-97109-6*) U of Wash Pr.

Lai, Honyi, tr. see Teiwes, Frederick C. & Sun, Warren, eds.

Lai, Juey H., ed. Polymers for Electronic Applications. 272p. 1989. 205.00 (*0-8493-4704-1*, TK) CRC Pr.

Lai, M. M. & Stohlman, S. A., eds. Coronaviruses. LC 87-22034. (Advances in Experimental Medicine & Biology Ser.: Vol. 218). (Illus.). 604p. 1987. 125.00 (*0-306-42672-2*, Plenum Pr) Plenum.

***Lai, Mary, et al.** Am I Covered for...? A Comprehensive Guide to Insuring Your Non-Profit Organization. 2nd ed. (Illus.). 286p. (C). 1992. pap. text ed. 14.95 (*0-614-01352-6*) Consort Human.

Lai, Ralph W., et al. Modern Proportionality Law for Science, Medicine, & Engineering Applications: A Graphical Description of the Law of Nature. (Illus.). 368p. (C). 1995. text ed. 85.00 (*0-9628526-2-7*); text ed. 28.50 (*0-9628526-1-9*) Toshi Co.

— Modern Proportionality Law for Science, Medicine, & Engineering Applications: A Graphical Description of the Law of Nature. (Illus.). 354p. (C). 1995. pap. 18.50 (*0-9628526-3-5*) Toshi Co.

Lai, Robert S. Writing MS-DOS Device Drivers. 2nd ed. 1992. pap. 29.95 (*0-201-60837-5*) Addison-Wesley.

Lai, Robert S. & Waite Group Staff. Writing MS-DOS Device Drivers. (Illus.). 400p. 1987. pap. 24.95 (*0-201-13185-4*) Addison-Wesley.

Lai, S. T. Gas Chromatography - Mass Spectrometry Operation. LC 88-90572. (Illus.). 153p. (Orig.). (C). 1988. pap. text ed. 55.00 (*0-945846-00-2*, R541) Realistic Syst.

Lai, T. C. Ch'i Pai-shih. LC 73-76338. (Illus.). 208p. 1973. 20.00 (*0-295-95315-2*) U of Wash Pr.

Lai, T. L. & Siegmund, D., eds. Herbert Robbins: Selected Papers. (Illus.). 560p. 1985. 72.00 (*0-387-96137-2*) Spr-Verlag.

Lai Tse-Han, et al. A Tragic Beginning: The Taiwan Uprising of February 28, 1947. LC 90-39218. (Illus.). 288p. 1991. 35.00 (*0-8047-1829-6*) Stanford U Pr.

Lai, Violet. He Was a Ram: Wong Aloiau of Hawaii. LC 85-972. (Illus.). 320p. 1985. text ed. 25.00 (*0-8248-0991-2*) UH Pr.

Lai, W. Michael, jt. auth. see Lin, S. P.

Lai, W. Michael, et al. Introduction to Continuum Mechanics. LC 72-10904. (C). 1978. text ed. 105.00 (*0-08-022698-1*, Pergamon Pr) Elsevier.

— Introduction to Continuum Mechanics. 3rd ed. LC 93-30117. 1994. text ed. 100.00 (*0-08-041700-0*, Pergamon Pr); Flexicover. pap. text ed. 40.00 (*0-08-041701-9*) Elsevier.

Lai, Walton L. Indentured Labor, Caribbean Sugar: Chinese & Indian Migrants to the British West Indies, 1838-1918. LC 92-33812. (Studies in Atlantic History & Culture). (Illus.). 384p. (C). 1993. text ed. 39.95 (*0-8018-4465-7*) Johns Hopkins.

Lai, Y. Yang, tr. see Shen, Terry C.

Lai Yen-Jen, tr. see Huang Su Huei.

Lai, Young-Jou & Hwang, Ching-Lai. Fuzzy Mathematical Programming: Methods & Applications. LC 92-27311. (Lecture Notes in Economics & Mathematical Systems Ser.: Vol. 394). 1993. 60.00 (*0-387-56098-X*) Spr-Verlag.

Laib, Nevin K. Rhetoric & Style: Strategies for Advanced Writers. LC 92-22827. 408p. (C). 1993. pap. text ed. write for info. (*0-13-478967-9*) P-H.

Laible, J., et al, eds. Finite Elements in Water Resources: Proceedings of the 5th International Conference, Burlington, Vermont, June 1984. 800p. 1984. 179.00 (*0-387-13468-9*) Spr-Verlag.

Laibman, David. Value, Technical Change, & Crisis: Explorations in Marxist Economic Theory. LC 91-11246. 400p. 1992. 62.95 (*0-87332-735-7*); pap. text ed. 25.95 (*0-87332-736-5*) M E Sharpe.

Laibman, David, ed. Science & Society General Index: Volumes 26-50 (1962 to 1986-87) LC 88-83178. 230p. 1989. lib. bdg. 50.00 (*0-89862-380-4*) Guilford Pr.

Laibman, David, et al. Soviet Union Socialist or Social-Imperialist: Essays Toward the Debate on the Nature of Soviet Society. LC 83-559. 210p. (Orig.). 1983. pap. 6.95 (*0-89851-062-7*) RCP Pubns.

Laibson. Year Book of Ophthalmology, 1993. 450p. 1993. 64.95 (*0-8151-5269-8*, Yr Bk Med Pubs) Mosby Yr Bk.

— Year Book of Ophthalmology, 1994. 253p. 1994. 64.95 (*0-8151-5270-1*, Yr Bk Med Pubs) Mosby Yr Bk.

— Year Book of Ophthalmology, 1995. 253p. 1995. 64.95 (*0-8151-5271-X*, Yr Bk Med Pubs) Mosby Yr Bk.

— Year Book of Ophthalmology, 1996. 253p. 1996. 64.95 (*0-8151-5272-8*, Yr Bk Med Pubs) Mosby Yr Bk.
— Yearbook of Ophthalmology, 1990. 280p. 1990. 57.95 (*0-8151-5266-3*, Yr Bk Med Pubs) Mosby Yr Bk.
— Yearbook of Ophthalmology, 1991. 292p. 1991. 57.95 (*0-8151-5267-1*) Mosby Yr Bk.
— Yearbook of Ophthalmology, 1992. 336p. 1992. 59.95 (*0-8151-5268-X*) Mosby Yr Bk.
Laibson, Peter R., ed. Year Book of Ophthalmology, 1989. (Illus.). 256p. 1989. 57.95 (*0-8151-5265-5*, Yr Bk Med Pubs) Mosby Yr Bk.
***Laibstain, Harry.** Investing, Collecting & Trading in Certified Commemoratives: In-Depth Analysis of Gold & Silver Issues: 1892 - 1954. (Illus.). 176p. 1995. spiral bd. 32.50 (*0-614-03960-6*) DLRC Pr.
***Laibstain, Harry & Lawrence, David.** The Complete Guide to Barber Quarters. 2nd ed. LC 94-80033. (Illus.). 176p. 1995. 49.95 (*1-880731-50-9*); pap. 29.95 (*1-880731-24-X*) DLRC Pr.
Laidi, Chen, tr. see Yanchi, Liu.
Laidi, Zaki. The Superpowers & Africa: The Constraints of a Rivalry, 1960-1990. Baudoin, Patricia, tr. LC 90-10832. (Illus.). 256p. 1990. pap. text ed. 14.95 (*0-226-46782-1*) U Ch Pr.
— The Superpowers & Africa: The Constraints of a Rivalry, 1960-1990. Baudoin, Patricia, tr. LC 90-10832. (Illus.). 256p. 1990. lib. bdg. 45.00 (*0-226-46781-3*) U Ch Pr.
***Laidi, Zaki, ed.** Power & Purpose after the Cold War. McPhail, Helen, tr. (World Time Ser.). 256p. 1995. 45.95 (*0-85496-807-5*); pap. 19.95 (*1-85973-077-9*) Berg Pubs.
Laidi, Zaki, ed. see De Senarclens, Pierre.
Laidig, Wyn D., jt. ed. see Burquest, Donald A.
Laidlaw. Vitamins & Cancer Prevention Contemporary Issues in Clinical Nutrition, Vol. 14. (Contemporary Issues in Clinical Nutrition Ser.). 1991. text ed. 82.95 (*0-471-56066-9*) Wiley.
Laidlaw, Angus, ed. see Russell, A. G. & Russell, Goldie.
Laidlaw, Brett. Blue Bel Air. 320p. 1993. 21.95 (*0-393-03406-2*) Norton.
Laidlaw, G. Norman. Elysian Encounter: Diderot & Gide. LC 63-19193. 1963. 34.95 (*0-8156-2054-3*) Syracuse U Pr.
Laidlaw, Harry H. Contemporary Queen Rearing. LC 79-50568. (Illus.). (C). 1979. 11.40 (*0-915698-05-6*) Dadant & Sons.
— Instrumental Insemination of Honey Bee Queens: Pictorial Instructional Manual. (Illus.). (C). 1977. 14.40 (*0-915698-03-X*) Dadant & Sons.
***Laidlaw, James.** Riches & Renunciation: Religion, Economy, & Society among the Jains. (Oxford Studies in Social & Cultural Anthropology). (Illus.). 400p. 1995. 65.00 (*0-19-828031-9*); pap. 24.95 (*0-19-828042-4*) OUP.
Laidlaw, James A., jt. auth. see Humphrey, Caroline.
Laidlaw, John, et al, eds. A Textbook of Epilepsy. 4th ed. LC 92-12309. 768p. 1993. 185.00 (*0-443-04473-2*) Churchill.
Laidlaw, L. & Roberts, R. Law Relating to Banking Services. (C). 1989. 190.00 (*0-85297-277-6*, Pub. by Inst Bankers UK) St Mut.
Laidlaw, Marc. Dad's Nuke. LC 85-80882. 251p. 1986. 15.95 (*0-917657-52-7*) D I Fine.
— The Orchid Eater. 240p. 1994. 19.95 (*0-312-10515-0*) St Martin.
— The 37th Mandala. 384p. 1995. 22.95 (*0-312-13021-X*) St Martin.
Laidlaw, R. A. La Razon Por Que? (The Reason Why) (SPA.). Date not set. 1.79 (*1-56063-004-3*, 498100) Editorial Unilit.
Laidlaw, Robert A. The Reason Why. 48p. 1975. pap. 3.99 (*0-310-27112-6*, 18243P) Zondervan.
— The Reason Why. LC 93-70313. 60p. reprint ed. pap. 1.50 (*0-88270-649-7*) Bridge Pub.
Laidlaw, Toni A. Healing Voices: Feminist Approaches to Therapy with Women. LC 89-43458. (Social & Behavioral Science Ser.). 367p. 1992. reprint ed. pap. 16.95 (*1-55542-418-X*) Jossey-Bass.
Laidlaw, Toni A., et al. Healing Voices: Feminist Approaches to Therapy with Women. LC 89-43458. (Social & Behavioral Sciences Ser.). 367p. 1990. 30.95x (*1-55542-225-X*) Jossey-Bass.
Laidler & Meiser. Physical Chemistry. 1982. text ed. 49.50 (*0-8053-5682-7*) Benjamin-Cummings.
— Physical Chemistry. (C). 1982. teacher ed, pap. text ed. 16.25 (*0-8053-5683-5*) Benjamin-Cummings.
Laidler, ed. see International Congress of Pure & Applied Chemistry 28th, Vancouver, BC, Canada, 16-22 August 1981.
Laidler, D. & Purdy, D. L., eds. Inflation & Labor Markets. (Studies in Inflation: No. II). 272p. (C). 1993. reprint ed. text ed. 54.95 (*0-7512-0199-5*, Pub. by Gregg Revivals UK) Ashgate Pub Co.
Laidler, David. Essays on Money & Inflation. (Studies in Inorganic Chemistry: No. III). 272p. (C). 1993. reprint ed. text ed. 54.95 (*0-7512-0198-7*, Pub. by Gregg Revivals UK) Ashgate Pub Co.
— The Golden Age of the Quantity Theory. 192p. 1991. text ed. 39.50 (*0-691-04295-0*) Princeton U Pr.
Laidler, David E. The Demand for Money: Theories, Evidence, & Problems. 3rd ed. 178p. (C). 1990. pap. text ed. 19.50 (*0-06-043827-4*) HarpCollege.
— The Demand for Money: Theories, Evidence, & Problems. 4th ed. LC 92-11945. (C). 1992. 38.00 (*0-06-501098-1*) HarpCollege.
— Monetarist Perspectives. 232p. 1983. 32.00 (*0-674-58240-3*) HUP.
— Taking Money Seriously. 200p. 1990. pap. 29.95 (*0-262-12148-4*) MIT Pr.
Laidler, Harry W. Social-Economic Movements: An Historical & Comparative Survey of Socialism. (Essay Index Reprint Ser.). 1977. reprint ed. 48.95 (*0-518-10149-5*) Ayer.
Laidler, Harry W. & Thomas, Norman. The Socialism of Our Times: A Symposium, Prelude to Depression. LC 76-27725. 1976. reprint ed. lib. bdg. 45.00 (*0-306-70850-7*) Da Capo.
Laidler, John, jt. auth. see Donaghy, Peter.
Laidler, Keith J. Reaction Kinetics, 2 vols., 1. LC 62-22037. 1963. pap. 93.00 (*0-08-009833-9*, Pub. by Pergamon Repr UK) Franklin.
— Reaction Kinetics, 2 vols., 2. LC 62-22037. 1963. 63.00 (*0-08-009836-3*, Pub. by Pergamon Repr UK); pap. 60.00 (*0-08-009835-5*, Pub. by Pergamon Repr UK) Franklin.
— The World of Physical Chemistry. (Illus.). 448p. 1995. pap. 39.95 (*0-19-855919-4*) OUP.
Laidler, Keith J. & Keith, J. Chemical Kinetics. 3rd ed. 531p. (C). 1990. text ed. 80.00 (*0-06-043862-2*) HarpCollege.
Laidler, Keith J., jt. ed. see Back, M.
Laidler, Kieth & Laidler, Liz. Pandas: Giants of the Bamboo Forest. (Illus.). 208p. 1994. 29.95 (*0-563-36361-4*, BBC-Parkwest) Parkwest Pubns.
Laidler, Liz, jt. auth. see Laidler, Kieth.
***Laidler, P.** Stroke Rehabilitation: Structure & Strategy. 336p. 1994. 44.95 (*1-56593-208-0*, 0522) Singular Publishing.
Laidlow, Philip. Tolley's Tax Planning for Post Death Variations. 150p. 1993. 90.00 (*0-85459-684-4*, Pub. by Tolley Pubng UK) St Mut.
Laidman, Hugh. Animals: How to Draw Them. LC 75-11930. (Illus.). 160p. (YA). (gr. 7 up). 1979. pap. 12.95 (*0-685-46950-6*, Dutton) NAL-Dutton.
Laifer, Miryam. Edmond Jabes: Un Judaisme Apres Dieu. (American University Studies: Romance Languages & Literature: Ser. II, Vol. 39). 151p. 1986. pap. 33.70 (*0-8204-0283-4*) P Lang Pubs.
Laignel-Lavastine, Maxime. French Medicine. LC 75-23666. (Clio Medica Ser.: 15). (Illus.). reprint ed. 37.50 (*0-404-58915-4*) AMS Pr.
Laik, Judy. Under Whose Influence? LC 93-86233. (Decision Is Yours Ser.). (Illus.). 64p. (J). (gr. 5-7). 1994. lib. bdg. 16.95 (*0-943990-98-X*); pap. 5.95 (*0-943990-97-1*) Parenting Pr.
Laik, Madeleine. Deck Chairs. Schein, Gideon Y., tr. (Publications Ser.: No. 6). 120p. (Orig.). 1984. pap. text ed. 8.95 (*0-913745-05-7*) Ubu Repertory.
Laikari, H., ed. River Basin Management V: Proceedings of the Conference Held in Rovaniemi, Finland, 31 July-4 August 1989. (Advances in Water Pollution Control Ser.: Vol. 9). (Illus.). 438p. 1989. 140.00 (*0-08-037379-8*, Pergamon Pr) Elsevier.
Laiken, Deidre S. Death among Strangers. 256p. 1988. pap. 3.95 (*0-380-70521-4*) Avon.
— Killing Time in Buffalo. 1990. 18.95 (*0-316-51223-0*) Little.
Laiken, Nora, et al. Interpretation of Electrocardiograms: A Self-Instructional Approach. 2nd ed. (Illus.). 264p. 1988. spiral bd. 33.50 (*0-88167-388-9*) Raven.
Laikin, Milton. Lens Design. (Optical Engineering Ser.: Vol. 27). 344p. 1991. 125.00 (*0-8247-8403-0*) Dekker.
— Lens Design. 2nd expanded rev. ed. LC 94-44816. (Optical Engineering Ser.: Vol. 48). 1995. write for info. (*0-8247-9602-0*) Dekker.
Lail, Steve. Six Flags over PTL: Fun with Jim & Tammy. (Illus.). 55p. (Orig.). 1985. pap. 4.95 (*0-318-22517-4*) Lail Press.
— Six More Flags over PTL: More Fun with Jim & Tammy. (Illus.). 48p. (Orig.). 1986. pap. 4.95 (*0-9618697-0-4*) Lail Press.
— The Truth about Rainbows. (Orig.). (C). 1987. pap. 5.95 (*0-9618697-2-0*) Lail Press.
Laili, Anthony F. Tailored Urologic Imaging. LC 80-16566. (Illus.). 335p. reprint ed. pap. 95.50 (*0-685-23362-6*, 2032298) Bks Demand.
Laiman. To Love & to Cherish. 1994. mass mkt. 5.50 (*0-671-86484-X*) PB.
Laiman, Leah. For Better, for Worse. Marrow, Linda, ed. 304p. (Orig.). 1994. mass mkt. 5.50 (*0-671-86483-1*) PB.
— For Richer, for Poorer. Marrow, Linda, ed. 320p. (Orig.). 1994. mass mkt. 5.50 (*0-671-86482-3*) PB.
Lain. Advertising Survival Kit. 64p. 1992. 1.75 (*0-318-60010-2*) Quill & Scroll.
Lain, Anna. Prism. 384p. 1988. mass mkt. 4.50 (*0-8217-2377-4*) Zebra.
Lain Entralgo, Pedro. Tan Solo Hombres. (Nueva Austral Ser.: Vol. 250). (SPA.). 1991. pap. text ed. 24.95x (*84-239-7250-X*) Elliots Bks.
Lain, Henry B. His Wise Counsel. 96p. (Orig.). 1994. pap. 6.99 (*1-56043-813-4*) Destiny Image.
Lain, J. Brooklyn City Directory, 1859. 1972. 59.95 (*0-87968-796-7*) Gordon Pr.
Laine, Andrew, ed. Wavelet Theory & Application. LC 93-10594. 140p. (C). 1993. lib. bdg. 95.00 (*0-7923-9357-0*) Kluwer Ac.
Laine, Claude, ed. Combinatory Vocabulary of CAD-CAM in Mechanical Engineering. 145p. (Orig.). 1993. pap. 20.75 (*0-660-58029-2*, Pub. by Canada Commun Grp CN) Accents Pubns.
Laine, Edward W., ed. see Sillanpaa, Nelma.
Laine, I., et al, eds. Complex Analysis. (Lecture Notes in Mathematics Ser.: Vol. 1351). 415p. 1988. pap. 47.90 (*0-387-50370-6*) Spr-Verlag.
Laine, Ilpo. Nevalinna Theory & Complex Differential Equations. LC 92-35852. (Studies in Mathematics: Vol. 15). viii, 341p. (C). 1992. lib. bdg. 89.95 (*3-11-013422-5*) De Gruyter.
Laine, Michael, ed. A Cultivated Mind: Essays on J. S. Mill Presented to John M. Robson. 192p. 1991. 60.00 (*0-8020-5915-5*) U of Toronto Pr.
Laine, Michael, ed. see Robson, John M.
Laine, Pascal. Dentelliere. (Folio Ser.: No. 726). (Orig.). (FRE.). pap. 8.95 (*2-07-036726-6*) Schoenhof.
— Jeanne du Bon Plaisir Ou les Hasards de la Fidelite. (Folio Ser.: No. 1730). (FRE.). 1986. pap. 8.95 (*2-07-037730-X*) Schoenhof.
— Monsieur Vous Oubliez Votre Cadavre. (Folio Ser.: No. 2186). (FRE.). 1970. pap. 9.95 (*2-07-038276-1*) Schoenhof.
— Petites Egarees. (Folio Ser.: No. 2170). (FRE.). pap. 14.95 (*2-07-038259-1*) Schoenhof.
— Plutot Deux Fois Qu'une. (Folio Ser.: No. 2063). (FRE.). pap. 9.95 (*2-07-038150-1*) Schoenhof.
— Trois Petits Meurtres...et Puis S'en Va. (Folio Ser.: No. 2026). 281p. (FRE.). 1985. pap. 9.95 (*2-07-038114-5*) Schoenhof.
Laine, Richard M., ed. Inorganic & Organometallic Polymers with Special Properties: Proceedings of the NATO Advanced Research Workshop, Cap d'Agde, France, September 9-14, 1990. (C). 1991. lib. bdg. 154.50 (*0-7923-1514-6*) Kluwer Ac.
— Transformation of Organometallics into Common & Exotic Materials: Design & Activation. (C). 1988. lib. bdg. 125.50 (*90-247-3661-7*) Kluwer Ac.
Laine, Richard M., jt. ed. see Harrod, John F.
Laine, Tom, ed. see Brass, Perry.
Lainen, William. Preparing Our Hearts. Hayes, Theresa, ed. 112p. 1994. pap. 6.99 (*0-7847-0225-X*, 18-03040) Standard Pub.
Laing. Fertility & Infertility in Veterinary Practice. 4th ed. 1989. text ed. 64.95 (*0-7020-1264-5*) Saunders.
***Laing, Adrian C.** R. D. Laing: A Biography. 248p. 1995. 50.00 (*0-7206-0934-8*, Pub. by P Owen Ltd UK) Dufour.
Laing, Alastair, ed. see Braham, Allan & Hager, Hellmut.
Laing, Alastair, ed. see Branner, Robert.
Laing, Alastair, ed. see Downes, Kerry.
Laing, Alastair, ed. see Garstang, Donald.
Laing, Alastair, ed. see Herrmann, Wolfgang.
Laing, Alastair, ed. see Leach, Peter.
Laing, Alastair, ed. see Stillman, Damie.
Laing, Alastair, ed. see Tadgell, Christopher.
Laing, Alastair, ed. see Watkin, David.
Laing, Alice F., jt. auth. see Chazan, Maurice.
Laing, Alison. Speaking As a Woman. 40p. 1989. pap. 10.00 (*1-880715-03-1*) Creat Des Srvs.
Laing, B. Kojo. Search Sweet Country. 312p. 1988. reprint ed. pap. 9.95 (*0-571-12996-X*) Faber & Faber.
Laing, Christine, jt. auth. see Bolotin, Norman.
Laing, D. G., et al, eds. The Human Sense of Smell. (Illus.). 395p. 1991. 159.00 (*0-387-53355-9*) Spr-Verlag.
Laing, Dave. One Chord Wonders: Power & Meaning in Punk Rock. 192p. 1985. 34.00 (*0-335-15065-9*, Open Univ Pr) Taylor & Francis.
Laing, Dave, jt. auth. see Hardy, Phil.
Laing, David. The Earth System: An Introduction to Earth Science. 608p. (C). 1991. pap. write for info. (*0-697-07952-X*) Wm C Brown Pubs.
Laing, David, ed. Collection of Ancient Scottish Prophecies in Alliterative Verse. LC 70-144433. (Bannatyne Club, Edinburgh. Publications: No. 44). reprint ed. 19.50 (*0-404-52754-X*) AMS Pr.
— Original Letters Relating to the Ecclesiastical Affairs of Scotland, 2 Vols. LC 73-171637. (Bannatyne Club, Edinburgh. Publications: No. 92). reprint ed. 95.00 (*0-404-52833-3*) AMS Pr.
— Registrum Cartarum Ecclesie Sancti Egidii De Edinburgh. LC 76-174803. (Bannatyne Club, Edinburgh. Publications: No. 105). reprint ed. 47.50 (*0-404-52860-0*) AMS Pr.
— Registrum Domus De Soltre. LC 77-171638. (Bannatyne Club, Edinburgh. Publications: No. 109). reprint ed. 42.50 (*0-404-52863-5*) AMS Pr.
— Royal Letters, Charters, & Tracts. LC 70-171639. (Bannatyne Club, Edinburgh. Publications: No. 114). reprint ed. 42.50 (*0-404-52869-4*) AMS Pr.
Laing, David & Lampiris, Nicholas. Aspen High Country: The Geology, a Pictorial Guide to Roads & Trails. (Illus.). 144p. (Orig.). (J). (gr. 9-12). 1980. pap. write for info. (*0-9604274-0-6*) Thunder River.
Laing, David, ed. see Baillie, Robert.
Laing, David, ed. see Bannatyne Club Staff.
Laing, David, ed. see Barbour, John.
Laing, David, ed. see Clerk, John.
Laing, David, ed. see Colville, John.
Laing, David, ed. see Ferguson, David.
Laing, David, ed. see Knox, John.
Laing, David, ed. see Rolland, John.
Laing, Ellen J. The Winking Owl: Art in the People's Republic of China. 250p. 1988. 65.00 (*0-520-06097-0*) U CA Pr.
Laing, G. S. Accident & Emergency Medicine. 225p. 1988. pap. 29.50 (*0-387-19508-4*) Spr-Verlag.
Laing, Geri, jt. auth. see Laing, Sam.
Laing, Gordon J., jt. auth. see Shorey, Paul.
Laing, Gregory H., jt. auth. see Curtis, Howard W.
Laing, Henry. Descriptive Catalogue of Impressions from Ancient Scottish Seals. LC 75-171640. (Maitland Club, Glasgow. Publications: No. 68). reprint ed. 47.50 (*0-404-53081-8*) AMS Pr.
Laing, Jane. Cicely Mary Barker & Her Art. (Illus.). 128p. (J). 1995. 35.00 (*0-7232-4051-5*) Warne.
Laing, Jennifer. The Art of Making Teddy Bears. (Illus.). 76p. 1993. pap. 12.95 (*1-86351-099-0*, Pub. by S Milner AT) Sterling.
Laing, Jennifer, jt. auth. see Laing, Lloyd.
Laing, John. Do-It-Yourself Graphic Design. (Illus.). 160p. 1985. pap. 15.00 (*0-02-011550-4*, Pub. by Gebrueder Borntraeger GW) Macmillan.
— Encyclopedia of Signs & Symbols. 1993. 19.99 (*0-517-07696-9*) Random Hse Value.
— One Cool Cat. (Methuen Young Drama Ser.). 43p. (J). 1988. pap. 5.95 (*0-413-54220-3*, A0197) Heinemann.
Laing, John, jt. auth. see Halkett, Samuel.
Laing, Joyce, jt. ed. see Carroll, Christopher.
Laing, Kojo. Godhorse. (African Writers Ser.). (Illus.). 57p. (Orig.). 1989. pap. 8.95 (*0-435-90552-X*) Heinemann.
— Major Gentl & the Achimoto Wars. (African Writers Ser.). 185p. 1992. pap. 8.95 (*0-435-90978-9*, 90978) Heinemann.
Laing, Linda. Guide to Adirondack Trails: Southern Region. 2nd ed. Burdick, Neal, ed. LC 93-28567. (Forest Preserve Ser.: Vol. VII). (Illus.). 256p. 1994. pap. 16.95 (*0-935272-65-8*) ADK Mtn Club.
Laing, Lloyd & Laing, Jennifer. Ancient Art: The Challenge to Modern Thought. (Illus.). 256p. (C). 1993. text ed. 45.00 (*0-7165-2473-2*, Pub. by Irish Acad Pr IE) Intl Spec Bk.
— Art of the Celts: From 700 B. C. to the Celtic Revival. LC 91-66018. (World of Art Ser.). (Illus.). 216p. 1992. pap. 12.95 (*0-500-20256-7*) Thames Hudson.
— Celtic Britain & Ireland: Art & Society. LC 95-16925. 1995. write for info. (*0-312-12613-1*) St Martin.
— Photographers Britain: Picts & the Scots. LC 92-35782. 1993. pap. 34.00 (*0-86299-885-9*) A Sutton Pub.
Laing, Margaret. Catalogue of Sources for a Linguistic Atlas of Early Medieval English. LC 93-18969. 1993. 53.00 (*0-85991-384-8*, DS Brewer) Boydell & Brewer.
— Edward Heath: Prime Minister. LC 72-95089. 258p. 1973. 30.00 (*0-89388-086-8*) Okpaku Communications.
— Middle English Dialectology: Essays on Some Principles & Problems. 272p. 1989. text ed. 50.00 (*0-08-036404-7*, Pub. by Aberdeen U Pr) Macmillan.
Laing, Margaret & Williamson, Keith, eds. Speaking in Our Tongues: Proceedings of a Colloquium on Medieval Dialectology & Related Disciplines. LC 93-38900. (Illus.). 144p. (C). 1994. text ed. 53.00 (*0-85991-403-8*, DS Brewer) Boydell & Brewer.
Laing, Martha. Grandma Moses: The Grand Old Lady of American Art. Rahmas, D. Steve, ed. LC 71-190231. (Outstanding Personalities Ser.: No. 13). 32p. (Orig.). (J). (gr. 7-9). 1972. lib. bdg. 4.95 (*0-87157-513-2*) SamHar Pr.
Laing, R. D. Knots. 96p. 1972. pap. 9.00 (*0-394-71776-7*, Vin) Random.
— The Politics of Experience. 1981. pap. 2.50 (*0-345-29815-2*) Ballantine.
— Politics of Experience. 1983. pap. 10.00 (*0-394-71475-X*) Pantheon.
— The Politics of the Family & Other Essays. 1972. pap. 9.00 (*0-394-71809-7*, Vin) Random.
— Self & Others. 1972. mass mkt. 5.95 (*0-14-021376-7*, Penguin Bks) Viking Penguin.
Laing, R. D. & Esterson, A. Sanity, Madness & the Family. 1970. mass mkt. 6.95 (*0-14-021157-8*, Penguin Bks) Viking Penguin.
Laing, R. D., jt. auth. see Russell, Roberta.
***Laing Research Services Staff.** Correlating Museum & Exhibition Attendance with Book & Catalog Sales. 105p. 1991. 95.00 (*0-938106-07-4*) Laing Res Servs.
— Sales & Distribution Practices of Independent Presses, 1989-1990. 56p. 1990. 45.00 (*0-938106-12-0*) Laing Res Servs.
— Survey of Independent Presses, 1989-1990: Sorted & Analyzed by Number of Titles in Print. 70p. 1990. 95.00 (*0-938106-08-2*) Laing Res Servs.
— Survey of Independent Presses, 1989-1990: Sorted & Analyzed by Publisher's Annual Gross Revenue. 70p. 1990. 95.00 (*0-938106-11-2*) Laing Res Servs.
— Survey of University Presses, 1989-1990. 70p. 1990. 95.00 (*0-938106-09-0*) Laing Res Servs.
Laing, Robert A., jt. ed. see Hirsch, Christian R.
***Laing, Sam.** How Sweet Is Winning...If You Lose with Your Kids. 24p. 1994. pap. 1.99 (*1-884553-27-3*) Discipleshp.
***Laing, Sam & Laing, Geri.** Raising Awesome Kids in Troubled Times. 224p. 1994. pap. 10.99 (*1-884553-23-0*) Discipleshp.
Laing, Samuel, tr. see Snorri Sturluson.
Laing, Stuart, jt. auth. see Mercer, David.
Laing, Susan, jt. auth. see Bruess, Clint E.
***Laing, Susan J.** Nutrition & Body Image. (Comprehensive Health for Middle Grades Ser.). (J). (gr. 6-9). 1996. 24.00 (*1-56071-470-0*, H572) ETR Assocs.
Lainhart, Ann S. State Census Records. 116p. 1992. 17.95 (*0-8063-1362-5*, 3275) Genealog Pub.
Lainhart, Ann S., ed. First Boston City Directory (1789) Including Extensive Annotations by John Haven Dexter (1791-1876) 152p. 1989. 20.00 (*0-88082-020-9*, S2-76750) New Eng Hist.
Lainiotis, jt. ed. see Ray.
Lainiotis, D. G. & Tzannes, Nicolaos S., eds. A Selection of Papers from Info II, 3 vols. 1980. lib. bdg. write for info. (*0-318-54001-0*) Kluwer Ac.
— A Selection of Papers from Info II, 3 vols., Vol. 1. 530p. 1980. lib. bdg. 106.50 (*90-277-1140-2*) Kluwer Ac.
— A Selection of Papers from Info II, 3 vols., Vol. 2. 600p. 1980. lib. bdg. 106.50 (*90-277-1129-1*) Kluwer Ac.
— A Selection of Papers from Info II, 3 vols., Vol. 3. 530p. 1980. lib. bdg. 106.50 (*90-277-1143-7*) Kluwer Ac.
***Lainoff.** Hannah Arendt. 1998. text ed. 22.95 (*0-8057-4027-9*) Macmillan.
Laiou, Angeliki E. Constantinople & the Latins: The Foreign Policy of Andronicus the 2nd, 1282-1328. LC 78-176042. (Historical Studies: No. 88). 400p. 1972. 27.50 (*0-674-16535-7*) HUP.
— Gender, Society & Economic Life in Byzantium. (Collected Studies: Vol. CS370). 336p. 1992. 95.00 (*0-86078-322-7*, Pub. by Variorum UK) Ashgate Pub Co.

An Asterisk (*) at the beginning of an entry indicates that the title is appearing in BIP for the first time.

Laiou, Angeliki E., ed. Consent & Coercion to Sex & Marriage in Ancient & Medieval Societies. LC 93-3070. 308p. 1993. 28.00 (*0-88402-213-7*, Dumbarton Rsch Lib) Dumbarton Oaks.

— Dumbarton Oaks Papers, No. 44. LC 42-6499. (Illus.). 396p. 1991. 85.00 (*0-88402-189-0*, DP44) Dumbarton Oaks.

— Dumbarton Oaks Papers, No. 45. LC 42-6499. (Illus.). 272p. 1992. 60.00 (*0-88402-196-3*, DP45) Dumbarton Oaks.

Laiou, Angeliki E. & Maguire, Henry, eds. Byzantium, a World Civilization. LC 92-16848. (Illus.). 200p. 1992. 30.00x (*0-88402-200-5*, LMBCP); pap. 17.00x (*0-88402-215-3*, LMBC) Dumbarton Oaks.

Laiou, Angeliki E. & Simon, Dieter, eds. Law & Society in Byzantium: Ninth-Twelfth Centuries. LC 93-29343. (Illus.). 308p. 1994. 35.00x (*0-88402-222-6*) Dumbarton Oaks.

Lair, Cynthia. Feeding the Whole Family: Down-to-Earth Cookbook & Whole Foods Guide. Russell, Jenifer & Geiger, Lura J., eds. (Family Ser.). 288p. (Orig.). 1994. pap. 19.95 (*0-931055-97-0*) LuraMedia.

Lair, Jess. I Ain't Much Baby, but I'm All I've Got. 1985. mass mkt. 4.95 (*0-449-20802-8*, Crest) Fawcett.

Laird. The Alphabet Zoo. LC 74-190264. (Illus.). 32p. (J). (ps-2). 1972. lib. bdg. 9.95 (*0-87783-053-3*) Oddo.

— Webster's New World Thesaurus. 1995. pap. 11.00 (*0-671-89450-1*) PB.

Laird, A. W. Ranking Baseball's Elite: An Analysis Derived from Player Statistics, 1893-1987. LC 89-43655. (Illus.). 238p. 1990. lib. bdg. 27.50x (*0-89950-497-3*) McFarland & Co.

Laird, Alma. Complete George Washington Anniversary Programs for Every School Grade: New Ways to Honor the Father of Our Country. 1977. 15.95 (*0-8369-6389-X*, 7453) Ayer.

Laird, Antonia B. Back of Beyond. LC 88-81681. 84p. 1988. 8.50 (*0-8233-0450-7*) Golden Quill.

— Echo of My Heart. LC 82-82298. 84p. 1982. 5.50 (*0-8233-0343-8*) Golden Quill.

— Shadowed Light. LC 92-81641. 80p. 1992. 11.00 (*0-8233-0480-9*) Golden Quill.

Laird, Archibald. The Near Great--Chronicle of the Vice-Presidents. (Illus.). 1980. 17.50 (*0-8158-0381-8*) Chris Mass.

— Profitable Company: Milestones & Monuments of the Signers of the Declaration of Independence. LC 84-71719. 1987. 19.50 (*0-8158-0425-3*) Chris Mass.

Laird, Betty A. & Laird, Roy D., eds. To Live Long Enough: The Memoirs of Naum Jasny, Scientific Analyst. LC 75-33900. x, 190p. 1976. 19.95 (*0-7006-0140-6*) U Pr of KS.

Laird, Betty A., jt. auth. see Laird, Roy D.

***Laird, Brian A.** Bowman's Line. LC 95-2822. 224p. 1995. 20.95 (*0-312-13033-3*) St Martin.

Laird-Brown, May, tr. see Steiner, Rudolf.

Laird, Carlton W. Never Vote for the Incumbent. 1993. 16. 95 (*0-533-10348-7*) Vantage.

Laird, Carobeth. Encounter with an Angry God. 1983. pap. 2.25 (*0-345-28464-X*) Ballantine.

— Encounter with an Angry God: Recollections of My Life with John Peabody Harrington. LC 93-23825. 205p. 1993. reprint ed. pap. 11.95 (*0-8263-1414-7*) U of NM Pr.

— Limbo. LC 79-10937. 190p. 1979. pap. 11.95 (*0-88316-536-8*) Chandler & Sharp.

— Mirror & Pattern. LC 83-62710. 1984. 25.00 (*0-939046-30-X*) Malki Mus Pr.

Laird, Charlton. Webster's New World Thesaurus. rev. ed. 512p. 1990. Trade pbk. pap. 10.95 (*0-446-39165-4*); Mass market pbk. mass mkt. 4.50 (*0-446-36027-9*) Warner Bks.

Laird, Charlton, ed. Walter Van Tilburg Clark: Critiques. LC 83-6789. (Illus.). 312p. 1983. 24.95 (*0-87417-077-X*) U of Nev Pr.

Laird, Charlton G. Iowa Legends of Buried Treasure. Hutchinson, Stephen K., ed. LC 90-19777. 187p. 1990. pap. 8.95 (*0-934988-23-4*) Foun Bks.

— Webster's New World Thesaurus. 854p. (YA). (gr. 9-12). 1987. pap. 12.00 (*0-13-948126-5*) P-H.

— Webster's New World Thesaurus. rev. ed. 854p. 1985. 16. 00 (*0-671-60437-6*, Websters New Wrld) P-H Gen Ref & Trav.

Laird, Charlton G., ed. World Through Literature. LC 77-99639. (Essay Index Reprint Ser.). 1977. 36.95 (*0-8369-1359-0*) Ayer.

Laird, Charlton G., jt. auth. see Gorrell, Robert M.

Laird, Charlton G., et al. Modern English Reader. 2nd ed. (Illus.). 416p. 1977. pap. text ed. write for info. (*0-13-594176-8*) P-H.

***Laird, Christa.** But Can the Phoenix Sing? LC 94-28422. (YA). (gr. 7 up). 1995. 15.00 (*0-688-13612-5*) Greenwillow.

— Shadow of the Wall. LC 89-34469. (YA). (gr. 7 up). 1990. 12.95 (*0-688-09336-1*) Greenwillow.

Laird, Donald A. What Makes People Buy. LC 75-39254. (Getting & Spending: the Consumer's Dilemma Ser.). 1976. reprint ed. 23.95 (*0-405-08027-1*) Ayer.

Laird, Donald A., et al. Psychology: Human Relations & Motivation. 6th ed. LC 82-217. 416p. 1983. text ed. 35. 00 (*0-07-036018-9*) McGraw.

Laird, Donivee. The Three Little Hawaiian Pigs & the Magic Shark. LC 81-67047. (Illus.). 40p. (J). (ps-3). 1981. 7.95 (*0-940350-19-X*) Barnaby Bks.

Laird, Donivee & Jossem, Carol. Keaka & the Liliko'i Vine. 1985. 7.95 (*0-940350-22-X*) Barnaby Bks.

— Ula Li'i & the Magic Shark. 7.95 (*0-940350-23-8*) Barnaby Bks.

— Will Wai Kula & the Three Mongooses. 1985. 7.95 (*0-940350-24-6*) Barnaby Bks.

Laird, Donivee M. Fantastic Hawaiian Energy Adventure. (Illus.). 32p. (J). (gr. 3-5). 1989. write for info. (*0-940350-16-5*) Barnaby Bks.

— Hau Kea & the Seven Menehune. (Illus.). 50p. (J). (gr. k-4). 1995. 7.95 (*0-940350-26-2*) Barnaby Bks.

— Keaka & the Liliko'i Vine. LC 82-72452. (Illus.). 42p. (J). (gr. k-3). 1982. 7.95 (*0-940350-10-6*) Barnaby Bks.

— Ula Li'i & the Magic Shark. LC 86-3390. (Illus.). 42p. (J). (gr. k-3). 1985. 7.95 (*0-940350-12-2*) Barnaby Bks.

— Will Wai Kula & the Three Mongooses. LC 83-8805. (Illus.). 44p. (J). (gr. k-3). 1983. 7.95 (*0-940350-13-0*) Barnaby Bks.

Laird, Dugan. Approaches to Training & Development. 2nd ed. LC 84-24480. 320p. 1985. 24.95 (*0-201-04498-6*) Addison-Wesley.

Laird, Edgar & Fischer, Robert, eds. Pelerin de Prusse on the Astrolabe: Text & Translation of His Practique de Astralabe. LC 94-8986. (Medieval & Renaissance Texts & Studies: Vol. 127). 1994. 20.00 (*0-86698-132-2*) MRTS.

Laird, Elizabeth. American Homes. (American Background Readers Ser.). (Illus.). 31p. (YA). 1989. pap. text ed. 5.25 (*0-582-01716-5*, 78664) Longman.

— Americans on the Move. (American Background Readers Ser.). (Illus.). 31p. (Orig.). (YA). 1989. pap. text ed. 5.25 (*0-582-01715-7*, 78663) Longman.

— Children's Treasury of Graces, Hymns & Prayers, 3 vols. (Illus.). (J). 1991. 7.99 (*0-517-05384-5*) Random Hse Value.

— The Day Patch Stood Guard. LC 90-11153. (Illus.). 32p. (J). (gr. k up). 1991. 11.95 (*0-688-10239-5*, Tambourine Bks); lib. bdg. 11.88 (*0-688-10240-9*, Tambourine Bks) Morrow.

— The Day Sidney Ran Off. LC 90-11154. (Illus.). 32p. (J). (gr. k up). 1991. 11.95 (*0-688-10241-7*, Tambourine Bks); lib. bdg. 11.88 (*0-688-10242-5*, Tambourine Bks) Morrow.

— The Day the Ducks Went Skating. LC 90-25899. (Illus.). 32p. (J). (gr. k up). 1991. 11.95 (*0-688-10246-8*, Tambourine Bks); lib. bdg. 11.88 (*0-688-10247-6*, Tambourine Bks) Morrow.

— The Day Veronica Was Nosy. LC 90-24063. (Illus.). 32p. (J). (gr. k up). 1991. 11.95 (*0-688-10248-4*, Tambourine Bks); lib. bdg. 11.88 (*0-688-10249-2*, Tambourine Bks) Morrow.

— Faces of the U. S. A. 1987. pap. text ed. 12.95 (*0-582-74923-9*, 78237) Longman.

— Faces of the U. S. A. (YA). 1987. audio 24.95 (*0-582-01896-X*, 78271) Longman.

— Kiss the Dust. LC 91-43517. 284p. (J). (gr. 5 up). 1992. 15.00 (*0-525-44893-4*, DCB) Dutton Child Bks.

— Kiss the Dust. 288p. (J). (gr. 5 up). 1994. pap. 3.99 (*0-14-036855-8*) Puffin Bks.

Laird, Elizabeth, jt. auth. see Ichikawa, Satomi.

Laird-Fryer, Barbara, ed. Blood Group Systems: Kell. LC 90-949. (C). 1990. text ed. 35.00 (*0-915355-80-9*) Am Assn Blood.

Laird-Fryer, Barbara, jt. ed. see Kasprisin, Christina.

Laird-Fryer, Barbara, jt. ed. see Moulds, JoAnn M.

Laird-Fryer, Barbara, jt. auth. see Unger, Phyllis.

Laird, Gearld F. & Dunn, Louise M. Frames & Framing: The Ultimate Illustrated How-to-Do-It Guide. (Illus.). 208p. 1987. pap. 14.95 (*0-8306-2909-2*) TAB Bks.

Laird, Gerald F. & Dunn, Louise M. Frames & Framing: The Ultimate Illustrated How to Guide. 1988. pap. 15.95 (*0-07-155848-9*) McGraw.

Laird, Holly A. Self & Sequence: The Poetry of D. H. Lawrence. LC 87-23047. 228p. 1988. 35.00 (*0-8139-1147-8*) U Pr of Va.

Laird, Hugh E., jt. ed. see Jobe, Phillip C.

Laird, J. T., ed. On All Fronts: Australian Stories of World War II. 250p. (Orig.). 1989. pap. 16.95 (*0-7022-2160-0*, Pub. by Univ Queensland Pr AT) Intl Spec Bk.

Laird, James D. & Thompson, Nicholas S. Psychology. (C). 1991. text ed. 54.36 (*0-395-47090-0*) HM.

Laird, Jean E. The Homemaker's Book of Energy Savers. LC 82-1295. 1982. pap. write for info. (*0-672-52712-X*) Macmillan.

— Your Condo-Co-Op: Tips for Living Comfortably in a Small Space. 1983. pap. write for info. (*0-8289-0515-0*) Viking Penguin.

Laird, Joan. Ageless Exercise: A Gentle Approach for the Inactive or Physically Limited. LC 93-60903. (Illus.). 64p. 1994. spiral bd. 10.95 (*0-9638390-0-4*) Angelwood Pr.

Laird, Joan, intro. Revisioning Social Work Education: A Social Constructionist Approach. LC 94-2853. (Journal of Teaching in Social Work). (Illus.). 326p. 1994. lib. bdg. 49.95 (*1-56024-615-4*) Haworth Pr.

Laird, Joan & Hartman, Ann, eds. A Handbook of Child Welfare: Context, Knowledge & Practice. 752p. (C). 1985. text ed. 60.00 (*0-02-918090-2*) Free Pr.

Laird, Joan, jt. auth. see Hartman, Ann.

Laird, John. Enquiry into Moral Notions. LC 76-114045. reprint ed. 22.50 (*0-404-03802-6*) AMS Pr.

— Idea of the Soul. LC 76-107811. (Select Bibliographies Reprint Ser.). 1977. 20.95 (*0-8369-5207-3*) Ayer.

— Idea of Value. LC 68-58973. (Reprints of Economic Classics Ser.). 1969. reprint ed. 39.50 (*0-678-00460-9*) Kelley.

— A Study in Realism. LC 77-152991. (Select Bibliographies Reprint Ser.). 1977. reprint ed. 20.95 (*0-8369-5743-1*) Ayer.

— Theism & Cosmology. LC 74-84317. (Essay Index Reprint Ser.). 1977. 23.95 (*0-8369-1147-4*) Ayer.

Laird, John, ed. Machine Learning International Workshop on Machine Learning: Proceedings. 467p. (C). 1988. pap. text ed. 19.95 (*0-934613-64-8*) Morgan Kaufmann.

Laird, John, et al. Universal Subgoaling & Chunking: The Automatic Generation & Learning of Goal Hierarchies. 1986. lib. bdg. 68.00 (*0-89838-213-0*) Kluwer Ac.

Laird, Judy M. Men of Evil: True Stories & Barbed Events of Life. rev. ed. LC 90-56285. (Illus.). 200p. 1991. 31.50 (*1-55914-368-1*); pap. 26.50 (*1-55914-369-X*) ABBE Pubs Assn.

— Women of Evil: True Stories & Barbed Events of Life. LC 89-7730. 150p. 1990. 27.50 (*1-55914-178-6*); pap. 24.50 (*1-55914-179-4*) ABBE Pubs Assn.

Laird, M. R., intro. Conservative Papers. LC 74-117774. (Essay Index Reprint Ser.). 1977. 21.95 (*0-8369-1748-0*) Ayer.

Laird, MacGregor & Oldfield, R. A. Narrative of an Expedition into the Interior of Africa, 2 vols., Set. (Illus.). 1971. reprint ed. 90.00 (*0-7146-1826-8*, Pub. by F Cass Pubs UK) Intl Spec Bk.

Laird, Margaret. We Are the World We Walk Through. 297p. 1993. pap. 12.95 (*0-9638172-0-5*) M Laird Fnd.

Laird, Mark. The Formal Garden: Traditions of Art & Nature Through Five Centuries. LC 92-70867. (Illus.). 240p. 1992. 55.00 (*0-500-01542-2*) Thames Hudson.

Laird, Marshall. Biocontrol of Medical & Veterinary Pests. LC 81-12083. 256p. 1981. text ed. 69.50 (*0-275-91346-5*, C1346, Praeger Pubs) Greenwood.

Laird, Marshall, ed. Blackflies: The Future for Biological Methods in Integrated Control. LC 81-66373. 1982. text ed. 157.00 (*0-12-434060-1*) Acad Pr.

— Commerce & the Spread of Pests & Disease Vectors. LC 83-16627. (Illus.). 368p. 1984. text ed. 59.95 (*0-275-91208-6*, C1208, Praeger Pubs) Greenwood.

— The Natural History of Larval Mosquito Habitats. 555p. 1988. text ed. 187.00 (*0-12-434005-9*) Acad Pr.

Laird, Marshall & Miles, James W., eds. Integrated Mosquito Control Methodologies, Vol. 2. 1985. text ed. 204.00 (*0-12-434002-4*) Acad Pr.

— Integrated Mosquito Control Methodologies: Experience & Components from Conventional Chemical Control, Vol. 1. 1983. text ed. 139.00 (*0-12-434001-6*) Acad Pr.

Laird, Marshall, et al, eds. Safety of Microbial Insecticides. 288p. 1990. 190.00 (*0-8493-4793-9*, SB933) CRC Pr.

***Laird, Nick L. & Roosevelt, Rita K.** Quantifying Impacts (QI) Handbook: A Comprehensive Guide to Quantifying Bottom-Line Impacts on Public & Government Affairs Activities. (Illus.). 82p. (Orig.). (C). 1994. pap. text ed. 29.95 (*0-9644865-0-4*) Laird & Assoc.

Laird, Peter, jt. auth. see Eastman, Kevin.

Laird, Philip D. Learning from Good & Bad Data. (C). 1988. lib. bdg. 60.50 (*0-89838-263-7*) Kluwer Ac.

Laird, R. F. The Boomer Bible. LC 91-50385. 880p. (Orig.). 1991. pap. 14.95 (*1-56305-075-7*, 3075) Workman Pub.

***Laird, Rebecca.** Leslie Weatherhead's the Will of God a Workbook. 96p. (Orig.). 1995. pap. 7.95 (*0-687-00840-9*) Abingdon.

— Ordained Women in the Church of the Nazarene: The First Generation. 162p. (Orig.). 1993. per. 9.95 (*0-8341-1452-6*, 85257) Beacon Hill.

— Robinson Rabbit, What Do You Hear? LC 89-82550. (Illus.). 32p. (J). (ps-00). 1990. pap. 5.99 (*0-8066-2463-9*, 9-2463) Augsburg Fortress.

Laird, Rebecca, jt. auth. see Williams, Cecil.

Laird, Rick. Improvising Jazz Bass. 1980. pap. 12.95 (*0-8256-4091-1*) Music Sales.

— Jazz Riffs for Bass, EFS205. (Illus.). 48p. 1978. pap. 9.95 (*0-8256-2205-0*, AM24605) Music Sales.

Laird, Robbin. Bonn & Moscow: A Partnership in Progress? (C). 1990. 65.00 (*0-907967-97-3*, Pub. by Inst Euro Def & Strat UK) St Mut.

Laird, Robbin & Clark, Susan. Britain's Security Policy: The Modern Soviet View. (C). 1990. 40.00 (*0-907967-89-2*, Pub. by Inst Euro Def & Strat UK) St Mut.

Laird, Robbin F., ed. West European Arms Control Policy. LC 89-16819. (Duke Press Policy Studies). 210p. 1990. lib. bdg. 41.95 (*0-8223-0955-6*) Duke.

Laird, Robbin F. & Clark, Susan L. The U. S. S. R. & the Western Alliance. 288p. 1989. 55.00 (*0-04-445392-2*) Routledge Chapman & Hall.

Laird, Robbin F. & Hoffmann, Erik P., eds. Soviet Foreign Policy in a Changing World. LC 85-18712. 993p. (Orig.). 1986. lib. bdg. 67.95 (*0-202-24166-1*); pap. text ed. 34.95 (*0-202-24167-X*) Aldine de Gruyter.

Laird, Robbin F., jt. auth. see Hoffmann, Erik P.

Laird, Robbin F., jt. ed. see Hoffmann, Erik P.

Laird, Ronald A. Some Low Level Walks in Strathspey. (C). 1986. pap. 29.00 (*0-906664-11-X*, Pub. by Mercat Pr Bks UK) St Mut.

Laird, Roy D. The Soviet Legacy. LC 92-41617. 240p. 1993. text ed. 49.95 (*0-275-94558-8*, C4558, Praeger Pubs) Greenwood.

Laird, Roy D. & Laird, Betty A. A Soviet Lexicon: Important Concepts, Terms, & Phrases. 224p. (C). 1987. pap. 16.95 (*0-669-16739-8*) Free Pr.

Laird, Roy D., jt. ed. see Laird, Betty A.

Laird, Sally, tr. see Petrushevskaya, Ludmilla.

Laird, Sally, tr. see Sorokin, Vladimir.

***Laird, Suzanne.** Choices in Child Care: What's Best for Your Child. (Illus.). 138p. (Orig.). 1992. pap. 12.95 (*1-55059-043-X*) Temeron Bks.

Laird, Thomas. Blue Collar & Other Stories. Danbury, Richard S., III, ed. 120p. (Orig.). 1994. pap. 8.95 (*0-89754-086-7*) Dan River Pr.

Laird, W. David. Hopi Bibliography: Comprehensive & Annotated. LC 77-95563. 735p. 1977. pap. 35.00 (*0-8165-0566-7*) U of Ariz Pr.

Laird, Walter. Ballroom Dance Pack. LC 93-26744. 1994. 24.95 (*1-56458-483-6*) Dorling Kindersley.

— Technique of Latin Dancing. (Ballroom Dance Ser.). 1984. lib. bdg. 79.95 (*0-87700-510-9*) Revisionist Pr.

Lairdon, Roberts, ed. I Saw Heaven. 31p. 1983. pap. 2.00 (*0-915693-00-3*) Christian Pub.

Lairson, Thomas & Skidmore, David. International Political Economy: The Struggle for Power & Wealth. LC 92-81265. 416p. (C). 1993. pap. text ed. 26.75 (*0-03-054589-7*) HB Coll Pubs.

Laisney, Francois, tr. see Laffont, Jean-Jacques & Moreaux, Michel, eds.

Laistner, Max. Thought & Letters in Western Europe, A. D. 500-900. 1972. 59.95 (*0-8490-1207-4*) Gordon Pr.

Laistner, Max L. The Greater Roman Historians. (Sather Classical Lectures: No. 21). 1947. 29.95 (*0-520-03365-5*) U CA Pr.

— Greek Economics. LC 79-171641. (Library of Greek Thought: No. 3). reprint ed. 41.00 (*0-404-07802-8*) AMS Pr.

Lait, J. E., jt. auth. see Samarasekera, F. V.

Lait, Jack. Beef, Iron & Wine. LC 78-116960. (Short Story Index Reprint Ser.). 1977. 21.95 (*0-8369-3464-4*) Ayer.

Laita, Luis M. & Gil de Montes, Carmen. Cortina - Holt Traveler's Spanish Dictionary: English-Spanish - Spanish-English. Berberi, Dilaver & Winje, Edel A., eds. LC 93-3673. 1993. pap. 6.95 (*0-8327-0721-X*) Cortina.

Laitala, Everett. Engineering & Organization. LC 59-8887. (Irwin Series in Industrial Engineering & Management). 407p. reprint ed. pap. 116.00 (*0-317-10777-1*, 2001044) Bks Demand.

Laite, Ben. Maritime Air Operations. (Air Power: Aircraft Weapons & Technology Ser.: Vol. 11). (Illus.). 200p. 1991. 40.00 (*0-08-040705-6*, Pub. by Brasseys UK); 25. 00 (*0-08-040706-4*, Pub. by Brasseys UK) Brasseys Inc.

Laithwaite, E. R. History of Linear Electric Motors. (Illus.). 1987. 30.00 (*0-333-39928-5*) San Francisco Pr.

Laithwaite, Eric. An Inventor in the Garden of Eden. (Illus.). 250p. (C). 1994. 24.95 (*0-521-44106-4*) Cambridge U Pr.

Laitier, Gabriel. Dictionnaire de Physique. 276p. (FRE.). 1968. pap. 55.00 (*0-8288-6632-5*, M-6328) Fr & Eur.

Laitin, David, ed. see Anderson, Benedict R.

Laitin, David, ed. see Desan, Suzanne.

Laitin, David, ed. see Given, James B.

Laitin, David D. Hegemony & Culture: Politics & Religious Change among the Yoruba. (Illus.). xiv, 252p. 1986. pap. text ed. 15.95 (*0-226-46790-2*) U Ch Pr.

— Language Repertoires & State Construction in Africa. (Studies in Comparative Politics). (Illus.). 176p. (C). 1992. 49.95 (*0-521-41343-5*) Cambridge U Pr.

Laitin, David D. Politics, Language, & Thought: The Somali Experience. LC 76-22958. (Illus.). 1977. lib. bdg. 23.00 (*0-226-46791-0*) U Ch Pr.

Laitin, Ken & Laitin, Steve. Playing Soccer. LC 79-63980. (Illus.). (J). (gr. 2-7). 1979. pap. 9.95 (*0-916802-22-1*) Soccer for Am.

Laitin, Steve, jt. auth. see Laitin, Ken.

Laitinen. Chinese Nationalism in the Qing Dynasty: A Study of Anti-Manchu Activities. (C). 1990. pap. 29.95 (*0-7007-0213-X*, Pub. by Curzon Pr UK) Humanities.

Laitl, J., jt. auth. see Janos, K.

Laitos, Jan G. Natural Resources Law: Cases & Materials. LC 85-13787. (American Casebook Ser.). 938p. (C). 1985. text ed. 49.00 (*0-314-90413-1*); teacher ed. pap. text ed. write for info. (*0-314-95851-7*) West Pub.

Laitos, Jan G. & Tomain, Joseph P. Energy & Natural Resources Law in a Nutshell. (Nutshell Ser.). 554p. 1992. pap. text ed. 18.50 (*0-314-00118-2*) West Pub.

Laity, Annabel, tr. see Nhat Hanh, Thich.

Laity, Annabel, tr. see Thich Nhat Hanh.

Laity, Edward. Priesthood, Old & New. 1980. 4.50 (*0-86544-012-3*) Salv Army Suppl South.

— Tabernacle Types & Teaching. 1980. pap. 3.95 (*0-86544-011-5*) Salv Army Suppl South.

Laity, Sally. Second Spring & The Kiss Goodbye, 2 bks. in 1. (Romance Reader Ser.: No. 10). 1992. 7.95 (*1-55748-258-6*) Barbour & Co.

***Laity, Sally & Crawford, Dianna.** The Tempering Blaze. LC 94-23236. (Freedom's Holy Light Ser.: Vol. 3). 1995. 9.99 (*0-8423-6902-3*) Tyndale.

Laity, Sally, jt. auth. see Crawford, Dianna.

Laizer, Sheri. Into Kurdistan: Frontiers under Fire. LC 91-8856. (Illus.). 128p. (C). 1991. text ed. 45.00 (*0-86232-898-5*, Pub. by Zed Books UK); pap. 15.00 (*0-86232-899-3*, Pub. by Zed Books UK) Humanities.

Laj, Carlo, jt. ed. see Kissel, Catherine.

***Laje, Zilia L.** La Cortina De Bagazo. LC 95-94272. 576p. (Orig.). (SPA.). 1995. pap. 19.00 (*0-9646224-0-8*) Z L Laje.

Lajimi, Ahmed & Tanlak, Acar. International Directory of Islamic Cultural Institutions. 344p. 1987. pap. 59.50 (*0-7103-0201-0*, 02010, Pub. by Kegan Paul Intl UK) Routledge Chapman & Hall.

Lajoie, Bob, jt. auth. see Lajoie, Gesele.

Lajoie, Gesele & Lajoie, Bob. Tennis Handbook. (Illus.). 46p. pap. 5.95 (*0-318-32568-3*) Hancock House.

LaJoie, Jim & Plumb, Ron. Year of the 'Cats: A Look Back at Northern Michigan University's 1990-91 Championship Hockey Season. 150p. 1991. pap. 9.95 (*0-9630901-0-0*) J LaJoie.

Lajoie, Susanne & Derry, Sharon. Computers As Cognitive Tools. (Technology & Education Ser.). 416p. 1993. text ed. 79.95 (*0-8058-1081-1*); pap. 32.50 (*0-8058-1082-X*) L Erlbaum Assocs.

Lajole, David G., ed. see Sprunt, Hugh H., et al.

Lajolo, Davide. An Absurd Vice: A Biography of Cesare Pavese. Pietralunga, Mario & Pietralunga, Mark, trs. LC 82-14482. 288p. (ITA.). 1983. 18.50 (*0-8112-0850-8*); pap. 9.25 (*0-8112-0851-6*, NDP545) New Directions.

Lajos, B. Pszichologiai Ertelmezo Szotar: Explanatory Psychological Dictionary. (HUN.). 1981. 24.95 (*0-8288-2220-4*, M172) Fr & Eur.

Lajos, Fury. Vasarnap Farkaspusztan. 1978. boxed 12.00 (*0-912404-11-6*) Alpha Pubns.

Lajos, Ivicsics. Hydraulic Models. 1980. 34.00 (*0-918334-38-1*) WRP.

LaJoy, Maureen. Bitty Business Book: Everyday Success Strategies for the Office. 84p. (Orig.). 1989. pap. 9.95 (*0-9623686-1-X*) Castalia MN.

— Power in the Workplace. (Illus.). 84p. (Orig.). 1990. pap. 9.95 (0-9623686-4-4) Castalia MN.
— Your Ten-Week Novel Writing Kit. 54p. (Orig.). 1990. pap. 20.00 (1-878723-00-6) Castalia MN.
LaJoyce, Martin. Mother Eve's Garden Club. 150p. 1993. pap. 7.99 (0-945564-73-2, Multnomah Bks) Questar Pubs.
— A Single Worry. LC 93-18944. 200p. (Orig.). 1993. pap. 6.99 (1-56722-011-8) Word Aflame.
Lajpat, Lala, jt. auth. see Lajpat, Rai.
Lajpat, Rai & Lajpat, Lala. The Arma Samaj: An Account of Its Origin, Doctrines & Activities. (C). 1989. 47.00 (81-85199-30-2, Pub. by Renaiss Publng Hse II) S Asia.
Lajpat Rai, Lala. Unhappy India. 2nd enl. rev. ed. LC 72-171642. reprint ed. 49.50 (0-404-03803-4) AMS Pr.
Lajpuri, Abdur R. Fatawa Rahimiyah, 3 vols., Set. 1992. 74. 85 (1-56744-453-9) Kazi Pubns.
— Fatawa Rahimiyah, Vol. 1. 360p. 1992. 24.95 (1-56744-450-4) Kazi Pubns.
— Fatawa Rahimiyah, Vol. 2. 354p. 1992. 24.95 (1-56744-451-2) Kazi Pubns.
— Fatawa Rahimiyah, Vol. 3. 250p. 1992. 24.95 (1-56744-452-0) Kazi Pubns.
Lajtha, Abel, ed. Handbook of Neurochemistry, Vol. 1: Chemical Architecture of the Nervous Syste. LC 68-28097. 508p. reprint ed. pap. 144.80 (0-317-27114-8, 2024701) Bks Demand.
— Handbook of Neurochemistry, Vol. 1: Chemical & Cellular Architecture. 2nd ed. LC 82-493. 516p. 1982. 120.00 (0-306-40861-9, Plenum Pr) Plenum.
— Handbook of Neurochemistry, Vol. 10: Pathological Neurochemistry. 2nd ed. LC 82-493. 822p. 1985. 130.00 (0-306-41744-8, Plenum Pr) Plenum.
— Handbook of Neurochemistry, Vol. 2: Experimental Neurochemistry. 2nd ed. LC 82-493. 498p. 1983. 120.00 (0-306-40972-0, Plenum Pr) Plenum.
— Handbook of Neurochemistry, Vol. 3: Metabolism in the Nervous System. 2nd ed. LC 82-493. 724p. 120.00 (0-306-41153-9, Plenum Pr) Plenum.
— Handbook of Neurochemistry, Vol. 4: Enzymes in the Nervous System. LC 82-493. 572p. 1983. 120.00 (0-306-41210-1, Plenum Pr) Plenum.
— Handbook of Neurochemistry, Vol. 5: Metabolic Turnover in the Nervous System. 2nd ed. LC 82-493. 518p. 1983. 120.00 (0-306-41323-X, Plenum Pr) Plenum.
— Handbook of Neurochemistry, Vol. 6: Receptors in the Nervous System. 2nd ed. LC 82-493. 694p. 1984. 130.00 (0-306-41411-2, Plenum Pr) Plenum.
— Handbook of Neurochemistry, Vol. 7: Structural Elements of the Nervous System. 2nd ed. LC 82-493. 734p. 1984. 130.00 (0-306-41440-6, Plenum Pr) Plenum.
— Handbook of Neurochemistry, Vol. 8: Neurochemical Systems. 2nd ed. LC 82-493. 700p. 1985. 130.00 (0-306-41579-8, Plenum Pr) Plenum.
— The Handbook of Neurochemistry, Vol. 9: Alterations of Metabolites in the Nervous System. 2nd ed. LC 82-493. 622p. 1985. 130.00 (0-306-41743-X, Plenum Pr) Plenum.
— Protein Metabolism of the Nervous System. LC 74-85373. 754p. reprint ed. pap. 180.00 (0-317-30347-3, 2024718) Bks Demand.
Lajtha, Abel, jt. ed. see Abood, Leo G.
Lajtha, K. & Michener, R. Stable Isotopes in Ecology and Environmental Science. (Illus.). 250p. 1994. 32.95 (0-632-03154-9) Blackwell Sci.
Laka, Itzial. On Syntax of Negation. LC 94-598. (Outstanding Dissertations in Linguistics Ser.). 1994. write for info. (0-8153-0696-2) Garland.
Laka, Itziar. On the Syntax of Negation. LC 94-598. (Outstanding Dissertations in Linguistics Ser.). 200p. 1994. 55.00 (0-8153-1728-X) Garland.
Lakatos, Geza. As I Saw It: The Tragedy of Hungary. Fenyo, Mario D., tr. Orig. Title: Ahony en Lattam. (Illus.). 250p. 1993. write for info. (0-318-72265-8) Universe Pub Co.
Lakatos, Imre. Philosophical Papers: Mathematics, Science & Epistemology, Vol. 2. Worrall, J. & Currie, Gregory, eds. LC 77-14374. 295p. 1980. pap. 29.95 (0-521-28030-3) Cambridge U Pr.
— Philosophical Papers: The Methodology of Scientific Research Programmes, Vol. 1. Worrall, J. & Currie, Gregory, eds. LC 77-71415. 1980. pap. 29.95 (0-521-28031-1) Cambridge U Pr.
***Lake.** How to Be More Productive in Windows 95. 1995. pap. text ed. 24.95 (1-56276-288-5) Ziff-Davis.
— Images of the Past. (Jersey Heritage Editions Ser.). 1991. write for info. (0-86120-018-7, Pub. by Aris & Phillips UK) David Brown.
— Lowriders & Other Customized Cars. (J). 1995. pap. 5.95 (0-516-40217-X) Childrens.
— These Haunted Islands: A Story of Witchcraft in the Channel Islands. 1991. write for info. (0-318-68515-9, Pub. by Aris & Phillips UK) David Brown.
Lake, A. L. Gold Fever. (Wild West in American History Ser.). (Illus.). 32p. (J). (gr. 3-8). 1990. lib. bdg. 18.00 (0-86625-374-2); lib. bdg. 13.50 (0-685-34710-9) Rourke Corp.
— Pony Express. (Wild West in American History Ser.). (Illus.). 32p. (J). (gr. 3-8). 1990. 13.50 (0-685-58648-0); lib. bdg. 18.00 (0-86625-368-8) Rourke Corp.
— Women of the West. (Wild West in American History Ser.). (Illus.). 32p. (J). (gr. 3-8). 1990. lib. bdg. 18.00 (0-86625-373-4); lib. bdg. 13.50 (0-685-58656-1) Rourke Corp.
***Lake, Alexander.** Killers in Africa: The Truth about Animals Lying in Wait & Hunters Lying in Print. Resnick, Mike, ed. & intro. by. 320p. Date not set. pap. text ed. 12.95 (1-57090-013-2) Alexander Bks.
Lake, Alizarin. An Alizarin Lake Reader. (Orig.). 1993. pap. text ed. 4.95 (1-56333-106-3) Masquerade.
— Diary of an Angel. rev. ed. 192p. (Orig.). 1991. mass mkt. 4.95 (1-878320-71-8) Masquerade.
— The Erotic Adventures of Harry Temple. (Orig.). 1993. pap. text ed. 4.95 (1-56333-127-6) Masquerade.
— Erotomania. (Orig.). 1993. pap. text ed. 4.95 (1-56333-128-4) Masquerade.
— More Erotic Adventures of Harry Temple. (Orig.). 1991. mass mkt. 4.95 (1-878320-67-X) Masquerade.
Lake, Anthony. Somoza Falling: A Case Study of Washington at Work. LC 90-34788. 336p. (Orig.). 1990. reprint ed. pap. 16.95 (0-87023-733-0) U of Mass Pr.
— The "Tar Baby" Option: American Policy Toward Southern Rhodesia. LC 76-2455. 316p. 1976. text ed. 43.00x (0-231-04066-0) Col U Pr.
— Third World Radical Regimes: U. S. Policy under Carter & Reagan. LC 85-81057. (Headline Ser.: No. 272). (Illus.). 56p. (Orig.). 1985. pap. 5.95 (0-87124-099-8) Foreign Policy.
Lake, Anthony, et al. After the Wars: Reconstruction in Afghanistan, Indochina, Central America, Southern Africa, & the Horn of Africa. (U. S. Third World Policy Perspectives Ser.: No. 16). 240p. (C). 1990. 32.95 (0-88738-392-0); pap. 17.95 (0-88738-880-9) Transaction Pubs.
Lake, Austen, jt. auth. see Atkinson, Leroy.
Lake, Brian D., jt. ed. see Filipe, M. Isabel.
Lake, Brian G., jt. ed. see Gibson, G. Gordan.
Lake, Bruce. Fifteen Hundred Feet over Vietnam: A Marine Helicopter Pilot's Diary. 372p. (Orig.). 1990. pap. 14.00 (0-9623500-2-8) Ministry Two.
Lake, Carlton. Confessions of a Literary Archaeologist. LC 89-13707. (Illus.). 256p. 1990. pap. 21.95 (0-8112-1130-4) New Directions.
— No Symbols Where None Intended: Samuel Beckett at the Harry Ransom Humanities Research Center. (Illus.). 185p. 1984. 20.00 (0-87959-101-3) U of Tex H Ransom Ctr.
Lake, Carlton & Ashton, Linda. Henri-Pierre Roche: An Introduction. (Illus.). 240p. 1991. 20.00 (0-87959-113-7) U of Tex H Ransom Ctr.
Lake, Carney. Reflected Glory: An Account of a British Soldier in Northern Ireland. 240p. 1994. 39.50 (0-85052-366-4, Pub. by L Cooper Bks UK) Trans-Atl Phila.
***Lake, Carol.** Cherry Blossom Tea: A Collection of Short Stories. 124p. 1994. pap. 8.95 (0-9642362-4-9) White Hart Pr.
— The Horse Is Out of Order: And Other Essays about the Writing Life. 70p. 1994. pap. 5.95 (0-9642362-2-2) White Hart Pr.
— Rosehill: Portraits from a Midlands City. 192p. 1991. 22. 95 (0-7475-0301-X, Pub. by Bloomsbury Pub Ltd UK); pap. 11.95 (0-7475-0578-0, Pub. by Bloomsbury Pub Ltd UK) Trafalgar.
Lake, Carol, ed. Clinical Monitoring for Anesthesia & Critical Care. 2nd ed. 1994. write for info. (0-318-72429-4) Saunders.
Lake, Carol L. Advances in Anesthesia, Vol. 11. 350p. 1993. 59.95 (0-8151-8276-7, Yr Bk Med Pubs) Mosby Yr Bk.
— Advances in Anesthesia, Vol. 12. 350p. 1994. 59.95 (0-8151-8277-5, Yr Bk Med Pubs) Mosby Yr Bk.
— Advances in Anesthesia, Vol. 13. 350p. 1995. 59.95 (0-8151-8278-3, Yr Bk Med Pubs) Mosby Yr Bk.
— Advances in Anesthesia, Vol. 14. 350p. 1996. write for info. (0-8151-5277-9, Yr Bk Med Pubs) Mosby Yr Bk.
— Advances in Anesthesia, Vol. 15. 350p. 1997. write for info. (0-8151-5278-7, Yr Bk Med Pubs) Mosby Yr Bk.
— Cardiovascular Anesthesia. (Illus.). 480p. 1984. 98.00 (0-387-96028-7) Spr-Verlag.
— Pediatric Cardiac Anesthesia. 2nd ed. (Illus.). 640p. 1993. boxed 110.00 (0-8385-7812-8, A7812-9) Appleton & Lange.
***Lake, Carol L. & Moore, Roger A.** Blood: Hemostasis, Transfusion, & Alternatives in the Perioperative Period. 496p. 1995. 125.00 (0-7817-0267-4) Raven.
Lake, Catherine A. Linking Up. 300p. 1988. pap. 9.95 (0-89865-625-7) Donning Co.
Lake, Celinda & Harper, Pat. Public Opinion Polling: A Handbook for Public Interest & Citizen Advocacy Groups. LC 87-3157. 162p. (Orig.). 1987. pap. 19.95 (0-933280-32-7) Island Pr.
Lake, D. J. & Hammond, G. P. Hammond's Edition of the Atlas of Shenandoah & Page Counties, Virginia: With Added Maps & Data. rev. ed. LC 90-93379. (Illus.). 60p. 1990. pap. text ed. 26.00 (1-878014-03-X) G P Hammond Pub.
Lake, Dale, jt. auth. see Ulrich, Dave.
Lake, Dale G. Perceiving & Behaving. LC 72-77891. 116p. reprint ed. pap. 33.10 (0-317-41889-0, 2026038) Bks Demand.
Lake, David, ed. The International Political Economy of Trade, 2 vols., Set. (Library of International Political Economy: Vol. 1). 1056p. 1992. 299.95 (1-85278-583-7, Pub. by E Elgar Pub UK) Ashgate Pub Co.
Lake, David, ed. see Wells, H. G.
Lake, David A. Power, Protection, & Free Trade: International Sources of U. S. Commercial Strategy, 1887-1939. LC 87-47869. (Cornell Studies in Political Economy). 264p. 1988. 36.50 (0-8014-2134-9) Cornell U Pr.
— Power, Protection, & Free Trade: International Sources of U. S. Commercial Strategy, 1887-1939. LC 87-47869. (Cornell Studies in Political Economy). 264p. 1990. reprint ed. pap. 14.95 (0-8014-9753-1) Cornell U Pr.
Lake, David A., jt. auth. see Frieden, Jeffry A.
Lake, David C. Feelings Are for Sharing. LC 86-80550. 128p. 1987. 10.50 (0-9616471-0-8) Intl Enlightenment.
Lake, David J. The Canon of Thomas Middleton's Plays: Internal Evidence for the Major Problems of Authorship. LC 74-25661. 314p. reprint ed. pap. 89.50 (0-317-20601-X, 2024487) Bks Demand.
Lake, E. & Porter, F. Livy: Hannibal the Scourge of Rome: Selections from Book XXI. 122p. 1984. reprint ed. 14.95 (0-86292-131-7, Pub. by Brstl Class Pr UK) Focus Info Gr.
***Lake, E. D.** Lowriders & Other Customized Cars. (Wheels Ser.). 48p. (J). (gr. 3-4). 1994. lib. bdg. 13.35 (1-56065-217-9) Capstone Pr.
Lake, Elizabeth, ed. see DuChateau, Wally.
Lake, Elizabeth, ed. see Hunt, Glen & Smith, Eugene.
Lake, Elizabeth, ed. see Messina, John.
Lake, Gina. Extraterrestrial Vision. Benjamin, Sara, ed. 192p. (Orig.). 1995. pap. 13.95 (1-880666-19-7) Oughten Hse.
— Pathways to Self-Discovery: Tools to Help You Access Your Higher Self for Guidance & Healing. McClure, Vimala, ed. 208p. (Orig.). 1994. pap. 12.00 (0-945934-11-4) New Wrld Lib.
Lake, H. S., tr. see Lievegoed, Bernard.
Lake, J. Spencer. Nature in Architecture: The Work of Sim Bruce Richards (An Exhibit Catalog) (Illus.). 36p. 1984. pap. 3.00 (0-918969-00-X) San Diego Soc Nat Hist.
Lake, J. W. Mythos of the Ark. 1993. reprint ed. pap. 8.95 (1-55818-199-7, Sure Fire) Holmes Pub.
— Tree & Serpent Worship. 1994. reprint ed. pap. 7.95 (1-55818-274-8, Sure Fire) Holmes Pub.
Lake, Jane. Riding Western. 88p. (C). 1990. pap. 21.00 (0-85131-432-5, Pub. by J A Allen & Co UK) St Mut.
Lake, Janet & Zilker, Sandra. Nourish & Flourish: How to Feast Nutritiously. 174p. 1990. text ed. 12.50 (0-9640010-1-2) Peace Pubng.
Lake, John G. Adventures in God. rev. ed. 96p. 1991. pap. 4.95 (0-89274-819-2, HH-819) Harrison Hse.
Lake, Jon. SU-27 Flanker Sukoi Ftr. (Osprey Colour Library). (Illus.). 128p. 1992. pap. 15.95 (1-85532-152-1, Pub. by Osprey Pubng Ltd UK) Motorbooks Intl.
— Sukhoi Su-27 'Flanker' (World Air Power Journal Special Ser.). (Illus.). 72p. 1994. pap. 9.95 (1-880588-12-9) AIRtime Pub.
Lake, Jon, ed. Phantom: Spirit in the Skies. 1993. 29.95 (1-880588-04-8) AIRtime Pub.
Lake, Jon, ed. see Aerospace Publishing Ltd. Staff.
Lake, Jon, jt. ed. see Donald, David.
Lake, Jon, jt. auth. see Dorr, Robert.
Lake, Julie, jt. auth. see Bailey, Ralph.
Lake, Kirsopp & New, Silva, eds. Six Collations of New Testament Manuscripts. (Harvard Theological Studies: Vol. 17). 1932. 26.00 (0-527-01017-0) Periodicals Srv.
Lake, Larry W. Enhanced Oil Recovery. 600p. 1988. text ed. 98.00 (0-13-281601-6) P-H.
Lake, Larry W., Jr. & Carroll, Herbert B. Reservoir Characterization. 1986. text ed. 105.00 (0-12-434065-2) Acad Pr.
Lake, Larry W., et al, eds. Reservoir Characterization, No. II. (Illus.). 726p. 1991. text ed. 109.00 (0-12-434066-0) Acad Pr.
Lake, Laura M. Environmental Regulation: The Political Effects of Implementation. LC 82-12305. 160p. 1982. text ed. 45.00 (0-275-90844-5, C0844, Praeger Pubs) Greenwood.
Lake, Linda K., jt. auth. see Connor, Patrick E.
Lake, M. D. Amends for a Murder. large type ed. 1991. 17. 95 (0-7451-8227-5, AH0252, Curley Lrg Print) Chivers N Amer.
— Amends for Murder. 224p. (Orig.). 1989. mass mkt. 4.99 (0-380-75865-2) Avon.
— Cold Comfort. 1990. mass mkt. 4.99 (0-380-76032-0) Avon.
— A Gift for Murder. 256p. (Orig.). 1992. mass mkt. 4.50 (0-380-76855-0) Avon.
— Murder by Mail. 256p. (Orig.). 1993. mass mkt. 4.99 (0-380-76856-9) Avon.
— Once Upon a Crime. 288p. (Orig.). 1995. mass mkt. 4.99 (0-380-77520-4) Avon.
— Poisoned Ivy. 256p. 1992. mass mkt. 4.99 (0-380-76573-X) Avon.
Lake, Margaret, tr. see Tsuji, Masanobu.
Lake, Marilyn, jt. ed. see Damousi, Joy.
Lake, Marilyn, jt. ed. see Holmes, Katie.
Lake, Matthew. Breaking into Windows. 1993. disk, pap. 24. 95 (1-56276-144-7) Ziff-Davis.
Lake, Monte B. Immigration Act of 1990: An Employer's Handbook. 354p. (Orig.). 1992. pap. 50.00 (0-916559-37-8) EPF.
Lake, Neal E. The Preacher's Notebook. 1993. pap. 5.95 (1-55673-594-4, 7993) CSS OH.
Lake of the Ozarks General Hospital Auxiliary Staff. A Taste of the Lake. LC 93-70696. 1993. write for info. (0-87197-369-3) Favorite Recipes.
Lake, P. S., jt. ed. see McComb, A. J.
Lake, Patricia, jt. auth. see Miller, Somi A.
Lake, Paul. Among the Immortals: A Novel. 302p. 1994. pap. 14.95 (0-934257-73-6) Story Line.
— Another Kind of Travel. (Phoenix Poets Ser.). 80p. 1987. pap. 7.95 (0-226-46808-9) U Ch Pr.
— Bull Dancing, Vol. 5. 1977. pap. 3.95 (0-685-50008-X) New Poets Chestnut Hills.
Lake, Peter & Dowling, Maria. Protestantism & the National Church in 16th Century England. 224p. 1987. lib. bdg. 55.00 (0-7099-1681-7, Pub. by Croom Helm UK) Routledge Chapman & Hall.
Lake, Peter, jt. ed. see Sharpe, Kevin.
Lake, R., jt. auth. see Young, B.
***Lake, Ralph B. & Draetta, Ugo.** Letters of Intent & Other Pre-Contractual Documents: Comparat Analysis & Forms. 2nd ed. 350p. 1994. boxed 95.00 (0-250-40740-X) Michie Butterworth.
Lake, Ralph B., et al. Breach & Adaptation of International Contracts: An Introduction to Lex Mercatoria. 240p. 1992. boxed 105.00 (0-88063-750-1) Michie Butterworth.
Lake, Robert. Backshooter. 1990. pap. 2.95 (0-8217-2875-X) Zebra.
— Blood Trail to Kansas. 1991. pap. 3.50 (0-8217-3541-1) Zebra.
— Mountain Man's Vengeance. 1991. pap. 3.50 (0-8217-3619-1) Zebra.
— Texas Iron. 288p. 1991. pap. 3.50 (0-8217-3320-6) Zebra.
Lake, Robert W., ed. Readings in Urban Analysis: Perspectives on Urban Form & Structure. LC 82-19723. 341p. 1983. pap. text ed. 2.00 (0-88285-082-2) Ctr Urban Pol Res.
Lake, Robert W. & Fitzgerald, Thomas E., Jr. Real Estate Tax Delinquency: Private Disinvestment & Public Response. LC 79-12207. 268p. 1979. 1.00 (0-88285-046-6) Ctr Urban Pol Res.
Lake, Russell W. Thank God for Prayer. LC 83-50397. 293p. 1983. 6.95 (0-87159-159-6) Unity Bks.
Lake, Sara E., tr. see Clavigero, Francisco J.
Lake, Steven & Feldman, Ruth D. Rematch: Winning Legal Battles with Your Ex. 224p. 1989. 9.95 (1-55652-053-0) Chicago Review.
Lake, Stuart N. Wyatt Earp: Frontier Marshall. Grad, Doug, ed. 416p. 1994. reprint ed. mass mkt. 5.50 (0-671-88537-5) PB.
Lake, Susan E. Unit Based Planning: A Guide for the Secondary English Teacher. 135p. (Orig.). (C). 1994. pap. 15.00 (1-881459-10-1) Eagle Pr SC.
Lake, Thomas T. Endo Nasal, Aural & Allied Techniques: Ear, Eye, Nose & Throat. 109p. 1976. reprint ed. spiral bd. 9.35 (0-7873-0521-9) Mokelumne.
— The Fundamentals of Applied Psychiatry for Non-Medical Physicians. 102p. 1961. reprint ed. spiral bd. 8.25 (0-7873-0520-0) Mokelumne.
— Treatment by Neuropathy & the Encyclopedia of Physical & Manipulative Therapeutics. 684p. 1972. reprint ed. spiral bd. 30.25 (0-7873-0519-7) Mokelumne.
Lake, Tony. Overcoming Nervous Breakdown. 107p. 1989. reprint ed. pap. 7.95 (1-878290-01-0) Intl Hlth MD.
Lake, Vicki. Firming up Your Flabby Faith. 96p. 1990. pap. 5.99 (0-89693-783-6) SP Pubns.
Lakefront Partnership Staff, comp. Chicago Celebrity Chefs. (Celebrity Chef Ser.). 264p. (Orig.). 1989. pap. 9.95 (0-89716-306-0) P B Pubng.
Lakein, Alan. How to Get Control of Your Time & Your Life. 10.95 (0-317-63116-0) McKay.
— How to Get Control of Your Time & Your Life. 160p. 1989. pap. 4.50 (0-451-15802-4, Sig) NAL-Dutton.
Lakela, Olga, et al. Plants of the Tampa Bay Area. rev. suppl. ed. 1976. pap. 7.95 (0-916224-10-4) Banyan Bks.
Lakeland, Ana. The Rag Doll Handbook. (Illus.). 128p. 1994. 19.95 (0-7134-6657-X, Pub. by Batsford UK) Trafalgar.
Lakeland, Jo, tr. see Mernissi, Fatima.
Lakeland, Mary J., tr. see Mernissi, Fatima.
Lakeland, Paul. Freedom in Christ: An Introduction to Political Theology. 2nd ed. LC 86-80021. 151p. reprint ed. pap. 43.10 (0-7837-5609-7, 2045515) Bks Demand.
— The Politics of Salvation: The Hegelian Idea of the State. LC 83-17875. (SUNY Series in Hegelian Studies). 197p. 1985. 64.50 (0-87395-846-2); pap. 21.95 (0-87395-847-0) State U NY Pr.
***Lakeman, Sandra D.** Natural Light & the Italian Piazza: Siena, As a Case Study. LC 93-206345. (Illus.). 110p. 1995. pap. 24.95 (0-295-97418-4) U of Wash Pr.
Lakemeyer, Gerhard & Nebel, Bernhard, eds. Foundations of Knowledge Representation & Reasoning. LC 94-20768. (Lecture Notes in Computer Science, Vol. 810; Lecture Notes in Artificial Intelligence). 1994. 52.00 (0-387-58107-3) Spr-Verlag.
Laken, William D. & Sanchez, David A. Topics in Ordinary Differential Equations. 160p. 1982. reprint ed. pap. 5.95 (0-486-61606-1) Dover.
Laker, Kenneth R. Design of Analog Integrated Circuits & Systems. 1994. text ed. write for info. (0-07-036060-X) McGraw.
Laker, Mark. Nursing Home Activities for the Handicapped. 98p. 1980. spiral bd., pap. 21.95x (0-398-04074-5) C C Thomas.
Laker, Rosalind. The Golden Tulip. large type ed. LC 92-176081. (General Ser.). 896p. 1993. pap. 18.95 (0-8161-5574-7) G K Hall.
— Jewelled Path. 576p. 1985. pap. 3.95 (0-8217-1504-6) Zebra.
— Orchids & Diamonds. LC 94-19000. 1995. 23.95 (0-385-47281-1) Doubleday.
— Orchids & Diamonds. large type ed. LC 94-45639. 559p. 1995. 22.95 (0-7862-0403-6) Thorndike Pr.
— Portrait of Eliza. large type ed. (Dales Ser.). 155p. 1994. pap. 16.95 (1-85389-417-6, Dales) Ulverscroft.
— The Sugar Pavilion. LC 93-13713. 1994. 22.50 (0-385-46826-1) Doubleday.
— The Sugar Pavilion. LC 94-1780. 1994. 23.95 (0-7862-0225-4) Thorndike Pr.
— The Venetian Mask. large type ed. 691p. 1993. reprint ed. lib. bdg. 22.95 (1-56054-585-2) Thorndike Pr.
Lakes, R. S., jt. auth. see Park, J. B.
Lakes Region General Hospital Auxiliary Staff. Lakes Region Cuisine. LC 93-70329. 1993. write for info. (0-87197-365-0) Favorite Recipes.
***Lakes, Richard D.** Critical Education for Work: Multidisciplinary Approaches. 224p. (Orig.). 1994. pap. text ed. 19.95 (1-56750-110-9) Ablex Pub.
***Lakes, Richard D., ed.** Critical Education for Work: Multidisciplinary Approaches. 224p. (Orig.). 1994. 37.50 (1-56750-109-5) Ablex Pub.
Lakeway, Ruth C. & White, Robert C., Jr. Italian Art Song. LC 87-46370. (Illus.). 416p. 1989. 29.95 (0-253-33154-4) Ind U Pr.
***Lakey, Berit, et al.** Changing Currents: A Guide for Leading Grassroots & Nonprofit Organizations. 224p. 1995. pap. 14.95 (0-86571-328-6) New Soc Pubs.

An Asterisk (*) at the beginning of an entry indicates that the title is appearing in BIP for the first time.

— Changing Currents: A Guide for Leading Grassroots & Nonprofit Organizations. 224p. 1995. lib. bdg. 39.95 (*0-86571-327-8*) New Soc Pubs.

Lakey, George. Non-Violent Action: How it Works. LC 63-17661. (C). 1963. pap. 3.00 (*0-87574-129-0*) Pendle Hill.

— Powerful Peacemaking: A Strategy for a Living Revolution. rev. ed. 266p. 1987. 34.95 (*0-86571-096-1*); pap. 12.95 (*0-86571-097-X*) New Soc Pubs.

Lakey, George, jt. auth. see Kokopeli, Bruce.

Lakey, J. R. A., jt. auth. see Duchene, A. S.

Lakey, Steven D. Bamboo Horses: Wooden Dragons - Twenty-Two Hornet. LC 80-69812. 60p. (Orig.). 1980. text ed. 4.95 (*0-685-01609-9*, 0003); pap. text ed. 3.25 (*0-936748-04-4*) Fade In.

— The Nickel Chimera. LC 80-65824. (Illus.). 60p. (C). 1980. 4.95 (*0-936748-00-1*); pap. 2.95 (*0-936748-01-X*) Fade In.

Lakha, Salim. Capitalism & Class in Colonial India. 240p. 1988. text ed. 25.00 (*81-207-0842-3*, Pub. by Sterling Pubs II) Apt Bks.

Lakha, Salim, jt. ed. see Pinches, Michael.

Lakhakia, A., ed. Selected Papers on Natural Optical Activity. 624p. 1990. 106.00 (*0-8194-0435-7*, VOL. MS15/HC); pap. 91.00 (*0-8194-0436-5*, VOL. MS15) SPIE.

Lakhan, V. C. & Trenhaile, Alan S., eds. Applications in Coastal Modeling. (Elsevier Oceanography Ser.: No. 49). 388p. 1989. 113.00 (*0-444-87452-6*) Elsevier.

Lakhani, Fatima. Indian Recipes for a Healthy Heart: 140 Low-Fat, Low-Cholesterol, Low-Sodium Gourmet Dishes from India Featuring 104 Vegetarian Recipes & a Recipe for Overall Fitness. LC 91-92185. 304p. (Orig.). 1992. pap. 14.95 (*0-9630235-0-0*) Fahil Pub.

Lakhanpal, P. L. A Rebel at Law. (C). 1987. 125.00 (*0-685-36505-0*) St Mut.

Lakhanpal, T. N. & Mukerji, K. G. Taxonomy of the Indian Myxomycetes. (Bibliotheca Mycologica Ser.: No. 78). (Illus.). 532p. 1981. lib. bdg. 72.00 (*3-7682-1287-4*) Lubrecht & Cramer.

Lakhanpal, T. N., jt. auth. see Monga, Pradeep.

Lakhno, V. D. Spin Wave Amplification: Electron Mechanisms. 148p. (C). 1992. text ed. 89.00 (*1-56072-067-0*) Nova Sci Pubs.

Lakhno, Victor D. Excited Polaron States in Condensed Media. (Proceedings in Nonlinear Science Ser.). 192p. 1992. text ed. 115.00 (*0-471-93563-4*) Wiley.

***Lakhno, Victor D., ed.** Polarons & Applications. (Proceedings in Nonlinear Science). 1994. text ed. 96.95 (*0-471-95514-0*) Wiley.

Lakhotia, R. N. Tax Planning Through Trusts & Wills. 2nd ed. (C). 1988. 60.00 (*0-685-27884-0*) St Mut.

— Zero to Hero in Income Tax. (C). 1990. 65.00 (*0-89771-267-6*) St Mut.

Lakhovsky, G. The Secret of Life: Cosmic Rays & Radiations & Radiations of Living Beings & Electro-Magnetic Waves. (Alternative Energy Ser.). 1991. lib. bdg. 79.95 (*0-8490-4275-5*) Gordon Pr.

Lakhovsky, Georges. The Secret of Life. 208p. 1991. pap. 9.95 (*0-932298-86-9*) Tri-State Pr Corp.

— The Secret of Life. 213p. 1970. reprint ed. spiral bd. 9.35 (*0-7873-0522-7*) Mokelumne.

— The Secret of Life: Electricity, Radiation & Your Body. Clement, Mark, tr. (Illus.). 1988. reprint ed. pap. 9.95 (*0-939482-08-8*) Noontide.

Lakhtakia, Akhlesh. Beltrami Fields in Chiral Media: Contemporary Chemical Physics Ser. 556p. 1994. text ed. 86.00 (*981-02-1403-0*) World Scientific Pub.

Lakhtakia, Akhlesh, ed. Essays on the Formal Aspects of Electromagnetic Theory. 550p. 1993. text ed. 140.00 (*981-02-0854-5*) World Scientific Pub.

Lakhtakia, Akhlesh, et al. Time-Harmonic Electromagnetic Fields in Chiral Media. (Lecture Notes in Physics Ser.: Vol. 335). vii, 121p. 1989. 31.00 (*0-387-51317-5*) Spr-Verlag.

Lakhtin, Y. Engineering Physical Metallurgy. (Russian Monographs & Texts on the Physical Sciences). 472p. 1965. text ed. 255.00 (*0-677-20240-7*) Gordon & Breach.

Laki, Koloman. Fibrinogen. LC 67-22482. 412p. reprint ed. pap. 117.50 (*0-685-16147-1*, 2027096) Bks Demand.

Laki, Koloman, ed. Contractile Proteins & Muscle. LC 72-134784. (Illus.). 622p. reprint ed. pap. 177.30 (*0-7837-0949-8*, 2041254) Bks Demand.

Lakin, Joan, jt. auth. see Meyers, Susan.

Lakin, K. M., jt. auth. see Chazov, E. I.

Lakin, Leonard & Beane, Leona. Materials in the Law of Business Contracts. 3rd ed. 272p. (C). 1994. per., pap. text ed. 28.95 (*0-8403-9236-2*) Kendall-Hunt.

Lakin, M. Personality Factors in Mothers of Excessively Crying Infants. (SRCD M: Vol. 22, No. 1). 1957. pap. 14.00 (*0-527-01569-5*) Periodicals Srv.

Lakin, Martin. Coping with Ethical Dilemmas. (Practitioner Guidebook Ser.). (C). 1991. 31.95 (*0-205-14402-0*, H4402, Longwood Div); pap. 21.95 (*0-205-14401-2*, H4401) Allyn.

— Ethical Issues in the Psychotherapies. 192p. 1988. 27.95 (*0-19-504446-0*) OUP.

— The Helping Group: Therapeutic Principles & Issues. 288p. 1987. 19.95 (*0-317-66348-8*, Pergamon Pr) Elsevier.

***Lakin, Pat.** Aware & Alert. LC 94-19718. (My Community Ser.). (Illus.). (J). 1995. lib. bdg. write for info. (*0-8114-8261-8*) Raintree Steck-V.

— Car Tunes. 32p. (J). (gr. 1-6). 1987. 6.95 (*0-394-88771-9*) Random Bks Yng Read.

— Information, Please. LC 94-22495. (My Community Ser.). (Illus.). (J). 1995. lib. bdg. write for info. (*0-8114-8260-X*) Raintree Steck-V.

— Red Letter Day: The Mail Carrier. LC 94-28680. (My Community Ser.). (Illus.). (J). 1995. lib. bdg. write for info. (*0-8114-8264-2*) Raintree Steck-V.

— Signs of Protest. LC 94-19717. (My Community Ser.). (Illus.). (J). 1995. lib. bdg. write for info. (*0-8114-8263-4*) Raintree Steck-V.

— A Summer Job. LC 94-19720. (My Community Ser.). (Illus.). (J). 1995. lib. bdg. write for info. (*0-8114-8259-6*) Raintree Steck-V.

— Where There's Smoke. LC 94-19706. (My Community Ser.). (Illus.). (J). 1995. lib. bdg. write for info. (*0-8114-8262-6*) Raintree Steck-V.

Lakin, Patricia. The Birthday Mystery: Adventure Mystery for Kids. (Puzzling Pen Pal Mysteries Ser.). (Illus.). 13p. (J). (gr. 3-6). 1991. 14.00 (*0-922242-21-6*) Lombard Mktg.

— The Case of the Stolen Jewels: Adventure Mystery for Kids Ages 8-12. (Illus.). 24p. (J). (gr. 3-4). 1992. 14.00 (*0-922242-33-X*) Lombard Mktg.

— Creativity: Around the World. LC 94-41207. (We All Share Ser.). (J). 1995. lib. bdg. 13.95 (*1-56711-142-4*) Blackbirch.

— Dad & Me in the Morning. LC 93-36169. (J). (ps-3). 1994. 14.95 (*0-8075-1419-5*) A Whitman.

— Don't Forget. LC 93-20341. (Illus.). 32p. (J). 1994. 14.00 (*0-688-12075-X*, Tambourine Bks); lib. bdg. 13.93 (*0-688-12076-8*, Tambourine Bks) Morrow.

— Family: Around the World. Glassman, Bruce, ed. LC 94-41713. (We All Share Ser.). (Illus.). 32p. (J). (gr. 2-5). 1995. lib. bdg. 13.95 (*1-56711-143-2*) Blackbirch.

— Get Ready to Read! LC 93-49842. (My School Ser.). (Illus.). (J). 1994. lib. bdg. 19.97 (*0-8114-3866-X*) Raintree Steck-V.

— A Good Sport! LC 93-49845. (My School Ser.). (Illus.). (J). 1994. lib. bdg. 19.97 (*0-8114-3870-8*) Raintree Steck-V.

— Growing Up: Around the World. Glassman, Bruce, ed. (We All Share Ser.). (Illus.). 32p. (J). (gr. 2-5). 1995. lib. bdg. 14.95 (*1-56711-144-0*) Blackbirch.

— Jennifer Capriati. LC 93-18131. (Winning Spirit Ser.). (J). 1993. 15.93 (*0-86592-090-7*); 11.95 (*0-685-66545-3*) Rourke Enter.

— The Mystery Illness. LC 93-49843. (My School Ser.). (Illus.). (J). 1994. lib. bdg. 19.97 (*0-8114-3867-8*) Raintree Steck-V.

— The Palace of Stars. LC 92-36796. (Illus.). 32p. (J). (ps up). 1993. 14.00 (*0-688-11176-9*, Tambourine Bks); lib. bdg. 13.93 (*0-688-11177-7*, Tambourine Bks) Morrow.

— Play: Around the World. Glassman, Bruce, ed. LC 94-38497. (We All Share Ser.). (Illus.). 32p. (J). (gr. 2-5). 1995. lib. bdg. 13.95 (*1-56711-141-6*) Blackbirch.

— Trash & Treasure. LC 93-49844. (My School Ser.). (Illus.). (J). 1994. lib. bdg. 19.97 (*0-8114-3865-1*) Raintree Steck-V.

— A True Partnership. LC 94-660. (My School Ser.). (J). (gr. 5 up). 1994. lib. bdg. 19.97 (*0-8114-3869-4*) Raintree Steck-V.

— Twick or Tweet. (J). Date not set. 2.50 (*0-679-87258-2*) Random.

— Up a Tree. LC 93-49847. (My School Ser.). (Illus.). (J). 1994. lib. bdg. 19.97 (*0-8114-3868-6*) Raintree Steck-V.

Lakin, Patty. Menace or Tennis: Adventure Mystery for Kids Ages 8-12. (Illus.). 24p. (J). (gr. 4-8). 1992. 14.00 (*0-922242-35-6*) Lombard Mktg.

Lakin, R. D. American Passport. 60p. 1992. 30.00 (*0-930126-38-6*) Typographeum.

— The Macdowell Poems. limited ed. 1977. bds. 15.00 (*0-930126-00-9*) Typographeum.

Lakin, Ruth. Kettle River Country. rev. ed. (Illus.). 300p. (Orig.). (C). 1987. pap. write for info. (*0-318-62465-6*) Statesman Exam.

Laking, Barbara, ed. Dried Flower Designs. (Plants & Gardens Ser.). (Illus.). 1989. ring bd. 3.95 (*0-945352-34-4*, Sterling) Bklyn Botanic.

Laking, Guy F. A Record of European Armour & Arms Through Seven Centuries, 5 vols. LC 79-8365. (Illus.). reprint ed. 295.00 (*0-404-18344-1*) AMS Pr.

Lakins, Jean. Something New. 1994. 10.95 (*0-8062-5023-2*) Carlton.

Lakis, Stephen G. The MPA Pocket Reference. rev. ed. Swan, Marc, ed. 60p. 1991. pap. write for info. (*0-318-64805-9*) Ctr Leader Stu.

— The Political Almanac - Massachusetts, 2 vols. rev. ed. Gustafson, Carl S., ed. 1991. Vol. II, The Executive Branch, 220p. write for info. (*0-318-64804-0*) Ctr Leader Stu.

— The Political Almanac - Massachusetts, 2 vols., Vol. I. rev. ed. Gustafson, Carl S., ed. 280p. 1991. pap. write for info. (*0-318-64803-2*) Ctr Leader Stu.

Lakke, J. P., et al, eds. Parenteral Drug Therapy in Spasticity & Parkinson's Disease. (New Trends in Clinical Neurology Ser.). (Illus.). 300p. (C). 1991. 78.00 (*1-85070-359-0*) Prthnon Pub.

Lakner, Armand A. & Anderson, Ronald T. Reliability Engineering for Nuclear & Other High Technology Systems: A Practical Guide. (Illus.). 418p. 1985. 142.25 (*0-85334-286-5*, Pub. by Elsevier Applied Sci UK) Elsevier.

Lako, G. Swedish-Hungarian Dictionary: Sved-Magyar Szotar. 4th ed. 1024p. (HUN & SWE.). 1985. 49.95 (*0-8288-1674-3*, M8583) Fr & Eur.

***Lako, Gy. & Feher, J.** Swedish-Hungarian Concise Dictionary. 1024p. 1992. 45.00x (*963-05-6400-9*, Pub. by Akad Kiado HU) St Mut.

Lako, Gyorgy. The Proto-Finno-Ugric Antecedents of the Hungarian Phonetic Stock. LC 67-66163. (Uralic & Altaic Ser.: Vol. 80). 1966. reprint ed. spiral bd. 12.00 (*0-87750-030-4*) Res Inst Inner Asian Studies.

Lakoff, George. Women, Fire & Dangerous Things. LC 86-19136. xxvi, 614p. 1990. pap. 19.95 (*0-226-46804-6*) U Ch Pr.

Lakoff, George & Johnson, Mark. Metaphors We Live By. LC 80-10783. xiv, 242p. 1981. pap. 10.95 (*0-226-46801-1*) U Ch Pr.

Lakoff, George & Turner, Mark. More Than Cool Reason: A Field Guide to Poetic Metaphor. LC 88-29306. 240p. 1989. pap. text ed. 12.95 (*0-226-46812-7*) U Ch Pr.

Lakoff, George, ed. see Borkin, Ann.

Lakoff, Robin T. & Coyne, James C. Father Knows Best: The Use & Abuse of Power in Freud's Case of Dora. (Athene Ser.). 160p. (C). 1992. text ed. 36.00 (*0-8077-6267-9*); pap. text ed. 16.95 (*0-8077-6266-0*) Tchrs Coll.

Lakoff, Sanford & Willoughby, Randy, eds. Strategic Defense & the Western Alliance. 240p. 1987. text ed. 35.00 (*0-669-15839-9*) Free Pr.

Lakoff, Sanford & York, Herbert F. A Shield in Space? Technology, Politics, & the Strategic Defense Initiative. (California Studies in Global Conflict & Cooperation: Vol. 1). 1989. 42.50 (*0-520-06650-2*) U CA Pr.

Lakomski, Gabriele, jt. auth. see Evers, Colin W.

Lakond, Wladimir, tr. see Tchaikovsky, Petr I.

Lakonishok, Josef, jt. auth. see Haugen, Robert.

Lakos, Amos. International Negotiations: A Bibliography. (Special Studies in International Relations: No. 14). 417p. (C). 1989. text ed. 88.50 (*0-8133-7558-4*) Westview.

— Terrorism, 1980-1990: A Bibliography. 443p. (C). 1991. pap. text ed. 75.50 (*0-8133-8035-9*) Westview.

***Lakos, John S.** Large-Scale Software Development in C Plus Plus. (Professional Computing Ser.). 1995. pap. 33.50 (*0-201-63362-0*) Addison-Wesley.

Lakoski, Joan M., et al. Cocaine: Pharmacology, Physiology & Clinical Strategies. 500p. 1990. 65.00 (*0-936923-42-3*); pap. 32.50 (*0-936923-43-1*) Telford Pr.

— Cocaine: Pharmacology, Physiology & Clinical Strategies. 1991. 98.95 (*0-8493-8813-9*, QP801) CRC Pr.

Lakowicz, ed. Time-Resolved Laser Spectroscopy in Biochemistry. 1988. 65.00 (*0-89252-944-X*, 909) SPIE.

Lakowicz, J., ed. Time-Resolved Laser Spectroscopy in Biochemistry II. 1990. 109.00 (*0-8194-0245-1*, VOL. 1204) SPIE.

Lakowicz, J. R., ed. Time-Resolved Laser Spectroscopy in Biochemistry III. 1992. 100.00 (*0-8194-0786-0*, 1640) SPIE.

— Topics in Fluorescence Spectroscopy, 4. (Illus.). 530p. (C). 1994. 95.00 (*0-306-44784-3*, Plenum Pr) Plenum.

Lakowicz, Joseph R. Principles of Fluorescence Spectroscopy. LC 85-28251. 510p. 1983. 49.50 (*0-306-41285-3*, Plenum Pr) Plenum.

Lakowicz, Joseph R., ed. Topics in Fluorescence Spectroscopy, Vol. 1: Techniques. (Illus.). 460p. 1991. 79.50 (*0-306-43874-7*, Plenum Pr) Plenum.

— Topics in Fluorescence Spectroscopy, Vol. 2: Principles. (Illus.). 466p. 1991. 79.50 (*0-306-43875-5*, Plenum Pr) Plenum.

— Topics in Fluorescence Spectroscopy, Vol. 3: Biochemical Applications. (Illus.). 406p. 1991. 79.50 (*0-306-43954-9*, Plenum Pr) Plenum.

Lakritz, Esther. Developing Library Skills. 112p. (J). (gr. 4-8). 1989. 10.95 (*0-86653-481-4*, GA1081) Good Apple.

— To Track a Copycat. Jones, M. L., ed. 210p. (Orig.). 1995. pap. 8.95 (*1-882270-34-7*) Old Rugged Cross.

***Laks, Andre & Schofield, Malcolm, eds.** Justice & Generosity: Studies in Hellenistic Social & Political Philosophy. (Proceedings of the Sixth Symposium Hellenisticum Ser.). (Illus.). 366p. (C). 1995. 64.95 (*0-521-45293-7*) Cambridge U Pr.

Laks, Batya. Electra: A Gender Sensitive Study of the Plays - Aeschylus' Oresteia Through Sam Shepard's Curse of the Starving Class, Based on the Myth. (Illus.). 192p. 1995. lib. bdg. 28.50 (*0-89950-924-X*) McFarland & Co.

Laks, Hillel, jt. auth. see Kapoor, Amar S.

Laks, Michael M., ed. Computerized Interpretation of the Electrocardiogram, No. VII. 414p. (Orig.). 1983. pap. 30.00 (*0-939204-19-3*, 82-09) Eng Found.

Laks, Peter E., jt. ed. see Hemingway, Richard W.

Lakshamma, C. Impact of Ramanuja's Teaching on Life & Conditions in Society. 1990. 39.00 (*81-85067-46-5*, Pub. by Sundeep II) S Asia.

***Lakshiaiminarayanan, Venkataraman.** Electronic Circuit Design Ideas. (EDN Ser.). (Illus.). 288p. 1994. pap. 29.95 (*0-7506-2047-1*) Buttrwrth-Heinemann.

Lakshiminarayana, B., ed. see Joint Fluids Engineering Gas Turbine Conference & Products Show Staff.

Lakshman Sarup, jt. auth. see Woolner, A. C.

Lakshman, W. D., ed. Public Enterprises & Employment in Developing Countries. (ICPE Bks.). 182p. 1984. pap. 20.00 (*92-9038-031-4*, Pub. by Intl Ctr Pub Ent XV) Kumarian Pr.

Lakshmana Rao, V. Industrial Entrepreneurship in India. (C). 1987. 26.00 (*81-85076-05-7*, Pub. by Chugh Pubns II) S Asia.

Lakshmana Ras, V. Economic Development of India. (C). 1987. 35.00 (*81-85076-27-8*, Pub. by Chugh Pubns II) S Asia.

Lakshmanan, M. Solitons. (Nonlinear Dynamics Ser.). (Illus.). 420p. 1988. 66.00 (*0-387-18588-7*) Spr-Verlag.

Lakshmanan, M. & Daniel, M., eds. Symmetries & Singularity Structures: Integrability & Chaos in Nonlinear Dynamical Systems. (Research Reports in Physics). (Illus.). 256p. 1991. pap. 64.00 (*0-387-53092-4*) Spr-Verlag.

Lakshmanan, T. R & Chatterjee, Lata. Urbanization & Environmental Quality. Natoli, Salvatore, ed. LC 76-57032. (Resource Papers for College Geography). (C). 1977. pap. text ed. 10.00 (*0-89291-122-0*) Assn Am Geographers.

Lakshmanan, T. R. & Johansson, B. B., eds. Large Scale Energy Projects, Assessment of Regional Consequences: An International Comparison of Experiences with Models & Methods. (Studies in Regional Science & Urban Economics: Vol. 12). 330p. 1985. 97.50 (*0-444-87724-X*, North Holland) Elsevier.

Lakshmanan, T. R. & Nijkamp, Peter, eds. Structure & Change in the Space Economy: Festschrift in Honor of Martin H. Beckmann. LC 93-16821. 1993. 109.00 (*0-387-56490-X*) Spr-Verlag.

***Lakshmanan, Usha.** Universal Grammar in Child Second Language Acquisition: Null Subjects & Morphological Uniformity. LC 94-26067. (Language Acquisition & Language Disorders (LALD) Ser.: 10). 1994. 35.00 (*1-55619-247-9*) Benjamins North Am.

Lakshmanan, V. I., intro. Advanced Materials - Application of Mineral & Metallurgical Processing Principles. LC 89-63668. (Illus.). 248p. (Orig.). 1990. pap. 58.50 (*0-87335-089-8*) SMM&E Inc.

Lakshmanan, V. I., et al, eds. Emerging Separation Technologies for Metals & Fuels. (Illus.). 480p. 1993. 84.00 (*0-87339-205-1*) Minerals Metals.

Lakshmanna, C., et al, eds. Social Action & Social Change. 1990. 37.00 (*0-685-40054-9*, Pub. by Ajanta II) S Asia.

Lakshmi. Ripples in the River. Ananthakrishnan, Indira, tr. (C). 1992. text ed. 4.00 (*81-7201-045-1*, Pub. by National Sahitya Akademi) S Asia.

Lakshmi, J. Vijaya & Kumari, M. Krishna. Kamesvara Temple at Gallavalli. (C). 1991. 55.00 (*0-8364-2771-8*, Pub. by Agam Kala Prakashan) S Asia.

Lakshmi, K. P. Communications Across the Borders: The U. S., the Non-Aligned & the New Information Order. (C). 1993. text ed. 16.00 (*81-7027-204-1*, Pub. by Radiant Pubs II) S Asia.

Lakshmi Narasu, Pokala. The Essence of Buddhism. 3rd enl. rev. ed. LC 78-72459. reprint ed. 32.50 (*0-404-17327-6*) AMS Pr.

Lakshmi, S. Challenges in Indian Education. rev. ed. 200p. 1992. text ed. 27.50 (*81-207-1143-2*, Pub. by Sterling Pubs II) Apt Bks.

— Innovations in Education. rev. ed. 208p. 1992. 27.50 (*81-207-1371-0*, Pub. by Sterling Pubs II) Apt Bks.

Lakshmikantham. Nonlinear Analysis & Applications. (Lecture Notes in Pure & Applied Mathematics Ser.: Vol. 109). 680p. 1987. 160.00 (*0-8247-7810-3*) Dekker.

— Trends in Theory & Practice of Nonlinear Differential Equations. (Lecture Notes in Pure & Applied Mathematics Ser.: Vol. 90). 592p. 1984. 140.00 (*0-8247-7130-3*) Dekker.

Lakshmikantham, et al. Stability Analysis of Nonlinear Systems. (Pure & Applied Mathematics Ser.: Vol. 125). 336p. 1989. 140.00 (*0-8247-8067-1*) Dekker.

Lakshmikantham, V. Nonlinear Differential Equations in Abstract Spaces. LC 80-41838. (I.S. Nonlinear Mathematics Series: Theory, Methods & Applications: Vol. 2). 272p. 1981. 125.00 (*0-08-025038-6*, Pergamon Pr) Elsevier.

— Theory of Differential Equations with Unbounded Delay. LC 94-27710. (Mathematics & Its Applications Ser.). 350p. (C). 1994. lib. bdg. 160.00 (*0-7923-3003-X*) Kluwer Ac.

Lakshmikantham, V., ed. Trends in the Theory & Practice of Non-Linear Analysis. (Mathematical Studies: Vol. 110). 1985. 110.25 (*0-444-87704-5*, North Holland) Elsevier.

Lakshmikantham, V. & Trigiante, D. Theory of Difference Equations: Numerical Methods & Applications. (Mathematics in Science & Engineering Ser.). 242p. 1988. text ed. 72.00 (*0-12-434100-4*) Acad Pr.

Lakshmikantham, V. & Xinzhi Liu. Stability Analysis in Terms of Two Measures. LC 93-14063. 250p. 1993. text ed. 61.00 (*981-02-1389-1*) World Scientific Pub.

Lakshmikantham, V., jt. auth. see Agarwal, Ravi P.

Lakshmikantham, V., jt. auth. see Heikkila, Seppo.

Lakshmikantham, V., et al. Practical Stability of Nonlinear Systems. 220p. (C). 1990. text ed. 53.00 (*981-02-0351-9*); pap. text ed. 36.00 (*981-02-0356-X*) World Scientific Pub.

— Vector Lyapunov Functions & Stability Analysis of Nonlinear Systems. (C). 1991. lib. bdg. 79.00 (*0-7923-1152-3*) Kluwer Ac.

Lakshmilcantham, V., et al, eds. Theory of Impulsive Differential Equations. 288p. (C). 1989. text ed. 74.00 (*9971-5-0970-9*) World Scientific Pub.

***Lakshminarayana, Budugur.** Fluid Dynamics & Heat Transfer of Turbomachinery. LC 94-41844. 1995. text ed. 79.95 (*0-471-85546-4*) Wiley.

Lakshminarayana, H. & Tyagi, S. S. Changes in Agrarian Structure in India. 163p. 1982. 21.95 (*0-318-36789-0*) Asia Bk Corp.

Lakshminarayana, H. D. Democracy in Rural India: Problems & Process. 180p. 1980. 15.95 (*0-940500-42-6*) Asia Bk Corp.

Lakshminarayana, J. S., jt. ed. see Nriagu, Jerome O.

Lakshminarayanaiah, N. Equations of Membrane Biophysics (Monograph) 1984. text ed. 109.00 (*0-12-434260-4*) Acad Pr.

Lakshminath, A. Precedent in the Indian Legal System. (C). 1989. 125.00 (*0-89771-768-6*, Pub. by Eastern Book II); 125.00 (*0-89771-759-7*, Pub. by Eastern Book II) St Mut.

— Precedent in the Indian Legal System. (C). 1990. text ed. 125.00 (*0-89771-485-7*) St Mut.

Lakshmiswaramma, M., jt. auth. see Chandra, Shanta K.

Lakshmivarahan, S. Learning Algorithms Theory & Applications. 279p. 1981. pap. 52.00 (*0-387-90640-1*) Spr-Verlag.

Lakshmivarahan, S. & Dhall, S. K. Analysis & Design of Parallel Algorithms: Arithmetic & Matrix Problems. 1990. text ed. write for info. (*0-07-036139-8*) McGraw.

— Parallel Computing Using the Prefix Problem. 304p. 1994. 59.95 (*0-19-508849-2*) OUP.

***Lakso.** Tasting Trouble. (Loveswept Ser.: No. 739). 1995. mass mkt. (*0-553-44423-9*, Loveswept) Bantam.

***Lakso, Elaine.** High Spirits. (Loveswept Ser.: No. 713). 1994. pap. 3.50 (*0-553-44422-0*, Loveswept) Bantam.

Lakusta, Boris H. West's California Code Forms with Practice Commentaries-Public Utilities: Contains Pocket Parts. 3rd ed. LC 82-50923. (Illus.). xi, 366p. 1984. 32.00 (0-685-07262-2) West Pub.

Lal. Genetic Engineering of Plants for Crop Improvement. 1993. 104.00 (0-8493-6424-8, SB123) CRC Pr.

Lal, A. K. Urban Family: A Study of Hindu Social System. 1990. 21.00 (0-317-99587-1, Pub. by Concept II) S Asia.

Lal, B. K. Contemporary Indian Philosophy. 364p. 1978. 15.95 (0-318-37017-4) Asia Bk Corp.

Lal, Barbara B. The Romance of Culture in an Urban Civilization: Robert E. Park & the Chicago School. 176p. 1990. 49.95 (0-415-02877-9, A3714) Routledge.

Lal, Basant K. Contemporary Indian Philosophy. xxi, 345p. (C). 1992. 16.00 (81-208-0260-8, Pub. by Motilal Banarsidass II) S Asia.

Lal, Bhawani. Extraordinary Trials from Law Courts. 135p. 1961. pap. 80.00 (0-317-54587-6) St Mut.

— Extraordinary Trials from Law Courts. (C). 1961. 6.00 (0-685-39529-4) St Mut.

Lal-Bhawani. Interpretation of Statutes. 326p. 1964. pap. 75.00 (0-317-54586-8) St Mut.

Lal, Brij V. Broken Waves: A History of the Fiji Islands in the Twentieth Century. LC 92-17786. (Pacific Islands Monograph Ser.: No. 11). (Illus.). 424p. 1992. text ed. 38.00 (0-8248-1418-5) UH Pr.

Lal, Brij V., et al, eds. Plantation Workers: Resistance & Accommodation. LC 93-10913. 352p. (C). 1993. text ed. 38.00 (0-8248-1496-7) UH Pr.

Lal, D. Market Access for Semi-Manufactures from Developing Countries, No. 5. (Commercial Policy Issues Ser.). 59p. 1979. lib. bdg. 16.50 (90-286-0548-7) Kluwer Ac.

Lal, Deepak. Against Dirigisme: The Case for Unshackling Economic Markets. LC 94-1702. 1994. pap. 14.95 (1-55815-324-1) ICS Pr.

— Development Economics, 4 vols., Set. (International Library of Critical Writings in Business History: No. 18). 1860p. 1992. text ed. 559.95 (1-85278-196-3, Pub. by E Elgar Pub UK) Ashgate Pub Co.

— The Hindu Equilibrium, Vol. I: Cultural Stability & Economic Stagnation in India, 1500 B.C. - 1980 A.D. (Illus.). 374p. 1989. 79.00 (0-19-828498-5) OUP.

— The Hindu Equilibrium, Vol. II: Aspects of Indian Labour. (Illus.). 218p. 1989. 49.95 (0-19-828499-3) OUP.

— India. 51p. 1988. pap. 5.00 (1-55815-016-1) ICS Pr.

— A Liberal International Economic Order: The International Monetary System & Economic Development. LC 80-22523. (Essays in International Finance Ser.: No. 139). 50p. reprint ed. pap. 25.00 (0-685-23684-6, 2032118) Bks Demand.

— Political Economy & Public Policy. 36p. 1990. pap. 5.00 (1-55815-101-X) ICS Pr.

— The Poverty of "Development Economics" (Illus.). 144p. 1986. pap. 12.95 (0-674-69471-6) HUP.

— The Repressed Economy: Causes, Consequences, Reform. (Economists of the Twentieth Century Ser.). 592p. 1993. 89.95 (1-85278-888-7, Pub. by E Elgar Pub UK) Ashgate Pub Co.

Lal, Deepak, jt. ed. see Scott, Maurice F.

Lal, H. City & Urban Fringe. 1987. 18.50 (81-7022-190-0, Pub. by Concept II) S Asia.

Lal, H., jt. ed. see Marangos, P. J.

Lal, Harbans, jt. ed. see Van Bever, William.

Lal, J. B. Environmental Conservation. 126p. 1987. 85.00 (0-685-21853-8, Pub. by Intl Bk Distr II); 65.00 (0-685-49628-7, Pub. by Intl Bk Distr II) St Mut.

— India's Forest. (C). 1987. 135.00 (0-685-21841-4, Pub. by Intl Bk Distr II) St Mut.

Lal, Joginder & Mark, James E., eds. Advances in Elastomers & Rubber Elasticity. LC 86-25416. 454p. 1986. 95.00 (0-306-42472-X, Plenum Pr) Plenum.

Lal, Joginder, jt. ed. see Mark, James E.

Lal, K., ed. Synthesis, Crystal Growth & Characterization: Proceedings of the International School on Synthesis Crystal Growth, October, '81. 400p. 1984. 107.75 (0-444-86435-0, 1-497-83, North Holland) Elsevier.

Lal, K., jt. auth. see Aagrawal, A. N.

Lal, K. B. Struggle for Change: International Economic Relations. 1984. 22.50 (0-8364-1226-5, Pub. by Allied II) S Asia.

Lal, K. M. Population Settlements: Development & Planning. 1988. 32.00 (81-85076-48-0, Pub. by Chugh Pubns II) S Asia.

Lal, K. S. Legacy of Muslim Rule in India. (C). 1992. 34.00 (81-85689-03-2, Pub. by Aditya Prakashan II) S Asia.

— The Mughal Harem. (C). 1988. 72.00 (81-85179-03-4, Pub. by Aditya Prakashan II) S Asia.

— Muslim Slave System in Medieval India. (C). 1995. 17.50x (81-85689-67-9, Pub. by Aditya Prakashan II) S Asia.

Lal, L., jt. auth. see Goyal, G.

Lal, Lakskshmi. The Ramayana. 179p. 1992. pap. 7.95 (0-86311-283-8, Pub. by Orient Longman Ltd II) Apt Bks.

Lal, Mohan. Rural Industrialisation & Regional Development. 168p. 1987. 21.00 (0-8364-2031-4, Pub. by Deep) S Asia.

Lal, Mukandi. Garhwal Painting. (Illus.). 120p. 1982. 55.00 (0-318-36335-6) Asia Bk Corp.

Lal, Muni. Mini Mughals. (Illus.). 340p. 1990. text ed. 37.50 (81-220-0174-2, Pub. by Konark Pubs Pvt Ltd II) Advent Bks Div.

— Mughal Glory: Stories of Love, Loyalty, Honour, Courage... 127p. 1989. text ed. 15.95 (81-220-0076-2, Pub. by Konark Pubs Pvt Ltd II) Advent Bks Div.

Lal, Nathuni. Benami Transactions. (C). 1990. 125.00 (0-89771-268-4) St Mut.

— Law of Arbitration. 4th rev. ed. (C). 1983. 85.00 (0-685-39801-3) St Mut.

Lal, P. An Annotated Mahabharata Bibliography. 31p. 1973. 10.00 (0-88253-306-1) Ind-US Inc.

— Change! They Said. (Writers Workshop Redbird Ser.). 24p. 1973. 5.00 (0-317-42433-5); 4.00 (0-89253-697-7) Ind-US Inc.

— The Concept of an Indian Literature: Six Essays by P. Lal. 49p. 1973. 10.00 (0-88253-303-7) Ind-US Inc.

— David McCutchion: Shraddanjali. 15.00 (0-89253-671-3); 6.75 (0-89253-672-1) Ind-US Inc.

— Draupadi & Jayadratha & Other Poems. 18p. 1973. 6.00 (0-88253-271-5); 4.00 (0-89253-540-7) Ind-US Inc.

— The First Writers Workshop Story Anthology. 9.00 (0-89253-762-0) Ind-US Inc.

— The Lemon Tree of Modern Sex. (Writers Workshop Greybird Ser.). 106p. 1975. 12.00 (0-88253-572-2); pap. text ed. 6.75 (0-88253-571-4) Ind-US Inc.

— Love's the First. 32p. 1973. 5.00 (0-88253-263-4); 4.00 (0-685-02469-5) Ind-US Inc.

— The Mahabharata of Vyasa. 400p. 1980. 15.95 (0-7069-1033-8); 29.95 (0-318-37171-5) Asia Bk Corp.

— The Man of Dharma & the Rasa of Silence. (Redbird Ser.). 61p. 1975. 8.00 (0-88253-831-4); pap. 4.80 (0-88253-832-2) Ind-US Inc.

— The Parrot's Death & Other Poems. 13p. 1973. 5.00 (0-88253-268-5); pap. 4.00 (0-88253-806-3) Ind-US Inc.

— T. S. Eliot: Homage from India. 12.00 (0-88253-300-2) Ind-US Inc.

— Transcreation: Two Essays. 29p. 1973. 8.00 (0-88253-269-3) Ind-US Inc.

— Yakshi from Didarganj. 42p. 1973. 8.00 (0-88253-267-7); 4.00 (0-89253-518-0) Ind-US Inc.

Lal, P., ed. The First Writers Workshop Literary Reader: An Anthology. (Writers Workshop Greybird Ser.). 107p. 1975. 15.00 (0-88253-542-0); pap. text ed. 6.75 (0-88253-541-2) Ind-US Inc.

— Great Sanskrit Plays in Modern Translation. LC 63-21383. 1957. pap. 12.95 (0-8112-0079-5, NDP142) New Directions.

— New English Poetry by Indian Women. (Writers Workshop Redbird Ser.). 1977. 8.00 (0-89253-804-X); text ed. 14.00 (0-89253-803-1) Ind-US Inc.

— The Second Writers Workshop Literary Reader: An Anthology. 72p. 1975. 15.00 (0-88253-624-9); pap. text ed. 6.75 (0-88253-623-0) Ind-US Inc.

Lal, P., tr. The Avyakta Upanisad. 25p. 1973. 8.00 (0-88253-272-3) Ind-US Inc.

— Avyakta Upanishad. (Writers Workshop Ser.). 1969. 4.00 (0-86578-006-4) Ind-US Inc.

— The Brhadaranyaka Upanisad. (Saffronbird Ser.). 117p. (ENG.). (C). 1975. pap. text ed. 6.75 (0-88253-828-4) Ind-US Inc.

— The Golden Womb of the Sun (Rig Veda) 40p. 1973. 6.75 (0-89253-787-6) Ind-US Inc.

Lal, P, tr. Isa Upanishad. 2nd ed. (Writers Workshop Saffronbird Ser.). 1971. 8.00 (0-317-42449-1) Ind-US Inc.

Lal, P., tr. The Japji (Adi Granth), Vol. 1. 38p. 1973. 4.80 (0-88253-262-6); pap. text ed. 4.00 (0-89253-788-4) Ind-US Inc.

— Mahabharata, 114 vols. 1973. Price per vol. 6.00 (0-685-73347-5) Ind-US Inc.

— More Songs from the Jap-Ji: Selections from the Adi-Granth, Vol.2. 20p. 1975. 4.80 (0-88253-708-3); pap. text ed. 4.00 (0-89253-789-2) Ind-US Inc.

— Sanskrit Love Lyrics. 31p. 1973. 6.75 (0-88253-265-0); 4.80 (0-89253-525-3) Ind-US Inc.

— Some Sanskrit Poems. 16p. 1973. 8.00 (0-88253-266-9); 4.00 (0-89253-520-2) Ind-US Inc.

Lal, P., tr. see Das, Jibanananda.

Lal, P., ed. see Derozio, Henry.

Lal, P., jt. auth. see Devi, Shyamasree.

Lal, P., tr. see Mahendravarman.

Lal, P., tr. see Premchand, A.

Lal, P., tr. see Roy, Tarapada.

Lal, P., jt. auth. see Shastri, P. N.

Lal, P., jt. ed. see Shastri, P. N.

Lal, P., tr. see Upanisads.

Lal, P. C. My Years with the Indian Air Force. 1986. 36.00 (0-317-68054-4, Pub. by Lancer II) S Asia.

Lal, Premila. Complete Book of Indian Cookery. 1994. pap. 11.95 (0-572-01938-6, Pub. by W Foulsham UK) Trans-Atl Phila.

Lal, R. Soil Erosion in the Tropics: Principles & Management. 1990. text ed. 93.00 (0-07-036087-1) McGraw.

— Soil Physical Properties & Crop Production in the Tropics. 551p. (C). 1989. 65.00 (0-685-61469-7, Pub. by Intl Bk Distr II); pap. 45.00 (0-685-61470-0, Pub. by Intl Bk Distr II) St Mut.

— Tropical Ecology & Physical Edaphology. LC 85-16906. 732p. 1987. text ed. 345.00 (0-471-90815-0, Wiley-Interscience) Wiley.

Lal, R., ed. Soil Physical Properties & Crop Production in the Tropics. 551p. 1989. 325.00 (81-7089-104-3, Pub. by Intl Bk Distr II) St Mut.

— Tropical Agricultural Hydrology Watershed Management & Land Use. 482p. 1990. 250.00 (81-7089-120-5, Pub. by Intl Bk Distr II) St Mut.

Lal, R. & Russell, E. W., eds. Tropical Agricultural Hydrology: Watershed Management & Land Use. LC 80-41590. (Wiley-Interscience Publication Ser.). 518p. reprint ed. pap. 147.70 (0-7837-3226-0, 2043243) Bks Demand.

Lal, R. & Stewart, B. A., eds. Soil Degradation. (Advances in Soil Science Ser.: Vol. 11). (Illus.). 352p. 1989. 109.00 (0-387-97126-2) Spr-Verlag.

— Soil Processes & Water Quality. LC 94-13702. (Advances in Soil Science Ser.). 416p. 1994. 69.95 (0-87371-980-8, L980) Lewis Pubs.

— Soil Restoration. (Advances in Soil Science Ser.: Vol. 17). (Illus.). 440p. 1991. 129.00 (0-387-97657-4) Spr-Verlag.

Lal, R., ed. see International Conference on Soil Conservation & Management in the Humid Tropics (1975: Ibadan, Nigeria) Staff.

Lal, R., et al, eds. Land Clearing & Development in the Tropics: Proceedings of a Conference Organized by the International Institute of Tropical Agriculture, Ibadan, Nigeria, November 1982. 488p. (C). 1984. text ed. 95.00 (90-6191-536-8, Pub. by A A Balkema NE) Ashgate Pub Co.

Lal, R. B. Crystal Growth in Space & Related Optical Diagnostics. 1992. 62.00 (0-8194-0685-6, 1557) SPIE.

— Principles & Practices of Range Management. (C). 1989. text ed. 125.00 (0-89771-578-0, Pub. by Intl Bk Distr II) St Mut.

— Principles & Practices of Range Management. 120p. 1990. 100.00 (81-7089-129-9, Pub. by Intl Bk Distr II) St Mut.

Lal, R. M. & Lal, Sukayna, eds. Crop Improvement Utilizing Biotechnology. 368p. 1989. 270.00 (0-8493-5082-4, SB123) CRC Pr.

Lal, Ramji. Political India, 1935-42: Anatomy of Indian Politics. 308p. 1986. 28.00 (81-202-0160-4, Pub. by Ajanta II) S Asia.

***Lal, Ratan, ed.** Soil Management & Greenhouse Effect. 400p. 1995. 79.95 (1-56670-117-1, L1117) Lewis Pubs.

Lal, Rattan, ed. Soil Erosion Research Methods. 2nd ed. (Illus.). 280p. (Orig.). 1994. pap. text ed. 39.95 (1-884015-09-3) St Lucie Pr.

Lal, Rattan, et al, eds. Sustainable Agricultural Systems. (Illus.). 696p. 1990. 60.00 (0-935734-21-X) Soil & Water Conserv.

***Lal, Rattan & Stewart, B. A., eds.** Soil Management: Experimental Basis for Sustainability. (Advances in Soil Science Ser.). 576p. 1995. 79.95 (1-55670-076-8, L1076) Lewis Pubs.

— Sustainable Management of Soils. LC 94-42105. (Advances in Soil Science Ser.). 1995. write for info. (1-56670-076-0) Lewis Pubs.

***Lal, Rattan, et al, eds.** Soils & Global Change. 464p. 1995. 85.00 (1-56670-118-X, L1118) Lewis Pubs.

Lal, Rup, ed. Pesticides & Nitrogen Cycle: Pesticides, Chemists & Soil Scientists, 3 vol., Set. 1988. 90.00 (0-8493-4350-X, QH545, CRC Reprint) Franklin.

Lal, S. K. Rural Social Transformation. (C). 1992. text ed. 32.00 (81-7033-159-5, Pub. by Rawat II) S Asia.

Lal, Sheo K. & Nahar, Umed R. Extent of Untouchability & Pattern of Discrimination. 1990. 19.50 (81-7099-221-4, Pub. by Mittal II) S Asia.

Lal, Shirley R., et al. Handbook on Gangs in Schools: Strategies to Reduce Gang-Related Activities. Herman, Janice L., ed. 88p. 1993. pap. 15.00 (0-8039-6071-9) Corwin Pr.

Lal, Shiv. Bangla-Pak Politics. 430p. 1986. 120.00 (0-317-61939-X, Pub. by Archives Pubs II) St Mut.

— British History of Elections (Olden Days) 260p. 1986. 125.00 (0-317-61940-3, Pub. by Archives Pubs II) St Mut.

— British History of Elections (Recent) 224p. 1986. 130.00 (0-317-61942-X, Pub. by Archives Pubs II) St Mut.

— The Death of Party System in India, 1982. 268p. 1986. 130.00 (0-317-61943-8, Pub. by Archives Pubs II) St Mut.

— Documents on Muslim States: Iran: Selected Political Documents. 224p. 1986. 150.00 (0-317-61944-6, Pub. by Archives Pubs II) St Mut.

— Documents on Muslim States: Morocco & Other African Nations. 300p. 1986. 120.00 (0-317-61945-4, Pub. by Archives Pubs II) St Mut.

— Documents on Muslim States: Politics in Iraq. 160p. 1986. 120.00 (0-317-61947-0, Pub. by Archives Pubs II) St Mut.

— Documents on Muslim States: Select Constitutions. 248p. 1986. 120.00 (0-317-61948-9, Pub. by Archives Pubs II) St Mut.

— Elections & the Constitution: The Question of Amendment. 412p. 1977. 120.00 (0-317-61949-7, Pub. by Archives Pubs II) St Mut.

— Global Election Records, 7 vols., Set. 1986. 1,850.00 (0-317-61955-1, Pub. by Archives Pubs II) St Mut.

— Indian Political Thought. (C). 1989. 540.00 (0-685-36475-5) St Mut.

— India's Freedom Fighters in South-East Asia. 224p. 1986. 130.00 (0-317-61958-6, Pub. by Archives Pubs II) St Mut.

— International Encyclopedia of Politics & Laws. 14000p. 1987. 3,900.00 (0-685-18847-7, Pub. by Archives Pubs II) St Mut.

— Malaysian Democracy: An Indian Perspective (1982) 432p. 1986. 120.00 (0-317-61966-7, Pub. by Archives Pubs II) St Mut.

— A Non-Muslim among Muslim States: Israel. 152p. 1986. 125.00 (0-317-61993-4, Pub. by Archives Pubs II) St Mut.

— Politico-Legal India, 5 vols., Set. 1986. 1,950.00 (81-7051-000-7, Pub. by Archives Pubs II) St Mut.

— The Two Leftist Parties of India, 1982. 200p. 1986. 165.00 (0-317-61987-X, Pub. by Archives Pubs II) St Mut.

***Lal, Shyam.** Tribals & Christian Missionaries. (C). 1994. text ed. 22.00 (81-85445-58-3, Pub. by Manas Pubns II) S Asia.

Lal, Sukayna, jt. ed. see Lal, R. M.

Lal, Victor. Fiji: Coups in Paradise. LC 88-14217. 256p. (C). 1990. text ed. 55.00 (0-86232-776-8, Pub. by Zed Books UK); pap. 17.50 (0-86232-777-6, Pub. by Zed Books UK) Humanities.

Lala, Chhaganlal. Philosophy of Bhakti. (C). 1989. 28.50 (81-7018-557-2, Pub. by BR Pub II) S Asia.

Lala, Marco. The Ultimate Weapon. (Illus.). 70p. (Orig.). 1987. pap. 12.95 (0-939427-82-6, 05052) Alpha Pubns OH.

Lala, P., ed. Satellite Perturbations & Orbital Determination. (Advances in Space Research Ser.: Vol. 1, No. 6). (Illus.). 95p. 1981. pap. 14.50 (0-08-028380-2, Pergamon Pr) Elsevier.

Lala, Paras. Digital System Design Using Programmable Logic Devices. 288p. 1990. boxed 44.00 (0-685-44717-0) P-H.

Lalagia. Spanish Dancing. Ivanova, Ana, ed. (Illus.). 168p. (Orig.). 1995. pap. 19.95 (0-903102-88-9, Pub. by Dance Bks UK) Princeton Bk Co.

Lalaguna, Juan. A Traveller's History of Spain. LC 89-15344. (Traveller's History Ser.). (Illus.). 306p. 1990. pap. 11.95 (0-940793-50-4) Interlink Pub.

— Traveller's History of Spain. rev. ed. LC 89-15344. 1994. pap. 13.95 (1-56656-148-5) Interlink Pub.

Lalance, Richard. The Tennis Trek. 2nd ed. 160p. (C). 1994. per. 16.50 (0-8403-9237-0) Kendall-Hunt.

Laland, John F., 2nd, tr. see Gutt, Martin.

***Laland, Stephanie.** Fifty-One Ways to Entertain Your Housecat While You're Out. 112p. (Orig.). 1994. pap. 7.50 (0-380-77431-3) Avon.

LaLande, John, et al. Activities Manual: First Year German. 176p. (GER.). (C). 1985. pap. text ed. write for info. (0-07-554344-3) McGraw.

Lalande, John F., II, tr. see Gutl, Martin.

Lalande, Michel R. De Profundis: Grand Motet for Soloists, Chorus, Woodwinds, Strings, & Continuo. Anthony, James R., ed. LC 79-29740. (Early Musical Masterworks Ser.). 182p. reprint ed. pap. 51.90 (0-8357-3897-3, 2036629) Bks Demand.

Lalande, Sebastien, jt. auth. see Courbis, Paul.

LaLanne, Elaine & Benyo, Richard. The Joy of Juicing: The Complete Guide to Healthy & Delicious Fresh Fruit & Vegetable Juices. 320p. 1992. pap. 10.00 (0-452-26928-8, Plume) NAL-Dutton.

Lalanne, Jack. Revitalize Your Health: Improve Your Health, Your Sex Life, & Your Looks after Age Fifty. 1995. pap. 13.95 (0-8038-9356-6) Hastings.

Lalanne, Maxime. The Technique of Etching. Koehler, S. R., tr. Orig. Title: The Treatise. (Illus.). 120p. 1982. reprint ed. pap. 4.95 (0-486-24182-3) Dover.

Lalanne, Michel, et al. Mechanical Vibrations for Engineers. Nelson, Frederick C., tr. & adapt. by. LC 83-6908. (Illus.). 274p. reprint ed. pap. 78.10 (0-8357-3097-2, 2039354) Bks Demand.

LaLanne, Michel, et al. Rotordynamics Prediction in Engineering. 1990. text ed. 84.95 (0-471-92633-7) Wiley.

Lalanne, P. & Chavel, P., eds. Perspectives for Parallel Optical Interconnects: Project 3199 WOIT. (ESPRIT Basic Research Ser.). xiii, 417p. 1993. 89.00 (0-387-56786-0) Spr-Verlag.

Lalbachan, Pamela. The Complete Caribbean Cookbook. (Illus.). 304p. 1994. 34.95 (0-8048-3038-X) C E Tuttle.

Lale, Cissy S., jt. auth. see Knight, Oliver.

Laleger, Grace E. Vocational Interests of High School Girls As Inventoried by the Strong & Manson Blanks. LC 76-176970. (Columbia University. Teachers College. Contributions to Education Ser.: No. 857). reprint ed. 37.50 (0-404-55857-7) AMS Pr.

Lalement, Rene. Reduction & Resolution: Computation & Logic. 400p. 1993. pap. text ed. 44.00 (0-13-770009-1) P-H.

Laliberte, Norman, jt. auth. see Mogelon, Alex.

Lalic, Ivan V. The Passionate Measure. (C). 1989. 23.00 (0-948268-60-3, Pub. by Dedalus Pr IE) St Mut.

— Roll Call of Mirrors: Selected Poems of Ivan V. Lalic. Simic, Charles, tr. LC 87-21185. (Wesleyan Poetry in Translation Ser.). 80p. 1988. 22.50 (0-8195-2151-5, Wesleyan Univ Pr); pap. 10.95 (0-8195-1152-8, Wesleyan Univ Pr) U Pr of New Eng.

Lalich, Janja, jt. auth. see Singer, Margaret T.

Lalich, Janja, jt. auth. see Tobias, Madeleine L.

Lalich, Richard, jt. auth. see Stovall, Pamela.

***Lalicki, Barbara.** If There Were Dreams to Sell. (J). (gr. 1-8). 1994. 15.95 (0-02-751251-7, Aladdin Paperbacks) S&S Childrens.

Lalini, V. Rural Leadership in India. 1991. 28.50 (0-685-40469-2, Pub. by Gian Publng Hse II) S Asia.

Lalique, Marie-Claude. Lalique. 640p. (FRE.). 1993. lib. bdg. 295.00 (0-7859-3655-6, 2883000018) Fr & Eur.

Lalique, Rene. Lalique Glass: The Complete Illustrated Catalogue for 1932. (Illus.). 160p. 1981. reprint ed. pap. 11.95 (0-486-24122-X) Dover.

Lalita, K., jt. ed. see Tharu, Susie.

Lalitananda, Swami. Yoga in Life. (Illus.). 1972. pap. 4.99 (0-934664-17-X) Yoga Res Foun.

— Yoga Mystic Songs for Meditation, 7 Vols. 1975. pap. 4.99 (0-934664-19-6) Yoga Res Foun.

Lalitananda, Swami, ed. Yoga Quotations from the Wisdom of Swami Jyotir Maya Nanda. (Illus.). 1974. pap. 6.95 (0-934664-27-7) Yoga Res Foun.

Lalive D'Epinay, Th., jt. ed. see Rodd, Mike G.

Lalkaka, R. & Mingyu, Wu. Managing Science Policy & Technology Acquisitions: Strategies for China. 544p. 1984. 40.00 (0-86346-050-X, Tycooly Pub) Weidner & Sons.

Lall, Arthur. The Emergence of Modern India. LC 80-25028. 288p. 1981. text ed. 40.00 (0-231-03430-X) Col U Pr.

— How Communist China Negotiates. LC 67-29051. 291p. 1968. pap. text ed. 17.00 (0-231-08592-3) Col U Pr.

— Modern International Negotiation. LC 66-17587. 404p. 1966. text ed. 52.50 (0-231-02935-7) Col U Pr.

Lall, B. Kent & Jones, Daniel L., Jr., eds. Major Development & Transportation Projects: Public-Private Partnerships. LC 90-980. 381p. 1990. pap. text ed. 37.00 (0-87262-764-0) Am Soc Civil Eng.

Lall, Betty G. Security Without Starwars: Verifying a Ban on Ballistic Missle Defense. 106p. 1987. pap. 6.00 (0-87871-052-3) CEP.

An Asterisk (*) at the beginning of an entry indicates that the title is appearing in BIP for the first time.

L

Lall, Betty G. & Brandes, Paul. Banning Nuclear Tests: Verification, Compliance, Savings. 83p. 1987. pap. 3.00 (*0-87871-053-1*) CEP.

Lall, Betty G. & Chollick, Eugene. The Intermediate Nuclear Forces Treaty: Verification Breakthrough. 58p. 1988. 3.00 (*0-87871-054-X*) CEP.

Lall, Bhagirath, jt. ed. see Marks, George V.

Lall, Chaman. Soft Magnetism: Fundamentals for Powder Metallurgy & Metal Injection Molding. LC 92-19313. (Monographs in P-M Ser.: No. 2). (Illus.). (C). 1992. pap. 60.00 (*1-878954-17-2*) Metal Powder.

***Lall, Chaman & Neupaver, Albert J., comps.** Advances in Powder Metallurgy & Particulate Materials - 1994: Proceedings of the 1994 International Conference & Exhibition on Powder Metallurgy & Particulate Materials, May 8-11, Toronto, Canada, 7 vols., Set. (Advances Ser.). 2400p. 1994. 750.00 (*1-878954-44-X*) Metal Powder.

Lall, Emmanuel N. Poetry of Encounter: Three Indo-Anglian Poets, Dom Moraes, A. K. Ramanujan, & Nissim Ezekiel. 120p. 1984. 14.00 (*0-86578-221-0*) Ind-US Inc.

***Lall, J. S., ed.** Selections from the Himalaya: Aspects of Change. (Oxford India Paperbacks Ser.). (Illus.). 220p. 1995. pap. 12.95 (*0-19-563263-X*) OUP.

Lall, K. B. Struggle for Change: (International Economic Relations) 327p. 1983. 34.95 (*0-318-37215-0*) Asia Bk Corp.

Lall, K. B., ed. The EEC in the Global Systems. 1984. 20.00 (*0-8364-1177-3*, Pub. by Allied II) S Asia.

Lall, K. B., et al, eds. EC '92: United Germany & the Changing World Order. 260p. 1992. 30.00 (*81-7027-188-6*, Pub. by Radiant Pubs II) S Asia.

— The European Community & SAARC. 114p. 1992. 25.00 (*81-7027-190-8*, Pub. by Radiant Pubs II) S Asia.

— European Union & Transformation of Europe's Economy. 262p. 1992. 35.00 (*81-7027-189-4*, Pub. by Radiant Pubs II) S Asia.

— India, Germany & the European Community. 164p. 1992. 27.50 (*81-7027-191-6*, Pub. by Radiant Pubs II) S Asia.

Lall, Kesar. An Encounter with the Yeti & Other Stories. 1991. 20.00 (*0-7855-0268-8*, Pub. by Ratna Pustak Bhandar) St Mut.

— Folk Tales from the Himalayan Kingdom of Nepal-Black Rice & Other Stories. 1993. 20.00 (*0-7855-0274-2*, Pub. by Ratna Pustak Bhandar) St Mut.

— Folk Tales from the Kingdom of Nepal. 1991. 20.00 (*0-7855-0275-0*, Pub. by Ratna Pustak Bhandar) St Mut.

— Nepal: Off the Beaten Path. 1992. 30.00 (*0-7855-0280-7*, Pub. by Ratna Pustak Bhandar) St Mut.

— Nepal Miscellany. 1993. 20.00 (*0-7855-0279-3*, Pub. by Ratna Pustak Bhandar) St Mut.

— Nepalese Customs & Manners. 1992. 20.00 (*0-7855-0282-3*, Pub. by Ratna Pustak Bhandar) St Mut.

— The Seven Sisters & Other Nepalese Tales. 1988. 20.00 (*0-7855-0286-6*, Pub. by Ratna Pustak Bhandar) St Mut.

— The Seven Sisters & Other Nepalese Tales. (Illus.). (C). 1988. 35.00 (*0-89771-082-7*, Pub. by Ratna Pustak Bhandar) St Mut.

Lall, Kesar, ed. The Nepalese Customs & Manners. 76p. (C). 1990. 35.00 (*0-89771-073-8*, Pub. by Ratna Pustak Bhandar) St Mut.

Lall, Kessar. Nepal off the Beaten Path. (C). 1992. 21.00 (*0-7855-0200-9*, Pub. by Ratna Pustak Bhandar) St Mut.

Lall, Pradeep, ed. see Hakim, Edward.

Lall, Rajiv, jt. auth. see Harrold, Peter.

Lall, Samuel B. Cactus Love. 4.80 (*0-89253-578-4*) Ind-US Inc.

Lall, Sanjaya. Building Industrial Competitiveness in Developing Countries. 75p. (Orig.). 1990. pap. 19.00 (*92-64-13397-6*) OECD.

Lall, Sanjaya, ed. Conflict & Bargaining. 1976. pap. 19.75 (*0-08-021060-0*, Pergamon Pr) Elsevier.

Lall, Sanjaya, jt. ed. see Balasubramanyam, V. N.

Lall, Sanjaya, et al. Technology & Enterprise Development: Ghana under Structural Adjustment. LC 93-47038. 1994. text ed. 69.95 (*0-312-12149-0*) St Martin.

Lalla, Barbara & D'Costa, Jean. Language in Exile: Three Hundred Years of Jamaican Creole. 276p. 1990. 41.95 (*0-8173-0447-9*) U of Ala Pr.

Lalla, Barbara, jt. auth. see D'Costa, Jean.

Lalleman, J. A. Dutch Language Proficiency of Turkish Children Born in the Netherlands. (Functional Grammar Ser.). xvi, 237p. 1986. pap. 53.85 (*90-6765-160-5*) Mouton.

Lalleman, Josine A., jt. auth. see Jordens, Peter.

Lallemand, Henri. Gallery of Art: Cezanne. 144p. 1994. 14.98 (*0-8317-5778-7*) Smithmark.

— Gallery of Art: Manet. 144p. 1994. 14.98 (*0-8317-5776-0*) Smithmark.

— Gallery of Art: Monet. 144p. 1994. 14.98 (*0-8317-5777-9*) Smithmark.

Lallemant, S. Z., jt. ed. see Dallapiccola, A. L.

Lalley, Edward P. Corporate Uncertainty & Risk Management. LC 82-60961. (Illus.). 187p. 1982. 19.95 (*0-937802-03-4*) RMSP.

Lalley, Jacqueline, ed. see Larner, Mary.

Lalli, Anthony F. Tailored Urologic Imaging. (Illus.). 323p. 1980. 63.50 (*0-8151-5276-0*, BKC-1, Yr Bk Med Pubs) Mosby Yr Bk.

Lalli, Carol M. & Gilmer, Ronald W. Pelagic Snails: The Biology of Holoplanktonic Gastropod Mollusks. LC 88-20116. (Illus.). 288p. 1989. 52.50 (*0-8047-1490-8*) Stanford U Pr.

Lalli, Carol M. & Parsons, Timothy R. Biological Oceanography: An Introduction. LC 92-19068. 1993. text ed. 95.00 (*0-08-041013-8*, Pergamon Pr); pap. text ed. 34.50 (*0-08-041014-6*, Pergamon Pr) Elsevier.

Lalli, Carole. Chicken Salads: More Than Fifty Scrumptious Recipes for an American Classic. 128p. (Orig.). 1994. pap. 10.00 (*0-06-095062-5*, PL) HarpC.

Lalli, Cele G. Modern Bride Guide to Etiquette: Answers to the Questions Today's Couples Really Ask. 240p. (Orig.). 1993. pap. text ed. 14.95 (*0-471-58299-9*) Wiley.

Lalli, Cele G. & Dahl, Stephanie H. Modern Bride Wedding Celebrations: The Complete Wedding Planner for Today's Bride. 256p. 1992. pap. text ed. 14.95 (*0-471-56882-1*) Wiley.

***Lalli, Judy.** At I'm Getting Better. 5th ed. (Illus.). 57p. (J). (gr. k-6). 1994. 5.95 (*0-935648-15-1*) Halldin Pub.

— Feelings Alphabet. LC 83-51343. (Creative Teaching Ser.). (Illus.). 74p. (Orig.). (ps-3). 1984. pap. 7.95 (*0-935266-15-1*, BW6615-1) B L Winch.

— Feelings Alphabet: An Album of Emotions from A to Z. (Illus.). 72p. 1991. pap. 7.95 (*0-915190-82-6*, JP-9082-6) Jalmar Pr.

***Lallier, Adalbert.** Sovereignty Association: Economic Realism or Utopia? 87p. 1995. 29.00 (*0-8095-4864-X*) Borgo Pr.

Lallier, Adalbert G. The Economics of Marx's Grundrisse: An Annotated Summary. LC 88-4613. 300p. 1989. text ed. 55.00 (*0-312-02038-4*) St Martin.

***Lallier-Verges, Elisabeth, et al, eds.** Organic Matter Accumulation: The Organic Cyclicities of the Kimmeridge Clay Formation (Yorkshire, GB) & the Recent Maar Sediments (Lac du Bouchet, France) LC 95-12984. (Lecture Notes in Earth Sciences Ser.: Vol. 57). 1995. write for info. (*0-387-59170-2*) Spr-Verlag.

Lalljee, Yousuf N. Know Your Islam. LC 81-51707. 256p. 1981. pap. 7.00 (*0-940368-02-1*, 60) Tahrike Tarsile Quran.

Lally, Dale V., Jr., tr. see Klauprecht, Emil.

Lally, Dick. Boston Red Sox. (J). 1991. pap. 2.99 (*0-517-05790-5*) Random Hse Value.

— The Chicago Cubs. (J). 1991. pap. 2.99 (*0-517-05791-3*) Random Hse Value.

Lally, Frank E. As Lord Acton Says. 1942. 20.00 (*0-686-17394-5*) R S Barnes.

Lally, J. Ronald, ed. Infant - Toddler Caregiving: A Guide to Social-Emotional Growth & Socialization. (Program for Infant - Toddler Caregivers Ser.). (Illus.). 104p. 1990. pap. 12.50 (*0-8011-0876-4*) Calif Education.

— Trainer's Manual, Module One: Social-Emotional Growth & Socialization. (Program for Infant - Toddler Caregivers Ser.). (Illus.). 164p. 1993. pap. 20.00 (*0-8011-1084-X*) Calif Education.

Lally, J. Ronald & Stewart, Jay. Infant - Toddler Caregiving: A Guide to Setting up Environments. (Program for Infant - Toddler Caregivers Ser.). (Illus.). 78p. 1990. pap. 12.50 (*0-8011-0879-9*) Calif Education.

Lally, J. Ronald, jt. auth. see Honig, Alice S.

Lally, J. Ronald, et al, eds. Infant - Toddler Caregiving: A Guide to Language Development & Communication. (Program for Infant - Toddler Caregivers Ser.). (Illus.). 78p. 1991. pap. 12.50 (*0-8011-0880-2*) Calif Education.

Lally, James, jt. auth. see Baldock, Cora V.

***Lally, Kelly A.** The Historic Architecture of Wake County, North Carolina. LC 93-85281. (Illus.). 448p. 1994. 35.00 (*0-9639198-0-6*) Wake County.

Lally, Kevin. Wilder Times: The Life & Times of Billy Wilder. 1996. 30.00 (*0-8050-3119-7*) H Holt & Co.

— Wilder Times: The Life & Times of Billy Wilder. 1996. pap. 14.95 (*0-8050-3120-0*) H Holt & Co.

Lally, Margaret. Juliana's Room. 64p. (Orig.). 1988. pap. 4.95 (*0-933248-10-5*) Bits Pr.

— The Nursery Teacher in Action. 194p. 1991. pap. 27.00 (*1-85396-131-0*, Pub. by P Chapman Pub UK) Taylor & Francis.

Lally, Maureen & Stimpson, Cynthia, eds. Where Shall We Meet? 2nd ed. 54p. pap. 11.95 (*0-685-44384-1*) WOW Pub.

Lally, Michael. Attitude: Uncollected Poems of the Seventies. 1982. pap. 7.50 (*0-914610-31-7*) Hanging Loose.

— Mentally, He's a Sick Man. (Salt Lick Samplers Ser.). reprint ed. pap. 25.00 (*0-7837-9160-7*, 2049860) Bks Demand.

Lally, Steven, jt. auth. see Gehani, Narain.

Lalman, David, jt. auth. see Bueno de Mesquita, Bruce.

Lalo, Eduardo. En el Burger King de la Calle San Francisco. (Illus.). 98p. 1986. pap. 7.00 (*0-317-01397-1*) Ed Astrolabio.

LaLoca. Adventures on the Isle of Adolescence. 128p. (Orig.). 1989. pap. 5.95 (*0-87286-236-4*) City Lights.

L'Aloge, Bob. Ghosts & Mysteries of the Old West: True Accounts of New Mexico & the Old West. rev. ed. LC 91-66180. (Illus.). 120p. 1991. pap. 9.95 (*0-9622940-5-5*) Yucca Tree Pr.

— The Incident of New Mexico's Nightriders: A True Account of the Socorro Vigilantes. LC 92-74693. (Illus.). 208p. (Orig.). 1993. pap. 10.95 (*1-881325-03-2*) Yucca Tree Pr.

— Knights of the Sixgun: A Diary of Gunfighters, Outlaws & Villains in New Mexico. LC 91-65342. (Illus.). 192p. (Orig.). 1991. pap. 9.95 (*0-9622940-3-9*) Yucca Tree Pr.

— Riders along the Rio Grande: A Collection of Outlaws, Prostitutes & Vigilantes. LC 92-60658. (Illus.). 212p. Date not set. pap. 9.95 (*1-881481-00-X*) Yucca Tree Pr.

— Yesterdays...Today! Vol. 1: Authentic Accounts of the Old West. Nelson-L'Aloge, Virginia, ed. (Illus.). 208p. (Orig.). (YA). (gr. 5 up). Date not set. pap. text ed. 25.90 (*0-938147-96-X*) Flying Eagle.

— Yesterdays...Today! Vol. 2: Authentic Accounts of the Past. Nelson-L'Aloge, Virginia, ed. (Illus.). 256p. (Orig.). (YA). (gr. 5 up). Date not set. pap. text ed. 25.90 (*0-614-05251-3*) Flying Eagle.

Lalond, David E. & Ross, John. Principles of Electronic Devices & Circuits: Transparencies. 1994. 69.95 (*0-8273-6421-0*) Delmar.

LaLond, David E. & Ross, John A. Experiments in Electronics Devices & Circuits. 310p. 1994. student ed 26.95 (*0-8273-4664-6*) Delmar.

— Experiments in Principles of Electronic Devices & Circuits. 88p. 1994. teacher ed 20.00 (*0-8273-4665-4*) Delmar.

— Principles of Electronic Controls & Devices: Printed Test Bank. 182p. 1994. 29.95 (*0-8273-6385-0*) Delmar.

— Principles of Electronic Devices & Circuits: Computerized Testmaker & Testbank for DOS Compatible Computers. 1994. 39.95 (*0-8273-6510-1*) Delmar.

LaLond, David L. & Ross, John A. Principles of Electronic Devices & Circuits. LC 92-36004. 1042p. 1994. text ed. 59.95 (*0-8273-4663-8*) Delmar.

LaLonde, Bernard J. Council of Logistics Management Supplement to Bibliography on Logistics & Physical Distribution Management. 1988. 15.00 (*0-318-33304-X*) Coun Logistics Mgt.

Lalonde, Beverly, ed. see Birmingham, Kelly J.

LaLonde, Beverly, ed. see Blackwell, Thomas T.

LaLonde, Cheryl, jt. auth. see Demling, Robert.

Lalonde, Gerald V., et al. Inscriptions. Horoi. Poletai Records, Leases of Public Lands. LC 90-49463. (Athenian Agora Ser.: Vol. 19). (Illus.). xiv, 245p. 1991. 90.00 (*0-87661-219-2*) Am Sch Athens.

Lalonde, Lawrence J. Legends of BAKA. 52p. 1984. pap. write for info. (*0-9608136-0-8*) L J Lalonde.

Lalonde, M., et al, eds. Frankia & Actinorhizal Plants. (Developments in Plant & Social Sciences Ser.). 1985. lib. bdg. 97.50 (*90-247-3214-X*) Kluwer Ac.

***Lalonde, Marc P., ed.** The Promise of Critical Theology: Essays in Honour of Charles Davis. (Editions SR Ser.: Vol. 16). 152p. (C). 1995. pap. 22.50 (*0-88920-254-0*, Pub. by Wilfrid Laurier CN) Humanities.

Lalonde, Patti, jt. auth. see Lalonde, Peter.

Lalonde, Peter. The Mark of the Beast: Your Money, Computers, & the End of the World. 1994. pap. 9.99 (*1-56507-218-9*) Harvest Hse.

— One World under Antichrist. 1991. pap. 8.99 (*0-89081-931-9*) Harvest Hse.

***Lalonde, Peter & Lalonde, Patti.** Left Behind. (Orig.). 1995. pap. 8.99 (*1-56507-364-9*) Harvest Hse.

Lalonde, Wilf R. Discovering Programming with Smalltalk. (C). 1994. pap. text ed. 40.95 (*0-8053-2720-7*) Benjamin-Cummings.

Lalonde, Wilf R. & Pugh, John R. Inside SmallTalk, Vol. II. 576p. 1990. text ed. 62.00 (*0-13-465964-3*) P-H.

— Smalltalk in Action. 1993. pap. text ed. 34.80 (*0-13-814039-1*) P-H.

LaLonde, Wilf R., jt. auth. see Pugh, John R.

LaLonde, William S. Professional Engineers' Examination Question & Answer Book. 1984. text ed. 45.00 (*0-07-036099-5*) McGraw.

LaLong, David. The Eight Thousand Eighty, Eight Thousand Eighty-Five, & Seven Hundred Eighty: Hardware, Software, Programming, Interfacing & Troubleshooting. (Illus.). 416p. 1988. text ed. 54.20 (*0-13-247008-X*) P-H.

Lalor, et al. Mathematics: Back to Basics. (C). 1977. 10.50 (*0-916060-03-9*) Math Alternatives.

Lalor, Brian. Dublin Bay: From Killiney to Howth. LC 89-82063. (Illus.). 160p. 1990. 45.00 (*0-86278-203-1*, Pub. by OBrien Pr IE) Dufour.

— Dublin Drawn & Quartered. (Illus.). 64p. 1991. 10.95 (*0-86278-251-1*, Pub. by OBrien Pr IE) Dufour.

— Ireland. 7th ed. (Blue Guide Ser.). (Illus.). 464p. 1995. pap. 19.95 (*0-393-31343-3*, Norton Paperbks) Norton.

— Ultimate Dublin Guide: An A-Z of Everything. (Illus.). 309p. (Orig.). 1991. pap. 14.95 (*0-86278-220-1*, Pub. by OBrien Pr IE) Dufour.

— West of West. (Illus.). 160p. (Orig.). 1990. pap. 19.95 (*0-86322-109-2*, Pub. by Brandon Bk Pubs IE) Irish Bks Media.

Lalor, Francis R. Leisuregrams. LC 80-83525. 1981. 7.95 (*0-87212-144-5*) Libra.

Lalor, John J., tr. see Nohl, Louis.

Lalou, Elizabeth, ed. see Bautier, Robert-Henri.

Lalou, Rene. Roman Francais Depuis Nineteen Hundred. 127p. 1966. 9.95 (*0-8288-7413-1*) Fr & Eur.

— Theatre en France Depuis Nineteen Hundred. 127p. 1951. 9.95 (*0-8288-7412-3*) Fr & Eur.

Lalouette, Jaques. Agawa Poems. 1986. 5.00 (*0-920806-85-6*, Pub. by Penumbra Pr CN) U of Toronto Pr.

Lalov, I. J. Modern Problems of Surface Physics - Proceedings of the 1st International School on Cmp. 924p. 1982. pap. 67.00 (*0-317-03969-5*) World Scientific Pub.

Laloy. La Musique Chinoise. 1993. pap. 18.50 (*0-910704-75-9*) Hawley.

Laloy, J. R., jt. auth. see Dany, M.

Lalrymple, Douglas J., et al. Cases in Marketing Management. 608p. (C). 1991. Net. text ed. write for info. (*0-471-54746-8*) Wiley.

Lalumia, Joseph. Ettore Majorana & the Atomic Bomb. 80p. 1993. pap. 12.95 (*1-880365-96-0*) Prof Pr NC.

— Ettore Majorana & the Atomic Bomb. 80p. 1993. pap. 12.95 (*1-880365-67-7*) Prof Pr NC.

Lalumia, Matthew P. Realism & Politics in Victorian Art of the Crimean War. LC 83-24284. (Studies in the Fine Arts: Iconography: No. 9). (Illus.). 304p. reprint ed. pap. 86.70 (*0-8357-1499-3*, 2070502) Bks Demand.

Lalumiere, Guy. Macrobiotic Home Food Processing. (Illus.). 96p. (Orig.). 1993. pap. 8.95 (*1-882984-00-5*) One Peaceful World.

Laluzerne & Tsuk. Tell Me about It! 1993. pap. 17.95 (*0-8384-3608-0*) Heinle & Heinle.

— Tell Me about It! 1993. teacher ed, pap. 7.95 (*0-8384-4202-1*) Heinle & Heinle.

— Tell Me about It! 1993. audio 20.00 (*0-8384-3609-9*) Heinle & Heinle.

***Lalvani, Suren.** Photography, Vision, & the Production of Modern Bodies. LC 95-5271. (Interruptions Ser.). (Illus.). 192p. (C). 1995. text ed. 49.50x (*0-7914-2727-7*); pap. 16.95x (*0-7914-2718-8*) State U NY Pr.

***Lalwani, Rajesh.** Power Programming with Gupta SQLWindows. LC 94-33563. 328p. 1994. 29.95 (*0-13-191545-2*) P-H.

— Power Programming with SQL Windows. 1994. disk, pap. 29.95 (*0-13-179306-3*) P-H.

Lam, jt. auth. see Fong.

Lam, Alice C. Women & Japanese Management: Discrimination & Reform. LC 91-48163. 1992. 35.00 (*0-415-06335-3*, A7652) Routledge.

Lam, Alven H. S. & Robinson, Dennis W., eds. Land Systems Technology: Background Papers Prepared for the Lincoln Institute of Land Policy Seminar on Land Systems Technology. (Lincoln Institute of Land Policy Monograph Ser.: No. 86-11). (Illus.). 52p. reprint ed. pap. 25.00 (*0-7837-5755-7*, 2045417) Bks Demand.

Lam, Arthur M., ed. Anesthetic Management of Acute Head Injury. LC 93-49496. 344p. 1995. text ed. 55.00 (*0-07-036127-4*) Hlth Prof Div.

Lam, Arthur M., jt. auth. see Chung, David C.

Lam, Chan F. Techniques for the Analysis & Modelling of Enzyme Kinetic Mechanisms. LC 81-188222. (Medical Computing Ser.: No. 4). (Illus.). 412p. reprint ed. pap. 117.50 (*0-8357-7049-4*, 2033343) Bks Demand.

Lam, Chun H. & Hempel, George H. Microcomputer Applications in Banking. LC 85-32322. 221p. 1986. text ed. 55.00 (*0-89930-117-7*, HMI/, Quorum Bks) Greenwood.

Lam, D. C., et al. Effluent Transport & Diffusion Models for the Coastal Zone. (Lecture Notes on Coastal & Estuarine Studies: Vol. 5). (Illus.). 170p. 1984. pap. 39.00 (*0-387-90928-1*) Spr-Verlag.

Lam, Dominic M. & Bray, Garth M., eds. Regeneration & Plasticity in the Mammalian Visual System, Vol. 4. (Illus.). 276p. 1992. 78.00 (*0-262-12169-7*, Bradford Bks) MIT Pr.

Lam, Dominic M. & Gilbert, Charles D., eds. Neural Mechanisms of Visual Perception: Proceedings Retina. (Research Foundation Symposia Ser.: Vol. 2). (Illus.). 300p. 1991. 70.00 (*0-262-12160-3*) MIT Pr.

— Proceedings of the Retina Research Foundation Symposia, Vol. 1: Cellular & Molecular Biology of the Retina. (Illus.). 200p. 1991. 45.00 (*0-262-62083-9*) MIT Pr.

Lam, Dominic M. & Shatz, Carla J., eds. Development of the Visual System. (Bradford - Proceedings of the Retina Foundation Symposium Ser.: Vol. 3). (Illus.). 256p. 1991. 70.00 (*0-262-12154-9*, Bradford Bks) MIT Pr.

Lam, J., et al, eds. Chemistry & Biology of Naturally Occurring Acetylenes & Related Compounds: Proceedings of a Conference. (Bioactive Molecules Ser.: No. 7). 384p. 1989. 100.00 (*0-444-87115-2*) Elsevier.

Lam, James C. Life of Goodrich. LC 87-82702. 160p. 1987. pap. text ed. 3.20 (*0-685-18343-2*) Evangel Lit.

Lam, Joseph S., jt. ed. see Yung, Bell.

Lam, K. D., et al. Total Quality: A Textbook of Strategic Quality Leadership & Planning. 360p. (C). 1992. pap. 35.00 (*0-9622176-9-7*) Air Acad Pr.

Lam, K. Y., jt. auth. see Tay, A. A.

Lam Kam Chuen. Step-by-Step Tai Chi. LC 94-7581. 1994. 14.00 (*0-671-89247-9*) S&S Trade.

— The Way of Energy: A Gaia Original. (Illus.). 192p. (Orig.). 1991. pap. 14.95 (*0-671-73645-0*, Fireside) S&S Trade.

Lam, Kwon W. & Mancuso, Ted. Northern Sil Lum Form Number Seven: Plum Flower Fist (or Moi Fah) LC 83-50020. (Illus.). 150p. 1984. pap. 8.95 (*0-86568-044-2*, 213) Unique Pubns.

Lam, Lai S. Mao Tse-Tung's Purposive Contention with the Superpowers: The Theory of Ch'i. LC 94-13504. 216p. 1994. text ed. 89.95 (*0-7734-2289-7*) E Mellen.

Lam Lai Sing. The Role of Ch'i in Mao Tse-Tung's Leadership Style. LC 93-29019. 336p. 1993. text ed. 99.95 (*0-7734-2224-2*, Mellen Univ Pr) E Mellen.

Lam, Lui, ed. Nonlinear Physics for Beginners. 250p. (C). 1995. text ed. 55.00 (*981-02-0140-0*); pap. text ed. 21.00 (*981-02-0141-9*) World Scientific Pub.

Lam, Lui & Morris, H. C., eds. Nonlinear Structures in Physical Systems: Pattern Formation, Chaos, & Waves: Proceedings of the Second Woodward Conference, San Jose State University, November 17-18, 1989. (Woodward Conference Ser.). (Illus.). x, 331p. 1990. 59.00 (*0-387-97344-3*) Spr-Verlag.

— Wave Phenomena. (Illus.). xii, 275p. 1988. 65.00 (*0-387-96921-7*) Spr-Verlag.

Lam, Lui & Naroditsky, V., eds. Modeling Complex Phenomena. (Woodward Conference Ser.). (Illus.). 320p. 1992. 65.00 (*0-387-97821-6*) Spr-Verlag.

Lam, Lui, jt. ed. see Shibaev, Valery.

Lam, Lui, et al, eds. Solitons in Liquid Crystals. (Partially Ordered Systems Ser.). (Illus.). 368p. 1991. 76.00 (*0-387-96878-4*) Spr-Verlag.

***Lam, Martin & Shimizu, Kaoru.** Kanji from the Start: A Comprehensive Japanese Reader. Hirowatari, Taro & Hulbert, Paul, eds. 360p. 1995. pap. 25.00 (*0-614-02578-8*) Kodansha.

Lam, Michael, jt. auth. see Markowitz, Morris J.

Lam, Monica S. A Systolic Array Optimizing Compiler. (C). 1988. lib. bdg. 61.00 (*0-89838-300-5*) Kluwer Ac.

Lam, Nina S., ed. see De Cola, Lee.

Lam, Richard B., jt. auth. see Cooper, James W.

Lam, Roger. The Cuckoo Clock Adventure. Gibb, George, ed. LC 82-99848. (Illus.). (Orig.). (J). (gr. 5-12). 1983. pap. 2.25 (*0-943310-01-6*) Six Pr.

L

Lam, S. & Malikin, G., eds. Analytical Applications of Immobilized Enzyme Reactors. (Illus.). 288p. 1993. 99.00 (*0-7514-0026-2*, Pub. by Blackie Acad & Prof UK) Routledge Chapman & Hall.

Lam, Sau-Hai, jt. auth. see Li, Wen-Hsiung.

Lam, Shui F. & Chan, K. Hung. Computer Capacity Planning: Theory & Practice. 214p. 1987. text ed. 54.00 (*0-12-434430-5*) Acad Pr.

Lam, T. Y. The Algebraic Theory of Quadratic Forms. 343p. (C). 1980. pap. text ed. 36.75 (*0-8053-5666-5*, Adv Bk Prog) Addison-Wesley.

— Exercises in Classical Ring Theory. LC 94-19976. (Problem Books in Mathematics Ser.). 1994. 49.00 (*0-387-94317-X*) Spr-Verlag.

— A First Course in Noncommutative Ring. (Graduate Texts in Mathematics Ser.: Vol. 131). xv, 397p. 1991. 49.00 (*0-387-97523-3*) Spr-Verlag.

— Orderings, Valuations & Quadratic Forms. LC 83-11729. (CBMS Regional Conference Series in Mathematics: No. 52). 143p. 1983. pap. 25.00 (*0-8218-0702-1*, CBMS-52) Am Math.

Lam, Tony. How to Beat Stress. 88p. 6.75 (*0-317-31556-0*) Chans Corp.

— Vietnamese Cooking. 1993. 12.98 (*1-55521-907-1*) Bk Sales Inc.

Lam, William K. & Brayton, Robert K. Timed Boolean Functions: A Unified Formalism for Exact Timing Analysis. LC 94-8519. (International Series in Engineering Computer Science, Computer Architecture & Digital Signal Processing Ser.). 296p. (C). 1994. lib. bdg. 95.00 (*0-7923-9454-2*) Kluwer Ac.

***Lam, Willy Wo-Lap.** China after Deng Xiaoping. LC 95-12275. xviii,497p. 1995. write for info. (*0-471-13114-8*) Wiley.

***Lam, Y. L., ed.** Canadian Public Education System: Issues & Prospects. 337p. (Orig.). (C). 1990. pap. text ed. 21.95x (*1-55059-019-7*) Temeron Bks.

***Lama.** Arising from Flames. (Timeless Wisdom Ser.). 1995. 15.95 (*1-882519-01-9*) WisdomKeepers.

***Lama, Dalai.** Disarmament, Peace, & Compassion. 24p. (Orig.). 1995. pap. 3.50 (*1-884519-13-X*) Open Media.

— Freedom in Exile. large type ed. 432p. 1991. 23.95 (*1-85089-531-7*, Pub. by ISIS UK) Transaction Pubs.

— The Meaning of Life: From a Buddhist Perspective. Hopkins, Jeffrey, ed. & tr. by. LC 91-30315. (Illus.). 114p. 1993. pap. 12.50 (*0-86171-096-7*) Wisdom MA.

— The Power of Compassion. 1995. 12.00 (*0-7225-3210-5*) Thorsons SF.

— Stallion on a Frozen Lake: Love Poems of the Sixth Dalai Lama. Barks, Coleman, tr. & intro. by. 72p. (C). 1993. pap. 8.00 (*0-9618916-5-3*) Maypop.

— The Turquoise Bee: The Tantric Lovesongs of the Sixth Dalai Lama, 1683-1706. Fields, Rick & Cutillo, Brian, trs. LC 93-31473. (Illus.). 144p. 1994. 15.00 (*0-06-250310-3*) Harper SF.

— The World of Tibetan Buddhism: An Overview of Its Philosophyy & Practice. Jinpa, Geshe T., ed. & tr. by. LC 94-30512. 224p. (Orig.). 1994. pap. 14.00 (*0-86171-097-5*) Wisdom MA.

Lama, Dalai, et al. Deity Yoga: In Action & Performance Tantras. LC 87-16562. 274p. 1987. reprint ed. pap. 18.95 (*0-937938-50-5*) Snow Lion Pubns.

LAMA Development Committee Staff. Staff Development: A Practical Guide. 2nd ed. Lipow, Anne G. & Carver, Deborah A., eds. LC 91-18962. 104p. (C). 1991. pap. text ed. 25.00 (*0-8389-3402-1*) ALA.

***Lama, Mahendra P., ed.** Sikkim: Society, Polity, Economy, Environment. (C). 1994. text ed. 30.00 (*81-7387-013-6*, Pub. by Indus Pub II) S Asia.

Lama Mi-pham. Golden Zephyr. Kawamura, Leslie S., tr. LC 75-5259. (Tibetan Translation Ser.: Vol. 4). (Illus.). 192p. (Orig.). 1975. pap. 12.95 (*0-913546-21-6*) Dharma Pub.

Lama, R. D. & Vutukuri, V. S. Handbook on Mechanical Properties of Rocks, Vol. III. (Rock & Soil Mechanics Ser.). (Illus.). (C). 1978. 65.00 (*0-87849-022-1*, Pub. by Trans Tech GW) LPS Dist Ctr.

— Handbook on Mechanical Properties of Rocks, Vol. IV. (Rock & Soil Mechanics Ser.). (Illus.). (C). 1978. 65.00 (*0-87849-023-X*, Pub. by Trans Tech GW) LPS Dist Ctr.

Lama Yongden. Mipam: The Lama of the Five Wisdoms: A Tibetan Novel by Lama Yongden. Lloyd, Percy, tr. LC 86-30062. 340p. 1987. 29.50 (*0-88706-531-7*); pap. 9.95 (*0-88706-532-5*) State U NY Pr.

LaMac, Liz. The Story of Dummyland: Little King Joe & the Witch's Maze. (Illus.). 130p. (J). (gr. 4-5). 1990. 9.95 (*0-927278-03-0*) L LaMac Productions.

Lamac, Miroslav. Frantisek Kupka. 86p. 1984. 49.00 (*0-317-61269-7*, Pub. by Collets UK) Pro-Am Music.

— Osma a Skupina Vytvarnych Umelcu 1907-1917, Cesky Kubismus. (Illus.). 544p. (CZE.). 1988. 70.00 (*0-317-03838-9*) Szwede Slavic.

Lamacz, Margaret, jt. auth. see Money, John.

LaMadrid, Enrique & Del Valle, Mario, eds. An Eye Through the Wall: Mexican Poetry-1970-1985. Brandi, John et al, trs. (Poetry Ser.). (Illus.). 220p. (Orig.). (ENG & SPA.). 1985. pap. 10.00 (*0-940510-14-6*) Tooth of Time.

Lamadrid, Enrique E., et al. Communicating in Spanish: A First Course. 2nd ed. LC 83-81321. 768p. 1984. vhs write for info. (*0-395-32715-6*); disk write for info. (*0-318-57690-2*) HM.

— Communicating in Spanish: A First Course, 2 Vols. 2nd ed. LC 83-81321. 768p. (C). 1984. text ed. 49.56 (*0-395-32707-5*); teacher ed, pap. 17.16 (*0-395-32708-3*) HM.

— Communicating in Spanish: A First Course, 2 Vols. 2nd ed. LC 83-81321. 768p. (C). 1984. student ed, pap. 19.56 (*0-395-32709-1*); pap. 4.36 (*0-395-32713-X*) HM.

— Communicating in Spanish: A First Course, 2 Vols., Pt. I. 2nd ed. LC 83-81321. 768p. (C). 1984. audio 22.76 (*0-395-32711-3*) HM.

— Communicating in Spanish: A First Course, 2 Vols., Pt. II. 2nd ed. LC 83-81321. 768p. (C). 1984. audio 22.76 (*0-395-32712-1*) HM.

***Lamadrid, Enrique R.** Tesoros del Espiritu - Treasures of the Spirit: A Portrait in Sound of Hispanic New Mexico. LC 94-20165. 192p. 1995. pap. 24.95 (*0-929820-05-3*) U of NM Pr.

Lamadrid, Enrique R., ed. En Breve: Minimalism in Mexican Poetry 1900-1985. Mares, E. A., tr. 80p. 1988. pap. 6.00 (*0-940510-17-0*) Tooth of Time.

Lamadriz, Rico, et al. Secrets of Cuban Entertaining: A Menu Cookbook. 133p. 5.95 (*0-941072-00-2*) Kennedy & Co.

Lamagna, Joseph. Lamagna Genealogy. (Illus.). 44p. (Orig.). 1992. pap. write for info. (*0-9610464-2-2*) J Lamagna.

— The Wild Game Cookbook for Beginner & Expert. 2nd ed. LC 91-73310. (Illus.). 112p. 1991. pap. 9.95 (*0-9627935-4-X*) Delancey Pr PA.

Lamagna, Joseph & Pisano, Carmen T. Coins-Coins-Coins: The Collector's Guide. 56p. (Orig.). 1988. pap. 8.50 (*0-9610464-1-4*) J Lamagna.

Lamal, P. A., ed. Behavioral Analysis of Societies & Cultural Practices. (Series in Health Psychology & Behavioral Medicine). 325p. 1991. 57.00 (*1-56032-123-7*) Hemisp Pub.

***Laman, Jennifer.** When Health Care Is Not Enough: Support Services for Pregnant Women & Infants. (State Legislative Report Ser.: Vol. 19, No. 8). 9p. 1994. 5.00 (*1-55516-226-6*, 7302-1908) Natl Conf State Legis.

Lamanat of Shah Waliullah of Deli, jt. auth. see Sata'at.

Lamancusa, Jim. Dynamite Crafts for Special Occasions. 1993. pap. text ed. 12.95 (*0-07-036159-2*) McGraw.

— Dynamite Crafts for Special Occasions. (J). (gr. 4-7). 1993. pap. 12.95 (*0-8306-4272-2*) TAB Bks.

Lamancusa, Joe. Kid Cash: Creative Money-Making Ideas. 1993. pap. text ed. 9.95 (*0-07-036158-4*) McGraw.

— Kid Cash: Creative Money-Making Ideas. (J). (gr. 4-7). 1993. pap. 9.95 (*0-8306-4265-X*) TAB Bks.

Lamancusa, Kathy. Bridal Creations. (Illus.). 28p. (Orig.). 1987. pap. 5.95 (*0-933491-18-2*) Hot off Pr.

— The Bride's Bouquet. (Illus.). 28p. (Orig.). 1986. pap. 5.95 (*0-933491-10-7*) Hot off Pr.

— Decorative Painting. 1991. 19.95 (*0-8306-1933-X*); pap. 10.95 (*0-8306-1931-3*) TAB Bks.

— Floral Fundamentals, Vol. 1. (Illus.). 28p. (Orig.). 1985. pap. 5.95 (*0-933491-08-5*) Hot off Pr.

— Floral Fundamentals, Vol. 2. (Illus.). 28p. (Orig.). 1986. pap. 5.95 (*0-933491-09-3*) Hot off Pr.

— Floral Fundamentals, Vol. 3. (Illus.). 28p. (Orig.). 1987. pap. 5.95 (*0-933491-17-4*) Hot off Pr.

— For Your Wedding Day. (Illus.). 28p. (Orig.). 1988. pap. text ed. 5.95 (*0-685-22198-9*) Hot off Pr.

— Great Ideas for Gift Baskets, Bags, & Boxes. 1993. text ed. write for info. (*0-07-027795-8*) McGraw.

— Great Ideas for Gift Baskets, Bags, & Boxes. (Illus.). 144p. 1992. pap. 12.95 (*0-8306-4035-5*, 3899) TAB Bks.

— Great Ideas for Gift Baskets, Bags & Boxes. 1992. pap. 12.95 (*0-07-157848-X*) McGraw.

— Kathy Lamancusa's Guide to Decorative Painting. 1991. text ed. 19.95 (*0-07-157598-7*); pap. text ed. 10.95 (*0-685-72251-1*) McGraw.

— Kathy Lamancusa's Guide to Floral Design. (Creative Home Design Ser.). (Illus.). 128p. 1990. 21.95 (*0-8306-7491-8*, 3491); pap. 12.95 (*0-8306-3491-6*) TAB Bks.

— Kathy Lamancusa's Guide to Wearable Art. 1992. pap. 10.95 (*0-07-157850-1*) McGraw.

— Kathy Lamancusa's Guide to Wreath Making. (Creative Home Design Ser.). (Illus.). 128p. 1991. 19.95 (*0-8306-6492-0*, 3492); pap. 10.95 (*0-8306-3492-4*) TAB Bks.

— Wearable Art. (Creative Home Design Ser.). 128p. 1992. 19.95 (*0-8306-4027-4*, 3900); pap. 10.95 (*0-8306-4026-6*, 3900) TAB Bks.

LaManna, Manfred, jt. ed. see Norman, George.

Lamanna, Mary A. & Riedmann, Agnes. Marriages & Families: Making Choices & Facing Change. 4th ed. 711p. (C). 1991. text ed. 48.95 (*0-534-12720-7*) Intl Thomson.

— Marriages & Families: Making Choices & Facing Change. 5th ed. 709p. (C). 1994. text ed. 48.95 (*0-534-18738-2*) Intl Thomson.

Lamantia, Philip. Meadowlark West. 104p. (Orig.). 1986. pap. 4.95 (*0-87286-176-7*) City Lights.

— Touch of the Marvelous. 1966. pap. 1.95 (*0-685-04678-8*) Oyez.

Lamar. Papers of Mirabeau Buonaparte, 6 vols., Set. 1993. reprint ed. lib. bdg. 450.00 (*0-7812-5941-X*) Rprt Serv.

Lamar, ed. see Bagley, Constance E. & Haubegger, Christi A.

Lamar, Celita. Our Voices, Ourselves: Women Writing for the French Theatre. LC 90-21539. (Currents in Romance Languages & Literature Ser.: Vol. 5). 213p. (C). 1991. text ed. 37.00 (*0-8204-1499-9*) P Lang Pubs.

Lamar, Christine. A Guide to Genealogical Materials at the Rhode Island Historical Society Library. rev. ed. 30p. (Orig.). 1985. pap. 2.50 (*0-917012-78-X*) RI Pubns Soc.

Lamar, Curt, ed. History of Rosedale, Mississippi, 1876-1976. LC 76-25443. 1976. 15.00 (*0-87152-246-2*) Reprint.

LaMar, D. F. Transcending Turmoil: Survivors of Dysfunctional Families. (Illus.). 320p. 1992. 27.95 (*0-306-44127-6*, Plenum Insight) Plenum.

Lamar, H., ed. A Reader's Encyclopedia of the American West. 2nd ed. Date not set. 50.00 (*0-06-270048-0*, Harper Ref) HarpC.

Lamar, H. Arthur. I Saw Stars: Memories of Adm. Nimitz's Flag Lt. 1975. pap. 2.00 (*0-934841-03-9*) Adm Nimitz Foun.

Lamar, Howard & Thompson, Leonard, eds. The Frontier in History: North America & Southern Africa Compared. (Illus.). 336p. (C). 1981. pap. 18.00 (*0-300-02742-7*, Y-406) Yale U Pr.

Lamar, Howard R. The Trader on the American Frontier: Myth's Victim. LC 76-51650. (Essays on the American West, Sponsored by Elma Dill Russell Spencer Foundation Ser.: No.2). (Illus.). 56p. 1977. 9.95 (*0-89096-033-X*) Tex A&M Univ Pr.

Lamar, Howard R., ed. see Perlot, Jean N.

Lamar, Jake. Bourgeois Blues: An American Memoir. LC 92-53557. 176p. 1992. pap. 9.00 (*0-452-26911-3*, Plume) NAL-Dutton.

Lamar, Laura. Desktop Design. Gerould, Phil, ed. LC 89-81517. 1990. pap. 9.95 (*1-56052-001-9*) Crisp Pubns.

Lamar, Mirabeau B. Papers, 6 Vols., Set. Gulick, C. A. et al, eds. LC 76-171643. reprint ed. 560.00 (*0-404-03820-4*) AMS Pr.

Lamar, N. How to Speak the Written Word. 1987. 13.95 (*0-933062-25-7*) R H Sommer.

LaMar, Nat R., ed. see Read, Joan R.

Lamar, Rene, ed. see Butler, Samuel.

LaMar, Steve. The Book of Baseball Lists. LC 92-51044. 508p. 1993. lib. bdg. 39.95 (*0-89950-661-5*) McFarland & Co.

LaMar, Virginia, ed. see Shakespeare, William.

LaMar, Virginia A. Travel & Roads in England. LC 61-1916. (Folger Guides to the Age of Shakespeare Ser.). 1961. 4.95 (*0-918016-23-1*) Folger Bks.

Lamar, William W., jt. auth. see Campbell, Jonathan.

LaMarca, George A. Iowa Pleading & Causes of Action, 1989-1993, 2 vols. suppl. ed. 700p. 1993. 60.00 (*0-250-40797-3*) Butterworth Legal Pubs.

— Iowa Pleading & Causes of Action, 1989-1993, 2 vols., Set. 700p. 1994. ring bd. 160.00 (*0-86678-784-4*) Michie Butterworth.

***Lamarche, Gara, ed.** Speech & Equality: Do We Really Have to Choose? 150p. 1995. 40.00 (*0-8147-5091-5*); pap. 16.50 (*0-8147-5105-9*) NYU Pr.

LaMarche, Robert J., jt. auth. see Connors, Jimmy.

Lamarck, J. B. Memoirs sur les Fossiles des Environs de Paris. 380p. 1980. 12.50 (*0-87710-374-7*) Paleo Res.

— Philosophie Zoologique, 2 vols. in 1. 1960. reprint ed. 75.00 (*3-7682-0028-0*) Lubrecht & Cramer.

Lamarck, Jean B. Zoological Philosophy: An Exposition with Regard to the Natural History of Animals. Elliot, Hugh, tr. LC 82-45842. reprint ed. 57.50 (*0-404-19353-6*) AMS Pr.

Lamare, James W. California Politics: Economics, Power, & Policy. Perlee, ed. LC 93-25933. 250p. (C). 1993. pap. text ed. 27.75 (*0-314-02677-0*) West Pub.

— Texas Politics: Economics, Power & Policy. 4th ed. Perlee, Clyde, ed. 294p. (C). 1991. pap. text ed. 31.50 (*0-314-81933-9*) West Pub.

— Texas Politics: Economics, Power, & Policy. 5th ed. Perlee, ed. LC 94-4546. 250p. (C). 1994. pap. text ed. 35.00 (*0-314-02849-8*) West Pub.

— What Rules America? 203p. (C). 1988. pap. text ed. 28.75 (*0-314-64228-5*) West Pub.

Lamare, James W., ed. International Crisis & Domestic Politics: Major Political Conflicts in the 1980s. LC 90-7803. 200p. 1991. text ed. 49.95 (*0-275-93304-0*, C3304, Praeger Pubs) Greenwood.

Lamarechal, C., jt. auth. see Balinski, M. L.

Lamarque, C. H., jt. ed. see Jezequel, L.

Lamarque, Martin, tr. see Werner, David.

Lamarque, Peter & Olsen, Stein H. Truth, Fiction, & Literature: A Philosophical Perspective. (Clarendon Library of Logic & Philosophy). 440p. 1994. 60.00 (*0-19-824082-1*) OUP.

LaMarre, ed. see Barrow, Georgia M. & Shuttlesworth, Guy.

LaMarre, ed. see Chalfant, H. Paul & LaBeff, Emily E.

Lamarre, ed. see Crew, Robert E.

LaMarre, ed. see Fogel, Alan.

LaMarre, ed. see Hatch, Kathryn L.

LaMarre, ed. see Heffernan, Joseph, et al.

LaMarre, ed. see Hessler, Richard.

LaMarre, ed. see Holman, John & Quinn, James.

LaMarre, ed. see Jackson, Richard H. & Hudman, Lloyd E.

LaMarre, ed. see Norris, Robert E.

LaMarre, ed. see Stone, William.

Lamarre, Paul. E.I.D.I.A. Catalogue Everything I Do Is Art: My Life Is Not My Own. (Illus.). 40p. (C). 1989. pap. 12.00 (*0-9619021-2-4*) Eidia Bks.

Lamarre, Paul & Wolf, Melissa. Starving Artists' Cookbook. (Illus.). 272p. 1991. pap. 13.50 (*0-9619021-0-8*) Eidia Bks.

— The Starving Artists' Cookbook: Food, Sex, Art. (Illus.). 162p. (Orig.). (C). 1991. pap. 60.00 (*0-9619021-1-6*, TXU 290827) Eidia Bks.

***LaMarsh, Jeannenne.** Changing the Way We Change: Gaining Control of Major Manufacturing Operational Change. (Engineering Process Improvement). 224p. 1995. 26.95 (*0-201-63364-7*) Addison-Wesley.

Lamarsh, John R. Introduction to Nuclear Engineering. 2nd ed. LC 82-8678. (Nuclear Science & Engineering Ser.). (Illus.). 652p. (C). 1983. text ed. 65.75 (*0-201-14200-7*) Addison-Wesley.

— Introduction to Nuclear Reactor Theory. 1966. write for info. (*0-201-04120-0*) Addison-Wesley.

Lamartine, Alphonse. Oeuvres Poetiques Completes. deluxe ed. Guyard, ed. (Pleiade Ser.). (FRE.). 1963. 93.95 (*2-07-010298-X*) Schoenhof.

Lamartine, Alphonse D. Le Livre du Centenaire. 380p. (FRE.). 1971. pap. 49.95 (*0-686-54277-0*, 2082103161) Fr & Eur.

— Le Manuscrit de Ma Mere. 200p. 65.00 (*0-686-54278-9*) Fr & Eur.

— Sur la Politique Rationnelle. 164p. 1978. reprint ed. 49.95 (*0-7859-5361-2*) Fr & Eur.

Lamartine, Alphonse de. Graziella. (Folio Ser.: No. 1085). (FRE.). 8.95 (*2-07-037085-2*) Schoenhof.

— A Pilgrimage to the Holy Land. LC 78-14368. 1978. reprint ed. 75.00 (*0-8201-1323-9*) Schol Facsimiles.

Lamartine, Alphonse M. Histoire des Girondins, 8 Vols, Set. 3rd ed. LC 70-171644. reprint ed. 280.00 (*0-404-07330-1*) AMS Pr.

— History of the French Revolution of 1848, 2 Vols in 1. LC 73-171645. reprint ed. 62.50 (*0-404-07138-4*) AMS Pr.

Lamas, G., et al. Bibliography of Butterflies, Vol. 124. (Atlas of Neotropical Lepidoptera Ser.). 1995. 42.95 (*0-945417-31-4*) Sci Pubs.

Lamaute, Denise. Tax-Cutting Tactics for Investors: Legal Loopholes for the 1990s. 1990. pap. text ed. 14.95 (*0-07-155955-8*) McGraw.

— Tax-Cutting Tactics for Investors: Legal Loopholes for the 1990s. 220p. 1989. 22.95 (*0-8306-4048-7*, Liberty Hse); pap. 14.95 (*0-8306-3048-1*, Liberty Hse) TAB Bks.

Lamaute, Denise, jt. auth. see Hunnisett, Henry.

Lamay, Craig, jt. auth. see Minow, Newton.

LaMay, Craig L. & Dennis, Everette E., eds. Media & the Environment. LC 91-23442. 266p. (Orig.). 1991. 35.00 (*1-55963-131-7*); pap. 17.95 (*1-55963-130-9*) Island Pr.

LaMay, Craig L., jt. ed. see Dennis, Everette E.

Lamaze. Journal Perinatal Education, 1993, No. 2. 72p. (C). 1993. pap. text ed. write for info. (*0-318-72517-7*) Jones & Bartlett.

— Journal Perinatal Education 1993, No. 3. (C). 1993. pap. text ed. write for info. (*0-318-72518-5*) Jones & Bartlett.

— Journal Perinatal Education 1993, No. 4. (C). 1993. pap. text ed. write for info. (*0-318-72519-3*) Jones & Bartlett.

Lamaze Childbirth Preparation Associaton of Ann Arbor, Inc. Staff. Journey into Life. Schumann, Mary J., ed. LC 83-13010. (Illus.). 240p. (Orig.). 1983. pap. 10.95 (*0-931114-22-5*) High-Scope.

***Lamb.** Breaking Away. Date not set. write for info. (*0-8129-2579-3*, Times Bks) Random.

— Colorful Cacti of American Desert. 11.95 (*0-02-567670-9*) Macmillan.

— Maiden of Inverness. Tolley, Carolyn, ed. 368p. (Orig.). 1995. mass mkt. 5.99 (*0-671-88220-1*) PB.

— MicroFocus Workbench & Toolset Developer's Guide. 1995. pap. text ed. 40.00 (*0-07-036122-3*) McGraw.

— SAPT: Diagnostic Radiology of the Dog & Cat. 144p. 1993. pap. 26.50 (*0-8151-5323-6*, Yr Bk Med Pubs) Mosby Yr Bk.

— She's Come Undone. 1994. 3.99 (*0-517-13633-3*) Random Hse Value.

Lamb & Kenaga, eds. Avian & Mammalian Wildlife Toxicology: Second Conference - STP 757. 170p. 1981. pap. 18.50 (*0-8031-0759-5*, 04-757000-48) ASTM.

Lamb, jt. auth. see Bornstein.

Lamb, et al. Principles of Marketing. 2nd ed. (C). 1994. text ed. 58.95 (*0-538-82982-6*, SB61BA) S-W Pub.

Lamb, et al, eds. Hand Management. 112p. 1989. 9.00 (*0-912452-72-2*, P-69) Am Phys Therapy Assn.

Lamb, A. F. Pinus Caribaea, Vol. 1. 1978. 50.00 (*0-85074-015-0*) St Mut.

Lamb, Albert, ed. see Neill, A. S.

Lamb, Andrew. Jerome Kern in Edwardian London. LC 85-80274. (I.S.A.M. Monographs: No. 22). (Illus.). 96p. 1985. pap. 10.00 (*0-914678-24-8*) Inst Am Music.

— U-Musik und Osterreich: Max Schonherr in Seinen Schriften und Erinnerungen - Light Music from Austria: Writings & Reminiscences of Max Schonherr. LC 91-29172. (Austrian Culture Ser.: Vol. 6). 262p. (ENG & GER.). (C). 1992. text ed. 62.95 (*0-8204-1671-1*) P Lang Pubs.

Lamb, Andrew, jt. auth. see Ganzl, Kurt.

Lamb, Annette. Emerging Technologies & Instruction: Hypertext, Hypermedia, & Interactive Multimedia. Milheim, William D., ed. LC 91-4704. (Educational Technology Selected Bibliography Ser.: Vol. 4). 64p. 1991. 19.95 (*0-87778-234-2*) Educ Tech Pubns.

— IBM LinkWay Authoring Tool for Presentations, Tutorials, & Information Exploration. Saari, Joani, ed. 800p. 1993. pap. text ed. 49.95 (*0-89262-353-5*); 50.00 (*0-89262-356-X*) Career Pub.

— IBM LinkWay Creativity Tool. Saari, Joani, ed. 700p. 1992. pap. text ed. 39.95 (*0-89262-368-3*); 50.00 (*0-89262-328-4*) Career Pub.

— Powerful Presentations: Using Your Macintosh for the Classroom of the Future. Schach, Mickey, ed. 480p. 1991. 39.95 (*0-89262-393-4*); student ed 50.00 (*0-89262-401-9*) Career Pub.

— Powerful Presentations Using Your IBM & Express Publisher. Saari, Joani, ed. 480p. 1993. 39.95 (*0-89262-394-2*); student ed 50.00 (*0-89262-406-X*) Career Pub.

***Lamb, Annette & Johnson, Larry.** Strap on Your Spurs: Technology & Change Cowboy Style. (Illus.). 173p. (C). 1994. pap. text ed. 19.95 (*0-9641581-0-8*) Vision to Action.

Lamb, Annette & Myers, Dennis. Hypercard (Mac) Creativity Tool. Schach, Mickey, ed. 704p. 1991. 39.95 (*0-89262-326-8*); 50.00 (*0-685-67733-8*); write for info. (*0-318-68799-2*) Career Pub.

Lamb, Annette, jt. auth. see Myers, Dennis.

Lamb, Arnette. The Betrothal. Tolley, Carolyn, ed. 384p. (Orig.). 1992. mass mkt. 5.50 (*0-671-73002-9*, Pocket Star Bks) PB.

— The Betrothal. large type ed. LC 92-27928. 521p. (Orig.). 1992. reprint ed. lib. bdg. 17.95 (*1-56054-546-1*) Thorndike Pr.

— Border Bride. Tolley, Carolyn, ed. 320p. (Orig.). 1993. mass mkt. 5.99 (*0-671-77933-8*) PB.

An Asterisk (*) at the beginning of an entry indicates that the title is appearing in BIP for the first time.

— Border Lord. Tolley, Carolyn, ed. 336p. (Orig.). 1993. mass mkt. 5.99 (*0-671-77932-X*) PB.
— Chieftain. 1994. mass mkt. 5.50 (*0-671-77937-0*) PB.
— Chieftain. large type ed. LC 95-2474. 419p. 1995. 18.95 (*0-7838-1279-5*) Hall.
Lamb, Arthur W. Take Back Your Life: How to Regain Your Personal Freedom. 168p. 1992. pap. 12.95 (*0-9631757-6-9*) Pin Oak Pr.
Lamb, Beth & Logsdon, Phyllis. Positively Kindergarten: A Classroom-Proven, Theme-Based, Developmental Guide for the Kindergarten Teacher. 141p. (Orig.). 1991. pap. 14.95 (*0-935493-48-4*) Modern Learn Pr.
Lamb, Bob. Overcoming Blood. 224p. 1993. pap. 4.99 (*0-88368-270-2*) Whitaker Hse.
Lamb, Caroline. Glenarvon. LC 93-17429. 264p. 1993. reprint ed. 80.00 (*1-85477-132-9*, Pub. by Woodstock Bks UK) Cassell.
Lamb, Caroline P. Glenarvon, 3 vols. in 1. LC 71-161933. 1972. reprint ed. 50.00 (*0-8201-1093-0*) Schol Facsimiles.
— Glenarvon, 3 vols., Set. 3rd ed. LC 70-37709. reprint ed. 97.50 (*0-404-56767-3*) AMS Pr.
Lamb, Cecile, jt. auth. see Stagg, Mildred A.
Lamb, Charles. Charles Lamb: Prose & Poetry. LC 77-28850. 216p. 1978. reprint ed. text ed. 35.00 (*0-313-20274-5*, LAPP0, Greenwood Pr) Greenwood.
— Elia. LC 91-31468. 358p. 1991. reprint ed. 55.00 (*1-85477-074-8*, Pub. by Woodstock Bks UK) Cassell.
— Illustrated Tales from Shakespeare. 1994. 9.98 (*0-681-45333-8*) Longmeadow Pr.
— Lamb & Hazlitt. LC 76-168954. reprint ed. 30.00 (*0-404-07359-X*) AMS Pr.
— Lamb's Criticism: A Selection from the Literary Criticism of Charles Lamb. (BCL1-PR English Literature Ser.). 1992. reprint ed. lib. bdg. 69.00 (*0-7812-7015-4*) Rprt Serv.
— Life, Letters & Writings of Charles Lamb, 6 vols, Set. Fitzgerald, Percy H., ed. LC 77-148887. (Select Bibliographies Reprint Ser.). 1977. reprint ed. 192.95 (*0-8369-5654-0*) Ayer.
— Rosamund Gray. LC 91-16915. 146p. 1991. reprint ed. 43.00 (*1-85477-075-6*, Pub. by Woodstock Bks UK) Cassell.
— Selected Essays. Nabholtz, John R., ed. (Crofts Classics Ser.). 192p. 1967. pap. text ed. write for info. (*0-88295-052-5*) Harlan Davidson.
— The Works of Charles & Mary Lamb, 7 vols., Set. (BCL1-PR English Literature Ser.). 1992. reprint ed. lib. bdg. 630.00 (*0-7812-7584-9*) Rprt Serv.
Lamb, Charles & Lamb, Mary. Lamb's Poetry for Children. LC 78-108585. (Granger Index Reprint Ser.). 1977. 19.95 (*0-8369-6113-7*) Ayer.
— Letters of Charles & Mary Lamb, 3 Vols. Lucas, E. V., ed. LC 68-59268. reprint ed. write for info. (*0-404-03840-9*) AMS Pr.
— Tales from Shakespeare. (Illus.). 318p. 1993. pap. 6.95 (*0-460-87283-4*, Everyman's Classic Lib) C E Tuttle.
— Tales from Shakespeare. LC 79-89991. (Illus.). 1988. 40.00 (*0-918016-04-5*) Folger Bks.
— Tales from Shakespeare. 336p. 1986. pap. 5.95 (*0-451-52391-1*, Sig Classics) NAL-Dutton.
— Tales from Shakespeare. (J). (gr. 5 up). 1988. pap. 3.99 (*0-14-035088-8*, Puffin) Puffin Bks.
— Tales from Shakespeare. (Puffin Classics Ser.). 352p. (J). 1995. pap. 3.99 (*0-14-036677-6*) Puffin Bks.
— Tales from Shakespeare. (J). (gr. k-6). 1986. 8.98 (*0-685-16860-3*, 621568) Random Hse Value.
— Tales from Shakespeare. (Children's Classics Ser.). 1988. 12.99 (*0-517-62156-8*) Random Hse Value.
— Tales from Shakespeare. rev. ed. Briggs, Julia, ed. 318p. 1995. pap. 6.95 (*0-460-87538-8*, Everyman's Classic Lib) C E Tuttle.
— Tales from Shakespeare. 1993. reprint ed. lib. bdg. 24.95 (*1-56849-117-4*) Buccaneer Bks.
— Works of Charles & Mary Lamb, Set. Lucas, E. V., ed. LC 68-59332. (Illus.). reprint ed. write for info. (*0-404-03830-1*) AMS Pr.
— The Works of Charles & Mary Lamb, 7 vols., Set. Lucas, E. V., ed. LC 70-115252. 1905. reprint ed. 450.00 (*0-403-00366-0*) Scholarly.
Lamb, Charles & Lamb, Mary A. The Letters of Charles & Mary Anne Lamb, 3 vols. Marrs, Edwin W., Jr., ed. (Illus.). write for info. (*0-318-51448-6*) Cornell U Pr.
— The Letters of Charles & Mary Anne Lamb, Vol. I: 1796-1801. Marrs, Edwin W., Jr., ed. (Illus.). 352p. 1975. Vol. I, 1796-1801, 352 p., 1975. 57.50x (*0-8014-0930-6*) Cornell U Pr.
— The Letters of Charles & Mary Anne Lamb, Vol. II: 1801-1809. Marrs, Edwin W., Jr., ed. (Illus.). 336p. 1976. Vol. II, 1801-1809, 336 p., 1976. 57.50x (*0-8014-0977-2*) Cornell U Pr.
— The Letters of Charles & Mary Anne Lamb, Vol. III: 1809-1817. Marrs, Edwin W., Jr., ed. (Illus.). 320p. 1978. Vol. III, 1809-1817, 320 p., 1978. 57.50x (*0-8014-1129-7*) Cornell U Pr.
Lamb, Charles, jt. auth. see Lamb, Mary.
Lamb, Charles, et al. Principles of Marketing. (C). 1992. text ed. 60.95 (*0-538-81368-7*, SB61AA) S-W Pub.
Lamb, Charles M. & Halpern, Stephen C., eds. The Burger Court: Political & Judicial Profiles. (Illus.). 528p. 1991. 49.95 (*0-252-01733-1*); pap. 19.95 (*0-252-06135-7*) U of Ill Pr.
Lamb, Charles M., jt. ed. see Goldman, Sheldon.
Lamb, Charles R., jt. auth. see Coleman, Patrick K.
Lamb, Charles W., Jr., jt. auth. see Cravens, David W.
Lamb, Charles W., jt. auth. see Crompton, John L.
***Lamb, Charles W., Jr., et al.** Marketing. 3rd ed. LC 95-2874. 1996. pap. 57.95 (*0-538-84948-7*) S-W Pub.
Lamb, Charlotte. Besieged. (Presents Ser.). 1992. pap. 2.89 (*0-373-11498-2*, 1-11498-2) Harlequin Bks.
— Dark Fate. large type ed. (Harlequin Romance Ser.). 1995. 18.95 (*0-263-14075-X*, Pub. by Mills & Boon UK) Thorndike Pr.
— Dark Music. (Presents Ser.: No. 1410). 1991. pap. 2.79 (*0-373-11410-9*) Harlequin Bks.
— Dark Pursuit. (Presents Ser.: No. 1370). 1991. pap. 2.75 (*0-373-11370-6*) Harlequin Bks.
— Dreaming. (Presents Ser.). 1994. mass mkt. 2.99 (*0-373-11618-7*, 1-11618-5) Harlequin Bks.
— Dreaming. large type ed. 1994. 17.95 (*0-263-13588-8*, Pub. by Mills & Boon Ltd UK) Chivers N Amer.
— Dying for You. (Presents Ser.). 1995. mass mkt. 3.25 (*0-373-11743-4*, 1-11743-1) Harlequin Bks.
— Falling in Love. large type ed. (Harlequin Ser.). 1994. 18.95 (*0-263-13767-8*) Thorndike Pr.
— Falling in Love: (Presents Plus) (Presents Ser.). 1994. mass mkt. 2.99 (*0-373-11672-1*, 1-11672-2) Harlequin Bks.
— Fire in the Blood. 1994. mass mkt. 2.99 (*0-373-11658-6*, 1-11658-1) Harlequin Bks.
— Fire in the Blood. large type ed. (Harlequin Ser.). 1994. 18.95 (*0-263-13659-0*) Thorndike Pr.
— Forbidden Fruit. large type ed. 1992. reprint ed. lib. bdg. 18.95 (*0-263-13037-1*, Pub. by Mills & Boon UK) Thorndike Pr.
— Forbidden Fruit: Presents Plus. (Presents Ser.). 1993. mass mkt. 2.99 (*0-373-11584-9*, 1-11584-9) Harlequin Bks.
— Guilty Love. (Presents Ser.). 1994. mass mkt. 2.99 (*0-373-11706-X*, 1-11706-8) Harlequin Bks.
— Guilty Love. large type ed. (Harlequin Romance Ser.). 1994. 18.95 (*0-263-13874-7*) Thorndike Pr.
— Heart on Fire. large type ed. 285p. 1991. reprint ed. lib. bdg. 18.95 (*0-263-12693-5*) Thorndike Pr.
— Rites of Possession. (Presents Ser.: No. 1345). 1991. pap. 2.75 (*0-373-11345-5*) Harlequin Bks.
— Rites of Possession. large type ed. 1990. reprint ed. lib. bdg. 18.95 (*0-263-12270-0*, Pub. by Mills & Boon UK) Thorndike Pr.
— Runaway Wife. large type ed. 1990. reprint ed. lib. bdg. 18.95 (*0-263-12078-3*, Pub. by Mills & Boon UK) Thorndike Pr.
— Sensation. large type ed. (Nightingale Ser.). 231p. 1990. pap. 12.95 (*0-8161-4959-3*) G K Hall.
— Shotgun Wedding. large type ed. 285p. 1991. reprint ed. lib. bdg. 18.95 (*0-263-12805-9*) Thorndike Pr.
— Sleeping Partners. (Presents Ser.). 1993. mass mkt. 2.99 (*0-373-11560-1*, 1-11560-9) Harlequin Bks.
— Sleeping Partners. large type ed. 285p. 1992. reprint ed. lib. bdg. 18.95 (*0-263-12838-5*) Thorndike Pr.
— Spellbinding. (Presents Ser.: No. 1393). 1991. pap. 2.79 (*0-373-11393-5*) Harlequin Bks.
— Spellbinding. 1994. 15.95 (*0-263-12418-5*, Pub. by Mills & Boon UK) Thorndike Pr.
— Surrender. (Presents Ser.). 1993. pap. 2.89 (*0-373-11540-7*, 1-11540-1) Harlequin Bks.
— A Sweet Addiction. (Presents Ser.). 1993. pap. 2.89 (*0-373-11530-X*, 1-11530-2) Harlequin Bks.
— Un Tendre Secret. (FRE.). 1994. pap. 3.50 (*0-373-34438-4*, 1-34438-1) Harlequin Bks.
— The Threat of Love. large type ed. 1991. reprint ed. lib. bdg. 18.95 (*0-263-12623-4*) Thorndike Pr.
— Vampire Lover: (Presents Plus) (Presents Ser.). 1995. pap. 3.25 (*0-373-11720-5*, 1-11720-9) Harlequin Bks.
— Wounds of Passion. 1994. mass mkt. 2.99 (*0-373-11687-X*, 1-11687-0) Harlequin Bks.
— Wounds of Passion. large type ed. (Harlequin Ser.). 1994. 18.95 (*0-263-13777-5*) Thorndike Pr.
***Lamb, Charlotte & Clair, Daphne.** Body & Soul. (Presents Ser.). 1995. mass mkt. 3.25 (*0-373-11733-7*, 1-11733-2) Harlequin Bks.
Lamb, Christopher J. Belief Systems & Decision Making in the Mayaguez Crisis. LC 88-12039. 328p. 1989. text ed. 29.95 (*0-8130-0900-6*) U Press Fla.
— How to Think about Arms Control, Disarmament & Defense. (Illus.). 400p. (C). 1988. pap. text ed. write for info. (*0-13-435462-1*) P-H.
Lamb, Clarice, jt. auth. see Nunan, David.
Lamb County History Book Comm. Staff, jt. auth. see Ogletree, Madema.
Lamb, D. Exploiting the Tropical Rain Forest. (Man & the Biosphere Ser.). 250p. 1990. 67.00 (*92-3-102646-1*, U6461) UNIPUB.
Lamb, D., et al. The Practice of Hand Surgery. 2nd ed. 1989. 235.00 (*0-632-01805-4*) Blackwell Sci.
Lamb, D. J. Appearance & Aesthetics in Dental Practice. (Dental Practitioners' Handbook Ser.: No. 37). (Illus.). 128p. 1988. pap. 24.95 (*0-7236-0753-2*, Pub. by John Wright UK) Buttrwrth-Heinemann.
— Problems & Solutions in Complete Denture Fabrication. (Illus.). 168p. 1993. text ed. 48.00 (*1-85097-021-1*) Quint Pub Co.
Lamb, Dana & Lamb, Ginger. Quest for the Lost City. LC 84-50124. (Illus.). 352p. (Orig.). 1984. reprint ed. pap. 10.95 (*0-915643-00-6*) Santa Barb Pr.
Lamb, Daniel S., ed. Howard University Medical Department, Washington, D. C. LC 78-37309. (Black Heritage Library Collection). 1977. reprint ed. 44.95 (*0-8369-8946-5*) Ayer.
Lamb, David. The Africans. LC 81-48271. (Illus.). 384p. 1983. 17.95 (*0-394-51887-X*) Random.
— The Africans. 1987. pap. 12.00 (*0-394-75308-9*, Vin) Random.
— The Arabs: Journeys Beyond the Mirage. LC 86-10136. (Illus.). 320p. 1987. 19.95 (*0-394-54433-1*) Random.
— The Arabs: Journeys Beyond the Mirage. LC 87-45914. 320p. 1988. pap. 13.00 (*0-394-75758-0*, Pub. by Avebury Pub UK) Random.
— Discovery, Creativity & Problem-Solving. 168p. 1991. text ed. 49.95 (*1-85628-043-8*, Pub. by Avebury Pub UK) Ashgate Pub Co.
— Do Platanos Go Wit' Collard Greens? LC 94-96061. 140p. (Orig.). 1994. pap. 8.95 (*0-9640692-1-0*) I Write.
— Down the Slippery Slope: Arguing in Applied Ethics. 112p. (C). 1988. text ed. 45.50 (*0-7099-4166-8*) Routledge Chapman & Hall.
— Hegel: From Foundation to System. (Philosophy Library.: No. 1). 252p. 1980. lib. bdg. 70.00 (*90-247-2359-0*) Kluwer Ac.
— Organ Transplants & Ethics. 176p. 1990. 59.95 (*0-415-03716-6*, A4686) Routledge.
— A Sense of Place. 1993. 22.00 (*0-8129-2159-3*, Times Bks) Random.
— A Sense of Place: Listening to Americans. large type ed. LC 93-24125. 1993. 21.95 (*0-7862-0005-7*) Thorndike Pr.
— Stolen Season: A Journey Through America & Baseball's Minor Leagues. 1991. 19.50 (*0-394-57608-X*) Random.
— Stolen Season: A Journey Through America & Baseball's Minor Leagues. 1992. reprint ed. pap. 9.99 (*0-446-39415-7*) Warner Bks.
Lamb, David, ed. Hegel & Modern Philosophy. 272p. 1987. lib. bdg. 62.00 (*0-7099-4168-4*, Pub. by Croom Helm UK) Routledge Chapman & Hall.
— New Horizons in the Philosophy of Science. (Philosophy of Science Ser.). 200p. 1992. 59.95 (*1-85628-296-1*, Pub. by Avebury Pub UK) Ashgate Pub Co.
— Perspectives in Exercise Science & Sports Medicine, Vol. 7: Physiology & Nutrition of Competitive Sport. LC 88-70343. (Illus.). 400p. (C). 1994. text ed. 45.00 (*1-884125-09-3*) Cooper Pubng.
Lamb, David & Williams, Melvin, eds. Perspectives in Exercise Science & Sports Medicine, Vol. 4: Ergogenics: Enhancement of Athletic Performance. LC 88-70343. (Illus.). 444p. reprint ed. text ed. 45.00 (*1-884125-08-5*) Cooper Pubng.
Lamb, David, jt. ed. see Gisolfi, Carl.
Lamb, David, et al, eds. Explorations in Medicine. (Avebury Series in Philosophy). 180p. 1987. text ed. 68.95 (*0-566-05346-2*, Pub. by Avebury Pub UK) Ashgate Pub Co.
— Perspectives in Exercise Science & Sports Medicine, Vol. 8: Exercise in Older Adults. LC 88-70343. (Illus.). 400p. 1995. text ed. 45.00 (*1-884125-20-4*) Cooper Pubng.
Lamb, David A. Software Engineering: Planning for Change. (Illus.). 256p. 1987. text ed. 59.00 (*0-13-822982-1*) P-H.
Lamb, David R. Physiology of Exercises: Responses & Adaptations. 2nd ed. 464p. (C). 1984. text ed. write for info. (*0-02-367210-2*) Macmillan.
Lamb, David R. & Gisolfi, Carl V. Energy Metabolism in Exercise & Sport, Vol. 5. (Perspective Ser.). 495p. (C). 1992. boxed write for info. (*0-697-16275-3*) Brown & Benchmark.
— Exercise, Heat & Thermoregulation. (Perspectives Ser.: Vol. 6). 408p. 1993. boxed write for info. (*0-697-20492-8*) Brown & Benchmark.
Lamb, David R. & Gisolfi, Carl V., eds. The Perspective Series, Vol. II: Youth Exercise Sport. (Illus.). 590p. 1989. boxed write for info. (*0-697-14815-7*) Brown & Benchmark.
Lamb, David R. & Murray, Robert, eds. The Perspective Series, Vol. I: Prolonged Exercise. (Illus.). 494p. 1988. boxed write for info. (*0-697-14818-1*) Brown & Benchmark.
Lamb, Donald Q. & Patterson, Joseph, eds. Cataclysmic Variables & Low-Mass X-Ray Binaries. 1985. lib. bdg. 134.50 (*90-277-1947-0*) Kluwer Ac.
Lamb, Doris. Psychotherapy with Adolescent Girls. 2nd ed. LC 86-12211. 278p. 1986. 45.00 (*0-306-42242-5*, Plenum Pr) Plenum.
— Psychotherapy with Adolescent Girls. LC 78-62560. (Jossey-Bass Social & Behavioral Science Ser.). 224p. reprint ed. pap. 63.90 (*0-8357-4900-2*, 2037830) Bks Demand.
***Lamb, Doug.** Pepper Sprays: Practical Self-Defense for Anyone, Anywhere. (Illus.). 120p. 1994. pap. 15.00 (*0-87364-794-7*) Paladin Pr.
Lamb, Douglas W. & Hooper, Geoffrey. Hand Conditions. LC 93-29874. (Colour Guide Ser.). (Orig.). 1994. pap. 19.95 (*0-443-04972-6*) Churchill.
Lamb, Douglas W. & Law, Hamish. Upper Limb Deficiencies in Children. 152p. 1987. 100.00 (*0-316-51269-9*, Little Med Div) Little.
Lamb, Elizabeth S. Casting into a Cloud: Southwest Haiku. (Xtras Ser.: No. 11). (Illus.). 72p. (Orig.). 1985. pap. 3.95 (*0-89120-024-X*) From Here.
— Thirty-Nine Blossoms. 28p. 1982. pap. 2.00 (*0-913719-59-5*) High-Coo Pr.
Lamb, F. Bruce. Rio Tigre & Beyond: The Amazon Jungle Medicine of Manuel Cordova. (Illus.). 256p. (Orig.). 1985. pap. 14.95 (*0-938190-59-8*) North Atlantic.
Lamb, F. Bruce & Cordova-Rios, Manuel. Wizard of the Upper Amazon. 204p. 1987. reprint ed. pap. 12.95 (*0-938190-80-6*) North Atlantic.
Lamb, F. Bruce & Rios, Manual C. Kidnapped in the Amazon Jungle. LC 93-44837. (Illus.). 158p. (Orig.). (YA). 1994. pap. 14.95 (*1-55643-173-2*) North Atlantic.
Lamb-Faffelberger, Margarete. Valie Export und Elfriede Jelinek im Spiegel der Presse: Zur Rezeption der Feministischen Avantgarde Osterreichs. LC 92-20676. 224p. (C). 1993. text ed. 39.95 (*0-8204-1980-X*) P Lang Pubs.
Lamb, Franklin, ed. Reason Not the Need: Eyewitness Chronicles of Israel's War in Lebanon. 936p. 1986. 60.00 (*0-85124-432-7*, Bertrand Russell Soc); pap. 40.00 (*0-85124-433-5*, Bertrand Russell Soc) St Mut.
Lamb, G. F., ed. Larousse Shakespeare Quotations. LC 94-75738. 368p. 1994. pap. 10.95 (*0-7523-5004-8*) LKC.
Lamb, G. L., Jr. Elements of Soliton Theory. (Illus.). 304p. 1994. reprint ed. pap. 9.95 (*0-486-68077-0*) Dover.
— Introductory Applications of Partial Differential Equations with Emphasis on Wave Propagation & Diffusion. LC 94-33111. 1995. text ed. 69.95 (*0-471-31123-5*) Wiley.
Lamb, Geoffrey. Managing Economic Policy Change: Institutional Dimensions. 38p. 1987. 6.95 (*0-8213-0921-8*, 20014) World Bank.
Lamb, Geoffrey & Kallab, Valeriana, eds. Military Expenditure & Economic Development: A Symposium on Research Issues. LC 92-34610. (Discussion Paper Ser.: No. 185). 163p. 1993. 10.95 (*0-8213-2289-3*, 12289) World Bank.
Lamb, Geoffrey & Weaving, Rachel, eds. Managing Policy Reform in the Real World: Asian Experiences. (EDI Seminar Ser.). 136p. 1992. 9.95 (*0-8213-1964-7*, 11964) World Bank.
Lamb, George. Dixon: A Pictorial History. (Illus.). 200p. 1987. 30.00 (*0-685-20016-7*) G Bradley.
Lamb, Ginger, jt. auth. see Lamb, Dana.
Lamb, Gordon H. Choral Techniques. 3rd ed. 316p. (C). 1988. spiral bd. write for info. (*0-697-00612-3*) Brown & Benchmark.
Lamb, H. H. Climate: Present, Past & Future, Vol. 2. 835p. 1977. 150.00 (*0-416-11540-3*, NO.2283) Routledge Chapman & Hall.
— Climate, History & the Modern World. (Illus.). 480p. 1982. pap. 29.95 (*0-416-33440-7*, NO. 3696) Routledge Chapman & Hall.
— Climate, History & the Modern World. 2nd ed. LC 94-44666. 1995. write for info. (*0-415-12734-3*); pap. write for info. (*0-415-12735-1*) Routledge.
— Climatic History & the Future. LC 84-15955. (Illus.). 884p. 1985. pap. text ed. 39.50x (*0-691-02387-5*) Princeton U Pr.
Lamb, H. Richard. Rehabilitation in Community Mental Health. LC 76-168989. (Jossey-Bass Behavioral Science Ser.). 222p. reprint ed. pap. 63.30 (*0-685-16195-1*, 2027760) Bks Demand.
— Treating the Long-Term Mentally Ill. LC 82-48391. (Jossey-Bass Social & Behavioral Science Ser.). 270p. reprint ed. pap. 77.00 (*0-7837-6514-2*, 2045626) Bks Demand.
Lamb, H. Richard, ed. The Homeless Mentally Ill. LC 84-16916. 280p. 1984. text ed. 23.00 (*0-89042-200-1*, 42-200-1) Am Psychiatric.
Lamb, H. Richard, ed. see American Psychiatric Association Staff.
Lamb, H. Richard, et al. Community Survival for Long-Term Patients. LC 75-44883. (Jossey-Bass Behavioral Science Ser.). 208p. reprint ed. pap. 59.30 (*0-8357-4992-4*, 2037925) Bks Demand.
Lamb, H. Richard, et al, eds. Handbook of Community Mental Health Practices: The San Mateo Experience. LC 72-92886. (Jossey-Bass Behavioral Sciences Ser.). 512p. reprint ed. 146.00 (*0-8357-9323-0*, 2013930) Bks Demand.
— Treating the Homeless Mentally Ill. LC 92-10470. 300p. 1992. text ed. 35.00 (*0-89042-236-2*) Am Psychiatric.
Lamb, Harold. Durandal. (Illus.). 1981. 15.00 (*0-937986-45-3*); 35.00 (*0-937986-64-X*) D M Grant.
— Emperor of All Men. 20.95 (*0-88411-798-7*, Aeonian Pr) Amereon Ltd.
— Marching Sands. LC 73-13258. (Classics of Science Fiction Ser.). 320p. 1986. reprint ed. 22.00 (*0-88355-113-6*) Hyperion Conn.
— The Sea of the Ravens. (Illus.). 1983. 15.00 (*0-937986-58-5*); 35.00 (*0-937986-59-3*) D M Grant.
— Tamerlane the Earth Shaker. 1976. 24.95 (*0-8488-1072-4*) Amereon Ltd.
— The Three Palladins. 1977. 12.00 (*0-686-27901-8*) D M Grant.
Lamb, Helen B. Studies on India & Vietnam. Lamont, Corliss, ed. LC 76-1668. 288p. 1976. 16.50 (*0-85345-384-5*) Monthly Rev.
— Studies on India & Vietnam. Lamont, Corliss, ed. LC 76-1668. 267p. reprint ed. pap. 76.10 (*0-7837-3922-2*, 2043770) Bks Demand.
— Vietnam's Will to Live: Resistance to Foreign Aggression from Early Times Through the Nineteenth Century. LC 72-81760. reprint ed. pap. 100.40 (*0-7837-9612-9*, 2060369) Bks Demand.
Lamb, Horace. Hydrodynamics. (Cambridge Mathematical Library). (Illus.). 750p. (C). 1993. pap. 17.95 (*0-521-45868-4*) Cambridge U Pr.
— Hydrodynamics. 6th ed. (Illus.). 1932. pap. text ed. 16.95 (*0-486-60256-7*) Dover.
Lamb, Howard. The Fatbook. 133p. 1982. ring bd. 39.95 (*0-9609150-0-1*) H Lamb.
Lamb, Hubert H. Climate: Present, Past & Future, Vol. 1. (Illus.). 1972. 165.00 (*0-416-11530-6*, NO.2785) Routledge Chapman & Hall.
— Historic Storms of the North Sea. 1991. 105.00 (*0-521-37522-3*) Cambridge U Pr.
— Weather, Climate & Human Affairs. 416p. 1988. text ed. 99.00 (*0-415-00674-0*) Routledge.
Lamb, I. Mackenzie & Zimmerman, Martin H. Benthic Marine Algae of the Antarctic Peninsula: Paper 4 in Biology of the Antarctic Seas V. Pawson, David L., ed. (Antarctic Research Ser.: Vol. 23). 104p. 1977. pap. 53.00 (*0-87590-128-X*) Am Geophysical.
Lamb, J. Dayne. A Question of Preference. (Teal Stewart Mystery Ser.). 304p. 1994. 16.95 (*0-8217-4631-6*) Zebra.
— Questionable Behavior. 288p. 1993. mass mkt. 3.99 (*0-8217-4333-3*) Zebra.
Lamb, J. F., et al. Essentials of Physiology. 3rd ed. (Essentials Ser.). (Illus.). 303p. 1992. pap. 36.95 (*0-632-03135-2*) Blackwell Sci.
Lamb, J. Parker. KATY Diesels to the Gulf. (Illus.). 108p. (Orig.). 1991. pap. 39.95 (*0-944119-05-0*) Andover Junction.
Lamb, J. R., jt. auth. see Owen, M. J.

L

Lamb, Jackie & Lamb, Wesley. Parent Education & Elementary Counseling. LC 77-12942. (New Vistas in Counseling Ser.: Vol. V). 151p. 1978. 29.95 (0-87705-318-9) Human Sci Pr.

Lamb, James C., IV & Foster, Paul M., eds. Physiology & Toxicology of Male Reproduction. 270p. 1988. text ed. 125.00 (0-12-434440-2) Acad Pr.

Lamb, Jane C., tr. see Coblence, Jean-Michel.

Lamb, Jane M. Sharing with Thumpy: My Story of Love & Grief. (Illus.). 48p. (J). (gr. k-12). 1985. student ed. pap. 8.95 (0-918533-10-4) Prairie Lark.

Lamb, Jane M., ed. Bittersweet...Hellogoodbye: A Resource in Planning Farewell Rituals When a Baby Dies. (Illus.). 220p. (Orig.). 1989. pap. 15.00 (0-918533-68-6) Prairie Lark.

Lamb, Jessia. Highland Rogue. Tolley, Carolyn, ed. 304p. (Orig.). 1991. mass mkt. 5.50 (0-671-73001-0) PB.

***Lamb, John L.** The End of the Summer. LC 94-46865. 1995. 18.95 (0-684-80358-5) S&S Trade.

***Lamb, Jonathan.** The Rhetoric of Suffering: Reading the Book of Job in the Eighteenth Century. (Illus.). 352p. 1995. 65.00 (0-19-818264-3) OUP.

— Sterne's Fiction & the Double Principle. (Cambridge Studies in Eighteenth-Century English Literature & Thought: No. 3). (C). 1989. 54.95 (0-521-37273-9) Cambridge U Pr.

Lamb, Joyce, jt. auth. see Nation, Edna.

Lamb, Karl A. As Orange Goes: Twelve California Families & the Future of American Politics. (C). 1974. pap. text ed. 6.95 (0-393-09235-6) Norton.

— As Orange Goes: Twelve California Families & the Future of American Politics. (C). 1974. text ed. 8.95 (0-393-05520-5) Norton.

Lamb, Kathleen, jt. auth. see Westerbeck, Colin.

***Lamb, Kathryn.** One Ewe over the Cuckoo's Nest. (Illus.). 96p. 1991. pap. 8.95 (0-85236-227-7, Pub. by Farming Pr UK) Diamond Farm Bk.

***Lamb, Keith W.** The Lord's Freedman. 266p. (Orig.). 1995. pap. 9.99 (1-56043-829-0) Destiny Image.

Lamb, Lawrence E. The Weighting Game: The Truth about Weight Control. 196p. 1988. 15.95 (0-8184-0487-6) Carol Pub Group.

— Weighting Game: The Truth about Weight Control. 1991. pap. 10.95 (0-8184-0551-1) Carol Pub Group.

Lamb, Linda. Learning the Vi Editor. 5th rev. ed. (Nutshell Handbook Ser.). 192p. 1990. reprint ed. pap. 21.95 (0-937175-67-6) OReilly & Assocs.

***Lamb, Linda & Peek, Jerry.** Using Email Effectively. 170p. 1995. pap. text ed. 19.95 (1-56592-103-8) OReilly & Assocs.

Lamb, M., jt. auth. see Checkland, O.

Lamb, M. L., tr. see St. Thomas Aquinas.

Lamb, M. W. & Harden, M. L. Meaning of Human Nutrition. (C). 1974. 118.00 (0-08-017078-1, Pub. by Pergamon Repr UK) Franklin.

Lamb, Malcolm. Directory of Officials & Organizations in China: A Quarter Century Guide. LC 94-12103. (Contemporary China Papers - Australian National University Ser.). 1392p. 1994. text ed. 160.00 (1-56324-427-6) M E Sharpe.

Lamb, Margaret. Antony & Cleopatra on the English Stage. LC 78-66803. 248p. 1970. 32.50 (0-8386-2198-8) Fairleigh Dickinson.

Lamb, Marion J., jt. auth. see Jablonka, Eva.

Lamb, Marjorie. Two Minutes a Day for a Greener Planet. 1991. mass mkt. 4.95 (0-06-104021-5, Harp PBks) HarpC.

Lamb, Martha J. Wall Street in History. LC 92-71285. (Illus.). 95p. (Orig.). 1992. reprint ed. pap. 14.00 (0-87034-104-9) Fraser Pub Co.

***Lamb, Mary & Lamb, Charles.** Mrs. Leicester's School, 1809. LC 94-44530. (Revolution & Romanticism, 1789-1834, Ser.). 1995. 48.00 (1-85477-182-5, Pub. by Woodstock Bks UK) Cassell.

Lamb, Mary, jt. auth. see Lamb, Charles.

Lamb, Mary A., jt. auth. see Lamb, Charles.

Lamb, Mary E. Gender & Authorship in the Sidney Circle. LC 90-50092. 288p. (Orig.). (C). 1991. text ed. 37.50 (0-299-12690-0); pap. text ed. 14.95 (0-299-12694-3) U of Wis Pr.

Lamb, Matthew L. History, Method & Theology: A Dialectical Comparison of Wilhelm Dilthey's Critique of Historical Reason & Bernard Lonergan's Meta-Methodology. LC 78-18707. (American Academy of Religion. Dissertation Ser.: No. 25). 562p. reprint ed. pap. 160.20 (0-7837-5463-9, 2045228) Bks Demand.

Lamb, Matthew L., ed. Creativity & Method: Studies in Honor of Rev. Bernard Lonergan, S.J. LC 81-80327. 600p. 1981. pap. 20.00 (0-685-03299-X) Marquette.

Lamb, May W. Life in Alaska: The Reminiscences of a Kansas Woman, 1916-1919. Zimmerman, Dorothy W., ed. LC 87-30023. (Illus.). x, 171p. 1988. pap. 8.95 (0-8032-7927-2) U of Nebr Pr.

Lamb, Michael & Keller, Heidi, eds. Infant Development: Perspectives from German-Speaking Countries. 400p. 1991. text ed. 79.95 (0-8058-0666-0) L Erlbaum Assocs.

Lamb, Michael, et al, eds. Infant-Mother Attachment: The Origins & Developmental Significance of Individual Differences in Strange Situation Behavior. 328p. (C). 1985. text ed. 79.95 (0-89859-654-8) L Erlbaum Assocs.

Lamb, Michael E., ed. Nontraditional Families: Parenting & Child Development. (Illus.). 372p. 1982. text ed. 79.95 (0-89859-178-3) L Erlbaum Assocs.

Lamb, Michael E. & Brown, Ann L., eds. Advances in Developmental Psychology, Vol. 1. (Advances in Developmental Psychology Ser.). 256p. 1981. text ed. 49.95 (0-89859-103-1) L Erlbaum Assocs.

— Advances in Developmental Psychology, Vol. 2. 224p. (C). 1982. text ed. 49.95 (0-89859-244-5) L Erlbaum Assocs.

Lamb, Michael E. & Sagi, Abraham, eds. Fatherhood & Family Policy. 288p. (C). 1983. text ed. 49.95 (0-89859-190-2) L Erlbaum Assocs.

Lamb, Michael E. & Sherrod, Lonnie R., eds. Infant Social Cognition: Theoretical & Empirical Considerations. LC 80-21137. 448p. 1981. text ed. 79.95 (0-89859-058-2) L Erlbaum Assocs.

Lamb, Michael E. & Sutton-Smith, Brian, eds. Sibling Relationships: Their Nature & Significance Across the Lifespan. 416p. 1982. 79.95 (0-89859-189-9) L Erlbaum Assocs.

Lamb, Michael E., jt. auth. see Bornstein, Marc H.

Lamb, Michael E., jt. ed. see Bornstein, Marc H.

Lamb, Michael E., jt. ed. see Elster, Arthur B.

Lamb, Michael E., jt. ed. see Ketterlinus, Robert D.

Lamb, Michael E., et al, eds. Advances in Developmental Psychology, Vol. 3. 312p. (C). 1984. text ed. 59.95 (0-89859-366-2) L Erlbaum Assocs.

— Advances in Developmental Psychology, Vol. 4. 376p. 1986. 79.95 (0-89859-675-0) L Erlbaum Assocs.

— Child Care in Context: Cross-Cultural Perspectives. 560p. 1991. text ed. 89.95 (0-8058-0797-7); pap. 39.95 (0-8058-0798-5) L Erlbaum Assocs.

— Social Interaction Analysis: Methodological Issues. LC 78-53287. (Illus.). 336p. 1979. 32.50 (0-299-07590-7) U of Wis Pr.

***Lamb, Nancy.** Alison Goes for the Gold. Bodnar, Judit & Gould, Betsy, eds. (Magic Attic Club Ser.). (Illus.). 64p. (Orig.). (J). (gr. 2-6). 1995. 12.95 (1-57513-002-5); pap. 5.95 (1-57513-003-3) Magic Attic Club.

— Alison on the Trail. Bodnar, Judit & Gould, Betsy, eds. (Magic Attic Club Ser.). (Illus.). 64p. (Orig.). (J). (gr. 2-6). 1995. 12.95 (1-57513-010-6); pap. 5.95 (1-57513-011-4) Magic Attic Club.

— The Great Mosquito, Bull, & Coffin Caper. LC 91-31125. (Illus.). 160p. (J). (gr. 3 up). 1992. 12.00 (0-688-10933-0) Lothrop.

— The Great Mosquito, Bull, & Coffin Caper. LC 91-31125. (Illus.). 128p. (J). (gr. 5 up). 1994. reprint ed. pap. 4.95 (0-688-12944-7, Pub. by Beech Tree Bks) Morrow.

***Lamb, Nancy & Singer, Muff.** The Vampires Went Thataway! LC 95-14844. (Illus.). 80p. (J). (gr. 1-3). 1995. lib. bdg. 11.50 (0-8167-3950-1, Little Rainbow); pap. 2.95 (0-8167-3718-5, Little Rainbow) Troll Assocs.

— The World's Greatest Toe Show. LC 93-28440. (Illus.). 64p. (J). (gr. 2-5). 1993. lib. bdg. 13.95 (0-8167-3322-8); pap. 3.95 (0-8167-3323-6) BrdgeWater.

Lamb, Norman. Guide to Teaching Strings. 5th ed. 208p. (C). 1990. ring bd. write for info. (0-697-05861-1) Brown & Benchmark.

Lamb, Norman & Cook, Susan J. Guide to Teaching Strings. 6th ed. 224p. 1994. spiral bd. write for info. (0-697-12499-1) Brown & Benchmark.

***Lamb, Paul.** Diary of the Trail. iii, 239p. (Orig.). 1995. pap. text ed. 10.00 (0-9639719-1-3) Lambs Fold Ranch.

— Memories from the Trail. iii, 122p. (Orig.). 1994. pap. text ed. 10.00 (0-9639719-0-5) Lambs Fold Ranch.

— Roses on the Trail. iii, 150p. (Orig.). 1995. pap. text ed. 10.00 (0-9639719-3-X) Lambs Fold Ranch.

Lamb, Peter, ed. see International Conference on Applications of Statistics & Probabilities to Soil & Structural Engineering Staff.

Lamb, Peter J., jt. auth. see Hastenrath, Stefan.

Lamb, Philip. NYAT! (National Yiddish Art Theater) 120p. 1987. pap. 6.95 (0-918537-02-9) Justin Bks.

Lamb, R. Bruce. The Wild Bunch: An Annotated Bibliography. LC 93-77746. (Illus.). 160p. 1993. 23.50 (1-881019-05-5) High Plns WY.

Lamb, Richard. Churchill As War Leader. 416p. 1993. 22.95 (0-88184-937-5) Carroll & Graf.

— Following Jesus in the Real World: Discipleship for the Post-College Years. LC 94-45410. 221p. (Orig.). 1995. pap. text ed. 10.99 (0-8308-1608-9, 1608) InterVarsity.

— Pascal: Programming with Style, A Brief Introduction. 208p. (C). 1987. pap. text ed. 17.25 (0-8053-5835-8) Benjamin-Cummings.

— Pascal: Structure & Style. (Illus.). 500p. (C). 1986. teacher ed 10.75 (0-8053-5831-5); pap. text ed. 40.95 (0-8053-5830-7) Benjamin-Cummings.

— War in Italy, 1943-1945: A Brutal Story. 336p. 1994. 23.95 (0-312-11093-6, Pub. by Thomas Dunne Bks) St Martin.

Lamb, Richard & Mittelberger, Ernest. In Celebration of Wine & Life. 2nd ed. (Illus.). 245p. 1980. 19.95 (0-932664-12-1); pap. 9.95 (0-932664-13-X) Wine Appreciation.

***Lamb, Richard G.** Availability Engineering & Manufacturing Plant Performance. 1995. text ed. 65.00 (0-13-324112-2) P-H.

Lamb, Richard L. Metropolitan Impacts on Rural America. LC 74-84782. (Research Papers Ser.: No. 162). (Illus.). 196p. pap. 12.00 (0-89065-069-1) U Chicago Comm Geo.

Lamb, Rob K. Cooperative Processing Using CICS. LC 92-20806. 1993. text ed. 45.00 (0-07-036111-8) McGraw.

Lamb, Robert. Advances in Strategic Management, Vol. 3. 1985. 73.25 (0-89232-506-2) Jai Pr.

— Striking Out. LC 90-53327. 264p. 1991. 22.00 (1-877946-06-0) Permanent Pr.

Lamb, Robert & Rappaport, Stephen P. Municipal Bonds: The Comprehensive Review of Municipal Securities & Public Finance. LC 86-27539. 1987. text ed. 34.95 (0-07-036084-7) McGraw.

Lamb, Robert & Shrivastava, Paul, eds. Advances in Strategic Management, Vol. 4. 1986. 73.25 (0-89232-668-9) Jai Pr.

— Advances in Strategic Management, Vol. 5. 1988. 73.25 (0-89232-766-9) Jai Pr.

Lamb, Robert, et al, eds. Business, Media & the Law: The Troubled Confluence. LC 78-55569. 1980. 27.50x (0-8147-0565-0) NYU Pr.

Lamb, Robert B. The Mule in Southern Agriculture. LC 63-63464. (University of California Publications in Social Welfare: vol. 15). 106p. reprint ed. pap. 30.30 (0-317-29513-6, 2021272) Bks Demand.

Lamb, Robert B., ed. Advances in Applied Business Strategy, Vol. 1. 1984. 73.25 (0-89232-402-3) Jai Pr.

— Advances in Applied Business Strategy, Vol. 2. 1991. 73.25 (0-89232-576-3) Jai Pr.

— Advances in Strategic Management, Vol. 1. 1983. 73.25 (0-89232-408-2) Jai Pr.

— Advances in Strategic Management, Vol. 2. 1983. 73.25 (0-89232-409-0) Jai Pr.

Lamb, Robert O., jt. ed. see Hoddinott, Keith B.

Lamb, Robert P., jt. auth. see Swaggart, Jimmy.

Lamb, Roger. Original & Authentic Journal of Occurrences During the Late American War. LC 67-29033. (Eyewitness Accounts of the American Revolution Ser., No. 1). 1968. reprint ed. 19.95 (0-405-01118-0) Ayer.

Lamb, Roy K. Microfocus Workbench & Toolset Developer's Guide. 1994. pap. text ed. 39.95 (0-07-026122-9) McGraw.

Lamb, Russell. France. (Illus.). 144p. 1992. 39.95 (1-55868-097-7) Gr Arts Ctr Pub.

Lamb, Ruth D. American Chamber of Horrors: The Truth about Food & Drugs. LC 75-39255. (Getting & Spending The Consumer's Dilemma Ser.). (Illus.). 1976. reprint ed. 35.95 (0-405-08028-X) Ayer.

Lamb, Ruth S. America Latina: Contrastes E Confrontos. 69p. (POR.). 1973. pap. 4.00 (0-912434-05-8) Ocelot Pr.

— Antologia del Cuento Guatemalteco. 1958. pap. 5.00 (0-912434-00-7) Ocelot Pr.

— Latin America: Sites & Insights. (J). (gr. 9-12). 1963. pap. 4.00 (0-912434-02-3) Ocelot Pr.

— Mexican Americans: Sons of the Southwest. LC 75-99258. (Illus.). (Orig.). 1970. pap. text ed. 8.95 (0-912434-03-1) Ocelot Pr.

— Mexican Theater of the Twentieth Century: Bibliography & Study. 2nd ed. 140p. 1975. pap. 8.95 (0-912434-18-X) Ocelot Pr.

— The World of Romanian Theater. (Illus.). 136p. 1976. pap. 8.95 (0-912434-20-1) Ocelot Pr.

Lamb, Samuel H. Native Trees & Shrubs of the Hawaiian Islands. LC 80-19715. 160p. 1981. pap. 14.95 (0-913270-91-1) Sunstone Pr.

— Woody Plants of the Southwest. LC 76-357696. (Illus.). 1977. pap. 12.95 (0-913270-50-4) Sunstone Pr.

Lamb, Samuel H., jt. auth. see Miller, Howard A.

Lamb, Sandra & Bellows, Dena. Parties for Home & School: A Piece of Cake. (Illus.). 144p. (J). (ps-4). 1985. student ed 12.95 (0-86653-328-1, GA 647) Good Apple.

Lamb, Sandra E. Rape in America: A Reference Handbook. (Contemporary World Issues Ser.). 225p. 1995. lib. bdg. 39.50 (0-87436-730-1) ABC-CLIO.

Lamb, Sharon, jt. ed. see Kagan, Jerome.

Lamb, Sidney. Canterbury Tales Prologue: Complete Study Guide. 1966. pap. 4.95 (0-8220-1404-1) Cliffs.

— Canterbury Tales, The Wife of Bath: Complete Study Guide. 1983. pap. 4.95 (0-8220-1408-4) Cliffs.

— Hamlet: Complete Study Guide. 1964. pap. 4.95 (0-8220-1415-7) Cliffs.

— Julius Caesar Complete Study Guide. 1964. pap. 4.95 (0-8220-1418-1) Cliffs.

— King Henry IV Complete Study Guide. 1965. pap. 4.95 (0-8220-1424-6) Cliffs.

— King Lear Complete Study Guide. 1964. pap. 4.95 (0-8220-1421-1) Cliffs.

— Merchant of Venice Complete Study Guide. 1965. pap. 4.95 (0-8220-1430-0) Cliffs.

— Othello Complete Study Guide. 1966. pap. 4.95 (0-8220-1433-5) Cliffs.

— Romeo & Juliet: Complete Study Guide. 1965. pap. 4.95 (0-8220-1437-8) Cliffs.

— Tempest Complete Study Guide. 1965. pap. 4.95 (0-8220-1440-8) Cliffs.

— Twelfth Night: Complete Study Guide. 1965. pap. 4.95 (0-8220-1444-0) Cliffs.

Lamb, Susan. Guide to Navajo Rugs. Foreman, Ronald J. & Priehs, T. J., eds. LC 92-62470. (Illus.). 32p. (Orig.). 1992. pap. 3.95 (1-877856-26-6) SW Pks Mnmts.

— Montezuma Castle National Monument. Foreman, Ronald J. & Priehs, T. J., eds. LC 92-62157. (Illus.). 16p. (Orig.). (YA). 1992. pap. 2.95 (1-877856-19-3) SW Pks Mnmts.

— Petroglyph National Monument. Foreman, Ronald J., ed. LC 92-62155. (Illus.). 16p. (Orig.). (YA). 1993. pap. 2.95 (1-877856-22-3) SW Pks Mnmts.

— Tumacacori National Historical Park. Priehs, T. J. & Scott, Sandra, eds. LC 93-86297. (Illus.). 16p. (Orig.). 1993. pap. 2.95 (1-877856-37-1) SW Pks Mnmts.

***Lamb, Susan, ed.** Best of Grand Canyon Nature Notes. 168p. 1994. pap. 11.95 (0-938216-49-X) GCNHA.

Lamb, Sydney M. & Mitchell, E. Douglas, eds. Sprung from Some Common Source: Investigations into the Prehistory of Languages. LC 90-46495. (Illus.). 432p. 1991. 47.50 (0-8047-1897-0) Stanford U Pr.

Lamb, Sydney M. & Newell, Leonard E. Outline of Straficational Grammar. LC 66-28562. (Illus.). 115p. reprint ed. pap. 32.80 (0-7837-6331-X, 2046044) Bks Demand.

Lamb, Toni, ed. see Molina, Tarea.

***Lamb, Trevor.** Colour: Art & Science. Bourriau, Janine, ed. (Darwin College Lectures). (Illus.). 246p. (C). 1995. 59.95 (0-521-49645-4); pap. 24.95 (0-521-49963-1) Cambridge U Pr.

***Lamb, Ursula.** Cosmographers and Pilots of the Spanish Maritime Empire. (Jvariorum Collected Studies Ser.: Vol. 499). 280p. 1995. 82.50 (0-86078-473-8, Pub. by Variorum UK) Ashgate Pub Co.

Lamb, V. B. The Betrayal of Richard the Third. (Illus.). 160p. (C). 1990. pap. 14.00 (0-86299-778-X) A Sutton Pub.

Lamb, V. R., jt. auth. see Rieber, J. E.

Lamb, W. R., tr. Lysias. LC 76-29460. reprint ed. 45.00 (0-404-15315-1) AMS Pr.

Lamb, Wallace E. Historic Lake George Illustrated. 3rd ed. LC 47-204. (Lake George Facts & Anecdotes Ser.). (Illus.). 52p. (Orig.). 1984. reprint ed. pap. text ed. 4.25 (0-317-06216-6) Lake George Hist.

Lamb, Wally. She's Come Undone. Regan, Judith, ed. 480p. 1993. reprint ed. mass mkt. 5.99 (0-671-75921-3, Pocket Star Bks) PB.

Lamb, Walter. Always Begin Where You Are: Themes in Poetry & Song. LC 78-32108. (Illus.). 1979. text ed. 15.20 (0-07-035921-0) McGraw.

Lamb, Warren & Watson, Elizabeth. Body Code: The Meaning in Movement. LC 87-60416. (Illus.). 190p. 1995. reprint ed. pap. 12.95 (0-916622-50-9) Princeton Bk Co.

***Lamb, Wendy.** Ten Out of Ten: Ten Winning Plays Selected from the Young Playwrights Festival 1982-1991. (YA). 1995. pap. 4.99 (0-440-21914-0) Dell.

Lamb, Wendy, ed. Ten Out of Ten: Ten Winning Plays Selected from the Young Playwrights Festival 1982-1991. LC 92-7944. 320p. (J). (gr. 7 up). 1992. 18.00 (0-385-30811-6) Delacorte.

Lamb, Wesley, jt. auth. see Lamb, Jackie.

Lamba, ed. Antibiotics & Microbial Transformations. 1987. 87.00 (0-8493-6408-6, QR88) CRC Pr.

Lamba, B. P. Graham Greene: His Mind & Art. LC 87-70632. 150p. 1987. text ed. 13.95 (0-86590-793-5) Apt Bks.

Lamba, P. S., ed. Impact of Urbanization & Industrialization on Rural Society. (C). 1992. 19.00 (81-224-0412-X, Pub. by Wiley Eastern II) S Asia.

Lambakis, Steven J. Winston Churchill - Architect of Peace: A Study of Statesmanship & the Origins of the Cold War. LC 92-42674. (Contributions in Political Science Ser.: No. 322). 208p. 1993. text ed. 49.95 (0-313-28823-2, GM8823, Greenwood Pr) Greenwood.

Lambard, Neil. Pocket Dictionary of Banjo Chords. 1966. pap. 2.95 (0-934286-19-1) Kenyon.

Lambarde, William. William Lambarde & Local Government: His "Ephemeris" & Twenty-Nine Charges to Juries & Commissions. Read, Conyers, ed. (Documents Ser.). 1978. 29.50 (0-918016-36-3) Folger Bks.

Lambden, John, jt. auth. see Targett, David.

Lambdin. Introduction to Biblical Hebrew. (C). 1985. pap. text ed. 25.00 (0-684-41322-1, Scribners) S&S Trade.

Lambdin, Dewey. For King & Country: The Naval Adventures of Alan Lewrie. LC 94-71111. 1088p. 1994. pap. 19.95 (1-55611-413-3, Primus) D I Fine.

— The French Admiral. (Midshipman Alan Lewrie Adventure Ser.). 1990. 19.95 (1-55611-208-4) D I Fine.

— French Admiral. 1991. mass mkt. 4.95 (1-55817-491-5, Pinnacle NY) Windsor NY.

— The Gun Ketch: An Alan Lewrie Naval Adventure. LC 92-54471. 1993. 21.95 (1-55611-356-0) D I Fine.

— The King's Coat. 384p. 1989. 19.95 (1-55611-142-8) D I Fine.

— King's Coat. 1990. pap. 3.95 (1-55817-389-7, Pinnacle NY) Windsor NY.

— King's Commission. 1991. 21.95 (1-55611-187-8) D I Fine.

— King's Privateer: An Alan Lewrie Naval Adventure. 1992. 21.95 (1-55611-324-2) D I Fine.

***Lambdin, Edward D.** The Cloud Master. 208p. 1994. per., pap. 8.95 (0-9643419-0-5) Wrd Weaver Pub.

Lambdin, Thomas O. Introduction to Classical Ethiopic (Ge'ez) LC 78-12895. (Harvard Semitic Studies). 452p. 1994. 44.95 (0-89130-263-8, 040424) Scholars Pr GA.

— Introduction to Classical Ethiopic (Ge'ez) LC 78-12895. (Harvard Semitic Studies: No. 24). 462p. reprint ed. pap. 131.70 (0-7837-5409-4, 2045173) Bks Demand.

— Introduction to Sahidic Coptic: A New Coptic Grammar. LC 82-14282. xvii, 377p. 1983. 45.00 (0-86554-048-9, MUP-H55) Mercer Univ Pr.

Lambdin, William S., jt. auth. see Bronaugh, Edwin L.

Lambe, John. A Briefe Description of the Notorious Life of J. Lambe. LC 76-57394. (English Experience Ser.: No. 811). 1977. reprint ed. lib. bdg. 15.00 (90-221-0811-2) Walter J Johnson.

Lambe, Philip C. & Hansen, Lawrence A., eds. Design & Performance of Earth Retaining Structures. LC 90-771. 904p. 1990. pap. text ed. 70.00 (0-87262-761-6) Am Soc Civil Eng.

Lambe, T. William & Whitman, Robert V. Soil Mechanics. LC 68-30915. (Geotechnical Engineering Ser.). 553p. (C). 1969. text ed. 89.95 (0-471-51192-7) Wiley.

Lambeck. Hydraulic Pumps & Motors: Selection & Application for Hydraulic Power Control Systems. (Fluid Power & Control Ser.: Vol. 1). 176p. 1983. 99.75 (0-8247-7014-5) Dekker.

Lambeck, Kurt. Geophysical Geodesy: The Slow Deformation of the Earth. (Illus.). 740p. 1988. 160.00 (0-19-854438-3); pap. 60.00 (0-19-854437-5) OUP.

Lambee, Joshua B. What I Saw at the Dance: A Poem to A Friend. Darden, Daniel Y., ed. LC 93-91549. 355p. (Orig.). (C). 1994. 27.00 (0-9637078-0-9); text ed. 24.00 (0-9637078-2-5); lib. bdg. 30.00 (0-9637078-1-7); pap. 15.95 (0-9637078-3-3); pap. text ed. 12.95 (0-9637078-4-1) HourGlass TX.

Lambeis, Barbara & Ratliff, Susan. Making More Money Retailing: Low Cost Ideas for Successful Merchandising & Boosting Profits from Your Retail Store. 140p. 1994. pap. 10.95 (0-9624798-8-8) Mktg Methods Pr.

Lambek, J. & Scott, P. J. Introduction to Higher-Order Categorical Logic. (Cambridge Studies in Advanced Mathematics). 304p. 1988. pap. 34.95 (0-521-35653-9) Cambridge U Pr.

An Asterisk (*) at the beginning of an entry indicates that the title is appearing in BIP for the first time.

Lambek, Joachim. Lectures in Rings & Modules. 3rd ed. LC 75-41494. viii, 184p. 1986. 16.95 (*0-8284-2283-4*) Chelsea Pub.

Lambek, Michael. Human Spirits: A Cultural Account of Trance in Mayotte. LC 81-1842. (Cambridge Studies in Cultural Systems). (Illus.). 272p. 1981. 39.50 (*0-521-23844-7*); pap. 21.95 (*0-521-28255-1*) Cambridge U Pr.

— Knowledge & Practice in Mayotte: Local Discourses of Islam, Sorcery, & Spirit Possession. (Anthropological Horizons Ser.: No. 3). 656p. 1993. 70.00 (*0-8020-2960-4*); pap. 24.95 (*0-8020-7783-8*) U of Toronto Pr.

Lambek, Ruth. A Passion for the Divine. 1979. pap. 5.95 (*0-87516-289-4*) DeVorss.

Lambelet, Philippe, jt. ed. see Keller, Walter.

Lambell, Ronald. French Period Houses & Their Details. LC 92-28317. 1992. 49.95 (*0-7506-1527-3*, Butterwrth Archit) Buttrwrth-Heinemann.

Lamberg-Karlovsky, C. C., ed. Archaeological Thought in America. (Illus.). 350p. (C). 1991. pap. 27.95 (*0-521-40643-9*) Cambridge U Pr.

***Lamberg-Karlovsky, C. C. & Sabloff, Jeremy A.** Ancient Civilizations: The Near East & Mesoamerica. 2nd ed. (Illus.). 406p. (Orig.). (C). 1995. pap. text ed. 24.95x (*0-88133-834-6*) Waveland Pr.

— Ancient Civilizations: The Near East & Mesoamerica. (Illus.). 350p. (Orig.). (C). 1987. reprint ed. pap. text ed. 20.95 (*0-88133-301-8*) Waveland Pr.

Lamberg, Lynn. Drugs & Sleep. (Encyclopedia of Psychoactive Drugs Ser.: No. 2). (Illus.). 128p. 1988. lib. bdg. 19.95 (*1-55546-213-8*) Chelsea Hse.

— Skin Disorders. (Medical Disorders & Their Treatment Ser.). (Illus.). 112p. (YA). (gr. 6-12). 1990. 18.95 (*0-7910-0076-1*) Chelsea Hse.

Lamberg, Lynne. Bodyrhythms: Biological Clocks & Peak Performance. LC 93-40320. 1994. 25.00 (*0-87795-991-9*) Morrow.

Lamberg, Lynne, jt auth. see Cartwright, Rosalind D.

Lambers, H., et al, eds. Fundamental, Ecological & Agricultural Aspects of Nitrogen Fixation. (Developments in Plant & Soil Sciences Ser.). 1986. lib. bdg. 201.50 (*90-247-3258-1*) Kluwer Ac.

Lamberson, L. R., jt. auth. see Kapur, K. C.

***Lambert.** The Constructivist Leader. 240p. (C). 1995. text ed. 44.00x (*0-8077-3463-2*); pap. text ed. 21.95x (*0-8077-3462-4*) Tchrs Coll.

— The Long Campaign: History of the Fifteenth Fighter Group World War II. 1982. 45.00 (*0-89745-032-9*) Beachcomber Bks.

— Running Time. 1983. 15.95 (*0-02-567680-6*) Macmillan.

— Soldering for Electronic Assemblies. (Manufacturing Engineering & Materials Processing Ser.: Vol. 25). 368p. 1988. 115.00 (*0-8247-7681-X*) Dekker.

Lambert, Alan & Scott-Hughes, Brian. Junior Drama Workshop. (Drama Anthologies Ser.). (Illus.). 96p. (Orig.). (YA). 1990. pap. 15.00 (*0-333-43459-5*, Pub. by Macmillan Ed UK) Players Pr.

Lambert, Alan, jt. auth. see O'Neill, Cecily.

Lambert, Andrew. Warrior: The World's First Ironclad Then & Now. LC 86-63792. 192p. 1987. 29.95 (*0-87021-986-3*) Naval Inst Pr.

Lambert, Andrew, ed. Warship, Vol. IX. LC 78-55455. (Illus.). 288p. 1986. 39.95 (*0-87021-984-7*) Naval Inst Pr.

— Warship, Vol. X. LC 78-55455. (Illus.). 288p. 1987. 39.95 (*0-87021-985-5*) Naval Inst Pr.

Lambert, Andrew & Badsey, Stephen. The Crimean War from the Times War Correspondents. (Illus.). 352p. 1994. 36.00 (*0-7509-0043-1*) A Sutton Pub.

Lambert, Andrew, jt. ed. see Gardiner, Robert.

Lambert, Andrew D. The Crimean War: British Grand Strategy Against Russia, 1853-56. LC 89-12701. (War, Armed Forces & Society Ser.). 391p. 1991. reprint ed. text ed. 24.95 (*0-7190-3564-3*, Pub. by Manchester Univ Pr UK) St Martin.

Lambert, Angela. Nineteen Thirty-Nine: The Last Season of Peace. large type ed. 387p. 1990. 10.97 (*0-685-56331-6*, Pub. by ISIS UK) Transaction Pubs.

***Lambert, Anthony.** Bradt Guide to Switzerland by Rail. (Illus.). 240p. (Orig.). 1995. pap. 15.95 (*1-56440-701-2*, Pub. by Bradt Pubns UK) Globe Pequot.

Lambert, Anthony J. Victorian & Edwardian Country House Life. LC 80-26606. (Illus.). 120p. 1981. 29.50 (*0-8419-0684-X*) Holmes & Meier.

Lambert, Audrey M. The Making of the Dutch Landscape: An Historical Geography of the Netherlands (Monograph) 2nd ed. 1985. text ed. 121.00 (*0-12-434645-6*) Acad Pr.

Lambert, B. Homecoming of the Alien Heart: A Search Inward. (Illus.). 200p. (Orig.). 1993. pap. 10.99 (*1-881542-11-4*) Blue Star Prodns.

Lambert, Barrie. How Safe Is Safe? Radiation Controversies Explained. (Illus.). 208p. 1990. pap. text ed. 14.95 (*0-04-440347-X*) Routledge Chapman & Hall.

Lambert, Brian K., ed. Milling, Methods & Machines. LC 82-61032. (Manufacturing Update Ser.). (Illus.). 268p. reprint ed. pap. 76.40 (*0-8357-6483-4*, 2035854) Bks Demand.

Lambert, Byron C. The Rise of the Anti-Mission Baptists: Sources & Leaders, 1800-1840. Gaustad, Edwin S., ed. LC 79-52573. (Baptist Tradition Ser.). 1980. lib. bdg. 42.95 (*0-405-12441-4*) Ayer.

Lambert, C., jt. ed. see Healey, P.

Lambert, Camille, Jr. & Freeman, Howard E. The Clinic Habit. 1967. pap. 17.95x (*0-8084-0083-5*) NCUP.

Lambert, Carrole, ed. The Empty Cross. LC 90-34401. (Studies in Comparative Literature). 352p. 1990. reprint ed. 25.00 (*0-8240-0002-1*) Garland.

Lambert, Charles, tr. see Calabrese, Omar.

Lambert, Charles, tr. see Vernant, Jean-Pierre, ed.

Lambert, Charles E. & Stone, Donald. Orthopaedic Physician's Assistant Techniques. LC 74-77819. (Allied Health Ser.). 1975. pap. 7.05 (*0-672-61388-3*, Bobbs) Macmillan.

Lambert, Charles J. Sweet Waters, a Chilean Farm. LC 75-14091. (Illus.). 212p. 1975. reprint ed. text ed. 55.00 (*0-8371-8201-8*, LASWA, Greenwood Pr) Greenwood.

Lambert, Cindy, ed. see James, Mark.

Lambert, Clark. The Business Presentations Workbook. 264p. 1988. spiral bd. 39.95 (*0-13-107467-9*) P-H.

— The Business Presentations Workbook. 264p. 1989. pap. 12.95 (*0-13-107518-7*) P-H.

— Secrets of a Successful Trainer: A Simplified Guide for Survival. LC 85-22596. 333p. 1986. text ed. 49.95 (*0-471-80143-7*) Wiley.

Lambert, Constant. Music Ho. 1967. 8.95 (*0-8079-0086-9*) October.

— Music Ho! a Study of Music in Decline. (Music Book Index Ser.). 342p. 1992. reprint ed. lib. bdg. 89.00 (*0-7812-9507-6*) Rprt Serv.

Lambert, D. Shakespeare Documents: A Chronological Catalogue. 1972. 59.95 (*0-8490-1034-9*) Gordon Pr.

Lambert, D. L., ed. Frontiers of Stellar Evolution. (ASP Conference Series Publications: Vol. 20). 626p. 1991. 25.00 (*0-937707-39-2*) Astron Soc Pacific.

Lambert, D. W. Unbribed Soul. 1979. pap. 4.25 (*0-87508-305-6*) Chr Lit.

***Lambert, D. Warren.** When the Ripe Pears Fell: The Battle of Richmond, Kentucky. LC 95-14688. 1995. text ed. write for info. (*0-9615162-3-2*) Madison Cty KY Hist.

Lambert, Dale. The Pacific Northwest: Past, Present & Future. (Illus.). 480p. (gr. 8-12). 1986. teacher ed 7.95 (*0-685-10071-5*); student ed 3.95 (*0-939688-17-4*); teacher ed 2.95 (*0-939688-18-2*); text ed. 19.95 (*0-939688-14-X*); 9.95 (*0-939688-16-6*) Directed Media.

Lambert, Darwin. Great Basin Drama: The Story of a National Park. (Illus.). 200p. 1991. pap. 12.95 (*0-911797-95-5*) R Rinehart.

— The Undying Past of Shenandoah National Park. 1989. 29.95 (*0-911797-58-0*); pap. 16.95 (*0-911797-57-2*) R Rinehart.

Lambert, David. Celebrating Christmas As If It Matters. 160p. 1992. pap. 9.99 (*0-310-54441-6*) Zondervan.

— The Children's Animal Atlas. LC 91-30147. (Children's Atlases Ser.). (Illus.). 96p. (J). (gr. 2-6). 1992. 16.95 (*1-56294-101-1*); lib. bdg. 18.90 (*1-56294-167-4*) Millbrook Pr.

— Children's Animal Atlas. (Children's Atlases Ser.). (J). (gr. 4-7). 1993. pap. 12.95 (*1-56294-720-6*) Millbrook Pr.

— Dictionnaire Francais-Anglais de l'Economie. 264p. (ENG & FRE.). 1975. pap. 49.95 (*0-8288-5857-8*, M63299) Fr & Eur.

— Fires & Floods. LC 92-8687. (Repairing the Damage Ser.). (Illus.). 48p. (YA). (gr. 6 up). 1992. text ed. 13.95 (*0-02-751350-5*, Mac Bks Young Read) S&S Childrens.

— Forests. LC 89-20311. (Our Planet Ser.). (Illus.). 32p. (J). (gr. 4-6). 1990. lib. bdg. 11.59 (*0-8167-1971-X*); pap. text ed. 3.95 (*0-8167-1972-1*) Troll Assocs.

— Joy in Suffering: Receiving Your Reward. (Beatitudes Ser.). 64p. 1993. Saddle stitch bdg. 4.99 (*0-310-59673-4*) Zondervan.

— Polar Regions. (Our World Ser.). (Illus.). 48p. (J). (gr. 5-8). 1987. lib. bdg. 12.95 (*0-382-09502-2*) Silver Burdett Pr.

— Seas & Oceans. LC 93-6352. (New View Ser.). (J). 1994. lib. bdg. 19.97 (*0-8114-9245-1*) Raintree Steck-V.

— Seas & Oceans. (Our World Ser.). (Illus.). 48p. (J). (gr. 5-8). 1987. lib. bdg. 12.95 (*0-382-09503-0*) Silver Burdett Pr.

— Showing Mercy: Getting What You Give. (Beatitudes Ser.). 64p. 1993. Saddle stitch. 4.99 (*0-310-59663-7*) Zondervan.

— Stars & Planets. LC 93-28282. (New View Ser.). (Illus.). (J). 1994. lib. bdg. 19.97 (*0-8114-9246-X*) Raintree Steck-V.

— The Ultimate Dinosaur Book. LC 93-21885. (Illus.). 192p. 1993. 29.95 (*1-56458-304-X*) Dorling Kindersley.

— Weather. LC 89-20304. (Our Planet Ser.). (Illus.). 32p. (J). (gr. 4-6). 1990. lib. bdg. 11.59 (*0-8167-1979-5*); pap. text ed. 3.95 (*0-8167-1980-9*) Troll Assocs.

— The World's Population. LC 93-716. (Young Geographer Ser.). (Illus.). 32p. (J). (gr. 4-6). 1993. 14.95 (*1-56847-050-9*) Thomson Lrning.

Lambert, David & McConnell, Anita. Seas & Oceans. LC 84-1654. (World of Science Ser.). (Illus.). 64p. (YA). (gr. 7 up). 1985. 15.95 (*0-8160-1064-1*) Facts on File.

Lambert, David & Osmond, Tony. Great Discoveries & Inventions. (World of Science Ser.). 64p. 1986. 15.95 (*0-8160-1062-5*) Facts on File.

Lambert, David, jt. auth. see Davis, Ken.

Lambert, David, jt. auth. see Diagram Group Staff.

Lambert, David, tr. see Lavigne, Marie.

Lambert, David, et al. The Field Guide to Prehistoric Life. LC 84-21237. (Illus.). 256p. reprint ed. pap. 73.00 (*0-8357-4250-4*, 2037040) Bks Demand.

Lambert, David M. & Spencer, Hamish G., eds. Speciation & the Recognition Concept: Theory & Application. (Illus.). 528p. 1994. text ed. 65.00 (*0-8018-4740-0*); pap. text ed. 35.00 (*0-8018-4741-9*) Johns Hopkins.

Lambert, Dean M. The Advent Jesse Tree. 96p. 1990. 9.95 (*0-687-00908-1*) Abingdon.

Lambert, Della M. Fires of My Heart & Other Poems. 1993. 8.95 (*0-533-10120-4*) Vantage.

Lambert, Derek. The Banya. 359p. 1992. 24.95 (*1-85619-044-7*, Sinclair-Stevenson) Trafalgar.

— Triad. 207p. 1991. 18.95 (*0-8027-1176-6*) Walker & Co.

— Vendetta. 176p. 1990. 16.95 (*0-8027-1120-0*) Walker & Co.

***Lambert, Don.** The Life & Art of Elizabeth "Grandma" Layton. Brady, Georgia, ed. LC 95-13661. (Illus.). 144p. 1995. 29.92 (*1-56796-116-9*) WRS Group.

Lambert, Douglas M. The Product Abandonment Decision. 224p. 22.95 (*0-86641-114-3*, 84166) Inst Mgmt Account.

Lambert, Douglas M. & Stock, James R. Strategic Logistics Management. 3rd ed. 820p. (C). 1992. text ed. 62.95 (*0-256-08838-1*) Irwin.

Lambert, Elizabeth. Wings of Desire. 384p. (Orig.). 1989. pap. 3.95 (*0-380-75599-8*) Avon.

***Lambert, Ellen Z.** The Face of Love: Feminism & the Beauty Question. 256p. 1995. 24.00 (*0-8070-6500-5*) Beacon Pr.

— Placing Sorrow: A Study of the Pastoral Elegy Convention from Theocritus to Milton. LC 76-23154. (Studies in Comparative Literature: No. 60). xxxiv, 231p. 1977. 30.00 (*0-8078-7060-9*) U of NC Pr.

Lambert, Erin, jt. auth. see Lambert, Lee R.

Lambert, F. J., jt. ed. see Antoniou, I.

Lambert, Frank. Pedlar in Divinity: George Whitefield & the Transatlantic Revivals, 1737-1770. LC 93-1345. (Illus.). 264p. 1994. text ed. 24.95 (*0-691-03296-3*) Princeton U Pr.

Lambert, Frederick. Letter Forms: 110 Complete Alphabets. 128p. 1972. pap. 5.95 (*0-486-22872-X*) Dover.

Lambert, Gavin. The Dangerous Edge. LC 76-2377. 272p. 1976. 18.95 (*0-670-25581-5*) Boulevard.

— Norma Shearer. 1990. 24.95 (*0-394-55158-3*) Knopf.

Lambert-Gocs, Miles. Wines of Greece. (Books on Wine Ser.). (Illus.). 336p. 1990. 24.95 (*0-571-15387-9*); pap. 13.95 (*0-571-15388-7*) Faber & Faber.

Lambert, Gussie. Facts from Acts: (Quiz Book) 1988. 2.25 (*0-89315-056-8*) Lambert Bk.

***Lambert, H. E.** Kikuyu Social & Political. (Classics in African Anthropology Ser.). (C). 1995. pap. text ed. 64.50 (*3-89473-686-0*); pap. text ed. 25.50 (*3-89473-879-0*) Westview.

— Kikuyu Social & Political Institutions. 157p. reprint ed. pap. 44.80 (*0-317-29886-0*, 2019419) Bks Demand.

Lambert, Hannah E. & Blake, Peter R., eds. Gynaecological Oncology. (Illus.). 248p. 1992. pap. 35.00 (*0-19-262203-X*) OUP.

Lambert, Harold P. Infections of the Central Nervous System. (Illus.). 416p. (C). 1991. 92.00 (*1-55664-206-7*) Mosby Yr Bk.

Lambert, Harold P. & O'Grady, Francis, eds. Antibiotic & Chemotherapy. 6th ed. (Illus.). 561p. 1991. text ed. 149.95 (*0-443-03203-3*) Churchill.

Lambert, Herbert, ed. see Christensen, James L.

Lambert, Herbert, ed. see Harrison, Russell F.

Lambert, Herbert H., ed. see Barlett, David L.

Lambert, Hugh K., jt. auth. see Parker, Watson.

Lambert, Isaac E. The Public Accepts: Stories Behind Famous Trade-Marks, Names, & Slogans. LC 75-39256. (Getting & Spending: the Consumer's Dilemma Ser.). (Illus.). 1976. reprint ed. 20.95 (*0-405-08029-8*) Ayer.

Lambert, J. D. Numerical Methods for Ordinary Differential Systems: The Initial Value Problem. 293p. 1991. text ed. 69.95 (*0-471-92990-5*) Wiley.

Lambert, J. H. Qvod Temptabam. (C). 1982. pap. text ed. 39.00 (*0-900269-08-1*, Pub. by Old Vicarage UK) St Mut.

Lambert, J. Karel, ed. Philosophical Applications of Free Logic. 320p. 1991. 59.00 (*0-19-506131-4*) OUP.

Lambert, Jacques. Latin America: Social Structures & Political Institutions. Katel, Helen, tr. LC 67-29784. 1968. pap. 13.00 (*0-520-00690-9*) U CA Pr.

Lambert, James F. Luther's Hymns. LC 83-45646. reprint ed. 34.50 (*0-404-19855-4*) AMS Pr.

Lambert, Janet. Candy Kane. 18.95 (*0-8488-0125-3*, Amereon Hse) Amereon Ltd.

— Confusion: By Cupid. 18.95 (*0-8488-0127-X*, Amereon Hse) Amereon Ltd.

— Don't Cry, Little Girl. 18.95 (*0-8488-0131-8*, Amereon Hse) Amereon Ltd.

— Just Jennifer. 1976. 18.95 (*0-8488-0126-1*, Amereon Hse) Amereon Ltd.

— Little Miss Atlas. 18.95 (*0-8488-0129-6*, Amereon Hse) Amereon Ltd.

— Myself & I. 18.95 (*0-8488-0128-8*, Amereon Hse) Amereon Ltd.

— Practically Perfect. 18.95 (*0-8488-0130-X*, Amereon Hse) Amereon Ltd.

***Lambert, Jean-Clarence.** Los Artistas Cobra. Vol. 1. (Illus.). (SPA.). 1993. write for info. (*0-614-00039-4*) Elliots Bks.

— Los Artistas Cobra. Vol. 1. (Illus.). (SPA.). 1993. write for info. (*0-614-00145-5*) Elliots Bks.

— Los Artistas Cobra. Vol. 1. (Illus.). (SPA.). 1993. write for info. (*0-614-00250-8*) Elliots Bks.

— Cobra. LC 83-21419. (Illus.). 264p. 125.00 (*0-89659-416-5*) Abbeville Pr.

— La Imaginacion Material. Vol. 2. (Illus.). (SPA.). 1993. write for info. (*0-614-00040-8*) Elliots Bks.

— La Imaginacion Material. Vol. 2. (Illus.). (SPA.). 1993. write for info. (*0-614-00146-3*) Elliots Bks.

— La Imaginacion Material. Vol. 2. (Illus.). (SPA.). 1993. write for info. (*0-614-00251-6*) Elliots Bks.

— Karel Appel: Works on Paper. LC 79-92227. (Illus.). 256p. 1980. 125.00 (*0-89659-069-0*) Abbeville Pr.

— Reino Imaginal, 2 vols. (Grandes Monografias). (Illus.). 358p. (SPA.). 1993. 225.00 (*84-343-0736-7*) Elliots Bks.

— Sugai. (Grandes Monografias). (Illus.). 224p. (SPA.). 1993. 175.00 (*84-343-0639-5*) Elliots Bks.

Lambert, Jean-Clarence, jt. ed. see Strahan, Bradley R.

Lambert, Jean-Paul. Disequilibrium Macroeconomic Models: Theory & Estimation of Rationing Models Using Business Survey Data. (Illus.). 200p. 1988. 49.95 (*0-521-32209-X*) Cambridge U Pr.

Lambert, Jeanette. African-American Legacies for the 21st Century: A Bibliography of Biographies for Children about Notable African-Americans. 25p. (Orig.). (J). (gr. k-8). 1994. pap. 4.95 (*0-9632736-3-9*) Edit Cetera.

— Black Images in Contemporary Children's Books: An Annotated Bibliography. 20p. (Orig.). 1991. pap. 5.50 (*0-9632736-0-4*) Edit Cetera.

— In First Place: A Bibliography of Books & Materials about Girls Involved in Sports. 25p. (Orig.). (J). (gr. k-9). 1994. pap. 5.95 (*0-9632736-2-0*) Edit Cetera.

— Twenty-First Century African-American Legacies: A Bibliography of Biographies for Children about Notable African-Americans. 25p. (Orig.). (J). (gr. k-8). 1994. pap. 5.95 (*0-9632736-1-2*) Edit Cetera.

Lambert, Jeremiah D. & Fesharaki, Fereidun, eds. Economic & Political Incentives to Petroleum Exploration: Developments in the Asia-Pacific Region. LC 89-34648. (Illus.). 180p. (C). 1989. lib. bdg. 52.00 (*0-935328-57-2*) Intl Law Inst.

Lambert, Jerry. Interfacing to the TRS-80 Computer: Models I, III & IV. (Illus.). 1984. text ed. 24.00 (*0-8359-3116-1*, Reston); pap. text ed. 16.95 (*0-8359-3115-3*, Reston) P-H.

Lambert, Jill. Scientific & Technical Journals. LC 85-116142. (Illus.). 191p. reprint ed. pap. 54.50 (*0-7837-5324-1*, 2045063) Bks Demand.

Lambert, Joanna, jt. auth. see Myers, Selma.

Lambert, Johann H. La Perspective Affranchie. (Perspective Ser.). (Illus.). 208p. (FRE.). (C). 1989. reprint ed. 135.00 (*1-85297-028-6*, Pub. by Archival Facs UK) St Mut.

Lambert, John. Solidarity & Survival: A Vision for Europe. 148p. 1994. 55.95 (*1-85628-871-4*, Pub. by Avebury Pub UK) Ashgate Pub Co.

Lambert, John & Hill, David. The Submarine Alliance. LC 86-60258. (Anatomy of the Ship Ser.). (Illus.). 96p. 1986. 36.95 (*0-87021-688-0*) Naval Inst Pr.

Lambert, John & Ross, Al. Allied Coastal Forces of World War II, Vol. 1. (Illus.). 256p. 1994. 43.95 (*1-55750-034-7*) Naval Inst Pr.

— Allied Coastal Forces of World War II, Vol. 2. (Illus.). 256p. 1994. 43.95 (*1-55750-035-5*) Naval Inst Pr.

Lambert, John, tr. see Toussaint, Jean-Philippe.

Lambert, John C. The Romance of Missionary Heroism, 1. 1979. pap. 4.99 (*0-88019-103-1*) Schmul Pub Co.

— The Romance of Missionary Heroism, 2. 1979. pap. 4.99 (*0-88019-104-X*) Schmul Pub Co.

Lambert, John W. The Pineapple Air Force: Pearl Harbor to Tokyo. LC 90-60558. (Illus.). 220p. (C). 1990. 44.95 (*0-9625860-0-5*) Phalanx Pub.

— Sortie: A Bibliography of Combat Aviation Unit Histories of World War II. 48p. (C). 1993. pap. 9.95 (*0-9625860-6-4*) Phalanx Pub.

Lambert, John W., ed. see Fry, Garry L.

Lambert, John W., ed. see Hagedorn, Dan.

Lambert, John W., ed. see Mullins, John D.

Lambert, John W., ed. see Olmsted, Merle.

Lambert, John W., ed. see Sakaida, Henry.

Lambert, John W., ed. see Van Osdol, William R.

***Lambert, Jonamay & Myers, Selma.** Activities for Diversity Training. 1994. ring bd. 139.95 (*0-87425-980-0*) Human Res Dev Pr.

Lambert, Jonamay, jt. auth. see Myers, Selma.

Lambert, Jonathan. Giant Jungle Pop-up Book: Animals of the Endangered Rain Forest. (Illus.). (J). (ps-3). 1992. 28.00 (*1-56021-183-0*) W J Fantasy.

— Twelve Days of Christmas. (J). (ps-3). 1992. pap. 12.00 (*0-671-78396-3*, S&S Bks Young Read) S&S Childrens.

Lambert, Jonathan, illus. Colors. (Early Learning Board Bks.). 18p. (J). (ps-1). 1992. bds. 1.95 (*0-681-41562-2*) Longmeadow Pr.

— Numbers. (Early Learning Board Bks.). 18p. (J). (ps-1). 1992. bds. 1.95 (*0-681-41563-0*) Longmeadow Pr.

— Opposites. (Early Learning Board Bks.). 18p. (J). (ps-1). 1992. bds. 1.95 (*0-681-41565-7*) Longmeadow Pr.

— Shapes. (Early Learning Board Bks.). 18p. (J). (ps-1). 1992. bds. 1.95 (*0-681-41564-9*) Longmeadow Pr.

Lambert, Joseph B. Physical Organic Chemistry Through Solved Problems. 1978. pap. text ed. 26.95 (*0-8162-4921-0*) Holden-Day.

Lambert, Joseph B., ed. Archaeological Chemistry, Vol. III. LC 83-15736. (Advances in Chemistry Ser.: No. 205). 487p. 1983. lib. bdg. 89.95 (*0-8412-0767-4*) Am Chemical.

Lambert, Joseph B. & Grupe, Gisela, eds. Prehistoric Human Bone: Archaeology at the Molecular Level. LC 93-21141. 1993. 136.00 (*0-387-55393-2*) Spr-Verlag.

Lambert, Joseph B. & Riddell, Frank G., eds. The Multinuclear Approach to NMR Spectroscopy. 1983. lib. bdg. 154.50 (*90-277-1582-3*) Kluwer Ac.

Lambert, Joseph B. & Takeuchi, Yoshito. Cyclic Organonitrogen Stereodynamics. (Methods in Stereochemical Analysis Ser.). 304p. 1991. text ed. 125.00 (*0-89573-773-6*) VCH Pubs.

Lambert, Joseph B. & Takeuchi, Yoshito, eds. Acyclic Organonitrogen Stereodynamics. (Methods in Stereochemical Analysis Ser.). 304p. 1991. text ed. 125.00 (*1-56081-555-8*) VCH Pubs.

— Organonitrogen Stereodynamics, 2 vols., Set, Pts. I & II. (Methods in Stereochemical Analysis Ser.). 692p. 1992. Set. text ed. 195.00 (*1-56081-556-6*) VCH Pubs.

Lambert, Joseph B., et al. Introduction to Organic Spectroscopy. 561p. (C). 1987. pap. write for info. (*0-02-367300-1*) Macmillan.

Lambert, Joseph C., tr. see Giraud, Marcel.

Lambert, Joseph J., ed. Terrorism & Hostages in International Law: A Commentary on the Hostages Convention 1979. 454p. (C). 1990. 220.00 (*0-949009-46-6*, Pub. by Grotius Pubns UK) St Mut.

Lambert, Judith & Peterson, Jane. From Course to Course: A Beginner's Guide to College Writing. (C). 1987. pap. text ed. 15.25 (*0-673-18328-9*) HarpCollege.

— From Course to Course: A Beginner's Guide to College Writing. LC 87-17290. (Illus.). 523p. reprint ed. pap. 149.10 (*0-7837-4744-6*, 2044553) Bks Demand.

L

Lambert, Judith & Wiener. The Advancing Writer, Bk. III. (C). 1994. text ed. 26.00 (*0-06-500303-9*) HarpCollege.

Lambert, K., ed. Philosophical Problems in Logic: Some Recent Developments. (Synthese Library: No. 29). 176p. 1970. lib. bdg. 62.00 (*90-277-0079-6*) Kluwer Ac.

Lambert, Karel. The Logical Way of Doing Things. LC 69-15450. 338p. reprint ed. pap. 96.40 (*0-317-08251-5*, 2013184) Bks Demand.

Lambert, Karel & Brittan, Gordon G., Jr. Introduction to the Philosophy of Science. rev. ed. xviii, 173p. 1987. pap. text ed. 15.00 (*0-924922-10-9*) Ridgeview.

— Introduction to the Philosophy of Science. 4th rev. ed. xviii, 173p. 1987. lib. bdg. 33.00 (*0-924922-60-5*) Ridgeview.

Lambert, Karel & Ulrih, William. The Nature of Argument. 282p. (C). 1988. reprint ed. pap. text ed. 24.00 (*0-8191-6747-9*) U Pr of Amer.

Lambert, Kathy. Martin Luther King, Jr. Civil Rights Leader. (Junior Black Americans of Achievement Ser.). (Illus.). 80p. (J). (gr. 3-6). 1993. lib. bdg. 14.95 (*0-7910-1759-1*) Chelsea Hse.

Lambert, Kathy K. Martin Luther King, Jr. Civil Rights Leader. (Junior Black Americans of Achievement Ser.). (Illus.). 80p. (J). (gr. 3-6). 1992. pap. 4.95 (*0-7910-1954-3*) Chelsea Hse.

Lambert, L. La Proteccion Espiritual (Spiritual Protection) (SPA.). Date not set. 3.50 (*1-56063-432-4*, 550016) Editorial Unilit.

Lambert, L., jt. auth. see Rowe, J.

Lambert, L., et al. Freeing Children for Adoption. (C). 1989. 39.00 (*0-903534-93-2*, Pub. by Brit Ag for Adopt & Fost UK) St Mut.

Lambert, L. Gary, jt. ed. see Hancock, Ralph C.

Lambert-Lagace, Louise. The Nutrition Challenge for Women. 192p. 1990. pap. 12.95 (*0-923521-06-2*) Bull Pub.

Lambert-Lagace, Louise & Meyer, Jean, intros. Feeding Your Baby: From Conception to Age Two. (Illus.). 320p. (Orig.). 1991. pap. 10.95 (*0-940625-37-7*) Surrey Bks.

Lambert, Laurie J., jt. auth. see Harper, Andrew C.

Lambert, Lee. Basic Library of the World's Greatest Music. (Illus.). 155p. (YA). (gr. 7 up). 1988. pap. text ed. 39.00 (*0-9621630-1-5*) L Lambert.

— Basic Library of the World's Greatest Music: Musical Learning System. (Illus.). 356p. (Orig.). 1990. teacher ed, pap. 29.00 (*0-9621630-0-7*) L Lambert.

Lambert, Lee R. & Lambert, Erin. The Other Kuwait: An American Father & Daughter's Personal Impressions. Berry, Connie & Wampler, Nan, eds. (Illus.). 250p. (Orig.). (C). 1992. pap. text ed. 16.95 (*0-9626397-1-0*) L R Lambert & Assocs.

***Lambert, Leo, et al, eds.** University Teaching: A Guide for Graduate Students. 200p. 1995. 15.00 (*0-8156-2637-1*) Syracuse U Pr.

Lambert, Lisa A. The Leakeys. LC 92-46046. (Biographies Ser.). (J). 1993. 19.93 (*0-86625-492-7*); 14.95 (*0-685-66536-4*) Rourke Pubns.

Lambert, M. Copper. (Spotlight on Resources Ser.). (Illus.). 48p. (J). (gr. 5 up). 1985. lib. bdg. 17.27 (*0-86592-270-5*); lib. bdg. 12.95 (*0-685-58324-4*) Rourke Corp.

— Iron & Steel. (Spotlight on Resources Ser.). (Illus.). 48p. (J). (gr. 5 up). 1985. 12.95 (*0-685-58325-2*); lib. bdg. 17.27 (*0-86592-268-3*) Rourke Corp.

— Plastics. (Spotlight on Resources Ser.). (Illus.). 48p. (J). (gr. 5 up). 1985. 12.95 (*0-685-58326-0*); lib. bdg. 17.27 (*0-86592-269-1*) Rourke Corp.

Lambert, M. W. & Laval, J., eds. DNA Repair Mechanisms & Their Biological Implications in Mammalian Cell. LC 89-72122. (NATO ASI Series A, Life Sciences: Vol. 182). (Illus.). 694p. 1990. 139.50 (*0-306-43411-3*, Plenum Pr) Plenum.

Lambert, Malcolm. Medieval Heresy: Popular Movements from the Gregorian Reform to the Reformation. rev. ed. 400p. 1992. reprint ed. 59.95 (*0-631-17431-1*); reprint ed. pap. 22.95 (*0-631-17432-X*) Blackwell Pubs.

Lambert, Margaret. English Popular Art. (C). 1989. text ed. 35.00 (*0-85036-372-1*, Pub. by Merlin Pr UK) Humanities.

***Lambert, Marjie.** Salsa Cooking. 1994. 17.98 (*0-7858-0023-9*) Bk Sales Inc.

— Southern Cooking. 1994. 17.98 (*0-7858-0025-5*) Bk Sales Inc.

Lambert, Mark. Dickens & the Suspended Quotation. LC 80-22072. 200p. reprint ed. pap. 57.00 (*0-8357-3751-9*, 2036477) Bks Demand.

— Farming & the Environment. LC 90-45614. (Conserving Our World Ser.). (Illus.). 48p. (J). (gr. 4-9). 1990. lib. bdg. 22.13 (*0-8114-2392-1*); pap. 5.95 (*0-8114-3453-2*) Raintree Steck-V.

— Homes in the Future. (Houses & Homes Ser.). (Illus.). 32p. (J). (gr. 2-5). 1989. 13.50 (*0-8225-2126-1*, Lerner Publctns) Lerner Group.

— Malory: Style & Vision in La Morte d'Arthur. LC 74-29727. (Yale Studies in English: No. 186). 241p. reprint ed. pap. 68.70 (*0-8357-8213-1*, 2033793) Bks Demand.

— Transportation. LC 93-24990. (Young Geographer Ser.). (Illus.). 32p. (J). (gr. 4-6). 1993. 14.95 (*1-56847-118-1*) Thomson Lrning.

Lambert, Mark & Insley, Jane. Communications & Transport. (World of Science Ser.). (Illus.). 64p. 1985. 15.95 (*0-8160-1073-0*) Facts on File.

Lambert, Mary H., ed. see Lambert, W. L.

***Lambert, Matthew.** Joey's Birthday Wish. LC 94-40451. (Publish-a-Book Ser.). (Illus.). (J). 1995. write for info. (*0-8114-7273-6*) Raintree Steck-V.

— My First Spring Day. (Publish-a-Book Contest Ser.). (Illus.). (J). 1994. lib. bdg. 19.97 (*0-8114-4459-7*) Raintree Steck-V.

Lambert, Maureen K. The Theory & Practice of Marriage at the Premier Institute of Marriage. (Illus.). 80p. 1994. pap. 12.00 (*0-8059-3558-4*) Dorrance.

Lambert, Mercedes. Dogtown: A Whitney Logan Mystery. 272p. 1992. mass mkt. 4.95 (*0-14-013928-1*, Penguin Bks) Viking Penguin.

***Lambert, Merryl.** Dolphin Sponsorship Kit. (Friends of the Ocean Ser.). 1994. 19.95 (*0-9641742-5-1*) Pequot Pubng.

— Grizzly Sponsorship Kit. 1995. 19.95 (*0-9641742-9-4*) Pequot Pubng.

— Rain Forest Preservation kit. (Friends of the Forest Ser.). 1991. 19.95 (*0-9641742-6-X*) Pequot Pubng.

— Siberian Tiger Sponsorship Kit. 1995. 19.95 (*0-9641742-7-8*) Pequot Pubng.

— Wetlands Preservation Kit. 1992. 19.95 (*0-614-06229-2*) Pequot Pubng.

— Whale Adoption Kit. (Friends of the Ocean Ser.). 1992. 19.95 (*0-9641742-3-5*) Pequot Pubng.

— Wild Mustang Sponsorship Kit. Date not set. pap. 19.95 (*1-886738-01-7*) Pequot Pubng.

— Wolf Sponsorship Kit. 1993. 19.95 (*0-9641742-4-3*) Pequot Pubng.

Lambert, Michael E., et al, eds. Eukaryotic Transposable Elements As Mutagenic Agents. (Banbury Report Ser.: No. 30). (Illus.). 362p. 1988. text ed. 77.00 (*0-87969-230-8*) Cold Spring Harbor.

Lambert, Michael J. The Effects of Psychotherapy, Vol. II. (Psychotherapy Research Review Ser.). 288p. 1982. 42.95 (*0-89885-099-1*) Human Sci Pr.

Lambert, Mike. Instant Guide to Fresh Water Birds. 1988. 3.99 (*0-517-66792-4*) Random Hse Value.

— Instant Guide to Sea Birds. 1988. 3.99 (*0-517-65524-1*) Random Hse Value.

Lambert, Miles. Fashion in Photographs, 1860-1880. (Illus.). 144p. (C). 1992. text ed. 82.50 (*0-7134-6392-9*) B&N Imports.

Lambert, Nancy. I Know I Think That There Are Angels. 31p. 1992. 4.95 (*1-882813-00-6*) Sneaker Pr.

Lambert, Neal. George Frederick Ruxton. LC 74-1974. (Western Writers Ser.: No. 15). 44p. 1974. pap. 3.95 (*0-88430-014-5*) Boise St U W Writ Ser.

Lambert, Neal E., ed. Literature of Belief. (Monograph Ser.: Vol. 5). 4.95 (*0-88494-409-3*) Bookcraft Inc.

Lambert, Nina. Players. 472p. 1994. pap. 16.95 (*0-7126-5569-7*, Pub. by Century UK) Trafalgar.

— Sisters & Strangers. 416p. 1995. 26.00 (*0-7126-5564-6*, Pub. by Century UK) Trafalgar.

Lambert, Norma K. Cumulative Indices to Military Affairs 1937-1969. (Libraries Bibliography: No. 6). 1979. 4.50 (*0-686-20808-0*) KSU.

Lambert, O. C. Catholicism Against Itself, Vol. 1. 1956. 11.95 (*0-89315-005-3*) Lambert Bk.

— Catholicism Against Itself, Vol. 2. 1965. 11.95 (*0-89315-006-1*) Lambert Bk.

— Russellism Unveiled. 1940. pap. 3.50 (*0-88027-090-X*) Firm Foun Pub.

Lambert Ortiz, Elisabeth. The Encyclopedia of Herbs, Spices & Flavorings. LC 92-6537. (Illus.). 288p. 1992. 34.95 (*1-56458-065-2*) Dorling Kindersley.

Lambert, P., jt. auth. see Pietruszka, M.

Lambert, P., et al. Color & Fiber. LC 86-61295. (Illus.). 255p. 1986. 49.50 (*0-88740-065-5*) Schiffer.

Lambert, P. Blud. Bathroom Humor: Passing Wind, Vol. 1. LC 88-81771. 200p. (Orig.). 1988. pap. 9.99 (*0-317-91202-X*) Fulcort Pr.

Lambert, P. H., et al, eds. From Antigen Presentation to Immunity & Allergy: Abstracts. (Journal: International Archives of Allergy & Applied Immunology: Vol. 83, Suppl. 1). iv, 44p. 1987. pap. 17.75 (*3-8055-4602-5*) S Karger.

Lambert, P. M. & Roger, E. H. Hospital Statistics in Europe. 200p. 1982. 48.75 (*0-444-86383-4*, North Holland) Elsevier.

Lambert, P. P., et al, eds. The Pathogenicity of Cationic Proteins. 396p. 1983. pap. text ed. 41.50 (*0-89004-689-1*) Raven.

Lambert, Patricia. Controlling Color: A Practical Introduction for Designers & Artists. 1991. pap. text ed. 16.95 (*0-07-036088-X*) McGraw.

— Controlling Color: A Practical Introduction for Designers & Artists. (Illus.). 96p. 1991. pap. 16.95 (*0-8306-3559-9*, NO. 3559, Design Pr) TAB Bks.

Lambert, Paul. ABCs of Child Care Work in Residential Care: The Linden Hill Manual. LC 77-73022. 76p. (C). 1977. pap. 12.95 (*0-87868-166-3*) Child Welfare.

Lambert, Paul F. & Franks, Kenny A., eds. Voices from the Oil Fields. LC 84-7327. (Illus.). 288p. 1984. 24.95 (*0-8061-1799-0*) U of Okla Pr.

Lambert, Paul F., jt. auth. see Franks, Kenny A.

Lambert, Paul H., et al, eds. Recent Advances in Systemic Lupus Erythematosus. 1984. text ed. 85.00 (*0-12-434620-0*) Acad Pr.

Lambert, Paulette, jt. auth. see Pietruszka, Marvin.

Lambert, Peter, jt. auth. see Hey, John.

Lambert, Peter G. My Poems (with a bit of Prose) LC 91-74115. 70p. 1992. 6.95 (*1-55523-469-0*) Winston-Derek.

Lambert, Peter J. Advanced Mathematics for Economists: Static & Dynamic Optimization. 224p. 1985. pap. 32.95 (*0-631-14139-1*) Blackwell Pubs.

— The Distribution & Redistribution of Income: A Mathematical Analysis. 2nd ed. LC 93-17870. 1993. text ed. 24.95 (*0-7190-4059-0*, Pub. by Manchester Univ Pr UK) St Martin.

***Lambert, Phyllis, ed.** Fortifications & the Synagogue: The Fortress of Babylon & the Ben Ezra Synagogue, Cairo. (Illus.). 240p. 1995. 65.00 (*0-297-83339-1*, Pub. by Weidenfeld) Trafalgar.

Lambert, Phyllis H. Turning Every Stone: Autism with Love - A Mother's Journal. (Illus.). 1990. pap. 14.95 (*0-9624737-4-X*) S P-Persephone Pr.

***Lambert, Pierre.** Dictionnaire Pratique des Mathematiques Vol. 1: Analyse. 284p. (FRE.). 1989. pap. 22.95 (*0-7859-7793-7*, 2218079429) Fr & Eur.

— Dictionnaire Pratique des Mathematiques Vol. 2: Algebre. 285p. (FRE.). 1990. pap. 22.95 (*0-7859-7786-4*, 2218025760) Fr & Eur.

Lambert, R. M., jt. ed. see Thomas, J. M.

***Lambert, Rae.** Mungo's World Tour. (Comes to Life Bks.). 16p. (J). (ps-2). 1995. write for info. (*1-57234-058-4*) YES Ent.

Lambert, Rebecca T., jt. auth. see McComish, Charles D.

Lambert, Rene. French-English, English-French Technical Aeronautics Dictionary. 304p. (ENG & FRE.). 1991. 95.00 (*0-8288-6957-X*, 2854281640) Fr & Eur.

Lambert, Richard D., ed. America's Most Challenging Objectives. LC 76-160739. (Annals Ser.: 396). 1971. 27.00 (*0-87761-140-8*); pap. 18.00 (*0-87761-139-4*) Am Acad Pol Soc Sci.

— China in the World Today. LC 72-78295. (Annals Ser.: 402). 300p. 1972. 27.00 (*0-685-00180-6*); pap. 18.00 (*0-87761-150-5*) Am Acad Pol Soc Sci.

— Foreign Language Instruction: A National Agenda. (Annals Ser.: Vol. 490). 1987. 26.00 (*0-8039-2931-5*); pap. 17.00 (*0-8039-2932-3*) Sage.

— New Directions in International Education. LC 80-65243. (Annals of the American Academy of Political & Social Science Ser.: No. 449). 1980. pap. text ed. 18.00 (*0-87761-251-X*) Am Acad Pol Soc Sci.

Lambert, Richard D. & Heston, Alan W., eds. The Annals Ninetieth Anniversary Index: 1976-1980. 192p. 1981. 26.00 (*0-8039-1762-7*); pap. 17.00 (*0-8039-1763-5*) Sage.

Lambert, Richard D., jt. ed. see Alexander, Herbert E.

Lambert, Richard D., jt. ed. see Altbach, Philip G.

Lambert, Richard D., ed. see American Academy of Political & Social Science Staff.

Lambert, Richard D., jt. ed. see Blake, David H.

Lambert, Richard D., ed. see Bradway, John S.

Lambert, Richard D., jt. ed. see Bressler, Marvin.

Lambert, Richard D., ed. see Charlesworth, James C.

Lambert, Richard D., jt. ed. see Charlesworth, James C.

Lambert, Richard D., jt. ed. see Clemente, Frank.

Lambert, Richard D., jt. ed. see Cook, Philip J.

Lambert, Richard D., ed. see Ferman, Louis A.

Lambert, Richard D., jt. ed. see Fox, Renee C.

Lambert, Richard D., jt. ed. see Fox, William T.

Lambert, Richard D., jt. ed. see Galnoor, Itzhal.

Lambert, Richard D., jt. ed. see Gordon, Milton M.

Lambert, Richard D., jt. ed. see Gross, Bertram M.

Lambert, Richard D., ed. see Hart, Parker T.

Lambert, Richard D., jt. ed. see Holland, Kenneth.

Lambert, Richard D., jt. ed. see Hollingsworth, J. Rogers.

Lambert, Richard D., jt. auth. see Jorden, Eleanor H.

Lambert, Richard D., jt. auth. see Lyons, Gene M.

Lambert, Richard D., jt. ed. see Mott, George F.

Lambert, Richard D., jt. ed. see Ornstein, Norman J.

Lambert, Richard D., jt. ed. see Park, Richard L.

Lambert, Richard D., ed. see Shur, Irene G. & Littell, Franklin H.

Lambert, Richard D., jt. ed. see Taeuber, Conrad.

Lambert, Richard D., jt. ed. see Weintraub, Sidney.

Lambert, Richard D., ed. see Wilcox, Wayne.

Lambert, Richard D., jt. ed. see Windmuller, John P.

Lambert, Richard D., jt. ed. see Wolfgang, Marvin E.

Lambert, Richard D., et al. The Role of the Scholarly Disciplines. 43p. pap. 10.95 (*0-915390-25-6*, Pub. by Change Mag) Transaction Pubs.

— The Transformation of an Indian Labor Market: The Case of Pune. LC 86-26900. (University of Pennsylvania Studies on South Asia: No. 3). x, 249p. 1986. 65.00 (*0-915027-63-1*) Benjamins North Am.

Lambert, Richard d., et al, eds. Language Planning Around the World: Contexts & Systemic Change. LC 94-5826. (National Foreign Language Center Monograph Ser.). 1994. 10.00 (*1-880671-03-4*) NFLC Pubns.

Lambert, Robert S. South Carolina Loyalists in the American Revolution. 362p. 1987. text ed. 29.95 (*0-87249-506-X*) U of SC Pr.

Lambert, Rosemary. The Twentieth Century. (Cambridge Introduction to Art Ser.). (C). 1981. pap. 11.95 (*0-521-29622-6*) Cambridge U Pr.

Lambert, Royston. Beloved & God: The Story of Hadrian & Antinous. 352p. reprint ed. pap. 9.95 (*0-8216-2003-7*) Carol Pub Group.

Lambert, Ruth D. One Hundred One Survival Tactics for New & Used Parents. (Illus.). (Orig.). 1991. pap. 11.95 (*0-927054-15-9*) H Sq Co.

Lambert, Ruth D. & Harrison, Henry S. Houses Cookbook. (Illus.). 1991. reprint ed. pap. 11.95 (*0-927054-16-7*) H Sq Co.

Lambert, S. D. The Phratries of Attica. LC 92-41140. (Monographs in Classical Antiquity). (Illus.). 400p. (C). 1993. text ed. 69.50 (*0-472-10388-1*) U of Mich Pr.

Lambert, Samuel W. When Mr. Pickwick Went Fishing. LC 74-3271. (Studies in Dickens: No. 52). 1974. lib. bdg. 47.95 (*0-8383-2063-5*) M S G Haskell Hse.

Lambert, Sheila. Bills & Acts: Legislative Procedures in Eighteenth-Century England. LC 78-163054. 256p. reprint ed. pap. 73.00 (*0-8357-7211-X*, 2031680) Bks Demand.

Lambert, Sheila, ed. The House of Commons Sessional Papers of the Eighteenth Century Pt. 1: George I & II, 20 vols., Set, incl. List Vol. I. 1975. Set. 2,200.00 (*0-8420-2014-4*) Scholarly Res Inc.

— The House of Commons Sessional Papers of the Eighteenth Century Pt. 2: George III, 127 vols., Set, incl. List Vol. II. 1975. Set. 13,690.00 (*0-8420-2016-0*) Scholarly Res Inc.

Lambert, Simon, ed. Managing Tertiary & Sixth Form Colleges. LC 88-2687. 134p. reprint ed. pap. 38.20 (*0-7837-5179-6*, 2044909) Bks Demand.

Lambert, Stephen. The Snowmaiden. (Illus.). 32p. (J). (gr. 1-3). 1992. 15.95 (*0-09-173861-X*, Pub. by Hutchnson UK) Trafalgar.

Lambert, Stephen, jt. auth. see DeGalan, Julie.

Lambert, Stephen E. & DeGalan, Julie. Great Jobs for English Majors. LC 93-45866. 1994. 11.95 (*0-8442-4350-7*, VGM Career Bks) NTC Pub Grp.

***Lambert, Stephen G. & Casey, William L.** Laser Communications in Space. LC 95-7139. 1995. write for info. (*0-89006-722-8*) Artech Hse.

Lambert, Steve. Internet Basics: Your Map to the Global Electronic Super Highway. 1993. 27.00 (*0-679-75023-1*) Random.

Lambert, Steve & Cox, Joyce. A Quick Course in Word for Windows: Version 2. (Quick Course Computer Book Ser.). (Illus.). 160p. 1992. pap. 12.95 (*1-879399-05-9*) Online Pr.

Lambert, Steve, jt. auth. see Cox, Joyce.

Lambert, Steve, jt. auth. see Wolverton, Van.

Lambert, Sylvie & Moser-Mercer, Barbara, eds. Bridging the Gap: Empirical Research in Simultaneous Interpretation. LC 94-9728. (Benjamins Translation Library: Vol. 3). 1994. 69.00 (*1-55619-481-1*) Benjamins North Am.

Lambert, Thomas F., Jr. The Case for Punitive Damages: A New Audit. (ATLA Monograph Ser.). 34p. (Orig.). 1988. pap. 6.00 (*0-941916-47-2*) ATLA Pr.

Lambert, Tom. Key Management Tools: 40 Time-Saving Techniques to Solve Everyday Business Problems. (Financial Times Management Ser.). 272p. 1993. 90.00x (*0-273-60384-1*, Pub. by Pitman Pubng UK) St Mut.

***Lambert, Tony.** Resurrection of the Chinese Church. 319p. (C). 1991. pap. 12.95 (*0-87788-728-4*) Shaw Pubs.

— Resurrection of the Chinese Church. 319p. (C). 1991. pap. 15.95 (*0-340-54997-1*) H & S Ltd.

Lambert, W. A., tr. see Luther, Martin.

***Lambert, W. C. & Van Vloten, W. A., eds.** Basic Mechanisms of Physiological & Aberrant Lymphoproliferation in the Skin. (NATO ASI Series A, Life Sciences: 265). (Illus.). 600p. 1994. 135.00 (*0-306-44736-3*, Plenum Pr) Plenum.

Lambert, W. L. Sandscripts, Vol. I: Word Pictures of Life. Lambert, Mary H., ed. & illus. by. LC 88-91181. 102p. (Orig.). (C). 1988. pap. 7.00 (*0-929357-00-0*) Sandscript Creations.

Lambert, Wallace E. Language, Psychology, & Culture: Essays by Wallace E. Lambert. Dil, Anwar S., ed. LC 71-183890. (Language Science & National Development Ser.). xvi, 368p. 1972. 47.50 (*0-8047-0803-7*) Stanford U Pr.

Lambert, Wallace E. & Klineberg, Otto. Children's Views of Foreign People: A Cross-National Study. LC 66-24057. (Century Psychology Ser.). (Illus.). 1967. 28.00 (*0-89197-076-2*) Irvington.

Lambert, Wallace E. & Taylor, Donald M. Coping with Cultural & Racial Diversity in Urban America. LC 89-16097. 214p. 1990. text ed. 49.95 (*0-275-93174-9*, C3174, Praeger Pubs) Greenwood.

Lambert, Walter N. Kinfolks & Custard Pie: Recollections & Recipes from an East Tennessean. LC 88-14342. (Illus.). 224p. 1988. 15.95 (*0-87049-585-2*) U of Tenn Pr.

Lambert, William R. Drink & Sobriety in Victorian Wales, C. 1820-C. 1895. xiv, 294p. 1984. 33.50 (*0-7083-0845-7*, Pub. by U of Wales UK) Bks Intl VA.

Lamberth, Wade C. & Doty, Donald, eds. Peripheral Vascular Surgery. (Illus.). 350p. 1987. 95.00 (*0-8151-5324-4*, WOV-1, Yr Bk Med Pubs) Mosby Yr Bk.

Lamberti, C. Diccionario Enciclopedico De Astronomia. 284p. 1989. 39.95 (*0-7859-6406-1*, 8486761131) Fr & Eur.

Lamberti, F. & Taylor, C. E., eds. Cyst Nematodes. LC 86-25381. (NATO ASI Series A, Life Sciences: Vol. 121). 478p. 1986. 110.00 (*0-306-42475-4*, Plenum Pr) Plenum.

— Root-Knot Nematodes: Meloidogyne Species: Systematics, Biology & Control. 1979. text ed. 151.00 (*0-12-434850-5*) Acad Pr.

***Lamberti, F., et al, eds.** Advances in Molecular Plant Nematology. (NATO ASI Series A, Life Sciences: 268). (C). 1994. 95.00 (*0-306-44822-X*, Plenum Pr) Plenum.

— Durable Resistance in Crops. LC 82-18980. (NATO ASI Series A, Life Sciences: Vol. 55). 464p. 1983. 115.00 (*0-306-41183-0*, Plenum Pr) Plenum.

Lamberti, Jean-Claude. Tocqueville & the Two Democracies. Goldhammer, Arthur, tr. LC 88-18758. 323p. 1989. 50.00 (*0-674-89435-9*) HUP.

Lamberti, Jean-Claude, ed. see De Tocqueville, Alexis.

Lamberti, Marjorie. State, Society, & the Elementary School in Imperial Germany. 302p. 1989. 49.95 (*0-19-505611-6*) OUP.

Lamberto, Charlanne, ed. see Overlook Hospital Auxilary Staff.

Lamberton, ed. Passive Infrared Systems & Technology. 184p. 1987. 43.00 (*0-89252-842-7*, 807) SPIE.

Lamberton, Don, et al. The Trouble with Technology. LC 83-10961. 200p. 1983. text ed. 29.95 (*0-312-81985-4*) St Martin.

Lamberton, Donald M. Theory of Profit. LC 70-1657. 1965. 27.50 (*0-678-06259-5*) Kelley.

Lamberton, Robert. Hesiod. LC 87-10595. 208p. (C). 1988. pap. 13.00 (*0-300-04069-5*) Yale U Pr.

— Homer the Theologian: Neoplatonist Allegorical Reading & the Growth of the Epic Tradition. LC 85-1184. (Transformation of the Classical Heritage Ser.: No. IX). 375p. (C). 1986. pap. 15.00 (*0-520-06607-3*) U CA Pr.

Lamberton, Robert, tr. Cave of Nymphs: Porphyry. LC 82-16969. 64p. (Orig.). 1983. 12.50 (*0-930794-71-0*); pap. 4.95 (*0-930794-72-9*) Station Hill Pr.

Lamberton, Robert, tr. see Blanchot, Maurice.

Lamberton, Robert, jt. ed. see Keaney, John J.

An Asterisk (*) at the beginning of an entry indicates that the title is appearing in BIP for the first time.

Lamberton, Robert D. & Rotroff, Susan I. Birds of the Athenian Agora. (Excavations of the Athenian Agora Picture Bks.: No. 22). (Illus.). 32p. 1985. pap. 3.00 (*0-87661-627-9*) Am Sch Athens.
Lamberton, Sharon, ed. see Behler, Quenda B.
Lamberton, Sharon, ed. see Behler, Quenda.
Lamberton, Sharon, ed. see Elkman, Richard.
Lamberton, Sharon, ed. see Rogers, Leon.
Lamberton, Sharon, ed. see Rogers, Leon & Weidman, Brent.
Lamberton, Sharon, ed. see Russell, Philip & Hemmer, Joe.
Lamberts, David W. & Potter, David E. Clinical Ocular Pharmacology. 560p. 1987. 89.95 (*0-316-51286-9*, Little Med Div) Little.
— Clinical Ophthalmic Pharmacology. 608p. 1987. text ed. 55.00 (*0-318-37135-9*) Little.
Lamberts, H. & Wood, M. ICPC: International Classification of Primary Care. 224p. 1988. pap. 31.95 (*0-19-261633-1*) OUP.
Lamberts, Henk, et al, eds. The International Classification of Primary Care in the European Community: With a Multi-Language Layer. (Illus.). 256p. 1993. 90.00 (*0-19-262298-6*) OUP.
Lamberts, J. J. A Short Introduction to English Usage. LC 80-28499. 400p. (C). 1981. reprint ed. lib. bdg. 29.50 (*0-89874-328-1*) Krieger.
Lamberts, W. J., jt. ed. see Van Wimersma Greidanus, T. B.
Lambertsen, Isaac, tr. Life of St. Anna of Novgorod. 16p. (Orig.). 1983. pap. 1.00 (*0-912927-06-2*, X006) St John Kronstadt.
— St. John of Kronstadt: Life, Service, & Akathist Hymn. 51p. (Orig.). 1983. pap. 4.00 (*0-912927-03-8*, X003) St John Kronstadt.
— Suffering of St. Eleutherius. 16p. (Orig.). 1983. pap. 1.00 (*0-912927-05-4*, X005) St John Kronstadt.
Lambertsen, Isaac E., tr. The Eleven Resurrectional Gospels of Matins: With the Resurrectional Exapostilaria & Their Theotokia & the Evangelical Stichera. (Illus.). 32p. (Orig.). 1992. pap. 4.00 (*0-912927-50-X*, X045) St John Kronstadt.
— The Holy Martyrs Adrian & Natalia: Account of Their Suffering, Liturgical Service, Akathist Hymn. 48p. (Orig.). 1989. pap. 3.50 (*0-912927-35-6*, X035) St John Kronstadt.
— The Holy Myrrh-Bearer Mary Magdalen: Life & Akathist Hymn. 48p. (Orig.). 1989. pap. 3.00 (*0-912927-34-8*, X034) St John Kronstadt.
— The Kazan' Icon of the Mother of God: History, Service, & Akathist Hymn. 48p. (Orig.). 1985. pap. 3.50 (*0-912927-13-5*, X013) St John Kronstadt.
— The Life of Our Holy Father Spyridon of Tremithus. 24p. (Orig.). 1982. pap. 1.50 (*0-912927-53-4*, Y002) St John Kronstadt.
— The Life of the Holy Apostle & Evangelist Luke: And the Liturgical Service in His Honor. 32p. (Orig.). 1989. pap. 2.50 (*0-912927-32-1*, X032) St John Kronstadt.
— Life of the Holy Prince Vladimir the Great of Kiev: With Liturgical Service, & Akathist Hymn. (Illus.). 48p. (Orig.). 1993. pap. 3.00 (*0-912927-55-0*, X046) St John Kronstadt.
— Prayers for the Blessing & Sanctification of Icons of Various Kinds, & of an Iconostasis. 24p. (Orig.). 1993. pap. 3.00 (*0-912927-51-8*, D014) St John Kronstadt.
— The Reigning, Kolomna Icon of the Mother of God: Account of Appearance, Liturgical Service, Akathist Hymn. (Illus.). 48p. (Orig.). 1989. pap. 4.00 (*0-912927-37-2*, X037) St John Kronstadt.
— The Rite of Holy Matrimony. 16p. (Orig.). 1991. pap. 2.00 (*0-912927-46-1*, D008) St John Kronstadt.
— Saints Euthymius, Ignatius & Acacius: Holy New Venerable-Martyrs of Athos. 32p. (Orig.). 1984. pap. 2.50 (*0-912927-10-0*, X010) St John Kronstadt.
— Service of Supplication Chanted in Time of Drought. 20p. (Orig.). 1991. pap. 2.00 (*0-912927-45-3*, D002) St John Kronstadt.
— The Service of the Lesser Sanctification of Water: Customarily Used on the 1st Day of August. 12p. (Orig.). 1992. pap. 3.00 (*0-912927-48-8*, D011) St John Kronstadt.
— St. Benedict of Nursia: Life from the Menology of St. Dimitri of Rostov, Orthodox Liturgical Service, Akathist Hymn, Rule for Monasteries. (Illus.). 80p. (Orig.). reprint ed. pap. 5.00 (*0-912927-38-0*, X038) St John Kronstadt.
— The Suffering of the Holy Venerable-Martyr Stephen the New. 32p. (Orig.). 1985. pap. 2.50 (*0-912927-14-3*, X014) St John Kronstadt.
— The Translation of the Precious Relics of Our Father among the Saints Nicholas, Archbishop of Myra in Lycia from Myra, to Bari in Italy: Account of the Translation, & the Liturgical Service for Its Commemoration. (Illus.). 32p. (Orig.). 1987. pap. 2.50 (*0-912927-26-7*, X026) St John Kronstadt.
— The Wonderworking Kurst-Root Icon of the Mother of God: Discovery & History, Recent Miracles, Liturgical Service, Akathist Hymn. (Illus.). 64p. (Orig.). 1989. pap. 3.50 (*0-912927-33-X*, X033) St John Kronstadt.
Lambertsen, Isaac E., tr. see Clader, Timothy, ed.
Lambertsen, Isaac E., tr. see Olson, Daniel, ed.
Lambertsen, Isaac E., tr. see Von Gardner, Ivan.
Lambertsen, Issac E. & Endres, Xenia, trs. The Lives of the Three Great Hierarchs: Basil the Great, Gregory the Theologian, & John Chrysostom. LC 89-104823. (Illus.). 192p. 1986. 15.50 (*0-935889-00-0*) Dormition Pubns.
Lambertsen, Issac E., jt. auth. see Holy Apostles Convent Staff.
Lamberty, B. George, jt. auth. see Cormack, George C.
Lamberty, G. & Coll, C. G., eds. Puerto Rican Women & Children: Issues in Health, Growth, & Development. (Topics in Social Psychiatry Ser.). (Illus.). 200p. 1994. 45.00 (*0-306-44615-4*, Plenum Pr) Plenum.
Lamberty, Kim, tr. see Committee for National Security & W. Averell Harriman Institute for Advanced Study of Soviet Union.
***Lambesis, B.** Healthy Senior Workbook. 1994. pap. 3.99 (*0-517-13382-2*) Random.
Lambesis, Barbara. One Hundred One Big Ideas for Promoting a Business on a Small Budget. LC 89-91071. 112p. (Orig.). 1989. pap. 9.95 (*0-9624798-0-2*) Mktg Methods Pr.
Lambesis, Barbara, ed. The Healthy Senior Workbook: Your Personal Health Management Planner. 160p. 1991. pap. 11.95 (*0-9624798-1-0*) Mktg Methods Pr.
Lambeth, et al. Solar Four. 96p. 1981. pap. 14.95 (*0-9601678-7-0*) Miami Dog Pr.
Lambeth, Courtney, jt. ed. see Im, Hun B.
Lambeth, Edmund B. Committed Journalism: An Ethic for the Profession. 2nd ed. LC 91-32569. 256p. 1992. text ed. 35.00 (*0-253-33220-6*); pap. text ed. 12.95 (*0-253-20719-3*, MB-719) Ind U Pr.
Lambeth, James & Delap, John. Solar Designing: 1979. (Illus.). 1977. 22.95 (*0-9601678-1-1*); pap. 11.95 (*0-9601678-2-X*) Miami Dog Pr.
Lambeth, Joseph A. Lambeth Method of Cake Decoration & Practical Pastries. LC 80-65654. (Illus.). 362p. 1980. reprint ed. 50.00 (*0-916096-23-8*) Books Bakers.
Lambeth, L. G., jt. auth. see Sainsbury, M.
Lambeth, R. J. Marine Insurance, Templeman on: Principles & Practice. 6th ed. (C). 1986. 600.00 (*0-685-32724-8*, Pub. by Witherby & Co UK) St Mut.
— Templeman on Marine Insurance: Its Principles & Practice. 6th ed. 628p. 1986. 89.50 (*0-273-02537-6*) Sheridan.
Lambi, Ivo N. The Navy & German Power Politics, Eighteen Sixty-Two to Nineteen Fourteen. 356p. (C). 1984. text ed. 65.00 (*0-04-943035-1*) Routledge Chapman & Hall.
***Lambiase, J. J., ed.** Hydrocarbon Habitat in Rift Basins. (Geological Society Special Publication: No. 80). 370p. (C). 1994. 108.00 (*1-897799-15-2*, Pub. by Geol Soc Pub Hse UK) AAPG.
Lambie, Dolores Z., et al. Home Teaching with Mothers & Infants: Ypsilanti-Carnegie Infant Education Project - an Experiment. LC 74-16863. (Monographs of the High-Scope Educational Research Foundation: No. 2). 129p. 1980. pap. 12.95 (*0-931114-01-2*) High-Scope.
Lambie, Jack. Composite Construction for Homebuilt Aircraft. Markowski, Michael A., ed. LC 83-51736. (Sport Aviation Ser.: No. 6). (Illus.). 320p. (Orig.). 1984. pap. 17.95 (*0-938716-14-X*) Markowski Intl.
— Composite Construction for Homebuilts & ARVs. (Illus.). 240p. 1984. pap. 19.95 (*0-685-24708-2*) Markowski Intl.
— Ultralight Airmanship: How to Master the Air in an Ultralight. Markowski, Michael A., ed. LC 81-71888. (Ultralight Aviation Ser.: No. 2). (Illus.). (Orig.). 1984. pap. 11.95 (*0-938716-02-6*) Markowski Intl.
Lambie, Rosemary & Daniels-Mohring, Debbie. Family Systems Within Educational Contexts: Understanding Students with Special Needs. LC 91-77050. 319p. 1993. pap. 29.95 (*0-89108-223-9*, 9204) Love Pub Co.
Lambie, William, jt. auth. see Carrington, Frank.
Lambin, H. Questions of Christians: Vol. 4: John's Response. LC 86-71749. 144p. 1986. pap. 3.95 (*0-914070-27-4*, 226) ACTA Pubns.
Lambin, H., jt. auth. see Massion, J.
Lambin, H. R., jt. auth. see Massion, J. C.
Lambin, Helen R. In the Beginning: A Humorous Survey of the Bible. (Illus.). 64p. (Orig.). 1991. pap. 3.95 (*0-87946-058-X*, 124) ACTA Pubns.
Lambin, Jean-Jacques. Marketing Strategy: A New European Approach. LC 93-21714. (Marketing for Professionals Ser.). 1993. 22.50 (*0-07-707795-4*) McGraw.
Lambin, Thomas O. An Introduction to Biblical Hebrew. 345p. (C). 1971. text ed. write for info. (*0-02-367250-1*, Scribners) S&S Trade.
Lambing, Peggy, jt. auth. see Kuehl, Charles.
Lambing, Peggy A. & Kuehl, Charles R. Small Business: Planning & Management. 3rd ed. LC 93-72828. 851p. (C). 1993. text ed. 51.00 (*0-03-097578-6*) Dryden Pr.
Lambing, Peggy A., jt. auth. see Kuehl, Charles R.
Lambiris, A. J. Frogs & Toads of the Natal Drakensberg. (Ukhahlamba Ser.: No. 3). 1989. pap. 11.95 (*0-86980-612-2*, Pub. by Univ Natal Pr SA) Intl Spec Bk.
Lambirth, Edwin. The Rivard House. 272p. 1985. reprint ed. pap. 3.25 (*0-8439-2220-6*) Dorchester Pub Co.
Lambkin, Romie. My Time in the War: An Irishwoman's Diary. (Illus.). 192p. 1993. 34.00 (*0-86327-351-3*, Pub. by Wolfhound Pr IE); pap. 17.95 (*0-86327-320-3*, Pub. by Wolfhound Pr IE) Dufour.
Lamble, J. W. & Abbott, A. C., eds. Receptors, Again. 322p. 1984. pap. 23.50 (*0-444-80593-1*, I-430-84) Elsevier.
Lamble, J. W. & Cuthbert, eds. More about Receptors. (Current Reviews in Biomedicine Ser.: Vol. 2). 180p. 1982. pap. 30.00 (*0-444-80428-5*) Elsevier.
Lamble, Phillip, tr. see Marx, Siegfried & Pfau, Werner.
***Lambley.** Middle Aged Rebel. 1995. pap. text ed. 14.95 (*1-85230-644-0*) Element MA.
Lambley, Peter. Insomnia & Other Sleeping Problems. 1989. pap. 3.95 (*1-55817-185-1*, Pinnacle NY) Windsor NY.
Lambo, T. A. & Day, Stacey B., eds. Issues in Contemporary International Health. LC 89-72169. (Illus.). 360p. 1990. 75.00 (*0-306-43344-3*, Plenum Med Bk) Plenum.
Lambooij, Ed E. Automatic Electronic Identification Systems for Farm Animals, No. EUR 13198. 144p. 1991. pap. 15.00 (*92-826-0526-4*, CD-NA-13198-EN-C, Pub. by Europ Com) UNIPUB.
Lamboon, Raymond E. Geology of Coshocton Co., Ohio. 245p. 1993. reprint ed. lib. bdg. 34.50 (*0-8328-2992-7*) Higginson Bk Co.
Lambooy, J. G., jt. ed. see Kuklinski, Antoni.
Lamboray, Jean-Louis & Elmendorf, A. Edward. Combatting AIDS & the Other Sexually Transmitted Diseases in Africa: A Review of the World Bank's Agenda for Action. LC 92-49522. (Discussion Paper Ser.: Vol. 181). 1992. 6.95 (*0-8213-2262-1*, 12262) World Bank.
Lambord, Creede & Lambord, Sharleen. Heart of Darkness. (Dark Conspiracy Ser.). 64p. (Orig.). (YA). 1991. pap. 10.00 (*0-685-61116-7*) Game Designers.
Lambord, Sharleen, jt. auth. see Lambord, Creede.
Lamborn, Alan. The Price of Power: Risk & Foreign Policy in Britain, France & Germany. (Studies in International Conflict: No. 4). 224p. (C). 1990. text ed. 55.00 (*0-04-445083-4*) Routledge Chapman & Hall.
Lamborn, E. Shakespeare, the Man. LC 76-30695. (Studies in Shakespeare: No. 24). 1977. lib. bdg. 75.00 (*0-8383-2173-9*) M S G Haskell Hse.
Lamborn, Edmund A. & Harrison, George B. Shakespeare: The Man & His Stage. LC 73-153336. reprint ed. 29.50 (*0-404-03805-0*) AMS Pr.
Lamborn, Florence, tr. see Lindgren, Astrid.
Lamborn, S. The Genealogy of the Lamborn Family with Extracts from History, Biographies & Anecdotes, Etc. (Illus.). 487p. reprint ed. lib. bdg. 81.00 (*0-8328-0745-1*); reprint ed. pap. 73.00 (*0-8328-0746-X*) Higginson Bk Co.
Lambot, Isobel. Blood Ties. large type ed. 1989. 17.95 (*0-7089-2092-6*) Ulverscroft.
— Come Back & Die. large type ed. 296p. 1989. 17.95 (*0-7089-1977-4*) Ulverscroft.
— The Identity Trap. large type ed. 288p. 1989. 17.95 (*0-7089-2013-6*) Ulverscroft.
— Still Waters Run Deadly. large type ed. 384p. 1989. 17.95 (*0-7089-2040-3*) Ulverscroft.
— Watcher on the Shore. large type ed. 336p. 1988. 15.95 (*0-7089-1914-6*) Ulverscroft.
Lambotte, H., jt. auth. see Taerwe, L.
***Lambou, Andreas.** Fountain Pens in the World. (Illus.). 328p. 1995. 180.00 (*0-302-00668-0*) Scala Books.
Lambourne, Cherie. Salads. Bourdreaux, Martina, ed. 64p. 1988. pap. 3.49 (*0-942320-08-5*) Am Cooking.
Lambourne, Lionel, ed. Madame Tussaud's Book of Victorian Masks. (Illus.). 48p. 1987. pap. 18.95 (*0-525-48359-4*, Dutton) NAL-Dutton.
Lambourne, Maureen. Birds of the World: Over Four Hundred of John Gould's Classic Bird Illustrations. LC 92-50130. (Illus.). 304p. 1992. 75.00 (*0-8478-1566-8*) Rizzoli Intl.
— Gould's Exotic Birds. (Victoria & Albert Natural History Illustrators Ser.). (Illus.). 64p. 1988. student ed 13.00 (*0-929655-58-3*) Abrams.
Lambourne, Mike. Down the Hatch! Find Out about Your Food. LC 91-22686. (Lighter Look Book Ser.). (Illus.). 40p. (J). (gr. 2-6). 1992. lib. bdg. 14.40 (*1-56294-150-X*) Millbrook Pr.
— Inside Story: The Latest News about Your Body. LC 91-22960. (Lighter Look Book Ser.). (Illus.). 40p. (J). (gr. 2-6). 1992. lib. bdg. 14.40 (*1-56294-148-8*) Millbrook Pr.
Lambourne, R., et al. Close Encounters? Science & Science Fiction. (Illus.). 200p. 1990. pap. 29.90 (*0-85274-141-3*) IOP Pub.
Lambourne, R. A., ed. Community, Church & Healing. (C). 1990. pap. 30.00 (*0-85305-279-4*, Pub. by J Arthur Ltd UK) St Mut.
Lambourne, Ron. Paint & Surface Coatings. 1993. pap. text ed. 205.00 (*0-13-030974-5*) P-H.
Lambra, G. N. & Greve, E. L., eds. Ocular Blood Flow in Glaucoma: Means, Methods & Measurements. LC 89-19833. (Illus.). 295p. 1989. lib. bdg. 75.00 (*90-6299-053-3*, Pub. by Kugler NE) Kugler Pubns.
***Lambrecht, Frank.** Pawa: A Memoir from the Belgian Congo 1945-1949. (Illus.). 112p. (Orig.). (C). 1994. pap. 17.95 (*0-9643780-0-0*) Lane & Assocs.
Lambrecht, Frank L. In the Shade of an Acacia Tree: Memoirs of a Health Officer in Africa: 1945-59. LC 90-56110. (Memoirs Ser.: Vol. 194). (Illus.). 420p. (C). 1991. 40.00 (*0-87169-194-9*, M194-LAF) Am Philos.
— Where the Mopane Bloom: A Biologist in Ngamiland, Botswana. LC 89-8101. 1990. 25.00 (*0-89341-577-4*, Longwood Academic) Hollowbrook.
***Lambrecht, J. Thomas.** 3-D Modeling Technology in Oral & Maxillofacial Surgery. LC 94-48366. 1995. text ed. 140.00 (*0-86715-287-7*) Quint Pub Co.
Lambrecht, Jan. Out of the Treasure: The Parables in the Gospel of Matthew. (Louvain Theological & Pastoral Monographs). 296p. (Orig.). (C). 1992. pap. 24.99 (*0-8028-0662-7*) Eerdmans.
— The Sermon on the Mount: Proclamation & Exhortation. LC 85-47751. (Good News Studies: Vol. 14). 255p. 1985. pap. 12.95 (*0-8146-5467-3*) Liturgical Pr.
— The Wretched "I" & Its Liberation: Paul in Romans 7 & 8. (Louvain Theological & Pastoral Monographs). 165p. 1993. pap. 24.99 (*0-8028-0570-1*) Eerdmans.
Lambrecht, Judith J. & Edgmand, Nina M. Microsoft Excel 5.0: A Professional Approach. LC 93-42004. 1994. write for info. (*0-02-801955-5*) Glencoe.
Lambrecht, K. & Quenstedt, W. A. Paleontologi: A Biographical & Bibliographical Register of Paleontologists, Pt. 72. Albritton, Claude C., Jr., ed. LC 77-6526. (History of Geology Ser.). 1978. reprint ed. lib. bdg. 44.95 (*0-405-10445-6*) Ayer.
Lambrecht, Knud. Information Structure & Sentence Form: Topic, Focus, & the Mental Representations of Discourse Referents. LC 93-30380. (Cambridge Studies in Linguistics: No. 71). 434p. (C). 1994. 54.95 (*0-521-38056-1*) Cambridge U Pr.
— Topic, Antitopic & Verb Agreement in Non-Standard French. (Pragmatics & Beyond Ser.: II: 6). vii, 113p. (Orig.). 1981. pap. 29.00x (*90-272-2526-5*) Benjamins North Am.
Lambrecht, Richard M. & Morcos, Nabil, eds. Nuclear & Radiochemistry Applications. LC 82-9111. (Illus.). 592p. 1982. 245.00 (*0-08-027544-3*, E125, Pub. by Pergamon Repr UK); 68.00 (*0-08-029389-1*, Pub. by Pergamon Repr UK) Franklin.
Lambrechts, Eric & Salu, Luc. Photography & Literature: An International Bibliography of Monographs. LC 91-34752. 320p. 1992. text ed. 100.00 (*0-7201-2113-2*, Z1023, Mansell Pub) Cassell.
Lambrechts, M. & Sansen, W. Biosensors: Microelectrochemical Devices. (Illus.). 320p. 1992. 112.00 (*0-7503-0112-0*) IOP Pub.
Lambrechtse, Rudi. Hiking the Escalante. LC 84-63000. (Illus.). 192p. (Orig.). 1985. pap. 7.50 (*0-915272-27-X*) Wasatch Pubs.
Lambrick, G. The Rollright Stones: Megaliths, Monuments, & Settlement in the Prehistoric Landscape. (Historical Buildings & Monuments Commission for England Archaeological Report Ser.: No. 6). (Illus.). 145p. 1988. pap. 40.00 (*1-85074-192-1*, HM4330, Pub. by HMSO UK) UNIPUB.
Lambright, Henry & Rahm, Dianne, eds. Technology & American Competitiveness. (Orig.). 1989. pap. 12.00 (*0-944285-12-0*) Pol Studies.
***Lambright, W. Henry.** Powering Apollo: James E. Webb of NASA. LC 94-29063. (New Series in NASA History). (Illus.). 296p. 1994. text ed. 35.95x (*0-8018-4902-0*) Johns Hopkins.
— Presidential Management of Science & Technology: The Johnson Presidency. (Administrative History of the Johnson Presidency Ser.). 238p. 1985. text ed. 25.00 (*0-292-76494-4*) U of Tex Pr.
Lambright, W. Henry & Rahm, Dianne, eds. Technology & U. S. Competitiveness: An Institutional Focus. LC 92-8845. (Contributions in Economics & Economic History Ser.: No. 139). 200p. 1992. text ed. 49.95 (*0-313-28560-8*, LRH, Greenwood Pr) Greenwood.
Lambris, J. D., ed. The Third Component of Complement. (Current Topics in Microbiology & Immunology Ser.: Vol. 153). (Illus.). 248p. 1989. 104.00 (*0-387-51513-5*) Spr-Verlag.
Lambropoulos, Peter, jt. auth. see Chin, S. L.
Lambropoulos, Peter, ed. see International Conference on Multiphoton Processes Staff, et al.
Lambropoulos, V., jt. auth. see Alexiou, M.
Lambropoulos, Vassilis. Literature As National Institution: Studies in the Politics of Modern Greek Criticism. 304p. 1988. text ed. 42.50 (*0-691-06731-7*) Princeton U Pr.
— The Rise of Eurocentrism: Anatomy of Interpretation. 480p. 1992. text ed. 35.00 (*0-691-06949-2*) Princeton U Pr.
Lambropoulos, Vassilis & Miller, David N., eds. Twentieth-Century Literary Theory: An Introductory Anthology. LC 86-5837. 521p. (Orig.). (C). 1987. 59.50 (*0-88706-265-2*); pap. 19.95 (*0-88706-266-0*) State U NY Pr.
Lambros, Anna V. Culture & the Literary Text: The Case of Flaubert's Madam Bovary. LC 94-1889. (American University Studies, Series II, Romance Languages & Literatures: Vol. 162). 1995. write for info. (*0-8204-2588-5*) P Lang Pubs.
Lambros, Nick. Americanization of Odysseus. 189p. 1988. pap. 8.95 (*0-89697-286-0*) Intl Univ Pr.
Lambros, Paul. The Coins of the Genoese Rulers of Chios (1314-1429) Barozzi, A., tr. (Illus.). 27p. 1968. pap. 5.00 (*0-916710-00-9*) Obol Intl.
— Gold Coins of Philippi. (Illus.). 1975. pap. 3.00 (*0-916710-20-3*) Obol Intl.
— Unpublished Coins of the Medieval Kingdom of Cyprus. Toumazou, Michael, tr. (Illus.). 170p. (ENG, FRE & GRE.). 1980. 30.00 (*0-916710-76-9*) Obol Intl.
— Unpublished Coins Struck at Glarentza in Imitation of Venetian by Robert of Taranto, Sovereign of the Peloponesse: 1346-1364. Gardiakos, B., tr. (Illus.). 30p. 1969. pap. 5.00 (*0-916710-01-7*) Obol Intl.
Lambros, Spyridon P., ed. Ecthesis Chronica & Chronicon Athenarum. LC 76-24931. (Byzantine Texts: No. 3). reprint ed. 30.00 (*0-404-60003-4*) AMS Pr.
Lambrou, Andreas. Fountain Pens: For Collectors. (Illus.). 208p. 1989. 50.00 (*0-85667-362-5*) Sothebys Pubns.
Lambrou, Evan C. AIDS: Scare or Scam? 1994. 10.95 (*0-533-10709-1*) Vantage.
Lambrou, Peter, jt. auth. see Alman, Brian M.
Lambroza, Shlomo. World Leaders - Boris Yeltsin. LC 92-46479. (Biographies Ser.). (J). 1993. 19.93 (*0-86625-482-X*); 14.95 (*0-685-66417-1*) Rourke Pubns.
Lambroza, Shlomo, jt. ed. see Klier, John D.
Lamb's Players Staff. Developing a Drama Group. 1989. 19.95 (*0-89066-185-5*) World Wide Pubs.
— Fifteen Surefire Scripts. 1989. pap. 9.95 (*0-89066-186-3*) World Wide Pubs.
Lambton, A. K. Theory & Practice in Medieval Persian Government. (Collected Studies: No. CS122). 332p. (C). 1980. reprint ed. lib. bdg. 89.95 (*0-86078-067-8*, Pub. by Variorum UK) Ashgate Pub Co.
Lambton, Ann K. Continuity & Change in Medieval Persia. 1988. 45.00 (*0-88706-133-8*) Mazda Pubs.
— Landlord & Peasant in Persia: A Study of Land Tenure & Land Revenue Administration. 550p. 1991. text ed. 59.50 (*1-85043-293-7*, Pub. by I B Tauris UK) St Martin.
— Persian Grammar. (C). 1953. pap. 39.95 (*0-521-09124-1*) Cambridge U Pr.
— Persian Vocabulary. (PER.). (C). 1953. pap. 39.95 (*0-521-09154-3*) Cambridge U Pr.
— Qajar Persia: Eleven Studies. 359p. 1988. 30.00 (*0-292-76900-8*) U of Tex Pr.
— State & Government in Medieval Islam: An Introduction to the Study of Islamic Political Theory; the Jurists. (London Oriental Ser.: No. 36). 1981. 59.00 (*0-19-713600-1*) OUP.

An Asterisk (*) at the beginning of an entry indicates that the title is appearing in BIP for the first time.

Lambton, George. Men & Horses I Have Known. 320p. 1990. pap. 34.00 (0-85131-031-1, Pub. by J A Allen & Co UK) St Mut.

***Lambton, Gunda.** Stealing the Show: Seven Women Artists in Canadian Public Art. (Illus.). 240p. 1994. 55.00 (0-7735-1188-1, Pub. by McGill CN); pap. 24.95 (0-7735-1189-X, Pub. by McGill CN) U of Toronto Pr.

Lambton, Lucinda. An Album of Curious Houses. 1989. 24. 95 (0-7011-3119-5) Random.

— Lucinda Lambton's Magnificent Menangerie: or Queer Pets & Their Goings On. 344p. 1994. 30.00 (0-00-217723-4, IntlDept) HarpC.

Lamdany, Ruben. The Market-Based Menu Approach in Action: The 1988 Brazil Financing Package. (Discussion Paper Ser.: No. 52). 56p. 1989. 6.95 (0-8213-1227-8, 20052) World Bank.

— Voluntary Debt-Reduction Operations: Bolivia, Mexico, & Beyond. 1989. 6.95 (0-8213-1159-X, 20042) World Bank.

Lamdany, Ruben & Underwood, John. Illustrative Effects of Voluntary Debt & Debt Service Reduction Operations. (Discussion Paper Ser.). 52p. 1989. 6.95 (0-8213-1400-9, 11400) World Bank.

Lamden, Charles W. The Securities & Exchange Commission: A Case Study in the Use of Accounting As an Instrument of Public Policy. Brief, Richard P., ed. LC 77-87302. (Development of Contemporary Accounting Thought Ser.). 1978. lib. bdg. 37.95 (0-405-10941-5) Ayer.

Lamdin, Douglas J., ed. The Managerial Economics Reader. LC 93-80416. 396p. 1994. pap. 30.00 (1-878975-37-4) Kolb Pub.

Lamdin, Griffith D. Odyssey to Guadalajara. LC 86-64031. (Hindsight Saga Ser.). (Illus.). 120p. 1987. pap. 6.95 (0-915433-14-1) Packrat WA.

Lamdin, Lois. Earn College Credit for What You Know. 2nd rev. ed. (Illus.). 256p. 1992. pap. 19.95 (0-9628073-2-X) CAEL.

Lamdin, Lois, ed. Roads to the Learning Society. 180p. (C). 1991. text ed. 25.00 (0-9628073-1-1) CAEL.

Lame Deer, pseud. & Erdoes, Richard. Lame Deer: Seeker of Visions. 1973. pap. 11.00 (0-671-21535-3, Touchstone Bks) S&S Trade.

Lame Deer & Erodes. Lame Deer, Seeker of Visions. Ng, Donna, ed. 550p. 1994. mass mkt. 5.50 (0-671-88802-1, WSP) PB.

Lamech, Ranjit, jt. auth. see Jenkins, Glenn.

***Lameer, Joep.** Al-Farabi & Aristotelian Syllogistics: Greek Theory & Islamic Practice. 1994. 74.50 (90-04-09884-4) E J Brill.

Lameijer, J. N., jt. auth. see Cockroft, A. N.

Lamelas, Diego. The Sale of Gibraltar in Fourteen Seventy-Four. (C). 1988. pap. text ed. 30.00 (0-948466-20-0, Pub. by Gibraltar Bks UK) St Mut.

Lamendola, Walter, jt. auth. see Glastonbury, Bryan.

Lamentowicz, Wojtek, et al. Eastern Europe & Democracy: The Case of Poland. (East-West Special Report Ser.). 45p. 1990. pap. text ed. 14.85 (0-8133-8088-X, LAMEASP) Westview.

Lamer, Hans. Woerterbuch der Antike. 8th ed. (GER.). 1976. 59.95 (0-8288-5768-7, M7042) Fr & Eur.

Lamer, Mirko. The World Fertilizer Economy. xvi, 715p. 1957. 75.00 (0-8047-0474-0) Stanford U Pr.

Lamer, Timothy W., jt. auth. see Pines, Burton Y.

Lamerisse, Albert. The Red Balloon. (Classic Short Stories Ser.). 32p. (J). (gr. 6). 1990. lib. bdg. 13.95 (0-88682-304-8) Creative Ed.

Lamers, C. B., ed. Clinical Impact of H Plus, K Plus-ATP-ase Inhibitors: Journal: Digestion, Vol. 44, Suppl. 1, 1989. 98p. 1989. pap. 29.75 (3-8055-5111-8) S Karger.

Lamers, Henny G. & De Loore, Camiel W., eds. Instabilities in Luminous Early Type Stars. (C). 1987. lib. bdg. 107. 00 (90-277-2522-5) Kluwer Ac.

Lamersdorf, W., ed. Office Knowledge: Representation, Management & Utilization. 1988. 72.00 (0-444-70451-5, North Holland) Elsevier.

Lametschwandtner, A., jt. auth. see Aharinejad, S. H.

Lamey. Diagnostic Picture Tests in Dentistry. 1989. 14.95 (0-7234-0982-X, Wolfe Pub) Mosby Yr Bk.

Lamey, Philip-John & Lewis, Michael A. Oral Medicine in Practice. (Illus.). 74p. 1991. pap. 42.50 (0-904588-32-7, Pub. by Brit Dental Assn UK) Ishiyaku Euro.

Lamey, Philip-John, jt. auth. see Lewis, Michael A.

Lamey, Robert. The Illustrated Guide to PSpice for DOS. LC 94-2662. (Illus.). 219p. 1994. pap. text ed. 39.95 (0-8273-6524-1) Delmar.

***Lamey, Robert W.** The Illustrated Guide to PSpice for Windows. LC 94-44412. 1995. 34.95 (0-8273-7068-7) Delmar.

Lamie, Edward L. Pascal Programming. LC 86-26779. 427p. reprint ed. pap. 121.70 (0-7837-2819-0, 2057653) Bks Demand.

Lamiell, James T. The Psychology of Personality: An Epistemological Inquiry. (Critical Assessments of Contemporary Psychology Ser.). (Illus.). 256p. 1987. text ed. 43.00 (0-231-06020-3) Col U Pr.

Lamigueiro, Fernando, ed. see Miranda, Juan C.

Laming, D. J., jt. ed. see Stow, D. A.

Laming, Donald, jt. ed. see Fischer, Gerhard H.

Laming, Peter B., jt. auth. see Rijsdijk, Jan F.

Laming, Peter R., ed. Brain Mechanisms of Behaviour in Lower Vertebrates. LC 80-41368. (Society for Experimental Biology Seminar Ser.: No. 9). 200p. 1981. 59.95 (0-521-23702-5); pap. 27.95 (0-521-28168-7) Cambridge U Pr.

Laming, R. G. Sensory Analysis. 1986. text ed. 131.00 (0-12-435455-6) Acad Pr.

Laming, Tim. Swing Wings. (Color Library). (Illus.). 128p. 1993. 15.95 (1-85532-373-7, Pub. by Osprey Pubng Ltd UK) Motorbooks Intl.

— Tiger Squadrons. (Osprey Colour Library). (Illus.). 128p. 1991. pap. 15.95 (1-85532-146-7, Pub. by Osprey Pubng Ltd UK) Motorbooks Intl.

Lamiroy, Beatrice. Les Verbes de Mouvement en Francais et en Espagnol: Etude Comparee de Leurs Infinitives. (Lingvisticae Investigationes Supplementa Ser.: No. 11). xiv, 323p. (FRE.). 1983. 62.00x (90-272-3121-4) Benjamins North Am.

Lamis, Alexander P. The Two-Party South. 2nd enl. ed. 464p. 1990. reprint ed. pap. 19.95 (0-19-506579-4) OUP.

Lamis, Alexander P., ed. Ohio Politics. LC 94-7637. (Illus.). 417p. 1994. text ed. 35.00x (0-87338-507-1); pap. 17.00 (0-87338-509-8) Kent St U Pr.

Lamis, Leroy. PC Art. 50p. (Orig.). (C). 1983. disk 50.00 (0-925999-27-X) PC Art.

Lamit, Gary. Descriptive Geometry. (Illus.). 464p. 1983. text ed. 79.00 (0-13-199802-1) P-H.

Lamit, L. Gary. Technical Drawing & Design. Conty, ed. LC 92-43902. 1184p. (C). 1993. text ed. 69.75 (0-314-01264-8) West Pub.

Lamit, L. Gary & Kitto, Kathleen L. Principles of Engineering Drawing. Conty, ed. LC 93-33033. 700p. (C). 1994. pap. text ed. 57.50 (0-314-02805-6) West Pub.

Lamit, Louis G. & Lloyd, Sandra J. Drafting for Electronics. 2nd ed. 592p. (C). 1993. write for info. (0-02-367342-7, Merrill Pub Co) Macmillan.

Lamit, Louis G. & Paige, Vernon. Computer-Aided Drafting & Design. 482p. (C). 1987. write for info. (0-675-20475-5, Merrill Pub Co) Macmillan.

Lamit, Louis G., et al. Workbook in Drafting for Electronics. 2nd ed. (Illus.). 256p. (C). 1993. pap. write for info. (0-02-367345-1) Macmillan.

***Lamke, Celia.** Nursing Approaches to HIV-AIDS Care. 3rd ed. 208p. (Orig.). (C). 1993. pap. 49.95 (1-878025-48-1) Western Schls.

***Lamke, Celia & Stein, Mary.** An Overview of HIV Infections & AIDS. 4th ed. LC 94-60086. (Illus.). 112p. (C). 1993. pap. 19.95 (1-878025-47-3) Western Schls.

Lamke, Robert, et al, eds. Perspectives on the AIDS Crisis & Thanatology: Thanatologic Aspects. LC 88-83830. (Current Thanatology Ser.). 140p. 1989. pap. 15.95 (0-930194-43-8) Ctr Thanatology.

Lamkin, Geraldine E. Lovey-a Book of Poems. 72p. 1983. pap. 5.00 (0-9612632-0-2) Lamkin.

Lamkin, Jean G. The Federal Manager's Guide to TQM. (Illus.). 50p. (Orig.). 1991. pap. text ed. 9.95 (0-936295-17-1) FPMI Comns.

Lamkin, Jeffrey C. The Massachusetts Eye & Ear Infirmary Review Manual for Ophthalmology. LC 92-49469. (Illus.). 672p. 1992. 69.95 (0-316-51293-1) Little.

Lamkin, Selma. Do It Right the First Time: Guide to Computer Installation. 1983. 15.00 (0-686-37906-3) Nikmal Pub.

Lamkin, Selma H. Accounting, Self-Instruction Manual. (Orig.). (C). 20.00 (0-686-32949-X) Nikmal Pub.

— How to Start & Succeed in Business: Small Business Development. abr. ed. 120p. 1991. pap. text ed. 35.00 (0-686-37907-1) Nikmal Pub.

— The Shoebox Syndrome (Record-Keeping) (Orig.). (C). 15.00 (0-686-32948-1) Nikmal Pub.

— Small Business Survival Manual: Applied Management for Small Non-Profit. (Orig.). (C). 20.00 (0-686-32947-3) Nikmal Pub.

Lamkin, Speed. Comes a Day. 1959. pap. 4.75 (0-8222-0231-X) Dramatists Play.

Lamley, Harry J., ed. see University of Hawaii (Honolulu), Asian Studies Program Staff.

***Lamm.** Corvette - America's Supercar. 1995. (0-7858-0341-6) Bk Sales Inc.

— Healing Obesity. 1995. 23.00 (0-684-81368-8) S&S Trade.

— The Power of Hope. 288p. 1995. text ed. 22.95 (0-89256-361-3, Rawson Assocs) Macmillan.

Lamm, C. Drew. Annirani & Mollymishi the Wild-Haired Doll. (Illus.). 24p. (J). (ps-2). 1990. 14.95 (1-55037-105-3, Pub. by Annick CN); pap. 5.95 (1-55037-106-1, Pub. by Annick CN) Firefly Bks Ltd.

— Cottontail at Clover Crescent. LC 94-28697. (Smithsonian's Backyard Ser.). (Illus.). 32p. (J). (ps-2). 1995. 15.95 (1-56899-108-8); 4.95 (1-56899-109-6) Soundprints.

— Cottontail at Clover Crescent. LC 94-28697. (Smithsonian's Backyard Ser.). (Illus.). 32p. (J). (ps-2). 1995. audio 19.95 (1-56899-112-6); audio write for info. (1-56899-113-4) Soundprints.

— Cottontail at Clover Crescent, Incl. 12" plush toy. LC 94-28697. (Smithsonian's Backyard Ser.). (Illus.). 32p. (J). (ps-2). 1995. 29.95 (1-56899-110-X) Soundprints.

— Cottontail at Clover Crescent, Mini-sized bk., incl. 6" plush toy. LC 94-28697. (Smithsonian's Backyard Ser.). (Illus.). 32p. (J). (ps-2). 1995. 12.95 (1-56899-111-8) Soundprints.

— Woodchuck at Blackberry Road. (Smithsonian's Backyard Ser.). (Illus.). 32p. (J). (ps-2). 1994. audio 19.95 (1-56899-091-X); 29.95 (1-56899-089-8); 4.95 (1-56899-088-X); 12.95 (1-56899-090-1); audio write for info. (1-56899-092-8) Soundprints.

— Woodchuck at Blackberry Road. (Smithsonian's Backyard Ser.). (Illus.). 32p. (J). (ps-2). 1994. 15.95 (1-56899-087-1) Soundprints.

***Lamm, D. L., ed.** Advances in the Treatment of Superficial Bladder Cancer: Optimizing BCG Immunotherapy: Optimizing BCG Immunotherapy. (Journal Ser.: Vol. 27, Suppl. 1, 1995). (Illus.). iv, 34p. 1995. pap. 20.00 (3-8055-6137-7) S Karger.

— BCG - A New Standard for Superficial Bladder Cancer: Journal: European Urology, Vol. 21, Suppl. 2, 1992. (Illus.). iv, 48p. 1992. pap. 14.50 (3-8055-5620-9) S Karger.

Lamm, David V. Contract Negotiation Cases: Government & Industry. 271p. (C). 1993. text ed. 37.50 (0-941448-06-1) Wordcraft MD.

— Instructors Manual to Accompany Contract Negotiation Cases: Government & Industry. 233p. (C). 1993. pap. 25.00 (0-941448-07-X) Wordcraft MD.

***Lamm, Donald L. & Paola, Angelo S.** Campbell's Urology: Review & Assessment. 304p. 1995. pap. text ed. 49.00 (0-7216-5158-5) Saunders.

Lamm, E., jt. auth. see Vasilenko, E.

Lamm, E., jt. ed. see Vasilenko, E.

Lamm, Geneva, jt. auth. see Judson, Martha.

Lamm, Jay. How to Restore British Sports Cars. (Illus.). 224p. 1992. pap. 24.95 (0-87938-567-7) Haynes Pubns.

Lamm, Jay W. All Wheel Drive High Performance Handbook. (Illus.). 144p. 1990. pap. 9.98 (0-87938-419-0) Motorbooks Intl.

Lamm, John W. Illustrated Shelby Buyers Guide. (MBI Illustrated Buyer's Guide Ser.). (Illus.). 176p. 1992. pap. 16.95 (0-87938-604-5) Motorbooks Intl.

Lamm, Kathryn. Ten Thousand Ideas for Term Papers, Projects, Reports & Speeches. 3rd ed. 1991. pap. 11.00 (0-13-904228-8) P-H.

Lamm, Lawrence, jt. ed. see Copeland, Lewis.

Lamm, Leonard J. The Idea of the Past: History, Science, & Practice in American Psychoanalysis. LC 92-44651. (Psychoanalytic Crosscurrents Ser.). 288p. (C). 1994. text ed. 40.00 (0-8147-5073-7) NYU Pr.

Lamm, Martin. August Strindberg. Carlson, Harry G., ed. LC 69-16323. 1972. 27.95 (0-405-08724-1) Ayer.

Lamm, Maurice. Becoming a Jew. 500p. 1991. 25.00 (0-8246-0350-8) Jonathan David.

— Jewish Way in Death & Mourning. rev. ed. LC 69-11684. 1972. pap. 12.95 (0-8246-0126-2) Jonathan David.

— Jewish Way in Love & Marriage. 1992. pap. 13.00 (0-8246-0353-2) Jonathan David.

— Living Torah in America. Cutter, William, ed. (Illus.). 182p. (YA). (gr. 8-10). Date not set. 30.00 (0-87441-513-6) Behrman.

— The Power of Hope: The One Essential of Life & Love. 1995. 17.00 (0-684-81228-2, Scribners) S&S Trade.

Lamm, Michael. Chevrolet Small Block V-8 Speed Equipment. (Illus.). 282p. 1989. pap. 6.98 (0-932128-05-X, Pub. by Lamm-Morada) Motorbooks Intl.

— Chevrolet, 1955. 1991. 14.95 (0-932128-06-8) Lamm-Morada Pub.

Lamm, Norman. Faith & Doubt. 1986. 11.95 (0-87068-138-9) Ktav.

— Faith & Doubt: Studies in Traditional Jewish. 1986. pap. 14.95 (0-685-33247-0) Ktav.

— A Hedge of Roses: Jewish Insights into Marriage. LC 66-19539. 1977. pap. 4.95 (0-87306-095-4) Feldheim.

— Torah Lishmah: The Study of Torah for Its Own Sake in the Work of Rabbi Hayyim of Volozhin & His Contemporaries. 1988. 25.00 (0-88125-117-8); pap. 16. 95 (0-88125-133-X) Ktav.

— Torah Umadda: The Encounter of Religious Learning & Worldly Knowledge in the Jewish Tradition. LC 89-18519. 264p. 1990. 35.00 (0-87668-810-5) Aronson.

— Torah Umadda: The Encounter of Religious Learning & Worldly Knowledge in the Jewish Tradition. LC 89-18519. 264p. 1994. pap. 20.00 (1-56821-231-3) Aronson.

Lamm, R. D. & Imhoff, G. The Immigration Time Bomb: The Fragmenting & Destruction of America by Immigration. 1986. lib. bdg. 79.95 (0-8490-3830-8) Gordon Pr.

Lamm, Richard D. & Grossman, Arnold. Nineteen Eighty-Eight: A Novel of Politics. 1986. pap. 3.95 (0-685-43593-8) St Martin.

***Lamm, Robert C. & Cross, Neal.** The Humanities in Western Culture: A Search for Human Values - Brief Version. 624p. (C). 1995. pap. write for info. (0-697-25425-9) Brown & Benchmark.

— Humanities in Western Culture, Vol. 1: A Search for Human Values. 496p. (C). 1993. pap. text ed. write for info. (0-697-10660-8) Brown & Benchmark.

— Humanities in Western Culture, Vol. 2: A Search for Human Values. 512p. (C). 1993. pap. text ed. write for info. (0-697-10667-5) Brown & Benchmark.

— Humanities Western Culture Vol. I: A Search for Human Values. 496p. (C). 1995. pap. write for info. (0-697-25427-5); audio write for info. (0-697-25428-3) Brown & Benchmark.

— Humanities Western Culture Vol. II: A Search for Human Values. 496p. (C). 1995. pap. write for info. (0-697-25429-1); audio write for info. (0-697-25430-5) Brown & Benchmark.

Lamm, Robert P., jt. auth. see Schaefer, Richard T.

***Lamm-Tennant, Joan.** Mutual Funds: Analysis, Allocation, & Performance Evaluation. 200p. (C). 1995. text ed. 35. 00 (0-943590-66-3) Amer College.

Lamm, Ursula, tr. see Bauer, Arnold.

Lamm, V., jt. auth. see Peteri, Z.

Lamm, Vanda. The Utilization of Nuclear Energy & International Law. 156p. 1984. 68.00 (0-569-08838-0, Pub. by Collets UK) Pro-Am Music.

Lamm, Vanda, jt. ed. see Peteri, Zoltan.

Lamma, E. & Mello, P., eds. Extensions of Logic Programming: Third International Workshop, ELP '92, Bologna, Italy, February 26-28, 1992, Proceedings. LC 92-45283. (Lecture Notes in Computer Science, Lecture Notes in Artificial Intelligence Ser.). 1993. 59.00 (0-387-56454-3) Spr-Verlag.

Lamman, D. R. Death of a Shark. LC 91-67764. 128p. (Orig.). 1994. pap. 9.00 (1-56002-163-2, Univ Edtns) Aegina Pr.

Lammas, David. Adhesives & Sealants. (Workshop Practice Ser.: No. 21). (Illus.). 144p. (Orig.). 1991. pap. 26.50 (0-85486-048-7, Pub. by Argus Books UK) Trans-Atl Phila.

Lamme, Ary J., III. America's Historic Landscapes: Community Power & the Preservation of Four National Historic Sites. LC 89-4925. (Illus.). 230p. 1990. text ed. 26.00x (0-87049-614-X) U of Tenn Pr.

— Geography of the United States. (C). 1995. pap. write for info. (0-02-367341-9) Macmillan.

Lamme, Linda, jt. ed. see Hoffman, Stevie.

Lamme, Linda L., et al. Literature-Based Moral Education: Children's Books & Activities to Enrich the K-5 Curriculum. 160p. 1992. pap. 24.50 (0-89774-723-2) Oryx Pr.

Lammens, Henri. Islam: Beliefs & Institutions. 1976. lib. bdg. 59.95 (0-8490-2080-8) Gordon Pr.

— Islam: Beliefs & Institutions. Ross, E. Denison, tr. 265p. reprint ed. text ed. 23.50 (0-685-13406-7) Coronet Bks.

***Lammens, Letty & Scholte, Els.** Beaded Animals in Jewelry. 56p. 1994. pap. 14.00 (0-916896-61-7) Lacis Pubns.

Lammer, Jutta. Cross-Stitch a Beautiful Christmas. LC 91-12851. (Illus.). 64p. 1992. pap. 9.95 (0-8069-8311-6) Sterling.

Lammermeyr, Horst U. Human Relations: The Key to Quality. (Illus.). 296p. 1990. text ed. 32.95 (0-527-91628-5, 916285) Qual Resc.

Lammers, Ann C. In God's Shadow: The Collaboration of Victor White & C. G. Jung. LC 94-15329. (Jung & Spirituality Ser.). 320p. 1994. pap. 19.95 (0-8091-3489-6) Paulist Pr.

Lammers, Cornelius J. & Szell, Gyorgy, eds. International Handbook of Participation in Organizations: For the Study of Organizational Democracy, Co-operation & Self-Management, Vol. 1: Organizational Democracy: Taking Stock. (Illus.). 376p. 1990. 105.00 (0-19-877259-9) OUP.

Lammers, Jeff & Blackburn, Ken. World Record Paper Airplane Kit. 32p. 1992. pap. 9.95 (0-9634845-0-8) Wrld Rec Paper.

Lammers, Johan G. Pollution of International Watercourses. 1984. lib. bdg. 263.50 (90-247-2955-6) Kluwer Ac.

Lammers, Johan G., jt. ed. see Kiss, A. C.

Lammers, Lawrence P., jt. auth. see Hardy, Owen B.

Lammers, Mark. Nordic Instrumental Music for Colleges & Universities. 236p. (Orig.). (C). 1991. pap. 15.00 (0-9630771-0-4) M Lammers.

***Lammers, Nadine B.** Birthday Stars. 32p. (J). (gr. k-5). 1994. pap. 5.95 (0-9642971-1-6) N B Lammers.

— Night Time Twinkles. 20p. (J). (gr. k-5). 1994. pap. 4.95 (0-9642971-0-8) N B Lammers.

Lammers, Stephen E. & Verhey, Allen, eds. On Moral Medicine: Theological Perspectives in Medical Ethics. 680p. 1987. pap. 19.99 (0-8028-0293-1) Eerdmans.

Lammers, Stephen E., jt. ed. see Verhey, Allen.

Lammers, Susan. All about Houseplants. rev. ed. ORTHO Books Editorial Staff, ed. LC 81-86183. (Illus.). 96p. (Orig.). 1982. pap. 9.95 (0-89721-002-6) Ortho Info.

Lammers, Susan, contrib. Programmers at Work: Interviews with 19 of Today's Most Brilliant Programmers. LC 86-5175. (At Work Ser.). 392p. 1986. 19.95 (1-55615-014-8); pap. 14.95 (0-914845-71-3) Microsoft.

Lammers, Susan, told to. Programmers at Work. 400p. 1989. pap. 9.95 (1-55615-211-6, Tempus Bks) Microsoft.

Lammers, Thomas G. Systematics of Clermontia (Campanulaceae- Lobelioideae) Anderson, Christiane, ed. (Systematic Botany Monographs: Vol. 32). (Illus.). 97p. 1991. Smyth-sewn, acid-free paper. pap. 13.00 (0-912861-32-0) Am Soc Plant.

Lammers, W., jt. auth. see Freye, Kurt.

***Lammers, Wayne.** Mangajin's Japanese Grammar Through Comics. (Illus.). 256p. (Orig.). (JPN.). (C). 1995. pap. 24.95 (0-9634335-5-5) Mangajin.

Lammers, Wayne & Morrison, Clinton D., trs. Treasures Three: Stories & Art by Students in Japan & Oregon. (Illus.). 258p. (Orig.). (J). (gr. k-12). 1994. pap. 15.95 (0-9616058-6-3) OR Students Writing.

Lammers, Wayne, jt. auth. see Simmons, Vaughan P.

Lammers, Wayne P., tr. & intro. The Tale of Matsura: Fujiwara Teika's Experiment in Fiction. LC 90-42197. (Michigan Monograph Series in Japanese Studies: No. 9). xii, 207p. 1992. 35.00 (0-939512-48-3) U MI Japan.

Lammers, Wayne P., tr. see Shono, Junzo.

Lammert, Charlotte. Mistress of Falcon Court. 1989. pap. 3.95 (0-8217-2659-5) Zebra.

Lammert, John M. Microbes. LC 92-9123. (YA). 1992. 12. 67 (0-86625-430-7); 12.50 (0-685-59398-3) Rourke Pubns.

Lammerts, Walter E., intro. Scientific Studies in Special Creation. 2nd ed. LC 70-150955. (Illus.). 343p. 1990. reprint ed. pap. 9.95 (0-940384-08-6) Creation Research.

***Lammertse, Friso.** Van Eyck to Bruegel, 1400-1550: Dutch & Flemish Painting in the Collection of the Museum. (Illus.). 298p. 1995. pap. 40.00 (90-6918-137-1) U of Wash Pr.

Lammey, William C. Karmic Tarot: A Profound System for Finding Your Life's Path. enl. rev. ed. Gross, Gina R. & Buryn, Ed, eds. (Illus.). 256p. 1993. pap. 16.95 (0-87877-136-0) Newcastle Pub.

Lammey, William L., ed. see Lawrence, Shirley B.

***Lammiman, Boyd.** Caught in the Crossfire: The Baptism That Demonstrates the Faith That Justifies. 1994. pap. 5.95 (1-56794-074-9) Star Bible.

Lammineur, P. & Cornillie, O. A. Industrial Robots, Vol. 2. (EPO Applied Technology Ser.: Vol. 2). (Illus.). 164p. 1984. 80.00 (0-08-031143-1, Pub. by Pergamon Repr UK) Franklin.

Lamming, D., ed. see McCall, G. J., et al.

Lamming, Douglas. A Scottish Internationalists' Who's Who, 1872-1986. 250p. 1987. 60.00 (0-907033-47-4) St Mut.

Lamming, Eric. Report of the Expert Group on Animal Feedingstuffs. 102p. 1992. pap. 35.00 (0-11-242936-X, HM2936X, Pub. by HMSO UK) UNIPUB.

Lamming, G. E., ed. Marshall's Physiology of Reproduction, Vol. 2: Reproduction Function in the Male. 4th ed. (Illus.). 704p. 1990. text ed. 125.00 (*0-443-01967-3*) Churchill.

Lamming, G. E., ed. see Easter School in Agricultural Science (14th 1967, University of Nottingham) Staff.

Lamming, G. E., ed. see Easter School in Agricultural Science (13th 1966, University of Nottingham) Staff.

***Lamming, George.** Conversations: Essays, Addresses, & Interviews 1953-1990. Drayton, Richard & Andaiye, eds. 300p. 1995. text ed. 42.50 (*0-472-09575-7*); pap. 14.95 (*0-472-06575-0*) U of Mich Pr.

— The Emigrants. LC 80-40599. 274p. 1987. pap. 6.95 (*0-8052-8036-7*) Schocken.

— The Emigrants. LC 94-2141. 280p. 1994. reprint ed. pap. 14.95 (*0-472-06470-3*, Ann Arbor Bks) U of Mich Pr.

— In the Castle of My Skin. (Ann Arbor Paperbacks Ser.). 314p. (C). 1991. reprint ed. text ed. 44.50 (*0-472-09468-8*); reprint ed. pap. text ed. 15.95 (*0-472-06468-1*) U of Mich Pr.

— Natives of My Person. (Ann Arbor Paperbacks Ser.). 256p. (C). 1992. reprint ed. text ed. 44.50 (*0-472-09467-X*); reprint ed. pap. text ed. 15.95 (*0-472-06467-3*) U of Mich Pr.

— The Pleasures of Exile. (Ann Arbor Paperbacks Ser.). 300p. (C). 1992. reprint ed. text ed. 44.50 (*0-472-09466-1*); reprint ed. pap. text ed. 15.95 (*0-472-06466-5*) U of Mich Pr.

Lamming, Richard. Beyond Partnership: Strategies for Innovation & Lean Supply. LC 92-38797. (Manufacturing Practitioner Ser.). 1993. pap. text ed. 36.95 (*0-13-143785-2*) P-H.

Lammon, Carol B., et al. Clinical Nursing Skills. LC 93-44872. (Illus.). 784p. 1995. pap. text ed. 40.00 (*0-7216-6680-9*) Saunders.

Lammond, D. Thomas Carlyle. LC 73-18127. (Studies in Thos. Carlyle: No. 53). 1974. lib. bdg. 49.95 (*0-8383-1740-5*) M S G Haskell Hse.

Lamnabhi-Lagarrigue, F., jt. ed. see Jacob, G.

***Lamoine, Georgees, ed.** Charges to the Grand Jury, 1689-1803. (Camden Fourth Ser.: No. 43). 648p. (C). 1995. 54.95 (*0-521-55163-3*) Cambridge U Pr.

Lamoine, Georges, ed. Charges to the Grand Jury in the Eighteenth Century, 1689-1803. (Royal Historical Society: Camden Fourth Ser.: No. 43). (C). 1992. text ed. 50.00 (*0-86193-130-0*, Royal Historical Soc) Boydell & Brewer.

Lamola, Angelo A., ed. Creation & Detection of the Excited State, 2 pts. LC 76-134785. (Illus.). 391p. reprint ed. Vol. 1, Pt. A, 391p. pap. 111.50 (*0-7837-0943-9*, 2041248); reprint ed. Vol. 1, Pt. B, 301p. pap. 85.80 (*0-7837-0944-7*, 2041248) Bks Demand.

Lamon, Lester C. Black Tennesseans, Nineteen Hundred to Nineteen Thirty. LC 76-49583. (Twentieth-Century America Ser.). 338p. reprint ed. pap. 96.40 (*0-8357-7299-3*, 2025561) Bks Demand.

— Blacks in Tennessee, 1791-1970. LC 81-3396. (Tennessee Three Star Ser.). (Illus.). 136p. 1981. pap. 4.95 (*0-87049-324-8*) U of Tenn Pr.

Lamon, Susan J., jt. ed. see Lesh, Richard A.

Lamon, Susan J., jt. ed. see Lesh, Richard.

Lamon, Ward H. Recollections of Abraham Lincoln, 1847-1865. Teillard, Dorothy L., ed. LC 94-18220. (Illus.). 380p. 1994. reprint ed. pap. 12.95 (*0-8032-7950-7*, Bison Books) U of Nebr Pr.

***Lamond, Angus I.** Pre-mRNA Processing. LC 95-998. (Molecular Biology Intelligence Unit Ser.). 220p. 1995. 99.00 (*1-57059-226-8*) R G Landes.

Lamond, Joseph F. & Klieger, Paul, eds. Significance of Testing & Properties of Concrete & Concrete-Making Materials. 4th ed. LC 94-16746. (Special Technical Publications: Vol. 169C). (Illus.). 630p. 1994. 110.00 (*0-8031-2053-2*, 0416903007) ASTM.

Lamond, Ross, jt. auth. see Jochle, Wolfgang.

***LaMonda, Barry.** Wormsly the Worm Can Do It: Can You Do It Too? (J). 1995. 8.95 (*0-8062-5220-0*) Carlton.

— Wormsly the Worm Goes to the Moon. 1995. 8.95 (*0-8062-5342-8*) Carlton.

Lamongie, Vivian E., tr. see Mugny, Gabriel & Perez, Juan A.

Lamonica. Nursing Leadership & Management. 1983. boxed 35.00 (*0-86720-391-9*) Jones & Bartlett.

Lamont, Alonzo D., Jr. That Serious He-Man Ball. 1992. pap. 4.75 (*0-8222-1127-0*) Dramatists Play.

Lamont, Billy. The Gallery of Light. 100p. 1993. pap. 9.95 (*0-9632881-0-5*); pap. 11.95 (*0-9632881-2-1*) Natl Post Modern.

Lamont-Brown, Raymond. Discovering Fife. 216p. (C). 1989. pap. text ed. 26.00 (*0-85976-204-1*, Pub. by J Donald) St Mut.

— Irish Grave Humour. 1987. pap. 9.95 (*0-86278-153-1*, Pub. by OBrien Pr IE) Dufour.

— The Life & Times of Berwick-upon-Tweed. 200p. (C). 1989. pap. text ed. 24.00 (*0-85976-233-5*, Pub. by J Donald) St Mut.

Lamont, Claire, ed. see Scott, Walter.

Lamont-Clarke, Ginette & Stevens, Florence. Et Si Papa se Perd au Zoo? LC 91-65364. (Illus.). 24p. (FRE.). (J). (ps-2). 1991. 12.95 (*0-88776-266-2*); pap. 6.95 (*0-88776-273-5*) Tundra Bks.

Lamont-Clarke, Ginette, jt. auth. see Stevens, Florence.

Lamont, Corliss. Freedom Is as Freedom Does. LC 74-171384. (Civil Liberties in American History Ser.). 1972. reprint ed. lib. bdg. 42.50 (*0-306-70497-8*) Da Capo.

— Freedom Is As Freedom Does: Civil Liberties in America. 352p. 1990. reprint ed. pap. text ed. 12.95 (*0-8264-0475-8*) Continuum.

— Freedom of Choice Affirmed. 224p. 1990. reprint ed. pap. text ed. 12.95 (*0-8264-0476-6*) Continuum.

— Humanist Funeral Service. 3rd ed. LC 77-76001. 48p. 1977. pap. 9.95 (*0-87975-090-1*) Prometheus Bks.

— A Humanist Wedding Service. 3rd ed. 29p. 6.95 (*0-87975-000-6*) Prometheus Bks.

— Illusion of Immortality. 4th ed. 320p. 1990. pap. text ed. 12.95 (*0-8044-6377-8*) Continuum.

— A Lifetime of Dissent. 414p. 1988. 27.95 (*0-87975-463-X*) Prometheus Bks.

— Lover's Credo. LC 82-13909. 1994. 7.95 (*0-87233-114-8*) Bauhan.

— The Philosophy of Humanism. 352p. 1990. pap. text ed. 12.95 (*0-8044-6379-4*) Continuum.

— Voice in the Wilderness: Collected Essays of Corliss Lamont. LC 74-75351. 327p. 1974. pap. 19.95 (*0-87975-060-X*) Prometheus Bks.

Lamont, Corliss, ed. Dear Corliss: Letters from Eminent Persons. 202p. (C). 1990. 21.95 (*0-87975-627-6*) Prometheus Bks.

— Man Answers Death. LC 79-99031. (Granger Index Reprint Ser.). 1977. 23.95 (*0-8369-6106-4*) Ayer.

Lamont, Corliss, ed. see Lamb, Helen B.

Lamont, Douglas. Forcing Our Hand: America's Trade Wars in the 1980s. 288p. 1986. text ed. 24.95 (*0-669-12668-3*) Free Pr.

— Winning Worldwide: Strategies for Dominating Global Markets. 336p. 1990. text ed. 30.00 (*1-55623-419-8*) Irwin Prof Pubng.

Lamont, Douglas, ed. Protectionism: Can American Business Overcome It? (ITT Key Issues Lecture Ser.). 127p. (Orig.). (C). 1986. pap. write for info. (*0-937137-01-4*) Bookscraft.

***Lamont, E.** Asteraceae. (Memoirs of the New York Botanical Garden Ser.: Vol. 72). (Illus.). 1995. pap. write for info. (*0-89327-391-0*) NY Botanical.

Lamont, Edward M. Ambassador from Wall Street: The Story of Thomas W. Lamont, J. P. Morgan's Chief Executive. 1993. 26.95 (*1-56833-018-9*) Madison Bks UPA.

LaMont, J. Thomas, ed. see Gorelick, Fred S.

Lamont, John. Diary. LC 78-171649. (Maitland Club, Glasgow. Publications: No. 7). reprint ed. 22.00 (*0-404-52933-X*) AMS Pr.

Lamont, Lansing. Breakup: The Coming End of Canada & the Stakes for America. LC 93-43809. 1994. 25.00 (*0-393-03634-0*) Norton.

Lamont, Lansing & Edmonds, J. Duncan. Friends So Different: Essays on Canada & the United States in the 1980's. 318p. 1989. 30.00 (*0-7766-0263-2*, Pub. by Univ Ottawa Pr CN) Paul & Co Pubs.

Lamont, Michele. Money, Morals, & Manners: The Culture of the French & the American Upper- Middle Class. LC 92-7270. (Morality & Society Ser.). (Illus.). 360p. 1992. 35.00 (*0-226-46815-1*) U Ch Pr.

— Money, Morals & Manners: The Culture of the French & the American Upper-Middle Class. (Morality & Society Ser.). xxx, 320p. 1994. pap. text ed. 12.95 (*0-226-46817-8*) U Ch Pr.

Lamont, Michele & Fournier, Marcel, eds. Cultivating Differences: Symbolic Boundaries & the Making of Inequality. LC 92-15204. 344p. (C). 1992. lib. bdg. 49.95 (*0-226-46813-5*); pap. text ed. 17.95 (*0-226-46814-3*) U Ch Pr.

Lamont, Norman. Financial Statement & Budget Report, 1990-1991. 73p. 1990. pap. 18.00 (*0-10-228690-6*, HM9660) UNIPUB.

***Lamont, Priscilla.** Out to Lunch. (Illus.). 32p. (J). (ps-2). 1995. 12.95 (*1-85697-564-9*, Kingfisher LKC) LKC.

Lamont, Rosette, et al, comments. CNL-Quarterly World Report: Shakespeare & the World, Vol. 4. (Illus.). 40p. 1982. pap. 4.95 (*0-918680-19-0*) Bagehot Council.

Lamont, Rosette, ed. Women on the Verge. 1993. pap. 14.95 (*1-55783-148-3*) Applause Theatre Bk Pubs.

Lamont, Rosette, tr. see Delbo, Charlotte.

Lamont, Rosette, tr. see Dunant, Ghislaine.

Lamont, Rosette, et al. New Literary Continents: Selected Papers of the Fifth NDEA Seminar on Foreign Area Studies, sponsored by Columbia University's School of International Affairs & the CNL, 1981. 1984. pap. 8.95 (*0-918680-25-5*) Bagehot Council.

Lamont, Rosette C. Ionesco's Imperatives: The Politics of Culture. LC 92-43167. (Theater: Theory - Text - Performance Ser.). 267p. (C). 1993. lib. bdg. 49.50 (*0-472-10310-9*) U of Mich Pr.

Lamont, Rosette C. & Friedman, Melvin J., eds. The Two Faces of Ionesco. LC 76-51038. 285p. 1978. 15.00 (*0-87875-116-X*) Whitston Pub.

Lamont, Rosette C., tr. see Delbo, Charlotte.

Lamont, Stewart. In Good Faith. 118p. (C). 1988. pap. text ed. 30.00 (*0-7152-0636-2*) St Mut.

— In Good Faith. 118p. (C). 1989. pap. 30.00 (*0-685-60685-6*, Pub. by St Andrew UK) St Mut.

Lamont, Susan J., jt. auth. see Schook, Lawrence B.

Lamont, Thomas W. Henry P. Davison: The Record of a Useful Life. LC 75-2644. (Wall Street & the Security Market Ser.). (Illus.). 1975. reprint ed. 39.95 (*0-405-06969-3*) Ayer.

Lamont, W. D. Law & the Moral Order: A Study in Ethics & Jurisprudence. 128p. 1981. text ed. 23.90 (*0-08-025742-9*, Pergamon Pr); pap. text ed. 12.95 (*0-08-025746-1*, Pergamon Pr) Elsevier.

Lamont, William. Puritanism & the English Revolution, 3 vols. (Modern Revivals in History Ser.). 810p. 1992. 171.95 (*0-7512-0004-2*, Pub. by Gregg Revivals UK) Ashgate Pub Co.

Lamont, William, ed. see Baxter, Richard.

Lamont, William D. Introduction to Green's Moral Philosophy. LC 78-20478. 1980. reprint ed. 21.45 (*0-88355-855-6*) Hyperion Conn.

LaMonte, Edward S. Politics & Welfare in Birmingham, 1900-1975. LC 94-7186. 320p. 1995. 32.95 (*0-8173-0754-0*) U of Ala Pr.

LaMonte, J. L. Feudal Monarchy in the Latin Kingdom of Jerusalem, 1100-1291. (Mediaeval Academy of America Publications: Vol. 11). 1932. 35.00 (*0-527-01685-3*) Periodicals Srv.

Lamoreau, John & Beebe, Ralph. Waging Peace. 1980. pap. 1.95 (*0-913342-31-9*) Barclay Pr.

***L'Amoreaux, Claudia.** Celebrating Women's Spirituality: Wall Calendar, 1996. (Illus.). 1995. 11.95 (*0-89594-729-3*) Crossing Pr.

***L'Amoreaux, Claudia, ed.** Celebrating Women's Spirituality: Engagement Calendar, 1996. (Illus.). 128p. 1995. spiral bd. 12.95 (*0-89594-728-5*) Crossing Pr.

LaMoreaux, James W. Medical Waste Solutions. 1994. write for info. (*0-87371-712-0*) Lewis Pubs.

Lamoreaux, Naomi. The Great Merger Movement in American Business, 1895-1904. (Illus.). 208p. 1988. pap. 15.95 (*0-521-35765-9*) Cambridge U Pr.

Lamoreaux, Naomi R. Insider Lending: Banks, Personal Connections, & Economic Development in Industrial New England. (Illus.). 224p. (C). 1994. 39.95 (*0-521-46096-4*) Cambridge U Pr.

***Lamoreaux, Naomi R. & Raff, Daniel M., eds.** Coordination & Information: Historical Perspectives on the Organization of Enterprise. LC 94-41674. 1995. pap. text ed. 22.50 (*0-226-46821-6*) U Ch Pr.

— Coordination & Information: Historical Perspectives on the Organization of Enterprise. LC 94-41674. (National Bureau of Economic Research Conference Report Ser.). 1995. lib. bdg. 68.00 (*0-226-46820-8*) U Ch Pr.

***Lamoreux, Diana J.** Red Bows on White Lambs. (Illus.). 128p. 1994. pap. 9.95 (*1-881576-40-X*) Providence Hse.

Lamorisse, Albert. The Red Balloon. LC 57-9229. (Illus.). 45p. (J). (ps-3). 1978. mass mkt. 7.95 (*0-385-14297-8*, Zephyr-BFYR) Doubleday.

Lamorisse, Albert, jt. auth. see Prevert, Jacques.

LaMorte, Kathy & Lewis, Sharen. Ecology Green Pages for Students & Teachers. Keeling, Jan, ed. (Illus.). 64p. (Orig.). (J). 1993. pap. text ed. 7.95 (*0-86530-269-3*) Incentive Pubns.

— U. S. Social Studies Yellow Pages for Students & Teachers. Keeling, Jan, ed. (Illus.). 64p. (Orig.). (J). 1993. pap. text ed. 7.95 (*0-86530-267-7*) Incentive Pubns.

— World Social Studies Yellow Pages for Students & Teachers. Newton, Rebecca, ed. (Illus.). 64p. (Orig.). (J). 1993. pap. text ed. 7.95 (*0-86530-268-5*) Incentive Pubns.

Lamorte, Michael. School Law. 3rd ed. 480p. (C). 1990. Casebound. boxed write for info. (*0-13-793704-0*) P-H.

Lamot, Clare, ed. see Scott, Walter.

***Lamothe, Andre.** Black Art of 3D Game Programming: Writing Your Own High-Speed 3D Polygon Video Games in C. 1000p. 1995. cd-rom, pap. 49.95 (*1-57169-004-2*) Waite Group Pr.

— Teach Yourself Game-Programming in 21 Days. 1994. cd-rom, pap. 39.99 (*0-672-30562-3*) Sams.

Lamothe, Andre, jt. auth. see Lampton, Christopher.

Lamothe, Richard, jt. auth. see Osteryoung, Jerome.

Lamothe, Solange, jt. auth. see Judge, Anne.

***Lamott.** Operating Instructions. 4.99 (*0-517-13778-X*) Random Hse Value.

Lamott, Anne. All New People. LC 89-15954. 192p. 1989. 16.95 (*0-86547-394-3*, North Pt Pr) FS&G.

— Bird by Bird: Instructions on Writing & Life. LC 94-5448. 1994. 21.00 (*0-679-43520-4*) Pantheon.

— Bird by Bird: Some Instructions on Writing & Life. LC 95-10225. 1995. write for info. (*0-385-48001-6*, Anchor NY) Doubleday.

— Hard Laughter. LC 86-62832. 304p. 1987. pap. 11.00 (*0-86547-280-7*, North Pt Pr) FS&G.

— Operating Instructions: A Journal of My Son's First Year. LC 92-30540. 240p. 1993. 21.00 (*0-679-42091-6*) Pantheon.

— Operating Instructions: A Journal of My Son's First Year. 272p. 1994. reprint ed. pap. 9.50 (*0-449-90928-X*, Columbine) Fawcett.

— Rosie. LC 88-34553. 288p. 1989. reprint ed. pap. 9.95 (*0-86547-390-0*, North Pt Pr) FS&G.

***LaMotta, Toni.** Recognition. LC 95-1339. 1995. write for info. (*0-527-76223-7*) Qual Resc.

Lamotte, Andree, jt. auth. see Calais-Germain, Blandine.

Lamotte, E. & Boin, S., trs. The Teaching of Vimalakirti. (C). 1976. 67.00 (*0-86013-077-0*, Pub. by Pali Text) Wisdom MA.

LaMotte, Ellen N. The Ethics of Opium. Grob, Gerald N., ed. LC 80-1260. (Addiction in America Ser.). 1981. reprint ed. lib. bdg. 20.95 (*0-405-13601-3*) Ayer.

Lamotte, Michel, jt. ed. see Garrigues, Philippe.

LaMotte, Victor S., jt. auth. see Magno, Joseph A.

Lamouliatte, H., jt. ed. see Megraud, F.

LaMountain, Dianne & Abramms, Bob. Cultural Diversity: A Workshop for Trainers. 250p. 1992. ring bd. 125.00 (*0-87425-190-7*) Human Res Dev Pr.

***Lamour.** Trouble Shooter. 1995. mass mkt. 4.99 (*0-553-57187-7*) Bantam.

L'Amour, Angelique, comp. A Trail of Memories: The Quotations of Louis L'Amour. LC 88-965. 224p. 1988. pap. 12.95 (*0-553-05271-3*) Bantam.

— A Trail of Memories: The Quotations of Louis L'Amour. large type ed. (General Ser.). 216p. 1989. lib. bdg. 20.95 (*0-8161-4728-0*, Large Print Bks) Hall.

L'Amour, L., see Tex Burns, pseud..

L'Amour, Louis. Bendigo-Shafter. 1983. mass mkt. 5.50 (*0-553-26446-X*) Bantam.

— Borden Chantry. 176p. (Orig.). 1989. 3.99 (*0-553-27863-0*) Bantam.

— Bowdrie. 1983. 3.99 (*0-553-28106-2*) Bantam.

— Bowdrie's Law. LC 85-824. (Orig.). 1984. mass mkt. 3.99 (*0-553-24550-3*) Bantam.

— Brionne. (Orig.). 1984. mass mkt. 3.99 (*0-553-28107-0*) Bantam.

— Brionne. large type ed. (Special Ser.). 192p. (Orig.). 1993. reprint ed. pap. 16.95 (*1-56054-653-0*) Thorndike Pr.

— Broken Gun. LC 85-2817. 1984. mass mkt. 3.99 (*0-553-24847-2*) Bantam.

— The Broken Gun. large type ed. (Special Ser.). 213p. 1993. reprint ed. pap. 16.95 (*1-56054-649-2*) Thorndike Pr.

— Buckskin Run. 1984. mass mkt. 3.99 (*0-553-24764-6*) Bantam.

— The Burning Hills. (Orig.). 1985. pap. 3.99 (*0-553-28210-7*) Bantam.

— The Californios. (Orig.). 1985. mass mkt. 3.99 (*0-553-25322-0*) Bantam.

— Callaghen. 192p. 1984. mass mkt. 3.99 (*0-553-24759-X*) Bantam.

— Catlow. 160p. (Orig.). 1984. pap. 3.99 (*0-553-24767-0*) Bantam.

— Chancy. (Orig.). 1984. 3.99 (*0-553-28085-6*) Bantam.

— The Cherokee Trail. 1982. pap. 3.99 (*0-553-27047-8*) Bantam.

— Comstock Lode. 1982. mass mkt. 5.50 (*0-553-27561-5*) Bantam.

— Comstock Lode. large type ed. (Special Ser.). 718p. 1993. reprint ed. pap. 16.95 (*1-56054-648-4*) Thorndike Pr.

— Conagher. 160p. (Orig.). 1982. mass mkt. 3.99 (*0-553-28101-1*) Bantam.

— Crossfire Trail. 176p. 1985. pap. 3.99 (*0-553-28099-6*) Bantam.

— Crossfire Trail. large type ed. LC 92-41743. (General Ser.). 1993. pap. 16.95 (*0-8161-5724-3*, Large Print Bks) Hall.

— Dark Canyon. (Illus.). 1985. 3.99 (*0-553-25324-7*) Bantam.

— Day Breakers, No. 3. 1984. mass mkt. 3.99 (*0-553-27674-3*) Bantam.

— Down the Long Hills. 1984. 3.99 (*0-553-28081-3*) Bantam.

— Down the Long Hills. large type ed. (Special Ser.). 222p. 1993. reprint ed. pap. 16.95 (*1-56054-651-4*) Thorndike Pr.

— Dutchman's Flat. 1986. mass mkt. 3.99 (*0-553-28111-9*) Bantam.

— Education of a Wandering Man. 1990. pap. 5.50 (*0-553-28652-8*) Bantam.

— Education of a Wandering Man. braille ed. 387p. 1990. vinyl bd. 30.96 (*1-56956-224-5*, BR8083) W A T Braille.

— Education of a Wandering Man. large type ed. LC 93-1971. 330p. 1993. reprint ed. pap. 17.95 (*0-8161-5797-9*) Hall.

— Empty Land. (Orig.). 1985. mass mkt. 3.99 (*0-553-25306-9*) Bantam.

— Fair Blows the Wind. 1982. mass mkt. 3.99 (*0-553-27629-8*) Bantam.

— Fallon. (Orig.). 1982. mass mkt. 3.99 (*0-553-28083-X*) Bantam.

— Fallon. large type ed. (Orig.). 1990. pap. 12.95 (*0-8161-5050-8*) G K Hall.

— The Ferguson Rifle. 192p. (Orig.). 1985. mass mkt. 3.99 (*0-553-25303-4*) Bantam.

— The First Fast Draw. 160p. 1985. mass mkt. 3.99 (*0-553-25224-0*) Bantam.

— First Fast Draw. 1989. lib. bdg. 15.95 (*0-8161-4414-1*) G K Hall.

— Flint. 192p. (Orig.). 1985. 3.99 (*0-553-25231-3*) Bantam.

— Frontier. LC 84-45178. 224p. 1984. 34.95 (*0-553-05078-8*) Bantam.

— Galloway. braille ed. 258p. (Orig.). 1994. text ed., vinyl bd. 20.64 (*1-56956-544-9*, BR9514) W A T Braille.

— Guns of the Timberlands. 160p. (Orig.). 1984. 3.99 (*0-553-24765-4*) Bantam.

— Hanging Woman Creek. 160p. (Orig.). 1984. mass mkt. 3.99 (*0-553-24762-X*) Bantam.

— The Haunted Mesa. (Orig.). 1988. mass mkt. 5.50 (*0-553-27022-2*) Bantam.

— Heller with a Gun. 1985. 3.99 (*0-553-25206-2*) Bantam.

— Heller with a Gun. 1984. pap. 2.50 (*0-449-12350-2*) Fawcett.

— High Graders. 1989. mass mkt. 3.99 (*0-553-27864-9*) Bantam.

— High Lonesome. 160p. (Orig.). 1982. mass mkt. 3.99 (*0-553-25972-5*) Bantam.

— Hills of Homicide. 1984. mass mkt. 3.99 (*0-553-24134-6*) Bantam.

— Hondo. 1991. 3.99 (*0-553-28090-2*) Bantam.

— Hondo. 1981. pap. 2.25 (*0-449-14255-8*, GM) Fawcett.

— Hondo. large type ed. LC 93-36323. (General Ser.). 1994. pap. write for info. (*0-8161-5796-0*, Large Print Bks) Hall.

— How the West Was Won. (YA). (gr. 7-12). 1984. mass mkt. 4.50 (*0-553-26913-5*) Bantam.

— The Iron Marshall. (Orig.). 1979. 3.99 (*0-553-24844-8*) Bantam.

— Jubal Sackett. 384p. (Orig.). 1986. mass mkt. 5.50 (*0-553-27739-1*) Bantam.

— The Key Lock Man. 1985. mass mkt. 3.99 (*0-553-28098-8*) Bantam.

— Kid Rodelo. (Orig.). 1984. mass mkt. 3.99 (*0-553-24748-4*) Bantam.

— Kilkenny. 1984. mass mkt. 3.99 (*0-553-24758-1*) Bantam.

— Killoe. 160p. (Orig.). 1982. mass mkt. 3.99 (*0-553-25742-0*) Bantam.

— Kilrone. (Western Ser.). 160p. 1981. 3.99 (*0-553-24867-7*) Bantam.

— Kiowa Trail. 160p. (Orig.). 1964. mass mkt. 3.99 (*0-553-24905-3*) Bantam.

— Lando. (Orig.). 1984. mass mkt. 3.99 (*0-553-27676-X*) Bantam.

— Lando. large type ed. (Special Ser.). 222p. (Orig.). 1993. reprint ed. pap. 16.95 (*1-56054-652-2*) Thorndike Pr.

— Last of the Breed. 1987. 5.50 (*0-553-28042-2*) Bantam.

L

— Last Stand at Papago Wells. 144p. (Orig.). 1986. 3.99 (0-553-25807-9) Bantam.
— Last Stand at Papago Wells. (Orig.). 1983. pap. 2.50 (0-449-12576-9, GM) Fawcett.
— The Law of the Desert Born. 1983. pap. 2.95 (0-88184-061-0) Carroll & Graf.
— Law of the Desert Born. 256p. (Orig.). 1984. mass mkt. 3.99 (0-553-24133-8) Bantam.
— Law of the Desert Born. 192p. (Orig.). 1983. 14.95 (0-671-06697-8) Boulevard.
— Law of the Desert Born. large type ed. (Special Ser.). 359p. (Orig.). 1993. reprint ed. pap. 16.95 (1-56054-646-8) Thorndike Pr.
— The Lonely Men. 1984. 3.99 (0-553-27677-8) Bantam.
— Lonely on the Mountain. (Orig.). 1984. mass mkt. 3.99 (0-553-27678-6) Bantam.
— The Lonesome Gods. 464p. (Orig.). 1984. mass mkt. 5.50 (0-553-27518-6) Bantam.
— Long Ride Home. 1989. 3.99 (0-553-28181-X) Bantam.
— Lonigan. 1988. 3.99 (0-553-27536-4) Bantam.
— Lonigan. large type ed. (General Ser.). 260p. 1989. lib. bdg. 18.95 (0-8161-4828-7) G K Hall.
— Louis L'Amour: The Sacketts, 4 vols., Set. 1990. Boxed set. boxed 17.50 (0-553-60928-9) Bantam.
— The Man Called Noon. 160p. 1985. pap. 3.99 (0-553-24753-0) Bantam.
— The Man Called Noon. large type ed. (Special Ser.). 271p. 1993. reprint ed. pap. 16.95 (1-56054-645-X) Thorndike Pr.
— The Man from Skibbereen. 192p. (Orig.). 1983. 3.99 (0-553-24906-1) Bantam.
— Man from the Broken Hills. 1975. mass mkt. 3.99 (0-553-27679-4) Bantam.
— Man Riding West. 1986. 2.95 (0-88184-251-6) Carroll & Graf.
— Matagorda. (Orig.). 1985. mass mkt. 3.99 (0-553-28108-9) Bantam.
— Milo Talon. 1981. mass mkt. 3.99 (0-553-24763-8) Bantam.
— Mojave Crossing. (Orig.). 1985. mass mkt. 3.99 (0-553-27680-8) Bantam.
— The Mountain Valley War. 208p. 1991. pap. 3.99 (0-553-25090-6) Bantam.
— Night over the Solomons. 1986. 3.99 (0-553-26602-0) Bantam.
— North to the Rails. (Orig.). 1983. mass mkt. 3.99 (0-553-28086-4) Bantam.
— The Outlaws of Mesquite. large type ed. 1990. 21.95 (0-385-41542-7, Bantam LT) BDD LT Grp.
Lamour, Louis. Outlaws of the Mesquite. 1991. pap. 3.99 (0-553-28714-1) Bantam.
L'Amour, Louis. Over on the Dry Side. 192p. (Orig.). 1985. pap. 3.99 (0-553-25321-2) Bantam.
— Passin' Through. 176p. (Orig.). 1985. pap. 3.99 (0-553-25320-4) Bantam.
— The Proving Trail. 1985. pap. 3.99 (0-553-25304-2) Bantam.
— The Quick & the Dead. 1982. 3.99 (0-553-28084-8) Bantam.
— Radigan. (Orig.). 1984. pap. 3.99 (0-553-28082-1) Bantam.
— Reilly's Luck. 224p. (Orig.). 1985. 3.99 (0-553-25305-0) Bantam.
— Ride the Dark Trail. 1984. mass mkt. 3.99 (0-553-27682-4) Bantam.
— Ride the River, No. 17. 1983. pap. 3.99 (0-553-27683-2) Bantam.
— The Rider of Lost Creek. 160p. (Orig.). 1982. mass mkt. 3.99 (0-553-25771-4) Bantam.
— Rider of Ruby Hills. 1986. 4.50 (0-553-28112-7) Bantam.
Lamour, Louis. Riders of High Rock. 1994. pap. 4.99 (0-553-56782-9) Bantam.
L'Amour, Louis. Riders of High Rock. large type ed. 1993. 24.95 (0-385-47040-1, Bantam LT) BDD LT Grp.
— Riding for the Brand. 1986. pap. 3.99 (0-553-28105-4) Bantam.
— Riding for the Brand. 192p. 1986. pap. 2.95 (0-88184-250-8) Carroll & Graf.
— Rivers West. 160p. (Orig.). 1983. 3.99 (0-553-25436-7) Bantam.
Lamour, Louis. Rustlers of West Fork: A Hopalong Cassidy Novel. 1992. mass mkt. 4.99 (0-553-29539-X) Bantam.
L'Amour, Louis. The Rustlers of West Fork: A Hopalong Cassidy Novel. large type ed. 1991. 22.00 (0-385-41996-1, Bantam LT) BDD LT Grp.
— The Rustlers of West Fork: A Hopalong Cassidy Novel. large type ed. LC 94-9291. 353p. 1994. pap. 17.95 (0-8161-5798-7) G K Hall.
— Sackett. 1984. pap. 3.99 (0-553-27684-0) Bantam.
— The Sackett Brand. 1985. pap. 3.99 (0-553-27685-9) Bantam.
— The Sackett Companion. LC 88-47530. 288p. 1988. 19.95 (0-553-05305-1) Bantam.
— The Sackett Companion: A Personal Guide to the Sackett Novels. 352p. 1992. pap. 10.00 (0-553-37102-9) Bantam.
— Sackett's Land. 1984. mass mkt. 3.99 (0-553-27686-7) Bantam.
— The Shadow Riders. 192p. 1982. mass mkt. 3.99 (0-553-23132-4) Bantam.
— Shalako. 176p. (Orig.). 1985. 3.99 (0-553-24858-8) Bantam.
— Showdown at Yellow Butte. 1983. 3.99 (0-553-27993-9) Bantam.
— Showdown at Yellow Butte. 192p. 1982. pap. 2.25 (0-449-14275-2, GM) Fawcett.
— Silver Canyon. 176p. (Orig.). 1957. mass mkt. 3.99 (0-553-24743-3) Bantam.
— Sitka. 1984. pap. 4.50 (0-553-27881-9) Bantam.
— The Sky-Liners. 1982. pap. 3.99 (0-553-27687-5) Bantam.
— The Sky-Liners. large type ed. (Special Ser.). 264p. 1993. reprint ed. pap. 16.95 (1-56054-650-6) Thorndike Pr.
— Smoke from This Altar. 1990. pap. 12.95 (0-553-07349-4) Bantam.
— Son of a Wanted Man. 176p. 1991. mass mkt. 3.99 (0-553-24457-4) Bantam.
— Son of a Wanted Man. large type ed. (Special Ser.). 269p. 1993. reprint ed. pap. 16.95 (1-56054-654-9) Thorndike Pr.
— The Strong Shall Live. 1985. 3.99 (0-553-25200-3) Bantam.
— The Strong Shall Live. large type ed. (Special Ser.). 242p. 1993. reprint ed. pap. 16.95 (1-56054-647-6) Thorndike Pr.
— Taggart. 160p. 1982. mass mkt. 3.99 (0-553-25477-4) Bantam.
— The Tall Stranger. 128p. 1986. 3.99 (0-553-28102-X) Bantam.
— The Tallest Stranger. large type ed. Bd. with Last Stand at Papago Wells. 12.00 (0-685-29824-8) Ulverscroft.
— The Tallest Stranger bd. with Last Stand at Papago Wells. large type ed. Bd. with Tallest Stranger. 1989. 12.00 (0-7089-0630-3) Ulverscroft.
— To Tame a Land. 1991. 3.99 (0-553-28031-7) Bantam.
— To Tame a Land. 1984. pap. 2.50 (0-449-12356-1) Fawcett.
— To the Far Blue Mountains. 1984. mass mkt. 3.99 (0-553-27688-3) Bantam.
— Trail of Memories: The Quotations of Louis L'Amour. 1993. pap. 9.95 (0-553-37303-X) Bantam.
— The Trail to Crazy Man. 1986. pap. 4.50 (0-553-28035-X) Bantam.
— Trail to Crazy Man. large type ed. (General Ser.). 584p. 1988. lib. bdg. 20.95 (0-8161-4351-X) G K Hall.
Lamour, Louis. Trail to Seven Pines. 1993. pap. 4.99 (0-553-56178-2) Bantam.
L'Amour, Louis. The Trail to Seven Pines. large type ed. LC 93-45637. 1994. pap. 17.95 (0-8161-5799-5, Large Print Bks) Hall.
— Trail to Seven Pines. large type ed. 1992. pap. 24.00 (0-385-42369-1, Bantam LT) BDD LT Grp.
— Treasure Mountain. (Orig.). 1984. 3.99 (0-553-27689-1) Bantam.
— Troubleshooter. 1994. pap. 19.95 (0-553-08912-9) Bantam.
— Tucker. 192p. 1984. mass mkt. 3.99 (0-553-25022-1) Bantam.
— Under the Sweetwater Rim. 1984. 3.99 (0-553-24760-3) Bantam.
— Utah Blaine. 1984. pap. 3.99 (0-553-24761-1) Bantam.
— Utah Blaine. 192p. 1982. pap. 2.50 (0-449-12357-X, GM) Fawcett.
— Valley of the Sun: Frontier Stories. LC 94-23224. 1995. pap. 19.95 (0-553-09962-0) Bantam.
— Walking Drum. 1985. pap. 5.50 (0-553-28040-6) Bantam.
— War Party. 160p. (Orig.). 1982. mass mkt. 3.99 (0-553-25393-X) Bantam.
— The Warrior's Path. (Orig.). 1984. mass mkt. 3.99 (0-553-27690-5) Bantam.
— West from Singapore. 1987. mass mkt. 3.99 (0-553-26353-6) Bantam.
— Westward the Tide. 224p. (Orig.). 1984. pap. 3.99 (0-553-24766-2) Bantam.
— Where the Long Grass Grows. 1985. pap. 3.99 (0-553-28172-0) Bantam.
— Yondering. rev. ed. (Orig.). 1989. pap. 3.99 (0-553-28203-4) Random Hse Value.
Lamoureux, Dorothy. The Arts & Crafts Studio of Dirk Van Erp. LC 89-61391. (Illus.). 60p. (Orig.). 1989. pap. 15.00 (1-877742-01-5) SF Craft & Folk.
***Lamoureux, Marie E.** Index to Clerical Biographies in William Buell Sprague's 'Annals of the American Pulpit' 25p. 1994. pap. 9.50 (0-944026-59-1) Am Antiquarian.
Lamoureux, Normand, jt. auth. see Comeau, Raymond F.
Lamoureux, Normand, jt. auth. see Comeau, Raymond.
Lamoureux, Normand J., jt. auth. see Comeau, Raymond F.
Lamoureux, Paul E., ed. Massachusetts Appellate Division Reports: 1980, 1981, 1982, 1983, 1984, 1985, 1986, 1987, 1988, 1989. 366p. 1984. 50.00 (0-318-03673-8) Lawyers Weekly.
Lamoureux, Vincent B. Guide to Ship Sanitation. 119p. (ENG, FRE & RUS.). 1967. pap. 5.60 (92-4-154010-9) World Health.
Lamp & Collett. Field Guide to Weeds in Australia. 3rd ed. 1990. 39.00 (0-909605-53-X, Pub. by Inkata Pr AT) Intl Spec Bk.
Lamp, C. O. Distant Love, Lasting Love. large type ed. 544p. 1984. 15.95 (0-7089-1129-3) Ulverscroft.
— Gentle Tigress. (Orig.). 1980. pap. 2.25 (0-8439-0727-4) Dorchester Pub Co.
***Lamp, David.** Astronomy for the Masses. 80p. (C). 1994. pap. text ed., spiral bd. 9.95 (0-7872-0304-1) Kendall-Hunt.
Lamp Light & Press Staff. Immune System Herbals, Approaches, Folklore: A How to Find or Locate Workbook. (Illus.). 70p. 1993. 25.95 (0-917593-28-6, Lamp Light Pr) Prosperity & Profits.
Lamp Light Press Staff. Advertising Black Markets: A Directory of Slang, Jargon & Chocolate Grammar. 70p. 1993. ring bd. 49.95 (0-917593-21-9, Lamp Light Pr) Prosperity & Profits.
— Advertising Cheaper with Telemarketing: Script Presentations Directory. 200p. (C). 1993. ring bd. 94.95 (0-917593-18-9, Lamp Light Pr) Prosperity & Profits.
— Advertising Food Businesses with Recipe Greetings: Samples Directory for Licensing. 60p. 1993. ring bd. 39.95 (0-917593-19-7, Lamp Light Pr) Prosperity & Profits.
— Business Theatre: Skits & Plays for Meetings, Conferences, Schools, Etc. 70p. 1993. ring bd. 19.95 (0-917593-32-4, Lamp Light Pr) Prosperity & Profits.
— Clip Art: Food Illustrations & Recipe Greeting Rhymes to Duplicate & Use. (Illus.). 50p. 1993. 49.95 (0-917593-12-X, Lamp Light Pr) Prosperity & Profits.
— Coffee Substitutes - Poetry, Greetings, Etc. (Illus.). 18p. (Orig.). (C). 1995. pap. text ed. 6.95 (0-917593-37-5, Lamp Light Pr) Prosperity & Profits.
— Copy Service Business Possibilities. 112p. (C). 1993. 32.95 (0-917593-14-6, Lamp Light Pr) Prosperity & Profits.
— Entrepreneur's Home School. (Illus.). 360p. 1993. ring bd. 179.00 (0-917593-16-2, Lamp Light Pr) Prosperity & Profits.
— Fragrantis Dictionary. rev. ed. (Illus.). 55p. 1993. ring bd. 23.95 (0-917593-33-2, Lamp Light Pr) Prosperity & Profits.
— Greeting Card Service Agency, Gift Shops: Greetings to Duplicate & Use. (Illus.). 60p. 1993. ring bd. 75.00 (0-917593-24-3, Lamp Light Pr) Prosperity & Profits.
— Greetings That Educate, Entertain & Rhyme to Duplicate & Use. (Illus.). 60p. 1993. ring bd. 29.95 (0-917593-23-5, Lamp Light Pr) Prosperity & Profits.
— Immune System Herbal Greetings to Duplicate & Use. (Illus.). 60p. 1993. 21.95 (0-917593-26-X, Lamp Light Pr) Prosperity & Profits.
— Index to Prayer Books, Pamphlets, Etc. 50p. 1984. pap. 2.50 (0-917593-01-4, Lamp Light Pr) Prosperity & Profits.
— Kids Businesses: Telemarketing Script Presentations. 75p. 1993. ring bd. 39.95 (0-917593-27-8, Lamp Light Pr) Prosperity & Profits.
— Love Theme Greetings to Duplicate & Use. (Illus.). 70p. 1993. ring bd. 29.95 (0-917593-22-7, Lamp Light Pr) Prosperity & Profits.
— Money Saving Frugal Consumer Workshop Notebook. (Illus.). 93p. 1993. ring bd. 37.95 (0-917593-15-4, Lamp Light Pr) Prosperity & Profits.
— Noah's Ark: A Story Rhyme. (Illus.). 23p. (J). (ps-6). 1992. pap. text ed. 6.95 (0-917593-11-1, Lamp Light Pr) Prosperity & Profits.
— Song Send Greetings to Duplicate & Use. (Illus.). 52p. 1993. 11.95 (0-917593-31-6, Lamp Light Pr) Prosperity & Profits.
— Tea Herbal Cookie Bag Greetings to Duplicate & Use. (Illus.). 58p. 1993. ring bd. 29.95 (0-917593-25-1, Lamp Light Pr) Prosperity & Profits.
Lamp Light Staff. Advertising with Flowers: Clip Art Directory. (Illus.). 60p. 1993. ring bd. 39.95 (0-917593-20-0, Lamp Light Pr) Prosperity & Profits.
— Make It Tasty Spice Recipe Greetings to Duplicate & Use. 60p. 1993. ring bd. 29.95 (0-917593-29-4, Lamp Light Pr) Prosperity & Profits.
Lamparczyk. Analysis & Characterization of Steroids. 1992. 139.95 (0-8493-3008-4, QP752) CRC Pr.
Lampard, Eric E. The History of Cities in the Economically Advanced Areas. (Reprint Series in Social Sciences). (C). 1993. reprint ed. pap. text ed. 4.50 (0-8290-2650-9, S-440) Irvington.
Lamparski, Richard. Lamparski's Hidden Hollywood: Where the Stars Lived, Loved & Died. 1981. pap. 8.95 (0-686-71142-4, Fireside) S&S Trade.
— Whatever Became of...? rev. ed. 1989. pap. 10.95 (0-517-57151-X, Crown) Crown Pub Group.
— Whatever Became of...? 11th rev. ed. 1989. 21.95 (0-517-57150-1, Crown) Crown Pub Group.
Lamparsky, D., jt. ed. see Muller, P. M.
Lampe, David, ed. The Legend of Being Irish: A Collection of Irish-American Poetry. 1988. 10.00 (0-934834-23-7) White Pine.
— Myths & Voices: New Canadian Short Fiction. 1993. pap. 17.00 (1-877727-28-8) White Pine.
Lampe, David, jt. auth. see Rosegrant, Susan.
Lampe, Diana. Embroider a Garden. (Illus.). 124p. 1994. 19.95 (1-86351-122-9, Pub. by S Milner AT) Sterling.
Lampe, Diana & Fisk, Jane. Embroidered Garden Flowers. (Illus.). 1992. 19.95 (1-86351-043-5, Pub. by S Milner AT) Sterling.
Lampe, G. W., ed. Patristic Greek Lexicon. 1616p. (GRE.). 1969. 285.00 (0-19-864213-X) OUP.
Lampe, John R. The Bulgarian Economy in the Twentieth Century. 256p. 1986. text ed. 45.00 (0-312-10785-4) St Martin.
Lampe, John R., ed. Creating Capital Markets in Eastern Europe. (Woodrow Wilson Center Press Ser.). 110p. (Orig.). 1992. pap. text ed. 10.95 (0-943875-42-0) Johns Hopkins.
Lampe, John R. & Jackson, Marvin R. Balkan Economic History, 1550-1950: From Imperial Borderlands to Developing Nations. LC 80-8844. (Illus.). 728p. 1982. 39.95 (0-253-30368-0) Ind U Pr.
Lampe, John R. & Nelson, Daniel N., eds. East European Security Reconsidered. (Woodrow Wilson Center Press Ser.). 175p. (Orig.). 1993. pap. text ed. 14.95 (0-943875-47-1) Johns Hopkins.
Lampe, John R., et al. Yugoslav-American Economic Relations since World War II. LC 90-38619. 262p. (C). 1991. text ed. 39.50 (0-8223-1061-9) Duke.
Lampe, Kenneth F. & McCann, Mary A. The AMA Handbook of Poisonous & Injurious Plants. LC 84-28532. (Illus.). 600p. (Orig.). 1985. pap. 28.00 (0-89970-183-3, OP25085) AMA.
Lampe, Kenneth F., ed. see Inter-American Conference in Toxicology & Occupational Medicine (5th: 1966: Coral Gables, FL) Staff.
Lampe, Philip E. Adultery in the United States: Close Encounters of the Sixth (or Seventh) Kind. LC 87-9641. 224p. 1988. 29.95 (0-87975-375-7) Prometheus Bks.
Lampe, Philip E., ed. Hispanics in the Church: Up from the Cellar. LC 93-33338. 1994. 54.95 (1-883255-19-8); pap. 34.95 (1-883255-18-X) Intl Scholars.
***Lampe, Susan.** Focus Charting: Documentation for Patient-Centered Care. 6th ed. 301p. 1994. pap. 25.00 (0-9621520-5-6) Creative Nursing.
***Lampe, Susan, ed.** Chart Forms. 260p. (Orig.). 1991. pap. 50.00 (0-9621520-8-0) Creative Nursing.
— Focus Charting, What We Have Learned: A Collection of Articles from Primarily Nursing Newsletter. 69p. 1992. pap. 10.00 (0-9621520-4-8) Creative Nursing.
Lampe, Thomas R. Idea to Marketplace: How to Turn Your Good Ideas into Moneymakers. (Illus.). 236p. (Orig.). 1991. reprint ed. pap. 9.95 (0-929923-44-8) Lowell Hse.
Lampe, Willard, jt. auth. see Armstrong, William H., III.
Lampel, Zvi. The Dynamics of Dispute: Machlokess in Talmudic Times. 270p. 1991. 17.95 (0-910818-96-7); pap. 13.95 (0-910818-99-1) Judaica Pr.
Lampen, Dorothy. Economic & Social Aspects of Federal Reclamation. Bruchey, Stuart, ed. LC 78-56686. (Management of Public Lands in the U. S. Ser.). (Illus.). 1979. reprint ed. lib. bdg. 15.95 (0-405-11338-2) Ayer.
Lampen, John. Findings: Poets & the Crisis of Faith. LC 93-85638. (Orig.). 1993. pap. 3.00 (0-87574-310-2) Pendle Hill.
Lampen, L. Finnish-Swedish Dictionary. 571p. (FIN & SWE.). 1980. 49.95 (0-8288-4699-5, M9655) Fr & Eur.
— Finnish-Swedish Dictionary: Ruotsalais-Suomalainen Suursanakirja. 6th ed. 857p. (FIN & SWE.). 1985. 150.00 (0-8288-1079-6, F64080) Fr & Eur.
— Finnish-Swedish-Finnish Dictionary: Suomi-Ruotsi-Suomi Taskusanakirja. 9th ed. 633p. (FIN & SWE.). 1987. 19.95 (0-8288-1693-X, M9647) Fr & Eur.
— Finnish-Swedish Students Dictionary: Suomalais-Ruotsalainen Opiskelusanakirja. 571p. (FIN & SWE.). 1985. 59.95 (0-8288-1679-4, M9656) Fr & Eur.
***Lampert.** The Fun Way to Advanced Bridge. Date not set. 8.95 (0-910791-77-5, 0575) Devyn Pr.
Lampert, ed. Optical Materials Technology for Energy Efficiency & Solar Energy Conversion, No. VI. 278p. 1987. 51.00 (0-89252-858-3, 823) SPIE.
Lampert, C. M. & Granqvist, C. G., eds. Large-Area Chromogenics: Materials & Devices for Transmittance Control (Advanced Institute - September 1988, Hamburg, FRG) (Proceedings Ser.: Vol. 1034). 585p. 1990. 99.00 (0-8194-0287-7); pap. 84.00 (0-8194-0069-6) SPIE.
Lampert, C. M., jt. auth. see Granqvist, C. G.
Lampert, C. M., jt. ed. see Granqvist, C. G.
Lampert, Carl M., jt. ed. see Granqvist, Claes G.
Lampert, Catherine. Rodin: Sculpture & Drawings. LC 86-50765. 256p. 1987. pap. 26.00 (0-300-03832-1) Yale U Pr.
Lampert, Dan & Woodley, Douglas R. Site Selection & Investigation. 170p. 1991. text ed. 64.95 (0-566-09090-2, Pub. by Gower UK) Ashgate Pub Co.
Lampert, Diane, jt. auth. see Farrow, Peter.
Lampert, E. The Apocalypse of History: Problems of Providence & Human Destiny. 1948. 49.50 (0-317-07646-9) Elliots Bks.
Lampert, Emily. A Little Touch of Monster. LC 85-26847. (Illus.). 32p. (J). (ps-3). 1986. lib. bdg. 12.95 (0-316-51287-7, 512877, Joy St Bks) Little.
Lampert, Erv, ed. see Anderson, Dorothy & Anderson, Robert.
Lampert, Erv, ed. see Anderson, Robert.
Lampert, Erv, ed. see Bruce, Hank & Bruce, Marlene.
Lampert, Eva, ed. see Anderson, Dorothy & Anderson, Robert.
Lampert, Eva, ed. see Anderson, Robert.
Lampert, F., et al, eds. Cancer in the First Year of Life: Leukemia, Neuroblastomas, Soft Tissue Sarcomas. (Beitraege zur Onkologie, Contributions to Oncology Ser.: Vol. 41). (Illus.). viii, 174p. 1991. 57.00 (3-8055-5233-5) S Karger.
Lampert, Harry. Fun Way to Serious Bridge. 1986. pap. 9.00 (0-671-63027-X) S&S Trade.
***Lampert, Jay.** Synthesis & Backward Reference in Husserl's Logical Investigations. LC 94-23102. (Phaenomenologica Ser.: Vol. 131). 1995. lib. bdg. 96.00 (0-7923-3105-2) Kluwer Ac.
Lampert, Junko. The Tofu Cookbook: Recipes for Traditional & Modern Cooking. LC 85-25546. (Illus.). 102p. (Orig.). 1986. pap. 12.95 (0-87701-383-7) Chronicle Bks.
***Lampert, Laurence.** Leo Strauss & Nietzsche. LC 95-10467. 1996. 22.50 (0-226-46825-9) U Ch Pr.
— Nietzsche & Modern Times: A Study of Bacon, Descartes, & Nietzsche. LC 92-27259. 480p. (C). 1993. text ed. 37.00 (0-300-05675-3) Yale U Pr.
— Nietzsche's Teaching: An Interpretation of "Thus Spake Zarathustra" LC 86-9209. 400p. (C). 1989. reprint ed. pap. 16.00 (0-300-04430-5) Yale U Pr.
Lampert, Lincoln M. Modern Dairy Products: Composition, Food Value, Processing, Chemistry, Bacteriology, Testing, Imitation Dairy Products. 425p. reprint ed. pap. 121.20 (0-7837-1961-2, 2042247) Bks Demand.
Lampert, Lyndon J., jt. auth. see Borneman, Walter R.
Lampert, M. A. & Mark, P. Current Injections in Solids. (Electrical Science Ser.). 1970. text ed. 151.00 (0-12-435350-9) Acad Pr.
Lampert, Martin D., jt. ed. see Edwards, Jane A.
Lampert, Nick & Ritterspoon, Gabor T., eds. Stalinism: Its Nature & Aftermath, Essays in Honor of Moshe Lewin. LC 91-15051. 200p. 1991. 62.95 (0-87332-876-0) M E Sharpe.
Lampert, Rachel & Rotman, Leslie. What's Remembered: Labanotation Score. (Educational Performance Collection). 231p. 1986. pap. write for info. (0-932582-46-X) Dance Notation.
Lampert, W., ed. Food Limitation & the Structure of Zooplankton Communities: Proceedings of an International Symposium, West Germany, 1984. (Advances in Limnology Ser.: No. 21). (Illus.). 497p. 1985. pap. text ed. 122.20 (3-510-47019-2) Lubrecht & Cramer.
Lamperti, Claudia M., ed. Woman Space: Future & Fantasy Stories by Women. LC 80-83471. 96p. (Orig.). 1981. pap. 4.95 (0-934678-04-9) New Victoria Pubs.

Lamperti, Giovanni B., jt. auth. see Brown, William E.

Lamperti, J. Stochastic Processes: A Survey of the Mathematical Theory. LC 77-24321. (Applied Mathematical Sciences Ser.: Vol. 23). 1977. pap. 32.50 (0-387-90275-9) Spr-Verlag.

Lamperti, John. What Are We Afraid Of? An Assessment of the "Communist Threat" in Central America. NARMIC-AFSC Staff, ed. LC 88-6690. 125p. (Orig.). 1988. 25.00 (0-89608-339-X); pap. 8.00 (0-89608-338-1) South End Pr.

Lamphear, F. Charles & Roesler, Theodore W. Input-Output Model of the Nebraska Economy, 1970. 1975. 2.50 (0-318-42808-3) Bur Busn Res U Nebr.

Lamphear, John. The Scattering Time: Turkana Responses to Colonial Rule. 336p. 1992. 72.00 (0-19-820226-1) OUP.

Lamphere, Louise. From Working Daughters to Working Mothers: Immigrant Women in a New England Industrial Community. LC 86-32952. (Anthropology of Contemporary Issues Ser.). (Illus.). 410p. 1987. 47.50 (0-8014-1945-X) Cornell U Pr.

— To Run after Them: Cultural & Social Bases of Cooperation in a Navajo Community. LC 77-22352. 230p. 1977. 15.95 (0-8165-0594-2); pap. 13.95 (0-8165-0369-9) U of Ariz Pr.

Lamphere, Louise, ed. Structuring Diversity: Ethnographic Perspectives on the New Immigration. LC 91-41183. (Illus.). 240p. 1992. lib. bdg. 38.00 (0-226-46818-6); pap. text ed. 15.00 (0-226-46819-4) U Ch Pr.

Lamphere, Louise, jt. ed. see Rosaldo, Michelle Z.

Lamphere, Louise, et al. Sunbelt Working Mothers: Reconciling Family & Factory. LC 92-56789. (Anthropology of Contemporary Issues Ser.). (Illus.). 352p. 1993. 42.50 (0-8014-2788-6); pap. 15.95 (0-8014-8066-3) Cornell U Pr.

Lamphere, Louise, et al, eds. Newcomers in the Workplace: Immigrants & the Restructuring of the U. S. Economy. LC 93-15205. (Labor & Social Change Ser.). 320p. (C). 1993. text ed. 44.95 (1-56639-124-5); pap. 19.95 (1-56639-131-8) Temple U Pr.

Lamphere, Robert J. The Secret War. 1994. 16.95 (0-533-10552-8) Vantage.

Lamphere, Robert J. & Schachtman, Thomas. The FBI-KGB War: A Special Agent's Story. LC 85-19407. (Illus.). 352p. 1986. 18.95 (0-394-54151-0) Random.

Lamphier, Mary J. The Pieceable Kingdom. LC 84-51255. (Illus.). 128p. (Orig.). 1985. pap. 14.95 (0-87069-426-X, Wallace-Hmestead) Chilton.

— Zany Characters of the Ad World, Collector's Identification & Value Guide. 176p. 1995. pap. 16.95 (0-89145-652-X, 3979) Collector Bks.

***Lampi, Heimo.** Death Stalks Meteora. 1994. pap. 10.95 (0-533-11072-6) Vantage.

Lamping, Alwena, jt. auth. see Durrant, Paul.

Lampiris, Nicholas, jt. auth. see Laing, David.

***Lampitt, Bob.** A Manager's Introduction to Tendering. (C). 1991. pap. 60.00x (0-85171-097-2, Pub. by IPM Hse UK) St Mut.

Lampitt, Dianah. The King's Women. 560p. (Orig.). 1993. pap. 5.99 (0-451-40389-4, Sig) NAL-Dutton.

***Lampitt, Dinah.** As Shadows Haunting. 544p. 1995. 5.99 (0-451-17865-3, Sig) NAL-Dutton.

***Lampkin, N. H. & Padel, S., eds.** The Economics of Organic Farming: An International Perspective. 480p. 1994. 90.00 (0-85198-911-X) CAB Intl.

Lampkin, Nicolas. Organic Farming. (Illus.). 720p. 1990. 48.95 (0-85236-191-2, Pub. by Farming Pr UK) Diamond Farm Bk.

Lampkin, Richard. Lampkin Genealogy: A Genealogcal History of the Ancestors of David P. Lampkin, Vol. 1. 870p. reprint ed. pap. 160.00 (0-8357-6288-2, AU00388) Bks Demand.

— Lampkin Genealogy: A Genealogcal History of the Ancestors of David P. Lampkin, Vol. 2. 868p. reprint ed. pap. 180.00 (0-8357-6289-0) Bks Demand.

Lampkin, Richard H. Selected Readings in Scripture & Morals: Twelve Canonical Scriptures Considered As Sources of True Propositions about the Morality of Eating Meat & of Drinking Alcohol, of Making War & of Making Love. 327p. reprint ed. pap. 93.20 (0-7837-2031-9, AU00418) Bks Demand.

— Variability in Recognizing Scientific Inquiry: An Analysis of High School Science Textbooks. LC 70-176971. (Columbia University. Teachers College. Contributions to Education Ser.: No. 955). reprint ed. 37.50 (0-404-55955-7) AMS Pr.

Lampkin, Rita. Easy Kana Workbook: Basic Practice in Hiragana & Katakana for Japanese Language Students. 1991. pap. 9.95 (0-8442-8532-3, Natl Textbk) NTC Pub Grp.

Lampkin, Rita L. & Christensen, John. The ABCs of ESL Business Letter Writing. (Illus.). 98p. 1989. text ed. 13.95 (1-877591-10-6); 15.95 (1-877591-09-2) Excellence Education.

Lampkin, Viola. Viola's Favorite Recipes. (Illus.). 74p. (Orig.). 1988. pap. write for info. (0-9621378-0-4) B Clagett.

Lampl-de Groot, Jeanne. Development of the Mind: Psychoanalytic Papers on Clinical & Theoretical Problems. LC 65-21749. 391p. 1965. text ed. 55.00 (0-8236-1240-6) Intl Univs Pr.

— Man & Mind. ix, 441p. 1985. text ed. 62.50x (0-8236-3087-0) Intl Univs Pr.

***Lampland, Martha.** The Object of Labor: Commodification of Agrarian Life in Socialist Hungary. LC 95-11554. 1996. lib. bdg. 39.95 (0-226-46829-1); pap. text ed. 14.95 (0-226-46830-5) U Ch Pr.

Lamplight Press Staff. Dude Ranches, Vacation Guest Ranches: A How to Find or Locate Reference & Planning Guide. rev. ed. (Illus.). 70p. 1995. ring bd. 19.95 (0-917593-13-8, Lamp Light Pr) Prosperity & Profits.

— Home Economics: Home School. 120p. 1993. ring bd. 25.95 (0-917593-17-0, Lamp Light Pr) Prosperity & Profits.

Lamplugh, Diana, et al. Working Alone: Surviving & Thriving. (Institute of Management Ser.). 208p. (Orig.). 1993. pap. 45.00x (0-273-60196-2, Pub. by Pitman Pubng UK) St Mut.

Lamplugh, F. The Gnosis of the Light: A Translation of the Untitled Apocalypse Contained in the Codex Brucianus. 89p. 1994. reprint ed. pap. 14.95 (1-56459-431-9) Kessinger Pub.

Lamplugh, George R. Politics on the Periphery: Factions & Parties in Georgia, 1783-1806. LC 85-40662. (Illus.). 224p. 1986. 38.50 (0-87413-288-6) U Delaware Pr.

Lamplugh, Rick. Job Search That Works. Gerould, Phil, ed. LC 91-70077. (Fifty-Minute Ser.). (Illus.). 110p. (Orig.). 1991. pap. 9.95 (1-56052-105-8) Crisp Pubns.

Lampman. Shadows in the Wind. 1994. mass mkt. 4.50 (0-06-108168-X, Harp PBks) HarpC.

Lampman & Peters, eds. Ferroalloys & Other Additives to Liquid Iron & Steel- STP 739. 216p. 1981. 24.75 (0-8031-0744-7, 04-739000-01) ASTM.

Lampman, Ben H. At the End of the Car Line. 1965. reprint ed. 20.00 (0-8323-0145-0) Binford Mort.

— Coming of the Pond Fishes. 177p. 1946. 20.00 (0-8323-0341-0) Binford Mort.

— How Could I Be Forgetting. (Illus.). 158p. 1956. pap. 4.95 (0-8323-0379-8) Binford Mort.

***Lampman, Carolyn.** Meadowlark. 1994. pap. 4.99 (0-06-108170-1, Harp PBks) HarpC.

— Murphy's Rainbow. 1993. mass mkt. 4.50 (0-06-108160-4, Harp PBks) HarpC.

— Willow Creek. 1994. mass mkt. 4.50 (0-06-108169-8) HarpC.

Lampman, Evelyn S. Treasure Mountain. (Eager Beaver Bks.). (Illus.). 207p. (J). (gr. 4). 1990. reprint ed. pap. 6.95 (0-87595-231-3) Oregon Hist.

Lampman, Henry P. The Wire Womb: Life in a Girls' Penal Institution. LC 72-90555. 191p. 1973. 24.95 (0-911012-23-0) Nelson-Hall.

Lampman, Hugh, jt. auth. see Zoller, Bettye P.

Lampman, Linda. Portland Guidebook. 1989. pap. 9.95 (0-9691246-5-1) Jhnstn Assocs.

Lampman, Richard M., jt. auth. see Campaigne, Barbara.

Lampman, Robert J. Changes in the Share of Wealth Held by Top Wealth-Holders, 1922-1956. (Occasional Papers: No. 71). 38p. 1960. reprint ed. 20.00 (0-87014-385-9) Natl Bur Econ Res.

— The Share of Top Wealth-Holders in National Wealth, 1922-56. LC 84-19118. xxvii, 286p. 1984. reprint ed. text ed. 79.50 (0-313-24425-1, LAST, Greenwood Pr) Greenwood.

— The Share of Top Wealth-Holders in National Wealth, 1922-56. (General Ser.: No. 74). 316p. 1962. reprint ed. 82.20 (0-87014-073-6) Natl Bur Econ Res.

— Social Welfare Spending: Accounting for Changes from Nineteen Fifty to Nineteen Seventy-Eight. (Institute for Research on Poverty Policy Analysis Ser.). 1984. text ed. 51.00 (0-12-435260-X) Acad Pr.

Lampmann, L. E., et al. CT Densitometry in Osteoporosis: The Impact on Management of the Patient. (Series in Radiology). 124p. 1984. lib. bdg. 80.50 (0-89838-633-0) Kluwer Ac.

***Lampner, Carl.** Recipes for Parent Survival: Revealing the Amazing Secrets of SUPERCHEF, the Great. (Illus.). 324p. 1995. pap. 19.95 (0-942963-63-6) Distinctive Pub.

Lampo, Richard G., jt. ed. see Williams, Mark F.

Lampola, R. Gastronomic Terms. 5th ed. 80p. (ENG & FIN.). 1985. 35.00 (0-8288-0844-9, F42684) Fr & Eur.

Lamport, F. J. German Classical Drama: Theatre, Humanity & Nation, 1750-1870. (C). 1992. pap. 18.95 (0-521-42828-9) Cambridge U Pr.

Lamport, F. J., tr. see Schiller, Friedrich.

Lamport, Leslie. Concurrent Program Verification. (Computer Science Ser.). (Illus.). 400p. (C). 1996. text ed. write for info. (0-201-50421-9) Addison-Wesley.

— LATEX: A Document Preparation System User's Guide & Reference Manual. 2nd ed. (Illus.). 242p. (C). 1994. pap. text ed. 35.50 (0-201-52983-1) Addison-Wesley.

Lamport, Nancy K., et al. Activity Analysis Handbook. 2nd ed. LC 92-60370. (Illus.). 150p. (Orig.). (C). 1993. student ed 26.00 (1-55642-215-6) SLACK Inc.

Lamport, Stanley W. California Practice Handbook: Attorney Ethics. Profesional Responsibility & Ethics Committee, Los Angeles County Bar Association Staff et al, eds. LC 93-6043. Date not set. write for info. (0-8205-1091-2) Bender.

***Lampou.** English-Greek & Greek-English Dictionary of Financial & Commercial Terms. 404p. (ENG & GRE.). Date not set. pap. 150.00 (0-7859-9055-0) Fr & Eur.

Lampp, James W. The Unicorn Caper. 1980. pap. 1.95 (0-8439-0817-3) Dorchester Pub Co.

Lamprati, L. M. Industrial Relations in Australia. 4th ed. 1985. pap. text ed. 26.95 (0-471-33390-5) Wiley.

Lamprecht. Lamprecht, der Pfaffe, Alexander: Gedicht Des Zwolften Jahrhunderts, 2 vols. cxxx, 1164p. 1971. reprint ed. Bd. I: Urtext und Ubersetzung Nebst Geschichtlichen und sprachlichen Erlauterungen. write for info. (0-318-71265-2, Pub. by Georg Olms GW); reprint ed. Bd. II: Ubersetzung Des Pseudo-Kallisthenes (nebst) Umfassenden Auszugen Aus Den Lateinischen, Franz. write for info. (0-318-71266-0, Pub. by Georg Olms GW) Lubrecht & Cramer.

— Lamprecht, der Pfaffe, Alexander: Gedicht Des Zwolften Jahrhunderts, 2 vols., Set. cxxx, 1164p. 1971. reprint ed. write for info. (0-318-71264-4, Pub. by Georg Olms GW) Lubrecht & Cramer.

***Lamprecht, E.** Heating & Cooling on Board. (Illus.). 112p. Date not set. pap. 18.50 (0-7136-3528-2) Sheridan.

Lamprecht, Gunther. Introduction to FORTRAN 77. vi, 150p. 1986. pap. 28.00 (3-528-03360-6, Pub. by Vieweg & Sohn GW) Ballen Bkslr.

Lamprecht, I. & Zotin, A. I., eds. Thermodynamics & Pattern Formation in Biology. xiii, 518p. (C). 1988. lib. bdg. 306.15 (0-89925-407-1) De Gruyter.

— Thermodynamics & Regulation of Biological Processes. LC 84-23302. (Illus.). xiv, 573p. 1985. 207.70 (0-89925-007-6) De Gruyter.

Lamprecht, James. ISO 9000: Preparing for Registration. LC 92-4932. (Quality & Reliability Ser.). (Illus.). 264p. 1992. 49.75 (0-8247-8741-2, 6562U) Dekker.

Lamprecht, James L. Implementing the ISO 9000 Series. LC 92-47141. (Quality & Reliability Ser.: Vol. 40). 280p. 1993. 49.75 (0-8247-9134-7) Dekker.

— ISO 9000 & the Service Sector: A Critical Interpretation of the 1994 Revisions. LC 94-27380. 1994. 35.00 (0-87389-313-1) ASQC Qual Pr.

Lamprecht, Sterling P. Metaphysics of Naturalism. LC 67-18049. (Century Philosophy Ser.). 1967. 39.50 (0-89197-302-8) Irvington.

Lamprecht, Sterling P., ed. see Hobbes, Thomas.

Lampreia, J. P., et al. Iteration Theory, ECIT 91. 372p. 1992. text ed. 95.00 (981-02-1109-0) World Scientific Pub.

Lamprey, Louise. Children of Ancient Gaul. LC 60-16708. (Illus.). (J). (gr. 7-11). 1968. 20.00 (0-8196-0109-8) Biblo.

— Children of Ancient Rome. LC 61-12876. (Illus.). (J). (gr. 7-11). 1967. 18.00 (0-8196-0114-4) Biblo.

***Lampright, Richard L.** Gold Placer Deposits Near Anchorage Alaska. (Illus.). 272p. (Orig.). 1995. pap. 29.95 (0-9645366-0-9) Iron Fire Pubns.

***Lampropoulos, George A., et al, eds.** Applications of Photonic Technology: Proceedings of an International Conference on Applications of Photonic Technology, Sensing, Signal Processing, & Communications, Held in Toronto, Ontario, Canada, June 21-23, 1994. 575p. 1995. 129.50 (0-306-45011-9) Plenum.

Lampros, Angelique, jt. auth. see Ballare, Antonia.

Lampson, B. W., et al, eds. Distributed Systems: Architecture & Implementation, An Advanced Course. (Springer Study Edition Ser.). 510p. 1988. pap. 41.00 (0-387-12116-1) Spr-Verlag.

Lampson, Butler W. Research in Man-Machine Communications Using Time Shared Computer Systems. LC 77-131392. 73p. 1969. 19.00 (0-403-04513-4) Scholarly.

Lampson, Marc. From Profanity Hill, King County Bar Association's Story. LC 93-71147. 24.95 (0-935503-10-2) Document Bk.

Lampson-Reiff, Kim, jt. auth. see Reiff, Dan.

***Lampton.** Sharks, Rays, & Eels: Golden Junior Guide. (J). 1995. 5.95 (0-307-11437-6, Golden Pr) Western Pub.

Lampton, Christopher. Bathtubs, Slides, Roller Coaster Rails: Simple Machines That Are Really Inclined Planes. (Gateway Simple Machines Ser.). (Illus.). 32p. (J). (gr. 2-4). 1991. lib. bdg. 13.40 (1-878841-23-8); pap. 4.95 (1-878841-44-0) Millbrook Pr.

— Blizzard. (Disaster! Ser.). (Illus.). 64p. (J). (gr. 4-6). 1991. lib. bdg. 13.90 (1-56294-029-5); pap. 5.95 (1-56294-775-3) Millbrook Pr.

— Blizzard: A Disaster Book. (J). (gr. 4-7). 1992. pap. 5.92 (0-395-63641-8) HM.

— Chemical Accident. (Disaster! Ser.). (Illus.). 48p. (J). (gr. 4-6). 1994. 13.90 (1-56294-316-2) Millbrook Pr.

— Coral Reefs in Danger. LC 91-41441. (Illus.). 64p. (J). (gr. 4-8). 1992. lib. bdg. 15.90 (1-56294-091-0) Millbrook Pr.

— DNA Fingerprinting. LC 91-16533. (Impact Bks.). (Illus.). 112p. (YA). (gr. 9-12). 1991. lib. bdg. 14.42 (0-531-13003-7) Watts.

— Drought. LC 91-18053. (Disaster! Ser.). (Illus.). 64p. (J). (gr. 4-6). 1992. lib. bdg. 13.90 (1-56294-125-9) Millbrook Pr.

— Drought. LC 91-18053. 1992. pap. 5.95 (1-878841-91-2) Millbrook Pr.

— Drought: A Disaster Book. (J). (gr. 4-7). 1992. pap. 5.92 (0-395-62465-7) HM.

— Earthquake. (Disaster! Ser.). (Illus.). 64p. (J). (gr. 4-6). 1991. lib. bdg. 13.90 (1-56294-031-7); pap. 5.95 (1-56294-777-X) Millbrook Pr.

— Earthquake: A Disaster Book. (J). (gr. 4-7). 1992. pap. 5.92 (0-395-63642-6) HM.

— Epidemic. LC 91-21413. 1992. pap. 5.95 (1-878841-92-0) Millbrook Pr.

— Epidemic. LC 91-21413. (Disaster! Ser.). (Illus.). 64p. (J). (gr. 4-6). 1992. lib. bdg. 13.90 (1-56294-126-7) Millbrook Pr.

— Epidemic: A Disaster Book. (J). (gr. 4-7). 1992. pap. 5.92 (0-395-62466-5) HM.

— Famine. LC 939-9428. (Disaster! Ser.). (Illus.). 48p. (J). (gr. 4-6). 1994. lib. bdg. 13.90 (1-56294-317-0) Millbrook Pr.

— Flights of Fantasy: Programming 3-D Video Games in Borland C Plus Plus. (Illus.). 560p. (Orig.). 1993. disk, pap. 34.95 (1-878739-18-2) Waite Group Pr.

— Forest Fire. (Disaster! Ser.). (Illus.). 64p. (J). (gr. 4-6). 1991. lib. bdg. 13.90 (1-56294-033-3); pap. 5.95 (1-56294-779-6) Millbrook Pr.

— Forest Fire: A Disaster Book. (J). (gr. 4-7). 1992. pap. 5.92 (0-395-63646-9) HM.

— Gardens of Imagination. 500p. 1994. disk, pap. 34.95 (1-878739-59-X) Waite Group Pr.

— Hurricane. (Disaster! Ser.). (Illus.). 64p. (J). (gr. 4-6). 1991. lib. bdg. 13.90 (1-56294-030-9); pap. 5.95 (1-56294-780-X) Millbrook Pr.

— Hurricane: A Disaster Book. (J). (gr. 4-7). 1992. pap. 5.92 (0-395-63643-4) HM.

— Insect Attack. LC 91-26155. (Disaster! Ser.). (Illus.). 64p. (J). (gr. 4-6). 1992. lib. bdg. 13.90 (1-56294-127-5) Millbrook Pr.

— Insect Attack. LC 91-26155. (Disaster! Ser.). 1992. pap. 5.95 (1-878841-93-9) Millbrook Pr.

— Insect Attack: A Disaster Book. (J). (gr. 4-7). 1992. pap. 5.92 (0-395-62467-3) HM.

— Jupiter. LC 93-31094. (J). 1994. text ed. 13.95 (0-89686-756-0, Crstwood Hse) Silver Burdett Pr.

— Marbles, Roller Skates, Doorknobs: Simple Machines That Are Really Wheels. LC 92-34332. (Gateway Simple Machines Ser.). (Illus.). 32p. (J). (gr. 2-4). 1991. lib. bdg. 13.40 (1-878841-24-6); pap. 4.95 (1-878841-45-9) Millbrook Pr.

— Mars. LC 93-30152. (J). 1994. text ed. 13.95 (0-89686-757-9, Crstwood Hse) Silver Burdett Pr.

— Mercury. LC 93-31290. (J). 1994. text ed. 13.95 (0-89686-758-7, Crstwood Hse) Silver Burdett Pr.

— Neptune. LC 93-31093. (J). 1994. text ed. 13.95 (0-89686-759-5, Crstwood Hse) Silver Burdett Pr.

— Nintendo Action Games. (Illus.). 72p. (J). (gr. 4-6). 1991. lib. bdg. 15.40 (1-878841-26-2); pap. 3.95 (1-878841-53-X) Millbrook Pr.

— Nintendo Role-Playing Games. (Illus.). 72p. (J). (gr. 4-6). 1991. lib. bdg. 15.40 (1-878841-25-4); pap. 3.95 (1-878841-52-1) Millbrook Pr.

— Nuclear Accident. LC 91-43564. (Disaster! Ser.). (Illus.). 48p. (J). (gr. 4-6). 1992. lib. bdg. 13.90 (1-56294-073-2); pap. 5.95 (1-56294-782-6) Millbrook Pr.

— Oil Spill. LC 91-43565. (Disaster! Ser.). (Illus.). 48p. (J). (gr. 4-6). 1992. lib. bdg. 13.90 (1-56294-071-6); pap. 5.95 (1-56294-783-4) Millbrook Pr.

— Pluto. LC 93-30151. (J). 1994. text ed. 13.95 (0-89686-760-9, Crstwood Hse) Silver Burdett Pr.

— Predicting AIDS & Other Epidemics. LC 89-8972. (Predicting Ser.). (Illus.). 144p. (YA). (gr. 9-12). 1989. lib. bdg. 14.77 (0-531-10785-X) Watts.

— Predicting Nuclear & Other Technological Disasters. LC 89-9160. (Predicting Ser.). (Illus.). 144p. (YA). (gr. 9-12). 1989. lib. bdg. 14.77 (0-531-10784-1) Watts.

— Rocketry: From Goddard to Space Travel. Kline, Marjory, ed. LC 87-21558. (First Bks.). (Illus.). 96p. (J). (gr. 7-9). 1988. lib. bdg. 11.62 (0-531-10483-4) Watts.

— Sailboats, Flag Poles, Cranes: Using Pulleys as Simple Machines. (Gateway Simple Machines Ser.). (Illus.). 32p. (J). (gr. 2-4). 1991. lib. bdg. 13.40 (1-56294-026-0) Millbrook Pr.

— Saturn. LC 93-30150. (J). 1994. text ed. 13.95 (0-89686-761-7, Crstwood Hse) Silver Burdett Pr.

— Science of Chaos: Complexity in the Natural World. LC 91-40896. (Venture Bks.). (Illus.). 128p. (YA). (gr. 7-12). 1992. lib. bdg. 14.28 (0-531-12513-0) Watts.

— Seesaws, Nutcrackers, Brooms: Simple Machines That Are Really Levers. (Gateway Simple Machines Ser.). (Illus.). 32p. (J). (gr. 2-4). 1991. lib. bdg. 13.40 (1-878841-22-X); pap. 4.95 (1-878841-43-2) Millbrook Pr.

— Telecommunications: From Telegraphs to Modems. LC 90-48230. (Venture Bks.). (Illus.). 96p. (J). (gr. 7-9). 1991. lib. bdg. 13.72 (0-531-12527-0) Watts.

— Thomas Alva Edison. LC 90-49178. (American Cavalcade Ser.). (Illus.). 88p. (J). (gr. 6-10). 1991. lib. bdg. 9.95 (1-55905-079-9) Marshall Cavendish.

— Tidal Wave. LC 91-21518. 1992. pap. 5.95 (1-878841-90-4) Millbrook Pr.

— Tidal Wave. LC 91-21518. (Disaster! Book Ser.). (Illus.). 64p. (J). (gr. 4-6). 1992. lib. bdg. 13.90 (1-56294-124-0) Millbrook Pr.

— Tidal Wave: A Disaster Book. (J). (gr. 4-7). 1992. pap. 5.92 (0-395-62464-9) HM.

— Tornado. (Disaster! Book Ser.). (Illus.). 64p. (J). (gr. 4-6). 1991. lib. bdg. 13.90 (1-56294-032-5); pap. 5.95 (1-56294-785-0) Millbrook Pr.

— Tornado: A Disaster Book. (J). (gr. 4-7). 1992. pap. 5.92 (0-395-63644-2) HM.

— Uranus. LC 93-31291. (J). 1994. text ed. 13.95 (0-89686-762-5, Crstwood Hse) Silver Burdett Pr.

— Venus. LC 93-31289. (J). 1994. text ed. 13.95 (0-89686-763-3, Crstwood Hse) Silver Burdett Pr.

— Volcano. (Disaster! Ser.). (Illus.). 64p. (J). (gr. 4-6). 1991. lib. bdg. 13.90 (1-56294-028-7); pap. 5.95 (1-56294-786-9) Millbrook Pr.

— Volcano: A Disaster Book. (J). (gr. 4-7). 1992. pap. 5.92 (0-395-63645-0) HM.

Lampton, Christopher & Kline, Marjory. Endangered Species. LC 87-25161. (Impact Ser.). (Illus.). 128p. (YA). (gr. 7-12). 1988. lib. bdg. 14.42 (0-531-10510-5) Watts.

***Lampton, Christopher & Lamothe, Andre.** Flights of Fantasy: Programming Advanced 3D Video Games in C-C Plus Plus. 2nd ed. 600p. 1995. disk, pap. 36.95 (1-57169-022-0) Waite Group Pr.

Lampton, Christopher F. Particle Physics: The New View of the Universe. LC 90-48049. (Illus.). 64p. (J). (gr. 6 up). 1991. lib. bdg. 15.95 (0-89490-328-4) Enslow Pubs.

Lampton, David M. Paths to Power: Elite Mobility in Contemporary China. (Michigan Monographs in Chinese Studies: No. 55). (Illus.). 379p. (Orig.). 1986. text ed. 22.00 (0-89264-063-4); pap. text ed. 14.00 (0-89264-064-2) Ctr Chinese Studies.

Lampton, David M., ed. Policy Implementation in Post-Mao China. LC 85-23218. (Studies on China: Vol. 7). 439p. 1987. 60.00 (0-520-05706-6) U CA Pr.

Lampton, David M. & Madancy, Joyce A. A Relationship Restored: Trends in U. S. - China Educational Exchanges, 1978-1984. LC 86-61028. 286p. reprint ed. pap. 81.60 (0-7837-1797-0, 2041998) Bks Demand.

***Lampton, David M. & Wilhelm, Alfred D., Jr., eds.** A Resurrection of the Republican Ideal. LC 95-3474. 306p. (C). 1995. pap. text ed. 32.50 (0-8191-9899-4) U Pr of Amer.

— U. S. & China Relations at a Crossroads. 306p. (Orig.). (C). 1995. lib. bdg. 49.50 (0-8191-9888-9) U Pr of Amer.

Lampton, David M., jt. ed. see Lieberthal, Kenneth G.

Lampton, Patrice. A Touch of Tiffany. (Illus.). 40p. 1989. pap. 13.95 (0-935133-25-9) CKE Pubns.

Lampugnani, Vittorio M. Berlin Tomorrow: International Architectural Visions. (Orig.). 1992. pap. 19.95 (*0-312-06783-6*) St Martin.

Lampugnani, Vittorio M., ed. Berlin Tomorrow: International Architectural Visions. (Illus.). 96p. (Orig.). 1991. pap. 21.95 (*0-312-07142-6*, Academy Edits) St Martin.

— Hong Kong Architecture: The Aesthetics of Density. (Illus.). 160p. 1993. 50.00 (*3-7913-1324-X*, Pub. by Prestel) TeNeues.

— Museum Architecture in Frankfurt, 1980-1990. (Illus.). 200p. 1990. 75.00 (*3-7913-1096-8*, Pub. by Prestel) TeNeues.

— Renzo Piano, 1987-1994. Kerr, David, tr. LC 95-3228. (Illus.). 272p. 1995. 49.50 (*0-8176-5159-4*) Birkhauser.

Lampugnani, Vittorio M., et al, eds. DAM Architecture Annual 1993. (Illus.). 200p. 1993. pap. 40.00 (*3-7913-1295-2*, Pub. by Prestel) TeNeues.

Lamqvist, Kurt, intro. Guilhem Ademar, Poesies du Troubadour Guilhem Ademar. LC 80-2180. reprint ed. 37.50 (*0-404-19006-5*) AMS Pr.

Lamrimpa, Gen. Shamatha Meditation: Tibetan Buddhist Teachings on the Cultivation of Meditative Quiescence. Sprager, Hart, ed. Wallace, B. Alan, tr. LC 92-28543. 1992. pap. 10.95 (*1-55939-006-9*) Snow Lion Pubns.

Lamsa, G. M., jt. auth. see Emhardt, William C.

Lamsa, George M. Gospel Light: An Indispensable Guide to the Teachings of Jesus & the Customs of His Time. LC 86-45020. 416p. 1986. pap. 17.00 (*0-06-064928-3*) Harper SF.

— Idioms in the Bible Explained & a Key to the Original Gospels. LC 85-42782. 128p. 1985. pap. 12.00 (*0-06-064927-5*) Harper SF.

— New Testament. 1989. pap. 10.95 (*0-06-064933-X*, PL) HarpC.

— New Testament Light. LC 87-45709. 384p. (Orig.). 1988. pap. 16.00 (*0-06-064932-1*, RD 713) Harper SF.

— Old Testament Light. LC 84-48774. 1008p. 1985. pap. 24.00 (*0-06-064925-9*) Harper SF.

Lamsa, George M., tr. Holy Bible. 1985. 40.00 (*0-06-064926-7*); pap. 20.95 (*0-685-17264-3*, RD 423) Harper SF.

— Holy Bible: From the Ancient Eastern Text. 1248p. 1985. pap. 30.00 (*0-06-064923-2*) Harper SF.

Lamson, jt. auth. see Tibbetts.

Lamson, Amy. Guide for the Beginning Therapist: Relationship Between Diagnosis & Treatment. 2nd ed. LC 78-4061. 130p. 1986. 32.95 (*0-89885-293-5*); pap. 19.95 (*0-89885-295-1*) Human Sci Pr.

— Psychology of Juvenile Crime. 123p. 1982. 32.95 (*0-89885-060-6*); pap. 18.95 (*0-89885-290-0*) Human Sci Pr.

Lamson, Byron S. Greater Works than These. 196p. 1987. 9.00 (*0-89367-124-X*) Light & Life.

Lamson, Byron S., ed. see Watson, C. Hoyt.

Lamson, C. & Vanderzwaag, D., eds. Transit Management in the Northwest Passage: Problems & Prospects. (Studies in Polar Research). (Illus.). 200p. 1988. 99.95 (*0-521-32065-8*) Cambridge U Pr.

Lamson, Christy. The Movie Critic's Journal. (Orig.). 1993. pap. 8.95 (*0-9638778-0-1*) Lamson Ent.

Lamson, Cynthia, ed. The Sea Has Many Voices: Oceans Policy for a Complex World. 368p. 1994. 44.95 (*0-7735-1112-1*, Pub. by McGill CN) U of Toronto Pr.

Lamson, Cynthia, jt. ed. see VanderZwaag, David L.

Lamson, David R. Two Years Experience Among the Shakers. LC 71-134418. reprint ed. 40.00 (*0-404-08477-X*) AMS Pr.

Lamson, Martha. Duval's Svengali on Singing. 1.00 (*0-8315-0111-1*) Speller.

Lamson, Mary S. Life & Education of Laura Dewey Bridgman: The Deaf, Dumb & Blind Girl. LC 74-21419. (Classics in Child Development Ser.). (Illus.). 420p. 1975. lib. bdg. 36.95 (*0-405-06469-1*) Ayer.

Lamson, Richard, jt. auth. see Bromley, Hank.

Lamson, Roy & Smith, Hallett, eds. Golden Hind. rev. ed. (Illus.). (C). 1956. text ed. 46.95 (*0-393-09483-9*) Norton.

Lamson-Scribner, F., tr. see Hackel, Eduard.

Lamson, W. Descendants of William Lamson of Ipswich, Massachusetts, 1634-1917. (Illus.). 414p. 1993. reprint ed. lib. bdg. 75.00 (*0-8328-3043-7*); reprint ed. pap. 65.00 (*0-8328-3044-5*) Higginson Bk Co.

Lamster, Frederick. Souls Made Great Through Love & Adversity: The Film Work of Frank Borzage. LC 80-28441. 242p. 1981. 22.50 (*0-8108-1404-8*) Scarecrow.

Lamy. Jersey Folk Lore. (Jersey Heritage Editions Ser.). 1991. write for info. (*0-86120-000-4*, Pub. by Aris & Phillips UK) David Brown.

Lamy, Bernard. Perspective Made Easie. (Perspective Ser.). (Illus.). 256p. (C). 1989. reprint ed. 135.00 (*1-85297-029-4*, Pub. by Archival Facs UK) St Mut.

Lamy, Jean & Lamy, Josette, eds. Invertebrate Oxygen-Binding Proteins: Structure, Active Site, & Function. LC 81-5570. (Illus.). 864p. reprint ed. pap. 180.00 (*0-7837-0790-8*, 2041104) Bks Demand.

Lamy, Josette, jt. ed. see Lamy, Jean.

Lamy, Lucie. Egyptian Mysteries: New Light on Ancient Knowledge. LC 88-51329. (Art & Imagination Ser.). (Illus.). 160p. 1989. pap. 15.95 (*0-500-81024-9*) Thames Hudson.

Lamy, M., jt. ed. see Thijs, L. G.

Lamy, Marge. Cross Country Ski Inns of the Northeastern U. S. & Quebec. 168p. 1991. pap. 16.95 (*0-9630607-0-8*) R Reid Assocs.

Lamy, P., jt. ed. see Giese, R. H.

Lamy, Paul, ed. Language Planning & Identity Planning. (International Journal of the Sociology of Language Ser.: No. 20). 1979. pap. text ed. 60.00 (*90-279-7768-2*) Mouton.

Lamy, Peter P. Prescribing for the Elderly. LC 78-55289. (Illus.). 714p. 1980. 59.95 (*0-88416-208-7*, Yr Bk Med Pubs) Mosby Yr Bk.

— Prescribing for the Elderly. LC 78-55289. 714p. reprint ed. pap. 180.00 (*0-8357-7865-7*, 2036282) Bks Demand.

Lamy, Steven L., et al. Teaching Global Awareness with Simulations & Games. (Illus.). 245p. (Orig.). (YA). (gr. 6-12). 1992. pap. text ed. 29.95 (*0-943804-15-9*) U of Denver Teach.

Lan, David. Flight. (Methuen New Theatrescripts Ser.). 1988. pap. 7.95 (*0-413-14590-5*, A0107, Pub. by Methuen UK) Heinemann.

— Guns & Rain: Guerillas & Spirit Mediums in Zimbabwe. LC 85-40287. (Perspectives on Southern Africa Ser.: No. 38). 1985. pap. 18.00 (*0-520-05589-6*) U CA Pr.

— ION: Euripides. 80p. 1995. pap. 11.95 (*0-413-69330-9*) Heinemann.

— Sergeant Ola & His Followers. 1988. pap. 4.95 (*0-413-47590-5*, A0260, Pub. by Methuen UK) Heinemann.

LAN Magazine Editors. LAN One Hundred Network Integrators: Market Report. (Illus.). 150p. 1994. pap. 397.00 (*0-87930-266-6*) Miller Freeman.

LAN Magazine Staff, ed. LAN Tutorial with Glossary of Terms: A Complete Introduction to Local Area Networks. 2nd ed. (LAN Magazine Networking Library). 320p. 1992. pap. 24.95 (*0-87930-261-5*) Miller Freeman.

***Lan, Martin & Shimizu, Kaoru.** Do-It-Yourself Japanese Through Comics: An Introduction to Japanese in Twelve Lessons. 360p. 1995. pap. 25.00 (*4-7700-1936-X*) Kodansha.

Lan, T. T. & Zhilian, Y., eds. Space Structures for Sports Buildings: Proceedings of the International Colloquium, Beijing, China, 27-30 October 1987. 662p. 1988. 128.00 (*1-85166-183-2*) Elsevier.

Lan-Ying, jt. auth. see Light.

Lana, Robert E. Assumptions of Social Psychology: A Reexamination. 160p. (C). 1991. text ed. 34.50 (*0-8058-1022-6*); pap. 16.50 (*0-8058-1023-4*) L Erlbaum Assocs.

***Lanada.** Kuntaw: The Ancient Pilipino Martial Arts. (Illus.). 1995. pap. text ed. 14.95 (*1-881116-62-X*) Black Forrest Pr.

Lanagan, Margo. Tankermen. (YA). 1993. pap. 6.95 (*1-86373-253-5*, Pub. by Allen & Unwin Aust Pty AT) IPG Chicago.

— Wildgame. 160p. (Orig.). (J). (gr. 4-8). 1993. pap. 7.95 (*1-86373-069-9*, Pub. by Allen & Unwin Aust Pty AT) IPG Chicago.

***Lanahan, Eleanor.** Scottie. 1995. 30.00 (*0-06-017179-0*, HarpT) HarpC.

Lanahan, M. A. Within a Delirium. 23p. 1986. pap. 30.00 (*0-7223-2046-9*, Pub. by A H S Ltd UK) St Mut.

Lanasa, Philip J., III, jt. auth. see Criscoe, Betty L.

LaNauze, John A. Alfred Deakin: A Biography, 2 Vols. 1965. 45.00 (*0-522-83884-7*) Intl Spec Bk.

LaNauze, T. A., ed. see Deakin, Alfred.

LaNave, Gregory, tr. Days of the Lord, Vol. 3: The Liturgical Year: Easter Triduum, Easter Season. 370p. (Orig.). 1993. pap. text ed. 17.95 (*0-8146-1901-0*) Liturgical Pr.

***Lanave, Kevin.** Christian Justice: Sharing God's Goodness. Allaire, Barbara, ed. (Illus.). 51p. (Orig.). 1995. teacher ed, spiral bd. 24.95 (*0-88489-331-6*) St Marys.

Lanbers, Hans, et al, eds. Causes & Consequences of Variation in Growth Rate & Productivity of Higher Plants. (Illus.). x, 364p. 1989. 115.00 (*90-5103-033-9*, Pub. by SPB Acad Pub NE) Koeltz Sci Bks.

Lancashire, Anne, ed. Editing Renaissance Dramatic Texts: English, Italian, & Spanish: Papers Given at the Eleventh Annual Conference on Editorial Problems, University of Toronto, 31 October-1 November, 1975. LC 76-7324. (Conference on Editorial Problems Ser.: No. 11). 1987. 29.50 (*0-404-63661-6*) AMS Pr.

Lancashire, Anne, ed. see Leech, Clifford.

Lancashire, Anne B., ed. see Lyly, John.

Lancashire, Ian. Dramatic Texts & Records of Britain: A Chronological Topography to 1558. (Studies in Early English Drama). 633p. 1984. 85.00 (*0-8020-5592-3*) U of Toronto Pr.

Lancashire, Ian, ed. Two Tudor Interludes: The Interlude of Youth, Hick Scorner. LC 79-3123. (Revels Plays Ser.). 303p. reprint ed. pap. 86.40 (*0-7837-0337-6*, 2040656) Bks Demand.

Lancaster. American Heritage History of the American Revolution: The History of America's Struggle for Independence. 384p. 1984. 17.95 (*0-517-44736-3*) Random Hse Value.

— The Jews in Spain. Date not set. write for info. (*0-85668-543-7*, Pub. by Aris & Phillips UK); pap. write for info. (*0-85668-544-5*, Pub. by Aris & Phillips UK) David Brown.

— Marketing. 1995. pap. write for info. (*0-7506-2055-2*, Focal) Buttrwrth-Heinemann.

Lancaster, Ann, ed. see Rosenbaum, Claire M.

Lancaster, Barbara M. Choosing Your New Home: A Consumer Guide to Living Styles for Retirees, New Jersey Edition, 1993. Gonzalez, Liane, ed. 259p. (Orig.). 1993. pap. text ed. 19.95 (*1-57108-000-7*) Lancashire Intl.

— Choosing Your New Home: A Consumer Guide to Living Styles for Retirees, New Jersey Edition, 1993. Gonzalez, Liane, ed. Pease, Suzanne, tr. & illus. by. 268p. (Orig.). 1994. pap. 24.95 (*1-57108-001-5*) Lancashire Intl.

— Choosing Your New Home: A Consumer Guide to Living Styles for Retirees, New Jersey Edition, 1993. LC 94-75143. (Illus.). 660p. (Orig.). 1994. pap. 29.95 (*1-57108-002-3*) Lancashire Intl.

— Guide to Living Styles for Retirees: Professional Edition 1994. Gonzalez, Liane, ed. 190p. (Orig.). 1994. ring bd. 89.95 (*1-57108-005-8*) Lancashire Intl.

Lancaster, Beverly, jt. auth. see Woods, Elsa.

Lancaster, Bill, jt. ed. see Coles, Robert.

Lancaster, Bob. The Jungles of Arkansas: A Personal History of the Wonder State. LC 89-30818. 245p. 1989. 22.00 (*1-55728-108-4*); pap. 12.95 (*1-55728-109-2*) U of Ark Pr.

Lancaster, Brian. The Elements of Judaism. 1993. pap. 9.95 (*1-85230-402-2*) Element MA.

— Mind, Brain & Human Potential: The Quest for an Understanding of Self. 204p. 1991. pap. 17.95 (*1-85230-209-7*) Element MA.

Lancaster-Brown, Peter. Skywatch: Eyes-on Activities for Getting to Know the Stars, Planets & Galaxies. (Illus.). 136p. 1994. pap. 7.95 (*0-8069-8628-X*) Sterling.

Lancaster, Bruce. The American Revolution. LC 85-3982. (American Heritage Library). (Illus.). 334p. 1985. pap. 12.95 (*0-8281-0281-3*) HM.

— Blind Journey. 1976. reprint ed. lib. bdg. 22.95 (*0-88411-685-9*, Aeonian Pr) Amereon Ltd.

— Bride of a Thousand Cedars. (Illus.). 344p. 1975. reprint ed. lib. bdg. 23.95 (*0-89190-883-8*, Rivercity Pr) Amereon Ltd.

— Bright to the Wanderer. (Illus.). 451p. 1975. reprint ed. lib. bdg. 27.95 (*0-89190-885-4*, Rivercity Pr) Amereon Ltd.

— For Us the Living. (Illus.). 556p. 1975. reprint ed. lib. bdg. 30.95 (*0-89190-882-X*, Rivercity Pr) Amereon Ltd.

— Guns of Burgoyne. (Illus.). 425p. 1975. reprint ed. lib. bdg. 25.95 (*0-89190-881-1*, Rivercity Pr) Amereon Ltd.

— Phantom Fortress. 1976. reprint ed. lib. bdg. 22.95 (*0-88411-683-2*, Aeonian Pr) Amereon Ltd.

— The Scarlet Patch. 1976. reprint ed. lib. bdg. 28.95 (*0-88411-682-4*, Aeonian Pr) Amereon Ltd.

— The Secret Road. 20.95 (*0-89190-217-1*, Am Repr) Amereon Ltd.

— Trumpet to Arms. 1976. reprint ed. lib. bdg. 24.95 (*0-88411-681-6*, Aeonian Pr) Amereon Ltd.

— Venture in the East. 1976. reprint ed. lib. bdg. 22.95 (*0-88411-684-0*, Aeonian Pr) Amereon Ltd.

— Wide Sleeve of Kwannon. (Illus.). 307p. 1975. reprint ed. lib. bdg. 22.95 (*0-89190-884-6*, Rivercity Pr) Amereon Ltd.

Lancaster, Carol. African Economic Reform: The External Dimension. LC 91-21933. (Policy Analysis in International Economics Ser.: No. 33). (Illus.). 82p. 1991. pap. 10.00 (*0-88132-096-X*) Inst Intl Eco.

— An Irresistable Force Meets an Immovable Object: The United States At UNCTAD I. (Pew Case Studies in International Affairs). 50p. (C). 1992. pap. text ed. 2.50 (*1-56927-108-9*) Geo U Inst Dplmcy.

— U. S. Aid to Sub-Saharan Africa: Challenges, Constraints, & Choices. (Significant Issues Ser.: Vol. 10, No. 16). 1988. pap. 6.95 (*0-89206-128-6*) CSI Studies.

Lancaster, Carol & Williamson, John, eds. African Debt & Financing. LC 86-7421. (Institute for International Economics. Special Report Ser.: No. 5). 236p. (Orig.). reprint ed. pap. 67.30 (*0-7837-4219-3*, 2043908) Bks Demand.

Lancaster, Carol J. United States & Africa: Into the Twenty-First Century. LC 93-19138. (Policy Essay Ser.: No. 7). (Illus.). 72p. (C). 1993. pap. text ed. 9.95 (*1-56517-010-5*) Overseas Dev Council.

Lancaster, Caroline, et al. Elegant Lodging: A Guide to Country Mansions & Manor Houses in Virginia, Maryland & Pennsylvania. 2nd ed. (Illus.). 184p. (Orig.). 1991. pap. 9.95 (*0-915168-23-5*) Wash Bk Trad.

Lancaster, Clay. Antebellum Architecture of Kentucky. LC 91-2419. (Illus.). 352p. 1991. 50.00 (*0-8131-1759-3*) U Pr of Ky.

— From Ur to Uncle Remus: Five Thousand Years of Animal Fable Illustration. (Illus.). 120p. Date not set. write for info. (*0-917519-06-X*) U of KY Libs.

— Holiday Island. Michael, Gayl, ed. (Illus.). 1992. pap. write for info. (*0-9607340-9-0*) Nantucket Hist Assn.

— Nantucket in the Nineteenth Century. LC 77-75512. (Illus.). 1979. pap. 9.95 (*0-486-23747-8*) Dover.

— Old Brooklyn Heights. (Illus.). 1980. pap. 7.95 (*0-486-23872-5*) Dover.

— Vestiges of the Venerable City: A Chronicle of Lexington, Kentucky. LC 78-61797. (Illus.). 282p. 1978. 14.95 (*0-912839-01-5*) Lexington-Fayette.

***Lancaster, Clay, intro.** Food for the Gods: Conversations with Vegetarian Representatives of the World's Religions (with Recipes from Each Tradition) (Illus.). 238p. 1996. pap. 14.95 (*0-9626169-2-3*) Pythago Bks.

Lancaster, Clay, jt. auth. see Gillon, Edmund V., Jr.

Lancaster, Dallas M., jt. intro. see Lancaster, Mary H.

Lancaster, Derek. Picture America: States & Capitals. Anderson, Stevens, ed. (Illus.). 136p. (YA). (gr. 5). 1991. pap. 4.95 (*1-880184-02-8*) Compact Classics.

***Lancaster, Don.** Blatant Opportunist Vol. I: Selected Reprints from Midnight Engineering. (Illus.). 144p. (Orig.). 1994. pap. 24.50 (*1-882193-21-0*) Synergetics Pr.

— The Case Against Patents: Selected Reprints from Midnight Engineering & Nuts & volts Magazines. 88p. (Orig.). 1994. pap. 12.50 (*1-882193-70-9*) Synergetics Pr.

— Don Lancaster's Active Filter Cookbook. (Illus.). 240p. (C). 1995. reprint ed. pap. 28.50 (*1-882193-31-8*) Synergetics Pr.

— Don Lancaster's CMOS Cookbook. (Illus.). 512p. (C). 1995. reprint ed. pap. 28.50 (*1-882193-33-4*) Synergetics Pr.

— Don Lancaster's TTL Cookbook. (Illus.). 335p. (C). 1995. reprint ed. pap. 28.50 (*1-882193-35-0*) Synergetics Pr.

— Hardware Hacker Vol. II. (Illus.). 152p. (Orig.). 1990. pap. 24.50 (*1-882193-02-4*) Synergetics Pr.

— Hardware Hacker Vol. III. (Illus.). 182p. (Orig.). 1994. pap. 24.50 (*1-882193-03-2*) Synergetics Pr.

— Hardware Hacker Vol. IV. (Illus.). 186p. (Orig.). 1994. pap. 24.50 (*1-882193-04-0*) Synergetics Pr.

— Incredible Secret Money Machine II. 2nd ed. (Illus.). 192p. 1992. pap. 18.50 (*1-882193-65-2*) Synergetics Pr.

— Resource Bin Vol. I: Selected Reprints from Nuts & Volts. 154p. (Orig.). 1994. pap. 24.50 (*1-882193-11-3*) Synergetics Pr.

Lancaster, Donald E. Active-Filter Cookbook. LC 74-33839. (Illus.). 1975. pap. 24.95 (*0-672-21168-8*) Sams.

— CMOS Cookbook. 2nd ed. 528p. 1988. pap. 24.95 (*0-672-22459-3*) Sams.

— TTL Cookbook. LC 73-90295. (Illus.). 336p. (Orig.). 1974. pap. 24.95 (*0-672-21035-5*) Sams.

Lancaster, E. M. Guide to Negro Marketing Information. 1991. lib. bdg. 77.95 (*0-8490-4511-8*) Gordon Pr.

Lancaster, F., jt. auth. see South Africa Council Automation Staff.

Lancaster, F. T. Administration of Public Solid Waste. 178p. 1992. spiral bd. 35.00 (*0-918334-79-9*) WRP.

Lancaster, F. W. If You Want to Evaluate Your Library... 193p. 1988. 34.50 (*0-87845-078-5*) U of Ill Lib Info Sci.

— If You Want to Evaluate Your Library. 2nd ed. (Illus.). (C). 1993. text ed. 39.50 (*0-87845-091-2*) U of Ill Lib Info Sci.

— Indexing & Abstracting in Theory & Practice. 1991. 39.50 (*0-87845-083-1*) U of Ill Lib Info Sci.

— Toward Paperless Information Systems. (Library & Information Science Ser.). 1978. text ed. 53.00 (*0-12-436050-5*) Acad Pr.

Lancaster, F. W., ed. Ethics & the Librarian: Proceedings of the 31st Allerton Institute. 1991. 20.00 (*0-87845-085-8*) U of Ill Lib Info Sci.

— Libraries & the Future: Essays on the Library in the Twenty-First Century. LC 92-42380. (Original Book Ser.). (Illus.). 189p. (C). 1993. lib. bdg. 29.95 (*1-56024-382-1*) Haworth Pr.

— What Is User Friendly? (Clinic on Library Applications of Data Processing, Proceedings: 1977). (C). 1988. text ed. 10.00 (*0-87845-076-9*) U of Ill Lib Info Sci.

Lancaster, F. W. & Fayen, E. G. Information Retrieval On-Line. LC 73-9697. (Information Sciences Ser.). 613p. reprint ed. pap. 174.80 (*0-8357-9911-5*, 2015840) Bks Demand.

Lancaster, F. W. & Warner, Amy. Information Retrieval Today. LC 93-77931. 350p. 1993. text ed. 54.95 (*0-87815-064-1*) Info Resources.

Lancaster, F. W., ed. see Clinic on Library Application of Data Processing Staff.

Lancaster, F. Wilfrid. Libraries & Librarians in an Age of Electronics. LC 82-81403. (Illus.). ix, 229p. 1982. text ed. 27.50 (*0-87815-040-4*) Info Resources.

— The Measurement & Evaluation of Library Services. LC 77-72081. xii, 395p. 1977. 39.50 (*0-87815-017-X*) Info Resources.

— Vocabulary Control for Information Retrieval. LC 78-186528. (Illus.). xiv, 233p. (C). 1972. text ed. 27.50 (*0-87815-006-4*) Info Resources.

— Vocabulary Control for Information Retrieval. 2nd ed. LC 84-82260. (Illus.). xvii, 270p. 1992. reprint ed. text ed. 27.50 (*0-87815-053-6*) Info Resources.

Lancaster, F. Wilfrid, jt. auth. see Baker, Sharon L.

Lancaster, F. Wilfrid, jt. auth. see Martyn, John.

Lancaster, Francine. Favorite Animal Songs, Set. (J). (gr. k up). 1985. audio, boxed 16.95 (*0-930647-01-7*) Lancaster Prodns.

— Favorite Hoilday Songs, Set. 1986. Boxed set incl. cassette & songbook. audio, boxed 16.95 (*0-930647-02-5*) Lancaster Prodns.

— Mother Goose & Other Nursery Songs: From the Collection of the Museum of Fine Arts, Boston. (J). (ps up). 1987. audio 16.95 (*0-930647-03-3*) Lancaster Prodns.

— Nursery Songs & Lullabies. (J). (gr. k up). 1984. 16.95 (*0-930647-00-9*); audio (*0-318-58469-7*) Lancaster Prodns.

Lancaster, Geoffrey & Jobber, David. Sales Technique & Management. 2nd ed. 273p. (Orig.). 1990. pap. 33.50 (*0-273-03190-2*, Pub. by Pitman Pub Ltd UK) Trans-Atl Phila.

— Selling & Sales Management. 3rd ed. 336p. (Orig.). 1994. pap. 48.50 (*0-273-60295-0*, Pub. by Pitman Pub Ltd UK) Trans-Atl Phila.

Lancaster, Geoffrey & Massingham, Lester. Essentials of Marketing: Text & Cases. 2nd ed. LC 93-19905. 1993. write for info. (*0-07-707728-8*) McGraw.

— Marketing Management. LC 92-25428. 1993. 16.95 (*0-07-707420-3*) McGraw.

Lancaster, Gordon. Introduction to Fields & Circuits. (Textbks. in Electrical & Electronic Engineering: No. 1). (Illus.). 408p. (C). 1992. pap. 39.95 (*0-19-853931-2*) OUP.

Lancaster, H. Carrington, ed. Creole Voices. (FRE.). 1990. 15.00 (*0-87498-009-7*) Assoc Pubs DC.

Lancaster, H. L. Lancaster Family: Thomas & Phebe Lancaster of Bucks County, Penn., & Their Descendants, 1711-1902. (Illus.). 302p. reprint ed. lib. bdg. 53.00 (*0-8328-0747-8*); reprint ed. pap. 45.00 (*0-8328-0748-6*) Higginson Bk Co.

Lancaster, H. O. Bibliography of Statistical Bibliographies. 1968. 18.00 (*0-934454-12-4*) Lubrecht & Cramer.

— Expectations of Life. (Illus.). 592p. 1990. 79.00 (*0-387-97105-X*) Spr-Verlag.

— Quantitative Methods in Biological & Medical Sciences: A Historical Essay. LC 94-8063. 1994. 69.00 (*0-387-94279-3*) Spr-Verlag.

Lancaster, Helen. Aging. 1980. pap. 6.50 (*0-8309-0290-2*) Herald Hse.

An Asterisk (*) at the beginning of an entry indicates that the title is appearing in BIP for the first time.

Lancaster, Henry C. Adventures of a Literary Historian: A Collection of His Writings Presented to H. C. Lancaster by His Former Students & Other Friends in Anticipation of His Sixtieth Birthday November 10, 1942. LC 68-14907. (Essay Index Reprint Ser.). 1977. 23.95 (*0-8369-0605-5*) Ayer.

— French Tragi-Comedy. LC 66-29465. 216p. 1966. reprint ed. 50.00 (*0-87752-059-3*) Gordian.

— History of French Dramatic Literature in the Seventeenth Century, 9 vols., Set. Incl. Pt. 1, Vol. 1. Pre-Classical Period, 1610-1634. LC 66-20028. 1966. 50.00x (*0-685-22670-0*); Pt. 1, Vol. 2. Pre-Classical Period, 1610-1634. LC 66-20028. 1966. 50.00 (*0-685-22671-9*); Pt. 2, Vol. 1. Period of Corneille, 1635-1651. LC 66-20028. 1966. 50.00 (*0-685-22672-7*); Pt. 2, Vol. 2. Period of Corneille, 1635-1651. LC 66-20028. 1966. 50.00 (*0-685-22673-5*); Pt. 3, Vol. 1. Period of Moliere, 1652-1672. LC 66-20028. 1966. 50.00 (*0-685-22674-3*); Pt. 3, Vol. 2. Period of Moliere, 1652-1672. LC 66-20028. 1966. 50.00 (*0-685-22675-1*); Pt. 4, Vol. 1. Period of Racine, 1673-1700. LC 66-20028. 1966. 50.00 (*0-685-22676-X*); Pt. 4, Vol. 2. Period of Racine, 1673-1700. LC 66-20028. 1966. 50.00 (*0-685-22677-8*); Pt. 5. Recapitulation, 1610-1700. LC 66-20028. 1966. 60.00 (*0-685-22678-6*); LC 66-20028. 3698p. 1966. reprint ed. 450.00 (*0-87752-060-7*) Gordian.

— Sunset: A History of Parisian Drama in the Last Years of Louis XIV, 1701-1715. LC 76-29737. 1977. reprint ed. text ed. 65.00 (*0-8371-9278-1*, LASH, Greenwood Pr) Greenwood.

Lancaster, J. F. Metallurgy of Welding. LC 92-38469. 1993. write for info. (*0-412-47810-2*) Chapman & Hall.

— Metallurgy of Welding. 4th ed. 352p. 1987. text ed. 105.00 (*0-04-669010-7*); pap. text ed. 44.95 (*0-04-669011-5*) Routledge Chapman & Hall.

Lancaster, Jack R., Jr., ed. Bioinorganic Chemistry of Nickel. LC 88-140028. 337p. 1988. lib. bdg. 115.00 (*0-89573-338-2*) VCH Pubs.

***Lancaster, James W.** Dumplings: A Collection of Poems. (Orig.). Date not set. write for info. (*0-614-03057-9*) Sewalls Pt.

Lancaster, Jane B., jt. auth. see Gelles, Richard J.

Lancaster, Jane B., et al, eds. Parenting Across the Life Span: Biosocial Dimensions. (Foundations of Human Behavior Ser.). (Illus.). 486p. (C). 1987. lib. bdg. 56.95 (*0-202-30332-2*) Aldine de Gruyter.

Lancaster, Jane F. Removal Aftershock: The Seminoles' Struggles to Survive in the West, 1836-1866. LC 94-129. (Illus.). 248p. (C). 1994. lib. bdg. 32.00 (*0-87049-845-2*); pap. text ed. 16.00 (*0-87049-846-0*) U of Tenn Pr.

Lancaster, Jeanette. Adult Psychiatric Nursing. 2nd ed. 1988. pap. 42.75 (*0-8385-0071-4*, A0071-9) Appleton & Lange.

— Adult Psychiatric Nursing. 3rd ed. (Current Clinical Nursing Ser.). 1988. pap. 41.00 (*0-444-01294-X*) Elsevier.

Lancaster, John. Art with Found Materials. LC 91-2875. (Fresh Start Ser.). (Illus.). 48p. (J). (gr. 5-8). 1991. lib. bdg. 12.95 (*0-531-14204-3*) Watts.

— Calligraphy Techniques. (Illus.). 144p. 1992. pap. 22.95 (*0-7134-4370-7*, Pub. by Batsford UK) Trafalgar.

— Decorated Lettering. LC 90-12036. (Fresh Start Ser.). (Illus.). 48p. (J). (gr. 5-8). 1990. lib. bdg. 12.95 (*0-531-14074-1*) Watts.

— Fabric Art. LC 90-12281. (Fresh Start Ser.). (Illus.). 48p. (J). (gr. 5-8). 1991. lib. bdg. 12.95 (*0-531-14102-0*) Watts.

— Handbook of Structural Welding. LC 92-29915. 430p. 1993. text ed. 65.50 (*0-07-031684-8*) McGraw.

Lancaster, John, jt. ed. see Maslen, Keith.

Lancaster, Joseph. Improvements in Education: As It Respects the Industrious Classes of the Community. 3rd ed. LC 68-56241. 1974. reprint ed. 35.00 (*0-678-00697-0*) Kelley.

Lancaster, Kathy. Keys to Adopting a Child. LC 94-5222. (Parenting Keys Ser.). 208p. (Orig.). 1994. pap. 5.95 (*0-8120-1925-3*) Barron.

Lancaster, Kelvin. Consumer Demand: A New Approach. LC 76-164502. (Columbia Studies in Economics: No. 5). 177p. 1971. text ed. 39.50 (*0-231-03357-5*) Col U Pr.

— Mathematical Economics. xiii, 411p. 1987. reprint ed. pap. text ed. 10.95 (*0-486-65391-9*) Dover.

— Variety, Equity, & Efficiency: Product Variety in an Industrial Society. LC 78-24616. 432p. 1979. text ed. 55.50 (*0-231-04616-2*) Col U Pr.

Lancaster, Kelvin J. Modern Consumer Theory. 288p. 1990. text ed. 59.95 (*1-85278-384-2*, Pub. by E Elgar Pub UK) Ashgate Pub Co.

Lancaster, Kent & Katz, Helen. Strategic Media Planning. 320p. 1989. disk 39.95 (*0-8442-3475-3*, NTC Busn Bks) NTC Pub Grp.

— Strategic Media Planning. 3rd ed. Knudsen, Anne, ed. Date not set. 79.95 (*0-8442-3537-7*, NTC Busn Bks) NTC Pub Grp.

Lancaster, L. & Yu, C. S. Assimilation of Buddhism in Korea: Religious Maturity & Innovation in the Silla Dynasty. LC 87-71274. 264p. (C). 1991. text ed. 45.00 (*0-89581-878-7*, Asian Human Pr) Jain Pub Co.

— Assimilation of Buddhism in Korea: Religious Maturity & Innovation in the Silla Dynasty. LC 87-71274. (Studies in Korean Religions & Culture: Vol. 4). 264p. (C). 1991. pap. text ed. 20.00 (*0-89581-889-2*, Asian Human Pr) Jain Pub Co.

— Introduction of Buddhism to Korea: New Cultural Patterns. LC 87-71273. 250p. (Orig.). (C). 1990. pap. text ed. 20.00 (*0-89581-888-4*, Asian Human Pr) Jain Pub Co.

Lancaster, Lane W. Government in Rural America. 2nd ed. LC 74-2686. (Illus.). 375p. 1974. reprint ed. text ed. 69.50 (*0-8371-7425-2*, LAGR, Greenwood Pr) Greenwood.

Lancaster, Lewis R., comp. The Korean Buddhist Canon: A Descriptive Catalogue. LC 75-40662. (Center for Korean Studies, UC Berkeley: No. 4). 1980. 80.00 (*0-520-03159-8*) U CA Pr.

Lancaster, Marshall. Raleigh: A Quirky, Unorthodox History of North Carolina's Capital. Jackson, Dot, ed. LC 92-72660. 266p. 1992. 19.95 (*1-878086-15-4*) Down Home NC.

Lancaster, Mary H. & Lancaster, Dallas M., intros. The Civil War Diary of Anne S. Frobel. LC 92-21439. 320p. 1992. pap. 14.95 (*0-939009-69-2*) EPM Pubns.

Lancaster, Michael. The New European Landscape. LC 94-15507. (Illus.). 144p. 1995. 64.95 (*0-7506-1546-X*, Butterwrth Archit) Buttrwrth-Heinemann.

Lancaster, Michael, jt. ed. see Goode, Patrick.

Lancaster, N. The Namib Sand Sea: Dune Forms, Processes & Sediments. 170p. (C). 1989. text ed. 85.00 (*90-6191-697-6*, Pub. by A A Balkema NE) Ashgate Pub Co.

Lancaster, N., jt. auth. see Deacon, Janette.

Lancaster, N., jt. ed. see Pye, K.

***Lancaster, Nicholas.** The Geomorphology of Desert Dunes. LC 94-47289. (Physical Environment Ser.). 1995. write for info. (*0-415-06093-1*) Routledge.

Lancaster, O. C. Effective Teaching & Learning. LC 73-82145. 368p. 1974. text ed. 83.00 (*0-677-04680-4*) Gordon & Breach.

Lancaster, Osbert. The Littlehampton Saga: Comprising the Saracen's Head, Drayneflete Revealed, the Littlehampton Bequest. (Illus.). 253p. 1993. reprint ed. pap. 15.95 (*0-7126-5248-5*, Pub. by Pimlico) Trafalgar.

— Sailing to Byzantium: An Architectural Companion. (Dorset Reprints Ser.). (Illus.). 182p. 1990. 19.95 (*0-88029-435-3*) Marboro Bks.

Lancaster, Osbert, jt. auth. see Scott-James, Anne.

Lancaster, Otis E. Jet Propulsion Engines. LC 58-5030. (High Speed Aerodynamics & Jet Propulsion Ser.: No. 12). (Illus.). 841p. reprint ed. pap. 180.00 (*0-8357-4398-5*, 2057068) Bks Demand.

***Lancaster, P. & Rodman, L.** Algebraic Riccati Equations. (Oxford Mathematical Monographs). 491p. 1995. 104.00 (*0-19-853795-6*) OUP.

Lancaster, Paul. Gentleman of the Press: The Life & Times of an Early Reporter, Julian Ralph of the Sun. LC 91-17818. (Illus.). 322p. 1992. 34.95 (*0-8156-2552-9*) Syracuse U Pr.

Lancaster, Peter & Salkauskas, Kestutis. Curve & Surface Fitting. (Computational Mathematics & Applications Ser.). 1986. text ed. 125.00 (*0-12-436060-2*); pap. text ed. 45.00 (*0-12-436061-0*) Acad Pr.

Lancaster, Peter & Tismenetsky, Miron. The Theory of Matrices. 2nd ed. (Computer Science & Applied Mathematics Ser.). (C). 1985. text ed. 69.00 (*0-12-435560-9*) Acad Pr.

Lancaster, Phil A. Merchandising New & Used Cars. 15.95 (*0-87359-030-9*, AM 202) Northwood Univ.

Lancaster, Phil A. & Wangberg, David I. Dealership Business Management. LC 81-83717. 315p. 1981. write for info. (*0-87359-027-9*) Northwood Univ.

Lancaster, Robert S. The Better Parts of a Life. (Illus.). 249p. (Orig.). 1990. pap. 14.95 (*0-9627687-1-5*) Proctors Hall Pr.

— The Better Parts of a Life. (Orig.). 1990. pap. 14.95 (*0-918769-33-7*) Univ South Pr.

Lancaster, Roger N. Life Is Hard: Machismo, Danger & the Intimacy of Power in Nicaragua. 370p. 1993. 25.00 (*0-520-07924-8*) U CA Pr.

— Life Is Hard: Machismo, Danger, & the Intimacy of Power in Nicaragua. LC 91-45764. 1994. pap. 14.00 (*0-520-08929-4*) U CA Pr.

— Thanks to God & the Revolution: Popular Religion & Class Consciousness in the New Nicaragua. 280p. 1988. text ed. 50.00 (*0-231-06730-5*); pap. text ed. 15.00 (*0-231-06731-3*) Col U Pr.

Lancaster, Ronald, et al. Fireworks: Principles & Practice. 2nd ed. (Illus.). 1992. 75.00 (*0-8206-0339-2*) Chem Pub.

Lancaster, Roy. Mediterranean Plants & Gardens. 1990. 15.95 (*0-903001-64-0*, Pub. by Burall Floraprint UK) J Markham & Assocs.

— A Plantsman in Nepal. (Illus.). 240p. Date not set. 69.50 (*1-85149-179-1*) Antique Collect.

— Roy Lacaster Travels in China: A Plantsman's Paradise. (Illus.). 520p. 1989. 79.50 (*1-85149-175-9*) Antique Collect.

— Trees for Your Garden. (Illus.). 1993. 35.00 (*0-85628-232-4*, Pub. by Aidan Ellis Pub UK) Antique Collect.

— What Plant Where? LC 95-8172. 256p. 1995. 24.95 (*0-7894-0151-7*, 6-70482) Dorling Kindersley.

***Lancaster, Ryan.** Top Forty Things Considerate Golfers Do. Westheimer, Mary, ed. (Illus.). 44p. (Orig.). 1994. pap. 10.00 (*1-885001-04-5*) Via Press.

Lancaster, Samuel. Lancaster Family of Maryland & Kentucky: History of English Ancestry, Emigration to Colony of Maryland, Pioneers of Kentucky. (Illus.). 200p. 1993. reprint ed. lib. bdg. 42.50 (*0-8328-3359-2*); reprint ed. pap. 32.50 (*0-8328-3360-6*) Higginson Bk Co.

Lancaster, Sheila. Dark Sweet Wanton. large type ed. 495p. 1981. 12.00 (*0-7089-0637-0*) Ulverscroft.

— Mistress of Fortune. large type ed. 576p. 1984. 15.95 (*0-7089-1113-7*) Ulverscroft.

Lancaster-Smith, M. Gastroenterology. (Management of Common Diseases in Family Practice Ser.). 1985. 22.00 (*0-88416-529-9*, Yr Bk Med Pubs) Mosby Yr Bk.

Lancaster, Theo, ed. The Corner. 128p. (C). 1988. pap. 35.00 (*0-7212-0769-3*, Pub. by Regency Press) St Mut.

Lancaster, Thomas D. Policy Stability & Democratic Change: Energy in Spain's Transition. LC 87-43185. (Illus.). 256p. 1990. lib. bdg. 30.00 (*0-271-00634-X*) Pa St U Pr.

Lancaster, Thomas D. & Prevost, Gary, eds. Politics & Change in Spain. LC 84-18107. 240p. 1985. text ed. 55.00 (*0-275-90133-5*, C0133, Praeger Pubs) Greenwood.

Lancaster, Tony. The Econometric Analysis of Transition Data. (Econometric Society Monographs: No. 17). (Illus.). 325p. (C). 1990. 64.95 (*0-521-26596-7*) Cambridge U Pr.

— The Econometric Analysis of Transition Data. (Econometric Society Monographs: No. 17). (Illus.). 368p. (C). 1992. pap. 19.95 (*0-521-43789-X*) Cambridge U Pr.

***Lancaster, William.** The Department Store: A Social History. 240p. 1995. 59.95 (*0-7185-1374-6*, Pub. by Leicester Univ Pr); pap. 18.95 (*0-7185-1985-X*, Pub. by Leicester Univ Pr) St Martin.

Lancaster, William W. If You're Waiting for Me, You're Backing Up. 64p. 1994. pap. 7.00 (*0-8059-3584-3*) Dorrance.

Lancaster, Yvonne E. From the Heart--Sketches from Life. (Illus.). 96p. 1986. pap. 7.95 (*0-940573-00-8*) Genesis Pub MA.

Lance, Algie L. Introduction to Microwave Theory & Measurements. 1964. text ed. 43.95 (*0-07-036104-5*) McGraw.

Lance, Donald M., jt. ed. see Glowka, Wayne.

***Lance, E. Christopher.** Hilbert C*-Modules: A Toolkit for Operator Algebraists. (London Mathematical Society Lecture Note Ser.: No. 210). 140p. (C). 1995. pap. 29.95 (*0-521-47910-X*) Cambridge U Pr.

Lance, Fran & King, Pat. Tell Your Secret. 128p. 1986. reprint ed. pap. 6.95 (*0-89221-142-3*) New Leaf.

Lance, Fran, jt. ed. see King, Pat.

Lance, G. N. & Deland, E. C. The Steady, Axially Symmetric Flow of a Viscous Fluid in a Deep Rotating Cylinder Heated from Below. LC 58-9085. (California University Publications in Engineering: Vol. 5, No. 6). 20p. reprint ed. pap. 25.00 (*0-317-10229-X*, 2021188) Bks Demand.

Lance, H. Darrell. The Old Testament & the Archaeologist. Tucker, Gene M., ed. LC 80-2387. (Guides to Biblical Scholarship: Old Testament Ser.). 112p. (Orig.). 1981. pap. 8.00 (*0-8006-0467-9*, 1-467, Fortress Pr) Augsburg Fortress.

Lance, H. Darrell, jt. ed. see Dever, William G.

Lance, J. & Pfaffenrath, V., eds. Sumatripian - From Molecule to Man: An Official Session at the 8th Migraine Trust Symposium - Journal: European Neurology, Vol. 31, No. 5, 1991. (Illus.). 72p. 1991. pap. 29.00 (*3-8055-5437-0*) S Karger.

Lance, James W. Mechanisms & Management of Headache. 4th ed. 272p. 1982. text ed. 49.95 (*0-407-26458-2*) Buttrwrth-Heinemann.

— Mechanisms & Management of Headache. 5th ed. 264p. 1993. text ed. 65.00 (*0-7506-0575-8*) Buttrwrth-Heinemann.

— Migraine & Other Headaches: A Renowned Physician's Guide to Diagnosis & Effective Treatment. (Illus.). 240p. 1986. pap. 14.00 (*0-684-18654-3*, Scribners) S&S Trade.

Lance, Janice. First Literature Experiences. (Illus.). 48p. 1991. pap. 5.95 (*1-879287-01-3*) Bk Lures.

Lance, Kathryn. Going to See Grassy Ella. LC 92-16237. (J). 1993. 12.00 (*0-688-12163-2*) Lothrop.

Lance, Keith C., et al. The Impact of School Library Media Centers on Academic Achievement. (Illus.). 125p. 1993. pap. text ed. 25.00 (*0-931510-48-1*) Hi Willow.

Lance, Larry R. & Hinton, John. Elementary Mathematics for Computing. LC 85-1258. 543p. 1986. teacher ed write for info. (*0-201-05124-9*); text ed. write for info. (*0-201-05123-0*) Addison-Wesley.

Lance, Larry R. & Hinton, John R. Computer Mathematics. Dennison, T. E., ed. 1992. pap. 24.00 (*0-923231-16-1*) Mohican Pub.

***Lance, Leonard L., et al.** Drug Information Handbook for the Allied Health Professional, 1995-96. 2nd ed. (Clinical Reference Library). 819p. 1995. pap. 27.75 (*0-916589-26-9*) Lexi-Comp.

— 1995 Quick Look Drug Book. 729p. 1995. pap. 34.00 (*0-683-07046-0*) Williams & Wilkins.

Lance, Leslie. Nurse Verena at Weirwater. large type ed. 1991. 21.95 (*0-7089-2463-8*) Ulverscroft.

— The Return of the Cuckoo. large type ed. 1990. 21.95 (*0-7089-2124-8*) Ulverscroft.

— Return to King's Mere. large type ed. 1976. 12.00 (*0-85456-481-0*) Ulverscroft.

— Spun by the Moon. large type ed. 336p. 1988. 15.95 (*0-7089-1900-6*) Ulverscroft.

— The Young Curmudgeon. large type ed. 352p. 1987. 16.95 (*0-7089-1686-4*) Ulverscroft.

Lance, Steven. Written Out of Television: The Encyclopedia of Cast Changes & Character Replacements, 1945-Present. LC 94-15370. 1995. write for info. (*0-8108-2902-9*) Scarecrow.

Lance, William L. Life Insurance, Spend It & Keep It: How to Make a Tax-Free Exchange of Your Life Insurance & Earn Tax-Deferred Interest. (Illus.). 52p. 1980. pap. 8.00 (*0-686-27280-3*) Truth Pub AZ.

Lancee, Charles T., ed. Echocardiology. (Developments in Cardiovascular Medicine Ser.: No. 1). 1979. lib. bdg. 145.50 (*90-247-2209-8*) Kluwer Ac.

Lancel, Serge. Carthage: A History. Nevill, Antonia, tr. (Illus.). 420p. 1994. 34.95 (*1-55786-468-3*) Blackwell Pubs.

Lancelle, George, jt. auth. see Frazer, Graham.

Lancelot, Claude, jt. auth. see Arnauld, Antoine.

Lancelot-Harrington, Katherine. America: Past & Present, Vols. 1-3. 2nd rev. ed. LC 92-31762. 1992. Vol. 2, The Challenge of New Frontiers. pap. 18.95 (*0-8384-3440-1*); Vol. 3, The Continuing Quest. pap. 18.95 (*0-8384-3441-X*) Heinle & Heinle.

— America: Past & Present, Vols. 1-3. 2nd rev. ed. LC 92-31762. 1992. Vol. 1, The Exploration of a Continent. pap. 18.95 (*0-8384-3439-8*) Heinle & Heinle.

Lancellotta, A. Geotechnical Engineering. (Illus.). 400p. (C). 1994. text ed. 95.00 (*90-5410-178-4*, Pub. by A A Balkema NE); pap. 60.00 (*90-5410-179-2*, Pub. by A A Balkema NE) Ashgate Pub Co.

***Lancer, Bob.** The Longtime Tales of Uncle Mo. (Illus.). 64p. (Orig.). (J). 1995. pap. 11.95 (*0-9628666-4-4*) Tools of the Tree.

— The Soulmate Process. 128p. (Orig.). (C). 1992. pap. 9.98 (*0-87554-501-7*) Valley Sun.

Lancer, Jack & Jones, Andrew. Multiple Choice Questions in Otolaryngology & Head & Neck Surgery. 162p. 1988. pap. 34.95 (*0-407-00761-X*) Buttrwrth-Heinemann.

Lancet, ed. see Danziger, Charles.

Lancet, ed. see Ekiguchi, Kunio.

Lancet, ed. see Kodansah Ltd. Staff.

Lancet, ed. see Kodansha Ltd. Staff.

Lancet, ed. see Oka, Isaburo.

Lancet, ed. see Richie, Donald.

Lancet, Barry, ed. Small Spaces: Stylish Ideas for Making More of Less in the Home. LC 92-36529. (Illus.). 96p. 1993. 27.00 (*4-7700-1495-3*) Kodansha.

Lancet, Barry, ed. see Kobayashi, Tadashi.

Lancet, Barry, ed. see Levy, Ran.

Lancet, Barry, ed. see Slivka, Rose & Tsujimoto, Karen.

Lanchbery, Edward, jt. auth. see Duke, Neville.

***Lanchester, F. W.** Aircraft in Warfare: The Dawn of the Fourth Arm. LC 95-77628. (Illus.). 224p. (C). 1995. 24.95 (*1-57321-002-1*) Lanchester Pr.

Lanchner, Carolyn. Joan Miro. (Illus.). 480p. 1993. 75.00 (*0-8109-6123-7*) Abrams.

— Joan Miro. (Illus.). 480p. 1993. 75.00 (*0-87070-434-6*) Mus of Modern Art.

— Joan Miro. (Illus.). 480p. 1993. pap. 37.50 (*0-87070-430-3*) Mus of Modern Art.

Lanchner, Carolyn & Rubin, William. Henri Rousseau. (Illus.). 272p. 1985. pap. 19.95 (*0-87070-565-2*) Mus of Modern Art.

Lanciani, Rodolfo. Ancient Rome in the Light of Recent Discoveries. LC 67-13335. (Illus.). 1972. reprint ed. 31.95 (*0-405-08725-X*, Pub. by Blom Pubns UK) Ayer.

— Destruction of Ancient Rome. LC 67-23855. (Illus.). 1972. reprint ed. 20.95 (*0-405-08726-8*, Pub. by Blom Pubns UK) Ayer.

— New Tales of Old Rome. LC 67-29707. (Illus.). 1972. reprint ed. 22.95 (*0-405-08727-6*, Pub. by Blom Pubns UK) Ayer.

— Pagan & Christian Rome. LC 67-23856. (Illus.). 1972. reprint ed. 39.95 (*0-405-08728-4*, Pub. by Blom Pubns UK) Ayer.

— Ruins & Excavations of Ancient Rome. LC 67-29706. (Illus.). 1972. reprint ed. 52.95 (*0-405-08729-2*, Pub. by Blom Pubns UK) Ayer.

Lanciaux, D. Operating Systems: Theory & Practice. 398p. 1979. 77.00 (*0-444-85300-6*, North Holland) Elsevier.

Lancini, G. & Lorenzetti, R. Biotechnology of Antibiotics & Other Bioactive Microbial Metabolites. (Illus.). 195p. (C). 1994. 59.50 (*0-306-44603-0*, Plenum Pr) Plenum.

Lancini, G. & Parenti, F. Antibiotics: An Integrated View. (Microbiology Ser.). (Illus.). 250p. 1982. 84.00 (*0-387-90630-4*) Spr-Verlag.

***Lancini, Giancarlo, et al.** Antibiotics - A Multidisciplinary Approach. 275p. 1995. 59.50 (*0-306-44924-2*) Plenum.

Lancioni, Judith A., jt. auth. see Kloskey, Thomas A.

Lancis, Antonio. Grau: Estadista y Politico (Cincuenta Anos en la Historia de Cuba) LC 85-80250. (Coleccion Cuba y Sus Jueces Ser.). (Illus.). 160p. (Orig.). (SPA.). 1985. pap. 9.95 (*0-89729-374-6*) Ediciones.

Lanctot, Barbara. A Walk Through Graceland Cemetery: A Chicago Architecture Foundation Walking Tour. 3rd ed. (Illus.). 68p. 1988. pap. 6.95 (*0-9620562-0-0*) Chi Arch Fndtn.

— A Walk Through Graceland Cemetery: A Chicago Architecture Foundation Walking Tour. 4th ed. (Illus.). 68p. 1992. reprint ed. pap. text ed. write for info. (*0-318-69176-0*) Chi Arch Fndtn.

Lanctot, Gustave. A History of Canada: From the Treaty of Utrecht to the Treaty of Paris, 1713-1763, Vol. 3. Cameron, Margaret M., tr. LC 63-2859. (Illus.). 318p. 1965. 34.00 (*0-674-39602-2*) HUP.

Lanctot, Guylaine. How to Have Great Legs at Any Age. (Illus.). 192p. (Orig.). 1988. pap. 6.95 (*0-942257-04-9*) New Chapter Pr.

Lanctot, Neil. Fair Dealing & Clean Playing: The Hilldale Club & the Development of Black Professional Baseball, 1910-1932. 304p. 1994. lib. bdg. 25.95 (*0-89950-988-6*) McFarland & Co.

Lancy, David. Cross-Cultural Studies in Cognition & Mathematics. (Developmental Psychology Ser.). 220p. 1983. text ed. 59.00 (*0-12-435620-6*) Acad Pr.

Lancy, David F. Children's Emergent Literacy: From Research to Practice. LC 93-23475. 416p. 1994. text ed. 65.00 (*0-275-94589-8*, Praeger Pubs) Greenwood.

— Qualitative Research in Education: An Introduction to the Major Traditions. LC 92-20128. 352p. (C). 1993. text ed. 39.95 (*0-8013-0309-5*, 78014) Longman.

Lancz, Gerald J., jt. auth. see Specter, Steven.

Lancz, Gerald J., jt. ed. see Specter, Steven.

Lanczik, M., jt. ed. see Beckmann, H.

Lanczos, Cornelius. Applied Analysis. (Illus.). 559p. 1988. reprint ed. pap. text ed. 12.95 (*0-486-65656-X*) Dover.

— The Variational Principles of Mechanics. 2nd ed. (Mathematical Expositions Ser.: No. 4). 393p. reprint ed. pap. 112.10 (*0-7837-0497-6*, 2040821) Bks Demand.

— The Variational Principles of Mechanics. 418p. 1986. reprint ed. pap. text ed. 11.95 (*0-486-65067-7*) Dover.

***Land.** Land O Lakes Treasury of Country Heritage Meals & Menus. 1994. 24.95 (*0-86573-957-9*) Cy De Cosse.

— Materials for Display & Printing Technologies. write for info. (0-444-00909-4) Elsevier.
Land, jt. auth. see De Launey.
Land, Ailsa H. & Powell, S. FORTRAN Codes for Mathematical Programming: Linear, Quadratic & Discrete. LC 73-2789. (Illus.). 265p. reprint ed. pap. 75. 60 (0-685-23421-5, 2032657) Bks Demand.
Land, Alexandra, tr. see Beaussant, Philippe.
Land, Aubrey C. Colonial Maryland: A History. LC 80-21732. (History of the American Colonies Ser.). 367p. 1981. lib. bdg. 35.00 (0-527-18713-5) Kraus Intl.
Land, Aubrey C. & Crowl, Phillip. The Old Line State, a History of Maryland. Radoff, Morris L. et al, eds. (C). 1971. 3.00 (0-942370-07-4); text ed. 5.00 (0-942370-08-2) MD St Archives.
Land, Aubrey G., et al, eds. Law, Society, & Politics in Early Maryland. LC 76-47374. (Illus.). 400p. 1977. 52.00x (0-8018-1872-9) Johns Hopkins.
***Land, Barbara.** Las Vegas with Kids: Where to Go, What to Do in America's Hottest Family Destination. LC 95-2703. 1995. pap. write for info. (0-7615-0014-6) Prima Pub.
Land, Barbara & Land, Myrick. A Short History of Reno. 160p. 1992. pap. 12.95 (0-938530-54-2) Lexikos.
Land, Barbara, jt. auth. see Land, Myrick.
***Land, Barbara N. & Land, Myrick E.** A Short History of Reno. LC 94-32428. (Illus.). 136p. 1995. 14.95 (0-87417-262-4) U of Nev Pr.
Land, D. G. & Nursten, H. E., eds. Progress in Flavour Research. (Illus.). 371p. 1979. 97.25 (0-85334-818-9, Pub. by Elsevier Applied Sci UK) Elsevier.
Land, Douglas S., jt. auth. see Siemer, Jeanne E.
Land, E. Waverly. Moves from Arm to Arm. Bayes, Ronald H., ed. 76p. (Orig.). 1993. pap. 8.95 (1-879934-07-8) St Andrews NC.
Land, Gary. The Essential of U. S. History since 1941. rev. ed. (Illus.). 112p. 1994. pap. text ed. 5.95 (0-87891-717-9) Res & Educ.
Land, Gary, ed. Adventism in America: A History. LC 86-29061. 311p. (Orig.). 1986. pap. 9.99 (0-8028-0237-0) Andrews Univ Pr.
Land, Gary, et al, eds. The World of Ellen G. White. 288p. 1987. 16.95 (0-8280-0395-5) Review & Herald.
Land, George. Grow or Die: The Principle of Transformation. 1991. 35.95 (0-9626605-1-5) Creative Ed.
Land, Helen, ed. AIDS: A Complete Guide to Psychosocial Intervention. LC 92-18565. 318p. 1992. pap. 25.95 (0-87304-258-1) Families Intl.
— AIDS: A Complete Guide to Psychosocial Intervention. 318p. 1992. pap. text ed. 25.95 (0-8261-4250-8) Springer Pub.
Land, Hilary & Ward, Sue. Social Security Review & Women. 1986. 20.00 (0-946088-26-8, Pub. by NCCL UK) St Mut.
***Land, Joe.** Unleashing the Power Within: How to Change Who You Are to Get What You Want. 208p. 1995. 22. 00 (0-345-40039-9) Ballantine.
Land, John. Lucifer Directive. 1990. mass mkt. 4.95 (0-8217-3354-0) Zebra.
Land, Jon. The Council of Ten. 352p. (Orig.). 1987. mass mkt. 5.99 (0-449-13117-3, GM) Fawcett.
— Day of the Delphi. 432p. (Orig.). 1993. mass mkt. 5.99 (0-8125-3434-4) Tor Bks.
— The Doomsday Spiral. 1983. pap. 2.95 (0-8217-1175-X) Zebra.
— The Eighth Trumpet. 1989. mass mkt. 5.95 (0-449-13398-2, GM) Fawcett.
— Fires of Midnight. 1995. 22.95 (0-312-85971-6) Forge NYC.
— Kingdom of the Seven. 432p. (Orig.). 1994. pap. 5.99 (0-8125-3435-2) Forge NYC.
— Labyrinth. 384p. (Orig.). 1985. mass mkt. 5.95 (0-449-12954-3, GM) Fawcett.
— The Ninth Dominion. (Orig.). 1991. mass mkt. 5.99 (0-449-14775-4, GM) Fawcett.
— Valhalla Testament. 352p. 1990. mass mkt. 5.95 (0-449-14634-0, GM) Fawcett.
— The Vengeance of the Tau. (Orig.). 1993. mass mkt. 5.99 (0-449-14776-2, GM) Fawcett.
— Vortex. 1984. pap. 3.50 (0-8217-1469-4) Zebra.
Land, Kenneth C. & Rogers, Andrei, eds. Multidimensional Mathematical Demography. LC 82-6821. (Studies in Population). 602p. 1982. text ed. 75.00 (0-12-435640-0) Acad Pr.
Land, Kenneth C. & Schneider, Stephen H., eds. Forecasting in the Social & Natural Sciences. (C). 1987. lib. bdg. 117.00 (90-277-2616-7) Kluwer Ac.
Land, Kenneth C. & Spilerman, Seymour, eds. Social Indicator Models. LC 74-79447. 412p. 1975. 45.00 (0-87154-505-5) Russell Sage.
Land, L. K., ed. see Cordy-Collins, Alana & Nicholson, H. B.
Land, L. S., jt. auth. see Bathurst, R. C.
Land, Leslie. The Yankee New England Cookbook. Orig. Title: Reading Between the Recipes. 288p. 1992. reprint ed. 7.99 (0-517-05793-X) Random Hse Value.
***Land, Lisa, ed.** Knowledge Based System Usage: Benefits Experienced & Lessons Learned. LC 94-31236. 1994. write for info. (0-07-709048-9) McGraw.
Land, Lois R. & Vaughan, Mary A. Music in Today's Classroom: Creating, Listening, Performing. 2nd ed. 246p. (C). 1978. pap. text ed. 26.75 (0-15-564895-0) HB Coll Pubs.
***Land, Lyton S.** Dolomitization. (Continuing Education Course Note Ser.: No. 24). (Illus.). 20p. 1983. pap. 9.00 (0-89181-173-7) AAPG.
Land, Mary. Louisiana Cookery. 1972. pap. 4.95 (0-87511-070-3) Claitors.
Land, Michael, jt. auth. see Turner, Sandra.
Land, Myrick. The Fine Art of Literary Mayhem: A Lively Account of Famous Writers & Their Feuds. 2nd rev. ed. LC 82-49332. 272p. 1983. pap. 9.95 (0-938530-11-9, 11-9) Lexikos.
Land, Myrick & Land, Barbara. Reno: A Sierra Mosaic. (Urban Tapestry Ser.). (Illus.). 300p. 1994. 39.50 (1-881096-07-6) Towery Pub.
Land, Myrick, jt. auth. see Land, Barbara.
Land, Myrick E. Writing for Magazines. 2nd ed. 220p. (C). 1992. text ed. write for info. (0-13-971193-7) P-H.
Land, Myrick E., jt. auth. see Land, Barbara N.
Land-Nellist, Cassandra. Colors in Hawaiian. (Hawaiian Treasures Ser.). (Illus.). 10p. (ENG & HAU.). (J). (ps). 1993. 3.95 (0-916630-72-2) Pr Pacifica.
— Counting Hawaiian Petroglyphs. (Hawaiian Treasures Ser.). (Illus.). 10p. (J). (ps). 1993. 3.95 (0-916630-74-9) Pr Pacifica.
— Gecko's Hawaiian Celebrations. (Hawaiian Treasures Ser.). (Illus.). 10p. (J). (ps). 1993. 3.95 (0-916630-71-4) Pr Pacifica.
— Hawai'i Pono'i. (Hawaiian Treasures Ser.). (Illus.). 10p. (J). (ps). 1993. 3.95 (0-916630-73-0) Pr Pacifica.
Land, Nick. The Thirst of Annihilation: Georges Bataille & Virulent Nihilism. LC 91-36365. 272p. 1992. 69.95 (0-415-05607-1, A7393) Routledge.
Land, Norman E. The Potted Tree: Essays in Venetian Art. LC 93-40775. 1994. 57.95 (1-879751-85-2) Camden Hse.
— The Viewer As Poet: The Renaissance Response to Art. LC 93-4469. 1994. 40.00 (0-271-01004-5) Pa St U Pr.
Land, Norman E., jt. auth. see Collins, Marcia.
***Land O Lakes Staff.** Baking. LC 95-13991. (Land O Lakes Collector Ser.). 128p. 1995. 14.95 (0-86573-967-6) Cy De Cosse.
— Chicken. LC 94-16805. (Land O Lakes Collector Ser.). 128p. 1994. pap. 9.95 (0-86573-953-6) Cy De Cosse.
— Grilling. LC 95-7312. (Land O Lakes Collector Ser.). 128p. 1995. 14.95 (0-86573-965-X) Cy De Cosse.
— Holiday. (Land O Lakes Collector Ser.). 128p. 1995. 14. 95 (0-86573-966-8) Cy De Cosse.
Land o'Lakes Staff. Chicken. LC 94-16805. (Land o'Lakes Collector Ser.). 128p. 1994. 14.95 (0-86573-952-8) Cy De Cosse.
— Cookies. LC 94-29050. (Land o'Lakes Collector Ser.). (Illus.). 128p. 1994. 14.95 (0-86573-954-4); pap. 9.95 (0-86573-955-2) Cy De Cosse.
Land, Pat, jt. auth. see Krzowski, Sue.
***Land, Peter A.** Managing to Get the Job Done: How to Make Sure Your Employees Are Ready, Willing, & Able to Succeed. 1994. text ed. 24.95 (0-471-11279-8) Wiley.
Land, Philip. Shaping Welfare Consensus: U. S. Catholic Bishops Contribution. 150p. (Orig.). (C). 1988. pap. text ed. 7.95 (0-934255-07-5) Center Concern.
Land, Philip, ed. Theology Meets Progress: Human Implications of Development. 1971. pap. 6.50 (0-8294-0326-4, Pub. by Gregorian Univ Pr IT) Loyola Univ Pr.
***Land, Philip S.** Catholic Social Teaching: As I Have Lived, Loved & Loathed It. LC 94-13207. 320p. 1994. pap. 15. 95 (0-8294-0808-8) Loyola Univ Pr.
Land Planning Committee, U.S. National Resources Board. Report of the Land Planning Committee, Pt. 2. LC 75-26322. (World Food Supply Ser.). (Illus.). 1976. reprint ed. 20.95 (0-405-07798-X) Ayer.
Land Planning, Public Works & Rural Land Use Committee, jt. auth. see United States National Resources Committee.
***Land, Ray & Percival, Fred, eds.** Aspects of Educational & Training Technology Vol. 28: Computer-Assisted & Open Access Education. 320p. 1995. text ed. 69.95 (0-89397-445-5) Nichols Pub.
Land, Richard D. & Moore, Louis A., eds. Citizen Christians. LC 93-6692. 1994. 12.99 (0-8054-1237-9) Broadman.
Land, Richard D., jt. ed. see Moore, Louis A.
Land, Richard D., jt. auth. see Moore, Louis.
Land, Robert D. Management of Organizations & Human Resources: Student Guide. (FLMI Insurance Education Program Ser.). 212p. 1989. student ed, pap. text ed. 10. 00 (0-939921-15-4) LOMA.
Land, Robert D., jt. auth. see Huggins, Kenneth.
Land, Stephen K. Challenge & Conventionality in the Fiction of E. M. Forster. LC 87-45795. (Studies in Modern Literature: No. 19). 1989. 34.50 (0-404-61589-9) AMS Pr.
— Paradox & Polarity in the Fiction of Joseph Conrad. LC 83-40160. 224p. 1985. text ed. 32.50 (0-312-59597-2) St Martin.
— The Philosophy of Language in Britain: Major Theories from Hobbes to Thomas Reid. LC 83-45287. (Studies in the Seventeenth Century: No. 2). 1986. 39.50 (0-404-61722-0) AMS Pr.
— Thomas Hardy: The Architecture of Fiction. LC 91-58170. (Studies in the Nineteenth Century: No. 12). 1992. 42.50 (0-404-61492-2) AMS Pr.
Land Trust Alliance & National Trust for Historic Preservation Staff. Appraising Easements: Guidelines for Valuation of Historic Preservation & Land Conservation Easements. rev. ed. 70p. 1990. pap. text ed. 17.00 (0-943915-05-8) Land Trust DC.
Land Trust Alliance Staff. Starting a Land Trust: A Guide to Forming a Land Conservation Organization. 200p. (Orig.). 1990. pap. 16.00 (0-943915-06-6) Land Trust DC.
Land Trust Exchange Staff, jt. auth. see Montana Land Reliance Staff.
Land, W., ed. Optimal Use of Sandimmun in Organ Transplantation. (Illus.). 40p. 1987. pap. 36.50 (0-387-17865-1) Spr-Verlag.
Land, W. & Dossetor, J. B., eds. Organ Replacement Therapy: Ethics, Justice & Commerce: First Joint Meeting of ESOT & EDTA - ERA Munich, December 1990. (Illus.). xxiii, 578p. 1991. 169.00 (0-387-53687-6) Spr-Verlag.
Land, W. A., jt. auth. see Delauney, W. E.
***Landa.** English-Serbocroatian Dictionary of Economics & Business. 358p. (ENG & SER.). 1986. 59.95 (0-7859-7511-X) Fr & Eur.
Landa, Bonnie L., jt. auth. see Halstead, Bruce W.
Landa, E. R. Buried Treasure to Buried Waste: The Rise & Fall of the Radium Industry. LC 87-22233. (Colorado School of Mines Quarterly Ser.: Vol. 82, No. 2). (Illus.). 336p. 1987. pap. text ed. 20.00 (0-918062-75-6) Colo Sch Mines.
Landa, Gertrude, see Aunt Naomi, pseud..
Landa, Henry C. Automotive Aerodymanics Handbook. 7th ed. (Illus.). 1990. 19.95 (0-931974-15-1) FICOA.
— Silencer Theory. (Illus.). 1979. pap. 11.00 (0-931974-09-7) FICOA.
— Solar Energy Handbook. 5th ed. (Illus.). (C). 1977. pap. 12.00 (0-931974-00-3) FICOA.
Landa, Janet T. Trust, Ethnicity, & Identity: Beyond the New Institutional Economics of Ethnic Trading Networks, Contract Law, & Gift-Changing. LC 94-1727. 250p. 1994. text ed. 49.50 (0-472-10361-X) U of Mich Pr.
Landa, Judah. How to Study Physics. (Illus.). 384p. 1994. 19.50 (0-9639716-0-3) Jay-El Pubns.
— Torah & Science. 1990. 39.50 (0-88125-320-0) Ktav.
Landa, L., ed. see Swift, Jonathan.
Landa, L. A., ed. see Swift, Jonathan.
Landa, L. N. Algorithmization in Learning & Instruction. Kopstein, Felix F., ed. Bennett, Virginia, tr. LC 73-11044. 752p. 1974. reprint ed. 44.95 (0-87778-063-3) Educ Tech Pubns.
— Instructional Regulation & Control: Cybernetics, Algorithmization & Heuristics in Education. Kopstein, Felix F., ed. Desch, Samuel, tr. LC 75-44383. 552p. 1976. 44.95 (0-87778-087-0) Educ Tech Pubns.
Landa, Louis, ed. see Defoe, Daniel.
Landa, Louis A. Essays in Eighteenth-Century English Literature. LC 80-7541. (Collected Essays Ser.). 270p. 1980. pap. 14.95 (0-691-01375-6) Princeton U Pr.
— Essays in Eighteenth-Century English Literature. LC 80-7541. (Princeton Series of Collected Essays). reprint ed. pap. 72.20 (0-7837-9365-0, 2060108) Bks Demand.
— Essays in Eighteenth-Century English Literature. LC 80-7541. (Princeton Series of Collected Essays: No. 3). 253p. reprint ed. pap. 72.20 (0-7837-1933-7, 2042148) Bks Demand.
Landa, M. English-Serbocroatian Economics & Business Studies Dict. 504p. (C). 1990. 150.00 (0-89771-929-8, Pub. by Collets) St Mut.
***Landa, Norbert.** Birthdays Are Best. (J). 1994. 3.99 (0-517-10209-9) Random Hse Value.
— How Does It Feel? LC 92-39238. (Illus.). 26p. (J). (ps-1). 1993. 14.95 (1-56566-032-3) Thomasson-Grant.
— Keeper of the Honeypot. (J). 1994. 3.99 (0-517-10213-7) Random Hse Value.
— No Pudding in the Treehouse. (J). 1994. 3.99 (0-517-10214-5) Random Hse Value.
— Rabbit & Chicken Count Eggs. LC 90-33436. (Illus.). (J). (ps). 1992. bds. 4.95 (0-688-09971-8, Tambourine Bks) Morrow.
— Rabbit & Chicken Find a Box. LC 90-33379. (Illus.). (J). (ps). 1992. bds. 4.95 (0-688-09968-8, Tambourine Bks) Morrow.
— Rabbit & Chicken Play Hide & Seek. LC 90-33484. (Illus.). (J). (ps). 1992. bds. 4.95 (0-688-09970-X, Tambourine Bks) Morrow.
— Rabbit & Chicken Play with Colors. LC 90-33485. (Illus.). (J). (ps). 1992. bds. 4.95 (0-688-09969-6, Tambourine Bks) Morrow.
— Where Is Santa Claus? (J). 1994. 3.99 (0-517-10215-3) Random Hse Value.
Landa, P. S., jt. auth. see Neimark, Yu. I.
Landa, Robin. Religious Art: A Workbook for Artists & Designers. 272p. 1985. 29.95 (0-13-773037-3); pap. 16. 95 (0-13-773029-2) P-H.
Landa, Ruth K. Creating Courseware: A Beginner's Guide. 380p. (C). 1984. pap. text ed. 26.50 (0-06-043837-1) HarpCollege.
Landahl, M. T. & Mollo-Christensen, E. Turbulence & Random Processes in Fluid Mechanics. 2nd ed. (Illus.). 170p. (C). 1992. 64.95 (0-521-41992-1); pap. 21.95 (0-521-42213-2) Cambridge U Pr.
Landahl, Marten, jt. auth. see Ashley, Holt.
Landais-Stamp, Paul & Rogers, Paul. Rocking the Boat: New Zealand, the United States & the Nuclear-Free Zone Controversy in the 1980s. 201p. 1989. 45.00 (0-85496-279-4) Berg Pubs.
Landau. Adaptive Control: The Model Reference Approach. (Control & Systems Theory Ser.: Vol. 8). 432p. 1979. 150.00 (0-8247-6548-6) Dekker.
— Courage to Be Gifted. pap. 10.00 (0-89824-527-3) Trillium Pr.
Landau, jt. auth. see Taussig.
Landau, et al. Family Mediation Handbook. 304p. 1987. pap. 45.00 (0-409-81161-0) Butterworth Legal Pubs.
— Quantum Electrodynamics. 2nd ed. (Course of Theoretical Physics Ser.: Vol. 4). (Illus.). 550p. 1982. pap. text ed. 54.00 (0-08-026504-9, Pergamon Pr) Elsevier.
Landau, Alan M. & Landau, Frieda W. Airborne Rangers. LC 92-7488. (Power Ser.). (Illus.). 128p. 1992. pap. 14. 95 (0-87938-606-1) Motorbooks Intl.
Landau, Asher F. Selected Judgments of the Supreme Court of Israel: Special Volume. 191p. 1971. 34.95 (0-87855-175-1) Transaction Pubs.
Landau, Asher F., ed. The Jerusalem Post Law Reports. 270p. (Orig.). 1993. pap. 17.50 (965-223-827-9) Gefen Bks.
Landau, Barbara & Gleitman, Lila R. Language & Experience: Evidence from the Blind Child. (Cognitive Science Ser.: Vol.). 272p. 1988. reprint ed. pap. 16.95 (0-674-51026-7) HUP.
Landau, Barbara, jt. ed. see Gleitman, Lila.
Landau, Carl & Landau, Katie. California Festivals. (Illus.). (Orig.). 1988. pap. 9.95 (0-929881-25-7) Landau Comns.
***Landau, Carol, et al.** The Complete Book of Menopause. 368p. (Orig.). 1995. pap. 15.00 (0-399-51906-8, Perigree Bks) Berkley Pub.
— The Complete Book of Menopause: Every Woman's Guide to Good Health. LC 93-38651. 352p. 1994. 22.95 (0-399-13946-X, Grosset-Putnam) Putnam Pub Group.
***Landau, D. P. & Mon, K. K., eds.** Computer Simulation Studies in Condensed-Matter Physics VII Vol. 78: Proceedings of the Seventh Workshop Athens, GA. (Physics Ser.). 244p. 1995. 107.00 (3-540-58481-1) Spr-Verlag.
Landau, D. P., jt. auth. see Family, F.
Landau, D. P., et al, eds. Computer Simulation Studies in Condensed Matter Physics. (Proceedings in Physics Ser.: Vol. 33). (Illus.). 240p. 1988. 70.00 (0-387-50449-4) Spr-Verlag.
— Computer Simulation Studies in Condensed Matter Physics III: Proceedings of the Third Workshop, Athens, GA, USA February 12-16, 1990. (Proceedings in Physics Ser.: Vol. 53). 224p. 1991. 64.00 (0-387-53607-8) Spr-Verlag.
— Computer Simulation Studies in Condensed-Matter Physics IV: Proceedings of the Fourth Workshop, Athens, GA, February 18-22, 1991. LC 92-39677. 1993. 109.00 (0-387-56309-1) Spr-Verlag.
— Computer Simulation Studies in Condensed-Matter Physics V: Proceedings of the Fifth Workshop, Athens, GA, USA, February 17-21, 1992. LC 93-18578. (Proceedings in Physics Ser.: Vol. 75). 1993. 69.00 (0-387-56474-8) Spr-Verlag.
— Computer Simulation Studies in Condensed-matter Physics VI. (Proceedings in Physics Ser.: Vol. 76). 225p. 1993. 98.00 (0-387-57143-4) Spr-Verlag.
Landau, David. Piety & Power: The World of Jewish Fundamentalism. LC 92-37540. 1992. 27.50 (0-8090-7605-5) Hill & Wang.
Landau, David & Parshall, Peter W. The Renaissance Print: 1471-1550. (Illus.). 448p. 1994. 65.00 (0-300-05739-3) Yale U Pr.
Landau, David, ed. see Peres, Shimon.
Landau, Diana, ed. Isak Dinesen's Africa: Images of the Wild Continent from the Writer's Life & Words. LC 85-8366. (Illus.). 160p. 1985. 35.00 (0-87156-821-7) Sierra.
Landau, Diana, jt. auth. see Halsey, David.
Landau, Edmund. Algebraische Zahlen. 2nd ed. 9.95 (0-8284-0062-8) Chelsea Pub.
— Differential & Integral Calculus. LC 65-4331. 372p. (C). 1981. text ed. 27.50 (0-8284-0078-4) Chelsea Pub.
— Elementare Zahlentheorie. LC 49-235. 14.95 (0-8284-0026-1) Chelsea Pub.
— Elementary Number Theory. 2nd ed. LC 57-8494. 1988. 19.95 (0-8284-0125-X) Chelsea Pub.
— Foundations of Analysis. 2nd ed. LC 60-15580. (gr. 9 up). 1960. text ed. 13.95 (0-8284-0079-2) Chelsea Pub.
— Grundlagen der Analysis: With Complete German-English Vocabulary. 4th ed. LC 60-7485. pap. 4.95 (0-8284-0141-1) Chelsea Pub.
— Handbuch der Lehre von der Verteilung der Primzahlen, 2 vols. in 1. 3rd ed. LC 73-21539. 1974. text ed. 55.00 (0-8284-0096-2) Chelsea Pub.
Landau, Elaine. Allergies. (Understanding Illness Ser.). (Illus.). 64p. (J). (gr. 5-8). 1994. lib. bdg. 15.98 (0-8050-2989-3) TFC Bks NY.
— Armed America. (Illus.). 128p. (YA). (gr. 6 up). 1990. lib. bdg. 12.98 (0-671-72386-3, Julian Messner); pap. 5.95 (0-671-72387-1, Julian Messner) Silver Burdett Pr.
— The Beauty Trap. LC 93-29641. (Open Door Bks.). (Illus.). 128p. (J). 1994. text ed. 13.95 (0-02-751389-0, New Dscvry Bks) Silver Burdett Pr.
— Big Brother Is Watching. (J). 1992. 14.95 (0-8027-8160-8); lib. bdg. 15.85 (0-8027-8161-6) Walker & Co.
— Bill Clinton. LC 92-39174. (Illus.). (J). (gr. 5-8). 1993. lib. bdg. 13.23 (0-531-11143-1); pap. 5.95 (0-531-15670-2) Watts.
— Blindness. (Understanding Illness Ser.). (Illus.). 64p. (J). (gr. 5-8). 1994. lib. bdg. 15.98 (0-8050-2992-3) TFC Bks NY.
— Breast Cancer. LC 95-3831. (Venture Bks.). (J). 1995. 14. 77 (0-531-11242-X) Watts.
— Cancer. (Understanding Illness Ser.). (Illus.). 64p. (J). (gr. 5-8). 1994. lib. bdg. 15.98 (0-8050-2990-7) TFC Bks NY.
— Chemical & Biological Warfare. 128p. (J). (gr. 5-9). 1991. 14.95 (0-525-67364-4, Lodestar Bks) Dutton Child Bks.
— The Cherokees. Rosoff, Iris, ed. LC 91-30262. (First Bks.). (Illus.). 64p. (J). (gr. 3-5). 1992. lib. bdg. 13.93 (0-531-20066-3) Watts.
— The Cherokees. (First Bks.). (Illus.). 64p. (J). (gr. 5-8). 1992. pap. 5.95 (0-531-15635-4) Watts.
— Child Abuse: An American Epidemic. LC 84-996. (Illus.). 128p. (J). (gr. 7 up). 1984. lib. bdg. 11.29 (0-671-47988-1, Julian Messner) Silver Burdett Pr.
— Child Abuse: An American Epidemic. rev. ed. 128p. (J). (gr. 7 up). 1990. lib. bdg. 12.98 (0-671-68874-X, Julian Messner); lib. bdg. 5.95 (0-671-68875-8, Julian Messner) Silver Burdett Pr.
— The Chilula. LC 93-31423. (First Book Ser.). (Illus.). 64p. (J). (gr. 5-8). 1994. lib. bdg. 13.93 (0-531-20132-5) Watts.

An Asterisk (*) at the beginning of an entry indicates that the title is appearing in BIP for the first time.

— The Chilula. LC 93-31423. (First Bks.). (Illus.). 64p. (J). (gr. 4-6). 1994. pap. 5.95 (*0-531-15685-0*) Watts.
— Colin Powell: Four Star General. LC 91-12860. (First Bks.). (Illus.). 64p. (J). (gr. 5-8). 1991. lib. bdg. 13.93 (*0-531-20143-0*) Watts.
— Cowboys. LC 90-31025. (First Bks.). (Illus.). 64p. (J). (gr. 5-8). 1990. lib. bdg. 13.93 (*0-531-10866-X*) Watts.
— Deafness. (Understanding Illness Ser.). (Illus.). 64p. (J). (gr. 5-8). 1994. lib. bdg. 15.98 (*0-8050-2993-1*) TFC Bks NY.
— Diabetes. (Understanding Illness Ser.). (Illus.). 64p. (J). (gr. 5-8). 1994. lib. bdg. 15.98 (*0-8050-2988-5*) TFC Bks NY.
— Different Drummer: Homosexuality in America. (YA). (gr. 7 up). 1986. lib. bdg. write for info. (*0-671-54997-9*, Julian Messner) Silver Burdett Pr.
— Dyslexia. (First Bks.). (Illus.). 64p. (J). (gr. 5-8). 1991. lib. bdg. 13.93 (*0-531-20030-2*) Watts.
— Endangered Plants. Rosoff, Iris, ed. LC 91-34926. (First Bks.). (Illus.). 64p. (J). (gr. 3-5). 1992. lib. bdg. 13.93 (*0-531-20134-1*) Watts.
— Endangered Plants. (First Bks.). (Illus.). 64p. (J). (gr. 5-8). 1992. pap. 5.95 (*0-531-15645-1*) Watts.
— Environmental Groups: The Earth Savers. LC 92-23679. (Better Earth Ser.). (Illus.). 112p. (J). (gr. 6 up). 1993. lib. bdg. 17.95 (*0-89490-396-9*) Enslow Pubs.
— Epilepsy. (Understanding Illness Ser.). (Illus.). 64p. (J). (gr. 5-8). 1994. lib. bdg. 15.98 (*0-8050-2991-5*) TFC Bks NY.
— Ghosts. (Mysteries of Science Ser.). (Illus.). 48p. (J). (gr. 3-6). 1995. 14.40 (*1-56294-544-0*) Millbrook Pr.
— The Homeless. (Teen Interest Collection). 128p. (J). (gr. 6-9). 1987. lib. bdg. 13.98 (*0-671-53492-0*, Julian Messner); lib. bdg. 9.74 (*0-685-47105-5*, Julian Messner) Silver Burdett Pr.
— Hooked: Talking about Addictions. LC 94-41680. (Illus.). 72p. (J). (gr. 4-6). 1995. lib. bdg. 15.90 (*1-56294-469-X*) Millbrook Pr.
— The Hopi. LC 93-31964. (First Book Ser.). (J). 1994. lib. bdg. 13.93 (*0-531-20098-1*) Watts.
— The Hopi. LC 93-31964. (First Bks.). (Illus.). 64p. (J). (gr. 4-6). 1994. pap. 5.95 (*0-531-15684-2*) Watts.
— Interesting Invertebrates: A Look at Some Animals Without Backbones. (First Bks.). (Illus.). 64p. (J). (gr. 5-8). 1991. lib. bdg. 13.93 (*0-531-20036-1*) Watts.
— Interracial Dating. LC 92-44814. (YA). (gr. 7 up). 1993. lib. bdg. 13.98 (*0-671-75258-8*, Julian Messner); lib. bdg. 7.95 (*0-671-75261-8*, Julian Messner) Silver Burdett Pr.
— Jupiter. LC 90-13099. (First Bks.). (Illus.). 64p. (J). (gr. 3-5). 1991. lib. bdg. 13.93 (*0-531-20015-9*) Watts.
— The Loch Ness Monster. LC 92-35145. (Mysteries of Science Ser.). (Illus.). 48p. (J). (gr. 3-6). 1993. lib. bdg. 14.40 (*1-56294-347-2*) Millbrook Pr.
— Lyme Disease. LC 89-70514. (First Bks.). (Illus.). (J). 1990. lib. bdg. 13.93 (*0-531-10931-3*) Watts.
— Mars. LC 90-13097. (First Bks.). (Illus.). 64p. (J). (gr. 3-5). 1991. lib. bdg. 13.93 (*0-531-20012-4*) Watts.
— Near-Death Experiences. (Mysteries of Science Ser.). (Illus.). 48p. (J). (gr. 3-6). 1995. 14.40 (*1-56294-543-2*) Millbrook Pr.
— Neptune. LC 90-13098. (First Bks.). (Illus.). 64p. (J). (gr. 3-5). 1991. lib. bdg. 13.93 (*0-531-20014-0*) Watts.
— On the Streets: The Lives of Adolescent Prostitutes. LC 86-21825. 112p. (YA). (gr. 9 up). 1987. lib. bdg. 12.98 (*0-671-62135-1*, Julian Messner) Silver Burdett Pr.
— The Pomo. LC 93-23264. (First Bks.). (Illus.). 64p. (J). (gr. 5-8). 1994. lib. bdg. 13.93 (*0-531-20123-6*) Watts.
— The Pomo. LC 93-23264. (First Bks.). (Illus.). 64p. (J). (gr. 4-6). 1994. pap. 5.95 (*0-531-15687-7*) Watts.
— Rabies. LC 92-26117. 64p. (J). (gr. 2-5). 1993. 14.99 (*0-525-67403-9*, Lodestar Bks) Dutton Child Bks.
— The Right to Die. (Impact Bks.). (Illus.). 208p. (YA). (gr. 7-12). 1993. lib. bdg. 14.42 (*0-531-13015-0*) Watts.
— Robert Fulton. LC 90-47865. (First Bks.). (Illus.). 64p. (J). (gr. 3-5). 1991. lib. bdg. 13.93 (*0-531-20016-7*) Watts.
— Sasquatch, Wild Man of the Woods. LC 92-35144. (Mysteries of Science Ser.). (Illus.). 48p. (J). (gr. 3-6). 1993. lib. bdg. 14.40 (*1-56294-348-0*) Millbrook Pr.
— Saturn. LC 90-13081. (First Bks.). (Illus.). 64p. (J). (gr. 3-5). 1991. lib. bdg. 13.93 (*0-531-20013-2*) Watts.
— Sexual Harassment. LC 92-43748. 128p. (J). (gr. 5 up). 1993. 14.95 (*0-8027-8265-5*); lib. bdg. 15.85 (*0-8027-8266-3*) Walker & Co.
— Sexually Transmitted Diseases. LC 85-4349. (Illus.). 96p. (J). (gr. 6 up). 1986. lib. bdg. 16.95 (*0-89490-115-X*) Enslow Pubs.
— Sibling Rivalry: Brothers & Sisters at Odds. (Illus.). 64p. (J). (gr. 4-6). 1994. 13.90 (*1-56294-328-6*) Millbrook Pr.
— The Sioux. LC 89-5654. (First Bks.). (Illus.). 64p. (J). (gr. 4-7). 1989. lib. bdg. 13.93 (*0-531-10754-X*) Watts.
— The Sioux. (Illus.). 64p. (J). (gr. 3 up). 1991. pap. 5.95 (*0-531-15606-0*) Watts.
— State Birds: Including the Commonwealth of Puerto Rico. LC 92-8949. (Illus.). 64p. (J). 1992. lib. bdg. 14.98 (*0-531-20058-2*); pap. 6.95 (*0-531-15629-X*) Watts.
— State Flowers: Including the Commonwealth of Puerto Rico. LC 92-8950. (YA). 1992. 14.98 (*0-531-20059-0*) Watts.
— State Flowers: Including the Commonwealth of Puerto Rico. (J). (gr. 4-7). 1992. pap. 6.95 (*0-531-15631-1*) Watts.
— Teenage Drinking. LC 94-40. (Issues in Focus Ser.). (Illus.). 104p. (YA). (gr. 6 up). 1994. lib. bdg. 17.95 (*0-89490-575-9*) Enslow Pubs.
— Teenage Violence. Steltenpohl, Jane, ed. (Illus.). 128p. (YA). (gr. 7 up). 1990. lib. bdg. 12.98 (*0-671-70153-3*, Julian Messner); pap. 5.95 (*0-671-70154-1*, Julian Messner) Silver Burdett Pr.
— Teenagers Talk about School. Steltenpohl, Jane, ed. LC 88-23065. 120p. (YA). (gr. 7 up). 1989. lib. bdg. 12.98 (*0-671-64568-4*, Julian Messner); pap. 5.95 (*0-671-68148-6*, Julian Messner) Silver Burdett Pr.
— Teens & the Death Penalty. LC 91-23351. (Issues in Focus Ser.). 112p. (J). (gr. 6 up). 1992. lib. bdg. 17.95 (*0-89490-297-0*) Enslow Pubs.
— Terrorism: America's Growing Threat. 128p. (J). (gr. 5-9). 1992. 15.00 (*0-525-67382-2*, Lodestar Bks) Dutton Child Bks.
— Tropical Rain Forests Around the World. LC 89-24810. (First Bks.). (J). (gr. 3-5). 1990. lib. bdg. 13.93 (*0-531-10896-1*) Watts.
— Tropical Rain Forests Around the World. (First Bks.). (Illus.). 64p. (J). (gr. 5-8). 1991. pap. 5.95 (*0-531-15600-1*) Watts.
— UFOs. (Mysteries of Science Ser.). (Illus.). 48p. (J). (gr. 3-6). 1995. 14.40 (*1-56294-542-4*) Millbrook Pr.
— The Warsaw Ghetto Uprising. LC 92-15851. (Illus.). 144p. (YA). (gr. 6 up). 1992. text ed. 14.95 (*0-02-751392-0*, Mac Bks Young Read) S&S Childrens.
— We Survived the Holocaust. LC 91-16982. (Non-Fiction Ser.). (Illus.). 144p. (YA). (gr. 9-12). 1991. 15.33 (*0-531-15229-4*); lib. bdg. 15.33 (*0-531-11115-6*) Watts.
— Weight: A Teenage Concern. 160p. (YA). (gr. 7 up). 1991. 15.00 (*0-525-67335-0*, Lodestar Bks) Dutton Child Bks.
— The White Power Movement: America's Racist Hate Groups. LC 92-40920. (Illus.). 96p. (YA). (gr. 7 up). 1993. lib. bdg. 15.90 (*1-56294-327-8*) Millbrook Pr.
— Why Are They Starving Themselves? Understanding Anorexia Nervosa & Bulimia. LC 82-24913. (Teen Survival Library). 160p. (J). (gr. 7 up). 1983. lib. bdg. 13.98 (*0-671-45582-6*, Julian Messner); pap. 5.95 (*0-671-49492-9*, Julian Messner) Silver Burdett Pr.
— Wildflowers Around the World. LC 90-13090. (First Book Ser.). (Illus.). 64p. (J). (gr. 3-5). 1991. lib. bdg. 13.93 (*0-531-20005-1*) Watts.
— Wildflowers Around the World. (First Bks.). 64p. (J). (gr. 5-8). 1992. pap. 5.95 (*0-531-15649-4*) Watts.
— Yeti, Abominable Snowman of the Himalayas. LC 92-35147. (Mysteries of Science Ser.). (Illus.). 48p. (J). (gr. 3-6). 1993. lib. bdg. 14.40 (*1-56294-349-9*) Millbrook Pr.
— Your Legal Rights. LC 94-42718. 128p. (YA). 1995. 13.95 (*0-8027-8359-7*); lib. bdg. 14.85 (*0-8027-8360-0*) Walker & Co.
*__Landau, Ellen, et al.__ Twenty-Five Years: A Retrospective. (Illus.). 78p. 1993. pap. text ed. 20.00 (*1-880353-04-0*) Cleveland Ctr.
__Landau, Ellen G.__ Jackson Pollock. (Illus.). 283p. 1989. 75.00 (*0-8109-3702-6*) Abrams.
*__Landau, Ellen G. & Grove, Jeffrey D.__ Lee Krasner: A Catalogue Raisonne. LC 94-41535. 1995. write for info. (*0-8109-3513-9*) Abrams.
__Landau, Elliott, et al.__ Child Development Through Literature. 1972. pap. text ed. write for info. (*0-13-130674-X*) P-H.
__Landau, Frieda W., jt. auth. see Landau, Alan M.__
__Landau, Fuller J. & Landau, Mann J.__ The Accounting Profession in Canada. (Professional Accounting in Foreign Countries Ser.). 75p. reprint ed. pap. 25.00 (*0-7837-0278-7*, 2040599) Bks Demand.
__Landau, George W., et al.__ Latin America at a Crossroads: The Challenge to the Trilateral Countries. (Triangle Papers). 1990. 6.00 (*0-930503-62-7*) Trilateral Comm.
__Landau, Gertrude, jt. auth. see Kubie, Susan H.__
__Landau, H.__ Moments in Mathematics. LC 87-19384. (PSAPM Ser.: Vol. 37). 154p. 1987. 33.00 (*0-8218-0114-7*, PSAPM-37) Am Math.
__Landau, Ioan D.__ System Identification & Control Design Using P.I.M. Plus Software. 272p. 1990. text ed. 69.00 (*0-13-880782-5*) P-H.
__Landau, Ioan D., jt. auth. see IFAC Symposium Staff.__
__Landau, Jacob, jt. auth. see Hoffmann, E. T.__
__Landau, Jacob M.__ The Arab Minority in Israel, 1967-1991: Political Aspects. LC 92-26238. (Illus.). 256p. 1993. 38.00 (*0-19-827712-1*, Clarendon Pr) OUP.
— The Hejaz Railway & the Muslim Pilgrimage: A Case of Ottoman Political Propaganda. LC 78-12918. 295p. reprint ed. pap. 84.10 (*0-685-15770-9*, 2027676) Bks Demand.
— Middle Eastern Themes: Papers in History & Politics. 309p. 1973. 35.00 (*0-7146-2969-3*, Pub. by F Cass Pubs UK) Intl Spec Bk.
— Pan-Turkism: From Irredentism to Cooperation. 2nd rev. ed. LC 94-42974. 256p. 1995. text ed. 35.00 (*0-253-32869-1*); pap. 14.95 (*0-253-20960-9*) Ind U Pr.
— Parliaments & Parties in Egypt. LC 79-1632. 1981. reprint ed. 22.00 (*0-88355-936-6*) Hyperion Conn.
— The Politics of Pan-Islam: Ideology & Organization. 448p. 1990. 95.00 (*0-19-827709-1*) OUP.
— The Politics of Pan-Islam: Ideology & Organization. 448p. 1994. reprint ed. pap. 19.95 (*0-19-827948-5*) OUP.
__Landau, Jacob M., jt. ed. see Heper, Metin.__
__Landau, Jeremy, jt. auth. see Burns, Michael.__
__Landau, Julie, tr.__ Beyond Spring: Tzu Poems of the Sung Dynasty. (Translations from the Asian Classics Ser.). 1994. write for info. (*0-231-09678-X*) Col U Pr.
__Landau, Katie, jt. auth. see Landau, Carl.__
__Landau, Kurt & Rohmert, Walter, eds.__ Recent Developments in Job Analysis: Proceedings of the International Symposium on Job Analysis. 290p. 1989. 99.00 (*0-85066-790-9*) Taylor & Francis.
__Landau, Kurt, jt. auth. see Rohmert, Walter.__
__Landau, L. D.__ Course of Theoretical Physics: The Classical Theory of Fields, Vol. 2. LC 75-4737. (Course of Theoretical Physics Ser.). (Illus.). 1980. pap. text ed. 36.00 (*0-08-025072-6*, Pergamon Pr) Elsevier.
— Electrodynamics of Continuous Media. 2nd ed. Landau, L. D. . & Lipshitz, E. M., eds. Sykes, L. D. et al, trs. (Course of Theoretical Physics Ser.: Vol. 8). 600p. 1984. pap. text ed. 48.00 (*0-08-030275-0*, Pergamon Pr) Elsevier.
— Fluid Mechanics. (Course of Theoretical Physics Ser.: No. 6). 536p. 1959. pap. 22.00 (*0-317-66821-8*, Pergamon Pr) Elsevier.
__Landau, L. D. & Lifshitz, E. M.__ Course of Theoretical Physics: Fluid Mechanics. 2nd ed. LC 86-30498. (Course of Theoretical Physics Ser.: No. 6). (Illus.). 551p. 1987. text ed. 130.00 (*0-08-033933-6*, Pergamon Pr); pap. text ed. 48.00 (*0-08-033932-8*, Pergamon Pr) Elsevier.
— Course on Theoretical Physics: Statistical Physics, Vol. 5, Pt. 1. 3rd ed. (Illus.). 1980. text ed. 160.00 (*0-08-023039-3*, Pergamon Pr); pap. text ed. 40.00 (*0-08-023038-5*, Pergamon Pr) Elsevier.
— Quantum Mechanics. LC 74-167927. (Shorter Course Theoretical Physics Ser.: Vol. 2). 1974. 154.00 (*0-08-017801-4*, Pub. by Pergamon Repr UK) Franklin.
__Landau, L. D., jt. ed. see Khalatnikov, I. M.__
__Landau, L. D. ., ed. see Landau, L. D.__
__Landau, L. D., et al.__ Theory of Elasticity. 3rd ed. Sykes, J. B. & Reid, W. H., trs. (Course of Theoretical Physics Ser.: Vol. 7). (Illus.). 235p. 1986. text ed. 120.00 (*0-08-033917-4*, Pergamon Pr); pap. text ed. 37.00 (*0-08-033916-6*, Pergamon Pr) Elsevier.
__Landau, Lev Davidovich & Smorodinskii, Iakov Abramovich.__ Lectures on Nuclear Theory. LC 92-47392. (Illus.). 108p. (ENG & RUS.). 1993. reprint ed. pap. 5.95 (*0-486-67513-0*) Dover.
__Landau, Lois & Myers, Laura G.__ Too Many Tomatoes, Squash, Beans, & Other Good Things: A Cookbook for When Your Garden Explodes. LC 75-34581. (Illus.). 288p. 1991. reprint ed. pap. 15.00 (*0-06-096857-5*, PL) HarpC.
__Landau, Madeline.__ Race, Poverty & the Cities: Hyperinnovation in Complex Policy Systems. LC 88-1298. 73p. (Orig.). 1988. pap. 9.95 (*0-87772-316-8*) UCB IGS.
__Landau, Mann J., jt. auth. see Landau, Fuller J.__
__Landau, Marcia G., jt. auth. see Klein, Robert A.__
__Landau, Marsha, jt. ed. see Lesh, Richard.__
__Landau, Matthew.__ Introduction to Aquaculture. 464p. (C). 1991. Net. text ed. write for info. (*0-471-61146-8*) Wiley.
— Poisonous & Venomous Animals. 84p. 1995. per., pap. text ed. 27.95 (*0-7872-0731-4*) Kendall-Hunt.
__Landau, Michael, jt. auth. see Lindey, Alexander.__
__Landau, Misia.__ Narratives of Human Evolution. 216p. (C). 1991. text ed. 27.00 (*0-300-04940-4*) Yale U Pr.
— Narratives of Human Evolution. 216p. (C). 1993. reprint ed. pap. text ed. 14.00 (*0-300-05431-9*) Yale U Pr.
__Landau, Nathan.__ Heavenly Deceptor. 337p. (Orig.). 1994. pap. 6.50 (*0-9620285-1-7*) Sound Music Pub.
__Landau, Norman J., et al.__ Premises Liability: Law & Practice, 3 vols. 1987. Looseleaf updates avail. write for info. (*0-8205-1568-X*) Bender.
*__Landau, Paul S.__ The Realm of the Word: Language, Gender & Christianity in a Southern African Kingdom. LC 94-24942. (Social History of Africa Ser.). 224p. 1995. 55.00 (*0-435-08963-3*); pap. 24.95 (*0-435-08965-X*) Heinemann.
__Landau, Ralph.__ Uncaging Animal Spirits: Essays on Engineering, Entrepreneurship & Economics. Gottron, Martha V., ed. LC 94-817. 1994. 42.50 (*0-262-21283-8*) MIT Pr.
— Uncaging Animal Spirits: Essays on Engineering, Entrepreneurship, & Economics. Gottron, Martha V., ed. (Illus.). 380p. 1994. 42.50 (*0-262-12183-2*) MIT Pr.
__Landau, Ralph, jt. ed. see Jorgenson, Dale W.__
__Landau, Robert I.__ Corporate Trust Administration & Management. 4th ed. 424p. 1992. text ed. 50.00 (*0-231-07670-3*) Col U Pr.
__Landau, Robert I. & Kennedy, Joseph C.__ Corporate Trust Administration & Management. 3rd ed. LC 85-2607. 1985. text ed. 49.00 (*0-231-05962-0*) Col U Pr.
__Landau, Robert M., et al, eds.__ Emerging Office Systems. LC 82-4086. (Communication & Information Science Ser.). 336p. 1982. 65.00 (*0-89391-075-9*) Ablex Pub.
__Landau, Rom.__ Ignace Paderewski: Musician & Statesman. LC 74-24137. reprint ed. 37.50 (*0-404-12999-4*) AMS Pr.
__Landau, Ronald I.__ The Hour of the Milk Is No Longer White. LC 92-90089. 156p. (Orig.). 1992. pap. 8.95 (*1-881215-00-8*) Landau & Assocs.
__Landau, Ronnie S.__ The Nazi Holocaust. 372p. 1994. 27.50 (*1-56663-054-1*); pap. 12.95 (*1-56663-052-5*) I R Dee.
__Landau, Rubin H.__ Quantum Mechanics. 1990. text ed. 79.95 (*0-471-63727-0*) Wiley.
__Landau, Rubin H., et al.__ A Scientist's & Engineer's Guide to Workstations & Supercomputers: Coping with UNIX, RISC, Vectors, & Programming. LC 92-19556. 416p. 1992. 59.95 (*0-471-53271-1*) Wiley.
__Landau, Saul.__ The Dangerous Doctrine: National Security & U. S. Foreign Policy. (Pacca Book). 201p. (C). 1988. pap. text ed. 19.95 (*0-8133-7508-8*) Westview.
— The Guerilla Wars of Central America: Nicaragua, El Salvador, & Guatemala. LC 93-24379. 1993. text ed. 35.00 (*0-312-10373-5*) St Martin.
— The Guerrilla Wars of Central America: Nicaragua, El Salvador & Guatemala. 211p. 1993. 35.00 (*0-297-82114-8*) Inst Policy Stud.
— My Dad Was Not Hamlet. Ferry, Carol, ed. 85p. (Orig.). 1993. pap. 9.95 (*0-89758-049-4*) Inst Policy Stud.
__Landau, Sidney I.__ Dictionaries: The Art & Craft of Lexicography. 384p. (C). 1989. pap. 18.95 (*0-521-36725-5*) Cambridge U Pr.
__Landau, Sidney I., ed.__ International Dictionary of Medicine & Biology. (Illus.). 3200p. 1986. text ed. 495.00 (*0-471-01849-X*) Churchill.
__Landau, Sidney I. & Bogus, Ronald.__ Doubleday Roget's Thesaurus in Dictionary Form. rev. ed. LC 86-24184. 816p. 1987. Thumb-indexed. pap. 14.00 (*0-385-23997-1*) Doubleday.
__Landau, Sidney M.__ Bantam College Roget's Thesaurus Dictionary Form. 1990. mass mkt. 4.99 (*0-553-28769-9*) Bantam.
__Landau, Sol.__ Turning Points. 1986. 13.95 (*0-88282-017-6*) New Horizon NJ.
— Turning Points: Self-Renewal at Mid-Life. 1992. pap. 11.95 (*0-88282-109-1*) New Horizon NJ.
__Landau-Stanton, Judith & Clements, Colleen D.__ AIDS, Health, & Mental Health: A Primary Sourcebook. LC 92-30578. 360p. 1993. text ed. 39.95 (*0-87630-688-1*) Brunner-Mazel.
__Landau, Ted.__ Sad Macs, Bombs, & Other Disasters: And What to Do about Them. LC 92-38361. 1993. pap. 24.95 (*0-201-62207-6*) Addison-Wesley.
— Sad Macs, Bombs & Other Disasters: And What to Do about Them. 2nd ed. LC 95-6088. 1995. pap. 34.95 (*0-201-40958-5*) Addison-Wesley.
— The Simple Process of Getting Healthy: The Total Book for Good Health & Well-Being. 66p. (Orig.). 1994. pap. 10.95 (*0-9640599-0-8*) Apollo Pub OR.
__Landau, Yehezkel, jt. ed. see Burrell, David.__
__Landauer Associates, Inc. Staff, jt. auth. see Society of Industrial.__
__Landauer, Gustav.__ For Socialism. Parent, David J., tr. LC 78-51081. (C). 1978. 25.00 (*0-914386-10-7*); pap. 14.00 (*0-914386-11-5*) Telos Pr.
__Landauer, Inc. Staff & Yim, Man-Sung.__ A Guide to Personnel Monitoring for Radiation in the Hospital Environment. LC 93-80627. (Illus.). 60p. (Orig.). 1994. pap. text ed. 40.00 (*0-9639768-0-X*) Landauer.
__Landauer, Lyndall B.__ Beyond the Lagoon: A Biography of Charles Melville Scammon. LC 85-81389. 1986. 19.95 (*0-933185-00-6*) Ransom Dist Co.
__Landauer, Susan.__ Paper Trails: Prints, Drawings & Watercolors of the San Francisco School of Abstract Expressionism. LC 92-73567. (Illus.). (C). 1993. pap. 12.00 (*0-945952-00-7*) Art Mus Santa Cruz.
— The San Francisco School of Abstract Expressionism. LC 94-47988. Date not set. write for info. (*0-520-08610-4*); pap. write for info. (*0-520-08611-2*) U CA Pr.
__Landauer, Susan, jt. ed. see Driesbach, Janice T.__
__Landauer, Susan, et al.__ Clyfford Still. Kellein, Thomas, ed. (Illus.). 176p. 1992. 60.00 (*3-7913-1187-5*, Pub. by Prestel) TeNeues.
*__Landauer, Thomas K.__ The Trouble with Computers: Usefulness, Useability & Productivity. (Illus.). 360p. 1995. 27.50 (*0-262-12186-7*, Bradford Bks) MIT Pr.
__Landauro, Antonio.__ Arte Contemporaneo: Movimientos y Artistas. (Illus.). 160p. (Orig.). (SPA.). (C). 1994. pap. text ed. write for info. (*1-56259-031-6*) Editorial Amer.
__Landaw, Jonathan.__ The Story of Buddha. (Illus.). (J). (gr. 3-10). 1979. 7.95 (*0-89744-140-0*) Auromere.
__Landaw, Jonathan & Brooke, Janet.__ Prince Siddhartha. rev. ed. (Children's Book Ser.). (Illus.). 144p. (J). (gr. 1-8). 1993. 15.95 (*0-86171-016-9*) Wisdom MA.
__Landaw, Jonathan & Weber, Andy.__ Images of Enlightenment: Tibetan Art in Practice. LC 93-40283. 1994. pap. 24.95 (*1-55939-024-7*) Snow Lion Pubns.
__Landaw, Jonathan, ed. see Yeshe, Lama T.__
__Landaw, Jonathan, ed. see Yeshe, Lama T. & Rinpoche, Zopa.__
__Landay, Alan L., et al, eds.__ Clinical Flow Cytometry. LC 93-9300. (Annals Ser.: Vol. 677). 1993. write for info. (*0-89766-767-0*); pap. write for info. (*0-89766-768-9*) NY Acad Sci.
__Landberg, Peter T.__ Thermodynamics & Statistical Mechanics. 1990. pap. 12.95 (*0-486-66493-7*) Dover.
__Lande.__ Blueprinting. Date not set. pap. 49.95 (*0-06-251049-5*, PL) HarpC.
— National Transportation Policy. 224p. 1992. 95.00 (*0-409-89721-3*) Butterworth Legal Pubs.
— Railway Law & the National Transportation Act. 240p. 1989. 100.00 (*0-409-80661-7*) Butterworth Legal Pubs.
__Lande, Adam, et al, eds.__ Aortitis: Clinical, Pathologic, & Radiographic Aspects. (Illus.). 288p. 1986. text ed. 83.00 (*0-88167-141-X*) Raven.
__Lande, Boris & Shtager, Evgenii.__ Microwave Radar Signatures of Sea Vessels: Krylov Shipbuilding Institute R&D. (Foreign Technology Assessment Ser.). 380p. (Orig.). 1994. pap. 55.00 (*1-881874-16-8*) Global Cnslts.
__Lande, Carl H., ed.__ Rebuilding a Nation: Philippine Challenges & American Policy. LC 86-32610. (Illus.). 592p. 1987. 37.95 (*0-88702-023-2*); pap. 22.95 (*0-88702-024-0*) Washington Inst Pr.
__Lande, D. A.__ From Somewhere in England the Life & Times of 8th Air Force Fighter, Bomber & Ground Crews. (Illus.). 176p. 1991. 29.95 (*0-87938-448-4*) Motorbooks Intl.
*__Lande, Debra, ed.__ A Wedding Book. (Illus.). 72p. 1994. 25.00 (*0-8118-0783-5*) Chronicle Bks.
*__Lande, E. B.__ Every Mother Is a Working Mother. 1994. pap. 3.99 (*0-517-13380-6*) Random.
__Lande, Ellen B.__ The Every Mother Is a Working Mother Daybook: How to Keep Track of Your Kids' Lives & Still Have a Life of Your Own. (Illus.). 184p. (Orig.). 1993. pap. 12.95 (*0-9636210-4-1*) Lansdowne Pr.
__Lande, James E. T. & Dewitt, Katherine, Jr.__ Chappaquiddick: The Real Story. 304p. 1994. mass mkt. 5.99 (*0-312-95276-7*) St Martin.
__Lande, Jeffery, et al, eds.__ Caring for the Children: Challenge to America. 336p. (C). 1989. text ed. 69.95 (*0-8058-0255-X*); pap. 29.95 (*0-8058-0256-8*) L Erlbaum Assocs.
__Lande, Marilyn.__ Edible Flowers: A Recipe Collection. 58p. 1993. pap. text ed. 5.95 (*0-9637596-0-4*) Lan-Design.
— Edible Flowers: A Recipe Collection. rev. ed. 59p. 1994. write for info. (*0-9637596-1-2*) Lan-Design.

***Lande, Nathaniel.** Dispatches from the Front: News Accounts of American Wars, 1776-1991. 336p. 1995. 35.00 (0-8050-3664-4) H Holt & Co.

Lande, Rivian & Knox, Marlys. Concepts of Genetics. (Orig.). 1980. write for info. (0-8087-3826-7) Burgess MN Intl.

Lande, Saul, ed. Progress in Peptide Research, Vol. 2. LC 76-153298. 404p. 1972. text ed. 316.00 (0-677-13610-2) Gordon & Breach.

Lande, Stephen L. & Crigler, Jeffrey C. The Guide to Buying American. LC 93-45555. 1994. 12.95 (0-8065-1512-0, Citadel Pr) Carol Pub Group.

Landeck, Michael. International Trade: Regional & Global Issues. LC 93-14617. 1994. text ed. 79.95 (0-312-10257-7) St Martin.

Landecker, T. L., jt. ed. see Roger, R. S.

Landefeld, C. F., jt. ed. see Katz, S.

Landefeld, Stewart M., et al. Washington Corporation Law & Practice. (National Corporation Law Ser.). 1991. ring bd. 126.00 (0-13-109398-3) Aspen Law.

Landeira, Ricardo. An Annotated Bibliography of Gabriel Miro. LC 78-70765. 200p. 1978. pap. 12.00 (0-89295-005-6) Society Sp & Sp-Am.

— Jose de Espronceda. LC 84-50239. 159p. 1985. pap. text ed. 25.00 (0-89295-032-3) Society Sp & Sp-Am.

Landeira, Ricardo & Gonzalez-del-Valle, Luis T., eds. Nuevos y Novisimos: Algunas Perspectivas Criticas sobre la Narrativa Espanola desde la Decada de los 60. LC 87-61581. 228p. (SPA.). 1987. pap. 30.00 (0-89295-051-X) Society Sp & Sp-Am.

Landeira, Ricardo, jt. auth. see Cardwell, Richard A.

Landeira, Richardo. The Modern Spanish Novel, Eighteen Ninety-Eight to Nineteen Thirty-Six. (Twayne's World Authors Ser.: No. 764). 184p. 1985. lib. bdg. 30.95 (0-8057-6603-0, Twayne) Macmillan.

Landek, Dan. Fast Track to SCSI: A Product Guide. 1990. pap. text ed. 52.00 (0-13-307000-X) P-H.

Landekich, Stephen. Corporate Codes of Conduct. Barth, Claire, ed. (Bold Step Ser.). 130p. (Orig.). 1989. pap. 24.95 (0-86641-175-5, 89237) Inst Mgmt Account.

Landel, jt. ed. see Nielson, L.

Landel, Robert D. Managing Productivity Through People. (C). 1986. teacher ed write for info. (0-8359-4165-5, Reston) P-H.

Landel, Robert D. & Freeland, James R. Aggregate Production Planning: Text & Cases. (C). 1984. teacher ed write for info. (0-8359-0032-0, Reston) P-H.

Landelius, Otto R. Swedish Place-Names in North America. Jarvi, Raymond, ed. Franzen, Karin, tr. LC 84-14192. 376p. 1985. text ed. 29.95 (0-8093-1204-2) S Ill U Pr.

Landell-Mills, Joslin. The Fund's International Banking Statistics. v, 54p. 1986. pap. 5.00 (1-55775-113-7); pap. 5.00 (1-55775-114-5) Intl Monetary.

— The Fund's International Banking Statistics. LC 86-20145. 60p. reprint ed. pap. 25.00 (0-685-23546-7, 2029093) Bks Demand.

Landell-Mills, Pierre, jt. auth. see Binswanger, Hans P.

Landell-Mills, Pierre, jt. ed. see Serageldin, Ismail.

Landels, John. Engineering in the Ancient World. LC 76-52030. 1978. pap. 14.00 (0-520-04127-5) U CA Pr.

***Landen, Todd.** Mates Don't Grow on Trees: How to Meet the Man or Woman for You. LC 94-74071. (Illus.). 208p. (Orig.). 1995. pap. 14.95 (0-9644671-4-3) Dancing Hearts.

Lander, Bernard. Towards an Understanding of Juvenile Delinquency. LC 72-120208. (Columbia University. Studies in the Social Sciences: No. 578). reprint ed. 20.00 (0-404-51578-9) AMS Pr.

Lander, Bruce, jt. auth. see Cull, Brian.

Lander, Cyril W. Power Electronics. 3rd ed. LC 92-44563. 1994. pap. text ed. 44.69 (0-07-707714-8) McGraw.

Lander, Eric S., ed. Calculating the Secrets of Life: Contributions of the Mathematical Sciences to Molecular Biology. 296p. (Orig.). (C). 1995. text ed. 27.95 (0-309-04886-9) Natl Acad Pr.

Lander, Ernest M., Jr. South Carolina: An Illustrated History of the Palmetto State. (Illus.). 208p. (YA). (gr. 7 up). 1988. 32.95 (0-89781-262-X) Preferred Mktg.

***Lander, Ernest M.** The Textile Industry in Antebellum South Carolina. LC 69-12590. 140p. 1969. pap. 39.90 (0-7837-8522-4, 2049331) Bks Demand.

Lander, Ernest M., Jr. & McGee, Charles M., Jr. A Rebel Came Home: The Diary & Letters of Floride Clemson, 1863-1866. rev. ed. Bleser, Carol & Fox-Genovese, Elizabeth, eds. (Women's Diaries & Letters of the Nineteenth-Century South Ser.). 205p. 1989. reprint ed. 29.95 (0-87249-642-2) U of SC Pr.

Lander, G. H., jt. auth. see Freedman, A. J.

Lander, G. H., jt. auth. see Freeman, A. J.

Lander, J. R. English Justices of the Peace 1461-1509. 256p. (C). 1990. text ed. 45.00 (0-86299-488-8) A Sutton Pub.

— Government & Community: England, 1450-1509. (New History of England Ser.). 413p. 1980. 37.50 (0-674-35793-0) HUP.

— Government & Community: England, 1450-1509. LC 80-15. (New History of England Ser.). 413p. 1981. pap. 16.95 (0-674-35794-9) HUP.

— The Limitations of English Monarchy in the Later Middle Ages. (Joanne Goodman Lectures). (Illus.). 104p. 1989. 25.00 (0-8020-5807-8); pap. 15.95 (0-8020-6724-7) U of Toronto Pr.

— The Wars of the Roses. (Illus.). 256p. (C). 1992. pap. text ed. 20.00 (0-7509-0018-0) A Sutton Pub.

Lander, Jack R. How to Get Hired Faster, for More Money, Whether You Are Presently Working or Not. LC 79-56038. (Illus.). 80p. 1980. pap. 5.95 (0-935722-00-9) Stonewall Co.

Lander, Kerstin, tr. see Cutburth, Ronald W.

Lander, L., ed. Chemicals in the Aquatic Environment. (Environmental Management Ser.). (Illus.). 430p. 1989. 181.00 (0-387-50863-5, 3090) Spr-Verlag.

Lander, Patricia S. & Charbonneau, Claudette. The Land & People of Finland. LC 88-27144. (Portraits of the Nations Ser.). (Illus.). 224p. (J). (gr. 6 up). 1990. 18.00 (0-397-32357-3, Lipp Jr Bks); lib. bdg. 17.89 (0-397-32358-1, Lipp Jr Bks) HarpC Child Bks.

Lander, Patricia S., jt. auth. see Charbonneau, Claudette.

Lander, R. L., ed. Sixth International Workshop on Photon-Photon Collision. 520p. 1985. 89.00 (9971-978-22-9) World Scientific Pub.

Lander, Richard. Captain Clapperton's Last Expedition to Africa, 2 vols., Set. (Illus.). 1967. 65.00 (0-7146-1827-6, Pub. by F Cass Pubs UK) Intl Spec Bk.

Landers. Federal Rules of Civil Procedure: With Selected Statutes & Cases, 1989. 1989. 16.00 (0-316-51364-4) Little.

Landers, jt. auth. see Kelly.

Landers, Andy. Women's Basketball Drills - Defensive Drills. (Orig.). (YA). (gr. 7 up). 1989. pap. 6.95 (0-932741-56-8) Championship Bks & Vid Prodns.

***Landers, Bertha.** Jubilee Celebrations Two. 1995. pap. 9.95 (0-87178-475-0) Brethren.

***Landers, Clare B., ed.** If I Were a Door: Writings by ESL Students. 54p. (Orig.). Date not set. pap. text ed. 8.00 (0-9640528-2-2, Voices Commun Pr) Jacar Pr Lit.

Landers, Clifford, tr. see Phillips, Lisa.

Landers, Clifford E., tr. see Amado, Jorge.

Landers, Daniel M., ed. Sport & Elite Performers. LC 85-18115. 212p. (C). 1986. text ed. 36.00x (0-87322-015-3, BLAN0015) Human Kinetics.

Landers, Daniel M., ed. see North American Society for the Psychology of Sport & Physical Activity Staff.

Landers, Dennis R., jt. ed. see Klein, Sanford L.

Landers, Gunnard. The Deer Killers. 209p. 1990. 21.95 (0-8027-1134-0) Walker & Co.

— The Violators. 250p. 1991. 19.95 (0-8027-1179-0) Walker & Co.

Landers-Henry, Joanne. Robert Fulton: Steamboat Builder. (Discovery Biographies Ser.). (Illus.). 80p. (J). (gr. 2-6). 1991. reprint ed. lib. bdg. 12.95 (0-7910-1411-8) Chelsea Hse.

Landers, Jack, jt. auth. see Polette, Doug.

Landers, Jack M. Home Repair & Maintenance. LC 85-27118. 384p. 1991. 31.40 (0-87006-820-2) Goodheart.

Landers, James P. Handbook of High Performance Capillary Electrophoresis. 1993. 99.50 (0-8493-8690-X) CRC Pr.

Landers, Jane L., jt. ed. see Colburn, David R.

Landers, Jeanette, ed. see Johnston, John P.

Landers, John. Death & the Metropolis: Studies in the Demographic History of London, 1670-1830. LC 92-10887. (Studies in Population, Economy & Society in Past Time: No. 20). 368p. (C). 1993. 64.95 (0-521-35599-0) Cambridge U Pr.

Landers, John & Reynolds, Vernon, eds. Fertility & Resources. (Society for the Study of Human Biology Symposium Ser.: No. 31). 200p. (C). 1990. 74.95 (0-521-39526-7) Cambridge U Pr.

Landers, John L. Dying for Life: The Journey to Transplant. LC 93-29983. 192p. 1994. pap. 12.95 (0-942963-39-3) Distinctive Pub.

Landers, John M., jt. auth. see Baker, Robert A.

Landers, Jonathan M. Civil Procedure: Adaptable to Courses Utilizing Materials by Landers. LC 87-130239. (Legalines Ser.). 257p. 10.95 (0-685-19020-X) HarBrace.

Landers, Jonathan M. & Martin, James A. Federal Rules of Civil Procedure with Selected Statutes & Cases: 1988 Edition. 1988. pap. text ed. write for info. (0-318-63385-X) Little.

***Landers, Kirk & Ritt, Michael J., Jr.** A Lifetime of Riches: The Biography of Napoleon Hill. LC 94-48789. 1995. 24.95 (0-525-94001-4, Dutton) NAL-Dutton.

Landers, Lynda S. Angel in Blue Jeans. 192p. 1992. 13.95 (0-8034-8975-7, Avalon Bks) Bouregy.

***Landers, Robert & Pate, Russ.** Greener Pastures: The Robert Landers Story. 275p. 1995. 19.95 (0-9646738-0-0) Harvest TX.

Landers, Robert, jt. ed. see Chase, Leslie R.

Landers, Robert K. Honest Writer. 1996. 35.00 (0-8050-2580-4) H Holt & Co.

Landers, Sam, jt. auth. see Maday, Tom.

Landers, Susan. Advanced First Aid. (C). 1993. student ed 14.00 (1-881592-00-6) Hayden-McNeil.

Landers, Thomas L., et al. Electronics Manufacturing Processes. LC 93-5980. 1994. text ed. 69.00 (0-13-176470-5) P-H.

Landes, Alison. Pariswalks. 4th ed. (Orig.). 1991. pap. 12.95 (0-8050-1186-2, Owl) H Holt & Co.

***Landes, Alison, ed.** Child Abuse: Betraying a Trust. (Information Plus Reference Ser.). (Illus.). 124p. (YA). (gr. 9-12). 1995. pap. 22.95 (1-878623-95-8) Info Plus TX.

— Violent Relationships: Battering & Abuse among Adults. (Information Plus Reference Ser.). (Illus.). 168p. (YA). (gr. 9-12). 1995. pap. text ed. 22.95 (1-878623-96-6) Info Plus TX.

***Landes, Alison, et al.** Abortion: An Eternal Social & Moral Issue. rev. ed. (Reference Ser.). 168p. 1994. pap. text ed. 22.95 (1-878623-65-6) Info Plus TX.

***Landes, Alison, et al, eds.** Death & Dying: Who Decides. (Reference Ser.). 168p. 1994. pap. text ed. 21.95 (1-878623-81-8) Info Plus TX.

— Illegal Drugs & Alcohol - America's Anguish. (Information Plus Ser.). 208p. 1993. pap. text ed. 23.95 (1-878623-57-5) Info Plus TX.

— Minorities - A Changing Role in American Society. rev. ed. (Reference Ser.). 172p. 1994. pap. text ed. 22.95 (1-878623-83-4) Info Plus TX.

Landes, Burton R. A Study of the International Press & Other Media in the Shaping of Public Opinion: The Sarah Churchill Cause. 5th ed. 400p. 1985. pap. 25.00 (0-915568-08-X) B R Landes.

— Study-Sarah Churchill. (Orig.). 1991. reprint ed. pap. write for info. (0-318-68562-0) B R Landes.

Landes, Daniel, ed. Confronting Omnicide: Jewish Reflections on Weapons of Mass Destruction. LC 90-48358. 312p. 1991. 40.00 (0-87668-851-2) Aronson.

Landes, David S. Bankers & Pashas: International Finance & Economic Imperialism in Egypt. (Illus.). 370p. 1980. pap. 17.50 (0-674-06165-9) HUP.

— Revolution in Time: Clocks & the Making of the Modern World. (Illus.). 502p. 1985. pap. text ed. 12.95 (0-674-76802-7) Belknap Pr.

— Revolution in Time: Clocks & the Making of the Modern World. LC 83-8489. (Illus.). 502p. 1983. 32.00 (0-674-76800-0) HUP.

— Unbound Prometheus: Technological Change & Industrial Development in Western Europe from 1750 to the Present. (C). 1969. pap. 19.95 (0-521-09418-6) Cambridge U Pr.

Landes, Deborah. Competence in Cloze: Level B, Science. 56p. 1990. student ed 4.25 (0-910307-81-4) Comp Pr.

— Competence in Cloze: Level B, Social Studies. 55p. 1989. student ed 4.25 (0-910307-84-9) Comp Pr.

Landes, George M. Students Vocabulary Bible Hebrew. (C). 1985. pap. text ed. 5.50 (0-684-41323-X, Scribners) S&S Trade.

— A Student's Vocabulary of Biblical Hebrew. 56p. (Orig.). (C). 1961. pap. write for info. (0-02-367410-5, Scribners) S&S Trade.

Landes, George M., ed. Report on Archaeological Work at Suwannet eth-Thaniya, Tananir, & Khirbet Minha. LC 75-30540. (American Schools of Oriental Research, Supplement Ser.: Vol. 21). 117p. 1975. text ed. 13.50 (0-89757-317-X); pap. text ed. 10.00 (0-89757-321-8) Am Sch Orient Res.

Landes, J. D., et al, eds. Elastic-Plastic Fracture - STP 668. 786p. 1979. 58.75 (0-8031-0330-1, 04-668000-30) ASTM.

— Nonlinear Fracture Mechanics, Vol. II: Elastic-Plastic Fracture. LC 88-38147. (Special Technical Publication Ser.: No. STP 995). (Illus.). 625p. 1989. text ed. 78.00 (0-8031-1257-2, 04-995002-30) ASTM.

Landes, Joan, jt. auth. see Levine, Sura.

Landes, Joan B. Women & the Public Sphere in the Age of the French Revolution. LC 88-3723. (Illus.). 296p. 1988. 37.95 (0-8014-2141-1); pap. 13.95 (0-8014-9481-8) Cornell U Pr.

Landes, JoAnn. Gi-Gi & Argo. (Illus.). 24p. (J). 1995. pap. 8.00 (0-8059-3611-4) Dorrance.

Landes, John D., ed. see Metallurgical Society of AIME Staff.

Landes, Kenneth K. Petroleum Geology. 2nd ed. LC 74-26700. 458p. 1975. reprint ed. 39.50 (0-88275-226-X) Krieger.

— Plane Table Manual for Geologists. 1951. 3.50 (0-911586-17-2) Wahr.

Landes-Levi, Louise. Extinction. 1990. pap. 9.00 (0-916258-24-6) Woodbine Pr.

— Extinction. 32p. 1992. reprint ed. pap. 9.00 (1-880516-10-1) Left Hand Bks.

Landes, Paula F. Augustine on Romans: Propositions from the Epistle to the Romans & Unfinished Commentary on the Epistle to the Romans. LC 82-10259. (Society of Biblical Literature Texts & Translations Ser.). 124p. (C). 1982. pap. 18.95 (0-89130-583-1, 06-02-23) Scholars Pr GA.

Landes, Richard, jt. ed. see Head, Thomas.

***Landes, Richard A.** Relics, Apocalypse, & the Deceits of History: Ademar of Chabannes, 989-1034. LC 94-39890. (Harvard Historical Studies). (Illus.). 416p. 1995. text ed. 55.00 (0-674-75530-8, LANREL) HUP.

Landes, Ronald G. The Canadian Polity: A Comparative Introduction. 3rd ed. 450p. 1991. pap. text ed. 45.00 (0-13-116740-5) P-H.

Landes, Ruth. City of Women. 287p. 1994. 35.00x (0-8263-1555-0); pap. 17.95 (0-8263-1556-9) U of NM Pr.

— Mystic Lake Sioux: Sociology of the Mdewakantonwan Santee. 234p. 1968. text ed. 25.00 (0-299-05040-8) U of Wis Pr.

— The Mystic Lake Sioux: Sociology of the Mdewakantonwan Santee. LC 68-9019. 232p. reprint ed. pap. 66.20 (0-7837-5589-9, 2045382) Bks Demand.

— Ojibwa Sociology. LC 79-84467. (Columbia Univ. Contributions to Anthropology Ser.: Vol. 29). reprint ed. 22.00 (0-404-50579-1) AMS Pr.

— Ojibwa Woman. LC 70-82362. (Columbia Univ. Contributions to Anthropology Ser.: Vol. 31). reprint ed. 27.50 (0-404-50581-3) AMS Pr.

Landes, William A., ed. see Morton, Carlos.

Landes, William-Alan. Aladdin n' His Magic Lamp. rev. ed. LC 89-43679. (Wondrawhopper Ser.). 52p. (J). (gr. 3-12). 1985. pap. 6.00 (0-88734-102-0); 30.00 (0-88734-003-2) Players Pr.

— Aladdin n' His Magic Lamp: Music & Lyrics. rev. ed. (Wondrawhopper Ser.). (J). (gr. 3-12). 1985. pap. text ed. 15.00 (0-88734-002-4) Players Pr.

— Alice n' Wonderland. LC 89-63870. (Wondrawhopper Ser.). (Orig.). (J). (gr. 3 up). 1984. pap. 6.00 (0-88734-112-8) Players Pr.

— The Ambassador. LC 92-50271. 50p. (Orig.). 1992. pap. 5.00 (0-88734-123-3) Players Pr.

— Jack 'n the Beanstalk. LC 89-43681. (Wondrawhopper Ser.). (J). (gr. 3-12). 1985. teacher ed 30.00 (0-88734-001-6) Players Pr.

— Jack 'n the Beanstalk. rev. ed. LC 89-43681. (Wondrawhopper Ser.). (J). (gr. 3-12). 1985. pap. 6.00 (0-88734-101-2) Players Pr.

— Jack 'n the Beanstalk: Music & Lyrics. rev. ed. (Wondrawhopper Ser.). (J). (gr. 3-12). 1985. pap. text ed. 15.00 (0-88734-000-8) Players Pr.

— Monologues & Scenes from World Theatre - American, Vol. 5. LC 93-16180. (World Theatre Ser.: Vol. 5). 62p. (Orig.). 1993. pap. 8.00 (0-88734-129-2) Players Pr.

— Monologues & Scenes from World Theatre - Ancient Greek & Roman, Vol. 1. LC 93-16180. 100p. (Orig.). 1996. pap. 8.00 (0-88734-125-X) Players Pr.

— Monologues & Scenes from World Theatre - Belgian, Austrian, Scandinavian, Irish, Vol. 3. LC 93-16180. 100p. (Orig.). 1993. pap. 8.00 (0-88734-127-6) Players Pr.

— Monologues & Scenes from World Theatre - German, French, Spanish, Italian, Russian, Vol. 2. 100p. (Orig.). 1993. pap. 8.00 (0-88734-126-8) Players Pr.

— A New Competitor. LC 91-58033. 24p. (Orig.). 1991. pap. 5.00 (0-88734-121-7) Players Pr.

— Performance One: Monologues for Women. 128p. (Orig.). 1991. pap. 10.00 (0-88734-122-5) Players Pr.

— Peter N' the Wolf. rev. ed. LC 89-69871. (Wondrawhopper Ser.). (J). (gr. 3-12). 1988. teacher ed 30.00 (0-88734-013-X); pap. 6.00 (0-88734-106-3) Players Pr.

— Pyramus & Thisbe. rev. ed. LC 90-53083. (J). (gr. 3 up). 1984. pap. 5.00 (0-88734-103-9) Players Pr.

— Rapunzel 'N the Witch. LC 89-43682. (Wondrawhopper Ser.). (J). (gr. 3-12). 1985. teacher ed 30.00 (0-88734-007-5) Players Pr.

— Rapunzel 'N the Witch. rev. ed. LC 89-43682. (Wondrawhopper Ser.). (J). (gr. 3-12). 1985. pap. 6.00 (0-88734-107-1) Players Pr.

— Rapunzel 'N the Witch: Music & Lyrics. rev. ed. (Wondrawhopper Ser.). (J). (gr. 3-12). 1985. pap. 15.00 (0-88734-006-7) Players Pr.

— Rhyme Tyme. LC 87-62593. (Wondrawhopper Ser.). 1988. teacher ed, pap. 30.00 (0-88734-009-1) Players Pr.

— Rhyme Tyme. rev. ed. LC 89-63869. (Wondrawhopper Ser.). (J). (gr. 3-12). 1985. pap. 6.00 (0-88734-108-X) Players Pr.

— Rumpelstiltskin. LC 89-43683. (Wondrawhopper Ser.). 52p. (J). (gr. 3-12). 1985. teacher ed 30.00 (0-88734-005-9) Players Pr.

— Rumpelstiltskin. rev. ed. LC 89-43683. (Wondrawhopper Ser.). 52p. (J). (gr. 3-12). 1985. pap. 6.00 (0-88734-104-7) Players Pr.

Landes, William-Alan & Lasky, Mark A. Grandpa's Bedtime Story. rev. ed. LC 89-63868. (J). (gr. 3-12). 1985. pap. 6.00 (0-88734-505-0) Players Pr.

Landes, William-Alan & Rizzo, Jeff. Rhyme Tyme: Music & Lyrics. rev. ed. (Wondrawhopper Ser.). (J). (gr. 3-12). 1985. pap. text ed. 15.00 (0-88734-008-3) Players Pr.

— Rumpelstiltskin: Music & Lyrics. rev. ed. (Wondrawhopper Ser.). (J). (gr. 3-12). 1985. pap. text ed. 15.00 (0-88734-004-0) Players Pr.

Landes, William-Alan & Standish, Marilyn. Diary of a Madman. rev. ed. LC 90-52545. 1985. pap. 5.00 (0-88734-109-8) Players Pr.

— The Wizard of Oz. LC 89-63872. (Wondrawhopper Ser.). (J). (gr. 3-12). 1985. teacher ed 30.00 (0-88734-011-3) Players Pr.

— The Wizard of Oz. rev. ed. LC 89-63872. (Wondrawhopper Ser.). (J). (gr. 3-12). 1985. pap. 6.00 (0-88734-105-5) Players Pr.

— The Wizard of Oz: Music & Lyrics. rev. ed. (Wondrawhopper Ser.). (J). (gr. 3-12). 1985. pap. text ed. 15.00 (0-88734-010-5) Players Pr.

Landes, William-Alan, ed. see Barrie, James M.

Landes, William-Alan, jt. auth. see Brooke, Iris.

Landes, William-Alan, ed. see Chekhov, Anton.

Landes, William-Alan, ed. see Chekov, Anton.

Landes, William-Alan, ed. see Dunseny, Edward J.

Landes, William-Alan, jt. auth. see Evans, Mary.

Landes, William-Alan, jt. auth. see Jans, Martin.

Landes, William-Alan, ed. see Shaw, George Bernard.

Landes, William-Alan, ed. see Wilde, Oscar.

Landes, William M. & Posner, Richard A. The Economic Structure of Tort Law. LC 86-18450. (Illus.). 352p. 1987. 37.50 (0-674-23051-5) HUP.

Landes, William M., jt. ed. see Becker, Gary S.

Landes, William M., ed. see Universities-National Bureau Staff.

Landesberg, Joseph, jt. auth. see Bettelheim, Frederick.

Landesco, John. Illinois Crime Survey. unexpurgated ed. Incl. Organized Crime in Chicago. LC 68-55774. 1968. (0-318-54973-5); LC 68-55774. (Crimson Crystal Adventures Ser.: No. 9). 1968. 40.00 (0-87585-009-X) Patterson Smith.

— Organized Crime in Chicago (unexpurgated) 1968. reprint ed. write for info. (0-318-62185-1) Patterson Smith.

Landesman, Alter F. Brownsville. 430p. 1989. 27.50 (0-8197-0151-3); pap. 16.95 (0-8197-0563-2) Bloch.

Landesman, Bill, jt. auth. see Berman, Kathleen.

Landesman, Charles. Color & Consciousness: An Essay in Metaphysics. LC 88-29442. 149p. (C). 1989. 24.95 (0-87722-616-4) Temple U Pr.

— Discourse & Its Presuppositions. LC 72-75201. 174p. reprint ed. pap. 49.60 (0-317-29272-2, 2022010) Bks Demand.

— The Eye & the Mind: Reflections on Perception & the Problem of Knowledge. (Philosophical Studies in Philosophy Ser.). 170p. (C). 1993. lib. bdg. 89.00 (0-7923-2586-9) Kluwer Ac.

Landesman, Dovid. A Practical Guide to Torah Learning. LC 94-32902. 1995. write for info. (1-56821-320-4) Aronson.

Landesman, Edward M. & Hestenes, Magnus R. Linear Algebra for Mathematics, Science, & Engineering. 540p. (C). 1992. text ed. write for info. (0-13-529561-0) P-H.

Landesman, Fran. Ballad of the Sad Young Men. LC 81-85724. 64p. 1982. 16.00 (0-932966-18-7) Permanent Pr.

— Invade My Privacy. LC 83-63244. 64p. (Orig.). 1984. pap. 16.00 (0-932966-44-6) Permanent Pr.

An Asterisk (*) at the beginning of an entry indicates that the title is appearing in BIP for the first time.

— More Truth Than Poetry. LC 80-85345. 64p. (Orig.). 1981. pap. 16.00 (*0-932966-13-6*) Permanent Pr.

Landesman, Jay. Rebel Without Applause. LC 86-62451. 286p. 1987. 22.00 (*0-932966-75-6*) Permanent Pr.

***Landesman, Peter.** The Raven. 360p. 1995. 23.00 (*1-880909-37-5*) Baskerville.

***Landesmann, Michael A. & Szekely, Istvan P., eds.** Industrial Restructuring & Trade Reorientation in Eastern Europe. (Department of Applied Economics Occasional Papers: No. 60). 350p. (C). 1995. 59.95 (*0-521-48085-X*) Cambridge U Pr.

Landess. Jesse Jackson & Politics. 1988. pap. 8.95 (*0-915463-50-4*) Green Hill.

Landfester, Manfred. Das Griechische Nomen "Philos" und Seine Ableitungen. Bd. 11. xi, 196p. (GER.). 1966. write for info. (*0-318-70616-4*, Pub. by Georg Olms GW) Lubrecht & Cramer.

— Handlungsverlauf und Komik in den Fruehen Komoedien des Aristophanes. (Untersuchungen zur Antiken Literatur und Geschichte Ser.: Vol. 17). (C). 1977. 115. 40 (*3-11-006950-4*) De Gruyter.

Landfield, Alvin W. & Epting, Franz R. Personal Construct Psychology: Clinical & Personality Assessment. LC 86-10477. 327p. 1986. 51.95 (*0-89885-315-X*); pap. 24.95 (*0-89885-318-4*) Human Sci Pr.

Landfield, Alvin W., jt. ed. see Epting, Franz.

Landfield, Alvin W., ed. see Nebraska Symposium on Motivation Staff.

Landfield, Lonie, ed. see Andringa, Patty P.

***Landfield, Philip W.** Brain Corticosteroid Receptors: Studies on the Mechanism, Function, & Neurotoxicity of Corticosteroid Action. de Kloet, E. Ronald et al, eds. (Annals of the New York Academy of Sciences: 746). 1994. pap. write for info. (*0-89766-908-8*) NY Acad Sci.

Landfried, Christine, ed. Constitutional Review & Legislation: An International Comparison. 266p. 1988. 69.50 (*3-7890-1640-3*, Pub. by Nomos Verlags GW) Intl Bk Import.

Landgarten, Helen. Magazine Photo Collage: A Multicultural Assessment & Treatment Technique. LC 93-16792. (Illus.). 224p. 1993. 28.95 (*0-87630-706-3*) Brunner-Mazel.

Landgarten, Helen B. Clinical Art Therapy: A Comprehensive Guide. LC 80-22564. 416p. 1981. 33.95 (*0-87630-237-1*) Brunner-Mazel.

— Family Art Psychotherapy: A Clinical Guide & Casebook. LC 86-28380. (Illus.). 320p. 1987. 36.95 (*0-87630-456-0*) Brunner-Mazel.

Landgarten, Helen B. & Lubbers, Darcy, eds. Adult Art Psychotherapy: Issues & Applications. LC 90-15103. (Illus.). 224p. 1991. 27.95 (*0-87630-593-1*) Brunner-Mazel.

Landgraf, Anne K. Na Wahi Pana o Koolau Poko: Legendary Places of Koolau Poko. Meinecke, Kalani, tr. LC 94-12427. (Illus.). 176p. (C). 1994. text ed. 32.00 (*0-8248-1578-5*) UH Pr.

Landgraf, Arthur. Commentarius Cantabrigiensis in Epistolas Pauli e Schola Petri Abaelardi, 3 vols. Incl. Vol. 1. In Epistolam Ad Romanos. 223p. 1937. 17.95 (*0-268-00133-2*); Vol. 2. In Epistolam Ad Corinthios Iam et Iiam, Ad Galatas et Ad Ephesios. 1223p. 1960. 17.95 (*0-268-00134-0*); Vol. 3. In Epistolam ad Philippenses, ad Colossenses, ad Thessalonicenses Primam et Secundam, ed Timotheam Priman et Secundam, ad Titum et Philemonem. 447p. 1944. 17.95 (*0-268-00132-4*); (Mediaeval Studies Ser.: No. 2). write for info. (*0-318-56117-4*) U of Notre Dame Pr.

Landgraf, Gustav. Kommentar Zu Ciceros Rede Pro Sexto Roscio Amerino. vii, 290p. 1978. reprint ed. write for info. (*3-487-01183-2*, Pub. by Georg Olms GW) Lubrecht & Cramer.

Landgraf, John R. Creative Singlehood & Pastoral Care. LC 82-7439. (Creative Pastoral Care & Counseling Ser.). 95p. reprint ed. pap. 27.10 (*0-685-23502-5*, 2029098) Bks Demand.

— Singling: A New Way to Live the Single Life. 180p. (Orig.). 1990. pap. 11.99 (*0-664-25086-6*) Westminster John Knox.

Landgraf, Otto. Oldtimer Sewing Machine. Forsdyke, Graham, tr. (Illus.). 192p. 1992. reprint ed. 49.00 (*3-926879-06-8*, Pub. by Weppert GmbH GW) A Stitch Back.

Landgraf, R., jt. ed. see Mitchell, M. R.

Landgraf, R. W., jt. ed. see Mitchell, M. R.

***Landgraf, Sherry.** Love's Voyage. Bradbury, Dianne & Bare, Wanda, eds. LC 95-67506. 436p. 1995. 23.95 (*0-9644981-0-3*) Donnabelle Pub.

Landgrebe, A. R., jt. ed. see Doddapaneni, N.

Landgrebe, A. R., et al, eds. Proceedings of the Workshop on Direct Methanol-Air Fuel Cells. LC 92-81870. (Proceedings Ser.: Vol. 92-14). 240p. 1992. 46.00 (*1-56677-015-7*) Electrochem Soc.

Landgrebe, John A. Theory & Practice in the Organic Laboratory: With Microscale & Standard Scale Experiments. 4th ed. LC 92-32949. 1993. text ed. 54.95 (*0-534-16854-X*) Brooks-Cole.

Landgren, Signe. New Thinking in Arms Control: Soviet Initiatives & US Responses, 1985-91. (SIPRI Pubns.). 312p. 1995. 45.00 (*0-19-829148-5*) OUP.

— Sufficient Defence? The Post-Soviet States & Security. (SIPRI Publication Ser.). 100p. 1995. pap. 22.00 (*0-19-829167-1*) OUP.

Landham, Sonny. The Total Man. LC 79-11128. 1981. 21.95 (*0-87949-157-4*) Ashley Bks.

Landi, Sheila. The Textile Conservator's Manual. 2nd ed. 368p. 1992. 130.00 (*0-7506-0352-6*) Buttrwrth-Heinemann.

Landies, Douglas C. Sensitive Spots: Nine Drawings. (Illus.). 1978. 3.00 (*0-686-75952-4*) Luna Bisonte.

Landin, Les & Gardner, Mary. Homework Sweet Homework. (YA). 1990. pap. 6.99 (*0-8224-3603-5*) Fearon Teach Aids.

Landin, Les & Thibault, Frank. Creative Chalkboard Activities. (J). (gr. 1-6). 1986. pap. 5.99 (*0-8224-1636-0*) Fearon Teach Aids.

Landin, Leslie. One Hundred Blackboard Games. rev. ed. (gr. 1-6). 1994. pap. 6.99 (*0-86653-919-0*) Fearon Teach Aids.

Landin, Leslie & Meredith, Paul. One Hundred Activities for Gifted Children. 1957. pap. 5.99 (*0-8224-5050-X*) Fearon Teach Aids.

Landing, B. H., et al, eds. Genetic Metabolic Diseases. (Perspectives in Pediatric Pathology Ser.: Vol. 17). (Illus.). xiv, 190p. 1993. 192.00 (*3-8055-5581-4*) S Karger.

Landing, Benjamin H. Factors in the Distribution of Butterfly Color & Behavior Patterns: Selected Aspects. (Illus.). ii, 200p. 1984. 17.95 (*0-911836-13-6*) Entomological Repr.

Landing, Devora. What Can Little Fish Do? (J). 1994. 6.95 (*0-533-08531-4*) Vantage.

Landing, Ed, ed. Dynamic Stratigraphy & Depositional Environments of the Hamilton Group (Middle Devonian) in New York State, Pt. II. (Bulletin Ser.: No. 469). (Illus.). 177p. (Orig.). (C). 1991. pap. text ed. 20. 00 (*1-55557-183-2*) NYS Museum.

— Studies in Stratigraphy & Paleontology in Honor of Donald W. Fisher. (Bulletin Ser.: No. 481). (Illus.). 380p. 1994. 25.00 (*1-55557-196-4*) NYS Museum.

Landini, M. P. Progress in Cytomegalovirus Research. (International Congress Ser.: Vol. 978). 1991. 118.00 (*0-444-89337-7*) Elsevier.

Landini, Michael J., Jr. ADA Source Book: What You Need to Know about the Americans with Disabilities Act: A Guide for Small & Medium Size Business. 70p. 1991. 9.95 (*0-88713-624-9*) Nat Alliance.

Landis. Environmental Toxicology. 1995. 59.95 (*0-87371-515-2*) Lewis Pubs.

Landis, Alison, et al, eds. Immigration & Illegal Aliens: Burden or Blessing? rev. ed. 148p. 1993. pap. text ed. 21.95 (*1-878623-58-3*) Info Plus TX.

Landis, Andy. Social Security, the Inside Story: An Expert Explains Your Rights & Benefits. LC 92-63250. (Illus.). 270p. (Orig.). 1993. pap. 14.95 (*0-931213-09-6*) Mount Vernon Pr.

Landis, Arthur H. Spain, the Unfinished Revolution. LC 75-21091. 463p. reprint ed. pap. 132.00 (*0-7837-0583-2*, 2040927) Bks Demand.

Landis, Benson Y. An Outline of the Bible: Book by Book. (Illus.). 192p. (Orig.). 1971. pap. 12.00 (*0-06-463263-6*, EH 263, Harper Ref) HarpC.

— Professional Codes: A Sociological Analysis to Determine Applications to the Educational Profession. LC 70-176974. (Columbia University. Teachers College. Contributions to Education Ser.: No. 267). reprint ed. 37.50 (*0-404-55267-6*) AMS Pr.

Landis, Bernard. Ego Boundaries. LC 70-138248. (Psychological Issues Monograph: No. 24, Vol. 6, No. 4). 177p. 1970. text ed. 26.00 (*0-8236-1570-7*) Intl Univs Pr.

Landis, Bill. Anger. Date not set. pap. 12.95 (*0-06-092214-1*) HarpC.

— Anger: The Unauthorized Biography of Kenneth Anger. 320p. Date not set. 25.00 (*0-06-016700-9*, HarpT) HarpC.

Landis, Brook I. Value Judgments in Arbitration: A Case Study of Saul Wallen. LC 77-8131. (Cornell Studies in Industrial & Labor Relations: No. 19). 200p. 1977. 10.00 (*0-87546-063-1*) ILR Pr.

Landis, Carney & Bolles, M. Marjorie. Personality & Sexuality in the Physically Handicapped Woman. Phillips, William R. & Rosebberg, Janet, eds. LC 79-6912. (Physically Handicapped in Society Ser.). 1980. reprint ed. lib. bdg. 19.95 (*0-405-13121-6*) Ayer.

Landis, Carney & Page, James D. Modern Society & Mental Disease. Grob, Gerald N., ed. LC 78-22571. (Historical Issues in Mental Health Ser.). (Illus.). 1980. reprint ed. lib. bdg. 18.95 (*0-405-11924-0*) Ayer.

Landis, Carolyn P., jt. auth. see Poage, James.

Landis, Carolyn P., jt. auth. see Rowell, Harry.

Landis, Charles. Twenty-Two Caliber Varmint Rifles. 1991. 32.00 (*0-935632-60-3*) Wolfe Pub Co.

— Woodchucks & Woodchuck Rifle. (Library Classics Ser.). 402p. 1988. reprint ed. 42.00 (*0-935632-62-X*) Wolfe Pub Co.

***Landis, Charles S.** Hunting with the Twenty-Two. 429p. 1993. 45.00 (*1-884849-01-6*) R&R Bks.

Landis, Dennis C. The Literature of the Encounter: A Selection of Books from European Americana. (Illus.). 96p. 1991. pap. 30.00 (*0-916617-36-X*) J C Brown.

Landis, Dennis C., ed. European Americana: A Chronological Guide to Works Printed in Europe Relating to the Americas, 1726-1750, Vol. VI. 852p. 1988. 310.00 (*0-685-45362-6*) Readex Bks.

Landis, Dennis C., jt. auth. see Alden, John.

Landis, Dick, intro. Multichip Module Compendium, 1992, Vol. 3. (Illus.). 427p. 1994. pap. text ed. 35.00 (*1-880433-13-3*) Intl Elect Pack.

— Selections from the I. E. P. S. Conference, 1991. (Illus.). 150p. Date not set. pap. text ed. write for info. (*1-880433-12-5*) Intl Elect Pack.

Landis, Dick & Schmisseur, Edward. Agricultural Database Management. (C). 1985. text ed. 23.95 (*0-8359-9130-X*, Reston); pap. 19.95 (*0-8359-9129-6*, Reston) P-H.

— Spreadsheet Software for Farm Business Management. 1985. pap. text ed. 22.00 (*0-8359-6955-X*, Reston) P-H.

***Landis, Dwight.** Trout Streams of Pennsylvania: An Angler's Guide. 2nd ed. LC 95-75138. (Illus.). 248p. (Orig.). 1995. pap. 18.95 (*1-879475-01-4*) Hempstead-Lyndell.

Landis, Dylan. Checklist for Your New Baby. 112p. (Orig.). 1993. pap. 3.99 (*0-425-13679-5*) Berkley Pub.

— Checklist for Your New Baby: The Indispensable Guide to What to Buy Before Your Baby Arrives. 96p. 1991. pap. 5.95 (*0-399-51657-3*, Perigree Bks) Berkley Pub.

— Your Health & Medical Workbook. 176p. (Orig.). 1995. pap. 9.00 (*0-425-15839-X*, Berkley Trade) Berkley Pub.

— Your Healthy Pregnancy Workbook. 240p. (Orig.). 1995. pap. 12.00 (*0-425-14952-8*, Berkley Trade) Berkley Pub.

Landis, Frederick, illus. The Emperors New Clothes. 52p. (LAT.). (YA). (gr. 9-12). 3.55 (*0-939507-04-8*, B710) Amer Classical.

***Landis, J. D.** Lying in Bed: A Novel. LC 94-43078. 296p. 1995. 19.95 (*1-56512-068-X*) Algonquin Bks.

Landis, James D. The Band Never Dances. LC 88-28401. 288p. (YA). (gr. 7 up). 1989. lib. bdg. 13.89 (*0-06-023722-8*) HarpC Child Bks.

— The Band Never Dances. LC 88-28401. (Trophy Keypoint Bk.). 288p. (YA). (gr. 7 up). 1993. pap. 3.95 (*0-06-447075-X*, Trophy) HarpC Child Bks.

Landis, James M., jt. auth. see Frankfurter, Felix.

Landis, Jean M., jt. auth. see Simon, Rita J.

***Landis, Jill M.** After All. 336p. (Orig.). 1995. pap. text ed. 5.50 (*0-515-11501-0*) Jove Pubns.

— Come Spring. 384p. (Orig.). 1992. mass mkt. 5.50 (*0-515-10861-8*) Jove Pubns.

— Jade. 1991. pap. 5.50 (*0-515-10591-0*) Jove Pubns.

— Past Promises. 1993. mass mkt. 4.99 (*0-515-11207-0*) Jove Pubns.

— Rose. 1990. mass mkt. 5.50 (*0-515-10346-2*) Jove Pubns.

— Sunflower. 1992. mass mkt. 5.50 (*0-515-10659-3*) Jove Pubns.

— Until Tomorrow. 368p. (Orig.). 1994. pap. text ed. 4.99 (*0-515-11403-0*); 159.68 (*0-515-11439-1*); 205.60 (*0-515-11440-5*) Jove Pubns.

— Wild Flower. 1989. mass mkt. 5.50 (*0-515-10102-8*) Jove Pubns.

Landis, Jill M., et al. Sweet Hearts. 320p. (Orig.). 1993. mass mkt. 4.99 (*1-55773-855-6*) Diamond.

Landis, John T. Mayflower Descendants & Their Marriages for Two Generations after the Landing. 37p. 1990. reprint ed. pap. 5.00 (*0-685-60390-3*, 3280) Clearfield Co.

Landis, Joseph C., ed. & tr. Three Great Jewish Plays. 272p. 1986. pap. 8.95 (*0-936839-04-X*) Applause Theatre Bk Pubs.

Landis, Judson R. Sociology: Concepts & Characteristics. 8th ed. 483p. (C). 1992. pap. 30.95 (*0-534-17256-3*) Intl Thomson.

— Sociology: Concepts & Characteristics. 9th ed. LC 94-35558. 1995. pap. 30.95 (*0-534-23754-1*) Intl Thomson.

— Sociology: Concepts & Characteristics. 9th ed. 1995. pap. 30.95 (*0-534-23755-X*) Intl Thomson.

Landis, Judson T., et al. Personal Adjustment, Marriage & Family Living. 6th ed. 1975. text ed. 26.48 (*0-13-657338-X*) P-H.

Landis, Mark. Joseph McCarthy: The Politics of Chaos. LC 85-63422. 176p. 1987. 32.50 (*0-941664-19-8*) Susquehanna U Pr.

Landis, Mary. Anthony Gets Ready for Church. (Jewel Bks.). (J). 1990. pap. 2.15 (*0-317-02906-1*) Rod & Staff.

— God's Wonderful Trees. (Jewel Bks.). (J). 1990. pap. 2.15 (*0-317-02907-X*) Rod & Staff.

— God's Wonderful Water. (Jewel Bks.). (J). 1990. pap. 2.15 (*0-317-02908-8*) Rod & Staff.

— My Thank You Book. (Jewel Bks.). (J). 1990. pap. 2.15 (*0-317-02909-6*) Rod & Staff.

Landis, Mary M. ABC Book of God's Creatures. (Jewel Bks.). 1993. pap. 2.15 (*0-317-05265-9*) Rod & Staff.

— Betty's Secret & Other Stories by Grandmother Lois. 181p. 1972. 5.60 (*0-686-05593-4*) Rod & Staff.

— The Coon Tree Summer: Merry Brook Farm Story. (J). (gr. 5 up). 1978. 9.05 (*0-686-22987-8*) Rod & Staff.

— David & Susan at the Little Green House. 1975. 6.70 (*0-686-11146-X*) Rod & Staff.

— David & Susan at Wild Rose Cottage. 1979. 7.85 (*0-686-22988-6*) Rod & Staff.

— Dear Princess. 1973. 8.00 (*0-317-00267-8*) Rod & Staff.

— God's Gifts. (Jewel Bks.). 1989. pap. 2.15 (*0-317-02024-2*) Rod & Staff.

— Health for the Glory of God. (J). (gr. 4-5). 1976. write for info. (*0-686-15484-3*); teacher ed write for info. (*0-686-15485-1*) Rod & Staff.

— Helping Mother. (Jewel Bks.). 1989. pap. 2.15 (*0-317-02025-0*) Rod & Staff.

— Ice Slide Winter: Merry Brook Farm Story. (J). (gr. 5 up). 1981. 8.50 (*0-686-30772-0*) Rod & Staff.

— Liebe Prinzessiin. (GER.). 1983. pap. 5.05 (*0-318-01333-9*) Rod & Staff.

— The Missing Popcorn & Other Stories. (J). (gr. 3-6). 1976. 6.55 (*0-686-15480-0*) Rod & Staff.

— My Blue Book of God's Different Things. (Jewel Bks.). 1993. pap. 2.15 (*0-317-05267-5*) Rod & Staff.

— My Green Book of God's Different Things. (Jewel Bks.). 1993. pap. 2.15 (*0-317-05268-3*) Rod & Staff.

— Rainbow Promise. 195p. 1992. 7.10 (*0-317-05260-8*) Rod & Staff.

— Summer Days with the Treelo Triplets. 192p. 1971. 7.05 (*0-686-05591-8*) Rod & Staff.

— Trouble at Windy Acres. (J). (gr. 5-10). 1976. 7.15 (*0-686-15486-X*) Rod & Staff.

— Die Truhe im Dachgeschoss. (GER.). 1980. pap. 2.60 (*0-686-32322-X*) Rod & Staff.

Landis, Michael & Moholt, Ray. Patios & Decks: How to Plan, Build & Enjoy. LC 82-84041. (Illus.). 192p. 1983. pap. 12.95 (*0-89586-162-3*) Price Stern.

Landis, Milton W. & Taylor, Carl B. The Early History of Cogan House Township (Lycoming County, Pa.) LC 81-50694. (Illus.). 285p. 1982. pap. 16.50 (*0-9605948-0-9*) C B Taylor.

Landis, Paul. Once Saved, Always Saved: Truth or Delusion? 143p. 1991. pap. 4.05 (*0-317-04649-7*) Rod & Staff.

Landis, Paul, ed. see Browning, Elizabeth Barrett.

Landis, Paul H. Three Iron Mining Towns: A Study in Cultural Change. LC 72-112555. (Rise of Urban America Ser.). 1974. reprint ed. 16.95 (*0-405-02462-2*) Ayer.

— Your Marriage & Family Living. 4th ed. (Illus.). (J). (gr. 10-12). 1976. text ed. 32.00 (*0-07-036187-8*) McGraw.

Landis, Paul M. Keuscheit Im Christlichen Neim. (GER.). 1980. pap. 1.25 (*0-686-32326-2*) Rod & Staff.

— Pureza en el Hogar Cristiano. (SPA.). 1978. pap. 0.65 (*0-686-32330-0*) Rod & Staff.

— Purity in the Christian Home. 1978. 1.40 (*0-686-25260-8*) Rod & Staff.

***Landis, Raymond B.** Studying Engineering: A Road Map to a Successful Career. (C). 1995. pap. text ed. 22.95 (*0-9646969-0-8*) Discover CA.

Landis, Robyn. BodyFueling: The Ground-Breaking Approach to Eating for Health, Energy, Fitness, & Fat Loss. 320p. 1994. 21.95 (*0-446-51767-4*) Warner Bks.

— BodyFueling: The Ground-Breaking Approach to Eating for Health, Energy, Fitness, & Fat Loss. 368p. 1995. mass mkt. 5.99 (*0-446-60194-2*) Warner Bks.

Landis, Scott. Design Book Five. 1990. pap. 19.95 (*0-942391-28-4*) Taunton.

— Design Book, No. 6: Fine Woodworking. 186p. 1992. pap. 25.95 (*1-56158-017-1*) Taunton.

— The Workbench Book. LC 86-51321. (Illus.). 256p. 1987. 34.95 (*0-918804-76-0*) Taunton.

— The Workshop Book. (C). 1991. 34.95 (*0-942391-37-3*) Taunton.

Landis, Scott & Wilson, Edward O., eds. Conservation by Design. (Illus.). 160p. (Orig.). 1993. pap. 30.00 (*0-9638593-0-7*) Woodwrks Alliance.

***Landis, Stephan.** Das Verhaeltnis des Johannesevangeliums zu den Synoptikern: Am Beispiel von Mt. 8, 5-13; Lk. 7, 1-10; Joh. 4, 46-54. (Beihefte zur Zeitschrift fuer die Neutestamentliche Wissenschaft Ser.: Bd. 74). 85p. (GER.). (C). 1994. pap. text ed. 36.95 (*3-11-014389-5*) De Gruyter.

Landis, Susan M. But Why Don't We Go to War? Finding Jesus' Path to Peace. 224p. (Orig.). 1993. pap. 9.95 (*0-8361-3647-0*) Herald Pr.

Landis, Teresa J. Aerobic Exercise for Life. 80p. (C). 1991. pap. text ed. 12.95 (*0-8403-6281-1*) Kendall-Hunt.

Landis, Thomas D. & Nisley, Rebecca G. Container Tree Nursery Manual, Vol. 4: Seedling Nutrition & Irrigation. (Agriculture Handbook Ser.: No. 674). (Illus.). 125p. 1989. per., pap. 15.00 (*0-16-000112-9*, S/N 001-001-006) USGPO.

Landis, Thomas D., jt. ed. see Duryea, Mary L.

Landis, W. G. & Van der Schalie, W. H., eds. Aquatic Toxicology & Risk Assessment, Vol. 13. (Special Technical Publication Ser.: No. 1096). (Illus.). 380p. 1990. text ed. 86.00 (*0-8031-1460-5*, 04-010960-16) ASTM.

Landis, Wayne G., et al, eds. Environmental Toxicology & Risk Assessment, STP 1179. LC 92-46581. (Special Technical Publication Ser.: No. STP 1179). (Illus.). 240p. 1993. 92.00 (*0-8031-1860-0*, 04-011790-16) ASTM.

Landkof, N. S. Foundations of Modern Potential Theory. Doohovskoy, A. P., tr. LC 77-186131. (Grundlehren der Mathematischen Wissenschaften Ser.: Vol. 180). 440p. 1973. 65.00 (*0-387-05394-8*) Spr-Verlag.

Landman, jt. auth. see Danzi.

Landman, Annlee. Learning to Quilt the Traditional Way. LC 93-40986. (Illus.). 128p. 1994. 19.95 (*0-8069-0629-4*) Sterling.

Landman, Fred. Structures for Semantics. 384p. (C). 1991. lib. bdg. 129.00 (*0-7923-1239-2*) Kluwer Ac.

Landman, Hedy, ed. see Preisner, Olga K.

Landman, Hedy B. Chinese Jade Carvings from the Collection of Dr. & Mrs. Harold L. Tonkin: Exhibition Catalogue. (Illus.). 48p. 1983. pap. 6.75 (*0-911209-28-X*) Palmer Mus Art.

— Selection IV: Glass from the Museum's Collection. LC 73-94132. (Illus.). 144p. 1974. 6.50 (*0-911517-36-7*) Mus of Art RI.

Landman, Hedy B., jt. auth. see Preisner, Olga K.

Landman, Janet. Regret. 320p. 1993. 25.00 (*0-19-507178-6*) OUP.

Landman, Jessica. A Citizen's Handbook on Water Quality Standards. 1987. 4.00 (*0-318-23632-X*) NRDC Newsletter.

Landman, Jessica, jt. auth. see Adler, Robert.

Landman, L., ed. Messianism in the Talmudic Era. 59.50 (*0-87068-445-0*) Ktav.

Landman, Leo, ed. Scholars & Scholarship: The Interaction Between Judaism & Other Cultures. 1991. 25.00 (*0-88125-344-8*) Ktav.

Landman, N. H., jt. ed. see Saunders, W. B.

Landman, Ruth & Halpern, Katherine S., eds. Applied Anthropologist & Public Servant: The Life & Work of Philleo Nash. 1989. 7.50 (*0-913167-28-2*) Am Anthro Assn.

Landman, Ruth H. Creating Community in the City: Cooperatives & Community Gardens in Washington, D. C. LC 92-42899. (Contemporary Urban Studies). 168p. 1993. text ed. 45.00 (*0-89789-316-6*, H316, Bergin & Garvey) Greenwood.

Landman, T. & Veltman, F., eds. Varieties of Formal Semantics: Proceedings of the 4th Amsterdam Colloquium. (Groningen-Amsterdam Studies in Semantics). xii, 425p. 1985. pap. 75.40 (*90-6765-007-2*) Mouton.

Landman, Uzi, ed. Aspects of the Kinetics & Dynamics of Surface Reactions. LC 80-68004. (AIP Conference Proceedings Ser.: No. 61). 343p. 1980. lib. bdg. 22.25 (*0-88318-160-6*) Am Inst Physics.

***Landmann, Eric & Hynek, Don.** Climber's Guide to Gibraltar Rock. 2nd ed. (Illus.). 64p. 1993. pap. text ed. write for info. (*0-9619571-5-8*) Granite WI.

Landmann, Eric, jt. auth. see Hynek, Don.

***Landmann, G. & Bonneau, M., eds.** Forest Decline & Atmospheric Deposition Effects in the Mountains of France. LC 95-6104. 1995. write for info. (*3-540-58874-4*) Spr-Verlag.

Landmann, Michael. Fundamental Anthropology. Parent, David J., ed. & tr. by. (Current Continental Research Ser.: No. 403). 354p. (Orig.). 1985. lib. bdg. 52.50 (*0-8191-4842-3*); pap. text ed. 32.00 (*0-8191-4843-1*) U Pr of Amer.

— Philosophische Anthropologie: Menschliche Selbstdeutung in Geschichte und Gegenwart. 5th ed. (Sammlung Goeschen Ser.: Vol. 2201). 228p. (C). 1976. pap. 12.95 (*3-11-002739-9*) De Gruyter.

— Philosophische Anthropologie: Menschliche Selbstdeutung in Geschichte und Gegenwart. 5th ed. (Sammlung Goeschen Ser.: Vol. 2201). 228p. (C). 1976. pap. 12.95 (*3-11-008997-1*) De Gruyter.

— Reform of the Hebrew Alphabet. Parent, David J., tr. LC 76-14595. (Illinois Language & Culture Ser.: Vol. 1). 345p. reprint ed. pap. 98.40 (*0-317-09443-2*, 2013715) Bks Demand.

Landmark, B. Arctic Communications: Proceedings of the 8th Meeting Agard Ionospheric Research Comm Athens 7-63. LC 64-17190. (Agardograph Ser.: No. 78). 1964. 131.00 (*0-08-010828-8*, Pub. by Pergamon Repr UK) Franklin.

Landmesser, Lynn T., ed. The Assembly of the Nervous System. 1989. text ed. 171.95 (*0-471-56232-7*) Wiley.

Lando, Gail & Sandness, Grace, eds. Pearls of Great Price: Writings of Southeast Asians. (Illus.). 80p. 1985. pap. 6.95 (*0-931323-03-7*) Mini-World Pubns.

Lando, Gail, ed. see Cherne, Jacqolyn.

Lando, Miriam. Funny Friday. 176p. (J). 1992. write for info. (*0-318-69354-2*) CIS Comm.

Lando, Ole & Beale, Hugh, eds. The Principles of European Contract Law: Prepared by the Commission on European Contract Law, Chairman, Ole Lando. LC 94-21316. 1994. lib. bdg. 153.00 (*0-7923-2957-0*) Kluwer Ac.

Landolfi, Tommaso. An Autumn Story. Neugroschel, Joachim, tr. LC 88-83031. 145p. 1989. 20.00 (*0-941419-27-4*, Eridanos Library); pap. 11.00 (*0-941419-26-6*, Eridanos Library) Marsilio Pubs.

— Gogol's Wife & Other Stories. LC 63-21382. 1963. pap. 8.95 (*0-8112-0080-9*, NDP155) New Directions.

Landolphi, Suzi. Hot, Sexy & Safer. 176p. (Orig.). 1994. pap. 12.00 (*0-399-51882-7*, Perigee Bks) Berkley Pub.

Landolt, A. M., ed. Complications in Neurosurgery I. (Progress in Neurological Surgery Ser.: Vol. 11). (Illus.). x, 174p. 1984. 78.50 (*3-8055-3691-7*) S Karger.

— Intensive Care & Monitoring of the Neurosurgical Patient. (Progress in Neurological Surgery Ser.: Vol. 12). (Illus.). xiv, 202p. 1987. 106.50 (*3-8055-4414-6*) S Karger.

Landolt, A. M., et al, eds. Advances in Pituitary Adenoma Research: Proceedings of the 4th European Workshop on Pituitary Adenomas, University of Zurich-Irchel, Zurich, Switzerland, September 13-16, 1987. (Advances in the Biosciences Ser.: Vol. 69). 500p. 1988. 110.00 (*0-08-035596-X*, Pergamon Pr) Elsevier.

Landolt, C., ed. The Paul E. Queneau International Symposium-Extractive Metallurgy of Copper, Nickel & Cobalt: Copper & Nickel Smelter Operations, Vol. 2. (Illus.). 416p. 1993. 68.00 (*0-87339-219-1*, 452) Minerals Metals.

Landolt, C., jt. ed. see Tyroler, G.

Landolt, C. A., ed. see Metallurgical Society of AIME Staff.

Landolt, E. A Manual of Examination of the Eyes. LC 78-20773. (Classics in Ophthalmology Ser.). 328p. 1979. reprint ed. lib. bdg. 31.50 (*0-88275-843-8*) Krieger.

Landolt, R., ed. Aktuelle Probleme der Paediatrischen Hepatologie. (Paediatrische Fortbildungskurse fuer die Praxis Ser.: Band 44). (Illus.). 1977. 76.00 (*3-8055-2662-8*) S Karger.

Landolt, Robert G. The Mexican-American Workers of San Antonio, Texas. Cortes, Carlos E., ed. LC 76-1291. (Chicano Heritage Ser.). (Illus.). 1977. 33.95 (*0-405-09509-0*) Ayer.

Landon, Alicia. The Worm Queen: Memoirs of Santa Ynez Valley. LC 91-29351. (Illus.). 112p. (Orig.). 1992. pap. 9.95 (*1-56474-006-4*) Fithian Pr.

Landon, B. A. & Goodall, J. D. An Atlas of Trauma Management: The First Hour. (Encyclopedia of Visual Medicine Ser.). (Illus.). 100p. 1993. 70.00 (*1-85070-411-2*) Prthnon Pub.

Landon, Brooks. The Aesthetics of Ambivalence: Rethinking Science Fiction Film in the Age of Electronic (Re) Production. LC 92-4048. (Contributions to the Study of Science Fiction & Fantasy Ser.: No. 52). 224p. 1992. text ed. 49.95 (*0-313-25687-X*, LAA/, Greenwood Pr) Greenwood.

— Thomas Berger. (United States Authors Ser.: No. 550). 200p. 1989. text ed. 21.95 (*0-8057-7540-4*, TUSAS 550, Pub. by Royal Botanic Garden UK) Macmillan.

Landon, Donald L. Country Lawyers: The Impact of Context on Professional Practice. LC 89-16220. 192p. 1990. text ed. 49.95 (*0-275-93042-4*, C3042, Praeger Pubs) Greenwood.

Landon, H. C. Beethoven: His Life, Work & World. LC 92-64271. (Illus.). 248p. 1993. 40.00 (*0-500-01540-6*) Thames Hudson.

— Haydn at Eszterhaza 1766-1790. LC 94-61475. (Haydn: Chronicle & Works). (Illus.). 819p. 1995. 100.00 (*0-500-01168-0*) Thames Hudson.

— Haydn: The Early Years 1732-1765. LC 94-61473. (Haydn: Chronicle & Works). (Illus.). 676p. 1995. 100.00 (*0-500-01169-9*) Thames Hudson.

— Haydn: The Late Years 1801-1809. LC 94-61478. (Haydn: Chronicle & Works). (Illus.). 523p. 1995. 100.00 (*0-500-01167-2*) Thames Hudson.

— Haydn: The Years of "The Creation" 1796-1800. LC 94-61477. (Haydn: Chronicle & Works). (Illus.). 676p. 1995. 100.00 (*0-500-01166-4*) Thames Hudson.

— Haydn: Chronicle & Works. Incl. Vol. V. Haydn: The Late Years 1801-1809. LC 76-14630. (Illus.). 496p. 1977. 70.00 (*0-253-37005-1*); LC 76-14630. write for info. (*0-318-53523-8*) Ind U Pr.

— Haydn in England 1791-1795. LC 94-61476. (Haydn: Chronicle & Works). (Illus.). 667p. 1995. 100.00 (*0-500-01164-8*) Thames Hudson.

— Mozart: The Golden Years. 256p. 1989. write for info. (*0-318-66745-2*) Macmillan.

— Mozart: The Golden Years. 271p. 1989. text ed. 29.95 (*0-02-872025-3*) Schirmer Bks.

— Mozart & Vienna. 208p. 1991. text ed. 22.50 (*0-02-871317-6*) Schirmer Bks.

— Mozart & Vienna. 208p. 1994. pap. 12.00 (*0-02-872026-1*) Schirmer Bks.

— The Mozart Essays. LC 94-61396. (Illus.). 240p. 1995. 29.95 (*0-500-01653-4*) Thames Hudson.

— Seventeen Ninety-One: Mozart's Last Year. LC 88-3169. (Illus.). 256p. 1988. 19.95 (*0-02-872592-1*) Macmillan.

— Seventeen Ninety-One: Mozart's Last Year. (Illus.). 240p. 1990. pap. 13.95 (*0-02-871315-X*) Schirmer Bks.

— Vivaldi. LC 93-60428. (Illus.). 240p. 1993. 24.95 (*0-500-01576-7*) Thames Hudson.

Landon, H. C., ed. The Mozart Compendium. (Illus.). 452p. 1990. text ed. 34.95 (*0-02-871321-4*) Schirmer Bks.

Landon, H. C. & Norwich, John J. Five Centuries of Music in Venice. 200p. 1991. text ed. 29.95 (*0-02-871318-4*) Schirmer Bks.

Landon, H. C. & Wyn Jones, David. Haydn: His Life & Music. LC 88-2685. (Illus.). 384p. 1988. 45.00 (*0-253-37265-8*) Ind U Pr.

Landon, Harold R., ed. Reinhold Niebuhr: A Prophetic Voice in Our Time. (Essay Index Reprint Ser.). 1977. reprint ed. 13.95 (*0-518-10150-9*) Ayer.

Landon, Harry F. History of the North Country, 3 vols., Set. 1993. reprint ed. lib. bdg. 225.00 (*0-7812-5188-5*) Rprt Serv.

Landon, Howard C. & Mitchell, Donald, eds. The Mozart Companion. LC 81-4227. (Illus.). xv, 397p. 1981. reprint ed. text ed. 35.00 (*0-313-23084-6*, LAMC, Greenwood Pr) Greenwood.

***Landon, J. & Chard, T., eds.** Therapeutic Antibodies. LC 94-38225. (Illus.). 240p. 1994. text ed. 98.00 (*0-387-19722-2*) Spr-Verlag.

Landon, J. R., ed. Booker Tropical Soil Manual: A Handbook for Soil Survey & Agricultural Land Evaluation in the Tropics & Sub-Tropics. 474p. 1991. pap. text ed. 67.95 (*0-470-21713-8*) Halsted Pr.

Landon, James O. Landon Genealogy. Boardman Genealogy. 383p. 1993. reprint ed. lib. bdg. 69.50 (*0-8328-2986-2*); reprint ed. pap. 59.50 (*0-8328-2987-0*) Higginson Bk Co.

Landon, John C., jt. ed. see Erwin, J.

Landon, John W. Behold the Mighty Wurlitzer: The History of the Theatre Pipe Organ. LC 83-5557. (Contributions to the Study of Popular Culture Ser.: No. 6). xv, 231p. 1983. text ed. 55.00 (*0-313-23827-8*, LPO/, Greenwood Pr) Greenwood.

— The Development of Social Welfare. LC 85-14254. 210p. 1985. 34.95 (*0-89885-258-7*) Human Sci Pr.

Landon, Joseph W. Clinical Practice in Music Education. (Contemporary Music Education Ser.). (Illus.). 128p. (Orig.). 1988. pap. 8.95 (*0-943988-03-9*, 943E) Music Educ Pubns.

— How to Write Learning Activity Packages for Music Education. (Contemporary Music Education Ser.). (Illus.). 109p. (Orig.). 1973. reprint ed. pap. 6.95 (*0-930424-01-8*) Music Educ Pubns.

— Leadership for Learning in Music Education. LC 75-305303. (Contemporary Music Education Ser.). 306p. (Orig.). 1975. reprint ed. pap. 12.95 (*0-943988-02-0*) Music Educ Pubns.

— Music Lab. (Mini-Modular Series in Music Education). (Illus.). 182p. (Orig.). (J). (gr. 3-8). 1982. pap. 14.95 (*0-943988-00-4*) Music Educ Pubns.

Landon, Joyce & Norman, Gene. Electronic Mail: A Guide to Electronic Communications. (Electronic Mail Ser.). (Illus.). 100p. 1987. pap. 12.95 (*0-939303-01-9*) Educ Lrn Syst.

Landon, Kenneth P., Jr. God of Glory: The Promise of Relationship. 1000p. (Orig.). 1992. pap. 24.95 (*1-877607-50-9*) Redeemer Bks.

Landon, Kenneth P. Siam in Transition: A Brief Survey of Cultural Trends in the Five Years Since the Revolution of 1932. LC 68-57615. (Illus.). 328p. 1969. reprint ed. text ed. 38.50 (*0-8371-0521-8*, LASI, Greenwood Pr) Greenwood.

Landon, Letitia. Fate of Adelaide. LC 90-8961. 204p. 1990. reprint ed. 50.00 (*0-8201-1447-2*) Schol Facsimiles.

— Poetical Works of Letitia Elizabeth Landon "L. E. L." LC 90-8789. 1990. 75.00 (*0-8201-1443-X*) Schol Facsimiles.

Landon, Letitia E. Ethel Churchill. LC 92-16474. 1992. 90.00 (*0-8201-1464-2*) Schol Facsimiles.

Landon, Linda L. Earth Angel Child: You May Be One. (Illus.). (Orig.). (J). (gr. 3 up). 1992. pap. 8.80 (*0-9633759-0-3*) Harmony Hill.

Landon, Lucinda. Meg MacKintosh & the Case of the Curious Whale Watch. (Illus.). 48p. (J). (gr. 2-5). 1987. 14.95 (*0-316-51362-8*, Joy St Bks) Little.

— Meg MacKintosh & the Case of the Missing Babe Ruth Baseball: A Solve-It-Yourself Mystery. LC 85-20055. (Illus.). 48p. (J). (gr. 2-5). 1986. 14.95 (*0-316-51318-0*, 513180, Joy St Bks) Little.

— Meg Mackintosh & the Mystery at the Medieval Castle. (J). (ps-3). 1993. mass mkt. 4.95 (*0-316-51376-8*) Little.

— Meg MacKintosh & the Mystery in the Locked Library: A Solve-It-Yourself Mystery. LC 92-19948. (J). 1993. 14.95 (*0-316-51374-1*, Joy St Bks) Little.

Landon, Margaret. Anna & the King of Siam. 360p. 1990. reprint ed. lib. bdg. 25.95 (*0-89966-753-8*) Buccaneer Bks.

Landon, Michael de L. Erin & Britannia: The Historical Background to a Modern Tragedy. LC 79-27005. (Illus.). 288p. (C). 1981. text ed. 27.95 (*0-88229-643-4*) Nelson-Hall.

Landon, P. Nepal, 2 vols., Set. (C). 1988. 500.00 (*0-7855-0061-8*, Pub. by Print Hse II) St Mut.

Landon, Perceval. Nepal, 2 vols., Set. 1993. 223.00 (*0-7855-0263-7*, Pub. by Ratna Pustak Bhandar) St Mut.

— Nepal, 2 vols., Set. (C). 1993. reprint ed. text ed. 70.00 (*81-206-0723-6*, Pub. by Asian Educ Servs II) S Asia.

— The Opening of Tibet: An Account of Lhasa & the Country & People of Central Tibet & of the Mission Sent There by the English Government in the 1903-1904. 1990. reprint ed. 68.50 (*81-85326-26-6*, Pub. by Vintage II) S Asia.

Landon, Perceval, ed. Nepal, 2 vols., Set. 358p. (C). 1987. 600.00 (*0-89771-068-1*, Pub. by Ratna Pustak Bhandar) St Mut.

Landon, Randy J. Amy. LC 85-63064. (Illus.). 44p. 1986. 12.00 (*0-936563-07-9*); pap. 4.50 (*0-936563-08-7*) Signpost.

Landon, Richard, ed. Editing & Editors: A Retrospective: Papers Given at the Twenty-First Annual Conference on Editorial Problems, University of Toronto, 1-2 November, 1985. LC 87-45816. (Conference on Editorial Problems Ser.: No. 21). 1987. 37.50 (*0-404-63671-3*) AMS Pr.

— Editing Editord: A Retrospective: Papers Given at the Twenty-First Annual Conference on Editorial Problems, University of Toronto, 1-2 Novmeber, 1985. (Conference on Editorial Problems Ser.: No. 21). 1988. 37.50 (*0-318-36026-8*) AMS Pr.

Landon, Robbins H. & Chapman, Roger. Studies in Eighteenth Century Music: A Tribute to Karl Geiringer on His 70th Birthday. (Music Reprint Ser.). 1979. reprint ed. lib. bdg. 49.50 (*0-306-79519-1*) Da Capo.

Landon, Robert P. Basic Surveying for Technicians. 299p. 1994. text ed. 39.95 (*0-8273-3941-0*) Delmar.

— Practical Surveying for Technicians: Instructor's Guide. 36p. 1994. 12.00 (*0-8273-3942-9*) Delmar.

***Landon, Susan M., ed.** Interior Rift Basins. (AAPG Memoir Ser.: No. 59). (Illus.). xi, 276p. 1994. 105.00 (*0-89181-339-X*) AAPG.

Landon, Will. Glacier Panorama. (Illus.). 160p. 1992. 50.00 (*1-56044-114-3*) Falcon Pr MT.

Landon, William, jt. auth. see Frazee, Irving A.

Landone, B. Do Four Things Now: The Way to a New Life Beyond Your Dreams. 1991. lib. bdg. 98.99 (*0-8490-5132-0*) Gordon Pr.

— How to Change Any Habit. (Self-Help Ser.). 1991. lib. bdg. 79.75 (*0-8490-4289-5*) Gordon Pr.

— How to Turn Your Desires & Ideals into Realities. (Self-Help Ser.). 1991. lib. bdg. 79.75 (*0-8490-4290-9*) Gordon Pr.

— The Means Which Guarantee Leadership: How to Become a Leader. 1991. lib. bdg. 79.95 (*0-8490-4993-8*) Gordon Pr.

— Your Electronic Body: The Electronic Potentials of Food. (Alternative Medicine Ser.). 1991. lib. bdg. 79.95 (*0-8490-4300-X*) Gordon Pr.

— Your Path Direct to the Goal You Desire. (Self-Help Ser.). 1991. lib. bdg. 75.00 (*0-8490-4292-5*) Gordon Pr.

Landone, Brown. The A-B-C of Truth. 98p. 1926. reprint ed. spiral bd. 4.40 (*0-7873-1108-1*) Mokelumne.

— Basic Vivid Thinking. 63p. 1966. reprint ed. spiral bd. 5.50 (*0-7873-1254-1*) Mokelumne.

— Beginning Youth. 62p. 1966. reprint ed. spiral bd. 5.50 (*0-7873-1130-8*) Mokelumne.

— Body Purification. 69p. 1994. reprint ed. spiral bd. 5.50 (*0-7873-1132-4*) Mokelumne.

— Body Purification: How to Transform Your Body. 1992. lib. bdg. 79.95 (*0-8490-5278-5*) Gordon Pr.

— The Breath of Youth. 75p. 1966. reprint ed. spiral bd. 4.40 (*0-7873-1147-2*) Mokelumne.

— The Christ Men Can Follow. 24p. 1966. reprint ed. spiral bd. 2.20 (*0-7873-1255-X*) Mokelumne.

— Deep, Deep Down in Your Heart. 249p. 1971. reprint ed. spiral bd. 8.80 (*0-7873-1251-7*) Mokelumne.

— Do Four Things Now. 528p. 1967. reprint ed. spiral bd. 16.50 (*0-7873-1253-3*) Mokelumne.

— Greater Spiritual Responsiveness of Body & Awakening the Brain of Spirit, Pt. 1. 150p. (Orig.). 1994. reprint ed. spiral bd. 8.80 (*0-7873-1105-7*) Mokelumne.

— Hope & Certainty. 36p. 1994. reprint ed. spiral bd. 2.75 (*0-7873-1181-2*) Mokelumne.

— How to Change Any Habit: A Course of 8 Lessons. 50p. 1966. reprint ed. spiral bd. 5.50 (*0-7873-1071-9*) Mokelumne.

— How to Turn Your Desires & Ideals into Realities. 159p. 1994. reprint ed. spiral bd. 4.40 (*0-7873-1185-5*) Mokelumne.

— I Reveal, the Landone Epistles. 138p. 1974. reprint ed. spiral bd. 11.00 (*0-7873-0524-3*) Mokelumne.

— Landone Assorted Titles, No. 1. 40p. 1968. reprint ed. spiral bd. 4.40 (*0-7873-1249-5*) Mokelumne.

— Landone Assorted Titles, No. 2. 35p. 1994. reprint ed. spiral bd. 3.30 (*0-7873-1043-3*) Mokelumne.

— Landone Assorted Titles, No. 3. 64p. 1994. reprint ed. spiral bd. 3.30 (*0-7873-1042-5*) Mokelumne.

— Landone Menus for Thirty One Days. 40p. 1994. reprint ed. spiral bd. 4.40 (*0-7873-1101-4*) Mokelumne.

— The Means Which Guarantee Leadership. 299p. 1976. reprint ed. spiral bd. 13.75 (*0-7873-0530-8*) Mokelumne.

— The Methods of Truth Which I Use. 102p. 1971. reprint ed. spiral bd. 4.95 (*0-7873-0528-6*) Mokelumne.

— Mysterious Catalytic Foods. 63p. 1994. reprint ed. spiral bd. 7.15 (*0-7873-1033-6*) Mokelumne.

— Powers That Turn Failure Into Success. 73p. 1985. reprint ed. spiral bd. 8.80 (*0-7873-1250-9*) Mokelumne.

— Proof of Proofs, They Live. 149p. 1972. reprint ed. spiral bd. 6.60 (*0-7873-0526-X*) Mokelumne.

— Prophecies of Melchi-Zedek in the Great Pyramid & the Seven Temples. 179p. 1970. reprint ed. spiral bd. 8.80 (*0-7873-0523-5*) Mokelumne.

— Sexual Revelations of the Bible. 260p. 1972. reprint ed. spiral bd. 11.00 (*0-7873-0527-8*) Mokelumne.

— Soul Catalysts & How to Use Them. 62p. 1971. reprint ed. spiral bd. 3.30 (*0-7873-1044-1*) Mokelumne.

— Spiritual Revelations of the Bible. 259p. (Orig.). 1972. reprint ed. spiral bd. 11.00 (*0-7873-1097-2*) Mokelumne.

— The Success Process. 233p. 1981. 12.00 (*0-89540-181-9*, SB-181) Sun Pub.

— Transformation of Your Life in Twenty-Four Hours. 16p. 1976. reprint ed. spiral bd. 3.30 (*0-7873-0531-6*) Mokelumne.

— Truth & Its Magnificent Simplicity. 62p. 1994. reprint ed. spiral bd. 5.50 (*0-7873-1086-7*) Mokelumne.

— Unconsciously Freeing the Body: (A Course of 16 Lessons) 36p. 1966. reprint ed. spiral bd. 5.50 (*0-7873-0525-1*) Mokelumne.

— Unknown Powers. 17p. 1994. reprint ed. spiral bd. 4.40 (*0-7873-1252-5*) Mokelumne.

— Your Ears: Reactivating Them. 28p. 1976. reprint ed. spiral bd. 5.50 (*0-7873-0532-4*) Mokelumne.

— Your Electronic Body & Electronic Potentials of Food. 249p. 1966. reprint ed. spiral bd. 19.25 (*0-7873-1072-7*) Mokelumne.

— Your Eyes - Rejuvenating Them. 47p. reprint ed. spiral bd. 5.50 (*0-7873-1074-3*) Mokelumne.

— Your Path Direct to the Goal You Desire. 518p. 1968. reprint ed. spiral bd. 22.00 (*0-7873-0529-4*) Mokelumne.

Landone Foundation Staff. He Lives. 127p. 1994. reprint ed. spiral bd. 4.40 (*0-7873-1013-1*) Mokelumne.

Landor, A. H. Tibet & Nepal Painted & Described. (C). 1994. 48.50 (*81-206-0852-6*, Pub. by Asian Educ Servs II) S Asia.

Landor, Gina & Cleaver, Paul. How to Play the Penny Whistle. (Illus.). 40p. 1980. pap. 4.95 (*0-86001-780-X*, AM27137) Music Sales.

Landor, John. Clio Chirugica: The Stomach. (Surgery Ser.). (Illus.). 350p. 1984. 65.00 (*0-941432-10-6*); pap. 35.00 (*0-941432-11-4*) R G Landes.

Landor, Lynn. Children's Own Stories: A Literature-Based Language Arts Program. (Illus.). 118p. 1990. pap. 20.00 (*0-936434-25-2*, Pub. by Zellerbach Fam Fund) SF Study Ctr.

Landor, Walter S. Citation & Examination of William Shakespeare. LC 73-16141. (Studies in Shakespeare: No. 24). 1974. reprint ed. lib. bdg. 59.95 (*0-8383-1721-9*) M S G Haskell Hse.

— Complete Works, 16 vols., Set. (BCL1-PR English Literature Ser.). 1992. reprint ed. lib. bdg. 1,440.00 (*0-7812-7587-3*) Rprt Serv.

— Gebir. LC 93-17427. 92p. 1993. reprint ed. 40.00 (*1-85477-128-0*, Pub. by Woodstock Bks UK) Cassell.

— Imaginary Conversations; Poems, Dialogues in Verse, & Epigrams, Longer Prose Works, 10 Vols, Set. Crump, Charles G., ed. LC 70-171652. (Illus.). 4126p. 1983. reprint ed. 675.00 (*0-404-07680-7*) AMS Pr.

— Poetry & Prose. LC 76-29435. reprint ed. 24.50 (*0-404-15314-3*) AMS Pr.

— Selected Imaginary Conversations of Literary Men & Statesmen. Proudfit, Charles L., ed. LC 69-10272. 302p. reprint ed. pap. 86.10 (*0-7837-6030-2*, 2045842) Bks Demand.

Landorf, Joyce. He Began with Eve. large type ed. (Large Print Inspirational Ser.). 1985. pap. 11.95 (*0-8027-2511-2*) Walker & Co.

— I Came to Love You Late. 192p. 1981. pap. 4.99 (*0-8007-8411-1*) Revell.

— Irregular People. large type ed. 1986. pap. 10.95 (*0-8027-2525-2*) Walker & Co.

— Mourning Song. LC 74-9938. 192p. 1974. 14.99 (*0-8007-0680-3*) Revell.

— Pros & Contras Liberacion de la Mujer: To Lib or Not to Lib. (SPA.). 2.95 (*84-7228-258-9*, 220725, Pub. by Edit Clie SP) TSELF.

Landow, Gayle, ed. see Anderson, G. Elaine.

Landow, George P. Elegant Jeremiahs: The Sage from Carlyle to Mailer. LC 86-47644. 184p. 1986. 25.95 (*0-8014-1905-0*) Cornell U Pr.

— Hypertext: The Convergence of Contemporary Critical Theory & Technology. LC 91-20068. (Parallax: Re-Visions of Culture & Society Ser.). (Illus.). 240p. 1991. text ed. 48.50 (*0-8018-4280-8*); pap. text ed. 15.95 (*0-8018-4281-6*) Johns Hopkins.

Landow, George P., ed. Hyper-Text-Theory. 377p. 1994. text ed. 38.50 (*0-8018-4837-7*); pap. text ed. 16.95 (*0-8018-4838-5*) Johns Hopkins.

Landow, George P. & Delany, Paul, eds. The Digital Word: Text-Based Computing in the Humanities. LC 92-33742. (Technical Communication & Information Systems Ser.). (Illus.). 366p. 1993. 42.50 (*0-262-12176-X*) MIT Pr.

Landow, George P., jt. auth. see Delany, Paul.

Landow, R. Kenneth. Handbook of Dermatologic Treatment. LC 83-80541. 219p. 1983. pap. text ed. 14.95 (*0-930010-09-4*) Jones Med.

Landowska, Wanda. Music of the Past. 185p. 1990. reprint ed. lib. bdg. 59.00 (*0-7812-9012-0*) Rprt Serv.

An Asterisk (*) at the beginning of an entry indicates that the title is appearing in BIP for the first time.

— Music of the Past. LC 75-181199. 184p. 1924. reprint ed. 39.00 (*0-403-01609-6*) Scholarly.

Landphair, H. C. & Klatt, F. Landscape Architecture Construction. 2nd ed. 448p. 1987. 48.25 (*0-444-01286-9*) P-H.

Landphair, H. C. & Motloch, J. L. Site Reconnaissance & Engineering: An Introduction for Architects, Landscape Architects & Planners. xxi, 300p. 1985. 45.00 (*0-444-00900-0*) P-H.

Landphair, Ted, jt. auth. see Highsmith, Carol M.

Landre, Debra. Explorations in Statistics & Probability. 288p. (C). 1992. pap. text ed. 14.95 (*0-8403-8099-2*) Kendall-Hunt.

Landre, Debra A. Explorations in College Algebra. 224p. 1992. per. 14.95 (*0-8403-7925-0*) Kendall-Hunt.

— Explorations in Elementary Algebra. 256p. (C). 1992. pap. text ed. 14.95 (*0-8403-7601-4*) Kendall-Hunt.

— Explorations in Intermediate Algebra. 288p. (C). 1992. pap. text ed. 14.95 (*0-8403-7844-0*) Kendall-Hunt.

Landreau, Anthony N. & Pickering, W. R. From the Bosporus to Samarkand: Flat-Woven Rugs. LC 71-81238. (Illus.). 1969. pap. 15.00 (*0-87405-001-4*) Textile Mus.

Landreau, Anthony N. & Yohe, Ralph S. Flowers of the Yayla: Yoruk Weaving of the Toros Mountains. LC 83-51062. (Illus.). 112p. 1983. pap. 27.50 (*0-295-96982-2*) U of Wash Pr.

Landreau, Anthony N., et al. Flowers of the Yayla: Yoruk Weaving of the Toros Mountains. LC 83-51062. (Illus.). 112p. 1983. pap. 18.50 (*0-87405-021-9*) Textile Mus.

Landregan, Steve. Speak Lord! Reflections on the Ordination Rite for Deacons. 52p. (Orig.). 1987. pap. 2.95 (*1-55586-150-4*) US Catholic.

Landreneau, Raymond L., Jr. The Cajun French Language, Vol. I. LC 89-71246. 112p. 1990. pap. 19.95 (*0-913845-03-5*) Chicot Pr.

Landres, Miriam D., ed. see Kabaker, Betty.

Landreth, Bill. The Bank Secrecy Act: Exemption Regulations Clarified. Zimmerman, Carolyn, ed. LC 88-70571. (Orig.). 1988. pap. 10.00 (*0-317-91177-5*) Amherst Ent.

— Out of the Inner Circle: The True Story of a Computer Intruder Capable of Cracking the Nation's Most Secure Computer Systems. LC 84-25402. 240p. 1989. reprint ed. pap. 9.95 (*1-55615-223-X*, Tempus Bks) Microsoft.

Landreth, Frank, ed. see Talania, Frank.

Landreth, Frank, ed. see Talania, Franquintin.

Landreth, Garry, jt. auth. see Berg, Robert.

***Landreth, Garry L.** Play Therapy: Dynamics of the Process of Counseling with Children. 380p. 1982. pap. 31.95 (*0-398-06221-8*) C C Thomas.

— Play Therapy: Dynamics of the Process of Counseling with Children. 380p. (C). 1982. 53.95x (*0-398-04716-2*) C C Thomas.

— Play Therapy: The Art of the Relationship. LC 91-70335. xviii, 382p. 1991. 32.95 (*1-55959-017-3*) Accel Devel.

Landreth, Jane. Gems of Nature. 161p. 1994. pap. text ed. 5.25 (*1-885022-01-8*) Precious Gems.

— Gems of the Home. 151p. 1994. pap. text ed. 5.25 (*1-885022-02-6*) Precious Gems.

— Magnify the Lord. 20p. 1994. 1.25 (*1-885022-00-X*) Precious Gems.

Landreth, Marsha. A Clinic for Murder. LC 93-1440. (Dr. Sam Turner Mystery Ser.). 1993. 19.95 (*0-8027-3241-0*) Walker & Co.

— French Creek. LC 92-3227. 1992. 16.95 (*0-87131-696-X*) M Evans.

— The Holiday Murders. LC 92-14826. 243p. 1992. 19.95 (*0-8027-1246-0*) Walker & Co.

— Vial Murders. LC 94-16398. (Doctor Samantha Turner Mystery Ser.). 1994. 19.95 (*0-8027-3199-6*) Walker & Co.

— William T. Sherman. 1994. 8.98 (*0-681-45386-9*) Longmeadow Pr.

Landreth, Oliver L. European Corporate Strategy: Heading for Two Thousand. LC 91-42563. 204p. 1992. text ed. 69.95 (*0-312-07916-8*) St Martin.

Landreth, Patrick, jt. auth. see Linehan, Patricia.

Landrey, David, ed. see Oppenheimer, Joel.

Landrey, Wanda. Outlaws in the Big Thicket. 1979. pap. 12.95 (*0-89015-144-X*) Sunbelt Media.

Landrey, Wanda A. Boardin' in the Thicket: Reminiscences & Recipes of Early Big Thicket Boarding Houses. LC 89-24868. (Illus.). 200p. 1989. 19.95 (*0-929398-07-6*) UNTX Pr.

Landrigan, Philip J. & Kazemi, Homayoun, eds. The Third Wave of Asbestos Disease, Exposure to Asbestos in Place: Public Health Control. LC 92-6138. (Annals Ser.: Vol. 643). 628p. 1992. pap. 190.00 (*0-89766-678-X*, Q11) NY Acad Sci.

Landrigan, Philip J., jt. auth. see Needleman, Herbert L.

Landrine, Hope. The Politics of Madness: A Theory of the Function of Madness in a Stratified Society. LC 91-16889. (American University Studies: Psychology: Ser. VIII, Vol. 22). 217p. 1992. 44.95 (*0-8204-1571-5*) P Lang Pubs.

Landrith, Thomas A. Preface & Other Poems. 1994. 12.95 (*0-533-10999-X*) Vantage.

Landrock, Arthur H. Adhesives Technology Handbook. LC 85-15329. (Illus.). 444p. 1986. 64.00 (*0-8155-1040-3*) Noyes.

***Landrock, Arthur H., ed.** Handbook of Plastic Foams. LC 94-15236. (Illus.). 488p. 1995. 84.00 (*0-8155-1357-7*) Noyes.

***Landrum, et al.** Outcome Oriented Rehabilitation: Principles, Strategies & Tools for Effective Program Management. 256p. 1995. 52.00 (*0-8342-0665-X*) Aspen Pub.

***Landrum, Carl.** Gem City: A Pictorial History. (Illinois Pictorial History Ser.). (Illus.). 1992. write for info. (*0-943963-26-5*) G Bradley.

Landrum, Gene N. Profiles of Female Genius: Thirteen Creative Women Who Changed the World. (Illus.). 437p. (C). 1994. 24.95 (*0-87975-892-9*) Prometheus Bks.

— Profiles of Genius: Thirteen Creative Men Who Changed the World. 263p. (C). 1993. 23.95 (*0-87975-832-5*) Prometheus Bks.

Landrum, Graham. The Famous D. A. R. Murder Mystery. 208p. 1992. 18.95 (*0-312-06968-5*, Pub. by Thomas Dunne Bks) St Martin.

— The Famous Dar Murder Mystery. large type ed. LC 92-14498. 292p. 1992. reprint ed. lib. bdg. 19.95 (*1-56054-444-9*) Thorndike Pr.

— The Rotary Club Murder Mystery. 224p. 1993. 17.95 (*0-312-09375-6*, Pub. by Thomas Dunne Bks) St Martin.

— The Sensational Music Club Mystery tc. large type ed. LC 95-2758. 250p. 1995. 20.95 (*0-7838-1278-7*) Hall.

Landrum, J. B. History of Spartanburg County (South Carolina), Embracing an Account of Many Important Events, & Biographical Sketches of Statesmen, Divines & Other Public Men & the Names of Many Others Worthy of Record in the History of Their County. (Illus.). 789p. 1991. reprint ed. pap. text ed. 43.00 (*1-55613-514-9*) Heritage Bk.

Landrum, Jeff. Reflections of a Boomtown: A Photographic Essay of the Burkburnett Oil Boom 1912-1982. (Illus.). 1982. 24.95 (*0-9611894-0-1*) J Landrum Pub.

***Landrum, John.** Colonial & Revolutionary History of Upper South Carolina. LC 61-1396. (Illus.). 376p. 1995. 35.00 (*0-87152-001-X*) Reprint.

— History of Spartanburg County. LC 77-13343. (Illus.). 800p. 1995. reprint ed. 45.00 (*0-87152-255-1*) Reprint.

Landrum, John F. Out of Court: How to Protect Your Business from Litigation. 160p. 1992. pap. 14.95 (*0-9633730-9-9*) Headwaters LA.

Landrum, L. R. Campomanesia et al (Myrtaceae) (Flora Neotropica Monograph: No. 45). (Illus.). 180p. 1986. pap. text ed. 35.50 (*0-89327-301-5*) NY Botanical.

Landrum, L. Wayne. Biscayne: The Story Behind the Scenery. (Illus.). 48p. 1990. pap. 6.95 (*0-88714-048-3*) KC Pubns.

Landrum, Larry, et al, eds. Dimensions of Detective Criticism. LC 76-14646. 1976. 16.95 (*0-87972-123-5*); pap. 9.95 (*0-87972-124-3*) Bowling Green Univ.

Landrum, Leslie R. The Life & Botanical Accomplishments of Boris Alexander Krukoff. LC 86-838. (Advances in Economic Botany Ser.: Vol. 2). (Illus.). 96p. (Orig.). 1986. pap. 17.50 (*0-89327-298-1*) NY Botanical.

— Myrceugenia (Myrtaceae) LC 81-11282. (Flora Neotropica Monograph Ser.: No. 29). (Illus.). 137p. 1981. pap. 20.00 (*0-89327-236-1*) NY Botanical.

Landrum, Lester C. Get What's Rightfully Yours or How Not to Get Stiffed by Those Dead Checks. (Illus.). 60p. 1986. pap. 14.95 (*0-910531-11-0*) Wolcotts.

Landrum, Michael. Alternative Dispute Resolution: How to Prepare the Case & Represent Your Client. 1988. audio 150.00 (*1-55917-009-3*); vhs 750.00 (*1-55917-010-7*) Natl Prac Inst.

Landrum, Phil, jt. auth. see Huggins, Kevin.

***Landrum, R. Eric.** Intro to Psychology. 192p. (C). 1994. pap. text ed., ring bd. 19.95 (*0-8403-9938-3*) Kendall-Hunt.

Landry, Alma. Psychic Development. 1992. 12.95 (*0-533-09646-4*) Vantage.

Landry, Anne G. Represented Discourse in the Novels of Francois Mauriac: Catholic University of America. LC 70-128933. (Studies in Romance Languages & Literatures: No. 44). reprint ed. 37.50 (*0-404-50344-6*) AMS Pr.

Landry, Anthony J., jt. auth. see Nardo, Valentino W.

Landry, Bart. The New Black Middle Class. 1987. 35.00 (*0-520-05942-5*); pap. 113.00 (*0-520-06465-8*) U CA Pr.

***Landry, Bernard.** A Phylogenetic Analysis of the Major Lineages of the Crambinae & of the Genera of Crambini of North America (Lepidoptera: Pyralidae) Gupta, Virendra K., ed. (Memoirs on Entomology, International Ser.: Vol. 56). (Illus.). 248p. 1995. 45.00x (*1-56665-056-9*) Assoc Pubs FL.

Landry, Donna. The Muses of Resistance: Laboring-Class Women's Poetry in Britain 1739-1796. (Illus.). 320p. (C). 1990. 64.95 (*0-521-37412-X*) Cambridge U Pr.

Landry, Donna & Maclean, Gerald. Materialist Feminisms. LC 92-45623. 280p. 1993. 49.95 (*1-55786-184-6*); pap. 19.95 (*1-55786-185-4*) Blackwell Pubs.

Landry, Donna, ed. see Spivak, Gayatri C.

Landry, Dorothy B. Family Fallout: A Handbook for Families of Adult Sexual Abuse Survivors. (Safer Society Ser.: No. 8). 76p. 1991. pap. 12.95 (*1-884444-05-9*) Safer Soc.

Landry, Ed. Caribbean Adventures: Classic Cajun Cooking & Tales from the Reign of the Pirates. (Illus.). 128p. 1994. pap. 11.95 (*0-9630244-1-8*) Adlai Hse.

Landry, Elaine M., et al. Curriculum for Negotiation & Conflict Management: Instructor's Manual. 524p. (C). 1991. 35.00 (*1-880711-01-X*) Prog Negot HLS.

Landry, Garrie, jt. auth. see Reese, William D.

Landry, Gordon. The Mortality of Man. 51p. (Orig.). 1990. pap. text ed. 2.95 (*0-945517-11-4*) Ministry Schl Pubns.

Landry, Greg & Landry, Nancy, eds. Directory of Newsletters Related to Health, Medicine, Nutrition, & Sports. 48p. (Orig.). 1988. write for info. (*0-929363-00-0*) FIT Pub.

Landry, Gregory L. AIDS in Sport. 32p. 1989. pap. (*0-88011-353-7*, PLAN0353) Human Kinetics.

Landry, Hilton. Interpretations in Shakespeare's Sonnets. LC 76-1901. (Perspectives in Criticism Ser.: No. 14). (Illus.). 185p. 1976. reprint ed. text ed. 65.00 (*0-8371-8749-4*, LAIS, Greenwood Pr) Greenwood.

Landry, Hilton, et al. A Concordance to the Poems of Hart Crane. LC 72-10663. (Concordances Ser.: No. 4). 1973. 20.00 (*0-8108-0564-2*) Scarecrow.

Landry, Hilton J., ed. New Essays on Shakespeare's Sonnets. LC 71-16167. (Studies in the Renaissance: No. 1). 1976. 34.50 (*0-404-09028-1*) AMS Pr.

Landry, J., jt. auth. see Fontenot, M. A.

Landry, Janice L. & Fesmire, Anna H. Explorations: Travel Geography & Destination Study. LC 93-42293. 352p. 1994. pap. text ed. 39.60 (*0-13-203647-9*) P-H Gen Ref & Trav.

Landry, Judith, tr. see Nodier, Charles.

Landry, Julie. A Christmas for Carol. 16p. (Orig.). 1991. pap. 2.50 (*0-88680-360-8*) I E Clark.

Landry, Juliette, ed. see Mooney, Blake.

Landry, M. R. & Hickey, B. M., eds. Coastal Oceanography of Washington & Oregon. (Oceanography Ser.: No. 47). 607p. 1989. 177.25 (*0-444-87308-2*) Elsevier.

Landry, Margie & Boulet, Ann, eds. Down the Bayou Cookbook: A Collection of Favarite Cajun Recipes. (Illus.). 256p. 1989. reprint ed. 12.95 (*0-9613375-0-8*) Larose Civic.

Landry, Mim J. Understanding Drugs of Abuse: The Process of Addiction, Treatment & Recovery. LC 93-26208. 400p. 1993. 21.95 (*0-88048-533-7*) Am Psychiatric.

Landry, Nancy, jt. ed. see Landry, Greg.

Landry, Paul. Kept in the Pocket of My Poems. 1993. pap. 3.00 (*0-929730-46-1*) Zeitgeist Pr.

Landry, Paul & McNair, Mattie. The Outward Bound Canoeing Handbook. (Illus.). 224p. 1992. pap. 12.95 (*1-55821-149-7*) Lyons & Burford.

***Landry, Pierre B. & Champ, Claire, eds.** Canadian Art Vol. II (G-K) Catalogue of the National Gallery of Canada. 416p. 1995. pap. 74.95 (*0-88884-638-X*) U Ch Pr.

Landry, Pierre B., jt. auth. see Hill, Charles C.

Landry, Roger. Hot Prospects. 1990. pap. 12.95 (*0-446-39129-8*) Warner Bks.

Landry, Sarah. Field Guide to Fishes Coloring Book. (J). 1987. pap. 5.95 (*0-395-44095-5*) HM.

Landry, Sarah, illus. & text. Peterson First Guide to Urban Wildlife. LC 93-31279. 1994. pap. 4.95 (*0-395-67069-1*) HM.

Landry, Terri. Kevin Graham's Fish & Seafood Cookbook: Body Conscious Cuisine. LC 93-17374. 208p. 1993. 35.00 (*1-55670-265-5*) Stewart Tabori & Chang.

Landry, Tom. The Ballad of Tont Lala. deluxe ed. (Illus.). 32p. (J). (gr. k-8). 6.00 (*0-931108-11-X*) Little Cajun Bks.

Landry, Tom & Lewis, Gregg. Tom Landry. 304p. 1991. mass mkt. 5.50 (*0-06-104057-6*, Harp PBks) HarpC.

— Tom Landry. large type ed. (Illus.). 336p. 1991. reprint ed. pap. 15.95 (*0-8027-2659-3*) Walker & Co.

Landry, William F. Crime Prevention 101: An Expert's Own Unique Crime Prevention How-to's Made Simple for Your Everyday Use. (Illus.). 256p. (Orig.). 1992. pap. 25.00 (*0-9624810-9-2*) Royal Heart Pub.

— Crime-Safety Made Easy: How to "Non-Violently" Safeguard Yourself, Your Loved Ones, Your Possessions, & Where You Live. (Illus.). 254p. (Orig.). 1989. pap. text ed. 19.95 (*0-9624810-0-9*) Royal Heart Pub.

***Lands, Lark.** Positively Well: Living with HIV As a Chronic, Manageable, Survivable Disease. 650p. (Orig.). 1995. pap. 24.95 (*0-8290-5200-3*) Irvington.

Lands, Merrilee, ed. Mayi: Some Bush Fruits of Dampeirland. (C). 1990. 30.00 (*0-685-52929-0*, Pub. by Pascoe Pub AT) St Mut.

***Lands, Neil.** Dordogne. (Visitors Guides Ser.). (Illus.). 256p. (Orig.). 1990. pap. 13.95 (*0-8169-0505-3*) Hunter NJ.

Lands, W. E., ed. Polyunsaturated Fatty Acids & Eicosanoids. 592p. 1987. 40.00 (*0-935315-15-2*) AOCS Pr.

Lands, William E. Fish & Human Health. 1986. text ed. 60.00 (*0-12-435645-1*) Acad Pr.

Lands, William E., ed. Biochemistry of Arachidonic Acid Metabolism. LC 85-4853. (Prostaglandins, Leukotrienes, & Cancer Ser.). 1985. lib. bdg. 118.00 (*0-89838-717-5*) Kluwer Ac.

Lands, William E., jt. ed. see Colowick, Sidney P.

Landsbaum, Jerome B. Measuring & Motivating Maintenance Programs. 1992. text ed. 37.80 (*0-13-567827-7*) P-H.

Landsberg, H. E., ed. Advances in Geophysics, Vol. 26. (Serial Publication Ser.). 1984. text ed. 142.00 (*0-12-018826-0*) Acad Pr.

— Advances in Geophysics, Vols. 1-17. Incl. Vol. 12. 1967. (*0-12-018812-0*); write for info. (*0-318-50185-6*) Acad Pr.

— General Climatology. (World Survey of Climatology Ser.: Vol. 3). 408p. 1981. 164.00 (*0-444-41776-1*) Elsevier.

Landsberg, H. E. & Wallen, C. C., eds. Climates of Central & Southern Europe. (World Survey of Climatology Ser.: Vol. 6). 1977. 146.25 (*0-444-41336-7*) Elsevier.

Landsberg, H. E., ed. see Flohn, H.

Landsberg, H. H., jt. auth. see Clawson, M.

Landsberg, Hans H. Natural Resources for U. S. Growth: A Look Ahead to the Year 2000. LC 64-24348. 269p. reprint ed. pap. 76.70 (*0-7837-3120-5*, 2042867) Bks Demand.

Landsberg, Hans H., ed. High Energy Costs, Assessing the Burden: Proceedings of a Conference Organized by Resources for the Future & the Brookings Institution, October 9-10, 1980, Washington, D. C. LC 82-48020. 406p. 1982. 27.95 (*0-8018-2921-6*) Resources Future.

Landsberg, Hans H. & Dukert, Joseph M. High Energy Costs: Uneven, Unfair, Unavoidable? LC 81-15648. 104p. 1981. pap. 9.95 (*0-8018-2782-5*) Resources Future.

Landsberg, Hans H., jt. auth. see Barger, Harold.

Landsberg, Hans H., jt. auth. see Netschert, Bruce C.

Landsberg, Hans H., jt. ed. see Olson, Mancur, Jr.

Landsberg, Hans H., et al. Energy & the Social Sciences: An Examination of Research Needs. LC 74-16949. (Resources for the Future, RFF Working Papers: EN-3). 786p. reprint ed. pap. 180.00 (*0-317-26469-9*, 2023804) Bks Demand.

— Resources in America's Future: Patterns of Requirements & Availabilities 1960-2000. LC 62-7233. 1017p. 1963. 50.00 (*0-8018-0357-8*) Resources Future.

Landsberg, Helmut. The Urban Climate. LC 80-2766. (International Geophysics Ser.). 1981. text ed. 65.00 (*0-12-435960-4*) Acad Pr.

Landsberg, J. J. Physiological Ecology of Forest Production. (Applied Botany & Crop Science Ser.). 1986. text ed. 103.00 (*0-12-435965-5*) Acad Pr.

Landsberg, J. J., jt. ed. see Pereira, J. S.

Landsberg, Marge E. The Genesis of Language & Speech: A Different Judgement of Evidence. xiv, 278p. (C). 1988. lib. bdg. 90.75 (*0-89925-370-9*) Mouton.

Landsberg, Melvin. Dos Passos Path to U. S. A. A Political Biography, 1912-1936. LC 72-75880. (Illus.). 304p. reprint ed. pap. 86.70 (*0-8357-9058-4*, 2012202) Bks Demand.

— John Dos Passos' Correspondence with Arthur E. McComb. (Illus.). 312p. 1991. text ed. 39.95 (*0-87081-137-1*) Univ Pr Colo.

Landsberg, P. T., ed. The Enigma of Time: A Selection of Thought-Provoking Articles. (Illus.). 260p. 1983. pap. 24.90 (*0-85274-547-8*) IOP Pub.

Landsberg, Paul-Louis. The Experience of Death: The Moral Problem of Suicide. Kastenbaum, Robert, ed. LC 76-19579. (Death & Dying Ser.). 1979. reprint ed. lib. bdg. 21.95 (*0-405-09576-7*) Ayer.

Landsberg, Peter T. Recombination in Semiconductors. (Illus.). 600p. (C). 1992. 180.00 (*0-521-36122-2*) Cambridge U Pr.

Landsberg, Peter T. & Moss, T. S., eds. Basic Properties of Semiconductors. LC 92-32392. (Handbook On Semiconductors Ser.: Vol. 1). write for info. (*0-444-88855-1*, North Holland) Elsevier.

— Basic Properties of Semiconductors, Set. write for info. (*0-318-70113-8*, North Holland) Elsevier.

Landsberg, Peter T. & Willoughby, A. F, eds. Recombination in Semiconductors: Selected Proceedings of the International Conference Held at the University of Southampton, England. 30 August - 1st September 1978. 1979. pap. 63.00 (*0-08-024226-X*, Pergamon Pr) Elsevier.

Landsberg, Peter T., jt. auth. see IUPAC Staff.

Landsberg, Steven E. Price Theory & Applications. 2nd ed. 736p. (C). 1992. text ed. 56.00 (*0-03-072252-7*) Dryden Pr.

Landsberger, Benno. Die Fauna des alten Mesopotamien nach der 14. LC 78-72747. (Ancient Mesopotamian Texts & Studies). reprint ed. 34.50 (*0-404-18190-2*) AMS Pr.

Landsberger, Frank R., jt. ed. see Scanu, Angelo M.

Landsberger, Kurt. William Steinitz, Chess Champion: A Biography of the Bohemian Caesar. LC 92-50376. 539p. 1992. lib. bdg. 49.50 (*0-89950-758-1*) McFarland & Co.

***Landsberger, Stefan L.** Chinese Propaganda Posters: From Revolution to Modernization. (Illus.). 204p. 1995. 85.00 (*1-56324-688-0*) M E Sharpe.

Landsbergis, Algirdas. The Last Picnic. 1977. pap. 4.00 (*0-87141-051-6*) Manyland.

***Landsburg, Stephen E.** Armchair Economist: Economics & Everyday Life. 1995. pap. 12.00 (*0-02-917776-6*) Free Pr.

Landsburg, Steven E. The Armchair Economist: The Economics of Everyday Experience. 260p. 1993. text ed. 22.95 (*0-02-917775-8*) Free Pr.

— Instructor's Manual with Transparency Masters to Accompany Price Theory & Applications. 2nd ed. 263p. (C). 1992. teacher ed, pap. text ed. 6.75 (*0-03-072253-5*) Dryden Pr.

— Price Theory & Application. LC 88-18071. (Illus.). 672p. (C). 1989. text ed. 56.25 (*0-03-020589-1*) Dryden Pr.

— Price Theory & Applications. 3rd ed. LC 94-32600. 600p. 1994. text ed. 60.25 (*0-314-04059-5*) West Pub.

Landscape Architecture Magazine Editors. Home Landscape, 1982. (Illus.). 1983. pap. 7.95 (*0-07-036194-0*) McGraw.

Landscape Architecture Magazine Staff. Profiles in Landscape Architecture. 104p. 1992. 16.95 (*0-941236-18-8*) Am Landscape Arch.

***Landsdown & Walker.** Your Child's Development. 1994. pap. 7.99 (*0-517-09503-3*) Random.

Landsdowne, ed. see Petty, William.

Landshoff, D. I., jt. auth. see Eden, Richard.

Landshoff, Ludwig. Johann Rudolf Zumsteeg (1760-1802) 215p. reprint ed. write for info. (*0-318-71923-1*, Pub. by Georg Olms GW) Lubrecht & Cramer.

Landshut, Siegfried. The Jewish Communities in the Muslim Countries of the Middle East. LC 75-6443. (Rise of Jewish Nationalism & the Middle East Ser.). 102p. 1976. reprint ed. 15.00 (*0-88355-330-9*) Hyperion Conn.

— Politisches Woerterbuch. (GER.). 1958. pap. 75.00 (*0-8288-6852-2*, M-7589) Fr & Eur.

Landskron, Jerry. Remington Rolling Block Pistols. LC 81-50481. (Illus.). 304p. 1981. 34.95 (*0-940028-01-8*) Rolling Block.

— Remington Rolling Block Pistols. deluxe ed. LC 81-50481. (Illus.). 304p. 1981. 39.95 (*0-940028-00-X*) Rolling Block.

Landsman, Julie. Basic Needs: A Year with Street Kids in a City School. LC 93-16148. 200p. (Orig.). 1993. pap. 12.95 (*0-915943-65-4*) Milkweed Ed.

— From Darkness to Light: Teens Write about How They Triumphed over Trouble. (YA). 1994. pap. 8.95 (*0-925190-36-5*) Fairview Press.

An Asterisk (*) at the beginning of an entry indicates that the title is appearing in BIP for the first time.

— Tips for Creating a Manageable Classroom: Understanding Your Students' Basic Needs. LC 94-31920. 1994. pap. 3.50 (*1-57131-200-5*) Milkweed Ed.

Landsman, Michael. Attitude of a Servant: Servant Heart - A Sign of Strength & Inner Peace Like Jesus. 1991. 3.50 (*0-88270-700-0*) Bridge Pub.

— Lord, Increase Our Faith. 186p. (Orig.). 1994. pap. 5.95 (*0-88270-718-3*) Bridge Pub.

— Supportive Ministries. 32p. 1992. pap. 2.45 (*0-88270-702-7*) Bridge Pub.

Landsman, Miriam J., jt. auth. see Nelson, Kristine E.

Landsman, Ned. Scotland & Its First American Colony, 1683-1760. LC 84-42891. (Illus.). 352p. 1985. text ed. 55.00 (*0-691-04724-3*) Princeton U Pr.

Landsman, Sandra G. Found: A Place for Me: The Development, Diagnosis & Treatment of Manic-Depressive Structure. (Illus.). xvi, 149p. (Orig.). 1985. pap. text ed. 14.95 (*0-935571-01-9*) Treehouse.

— I'm Special: An Experiential Workbook for the Child in Us All. (J). (gr. k up). 1986. pap. 6.95 (*0-935571-02-7*) Treehouse.

Landsman, Stephan A. Adversarial Justice: The American Approach to Adjudication. (American Casebook Ser.). 217p. (C). 1990. reprint ed. pap. text ed. 18.50 (*0-314-36115-4*) West Pub.

Landsman, Susan. A History Mystery: What Happened to Amelia Earhart? 96p. (Orig.). (J). 1991. pap. 3.50 (*0-380-76221-8*, Camelot) Avon.

— A History Mystery: Who Shot JFK? 96p. (Orig.). (YA). 1992. pap. 3.50 (*0-380-77063-6*, Camelot) Avon.

— Survival! In the Desert. 112p. (Orig.). (J). 1993. pap. 3.50 (*0-380-76601-9*, Camelot) Avon.

— Survival! In the Jungle. 112p. (Orig.). (YA). 1993. pap. 3.50 (*0-380-76605-1*, Camelot) Avon.

— Survival! at Sea. 112p. (Orig.). 1993. pap. 3.50 (*0-380-76603-5*, Camelot) Avon.

Landsman, Ted, jt. auth. see Jourard, Sidney M.

Landsman, Wayne R., jt. auth. see Beaver, William H.

Landsmann, Liliana T., ed. Advances in Infancy Research, Vol. 7. LC 90-49579. 213p. 1991. 65.00 (*0-89391-666-8*, RJ131, CRC Reprint) Franklin.

Landsmann, Liliana T. & Strauss, Sidney, eds. Culture, Schooling, & Psychological Development. (Human Development Ser.: Vol. 4). 224p. (C). 1991. text ed. 49.50 (*0-89391-529-7*) Ablex Pub.

Landsness, Ruthanne N., tr. see Paulus, Trina.

Landstone, Hetty, tr. see Schnitzler, Arthur.

Landstorfer, F. M. & Sacher, R. R. Optimisation of Wire Antennas. LC 84-27750. (Antenna Ser.). 174p. 1985. text ed. 180.00 (*0-471-90716-2*) Wiley.

Landstrom, Elsie H. Friends, Let Us Pray. LC 79-146679. (Orig.). 1970. pap. 3.00 (*0-87574-174-6*) Pendle Hill.

Landstrom, Elsie H., ed. Hyla Doc in Africa: 1950-1961. LC 93-6280. (Illus.). 104p. (Orig.). 1994. pap. 10.50 (*0-936609-32-X*) QED Ft Bragg.

Landstrom, Elsie H., ed. see Watters, Hyla S.

Landstrom, Lena, jt. auth. see Landstrom, Olof.

Landstrom, Olof & Landstrom, Lena. Will Gets a Haircut. LC 93-660. (Illus.). (J). 1993. reprint ed. 13.00 (*91-29-62075-9*, Pub. by R & S Bks) FS&G.

— Will Goes to the Beach. Wiberg, Carla, tr. (Illus.). 32p. (J). Date not set. 13.00 (*91-29-62914-4*) FS&G.

— Will Goes to the Post Office. (Illus.). 32p. (J). 1994. 13.00 (*91-29-62950-0*) FS&G.

— Will's New Cap. Fisher, Richard E., tr. 32p. (J). (ps-2). 1992. 13.00 (*91-29-62062-7*, Pub. by R & S Bks) FS&G.

Landsverk, Helen P., jt. auth. see Wardian, Jeanne F.

Landsverk, O. G. Runic Records of the Norsemen in America. (Library of Scandinavian Literature). 1974. lib. bdg. 39.50 (*0-8057-5457-1*) Irvington.

Landt, Dennis. Santa Fe. 1987. 35.00 (*0-917001-06-0*) Herring Pr.

Landtman, Gunnar. The Folk-Tales of the Kiwai Papuans. LC 78-63204. (Folktale Ser.). 1980. reprint ed. 42.50 (*0-404-16139-1*) AMS Pr.

— The Origin of the Inequality of the Social Classes. LC 75-100511. reprint ed. 37.50 (*0-404-00623-X*) AMS Pr.

— Origin of the Inequality of the Social Classes. LC 68-56332. (Illus.). 444p. 1969. reprint ed. text ed. 75.00 (*0-8371-0522-6*, LASC, Greenwood Pr) Greenwood.

Landua, R., et al, eds. Medium-Energy Antiprotons & the Quark-Gluon Structure of Hadrons. (Ettore Majorana International Science Series, Life Sciences: Vol. 58). (Illus.). 248p. 1992. 79.50 (*0-306-44087-3*, Plenum Pr) Plenum.

Landucci, Luca. Florentine Diary from Fourteen Fifteen to Fifteen Forty-Two. LC 76-88827. (Art Histories Collection Ser.). (Illus.). reprint ed. 23.50 (*0-405-02225-5*) Ayer.

— A Florentine Diary from Fourteen Fifty to Fifteen Sixteen. Rosen Jervis, Alice De, tr. LC 75-169766. (Select Bibliographies Reprint Ser.). 1977. reprint ed. 25.95 (*0-8369-5986-8*) Ayer.

Landva, Arvid & Knowles, G. David. Geotechnics of Waste Fills: Theory & Practices. LC 90-44937. (Special Technical Publication Ser.: No. 1070). (Illus.). 370p. 1990. text ed. 45.00 (*0-8031-1285-8*, 04-010700-38) ASTM.

Landvater, Darryl V. MRP II Standard System - A Handbook for Manufacturing Software Survival. LC 88-50484. 250p. 1993. LC 88-050484. student ed, pap. 67.50 (*0-939246-13-9*) Oliver Wight.

— Planning & Control in the Age of Lean Production. LC 93-60674. 200p. 1995. 75.00 (*0-939246-40-6*, Pub. by Pitman Pubng UK) St Mut.

— World Class Production & Inventory Management. LC 92-61829. 280p. 1993. 114.00 (*0-939246-19-8*, TM7525) Oliver Wight.

Landvater, Darryl V. & Gray, Christopher D. MRP II Standard System - A Handbook for Manufacturing Software Survival. LC 88-50485. 350p. 1993. LC 88-050485. 201.00 (*0-939246-12-0*) Oliver Wight.

***Landvik, Lorna.** Patty Jane's House of Curl: A Novel. 256p. 1995. 19.95 (*1-882593-12-X*) Bridge Wrks.

Landweber, Lawrence H., jt. auth. see Brainerd, Walter S.

Landweber, Peter S., tr. see Hirzebruch, Friedrich, et al.

Landwehr, B. J., jt. auth. see Hart, J. Dennis.

Landwehr, Bernard J. Basic Business Statistics. LC 84-26195. 246p. (C). 1985. lib. bdg. 24.50 (*0-89874-823-2*) Krieger.

Landwehr, Carl E., ed. Database Security: Status & Prospects. 330p. 1988. 77.00 (*0-444-70479-5*, North Holland) Elsevier.

— Database Security, Vol. 2 - Status & Prospects: Results of the IFIP WG11.3 Workshop, Kingston, Ontario, Canada, 5-7 October 1988. 282p. 1989. 72.00 (*0-444-87483-6*, North Holland) Elsevier.

Landwehr, Carl E., et al, eds. Dependable Computing for Critical Applications 3. LC 93-9046. (Dependable Computing & Fault-Tolerant Systems Ser.: Vol. 8). (Illus.). xii, 382p. 1993. 139.00 (*0-387-82481-2*) Spr-Verlag.

Landwehr, Carl E & Jajodia, Sushil, eds. Database Security, Vol. V: Status & Prospects, Results of the IFIP WG 11.3 Workshop on Database Security, Shepherdstown, West Virginia, U. S. A., 4-7 November, 1991. LC 92-10324. (IFIP Transactions A: Computer Science & Technology Ser.: Vol. A-6). 1992. write for info. (*0-444-89518-3*, North Holland) Elsevier.

Landwehr, Carl E., jt. ed. see Jajodia, Sushil.

Landwehr, Carl E., jt. ed. see Keefe, Thomas F.

Landwehr, Carl E., jt. ed. see Spooner, D. L.

Landwehr, G., ed. Application of High Magnetic Fields in Semiconductor Physics: Proceedings, Grenoble, France, 1982. (Lecture Notes in Physics Ser.: Vol. 177). 552p. 1983. pap. 49.00 (*0-387-11996-5*) Spr-Verlag.

— High Magnetic Fields in Semiconductor Physics. (Solid-State Sciences Ser.: Vol. 71). (Illus.). 560p. 1987. 77.00 (*0-387-17872-4*) Spr-Verlag.

— High Magnetic Fields in Semiconductor Physics II. (Solid-State Sciences Ser.: Vol. 87). (Illus.). 648p. 1989. 95.00 (*0-387-51227-6*) Spr-Verlag.

Landwehr, G. & Rashba, E. I., eds. Landau Level Spectroscopy, 2 pts., Pt. 1. 1300p. 1990. 283.00 (*0-444-88535-8*, North Holland) Elsevier.

— Landau Level Spectroscopy, 2 pts., Pt. 2. 1300p. 1990. 283.00 (*0-444-88873-X*, North Holland) Elsevier.

— Landau Level Spectroscopy, 2 pts., Set. 1300p. 1990. 511.50 (*0-444-88874-8*, North Holland) Elsevier.

Landwehr, G., et al, eds. High Magnetic Fields in Semiconductor Physics Three: Quantum Hall Effect, Transport & Optics - Proceedings at the International Conference, Wurzburg, FRG, July 30 to August 3, 1990. (Solid-State Sciences Ser.: Vol. 101). (Illus.). 744p. 1992. 113.00 (*0-387-53618-3*) Spr-Verlag.

***Landwehr, James M. & Watkins, Ann E.** Exploring Data: Student. rev. ed. (Quantitative Literacy Ser.). (Illus.). 181p. 1994. teacher ed 15.95 (*0-614-01250-3*); pap. text ed. 10.50 (*0-86651-610-7*) Seymour Pubns.

Landwehr, John. Splendid Ceremonies: State Entries & Royal Funerals in the Low Countries, 1515-1791--A Bibliography. (Illus.). 350p. 1971. text ed. 87.50 (*90-6004-287-5*, Pub. by B De Graaf NE) Coronet Bks.

Landwehr, K., ed. Ecological Perception Research, Visual Communication, & Aesthetics. (Recent Research in Psychology Ser.). viii, 143p. 1990. pap. 31.00 (*0-387-52200-X*) Spr-Verlag.

Landwehr, M. & Southwestern Legal Foundation Staff. Oil & Gas Accounting. 1978. Looseleaf updates avail. write for info. (*0-8205-1659-7*) Bender.

Landwehr, Richard. Fighting for Freedom: The Ukrainian Volunteer Division of the Waffen-SS. (Illus.). 224p. 1985. 24.95 (*0-918184-05-3*) Bibliophile.

— Romanian Volunteers of the Waffen-SS 1944-1945. (Eastern Front Battle Ser.). (Illus.). 148p. 1991. 20.00 (*0-918184-08-8*) Bibliophile.

Landwehr, Sheldon, ed. see Landwehr, Sheldon, & Associates Staff.

Landwehr, Sheldon, & Associates Staff. Who's Who in America's Restaurants: New York & Eastern States Limited, 1983 - 1984. Landwehr, Sheldon, ed. LC 82-645944. (Illus.). 272p. 1983. 129.50 (*0-910297-01-0*); pap. 14.95 (*0-910297-02-9*) Whos Who Rest.

— Who's Who in America's Restaurants 1985. Landwehr, Sheldon, ed. LC 82-645944. (Illus.). 435p. 1984. 49.95 (*0-910297-03-7*); pap. 14.95 (*0-910297-04-5*) Whos Who Rest.

— Who's Who in America's Restaurants 1986-1987. LC 82-645944. (Illus.). 401p. 1985. 49.95 (*0-910297-05-3*); pap. 14.95 (*0-910297-06-1*) Whos Who Rest.

Landwehr, William C. Watercolor U. S. A. 1986: The Monumental Image. LC 86-61583. (Illus.). 80p. (Orig.). 1986. pap. text ed. 15.00 (*0-934306-06-0*) Springfield.

Landwehr, William C., ed. see Albin, Edgar A., et al.

Landy, Alice S. The Heath Introduction to Literature. 3rd ed. LC 87-80091. 1085p. (C). 1988. pap. text ed. 12.00 (*0-669-14809-1*); Instr.'s guide. teacher ed 2.00 (*0-669-14810-5*) Heath.

— The Heath Introduction to Literature. 4th ed. 1142p. (C). 1992. pap. text ed. write for info. (*0-669-24409-0*); Instr.'s ed. teacher ed write for info. (*0-669-24410-4*) Heath.

— To Read a Poem. 348p. 1979. pap. text ed. 11.50 (*0-669-01535-0*) Heath.

Landy, Alice S. & Sommer, Robert F. Heath Literature for Composition. LC 89-84719. 990p. (C). 1990. pap. text ed. 12.50 (*0-669-20884-1*); Instr.'s guide. teacher ed 2.00 (*0-669-24535-6*) Heath.

Landy, Edward, et al, eds. Guidance in American Education, 3 vols., 1. LC 64-54998. 1990. pap. 3.95 (*0-674-36500-3*) HUP.

— Guidance in American Education, 3 vols., 2. LC 64-54998. 1990. pap. 7.95 (*0-674-36501-1*) HUP.

— Guidance in American Education, 3 vols., 3. LC 64-54998. 1990. 14.00 (*0-674-36503-8*) HUP.

Landy, Elliott. Woodstock Vision. (Illus.). 128p. 1994. pap. text ed. 19.95 (*0-8264-0662-9*) Continuum.

— Woodstock Vision. (Illus.). 128p. 1994. 39.50 (*0-8264-0663-7*) Continuum.

— Woodstock 1969: The First Festival. (Illus.). 1994. 39.95 (*0-916290-75-1*); pap. 24.95 (*0-916290-74-3*) Squarebooks.

Landy, Frank J. Psychology: The Science of People. 2nd ed. (Illus.). 672p. (C). 1987. Study guide with practice tests & software activity. student ed, pap. text ed. write for info. (*0-318-61592-4*) P-H.

— The Psychology of Work Behavior. 4th ed. 758p. (C). 1989. text ed. 53.95 (*0-534-11091-6*) Brooks-Cole.

Landy, Frank J. & Farr, James F. The Measurement of Work Performance: Methods, Theory & Applications (Monograph) LC 82-22657. (Organizational & Occupational Psychology Ser.). 1983. text ed. 59.00 (*0-12-435660-5*) Acad Pr.

Landy, Frank J., et al, eds. Performance Measurement & Theory. 416p. 1983. text ed. 79.95 (*0-89859-246-1*) L Erlbaum Assocs.

Landy, Gene K. The Software Developer's & Marketer's Legal Companion: Protect Your Software & Your Business. LC 93-19050. 1993. pap. 34.95 (*0-201-62276-9*) Addison-Wesley.

***Landy, Gerald.** Military Paintings of Terence Cuneo. (Illus.). 192p. Date not set. 60.00 (*1-872727-51-4*) Pincushion Pr.

Landy, Jacob. Architecture of Minard Lafever. LC 69-19461. (Illus.). 313p. 1970. text ed. 63.00 (*0-231-03132-7*) Col U Pr.

— The Architecture of Minard Lafever. LC 69-19461. 227p. reprint ed. pap. 64.70 (*0-7837-0420-8*, 2040743) Bks Demand.

Landy, Joanne. Ready to Use Physical Education Activities. (J). (gr. 5-9). 1993. pap. 27.95 (*0-685-63549-X*) P-H.

— Ready-to-Use Physical Education Activities for Grades 5-6. 1993. pap. 27.95 (*0-13-673070-1*) P-H.

Landy, Joanne, jt. auth. see Landy, Maxwell J.

Landy, Laura. Something Ventured, Something Gained: A Business Development Guide for Nonprofit Organizations. LC 89-15139. 150p. 1989. pap. 19.95 (*0-915400-81-2*, ACA Bks) Am Council Arts.

Landy, Lynne, jt. auth. see Pyke, Kaye.

Landy, M., jt. ed. see Forster, O.

Landy, Marc, ed. Environmental Impact Statement Directory: The National Network of EIS-Related Agencies & Organizations. LC 80-27909. 380p. 1981. 110.00 (*0-306-65195-5*, IFI-Plenum) Plenum.

— Modern Presidents & the Presidency. LC 84-47857. 256p. 1984. text ed. 27.95 (*0-669-08683-5*); text ed. 14.95 (*0-669-09468-4*) Free Pr.

Landy, Marc, ed. see De Jouvenel, Bertrand.

Landy, Marc K. The Politics of Environmental Reform: Controlling Kentucky Strip Mining. LC 76-15907. (RFF Working Paper Ser.: PD-2). (Illus.). 414p. reprint ed. pap. 118.00 (*0-685-20403-0*, 2030208) Bks Demand.

***Landy, Marc K. & Levin, Martin A., eds.** The New Politics of Public Policy. LC 94-24379. 384p. 1994. text ed. 48.50x (*0-8018-4877-6*); pap. text ed. 16.95x (*0-8018-4878-4*) Johns Hopkins.

Landy, Marc K., et al. The Environmental Protection Agency: From Nixon to Clinton. exp. ed. 368p. (C). 1994. pap. text ed. 17.95 (*0-19-508673-2*) OUP.

Landy, Marcia. British Genres: Cinema & Society, 1930-1960. (Illus.). 620p. 1991. text ed. 75.00 (*0-691-03176-2*); pap. text ed. 23.95 (*0-685-48016-X*) Princeton U Pr.

— Culture, Politics, & the Writings of Antonio Gramsci. LC 93-43616. 1994. text ed. 44.95 (*0-8166-2390-2*); pap. text ed. 18.95 (*0-8166-2391-0*) U of Minn Pr.

— Fascism in Film: The Italian Commercial Cinema, 1931-1943. LC 85-43296. 369p. reprint ed. pap. 105.20 (*0-7837-0095-4*, 2040373) Bks Demand.

Landy, Marcia, ed. Imitations of Life: A Reader on Film & Television Melodrama. LC 90-39379. (Contemporary Film & Television Ser.). (Illus.). 619p. (C). 1991. text ed. 45.00 (*0-8143-2064-3*); pap. text ed. 21.95 (*0-8143-2065-1*) Wayne St U Pr.

Landy, Maxwell J. Ready-To-Use Physical Education Activities for Grades 3-4, Vol. 2. (J). (gr. 3-4). 1993. pap. 27.95 (*0-13-673088-4*) P-H.

Landy, Maxwell J. & Landy, Joanne. Ready-to-Use P.E. Activities, Vol. 1. LC 92-21049. 1992. write for info. (*0-13-673054-X*, Parker Publishing Co) P-H.

Landy, Michael S. & Movshon, J. Anthony, eds. Computational Models of Visual Processing. (Illus.). 432p. 1991. 60.00 (*0-262-12155-7*) MIT Pr.

***Landy, Robert J.** Drama Therapy: Concepts, Theories & Practices. 2nd ed. LC 94-28228. 244p. (C). 1994. text ed. 58.95x (*0-398-05928-4*) C C Thomas.

— Drama Therapy: Concepts, Theories & Practices. 2nd ed. LC 94-28228. 244p. (C). 1994. pap. 33.95x (*0-398-05947-0*) C C Thomas.

— Handbook of Educational Drama & Theatre. LC 82-6111. xiv, 282p. 1982. text ed. 69.50 (*0-313-22947-3*, LHE/, Greenwood Pr) Greenwood.

— Persona & Performance: The Use of Role in Drama, Therapy, & Everyday Life. 310p. 1993. lib. bdg. 24.95 (*0-89862-023-6*) Guilford Pr.

Landy, Uta & Ratnam, S. S., eds. Prevention & Treatment of Contraceptive Failure. LC 86-25318. 256p. 1986. 69.50 (*0-306-42477-0*, Plenum Pr) Plenum.

Landynski, Jacob W. Search & Seizure & the Supreme Court: A Study in Constitutional Interpretation. LC 65-13523. (Johns Hopkins University Studies in Historical & Political Science: Ser. 84: No. 1). 296p. reprint ed. pap. 84.40 (*0-317-09094-1*, 2005193) Bks Demand.

Landzberg, Abraham H., ed. Electronics Manufacturing Diagnostics Handbook. LC 92-18936. 1993. text ed. 99.95 (*0-442-00471-0*) Van Nos Reinhold.

Lane. Arabian Society in the Middle Ages: Studies from the 1001 Nights. (C). 1987. pap. 19.95 (*0-7007-0195-8*, Pub. by Curzon Pr UK) Humanities.

— Arabic-English Lexicon, Vol. 1. 1995. 275.00 (*0-946621-03-9*) Artium Bks.

— Heparin. 1989. 135.95 (*0-8493-7100-7*, R) CRC Pr.

Lane & Otten, eds. Fracture Mechanics: 13th Conference - STP 743. 650p. 1981. 58.50 (*0-8031-0732-3*, 04-743000-30) ASTM.

Lane, et al. Writing Clearly. 1993. pap. 19.95 (*0-8384-3849-0*); teacher ed, pap. 19.95 (*0-8384-4207-2*) Heinle & Heinle.

Lane, A. & Catrice, R. Formulaire International: Modeles D'actes, Formules et Locutions Pour la Pratique Jurisdiques. 724p. (FRE & GER.). 1969. 89.95 (*0-8288-6598-1*, M-6330) Fr & Eur.

Lane, A. T. Solidarity or Survival? American Labor & European Immigrants, 1830-1924. LC 86-25735. (Contributions in Labor Studies: No. 21). 242p. 1987. text ed. 55.00 (*0-313-25544-X*, LSV/, Greenwood Pr) Greenwood.

***Lane, A. Thomas.** Biographical Dictionary of European Labor Leaders. LC 94-24945. 1204p. 1995. text ed. 225.00 (*0-313-26456-2*, Greenwood Pr) Greenwood.

Lane, Abbe. But Where Is Love? 512p. 1994. mass mkt. 5.99 (*0-446-60035-0*) Warner Bks.

Lane, Alan, jt. ed. see Edwards, Nancy.

Lane, Alex. Turbo C Plus Plus by Example. 1992. pap. 29.95 (*1-55851-123-7*); pap. 39.95 (*1-55851-141-5*) M&T Bks.

Lane, Alfred H. Gifts & Exchange Manual. LC 79-7590. 121p. 1980. text ed. 42.95 (*0-313-21389-5*, LGE/, Greenwood Pr) Greenwood.

Lane, Alice. Atlantii! (Illus.). 296p. (Orig.). 1993. pap. 14.95 (*0-9636665-0-9*) Altre Pub.

***Lane, Ambrose I.** Return of the Buffalo: The Story Behind America's Indian Gaming Explosion. LC 95-11677. 1995. text ed. write for info. (*0-89789-432-4*, Bergin & Garvey); pap. text ed. write for info. (*0-89789-433-2*, Bergin & Garvey) Greenwood.

Lane, Andrew. Motoring Costume. (Album Ser.). 32p. 1989. pap. 25.00x (*0-85263-872-8*, Pub. by Shire Pubns UK) Lubrecht & Cramer.

***Lane, Ann & Temperley, Howard, eds.** The Rise & Fall of the Grand Alliance, 1941-1945. LC 95-13886. 1995. write for info. (*0-312-12674-3*) St Martin.

Lane, Ann J., ed. The Charlotte Perkins Gilman Reader: "The Yellow Wallpaper" & Other Fiction. 1980. pap. 14.00 (*0-394-73933-7*) Pantheon.

— The Debate over Slavery: Stanley Elkins & His Critics. LC 79-141518. (Illini Book Ser.: No. IB-73). 384p. reprint ed. pap. 109.50 (*0-317-09737-7*, 2022257) Bks Demand.

— Mary Ritter Beard: A Sourcebook. 252p. 1988. reprint ed. pap. 12.95 (*1-55553-029-X*) NE U Pr.

Lane, Art, jt. auth. see Lane, Kit.

Lane, Arthur E. An Adequate Response: The War Poetry of Wilfred Owen & Siegfried Sassoon. LC 74-39905. 191p. reprint ed. pap. 54.50 (*0-7837-3795-5*, 2043615) Bks Demand.

Lane, Barbara. Background of Treaty-Making in Western Washington. (Treaty Manuscripts Ser.: No. 3). 32p. 15.00 (*0-944253-25-3*) Inst Dev Indian Law.

Lane, Barbara, jt. auth. see Lane, Robert B.

Lane, Barbara G. Flemish Painting Outside Bruges, 1400-1500: An Annotated Bibliography. (Reference Publications in Art History). 286p. 1986. lib. bdg. 55.00 (*0-8161-8600-6*, Hall Reference) Macmillan.

Lane, Barbara M. Architecture & Politics in Germany, 1918-1945. LC 85-8550. 292p. 1985. pap. 17.50 (*0-674-04370-7*) HUP.

Lane, Barry. After "The End" Teaching & Learning Creative Revision. LC 92-32704. 230p. 1992. pap. text ed. 18.00 (*0-435-08714-2*, 08714) Heinemann.

— Writing As a Road to Self-Discovery. (Illus.). 208p. 1993. 16.95 (*0-89879-537-0*) Writers Digest.

Lane, Barry, jt. auth. see Ballenger, Bruce.

Lane, Barry, ed. see Boise, Ruth.

Lane, Barry, ed. see Champine, Rosa B.

Lane, Barry, ed. see Cram, Lillian.

Lane, Barry, ed. see Gaboriault, Randy.

Lane, Barry, ed. see Gulliver, Deborah.

Lane, Belden. Landscapes of the Sacred: Geography & Narrative in American Spirituality. (Isaac Hecker Studies in Religion & American Culture: Vol. 2). 256p. (Orig.). 1988. pap. 14.95 (*0-8091-2988-4*) Paulist Pr.

Lane, Belden C. Storytelling: Study Guide, The Enchantment of Theology Cassette Tapes. LC 86-6079. 24p. (Orig.). 1982. pap. 2.50 (*0-8272-3419-8*, 10S2113) Chalice Pr.

Lane, Ben, ed. see Fogle, Jeanne S.

Lane, Beverly. Sweet Victory. 224p. (Orig.). 1993. pap. 2.95 (*1-56597-046-2*, Kismet) Meteor Pub.

***Lane, Brian.** Chronicle of 20th Century Murder, Vol. II. 288p. 1995. pap. text ed. 7.99 (*0-425-14832-7*) Jove Pubns.

— Chronicle of 20th Century Murder Vol. I. 288p. (Orig.). 1995. pap. text ed. 5.99 (*0-425-14649-9*) Berkley Pub.

— Murder Update: Modern Murders That Made the Headlines. 224p. 1991. pap. 9.95 (*0-88184-740-2*) Carroll & Graf.

Lane, Brian, ed. The Murder Club Regional Guides, 2 vols. (C). 1989. pap. write for info. (*0-318-65235-8*) St Mut.

An Asterisk (*) at the beginning of an entry indicates that the title is appearing in BIP for the first time.

— The Murder Club Regional Guides, 2 vols., No. 5: Eastern & Home Countries. (C). 1989. No. 5, Eastern & Home Countries. pap. 39.00 (*0-245-54679-0*) St Mut.

— The Murder Club Regional Guides, 2 vols., No. 6: South-West England & Wales. (C). 1989. No. 6, South-West England & Wales. pap. 39.00 (*0-245-54686-3*) St Mut.

Lane, Brian & Gregg, Wilfred. The Encyclopedia of Serial Killers. 416p. (Orig.). 1994. mass mkt. 5.99 (*1-55773-974-9*) Diamond.

Lane, Brigitte. Franco-American Folk Traditions & Popular Culture in a Former Milltown: Aspects of Ethnic Urban Folklore & the Dynamics of Folklore Change in Lowell, Massachusetts. LC 90-39059. (Harvard Dissertations in Folklore & Oral Literature Ser.). 632p. 1990. reprint ed. 120.00 (*0-8240-2674-8*) Garland.

Lane, Byron D. Managing People. rev. ed. (Successful Business Library). (Illus.). 239p. 1990. pap. 19.95 (*1-55571-090-5*) Oasis Pr OR.

— Managing People. 2nd rev. ed. (Successful Business Library). (Illus.). 239p. 1990. ring bd. 39.95 (*1-55571-117-0*) Oasis Pr OR.

Lane, C. E. & Steinberg, R. Discovery of the Neutrino, Franklin Symposium Proceedings in Celebration. 232p. 1993. text ed. 91.00 (*981-02-1567-3*) World Scientific Pub.

Lane, Calvin W. Evelyn Waugh. (English Authors Ser.: No. 301). 192p. (C). 1981. text ed. 21.95 (*0-8057-6793-2*, Pub. by Royal Botanic Garden UK) Macmillan.

Lane, Caren B. & Mancuso, George A. Purchasing Magazine's Guide to the PWB Marketplace. LC 93-30039. 1993. write for info. (*0-13-090242-X*) P-H.

Lane, Carl D. The Boatman's Manual. 4th enl. rev. ed. (Illus.). 1979. 25.95 (*0-393-03190-X*) Norton.

Lane, Carla, jt. auth. see Portway, Patrick.

***Lane, Carole A.** Naked in Cyberspace: How to Find Personal Information Online. 256p. 1995. pap. 27.95 (*0-910965-17-X*, Pembrtn Pr Bks) Online.

Lane, Charles. Cooper Henderson & the Open Road. 128p. 1990. 100.00 (*0-85131-392-2*, Pub. by J A Allen & Co UK) St Mut.

— Harry Hall's Classic Winners. 150p. 1990. 100.00 (*0-85131-471-6*, Pub. by J A Allen & Co UK) St Mut.

— A Voluntary Political Government: Letters from Charles Lane. LC 82-19787. 104p. (Orig.). 1982. pap. 5.95 (*0-9602574-3-8*) M E Coughlin.

Lane, Charles E., jt. ed. see Humm, Harold J.

Lane, Charles S. New Hampshire's First Tourists in the Lakes & Mountains. rev. ed. (Illus.). 207p. 1993. pap. 18.00 (*0-9637214-1-0*) Old Print Barn.

Lane, Chris, jt. auth. see Lee, Melinda.

Lane, Christel. Christian Religion in the Soviet Union: A Sociological Study. LC 77-801. 256p. 1978. 59.50 (*0-87395-327-4*) State U NY Pr.

— Industry & Society in Europe: Stability & Change in Britain, Germany & France. LC 94-43574. (Illus.). 256p. 1995. 63.95 (*1-85278-394-X*, Pub. by E Elgar Pub UK) Ashgate Pub Co.

— Management & Labour in Europe: The Industrial Enterprise in Germany, Britain & France. 368p. 1989. text ed. 69.95 (*1-85278-058-4*, Pub. by E Elgar Pub UK); pap. text ed. 22.95 (*1-85278-208-0*, Pub. by E Elgar Pub UK) Ashgate Pub Co.

— The Rites of Rulers: Ritual in Industrial Society-the Soviet Case. LC 80-41747. (Illus.). 338p. 1981. 74.95 (*0-521-22608-2*) Cambridge U Pr.

***Lane, Christoper.** The Ruling Passion: British Colonial Allegory & the Paradox of Homosexual Desire. LC 95-6484. 1995. write for info. (*0-8223-1677-3*) Duke.

Lane, Christopher. Eden's Gate. LC 94-14746. 1994. pap. 11.99 (*0-310-41161-0*) Zondervan.

— Kingdom Parables. (Illus.). 192p. (J). 1994. 14.99 (*1-56476-275-0*, Victor Books) SP Pubns.

— The Ruling Passion: British Colonial Allegory & the Paradox of Homosexual Desire. LC 95-6484. 1995. pap. write for info. (*0-8223-1689-7*) Duke.

— Stardust: I Climbed a Rainbow Once. (Illus.). 1993. 4.50 (*0-8378-5304-4*) Gibson.

— Stardust: I Saw an Angel Yesterday. (Illus.). 1993. 4.50 (*0-8378-5305-2*) Gibson.

Lane, Christopher W. Impressions of Niagara: The Charles Rand Penney Collection. 198p. 1993. 50.00 (*0-9636924-0-2*); pap. 29.50 (*0-9636924-1-0*) Phila Prnt Shop.

Lane, Christy. Christy Lane's Complete Book of Line Dancing. LC 94-18038. (Illus.). 160p. 1994. pap. 13.95 (*0-87322-719-0*, PLAN0719) Human Kinetics.

Lane, Clinton F. & Kabalka, George W. A New Hydroboration Reagent. 1976. pap. 12.75 (*0-08-021330-8*, Pergamon Pr) Elsevier.

Lane, Cristy & Stevens, Laura A. How to Help Your Own Troubled Marriage. 1989. pap. 9.95 (*0-317-93509-7*) L S Records.

Lane, D. & Acland, J., eds. Industrial Robotics. (Bibliography Ser.). 1981. pap. 49.00 (*0-85296-249-5*, BI011) Inst Elect Eng.

Lane, D. & Cooper. Cones's Veterinary Nursing, 2 vols. 2nd ed. 1994. text ed. 130.00 (*0-08-042288-8*) Elsevier.

***Lane, D. A., et al, eds.** Fibrinogen: Fibrin Formation & Fibrinolysis: Proceedings of a Workshop on Fibrinogen, London, England, April 2-3, 1985. (Illus.). xviii, 396p. 1986. 192.35 (*3-11-010597-7*) De Gruyter.

— Fibrinogen, Vol. 4: Fibrin Formation & Fibrinolysis: Proceedings of a Workshop on Fibrinogen, London, England, April 2-3, 1985. (Illus.). xviii, 396p. 1986. 192.35 (*0-89925-152-8*) De Gruyter.

— Heparin & Related Polysaccharides. (Advances in Experimental Medicine & Biology Ser.: Vol. 313). (Illus.). 360p. (C). 1992. 85.00 (*0-306-44212-4*, Plenum Pr) Plenum.

Lane, D. R. Jones' Animal Nursing. 3rd ed. (Illus.). 1980. text ed. 74.00 (*0-08-024945-0*, Pergamon Pr); pap. text ed. 40.00 (*0-08-024944-2*, Pergamon Pr) Elsevier.

Lane, D. R., ed. Jones' Animal Nursing. 4th ed. (Illus.). 620p. 1985. text ed. 100.00 (*0-08-031982-3*, Pergamon Pr); pap. text ed. 51.00 (*0-08-031983-1*, Pergamon Pr) Elsevier.

— Jones' Animal Nursing. 5th ed. (Illus.). 800p. 1989. text ed. 140.00 (*0-08-036158-7*, 0901; 0902; 0904, Pergamon Pr); pap. text ed. 50.00 (*0-08-036157-9*, 0901; 0902; 0904, Pergamon Pr) Elsevier.

Lane, Dame E. Hear the Other Side. 1985. 38.00 (*0-406-50240-4*, U.K.) Butterworth Legal Pubs.

Lane, David. Landlord-Tenant Rights in British Columbia: Canadian Edition. 7th ed. (Legal Ser.). 144p. 1991. 8.95 (*0-88908-459-9*) Self-Counsel Pr.

— The Roots of Russian Communism: A Social & Historical Study of Russian Social Democracy 1898-1907. LC 74-15196. 1975. pap. text ed. 14.95 (*0-271-01178-5*) Pa St U Pr.

— Soviet Society under Perestroika. 256p. 1990. text ed. 75.00 (*0-04-445166-0*); pap. text ed. 22.95 (*0-04-445167-9*) Routledge Chapman & Hall.

— Soviet Society under Perestroika. 300p. 1992. pap. 14.95 (*0-00-302060-6*, A8325) Routledge Chapman & Hall.

— Transistor Radios: A Wallace-Homestead Price Guide. 176p. 1994. pap. 19.95 (*0-87069-712-9*) Chilton.

Lane, David, ed. Russia in Flux: The Political & Social Consequences of Reform. 240p. 1992. 64.95 (*1-85278-680-9*, Pub. by E Elgar Pub UK); pap. 22.95 (*1-85278-713-9*, Pub. by E Elgar Pub UK) Ashgate Pub Co.

— Russia in Transition: Policies, Classes & Inequalities. 292p. (C). 1996. pap. text ed. 18.95 (*0-582-27566-0*) Longman.

Lane, David & O'Dell, Felicity. The Soviet Industrial Worker: Social Class, Education & Control. LC 78-60509. 180p. 1978. text ed. 35.00 (*0-312-74841-8*) St Martin.

Lane, David & Stratford, Brian, eds. Current Approaches to Down's Syndrome. LC 85-8842. 447p. 1985. text ed. 75.00 (*0-275-90212-9*, C0212, Praeger Pubs) Greenwood.

Lane, David, jt. auth. see Harlow, Ed.

Lane, David, jt. ed. see Harlow, Ed.

Lane, David, jt. auth. see Talsky, Aaron.

Lane, David A. & Miller, Andrew, eds. Child & Adolescent Therapy: A Handbook. LC 92-18914. (Psychotherapy Handbooks Ser.). 1993. 99.00 (*0-335-09891-6*, Open Univ Pr); pap. 36.00 (*0-335-09890-8*, Open Univ Pr) Taylor & Francis.

Lane, David C. Clash of the Archetypes: The Mummy Meets the Wolfman. (Occam's Razor Ser.). 1992. pap. 2.00 (*1-56543-006-9*) Mt SA Coll Philos.

— Exposing Cults: When the Skeptical Mind Confronts the Mystical. LC 94-9197. (Garland Reference Library of Social Science, Religious Information Systems Ser.: Vol. 890, Vol. 10). 304p. 1994. 45.00 (*0-8153-1275-X*, SS890) Garland.

— Gurus, Swamis, & Vegetarianism. (Occam's Razor Ser.). 53p. (Orig.). 1992. pap. text ed. 2.00 (*1-56543-011-5*) Mt SA Coll Philos.

— Inner Visions & Running Trains: A Comparative Study of the Unknowing Sage and the Tibetan Book of the Dead. (Jewels of India Ser.). 60p. 1992. pap. 2.00 (*1-56543-007-7*) Mt SA Coll Philos.

— The Making of a Spiritual Movement: The Untold Story of Paul Twitchell & Eckankar. rev. ed. (Understanding Cults & Spiritual Movements Ser.). 211p. 1994. pap. 15.00 (*0-9611124-6-8*) Del Mar Pr.

— The Making of a Spiritual Movement: The Untold Story of Paul Twitchell & Eckankar. 4th rev. ed. (Understanding Cults & Spiritual Movements Ser.: No. 1). (Illus.). 171p. 1989. pap. 19.95 (*0-685-26797-0*) Del Mar Pr.

— The Mystical Dimension: An Essay on Unknowingness. (Jewels of India Ser.). (Orig.). 1992. pap. 2.00 (*1-56543-010-7*) Mt SA Coll Philos.

— Why I Don't Eat Faces: The Hierarchical Principle Behind Vegetarianism. (Occam's Razor Ser.). 54p. (Orig.). 1992. pap. 4.95 (*1-56543-019-0*) Mt SA Coll Philos.

Lane, David C., ed. The Teachings of Jesus: A Dialogue Between an Indian Mystic & a Group of Christian Fundamentalists. (Jewels of India Ser.). 50p. 1992. pap. 2.00 (*1-56543-005-0*) Mt SA Coll Philos.

— Understanding Cults & Spiritual Movements. (Understanding Cults & Spiritual Movements Ser.). (Illus.). 200p. (Orig.). 1989. pap. 21.95 (*0-9611124-2-5*) Del Mar Pr.

— The Unknowing Sage: The Life & Work of Baba Fagir Chand. (Enchanted Land Book Ser.). (Illus.). 63p. (Orig.). 1989. pap. 11.95 (*0-9611124-1-7*) Del Mar Pr.

Lane, David C., ed. see Chano, Fagir.

Lane, David C., ed. see Juergensmeyer, Mark.

Lane, David H. A Book for Music Teachers. 80p. (Orig.). 1987. pap. 6.95 (*0-934009-01-5*) Presser Co.

Lane, David J. The Peshitta of Leviticus. LC 94-569. (Monographs of the Peshitta Institute Leiden: Vol. 6). 1994. 71.50 (*90-04-10020-2*) E J Brill.

Lane, David M. Hyperstat: Macintosh Hypermedia for Analyzing Data & Learning Statistics. (Illus.). 128p. 1993. disk 59.95 (*0-12-436130-7*, AP Prof) Acad Pr.

Lane-Davies, A. Holy Wells of Cornwall. pap. 3.95 (*0-89979-021-6*) British Am Bks.

***Lane, Deforia.** Music as Medicine: Deforia Lane's Life of Music, Healing & Faith. 208p. 1995. 24.99 (*0-310-21089-5*) Zondervan.

— Music as Medicine: Deforia Lane's Life of Music, Healing & Faith. 2nd ed. 208p. 1995. pap. 16.99 (*0-310-43210-3*) Zondervan.

Lane, Denis. Cloud & the Silver Lining. 1985. pap. 3.99 (*0-85234-193-8*, Pub. by Evangel Pr UK) Presby & Reformed.

— God's Powerful Weapon. 1977. pap. 1.25 (*9971-972-21-2*) OMF Bks.

— Keeping Body & Soul Together. 1982. pap. 2.25 (*0-85363-144-1*) OMF Bks.

— Man & His God. 1981. pap. 4.99 (*0-85234-155-5*, Pub. by Evangel Pr UK) Presby & Reformed.

— Preach the Word. 1986. pap. 7.99 (*0-85234-221-7*, Pub. by Evangel Pr UK) Presby & Reformed.

— Tuning God's New Instrument. 100p. (Orig.). (C). 1990. pap. text ed. 6.95 (*9971-972-97-2*) OMF Bks.

Lane, Denis, ed. In the Spirit of Powys: New Essays. LC 89-42925. 272p. 1990. 39.50 (*0-8387-5173-3*) Bucknell U Pr.

Lane, Denis & Stein, Rita, eds. Modern British Literature, Vol. V: Supplement, Vol. 5, Suppl. 2. (Library of Literary Criticism). 600p. 1985. 75.00 (*0-8044-3140-X*, F Ungar Bks) Continuum.

Lane, Dermont A. The Reality of Jesus. LC 77-70635. (Exploration Book Ser.). 180p. 1977. pap. 9.95 (*0-8091-2020-8*) Paulist Pr.

Lane, Dermot. Christ at the Centre: Selected Issues in Christology. 154p. 1989. pap. 24.00 (*1-85390-058-3*, Pub. by Veritas IE) St Mut.

Lane, Dermot A. The Experience of God: An Invitation to Do Theology. LC 81-80873. 96p. (Orig.). 1981. pap. 5.95 (*0-8091-2394-0*) Paulist Pr.

— The Experience of God: An Invitation to Do Theology. 86p. (Orig.). 1989. pap. 22.00 (*0-86217-179-2*, Pub. by Veritas IE) St Mut.

Lane, Derwood. Saragosa: The Town Killed by a Tornado. (Illus.). 288p. 1989. pap. 12.95 (*0-89015-672-7*) Sunbelt Media.

Lane, Don. Trial & Error. 325p. (C). 1990. 90.00 (*0-86439-154-4*, Pub. by Boolarong Pubns AT) St Mut.

***Lane, Dorothy F.** The Island as Site of Resistance: An Examination of Caribbean & New Zealand Texts. LC 94-3675. (Studies of World Literature in English: 6). 1995. write for info. (*0-8204-2642-3*) P Lang Pubs.

Lane, E. W. Arabic English Lexicon, 8 vols. (ARA & ENG.). 1985. reprint ed. 195.00 (*0-8288-8455-2*) Fr & Eur.

— Manners & Customs of the Modern Egyptians. 616p. 1986. 360.00 (*1-85077-115-4*, Darf Pubs Ltd) St Mut.

Lane, Eamonn, jt. auth. see Collins, Denis.

Lane, Edmund C., ed. Do Not Be Afraid: I Am with You. 1991. pap. 2.50 (*0-8189-0617-0*) Alba.

Lane, Edmund C., tr. see Benigni, Maria L.

Lane, Edmund C., tr. see Giudici, Maria P.

Lane, Edmund C., tr. see Haring, Bernard & Salvoldi, Valentin.

Lane, Edmund C., tr. see Marcucci, Domenico.

Lane, Edmund C., tr. see Pasquero, Fedele.

Lane, Edmund C., tr. see Romano, Giuseppe.

Lane, Edmund C., tr. see Tarzia, Antonio.

Lane, Edward, jt. auth. see Qamus, Madd A.

Lane, Edward W. Arabian Society in the Middle Ages: Studies from One Thousand & One Nights. 300p. 1989. text ed. 27.50 (*81-207-0939-X*, Pub. by Sterling Pubs II) Apt Bks.

— Arabic-English Lexicon, 2 vols., Set. 1984. reprint ed. 320.00x (*0-946621-04-7*) Intl Bk Ctr.

Lane, Elizabeth. MacKenna's Promise. (Historical Ser.). 1994. mass mkt. 3.99 (*0-373-28816-6*, 1-28816-6) Harlequin Bks.

— Wild Wings, Wild Heart. (Special Edition Ser.). 1995. pap. 3.50 (*0-373-09936-3*, 1-09936-5) Silhouette.

Lane, Eric, ed. Telling Tales: And Other New One-Act Plays. 350p. (Orig.). 1993. pap. 15.00 (*0-14-048237-7*, Penguin Bks) Viking Penguin.

Lane, Eric & Brenson, Ian, intros. Oberammergau: Passion Play. 232p. 1985. pap. 7.95 (*0-946626-05-7*, Pub. by Dedalus Bks UK) Hippocrene Bks.

Lane, Eric & Lane, Joyce. Eve's Story: A Christian Woman's Search for Fullness & Equality. 1984. pap. 5.99 (*0-85234-181-4*, Pub. by Evangel Pr UK) Presby & Reformed.

***Lane, Eric & Shengold, Nina, eds.** The Actor's Book of Gay & Lesbian Plays. 400p. 1995. pap. 13.95 (*0-14-024552-9*, Penguin Bks) Viking Penguin.

— The Actor's Book of Scenes from New Plays. 448p. 1988. pap. 10.95 (*0-14-010487-9*, Penguin Bks) Viking Penguin.

Lane, Eric, jt. ed. see Shengold, Nina.

Lane, Ermot. The Reality of Jesus. 180p. 1989. pap. 22.00 (*0-901810-85-1*, Pub. by Veritas IE) St Mut.

Lane, Ernest P. Metric Differential Geometry of Curves & Surfaces. LC 40-12579. 224p. reprint ed. pap. 63.90 (*0-317-20710-5*, 2024120) Bks Demand.

Lane, Eugene N., jt. ed. see MacMullen, Ramsay.

Lane, Evelyn C. Bishop & Burroughs Families in Early Massachusetts, Vital Records from Printed Sources. LC 91-75314. 122p. 1991. pap. 18.75 (*0-9626201-4-9*) E C Lane.

— Carrier - Currier Families in Early Massachusetts: Vital Records from Printed Sources. 117p. (Orig.). 1992. pap. 18.50 (*0-9626201-5-7*) E C Lane.

— Nurse & Esty Families in Early Massachusetts: Vital Records from Printed Sources. LC 91-90438. 150p. (Orig.). 1991. pap. 21.50 (*0-9626201-3-0*) E C Lane.

— Proctor Family in Early Massachusetts: Vital Records from Printed Sources. LC 91-61377. 125p. 1991. pap. 18.75 (*0-9626201-2-2*) E C Lane.

— Towne Family in Early Massachusetts Vital Records from Printed Sources. 103p. 1991. pap. 15.00 (*0-9626201-1-4*) E C Lane.

Lane, Ferdinand. Mysterious Sea. LC 73-128268. (Essay Index Reprint Ser.). 1977. 24.95 (*0-8369-1971-8*) Ayer.

Lane, Francis E. American Charities & the Child of the Immigrant: Study of Typical Child Caring Institutions New York & Massachusetts-1845-1880, Vol. 6. LC 74-1691. (Children & Youth Ser.). 188p. 1974. reprint ed. 20.95 (*0-405-05967-1*) Ayer.

Lane, Franklin K. The Letters of Franklin K. Lane, Personal & Political. (American Biography Ser.). 473p. 1991. reprint ed. lib. bdg. 89.00 (*0-7812-8237-3*) Rprt Serv.

Lane, Fred, ed. Medical Trial Technique Quarterly, 38 vols. LC 72-136152. 1954. 1,100.00 (*0-318-42410-X*) Clark Boardman Callaghan.

Lane, Fred & Birnbaum, David A. Lane Medical Litigation Guide, 4 vols. LC 81-10167. 1981. ring bd. 525.00 (*0-685-09243-7*) Clark Boardman Callaghan.

Lane, Fred, jt. auth. see Goldstein, Irving.

Lane, Frederic C. Andrea Barbarigo, Merchant of Venice, 1418-1449. LC 78-64194. (Johns Hopkins University. Studies in the Social Sciences. Thirtieth Ser. 1912: 1). reprint ed. 37.50 (*0-404-61300-4*) AMS Pr.

— Studies in Venetian Social & Economic History. Kohl, Benjamin G. & Mueller, Reinhold C., eds. (Collected Studies: No. CS254). (Illus.). 346p. (ENG, FRE & ITA.). (C). 1987. reprint ed. lib. bdg. 95.00 (*0-86078-202-6*, Pub. by Variorum UK) Ashgate Pub Co.

— Venetian Ships & Shipbuilders of the Renaissance. 1979. 28.95 (*0-405-10609-2*) Ayer.

— Venetian Ships & Shipbuilders of the Renaissance. LC 92-11280. (Softshell Bks.). (Illus.). 296p. 1992. reprint ed. pap. text ed. 15.95 (*0-8018-4514-9*) Johns Hopkins.

— Venice: A Maritime Republic. LC 72-12342. (Illus.). 518p. 1973. pap. 16.95 (*0-8018-1460-X*) Johns Hopkins.

— Venice & History: The Collected Papers of Frederic C. Lane. LC 66-14160. 582p. reprint ed. pap. 165.90 (*0-317-30121-7*, 2025304) Bks Demand.

Lane, Frederic C. & Mueller, Reinhold. Money & Banking in Medieval & Renaissance Venice, Vol. I: Coins & Moneys of Account. LC 84-47947. (Illus.). 712p. (C). 1985. text ed. 68.00 (*0-8018-3157-1*) Johns Hopkins.

Lane, Frederick C. Profits from Power: Readings in Protection Rent & Violence-Controlling Enterprises. LC 79-13860. 128p. 1979. 59.50 (*0-87395-403-3*); pap. 19.95 (*0-87395-420-3*) State U NY Pr.

Lane, Frederick S., 3rd, jt. auth. see Berger, Richie E.

***Lane, Fredrick S.** Current Issues in Public Administration. 5th ed. 496p. 1993. pap. text ed. 21.00 (*0-312-08413-7*) St Martin.

Lane, G. S. Words for Clothing in the Principal Indo-European Languages. (LD Ser.: No. 9). 1931. pap. 16.00 (*0-527-00755-2*) Periodicals Srv.

Lane, Gary. Beating the French. (Batsford Chess Library Ser.). 144p. 1994. pap. 16.95 (*0-8050-3292-4*) H Holt & Co.

— A Concordance to Personae: Concordance to the Poems of Ezra Pound. LC 72-6462. (Reference Ser.: No. 44). (C). 1972. lib. bdg. 75.00 (*0-8383-1613-1*) M S G Haskell Hse.

— A Concordance to the Poems of Hart Crane. LC 72-1872. (Reference Ser.: No. 44). 356p. (C). 1972. lib. bdg. 75.00 (*0-8383-1437-6*) M S G Haskell Hse.

— A Concordance to the Poems of Marianne Moore. LC 72-6438. (Reference Ser.: No. 44). 1972. lib. bdg. 75.00 (*0-8383-1588-7*) M S G Haskell Hse.

— The C3 Sicilian: Analysis & Complete Games. (Illus.). 208p. 1990. pap. 22.95 (*1-85223-318-4*, Pub. by Crowood Pr UK) Trafalgar.

— The Ruy Lopez for the Tournament Player. 240p. 1992. pap. 19.95 (*0-8050-2317-8*, Pub. by Batsford Chess UK) H Holt & Co.

— Sylvia Plath: New Views on the Poetry. LC 78-20515. 280p. reprint ed. pap. 79.80 (*0-685-15476-9*, 2026323) Bks Demand.

— Winning with the Bishop's Opening. (Batsford Chess Library). 120p. 1993. pap. 19.95 (*0-8050-2636-3*, Owl) H Holt & Co.

— Winning with the Closed Sicilian. (Batsford Chess Library). 160p. 1993. pap. 19.95 (*0-8050-2637-1*, Owl) H Holt & Co.

— Winning with the Fischer-Sozin Attack. (Batsford Chess Library). 1994. pap. 19.95 (*0-8050-3576-1*) H Holt & Co.

— Winning with the Scotch. (Batsford Chess Library). 160p. 1993. pap. 19.95 (*0-8050-2940-0*) H Holt & Co.

Lane, Gary, ed. A Word-Index to James Joyce's Dubliners. LC 71-183760. (Reference Ser.: No. 44). 270p. 1972. lib. bdg. 75.00 (*0-8383-1384-1*) M S G Haskell Hse.

Lane, George, jt. auth. see Gerl, George.

Lane, George A. Chicago Churches & Synagogues. 255p. 1981. 25.00 (*0-8294-0373-6*) Loyola Univ Pr.

— Christian Spirituality: An Historical Sketch. 88p. 1984. pap. 4.95 (*0-8294-0450-3*) Loyola Univ Pr.

Lane, George A., ed. Solar Heat Storage--Latent Heat Materials: Vol. 1, Background & Scientific Principles. 288p. 1986. 168.00 (*0-8493-6585-6*, TJ810, CRC Reprint) Franklin.

— Solar Heat Storage--Latent Heat Materials: Vol. 1, Background & Scientific Principles, II. 288p. 1986. 204.00 (*0-8493-6586-4*, TJ810, CRC Reprint) Franklin.

Lane, George M. A Latin Grammar for Schools & Colleges. rev. ed. LC 78-107458. reprint ed. 19.50 (*0-404-00634-5*) AMS Pr.

***Lane, Gerald R., et al, eds.** Technologies for Advanced Land Combat: Proceedings of a Conference Held 17-18 April, 1995, Orlando, Florida. LC 95-9816. (Critical Reviews of Optical Science Technology Ser.: Vol. 59). 1995. pap. write for info. (*0-8194-1851-X*) SPIE.

Lane, Gerd R. & Mels, Reinhard. Chronograph Wristwatches: Stop Watches. (Illus.). 256p. 1993. 79.95 (*0-88740-502-9*) Schiffer.

Lane, Gilles. Government, Justice, & Contempt. LC 92-34527. 144p. (Orig.). (C). 1993. lib. bdg. 34.50 (0-8191-8956-1); pap. text ed. 16.50 (0-8191-8957-X) U Pr of Amer.

Lane, Harlan. Mask of Benevolence: Disabling the Deaf Community. 1992. 25.00 (0-679-40462-7) Knopf.

— The Mask of Benevolence: Disabling the Deaf Community. LC 93-13107. 1993. pap. 13.00 (0-679-73614-X, Vin) Random.

— When the Mind Hears. 1989. pap. 15.96 (0-679-72023-5) McKay.

— When the Mind Hears: A History of the Deaf. LC 83-43201. 608p. 1984. 29.95 (0-394-50878-5) Random.

— When the Mind Hears: A History of the Deaf. 1989. pap. 16.95 (0-685-27139-0, Vin) Random.

— The Wild Boy of Aveyron. (Illus.). 384p. 1979. pap. 15.95 (0-674-95300-2) HUP.

Lane, Harlan, ed. The Deaf Experience: Classics in Language & Education. Philip, Franklin, tr. (Illus.). 384p. 1984. 32.00 (0-674-19460-8) HUP.

Lane, Harlan & Grosjean, Francois, eds. Recent Perspectives on American Sign Language. 176p. 1989. reprint ed. pap. 34.50 (0-8058-0560-5) L Erlbaum Assocs.

Lane, Harlan, jt. ed. see Fischer, Renate.

Lane, Harlan, jt. tr. see Philip, Franklin.

Lane, Harlan, jt. auth. see Phillip, F.

Lane, Harold, contrib. Five Hundred Hymns for Instruments, Bk. C. 316p. 1976. spiral bd. 19.95 (0-685-68382-6, MB-329) Lillenas.

— Five Hundred Hymns for Instruments, Bk. D. 316p. 1976. spiral bd. 19.95 (0-685-68383-4, MB-330) Lillenas.

— Five Hundred Hymns for Instruments, Bk. A. 316p. 1976. spiral bd. 19.95 (0-685-68379-6, MB-327) Lillenas.

— Five Hundred Hymns for Instruments, Bk. B. 316p. 1976. spiral bd. 19.95 (0-8341-9185-7, MB-328) Lillenas.

— Five Hundred Hymns for Instruments, Bk. E. 316p. 1976. spiral bd. 19.95 (0-8341-9184-9, MB-331) Lillenas.

— Five Hundred Hymns for Instruments, Bk. F. 316p. 1976. spiral bd. 19.95 (0-8341-9183-0, MB-332) Lillenas.

Lane, Harold & Van Hartesvelt, Mark. Essentials of Hospitality Administration. (C). 1983. teacher ed write for info. (0-8359-1772-X, Reston) P-H.

Lane, Harold A. & Straka, Joseph J. Late Mississippian & Early Pennsylvanian Conodonts, Arkansas & Oklahoma. (Geological Society of America, Special Paper Ser.: No. 152). 204p. reprint ed. pap. 58.20 (0-317-51968-9, 2027370) Bks Demand.

Lane, Harole. Hospitality World. 1990. text ed. write for info. (0-442-00118-5) Van Nos Reinhold.

Lane, Helen, tr. see Anderson, et al.

Lane, Helen, tr. see Bastos, Augusto R.

Lane, Helen, tr. see Garcia-Ponce, Juan.

Lane, Helen, tr. see Goytisolo, Juan.

Lane, Helen, tr. see Llosa, Mario V.

Lane, Helen, tr. see Merino, Jose M.

Lane, Helen, tr. see Merino, Jose Maria.

Lane, Helen, tr. see Paz, Octavio.

Lane, Helen, tr. see Pinon, Nelida.

Lane, Helen, tr. see Valenzuela, Luisa.

Lane, Helen, tr. see Vargas Llosa, Mario.

***Lane, Helen H.** History of Dighton, the South Purchase, 1712. 263p. 1995. reprint ed. lib. bdg. 35.00 (0-8328-4696-1) Higginson Bk Co.

Lane, Helen R., tr. see Breton, Andre.

Lane, Helen R., tr. see Burch, Noel.

Lane, Helen R., tr. see Fernandez-Santos, Jesus.

Lane, Helen R., tr. see Friedlander, Saul.

Lane, Helen R., tr. see Gaite, Carmen M.

Lane, Helen R., tr. see Goytisolo, Juan.

Lane, Helen R., tr. see Poniatowska, Elena.

Lane, Helen R., tr. see Quijano, Anibal.

Lane, Helen R., tr. see Rebolledo, Francisco.

Lane, Helen R., tr. see Revel, Jean-Francois.

Lane, Helen R., tr. see Simon, Claude.

Lane, Helen R., tr. see Vargas Llosa, Mario.

Lane, Henry W. & DiStefano, Joseph J. International Management Behavior. 2nd ed. 478p. (C). 1992. text ed. 36.95 (0-534-92933-8) Intl Thomson.

Lane, Henry W., et al. Managing Large Research & Development Programs. LC 81-849. 166p. 1982. pap. 21.95 (0-87395-474-2) State U NY Pr.

Lane, Henry W., et al, eds. Managing Large Research & Development Programs. LC 81-849. 166p. 1982. 64.50 (0-87395-473-4) State U NY Pr.

Lane, I. William & Comac, Linda. Sharks Don't Get Cancer: How Shark Cartilage Could Save Your Life. LC 92-782. 216p. 1993. pap. 11.95 (0-89529-520-2) Avery Pub.

Lane, Irving, jt. auth. see Siegel, Laurence.

Lane, Irving M. & Messe, Lawrence A. Equity & the Distribution of Rewards. LC 71-131014. 129p. 1970. 19.50 (0-685-38425-X) Scholarly.

Lane, J. A. Microwave Power Measurement. (IEE Monograph Ser.: No. 12). (Illus.). 80p. reprint ed. pap. 25.00 (0-8357-8952-7, 2033454) Bks Demand.

Lane, J. D., ed. Robotic Welding. (International Trends in Manufacturing Technology Ser.). (Illus.). 380p. 1987. 90.00 (0-387-16676-9) Spr-Verlag.

Lane, J. D. & King, R. H. Automatic Steering of an Articulated Haul Truck for Underground Mining. 1994. write for info. (0-318-72529-0) US Interior.

Lane, J. D., jt. auth. see Smith, J. E.

Lane, J. Eric. Moment of Encounter. LC 83-49361. (American University Studies: History: Ser. IX, Vol. 6). 163p. (Orig.). (C). 1984. pap. text ed. 17.55 (0-8204-0090-4) P Lang Pubs.

Lane, J. S. On Optimal Population Paths. LC 77-704. (Lecture Notes in Economics & Mathematical Systems Ser.: Vol. 142). 1977. pap. 26.00 (0-387-08070-8) Spr-Verlag.

Lane, Jack, jt. auth. see O'Sullivan, Maurice.

Lane, Jack, jt. ed. see O'Sullivan, Maurice.

Lane, James B. City of the Century: A History of Gary, Indiana. LC 77-23622. (Illus.). 416p. 1978. 20.00 (0-253-11187-0) Ind U Pr.

Lane, James B. & Escobar, Edward J., eds. Forging a Community: The Latino Experience in Northwest Indiana, 1919-1975. LC 87-10292. (Illus.). 306p. 1987. 29.95 (0-253-32382-7); pap. 9.95 (0-253-21213-8) Ind U Pr.

***Lane, James M.** The Complete Golfer's Almanac, 1995. (Orig.). 1995. pap. 13.95 (0-399-52151-8, Perigree Bks) Berkley Pub.

— Guide to Golf Schools & Resorts. 300p. 1995. pap. 12.95 (1-56079-476-3) Petersons Guides.

Lane, James R., jt. ed. see Andres, Rachel.

Lane, James W. Masters in Modern Art. LC 67-22100. (Essay Index Reprint Ser.). 1977. 19.95 (0-8369-1332-9) Ayer.

Lane, Jan-Erik. Bureaucracy & Public Choice. (Modern Politics Ser.: Vol. 15). (Illus.). 320p. (C). 1987. text ed. 45.00 (0-8039-8067-1); pap. text ed. 17.95 (0-8039-8068-X) Sage.

— Institutional Reform: A Public Policy Perspective. 256p. 1990. text ed. 52.95 (1-85521-002-9, Pub. by Dartmth Pub UK) Ashgate Pub Co.

— The Public Sector: Concepts, Models & Approaches. (Illus.). 240p. (C). 1993. text ed. 65.00 (0-8039-8818-4); pap. text ed. 21.95 (0-8039-8819-2) Sage.

Lane, Jan-Erik, ed. Understanding the Swedish Model. 1991. text ed. 30.00 (0-7146-3445-X, Pub. by F Cass Pubs UK) Intl Spec Bk.

***Lane, Jan-Erik & Errson, Svante.** Comparative Politics: An Introduction & New Approach. LC 94-32597. 1995. 52.95 (0-7456-1256-3); pap. 21.95 (0-7456-1257-1) Blackwell Pubs.

Lane, Jan-Erik & Ersson, Svante. Comparative Political Economy. 1990. text ed. 49.00 (0-86187-795-0, Pub. by Pinter Pubs UK); pap. text ed. 14.50 (0-685-47273-6, Pub. by Pinter Pubs UK); pap. text ed. 14.50 (0-86187-858-2, Pub. by Pinter Pubs UK) St Martin.

— Politics & Society in Western Europe. rev. ed. (Illus.). 320p. (C). 1991. pap. text ed. 19.95 (0-8039-8407-3) Sage.

— Politics & Society in Western Europe. 2nd rev. ed. (Illus.). 320p. (C). 1991. text ed. 55.00 (0-8039-8406-5) Sage.

Lane, Jan-Erik & Ersson, Svante O. Politics & Society in Western Europe. 3rd ed. 432p. 1994. 69.95 (0-8039-7795-6); pap. 21.95 (0-8039-7796-4) Sage.

***Lane, Jan-Erik, et al.** Political Data Handbook: OECD Countries. 2nd ed. (Comparative European Politics Ser.). (Illus.). 272p. 1995. 65.00 (0-19-828053-X) OUP.

Lane, Jane. A Call of Trumpets. large type ed. (Shadows of the Crown Ser.). 1974. 15.95 (0-85456-615-5) Ulverscroft.

— The Young & Lonely King. large type ed. (Shadows of the Crown Ser.). 1974. 15.95 (0-85456-613-9) Ulverscroft.

Lane, Jay, ed. see Horwitz, Ken.

Lane, Jay, ed. see Martinson, Linda.

Lane, Jay, ed. see Northwest Seafood Consultants Staff.

Lane, Jay, ed. see Rezvani, Kate A.

Lane, Jay B., ed. Cousins' Cuisine: An All-American Family Cookbook. (Illus.). 134p. (Orig.). 1988. pap. 5.95 (0-934363-05-6) Lance Pubns.

Lane, Jeremy. Yellow Men Sleep. (Illus.). 1983. 15.00 (0-937986-99-2) D M Grant.

Lane, John. Against Information. Crowe, Thomas R., ed. (Illus.). 8p. 1994. 1.00 (1-883197-04-X) New Native Pr.

— Against Information & Other Poems. LC 94-69299. 68p. (Orig.). 1995. pap. 7.95 (1-883197-06-6) New Native Pr.

— Body Poems. limited ed. 20p. 1991. pap. 4.50 (0-685-64796-X) New Native Pr.

— The Living Tree: Art & the Sacred. (Illus.). (Orig.). 1992. pap. 19.95 (1-870098-15-3, Pub. by Green Bks UK) Seven Hills Bk.

— Weed Time: Essays from the Edge of a Country Yard. 70p. (Orig.). Date not set. pap. 8.00 (0-9638731-3-X) Holocene Pr.

Lane, John, ed. Management Techniques for School Districts. (Illus.). 114p. (Orig.). 1985. pap. 15.00 (0-910170-40-1) Assn Sch Busn.

— Marketing Techniques for School Districts. (Illus.). 199p. (Orig.). 1986. pap. 16.00 (0-910170-43-6) Assn Sch Busn.

Lane, John, jt. ed. see Stevenson, Kenneth.

Lane, John E., jt. auth. see Hammel, Eric.

Lane, John H., Jr. Voluntary Associations among Mexican Americans in San Antonio, Texas: Organizational & Leadership Characteristics. Cortes, Carlos E., ed. LC 76-1292. (Chicano Heritage Ser.). 1977. 20.95 (0-405-09510-4) Ayer.

***Lane, John J., ed.** Ferment in Education: A Look Abroad. 220p. 1995. 26.00 (0-226-46862-3) U Ch Pr.

Lane, John J. & Epps, Edgar G., eds. Restructuring the Schools: Problems & Prospects. LC 91-66584. (NSSE Series on Contemporary Educational Issues). 217p. 1992. 29.25 (0-8211-1116-7); text ed. 26.25 (0-685-67389-8) McCutchan.

Lane, John J. & Walberg, Herbert J., eds. Effective School Leadership: Policy & Process. LC 86-63774. (NSSE Series on Contemporary Educational Issues). 218p. (C). 1987. 30.50 (0-8211-1115-9); text ed. write for info. (0-685-17950-8) McCutchan.

Lane, John J., jt. ed. see Walberg, Herbert J.

Lane, John R. & Larsen, Susan C., eds. Abstract Painting & Sculpture in America 1927-1944. LC 83-3850. (Illus.). 256p. 1983. pap. text ed. 24.95 (0-88039-006-9) Mus Art Carnegie.

Lane, John R., et al, eds. Carnegie International, 1985. LC 85-25870. (Illus.). 256p. (Orig.). 1985. pap. 10.00 (0-88039-011-5) Mus Art Carnegie.

***Lane, Joseph M.** Metabolic Bone Disease: Outcomes Research. Keller, Robert B., ed. (Current Opinion in Orthopedics Ser.). (Illus.). 91p. (Orig.). 1994. pap. text ed. 59.95 (1-85922-652-3) Current Science.

Lane, Joseph M. & Healey, John H., eds. Diagnosis & Management of Pathologic Fractures. LC 92-48561. 192p. 1993. 115.50 (0-7817-0062-0) Raven.

Lane, Joseph P., jt. auth. see Mann, William C.

Lane, Joyce, jt. auth. see Adams, Russ.

Lane, Joyce, jt. auth. see Lane, Eric.

Lane, Julie. The Life & Adventures of Santa Claus. (Illus.). 144p. (J). 1987. 12.95 (0-685-19459-0) Equity Pubng NH.

— The Life & Adventures of Santa Claus. rev. ed. (Illus.). 154p. (J). 1985. pap. 10.00 (0-9615664-1-8) Parkhurst Brook Pubs.

Lane, K. A., ed. Machine Tools, 1984: Proceedings of the International Conference, Birmingham, U. K., June 26-28, 1984. 650p. 1984. 120.50 (0-444-87542-5, North Holland) Elsevier.

***Lane, Karen.** The Medical Assisting Examination Guide: A Comprehensive Review for Certification. 2nd ed. (Illus.). 340p. (C). 1995. pap. text ed. 28.00 (0-8036-0039-9) Davis Co.

— Medical Assisting Examination Guide Comprehensive Review for Certification. (Illus.). 192p. (C). 1991. pap. 27.95 (0-8036-5464-2) Davis Co.

— Medications: A Guide for the Health Professions. (Illus.). 322p. 1992. pap. text ed. 24.95 (0-8036-5466-9) Davis Co.

Lane, Karen, ed. Saunders Manual of Medical Assisting Practice. LC 92-49703. (Illus.). 888p. 1992. text ed. 44.50 (0-7216-3063-4) Saunders.

Lane, Keith & Speed, Sandra M. Black Relationships the Truth: A Practical Guide to Loving Relationships in the 90s. LC 94-71753. 200p. 1994. pap. 15.00 (0-9641951-9-4) Creative Commun.

Lane, Kel. Shadows: A Book of Verse. LC 91-90777. 61p. (Orig.). 1992. pap. 7.00 (0-9631621-0-1) K Lane.

Lane, Kelley, et al. Managing in Mexico: A Cultural Perspective. 14p. (SPA.). (C). 1985. pap. text ed. 5.25 (0-937795-05-4) Border Res Inst.

Lane, Kenneth A. Developing Your Child for Success. LC 90-62570. (Illus.). 230p. 1991. per. 24.95 (1-878145-00-2) Learning Potentials.

— Reversal Errors: Theories & Procedures. Corngold, Sally M., ed. LC 88-50982. (Illus.). 153p. (Orig.). 1988. pap. 15.00 (0-929780-00-0) VisionExtension.

Lane, Kenneth S. Field Test Sections Save Cost in Tunnel Support: Report from Underground Construction Research Council. LC 76-378194. 64p. reprint ed. pap. 25.00 (0-317-08502-6, 2014477) Bks Demand.

Lane, Kenneth S., ed. see North American Rapid Excavation & Tunneling Conference Staff.

Lane, Kit. Beyond B., M., & D. A Guide to Collecting & Publishing Family History. LC 90-60630. 52p. (Orig.). 1990. pap. 3.84 (1-877703-18-4) Pavilion Pr.

— Built on the Banks of the Kalamazoo. LC 93-83589. (Saugatuck Maritime Ser.). (Illus.). 288p. 1993. pap. 17.50 (1-877703-00-1) Pavilion Pr.

— Buried Singapore: Michigan's Imaginary Pompeii. LC 93-83589. (Illus.). 64p. 1994. pap. 5.50 (1-877703-09-5) Pavilion Pr.

— The Day the Elephant Died & Other Tales of Saugatuck. LC 90-61362. (Illus.). 72p. (Orig.). 1990. pap. 5.50 (1-877703-19-2) Pavilion Pr.

— The Dustless Road to Happyland: Chicago-Saugatuck Passenger Boats 1859-1929. LC 95-68184. (Saugatuck Maritime Ser.: Vol. 2). (Illus.). 160p. (Orig.). 1995. pap. 15.50 (1-877703-01-X) Pavilion Pr.

— John Allen: Michigan's Pioneer Promoter. (Illus.). 224p. 1989. 19.50 (1-877703-17-6); pap. 11.50 (1-877703-16-8) Pavilion Pr.

— The Letters of William G. Butler & Other Tales of Saugatuck. LC 94-66962. (Illus.). 80p. (Orig.). 1994. pap. 5.50 (1-877703-23-0) Pavilion Pr.

— Lucius Lyon: An Eminently Useful Citizen. LC 91-60196. (Illus.). 352p. 1991. 19.50 (1-877703-21-4) Pavilion Pr.

— Michigan's Victorian Poets. 52p. 1993. pap. 4.00 (1-877703-10-9) Pavilion Pr.

— The Popcorn Millionaire & Other Tales of Saugatuck. LC 91-60187. (Illus.). 94p. (Orig.). 1991. pap. 5.50 (1-877703-20-6) Pavilion Pr.

— Western Allegan County, Michigan. (Illus.). 541p. 1988. 64.50 (0-88107-122-6) Curtis Media.

— The Wreck of the Hippocampus & Other Tales of Saugatuck. LC 92-80010. (Illus.). 96p. (Orig.). 1992. pap. 5.50 (1-877703-22-2) Pavilion Pr.

Lane, Kit & Lane, Art. Australia: A Traveler's Preview. LC 89-62874. (Illus.). 80p. (Orig.). 1989. pap. 5.95 (1-877703-15-X) Pavilion Pr.

— Fiji: A Traveler's Preview. LC 89-62878. (Illus.). 64p. (Orig.). 1989. pap. 5.95 (1-877703-14-1) Pavilion Pr.

— Galapagos Islands: A Traveler's Preview. LC 89-62879. (Illus.). 64p. (Orig.). 1989. pap. 5.95 (1-877703-13-3) Pavilion Pr.

— Winter on Spain's Costa del Sol: A Traveler's Preview. LC 90-62946. (Illus.). (Orig.). 1990. pap. 5.95 (1-877703-12-5) Pavilion Pr.

Lane, Kristi. Feelings Are Real: Intermediate Workbook. vii, 48p. (J). (gr. 4-6). 1991. 6.95 (1-55959-016-5) Accel Devel.

— Feelings Are Real: Leader Manual. x, 150p. (Orig.). 1991. pap. text ed. 12.95 (1-55959-014-9) Accel Devel.

— Feelings Are Real: Primary Workbook. viii, 40p. (J). (gr. 2-3). 1991. 6.95 (1-55959-015-7) Accel Devel.

Lane, Larry. Claim Your Money from Insurance Companies. LC 93-85361. (Illus.). 310p. 1993. pap. 14.95 (0-9622317-2-X) Tailight Studio.

Lane, Larry M. & Wolf, James F. The Human Resource Crisis in the Public Sector: Rebuilding the Capacity to Govern. LC 90-32647. 248p. 1990. text ed. 55.00 (0-89930-491-5, WRJ/, Quorum Bks) Greenwood.

Lane, Lea, jt. auth. see Linde, Shirley.

Lane, Leonard G. Gallaudet Survival Guide to Signing. LC 89-25686. (Illus.). 224p. (Orig.). 1990. pap. 5.95 (0-930323-67-X) Gallaudet Univ Pr.

Lane, LeRoy E. By All Means, Communicate: An Introduction to Basic Speech. 384p. (C). 1987. pap. text ed. write for info. (0-13-109612-5) P-H.

Lane, Leroy L. By All Means Communicate. 2nd ed. 384p. (C). 1990. pap. text ed. write for info. (0-13-109687-7) P-H.

Lane, Linda. Focus on Pronunciation: Principles & Practice for Effective Communication. LC 92-33239. 1993. teacher ed 14.95 (0-8013-1098-9, 79556); pap. text ed. 23.70 (0-8013-0806-2, 7866) Longman.

— Focus on Pronunciation: Principles & Practice for Effective Communication, 4 cass., Set. LC 92-33239. 1993. audio 66.00 (0-8013-0807-0, 78867) Longman.

Lane, Linda & Andrews, Nancy L. Malibu 90265. 1991. mass mkt. 4.95 (0-8217-3488-1) Zebra.

Lane, Lois W. Posey with the Insane & Sane. LC 92-85409. 107p. 1993. pap. 5.95 (1-55523-548-4) Winston-Derek.

***Lane, Maggie.** Jane Austen & Food. LC 95-5995. 1995. 40.00 (1-85285-124-4) Hambledon Press.

— Jane Austen's Family: Through Five Generations. (Illus.). 276p. 1984. text ed. 37.50 (0-7090-1744-8) Trans-Atl Phila.

— Literary Daughters. LC 88-34348. (Illus.). 222p. 1989. text ed. 35.00 (0-312-02853-9) St Martin.

Lane, Marc J. Legal Handbook for Small Business. rev. ed. LC 88-48039. 272p. 1989. 19.95 (0-8144-5951-X) AMACOM.

— Purchase & Sale of Small Businesses: Tax & Legal Aspects. 2nd ed. (Business Practice Library). 781p. 1991. text ed. 121.00 (0-471-52084-5) Wiley.

— Purchase & Sale of Small Businesses: Tax & Legal Aspects, Vol. 2. 2nd ed. (Business Practice Library). 1188p. 1991. text ed. 242.00 (0-471-52083-7); text ed. 121.00 (0-471-52085-3) Wiley.

— Taxation for Engineering & Technical Consultants. LC 80-12065. 182p. reprint ed. pap. 51.90 (0-317-07941-7, 2055530) Bks Demand.

— Taxation for Small Manufacturers. LC 80-11621. 174p. reprint ed. pap. 49.60 (0-317-07945-X, 2055532) Bks Demand.

— Taxation for the Computer Industry. LC 80-12070. 189p. reprint ed. pap. 53.90 (0-317-07943-3, 2055531) Bks Demand.

Lane, Marcia. Picturing the Rose: A Way of Looking at Fairy Tales. LC 93-5777. 121p. 1994. 30.00 (0-8242-0848-X) Wilson.

Lane, Margaret. The Beaver. LC 81-67074. (Illus.). 32p. (J). (gr. k-4). 1981. 13.99 (0-8037-0624-3) Dial Bks Young.

— The Beaver. (Illus.). 32p. (J). (gr. k-4). 1993. pap. 4.99 (0-14-054925-0, Puff Pied Piper) Puffin Bks.

— Bronte Story. LC 75-108394. (Illus.). 368p. 1971. reprint ed. text ed. 35.00 (0-8371-3817-5, LABS, Greenwood Pr) Greenwood.

— The Fish: The Story of the Stickleback. LC 81-5545. (Illus.). 32p. (J). (ps-4). 1981. 13.99 (0-8037-2580-9) Dial Bks Young.

— The Fish: The Story of the Stickleback. (Illus.). 32p. (J). (gr. k-4). 1994. pap. 4.99 (0-14-055276-6, Puff Pied Piper) Puffin Bks.

— The Fox. LC 82-71355. (Illus.). 32p. (J). (ps-4). 1981. 13.99 (0-8037-2491-8) Dial Bks Young.

— The Fox. (Illus.). 32p. (J). (gr. k-4). 1994. pap. 4.99 (0-14-050337-4, Puff Pied Piper) Puffin Bks.

— The Frog. LC 81-1228. (Illus.). 32p. (J). (gr. k-4). 1981. 13.99 (0-8037-2711-9) Dial Bks Young.

— The Frog. (Illus.). 32p. (J). (gr. k-4). 1994. pap. 4.99 (0-14-050340-4, Puff Pied Piper) Puffin Bks.

— The Spider. LC 82-71354. (Illus.). 32p. (J). (ps-4). 1983. 13.99 (0-8037-8303-5, 0339-110) Dial Bks Young.

— The Spider. (Illus.). 32p. (J). (gr. k-4). 1994. pap. 4.99 (0-14-055277-4, Puff Pied Piper) Puffin Bks.

— The Squirrel. LC 81-1229. (Illus.). 32p. (J). (gr. k-4). 1981. 13.99 (0-8037-8230-6) Dial Bks Young.

— The Squirrel. (Illus.). 32p. (J). (gr. k-4). 1993. pap. 4.99 (0-14-054926-9, Puff Pied Piper) Puffin Bks.

Lane, Margaret T. State Publications & Depository Libraries: A Reference Handbook. LC 80-24688. (Illus.). 560p. 1981. text ed. 105.00 (0-313-22118-9, LSP/, Greenwood Pr) Greenwood.

Lane, Mark. Chicago Eyewitness. LC 68-58740. (Illus.). (Orig.). 1968. 14.95 (0-8392-5013-4); pap. 10.95 (0-686-66377-2) Astor-Honor.

— Plausible Denial: Was the CIA Involved in the Assassination of JFK? (Illus.). 432p. 1992. pap. 13.95 (1-56025-048-8) Thunders Mouth.

— Rush to Judgment. 512p. 1992. pap. 13.95 (1-56025-043-7) Thunders Mouth.

Lane, Mark & Gregory, Dick. Murder in Memphis: The FBI & the Assassination of Martin Luther King. 336p. 1993. pap. 13.95 (1-56025-056-9) Thunders Mouth.

Lane, Martha, jt. auth. see Steen, Arleen.

Lane, Martha A. Emergency English: A Handbook for Tutors. rev. ed. 1991. pap. 8.99 (0-8066-2584-8, 10-25848) Augsburg Fortress.

— Emergency English Workbook. rev. ed. 228p. 1991. pap. 11.99 (0-8066-2585-6, 10-25856) Augsburg Fortress.

Lane, Martha L., jt. auth. see Steen, Arlene.

Lane, Martha S. Malawi. LC 89-25433. (Enchantment of the World Ser.). (Illus.). 128p. (J). (gr. 5-9). 1990. lib. bdg. 20.55 (0-516-02720-4) Childrens.

An Asterisk (*) at the beginning of an entry indicates that the title is appearing in BIP for the first time.

Lane, Mary. Pot Pourri: A Practical Guide. 100p. 1985. 60.00 (0-685-12458-4, Pub. by Bishopsgate Pr Ltd UK); pap. 21.00 (0-685-12459-2, Pub. by Bishopsgte Pr UK) St Mut.
— Soaring on a Grasshopper's Back. Wilson, Christine & Wilson, Austin, eds. (Illus.). 141p. 1983. 9.95 (0-9612144-0-6) Vireo Pr.
Lane, Mary B. & Signer, Sheila. Infant - Toddler Caregiving: A Guide to Creating Partnerships with Parents. (Program for Infant - Toddler Caregivers Ser.). (Illus.). 102p. 1990. pap. 12.50 (0-8011-0878-0) Calif Education.
Lane, Mary C. Melbo Years: A History of the School of Education of the University of Southern California, 1953-73. LC 74-12808. (Illus.). 350p. 1974. 25.00 (0-88474-017-X) U of S Cal Pr.
Lane, Mary E. A Guide to the Antiquities of the Fayyum. 1985. pap. 17.50 (977-424-042-1, Pub. by Am Univ Cairo Pr UA) Col U Pr.
Lane, Mary H., ed. see Proctor, Elizabeth M.
***Lane, Mary L. & Weinberger, Scott R.** Flying with Baby: A Parent's Guide to Making Air Travel with an Infant or Toddler Easy. 20p. (Orig.). 1994. pap. 5.95 (0-9643266-0-4) Third St Pr.
Lane, Mary T. & Wileman, Ralph E. A Structure for Population Education: Goals, Generalizations, & Behavioral Objectives. 2nd ed. LC 74-77985. 1978. pap. 4.00 (0-89055-128-6) Carolina Pop Ctr.
Lane, Max, tr. see Rendra, Willibordus S.
Lane, Max, tr. see Toer, Pramoedya A.
Lane, Mervin, ed. Black Mountain College: Sprouted Seeds- An Anthology of Personal Accounts. LC 90-35968. (Illus.). 368p. 1990. 35.00 (0-87049-663-8) U of Tenn Pr.
Lane, Michael. A Man's View of Life & Love. Allums, Betty, ed. 57p. (Orig.). 1988. pap. 8.00 (0-932211-02-X) BA Cross Ctrl.
— Pink Highways: Tales of Queer Madness on the Open Road. LC 94-20515. 1995. 19.95 (1-55972-263-0, Birch Ln Pr) Carol Pub Group.
Lane, Michael & Crotty, Jim. Mad Monks on the Road: A Forty-Seven-Thousand-Hour Dashboard Adventure Across America - from Paradise, California, to Royal, Arkansas, & up the New Jersey Turnpike. (Illus.). 288p. (Orig.). 1993. pap. 11.00 (0-671-76797-6, Fireside) S&S Trade.
Lane, Michael K., et al. Style Manual for Political Science. (C). 1993. pap. 4.00 (1-878147-09-9) Am Political.
Lane, Mike, ed. see Vitale, Mike.
Lane, Mills. Architecture of the Old South. LC 93-1550. 1993. 55.00 (1-55859-044-7) Abbeville Pr.
— Architecture of the Old South: Georgia. (Illus.). 264p. 1990. 34.95 (1-55859-021-8) Abbeville Pr.
— Architecture of the Old South: Kentucky & Tennessee. (Illus.). 245p. 1993. 55.00 (0-88322-022-9) Beehive GA.
— Architecture of the Old South: Louisiana. (Illus.). 264p. 1990. 34.95 (1-55859-022-6) Abbeville Pr.
— Architecture of the Old South: Mississippi & Alabama. (Illus.). 264p. 1989. 34.95 (1-55859-008-0) Abbeville Pr.
— Architecture of the Old South: North Carolina. (Illus.). 264p. 1990. 34.95 (1-55859-009-9) Abbeville Pr.
— Architecture of the Old South: South Carolina. (Illus.). 264p. 1989. 34.95 (1-55859-004-8) Abbeville Pr.
— Architecture of the Old South: Virginia. (Illus.). 240p. 1989. 34.95 (0-89659-970-1) Abbeville Pr.
— The People of Georgia: An Illustrated History. 2nd ed. (Illus.). 312p. 1992. 50.00 (0-88322-000-8) Beehive GA.
— Savannah Revisited: History & Architecture. 4th ed. (Illus.). 218p. 1994. 35.00 (0-88322-021-0) Beehive GA.
***Lane, Mills, ed.** Dear Mother: Don't Grieve about Me, If I Get Killed, I'll Only be Dead: Letters from Georgia Soldiers in the Civil War. (Illus.). 356p. 1990. 35.00 (0-88322-009-1) Beehive GA.
— General Oglethorpe's Georgia: Colonial Letters 1733-1743, 2 vols., Set. 674p. 1990. 60.00 (0-88322-001-6) Beehive GA.
— Georgia, History Written by Those Who Lived It. (Documentary History Ser.). 360p. 1995. 40.00 (0-88322-020-2) Beehive GA.
— Neither More nor Less Than Men: Slavery in Georgia. (A Documentary History Ser.). 248p. 1993. 35.00 (0-88322-016-4) Beehive GA.
— The Rambler in Georgia: Travellers' Accounts of Frontier Georgia. (Illus.). 233p. 1990. 30.00 (0-88322-003-2) Beehive GA.
— Standing upon the Mouth of a Volcano: New South Georgia. (A Documentary History Ser.). 245p. 1993. 35.00 (0-88322-018-0) Beehive GA.
— Times That Prove People's Principles: Civil War Georgia. (Documentary History Ser.). 276p. 1993. 35.00 (0-88322-017-2) Beehive GA.
Lane, N. E. Skill Acquisition Rates & Patterns. (Recent Research in Psychology Ser.). (Illus.). 170p. 1987. pap. 46.00 (0-387-96579-3) Spr-Verlag.
Lane, N. Gary. Life of the Past. 3rd ed. (Illus.). 352p. (C). 1992. pap. write for info. (0-02-367405-9) Macmillan.
Lane, Nancy. How to Have a Happy New Rear! (Illus.). (Orig.). 1983. pap. 4.95 (0-912171-00-6, 50M) World Pr Ltd.
— Saving Face. write for info. (0-318-58989-3) World Pr Ltd.
— Understanding Eugene Ionesco. Hardin, James N., ed. LC 93-42291. (Understanding Modern European & Latin American Literature Ser.). 200p. (C). 1994. text ed. 34.95 (0-87249-981-2) U of SC Pr.
Lane, Nancy, jt. ed. see Chisholm, Margaret.
Lane, Norman, jt. auth. see Irwin, Robert.
Lane, Norman H. & Zaritsky, Howard M. Federal Income Taxation of Estates & Trusts. 1988. Supplemented semi-annually; write for info. 135.00 (0-7913-0012-9, FIET) Warren Gorham & Lamont.
***Lane, P. H.** Commentary on the Australian Constitution: With Sixth Cumulative Supplement. suppl. ed. 298p. 1994. pap. 75.00 (0-455-21278-3, Pub. by Law Bk Co) W W Gaunt.
— A Digest of Australian Constitutional Cases. 3rd ed. xxi, 487p. 1988. 102.00 (0-455-20812-3, Pub. by Law Bk Co); pap. 63.00 (0-455-20813-1, Pub. by Law Bk Co) W W Gaunt.
— A Digest of Australian Constitutional Cases. 4th ed. 483p. 1992. 110.00 (0-455-21145-0, Pub. by Law Bk Co); pap. 68.00 (0-455-21146-9, Pub. by Law Bk Co) W W Gaunt.
— An Introduction to the Australian Constitution. 5th ed. ix, 276p. 1990. pap. 32.00 (0-455-21012-8, Pub. by Law Bk Co) W W Gaunt.
— Introduction to the Australian Constitutions. 6th ed. 320p. 1994. text ed. 36.00 (0-455-21260-0, Pub. by Law Bk Co) W W Gaunt.
— Lane's Commentary on the Australian Constitution. suppl. ed. 766p. 1986. 195.00 (0-455-20701-1, Pub. by Law Bk Co) W W Gaunt.
— Lane's Commentary on the Australian Constitution. suppl. ed. xxxviii, 766p. 1991. pap. 54.00 (0-455-21045-4, Pub. by Law Bk Co) W W Gaunt.
— A Manual of Australian Constitutional Law. 4th ed. xxii, 565p. 1987. pap. 74.50 (0-455-20771-2, Pub. by Law Bk Co) W W Gaunt.
Lane-Palagyi, Addyse. The East River & the Unicorn Tapestries. 160p. 1992. 24.95 (1-56538-026-6); pap. 12.95 (1-56538-025-8) Addison-Pacific.
***Lane, Pamela S.** Conflict Resolution for Kids: A Group Facilitator's Guide. 80p. 1995. spiral bd. 12.95x (1-56032-387-6) Accel Devel.
***Lane, Patrick.** Woman in the Dust: Drawings & Poems. (Illus.). 80p. 1995. 27.00 (0-8095-4921-2) Borgo Pr.
Lane, Patrick R., jt. auth. see Pollack, Cecelia.
Lane, Peggy. Facets of Life. Teasley, Jamie, ed. LC 89-51761. 44p. 1990. 5.95 (1-55523-293-0) Winston-Derek.
Lane, Peter. Ceramic Form. LC 87-26427. (Illus.). 224p. (C). 1988. 35.00 (0-8478-0889-0) Rizzoli Intl.
— Contemporary Porcelain. 224p. 1995. 39.95 (0-8019-8635-4) Chilton.
— Europe since Nineteen Forty-Five: An Introduction. LC 85-6012. (Illus.). 304p. 1985. 45.00 (0-389-20575-3, N8134) B&N Imports.
— Success in British History Seventeen Sixty to Nineteen Fourteen. (Success Ser.). (Illus.). 1978. pap. 12.00 (0-7195-3483-6) Transatl Arts.
Lane, Peter, et al. Genstat Five: A Second Course. (Illus.). 256p. 1989. 65.00 (0-19-852201-0); pap. 29.95 (0-19-852218-5) OUP.
— Genstat 5: An Introduction. (Illus.). 176p. 1988. 45.00 (0-19-852209-6) OUP.
Lane, Peter B. The United States & the Balkan Crisis of 1940-41. LC 88-11062. (Modern American History Ser.). 336p. 1988. 20.00 (0-8240-4332-4) Garland.
Lane, Pinkie G. Girl at the Window: Poems by Pinkie Gordon Lane. LC 91-4197. 64p. 1991. text ed. 14.95 (0-8071-1713-7); pap. 7.95 (0-8071-1714-5) La State U Pr.
— I Never Scream: New & Selected Poems. LC 85-80139. 104p. (Orig.). 1985. per. 7.50 (0-916418-58-8) Lotus.
Lane-Poole, E. W. Arabic-English Lexicon, Vol. I. 1500p. (C). 1993. text ed. 165.00 (1-56744-491-1) Kazi Pubns.
— Arabic-English Lexicon, Vol. II. 1520p. (C). 1993. text ed. 165.00 (1-56744-492-X) Kazi Pubns.
Lane-Poole, S. The Barbary Corsairs. 334p. 1984. 200.00 (1-85077-018-2, Darf Pubs Ltd) St Mut.
— History of Egypt in the Middle Ages. LC 68-25246. (World History Ser.: No. 48). (C). 1969. reprint ed. lib. bdg. 75.00 (0-8383-0210-6) M S G Haskell Hse.
— Medieval India, Under Mohammedan Rule. LC 70-132442. (World History Ser.: No. 48). 1970. reprint ed. lib. bdg. 75.00 (0-8383-1196-2) M S G Haskell Hse.
— The Moors in Spain. 304p. 1984. 190.00 (1-85077-042-5, Darf Pubs Ltd) St Mut.
— Saladin. 528p. 1985. 300.00 (1-85077-068-9, Darf Pubs Ltd) St Mut.
— The Story of Cairo. (Mediaeval Towns Ser.: Vol. 11). 1974. reprint ed. pap. 40.00 (0-8115-0853-6) Periodicals Srv.
— Turkey. 400p. 1986. 300.00 (1-85077-130-8, Darf Pubs Ltd) St Mut.
Lane-Poole, Stanley. Cairo: Sketches of Its History, Monuments & Social Life. LC 73-6286. (Middle East Ser.). 1979. reprint ed. 33.95 (0-405-05345-2) Ayer.
— History of Egypt in the Middle Ages. (Illus.). 382p. 1968. reprint ed. 35.00 (0-7146-1686-9, Pub. by F Cass Pubs UK) Intl Spec Bk.
— History of India from the Reign of Akbar the Great to the Fall of the Moghul Empire. LC 72-14391. (History of India Ser.: No. 4). reprint ed. 90.00 (0-404-09004-4) AMS Pr.
— The Life of the Right Honourable Stratford Canning, Viscount Stratford de Redcliffe, 2 vols. LC 73-171653. reprint ed. 115.00 (0-404-07387-5) AMS Pr.
— Mediaeval India: Under Mohammed Rule. 1990. reprint ed. 12.50 (0-8364-2517-0, Pub. by Low Price II) S Asia.
— Mediaeval India from the Mohammedan Conquest to the Reign of Akbar the Great. LC 72-14391. (History of India Ser.: No. 3). reprint ed. 90.00 (0-404-09003-6) AMS Pr.
— The Moors in Spain. 212p. 1924. pap. text ed. 49.95 (0-916157-31-8) African Islam Miss Pubns.
— The Moors in Spain. LC 90-81538. (Illus.). 274p. 1990. reprint ed. pap. 14.95 (0-933121-19-9) Black Classic.
— Saladin: And the Fall of the Kingdom of Jerusalem, Vol. 1. 1991. pap. text ed. 15.00 (0-916157-93-8) African Islam Miss Pubns.
— Saladin: And the Fall of the Kingdom of Jerusalem, Vol. 2. 1991. pap. text ed. 15.00 (0-916157-94-6) African Islam Miss Pubns.
— Saladin: And the Fall of the Kingdom of Jerusalem, Vol. 3. 1991. pap. text ed. 15.00 (0-916157-95-4) African Islam Miss Pubns.
— Saladin & the Fall of the Kingdom of Jerusalem. LC 73-14453. (Heroes of the Nations Ser.). reprint ed. 37.50 (0-404-58270-2) AMS Pr.
— Social Life in Egypt: A Description of the Country & Its People. LC 77-87653. (Illus.). reprint ed. 24.50 (0-404-16414-5) AMS Pr.
— The Speeches & Table Talk of the Prophet Muhammad. 189p. 1979. 9.95 (0-318-36781-5) Asia Bk Corp.
— The Story of the Barbary Corsairs. LC 73-97416. (Illus.). 316p. 1970. reprint ed. text ed. 38.50 (0-8371-3231-2, LBC&, Negro U Pr) Greenwood.
— Studies in a Mosque, Vol. 1. Obaba, Al I., ed. 184p. 1990. pap. text ed. 18.00 (0-916157-22-9) African Islam Miss Pubns.
— Studies in a Mosque, Vol. II. 136p. 1990. pap. text ed. 18.00 (0-916157-58-X) African Islam Miss Pubns.
Lane, R. W. & Otten, G., eds. Power Plant Instrumentation for Measurement of High-Purity Water Quality - STP 742. 235p. 1981. 26.50 (0-8031-0798-6, 04-742000-16) ASTM.
Lane, R. Wilder. The Discovery of Freedom: Man's Struggle Against Authority. 3rd ed. 284p. 1984. pap. 12.95 (0-930073-00-2) Fox & Wilkes.
Lane, Richard. Fun Songs for Children. (Illus.). 56p. 1987. pap. 7.95 (0-8256-1094-X, AM63876) Music Sales.
— The Golden Age of Australian Radio Drama. 496p. Date not set. 49.95 (0-522-84556-8) Intl Spec Bk.
— Images from the Floating World. (Illus.). 368p. 1988. 125.00 (0-914427-01-6, Tabard Pr) W S Konecky Assocs.
— Lane's English As a Second Language, 6 bks. Incl. Bk. 1. 76p. 1995. pap. text ed. 9.25 (0-935606-01-7); Bk. 2. 83p. 1987. pap. text ed. 9.25 (0-686-83956-0); Bk. 3. 82p. 1987. pap. text ed. 9.25 (0-686-83957-9); Bk. 4. 84p. 1987. pap. text ed. 9.25 (0-686-83959-5); Bk. 5. 95p. 1987. pap. text ed. 9.95 (0-685-73576-1); Bk. 6. 105p. 1987. pap. text ed. 9.25 (0-686-83961-7); Lane's English Pronunciation Guide. 44p. 1995. per., pap. text ed. 9.25 (0-935606-04-1); Lane's English Pronunciation Guide. 44p. audio 49.95 (0-685-42604-1); Lane's English Pronunciation Guide. 1987. audio 49.95 (0-685-07059-X); (Illus.). 120p. 1987. Set pap. text ed. 9.25 (0-685-07057-3) Lane Pr.
Lane, Richard, ed. Masterpieces of Japanese Prints: The European Collections Ukiyo-e from the Victoria & Albert Museum. (Illus.). 160p. 1991. 40.00 (4-7700-1613-1) Kodansha.
Lane, Richard, ed. see Tuttle, Tom.
Lane, Richard B., jt. auth. see Grossman, Stanley I.
Lane, Richard G. Keno: 11-2 System. 88p. 1992. per. write for info. (0-9631267-7-6) Pubns Pr.
Lane, Richard H. & Douglass, William A. Basque Sheepherders of the American West: A Photographic Documentary. LC 85-291. (Basque Book Ser.). (Illus.). 200p. 1985. 40.00 (0-87417-089-3) U of Nev Pr.
Lane, Richard L., ed. see Freeman, G. D.
Lane, Richard P. & Crosske, Roger W., eds. Medical Insects & Arachnids. LC 92-49000. 1993. write for info. (0-04-124000-6) Chapman & Hall.
Lane, Robert. Shepheards Devises: Edmund Spenser's Shepheardes Calender & the Institutions of Elizabethan Society. LC 92-27594. (Illus.). 256p. 1993. 40.00 (0-8203-1514-1) U of Ga Pr.
Lane, Robert B. & Lane, Barbara. Chehalis River Treaty Council & the Treaty of Olympia. (Treaty Manuscripts Ser.: No. 1). 77p. 15.00 (0-944253-23-7) Inst Dev Indian Law.
— The Treaties of Puget Sound, 1854-1855. (Treaty Manuscripts Ser.: No. 6). 60p. 12.50 (0-944253-28-8) Inst Dev Indian Law.
— Western Washington Treaty Proceedings. (Treaty Manuscripts Ser.: No. 2). 67p. 12.50 (0-944253-24-5) Inst Dev Indian Law.
Lane, Robert C., ed. Psychoanalytic Approaches to Supervision. LC 90-1971. (Current Issues in Psychoanalytic Practice Ser.: No. 2). 224p. 1990. 28.95 (0-87630-603-2) Brunner-Mazel.
Lane, Robert C. & Meisels, Murray, eds. A History of the Division of Psychoanalysis of the American Psychological Association. 384p. 1993. pap. text ed. 49.95 (0-8058-1323-3) L Erlbaum Assocs.
Lane, Robert C., jt. auth. see Edward, David A.
Lane, Robert D. Reading the Bible: Intention, Text, Interpretation. 222p. (Orig.). (C). 1993. pap. text ed. 19.75 (0-8191-9114-0) U Pr of Amer.
Lane, Robert E. The Fear of Equality. (Reprint Series in Social Sciences). (C). 1993. reprint ed. pap. text ed. 1.00 (0-8290-2734-3, PS-162) Irvington.
— The Market Experience. 586p. (C). 1991. pap. 29.95 (0-521-40737-0) Cambridge U Pr.
— Political Man. LC 75-158930. (Illus.). 1972. pap. 12.95 (0-02-917810-X) Free Pr.
Lane, Robert G. A Solitary Dance. LC 82-81020. (Illus.). 240p. (Orig.). (C). 1983. 14.95 (0-943104-82-3); pap. 8.95 (0-943104-83-1) Serrell-Simons.
Lane, Robert S., jt. auth. see Middlekauff, Woodrow S.
Lane, Robert W. Beyond the Schoolhouse Gate: Free Speech & the Inculcation of Values. LC 94-16430. 224p. (C). 1994. text ed. 49.95 (1-56639-274-8) Temple U Pr.
— Beyond the Schoolhouse Gate: Free Speech & the Inculcation of Values. LC 94-16430. 224p. (C). 1995. pap. text ed. 17.95 (1-56639-275-6) Temple U Pr.
Lane, Rodney, jt. ed. see Cella, Charles P.
Lane, Roger. Roots of Violence in Black Philadelphia, 1860-1900. (Illus.). 224p. 1986. 35.00 (0-674-77990-8) HUP.
— Roots of Violence in Black Philadelphia, 1860-1900. 224p. 1989. reprint ed. pap. 14.95 (0-674-77978-9) HUP.
— Violent Death in the City: Suicide, Accident, & Murder in Nineteenth-Century Philadelphia. LC 79-11836. (Commonwealth Fund Publications). 202p. 1979. 32.00 (0-674-93946-8) HUP.
— William Dorsey's Philadelphia & Ours: On the Past & Future of the Black City in America. (Illus.). 512p. 1991. 39.95 (0-19-506566-2, 11827) OUP.
Lane, Roger & Turner, John J., Jr., eds. Riot, Rout, & Tumult: Readings in American Social & Political Violence. LC 77-84752. (Contributions in American History Ser.: No. 69). 399p. 1978. text ed. 49.95 (0-8371-9845-3, LRR/, Greenwood Pr) Greenwood.
— Riot, Rout, & Tumult: Readings in American Social & Political Violence. LC 82-42513. 416p. (C). 1984. reprint ed. pap. text ed. 29.00 (0-8191-2666-7) U Pr of Amer.
Lane, Ron. An Introduction to Utilities. LC 75-19284. 176p. reprint ed. pap. 50.20 (0-317-08595-6, 2010397) Bks Demand.
Lane, Ronald J. & Cross, Tim L. Microcomputer Applications for Agricultural Financial Management. (C). 1986. 32.00 (0-8359-4410-7, Reston); pap. text ed. 21.95 (0-8359-4409-3, Reston) P-H.
Lane, Rosalie. The Picture Knitting Book. (Illus.). 128p. 1994. 24.95 (0-7153-0136-5, Pub. by D & C Pub UK) Sterling.
Lane, Rose W. Discovery of Freedom: Man's Struggle Against Authority. LC 73-172216. (Right Wing Individualist Tradition in America Ser.). 1979. reprint ed. 21.95 (0-405-00425-7) Ayer.
— Free Land. LC 84-7493. iv, 332p. 1984. reprint ed. pap. 10.95 (0-8032-7914-0, Bison Books) U of Nebr Pr.
— Let the Hurricane Roar. LC 85-42742. (Trophy Bk.). 128p. (J). (gr. 5-9). 1985. pap. 3.50 (0-06-440158-8, Trophy) HarpC Child Bks.
— Old Home Town. LC 85-8645. xvii, 309p. 1985. reprint ed. pap. 10.00 (0-8032-7917-5, Bison Books) U of Nebr Pr.
— Young Pioneers. 1976. 15.95 (0-8488-0557-7) Amereon Ltd.
Lane, Rose W., jt. auth. see Wilder, Laura I.
Lane, Rose W., ed. see Wilder, Laura I.
Lane, Rose W., jt. auth. see Wilder, Laura Ingalls.
Lane, Roumelia. Sea of Zanj. large type ed. 1977. 12.00 (0-7089-0067-4) Ulverscroft.
Lane, Russel M., et al. Sport Medicine: Protection, Treatment & Nutrition. LC 73-10420. (Sport Medicine Ser.: Vol. 2). 1974. 29.00 (0-8422-7140-6) Irvington.
Lane, Russell W. Control of Scale & Corrosion in Building Water Systems. LC 92-35156. 1993. text ed. 47.00 (0-07-036217-3) McGraw.
Lane, Ruth. Scenebook for Student Actors. 264p. (C). 1973. Spiralbound. pap. 20.95 (0-8221-0099-1) Intl Thomson.
Lane, S. Mac. Mathematics: Form & Function. (Illus.). xi, 476p. 1985. 49.00 (0-387-96217-4) Spr-Verlag.
Lane, Sandy, jt. ed. see Ryan, Gail D.
Lane, Sarah & Turkovich, Marilyn. Days of the Dead (Los Dias de los Muertos) 39p. (J). (gr. 6-12). 1991. pap. 10.95 (0-930141-42-3) World Eagle.
Lane, Sarah, et al. The Cora: People of the Sierra Madre. 51p. (J). (gr. 6-12). 1989. pap. 9.95 (0-941379-06-X, 5114) World Eagle.
Lane, Scott E. Gambling Card Sharps: How to Beat a Cheater. 230p. 1992. pap. 19.95 (0-9635261-0-3) CAD-Cam Pubn.
Lane, Sharon, et al, eds. The Seattle Times Cookbook. (Illus.). 436p. 1985. 18.95 (0-89716-144-0) P B Pubng.
Lane, Shirley. Reading Sentences, Grade 2. Hoffman, Joan, ed. (I Know It! Bks.). (Illus.). 32p. (J). (gr. 2). 1979. student ed 1.99 (0-938256-09-2) Sch Zone Pub Co.
— Reading Stories, Grade 2. Hoffman, Joan, ed. (I Know It! Bks.). (Illus.). 32p. (J). (gr. 2). 1979. student ed 1.99 (0-938256-10-6) Sch Zone Pub Co.
Lane, Simon. Still Life with Books: A Novel. LC 93-18948. 144p. 1993. 17.95 (1-882593-02-2) Bridge Wrks.
Lane, Susan. How to Make Money in Newspaper Syndication. Hasten, Elizabeth, ed. 132p. (Orig.). 1987. pap. 17.95 (0-9615800-3-8) Newspaper Syn.
Lane, Susan & Hasten, Elizabeth. The Guide to Newspaper Syndication, 1992-1993. 179p. (Orig.). 1992. pap. 19.95 (0-9615800-4-6) Newspaper Syn.
Lane, Sylvia, jt. ed. see Adelman, Irma.
Lane, T. A. & Myllylae, G., eds. Leukocyte-Depleted Blood Products. (Current Studies in Hematology & Blood Transfusion: No. 60). (Illus.). viii, 150p. 1994. 137.75 (3-8055-5862-7) S Karger.
Lane, Tamar. What's Wrong with the Movies? LC 78-160237. (Moving Pictures Ser.). 254p. 1971. reprint ed. lib. bdg. 29.95 (0-89198-038-5) Ozer.
Lane, Terry S., jt. auth. see Feins, Judith D.
Lane, Theodore. Measuring Changes in Alaska's Labor Market: Hours Worked vs People Employed. (Occasional Paper Ser.: No. 16). 13p. 1982. pap. write for info. (0-88353-035-X) U Alaska Inst Res.
Lane, Theodore, ed. Developing America's Northern Frontier. LC 86-28233. (Illus.). 270p. (Orig.). 1987. pap. text ed. 25.00 (0-8191-6082-2, Inst Soc Econ Res) U Pr of Amer.
Lane, Thomas. The Artists' Manifesto: The Time has Come. 1992. 19.95 (0-9631537-0-6) Wildfire Pr.
— A Priesthood in Tune: Theological Reflections on Ministry. 320p. (Orig.). 1993. pap. 12.95 (1-85607-068-9, Pub. by Columba Pr IE) Twenty-Third.
— Way of Quality: Dialogues on Kaizen Thinking. 1993. 21.95 (0-9636387-0-X) Dialogos Pr.
Lane, Thomas, jt. ed. see Hiden, John.
Lane, Tony. Grey Dawn Breaking: British Merchant Seafarers in the Late Twentieth Century. LC 88-31960. (Illus.). 224p. 1988. text ed. 65.00 (0-7190-1876-5, Pub. by Manchester Univ Pr UK) St Martin.

L

Lane, Tony, ed. see Calvin, John.
Lane, Tracy. The Living Organization: Systems of Behavior. LC 88-39746. 229p. 1989. text ed. 55.00 (*0-275-93084-X*, C3084, Praeger Pubs) Greenwood.
Lane, V. P. Security of Computer Based Information Systems. (Computer Science Ser.). (Illus.). 192p. (Orig.). (C). 1985. pap. text ed. 27.50 (*0-333-36437-6*, Pub. by Macmill Press UK) Scholium Intl.
Lane, Vera W. & Molyneaux, Dorothy. The Dynamics of Communicative Development. 432p. (C). 1992. text ed. write for info. (*0-13-222019-9*) P-H.
Lane, Vera W., jt. auth. see Molyneaux, Dorothy.
Lane, Victoria. Shattered Images. 1993. 18.95 (*0-533-10333-9*) Vantage.
Lane, W. Ben & Wright, Paul S., eds. The Presbyterian Elder. rev. ed. LC 92-13900. 1992. pap. 5.99 (*0-664-25427-6*) Westminster John Knox.
Lane, W. Ben, ed. see Fogle, Jeanne S.
Lane, W. Ronald, jt. auth. see Russell, J. Thomas.
Lane, Wheaton J., jt. ed. see Labatut, Jean.
Lane, Wilbur. Evening Devotions. 1993. 8.95 (*0-533-10380-0*) Vantage.
Lane, William. Moonlight Standing in As Cordelia. 1980. pap. 4.50 (*0-914610-20-1*) Hanging Loose.
— Praying with the Saints: Saints' Lives & Prayers. 67p. (Orig.). 1989. pap. 5.95 (*1-85390-034-6*, Pub. by Veritas Publns IE) Ignatius Pr.
— WBC, Vol. 47A: Hebrews. 1991. 24.99 (*0-8499-0246-0*) Word Inc.
Lane, William, ed. A Book of New Testament Prayers. 95p. 1988. reprint ed. pap. 5.95 (*1-85390-046-X*, Pub. by Veritas Publns IE) Ignatius Pr.
***Lane, William, et al.** The Newspaperman's Guide to the Law. 5th ed. 352p. 1990. pap. 86.00 (*0-409-05769-X*, SA); boxed 126.00 (*0-409-05770-3*, SA) Butterworth Legal Pubs.
Lane, William C. Tip, Tap, Toe: The Great Tapdancers. write for info. (*0-318-58990-7*) World Pr Ltd.
Lane, William L. Commentary on the Gospel of Mark. (New International Commentary on the New Testament Ser.). 1974. 27.99 (*0-8028-2502-8*) Eerdmans.
— Hebrews: A Call to Commitment. 192p. 1988. pap. text ed. 9.95 (*0-943575-03-6*) Hendrickson MA.
Lane, William L., et al. The New Testament Speaks. 1969. text ed. 20.00 (*0-06-064917-8*) Harper SF.
Lane-Williams, Mildred. Dust on Their Feet. 1992. 10.95 (*0-533-10194-8*) Vantage.
Lane, Winthrop D. Civil War in West Virginia: A Story of the Industrial Conflict in the Coal Mines. LC 76-89745. (American Labor Ser.). reprint ed. 17.95 (*0-405-02133-X*) Ayer.
***Lane, Yvette O., et al.** I Can Go Anywhere from Home If You Guide Me. (Illus.). 5p. (YA). 1994. pap. 10.00 (*0-913491-31-4*) SCP Third.
Lanecki, Francois. French-English Vocabulary of the Industrial Sewing Machine. 87p. (ENG & FRE.). 1981. reprint ed. pap. 19.95 (*0-8288-0743-4*, M6331) Fr & Eur.
— Lexique de la Machine a Coudre Familiale. Dupre, Celine, ed. 12p. (FRE.). 1974. pap. 9.95 (*0-7859-0800-5*, M-9229) Fr & Eur.
Lanegran, David & Palm, Risa I. An Invitation to Geography. 2nd ed. (Geography Ser.). (Illus.). 1978. text ed. write for info. (*0-07-036216-5*) McGraw.
Laneham, Robert. Captain Cox, His Ballads & Books, or Robert Laneham's Letter. Furnivall, Frederick J., ed. LC 68-57998. (Ballad Society, London. Publications: No. 7). reprint ed. 30.00 (*0-404-50823-5*) AMS Pr.
***Laner, Mary R.** Dating: Delights, Discontents & Dilemmas. 2nd ed. 290p. (C). 1995. pap. text ed. 15.95 (*1-879215-26-8*) Sheffield WI.
Lanes, Douglas M., jt. auth. see Horowitz, Karen.
Lanes, Selma G. The Art of Maurice Sendak. (Illus.). 278p. 1984. pap. 34.98 (*0-8109-8063-0*, Abradale Pr) Abrams.
Lanes, Selma G., jt. auth. see Gish, Lillian.
Laney, Al. Following the Leaders: A Reminiscence. 165p. 1991. 28.00 (*0-940889-34-X*) Classics Golf.
Laney-Cummings, Karen, jt. auth. see Estes, Mark.
Laney, Dolores, ed. see Ceasor, Ebraska D.
Laney, J. C. Site Safety. LC 81-19540. (Site Practice Ser.). (Illus.). 226p. reprint ed. pap. 64.50 (*0-8357-3536-2*, 2034484) Bks Demand.
Laney, J. Carl. Cuando en la Iglesia Hay Pecado. 176p. (Orig.). (SPA.). 1991. pap. 4.95 (*0-88113-050-8*) Edit Betania.
— The Divorce Myth. LC 81-7690. 160p. 1986. pap. 7.99 (*0-87123-892-6*) Bethany Hse.
— Ezra-Nehemiah. (Everyman's Bible Commentary Ser.). (Orig.). 1982. pap. 7.99 (*0-8024-2014-1*) Moody.
— First & Second Samuel. (Everyman's Bible Commentary Ser.). 1982. pap. 7.99 (*0-8024-2010-9*) Moody.
— A Guide to Church Discipline. LC 85-15121. 176p. 1985. 8.99 (*1-55661-108-0*) Bethany Hse.
— Zechariah. (Everyman's Bible Commentary Ser.). (Orig.). (C). 1984. pap. 7.99 (*0-8024-0445-6*) Moody.
Laney, Joan & Mosser, David. Devotional Companion to the International Lessons 94-95. 112p. (Orig.). 1994. pap. 8.95 (*0-687-08635-3*) Abingdon.
Laney, L. Carl. John. 1992. pap. 18.99 (*0-8024-5621-9*) Moody.
Laney, Shelby C. TWO. LC 91-67929. 96p. 1993. pap. 8.00 (*1-56002-188-8*, Univ Edtns) Aegina Pr.
Laney, William R. & Gibilisco, Joseph A., eds. Diagnosis & Treatment in Prosthodontics. LC 82-15171. 575p. reprint ed. pap. 163.90 (*0-685-20935-0*, 2056516) Bks Demand.
Laney, William R. & Tolman, Dan E., eds. Tissue Integration in Oral, Orthopedic, & Maxillofacial Reconstruction. (Illus.). 396p. 1992. text ed. 68.00 (*0-86715-251-6*) Quint Pub Co.
Laney, William R., jt. auth. see Taylor, Thomas D.
Lanfear, Kenneth J., jt. ed. see Harlin, John M.
Lanfear, Vincent W. Business Fluctuations & the American Labor Movement, 1915-1922. LC 68-57572. (Columbia University. Studies in the Social Sciences: No. 247). reprint ed. 20.00 (*0-404-51247-X*) AMS Pr.
Lanford, Mickey. Inside Passage to Death. 240p. (Orig.). 1986. pap. 2.95 (*0-8439-5010-2*) Dorchester Pub Co.
Lanfranc De Milan, Guido. Text & Concordance of Biblioteca Nacional, MS2165: Arte Complida de Cirugia. Wasick, Cynthia M. & Ardemagni, Enrica, eds. (Medieval Spanish Medical Texts Ser.: No. 26). 10p. (SPA.). 1988. 10.00 (*0-940639-25-4*) Hispanic Seminary.
Lanfranchi, Giovanni B. & Parpola, Simo, eds. The Correspondence of Sargon the Second, Pt. II: Letters from the Northern & Northeastern Provinces. (State Archives of Assyria Ser.: Vol. V). xxxvii, 272p. 1991. text ed. 55.00 (*951-570-079-5*, Pub. by Helsinki Univ Pr FI); pap. text ed. 44.00 (*951-570-078-7*, Pub. by Helsinki Univ Pr FI) Eisenbrauns.
Lanfranco of Milan. Lanfrank's Science of Cirurgie. Fleischhacker, R. V., ed. (EETS, OS Ser.: No. 102). 1969. 50.00 (*0-527-00103-1*) Periodicals Srv.
Lanfrey, Pierre. History of Napoleon First, 4 Vols, 1. 2nd ed. LC 77-171654. reprint ed. write for info. (*0-404-07341-7*) AMS Pr.
— History of Napoleon First, 4 Vols, 2. 2nd ed. LC 77-171654. reprint ed. write for info. (*0-404-07342-5*) AMS Pr.
— History of Napoleon First, 4 Vols, 3. 2nd ed. LC 77-171654. reprint ed. write for info. (*0-404-07343-3*) AMS Pr.
— History of Napoleon First, 4 Vols, 4. 2nd ed. LC 77-171654. reprint ed. write for info. (*0-404-07344-1*) AMS Pr.
— History of Napoleon First, 4 Vols, Set. 2nd ed. LC 77-171654. reprint ed. 175.00 (*0-404-07340-9*) AMS Pr.
Lanfur, J. Depths of Hell. LC 85-90917. 145p. (Orig.). 1985. pap. 2.00 (*0-9615034-0-8*) J Lanfur.
Lang. Cost Analysis for Capital Investment Decisions. (Cost Engineering Ser.: Vol. 14). 400p. 1989. 175.00 (*0-8247-7894-4*) Dekker.
— Principles of Air Conditioning. 5th ed. 28p. 1995. teacher ed 10.00 (*0-8273-6592-6*) Delmar.
— Teach Yourself Critical Path Analysis. (Teach Yourself Ser.). 1977. pap. 6.95 (*0-679-10504-2*) McKay.
Lang, jt. auth. see Blass.
Lang, jt. ed. see Kalivas.
Lang, et al. Wax-up for Functional Occlusion. (Illus.). 28p. 1989. ring bd. 20.00 (*0-86715-217-6*) Quint Pub Co.
Lang, A. Books & Bookmen. 1976. lib. bdg. 59.95 (*0-8490-1534-0*) Gordon Pr.
Lang, A. G., jt. auth. see Amos, H. D.
Lang, A. L. Memoirs of Robert E. Lee. 1992. 10.98 (*0-89009-694-5*) Bk Sales Inc.
Lang, Alan R. Alcohol: Teenage Drinking. (Encyclopedia of Psychoactive Drugs Ser.: No. 1). (Illus.). (YA). (gr. 5 up). 1992. lib. bdg. 19.95 (*0-685-52236-9*) Chelsea Hse.
Lang, Albert R., jt. ed. see Bower, Gordon H.
Lang, Aldon S. Financial History of the Public Lands in Texas. Bruchey, Stuart, ed. LC 78-56692. (Management of Public Lands in the U. S. Ser.). 1979. reprint ed. lib. bdg. 19.95 (*0-405-11339-0*) Ayer.
Lang, Amei. Die Geriefte Drehscheibenkeramik der Heuneburg 1950-1970 & Verwandte Gruppen Heuneburgstudien 3. LC 74-76528. (Roemisch-Germanische Forschungen Ser.: Vol. 34). (Illus.). x, 114p. (C). 1974. 84.60 (*3-11-004516-8*) De Gruyter.
Lang, Amy S. Prophetic Woman: Anne Hutchinson & the Problem of Dissent in the Literature of New England. 236p. 1987. pap. 12.00 (*0-520-06608-1*) U CA Pr.
Lang, Andrew. Adventures among Books. LC 73-105023. (Essay Index Reprint Ser.). 1977. 23.95 (*0-8369-1474-0*) Ayer.
— Aladdin. (Illus.). 32p. (J). (gr. k-3). 1983. pap. 5.99 (*0-14-050389-7*, Puffin) Puffin Bks.
— Alfred Tennyson. 2nd ed. LC 70-111615. reprint ed. 27.50 (*0-404-03856-5*) AMS Pr.
— Andrew Lang Fairy Tale Book. 496p. 1987. 28.95 (*0-89966-601-9*) Buccaneer Bks.
— The Arabian Nights Entertainments. (Illus.). 19.25 (*0-8446-0752-5*) Peter Smith.
— The Blue Fairy Book. 25.95 (*0-89190-089-6*, Am Repr) Amereon Ltd.
— The Blue Fairy Book. (J). 19.25 (*0-8446-5495-7*) Peter Smith.
— Blue Poetry Book. LC 77-80375. (Granger Index Reprint Ser.). 1977. 25.95 (*0-8369-6080-7*) Ayer.
— Book of Dreams & Ghosts. LC 71-108815. reprint ed. 37.50 (*0-404-03848-4*) AMS Pr.
— Books & Bookmen. LC 76-115093. (Illus.). reprint ed. 37.50 (*0-404-03818-2*) AMS Pr.
— The Brown Fairy Book. (J). 19.25 (*0-8446-5496-5*) Peter Smith.
— Cock Lane & Common-Sense. LC 74-110572. reprint ed. 39.50 (*0-404-03846-8*) AMS Pr.
— The Crimson Fairy Book. LC 67-17988. (Illus.). (J). (gr. 4-8). 19.25 (*0-8446-0753-3*) Peter Smith.
— Custom & Myth. 2nd rev. ed. LC 68-59267. reprint ed. 37.50 (*0-404-03817-4*) AMS Pr.
— Custom & Myth. (Illus.). 1977. reprint ed. 14.95 (*0-85409-969-7*) Charles River Bks.
— Disentanglers. LC 71-112938. reprint ed. 39.50 (*0-404-03859-X*) AMS Pr.
— Essays in Little. 2nd ed. LC 68-59265. reprint ed. 37.50 (*0-404-03839-5*) AMS Pr.
— The Flying Ship. LC 94-42963. (Illus.). (J). (gr. 2 up). 1995. 16.00 (*0-688-11404-0*); lib. bdg. 15.93 (*0-688-11405-9*) Morrow Jr Bks.
— Green Fairy Book. LC 34-28314. (Airmont Classics Ser.). (Illus.). (J). (gr. 4 up). 1969. pap. 2.95 (*0-8049-0197-X*, CL-197) Airmont.
— History of English Literature. LC 75-95357. reprint ed. 38.00 (*0-404-03872-7*) AMS Pr.
— History of Scotland, 4 Vols, Set. LC 78-109917. reprint ed. 375.00 (*0-404-03860-3*) AMS Pr.
— Homer & His Age. LC 68-59285. reprint ed. 37.50 (*0-404-03867-0*) AMS Pr.
— Homer & the Epic. LC 71-109918. reprint ed. 38.00 (*0-404-03845-X*) AMS Pr.
— How to Fail in Literature. LC 78-101919. reprint ed. 37.50 (*0-404-03837-9*) AMS Pr.
— Lang's Ballads of Books. LC 75-75714. (Granger Index Reprint Ser.). 1977. 18.95 (*0-8369-6024-6*) Ayer.
— Letters on Literature. LC 68-54277. reprint ed. 37.50 (*0-404-03836-0*) AMS Pr.
— Letters to Dead Authors. LC 68-59284. reprint ed. 37.50 (*0-404-03819-0*) AMS Pr.
— Library. LC 68-59288. reprint ed. 40.00 (*0-404-03816-6*) AMS Pr.
— Library: With a Chapter on Modern English Illustrated Books by Austin Dobson. 2nd enl. ed. LC 72-1657. reprint ed. 10.00 (*0-404-03844-1*) AMS Pr.
— Life & Letters of John Gibson Lockhart, 2 Vols. LC 79-110131. 1970. reprint ed. 74.50 (*0-404-03849-2*) AMS Pr.
— The Lilac Fairy Book. (Illus.). (J). (gr. 4-12). 19.25 (*0-8446-2425-X*) Peter Smith.
— Magic & Religion. 1972. 59.95 (*0-8490-0576-0*) Gordon Pr.
— Magic & Religion. LC 76-137255. reprint ed. 29.50 (*0-404-03857-3*) AMS Pr.
— Magic & Religion. LC 69-13964. 316p. 1969. reprint ed. text ed. 59.75 (*0-8371-0933-7*, LAMR) Greenwood.
— Making of Religion. LC 68-59286. reprint ed. 51.50 (*0-404-03854-9*) AMS Pr.
— Mark of Cain. LC 68-54278. reprint ed. 37.50 (*0-404-03828-X*) AMS Pr.
— Modern Mythology. LC 68-54279. reprint ed. 40.00 (*0-404-03852-2*) AMS Pr.
— A Monk of Fife. LC 68-59287. reprint ed. 37.50 (*0-404-03847-6*) AMS Pr.
— More Favorite Fairy Tales. 1976. 20.95 (*0-8488-0822-3*) Amereon Ltd.
— Mystery of Mary Stuart. LC 78-111771. reprint ed. 20.00 (*0-404-03858-1*) AMS Pr.
— Myth, Ritual & Religion, 2 vols. 1993. 59.00 (*1-881338-46-0*) Nataraj Bks.
— Myth, Ritual & Religion, 2 Vols in 1. LC 68-54280. reprint ed. 55.00 (*0-404-03868-9*) AMS Pr.
— Old Friends. LC 70-101914. reprint ed. 37.50 (*0-404-03838-7*) AMS Pr.
— Olive Fairy Book. 22.95 (*0-89190-086-1*, Am Repr) Amereon Ltd.
— The Olive Fairy Book. (Illus.). (J). (gr. 2 up). 19.25 (*0-8446-0754-1*) Peter Smith.
— The Orange Fairy Book. (Illus.). (J). (gr. 4-12). 19.25 (*0-8446-4770-5*) Peter Smith.
— Pickle the Spy. LC 72-110132. reprint ed. 37.50 (*0-404-03853-0*) AMS Pr.
— Pink Fairy Book. (Illus.). 360p. (J). (gr. 4-6). 1966. pap. 6.95 (*0-486-21792-2*) Dover.
— The Pink Fairy Book. (Illus.). (J). (gr. 2 up). 19.25 (*0-8446-0755-X*) Peter Smith.
— Prince Charles Edward. LC 01-25240. reprint ed. 105.00 (*0-404-03855-7*) AMS Pr.
— The Rainbow Fairy Book. LC 92-33449. (Books of Wonder). (Illus.). 288p. (J). 1993. 20.00 (*0-688-10878-4*) Morrow Jr Bks.
— Red Fairy Book. 1976. 15.95 (*0-8488-1403-7*) Amereon Ltd.
— The Red Fairy Book. (Illus.). (J). (gr. 2 up). 19.25 (*0-8446-0756-8*) Peter Smith.
— The Red Fairy Book. 1987. reprint ed. lib. bdg. 16.95 (*0-89966-602-7*) Buccaneer Bks.
— Secret of the Totem. LC 70-115094. 1970. reprint ed. 24.50 (*0-404-03866-2*) AMS Pr.
— Shakespeare, Bacon & the Great Unknown. LC 75-75982. reprint ed. 40.00 (*0-404-03871-9*) AMS Pr.
— Sir Walter Scott & the Border Minstrelsy. LC 68-59266. reprint ed. 37.50 (*0-404-03869-7*) AMS Pr.
— Valet's Tragedy & Other Studies. LC 75-112939. (Illus.). reprint ed. 39.00 (*0-404-03865-4*) AMS Pr.
— The Violet Fairy Book. (Illus.). (J). (gr. 2 up). 19.25 (*0-8446-0757-6*) Peter Smith.
— World of Homer. LC 68-54281. reprint ed. 37.50 (*0-404-03870-0*) AMS Pr.
— The Yellow Fairy Book. (Illus.). (J). (gr. 2 up). 19.25 (*0-8446-0758-4*) Peter Smith.
Lang, Andrew, ed. The Arabian Nights Entertainments. 25.95 (*0-89190-085-3*, Am Repr) Amereon Ltd.
— Arabian Nights Entertainments. LC 69-17098. (Illus.). xv, 424p. (J). (gr. k-6). 1969. reprint ed. pap. 6.95 (*0-486-22289-6*) Dover.
— Blue Fairy Book. LC 34-28315. (Airmont Classics Ser.). (Illus.). (J). (gr. 4 up). 1969. pap. 2.95 (*0-8049-0196-1*, CL-196) Airmont.
— Blue Fairy Book. LC 34-28315. (Illus.). 390p. (J). (gr. 1-6). 1965. pap. 6.95 (*0-486-21437-0*) Dover.
— The Blue Fairy Book. (Illus.). (J). 1994. 8.98 (*1-56731-059-1*, MJF Bks) Fine Comms.
— Brown Fairy Book. (Illus.). (J). (gr. 1-6). pap. 6.95 (*0-486-21438-9*) Dover.
— The Chronicles of Pantouflia. 18.95 (*0-89190-088-8*, Am Repr) Amereon Ltd.
— Crimson Fairy Book. LC 67-17988. (Illus.). 371p. (J). (gr. 4-6). 1966. pap. 6.95 (*0-486-21799-X*) Dover.
— Green Fairy Book. LC 34-28314. (Illus.). 366p. (J). (gr. 4-6). 1965. pap. 6.95 (*0-486-21439-7*) Dover.
— The Green Fairy Book. (Illus.). (J). (gr. 4 up). 19.25 (*0-8446-5056-0*) Peter Smith.
— Grey Fairy Book. LC 67-17983. (Illus.). 387p. (J). (gr. 4-6). 1900. pap. 6.95 (*0-486-21791-4*) Dover.
— Grey Fairy Book. (Illus.). (J). (gr. 4 up). 19.25 (*0-8446-2424-1*) Peter Smith.
— Lilac Fairy Book. (Illus.). 367p. (J). (ps-4). 1968. pap. 6.95 (*0-486-21907-0*) Dover.
— The Lilac Fairy Book. 24.95 (*0-89190-084-5*, Am Repr) Amereon Ltd.
— The Nursery Rhyme Book. 21.95 (*0-89190-082-9*, Am Repr) Amereon Ltd.
— Olive Fairy Book. (Illus.). 330p. (J). (gr. 4-6). 1966. pap. 5.95 (*0-486-21908-9*) Dover.
— Orange Fairy Book. (Illus.). 358p. (J). (gr. 1-6). 1968. pap. 6.95 (*0-486-21909-7*) Dover.
— The Orange Fairy Book. 24.95 (*0-89190-083-7*, Am Repr) Amereon Ltd.
— The Pink Fairy Book. 24.95 (*0-89190-080-2*, Am Repr) Amereon Ltd.
— Red Fairy Book. (Illus.). 367p. (J). (gr. 4-6). pap. 6.95 (*0-486-21673-X*) Dover.
— The Red Fairy Book. (Illus.). (J). 1994. 8.98 (*1-56731-060-5*, MJF Bks) Fine Comms.
— Violet Fairy Book. (Illus.). (J). (gr. 4-6). pap. 6.95 (*0-486-21675-6*) Dover.
— The Violet Fairy Book. 25.95 (*0-89190-081-0*, Am Repr) Amereon Ltd.
— Yellow Fairy Book. (Illus.). 321p. (J). (gr. 4-6). pap. 6.95 (*0-486-21674-8*) Dover.
Lang, Andrew & Henley, W. E. Pictures at Play or Dialogues of the Galleries. LC 70-112940. (Illus.). reprint ed. 37.50 (*0-404-03829-8*) AMS Pr.
Lang, Andrew, tr. see De Saint-Pierre, Bernardin J.
Lang, Andrew, tr. see Homer.
Lang, Andrew G. Estate Agency Law & Practice in N. S. W. 3rd ed. xxx, 513p. 1988. pap. 49.50 (*0-455-20768-2*, Pub. by Law Bk Co) W W Gaunt.
— Residential Tenancies Law & Practice (N. S. W.) 2nd ed. xxiii, 328p. 1990. pap. 39.00 (*0-455-20798-4*, Pub. by Law Bk Co) W W Gaunt.
***Lang, Andrew S.** A Practical Guide to Association Financial Management. LC 95-13207. 1995. 119.00 (*0-8342-0431-2*) Aspen Pub.
— A Practical Guide to Nonprofit Financial Management. LC 95-13206. 1995. 119.00 (*0-8342-0430-4*) Aspen Pub.
Lang, Annie, ed. Measuring Psychological Responses to Media Messages. (LEA's Communication Ser.). 256p. 1994. text ed. 49.95 (*0-8058-0717-9*) L Erlbaum Assocs.
Lang, Anthony E. & Weiner, William J. Drug-Induced Movement Disorders. (Illus.). 416p. 1992. 70.00 (*0-87993-525-1*) Futura Pub.
Lang, Anthony E., jt. auth. see Weiner, William J.
Lang, Anthony E., jt. ed. see Weiner, William J.
Lang, Aubrey. Eagles. (Sierra Club Wildlife Library). 64p. (J). (gr. 3-6). 1990. 15.95 (*0-316-51387-3*) Little.
— Eagles. (Sierra Club Bks.). (Illus.). (J). (gr. 3-6). 1995. pap. 7.95 (*0-316-51383-0*) Little.
— Rudy Visits the North. LC 91-75423. (Illus.). 40p. (J). (ps-2). 1992. lib. bdg. 14.89 (*1-56282-208-X*) Hyprn Child.
***Lang, Barbara F. & Halter, Mary.** Making Choices Curriculum: Life Skills for Adolelscents. 1995. student ed, teacher ed 69.95 (*0-911655-49-2*) Advocacy Pr.
— Making Choices Workbook: Life Skills for Adolescents. 1994. student ed, pap. 8.95 (*0-911655-37-9*) Advocacy Pr.
Lang, Berel. Act & Idea in the Nazi Genocide. 328p. 1990. lib. bdg. 49.95 (*0-226-46868-2*); pap. 14.95 (*0-226-46869-0*) U Ch Pr.
— The Anatomy of Philosophical Style: Literary Philosophy & the Philosophy of Literature. (C). 1990. pap. text ed. 21.95 (*0-631-17546-6*) Blackwell Pubs.
— Art & Inquiry. LC 74-18240. 227p. 1975. lib. bdg. 24.00 (*0-8143-1531-3*) Ridgeview.
— Art & Inquiry. LC 74-18240. 229p. reprint ed. pap. 65.30 (*0-8357-5756-0*, 2032712) Bks Demand.
— Mind's Bodies: Thought in the Art. 128p. 1995. text ed. 39.50x (*0-7914-2553-3*); pap. 12.95x (*0-7914-2554-1*) State U NY Pr.
— Philosophy & the Art of Writing: Studies in Philosophical & Literary Style. LC 81-65865. 248p. 1983. 35.00 (*0-8387-5030-3*) Bucknell U Pr.
— Writing & the Moral Self. 160p. 1991. 42.50 (*0-415-90295-9*, A4289, Routledge NY); pap. 13.95 (*0-415-90296-7*, A4293, Routledge NY) Routledge.
Lang, Berel, ed. The Concept of Style. rev. ed. LC 86-16233. (Illus.). 320p. 1987. pap. 17.95 (*0-8014-9439-7*) Cornell U Pr.
— Writing & the Holocaust. LC 88-11249. 301p. 1989. 45.00 (*0-8419-1184-3*); pap. 19.95 (*0-8419-1185-1*) Holmes & Meier.
Lang, Berel, intro. Philosophical Style: An Anthology about the Reading & Writing of Philosophy. LC 79-20424. 560p. 1980. reprint ed. lib. bdg. 21.50 (*0-88229-230-7*) Hackett Pub.
Lang, Berel, et al. The Death of Art. (World of Art Ser.). 220p. 1984. 55.00 (*0-930586-38-7*) Haven Pubns.
Lang, Berel, et al, eds. The Philosopher in the Community: Essays in Memory of Bertram Morris. LC 84-13224. (Illus.). 190p. (Orig.). 1984. lib. bdg. 48.00 (*0-8191-4187-9*); pap. text ed. 20.50 (*0-8191-4188-7*) U Pr of Amer.
Lang, Bernhard. Wisdom & the Book of Proverbs. LC 85-21527. 204p. 1985. pap. 10.95 (*0-8298-0568-0*) Pilgrim OH.
Lang, Bob. Uncle Bobby's Finally Sober. 77p. (Orig.). 1987. pap. 2.95 (*0-9618264-0-1*) Psalm Thirty Pubs.
Lang, C. B., jt. ed. see Gausterer, H.
Lang, C. B., jt. ed. see Mitter, H.
Lang, Candace D. Irony-Humor: Critical Paradigms. LC 87-45483. 256p. 1988. text ed. 37.50x (*0-8018-3528-3*) Johns Hopkins.
Lang-Carlin, Alexandra. Dark Destiny. 400p. 1984. pap. 3.75 (*0-8439-2111-0*) Dorchester Pub Co.

An Asterisk (*) at the beginning of an entry indicates that the title is appearing in BIP for the first time.

— Wings of Love. 400p. (Orig.). 1987. pap. 3.95 (*0-8439-2501-9*) Dorchester Pub Co.

Lang, Carol E., jt. auth. see Queen, Pat.

Lang, Caroline. Keep Smiling Through: Women in the Second World War. (Women in History Ser.). (Illus.). 48p. (C). 1989. pap. 8.95 (*0-521-37747-1*) Cambridge U Pr.

Lang, Cecil Y. The Pre-Raphaelites & Their Circle. 2nd ed. LC 75-12233. xxix, 592p. 1975. pap. text ed. 16.95 (*0-226-46866-6*, P651) U Ch Pr.

Lang, Cecil Y., ed. see Swinburne, Algernon C.

Lang, Cecil Y., ed. see Tennyson, Alfred.

Lang, Cynthia. Case Method Teaching in Community College: A Guide for Teaching & Faculty Development. 106p. (C). 1986. write for info. (*0-89292-092-0*) Educ Dev Ctr.

Lang, Daniel A. The Disabled Physician: Problem - Solving Strategies for the Medical Staff. LC 89-6673. 148p. (Orig.). 1989. 37.50 (*1-55648-033-4*, 145103) AHPI.

— Medical Staff Peer Review: A Strategy for Motivation & Performance. LC 90-14532. 145p. (Orig.). 1991. 42.50 (*1-55648-065-2*, 145157) AHPI.

***Lang, Daniel A., et al.** Managing Medical Staff Change Through Bylaws & Other Strategies. LC 95-13933. 1995. write for info. (*1-55648-138-1*) AHPI.

Lang, Daniel G. Foreign Policy in the Early Republic: The Law of Nations & the Balance of Power. LC 85-11341. (Political Traditions in Foreign Policy Ser.). 175p. 1985. text ed. 27.50 (*0-8071-1255-0*) La State U Pr.

Lang, Daniel G., jt. ed. see Clinton, David.

Lang, Darrel & Stinston, Bill. Lazy Dogs & Snoozing Frogs: Relaxation & Quieting Activities for Children. 53p. 1988. 10.95 (*0-9611456-4-1*) Coulee Pr.

Lang, David & Odell, John. Korean Joggers: (Shoe Exports) (Pew Case Studies in International Affairs). 50p. (C). 1992. pap. text ed. 2.50 (*1-56927-129-1*) Geo U Inst Dplmcy.

Lang, David M., ed. Lives & Legends of the Georgian Saints. 179p. 1976. pap. 8.95 (*0-913836-29-X*) St Vladimirs.

***Lang, Denise.** The Dark Son. (Illus.). 416p. (Orig.). 1995. mass mkt. 5.99 (*0-380-77595-6*) Avon.

— How to Stop Your Relatives from Driving You Crazy. 272p. 1992. pap. 11.00 (*0-671-78911-2*, Fireside) S&S Trade.

Lang, Denise & DeSilva, Derrick M., Jr. Coping with Lyme Disease: A Practical Guide to Dealing with Diagnosis & Treatment. LC 93-16442. 288p. (Orig.). 1993. pap. 12.95 (*0-8050-2650-9*, Owl) H Holt & Co.

Lang, Denise V. But Everyone Else Looks So Sure of Themselves: A Guide to Surviving the Teen Years. LC 90-39087. (Illus.). 160p. (Orig.). (YA). (gr. 7 up). 1991. pap. 9.95 (*1-55870-177-X*) Shoe Tree Pr.

Lang, Doe. The Secret of Charisma. 370p. reprint ed. pap. 12.95 (*0-934297-00-2*) New Choices.

— Secrets of Charisma: New Ways to Capture the Magic Skills of Leaders & Lovers. 362p. 1993. reprint ed. pap. 5.50 (*0-944007-41-4*, S P I Bks) Sure Sellers.

Lang, Donna. Decorating with Fabric. 1989. pap. 22.00 (*0-517-57378-4*, C P Pubs) Crown Pub Group.

— Decorating with Paper: Extraordinary Ways to Use 1993 Papers Throughout Your Home. 1993. 24.00 (*0-517-88124-1*, C P Pubs) Crown Pub Group.

Lang, Donna & Robertson, Lucretia. Decorating with Paper: Creative Looks with Wallpaper, Art Prints, Giftwrap & More. LC 92-30331. (Illus.). 224p. 1993. 35.00 (*0-517-57753-4*, C P Pubs) Crown Pub Group.

Lang, E., ed. Beta-Blockers in the Elderly. (Illus.). 107p. 1982. pap. 32.00 (*0-387-11682-6*) Spr-Verlag.

— Coatings for High Temperature Applications. (Illus.). 448p. 1984. 124.25 (*0-85334-221-0*, Pub. by Elsevier Applied Sci UK) Elsevier.

— The Role of Active Elements in the Oxidation Behavior of High Temperature Metals & Alloys: Proceedings of the European Colloquim Organized by Commission of the European Communities, Directorate General, Science, Research & Development, Held at the Institute of Advanced Materials, Petten, the Netherlands. 374p. 1989. 81.00 (*1-85166-420-3*) Elsevier.

Lang, E., jt. ed. see Bierwisch, Manfred.

Lang, E., et al. Modelling Spatial Knowledge on a Linguistic Basis: Theory - Prototype - Integration. (Lecture Notes in Artifical Intelligence, Subseries of Lecture Notes in Computer Science: Vol. 481). ix, 138p. 1991. pap. 23.00 (*0-387-53718-X*) Spr-Verlag.

Lang, E. K., et al, eds. Radiology of the Upper Urinary Tract. (Medical Radiology, Diagnostic Imaging & Radiation Oncology Ser.). (Illus.). 384p. 1991. 269.00 (*0-387-52546-7*) Spr-Verlag.

Lang, E. M., tr. see Lepelletier, Edmond A.

Lang, Edgar A. Ludwig Tieck's Early Concept of Catholic Clergy & Church. LC 74-140044. (Catholic University Studies in German: No. 8). reprint ed. 37.50 (*0-404-50228-8*) AMS Pr.

Lang, Edith M. The Effects of Net Interregional Migration on Agricultural Income Growth: The United States, 1850-1860. LC 75-2585. (Dissertations in American Economic History Ser.). (Illus.). 1975. 23.95 (*0-405-07205-8*) Ayer.

Lang, Edith M. & West, George. Musical Accompaniment of Moving Pictures. LC 72-124014. (Literature of Cinema, Ser. 1). 1975. reprint ed. 11.95 (*0-405-01620-4*) Ayer.

Lang, Eleanor M., ed. Art of the Real World. (Masterworks of Literature Ser.). 1979. pap. 13.95 (*0-8084-0424-5*) NCUP.

Lang, Erich K. Roentgenographic Diagnosis of Renal Mass Lesions. LC 70-125008. (Illus.). 190p. 1971. 10.60 (*0-87527-047-6*) Green.

Lang, Erich K., ed. Radiology of the Lower Urinary Tract. LC 93-49790. (Medical Radiology. Diagnostic Imaging & Radiation Oncology Ser.). 1994. write for info. (*0-387-53720-1*) Spr-Verlag.

Lang, Ewald. The Semantics of Coordination. LC 84-14541. (Studies in Language Companion: No. 9). 300p. 1984. 91.00x (*90-272-3008-0*) Benjamins North Am.

Lang, F., ed. Cell Volume Regulation. (Journal: Renal Physiology & Biochemistry: Vol. 11, No. 3-5, 1988). (Illus.). 180p. 1989. pap. 109.75 (*3-8055-4986-5*) S Karger.

— Ion Channels in Renal Epithelia. (Journal: Renal Physiology & Biochemistry: Vol. 13, No. 1-2, 1990). (Illus.). 128p. 1990. pap. 104.00 (*3-8055-5163-0*) S Karger.

— Ion Transport in the Regulation of Cell Proliferation in Cellular Physiology & Biochemistry: Journal: Cellular Physiology & Biochemistry, Vol. 2, No. 3, 1992. (Illus.). 92p. 1992. pap. 35.25 (*3-8055-5638-1*) S Karger.

— The Molecules of Transport Ion Channels. (Journal: Cellular Physiology & Biochemistry: Vol. 3, No. 5-6, 1993). (Illus.). 164p. 1993. pap. 69.75 (*3-8055-5848-1*) S Karger.

— Physiology of Diuretic Action. (Journal: Renal Physiology & Biochemistry: Vol. 10, No. 3, 1987). 92p. 1988. pap. 45.75 (*3-8055-4769-2*) S Karger.

Lang, Franz. Performing Arts Resources, Vol. 9: An Essay on Stage Performance, A Translation of Franz Lang's Dissertatio de Actione Scenica (1727) by Alfred Siemon Golding. Cocuzza, Gininne & Cohen-Stratyner, Barbarba N., eds. Golding, Alfred S., tr. LC 75-646287. (Illus.). 128p. 1984. reprint ed. 25.00 (*0-932610-05-6*) Theatre Lib.

Lang, Frieda A. Parent-Group Counseling: A Counselor's Handbook & Practical Guide. 240p. (Orig.). 1988. text ed. 27.95 (*0-669-18015-7*) Free Pr.

Lang, Fritz. Metropolis. (Classic Screenplay Ser.). (Illus.). 144p. 1990. pap. 9.95 (*0-571-12601-4*) Faber & Faber.

Lang, Fritz & Muth, Jon. M, Vol. 1. (Illus.). 1990. pap. 5.95 (*1-56060-055-1*) Eclipse Bks.

— M, Vol. 2. (Illus.). 1990. pap. 4.95 (*1-56060-056-X*) Eclipse Bks.

— M, Vol. 3. (Illus.). 1990. pap. 4.95 (*1-56060-057-8*) Eclipse Bks.

***Lang, G.** Metallurgy of Non-Ferrous Metals: Glossary of Technical Terms English-French-German-Spanish. 633p. (ENG, FRE & GER.). 1994. pap. 180.00x (*3-87017-223-1*) IBD Ltd.

Lang, G., ed. Swiss Lake & Mire Environments During the last 15,000 Years. (Dissertationes Botanicae Ser.: No. 87). (Illus.). 428p. 1985. pap. 104.00 (*3-7682-1447-8*) Lubrecht & Cramer.

***Lang, G. & Nitsche, J.** Extrusion of Metals: Glossary of Technical Terms English-French-German-Spanish. 295p. (ENG, FRE & GER.). 1991. pap. 140.00x (*3-87017-192-8*) IBD Ltd.

Lang, G. & Schluchter, Ch., eds. Lake, Mire & River Environment During the Last 150000 Years: Proceedings of the INQUA-IGCP 158 Meetings on the Palaeohydrological Changes During the Last 150000 Years, Bern, June, 1985. (Illus.). 248p. (C). 1988. text ed. 70.00 (*90-6191-849-9*, Pub. by A A Balkema NE) Ashgate Pub Co.

Lang, G. P., jt. auth. see Amos, H. D.

Lang, Gehard & Heiss, George D. A Practical Guide to Research Methods. 4th ed. 204p. (Orig.). (C). 1990. lib. bdg. 43.50 (*0-8191-7973-6*); pap. text ed. 22.00 (*0-8191-7974-4*) U Pr of Amer.

Lang, George. The Cafe des Artistes Cookbook: Favorite Recipes from One of New York's Most Romantic Restaurants. (Illus.). 96p. 1984. 14.00 (*0-517-55307-4*, C P Pubs) Crown Pub Group.

— George Lang's Cuisine of Hungary. LC 94-14864. 1994. 12.99 (*0-517-11868-8*) Random Hse Value.

— Lang's Compendium of Culinary. 1994. 6.99 (*0-517-11951-X*) Random Hse Value.

Lang, George, ed. see Ngate, Jonathan.

Lang, George, ed. see Priebe, Richard K.

***Lang, George, et al, comps.** Medal of Honor Recipients, 1863-1994, 2 vols. (Illus.). 352p. 1995. 80.00 (*0-8160-3259-9*) Facts on File.

Lang, Gerhard & Heiss, George D. A Practical Guide to Research Methods. 5th ed. LC 93-40438. 202p. (Orig.). (C). Date not set. lib. bdg. 48.50 (*0-8191-9383-6*); pap. text ed. 23.50 (*0-8191-9384-4*) U Pr of Amer.

***Lang, Gerhard K. & Gotfried.** Corneal & External Disorders & Refractive Disorders. Naumann, O. H., ed. (Current Opinion in Ophthalmology Ser.). (Illus.). (Orig.). 1994. pap. text ed. 59.95 (*1-85922-627-2*) Current Science.

Lang, Gerhard K. & Naumann, Gottfried O. Corneal & External Disorders: Refractive Surgery. (Current Opinion in Ophthalmology Ser.). (Illus.). 115p. (Orig.). 1993. pap. text ed. 59.95 (*1-870485-70-X*) Current Science.

Lang, Gernot. Glossary of Technical Terms: Extrusion of Metals. 800p. (ENG & GER.). 1982. 195.00 (*0-8288-0595-4*, M6604) Fr & Eur.

— Glossary of Technical Terms: Non-Ferrous Metal Casting German-English - English-German. 442p. 1985. lib. bdg. 39.00 (*3-88355-094-9*, Pub. by DGM Metallurgy Info GW) IR Pubns.

Lang, Gernot, tr. see Laue, Kurt & Stenger, Helmut.

Lang, Gerrit, et al. Personal Conversations: Roles & Skills for Counsellors. (International Library of Psychology). 176p. 1990. 49.95 (*0-415-03477-9*, A4149); pap. 14.95 (*0-415-03478-7*, A4153) Routledge.

Lang, Gladys E. & Lang, Kurt. The Battle for Public Opinion: The President, the Press & the Polls During Watergate. 360p. 1983. text ed. 61.00 (*0-231-05548-X*); pap. text ed. 20.00 (*0-231-05549-8*) Col U Pr.

— Etched in Memory: The Building & Survival of Artistic Reputation. LC 89-70715. (H. Eugene & Lillian Youngs Lehman Ser.). (Illus.). xxii, 484p. (C). 1990. 19.95 (*0-8078-1908-5*) U of NC Pr.

Lang, Gladys E., jt. auth. see Lang, Kurt.

Lang, Gladys E., jt. ed. see Lang, Kurt.

Lang, Glenna, illus. My Shadow. LC 88-46107. 32p. (J). (gr. 1 up). 1989. 14.95 (*0-87923-788-0*) Godine.

Lang, Gordon. Miller's Antiques Checklist: Porcelain. Miller, Judith & Miller, Martin, eds. (Illus.). 192p. 1991. 13.95 (*0-85533-894-6*, Pub. by Millers Pubns UK) Antique Collect.

— Miller's Antiques Checklist: Pottery. (Illus.). 192p. 1995. 14.95 (*1-85732-408-0*, Pub. by Millers Pubns UK) Antique Collect.

Lang, Gordon, jt. auth. see Caplan, Sandi.

Lang, Gottfried O. A Study in Culture Contact & Culture Change: The Whiterock Utes in Transition. (Utah Anthropological Papers: No. 15). reprint ed. 10.50 (*0-404-60615-6*) AMS Pr.

Lang, Grace. Love a Hostage. large type ed. (Linford Romance Library). 272p. 1993. pap. 14.95 (*0-7089-7324-8*, Linford) Ulverscroft.

— Springboard to Love. large type ed. (Linford Romance Library). 1991. pap. 13.95 (*0-7089-7062-1*) Ulverscroft.

Lang, Graeme & Ragvald, Lars. The Rise of a Refugee God: Hong Kong's Wong Tai Sin. LC 92-47422. 1993. pap. write for info. (*0-19-585744-5*) OUP.

— The Rise of a Refugee God: Hong Kong's Wong Tai Sin. LC 92-47422. 1993. 58.00 (*0-19-585755-0*) OUP.

***Lang, Greg & Berberich, Chris.** All Children Are Special: Creating an Inclusive Classroom. (Illus.). 152p. (Orig.). (C). 1995. pap. text ed. 18.50 (*1-57110-017-2*) Stenhse Pubs.

Lang, H. Jack. Dear Wit. 256p. 1990. 17.95 (*0-685-31178-3*, Websters New Wrld); pap. 9.95 (*0-685-31179-1*, Websters New Wrld) P-H Gen Ref & Trav.

— Dear Wit: Letters from the World's Wits. 1990. 17.95 (*0-13-961707-8*) P-H.

Lang, Hans J. & Merino, Donald N. The Selection Process for Capital Projects. (Engineering & Technology Management Ser.). 600p. 1993. text ed. 79.95 (*0-471-63425-5*) Wiley.

Lang, Harry G. Silence of the Spheres: The Deaf Experience in the History of Science. LC 93-20838. 187p. 1994. text ed. 49.95 (*0-89789-368-9*, Bergin & Garvey) Greenwood.

***Lang, Harry G. & Meath-Lang, Bonnie.** Deaf Persons in the Arts & Sciences: A Biographical Dictionary. LC 94-24206. 496p. 1995. text ed. 69.50 (*0-313-29170-5*, Greenwood Pr) Greenwood.

Lang, Helen S. Aristotle's Physics & Its Medieval Varieties. LC 91-35652. (Ancient Greek Philosophy Ser.). 322p. (C). 1992. 59.50 (*0-7914-1083-8*); pap. 19.95 (*0-7914-1084-6*) State U NY Pr.

Lang, Henry R., frwd. Cancionero De Baena. 380p. 1971. reprint ed. 25.00 (*0-87535-116-6*) Hispanic Soc.

Lang, Herbert H., ed. see Nixon, Pat I.

***Lang, Herbert O.** History of Tuolumne County Ca. with Biographies. 557p. 1995. reprint ed. lib. bdg. 55.00 (*0-8328-4456-X*) Higginson Bk Co.

Lang, Hilary & Ward, Sue. Women Won't Benefit. (C). 1988. 25.00 (*0-685-33954-8*, Pub. by NCCL UK) St Mut.

Lang-Hinrichs, C. Extrachromosomale in-vitro-Genetik bei Pilzen Chondriom-Vektoren bei Hefen- (Bibliotheca Mycologica Ser.: Vol. 102). (Illus.). 124p. (GER.). 1986. pap. 35.00 (*3-443-59003-9*) Lubrecht & Cramer.

Lang, I. L., jt. auth. see Magay, T.

***Lang, I. M., et al.** Hungarian-English & English Hungarian Dictionary for Tourists. 630p. (C). 1991. pap. 21.00x (*963-05-5984-6*, Pub. by Akad Kiado HU) St Mut.

Lang, Iain. Jazz in Perspective. LC 76-6985. (Roots of Jazz Ser.). 1976. lib. bdg. 22.50 (*0-306-70814-0*) Da Capo.

Lang, Isa. Index to Federal Tax Articles, 5 vols., Set. Goldstein, Gersham et al, eds. 1976. 385.00 (*0-88262-018-5*, IFTA) Warren Gorham & Lamont.

Lang, J. Clinical Anatomy of the Nose & Paranasal Sinuses. (Illus.). 144p. 1989. text ed. 119.00 (*0-86577-330-0*) Thieme Med Pubs.

— Topographische Anatomie des Plexus Brachialis und Thoracic-Outlet-Syndrom. (Illus.). 74p. (GER.). 1985. pap. 43.85 (*3-11-010160-2*) De Gruyter.

Lang, J., jt. ed. see Brown, R.

Lang, J. Spencer. To Awaken a Sleeping Giant. Goodman, Sharon L., ed. (Orig.). 1986. pap. 4.00 (*0-935369-07-4*) In Tradition Pub.

Lang, J. Stephen. Best of Bible Trivia I: Kings, Criminals, Saints & Sinners. 1990. pap. 4.99 (*0-8423-0464-9*) Tyndale.

— Best of Bible Trivia II: Palaces, Poisons, Feasts & Beasts. 176p. 1990. pap. 3.95 (*0-8423-0465-7*) Tyndale.

— The Complete Book of Bible Trivia. 400p. 1988. pap. 11.99 (*0-8423-0421-5*) Tyndale.

— The Whimsical, Quizzical Bible Trivia Book. LC 94-40271. 1995. 10.99 (*0-8423-8001-9*) Tyndale.

Lang, James. Inside Development in Latin America: A Report from the Dominican Republic, Colombia, & Brazil. LC 87-5950. xx, 307p. (C). 1988. 49.95 (*0-8078-1753-8*); pap. 14.95 (*0-8078-4195-1*) U of NC Pr.

Lang, James T. Corpus of Anglo-Saxon Stone Sculpture Vol. III: York & Eastern Yorkshire. (British Academy Ser.). (Illus.). 456p. 1991. 195.00 (*0-19-726079-9*) OUP.

Lang, Jeffery. American Express Guide to Corporate Travel Management. 196p. 1993. 29.95 (*0-8144-0204-6*) AMACOM.

***Lang, Jeffrey.** Struggling to Surrender: Some Impressions of an American Convert to Islam. LC 94-29827. 1994. write for info. (*0-915957-19-1*) Amana Corp.

Lang, Jeffrey B. American Express Guide to Corporate Travel Management. 1993. 29.95 (*0-8100-0204-3*) Northwest Pub.

Lang, Jenifer. Jenifer Lang Cooks for Kids: One Hundred & Fifty-Three Recipes & Ideas for Good Food That Kids Love to Eat. (Illus.). 192p. 1991. 22.50 (*0-517-58417-4*, Harmony) Crown Pub Group.

— Jenifer Lang Cooks for Kids: 153 Recipes & Ideas for Good Food Kids Love to Eat. 1993. 10.00 (*0-517-88027-X*, Crown) Crown Pub Group.

Lang, Jenifer H., ed. Larousse Gastronomique: The New American Edition of the World's Greatest Culinary Encyclopedia. (Illus.). 1988. 60.00 (*0-517-57032-7*, Crown) Crown Pub Group.

***Lang, Jennifer.** The Crowning City. 416p. 1995. pap. 11.95 (*0-7472-4494-4*, Pub. by Headline UK) Trafalgar.

— The Peacock & the Pearl. LC 92-34394. 1992. 22.95 (*0-312-08871-X*) St Martin.

***Lang, Jim.** Great Careers for People Who Want to be Entrepreneurs, Vol. 1. (Career Connections, Series 2: Communications, the Arts, & Entrepreneurship). 48p. 1994. 17.95 (*0-8103-9967-9*, UXL) Gale.

— Make Your Own Breaks: Become an Entrepreneur & Create Your Own Future. 214p. 1994. pap. text ed. 15.95 (*1-880030-25-X*) DBM Pub.

Lang, Joan, ed. see Zagat, Eugene H., Jr. & Zagat, Nina S.

Lang, Joan, ed. see Zagat Survey Staff.

Lang, Joel. Greater Hartford Horizons. LC 91-65842. (Urban Tapestry Ser.). (Illus.). 248p. 1991. 39.50 (*0-9628128-1-1*) Towery Pub.

Lang, Johannes. Clinical Anatomy of the Cervical Spine. (Illus.). 188p. 1993. text ed. 129.00 (*0-86577-486-2*) Thieme Med Pubs.

— Clinical Anatomy of the Masticatory Apparatus & the Peripharyngeal Spaces. (Illus.). 220p. 1994. 149.00 (*0-86577-551-6*) Thieme Med Pubs.

— Clinical Anatomy of the Masticatory Apparatus & the Peripharyngeal Spaces. Telger, Terry C., tr. 1994. write for info. (*3-13-799101-3*) Thieme Med Pubs.

— Clinical Anatomy of the Posterior Cranial Fossa & Its Forimina. (Illus.). 166p. 1991. text ed. 109.00 (*0-86577-379-3*) Thieme Med Pubs.

Lang, Johannes G. Current, Voltage, Resistance. (Siemens Programmed Instruction Ser.: 9). 71p. reprint ed. pap. 25.00 (*0-317-27766-9*, 2052086) Bks Demand.

— The Electric Field. (Siemens Programmed Instruction Ser.: 2). 64p. reprint ed. pap. 25.00 (*0-685-10685-3*, 2052079) Bks Demand.

— The Magnetic Field. (Siemens Programmed Instruction Ser.: No. 3). 67p. reprint ed. pap. 25.00 (*0-317-26183-5*, 2052080) Bks Demand.

***Lang, John, ed.** Pale Moon: Myths & Legends of Native Americans. 160p. 1995. 11.95 (*1-57034-014-5*) ICS Bks.

Lang, John D. & Taylor, Samuel, Jr. Report of a Visit to Some of the Tribes of Indians, Located West of the Mississippi River. 34p. 1973. 7.50 (*0-87770-123-7*) Ye Galleon.

Lang, John T. Digest of State Lotteries. (Illus.). 96p. (Orig.). 1983. pap. write for info. (*0-913397-00-8*) Hilltop Publishing.

Lang, Jon T. Urban Design: The American Experience. LC 93-15893. 509p. 1994. pap. 59.95 (*0-442-01360-4*) Van Nos Reinhold.

Lang, Josephine. Selected Songs. LC 82-2435. (Women Composers Ser.). 1982. 29.50 (*0-306-76097-5*) Da Capo.

Lang, Jovian. Dictionary of the Liturgy. 1989. 9.95 (*0-89942-273-X*) Catholic Bk Pub.

Lang, Jovian P., ed. Unequal Access to Information: Problems & Needs of the World's Information Poor. LC 87-34577. 250p. 1988. pap. 35.00 (*0-87650-239-7*) Pierian.

Lang, Jovian P., ed. see ALA, Reference & Adult Services Division Ad Hoc Committee.

Lang, Julian. Ararapikva: Traditional Karuk Indian Literature from Northwestern California. (Illus.). 112p. 1993. 30.00 (*0-930588-69-X*); pap. 10.95 (*0-930588-65-7*) Heyday Bks.

Lang, Julian, ed. Ararapikva: Traditional Karuk Indian Literature from Northwestern California. 122p. (C). 1993. reprint ed. lib. bdg. 29.00x (*0-8095-4981-6*) Borgo Pr.

Lang, K. Monographie der Harpacticiden. (Illus.). 1682p. (GER.). 1975. reprint ed. lib. bdg. 421.50 (*3-87429-089-1*) Koeltz Sci Bks.

Lang, Karl R., jt. auth. see Donohue, D. A.

Lang, Kathy. The Writer's Guide to Desktop Publishing: Using a Computer to Prepare Reports, Articles & Books. 184p. 1987. pap. text ed. 37.00 (*0-12-436275-3*) Acad Pr.

Lang, Kenneth R. Astrophysical Data: Planets & Stars. (Illus.). 956p. 1993. 59.00 (*0-387-97109-2*) Spr-Verlag.

— Sun, Earth, & Sky. LC 95-6109. 1995. write for info. (*3-540-58778-0*) Spr-Verlag.

— Wanderers in Space: Exploration & Discovery in the Solar System. 1991. pap. 24.95 (*0-521-42252-3*) Cambridge U Pr.

Lang, Kenneth R. & Gingerich, Owen, eds. A Source Book in Astronomy & Astrophysics, 1900-1975. LC 78-9463. (Source Books in the History of the Sciences). 942p. 1979. 90.00 (*0-674-82200-5*) HUP.

— Source Book on Astronomy & Astrophysics. 922p. 1980. 41.95 (*0-318-13544-2*, B0163) HUP.

Lang, Klaus. The Karajan Dossier. 240p. 1993. 22.95 (*0-571-16408-0*) Faber & Faber.

Lang, Klaus, et al. International Construction Terminology. 131p. (ENG & FRE.). 1980. pap. write for info. (*0-7859-4855-4*) Fr & Eur.

Lang, Kurt & Lang, Gladys E. The Unique Perspective of Television & Its Effect: A Pilot Study. (Reprint Series in Social Sciences). (C). 1993. reprint ed. pap. text ed. 1.00 (*0-8290-3797-7*, S-160) Irvington.

Lang, Kurt & Lang, Gladys E., eds. Research in Social Movement, Conflict & Change, Vol. 9. 280p. 1986. 73. 25 (*0-89232-594-1*) Jai Pr.

Lang, Kurt, jt. auth. see Lang, Gladys E.

Lang, L. Absorption Spectra in the Ultraviolet & Visible Region, Vol. XXIV. 420p. 1982. 295.00 (*0-569-08738-4*, Pub. by Collets UK) Pro-Am Music.

Lang, L., et al, eds. Absorption Spectra in the Infrared Region, 2 vols., 1. LC 75-647671. reprint ed. pap. 80.00 (*0-8357-5021-3*, 2025747) Bks Demand.

— Absorption Spectra in the Infrared Region, 2 vols., 2. LC 75-647671. 319p. reprint ed. pap. 91.00 (*0-8357-5022-1*) Bks Demand.

Lang, Larry R. Strategy for Personal Finance. 4th ed. 640p. 1988. text ed. write for info. (*0-07-036317-X*) McGraw.

— Strategy for Personal Finance. 5th ed. LC 92-37247. (Series in Finance). 1993. text ed. write for info. (*0-07-036400-1*) McGraw.

— Strategy for Personal Finance. 5th ed. LC 92-37247. (Series in Finance). 1993. Wkbk. student ed. pap. text ed. write for info. (*0-07-036402-8*) McGraw.

Lang, Laszlo. International Regimes & the Political Economy of East-West Relations. 75p. (C). 1990. pap. text ed. 14.85 (*0-8133-7946-6*) Westview.

Lang, Leonora B., tr. see Rambaud, Alfred N.

***Lang, Lucy.** Tomorrow Is Beautiful. (American Autobiography Ser.). 303p. 1995. reprint ed. lib. bdg. 99. 00 (*0-7812-8573-9*) Rprt Serv.

***Lang, M. & Khoury, C.** Federal Tax Elections. 1992. 155. 00 (*0-7913-0864-2*) Warren Gorham & Lamont.

Lang, M. F. Spanish Word Formation: Productive Derivational Morphology in the Modern Lexis. (Romance Linguistics Ser.). 304p. 1990. 65.00 (*0-415-04143-0*, A4105) Routledge.

Lang, Mabel. The Athenian Citizen. (Excavations of the Athenian Agora Picture Bks.: No. 4). (Illus.). 32p. 1987. pap. 3.00 (*0-87661-632-5*) Am Sch Athens.

— Cure & Cult in Ancient Corinth: A Guide to the Asklepieion. (American Excavations in Old Corinth, Corinth Notes Ser.: No. 1). (Illus.). 32p. 1977. pap. 3.00 (*0-87661-670-8*) Am Sch Athens.

— Graffiti & Dipinti. LC 75-40229. (Athenian Agora Ser.: Vol. 21). (Illus.). x, 116p. 1976. 35.00 (*0-87661-221-4*) Am Sch Athens.

— Graffiti in the Athenian Agora. (Excavations of the Athenian Agora Picture Bks.: No. 14). (Illus.). 1988. pap. 3.00 (*0-87661-633-3*) Am Sch Athens.

— Herodotean Narrative & Discourse. (Martin Classical Lectures: No. 28). (Illus.). 192p. 1984. 20.00 (*0-674-38985-9*) HUP.

— Life, Death & Litigation in the Athenian Agora. (Excavations of the Athenian Agora Picture Bks.: No. 23). (Illus.). 32p. 1994. pap. 3.00 (*0-87661-637-6*) Am Sch Athens.

— Socrates in the Agora. (Excavations of the Athenian Agora Picture Bks.: No. 17). (Illus.). 32p. 1978. pap. 3.00 (*0-87661-617-1*) Am Sch Athens.

— Waterworks in the Athenian Agora. LC 69-22670. (Excavations of the Athenian Agora Picture Bks.: No. 11). (Illus.). 32p. 1968. pap. 3.00 (*0-87661-611-2*) Am Sch Athens.

Lang, Mabel L. Ostraka. LC 90-46998. (Athenian Agora Ser.: Vol. 25). (Illus.). xvi, 188p. 1990. 55.00 (*0-87661-225-7*) Am Sch Athens.

***Lang, Marilyn, ed.** National Directory of Health Care Critical Pathways. 136p. 1995. pap. text ed. 98.00 (*0-9645360-0-5*) Cor Hlthcare.

Lang, Marshall. Gedeon y los Jueces: Gideon & Judges. (SPA.). 6.95 (*84-7645-005-2*, 223079, Pub. by Edit Clie SP) TSELF.

Lang, Marvel, ed. Contemporary Urban America: Problems, Issues, & Alternatives. 480p. (Orig.). (C). 1991. lib. bdg. 58.00 (*0-8191-8261-3*); pap. text ed. 32.00 (*0-8191-8262-1*) U Pr of Amer.

Lang, Marvel & Ford, Clinita A., eds. Strategies for Retaining Minority Students in Higher Education. (Illus.). 180p. (C). 1992. text ed. 39.95x (*0-398-05820-2*) C C Thomas.

— Strategies for Retaining Minority Students in Higher Education. (Illus.). 180p. 1992. pap. 24.95 (*0-398-06222-6*) C C Thomas.

Lang, Meredith. Defender of the Faith: The High Court of Mississippi, 1817-1875. LC 77-7971. 184p. reprint ed. pap. 52.50 (*0-7837-1063-1*, 2041585) Bks Demand.

Lang, Michael, jt. auth. see Young, Jean.

Lang, Michael B. & Khoury, Colleen A. Federal Tax Elections. 1991. ring bd. 105.00 (*0-685-69572-7*, FTE) Warren Gorham & Lamont.

Lang, Michael H. Homelessness Amid Affluence: Structure & Paradox in the American Political Economy. LC 89-32271. 247p. 1989. text ed. 49.95 (*0-275-93167-6*, C3167, Praeger Pubs) Greenwood.

Lang, Mike. Grand Prix Race by Race Account of F-1 World Championship Motor Racing, Vol. 4. (Illus.). 256p. 1992. 49.95 (*0-85429-733-2*) Haynes Pubns.

— Grand Prix, 1950-73, Vols. 1 & 2. (Illus.). 548p. 1991. 39. 95 (*0-85429-861-4*, Pub. by G T Foulis Ltd) Haynes Pubns.

— Grand Prix! 1974 to 1980, Vol. 3. 400p. 35.95 (*0-85429-380-9*, F380, Pub. by G T Foulis Ltd) Haynes Pubns.

Lang, Natalie, ed. see Jones, Lawrence K.

Lang, Natalie, ed. see Kaminski, Robert & Sierra, Judy.

Lang, Natalie, ed. see National Conference of State Legislatures Staff.

Lang, Norma, jt. ed. see Werley, Harriet.

Lang, Norma, et al. Quality of Health Care for Older People in America: A Review of Nursing Studies. 131p. (Orig.). (C). 1990. pap. 23.95 (*1-55810-060-1*, GE-13) Am Nurses Pub.

Lang, Norma C. & Sulman, Joanne, eds. Collectivity in Social Group Work: Concept & Practice. LC 86-31898. (Social Work with Groups Ser.: Vol. 9, No. 4). 125p. 1987. text ed. 29.95 (*0-86656-661-9*) Haworth Pr.

Lang, Norman. Call of the Cuckoo. 1993. mass mkt. 4.99 (*0-06-100622-X*, Harp PBks) HarpC.

— Last Ramadan. (Orig.). 1991. mass mkt. 4.99 (*0-06-100296-8*, Harp PBks) HarpC.

Lang, Olga. Chinese Family & Society. (Illus.). 395p. 1985. reprint ed. pap. 18.00 (*0-89986-373-6*) Oriental Bk Store.

— Pa Chin & His Writings: Chinese Youth Between the Two Revolutions. LC 67-17314. (Harvard East Asian Ser.: No. 28). 418p. 1967. reprint ed. pap. 119.20 (*0-7837-4115-4*, 2057938) Bks Demand.

Lang, Ossian H., ed. Educational Creeds of the Nineteenth Century. LC 78-165722. (American Education Ser, No. 2). (Illus.). 1972. reprint ed. 17.95 (*0-405-03711-2*) Ayer.

Lang, Otto. A Bird of Passage: The Story of My Life. Pavelich, Marnie H., ed. (Illus.). 416p. 1994. 40.00 (*1-56044-294-8*); pap. 24.00 (*1-56044-281-6*) Falcon Pr MT.

Lang, Paul. Die Speusippi Academici Scriptis. 89p. 1965. reprint ed. write for info. (*0-318-70952-X*, Pub. by Georg Olms GW) Lubrecht & Cramer.

Lang, Paul, jt. auth. see Lang, Susan S.

Lang, Paul H. Church Ushering. rev. ed. 1957. pap. 1.95 (*0-570-03522-8*, 14-1141) Concordia.

— What an Altar Guild Should Know. 1964. ring bd. 8.95 (*0-570-03501-5*, 14-1528) Concordia.

Lang, Paul H., ed. Haydn Commemorative Issue of "The Musical Quarterly." LC 82-1590. (Music Reprint Ser.). 1983. reprint ed. lib. bdg. 29.50 (*0-306-76156-4*) Da Capo.

— Music in Western Civilization. (Illus.). (C). 1940. text ed. 35.95 (*0-393-09428-6*) Norton.

— One Hundred Years of Music in America. LC 84-1798. (Music Reprint Ser.). 322p. 1984. reprint ed. lib. bdg. 39. 50 (*0-306-76242-0*) Da Capo.

— Symphony, Eighteen Hundred to Nineteen Hundred. LC 75-77392. (Music Anthology Ser.). (C). 1969. pap. text ed. 19.95 (*0-393-09865-6*) Norton.

***Lang, Paul S. & Lang, Susan S.** Teen Fathers. (Changing Family Ser.). 128p. (YA). (gr. 9-12). 1995. lib. bdg. 14. 49 (*0-531-11216-0*) Watts.

***Lang, Peter, ed.** Mortal City: Storefront Books. (Illus.). 112p. (Orig.). 1995. pap. 11.95 (*1-56898-046-9*) Princeton Arch.

Lang, Peter, ed. see McGuiness, John.

Lang, Peter, ed. see Whitaker, Patrick.

Lang, Richard W. & Harris, Arthur. The Faunal Remains from Arroyo Hondo Pueblo, New Mexico: A Study in Short-Term Subsistence Change. LC 84-10514. (Arroyo Hondo Archaeological Ser.: Vol. 5). (Illus.). 325p. 1984. pap. 15.00 (*0-933452-09-8*) Schol Am Res.

Lang, Robert. American Film Melodrama: Griffith, Vidor, Minelli. 246p. 1989. text ed. 49.50 (*0-691-04759-6*) Princeton U Pr.

Lang, Robert & Kunselman, Joan. Heinrich Schenker, Oswald Jonas, Moriz Violin: A Checklist of Manuscripts & Other Papers in the Oswald Jonas Memorial Collection. LC 94-9207. (Catalogs & Bibliographies Ser.: Vol. 10). 1994. 32.00 (*0-520-09790-4*) U CA Pr.

Lang, Robert, ed. see Griffith, D. W.

Lang, Robert, jt. auth. see Montroll, John.

Lang, Robert, tr. see Ninio, Jacques.

Lang, Robert J. The Complete Book of Origami. 160p. 1989. pap. 6.95 (*0-486-25837-8*) Dover.

— Investment Software Reference Guide. 3rd rev. ed. 128p. 1988. pap. text ed. 11.95 (*0-929777-00-X*) SCIX Corp.

— Origami Insects & Their Kin: Step-by-Step Instructions in Over 1500 Diagrams. LC 95-50. (Illus.). 1995. pap. write for info. (*0-486-28602-9*) Dover.

— Origami Zoo. 1990. pap. 14.95 (*0-312-04015-6*) St Martin.

***Lang, S.** Introduction to Diophantine Approximations. 2nd ed. 136p. 1995. 39.00 (*0-387-94456-7*) Spr-Verlag.

Lang, S., et al. Solutions Manual for Geometry: A High School Course. LC 93-38093. 1994. 29.95 (*0-387-94181-9*) Spr-Verlag.

Lang, S. B. Pyroelectricity, 2 pts., Set. 366p. 1981. text ed. 371.00 (*0-677-40335-6*) Gordon & Breach.

Lang, S. B., jt. auth. see Das Gupta, D. K.

Lang, Sean. The Second World War: Conflict & Cooperation. (History Programme Ser.). 96p. (C). 1993. pap. 10.25 (*0-521-43826-8*) Cambridge U Pr.

— The Second World War: Conflict & Cooperation. (History Programme Ser.). 96p. (C). 1994. pap. 16.95 (*0-521-43827-6*) Cambridge U Pr.

Lang, Serge. Algebraic Number Theory. 2nd ed. LC 93-50625. (Graduate Texts in Mathematics Ser.: Vol. 110). 376p. 1994. text ed. 39.00 (*0-387-94225-4*) Spr-Verlag.

— Differential & Riemannian Manifolds. LC 94-20828. 1995. 49.50 (*0-387-94338-2*) Spr-Verlag.

Lang, Serge, jt. auth. see Jorgenson, Jay.

Lang, Serge A. Abelian Varieties. 260p. 1983. reprint ed. pap. 29.80 (*0-387-90875-7*) Spr-Verlag.

— Algebra. 2nd ed. 714p. (C). 1984. text ed. 63.50 (*0-201-05487-6*, Adv Bk Prog) Addison-Wesley.

— Algebra. 3rd ed. (Illus.). 892p. (C). 1993. text ed. 64.50 (*0-201-55540-9*) Addison-Wesley.

— Algebraic Number Theory. (Graduate Texts in Mathematics Ser.: Vol. 110). 370p. 1993. reprint ed. 29. 80 (*0-387-96375-8*) Spr-Verlag.

— Basic Mathematics. (Illus.). xv, 475p. 1988. pap. 29.80 (*0-387-96787-7*) Spr-Verlag.

— The Beauty of Doing Mathematics. (Illus.). xi, 127p. 1994. pap. 26.00 (*0-387-96149-6*) Spr-Verlag.

— Calculus of Several Variables. 2nd ed. LC 78-55822. (Mathematics Ser.). (Illus.). 1979. text ed. write for info. (*0-201-04299-1*) Addison-Wesley.

— Calculus of Several Variables. 3rd ed. (Undergraduate Texts in Mathematics Ser.). (Illus.). 590p. 1988. 49.00 (*0-387-96405-3*) Spr-Verlag.

— Complex Analysis. (Graduate Texts in Mathematics Ser.: Vol. 103). (Illus.). 385p. 1988. 49.00 (*0-387-96085-6*) Spr-Verlag.

— Complex Analysis. 3rd ed. LC 92-21625. (Graduate Texts in Mathematics Ser.: Vol. 103). (Illus.). 400p. 1995. 59. 00 (*0-387-97886-0*) Spr-Verlag.

— Complex Multiplications. (Grundlehren der Mathematischen Wissenschaften Ser.: Vol. 255). 192p. 1983. 72.00 (*0-387-90786-6*) Spr-Verlag.

— Cyclotomic Fields First & Second. (Graduate Texts in Mathematics Ser.: Vol. 121). (Illus.). 432p. 1989. 49.90 (*0-387-96671-4*, 1209) Spr-Verlag.

— Cyclotonic Fields: Two. (Graduate Texts in Mathematics Ser.: Vol. 69). 288p. 1980. 36.00 (*0-387-90447-6*) Spr-Verlag.

— Differential Manifolds. 2nd ed. (Illus.). ix, 230p. 1988. pap. 29.80 (*0-387-96113-5*) Spr-Verlag.

— Elliptic Curves: Diophantine Analysis. LC 77-21139. (Grundlehren der Mathematischen Wissenschaften Ser.: Vol. 231). 1979. 79.00 (*0-387-08489-4*) Spr-Verlag.

— Elliptic Functions. 2nd ed. (Graduate Texts in Mathematics Ser.: Vol. 112). 340p. 1987. 39.90 (*0-387-96508-4*) Spr-Verlag.

— First Course in Calculus. 4th ed. LC 77-76193. (Mathematics Ser.). (Illus.). 1978. text ed. write for info. (*0-201-04149-9*) Addison-Wesley.

— A First Course in Calculus. 5th ed. (Undergraduate Texts in Mathematics Ser.). (Illus.). xv, 727p. 1993. reprint ed. 39.95 (*0-387-96201-8*) Spr-Verlag.

— Fundamentals of Diophantine Geometry. (Illus.). 400p. 1983. 69.00 (*0-387-90837-4*) Spr-Verlag.

— Introduction to Algebraic & Abelian Functions. (Graduate Texts in Mathematics Ser.: Vol. 89). (Illus.). 176p. 1982. 49.00 (*0-387-90710-6*) Spr-Verlag.

— Introduction to Arakelov Theory. (Illus.). x, 187p. 1988. 49.95 (*0-387-96793-1*) Spr-Verlag.

— Introduction to Complex Hyperbolic Spaces. (Illus.). 300p. 1987. 59.90 (*0-387-96447-9*) Spr-Verlag.

— Introduction to Linear Algebra. LC 77-100872. (Mathematics Ser.). (C). 1970. pap. write for info. (*0-201-04206-1*) Addison-Wesley.

— Introduction to Linear Algebra. 2nd ed. (Undergraduate Texts in Mathematics Ser.). (Illus.). viii, 291p. 1993. 38. 00 (*0-387-96205-0*) Spr-Verlag.

— Introduction to Modular Forms. (Grundlehren der Mathematischen Wissenschaften Ser.: Vol. 222). (Illus.). 1987. 69.00 (*0-387-07833-9*) Spr-Verlag.

— Linear Algebra. 3rd ed. (Undergraduate Texts in Mathematics Ser.). (Illus.). 200p. 1994. 39.80 (*0-387-96412-6*) Spr-Verlag.

— Math! Encounters with High School. (Illus.). 150p. 1985. pap. 26.00 (*0-387-96129-1*) Spr-Verlag.

— Number Theory III: Diophantine Geometry. (Encyclopaedia of Mathematical Sciences Ser.: Vol. 60). (Illus.). 304p. 1991. 65.00 (*0-387-53004-5*) Spr-Verlag.

— Real Analysis. 2nd ed. (C). 1983. 45.95 (*0-201-14179-5*, Adv Bk Prog) Addison-Wesley.

— Real Analysis. 3rd ed. LC 92-21208. 600p. 1993. 49.90 (*0-387-94001-4*) Spr-Verlag.

— SL Two (IR) (Graduate Texts in Mathematics Ser.: Vol. 105). (Illus.). xiv, 428p. 1985. reprint ed. 49.00 (*0-387-96198-4*) Spr-Verlag.

— Undergraduate Algebra. (Undergraduate Texts in Mathematics Ser.). (Illus.). 250p. 1986. 36.00 (*0-387-96404-5*) Spr-Verlag.

— Undergraduate Algebra. 2nd ed. Ewing, J. H. et al, eds. (Undergraduate Texts in Mathematics Ser.). (Illus.). xi, 367p. 1994. text ed. 39.80 (*0-387-97279-X*) Spr-Verlag.

— Undergraduate Analysis. (Undergraduate Texts in Mathematics Ser.). (Illus.). 545p. 1995. reprint ed. 45.00 (*0-387-90800-5*) Spr-Verlag.

Lang, Serge A., ed. The File: A Case Study in Correction (1977 - 1979) 712p. 1981. pap. 49.00 (*0-387-90607-X*) Spr-Verlag.

Lang, Serge A. & Cherry, W. Topics in Nevanlinna Theory. Dold, A. et al, eds. (Lecture Notes in Mathematics Ser.: Vol. 1433). (Illus.). ii, 174p. 1990. pap. 26.00 (*0-387-52785-0*) Spr-Verlag.

Lang, Serge A. & Murrow, Gene. Geometry: A High School Course. 2nd ed. (Illus.). 464p. 1991. pap. text ed. 29.80 (*0-387-90727-0*) Spr-Verlag.

— Geometry: A High School Course. 2nd ed. (Illus.). xii, 394p. 1994. 39.95 (*0-387-96654-4*) Spr-Verlag.

Lang, Serge A., ed. see Artin, Emil.

Lang, Serge A., jt. auth. see Fulton, W.

Lang, Serge A., jt. auth. see Kubert, D. S.

Lang Shih Fan, ed. Advances in Fluidization Engineering. LC 90-837. (AIChE Symposium Ser.: Vol. 86, No. 276). 136p. 1990. pap. 52.00 (*0-8169-0488-X*) Am Inst Chem Eng.

Lang, Sidney B. Sourcebook of Pyroelectricity. (Ferroelectricity & Related Phenomena Ser.). 578p. 1974. text ed. 303.00 (*0-677-01580-1*) Gordon & Breach.

Lang, Simon. EINAI, No. 2: Timeslide. 272p. (Orig.). 1993. mass mkt. 4.99 (*0-441-80928-6*) Ace Bks.

— Hopeship. 240p. (Orig.). 1994. mass mkt. 4.99 (*0-441-34306-6*) Ace Bks.

Lang-Sims, Lois. Letters to Lalage: The Letters of Charles Williams to Lois Lang-Sims. LC 89-33241. 97p. 1990. pap. 16.50 (*0-87338-398-2*) Kent St U Pr.

Lang, Stephen & Teninga, Adelaide. Living Long & Loving It! (Friendship Ser.). (Illus.). 48p. (Orig.). 1993. reprint ed. pap. write for info. (*1-882536-11-8*, A100-0035) Bible League.

— Shall We? (Friendship Ser.). (Illus.). 48p. (Orig.). 1993. reprint ed. pap. write for info. (*1-882536-10-X*, A100-0034) Bible League.

Lang, Stephen A. An Investigation of Image Processing Techniques at Pincevent Habitation, No. 1: An Upper Magdalenian Site in Northern France. (Anthropological Research Papers: No. 43). vii, 110p. (Orig.). 1992. 25.00 (*0-936249-13-7*) AZ Univ ARP.

Lang, Stephen J. The Best of Bible Trivia III: Angels, Demons, Scrolls, & Scribes. 1991. pap. 3.95 (*0-8423-0466-5*) Tyndale.

— The Illustrated Book of Bible Trivia. (Illus.). (J). 1991. lib. bdg. 12.99 (*0-8423-1613-2*) Tyndale.

Lang, Steven & Spectre, Peter H. On the Hawser: A Tugboat Album. LC 79-67416. (Illus.). 522p. 1980. 60.00 (*0-89272-071-9*, PIC436) Down East.

Lang, Susan. The Ortho Book of Gardening Basics. Rae, Norman, ed. LC 90-86169. (Illus.). 504p. 1991. 24.95 (*0-89721-233-9*) Ortho Info.

Lang, Susan, ed. see Wolf, Rex & McNair, James.

Lang, Susan M., ed. AOTCB Study Guide for the COTA Certification Examination. 72p. (Orig.). (C). 1994. pap. text ed. 20.00 (*0-9639373-0-8*) Am Occupat Ther.

— AOTCB Study Guide for the OTR Certification Examination. 76p. (Orig.). (C). 1994. pap. text ed. 20.00 (*0-9639373-1-6*) Am Occupat Ther.

Lang, Susan S. Teen Violence. (Violence in America Ser.). (Illus.). 176p. (YA). (gr. 9-12). 1994. lib. bdg. 14.77 (*0-531-11202-0*) Watts.

Lang, Susan S. & Lang, Paul. Censorship. (Illus.). 96p. (YA). (gr. 9-12). 1993. lib. bdg. 14.21 (*0-531-10999-2*) Watts.

Lang, Susan S. & Patt, Richard B. You Don't Have to Suffer: A Complete Guide to Relieving Cancer Pain for Patients & Their Families. (Illus.). 384p. 1994. 25.00 (*0-19-508418-7*) OUP.

— You Don't Have to Suffer: A Complete Guide to Relieving Cancer Pain for Patients & Their Families. (Illus.). 384p. 1995. pap. 10.95 (*0-19-508419-5*) OUP.

Lang, Susan S., jt. auth. see Cayuga Nature Center Staff.

Lang, Susan S., jt. auth. see Lang, Paul S.

Lang, Susan S., jt. auth. see Robbins, Lawrence.

Lang, Susanna, tr. see Bonnefoy, Yves.

***Lang, Tam, et al.** The Light of the Capital: Three Modern Vietnamese Classics from Old Hanoi. Lockhart, Greg & Lockhart, Monique, trs. (Oxford in Asia Paperbacks Ser.). 200p. 1995. pap. 12.95 (*967-65-3093-X*) OUP.

Lang, Terri & Schoenholz, Deborah L. The World's Best Colorbook of Dragons. (Modern Mythologies Ser.: Vol. 1). (Illus.). 64p. (Orig.). 1988. ring bd. 14.50 (*0-317-91171-6*) Uptown Bkworks.

Lang, Thomas A., jt. auth. see Reed, Rosalind.

Lang, Tim & Hines, Colin. The New Protectionism: Protecting the Future Against Free Trade. LC 93-28024. 208p. 1994. 11.95 (*1-56584-135-2*) New Press NY.

— The New Protectionism: Protecting the Future Against Free Trade. 176p. (Orig.). 1993. pap. write for info. (*1-85383-165-4*, Pub. by Erthscan Pubns UK) Island Pr.

***Lang, Timothy.** The Victorians & the Stuart Heritage: Interpretations of a Discordant Past. 215p. (C). 1995. 49.95 (*0-521-47464-7*) Cambridge U Pr.

Lang, Tom & Zier, Don. Jo, the Japanese Short Staff. LC 84-52443. (Illus.). 112p. (Orig.). 1985. pap. 12.95 (*0-86568-058-2*, 310) Unique Pubns.

Lang, Tomas, jt. auth. see Ercegovac, Milos D.

Lang, Tomas, jt. auth. see Moreno, Jaime H.

Lang, Tran T. Computerised Instrumentation. 240p. 1991. text ed. 175.00 (*0-471-92504-7*) Wiley.

— Electronics of Measuring Systems: Practical Implementation of Analogue & Digital Techniques. LC 86-26786. 318p. 1987. text ed. 200.00 (*0-471-91157-7*) Wiley.

Lang, V. Paul. Principles of Air Conditioning. 4th ed. LC 86-32988. 384p. (C). 1987. teacher ed 12.00 (*0-8273-2760-9*); pap. text ed. 32.95 (*0-8273-2759-5*) Delmar.

— Principles of Air Conditioning. 5th ed. LC 94-44734. 1995. 36.95 (*0-8273-6591-8*) Delmar.

Lang, Virgil R. & Krug, Samuel E. Perspectives on the Executive Personality. LC 78-27205. 1983. pap. text ed. 12.50 (*0-918296-12-9*) Inst Personality & Ability.

Lang, Virginia L. Cats. 1994. 7.50 (*0-934536-56-2*) Rose Shell Pr.

Lang, W. History of Seneca County, Ohio. (Illus.). 691p. 1993. reprint ed. lib. bdg. 69.50 (*0-8328-3228-6*) Higginson Bk Co.

Lang, W. Harold. Islands of the Pacific. Kubat, Frank J., Jr., ed. LC 87-83228. (Illus.). 168p. (YA). 1988. 44.95 (*0-945201-00-1*) Gannam-Kubat.

Lang, Walt. United States Military Almanac. 1989. 24.99 (*0-517-68846-8*) Random Hse Value.

Lang, Walter A. J. Job & Science. 2nd rev. ed. (Illus.). 541p. (C). 1993. reprint ed. pap. 29.95 (*0-9633724-0-8*) Genesis Inst.

Lang-Wescott, Martha. Derivative Angles. (Illus.). 30p. (Orig.). 1992. pap. text ed. 7.95 (*0-9619852-0-8*) Treehouse Mtn.

— The Mechanics of Free Will: The Astrology of Perception, Reality & Will. LC 87-51613. (Illus.). 226p. (Orig.). 1987. pap. 19.95 (*0-9619852-5-9*) Treehouse Mtn.

— Mechanics of the Future: Asteroids. (Illus.). 244p. 1991. pap. text ed. 22.95 (*0-9619852-1-6*) Treehouse Mtn.

— The Orders of Light. (Illus.). 320p. (Orig.). 1993. pap. 25. 00 (*0-9619852-3-2*) Treehouse Mtn.

Lang-Wescott, Martha, ed. Asteroid Mechanics, 2 vols., Vol. 2, 80p. (Orig.). 1991. pap. 15.95 (*0-9619852-4-0*) Treehouse Mtn.

Lang, William L., ed. Centennial West: Essays on the Northern Tier States. LC 90-6167. 300p. 1991. 30.00 (*0-295-96965-2*); pap. 17.50 (*0-295-96966-0*) U of Wash Pr.
— Stories from an Open Country: Essays on the Yellowstone Valley. (Illus.). 256p. 1995. pap. 19.95 (*0-9628215-1-9*) Westn Heritage Ctr.
***Lang, Winfried, ed.** Sustainable Development & International Law. LC 95-7301. 1995. lib. bdg. 120.00 (*1-85966-179-3*, Pub. by Graham & Trotman UK) Kluwer Ac.
Langa Mora, Enriaue. Diccionario de Hacienda Publica. 448p. 1990. pap. 45.00 (*0-7859-5975-0*, 8436802489) Fr & Eur.
Langacker, Paul. Precision Tests of the Standard Electroweak Model. 1032p. 1995. text ed. 162.00 (*981-02-1284-4*) World Scientific Pub.
Langacker, Paul, jt. ed. see Cvetic, Mirjam.
Langacker, Ronald W. Concept, Image, & Symbol: The Cognitive Basis of Grammar. 1990. 105.75 (*3-11-012599-4*) Mouton.
— Concept, Image & Symbol: The Cognitive Basis of Grammar. (Cognitive Linguistics Research Ser.: No. 1). (Illus.). x, 395p. (Orig.). (C). 1991. pap. text ed. 29.95 (*3-11-012863-2*, 152-91) Mouton.
— Foundations of Cognitive Grammar: Vol. I, Theoretical Prerequisites. LC 84-51300. 528p. 1987. 52.50 (*0-8047-1261-1*) Stanford U Pr.
— Foundations of Cognitive Grammar, Vol. II: Descriptive Application. LC 84-51300. 608p. 1991. 57.50 (*0-8047-1909-8*) Stanford U Pr.
— Language & Its Structure: Some Fundamental Linguistic Concepts. 2nd ed. LC 68-27167. 275p. (C). 1973. pap. text ed. 25.50 (*0-15-549192-X*) HB Coll Pubs.
Langacker, Ronald W., ed. see Beller, Patricia, et al.
Langacker, Ronald W., ed. see Hyde, Villiana.
Langan, Bernie, ed. see Mayans, Ernesto.
***Langan, Celeste.** Romantic Vagrancy: Wordsworth & the Simulation of Freedom. (Cambridge Studies in Romanticism: No. 15). (Illus.). 302p. (C). 1995. write for info. (*0-521-47507-4*) Cambridge U Pr.
Langan-Fox, Janice, jt. auth. see Poole, Millicent E.
Langan, John. College Writing Skills. 1984. text ed. write for info. (*0-07-036286-6*) McGraw.
— College Writing Skills. 3rd ed. 1992. pap. text ed. write for info. (*0-07-036382-X*) McGraw.
— College Writing Skills with Readings. 3rd ed. LC 92-9865. 1992. pap. text ed. write for info. (*0-07-036384-6*) McGraw.
— English Skills. 4th ed. 544p. (C). 1988. pap. write for info. (*0-318-63988-2*) McGraw.
— English Skills. 5th ed. LC 92-26672. 1992. pap. text ed. write for info. (*0-07-036393-5*) McGraw.
— English Skills with Readings. 2nd ed. 1991. pap. text ed. write for info. (*0-07-036374-9*) McGraw.
— English Skills with Readings. 3rd ed. LC 94-17411. 1994. 18.50 (*0-07-036418-4*) McGraw.
— Guide to the Langan System. 1989. pap. text ed. write for info. (*0-07-036343-9*) McGraw.
— Reading & Study Skills: A Workbook for Writers, Form A. 5th ed. 1992. text ed. write for info. (*0-07-036383-8*) McGraw.
— Reading & Study Skills: A Workbook for Writers, Form B. 4th ed. 1990. pap. text ed. write for info. (*0-07-036346-3*) McGraw.
— Reading & Study Skills: A Workbook for Writers, Form B. 5th ed. LC 93-36861. 1994. pap. text ed. write for info. (*0-07-036413-3*) McGraw.
— Reading & Study Skills: Form B. 3rd ed. 576p. 1986. Ditto masters. write for info. (*0-07-036316-1*) McGraw.
— Sentence Skills, Form C. 4th ed. 1991. pap. text ed. write for info. (*0-07-036377-3*) McGraw.
— Sentence Skills: A Workbook for Writers. 5th ed. LC 94-31072. (Langan Ser.). 1994. write for info. (*0-07-036424-9*) McGraw.
— Sentence Skills: A Workbook for Writers : Form C. 5th ed. 1994. pap. text ed. write for info. (*0-07-036423-0*) McGraw.
— Sentence Skills: A Workbook for Writers, Form A. 3rd ed. 496p. (C). 1986. pap. text ed. write for info. (*0-07-036305-6*) McGraw.
— Sentence Skills: A Workbook for Writers, Form B. 4th ed. 1990. pap. text ed. write for info. (*0-07-036344-7*) McGraw.
— Sentence Skills: A Workbook for Writers: Form B. 5th ed. LC 93-28530. 1994. pap. text ed. write for info. (*0-07-036410-9*) McGraw.
— Sentence Skills: Form A. 5th ed. 1993. pap. text ed. write for info. (*0-07-036396-X*) McGraw.
— Ten Steps to Advancing College Reading Skills. 2nd ed. 496p. (C). 1993. pap. text ed. 16.00 (*0-944210-56-2*) Townsend NJ.
— Ten Steps to Building College Reading Skills, Form A. 2nd ed. 430p. (C). 1993. pap. text ed. 16.00 (*0-944210-58-9*) Townsend NJ.
— Ten Steps to Improving College Reading Skills. 2nd ed. (C). 1992. pap. text ed. 16.00 (*0-944210-52-X*) Townsend NJ.
Langan, John & Nadell, Judith. Doing Well in College: A Concise Guide to Reading, Writing & Study Skills. Talkington, William A., ed. (Illus.). 208p. (Orig.). 1980. text ed. write for info. (*0-07-036262-9*) McGraw.
Langan, John, jt. ed. see Hennelly, Alfred T.
Langan, John, jt. ed. see Weigel, George.
Langan, John, et al. Improving Reading Comprehension Skills. (C). 1992. pap. text ed. 16.00 (*0-944210-54-6*) Townsend NJ.
Langan, John P., ed. Catholic Universities in Church & Society: A Dialogue on Ex corde Ecclesiae. LC 93-22154. 240p. (Orig.). 1993. pap. 14.95 (*0-87840-544-5*) Georgetown U Pr.
Langan, Katherine, tr. see Pike, Kenneth L.
Langan, Mary & Day, Lesley, eds. Women, Oppression & Social Work: Issues in Anti-Discriminatory Practice. LC 92-288. 256p. 1992. 69.95 (*0-415-08030-4*, A9592) Routledge.
Langan, Mary & Lee, Phil, eds. Radical Social Work Today. 276p. 1989. text ed. 65.00 (*0-04-445368-X*); pap. text ed. 19.95 (*0-04-445321-3*) Routledge Chapman & Hall.
Langan, Peter. A Life with Food. (Illus.). 128p. 1992. 39.95 (*0-7475-0220-X*, Pub. by Bloomsbury Pub Ltd UK) Trafalgar.
Langan, Ruth. All That Glitters. 1994. mass mkt. 4.99 (*0-06-108177-9*, Harp PBks) HarpC.
— Angel. 1994. mass mkt. 3.99 (*0-373-28845-X*, 1-28845-5) Harlequin Bks.
— Deception. (Historical Ser.). 1993. mass mkt. 3.99 (*0-373-28796-8*, 1-28796-0) Harlequin Bks.
— Highland Heart. (Historical Ser.: No. 711). 1992. mass mkt. 3.99 (*0-373-28711-9*, 1-28711-9) Harlequin Bks.
— Highland Heaven. (Historical Ser.). 1995. pap. 4.50 (*0-373-28869-7*, 1-28869-5) Harlequin Bks.
— The Highlander. (Historical Ser.). 1994. mass mkt. 3.99 (*0-373-28828-X*, 1-28828-1) Harlequin Bks.
— Texas Hero. (Historical Ser.). 1993. mass mkt. 3.99 (*0-373-28780-1*, 1-28780-4) Harlequin Bks.
— To Love a Dreamer. (Men Made in America Ser.). 1994. pap. 3.99 (*0-373-45192-X*, 1-45192-1) Harlequin Bks.
Langan, Ruth R. Addy Starr. 352p. 1992. 19.00 (*0-7278-4370-2*) Severn Hse.
— Addy Starr. 368p. 1994. mass mkt. 4.99 (*0-505-51989-5*, Love Spell) Dorchester Pub Co.
Langan, Thomas. The Meaning of Heidegger: A Critical Study of an Existentialist Phenomenology. LC 83-12737. ix, 246p. (C). 1983. reprint ed. text ed. 55.00 (*0-313-24124-4*, LAMH, Greenwood Pr) Greenwood.
— Self-Discovery. LC 84-82059. 64p. (Orig.). 1985. pap. text ed. 3.50 (*0-910727-06-6*) Golden Phoenix.
— Tradition & Authenticity in the Search for Ecumenic Wisdom. 256p. (C). 1992. text ed. 34.95 (*0-8262-0800-2*) U of Mo Pr.
Langan, Thomas D. The Meaning of Heidegger. LC 59-9976. 258p. (C). reprint ed. 73.60 (*0-8357-9067-3*, 2006114) Bks Demand.
Langanke, K., et al, eds. Computational Nuclear Physics 1: Nuclear Structure. (Illus.). xii, 209p. 1991. text ed., 5.25 hd 64.50 (*0-387-53571-3*) Spr-Verlag.
— Computational Nuclear Physics 2. LC 92-37450. 216p. 1993. 79.00 (*0-387-97954-9*) Spr-Verlag.
Langard, S. Biological & Environmental Aspects of Chromium. (Topics in Environmental Health Ser.). 1983. 142.00 (*0-444-80441-2*, I-008-83) Elsevier.
Langbaine, Gerard. An Account of the English Dramatick Poets. (Anglistica & Americana Ser.: No. 9). 556p. 1968. reprint ed. 89.70 (*0-685-66488-0*, 05102000, Pub. by Georg Olms GW) Lubrecht & Cramer.
— An Account of the English Dramatick Poets. No. 9. 556p. 1968. reprint ed. write for info. (*0-318-71924-X*, Pub. by Georg Olms GW) Lubrecht & Cramer.
— An Account of the English Dramatick Poets, 1691, 2 vols., Set. LC 92-22686. (Augustan Reprints Ser.: No. 5 (1971)). 1992. 75.00 (*0-404-70105-1*) AMS Pr.
— The Lives & Characters of the English Dramatic Poets. LC 70-144618. reprint ed. 49.50 (*0-404-02769-5*) AMS Pr.
— Momus Trimphans: or The Plagiaries of the English Stage: Expos'd in a Catalogue of All the Comedies, Tragi- Comedies, Masques, Tragedies, Opera's, Pastorals, Interludes. LC 92-24820. (Augustan Reprints Ser.: No. 150 (1971)). reprint ed. 12.00 (*0-404-70150-7*, PR625) AMS Pr.
— Momus Triumphans. LC 74-121838. reprint ed. 37.50 (*0-404-03873-5*) AMS Pr.
— Momus Truimphans: The Plagiaries of the English Stage-Expos'd in a Catalogue. Bd. with Lives & Characters of the English Dramatic Poets. (English Stage Ser.: Vol. 19). 1974. Set lib. bdg. 61.00 (*0-8240-0602-X*) Garland.
Langbart, David A., jt. auth. see Haines, Gerald K.
Langbauer, Laurie. Women & Romance: The Consolations of Gender in the English Novel. LC 90-55116. (Reading Women Writing Ser.). 288p. 1990. 38.95 (*0-8014-2421-6*); pap. 13.95 (*0-8014-9692-6*) Cornell U Pr.
Langbaum, Francesca L., ed. The Random House Basic Dictionary: French. (ENG & FRE.). 1986. mass mkt. 3.99 (*0-345-33712-3*) Ballantine.
Langbaum, Francesca V., jt. auth. see Hall, Robert A., Jr.
Langbaum, Robert. The Mysteries of Identity: A Theme in Modern Literature. LC 81-21894. (Phoenix Ser.). (C). 1982. pap. text ed. 12.00 (*0-226-46873-9*) U Ch Pr.
— The Poetry of Experience: The Dramatic Monologue in Modern Literary Tradition. LC 85-14861. 252p. 1986. reprint ed. pap. text ed. 9.95 (*0-226-46872-0*) U Ch Pr.
— Thomas Hardy in Our Time. LC 94-14199. 1994. write for info. (*0-312-12200-4*) St Martin.
— The Word from Below: Essays on Modern Literature & Culture. LC 87-40140. 288p. 1988. text ed. 35.00 (*0-299-11180-6*) U of Wis Pr.
— Word from Below: Essays on Modern Literature & Culture. LC 87-40140. 288p. 1987. pap. text ed. 14.95 (*0-299-11184-9*) U of Wis Pr.
Langbaum, Robert, ed. Victorian Age: Essays in History & in Social & Literary Criticism. 320p. (C). 1983. reprint ed. pap. 8.00 (*0-89733-055-2*) Academy Chi Pubs.
Langbaum, Robert, ed. see Shakespeare, William.
Langbein, D. Theory of Van der Waals Attraction. LC 25-9130. (Tracts in Modern Physics Ser.: Vol. 72). (Illus.). 150p. 1974. 53.00 (*0-387-06742-6*) Spr-Verlag.
Langbein, Hermann. Against All Hope: Resistance in the Nazi Concentration Camps, 1938-1945. Zohn, Henry, tr. LC 93-16247. 1993. 29.95 (*1-55778-363-2*) Paragon Hse.
Langbein, John H. Prosecuting Crime in the Renaissance: England, Germany, France. LC 73-81670. (Studies in Legal History). (Illus.). 330p. reprint ed. pap. 94.10 (*0-7837-4165-0*, 2059013) Bks Demand.
Langbein, John H. & Waggoner, Lawrence W. Selected Statutes on Trusts & Estates. 851p. 1993. pap. text ed. 21.95 (*1-56662-144-5*) Foundation Pr.
— Selected Statutes on Trusts & Estates. 1,992th ed. 809p. 1991. pap. text ed. 20.95 (*0-88277-961-3*) Foundation Pr.
Langbein, John H. & Wolk, Bruce A. Pension & Employee Benefit Law. (University Casebook Ser.). 673p. 1990. text ed. 37.95 (*0-88277-780-7*) Foundation Pr.
— Pension & Employee Benefit Law. 2nd ed. (Illus.). 912p. 1995. text ed. 44.95 (*1-56662-243-3*) Foundation Pr.
— Pension & Employee Benefit Law: Teacher's Manual. (University Casebook Ser.). 202p. 1990. pap. text ed. write for info. (*0-88277-848-X*) Foundation Pr.
— Pension & Employee Benefit Law: 1994 Supplement. (University Casebook Ser.). 175p. 1994. pap. text ed. 9.00 (*1-56662-203-4*) Foundation Pr.
— Pension & Employee Benefit Law, 1991 Supplement. 87p. (C). 1991. pap. text ed. write for info. (*0-318-68679-1*) Foundation Pr.
— Supplement to Pension & Employee Benefit Lalw, 1993. (University Casebook Ser.). 144p. 1993. pap. text ed. 8.95 (*1-56662-104-6*) Foundation Pr.
Langbein, Laura I. & Lichtman, Allan J. Ecological Inference. LC 77-93283. (Quantitative Applications in the Social Sciences Ser.: Vol. 10). 70p. 1978. pap. 9.95 (*0-8039-0941-1*) Sage.
Langbein, Stanley. Taxation & Regulation of Bank & Thrift Acquisitions. LC 92-30608. (Tax & Estate Planning Ser.). 1993. text ed. 190.00 (*0-07-172152-5*) Shepards-McGraw.
Langberg, Diane. Feeling Good, Feeling Bad. 238p. (Orig.). 1991. pap. 8.99 (*0-89283-713-6*, Vine Bks) Servant.
Langberg, Diane M. Counsel for Pastor's Wives. 128p. (Orig.). 1988. pap. 9.99 (*0-310-37621-1*, 12086P) Zondervan.
***Langberg, Mike.** CD-ROM Superguide. 352p. (Orig.). 1995. pap. 20.00 (*0-345-39278-7*) Ballantine.
Langbert, Mitchell, jt. auth. see Handel, Bernard.
Langbort. Building Success in Math. 1985. pap. 17.25 (*0-534-03394-6*) Seymour Pubns.
Langbridge, R. Charlotte Bronte: A Psychological Study. LC 72-3280. (English Literature Ser.: No. 33). 1972. reprint ed. lib. bdg. 75.00 (*0-8383-1529-1*) M S G Haskell Hse.
Langcaon, Jeff. Where's Kimo? (Illus.). 24p. (J). (gr. k-2). 1993. pap. 6.95 (*1-880188-65-1*) Bess Pr.
Langdale, Cecily. Gwen John. 252p. (C). 1989. reprint ed. 30.00 (*0-300-04484-4*) Yale U Pr.
Langdana, Farrokh K. Sustaining Domestic Budget Deficits in Open Economies. 208p. 1990. 58.00 (*0-415-03735-2*, A3700) Routledge.
Langdana, Farrokh K., jt. auth. see Burdekin, Richard C.
Langdell, C. C. A Summary of the Law of Contracts. xiv, 278p. 1980. reprint ed. lib. bdg. 26.00 (*0-8377-0809-5*) Rothman.
Langdell, Tim. Virtual Reality Beyond Imagination. 1994. pap. 24.95 (*0-672-30458-9*) Sams.
Langdon & Stout. Teaching Moral & Spiritual Values. 1979. 7.95 (*0-933062-02-8*) R H Sommer.
Langdon, jt. auth. see U. C. F. Wellness Institute Staff.
Langdon, A. B., jt. auth. see Birdsall, C. K.
Langdon, Agnes, jt. auth. see Hoffmann, Dirk.
Langdon, Agnes D., jt. ed. see Guilloton, Doris S.
Langdon, Agnes D., et al. Alternativen: A Multi-Option German Reader. LC 88-19101. (Illus.). 272p. (GER.). (C). 1989. pap. text ed. 21.75 (*0-03-003732-8*) HB Coll Pubs.
Langdon, Arthur G. Old Cornish Crosses. 1977. lib. bdg. 134.95 (*0-8490-2367-X*) Gordon Pr.
Langdon, Barbara R. Fairfield County Marriages Seventeen Seventy-Five to Eighteen Seventy-Nine: Implied in Fairfield County, S. C. Probate Records. 262p. (Orig.). 1986. pap. 20.00 (*0-938741-03-9*) Langdon & Langdon.
— York County Marriages Seventeen Seventy to Eighteen Sixty-Nine: Implied in York County, S. C. Probate Records. rev. ed. 100p. (Orig.). 1986. reprint ed. pap. text ed. 15.00 (*0-938741-00-4*) Langdon & Langdon.
Langdon, Barbara R. & Langdon, Shirley P. Barnwell County Marriages Seventeen Seventy-Five to Eighteen Seventy-Nine: Implied in Barnwell County, S. C. Probate & Equity Records. rev. ed. 188p. (Orig.). 1987. reprint ed. pap. text ed. 20.00 (*0-938741-01-2*) Langdon & Langdon.
— Chester County Marriages Seventeen Seventy-Eight to Eighteen Seventy-Nine: Implied in Chester County, S. C. Probate & Equity Records. 221p. (Orig.). 1985. pap. text ed. 20.00 (*0-938741-02-0*) Langdon & Langdon.
Langdon-Brown, Walter. Thus We Are Men. LC 79-86768. (Essay Index Reprint Ser.). 1977. 23.95 (*0-8369-1148-2*) Ayer.
Langdon-Dahm, Martha. Trade Secrets: Twenty-Five Proven Success Tools for Working, Dealing & Winning with People. LC 85-82343. 211p. (Orig.). 1986. pap. 14.95 (*0-936585-00-5*) Learn Deve.
***Langdon, Danny.** The New Language of Work. 300p. 1995. 27.95 (*0-87425-990-8*) Human Res Dev Pr.
Langdon, Danny G. The Adjunct Study Guide. LC 77-25457. (Instructional Design Library). (Illus.). 100p. 1978. 23.95 (*0-87778-105-2*) Educ Tech Pubns.
— The Audio Workbook. LC 77-25109. (Instructional Design Library). (Illus.). 80p. 1978. 23.95 (*0-87778-109-5*) Educ Tech Pubns.
— The Construct Lesson Plan: Improving Group Instruction. LC 77-25406. (Instructional Design Library). (Illus.). 96p. 1978. 23.95 (*0-87778-111-7*) Educ Tech Pubns.
— Interactive Instructional Designs for Individualized Learning. LC 72-89577. 176p. 1973. pap. 19.95 (*0-87778-041-2*) Educ Tech Pubns.
Langdon, Danny G., ed. see Alden, Jay.
Langdon, Danny G., ed. see Broadwell, Martin M.
Langdon, Danny G., ed. see Bullock, Donald H.
Langdon, Danny G., ed. see Caskey, Owen L.
Langdon, Danny G., ed. see DeVries, David L., et al.
Langdon, Danny G., ed. see Dormant, Diane.
Langdon, Danny G., ed. see Endsley, William R.
Langdon, Danny G., ed. see Engelmann, Siegfried.
Langdon, Danny G., ed. see Esbensen, Thorwald.
Langdon, Danny G., ed. see Feldhusen, John F.
Langdon, Danny G., ed. see Godfrey, Robert C.
Langdon, Danny G., ed. see Horabin, Ivan & Lewis, Brian.
Langdon, Danny G., ed. see Kapfer, Philip G. & Kapfer, Miriam B.
Langdon, Danny G., ed. see Lauridsen, David.
Langdon, Danny G., ed. see Merrill, M. David, et al.
Langdon, Danny G., ed. see Norton, Margaret, et al.
Langdon, Danny G., ed. see Parker, Lorne A. & Monson, Mavis K.
Langdon, Danny G., ed. see Rahmlow, Harold F., et al.
Langdon, Danny G., ed. see Rahmlow, Harold F.
Langdon, Danny G., ed. see Russell, James D.
Langdon, Danny G., ed. see Sherman, J. Gilmour & Ruskin, Robert S.
Langdon, Danny G., ed. see Sherman, Thomas M.
Langdon, Danny G., ed. see Stolovitch, Harold D.
Langdon, Danny G., ed. see Stolovitch, Harold D. & Thiagarajan, Sivasailam.
Langdon, Danny G., ed. see Thiagarajan, Sivasailam.
Langdon, Danny G., ed. see Thiagarajan, Sivasailam & Stolovitch, Harold D.
Langdon, Danny G., ed. see Thiagarajan, Sivasailam.
Langdon, Danny G., ed. see Von Harrison, Grant & Guymon, Ronald E.
Langdon, Danny G., ed. see Wales, Charles E. & Stager, Robert A.
Langdon, Danny G., ed. see Wohlking, Wallace & Gill, Patricia J.
Langdon, Danny G., ed. see Wydra, Frank T.
Langdon-Davies, J. Air Raid. LC 74-16278. (World History Ser.: No. 48). 1974. lib. bdg. 51.95 (*0-8383-1839-8*) M S G Haskell Hse.
Langdon-Davies, John. Seeds of Life. 1955. 9.95 (*0-8159-6808-6*) Devin.
Langdon, Davis, et al. European Construction Cost Handbook. 400p. 1993. 139.95 (*0-87629-282-1*, 67300) R S Means.
***Langdon, Davis, Seah International Staff.** Asia-Pacific Construction Costs Handbook. 1994. 139.95 (*0-87629-346-1*) R S Means.
Langdon, E. Jean & Baer, Gerhard, eds. Portals of Power: Shamanism in South America. LC 91-42609. (Illus.). 360p. 1992. 37.50x (*0-8263-1345-0*) U of NM Pr.
Langdon, Emma F. Cripple Creek Strike: A History of Industrial Wars in Colorado 1903-4-5. LC 75-90402. (Mass Violence in America Ser.). (Illus.). 1975. reprint ed. 46.95 (*0-405-01322-1*) Ayer.
Langdon, Frank, jt. ed. see Akaha, Tsuneo.
Langdon, Frank C. & Ross, Douglas A., eds. Superpower Maritime Strategy in the Pacific. 252p. 1990. 59.95 (*0-415-04387-5*, A4136) Routledge.
Langdon, George D. Pilgrim Colony: A History of New Plymouth, 1620-1691. LC 66-21526. (Yale Publications in American Studies: No. 12). 268p. reprint ed. pap. 76. 40 (*0-8357-8268-9*, 2033796) Bks Demand.
Langdon, Glen G., Jr. Computer Design. LC 81-71785. (Illus.). 577p. (C). 1982. 39.00 (*0-9607864-0-6*) Computeach.
Langdon, Guy & Hecklingbottom, David, eds. Computer Handbook: The Sinclair QL. (C). 1985. pap. text ed. 40. 00 (*0-273-02244-X*, Pub. by Pitman Pubng UK) St Mut.
Langdon, Harry. Children Celebrate: Thirty-Nine Plays for Feasts. 104p. 1993. 7.95 (*0-86716-165-5*) St Anthony Mess Pr.
Langdon, Helen. Holbein. (Color Library). (Illus.). 128p. (C). 1994. pap. 14.95 (*0-7148-2867-X*, Pub. by Phaidon Press UK) Chronicle Bks.
— Holbein. (Color Library). (Illus.). 128p. (C). 1994. reprint ed. 19.95 (*0-7148-3218-9*, Pub. by Phaidon Press UK) Chronicle Bks.
Langdon, Henrette W. Hispanic Children & Adults with Communication Disorders: Assessment & Intervention. LC 91-42491. (Excellence in Practice Ser.). 450p. 1992. 54.00 (*0-8342-0288-3*) Aspen Pub.
Langdon, Ida. Milton's Theory of Poetry & Fine Art: And Essay. (BCL1-PR English Literature Ser.). 342p. 1992. reprint ed. lib. bdg. 89.00 (*0-7812-7385-4*) Rprt Serv.
Langdon, J. H. Functional Morphology of the Miocene Hominoid Foot. (Contributions to Primatology Ser.: Vol. 22). (Illus.). x, 226p. 1986. 78.50 (*3-8055-4258-5*) S Karger.
Langdon, John H. Human Dissection for the Health Sciences. LC 93-1842. (Spiral Manual Ser.). 336p. 1993. 33.95 (*0-316-51394-6*) Little.
Langdon, John S. Byzantium's Last Imperial Offensive in Asia Minor: The Documentary Evidence for & Hagiographical Lore about John III Ducas Vatatzes's Crusade Against the Turks, 1222 or 1225 to 1231. (Hellenism: Ancient, Mediaeval, Modern Ser.: No. 7). (Illus.). 172p. 1992. text ed. 45.00 (*0-89241-497-9*) Caratzas.
Langdon, John S., et al, eds. To Hellenikon, Studies in Honor of Speros Vryonis, Jr., 2 vols., Set. 1018p. Date not set. lib. bdg. 140.00 (*0-89241-504-5*) Caratzas.
— To Hellenikon, Studies in Honor of Speros Vryonis, Jr., Vol. I: Hellenic Antiquity & Byzantium. 522p. 1993. lib. bdg. 75.00 (*0-89241-512-6*) Caratzas.

L

Langdon, John W. July, Nineteen Fourteen: The Long Debate, 1918-1990. 206p. 1991. 49.95 (0-85496-680-3) Berg Pubs.

***Langdon, Ken.** Key Accounts Are Different: Solution Selling for Key Account Managers. 320p. 1995. pap. 19.95 (0-273-61780-X, Pub. by Pitman Pub UK) Natl Bk Netwk.

Langdon, Margaret. Comparative Hokan-Coahuiltecan Studies. LC 72-94480. (Janua Linguarum, Ser. Critica: No. 4). (Illus.). 114p. 1974. pap. text ed. 58.50 (90-279-2717-0) Mouton.

Langdon, Margaret & Silver, Shirley. American Indian & Indoeuropean Studies: Papers in Honor of Madison S. Beeler. Klar, Kathryn et al, eds. (Trends in Linguistics, Studies & Monographs: No. 16). 495p. 1980. 103.85 (90-279-7876-X) Mouton.

Langdon, Margaret, ed. see Conference on Hokan Languages, San Diego, California, April, 1970.

Langdon, Merle K. A Sanctuary of Zeus on Mount Hymettos, No. 16. LC 76-16777. (Hesperia Supplement Ser.: No. 16). (Illus.). xi, 118p. 1976. pap. 15.00 (0-87661-516-7) Am Sch Athens.

Langdon, Michael J. Where Leadership Begins: Key Skills of Today's Best Managers. LC 92-44801. 148p. 1993. pap. 9.95 (0-87389-191-0) ASQC Qual Pr.

***Langdon, Philip.** A Better Place to Live. 1995. pap. 14.00 (0-06-097661-6, PL) HarpC.

— A Better Place to Live: Reshaping the American Suburb. LC 93-42348. (Illus.). 288p. 1994. text ed. 29.95 (0-87023-914-7) U of Mass Pr.

Langdon, Philip, jt. auth. see Thomas, Steve.

Langdon, Richard & Rothwell, Roy G., eds. Design & Innovation: Policy & Management. LC 85-26109. 220p. 1986. text ed. 29.95 (0-312-19448-X) St Martin.

Langdon, S. Babylonian Menologies & the Semitic Calendars. (British Academy, London, Schweich Lectures on Biblical Archaeology Series, 1930). 1972. reprint ed. pap. 20.00 (0-8115-1275-4) Periodicals Srv.

Langdon, Samuel, tr. Hymn to Ishtar As Venus & Idin-Dagan As Tammuz. 1993. pap. 5.95 (1-55818-201-2, Pub. by Alexandrian Pr) Holmes Pub.

Langdon, Shirley P., jt. auth. see Langdon, Barbara R.

Langdon, Stephen H. Babylonian Liturgies. LC 78-72746. (Ancient Mesopotamian Texts & Studies). (Illus.). reprint ed. 37.50 (0-404-18191-0) AMS Pr.

— Babylonian Menologies & the Semitic Calendars. LC 78-72744. (Ancient Mesopotamian Texts & Studies). reprint ed. 21.50 (0-404-18192-9) AMS Pr.

— Babylonian Wisdom. 1976. lib. bdg. 34.95 (0-8490-1468-9) Gordon Pr.

— Sumerian Grammatical Texts. LC 17-16093. (University of Pennsylvania, the University Museum, Publications of the Babylonian Section: Vol. 12, No. 1). 103p. reprint ed. pap. 29.40 (0-317-28543-2, 2052028) Bks Demand.

— Sumerian Liturgical Texts. LC 17-16092. (University of Pennsylvania, the University Museum, Publications of the Babylonian Section: Vol. 10, No. 2). 163p. reprint ed. pap. 46.50 (0-317-28546-7, 2052026) Bks Demand.

— Tammuz & Ishtar. LC 78-72750. (Ancient Mesopotamian Texts & Studies). reprint ed. 34.50 (0-404-18193-7) AMS Pr.

***Langdon, Steve J.** The Native People of Alaska. 3rd rev. ed. Bovy, Edward, ed. (Illus.). 96p. (Orig.). 1994. pap. text ed. 7.95 (0-936425-17-2) Greatland Graphics.

Langdon, Steve J., ed. Contemporary Alaskan Native Economies. (Illus.). 194p. (Orig.). (C). 1986. pap. text ed. 23.00 (0-8191-5117-3) U Pr of Amer.

Langdon, Steven W. Multinational Corporations in the Political Economy of Kenya. 220p. 1981. text ed. 35.00 (0-312-55254-8) St Martin.

Langdon, T. G., et al, eds. Hot Deformation of Aluminum Alloys. (Illus.). 420p. 1991. 118.00 (0-87339-169-1, 412) Minerals Metals.

***Langdon, Terence G., ed.** Superplasticity in Advanced Materials: ICSAM-94. (Materials Science Forum Ser.: Vols. 170-172). (Illus.). 824p. (C). 1995. 210.00 (0-87849-685-8, Inform) LPS Dist Ctr.

Langdon, William. Everyday Things in American Life, 2 vols. Incl. Vol. 1. Everyday Things, 1607-1676. 416p. 1981. text ed. 55.00 (0-684-17415-4); Vol. 2. Everyday Things, 1776-1876. (Illus.). 448p. 1981. text ed. 45.00 (0-684-17416-2); write for info. (0-318-55713-4) Macmillan.

Langdon, William C. Everyday Things in American Life, 2 vols., Set. (BCL1 - U. S. History Ser.). 1991. reprint ed. lib. bdg. 150.00 (0-7812-6003-5) Rprt Serv.

Langdon, William G., Jr. Bits & Bitting Manual: Getting the Horse to Understand Man, the Bit, the Rein, & the Leg. LC 93-206482. (Illus.). 113p. 1989. spiral bd. 29.95 (1-883714-03-6) Langdon Ent.

— Bits, Patterns & Reining: Teaching Horses to Rein. LC 93-206517. 157p. 1990. spiral bd. 29.95 (1-883714-04-4) Langdon Ent.

— Fouler. LC 93-206461. (Illus.). 80p. 1992. spiral bd. 29.95 (1-883714-02-8) Langdon Ent.

— Polo a Way of Life. LC 93-206495. (Illus.). 219p. 1964. spiral bd. 29.95 (1-883714-00-1) Langdon Ent.

— Ride Right: An Informative Training Manual for the Serious Rider That Wants to Improve. LC 93-91892. (Illus.). 122p. 1993. spiral bd. 29.95 (1-883714-06-0) Langdon Ent.

— Team Play Polo. LC 93-206527. (Illus.). 128p. 1985. spiral bd. 29.95 (1-883714-01-X) Langdon Ent.

— Training with Bits: Bitting Techniques to Make Training Understandable for the Horse. LC 93-199250. (Illus.). 100p. (Orig.). 1992. spiral bd. 29.95 (1-883714-05-2) Langdon Ent.

Lange. Basic Radiopharmacy C. 1991. write for info. (0-8151-5302-3, Yr Bk Med Pubs) Mosby Yr Bk.

— Design Dimensioning with Computer Graphics Applications. (Mechanical Engineering Ser.: Vol. 31). 344p. 1984. 75.00 (0-8247-7119-2) Dekker.

— Solving Mechanical Design Problems with Computer Graphics. (Mechanical Engineering Ser.: Vol. 48). 408p. 1986. 125.00 (0-8247-7479-5) Dekker.

— The Sorrows of Young Werther, the New Melusina, Novelle. 177p. (C). 1949. pap. text ed. 18.50 (0-03-008900-X) HB Coll Pubs.

Lange, A. H. Catechetical Review. 1968. pap. 0.75 (0-570-03520-1, 14-1102) Concordia.

Lange, Adrianne. El Manual de la Super Mama. 224p. (Orig.). (SPA.). 1987. pap. 4.95 (0-939193-11-6) Edit Concepts.

— Manual de la Super-Mama. Creative Publishing Concepts Staff, ed. (Orig.). (SPA.). 1990. pap. write for info. (0-944499-82-1) Editorial Amer.

Lange, Andre & Soudart, E. A. Treatise on Cryptography: With Problems in French. 18.1p. 1981. pap. 26.80 (0-89412-055-7) Aegean Park Pr.

Lange, Art. Evidence. LC 81-11377. 1981. pap. 3.50 (0-916328-15-5) Yellow Pr.

Lange, Art & Mackey, Nathaniel, eds. Moment's Notice: Jazz in Poetry & Prose. LC 93-10151. 384p. (Orig.). 1993. pap. 17.50 (1-56689-001-2) Coffee Hse.

Lange, Arthur, jt. auth. see Ellis, Albert.

Lange, Arthur J. & Jakubowski, Patricia. Responsible Assertive Behavior: Cognitive-Behavioral Procedures for Trainers. LC 76-1703. (Orig.). (C). 1976. pap. text ed. 19.95 (0-87822-174-3, 1743) Res Press.

Lange, Arthur J., jt. auth. see Jakubowski, Patricia.

Lange-Bertalot, H. Eighty-Five New Taxa & Much More Than One Hundred Taxonomic Clarifications Supplementary to Suesswasserflora von Mitteleuropa, Vol. 2/1-4. (Bibliotheca Diatomologica Ser.: Vol. 27). (Illus.). 454p. (GER.). 1993. lib. bdg. 167.95 (3-443-57018-6, Pub. by Cramer-Borntraeger GW) Lubrecht & Cramer.

Lange-Bertalot, H. & Krammer, K. Achnantes, eine Monographie der Gattung: Mit Definitio der Gattung Cocconeis und Nachtraegen zu den Naviculaceae. (Bibliotheca Diatomologica Ser.: Vol. 18). (Illus.). 392p. (GER.). 1989. lib. bdg. 152.00 (3-443-57009-7, Pub. by Cramer GW) Lubrecht & Cramer.

— Bacillariaceae, Epithemiaceae, Surirellaceae. Neue und Wenig Bekannte Taxa, Neue Kombinationen Und Synonyme, Sowie Bemerkungen und und Ergaenzungen zu den Naviculaceae. (Bibliotheca Diatomologica Ser.: Vol. 15). (Illus.). 272p. (GER.). 1988. lib. bdg. 92.00 (3-443-57006-2) Lubrecht & Cramer.

***Lange-Bertalot, H. & Moser, Gerd.** Brachysira. Monographie der Gattug. Wichtige Indikator-Species Fuer das Gewaesser-Monitoring und Naviculadicta No. Gen. Ein Loesungsvorschlag Zu Dem Problem Navicula Sensu Lato Ohne Navicula Sensu Strictu Vol. 29. (Bibliotheca Diatomologica Ser.). (Illus.). 212p. (GER.). 1994. lib. bdg. 105.00x (3-443-57020-8) Lubrecht & Cramer.

Lange-Bertalot, H., jt. auth. see Krammer, K.

Lange-Bertalot, H., ed. see Pascher, A.

Lange, Bertalot H.

Lange-Bertalot, Horst, jt. auth. see Reichardt, Irwin.

Lange, Brian M., et al. Dental Management of the Handicapped: Approaches for Dental Auxiliaries. LC 82-23939. 182p. reprint ed. pap. 51.90 (0-7837-2852-2, 2057620) Bks Demand.

Lange, Charles E. The Humerus of the Long Arm of the Law. 103p. (C). 1989. 67.00 (0-7223-2219-4, Pub. by A H S Ltd UK) St Mut.

Lange, Charles H., ed. see Bandelier, Adolph F.

Lange, Dale L. Foreign Language Education: A Reappraisal. (ACTFL Review Ser.: Vol. 4). 1972. pap. 21.25 (0-8442-9347-4, Natl Textbk) NTC Pub Grp.

Lange, David W. The Complete Guide to Buffalo Nickels. 130p. (Orig.). 1993. 44.95 (1-880731-13-4); pap. 24.95 (1-880731-14-2) DLRC Pr.

— The Complete Guide to Mercury Dimes. (Illus.). 180p. Date not set. 49.95 (1-880731-19-3); pap. 29.95 (1-880731-17-7) DLRC Pr.

Lange, Dierk. A Sudanic Chronicle: The Borno Expeditions of Idris Alauma (1564-1576) (Illus.). 250p. (Orig.). 1987. pap. 49.50 (3-515-04926-6) Coronet Bks.

Lange, Dieter & Born, Gary. The Extraterritorial Application of National Laws. LC 87-3300. 1987. 38.00 (90-6544-306-1) Kluwer Law Tax Pubs.

***Lange, Dorothea.** Photographs of a Lifetime. 182p. Date not set. 50.00 (0-89381-657-4) FS&G.

Lange, Dorothea & Taylor, Paul S. An American Exodus: A Record of Human Erosion. LC 74-30641. (American Farmers & the Rise of Agribusiness Ser.). (Illus.). 1979. reprint ed. 23.95 (0-405-06811-5) Ayer.

Lange, Dorothea, et al. The Thunderbird Remembered: Maynard Dixon, the Man & the Artist. LC 94-75152. (Gene Autry Western Heritage Museum Ser.). (Illus.). 112p. 1994. pap. 19.95 (0-295-97388-9) U of Wash Pr.

Lange, Ed. Family Naturism in America. LC 87-30329. (Nudist Pictorial Classic Ser.). (Illus.). 100p. (Orig.). 1989. pap. 24.95 (0-910550-54-9) Elysium.

— Family Naturism in Europe. LC 88-6954. (Illus.). 1983. 29.95 (0-910550-21-2); pap. 24.95 (0-910550-20-4) Elysium.

— N Is for Naked. Bancroft, Iris, ed. (Vintage Nudist Classics Ser.). (Illus.). 64p. (Orig.). 1995. pap. 21.95 (1-55599-052-5, Sun West) Elysium.

— Nudist Magazines of the Fifties & Sixties, Bk. 3. Bancroft, Iris, ed. (Nudist Nostalgia Ser.). (Illus.). 100p. (C). 1994. 29.95 (1-55599-050-9) Elysium.

— Nudist Magazines of the Fifties & Sixties, Bk. 3. Bancroft, Iris, ed. (Nudist Nostalgia Ser.). (Illus.). 100p. (C). 1995. pap. 24.95 (1-55599-051-7) Elysium.

— Nudist Nudes. LC 91-9296. (Illus.). 1991. pap. 14.95 (1-55599-043-6) Elysium.

Lange, Ed, ed. Fun in the Sun, Bk. 2: Nudist-Naturist Recreation. LC 90-49181. (Illus.). 64p. 1990. 26.95 (1-55599-035-5); pap. 21.95 (1-55599-036-3) Elysium.

— The Shameless Nude: A Historic Look at Nudism in the Sixties. LC 91-11562. (Illus.). 140p. 1991. 29.95 (1-55599-037-1) Elysium.

Lange, Ed & Sohler, Stan. Nudist Magazines of the Fifties & Sixties, Bk. 2. Bancroft, Iris, ed. (Nudist Nostalgia Ser.). (Illus.). 100p. 1993. 29.95 (1-55599-047-9); pap. 24.95 (1-55599-048-7) Elysium.

Lange, Ed, jt. auth. see Sohler, Stan.

***Lange, Emma.** A Certain Reputation. (Signet Regency Romance Ser.). 224p. (Orig.). 1995. mass mkt., pap. 3.99 (0-451-18398-3) NAL-Dutton.

— The Cost of Honor. 224p. 1988. pap. 3.99 (0-451-15188-7, Sig) NAL-Dutton.

— The Earl's Return. (Regency Romance Ser.). 224p. (Orig.). 1993. pap. 3.99 (0-451-17560-3, Sig) NAL-Dutton.

— Exeter's Daughter. (Regency Romance Ser.). 224p. 1995. pap. 3.99 (0-451-18509-9, Sig) NAL-Dutton.

— A Heart in Peril. (Signet Regency Romance Ser.). 224p. (Orig.). 1994. pap. 3.99 (0-451-18107-7, Sig) NAL-Dutton.

— Irish Earl's Ruse. (Signet Regency Romance Ser.). 224p. 1992. 3.99 (0-451-17257-4) NAL-Dutton.

— A Second Match. 224p. 1993. pap. 3.99 (0-451-17737-1, Sig) NAL-Dutton.

— The Unmanageable Miss Marlowe. (Regency Romance Ser.). 224p. (Orig.). 1991. pap. 3.99 (0-451-17045-8, Sig) NAL-Dutton.

Lange, Emma, et al. A Regency Valentine, Vol. 2. large type ed. (Nightingale Series Large Print Bks.). 296p. 1992. pap. 14.95 (0-8161-5272-1, Nightingale) Hall.

Lange, Ernst. And Yet It Moves: Dream & Reality in the Ecumenical Movement. Robertson, Edwin, tr. 181p. reprint ed. pap. 51.60 (0-7837-5993-2, 2045803) Bks Demand.

Lange, F. G. Handbook of Safety & Accident Prevention. 1991. lib. bdg. 125.95 (0-8490-4526-6) Gordon Pr.

Lange, Frederick, et al. Yellow Jacket: A Four Corners Anasazi Ceremonial Center. rev. ed. LC 86-82465. (Illus.). 72p. (Orig.). 1986. pap. 5.95 (1-55566-005-3) Johnson Bks.

Lange, Frederick A. The History of Materialism: Criticism of Its Present Importance. LC 73-14163. (Perspectives in Social Inquiry Ser.). 380p. 1980. reprint ed. 30.95 (0-405-05508-0) Ayer.

***Lange, Frederick W., ed.** Paths to Central American Prehistory. (Illus.). 448p. 1995. 45.00x (0-87081-402-8) Univ Pr Colo.

— Precolumbian Jade: New Geological & Cultural Interpretations. LC 92-34099. (Illus.). 416p. (C). 1993. text ed. 45.00 (0-87480-393-4) U of Utah Pr.

— Wealth & Hierarchy in the Intermediate Area. LC 90-43419. (Illus.). 476p. 1992. 36.00 (0-88402-191-2) Dumbarton Oaks.

Lange, Frederick W., jt. ed. see Bishop, Ronald L.

Lange, Frederick W., jt. auth. see Handler, Jerome S.

Lange, Frederick W., et al. The Archaeology of Pacific Nicaragua. LC 90-23536. (Illus.). 344p. 1992. 49.95x (0-8263-1260-8) U of NM Pr.

Lange, Glenn-Marie, jt. auth. see Duchin, Faye.

Lange, Guenter A., ed. Systematic Analysis of Technical Failures: Lectures of an Advanced Study Seminar. (Illus.). 405p. 1986. lib. bdg. 56.00 (3-88355-091-4, Pub. by DGM Metallurgy Info GW) IR Pubns.

Lange, H., jt. ed. see Barth, W. P.

Lange, H., jt. auth. see Rosler, H. J.

Lange, Helene. Higher Education of Women in Europe. 1977. lib. bdg. 59.95 (0-8490-1949-4) Gordon Pr.

Lange, Herbert. Vox--Enciclopedia Cultural, Tomo 8: Plantas. 210p. (SPA.). 1977. 49.95 (0-7859-0903-6, S-50501) Fr & Eur.

Lange, Herbert & Birkenhake, Christina. Complex Abelian Varieties. LC 92-23806. (Grundlehren der Mathematischen Wissenschaften Ser.: Vol. 302). 1992. 109.00 (0-387-54747-9) Spr-Verlag.

Lange, J. M., jt. auth. see Willkomm, H. M.

Lange, James & Dewitt, Katherine, Jr. Chappaquiddick: The Real Story. LC 92-41155. 1993. 21.95 (0-312-08749-7, Pub. by Thomas Dunne Bks) St Martin.

Lange, Jeffrey, jt. ed. see Coleman, Jules.

Lange, Johannes. Crime & Destiny. Haldane, Charlotte, tr. (Historical Foundations of Forensic Psychiatry & Psychology Ser.). 250p. 1983. reprint ed. lib. bdg. 25.00 (0-306-76209-9) Da Capo.

Lange, John. Cognitivity Paradox: An Inquiry Concerning the Claims of Philosophy. LC 72-90952. 1970. 29.95 (0-691-07159-4); pap. 12.95 (0-691-01967-3) Princeton U Pr.

Lange, John, ed. see Lewis, Clarence I.

Lange, K. Robert, ed. Handbook for Detergent Formulators. LC 93-49047. (C). 1994. text ed. write for info. (1-56990-167-8) Hanser-Gardner.

***Lange, Kelly.** Trophy Wife. 1995. 23.00 (0-684-80191-4) S&S Trade.

Lange, Klaus. International Construction Contracts Terminology. 131p. (ENG, FRE & GER.). 1980. pap. 39.95 (0-8288-0223-8, M15022) Fr & Eur.

Lange, Kofi R., tr. see Christaller, J. G.

Lange-Kowal, Ernst E. Langenscheidt French-German Dictionary: Langenscheidt Handwoerterbuch Franzoesisch-Deutsch. 12th ed. 640p. (FRE & GER.). 1982. 59.95 (0-8288-0341-2, M6155) Fr & Eur.

— Langenscheidt French-German, German-French Pocket Dictionary: Langenscheidt Taschenwoerterbuch Franzoesisch-Deutsch-Franzoesisch. 1216p. (FRE & GER.). 1982. 39.95 (0-8288-0343-9, M8010) Fr & Eur.

— Langenscheidt French-German Pocket Dictionary: Langenscheidt Taschenwoerterbuch Franzoesisch-Deutsch. 575p. (FRE & GER.). 1982. 24.95 (0-8288-0344-7, M8220) Fr & Eur.

— Langenscheidt German-French, French-German Dictionary: Langenscheidt Handwoerterbuch Franzoesisch-Deutsch-Franzoesisch. 14th ed. 1314p. (FRE & GER.). 1983. 85.00 (0-8288-0342-0, M15629) Fr & Eur.

Lange-Kowal, Ernst E., jt. auth. see Larousse Staff.

***Lange, Kurt.** Handbook of Metal Forming. LC 83-19897. 1176p. 1995. 125.00 (0-87263-457-4) SME.

Lange, Lou A. The Riddle of Liberty: Emerson on Alienation, Freedom & Obedience. LC 86-6605. (Studies in Humanities Ser.). (C). 1986. 30.95 (1-55540-019-1, 00-01-11) Scholars Pr GA.

Lange, Ludwig. Romiscshe Alterthumer, 3 vols., Set. xxxvi, 2366p. 1974. reprint ed. write for info. (3-487-05235-0, Pub. by Georg Olms GW) Lubrecht & Cramer.

Lange, Ludwig P. & Benton, Arnold. The Multimeter. 51p. 1975. 15.00 (0-318-41565-8, PT8) Am Assn Physics.

Lange, Lynda, jt. ed. see Clark, Lorenne.

Lange, Margo. Quest for Health & Happiness: A Woman's Guide: Fitness Tips for the Body-Mind-Heart-Soul Plus Dream Planner & Daily Diary. 296p. (Orig.). 1993. student ed, pap. 15.95 (0-9635020-9-3) M Lange Comm.

Lange, Marie A. & Mandt, Jinger, eds. Classified Directory of Wisconsin Manufacturers, 1994. 53th ed. 1100p. 1993. 120.00 (0-942198-20-4) WMC Serv.

— Wisconsin Services Directory, 1994. 6th ed. 1000p. 1994. 120.00 (0-942198-19-0) WMC Serv.

Lange, Monique. The Bathing Huts. Beaumont, Barbara, tr. LC 84-29287. 128p. 1986. 13.95 (0-7145-2821-8) M Boyars Pubs.

— Cannibals in Sicily & the Bathing Huts. Beaumont, Barbara, tr. (Iris Ser.). 112p. 1988. 18.95 (0-7145-2879-X) M Boyars Pubs.

— Piaf. Orig. Title: Histoire De Piaf. 252p. 1983. pap. 11.95 (0-394-62428-9) Seaver Bks.

Lange, Nicholas de. Atlas of the Jewish World. (Cultural Atlas Ser.). (Illus.). 240p. 1984. 45.00 (0-87196-043-5) Facts on File.

Lange, Nicholas T. Case Studies in Biometry. (Series in Probability & Mathematical Statistics). 1994. 69.95 (0-471-58885-7); pap. 39.95 (0-471-58925-X) Wiley.

Lange, O. L., et al. Physiological Plant Ecology II: Water Relations & Carbon Assimilation. (Encyclopedia of Plant Physiology Ser.: Vol. 12 B). (Illus.). 153p. 1982. 293.00 (0-387-10906-4) Spr-Verlag.

Lange, O. L., et al, eds. Physiological Plant Biology IV: Ecosystems Processes - Mineral Cycling, Productivity, & Man's Influence. (Encyclopedia of Plant Physiology Ser.: Vol. 12 D). (Illus.). 690p. 1983. 293.00 (0-387-10908-0) Spr-Verlag.

— Physiological Plant Ecology I: Responses to the Physical Environment. (Encyclopedia of Plant Physiology Ser.: Vol. 12 A). (Illus.). 625p. 1981. 238.00 (0-387-10763-0) Spr-Verlag.

— Physiological Plant Ecology III: Responses to the Chemical & Biological Environment. (Encyclopedia of Plant Physiology Ser.: Vol. 12C). (Illus.). 850p. 1983. 293.00 (0-387-10907-2) Spr-Verlag.

Lange, Oscar & Taylor, Fred M. On the Economic Theory of Socialism. Lippincott, Benjamin E., ed. LC 76-11295. (Reprints of Economic Classics Ser.). vii, 143p. 1970. reprint ed. 25.00 (0-678-00613-X) Kelley.

Lange, Oscar R. Price Flexibility & Employment. LC 78-6631. (Cowles Commission for Research in Economics, Monograph Ser.: No. 8). (Illus.). 114p. 1978. reprint ed. text ed. 35.00 (0-313-20480-2, LAPF, Greenwood Pr) Greenwood.

Lange, Oskar. Introduction to Econometrics. 4th rev. ed. LC 77-30671. 1978. text ed. 186.00 (0-08-022988-3, Pub. by Pergamon Repr UK) Franklin.

— Introduction to Economic Cybernetics. Banasinski, Antoni, ed. Stadler, Jozef, tr. LC 73-106449. (Illus.). 200p. 1970. 86.00 (0-08-006652-6, Pub. by Pergamon Repr UK) Franklin.

— On Political Economy & Econometrics. 1965. 277.00 (0-08-011588-8, Pub. by Pergamon Repr UK) Franklin.

— Optimal Decisions. LC 76-143810. 304p. 1972. 129.00 (0-08-016053-0, Pub. by Pergamon Repr UK) Franklin.

— Papers in Economics & Sociology, 1930-1960. Knightsfield, P. F., tr. LC 68-22080. 1970. 252.00 (0-08-012352-X, Pub. by Pergamon Repr UK) Franklin.

— Political Economy, 2 vols., Vol. 1. LC 65-367. 1963. 154.00 (0-08-013561-7, Pub. by Pergamon Repr UK) Franklin.

— Political Economy, 2 vols., Vol. 2. LC 65-367. 1972. 112.00 (0-08-016572-9, Pub. by Pergamon Repr UK) Franklin.

— Wholes & Parts: General Theory of System Behaviour. LC 63-23236. 1965. 37.00 (0-08-011173-4, Pub. by Pergamon Repr UK) Franklin.

Lange, Oskar & Banasinski, Antoni. Theory of Reproduction & Accumulation. 1969. 82.00 (0-08-012256-6, Pub. by Pergamon Repr UK) Franklin.

Lange, Oskar, et al, eds. Studies in Mathematical Economics & Econometrics in Memory of Henry Schultz. LC 68-8498. (Essay Index Reprint Ser.). 1977. 23.95 (0-8369-0916-X) Ayer.

Lange, Peter. Union Democracy & Liberal Corporatism: Exit Voice & Wage Regulation in Postwar Europe. (Western Societies Papers). 117p. 1984. 11.95 (0-8014-9636-5) Cornell U Pr.

Lange, Peter & Regini, Marino, eds. State, Market & Social Regulation: New Perspectives on Italy. (Illus.). (C). 1989. 59.95 (0-521-35453-6) Cambridge U Pr.

An Asterisk (*) at the beginning of an entry indicates that the title is appearing in BIP for the first time.

Lange, Ridgley & Wang, Shengwang, eds. New Approaches in Spectral Decomposition. LC 92-6183. (Contemporary Mathematics Ser.: Vol. 128). 273p. 1992. 44.00 (*0-8218-5139-X*, CONM/128C) Am Math.

Lange, Robert C. Nuclear Medicine for Technicians. LC 75-95732. 180p. reprint ed. pap. 51.30 (*0-317-26173-8*, 2024266) Bks Demand.

Lange, Rod, jt. auth. see Laban, Rudolf.

Lange, Roland. Five Hundred One Japanese Verbs. 1988. pap. 10.95 (*0-8120-3991-2*) Barron.

— Japanese Verbs. 350p. 1991. spiral bd. 5.95 (*0-8120-4525-4*) Barron.

Lange, S. Techniques & Indications in Radiology: Kidney & Urinary Tract. (Flexibook Ser.). (Illus.). 233p. 1987. pap. text ed. 27.00 (*0-86577-262-2*) Thieme Med Pubs.

Lange, S., et al. Zerebrale und Spinale Computertomographie. 2nd enl. rev. ed. (Illus.). 266p. 1988. 66.75 (*3-8055-4591-6*) S Karger.

Lange, Sebastian. Radiology of Chest Diseases. (Illus.). 300p. 1989. text ed. 69.00 (*0-86577-313-0*) Thieme Med Pubs.

— Teaching Atlas of Urologic Radiology. LC 94-35149. (Illus.). 300p. (ENG.). 1994. 99.00 (*0-86577-540-0*) Thieme Med Pubs.

Lange, Sebastian & Stark, Paul. Teaching Atlas of Thoracic Radiology. LC 92-49323. 1993. 99.00 (*0-86577-467-6*) Thieme Med Pubs.

Lange, Stella, tr. see Pieper, Josef.

***Lange, Steve.** Going for the Gold: 1996 Women's Gymnastics Calendar. Quiner, Barry, ed. (Illus.). 24p. (Orig.). (J). (gr. 2 up). 1995. pap. 8.95 (*0-9643460-2-8*) Bradford Bk.

Lange, Suzanne. The Year. LC 78-120787. (J). (gr. 8 up). 1970. 22.95 (*0-87599-173-4*) S G Phillips.

Lange, V. N. Physical Paradoxes & Sophisms. 232p. (C). 1987. 25.00 (*0-685-36861-0*, Pub. by Collets) St Mut.

Lange, Victor. Classical Age of German Literature, 1740-1815. LC 82-15734. 256p. (Orig.). (C). 1982. 35.00 (*0-8419-0853-2*); pap. 19.50 (*0-8419-0854-0*) Holmes & Meier.

Lange, Victor, jt. ed. see Amacher, Richard E.

Lange, Victor, jt. ed. see Blackall, Eric A.

Lange, Victor, tr. see Blackall, Eric A. & Lange, Victor, eds.

Lange, Victor, tr. see Goethe, Johann Wolfgang Von.

Lange, Victor, ed. see Goethe, Johann Wolfgang Von.

Lange, Victor, ed. see Hoffmann, E. T.

Lange, W. Efficiency in Plant Breeding. 383p. 1990. 180.00 (*81-7089-125-6*, Pub. by Intl Bk Distr II) St Mut.

Lange, W., jt. ed. see Masihi, K. N.

Lange, W. Robert. International Health Guide for Senior Citizen Travelers. LC 88-15210. 70p. (Orig.). 1990. pap. 4.95 (*0-87576-139-9*) Pilot Bks.

Lange, Walter H., et al. Business & Consumer Mathematics. 5th ed. 752p. (C). 1991. pap. text ed. 51.95 (*0-256-09135-8*) Irwin.

***Lange, Wolfgang.** Woerterbuch Georgisch-Deutsch, Deutsch-Georgisch. 161p. (GEO & GER.). 1987. 39.95 (*0-7859-8523-9*, 3871188506) Fr & Eur.

***Langedyk.** Estimating & Bidding for Builders & Remodelers with CD-ROM. rev. ed. 272p. 1995. cd-rom, pap. text ed. 62.55 (*1-57218-010-2*) Craftsman.

Langefors, B., et al, eds. Trends in Information Systems: TC 8 Anthology. 450p. 1986. 79.50 (*0-444-87949-8*, North Holland) Elsevier.

Langeheine, R. & Rost, J., eds. Latent Trait & Latent Class Models. LC 88-4141. (Illus.). 328p. 1988. 59.50 (*0-306-42727-3*, Plenum Pr) Plenum.

Langeher, Frances. Painting Reasons on the Mirror. (Illus.). (Orig.). 1989. pap. text ed. 6.50 (*0-9623824-0-X*) Broken Mirrors Pr.

Langehough, Mabel. The Innkeeper. 1973. 4.25 (*0-685-68593-4*, MC-245) Lillenas.

***Langel, Randy.** Client-Server: The 10 Percent You Need to Know. LC 94-79114. (Orig.). 1994. per., pap. 29.95 (*0-9643104-0-6*) IBM So Calif.

Langelaan, James S. The Philosophy & Theology of Love: According to St. Francis de Sales. LC 94-13278. (Toronto Studies in Theology: Vol. 67). 234p. 1994. text ed. 89.95 (*0-7734-9100-7*) E Mellen.

Langelan, Martha J. Back Off! How to Confront & Stop Sexual Harassment & Harassers. 224p. (Orig.). 1993. pap. 12.00 (*0-671-78856-6*, Fireside) S&S Trade.

Langeler, B., jt. auth. see Bendow, B.

Langellier, Alice & Langellier, Paul. Billet Circulaire. LC 66-12110. (FRE.). (C). 1966. reprint ed. pap. text ed. 6.95 (*0-89197-516-0*) Irvington.

Langellier, J. Phillip. Parade Ground Soldiers: Military Uniforms & Headress, 1837-1910, in the Collections of the State Historical Society of Wisconsin. LC 78-4681. 132p. 1978. pap. 5.00 (*0-87020-174-3*) State Hist Soc Wis.

***Langellier, John.** U. S. Dragoons 1833-55. (Osprey Men-at-Arms Ser.). (Illus.). 48p. 1995. pap. 11.95 (*1-85532-389-3*, Pub. by Osprey UK) Stackpole.

Langellier, John, ed. Armed Forces on the West Coast. (Illus.). 76p. (Orig.). 1981. pap. text ed. 15.00 (*0-89745-023-X*) Sunflower U Pr.

***Langellier, John P.** The Bluecoats: The U. S. Army in the West, 1848-1897. LC 95-15138. (G. I. Ser.: Vol. 2). (Illus.). 80p. 1995. pap. 12.95 (*1-85367-221-1*, Pub. by Greenhill Bks UK) Stackpole.

— The War in Europe: From the Kasserine Pass to Berlin, 1941-1945. LC 95-15139. (G. I.: Illustrated History of the American Soldier, His Uniform & His Equipment Ser.: Vol. 1). (Illus.). 80p. 1995. pap. 12.95 (*1-85367-220-3*, Pub. by Greenhill Bks UK) Stackpole.

Langellier, John P., comp. Myles Keogh: The Life & Legend of an Irish Dragoon with the Seventh Cavalry. LC 91-65910. (Montana & the West Ser.: Vol. 9). (Illus.). 206p. 75.00 (*0-912783-21-4*) Upton Sons.

— Myles Keogh: The Life & Legend of an Irish Dragoon with the Seventh Cavalry. deluxe limited ed. LC 91-65910. (Montana & the West Ser.: Vol. 9). (Illus.). 206p. ring bd. 150.00 (*0-685-54504-0*) Upton Sons.

Langellier, John P., ed. see Dixon, Daniel, et al.

Langellier, Paul, jt. auth. see Langellier, Alice.

Langeluttig, Albert. Department of Justice of the United States. (Brookings Institution Reprint Ser.). reprint ed. lib. bdg. 39.50 (*0-697-00161-X*) Irvington.

Langeman, LaVera. Cat Quilts & Crafts. LC 92-8556. (New Ser.). (Illus.). 96p. 1992. 12.95 (*0-8019-8355-X*) Chilton.

Langemo, Amanda, tr. see Stigen, Terje.

Langemo, Mark, jt. auth. see Brathal, Daniel A.

Langen, Annette. Letters from Felix: A Little Rabbit on a World Tour. (J). 1994. 16.95 (*1-55859-886-3*) Abbeville Pr.

Langen, P. Antimetabolites of Nucleic Acid Metabolism. 286p. 1975. text ed. 190.00 (*0-677-30760-8*) Gordon & Breach.

Langen, P., ed. see Flaccus, Valerius.

Langen, P., jt. ed. see Skoda, J.

Langen, Peter. Beitrage Zur Kritik und Erklarung Des Plautus. iv, 348p. (GER.). 1973. reprint ed. write for info. (*3-487-04991-0*, Pub. by Georg Olms GW) Lubrecht & Cramer.

— Plautinische Studien. Bd. V, 1. vi, 400p. 1970. reprint ed. write for info. (*0-318-71159-1*, Pub. by Georg Olms GW) Lubrecht & Cramer.

Langen, Victor, ed. The Gospel Harmony, Bk. II: New Life for All. (Global Harmony Ser.). 72p. (Orig.). 1994. pap. write for info. (*0-942495-34-9*) Amherst Pr.

— The Gospel Harmony, Bk. III: Change Is Necessary. (Gospel Harmony Ser.). 64p. (Orig.). 1994. pap. write for info. (*0-942495-35-7*) Amherst Pr.

— The Gospel Harmony, Bk. IV: Glorious Visions. (Gospel Harmony Ser.). 64p. (Orig.). 1994. pap. write for info. (*0-942495-36-5*) Amherst Pr.

Langenbach, A. Monotone Potentialoperatoren in Theorie & Anwendung. (GER.). 1977. 37.80 (*3-540-08071-6*) Spr-Verlag.

Langenbach, Michael. Curriculum Models in Adult Education. 240p. 1993. 24.00 (*0-89464-784-9*) Krieger.

Langenbach, Michael, et al. An Introduction to Educational Research. LC 93-22189. 1993. text ed. write for info. (*0-205-13902-7*) Allyn.

Langenbach, Randolph, jt. auth. see Hareven, Tamara K.

Langenbach, Robert, et al, eds. Tumor Promoters: Biological Approaches for Mechanistic Studies & Assay Systems. (Progress in Cancer Research & Therapy Ser.: Vol. 34). 480p. 1988. text ed. 121.50 (*0-88167-451-6*) Raven.

Langenbeck, ed. In-Process Optical Metrology for Precision Machining. 225p. 1987. 43.00 (*0-89252-837-0*, 802) SPIE.

Langenbeck, P., ed. Micromachining Optical Components & Precision Engineering, Vol. 1015. 1989. 45.00 (*0-8194-0050-5*) SPIE.

Langenbeck, P., jt. ed. see Macleod, H. A.

Langenberg, D. N. & Larken, A. I., eds. Nonequilibrium Superconductivity. (Modern Problems in Condensed Matter Sciences Ser.: Vol. 12). 710p. 1986. 120.50 (*0-317-45880-9*, North Holland) Elsevier.

Langenbrunner, Jim. I Love the Lady Choir Director by Uncle Jim but He Was Kicked-Out for Misbehaving. (Illus.). 1989. write for info. (*0-318-65114-9*) J Langenbrunner.

Langenderfer, et al. Personal Income Taxation 1994 Edition. 94th rev. ed. (C). 1994. pap. 30.95 (*0-538-81633-3*) S-W Pub.

Langenderfer, Harold Q. The Federal Income Tax, 1861 to 1872. Brief, Richard P., ed. LC 80-1500. (Dimensions of Accounting Theory & Practice Ser.). 1980. lib. bdg. 88. 95 (*0-405-13493-2*) Ayer.

— Federal Income Taxation. (C). 1991. text ed. write for info. (*0-538-80675-3*, AG60B8H81C) S-W Pub.

— Federal Income Taxation, 1993. 1992. pap. write for info. (*0-538-81616-3*) S-W Pub.

— Personal Income Taxation, 1993. 1992. pap. write for info. (*0-538-81617-1*) S-W Pub.

Langenderfer, Harold Q., et al. Federal Income Taxation: 1994 Edition. 94th ed. (C). 1994. pap. 33.95 (*0-538-81632-5*, AG60DB) S-W Pub.

— Federal Income Taxation, 1991. 576p. 1992. pap. text ed. write for info. (*0-538-81610-4*, AG60A8H810); pap. text ed. write for info. (*0-538-81611-2*, AG60A8H88C) S-W Pub.

— Personal Income Taxation, Copyright 1991. 320p. 1991. pap. text ed. write for info. (*0-538-80676-1*, AG60A81) S-W Pub.

Langendoen, D. Terence, jt. ed. see Fillmore, Charles J.

Langendoen, David, ed. see Home Office Computing Staff.

Langendorf, Adele. Denial. (Orig.). 1986. pap. 6.00 (*0-912449-19-5*) Floating Island.

Langendorf, Hans. Legal Dictionary: Part 1, Dutch-German. 365p. (DUT & GER.). 1978. lib. bdg. 44.00 (*90-268-0707-4*) Kluwer Ac.

— Woerterbuch der Deutschen und Nierderlaendischen Rechtssprache, Vol. 1. 365p. (DUT & GER.). 1991. 85. 00 (*0-8288-5771-7*, M7025) Fr & Eur.

— Woerterbuch der Deutschen und Nierderlaendischen Rechtssprache, Vol 2. 426p. (DUT & GER.). 1989. 125. 00 (*0-8288-5772-5*, M7026) Fr & Eur.

Langendorf, Hans, ed. Legal Dictionary: Dutch-German. 1991. text ed. 46.00 (*90-6544-563-3*) Kluwer Law Tax Pubs.

Langendorf, Pat. It's Not a Bad Start. LC 92-60342. 208p. (Orig.). 1992. pap. 14.95 (*0-9625714-5-8*) Spruce Gulch Pr.

Langendorf, Patricia. Logging the Rockies: The Langendorf Olson Story. large type ed. (Illus.). 249p. (Orig.). 1992. lib. bdg. 40.00 (*0-9625714-8-2*); pap. 22.50 (*0-9625714-9-0*) Spruce Gulch Pr.

Langendorf, Richard, jt. auth. see Pick, Alfred.

Langendorfer, Stephen J. & Bruya, Lawrence D. Aquatic Readiness: Developing Water Competence in Young Children. LC 93-42159. (Illus.). 224p. 1995. pap. text ed. 28.00 (*0-87322-663-1*, BLAN0663) Human Kinetics.

Langendorff, T., jt. ed. see Zurcher, E.

Langenes, Bill, jt. auth. see Ewing, David.

Langenfeld, Robert. George Moore: An Annotated Secondary Bibliography of Writings about Him. LC 84-48436. (Studies in Modern Literature: No. 13). 1987. 76. 50 (*0-404-61583-X*) AMS Pr.

Langenfeld, Robert, ed. Reconsidering Aubrey Beardsley. LC 89-34603. (Nineteenth-Century Studies). 526p. 1991. 50.00 (*0-8357-1979-0*) Univ Rochester Pr.

Langenheim, Ralph L., Jr., jt. auth. see Frost, Stanley H.

***Langenheim, Victoria E.** Gravity of the New Madrid Seismic Zone. 1996. write for info. (*0-615-00254-4*) USGPO.

Langenkamp, R. D. Handbook of Oil Industry Terms & Phrases. 4th ed. 360p. 1984. 15.00 (*0-87814-258-4*, P4349) PennWell Bks.

— Handbook of Oil Industry Terms & Phrases. 5th ed. LC 94-13887. 400p. 1994. 49.95 (*0-87814-421-8*, P4557) PennWell Bks.

***Langenkamp, Robert D.** The Illustrated Petroleum Reference Dictionary. LC 94-34489. (Illus.). 1994. write for info. (*0-87814-423-4*) PennWell Bks.

Langenscheidt Editorial Staff, ed. Computergestuetzter Fremdsprachenunterricht: Ein Handbuch. 128p. 1985. pap. 21.50 (*3-468-49434-3*) Langenscheidt.

Langenscheidt, Florian. Wish I May, Wish I Might. 1993. 8.95 (*1-55859-638-0*) Abbeville Pr.

***Langenscheidt Staff.** CC-ROM Bibliothek. 695p. (ENG & GER.). 1994. write for info. (*0-614-00359-8*, 3468909012) Fr & Eur.

— Glossaire Europeen de Terminologie Juridique & Administrative, No. 15: Termes de Droit Anglais des Obligations, Anglais-Francais. 36p. (ENG & FRE.). pap. 29.95 (*0-7859-0416-6*, M9482) Fr & Eur.

— Glossaire Europeen de Terminologie Juridique et Administrative. 127p. (ENG & GER.). 1973. pap. 14.95 (*0-685-57825-9*, M-9485) Fr & Eur.

— Glossaire Europeen de Terminologie Juridique et Administrative: Regional Policy. 111p. (FRE.). write for info. (*0-7859-0417-4*, M9484) Fr & Eur.

— Glossaire Europeen de Terminologie Juridique et Administrative, No. 1: Terminologie Administrative et Secretariat. (FRE & GER.). write for info. (*0-318-56667-2*, M-9495) Fr & Eur.

— Glossaire Europeen de Terminologie Juridique et Administrative, No. 10: Marches Publics. 72p. (FRE & GER.). 1972. pap. 12.95 (*0-8288-6395-4*, M-9479) Fr & Eur.

— Glossaire Europeen de Terminologie Juridique et Administrative, No. 11: Jeunesse. (Allemand-Francais Ser.). 109p. (FRE & GER.). 1972. pap. 12.95 (*0-8288-6394-6*, M-9478) Fr & Eur.

— Glossaire Europeen de Terminologie Juridique et Administrative, No. 13: Law of Establishment. 100p. (FRE.). 1973. pap. 12.95 (*0-8288-6295-8*, M-9480) Fr & Eur.

— Glossaire Europeen de Terminologie Juridique et Administrative, No. 19: Droit du Mariage. 96p. (FRE & GER.). 1973. pap. 14.95 (*0-8288-6294-X*, M-9486) Fr & Eur.

— Glossaire Europeen de Terminologie Juridique et Administrative, No. 2: Terminologie de Reunions. (GER & ITA.). write for info. (*0-318-56674-5*, M-9497) Fr & Eur.

— Glossaire Europeen de Terminologie Juridique et Administrative, No. 20: Local Government. 96p. (GER & ITA.). 1975. pap. 14.95 (*0-8288-5890-X*, M9487) Fr & Eur.

— Glossaire Europeen de Terminologie Juridique et Administrative, No. 21: Droits D'Etablissement. 146p. (FRE & GER.). 1976. pap. 18.95 (*0-8288-5671-0*, M9488) Fr & Eur.

— Glossaire Europeen de Terminologie Juridique et Administrative, No. 22: Civil Service Organizations. 83p. (ENG & GER.). 1976. pap. 24.95 (*0-8288-5672-9*, M9489) Fr & Eur.

— Glossaire Europeen de Terminologie Juridique et Administrative, No. 23: Eductions et Enseignment. 168p. (FRE & GER.). pap. 18.95 (*0-7859-0418-2*, M9490) Fr & Eur.

— Glossaire Europeen de Terminologie Juridique et Administrative, No. 24: Office Terminology, German-Italian. 79p. (GER & ITA.). 1979. pap. 14.95 (*0-8288-4806-8*, M9491) Fr & Eur.

— Glossaire Europeen de Terminologie Juridique et Administrative, No. 25: Conference Terminology, German-Italian. 72p. (GER & ITA.). 1979. pap. 24.95 (*0-8288-4805-X*, M9492) Fr & Eur.

— Glossaire Europeen de Terminologie Juridique et Administrative, No. 26: Budgeting & Auditing, German-Italian. 144p. (GER & ITA.). 1980. pap. 19.95 (*3-468-49076-3*) Fr & Eur.

— Glossaire Europeen de Terminologie Juridique et Administrative, No. 27: Motor, Insurance, German-Italian. 152p. (GER & ITA.). 1980. pap. 19.95 (*0-8288-4703-7*, M9494) Fr & Eur.

— Glossaire Europeen de Terminologie Juridique et Administrative, No. 29: Environment Policy Protection & Management of the Environment. 160p. (ENG & GER.). pap. 22.50 (*0-7859-0419-0*, M9496) Fr & Eur.

— Glossaire Europeen de Terminologie Juridique et Administrative, No. 3: Renumeration. (FRE & GER.). write for info. (*0-318-56668-0*, M-9498) Fr & Eur.

— Glossaire Europeen de Terminologie Juridique et Administrative, No. 4: Oroit Administratif. (FRE & GER.). write for info. (*0-318-56662-1*, M-9499) Fr & Eur.

— Glossaire Europeen de Terminologie Juridique et Administrative, No. 6: Droits des Collectivites Locales. (FRE & GER.). write for info. (*0-318-56665-6*) Fr & Eur.

— Glossaire Europeen de Terminologie Juridique et Administrative, No. 7: Budget. (FRE & GER.). write for info. (*0-318-56675-3*, M-9603) Fr & Eur.

— Glossaire Europeen de Terminologie Juridique et Administrative, No. 8: Oroit de al Fonction Publique. (FRE & GER.). write for info. (*0-318-56663-X*, M-9604) Fr & Eur.

— Glossaire Europeen de Terminologie Juridique et Administrative, No. 9: Amenagement du Territoie. (FRE & GER.). write for info. (*0-318-56676-1*, M-9605) Fr & Eur.

— Langenscheidt Picture Dictionary. (J). (gr. 4-7). 1993. English. 19.95 (*0-88729-850-8*); FRE-ENG. 19.95 (*0-88729-851-6*); GER-ENG. 19.95 (*0-88729-852-4*); ITA-ENG. 19.95 (*0-88729-853-2*); SPA-ENG. 19.95 (*0-88729-854-0*); JPN-ENG. 24.95 (*0-88729-855-9*); GRE-ENG. 19.95 (*0-88729-862-1*); HEB-ENG. 19.95 (*0-88729-863-X*); 19.95 (*0-88729-864-8*); POR-ENG. 19.95 (*0-88729-865-6*); RUS-ENG. 19.95 (*0-88729-866-4*); CHI-ENG. 19.95 (*0-88729-867-2*); ENG. pap. 14.95 (*0-88729-856-7*); FRE-ENG. pap. 14. 95 (*0-88729-857-5*); GER-ENG. pap. 14.95 (*0-88729-858-3*); ITA-ENG. pap. 14.95 (*0-88729-859-1*); SPA-ENG. pap. 14.95 (*0-88729-860-5*); JPN-ENG. pap. write for info. (*0-88729-861-3*); POL-ENG. write for info. (*0-318-71677-1*) Langenscheidt.

— Langenscheidt Universal Dictionary Spanish. 380p. 1994. pap. 4.95 (*0-88729-064-7*) Langenscheidt.

— Langenscheidt Universal Spanish-German, German-Spanish Dictionary: Langenscheidt Universal Woerterbuch Spanisch-Deutsch-Spanisch. 480p. (GER & SPA.). 1983. 14.95 (*0-8288-0350-1*, S39870) Fr & Eur.

— PC-Woerterbuch English. 495p. (FRE & GER.). 1994. write for info. (*0-614-00362-8*, 3468909128); write for info. (*0-614-00363-6*, 3468909128) Fr & Eur.

— PC-Woerterbuch Franzoesich. 495p. (FRE & GER.). 1994. 150.00 (*0-614-00361-X*, 3468909187) Fr & Eur.

— Presupuesto Publico y Fiscalization Glossary German & Spanish, Europa-Glossar der Rechts und Verwaltungssprache No. 28. 183p. (GER & SPA.). Date not set. pap. 22.50 (*0-7859-7565-9*, 346849078X) Fr & Eur.

— Super Mario Super Englisch: Woerterbuch Fur Kids: English-German, German-English. 2nd ed. 576p. (ENG & GER.). 1993. 29.95 (*0-7859-8390-2*, 3468203705) Fr & Eur.

— Woerterbuch Franzoesich Langenscheidt CD-ROM. 125p. (FRE & GER.). 1994. write for info. (*0-614-00360-1*, 3468906153) Fr & Eur.

***Langensiepen, Bernd & Guleryuz, Ahmet.** The Ottoman Steam Navy, 1828-1923. Cooper, J., tr. LC 94-69766. (Illus.). 208p. 1995. 49.95 (*1-55750-659-0*) Naval Inst Pr.

Langenus, Gustave. Complete Method for the Clarinet, 3 pts. (Illus.). 88p. Pt. 1, 1923, 88p. pap. 12.00 (*0-8258-0240-7*, 0-1402); Pt. 2, 1916, 85p. pap. 13.00 (*0-8258-0241-5*, 0-1403); Pt. 3, Virtuoso Studies & Duos, 1943, 118p. pap. 13.00 (*0-8258-0242-3*, 0-1404) Fischer Inc NY.

Langenus, Gustave, ed. see Baermann, Carl.

Langenus, Ron. Merlin's Return. Delmonte, Niesje C., tr. (Illus.). 175p. (J). (gr. 5-8). 1994. pap. 7.95 (*0-86327-383-1*, Pub. by Wolfhound Pr IE) Dufour.

— Mission West: Journey of Mystery & Adventure to the Edge of the World. (Illus.). 128p. (Orig.). (YA). 1990. pap. 8.95 (*0-86327-239-8*, Pub. by Wolfhound Pr IE) Dufour.

Langer. Arthritis. 1989. pap. 1.95 (*0-87983-411-0*) Keats.

— Dental Problems. 1989. pap. 1.95 (*0-87983-414-5*) Keats.

— Envisioning Literature: Literary Understanding & Literature Instruction. (Language & Literacy Ser.). 192p. (C). 1995. text ed. 39.00x (*0-8077-3465-9*); pap. text ed. 17.95x (*0-8077-3464-0*) Tchrs Coll.

— Fatigue. 1989. pap. 1.95 (*0-87983-373-4*) Keats.

— Life Extension. 1989. pap. 1.95 (*0-87983-413-7*) Keats.

— Osteoporosis. 1989. pap. 1.95 (*0-87983-416-1*) Keats.

Langer, jt. auth. see Chasin.

Langer, Anja & Reynolds, Bill. Body Flex - Body Magic. (Illus.). 368p. 1992. pap. 14.95 (*0-8092-3930-2*) Contemp Bks.

Langer, Audrey R. Ashes under Uricon. 350p. (Orig.). 1989. pap. 8.95 (*0-929827-01-5*) New Saga Pubs.

— The Woman, Inge. 320p. (Orig.). 1988. pap. 7.95 (*0-929827-00-7*) New Saga Pubs.

Langer, Audrey R., jt. auth. see Sargeant, Roger E.

Langer, Burkhard. Zur Energieabhaengigkeit Von Photoelektronensatelliten. LC 92-37269. (Studies of Vacuum Ultraviolet & X-Ray Processes: No. 2). 1992. 45.00 (*0-404-69952-9*) AMS Pr.

Langer, Cassandra. Feminist Art Criticism: An Annotated Bibliography. LC 93-822. 250p. 1993. lib. bdg. 55.00 (*0-8161-8948-X*, Hall Reference) Macmillan.

— Mother & Child in Art. (Illus.). 160p. 1991. 19.99 (*0-517-05665-8*, Crescent) Random Hse Value.

Langer, Cassandra, et al, eds. New Feminist Criticism: Art, Identity, Action. LC 92-56247. (Illus.). 272p. (Orig.). 1994. pap. 15.00 (*0-06-430909-6*, PL) HarpC.

Langer, E. Death of Mulageta Seraw. Date not set. 22.95 (*0-06-019019-1*, HarpT) HarpC.

— Die Gattung Hyphodontia John Eriksson. (Bibliotheca Mycologica Ser.: Vol. 154). (Illus.). 298p. (GER.). 1994. pap. 85.00 (*3-443-59055-1*, Pub. by Cramer-Borntraeger GW) Lubrecht & Cramer.

L

Langer, Elinor. Josephine Herbst. 384p. 1994. reprint ed. pap. text ed. 14.95 (*1-55553-183-0*) NE U Pr.

Langer, Ellen, jt. ed. see Schank, Roger C.

Langer, Ellen J. Mindfulness. 1989. 16.30 (*0-201-09502-5*) Addison-Wesley.

— Mindfulness. 1990. pap. 10.58 (*0-201-52341-8*) Addison-Wesley.

— The Psychology of Control. LC 83-11224. (Illus.). 311p. reprint ed. pap. 88.70 (*0-8357-4816-2*, 2037753) Bks Demand.

Langer, Ellen J., jt. ed. see Alexander, Charles N.

Langer, Erick D. Economic Change & Rural Resistance in Southern Bolivia, 1880-1930. LC 88-31117. 288p. 1989. 45.00 (*0-8047-1491-6*) Stanford U Pr.

— The New Latin American Mission History. Jackson, Robert H., ed. LC 94-43080. (Latin American Studies Ser.). (Illus.). 240p. 1995. pap. text ed. 16.95 (*0-8032-7953-1*) U of Nebr Pr.

Langer, Erick D., jt. auth. see Jackson, Robert H.

Langer, Fritz. Intellektualmythologie: Betrachtungen Uber das Wesen das Mythus und Die Mythologische Methode. Bolle, Kees W., ed. LC 77-79136. (Mythology Ser.). (GER.). 1978. reprint ed. lib. bdg. 23.95 (*0-405-10546-0*) Ayer.

Langer, Gary F. The Coming of Age of Political Economy, 1815-1825. LC 86-31802. (Contributions in Economics & Economic History Ser.: No. 72). (Illus.). 236p. 1987. text ed. 55.00 (*0-313-25645-4*, LCA/, Greenwood Pr) Greenwood.

Langer, Glenn A. Calcium & the Heart. 400p. 1990. 98.50 (*0-88167-617-9*) Raven.

Langer, J. A., ed. see ASTM Committee D-18 on Soil & Rock.

***Langer, J. B.** The Adventures of Missus Beckaling. 160p. 1996. pap. 7.95 (*0-7610-0506-4*) NW Pub.

Langer, Jiri. Nine Gates to the Chasidic Mysteries. Jolly, Stephen, tr. LC 92-28679. 312p. 1993. 30.00 (*0-87668-249-2*) Aronson.

Langer, Josef. Emerging Sociology: An International Perspective. 157p. 1992. 59.95 (*1-85628-279-1*, Pub. by Avebury Pub UK) Ashgate Pub Co.

Langer, Judith. Children Reading & Writing: Structures & Strategies. Farr, Marcia, ed. LC 85-31564. (Writing Research Ser.: Vol. 7). 200p. 1986. text ed. 39.50 (*0-89391-302-2*); pap. 24.50 (*0-89391-303-0*) Ablex Pub.

Langer, Judith, ed. Language, Literacy & Culture: Issues of Society & Schooling. LC 87-11450. 256p. (C). 1987. text ed. 39.50 (*0-89391-437-1*) Ablex Pub.

Langer, Judith A. Literature Instruction: A Focus on Student Response. 211p. 1992. pap. 14.95 (*0-8141-3318-5*) NCTE.

Langer, Judith A. & Smith-Burke, M. Trika, eds. Reader Meets Author - Bridging the Gap: A Psycholinguistic & Sociolinguistic Perspective. LC 81-20769. (Illus.). 250p. reprint ed. pap. 71.30 (*0-8357-4310-1*, 2037108) Bks Demand.

Langer, Judith A., jt. ed. see Flood, James.

Langer-Kaneko, Christiane. Das Reine Land: Zur Begegnung von Amida-Buddhismus und Christentum. (Zeitschrift fur Religions- und Geistesgeschichte Ser.: Vol. 29). xii, 194p. 1986. 40.00 (*90-04-07786-3*) E J Brill.

Langer, Lawrence L. Admitting the Holocaust: Collected Essays. LC 94-13368. 202p. 1995. 23.00 (*0-19-509357-7*) OUP.

— Art from the Ashes: A Holocaust Anthology. (Illus.). 694p. 1995. 30.00 (*0-19-507559-5*) OUP.

— Art from the Ashes: A Holocaust Anthology. (Illus.). 720p. (C). 1995. reprint ed. pap. text ed. 17.95 (*0-19-507732-6*) OUP.

— The Holocaust & the Literary Imagination. LC 75-8443. 336p. 1977. pap. 16.00 (*0-300-02121-6*) Yale U Pr.

— Holocaust Testimonies: The Ruins of Memory. 240p. (C). 1991. text ed. 32.00 (*0-300-04966-8*) Yale U Pr.

— Holocaust Testimonies: The Ruins of Memory. LC 90-44768. (C). 1993. pap. 13.00 (*0-300-05247-2*) Yale U Pr.

— Versions of Survival: The Holocaust & the Human Spirit. LC 81-14560. (SUNY Series in Modern Jewish Literature & Culture). 280p. (C). 1982. 19.95 (*0-87395-583-8*) State U NY Pr.

Langer, M., jt. auth. see Hardy, H. R.

Langer, M., jt. auth. see Hardy, H. R., Jr.

Langer, Maria. Auditing Microcomputers. Campbell, Lee A., ed. 71p. 1991. Tool kit. 200.00 (*0-89413-238-5*) Inst Inter Aud.

— The Endocrine & the Liver: Proceedings of the Serono Symposia, No. 51. 1983. text ed. 184.00 (*0-12-436580-9*) Acad Pr.

— Integrating PCs into the Internal Audit Process. Campbell, Lee A., ed. 99p. 1991. Self-study. student ed, pap. text ed. 130.00 (*0-89413-255-5*) Inst Inter Aud.

— Mac Power Toolkit. (Macintosh Library). (Illus.). 304p. (Orig.). 1993. Incl. 2 double density disks. disk 34.95 (*1-56830-002-6*) Hayden.

— The Macintosh Bible Guide to Word 6. (Illus.). 776p. 1995. 24.95 (*1-56609-073-3*) Peachpit Pr.

— Macintosh Slick Tricks. (Slick Tricks Ser.). 1994. pap. 16.00 (*0-679-75606-X*, Random) Random.

— Murphy's Law of Macs. LC 93-84943. 354p. 1993. pap. 16.99 (*0-7821-1318-4*) Sybex.

Langer, Maria L. FileMaker Pro 2.0 for the Mac in a Nutshell. LC 92-83713. 270p. 1992. pap. 17.95 (*0-7821-1214-5*) Sybex.

Langer, Maria L., jt. auth. see David, Bernard J.

Langer, Marie. Motherhood & Sexuality. Hollander, Nancy C., tr. LC 91-43985. (Feminism & Psychoanalysis Ser.). 305p. 1992. reprint ed. lib. bdg. 36.95 (*0-89862-093-7*) Guilford Pr.

Langer, Marshall J. Practical International Tax Planning. 3rd ed. 454p. 1988. 185.00 (*0-685-69476-3*) PLI.

Langer, Michael, jt. auth. see Dietz, Robert.

Langer, Monika. Merleau-Ponty's Phenomenology of Perception: A Guide & Commentary. 1989. pap. 19.95 (*0-8130-0926-X*) U Press Fla.

Langer, P. & Greer, M. A. Antithyroid Substances & Naturally Occuring Goitrogens. (Illus.). 1977. 59.25 (*3-8055-2659-8*) S Karger.

Langer, Paul, jt. auth. see Swearingen, A. Rodger.

Langer, Paul F. & Zasloff, Joseph J. North Vietnam & the Pathet Lao: Partners in the Struggle for Laos. LC 73-134326. (Rand Corporation Research Studies). 276p. 1970. 29.00 (*0-674-62675-3*) HUP.

Langer, Paul H., jt. ed. see Gupta, Dinesh C.

Langer, Peter. The Mammalian Herbivore Stomach: Comparative Anatomy, Function & Evolution. 552p. 1988. lib. bdg. 250.00 (*0-89574-254-3*, Pub. by Gustav Fischer Verlag) VCH Pubs.

Langer, Peter, jt. ed. see Chivers, David J.

Langer, R. E., ed. see Applied Mathematics Symposium Staff.

Langer, R. H., ed. Pastures: Their Ecology & Management. (Illus.). 512p. 1990. pap. 59.95 (*0-19-558174-1*) OUP.

Langer, R. H., jt. auth. see Hill, G. D.

Langer, R. S., jt. ed. see Peppas, N. A.

Langer, Richard W. The After-Dinner Gardening Book. rev. ed. (Illus.). 208p. 1992. pap. 9.95 (*0-89815-450-2*) Ten Speed Pr.

— Bread Machine Bakery Book: How to Bake Wonderful Homemade Breads with Your Bread Machines. 1991. pap. 10.95 (*0-316-51388-1*) Little.

— Bread Machine Sweets & Treats: Featuring Tea Breads, Coffee Cakes, & Festive Desserts for all Occasions. LC 93-16014. (Illus.). 1993. pap. 10.95 (*0-316-51391-1*) Little.

— Grow It! 1994. 21.50 (*0-8446-6725-0*) Peter Smith.

— Grow It! The Beginner's Complete Organic Small-Farm Guide. 1994. pap. 12.00 (*0-374-52390-8*, Noonday) FS&G.

— Grow It Indoors: How to Make Houseplants Thrive. (Illus.). 384p. 1995. pap. 16.95 (*0-8117-2480-8*) Stackpole.

— More Recipes for Your Bread Machine Bakery. LC 92-25406. 1992. pap. 10.95 (*0-316-51390-3*) Little.

Langer, Robert, jt. ed. see Cleland, Jeffrey L.

Langer, Robert S. & Wise, Donald L., eds. Medical Applications of Controlled Release, 2 vols., Vol. I: Classes of Systems. 272p. 1985. 168.00 (*0-8493-5405-6*, RS201, CRC Reprint) Franklin.

— Medical Applications of Controlled Release, 2 vols., Vol. II: Applications & Evaluation. 248p. 1985. 168.00 (*0-8493-5406-4*, RS201, CRC Reprint) Franklin.

Langer, Rudolph E. Electromagnetic Waves: Proceedings of a Symposium Conducted by the Mathematics Research Center, United States Army, at the University of Wisconsin, Madison, April 10-12, 1961. LC 62-60005. (Publication of the Mathematics Research Center, U. S. Army, the University of Wisconsin Ser.: No. 6). 408p. reprint ed. pap. 116.30 (*0-7837-6660-2*, 2046272) Bks Demand.

Langer, Rudolph E., ed. Boundary Problems in Differential Equations: Proceedings of a Symposium Conducted by the Mathematics Research Center at the University of Wisconsin, Madison, April 20-22, 1959. LC 60-60003. (U. S. Army. Mathematics Research Center Publication Ser.: No. 2). 334p. reprint ed. pap. 95.20 (*0-8357-7368-X*, 2021137) Bks Demand.

— Electromagnetic Waves. (Mathematics Research Center Publications: No. 6). (Illus.). 408p. 1962. 17.50 (*0-299-02500-4*) U of Wis Pr.

— Nonlinear Problems: Proceedings of a Symposium Conducted by the Mathematics Research Center, United States Army, at the University of Wisconsin, Madison, April 30-May 2, 1962. LC 63-8971. (U. S. Army. Mathematics Research Center Publication Ser.: No. 8). 336p. reprint ed. pap. 95.80 (*0-317-09187-5*, 2021138) Bks Demand.

— On Numerical Approximation: Proceedings of a Symposium Conducted by the Mathematics Research Center, United States Army, at the University of Wisconsin, Madison, April 21-23 1958. LC 59-9018. (Army Mathematics Research Center Ser.: No. 1). 474p. reprint ed. pap. 135.10 (*0-317-09181-6*, 2021136) Bks Demand.

— Partial Differential Equations & Continuum Mechanics. (Mathematics Research Center Publications: No. 5). (Illus.). 414p. 1961. 17.00 (*0-299-02350-8*) U of Wis Pr.

— Partial Differential Equations & Continuum Mechanics. LC 61-600003. (U. S. Army. Mathematics Research Center Publication Ser.: No. 5). 413p. reprint ed. pap. 117.80 (*0-317-09147-6*, 2015364) Bks Demand.

Langer, Rudolph Ernest, ed. Frontiers of Numerical Mathematics: A Symposium Conducted by the Mathematics Research Center, United States Army & the National Bureau of Standards at the University of Wisconsin, Madison, Wisconsin, October 30 & 31, 1959. LC 60-60026. (U. S. Army. Mathematics Research Center Publication Ser.: No. 4). 144p. reprint ed. pap. 41.10 (*0-317-08424-0*, 2004656) Bks Demand.

Langer, Russell D. Accounting As a Variable in Mergers. Brief, Richard P., ed. LC 77-87303. (Development of Contemporary Accounting Thought Ser.). 1978. lib. bdg. 26.95 (*0-405-10942-3*) Ayer.

Langer, S. Z. & Church, M. K., eds. New Developments in the Therapy of Allergic Disorders & Asthma. (International Academy for Biomedical & Drug Research Ser.: Vol. 6). (Illus.). vi, 136p. 1994. 128.00 (*3-8055-5748-5*) S Karger.

Langer, S. Z., ed. see Brunello, N., et al.

Langer, S. Z., et al. Presynadtic Receptors: Proceedings of the Satellite Symposium, Paris, July 22-23 1978, 7th International Congress of Pharmacology. (Illus.). 414p. 1979. 81.00 (*0-08-023190-X*, Pergamon Pr) Elsevier.

***Langer, S. Z., et al, eds.** Critical Issues in the Treatment of Affective Disorders. (International Academy for Biomedical & Drug Research Ser.: Vol. 9). (Illus.). viii, 198p. 1995. 179.25 (*3-8055-6032-X*) S Karger.

— New Vistas in Depression. (Illus.). 339p. 1982. 81.00 (*0-08-027388-2*, Pergamon Pr) Elsevier.

— Presynaptic Receptors & Neuronal Transporters: Proceedings of the Official Satellite Symposium to the IUPHAR 1990 Congress Held in Rouen, France, 26-29 June 1990. (Advances in the Biosciences Ser.: No. 82). (Illus.). 352p. 1992. 200.00 (*0-08-041165-7*, Pergamon Pr) Elsevier.

— Serotonin Receptor Subtypes: Pharmacological Significance & Clinical Implications. (International Academy for Biomedical & Drug Research Ser.: Vol. 1). (Illus.). x, 146p. 1992. 108.00 (*3-8055-5550-4*) S Karger.

Langer, Sheldon, et al. A Practical Manual for a Basic Approach to Clinical Electrodynography. 68p. 1988. pap. text ed. 24.00 (*0-317-91266-6*) Langer Found BSMR.

— A Practical Manual for a Basic Approach to Clinical Electrodynography. 68p. 1988. pap. text ed. 24.00 (*0-936445-02-5*) Langer Found BSMR.

Langer, Shirley, tr. see Morgan, Allen.

Langer, Shirley, tr. see Munsch, Robert.

Langer, Stephen. Solved: The Riddle of Illness. 206p. (Orig.). 1984. 17.95 (*0-87983-370-X*); pap. 10.95 (*0-87983-357-2*) Keats.

Langer, Stephen & Scheer, James F. Solved: the Riddle of Weight Loss: Restore Healthy Body Chemistry & Lose Weight Naturally. Orig. Title: How to Win at Weight Loss. 256p. (Orig.). 1989. pap. 9.95 (*0-89281-296-6*, Heal Arts VT) Inner Tradit.

Langer, Stephen E. & Scheer, James F. How to Win at Weight Loss. rev. ed. 316p. 1994. 29.98 (*0-941683-11-7*) Instant Improve.

— Solved: The Riddle of Illness. 2nd expanded rev. ed. LC 95-2608. 208p. 1995. pap. 12.95 (*0-87983-667-9*) Keats.

Langer, Steven, ed. Available Pay Survey Reports for Other Countries: An Annotated Bibliography. 4th ed. 1995. pap. 160.00 (*0-916506-39-8*) Abbott Langer Assocs.

— Available Pay Survey Reports for the U. S. An Annotated Bibliography. 4th ed. 1995. pap. 450.00 (*0-317-55987-7*) Abbott Langer Assocs.

— Compensation & Benefits in Consulting Engineering & Land Surveying Firms in California. 3rd ed. 229p. 1994. pap. 395.00 (*0-614-05745-0*) Abbott Langer Assocs.

— Compensation & Benefits in Consulting Engineering Firms - 1995 National Edition. 467p. 1995. pap. 495.00 (*0-614-05741-8*) Abbott Langer Assocs.

— Compensation & Benefits in Consulting Engineering Firms in Indiana. 2nd ed. 208p. 1994. pap. 395.00 (*0-614-05742-6*) Abbott Langer Assocs.

— Compensation & Benefits in Consulting Engineering Firms in New England. 3rd ed. 225p. 1994. pap. 395.00 (*0-614-05744-2*) Abbott Langer Assocs.

— Compensation & Benefits in Consulting Engineering Firms in Utah. 202p. 1994. pap. 395.00 (*0-614-05743-4*) Abbott Langer Assocs.

— Compensation & Benefits in Engineering Firms in the Geotechnical Field. 6th ed. 307p. 1994. pap. 395.00 (*0-614-05746-9*) Abbott Langer Assocs.

— Compensation in Food & Beverage Processing. 1995. pap. 450.00 (*0-614-05751-5*) Abbott Langer Assocs.

— Compensation in Manufacturing. 14th ed. 622p. 1994. pap. 450.00 (*0-916506-25-8*) Abbott Langer Assocs.

— Compensation in Medical Equipment Manufacturing. 198p. 1994. pap. 450.00 (*0-614-05750-7*) Abbott Langer Assocs.

— Compensation in Nonprofit Organizations. 7th ed. 1233p. 1994. pap. 225.00 (*0-614-05748-5*) Abbott Langer Assocs.

— Compensation in Research & Development. 9th ed. 573p. 1995. pap. 650.00 (*0-916506-34-7*) Abbott Langer Assocs.

— Compensation in the Accounting-Financial Field. 14th ed. 353p. 1995. pap. 495.00 (*0-317-55984-2*) Abbott Langer Assocs.

— Compensation in the Human Resources Field. 16th ed. 1071p. 1994. pap. 500.00 (*0-916506-31-2*) Abbott Langer Assocs.

— Compensation in the MIS-dp Field. 12th ed. 687p. 1995. pap. 750.00 (*0-916506-37-1*) Abbott Langer Assocs.

— Compensation in the Security-Loss Prevention Field. 8th ed. 367p. 1994. pap. 395.00 (*0-916506-23-1*) Abbott Langer Assocs.

— Compensation of Plant & Facilities Managers & Engineers. 438p. 1994. pap. 150.00 (*0-614-05752-3*) Abbott Langer Assocs.

— Compensation of Professional Geologists. 437p. 1994. pap. 150.00 (*0-614-05747-7*) Abbott Langer Assocs.

— Fringe Benefits & Working Conditions in Nonprofit Organizations. 7th ed. 1233p. 1994. pap. 125.00 (*0-614-05749-3*) Abbott Langer Assocs.

— Income in Sales-Marketing Management. 15th ed. 1071p. 1994. pap. 395.00 (*0-317-55980-X*) Abbott Langer Assocs.

— Inter-City Wage Salary Differentials - 1995. 1995. pap. 225.00 (*0-317-55986-9*) Abbott Langer Assocs.

— Salaries & Bonuses in the Service Department - 1994. 74p. 1994. pap. 295.00 (*0-317-55974-5*) Abbott Langer Assocs.

Langer, Susanne K. Feeling & Form. 431p. (C). 1977. pap. write for info. (*0-02-367500-4*, Scribners) S&S Trade.

— Introduction to Symbolic Logic. 3rd ed. 1953. pap. text ed. 9.95 (*0-486-60164-1*) Dover.

— Mind: An Essay on Human Feeling. Incl. LC 66-26686. (Illus.). 512p. 1967. 45.00 (*0-8018-0360-8*); LC 66-26686. 412p. 1973. 40.00 (*0-8018-1428-6*); LC 66-26686. 412p. 1973. pap. 15.95 (*0-8018-1607-6*); Vol. III. LC 66-26686. 264p. 32.00 (*0-8018-2756-6*); Vol. III. LC 66-26686. 264p. pap. 15.95 (*0-8018-2511-3*); Set. LC 66-26686. 264p. pap. 45.00 (*0-8018-2555-5*); LC 66-26686. write for info. (*0-318-53779-6*) Johns Hopkins.

— Philosophical Sketches. 1979. 21.95 (*0-405-10610-6*) Ayer.

— Philosophy in a New Key: A Study in the Symbolism of Reason, Rite & Art. 3rd ed. LC 57-1386. 330p. 1957. pap. text ed. 12.95 (*0-674-66503-1*) HUP.

— Problems of Art. 184p. (C). 1977. pap. write for info. (*0-02-367510-1*, Scribners) S&S Trade.

— Problems of Art. 1985. 15.00 (*0-684-15346-7*, Scribners) S&S Trade.

— Reflections on Art. 1979. 25.95 (*0-405-10611-4*) Ayer.

Langer, Susanne K. & Danto, Arthur C. Mind: An Essay on Human Feeling. abr. ed. LC 88-45414. 464p. (C). 1988. text ed. 50.00 (*0-8018-3705-7*); pap. 16.95 (*0-8018-3706-5*) Johns Hopkins.

Langer, Susanne K., tr. see Cassirer, Ernst.

Langer, Ullrich. Divine & Poetic Freedom in the Renaissance: Nominalist Theology & Literature in France & Italy. 224p. (C). 1990. text ed. 35.00 (*0-691-06853-4*) Princeton U Pr.

— Invention, Death, & Self-Definitions in the Poetry of Pierre de Ronsard. (Stanford French & Italian Studies: Vol. 45). 128p. (Orig.). 1986. pap. 46.50 (*0-915838-61-3*) Anma Libri.

Langer, Walter C. The Mind of Adolf Hitler: The Secret Wartime Report. 1985. pap. 8.95 (*0-452-00740-5*, Mer) NAL-Dutton.

— The Mind of Adolf Hitler: The Secret Wartime Report. 1989. pap. 9.95 (*0-452-00940-5*) NAL-Dutton.

Langer, William L. European Alliances & Alignments, 1871-1890. LC 77-1767. 509p. 1977. reprint ed. text ed. 45.50 (*0-8371-9518-7*, LAEA, Greenwood Pr) Greenwood.

— Explorations in Crisis: Papers on International History. Schorske, Carl E. & Schorske, Elizabeth, eds. LC 69-18036. 561p. reprint ed. pap. 159.90 (*0-7837-2291-5*, 2057379) Bks Demand.

— In & Out of the Ivory Tower: The Autobiography of William L. Langer. LC 77-20035. 1978. 20.00 (*0-88202-177-X*) Watson Pub Intl.

Langer, William L., ed. An Encyclopedia of World History. 5th ed. 1973. 45.00 (*0-395-13592-3*) HM.

— Perspectives in Western Civilization: Essays from Horizon, 2 Vols, 1. (Illus.). (C). 1990. pap. text ed. 28.50 (*0-06-043841-X*) HarpCollege.

— Perspectives in Western Civilization: Essays from Horizon, 2 Vols, 2. (Illus.). (C). 1990. pap. text ed. 20.75 (*0-06-043835-5*) HarpCollege.

Langer, William L. & Gleason, S. Everett. The Challenge to Isolation: The World Crisis of 1937-1940 & American Foreign Policy, Vol. 1. 15.00 (*0-8446-0759-2*) Peter Smith.

Langeraar, W. Surveying & Charting of the Seas. (Elsevier Oceanography Ser.: No. 37). 612p. 1984. 89.75 (*0-444-42278-1*, I-540-83) Elsevier.

Langerbeck, Hermann. Neue Philologische Untersuchungen, Heft 10: Doxis Epirhysmie. 132p. 1967. write for info. (*3-296-14190-1*, Pub. by Georg Olms GW) Lubrecht & Cramer.

Langerhorst, Christina T. Automated Perimetry in Glaucoma: Fluctuation Behavior & General & Local Reduction of Sensitivity. (Illus.). 172p. 1988. pap. text ed. 45.00 (*90-6299-025-8*, Pub. by Kugler NE) Kugler Pubns.

Langerman. OSHA Bloodborne Pathogens Exposure Control Plan. 1992. 89.95 (*0-87371-802-X*, RA642) Lewis Pubs.

Langerman, Jean. No Carrots for Harry! LC 89-3373. (Illus.). (J). (ps-3). 1989. 5.95 (*0-8193-1190-1*) Parents.

— No Carrots for Harry! (Sunny Day Bks.). (Illus.). 48p. (J). (ps-2). 1992. pap. 2.95 (*0-448-40320-X*, G&D) Putnam Pub Group.

— No Carrots for Harry. (Parents Magazine Press Read-Aloud Library). (Illus.). 42p. (J). (ps-3). 1992. lib. bdg. 14.60 (*0-8368-0876-2*) Gareth Stevens Inc.

Langerman, Neal. Hazardous Chemical Labels: Use, Design, & Requirements. 1994. 59.95 (*0-87371-917-4*) Lewis Pubs.

Langerman, Phillip D., ed. see Adult Education Association Staff.

Langermann, Tzvi. Ibn Al-Haytham's: On the Configuration of the World. LC 90-3248. (Harvard Dissertations in the History of Science Ser.: Vol. 3). 392p. 1990. 117.00 (*0-8240-0041-2*) Garland.

Langeston, Lynne E. Marriage Therapy - Index of New Information for the Married, Divorced, Live-ins & Professional Counselors. 180p. 1993. 49.50 (*1-55914-876-4*); pap. 39.50 (*1-55914-877-2*) ABBE Pubs Assn.

Langevin, ed. Light Scattering by Liquid Surfaces & Complementary Techniques. (Surfactant Science Ser.: Vol. 41). 472p. 1991. 165.00 (*0-8247-8607-6*) Dekker.

Langevin, D., ed. see Meunier, J.

Langevin, Don. How-to-Grow World Class Giant Pumpkins. LC 93-71941. (Illus.). 128p. (Orig.). 1993. pap. 14.95 (*0-9632793-4-3*) Annedawn Pub.

Langevin, Don, jt. auth. see Wiberg, Hugh.

Langevin, Donald G. The Growing & Marketing of Fall Mums: How You Can Turn Your Backyard into ... a Money-Making, Growing Machine! LC 92-71432. (Illus.). 224p. (Orig.). 1992. pap. text ed. 16.95 (*0-9632793-3-5*) Annedawn Pub.

Langevin, Leo J. Advanced VSE Systems Programming Techniques. LC 90-8529. 224p. 1990. 34.95 (*0-89435-365-9*) Wiley.

An Asterisk (*) at the beginning of an entry indicates that the title is appearing in BIP for the first time.

— Advanced VSE Systems Programming Techniques. 203p. 1993. text ed. 42.95 (*0-471-58029-5*) Wiley.
— DOS - VSE - SP Guide for Systems Programming: Concepts, Programs, Macros, Subroutines. 456p. 1993. pap. text ed. 39.95 (*0-471-56021-9*) Wiley.
— DOS-VSE-SP Guide for Systems Programming: Programs, Macros, Subroutines. LC 89-10368. 1989. 39.95 (*0-89435-299-7*) Wiley.
— VSE JCL & Subroutines for Application Programmers. 1992. 34.95 (*0-471-58028-7*, GC4019) Wiley.
— VSE JCL & Subroutines for Application Programmers. 1992. 34.95 (*0-89435-401-9*) Wiley.
Langevin, M. & Waldschmidt, M., eds. Cinquante Ans de Polynomes - Fifty Years of Polynomials. (Lecture Notes in Mathematics Ser.: Vol. 1415). ix, 235p. 1990. pap. 34.80 (*0-387-52190-9*, 3899) Spr-Verlag.
Langevin, R. Sexual Strands: Understanding & Treating Sexual Anomalies in Men. (Illus.). 560p. (C). 1983. text ed. 99.95 (*0-89859-205-4*) L Erlbaum Assocs.
Langevin, Ron, ed. Erotic Preference, Gender Identity, & Aggression in Men: New Research Studies. 376p. 1984. text ed. 79.95 (*0-89859-445-6*) L Erlbaum Assocs.
Langevoort, Donald C. Insider Trading: Regulation, Enforcement & Prevention. LC 91-27756. (Securities Law Ser.). 1991. ring bd. 145.00 (*0-87632-758-7*) Clark Boardman Callaghan.
***Langeweg, Kick.** King's Indian: Saemisch Variation. (Electronic Chessbooks Ser.). 80p. 1995. disk, pap. 25.00 (*0-917237-12-9*) Chess Combi.
Langeweg, Kick, ed. Sicilian Defense - 2.F4: 2.F4. (Electronic Chessbook Ser.). 64p. 1994. disk 25.00 (*0-917237-04-8*, Interchess) Chess Combi.
***Langewiesche.** Cutting for Sign. 1995. pap. 12.00 (*0-679-75963-8*) Random.
Langewiesche, Karl R. Carl Larsson: Fifty Paintings. Rice, Alan L., tr. (Illus.). 104p. 1985. 19.95 (*0-940607-05-0*) Pictura NJ.
— Carl Larsson: On the Sunny Side. Rice, Alan L., tr. (Illus.). 62p. 1984. reprint ed. 19.95 (*0-940607-06-9*) Pictura NJ.
Langewiesche, William. Cutting for Sign. LC 93-9040. 288p. 1994. 23.00 (*0-679-41113-5*) Pantheon.
Langewiesche, Wolfgang. Stick & Rudder. (Illus.). 1944. text ed. 19.95 (*0-07-036240-8*) McGraw.
— Stick & Rudder: Fiftieth Anniversary. LC 94-18945. 1994. text ed. 50.00 (*0-07-036242-4*) TAB Bks.
Langfeldt, T. & Porter, M. Sexuality & Family Planning: Report of a Consultation & Research Findings. 62p. 1986. pap. 4.80 (*92-890-1042-8*) World Health.
Langfield, Weldon. How to Survive & Prosper: A Guidebook for Christian Men. 1992. pap. write for info. (*0-9634097-0-0*) W Langfield Pubns.
Langfitt, Thomas W., et al, eds. Partners in the Research Enterprise: University-Corporate Relations in Science & Technology. LC 83-3508. (Illus.). 224p. 1983. pap. text ed. 25.95x (*0-8122-1150-2*) U of Pa Pr.
Langford, jt. auth. see Perreau.
***Langford, A. T.** Why Men Marry: Insights from Marrying Men. LC 94-42508. 1995. 18.95 (*1-57101-008-4*) MasterMedia Ltd.
— Why Men Marry: Insights from Marrying Men. 200p. 1995. 18.95 (*1-57101-022-X*) MasterMedia Ltd.
Langford, Alec J. Invitations to Communion. LC 86-6116. 112p. (Orig.). 1986. pap. 7.99 (*0-8272-1607-6*) Chalice Pr.
Langford, Alton, illus. Caribou Country: From an Original Article Which Appeared in Ranger Rick Magazine, Copyright National Wildlife Federation. LC 92-7732. (Adventures of Ranger Rick Ser.). 20p. (J). (gr. k-3). 1992. 6.95 (*0-924483-53-9*); audio 35.95 (*0-924483-50-4*); 21.95 (*0-924483-51-2*); audio 9.95 (*0-924483-52-0*); audio write for info. (*0-924483-80-6*) Soundprints.
— Deputy Scarlett: From an Original Article Which Appeared in Ranger Rick Magazine, copyright National Wildlife Federation. LC 92-8024. (Adventures of Ranger Rick Ser.). 20p. (J). (gr. k-3). 1992. 6.95 (*0-924483-49-0*); audio 35.95 (*0-924483-46-6*); 21.95 (*0-924483-47-4*); audio 9.95 (*0-924483-48-2*); audio write for info. (*0-924483-79-2*) Soundprints.
— Rick's First Adventure: From an Original Article Which Appeared in Ranger Rick Magazine, Copyright National Wildlife Federation. LC 92-11868. (Adventures of Ranger Rick Ser.). 20p. (J). (gr. k-3). 1992. 6.95 (*0-924483-45-8*); digital audio 35.95 (*0-924483-42-3*); 21.95 (*0-924483-43-1*); digital audio 9.95 (*0-924483-44-X*); audio write for info. (*0-924483-78-4*) Soundprints.
Langford, Andy. Blueprints for Worship: A User's Guide for United Methodist Congregations. LC 92-41992. 96p. (Orig.). 1993. pap. 9.95 (*0-687-03312-8*) Abingdon.
Langford, Andy, ed. The United Methodist Book of Worship. LC 92-28537. 1992. 24.95 (*0-687-03572-4*); pap. 49.95 (*0-687-03573-2*) Abingdon.
Langford, Andy, jt. auth. see Willimon, William H.
Langford, Anne. Meditation for Little People. LC 75-46191. (Illus.). 40p. (J). (gr. k-4). 1976. reprint ed. pap. 6.95 (*0-87516-211-8*) DeVorss.
Langford, Carl T. Hizzoner the Mayor. LC 75-40537. 1976. 8.95 (*0-88435-005-3*) Chateau Pub.
***Langford, Cooper H. & Beebe, Ralph A.** The Development of Chemical Principles. unabridged ed. (Illus.). 384p. 1995. pap. text ed. 9.95 (*0-486-68359-1*) Dover.
Langford, David. Let's Hear It for the Deaf Man. 64p. 1992. write for info. (*0-915368-50-1*) New Eng SF Assoc.
***Langford, David & Cleary, Barbara.** Orchestrating Learning with Quality. LC 94-45285. 1995. pap. 22.00 (*0-87389-321-2*) ASQC Qual Pr.
Langford, David & Male, Steven. Strategic Management in Construction. 144p. 1991. text ed. 64.95 (*0-566-09015-5*, Pub. by Gower UK) Ashgate Pub Co.
***Langford, Diane.** Shame about the Street. 1995. pap. 11.99 (*1-85242-269-6*) Serpents Tail.
***Langford, Duncan.** Practical Computer Ethics. LC 95-2503. 1995. pap. write for info. (*0-07-709012-8*) McGraw.
Langford, Eulalie T. Heritage. 523p. 1991. 39.95 (*0-9630972-0-2*) E T Langford.
Langford, Gary & Langford, Lauren. The Psychic Almanac, Nineteen Ninety-One A. D. 224p. (Orig.). pap. text ed. 6.95 (*0-9627408-0-2*) Forest Light Pr.
Langford, Gerald. Alias O. Henry: A Biography of William Sidney Porter. LC 83-1743. (Illus.). xix, 294p. 1983. reprint ed. text ed. 48.50 (*0-313-23964-9*, LAAL, Greenwood Pr) Greenwood.
Langford, H. G., jt. ed. see Blaufox, M. D.
Langford, Howard D. Educational Service: Its Functions & Possibilities. LC 74-176975. (Columbia University. Teachers College. Contributions to Education Ser.: No. 509). reprint ed. 37.50 (*0-404-55509-8*) AMS Pr.
Langford, J. A. Prison Books & Their Authors. 1972. 59.95 (*0-8490-0892-1*) Gordon Pr.
Langford, J. O. & Gipson, Fred. Big Bend: A Homesteader's Story. (Illus.). 1974. reprint ed. pap. 8.95 (*0-292-70734-7*) U of Tex Pr.
Langford, James R., jt. ed. see Rouner, Leroy S.
Langford, Jerome J. Galileo, Science & the Church. 3rd ed. 230p. (C). 1992. pap. 15.95 (*0-472-06510-6*) U of Mich Pr.
Langford, Jim. The Cub Fan's Guide to Life: The Ultimate Self-Help Book. rev. ed. LC 84-12695. (Illus.). 96p. 1984. pap. 4.95 (*0-912083-08-5*) Diamond Communications.
— The Cubs Fans' Little Book of Wisdom: One Hundred One Truths Learned the Hard Way. LC 93-37864. 1993. 5.95 (*0-912083-68-9*) Diamond Communications.
— Runs, Hits & Errors: A Treasury of Cub History & Humor. LC 87-27272. (Illus.). 219p. 1987. 14.95 (*0-912083-22-0*) Diamond Communications.
Langford, Jim, jt. auth. see Walton, Jerome.
Langford, Joel. Silver: Practical Guide to Collecting Silverware. 1991. 12.98 (*1-55521-710-9*) Bk Sales Inc.
Langford, John W. Logistics: Principles & Applications. 1994. text ed. 65.00 (*0-07-036415-X*) McGraw.
— Transport in Transition: The Reorganization of the Federal Transport Portfolio. LC 76-381003. (Canadian Public Administration Ser.). 283p. reprint ed. pap. 80.70 (*0-7837-1165-4*, 2041694) Bks Demand.
Langford, John W. & Brownsey, K. Lorne. Economic Policy-Making in the Asia-Pacific Region. 342p. 1990. pap. text ed. 26.95 (*0-88645-104-3*, Pub. by Inst Res Pub CN) Ashgate Pub Co.
Langford, John W. & Brownsey, K. Lorne, eds. The Changing Shape of Government in the Asia-Pacific Region. 326p. 1988. pap. text ed. 22.00 (*0-88645-060-8*, Pub. by Inst SE Asian Studies SI) Ashgate Pub Co.
Langford, John W., jt. auth. see Kernaghan, Kenneth.
Langford, Laura C. The Ladies of the White House. LC 70-171655. (Illus.). reprint ed. 76.50 (*0-404-04608-8*) AMS Pr.
Langford, Lauren, jt. auth. see Langford, Gary.
Langford, Mark, et al, photos. San Antonio: Portrait of the Fiesta City. (Illus.). 96p. 1992. pap. 16.95 (*0-89658-204-3*) Voyageur Pr.
***Langford, Martha.** George Steeves: 1979-1993. 115p. 1994. pap. text ed. 34.95 (*0-88884-566-9*) U Ch Pr.
— Tom Gibson: False Evidence Appearing Real. 109p. 1994. pap. text ed. 25.00 (*0-88884-567-7*) U Ch Pr.
Langford, Martha, ed. Beau: A Reflection on the Nature of Beauty in Photography. (Illus.). 112p. 1992. 39.95 (*0-88884-562-6*) U Ch Pr.
Langford, Mary. That Nothing Be Wasted: My Experience with the Suicide of My Son. 64p. (Orig.). 1989. pap. text ed. 2.95 (*0-936625-61-9*, New Hope AL) Womans Mission Union.
Langford, Michael. Advanced Photography. 5th ed. (Illus.). 320p. 1989. pap. 25.00 (*0-240-51088-7*, Focal) Buttrwrth-Heinemann.
— Basic Photography. 5th ed. (Illus.). 320p. (C). 1986. pap. 18.95 (*0-240-51257-X*, Focal) Buttrwrth-Heinemann.
— Creative Photography. LC 90-23348. (Home Handbooks Ser.). (Illus.). 240p. (Orig.). 1991. pap. 16.00 (*0-89577-379-1*, Random) RD Assn.
— The Darkroom Handbook. LC 83-49188. 120p. 1984. pap. 26.00 (*0-394-72468-2*) Knopf.
— Learn Photography in a Weekend. LC 92-53044. 1992. 15.50 (*0-679-41674-9*) Knopf.
— Michael Langford's 35 Millimeter Handbook. 3rd ed. LC 92-54920. 1993. pap. 20.00 (*0-679-74634-X*) Knopf.
— Starting Photography. 2nd ed. LC 93-17759. (Illus.). 160p. (YA). (gr. 7 up). 1993. pap. 9.95 (*0-240-51348-7*, Focal) Buttrwrth-Heinemann.
— The Step-by-Step Guide to Photography. LC 78-54894. (Illus.). 1978. 24.95 (*0-394-41604-X*) Knopf.
— Step by Step Guide to Photography. LC 78-54894. (C). 1979. pap. text ed. write for info. (*0-07-553591-2*) McGraw.
— Story of Photography. (Illus.). 163p. 1980. pap. 26.95 (*0-240-51044-5*, Focal) Buttrwrth-Heinemann.
Langford, Michele K., ed. Contours of the Fantastic: Selected Essays from the Eighth International Conference on the Fantastic in the Arts. LC 89-23308. (Contributions to the Study of Science Fiction & Fantasy Ser.: No. 41). 256p. 1990. text ed. 55.00 (*0-313-26647-6*, LCN/) Greenwood.
Langford, N. P. The Ascent of Mt. Hayden. Jones, William R., ed. (Illus.). 1980. reprint ed. pap. 3.95 (*0-89646-066-5*) Vistabooks.
Langford, Nathaniel P. Discovery of Yellowstone Park: Journal of the Washburn Expedition to the Yellowstone & Firehole Rivers in the Year 1870. LC 78-93106. (Illus.). lxii, 147p. 1972. pap. 8.95 (*0-8032-5705-8*) U of Nebr Pr.
— The Discovery of Yellowstone Park, Journal of the Washburn Expedition to the Yellowstone & Firehole Rivers in the Year 1870. (American Biography Ser.). 125p. 1991. reprint ed. lib. bdg. 59.00 (*0-7812-8238-1*) Rprt Serv.
— Vigilante Days & Ways. (Sweetgrass Bks.). 400p. reprint ed. pap. 13.95 (*1-56037-038-6*) Am Wrld Geog.
— Vigilante Days & Ways. LC 71-160979. (Select Bibliographies Reprint Ser.). 1977. reprint ed. 42.95 (*0-8369-5847-0*) Ayer.
— Vigilante Days & Ways, 2 Vols, Set. LC 76-156021. reprint ed. 95.00 (*0-404-09121-0*) AMS Pr.
Langford, Paul. A Polite & Commercial People: England 1727-1783. (New Oxford History of England Ser.). (Illus.). 824p. 1989. 55.00 (*0-19-822828-7*) OUP.
— A Polite & Commercial People: England, 1727-1783. (New Oxford History of England Ser.). (Illus.). 832p. 1994. reprint ed. pap. 18.95 (*0-19-285253-1*) OUP.
— Public Life & Propertied Englishmen, 1689-1798. (Illus.). 632p. 1994. reprint ed. pap. 29.95 (*0-19-820534-1*) OUP.
— Public Life & Propertied Englishmen, 1689-1798: The Ford Lectures Delivered in the University of Oxford, 1990. (Illus.). 632p. 1991. 89.00 (*0-19-820149-4*) OUP.
— Walpole & the Robinocracy. LC 85-6609. (English Satirical Print Ser.). 252p. 1986. lib. bdg. 100.00 (*0-85964-175-9*) Chadwyck-Healey.
Langford, Paul & Harvie, Christopher T. The Oxford History of Britain, Vol. 4: The Eighteenth Century & the Age of Industry. Morgan, Kenneth O., ed. (Illus.). 160p. 1992. pap. 10.95 (*0-19-285266-3*) OUP.
Langford, Peter. Children's Thinking & Learning in the Elementary School. LC 88-51818. 176p. 1989. 24.50 (*0-87762-604-9*) Technomic.
— Concept Development in the Primary School. 144p. 1987. lib. bdg. 45.00 (*0-7099-4162-5*, Pub. by Croom Helm UK) Routledge Chapman & Hall.
— Concept Development in the Secondary School. 192p. 1987. lib. bdg. 42.50 (*0-7099-4163-3*, Pub. by Croom Helm UK) Routledge Chapman & Hall.
Langford, R. Everett, jt. auth. see Campbell, Reginald L.
***Langford, R. P. & Combes, J. M.** Depositional Environments of Unstable Shelf-Margin Deltas of the Oligocene Vicksburg Formation, McAllen Ranch Field, South Texas. (Illus.). 60p. 1994. 5.00 (*0-614-01868-4*) Bur Econ Geology.
***Langford, R. P., et al.** Reservoir Heterogeneity & Permeability Barriers in the Vicksburg S Reservoir, McAllen Ranch Gas Field. (Report of Investigations Ser.: No. RI 222). (Illus.). 64p. 1994. 7.00 (*0-614-06201-2*) Bur Econ Geology.
— Use of Dipmeters in Stratigraphic & Depositional Interpretation of Natural Gas Reservoirs of the Oligocene Vicksburg Formation: An Example from McAllen Ranch Field, Hidalgo County, Texas. (Illus.). 39p. 1994. 5.50 (*0-614-01871-4*) Bur Econ Geology.
Langford, Roland E., jt. auth. see Campbell, Reginald L.
Langford, T. E., ed. Ecological Effects of Thermal Discharges. (Pollution Monitoring Ser.). 470p. 1990. 138.00 (*1-85166-451-3*) Elsevier.
Langford, T. E., jt. auth. see Dibble.
Langford, Teddy L. Managing & Being Managed: Preparation for Reintegrated Professional Nursing Practice. rev. ed. (Illus.). 352p. (C). 1990. pap. text ed. 26.95 (*0-9626604-1-8*) Landover Pub.
Langford, Thomas A. God Made Known. Brockwell, Charles W., ed. (We Believe Ser.). 144p. (Orig.). 1992. pap. 8.95 (*0-687-17976-9*) Abingdon.
— Practical Divinity: Theology in the Wesleyan Tradition. LC 82-20653. 304p. (Orig.). 1983. pap. 13.95 (*0-687-33326-1*) Abingdon.
— Wesleyan Theology: A Sourcebook. LC 84-7170. 320p. (C). 1984. lib. bdg. 30.00 (*0-939464-40-3*); pap. 14.95 (*0-939464-41-1*) Labyrinth Pr.
Langford, Thomas A. & Poteat, William H., eds. Intellect & Hope: Essays in the Thought of Michael Polyani. LC 68-23393. (Lilly Endowment Research Program in Christianity & Politics Ser). (Illus.). xi, 464p. 1968. 48.00 (*0-8223-0105-9*) Duke.
Langford, Thomas W., Jr., jt. auth. see Isard, Walter.
Langford, Walter M. Legends of Baseball: An Oral History of The Game's Golden Age. LC 87-5354. (Orig.). 1987. lib. bdg. 17.95 (*0-912083-25-5*); pap. 8.95 (*0-912083-20-4*) Diamond Communications.
— The Mexican Novel Comes of Age. LC 77-160486. 239p. 1971. text ed. 18.95 (*0-8290-2401-8*) Irvington.
— The Mexican Novel Comes of Age. LC 77-160486. 239p. 1971. 19.95 (*0-268-00450-1*) U of Notre Dame Pr.
Langfors, Arthur, ed. see Amauri, Maurice & DeCraon, Pierre.
Langguth, A. J. Patriots: The Men Who Started the American Revolution. 1989. pap. 16.00 (*0-671-67562-1*, Touchstone Bks) S&S Trade.
Langguth, Aj. Noise of War: Caesar, Pompey, Octavian & the Struggle for Rome. 1994. 25.00 (*0-671-70829-5*) S&S Trade.
Langhaar, Henry L. Energy Methods in Applied Mechanics. LC 88-38817. 364p. (C). 1989. reprint ed. lib. bdg. 43.50 (*0-89464-364-9*) Krieger.
***Langham, Barbara A.** The Complete Worker's Compensation Guide for Texas Physicians. (Illus.). 150p. 1994. student ed 149.00 (*0-9640262-3-6*) TX Med Assn.
— The Pecan Tree: A True Friend. LC 94-96074. (Illus.). 32p. (J). (gr. k-3). 1994. lib. bdg. 12.95 (*0-9640804-0-0*) B A Langham.
Langham, Derald G. Circle Gardening. (Illus.). 1978. pap. 9.95 (*0-8159-5215-5*) Devin.
Langham, Ian G. The Building of British Social Anthropology. 420p. 1981. lib. bdg. 136.50 (*90-277-1264-6*) Kluwer Ac.
Langham, Ian G., jt. auth. see Oldroyd, David R.
Langham, Josephine & Chrichley, Janine. Radio Research: An Annotated Bibliography 1975-1988. 368p. 1990. text ed. 69.95 (*0-566-07130-4*, Pub. by Avebury Pub UK) Ashgate Pub Co.
Langham, M. J., jt. auth. see Hussey, David E.
Langham, Marion. Belleek-Irish Porcelain: An Illustrated Guide to Over 2000 Pieces. 1993. 79.95 (*1-870948-77-7*, Pub. by Quiller Pr UK) St Mut.
Langham, Thomas A. Border Trials: Ricardo Flores Magon & the Mexican Liberals. (Southwestern Studies: No. 65). 1981. pap. 10.00 (*0-87404-123-6*) Tex Western.
Langham, Tony, jt. auth. see Breese, Gillian.
Langham, Tony, tr. see Zoeteman, Kees.
Langhammer, Rolf J. Trade in Services Between ASEAN & EC Member States: Case Studies for West Germany, France & the Netherlands. 67p. 1991. pap. text ed. 10.00 (*981-3035-75-7*, Pub. by Inst SE Asian Studies SI) Ashgate Pub Co.
Langhammer, Rolf J. & Hiemenz, Ulrich. Regional Integration among Developing Countries: Opportunities, Obstacles & Options. 112p. (Orig.). (C). 1992. pap. text ed. 34.50 (*0-472-10376-8*) U of Mich Pr.
Langhammer, Rolf J. & Rieger, Hans C., eds. ASEAN & the EC: Trade in Tropical Agricultural Products. 185p. 1988. pap. text ed. 13.75 (*9971-988-81-X*, Pub. by Inst SE Asian Studies SI) Ashgate Pub Co.
Langhammer, Rolf J. & Sapir, Andre. Economic Impact of Generalized Tariff Preferences. (Thames Essays Ser.: Vol. 49). 80p. 1987. pap. text ed. 22.95 (*0-566-05338-1*) Ashgate Pub Co.
Langhans, Edward A. Eighteenth Century British & Irish Promptbooks: A Descriptive Bibliography. LC 87-23638. (Bibliographies & Indexes in the Performing Arts Ser.: No. 6). 304p. 1987. text ed. 75.00 (*0-313-24029-9*, LEB/, Greenwood Pr) Greenwood.
— An International Dictionary of Theatre Language. Trapido, Joel & Brandon, James R., eds. LC 83-22756. xxxvi, 1032p. 1985. text ed. 105.00 (*0-313-22980-5*, TDT/, Greenwood Pr) Greenwood.
— Restoration Promptbooks. LC 80-15626. 563p. 1981. 100.00 (*0-8093-0885-1*) S Ill U Pr.
Langhans, Robert W. Greenhouse Management: Guide to Structures, Environmental Control, Materials Handling, Crop Programming & Business Analysis. 3rd ed. (Illus.). 274p. 1990. 30.00 (*0-9604006-2-1*) Halcyon Ithaca.
Langhans, Robert W., ed. A Growth Chamber Manual: Environmental Control for Plants. LC 77-90906. (Comstock Book Ser.). (Illus.). 240p. 1978. 39.95 (*0-8014-1169-6*) Cornell U Pr.
Langhart, Nicholas. Houses of Southold: First Three Hundred Fifty Years. 1976. 25.95 (*0-8488-0870-3*) Amereon Ltd.
***Langhoff, June.** Telecom Made Easy: Money-Saving, Profit-Building Solutions for Home Businesses, Telecommuters & Small Organizations. LC 94-74496. (Illus.). 384p. (Orig.). 1995. pap. 19.95 (*0-9632790-2-5*) Aegis Pub Grp.
***Langhoff, Stephen R., ed.** Quantum Mechanical Electronic Structure Calculations with Chemical Accuracy. LC 94-39289. (Understanding Chemical Reactivity Ser.: Vol. 13). 1995. lib. bdg. 208.00 (*0-7923-3264-4*) Kluwer Ac.
Langholf, Volker. Medical Theories in Hippocrates: Early Texts & the "Epidemics" (Untersuchungen zur Antiken Literatur und Geschichte Ser.: No. 34). vi, 285p. (C). 1990. lib. bdg. 127.70 (*3-11-011956-0*) De Gruyter.
Langholm, Odd. Economics in the Medieval Schools: Wealth, Exchange, Value, Money & Usury According to the Paris Theological Tradition, 1200-1350. LC 91-24347. (STGM Ser.: No. 29). viii, 633p. 1992. 151.50 (*90-04-09422-9*) E J Brill.
Langholm, Tore. Partiality, Truth & Persistence. LC 88-15015. (CSLI Lecture Notes Ser.: No. 15). 155p. 1988. 29.95 (*0-937073-35-0*); pap. 12.95 (*0-937073-34-2*) Ctr Study Language.
Langholz, Gideon, jt. ed. see Kandel, Abraham.
Langhorn, Richard & Hamilton, Keith. The Practice of Diplomacy: Its Evolution, Theory & Administration. LC 94-15093. 240p. 1994. 59.95x (*0-415-10474-2*, B4096); pap. 17.95 (*0-415-10475-0*, B4100) Routledge.
Langhorne, Elizabeth. Monticello: A Family Story. (Illus.). 304p. 1987. 21.95 (*0-912697-58-X*) Algonquin Bks.
— Worlds Collide on Vieques: An Intimate Portrait from the Time of Columbus. LC 92-28718. (Illus.). 100p. 1992. 12.95 (*0-944957-36-6*) Rivercross Pub.
Langhorne, Elizabeth, et al. A Virginia Family & Its Plantation Houses. LC 86-28072. (Illus.). 176p. 1987. 28.50 (*0-8139-1127-3*) U Pr of Va.
Langhorne, Karyn E., jt. auth. see Martin, Eric R.
***Langiahr, Jenet & Sebree, Anita.** Newborn Video. 32p. Date not set. vhs 19.95 (*0-8431-2288-9*) Price Stern.
Langill, Ellen. Carroll College: The First Century, 1846-1946. LC 79-54879. (Illus.). 1980. text ed. 20.95 (*0-916120-06-6*) Carroll Coll.
— Pompey Poems... Celebrating a Cat. LC 86-91603. (Illus.). 64p. (Orig.). (YA). (gr. 7-12). 1986. 10.25 (*0-943864-28-3*); pap. 3.50 (*0-943864-26-7*) Davenport.
Langill, Ellen D. Foley & Lardner: Attorneys at Law, 1842-1992. LC 92-20157. (Illus.). 245p. 1992. 35.00 (*0-87020-267-7*) State Hist Soc Wis.
Langill, Ellen D. & Loerke, Jean Penn, eds. From Farmland to Freeways: A History of Waukesha County, Wisconsin. (Illus.). 480p. 1984. 30.00 (*0-685-09626-2*) Waukesha.
Langille, Carol. All That Glitters on Water. Raymond, Clarinda H., ed. 64p. 1990. pap. 5.95 (*0-932616-29-1*) New Poets Chestnut Hills.
Langille, Peter. Changing the Guard: Canada's Defense in Transition. 224p. 1990. 32.50 (*0-8020-5870-1*) U of Toronto Pr.

Langilotti, Frank T. Adjunctive Therapy: 1985 Edition. (Illus.). 152p. 1985. 30.00 (*0-938470-03-5*) NY Chiro Coll.

Langin, Bernd G. Plain & Amish. Thiessen, Jack, tr. (Illus.). 416p. 1994. pap. 15.95 (*0-8361-3665-9*) Herald Pr.

Langin, Chester. An Easy Course in Using DOS. 336p. 1992. pap. 19.95 (*0-931011-40-X*) Grapevine Pubns.

Langius, Gregor. Eine Ausgewaehlte Sammlung Motetten Zu 4, 5, 6 und 8 Stimmen. Starke, Reinhold, ed. Vol. XXV. (GER & LAT.). 1967. reprint ed. write for info. (*0-318-51196-7*) Broude.

Langjahr, Stephen W. & Brister, Robert D. Coloring Atlas of Human Anatomy. 2nd ed. 202p. (C). 1992. spiral bd. 20.50 (*0-8053-4020-3*); write for info. (*0-8053-4021-1*) Benjamin-Cummings.

Langkamp, P. J. Germination of Australian Native Plant Seed. (Illus.). 236p. 1987. 67.00 (*0-909605-49-1*, Pub. by Inkata Pr AT) Intl Spec Bk.

Langkau, David A. Civil War Veterans of Winnebago Co, WI, Vol. I: A-H. 378p. (Orig.). 1994. pap. text ed. 27.50 (*1-55613-911-X*) Heritage Bk.

— Civil War Veterans of Winnebago County, Wisconsin Vol. 2, I-T. 384p. (Orig.). 1994. pap. text ed. 27.50 (*0-7884-0035-5*) Heritage Bk.

***Langkein, John H. & Waggoner, Laurence W.** Selected Statutes on Trusts & Estates, 1995. 908p. 1994. pap. text ed. 21.95 (*1-56662-237-9*) Foundation Pr.

Langlais, F. & Tomeno, B., eds. Limb Salvage: Major Reconstruction in Oncologic & Nontumoral Conditions, 5th International Symposium - St. Malo. ISOLS-GETO. (Illus.). 880p. 1991. 173.00 (*0-387-52861-X*) Spr-Verlag.

Langlais, Jacques & Rome, David. Jews & French Quebecers: Two Hundred Years of Shared History. 256p. (C). 1991. pap. 29.95 (*0-88920-998-7*, Pub. by Wilfrid Laurier CN) Humanities.

Langlais, R. Road News from Tibet. 227p. 1993. pap. 39.00 (*0-387-56965-0*) Spr-Verlag.

Langlais, Robert P. & Miller, Craig S. Color Atlas of Common Oral Diseases. LC 89-12561. (Illus.). 182p. 1992. text ed. 36.95 (*0-8121-1249-0*) Williams & Wilkins.

Langlais, Robert P., et al. Diagnostic Imaging of the Jaws. (Illus.). 715p. (C). 1994. pap. text ed. 62.95 (*0-683-04849-X*) Williams & Wilkins.

Langland, Elizabeth. Anne Bronte: The Other One. (C). 1989. text ed. 58.00 (*0-389-20865-5*, N8423); pap. text ed. 22.50 (*0-389-20866-3*, N8424) B&N Imports.

— Nobody's Angels: Middle-Class Women & Domestic Ideology in Victorian Culture. LC 94-24393. (Reading Women Writing). 288p. 1995. 39.50x (*0-8014-3045-3*); pap. 15.95x (*0-8014-8220-8*) Cornell U Pr.

— Society in the Novel. LC 83-23597. 279p. reprint ed. pap. 79.60 (*0-7837-2067-X*, 2042342) Bks Demand.

Langland, Elizabeth & Gove, Walter, eds. A Feminist Perspective in the Academy: The Difference It Makes. LC 82-17520. 168p. 1983. pap. 5.95 (*0-226-46875-5*) U Ch Pr.

Langland, Elizabeth, jt. ed. see Claridge, Laura.

Langland, Joseph. Selected Poems. LC 90-24604. 128p. 1991. lib. bdg. 20.00 (*0-87023-747-0*) U of Mass Pr.

— Selected Poems. LC 90-24604. 1992. pap. 10.95 (*0-87023-800-0*) U of Mass Pr.

— Twelve Poems: With Preludes & Postludes. 40p. (Orig.). 1988. pap. 6.00 (*0-938566-37-7*) Adastra Pr.

Langland, Olaf E., et al. Radiology for Dental Hygienists & Dental Assistants. (Illus.). 252p. (C). 1988. text ed. 42.95 (*0-398-05470-3*) C C Thomas.

— Textbook of Dental Radiology. 2nd ed. (Illus.). 684p. (C). 1984. 67.95x (*0-398-04910-6*) C C Thomas.

Langland, William. Piers Plowman. Kirk, Elizabeth D. & Anderson, Judith H., eds. Donaldson, E. Talbot, tr. (C). 1990. pap. text ed. 8.95 (*0-393-96011-0*) Norton.

— Piers Plowman: A Facsimile of the Z-Text in Bodleian Library, Oxford, MS Bodley 851. Rigg, A. G., ed. (Illus.). 96p. (C). 1993. text ed. 135.00 (*0-85991-396-1*, DS Brewer) Boydell & Brewer.

— Piers Plowman: A New Translation of the B-Text. Schmidt, A. V., tr. & intro. by. (World's Classics Ser.). 400p. 1992. pap. 6.95 (*0-19-282587-9*) OUP.

— Piers Plowman Glossary, Pt. 4. Skeat, W. W., ed. (EETS, OS Ser.: No. 81). 1974. reprint ed. 58.00 (*0-527-00060-4*) Periodicals Srv.

— Piers the Ploughman. Goodridge, J. F., tr. (Classics Ser.). (Orig.). 1959. mass mkt. 9.95 (*0-14-044087-9*, Penguin Classics) Viking Penguin.

— Piers the Plowman: A Critical Edition of the A-Version. Knott, Thomas A. & Fowler, David C., eds. 316p. reprint ed. pap. 90.10 (*0-317-19926-9*, 2023122) Bks Demand.

— The Vision of Piers Plowman. 352p. 1991. pap. 8.50 (*0-460-87094-7*, Everyman's Classic Lib) C E Tuttle.

— Vision of Piers Plowman. Wells, Henry W., tr. LC 68-55324. 304p. 1969. reprint ed. text ed. 38.50 (*0-8371-0525-0*, LAPP, Greenwood Pr) Greenwood.

— Vision of Piers the Plowman. Skeat, W. W., ed. LC 66-26827. (Medieval Library). reprint ed. 45.00 (*0-8154-0134-5*) Cooper Sq.

— The Vision of William Concerning Piers Plowman, Pt. 4. Skeat, W. W., ed. (EETS, OS Ser.: No. 67). 1974. reprint ed. 62.00 (*0-527-00059-0*) Periodicals Srv.

— The Vision of William Concerning Piers the Plowman. (BCL1-PR English Literature Ser.). 216p. 1992. reprint ed. lib. bdg. 79.00 (*0-7812-7183-5*) Rprt Serv.

— Vision of William Concerning Piers the Plowman, in Three Parallel Texts, Together with Richard the Redeless, 2 Vols. Skeat, Walter W., ed. 1986. 125.00 (*0-19-811366-8*) OUP.

Langlands, R. Base Change for GL (2) LC 79-28820. (Annals of Mathematics Studies: No. 96). 225p. 1980. 49.50 (*0-691-08263-4*); pap. 19.95 (*0-691-08272-3*) Princeton U Pr.

Langlands, Robert P. Euler Products. LC 72-151580. (Yale Mathematical Monographs: Vol. 1). 59p. reprint ed. pap. 25.00 (*0-317-09487-4*, 2016790) Bks Demand.

Langley. Babes in the Woods. 1987. pap. 6.95 (*0-930096-90-8*) G Gannett.

***Langley, Aidan & Mulcahy, Richard.** Unapproved Pension Schemes. 140p. 1994. boxed 143.00 (*0-406-02982-2*, UK) Butterworth Legal Pubs.

Langley, Albert M., Jr., jt. auth. see Beckum, William F., Jr.

Langley, Albert M., Jr., et al. Seaboard Air Line Railway Album. LC 88-50417. (Illus.). 184p. (Orig.). 1988. pap. 27.95 (*0-9615257-2-X*) Union Sta.

***Langley, Andrew.** Discovering the New World: The Voyages of Christopher Columbus. LC 94-43535. (Great Explorers Ser.). (Illus.). 32p. (YA). (gr. 4 up). 1995. lib. bdg. 14.95 (*0-7910-2821-6*) Chelsea Hse.

— Exploring the Pacific: The Expeditions of Captain Hook. LC 94-43513. (Great Explorers Ser.). (Illus.). 32p. (YA). (gr. 4 up). 1995. lib. bdg. 14.95 (*0-7910-2819-4*) Chelsea Hse.

— Grasslands. LC 93-77346. (Nature Search Ser.). (Illus.). 32p. (J). (gr. 4-7). 1993. 14.00 (*0-89577-515-8*) RD Assn.

— The Great Polar Adventure: The Journey of Roald Amundsen. LC 94-43511. (Great Explorers Ser.). (Illus.). 32p. (J). (gr. 4 up). 1995. lib. bdg. 14.95 (*0-7910-2820-8*) Chelsea Hse.

— The Industrial Revolution. (See Through History Ser.). (Illus.). 48p. (J). (gr. 3-7). 1994. 15.99 (*0-670-85835-8*) Viking Child Bks.

— Into Space: The Missions of Neil Armstrong. LC 94-43512. (Great Explorers Ser.). (Illus.). 32p. (YA). (gr. 4 up). 1995. lib. bdg. 14.95 (*0-7910-2822-4*) Chelsea Hse.

— Paper. LC 93-6818. (Resources Ser.). (Illus.). 32p. (J). (gr. 3-6). 1993. 13.95 (*1-56847-047-9*) Thomson Lrning.

— Passport to Great Britain. LC 93-21187. (J). 1994. lib. bdg. 14.77 (*0-531-14297-3*) Watts.

— Sports & Politics. (World Issues Ser.). (Illus.). 48p. (J). (gr. 5 up). 1990. lib. bdg. 18.60 (*0-86592-117-2*); lib. bdg. 13.95 (*0-685-46458-X*) Rourke Corp.

— Steel. LC 93-6834. (Resources Ser.). 32p. (J). (gr. 3-6). 1993. 13.95 (*1-56847-044-4*) Thomson Lrning.

— Travel Games for Kids. rev. ed. LC 90-84702. (Illus.). 112p. (J). (gr. k-8). 1992. pap. 10.95 (*0-936399-09-0*) Berkshire Hse.

— Wetlands. LC 92-62551. (Nature Search Ser.). (Illus.). 32p. (J). (gr. 4-7). 1993. 14.00 (*0-89577-482-8*) RD Assn.

Langley, Andy. The Hungry Mice. (Window Board Bks.). (Illus.). 8p. (J). 1992. bds. 3.95 (*0-681-41517-7*) Longmeadow Pr.

— The Naughty Mice. (Window Board Bks.). (Illus.). 8p. (J). 1992. bds. 3.95 (*0-681-41516-9*) Longmeadow Pr.

Langley, B. Electric Controls for Refrigeration & Air Conditioning Controls. 2nd ed. 1987. pap. text ed. 55.00 (*0-13-247503-0*) P-H.

Langley, Batty. Builder's Director. LC 69-16324. (Illus.). 1972. reprint ed. 15.95 (*0-405-08730-6*, Pub. by Blom Pubns UK) Ayer.

— Builder's Jewel. LC 69-16325. (Illus.). 1972. reprint ed. 12.95 (*0-405-08731-4*, Pub. by Blom Pubns UK) Ayer.

— City & Country Builder's & Workman's Treasury of Designs. LC 67-18424. (Illus.). 1972. reprint ed. 31.95 (*0-405-08732-2*, Pub. by Blom Pubns UK) Ayer.

Langley, Batty & Langley, Thomas. Gothic Architecture. LC 73-172512. 1972. reprint ed. 18.95 (*0-405-08733-0*, Pub. by Blom Pubns UK) Ayer.

Langley, Beryl & Stapp, Joyce. For Women Only: A Guide to Emotional Well-Being. 1992. pap. 4.50 (*0-425-13239-0*) Berkley Pub.

Langley, Beryl W. & Stapp, E. Joyce. A Woman's Guide to Mental Health. 144p. (Orig.). 1990. pap. 7.95 (*0-929162-23-4*) PIA Pr.

Langley, Beth & Lombardino, Linda, eds. Neurodevelopmental Strategies for Managing Communication Disorders in Children with Severe Motor Dysfunction. LC 90-9166. 342p. 1991. text ed. 37.00 (*0-89079-422-7*, 1942) PRO-ED.

Langley, Bill & Dias, Ron, illus. Walt Disney's Lady & the Tramp. (Big Golden Book Ser.). 24p. (J). (ps-3). 1993. 3.50 (*0-307-12367-7*, 12367, Golden Pr) Western Pub.

— Walt Disney's One Hundred One Dalmatians. (J). (ps-2). 1991. write for info. (*0-307-12346-4*, Golden Pr) Western Pub.

Langley, Bill & Wakeman, Diana, illus. Winnie the Pooh & the Blustery Day. LC 92-55130. (Many Adventures of Winnie the Pooh Ser.). 48p. (J). (ps-00). 1993. 12.95 (*1-56282-488-0*) Disney Pr.

Langley, Billy & Fairmont, Press. Fundamentals of Air Conditioning Systems. 1994. text ed. 51.75 (*0-13-147422-7*) P-H.

Langley, Billy C. Air Conditioning & Refrigeration Trouble-Shooting Handbook. (Illus.). 650p. 1980. text ed. 82.00 (*0-8359-0204-8*, Reston) P-H.

— Basic Refrigeration. 416p. (C). 1982. write for info. (*0-8359-0418-0*, Reston) P-H.

— Boiler Operations. 417p. (C). 1988. text ed. 39.00 (*0-15-505526-7*) SCP.

— Comfort Heating. 3rd ed. (C). 1985. teacher ed write for info. (*0-8359-0888-7*, Reston); text ed. 65.00 (*0-8359-0887-9*, Reston) P-H.

— Comfort Heating. 4th ed. LC 93-8220. 518p. 1994. text ed. 56.00 (*0-13-151879-8*) P-H.

— Control Systems for Air Conditioning & Refrigeration. (Illus.). 192p. (C). 1985. text ed. 63.00 (*0-13-171679-4*) P-H.

— Cooling Systems Troubleshooting Handbook. (Illus.). 320p. (C). 1986. text ed. 78.00 (*0-8359-1036-9*, Reston) P-H.

— Electricity for Refrigeration & Air Conditioning. (C). 1984. text ed. 32.00 (*0-8359-1601-4*, Reston); teacher ed write for info. (*0-8359-1791-6*, Reston) P-H.

— Fundamentals of Air Conditioning Systems. LC 94-23108. 1994. write for info. (*0-88173-176-5*) Fairmont Pr.

— Fundamentals of Refrigeration. LC 94-42864. 1995. write for info. (*0-8273-6529-2*) Delmar.

— Heat Pump Technology. 2nd ed. 416p. 1988. text ed. 73.00 (*0-13-385766-2*) P-H.

— Heating System Troubleshooting Handbook. (Illus.). 572p. 1987. text ed. 60.00 (*0-8359-2805-5*) P-H.

— Heating, Ventilating, Air Conditioning & Refrigeration. 600p. 1990. pap. text ed. 63.00 (*0-13-385634-8*) P-H.

— High-Efficiency Gas Furnace Troubleshooting Handbook. 240p. (C). 1991. text ed. write for info. (*0-13-388653-0*) P-H.

— Major Appliances: Operation, Maintenance, Troubleshooting & Repair. 350p. 1993. text ed. 49.00 (*0-13-544834-4*) P-H.

— Operating at Peak Efficiency: A Technician's guide to Servicing HVAC/R Equipment. LC 95-15991. 1995. pap. write for info. (*1-885863-07-1*) Busn News.

— Principles & Service of Automotive Air Conditioning. (C). 1984. pap. 27.00 (*0-8359-5615-6*, Reston) P-H.

— Refrigerant Management: The Recovery, Recycling & Reclaiming of CFCs. LC 92-40577. 155p. 1994. pap. text ed. 29.95 (*0-8273-5590-4*) Delmar.

— Refrigeration & Air Conditioning. 3rd ed. 1985. text ed. 76.00 (*0-8359-6629-1*, Reston) P-H.

— Solid State Electronic Controls in Air Conditioning & Refrigeration. 304p. 1988. text ed. 65.00 (*0-13-823360-8*) P-H.

Langley, Bob. Autumn Tiger. 252p. 1986. 15.95 (*0-8027-0884-6*) Walker & Co.

— Autumn Tiger. large type ed. 480p. 1983. 15.95 (*0-7089-0959-0*) Ulverscroft.

— Avenge the Belgrano. LC 87-34461. 1988. 18.95 (*0-8027-1030-1*) Walker & Co.

— Avenge the Belgrano. large type ed. 1990. 21.95 (*0-7089-2140-X*) Ulverscroft.

— Blood River. large type ed. 1991. 21.95 (*0-7089-2431-X*) Ulverscroft.

— The Churchill Diamonds. 240p. 1986. 15.95 (*0-8027-0934-6*) Walker & Co.

— The Churchill Diamonds. large type ed. 448p. 1987. 16.95 (*0-7089-1687-2*) Ulverscroft.

— Conquistadores. large type ed. 448p. 1987. 16.95 (*0-7089-1627-9*) Ulverscroft.

— East of Everest. 252p. 1987. 16.95 (*0-8027-0961-3*) Walker & Co.

— Falklands Gambit. LC 85-20179. 272p. 1985. 15.95 (*0-8027-0871-4*) Walker & Co.

— The Hour of the Argentine. 1987. 16.95 (*0-8027-0992-3*) Walker & Co.

— Hour of the Gaucho. large type ed. 488p. 1988. 16.95 (*0-7089-1904-9*) Ulverscroft.

— Traverse of the Gods. large type ed. 464p. 1982. 15.95 (*0-7089-0879-9*) Ulverscroft.

Langley, Christopher. Women! from Mars. LC 76-15099. 1976. 15.00 (*0-87832-018-0*) Piper.

Langley, Dorothy. Fool's Mate. LC 78-139787. 1970. 4.95 (*0-913676-01-2*) Traumwald Pr.

— Swamp Angel. 237p. 1982. pap. 9.00 (*0-89733-061-7*) Academy Chi Pubs.

— Tom Sawyer Comes Home. LC 73-78123. 1973. 7.95 (*0-913676-02-0*) Traumwald Pr.

***Langley, Emma.** Full Release. 1995. 13.95 (*0-8062-5376-2*) Carlton.

Langley, Ernest. The Poetry of Giacomo Da Lentino: Sicilian Poet of the Thirteenth Century. 1977. lib. bdg. 59.95 (*0-8490-2448-X*) Gordon Pr.

Langley, F. A., jt. auth. see Fox, H.

Langley, F. P. & Caldicott, D. A. Workbook in Accounting. 3rd ed. (C). 1981. pap. 18.50 (*0-408-10680-8*) Buttrwrth-Heinemann.

Langley, F. P. & Harden, Geoff. Introduction to Accounting for Business Studies. 5th ed. 1990. U.K. pap. 30.00 (*0-406-51370-8*) Butterworth Legal Pubs.

***Langley, F. P. & Hardern, G. S.** Introduction to Accounting for Business Studies. 6th ed. 400p. 1994. pap. text ed. 29.00 (*0-406-03252-1*, UK) Butterworth Legal Pubs.

Langley, Florence. Glimpse of the Past: A History of Wilmot, New Hampshire. LC 86-22491. (Illus.). 160p. 1986. 14.95 (*0-914659-21-9*) Phoenix Pub.

— When School Bells Rang. LC 76-50006. (Illus.). 80p. 1976. 6.95 (*0-914016-34-2*) Phoenix Pub.

— With Prayer & Psalm: The History of Wilmot, New Hampshire Churches. LC 81-5116. 80p. 1981. 7.95 (*0-914016-77-6*) Phoenix Pub.

Langley, G. H. Sri Aurobindo. 1972. 59.95 (*0-8490-1119-1*) Gordon Pr.

Langley, Garda. Understanding Horses. (Illus.). 256p. 1990. 19.95 (*0-943955-20-3*, Trafalgar Sq Pub) Trafalgar.

Langley, Gilbert W. Tricks Your Cat Can Do. (Orig.). 1991. 4.98 (*1-55521-755-9*) Bk Sales Inc.

Langley, Glynis. The Age of Dinosaurs. (Illus.). 64p. (J). (gr. k-5). 1992. per. 6.95 (*0-8249-8537-0*, Ideals Child) Hambleton-Hill.

Langley, Graham. International Dictionary of Telecommunications. 420p. (C). 1986. text ed. 350.00 (*0-685-40848-5*, Pub. by Pitman Pubng UK) St Mut.

— Telecommunications Primer. 192p. (C). 1990. pap. text ed. 125.00 (*0-273-03187-2*, Pub. by Pitman Pubng UK) St Mut.

— Telephony's Dictionary. 2nd ed. 416p. 1986. 40.00 (*0-917845-04-8*) Intertec IL.

Langley, Graham & Ronayne, John. Telecommunications Primer. 4th ed. 240p. 1993. pap. 36.50 (*0-273-60157-1*, Pub. by Pitman Pub Ltd UK) Trans-Atl Phila.

***Langley, Harold D.** A History of Medicine in the Early U. S. Navy. LC 94-31383. (Illus.). 472p. 1995. text ed. 49.95x (*0-8018-4876-8*) Johns Hopkins.

— Social Reform in the United States Navy, 1798-1862. LC 67-10440. 323p. reprint ed. pap. 92.10 (*0-7837-5741-7*, 2045402) Bks Demand.

Langley, Harold G. Social Reform in the United States Navy, Seventeen Ninety-Eight to Eighteen Sixty-Two. LC 67-10440. (Illus.). 323p. reprint ed. pap. 92.10 (*0-317-08240-X*, 2015037) Bks Demand.

Langley, James. The New Bike Book: How to Get the Most Out of Your New Bicycle. LC 89-81204. (Illus.). 128p. (Orig.). (J). 1990. pap. 4.95 (*0-933201-28-1*) Bicycle Books.

Langley, James, et al, eds. Earl O. Heady: His Impact on Agricultural Economics. LC 94-5800. 184p. 1994. 34.95 (*0-8138-2249-1*) Iowa St U Pr.

Langley, James M., ed. Living with Art Two. LC 83-62194. (Illus.). 134p. (Orig.). 1983. pap. 15.00 (*0-940784-05-X*) Miami Univ Art.

Langley, Jeff, jt. auth. see Near, Holly.

Langley, Joan & Langley, Wright. Key West Images of the Past. LC 81-71478. (Illus.). 132p. 1982. 21.95 (*0-9609272-1-2*); pap. 13.95 (*0-9609272-0-4*) Images Key.

— Old Key West in 3-D. LC 85-82420. (Illus.). 64p. 1986. pap. 14.95 (*0-911607-04-8*) Langley Pr Inc.

Langley, Jonathan. Goldilocks & the Three Bears. LC 91-33155. (Illus.). 32p. (J). (gr. k-3). 1993. lib. bdg. 10.89 (*0-06-020815-5*) HarpC Child Bks.

— The Three Billy Goats Gruff. LC 92-4842. (Illus.). 32p. (J). (ps-3). Date not set. 15.00 (*0-06-021224-1*); lib. bdg. 14.89 (*0-06-021474-0*) HarpC Child Bks.

***Langley, Jonathan, illus.** Hey Diddle, Diddle: And Other Mother Goose Rhymes Pop up Book. 10p. (J). (ps-k). 1995. 4.95 (*0-694-00634-3*, Festival) HarpC Child Bks.

— Old King Cole: And Other Mother Goose Rhymes Pop-Up Book. 10p. (J). (ps). 1995. 4.95 (*0-694-00635-1*, Festival) HarpC Child Bks.

— Rain, Rain, Go Away! A Book of Nursery Rhymes. LC 89-34594. 96p. (J). (ps-1). 1991. 12.95 (*0-8037-0762-2*) Dial Bks Young.

Langley, Julia, jt. auth. see Elphinstone, Margaret.

Langley, Keith, jt. ed. see Gratzl, Manfred.

Langley, L. L., et al. Dynamic Anatomy & Physiology. 5th ed. (Illus.). 1980. text ed. 43.95 (*0-07-036275-0*) McGraw.

Langley, Lee. Persistent Rumours. LC 94-6454. 328p. 1994. 21.95 (*1-57131-001-0*) Milkweed Ed.

Langley, Lester D. America & the Americas: The United States in the Western Hemisphere. LC 89-31968. (United States & the Americas Ser.). 304p. 1989. 35.00 (*0-8203-1103-0*); pap. 15.00 (*0-8203-1104-9*) U of Ga Pr.

— The Banana Wars: United States Intervention in the Caribbean, 1898-1934. 2nd ed. 264p. (C). 1988. reprint ed. pap. 19.95 (*0-534-10909-8*) Intl Thomson.

— Mexico & the United States. (Twayne's International History Ser.: No. 8). 160p. 1991. text ed. 27.95 (*0-8057-7912-4*, Twayne); pap. 13.95 (*0-8057-9209-0*, Twayne) Macmillan.

— The United States & the Caribbean in the Twentieth Century. 4th ed. LC 89-4660. 360p. 1989. pap. 15.00 (*0-8203-1154-5*) U of Ga Pr.

Langley, Lester D. & Schoonover, Thomas D. The Banana Men: American Mercenaries & Entrepreneurs in Central America, 1880-1930. LC 94-12864. (Illus.). 224p. 1995. 29.95 (*0-8131-1891-3*) U Pr of Ky.

Langley, Michael H. Self-Management Therapy for Borderline Personality Disorder: A Therapist-Guided Approach. LC 93-34656. 216p. 1993. 29.95 (*0-8261-8300-X*) Springer Pub.

Langley, Mike, ed. Rewarding the Sales Force. 100p. (C). 1987. 45.00 (*0-85292-380-5*) St Mut.

Langley, Myrtle. World Religions. (Lion Manuals Ser.). (Illus.). 128p. 1994. 12.95 (*0-7459-2541-3*) Lion USA.

Langley, Myrtle S. The Nandi of Kenya: Life Crisis Rituals in a Period of Change. LC 78-31186. 1979. text ed. 29.95 (*0-312-55884-8*) St Martin.

Langley, Nina, jt. ed. see Shipley, Betty.

Langley, Noel. Edgar Cayce on Reincarnation. 288p. 1989. mass mkt. 5.50 (*0-446-35784-7*) Warner Bks.

***Langley, Pat.** Elements of Machine Learning. 1995. 44.95 (*1-55860-301-8*) Morgan Kaufmann.

Langley, Pat, ed. Machine Learning International Workshop, 4th, Irvine, CA: Proceedings. LC 87-3803. 416p. (Orig.). (C). 1987. pap. text ed. 34.95 (*0-934613-41-9*) Morgan Kaufmann.

Langley, Pat, jt. ed. see Shrager, Jeff.

Langley, Patrick, et al. Scientific Discovery: Computational Explorations of the Creative Processes. (Illus.). 344p. 1987. pap. 17.50 (*0-262-62052-9*) MIT Pr.

Langley, Phillip D., jt. auth. see Boyle, Gregory J.

Langley-Price, Pat & Ouvry, Philip. Competent Crew: An Introduction to the Practice & Theory of Sailing. 2nd ed. (Illus.). 190p. 1991. pap. 19.95 (*0-7136-3421-9*, Adlard Coles) Sheridan.

— Ocean Yachtmaster. (Illus.). 192p. 1984. 35.00 (*0-229-11695-7*, Adlard Coles) Sheridan.

— Ocean Yachtmaster. (Illus.). 192p. 1984. 35.00 (*0-7136-3596-7*) Sheridan.

Langley, Ray. Pool Players Bible. (Illus.). 1981. 6.00 (*0-686-29667-2*) Langley.

Langley Research Center Staff. Variable Sweep Wings: From Theory to Practice, a Symposium of the Langley Research Center, Hampton, Virginia, March 1981. 1981. pap. 18.00 (*0-89126-103-6*) MA-AH Pub.

An Asterisk (*) at the beginning of an entry indicates that the title is appearing in BIP for the first time.

Langley, Robert, et al, eds. Surface Conditioning of Vacuum Systems: AVS Series 8. LC 89-82542. (AIP Conference Proceedings Ser.: No. 199). (Illus.). 184p. 1989. lib. bdg. 70.00 (*0-88318-756-6*) Am Inst Physics.

Langley, Roland, ed. see Dunnavant, Robert, Jr.

Langley, Russell A. Practical Statistics Simply Explained. 2nd ed. 1971. pap. 7.95 (*0-486-22729-4*) Dover.

Langley, Stephen. Theatre Management & Production in America: Commercial, Stock, Resident, College, Community, Theatre & Presenting Organizations. (Illus.). 702p. (C). 1990. 37.50 (*0-89676-115-0*) Drama Bk.

Langley, Stephen & Abruzzo, James. Jobs in Arts & Media Management. rev. ed. LC 92-5885. 230p. (Orig.). 1992. pap. 21.95 (*0-915400-99-5*, ACA Bks) Am Council Arts.

— Jobs in Arts & Media Management: What They Are & How to Get One. rev. ed. LC 89-38745. 281p. 1990. reprint ed. pap. 21.95 (*0-915400-80-4*, ACA Bks) Am Council Arts.

Langley, Tania. Dawn. 224p. 1980. pap. 1.75 (*0-449-50049-7*, Coventry) Fawcett.

— The London Linnet. large type ed. 416p. 1986. 15.95 (*0-7089-1543-4*) Ulverscroft.

Langley, Thomas, jt. auth. see Langley, Batty.

Langley, Tom, jt. auth. see King, Bob.

Langley, Virginia. Thar She Blows. (J). (gr. 2-5). 1986. pap. 6.95 (*0-930096-87-8*) G Gannett.

Langley, Winston E., ed. Human Rights: Sixty Major Global Instruments Introduced, Reprinted & Indexed. LC 92-53503. 383p. 1992. lib. bdg. 72.00x (*0-89950-669-0*) McFarland & Co.

— Women's Rights in International Documents: A Sourcebook with Commentary. LC 90-53501. 216p. 1991. lib. bdg. 43.50x (*0-89950-548-1*) McFarland & Co.

Langley, Winston E. & Fox, Vivan C., eds. Women's Rights in America: A Documentary History. LC 94-7429. (Primary Documents in American History & Contemporary Issues Ser.). 400p. 1994. text ed. 49.95 (*0-313-28755-4*, Greenwood Pr) Greenwood.

Langley, Winston E., jt. ed. see Glasgow, Roy A.

Langley, Wright, jt. auth. see Langley, Joan.

Langley, Wright, jt. auth. see Windhorn, Stan.

Langlois, Bill & O'Connor, John. Surviving the Age of Fear. (Illus.). 256p. 1993. pap. 12.95 (*1-56796-013-8*) WRS Group.

Langlois, Donald & McAdams, Richard. Performance Appraisal of School Management: Evaluating the Administrative Team. LC 91-67571. 175p. 1992. text ed. 39.00 (*0-87762-892-0*) Technomic.

Langlois, E., ed. see De Lorris, Guillaume & De Meur, Jean.

Langlois, E., jt. auth. see Paris, G.

Langlois, Ethel G., ed. Scholarly Publishing in an Era of Change. 86p. 1980. 18.00 (*0-318-16605-4*); 22.00 (*0-318-16606-2*) Soc Schol Pub.

Langlois, Janet L. Belle Gunness: The Lady Bluebeard. LC 84-43172. (Illus.). 188p. 1985. 24.95 (*0-253-31157-8*) Ind U Pr.

Langlois, Jennifer & Ashley, David. A Basic Microbiology Dictionary. (Illus.). 150p. Date not set. lib. bdg. 25.00 (*1-56308-112-1*) Libs Unl.

Langlois, John D., Jr., ed. China under Mongol Rule. LC 80-8559. (Illus.). 515p. reprint ed. pap. 146.80 (*0-7837-6497-9*, 2046587) Bks Demand.

Langlois, Richard N., ed. Economics As a Process: Essays in "The New Institutional Economics" (Illus.). 288p. (C). 1989. pap. 19.95 (*0-521-37859-1*) Cambridge U Pr.

***Langlois, Richard N. & Robertson, Paul.** Firms, Markets & Economic Change. LC 94-23752. 224p. 1995. pap. 22.95 (*0-415-12385-2*, C0413) Routledge.

— Firms, Markets & Economic Change: A Dynamic Theory of Business Institutions. LC 94-23752. 224p. 1995. 65.00 (*0-415-12119-1*, C0412) Routledge.

Langlois, Richard N., jt. ed. see Fusfeld, Herbert I.

Langlois, Simon, et al. Recent Social Trends in Quebec, 1960-1990. 1991. 70.00 (*0-7735-0879-1*, Pub. by McGill CN) U of Toronto Pr.

***Langlois, Simon, et al, eds.** Convergence or Divergence? Comparing Recent Social Trends in Industrial Societies. (Comparative Charting of Social Change Ser.). 360p. 1995. 55.00 (*0-7735-1264-0*) U of Toronto Pr.

Langlois, T. H. A Study of the Small-Mouth Bass, Micropterus Dolomieu (Lacepede) in Rearing Ponds in Ohio. (Bulletin Ser.: No. 33). 1936. 2.00 (*0-86727-032-2*) Ohio Bio Survey.

Langlos, Ruth & Niemiee, Dennis. Murder, No Doubt: A Widow's Nightmare. 1993. 22.95 (*0-88282-078-8*) New Horizon NJ.

***Langmaack, H., et al, eds.** Formal Techniques in Real-Time & Fault-Tolerant Systems: Proceedings of the Third International Symposium Organized Jointly with the Working Group Provably Correct Systems - ProCos, Lubeck, Germany, September 19-23, 1994. (Lecture Notes in Computer Science: Vol. 863). xiv, 787p. 1994. 102.00 (*3-540-58468-4*) Spr-Verlag.

— Formal Techniques in Real-Time & Fault-Tolerant Systems: Third International Symposium Organized Jointly with the Working Group Provably Correct Systems, ProCoS, Lubeck, Germany, September 19-23, 1994 Proceedings. LC 94-33384. (Lecture Notes in Science Ser.: 863). 1994. 102.00 (*0-387-58468-4*) Spr-Verlag.

Langmaid, Roy, jt. auth. see Gordon, Wendy.

***Langman, Larry.** A Guide to American Crime Films of the Thirties. LC 94-41519. (Bibliographies & Indexes in the Performing Arts Ser.: Vol. 18). 392p. 1995. text ed. 79.50 (*0-313-29532-8*, Greenwood Pr) Greenwood.

— A Guide to American Film Directors: The Sound Era, 1929-1979, 2 vols., Set. LC 81-14536. 1981. 45.00 (*0-8108-1467-6*) Scarecrow.

— A Guide to American Screenwriters: The Sound Era, 1929-1982, 2 vols. LC 84-48018. (Reference Library of the Humanities: Vol. 501). 1346p. 1984. lib. bdg. 113.00 (*0-8240-8927-8*) Garland.

— A Guide to Silent Westerns. LC 92-23783. (Bibliographies & Indexes in the Performing Arts Ser.: No. 13). 616p. 1992. text ed. 79.50 (*0-313-27858-X*, LSD, Greenwood Pr) Greenwood.

— An Illustrated Dictionary of Word Processing. LC 85-43344. (Illus.). 304p. 1986. pap. 34.50 (*0-89774-286-9*) Oryx Pr.

Langman, Larry, comp. Encyclopedia of American Film Comedy. LC 87-11837. (Illus.). 639p. 1987. 75.00 (*0-8240-8496-9*) Garland.

Langman, Larry & Ebner, David. Encyclopedia of American Spy Films. LC 90-3577. (Reference Library of the Humanities: Vol. 1187). (Illus.). 352p. 1990. 60.00 (*0-8240-5533-0*, H1189) Garland.

Langman, Larry & Finn, Daniel. A Guide to American Silent Crime Films. LC 93-41436. (Bibliographies & Indexes in the Performing Arts Ser.: No. 15). 351p. 1994. text ed. 69.50 (*0-313-28858-5*, Greenwood Pr) Greenwood.

Langman, Larry & Gold, Paul, comps. Comedy Quotes from the Movies: Over 4000 Bits of Humorous Dialogue from All Film Genres, Topically Arranged & Indexed. LC 92-56659. 1993. lib. bdg. 42.00 (*0-89950-863-4*) McFarland & Co.

Langman, Larry & Molinari, Joseph. The New Video Encyclopedia. LC 90-3605. (Illus.). 328p. 1990. 55.00 (*0-8240-8244-3*, H1221) Garland.

Langman, Larry & Spinelli, Paul. The Complete Video Book. 1984. pap. 3.95 (*0-685-07892-2*) Zebra.

Langman, Rodney E. The Immune System. 209p. 1989. text ed. 73.00 (*0-12-436585-X*); pap. text ed. 40.00 (*0-12-436586-8*) Acad Pr.

Langmesser, August. Eine Moderne Orientreise. 178p. reprint ed. write for info. (*0-318-71527-9*, Pub. by Georg Olms GW) Lubrecht & Cramer.

Langmore, Diane. Missionary Lives: Papua, 1874-1914. LC 88-26131. (Pacific Islands Monograph Ser.: No. 6). (Illus.). 430p. 1989. text ed. 35.00 (*0-8248-1163-1*) UH Pr.

— Tamate-A King: James Chalmers in New Guinea, 1877-1901. (Illus.). xvi, 169p. 1974. 29.95 (*0-522-84079-5*) Intl Spec Bk.

***Langmore, John & Quiggin, John.** Work for All Full Employment in the Nineties: Full Employment in the Nineties. 400p. Date not set. pap. 24.95 (*0-522-84641-6*) Intl Spec Bk.

Langmuir, Elizabeth C. & Chojnacki, Stanislaw. Ethiopia, the Christian Art of an African Nation. (Illus.). 1978. 6.95 (*0-87577-057-6*, Peabody Museum) Peabody Essex Mus.

Langmuir, Erika. The National Gallery Companion Guide. (National Gallery Publications). (Illus.). 336p. 1994. pap. text ed. 20.00 (*0-300-06133-1*) Yale U Pr.

— The Pan Art Dictionary, Vol. 1: 1300-1800. 385p. (Orig.). 1989. pap. 21.50 (*0-330-30923-4*, Pub. by Pan Books UK) Trans-Atl Phila.

Langmuir, G. E., ed. West Highland Steamers. (C). 1987. 175.00 (*0-85174-505-9*, Pub. by Brwn Son Ferg) St Mut.

Langmuir, Gavin I. History, Religion, & Antisemitism. 391p. 1990. 45.00 (*0-520-06141-1*) U CA Pr.

— History, Religion, & Antisemitism. 1993. pap. 15.00 (*0-520-07728-8*) U CA Pr.

— Toward a Definition of Antisemitism. 427p. 1990. 45.00 (*0-520-06144-6*) U CA Pr.

Langner, Lawrence & Robinson, Julian. The Importance of Wearing Clothes. rev. ed. Moran, Chris, ed. (Illus.). 400p. (C). 1991. 24.95 (*1-55599-039-8*) Elysium.

Langness, Anna P., jt. auth. see Thurman, Leon.

Langness, L. L. The Study of Culture. rev. ed. LC 86-32716. (Publications in Anthropology & Related Fields). (Illus.). 288p. 1987. pap. 16.95x (*0-88316-556-2*) Chandler & Sharp.

Langness, L. L. & Frank, Gelya F. Lives: An Anthropological Approach to Biography. Edgerton, R. B., ed. LC 81-15460. (Chandler & Sharp Publications in Anthropology Ser.). 232p. (Orig.). (C). 1981. pap. 14.95 (*0-88316-542-2*) Chandler & Sharp.

Langness, L. L. & Hays, Terence E., eds. Anthropology in the High Valleys. LC 86-26415. (Publications in Anthropology & Related Fields). 384p. 1987. 24.95 (*0-88316-555-4*) Chandler & Sharp.

Langness, L. L., ed. see Eastman, Carol M.

Langness, L. L., ed. see Jones, Rex L. & Jones, Shirley K.

Langness, L. L., ed. see Kearney, Michael.

Langness, L. L., ed. see Lindenbaum, Shirley.

Langness, L. L., ed. see Marshall, Mac.

Langness, L. L., ed. see Meggitt, Mervyn.

Langness, L. L., ed. see Schuster, Ilsa M.

Langness, Lewis L. Other Fields, Other Grasshoppers: Readings in Cultural Anthropology. LC 76-55310. (C). 1990. pap. text ed. 25.50 (*0-397-47363-X*) HarpCollege.

Langness, Lewis L. & Levine, Harold, eds. Culture & Retardation. 1986. lib. bdg. 99.50 (*90-277-2177-7*) Kluwer Ac.

— Culture & Retardation. 1987. pap. text ed. 41.50 (*90-277-2178-5*) Kluwer Ac.

Langness, Lewis L., ed. see Spiro, Melford E.

Lango, John W. Whitehead's Ontology. LC 78-171184. 102p. 1972. 49.50 (*0-87395-093-3*) State U NY Pr.

— Whitehead's Ontology. LC 78-741184. 112p. reprint ed. pap. 32.00 (*0-317-09030-5*, 2010958) Bks Demand.

Langomo, Amando, tr. see Stigen, Terge.

Langone, Jerry R. The Right Stats. (Illus.). 32p. 1994. 6.95 (*0-8059-3531-2*) Dorrance.

***Langone, John.** Harvard Med: The Story Behind America's Premier Medical School & the Making of America's Doctors. 416p. 1995. 25.00 (*0-517-59306-8*, Crown) Crown Pub Group.

— Tough Choices: A Book about Substance Abuse. LC 94-17580. (J). 1995. 14.95 (*0-316-51407-1*) Little.

Langone, John J. AIDS: The Facts. 192p. 1988. pap. 8.95 (*0-316-51412-8*) Little.

— AIDS: The Facts. rev. ed. 1991. pap. 10.95 (*0-316-51414-4*) Little.

— Dead End: A Book about Suicide. LC 85-25620. (J). (gr. 6 up). 1986. 14.95 (*0-316-51432-2*) Little.

— In the Shogun's Shadow: Understanding a Changing Japan. LC 93-23999. (Illus.). (J). 1994. 16.95 (*0-316-51409-8*) Little.

— Our Endangered Earth: Our Fragile Environment & What We Can Do to Save It. (YA). (gr. 6 up). 1992. 16.95 (*0-316-51415-2*) Little.

— Spreading Poison: A Book about Racism & Prejudice. LC 92-17847. (J). 1993. 15.95 (*0-316-51410-1*) Little.

— Teaching Students with Mild & Moderate Learning Problems. 472p. 1990. teacher ed write for info. (*0-318-66390-2*, H23633); pap. text ed. 44.00 (*0-205-12362-7*, H23625) Allyn.

Langone, John J. & Van Vunakis, Helen, eds. Methods in Enzymology: Immunochemical Techniques, Vol. 74, Pt. C. 1981. text ed. 137.00 (*0-12-181974-4*) Acad Pr.

Langone, John J., jt. ed. see Colowick, Sidney P.

Langone, John J., et al, eds. Methods in Enzymology, Vol. 178: Antibodies, Antigens, & Molecular Mimicry. 835p. 1989. text ed. 130.00 (*0-12-182079-3*) Acad Pr.

Langone, Michael D., ed. Recovery from Cults: Help for Victims of Psychological & Spiritual Abuse. 400p. (C). 1994. 37.00 (*0-393-70164-6*) Norton.

— Recovery from Cults: Help for Victims of Psychological & Spiritual Abuse. 432p. 1995. pap. 17.95 (*0-393-31321-2*, Norton Paperbks) Norton.

Langone, Michael D. & Blood, Linda O. Satanism & Occult-Related Violence: What You Should Know. 110p. (Orig.). 1990. pap. text ed. 11.95 (*0-685-56246-8*) Am Family Foun.

Langone, Michael D., jt. auth. see Ross, Joan C.

Langoni, Carlos G. The Development Crisis: Blueprint for Change. LC 87-29350. 158p. 1987. 22.95 (*0-917616-95-2*); pap. 12.95 (*0-917616-94-4*) ICS Pr.

Langoni, Carlos G., jt. auth. see Shepherd, Geoffrey.

Langord, A. C., ed. see Society of Photographic Scientists & Engineers Staff.

Langosch, Karl, ed. Nibelunge Not in Auswahl: Mit kurzem Woerterbuch. 11th ed. (Sammlung Goeschen Ser.: No. 1). (C). 1966. 6.00 (*3-11-002722-4*) De Gruyter.

Langouche, F., et al. Functional Integration & Semiclassical Expansions. 1982. lib. bdg. 90.00 (*90-277-1472-X*) Kluwer Ac.

Langouche, G., ed. Hyperfine Interaction of Defects in Semiconductors. LC 92-9203. 1992. write for info. (*0-444-89134-X*) Elsevier.

***Langouche, G., et al, eds.** Nuclear Methods in Semiconductor Physics: Proceedings of Symposium F, E-MRS Spring Conference, Strasbourg, France, 28-30 May, 1991. (European Materials Research Society Symposia Proceedings Ser.: 25). x, 260p. 1992. 168.50 (*0-444-89420-9*) Elsevier.

Langran, Gail. Time in Geographic Information Systems. (Technical Issues in GIS Ser.). 180p. 1992. 90.00 (*0-7484-0003-6*, Pub. by Tay Francis Ltd UK); pap. 39.95 (*0-7484-0059-1*, Pub. by Tay Francis Ltd UK) Taylor & Francis.

Langran, Robert. The United States Supreme Court: An Historical & Political Analysis. 2nd ed. 1992. 30.00 (*0-536-57699-8*) Ginn Pr.

Langrana, N. A., et al, eds. Nineteen Ninety-Three Bioengineering Conference. LC 93-71951. (BED Ser.: Vol. 24). 677p. 1993. 70.00 (*0-7918-0682-0*) ASME.

Langrand, Olivier. Guide to the Birds of Madagascar. 456p. (C). 1990. 55.00 (*0-300-04310-4*) Yale U Pr.

Langrehr, D., jt. ed. see Miranda, D. R.

Langrehr, John. Sharing Thinking Strategies. Presseisen, Barbara, ed. 121p. (Orig.). 1990. teacher ed 22.95 (*1-879639-09-2*) Natl Educ Serv.

— Teaching Students to Think. 122p. 1988. Manual 122 p. teacher ed 21.95 (*1-879639-12-2*); Wkbk 110 p. student ed 9.95 (*1-879639-13-0*) Natl Educ Serv.

Langrick, Roger. Barter Systems: A Business Guide for Trade Exchanges. 192p. 1994. 14.95 (*0-681-45230-7*) Longmeadow Pr.

Langridge, Derek, ed. Classification: Its Kinds, Elements, Systems & Applications. 100p. 1992. 50.00 (*0-86291-622-4*) Bowker-Saur.

— Subject Analysis: Principles & Procedures. 146p. 1989. lib. bdg. 32.50 (*0-408-03031-3*) Bowker-Saur.

Langridge, Derek & Herman, Esther, eds. Universe of Knowledge. LC 68-66990. (Student Contribution Ser.: No. 2). 1969. pap. 3.50 (*0-911808-04-3*) U of Md Lib Serv.

Langridge, J. Molecular Genetics & Comparative Evolution. 1991. text ed. 114.95 (*0-471-92876-3*) Wiley.

Langrish, Bob, jt. auth. see Oliver, Robert.

Langronet, Michel. Enciclopedia Juvenil Larousse: Childrens Larousse Encyclopedia, 8 vols., Set. 4th ed. 1552p. (SPA.). (J). 1978. 495.00 (*0-8288-5226-X*, S50479) Fr & Eur.

— Enciclopedia Juvenil Larousse (Spanish Edition), 8 vols., Set. 4th ed. (SPA.). 1978. 495.00 (*0-8288-8233-9*, 8471782413) Fr & Eur.

***Langs, Robert.** Clinical Practice & the Architecture of the Mind. 160p. 1995. pap. 22.95 (*1-85575-088-0*) Brunner-Mazel.

— Clinical Workbook for Psychotherapists. 506p. 1992. pap. 52.50 (*1-85575-004-X*, Pub. by Karnac Bks UK) Brunner-Mazel.

— Decoding Your Dreams. 256p. 1989. pap. 10.00 (*0-345-36431-7*, Ballantine Trade) Ballantine.

— Doing Supervision & Being Supervised: The Supervision of Psychotherapy in Light of the Evolution & Architecture of the Human Mind. 262p. 1994. pap. 36.50 (*1-85575-060-0*, Pub. by Karnac Bks UK) Brunner-Mazel.

— The Dream Workbook: Simple Exercises to Unravel the Secrets to Your Dreams. 208p. (Orig.). 1994. pap. text ed. 14.00 (*0-9641509-1-3*) Allian Pubng.

— Interactions: The Realm of Transference & Countertransference. LC 80-68042. 592p. 1980. 50.00 (*0-87668-425-8*) Aronson.

— The Listening Process. rev. ed. LC 91-43378. 456p. 1992. 45.00x (*0-87668-520-3*) Aronson.

— Madness & Cure. 296p. (C). 1995. text ed. 38.95 (*0-89876-218-9*) Gardner Pr.

— A Primer of Psychotherapy. LC 86-22869. 256p. (C). 1993. reprint ed. pap. text ed. 29.50 (*0-89876-197-2*) Gardner Pr.

— The Psychotherapeutic Conspiracy. LC 81-20601. 352p. 1982. 30.00 (*0-87668-488-6*) Aronson.

— Psychotherapy: A Basic Text. LC 81-17663. 800p. 1982. 60.00 (*0-87668-466-5*) Aronson.

— Resistances & Interventions: The Nature of Therapeutic Work. LC 80-69667. 800p. 1981. 50.00 (*0-87668-433-9*) Aronson.

— Science, Systems, & Psychoanalysis. 262p. 1992. pap. 34.50 (*1-85575-036-8*, Pub. by Karnac Bks UK) Brunner-Mazel.

— The Therapeutic Environment. LC 79-64458. 592p. 1979. 50.00 (*0-87668-385-5*) Aronson.

— Unconscious Communication in Everyday Life. LC 82-1669. 224p. 1993. pap. 27.50x (*1-56821-106-6*) Aronson.

— Workbooks for Psychotherapists: Intervening & Validating, Vol. 3. LC 84-62354. (Workbooks for Psychotherapists Ser.). 302p. 1985. pap. text ed. 33.50 (*0-931231-03-5*) Newconcept Pr.

— Workbooks for Psychotherapists: Listening & Formulating, Vol. 2. LC 84-62354. (Workbooks for Psychotherapists Ser.). 304p. 1985. pap. text ed. 36.00 (*0-931231-02-7*) Newconcept Pr.

— Workbooks for Psychotherapists: Understanding Unconscious Communication, Vol. 1. LC 84-62354. (Workbooks for Psychotherapists Ser.). 144p. 1985. pap. text ed. 20.00 (*0-931231-01-9*) Newconcept Pr.

Langs, Robert, ed. Classics in Psychoanalytic Technique. rev. ed. LC 90-38548. 512p. 1990. 80.00 (*0-87668-744-3*) Aronson.

— Contemporary Theories in Psychoanalysis. 296p. (C). 1995. text ed. write for info. (*0-89876-216-2*) Gardner Pr.

— The Yearbook of Psychoanalysis & Psychotherapy, Vol. 1-1985. 432p. 1985. text ed. 49.95 (*0-931231-04-3*) Newconcept Pr.

— The Yearbook of Psychoanalysis & Psychotherapy, Vol. 2. LC 86-641022. 356p. 1987. text ed. 45.00 (*0-89876-141-7*) Gardner Pr.

Langs, Robert & Badalamenti, Rosalyn T. Physics of the Mind. Date not set. write for info. (*0-345-37081-3*, Ballantine Trade) Ballantine.

Langs, Robert & Searles, Harold. Intrapsychic & Interpersonal Dimensions of Treatment. LC 80-7480. 336p. 1980. 35.00 (*0-87668-404-5*) Aronson.

Langs, Robert & Stone, Leo. The Therapeutic Experience & Its Setting: A Clinical Dialogue. LC 80-667. 382p. 1980. 40.00 (*0-87668-405-3*) Aronson.

Langs, Robert J. The Bipersonal Field. LC 75-42530. 480p. 1976. 40.00 (*0-87668-246-8*) Aronson.

— Empowered Psychotherapy: Teaching Self Processing - A New Approach to the Human Psyche & Its Reintegration. 240p. 1994. pap. 32.50 (*1-85575-057-0*, Pub. by Karnac Bks UK) Brunner-Mazel.

— The Technique of Psychoanalytic Psychotherapy, Vol. 1: The Initial Contact, Theoretical Framework, Understanding the Patient's Communications, the Therapist's Interventions. LC 72-96542. 672p. 1973. 55.00 (*0-87668-104-6*) Aronson.

— The Technique of Psychoanalytic Psychotherapy, Vol. 2: The Patient's Responses to Intervention, the Patient-Therapist Relationship, the Phases of Psychotherapy. LC 72-96542. 544p. 1974. 50.00 (*0-87668-105-4*) Aronson.

Langs, Robert J., ed. Technique in Transition. LC 78-65121. 744p. 1978. 60.00 (*0-87668-349-9*) Aronson.

Langsam, Walter C., ed. Historic Documents of World War II. LC 76-56108. 192p. 1977. reprint ed. text ed. 45.00 (*0-8371-9426-1*, LAHD, Greenwood Pr) Greenwood.

Langsdon, L. R., Sr. Everyman Says - One-Liners for Writing, Speaking & Daily Living: Common Sense Strategies for Winning at the Game of Life. 327p. 1989. 18.95 (*0-9619098-0-3*) Angel Par Pr.

Langsdorf, Lenore & Smith, Andrew R., eds. Recovering Pragmatism's Voice: The Classical Tradition, Rorty, & the Philosophy of Communication. LC 94-1571. (SUNY Series in the Philosophy of the Social Sciences). 336p. 1994. 57.50 (*0-7914-2213-5*); pap. 18.95 (*0-7914-2214-3*) State U NY Pr.

Langsdorf, Lenore, jt. ed. see Angus, Ian.

***Langsdorf, Lenore, et al, eds.** Phenomenology, Interpretation, & Community. (Selected Studies in Phenomenology & Existential Philosophy: Vol. 19). 288p. (C). 1996. text ed. 59.50x (*0-7914-2865-6*); pap. 19.95x (*0-7914-2866-4*) State U NY Pr.

Langsdorff, Georg. Langsdorff's Narrative of the Rezanov Voyage. 1988. 29.95 (*0-87770-449-X*) Ye Galleon.

***Langsen, Richard C.** What Is Alcoholism? A Guide for Children. LC 94-39449. (Illus.). (J). 1996. 14.99 (*0-8037-1686-9*) Dial Bks Young.

Langseth, Jo-Ann, jt. ed. see Stahl, R. James.

L

Langseth, Marcus G. & Mammerickx, Jacqueline. Ocean Margin Drilling Program Atlases, Vol. 8. (Regional Atlas Ser.). 1985. pap. 195.00 (*0-86720-258-0*) Jones & Bartlett.

Langsford, Alwyn. Distributed Systems Management. (C). 1993. text ed. 43.95 (*0-201-63176-8*) Addison-Wesley.

Langshaw, Deborah. Finding a Job without Losing Your Mind! A Survivor's Manual for Job Hunters & Their Families. 96p. (Orig.). 1993. pap. 9.95 (*0-9633939-0-1*) SimonWood Pr.

Langsjoen, Arne, et al. Experiments in General, Organic, & Biological Chemistry. 288p. (C). 1988. student ed, pap. text ed. 27.00 (*0-15-525901-6*) SCP.

Langsley, Donald G. Legal Aspects of Certification & Accreditation. LC 83-72022. 308p. 1983. 34.95 (*0-685-43155-X*) Am Bd Med Spec.

Langsley, Donald G., ed. Health Policy Issues Affecting Medical Education. 1990. lib. bdg. write for info. (*0-934277-13-3*) Am Bd Med Spec.

— How to Select Residents. LC 87-73378. 300p. 1988. lib. bdg. 39.95 (*0-934277-11-7*) Am Bd Med Spec.

Langsley, Donald G. & Darragh, James H., eds. Trends in Specialization: Tomorrow's Medicine. LC 85-73107. (Illus.). 128p. 1985. lib. bdg. 29.95 (*0-934277-06-0*) Am Bd Med Spec.

Langsley, Donald G. & Lloyd, John S., eds. Recertification for Medical Specialists. LC 87-72510. 276p. 1987. lib. bdg. 39.95 (*0-934277-10-9*) Am Bd Med Spec.

Langsley, Donald G. & Signer, Mona, eds. Hospital Privileges & Specialty Medicine. LC 86-70590. (Illus.). 352p. 1986. lib. bdg. 34.95 (*0-934277-08-7*) Am Bd Med Spec.

Langsner, Drew. Green Woodworking. Hylton, Bill, ed. LC 87-9466. 320p. 1987. pap. 14.95 (*0-87857-689-4*, 14-668-1) Rodale Pr Inc.

— Green Woodworking: A Hands-on-Approach. 2nd ed. Thompson, Elaine, ed. LC 94-42309. (Country Workshop Handbook Ser.). (Illus.). 176p. (Orig.). 1995. reprint ed. pap. 15.95 (*0-937274-82-8*, Lark Bks) Sterling.

Langstaff, Bard & McConnaughy, James, eds. Fifty Years on Fifty-Seventh Street. (Illus.). 72p. (Orig.). 1986. pap. write for info. (*0-9616646-1-0*) S J Shrubsole.

Langstaff, Eleanor, jt. auth. see McDonough, Kristin.

Langstaff, Eleanor D. Panama. (World Bibliographical Ser.: No. 14). 184p. 1982. lib. bdg. 28.00 (*0-903450-26-7*) ABC-CLIO.

Langstaff, J. David Copperfield's Library. 1972. 59.95 (*0-87968-998-6*) Gordon Pr.

***Langstaff, John.** Annotated Bibliography Bk. IV. (Music Makes a Difference Ser.). 12p. 1994. pap. 1.95 (*1-886380-03-1*) Langstaff Vid.

— I Have a Song to Sing. (J). (ps up). 1994. text ed. 17.95 (*0-689-50591-4*, Mac Bks Young Read) S&S Childrens.

— Oh, A-Hunting We Will Go. LC 74-76274. (Illus.). 32p. (J). (ps-3). 1974. text ed. 14.95 (*0-689-50007-6*, McElderry) S&S Childrens.

— Oh, A-Hunting We Will Go. LC 91-1987. (Illus.). 32p. (J). (gr. k-3). 1991. reprint ed. pap. 4.95 (*0-689-71503-X*, Aladdin Paperbacks) S&S Childrens.

— Over in the Meadow. (Illus.). (J). (ps-1). 1992. pap. 19.95 (*0-15-258853-1*) HarBrace.

— What a Morning! The Christmas Story in Black Spirituals. LC 87-750130. (Illus.). 32p. (J). 1987. text ed. 14.95 (*0-689-50422-5*, McElderry) S&S Childrens.

Langstaff, John & Bryan, Ashley. Climbing Jacob's Ladder: Heroes of the Bible in African-American Spirituals. LC 90-27297. (Illus.). 24p. (J). 1991. text ed. 14.95 (*0-689-50494-2*, McElderry) S&S Childrens.

Langstaff, John & Rojankovsky, Feodor. Frog Went A-Courtin' LC 55-5237. (Illus.). (J). (ps-3). 1955. 14.95 (*0-15-230214-X*, HB Juv Bks) HarBrace.

— Frog Went A-Courtin' LC 55-5237. (Illus.). 32p. (J). (ps-3). 1972. pap. 4.95 (*0-15-633900-5*, Voyager Bks) HarBrace.

— Over in the Meadow. LC 57-8587. (Illus.). (J). (ps-3). 1957. 14.95 (*0-15-258854-X*, HB Juv Bks) HarBrace.

— Over in the Meadow. LC 57-8587. (Illus.). 32p. (J). (ps-3). 1973. reprint ed. pap. 3.95 (*0-15-670500-1*, Voyager Bks) HarBrace.

Langstaff, John, jt. auth. see Langstaff, Nancy.

Langstaff, John, jt. auth. see Mayer, Elizabeth L.

Langstaff, Launcelott. Salmagundi. 1972. reprint ed. lib. bdg. 39.50 (*0-8422-8162-2*) Irvington.

Langstaff, Nancy & Langstaff, John. Sally Go Round the Moon & Other Revels Songs & Singing Games for Young Children. LC 86-90535. (Illus.). 127p. (J). (ps-1). 1986. pap. 12.95 (*0-9618334-0-8*) Revels Pubns.

Langstaff, Nancy & Sproul, Adelaide. Exploring with Clay. Cohen, Monroe D., ed. LC 79-17398. 48p. 1979. pap. 7.15 (*0-87173-093-6*) ACEI.

***Langsten, P., ed.** Advanced Computer Applications 1994: Proceedings of the Pressure Vessels & Piping Conference, Minneapolis, MN, 1994. LC 94-71262. (PVP Ser.: Vol. 274). 147p. 1994. pap. 50.00 (*0-7918-1197-2*) ASME.

Langston, Diane J. & Smith, Adeline M. Free Magazines for Libraries. 4th ed. 303p. 1994. pap. 28.50 (*0-89950-947-9*) McFarland & Co.

Langston, Donna. Kaida: Poems of a Working Feminist. 1985. pap. 6.00 (*0-317-20172-7*) Quixote.

Langston, Eugene, tr. see Niwano, Nikkyo.

Langston, Evelyn. Lord, Help Me Love This Hyperactive Child. LC 92-46037. 1992. pap. 8.99 (*0-8054-6064-0*) Broadman.

***Langston, J. William & Palfreman, Jon.** The Case of the Frozen Addicts. 304p. 1995. 25.00 (*0-679-42465-2*) Pantheon.

Langston, J. William & Young, Anne, eds. Neurotoxins & Neurodegenerative Disease. LC 92-16494. (Annals Ser.: Vol. 648). 1992. write for info. (*0-89766-695-X*); pap. write for info. (*0-89766-696-8*) NY Acad Sci.

Langston, Jack M. Lexigrow: A New & Easy Gardening Concept. LC 82-90041. (Illus.). 160p. (Orig.). 1982. pap. 14.95 (*0-910387-00-1*) Lexigrow Intl.

Langston, John M. Freedom & Citizenship. LC 74-79012. (Black Heritage Library Collection). 1977. 29.95 (*0-8369-8618-0*) Ayer.

— From the Virginia Plantation to the National Capitol. LC 69-18567. (American Negro: His History & Literature, Ser. No. 2). 1968. reprint ed. 25.95 (*0-405-01877-0*) Ayer.

Langston, Kathleen U. Psychology of Alcoholism: Medical & Scientific Guide for Reference & Research. LC 83-46097. 150p. 1985. 37.50 (*0-88164-126-X*); pap. 34.50 (*0-88164-127-8*) ABBE Pubs Assn.

Langston, L. H. Practical Bank Operation, 2 vols., Set. Bruchey, Stuart, ed. LC 80-1159. (Rise of Commercial Banking Ser.). (Illus.). 1981. reprint ed. lib. bdg. 71.95 (*0-405-13666-8*) Ayer.

***Langston, Laura.** The Magic Ear. (Illus.). 32p. (J). 1995. 12.95 (*1-55143-035-5*) Orca Bk Pubs.

— No Such Thing As Far Away. (Illus.). 32p. (J). (gr. 1-4). 1994. lib. bdg. 14.95 (*1-55143-010-X*) Orca Bk Pubs.

— Pay Dirt! The Search for Gold in British Columbia. (Illus.). 76p. (Orig.). (YA). (gr. 8-12). 1995. pap. 8.95 (*1-55143-029-0*) Orca Bk Pubs.

***Langston, Loup & Corral, Pablo, eds.** Discovering Ecuador & the Galapagos Islands. 49.95 (*0-9644049-0-7*) Descubriendo Ecu.

Langston, Lucille, see Wynne Gibson, pseud..

Langston, Melissa & Durso, Asunta. Thick to Thin: Your Thirty-Day Diet Companion. (Orig.). 1992. pap. 2.95 (*0-399-51703-0*, Perigree Bks) Berkley Pub.

***Langston, Nancy.** Forest Dreams, Forest Nightmares: The Paradox of Old Growth in the Inland West. (Weyerhaeuser Environmental Bks.). (Illus.). 400p. (C). 1995. 24.95 (*0-295-97456-7*) U of Wash Pr.

Langston, Nanda, et al. From the Heart: Recipes from The Taste of Health Restaurant. (Illus.). 130p. (Orig.). 1989. pap. 9.95 (*0-942333-10-1*) Bio-Comms Pr.

Langston, Ruth C., ed. The North Carolina Historical Review: Supplement to Fifty-Year Index, 1974-1983. 243p. (Orig.). 1989. pap. 30.00 (*0-86526-213-6*) NC Archives.

Langston, Ruth C., jt. ed. see Crabtree, Beth G.

Langston, Teresa A. Parenting Without Pressure: A Whole Family Approach To. LC 94-65638. 160p. 1994. pap. 12.00 (*0-89109-750-3*) Pinon Press.

Langston, Thomas S. Ideologues & Presidents: From the New Deal to the Reagan Revolution. 272p. 1992. text ed. 38.00x (*0-8018-4361-8*) Johns Hopkins.

— With Reverence & Contempt: How Americans Think about Their President. LC 94-34134. (Interpreting American Politics Ser.). 192p. 1994. 24.95 (*0-8018-5016-9*) Johns Hopkins.

— With Reverence & Contempt: How Americans Think about Their President. LC 94-34134. (Interpreting American Politics Ser.). 1995. pap. write for info. (*0-8018-5017-7*) Johns Hopkins.

Langstraat, Patricia, jt. auth. see Mazor, Stanley.

Langstrom, Carla T. Methods & Instrumentation for Medical Automation. LC 84-45004. 150p. 1985. 37.50 (*0-88164-182-0*); pap. 34.50 (*0-88164-183-9*) ABBE Pubs Assn.

Langstrom, Kathleen U. Drug Therapy Factors & Adverse Effects: Medical Analysis Index with Research Bibliography. LC 88-47785. 173p. 1988. 39.50 (*0-88164-708-X*); pap. 34.50 (*0-88164-709-8*) ABBE Pubs Assn.

— Therapy of Alcoholism: Medical Research Reference Analysis with Bibliography. LC 84-45986. 150p. 1987. 37.50 (*0-88164-294-0*); pap. 34.50 (*0-88164-295-9*) ABBE Pubs Assn.

Langstron, Kathleen U. Drugs in All Phases of Life & Medicine: Subject Analysis Index With Research Bibliography. LC 85-47581. 150p. 1987. 39.50 (*0-88164-336-X*); pap. 34.50 (*0-88164-337-8*) ABBE Pubs Assn.

Langthaler, Rudolf. Kants Ethik Als "System der Zwecke" Perspektiven Einer Modifizierten Idee der "Moralischen Teleologie & Ethikotheologie. (Kantstudien-Ergaenzungsheft Ser.: Band 125). xiv, 428p. (C). 1990. lib. bdg. 129.25 (*3-11-012620-6*) De Gruyter.

— Organismus und Umwelt. (Studien und Materialien Zur Geschichte der Philosophie Ser.: Bd. 34). 270p. (GER.). 1992. write for info. (*3-487-09638-2*, Pub. by Georg Olms GW) Lubrecht & Cramer.

Langthorp, Herb, jt. auth. see American Production.

Langton, Brenda & Stuart, Margaret. The Cafe Brenda Cookbook: Redefining Seafood & Vegetarian Cuisine. (Illus.). 240p. (Orig.). 1992. pap. 17.95 (*0-89658-205-1*) Voyageur Pr.

Langton, Charan. Join a Club: Directory of Clubs & Associations of Greater Los Angeles. (Illus.). 270p. (Orig.). 1983. pap. 10.00 (*0-913063-00-2*) Shartec Syst.

Langton, Christopher. An Introduction into Physicke. LC 75-25797. (English Experience Ser.: No. 281). 1970. reprint ed. 16.00 (*90-221-0281-5*) Walter J Johnson.

Langton, Christopher G. Artificial Life III. (Illus.). (C). 1993. 55.95 (*0-201-62492-3*) Addison-Wesley.

— Artificial Life III. (Proceedings, Santa Fe Institute Studies in the Sciences of Complexity: Vol. 17). (Illus.). 599p. (C). 1993. pap. 34.95 (*0-201-62494-X*) Addison-Wesley.

***Langton, Christopher G., ed.** Artificial Life: An Overview. (Complex Adaptive Systems Ser.). (Illus.). 336p. 1995. 42.00 (*0-262-12189-1*, Bradford Bks) MIT Pr.

— Artificial Life: Proceedings of an Interdisciplinary Workshop on the Synthesis & Simulation of Living Systems. (Santa Fe Institute Ser.). 688p. (C). 1989. pap. 34.95 (*0-201-09356-1*, Adv Bk Prog) Addison-Wesley.

Langton, Christopher G., et al. Artificial Life II. (Santa Fe Institute Ser.). (Illus.). 500p. (C). 1992. 54.95 (*0-201-52570-4*, Adv Bk Prog); pap. 34.95 (*0-201-52571-2*, Adv Bk Prog) Addison-Wesley.

Langton, Daniel J. The Inheritance. 48p. 1988. pap. text ed. 10.00 (*0-9615838-1-9*) Cheltenham Pr.

— Life Forms. 245p. 1995. pap. text ed. 15.00 (*0-9615838-2-7*) Cheltenham Pr.

— Querencia. 64p. 1976. 10.00 (*0-317-89523-0*) Cheltenham Pr.

— Querencia: Poems. LC 76-740443. (Devins Award Breakthrough Ser.). 64p. 1976. 14.95 (*0-8262-0192-X*) U of Mo Pr.

Langton, Daniel J. & Stock, Robert. The Hogarth-Selkirk Letters. 70p. 1985. pap. 7.00 (*0-9615838-0-0*) Cheltenham Pr.

Langton, Dawn, jt. auth. see DiLeo, Dale.

Langton, Edward. Essentials of Demonology: A Study of Jewish & Christian Doctrine. LC 79-8108. (Illus.). 272p. reprint ed. 27.50 (*0-404-18419-7*) AMS Pr.

— Satan, a Portrait: A Study of the Character of Satan Through All the Ages. 1976. lib. bdg. 59.95 (*0-8490-2568-0*) Gordon Pr.

Langton, H. H., ed. see Campbell, Patrick.

Langton, H. H., tr. see Sagard-Theodat, Gabriel.

Langton, Jane. The Dante Game. (Homer Kelly Mystery Ser.). (Illus.). 336p. 1992. mass mkt. 5.95 (*0-14-013887-0*, Penguin Bks) Viking Penguin.

— Dark Nantucket Noon. (Black Dagger Crime Ser.). (Illus.). 304p. 1993. 16.50 (*0-7451-8604-1*, Black Dagger) Chivers N Amer.

— Dark Nantucket Noon. (Fiction Ser.). 304p. 1981. mass mkt. 5.95 (*0-14-005836-2*, Penguin Bks) Viking Penguin.

— The Diamond in the Window. (J). (gr. 5 up). 17.50 (*0-8446-6414-6*) Peter Smith.

— The Diamond in the Window. LC 62-7312. (Trophy Bk.). (Illus.). 256p. (J). (gr. 5 up). 1973. reprint ed. pap. 3.95 (*0-06-440042-5*, Trophy) HarpC Child Bks.

— Divine Inspiration: A Homer Kelly Mystery. (Illus.). 416p. 1994. reprint ed. mass mkt. 5.95 (*0-14-017376-5*, Penguin Bks) Viking Penguin.

— Emily Dickinson Is Dead. (Crime Ser.). 256p. 1985. mass mkt. 5.95 (*0-14-007771-5*, Penguin Bks) Viking Penguin.

— Emily Dickinson Is Dead. large type ed. 448p. 1992. pap. 14.95 (*0-7089-7162-8*, Trailtree Bookshop) Ulverscroft.

— Fledgling. LC 79-2008. (Ursula Nordstrom Bk.). 192p. (J). (gr. 3-7). 1980. lib. bdg. 14.89 (*0-06-023679-5*) HarpC Child Bks.

— The Fledgling. LC 79-2008. (Trophy Bk.). 192p. (J). (gr. 3-7). 1981. pap. 3.95 (*0-06-440121-9*, Trophy) HarpC Child Bks.

— Fragile Flag. LC 83-49471. (Trophy Bk.). 288p. (J). (gr. 5 up). 1989. pap. 4.95 (*0-06-440311-4*, Trophy) HarpC Child Bks.

— God in Concord. large type ed. LC 92-27925. (Illus.). 529p. 1993. reprint ed. lib. bdg. 19.95 (*1-56054-534-8*) Thorndike Pr.

— God in Concord: A Homer Kelly Mystery. (Illus.). 352p. 1993. mass mkt. 5.95 (*0-14-016594-0*, Penguin Bks) Viking Penguin.

— Good & Dead. 256p. 1989. pap. 3.95 (*0-14-010088-1*, Penguin Bks); mass mkt. 5.95 (*0-14-012687-2*, Penguin Bks) Viking Penguin.

— The Memorial Hall Murder. (Fiction Ser.). 272p. 1981. mass mkt. 5.95 (*0-14-005704-8*, Penguin Bks) Viking Penguin.

— Murder at the Gardner. 352p. 1989. mass mkt. 5.95 (*0-14-011382-7*, Penguin Bks) Viking Penguin.

— Murder at the Gardner. large type ed. LC 88-14728. 468p. 1988. reprint ed. bds. 7.95 (*0-89621-170-3*) Thorndike Pr.

— Natural Enemy. (Illus.). 228p. 1987. pap. 3.95 (*0-14-009345-1*, Penguin Bks) Viking Penguin.

— Natural Enemy. (Homer Kelly Mystery Ser.). 288p. 1990. mass mkt. 5.95 (*0-14-013393-3*, Penguin Bks) Viking Penguin.

— The Queen's Necklace: A Swedish Folktale. (Illus.). 40p. (J). (gr. k-3). 1994. 15.95 (*0-7868-0011-9*); lib. bdg. 15.89 (*0-7868-2007-1*) Hyprn Child.

— The Shortest Day: Murder at the Revels. LC 95-14266. (Homer Kelly Mystery Ser.). (Illus.). 288p. 1995. 19.95 (*0-670-84710-0*, Viking) Viking Penguin.

— The Transcendental Murder. 256p. 1990. mass mkt. 5.95 (*0-14-014852-3*, Penguin Bks) Viking Penguin.

— The Transcendental Murder. 256p. 1990. pap. 3.95 (*0-14-011384-3*, Penguin Bks) Viking Penguin.

Langton, Jane, ret. Salt. LC 91-74007. (Illus.). 40p. (J). (ps-4). 1994. 5.95 (*1-56282-681-6*) Hyprn Ppbks.

Langton, Jean H. I Have Called You By Name. 1986. pap. 1.95 (*0-8198-3614-1*) Pauline Bks.

Langton, Jeffrey H. The Victor Story: History of a Bitter Root Valley Town. LC 85-61259. (Illus.). 126p. 1985. 14.95 (*0-933126-62-X*) Pictorial Hist.

Langton, John. Geographical Change & Industrial Revolution: Coalmining in South West Lancashire, 1590-1799. LC 78-67428. (Cambridge Geographical Studies: Vol. 11). 336p. reprint ed. pap. 95.80 (*0-685-16068-8*, 2027241) Bks Demand.

Langton, John & Morris, R. J. Atlas of Industrializing Britain. 280p. 1987. 35.00 (*0-416-30290-4*, 1123); pap. 15.95 (*0-416-30300-5*, 1132) Routledge Chapman & Hall.

Langton, John, jt. auth. see Hoppe, Goran.

***Langton, Loup & Corral, Pablo, eds.** Descubriendo Ecuador. 238p. (SPA.). 60.00 (*0-9644049-1-5*) Descubriendo Ecu.

Langton, Mandy & Pilgrim, Anne. The Pony Puzzle Book. 86p. (C). 1990. 21.00 (*0-85131-535-6*, Pub. by J A Allen & Co UK) St Mut.

Langton, Mark, jt. auth. see Nasenauer, Jim.

Langton, Phyllis A. Jurisdiction Competition Between Obstetricians & Nurse Midwives in Washington, Vol. O7. 1991. 4.00 (*0-317-04773-6*) GWU CWAS.

Langton, Robert. Childhood & Youth of Charles Dickens. LC 76-148809. reprint ed. 34.50 (*0-404-08875-9*) AMS Pr.

Langton, Roger W. If I Don't Find Pleasure I Will Die. 1977. pap. 2.00 (*0-916296-04-0*) Poor Souls Pr.

Langton, Stuart & Miller, Frederick T. Youth Community Service: A New Era for America's Ethoss of Community Service. (IRE Report: No. 14). 20p. (Orig.). 1988. pap. 5.00 (*0-917754-26-3*, 14P) Inst Responsive.

Langton, Stuart, jt. ed. see DeSario, Jack.

Langtry, J. O. & Ball, D., eds. A Vulnerable Country: Civil Resources in the Defence of Australia. 704p. 1986. 62.00 (*0-08-033045-2*, K122,K120,K115, Pergamon Pr) Elsevier.

Langtry, Lillie. The Days I Knew. LC 79-8067. (Illus.). 336p. reprint ed. 29.50 (*0-404-18378-6*) AMS Pr.

— The Days I Knew. (Illus.). 338p. 1977. reprint ed. lib. bdg. 24.95 (*0-89966-927-1*) Buccaneer Bks.

Language & Reading in Mathematics Group Staff. Children Reading Mathematics. Shuard, Hilary & Rothery, Andrew, eds. (Illus.). 170p. 1990. pap. text ed. 18.00 (*0-7195-4093-3*, 00653, Pub. by John Murray Ltd UK) Heinemann.

Language Inc. Staff, tr. see UNICEF Staff.

Language Institute, Beijing Staff. New Chinese Three Hundred: A Beginning Language Course. (C & T Asian Language Ser.). 351p. (C). 1984. pap. 14.95 (*0-88727-001-8*) Cheng & Tsui.

Language Rsrch Inst of Seoul Natl Univ Staff. Korean Through English, Bk. 1. LC 93-79442. (Illus.). 138p. (Orig.). (ENG & KOR.). 1993. pap. text ed. 16.50x (*1-56591-015-X*) Hollym Intl.

— Korean Through English, Bk. 2. LC 93-79442. (Illus.). 140p. (Orig.). (ENG & KOR.). 1993. pap. text ed. 16.50x (*1-56591-016-8*) Hollym Intl.

— Korean Through English, Bk. 3. LC 93-79442. 189p. (Orig.). (ENG & KOR.). 1993. pap. text ed. 18.50x (*1-56591-017-6*) Hollym Intl.

Language Services Division of the Foreign Office of the Federal Republic of Germany Staff, ed. Disarmament Terminology: English, German, French, Spanish, Russian. LC 82-14931. (Terminological Ser.: Vol. 1). 645p. 1982. pap. 81.55 (*3-11-008858-4*) De Gruyter.

Language Studies Centre Staff & Jenkins, Carol. Mathwords: A Word Book for Mathematics. (Illus.). 64p. (C). 1994. 16.50 (*0-521-45527-8*) Cambridge U Pr.

***Language Systems Corporation Staff.** LS Fortran: Language Reference. 1994. pap. write for info. (*1-885644-02-7*) LSC VA.

— LS Fortran: Macintosh User's Guide. 1995. pap. write for info. (*1-885644-03-5*) LSC VA.

— LS Fortran: Power Macintosh User's Guide. 1994. pap. write for info. (*1-885644-04-3*) LSC VA.

— LS Fortran Personal: Language Reference. 1994. cd-rom write for info. (*1-885644-09-4*) LSC VA.

Langui, Emile, frwd. La Belle Epoque. (Illus.). 1970. pap. 8.50 (*0-88397-016-3*) Art Srvc Intl.

Languilli, Nino. Possibility, Necessity & Existence: Abbagnano & His Predecessors. (Themes in the History of Philosophy Ser.). 250p. (C). 1992. 44.95 (*0-87722-921-X*) Temple U Pr.

Langum, David J. Crossing over the Line: Legislating Morality & the Mann Act. LC 94-13292. (Chicago Series in Sexuality, History, & Society). (Illus.). 264p. 1994. 24.95 (*0-226-46880-1*) U Ch Pr.

— Law & Community on the Mexican California Frontier: Anglo-American Expatriates & the Clash of Legal Traditions, 1821-1846. LC 86-19341. (Illus.). 320p. 1987. 35.00 (*0-8061-2037-1*) U of Okla Pr.

Langum, David J., ed. The Law in the West. (Illus.). 96p. 1985. pap. 15.00 (*0-89745-068-X*) Sunflower U Pr.

Langum, David J., jt. auth. see Hague, Harlan.

Langvardt, Arlen W. Creditors' Remedies Forms, 1990. (Nebraska Legal Forms Ser.). 140p. disk, ring bd. 85.00 (*0-685-49522-1*) Butterworth Legal Pubs.

— Creditors' Remedies Forms, 1990. (Nebraska Legal Forms Ser.). 140p. ring bd. 50.00 (*0-86678-026-2*) Michie Butterworth.

— Creditors' Remedies Forms, 1990. suppl. ed. (Nebraska Legal Forms Ser.). 140p. 1993. 34.50 (*0-685-74348-9*) Butterworth Legal Pubs.

Langville, Alan R., comp. Modern World Rulers: A Chronology. LC 79-19294. 372p. 1979. 32.50 (*0-8108-1251-7*) Scarecrow.

Langway, C. C. Jr., et al, eds. Greenland Ice Core: Geophysics, Geochemistry, & the Environment. (Geophysical Monograph Ser.: Vol.33). 118p. 1985. 19.00 (*0-87590-057-7*) Am Geophysical.

Langwell, William H. The Conservation of Books & Documents. LC 73-2640. 114p. 1974. reprint ed. text ed. 35.00 (*0-8371-6810-4*, LACB, Greenwood Pr) Greenwood.

Langwick, John. Eastern European Technological Business Opportunities: An Executive Report. 304p. (C). 1993. pap. text ed. 95.00 (*0-13-605890-6*) P-H.

Langwick, John J. Eastern European Technological Business Opportunities: An Executive Report. LC 92-39409. 1993. write for info. (*0-88173-170-6*) Fairmont Pr.

Langworth, R. Illustrated Oldsmobile Buyer's Guide. (Buyer's Guide Ser.). (Illus.). 160p. 1987. pap. 16.95 (*0-87938-270-8*) Motorbooks Intl.

Langworth, R. M. Great American Convertibles. 1991. 29.99 (*0-517-03584-7*) Random Hse Value.

An Asterisk (*) at the beginning of an entry indicates that the title is appearing in BIP for the first time.

— New Complete Book of Collectible Cars, 1930-90. 576p. 1989. 19.98 (*1-56173-303-2*) Pubns Intl Ltd.

Langworth, Richard. Illustrated Buick Buyer's Guide. (Illus.). 1989. pap. 16.95 (*0-87938-318-6*) Motorbooks Intl.

— Illustrated Cadillac Buyer's Guide. 2nd ed. (Illus.). 1993. pap. 16.95 (*0-87938-744-0*) Motorbooks Intl.

— Illustrated Packard Buyers Guide. (Motorbooks Illustrated Buyer's Guide Ser.). (Illus.). 160p. 1991. pap. 16.95 (*0-87938-427-1*) Motorbooks Intl.

Langworth, Richard M. Chrysler & Imperial, 1946-1975: The Classic Postwar Years. LC 92-33788. (MBI Ser.). (Illus.). 200p. 1993. 24.95 (*0-87938-728-9*) Motorbooks Intl.

— Fifty Years of American Automobiles. 1989. 49.99 (*0-517-68640-6*) Random Hse Value.

— Great American Automobiles of the '50s. 1989. 29.99 (*0-517-67556-0*) Random Hse Value.

— Hudson, 1946-1957: The Classic Postwar Years. rev. ed. LC 92-33789. (MBI Ser.). (Illus.). 200p. 1993. 24.95 (*0-87938-729-7*) Motorbooks Intl.

***Langworth, Richard M. & Redburn, H. Ashley.** Churchill Bibliographic Data: Surveys of Works by & about Sir Winston Churchill. (Educational Ser.: No. 4). (Illus.). 52p. 1992. pap. 10.00 (*0-614-04945-8*) Intl Churchill Soc.

Langworth, Richard M., ed. see Cooke, Alistair, et al.

Langworth, Richard M., jt. auth. see Hall, Asa E.

Langworth, Richard M., ed. see Russell, Douglas S.

Langworth, Richard R. Illustrated Studebaker Buyer's Guide. 1991. pap. 16.95 (*0-87938-490-5*) Motorbooks Intl.

Langworthy. Chemical Feed Systems Pocket Guide. 1995. write for info. (*0-87371-543-8*) Lewis Pubs.

Langworthy, Franklin. Scenery of the Plains, Mountains & Mines. LC 76-87645. (American Scene Ser.). (Illus.). 292p. 1972. reprint ed. lib. bdg. 39.50 (*0-306-71785-9*) Da Capo.

Langworthy, Harry W., ed. see Wiese, Carl.

Langworthy, J. Lamont & McNeil, Katherine. Hillside Homes. LC 82-82433. (Illus.). 128p. (Orig.). 1983. pap. 10.00 (*0-9609334-0-9*) IO.

Langworthy, Robert H. The Structure of Police Organizations. LC 86-21173. 176p. 1986. text ed. 49.95 (*0-275-92328-2*, C2328, Praeger Pubs) Greenwood.

Langworthy, Robert H. & Travis, Lawrence F., III. Policing in America. LC 93-19210. (Criminal Justice Ser.). 490p. (C). 1994. text ed. write for info. (*0-02-367421-0*) Macmillan.

Langworthy, Robert J., jt. ed. see McCarthy, Belinda.

Lanham, B. J., jt. auth. see Titow, W. V.

Lanham, David, et al. Criminal Fraud. xli, 629p. 1987. 96.00 (*0-455-20745-3*, Pub. by Law Bk Co) W W Gaunt.

Lanham, Edwin. Wind Blew West. 1993. reprint ed. lib. bdg. 75.00 (*0-7812-5968-1*) Rprt Serv.

Lanham, Edwin & Stewart, Alan. Murder on My Street. Stewart, Alan, ed. (Black Dagger Crime Ser.). 200p. 1990. reprint ed. text ed. 16.50 (*0-86220-770-3*, Black Dagger) Chivers N Amer.

Lanham, Frank W. The Meaning of School Accounts. 4th ed. 115p. (C). 1983. pap. text ed. 10.95 (*1-55996-132-5*, MSC102) Univ Council Educ Admin.

Lanham, John C., Jr., ed. see Hannon, Charles-Louis.

Lanham, L. W. & MacDonald, C. A. The Standard in South African English & Its Social History. (Varieties of English Around the World Text Ser.: Vol. G1). 96p. (Orig.). 1979. pap. 33.00 (*3-87276-210-9*) Benjamins North Am.

Lanham, Richard A. The Electronic Word: Democracy, Technology, & the Arts. 256p. 1993. 22.50 (*0-226-46883-6*); lib. bdg. 19.95 (*0-226-46884-4*) U Ch Pr.

— The Electronic Word: Democracy, Technology & the Arts. 302p. 1994. pap. 11.95 (*0-226-46885-2*) U Ch Pr.

— A Handlist of Rhetorical Terms. 2nd ed. 168p. 1992. 35.00 (*0-520-07668-0*); pap. 14.00 (*0-520-07669-9*) U CA Pr.

— Literacy & the Survival of Humanism. LC 83-3618. 208p. 1983. 35.00 (*0-300-02968-3*) Yale U Pr.

— Revising Business Prose. 3rd ed. (Illus.). 160p. (C). 1992. pap. write for info. (*0-02-367465-2*) Macmillan.

— The Revising Business Prose Self-Teaching Exercise Book. 96p. (C). 1987. pap. write for info. (*0-02-367480-6*) Macmillan.

— Revising Prose. 1984. pap. 10.50 (*0-684-15987-2*, Scribners) S&S Trade.

— Revising Prose. 3rd ed. (Illus.). 144p. (C). 1992. pap. write for info. (*0-02-367445-8*) Macmillan.

— The Revising Prose Self-Teaching Exercise Book. 96p. (C). 1987. pap. write for info. (*0-02-367490-3*) Macmillan.

— Style: An Anti-Textbook. LC 73-86906. 144p. 1978. pap. 10.00 (*0-300-02243-3*) Yale U Pr.

— Tristram Shandy: The Games of Pleasure. LC 70-174461. 184p. reprint ed. pap. 52.50 (*0-685-23669-2*, 2029048) Bks Demand.

Lanham, Url. The Bone Hunters: The Heroic Age of Paleontology in the American West. Orig. Title: The Bone Hunters. (Illus.). 304p. 1991. reprint ed. pap. 10.95 (*0-486-26917-5*) Dover.

Lanham, Url N. The Fishes. LC 62-9366. (Illus.). 116p. 1967. reprint ed. pap. text ed. 16.00 (*0-231-08581-8*) Col U Pr.

— The Insects. LC 64-14235. (Illus.). 1967. pap. text ed. 16.00 (*0-231-08582-6*) Col U Pr.

— Origins of Modern Biology. LC 68-24478. 273p. (J). (gr. 11-12). 1971. text ed. 46.50 (*0-231-02872-5*); pap. text ed. 18.00 (*0-231-08660-1*) Col U Pr.

Lanhei Kim Park. The Heavenly Pomegranate. 76p. (J). (gr. 5-7). 1973. pap. text ed. 3.00 (*0-686-05501-2*) Simpson Pub.

Lanher, Jean & Litaize, Alain. Dictionnaire du Francais Regional de Lorraine. 160p. (FRE.). 1990. 125.00 (*0-8288-9479-5*) Fr & Eur.

Lanidey, jt. auth. see Weil.

***Lanier.** Complete Guide to Bed & Breakfasts, Inns & Guesthouses. 12th ed. 1995. pap. text ed. 16.95 (*0-89815-666-1*) Ten Speed Pr.

— Elegant Small Hotels. 9th ed. 1994. pap. text ed. 19.95 (*0-89815-665-3*) Ten Speed Pr.

Lanier & Lee, eds. Surimi Technology. (Food Science & Technology Ser.: Vol. 50). 536p. 1992. 185.00 (*0-8247-8470-7*) Dekker.

Lanier, Alison. Living in the U. S. A. 4th ed. LC 87-46327. 230p. 1988. pap. text ed. 12.95 (*0-933662-69-6*) Intercult Pr.

Lanier, Alison R. The Rising Sun on Main Street: Working with the Japanese. 2nd ed. LC 92-70978. 290p. 1992. pap. 12.95 (*0-945510-11-X*) Intl Info Assocs.

— Your Manager Abroad: How Welcome? How Prepared? LC 75-26584. (AMA Management Briefing Ser.). 51p. reprint ed. pap. 25.00 (*0-317-09625-7*, 2050195) Bks Demand.

***Lanier, Bob.** Children & Asthma: The New Epidemic & How to Treat It. 1992. 23.95 (*1-56530-027-0*) Summit TX.

Lanier, Clifford. Thorn-Fruit. 1973. reprint ed. lib. bdg. 35.00 (*0-8490-1206-6*) Gordon Pr.

Lanier, Doris. Absinthe - The Cocaine of the Nineteenth Century: A History of the Hallucinogenic Drug & Its Effect on Artists & Writers in Europe & the United States. (Illus.). 192p. 1995. lib. bdg. 29.95 (*0-89950-989-4*) McFarland & Co.

Lanier-Graham, Susan D. The Ecology of War: Environmental Impacts of Weaponry & Warfare. LC 92-43568. (Illus.). 208p. 1993. 22.95 (*0-8027-1262-2*) Walker & Co.

— The Nature Directory: A Guide to Environmental Organizations. 304p. 1991. 22.95 (*0-8027-1151-0*); pap. 12.95 (*0-8027-7348-6*) Walker & Co.

Lanier, Henry W. A. B. Frost: American Sportsman's Artist. 2nd ed. (Fifty Greatest Bks.). (Illus.). 170p. 1990. reprint ed. 39.95 (*1-56416-003-3*) Derrydale Pr.

Lanier, Henry W., ed. see Lanier, Sidney.

Lanier, Henry W., ed. see Wilkins Freeman, Mary E.

Lanier, Jean. The Awakening of Adam. 1973. pap. 2.25 (*0-913456-63-2*) Interbk Inc.

— The Evolution of Eve. 2nd ed. 96p. 1973. pap. 2.25 (*0-913456-62-4*) Interbk Inc.

— Paraphrases for Pilgrims. 1977. pap. 1.75 (*0-89192-187-7*) Interbk Inc.

— The Wisdom of Being Human. (Illus.). 151p. (Orig.). 1989. 13.95 (*0-941255-40-9*); pap. 7.95 (*0-941255-39-5*) Integral Pub.

Lanier, Laura. All Things Bright & Beautiful. (Illus.). 64p. 1993. 9.50 (*0-8378-6946-3*) Gibson.

Lanier, Pamela. All Suite Hotel Guide. 5th ed. (Orig.). 1991. pap. 14.95 (*0-89815-445-6*) Ten Speed Pr.

— All Suite Hotel Guide. 6th ed. (Illus.). 236p. (Orig.). 1992. pap. 14.95 (*0-89815-512-6*) Ten Speed Pr.

— All-Suite Hotel Guide. 7th ed. 1993. pap. 14.95 (*0-89815-580-0*) Ten Speed Pr.

— All-Suite Hotel Guide. 8th ed. 336p. 1995. pap. 14.95 (*0-89815-725-0*) Ten Speed Pr.

— Complete Guide to Bed & Breakfasts, Inns & Guesthouses. 1993. pap. 16.95 (*0-89815-530-4*) Ten Speed Pr.

— Complete Guide to Bed & Breakfasts, Inns & Guesthouses. 11th ed. 1994. pap. 16.95 (*0-89815-582-7*) Ten Speed Pr.

— Complete Guide to Bed & Breakfasts, Inns & Guesthouses: Southern Edition. 1993. pap. 7.95 (*0-89815-532-0*) Ten Speed Pr.

— Complete Guide to Bed & Breakfasts, Inns & Guesthouses: Western Edition. 1993. pap. 7.95 (*0-89815-531-2*) Ten Speed Pr.

— Condo Vacations: The Complete Guide. 4th ed. 496p. 1992. pap. 14.95 (*0-89815-461-8*) Ten Speed Pr.

— Condo Vacations: The Complete Guide. 5th ed. 1993. pap. 14.95 (*0-89815-551-7*) Ten Speed Pr.

— Elegant Hotels of the Pacific Rim. 1993. pap. 14.95 (*0-89815-583-5*) Ten Speed Pr.

— Elegant Small Hotels. 5th ed. 236p. (Orig.). 1995. pap. 14.95 (*0-89815-768-4*) Ten Speed Pr.

— Elegant Small Hotels: A Connoisseur's Guide. 8th ed. 1993. pap. 19.95 (*0-89815-581-9*) Ten Speed Pr.

— Golf Courses: The Complete Guide. 5th ed. 512p. (Orig.). 1995. pap. 14.95 (*0-89815-732-3*) Ten Speed Pr.

— Golf Resorts: The Complete Guide. 5th ed. 1993. pap. 14.95 (*0-89815-533-9*) Ten Speed Pr.

— Golf Resorts: The Complete Guide. 6th ed. 320p. 1995. pap. 14.95 (*0-89815-726-9*) Ten Speed Pr.

— Golf Resorts International. 3rd ed. (Orig.). 1993. pap. 19.95 (*0-89815-534-7*) Ten Speed Pr.

— Twenty-Two Days in Alaska: The Itinerary Planner. (Illus.). 128p. (Orig.). 1988. pap. 7.95 (*0-912528-68-0*) John Muir.

Lanier, Parks, Jr., ed. The Poetics of Appalachian Space. LC 90-45244. (Illus.). 232p. 1991. text ed. 26.00x (*0-87049-692-1*) U of Tenn Pr.

Lanier Publishing Staff. Back Almanac. LC 92-25976. 182p. 1992. pap. 14.95 (*0-685-70014-3*) Celestial Arts.

***Lanier, Roxanne.** The Islands Are Asking. 64p. (Orig.). Date not set. pap. 10.00 (*0-9646377-0-7*) Skimming Stone Pr.

Lanier, Roy, Jr. Epistles of John. 1992. pap. 8.95 (*0-89137-136-2*) Quality Pubns.

Lanier, Roy, Sr. The Timeless Trinity. 1974. 11.95 (*0-89137-551-1*) Quality Pubns.

— Twenty Years of the Problem Page, Vol. I. 1985. pap. 7.50 (*0-89137-549-X*) Quality Pubns.

— Twenty Years of the Problem Page, Vol. II. 1985. pap. 7.50 (*0-89137-555-4*) Quality Pubns.

Lanier, Roy H., Jr. Cross Questions & Scripture Answers. 1960. pap. 2.75 (*0-89137-618-6*) Quality Pubns.

Lanier, S. Music & Poetry. LC 68-25292. (Studies in Poetry: No. 38). (C). 1969. reprint ed. lib. bdg. 49.95 (*0-8383-0306-4*) M S G Haskell Hse.

Lanier, Sidney. The Boy's King Arthur. LC 73-13451. (Illustrated Classics Ser.). (Illus.). 336p. (J). 1989. text ed. 24.95 (*0-684-19111-3*, C Scribner Sons Young) S&S Childrens.

— The Boy's King Arthur. deluxe ed. LC 73-13451. (Illustrated Classics Ser.). (Illus.). 336p. (J). 1989. 75.00 (*0-684-19118-0*, C Scribner Sons Young) S&S Childrens.

— The Centennial Edition of the Works of Sidney Lanier, Vol. 10: Letters 1878-1881. Anderson, C. R. & Starke, A. H., eds. LC 46-2793. (Illus.). 558p. reprint ed. pap. 159.10 (*0-7837-3396-8*, 2043354) Bks Demand.

— Collected Writings. 1972. 600.00 (*0-87968-906-4*) Gordon Pr.

— Florida: Its Scenery, Climate & History. A Facsimile Reproduction of the 1875 Edition, with Introduction & Index by Jerrell H. Shofner. LC 72-14330. (Bicentennial Floridian Facsimile Ser.). 318p. reprint ed. pap. 90.70 (*0-8357-6922-4*, 2037981) Bks Demand.

— Letters. 1972. 59.95 (*0-8490-0510-8*) Gordon Pr.

— Letters: Selections from His Correspondence. Lanier, Henry W., ed. LC 71-37890. (Select Bibliographies Reprint Ser.). 1977. reprint ed. 23.95 (*0-8369-6727-5*) Ayer.

— Music & Poetry. 1973. lib. bdg. 250.00 (*0-87968-028-8*) Gordon Pr.

— Music & Poetry. LC 74-171656. reprint ed. 5.00 (*0-404-03874-3*) AMS Pr.

— Poems & Letters. (American Autobiography Ser.). 227p. 1995. reprint ed. lib. bdg. 79.00 (*0-7812-8574-7*) Rprt Serv.

— Poems of Sidney Lanier. LC 80-29576. 314p. 1981. reprint ed. 24.95 (*0-8203-0560-X*) U of Ga Pr.

— Selected Poems. LC 83-48838. reprint ed. 21.50 (*0-404-20151-2*) AMS Pr.

— Shakespeare & His Forerunners, 2 vols. (BCL1-PR English Literature Ser.). 1992. reprint ed. lib. bdg. 99.00 (*0-7812-7289-0*) Rprt Serv.

— Shakspere & His Forerunners, 2 Vols. LC 74-171656. reprint ed. 95.00 (*0-404-03875-1*) AMS Pr.

— Sidney Lanier: Poems & Letters. LC 76-83323. 239p. reprint ed. pap. 68.20 (*0-317-39701-X*, 2025824) Bks Demand.

Lanier, Sidney, ed. Music & Poetry: Essays upon Some Aspects & Interrelations of the Two Arts. 248p. 1990. reprint ed. lib. bdg. 69.00 (*0-7812-9013-9*) Rprt Serv.

Lanier, Sidney, ed. see Mallory, Thomas.

Lanier, Sterling E. The Curious Quests of Brigadier Fellowes. (Illus.). 1986. 30.00 (*0-937986-89-5*) D M Grant.

— Hiero's Journey. 336p. 1983. pap. 5.99 (*0-345-30841-7*, Del Rey) Ballantine.

Lanier, Susan. Computerized Accounting: 3.5 Version. 400p. (C). 1992. write for info. (*0-13-159609-8*) P-H.

— Computerized Accounting: 5.25 Version. 400p. (C). 1992. pap. text ed. write for info. (*0-13-156472-2*) P-H.

Lanier, Vincent. The Arts We See: A Simplified Introduction to the Visual Arts. (Orig.). 1982. pap. text ed. 13.95 (*0-8077-2699-0*) Tchrs Coll.

— Essays in Art Education: The Development of One Point of View. 2nd ed. 144p. 1976. pap. text ed. 6.95 (*0-8422-0516-0*) Irvington.

— The World of Art Education. 56p. 1991. pap. 15.00 (*0-937652-57-1*) Natl Art Ed.

***Lanier, Virginia.** Death in Bloodhound Red. LC 94-43196. 462p. 1995. 19.95 (*1-56164-076-X*) Pineapple Pr.

***Lanig & Chase.** A Practical Guide to Health Promotion Strategies after Spinal Cord Injury. 250p. 1995. 59.00 (*0-8342-0628-5*) Aspen Pub.

Lanigan, Anne. Complete Yogurt Cookbook. Adler, Andrew & Adler, Roger, eds. (Illus.). 1978. 9.95 (*0-916844-02-1*); pap. text ed. 5.95 (*0-916844-03-X*) Turtle Pr.

Lanigan, Anni, jt. auth. see Cohen, Matthew M.

Lanigan, Catherine. All or Nothing. 400p. (Orig.). 1989. mass mkt. 4.50 (*0-380-75459-2*) Avon.

— At Long Last Love. 416p. (Orig.). 1994. mass mkt. 4.99 (*0-380-76948-4*) Avon.

— A Promise Made. 496p. (Orig.). 1990. mass mkt. 4.95 (*0-380-75694-3*) Avon.

— The Way of the Wicked. 448p. (Orig.). 1993. mass mkt. 4.99 (*0-380-76947-6*) Avon.

— Web of Deceit. 400p. 1987. mass mkt. 4.50 (*0-380-75311-1*) Avon.

Lanigan, Ernest J. The Baseball Cyclopedia. 216p. 1988. reprint ed. pap. 12.50 (*0-944786-26-X*) Horton Pub.

— The Sporting News Record Book, 1932. 1989. reprint ed. pap. 3.50 (*0-944786-42-1*) Horton Pub.

— The Sporting News Record Book, 1934. 1989. reprint ed. pap. 3.50 (*0-944786-44-8*) Horton Pub.

Lanigan, Ernest J., ed. The Sporting News Record Book, 1929. 100p. 1988. reprint ed. pap. 3.50 (*0-944786-09-X*) Horton Pub.

— The Sporting News Record Book, 1930. 100p. 1988. reprint ed. pap. 3.50 (*0-944786-10-3*) Horton Pub.

— The Sporting News Record Book, 1931. 100p. 1989. reprint ed. pap. 3.50 (*0-944786-41-3*) Horton Pub.

— The Sporting News Record Book, 1933. 1989. reprint ed. pap. 3.50 (*0-944786-43-X*) Horton Pub.

— The Sporting News Record Book, 1935. 1989. reprint ed. pap. 3.50 (*0-944786-45-6*) Horton Pub.

— The Sporting News Record Book, 1936. 1989. reprint ed. pap. 3.50 (*0-944786-47-2*) Horton Pub.

— The Sporting News Record Book, 1937. 1989. reprint ed. pap. 5.00 (*0-944786-48-0*) Horton Pub.

— The Sporting News Record Book, 1938. 1989. reprint ed. pap. 5.00 (*0-944786-49-9*) Horton Pub.

— The Sporting News Record Book, 1939. 1989. reprint ed. pap. 5.00 (*0-944786-50-2*) Horton Pub.

— The Sporting News Record Book, 1940. 1989. reprint ed. pap. 5.00 (*0-944786-51-0*) Horton Pub.

Lanigan, Katherine & Tyler, Gerald, eds. Kilkenny: Its Architecture & History. 120p. 1982. 35.00 (*0-905140-41-9*) St Mut.

Lanigan, Mike. Engineers in Business: The Principles of Management & Product Design. LC 92-11533. (C). 1992. pap. text ed. 34.95 (*0-201-41695-6*) Addison-Wesley.

Lanigan, Richard L. The Human Science of Communicology: A Phenomenology of Discourse in Foucault & Merleau-Ponty. LC 91-47094. (Illus.). 288p. (C). 1992. text ed. 34.95x (*0-8207-0242-0*) Duquesne.

— Phenomenology of Communication. LC 87-24587. 288p. 1988. text ed. 19.50 (*0-8207-0185-8*) Duquesne.

— Semiotic Phenomenology of Rhetoric: Eidetic Practice in Henry Grattan's Discourse on Tolerance. (Current Continental Research Ser.: No. 203). (Illus.). 248p. (Orig.). 1984. 52.00 (*0-8191-4294-8*, Ctr Adv Res); pap. 23.00 (*0-8191-4295-6*, Ctr Adv Res) U Pr of Amer.

— Speaking & Semiology: Maurice Merleau-Ponty's Phenomenological Theory of Existential Communication. 2nd ed. LC 91-30860. (Approaches to Semiotics Ser.: No. 22). vi, 257p. 1991. lib. bdg. 106.15 (*3-11-012864-0*) Mouton.

Lanigan, Suds. Man Walked into a Bar. 1988. pap. 2.95 (*0-312-91276-5*) St Martin.

— Minister, a Rabbi & a Priest. 1990. pap. 2.95 (*0-312-92136-5*) St Martin.

***Laning, Charlotte.** Bearded Collie. (Illus.). 188p. (SWE.). 1995. 40.00 (*0-9644628-1-8*) C Laning.

Lanir, Zvi. Israeli Defense in the 1980's. LC 83-23124. 272p. 1984. text ed. 49.95 (*0-275-91209-4*, C1209, Praeger Pubs) Greenwood.

***Lanius, Roger E. & Hallwas, John E., eds.** Cultures in Conflict: A Documentary History of the Mormon War in Illinois. (Illus.). 1995. 37.95x (*0-87421-186-7*) Utah St U Pr.

Lanjalley, Paul & Corriez, Paul. Histoire de la Revolution Du 18 Mars. LC 78-171657. reprint ed. 76.50 (*0-404-07139-2*) AMS Pr.

Lanjouw, G. J., jt. auth. see Kuipers, S. K.

Lank, David. From the Wild. Hume, Christopher, ed. (Illus.). 192p. 1987. 45.00 (*0-942802-57-8*) NorthWord.

Lank, Edith. Essentials of New Jersey Real Estate. 368p. 1991. pap. 29.95 (*0-7931-0194-8*, 400-463A) Dearborn Finan.

— Essentials of New Jersey Real Estate: Update 1995. 1995. pap. 29.95 (*0-7931-1286-9*, Real Estate Ed) Dearborn Finan.

— Homebuyer's Kit. 3rd ed. LC 94-22977. 194p. 1994. pap. 15.95 (*0-7931-1114-5*, 1913-0603, Real Estate Ed) Dearborn Finan.

— Homeseller's Kit. 3rd ed. 224p. 1994. pap. 15.95 (*0-7931-1113-7*, 191305-03, Real Estate Ed) Dearborn Finan.

— The 201 Questions Every Homebuyer & Homeseller Must Ask. 240p. (Orig.). 1995. pap. 15.95 (*0-7931-1434-9*, 1913-3501, Real Estate Ed) Dearborn Finan.

Lank, Edith, ed. Modern Real Estate Practice Study Guide. 13th ed. LC 93-36187. 230p. 1994. pap. 13.95 (*0-7931-0728-8*, 1510-0213) Dearborn Finan.

Lank, Elizabeth, jt. auth. see Mayo, Andrew.

Lankard, David R., ed. see American Concrete Institute Staff.

Lankavatara-Sutra. Self-Realization of Noble Wisdom. Goddard, Dwight, ed. Suzuki, D. T., tr. LC 78-72461. reprint ed. 23.00 (*0-404-17333-0*) AMS Pr.

Lankenau, Walter C., ed. see Ronfor, Philip A.

Lanker, Brian, photos. I Dream a World: Portraits of Black Women Who Changed America. LC 88-32697. (Illus.). 160p. 1989. 40.00 (*1-55670-063-6*); pap. 24.95 (*1-55670-092-X*) Stewart Tabori & Chang.

— I Dream a World: Wall Calendar for 1996. (Illus.). 24p. 1995. 9.95 (*1-55670-412-7*) Stewart Tabori & Chang.

Lankester, Colin & Mantin, Peter. From Romanov to Gorbachev: Russia in the 20th Century. 96p. (Orig.). 1989. pap. 14.95 (*0-317-05921-1*, Pub. by Stanley Thornes UK) Trans-Atl Phila.

Lankester, Colin, jt. auth. see Mantin, Peter.

Lankester, Edwin R. Diversions of a Naturalist. LC 77-105024. (Essay Index Reprint Ser.). 1977. 29.95 (*0-8369-1471-6*) Ayer.

— Great & Small Things. LC 72-5630. (Essay Index Reprint Ser.). 1977. reprint ed. 23.95 (*0-8369-2995-0*) Ayer.

— Science from an Easy Chair, First Series. LC 79-152185. (Essay Index Reprint Ser.). 1977. 26.95 (*0-8369-2194-1*) Ayer.

— Science from an Easy Chair, Second Series. LC 79-152185. (Essay Index Reprint Ser.). 1977. 23.95 (*0-8369-2210-7*) Ayer.

— Secrets of Earth & Sea. LC 76-93352. (Essay Index Reprint Ser.). 1977. 21.95 (*0-8369-1301-9*) Ayer.

Lankester, Edwin R., ed. see Ray, John.

***Lankevich, George.** Chief Justices of the U. S. 1995. 20.00 (*0-614-06203-9*) Bronx County.

Lankevich, George J. World & West: Readings in Contemporary History. 3rd ed. (Illus.). 218p. 1992. pap. text ed. 10.95 (*0-89529-572-5*) Avery Pub.

Lankevich, George J., ed. United Nations Archives, New York: United Nations War Crimes Commission. LC 89-16915. (Archives of the Holocaust Ser.: Vol. 16). 400p. 1990. reprint ed. 100.00 (*0-8240-5498-9*) Garland.

Lankford, E. Louis. Aesthetics: Issues & Inquiry. 106p. 1992. pap. 15.00 (*0-937652-60-1*) Natl Art Ed.

Lankford, J., jt. ed. see Ritchie, R. O.

An Asterisk (*) at the beginning of an entry indicates that the title is appearing in BIP for the first time.

Lankford, J., et al. Fatigue Mechanisms: Advances in Quantitative Measurement of Physical Damage- STP 811. LC 82-73773. 498p. 1983. text ed. 50.00 (*0-8031-0250-X*, 04-811000-30) ASTM.

***Lankford, Jefferson L. & Blaze, Douglas A.** The Law of Negligence in Arizona. 597p. 1992. 80.00 (*0-87473-780-X*) Michie Butterworth.

Lankford, Kurt, jt. auth. see Litz, Brian.

Lankford, Larry G., jt. auth. see Hearn, Eldon D.

Lankford, Larry G., jt. auth. see Hearn, Eldon.

Lankford, Mary D. Christmas Around the World. LC 93-38566. (Illus.). 48p. (J). (gr. 2 up). 1995. 16.00 (*0-688-12166-7*); lib. bdg. 15.93 (*0-688-12167-5*) Morrow Jr Bks.

— Films for Learning, Thinking & Doing. 228p. 1991. lib. bdg. 24.50 (*0-87287-626-8*) Libs Unl.

— Hopscotch Around the World. LC 91-17152. (Illus.). 48p. (J). (gr. 4 up). 1992. 16.00 (*0-688-08419-7*); lib. bdg. 15.93 (*0-688-08420-6*) Morrow Jr Bks.

— Is It Dark? Is It Light? LC 90-21492. (Illus.). 32p. (J). (ps-2). 1991. 13.00 (*0-679-81579-1*); lib. bdg. 13.99 (*0-679-91579-6*) Knopf Bks Yng Read.

— Jacks. (Illus.). 1996. write for info. (*0-688-13707-5*); lib. bdg. write for info. (*0-688-13708-3*) Morrow Jr Bks.

— Quinceanera: A Latina's Journey to Womanhood. (Illus.). 48p. (J). (gr. 6-9). 1994. lib. bdg. 14.90 (*1-56294-363-4*) Millbrook Pr.

— Successful Field Trips. 175p. 1992. pap. text ed. 35.00 (*0-87436-638-0*) ABC-CLIO.

***Lankford, Nelson D.** Last American Aristocrat: The Biography of David K. E. Bruce, Vol. 1. 1995. 24.95 (*0-316-51501-9*) Little.

Lankford, Nelson D., ed. OSS Against the Reich: The World War II Diaries of Colonel David K. E. Bruce. LC 90-47719. (Illus.). 256p. 1991. 28.50 (*0-87338-427-X*) Kent St U Pr.

Lankford, Nelson D., intro. An Irishman in Dixie: Thomas Conolly's Diary of the Fall of the Confederacy. 165p. 1988. 29.95 (*0-87249-555-8*) U of SC Pr.

Lankford, Nelson D., ed. see Hilldrup, Robert P.

Lankford, P. Toxicity Reduction in Industrial Effluence. 1990. text ed. 72.95 (*0-442-00234-3*) Van Nos Reinhold.

Lankford, Philip M. Regional Incomes in the United States 1929-1967: Level, Distribution, Stability, & Growth. LC 72-91224. (Research Papers Ser.: No. 145). (Illus.). 137p. 1973. pap. 12.00 (*0-89065-052-7*) U Chicago Comm Geo.

Lankford, Robert D. Dream Weaver: Survive until Dawn, Vol. 1, Issue 1. (Illus.). 24p. (YA). (gr. 11 up). 1987. pap. 1.95 (*0-9621811-0-2*) Lankford Comics.

— Dream Weaver in the Face of Fear, Vol. 1, No. 3. (Illus.). 48p. (YA). (gr. 11 up). 1991. pap. 2.75 (*0-9621811-2-9*) Lankford Comics.

— Dreamweaver, Vol. 1. 2nd ed. (Illus.). 24p. (YA). (gr. 10 up). 1988. pap. 1.95 (*0-685-44540-2*) Lankford Comics.

— Dreamweaver, Vol. 1. 4th ed. (Illus.). 24p. (YA). (gr. 10 up). 1989. pap. 1.95 (*0-317-93324-8*) Lankford Comics.

Lankford, T. Randall. Integrated Science for Health Students. 3rd ed. (C). 1984. teacher ed write for info. (*0-8359-3101-3*, Reston); text ed. 38.95 (*0-8359-3106-4*, Reston) P-H.

Lankford, T. Randall & Gribble, Paula V. Foundations of Normal & Therapeutic Nutrition. 2nd ed. LC 93-35725. 656p. 1994. pap. text ed. 32.95 (*0-8273-5268-9*) Delmar.

Lankford, T. Randall & Jacobs-Steward, Paula M. Foundations of Normal & Therapeutic Nutrition. LC 85-22664. 736p. 1986. teacher ed 12.00 (*0-8273-4283-7*) Delmar.

Lankford, Terry T. Pilot's Guide to Weather Reports, Forecasts & Flight Planning. (Practical Flying Ser.). (Illus.). 416p. 1990. 29.95 (*0-8306-7582-5*, 3582); pap. 19.95 (*0-8306-6582-X*) TAB Bks.

— The Pilot's Guide to Weather Reports, Forecasts & Flight Planning. 1991. pap. text ed. 19.95 (*0-07-156003-3*) McGraw.

— Pilot's Guide to Weather Reports, Forecasts, & Flight Planning. 2nd ed. LC 95-1617. 1995. pap. text ed. 19.95 (*0-07-036427-3*) TAB Bks.

— Understanding Aeronautical Charts. 1992. 27.95 (*0-07-157800-5*); pap. 17.95 (*0-07-157799-8*) McGraw.

— Understanding Aeronautical Charts. (Practical Flying Ser.). 320p. 1992. 27.95 (*0-8306-3912-8*, 1041); pap. 17.95 (*0-8306-3911-X*, 1041) TAB Bks.

Lankheit, Klaus, ed. see Marc, Franz.

Lankhorst, Gustaaf J. Management of Ankle Injuries. LC 91-7077. (Illus.). 52p. 1991. text ed. 16.00 (*0-88937-064-8*) Hogrefe & Huber Pubs.

Lankin, Eliahu. To Win the Promised Land: Story of a Freedom Fighter. Hershberg, Artziah, tr. (Illus.). 400p. 1992. 25.00 (*0-917883-05-5*) Benmir Bks.

Lankisch, P. G., ed. Pancreatic Enzymes in Health & Disease. (Illus.). 224p. 1991. pap. 78.00 (*0-387-53187-4*) Spr-Verlag.

Lankow, Edward. How to Breathe Right. 1984. spiral bd. 5.50 (*0-7873-0990-7*) Mokelumne.

Lankowitz, Stanley, jt. auth. see Ellis, David B.

Lankowski, Carl. Germany & the European Community. 1993. text ed. 49.95 (*0-312-06035-1*) St Martin.

Lanks, Karl W. Academic Environment: A Handbook for Evaluating Faculty Employment Opportunities. LC 90-81847. 138p. (Orig.). (C). 1990. pap. text ed. 12.95 (*0-9626658-0-0*) Faculty Brooklyn.

Lankshear, Colin & Lawler, Moira. Literacy, Schooling & Revolution. (Education Policy Perspectives Ser.). 250p. 1989. 90.00 (*1-85000-239-8*, Falmer Pr); pap. 39.50 (*1-85000-589-3*, Falmer Pr) Taylor & Francis.

Lankshear, Colin & McLaren, Peter L., eds. Critical Literacy: Politics, Praxis, & the Postmodern. LC 91-39669. (SUNY Series, Teacher Empowerment & School Reform). 443p. (C). 1993. 64.50 (*0-7914-1229-6*); pap. 21.95 (*0-7914-1230-X*) State U NY Pr.

Lankshear, Colin, jt. ed. see McLaren, Peter.

Lankton, Carol & Lankton, Stephen R. Tales of Enchantment: Goal-Oriented Metaphors for Adults & Children in Therapy. LC 89-720. 432p. 1989. 41.95 (*0-87630-504-4*) Brunner-Mazel.

Lankton, Carol H., jt. auth. see Lankton, Stephen R.

Lankton, Larry. Cradle to Grave: Life, Work, & Death at the Lake Superior Copper Mines. (Illus.). 352p. 1993. reprint ed. pap. 16.95 (*0-19-508357-1*) OUP.

Lankton, Stephen. Practical Magic: A Translation of Basic Neuro-Linguistic Programming into Clinical Psychotherapy. LC 80-50148. 1980. 15.95 (*0-916990-08-7*) META Pubns.

Lankton, Stephen & Zeig, Jeffrey K., eds. Research, Comparisons, & Medical Applications of Ericksonian Techniques. LC 88-2896. (Ericksonian Monographs: No. 4). 132p. 1988. 26.95 (*0-87630-510-9*) Brunner-Mazel.

Lankton, Stephen R. The Blammo-Surprise! Book: A Story to Help Children Overcome Fears. LC 88-13566. (Illus.). 48p. (J). (gr. 1 up). 1988. pap. 8.95 (*0-945354-10-X*) Magination Pr.

Lankton, Stephen R., ed. The Broader Implications of Ericksonian Therapy. LC 89-71310. (Ericksonian Monographs: No. 7). 128p. 1990. 26.95 (*0-87630-582-6*) Brunner-Mazel.

— Central Themes & Principles of Ericksonian Therapy. LC 87-13831. (Ericksonian Monographs: No. 2). 152p. 1987. 26.95 (*0-87630-470-6*) Brunner-Mazel.

— Elements & Dimensions of an Ericksonian Approach. LC 85-17454. (Ericksonian Monographs: No. 1). 152p. 1985. 26.95 (*0-87630-411-0*) Brunner-Mazel.

— Ericksonian Hypnosis: Application, Preparation & Research. LC 88-242445. (Ericksonian Monographs: No. 5). 140p. 1988. 26.95 (*0-87630-523-0*) Brunner-Mazel.

Lankton, Stephen R. & Erickson, Kristina K., eds. The Essence of a Single-Session Success. LC 93-11832. (Ericksonian Monographs: No. 9). 184p. 1993. 26.95 (*0-87630-727-6*) Brunner-Mazel.

Lankton, Stephen R. & Lankton, Carol H. The Answer Within: A Clinical Framework of Ericksonian Hypnotherapy. LC 82-20637. 392p. 1983. 32.95 (*0-87630-320-3*) Brunner-Mazel.

— Enchantment & Intervention in Family Therapy: Training in Ericksonian Approaches. LC 86-4240. 336p. 1986. 32.95 (*0-87630-428-5*); audio 12.95 (*0-87630-467-6*) Brunner-Mazel.

Lankton, Stephen R. & Zeig, Jeffrey K., eds. Ericksonian Monographs No. 10: Difficult Contexts for Therapy. LC 94-5346. (Ericksonian Monographs: No. 10). 160p. 1995. 26.95 (*0-87630-749-7*) Brunner-Mazel.

— Extrapolations: Demonstrations of Ericksonian Therapy. LC 89-37590. (Ericksonian Monographs: No. 6). 136p. 1989. 26.95 (*0-87630-567-2*) Brunner-Mazel.

— Treatment of Special Populations with Ericksonian Approaches. LC 87-35514. (Ericksonian Monographs: No. 3). 160p. 1988. 26.95 (*0-87630-494-3*) Brunner-Mazel.

Lankton, Stephen R., jt. auth. see Lankton, Carol.

Lankton, Stephen R., ed. see Zeig, Jeffrey K.

Lankton, Stephen R., et al, eds. Views on Ericksonian Brief Therapy, Process & Action. LC 91-16001. (Ericksonian Monographs: No. 8). 128p. 1991. 26.95 (*0-87630-646-6*) Brunner-Mazel.

Lanllier, Jan. Five Centuries of Jewelry. 1989. 24.99 (*0-517-67240-5*) Random Hse Value.

Lanly, Andre, ed. see Villon, Francois.

Lanman, Barry A. & Mehaffy, George L. Oral History in the Secondary School Classroom. (Oral History Association Pamphlet Ser.: No. 2). 39p. (Orig.). 1988. teacher ed 5.00 (*0-317-03930-X*); pap. 5.00 (*0-317-03929-6*) Oral Hist.

Lanman, Charles. Beginnings of Hindu Pantheism. 1972. 35.00 (*0-87968-719-3*) Gordon Pr.

— Biographical Annals of the Civil Government of the United States. 1976. reprint ed. 75.00 (*1-55888-934-5*) Omnigraphics Inc.

— A Canoe Voyage up the Mississippi & Around Lake Superior in 1846. LC 77-85592. 1978. reprint ed. 17.50 (*0-912382-22-8*); reprint ed. 8.00 (*0-912382-23-6*) Black Letter.

Lanman, Charles R. Sanskrit Reader: Text & Vocabulary & Notes. LC 11-24320. 425p. 1984. 44.00 (*0-674-78900-8*) HUP.

Lanman, Jonathan T. On the Origin of Portolan Charts. (Illus.). 56p. 1987. pap. 8.00 (*0-911028-37-4*) Newberry.

Lanmann, Charles R. Sanskrit Reader with Vocabulary & Notes. (C). 1983. reprint ed. 16.00 (*0-8364-2860-9*) S Asia.

Lanmon, Dwight P. Glass from Six Centuries. LC 78-62279. (Illus.). 134p. 1976. pap. 10.00 (*0-317-13582-1*) Wadsworth Atheneum.

Lanmon, Dwight P. & Whitehouse, David B. Glass. (Robert Lehman Collection: Vol. 11). (Illus.). 358p. 1993. 110.00 (*0-691-03405-2*) Princeton U Pr.

Lanmon, Dwight P., et al. John Frederick Amelung: Early American Glassmaker. LC 86-72706. (Illus.). 243p. 1991. 65.00 (*0-87290-075-4*) Corning.

Lanmon, Lorraine W. Quarry Farm: A Study of the "Picturesque" (Quarry Farm Papers: No. 3). 36p. 1991. pap. 5.00 (*1-880817-03-9*) EC Ctr Mark T Stu.

— William Lescaze, Architect. LC 83-45295. 216p. 1987. 55.00 (*0-87982-506-5*) Art Alliance.

Lanmuir, G. E., jt. auth. see Duckworth, C. L.

Lann, Irma S., et al, eds. Strategies for Studying Suicide & Suicidal Behavior. 164p. 1989. lib. bdg. 19.95 (*0-89862-383-9*) Guilford Pr.

Lannan Museum Staff. Edward Ruscha. Clearwater, Bonnie et al, eds. 1988. pap. 24.95 (*0-8109-2405-6*) Abrams.

***Lanner.** Galoppe. (Illus.). 1973. pap. 65.00 (*0-8450-1017-4*) Broude.

— Quadrillen, Marsche & Andere Werkes. (Illus.). 1973. pap. 65.00 (*0-8450-1018-2*) Broude.

— Walzer Nr. 1-30. (Illus.). 1973. pap. 65.00 (*0-8450-1011-5*) Broude.

— Walzer Nr. 31-51. 1973. pap. 65.00 (*0-8450-1012-3*) Broude.

— Walzer Nr. 52-70. (Illus.). 1973. pap. 65.00 (*0-8450-1013-1*) Broude.

— Walzer Nr. 71-93. 1973. pap. 65.00 (*0-8450-1014-X*) Broude.

— Walzer Nr. 94-106: Anhang. (Illus.). 1973. pap. 65.00 (*0-8450-1015-8*) Broude.

Lanner, Ron. Autumn Leaves. (Illus.). 1990. 19.50 (*1-55971-078-0*, 0191) NorthWord.

Lanner, Ronald M. The Pinon Pine: A Natural & Cultural History. LC 81-119. (Illus.). 224p. 1981. 21.95 (*0-87417-065-6*); pap. 13.95 (*0-87417-066-4*) U of Nev Pr.

Lannering, J. Studies in the Prose Style of Joseph Addison. (Essays & Studies on English Language & Literature: Vol. 9). 1974. reprint ed. pap. 20.00 (*0-8115-0207-4*) Periodicals Srv.

Lanners, Edi. Secrets of One Hundred Twenty-Three Classic Science Tricks & Experiments. (Illus.). 196p. (Orig.). 1987. pap. 8.95 (*0-8306-2821-5*) TAB Bks.

— Secrets of 123 Classic Science Tricks & Experiments. 1987. pap. text ed. 9.95 (*0-07-157345-3*) McGraw.

Lannert. Mexican Americans. (American Voices Ser.). (J). 1991. 13.95 (*0-86593-139-9*); lib. bdg. 18.60 (*0-685-59187-5*) Rourke Corp.

Lannestock, Gustaf, tr. see Boye, Karin.

Lanni, Deborah. What's a Duck Like You Doing in a Place Like This? (Illus.). iv, 23p. (Orig.). (J). (gr. 3-6). 1984. pap. 2.00 (*0-942788-12-5*) Iris Visual.

Lanning, David D., jt. ed. see White, James D.

Lanning, George, jt. auth. see Macauley, Robie.

Lanning, Jim & Lanning, Judy. Texas Cowboys: Memories of the Early Days. LC 83-40494. (Illus.). 256p. 1984. 15.95 (*0-89096-184-0*) Tex A&M Univ Pr.

***Lanning, Jim & Lanning, Judy, eds.** Texas Cowboys: Memories of the Early Days. LC 83-40494. (Illus.). 256p. (Orig.). 1995. pap. 12.95 (*0-89096-658-3*) Tex A&M Univ Pr.

Lanning, John T. The Royal Protomedicato: The Regulation of the Medical Profession in the Spanish Empire. TePaske, John J., ed. LC 85-4611. v, 485p. (C). 1985. 48.00 (*0-8223-0651-4*) Duke.

Lanning, Joyce A., jt. auth. see Juster, Robert J.

Lanning, Judy, jt. auth. see Lanning, Jim.

Lanning, Judy, jt. ed. see Lanning, Jim.

Lanning, K. Consistency, Scalability, & Personality Measurement. (Recent Research in Psychology Ser.). (Illus.). viii, 157p. 1990. pap. 36.00 (*0-387-97438-5*) Spr-Verlag.

Lanning, Lee. The Only War We Had: A Platoon Leader's Journal of Vietnam. 304p. (Orig.). 1987. mass mkt. 5.99 (*0-8041-0005-5*) Ivy Books.

Lanning, Lee & Hart, Nett. Ripening: An Almanac of Lesbian Lore & Vision, Vol. 1. 160p. 1992. reprint ed. pap. 8.95 (*0-9615605-2-5*) Word Weavers.

Lanning, Linda M. Waiting Wife. 1997. mass mkt. write for info. (*0-8041-0937-0*) Ivy Books.

Lanning, Michael L. The Battles of Peace. (Orig.). 1992. mass mkt. 4.99 (*0-8041-0609-6*) Ivy Books.

— Inside the LRRPS: Rangers in Vietnam. 256p. 1988. mass mkt. 4.95 (*0-8041-0166-3*) Ivy Books.

— Vietnam at the Movies. (Illus.). 400p. 1994. pap. 12.50 (*0-449-90891-7*, ExPress) Fawcett.

— Vietnam at the Movies. 1992. pap. write for info. (*0-8041-1006-9*) Ivy Books.

— Vietnam Nineteen Sixty-Nine to Nineteen Seventy: A Company Commander's Journal. 320p. 1988. mass mkt. 4.95 (*0-8041-0187-6*) Ivy Books.

Lanning, Michael L. & Cragg, Dan. Inside the VC & the NVA: The Real Story of North Vietnam's Armed Forces. 1994. mass mkt. 5.99 (*0-8041-0500-6*) Ivy Books.

Lanning, Michael L. & Stubbe, Ray W. Inside Force Recon: Recon Marines in Vietnam. 304p. 1989. mass mkt. 5.99 (*0-8041-0301-1*) Ivy Books.

Lanning, Rosemary, tr. see Hanel, Wolfram.

Lanning, Rosemary, tr. see Lussert, Anneliese.

Lanning, Rosemary, tr. see Ostheeren, Ingrid.

Lanning, Rosemary, tr. see Pfister, Marcus.

Lanning, Rosemary, tr. see Scheffler, Ursel.

Lanning, Rosemary, tr. see Scheidl, Gerda M.

Lanning, Rosemary, tr. see Siegenthaler, Kathrin & Pfister, Marcus.

Lanning, Rosemary, tr. see Waas, Uli.

Lannon, Frances. Privilege, Persecution & Prophecy: The Catholic Church in Spain, 1875-1975. (Illus.). 350p. 1987. 69.00 (*0-19-821923-7*) OUP.

Lannon, John M. Technical Writing. 5th ed. (C). 1991. text ed. 7.20 (*0-673-49882-4*) HarpCollege.

— Technical Writing. 6th ed. (C). 1993. pap. 33.00 (*0-673-52294-6*) HarpCollege.

— The Writing Process. 4th ed. (C). 1991. text ed. 30.50 (*0-673-52133-8*) HarpCollege.

— The Writing Process: A Concise Rhetoric. 5th ed. LC 94-18589. (C). 1995. 23.50 (*0-673-52399-3*) HarpC.

Lannon, John M., jt. auth. see Dumont, Raymond A.

Lannon, Kathleen, ed. InfoMap Project Manager's Guide. (Illus.). 100p. (Orig.). 1990. pap. 39.95 (*0-9606408-5-1*) Info Mgmt Pr.

Lannon, Margaret C. & Arcangelo, Virginia P. Essentials of Clinical Pharmacology & Dosage Calculation. 2nd ed. LC 64-4701. (Illus.). 306p. 1986. text ed. 21.50 (*0-397-54531-2*, Lippincott Nursing) Lippincott.

Lannon, Maurice. Polyester & Fiberglass. 8th ed. 1969. 6.00 (*0-685-11725-1*) Gem O Lite.

Lannoo, M. & Bourgoin, J. Point Defects in Semiconductors I. (Solid-State Sciences Ser.: Vol. 22). (Illus.). 260p. 1981. 53.00 (*0-387-10518-2*) Spr-Verlag.

Lannoo, M. & Friedel, P. Atomic & Electronic Structure of Surfaces: Theoretical Foundations. Ertl, G. & Gomer, R., eds. (Surface Sciences Ser.: Vol. 16). (Illus.). 272p. 1991. 64.00 (*0-387-52682-X*) Spr-Verlag.

Lannoo, M., jt. auth. see Bourgoin, J.

Lannoy, Richard. The Speaking Tree: A Study of Indian Culture & Society. LC 74-158205. (Illus.). 1974. pap. 13.95 (*0-19-519754-2*) OUP.

Lannoy, Violet D. Pears from the Willow Tree. LC 86-50770. 151p. (Orig.). 1989. 28.00 (*0-89410-564-7*); pap. 14.50 (*0-89410-565-5*) Three Continents.

L'Annunziata, Michael F. Radionuclide Tracers. 485p. 1987. text ed. 186.00 (*0-12-436252-4*) Acad Pr.

L'Annunziata, Michael F. & Legg, Joe. Isotopes & Radiation in Agricultural Sciences: Soil-Plant-Water Relationships, Vol. 1. 1984. text ed. 137.00 (*0-12-436601-5*) Acad Pr.

L'Annunziata, Michael F. & Legg, Joe, eds. Isotopes & Radiation in Agricultural Sciences: Animals, Plants, Food & the Environment, Vol. 2. 1984. text ed. 137.00 (*0-12-436602-3*) Acad Pr.

Lannutti, J. E. & Williams, P. K., eds. Current Trends in the Theory of Fields: Tallahassee, 1979. (AIP Conference Proceedings Ser.: No. 48). (Illus.). 1978. lib. bdg. 16.25 (*0-88318-147-9*) Am Inst Physics.

Lano, K. & Haughton, H., eds. Object-Oriented Specification Case Studies. LC 93-21698. (Object Oriented Ser.). 1993. pap. text ed. 47.00 (*0-13-097015-8*) P-H.

Lano, Kevin & Haughton, Howard. Reverse Engineering & Software Maintenance: A Practical Approach. LC 93-29541. (International Series in Software Engineering). 1993. write for info. (*0-07-707897-7*) McGraw.

Lano, Kevin, jt. auth. see Haughton, Howard.

Lanoix, J. N., jt. auth. see Wagner, E. G.

Lanon, Frances & Preston, Paul, eds. Elites & Power in Twentieth-Century Spain: Essays in Honour of Sir Raymond Carr. (Illus.). 328p. 1991. 85.00 (*0-19-822880-5*) OUP.

Lanot, Marra P. Passion & Compassion: Mga Tula Sa Ingles at Pilipino. 153p. 1981. pap. 8.75 (*0-686-32581-8*, Pub. by New Day Pub PH) Cellar.

Lanotte, L., ed. Magnetoelastic Effects & Applications: Proceedings of the First International Meeting on Magnetoelastic Effects & Applications, Naples, Italy, 24-26 May, 1993. LC 93-34426. (Studies in Applied Electromagnetics in Materials: No. 4). 1993. write for info. (*0-444-81711-5*) Elsevier.

***Lanoue, David G. & Wilson, Vivian A., eds.** Bard South: Teaching Writing at Historically Black Colleges & Universities. (Occasional Publication Ser.: No. 1). 63p. 1988. pap. 6.95 (*1-883275-03-2*) Xavier Rev.

Lanoue, David J. From Camelot to the Teflon President: Economics & Presidential Popularity Since 1960. LC 88-10251. (Contributions in Political Science Ser.: No. 222). 137p. 1988. text ed. 45.00 (*0-313-26393-0*, LFM/, Greenwood Pr) Greenwood.

Lanoue, David J. & Schrott, Peter R. The Joint Press Conference: The History, Impact, & Prospects of American Presidential Debates. LC 90-45322. (Contributions to the Study of Mass Media & Communications Ser.: No. 26). 184p. 1991. text ed. 47.95 (*0-313-27248-4*, LPA, Greenwood Pr) Greenwood.

Lanoue, F. Drownproofing: A New Technique for Water Safety. 1978. pap. 3.95 (*0-685-03844-0*) P-H.

LaNoue, George R. & Lee, Barbara A. Academics in Court: The Consequences of Faculty Discrimination Litigation. LC 87-5047. 1987. text ed. 42.50 (*0-472-10086-6*); pap. text ed. 19.95 (*0-472-08070-9*) U of Mich Pr.

Lanoue, Guy. Brothers: The Politics of Violence among the Sekani of Northern British Columbia. 250p. 1992. 49.50 (*0-85496-746-X*) Berg Pubs.

Lanouette, William & Silard, Bela. Genius in the Shadows: A Biography of Leo Szilard; the Man Behind the Bomb. Stewart, Robert, ed. (Illus.). 640p. 1993. text ed. 35.00 (*0-684-19011-7*, Scribners) S&S Trade.

— Genius in the Shadows: A Biography of Leo Szilard, the Man Behind the Bomb. (Illus.). 603p. 1994. pap. 18.95 (*0-226-46888-7*) U Ch Pr.

Lanoux, ed. see Zola, Emile.

Lanoux, Armand, ed. see Zola, Emile.

Lanoux, Rene, ed. see Zola, Emile.

Lanphear, Roger G. Gay Spirituality: Experiences in Self Realization for Gay Men, Lesbians, & Enlightened Heterosexuals. 160p. (Orig.). 1990. pap. 9.95 (*0-9625800-0-7*) Unified Pubns.

— Keep Your Self Alive: A Twenty-First Century Guide to Perfect Health & Freedom from Stress. 141p. (Orig.). 1992. pap. 9.95 (*0-9625800-2-3*) Unified Pubns.

— Money Making: New Techniques for Easy & Direct Flow of Wealth. 160p. (Orig.). 1991. pap. 9.95 (*0-9625800-1-5*) Unified Pubns.

— UNIFIED--A Course on Truth & Practical Guidance from Babaji. LC 86-72570. 160p. (Orig.). 1987. pap. 8.95 (*0-87516-585-0*) DeVorss.

***Lanphere, M. A., et al, eds.** Abstracts of the Eighth International Conference on Geochronology, Cosmochronology & Isotope Geology. (Illus.). 384p. (Orig.). (C). 1994. pap. text ed. 75.00x (*0-7881-1349-6*) Diane Pub.

Lanphere, Roberta, jt. auth. see Drnei, Herta.

Lanquetin, P., jt. auth. see Boidin, J.

Lanre. Design Consultants Including Design Colleges '94. 1993. 125.00 (*0-9518494-3-3*, Pub. by Janvier Pubng Ltd UK) St Mut.

— The Professional & Business Guide to Design Services '94. 1993. 185.00 (*0-9518494-1-7*, Pub. by Janvier Pubng Ltd UK) St Mut.

An Asterisk (*) at the beginning of an entry indicates that the title is appearing in BIP for the first time.

— The Visual Index of Creative Services '93-'94. 1993. pap. 135.00 (*0-9518494-2-5*, Pub. by Janvier Pubng Ltd UK) St Mut.

Lanros, Nedell E. Assessment & Intervention in Emergency Nursing. 3rd ed. (Illus.). 669p. 1988. boxed, pap. 44.95 (*0-8385-0435-3*, A0435-6) Appleton & Lange.

Lansberg, H. E., ed. see Orvig, S.

Lansberg, Hans H., ed. Making National Energy Policy. 148p. 1993. pap. 22.50 (*0-915707-70-5*) Resources Future.

Lansberg, P. J., jt. auth. see Defesche, J. C.

Lansberry, J. Robert. Police Lieutenants & Captains Handbook, Vol. II. 88p. (Orig.). 1971. pap. 21.95 (*0-685-46276-5*, DH008) Davis Pub Law.

— Police Sergeants Handbook, Vol. II. 279p. (Orig.). 1972. pap. 21.95 (*1-56325-050-0*, DH012) Davis Pub Law.

Lansberry, J. Robert & Hendel, Ralph E. Police Lieutenant's & Captains Handbook, Vol. I. (Illus.). 225p. (Orig.). 1971. pap. 21.95 (*1-56325-023-3*, DH007) Davis Pub Law.

Lansbury, Angela. Angela Lansbury's Positive Moves. large type ed. 160p. 1991. reprint ed. lib. bdg. 21.95 (*1-56054-124-5*) Thorndike Pr.

— Angela Lansbury's Positive Moves. large type ed. 160p. 1991. pap. 14.95 (*1-56054-990-4*) Thorndike Pr.

— Family Matters: Wedding Speeches & Toasts. rev. ed. 96p. 1994. pap. 6.95 (*0-7063-7218-2*, Pub. by Ward Lock UK) Sterling.

Lansbury, Coral. The Grotto. 608p. 1990. mass mkt. 5.95 (*0-8041-0648-7*) Ivy Books.

— The Old Brown Dog: Women, Workers & Vivisection in Edwardian England. LC 85-40369. 232p. 1985. text ed. 24.00 (*0-299-10250-5*) U of Wis Pr.

— The Reasonable Man: Trollope's Legal Fiction. LC 80-8560. 240p. pap. 68.40 (*0-8357-4649-6*, 2037579) Bks Demand.

Lansbury, George. My Pilgrimage for Peace. Bd. with Peace Through Economic Cooperation. LC 70-147723. LC 70-147723. (Library of War & Peace; Peace Leaders: Biographies & Memoirs). 1972. Set lib. bdg. 46.00 (*0-8240-0251-2*) Garland.

***Lansbury, James.** Korzeniowski. (Ninety's Title Ser.). 176p. (Orig.). 1995. pap. 11.99 (*1-85242-240-8*) Serpents Tail.

***Lansbury, R.** International & Comparative Industrial. 1994. 24.95 (*1-86373-370-1*) IPG Chicago.

Lansbury, Russel D., jt. auth. see Graversen, Gert.

Lansbury, Russell, jt. ed. see Bamber, Greg J.

Lansche, Jerry. The Forgotten Championships: Postseason Baseball, 1882-1981. LC 89-42584. 376p. 1989. lib. bdg. 38.50 (*0-89950-414-0*) McFarland & Co.

— Stan "The Man" Musial: Born to Be a Ball Player. LC 93-45459. 240p. 1994. 19.95 (*0-87833-846-2*) Taylor Pub.

Lansdale, Bruce. Metamorphosis, or, Why I Love Greece. LC 78-75129. (Illus.). 128p. 1979. 30.00 (*0-89241-083-3*) Caratzas.

***Lansdale, Edward G.** In the Midst of Wars: An American's Mission to Southeast Asia. LC 91-70451. 386p. 1991. pap. 19.95 (*0-8232-1314-5*) Fordham.

Lansdale, Joe B. Mucho Mojo. 304p. 1995. mass mkt. 5.99 (*0-446-40187-0*, Mysterious Paperbk) Warner Bks.

Lansdale, Joe R. Act of Love. 1990. pap. 3.95 (*0-8217-3080-0*) Zebra.

— Best Sellers Guaranteed. 224p. (Orig.). 1993. pap. 4.50 (*0-441-05502-8*) Ace Bks.

— By Bizarre Hands. 256p. 1991. mass mkt. 3.99 (*0-380-71205-9*) Avon.

— Cold in July. 208p. 1995. mass mkt. 5.50 (*0-446-40430-6*, Mysterious Paperbk) Warner Bks.

— Dead in the West. LC 85-27887. (Illus.). 136p. (Orig.). 1986. pap. 6.95 (*0-917053-04-4*) Space And.

— Johan Hex: Two Gun Mojo. Kahan, Bob, ed. 160p. 1994. pap. 12.95 (*1-56389-162-X*, Vertigo) DC Comics.

— Mucho Mojo. 320p. 1994. 19.95 (*0-89296-490-1*) Mysterious Pr.

— The Nightrunners. 248p. 1995. mass mkt. 4.95 (*0-7867-0289-3*) Carroll & Graf.

— Savage Season. 192p. 1995. mass mkt. 5.50 (*0-446-40431-4*, Mysterious Paperbk) Warner Bks.

— The Two-Bear Mambo. 288p. 1995. write for info. (*0-89296-491-X*) Mysterious Pr.

— The Two-Bear Mambo. 1996. mass mkt. write for info. (*0-446-40188-9*, Mysterious Paperbk) Warner Bks.

***Lansdale, Joe R. & Klaw, Richard, eds.** Weird Business. (Illus.). 420p. 1995. 29.95 (*1-885418-02-7*) MOJO Pr.

Lansdale, Joe R., jt. ed. see Lansdale, Karen.

Lansdale, Karen & Lansdale, Joe R., eds. Dark at Heart. 350p. 1992. 21.95 (*0-913165-64-6*) Dark Harvest.

Lansdale, Maria H. Paris: Its Sites, Monuments & History. 1977. lib. bdg. 59.95 (*0-8490-2413-7*) Gordon Pr.

Lansdale, Mark W. & Ormerod, Thomas C. Understanding Interfaces: A Handbook of Human-Computer Dialogue. (Computers & People Ser.). (Illus.). 304p. 1994. text ed. 45.00 (*0-12-528390-3*) Acad Pr.

Lansdell, Avril. Fashion a la Carte 1860-1900. 1989. pap. 25.00 (*0-85263-747-0*, Pub. by Shire UK) St Mut.

— Occupational Costume & Working Clothes, 1776-1976. 1990. 4.50 (*0-913714-07-0*) Legacy Books.

— Occupational Costumes. 1989. pap. 25.00 (*0-85263-689-X*, Pub. by Shire UK) St Mut.

— Seaside Fashions 1860-1939. 1989. pap. 25.00 (*0-7478-0066-9*, Pub. by Shire UK) St Mut.

— Wedding Fashions 1860-1980. 1989. pap. 25.00 (*0-85263-839-6*, Pub. by Shire UK) St Mut.

Lansdell, Henry. Russian Central Asia: Including Kuldja, Bokhara, Khiva & Merv. LC 79-115556. (Russia Observed, Series I). 1970. reprint ed. 70.95 (*0-405-03041-X*) Ayer.

— Through Siberia. LC 75-115555. (Russia Observed, Series I). 1970. reprint ed. 46.95 (*0-405-03042-8*) Ayer.

Lansdown, A. B. G., jt. auth. see Conning, D. M.

Lansdown, A. V. & Campbell, J. South African Criminal Law & Procedure, Vol. V: Criminal Procedure & Evidence. 1192p. 1982. write for info. (*0-7021-1257-7*, Pub. by Juta SA) W W Gaunt.

Lansdown, Andrew. Beyond the Open Door. (J). (gr. 4-7). 1993. pap. 2.95 (*0-590-47160-0*) Scholastic Inc.

Lansdown, J. & Earnshaw, R. A., eds. Computers in Art, Design & Animation. (Illus.). xvii, 305p. 1989. 89.00 (*0-387-96896-2*, 2321) Spr-Verlag.

Lansdown, Richard. Byron's Historical Dramas. (Illus.). 272p. 1992. 59.00 (*0-19-811252-1*) OUP.

Lansdown, Richard & Walker, Marjorie. Your Child's Development: From Birth Through Adolescence, a Complete Guide for Parents. LC 91-52722. (Illus.). 512p. 1991. 29.95 (*0-394-57814-7*) Knopf.

Lansdown, Richard & Yule, William, eds. Lead Toxicity: History & Environmental Impact. LC 86-2816. (Environmental Toxicology Ser.). 304p. 1986. text ed. 55.00 (*0-8018-3338-8*) Johns Hopkins.

Lansdown, Richard, jt. ed. see Richman, Naomi.

Lansdowne, J F. Lansdowne's Birds of the Forest. 1989. 49. 98 (*0-88486-027-2*) Arrowood Pr.

***Lansdowne, Judith A.** Amelia's Intrigue. 352p. 1995. pap. 3.99 (*0-8217-5013-5*) Zebra.

Lansdowne, Zachary. The Rays & Esoteric Psychology. 144p. (Orig.). 1989. pap. 8.95 (*0-87728-682-5*) Weiser.

Lansdowne, Zachary F. The Chakras & Esoteric Healing. LC 84-51108. 160p. 1986. pap. 8.95 (*0-87728-584-5*) Weiser.

— Rules for Spiritual Initiation. 128p. (Orig.). 1990. pap. 7.95 (*0-87728-707-4*) Weiser.

Lansdowne, Zachery. Ray Methods of Healing. (Illus.). 176p. (Orig.). 1993. pap. 10.95 (*0-87728-745-7*) Weiser.

Lanser, Susan S. Fictions of Authority: Women Writers & Narrative Voice. LC 91-55537. 304p. 1992. 39.95 (*0-8014-2377-5*); pap. 14.95 (*0-8014-8020-5*) Cornell U Pr.

Lansford, Kim D., ed. see Robertson, Lee.

Lansing, Alfred. Endurance: Shackleton's Incredible Voyage. 282p. 1986. pap. 9.95 (*0-88184-178-1*) Carroll & Graf.

— Endurance: Shackleton's Incredible Voyage. LC 94-71390. (Adventure Library). (Illus.). 320p. 1994. reprint ed. lib. bdg. 25.00 (*1-885283-00-8*) Advent Library.

Lansing, Carl. Legal Defense Handbook: For Christians in Ministry. LC 92-81119. 272p. (Orig.). 1992. pap. 15.00 (*0-89109-683-3*) NavPress.

Lansing, Carol. The Florentine Magnates: Lineage & Faction in a Medieval Commune. (Illus.). 285p. 1991. text ed. 49.50 (*0-691-03154-1*) Princeton U Pr.

Lansing Community College, Science Department Staff. The Science of the Water Planet. (C). 1993. student ed 12.00 (*1-881592-16-2*) Hayden-McNeil.

Lansing, Dorothy I. That Magnificent Cestrian-William Darlington: Being a Short Biography, 1782-1863. 87p. (Orig.). 1985. pap. 14.95 (*0-9619411-0-3*) Serpentine Pr.

***Lansing, Gerrit.** The Heavenly Tree Grows Downward. expanded rev. ed. 248p. 1995. pap. 16.95 (*1-883689-12-0*) Talisman Hse.

— The Heavenly Tree Grows Downward. expanded rev. ed. 248p. 1995. lib. bdg. 37.95 (*1-883689-13-9*) Talisman Hse.

Lansing, Gerritt. The Heavenly Tree Grows Downward. 15. 00 (*0-913028-47-9*); pap. 4.00 (*0-913028-40-1*) North Atlantic.

Lansing, J. Stephen. Priests & Programmers: Colonialism, Ecology & the Technologies of Power in the Balinese State. (Illus.). 1991. 39.50 (*0-691-09466-7*); pap. 14.95 (*0-691-02863-X*) Princeton U Pr.

— Three Worlds of Bali. LC 83-4117. (Illus.). 188p. 1983. text ed. 37.50 (*0-275-91720-7*, C1720, Praeger Pubs) Greenwood.

Lansing, Jewel. Campaigning for Office: A Woman Runs. LC 91-52962. 200p. 1991. pap. 9.95 (*0-88247-887-7*) R & E Pubs.

— One Hundred One Campaign Tips for Women Candidates & Their Staff. Parker, Diane, ed. LC 91-52961. 200p. 1991. pap. 9.95 (*0-88247-886-9*) R & E Pubs.

Lansing, John. The Black Eagles, No. 10: Cambodia Kill-Zone. 224p. 1986. pap. 2.50 (*0-8217-1953-X*) Zebra.

— The Black Eagles, No. 11: Duel on the Song Cai. 240p. 1987. pap. 2.50 (*0-8217-2048-1*) Zebra.

— Black Eagles No. 13: Encore at Dien Bien Phu. 1987. pap. 2.50 (*0-8217-2197-6*) Zebra.

— Black Eagles No. 14: Firestorm at Dong Nam. 1988. pap. 2.50 (*0-8217-2287-5*) Zebra.

— The Black Eagles, No. 15: Ho's Hellhounds. 256p. 1988. pap. 2.95 (*0-8217-2358-8*) Zebra.

— The Black Eagles, No. 16: Monsoon Hellhole. 256p. 1988. pap. 2.95 (*0-8217-2434-7*) Zebra.

— The Black Eagles, No. 17: Mau Len Death Zone. 256p. 1988. pap. 2.95 (*0-8217-2514-9*) Zebra.

— Black Eagles No. 18: Durong Warrior. 1989. pap. 2.95 (*0-8217-2631-5*) Zebra.

— Black Eagles No. 19: Hoa-Tien Kill. 1989. pap. 2.95 (*0-8217-2713-3*) Zebra.

— The Black Eagles, No. 4: Pungi Patrol. 240p. 1984. pap. 2.50 (*0-8217-1389-2*) Zebra.

— The Black Eagles, No. 7: Beyond the DMZ. 1985. pap. 2.50 (*0-8217-1610-7*) Zebra.

— Bo Binh Command. (Black Eagles Ser.: No. 20). 1990. pap. 2.95 (*0-8217-2992-6*) Zebra.

— Hanoi Hellground. (Black Eagles Ser.: Vol. 1). 1983. pap. 2.95 (*0-8217-1249-7*) Zebra.

— Mekong Massacre. (Black Eagles Ser.: No. 2). 1983. pap. 2.50 (*0-8217-1294-2*) Zebra.

— Nguy Hiem War Zone. (Black Eagles Ser.: No. 21). 1990. pap. 2.95 (*0-8217-3076-2*) Zebra.

— Nightmare in Laos. (Black Eagles Ser.: No. 3). 1984. pap. 2.50 (*0-8217-1341-8*) Zebra.

Lansing, John B. & Morgan, James N. Economic Survey Methods. LC 71-633672. 448p. 1971. pap. 16.00 (*0-87944-008-2*) Inst Soc Res.

Lansing, John B., et al. Planned Residential Environments. LC 76-632967. 283p. 1970. 20.00 (*0-87944-088-0*) Inst Soc Res.

— Planned Residential Environments: A Report Prepared for the U. S. Department of Transportation, Bureau of Public Road. LC 76-632967. (Illus.). 281p. reprint ed. pap. 80.10 (*0-7837-5243-1*, 2044977) Bks Demand.

Lansing, Karen E. Time to Be a Friend. LC 92-13010. 96p. (J). (gr. 4-8). 1993. pap. 4.95 (*0-8361-3614-4*) Herald Pr.

— Time to Fly. LC 91-14393. 104p. (Orig.). (J). (gr. 4-8). 1991. pap. 5.95 (*0-8361-3560-1*) Herald Pr.

Lansing, Marion F. Against All Odds. LC 78-84318. (Essay Index Reprint Ser.). 1977. 21.95 (*0-8369-1149-0*) Ayer.

— Liberators & Heroes of Mexico & Central America. LC 72-152186. (Essay Index Reprint Ser.). 1977. reprint ed. 28.95 (*0-8369-2237-9*) Ayer.

— Liberators & Heroes of South America. LC 76-156675. (Essay Index Reprint Ser.). 1977. reprint ed. 31.95 (*0-8369-2321-9*) Ayer.

Lansing, Mary R. City Tales. 1994. 8.95 (*0-8062-4806-8*) Carlton.

Lansing, Nan. Christmas Customs Cookbook. 346p. 1993. lib. bdg. write for info. (*0-9637976-3-8*) Nickoli Pub.

Lansing, Robert. Big Four, & Others of the Peace Conference. LC 73-177961. (Essay Index Reprint Ser.). 1977. reprint ed. 21.95 (*0-8369-2556-4*) Ayer.

— Peace Negotiations: A Personal Narrative. LC 74-110852. (Illus.). 328p. 1971. reprint ed. text ed. 59.75 (*0-8371-4519-8*, LAPN, Greenwood Pr) Greenwood.

— War Memoirs of Robert Lansing, Secretary of State. LC 78-110853. 383p. 1971. reprint ed. text ed. 65.00 (*0-8371-4520-1*, LAWM, Greenwood Pr) Greenwood.

Lansing, Ronald. Juggernaut: The Whitman Massacre Trial, 1850. 140p. 1993. pap. 15.95 (*0-9635086-0-1*) Ninth Judicial CHS.

Lansing, Stephen. The Balinese. Spindler, George & Spindler, Louise, eds. (Case Studies in Anthropology). (Illus.). 168p. (C). 1995. pap. text ed. write for info. (*0-15-500240-6*) HB Coll Pubs.

Lansky. Industrial Pneumatic Control. (Fluid Power & Control Ser.: Vol. 6). 264p. 1986. 120.00 (*0-8247-7494-9*) Dekker.

Lansky, Amy, ed. Foundations of Automatic Planning: The Classical Approach & Beyond: Papers from the 1993 Spring Symposium. (Technical Reports). (Illus.). 168p. (Orig.). (C). 1993. spiral bd. 25.00 (*0-929280-40-7*) Amer Artificial.

Lansky, Amy, jt. ed. see Georgeff, Michael.

Lansky, Bruce. A Bad Case of the Giggles: Kid's Favorite Funny Poems. 1994. pap. 14.00 (*0-671-89982-1*) Meadowbrook.

— A Bad Case of the Giggles: Kid's Favorite Funny Poems. LC 94-3336. (Illus.). (J). 1994. 14.00 (*0-88166-213-5*, 0671899821) Meadowbrook.

— Best Baby Name Book. rev. ed. 1989. pap. write for info. (*0-318-65142-4*) S&S Trade.

— The Best Baby Name Book in the Whole Wide World. LC 84-6632. 140p. 1990. reprint ed. pap. 5.00 (*0-915658-17-8*) Meadowbrook.

— Funny Side of Parenthood. 1994. pap. 5.95 (*0-671-88444-1*) Meadowbrook.

— Moms Say the Funniest Things: A Collection of Motherly Wit & Wisdom. LC 90-26455. (Illus.). 110p. 1992. pap. 6.00 (*0-88166-178-3*) Meadowbrook.

— Mother Murphy's Law. LC 86-5240. 96p. 1986. pap. 4.50 (*0-88166-080-9*) Meadowbrook.

— Mother Murphy's Law. 1986. 4.50 (*0-671-62274-9*) S&S Trade.

— The New Adventures of Mother Goose: Gentle Rhymes for Happy Times. (Illus.). 32p. (J). (ps-k). 1993. pap. 15. 00 (*0-671-87288-5*) S&S Trade.

— The New Adventures of Mother Goose: Gentle Rhymes for Happy Times. (Illus.). 32p. (J). 1993. 15.00 (*1-881662-01-2*) Meadowbrook.

— New Rhymes about Animals. 1995. pap. 4.95 (*0-671-51980-8*) Meadowbrook.

— New Rhymes about Animals: The New Adventures of Mother Goose Board Book Collection. (Illus.). 1995. bds. 4.95 (*0-88116-228-0*) Meadowbrook.

— New Rhymes for Bedtime. 1995. pap. 4.95 (*0-671-51978-6*) S&S Trade.

— New Rhymes for Bedtime: The New Adventures of Mother Goose Board Book Collection. (Illus.). 1995. bds. 4.95 (*0-88116-226-4*) Meadowbrook.

— New Rhymes for Mealtime. 1995. pap. 4.95 (*0-671-51979-4*) S&S Trade.

— New Rhymes for Mealtime: The New Adventures of Mother Goose Board Book Collection. (Illus.). 1995. bds. 4.95 (*0-88116-225-6*) Meadowbrook.

— New Rhymes for Playtime. 1995. pap. 4.95 (*0-671-51977-8*) S&S Trade.

— New Rhymes for Playtime: The New Adventures of Mother Goose Board Book Collection. (Illus.). 1995. bds. 4.95 (*0-88116-227-2*) Meadowbrook.

— Ten Thousand Baby Names. LC 85-717. 144p. 1985. pap. 3.50 (*0-88166-067-1*) Meadowbrook.

— 35,000+ Baby Names. LC 95-10295. 1995. pap. write for info. (*0-88166-216-X*) Meadowbrook.

— Twenty-Five Thousand Baby Names. 1995. pap. 4.95 (*0-671-51975-1*) Meadowbrook.

Lansky, Bruce, comp. If We'd Wanted Quiet, We Would Have Raised Goldfish: Poems for Parents. (Illus.). 80p. 1994. pap. 12.00 (*0-671-89457-9*) Meadowbrook.

— Kids Pick the Funniest Poems. LC 91-31072. (Illus.). 120p. (J). 1991. 14.00 (*0-88166-149-X*) Meadowbrook.

***Lansky, Bruce, ed. & Burch, Stephen.** Girls to the Rescue: Tales from Around the World. (Illus.). 96p. 1995. pap. 3.95 (*0-671-89979-1*) S&S Trade.

***Lansky, Bruce, sel.** For Better & for Worse: The Best Quotes about Marriage. 1995. pap. 6.00 (*0-88116-231-0*) Meadowbrook.

— For Better & for Worse: The Best Quotes about Marriage. LC 94-49093. 1995. 6.00 (*0-88166-231-3*) Meadowbrook.

— For Better & for Worse: The Best Quotes about Marriage. (Illus.). 1995. pap. 6.00 (*0-671-52702-9*) Meadowbrook.

— The Funny Side of Parenthood. (Illus.). 112p. 1994. pap. 5.95 (*0-88166-206-2*) Meadowbrook.

— If We'd Wanted Quiet, We Would Have Raised Goldfish: Poems for Parents. (Illus.). 96p. 1994. 12.00 (*0-88166-210-0*) Meadowbrook.

Lansky, Bruce & Jones, K. L. Dads Say the Dumbest Things. LC 89-29067. 112p. 1989. pap. 6.00 (*0-88166-131-7*) Meadowbrook.

Lansky, Bruce & Sinrod, Barry. The Baby Name Personality Survey. LC 88-27142. 230p. 1990. pap. 7.00 (*0-88166-164-3*) Meadowbrook.

— The Baby Name Personality Survey: Personality Profiles of the 1,500 Most Popular Names. 1990. pap. 8.00 (*0-671-68382-9*) Meadowbrook.

Lansky, Bryna. Tomorrow's Retiree: A Planning & Resource Publication. (Northeast Edition - 1990-1992 Ser.). 1990. pap. 12.95 (*0-9618885-0-4*) Tomorrows Retiree.

Lansky, Bryna, ed. Tomorrow's Retiree: A National Publication of Local Resources. (Midwest Edition - 1993-1994 Ser.). 144p. 1993. pap. 14.95 (*0-9618885-2-0*) Tomorrows Retiree.

— Tomorrow's Retiree: A National Publication of Local Resources. (West Edition - 1993-1994 Ser.). 1993. pap. 14.95 (*0-9618885-4-7*) Tomorrows Retiree.

— Tomorrow's Retiree: A National Publication of Local Resources. (South Edition - 1993-1994 Ser.). 1993. pap. 14.95 (*0-9618885-3-9*) Tomorrows Retiree.

— Tomorrow's Retiree: A National Publication of Local Resources. rev. ed. (Northeast Edition - 1993-1994 Ser.). 144p. 1993. pap. 14.95 (*0-9618885-1-2*) Tomorrows Retiree.

***Lansky, Melvin & Morrison, Andrew, eds.** New Perspectives on Shame. 1995. write for info. (*0-88163-169-8*) Analytic Pr.

Lansky, Melvin R. Fathers Who Fail: Shame & Psychopathology in the Family System. 272p. 1992. 36. 00 (*0-88163-105-1*) Analytic Pr.

Lansky, Melvin R., ed. Essential Papers on Dreams. (Essential Papers in Psychology). 488p. 1992. text ed. 60.00 (*0-8147-5061-3*); pap. text ed. 25.00 (*0-8147-5062-1*) NYU Pr.

— Family Approaches to Major Psychiatric Disorders. LC 85-18494. (Clinical Insights Ser.). 169p. reprint ed. pap. 48.20 (*0-8357-7838-X*, 2036212) Bks Demand.

***Lansky, Melvin R. & Bley, Carol R.** Posttraumatic Nightmares: Psychodynamic Explorations. LC 94-43415. 208p. 1995. 29.95 (*0-88163-193-0*) Analytic Pr.

Lansky, Mitch. Beyond the Beauty Strip: Saving What's Left of Our Forests. (Illus.). 400p. (Orig.). 1992. 35.00 (*0-88448-103-4*); pap. 19.95 (*0-88448-094-1*) Tilbury Hse.

Lansky, Vicki. Another Use for...101 Common Household Items. (Illus.). 160p. (Orig.). 1991. pap. 6.95 (*0-916773-30-2*) Book Peddlers.

— Baby Proofing Basics: How to Keep Your Child Safe. 150p. (Orig.). 1991. pap. 5.95 (*0-916773-28-0*) Book Peddlers.

— Baking Soda: Over Five Hundred Fabulous, Fun & Frugal Uses You've Probably Never Thought Of. (Illus.). 120p. (Orig.). 1995. pap. 6.95 (*0-916773-42-6*) Book Peddlers.

— The Best of Vicki Lansky's Practical Parenting. 84p. (Orig.). 1987. pap. 5.95 (*0-916773-05-1*) Book Peddlers.

— Birthday Parties: Best Party Tips & Ideas for Ages 1-8. (Illus.). 160p. 1989. reprint ed. pap. 8.95 (*0-916773-36-1*) Book Peddlers.

— Dear Babysitter Handbook. 60p. (J). (gr. 7 up). 1990. pap. 4.95 (*0-916773-16-7*) Book Peddlers.

— Don't Throw That Out! A Pennywise Parents Guide to Creative Uses for over 200 Household Items: A Pennywise Parents Guide for Creative Uses to over 200 Household Items. (Illus.). 112p. (Orig.). 1994. pap. 6.95 (*0-916773-40-X*) Book Peddlers.

— Feed Me, I'm Yours. 176p. 1982. mass mkt. 4.99 (*0-553-27251-9*) Bantam.

— Feed Me! I'm Yours. rev. ed. LC 86-8364. 132p. 1986. spiral bd. 8.00 (*0-88166-072-8*) Meadowbrook.

— Feed Me! I'm Yours. rev. ed. LC 86-8364. (Illus.). 130p. 1994. spiral bd. 8.00 (*0-88166-208-9*, 0671884433) Meadowbrook.

— Games Babies Play: From Birth to Twelve Months. 110p. (Orig.). 1993. pap. 8.95 (*0-916773-33-7*) Book Peddlers.

— Getting Your Child to Sleep...& Back to Sleep: Tips for Parents of Infants, Toddlers & Preschoolers. rev. ed. (Illus.). 140p. (Orig.). 1991. reprint ed. pap. 6.95 (*0-916773-19-1*) Book Peddlers.

— Koko Bear's Big Earache: Preparing for Ear Tube Surgery. 32p. (Orig.). (J). (ps). 1990. pap. 4.95 (*0-916773-26-4*) Book Peddlers.

— Koko Bear's New Babysitter. 32p. (Orig.). (J). (ps). 1989. pap. 3.95 (*0-916773-24-8*) Book Peddlers.

— Koko Bear's Potty. (J). 1986. pap. 3.99 (*0-553-34444-7*) Bantam.

— A New Baby at Koko Bear's House. (Illus.). 32p. (Orig.). (J). 1991. reprint ed. pap. 5.95 (*0-916773-22-1*) Book Peddlers.

— One Hundred One Ways to Be a Special Dad. LC 92-41271. 112p. 1993. 6.95 (*0-8092-3820-9*) Contemp Bks.

— 101 Ways to Be a Special Mom. (Illus.). 112p. 1995. 6.95 (*0-8092-3530-7*) Contemp Bks.

— One Hundred One Ways to Make Your Child Feel Special. (Illus.). 120p. (Orig.). 1991. 6.95 (*0-8092-3997-3*) Contemp Bks.

An Asterisk (*) at the beginning of an entry indicates that the title is appearing in BIP for the first time.

L

— One Hundred One Ways to Say I Love You. 1991. pap. 6.95 (*0-671-72350-2*) S&S Trade.
— One Hundred One Ways to Tell Your Child "I Love You" (Illus.). 112p. 1988. 6.95 (*0-8092-4527-2*) Contemp Bks.
— Practical Parenting Tips. enl. rev. ed. LC 92-17149. (Illus.). 192p. 1992. pap. 8.00 (*0-88166-192-9*) Meadowbrook.
— Practical Parenting Tips for the First Five Years. 1992. pap. 8.00 (*0-671-79205-9*) S&S Trade.
— The Taming of the C. A. N. D. Y. Monster. rev. ed. 156p. 1988. reprint ed. lib. bdg. 7.95 (*0-916773-08-6*); reprint ed. pap. 7.95 (*0-916773-07-8*) Book Peddlers.
— Toilet Training: A Practical Guide to Daytime & Nighttime Training. rev. ed. LC 92-35022. 1984. pap. 4.99 (*0-553-37140-1*) Bantam.
— Transparent Tape: Over 350 Super, Simple & Surprising Uses You've Probably Never Thought Of. (Illus.). 108p. 1995. pap. 6.95 (*0-916773-44-2*) Book Peddlers.
— Trouble-Free Travel with Children: Helpful Hints for Parents on the Go. 2nd rev. ed. (Illus.). 156p. 1991. reprint ed. pap. 6.95 (*0-916773-14-0*) Book Peddlers.
— Vicki Lansky's Divorce Book. 1991. pap. 4.99 (*0-451-16977-8*, Sig) NAL-Dutton.
— Vicki Lansky's Sing along Birthday Fun Book & Cassette. 48p. (J). (ps-1). 1989. pap. 5.95 (*0-590-63234-5*) Scholastic Inc.
— Welcoming Your Second Baby. 120p. 1990. pap. 5.95 (*0-916773-12-4*) Book Peddlers.
Lansky, Vicki, jt. auth. see Consumer Guide Editors.
Lansky, Vicky. Microwave Cooking for Kids. (J). 1992. 6.95 (*0-590-44203-1*) Scholastic Inc.
Lansky, Vicky, jt. auth. see Consumer Guide Editors.
Lansky, Z. J., jt. auth. see Pippenger, John J.
Lansley, Alfred, et al. Chula Vista: The Early Years, Vol. 2. (Illus.). 80p. (Orig.). Date not set. pap. 7.95 (*0-938711-17-2*) Tecolote Pubns.
Lansley, John, jt. ed. see Jones, Helen.
Lansley, P. & Harlow, P., eds. Managing Construction Worldwide, 3 vols., Set. 1300p. 1988. lib. bdg. 235.00 (*0-419-14030-1*, E & FN Spon) Routledge Chapman & Hall.
Lanslots, D. I. The Primitive Church. LC 79-67862. 295p. 1980. reprint ed. pap. 8.50 (*0-89555-134-9*) TAN Bks Pubs.
***Lansner.** How Money Works. 1995. pap. text ed. 19.95 (*1-56276-291-5*) Ziff-Davis.
Lanson, Gerald, jt. auth. see Stephens, Mitchell.
Lanson, Gustave. Bossuet. Mayer, J. P., ed. LC 78-67363. (European Political Thought Ser.). (FRE.). 1979. reprint ed. lib. bdg. 40.95 (*0-405-11711-6*) Ayer.
— Corneille. LC 75-41170. reprint ed. 36.00 (*0-404-14797-6*) AMS Pr.
Lansverk, Marvin D. The Wisdom of Many, the Vision of One: The Proverbs of William Blake. LC 93-35971. (American University Studies, IV, English Language & Literature: Vol. 142). 215p. (C). 1994. text ed. 38.95 (*0-8204-1781-5*) P Lang Pubs.
Lant, A. F., ed. Advanced Medicine, Eleven: Proceedings of the 11th Annual Symposium on Advanced Medicine 1975. (Illus.). 450p. (Orig.). 1975. pap. text ed. 42.00 (*0-8464-0112-6*) Beekman Pubs.
Lant, A. F., ed. see Advanced Medical Symposia Staff & Royal College of Physicians Staff.
Lant, Antonia C. Blackout: Reinventing Women for Wartime British Cinema. (Illus.). 262p. 1991. text ed. 55.00 (*0-691-05540-8*); pap. text ed. 16.95 (*0-691-00828-0*) Princeton U Pr.
Lant, Jeffrey. Cash Copy: How to Offer Your Products & Services so Your Prospects Buy Them ... Now! 3rd ed. 480p. 1992. pap. 35.00 (*0-940374-23-4*) JLA Pubns.
— Development Today: A Fund Raising guide for Nonprofit Organizations. 5th ed. 282p. 1993. pap. 24.95 (*0-940374-25-0*) JLA Pubns.
— How to Make a Whole Lot More Than One Million Dollars Writing, Commissioning, Publishing & Selling "How-to" Information. 2nd rev. ed. 552p. 1993. 39.95 (*0-940374-26-9*) JLA Pubns.
— How to Make at Least One Hundred Thousand Dollars Every Year As a Successful Consultant in Your Own Field. 2nd ed. 316p. 1992. pap. 35.00 (*0-940374-21-8*) JLA Pubns.
— Money Talks: The Complete Guide to Creating a Profitable Workshop or Seminar in Any Field. 3rd rev. ed. 302p. (Orig.). 1995. 35.00 (*0-940374-27-7*) JLA Pubns.
— Multi-Level Money: The Complete Guide to Generating, Closing & Working with All the Prospects You Need to Make Real Money Every Month in Network Marketing. 2nd ed. 250p. (Orig.). 1995. pap. 19.95 (*0-940374-28-5*) JLA Pubns.
— No More Cold Calls. 1993. pap. 39.95 (*0-940374-24-2*) JLA Pubns.
— The Unabashed Self-Promoter's Guide: What Every Man, Woman, Child & Organization in America Needs to Know About Getting Ahead by Exploiting the Media. 2nd ed. (Enterprise Ser.: Vol. 2). 366p. (Orig.). 1992. pap. 35.00 (*0-940374-18-8*) JLA Pubns.
Lant, Theresa. Executive Decision Making. LC 94-70912. 120p. (Orig.). 1994. pap. text ed. 15.00 (*0-910586-97-7*) Finan Exec.
Lanteri, Edouard. Modelling & Sculpting Animals. 352p. 1985. reprint ed. pap. 6.95 (*0-486-25007-5*) Dover.
— Modelling & Sculpting the Human Figure. 480p. 1985. reprint ed. pap. 8.95 (*0-486-25006-7*) Dover.
Lanterman, E., ed. see Society for Applied Spectroscopy Staff.
Lanterman, Ray, jt. auth. see Kyselka, Will.
Lantermann, Susanne, jt. auth. see Lantermann, Werner.
Lantermann, W., jt. auth. see Brockmann, J.
Lantermann, Werner. New Parrot Handbook. (Illus.). 144p. 1986. pap. 8.95 (*0-8120-3729-4*) Barron.
Lantermann, Werner & Lantermann, Susanne. Amazon Parrots. (Pet Owner's Manuals Ser.). 64p. 1988. pap. 5.95 (*0-8120-4035-X*) Barron.
— Cockatoos. (Illus.). 56p. 1989. pap. 5.95 (*0-8120-4159-3*) Barron.
Lantero, Erminie H. Feminine Aspects of Divinity. LC 73-84214. 36p. (Orig.). 1973. pap. 3.00 (*0-87574-191-6*) Pendle Hill.
Lanthall, Lisa-Theresa. My Home. (Illus.). (J). (ps). 1994. 5.99 (*0-553-09656-7*) Bantam.
Lanthony, Phillippe. Dictionnaire du Strabisme: Phisiologie et Clinique. 202p. (FRE.). 1983. 79.95 (*0-8288-1813-4*, M15412) Fr & Eur.
Lantier, Raymond, jt. auth. see Breuil, Henri.
Lantier-Sampon, Patricia. Airplanes. LC 91-50344. (Wings Ser.). (Illus.). 24p. (J). (ps-2). 1993. lib. bdg. 15.93 (*0-8368-0539-9*) Gareth Stevens Inc.
— Birds. LC 91-50345. (Wings Ser.). (Illus.). 24p. (J). (ps-2). 1991. lib. bdg. 15.93 (*0-8368-0541-0*) Gareth Stevens Inc.
— Flying Animals. LC 91-50346. (Wings Ser.). (Illus.). 24p. (J). (ps-2). 1991. lib. bdg. 15.93 (*0-8368-0540-2*) Gareth Stevens Inc.
— Flying Insects. LC 91-50347. (Wings Ser.). (Illus.). 24p. (J). (ps-2). 1991. lib. bdg. 15.93 (*0-8368-0542-9*) Gareth Stevens Inc.
— Wings, 4 vols., Set. (Illus.). 24p. (J). (ps-2). 1994. lib. bdg. 63.72 (*0-8368-0755-3*) Gareth Stevens Inc.
Lantier-Sampon, Patricia, adapt. The Wonder of Loons. LC 92-16945. (Animal Wonders Ser.). (J). 1992. lib. bdg. 18.60 (*0-8368-0856-8*) Gareth Stevens Inc.
Lantiere, Joseph. The Magician's Wand - An Illustrated History. (Illus.). 55p. (Orig.). 1990. pap. 7.00 (*0-9627695-2-5*) J Lantiere Bks.
— Professional Tarot Reading Secrets. (Illus.). 44p. (Orig.). 1992. pap. 12.50 (*0-9627695-3-3*) J Lantiere Bks.
— Springboards of Superstition. (Illus.). 58p. (Orig.). 1990. pap. 7.00 (*0-9627695-0-9*) J Lantiere Bks.
Lantigua, John. Burn Season. 1990. mass mkt. 4.50 (*0-06-100097-3*, Harp PBks) HarpC.
Lanting, Frans. Okavango: Africa's Last Eden. Eckstrom, Christine, ed. LC 93-10296. 1993. 45.00 (*0-8118-0527-1*) Chronicle Bks.
Lanting, Frans, photos. Madagascar: A World Out of Time. 144p. 1990. 40.00 (*0-89381-422-9*) Aperture.
Lanting, Frans, jt. photos see Cavagnaro, David.
Lanting, Fred L. The Total German Shepherd Dog. LC 89-18386. (Illus.). 368p. 1990. 34.95 (*0-931866-43-X*) Alpine Pubns.
***Lantis, David, et al.** California. 544p. (C). 1995. per., pap. text ed. 45.95 (*0-7872-1018-8*) Kendall-Hunt.
Lantis, David W., et al. California: Land of Contrast. 3rd ed. 496p. 1981. per. 16.95 (*0-8403-2493-6*) Kendall-Hunt.
— California: The Pacific Connection. (Illus.). 595p. (C). 1988. 35.00 (*0-9629915-1-1*); pap. text ed. 29.95 (*0-9620015-2-X*) Creekside Pr.
Lantis, Margaret. Alaskan Eskimo Ceremonialism. LC 84-45514. (American Ethnological Society Monographs: No. 11). 1988. reprint ed. 22.50 (*0-404-62911-3*) AMS Pr.
— Eskimo Childhood & Interpersonal Relationships. LC 84-45528. (American Ethnological Society Monographs: No. 33). 1988. reprint ed. 32.00 (*0-404-62932-6*) AMS Pr.
***Lanto, Sandra & Spera, Stefanie.** From Stress to Strength: Achieving Wellness at Work & in Life. 160p. 1995. pap. 11.00 (*1-880030-42-X*) DBM Pub.
Lantolf, James P. & Appel, Gabriela, eds. Vygotskian Approaches to Second Language Research. LC 93-49680. (Second Language Learning Ser.). 221p. 1994. 42.50 (*1-56750-024-2*); pap. 22.95 (*1-56750-025-0*) Ablex Pub.
Lantolf, James P. & Labarca, Angela. Research in Second Language Learning: Focus on the Classroom. DiPietro, Robert J., ed. LC 86-22300. (Delaware Symposia on Language Studies: Vol. 6). 240p. (C). 1987. text ed. 39.50 (*0-89391-363-4*) Ablex Pub.
Lantolf, James P., ed. see Colloquium on Hispanic & Luso-Brazilian Linguistics Staff.
Lanton, Sandy. Baby's Dinner. (Everyday Concept Ser.). (Illus.). 32p. (J). (ps-2). Date not set. 11.95 (*1-56065-145-8*) Capstone Pr.
— Bedtime. (Everyday Concept Ser.). (Illus.). 32p. (J). (ps-2). Date not set. 11.95 (*1-56065-141-5*) Capstone Pr.
— Daddy's Chair. LC 90-44908. (Illus.). 32p. (J). (gr. k-4). 1991. 12.95 (*0-929371-51-8*) Kar Ben.
— The Girl Who Wouldn't See. (Illus.). 32p. (J). (ps-2). Date not set. 11.95 (*1-56065-140-7*) Capstone Pr.
— Is That Our Car? (Everyday Concept Ser.). (Illus.). 32p. (J). (ps-2). Date not set. 11.95 (*1-56065-143-1*) Capstone Pr.
— That's Not the Way Mommy Does It. (Illus.). 32p. (J). (ps-2). Date not set. 11.95 (*1-56065-142-3*) Capstone Pr.
Lantos, I., jt. auth. see Hatala, P.
Lantran, Jean-Marie, jt. auth. see Abeille, Bernard.
Lantz, Alma E., et al. Re-Entry Programs for Female Scientists. LC 79-25364. 220p. 1980. text ed. 49.95 (*0-275-90510-1*, C0510, Praeger Pubs) Greenwood.
***Lantz, David L.** Bill Clinton You're No John F. Kennedy. (Illus.). 151p. (Orig.). Date not set. pap. text ed. 9.95 (*0-9639611-0-1*) Joshua Hse.
Lantz, Fran, et al. The One & Only, Brutally Honest, No Holds Barred, Tell It Like It Is Santa Barbara Restaurant Guide. 62p. (Orig.). 1988. pap. 4.95 (*0-317-91300-X*) Elan Pr.
Lantz, Frances. Mom, There's a Pig in My Bed! 144p. (Orig.). (J). (gr. 4). 1992. pap. 3.50 (*0-380-76112-2*, Camelot) Avon.
— Rock, Rap, & Rad: How to Be a Rock Or Rap Star. 224p. (Orig.). (YA). 1992. mass mkt. 3.99 (*0-380-76793-7*, Flare) Avon.
Lantz, Francess. Marissa's Dance. LC 93-43225. (Boys' School Girls Ser.). (Illus.). 128p. (J). (gr. 3-7). 1994. pap. text ed. 2.95 (*0-8167-3475-5*) Troll Assocs.
— Randy's Raiders. LC 93-44345. (Boys' School Girls Ser.). (Illus.). 176p. (J). (gr. 3-6). 1994. pap. 3.95 (*0-8167-3474-7*) Troll Assocs.
Lantz, Herman R. & Snyder, Eloise C. Marriage: An Examination of the Man-Woman Relationship. 2nd ed. LC 69-16038. (Illus.). 278p. reprint ed. pap. 79.30 (*0-317-09743-1*, 2013722) Bks Demand.
Lantz, James E. Existential Family Therapy: Using the Concepts of Viktor Frankl. LC 93-19993. 224p. 1994. 30.00 (*0-87668-578-5*) Aronson.
Lantz, Jim, jt. auth. see Harper, Karen.
***Lantz, John.** Nursing Care of the Elderly. 3rd ed. LC 95-13836. 290p. 1995. pap. text ed. 49.95 (*1-878025-70-8*) Western Schls.
Lantz, John, ed. Nursing Care of the Elderly. 2nd ed. LC 94-60084. 288p. (Orig.). (C). 1993. pap. text ed. 49.95 (*1-878025-46-5*) Western Schls.
Lantz, K. A., ed. see Leskov, Nikolai S.
Lantz, Karen, et al. Language Lessons for the Cirriculum, 3 vols. (Illus.). 1991. Fifth Grade Math. spiral bd. 27.95 (*1-55999-175-5*); Fifth Grade Language Arts. spiral bd. 27.95 (*1-55999-176-3*); Fifth Grade Science - Social Studies. spiral bd. 27.95 (*1-55999-177-1*) LinguiSystems.
— Language Lessons for the Cirriculum, 3 vols., Set. (Illus.). 1991. spiral bd. 74.85 (*1-55999-189-5*) LinguiSystems.
Lantz, Kenneth, tr. see Dostoyevsky, Fyodor.
Lantz, Norma R. After Stephen: From Hurting to Healed. LC 87-70625. (Illus.). 175p. (Orig.). 1987. pap. 9.95 (*0-942419-00-6*) Ana Pub.
Lantz, Peggy S. & Hale, Wendy A. The Young Naturalist's Guide to Florida. LC 94-15045. (Illus.). 128p. 1994. pap. 16.95 (*1-56164-051-4*) Pineapple Pr.
Lantz, Peggy S., ed. see Huegel, Craig N.
Lantz, Raymond C. Ottawa & Chippewa Indians of Michigan, 1855-1868: Including Some Swan Creek & Black River of the Sac & Fox Agency for the Years 1857, 1858 & 1865. x, 107p. (Orig.). 1993. pap. text ed. 14.00 (*1-55613-760-5*) Heritage Bk.
— Ottawa & Chippewa Indians of Michigan, 1870-1909. 296p. 1991. pap. 21.00 (*1-55613-531-9*) Heritage Bk.
— Potawatomi: Indians of Michigan, 1843-1904. 92p. 1992. pap. text ed. 14.00 (*1-55613-619-6*) Heritage Bk.
— Seminole Indians of Florida 1850-1874. 415p. (Orig.). 1994. pap. text ed. 30.00 (*0-7884-0034-7*) Heritage Bk.
Lantz, Walter. Chosen People, Promised Land: A Drama of the Spirit. 48p. 1982. 7.50 (*0-9610364-0-0*) W D Lantz.
— Chosen People, Promised Land: A Drama of the Spirit, No. I. suppl. ed. 17p. 1983. Supplement I, 1983, 17 pg. 2.50 (*0-9610364-1-9*) W D Lantz.
— Chosen People, Promised Land: A Drama of the Spirit, No. II. suppl. ed. 34p. 1983. Supplement II, 1983, 34 pg. 5.00 (*0-9610364-2-7*) W D Lantz.
Lantzeff, George V. & Pierce, Richard A. Eastward to Empire: Exploration & Conquest on the Russian Open Frontier, to Seventeen Fifty. LC 72-82244. 1973. 28.50 (*0-7735-0133-9*) Limestone Pr.
Lantzy, M. Louise, comp. Individuals with Disabilities Education Act: An Annotated Guide to Its Literature & Resources, 1980-1991. LC 92-9676. xi, 148p. 1992. ring bd. 37.50 (*0-8377-9274-6*) Rothman.
Lanusse, Armand, ed. Les Cenelles: Choix de Poesies Indigenes. (B. E. Ser.: No. 53). (FRE.). 1845. 30.00 (*0-8115-3004-3*) Periodicals Srv.
Lanuti, W. Vito. J. Williams & Sons Wedding Guide & Directory. Kukuda, Kenneth J., ed. (Orange County Edition (1990) Ser.). 178p. (Orig.). 1990. pap. 12.95 (*0-9626371-0-6*) J Williams & Sons.
Lanuza, Jose L., jt. auth. see Burri, Rene.
Lanyen, Milton & Bulmore, Lawrence. Cinnabar Hills. 1967. 22.20 (*0-912314-20-6*) Academy Santa Clara.
Lanyer, Aemelia. The Poems of Aemelia Lanyer: Salve Deus Rex Judaeorum. Woods, Susanne, ed. (Women Writers in English Ser.). (Illus.). 192p. 1993. 32.50 (*0-19-508037-8*); pap. 12.95 (*0-19-508361-X*) OUP.
Lanyi, Andrew A. Confessions of a Stockbroker: You, Too Can Find Tomorrow's Blue Chips Before Wall Street Finds Them. LC 92-25479. 1992. 19.95 (*0-13-175746-6*) P-H.
Lanyi, Gabriel. Manging Documentation Projects in an Imperfect World. 1994. pap. text ed. 29.95 (*0-935470-74-3*) Battelle.
Lanyi, M. Diagnosis & Differential Diagnosis of Breast Calcifications. (Illus.). 270p. 1987. 124.00 (*0-387-16949-0*) Spr-Verlag.
Lanyon, Barbara P., jt. auth. see Lanyon, Richard I.
Lanyon, Ellen. Transformations I: 1973-74. 1977. pap. 12.50 (*0-89439-005-8*) Printed Matter.
***Lanyon, Richard I. & Goodstein, Leonard.** Personality Assessment. 3rd ed. (Series on Personality Processes). Date not set. text ed. write for info. (*0-471-55562-2*) Wiley.
Lanyon, Richard I. & Goodstein, Leonard D. Personality Assessment. 2nd ed. 328p. (C). 1992. pap. text ed. 24.50 (*0-8191-8487-X*) U Pr of Amer.
Lanyon, Richard I. & Lanyon, Barbara P. Behavior Therapy: A Clinical Introduction. LC 77-83022. (Topics in Clinical Psychology Ser.: 7). 1978. pap. text ed. write for info. (*0-201-04100-6*) Addison-Wesley.
— Therapy: A Clinical Introduction. 192p. (C). 1978. pap. text ed. write for info. (*0-394-34770-6*) Random.
Lanyon, Richard I., jt. ed. see Goodstein, Leonard D.
Lanyon, W. E. & Tavolga, W. N. Animal Sound & Communications. 1960. 12.50 (*0-934454-07-8*) Lubrecht & Cramer.
Lanyon, Walter C. Abo Allah, Teacher, Healer. 77p. 1975. spiral bd. 4.40 (*0-7873-0533-2*) Mokelumne.
— And It Was Told of a Certain Potter. LC 78-163038. (Short Story Index Reprint Ser.). 1977. reprint ed. 13.95 (*0-8369-3952-2*) Ayer.
— Demonstration. reprint ed. 5.00 (*0-685-71646-5*); reprint ed. spiral bd. 5.00 (*0-7873-1000-X*) Mokelumne.
— London Notes & Lectures. 2nd ed. 213p. 1972. reprint ed. spiral bd. 8.80 (*0-7873-0534-0*) Mokelumne.
Lanyon, Wesley E. The Comparative Biology of the Meadowlarks (Sturnella) in Wisconsin. (Publications of the Nuttall Ornithological Club: No. 1). (Illus.). 66p. 1957. pap. 4.00 (*1-877973-10-6*) Nuttall Ornith.
Lanz, Henry. Physical Basis of Rime: An Essay on the Aesthetics of Sound. LC 69-10115. (Illus.). 365p. 1969. reprint ed. text ed. 65.00 (*0-8371-0136-0*, LABR, Greenwood Pr) Greenwood.
Lanz, K., jt. auth. see Achterberg, E.
Lanz, K., jt. auth. see Ahterberg, E.
***Lanz, Karen.** Employing & Managing People. 176p. (C). 1991. pap. 36.00x (*0-273-03513-4*, Pub. by Pitman Pubng UK) St Mut.
— Hiring & Firing: Employing & Managing People. (Pitman Small Business Bookshelf Ser.). 256p. (Orig.). 1988. pap. 22.50 (*0-273-02826-X*, Pub. by Pitman Pub Ltd UK) Trans-Atl Phila.
***Lanz, Klaus.** The Greenpeace Book of Water. LC 95-30497. (Illus.). 160p. 1995. 35.00 (*0-8069-4212-6*) Sterling.
Lanz, Maria E. Como Leer La Celestina. Date not set. 45.50 (*0-685-69534-4*) Scripta.
Lanza, Anna T. The Heart of Sicily: Recipes & Reminiscences of Life at Regaleali, a Country Estate. LC 92-45598. 1993. 40.00 (*0-517-58961-3*, C P Pubs) Crown Pub Group.
Lanza, Barbara. First Christmas Pop-up Book. (J). (ps-3). 1993. 6.95 (*0-307-12464-9*, Golden Pr) Western Pub.
Lanza, Carmela D. Long Island Girl. (Italian-American Women's Poetry Ser.: No. 3). 20p. (Orig.). 1992. pap. 3.00 (*1-883112-03-6*) Malafemmina.
Lanza, J. Art of Teaching Ballroom Dancing. (Ballroom Dance Ser.). 1986. lib. bdg. 99.95 (*0-8490-3326-8*) Gordon Pr.
Lanza, Janet, jt. auth. see Nelson, Tina.
Lanza, Janet R. & Wilson, Carolyn C. The Word Kit Adolescent: A Program to Build Expressive Vocabulary & Semantic Skills for Adolescents. 270p. 1991. student ed 99.95 (*1-55999-209-3*) LinguiSystems.
Lanza, Janet R., et al. Artic Blends to Go: A Language-Based Articulation Program, 5 bks., Set. 1992. 29.95 (*1-55999-236-0*) LinguiSystems.
— Artic to Go: A Two-in-One Therapy Program: Language Based Articulation Exercises, 5 booklets. 1988. 29.95 (*1-55999-016-3*) LinguiSystems.
Lanza, Joseph. Elevator Music: A Surreal History of Muzak, Easy-Listening, & Other Moodsong. (Illus.). 272p. 1994. 22.00 (*0-312-10540-1*) St Martin.
— Elevator Music: A Surreal History of Muzak, Easy-Listening, & Other Moodsong. 288p. 1995. pap. 11.00 (*0-312-13063-5*) St Martin.
— Fragile Geometry: The Films, Philosophy, & Misadventures of Nicolas Roeg. (Illus.). 176p. 1988. 35.00 (*1-55554-033-3*); pap. 12.95 (*1-55554-034-1*) PAJ Pubns.
Lanza, Michael L. Agrarianism & Reconstruction Politics: The Southern Homestead Act. LC 89-12137. 184p. 1990. text ed. 25.00 (*0-8071-1545-2*) La State U Pr.
***Lanza, Robert, ed.** One World: The Health & Survival of the Human Species in the 21st Century. 1995. 25.00 (*0-929173-16-3*) Health Press.
Lanza, Robert P. & Chick, William L., eds. Immunodulation of Pancreatic Islets, II. 130p. 1994. 89.95 (*1-57059-134-2*, LN9134) CRC Pr.
— Immunoisolation of Pancreatic Islets, III. 130p. 1994. 89.95 (*1-57059-135-0*, LN9135) CRC Pr.
— Procurement of Pancreatic Islets, Vol. I. 130p. 1994. 89.95 (*1-57059-133-4*, LN9133) CRC Pr.
Lanzafame, Raymond, ed. see Rochester General Hospital Laser Group Staff.
Lanzano, jt. auth. see Bodman.
Lanzano, Michael R., jt. auth. see Bodman, Jean W.
Lanzara, Joseph. Paradise Lost: The Novel. 240p. 1994. 24.95 (*0-9639621-4-0*) New Arts Lib.
Lanzarini, G., jt. ed. see Cantarelli, C.
Lanzarone & Kahn, Steven C. Personnel Director's Legal Guide, No. 2745. suppl. ed. 1200p. 1991. Supplement, 1991-1. text ed. 48.00 (*0-7913-1033-7*) Warren Gorham & Lamont.
— Personnel Director's Legal Guide, No. 2745. 2nd ed. 1200p. 1991. Supplemented annually. boxed 126.00 (*0-7913-0373-X*) Warren Gorham & Lamont.
Lanzarone, Michael R. Education Law: The Rights of Students & Teachers, 2 vols, Set. 1200p. Date not set. write for info. (*0-07-036372-2*) McGraw.
Lanzarotti, Sally, ed. see Avery, Virginia.
Lanze, W. Dabi das Abkuerzungsverzeichnis Fuer Den Ingenieur: Index of Abbreviations for Engineers. 2nd ed. 344p. (GER & RUS.). 1981. 75.00 (*0-8288-1164-4*, M15318) Fr & Eur.
Lanzen Harris, Laurie. Twentieth Century Literary Movements Dictionary. (Literary Movements Reference Ser.). 500p. 1995. lib. bdg. 70.00 (*1-55888-426-2*) Omnigraphics Inc.
Lanzen Harris, Laurie & Henderson, Helene, eds. Twentieth Century Literary Movements Index. (Literary Movements Reference Ser.). 419p. 1991. lib. bdg. 70.00 (*1-55888-306-1*) Omnigraphics Inc.
***Lanzer, P. & Roesch, J.** Vascular Diagnostics: Noninvasive & Invasive Techniques-Perinterventional Evaluation. 300p. 1994. 125.00 (*0-387-57939-7*) Spr-Verlag.
Lanzer, P. & Yoganathan, A. P., eds. Vascular Imaging by Color Doppler & Magnetic Resonance. (Illus.). xiii, 338p. 1991. 249.00 (*0-387-53320-6*) Spr-Verlag.

An Asterisk (*) at the beginning of an entry indicates that the title is appearing in BIP for the first time.

Lanzerotti, L. J. & Park, C., eds. Upper Atmosphere Research in Antarctica. (Antarctic Research Ser.: Vol. 29). (Illus.). 264p. 1977. 50.00 (*0-87590-141-7*) Am Geophysical.

Lanzi, G., et al, eds. Headache in Children & Adolescents: Proceedings of the 1st International Symposium on Headache in Children & Adolescents. (International Congress Ser.: No. 833). 372p. 1989. 107.75 (*0-444-81074-9*, Excerpta Medica) Elsevier.

Lanzilloti, Robert F. & Peles, Y. C. Research in Finance: Supplement Management under Government Intervention. 73.25 (*0-89232-427-9*) Jai Pr.

Lanzillotti, Robert F., et al. Phase II in Review: The Price Commission Experience. LC 75-5164. (Brookings INstitution Studies in Wage-Price Policy). 223p. reprint ed. pap. 63.60 (*0-317-26731-0*, 2025387) Bks Demand.

Lanzillotti, Robert F., ed. see Government-Mandated Costs Seminar Staff.

Lanzinger, Klaus. Jason's Voyage: The Search for the Old World in American Literature. A Study of Melville, Hawthorne, Henry James, & Thomas Wolfe. (American University Studies: American Literature: Ser. XXIV, Vol. 16). 243p. (C). 1989. text ed. 40.50 (*0-8204-0975-8*) P Lang Pubs.

***Lanzkowsky, Philip.** Manual of Pediatric Hematology & Oncology. 2nd ed. LC 94-32744. 1994. pap. 99.00 (*0-443-08969-8*) Churchill.

Lanzkowsky, Philip, et al. Manual of Pediatric Hematology & Oncology. LC 89-470. 468p. reprint ed. pap. 133.40 (*0-7837-1613-3*, 2041905) Bks Demand.

Lanzl. Clinical Radiotherapy Physics. 1994. write for info. (*0-8493-6891-X*) CRC Pr.

Lanzl, F., et al. Optics in Complex Systems (Aug 1990, Garmish, FRG), Vol. 1319. 1990. 100.00 (*0-8194-0380-6*) SPIE.

***Lanzmann, Claude.** Shoah: The Complete Text of the Acclaimed Holocaust Film. rev. ed. (Illus.). 208p. 1995. pap. write for info. (*0-306-80665-7*) Da Capo.

Lanzone, R. V. Dizionario Di Mitologia Egizia, 3 vols. 1312p. (ITA.). 1974. reprint ed. 590.00x (*90-272-0931-6*, 0932-4) Benjamins North Am.

— Dizzionario Di Mitologia Egizia, Vol. 4. xv, 205p. 1975. 105.00 (*90-272-0934-0*) Benjamins North Am.

Lao, Kenneth Q. Engineering Optics. (Electrical Engineering Ser.). 1991. text ed. write for info. (*0-442-00685-3*) Van Nos Reinhold.

Lao She. Rickshaw. James, Jean M., tr. LC 79-10658. Orig. Title: Lo-to Hsiang Tzu. (C). 1979. text ed. 12.00 (*0-8248-0616-6*); pap. text ed. 8.95 (*0-8248-0655-7*) UH Pr.

Lao-Tze. The Canon of Reason & Virtue. Carus, Paul, ed. LC 73-21701. 209p. 1974. pap. 6.95 (*0-87548-064-0*) Open Court.

Lao Tze. Treatise on Response & Retribution. Carus, Paul & Suzuki, D. T., trs. LC 06-28775. (Illus.). 139p. 1973. reprint ed. pap. 6.95 (*0-87548-244-9*) Open Court.

Lao-tzu. The Light of China: Selections. 1972. lib. bdg. 250. 00 (*0-87968-534-4*) Krishna Pr.

— Lyrical Translation of Lao Tzu's Tao-Te Ching in English & Korean. LC 90-91956. (Illus.). 300p. (Orig.). pap. 20. 00 (*0-942049-03-9*) One Mind Pr.

Lao Tzu. Tao Te Ching. (Classics Ser.). 1964. mass mkt. 6.95 (*0-14-044131-X*, Penguin Classics) Viking Penguin.

Lao-Tzu. Tao Te Ching. Addiss, Stephen & Lombardo, Stanley, trs. LC 93-21939. (Hackett Classics Ser.). (Illus.). 128p. (Orig.). (C). 1993. lib. bdg. 27.95 (*0-87220-233-X*); pap. text ed. 6.95 (*0-87220-232-1*) Hackett Pub.

***Lao Tzu.** Tao Te Ching. Walker, Brian B., tr. 112p. 1995. 16.95 (*0-312-13190-9*) St Martin.

— Tao Te Ching. 190p. 1987. reprint ed. lib. bdg. 23.95 (*0-89966-610-8*) Buccaneer Bks.

— Tao Te Ching: About the Way of Nature & Its Power. Miles, Thomas H., tr. LC 91-46362. (Illus.). 176p. (Orig.). 1992. pap. 8.95 (*0-89529-506-7*) Avery Pub.

— Tao Te Ching: An Illustrated Journey. LC 93-39655. (Illus.). 104p. 1994. pap. 12.95 (*0-8212-2075-6*) Bulfinch Pr.

— Tao Te Ching: The Classic Book of Integrity & the Way. 1990. 9.95 (*0-553-34935-X*) Bantam.

— The Way of Life. 1955. pap. 4.99 (*0-451-62674-5*, Ment) NAL-Dutton.

— Way of Life: Tao Te Ching. Blakney, R. B., tr. 1955. pap. 3.95 (*0-451-62563-3*, Ment) NAL-Dutton.

— Wen-tzu: Understanding the Mysteries. Cleary, Thomas, tr. LC 92-53700. (Dragon Editions Ser.). Orig. Title: Further Teachings of Lao-tzu. 168p. (Orig.). 1992. pap. 11.00 (*0-87773-862-9*) Shambhala Pubns.

Lao-zi. Dao de Jing: The Old Sage's Classic of the Way of Virtue. Byrne, Patrick M., tr. 162p. 1991. pap. 15.00 (*0-89540-160-6*, SB-160) Sun Pub.

Laor, Nathaniel & Agassi, Joseph. Diagnosis: Philosophical & Medical Perspectives. (C). 1990. lib. bdg. 79.00 (*0-7923-0845-X*) Kluwer Ac.

Laor, Nathaniel, jt. ed. see Jarvie, I. C.

Laosa, Luis M. & Sigel, Irving E., eds. Families As Learning Environments for Children. LC 82-18062. 414p. 1982. 65.00 (*0-306-40939-9*, Plenum Pr) Plenum.

Laosa, Luis M., jt. ed. see Sigel, Irving E.

Lap, M. Tamil-French Dictionary: Vocabulaire Tamoul-Francais. (FRE & TAM.). 1984. 24.95 (*0-8288-1727-8*, F109490) Fr & Eur.

LAP Staff. Catalogue of Films & Videos in the British Medical Association Library. 347p. 1993. 60.00 (*1-85604-082-8*, LAP0828, Pub. by Lib Assn Pub UK) UNIPUB.

Lapadula, Dorothy. Doing It Right: Making the Most of Your Life. 1990. 16.95 (*0-944007-57-0*) Sure Sellers.

— Doing It Right ... Now: Life Advice & More - for the Enterprising Woman. 1992. pap. 8.99 (*1-56171-165-9*, S P I Bks) Sure Sellers.

Lapage, S. P., et al, eds. International Code of Nomenclature of Bacteria, & Statutes of the International Committee on Systematic Bacteriology, & Statutes of the Bacteriology Section of the International Association of Microbiological Societies: Bacteriological Code. rev. ed. LC 75-20730. 216p. reprint ed. pap. 61.60 (*0-685-23712-5*, 2032233) Bks Demand.

LaPaglia, Nancy. Storytellers: The Image of the Two-Year College in American Fiction & in Women's Journals. LC 93-37645. 201p. 1994. pap. 15.95 (*1-879528-07-X*) LEPS Pr.

LaPaglia, Peter S., jt. auth. see Crutchfield, James A.

Lapaine, Daniel, et al. Interplay. 125p. (Orig.). 1987. pap. 12.95 (*0-936839-72-4*) Applause Theatre Bk Pubs.

Lapaire, Pierre J. Montherlant et la Parole: Etude d'un Langage Dramatique. LC 93-83301. 149p. (FRE.). 1993. lib. bdg. 33.95 (*0-917786-94-7*) Summa Pubns.

Lapaire, Sophie, ed. see Ching Hai.

LaPalma, Marina. Grammars for Jess. (Illus.). 56p. 1981. 4.50 (*0-932716-16-4*) Kelsey St Pr.

LaPalombara, Joseph. Democracy, Italian Style. LC 87-6124. 320p. (C). 1989. reprint ed. 14.00 (*0-300-04411-9*) Yale U Pr.

— The Initiative & Referendum in Oregon, 1938-1948. LC 50-62689. (Oregon State Monographs, Studies in Political Science: No. 1). 149p. reprint ed. pap. 42.50 (*0-7837-0157-8*, 2040454) Bks Demand.

LaPalombara, Joseph & Weiner, Myron, eds. Political Parties & Political Development. LC 66-10558. (Studies in Political Development: No. 6). (Illus.). 495p. reprint ed. pap. 141.10 (*0-8357-6271-8*, 2034647) Bks Demand.

LaPalombara, Joseph G. The Italian Labor Movement: Problems & Prospects. LC 82-11885. 192p. 1982. reprint ed. text ed. 59.75 (*0-313-23553-8*, LAIT, Greenwood Pr) Greenwood.

— Italy: The Politics of Planning. LC 66-17523. (National Planning Ser.: No. 7). 204p. reprint ed. pap. 58.20 (*0-317-29009-6*, 2020398) Bks Demand.

Lapape, Brice, jt. ed. see Steels, Luc.

Lapas, Raimundas M. It Happened on the Silver Screen: Ethnic Lithuanian Cinematographic Activities in the United States, 1909-1979. 1983. 19.95 (*0-685-09857-5*) Baltic Cinema.

— Ten, Ekrane Suzibus: Amerikos Lietuviu Kinematografija, 1909-1979. LC 81-69029. (Illus.). 386p. (ENG & LIT.). 19.95 (*0-941618-00-5*) Baltic Cinema.

Lapasta, Douglas, ed. see Neuweiler, Phillip F.

Lapati, Americo D. A High School Curriculum for Leadership. 1961. 17.95x (*0-8084-0375-3*) NCUP.

— Orestes A. Brownson. (Twayne's United States Authors Ser.). 1965. pap. 13.95 (*0-8084-0238-2*, T88) NCUP.

Lapati, Americo D., ed. see Brownson, Orestes A.

Lapatra, Jack, jt. auth. see Temes, Gabor C.

***LaPaz, Camilla & Elliot, Belinda.** 1001 Prescription Drugs: Good Effects & Side Effects. 1995. text ed. 27.95 (*0-915099-67-5*) FC&A Pub.

Lapchick, J. Michael. Brand Name Guide to Low-Fat & Fat-Free Foods: A Comprehensive Listing of More Than 1000 Packaged Low-Fat & Fat-Free Foods Found in Almost Every Grocery Store with Complete Nutrition Information. 190p. 1995. pap. 9.95 (*1-56561-045-8*) Chronimed.

Lapchick, J. Michael & Mo, Rosa A. The Brand Name Pocket Guide to Additive Free Foods: A Comprehensive Listing to More Than 1000 Preservative & Additive Free Foods Found in Almost Every Grocery Store - Complete with Nutrition Information. 160p. 1994. pap. 9.95 (*1-56561-040-7*, 004237) Chronimed.

Lapchick, Mike & Appleseth, Cindy. The Label Reader's Pocket Dictionary of Food Additives. 128p. (Orig.). 1993. pap. 4.95 (*1-56561-027-X*) Chronimed.

Lapchick, Richard E. Five Minutes to Midnight: Race & Sport in the 1990s. 352p. 1991. 29.95 (*0-8191-8066-1*); pap. 14.95 (*0-8191-8166-8*) Madison Bks UPA.

— Fractured Focus: Sport As a Reflection of Society. 416p. 1986. text ed. 35.00 (*0-669-12860-0*); text ed. 19.95 (*0-669-12288-2*) Free Pr.

— Pass to Play: Student Athletes & Academics. 48p. 1989. 7.95 (*0-8106-3339-6*) NEA.

— The Politics of Race & International Sport: The Case of South Africa. LC 74-11705. (Studies in Human Rights: No. 1). 268p. 1975. text ed. 38.50 (*0-8371-7691-3*, LPR/, Greenwood Pr) Greenwood.

Lapchick, Richard E. & Malekoff, Robert. On the Mark: Putting the Student Back in Student-Athlete. 240p. 1986. text ed. 16.95 (*0-669-13824-X*) Free Pr.

***Lapchick, Richard E. & Slaughter, John B., eds.** The Rules of the Game: Ethics in College Sport. LC 94-28029. (American Council on Education - Oryx Press Series on Higher Education). 272p. 1989. text ed. 19.95 (*0-89774-831-X*) Oryx Pr.

Lapchick, Richard E. & Urdang, Stephanie. Oppression & Resistance: The Struggle of Women in Southern Africa. LC 81-4267. (Contributions in Women's Studies: No. 29). (Illus.). xiv, 197p. 1982. text ed. 49.95 (*0-313-22960-0*, LWA/, Greenwood Pr) Greenwood.

Lape, Fred. A Farm & Village Boyhood. LC 80-17303. (York State Book Ser.). (Illus.). 175p. reprint ed. pap. 49.90 (*0-8357-3124-3*, 2039385) Bks Demand.

Lapedes, D. N. Encyclopedic Italian-English, English-Italian Scientific & Technical Dictionary: Dizionario Enciclopedico Scientifico e Tecnico: Inglese-Italiano, Italiano-Inglese. 2122p. (ENG & ITA.). 1980. 295.00 (*0-8288-4693-6*, M9201) Fr & Eur.

— Spanish & English Dictionary of Technical & Scientific Terminology: Diccionario de Terminos Cientificos y Tecnicos, 5 vols., Set. 2952p. (ENG & SPA.). 1981. 895. 00 (*0-8288-0668-3*, S38580) Fr & Eur.

Lapenna, Ivo. Soviet Penal Policy. LC 80-15755. (Background Bk.). 148p. 1980. reprint ed. text ed. 49.75 (*0-313-22570-2*, LASP, Greenwood Pr) Greenwood.

LaPenta, Anthony V., Jr. The Sniper. LC 75-16563. 1976. 21.95 (*0-87949-042-X*) Ashley Bks.

LaPenta, Barbara L., tr. see Tafuri, Manfredo.

***LaPenta, Marilyn.** Music, Songs, & Poems. Evento, Susan, ed. (Macmillan Early Skills Program - Conversion Ser.). 64p. (J). (ps-2). Date not set. pap. text ed. 9.95 (*1-56784-506-1*) Newbridge Comms.

— Our America. Evento, Susan, ed. (Macmillan Early Skills Program - Conversion Ser.). 64p. (J). (ps-2). Date not set. pap. text ed. 9.95 (*1-56784-513-4*) Newbridge Comms.

***LaPenta, Marilyn & Bielitz, Joan.** Activity Centers. Evento, Susan, ed. (Macmillan Early Skills Program - Conversion Ser.). 64p. (J). (ps-2). Date not set. pap. text ed. 9.95 (*1-56784-507-X*) Newbridge Comms.

LaPenta, Marilyn, jt. auth. see Bielitz, Joan.

Laperle, Patricia J. Under His Wings. LC 86-63915. (Illus.). 52p. (Orig.). 1987. pap. 7.75 (*0-910147-41-8*) World Poetry Pr.

Laperouse, Jean F. & Chinard, Gilbert. Le Voyage de Laperouse sur les Cotes de l'Alaska et de la California (1786) 1979. 21.95 (*0-405-10592-4*) Ayer.

***Lapeyre.** Practical Business Negotiations: French-English-Spanish. 174p. (ENG, FRE & SPA.). 1992. 24.95 (*0-7859-7513-6*, 8428319464) Fr & Eur.

— Secretary's International Dictionary: English-Spanish-French. 165p. (ENG, FRE & SPA.). 1992. 24.95 (*0-7859-7512-8*, 8428319456) Fr & Eur.

***Lapeyre, B.** The International Secretary Dictionary: English-Spanish-French. (ENG, FRE & SPA.). 1992. pap. 25.00 (*0-7859-8905-6*) Fr & Eur.

— Practical Business Negotiations in French-English-Spanish. (ENG, FRE & SPA.). 1992. pap. 22.00 (*0-7859-8919-6*) Fr & Eur.

Lapeyre, B. & Sheppard, P. The International Secretary Dictionary: English-Spanish-French. 165p. (ENG, FRE & SPA.). 1992. pap. 25.00 (*84-283-1945-6*, Pub. by Paraninfo) IBD Ltd.

— Practical Business Negotiations in French-English-Spanish. 174p. 1992. pap. 22.00 (*84-283-1946-4*) IBD Ltd.

Lapeyre, Benedicte & Sheppard, Pamela. Chairing Meetings in French As Well As in English. 87p. (ENG & FRE.). 1992. 39.95 (*0-7859-1001-8*, 2708114557) Fr & Eur.

— Taking the Floor in Meetings in French As Well As in English. 109p. (ENG & FRE.). 1992. 39.95 (*0-7859-1002-6*, 2708114565) Fr & Eur.

Lapeyrouse, Norton J. Formulas & Calculations for Drilling, Production & Workover. 224p. 1992. 45.00 (*0-88415-011-9*) Gulf Pub.

Lapeyrouse, Stephen L. Towards the Spiritual Convergence of America & Russia: American Mind & Russian Soul, American Individuality & Russian Community, & the Potent Alchemy of National Characteristics. LC 90-92072. 168p. (Orig.). 1991. pap. 12.95 (*0-9628048-0-0*) S Lapeyrouse.

***Lapham, Alice G.** Old Planters of Beverly in Massachusetts, & the Thousand Acre Grant of 1635. (Illus.). 133p. 1995. reprint ed. lib. bdg. 29.50 (*0-8328-4695-3*); reprint ed. pap. 19.50 (*0-8328-4703-8*) Higginson Bk Co.

Lapham, David D., tr. see Yoon, Suk-Joong.

Lapham, Increase A. The Antiquities of Wisconsin As Surveyed & Described. LC 72-5000. (Antiquities of the New World Ser.: Vol. 4). (Illus.). reprint ed. 42.50 (*0-404-57304-5*) AMS Pr.

— Wisconsin: Its Geography & Topography, History, Geology & Mineralogy. LC 74-107. (Mid-American Frontier Ser.). 1975. reprint ed. 21.95 (*0-405-06874-3*) Ayer.

Lapham, Lewis H. Fortune's Child. 1994. pap. 12.95 (*1-879957-21-3*) Harpers Mag Found.

— Imperial Masquerade. 1991. pap. 12.95 (*0-8021-3244-8*) Grove-Atltic.

— The Wish for Kings: The Passing of the Democratic Spirit in America. LC 92-27255. 213p. 1993. 22.00 (*0-8021-1446-6*) Grove-Atltic.

Lapham, Lewis H., ed. High Technology & Human Freedom. LC 85-8341. (International Symposia Ser.). (Illus.). 170p. (Orig.). 1986. 26.00 (*0-87474-598-5*, LAHT); pap. 12.95 (*0-87474-599-3*, LAHTP) Smithsonian.

Lapham, Lewis H., et al. Harper's Index Book. LC 86-33549. 144p. 1987. pap. 6.95 (*0-8050-0325-8*, Owl) H Holt & Co.

***Lapham, Robert W. & Agar, Heather.** Drug Calculations for Nurses: A Step by Step Approach. 176p. 1995. pap. 14.99 (*1-56593-600-0*, 1228) Singular Publishing.

Lapham, Samuel, Jr., jt. auth. see Simons, Albert.

Lapham, W. B. Clason, Clawson, Classon, Clesson, Clarson, Stephen Clason of Stamford, Connecticut, in 1654, & Some of His Descendants, Compiled from Data Chiefly Collected by Oliver B. Clason. (Illus.). 160p. 1993. reprint ed. lib. bdg. 34.00 (*0-8328-1358-3*); reprint ed. pap. 24.00 (*0-8328-1359-1*) Higginson Bk Co.

Lapham, William B. Centennial History of Norway, Oxford County, Maine. (Illus.). 822p. 1986. reprint ed. 55.00 (*0-89725-061-3*) Picton Pr.

— Genealogical Sketches of Robert & John Hazelton & Some of Their Descendants: With Brief Notices of Other New England Families Bearing This Name. (Illus.). 368p. 1989. reprint ed. lib. bdg. 63.00 (*0-8328-0649-8*); reprint ed. pap. 55.00 (*0-8328-0650-1*) Higginson Bk Co.

— History of Bethel, Formerly Sudbury Canada, Oxford County, Maine, 1768-1890, with a Brief Sketch of Hanover & Family Statistics. LC 81-82795. (Illus.). 827p. 1981. reprint ed. 50.00 (*0-89725-023-0*) Picton Pr.

— History of Rumford, Oxford County, Maine from Its First Settlement in 1779 to the Present Time. (Illus.). 432p. 1992. reprint ed. lib. bdg. 45.00 (*0-8328-2521-2*) Higginson Bk Co.

— History of Woodstock, Maine. LC 83-62055. (Illus.). 359p. 1983. reprint ed. 35.00 (*0-89725-041-9*) Picton Pr.

Lapham, William B. & Maxim, Silas P. History of Paris, Maine. (Illus.). 816p. 1992. reprint ed. lib. bdg. 44.50 (*0-8328-2528-X*) Higginson Bk Co.

LaPiana, David. Nonprofit Mergers: The Board Responsibility to Consider the Unthinkable. (Nonprofit Governance Ser.: No. 56). 26p. (Orig.). (C). 1994. pap. text ed. 12.00 (*0-925299-32-4*) Natl Ctr Nonprofit.

LaPiana, Maxine F. Westward Ho! (J). 1994. 7.95 (*0-8062-4925-0*) Carlton.

LaPiana, William P. Logic & Experience: The Origin of Modern American Legal Education. 264p. 1994. 42.00 (*0-19-507935-3*) OUP.

Lapick, Gaetan J. & Geller, Jack. Scientific Fur Servicing: Storage, Cleaning, Repairing & Restyling. (Illus.). 145p. reprint ed. pap. 41.40 (*0-317-10808-5*, 2011751) Bks Demand.

***Lapicque, F., et al, eds.** Electrochemical Engineering & Energy: Proceedings of the Third European Symposium, Held in Nancy, France, March 23-25, 1994. LC 94-44821. 270p. 1995. 89.50 (*0-306-44887-4*, Plenum Pr) Plenum.

Lapide, Phinn E. Hebrew in the Church: The Foundations of Jewish-Christian Dialogue. Rhodes, Erroll F., tr. LC 84-26044. 274p. reprint ed. pap. 78.10 (*0-685-23457-6*, 2032735) Bks Demand.

Lapide, Phinn E. & Moltmann, Jurgen. Jewish Monotheism & Christian Trinitarian Doctrine: A Dialogue by Pinchas Lapide & Jurgen Moltmann. Swidler, Leonard, tr. LC 80-8058. 93p. reprint ed. pap. 26.60 (*0-685-23577-7*, 2029107) Bks Demand.

Lapide, Pinchas. The Sermon on the Mount: Utopia or Program for Action? Swidler, Arlene, tr. LC 85-29810. 160p. (Orig.). reprint ed. pap. 45.60 (*0-8357-2681-9*, 2040217) Bks Demand.

Lapides, Kenneth, ed. Marx & Engels on Trade Unions. LC 86-25266. 264p. 1986. text ed. 55.00 (*0-275-92373-8*, C2373, Praeger Pubs) Greenwood.

Lapides, Paul D. Managing & Leasing Residential Properties. (Real Estate Practice Library). 648p. 1992. text ed. 123.00 (*0-471-55179-1*) Wiley.

— Managing & Leasing Residential Properties: Forms & Procedures. (Real Estate Practice Library). 496p. 1993. text ed. 123.00 (*0-471-58590-4*) Wiley.

***Lapides, Paul D. & Miller, E. Robert.** Managing & Leasing Residential Properties: Forms & Procedures, 1994 Supplement. 1993. pap. text ed. 45.00 (*0-614-00728-3*) Wiley.

Lapides, Paul D., jt. auth. see Rondeau, Edmond P.

Lapides, Robert, ed. Lodz Ghetto: Inside a Community under Siege. (Illus.). 528p. 1991. pap. 17.95 (*0-14-013228-7*) Viking Penguin.

Lapidge, M., jt. ed. see Rosier, James L.

Lapidge, Michael. Anglo-Latin Literature, 900-1066. LC 93-20227. 1993. boxed 65.00 (*1-85285-012-4*) Hambledon Press.

— Anglo-Saxon Litanies of the Saints. (Henry Bradshaw Society Ser.: No. CVI). 352p. (C). 1991. text ed. 50.00 (*1-870252-01-2*) Boydell & Brewer.

***Lapidge, Michael, ed.** Archbishop Theodore: Commemorative Studies on His Life & Influence. (Cambridge Studies on Anglo-Saxon England: No. 11). 354p. (C). 1995. 59.95 (*0-521-48077-9*) Cambridge U Pr.

Lapidge, Michael, intro. Bede & His World: The Jarrow Lectures, 1958-1993. (Illus.). 1000p. 1994. 245.00 (*0-86078-449-5*, Pub. by Variorum UK) Ashgate Pub Co.

Lapidge, Michael & Gneuss, Helmut, eds. Learning & Literature in Anglo-Saxon England: Studies Presented to Peter Clemoes on the Occasion of His 65th Birthday. (Illus.). 450p. 1985. 89.95 (*0-521-25902-9*) Cambridge U Pr.

Lapidge, Michael & Herren, Michael, trs. Aldhelm: The Prose Works. 210p. 1979. 52.25 (*0-8476-6090-7*) Rowman.

Lapidge, Michael, ed. see Aldhelm.

Lapidge, Michael, jt. auth. see Bischoff, Bernhard.

Lapidge, Michael, ed. see Blair, Peter H.

Lapidge, Michael, ed. see Esposito, Mario.

Lapidge, Michael, jt. tr. see Keynes, Simon.

Lapidge, Michael, tr. see Rosier, James L. & Lapidge, M., eds.

Lapidge, Michael, ed. see Wulfstan of Wincheste.

Lapidge, S., jt. auth. see Roberts, Arthur D.

Lapidot, Ema. Borges & Artificial Intelligence: An Analysis in the Style of Pierre Menard. LC 90-5917. (American University Studies: Latin American Literature: Ser. XXII, Vol. 11). 197p. (C). 1991. text ed. 39.95 (*0-8204-1376-3*) P Lang Pubs.

Lapidoth, Ruth, ed. The Jerusalem Question & Its Resolution: Selected Documents. 576p. (C). 1994. lib. bdg. 162.50 (*0-7923-2893-0*) Kluwer Ac.

Lapidoth, Ruth & Hirsh, Moshe. The Arab-Israel Conflict & Its Resolution: Selected Documents. 388p. (C). 1992. lib. bdg. 140.50 (*0-7923-1300-3*) Kluwer Ac.

Lapidus. In Pursuit of Gold: Alchemy in Theory & Practice. (Illus.). 180p. (Orig.). Date not set. 13.95 (*0-8464-4242-6*) Beekman Pubs.

Lapidus, B. A. & Shevtsoka, S. V. The Learner's Russian-English Dictionary. 550p. (ENG & RUS.). 1977. 19.95 (*0-8288-5452-1*, M9117) Fr & Eur.

Lapidus, Dorothy F. The Facts on File Dictionary of Geology & Geophysics. (Science Dictionaries Ser.). (Illus.). 347p. 1987. 24.95 (*0-87196-703-0*) Facts on File.

Lapidus, Gail, ed. The New Russia. 280p. (C). 1994. text ed. 57.00 (*0-8133-2076-3*); pap. text ed. 19.95 (*0-8133-2077-1*) Westview.

Lapidus, Gail, jt. ed. see Dallin, Alexander.

Lapidus, Gail W. State & Society in the Soviet Union. 300p. Date not set. text ed. 43.50 (*0-8133-0893-3*); pap. text ed. 18.50 (*0-8133-0894-1*) Westview.

L

— Women in Soviet Society: Equality, Development, & Social Change. LC 74-16710. 1978. pap. 12.00 (*0-520-03938-6*) U CA Pr.

Lapidus, Gail W., ed. The Nationality Question in the Soviet Union. LC 92-3618. (Articles on Russian & Soviet History, 1500-1991 Ser.: Vol. 11). 368p. 1992. 58.00 (*0-8153-0568-0*) Garland.

— Women, Work, & Family in the Soviet Union. LC 81-9281. 358p. reprint ed. pap. 102.10 (*0-8357-2620-7*, 2040108) Bks Demand.

Lapidus, Gail W. & Swanson, Guy E., eds. State & Welfare, U. S. A. - U. S. S. R. Contemporary Policy & Practice. LC 88-15444. (Research Ser.: No. 71). (Illus.). xxii, 467p. 1988. pap. 22.50 (*0-87725-171-1*) U of Cal IAS.

Lapidus, Gail W., et al, eds. From Union to Commonwealth: Nationalism & Separatism in the Soviet Republics. (Soviet Paperbacks Ser.: No. 6). 128p. (C). 1992. 49.95 (*0-521-41706-6*); pap. 14.95 (*0-521-42716-9*) Cambridge U Pr.

Lapidus, Ira M. Contemporary Islamic Movements in Historical Perspective. LC 83-82308. (Policy Papers in International Affairs Ser.: No. 18). viii, 66p. (C). 1983. pap. 6.50 (*0-87725-518-0*) U of Cal IAS.

— A History of Islamic Societies. (Illus.). 1000p. 1988. 84.95 (*0-521-22552-3*) Cambridge U Pr.

— A History of Islamic Societies. 1990. pap. 27.95 (*0-521-29549-1*) Cambridge U Pr.

Lapidus, Ira M., jt. auth. see Burke, Edmund, III.

Lapidus, Jacqueline. Ready to Survive. LC 75-9593. 24p. 1975. pap. 4.00 (*0-914610-04-X*) Hanging Loose.

— Starting Over. (Illus.). 1990. pap. 3.50 (*0-918314-03-8*) Out & Out.

— Ultimate Conspiracy. 84p. (Orig.). 1987. pap. 7.95 (*0-9619598-0-0*) Lynx Pubns.

Lapidus, Joellen. Lapidus on Dulcimer. (Illus.). 228p. (Orig.). 1978. pap. 9.95 (*0-89705-007-X*) Almo Pubns.

Lapidus, June, jt. auth. see Hartmann, Heidi.

Lapidus, Leon & Pinder, George F. Numerical Solution of Partial Differential Equations in Science & Engineering. LC 81-16491. 677p. 1982. text ed. 135.00 (*0-471-09866-3*) Wiley.

Lapidus, M. Bilingual Glossary of Business Terms. 213p. (ENG & SPA.). 1982. pap. 14.95 (*0-8288-0133-9*, S 19416) Fr & Eur.

Lapidus, M., jt. auth. see Johnson, G.

***Lapidus, Mikhail C., et al.** Business in the Russian Free Market. Jezmir, Leonid, tr. LC 95-94101. 244p. (Orig.). (C). 1995. pap. 18.00 (*0-9645464-1-8*) MIR Hse.

Lapidus, Roxanne, tr. see Finkielkraut, Alain.

Lapidus, Roxanne, tr. see Serres, Michael.

Lapiere & Krieg, eds. Connective Tissue Diseases of the Skin. (Basic & Clinical Dermatology Ser.: Vol. 9). 408p. 1993. 165.00 (*0-8247-9133-9*) Dekker.

Lapierre, jt. auth. see Collins.

LaPierre, Alexandra. Fanny Stevenson: A Romance of Destiny. Cosman, Carol, tr. (Illus.). 520p. 1995. 26.00 (*0-7867-0127-7*) Carroll & Graf.

Lapierre, Andre, ed. Names of French Canada. (International Library of Names). 400p. (C). text ed. write for info. (*0-8290-1214-1*) Irvington.

Lapierre, Dominique. Beyond Love. 416p. 1991. 22.95 (*0-446-51438-1*) Warner Bks.

— Beyond Love. 1992. pap. 12.99 (*0-446-39346-0*) Warner Bks.

— The City of Joy. 544p. 1988. mass mkt. 6.99 (*0-446-35556-9*) Warner Bks.

Lapierre, Dominique, jt. auth. see Collins, Larry.

LaPierre, Dominique

Lapierre, Dominique

Lapierre, Janet. The Cruel Mother. 1991. reprint ed. mass mkt. 3.95 (*0-373-26078-4*) Harlequin Bks.

— Grandmother's House. (Mystery Ser.). 1993. mass mkt. 3.99 (*0-373-26120-9*, 1-26120-5) Harlequin Bks.

— Grandmother's House. 288p. 1991. text ed. 19.95 (*0-684-19382-5*, Scribners) S&S Trade.

— Old Enemies: A Meg Halloran Novel. 256p. 1993. text ed. 20.00 (*0-684-19614-X*, Scribners) S&S Trade.

Lapierre, Ronald F. Homeowner's Bid Package: Your Guide to the Competitive Bidding of Home Improvement Work. (Illus.). 110p. (Orig.). 1991. pap. 13.95 (*0-9630496-0-7*) Systs Construct.

LaPierre, Wayne. Guns, Crime & Freedom. 264p. 1994. 22.95 (*0-89526-477-3*) Regnery Pub.

— Guns, Crime, & Freedom. 1995. 12.50 (*0-06-097674-8*, PL) HarpC.

Lapillone, B., jt. auth. see Chateau, B.

***Lapin, Daniel.** The Vampire, Dracula & Incest: The Vampire Myth, Stoker's Dracula, & Psychotherapy of Vampiric Sexual Abuse. 252p. (Orig.). 1995. pap. 14.95 (*0-9644983-0-8*) Gargoyle Pub.

Lapin, J. E. Portable C & UNIX Systems Programming. 208p. 1987. 30.95 (*0-13-686494-5*) P-H.

Lapin, Lawrence L. Business Statistics. LC 84-6690. (College Outline Ser.). 341p. (C). 1984. pap. text ed. 12.50 (*0-15-601553-6*) HB Coll Pubs.

— The Home Owner's Guide to Making a Fortune. (Illus.). 168p. 1981. 12.95 (*0-9605140-0-7*) Alamo Pr.

— Instructor's Manual to Accompany Statistics for Modern Business Decisions. 6th ed. 524p. (C). 1993. pap. text ed. 10.00 (*0-15-500629-0*) Dryden Pr.

— Quantitative Methods for Business Decisions. 5th ed. 850p. (C). 1990. text ed. 57.75 (*0-15-574331-7*) Dryden Pr.

— Quantitative Methods for Business Decisions, with Cases. 6th ed. LC 93-73933. 1250p. (C). 1994. text ed. 62.75 (*0-03-096916-6*) Dryden Pr.

— Quantitative Methods for Business Decisions, with Cases. 6th ed. LC 93-73933. (C). 1994. disk 21.50 (*0-03-097817-3*); disk 21.50 (*0-03-097818-1*); disk 21.50 (*0-03-094889-4*) Dryden Pr.

— Statistics for Modern Business Decisions. 5th ed. 1021p. (C). 1990. text ed. 56.00 (*0-15-583705-2*); disk write for info. (*0-318-67019-4*); disk 20.50 (*0-15-583710-9*); write for info. (*0-318-67020-8*) Dryden Pr.

— Statistics for Modern Business Decisions. 6th ed. LC 92-70669. 1263p. (C). 1993. text ed. 58.75 (*0-15-500004-7*) Dryden Pr.

Lapin, Lee. How to Get Anything on Anybody. (Illus.). 272p. (Orig.). 1987. 30.00 (*0-87364-594-4*) Paladin Pr.

—The Whole Spy Catalog: A Research Encyclopedia for Researchers, PIs, Spies & Generally Nosy People. (Illus.). 440p. (Orig.). 1995. pap. 44.95 (*1-880231-10-7*) ISECO. THE WHOLE EARTH CATALOG OF SPYING. Recommended by CIA directors, KGB officers & the world's most famous private detective. THE WHOLE SPY CATALOG is a hands-on encyclopedia of professional secrets, tricks, "inside" phone numbers & cutting edge techniques to trace, track, surveil & investigate anyone or anything... Is that guy (or woman) who bought you that last Scotch really a respected CEO or a serial rapist? Run his/her whole life down from the comfort of your living room. TEAR OUT fax forms included. Missing an old friend or ex-husband? A $5.00 phone call that instantly locates almost anyone. Going through a divorce, got a judgement? Find real property, bank accounts, stocks, bonds... SPIES R US What the major spy agencies are up to - How/ where to hire ex-KGB or ex-CIA agents, get a job or scholarship with the CIA, join a social club for "young intelligence professionals", subscribe to the FBI newsletter. PRIVATE DETECTIVES - AERIAL PHOTOGRAPHS - NIGHT VISION - ELECTRONIC SURVEILLANCE - VIDEO SURVEILLANCE. 440 pages (207 photos) large format, $44.95. Intelligence Incorporated, distributed by IPG. ISBN 1-880231-10-7. Major media interest, comprehensive ad/PR campaign. To order contact the publisher at (415) 851-3957. ***Publisher Provided Annotation.***

Lapin, Mark. Pledge of Allegiance. large type ed. LC 91-18381. 396p. 1991. reprint ed. lib. bdg. 19.95 (*1-56054-195-4*) Thorndike Pr.

Lapin, Pierre. The Tale of Peter Rabbit. (FRE.). 1973. 5.95 (*0-7232-3673-9*) Warne.

Lapina, Ronald P. Estimating Centrifugal Compressor Performance. LC 82-3124. (Process Compressor Technology Ser.: Vol. 1). 208p. 1982. 48.00 (*0-87201-101-1*) Gulf Pub.

— TI-59 Manual for Estimating Centrifugal Compressor Performance. LC 83-3124. (Process Compressor Technology Ser.: Vol. 2). 334p. 1983. 59.00 (*0-87201-100-3*) Gulf Pub.

Lapine, James. Twelve Dreams. 1982. pap. 4.75 (*0-8222-1176-9*) Dramatists Play.

Lapine, James & Sondheim, Stephen. Into the Woods. LC 89-4402. 160p. 1989. pap. 8.95 (*0-930452-93-3*) Theatre Comm.

— Passion. 144p. 1994. 22.50 (*1-55936-087-9*); pap. 10.95 (*1-55936-088-7*) Theatre Comm.

Lapine, James, jt. auth. see Finn, William.

Lapine, James, jt. auth. see Sondheim, Stephen.

Lapine, James, et al. Wordplays 5: New American Drama. (Wordplays Ser.). 188p. 1986. pap. 13.95x (*1-55554-007-4*) PAJ Pubns.

Lapine, Jennifer & Lapine, Susan. My First Hebrew Alphabet Book. (Illus.). 48p. (J). (ps-1). 1977. pap. 3.95 (*0-8197-0399-0*) Bloch.

Lapine, Kenneth M. Consumer Credit Law: Transaction & Forms, 3 vols. 1984. Update. write for info. (*0-8205-1084-X*) Bender.

Lapine, Susan, jt. auth. see Lapine, Jennifer.

Laping, Francis & Knight, Hans. Remember Hungary 1956: A Pictorial History of the Hungarian Revolution. (Illus.). 381p. 1992. 45.00 (*0-912404-01-9*) Alpha Pubns.

Lapinski, Mike. Western Hunting Guide. (Illus.). 172p. 1989. 17.95 (*0-912299-43-6*); pap. 12.95 (*0-912299-44-4*) Stoneydale Pr Pub.

— Whitetail Deer Hunting. (Illus.). 64p. 1988. pap. 3.50 (*0-912299-34-7*) Stoneydale Pr Pub.

Lapinski, Mike, et al. All about Elk. Miller, Bill, ed. LC 86-63878. (Hunter's Information Ser.). (Illus.). 253p. 1987. 15.95 (*0-914697-07-2*) N Amer Outdoor Grp.

Lapirov, Il'ia. Vek: Kniga Stikhov. LC 85-63414. 208p. (Orig.). (RUS.). 1986. pap. 14.00 (*0-89830-108-4*) Russica Pubs.

Lapis, K., ed. Developments of Cancer Chemotherapy. (Journal: Oncology: Vol. 37, Suppl. 1). (Illus.). iv, 120p. 1980. pap. 26.50 (*3-8055-1588-X*) S Karger.

***Lapis, K. & Eckhardt, S.** Lectures & Symposia of the 14th International Cancer Congress: Carcinogenesis & Tumour Progression, Vol. 4. 334p. (C). 1987. 168.00x (*963-05-4526-8*) St Mut.

— Lectures & Symposia of the 14th International Cancer Congress: Cytology, Pathology & Cancer Prognosis, Vol. 3. 219p. (C). 1987. 108.00x (*963-05-4525-X*) St Mut.

— Lectures & Symposia of the 14th International Cancer Congress: Epidemiology, Prevention, Diagnosis, Vol. 6. 365p. (C). 1987. 174.00x (*963-05-4528-4*) St Mut.

— Lectures & Symposia of the 14th International Cancer Congress: Molecular Biology & Differentiation of Cancer Cells (Oncogenes, Growth Factors, Receptors), Vol. 2. 361p. (C). 1987. 168.00x (*963-05-4524-1*) St Mut.

— Lectures & Symposia of the 14th International Cancer Congress: Novel Approaches in Cancer Therapy, Vol. 5. 387p. (C). 1987. 174.00x (*963-05-4527-6*) St Mut.

— Lectures & Symposia of the 14th International Cancer Congress: Oncological Surgery, Vol. 7. 223p. (C). 1987. 108.00x (*963-05-4529-2*) St Mut.

— Lectures & Symposia of the 14th International Cancer Congress, 13 vols., Set. (C). 1987. 1,875.00x (*963-05-4522-5*) St Mut.

— Lectures & Symposia of the 14th Intl. Cancer Congress: Cancer Research & Treatment Today: Results, Trends & Frontiers, Vol. 1. 266p. (C). 1987. 132.00x (*963-05-4523-3*) St Mut.

***Lapis, K. & Eckhardt, S., eds.** Lectures & Symposia of the 14th International Cancer Congress: Anticancer Drug Research, Vol. 9. 352p. (C). 1987. 168.00x (*963-05-4530-6*) St Mut.

— Lectures & Symposia of the 14th International Cancer Congress: Endocrine Aspects of Malignancies, Vol. 12. 293p. (C). 1987. 168.00x (*963-05-4534-9*) St Mut.

— Lectures & Symposia of the 14th International Cancer Congress: Medical Oncology, Vol. 11. 339p. (C). 1987. 168.00x (*963-05-4533-0*) St Mut.

— Lectures & Symposia of the 14th Intl. Cancer Congress: Education, Nursing, Organization, Vol. 13. 336p. (C). 1987. 168.00x (*963-05-4535-7*) St Mut.

— Lectures & Symposia of the 4th International Cancer Congress: Biological Response Modifiers, Leukemias & Lymphomas, Vol. 10. 133p. (C). 1987. 69.00x (*963-05-4532-2*) St Mut.

Lapis, K. & Jeney, A. Regulation & Control of Cell Proliferation. 512p. 1984. 310.00 (*0-569-08824-0*, Pub. by Collets UK) Pro-Am Music.

— Regulation & Control of Cell Proliferation. 512p. (C). 1984. 162.00x (*963-05-3246-8*, Pub. by Akad Kiado HU) St Mut.

Lapis, Karoly & Johannessen, Jan V. Liver Carcinogenesis. 1979. text ed. 35.00 (*0-07-036368-4*) McGraw.

Lapis, Karoly, et al, eds. Biochemistry & Molecular Genetics of Cancer Metastasis. (Developments in Oncology Ser.). 1986. lib. bdg. 85.00 (*0-89838-785-X*) Kluwer Ac.

Lapisardi, Frederick S., ed. see Gore-Booth, Eva.

Lapitskii, A., jt. auth. see Stupin, L.

Lapitsky, Alexander. Peace in One Hundred Languages: A One Word Multilingual Dictionary. 48p. 1993. pap. 9.95 (*0-915190-74-5*) Jalmar Pr.

Lapka, Fay S. Dark Is a Color. 264p. (Orig.). (YA). (gr. 9-12). 1990. pap. 6.99 (*0-87788-163-4*) Shaw Pubs.

— Hoverlight. (Young Adult Fiction Ser.). (Orig.). (YA). 1991. pap. 6.99 (*0-87788-352-1*) Shaw Pubs.

— The Sea, the Song & the Trumpetfish. (Young Adult Fiction Ser.). 160p. (Orig.). (YA). (gr. 7-12). 1991. pap. 6.99 (*0-87788-754-3*) Shaw Pubs.

Lapkus, Danas & Dokalskaite, Ona, intros. Ona Dokalskaite. LC 92-72672. (Illus.). 170p. 1993. 35.00 (*0-9617756-5-3*) Galerija.

Lapkus, Danas, ed. see Paskevicius, Mykolas.

LaPlaca, Annette. Are We Almost There? The Kids' Book of Travel Fun. (Illus.). 45p. (Orig.). (J). (gr. 1-5). 1992. student ed, pap. 4.99 (*0-87788-051-4*) Shaw Pubs.

— How Long 'til Christmas? The Kid's Book of Holiday Fun. (Illus.). 48p. (Orig.). (J). (gr. 3-6). 1993. pap. 4.99 (*0-87788-369-6*) Shaw Pubs.

— I Read It on the Refrigerator: Memos for Amazing Moms. (Illus.). 96p. (Orig.). 1992. pap. 4.99 (*0-87788-385-8*) Shaw Pubs.

— It Came from My Senior Yearbook: Pocket Guide to Life 101. 96p. (Orig.). 1992. pap. 4.99 (*0-87788-398-X*) Shaw Pubs.

LaPlaca, Annette, ed. Grandparents Have All the Fun: A Scrapbook of Chuckles & Inspirations. LC 92-30773. (Illus.). 112p. (Orig.). 1993. 4.99 (*0-87788-361-0*) Shaw Pubs.

LaPlaca, Annette, jt. auth. see LaPlaca, David.

LaPlaca, Annette H., jt. auth. see Heinrich, Joyce.

***LaPlaca, David, illus.** The Sunday Morning Fun Book. 48p. 1995. pap. 5.99 (*0-87788-569-9*) Shaw Pubs.

LaPlaca, David & LaPlaca, Annette. I Thought of It While Shaving: Ideas for Devoted Dads. 96p. (Orig.). 1992. pap. 4.99 (*0-87788-387-4*) Shaw Pubs.

Laplaca, Michael. Easter Decorations: Make & Color Your Own. (J). (ps-3). 1989. pap. 1.95 (*0-89375-647-4*) Troll Assocs.

LaPlaca, Michael. How to Draw Boats, Trains, & Planes. LC 81-52123. (Illus.). 32p. (J). (gr. 2-6). 1982. lib. bdg. 10.65 (*0-89375-682-2*); pap. text ed. 1.95 (*0-89375-497-8*) Troll Assocs.

— How to Draw Cars & Trucks. LC 81-52122. (Illus.). 32p. (J). (gr. 2-6). 1982. lib. bdg. 10.65 (*0-89375-681-4*); pap. text ed. 1.95 (*0-89375-498-6*) Troll Assocs.

— How to Draw Dinosaurs. LC 81-52118. (Illus.). 32p. (J). (gr. 2-6). 1982. lib. bdg. 10.65 (*0-89375-683-0*); pap. text ed. 1.95 (*0-89375-496-X*) Troll Assocs.

Laplace, Cyrille P. Voyage Autour du Monde par les Mers de l'Indeet de Chine, Tome 1. (Discovery of the Pacific & Australia Ser.). (Illus.). 602p. (FRE.). (C). 1989. reprint ed. 135.00 (*1-85297-001-4*, Pub. by Archival Facs UK) St Mut.

Laplace, Jean. Prayer According to the Scriptures. 85p. 1991. pap. 7.95 (*1-85390-167-9*, Pub. by Veritas Publns IE) Ignatius Pr.

LaPlace, Jean. Preparing for Spiritual Direction. 196p. 1975. 4.95 (*0-8199-0558-5*, Frncscn Herld) Franciscan Pr.

— Preparing for Spiritual Direction. 196p. 1975. 4.95 (*0-8199-0550-X*, Frncscn Herld) Franciscan Pr.

LaPlace, John. Health. 5th ed. (Illus.). 608p. (C). 1986. pap. text ed. write for info. (*0-13-384587-7*) P-H.

Laplace, P. S., jt. auth. see Lavoisier, A. L.

Laplace, Pierre S. Celestial Mechanics, Set. LC 69-11316. text ed. 250.00 (*0-8284-0194-2*) Chelsea Pub.

— Celestial Mechanics, Vol. 5. LC 63-11316. 1969. reprint ed. text ed. 39.50 (*0-8284-0214-0*) Chelsea Pub.

— Philosophical Essays on Probabilities, 13. Toomer, G. J., ed. Dale, Andrew I., tr. LC 94-25497. 270p. 1994. 59.00 (*0-387-94349-8*) Spr-Verlag.

Laplanche, J. & Pontalis, J. B. Vocabulary of Psychoanalysis (Vocabulaire de la Psychanalyse) 10th ed. 544p. (FRE.). 1990. 105.00 (*0-7859-4741-8*, M14530) Fr & Eur.

Laplanche, Jean. Life & Death in Psychoanalysis. LC 75-36928. 160p. reprint ed. pap. 45.60 (*0-317-20653-2*, 2024138) Bks Demand.

— Life & Death in Psychoanalysis. Mehlman, Jeffrey, tr. LC 75-36928. 160p. 1985. reprint ed. pap. text ed. 12.95 (*0-8018-2730-2*) Johns Hopkins.

— New Foundations for Psychoanalysis. Macey, David, tr. (Illus.). 192p. 1989. pap. text ed. 19.95 (*0-631-16662-9*) Blackwell Pubs.

— Das Vokabular der Psychoanalyse: The Vocabulary of Psychoanalysis, 2 vols. (GER.). 1973. pap. 49.95 (*0-8288-6340-7*, M-7680, Suhrkamp) Fr & Eur.

Laplanche, Jean & Pontalis, J-B. The Language of Psycho-Analysis. Micholson-Smith, Donald, tr. LC 73-18418. 510p. (C). 1974. text ed. 39.95 (*0-393-01105-4*) Norton.

Laplanche, Jean & Pontalis, Jean-Bertrand. Diccionario del Psicoanalisis. 3rd deluxe ed. Cervantes Gimeno, Fernando, ed. 558p. (SPA.). 1977. 65.50 (*0-7859-0894-3*, S-31445) Fr & Eur.

Laplanche, Jean, ed. see Pontalis, Jean-Baptiste.

LaPlant, Sarah, jt. auth. see Franklin, Carleen.

***LaPlante, Dan & LaPlante, Roberta.** New England's Best Family Getaways: Country Inns & Bed & Breakfasts. 2nd rev. ed. LC 94-69865. (Illus.). 300p. (Orig.). 1995. pap. 14.95 (*0-9632294-1-9*) Columbine Pub.

LaPlante, John D. Asian Art. 3rd ed. 304p. (C). 1992. pap. write for info. (*0-697-11591-7*) Brown & Benchmark.

LaPlante, Joseph A., jt. auth. see Tait, Colin C.

LaPlante, Josephine M. & Durham, Taylor R. An Introduction to Benefit-Cost Analysis for Evaluating Public Expenditure Alternatives. (Learning Packages in the Policy Sciences Ser.: No. 22). (Illus.). 74p. (C). 1983. pap. text ed. 10.50 (*0-936826-17-7*) PS Assocs Croton.

***Laplante, Lisa I. & Kinsley, Carol W., eds.** Things That Work in Community Service Learning Vol. 1. 160p. (Orig.). 1994. pap. 20.00 (*0-9644330-0-1*) Comm Srv Lrning.

Laplante, Lynda. Prime Suspect 3. 1994. mass mkt. 4.99 (*0-440-21496-3*) Dell.

***LaPlante, Philip.** Easy PC Maintenance & Repair. 2nd ed. 1995. text ed. 27.95 (*0-07-036432-X*, Windcrest) TAB Bks.

— Fractal Mania. 1993. pap. text ed. 29.95 (*0-07-036422-2*) McGraw.

***Laplante, Phillip.** Easy PC Maintenance & Repair. 2nd ed. 1995. pap. text ed. 17.95 (*0-07-036433-8*, Windcrest) TAB Bks.

— Fractal Mania. LC 93-8265. 158p. 1993. pap. text ed. 29.95 (*0-8306-4434-2*, Windcrest) TAB Bks.

Laplante, Phillip & Martin, Robert. Using UNIX. Gordon, Robert J., ed. LC 93-9501. 225p. (C). 1993. pap. text ed. 23.75 (*0-314-01262-1*) West Pub.

Laplante, Phillip A. Real-Time Systems Design & Analysis: An Engineer's Handbook. (Illus.). 360p. 1993. text ed. 49.95 (*0-7803-0402-0*, PC0297-2) Inst Electrical.

Laplante, Phillip A., jt. auth. see Dougherty, Edward R.

LaPlante, Richard. Mantis. 352p. 1993. 19.95 (*0-312-85531-1*) Tor Bks.

LaPlante, Roberta, jt. auth. see LaPlante, Dan.

LaPlantz, David. Artists Anodizing Aluminum. LC 87-61000. (Illus.). 200p. (Orig.). 1988. pap. 19.95 (*0-942002-03-2*) Press LaPlantz.

LaPlantz, David, ed. Jewelry - Metalwork 1991 Survey: Visions - Concepts - Communication. (Illus.). 160p. (Orig.). (C). 1991. pap. text ed. 19.95 (*0-942002-05-9*) Press LaPlantz.

LaPlantz, Shereen. The Mad Weave Book. LC 84-90630. (Illus.). 76p. (Orig.). 1984. pap. 6.95 (*0-942002-01-6*) Press LaPlantz.

— Twill Basketry: A Handbook of Designs, Techniques, & Styles. LC 92-29051. (Illus.). 144p. 1992. 19.95 (*0-937274-64-X*) Lark Books.

LaPlantz, Shereen, ed. Basketry Round Up 1991, No. 1. (Illus.). 112p. (Orig.). (C). 1990. pap. 18.95 (*0-942002-04-0*) Press LaPlantz.

Lapo, Andrey. Traces of Bygone Biospheres. (Illus.). 356p. 1988. pap. 8.95 (*0-907791-06-9*) Synerg AZ.

Lapoint, George M. Chess Points: How You Can Win Chess Games. (Illus.). 226p. (Orig.). (C). 1989. pap. 9.95 (*0-9623240-0-0*) Gemla Pub.

LaPoint, Velma, jt. auth. see Washington, Valora.

***Lapointe, Claude.** Out of Sight. (J). 1995. write for info. (*1-56846-106-2*) Creative Ed.

— Out of Sight. LC 94-38165. (Illus.). (J). 1995. write for info. (*1-56846-110-0*) Creative Ed.

An Asterisk (*) at the beginning of an entry indicates that the title is appearing in BIP for the first time.

LaPointe-Crump, Janice D. & Staley, Kimberly T. Discovering Jazz Dance: America's Energy & Soul. 224p. (C). 1992. pap. text ed. write for info. (0-697-11392-2) Brown & Benchmark.

Lapointe, Francois H., comp. Ludwig Wittgenstein: A Comprehensive Bibliography. LC 79-6565. 312p. 1980. text ed. 55.00 (0-313-22127-8, LAW/, Greenwood Pr) Greenwood.

— Soren Kierkegaard & His Critics: An International Bibliography of Criticism. LC 80-783. viii, 430p. 1980. text ed. 79.50 (0-313-22333-5, LKI/, Greenwood Pr) Greenwood.

Lapointe, Francois H., ed. George Lukacs & His Critics: An International Bibliography with Annotations, 1910-1982. LC 83-5613. ix, 403p. 1983. text ed. 65.00 (0-313-23891-X, LAG/, Greenwood Pr) Greenwood.

LaPointe, Leonard. Aphasia & Related Neurogenic Language Disorders. (Illus.). 256p. 1990. text ed. 46.00 (0-86577-314-9) Thieme Med Pubs.

LaPointe, Leonard L. Base-Ten Response Form. rev. ed. (Illus.). (C). 1991. ring bd. 51.50x (1-879105-28-4, 0212); 32.50 (1-879105-27-6, 0212) Singular Publishing.

LaPointe, P. R., jt. ed. see Barton, C. C.

Lapointe, Pierre. DBase Compiled for DOS Developer's Guide. 1994. 30.00 (0-679-75159-9) Random.

Lapolla, Garibaldi M. The Fire in the Flesh. LC 74-17935. (Italian American Experience Ser.). 362p. 1975. reprint ed. 24.95 (0-405-06407-1) Ayer.

— The Grand Gennaro. LC 74-17937. (Italian American Experience Ser.). 380p. 1975. reprint ed. 25.95 (0-405-06408-X) Ayer.

***LaPolla, Randy J. & Lowe, John B.** Bibliography of the International Conferences on Sino-Tibetan Languages & Linguistics I-XXV. Matisoff, James A., ed. LC 94-72182. (STEDT Monograph Ser.: 1A). 308p. (Orig.). (C). 1994. pap. text ed. 28.00 (0-944613-22-5) UC Berkeley Ctrs SE Asia.

Lapomarda, Vincent A. The Boston Mayor Who Became Truman's Secretary of Labor: Maurice J. Tobin & the Democratic Party. LC 93-40602. (American University Studies: Vol. 159). 360p. (C). 1995. text ed. 58.95 (0-8204-2448-X) P Lang Pubs.

— The Jesuit Heritage in New England. LC 76-42896. (Illus.). (Orig.). (C). 1977. pap. 8.00 (0-9606294-0-8) Jesuits Holy Cross.

— The Jesuits & the Third Reich. LC 88-27180. (Texts & Studies in Religion: Vol. 39). 392p. 1989. lib. bdg. 99.95 (0-88946-828-1) E Mellen.

— The Knights of Columbus in Massachusetts. 158p. (Orig.). 1982. pap. 10.00 (0-9608258-1-9) Mass State.

Laponce, J. A. The Government of the Fifth Republic. LC 76-2005. (Illus.). 415p. 1976. reprint ed. text ed. 75.00 (0-8371-8763-X, LAGF, Greenwood Pr) Greenwood.

— Languages & Their Territories. Martin-Sperry, A. D., tr. 275p. 1987. 37.50 (0-8020-5703-9); pap. 19.95 (0-8020-6631-3) U of Toronto Pr.

— Left & Right: The Topography of Political Perceptions. 284p. 1981. 40.00 (0-8020-5533-8) U of Toronto Pr.

Laponce, J. A. & Smoker, Paul, eds. Experimentation & Simulation in Political Science. LC 72-163827. 475p. reprint ed. pap. 135.40 (0-685-15804-7, 2026368) Bks Demand.

Laponce, J. A., jt. ed. see Berry, J. W.

Laponce, Jean & Meisel, John, eds. Debating the Constitution. 156p. 1994. pap. 19.00 (0-7766-0401-5, Pub. by Univ Ottawa Pr CN) Univ Ottawa Pr Co Pubs.

Laporta, Jose. Comunicacion Musical Evangelica: Christian Music Manual. (SPA.). 4.95 (84-7645-025-7, 223103, Pub. by Edit Clie SP) TSELF.

Laporte, Jean. Eucharistia in Philo. LC 82-25876. (Studies in the Bible & Early Christianity: Vol. 3). 274p. 1983. lib. bdg. 89.95 (0-88946-601-7) E Mellen.

LaPorte, Jean. The Role of Women in Early Christianity. LC 82-8281. (Studies in Women & Religion: Vol. 7). 196p. (C). 1982. lib. bdg. 79.95 (0-88946-545-2) E Mellen.

Laporte, Jean & Taylor, Finian. Understanding Our Biblical & Early Christian Tradition: An Introductory Textbook in Theology. LC 91-35645. 368p. 1991. pap. 34.95 (0-7734-9668-8) E Mellen.

LaPorte, Jean L. Tuttle - Tuthill: One Branch of the Eli Tuthill Family of Liberty Township of Michigan, Descendants of the Tuthill Family of Southold & Orient, Long Island, 1640, & of Tharston, England. (Illus.). 107p. 1992. lib. bdg. 25.00 (0-8328-2357-0); pap. 15.00 (0-8328-2358-9) Higginson Bk Co.

Laporte, L. F., ed. Establishment of a Geologic Framework for Paleoanthropology. (Special Paper Ser.: No. 242). (Illus.). 82p. 1990. pap. 22.50 (0-8137-2242-X) Geol Soc.

Laporte, Leo F. Ancient Environments. 2nd ed. (Foundations of the Earth Ser.). (Illus.). 1979. pap. text ed. write for info. (0-13-036384-7) P-H.

Laporte, Leo F., ed. Reefs in Time & Space: Selected Examples from the Recent & Ancient. LC 74-165238. (Society of Economic Paleontologists & Mineralogists, Special Publication Ser.: No. 18). 260p. reprint ed. pap. 74.10 (0-317-27147-4, 2024745) Bks Demand.

Laporte, Leo F., jt. auth. see Newton, Cathryn.

LaPorte, Margery, pseud. Circle of Blood. LC 88-72333. 143p. (Orig.). 1989. pap. 5.00 (0-916383-81-4) Aegina Pr.

LaPorte, Penny & Maurer, Jay. Structure Practice in Context: Workbooks 1-3, No. 1. 106p. (Orig.). 1985. Wkbk. 1. student ed, pap. text ed. 12.95 (0-582-79858-2, 12.95 WKBK. 3) Longman.

— Structure Practice in Context: Workbooks 1-3, No. 2. 106p. (Orig.). 1985. Wkbk. 2. student ed. pap. text ed. 12.95 (0-582-79859-0, 75105) Longman.

— Structure Practice in Context: Workbooks 1-3, No. 3. 106p. (Orig.). 1985. Wkbk. 3. student ed. pap. text ed. 12.95 (0-582-79860-4, 75106) Longman.

LaPorte, Penny & O'Neill, Robert. American Kernel Lessons: Advanced Teacher's Edition. 101p. 1982. 18.95 (0-582-79763-2, 75017) Longman.

LaPorte, Valerie & Rubin, Jeffrey, eds. Reform & Regulation in Long Term Care. LC 79-9761. 230p. 1979. text ed. 55.00 (0-275-90379-6, C0379, Praeger Pubs) Greenwood.

LaPorte, Valerie, jt. ed. see Rubin, Jeffrey.

***Lapos-Massey, Freeda.** A Royal Buggy Garden. (Illus.). 29p. (J). (gr. 3-6). 1994. lib. bdg. 13.75 (1-886272-00-X) Bugsy-n-Doc.

LaPosata. The Clinical Hemotasis Handbook. 348p. 1989. pap. 29.95 (0-8151-5540-9, Yr Bk Med Pubs) Mosby Yr Bk.

Laposata, Michael. SI Unit Conversion Guide. (Illus.). 110p. (Orig.). 1992. spiral bd. 14.95 (0-910133-38-7) MA Med Soc.

Lapouge, Gilles. The Battle of Wagram. Brownjohn, J. Maxwell, tr. 356p. (C). 1988. 19.95 (0-941533-32-8) New Amsterdam Bks.

— The Battle of Wagram. Brownjohn, J. Maxwell, tr. 356p. 1990. reprint ed. pap. 12.95 (1-56131-013-1) New Amsterdam Bks.

Lapp. Digital Communication & Signal Processing. Date not set. text ed. write for info. (0-318-72278-X) Van Nos Reinhold.

Lapp, Alvin K., et al. The Amish Cookbook. (Illus.). 433p. 1992. 11.25 (0-9637275-0-8) A K Lapp.

Lapp, Charles L., jt. auth. see Frank, William.

Lapp, Claudia. Honey. 1977. pap. 3.00 (0-916696-04-9) Cross Country.

***Lapp, Danielle C.** Don't Forget! Easy Exercises for a Better Memory. expanded ed. LC 95-798. 288p. (C). 1995. pap. 9.62 (0-201-48336-X) Addison-Wesley.

— Maximizing Your Memory Power. 1992. pap. 4.95 (0-8120-4799-0) Barron.

— Nearly Total Recall: A Guide to a Better Memory at Any Age. (Portable Stanford Book Ser.). 192p. (Orig.). 1992. pap. 12.95 (0-916318-51-6) Stanford Alumni Assn.

Lapp, David & Flood, James. Teaching Reading to Every Child. 3rd ed. 720p. (C). 1992. text ed. write for info. (0-02-367630-2) Macmillan.

Lapp, Diane, ed. Making Reading Possible Through Effective Classroom Management. LC 80-10444. 248p. reprint ed. pap. 70.70 (0-317-58123-6, 2029727) Bks Demand.

Lapp, Diane, jt. auth. see Anderson, Paul S.

Lapp, Diane, jt. auth. see Flood, James.

Lapp, Diane K., jt. auth. see Flood, James.

Lapp, Elizabeth. Journal of Tears. 1984. pap. 3.50 (0-87813-522-7) Christian Light.

Lapp, Henry, illus. A Craftsman's Handbook: Henry Lapp. LC 91-70663. 100p. 1991. pap. 15.95 (1-56148-014-2) Good Bks PA.

Lapp, Janet. Dancing with Tigers. 123p. 1994. pap. 10.95 (1-885365-01-2) Demeter Pr.

— Dancing with Tigers. 224p. 1995. boxed 22.95 (1-885365-02-0) Demeter Pr.

Lapp, John A. The Mennonite Church in India: Eighteen Ninety-Seven to Nineteen Sixty-Two. LC 75-186445. (Studies in Anabaptist & Mennonite History: No. 14). 248p. 1972. 12.95 (0-8361-1122-2) Herald Pr.

Lapp, John C. The Brazen Tower: Essays on Mythological Imagery in French Renaissance & Baroque, 1550-1670. (Stanford French & Italian Studies: No. 7). 198p. 1978. pap. 46.50 (0-915838-35-4) Anma Libri.

Lapp, John C., ed. see Corneille, Pierre.

Lapp, Marshall, jt. ed. see Stwalley, William C.

Lapp, Marshall, et al, eds. Advances in Laser Science, II. LC 87-71962. (Conference Proceeding Ser.: No. 160). 768p. 1987. lib. bdg. 85.00 (0-88318-360-9) Am Inst Physics.

Lapp, Nancy L., ed. see Lapp, Paul W.

Lapp, Nancy L., jt. ed. see Lapp, Paul W.

Lapp, Paul. The Excavations at Beth-Zur, 1957. (American Schools of Oriental Research Ser.: Vol. 38). 87p. 1968. text ed. 20.00 (0-89757-038-3) Am Sch Orient Res.

Lapp, Paul W. The Dhahr Mirzbaneh Tombs: Three Intermediate Bronze Age Cemeteries in Jordan. (American Schools of Oriental Research Publications of the Jerusalem School Archaeology: Vol. 4). x, 117p. 1966. pap. text ed. 12.50 (0-317-04129-0) Am Schls Oriental.

— The Tale of the Tell, Archeological Studies: Archaeological Studies by Paul W. Lapp. Lapp, Nancy L., ed. LC 75-5861. (Pittsburgh Theological Monograph Ser.: No. 5). 1975. pap. 9.25 (0-915138-05-0) Pickwick.

Lapp, Paul W. & Lapp, Nancy L., eds. Discoveries in the Wadi ed-Daliyeh. (Annual of the American Schools of Oriental Research Ser.: Vol. 41). (Illus.). 106p. 1974. text ed. 20.00 (0-89757-041-3) Am Sch Orient Res.

Lapp, Ralph E. Must We Hide? LC 81-6440. (Illus.). x, 182p. 1981. reprint ed. text ed. 49.75 (0-313-23102-8, LAMW, Greenwood Pr) Greenwood.

— My Life with Radiation-Hiroshima plus 50. 1995. pap. text ed. 10.00 (0-614-03716-6) Med Physics Pub.

— The Radiation Controversy. 2nd ed. LC 78-83841. (Illus.). 1979. pap. 4.95 (0-9603716-0-5) Reddy Comm.

Lapp, Rudolph M. Afro-Americans in California. 2nd ed. Hundley, Norris, Jr. & Schutz, John A., eds. (Golden State Ser.). (Illus.). 128p. 1987. pap. 10.00 (0-87835-152-3) MTL.

— Blacks in Gold Rush California. LC 76-30534. (Yale Western Americana Ser.: No. 13). (Illus.). 1977. 42.00 (0-300-01988-2) Yale U Pr.

Lapp, Sallie Y. Amish Cooking. 48p. 1982. 1.69 (0-9637275-2-4) A K Lapp.

— Amish Treats from My Kitchen. (Illus.). 47p. (Orig.). 1981. 3.29 (0-9637275-1-6) A K Lapp.

Lapp, T. Digital Communication & Signal Processing. 1988. text ed. write for info. (0-442-26042-3) Van Nos Reinhold.

Lapp, Warren A. & Silberman, Herbert A., eds. United States Large Cents 1793-1857. LC 74-27611. (Gleanings from the Numismatist Ser.). (Illus.). 640p. 1975. 50.00 (0-88000-058-9) Quarterman.

Lappan, Richard L. Child Custody Investigation. 35p. 1990. pap. text ed. 19.95 (0-918487-36-6) Thomas Pubns TX.

Lappas & Owens. Washington University Manual of Clinical Pharmacology for the Anesthesiologist. (Illus.). 400p. 1990. spiral bd. 29.95 (0-8016-3365-6) Mosby Yr Bk.

Lappe, Claus O., jt. auth. see Daly, Peter M.

Lappe, Frances M. Diet for a Small Planet. 20th ed. 528p. 1991. pap. 14.00 (0-345-37366-9, Ballantine Trade) Ballantine.

— Diet for a Small Planet: 10th Anniversary Edition. 1986. mass mkt. 6.99 (0-345-32120-0, Ballantine Trade) Ballantine.

Lappe, Frances M. & Collins, Joseph. Now We Can Speak: A Journey Through the New Nicaragua. LC 82-21289. 128p. (Orig.). 1982. pap. 4.95 (0-935028-14-5) Inst Food & Develop.

— World Hunger: Twelve Myths. 224p. 1986. pap. 10.95 (0-8021-5041-1) Grove-Atltic.

Lappe, Frances M. & Du Bois, Paul M. The Quickening of America: Rebuilding Our Nation, Remaking Our Lives. LC 93-35547. (Nonprofit Ser.). 350p. 1994. 18.00 (1-55542-605-0) Jossey-Bass.

Lappe, Frances M. & Schurman, Rachel. Taking Population Seriously. (Illus.). 90p. 1990. pap. 7.95 (0-935028-53-6) Inst Food & Develop.

Lappe, Frances M. & Schurmann, Rachel. Betraying the National Interest. (Food First Bks.). 160p. 1987. 18.95 (0-8021-0012-0); pap. 8.95 (0-8021-3027-5) Inst Food & Develop.

Lappe, Frances M., et al. Aid As Obstacle: Twenty Questions, Foreign Aid & the Hungry. (Illus.). 197p. (Orig.). 1980. pap. 5.95 (0-935028-07-2) Inst Food & Develop.

***Lappe, Marc.** Breakout: The Evolving Threat of Drug-Resistant Disease. LC 95-12016. Orig. Title: Revolutionary Medicine. (Illus.). 272p. 1995. pap. 14.00 (0-87156-382-7) Sierra.

— Broken Code: The Exploitation of DNA. LC 84-22190. (Illus.). 288p. (Orig.). 1985. 17.95 (0-87156-835-7) Sierra.

— Chemical Deception: The Toxic Threat to Health & the Environment. LC 90-9043. (Illus.). 420p. 1991. 27.00 (0-87156-603-6) Sierra.

— Chemical Deception: The Toxic Threat to Health & the Environment. LC 90-9043. 384p. 1992. reprint ed. pap. 15.00 (0-87156-511-0) Sierra.

— Evolutionary of Medicine: Rethinking the Origins of Disease. LC 94-5832. 384p. 1994. 30.00 (0-87156-519-6) Sierra.

— When Antibiotics Fail: Restoring the Ecology of the Body. 320p. (Orig.). (C). 1995. pap. 14.95 (1-55643-191-0) North Atlantic.

— When Antibiotics Fail: Restoring the Ecology of the Body. rev. ed. 288p. (Orig.). 1987. reprint ed. pap. 12.95 (0-938190-74-1) North Atlantic.

— When Antibiotics Fail: Restoring the Ecology of the Body. 2nd rev. ed. 288p. (Orig.). 1987. reprint ed. 25.00 (0-938190-75-X) North Atlantic.

Lappe, Marc & Morison, Robert S., eds. Ethical & Scientific Issues Posed by Human Uses of Molecular Genetics, Vol. 265. (Annals Ser.). 208p. 1976. 26.00 (0-89072-019-3) NY Acad Sci.

Lappe, Marc, jt. ed. see Murphy, Timothy F.

Lappe, Robert J., jt. auth. see McDonald, Hugh J.

Lapper, Richard. Honduras: State for Sale. (Latin America Bureau Ser.). 128p. (Orig.). 1985. pap. 7.00 (0-85345-697-6, Pub. by Lat Am Bur UK) Monthly Rev.

Lappin & Sauer. Alpha Olefins Applications Handbook. (Chemical Industries Ser.: Vol. 37). 480p. 1989. 155.00 (0-8247-7895-2) Dekker.

Lappin, Ben W. & Teicher, Morton I. Distant Partners: Community Change Through Project Renewal. 298p. (Orig.). (C). 1990. lib. bdg. 49.00 (0-8191-7760-1); pap. text ed. 25.50 (0-8191-7761-X) U Pr of Amer.

Lappin, Elena, ed. Jewish Voices, German Words: Growing up Jewish in Postwar Germany & Austria. Winston, Krishna, tr. LC 93-39950. 303p. 1994. 23.95 (0-945774-23-0, PT405.J48) Catbird Pr.

Lappin, Greg, et al. Tennis Doubles, No. 1: Winning Strategies for All Levels. (Illus.). 144p. (Orig.). 1985. pap. 9.95 (0-930425-00-6) KG Bks Co.

Lappin, Ivan M., jt. auth. see Blakely, Robert J.

Lappin, Kendall, tr. The Muse Spoke French: Selected Poems. LC 94-70671. 128p. (Orig.). 1994. pap. 9.95 (1-878580-59-0) Asylum Arts.

Lappin, Kendall, tr. see Baudelaire, Charles.

Lappin, Kendall, tr. see De Nerval, Gerard.

Lappin, Kendall E. Baudelaire Revisited: Forty-One Poems. LC 81-90014. (Illus.). 196p. 1981. 11.95 (0-9605710-1-9); pap. 7.95 (0-9605710-0-0) KEL Pubns.

Lappin, Linda. Wintering with the Abominable Snowman. 66p. 1975. pap. 8.00 (0-87711-060-3) Story Line.

Lappin, Linda, tr. see Careri, Giovanni.

Lappin, Linda, tr. see Petrucci, Armando.

Lappin, Peter. First Lady of the World: A Popular History of Devotion to Mary. 192p. 1988. 14.95 (0-89944-098-3); pap. 9.95 (0-89944-091-6) Don Bosco Multimedia.

— Stories of Don Bosco. 2nd ed. LC 78-72525. (Illus.). 272p. (J). (gr. 5-12). 1979. pap. 8.95 (0-89944-036-3) Don Bosco Multimedia.

— Zatti! 77p. 1987. pap. 2.50 (0-89944-090-8, D Bosco Pubns) Don Bosco Multimedia.

***Lappin-Scott, Hilary M. & Costerton, J. William, eds.** Microbial Biofilms. (Plant & Microbiotechnology Research Ser.: No. 5). (Illus.). 300p. (C). 1995. write for info. (0-521-45412-3) Cambridge U Pr.

Lappin, Shalom. Sorts, Ontology, & Metaphor: The Semantics of Sortal Structure. (Foundations of Communication & Cognition Ser.). 173p. 1981. 65.40 (3-11-008309-4) De Gruyter.

***Lappin, Shalom, ed. & intro.** The Handbook of Contemporary Semantic Theory. (Handbooks in Linguistics Ser.). 640p. 1996. write for info. (0-631-18752-9) Blackwell Pubs.

Lappin, Terence R., jt. ed. see Rich, Ivan N.

***Lapping, Brian & Radice, Giles.** More Power to the People: Young Fabian Essays on Democracy in Britain. 1968. pap. 49.50x (0-614-01798-X) Elliots Bks.

Lapping, Mark, ed. see Russell, Howard S.

Lapping, Mark B., et al. Rural Planning & Development in the United States. LC 89-2231. 342p. 1989. lib. bdg. 45.00 (0-89862-384-7); pap. text ed. 20.95 (0-89862-517-3) Guilford Pr.

Lapple, Alfred. The Catholic Church: A Brief History. (Orig.). 1985. pap. 6.95 (0-8091-9567-4) Paulist Pr.

Lappo-Danilevskii, J. A. Systemes des Equations Differentielles, 3 Vols. in 1. LC 53-7110. 35.00 (0-8284-0094-6) Chelsea Pub.

Laprade, Armand, ed. see Montherlant, Henri de.

Laprade, B. N., jt. ed. see Johnson, C. B.

Laprade, William T. England & the French Revolution, 1789-1797. LC 77-109922. reprint ed. 27.50 (0-404-03878-6) AMS Pr.

Laprie, J. C., jt. ed. see Avizienis, A.

Laprie, J. C., et al, eds. Dependability: Basic Concepts & Terminology. (Dependable Computing & Fault-Tolerant Systems Ser.: Vol. 5). (Illus.). xii, 268p. 1992. 89.00 (0-387-82296-8) Spr-Verlag.

Laprise, Susan, ed. see Parent-Child Nursing Department.

Laprisot, Sebastien. A Very Long Engagement. Coverdale, Linda, tr. LC 94-11290. 336p. 1994. pap. 10.95 (0-452-27297-1, Plume) NAL-Dutton.

Lapsanski, Duane. Evangelical Perfection: An Historical Examination of the Concept in the Early Franciscan Sources. (Theology Ser.). 1977. 15.00 (0-686-27933-6) Franciscan Inst.

Lapsansky, Emma J. Neighborhoods in Transition: William Penn's Dream & Urban Reality. LC 93-38423. (Studies in African American History & Culture). (Illus.). 216p. 1994. 55.00 (0-8153-1566-X) Garland.

Lapsley, D. K. & Power, F. Clark, eds. Self, Ego, & Identity. (Illus.). 280p. 1988. 54.00 (0-387-96588-2) Spr-Verlag.

Lapsley, Daniel K., jt. ed. see Power, F. Clark.

Lapsley, J. T., jt. auth. see Cooke, George M.

Lapsley, James N. Renewal in Late Life Through Pastoral Counseling. LC 92-19818. (Integration Ser.). 128p. 1992. pap. 9.95 (0-8091-3333-4) Paulist Pr.

Lapsley, Peter. Fly Fishing for Trout. (Illus.). 192p. Date not set. 39.95 (0-09-174824-0, Pub. by S Paul UK) Trafalgar.

Lapsley, Robert & Westlake, Michael. Film Theory: An Introduction. (Images of Culture Ser.). 256p. 1989. text ed. 17.95 (0-7190-2602-4, Pub. by Manchester Univ Pr UK) St Martin.

Laptev, I. The Planet of Reason: A Sociological Study of Man-Nature Relationship. Sayer, Jane, tr. 220p. 1977. 7.50 (0-317-53779-2, Pub. by Collets UK) Pro-Am Music.

Laptev, V., ed. Economic Law. 142p. (C). 1987. 30.00 (0-685-31522-3, Pub. by Collets UK) Pro-Am Music.

Lapuente, F. A., jt. auth. see Rogers, P. P.

***Lapuma.** Finding the Giddness Within, Vol. 1. 1995. 9.95 (1-878203-01-0) SoulSource.

LaPuma, Karen & Runkis, Walt. Awakening Female Power: The Way of the Goddess Warrior. 4th rev. ed. LC 89-51331. (Illus.). 240p. (Orig.). 1991. reprint ed. pap. 12.95 (1-878203-02-9) SoulSource.

Lapuz, Lourdes V. Filipino Marriages in Crisis. 1977. 4.75 (971-10-0301-5, Pub. by New Day Pub PH) Cellar.

Lapwood, E. R. Ordinary Differential Equations. LC 68-21278. 1968. 95.00 (0-08-012551-4, Pub. by Pergamon Repr UK) Franklin.

Lapwood, E. R. & Usami, T. Free Oscillations of the Earth. (Cambridge Monographs on Mechanics & Applied Mathematics). (Illus.). 168p. 1981. 89.95 (0-521-23536-7) Cambridge U Pr.

Laqua, H., jt. auth. see Lucke, K.

Laque, Carol F. The Fury of the Birds. (Orig.). 1992. pap. 12.00 (0-9619532-1-7) Circumference Pr.

— Midnight Noon. (Orig.). 1995. pap. 15.00 (0-9619532-2-5) Circumference Pr.

LaQue Center for Corrosion Technology, Inc. Staff. Optimizing Cleaning Techniques for Copper Alloy Condenser Tubing in Seawater Service. 48p. 1984. write for info. (0-318-60405-1) Intl Copper.

Laqueur, Maria & Dickinson, Donna. Breaking Out of Nine to Five: How to Revise Your Job to Fit You. 256p. (Orig.). 1994. pap. 12.95 (1-56079-351-1) Petersons Guides.

Laqueur, Richard. Epigraphische Untersuchungen Zu Den Griechischen Volksbeschlussen. iv, 211p. reprint ed. write for info. (0-318-72099-X, Pub. by Georg Olms GW) Lubrecht & Cramer.

Laqueur, Thomas. Making Sex: Body & Gender from the Greeks to Freud. (Illus.). 313p. 1990. text ed. 37.00 (0-674-54349-1) HUP.

— Making Sex: Body & Gender from the Greeks to Freud. (Illus.). 336p. 1992. pap. text ed. 14.00 (0-674-54355-6) HUP.

Laqueur, Thomas, jt. ed. see Gallagher, Catherine.

Laqueur, Thomas W. Religion & Respectability: Sunday Schools & Working Class Culture, 1780-1850. LC 75-29728. 308p. reprint ed. pap. 87.80 (*0-8357-8302-2*, 2033797) Bks Demand.

Laqueur, Walter. The Age of Terrorism. 1988. pap. 12.95 (*0-316-51479-9*) Little.

— America, Europe, & the Soviet Union: Selected Essays. LC 82-19423. 234p. 1983. 39.95x (*0-87855-362-2*) Transaction Pubs.

— Black Hundred: The Rise of the Extreme Right in Russia. (Illus.). 336p. 1994. reprint ed. pap. 15.00 (*0-06-092534-5*, PL) HarpC.

— The Dream That Failed: Reflections on the Soviet Union. 272p. 1994. 25.00 (*0-19-508978-2*) OUP.

— The Dream That Failed: Reflections on the Soviet Union. 248p. 1996. pap. 11.95 (*0-19-510282-7*) OUP.

— Europe in Our Time: A History, 1945-1992. 624p. 1993. pap. 14.95 (*0-14-013969-9*, Penguin Bks) Viking Penguin.

— Europe since Hitler: The Rebirth of Europe. rev. ed. 580p. 1982. pap. 10.95 (*0-14-021411-9*, Penguin Bks) Viking Penguin.

— Fate of the Revolution. rev. ed. 1987. pap. 10.95 (*0-02-034080-X*, Collier S&S) S&S Trade.

— History of Zionism. 1989. pap. 16.95 (*0-8052-0899-2*) Schocken.

— The Long Road to Freedom: Russia & Glasnost. 352p. 1990. pap. 10.95 (*0-02-034090-7*, Collier S&S) S&S Trade.

— Looking Forward, Looking Backward. LC 83-11038. 154p. 1983. pap. text ed. 9.95 (*0-275-91578-6*, B1578, Praeger Pubs) Greenwood.

— The Political Psychology of Appeasement: Finlandization & Other Unpopular Essays on World Affairs. LC 79-6854. 283p. 1980. text ed. 28.95 (*0-87855-336-3*) Transaction Pubs.

— Russia & Germany: A Century of Conflict. 379p. (C). 1990. pap. 19.95 (*0-88738-349-1*) Transaction Pubs.

— Soviet Realities: Culture & Politics from Stalin to Gorbachev. 305p. 1989. 39.95 (*0-88738-302-5*) Transaction Pubs.

— Soviet Union Two Thousand: Reform or Revolution? 224p. 1991. pap. 10.95 (*0-312-06471-3*) St Martin.

— Thursday's Child Has Far to Go: A Memoir of the Journeying Years. 416p. 1993. text ed. 30.00 (*0-684-19421-X*, Scribners) S&S Trade.

— U. S. Defense Posture. (Task Force on the Eighties Ser.). 24p. 1981. pap. 2.50 (*0-87495-036-8*) Am Jewish Comm.

— The Uses & Limits of Intelligence. rev. ed. LC 92-32932. 445p. (C). 1993. pap. 21.95 (*1-56000-594-7*) Transaction Pubs.

— Young Germany: A History of the German Youth Movement. 260p. 1984. 32.95 (*0-88738-002-6*); pap. 18.95 (*0-87855-960-4*) Transaction Pubs.

Laqueur, Walter, ed. Fascism: A Readers' Guide: Analysis, Interpretations & Bibliography. LC 75-13158. 1977. pap. 15.00 (*0-520-03642-5*) U CA Pr.

— Middle East in Transition: Studies in Contemporary History. LC 70-156676. (Essay Index Reprint Ser.). 1977. reprint ed. 31.95 (*0-8369-2367-7*) Ayer.

— The Pattern of Soviet Conduct in the Third World. 256p. 1983. 38.50 (*0-275-91031-8*, C1031, Praeger Pubs) Greenwood.

— The Second World War: Essays in Military & Political History. LC 81-86067. (Sage Readers in 20th Century History Ser.: No. 4). 413p. reprint ed. pap. 117.80 (*0-8357-8444-4*, 2034708) Bks Demand.

Laqueur, Walter & Bubin, Barry, eds. The Israel-Arab Reader: A Documentary History of the Middle East. rev. ed. (Pelican Ser.). 688p. 1984. pap. 10.95 (*0-14-022588-9*, Penguin Bks) Viking Penguin.

Laqueur, Walter & Hunter, Robert, eds. European Peace Movements & the Future of the Western Alliance. 385p. (C). 1985. 39.95 (*0-88738-035-2*) Transaction Pubs.

Laqueur, Walter & Roberts, Brad, eds. America in the World, 1962-1987: A Strategic & Political Reader. 350p. 1987. text ed. 39.95 (*0-312-01318-3*) St Martin.

Laqueur, Walter & Rubin, Barry. The Human Rights Reader. rev. ed. 448p. (Orig.). 1990. pap. 13.95 (*0-452-01026-8*, Mer) NAL-Dutton.

Laqueur, Walter & Rubin, Barry, eds. The Human Rights Reader. (Orig.). 1979. pap. 9.95 (*0-452-00853-0*, F661, Mer) NAL-Dutton.

— The Israel-Arab Reader: A Documentary History of the Middle East. rev. ed. 720p. 1995. pap. 15.95 (*0-14-024562-6*, Penguin Bks) Viking Penguin.

— The Israel-Arab Reader: A Documentary History of the Middle East Conflict. LC 84-8047. 720p. reprint ed. pap. 180.00 (*0-8357-5600-9*, 2035241) Bks Demand.

Laqueur, Walter & Sloss, L. European Security in the 1990s: Deterrence & Defense after the INF Treaty. LC 89-49472. (Issues in International Security Ser.). (Illus.). 223p. 1990. 35.00 (*0-306-43442-3*, Plenum Pr) Plenum.

Laqueur, Walter, ed. see Friend, Julius W.

Laqueur, Walter, ed. see George, Bruce, et al.

Laqueur, Walter, ed. see Hanson, Philip.

Laqueur, Walter, ed. see Lowenthal, Mark M.

Laqueur, Walter, ed. see Ter Haar, Barend.

Laqueur, Walter, et al, eds. Historians in Politics. LC 74-78421. (Sage Readers in 20th Century History Ser.: Vol. 1). 360p. reprint ed. pap. 102.60 (*0-317-09543-9*, 2021920) Bks Demand.

LaQuey, Tracy. Internet Companion: A Beginner's Guide to Global Networking. 2nd ed. 1994. pap. 12.95 (*0-201-40766-3*) Addison-Wesley.

— Internet Companion Plus: A Beginner's Start-up Kit for Global Networking. Set. 2nd ed. 1994. disk 19.95 (*0-201-40837-6*) Addison-Wesley.

LaQuey, Tracy & Ryer, Jeanne C. The Internet Companion: A Beginner's Guide to Global Networks. LC 92-31691. 1992. pap. 12.95 (*0-201-62224-6*) Addison-Wesley.

— The Internet Companion Plus: A Beginner's Start-up Kit for Global Networking. LC 93-35647. 1993. pap. 19.95 (*0-201-62719-1*) Addison-Wesley.

LaQuey, Tracy L. The Users' Directory of Computer Networks. (Illus.). 630p. (Orig.). 1990. pap. 35.95 (*1-55558-047-5*, EY-C200E-DP, Digital DEC) Buttrwrth-Heinemann.

Laquian, E. & Sobrevinas, Irene. Filipino Cooking Abroad. 194p. 1977. 11.95 (*0-318-36289-9*) Asia Bk Corp.

***Lara, Adair.** At Adair's House: More Columns from America's Favorite Former Single Mom. LC 94-33727. 1995. pap. 11.95 (*0-8118-0498-4*) Chronicle Bks.

— Slowing Down in a Speeded up World. 150p. (Orig.). 1994. pap. 8.95 (*0-943233-57-7*) Conari Press.

— Slowing down in a Speeded-up World. 150p. 1994. 25.00x (*0-8095-5878-5*) Borgo Pr.

— Welcome to Earth, Mom: Tales of a Single Mother. 192p. 1992. pap. 9.95 (*0-8118-0090-3*) Chronicle Bks.

Lara, Jesus. Diccionario de Qheshwa-Espanol, Espanol-Qheshwa. 3rd ed. 430p. (MIS & SPA.). 1990. pap. write for info. (*0-7859-4889-9*) Fr & Eur.

— Diccionario de Ro de Qheshwa-Espanol, Espanol-Qheshwa. (SPA.). 39.95 (*0-686-56703-X*) Fr & Eur.

— Quechua Peoples Poetry. Proser, Maria & Scully, James, eds. Scully, James, tr. LC 76-26704. Orig. Title: Poesia Popular Quechua. 68p. 1977. pap. 9.95 (*0-915306-09-3*) Curbstone.

Lara, Juan, jt. auth. see Neuberger, Egon.

***Lara, Silvia, et al.** Inside Costa Rica. 1995. pap. text ed. 11.95 (*0-911213-51-1*) Interhemisp Res Ctr.

***Larabee, Ellen.** Sermon Starters & Chancel Teasers: Four Short Interludes. (Christian Theatre Ser.). 33p. (Orig.). 1994. pap. 5.95 (*1-57514-132-9*, 1164) Encore Perform Pub.

Larabee, Kim. Behind the Mask. LC 88-83327. 200p. (Orig.). 1989. pap. 6.95 (*1-55583-151-6*) Alyson Pubns.

Laraby, Larry, ed. see Haines, John, et al.

Laragh, John H., ed. Frontiers in Hypertension Research. (Illus.). 628p. 1981. 94.00 (*0-387-90557-X*) Spr-Verlag.

Laragh, John H. & Brenner, Barry M. Hypertension: Pathophysiology, Diagnosis, & Management, 2 vols. 2nd ed. 3344p. 1995. 345.00 (*0-7817-0157-0*) Raven.

Laragh, John H., jt. auth. see Blumenfeld, Jon D.

Laragh, John H., jt. auth. see Brenner, Barry M.

Laragh, John H., jt. ed. see Brenner, Barry M.

Laragh, John H., jt. ed. see Davis, James O.

Laragh, John H., et al. Endocrine Mechanisms in Hypertension. (Perspectives in Hypertension Ser.: Vol. 2). 380p. 1989. 121.50 (*0-88167-479-6*, 1932) Raven.

Laraia. Quick Psychopharmacology Reference. 64p. 1990. pap. 8.95 (*0-8016-2729-X*) Mosby Yr Bk.

Laraia, Michele T. Quick Psychopharmacology Reference. 2nd ed. 64p. 1994. pap. 8.95 (*0-8016-8064-6*) Mosby Yr Bk.

Laraja, Taryn, jt. auth. see Lynch, Priscilla.

Laraki, Karim. Food Subsidies: A Case Study of Price Reform in Morocco. (Living Standards Measurement Study Working Paper Ser.). 72p. 1988. 7.95 (*0-8213-1116-6*, 11116) World Bank.

Laramee, Eve A. The Eroded Terrain of Memory. Ottmann, Klaus, ed. (Illus.). 4p. (Orig.). (C). 1990. pap. text ed. 5.00 (*0-929687-04-3*) E & C Zilkha Gal.

Laramore, Darryl, jt. auth. see Kennedy, Joyce L.

Laramore, Jon. A Guide for Social Security Advocates. 40p. 1984. pap. 4.00 (*0-685-23187-9*, 41,250) NCLS Inc.

Laramore, Robert D., jt. auth. see McPherson, George.

Larana, Enrique, et al, eds. New Social Movements: From Ideology to Identity. LC 93-37495. 384p. (C). 1994. text ed. 49.95 (*1-56639-186-5*); pap. text ed. 18.95 (*1-56639-187-3*) Temple U Pr.

Laraneta, M., jt. ed. see Peccei, R.

***Laraque, Paul.** Liberty Drum: Selected Poems. Hirschman, Jack, tr. & pref. by. 144p. (Orig.). (C). 1995. pap. 11.95 (*1-885214-05-7*) Azul Edits.

Larason, Lew. The Basket Collectors Book. (Illus.). 156p. (Orig.). 1978. pap. 6.95 (*0-936099-00-3*) Scorpio Pubns.

— Baskets - Baskets - Baskets: An Advisory for Collectors. (Illus.). 8p. (Orig.). 1988. pap. 1.95 (*0-936099-01-1*) Scorpio Pubns.

— Buying Antique Furniture: An Advisory. Guthrie, Pattie, ed. (Illus.). 174p. (Orig.). 1992. pap. text ed. 14.95 (*0-936099-02-X*) Scorpio Pubns.

Laraya-Cuasay, L. R. Interstitial Lung Diseases in Children, 3 vols., Vol. I. Hughes, W. T., ed. 224p. 1988. 119.00 (*0-8493-4301-1*, RJ436, CRC Reprint) Franklin.

— Interstitial Lung Diseases in Children, 3 vols., Vol. II. Hughes, W. T., ed. 208p. 1988. 126.00 (*0-8493-4302-X*, RJ436) CRC Pr.

— Interstitial Lung Diseases in Children, 3 vols., Vol. III. Hughes, W. T., ed. 224p. 1988. 116.00 (*0-8493-4303-8*, RJ436, CRC Reprint) Franklin.

***Larbalestier, Simon.** The Art & Craft of Collage. LC 94-22236. 1995. 17.95 (*0-8118-0806-8*) Chronicle Bks.

***Larbalestrie, Deborah E.** Paralegal Practice & Procedure: A Practical Guide for the Legal Assistant. 3rd ed. LC 94-28860. 1994. pap. text ed. write for info. (*0-13-108564-6*) P-H.

Larbalestrier, Deborah E. Paralegal Practice & Procedure: A Practical Guide for the Legal Assistant. LC 85-12407. 1986. text ed. 34.95 (*0-13-648726-2*); pap. 16.95 (*0-13-648718-1*) P-H.

— Paralegal Practice & Procedure: A Practical Guide for the Legal Assistant. 3rd ed. LC 94-28860. 1994. write for info. (*0-13-108572-7*) P-H.

— Paralegal's Handbook of Annotated Legal Forms, Clauses & Procedures. 384p. 1982. 39.50 (*0-13-648642-8*, Busn) P-H.

Larbaud, V. Oeuvres. (FRE.). 1957. lib. bdg. 110.00 (*0-8288-3519-5*, F10840) Fr & Eur.

— Les Poesies de A. O. Barnabooth: Poesies Divers. (FRE.). 1987. pap. 10.95 (*0-8288-3863-1*, F109090) Fr & Eur.

Larbaud, Valery. Childish Things. Wald, Catherine, tr. (Sun & Moon Classics Ser.: No. 19). 200p. (Orig.). 1990. pap. 13.95 (*1-55713-119-8*) Sun & Moon CA.

— The Diary of A. O. Barnabooth. Cannan, Gilbert, tr. LC 90-46619. (Recovered Classics Ser.). 336p. 1990. reprint ed. 18.00 (*0-929701-14-3*); reprint ed. pap. 10.00 (*0-929701-15-1*) McPherson & Co.

— An Homage to Jerome. Chezet, Jean-Paul de, tr. LC 83-63447. 64p. (Orig.). 1984. pap. 6.95 (*0-910395-09-8*) Marlboro Pr.

Larbig, Laura M. White Buffalo Poems. Sharenov, Evelyn, ed. 24p. (Orig.). 1994. pap. 5.50 (*0-9627791-4-8*) Willamette Bks OR.

Larcada, Luis I. La Imagen Que No Se Deteriora. Editorial Arcos Inc. Staff, ed. (Arcos Poetica Ser.: No. 1). (Illus.). 110p. (Orig.). (SPA.). 1989. lib. bdg. 10.00 (*0-937509-04-3*) Edit Arcos.

— La Peninsula y la Isla. LC 86-62103. (Senda de Estudios y Ensayos Ser.). (Illus.). 96p. (Orig.). (SPA.). 1987. pap. 8.95 (*0-918454-58-1*) Senda Nueva.

— El Piano de Cristal. Editorial Arcos Inc. Staff, ed. LC 86-80617. (Coleccion Narrativa y Ensayo Ser.). (Illus.). 117p. (Orig.). 1986. 7.50 (*0-937509-00-0*) Edit Arcos.

— Tierra del Sur. Editorial Arcos, Inc. Staff, ed. (Arcos Poetica Ser.: No. 3). (Illus.). 44p. (SPA.). 1993. lib. bdg. 6.00 (*0-937509-09-4*) Edit Arcos.

Larcada, Luis I., ed. see Guerra, Pedro L.

Larcan, A., et al, eds. Consumption Coagulpathies. 176p. 1987. 73.50 (*2-225-80981-X*, MA981, Yr Bk Med Pubs) Mosby Yr Bk.

Larche. From the Heartland: Introduction to Speech Communication. 1993. pap. 19.95 (*0-685-65897-X*) Burgess MN Intl.

***L'Arche Daybreak Community Staff.** Living the Beatitudes: Daily Reflections for Lent. 112p. 1994. 9.95 (*0-86716-231-7*) St Anthony Mess Pr.

***Larche, Doug.** O Christmas Three! Date not set. 5.00 (*0-87129-535-0*, O54) Dramatic Pub.

Larche, Douglas W., see Father Gander, pseud..

Larcher, F. R., tr. see St. Thomas Aquinas.

Larcher, Fabian R., tr. see St. Thomas Aquinas.

Larcher, Jean. Allover Patterns with Letter Forms. LC 85-4544. 48p. (Orig.). 1985. pap. 3.50 (*0-486-24908-5*) Dover.

— Fantastic Alphabets. LC 76-24153. (Pictorial Archive Ser.). 56p. (Orig.). 1976. pap. 4.95 (*0-486-23412-6*) Dover.

— Geometrical Designs & Optical Art. LC 74-79464. (Pictorial Archive Ser.). (Illus.). 80p. 1974. 5.95 (*0-486-23100-3*) Dover.

— Optical & Geometrical Allover Patterns: 70 Original Drawings. LC 78-72985. (Pictorial Archive Ser.). (Illus.). 1979. pap. 7.95 (*0-486-23758-3*) Dover.

— Ready-to-Use News Announcements. 1981. pap. 4.50 (*0-486-24173-4*) Dover.

Larcher, W. Physiological Plant Ecology. rev. ed. Biederman-Thorson, M. A., tr. LC 79-26396. (Illus.). 304p. 1980. 34.00 (*3-540-09795-3*) Spr-Verlag.

Larcher, W., jt. auth. see Sakai, A.

***Larcher, Walter.** Physiological Plant Ecology: Ecophysiology & Stress Physiology of Function Groups. 3rd ed. LC 94-24405. 1995. write for info. (*0-387-58116-2*) Spr-Verlag.

***Larchey, Eitenne-Loredan.** Dictionnaire de l'Argot Parisien. 252p. (FRE.). 1985. pap. 32.95 (*0-7859-8233-7*, 2905291036) Fr & Eur.

Larcom, Lucy. An Idyl of Work. LC 72-88503. ix, 183p. 1970. reprint ed. text ed. 52.50 (*0-8371-4968-1*, LAIW, Greenwood Pr) Greenwood.

— New England Girlhood. 12.00 (*0-8446-2431-4*) Peter Smith.

— A New England Girlhood. 274p. 1977. reprint ed. 22.50 (*0-87928-078-6*) Corner Hse.

— A New England Girlhood: Outlined from Memory. (Illus.). 300p. 1985. reprint ed. pap. 12.95 (*0-930350-82-0*) NE U Pr.

Larcom, Thomas A., ed. see Petty, William.

***Larcombe, Isobel.** Reintegration to School after Hospital Treatment: Needs & Services. 137p. (C). 1995. boxed, pap. text ed. 51.95 (*1-85628-990-7*, Pub. by Avebury Pub UK) Ashgate Pub Co.

Larcombe, Jennifer R. Leaning on a Spider's Web. LC 92-38137. 312p. (Orig.). 1993. pap. 9.99 (*0-8308-1374-8*, 1374) InterVarsity.

Larcombe, M. H. & Halsal, J. R. Robotics in Nuclear Engineering: Computer Assisted Teleoperation in Hazardous Environments with Particular Reference to Radiation Fields. 164p. 1984. pap. text ed. 76.50 (*0-86010-613-6*) G & T Inc.

Larcombe, Tony. Mathematical Learning Difficulties in the Secondary School: Pupil Needs & Teacher Roles. 128p. 1985. pap. 29.00 (*0-335-15020-9*, Open Univ Pr) Taylor & Francis.

Lardaro. Applied Econometrics. (C). 1992. text ed. 72.00 (*0-06-043847-9*) HarpCollege.

— Applied Econometrics. (C). 1993. student ed 18.75 (*0-06-501610-6*) HarpCollege.

Lardas, George D., tr. see St. Tikhon of Zadonsk.

Larde, Enrique. The Crown Prince Rudolf: His Mysterious Life after Mayerling. (Illus.). 112p. 1994. 11.00 (*0-8059-3580-0*) Dorrance.

Lardet, Pierre. L' Apologie de Jerome Contre Rufin: Un Commentaire. LC 93-13086. (Supplements to Vigiliae Christianae Ser.: Vol. 15). xxxii, 564p. (FRE.). 1993. 140.00 (*90-04-09457-1*) E J Brill.

Lardinois, A. P., jt. auth. see Oudemans, T. C.

***Lardinois, Robert, et al.** Deedo & Dido. LC 92-20879. (Our Feathered & Furry Friends Ser.). (Illus.). 42p. (J). (ps-2). 1992. audio, lib. bdg. 21.95 (*0-9629715-2-9*); audio 7.95 (*0-9629715-3-7*) Jewel Publishing.

— Deedo & Dido: Story. LC 92-20879. (Our Feathered & Furry Friends Ser.). (Illus.). 42p. (J). (ps-2). 1992. lib. bdg. 14.95 (*0-9629715-1-0*) Jewel Publishing.

***Lardner, D.** Manufacturing of Porcelain & Glass. 320p. 1994. pap. 25.00 (*0-87556-795-9*) Saifer.

— Steam Engine, 1888. (Illus.). 135p. 1989. pap. 20.00 (*0-87556-165-9*) Saifer.

Lardner, D., jt. auth. see Kater, Henry.

Lardner, Dionysius. Railway Economy: A Treatise on the New Art of Transport. LC 67-29509. (Reprints of Economic Classics Ser.). 1968. reprint ed. 45.00 (*0-678-00361-0*) Kelley.

***Lardner, George.** The Stalking of Kristin: A Father Investigates the Murder of His Daughter. LC 95-14575. 1995. 21.00 (*0-87113-613-9*, Atlntc Mnthly) Grove-Atltic.

***Lardner, James.** An Angry Man. Date not set. 25.00 (*0-394-57648-9*) Random.

Lardner, Jocelyn. How to Step by Step Develop a Personal Computer Hobby: With Step by Step Instructions in Language You Can Understand. 50p. 1991. pap. write for info. (*0-9630063-0-4*) Skorping Pubs.

Lardner, John. Strong Cigars & Lovely Women. 19.95 (*0-8488-0124-5*, Amereon Hse) Amereon Ltd.

Lardner, Kym. Arnold the Prickly Teddy. LC 92-31919. (Voyages Ser.). (Illus.). (J). 1993. 14.00 (*0-383-03552-X*) SRA Schl Grp.

Lardner, Nathaniel, jt. auth. see Wake, William.

Lardner, R. W. Mathematical Theory of Dislocations & Fracture. LC 75-190346. (Mathematical Expositions Ser.: No. 17). 375p. reprint ed. pap. 106.90 (*0-317-09423-8*, 2020498) Bks Demand.

Lardner, Ring, Jr. The Best Short Stories: Twenty-Five Stories from America's Foremost Humorist. LC 92-33701. 360p. 1993. pap. 10.00 (*0-02-022341-2*, Collier S&S) S&S Trade.

Lardner, Ring. The Best Short Stories of Ring Lardner. 1976. 23.95 (*0-89190-073-X*, Am Repr) Amereon Ltd.

Lardner, Ring, Jr. The Best Short Stories of Ring Lardner. 352p. 1976. text ed. 40.00 (*0-684-14743-2*, Scribners) S&S Trade.

— The Best Short Stories of Ring Lardner. LC 57-13394. 346p. 1985. lib. bdg. 22.50 (*0-685-04559-5*, Scribners); pap. 5.95 (*0-684-18363-3*, Scribners) S&S Trade.

Lardner, Ring. Haircut. (Short Stories Ser.). (J). (gr. 5 up). 1992. lib. bdg. 13.95 (*0-88682-499-0*) Creative Ed.

— Haircut & Other Stories. 190p. reprint ed. lib. bdg. 18.95 (*0-88411-583-6*, Aeonian Pr) Amereon Ltd.

Lardner, Ring, Jr. Haircut & Other Stories. 192p. 1991. pap. 9.95 (*0-02-022344-7*, Pub. by Gebrueder Borntraeger GW) Macmillan.

— Ring Around the Bases: The Complete Baseball Stories of Ring Lardner. (Illus.). 320p. 1992. text ed. 35.00 (*0-684-19374-4*, Scribners) S&S Trade.

— Some Champions: Previously Uncollected Autobiographical Sketches & Fiction. 208p. 1977. pap. 3.95 (*0-684-15065-4*, Scribners) S&S Trade.

— Some Champions: Sketches & Fiction from a Humorist's Career. Bruccoli, Matthew J. & Layman, Richard, eds. LC 92-33699. 205p. 1993. pap. 9.00 (*0-02-022343-9*, Pub. by Gebrueder Borntraeger GW) Macmillan.

Lardner, Ring. Story of the Wonder Man. 1976. 20.95 (*0-8488-1073-2*) Amereon Ltd.

— You Know Me Al. unabridged ed. (Thrift Editions Ser.). 128p. 1995. pap. text ed. 1.00 (*0-486-28513-8*) Dover.

— You Know Me Al. 218p. reprint ed. lib. bdg. 20.95 (*0-88411-584-4*, Aeonian Pr) Amereon Ltd.

— You Know Me Al. 1993. reprint ed. lib. bdg. 18.95 (*1-56849-207-3*) Buccaneer Bks.

Lardner, Ring, Jr. You Know Me Al. 1987. text ed. 30.00 (*0-02-568440-X*, Scribners) S&S Trade.

— You Know Me Al: A Busher's Letters. 224p. 1991. pap. 9.95 (*0-02-022342-0*, Pub. by Gebrueder Borntraeger GW) Macmillan.

Lardner, Ring, Jr. & Sheed, Wilfrid, intros. Haircut & Other Stories. LC 84-40002. 192p. 1984. pap. 6.95 (*0-394-72610-3*, Vin) Random.

Lardner, Ring W. How to Write Short Stories. 1971. reprint ed. 59.00 (*0-403-01063-2*) Scholarly.

— The Story of a Wonder Man: Being the Autobiography of Ring Lardner. LC 75-26216. (Illus.). 151p. 1975. reprint ed. text ed. 45.00 (*0-8371-8414-2*, LAWOM, Greenwood Pr) Greenwood.

— You Know Me Al. (Prairie State Bks.). 272p. 1992. pap. 10.95 (*0-252-06230-2*) U of Ill Pr.

Lardner, Robin W., jt. auth. see Arya, Jagdish C.

Lardner, Thomas J. & Archer, R. R. Mechanics of Solids: An Introduction. LC 93-2372. 1994. text ed. write for info. (*0-07-833358-X*) McGraw.

Lardo, Vincent. China House. 204p. (Orig.). 1983. pap. 6.95 (*0-932870-30-9*) Alyson Pubns.

— The Prince & the Pretender. 206p. (Orig.). 1984. pap. 5.95 (*0-932870-53-8*) Alyson Pubns.

Lardon, jt. auth. see Anonimo.

Lardy, Nicholas R. Agriculture in China's Modern Economic Development. LC 82-23555. (Illus.). 285p. 1983. 69.95 (*0-521-25246-6*) Cambridge U Pr.

— China in the World Economy. 156p. (Orig.). (C). 1994. pap. 16.95 (*0-88132-200-8*) Inst Intl Eco.

— China's Entry into the World Economy: Implications for Northeast Asia & the U. S. (Asian Agenda Report Ser.: No. 11). (Illus.). 76p. (Orig.). (C). 1987. lib. bdg. 27.00 (*0-8191-6371-6*, The Asia Society); pap. text ed. 10.50 (*0-8191-6372-4*, The Asia Society) U Pr of Amer.

— Economic Growth & Distribution in China. (Illus.). 1978. 64.95 (*0-521-21904-3*) Cambridge U Pr.

— Foreign Trade & Economic Reform in China: 1978-1990. (Illus.). 216p. (C). 1993. pap. 14.95 (*0-521-45835-8*) Cambridge U Pr.

An Asterisk (*) at the beginning of an entry indicates that the title is appearing in BIP for the first time.

— Foreign Trade & Economic Reform in China, 1978-1990. (Illus.). 222p. (C). 1991. 54.95 (0-521-41495-4) Cambridge U Pr.

Lardy, Nicholas R., ed. Chinese Economic Planning: Transations from Chi-Hua Ching-Chi. LC 78-52292. 280p. reprint ed. pap. 79.80 (0-317-29625-6, 2021858) Bks Demand.

Lardy, Nicholas R. & Lieberthal, Kenneth, eds. Chen Yun's Strategy for China's Development: A Non-Maoist Alternative. LC 82-16776. (China Book Project Ser.). 250p. 1983. 62.95 (0-87332-225-8) M E Sharpe.

Lare, Gary, jt. auth. see Schroeder, Don.

Lare, James, jt. ed. see Rossiter, Clinton.

LaRear, Paul, jt. auth. see Vockell, Edward.

*Lareau, Alan. Wild Stage: Literary Cabarets of the Weimar Republic. (Studies in German Literature, Lingistics, & Culture). 228p. 1995. 54.95 (1-879751-86-0) Camden Hse.

Lareau, Annette. Home Advantage: Social Class & Parental Intervention in Elementary Education. 220p. 1989. 70.00 (1-85000-312-2, Falmer Pr); pap. 30.00 (1-85000-317-3, Falmer Pr) Taylor & Francis.

Lareau, Peter N. Drafting the Union Contract: A Handbook for the Management Negotiator. 1988. write for info. (0-8205-1494-2) Bender.

Lareau, Thomas J. & Darmstadter, Joel. Energy & Household Expenditure Patterns. LC 83-17633. 161p. 1983. 15.95 (0-8018-3204-7) Resources Future.

Lareau, W. The Businessuses of American't & Change. 128p. 1992. 12.95 (0-8329-0501-1) New Win Pub.

Lareau, William. American Samurai. 1992. reprint ed. pap. 13.99 (0-446-39360-6) Warner Bks.

— American Samurai: Warrior for the Coming Dark Ages of American Business. 336p. 1991. 17.95 (0-8329-0458-9) New Win Pub.

— Conduct Expected: The Unwritten Rules for a Successful Business Career. 198p. 1986. pap. 12.95 (0-8329-0443-0) New Win Pub.

— Dancing with the Dinosaur. LC 93-33922. 256p. 1993. 14.95 (0-8329-0505-4) New Win Pub.

— Where Am I Now? Where Am I Going? Career Manual. LC 92-3981. 1992. pap. 12.95 (0-8329-0500-3) New Win Pub.

— Where Am I Now? Where Am I Going? The Career Manual. LC 92-3981. 256p. 1991. 17.95 (0-8329-0464-3) New Win Pub.

Larebo, Haile M. Italian Land Policy in Ethiopia 1935-1941. (Oxford Studies in African Affairs). (Illus.). 392p. 1994. 69.00 (0-19-820262-8) OUP.

Laredo, J. D., jt. ed. see Bard, M.

Laredo, Joseph, tr. see Camus, Albert.

Laredo, Ruth. The Ruth Laredo Becoming a Musician Book. (Illus.). 72p. 1992. pap. 11.95 (0-913574-99-6, EA00714) Eur-Am Music.

Laredo Texas School District Staff, tr. see Amundson, Kristen.

Laredo, Victor. Sephardic Spain. (Illus.). 1978. pap. 8.00 (84-399-8381-6) Edit Mensaje.

Laredu, tr. see Baichelor.

LaReine, Olympe. The Cajuns of the German Coast. LC 91-67752. 126p. 1993. pap. 8.00 (1-56002-160-8, Univ Edtns) Aegina Pr.

Larence. The Ark of the Covenant & Christianity. rev. ed. 112p. 1995. 11.95 (0-910653-13-5, 81-021, Red River Pr) Archival Servs.

*Larence, et al, eds. Archival Administration. 256p. 1995. 12.95 (0-614-07377-4, 82-003, Red River Pr) Archival Servs.

— Archival Services. 256p. 1995. 12.00 (0-910653-22-4) Archival Servs.

— Introduction to Archival Services. 96p. 1995. 10.95 (0-614-07376-6, 82-002, Red River Pr) Archival Servs.

— Introduction to Archival Services. 96p. 1995. 7.00 (0-910653-21-6) Archival Servs.

Larere, Philippe. Baptism in Water & Baptism in the Spirit. 96p. (Orig.). 1994. pap. text ed. 7.95 (0-8146-2225-9) Liturgical Pr.

— The Lord's Supper: Toward an Ecumenical Understanding of the Eucharist. Madigan, Patrick, tr. 96p. (Orig.). 1993. pap. text ed. 7.95 (0-8146-2226-7) Liturgical Pr.

Larew, Hiram & Capizzi, Joseph. Common Insect & Mite Galls of the Pacific Northwest. (Illus.). 80p. (Orig.). 1983. pap. 7.95 (0-87071-055-9) Oreg St U Pr.

Larew, James C. A Party Reborn: The Democrats of Iowa, 1950-1974. LC 80-51855. (Illus.). 216p. (C). 1980. 12.00 (0-89033-002-6); pap. 6.00 (0-686-69969-6) State Hist Iowa.

Larfeld, Wilhelm. Handbuch der Griechischen Epigraphik, 2 vols. in 3. 1971. reprint ed. write for info. (0-318-72100-7, Pub. by Georg Olms GW) Lubrecht & Cramer.

— Handbuch der Griechischen Epigraphik, 2 vols. in 3, Bd. I. xxii, 1561p. 1971. reprint ed. write for info. (0-318-70954-6, Pub. by Georg Olms GW) Lubrecht & Cramer.

— Handbuch der Griechischen Epigraphik, 2 vols. in 3, Bd. II, 1: Die Attischen Inschriften. xxii, 1561p. 1971. reprint ed. write for info. (0-318-70955-4, Pub. by Georg Olms GW) Lubrecht & Cramer.

— Handbuch der Griechischen Epigraphik, 2 vols. in 3, Bd. II, 2: Handbuch der Attischen Inschriften. xxii, 1561p. 1971. reprint ed. write for info. (0-318-70956-2, Pub. by Georg Olms GW) Lubrecht & Cramer.

— Handbuch der Griechischen Epigraphik, 2 vols. in 3, Set. xxii, 1561p. 1971. reprint ed. write for info. (0-318-70953-8, Pub. by Georg Olms GW) Lubrecht & Cramer.

Larg, D. John Ruskin. LC 74-1447. (John Ruskin Ser.: No. 87). 1974. lib. bdg. 41.95 (0-8383-2047-3) M S G Haskell Hse.

Largay, James A. & Livingston, John. Accounting for Changing Prices: Replacement Cost & General Price Level Adjustments. LC 76-7491. (Wiley Hamilton Publication). 317p. reprint ed. pap. 90.40 (0-8357-5065-5, 2025177) Bks Demand.

Largay, James A., III, jt. auth. see Huefner, Ronald J.

Large, A., jt. auth. see Armstrong, C. J.

Large, Andy, jt. auth. see Armstrong, Chris.

Large, B. J. & Hughes, I. E. Learning Pharmacology Through MCQ. 2nd ed. 1990. pap. text ed. 37.95 (0-471-92708-2) Wiley.

Large, Brian. Martinu. LC 75-45082. (Illus.). 198p. 1976. 45.00 (0-8419-0256-9) Holmes & Meier.

— Smetana. LC 84-1825. (Music Reprint Ser.). (Illus.). 524p. 1985. reprint ed. lib. bdg. 52.50 (0-306-76243-9) Da Capo.

Large, Brian, ed. see Wagner, Richard.

Large, Char. The Clustering Approach to Better Essay Writing. 59p. 1987. student ed, pap. 9.99 (0-89824-146-4) Trillium Pr.

Large, David C. Between Two Fires: Europe's Path in the 1930s. 1991. pap. 15.95 (0-393-30757-3) Norton.

— Germans to the Front: West German Rearmament in the Adenauer Era. LC 95-5401. 1995. write for info. (0-8078-2235-3); pap. write for info. (0-8078-4539-6) U of NC Pr.

Large, David C., ed. Contending with Hitler: Varieties of German Resistance in the Third Reich. (Publications of the German Historical Institute, Washington, D.C.). 208p. (C). 1992. 42.95 (0-521-41459-8) Cambridge U Pr.

— Contending with Hitler: Varieties of German Resistance in the Third Reich. (Publications of the German Historical Institute, Washington, D.C.). 205p. (C). 1994. pap. 13.95 (0-521-46668-7) Cambridge U Pr.

Large, David C. & Weber, William, eds. Wagnerism in European Culture & Politics. LC 83-45936. 304p. 1984. pap. 17.95 (0-8014-9283-1) Cornell U Pr.

Large, E. C. Asleep in the Afternoon: A Novel. Reginald, R. & Melville, Douglas, eds. LC 77-84241. (Lost Race & Adult Fantasy Ser.). 1978. reprint ed. lib. bdg. 33.95 (0-405-10991-1) Ayer.

Large, J. A., jt. auth. see Armstrong, C. J.

Large, J. Andrew, jt. auth. see Armstrong, Christopher J.

*Large, James. Titles & Symbols of Christ: 280 Titles & Symbols. (World Classic Reference Library). 578p. 1995. reprint ed. 14.99 (0-529-10335-4) World Bible.

*Large, Josaphat. Pe Set: Powem. Mafrou, Edisyon, ed. 1994. text ed. write for info. (0-9641162-0-0) Edit La Jeremienne.

Large, Judy, jt. auth. see Carey, Diana.

Large, Martin. Social Ecology: Exploring Post-Industrial Society. 163p. 1990. pap. 8.95 (0-9507062-2-1, 660, Pub. by Hawthorn Press UK) Anthroposophic.

— Who's Bringing Them up? Television & Child Development: How to Break the T. V. Habit. 192p. 1990. pap. 14.95 (1-869890-24-8, 317, Pub. by Hawthorn Press UK) Anthroposophic.

Large, Peter. The Micro Revolution Revisited. LC 84-2164. 224p. 1984. 33.00 (0-8476-7361-8) Rowman.

Large, Stephen. Emperor Hirohito & Showa Japan: A Political Biography. LC 91-47983. (Nissan Institute Japanese Studies). 288p. 1992. 35.00 (0-415-03203-2, A9581) Routledge.

Largen, Velda L. Guide to Good Food. rev. ed. LC 86-19452. (Illus.). 735p. 1992. text ed. 43.60 (0-87006-885-7) Goodheart.

Largent, Christopher, jt. auth. see Breton, Denise.

Largent, D. L. Leptonia & Related Genera of the West Coast. 1976. 52.00 (3-7682-1114-2) Lubrecht & Cramer.

Largent, David. How to Identify Mushrooms (to Genus I) Macroscopic Features. 2nd ed. (Illus.). 86p. (C). 1977. pap. 13.95 (0-916422-00-3) Mad River.

Largent, David, et al. How to Identify Mushrooms (to Genus III) Microscopic Features. (Illus.). 148p. (C). 1977. pap. 20.95x (0-916422-09-7) Mad River.

Largent, David L. Agaricales of California Five: Hygrophoraceae. (Illus.). 220p. (Orig.). 1985. pap. text ed. 67.95 (0-916422-54-2) Mad River.

— Entolomataceae of Western North America: Agaricales of California, Vol. 8. (Illus.). 550p. (Orig.). 1994. pap. 225.00x (0-916422-81-X) Mad River.

Largent, David L. & Baroni, Timothy J. How to Identify Mushrooms to Genus VI: The Modern Genera - Keys & Descriptions. 200p. (Orig.). 1988. pap. 22.95 (0-916422-76-3) Mad River.

Largent, David L. & Thiers, H. How to Identify Mushrooms (to Genus II): Field Identification of Genera. (Illus.). 32p. (C). 1977. pap. 4.25 (0-916422-08-9) Mad River.

Largent, R. Karl. Black Death. 368p. (Orig.). 1988. pap. 3.95 (0-8439-2591-4) Dorchester Pub Co.

— Black Death. 368p. 1995. mass mkt., pap. text ed. 4.99 (0-8439-3797-1) Dorchester Pub Co.

— Get the Job You Want: Workbook for the Rotten Resume Writer. Clemens, Matthew V., ed. (Rotten Writer Ser.). (Illus.). 206p. (Orig.). 1995. student ed 19.95 (0-9644770-1-7) Threadbare Pub.

— Getting Started... Handbook for the Beginning Novelist. 144p. 1992. pap. write for info. (1-882214-00-5) PowerHse Pr.

— The Lake. 368p. (Orig.). 1993. pap. 4.50 (0-8439-3455-7) Dorchester Pub Co.

— Pagoda. 1989. pap. 4.50 (0-8439-2756-9) Dorchester Pub Co.

— Prometheus Project. 1993. pap. 4.50 (0-8439-3391-7) Dorchester Pub Co.

— Red Ice. 448p. (Orig.). 1995. mass mkt., pap. text ed. 5.99 (0-8439-3774-2) Dorchester Pub Co.

— Red Tide. 448p. (Orig.). 1992. pap. 4.99 (0-8439-3366-6) Dorchester Pub Co.

— The Witch of Sixkill. 368p. (Orig.). 1990. pap. 4.50 (0-8439-2984-7) Dorchester Pub Co.

— Write Tight & Right: Workbook for the Rotten Business Writer. Clemens, Matthew V., ed. (Rotten Writer Ser.). (Illus.). 224p. (Orig.). 1995. student ed 19.95 (0-9644770-2-5) Threadbare Pub.

Largeut, Vera, ed. see University of North Carolina Woman's College Faculty Staff.

Largey, Dennis L. Anchors for the Soul. 9.95 (0-88494-692-4) Bookcraft Inc.

Larghi, Vincent. Some General Facts about Human Behavior. 1991. 13.95 (0-533-09330-9) Vantage.

Largus, Scribonius. Scribonius Largus - Concordantia in Scribonium Largum. Sconocchia, S., ed. (Alpha-Omega, Reihe A Ser.: Bd. XCII). xi, 390p. (GER.). 1988. write for info. (3-487-09116-X, Pub. by Georg Olms GW) Lubrecht & Cramer.

Lari, A. Niku, ed. Advances in Surface Treatments II: Technology, Applications, Effects. (Illus.). 294p. 1986. 118.00 (0-08-032535-1, Pub. by PPL UK) Franklin.

Lari, Suhail Z. A History of Sindh. 212p. 1995. 15.95 (0-19-577501-5) OUP.

Laric, Michael V. & Stiff, M. Ronald. Lotus 1-2-3 for Marketing & Sales. 256p. 1984. pap. 24.95 (0-685-08556-2) P-H.

— Marketing & Business Planning with the IBM PCs: A Guide to the Productive Use of Personal Computers for Business & Marketing Professionals. (Illus.). 224p. 1985. pap. 16.95 (0-13-557067-0) P-H.

Larijani, L. Casey. The Virtual Reality Primer. LC 93-26466. 1993. text ed. 40.00 (0-07-036417-6) McGraw.

— The Virtual Reality Primer. LC 93-26466. 1994. pap. text ed. 24.95 (0-07-036416-8) McGraw.

*Larikov, L. N., et al. Diffusion Processes in Ordered Alloys. Pednekar, S. P., tr. (Illus.). 184p. (C). 1981. text ed. 64.00 (0-614-01343-7, Pub. by Oxonion Pr Pvt Ltd) Science Pubs.

Larimer County Heritage Association Staff & Morris, Andrew J. History of Larimer County, Colorado. (Illus.). 1986. 60.00 (0-88107-046-7) Curtis Media.

Larimer, Louie V., Jr. The Legal Guide for Practicing Psychotherapy in Colorado. 1992. pap. 34.95 (0-9633550-0-7) Ctr Prof Develop.

Larimer, Tamela. Buck. LC 86-90774. 176p. (Orig.). (J). (gr. 7 up). 1986. pap. 2.50 (0-380-75172-0, Flare) Avon.

Larimore, Bertha B. Sprouting for All Seasons: How & What to Sprout, Including Delicious Easy-to-Prepare Recipes. LC 75-23564. (Illus.). 140p. (Orig.). 1993. reprint ed. pap. 10.98 (0-88290-055-2) Horizon Utah.

Larimore, Cindy. Horses--Oil. (How to Draw & Paint Ser.). (Illus.). 32p. (Orig.). 1990. pap. 5.95 (1-56010-065-6, HT-228) W Foster Pub.

Larimore, Helen. Older Women in Recovery: Sharing Experience, Strength & Hope. 1992. pap. 10.95 (1-55874-226-3) Health Comm.

Larin, I. V. Pasture Economy & Meadow Cultivation. 648p. 1962. text ed. 150.00 (0-7065-0205-1, Pub. by Keter Pub IS) Coronet Bks.

Larina, Anna. This I Cannot Forget: The Memoirs of Nikolai Bukharin's Widow. (Illus.). 352p. 1993. 24.95 (0-393-03025-3) Norton.

— This I Cannot Forget: The Memoirs of Nikolai Bukharin's Widow. 408p. 1994. pap. 15.00 (0-393-31234-8) Norton.

Larios, Julie. On the Stairs. LC 93-20588. (Illus.). (J). Date not set. write for info. (0-689-31643-7, Atheneum S&S) S&S Trade.

Larios, Richard, jt. auth. see De Ruiz, Dana C.

*Larish, John. Apple QuickTake 100 (H175) (Magic Lantern Guide Ser.). (Illus.). 174p. (Orig.). 1994. pap. 19.95 (1-883403-14-6) Saunders Photo.

— Digital Cameras: The New Era of Color Photography. 1995. 27.95 (0-941845-14-1) Micro Pub Pr.

— Digital Photography: Pictures of Tomorrow. 1994. pap. 27.95 (0-941845-08-7) Micro Pub Pr.

— Photo CD: Quality Photographs at Your Fingertips. 1994. pap. 27.95 (0-941845-09-5) Micro Pub Pr.

Larison, C. W. Silvia Dubois: A Biografy of the Slav Who Whipt Her Mistres & Gand Her Fredom. Lobdell, Jared C., tr. & intro. by. (Schomburg Library of Nineteenth-Century Black Women Writers). (Illus.). 168p. 1990. reprint ed. pap. 9.95 (0-19-506671-5) OUP.

— Silvia Dubois: A Biografy of the Slav Who Whipt Her Mistres & Gand Her Fredom. Lobdell, Jared C., tr. & intro. by. (Schomburg Library of Nineteenth-Century Black Women Writers). 288p. 1988. 29.95 (0-19-505239-0) OUP.

Larison, Julie, jt. auth. see Sexton, Tom.

Laritz, Kenneth F. Attorney's Guide to Social Security Disability Claims. LC 86-10210. (Regulatory Manual Ser.). 451p. 1986. text ed. 110.00 (0-07-008461-0) Shepards-McGraw.

LaRiviere, Ann. The Development Council: Cornerstone for Success Considerations. 50p. (Orig.). 1993. pap. 8.00 (1-55833-091-7) Natl Cath Educ.

Lariviere, Richard W. The Divyatattva of Raghunandana Bhattacarya: Ordeals in Classical Hindu Law. 1982. 22.00 (0-8364-0854-3, Pub. by Manohar II) S Asia.

Lariviere, Richard W., ed. & tr. The Naradasmrti, Pt. 1. LC 89-37780. (Studies on South Asia: No. 4). xxx, 328p. 1989. 30.00 (0-936115-06-8) U Penn South Asia.

— The Naradasmrti, Pt. 2. LC 89-37780. (Studies on South Asia: No. 5). xxxii, 250p. 1989. 30.00 (0-685-48877-2) U Penn South Asia.

— The Naradasmrti, Set. LC 89-37780. (Studies on South Asia: No. 4). xxx, 328p. 1989. 20.00 (0-936115-04-1) U Penn South Asia.

— The Naradasmrti, Set. LC 89-37780. (Studies on South Asia: No. 5). xxxii, 250p. 1989. 20.00 (0-936115-05-X) U Penn South Asia.

LaRivierre, John. Boardsailing Oregon: A Guide to the Best Windsurfing in Oregon. (Illus.). 304p. 1990. pap. 12.95 (0-89732-088-3) Menasha Ridge.

Lark Books Staff, tr. see Evers, Inge.

Lark, David L., et al. Protein-Carbohydrate Interactions in Biological Systems: The Molecular Biology of Molecular Pathogenicity. (Fems Symposia Publications). 1986. text ed. 137.00 (0-12-436665-1) Acad Pr.

Lark, Madeline. All for a Lark. large type ed. (Ulverscroft Ser.). 208p. 1994. 20.95 (0-7089-3046-8) Ulverscroft.

Lark, P. D., et al. The Handling of Chemical Data. LC 66-17264. 1960. 156.00 (0-08-011849-6, Pub. by Pergamon Repr UK) Franklin.

*Lark, Susan. Dr. Susan Lark's the Menstrual Cramps Self Help Book: Effective Solutions for Pain & Discomfort Due to Menstrual Cramps & PMS. LC 95-14861. 1995. write for info. (0-89087-771-8) Celestial Arts.

— The Womens' Health Companion: Self-Help Nutrition Guide & Cookbook. 400p. (Orig.). 1994. 26.95 (0-89087-733-5) Celestial Arts.

Lark, Susan M. Anemia & Heavy Menstrual Flow. 164p. 1993. pap. 12.95 (0-917010-49-3, Wstchstr Pub Co) Natl Nursing.

— Anxiety & Stress: A Self-Help Program. (Women's Health Ser.). 284p. 1993. pap. 12.95 (0-917010-55-8, Wstchstr Pub Co) Natl Nursing.

— Chronic Fatigue & Tiredness. 234p. 1993. pap. 12.95 (0-917010-52-3, Wstchstr Pub Co) Natl Nursing.

— The Estrogen Decision: A Self-Help Program. (Women's Health Ser.). 316p. 1994. pap. 14.95 (0-917010-56-6, Wstchstr Pub Co) Natl Nursing.

— Fibroid Tumors & Endometriosis: A Self-Help Program. (Women's Health Ser.). 264p. 1993. pap. 12.95 (0-917010-54-X, Wstchstr Pub Co) Natl Nursing.

Lark, Susan M. Menopause Self Help Book. LC 89-25292. 1990. pap. 16.95 (0-89087-592-8) Celestial Arts.

Lark, Susan M. Menstrual Cramps: A Self-Help Program. 224p. 1993. pap. 12.95 (0-917010-51-5, Wstchstr Pub Co) Natl Nursing.

— Premenstrual Syndrome Self-Help Book. LC 89-25292. 1989. pap. 16.95 (0-89087-587-1) Celestial Arts.

Lark, Virginia, ed. see Maze, Carol M.

Larka, Robert. Television's Private Eye. Sterling, Christopher H., ed. LC 78-21724. (Dissertations in Broadcasting Ser.). (Illus.). 1980. lib. bdg. 23.95 (0-405-11763-9) Ayer.

Larkcom, Joy. Oriental Vegetables: The Complete Guide for the Gardening Cook. (Illus.). 248p. 1991. 29.95 (4-7700-1619-0) Kodansha.

— Oriental Vegetables: The Complete Guide for the Gardening Cook. (Illus.). 240p. 1994. pap. 17.00 (1-56836-017-7) Kodansha.

— The Salad Garden: Salads from Seed to Table; A Complete, Illustrated, Year-Round Guide. LC 83-40382. (Home Gardening Book Shelf Ser.). (Illus.). 168p. 1984. pap. 12.95 (0-670-61573-0) Viking Penguin.

Larke, Joe. The Bullfrog & the Grasshopper & Other "Tails" (Illus.). 72p. (J). (gr. k-6). 1987. 10.00 (0-9620112-0-7) Grin A Bit.

— Can't Reach the Itch. (Illus.). 72p. (J). (gr. 1-6). 1988. 10.00 (0-9620112-1-5) Grin A Bit.

— Dopie Dope Goes to the Fair. (Illus.). 49p. (J). (gr. k-5). 1992. 13.95 (0-9620112-7-4) Grin A Bit.

— Dopie Dope Grin A Bit Poetry Series. (Illus.). (J). (gr. k-6). 1992. write for info. (0-9620112-9-0) Grin A Bit.

— Two Pigs in Wigs. (J). (ps-3). 1991. 11.95 (0-9620112-2-3) Grin A Bit.

Larke, Roy. Japanese Retailing. LC 93-50173. 1994. write for info. (0-415-08362-1) Routledge.

Larke, T. A. German Notebooks for the Returning Student. (Returning Student Ser.: No. 2). (C). 1983. ring bd. 9.95 (0-915559-00-5, DT1) Answer-Bk.

— Liechtenstein Index & Thesaurus. rev. ed. (Illus.). 70p. 1983. ring bd. 25.00 (0-9608460-4-2, FL1 REV) Answer-Bk.

— Swedish Notebooks for the Returning Student, 3 Vols., 1. (Returning Student Ser.: No. 1). (Illus.). 1981. ring bd. 4.95 (0-9608460-1-8, SV1) Answer-Bk.

— Swedish Notebooks for the Returning Student, 3 Vols., 2. (Returning Student Ser.: No. 1). (Illus.). 1981. ring bd. 4.95 (0-9608460-2-6, SV1) Answer-Bk.

— Swedish Notebooks for the Returning Student, 3 Vols., 3. (Returning Student Ser.: No. 1). (Illus.). 1981. ring bd. 4.95 (0-9608460-3-4, SV1) Answer-Bk.

— Swedish Notebooks for the Returning Student, 3 Vols., Set. (Returning Student Ser.: No. 1). (Illus.). 1981. ring bd. 12.95 (0-9608460-0-X, SV1) Answer-Bk.

Larken, A. I., jt. ed. see Langenberg, D. N.

Larken, H. W. Compositors Work in Printing. 3rd ed. 382p. 1969. 30.00 (0-905418-08-5, Pub. by Gresham Bks) St Mut.

— Modern Type Setting Techniques: Electric Composition. 192p. 1984. 60.00 (0-946095-10-8, Pub. by Gresham Bks UK) St Mut.

— Type Composition in the Private Press. 128p. 1983. 35.00 (0-946095-11-6, Pub. by Gresham Bks UK) St Mut.

Larkey, Edward. Pungent Sounds: Constructing Identity with Popular Music in Austria. LC 93-20113. (Austrian Culture Ser.: Vol. 9). 342p. (Orig.). (C). 1993. pap. text ed. 35.95 (0-8204-2170-7) P Lang Pubs.

Larkey, Jan. Flatter Your Figure. (Illus.). 96p. 1991. pap. 10.00 (0-671-76296-6) S&S Trade.

— Flatter Your Figure: A Style Workbook for Women of All Sizes, Shapes & Ages. rev. ed. (Illus.). 30p. 1987. pap. 9.95 (0-944749-01-1) J Larkey Image.

Larkey, Patrick, jt. auth. see Downs, George.

Larkey, Patrick D. Evaluating Public Programs: The Impact of General Revenue-Sharing on Municipal Fiscal Behavior. LC 78-51176. 1979. 42.50 (0-691-07601-4) Princeton U Pr.

— Evaluating Public Programs: The Impact of General Revenue Sharing on Municipal Government. LC 78-51176. reprint ed. pap. 80.70 (0-7837-9367-7, 2060110) Bks Demand.

Larkey, Patrick D., jt. ed. see Sproull, Lee S.

An Asterisk (*) at the beginning of an entry indicates that the title is appearing in BIP for the first time.

Larkham, Peter J. Conservation & the Changing Urban Landscape. (Progress in Planning Ser.: No. 37). 88p. 1992. pap. 66.00 (0-08-041852-X, Pergamon Pr) Elsevier.

Larkham, Peter J., jt. ed. see Ashworth, G. J.

Larkham, Peter J., jt. ed. see Whitehand, J. W.

Larkin. Sexual Harassment: High School Girls Speak Out. (NFS Canada Ser.). 1994. pap. 14.95 (0-929005-65-1, Pub. by Second Story Pr CN) InBook.

Larkin, Bruce D., ed. Vital Interests: The Soviet Issue in U. S. Central American Policy. LC 87-39458. 512p. (C). 1988. lib. bdg. 42.00 (1-55587-111-9); pap. text ed. 16. 95 (1-55587-112-7) Lynne Rienner.

Larkin, Bryant. Larkin's Dulcimer Book. LC 82-84550. (Illus.). 103p. 1982. pap. 9.95 (0-943644-00-3); digital audio 7.98 (0-685-06235-X) Ivory Pal.

— Larkin's Dulcimer Book, Set. LC 82-84550. (Illus.). 103p. 1982. 16.95 (0-685-06236-8) Ivory Pal.

***Larkin, Clarence.** The Book of Revelation: A Study of the Last Prophetic Book of Holy Scripture. (Illus.). 210p. 1995. pap. 15.00 (0-89540-303-X) Sun Pub.

***Larkin, David.** Farm: The Vernacular Tradition of Working Buildings. (Illus.). 240p. 1995. 60.00 (1-885254-08-3) Monacelli Pr.

— Farm: The Vernacular Tradition of Working Buildings, 4 vols., Set. (Illus.). 240p. 1995. 240.00 (1-885254-20-2) Monacelli Pr.

Larkin, David, ed. Frank Lloyd Wright: The Masterworks. LC 93-10434. (Illus.). 312p. 1993. 60.00 (0-8478-1715-6) Rizzoli Intl.

Larkin, David, ed. see Beveridge, Charles.

Larkin, David, jt. auth. see Frampton, Kenneth.

Larkin, David, ed. see Garrett, Wendell.

Larkin, David, ed. see Kennedy, Roger G.

Larkin, David, ed. see Rocheleau, Paul & Sprigg, June.

Larkin, David, jt. auth. see Romero, Orlando.

Larkin, David, jt. auth. see Roscoe, Gerald.

Larkin, David, jt. auth. see Spectre, Peter H.

Larkin, David, jt. auth. see Sprigg, June.

Larkin, David E., ed. Faeries. 1979. pap. 19.95 (0-553-34634-2) Bantam.

Larkin, Edward T. War in Goethe's Writings: Representation & Assessment. LC 92-10192. 268p. 1992. lib. bdg. 69.95 (0-7734-9540-1) E Mellen.

Larkin, Emmet. The Consolidation of the Roman Catholic Church in Ireland, 1860-1870. LC 86-25059. xxii, 714p. 1987. 65.00 (0-8078-1725-2) U of NC Pr.

— The Historical Dimensions of Irish Catholicism. LC 76-6350. (Irish Americans Ser.). 1976. 23.95 (0-405-09344-6) Ayer.

— James Larkin: Irish Labour Leader, 1876-1947. 306p. (C). 1989. pap. text ed. 19.95 (0-7453-0304-8) Westview.

— The Making of the Roman Catholic Church in Ireland, 1850-1860. LC 79-19560. (Illus.). 544p. reprint ed. pap. 155.10 (0-7837-6857-5, 2046686) Bks Demand.

— The Roman Catholic Church & the Home Rule Movement in Ireland, 1870-1874. LC 89-36347. xxii, 416p. (C). 1990. 65.00 (0-8078-1886-0) U of NC Pr.

— The Roman Catholic Church in Ireland & the Fall of Parnell, 1888-1891. LC 78-22056. xxi, 316p. 1979. 37.50 (0-8078-1352-4) U of NC Pr.

Larkin, Emmet, ed. Alexis de Tocqueville's Journey to Ireland. LC 89-23851. 157p. 1990. 26.95 (0-8132-0718-5); pap. 14.95 (0-8132-0719-3) Cath U Pr.

Larkin, Emmet J. The Roman Catholic Church & the Creation of the Modern Irish State, 1878-1886. LC 75-7169. (American Philosophical Society, Memoirs Ser.: Vol. 108). 436p. reprint ed. pap. 124.30 (0-317-29437-7, 2024293) Bks Demand.

Larkin, Ernest. Silent Presence. 1984. pap. 6.95 (0-87193-172-9) Dimension Bks.

Larkin, Ernest F., ed. Proceedings of the Nineteen Eighty-Six Conference of the American Academy of Advertising. 1986. pap. 25.00 (0-931030-09-9) Am Acad Advert.

***Larkin, Ernest F. & Larkin, Susan S.** College Newspaper Advertising Managers Handbook. 60p. 1994. pap. text ed. 25.00 (0-9644192-0-3) Assoc Collegiate Pr.

Larkin, F. Daniel. John B. Jervis: An American Engineering Pioneer. LC 89-26953. (History of Science & Technology Reprint Ser.). (Illus.). 212p. 1990. text ed. 27.95 (0-8138-0355-1) Iowa St U Pr.

Larkin, Frank J. Basic Coastal Navigation: An Introduction to Piloting. (Illus.). 250p. 1993. 29.95 (0-924486-39-2) Sheridan.

Larkin, Geraldine A. Twelve Simple Steps to a Winning Marketing Plan. 210p. 1992. 16.95 (1-55738-297-2) Probus Pub Co.

— Woman to Woman: Street Smarts for Women Entrepreneurs. LC 93-4260. 1993. 14.95 (0-13-706658-9) P-H.

Larkin, Greg. Working Writing. 480p. (C). 1985. pap. write for info. (0-675-20237-X, Merrill Pub Co) Macmillan.

Larkin, Gregory, jt. ed. see Kagan, Alfred.

Larkin, Henry. Carlyle & the Open Secret of His Life. LC 76-122621. (English Biography Ser.: No. 31). 1970. reprint ed. lib. bdg. 62.95 (0-8383-0905-4) M S G Haskell Hse.

Larkin, J. Donald & Larkin, Sue. The Larkin Guide: Enjoying the Riches of Retirement. LC 87-73134. 96p. 1988. spiral bd. 7.95 (0-9619643-0-8) Damike Pub.

Larkin, Jack. Children Everywhere. LC 87-22685. (Illus.). 47p. 1987. 6.95 (0-913387-02-9) Old Sturbridge.

— The Merriams of Brookfield: Printing in the Economy & Culture of Rural Massachusetts in the Early Nineteenth Century. 48p. 1986. pap. 5.00 (0-912296-84-4) Am Antiquarian.

— The Reshaping of Everyday Life, 1790-1840. LC 87-46152. (Everyday Life in Early America). 384p. 1989. reprint ed. pap. 13.00 (0-06-091606-0, PL) HarpC.

Larkin, James B., ed. see Martinez de Toledo, Alfonso.

Larkin, James F., jt. ed. see Hughes, Paul L.

Larkin, James J. Vehicle Leasing. 2nd rev. ed. 224p. 1985. text ed. 40.50 (0-915260-18-2) Atcom.

Larkin, Jill, et al, eds. Computer Assisted Instruction & Intelligent Tutoring Systems: Establishing Communication & Collaboration. 288p. (C). 1991. text ed. 59.95 (0-8058-0232-0); pap. 32.50 (0-8058-0233-9) L Erlbaum Assocs.

Larkin, Joan. Housework. (Illus.). 1976. pap. 3.50 (0-918314-02-X) Out & Out.

— A Long Sound. 89p. 1986. pap. 8.95 (0-9614886-1-1) Tilbury Hse.

Larkin, Joan, jt. ed. see Morse, Carl.

Larkin, John, ed. The Trial of William Drennan. 144p. 1991. 29.50 (0-7165-2457-0, Pub. by Irish Acad Pr IE) Intl Spec Bk.

Larkin, John, jt. auth. see Kramer, Kenneth P.

Larkin, John A. The Pampangans: Colonial Society in A Philippine Province. LC 74-165232. (Illus.). 358p. reprint ed. pap. 102.10 (0-7837-4814-0, 2044461) Bks Demand.

— Sugar & the Origins of Modern Philippine Society. 339p. 1994. 48.00 (0-520-07956-6) U CA Pr.

Larkin, John A., ed. Perspectives on Philippine Historiography: A Symposium. LC 78-59565. (Monograph Ser.: No. 21). iv, 74p. 1979. pap. 9.50 (0-938692-09-7) Yale U SE Asia.

***Larkin, Joseph M. & Sleeter, Christine E., eds.** Developing Multicultural Teacher Education Curricula. (SUNY Series, Social Context of Education & SUNY Series, Teacher Empowerment & School Reform.). 352p. 1995. text ed. 64.50x (0-7914-2593-2) State U NY Pr.

— Developing Multicultural Teacher Education Curricula. (Social Context of Education Series & Teacher Preparation & Development Ser.). 352p. 1995. pap. 21. 95x (0-7914-2594-0) State U NY Pr.

Larkin, Judy, jt. auth. see McFarland, Kathleen.

Larkin, Kara. Home Ties. 1994. pap. 2.75 (0-373-19047-6, 1-19047-9) Harlequin Bks.

Larkin, Kenneth J. Barron's Regents Exams & Answers, Comprehensive Latin. 1992. pap. 5.95 (0-8120-3345-0) Barron.

Larkin, Kevin, ed. The West Virginia Journal of Psychological Reach & Practice: The Journal of the West Virginia Psychological Association. (C). 1992. pap. text ed. write for info. (0-9634170-4-5) WVa Psychol Assn.

— The West Virginia Journal of Psychological Research & Practice: The Journal of the West Virginia Psychological Association. 1992. write for info. (0-9634170-0-2) WVa Psychol Assn.

Larkin, Larry. Full Speed Ahead. LC 72-80818. (Illus.). 146p. reprint ed. 14.00 (0-686-36269-1) Larkin.

Larkin, Margaret, ed. Singing Cowboy. LC 78-31779. (Music Reprint Ser.). 176p. 1979. reprint ed. 27.50 (0-306-79555-8) Da Capo.

***Larkin, Mary A.** Ties of Love & Hate. large type ed. (Dales Large Print Ser.). 1994. pap. 16.95 (1-85389-500-8, Pub. by Magna Print Bks) Ulverscroft.

— The Wasted Years. large type ed. 569p. 1994. 19.95 (0-7505-0598-2) Ulverscroft.

— White Clapboard. (Illus.). 12p. (Orig.). (C). 1988. pap. 7.00 (0-9620840-0-X) C O Allen.

Larkin, Mary A., frwd. Proceedings of the Inter-American Conference on Migration Trends & Policies, February 4-6, 1986. (Illus.). 168p. (Orig.). 1987. pap. text ed. 7.50 (0-924046-00-7) Ctr EPRA.

Larkin, Mary A., prol. Informe: Conferencia Inter-Americana Sobre las Direcciones y Politicas Migratorias, 4-6 de Febrero del 1986. (Illus.). 181p. (SPA.). 1988. pap. text ed. 7.50 (0-924046-01-5) Ctr EPRA.

Larkin, Mary Ann. The Coil of the Skin. LC 82-70066. (Series Seven). 50p. (Orig.). 1980. pap. 7.00 (0-931846-20-X) Wash Writers Pub.

Larkin, Maureen, jt. auth. see Schneider, Meir.

Larkin, Maurice. France Since the Popular Front: Government & People, 1936-1986. (Illus.). 456p. 1988. pap. 22.00 (0-19-873035-7) OUP.

— Man & Society in Nineteenth-Century Realism: Determinism & Literature. 201p. 1977. 34.50 (0-87471-956-9) Rowman.

— Religion, Politics & Preferment in France since Eighteen Ninety: "La Belle Epoque" & Its Legacy. 220p. (C). 1995. 49.95 (0-521-41916-6) Cambridge U Pr.

Larkin, Miriam T. Language in the Philosophy of Aristotle. LC 74-165145. (Janua Linguarum, Ser. Minor: No. 87). 113p. 1971. pap. text ed. 34.65 (90-279-1843-0) Mouton.

Larkin, M.J., jt. auth. see Patrick, S.

Larkin, Murl A. Civil Evidence Trial Manual for Texas Lawyers, 1986-93. 2nd ed. 950p. 1991. ring bd. 170.00 (0-409-25658-7) Michie Butterworth.

— Civil Evidence Trial Manual for Texas Lawyers, 1986-93. 2nd suppl. ed. 950p. 1994. 50.00 (0-250-42764-8) Butterworth Legal Pubs.

— Criminal Evidence Trial Manual for Texas Lawyers. 2nd ed. 1300p. 1994. ring bd. 170.00 (1-56257-958-4) Michie Butterworth.

— Criminal Evidence Trial Manual for Texas Lawyers. 2nd suppl. ed. 1300p. 1994. 50.00 (0-685-70861-6) Butterworth Legal Pubs.

— Federal Testimonial Privileges. LC 82-12958. (Federal Court Rules Ser.). 1982. ring bd. 145.00 (0-87632-319-0) Clark Boardman Callaghan.

— New Mexico Rules of Evidence. 480p. 1994. ring bd. 125. 00 (0-614-05925-9) Michie Butterworth.

— New Mexico Rules of Evidence, 1983, 1986, 1991. rev. ed. 480p. 1991. ring bd. 125.00 (0-409-25133-X) Butterworth Legal Pubs.

— New Mexico Rules of Evidence, 1983, 1986, 1991. suppl. ed. 480p. 1993. 57.50 (0-685-49752-6) Butterworth Legal Pubs.

Larkin, P. J. African Heritage. 64p. (C). 1988. 50.00 (0-685-33811-8, Pub. by S Thornes Pubs UK) St Mut.

— African Heritage. rev. ed. (Illus.). 64p. 1980. pap. 10.95 (0-7175-0613-4) Dufour.

— Age of Discovery. 64p. (C). 1988. 35.00 (0-685-33808-8, Pub. by S Thornes Pubs UK) St Mut.

— Age of Discovery. rev. ed. (Illus.). 64p. 1976. pap. 9.95 (0-7175-0761-0) Dufour.

— The Ancient World. 64p. (C). 1988. 35.00 (0-685-33810-X, Pub. by S Thornes Pubs UK) St Mut.

— The Ancient World. (Illus.). 64p. 1971. reprint ed. pap. 10.95 (0-7175-0588-X) Dufour.

— Britain's Heritage Bk. 3: German Kings from Hanover to Parliament & Reform. 64p. (C). 1988. 29.00 (0-7175-0004-7, Pub. by S Thornes Pubs UK) St Mut.

— European Heritage. (Illus.). 64p. 1981. pap. 9.95 (0-7175-0882-X) Dufour.

— Island Story, Bk. 1: Britain from the Romans to the Wars of the Roses. 72p. (C). 1983. 45.00 (0-7175-1019-0, Pub. by S Thornes Pubs UK) St Mut.

— Island Story, Bk. 2: Britain from the Tudors to Queen Anne. 72p. (C). 1984. 35.00 (0-7175-1229-0, Pub. by S Thornes Pubs UK) St Mut.

— Island Story, Bk. 3: Georgian & Victorian Britain. 72p. (C). 1985. 45.00 (0-7175-1295-9, Pub. by S Thornes Pubs UK) St Mut.

— Medieval World. (Illus.). 64p. 1974. pap. 10.95 (0-7175-0663-0) Dufour.

— Medieval World. 64p. (C). 1988. 35.00 (0-685-33809-6, Pub. by S Thornes Pubs UK) St Mut.

— U. S. A. & Russia. (World History in 20th Century Ser.). (Illus.). 158p. 1977. pap. 10.95 (0-7175-0063-2) Dufour.

Larkin, P. J., ed. American Heritage. 64p. (C). 1988. 30.00 (0-685-33812-6, Pub. by S Thornes Pubs UK) St Mut.

— Britain's Heritage Bk. 2: The Tudors & the Stuarts. 64p. (C). 1986. 29.00 (0-7175-0002-0, Pub. by S Thornes Pubs UK) St Mut.

— Britain's Heritage Bk. 4: Queen Victoria to the Welfare State. 64p. (C). 1983. 29.00 (0-7175-0006-3, Pub. by S Thornes Pubs UK) St Mut.

Larkin, Patricia. Everything You Need to Know When A Parent Doesn't Speak English. LC 94-1905. (J). 1994. 15.95 (0-8239-1691-X) Rosen Group.

Larkin, Patricia & Backer, Barbara. Problem-Oriented Nursing Assessment. (C). 1977. text ed. 17.95 (0-07-036450-8) McGraw.

Larkin, Patricia, jt. auth. see Crudi.

Larkin, Peter A. Freshwater Pollution, Canadian Style. LC 73-94316. (Environmental Damage & Control in Canada Ser.: No. 3). 168p. reprint ed. pap. 47.90 (0-7837-1032-1, 2041343) Bks Demand.

Larkin, Philip. All What Jazz: A Record Diary. 316p. 1985. 19.95 (0-374-10340-2); pap. 9.95 (0-374-51908-0) FS&G.

— Collected Poems. 1993. pap. 15.00 (0-374-52275-8, Noonday) FS&G.

— A Girl in Winter. LC 75-27291. 256p. 1985. pap. 11.95 (0-87951-217-2) Overlook Pr.

— High Windows. LC 74-9800. 42p. 1983. pap. 9.00 (0-374-51212-4) FS&G.

— Jill. LC 75-27292. (Tusk Bks.). 256p. 1984. 22.50 (0-87951-038-2); pap. 11.95 (0-87951-961-4) Overlook Pr.

— The North Ship. 48p. 1974. pap. 8.95 (0-571-10503-3) Faber & Faber.

— Required Writing: Miscellaneous Pieces 1955-1982. LC 84-4099. 336p. (C). 1984. pap. 9.95 (0-374-51840-8) FS&G.

— Selected Letters: 1940-1985. Thwaite, Anthony, ed. 1993. 40.00 (0-374-25829-5) FS&G.

— The Whitsun Weddings. 46p. 1971. pap. 7.95 (0-571-09710-3) Faber & Faber.

Larkin, Philip, ed. The Oxford Book of Twentieth Century English Verse. 1973. 35.00 (0-19-812137-7) OUP.

Larkin, Ralph W. Suburban Youth in Cultural Crisis. LC 78-10742. 1979. pap. text ed. 14.95 (0-19-502523-7) OUP.

Larkin, Ralph W., jt. auth. see Foss, Daniel A.

Larkin, Robert P. & Peters, Gary L. Biographical Dictionary of Geography. LC 92-18364. 384p. 1993. text ed. 69.50 (0-313-27622-6, LBG, Greenwood Pr) Greenwood.

— Dictionary of Concepts in Human Geography. LC 82-24258. (Reference Sources for the Social Sciences & Humanities Ser.: No. 2). viii, 286p. 1983. text ed. 59.95 (0-313-22729-2, LHG, Greenwood Pr) Greenwood.

Larkin, Robert P., jt. auth. see Peters, Gary L.

***Larkin, Rochelle.** My First Little 12 Story Book Set. (J). (ps-2). 1994. 29.95 (1-886520-00-3) Micro R&D.

Larkin, Sandar, jt. auth. see Larkin, T. J.

Larkin, Sharon, jt. auth. see Swain, Merrill.

Larkin, Stillman C. The Pioneer History of Meigs County, Ohio. (Illus.). 224p. 1989. reprint ed. pap. 15.00 (1-55613-214-X) Heritage Bk.

— Pioneer History of Meigs County, Ohio. 208p. 1995. reprint ed. lib. bdg. 31.00 (0-8328-4479-9) Higginson Bk Co.

Larkin, Sue, jt. auth. see Larkin, J. Donald.

Larkin, Susan S., jt. auth. see Larkin, Ernest F.

Larkin, T. J. & Larkin, Sandar. Communicating Change: Winning Employee Support for New Business Goals. 224p. 1994. text ed. 22.95 (0-07-036452-4) McGraw.

Larkin, Troy J. Tax Break: How to Reduce the Taxes on Your Home. Graviet, Lois, ed. 100p. (Orig.). 1992. pap. 29.95 (0-9632424-0-7) CITTA.

Larkin, William. Get Real about Yourself: Twenty-Five Ways to Grow Whole & Holy. 160p. (Orig.). 1995. pap. 9.95 (0-89622-606-9) Twenty-Third.

***Larkin, William J., Jr.** Acts. LC 95-12621. (New Testament Commentary Ser.: Vol. 5). 1995. write for info. (0-8308-1805-7) InterVarsity.

— Culture & Biblical Hermeneutics: Interpreting & Applying the Authoritative Word in a Relativistic Age. 402p. (Orig.). (C). 1993. reprint ed. pap. text ed. 30.00 (0-8191-9219-8) U Pr of Amer.

Larking, Lambert B., ed. Proceedings Principally in the County of Kent, in Connection with the Parliaments Called in 1640, & Especially with the Committee of Religion Appointed in That Year. (Camden Society, London. Publications, First Ser.: No. 80a). reprint ed. 70.00 (0-404-50180-X) AMS Pr.

Larking, Lambert B., ed. see Philippus De Thame.

Larkins, B. A., jt. ed. see Herrmann, R. G.

Larkins, Ernest R. The Impact of Taxes on U. S. Citizens Working Abroad. LC 83-9201. (Research for Business Decisions Ser.: No. 66). 143p. reprint ed. pap. 40.80 (0-8357-1487-X, 2070399) Bks Demand.

***Larkins, Mary J.** Follow Your Dreams. 40p. 1994. per., pap. 7.00 (0-8059-3644-0) Dorrance.

Larkins, Patricia. Opportunities in Speech-Language Pathology Careers. (Illus.). 160p. 1988. 13.95 (0-8442-6013-4, VGM Career Bks); pap. 10.95 (0-8442-6014-2, VGM Career Bks) NTC Pub Grp.

Larkins, R. G., et al, eds. Diabetes Nineteen Eighty-Eight: Proceedings of the Thirteenth Congress of the International Diabetes Federation, Sydney, 20-25 Nov., 1988. (International Congress Ser.: No. 800). 1246p. 1989. 205.25 (0-444-81086-2) Elsevier.

Larkins, Richard & Smallwood, Richard. Clinical Skills: The Interview, Physical Examination & Assessment of the Patient's Problems. 250p. Date not set. pap. 34.95 (0-522-84467-7) Intl Spec Bk.

Larkins, Richard G., jt. auth. see Kincaid-Smith, Priscilla.

Larkins, William T. The Ford Tri-Motor 1926-1992. LC 92-60363. (Illus.). 288p. 1992. 49.95 (0-88740-416-2) Schiffer.

— U. S. Navy Aircraft 1921-1941, U. S. Marine Corps Aircraft 1914-1959: Two Classics in One Volume. LC 88-17753. (Illus.). 608p. 1995. 39.95 (0-88740-742-0) Schiffer.

Larkum, A. W., et al, eds. Biology of Seagrasses: A Treatise of Seagrasses with Special Reference to the Australian Region. (Aquatic Plant Studies: No. 2). 885p. 1989. 174. 50 (0-444-87403-8) Elsevier.

Larlan, David, ed. see Garrett, Wendell.

Larlham, Peter F. Black Theater, Dance, & Ritual in South Africa. Brockett, Oscar, ed. LC 85-8758. (Theater & Dramatic Studies: No. 29). 172p. reprint ed. 54.50 (0-8357-1658-9, 2070473) Bks Demand.

Larmer, Robert A. Water into Wine: An Investigation of the Concept of Miracle. 160p. 1987. 39.95 (0-7735-0615-2, Pub. by McGill CN) U of Toronto Pr.

***Larminie, Vivienne.** Wealth, Kinship & Culture: The 17th-Century Newdigates of Arbury & Their World. (Royal Historical Society Studies in History: No. 72). (Illus.). 384p. (C). 1995. text ed. 71.00 (0-86193-231-5, Royal Historical Soc) Boydell & Brewer.

Larminie, William, comp. West Irish Folk-Tales & Romances. LC 72-4191. (Select Bibliographies Reprint Ser.). 1977. reprint ed. 19.95 (0-8369-6888-3) Ayer.

Larmore, Charles E. Patterns of Moral Complexity. 140p. 1987. pap. 16.95 (0-521-33891-3) Cambridge U Pr.

Larmore, Lewis & Gervais, Robert L., eds. Space Shuttles & Interplanetary Missions: Proceedings of the Annual Meeting, 16th, Anaheim, California, 1970. (Advances in the Astronautical Sciences Ser.: Vol. 28). 1970. 35.00 (0-87703-055-3, Pub. by Am Astro Soc) Univelt Inc.

— Space Stations: Proceedings of the Annual Meeting, 16th, Anaheim, California, 1970. (Advances in the Astronautical Sciences Ser.: Vol. 27). 1970. 45.00 (0-87703-054-5, Pub. by Am Astro Soc) Univelt Inc.

Larmour, A. S. Step by Step. 211p. 1986. 50.00 (0-7212-0736-7, Pub. by Regency Press) St Mut.

Larmour, Peter, jt. auth. see Colebatch, Hal.

Larmour, Peter, et al, eds. Land, People & Government: Public Lands Policy in the South. LC 82-188428. 203p. reprint ed. pap. 57.90 (0-7837-3945-1, 2043710) Bks Demand.

Larmour, Peter J. The French Radical Party in the 1930's. viii, 328p. 1964. 42.50 (0-8047-0206-3) Stanford U Pr.

— The French Radical Party in the 1930's. fac. ed. LC 64-14554. (Illus.). 111p. 1964. reprint ed. pap. 30.00 (0-7837-7916-X, 2047672) Bks Demand.

Larmouth, John. Understanding OSI. 300p. 1994. pap. text ed. 33.00 (0-13-927765-X) P-H.

***Larmouth, Thomas E. & Murray, Carmin R.** Legal & Ethical Issues in Surreptitious Recording. (Publication of the American Dialect Society: No. 76). 88p. 1991. pap. 11.00 (0-8173-0540-8) U of Ala Pr.

Larn, Richard. Shipwrecks Around Land's End. (C). 1989. pap. 24.95 (0-85025-307-1, Pub. by Tor Mark Pr UK) St Mut.

— Shipwrecks Around the Lizard. (C). 1990. pap. 24.95 (0-85025-306-3, Pub. by Tor Mark Pr UK) St Mut.

— Shipwrecks North Coast: St. Ives to Bude. (C). 1990. pap. 35.00 (0-85025-324-1, Pub. by Tor Mark Pr UK) St Mut.

Larn, Richard & Whistler, Rex. Commercial Diving Manual. (Illus.). 512p. 1993. 39.95 (0-7153-0100-4, Pub. by D & C Pub UK) Sterling.

Larned, E. D. Church Records of Killingly, Connecticut. 56p. 1984. pap. 7.00 (0-912606-22-3) Hunterdon Hse.

Larned, Ellen D. Historic Gleanings in Windham County, Connecticut. 254p. 1992. reprint ed. pap. 19.50 (1-55613-659-5) Heritage Bk.

— History of Windham County, 2 vols. (Illus.). 1181p. 1995. reprint ed. lib. bdg. 109.00 (0-8328-4488-8) Higginson Bk Co.

An Asterisk (*) at the beginning of an entry indicates that the title is appearing in BIP for the first time.

***Larned, J. N., ed.** The Literature of American History: A Bibliographical Guide. 588p. 1995. reprint ed. lib. bdg. 64.50 (*0-8328-4506-X*) Higginson Bk Co.
— Literature of American History, a Bibliographical Guide. 588p. 1995. reprint ed. lib. bdg. 59.95 (*0-8328-4487-X*) Higginson Bk Co.
Larned, Joseph N. Life & Work of William Pryor Letchworth, Student & Minister of Public Benevolence. LC 71-172592. (Criminology, Law Enforcement, & Social Problems Ser.: No. 182). (Illus.). 1974. reprint ed. 24.00 (*0-87585-182-7*) Patterson Smith.
Larned, Josephus N. Books, Culture & Character. LC 70-90650. (Essay Index Reprint Ser.). 1977. 19.95 (*0-8369-1211-X*) Ayer.
— Study of Greatness in Men. LC 73-156677. (Essay Index Reprint Ser.). 1977. reprint ed. 23.95 (*0-8369-2557-2*) Ayer.
Larned, Josephus N., et al. English Leadership. LC 70-93353. (Essay Index Reprint Ser.). 1977. 26.95 (*0-8369-1416-3*) Ayer.
Larned, W. T. American Indian Fairy Tales. LC 93-46940. (J). 1994. 8.99 (*0-517-10177-7*, Derrydale Bks) Random Hse Value.
Larner, Christina. Enemies of God: The Witch-Hunt in Scotland. LC 81-47605. 256p. reprint ed. pap. 73.00 (*0-7837-2186-2*, 2042524) Bks Demand.
Larner, Mary. In the Neighborhood: Programs That Strengthen Family Day Care for Low-Income Families. 96p. (Orig.). 1994. pap. 12.95 (*0-926582-12-7*) NCCP.
— Linking Family Support & Early Childhood Programs: Issues, Experience, Opportunities. Lalley, Jacqueline, ed. (Guidelines for Effective Practice Ser.). 40p. (Orig.). 1995. pap. 7.00 (*1-885429-09-6*) Family Resource.
Larner, Mary, et al, eds. Fair Start for Children: Lessons Learned from Seven Demonstration Programs. 288p. (C). 1993. text ed. 30.00 (*0-300-05206-5*) Yale U Pr.
Larner, Robert J. & Meehan, James W., Jr., eds. Economics & Antitrust Policy. LC 88-18515. 250p. 1989. text ed. 59.95 (*0-89930-386-2*, LRA/, Quorum Bks) Greenwood.
Larocca. Handbook of Home Care IV Therapy. 4th ed. 192p. 1993. spiral bd. 26.95 (*0-685-65363-3*) Mosby Yr Bk.
Larocca, Felix E. Facilitator's Training Manual: A Primer: The Bash Approach. 2nd rev. ed. (Illus.). (C). 1989. pap. text ed. 7.50 (*0-317-93544-5*) Bash Inc.
Larocca, Felix E., ed. Eating Disorders. LC 85-81895. (New Directions for Mental Health Services Ser.: No. MHS 31). (Orig.). 1986. pap. 17.95 (*1-55542-988-2*) Jossey-Bass.
LaRocca, Joanne C. Pocket Guide to Intravenous Therapy. 2nd ed. LC 92-49181. 300p. 1992. spiral bd. 19.95 (*0-8016-6688-0*) Mosby Yr Bk.
Larocca, Joanne C. Pocket Guide to IV Therapy. 2nd ed. 1993. pap. 19.95 (*0-8016-6910-3*) Mosby Yr Bk.
LaRocco, Lesli, ed. see Zoshchenko, Mikhail.
LaRocco, Rich, ed. see Darner, Kirt I.
Laroche, Michel, jt. auth. see Kirpalani, Vishnu H.
***LaRochelle, David.** The Case of the Missing Lynx. (Mad Mysteries Ser.). (Illus.). 48p. (Orig.). (J). (gr. 2 up). 1995. pap. 2.95 (*0-8431-3797-5*) Price Stern.
— A Christmas Guest. (Carolrhoda Picture Bks.). (Illus.). 32p. (J). (ps-3). 1989. reprint ed. pap. 5.95 (*0-685-25636-7*, Lerner Publctns) Lerner Group.
— The Evening King. LC 91-1970. (Illus.). 32p. (J). (ps-2). 1993. text ed. 14.95 (*0-689-31640-2*, Atheneum Bks Young) S&S Childrens.
— The Invisible Suit Case. (Mad Mysteries Ser.). (Illus.). 48p. (Orig.). (J). (gr. 2 up). 1995. pap. 2.95 (*0-8431-3798-3*) Price Stern.
LaRochelle, Jeffrey, jt. auth. see Laforest, Thomas J.
LaRochelle, Jeffrey, jt. auth. see Laforest, Thomas.
Larock, Bruce E., jt. auth. see Newman, Donald G.
Larock, R. C. Organomercury Compounds in Organic Synthesis. (Reactivity & Structure Ser.: Vol. 22). 420p. 1985. 220.00 (*0-387-13749-1*) Spr-Verlag.
Larock, Richard C. Comprehensive Organic Transformations: A Guide to Functional Group Preparations. LC 89-30333. 1160p. 1989. lib. bdg. 60.00 (*0-89573-710-8*) VCH Pubs.
Larocque, Jean-Paul. Life with Me. (Illus.). 14p. (J). (gr. k-3). 1994. pap. 11.95 (*1-895583-67-5*) MAYA Pubs.
— Numbers Time. (Illus.). 17p. (J). (gr. k-3). 1993. pap. 11.95 (*1-895583-62-4*) MAYA Pubs.
— Our Night Out. (Illus.). 12p. (J). (gr. k-3). 1994. pap. 10.95 (*1-895583-66-7*) MAYA Pubs.
— What I Like to Eat. (Illus.). 18p. (J). (gr. k-3). 1995. pap. 10.95 (*1-895583-74-8*) MAYA Pubs.
— What Is Two Plus Two. (Illus.). 12p. (J). (gr. k-3). 1993. pap. 10.95 (*1-895583-63-2*) MAYA Pubs.
— Wille Wacka Land. (Illus.). 12p. (J). (gr. 1-3). 1992. pap. 6.95 (*1-895583-04-7*) MAYA Pubs.
LaRocque, L. E. Boiler Operator's Dictionary. LC 87-18417. 151p. 1988. pap. 12.95 (*0-912524-41-3*) Busn News.
— Starting in Heating & Air Conditioning Service. Turpin, Joanna, ed. LC 92-11928. (Illus.). 180p. (C). 1992. 39.95 (*0-912524-63-4*) Busn News.
LaRocque, Lionel. Boilers Simplified. LC 87-685. 240p. 1987. 27.95 (*0-912524-40-5*) Busn News.
LaRoe, Ross M., jt. auth. see Pool, John C.
Larom, Peter, jt. auth. see Rousmaniere, Leah R.
Laron, Z., ed. European Society for Pediatric Endocrinology (ESPE) & Lawson Wilkins Pediatric Endocrinology Society (LWPES) Abstracts: Third Joint Meeting, Jerusalem, October - November 1989. (Journal: Hormone Research: Vol. 31, Suppl. 1). viii, 84p. 1989. 37.00 (*3-8055-5117-7*) S Karger.
— Prognosis of Diabetes in Children. (Pediatric & Adolescent Endocrinology Ser.: Vol. 18). xiv, 304p. 1989. 199.25 (*3-8055-4702-1*) S Karger.
— Third Joint Meeting of the European Society for Paediatric Endocrinology (ESPE) & the Lawson Wilkins Pediatric Endocrine Society (LWPES) Proceedings of the Plenary Lectures & Symposia, Jerusalem, October - November 1989. (Journal: Hormone Research: Vol. 33, No. 2-4, 1990). (Illus.). 116p. 1990. pap. 105.00 (*3-8055-5289-0*) S Karger.
Laron, Z. & Butenandt, O., eds. Evaluation of Growth Hormone Secretion. (Pediatric & Adolescent Endocrinology Ser.: Vol. 12). (Illus.). viii, 200p. 1983. 121.75 (*3-8055-3623-2*) S Karger.
Laron, Z. & Galatzer, A., eds. Psychological Aspects of Diabetes in Children & Adolescents. (Pediatric & Adolescent Endocrinology Ser.: Vol. 10). xvi, 248p. 1983. 147.25 (*3-8055-3575-9*) S Karger.
— Recent Progress in Medico-Social Problems in Juvenile Diabetics, Pt. II. (Pediatric & Adolescent Endocrinology Ser.: Vol. 11). (Illus.). x, 210p. 1983. 122.50 (*3-8055-3594-5*) S Karger.
Laron, Z. & Karp, M., eds. Future Trends in Juvenile Diabetes. (Pediatric & Adolescent Endocrinology Ser.: Vol. 15). (Illus.). xiv, 410p. 1986. 280.00 (*3-8055-3958-4*) S Karger.
— Prediabetes - Are We Ready to Intervene? (Pediatric & Adolescent Endocrinology Ser.: Vol. 23). (Illus.). x, 192p. 1993. 196.00 (*3-8055-5665-9*) S Karger.
Laron, Z. & Parks, J. S., eds. Lessons from Laron Syndrome (LS) 1966-1992: A Model of GH & IGF-I Action & Interaction. (Pediatric & Adolescent Endocrinology Ser.: Vol. 24). (Illus.). x, 368p. 1993. 296.00 (*3-8055-5671-3*) S Karger.
Laron, Z., ed. see International Beilinson Symposium Staff.
Laron, Zvi, ed. The Adipose Child. (Pediatric & Adolescent Endocrinology Ser.: Vol.1). 250p. 1976. 71.25 (*3-8055-2343-2*) S Karger.
Laron, Zvi, ed. see International Beilinson Symposium Staff.
LaRondelle, Hans K. The Good News about Armageddon. Coffen, Richard, ed. 32p. (Orig.). 1991. pap. 0.79 (*0-8280-0590-7*) Review & Herald.
— The Israel of God in Prophecy: Principles of Prophetic Interpretation. LC 82-74358. 240p. 1983. pap. 15.99 (*0-943872-14-6*) Andrews Univ Pr.
— Perfection & Perfectionism: A Dogmatic-Ethical Study of Biblical Perfection & Phenomenal Perfectionism. LC 82-74358. vii, 372p. 1979. pap. 16.99 (*0-943872-03-0*) Andrews Univ Pr.
Larone, Davise H. Medically Important Fungi: A Guide to Identification. 2nd ed. LC 92-48471. (Illus.). 240p. 1993. pap. 29.95 (*1-55581-058-6*) Am Soc Microbio.
***Larone, Davise H., ed.** Medically Important Fungi: A Guide to Identification. 3rd ed. LC 94-40202. 1995. write for info. (*1-55581-091-8*) Am Soc Microbio.
Laroque, Didier. Nemo. (Illus.). 108p. (ENG & SPA.). 1993. pap. 28.95 (*84-252-1530-7*) Rizzoli Intl.
Laroque, Francois. The Age of Shakespeare. Campbell, Alexandra, tr. (Illus.). 192p. 1993. pap. 12.95 (*0-8109-2890-6*) Abrams.
— The Journal of Francois Laroque. 102p. 1981. 14.95 (*0-87770-262-4*) Ye Galleon.
— Shakespeare's Festive World: Elizabethan Seasonal Entertainment & the Professional Stage. Lloyd, Janet, tr. (European Studies in English Literature). (Illus.). 439p. (C). 1993. pap. 19.95 (*0-521-45786-6*) Cambridge U Pr.
Laroque, P. The Social Institutions of France. 815p. 1983. text ed. 611.00 (*0-677-30970-8*) Gordon & Breach.
Laros, Russell K., ed. Blood Disorders in Pregnancy. LC 85-24012. 257p. reprint ed. pap. 73.30 (*0-7837-2724-0*, 2043104) Bks Demand.
LaRosa, Benedict D. Gun Control: A Historical Perspective. 14p. (Orig.). 1992. pap. 2.50 (*0-9627423-1-7*) Candlestick.
— Gun Control: A Historical Perspective. 2nd ed. 14p. (Orig.). 1992. pap. 2.50 (*0-9627423-2-5*) Candlestick.
LaRosa, Judith H., jt. auth. see Alexander, Linda L.
LaRose, Mary K., tr. see Descamps-Lequime, Sophie & Vernerey, Denise.
LaRose, Mary K., tr. see Guittard, Charles.
LaRose, Mary K., tr. see Koenig, Viviane.
LaRose, Mary K., tr. see Moktefi, Mokhtar.
LaRose, Robert, jt. auth. see Strubhaar, Joseph.
LaRose-Weaver, Diane & Cusick, Dawn. Glorious Christmas Crafts: Celebrate the Holidays with More Than 120 Festive Projects to Make. (Illus.). 160p. 1993. pap. 14.95 (*0-8069-8379-5*) Sterling.
Larossa. Social History of Fatherhood. 1992. lib. bdg. 34.95 (*0-226-46903-4*) U Ch Pr.
LaRossa, Ralph. Conflict & Power in Marriage: Expecting the First Child. LC 77-8566. (Sage Library of Social Research: No. 50). 176p. reprint ed. pap. 50.20 (*0-8357-8445-2*, 2034709) Bks Demand.
LaRossa, Ralph, ed. Family Case Studies: A Sociological Perspective. 260p. (C). 1984. pap. 14.95 (*0-02-918010-4*) Free Pr.
LaRouche, Janice & Ryan, Regina. Janice LaRouche's Strategies for Women at Work. 400p. 1984. pap. 9.95 (*0-380-86744-3*) Avon.
Larouche, L. & Pilon, J. Terminologie de la Gestion: Les Organigrammes: Management Terminology. Cote, M., ed. 223p. 1974. pap. 24.95 (*0-8288-6215-X*, M-9220) Fr & Eur.
LaRouche, Lyndon H., Jr. La Ciencia de la Economia Christiana. Small, Dennis & Lozano, Salvador, trs. LC 93-83889. (Illus.). 300p. (Orig.). (SPA.). 1993. pap. 10.00 (*1-882985-00-1*) Schiller Inst.
— Cold Fusion: A Challenge to United States Science Policy. Gallagher, Paul, ed. LC 92-60722. (Illus.). 173p. (Orig.). (C). 1992. pap. 20.00 (*0-9621095-7-6*) Schiller Inst.
— The Power of Reason - 1988: An Autobiography. LC 87-7894. (Illus.). 331p. (Orig.). 1987. pap. 10.00 (*0-943235-00-6*) Exec Intel Review.
— The Science of Christian Economy: The Prison Writings of Lyndon LaRouche. Wertz, Marianna, ed. LC 91-62722. (Illus.). 600p. (Orig.). (C). 1992. pap. 15.00 (*0-9621095-6-8*) Schiller Inst.
— Selections from Lyndon H. LaRouche, Jr. Wei, Ray, ed. & tr. by. Chu, Andy, tr. LC 92-62931. 140p. (Orig.). (CHI.). 1992. pap. 7.00 (*0-9621095-9-2*) Schiller Inst.
— So, You Wish to Learn All about Economics? A Text on Elementary Mathematical Economics. 192p. (Orig.). 1995. pap. 10.00 (*0-933488-35-1*) Exec Intel Review.
— So, You Wish to Learn All about Economics? A Text on Elementary Mathematical Economics. 2nd ed. Huth, Christina, ed. (Illus.). 192p. (Orig.). 1995. pap. 10.00 (*0-943235-13-8*) Exec Intel Review.
LaRoue, Samuel D., Jr. & Uguccioni, Ellen J. Coral Gables in Postcards: Scenes from Florida's Yesterday. LC 88-71025. (Illus.). 56p. (Orig.). 1988. pap. 12.95 (*0-9620565-0-2*) Dade Heritage Trust.
Laroui, Abdallah. The Crisis of the Arab Intellectual: Traditionalism or Historicism? Cammell, Diarmid, tr. LC 74-29796. 1977. 45.00 (*0-520-02971-2*) U CA Pr.
Larousse. Petit Larousse Illustre: 1994. (Illus.). 59.95 (*0-685-74790-5*) Schoenhof.
— Petit Larousse Illustre 1995. 1784p. 1994. write for info. (*0-7859-8753-3*) Fr & Eur.
***Larousse, David P.** The Hors D'Oeuvres Bible. LC 94-25399. 1995. text ed. 45.00 (*0-471-01312-9*) Wiley.
— The Sauce Bible: A Guide to the Saucier's Craft. 400p. 1993. text ed. 54.95 (*0-471-57228-4*) Wiley.
— A Taste for All Seasons: A Celebration of American Food. (Illus.). 192p. 1990. 24.95 (*1-55832-020-2*) Harvard Common Pr.
Larousse, David P. & Gibson, Alan R. The Pillar House Cookbook. (Illus.). 144p. (Orig.). 1988. pap. 14.95 (*1-55832-005-9*) Harvard Common Pr.
Larousse Editorial Staff. Larousse Concise Spanish-English English-Spanish Dictionary. LC 93-86204. 1248p. (ENG & SPA.). 1994. 16.95 (*2-03-420400-X*, Larousse LKC); pap. 9.95 (*2-03-420600-2*, Larousse LKC) LKC.
— The Larousse French-English English-French Dictionary. unabridged ed. LC 93-86202. (Illus.). 2064p. (ENG & FRE.). 1994. 40.00 (*2-03-420100-0*, Larousse LKC) LKC.
— Larousse Pocket French-English English-French Dictionary. LC 93-86205. 768p. (Orig.). (ENG & FRE.). 1994. pap. 4.50 (*2-03-420700-9*, Larousse LKC) LKC.
— Larousse Pocket Spanish-English English-Spanish Dictionary. LC 93-86206. 768p. (Orig.). (ENG & SPA.). 1994. pap. 4.50 (*2-03-420800-5*, Larousse LKC) LKC.
— The Larousse Spanish-English English-Spanish Dictionary. unabridged ed. LC 93-86201. (Illus.). 1592p. (ENG & SPA.). 1994. 40.00 (*2-03-420200-7*, Larousse LKC) LKC.
Larousse, Pierre, jt. auth. see Clement, Felix.
***Larousse, Pierre.** Grand Dictionnaire Universel du XIX Siecle, 24 vols. fac. ed. (FRE.). 1990. write for info. (*0-7859-8661-8*, 286971193x) Fr & Eur.
***Larousse Staff.** Allemand: Guide de Conversation et Dictionnaire. 187p. (FRE.). 1991. pap. 16.95 (*0-7859-7656-6*, 2034035046) Fr & Eur.
— Anglais: Guide de Conversation et Dictionnaire. 175p. (ENG & FRE.). 1991. pap. 16.95 (*0-7859-7655-8*, 2034035011) Fr & Eur.
— Diccionario Enciclopedia Larousse: Larousse Encyclopedia Dictionary (Spanish Edition), 12 vols., Set. (SPA.). 995.00 (*0-8288-8245-2*) Fr & Eur.
— Diccionario Enciclopedico Larousse: Larousse Encyclopedia Dictionary: Spanish Edition, 12 vols. 1992. write for info. (*0-7859-5231-4*) Fr & Eur.
— Dictionnaire de la Medecine Larousse. (FRE.). 1990. pap. 16.95 (*0-7859-7850-X*, 2253037842) Fr & Eur.
— Dictionnaire de la Peinture Allemande et d'Europe Centrale. 414p. (FRE.). 1990. pap. 79.95 (*0-7859-7693-0*, 2037400179) Fr & Eur.
— Dictionnaire de la Peinture Francaise. 520p. (FRE.). 1989. pap. 89.95 (*0-8288-2596-3*, 203740011X) Fr & Eur.
— Dictionnaire de la Peinture Italienne. 528p. (FRE.). 1989. pap. 79.95 (*0-7859-5540-2*, 2037400136) Fr & Eur.
— Dictionnaire des Difficultes de la Langue Francaise. 435p. (FRE.). 1992. 55.00 (*0-7859-0962-1*, 2033409023) Fr & Eur.
— Dictionnaire des Jeux de Lettres. 1088p. (FRE.). 1994. pap. 32.95 (*0-7859-7689-2*, 2037300913) Fr & Eur.
— Dictionnaire des Mots Croises. rev. ed. 904p. (FRE.). 1991. pap. 32.95 (*0-7859-7690-6*, 2037302150) Fr & Eur.
— Dictionnaire des Termes Techniques, l'Atelier du Peintre. 408p. (FRE.). 1990. pap. 79.95 (*0-7859-7696-5*, 2037400667) Fr & Eur.
— Dictionnaire du Francais Contemporain Manual et Travaux Pratiques. 29.95 (*0-317-45626-1*) Fr & Eur.
— Dictionnaire Encyclopedique Larousse L1. (FRE.). 1979. 250.00 (*0-7859-0127-2*, M7733) Fr & Eur.
— Dictionnaire Europa. 1959. write for info. (*0-7859-7649-3*, 2034010329) Fr & Eur.
— Dictionnaire General pour la Maitrise de la Langue Francaise. 1993. write for info. (*0-7859-7641-8*, 2033203026) Fr & Eur.
— Dictionnaire Larousse Bilingue de Poche. Date not set. write for info. (*0-7859-8605-7*, 203401104X) Fr & Eur.
— Dictionnaire Moderne Larousse Saturne Francais-Anglais, Anglais-Francais. 49.95 (*0-317-45631-8*) Fr & Eur.
— Dictionnaire Moderne Larousse Saturne Francais-Anglais, Anglais-Francaise. (ENG & FRE.). write for info. (*0-8288-7839-0*) Fr & Eur.
— Dictionnaire Pratique des Medicaments. (FRE.). 1989. write for info. (*0-7859-8609-X*, 203510128X) Fr & Eur.
— Dictionnaire Sachs No. 2. Date not set. write for info. (*0-7859-7634-5*, 2030281034) Fr & Eur.
— Dictionnaire Sachs-Villate No. 1. Date not set. write for info. (*0-7859-7633-7*, 2030281034) Fr & Eur.
— Dictionnaire Sachs-Villate Francais-Allemand, Allemand-Francais. (FRE & GER.). Date not set. 450.00 (*0-7859-7632-9*) Fr & Eur.
— French Collegiate Dictionary. 1092p. (FRE.). 1991. 39.95 (*0-8288-6960-X*, 2033202178) Fr & Eur.
— French-English, English-French Dictionary. 1984. mass mkt. 4.99 (*0-671-45851-5*) PB.
— Grammaire Anglaise. 256p. (ENG & FRE.). 1992. pap. 15.95 (*0-7859-0963-X*, 2034060024) Fr & Eur.
— Gran Enciclopedia Larousse, 24 vols., Set. 10740p. (SPA.). 2,495.00 (*0-8288-8250-9*, S12308) Fr & Eur.
— Gran Enciclopedia Larousse: Atlas Historico: Larousse Historical Atlas. (Illus.). (SPA.). 125.00 (*0-8288-8248-7*) Fr & Eur.
— Gran Enciclopedia Larousse Atlas Geografico: Geographical Atlas. (Illus.). (SPA.). 125.00 (*0-8288-8247-9*) Fr & Eur.
— Gran Enciclopedia Larousse Color, 24 vols. 10740p. (SPA.). 1992. 3,995.00 (*0-7859-5123-7*) Fr & Eur.
— Grand Dictionnaire Encyclopedique Larousse, 10 vols. 1, 250.00 (*0-685-13389-3*) Fr & Eur.
— Grand Dictionnaire Francais-Espagnol, Espagnol-Francais. 1500p. (FRE & SPA.). 1992. 105.00 (*0-7859-7660-4*, 2034513282) Fr & Eur.
— Grand Larousse Annuel: 1993. 576p. 1993. 250.00 (*0-7859-5598-4*, 2031002937) Fr & Eur.
— Grand Larousse Encyclopedique, 15 vols., Set. 11200p. (FRE.). 1985. 2,995.00 (*0-8288-6775-5*, F42400) Fr & Eur.
— Grand Larousse Encyclopedique: Supplement. 1088p. (FRE.). 1975. 89.50 (*0-8288-5893-4*, M6288) Fr & Eur.
— Le Grand Larousse in 5 Volumes, Vol. 5. 3560p. (FRE.). 1992. 995.00 (*0-8288-1941-6*, M522) Fr & Eur.
— Grand Larousse Universel, 15 vols. 11130p. (FRE.). 1988. 2,295.00 (*0-8288-1940-8*, F12840) Fr & Eur.
— La Grande Encyclopedie, 22 vols. & index. 1,995.00 (*0-317-45639-3*) Fr & Eur.
— Grande Encyclopedie, 22 vols., Set. (FRE.). 2,995.00 (*0-8288-7841-2*, M8689) Fr & Eur.
— La Grande Encyclopedie, Vol. 2: Amiens-Austen. 1976. Vol. 2 Amiens-Austen. 160.00 (*0-7859-5579-8*, 2030009024) Fr & Eur.
— Grande Encyclopedie Larousse, Index. 650p. (FRE.). 1978. 150.00 (*0-8288-5247-2*, M6292) Fr & Eur.
— Italien: Guide de Conversation et Dictionnaire. 174p. (FRE & ITA.). 1991. pap. 16.95 (*0-7859-8606-5*, 203403502x) Fr & Eur.
— Larousse: Pluridictionnaire. 45.00 (*0-317-45660-1*) Fr & Eur.
— Larousse Business Dictionary English-French - Francais-Anglais. 336p. 1990. pap. 59.95 (*0-8288-2394-4*, F137232) Fr & Eur.
— Larousse de Poche. 8.95 (*0-317-45661-X*); 18.95 (*0-8288-7843-9*, M9357) Fr & Eur.
— Larousse de Poche: Dictionnaire des Noms Communs et des Noms Propres. 864p. (FRE.). 1993. pap. 19.95 (*0-7859-7638-8*, 2033201066) Fr & Eur.
— Larousse Dictionary of Literature: Larousse Dictionnaire des Litteratures, 2 vols., Set. 1888p. (FRE.). 1986. 250.00 (*0-8288-1564-X*, F41450) Fr & Eur.
— Larousse Dictionary of Music: Larousse de la Musique, 2 vols., Set. 1803p. 1982. 295.00 (*0-8288-2169-0*, M14302) Fr & Eur.
— Larousse Dictionnaire Compact Francais-Anglias, Anglias Francais. 1000p. 1993. pap. 49.95 (*0-7859-5599-2*, 2034016319) Fr & Eur.
— Larousse Dictionnaire Complet des Mots Croises. (FRE.). Date not set. 55.00 (*0-7859-7643-4*, 2033402010) Fr & Eur.
— Larousse Dictionnaire de la Peinture Espagnole et Portugais du Moyen Age a nos Jours. 319p. (FRE.). 1989. pap. 69.95 (*0-7859-7692-2*, 2037400160) Fr & Eur.
— Larousse Dictionnaire de la Peinture Flamande et Hollandaise du Moyen Age a nos Jours. 493p. (FRE.). 1989. pap. 79.95 (*0-7859-7691-4*, 2037400152) Fr & Eur.
— Larousse Dictionnaire de la Prononciation. 37.50 (*0-317-45654-7*) Fr & Eur.
— Larousse Dictionnaire de la Sociologie. 288p. (FRE.). 1993. pap. 29.95 (*0-7859-7728-7*, 2097202276) Fr & Eur.
— Larousse Dictionnaire de l'Ancien Francais. 39.95 (*0-317-45644-X*) Fr & Eur.
— Larousse Dictionnaire de Linguistique. (FRE.). 37.50 (*0-8288-7846-3*) Fr & Eur.
— Larousse Dictionnaire de Psychologie. 273p. (FRE.). 1991. pap. 28.95 (*0-7859-7684-1*, 2037202164) Fr & Eur.
— Larousse Dictionnaire des Anglicismes. 37.50 (*0-317-45645-8*); write for info. (*0-8288-7847-1*) Fr & Eur.
— Larousse Dictionnaire des Courants Picturaux Tendences, Mouvements, Ecoles, Genres, du Moyen Age a nos Jours. 448p. (FRE.). 1990. pap. 79.95 (*0-7859-7694-9*, 2037400616) Fr & Eur.
— Larousse Dictionnaire des Difficultes de la Langue Francaise. 37.50 (*0-317-45646-6*); write for info. (*0-8288-7848-X*) Fr & Eur.
— Larousse Dictionnaire des Locutions Francaises. 37.50 (*0-317-45651-2*) Fr & Eur.
— Larousse Dictionnaire des Mots Croises. 39.95 (*0-317-45652-0*) Fr & Eur.
— Larousse Dictionnaire des Mots Croises. 1956p. (FRE.). 1992. 59.95 (*0-8288-2339-1*, F136840) Fr & Eur.

— Larousse Dictionnaire des Noms de Famille et Prenoms de France. 37.50 (*0-317-45653-9*); write for info. (*0-8288-7851-X*) Fr & Eur.

— Larousse Dictionnaire des Proverbs, Sentences et Maximes. (FRE.). 37.50 (*0-8288-7852-8*) Fr & Eur.

— Larousse Dictionnaire des Rimes Orales et Ecrites. 37.50 (*0-317-45656-3*) Fr & Eur.

— Larousse Dictionnaire des Rimes Orales et Ecrites. 576p. (FRE.). 1992. 27.95 (*0-8288-7401-8*, F12341) Fr & Eur.

— Larousse Dictionnaire des Verbes Francais. (FRE.). 37.50 (*0-8288-7853-6*) Fr & Eur.

— Larousse Dictionnaire Du Francais Au College: 35,000 Mots Avec Etymologies. 1092p. (FRE.). 1991. 49.95 (*0-7859-7640-X*, 2033202178) Fr & Eur.

— Larousse Dictionnaire du Francais Classique. 39.95 (*0-317-45648-2*) Fr & Eur.

— Larousse Dictionnaire du Francais Contemporain Illustre. 29.95 (*0-317-45649-0*); write for info. (*0-8288-7855-2*) Fr & Eur.

— Larousse Dictionnaire Etymologique. 39.95 (*0-317-45647-4*) Fr & Eur.

— Larousse Dictionnaire Francais. 767p. (FRE.). 1991. 32.95 (*0-7859-7639-6*, 2033201392) Fr & Eur.

— Larousse Dictionnaire Analogique. 39.95 (*0-317-45643-1*) Fr & Eur.

— Larousse Francais - Anglais-Anglais - Francais de Poche. 8.95 (*0-317-45658-X*) Fr & Eur.

— Larousse Francais-Anglais, Anglais-Francais de Poche. (ENG & FRE.). write for info. (*0-8288-7858-7*) Fr & Eur.

— Larousse Illustrated International Encyclopedia. 1975. text ed. 11.50 (*0-07-036479-6*) McGraw.

— Larousse "L3", 3 vols. 495.00 (*0-317-45659-8*) Fr & Eur.

— Larousse L3, 3 vols., Set. 595.00 (*0-8288-7842-0*, M6473) Fr & Eur.

— Larousse Mercury French-Spanish, Spanish-French Dictionary: Dictionnaire Mercure Francais-Espagnol-Francais. (FRE & SPA.). 1981. 35.00 (*0-8288-0739-6*, S34571) Fr & Eur.

— Larousse pour Tous. 18.95 (*0-317-45662-8*) Fr & Eur.

— Larousse Practical English-Spanish Technical-Scientific Vocabulary: Vocabulario Pratico Larousse Tecnico-Cientifico Ingles-Espanol. 670p. (ENG & SPA.). 1984. 9.95 (*0-8288-0663-2*, F13910) Fr & Eur.

— Larousse Spanish Dictionary. 1983. pap. 5.99 (*0-451-16809-7*) NAL-Dutton.

— Larousse Universel L2, 2 vols., Set. 1800p. (FRE.). 1969. 395.00 (*0-8288-6609-0*, F128509); 295.00 (*0-685-62924-4*, F12850) Fr & Eur.

— Mon Dictionnaire Francais - Anglais-Anglais - Anglais-Francais en Couleurs. 24.95 (*0-317-45756-X*) Fr & Eur.

— Nouveau Dictionnaire Larousse des Mots Croises. (FRE.). 1981. 24.95 (*0-8288-2340-5*, F 136830) Fr & Eur.

— Nouveau Larousse Elementaire. 35.00 (*0-317-45759-4*) Fr & Eur.

— Nouveau Petit Larousse. write for info. (*0-8288-7835-8*) Fr & Eur.

— Petit Larousse en Couleurs. 95.00 (*0-317-45760-8*) Fr & Eur.

— Petit Larousse Illustre. 39.95 (*0-317-45763-2*) Fr & Eur.

— Petit Larousse Illustre. (Illus.). 1872p. write for info. (*0-7859-3734-X*) Fr & Eur.

— Portugais: Guide de Conversation et Dictionnaire. 192p. (FRE & POR.). 1992. pap. 16.95 (*0-7859-7657-4*, 2034035054) Fr & Eur.

Larousse Staff & Dauzat, Albert. Larousse Dictionnaire Etymologique. 626p. (FRE.). 1985. pap. 27.95 (*0-7859-4539-3*) Fr & Eur.

Larousse Staff & Garcia-Pelayo, Ramon. Pequena Enciclopedia Tematica Larousse en Color. Small Thematic Larousse Encyclopedia in Color, 2 vols., Set. 1096p. 1978. 175.00 (*0-8288-5260-X*, S30235) Fr & Eur.

Larousse Staff & Lange-Kowal, Ernst E. Mercury Larousse French-German, German-French Dictionary: Dictionnaire Mercure Francais-Allemand-Francais. 3rd ed. 1206p. (FRE & GER.). 1964. 55.00 (*0-7859-4826-0*) Fr & Eur.

LaRoux, Madame. The Practice of Classical Palmistry. (Illus.). 288p. 1993. pap. 14.95 (*0-87728-720-1*) Weiser.

Laroy, C., jt. auth. see Cranmer, D.

Larpenter, Carl. Electricians' Pocket Reference & Record. 1964. 1.50 (*0-87511-071-1*) Claitors.

Larpenteur, Charles. Forty Years a Fur Trader on the Upper Missouri: The Personal Narrative of Charles Larpenteur, 1833-1872. LC 88-38637. (Illus.). xxviii, 388p. 1989. reprint ed. pap. 9.95 (*0-8032-7930-2*) U of Nebr Pr.

Larrabee, Carroll B. How to Package for Profit: A Manual of Packaging. LC 75-39257. (Getting & Spending: the Consumer's Dilemma Ser.). (Illus.). 1976. reprint ed. 20.95 (*0-405-08030-1*) Ayer.

Larrabee, Denise M. Anne Hampton Brewster: Nineteenth-Century Author & "Social Outlaw" 32p. (Orig.). 1992. pap. 3.50 (*0-914076-84-1*) Lib Co Phila.

— By a Lady: American Women Poets of the 18th & 19th Centuries. 24p. (Orig.). 1988. pap. 2.00 (*0-914076-53-1*) Lib Co Phila.

Larrabee, Elizabeth. Random Pieces: Vignettes from the Thirties. 96p. 1993. pap. 7.95 (*0-9636690-0-1*) Withee Pub.

Larrabee, Eric. Commander in Chief - Franklin Delano Roosevelt: His Lieutenants & Their War. 1988. pap. 16.95 (*0-671-66382-8*, Touchstone Bks) S&S Trade.

Larrabee, Eric, ed. see American Studies Association Staff.

Larrabee, F. Stephen. Eastern European Security After the Cold War. LC 93-38122. 1993. write for info. (*0-8330-1471-4*, MR-254-USDP) Rand Corp.

Larrabee, F. Stephen, ed. The Two German States & European Security. 286p. 1989. text ed. 45.00 (*0-312-02683-8*); pap. 15.95 (*0-312-02820-2*) St Martin.

— The Volatile Powder Keg: Balkan Security after the Cold War. 300p. (Orig.). (C). 1994. lib. bdg. 61.00 (*1-879383-22-5*); pap. text ed. 26.50 (*1-879383-23-3*) Am Univ Pr.

Larrabee, F. Stephen, jt. auth. see Szayna, Thomas S.

Larrabee, Graydon B., jt. ed. see Kane, Philip F.

Larrabee, James, ed. Philosophy, B-BJ. (LC Cumulative Classification Ser.). 300p. 1985. ring bd. 38.00 (*0-933949-14-6*); fiche 13.00 (*0-933949-18-9*) Livia Pr.

— Religion, BL-BX. LC 85-6863. (LC Cumulative Classification Ser.). 1000p. 1985. ring bd. 105.00 (*0-933949-11-1*); fiche write for info. (*0-933949-15-4*) Livia Pr.

— Religion, BL-BX, Vol. 1. LC 85-6863. (LC Cumulative Classification Ser.). 1000p. 1985. write for info. (*0-933949-12-X*); fiche write for info. (*0-933949-16-2*) Livia Pr.

— Religion, BL-BX, Vol. 2. LC 85-6863. (LC Cumulative Classification Ser.). 1000p. 1985. write for info. (*0-933949-13-8*); fiche write for info. (*0-933949-17-0*) Livia Pr.

Larrabee, Jean G. Coaching Swimming Effectively. LC 86-18594. (Illus.). 112p. (Orig.). 1987. pap. 18.00 (*0-87322-080-3*, BLAR0080) Human Kinetics.

***Larrabee, Larry.** Satisfaction in Parenting. Goc, Michael J., ed. 128p. (Orig.). 1995. pap. 12.00x (*0-938627-24-4*) New Past Pr.

Larrabee, Lisa. Grandmother Five Baskets. LC 93-10451. (Illus.). 64p. (J). (gr. 3-7). 1993. pap. 9.95 (*0-943173-90-6*) Harbinger AZ.

Larrabee, Margery. All the Time in the World. 1971. pap. 2.00 (*0-911214-21-6*) Rational Isl.

Larrabee, Mary J., ed. An Ethic of Care: Feminist & Interdisciplinary Perspectives. LC 92-13206. (Thinking Gender Ser.). 1992. 49.95 (*0-415-90567-2*, A7152, Routledge NY); pap. 15.95 (*0-415-90568-0*, A7156, Routledge NY) Routledge.

Larrabee, Stephen, ed. Conventional Arms Control & East-West Security. LC 89-7685. (Duke Press Policy Studies). 491p. 1989. lib. bdg. 70.50 (*0-8223-0980-7*); pap. text ed. 21.95 (*0-8223-0992-0*) Duke.

Larrabee, Stephen A. English Bards & Crecian Marbles: The Relationship Between Sculpture & Poetry Especially. 1988. reprint ed. lib. bdg. 69.00 (*0-7812-0062-8*) Rprt Serv.

— English Bards & Grecian Marbles: The Relationship Between Sculpture & Poetry Especially in the Romantic Period. reprint ed. 59.00 (*0-403-08621-3*) Somerset Pub.

Larrabee, Wayne F., Jr. Principles of Facial Reconstruction. 1995. 86.00 (*0-7817-0150-3*) Raven.

Larrabee, Wayne F., Jr. & Makielski, Kathleen H. Surgical Anatomy of the Face. LC 92-21808. 240p. 1993. 152.50 (*0-88167-945-3*) Raven.

— Surgical Anatomy of the Face, Set. LC 92-21808. 240p. 1993. sl. 184.00 (*0-7817-0053-1*) Raven.

Larrabee, William. Railroad Question. LC 76-150190. (Select Bibliographies Reprint Ser.). 1977. 25.95 (*0-8369-5703-2*) Ayer.

Larrain, B., jt. auth. see Sachs, Jeffrey.

Larrain, Carlos J. Struktur der Reden in der Odyssee 1-8. (Spudasmata Ser.: Bd. 41). xi, 497p. (GER.). 1987. write for info. (*3-487-07831-7*, Pub. by Georg Olms GW) Lubrecht & Cramer.

Larrain, Felipe & Velasco, Andres. Can Swaps Solve the Debt Crisis? Lessons from the Chilean Experience. Riccardi, Margaret B., ed. LC 90-21355. (Studies in International Finance: No. 69). 50p. (Orig.). 1990. pap. text ed. 11.00 (*0-88165-241-5*) Princeton U Int Finan Econ.

Larrain, Felipe, jt. ed. see Edwards, Sebastian.

Larrain, Jorge. Ideology & Cultural Identity: Modernity & the Third World Presence. 220p. (C). 1994. text ed. 49.95 (*0-7456-1315-2*); pap. text ed. 19.95x (*0-7456-1316-0*) Blackwell Pubs.

— A Reconstruction of Historical Materialism. Bottomore, Thomas B. & Mulkay, Michael, eds. LC 85-18699. (Controversies in Sociology Ser.: No. 19). 120p. 1986. text ed. 44.95 (*0-04-301207-8*); pap. text ed. 17.95 (*0-04-301208-6*) Routledge Chapman & Hall.

— Theories of Development: Capitalism, Colonialism & Dependency. (Illus.). 220p. (C). 1989. pap. text ed. 24.95 (*0-685-27154-4*) Blackwell Pubs.

Larrain, Jorge A. The Concept of Ideology. (Modern Revivals in Philosophy Ser.). 256p. 1992. 58.95 (*0-7512-0049-2*, Pub. by Gregg Pub UK) Ashgate Pub Co.

— Marxism & Ideology. (Modern Revivals in Philosophy Ser.). 272p. 1992. 56.95 (*0-7512-0013-1*, Pub. by Gregg Revivals UK) Ashgate Pub Co.

— A Reconstruction of Historical Materialism. (Modern Revivals in Philosophy Ser.). 138p. 1992. 48.95 (*0-7512-0048-4*, Pub. by Gregg Pub UK) Ashgate Pub Co.

Larrain, Virginia. Timeless Voices. LC 78-54476. 128p. (Orig.). 1990. pap. 6.95 (*0-89087-231-7*) Celestial Arts.

Larralde, Signa, jt. auth. see Sebastian, Lynne.

Larranaga, Ignacio. The Silence of Mary. Gaudet, V., tr. LC 91-34526. 215p. (Orig.). 1991. pap. 12.95 (*0-8198-6911-2*) Pauline Bks.

Larranaga, Osvaldo, jt. ed. see Aedo, Cristian.

Larranaga, Robert D. The King's Shadow. (Picture Bks.). (Illus.). 32p. (J). (ps-3). 1991. lib. bdg. 18.95 (*0-87614-688-4*, Carolrhoda) Lerner Group.

Larrauri, Augustin. Dictionnaire d'Oto-Rhino-Laryngologie, 5 vols. (ENG, FRE, GER, ITA & SPA.). 1971. 95.00 (*0-8288-6442-X*, M-6338) Fr & Eur.

Larre, Claude. Rooted in Spirit: The Heart of Chinese Medicine. De la Vallee, Elisabeth R., tr. LC 93-33271. 1992. 39.95 (*0-88268-120-6*); pap. 19.95 (*0-88268-114-1*) Station Hill Pr.

Larre, Claude, et al. Survey of Traditional Chinese Medicine. Stang, Sarah E., tr. (Illus.). 231p. (Orig.). (FRE.). 1986. pap. 15.00 (*0-912381-00-0*) Trad Acupuncture.

Larrea, Juan. Guernica: Pablo Picasso. LC 73-91376. (Contemporary Art Ser.). (Illus.). 1970. reprint ed. 18.95 (*0-405-00731-0*) Ayer.

Larreche, Jean-Claude. MARKOPS. 2nd ed. 180p. 1992. Incl. 5 1/4" disk. disk 32.50 (*0-89426-202-5*); Incl. 3 1/2" disk. disk 32.50 (*0-89426-203-3*); Instr. manual incl. 5 1/4" disk. teacher ed, disk 32.50 (*0-89426-204-1*); Instr. manual incl. 3 1/2" disk. teacher ed, disk 32.50 (*0-89426-205-X*); Instr. manual incl. 5 1/4" disk. teacher ed, disk 32.50 (*0-685-74392-6*); pap. 32.50 (*0-685-74391-8*) Boyd & Fraser.

Larreche, Jean-Claude & Gatignon, Hubert A. MARKSTRAT 2. 2nd ed. 240p. (C). 1990. Incl. 5 1/4 diskette. disk 38.50 (*0-89426-124-X*); Incl. 3 1/2 disk. disk 38.50 (*0-89426-164-9*); Teaching notes. pap. text ed. 38.50 (*0-89426-125-8*) Boyd & Fraser.

Larreche, Jean-Claude, jt. auth. see Cook, Victor J.

Larremore, Thomas A. & Hopkins, Amy. The Marion Press: A Survey & a Checklist. LC 85-51272. 293p. 1981. reprint ed. 35.00 (*0-938768-04-2*) Oak Knoll.

Larreta, Enrique. The Glory of Don Ramiro. Walton, L. B., tr. 1977. pap. 250.00 (*0-8490-1891-9*) Gordon Pr.

Larrick, Geary. Analytical & Biographical Writings in Percussion Music. (American University Studies: Fine Arts: Ser. XX, Vol. 10). 227p. (C). 1989. text ed. 38.60 (*0-8204-0876-X*) P Lang Pubs.

— Biographical Essays on Twentieth-Century Percussionists. LC 92-18731. 336p. 1992. lib. bdg. 99.95 (*0-7734-9559-2*) E Mellen.

— Musical References & Song Texts in the Bible. LC 90-13480. (Studies in the History & Interpretation of Music: Vol. 9). (Illus.). 172p. 1990. lib. bdg. 79.95 (*0-88946-492-8*) E Mellen.

Larrick, J. W. & Burck, K. B. Gene Therapy: Application of Molecular Biology. 284p. 1991. 39.50 (*0-8385-3104-0*, A3104-5) Appleton & Lange.

Larrick, Nancy. Bring Me All of Your Dreams. LC 79-26892. 128p. (YA). (gr. 10 up). 1988. pap. 6.95 (*0-87131-550-5*) M Evans.

— Crazy to Be Alive in Such a Strange World: Poems about People. LC 76-49667. (Illus.). 192p. (J). (gr. 5 up). 1989. pap. 6.95 (*0-87131-566-1*) M Evans.

— When the Dark Comes Dancing: A Bedtime Poetry Book. LC 81-428. (Illus.). (J). (ps-2). 1983. 17.95 (*0-399-20807-0*, Philomel Bks) Putnam Pub Group.

Larrick, Nancy, ed. Mice Are Nice. (Illus.). 48p. (J). 1990. 15.95 (*0-399-21495-X*, Philomel Bks) Putnam Pub Group.

— Night of the Whippoorwill. (Illus.). 72p. (J). (ps up). 1992. 19.95 (*0-399-21874-2*, Philomel Bks) Putnam Pub Group.

— Piping Down the Valleys Wild. 247p. (J). (gr. 10 up). 1982. mass mkt. 4.99 (*0-440-46952-X*, YB) Dell.

Larrick, Nancy, sel. Room for Me & a Mountain Lion: Poetry of Open Spaces. LC 73-87710. (Illus.). 192p. (J). (gr. 5 up). 1989. pap. 6.95 (*0-87131-569-6*) M Evans.

Larrie, Reginald. Corners of Black History. (Illus.). 70p. 1986. reprint ed. 9.95 (*0-9615662-0-5*); reprint ed. teacher ed write for info. (*0-9615662-1-3*) Olympian King Co.

***Larrieu, Robert.** Dictionnaire Espagnol-Francais et Francais-Espagnol. 1978. write for info. (*0-7859-8006-7*, 2-7370-0109-9) Fr & Eur.

Larrieu, Robert, jt. ed. see Salva, Vicente.

Larrieu, V. Principles of Linear Algebra. 282p. 1972. text ed. 198.00 (*0-677-01610-7*); pap. text ed. 76.00 (*0-677-01615-8*) Gordon & Breach.

Larrigan, Tex. Buckmaster. large type ed. (Linford Western Library). 272p. 1993. pap. 14.95 (*0-7089-7443-0*, Linford) Ulverscroft.

— Buckmaster & the Cattlelifters. large type ed. (Linford Western Library). 272p. 1992. pap. 14.95 (*0-7089-7176-8*, Linford) Ulverscroft.

— Buscadero. large type ed. (Linford Western Library). 288p. 1994. pap. 14.95 (*0-7089-7496-1*, Linford) Ulverscroft.

Larrimer, Don. Bio-Bibliography of Justice Tom C. Clark. (Legal Bibliography Ser.: No. 27). 37p. (Orig.). 1985. pap. 20.00 (*0-935630-10-4*) U of Tex Tarlton Law Lib.

Larrington, Carolyne. Feminist Companion to Mythology. 1992. pap. 24.00 (*0-04-440850-1*) Thorsons SF.

— A Store of Common Sense: Gnomic Theme & Style in Old Icelandic & Old English Wisdom Poetry. LC 92-11139. (Oxford English Monographs). 256p. 1993. 49.95 (*0-19-811982-8*, Old Oregon Bk Store) OUP.

— Women & Writing in Early Europe: A Sourcebook. LC 94-30485. 272p. 1995. 65.00x (*0-415-10684-2*, B3162); pap. 17.95 (*0-415-10685-0*, B3166) Routledge.

Larrison, Earl J. Mammals of the Northwest (Washington, Oregon, Idaho, & British Columbia) LC 73-94501. (Trailside Ser.). (Illus.). 1976. pap. 8.95 (*0-914516-04-3*) Seattle Audubon Soc.

Larrison, Earl J., jt. auth. see Christensen, James R.

Larrison, Earl J., jt. auth. see Higman, Harry W.

Larrison, Roxann. A Garden of Bitter Herbs. (Orig.). (YA). 1993. pap. 3.95 (*0-87067-389-0*) Holloway.

Larrissy, Edward. Reading Twentieth Century Poetry: The Language of Gender & Objects. 192p. (C). 1991. pap. text ed. 18.95 (*0-631-15359-4*) Blackwell Pubs.

Larriva, Barbara. Poppy. 160p. 1990. pap. 3.95 (*0-345-36518-6*) Ballantine.

Larrivee, Barbara. Strategies for Effective Classroom Management: Creating a Collaborative Climate. LC 92-20127. 1992. teacher ed 99.95 (*0-205-13942-6*) Allyn.

— Strategies for Effective Classroom Management: Creating a Collaborative Climate. (C). 1993. teacher ed, pap. text ed. 29.95 (*0-205-13941-8*, H39415) Allyn.

Larrivee-Cohen, Donna, jt. ed. see Baird, Mary.

Larrondo, Rosi, ed. Data for Discovery: Proceedings of the Twelfth International CODATA Conference, 15-19 July 1990, Columbus, Ohio, U. S. A. LC 92-34429. 1993. 95.00 (*1-56700-002-9*) Begell Hse.

Larrouturou, Bernard, jt. auth. see Berestycki, Henri.

Larrouturou, Bernard, jt. ed. see Dervieux, A.

Larrouturou, Bernard, ed. see Temam, Roger, et al.

Larrowe, Charles P. Harry Bridges: The Rise & Fall of Radical Labor in the United States. rev. ed. LC 72-78321. 432p. 1977. pap. 8.95 (*0-88208-032-6*) L Hill Bks.

— Shape-up & Hiring Hall. LC 75-46614. (Illus.). 250p. 1976. reprint ed. text ed. 65.00 (*0-8371-8750-8*, LASU, Greenwood Pr) Greenwood.

Larrson, Borje, jt. ed. see Amaldi, Ugo.

Larrucea De Tovar, C., jt. auth. see Tovar, A.

Larry, Charles. Peboan & Seegwun. 32p. (J). (ps-3). 1993. 16.00 (*0-374-35773-0*) FS&G.

Lars, Melvin. Reflections of Life. 55p. (Orig.). 1993. pap. 10.00 (*0-9638218-0-6*) M Lars.

Larschan, Edward J. & Larschan, Richard J. The Diagnosis Is Cancer: A Psychological & Legal Resource Handbook for Cancer Patients, Their Families & Helping Professionals. 144p. 1986. pap. 9.95 (*0-915950-77-4*) Bull Pub.

Larschan, Richard J., jt. auth. see Larschan, Edward J.

Larsen. Knocking on Heaven's Door. Date not set. pap. 10.00 (*0-06-250984-5*, PL) HarpC.

— Long Walk Home. Date not set. pap. 10.00 (*0-06-250980-2*, PL) HarpC.

— New Lead & Targets in Drug Research. (ABS Ser.: No. 33). 500p. 1992. 89.50 (*87-16-10810-8*) Mosby Yr Bk.

— Space. Date not set. pap. 10.00 (*0-06-250979-9*, PL) HarpC.

— Vision Catcher. Date not set. pap. 10.00 (*0-06-250978-0*, PL) HarpC.

Larsen, jt. auth. see McEwen.

Larsen, Agnessa. Graffiti on My Heart. 416p. (Orig.). 1994. pap. text ed. 15.95 (*0-89716-509-8*) P B Pubng.

Larsen, Al. God: For Thine is the Kingdom & the Power & the Glory Forever, Amen. LC 92-90449. (Illus.). xxviii, 254p. (Orig.). (C). 1992. pap. text ed. 12.95 (*0-9633252-1-3*) A Larsen.

Larsen, Allan, ed. Aerodynamics of Large Bridges: Proceedings of the First International Symposium, Copenhagen, Denmark, 19-21 February 1992. (Illus.). 313p. (C). 1992. text ed. 85.00 (*90-5410-042-7*, Pub. by A A Balkema NE) Ashgate Pub Co.

Larsen, Anita. Amelia Earhart: Missing, Declared Dead. LC 91-19246. (History's Mysteries Ser.). (Illus.). 48p. (J). (gr. 5-6). 1992. text ed. 11.95 (*0-89686-613-0*, Crstwood Hse) Silver Burdett Pr.

— Montezuma's Missing Treasure. LC 91-19259. (History's Mysteries Ser.). (Illus.). 48p. (J). (gr. 5-6). 1992. text ed. 11.95 (*0-89686-615-7*, Crstwood Hse) Silver Burdett Pr.

— Psychic Sleuths: How Psychic Information Is Used to Solve Crimes. LC 93-40593. (J). 1994. text ed. 14.95 (*0-02-751645-8*, New Dscvry Bks) Silver Burdett Pr.

— Raoul Wallenberg: Missing Diplomat. LC 91-19937. (History's Mysteries Ser.). (Illus.). 48p. (J). (gr. 5-6). 1992. text ed. 11.95 (*0-89686-616-5*, Crstwood Hse) Silver Burdett Pr.

— The Roanoke Missing Persons Case. LC 91-19524. (History's Mysteries Ser.). (Illus.). 48p. (J). (gr. 5-6). 1992. text ed. 11.95 (*0-89686-619-X*, Crstwood Hse) Silver Burdett Pr.

— The Rosenbergs. LC 91-22311. (History's Mysteries Ser.). (Illus.). 48p. (J). (gr. 5-6). 1992. text ed. 11.95 (*0-89686-612-2*, Crstwood Hse) Silver Burdett Pr.

— True Crimes & How They Were Solved. (J). (gr. 4-7). 1993. pap. 2.95 (*0-590-46856-1*) Scholastic Inc.

Larsen, Anne R. & Winn, Colette H., eds. Renaissance Women Writers: French Texts - American Contexts. LC 93-26577. (Illus.). 242p. 1994. text ed. 39.95 (*0-8143-2473-8*) Wayne St U Pr.

Larsen, B., jt. ed. see Galask, R. P.

Larsen, Bent. Bent Larsen: Master of Counter-Attack. (Illus.). 1992. pap. 19.95 (*0-7134-6901-3*, Pub. by Batsford UK) Trafalgar.

Larsen, Bev. Darla: Faith over Fire. 130p. (Orig.). 1991. pap. 12.00 (*0-929690-13-3*) Herit Pubs AZ.

Larsen, Bruce. What God Wants to Know: Finding Answers in God's Vital Questions. LC 92-56107. 160p. 1994. reprint ed. pap. 8.00 (*0-06-065013-3*) Harper SF.

Larsen, C. M. Floating Production Systems Research & Development Program. (C). 1989. 95.00 (*0-89771-722-8*, Pub. by Lorne & MacLean Marine) St Mut.

Larsen, Carl. Even the Dog Won't Eat My Meat Loaf. LC 79-19887. 1980. pap. 5.95 (*0-89645-011-2*) Media Ventures.

Larsen, Carl M. Floating Production Systems Research & Development Program. 1989. 150.00 (*90-6314-580-2*, Pub. by Lorne & MacLean Marine) St Mut.

Larsen, Chris, jt. auth. see Kolbrek, Loyal.

Larsen, Clark, et al. Human Origins: The Fossil Record. 2nd rev. ed. (Illus.). 207p. (Orig.). (C). 1991. pap. text ed. 15.95 (*0-88133-575-4*) Waveland Pr.

Larsen, Clark S. Native American Demography in the Spanish Borderlands. LC 90-22357. (Spanish Borderlands Sourcebooks Ser.: Vol. 2). 478p. 1991. reprint ed. 77.00 (*0-8240-0781-6*) Garland.

Larsen, Clark S. & Milner, George R., eds. In the Wake of Contact: Biological Responses to Conquest. LC 93-15716. 216p. 1993. text ed. 89.00 (*0-471-30544-8*, Wiley-Liss) Wiley.

***Larsen, Claudia.** The Little Angel's Bible Stories. (Illus.). 160p. (J). (ps-2). 1994. 10.99 (*0-7814-0185-2*) Chariot Family.

An Asterisk (*) at the beginning of an entry indicates that the title is appearing in BIP for the first time.

Larsen, Curtis E. Life & Land Use on the Bahrain Islands: The Geoarcheology of an Ancient Society. LC 83-5085. (Prehistoric Archeology & Ecology Ser.). (Illus.). 320p. 1984. lib. bdg. 20.00 (*0-226-46905-0*); pap. text ed. 9.00 (*0-226-46906-9*) U Ch Pr.

Larsen, Cynthia & Shannon, Paul. The Synchronicity Guidebook...High-Tech Meditation. LC 93-74177. (Illus.). 120p. (Orig.). 1994. pap. write for info. (*1-884068-20-0*) Amethyst Pub.

Larsen, Dale. What Happens When God Answers Prayer: Leaders Guide. 72p. (Orig.). 1994. pap. 5.99 (*1-56476-251-3*, Victor Books) SP Pubns.

Larsen, Dale & Larsen, Sandy. Discovering Myself: Who Am I Anyway? (Bible Discovery Guide Ser.). (Illus.). 32p. (Orig.). (YA). (gr. 7-10). 1987. Camper Ed. 1.50 (*0-87788-178-2*); Counselor Ed. 3.50 (*0-87788-179-0*) Shaw Pubs.

— How to Spend Less & Enjoy It More. LC 93-42735. (Saltshaker Bks.). 144p. 1994. pap. 7.99 (*0-8308-1634-8*, 1634, Saltshaker Bk) InterVarsity.

— It's Up to Me: Choosing God's Way. (Bible Discovery Guide Ser.). (Illus.). 32p. (J). (gr. 4-6). 1989. 1.50 (*0-87788-404-8*); teacher ed 3.50 (*0-87788-405-6*) Shaw Pubs.

— Joseph: From Pit to Pyramid. (Bible Discovery Guide Ser.). (Illus.). 32p. (J). (gr. 4-6). 1989. student ed 1.50 (*0-87788-435-8*); teacher ed 3.50 (*0-87788-436-6*) Shaw Pubs.

— Managing Money: A NetWork Discussion Guide. 48p. 1993. 4.99 (*0-87788-520-6*) Shaw Pubs.

— Maturing in Christ. (Teamwork Discipleship Guides Ser.). 96p. (Orig.). 1993. pap. 4.99 (*0-8308-1127-3*, 1127) InterVarsity.

— Moneywise: Biblical Spending, Saving, Sharing. 64p. 1992. 4.99 (*0-87788-550-8*) Shaw Pubs.

— One Body, One Spirit: Building Relationships in the Church. (Fisherman Bible Studyguide Ser.). 64p. (Orig.). 1988. 4.99 (*0-87788-619-9*) Shaw Pubs.

— Patching Your Parachute: How You Can Beat Unemployment. LC 93-18097. 138p. (Orig.). 1993. pap. 7.99 (*0-8308-1347-0*, 1347) InterVarsity.

— Teamwork Discipleship Guides Series, Set. (Orig.). 1993. pap. 9.98 (*0-8308-1125-7*, 1125) InterVarsity.

— Tending Creation. (NetWork Discussion Guides Ser.). 48p. (Orig.). 1991. 4.99 (*0-87788-806-X*) Shaw Pubs.

— While Creation Waits: A Christian Response to the Environmental Challenge. 200p. 1992. pap. 8.99 (*0-87788-949-X*) Shaw Pubs.

Larsen, Dale, jt. auth. see Larsen, Sandy.

Larsen, Dan. David Livingstone. (Young Reader's Christian Library). (J). (gr. 3 up). 1992. per., pap. 2.50 (*1-55748-259-4*) Barbour & Co.

— Jesus. (Young Reader's Christian Library). (Illus.). 224p. (J). (gr. 4-8). 1989. pap. text ed. 2.50 (*1-55748-100-8*) Barbour & Co.

— Jesus. (Illustrated Christian Classics Ser.). (J). (gr. 3 up). 1992. 9.95 (*1-55748-274-8*) Barbour & Co.

Larsen, Dan, ed. see Bunyan, John.

***Larsen, David.** Jews, Gentiles, & the Church: A New Perspective on History & Prophecy. 352p. 1995. 19.99 (*0-929239-42-3*) Discovery Hse Pubs.

Larsen, David & Larsen, Sandy. Starting with Christ. (Teamwork Discipleship Guides Ser.). 96p. (Orig.). 1993. pap. 4.99 (*0-8308-1126-5*, 1126) InterVarsity.

Larsen, David C. Who Gets It When You Go? Wills, Probate & Inheritance Taxes for the Hawaii Resident. rev. ed. LC 86-11258. (Illus.). 128p. 1986. pap. 8.50 (*0-8248-1089-9*) UH Pr.

Larsen, David G., ed. see Berlin, Howard M.

Larsen, David L. The Anatomy of Preaching: Identifying the Issues in Preaching Today. LC 89-39248. 208p. (Orig.). 1989. pap. text ed. 11.99 (*0-8010-5657-8*) Baker Bk.

— Caring for the Flock: Pastoral Ministry in the Local Congregation. LC 91-2175. 256p. (Orig.). 1991. pap. 10.99 (*0-89107-609-3*) Crossway Bks.

— The Evangelism Mandate: Restoring the Centrality of Gospel Preaching. LC 92-24662. 256p. (Orig.). 1992. pap. 12.99 (*0-89107-678-6*) Crossway Bks.

— Telling the Old, Old Story: The Art of Narrative Preaching. LC 94-42394. 320p. (Orig.). 1995. pap. 14.99 (*0-89107-836-3*) Crossway Bks.

Larsen, Dean L. Free to Act. 9.95 (*0-88494-712-2*) Bookcraft Inc.

Larsen, Deborah. Stitching Porcelain: After Matteo Ricci in Sixteenth-Century China. LC 90-21176. 80p. (Orig.). 1991. pap. 9.95 (*0-8112-1161-4*, NDP710) New Directions.

Larsen, Dinah, ed. see Ray, Dorothy J.

Larsen, Donald, jt. ed. see Staum, M.

Larsen, E. A., jt. auth. see Mosich, A. N.

Larsen, E. John. Modern Advanced Accounting. 6th ed. LC 93-27419. 1994. text ed. write for info. (*0-07-036595-4*); Study guide. student ed, pap. text ed. write for info. (*0-07-036599-7*); Accounting worksheets. pap. text ed. write for info. (*0-07-036600-4*) McGraw.

Larsen, E. John, jt. auth. see Mosich, A. N.

Larsen, Earnest. Love Is a Hunger. LC 90-19445. (Illus.). 160p. 1979. pap. 8.95 (*0-89638-251-6*) Hazelden.

Larsen, Earnie. Differences in the Way Men & Women Perceive Love. 19p. 1986. 1.00 (*0-936098-50-3*) Intl Marriage.

— From Anger to Forgiveness. (Orig.). 1992. mass mkt. 4.99 (*0-345-37982-9*) Ballantine.

— I Should Be Happy...Why Do I Hurt?, 5 pamphlets, Set. 81p. 1986. pap. 5.00 (*0-936098-42-2*) Intl Marriage.

— Old Patterns, New Truths: Beyond the Adult Child Syndrome. 112p. (Orig.). 1988. student ed, pap. 11.00 (*0-89486-539-0*, 5044A) Hazelden.

— Recovering Catholics & the God Who Loves Them, 5 pamphlets, Set. 64p. 1990. pap. 5.00 (*0-936098-61-9*) Intl Marriage.

— Something's Missing in My Life!, 3 pamphlets, Set. 37p. (Orig.). 1987. pap. 3.00 (*0-936098-55-4*) Intl Marriage.

— Stage II Relationships. 1987. pap. 10.00 (*0-06-254808-5*, PL-4199) Harper SF.

— Stage Two Recovery: Life Beyond Addiction. 96p. 1984. pap. 10.00 (*0-86683-460-5*) Harper SF.

Larsen, Earnie & Goodstein, Jeanette. Who's Driving Your Bus? Codependent Business Behaviors of Workaholics, Perfectionists, Martyrs, Tap Dancers, Caretakers, & People Pleasers. Padgett, JoAnn, ed. LC 92-51019. 180p. 1993. 29.95 (*0-88390-372-5*); pap. 12.95 (*0-89384-202-8*) Pfeiffer & Co.

Larsen, Earnie & Hegarty, Carol L. Believing in Myself: Self-Esteem: Daily Meditations. 384p. 1991. pap. 9.00 (*0-671-76616-3*, Fireside) S&S Trade.

— Days of Healing, Days of Joy: Daily Meditations for Adult Children. 400p. (Orig.). 1989. pap. 9.00 (*0-89486-455-6*, 5024A) Hazelden.

— Days of Healing, Days of Joy: Daily Meditations for Adult Children. LC 86-43009. (Orig.). 1987. reprint ed. pap. 10.00 (*0-06-255449-2*, Hazelden SF) Harper SF.

Larsen, Earnie & Parnegg, Janee. Recovering Catholics: What to Do When Religion Comes Between You & God. LC 91-58903. 1992. pap. 10.00 (*0-06-064955-0*) Harper SF.

Larsen, Earnie, jt. auth. see Goodstein, Jeanette.

***Larsen, Ellen.** Thankful & Teachable. Bible, Debbie, ed. (Value Builders Ser.). (J). 1995. 7.95 (*0-7814-5087-X*, 08722) Cook.

Larsen, Eric. An American Memory. 240p. 1988. 12.95 (*0-912697-68-7*) Algonquin Bks.

— I Am Zoe Handke. 224p. 1992. 16.95 (*0-945575-86-6*) Algonquin Bks.

— Spider-Man: Revenge of Sinister Six. (Spider-Man Ser.). 128p. 1994. pap. 15.95 (*0-7851-0047-4*) Marvel Entmnt.

Larsen, Erling. James Agee. LC 78-633324. (University of Minnesota Pamphlets on American Writers Ser.: No. 95). 47p. (Orig.). reprint ed. pap. 25.00 (*0-7837-2877-8*, 2057578) Bks Demand.

Larsen-Freeman, Diane. Techniques & Principles in Language Teaching. (Techniques in Teaching English As a Second Language Ser.). 142p. 1986. pap. 10.50 (*0-19-434133-X*) OUP.

Larsen-Freeman, Diane, jt. auth. see Celce-Murcia, Marianne.

Larsen, G. & Chilingar, G. V., eds. Diagenesis in Sediments & Sedimentary Rocks, Vol. 2. (Developments in Sedimentology Ser.: Vol. 25B). 572p. 1983. 159.00 (*0-444-42013-4*) Elsevier.

Larsen, Gaylord. Dorothy & Agatha. 304p. 1992. pap. 3.99 (*0-451-40314-2*, Onyx) NAL-Dutton.

Larsen, Glenn H. & Larsen, Kristopher A. Mastering Harvard Graphics 3 for DOS. LC 91-65970. 538p. 1991. 29.99 (*0-89588-870-X*) Sybex.

Larsen, Gloria P. Korea Coloring Book. 32p. (J). (gr. k-6). 1992. 4.95 (*0-9636374-0-1*) Shared Wrld.

Larsen, Gwynne & Leeburg, Verlene. First Look at DOS. 1992. pap. text ed. write for info. (*0-07-036585-7*) McGraw.

— First Look at NetWare 2.2. 1992. pap. text ed. write for info. (*0-07-036586-5*) McGraw.

— First Look at WordPerfect 5.1. 1992. pap. text ed. write for info. (*0-07-036587-3*) McGraw.

Larsen, Gwynne & Shaw, Kenneth. First Look at WordPerfect 6.0 for Windows. 1994. pap. text ed. write for info. (*0-07-036601-2*) McGraw.

— Using WordPerfect 6.0 for Windows. 1995. pap. text ed. write for info. (*0-07-036602-0*) McGraw.

Larsen, Gwynne, jt. auth. see Leeburg, Verlene.

Larsen, Gwynne, et al. Using Microsoft Works: An Introduction to Computing. LC 92-25313. 1993. write for info. (*0-87835-884-6*) Boyd & Fraser.

— Using Microsoft Works 3.0 for Windows: An Introduction to Computing. LC 94-21639. 583p. 1994. 36.00 (*0-87709-845-X*) Boyd & Fraser.

Larsen, H. A. Knut Hamsun. 1971. 59.95 (*0-87968-385-6*) Gordon Pr.

Larsen, H. Hartvig, et al, eds. Marketing & Semiotics: Selected Papers from the Copenhagen Symposium. 240p. (Orig.). 1991. pap. 96.00x (*87-17-03591-0*, Pub. by Almqv & Wiksell SW) Coronet Bks.

Larsen, Hal S., jt. auth. see Rice-Spearman, Lori.

Larsen, Hanna A., ed. Norway's Best Stories: An Introduction to Modern Norwegian Fiction. Orbeck, Anders, tr. LC 75-169557. (Short Story Index Reprint Ser.). 1977. reprint ed. 23.95 (*0-8369-4019-9*) Ayer.

— Sweden's Best Stories: An Introduction to Swedish Fiction. Stork, Charles W., tr. LC 70-37276. (Short Story Index Reprint Ser.). 1977. reprint ed. 23.95 (*0-8369-4087-3*) Ayer.

— Told in Norway: An Introduction to Modern Norwegian Fiction. Orbeck, Anders, tr. LC 72-3366. (Short Story Index Reprint Ser.). 1977. reprint ed. 23.95 (*0-8369-4152-7*) Ayer.

Larsen, Heidi. A Woman's Little Black Book. (Illus.). 86p. (Orig.). 1992. pap. 7.95 (*1-56684-007-4*) Pubs Dist Ctr Inc.

Larsen, Henning. An Old Icelandic Medical Miscellany. LC 75-23736. reprint ed. 40.00 (*0-404-13293-6*) AMS Pr.

Larsen, Henry D. Nautical Knowledge. LC 92-27896. 1992. write for info. (*0-934523-05-3*) Middle Coast Pub.

Larsen, Homer. You'll Be Surprised What the Lord Can Do. Giles, Connie G. & Heatherley, Francis W., eds. 144p. (Orig.). 1993. pap. 8.95 (*0-929488-99-7*) Balcony Pub Inc.

Larsen, Hovis J. Telecommunications: Index of New Information with Authors, Subjects & References. 1994. 49.50 (*1-55914-994-9*); pap. 39.50 (*1-55914-995-7*) ABBE Pubs Assn.

Larsen, J. A. The Northern Forest Border in Canada & Alaska. (Ecological Studies: Vol. 70). (Illus.). 260p. 1988. 119.00 (*0-387-96753-2*) Spr-Verlag.

***Larsen, Jack L.** Folk Art from the Global Village: The Girard Collection at the Museum of International Folk Art. (Illus.). 1995. bds. 19.95 (*0-89013-273-9*) Museum NM Pr.

— Furnishing Fabrics: An International Sourcebook. 240p. (C). 1989. 185.00 (*0-685-46413-X*, Pub. by Textile Institue UK) St Mut.

— Material Wealth: Living with Luxurious Fabrics. (Illus.). 240p. 1989. 29.98 (*1-55859-007-2*); 125.00 (*1-55859-112-5*) Abbeville Pr.

— The Tactile Vessel: New Basket Form. (Illus.). 100p. (Orig.). 1989. pap. 19.95 (*0-9616623-3-6*) Erie Art Mus.

Larsen, Jack L. & Weeks, Jeanne. Fabrics for Interiors. 1975. pap. 24.95 (*0-442-24684-6*) Van Nos Reinhold.

Larsen, Jacob, jt. ed. see Patterson, David J.

***Larsen, James.** QuickSteps to Learning: Word 2.0 for Windows Beginning. 1993. spiral bd. 22.95 (*1-56951-003-2*) Sftware Trng.

***Larsen, James & Sunny, Bethany.** Quick Steps to Learning: Word for Windows 6.0 Level I. 221p. 1994. spiral bd., pap. 22.95 (*1-56951-045-8*) Sftware Trng.

Larsen, James E. Real Estate Principles & Practices. Bruckner, ed. LC 93-44421. 600p. (C). 1994. text ed. 58.00 (*0-314-02823-4*) West Pub.

Larsen, James M. & Allison, John E., eds. Small-Crack Test Methods. LC 92-10509. (STP Ser.: Vol. 1149). (Illus.). 230p. 1992. text ed. 72.00 (*0-8031-1469-9*, 04-011490-30) ASTM.

Larsen, Jeanne. James Cook in Search of Terra Incognita. (Virginia Commonwealth University Series for Contemporary Poetry). 81p. 1980. text ed. 10.95 (*0-8139-0849-3*) U Pr of Va.

Larsen, Jeanne, tr. Brocade River Poems: Selected Works of the Tang Bynasty Courtesan Xue Tao. 116p. 1987. pap. text ed. 10.95 (*0-691-01434-5*) Princeton U Pr.

Larsen, Jens P. Handel, Haydn, & the Viennese Classical Style. Krhamer, Ulrich, tr. LC 88-1206. (Studies in Musicology: No. 100). 344p. reprint ed. pap. 98.10 (*0-8357-1851-4*, 2070652) Bks Demand.

— Handel's Messiah. 1990. pap. 9.95 (*0-393-30628-3*) Norton.

— Handel's Messiah: Origins, Composition, Sources. 2nd ed. LC 88-10128. 336p. 1990. reprint ed. text ed. 75.00 (*0-313-24426-X*, LAHM, Greenwood Pr) Greenwood.

— Die Haydn-Uberlieferung. 1990. reprint ed. 41.00 (*3-262-01419-2*) Periodicals Srv.

Larsen, Jens P. & Feder, Georg. The New Grove Haydn. (New Grove Composer Biography Ser.). (Illus.). 1983. pap. 16.95 (*0-393-30085-4*) Norton.

Larsen, Jens P., et al, eds. Haydn Studies. (C). 1981. text ed. 35.00 (*0-393-01454-1*) Norton.

***Larsen, Jo A.** How Do You Want Your Room...Plain or Padded? Sanity-Preserving Tactics for the 90's Woman. (Illus.). (Orig.). 1995. pap. 13.95 (*0-87579-972-8*, Shadow Mount) Deseret Bk.

Larsen, Jo A., jt. auth. see Hepworth, Dean H.

Larsen, Joan S. Lovin' Dutch Ovens: A Cook Book for the Dutch Oven Enthusiast. Bessey, Carolyn & Ware, Julie, eds. LC 91-90722. (Illus.). 241p. 1991. 19.95 (*1-880415-03-8*) L F S Pubns.

Larsen, JoAnn. I'm a Day Late & a Dollar Short...& It's Okay! A Woman's Survival Guide for the '90s. LC 91-16535. 324p. 1991. pap. 9.95 (*0-87579-480-7*) Deseret Bk.

Larsen, John C., ed. Researcher's Guide to Archives & Regional History Sources. LC 88-15081. xiv, 167p. (C). 1988. lib. bdg. 29.50 (*0-208-02144-2*, Lib Prof Pubns) Shoe String.

Larsen, John E. Modern Advanced Accounting. 5th ed. 1991. text ed. write for info. (*0-07-036556-3*); Working papers. pap. text ed. write for info. (*0-07-036560-1*); Study guide. student ed, pap. text ed. write for info. (*0-07-036561-X*) McGraw.

Larsen, John M. Between Us Friends. LC 83-61454. 112p. 1983. pap. 7.95 (*0-89390-050-8*) Resource Pubns.

Larsen, K. G. & Skou, A., eds. Computer Aided Verification. (Lecture Notes in Computer Science Ser.: Vol. 575). 487p. 1992. pap. 61.00 (*0-387-55179-4*) Spr-Verlag.

Larsen, Kai & Holm-Nielson, Lauritz B., eds. Tropical Botany. LC 79-41003. 1980. text ed. 200.00 (*0-12-437350-X*) Acad Pr.

Larsen, Karen K. Make Your Own Decorative Boxes with Easy-to-Use Patterns. (Illus.). 32p. 1993. reprint ed. pap. text ed. 2.95 (*0-486-27814-X*) Dover.

Larsen, Karl V. See & Draw. LC 91-73904. (Illus.). 152p. 1993. 23.95 (*0-87192-242-8*) Davis Mass.

Larsen, Kent P. A Touch of Larceny: The Insurance Agent's Survival Guide. LC 84-60877. 120p. (Orig.). 1984. pap. 7.95 (*0-913581-01-1*) Publitec.

Larsen, Knud, ed. Dialectics & Ideology in Psychology. LC 85-22991. (Publications for the Advancement of Theory & History in Psychology, the PATH Ser.). 296p. 1986. text ed. 47.50 (*0-89391-222-0*) Ablex Pub.

Larsen, Knud S. Aggression: Myths & Models. LC 76-5882. 416p. 1976. 37.95 (*0-911012-71-0*) Nelson-Hall.

Larsen, Knud S., ed. Conflict & Social Psychology. 272p. (C). 1993. text ed. 65.00 (*0-8039-8745-5*) Sage.

Larsen, Kristopher A., jt. auth. see Larsen, Glenn H.

Larsen, Larry. An Angler's Guide to Bass Patterns: Productive Methods, Places & Times. LC 89-92685. (Bass Series Library). (Illus.). 160p. (Orig.). 1990. pap. 9.95 (*0-936513-07-1*, BSL8) Larsens Outdoor.

— Bass Fishing Facts: Angler's Guide to Bass Lifestyles & Behavior. LC 88-91464. (Bass Series Library). (Illus.). 135p. (Orig.). 1989. pap. 9.95 (*0-936513-05-5*, BSL6) Larsens Outdoor.

— Bass Guide Tips: An Angler's Guide. LC 90-63531. (Bass Series Library). (Illus.). 160p. 1991. text ed. 9.95 (*0-936513-10-1*) Larsens Outdoor.

— Bass Lures: Tricks & Techniques. LC 87-82758. (Illus.). 128p. (Orig.). 1988. pap. 9.95 (*0-936513-02-0*) Larsens Outdoor.

— Bass Pro Strategies. LC 87-82757. (Illus.). 128p. (Orig.). 1988. pap. 9.95 (*0-936513-01-2*) Larsens Outdoor.

— Crappie Tactics. LC 93-79800. (Freshwater Library). (Illus.). 160p. (Orig.). 1993. pap. text ed. 9.95 (*0-936513-40-3*) Larsens Outdoor.

— Follow the Forage for Better Bass Angling, Vol. 1: Bass-Prey Relationship. 2nd rev. ed. LC 88-92905. (Bass Series Library). (Illus.). 143p. 1989. pap. 9.95 (*0-936513-03-9*, BSL1) Larsens Outdoor.

— Follow the Forage for Better Bass Angling, Vol. 2: Techniques. 2nd rev. ed. LC 88-92906. (Bass Series Library). (Illus.). 144p. 1989. pap. 9.95 (*0-936513-04-7*, BSL2) Larsens Outdoor.

— Guide to Central Florida Bass Waters. LC 91-76768. (Illus.). 192p. (Orig.). 1991. pap. 12.95 (*0-936513-19-5*) Larsens Outdoor.

— Guide to North Florida Bass Waters. LC 91-76436. (Bass Water Ser.). (Illus.). 192p. (Orig.). 1991. pap. 12.95 (*0-936513-15-2*) Larsens Outdoor.

— Guide to South Florida Bass Waters. LC 92-71319. (Bass Water Ser.). (Illus.). 192p. (Orig.). 1992. pap. 12.95 (*0-936513-20-9*) Larsens Outdoor.

— Larry Larsen on Bass Tactics. LC 92-74325. (Larsen on Bass Ser.). (Illus.). 228p. (Orig.). (C). 1992. pap. text ed. 12.95 (*0-936513-27-6*) Larsens Outdoor.

— Mastering Largemouth Bass. LC 89-63111. (Complete Angler's Library). 261p. 1989. write for info. (*0-914697-24-2*) N Amer Outdoor Grp.

— Peacock Bass Explosions: Where, When & How to Catch America's Greatest Gamefish. LC 93-79801. (Illus.). 192p. (Orig.). 1993. pap. text ed. 12.95 (*0-936513-35-7*) Larsens Outdoor.

— Shallow Water Bass. LC 85-82041. (Illus.). 160p. (Orig.). 1986. pap. 9.95 (*0-936513-00-4*) Larsens Outdoor.

— Trophy Bass: An Angler's Guide. LC 89-92683. (Bass Series Library). (Illus.). 160p. (Orig.). 1990. pap. 9.95 (*0-936513-06-3*, BSL7) Larsens Outdoor.

Larsen, Larry & O'Keefe, M. Timothy. Fish & Dive Florida & the Keys: A Candid Destination Guide. Larsen, Lilliam M., ed. LC 92-90226. (Outdoor Travel Ser.). (Illus.). 192p. (Orig.). 1992. pap. 11.95 (*0-936513-26-8*) Larsens Outdoor.

— Fish & Dive the Caribbean: A Truthful Destination Guide from Cancun to the British Virgin Islands. Larsen, Lilliam M., ed. LC 91-76441. (Outdoor Travel Ser.). (Illus.). 192p. (Orig.). 1991. pap. 11.95 (*0-936513-17-9*) Larsens Outdoor.

Larsen, Larry, jt. ed. see Forsse, Ken.

Larsen, Larry L. The Winner Within: Habits of the Happy, Healthy, Wealthy, & Wise. French, Florence E., ed. LC 92-97556. (Illus.). 212p. (Orig.). 1993. pap. 15.00 (*0-9634716-0-0*) Achieve Bk.

Larsen, Lawrence E. & Jacobi, John H., eds. Medical Applications of Microwave Imaging. LC 85-23923. 240p. 1986. 49.95 (*0-87942-196-7*, PC01941) Inst Electrical.

Larsen, Lawrence H. Federal Justice in Western Missouri: The Judges, the Cases, the Times. (Illus.). 304p. 1994. 42.50 (*0-8262-0973-4*) U of Mo Pr.

— The President Wore Spats: A Biography of Glenn Frank. LC 65-63009. (Illus.). 198p. 1965. 4.50 (*0-87020-056-9*) State Hist Soc Wis.

— The Rise of the Urban South. LC 84-25596. 232p. 1985. 25.00 (*0-8131-1538-8*) U Pr of Ky.

— The Urban South: A History. LC 89-34162. 224p. 1990. text ed. 25.00 (*0-8131-0309-6*) U Pr of Ky.

— Wall of Flames: The Minnesota Forest Fire of 1894. LC 84-61133. 187p. 1984. 9.85 (*0-911042-29-6*) N Dak Inst.

Larsen, Lawrence H. & Hulston, Nancy J. The University of Kansas Medical Center: A Pictorial History. LC 91-44669. (Illus.). x, 222p. 1992. 35.00 (*0-7006-0539-8*) U Pr of KS.

Larsen, Lawrence H., jt. auth. see Glaab, Charles N.

Larsen, Lawrence P. Macro 86 Assembly Language Programming. LC 84-19295. (Macro-86 Software Design Ser.). (Illus.). 900p. 1984. ring bd. 59.95 (*0-87119-100-8*, EC-1201) Heathkit-Zenith Ed.

Larsen, Lee A. Marionette County. 418p. 1994. pap. 12.95 (*1-56901-148-6*) NW Pub.

Larsen, Leif, jt. auth. see Elboth, David.

Larsen, Lilliam M., ed. see Larsen, Larry & O'Keefe, M. Timothy.

Larsen, Linda J. Renaissance: A Thematic Unit. Coan, Sharon & Levin, Ina M., eds. (Thematic Units Ser.). (Illus.). 80p. 1994. student ed 8.95 (*1-55734-580-5*) Tchr Create Mat.

— Wolves - a Thematic Unit. (Thematic Units Ser.). (Illus.). 80p. (Orig.). 1994. student ed, pap. 8.95 (*1-55734-583-X*) Tchr Create Mat.

Larsen, Lucretia. The Wholesome Ways of Our Olden Days. 116p. 1985. 14.95 (*0-87770-360-4*) Ye Galleon.

Larsen, Ludwig B. The Little Book: Key to the Bible & Heaven. 280p. 1974. reprint ed. spiral bd. 7.70 (*0-7873-0535-9*) Mokelumne.

Larsen, M. J. & Cobb-Poulle, L. A. Phellinus (Hymenochaetaceae) A Survey of the World Taxa 1990. (Synopsis Fungorum Ser.: No. 3). 206p. 1990. pap. text ed. 60.00 (*82-90724-07-1*, Pub. by Fungi-Flora NO) Lubrecht & Cramer.

Larsen, M. T., ed. see Copenhagen University, Center for Research in the Humanities Staff.

Larsen, M. T., jt. ed. see Harbsmeier, Michael.

Larsen, Madelyn, ed. see Harrison, Sally.

Larsen, Madelyn, ed. see Imus, Brenda.

Larsen, Madelyn, ed. see Snader, Meredith L., et al.

Larsen, Margie, jt. auth. see Dudko, Mary A.

Larsen, Marianne. Selected Poems. LC 82-5083. 50p. 1982. pap. 7.95 (0-915306-29-8) Curbstone.

Larsen, Maurice A., jt. ed. see Randolph, Alan D.

Larsen, Michael. Dave Godfrey & His Works. (Canadian Author Studies). 55p. (C). 1989. pap. text ed. 9.95 (0-920763-87-1, Pub. by ECW Press CN) Genl Dist Srvs.

— How to Write a Book Proposal. 136p. 1990. pap. 11.99 (0-89879-419-6) Writers Digest.

— Worry Bead Book. 1989. pap. 8.95 (0-312-03455-5) St Martin.

Larsen, Michael & Pomada, Elizabeth. Daughters of Painted Ladies. (Illus.). 144p. 1987. 29.95 (0-525-24609-6, Dutton); pap. 15.95 (0-525-48337-3, Dutton) NAL-Dutton.

Larsen, Michael, jt. auth. see Bennett, Hal Z.

Larsen, Michael, jt. auth. see Pomada, Elizabeth.

Larsen, Michael J. A Contribution to the Taxonomy of the Genus Tomentella. (Mycologia Memoirs Ser.: No. 4). (Illus.). 145p. 1974. pap. text ed. 12.50 (0-945345-40-2) Lubrecht & Cramer.

Larsen, Miriam C., comp. Oddball Sayings, Witty Expressions & Downhome Folklore: A Collection of Clever Phrases. LC 93-43757. 100p. 1995. pap. 6.95 (1-56875-077-3) R & E Pubs.

***Larsen, Naomi H.** Thoughts from My Rocking Chair. (Illus.). 39p. (Orig.). 1994. pap. 7.95 (1-884498-00-0) CompuVisuals.

Larsen, Neil. Modernism & Hegemony: A Materialist Critique of Aesthetic Agencies. 150p. 1989. text ed. 39.95 (0-8166-1784-8); pap. text ed. 14.95 (0-8166-1785-6) U of Minn Pr.

— Reading North by South: On Latin American Literature, Culture & Politics. LC 94-43194. 1995. text ed. 44.95 (0-8166-2583-2); text ed. 18.95 (0-8166-2584-0) U of Minn Pr.

Larsen, Nella. Passing. LC 76-92233. (American Negro: His History & Literature, Ser. No. 3). 1970. reprint ed. 27.95 (0-405-01930-0) Ayer.

— Passing. LC 69-18567. 226p. 1990. reprint ed. pap. 19.95 (0-88143-119-2) Ayer.

— Passing. LC 73-82056. 215p. 1969. reprint ed. text ed. 38.50 (0-8371-1541-8, LAP&, Greenwood Pr) Greenwood.

— Quicksand. LC 74-75553. 312p. 1970. reprint ed. text ed. 39.75 (0-8371-1127-7, LAQ&, Greenwood Pr) Greenwood.

Larsen, Otto N. Milestones & Millstones: Social Science at the National Science Foundation, 1945-1991. 292p. (C). 1991. text ed. 39.95 (0-88738-441-2) Transaction Pubs.

— Voicing Social Concern: The Mass Media, Violence, Pornography, Censorship, Organization, Social Science, the Ultramultiversity. 318p. Date not set. lib. bdg. 32.50 (0-8191-9437-9) U Pr of Amer.

Larsen, Otto N., jt. auth. see De Fleur, Melvin L.

Larsen, Otto N., jt. auth. see Medalia, Nahum Z.

Larsen, P. G., ed. see First International Symposium of Formal Methods Europe Staff.

Larsen, P. K. & Dobson, P. J., eds. Reflection High-Energy Electron Diffraction & Reflection Electron Imaging of Surfaces. LC 88-28843. (NATO ASI Series B, Physics: Vol. 188). (Illus.). 556p. 1988. 125.00 (0-306-43035-5, Plenum Pr) Plenum.

Larsen, P. K., ed. see Moan, T., et al.

***Larsen, Paul.** To the Third Power: The Inside Story of Bill Koch's Winning Strategies for the America's Cup. (Illus.). 256p. 1995. 24.95 (0-88448-147-6) Tilbury Hse.

Larsen, Paul, jt. auth. see Marshall, Roger.

Larsen, Paul, tr. see Nissen, Hans J., et al.

***Larsen, Paul C.** To the Third Power: The Inside Story of Bill Koch's Winning Strategies for the America's Cup. (Illus.). 504p. 1995. 100.00 (0-9644058-0-6) Tilbury Hse.

Larsen, Paul E. The Mission of a Covenant. 1985. pap. 6.95 (0-910452-61-X) Covenant.

Larsen, Paul L. Why Do We Wear Ashes? 1991. pap. 5.25 (1-55673-284-8, 9117) CSS OH.

***Larsen, Paula B.** Beauty at Dawn: Notes to My Sisters. LC 94-7824. (Women's Wisdom Ser.). (Illus.). 64p. (Orig.). 1994. 7.95 (0-89243-692-1, Triumph Books) Liguori Pubns.

— Gammaw...Gammaw... Thunder in an Infant's Voice. LC 94-7303. (Women's Wisdom Ser.). (Illus.). 48p. 1994. 7.95 (0-89243-693-X, Triumph Books) Liguori Pubns.

Larsen, Phyllis. Ghirardelli Original Chocolate Cookbook. 3rd rev. ed. Allen, Vera, ed. (Illus.). (Orig.). 6.00 (0-9610218-0-2) Ghirardelli Choc.

Larsen, Poul S., jt. auth. see Garby, Lars.

Larsen, R. M., et al, eds. Structural & Tectonic Modelling Had Its Application to Petroleum Geology. 549p. 1992. 165.50 (0-444-88607-9) Elsevier.

Larsen, Ray R., jt. ed. see Chance, Michael R.

Larsen, Rayola C. Alphabet Talk: Gospel Rhymes for Each Letter of the Alphabet. LC 89-83429. (Illus.). 32p. (Orig.). (J). (gr. k-3). 1989. reprint ed. pap. 4.98 (0-88290-147-8) Horizon Utah.

Larsen, Rebecca. Franklin D. Roosevelt: Man of Destiny. (Non-Fiction Ser.). (Illus.). 224p. (YA). (gr. 9-12). 1991. lib. bdg. 16.38 (0-531-11068-0) Watts.

— Oppenheimer & the Atomic Bomb. LC 88-16981. (Illus.). 192p. (YA). (gr. 6-12). 1988. lib. bdg. 15.47 (0-531-10607-1) Watts.

— Paul Robeson: Hero Before His Time. LC 89-8880. (Illus.). 158p. (J). (gr. 6-9). 1989. lib. bdg. 15.33 (0-531-10779-5) Watts.

— Richard Nixon: The Rise & Fall of a President. (Illus.). 224p. (YA). (gr. 9-12). 1991. lib. bdg. 16.38 (0-531-10997-6) Watts.

— Ronald Reagan. (Impact Biographies Ser.). (Illus.). 128p. (YA). (gr. 7-12). 1994. lib. bdg. 15.44 (0-531-11191-1) Watts.

Larsen, Richard. Ted Bundy: The Deliberate Stranger. 1990. mass mkt. 5.50 (0-671-72866-0) PB.

Larsen, Richard J. Statistics for the Health Sciences. (Illus.). (C). 1986. reprint ed. 21.95 (0-935005-10-2); reprint ed. pap. text ed. 14.95 (0-935005-04-8) Lincoln-Rembrandt.

Larsen, Richard J. & Marx, Morris L. An Introduction to Mathematical Statistics & Its Applications. 2nd ed. (Illus.). 640p. (C). 1985. text ed. write for info. (0-13-487174-X) P-H.

— Statistics. 800p. (C). 1990. text ed. write for info. (0-13-844085-9) P-H.

Larsen, Robert P., jt. auth. see Wrenn, C. Gilbert.

Larsen, Robin, jt. auth. see Larsen, Stephen C.

Larsen, Robin, et al, eds. Emanuel Swedenborg: A Continuing Vision. LC 87-51521. (Illus.). 558p. 1988. 75.00 (0-87785-136-0); pap. 50.00 (0-87785-137-9) Swedenborg.

Larsen, Ronald. Banach Algebras: An Introduction. LC 73-84868. (Pure & Applied Mathematics Ser.: No. 24). 359p. reprint ed. pap. 102.40 (0-8357-6032-4, 2034545) Bks Demand.

— Functional Analysis: An Introduction. LC 72-90375. (Pure & Applied Mathematics Ser.: Vol. 15). 515p. reprint ed. pap. 146.80 (0-685-16163-3, 2027099) Bks Demand.

— Introduction to the Theory of Multipliers. LC 78-134023. (Grundlehren der Mathematischen Wissenschaften Ser.: Vol. 175). 1971. 89.00 (0-387-05120-1) Spr-Verlag.

— A Potter's Companion: Imagination, Originality, & Craft. (Illus.). 192p. (Orig.). 1992. pap. 17.95 (0-89281-445-4, Park St Pr) Inner Tradit.

Larsen, Ronald J. The Puerto Ricans in America. (In America Ser.). (Illus.). 80p. (J). (gr. 5 up). 1989. pap. 5.95 (0-8225-1036-7, Lerner Publctns) Lerner Group.

— The Puerto Ricans in America. (In America Ser.). (Illus.). 80p. (YA). (gr. 5 up). 1989. lib. bdg. 17.50 (0-8225-0238-0, Lerner Publctns) Lerner Group.

Larsen, Roy A., ed. Introduction to Floriculture. 2nd ed. (Illus.). 636p. 1992. text ed. 49.95 (0-12-437651-7) Acad Pr.

Larsen, S. Spotlight on Films. 1976. lib. bdg. 69.95 (0-8490-2662-8) Gordon Pr.

Larsen, Sally G., jt. auth. see Helman, Iris B.

Larsen, Sandra A., et al, eds. Manual of Tests for Syphilis. 8th ed. 208p. 1990. 30.00 (0-87553-174-1) Am Pub Health.

Larsen, Sandy. Choosing: Which Way Do I Go? (Bible Discovery Guide for Campers Ser.). (Illus.). 32p. (J). (gr. 7-10). 1985. 1.50 (0-87788-115-4); 3.50 (0-87788-116-2) Shaw Pubs.

— Eye-Opening Bible Studies. (Bible Discovery Guide for Campers Ser.). 32p. (J). (gr. 6-10). 1986. 1.95 (0-87788-247-9) Shaw Pubs.

— Forgiving: Lightening Your Load. (Bible Discovery Guide Ser.). (Illus.). 32p. (J). (gr. 6-8). 1985. 1.50 (0-87788-279-7); 3.50 (0-87788-280-0) Shaw Pubs.

— Standing Strong: Notes from Joseph's Journal. (Bible Discovery Guide Ser.). (Illus.). 32p. (Orig.). 1986. student ed 1.50 (0-87788-784-5); teacher ed 3.50 (0-87788-785-3) Shaw Pubs.

— Sticking Together: Friendships for Life. (Bible Discovery Guide Ser.). 32p. (Orig.). 1987. student ed 1.50 (0-87788-787-X); teacher ed 3.50 (0-87788-788-8) Shaw Pubs.

Larsen, Sandy & Larsen, Dale. Celebrating Creation: Exploring God's World. (Bible Discovery Guide Ser.). 32p. (YA). (gr. 7-10). 1988. Camper. 1.50 (0-87788-109-X); Counselor. 3.50 (0-87788-110-3) Shaw Pubs.

Larsen, Sandy, jt. auth. see Larsen, Dale.

Larsen, Sandy, jt. auth. see Larsen, David.

Larsen, Sonja & Hoffman, G. L. Signs that Sell: The Handbook of Successful Merchandise Signing. (Illus.). 200p. (C). 1991. 29.95 (0-9629666-0-6); pap. text ed. write for info. (0-9629666-1-4) Insignia Systs.

Larsen, Stephen. The Shaman's Doorway: Opening Imagination to Power & Myth. (Illus.). 260p. (Orig.). 1988. reprint ed. pap. 10.95 (0-88268-072-2) Station Hill Pr.

Larsen, Stephen, ed. see Blackmer, Carolyn.

Larsen, Stephen, ed. see Mutwa, Credo.

Larsen, Stephen C. & Larsen, Robin. A Fire in the Mind: The Life of Joseph Campbell. 1991. 30.00 (0-385-26635-9) Doubleday.

— A Fire in the Mind: The Life of Joseph Campbell. LC 92-23556. 1993. reprint ed. 15.95 (0-385-26636-7, Anchor NY) Doubleday.

Larsen, Susan. Boldstrokes & Quiet Gestures: Twentieth Century Drawings & Watercolors from the Santa Barbara Museum of Art. 1992. 25.00 (1-882603-00-1) Mid Am Arts.

Larsen, Susan, et al. Richard Diebenkorn: Works on Paper from the Harry W. & Margaret Anderson Collection. LC 92-73206. (Illus.). 96p. (Orig.). (C). 1993. pap. 15.00 (0-945192-11-8) USC Fisher Gallery.

Larsen, Susan C. Jean Arp Centenary Exhibition: Sculpture, Reliefs, & Graphic Work. Hunter, Sam & Matinko-Wald, Ruth, eds. LC 87-60011. 64p. (Orig.). (C). 1987. pap. write for info. (0-942461-01-0) Mus Art Fl.

— Variations: Five Los Angeles Painters. LC 80-69334. (Illus.). 51p. (Orig.). 1980. pap. write for info. (0-911291-05-9) Fellows Cont Art.

Larsen, Susan C., text. Vija Celmins: A Survey Exhibition. LC 79-92204. (Illus.). 96p. (Orig.). 1980. pap. 16.00 (0-911291-04-0) Fellows Cont Art.

Larsen, Susan C., jt. auth. see Armstrong, Tom.

Larsen, Susan C., jt. ed. see Lane, John R.

Larsen, T., jt. auth. see Engberg, J.

Larsen, Torben. Butterflies of Saudi Arabia & Its Neighbors. 1983. 49.95 (0-86685-542-4) Intl Bk Ctr.

Larsen, Torben B. The Butterflies of Kenya & Their Natural History. (Illus.). 128p. 1992. 195.00 (0-19-854011-6) OUP.

Larsen, Wanwadee. Confessions of a Mail Order Bride. 1991. mass mkt. 4.50 (0-06-100136-8, Harp PBks) HarpC.

— Confessions of a Mail Order Bride: American Life Through Thai Eyes. LC 89-43331. 324p. 1989. 21.95 (0-88282-051-6) New Horizon NJ.

Larsen, Wendy U., jt. auth. see Babcock, Richard F.

Larsen, William J. Human Embryology. (Illus.). 479p. 1993. text ed. 35.00 (0-443-08724-5) Churchill.

— Study Guide for Human Embryology. (Illus.). 272p. 1993. pap. 21.95 (0-443-08944-2) Churchill.

Larsgaard, Mary L. Map Librarianship: An Introduction. 2nd ed. LC 86-21381. 400p. 1986. lib. bdg. 43.50 (0-87287-537-7) Libs Unl.

— Topographic Mapping of Africa, Antarctica, & Eurasia. LC 92-39327. (Occasional Papers: No. 14). (Illus.). 1992. 45.00 (0-939112-29-9) Western Assn Map.

Larsh, Ed & Nichols, Robert. Leadville U. S. A. LC 92-25236. (Illus.). 300p. (Orig.). 1993. 22.95 (1-55566-097-5) Johnson Bks.

Larsh, Edward & Nichols, Robert. Let's Take the Aspen Train. Larsh, Jane, ed. (Illus.). 160p. (C). 1988. 34.95 (0-9620872-0-3) Larsh & Nichols.

Larsh, Jane, ed. see Larsh, Edward & Nichols, Robert.

***Larson.** Annals of the Mormon Battalion. Shawgo, Bob, ed. (Illus.). 650p. 1994. 75.00 (0-910523-40-1) Grandin Bk Co.

— Divergent Realities. 1995. pap. 16.00 (0-465-01663-4) Basic.

— Hidden Spirits. 16.00 (0-679-85803-2) Random.

— Math K: An Incremental Development. (J). (gr. k). 1991. Classroom kit. teacher ed 125.00 (0-939798-84-0); Ready-made student material. 175.00 (0-939798-90-5) Saxon Pubs OK.

— Math K: An Incremental Development, Manipulative kit. 1991. 340.00 (1-56577-001-3) Saxon Pubs OK.

— Math 1: An Incremental Development. (J). (gr. 1). 1991. 568.00 (0-939798-26-3); 465.00 (0-939798-85-9); teacher ed 125.00 (0-939798-27-1); 22.75 (0-939798-81-6); 365.00 (0-939798-68-9); 468.00 (0-939798-67-0); 320.00 (1-56577-002-1) Saxon Pubs OK.

— Math 2: An Incremental Development. (J). (gr. 2). 1991. 584.00 (0-939798-28-X); 475.00 (0-939798-86-7); teacher ed 125.00 (0-939798-29-8); 23.00 (0-939798-82-4); 375.00 (0-939798-69-7); 484.00 (0-939798-88-3); 360.00 (1-56577-003-X) Saxon Pubs OK.

— Math 3: An Incremental Development. (J). (gr. 3). 1991. 592.00 (0-939798-30-1); 480.00 (0-939798-87-5); teacher ed 125.00 (0-939798-31-X); student ed 23.50 (0-939798-83-2); 380.00 (0-939798-70-0); 492.00 (0-939798-89-1); 265.00 (1-56577-004-8) Saxon Pubs OK.

— Workers' Compensation Law. 1992. write for info. (0-8205-0281-2, 512); teacher ed write for info. (0-8205-0282-0) Bender.

Larson & Casti. Principles of Dynamic Programming Pt. 1: Basic Analytical & Computational Methods. (Control & Systems Theory Ser.: Vol. 7). 344p. 1978. 89.75 (0-8247-6589-3) Dekker.

Larson & Pitman. Bedrock Geology of the World. (C). 1995. pap. text ed. write for info. (0-7167-1716-6) W H Freeman.

Larson & Ponce, eds. Hymnal Companion Two. 1992. 29.95 (0-87162-622-5, D4711) Warner Pr.

Larson, jt. auth. see Dunn, Susan.

Larson, jt. auth. see Hulse.

Larson, jt. auth. see Pyle.

Larson, A. Karl, ed. see Walker, Charles L.

Larson, Agnes M. History of the White Pine Industry in Minnesota. LC 72-2875. (Use & Abuse of America's Natural Resources Ser.). (Illus.). 468p. 1972. reprint ed. 35.95 (0-405-04516-6) Ayer.

— John A. Johnson: An Uncommon American. 312p. 1969. 10.00 (0-87732-049-7) Norwegian-Am Hist Assn.

Larson, Allan L. The Human Triad: An Introductory Essay on Politics, Society, & Culture. LC 87-30485. xii, 148p. (Orig.). 1988. pap. 12.95 (0-88280-119-8) ETC Pubns.

— Soviet Society in Historical Perspective: Polity, Ideology, & Economy. (C). 1995. lib. bdg. write for info. (0-89464-793-8) Krieger.

Larson, Anna A., tr. see Jacobsen, J. P.

Larson, Arthur. A Republican Looks at His Party. LC 74-12630. 210p. 1974. reprint ed. text ed. 35.00 (0-8371-7737-5, LARE, Greenwood Pr) Greenwood.

— Workmen's Compensation: Desk Edition, 3 vols., Set. 1972. ring bd. write for info. (0-8205-1347-4) Bender.

— Workmen's Compensation Law, 11 vols. 1952. write for info. (0-8205-1340-7) Bender.

Larson, Arthur & Larson, Lex K. Employment Discrimination, 5 vols. 1975. Updates available. ring bd. write for info. (0-8205-1626-0) Bender.

Larson, Arthur D. Civil-Military Relations & Militarism: A Classified Bibliography Covering the United States & Other Nations of the World (with Introductory Notes) LC 71-31050. (Libraries Bibliography: No. 9). 1971. reprint ed. 4.00 (0-686-20807-2) KSU.

Larson, B. C., et al, eds. Characterization of the Structure & Chemistry of Defects in Materials: Materials Research Society Symposium Proceedings, Vol. 138. 1989. text ed. 54.00 (1-55899-011-9) Materials Res.

Larson, Barbara. Prairie Collection Cookbook Centennial Edition. Gonzalez, Helga, ed. (Illus.). 224p. 1988. 13.95 (0-318-35132-3) Bismarck Mandan.

Larson, Bob. Larson's Book of Rock. 160p. 1987. pap. 7.99 (0-8423-5687-8) Tyndale.

— Larson's New Book of Cults. 1989. pap. 12.99 (0-8423-2860-2) Tyndale.

Larson, Bob, jt. auth. see Gurley, Heather.

Larson, Boyd. Transistor Fundamentals & Servicing. (Illus.). 480p. 1974. text ed. 82.00 (0-13-929992-0) P-H.

Larson, Brian, jt. auth. see Galli, Mark.

Larson, Brooke. Colonialism & Agrarian Transformation in Bolivia: Cochabamba, 1550-1900. (Illus.). 424p. 1988. pap. text ed. 26.95 (0-691-10241-4) Princeton U Pr.

***Larson, Brooke, et al, eds.** Ethnicity, Markets, & Migration in the Andes: At the Crossroads of History & Anthropology. LC 95-864. 1995. write for info. (0-8223-1633-1); pap. write for info. (0-8223-1647-1) Duke.

Larson, Bruce. Atrevete Con la Vida: Dare to Live Now. (SPA.). 3.95 (84-7228-141-8, 220054, Pub. by Edit Clie SP) TSELF.

— A Call to Holy Living: Walking with God in Joy, Praise, & Gratitude. LC 87-34579. (Christian Growth Bks.). (Illus.). 128p. (Orig.). 1988. pap. 9.99 (0-8066-2305-5, 10-0963, Augsburg) Augsburg Fortress.

— CC, NT, Vol. 3: Luke. 347p. 1983. write for info. (0-8499-0156-1) Word Inc.

— Communicator's Commentary, Vol. 3: Luke. 346p. 1991. reprint ed. pap. 10.99 (0-8499-3276-9) Word Inc.

— Database Experts' Guide to Database 2. 352p. 1988. text ed. 44.95 (0-07-036488-5); pap. text ed. 34.95 (0-07-023267-9) McGraw.

— Don De la Libertad: Setting Men Free. (SPA.). 4.25 (84-7228-132-9, 220318, Pub. by Edit Clie SP) TSELF.

— Living out the Book of Acts. 168p. 1989. 8.99 (0-8499-3149-5) Word Inc.

— Parabolas de la Vida Moderna: Thirty Days to a New You. (SPA.). 3.95 (84-7228-048-9, 220670, Pub. by Edit Clie SP) TSELF.

— There's a Lot More to Health Than Not Being Sick. 144p. 1991. write for info. (1-879989-00-X) New Hope Pub.

— Vida Cristiana el Crecimiento: Living in the Growing Edge. (SPA.). 3.25 (84-7228-672-X, 220947, Pub. by Edit Clie SP) TSELF.

Larson, Bruce, jt. auth. see Henson, Sarah.

Larson, Bruce L. Lactation. LC 85-58. (Illus.). 288p. reprint ed. pap. 82.10 (0-8357-6753-1, 2035409) Bks Demand.

— SQL Solutions for IBM DBMSS. 1991. text ed. 49.95 (0-442-00119-3) Van Nos Reinhold.

Larson, Bruce R., jt. auth. see Abrahams, Paul W.

Larson, C. D. Mastery of Fate. 106p. 1963. reprint ed. spiral bd. 3.30 (0-7873-0536-7) Mokelumne.

Larson, C. F., jt. ed. see Smith, W. Novis.

***Larson, C. Kay.** Til I Come Marching Home: A Brief History of American Women in World War II. (Illus.). (Orig.). 1995. pap. 10.00 (0-9634895-2-6) Minerva Ctr.

Larson, C. Philip, Jr., jt. auth. see Cullen, Stuart C.

Larson, Calvin J. Pure & Applied Sociological Theory: Problems & Issues. LC 91-78389. 212p. (C). 1992. text ed. 28.00 (0-03-055348-2) HB Coll Pubs.

— Sociological Theory: From the Enlightenment to the Present. LC 86-80124. 247p. (Orig.). 1987. lib. bdg. 34.95 (0-930390-72-5); pap. text ed. 15.95 (0-930390-71-7) Gen Hall.

Larson, Carl E. & LaFasto, Frank M. Teamwork: What Must Go Right - What Can Go Wrong. (Series in Interpersonal Communication). 152p. (C). 1989. text ed. 48.00 (0-8039-3289-8); pap. text ed. 22.95 (0-8039-3290-1) Sage.

Larson, Carl E., jt. auth. see Chrislip, David D.

Larson, Carl F., comp. American Regional Theatre History to 1900: A Bibliography. LC 79-11282. 200p. 1979. 22.00 (0-8108-1216-9) Scarecrow.

Larson, Carol A. Sharing Time: A Guide to Quality Kindergarten Enrichment. 64p. 1990. 8.00 (0-911943-22-6) Leadership Pub.

Larson, Carole. Forgotten Frontier: The Story of Southeastern New Mexico. LC 93-3631. (Illus.). 329p. 1993. 35.00x (0-8263-1439-2); pap. 18.95 (0-8263-1440-6) U of NM Pr.

Larson, Carolyn, ed. see Old World Wisconsin Staff.

Larson, Catherine. Language & the Comedia: Theory & Practice. LC 89-46406. 1991. 35.00 (0-8387-5180-6) Bucknell U Pr.

Larson, Cedric. Who: Sixty Years of American Eminence. (Illus.). 1958. 25.00 (0-8392-1131-7) Astor-Honor.

Larson, Cedric, jt. auth. see Mock, James R.

Larson, Charles. Innovative Billing & Collection Methods That Work. 192p. 1994. text ed. 50.00 (1-55623-032-X) Irwin Prof Pubng.

Larson, Charles A. Drafting California Revocable Living Trusts: June 1993 Update. 2nd ed. Archer, Carine, ed. LC 84-71499. 179p. 1993. pap. text ed. 28.00 (0-88124-650-6, ES-38837) Cont Ed Bar-CA.

Larson, Charles M. By His Own Hand Upon Papyrus: A New Look at the Joseph Smith Papyri. 240p. (Orig.). 1990. pap. text ed. 11.95 (0-9620963-2-6) Inst Rel Rsch.

Larson, Charles R. The Emergence of African Fiction. rev. ed. LC 71-180489. 305p. 1972. 15.00 (0-253-31945-5); pap. 5.00 (0-253-20149-7) Three Continents.

— Invisible Darkness: Jean Toomer & Nella Larsen. LC 93-15637. (Illus.). 255p. 1993. text ed. 34.95x (0-87745-425-6); pap. 14.95 (0-87745-437-X) U of Iowa Pr.

Larson, Charles R. & Golden, Marita, frwds. An Intimation of Things Distant: The Collected Fiction of Nella Larsen. 336p. 1992. mass mkt. 9.50 (0-385-42149-4) Doubleday.

Larson, Charles R., jt. auth. see Rubenstein, Roberta.

Larson, Charles R., ed. see Thurman, Wallace.

Larson, Charles U. Persuasion: Reception & Responsibility. 6th ed. 422p. (C). 1992. pap. 32.95 (0-534-14982-0) Intl Thomson.

— Persuasion: Reception & Responsibility. 7th ed. LC 94-12354. 447p. 1995. pap. 32.95 (0-534-23070-9) Intl Thomson.

Larson, Christian D. Leave It to God. 1940. pap. 3.00 (0-87516-191-X) DeVorss.

An Asterisk (*) at the beginning of an entry indicates that the title is appearing in BIP for the first time.

— The Pathway of Roses: Paths to the Life Beautiful. 368p. 1994. reprint ed. pap. 9.95 (*0-87877-187-5*) Newcastle Pub.

Larson, Christopher. Tropic of Deceit. LC 92-22214. 1993. 23.00 (*0-688-12164-0*) Morrow.

***Larson, Claudine W.** An Unplanned Audition. (Illus.). 24p. (J). (gr. 3-5). 1995. pap. 7.00 (*0-8059-3699-8*) Dorrance.

Larson, Colleen L. & Preskill, Hallie, eds. Organizations in Transition: Opportunities & Challenges for Evaluation. LC 85-644749. (New Directions for Program Evaluation Ser.: No. PE 49). 1991. 17.95 (*1-55542-795-2*) Jossey-Bass.

Larson, Constant. History of Douglas & Grant Counties, Minnesota, Vol. 1. (Illus.). 509p. 1994. reprint ed. lib. bdg. 52.50 (*0-8328-3840-3*) Higginson Bk Co.

— History of Douglas & Grant Counties, Minnesota, Vol. 2. (Illus.). 693p. 1994. reprint ed. lib. bdg. 69.50 (*0-8328-3841-1*) Higginson Bk Co.

Larson, Craig B. Illustrations for Preaching & Teaching: From Leadership Journal. LC 93-23484. 288p. 1994. 14.99 (*0-8010-5691-8*) Baker Bk.

— Running the Midnight Marathon. LC 90-21923. 1991. pap. 7.99 (*0-8007-5394-1*) Revell.

Larson, D. H. & Fejer, M. Improving Glass Melting Furnace Operation Using Improved Combustion Control Methods. 66p. 1973. pap. 6.00 (*0-318-12639-7*, L10373) Am Gas Assn.

Larson, Dale G. The Helper's Journey: Working with People Facing Grief, Loss, & Life-Threatening Illness. LC 93-84096. 292p. (Orig.). (C). 1993. pap. text ed. 17.95 (*0-87822-344-4*, 4668) Res Press.

***Larson, Dale L.** Connect Your Amiga! A Guide to the Internet, LANs, BBSs & Online Services. 256p. (Orig.). 1994. pap. 24.95 (*1-885876-02-5*) Intangible Assets.

Larson, Dan, ed. see Wallace, Lew.

Larson, David. Crosscountry Skier's Log. (Illus.). 72p. (Orig.). 1984. spiral bd., pap. 3.00 (*0-9613928-0-0*) Larson Joliet.

Larson, David, jt. auth. see Galuppi, Baldassare.

Larson, David E., ed. Mayo Clinic Family Health Book: The Ultimate Home Medical Reference. (Illus.). 1392p. 1990. 40.00 (*0-688-07819-2*) Morrow.

Larson, David L. Security Issues & the Law of the Sea. LC 93-20257. (C). 1994. lib. bdg. 47.50 (*0-8191-9089-6*) U Pr of Amer.

Larson, David R., ed. Abortion: Ethical Issues & Options. LC 92-28584. (C). 1992. 9.95 (*1-881127-00-1*) LLU Ctr Christ Bio.

Larson, Deborah A. John Donne & Twentieth-Century Criticism. LC 87-46423. 208p. 1989. 36.50 (*0-8386-3338-2*) Fairleigh Dickinson.

Larson, Deborah W. Negotiation the Austrian State Treaty, 1953-1955. (Pew Case Studies in International Affairs). 50p. (C). 1988. pap. text ed. 2.50 (*1-56927-432-0*) Geo U Inst Dplmcy.

— Origins of Containment: A Psychological Explanation. LC 85-42691. 420p. 1989. 55.00 (*0-691-07691-X*); pap. text ed. 17.95 (*0-691-02303-4*) Princeton U Pr.

Larson, Dewey B. Beyond Newton. LC 63-22695. (Illus.). 1964. 15.00 (*0-913138-03-7*) North Pacific.

— Beyond Space & Time. 385p. 1995. 30.00 (*0-913138-12-6*) North Pacific.

— The Neglected Facts of Science. 140p. 1982. pap. 7.50 (*0-913138-10-X*) North Pacific.

— New Light on Space & Time. LC 65-24256. (Illus.). 1964. reprint ed. pap. 11.00 (*0-913138-08-8*) North Pacific.

— Nothing but Motion. LC 79-88078. (Illus.). 289p. 1979. 18.00 (*0-913138-07-X*) North Pacific.

— The Road to Full Employment. LC 75-44558. 1976. 11.00 (*0-913138-06-1*) North Pacific.

— Universe of Motion. LC 84-60388. (Illus.). 460p. 1984. 28.00 (*0-913138-11-8*) North Pacific.

Larson, Don W. Medical Cost Crisis: A Common-Sense Solution. 240p. 1993. 24.00 (*0-9635576-0-2*) Bond Pub MN.

Larson, Donald N. & Smalley, William A. Becoming Bilingual: A Guide to Language Learning. LC 84-15383. 450p. 1984. reprint ed. pap. text ed. 34.00 (*0-8191-4246-8*) U Pr of Amer.

Larson, Donald R. The Honor Plays of Lope De Vega. 272p. 1978. 26.50 (*0-674-40628-1*) HUP.

Larson, Doris, jt. auth. see Larson, Roland.

Larson, Dorothy W. Bright Shadows. LC 92-81679. (Illus.). 96p. (J). (gr. 4-6). 1992. 14.95 (*0-9621779-0-3*) Sandstone Pub.

***Larson, Duane H.** Times of Trinity: A Proposal for Theistic Cosmology. LC 94-37760. (Worcester Polytechnic Institute Studies in Science, Technology & Culture: Vol. 17). 1995. write for info. (*0-8204-2706-3*) P Lang Pubs.

Larson, E. Great Ideas in Engineering. 1967. 81.00 (*0-08-007078-7*, Pub. by Pergamon Repr UK) Franklin.

Larson, E. Dixon. Remington Tips. 1975. 4.95 (*0-913150-34-7*) Pioneer Pr.

***Larson, Edward J.** Sex, Race & Science: Eugenics in the Deep South. LC 94-28124. 251p. 1994. text ed. 35.00x (*0-8018-4938-1*) Johns Hopkins.

— Trial & Error: The American Controversy Over Creation & Evolution. LC 85-7144. 254p. 1989. pap. 10.95 (*0-19-506143-8*) OUP.

Larson, Edwin E., jt. auth. see Birkeland, Peter W.

***Larson, Effie R.** The Word Surprises. 1995. 12.95 (*0-533-11473-X*) Vantage.

***Larson, Ellen.** Accepting & Peaceful. Bible, Debbie, ed. (Value Builders Ser.). (J). 1995. 7.95 (*0-7814-5093-4*, 10074) Cook.

— Attentive & Committed. Bible, Debbie, ed. (Value Builders Ser.). (J). 1995. 7.95 (*0-7814-5100-0*, 10454) Cook.

— Compassionate & Trusting. Bible, Debbie, ed. (Value Builders Ser.). (J). 1995. 7.95 (*0-7814-5095-0*, 10090) Cook.

— Concern & Reverence. Bible, Debbie, ed. (Value Builders Ser.). (J). 1995. 7.95 (*0-7814-5094-2*, 10082) Cook.

— Conviction & Sincerity. Bible, Debbie, ed. (Value Builders Ser.). (J). 1995. 7.95 (*0-7814-5102-7*, 10488) Cook.

— Cooperative & Humble. Bible, Debbie, ed. (Value Builders Ser.). (J). 1995. 7.95 (*0-7814-5089-6*, 09563) Cook.

— Courageous & Holy. Bible, Debbie, ed. (Value Builders Ser.). (J). 1995. 7.95 (*0-7814-5096-9*, 10173) Cook.

— Faith & Wisdom. Bible, Debbie, ed. (Value Builders Ser.). (J). 1995. 7.95 (*0-7814-5088-8*, 08854) Cook.

— Forgiving & Hopeful. Bible, Debbie, ed. (Value Builders Ser.). (J). 1995. 7.95 (*0-7814-5092-6*, 09977) Cook.

— Friendly & Consistent. Bible, Debbie, ed. (Value Builders Ser.). (J). 1995. 7.95 (*0-7814-5104-3*, 10512) Cook.

— Generosity & Initiative. Bible, Debbie, ed. (Value Builders Ser.). (J). 1995. 7.95 (*0-7814-5098-5*, 10405) Cook.

— Gentle & Resourceful. Bible, Debbie, ed. (Value Builders Ser.). (J). 1995. 7.95 (*0-7814-5107-8*, 10868) Cook.

— Helpful & Confident. Bible, Debbie, ed. (Value Builders Ser.). (J). 1995. 7.95 (*0-7814-5085-3*, 08706) Cook.

— Honest & Respectful Writing. Bible, Debbie, ed. (Value Builders Ser.). (J). 1995. 7.95 (*0-7814-5099-3*, 10447) Cook.

— Kind & Purposeful. Bible, Debbie, ed. (Value Builders Ser.). (J). 1995. 7.95 (*0-7814-5101-9*, 10470) Cook.

— Loving & Persevering. Bible, Debbie, ed. (Value Builders Ser.). (J). 1995. 7.95 (*0-7814-5097-7*, 10280) Cook.

— Loyal & Self-Disciplined. Bible, Debbie, ed. (Value Builders Ser.). (J). 1995. 7.95 (*0-7814-5105-1*, 10561) Cook.

— Obedient & Worshipful. Bible, Debbie, ed. (Value Builders Ser.). (J). 1995. 7.95 (*0-7814-5086-1*, 08714) Cook.

— Patience & Empathy. Bible, Debbie, ed. (Value Builders Ser.). (J). 1995. 7.95 (*0-7814-5103-5*, 10504) Cook.

— Repentant & Joyful. Bible, Debbie, ed. (Value Builders Ser.). (J). 1995. 7.95 (*0-7814-5090-X*, 09720) Cook.

— Responsible & Merciful. Bible, Debbie, ed. (Value Builders Ser.). (J). 1995. 7.95 (*0-7814-5091-8*, 09951) Cook.

— Stewardship & Fairness. Bible, Debbie, ed. (Value Builders Ser.). (J). 1995. 7.95 (*0-7814-5106-X*, 10777) Cook.

— Unselfish & Prayerful. Bible, Debbie, ed. (Value Builders Ser.). (J). 1995. 7.95 (*0-7814-5108-6*, 10884) Cook.

Larson, Ellen & Esterline, David. More Than a Story. 96p. 1991. pap. 5.99 (*0-89693-813-1*) SP Pubns.

Larson, Ellen E. Recruiting Help & Hope for Finding Volunteers. Brewer, Karen, ed. 96p. (Orig.). 1994. pap. 12.99 (*0-7847-0232-2*, 18-03242) Standard Pub.

Larson, Emil L. One-Room & Consolidated Schools of Connecticut: A Comparative Study of Teachers, Costs & Holding Power. LC 78-176976. (Columbia University. Teachers College. Contributions to Education Ser.: No. 182). reprint ed. 37.50 (*0-404-55182-3*) AMS Pr.

Larson, Eric, jt. auth. see Kantor, Herman I.

Larson, Eric B. & Lilies, W. Conrad, Jr. Manual of Admitting Orders & Therapeutics. 3rd ed. LC 93-26134. 1994. pap. text ed. 25.50 (*0-7216-5268-9*) Saunders.

Larson, Eric B., jt. auth. see Metz, Robert J.

Larson, Eric B., jt. auth. see Ramsey, Paul G.

Larson, Eric M. Variations of the Smooth Bore H & R Handy-Gun: A Pocket Guide to Their Identification. LC 93-91518. (Illus.). 64p. (Orig.). 1993. pap. 10.00 (*0-9636465-0-8*) E M Larson.

***Larson, Eric V. & Kent, Glenn A.** A New Methodology for Assessing Multi-Layer Missile Defense Options. LC 94-32983. 1994. write for info. (*0-8330-1579-6*, MR390AF) Rand Corp.

Larson, Eric V. & Palmer, Adele R. The Decisionmaking Context in the U. S. Department of the Navy: A Primer for Cost Analysis. LC 93-48871. (MR-255-PA&E Ser.). 189p. 1994. pap. text ed. 15.00 (*0-8330-1502-8*) Rand Corp.

Larson, Eric V., jt. auth. see Palmer, Adele R.

Larson, Erik. Lethal Passage. 1994. 21.00 (*0-517-59677-6*, Crown) Crown Pub Group.

— Lethal Passage. 1995. 22.95 (*0-8050-2531-6*) H Holt & Co.

— Lethal Passage: The Journey of a Gun. 1995. pap. 12.00 (*0-679-75927-1*, Vin) Random.

— The Naked Consumer: How Our Private Lives Become Public Commodities. 288p. 1994. pap. 10.95 (*0-14-023303-2*, Penguin Bks) Viking Penguin.

Larson, Esther E. Swedish Commentators on America: Sixteen Thirty-Eight to Eighteen Sixty-Five. Scott, Franklyn D., ed. LC 78-15194. (Scandinavians in America Ser.). 1979. reprint ed. lib. bdg. 17.95 (*0-405-11647-0*) Ayer.

Larson, Everette E., jt. auth. see Perl, Raphael.

Larson, Frances D. The Genealogist's Dictionary. rev. ed. (Illus.). 129p. (C). 1989. pap. 10.00 (*0-317-93982-3*) Camano Pub.

Larson, G. J. & Bhattacharya, R. S. Encyclopaedia of Indian Philosophies, Vol. 4. 1987. 64.95 (*81-208-0311-6*) Asia Bk Corp.

Larson, Gary. Beyond the Far Side. (Orig.). 1983. pap. text ed. 6.95 (*0-8362-1149-9*) Andrews & McMeel.

— Bride of the Far Side. (Illus.). 104p. (Orig.). 1985. pap. 6.95 (*0-8362-2066-8*) Andrews & McMeel.

— The Chickens Are Restless. (Illus.). 96p. (Orig.). 1993. pap. 8.95 (*0-8362-1717-9*) Andrews & McMeel.

— Cows of Our Planet: A Far Side Collection. (Illus.). 96p. (Orig.). 1992. pap. 8.95 (*0-8362-1701-2*) Andrews & McMeel.

— Curse of Madame C: A Far Side Collection. 1994. pap. 8.95 (*0-8362-1763-2*) Andrews & McMeel.

— The Far Side. LC 82-72418. (Illus.). 104p. (Orig.). 1982. pap. 6.95 (*0-8362-1200-2*) Andrews & McMeel.

— The Far Side Gallery. (Illus.). 208p. (Orig.). 1984. pap. 10.95 (*0-8362-2062-5*) Andrews & McMeel.

— Far Side Gallery Five. (Illus.). 160p. 1995. pap. 12.95 (*0-8362-0425-5*) Andrews & McMeel.

— Far Side Gallery 2. (Illus.). 192p. (Orig.). 1986. pap. 10.95 (*0-8362-2085-4*) Andrews & McMeel.

— Far Side Gallery 4. (Illus.). 168p. (Orig.). 1993. 19.95 (*0-8362-1726-8*); pap. 12.95 (*0-8362-1724-1*) Andrews & McMeel.

— Far Side Gallery 5. (Illus.). 160p. 1995. 19.95 (*0-8362-0426-3*) Andrews & McMeel.

— The Far Side Observer. (Illus.). 104p. (Orig.). 1987. pap. 6.95 (*0-8362-2098-6*) Andrews & McMeel.

— Hound of the Far Side. (Illus.). 104p. (Orig.). 1987. pap. 6.95 (*0-8362-2087-0*) Andrews & McMeel.

— In Search of the Far Side. (Illus.). 104p. (Orig.). 1984. pap. 6.95 (*0-8362-2060-9*) Andrews & McMeel.

— It Came from the Far Side. 104p. 1985. pap. 6.95 (*0-8362-2073-0*) Andrews & McMeel.

— Night of the Crash-Test Dummies. 1988. pap. 6.95 (*0-8362-2049-8*) Andrews & McMeel.

— PreHistory of the Far Side: A Tenth Anniversary Exhibit. 256p. 1989. pap. 12.95 (*0-8362-1851-5*) Andrews & McMeel.

— Prehistory of the Far Side: A Tenth Anniversary Exhibit. 256p. 1989. 19.95 (*0-8362-1861-2*) Andrews & McMeel.

— Unnatural Selections: A Far Side Collection. (Illus.). 96p. (Orig.). 1991. pap. 8.95 (*0-8362-1881-7*) Andrews & McMeel.

— Valley of the Far Side. (Illus.). 104p. (Orig.). 1985. pap. 6.95 (*0-8362-2067-6*) Andrews & McMeel.

— Wiener Dog Art: A Far Side Collection. 112p. 1990. pap. 7.95 (*0-8362-1865-5*) Andrews & McMeel.

— Wildlife Preserves: A Far Side Collection. (Illus.). 104p. (Orig.). 1989. pap. 6.95 (*0-8362-1842-6*) Andrews & McMeel.

Larson, Gary & Gould, Stephen J. Far Side Gallery 3. 192p. 1988. 19.95 (*0-8362-1810-8*); pap. 10.95 (*0-8362-1831-0*) Andrews & McMeel.

Larson, Gary L., et al, eds. Crater Lake: An Ecosystem Study. LC 89-63688. (Illus.). 221p. 1991. 27.95 (*0-934394-07-5*) AAASPD.

Larson, Gary N., ed. see Unger, Merrill F.

Larson, Gaylen & Littauer, Marita. Too Much Is Never Enough: Behaviors You Never Thought Were Addictions: How to Recognize & Overcome Them: A Christian's Guide. LC 92-5729. (Lifeline Ser.). 125p. 1992. pap. 2.99 (*0-8163-1109-9*) Pacific Pr Pub Assn.

***Larson, Gene & Snyder, Jeffrey B.** Power Carving Birds, Fish & Penguins: Using Beautiful Hardwoods. (Illus.). 64p. (Orig.). 1994. pap. 12.95 (*0-88740-565-7*) Schiffer.

Larson, George A. & Pridmore, Jay. Chicago Architecture & Design. LC 93-18306. (Illus.). 1993. 49.50 (*0-8109-3192-3*) Abrams.

Larson, Georgianna & Kahn, Judith A. Special Needs - Special Solutions: How to Get Quality Care for a Child with Special Health Needs. (Illus.). 96p. 1991. pap. 7.95 (*0-9629995-0-4*) Lifeline Pr.

Larson, Gerald J. India's Agony over Religion. LC 94-18318. (SUNY Series in Religious Studies). 393p. (C). 1995. text ed. 59.50 (*0-7914-2411-1*); pap. text ed. 19.95 (*0-7914-2412-X*) State U NY Pr.

Larson, Gerald J., et al, eds. Samkhya: A Dualist Tradition in Indian Philosophy. LC 85-43199. (Encyclopedia of Indian Philosophies: Vol. 4). 800p. 1987. 84.00 (*0-691-07301-5*) Princeton U Pr.

Larson, Gerald J. & Deutsch, Eliot, eds. Interpreting Across Boundaries: New Essays in Comparative Philosophy. 328p. 1988. text ed. 47.50 (*0-691-07319-8*) Princeton U Pr.

Larson, Gerald J., et al, eds. Myth in Indo-European Antiquity. LC 72-93522. (Publications of the UCSR Institute of Religious Studies). 205p. reprint ed. pap. 58.50 (*0-685-23602-1*, 2029049) Bks Demand.

Larson, Gerald L., ed. Advances in Silicon Chemistry, Vol. 1. 1991. 90.25 (*1-55938-176-0*) Jai Pr.

— Advances in Silicon Chemistry, Vol. 2. 1992. 90.25 (*1-55938-177-9*) Jai Pr.

Larson, Gladys N. The Pilgrim's Progress. 1991. 7.95 (*0-910452-36-9*) Covenant.

Larson, H. M., jt. auth. see Gras, N. S.

Larson, Hal. If He Loves Me, Why Doesn't He Tell Me? LC 93-24300. 128p. 1994. 12.95 (*1-879904-11-X*) Halo Bks.

Larson, Hal & Larson, Susan. Suddenly Single! A Lifeline for Anyone Who Has Lost a Love. 2nd ed. LC 92-34631. 256p. (Orig.). 1993. 13.95 (*1-879904-09-8*) Halo Bks.

Larson, Harold J. Introduction to Probability. (Illus.). 328p. (C). 1995. text ed. 60.25 (*0-201-51286-6*) Addison-Wesley.

— Introduction to Probability Theory & Statistical Inference. 3rd ed. LC 81-16246. 637p. (C). 1982. Net. text ed. write for info. (*0-471-05909-9*) Wiley.

— Statistics: An Introduction. LC 83-8414. 428p. 1983. reprint ed. 42.50 (*0-89874-639-6*) Krieger.

Larson, Harold J. & Shubert, Bruno O. Probabilistic Models in Engineering Science: Random Noise, Signals & Dynamic Systems. LC 89-2828. 750p. (C). 1989. reprint ed. lib. bdg. 79.50 (*0-89464-373-8*) Krieger.

Larson, Heidi. Wedding Time. (Way We Live Ser.). (Illus.). 25p. (J). (gr. 2-4). 1991. 13.95 (*0-237-60146-X*, Pub. by Evans Bros Ltd UK) Trafalgar.

Larson, Henrietta M. Guide to Business History: Materials for the Study of American Business History & Suggestions for Their Use. 1811p. 1964. reprint ed. 22.50 (*0-910324-04-2*) Canner.

— Wheat Market & the Farmer in Minnesota, 1858-1900. LC 70-82232. (Columbia University. Studies in the Social Sciences: No. 269). reprint ed. 21.00 (*0-404-51269-0*) AMS Pr.

Larson, Henrietta M. & Porter, Kenneth W. History of Humble Oil & Refining Company: A Study in Industrial Growth. LC 75-41768. (Companies & Men: Business Enterprises in America Ser.). (Illus.). 1976. reprint ed. 82.95 (*0-405-08083-2*) Ayer.

***Larson, Ingrid D.** The Adventures of Herman & Hurby. LC 94-90281. (Illus.). 64p. (Orig.). (J). 1995. pap. 10.00 (*1-56002-485-2*, Univ Edtns) Aegina Pr.

Larson, J. & Unger, C., eds. Engineering for Human-Computer Interaction: Proceedings of the Working Conference on Engineering for Human-Computer Interaction, Ellivuori, Finland, 10-14 August 1992. LC 92-40525. (IFIP Transactions A: Computer Science & Technology Ser.: Vol. A-18). 1992. write for info. (*0-444-89904-9*, North Holland) Elsevier.

Larson, J. R., jt. auth. see Mitchell, Terence R.

Larson, Jack L., jt. auth. see DeBruyn, Robert L.

***Larson, Jackie & Comstock, Cheri.** The New Rules of the Job Search Game: Why Todays Managers Hire & Why They Don't. 1994. pap. 10.00 (*1-55850-404-4*) Adams Pubng.

Larson, James. Database Management. LC 86-45873. 440p. 1987. pap. 7.95 (*0-8186-0714-9*, 714) IEEE Comp Soc.

— Television's Window on the World. Voigt, Melvin J., ed. LC 84-15859. (Communication & Information Science Ser.). 224p. 1984. text ed. 47.50 (*0-89391-142-9*); pap. 26.50 (*0-89391-312-X*) Ablex Pub.

Larson, James, jt. tr. see Nathan, Leonard.

***Larson, James A.** Database Directions: Beyond Relational Introduction to Distributed Multimedia & Object. 1995. pap. text ed. 39.00 (*0-13-290867-0*) P-H.

— Interactive Software: Tools for Building Interactive User Interface. 368p. 1991. text ed. 55.00 (*0-13-924044-6*) P-H.

— Treasury Auction Results As Interest Rate Predictors. rev. ed. LC 93-41567. (Financial Sector of the American Economy Ser.). 152p. 1994. 40.00 (*0-8153-1682-8*) Garland.

Larson, James F. Global Television & Foreign Policy. LC 87-72369. (Headline Ser.: No. 283). (Illus.). 72p. (Orig.). 1988. pap. 5.95 (*0-87124-117-X*) Foreign Policy.

— The Telecommunications Revolution in Korea. (Illus.). 1996. 49.95 (*0-19-586785-8*) OUP.

Larson, James F. & Park, Heung S. Global Television & the Politics of the Seoul Olympics. LC 93-24871. (Politics in Asia & the Pacific Ser.). 281p. 1993. text ed. 58.00 (*0-8133-1693-6*) Westview.

— Global Television & the Politics of the Seoul Olympics. LC 93-24871. (Politics in Asia & the Pacific Ser.). 281p. (C). 1993. pap. text ed. 19.95 (*0-8133-1694-4*) Westview.

Larson, James L. Interpreting Nature: The Science of Living Form from Linnaeus to Kant. LC 94-2904. 256p. 1994. text ed. 40.00x (*0-8018-4840-7*) Johns Hopkins.

Larson, James S. The Measurement of Health: Concepts & Indicators. LC 90-44840. (Contributions in Medical Studies: No. 31). 192p. 1991. text ed. 47.95 (*0-313-27339-1*, LMH, Greenwood Pr) Greenwood.

— Why Government Programs Fail: Improving Policy Implementation. LC 79-26917. 140p. 1980. text ed. 45.00 (*0-275-90511-X*, C0511, Praeger Pubs) Greenwood.

Larson, Janet E. The Versatile Border Collie. LC 89-18386. (Illus.). 160p. 1987. 24.95 (*0-931866-14-6*) Alpine Pubns.

Larson, Janet L. Dickens & the Broken Scripture. LC 84-24001. (Illus.). 376p. 1986. 30.00 (*0-8203-0769-6*) U of Ga Pr.

***Larson, Jay L.** Earth Data & New Weapons. (Illus.). 133p. (Orig.). (C). 1994. pap. text ed. 40.00x (*0-7881-1214-7*) Diane Pub.

Larson, Jay L. & Pelletiere, George A. Earth Data & New Weapons. LC 89-13151. (Illus.). 141p. (Orig.). 1989. per., pap. 3.75 (*0-16-001722-X*, S/N 008-020-011) USGPO.

Larson, Jean L., jt. auth. see Fontana, Marjorie A.

Larson, Jeanne & Cyrus-Micheels, Madge, eds. Seeds of Peace: A Catalogue of Quotations. (Illus.). 288p. 1987. 39.95 (*0-86571-098-8*); pap. 14.95 (*0-86571-099-6*) New Soc Pubs.

Larson, Jeffry H., et al. Effective Stepparenting. LC 84-8044. (Workshop Models for Family Life Education Ser.). 158p. 1984. 19.95 (*0-87304-211-5*) Families Intl.

Larson, Jennifer. Greek Heroine Cults. LC 94-11044. (Wisconsin Studies in Classics). 1995. 37.00 (*0-299-14370-8*); pap. 17.95 (*0-299-14374-0*) U of Wis Pr.

Larson, Jennifer, jt. auth. see Goldstein, Margaret J.

Larson, Jerry W., jt. auth. see Wilkins, Ernest J.

Larson, Jim. Disfrute Ensenando: Make Learning a Joy. (SPA.). 3.95 (*84-7228-401-8*, 220317, Pub. by Edit Clie SP) TSELF.

— Walking in God's Light. LC 84-9963. 1984. pap. 5.99 (*0-8307-0953-3*, S181216) Regal.

Larson, Joan M. Seven Weeks to Sobriety: The Proven Program to Fight Alcoholism Through Nutrition. (Illus.). 336p. 1993. pap. 11.00 (*0-449-90896-8*, Columbine) Fawcett.

Larson, Jody B., ed. see Vallangca, Caridad C.

Larson, John. How to Train a Guard Dog. LC 86-81033. (Illus.). 112p. (Orig.). 1987. pap. 10.00 (*0-918751-05-5*, 02) J O Flores.

Larson, John A., jt. auth. see Northrup, Herbert R.

Larson, John A., et al. Lying & Its Detection: A Study of Deception & Deception Tests. LC 69-16241. (Criminology, Law Enforcement, & Social Problems Ser.: No. 78). 1969. reprint ed. 30.00 (*0-87585-078-2*) Patterson Smith.

***Larson, John C. & Fleming, Jeff.** Insight: In Site: Incite: Memory: Artist & the Community: Fred Wilson. Margolis, Nancy H., ed. (Illus.). 32p. 1994. 8.00 (*0-9611560-5-8*) SEC Contemp Art-Ava.

An Asterisk (*) at the beginning of an entry indicates that the title is appearing in BIP for the first time.

Larson, John L. Bonds of Enterprise: John Murray Forbes & Western Development in America's Railway Age. 1984. text ed. 30.00 (*0-07-103279-7*) McGraw.

***Larson, John W.** South Dakota Evidence. 960p. 1991. 95.00 (*0-87473-748-6*) Michie Butterworth.

Larson, Jonathan A. Elegant Technology: Economic Prosperity from an Environmental Blueprint. 271p. 1992. 19.95 (*0-913215-58-9*) Riverdale Co.

Larson, Joyce E., ed. New Foundations for Asian & Pacific Security. 300p. (C). 1980. text ed. 32.95 (*0-87855-413-0*); pap. text ed. 18.95 (*0-87855-845-4*) Transaction Pubs.

Larson, Judy L. & Payne, Cynthia, eds. Graphic Arts & the South: Proceedings of the 1990 North American Print Conference. LC 92-25584. (Illus.). 296p. 1993. 40.00 (*1-55728-266-8*) U of Ark Pr.

Larson, Judy L., et al. American Paintings at the High Museum of Art. LC 94-13850. (Illus.). 220p. 1994. 50.00 (*1-55595-094-9*) Hudson Hills.

Larson, Katharine M., ed. see Walker, Charles L.

Larson, Kelli A. Ernest Hemingway: A Reference Guide, 1974-1989. 352p. 1990. text ed. 50.00 (*0-8161-8944-7*, Hall Reference) Macmillan.

— Guide to the Poetry of William Carlos Williams. LC 94-40682. (Guides to 20th Century Poets Ser.). 1995. write for info. (*0-8161-1986-4*) G K Hall.

Larson, Kenneth H., jt. ed. see Krebs, Mary J.

***Larson, Kermit & Terry, Jack.** Fundamental Accounting Principles & General Ledger Applications. 12th ed. (C). 1990. text ed., disk 64.95 (*0-256-08413-0*) Irwin.

***Larson, Kermit, et al.** Comptabilite Financiere. 2nd ed. 448p. (FRE.). (C). 1992. text ed. 30.95 (*0-256-10853-6*) Irwin.

— Comptabilite Financiere Tome, Vol. 2. 528p. (C). 1988. text ed. 32.95 (*0-256-06629-9*) Irwin.

— Financial Accounting Principles: Canadian Version. 416p. (C). 1991. student ed, text ed. 17.95 (*0-256-09387-3*) Irwin.

— Financial Accounting Principles: Canadian Version. 1064p. (C). 1991. text ed. 49.95 (*0-256-09386-5*) Irwin.

— Financial Accounting Principles (Canadian) 2nd ed. (C). 1993. 43.95 (*0-256-13415-4*) Richard D Strahin.

— Fundamental Accounting Principles: Canadian Version. 7th ed. 1492p. (C). 1993. text ed. 48.95 (*0-256-10721-1*) Irwin.

Larson, Kermit D., et al. Fundamental Accounting Principles, Chapters 1-16. 13th ed. LC 93-16833. 1898p. (C). 1993. text ed. 66.95 (*0-256-14564-4*) Irwin.

Larson, Kermit D. & Miller, Paul B. Financial Accounting. 5th ed. 1036p. (C). 1991. text ed. 49.95 (*0-256-09193-5*) Irwin.

— Financial Accounting. 6th ed. LC 94-22610. 714p. (C). 1994. text ed. 49.95 (*0-256-13338-7*) Irwin.

— Financial Accounting: F.A.S.T. Edition. 6th ed. LC 94-22610. (C). 1994. write for info. (*0-256-13378-6*) Irwin.

— Fundamental Accounting Principles. 13th ed. LC 92-21073. 1600p. (C). 1992. text ed. 65.95 (*0-256-10128-0*) Irwin.

Larson, Kermit D. & Pyle, William E. Fundamental Accounting Principles, 1. 12th ed. (C). 1989. 18.95 (*0-256-08065-8*); student ed 20.95 (*0-256-08224-3*); 21.50 (*0-256-08063-1*) Irwin.

— Fundamental Accounting Principles, 2. 12th ed. 69p. (C). 1989. 20.95 (*0-256-08066-6*); student ed 20.95 (*0-256-08225-1*) Irwin.

— Fundamental Accounting Principles, 3. 12th ed. (C). 1989. 18.95 (*0-256-08067-4*) Irwin.

— Fundamental Accounting Principles, Set. 12th ed. (C). 1989. text ed. 59.95 (*0-256-07342-2*) Irwin.

Larson, Kermit D., et al. Fundamentals of Financial & Managerial Accounting. LC 93-36781. 1993. teacher ed write for info. (*0-256-15502-X*) Irwin.

— Fundamentals of Financial & Managerial Accounting. LC 93-36781. 1362p. (C). 1993. text ed. 65.95 (*0-256-11023-9*) Irwin.

Larson, Kerry C. Whitman's Drama of Consensus. 296p. 1988. lib. bdg. 45.00 (*0-226-46907-7*); pap. text ed. 15.95 (*0-226-46908-5*) U Ch Pr.

Larson, Kirby. Second-Grade Pig Pals. LC 93-16061. (Illus.). 96p. (J). (gr. 1-5). 1994. 14.95 (*0-8234-1107-9*) Holiday.

Larson, Knute. Growing Adults on Sunday Morning. (Equipped for Ministry Ser.). 120p. 1991. pap. 7.99 (*0-89693-822-0*) SP Pubns.

Larson, L., et al. Comparative Negligence, 3 vols. 1984. Updates. ring bd. write for info. (*0-8205-1226-5*) Bender.

Larson, L. C. Problem-Solving Through Problems. Halmos, P. R., ed. (Problem Books in Mathematics). (Illus.). xi, 332p. 1994. reprint ed. pap. 39.95 (*0-387-96171-2*) Spr-Verlag.

Larson, L. H., et al. An Unusual Rattle from the Etowah Site. (Missouri Archaeologist Ser.: Vol. 19, No. 4). 1957. 1.00 (*0-943414-79-2*, 111904) MO Arch Soc.

Larson, Larry & Lee, Levi. Some Things You Need to Know... 1986. pap. 4.75 (*0-8222-1056-8*) Dramatists Play.

Larson, Larry L., et al. Commercial & Experimental Organic Insecticides. rev. ed. 105p. 1985. 23.00 (*0-938522-28-0*) Entomol Soc.

Larson, Lars L., jt. ed. see Hunt, James G.

Larson, Laurence M. Canute the Great, Nine Ninety-Five to Ten Thirty-Five. LC 71-111764. (Heroes of the Nations Ser.). reprint ed. 30.00 (*0-404-03879-4*) AMS Pr.

— The Changing West. 180p. 1937. 10.00 (*0-87732-018-7*) Norwegian-Am Hist Assn.

— Changing West, & Other Essays. LC 68-16946. (Essay Index Reprint Ser.). (Illus.). 1977. reprint ed. 19.95 (*0-8369-0606-3*) Ayer.

— King's Household in England Before the Norman Conquest. 1904. 7.00 (*0-403-00042-4*) Scholarly.

— The King's Household in England Before the Norman Conquest. LC 75-99885. reprint ed. 29.50 (*0-404-00617-5*) AMS Pr.

— King's Household in England Before the Norman Conquest. LC 69-13967. 211p. 1970. reprint ed. text ed. 55.00 (*0-8371-1805-0*, LAKH, Greenwood Pr) Greenwood.

— Log Book of a Young Immigrant. 318p. 1939. 12.00 (*0-87732-021-7*) Norwegian-Am Hist Assn.

Larson, Laurence M., tr. The King's Mirror. LC 72-1542. (Library of Scandinavian Literature: Vol. 15). 1917. 11.50 (*0-89067-008-0*) Am Scandinavian.

— The King's Mirror (Speculum Regale--Konungs Skuggsja) LC 72-1542. 1917. lib. bdg. 7.50 (*0-8057-3328-0*); pap. 12.95 (*0-685-02669-8*) Irvington.

Larson, LeRoy. Reflections from the North Woods. LC 86-62069. (Orig.). 1986. write for info. (*0-9617181-0-2*) Banjar Pubns.

Larson, Lester. Farm Tractors: 1950-1975. LC 81-69655. 184p. (Orig.). 1981. pap. 15.95 (*0-916150-36-4*, HO981) Am Soc Ag Eng.

Larson, Lewis H. Aboriginal Subsistence Technology on the Southeastern Coastal Plain During the Late Prehistoric Period. LC 80-16279. (Ripley P. Bullen Monographs in Anthropology & History: No. 2). (Illus.). 1980. 32.95 (*0-8130-0675-9*) U Press Fla.

Larson, Lex K. Employment Screening. 1988. Looseleaf updates available. write for info. (*0-8205-1464-0*) Bender.

Larson, Lex K. & Borowsky, Philip. Unjust Dismissal, 2 vols. 1985. Updates available. ring bd. write for info. (*0-8205-1779-8*) Bender.

Larson, Lex K., jt. auth. see Larson, Arthur.

Larson, Linda, jt. auth. see Baeckler, Virginia.

Larson, Linda S. & Kelly, Mona M. Conch Cats at Ernest Hemingway Home & Museum. (Illus.). 20p. (Orig.). 1993. pap. 5.95 (*0-9636896-0-6*) Conch Cats.

Larson, Loren C. Algebra & Trigonometry Refresher for Calculus Students. LC 79-20633. (Mathematical Sciences Ser.). (Illus.). 192p. (C). 1995. pap. text ed. write for info. (*0-7167-1110-9*) W H Freeman.

Larson, Louise L. Sweet Bamboo: A Saga of a Chinese American Family. LC 89-62055. (Illus.). viii, 227p. (Orig.). 1990. pap. 12.95 (*0-930377-02-8*) Chinese Hist CA.

Larson, Magali S. Behind the Postmodern Facade: Architectural Change in Late Twentieth-Century America. LC 92-25694. 1993. 35.00 (*0-520-08135-8*) U CA Pr.

— Behind the Postmodern Facade: Architectural Change in Late Twentieth-Century America. (Illus.). 319p. 1995. pap. 15.00 (*0-520-20161-2*) U CA Pr.

Larson, Margaret M. & Cote, Dolores Y. The Polyurethane Industry Directory & Buyer's Guide, 1993. 1993. 195.00 (*0-9637205-0-3*) Larson Pubng.

Larson, Mark. Complete Guide to Baseball Memorabilia. LC 92-71451. (Illus.). 464p. 1992. pap. 14.95 (*0-87341-190-0*) Krause Pubns.

— SCD Baseball Cards: Questions & Answers. 2nd ed. LC 90-60580. (Illus.). 272p. 1992. pap. 5.95 (*0-87341-216-8*) Krause Pubns.

— SCD Minor League Baseball Card Price Guide. LC 92-74798. (Illus.). 480p. (Orig.). 1993. pap. 14.95 (*0-87341-239-7*) Krause Pubns.

Larson, Mark, ed. Getting Started in Card Collecting. LC 93-77553. 208p. 1993. pap. 6.95 (*0-87341-263-X*) Krause Pubns.

— SCD - The Sports Card Explosion. LC 93-77541. (Illus.). 304p. (Orig.). 1993. pap. 16.95 (*0-87341-254-0*) Krause Pubns.

Larson, Mark, jt. auth. see Amberg, Jay.

Larson, Mark, jt. auth. see Wagner, Betty Jane.

Larson, Mark, et al, eds. Mickey Mantle Memorabilia. LC 93-77548. 208p. (Orig.). 1993. pap. 14.95 (*0-87341-261-3*) Krause Pubns.

Larson, Martin. How to Defend Yourself Against the Internal Revenue Service. rev. ed. 1985. 175.00 (*0-935036-08-3*) Liberty Lobby.

— Martin Larson's Best. 1982. 5.95 (*0-935036-02-4*) Liberty Lobby.

Larson, Martin A. The Continuing Tax Rebellion: What Millions of Americans Are Doing to Restore Constitutional Government. rev. ed. LC 79-89020. 1979. pap. 12.95 (*0-8159-5220-1*) Devin.

— The Essence-Christian Faith. 273p. 10.95 (*0-318-17118-X*) Atheist Assn.

— The Essene-Christian Faith. 273p. 1989. pap. 15.00 (*0-939482-16-9*) Truth Seeker.

— The IRS vs. the Middle Class or How the Average Citizen Can Protect Himself Against the Federal Tax Collector. LC 79-67271. (Orig.). 1980. 12.95 (*0-8159-5824-2*); pap. 6.95 (*0-8159-5827-7*) Devin.

— Jefferson: Magnificent Populist. 390p. 13.50 (*0-318-17117-1*) Atheist Assn.

— Modernity of Milton: A Theological & Philosophical Interpretation. LC 76-124764. reprint ed. 37.00 (*0-404-03880-8*) AMS Pr.

— The Story of Christian Origins. 711p. 12.50 (*0-318-17119-8*) Atheist Assn.

— The Story of Christian Origins. LC 76-40842. 711p. 1977. 15.00 (*0-88331-090-2*) Truth Seeker.

— The Story of Christian Origins: The Source & Establishment of Western Religion. LC 76-40842. 712p. 1988. reprint ed. pap. 12.50 (*0-945027-00-1*) Sparrow Hawk Pr.

— Tax Revolt: The Battle for the Constitution. LC 84-14219. 304p. 1985. 16.95 (*0-8159-6922-8*) Devin.

Larson, Mary Lou, jt. ed. see Francis, Julie E.

Larson, Mildred L. Meaning-Based Translation: A Guide to Cross-Language Equivalence. 548p. (Orig.). 1985. pap. text ed. 36.00 (*0-8191-4301-4*, Summer Instit Ling) U Pr of Amer.

Larson, Mildred L. & Davis, Patricia M. Bilingual Education: An Experience in Peruvian Amazonia. LC 81-51059. 435p. reprint ed. pap. 124.00 (*0-8357-3358-0*, 2039595) Bks Demand.

Larson, Mildred L. & Davis, Patricia M., eds. Bilingual Education: An Experience in Peruvian Amazonia. LC 81-51059. 417p. 1981. pap. 12.00 (*0-88312-918-3*); fiche 20.00 (*0-88312-596-X*) Summer Instit Ling.

Larson, Mobby. Prayers of a Christian Educator. (Greeting Book Line Ser.). 32p. (Orig.). 1985. pap. 1.95 (*0-89622-277-2*) Twenty-Third.

— Prayers of a New Mother. (Greeting Book Line Ser.). 32p. (Orig.). 1985. pap. 1.95 (*0-89622-230-6*) Twenty-Third.

— Why Can't We Talk? Prayers for Parents & Teenagers. LC 90-70621. 64p. (Orig.). 1990. pap. 5.95 (*0-89622-475-9*) Twenty-Third.

Larson, Muriel. Joy Every Morning. (Quiet Time Books for Women). 1979. pap. 3.99 (*0-8024-4396-6*) Moody.

— Petals of Praise. (Quiet Time Books for Women). pap. 3.99 (*0-8024-6474-2*) Moody.

***Larson, Nancy.** Math K Home Study Kit. 1994. 55.00 (*1-56577-036-6*) Saxon Pubs OK.

— Math One Home Study Kit. 1994. 85.00 (*1-56577-037-4*) Saxon Pubs OK.

— Math Three Home Study Kit. 1994. 90.00 (*1-56577-039-0*) Saxon Pubs OK.

— Math Two Home Study Kit. 1994. 87.50 (*1-56577-038-2*) Saxon Pubs OK.

Larson, Nella. Quicksand & Passing. McDowell, Deborah, ed. (American Women Writers Ser.). 300p. (C). 1986. text ed. 35.00 (*0-8135-1169-0*); pap. text ed. 10.00 (*0-8135-1170-4*) Rutgers U Pr.

Larson, Noel, jt. auth. see Maddock, James W.

Larson, Noel R., jt. auth. see Maddock, James W.

***Larson, Nola, et al.** Transition Magician: Strategies for Guiding Your Children in Early Childhood Programs. (Illus.). 126p. (Orig.). 1994. pap. 17.95 (*0-934140-81-2*) Redleaf Pr.

Larson, Norine, ed. see Boylan, Bob.

Larson, Olaf F., et al. Sociology in Government: The Galpin-Taylor Years in the U. S. Department of Agriculture, 1919-1953. (Rural Studies). (C). 1996. pap. text ed. 49.00 (*0-8133-8793-0*) Westview.

Larson, Orville K. Scene Design in the American Theatre: Nineteen-Fifteen to Nineteen Sixty. LC 88-27628. (Illus.). 405p. (C). 1989. 50.00 (*1-55728-064-9*); pap. 35.00 (*1-55728-065-7*) U of Ark Pr.

Larson, Orville K., ed. Scene Design for Stage & Screen. LC 76-10460. (Illus.). 334p. 1976. reprint ed. text ed. 35.00 (*0-8371-8320-0*, LASS, Greenwood Pr) Greenwood.

— The Theatrical Writings of Fabrizio Carini Motta. LC 87-4296. (Illus.). 145p. (C). 1987. text ed. 19.95 (*0-8093-1337-5*) S Ill U Pr.

Larson, Paul. Nothing Ventured, Nothing Gained: The Montana Entrepreneur's Guide. (Illus.). 300p. (Orig.). 1989. pap. 19.95 (*0-685-29454-4*) University MT.

Larson, Paul C. Municipal Monument: A Centennial History of the Municipal Building Serving Minneapolis & Hennepin County, Minnesota. 128p. 1991. 18.95 (*0-9630086-0-9*) Muni Bldg Comm.

Larson, Paul C., et al. The Spirit of H. H. Richardson on the Midland Prairies. (Illus.). 176p. 1988. pap. 24.95 (*0-938713-02-7*) Univ MN Art Mus.

Larson, Pedro. Crecimiento de la Iglesia: Church Growth. 272p. (Orig.). (SPA.). 1990. pap. 7.50 (*0-311-17031-5*) Casa Bautista.

Larson, Philip R. The Vascular Cambium: Development & Structure. LC 94-7963. (Springer Series in Wood Science). 1994. write for info. (*3-540-57165-5*) Spr-Verlag.

— The Vascular Cambium: Development & Structure. LC 94-7963. (Springer Series in Wood Science). 1994. 290.00 (*0-387-57165-5*) Spr-Verlag.

Larson, R. Su Hijo y el Rock (Your Kids & Rock) (SPA.). Date not set. 2.49 (*0-945792-75-1*, 498047) Editorial Unilit.

Larson, R. M. & Nasr, H. N., eds. Model-Based Vision Development & Tools. 1992. 53.00 (*0-8194-0746-1*, 1609) SPIE.

Larson, Randall D. The Complete Robert Bloch: An Illustrated International Bibliography. LC 87-20858. (Illus.). x, 126p. 1987. lib. bdg. 25.00x (*0-8095-6106-9*) Borgo Pr.

— Films into Books: An Analytical Bibliography of Film Novelization, Movie, & TV Tie-ins. LC 94-24274. 623p. 1995. 69.50 (*0-8108-2928-2*) Scarecrow.

— Music from the House of Hammer: Music in the Hammer Horror Films, 1950-1980. 1995. write for info. (*0-8108-2975-4*) Scarecrow.

— Musique Fantastique: A Survey of Film Music in the Fantastic Cinema. LC 84-13954. 602p. 1984. 45.00 (*0-8108-1728-4*) Scarecrow.

— Robert Bloch. Schlobin, Roger C., ed. LC 86-5751. (Starmont Reader's Guide Ser.: Vol. 37). iv, 148p. 1986. 27.00x (*0-930261-59-3*); pap. text ed. 17.00x (*0-930261-58-5*) Borgo Pr.

— The Work of Joseph Payne Brennan: An Annotated Bibliography & Guide. Clarke, Boden, ed. (Bibliographies of Modern Authors Ser.: No. 26). 128p. Date not set. lib. bdg. write for info. (*0-8095-0521-5*); pap. write for info. (*0-8095-1521-0*) Borgo Pr.

Larson, Randall D., ed. Film Music Around the World. LC 87-31964. 74p. 1987. lib. bdg. 23.00x (*0-8095-6700-8*) Borgo Pr.

— The Robert Bloch Companion. LC 89-26126. (Starmont Studies in Literary Criticism: No. 32). iv, 157p. (Orig.). 1989. 29.00x (*1-55742-147-1*); pap. 19.00x (*1-55742-146-3*) Borgo Pr.

Larson, Randy. Hot Fudge Monday: Tasty Ways to Teach Parts of Speech to Students Who Have a Hard Time Swallowing Anything to Do with Grammar. 127p. 1993. 18.95 (*1-877673-17-X*, HOT) Cottonwood Pr.

— Short & Sweet: Quick Creative Writing Activities That Encourage Imagination, Humor & Enthusiasm about Writing. 36p. 1993. 10.95 (*1-877673-19-6*, SS) Cottonwood Pr.

Larson, Ray & Larson, Rebecca. When the Womb Is Empty. 200p. (Orig.). 1988. 8.99 (*0-88368-198-6*) Whitaker Hse.

Larson, Raymond, intro. The Apology & Crito of Plato & the Apology & Symposium of Xenophon. 122p. (C). 1980. pap. 9.00 (*0-87291-141-1*) Coronado Pr.

Larson, Raymond, ed. see Plato.

Larson, Rebecca, jt. auth. see Larson, Ray.

Larson, Rebecca D. Blue & Gray Roses of Intrigue. (Illus.). 72p. (C). 1993. pap. text ed. 5.95 (*0-939631-46-6*) Thomas Publications.

Larson, Reed & Richards, Maryse H. Divergent Realities: The Emotional Lives of Mothers, Fathers, & Adolescents. LC 93-46394. 256p. 1994. 26.00 (*0-465-01662-6*) Basic.

Larson, Reed, jt. auth. see Csikszentmihalyi, Mihaly.

Larson, Renae, ed. see Grein, Judith H.

***Larson, Richard & Segal, Gabriel.** Knowledge of Meaning: An Introduction to Semantic Theory. LC 95-5324. (Illus.). 368p. 1995. 70.00 (*0-262-12193-X*, Bradford Bks); pap. 35.00x (*0-262-62100-2*, Bradford Bks) MIT Pr.

Larson, Richard, et al. Introduction to Sociology: Order & Change in Society. 464p. (C). 1994. per. 25.95 (*0-8403-9275-3*) Kendall-Hunt.

Larson, Richard A., ed. Biohazards of Drinking Water Treatment. (Illus.). 294p. 1988. 79.95 (*0-87371-110-6*, TD433) Lewis Pubs.

Larson, Richard A. & Weber, Eric J. Reaction Mechanisms in Environmental Organic Chemistry. 480p. 1994. 69.95 (*0-87371-258-7*, TD156) Lewis Pubs.

Larson, Richard K. Control & Grammar. (Studies in Linguistics & Philosophy). 352p. (C). 1992. lib. bdg. 125.00 (*0-7923-1692-4*) Kluwer Ac.

Larson, Rick. Principles of Minnesota Real Estate. 2nd ed. (Illus.). 450p. 1992. pap. 32.95 (*0-915799-90-1*) Rockwell WA.

Larson, Robert. Changing Schools from the Inside Out. LC 91-68578. 170p. 1992. pap. text ed. 35.00 (*0-87762-901-3*) Technomic.

Larson, Robert C., jt. auth. see Engstrom, Ted W.

Larson, Robert E. & Casti, John L. Principles of Dynamic Programming, Part Two Pt.2: Advanced Theory & Applications. (Control & Systems Theory Ser.: Vol. 7). 512p. 1982. 125.00 (*0-8247-6590-7*) Dekker.

Larson, Robert H. The British Army & the Theory of Armored Warfare 1918-1940. LC 83-47509. (Illus.). 272p. 1984. 45.00 (*0-87413-219-3*) U Delaware Pr.

Larson, Robert H., et al. Williamsport: Frontier Village to Regional Center. LC 84-21930. (Illus.). 208p. 1984. 22.95 (*0-89781-110-0*) Preferred Mktg.

Larson, Robert L. Goal Setting in Planning: Myths & Realities. (Occasional Papers: No. 3). (Illus.). 41p. (Orig.). 1980. pap. text ed. 2.50 (*0-944277-04-7*, L37) U VT Ctr Rsch VT.

Larson, Robert L. & Grana, William A. The Knee: Form, Function, Pathology, & Treatment. (Illus.). 715p. 1992. text ed. 138.00 (*0-7216-3495-8*) Saunders.

Larson, Robert W. New Mexico's Quest for Statehood, 1846-1912. LC 68-23022. 415p. reprint ed. pap. 118.30 (*0-317-55792-0*, 2029315) Bks Demand.

— Populism in the Mountain West. LC 86-16160. 220p. reprint ed. pap. 62.70 (*0-7837-5854-5*, 2045573) Bks Demand.

— Shaping Educational Change: The First Century of the University of Northern Colorado at Greeley. LC 88-352. (Illus.). 504p. (C). 1989. 39.95 (*0-87081-172-X*) Univ Pr Colo.

Larson, Rodger, et al. Scars, Pleasure & Sacrifice: Argentina - Colombia Video Creations. (Illus.). 64p. (Orig.). (ENG & SPA.). 1994. pap. write for info. (*1-883592-08-9*) Perm Mission.

Larson, Roger. No Winners. 1979. pap. 3.95 (*0-9602468-0-0*) Ipse Dixit Pr.

Larson, Roland & Larson, Doris. I Need to Have You Know Me. (Orig.). 1980. pap. 7.95 (*0-03-053431-3*) Harper SF.

Larson, Roland E. Algebra & Trigonometry. 2nd ed. 736p. (C). 1990. teacher ed 2.00 (*0-669-16270-1*); text ed. 33.00 (*0-669-16269-8*); 8.50 (*0-669-16271-X*); 10.50 (*0-669-16272-8*) Heath.

— College Algebra. 2nd ed. 576p. (C). 1990. student ed 8.50 (*0-669-16275-2*); teacher ed 10.50 (*0-669-16276-0*); teacher ed 2.00 (*0-669-16274-4*); text ed. 32.50 (*0-669-16273-6*) Heath.

— Precalculus. 2nd ed. 736p. (C). 1990. text ed. 33.00 (*0-669-16277-9*); Study & solutions guide. student ed 8.50 (*0-669-17345-2*); Study guide. student ed 10.50 (*0-685-58267-1*); Instr.'s guide. teacher ed 2.00 (*0-685-67669-2*); Transparencies. trans. 60.00 (*0-669-17346-0*) Heath.

— Trigonometry. 2nd ed. 400p. (C). 1990. teacher ed 2.00 (*0-669-16267-1*); text ed. 31.50 (*0-669-16266-3*); teacher ed 8.00 (*0-669-16268-X*); teacher ed 8.50 (*0-669-19540-5*) Heath.

Larson, Roland E. & Edwards, Bruce H. Elementary Linear Algebra. LC 87-81233. 528p. (C). 1988. text ed. 34.00 (*0-669-14583-1*); Student soln. guide. student ed 10.00 (*0-669-14581-5*); Even-numbered answers. 2.00 (*0-669-14582-3*) Heath.

An Asterisk (*) at the beginning of an entry indicates that the title is appearing in BIP for the first time.

— Elementary Linear Algebra. 2nd ed. LC 90-81475. 592p. (C). 1991. text ed. write for info. (*0-669-24592-5*); Study & solutions guide. student ed write for info. (*0-669-27143-8*); Complete solutions guide. teacher ed write for info. (*0-669-27145-4*); Answers to even-numbered exercises. write for info. (*0-669-27142-X*); Test item file. write for info. (*0-669-27146-2*) Heath.

— Finite Mathematics. LC 90-83169. 500p. (C). 1991. text ed. write for info. (*0-669-16801-7*); Student solutions guide. student ed write for info. (*0-669-16803-3*); Instr.'s guide. teacher ed write for info. (*0-669-16802-5*); Complete solutions guide. teacher ed write for info. (*0-669-27154-3*); Transparencies. trans. write for info. (*0-669-27337-6*); Test item file. write for info. (*0-669-27155-1*) Heath.

— Finite Mathematics with Calculus. 926p. (C). 1991. text ed. write for info. (*0-669-16804-1*); Student solutions guide. student ed write for info. (*0-669-16806-8*); Instr.'s guide. teacher ed write for info. (*0-669-16805-X*); Complete solutions guide. teacher ed write for info. (*0-669-27156-X*); Transparencies. trans. write for info. (*0-318-68395-4*); Test item file. write for info. (*0-669-27157-8*) Heath.

Larson, Roland E. & Hostetler, Robert P. Algebra & Trigonometry. 3rd annot. ed. 818p. (C). 1993. Instr.'s annotated ed. teacher ed write for info. (*0-669-33234-8*) Heath.

— Algebra & Trigonometry. 3rd ed. 818p. (C). 1993. text ed. write for info. (*0-669-28298-7*); Study & soultions guide. student ed write for info. (*0-669-28300-2*); Transparencies. trans. write for info. (*0-318-70104-9*); Complete solutions guide. write for info. (*0-669-28301-0*); Test item file/Resource guide. write for info. (*0-669-28302-9*) Heath.

— Brief Calculus with Application. 2nd ed. LC 86-82096. 640p. (C). 1987. text ed. 37.00 (*0-669-12060-X*); Student soln. guide. student ed 8.50 (*0-669-12061-8*); Matrices suppl. 2.50 (*0-669-13013-3*); Answer key. 2.00 (*0-669-12063-4*) Heath.

— Brief Calculus with Applications Alternate. 2nd ed. LC 86-82095. 512p. (C). 1990. text ed. 35.00 (*0-669-12186-X*); Student soln. guide. student ed 8.50 (*0-669-12187-8*); Answer key. 2.00 (*0-669-12188-6*) Heath.

— Calculus with Analytic Geometry, 3 vols. 3rd ed. LC 85-80719. 1013p. (C). 1986. text ed. 45.50 (*0-669-09568-0*); Study & soln. guide. student ed 12.00 (*0-669-10098-6*); Transparencies. trans. 50.00 (*0-669-10102-8*); Vol. I, sol. guide. 10.50 (*0-669-10099-4*); Vol. II, sol. guide. 10.50 (*0-669-10100-1*); Vol. III, sol. guide. 10.50 (*0-669-10101-X*) Heath.

— Calculus with Analytic Geometry. 5th alternate ed. 1123p. (C). 1994. text ed. write for info. (*0-669-34227-0*) Heath.

— Calculus with Analytic Geometry Alternate with Late Trigonometry. 4th alternate ed. 1113p. (C). 1990. text ed. 44.50 (*0-669-17843-8*); Instr.'s guide. teacher ed 2.00 (*0-669-21738-7*); Transparencies. trans. 60.00 (*0-669-16412-7*); Study & solutions guide. 12.00 (*0-669-17844-6*); Complete Solutions Guide, Vol. I. 10.50 (*0-669-17845-4*); Solutions, Vol. II. 10.50 (*0-669-17846-2*); Solutions, Vol. III. 10.50 (*0-669-17847-0*); Test item file. 2.00 (*0-669-21817-0*) Heath.

— College Algebra. 3rd ed. 620p. (C). 1993. Instr.'s annotated ed. student ed write for info. (*0-669-33235-6*); text ed. write for info. (*0-669-28304-5*); Study & solutions guide. student ed, text ed. write for info. (*0-669-28306-1*); Complete solutions guide. teacher ed, text ed. write for info. (*0-669-28307-X*); Transparencies. trans. write for info. (*0-669-28322-3*); College Algebra videotapes. vhs write for info. (*0-669-28580-3*); Test item file/Resource guide. write for info. (*0-669-28309-6*) Heath.

— Elementary Algebra. 551p. (C). 1992. text ed. write for info. (*0-669-18763-1*); Student solutions guide. student ed write for info. (*0-669-18766-6*); Study guide. student ed write for info. (*0-669-18765-8*); Instr.'s guide. teacher ed write for info. (*0-669-18764-X*); Complete solutions guide. teacher ed write for info. (*0-669-27886-6*); Test item file. write for info. (*0-669-28279-0*) Heath.

— Elementary Algebra. annot. ed. 551p. (C). 1992. Instr.'s annotated ed. teacher ed write for info. (*0-669-33041-8*) Heath.

— Interactive Calculus: CD-ROM for Windows. (C). 1994. cd-rom write for info. (*0-669-35712-X*) Heath.

— Intermediate Algebra. 726p. (C). 1992. text ed. write for info. (*0-669-18767-4*); Study guide. student ed write for info. (*0-669-18769-0*); Instr.'s guide. teacher ed write for info. (*0-669-18768-2*); Student solutions guide. write for info. (*0-669-18771-2*); Complete solutions guide. write for info. (*0-669-27897-1*); Test item file. write for info. (*0-669-28280-4*) Heath.

— Intermediate Algebra. annot. ed. 726p. (C). 1992. Instr.'s annotated ed. teacher ed write for info. (*0-669-33039-6*) Heath.

— Precalculus. 826p. (C). 1993. Study & soultions guide. student ed write for info. (*0-669-28312-6*); Complete solutions guide. teacher ed write for info. (*0-669-28313-4*); Test item file/Resource guide. write for info. (*0-669-28314-2*); The Algebra of Calculus. write for info. (*0-669-21885-5*) Heath.

— Precalculus. annot. ed. 826p. (C). 1993. Instr.'s annotated ed. teacher ed write for info. (*0-669-33236-4*) Heath.

— Precalculus. 3rd ed. 826p. (C). 1993. text ed. write for info. (*0-669-28310-X*) Heath.

— Trigonometry. 3rd annot. ed. 592p. (C). 1993. Instr.'s annotated ed. teacher ed write for info. (*0-669-33237-2*) Heath.

— Trigonometry. 3rd ed. 592p. (C). 1993. text ed. write for info. (*0-669-28317-7*); Study & solutions guide. student ed write for info. (*0-669-28319-3*); Instr.'s guide. teacher ed write for info. (*0-669-28318-5*); Transparencies. trans. write for info. (*0-318-70103-0*); Test item file/Resource guide. write for info. (*0-669-28321-5*) Heath.

— Trigonometry: A Graphing Approach. 500p. (C). 1995. text ed. write for info. (*0-669-28296-0*) Heath.

Larson, Roland E., et al. Brief Calculus with Applications. 3rd ed. LC 89-81072. 812p. (C). 1991. text ed. 37.00 (*0-669-21767-0*); Study guide & workbook. student ed 12.00 (*0-669-24500-3*); Student solutions guide. student ed 8.50 (*0-669-21769-7*); Instr.'s guide. teacher ed 2.00 (*0-669-21768-9*); Transparencies. trans. write for info. (*0-669-27336-8*); Systems of equations, matrices & determinants. write for info. (*0-669-21770-0*); Complete solutions guide. write for info. (*0-669-27149-7*); Test item file. write for info. (*0-669-27150-0*) Heath.

— Brief Calculus with Applications. 4th ed. 736p. (C). 1995. text ed. write for info. (*0-669-35165-2*) Heath.

— Brief Calculus with Applications: Alternate Third Edition. LC 89-81072. 648p. (C). 1990. text ed. 35.00 (*0-669-21763-8*); Student solutions guide. student ed 8.50 (*0-669-21764-6*); Study guide & workbook. student ed write for info. (*0-318-68032-7*); Instr.'s guide. teacher ed 2.00 (*0-669-21765-4*); Complete solutions guide. write for info. (*0-669-27147-0*); Test item file. write for info. (*0-669-27148-9*) Heath.

— Calculus: Early Transcendental Functions. 1128p. (C). 1995. text ed. write for info. (*0-669-39349-5*) Heath.

— Calculus of a Single Variable. 4th ed. 707p. (C). 1990. text ed. write for info. (*0-669-24591-7*); Instr.'s guide. teacher ed write for info. (*0-669-21737-9*); Calculus Applications in Engineering & Science. write for info. (*0-669-21676-3*); Graphics Calculator Suppl. write for info. (*0-669-28905-1*); Test item file. write for info. (*0-318-70107-3*) Heath.

— Calculus of a Single Variable. 5th ed. 713p. (C). 1994. text ed. write for info. (*0-669-35250-0*) Heath.

— Calculus of a Single Variable: Early Transcendental Functions. 714p. (C). 1995. text ed. write for info. (*0-669-39348-7*) Heath.

— Calculus with Analytic Geometry. 4th ed. 1083p. (C). 1993. text ed. write for info. (*0-669-16406-2*); Study & solutions guide. write for info. (*0-669-16407-0*); Complete solutions guide, Vol. I. write for info. (*0-669-16408-9*); Solutions, Vol. II. write for info. (*0-669-16409-7*); Solutions, Vol. III. write for info. (*0-669-16411-9*); Test item file. write for info. (*0-669-21828-6*); Computer Projects for Calculus. write for info. (*0-669-28499-8*) Heath.

— Calculus with Analytic Geometry. 5th ed. 1127p. (C). 1994. text ed. write for info. (*0-669-35335-3*) Heath.

— College Algebra: A Graphing Approach. 688p. (C). 1993. text ed. write for info. (*0-669-28294-4*); Instr.'s guide. teacher ed write for info. (*0-669-33231-3*); Study & solutions guide. write for info. (*0-669-28295-2*); Test item file/Resource guide. write for info. (*0-318-70105-7*) Heath.

— College Algebra: Concepts & Models. 678p. (C). 1992. text ed. write for info. (*0-669-18758-5*); Instr.'s guide. teacher ed write for info. (*0-669-18759-3*); Transparencies. trans. write for info. (*0-318-70102-2*); Study & solutions guide. write for info. (*0-669-18760-7*); Complete solutions guide. write for info. (*0-669-18761-5*); Test item file. write for info. (*0-669-28087-9*) Heath.

— Elementary Algebra: Concepts & Models. 792p. (C). 1993. text ed. write for info. (*0-669-36074-0*) Heath.

— Intermediate Algebra: Concepts & Models. 932p. (C). 1993. text ed. write for info. (*0-669-36075-9*) Heath.

— Intermediate Algebra: Graphs & Functions. 800p. (C). 1994. text ed. write for info. (*0-669-33755-2*) Heath.

— Multivariable Calculus. 5th ed. 413p. (C). 1994. text ed. write for info. (*0-669-39345-2*) Heath.

— Precalculus: A Graphing Approach. 826p. (C). 1993. text ed. write for info. (*0-669-28500-5*); Study & solutions guide. student ed write for info. (*0-669-28501-3*); Instr.'s guide. teacher ed write for info. (*0-669-33232-1*); Test item file/Resource guide. write for info. (*0-318-70106-5*) Heath.

— Precalculus: Functions & Graphs: A Graphing Approach. 750p. (C). 1994. text ed. write for info. (*0-669-35206-3*) Heath.

— Precalculus with Limits: A Graphing Approach. 932p. (C). 1994. text ed. write for info. (*0-669-35251-9*) Heath.

***Larson, Ron.** Swamp Song: A Natural History of Florida's Swamps. LC 95-9806. (Illus.). 248p. 1995. pap. 19.95 (*0-8130-1355-0*) U Press Fla.

— Upper Mississippi River History: Fact-Fiction-Legend. LC 94-92055. (Illus.). 140p. 1995. 45.00 (*0-9640937-0-7*) Steamboat Pr.

***Larson, Ronal & West, Ronald E., eds.** Implementation of Solar Thermal Technology. (Illus.). 1000p. 1996. 85.00 (*0-262-12187-5*) MIT Pr.

Larson, Ronald. Constitutive Equations for Polymer Melts & Solutions. (Illus.). 384p. 1988. text ed. 59.95 (*0-409-90119-9*) Buttrwrth-Heinemann.

Larson, Ronald C., jt. ed. see Garrett, Jessie A.

Larson, Rory, tr. see Kappeler, Max.

Larson, Ross. Fantasy & Imagination in the Mexican Narrative. LC 77-3019. 208p. 1977. pap. 2.00 (*0-87918-032-3*) ASU Lat Am St.

Larson, Roy A. Production of Florist Azaleas. Armitage, Allan M., ed. LC 92-41795. (Growers Handbook Ser.: Vol. 6). (Illus.). 1993. pap. 17.95 (*0-88192-230-7*) Timber.

Larson, Russ. Beginner's Guide to Large Scale Model Railroading. Miller, Allan, ed. (Illus.). 96p. (Orig.). 1995. pap. 16.95 (*0-89024-110-4*) Kalmbach.

***Larson, Russ & Horowitz, Mark.** Beginner's Guide to Large Scale Model Railroading. Johnson, Kent, ed. (Illus.). 96p. (Orig.). 1995. pap. 16.95 (*0-89778-397-2*) Greenberg Bks.

Larson, Russell. The Beginner's Guide to N Scale Model Railroading. Emmerich, Michael, ed. (Illus.). 104p. (Orig.). 1990. pap. text ed. 11.95 (*0-89024-098-1*) Kalmbach.

Larson, Russell J. Africa by Four: Coloring Book. (Illus.). 14p. (Orig.). (J). (gr. k-6). 1992. pap. text ed. 1.85 (*1-881087-01-8*) Storm Moutain.

— USA Coloring Book. (Illus.). 50p. (Orig.). (J). (gr. k-6). 1992. pap. text ed. 4.95 (*1-881087-00-X*) Storm Moutain.

Larson, Rustin. Tiresias Strung Out on a Half Can of Pepsi. 25p. (Orig.). 1993. pap. 5.00 (*0-9619744-6-X*) Blue Light Pr.

Larson, Sarah L. Making Meaning: A Guide for Passing the Regent's Essay. 160p. 1993. per. 17.95 (*0-8403-9018-1*) Kendall-Hunt.

Larson, Shirley. Out of the Fire. 368p. (Orig.). 1992. pap. 4.50 (*0-8439-3200-7*) Dorchester Pub Co.

***Larson, Sidner J.** Catch Colt. LC 94-32267. (American Indian Lives Ser.). x, 164p. 1995. 21.00 (*0-8032-2908-9*) U of Nebr Pr.

Larson, Sidney, jt. auth. see Overby, Osmund.

Larson, Simeon & Nissen, Bruce, eds. Theories of the Labor Movement. LC 86-32414. 408p. (C). 1987. text ed. 49.95 (*0-8143-1815-0*); pap. text ed. 18.95 (*0-8143-1816-9*) Wayne St U Pr.

Larson, Stan. Quest for the Gold Plates: Thomas Stuart Ferguson's Archaeological Search for the Book of Mormon. (Illus.). 224p. 1995. text ed. 19.95 (*0-9634732-1-2*) Freethinker.

Larson, Stan, ed. Prisoner for Polygamy: The Memoirs & Letters of Rudger Clawson at the Utah Territorial Penitentiary, 1884-87. (Illus.). 240p. (C). 1993. 24.95 (*0-252-01861-3*) U of Ill Pr.

Larson, Stan, ed. see Roberts, B. H.

Larson, Stephanie G. Creating Consent of the Governed: A Member of Congress & the Local Media. LC 91-40750. 232p. (C). 1992. 27.50 (*0-8093-1787-7*) S Ill U Pr.

Larson, Steven. Desktop Publishing: Essential Applications. 1990. teacher ed (*0-318-66849-1*); pap. 10.50 (*0-07-036491-5*) McGraw.

— Desktop Publishing Applications. 1989. pap. 15.40 (*0-07-036484-2*) McGraw.

***Larson, Steven B.** Using DOS in Court Reporting. 122p. 1994. pap. text ed. 21.95 (*1-881859-07-X*) Natl Ct Report.

Larson, Steven B., jt. auth. see Nordenstam, Garry.

Larson, Steven M. & Kaplan, William. Nuclear Medicine in Oncology. (Illus.). 500p. 1994. 135.00 (*0-397-51375-5*) Lippincott.

Larson, Susan, illus. You Are My Friend: A Celebration of Friendship. LC 90-3028. 156p. (Orig.). 1991. pap. 9.95 (*0-9622874-8-2*) Halo Bks.

Larson, Susan, jt. auth. see Larson, Hal.

Larson, Susan C., text. Sunshine & Shadow: Recent Painting in Southern California. LC 84-73006. (Illus.). 75p. (Orig.). 1985. pap. 10.00 (*0-911291-10-5*) Fellows Cont Art.

Larson, T. A. History of Wyoming. rev. ed. (Illus.). xiv, 695p. 1978. reprint ed. pap. 23.00x (*0-8032-7936-1*) U of Nebr Pr.

Larson, Taft A. Wyoming: A History. LC 77-3592. (States & the Nation Ser.). (Illus.). 1984. pap. 10.95 (*0-393-30183-4*) Norton.

***Larson Texts, Inc. (Meridian Creative Group) Staff.** CBL Explorations in Calculus for the TI-82: Calculator-Based Laboratory. 112p. (Orig.). (C). 1995. pap. text ed. write for info. (*0-9639121-1-9*) Meridian Creative.

Larson, Thomas B. Soviet-American Rivalry. (C). 1978. text ed. 19.95 (*0-393-05689-9*) Norton.

Larson, Verna. Bearables of Bernie Bear. Pappas, Debra S., ed. (Illus.). 30p. (Orig.). (J). 1994. pap. 8.95 (*1-56550-022-9*) Vis Bks Intl.

***Larson, Vicki L. & McKinley, Nancy.** Language Disorders in Older Students: Preadolescents & Adolescents. LC 94-34928. 1995. pap. 37.00 (*0-930599-29-2*) Thinking Pubns.

Larson, Vicki L. & McKinley, Nancy L. Communication Assessment & Intervention Strategies for Adolescents. LC 86-51418. 387p. (YA). (gr. 5-12). 1987. text ed. 39.00 (*0-930599-07-1*) Thinking Pubns.

— Giving Your Child the Gift of Humor. Joubert, Vivian, ed. 128p. (Orig.). 1990. pap. 10.95 (*0-9622880-0-4*) Maxing Pub.

Larson, Virginia. How to Write a Winning Proposal. 2nd rev. ed. (Illus.). 68p. 1986. pap. 9.95 (*0-931954-01-0*) Classic Hse.

Larson, Virginia, tr. see Horie, Michiaki & Horie, Hildegard.

Larson, W. E., et al, eds. Mechanics & Related Processes in Structured Agricultural Soils. (C). 1989. lib. bdg. 105.50 (*0-7923-0342-3*) Kluwer Ac.

Larson, Wanda Z. Miracle at Blowing Rock. Bard, Ruth, ed. (Illus.). 20p. (Orig.). 1992. pap. 4.95 (*0-9628584-2-0*) Blue Uncrn.

— Our Flag: Born Through Valor. (Illus.). 64p. (J). (gr. 1 up). 1995. pap. 12.00 (*0-9628584-1-2*) Blue Uncrn.

— Portlandia. (Illus.). 1991. pap. 8.95 (*0-9628584-0-4*) Blue Uncrn.

Larson, Wendy. Air. (My World Poke & Look Bks.). (Illus.). 14p. (J). (ps-1). 1994. bds. 4.95 (*0-448-40569-5*, G&D) Putnam Pub Group.

— Earth. (My World Poke & Look Bks.). (Illus.). 14p. (J). (ps-1). 1994. bds. 4.95 (*0-448-40570-9*, G&D) Putnam Pub Group.

— Literary Authority & the Modern Chinese Writer: Ambivalence & Autobiography. LC 90-27835. 222p. 1991. text ed. 36.95 (*0-8223-1113-5*) Duke.

— Puppy Love. (J). (gr. 4-8). 1993. pap. 2.50 (*0-448-40463-X*, G&D) Putnam Pub Group.

— Sun. (My World Poke & Look Bks.). (Illus.). 14p. (J). (ps-1). 1994. bds. 4.95 (*0-448-40571-7*, G&D) Putnam Pub Group.

— Water. (My World Poke & Look Bks.). (Illus.). 14p. (J). (ps-1). 1994. bds. 4.95 (*0-448-40572-5*, G&D) Putnam Pub Group.

Larson, Wendy, adapt. Little Rascals: The Junior Novelization. LC 94-12797. 64p. (J). (ps-2). 1994. 4.50 (*0-8431-3095-4*) Price Stern.

Larson, Wendy & Wedell-Wedellsborg, Anne, eds. Inside Out: Modernism & Postmodernism in Chinese Literary Culture. 203p. 1993. 52.50 (*87-7288-427-4*, Pub. by Aarhus Univ Pr DK) Coronet Bks.

Larson, Wendy, tr. see Wang, Meng.

***Larson, Wendy A.** When Crisis Strikes on Campus. 254p. 1994. vhs 79.95 (*0-89964-297-7*) Coun Adv & Supp Ed.

***Larson, Wendy A., ed.** 1975-1993 CASE Currents Index. 134p. 1993. 18.00 (*0-89964-300-0*) Coun Adv & Supp Ed.

Larson, Wiley J. & Wertz, James R., eds. Space Mission Analysis & Design. 2nd ed. LC 92-64312. (Space Technology Library). 1992. lib. bdg. 140.50 (*0-7923-1998-2*); pap. 44.75 (*1-881883-01-9*) Kluwer Ac.

Larson, Wiley J., jt. ed. see Sarafin, Thomas P.

Larson, Wiley J., jt. ed. see Wertz, James R.

Larson, William C., ed. see Society of Mining Engineers of AIME Staff.

***Larsson.** Principles of Yacht Design. 1995. text ed. 39.95 (*0-07-036492-3*) Intl Marine.

Larsson & Friberg. Food Emulsions. 2nd rev. ed. (Food Science & Technology Ser.: Vol. 38). 504p. 1990. 175.00 (*0-8247-8306-9*) Dekker.

Larsson, jt. auth. see Eliasson.

Larsson, Agne, et al, eds. Functions of Glutathione: Biochemical, Physiological, Toxicological, & Clinical Aspects: Fifth Karolinska Institute Nobel Conference. (Illus.). 424p. 1983. text ed. 127.00 (*0-89004-908-4*) Raven.

Larsson, Anita. Women Householders & Housing Strategies: The Case of Gaborone, Botswana. (Illus.). 180p. (Orig.). 1989. pap. 40.00x (*91-540-9339-2*, Pub. by Almqv & Wiksell SW) Coronet Bks.

Larsson, B., jt. ed. see Carlsson, H.

Larsson, Birgitta. Conversion to Greater Freedom? Women, Church & Social Change in North-Western Tanzania under Colonial Rule. (Studia Historica Upsaliensia: No. 162). (Illus.). 230p. (Orig.). 1991. pap. 46.50x (*91-554-2684-0*, Pub. by Almqv & Wiksell SW) Coronet Bks.

Larsson, Borje, jt. auth. see Kullander, Sven.

Larsson, C. & Moller, I. M., eds. The Plant Plasma Membrane. (Illus.). 432p. 1990. 194.00 (*0-387-50836-8*) Spr-Verlag.

Larsson, Clotye M., ed. Marriage Across the Color Line. 1965. 4.95 (*0-87485-014-2*) Johnson Chi.

Larsson, Gerhard. Land Readjustment: A Modern Approach to Urbanization. LC 93-1214. 154p. 1993. 59.95 (*1-85628-507-3*, Pub. by Avebury Pub UK) Ashgate Pub Co.

— Land Registration & Cadastral Systems: Tools for Land Information & Management. 175p. 1991. pap. text ed. 51.95 (*0-470-21798-7*) Halsted Pr.

Larsson, Gunnar & Astrand, Hans, eds. Gustavian Opera: Swedish Opera, Dance & Theatre 1771-1809. (Royal Swedish Academy of Music Ser.: No. 66). (Illus.). 492p. 1991. 121.00x (*91-85428-64-7*, Pub. by Almqv & Wiksell SW) Coronet Bks.

Larsson, Hans, jt. auth. see Olsen, Klaus M.

Larsson, Jytte T. Catalogue of the Rischel & Birket-Smith Collection of Guitar Music in the Royal Library of Copenhagen. Danner, Peter, ed. LC 89-80417. 272p. 1989. 45.00 (*0-936186-20-8*); pap. 29.00 (*0-936186-33-X*) Edit Orphee.

Larsson, Kare. Lipids-Molecular Organization, Physical Function & Technical Applications. (Oily Press Lipid Library Ser.). (Illus.). 235p. (C). 1994. 55.00 (*0-9514171-4-2*, Pub. by Oily Pr UK) Matreya.

Larsson, L. H., ed. Advances in Elasto-Plastic Fracture Mechanics. (Illus.). 428p. 1980. 97.25 (*0-85334-889-8*, Pub. by Elsevier Applied Sci UK) Elsevier.

— Subcritical Crack Growth Due to Fatigue, Stress Corrosion & Creep: Selected Proceedings of the Third Advanced Seminar on Fracture Mechanics (ASFM 3), Joint Research Centre, Ispra, Italy, 19-23 October 1981. (Illus.). 640p. 1985. 194.50 (*0-85334-289-X*, Pub. by Elsevier Applied Sci UK) Elsevier.

Larsson, L. H., jt. ed. see Herrmann, K. P.

Larsson, Lars, et al, eds. The Archaeology of the Cultural Landscape: Field Work & Research in a South Swedish Rural Region. (Acta Archaeologica Ludensia Ser.: Vol. 4.0, No. 19). (Illus.). 498p. 1993. 120.00x (*91-22-01550-7*, Pub. by Almqv & Wiksell SW) Coronet Bks.

Larsson, Lars-Gunnar. Proceedings of the Second Scandinavian Symposium on Aspectology. (Studia Uralica et Altaica Upsaliensia Ser.: No. 19). 130p. (Orig.). 1989. pap. 37.50x (*91-554-2412-0*, Pub. by Almqv & Wiksell SW) Coronet Bks.

Larsson, Lars-Inge. Immunocytochemistry: Theory & Practice. 256p. 1988. 228.00 (*0-8493-6078-1*, QR187) CRC Pr.

— Regulatory Peptides & Amines During Ontogeny & in Non-Endocrine Cancers: Occurrence & Possible Functional Significance. LC 88-10967. (Progress in Histochemistry & Cytochemistry Ser.: Vol. 17, No. 4). 222p. 1988. pap. 125.00 (0-89574-263-2, Pub. by Gustav Fischer Verlag) VCH Pubs.

Larsson, Lennart, Jr. Carpets from China, Xinjiang & Tibet. (Illus.). 141p. 1987. 60.00 (0-87556-748-7) Saifer.

Larsson, Olle & Major, James. World Cup Ski Technique: Learn & Improve. Smith, Doug, ed. LC 79-90395. (Illus.). (Orig.). 1979. pap. 18.95 (0-935240-00-4) Poudre Pr.

***Larsson, Petter & Weider, Lawrence J., eds.** Cladocera as Model Organisms in Biology. LC 95-13976. (Developments in Hydrobiology Ser.: No. 107). 1995. write for info. (0-7923-3471-X) Kluwer Ac.

Larsson, Staffan, jt. ed. see Ball, Stephen J.

Larsson, Thomas B. Bronze Age Metalwork in Southern Sweden: Aspects of Social & Spatial Organization 1800-500 B. C. (Illus.). xii, 200p. (Orig.). 1986. pap. text ed. 70.00x (91-7174-229-8) Coronet Bks.

Lart, Charles E. Huguenot Pedigrees, 2 vols. in 1. 258p. 1992. reprint ed. pap. 22.50 (0-685-60534-5, 3290) Clearfield Co.

Larter, Chris. Horses on Wings, Wheels & Waves. 192p. 1984. 39.00 (0-7212-0654-9, Pub. by Regency Press) St Mut.

***Lartey, Emmanuel Y., et al, eds.** The Church & Healing: Echoes from Africa. LC 94-26926. (African Pastoral Studies, Etudes Pastorales Africaines: 2). (ENG & FRE.). 1994. write for info. (3-631-47227-7) P Lang Pubs.

LaRue. Student's Guide to the Study of Law: An Introduction. 1988. write for info. (0-8205-0436-X, 684) Bender.

LaRue, Asenath, jt. auth. see Spar, J. Edward.

***LaRue, C. Steven.** Handel & His Singers: The Creation of the Royal Academy Operas, 1720-1728. (Oxford Monographs on Music). (Illus.). 224p. 1995. text ed. 49.95 (0-19-816315-0) OUP.

LaRue, Charles. Basic Biology. 2nd ed. (Illus.). 294p. 1992. teacher ed 12.99 (0-7916-0098-X); student ed 4.99 (0-7916-0099-8); text ed. 19.49 (0-7916-0097-1); 9.99 (0-7916-0107-2) Media Materials.

Larue, D. K. & Steel, R. J., eds. Cenozoic Marine Sedimentation, Pacific Margin U. S. A. (Illus.). 247p. (Orig.). 1983. pap. 8.00 (1-878861-44-1) Pac Section SEPM.

Larue, Gerald. Biblical vs. Secular Ethics. Hoffmann, R. Joseph, ed. 191p. 1988. text ed. 28.95 (0-87975-418-4) Prometheus Bks.

— Playing God. 256p. 1995. reprint ed. 19.95 (1-55921-145-8) Moyer Bell.

— Sex & the Bible. LC 83-60201. 173p. 1983. 26.95 (0-87975-206-8); pap. 19.95 (0-87975-229-7) Prometheus Bks.

Larue, Gerald, jt. ed. see Hoffmann, R. Joseph.

Larue, Gerald A. Ancient Myth & Modern Life. rev. ed. (Illus.). 304p. 1988. pap. 16.95 (0-913111-24-4) Centerline.

— Euthanasia & Religion: A Survey of the Attitudes of World Religions to the Right-to-Die. LC 84-62806. 155p. (Orig.). 1985. pap. 10.00 (0-9606030-1-8) Hemlock Soc.

— Freethought Across the Centuries: Toward a New Age of Enlightenment. 500p. (Orig.). 1995. pap. 15.00 (0-931779-03-0) Humanist Pr.

— Geroethics: A New Vision of Growing Old in America. (Golden Age Books - Perspectives on Aging Ser.). 267p. (C). 1992. 23.95 (0-87975-750-7) Prometheus Bks.

— The Supernatural, the Occult, & the Bible. 303p. (C). 1990. 23.95 (0-87975-615-2) Prometheus Bks.

— The Way of Ethical Humanism. 96p. 1989. pap. 10.95 (0-913111-22-8) Centerline.

— The Way of Positive Humanism. 96p. 1989. pap. 10.95 (0-913111-25-2) Centerline.

Larue, Gerald A. & Bayly, Rich, eds. Long-Term Care in an Aging Society: Choices & Challenges for the '90s. (Golden Age Books - Perspectives on Aging Ser.). 170p. (Orig.). 1992. 22.95 (0-87975-695-0); pap. 16.95 (0-87975-712-4) Prometheus Bks.

LaRue, James, ed. see McGinty, Patricia.

LaRue, James H. & Johnson, R. Scott, eds. Peaches, Plums & Nectarines: Growing & Handling for Fresh Market. LC 89-83832. (Illus.). 252p. (Orig.). 1989. pap. 42.50 (0-931876-88-5, 3331) ANR Pubns CA.

LaRue, Jan. A Catalogue of Eighteenth Century Symphonies: Vol. I, Thematic Identifier. LC 86-46404. 368p. 1988. 29.95 (0-253-31363-5) Ind U Pr.

— Guidelines for Style Analysis. 2nd ed. LC 92-25439. (Detroit Monographs in Musicology: No. 12). 1992. 35.00 (0-89990-062-3) Info Coord.

LaRue, Keith S. My Expression of Existence. 52p. 1993. 5.95 (0-8059-3411-1) Dorrance.

LaRue, L. H. Constitutional Law as Fiction: Narrative in the Rhetoric of Authority. LC 94-15750. 176p. 1995. 28.50 (0-271-01406-7); pap. 13.95 (0-271-01407-5) Pa St U Pr.

LaRue, L. H., ed. see Ritz, Wilfred J.

LaRue, Walt. Rodeo Cartoons from The Buckboard. LC 89-91854. (Illus.). x, 135p. 1989. 12.95 (0-9624489-0-7) G Logsdon Bks.

— Rodeo Cartoons from The Buckboard. deluxe limited ed. LC 89-91854. (Illus.). x, 135p. 1989. Leather bd., numbered & signed collector's ed. 50.00 (0-9624489-1-5) G Logsdon Bks.

LaRuffa, A. L. Monte Carmelo: An Italian-American Community in the Bronx. (Library of Anthropology). 192p. 1988. text ed. 42.00 (2-88124-253-7) Gordon & Breach.

LaRuffa, Anthony L. San Cipriano: Life in a Puerto Rican Community. LC 73-136765. (Library of Anthropology). (Illus.). 116p. 1971. text ed. 65.00 (0-677-03470-9) Gordon & Breach.

***LaRune, T. D.** LaRune's Rockpecker Notes: "A Mineral Prospector's Primer" LC 94-67809. (Illus.). 543p. (C). 1995. text ed. 36.00 (1-886499-00-4, Skill Ware); pap. text ed. 29.00 (1-886499-01-2, Skill Ware); disk 59.00 (1-886499-02-0, Skill Ware); disk 89.00 (1-886499-03-9, Skill Ware) Skill-Quest.

Larungu, Rute. African-American Cultures: Myths & Legends from Ghana for Children. LC 92-81116. (Illus.). 96p. (J). (gr. 3 up). 1992. lib. bdg. 14.95 (1-878893-21-1); pap. 8.95 (1-878893-20-3) Telcraft Bks.

Larus, Joel, jt. ed. see Lawrence, Robert M.

LaRusso, Carol S., intro. & sel. The Wisdom of Women. LC 92-17602. (Classic Wisdom Collection). 128p. 1992. 12.95 (1-880032-09-0) New Wrld Lib.

LaRusso, Carol S., ed. see Thoreau, Henry David.

Larvor, P., jt. ed. see Raymond, W. F.

Larwood, jt. auth. see McLimore.

Larwood, G. P., ed. Extinction & Survival in the Fossil Record. (Systematics Association Special Volume Ser.: Vol. 34). (Illus.). 376p. 1988. 90.00 (0-19-857708-7) OUP.

Larwood, G. P., jt. ed. see Taylor, P. D.

Larwood, Laurie, jt. ed. see Gattiker, U. E.

Larwood, Laurie, jt. ed. see Gutek, Barbara A.

Larwood, Laurie, jt. ed. see Rose, Suzanna.

Lary, Hal B. Imports of Manufactures from Less Developed Countries. (Studies in International Economic Relations: No. 4). 303p. 1968. 79.10 (0-87014-485-5) Natl Bur Econ Res.

— Imports of Manufactures from Less Developed Countries. LC 67-28434. (Studies in International Economic Relations: No. 4). (Illus.). 304p. reprint ed. pap. 86.70 (0-8357-7576-3, 2056897) Bks Demand.

— Problems of the United States As World Trader & Banker. (Economic Relations Ser.: No. 1). 191p. 1963. reprint ed. 49.70 (0-87014-153-8) Natl Bur Econ Res.

— Supplement to NBER Report Two: Tariff Preferences of Less Developed Countries. 12p. reprint ed. 20.00 (0-685-61343-7) Natl Bur Econ Res.

Lary, Hal B., et al. The United States in the World Economy. LC 75-26859. (Economic Series: No. 23). 216p. 1975. reprint ed. text ed. 55.00 (0-8371-8257-3, LAUS, Greenwood Pr) Greenwood.

Lary, N. M. Dostoevsky & Soviet Film: Visions of Demonic Realism. LC 86-47645. (Illus.). 280p. 1986. 32.95 (0-8014-1882-8) Cornell U Pr.

Larzelere, Alex. Castro's Ploy, America's Dilemma: The 1980 Cuban Boatlift. LC 88-28941. (Illus.). 581p. (Orig.). 1988. pap. 16.00 (0-318-42912-8, S/N 008-020-01144-4) USGPO.

Larzelere, Bob. The Harmony of Love. 3rd ed. LC 81-3189. 144p. (Orig.). 1982. pap. 15.00 (0-932654-03-7) Context Pubns.

Las Casas. Le Memorial de Sant-Helene: Chapitres 9-14, Vol. 2. 1520p. 41.50 (0-686-56533-9) Fr & Eur.

Las Cases. Le Memorial de Saint-Helene, Vol. 1. (FRE.). 1978. lib. bdg. 95.00 (0-8288-3520-9, F13311) Fr & Eur.

— Le Memorial de Saint-Helene, Vol. 2. (FRE.). 1978. lib. bdg. 95.00 (0-8288-3521-7, F13312) Fr & Eur.

Las Vergnas, Raymond. W. M. Thackeray (1811-1863) L'homme, le penseur, le romancier. LC 70-148810. reprint ed. 49.50 (0-404-08876-7) AMS Pr.

Lasa, Bernardo E. Diccionario Enciclopedica Vasco, Vol. 11: Ento-Esubi. 624p. 1980. 195.00 (0-7859-6475-4) Fr & Eur.

— Diccionario Enciclopedica Vasco, Vol. 14: Fortif-Gallet. 592p. 1982. 195.00 (0-7859-6070-8, 8470252143) Fr & Eur.

— Diccionario Enciclopedica Vasco, Vol. 16: Geol-Gruzeta. 592p. 1984. 195.00 (0-7859-6477-0) Fr & Eur.

— Diccionario Enciclopedica Vasco, Vol. 27: Mars-Mendix. 576p. 1989. 195.00 (0-7859-6478-9) Fr & Eur.

— Diccionario Espanol-Vasco, Vol. 3. 170p. 1965. pap. 19.95 (0-7859-6476-2) Fr & Eur.

Lasaga, A. C. & Kirkpatrick, R. J., eds. Kinetics of Geochemical Processes. (Reviews in Mineralogy Ser.: Vol. 8). 398p. 1981. per. 10.00 (0-939950-08-1) Mineralogical Soc.

Lasaga, Jose I. Vidas Cubanas (Cuban Lives), 2 vols. Duran, Nelson, tr. LC 84-189243. (Coleccion Cuba y Sus Jueces Ser.). (Illus.). (Orig.). (ENG & SPA.). 1988. Vol. 2: Paginas de la Historia de Cuba (Pages from Cuban History), 470p. pap. 12.00 (0-89729-407-6) Ediciones.

— Vidas Cubanas (Cuban Lives), 2 vols., 1. Duran, Nelson, tr. LC 84-189243. (Coleccion Cuba y Sus Jueces Ser.). (Illus.). (Orig.). (ENG & SPA.). 1988. pap. 12.00 (0-89729-165-4) Ediciones.

Lasagabaster, Jesus M., ed. see Baroja, Pio.

Lasagna. Year Book of Drug Therapy, 1993. 480p. 1993. 59.95 (0-8151-5291-4, Yr Bk Med Pubs) Mosby Yr Bk.

— Year Book of Drug Therapy, 1994. 350p. 1994. 59.95 (0-8151-5292-2, Yr Bk Med Pubs) Mosby Yr Bk.

— Year Book of Drug Therapy, 1995. 350p. 1995. 59.95 (0-8151-5293-0, Yr Bk Med Pubs) Mosby Yr Bk.

— Year Book of Drug Therapy, 1996. 350p. 1996. 59.95 (0-8151-5294-9, Yr Bk Med Pubs) Mosby Yr Bk.

— Yearbook of Drug Therapy, 1991. 347p. 1991. 57.95 (0-8151-4612-4, Yr Bk Med Pubs) Mosby Yr Bk.

— Yearbook of Drug Therapy, 1992. 426p. 1992. 59.95 (0-8151-4611-6) Mosby Yr Bk.

Lasagna, Louis. Phenylpropanolamine: A Review. LC 86-28963. 455p. reprint ed. pap. 129.70 (0-7837-2818-2, 2057654) Bks Demand.

Lasagna, Louis & Bearn, Alexander G., eds. Innovation & Acceleration in Clinical Drug Development (MEDAC 1986) 182p. 1987. text ed. 76.50 (0-88167-346-3) Raven.

Lasagna, Michele, jt. auth. see Faber, Gail.

Lasagne, Louis S. Doctor's Dilemmas. LC 70-105025. (Essay Index Reprint Ser.). 1977. 23.95 (0-8369-1669-7) Ayer.

Lasagne, Louis S., ed. Clinical Pharmacology, Set. 1966. 122.00 (0-08-012067-9, Pub. by Pergamon Repr UK) Franklin.

Lasagne, Louis S. & Acton, F. Clinical Pharmacology, Vol. 1. LC 66-22360. (International Encyclopedia of Pharmacology & Therapeutics Ser.: Sec. 6). 1966. 168.00 (0-08-012066-0, Pub. by Pergamon Repr UK) Franklin.

Lasagne, Louis S., et al, eds. Dose-Response Relationships in Clinical Pharmacology: Proceedings of Esteve Foundation Symposium III - Dose Response Relationships in Man, Son Vida, Mallorca, 12-15 Oct., 1988. (International Congress Ser.: No. 808). 348p. 1989. 102.75 (0-444-81084-6, Excerpta Medica) Elsevier.

LaSalle, Charles. Heads & Figures in Charcoal. (How to Draw & Paint Ser.). (Illus.). 32p. (Orig.). 1989. pap. 5.95 (1-56010-005-2, HT051) W Foster Pub.

LaSalle, David F. Applied Physics. 1993. 14.95 (0-8062-4559-X) Carlton.

LaSalle History Book Committee Staff. LaSalle County, Colorado. (Illus.). 178p. 1988. 30.00 (0-88107-108-0) Curtis Media.

LaSalle, J. & Gauld, I. D., eds. Hymenoptera & Biodiversity. 320p. 1993. text ed. 94.00 (0-85198-830-X) CAB Intl.

Lasalle, J. P. The Stability & Control of Discrete Processes. (Applied Mathematical Sciences Ser.: Vol. 62). (Illus.). 610p. 1986. pap. 39.00 (0-387-96411-8) Spr-Verlag.

LaSalle, J. P. The Stability of Dynamical Systems. (CBMS-NSF Regional Conference Ser.: No. 25). v, 76p. (Orig.). 1976. pap. text ed. 19.25 (0-89871-022-7) Soc Indus-Appl Math.

LaSalle Parish Genealogical Society Staff. LaSalle Parish, Louisiana. (Illus.). 295p. 1989. write for info. (0-88107-141-2) Curtis Media.

LaSalle, Patricia A. College & University Magazines: Building Credibility to Advance Your Institution. 121p. 1991. 32.00 (0-89964-284-5) Coun Adv & Supp Ed.

LaSalle, Peter. The Graves of Famous Writers & Other Stories. LC 79-3065. (Breakthrough Bks.). 96p. 1980. text ed. 14.95 (0-8262-0287-X) U of Mo Pr.

Lasana Okpara, Mzee, see Fred L. Hord, pseud..

Lasansky, Jeannette. Collecting Guide: Holiday Paper Honeycomb-Cards, Garlands, Centerpieces, & Other Tissue-Paper Fantasies of the 20th Century. Foster, Joseph G., ed. LC 92-44577. (Illus.). 48p. (Orig.). 1993. pap. 15.00 (0-917127-07-2) Oral Traditions.

— A Good Start: The Aussteier or Dowry. Foster, Joseph, ed. (Illus.). 88p. (Orig.). 1990. pap. 22.00 (0-917127-05-6) Oral Traditions.

— A Good Start: The Aussteier or Dowry. LC 89-48999. (Distributed for the Oral Traditions Project Ser.). (Illus.). 88p. (Orig.). 1990. pap. 24.95 (0-8122-8261-2) U of Pa Pr.

— Made of Mud: Stoneware Potteries in Central Pennsylvania, 1831-1929. LC 79-2708. (Illus.). 1979. pap. 12.50 (0-271-00228-X, Keystone Bks) Pa St U Pr.

— Pieced by Mother: Over One Hundred Years of Quiltmaking Traditions. Steffensen, Elsbeth & Foster, Joseph, eds. (Illus.). 120p. (Orig.). 1986. pap. 19.95 (0-917127-02-1) Oral Traditions.

— Redware Pottery in Central Pennsylvania, 1790-1904. Blair, Cathy et al, eds. (Illus.). 60p. 1989. reprint ed. pap. text ed. 14.50 (0-917127-04-8) Oral Traditions.

— Willow, Oak & Rye: Basket Traditions in Pennsylvania. LC 79-2709. (Illus.). 1979. pap. 12.50 (0-271-00229-8, Keystone Bks) Pa St U Pr.

Lasansky, Jeannette, ed. Bits & Pieces: Textile Traditions. LC 90-27530. (Distributed for the Oral Traditions Project Ser.). (Illus.). 120p. (Orig.). (C). 1991. pap. 24.95 (0-8122-1362-9) U of Pa Pr.

Lasansky, Jeannette, et al. On the Cutting Edge: Textile Collectors, Collections, & Traditions. LC 93-46431. 1994. 24.95 (0-917127-08-0) Oral Traditions.

— Pieced by Mother: Symposium Papers. (Illus.). 104p. (Orig.). 1988. pap. 19.95 (0-917127-03-X) Oral Traditions.

Lasansky, Jeannette, et al, eds. On the Cutting Edge: Textile Collectors, Collections, & Traditions. LC 93-46431. (Illus.). 120p. 1994. pap. 24.00 (0-8122-1518-4) U of Pa Pr.

Lasansky, Mauricio. The Nazi Drawings. LC 75-41656. (Illus.). 85p. 1976. 19.95 (0-87745-065-X) U of Iowa Pr.

LaSarre, Zulu. La Palabra. LC 93-199226. (Colecciom Luz Ser.). (Illus.). 76p. (SPA.). 1991. 12.50 (0-9634009-0-8) Luz Bilingual.

Lasarte, Pedro, ed. Satira Hecha Por Mateo Rosas De Oquendo a las Cosas Que Pasan En el Piru, Ano De 1598. (Colonial Latin American Literature Ser.: No. 2). cxx, 182p. 1990. 25.00 (0-940639-52-1) Hispanic Seminary.

Lasartemay, Eugene P. & Rudge, Mary. For Love of Jack London: His Life with Jennie Prentiss - A True Love Story. 1991. 16.95 (0-533-08838-0) Vantage.

***Lasater.** The New Pacific Community: Clinton's Strategic Options Toward Asia. (C). 1995. text ed. 49.95 (0-8133-8869-4) Westview.

Lasater, Dale. Falfurrias: Ed C. Lasater & the Development of South Texas. LC 84-40130. (Illus.). 318p. 1985. 22.50 (0-89096-209-X) Tex A&M Univ Pr.

***Lasater, Judith.** Relax & Renew: Restful Yoga for Stressful Times. (Illus.). 248p. (Orig.). 1995. pap. 19.95 (0-9627138-4-8) Rodmell Pr.

Lasater, Kaye, ed. see Hill, Harriet T.

Lasater, Laurence M. The Lasater Philosophy of Cattle Raising. 2nd ed. LC 79-190505. (Illus.). 69p. 1992. pap. 12.00 (0-87404-226-7) Tex Western.

Lasater, Martin. A Step Toward Democracy: December 1989 Elections in Taiwan, Republic of China. 100p. (C). 1990. pap. text ed. 9.75 (0-8447-7007-8, AEI Pr) Am Enterprise.

***Lasater, Martin L.** Changing of the Guard: Preside. (C). 1995. text ed. 44.95 (0-8133-8806-6) Westview.

— U. S. Interests in the New Taiwan. 258p. (C). 1993. text ed. 57.50 (0-8133-8396-X) Westview.

Lasater, Martin L., jt. ed. see Chang, Parris H.

Lasca, N. P. & Donahue, J., eds. Archaeological Geology of North America. (DNAG Centennial Special Volumes Ser.: Vol. 4). (Illus.). 543p. 1990. 62.50 (0-8137-5304-X) Geol Soc.

Lascelle, Joan, jt. auth. see Brown, Howard M.

Lascelles, G. Art of Falconry. 176p. 17.50 (0-87556-647-2) Saifer.

***Lascelles, Mary.** Jane Austen & Her Art. 240p. (C). 1995. pap. 22.50 (0-485-12113-1, Pub. by Athlone Pr UK) Humanities.

Lascelles, Mary, ed. see Johnson, Samuel.

Lascelles, P. T. & Donaldson, D. Diagnostic Function Tests in Chemical Pathology. 224p. 1990. lib. bdg. 65.00 (0-7462-0108-7) Kluwer Ac.

— Diagnostic Function Tests in Chemical Pathology. (C). 1990. lib. bdg. 55.00 (0-685-32873-2); pap. text ed. 43.50 (0-7462-0107-9) Kluwer Ac.

Lasch, Christopher. Culture of Narcissism: American Life in an Age of Diminishing Expectations. 1991. pap. 11.95 (0-393-30738-7) Norton.

— Haven in a Heartless World: The Family Besieged. 256p. 1995. pap. 12.95 (0-393-31303-4, Norton Paperbks) Norton.

— The Minimal Self: Psychic Survival in Troubled Times. LC 84-4103. 352p. 1984. reprint ed. 16.95 (0-393-01922-5) Norton.

— The Minimal Self: Psychic Survival in Troubled Times. LC 84-4103. 352p. 1985. reprint ed. pap. 11.95 (0-393-30263-6) Norton.

— The New Radicalism in America, Eighteen Eighty-Nine to Nineteen Sixty-Three: The Intellectual As a Social Type. 384p. 1986. reprint ed. pap. 8.95 (0-393-30319-5) Norton.

— The Revolt of the Elites & the Betrayal of Democracy. 276p. 1995. 22.00 (0-393-03699-5) Norton.

— The Revolt of the Elites & the Betrayal of Democracy. 256p. 1995. pap. 12.95 (0-393-31371-9, Norton Paperbks) Norton.

— The True & Only Heaven: Progress & Its Critics. 592p. 1991. pap. 14.95 (0-393-30795-6) Norton.

Lasch, Christopher, ed. see Addams, Jane.

Lasch-Quinn, Elisabeth. Black Neighbors: Race & the Limits of Reform in the American Settlement House Movement, 1890-1945. LC 93-18533. (Illus.). xiv, 226p. (C). 1993. 39.95 (0-8078-2114-4); pap. 14.95 (0-8078-4423-3) U of NC Pr.

Lascher, Edward L., Jr., jt. ed. see Williams, Shirley.

Laschet, Nikolaus J. Freemasonry: For He Who Knocks, the Door Will Be Opened. 1993. 18.50 (0-533-10512-9) Vantage.

Lasco, Dianna. Developing a Successful Women's Track & Field Program. LC 85-21790. 214p. 1986. text ed. 21.95 (0-13-205261-X, Busn) P-H.

Lascoe, O. D. Handbook of Fabrication Processes. 456p. 1988. 128.00 (0-87170-302-5, 6401U) ASM.

Lascoe, O. D., et al. Machine Shop Operations & Setups. 4th ed. (Illus.). 582p. 1973. 24.96 (0-8269-1842-5) Am Technical.

LasCola, Amy, ed. see Eichel, Carol.

Lascombe, J., ed. see Societe de Chimie Physique Staff.

Lascombe, Jean, ed. see International Conference on Raman Spectroscopy Staff, et al.

Lascombes, Andre, ed. Spectacle & Image in Renaissance Europe: Selected Papers of the 32nd Conference at the Centre d'Etudes Superieures de la Renaissance de Tours, 29 June-8 July 1989: Spectacle & Image dans l'Europe de la Renaissance: Choix de Communications du 32nd Colloque du Centre d'Etudes Superieures de la Ranaissance de Tours, 29 Juin-Juillet 1989. LC 92-44780. (Symbola et Emblemata, Studies in Renaissance & Baroque Symbolism: No. 4). (Illus.). viii, 367p. (FRE.). 1993. 91.50 (90-04-09774-0) E J Brill.

Lasdon, Susan. Making Victorians: The Drummond Children's World 1827-1832. (Illus.). 96p. 1985. 15.95 (0-575-03176-X, Pub. by V Gollancz UK) Trafalgar.

Lasdun, Denys, comp. Architecture in an Age of Scepticism. (Illus.). 1985. 50.00 (0-19-520445-X) OUP.

Lasdun, James. Jump Start. 1989. pap. 7.95 (0-393-30590-2) Norton.

— Three Evenings: Stories. 192p. 1992. 18.00 (0-374-20887-5) FS&G.

Lasdun, Susan. The English Park: Royal, Private & Public. 1992. 35.00 (0-86565-131-0) Vendome.

Laseau, Paul. The Architectural Drawing: Options for Design. (Illus.). 192p. 1990. 27.95 (0-8306-7008-4, 50008, Design Pr); pap. 18.95 (0-8306-8008-X, Design Pr) TAB Bks.

— Architectural Drawing: Options for Design. 1991. text ed. 27.95 (0-07-036497-4); pap. text ed. 18.95 (0-07-036496-6) McGraw.

— Graphic Thinking for Architects & Designers. 2nd ed. (Illus.). 256p. 1989. pap. 39.95 (0-442-25844-5) Van Nos Reinhold.

Laseau, Paul, jt. auth. see Crowe, Norman.

Laseau, Paul, jt. auth. see Eggink, Harry.

Laseau, Paul, et al, eds. Frank Lloyd Wright: Between Principle & Form. (Illus.). 208p. 1992. pap. 39.95 (0-442-23478-3) Van Nos Reinhold.

Lasegue, A. Musee Botanique de M. Benjamin Delessert. 1970. reprint ed. 65.00 (3-7682-0686-6) Lubrecht & Cramer.

An Asterisk (*) at the beginning of an entry indicates that the title is appearing in BIP for the first time.

Lasell, Vicki. The Complete Book on Taming & Training Your Guinea Pig. (Illus.). 32p. (Orig.). (J). (gr. 5-12). 1987. pap. 3.95 (*0-916005-06-2*) Silver Sea.

Lasenby, A. N., jt. ed. see Kaiser, N.

***Laser, Beate.** Wirking des Weizen-und Roggengenoms auf die Mitochondriale Genexpression Bei Titricale. (Dissertationes Botanicae Ser.: 218). (Illus.). 102p. (GER.). 1994. pap. 59.50 (*3-443-64132-6*) Lubrecht & Cramer.

Laser, Connie, ed. see Forsythe, Steven G.

Laser Tech Staff. Emergency Service Dive Team Standards & Procedures Manual. Cameron, E. C., ed. (Illus.). 50p. 1989. pap. 10.95 (*0-943155-08-8*) Laser Tech.

— Rapid Deployment Underwater Search & Rescue: Organizing, Training & Equipping an Emergency Service Dive Team. Tackett, Eric & Hunsinger, Ruth A., eds. (Illus.). 150p. (Orig.). 1987. teacher ed 15.95 (*0-943155-06-1*, 1021); pap. 16.95 (*0-318-22568-9*) Laser Tech.

LaSerna Ramos, Irene E. Revision del Genero Bistropogon L'Hrt. (Lamiaceae-Stachyoideae) Endemismo de la Region Macaronesica. (Phanerogamarum Monographiae: Vol. 18). (Illus.). 380p. (SPA.). 1984. lib. bdg. 97.50 (*3-7682-1399-4*) Lubrecht & Cramer.

Lash, Batton. Wolff & Byrd, Counselors of the Macabre: Supernatural Law. LC 92-61485. (Wolff & Byrd, Counselors of the Macabre Ser.: Vol. 2). (Illus.). 80p. (Orig.). 1992. pap. 7.95 (*0-9633954-0-8*) Exhibit A Pr.

Lash, Hannah, tr. see Oved, Yaacov.

Lash, James. The Royal Cricket of Japan: An Original Fantasy. Moe, Christian & Payne, Darwin R., eds. 44p. 1971. pap. 1.00 (*0-8093-0554-2*) S Ill U Pr.

Lash, James & Burger, Max M., eds. Cell & Tissue Interactions. LC 77-83689. (Society of General Physiologists Ser.: Vol. 32). 331p. 1977. 77.50 (*0-89004-180-6*) Raven.

Lash, Jamie S. Love Song to the Messiah. 16p. 1987. reprint ed. pap. 3.00 (*0-915775-05-0*) Love Song Mess Assn.

— Righteous Rhymes, Vol. 1. (Illus.). 24p. (J). (gr. 2-7). 1983. pap. 2.95 (*0-915775-00-X*) Love Song Mess Assn.

— Roots & Fruits. 1987. reprint ed. pap. 3.00 (*0-915775-04-2*) Love Song Mess Assn.

Lash, Jamie S., ed. Righteous Rhymes, Vol. 2. (Illus.). 24p. (J). 1987. pap. 2.95 (*0-915775-01-8*) Love Song Mess Assn.

Lash, Jamie S., jt. auth. see Lash, Neil A.

Lash, Jeffrey N. Destroyer of the Iron Horse: General Joseph E. Johnston & Confederate Rail Transport, 1861-1865. LC 90-5372. (Illus.). 240p. 1991. 28.50x (*0-87338-423-7*) Kent St U Pr.

***Lash, John.** The Hero. LC 94-61395. (Art & Imagination Ser.). (Illus.). 96p. 1995. pap. 15.95 (*0-500-81047-8*) Thames Hudson.

— Seeker's Handbook: The Complete Guide to Spiritual Traditions. 1991. 25.00 (*0-517-57797-6*, Harmony) Crown Pub Group.

— Tai Chi Journey. 1990. pap. 13.95 (*1-85230-120-1*) Element MA.

— Twins & the Double. LC 93-60203. (Art & Imagination Ser.). (Illus.). 96p. 1993. pap. 15.95 (*0-500-81042-7*) Thames Hudson.

Lash, John D. Cowboy Stories from East Texas. LC 90-28880. (Illus.). 80p. (J). (gr. 1-4). 1991. reprint ed. lib. bdg. 14.95 (*0-937460-66-4*) Hendrick-Long.

Lash, Joseph P. Dag Hammarskjold, Custodian of the Brushfire Peace. LC 73-22637. 304p. (C). 1974. reprint ed. text ed. 59.75 (*0-8371-6995-X*, LADJ, Greenwood Pr) Greenwood.

— Eleanor: The Years Alone. (Illus.). 368p. 1972. 14.95 (*0-393-07361-0*) Norton.

— Eleanor & Franklin. 1024p. (YA). (gr. 10). 1973. pap. 5.95 (*0-451-14076-1*, AE1231, Sig) NAL-Dutton.

— Helen & Teacher: The Story of Helen Keller & Anne Sullivan Macy. LC 79-25599. 879p. 1980. 19.95 (*0-89128-234-3*) Am Foun Blind.

Lash, Kenneth. A Lot for the Money. 116p. 1982. pap. 6.95 (*0-915996-09-X*) North Am Rev.

Lash, Linda. Complete Guide to Customer Service. (Training & Development Ser.). 1989. text ed. 37.50 (*0-471-62428-4*) Wiley.

Lash, Maryann, jt. auth. see Brackett, Babette.

Lash, Michele, et al. My Kind of Family: A Book for Kids in Single-Parent Homes. LC 90-31471. (Illus.). 208p. (J). (ps-6). 1990. spiral bd., pap. 16.95 (*0-914525-12-3*); spiral bd. 16.95 (*0-914525-13-1*) Waterfront Bks.

Lash, Neil A. & Lash, Jamie S. Looking for Leaven. (Jewish Jewels Ser.: Vol. 1). (Illus.). 21p. (Orig.). 1985. pap. 1.50 (*0-915775-02-6*) Love Song Mess Assn.

Lash, Nicholas. Believing Three Ways in One God: A Reading of the Apostles' Creed. LC 92-33909. (C). 1993. text ed. 21.95 (*0-268-00691-1*) U of Notre Dame Pr.

— Believing Three Ways in One God: A Reading of the Apostles' Creed. LC 92-33903. (C). 1993. pap. text ed. 12.95 (*0-268-00692-X*) U of Notre Dame Pr.

— Easter in Ordinary: Reflections on Human Experience & the Knowledge of God. LC 87-23738. 313p. (C). 1990. reprint ed. pap. text ed. 12.95 (*0-268-00926-0*) U of Notre Dame Pr.

— Theology on the Way to Emmaus. 256p. (C). 1986. pap. text ed. 18.95 (*0-334-02352-1*, SCM Pr) TPI PA.

Lash, Nicholas A. Banking Laws & Regulations: An Economic Perspective. (Illus.). 176p. (C). 1987. pap. text ed. 53.00 (*0-13-055609-2*) P-H.

Lash, Robert. Practice Questions & Solutions Based on Formwork for Concrete Structures (Tables Only) for Florida Contractor's Tests. 62p. 1977. pap. 7.00 (*0-935715-08-8*, 0477) Construct Bkstore.

Lash, Scott. The Militant Worker: Class & Radicalism in France & America. LC 83-25366. 260p. 1984. 36.50 (*0-8386-3224-6*) Fairleigh Dickinson.

— Post-Structuralist & Post-Modernist Sociology. (Schools of Thought in Sociology Ser.: No. 9). 480p. 1991. text ed. 159.95 (*1-85278-183-1*, Pub. by E Elgar Pub UK) Ashgate Pub Co.

— The Sociology of Postmodernism. (International Library of Sociology). 256p. 1990. 52.50 (*0-415-04784-6*, A4159); pap. 14.95 (*0-415-04785-4*, A4163) Routledge.

Lash, Scott & Friedman, Jonathan, eds. Modernity & Identity. 320p. (C). 1991. text ed. 64.95 (*0-631-17585-7*); pap. 21.95 (*0-631-17586-5*) Blackwell Pubs.

Lash, Scott & Urry, John. Economies of Signs & Space. (Theory, Culture & Society Ser.). 384p. (C). 1994. text ed. 69.95 (*0-8039-8471-5*); pap. text ed. 24.95 (*0-8039-8472-3*) Sage.

— The End of Organized Capitalism. LC 87-40366. 360p. (C). 1987. text ed. 45.00 (*0-299-11670-0*); pap. text ed. 17.50 (*0-299-11674-3*) U of Wis Pr.

Lash, Scott, jt. ed. see Whimster, Sam.

Lashbrook, Greg, jt. auth. see Johnson, Kathy.

Lashbrook, Marilyn. Alguien a Quien Amar (Creacion) Orig. Title: Someone to Love. 32p. (SPA.). 1994. pap. 3.25 (*0-8254-1427-X*) Kregel.

— Aunque Soy Pequeno (David) Orig. Title: I May Be Little. 32p. (SPA.). 1994. pap. 3.50 (*0-8254-1428-8*) Kregel.

— The Best Day Ever: The Story of Jesus. LC 90-63764. (Me Too! Readers Ser.). (Illus.). (J). (gr. k-3). 1991. 5.95 (*0-86606-444-3*, 875) Roper Pr.

— De Dos en Dos (Noe) Orig. Title: Two by Two. 32p. (SPA.). 1994. pap. 3.50 (*0-8254-1429-6*) Kregel.

— Digging for Buried Treasure. (Illus.). 12p. (J). (gr. k-6). 1984. pap. text ed. 4.25 (*1-55976-141-5*) CEF Press.

— Don't Rock the Boat: The Story of the Miraculous Catch. LC 88-63779. (Me Too! Bks.). (Illus.). 32p. (J). (ps). 1989. 5.95 (*0-86606-435-4*, 867) Roper Pr.

— Don't Stop...Fill Every Pot: The Story of the Widow's Oil. LC 93-86766. (Me Too! Bks.). (Illus.). 32p. (J). (ps). 1995. 5.95 (*0-86606-451-6*, 879) Roper Pr.

— Echa la Red! 32p. (SPA.). 1995. pap. 3.50 (*0-8254-1440-7*) Kregel.

— En la Rama de un Arbol (Zaqueo) 32p. (SPA.). 1995. pap. 3.50 (*0-8254-1441-5*) Kregel.

— Get Lost, Little Brother: The Story of Joseph. LC 87-62503. (Me Too! Bks.). (Illus.). 32p. (J). (ps). 1988. 5.95 (*0-86606-432-X*, 863) Roper Pr.

— God, Please Send Fire: Elijah & the Prophets of Baal. LC 90-60458. (Me Too! Readers Ser.). (Illus.). 32p. (J). (gr. k-3). 1990. 5.95 (*0-86606-440-0*, 871) Roper Pr.

— God Speaks to Me. (Illus.). 52p. (J). (gr. k-6). 1985. pap. text ed. 8.99 (*1-55976-030-3*) CEF Press.

— God's Happy Helpers: The Story of Tabitha & Friends. LC 94-66751. (Me Too! Bks.). (Illus.). 32p. (J). 1995. 5.95 (*0-86606-453-2*, 881) Roper Pr.

— Good, Better, Best: The Story of Mary & Martha. LC 94-66483. (Me Too! Bks.). (Illus.). (J). 1995. 5.95 (*0-86606-452-4*, 880) Roper Pr.

— The Great Shake-Up: Miracles at Philippi. LC 90-63768. (Me Too! Readers Ser.). (Illus.). 32p. (J). (gr. k-3). 1991. 5.95 (*0-86606-445-1*, 876) Roper Pr.

— Handcrafts Without Headaches. LC 86-61420. 96p. 1986. pap. 6.95 (*0-86606-425-7*, 831) Roper Pr.

— I Don't Want to: The Story of Jonah. LC 87-60264. (Me Too! Bks.). (Illus.). 32p. (J). (ps). 1987. 5.95 (*0-86606-428-1*, 844) Roper Pr.

— I May be Little: The Story of David's Growth. LC 87-60262. (Me Too! Bks.). (Illus.). 32p. (J). (ps). 1987. 5.95 (*0-86606-429-X*, 843) Roper Pr.

— I'll Pray Anyway: The Story of Daniel. LC 87-63502. (Me Too! Bks.). (Illus.). 32p. (J). (ps). 1988. 5.95 (*0-86606-430-3*, 861) Roper Pr.

— It's Not My Fault: Man's Big Mistake. LC 90-60459. (Me Too! Readers Ser.). (Illus.). 32p. (J). (gr. k-3). 1990. 5.95 (*0-86606-439-7*, 870) Roper Pr.

— El Muro Que No Se Cayo (Rahab) Orig. Title: Wall That Did Not Fall (Rahab). 32p. (SPA.). 1988. pap. 3.50 (*0-8254-1430-X*) Kregel.

— No Habla Arbol de Navidad (Cristo) Orig. Title: No Tree for Christmas. 32p. (SPA.). 1994. pap. 3.50 (*0-8254-1437-7*) Kregel.

— No Les Hizo Falta Un Barco (Moises) Orig. Title: Who Needs a Boat? (Moses). 32p. (SPA.). 1988. pap. 3.50 (*0-8254-1431-8*) Kregel.

— No Quiero (Jonas) Orig. Title: I Don't Want To. 32p. (SPA.). 1994. pap. 3.50 (*0-8254-1432-6*) Kregel.

— No Te Queremos Ver Mas, Hermanito (Jose) Orig. Title: Get Lost, Little Brother (Joseph). 32p. (SPA.). 1988. pap. 3.50 (*0-8254-1433-4*) Kregel.

— No Tree for Christmas: The Story of Jesus' Birth. LC 88-62025. (Me Too! Bks.). (Illus.). 32p. (J). (ps). 1989. 5.95 (*0-86606-434-6*, 866) Roper Pr.

— Nothing to Fear: Jesus Walks on Water. LC 90-61060. (Me Too! Readers Ser.). (Illus.). 32p. (J). (gr. k-3). 1991. 5.95 (*0-86606-443-5*, 874) Roper Pr.

— Now I See: The Story of the Man Born Blind. LC 88-62520. (Me Too! Bks.). (Illus.). 32p. (J). (ps). 1989. 5.95 (*0-86606-437-0*, 869) Roper Pr.

— Out on a Limb: The Story of Zacchaeus. LC 88-63782. (Me Too! Bks.). (Illus.). 32p. (J). (ps). 1989. 5.95 (*0-86606-436-2*, 868) Roper Pr.

— Puedo Ver (Ciego) Orig. Title: Now I See. 32p. (SPA.). 1994. pap. 3.50 (*0-8254-1439-3*) Kregel.

— Someone to Love: The Story of Creation. LC 87-60261. (Me Too! Bks.). (Illus.). 32p. (J). (ps). 1987. 5.95 (*0-86606-426-5*, 841) Roper Pr.

— Sowing & Growing: The Parable of the Sower & the Soils. LC 93-86767. (Me Too! Bks.). (Illus.). 32p. (J). (ps). 1995. 5.95 (*0-86606-450-8*, 878) Roper Pr.

— Too Bad, Ahab! Naboth's Vineyard. LC 90-60457. (Me Too! Readers Ser.). (Illus.). 32p. (J). (gr. k-3). 1990. 5.95 (*0-86606-441-9*, 872) Roper Pr.

— Two by Two: The Story of Noah's Faith. LC 87-60263. (Me Too! Bks.). (Illus.). 32p. (J). (ps). 1987. 5.95 (*0-86606-427-3*, 842) Roper Pr.

— Two Lads & a Dad: The Prodigal Son. LC 90-63769. (Me Too! Readers Ser.). (Illus.). (J). (gr. k-3). 1991. 5.95 (*0-86606-446-X*, 877) Roper Pr.

— The Wall That Did Not Fall: The Story of Rahab's Faith. LC 87-63420. (Me Too! Bks.). (Illus.). 32p. (J). (ps). 1988. 5.95 (*0-86606-433-8*, 864) Roper Pr.

— The Weak Strongman: Samson. LC 90-60456. (Me Too! Readers Ser.). (Illus.). 32p. (J). (gr. k-3). 1990. 5.95 (*0-86606-442-7*, 873) Roper Pr.

— Who Needs a Boat? The Story of Moses. LC 87-83295. (Me Too! Bks.). (Illus.). 32p. (J). (ps). 1988. 5.95 (*0-86606-431-1*, 862) Roper Pr.

— Yo Igual Voy a Orar (Daniel) Orig. Title: I'll Pray Anyway (Daniel). 32p. (SPA.). 1988. pap. 3.50 (*0-8254-1435-0*) Kregel.

Lashbrooke, E. C., Jr. Tax-Exempt Organizations. LC 84-22253. xi, 364p. 1985. text ed. 69.50 (*0-89930-083-9*, LTE/, Quorum Bks) Greenwood.

Lashbrooke, E. C., Jr. & Swygert, Michael I. The Legal Handbook of Business Transactions: A Guide for Managers & Entrepreneurs. LC 86-30595. 599p. 1987. text ed. 95.00 (*0-89930-179-7*, LLH/, Quorum Bks) Greenwood.

Lasher, Lawrence, ed. Conversations with Bernard Malamud. LC 90-49374. (Literary Conversations Ser.). 1991. 37.50 (*0-87805-489-8*); pap. 15.95 (*0-87805-490-1*) U Pr of Miss.

Lasher, Marcia. Scrap Quilt, Strips & Spider Webs. (Illus.). 64p. 1991. 8.95 (*0-922705-26-7*) Quilt Day.

Lasher, Margot. The Art & Practice of Compassion & Empathy. 224p. (Orig.). 1992. pap. 11.95 (*0-87477-710-0*) J P Tarcher.

Lasher, William & Hausman, Carl. Small Business Franchise Made Simple. LC 93-6709. 1994. pap. 12.00 (*0-385-42552-X*) Doubleday.

Lasher, William R. The Perfect Business Plan Made Simple. LC 93-35669. 1994. pap. 12.00 (*0-385-46934-9*) Doubleday.

***Lashgari, Deirdre, ed.** Violence, Silence, & Anger: Women's Writing As Transgression. 384p. (C). 1995. pap. text ed. 19.95 (*0-8139-1493-0*) U Pr of Va.

***Lashgari, Dierdre, ed.** Violence, Silence, & Anger: Women's Writing As Transgression. 384p. (C). 1995. text ed. 55.00 (*0-8139-1492-2*) U Pr of Va.

***Lashier, Kathleen.** Dad, Share Your Life with Me... (Memory-a-Day Ser.). 366p. (Orig.). 1992. pap. 8.95 (*1-56383-040-X*, 5054) G & R Pub.

— Grandma, Tell Me Your Memories... (Memory-a-Day Ser.). 366p. (Orig.). 1992. pap. 8.95 (*1-56383-037-X*, 5051) G & R Pub.

— Grandpa, Tell Me Your Memories... (Memory-a-Day Ser.). 366p. (Orig.). 1992. pap. 8.95 (*1-56383-038-8*, 5052) G & R Pub.

— Mom, Share Your Life with Me... (Memory-a-Day Ser.). 366p. (Orig.). 1992. pap. 8.95 (*1-56383-039-6*, 5053) G & R Pub.

Lashings, Edwina G. Chocolate & Chortles. 64p. (Orig.). 1975. pap. 2.95 (*0-938758-02-0*) MTM Pub Co.

Lashinsky, Herbert, tr. see Leontovich, M. A., ed.

***Lashley, Conrad.** Improving Study Skills: A Competence Approach. LC 95-14759. 1995. write for info. (*0-304-33336-0*) Cassell.

Lashley, Cynthia. Taking the "Sigh" Out of Science: A Handbook for Teachers & Parents of Young Children. (Illus.). 60p. (Orig.). 1992. spiral bd., pap. 7.95 (*0-9623249-6-5*) Intermountain.

Lashley, Marilyn. Public Television: Panacea, Pork Barrel, or Public Trust? LC 91-34482. (Contributions to the Study of Mass Media & Communications Ser.: No. 33). 176p. 1992. text ed. 42.95 (*0-313-27964-0*, LPT/, Greenwood Pr) Greenwood.

Lashley, Marilyn E. & Jackson, Melanie N., eds. African Americans & the New Policy Consensus: Retreat of the Liberal State? LC 94-872. (Contributions in Political Science Ser.: No. 347). 264p. 1994. text ed. 55.00 (*0-313-28880-1*, Greenwood Pr) Greenwood.

Lashley, Mary E., et al. Being Called to Care. LC 93-7296. 215p. 1994. 59.50 (*0-7914-1839-1*); pap. 19.95 (*0-7914-1840-5*) State U NY Pr.

***Lashley, Rickey D.** Policework: The Need for a Noble Character. LC 94-32921. 144p. 1995. text ed. 49.95 (*0-275-95013-1*, Praeger Pubs) Greenwood.

Lashman, Rebekah, jt. auth. see McCarthy, Karin.

Lashmore-Davies, C. N., jt. auth. see Manheimer, W. M.

***Lashner, William.** Hostile Witness: A Novel. 1995. 23.00 (*0-06-039146-4*) HarpC.

Lashof, Daniel & Tirpak, Dennis A. Policy Options for Stabilizing Global Climate. 825p. 1990. 115.00 (*1-56032-072-9*) Hemisp Pub.

Lasic, D. D. Liposomes: From Physics to Applications. LC 92-49031. 1993. 271.50 (*0-444-89548-5*) Elsevier.

***Lasic, D. D. & Martin, F. J., eds.** Stealth Liposomes. LC 94-32683. (Pharmacology & Toxicology Ser.). 1995. write for info. (*0-8493-8383-8*) CRC Pr.

Lasic, Vinko D. Pleterni Ukras Od Najstarijih Vremena Do Danas. Njegov Likovni Oblik I Znacenje, Supplement: The Principal Conclusions of this Research, the Twist or Guilloche as Ornament from Ancient or Guilloche as Ornament from Ancient Times to the Present, Its Exterior Form & Innter Meaning. Condic, Dusko, tr. 920p. (CRO.). Date not set. write for info. (*1-880829-02-9*) Z I R A L.

Lasiecka, I. & Triggiani, R. Differential & Algebraic Equations with Application to Boundary-Point Control Problems: Continuous Theory & Approximation Theory. Thoma, M. & Wyner, A., eds. (Lecture Notes in Control & Information Sciences Ser.: Vol. 164). 171p. 1991. pap. 33.00 (*0-387-54339-2*) Spr-Verlag.

Lasiecka, I. & Triggiani, R., eds. Control Problems for Systems Described by Partial Differential Equation & Applications. (Lecture Notes in Control & Information Sciences Ser.: Vol. 97). 400p. 1987. pap. 73.00 (*0-387-18054-0*) Spr-Verlag.

Lasiecka, I., jt. ed. see Kurzhanski, Alexander B.

Lasilla, Dennis R. & Kilpatrick, Bob G. Compensation Tax Guide. 2nd ed. 504p. Date not set. pap. 39.50 (*0-8080-0008-X*) Commerce.

Lasinski, Thomas, jt. auth. see Levi-Setti, Riccardo.

Lasio. Professor Lasio's The Office Passalong: Round Tuits & Other Silliness. Sharp, F. J., ed. LC 91-71394. (Illus.). 50p. 1991. 5.00 (*0-9629202-0-7*) Co Called W.

Lasjaunias, P. & Berenstein, A. Surgical Neuroangiography, Vol. 1. (Functional Anatomy of Craniofacial Arteries Ser.). (Illus.). 450p. 1994. 199.00 (*0-387-16534-7*) Spr-Verlag.

— Surgical Neuroangiography, Vol. 2. (Endovascular Treatment of Craniofacial Lesions Ser.). (Illus.). 450p. 1987. 199.00 (*0-387-16535-5*) Spr-Verlag.

Lasjaunias, P., jt. auth. see Berenstein, A.

Lasjaunias, P., et al, eds. Frontiers in European Radiology, Vol. 4. (Illus.). 165p. 1984. 62.20 (*0-387-13410-7*) Spr-Verlag.

Lask, Bryan F. Childhood Illness: The Psychosomatic Approach. 1989. text ed. 103.00 (*0-471-91821-0*) Wiley.

Lask, Bryan F. & Fosson, Abe. Childhood Illness the Psychosomatic Approach: Children Talking with Their Bodies. 156p. 1993. pap. text ed. 29.95 (*0-471-91822-9*) Wiley.

Lask, Gary P. & Moy, Ronald L. Principles & Techniques of Cutaneous Surgery. 608p. 1995. text ed. 150.00 (*0-07-036471-0*) Hlth Prof Div.

Lask, I. M., tr. see Ben-Amos, Dan, et al, eds.

Laska, Eugene M., et al, eds. Information Support to Mental Health Programs: An International Perspective. 301p. 1983. 40.95 (*0-89885-083-5*) Human Sci Pr.

***Laska, John A. & Juarez, Tina.** Grading & Marking in American Schools: Two Centuries of Debate. LC 92-5612. 162p. 1992. pap. 19.95 (*0-398-06223-4*) C C Thomas.

— Grading & Marking in American Schools: Two Centuries of Debate. LC 92-5612. 162p. (C). 1992. text ed. 36.95x (*0-398-05806-7*) C C Thomas.

Laska, John A., jt. auth. see Gillett, Margaret.

Laska, Lewis L. Tennessee Legal Research Handbook. LC 77-71305. x, 203p. 1977. lib. bdg. 36.00 (*0-930342-04-6*, 300860); pap. 25.00 (*0-89941-264-5*) W S Hein.

— The Tennessee State Constitution: A Reference Guide. LC 90-32454. (Reference Guides to the State Constitutions of the United States Ser.: No. 2). 216p. 1990. text ed. 59.95 (*0-313-26653-0*, LTO/, Greenwood Pr) Greenwood.

Laska, P. J. The Day the Eighties Began. LC 91-71452. 62p. (Orig.). 1991. pap. 8.00 (*0-9627891-1-9*) Igneus Pr.

Laska, Richard, jt. auth. see Paller, Alan.

Laska, Shirley. Floodproof Retrofitting: Homeowner Self-Help Behavior. (Monograph: No. 49). 280p. (Orig.). 1991. pap. 10.00 (*1-877943-04-5*) Natural Hazards.

Laska, Shirley & Puffer, Andrew, eds. Coastlines of the Gulf of Mexico. LC 93-14140. (Coastlines of the World Ser.). 1993. write for info. (*0-87262-960-0*) Am Soc Civil Eng.

Laska, Vera. Nazism Resistance & Holocaust in World War II: A Bibliography. LC 84-23586. 205p. 1985. 20.00 (*0-8108-1771-3*) Scarecrow.

Laska, Vera, ed. Women in the Resistance & in the Holocaust: The Voices of Eyewitnesses. LC 82-12018. (Contributions in Women's Studies: No. 37). xv, 330p. 1983. text ed. 55.00 (*0-313-23457-4*, LWH/, Greenwood Pr) Greenwood.

Laskar, A. L., et al, eds. Diffusion in Materials. (C). 1990. lib. bdg. 215.00 (*0-7923-0653-8*) Kluwer Ac.

— Diffusion in Solids. (Material Science Forum Ser.: Vol. 1). 290p. (C). 1984. pap. text ed. 78.00 (*0-87849-533-9*, Pub. by Trans Tech GW) LPS Dist Ctr.

Laskar, Amulya & Chandra, Suresh, eds. Superionic Solids & Solid Electrolytes: Recent Trends. (Materials Science & Technology Ser.). 711p. 1989. text ed. 132.00 (*0-12-437075-6*) Acad Pr.

Laskar, R. C., jt. ed. see Hedetniemi, S. T.

***Laskaris, George.** Color Atlas of Oral Diseases. 2nd ed. LC 94-9767. (Illus.). 400p. Date not set. 99.00 (*0-614-02693-8*) Thieme Med Pubs.

Laskaris, Vasilia, jt. auth. see Vaporis, Nomikos M.

Laske, R., jt. auth. see Franey, P.

Lasker, Albert D. The Lasker Story. 128p. 1987. 11.95 (*0-8442-3099-5*, NTC Busn Bks) NTC Pub Grp.

Lasker, Bruno. Filipino Immigration to the Continental United States & to Hawaii. LC 69-18783. (American Immigration Collection Ser., No. 1). (Illus.). 1976. reprint ed. 26.95 (*0-405-00531-8*) Ayer.

— Human Bondage in Southeast Asia. LC 79-138155. 406p. (C). 1972. reprint ed. lib. bdg. 26.00 (*0-8371-5612-2*, LAHU, Greenwood Pr) Greenwood.

— Peoples of Southeast Asia. LC 74-161765. (Institute of Pacific Relations Ser.). reprint ed. 30.00 (*0-404-09029-X*) AMS Pr.

Lasker, Bruno & Roman, Agnes. Propaganda from China & Japan: A Case Study in Propaganda Analysis. LC 75-30126. (Institute of Pacific Relations Ser.). reprint ed. 22.00 (*0-404-59537-5*) AMS Pr.

Lasker, Carrol, tr. see Small, Adam.

Lasker, D. J. Jewish Philosophical Polemics Against Christianity in the Middle Ages. 29.50 (*0-87068-498-1*) Ktav.

Lasker, Daniel J. Jewish Philosophical Polemics Against Christianity in the Middle Ages. 320p. 15.00 (*0-686-95177-8*) ADL.

Lasker, Daniel J., tr. see Crescas, Hasdai.

Lasker, Edward. Chess for Fun & Chess for Blood. 2nd ed. (Illus.). 1942. pap. 5.95 (*0-486-20146-5*) Dover.

An Asterisk (*) at the beginning of an entry indicates that the title is appearing in BIP for the first time.

— Chess Strategy. Du Mont, J., tr. (Illus.). 1959. pap. 5.95 (*0-486-20528-2*) Dover.

— Go & Go Moku. (Illus.). 1960. pap. 5.95 (*0-486-20613-0*) Dover.

— Modern Chess Strategy. rev. ed. 1979. 13.00 (*0-679-14022-0*, 9, Tarten) McKay.

Lasker, Emanual. Lasker's Chess Manual. (Illus.). 352p. 1992. reprint ed. 22.95 (*0-7134-6955-2*, Pub. by Batsford UK) Trafalgar.

Lasker, Emanuel. Common Sense in Chess. 1965. pap. 3.95 (*0-486-21440-0*) Dover.

— The Community of the Future. 1976. lib. bdg. 59.95 (*0-8490-1650-9*) Gordon Pr.

— Lasker's Manual of Chess. (YA). (gr. 7-12). pap. 6.95 (*0-486-20640-8*) Dover.

Lasker, G., jt. ed. see Mascie-Taylor, C. G.

Lasker, G. W. & Mascie-Taylor, C. G., eds. Atlas of British Surnames. LC 89-70574. 96p. 1990. pap. 14.95 (*0-8143-2253-0*) Wayne St U Pr.

Lasker, Gabriel W. Surnames & Genetic Structure. (Cambridge Studies in Biological Anthropology). 150p. 1985. 37.95 (*0-521-30285-4*) Cambridge U Pr.

Lasker, Gabriel W., ed. The Processes of Ongoing Human Evolution. LC 60-12566. 113p. reprint ed. pap. 32.30 (*0-7837-3783-1*, 2043602) Bks Demand.

Lasker, Gabriel W. & Mascie-Taylor, C. G., eds. Research Strategies in Human Biology: Field & Survey Studies. (Studies in Biological Anthropology: No. 14). (Illus.). 200p. (C). 1993. 64.95 (*0-521-43188-3*) Cambridge U Pr.

Lasker, Gabriel W. & Tyzzer, Robert N. Physical Anthropology. 3rd ed. (C). 1982. text ed. 44.75 (*0-03-047551-1*) HB Coll Pubs.

Lasker, Gabriel W., jt. ed. see Mascie-Taylor, C. G.

Lasker, George E. The Relation Between Major World Problems & Systems Learning: Proceedings of the Society for General Systems Research, 1983, Set, Vols. 1 & 2. 800p. 1983. Set. pap. text ed. 66.00 (*0-914105-28-0*) Intersystems Pubns.

Lasker, J., jt. auth. see Wallace, B.

Lasker, Joe. The Great Alexander the Great. (J). (ps-3). 1990. pap. 3.95 (*0-14-054318-X*, Puffin) Puffin Bks.

— He's My Brother. LC 73-7318. (Albert Whitman Concept Bks.). (Illus.). 40p. (J). (gr. 1-3). 1974. lib. bdg. 13.95 (*0-8075-3218-5*) A Whitman.

— Mothers Can Do Anything. LC 72-83684. (Albert Whitman Concept Bks.). (Illus.). 40p. (J). (gr. k-2). 1972. lib. bdg. 13.95 (*0-8075-5287-9*) A Whitman.

— Nick Joins In. Tucker, Kathleen, ed. LC 79-29637. (Albert Whitman Concept Bks.: Level 1). (Illus.). 32p. (J). (gr. 1-3). 1980. lib. bdg. 13.95 (*0-8075-5612-2*) A Whitman.

— Tournament of Knights. LC 85-48075. (Illus.). 32p. (J). (gr. 3 up). 1986. lib. bdg. 14.89 (*0-690-04542-5*, Crowell Jr Bks) HarpC Child Bks.

— A Tournament of Knights. LC 85-48075. (Trophy Picture Bk.). (Illus.). 32p. (J). (gr. 3 up). 1989. reprint ed. pap. 5.95 (*0-06-443192-4*, Trophy) HarpC Child Bks.

Lasker, Judith & Borg, Susan. In Search of Parenthood: Coping with Infertility & High-Tech Conception. LC 86-47863. 346p. reprint ed. pap. 98.70 (*0-7837-1384-3*, 2041560) Bks Demand.

Lasker, Judith N. & Borg, Susan. In Search of Parenthood: Coping with Infertility & High-Tech Conception. enl. rev. ed. LC 94-12494. 1994. lib. bdg. 44.95 (*1-56639-258-6*) Temple U Pr.

— In Search of Parenthood: Coping with Infertility & High-Tech Conception. rev. ed. LC 94-12494. 1995. pap. text ed. 18.95 (*1-56639-259-4*) Temple U Pr.

Lasker-Schuler, Else. Concert - Konzert: Das Konzert. Snook, Jean M., tr. LC 93-45427. (European Women Writers Ser.). xvi, 164p. 1994. text ed. 25.00 (*0-8032-2900-3*) U of Nebr Pr.

— Your Diamond Dreams Cut Open My Arteries: Poems by Else Lasker-Schuler. LC 82-2656. (Germanic Languages & Literatures Ser.: No. 100). ix, 317p. 1983. 30.00 (*0-8078-8100-7*) U of NC Pr.

Laskey, Carolyn T. Nurturing the Nurse on the Path to Success. Rezvan, Jerena B., ed. 210p. (Orig.). 1994. pap. 16.95 (*1-880254-11-5*) Vista.

***Laskey, Carolyn T. & Hutchings, Patty.** Poetry to Heal Your Inner Self. 136p. (Orig.). 1994. pap. 9.95 (*1-880254-29-8*) Vista.

Laskey, R. A., jt. ed. see Friday, L. E.

Laski, H. J., ed. see Laski, Harold J., et al.

Laski, Harold. The American Presidency. LC 80-50104. (Social Science Classics Ser.). 278p. 1980. 34.95 (*0-87855-390-8*); pap. 18.95 (*0-87855-821-7*) Transaction Pubs.

Laski, Harold J. American Democracy: A Commentary & an Interpretation. LC 74-122066. 1974. reprint ed. 57.50 (*0-678-03165-7*) Kelley.

— Danger of Being a Gentleman: And Other Essays. LC 72-1154. (Essay Index Reprint Ser.). 1977. reprint ed. 20.95 (*0-8369-2849-0*) Ayer.

— Democracy in Crisis. LC 70-97892. reprint ed. 19.25 (*0-404-03882-4*) AMS Pr.

— Dilemma of Our Times: An Historical Essay. LC 68-14930. 1968. reprint ed. 37.50 (*0-678-05062-7*) Kelley.

— Faith, Reason & Civilization: An Essay in Historical Analysis. LC 74-167375. (Essay Index Reprint Ser.). 1977. reprint ed. 18.95 (*0-8369-2662-5*) Ayer.

— Foundations of Sovereignty, & Other Essays. LC 68-22105. (Essay Index Reprint Ser.). 1977. 20.95 (*0-8369-0607-1*) Ayer.

— Liberty in the Modern State. rev. ed. LC 77-122064. 1972. reprint ed. 29.50 (*0-678-03166-5*) Kelley.

— Reflections on the Revolution of Our Time. 367p. 1968. reprint ed. 25.00 (*0-7146-1564-1*, Pub. by F Cass Pubs UK) Intl Spec Bk.

— Reflections on the Revolution of Our Times. LC 68-14931. 1968. reprint ed. 39.50 (*0-678-05063-5*) Kelley.

— The Rise of European Liberalism: An Essay in Interpretation. LC 83-45444. reprint ed. 31.50 (*0-404-20152-0*) AMS Pr.

— State in Theory & Practice. 336p. 1967. 49.50x (*0-614-01806-4*) Elliots Bks.

— Studies in Law & Politics. LC 68-22106. (Essay Index Reprint Ser.). 1977. 20.95 (*0-8369-0608-X*) Ayer.

Laski, Harold J., et al. A Century of Municipal Progress, 1835-1935. Laski, H. J. et al, eds. LC 75-41171. reprint ed. 29.50 (*0-685-14561-1*) AMS Pr.

— A Century of Municipal Progress, 1835-1935: From Self-Government to National Sovereignty. Laski, H. J. & Jennings, W. Ivor, eds. LC 75-41171. reprint ed. 45.00 (*0-404-14561-2*) AMS Pr.

Laski, Harold J., et al, eds. A Century of Municipal Progress, 1835-1935. LC 77-27362. 511p. 1978. reprint ed. text ed. 75.00 (*0-313-20192-7*, LACE, Greenwood Pr) Greenwood.

Laski, Kazimiera, jt. auth. see Brus, Wlodzimierz.

Laski, Marghanita. George Eliot. LC 86-51198. (Literary Lives Ser.). (Illus.). 128p. 1987. reprint ed. pap. 9.95 (*0-500-26023-0*) Thames Hudson.

— The Victorian Chaise Longue. 119p. 1984. pap. 5.00 (*0-89733-097-8*) Academy Chi Pubs.

Laskier, Michael M. The Alliance Israelite Universelle & the Jewish Communities of Morocco, 1862-1962. LC 82-5892. (Modern Jewish History Ser.). 384p. 1984. 64.50 (*0-87395-656-7*); pap. 21.95 (*0-87395-655-9*) State U NY Pr.

— The Jews of Egypt, 1920-1970: In the Midst of Zionism, Anti-Semitism, & the Middle East Conflict. 350p. 1991. text ed. 55.00x (*0-8147-5058-3*); pap. 18.50 (*0-8147-5078-8*) NYU Pr.

— North African Jewry in the Twentieth Century: The Jews of Morocco, Tunisia, & Algeria. LC 93-28377. 1994. 50.00 (*0-8147-5072-9*) NYU Pr.

Laskin. Billy Budd & Typee (Melville) (Book Notes Ser.). (C). 1984. pap. 2.50 (*0-8120-3404-X*) Barron.

Laskin, jt. auth. see Sarnet.

Laskin, A. & Lechevalier, H. Handbook of Microbiology, 2 vols., Set. 2nd ed. LC 77-12460. 1981. 888.00 (*0-8493-7200-3*) CRC Pr.

— Microbiak Composition Amino Acids, Proteins & Nucleic Acids. 2nd ed. LC 77-12460. (Handbook of Microbiology Ser.: Vol. 3). 1981. 146.00 (*0-8493-7203-8*) CRC Pr.

Laskin, Allan I. & Lechevalier, Hubert, eds. Handbook of Microbiology, Vol. VII. 2nd ed. 624p. 1984. 152.95 (*0-8493-7207-0*, QR6, CRC Reprint) Franklin.

Laskin, Allen, jt. ed. see Sandford, Paul A.

Laskin, Allen I., ed. Advances in Applied Microbiology, Vol. 29. (Serial Publication Ser.). 1983. text ed. 151.00 (*0-12-002629-5*) Acad Pr.

— Advances in Applied Microbiology, Vol. 32. (Serial Publication Ser.). 214p. 1987. text ed. 104.00 (*0-12-002632-5*) Acad Pr.

— Advances in Applied Microbiology, Vol. 33. (Serial Publication Ser.). 368p. 1988. text ed. 104.00 (*0-12-002633-3*) Acad Pr.

— Enzymes & Immobilized Cells in Biotechnology. (Biotechnology Ser.). 317p. 1985. text ed. 28.00 (*0-8053-6360-2*) Buttrwrth-Heinemann.

Laskin, Allen I. & Last, Jerold A., eds. Nucleic Acid Biosynthesis. LC 72-89529. (Methods in Molecular Biology Ser.: No. 4). (Illus.). 288p. reprint ed. pap. 82.10 (*0-7837-0781-9*, 2041095) Bks Demand.

Laskin, Allen I. & Lechevalier, Hubert. Handbook of Microbiology: Fungi, Algae, Protozoa & Viruses, Vol. II. 2nd ed. 888p. 1979. 151.95 (*0-8493-7202-X*, QR6, CRC Reprint) Franklin.

Laskin, Allen I. & Lechevalier, Hubert, eds. Handbook of Microbiology, Vol. V. 2nd ed. 936p. 1984. 185.95 (*0-8493-7205-4*, QR6, CRC Reprint) Franklin.

— Handbook of Microbiology, Vol. IX, Pt. A. 2nd ed. 544p. 1988. Pt. A, 544p. 289.95 (*0-8493-7210-0*, QR6) CRC Pr.

— Handbook of Microbiology, Vol. IX, Pt. B. 2nd ed. 224p. 1988. Pt. B, 224p. 185.95 (*0-8493-7211-9*, QR6) CRC Pr.

— Handbook of Microbiology: Bacteria, Vol. I. 2nd ed. 770p. 1977. 394.00 (*0-8493-7201-1*, QR6, CRC Reprint) Franklin.

— Handbook of Microbiology: Growth & Metabolism, Vol. VI. 2nd ed. 392p. 1984. 130.95 (*0-8493-7206-2*, QR6, CRC Reprint) Franklin.

— Handbook of Microbiology: Microbial Composition: Amino Acids, Proteins & Nucleic Acids, Vol. III. 2nd ed. 1000p. 1987. 185.95 (*0-8493-7208-9*, QR6) CRC Pr.

— Handbook of Microbiology: Microbial Composition: Carbohydrates, Lipids & Minerals, Vol. IV. 2nd ed. 744p. 1982. 135.00 (*0-8493-7204-6*, QR6, CRC Reprint) Franklin.

— Handbook of Microbiology, CRC, Vol. 3: Microbial Metabolism, Genetics & Immunology. LC 72-88766. (Handbook Ser.). 800p. 1974. 53.95 (*0-87819-584-X*, CRC Reprint) Franklin.

Laskin, Allen I., ed. see Last, Jerold A.

Laskin, Allen I., jt. ed. see Last, Jerold A.

Laskin, Allen I., jt. auth. see Neidleman, Saul L.

Laskin, Allen I., jt. ed. see Neidleman, Saul L.

Laskin, Allen I., et al, eds. Enzyme Engineering, Vol. 8. (Annals Ser.: Vol. 501). (Illus.). 573p. 1987. 143.00 (*0-89766-397-7*) NY Acad Sci.

Laskin, Allen I., jt. ed. see Neidleman, Saul.

Laskin, Amy. Maximizing Your Mac. 1992. pap. 24.95 (*1-55828-244-0*) MIS Press.

Laskin, D. & O'Neill, K. Little Girl Book. Date not set. pap. write for info. (*0-345-38678-7*) Ballantine.

Laskin, David. Eastern Islands: Accessible Islands of the East Coast. LC 89-39390. (Illus.). 288p. reprint ed. pap. 82.10 (*0-7837-6692-0*, 2046309) Bks Demand.

— Parents Book of Child Safety. (Parents Magazine Childcare Ser.). 320p. (Orig.). 1991. mass mkt. 4.99 (*0-345-35104-5*) Ballantine.

— Parents Books for New Fathers. 448p. 1988. mass mkt. 4.95 (*0-345-33707-7*) Ballantine.

Laskin, David, ed. An Angel a Week. 1992. mass mkt. 4.00 (*0-345-38075-4*) Ballantine.

***Laskin, David & Hughes, Holly.** The Reading Group Companion: Starting & Sustaining a Book Discussion Group. LC 94-30200. 1995. write for info. (*0-452-27201-7*) Macmillan.

Laskin, David & Laskin, Kathleen O. The Little Girl Book. 304p. (Orig.). 1992. pap. 8.00 (*0-345-36802-9*, Ballantine Trade) Ballantine.

Laskin, Davis. Common Life: Four Generations of American Literary Friendship & Influence. LC 93-40588. 1994. 27.50 (*0-671-72419-3*) S&S Trade.

Laskin, Debra L., jt. ed. see Schook, Larence B.

Laskin, Emma, jt. auth. see Gardner, Howard.

Laskin, Kathleen O., jt. auth. see Laskin, David.

Laskin, Myron, Jr., ed. European & American Painting, Sculpture, & Decorative Arts in the National Gallery of Canada, Vol. I: 1300-1800. (Illus.). 475p. 1987. 97.50 (*0-226-56336-7*, Pub. by Natl Mus Sci Tech CN) U Ch Pr.

Laskin, Pamela L. & Moskowitz, Addie A. Wish upon a Star: A Story for Children with a Parent Who Is Mentally Ill. LC 91-211. (Illus.). 32p. (J). (ps-2). 1991. 16.95 (*0-945354-30-4*); pap. 8.95 (*0-945354-29-0*) Magination Pr.

Laskin, R. S., ed. Total Knee Replacement. (Illus.). xvi, 268p. 1991. 155.00 (*0-387-19644-7*) Spr-Verlag.

Laskin, Sidney & Goldstein, Bernard D., eds. Benzene Toxicity: A Critical Evaluation. LC 77-17128. 152p. reprint ed. pap. 43.40 (*0-8357-7133-4*, 2055329) Bks Demand.

Lasko-McCarthey, Peggy & Knopf, Karl. Adapted Physical Education for Adults with Disabilities. 3rd ed. (Illus.). 250p. 1992. pap. 29.95 (*0-945483-13-9*) E Bowers Pub.

Lasko, Patricia M. Take His Word. 1993. 12.95 (*0-533-10647-8*) Vantage.

Lasko, Paul F. Molecular Genetics of Drosophilia Oogenesis. (Molecular Biology Intelligence Unit Ser.). 118p. 1994. 89.95 (*1-57059-032-X*, LN9032) R G Landes.

Lasko, Peter. Ars Sacra, 800-1200. (Pelican History of Art Ser.). (Illus.). 320p. 1995. 65.00 (*0-300-06048-3*) Yale U Pr.

— Ars Sacra, 800-1200. 2nd ed. LC 93-28559. 1994. 55.00 (*0-300-05367-3*) Yale U Pr.

Laskow, Leonard. Healing with Love: A Breakthrough Mind - Body Medical Program for Healing Yourself & Others. LC 91-55293. (Illus.). 368p. 1992. pap. 14.00 (*0-06-250513-0*) Harper SF.

Laskowski, J., ed. Mineral Processing: Developments in Mineral Processing, 2 vols., Set. (Developments in Mineral Processing Ser.). 2116p. 1981. 323.00 (*0-444-99775-X*) Elsevier.

Laskowski, J. S., ed. Frothing in Flotation: A Volume in Honor of Jan Leja. (Mineral Processing & Extractive Metallury Review Ser.: Vol. 5). 340p. 1989. text ed. 79.00 (*2-88124-297-9*) Gordon & Breach.

Laskowski, Larry. Heinrich Schenker: An Annotated Index to His Analyses of Musical Works. LC 78-16997. (Annotated Reference Tools in Music Ser.: No. 1, Harmonologia). 1978. lib. bdg. 48.00 (*0-918728-06-1*) Pendragon NY.

Laskowski, Leonard J. Dynamic Presentation Skills for the Business Professional. 112p. 1994. pap. text ed., spiral bd. 12.95 (*0-8403-9141-2*) Kendall-Hunt.

Laskowski, Lester P., jt. auth. see Tocci, Ronald J.

Laskowski, William E., Jr. Rupert Brooke. LC 93-40510. (Twayne's English Authors Ser.: No. 504). 1994. lib. bdg. 22.95 (*0-8057-7025-9*, Twayne) Macmillan.

Lasky, Barry S., ed. The New Careers Directory: Internships & Professional Opportunities in Technology & Social Change. rev. ed. 325p. (Orig.). 1993. pap. 18.00 (*0-9639007-0-6*) Student Pugwash.

Lasky, Betty. RKO: The Biggest Little Major of Them All. (Illus.). 240p. 1984. pap. 9.95 (*0-13-781444-5*) P-H.

— RKO: The Biggest Little Major of Them All. LC 88-64132. 256p. 1989. pap. 16.95 (*0-915677-41-5*) Roundtable Pub.

***Lasky, Celeste. Resurrection of a Woman. 465p. (Orig.). 1995. pap. 6.99 (*0-9643331-0-4*) Write On Pubns. An AWARD-WINNING novel based on a true story of a woman in the 1880s. Because of her father's greed, Leah Cullen--already in love--is forced to marry another man & bear him children. She is trapped in a loveless & abusive marriage. Add to this situation deceit, adultery & murder & the reader is treated to a riveting story that is as timely today as the late evening news. Here is a story of one woman's strength & courage in the face of unbelievable obstacles. TESTIMONIALS: "Dutiful daughter, wife & mother, Leah maintains her dignity & cherishes a romance she believed lost. Desperate to survive, her brave determination yields surprising rewards...TWO thumbs up!!!" --Peter Jewell, KLOV radio. "I read Celeste Lasky's intriguing book, THE RESURRECTION OF A WOMAN, with interest & satisfaction. From the point of therapy & healing, THE RESURRECTION OF A WOMAN will be beneficial reading."--Leonard Urban, Family Therapist. ISBN 0-9643331-0-4, $6.99 U.S., $8.99 Can. Distributors: Ingram Book Company, Baker & Taylor & Publishers Distribution Center. Also available through Write On Publications, 4421 N. Franklin Ave., Loveland, CO 80538. (970) 669-5592 or (970) 663-6717. FAX: (970) 663-6891.** *Publisher Provided Annotation.*

Lasky, Herbert. Guidelines for Handling Psychiatric Issues in Workers' Compensation Cases. (Illus.). 406p. 1988. 55.00 (*0-318-42782-6*) Lex Com Enterprises.

— Psychiatric Claims in Worker's Compensation & Civil Actions, 2 vols., Vol. 2. LC 92-41684. (Personal Injury Library). 1993. Set. text ed. 228.00 (*0-471-58490-8*) Wiley.

Lasky, Jane. L. A. Woman. 240p. (Orig.). 1990. pap. 12.95 (*0-446-38779-7*) Warner Bks.

Lasky, Judith & Silverman, Helen W., eds. Love: Psychoanalytic Perspectives. 224p. 1988. 45.00 (*0-8147-5036-2*) NYU Pr.

Lasky, Julie, jt. auth. see Heller, Steven.

Lasky, Kathryn. A Baby for Max. LC 86-22131. (Illus.). 48p. (J). (ps-2). 1987. pap. 4.95 (*0-689-71118-2*, Aladdin Paperbacks) S&S Childrens.

— Beyond the Burning Time. 176p. (YA). (gr. 7 up). 1994. 13.95 (*0-590-47331-X*, Blue Sky Press) Scholastic Inc.

— Beyond the Divide. LC 82-22867. 264p. (YA). (gr. 7 up). 1983. text ed. 15.95 (*0-02-751670-9*, Mac Bks Young Read) S&S Childrens.

— The Bone Wars. LC 88-13426. 378p. (J). (gr. 7 up). 1988. 12.95 (*0-688-07433-2*) Morrow Jr Bks.

— Cloud Eyes. LC 93-37805. (J). 1994. 14.95 (*0-15-219168-2*) HarBrace.

— Days of the Dead. LC 93-47957. (Illus.). 48p. (J). (gr. 3-7). 1994. 15.95 (*0-7868-0022-4*); lib. bdg. 15.89 (*0-7868-2018-7*) Hyprn Child.

— Dinosaur Dig. LC 89-13212. (Illus.). 64p. (J). (gr. 3 up). 1990. 13.95 (*0-688-08574-1*); lib. bdg. 13.88 (*0-688-08575-X*) Morrow Jr Bks.

— Double Trouble Squared. (J). (gr. 3 up). 1991. 14.95 (*0-15-224126-4*, HB Juv Bks) HarBrace.

— Double Trouble Squared. (J). (gr. 4-7). 1991. pap. 5.95 (*0-15-224127-2*) HarBrace.

— Fourth of July Bear. LC 90-37422. (Illus.). 40p. (J). (gr. k up). 1991. 13.95 (*0-688-08287-4*) Morrow Jr Bks.

— The Gates of the Wind. LC 94-8390. (J). 1995. write for info. (*0-15-204264-4*) HarBrace.

— I Have an Aunt on Marlborough Street. LC 91-279. (Illus.). 32p. (J). (gr. k-3). 1992. text ed. 13.95 (*0-02-751701-2*, Mac Bks Young Read) S&S Childrens.

— The Librarian Who Measured the Earth. LC 92-42656. (Illus.). (J). (gr. 1-5). 1994. 16.95 (*0-316-51526-4*, Joy St Bks) Little.

— A Life Between Two Comets: The Story of Mark Twain. LC 95-18479. (Illus.). (J). 1996. write for info. (*0-15-252110-0*) HarBrace.

— Lunch Bunnies. LC 92-31554. (Illus.). (J). 1993. 13.95 (*0-316-51525-6*, Joy St Bks) Little.

— Memoirs of a Book Bat. (J). (gr. 4 up). 1994. 10.95 (*0-15-215727-1*) HarBrace.

— My Island Grandma. LC 91-31000. (Illus.). 32p. (J). (ps up). 1993. 15.00 (*0-688-07946-6*); lib. bdg. 14.93 (*0-688-07948-2*) Morrow Jr Bks.

— The Night Journey. (Novels Ser.). (Illus.). 152p. (J). (gr. 5-9). 1986. pap. 4.99 (*0-14-032048-2*, Puffin) Puffin Bks.

— Pageant. LC 86-12087. 240p. (YA). (gr. 7 up). 1986. text ed. 14.95 (*0-02-751720-9*, Four Winds Pr) S&S Childrens.

— Pond Year. LC 94-14834. 32p. 1995. 13.95 (*1-56402-187-4*) Candlewick Pr.

— Sea Swan. LC 88-1444. (Illus.). 32p. (J). (gr. k-3). 1988. text ed. 14.95 (*0-02-751700-4*, Mac Bks Young Read) S&S Childrens.

— Shadows in the Water: A Starbuck Family Adventure. LC 92-8139. (J). 1992. 16.95 (*0-15-273533-X*, HB Juv Bks); pap. 6.95 (*0-15-273534-8*, HB Juv Bks) HarBrace.

— She's Wearing a Dead Bird on Her Head. LC 94-18204. (Illus.). 40p. (J). (gr. k-4). 1995. 14.95 (*0-7868-0065-8*); lib. bdg. 14.89 (*0-7868-2052-7*) Hyprn Child.

— The Solo. LC 92-44456. (Illus.). 32p. (J). (ps-2). 1994. text ed. 14.95 (*0-02-751664-4*, Mac Bks Young Read) S&S Childrens.

— Sugaring Time. LC 82-23928. (Illus.). 64p. (J). (gr. 3-7). 1983. lib. bdg. 13.95 (*0-02-751680-6*, Mac Bks Young Read) S&S Childrens.

— Sugaring Time. LC 86-3468. (Illus.). 64p. (J). (gr. 3-7). 1986. reprint ed. pap. 4.95 (*0-689-71081-X*, Aladdin Paperbacks) S&S Childrens.

— Surtsey: The Newest Place on Earth. LC 92-52990. (Illus.). 64p. (J). (gr. 3-7). 1992. 15.95 (*1-56282-300-0*); lib. bdg. 15.89 (*1-56282-301-9*) Hyprn Child.

— Surtsey: The Newest Place on Earth. (Illus.). 64p. (J). (gr. 3-7). 1994. pap. 6.95 (*0-7868-1004-1*) Hyprn Ppbks.

— The Tantrum. LC 92-3701. (Illus.). 32p. (J). (ps-1). 1993. lib. bdg. 13.95 (*0-02-751661-X*, Mac Bks Young Read) S&S Childrens.

— Think Like an Eagle: At Work with a Wildlife Photographer. (Illus.). 48p. (J). (gr. 3 up). 1992. 15.95 (*0-316-51519-1*, Joy St Bks) Little.

— Traces of Life: The Origins of Humankind. LC 89-12092. (Illus.). 144p. (J). (gr. 5 up). 1990. 16.95 (*0-688-07237-2*) Morrow Jr Bks.

An Asterisk (*) at the beginning of an entry indicates that the title is appearing in BIP for the first time.

— Voice in the Wind: A Starbuck Family Adventure. (J). (gr. 4-7). 1993. 10.95 (*0-15-294102-9*, HB Juv Bks); pap. 3.95 (*0-15-294103-7*, HB Juv Bks) HarBrace.

Lasky, Kathryn & Knight, Meribah. Searching for Laura Ingalls: A Reader's Journal. LC 92-26188. (Illus.). 48p. (J). (gr. 2-6). 1993. text ed. 15.95 (*0-02-751666-0*, Mac Bks Young Read) S&S Childrens.

***Lasky, Larry C. & Warkentin, Phyllis, eds.** Stem Cell & Marrow Processing for Transplantation. (Illus.). (C). Date not set. text ed. 35.00 (*1-56395-042-1*) Am Assn Blood.

Lasky, Lila & Mukerji, Rose. Art: Basic for Young Children. LC 80-82565. (Illus.). 164p. (Orig.). 1980. pap. text ed. 5.00 (*0-912674-73-3*, NAEYC NO. 106) Natl Assn Child Ed.

Lasky, Mark A., jt. auth. see Landes, William-Alan.

Lasky, Mark J. Three Essays on Productivity: The Impacts of Profitability, Business Cycles, & the Capital Stock on Productivity. LC 93-48968. (Studies on Industrial Productivity). 192p. 1994. 45.00 (*0-8153-1622-4*) Garland.

Lasky, Melvin J. On the Barricades, & Off. 256p. (Orig.). 1989. pap. 24.95 (*0-88738-726-8*) Transaction Pubs.

— Utopia & Revolution: On the Origins of a Metaphor or Some Illustrations of Political Temperament & Intellectual Climate & How Ideas, Ideals & Ideologies Have Been Historically Related. LC 75-27893. xiv, 726p. 1985. pap. text ed. 30.00 (*0-226-46911-5*) U Ch Pr.

— Voices in a Revolution: The Collapse of East German Communism. 188p. (C). 1992. 32.95 (*1-56000-030-9*) Transaction Pubs.

Lasky, Melvin J., ed. The Hungarian Revolution: A White Book. LC 70-119936. (Select Bibliographies Reprint Ser.). 1977. reprint ed. 28.95 (*0-8369-5379-7*) Ayer.

Lasky, Michael, jt. auth. see Harris, Robert A.

Lasky, Richard. Dynamics of Development & the Therapeutic Process. LC 92-17808. 488p. 1993. 50.00x (*0-87668-565-3*) Aronson.

— Psychology of Multiple Personality Disorders. Date not set. write for info. (*1-56821-061-2*) Aronson.

***Lasky, Ronald C., et al, eds.** Optoelectronics for Data Communication. (Illus.). 450p. 1995. boxed write for info. (*0-12-437160-4*) Acad Pr.

Lasky Schub, Joyce & Carr, Raymond, eds. Spain: Studies in Political Security. LC 85-16948. (Washington Papers: No. 117). 125p. 1985. text ed. 49.95 (*0-275-90192-0*, C0192, Praeger Pubs) Greenwood.

Lasky, Tamar, jt. auth. see Stolley, Paul D.

Lasky, Vivienne, jt. auth. see Freeman, Robert.

Laslett, Betsy. Arts & 504: A 504 Handbook for Accessible Arts Programming. (Illus.). 101p. 1985. pap. 5.00 (*0-16-004283-6*, S/N 036-000-00047-3) USGPO.

Laslett, John & Tyler, Mary. International Ladies Garment Workers Union in Los Angeles, 1907-1988. LC 89-50435. (Illus.). 167p. (Orig.). 1989. pap. 8.95 (*0-923145-02-8*) Ten Star Pr.

Laslett, John H. Nature's Noblemen: The Fortunes of the Independent Collier in Scotland & the American Midwest, 1855-1889. (Monograph & Research Ser.: No. 34). 87p. 1984. 6.00 (*0-89215-120-X*) U Cal LA Indus Rel.

Laslett, John H. & Lipset, Seymour M., eds. Failure of a Dream? Essays in the History of American Socialism. rev. ed. LC 77-80472. 592p. (C). 1984. pap. 15.00 (*0-520-04452-5*) U CA Pr.

Laslett, Peter. Family Life & Illicit Love in Earlier Generations. 1977. 22.95 (*0-521-21408-4*) Cambridge U Pr.

— A Fresh Map of Life: The Emergence of the Third Age. LC 90-47101. 213p. 1991. pap. 15.95 (*0-674-32327-0*, LASFRX) HUP.

— World We Have Lost. 3rd ed. (C). 1986. pap. text ed. 12.95 (*0-684-18079-0*, Scribners) S&S Trade.

— The World We Have Lost: England Before the Industrial Age. 3rd ed. LC 84-1242. 353p. (C). 1984. pap. write for info. (*0-02-367860-7*, Scribners) S&S Trade.

Laslett, Peter & Fishkin, James, eds. Philosophy, Politics & Society, Vol. 5. LC 78-64932. 1979. 45.00 (*0-300-02337-5*) Yale U Pr.

Laslett, Peter & Fishkin, James S., eds. Justice Between Age Groups & Generations. (Philosophy, Politics, & Society Ser.: No. 6). 272p. (C). 1992. text ed. 35.00 (*0-300-05073-9*) Yale U Pr.

Laslett, Peter, jt. ed. see Kertzer, David I.

Laslett, Peter, ed. see Locke, John.

Laslett, Peter, et al, eds. Bastardy & Its Comparative History: Studies in the History of Illegitimacy & Martial Nonconformism. (Studies in Social & Demographic History). (Illus.). 446p. 1980. 47.50 (*0-674-06338-4*) HUP.

Laslett, Robert & Smith, Colin J. Effective Classroom Management. 2nd ed. 160p. 1993. pap. 16.95 (*0-415-07152-6*, A7697) Routledge.

Lasley, John F. Genetics of Livestock Improvement. 4th ed. (Illus.). 528p. (C). 1986. text ed. 58.40 (*0-13-351206-1*) P-H.

Lasley, John F., jt. auth. see Campbell, John R.

Lasley, Mary. A Day at the Beach. (Story Puzzle Book Ser.). 4p. (J). (ps-2). 1990. 9.95 (*0-88679-843-4*) Educ Insights.

— A Day at the Park. (Story Puzzle Book Ser.). 4p. (J). (ps-2). 1990. 9.95 (*0-88679-841-8*) Educ Insights.

— Do-It-Yourself Story Puzzle Book. (Illus.). 2p. (J). (ps). 1988. 9.95 (*0-9622406-0-5*) MOL Bks.

***Lasley, Paul, et al.** Beyond the Amber Waves of Grain: An Examination of Social & Economic Restructuring in the Heartland. (Rural Studies Ser.). 256p. (C). 1995. pap. text ed. 39.95 (*0-8133-8930-5*) Westview.

***Lasley, Thomas.** Issues in Teacher Education: Background Papers from the National Commission for Excellence in Teacher Education, Vol. II. 1986. 14.00 (*0-89333-043-4*) AACTE.

Lasley, Thomas J. Teaching Peace: Toward Cultural Selflessness. LC 93-43730. 216p. 1994. text ed. 49.95 (*0-89789-371-9*, Bergin & Garvey) Greenwood.

***Laslie, Judy A.** Nine Chances to Feel Good About Yourself. (Orig.). 1995. pap. 14.95 (*0-614-05139-8*) Radnor Hse.

Laslo, Alexander J. The Interallied Victory Medals of World War I. LC 86-71991. (Illus.). 150p. (Orig.). 1986. pap. 15.95 (*0-9617320-0-8*) Dorado Publishing.

— The Interrallied Victory Medals of World War I. 2nd rev. ed. LC 91-76602. (Illus.). 130p. 1992. 29.95 (*0-9617320-1-6*) Dorado Publishing.

Laslo, Cynthia. The Rosen Photo Guide to a Career in the Circus. (Illus.). (YA). (gr. 7-12). 1988. lib. bdg. 12.95 (*0-8239-0819-4*) Rosen Group.

***Lasner, Mark S.** A Selective Checklist of the Published Work of Aubrey Beardsley. 1994. text ed. 75.00 (*0-9644734-0-2*) T G Boss.

Lasner, Mark S., jt. ed. see Stetz, Margaret D.

Lasnier, F. & Ang, T. Photovoltaic Engineering Handbook. (Illus.). 568p. 1990. 176.00 (*0-85274-311-4*) IOP Pub.

Lasnik, Howard. Essays on Anaphora. (C). 1989. pap. text ed. 34.00 (*1-55608-091-3*) Kluwer Ac.

— Essays on Restrictiveness & Learnability. (C). 1990. lib. bdg. 102.50 (*0-7923-0628-7*) Kluwer Ac.

Lasnik, Howard & Saito, Mamoru. Move A: Conditions on Its Application & Output. (Current Studies in Linguistics: No. 22). (Illus.). 270p. 1992. 35.00 (*0-262-12161-1*) MIT Pr.

— Move Alpha: Conditions on Its Application & Output. (Current Studies in Linguistics: No. 22). (Illus.). 240p. 1994. pap. 16.95x (*0-262-62091-X*) MIT Pr.

Lasnik, Howard & Uriagereka, Juan. A Course in GB Syntax: Lectures on Binding & Empty Categories. 220p. (Orig.). (C). 1988. 35.00 (*0-262-12130-1*, Bradford Bks); pap. 18.95 (*0-262-62060-X*, Bradford Bks) MIT Pr.

Lasnik, Howard, jt. ed. see Osherson, Daniel N.

Lasobre, Jacques & Sommer, H. Risk, Insurance, Reinsurance: Lexicon. 396p. (ENG & FRE.). 1981. 75.00 (*0-8288-0968-2*, M 6354) Fr & Eur.

Lasocki, David, comp. Fluting & Dancing: Articles & Reminiscences for Betty Bang Mather on Her 65th Birthday. LC 92-20693. (Illus.). 208p. (Orig.). 1992. pap. text ed. 25.00 (*0-941084-12-4*) McGinnis & Marx.

Lasocki, David & Mather, Betty B. The Classical Woodwind Cadenza: A Workbook. 1978. 10.00 (*0-941084-06-X*) McGinnis & Marx.

***Lasocki, David & Prior, Roger.** The Bassanos: Venetian Musicians & Instrument Makers in England, 1531-1665. 324p. 1995. 68.95 (*0-85967-943-8*, Pub. by Scolar Pr UK) Ashgate Pub Co.

Lasocki, David, jt. auth. see Griscom, Richard.

Lasocki, David, jt. auth. see Mather, Betty B.

Lasocki, David, jt. auth. see Mather, Betty Bang.

Lasok, D. & Bridge, J. W. Law & Institutions of the European Communities. 5th ed. 1991. pap. 52.00 (*0-406-60931-4*, U.K.) Butterworth Legal Pubs.

Lasok, D. & Stone, P. A. Conflict of Laws in the European Community. 1987. U.K. text ed. 68.00 (*0-86205-071-5*) Butterworth Legal Pubs.

Lasok, D., et al, eds. Fundamental Duties: A Volume of Essays by Present & Former Members of the Law Faculty of the University of Exeter to Commemorate the Silver Jubilee of the University. LC 80-40933. 269p. 1980. 120.00 (*0-08-024048-8*, Pub. by Pergamon Repr UK) Franklin.

Lasok, Dominik. The Customs Law of the European Economic Community. 2nd ed. 300p. 1991. pap. 108.00 (*90-6544-483-1*) Kluwer Law Tax Pubs.

— The Professions & Services in the European Economic Community. LC 86-15274. 396p. 1986. 133.00 (*90-6544-253-7*) Kluwer Law Tax Pubs.

Lasok, K. P. Lasok: The European Court of Justice - Practice & Procedure. 2nd ed. 1994. 270.00 (*0-406-00621-0*) Butterworth Legal Pubs.

LaSor, William S. Handbook of Biblical Hebrew. 1989. pap. 35.00 (*0-8028-0444-6*) Eerdmans.

LaSorda, Tommy & Fisher, David. The Artful Dodger. (Illus.). 368p. 1986. pap. 3.95 (*0-380-70085-9*) Avon.

Lasota, Andrzej & Mackey, Michael C. Chaos, Fractals, & Noise: Stochastic Aspects of Dynamics. LC 93-10432. (Applied Mathematical Sciences Ser.: Vol. 97). 1993. 49.00 (*0-387-94049-9*) Spr-Verlag.

LaSota, Marcia. Women & Business Ownership: A Bibliography. 180p. 1987. lib. bdg. 37.50 (*0-933474-45-8*) Media Mktg Group.

Laspada, Sebastian, jt. auth. see Mohan, Madan.

Lasry, George. Valuing Common Stock: The Power of Prudence. LC 78-24023. 270p. reprint ed. pap. 77.00 (*0-317-27196-2*, 2023930) Bks Demand.

Lass. Principles of Experimental Phonetics. 1994. 44.95 (*0-8016-7975-3*) Mosby Yr Bk.

Lass, A. H., jt. auth. see Flesch, Rudolf.

Lass, Abraham, jt. auth. see Cole, Sylvia.

Lass, Abraham H. Business Spelling & Word Power. 2nd ed. 1961. teacher ed 6.67 (*0-672-96013-3*, Bobbs) Macmillan.

— Business Spelling & Word Power. 7th ed. 1961. pap. text ed. 9.95 (*0-672-96012-5*, Bobbs); 3.95 (*0-672-96015-X*, Bobbs) Macmillan.

— Dictionary of Classical, Biblical, & Literary Allusions. 1988. mass mkt. 5.99 (*0-449-14565-4*) Fawcett.

— Secret Sharer & Other Great Stories. Trasman, N., ed. (Orig.). 1989. pap. 4.50 (*0-451-62540-4*) NAL-Dutton.

Lass, Abraham H. & Tasman, Norma L., eds. Secret Sharer & Other Great Stories. (Orig.). 1969. pap. 5.99 (*0-451-62667-2*, ME2084, Ment) NAL-Dutton.

— Twenty-One Great Stories. (Orig.). 1969. pap. 5.99 (*0-451-62785-7*, Sig) NAL-Dutton.

Lass, Abraham H., jt. ed. see Goldstone, Richard.

Lass, Abraham H., et al. The Facts on File Dictionary of Classical, Biblical, & Literary Allusions. 256p. 1987. 21.95 (*0-8160-1267-9*) Facts on File.

***Lass, Barbara.** Hawaiian Adze Production & Distribution: Implications for the Development of Chiefdoms. (Monograth Ser.: No. 37). (Illus.). 96p. (C). 1994. pap. 15.00x (*0-917956-81-8*) UCLA Arch.

Lass, Bonnie & Davis, Beth. The Remedial Reading Handbook. (Illus.). 224p. (C). 1985. pap. text ed. write for info. (*0-13-773474-3*) P-H.

Lass, Harry. Elements of Pure & Applied Mathematics. LC 56-8867. (International Pure & Applied Mathematics Ser.). 503p. reprint ed. pap. 143.40 (*0-317-28234-4*, 2055972) Bks Demand.

Lass, Norman J. Speech & Language: Advances in Basic Research & Practice, Vol. 7. (Serial Publication Ser.). 1982. text ed. 116.00 (*0-12-608607-9*) Acad Pr.

Lass, Norman J., ed. Experimental Phonetics. 552p. 1974. pap. text ed. 16.95 (*0-8422-0375-3*) Irvington.

— Speech & Hearing Science: Selected Readings. 382p. 1974. text ed. 49.50 (*0-8422-5154-5*); pap. text ed. 14.50 (*0-8422-0377-X*) Irvington.

— Speech & Language: Advances in Basic Research & Practice. (Serial Publication Ser.: Vol. 9). 1983. text ed. 116.00 (*0-12-608609-5*) Acad Pr.

— Speech & Language: Advances in Basic Research & Practice, Vol. 1. (Serial Publication Ser.). 1979. text ed. 116.00 (*0-12-608601-X*) Acad Pr.

— Speech & Language: Advances in Basic Research & Practice, Vol. 3. (Serial Publication Ser.). 1980. text ed. 116.00 (*0-12-608603-6*) Acad Pr.

— Speech & Language: Advances in Basic Research & Practice, Vol. 4. 1980. text ed. 116.00 (*0-12-608604-4*) Acad Pr.

— Speech & Language: Advances in Basic Research & Practice, Vol. 5. (Serial Publication Ser.). 1981. text ed. 116.00 (*0-12-608605-2*) Acad Pr.

— Speech & Language: Advances in Basic Research & Practice, Vol. 6. (Serial Publication Ser.). 496p. 1982. text ed. 116.00 (*0-12-608606-0*) Acad Pr.

— Speech & Language: Advances in Basic Research & Practice, Vol. 8. (Serial Publication Ser.). 1982. text ed. 116.00 (*0-12-608608-7*) Acad Pr.

— Speech & Language: Advances in Basic Research & Practice, Vol. 2. (Serial Publication Ser.). 1979. text ed. 116.00 (*0-12-608602-8*) Acad Pr.

Lass, Norman J., et al. Handbook of Speech-Language Pathology & Audiology. 1400p. 1988. 67.00 (*1-55664-037-4*) Mosby Yr Bk.

Lass, R. A., jt. auth. see Wood, G. A.

Lass, Roger. Old English: A Historical Linguistic Companion. LC 93-18182. 272p. (C). 1994. pap. 32.95 (*0-521-45848-X*) Cambridge U Pr.

— Old English: A Historical Linguistic Companion. LC 93-18182. 272p. (C). 1994. 74.95 (*0-521-43087-9*) Cambridge U Pr.

— On Explaining Language Change. LC 79-51825. (Cambridge Studies in Linguistics: No. 27). 200p. reprint ed. pap. 57.00 (*0-317-20626-5*, 2024580) Bks Demand.

Lass, William E. From the Missouri to the Great Salt Lake: An Account of Overland Freighting. LC 75-183071. (Nebraska State Historical Publications Ser.: Vol. 26). (Illus.). 312p. 1972. 7.95 (*0-686-18151-4*) Nebraska Hist.

— A History of Steamboating on the Upper Missouri River. LC 62-14663. (Illus.). 247p. reprint ed. pap. 70.40 (*0-8357-8168-2*, 2034163) Bks Demand.

— Minnesota's Boundary with Canada: Its Evolution since 1783. LC 80-21644. (Minnesota Public Affairs Center Publication Ser.). (Illus.). 141p. 1980. 16.50 (*0-87351-147-6*); pap. 8.75 (*0-87351-153-0*) Minn Hist.

***Lassaigne, Jacques & Weelen, Guy.** Vieira Da Silva. (Grandes Monografias). (Illus.). 340p. (SPA.). 1993. 175.00 (*84-343-0303-5*) Elliots Bks.

Lassaletta, Manuel. Mensajes De Luz Profetica (Messages of Prophetic Light) (SPA.). 1989. 3.99 (*0-945792-71-9*, 498452) Editorial Unilit.

Lassalle, Ferdinand. Die Philosophie Herakleitos Des Dunklen Von Ephesos, 2 vols. in 1. (Spudasmata Ser.: Bd. XLI). xxii, 858p. 1973. reprint ed. write for info. (*3-487-05004-8*, Pub. by Georg Olms GW) Lubrecht & Cramer.

Lassalle, George. George Lassalle's Middle Eastern Food East of Orphanides. (Illus.). 208p. 1993. pap. 15.95 (*1-85626-101-8*) Trafalgar.

Lassan, N. A. Advances & Technical Standards in Neurosurgery, Vol. 4. LC 74-10499. 1977. 73.00 (*0-387-81423-X*) Spr-Verlag.

***Lassanyi, Mary E.** Central & Eastern Europe: Going Global: A Bibliography & Directory. (Illus.). 95p. (Orig.). (C). 1995. pap. text ed. 35.00x (*0-7881-1531-6*) Diane Pub.

***Lassanyl, Mary E., ed.** South America's Economic Development & Emerging Markets: A Bibliography. 57p. (Orig.). (C). 1994. pap. text ed. 40.00x (*0-7881-1541-3*) Diane Pub.

Lassar, Terry. City Deal Making. LC 90-70877. 1990. 37.95 (*0-87420-704-5*) Urban Land.

Lassar, Terry J. Carrots & Sticks: New Zoning Downtown. LC 89-51454. 196p. (Orig.). 1989. pap. text ed. 56.95 (*0-87420-693-6*, C58) Urban Land.

Lassau, Jean-Pierre. Atlas of Neonatal Anatomy. (Illus.). 180p. 1982. 73.00 (*0-89352-139-6*, MA139, Yr Bk Med Pubs) Mosby Yr Bk.

***Lasse, Antonsen.** Per Kirkeby: Works from the Sixties. (Illus.). 50p. 1995. 25.00 (*1-885013-08-6*) M Werner.

Lassegue, Pierre. Lexique de Comptabilite. 3rd ed. 404p. 1993. pap. 39.95 (*0-7859-5622-0*, 2247015328) Fr & Eur.

Lassell, Michael. Decade Dance. LC 90-43181. 144p. (Orig.). 1990. pap. 7.95 (*1-55583-179-6*) Alyson Pubns.

— The Hard Way. (Orig.). 1995. pap. 12.95 (*1-56333-231-0*) Masquerade.

— The Name of Love: Great Gay Love Poems. LC 94-36026. 1994. 10.00 (*0-312-11863-5*, Stonewall Inn) St Martin.

— Poems for Lost & Un-Lost Boys. LC 85-73772. (Amelia Chapbooks Ser.). (Illus.). 92p. (Orig.). 1985. pap. 10.95 (*0-936545-00-3*) Amelia.

Lassen. Brain Work & Mental Activity. (ABS Ser.: No. 31). 550p. 1991. 89.50 (*87-16-10698-9*) Mosby Yr Bk.

Lassen, Cheryl A. Reaching the Assetless Poor: Projects & Strategies for Their Self-Reliant Development. (Special Series on Landlessness & Near-Landlessness: No. 6). 68p. (Orig.). (C). 1980. pap. text ed. 6.75 (*0-86731-073-1*) Cornell CIS RDC.

***Lassen, Mary M.** Community-Based Family Support in Public Housing. LC 95-76523. 172p. 1995. pap. text ed. 15.00 (*0-9630627-5-1*) Harvard Fam.

Lasser, Carol, ed. Educating Men & Women Together: Coeducation in a Changing World. LC 86-7126. (Illus.). 184p. 1987. 24.95 (*0-252-01346-8*) U of Ill Pr.

Lasser, Carol & Merrill, Marlene D., eds. Friends & Sisters: Letters Between Lucy Stone & Antoinette Brown Blackwell, 1846-93. LC 86-24984. (Women in American History Ser.). (Illus.). 314p. 1987. 29.95 (*0-252-01396-4*) U of Ill Pr.

Lasser, Dieter, jt. auth. see Hoschek, Josef.

Lasser, J. K. J. K. Lasser What New Tax Law Me. 1993. mass mkt. 4.99 (*0-671-88566-9*) PB.

Lasser, J. K., Law Institute Staff & Greisman, Bernard. J. K. Lasser's How You Can Profit from the New Tax Laws. rev. ed. 220p. write for info. (*0-318-60216-4*) S&S Trade.

Lasser, J. K., Tax Institute Staff. J. K. Lasser's Guide to Planning Your Successful Retirement. write for info. (*0-318-59619-9*) S&S Trade.

— J. K. Lasser's How to Avoid a Tax Audit of Your Return. rev. ed. write for info. (*0-318-59599-0*) S&S Trade.

— J. K. Lasser's Professional Edition of Your Income Tax. write for info. (*0-318-59616-4*) S&S Trade.

— J. K. Lasser's Successful Tax Planning for Real Estate. 390p. 1986. pap. 17.95 (*0-671-52894-7*) S&S Trade.

— J. K. Lasser's Your Income Tax Software 1991 & Pacioli 2000: Integrated Software to Simplify Your 1990 Tax Return & Your 1991 Tax Planning. 128p. 1991. boxed, disk 99.95 (*0-13-508334-6*, J K Lasser) P-H Gen Ref & Trav.

— J. K. Lasser's Your Income Tax, 1981. 1980. pap. 5.95 (*0-686-72557-3*, Fireside) S&S Trade.

— J. K. Lasser's Your Income Tax 1988. 1988. pap. write for info. (*0-318-62741-8*) S&S Trade.

— J. K. Lasser's Your Income Tax, 1994. 1993. pap. 14.00 (*0-671-86943-4*, J K Lasser) P-H Gen Ref & Trav.

— J. K. Lasser's 1986 Taxes Made Easy. 1986. pap. 3.95 (*0-317-40477-6*) P-H.

— Lasser's Your Income Tax 1982. pap. 5.95 (*0-686-91635-2*) S&S Trade.

— Your Nineteen Eighty-Six Money Saving Tax Guide. write for info. (*0-318-59611-3*) S&S Trade.

Lasser, William. The Limits of Judicial Power: The Supreme Court in American Politics. LC 88-40141. xi, 354p. (C). 1988. 37.50 (*0-8078-1810-0*); pap. 12.95 (*0-8078-4233-8*) U of NC Pr.

— Perspectives on American Government: A Comprehensive Reader. 775p. (C). 1992. pap. text ed. write for info. (*0-669-21875-8*); write for info. (*0-669-28289-8*) Heath.

***Lasserre, Guy.** Synopse des Lois du Pentateuque. 242p. 1994. text ed. 85.75 (*90-04-10202-7*) E J Brill.

Lasserre, Jean. War & the Gospel. Coburn, O., tr. 248p. 1962. 10.00 (*0-227-67635-1*) Attic Pr.

— War & the Gospel. LC 62-52667. 246p. reprint ed. pap. 70.20 (*0-7837-5106-0*, 2044805) Bks Demand.

Lasserre, Jean-Bernard, jt. auth. see Dauzere-Peres, Stephane.

Lasserre, P. & Martin, J. M., eds. Biogeochemical Processes at the Land-Sea Boundary. (Oceanography Ser.: No. 43). 224p. 1986. 79.50 (*0-444-42675-2*) Elsevier.

Lassers, Eugene W. The Famous & the Infamous: Presidential Trivia, Book 1. (Illus.). 66p. (Orig.). 1990. pap. 3.00 (*0-9626129-0-1*) E W Lassers.

Lasseter, Chriscilla A. The Corners of My Mind. 1993. 8.95 (*0-533-10399-1*) Vantage.

***Lasseter, Don.** Property of the Folsom Wolf. 512p. 1995. mass mkt. 4.99 (*0-7860-0090-2*, Pinnacle NY) Windsor NY.

— Property of the Folsom Wolf. 512p. 1995. pap. 4.99 (*0-8217-0090-1*) Zebra.

***Lasseter, John & Daly, Steve.** Toy Story: The Art & Making of the Animated Film. (Illus.). 136p. 1995. 39.95 (*0-7868-6180-0*) Hyperion.

Lassetter, jt. auth. see Creek.

Lassey, William R., jt. auth. see Carlson.

Lassez, Jean-Louis & Clard, Keith, eds. Logic Programming: Proceedings of the Fourth International Conference, 2 vols. (Logic Programming - Research Reports & Notes). 704p. (Orig.). 1987. pap. 60.00 (*0-262-12125-5*) MIT Pr.

Lassez, Jean-Louis & Plotkin, Gordon, eds. Computational Logic: Essays in Honor of Alan Robinson. (Illus.). 752p. 1991. 75.00 (*0-262-12156-5*) MIT Pr.

***Lassig, Jurgen.** Spiny. LC 94-40893. (Illus.). 64p. (J). (gr. 1-3). 1995. 13.95 (*1-55858-401-3*); lib. bdg. 13.88 (*1-55858-402-1*) North-South Bks NYC.

Lassik, Grace E. The Raccoon Connection. rev. ed. Carolock, G. M. et al, eds. (Illus.). 15p. (J). (ps-2). 1992. reprint ed. pap. 9.95 (*1-880926-00-8*) Four Star SC.

Lassila & Kilpatrick. Compensation Tax Guide. 480p. 1990. pap. 25.00 (*0-685-66965-3*, 5069) Commerce.

Lassiter, J. W. & Edwards, Hardy M. Animal Nutrition. (C). 1982. teacher ed write for info. (*0-8359-0223-4*, Reston) P-H.

Lassiter, James & Gilbertie, James. Survey of Economics. 2nd ed. 1992. pap. 47.25 (*1-56226-118-5*) CT Pub.

Lassiter, Kenneth T., ed. see Society of Photographic Scientists & Engineers Staff.

***Lassiter, Sybil M.** Multicultural Clients: Professional Handbook for Health Care Providers & Social Workers. LC 94-30927. 224p. 1995. text ed. 65.00 (*0-313-29140-3*, Greenwood Pr) Greenwood.

Lasslo, A., ed. Blood Platelet Function & Medicinal Chemistry. 336p. 1984. 71.25 (*0-444-00790-3*) Elsevier.

Lassman, F., et al, eds. Early Correlates of Speech, Language & Hearing. LC 79-11098. (Illus.). 872p. 1980. 71.00 (*0-88416-214-1*, Yr Bk Med Pubs) Mosby Yr Bk.

Lassman, Peter, ed. Politics & Social Theory. 240p. 1989. pap. text ed. 14.95 (*0-415-01799-8*) Routledge.

Lassman, Peter, ed. see Weber, Max.

Lassman, Peter, et al, eds. Max Weber's "Science As a Vocation" 240p. 1988. 55.00 (*0-04-301211-6*) Routledge Chapman & Hall.

Lassmann, K. Transactions of Two International Seminars on the Mathematical - Mechanical, No. EUR 13600. 276p. 1991. pap. 30.00 (*92-826-2886-8*, CD-NA-13660-EN-C) UNIPUB.

Lassner, Jacob. Demonizing the Queen of Sheba: Boundaries of Gender & Culture in Postbiblical Judaism & Medieval Islam. LC 93-7499. (Chicago Studies in the History of Judaism). 360p. 1993. lib. bdg. 49.95 (*0-226-46913-1*); pap. text ed. 19.95 (*0-226-46915-8*) U Ch Pr.

— Islamic Revolution & Historical Memory: An Inquiry into the Art of Abbasid Apologetics. (American Oriental Ser.: Vol. 66). 1986. 22.00 (*0-940490-66-8*) Am Orient Soc.

— The Topography of Baghdad in the Early Middle Ages: Text & Studies. LC 69-11339. 325p. reprint ed. pap. 92.70 (*0-7837-3580-4*, 2043439) Bks Demand.

Lassner, Jacob, jt. ed. see Fields, Philip.

Lassner, Jacob, tr. see Fields, Philip & Lassner, Jacob, eds.

Lassner, Joseph, et al, eds. Social Group Work: Competence & Values in Practice. LC 86-32012. (Social Work with Groups Supplement Ser.: No. 2). 230p. 1987. text ed. 44.95 (*0-86656-643-0*) Haworth Pr.

Lassner, Phyllis. Elizabeth Bowen. 204p. (C). 1989. text ed. 46.00 (*0-389-20878-7*); pap. 19.00 (*0-389-20879-5*) B&N Imports.

— Elizabeth Bowen: A Study of Short Fiction. (Twayne's Studies in Short Fiction: No. 27). 216p. 1991. text ed. 22.95 (*0-8057-8336-9*, Pub. by Royal Botanic Garden UK) Macmillan.

***Lasso.** Madrigale I: Das 1 & 2 Buch 5-Stimmiger Madrigale (1555 & 1557) (Illus.). 1973. pap. 85.00 (*0-8450-1902-3*) Broude.

— Madrigale II: Das 3 & 4, Buch 5-Stimmiger Madrigale (1562 & 1567) (Illus.). 1973. pap. 85.00 (*0-8450-1904-X*) Broude.

— Madrigale III: Die Beiden Madrigalsammlungen (1585 & 1587) (Illus.). 1973. pap. 85.00 (*0-8450-1906-6*) Broude.

— Madrigale IV: 4 & 5-Stimmige Madrigale aus Verschiedenen Drucken. (Illus.). 1973. pap. 85.00 (*0-8450-1908-2*) Broude.

— Magnum Opus Musicum I: Motetten fur 2, 3 & 4 Stimmen (Nr. 1-90) (Illus.). 1973. pap. 85.00 (*0-8450-1901-5*) Broude.

— Magnum Opus Musicum II: Motetten fur 4 & 5 Stimmen (Nr. 91-160) (Illus.). 1973. pap. 85.00 (*0-8450-1903-1*) Broude.

— Magnum Opus Musicum III: Motetten fur 5 Stimmen (Nr. 161-211) (Illus.). 1973. pap. 85.00 (*0-8450-1905-8*) Broude.

— Magnum Opus Musicum IV: Motetten fur 5 Stimmen (Nr. 212-248) 1973. 85.00 (*0-8450-1907-4*) Broude.

Lasso de La Vega, Javier & Robert Candau, Jose M., eds. Diccionario Enciclopedias Labor: Encyclopedia Dictionary of Labor, 9 vols. 7th ed. 6500p. (ENG, FRE, GER, POR & SPA.). 1978. 495.00 (*0-8288-5127-1*, S12269) Fr & Eur.

Lassoie & Hinckle. Techniques & Approaches in Forest Tree Ecophysiology. 1991. 322.00 (*0-8493-6866-9*, QK938) CRC Pr.

Lasson, Frans, ed. see Dinesen, Isak.

Lasson, Kenneth. Private Lives of Public Servants. LC 77-15758. 275p. reprint ed. pap. 78.40 (*0-685-16325-3*, 2056234) Bks Demand.

— Representing Yourself: What You Can Do Without a Lawyer. 2nd ed. LC 94-46383. 1995. 12.95 (*0-452-27451-6*, Plume) NAL-Dutton.

Lasson, Kenneth, jt. auth. see Cohen, William S.

Lasson, Kenneth, jt. auth. see Margulies, Sheldon.

Lasson, Nelson B. The History & Development of the Fourth Amendment to the United States Constitution. LC 78-64166. (Johns Hopkins University. Studies in the Social Sciences. Thirtieth Ser. 1912: 2). reprint ed. 34.50 (*0-404-61276-8*) AMS Pr.

— History & Development of the Fourth Amendment to the United States Constitution. LC 75-87389. (American Constitutional & Legal History Ser). 1970. reprint ed. lib. bdg. 27.50 (*0-306-71532-5*) Da Capo.

Lassonde, Maryse & Jeeves, Malcolm A., eds. 031994al Agenesis: A Natural Split Brain? LC 93-46518. (Advances in Behavioral Biology Ser.: Vol. 42). (Illus.). 308p. 1994. 89.50 (*0-306-44660-X*, Plenum Pr) Plenum.

Lassonde, Reid E. Thirty-Five Practical Ways to Improve Your Health: A Common Sense Approach for Wholesome Living. LC 91-68336. (Illus.). 142p. (Orig.). 1992. pap. 9.95 (*0-9631846-7-9*) Real-Life Pubns.

***Lassure, C.** Tech Vocabulary-Vocabulaire Anglais-Francais de la Haute Technologie. 223p. (ENG & FRE.). 1991. pap. 39.95 (*0-7859-7150-5*) Fr & Eur.

***Lassus, Jean.** Antioch-on-the-Orontes Vol. 5: Les Portiques D'Antioche. LC 35-1197. (Publications of the Committee for the Excavation of Antioch & Its Vicinity). pap. 64.50 (*0-7837-9368-5*, 2060111) Bks Demand.

— Excavations at Antioch 5: Les Portiques D'antioche. LC 35-1197. (Illus.). (FRE.). 1972. 90.00x (*0-691-03537-7*) Princeton U Pr.

***Lassus, Patrick.** Harmful Marine Algal Blooms. Date not set. 170.00 (*1-898298-11-4*) Spr-Verlag.

Lasswell, Harold D. Harold D. Lasswell on Political Sociology. LC 76-22961. (Heritage of Sociology Ser.). 1977. lib. bdg. 27.50 (*0-226-46920-4*) U Ch Pr.

— Jurisprudence for a Free Society: Studies in Law, Science & Policy, 2 vols., Set. 1612p. (C). 1992. lib. bdg. 594.00 (*0-7923-0989-8*) Kluwer Ac.

— National Security & Individual Freedom. LC 71-139193. (Civil Liberties in American History Ser.). 1971. reprint ed. lib. bdg. 32.50 (*0-306-70085-9*) Da Capo.

— Politics: Who Gets What, When & How. 21.75 (*0-8446-1277-4*) Peter Smith.

— Power & Personality. LC 75-22644. 262p. 1976. reprint ed. text ed. 59.75 (*0-8371-8374-X*, LAPOP, Greenwood Pr) Greenwood.

— A Pre-View of Policy Sciences. LC 78-165801. (Policy Sciences Book Ser.). 187p. reprint ed. pap. 53.30 (*0-685-15397-5*, 2026259) Bks Demand.

— Psychopathology & Politics. xxvi, 340p. 1986. pap. text ed. 18.95 (*0-226-46919-0*) U Ch Pr.

— The Signature of Power: Buildings, Communication, & Policy. 224p. (C). 1978. text ed. 39.95x (*0-87855-289-8*) Transaction Pubs.

Lasswell, Harold D. & Blumenstock, Dorothy. World Revolutionary Propaganda. LC 78-114887. (Select Bibliographies Reprint Ser.). 1977. 29.95 (*0-8369-5291-X*) Ayer.

Lasswell, Harold D. & Lerner, Daniel, eds. World Revolutionary Elites: Studies in Coercive Ideological Movements. LC 80-21600. xi, 478p. 1980. reprint ed. text ed. 79.50 (*0-313-22572-9*, LAWE, Greenwood Pr) Greenwood.

Lasswell, Harold D., jt. auth. see Arens, Richard.

Lasswell, Harold D., et al, eds. Emergence of Public Opinion in the West. LC 79-18790. (Propaganda & Communication in World History Ser.: Vol. 2). 576p. reprint ed. pap. 164.20 (*0-685-17121-3*, 2027027) Bks Demand.

— Propaganda & Communication in World History, Vol. 3. LC 79-21108. 576p. reprint ed. pap. 164.20 (*0-685-17867-6*, 2029588) Bks Demand.

— Propaganda & Promotional Activities: An Annotated Bibliography. LC 75-77979. 474p. reprint ed. pap. 135.10 (*0-317-10305-9*, 2020100) Bks Demand.

Lasswell, Marcia & Lasswell, Thomas. Marriage & the Family. 3rd ed. 592p. (C). 1991. text ed. 47.95 (*0-534-12870-X*) Intl Thomson.

Lasswell, Mary. Bread for the Living. 1976. 18.95 (*0-8488-1405-3*) Amereon Ltd.

— Bread for the Living. 1981. reprint ed. lib. bdg. 19.95 (*0-89966-438-5*) Buccaneer Bks.

— Mrs. Rasmussen's Book of One Arm Cookery. Date not set. 15.95 (*0-8488-1406-1*) Amereon Ltd.

— Mrs. Rasmussen's Book of One-Arm Cookery. 1981. reprint ed. lib. bdg. 16.95 (*0-89966-437-7*) Buccaneer Bks.

Lasswell, Thomas, jt. auth. see Lasswell, Marcia.

Last, jt. auth. see Pratt.

Last, B. F. & Van Veldhuizen, A. M. Developments in Paediatric Psychosocial Oncology. 183p. 1992. 41.00 (*90-265-1131-0*, Pub. by Swets Pub Serv NE) Taylor & Francis.

Last, B. F. & VanVeldhuizn. Children with Cancer. 1991. 43.00 (*90-265-1038-1*, Pub. by Swets Pub Serv NE) Taylor & Francis.

Last, Cynthia G., ed. Anxiety Across the Life Span: A Developmental Perspective. LC 92-49675. (Behavior Therapy & Behavioral Medicine Ser.: Vol. 26). 232p. 1993. 37.95 (*0-8261-6460-9*) Springer Pub.

Last, Cynthia G. & Hersen, Michel. Handbook of Child Psychiatric Diagnosis. 1989. text ed. 80.00 (*0-471-84887-5*) Wiley.

Last, Cynthia G. & Hersen, Michel, eds. Issues in Diagnostic Research. LC 86-30575. 360p. 1987. 59.50 (*0-306-42424-X*, Plenum Pr) Plenum.

Last, Cynthia G. & Herson, Michel, eds. Adult Behavior Therapy Casebook. LC 93-6252. 1994p. 1993. 59.50 (*0-306-44451-8*) Plenum.

Last, Cynthia G., jt. ed. see Hersen, M.

Last, Cynthia G., jt. auth. see Hersen, Michel.

Last, Cynthia G., jt. auth. see Klein, Rachel G.

Last, F. T., et al, eds. Land & Its Uses-Actual & Potential: An Environmental Appraisal. LC 85-28111. (NATO ASI Conference Series I, Ecology: Vol. 10). 610p. 1986. 110.00 (*0-306-42214-X*, Plenum Pr) Plenum.

Last, F. W. How to Play Tennis: An Illustrated Guide to All Aspects of the Game. 18.50 (*0-87559-112-4*) Shalom.

Last, George & Williams, Paul. An Introduction to ROV Operations. 300p. (C). 1993. 280.00 (*1-870945-23-9*, Pub. by Oilfield Pubns UK) St Mut.

Last, Jay T., jt. auth. see McClelland, Gordon T.

Last, Jerold, ed. Eukaryotes at the Subcellular Level: Development & Differentiation. LC 75-42541. (Methods in Molecular Biology Ser.: No. 8). (Illus.). 472p. reprint ed. pap. 134.60 (*0-7837-0838-6*, 2041152) Bks Demand.

Last, Jerold A. Subcellular Particles, Structures, & Organelles. Laskin, Allen I., ed. LC 73-90306. (Methods in Molecular Biology Ser.: No. 5). (Illus.). 325p. reprint ed. pap. 92.70 (*0-7837-0906-4*, 2041211) Bks Demand.

Last, Jerold A. & Laskin, Allen I., eds. Protein Biosynthesis in Bacterial Systems. LC 78-160517. (Methods in Molecular Biology Ser.: No. 1). 349p. reprint ed. pap. 99.50 (*0-7837-0745-2*, 2041065) Bks Demand.

— Protein Biosynthesis in Nonbacterial Systems. LC 78-189798. (Methods in Molecular Biology Ser.: No. 2). (Illus.). 352p. reprint ed. pap. 100.40 (*0-7837-0740-1*, 2041062) Bks Demand.

Last, Jerold A., jt. ed. see Laskin, Allen I.

Last, Joan. At the Keyboard, 4 Bks, Bk. 1. 1954. pap. 6.95 (*0-19-322280-9*) OUP.

— At the Keyboard, 4 Bks, Bk. 2. 1954. pap. 6.95 (*0-19-322281-7*) OUP.

— At the Keyboard, 4 Bks, Bk. 3. 1954. pap. 6.95 (*0-19-322282-5*) OUP.

— At the Keyboard, 4 Bks, Bk. 4. 1954. pap. 6.95 (*0-19-322283-3*) OUP.

— The Young Pianist: An Approach for Teachers & Students. 2nd ed. (Illus.). 1985. pap. 17.95 (*0-19-322287-6*) OUP.

Last, John M. Diccionario de Enfermeria. 15th ed. 400p. (SPA.). 1984. pap. 19.95 (*0-7859-5929-7*, 8434523728) Fr & Eur.

— Diccionario de Epidemiologia. 216p. (SPA.). 1989. 49.95 (*0-7859-3356-5*, 8434523728) Fr & Eur.

— A Dictionary of Epidemiology. 3rd ed. (Illus.). 208p. 1995. 35.00 (*0-19-509667-3*) OUP.

— A Dictionary of Epidemiology. 3rd ed. (Illus.). 208p. 1995. pap. 16.95 (*0-19-509668-1*) OUP.

— Maxcy-Rosenau-Last Public Health & Preventive Medicine. 13th ed. (Illus.). 1257p. (C). 1992. text ed. 120.00 (*0-8385-6188-8*, A6188-5) Appleton & Lange.

— Public Health & Human Ecology. 416p. 1987. pap. text ed. 42.95 (*0-8385-8045-9*, A8045-5) Appleton & Lange.

Last, John M., ed. A Dictionary of Epidemiology. 2nd ed. (Handbooks Sponsored by the IEA & WHO Ser.). (Illus.). 160p. 1988. pap. 14.95 (*0-19-505481-4*) OUP.

Last, Mary Z., jt. auth. see Pratt, Philip J.

Last, Murray & Chavunduka, Gordon L. The Professionalisation of African Medicine. (International African Institute Seminar Studies). (Illus.). 368p. 1988. text ed. 79.95 (*0-7190-1851-X*, Pub. by Manchester Univ Pr UK) St Martin.

Last, P. & Stevens, J. Sharks & Rays of Australia. (Illus.). 600p. 1993. 59.95 (*0-643-05143-0*, Pub. by CSIRO AT) Intl Spec Bk.

Last, P. R., et al. Fishes of Tasmania. (Illus.). 563p. 1983. pap. text ed. 75.00 (*0-7246-1143-6*, Pub. by Tasmanian Govt Print AT) Lubrecht & Cramer.

Last, Rex. MS-DOS 5 - 6 Masterclass. 250p. 1994. pap. 47.50 (*1-85058-322-6*, Pub. by Sigma Press UK) Coronet Bks.

Last, Rex W., jt. auth. see Barker, Christine R.

Last, W. M., jt. ed. see Renaut, R. W.

Laster, Ann A. & Pickett, Nell A. Occupational English. 4th ed. 576p. (C). 1990. pap. text ed. 40.00 (*0-06-043858-4*) HarpCollege.

Laster, Ann A., jt. auth. see Pickett, Nell A.

Laster, Ann A., jt. auth. see Pickett.

Laster, Clay. The Complete Handbook of Amateur Radio. 3rd ed. 1993. pap. text ed. 21.95 (*0-07-036594-6*) McGraw.

— The Complete Handbook of Amateur Radio. 3rd ed. LC 93-1556. 1993. pap. 19.60 (*0-8306-4354-0*) TAB Bks.

— Thyristor Theory & Application. (Illus.). 192p. 1986. pap. 10.95 (*0-685-13448-2*, 2665P) TAB Bks.

Laster, James, comp. Catalogue of Choral Music Arranged in Biblical Order. LC 82-16745. 269p. 1983. 39.50 (*0-8108-1592-3*) Scarecrow.

— A Discography of Treble Voice Recordings. LC 84-22179. 157p. 1984. 20.00 (*0-8108-1760-8*) Scarecrow.

Laster, James H., comp. Catalogue of Vocal Solos & Duets Arranged in Biblical Order. LC 84-14187. 212p. 1984. 25.00 (*0-8108-1748-9*) Scarecrow.

Laster, Janet F. Toward Excellence in Secondary Vocational Education: Using Cognitive Psychology in Curriculum Planning. 65p. 1985. 7.25 (*0-318-22221-3*, IN297) Ctr Educ Trng Employ.

Laster, Jim. The Birthday Gift That Beeped. Knight, George, ed. LC 83-176266. (Illus.). 56p. (J). (gr. k-4). 1983. 10.95 (*0-9612780-0-5*) J Laster Pub Co.

Laster, Kathy & Taylor, Veronica. Interpreters & the Legal System. 280p. 1994. pap. 39.00 (*1-86287-130-2*, Pub. by Federation Pr AU) W W Gaunt.

***Laster, Leonard.** Choices after Medical School. 300p. (C). 1995. pap. write for info. (*0-393-71030-0*) Norton.

Laster, Paul & Riccardo, Renee. Acceptable Entertainment. LC 88-80322. 1988. pap. 14.00 (*0-916365-25-5*) Ind Curators.

— Spiral of Artificiality. Bershad, Deborah, ed. (Illus.). 24p. (Orig.). 1987. pap. write for info. (*0-936739-09-6*) Hallwalls Inc.

Laster, Thomas G. How to Profit Through Politeness or Good Manners Can't Be All Bad. LC 82-80252. 150p. (Orig.). (C). 1982. 14.95 (*0-88247-654-8*); pap. 9.95 (*0-88247-653-X*) R & E Pubs.

Lastigzon, J. World Fertilizer Progress Into the 1980s. (Technical Bulletin Ser.: No. T-22). (Illus.). 64p. (Orig.). 1981. pap. 4.00 (*0-88090-021-0*) Intl Fertilizer.

Lasting, Ingeborg & Singer, Heidi. Living Language German All the Way: Learn at Home & on the Go. LC 93-22955. (ENG & GER.). 1994. Manual/cassette pkg. audio 60.00 (*0-517-58378-X*, Crown); Manual. 15.00 (*0-517-58379-8*, Crown) Crown Pub Group.

Lastiri, Santiago, jt. ed. see Ramirez, Bernardo.

Lastman, G. J. & Sinha, Naresh K. Microcomputer-Based Numerical Methods for Science & Engineering. 544p. (C). 1989. pap. 60.00 (*0-03-013792-6*); Solutions manual with instr.'s edition software. write for info. (*0-03-013789-6*) SCP.

Lastovka, M., ed. International Association of Logopedics & Phoniatrics, 21st Congress, Prague, August 1989: Main Reports. (Illus.). 96p. 1989. pap. 49.00 (*3-8055-5053-7*) S Karger.

Lastra, G. L., et al, eds. Applications of Computers to Engineering Design, Manufacturing & Management: Proceedings of the TC5 Conference on CAD-CAM Technology Transfer, Mexico City, Mexico 22-26 August, 1988. 338p. 1989. 82.00 (*0-444-87314-7*, North Holland) Elsevier.

Lastres, Helena M. The Advance Materials Revolution & the Japanese System of Innovation. LC 94-16019. 1994. text ed. 65.00 (*0-312-12055-9*) St Martin.

Lastrucci, Carlo. Scientific Approach. 257p. 1967. pap. 16.95 (*0-87073-042-8*) Schenkman Bks Inc.

Lasure, Linda L., jt. ed. see Bennett, J. W.

Laswell, J. Verne. Poems by the End of the Oregon Trail. Stiltner, E., ed. & intro. by. 76p. (Orig.). 1990. 7.75 (*1-878457-54-3*); pap. 7.75 (*0-685-30411-6*) Skunk Creek Computing Servs.

Laswell, Lawrence K. Collision: Theory vs. Reality in Expert Systems. LC 89-3723. (Illus.). 286p. 1989. pap. 29.95 (*0-89435-294-6*, BF2946) Wiley.

Laswell, Mary. Suds in Your Eye. adapted ed. 1944. pap. 4.75 (*0-8222-1095-9*) Dramatists Play.

Laszity, Radomir & Hidvegi, Mate, eds. Amino Acid Composition & Biological Value of Cereal Proteins. 1985. lib. bdg. 164.50 (*90-277-1937-3*) Kluwer Ac.

Laszlo. Physicians Guide to Cancer Care Complications: Prevention. (Fundamentals of Cancer Management Ser.: Vol. 2). 360p. 1986. 135.00 (*0-8247-7547-3*) Dekker.

Laszlo, E. Human Values & the Mind of Man. (Current Topics of Contemporary Thought Ser.). 184p. 1971. text ed. 77.00 (*0-677-14590-X*) Gordon & Breach.

Laszlo, E., ed. The New Evolutionary Paradigm: Transdisciplinary Studies. 208p. 1991. text ed. 62.00 (*2-88124-375-4*) Gordon & Breach.

Laszlo, E., jt. auth. see Stulman, J.

Laszlo, Ervin. The Choice, Evolution or Extinction? A Thinking Person's Guide to Global Issues. LC 93-29994. 224p. 1994. 17.95 (*0-87477-753-4*, J P T-Putnam) Putnam Pub Group.

— Co-Operation for Development: Strategies for the 1980's. 107p. 1984. pap. 10.00 (*0-86346-046-1*, Tycooly Pub) Weidner & Sons.

— Co-Operation in the 1980s: Principles & Prospects, Vol. 1. 208p. 1984. pap. 20.00 (*0-907567-73-8*, Tycooly Pub) Weidner & Sons.

— The Communist Idealogy in Hungary: Handbook for Basic Research. (Sovietica Ser.: No. 23). 351p. 1966. lib. bdg. 89.00 (*90-277-0056-7*) Kluwer Ac.

— The Inner Limits of Mankind. 160p. 1989. 14.95 (*1-85168-015-2*); pap. 7.95 (*1-85168-009-8*) Onewrld Pubns.

— The Interconnected Universe: Conceptual Foundations of Transdiciplinary Unified Theory. LC 95-1807. 170p. 1995. text ed. 32.00 (*981-02-2202-5*) World Scientific Pub.

— Introduction to Systems Philosophy - Toward a New Paradigm of Contemporary Thought. LC 76-156080. 350p. 1972. 108.00 (*0-677-03850-X*) Gordon & Breach.

— Multi-Cultural Planet: The Report of a Unesco International Expert Group. 1994. pap. 17.95 (*1-85168-042-X*) Onewrld Pubns.

— System, Structure & Experience: Toward a Scientific Theory of Mind. (Current Topics of Contemporary Thought Ser.: Vol. 1). 124p. 1969. text ed. 82.00 (*0-677-02360-X*) Gordon & Breach.

— The Systems View of the World. LC 71-188357. 131p. 1972. pap. 7.95 (*0-8076-0636-7*) Braziller.

— Vision 2020: Reordering Chaos for Global Survival. LC 93-30959. 1994. pap. text ed. 12.95 (*2-88124-612-5*) Gordon & Breach.

Laszlo, Ervin, ed. Europe in the Contemporary World. (Special Issue of the Journal World Futures). 308p. 1986. pap. text ed. 41.00 (*0-677-21520-7*) Gordon & Breach.

— Goals in a Global Community: Studies on the Conceptual Foundations, Vol. I. LC 77-79971. 1977. text ed. 146.00 (*0-08-022221-8*, Pub. by Pergamon Repr UK) Franklin.

— Philosophy in the Soviet Union: A Survey of the Mid-Sixties. (Sovietica Ser.: No.25). 208p. 1967. lib. bdg. 45.50 (*90-277-0057-5*) Kluwer Ac.

— The Relevance of General Systems Theory. LC 72-81355. 213p. 1972. 8.95 (*0-8076-0659-6*) Braziller.

Laszlo, Ervin & Bierman, Judah, eds. Goals in a Global Community, Vol. II. 1978. text ed. 130.00 (*0-08-022973-5*, Pergamon Pr) Elsevier.

Laszlo, Ervin & Kurtzman, Joel, eds. Political & Institutional Issues of the New International Economic Order. (Policy Studies on the New International Economic Order). 208p. 1981. 52.00 (*0-08-025122-6*, Pergamon Pr) Elsevier.

— The Structure of the World Economy & Prospects for a New International Economic Order. LC 79-23350. (Policy Studies on the New International Economic Order). 120p. 1980. 44.00 (*0-08-025119-6*, Pergamon Pr) Elsevier.

— The United States, Canada & the New International Economic Order. (Policy Studies). 1979. 52.00 (*0-08-025113-7*, Pergamon Pr) Elsevier.

Laszlo, Ervin & Wilbur, James B., eds. Human Values & Natural Science. (Current Topics of Contemporary Thought Ser.: Vol. 4). 306p. 1970. text ed. 99.00 (*0-677-13960-8*) Gordon & Breach.

— Value Theory in Philosophy & Social Science. LC 73-84239. (Current Topics of Contemporary Thought Ser.). 166p. 1973. text ed. 82.00 (*0-677-14160-2*) Gordon & Breach.

An Asterisk (*) at the beginning of an entry indicates that the title is appearing in BIP for the first time.

Laszlo, Ervin & Yoo, Jong Y., eds. World Encyclopedia of Peace, 4 vols. LC 86-25520. (Illus.). 1930p. 1986. 615.00 (*0-08-032685-4*, Pergamon Pr) Elsevier.

Laszlo, Ervin, jt. ed. see Gotesky, Rubin.

Laszlo, Ervin, ed. see Sutherland, John W.

Laszlo, Ervin, et al. R C D C (Regional Cooperation among Developing Countries) The New Imperative of Development in the 1980's. 75p. 1981. pap. 25.00 (*0-08-027556-7*, Pergamon Pr) Elsevier.

Laszlo, Ervin, et al, eds. The Evolution of Cognitive Maps: New Paradigms for the Twenty-First Century. LC 92-23607. (World Futures General Evolution Studies: Vol. 5). 1993. text ed. 75.00 (*2-88124-559-5*) Gordon & Breach.

Laszlo, F. & Janaky, T., eds. Clinical Application of Radioimmunoassay. 1992. pap. 32.00 (*963-05-6219-7*, Pub. by A K HU) Intl Spec Bk.

Laszlo, F. A. Recent Results in Peptide Hormone & Androgenic Steroid Research 9th Congress of the Hungarian Society of Endocrinology. 326p. 1979. 103.00 (*0-569-08624-8*, Pub. by Collets UK) Pro-Am Music.

— Renal Cortical Necrosis. (Contributions to Nephrology Ser.: Vol. 28). (Illus.). viii, 216p. 1981. pap. 60.00 (*3-8055-2109-X*) S Karger.

Laszlo, F. A. & Antoni, F. Biomedical Significance of Peptide Research. 280p. 1984. 150.00 (*0-569-08821-6*, Pub. by Collets UK) Pro-Am Music.

— Biomedical Significance of Peptide Research. 278p. (C). 1984. 87.00x (*963-05-3886-5*, Pub. by Akad Kiado HU) St Mut.

Laszlo, G. Dictionary of Technical Information: Power Electronics. 584p. (C). 1985. 125.00 (*0-685-60802-6*, Pub. by Collets) St Mut.

Laszlo, G., ed. Dictionary of Technical Information: Power Electronics. 584p. (C). 1985. 125.00 (*0-685-49865-4*, Pub. by Collets) St Mut.

Laszlo, Gabriel. Pulmonary Function: A Guide for Clinicians. (Illus.). 350p. (C). 1994. 69.95 (*0-521-43050-X*); pap. 37.95 (*0-521-44679-1*) Cambridge U Pr.

***Laszlo, Ivan.** Malmond. LC 94-78724. 216p. (Orig.). 1995. pap. 12.95 (*1-882897-00-5*) Lost Coast.

Laszlo, J. A., jt. ed. see Dintzis, F. R.

Laszlo, Janos, jt. ed. see Cupchik, Gerald C.

***Laszlo, John.** The Cure of Childhood Leukemia: Into the Age of Miracles. (Illus.). 300p. (C). 1995. text ed. 29.95 (*0-8135-2186-6*) Rutgers U Pr.

Laszlo, Judith I. & Bairstow, Phillip J. Perceptual Motor Behavior: Developmental Assessment & Therapy. 1985. text ed. 37.50 (*0-275-91650-2*, C1650, Praeger Pubs) Greenwood.

Laszlo, Judith L., jt. ed. see Van Rossum, Jacques H.

Laszlo, M. B., jt. auth. see Krompecher, I.

Laszlo, Pierre. Molecular Correlates of Biological Concepts: A History of Biochemistry. (Comprehensive Biochemistry Ser.: No. 34A). 492p. 1986. 162.00 (*0-444-80776-4*) Elsevier.

— Organic Reactions: Simplicity & Logic. LC 94-30633. 1994. text ed. 74.95 (*0-471-93933-1*); pap. text ed. 39.95 (*0-471-95278-8*) Wiley.

Laszlo, Pierre, ed. NMR of Newly Accessible Nuclei, Vol. 1: Chemical & Biochemical Applications. LC 83-4619. 1983. text ed. 126.00 (*0-12-437101-9*) Acad Pr.

— NMR of Newly Accessible Nuclei, Vol. 2: Chemically & Biochemically Important Elements. 1984. text ed. 138.00 (*0-12-437102-7*) Acad Pr.

— Preparative Chemistry Using Supported Reagents. 545p. 1987. text ed. 165.00 (*0-12-437105-1*) Acad Pr.

Laszlo, Pierre, jt. auth. see Balogh, M.

Laszok, Anthony A., ed. see Appleyard, et al.

Laszt, L. & Schaad, R. Luftverunreinigung und Herz-Kreislauf-System. (Illus.). viii, 140p. 1980. pap. 22.50 (*3-8055-3067-6*) S Karger.

Laszt, L., ed. see Symposia Angiologica Santoriana Staff.

Lasztity, Radomir. The Chemistry of Cereal Proteins. 216p. 1984. 139.95 (*0-8493-5140-5*, TP453, CRC Reprint) Franklin.

— The Chemistry of Cereal Proteins. 2nd ed. 300p. 1995. write for info. (*0-8493-2763-6*, 2763) CRC Pr.

***Lat-Kla, Loo-Wit.** Gold Hunting in the Cascade Mountains. LC 91-72915. (Illus.). vi, 56p. 1991. reprint ed. 45.00x (*0-9629954-0-1*) Bk Club Wash.

Lata Gairala, jt. auth. see Poonam Sharma.

Lata, Gene F., jt. auth. see Dryer, R. L.

Lataille, Jane I. Electrical Equipment in Hazardous (Classified) Locations. 1988. 5.35 (*0-685-38091-2*, TR 88-1) Society Fire Protect.

Latal, H. & Mitter, H., eds. Concepts & Trends in Particle Physics. (Illus.). 340p. 1987. 59.00 (*0-387-17372-2*) Spr-Verlag.

— Physics for a New Generation: Prospects for High-Energy Physics at New Accelerators; Proceedings of the XXVIII, Internationale Universitatswochen fur Kernphysik, Schladming, Austria, March 1989. (Illus.). 344p. 1990. 63.00 (*0-387-52378-2*) Spr-Verlag.

***Latal, Heimo & Schweiger, Wolfgang, eds.** Matter Under Extreme Conditions: Proceedings of the 33th Internationale Universit Atswochen fur Kern - und Teilchenphysik, Schladming, Austria, 27 February - 5 March 1994. (Lecture Notes in Physics: Vol. 440). 1994. write for info. (*3-540-58689-X*) Spr-Verlag.

Latane, John H. America As a World Power, 1897-1907. (History - United States Ser.). 350p. 1992. reprint ed. lib. bdg. 89.00 (*0-7812-6213-5*) Rprt Serv.

— America As a World Power, 1897-1907. LC 79-145131. (Illus.). 1971. reprint ed. 49.00 (*0-403-01064-0*) Scholarly.

— The Early Relations Between Maryland & Virginia. Bd. with Is History Past Politics? LC 78-63837. LC 78-63837. (Johns Hopkins University. Studies in the Social Sciences. Thirtieth Ser. 1912: 3-4). reprint ed. 11.50 (*0-404-61096-X*) AMS Pr.

Latanision, R. M. & Fischer, T. E. Advances in Mechanics & Physics of Surfaces, Vol. 1. 262p. 1981. text ed. 207.00 (*3-7186-0026-9*) Gordon & Breach.

— Advances in the Mechanics & Physics of Surfaces, Vol. 3. 352p. 1986. text ed. 226.00 (*3-7186-0251-2*) Gordon & Breach.

Latanision, R. M. & Fischer, T. E., eds. Advances in the Mechanics & Physics of Surfaces, Vol. 2. 374p. 1983. text ed. 222.00 (*3-7186-0156-7*) Gordon & Breach.

Latanision, R. M. & Jones, R. H., eds. Chemistry & Physics of Fracture. (C). 1987. lib. bdg. 216.50 (*90-247-3580-7*) Kluwer Ac.

Latapi, Agustin E., jt. ed. see De la Rocha, Mercedes G.

Latas, Michael. Job Series Now: The Series. 336p. 1993. Series. pap. 25.95 (*1-882904-05-2*) Job Srch Pubs.

— Job Series Now: The Series, 1. 336p. 1993. pap. 3.95 (*1-882904-10-9*) Job Srch Pubs.

Latash, Mark L. Control of Human Movement. LC 92-36991. (Illus.). 392p. 1993. text ed. 47.00x (*0-87322-455-8*, BLAT0455) Human Kinetics.

Latash, Mark L., ed. see Bernstein, N. A.

Latassa y Ortin, Felix D. Bibliotecas Antiguas y Nuevas, 3 vols. reprint ed. write for info. (*0-318-71836-7*, Pub. by Georg Olms GW) Lubrecht & Cramer.

Lataste, X., jt. ed. see Ferrari, M. D.

Lataste, X., jt. ed. see Lieberman, A.

Latawski, Paul, ed. Contemporary Nationalism in East Central Europe: Unfinished Business. LC 94-16291. 1994. write for info. (*0-312-12276-4*) St Martin.

— The Reconstruction of Poland, 1914-23. LC 91-19886. 217p. 1992. text ed. 69.95 (*0-312-06536-1*) St Martin.

Latch, Edward. Mosaic System of Chronology in the Elucidation of Mysteries Pertaining to the "Bible in Stone" Known As the Great Pyramyd of Egypt. 1987. reprint ed. pap. 5.95 (*0-916411-71-0*, Sure Fire) Holmes Pub.

Latcham, Jack, jt. auth. see Birch, Derek W.

Latcham, W. E., jt. auth. see Gabb, M. H.

Latchaw. MR & CT Imaging of the Head, Neck & Spine. (SPA.). 1992. 225.00 (*0-8016-6732-1*) Mosby Yr Bk.

Latchaw, Richard E. MR & CT Imaging of the Head, Neck & Spine. 2nd ed. 1216p. 1990. 235.00 (*0-8151-5330-9*, Yr Bk Med Pubs) Mosby Yr Bk.

Latchaw, Richard E., ed. Computed Tomography of the Head, Neck & Spine. (Illus.). 500p. 1984. 195.00 (*0-8151-5329-5*, Yr Bk Med Pubs) Mosby Yr Bk.

Latchem, Colin, et al, eds. Interactive Multimedia: Practice & Promise. 1992. 75.00 (*0-7494-0815-4*, Pub. by Kogan Page Educ UK) Taylor & Francis.

Latchman, D. S., ed. From Genetics to Gene Therapy. (University College, London, Molecular Pathology Ser.). 250p. 1994. 167.50x (*1-872748-36-8*, Pub. by Bios Scientific UK) Coronet Bks.

***Latchman, David, ed.** Eukaryotic Transcription Factors. (Illus.). 288p. 1994. pap. text ed. 39.95 (*0-12-437171-X*) Acad Pr.

***Latchman, David S.** Eukaryotic Transcription Factors. 2nd ed. (Illus.). 304p. 1995. boxed write for info. (*0-12-437172-8*) Acad Pr.

— Gene Regulation: A Eukaryotic Perspective. (Illus.). 220p. (C). 1990. text ed. 65.00 (*0-04-445242-X*); pap. text ed. 24.95 (*0-04-445243-8*) Routledge Chapman & Hall.

***Latchman, David S., ed.** Genetic Manipulation of the Nervous System: Viral Approaches. (Neuroscience Perspectives Ser.). (Illus.). 250p. 1995. boxed write for info. (*0-12-437165-5*) Acad Pr.

— PCR Applications in Pathology: Principles & Practice. (Modern Methods in Pathology Ser.). (Illus.). 288p. 1995. 49.95 (*0-19-854835-4*) OUP.

— Transcription Factors: A Practical Approach. LC 92-48702. (Practical Approach Ser.). (C). 1993. 70.00 (*0-19-963342-8*, IRL Pr); pap. 39.00 (*0-19-963341-X*, IRL Pr) OUP.

Late, N. T. Bay of Pigs: Can of Worms. 10p. (Orig.). 1994. pap. write for info. (*0-9641448-9-1*) N Late Pub.

— Biopsy Notes. 14p. (Orig.). 1994. pap. write for info. (*0-9641448-7-5*) N Late Pub.

— Intomorrow. 40p. (Orig.). 1995. pap. write for info. (*0-9641448-6-7*) N Late Pub.

— The Second Hand. 11p. (Orig.). (C). 1994. pap. write for info. (*0-9641448-3-2*) N Late Pub.

Late Night with David Letterman Writers Staff & Letterman, David. An Altogether New Book of Top Ten Lists: From "Late Night with David Letterman" Peters, Sally, ed. 160p. (Orig.). 1991. pap. 11.00 (*0-671-74901-3*) PB.

— The Late Night with David Letterman Book of Top Ten Lists. Wells, Leslie, ed. 160p. (Orig.). 1990. pap. 11.00 (*0-671-72671-4*) PB.

Lateef, K. Sarwar, jt. ed. see Boughton, James M.

Lategan, Bernard C. & Vorster, Willem S. Text & Reality: Aspects of Reference in Biblical Texts. 1985. 22.95 (*0-89130-822-9*, 06 06 14); pap. 16.95 (*0-89130-823-7*) Scholars Pr GA.

Lateiner, Alfred. Modern Techniques of Supervision. 15th rev. ed. LC 66-4182. 1978. One to nineteen copies. pap. 10.00 (*0-911722-00-9*); Twenty to forty-nine copies. pap. 8.00 (*0-318-54063-0*); Fifty or more copies. pap. 7.50 (*0-318-54064-9*) Lateiner.

Lateiner, Donald. The Historical Method of Herodotus. (Phoenix Supplementary Volumes Ser.: No. 23). 333p. 1989. 45.00 (*0-8020-5793-4*) U of Toronto Pr.

— The Historical Method of Herodotus. (Phoenix Supplementary Volumes Ser.: No. 23). 336p. 1992. pap. 19.95 (*0-8020-7684-X*) U of Toronto Pr.

— Sardonic Smile: Nonverbal Behavior in Homeric Epic. LC 95-1704. 1995. 44.50 (*0-472-10598-1*) U of Mich Pr.

Latela, Mary E. My Friend Is Dying: Prayers & Reflections. 64p. (Orig.). 1993. pap. text ed. 3.95 (*0-89243-517-8*) Liguori Pubns.

Latella, F. Skip, et al. Get in Shape, Stay in Shape. (Illus.). 128p. 1989. pap. 14.95 (*0-89043-243-0*) Consumer Reports.

Latella, Lisa. A Song for the Prince. (Illus.). 36p. (Orig.). (J). (gr. k up). 1984. pap. write for info. (*0-9608592-1-7*) Gallery Arts.

Laterrade, Remy. Dat Little Cajun Cookbook by Remy. 150p. (Orig.). 1993. spiral bd. 4.95 (*0-9632197-1-5*) Relco Ent.

— Dat Little New Orleans Cookbook. 150p. (Orig.). 1994. spiral bd., pap. 4.95 (*0-9632197-2-3*) Relco Ent.

— I Want Dat Cajun Cookbook: A Collection of Cajun Cuisine. 2nd rev. ed. (Illus.). 226p. 1995. reprint ed. 12.95 (*0-9632197-3-1*) Relco Ent.

***Laterrade, Remy & Arrigo, Joe.** Dat Little Plantation Dessert Cookbook. (Illus.). 151p. 1995. spiral bd., pap. 4.95 (*0-9632197-4-X*) Relco Ent.

Latessa, Edward J., jt. auth. see Vito, Gennaro F.

Latge, J. P. & Boucias, D., eds. Fungal Cell Wall & Immune Response. (NATO ASI Series H: Cell Biology: Vol. 53). (Illus.). 472p. 1991. 175.00 (*0-387-53147-5*) Spr-Verlag.

Latge, J. P., et al, eds. Fungal Antigens: Isolation, Purification, & Detection. (Illus.). 486p. 1989. 125.00 (*0-306-43115-7*, Plenum Pr) Plenum.

Lath, Mukund. Dattilam. (C). 1988. 48.50 (*81-208-0586-0*, Pub. by Motilal Banarsidass II) S Asia.

Lath, Mukund, jt. auth. see Callewaert, Winand.

Latham, A. J. H., comp. Africa, Asia, & South America since 1800: A Bibliographical Guide. LC 93-47152. 1994. text ed. write for info. (*0-7190-1877-3*, Pub. by Manchester Univ Pr UK) St Martin.

Latham, Aaron. The Frozen Leopard: Hunting My Dark Heart in Africa. (Destinations Ser.). (Illus.). 352p. 1992. pap. 12.00 (*0-671-79278-4*, Touchstone Bks) S&S Trade.

Latham, Agnes, ed. see Shakespeare, William.

Latham, Andrew, ed. see NATO Advanced Research Workshop on the Future of the Defence Firm Staff.

Latham, Barbara, jt. auth. see Carr, Harold.

***Latham-Bass, Leigh A.** Race the Tide. 1995. 10.95 (*0-533-11084-X*) Vantage.

Latham, Bill, jt. auth. see Lea, Thomas D.

Latham, Caroline. Katherine Hepburn. (American Women of Achievement Ser.). (Illus.). 112p. (YA). (gr. 5 up). 1988. 17.95 (*1-55546-658-3*); pap. 9.95 (*0-7910-0416-3*) Chelsea Hse.

— Michael Jackson: Thrill. 1984. pap. 2.95 (*0-8217-1430-9*) Zebra.

Latham, Caroline & Agresta, David. Dodge Dynasty: The Car & the Family That Rocked Detroit. (Illus.). 360p. 1989. 19.95 (*0-15-125320-X*) HarBrace.

***Latham, Cathy.** Measure Twice Cut Once: Construction Debris & Nonhazardous Industrial Waste Report. (Illus.). 89p. (Orig.). (C). 1994. pap. text ed. 45.00x (*0-7881-1067-5*) Diane Pub.

Latham, Charles, Jr. Dublin School, a New Beginning, 1970-1985. (Illus.). 1987. pap. 10.00 (*0-87233-089-3*) Bauhan.

Latham, Charles. William Fortune: A Hoosier Biography. (Illus.). 150p. 1994. 18.95 (*0-87820-837-2*) Guild Pr IN.

Latham, Charles W. Lithographic Offset Press Operating. rev. ed. LC 57-22887. 273p. reprint ed. pap. 77.90 (*0-7837-0365-1*, 2040687) Bks Demand.

Latham, D. & De Costa, L. A., eds. Large-Scale Structures & Peculiar Motions in the Universe. (ASP Conference Series Publications: Vol. 15). 406p. 1991. 25.00 (*0-937707-34-1*) Astron Soc Pacific.

Latham, D. W., jt. ed. see Davis Philip, A. G.

Latham, David. Sinclair Ross: An Annotated Bibliography. 395p. (C). 1981. pap. text ed. 9.00 (*0-920763-63-4*, Pub. by ECW Press CN) Genl Dist Srvs.

Latham, David & Latham, Sheila. An Annotated Critical Bibliography of William Morris. LC 90-47281. 220p. 1991. text ed. 49.95 (*0-312-05656-7*) St Martin.

Latham, Donald C., jt. auth. see Martin, Thomas L., Jr.

Latham, E. Famous Sayings & Their Authors. 1972. 59.95 (*0-8490-0155-2*) Gordon Pr.

Latham, Earl. The Communist Controversy in Washington: From the New Deal to McCarthy. LC 66-14447. 460p. reprint ed. pap. 131.10 (*0-685-09008-6*, 2002785) Bks Demand.

— The Group Basis of Politics: Notes for a Theory. (Reprint Series in Social Sciences). (C). 1993. reprint ed. pap. text ed. 1.00 (*0-8290-2753-X*, PS-164) Irvington.

— Politics of Railroad Coordination, 1933-1936. LC 59-9279. 348p. 1959. 34.50 (*0-674-68951-8*) HUP.

Latham, Earl, ed. The Declaration of Independence & the Constitution. 3rd ed. (Problems in American Civilization Ser.). 288p. (C). 1976. pap. text ed. 8.50 (*0-669-94888-8*) Heath.

— The Meaning of McCarthyism. 2nd ed. (Problems in American Civilization Ser.). 216p. (C). 1973. pap. text ed. 8.50 (*0-669-81851-8*) Heath.

Latham, Edward. A Dictionary of Names, Nicknames, & Surnames of Persons, Places & Things. LC 89-26513. 334p. 1990. reprint ed. lib. bdg. 48.00 (*1-55888-901-9*) Omnigraphics Inc.

Latham Foundation Staff. Universal Kinship: The Bond Between All Living Things. LC 91-50981. (Illus.). 200p. 1992. text ed. 22.95 (*0-88247-918-0*, 918); pap. text ed. 11.95 (*0-88247-917-2*, 917) R & E Pubs.

Latham, G. C., jt. auth. see Notcott, L. A.

Latham, Gary P. Increasing Productivity Through Performance Appraisal. 2nd ed. (C). 1994. pap. text ed. 26.95 (*0-201-51400-1*) Addison-Wesley.

Latham, Gary P., jt. auth. see Locke, Edwin A.

Latham, Gary P., jt. auth. see Mealiea, Laird W.

Latham, Glen I. The Power of Positive Parenting. 426p. 1994. pap. 14.95 (*1-56901-141-9*) NW Pub.

Latham, Hugh, tr. see Sehlin, Gunhild.

Latham, Hugh, tr. see Streit, Jacob.

Latham, J. D. From Muslim Spain to Barbary: Studies in the History & Culture of the Muslim West. (Collected Studies: No. CS246). (Illus.). 348p. (C). 1986. reprint ed. lib. bdg. 99.50 (*0-86078-194-1*, Pub. by Variorum UK) Ashgate Pub Co.

Latham, Jacqueline E., ed. Critics on Virginia Woolf. LC 77-124653. (Readings in Literary Criticism Ser.: No. 8). 1979. pap. 10.95 (*0-87024-170-2*) U of Miami Pr.

Latham, Jean L. Carry on, Mr. Bowditch. (Illus.). (J). (gr. 6 up). 1955. 14.95 (*0-395-06881-9*) HM.

— Carry on, Mr. Bowditch. LC 55-5219. (Illus.). 256p. (J). (gr. 6 up). 1973. pap. 5.95 (*0-395-13713-6*, Sandpiper) HM.

— David Glasgow Farragut: Our First Admiral. (Discovery Biographies Ser.). (Illus.). 80p. (J). (gr. 2-6). 1991. reprint ed. lib. bdg. 12.95 (*0-7910-1438-X*) Chelsea Hse.

— Eli Whitney: Great Inventor. (Discovery Biographies Ser.). (Illus.). 80p. (J). (gr. 2-6). 1991. reprint ed. lib. bdg. 12.95 (*0-7910-1453-3*) Chelsea Hse.

— Elizabeth Blackwell: Pioneer Woman Doctor. (Discovery Biographies Ser.). (Illus.). 80p. (J). (gr. 2-6). 1991. reprint ed. lib. bdg. 12.95 (*0-7910-1406-1*) Chelsea Hse.

— George W. Goethals: Panama Canal Engineer. (Discovery Biographies Ser.). (Illus.). 80p. (J). (gr. 2-6). 1991. reprint ed. lib. bdg. 12.95 (*0-7910-1440-1*) Chelsea Hse.

— Rachel Carson: Who Loved the Sea. (Discovery Biographies Ser.). (Illus.). 80p. (J). (gr. 2-6). 1991. reprint ed. lib. bdg. 12.95 (*0-7910-1408-8*) Chelsea Hse.

— Sam Houston: Hero of Texas. (Discovery Biographies Ser.). (Illus.). 80p. (J). (gr. 2-6). 1991. reprint ed. lib. bdg. 12.95 (*0-7910-1441-X*) Chelsea Hse.

— Samuel F. B. Morse. (Discovery Biographies Ser.). (Illus.). 80p. (J). (gr. 2-6). 1991. reprint ed. lib. bdg. 12.95 (*0-7910-1447-9*) Chelsea Hse.

Latham, Jean L., comp. Do's & Don'ts of Drama. rev. ed. 1983. 5.95 (*0-87129-311-0*, D22) Dramatic Pub.

Latham, John, jt. ed. see Ruhnke, Lothar H.

Latham, Joyce. Where I Belong: A Forest of Dean Childhood in the 1930s. LC 93-30086. 1993. 29.00 (*0-7509-0386-4*) A Sutton Pub.

Latham, Linnet, ed. see Pepys, Samuel.

Latham, Maxwell E., Jr. Abortion in the Church. LC 89-85219. (Illus.). 216p. (Orig.). 1990. pap. 6.95 (*1-878153-00-5*) Light The World.

Latham, Michael A. The Hawaii Guide. Suzuki-Latham, Kathea, ed. LC 85-61611. (Illus.). 160p. (Orig.). 1986. pap. 8.95 (*0-934997-00-4*) Pacific Pub HI.

Latham, Minor W. The Elizabethan Fairies: The Fairies of Folklore & the Fairies of Shakespeare. (BCL1-PR English Literature Ser.). 313p. 1992. reprint ed. lib. bdg. 89.00 (*0-7812-7033-2*) Rprt Serv.

Latham, N. & Amoni, I. J. Sketch Map History of West Africa. (Illus.). (C). 1978. 13.95 (*0-7175-0803-X*, Pub. by S Thornes UK) Dufour.

Latham, Norah. A Sketch Map History of West Africa. 96p. (C). 1978. 39.00 (*0-685-33807-X*, Pub. by S Thornes Pubs UK) St Mut.

Latham, Patricia H., jt. auth. see Latham, Peter S.

Latham, Peter. Brahms: Music Book Index. 230p. 1993. reprint ed. lib. bdg. 79.00 (*0-7812-9574-2*) Rprt Serv.

Latham, Peter S. Government Contract Disputes & Supplement. 2nd ed. (Illus.). 1000p. 1986. ring bd. 175.00 (*0-318-23582-X*) Fed Pubns Inc.

***Latham, Peter S. & Latham, Patricia H.** Attention Deficit Disorder & the Law. 143p. 1993. pap. text ed. 25.00 (*1-883560-00-4*) JKL Communs.

— Learning Disabilities & the Law. 178p. 1993. pap. text ed. 28.00 (*1-883560-02-0*) JKL Communs.

***Latham, Peter S., et al.** Succeeding in the Workplace: Attention Deficit Disorder & Learning Disabilities in the Workplace: a Guide for Success. 154p. (Orig.). 1994. pap. text ed. 25.00 (*1-883560-03-9*) JKL Communs.

Latham, R. E., tr. see Lucretius.

Latham, R. G. Two Dissertations on the Hamlet of Saxo Grammaticus & of Shakespear. LC 71-171658. reprint ed. 39.50 (*0-404-03883-2*) AMS Pr.

Latham, Richard T. The Law & the Commonwealth. LC 70-104250. vii, 632p. 1970. reprint ed. text ed. 85.00 (*0-8371-3974-0*, LALC, Greenwood Pr) Greenwood.

Latham, Robert. Catalogue of the Pepys Library at Magdalene College, Cambridge, Vol. 3: Pt. 1 - Prints & Drawings (General) Aspital, A., ed. (Illus.). 396p. 1980. 188.25 (*0-8476-3637-2*) Rowman.

Latham, Robert, ed. Catalogue of the Pepys Library at Magdalene College, Cambridge, 2 vols., Set. (Illus.). 840p. (C). 1991. 315.00 (*0-85991-304-X*) Boydell & Brewer.

— Catalogue of the Pepys Library at Magdalene College, Cambridge, IV: Music, Maps & Calligraphy. (Illus.). 192p. 1989. 216.00 (*0-85991-246-9*) Boydell & Brewer.

Latham, Robert & Beadle, Richard, eds. Catalogue of the Pepys Library at Magdalene College, Cambridge, Vol. 5: V.i. Medieval Manuscripts. 160p. (C). 1993. text ed. 171.00 (*0-85991-341-4*) Boydell & Brewer.

Latham, Robert & Smith, N. A., eds. Catalogue of the Pepys Library, Vol. 1. (Printed Bks.). 201p. 1978. 125.00 (*0-87471-819-8*) Rowman.

Latham, Robert & Weinstein, Helen, eds. Catalogue of the Pepys Library at Magdalene College, Cambridge, Vol. II: Ballads, 2 pts., Pt. 1: Catalogue. (Illus.). 256p. (C). 1993. text ed. 234.00 (*0-85991-315-5*) Boydell & Brewer.

— Catalogue of the Pepys Library at Magdalene College, Cambridge, Vol. II: Ballads, 2 pts., Pt. 2. (Illus.). 240p. (C). 1993. Pt 2 240p. text ed. 216.00 (*0-85991-333-3*) Boydell & Brewer.

Latham, Robert, jt. auth. see Collins, Robert A.

Latham, Robert, jt. ed. see Collins, Robert A.

L

Latham, Robert, ed. see Pepys, Samuel.

***Latham, Robert C., ed.** Samuel Pepys & the Second Dutch War: Pepys's Navy White Book & Brooke House Papers. (Navy Records Ser.: Vol. 133). 350p. 1995. 76.95 (*1-85928-136-2*) Ashgate Pub Co.

Latham, Robert G. The Ethnology of the British Colonies & Dependencies. LC 74-7976. reprint ed. 45.00 (*0-404-11866-6*) AMS Pr.

***Latham, Rodney V. & Ningshang Xu.** High Voltage Vacuum Insulation: Basic Concepts & Technological Practice. (Illus.). 596p. 1995. boxed 99.95 (*0-12-437175-2*) Acad Pr.

Latham, Ronald, tr. see Polo, Marco.

Latham, Ronald E., ed. Revised Medieval Latin Word-List from British & Irish Sources. (British Academy Ser.). 1965. 58.00 (*0-19-725891-3*) OUP.

Latham, Ronald E., tr. The Travels of Marco Polo. (Classics Ser.). 1958. pap. 9.95 (*0-14-044057-7*, Penguin Classics) Viking Penguin.

***Latham, Roy.** The Dictionary of Computer Graphics Technology & Applications. 2nd ed. LC 94-36569. 1995. 19.00 (*0-387-94405-2*) Spr-Verlag.

Latham, Sheila. W. O. Mitchell: An Annotated Bibliography. 364p. (C). 1981. pap. text ed. 9.00 (*0-920763-59-6*, Pub. by ECW Press CN) Genl Dist Srvs.

Latham, Sheila, jt. auth. see Latham, David.

Latham, Sheila, et al, eds. Library Services for Off-Campus & Distance Education: An Annotated Bibliography. LC 91-6399. 272p. 1991. 40.00 (*0-8389-2157-4*) ALA.

Latham, Tony. BBC Microcomputer Disk Companion. 1984. pap. 12.95 (*0-13-069311-1*) P-H.

***Latham, Violet.** Justice or Mercy: A Tragedy. (Illus.). 1994. pap. text ed. 7.00 (*0-938041-21-5*) Arc Pr AR.

Latham, William. How to Find Your Family Roots: The Complete Guide to Searching for Your Ancesters. LC 93-87392. 224p. 1994. 12.95 (*0-9639946-0-3*) Snta Monica.

Latham, William, jt. auth. see Todd, Stephen.

Latham, William R. Locational Behavior in Manufacturing Industries. (Studies in Applied Regional Science: No. 4). 1976. pap. text ed. 32.00 (*90-207-0638-1*) Kluwer Ac.

Latham, Williams. Epitaphs in Old Bridgewater, Massachusetts. vii, 259p. 1986. reprint ed. pap. 20.00 (*0-917890-91-4*) Heritage Bk.

Lathan, John & Kawakatsu, Heita, eds. Japanese Industrialization & the Asian Economy. LC 94-5183. 224p. 1994. 65.00 (*0-415-11501-9*, B4599) Routledge.

Lathan, Ronald E., tr. see Lucretius.

***Lathan, Virginia A.** The Deposition Handbook: A Guide to Help You Give a Winning Deposition. rev. ed. LC 93-71190. 100p. 1995. pap. 14.95 (*0-9636195-2-7*) Curry-Co Pubns.

— Preventing Sexual Harrassment. rev. ed. LC 95-68463. 55p. 1995. pap. 14.95 (*0-9636195-1-9*) Curry-Co Pubns.

Lathbury, Roger. An Editing Workbook. 262p. 1989. spiral bd. 27.95 (*0-8403-5130-5*) Kendall-Hunt.

Lathe, Robert F., tr. see Steiner, Rudolf.

Lathem, Edward C. Chronological Tables of American Newspapers, 1690-1820. LC 70-185613. 131p. 1972. 40.00 (*0-8271-7204-4*, U Pr of Va) Am Antiquarian.

— Robert Frost Poetry & Prose. LC 74-188990. 496p. 1984. pap. 14.95 (*0-8050-0245-6*, Owl) H Holt & Co.

Lathem, Edward C., ed. Concordance to the Poetry of Robert Frost. rev. ed. 640p. 1994. 65.00 (*0-88432-742-6*) Audio-Forum.

— The Poetry of Robert Frost. LC 68-24759. 632p. 1969. 27.50 (*0-8050-0502-1*) H Holt & Co.

— Seventy-Six United Statesiana: Seventy-Six Works of American Scholarship Relating to America as Published During Two Centuries from the Revolutionary Era of the United States Through the Nation's Bicentennial Year, 1776-1976. LC 76-151831. 170p. reprint ed. pap. 48.50 (*0-8357-2718-1*, 2039832) Bks Demand.

— Your Son, Calvin Coolidge. 244p. 1968. pap. 7.50 (*0-914960-35-0*) Academy Bks.

Lathem, Edward C., ed. see Frost, Robert.

Lathem, Edward C., ed. see Stegner, Wallace.

Lathem, Edward C., ed. see Thompson, Lawrence & Winnick, R. H.

***Lathen.** Right on the Money. 1995. mass mkt. 4.99 (*0-06-104295-1*, Harp PBks) HarpC.

***Lathen, Emma.** Accounting for Murder: A John Putnam Thatcher Mystery. 192p. 1995. pap. 7.00 (*1-57283-000-X*) S&S Trade.

— Banking on Death: A John Putnam Thatcher Mystery. 168p. 1993. reprint ed. pap. 6.95 (*1-883402-06-9*) S&S Trade.

— By Hook or by Crook. large type ed. LC 92-40909. (Nightingale Ser.). 1993. 14.95 (*0-8161-5707-3*) G K Hall.

— East Is East. 1994. pap. 4.99 (*0-06-104296-X*, PL) HarpC Child Bks.

— East Is East. 1994. mass mkt. 5.99 (*0-06-104297-8*, Harp PBks) HarpC.

— East Is East. large type ed. 422p. 1992. reprint ed. lib. bdg. 20.95 (*1-56054-421-X*) Thorndike Pr.

— Right on the Money: A John Putman Thatcher Mystery. 256p. 1993. 20.00 (*0-671-73708-2*) S&S Trade.

Lather, Patti. Feminist Research in Education: Within - Against. 116p. (C). 1991. pap. 60.00x (*0-7300-1256-5*, ESA846, Pub. by Deakin Univ AT) St Mut.

— Getting Smart: Feminist Research & Pedagogy within the Postmodern. (Critical Social Thought Ser.). 256p. 1991. 45.00 (*0-415-90377-7*, A2332, Routledge NY); pap. 14.95 (*0-415-90378-5*, A5173, Routledge NY) Routledge.

Lathers & Schraeder. Epilepsy & Sudden Death. (Neurological Disease & Therapy Ser.: Vol. 7). 552p. 1990. 180.00 (*0-8247-8308-5*) Dekker.

Lathers, Marie. The Aesthetics of Artifice: Villiers' Future Eve. LC 91-58691. (AMS Studies in the Nineteenth Century: No. 13). 1992. 39.50 (*0-404-61493-0*) AMS Pr.

Lathi, B. P. Linear Systems & Signals. LC 91-75492. 656p. (C). 1992. 69.95 (*0-941413-34-9*) Berkeley-Cambridge.

— Modern Digital & Analog Communications Systems. 2nd ed. 714p. (C). 1989. text ed. 69.25 (*0-03-027933-X*); Solutions manual. write for info. (*0-03-030992-1*) SCP.

— Signals & Systems. LC 86-72954. 531p. 1987. text ed. 44.95 (*0-941413-33-0*) Berkeley-Cambridge.

***Lathim, Rod & Wisehart, Cynthia.** Access Theater. 1996. write for info. (*0-614-05603-9*) WRS Group.

Lathlean, Judith & Vaughan, Barbara, eds. Unifying Nursing Practice & Theory. LC 93-48048. 1994. pap. 24.95 (*0-7506-1593-1*) Buttrwrth-Heinemann.

***Lathom.** Midnight Bell, Vol. 1. 1995. pap. 10.95 (*1-871438-30-6*) Atrium Pubs.

Lathom, Wanda & Eagle, Charles, eds. Music Therapy for Handicapped Children, 3 vol set. LC 84-72744. pap. text ed. 20.00 (*0-685-73900-7*) Meseraule Prnting.

— Music Therapy for Handicapped Children, 3 vol set, Set. LC 84-72744. pap. text ed. 42.00 (*0-685-73899-X*) Meseraule Prnting.

Lathouwers, L., jt. ed. see Broeckhove, J.

Lathrop, Alan K., jt. ed. see Kelly, Richard J.

Lathrop, Ann. Online & CD-ROM Databases in School Libraries: Readings. Tenopir, Carol, ed. (Database Searching Ser.). 250p. 1989. lib. bdg. 31.00 (*0-87287-756-6*) Libs Unl.

Lathrop, Ann & Goodson, Bobby. Courseware in the Classroom: Selecting, Organizing, & Using Educational Software. 1983. text ed. 12.95 (*0-201-20007-4*) Addison-Wesley.

Lathrop, Churchill & Elzea, Rowland, intros. Thomas George-A Retrospective: Paintings & Works on Paper. (Illus.). 32p. (Orig.). 1987. pap. 7.50 (*0-938766-04-X*) NJ State Mus.

Lathrop, Donald, jt. auth. see Gibson, Karen.

Lathrop, Dorothy B. Animals of the Bible. LC 86-46118. (Illus.). 68p. (J). (ps up). 1937. 16.00 (*0-397-31536-8*, Lipp Jr Bks); lib. bdg. 15.89 (*0-397-30047-6*, Lipp Jr Bks) HarpC Child Bks.

Lathrop, Elise. Early American Inns & Taverns. 1993. reprint ed. lib. bdg. 89.00 (*0-7812-5479-5*) Rprt Serv.

— Where Shakespeare Set His Stage. LC 70-128571. (Studies in Shakespeare: No. 24). 1970. reprint ed. lib. bdg. 59.95 (*0-8383-0907-0*) M S G Haskell Hse.

Lathrop, Elise L. Early American Inns & Taverns. LC 68-20234. (Illus.). 1972. reprint ed. 20.95 (*0-405-08734-9*, Pub. by Blom Pubns UK) Ayer.

Lathrop, Elsie. Early American Inns & Taverns. 365p. 1993. reprint ed. lib. bdg. 89.00 (*0-7812-5297-0*) Rprt Serv.

— Historic Houses of Early America. 464p. 1993. reprint ed. lib. bdg. 99.00 (*0-7812-5298-9*) Rprt Serv.

Lathrop, George P. Study of Hawthorne. LC 70-86168. reprint ed. 17.50 (*0-404-03884-0*) AMS Pr.

— Study of Hawthorne. LC 78-107178. 1970. reprint ed. 16.00 (*0-403-00237-0*) Scholarly.

— A Study of Hawthorne. (BCL1-PS American Literature Ser.). 350p. 1992. reprint ed. lib. bdg. 89.00 (*0-7812-6728-5*) Rprt Serv.

— Would You Kill Him? LC 73-104507. 388p. reprint ed. lib. bdg. 29.00 (*0-8398-1151-9*) Irvington.

— Would You Kill Him? 388p. (C). 1986. reprint ed. pap. text ed. 6.95 (*0-8290-1959-6*) Irvington.

Lathrop, Gordon & Ramshaw, Gail. Psalter for the Christian People: An Inclusive Language. 216p. (Orig.). 1993. pap. text ed. 14.95 (*0-8146-6134-3*, Pueblo Bks) Liturgical Pr.

Lathrop, Gordon & Ramshaw, Gail, eds. Lectionary for the Christian People, Cycle C. 288p. 1992. pap. 17.95 (*0-8146-6082-7*, Pueblo Bks) Liturgical Pr.

— Lectionary for the Christian People, Cycle A. 265p. 1992. pap. 17.95 (*0-8146-6079-7*, Pueblo Bks) Liturgical Pr.

— Lectionary for the Christian People, Cycle B. 273p. 1992. pap. 17.95 (*0-8146-6081-9*, Pueblo Bks) Liturgical Pr.

Lathrop, Gordon W. Holy Things: A Liturgical Theology. LC 93-19836. 240p. 1993. 27.00 (*0-8006-2727-X*, 1-2727) Augsburg Fortress.

Lathrop, Irvin T., jt. auth. see La Cour, Marshall.

Lathrop, J. Philip. Restructuring Health Care: The Patient-Focused Paradigm. LC 93-29550. (Health Ser.). 250p. 1993. 32.95 (*1-55542-594-1*) Jossey-Bass.

Lathrop, J. W., jt. auth. see IIASA International Workshop Staff.

Lathrop, Jacqueline P. Ancient Mexico: Cultural Traditions in the Land of the Feathered Serpent. 4th ed. 208p. (C). 1994. per., pap. text ed. 21.95 (*0-8403-6426-1*) Kendall-Hunt.

Lathrop, JoAnna. Willa Cather: A Checklist of Her Published Writing. LC 74-82561. 132p. reprint ed. pap. 37.70 (*0-7837-6031-0*, 2045843) Bks Demand.

Lathrop, Michael L. Insurance for Environmental Liability. 1992. write for info. (*0-8205-1833-6*) Bender.

Lathrop, Mitchell L. Environmental Insurance Coverage: State Law & Regulation, 2 vols. 810p. 1994. ring bd. 195.00 (*0-88063-362-X*) Michie Butterworth.

— Environmental Insurance Coverage: State Law & Regulation, 2 vols. suppl. ed. 810p. 1991. 60.00 (*1-56257-153-2*) Butterworth Legal Pubs.

— State Hazardous Waste Regulation, 1991-1992, 2 vols. 750p. 1992. ring bd. 160.00 (*0-88063-361-1*) Michie Butterworth.

— State Hazardous Waste Regulation, 1991-1992, 2 vols. suppl. ed. 1992. ring bd. 62.00 (*0-685-74334-9*) Butterworth Legal Pubs.

Lathrop, Richard. Don't Use a Resume. 64p. 1980. pap. 3.95 (*0-89815-027-2*) Ten Speed Pr.

— The Job Market: What Ails It & What Needs to Be Done about It to Reduce Unemployment. (Illus.). (Orig.). 1978. pap. 4.85 (*0-935234-00-4*) Natl Ctr Job Mkt.

— Who's Hiring Who. rev. ed. (Illus.). 272p. 1989. pap. 9.95 (*0-89815-298-4*) Ten Speed Pr.

Lathrop, Ron. Back-Yard Mechanic, Vol. 3. (Illus.). 92p. 1981. pap. 3.00 (*0-16-002156-1*, S/N 008-070-00463-1) USGPO.

Lathrop, Rose H. Memories of Hawthorne. 1972. 59.95 (*0-8490-0606-6*) Gordon Pr.

— Memories of Hawthorne. LC 79-96474. reprint ed. 10.00 (*0-404-03885-9*) AMS Pr.

— Memories of Hawthorne. (BCL1-PS American Literature Ser.). 482p. 1992. reprint ed. lib. bdg. 99.00 (*0-7812-6729-3*) Rprt Serv.

— Rose Hawthrone Lathrop: Selected Writings. LC 93-14622. (Sources of American Spirituality Ser.). 256p. 1993. 24.95 (*0-8091-0463-6*) Paulist Pr.

Lathrop, Tad, ed. see Wolper, Andrea.

Lathrop, Thomas. Curso de Gramatica Historica Espanola. Gutierrez, Juan & Blas, Ana, trs. 387p. 1992. pap. 19.00 (*84-344-8375-0*) Juan de la Cuesta.

Lathrop, Thomas & Dias, Eduardo. Brasil! Lingua e Cultura. (Illus.). 392p. (C). 1992. 14.95 (*0-942566-15-7*); text ed. 41.95 (*0-942566-08-4*) LinguaText.

Lathrop, Thomas, ed. see Armistead, Samuel.

Lathrop, Thomas, ed. see Avalle-Arce, J., et al.

Lathrop, Thomas, ed. see Avellaneda, Alonso F.

Lathrop, Thomas, ed. see Aylward, E. T.

Lathrop, Thomas, ed. see Case, Thomas.

Lathrop, Thomas, ed. see Clamurro, William.

Lathrop, Thomas, ed. see De Lasry, Benaim.

Lathrop, Thomas, ed. see Drake, D. & Finello, D.

Lathrop, Thomas, ed. see Eisenberg, Daniel.

Lathrop, Thomas, ed. see Flores, Robert.

Lathrop, Thomas, ed. see Grieve, Patricia.

Lathrop, Thomas, ed. see Hall, Kenneth.

Lathrop, Thomas, ed. see Hegyi, Ottmar.

Lathrop, Thomas, ed. see Iffland, James.

Lathrop, Thomas, ed. see Irving, Thomas B.

Lathrop, Thomas, ed. see Leonard, Irving.

Lathrop, Thomas, ed. see Lore, A. G.

Lathrop, Thomas, ed. see McGaha, Michael.

Lathrop, Thomas, ed. see Nelson, Ardis.

Lathrop, Thomas, ed. see Olinger, Paula.

Lathrop, Thomas, ed. see Parr, James.

Lathrop, Thomas, ed. see Parr, James, et al.

Lathrop, Thomas, ed. see Quevedo, Francisco.

Lathrop, Thomas, ed. see Riley, E. C.

Lathrop, Thomas, ed. see Rini, Joel.

Lathrop, Thomas, ed. see Rivers, Elias.

Lathrop, Thomas, ed. see Scavincky, Gary.

Lathrop, Thomas, ed. see Vidal, Hernan.

Lathrop, Thomas, ed. see Williamsen, Amy.

Lathrop, Thomas, et al, eds. La Coronica de Adramon. 300p. (SPA.). 1992. pap. 23.00 (*0-936388-59-5*) Juan de la Cuesta.

Lathrop, Thomas A., jt. auth. see Jensen, Frede.

***Lathrop, Wendy, ed.** Legal Topics in Boundary Surveying. 264p. 1990. pap. 65.00 (*0-614-06110-5*, S293) Am Congrs Survey.

Lathrop, Wendy R., ed. Stewardship of the Land. (Modulus: the Architectural Review of the University of Virginia Ser.: Vol. 20). (Illus.). 168p. (Orig.). 1991. pap. 24.95 (*1-878271-29-6*) Princeton Arch.

Lathrop, William G. The Brass Industry in the U. S. A Study of the Origin & the Development of the Brass Industry in the Naugatuck Valley & Its Subsequent Extension over the Nation. LC 72-5060. (Technology & Society Ser.). (Illus.). 230p. 1972. reprint ed. 17.95 (*0-405-04711-8*) Ayer.

Lathrope, Daniel J. The Alternative Minimum Tax. 1993. ring bd. 155.00 (*0-685-69582-4*, ALMT) Warren Gorham & Lamont.

— Alternative Minimum Tax. 672p. 1994. 155.00 (*0-7913-1978-4*) Warren Gorham & Lamont.

Lathrope, Daniel J., ed. see Lind, Stephen A. & Schwarz, Stephen.

Lathrope, Daniel J., jt. auth. see Schwarz, Stephen.

Latia, Douglas C. Non-Destructive Testing for Aircraft. (Illus.). 1994. pap. text ed. 25.95 (*0-89100-415-7*, EA-415) IAP.

Latif, Bilkees. Her India: The Fragrance of Forgotten Years. 264p. 1984. 17.00 (*0-86578-231-8*); pap. 9.90 (*0-86578-264-4*) Ind-US Inc.

Latif-Pembry, Rebecca C. Word Processing Using WANG Systems. 265p. (C). 1988. pap. text ed. 28.00 (*0-15-596668-5*, WANG) Dryden Pr.

Latif-Pembry, Rebecca C. & Royer, Harold L. Lotus 1-2-3 for Beginners. 2nd ed. 250p. (C). 1992. pap. text ed. write for info. (*0-13-517335-3*) P-H.

Latif, Rebecca C. IBM Displaywriter: Word Processing Production Techniques. (C). 1984. pap. text ed. write for info. (*0-8359-3039-4*, Reston) P-H.

— IBM Displaywriter: Word Processing Production Techniques Made Easy. (Illus.). 25p. 15.94 (*0-317-13055-2*) P-H.

— Phillips-Micom Word Processing: Production & Applications. (C). 1984. pap. text ed. write for info. (*0-8359-5534-6*, Reston) P-H.

Latif, S. A. Basics of Islamic Culture. pap. 4.25 (*0-935782-45-1*) Kazi Pubns.

— The Mind Al-Quran Builds. 200p. 1983. 7.50 (*1-56744-330-3*) Kazi Pubns.

***Latif, S. Abdul.** Muslim Mystic Movement in Bengal 1301-1550. (C). 1993. 14.00x (*81-7074-136-X*, Pub. by KP Bagchi IA) S Asia.

Latifi. Snakes of Iran. LC 90-63908. 1991. write for info. (*0-916984-22-2*) SSAR.

***Latifi, M.** L' Hotellerie en Francais. (FRE.). Date not set. pap. 34.95 (*0-7859-7570-5*) Fr & Eur.

***Latifi, Rifat.** Surgical Nutrition: Strategies in Critically Ill Patients. Dudrick, Stanley, ed. LC 95-4265. (Medical Intelligence Unit Ser.). 212p. 1995. write for info. (*1-57059-154-7*) R G Landes.

Latifi, Rifat, ed. Amino Acids in Critical Care & Cancer. 118p. 1994. 89.95 (*1-57059-027-3*, LN9027) CRC Pr.

Latil, M. Enhanced Oil Recovery. LC 79-56344. 236p. (Orig.). 1980. pap. 49.00 (*0-87201-775-3*) Gulf Pub.

Latimer, Carole. Wilderness Cuisine: How to Prepare & Enjoy Fine Food on the Trail & in Camp. LC 91-9288. 240p. (Orig.). 1990. pap. 12.95 (*0-89997-114-8*) Wilderness Pr.

***Latimer, Clare.** Clare's Kitchen: The In Way to Eat. (Illus.). 1995. 29.95 (*0-7475-1704-5*, Pub. by Bloomsbury Pub Ltd UK) Trafalgar.

Latimer, Dan. Contemporary Critical Theory. 669p. (C). 1988. pap. text ed. 29.50 (*0-15-513494-9*) HB Coll Pubs.

Latimer, E. Spain in the 19th Century. 1976. lib. bdg. 59.95 (*0-8490-2643-1*) Gordon Pr.

***Latimer, Frances B.** The 1860 Census for Northampton County, Virginia. 104p. Date not set. pap. text ed. 13.50 (*1-886706-07-7*) Hickory Hse.

— The Register of Free Negroes: Northampton County, Virginia, 1853-1861. xxiv, 82p. 1992. pap. text ed. 16.50 (*1-55613-622-6*) Heritage Bk.

Latimer, Francis B. Instruments of Freedom: Deeds & Wills of Emancipation, Northampton Co, VA 1782-1864. rev. ed. xli, 184p. (Orig.). 1994. pap. text ed. 20.00 (*1-55613-775-3*) Heritage Bk.

Latimer, Gordon, jt. auth. see Latimer, Norma.

Latimer, Heather. Curse of the Painted Cats: A Romantic Suspense Novel. 250p. (J). 1989. 18.95 (*0-943698-03-0*); pap. 4.95 (*0-943698-04-9*); audio 15.95 (*0-943698-06-5*) Papyrus Letterbox.

— Is Forever Too Long in Las Vegas? A Novel about the Dashing Wexford Males & the Women Who Love Them. Hutchison-Cleaves, Geoffrey, ed. 310p. 1995. 24.95 (*0-943698-16-2*); pap. 12.95 (*0-943698-15-4*) Papyrus Letterbox.

— Louis Wain - King of the Cat Artists, 1860-1939: A Dramatized Biography. Hutchison-Cleaves, Geoffrey, ed. LC 82-82032. (Illus.). 172p. 1992. reprint ed. 25.00 (*0-943698-02-2*); reprint ed. lib. bdg. 25.00 (*0-943698-01-4*) Papyrus Letterbox.

Latimer, Hugh. Selected Sermons of Hugh Latimer. Chester, Allan G., ed. (Documents Ser.). 1978. 29.50 (*0-918016-43-6*) Folger Bks.

— Sermons. LC 76-172301. reprint ed. 45.00 (*0-404-03886-7*) AMS Pr.

— Seven Sermons Before Edward the Sixth: 1549. Arber, Edward, ed. 208p. 1993. pap. 20.00 (*0-87556-144-6*) Saifer.

Latimer, Ian, jt. auth. see Hawkes, John.

Latimer, James W. The Pits of Middle Texas: People of the Smoke Pits...& Their Barbecue. (Illus.). 144p. (Orig.). 1993. pap. 12.95 (*0-9635939-0-0*) Literary Serv.

Latimer, Jane E. Beyond the Food Game: A Spiritual & Psychological Approach to Healing Emotional Eating. LC 93-10052. (Illus.). 1993. pap. 9.95 (*1-882109-01-5*) LivingQuest.

— The Healing Power of Inner Light-Fire: Accessing Higher Consciousness to Heal Your Life. LC 90-5492. 160p. (Orig.). 1990. pap. 9.95 (*1-882109-05-8*) LivingQuest.

— Living Binge Free: A Personal Guide to Victory over Compulsive Eating. LC 88-15899. 1991. pap. 11.95 (*1-882109-00-7*) LivingQuest.

Latimer, Jim. Fox under First Base. LC 89-27576. (Illus.). 32p. (J). (gr. k-2). 1991. text ed. 13.95 (*0-684-19053-2*, C Scribner Sons Young) S&S Childrens.

— Going the Moose Way Home. LC 87-9762. (Illus.). 32p. (J). (gr. 1-3). 1988. text ed. 13.95 (*0-684-18890-2*, C Scribner Sons Young) S&S Childrens.

— The Irish Piper. LC 90-34550. (Illus.). 32p. (J). (gr. 1-3). 1991. text ed. 13.95 (*0-684-19130-X*, C Scribner Sons Young) S&S Childrens.

— James Bear & the Goose Gathering. LC 92-26190. (Illus.). 32p. (J). (gr. k-2). 1994. text ed. 14.95 (*0-684-19526-7*, C Scribner Sons Young) S&S Childrens.

— James Bear's Pie. LC 90-36193. (Illus.). 32p. (J). (ps-2). 1992. text ed. 13.95 (*0-684-19226-8*, C Scribner Sons Young) S&S Childrens.

— Moose & Friends. LC 91-14047. (Illus.). 32p. (J). (gr. 1-3). 1993. text ed. 14.95 (*0-684-19335-3*, C Scribner Sons Young) S&S Childrens.

— Snail & Buffalo. LC 95-4276. (Illus.). 32p. (J). (ps-3). 1995. 14.95 (*0-531-09490-1*); lib. bdg. 14.99 (*0-531-08790-5*) Orchard Bks Watts.

— When Moose Was Young. LC 89-10059. (Illus.). 32p. (J). (gr. 1-3). 1990. text ed. 13.95 (*0-684-18932-1*, C Scribner Sons Young) S&S Childrens.

Latimer, Jonathan. The Dead Don't Care. (C). 1989. 35.00 (*0-948353-07-4*, Pub. by Oldcastle Bks UK) St Mut.

— The Dead Don't Care. LC 90-84278. 261p. 1990. reprint ed. pap. 7.95 (*1-55882-082-5*) Intl Polygonics.

— Headed for a Hearse. LC 80-12148. 306p. 1980. 18.95 (*0-8398-2652-4*) Boulevard.

— Headed for a Hearse. LC 90-80763. 306p. 1990. pap. 7.95 (*1-55882-069-8*) Intl Polygonics.

— Headed for a Hearse. (C). 1989. 35.00 (*0-948353-30-9*, Pub. by Oldcastle Bks UK) St Mut.

— The Lady in the Morgue. 192p. 1988. pap. 4.95 (*0-930330-79-X*) Intl Polygonics.

— Lady in the Morgue. (C). 1989. 35.00 (*0-948353-21-X*, Pub. by Oldcastle Bks UK) St Mut.

— Murder in the Madhouse. (C). 1989. 35.00 (*0-948353-28-7*, Pub. by Oldcastle Bks UK) St Mut.

— Murder in the Madhouse. LC 89-85727. 300p. 1989. reprint ed. pap. 7.95 (*1-55882-023-X*, Lib Crime Classics) Intl Polygonics.

— Red Gardenias. (C). 1989. 35.00 (*0-948353-39-2*, Pub. by Oldcastle Bks UK) St Mut.

An Asterisk (*) at the beginning of an entry indicates that the title is appearing in BIP for the first time.

— Red Gardenias. LC 91-70601. 280p. 1991. reprint ed. pap. 8.95 (*1-55882-094-9*, Lib Crime Classics) Intl Polygonics.
— The Search for My Great Uncle's Head. LC 89-85718. 297p. reprint ed. pap. 7.95 (*1-55882-052-3*, Lib Crime Classics) Intl Polygonics.
— Sinners & Shrouds. LC 82-21449. 1983. pap. 12.95 (*0-671-66450-6*); pap. 4.95 (*0-685-57776-7*) S&S Trade.
Latimer, Mansfield. Never Too Old to Play Tennis: And Never Too Old to Start. (Illus.). 176p. (Orig.). 1993. pap. 12.95 (*1-55870-288-1*) Betterway Bks.
Latimer, Margaret. Two Cities: New York & Brooklyn the Year the Great Bridge Opened. LC 83-71020. (Brooklyn Rediscovery Publication Ser.). (Illus.). 120p. (Orig.). 1983. pap. 4.00 (*0-933250-09-6*) Bklyn Educ.
Latimer, Margaret, ed. Brooklyn Almanac. (Brooklyn Rediscovery Publication Ser.). (Illus.). 102p. 1984. pap. 7.95 (*0-933250-11-8*) Bklyn Educ.
Latimer, Margaret, et al, intros. Bridge to the Future: A Centennial Celebration of the Brooklyn Bridge. LC 84-11444. (Annals Ser.: Vol. 424). 355p. 1984. lib. bdg. 75.00 (*0-89766-246-6*); pap. 75.00 (*0-89766-247-4*) NY Acad Sci.
Latimer, Margery. Guardian Angel, & Other Stories. LC 75-157783. (Short Story Index Reprint Ser.). 1977. reprint ed. 20.95 (*0-8369-3895-X*) Ayer.
— The Guardian Angel & Other Stories. LC 84-14175. 264p. 1984. reprint ed. pap. 8.95 (*0-935312-13-7*) Feminist Pr.
Latimer, Margery T., ed. see Toomer, Jean.
Latimer, Norma & Latimer, Gordon. Irish Country Cooking. (Traditional Cooking of Great Britain Ser.). (Illus.). 108p. (Orig.). 1985. pap. 6.95 (*0-941869-03-2*) Latimers.
— Scottish Fare. (Traditional Cooking of Great Britain Ser.). (Illus.). 105p. (Orig.). 1983. pap. 6.95 (*0-941869-02-4*) Latimers.
Latimer, Norma, et al. Eat, Sleep & Be Merrie in Britain. (Travel in Britain Ser.). (Illus.). 343p. (Orig.). 1985. pap. 12.95 (*0-941869-04-0*) Latimers.
— English Desserts, Puddings, Cakes & Scones. (Traditional Cooking of Great Britain Ser.). (Illus.). 123p. (Orig.). 1984. pap. 6.95 (*0-941869-01-6*) Latimers.
— Olde English Traditional Country Style Recipes. (Traditional Cooking of Great Britain Ser.). (Illus.). 105p. (Orig.). 1984. pap. 6.95 (*0-941869-00-8*) Latimers.
***Latimer, Paul.** Commercial Law Workbook. 350p. 1995. pap. 29.00 (*0-455-21290-2*, Pub. by Law Bk Co) W W Gaunt.
Latimer, Paul, jt. auth. see Hardy Ivamy, E. R.
Latimer, Paul R. Functional Gastrointestinal Disorders: A Behavioral Medicine Approach. 192p. 1983. 23.95 (*0-8261-4310-5*) Springer Pub.
Latimer, Paula. Mediate Your Divorce & Save Attorneys' Fees. 52p. (Orig.). 1993. pap. write for info. (*0-9636555-0-7*) P Latimer.
Latimer, Renate, tr. see Eisenreich, Herbert.
Latimer, Tirza T. The Perfume Atomizer: An Object with Atmosphere. LC 91-67016. (Illus.). 168p. 1992. text ed. 69.95 (*0-88740-382-4*) Schiffer.
Latimore, James. Weeding Out the Target Population: The Law of Accountability in a Manpower Program. LC 84-8952. (Contributions in Sociology Ser.: No. 54). (Illus.). x, 176p. 1985. text ed. 49.95 (*0-313-24495-2*, LWT/, Greenwood Pr) Greenwood.
Latimore, Sarah B. & Haskell, Grace C. Arthur Rackham: A Bibliography. 3rd ed. 111p. 1987. reprint ed. 21.00 (*0-935259-01-5*) San Marco Bk.
Latin American Conference Staff. Fiscal Policy for Industrialization & Development in Latin America. Geithman, David T., ed. LC 74-2231. 380p. reprint ed. pap. 108.30 (*0-7837-4954-6*, 2044620) Bks Demand.
— Man in the Amazon. Wagley, Charles, ed. LC 74-10857. (Illus.). 346p. reprint ed. pap. 98.70 (*0-7837-5011-0*, 2044678) Bks Demand.
— Universities in Transition: The U. S. Presence in Latin American Higher Education. Renner, Richard R., ed. LC 73-8234. 156p. reprint ed. pap. 44.50 (*0-7837-5085-4*, 2044783) Bks Demand.
Latin American Economic Institute Staff. Economic Defense of the Western Hemisphere. LC 68-57328. (Essay Index Reprint Ser.). 1977. 19.95 (*0-8369-0609-8*) Ayer.
Latin American Institute Staff, tr. see Adams, Clinton, et al.
Latin American School of Physics-University of Mexico, 1965 Staff. Many-Body Problems & Other Selected Topics in Theoretical Physics, 2 Vol. Set. Moshinsky, M. et al, eds. LC 65-29013. (Illus.). 967p. 1966. pap. text ed. 140.00 (*0-677-12935-1*) Gordon & Breach.
— Many-Body Problems & Other Selected Topics in Theoretical Physics, 2 Vol. Set. Moshinsky, M. et al, eds. LC 65-29013. (Illus.). 967p. 1966. text ed. 451.00 (*0-677-11500-8*) Gordon & Breach.
Latin Culture Productions Staff, ed. see Lacoren, Nestor R.
Latin, Howard A. Privacy: A Selected Bibliography & Topical Index of Social Science Materials. iv, 94p. (Orig.). 1976. pap. 7.50 (*0-8377-0805-2*) Rothman.
Latin, Richard, jt. auth. see Berg, Kris.
Lating, J. M., jt. ed. see Everly, G. S., Jr.
Latini, Brunetto. Brunetto Latini: The Book of the Treasure - Li Livres dou Treasure. Barrette, Paul & Baldwin, Spurgeon, trs. LC 92-21785. (Library of Medieval Literature: Series B, Vol. 90). 440p. 1992. 63.00 (*0-8153-0763-2*) Garland.
— Libro del Tesoro: Version Castellana de Li Livres dou Tresor. Baldwin, Spurgeon, tr. & intro. by. (Spanish Ser.: No. 46). viii, 260p. (SPA.). 1989. 25.00 (*0-940639-31-9*) Hispanic Seminary.
Latini, Roberto, jt. ed. see Tognoni, Gianni.

Latino, Frank. The Legend of Holly Boy: The Holly Boy. (Illus.). 38p. (J). (gr. 1-6). 1993. 15.95 (*0-9640474-0-3*); pap. 7.95 (*0-9640474-1-1*) F Latino Pub Co. "VOTED: 'BEST BOOK OF THE YEAR' CHILDREN'S INTEREST CATEGORY, BY THE NORTH AMERICAN BOOKDEALERS ASSOCIATION. THE LEGEND OF HOLLY BOY is a Christmas story about a little girl who was sad at Christmas time because her Dad cut up a holly tree to make wreaths. This child felt that at Christmas time "everyone & everybody should be happy," but the holly wreath could not be happy, all cut & tied. That evening she prayed to make the holly wreath happy...& it then turned into a little holly boy. Holly Boy told her he was never happier, because now he gives pleasure to other people, "& just like me, pleasure goes 'round & 'round." Holly Boy then takes Linda back in time to Bethlehem, where they see a little dying holly tree. The tree wishes he "could give himself to the baby Jesus," the star of Bethlehem becomes an angel that transforms the dying tree into the bright new holly boy. Then Holly Boy takes Linda to the woodland wonderland where he & all his friends lived. King Otto will not believe the story about the birth of Jesus & the new era of love, so he attacks & destroys Holly Boy & all his friends to prove that "everyone must die" & "only the strong survive." The animals then attack him with snowballs & he falls off a cliff. The star of Bethlehem, angel, revives every character & rewards them with everlasting life to be an evergreen plant. ***Publisher Provided Annotation.***

Latinus, Ioannes, et al. The First African Authors to Write in Latin, 3 wks., Set. (B. E. Ser.: No. 1). 1742. Three works in one unit. 50.00 (*0-8115-2952-5*) Periodicals Srv.
Latiolais, Michelle. Even Now. 1990. 18.95 (*0-374-14993-3*) FS&G.
Latiolais, P., et al, eds. Topology & Combinatorial Group Theory: Proceedings of the Fall Foliage Topology Seminars Held in New Hampshire, 1985-1988. (Lecture Notes in Mathematics Ser.: Vol. 1440). vi, 207p. 1990. pap. 30.00 (*0-387-52990-X*) Spr-Verlag.
Latkovich, V. J., ed. Proceedings of a Pressure Transducer-Packer Workshop. 53p. (Orig.). (C). 1994. pap. text ed. 50.00 (*0-7881-0804-2*) Diane Pub.
Latman, Alan & Lightstone, James F., eds. The Kaminstein Legislative History Project: A Compendium & Analytical Index of Materials Leading to the Copyright Act of 1976, 6 Vols. (Illus.). 1985. text ed. 95.00 (*0-8377-0732-3*) Rothman.
Latman, Alan, et al. Copyright for the Nineties. 3rd ed. (Contemporary Legal Education Ser.). 881p. 1989. 47.00 (*0-87473-444-4*) Michie Butterworth.
— Copyright for the Nineties. 3rd suppl. ed. (Contemporary Legal Education Ser.). 881p. 1989. 6.00 (*0-87473-773-7*) Michie Butterworth.
Latner, A. L. & Schwartz, M. K., eds. Advances in Clinical Chemistry, Vol. 23. (Serial Publication Ser.). 1983. text ed. 149.00 (*0-12-010323-0*) Acad Pr.
Latner, Joel. The Gestalt Therapy Book. rev. ed. LC 73-82442. 240p. 1984. reprint ed. pap. 18.50 (*0-939266-04-0*) Gestalt Journal.
Latombe, Jean-Claude. Robot Motion Planning. (International Series in Engineering & Computer Science, VLSI, Computer Architecture, & Digital Screen Processing). 672p. 1990. lib. bdg. 109.50 (*0-7923-9129-2*) Kluwer Ac.
Latona, Joseph C. & Nathan, Jay, eds. Cases & Readings in Production & Operations Management. LC 93-48384. 1994. pap. text ed. 34.80 (*0-205-13936-1*) Allyn.
Latond, D., et al. The Person with Aphasia: Psychosocial Issues. LC 92-49888. (Illus.). 306p. (Orig.). (C). 1992. pap. text ed. 47.50x (*1-56593-067-3*) Singular Publishing.
LaTorra, Michael. A Warrior Blends with Life: A Modern Tao. LC 93-12491. 1993. pap. 12.95 (*1-55643-160-0*) North Atlantic.
LaTorre, D. R. Calculator Enhancement for Linear Algebra. 130p. (C). 1990. pap. text ed. 8.00 (*0-15-505674-3*) HB Coll Pubs.
— Calculator Enhancement for Linear Algebra. (Clemson Calculator Enhancement Ser.). 192p. (C). 1992. pap. text ed. 12.00 (*0-03-092729-3*) SCP.
LaTorre, D. R., jt. auth. see Proctor, T.
Latorre, Dolores L. Cooking & Curing with Herbs in Mexico. (Illus.). 1977. 20.00 (*0-88426-051-8*) Encino Pr.
Latorre, Dolores L., ed. see McKellar, Margaret M.
Latorre, Felipe. Mexican Kickapoo Indians. 1991. pap. 10.95 (*0-486-26742-3*) Dover.
Latorre, J. & Monreal, M., eds. Clinical Atlas of Vascular Disorders. 128p. 1988. 24.95 (*0-8151-5325-2*, CDA-1, Yr Bk Med Pubs) Mosby Yr Bk.
Latorre, Ramon, ed. Ionic Channels in Cells & Model Systems. LC 86-12265. (Centro de Estudios Cientificos de Santiago Ser.). 462p. 1986. 85.00 (*0-306-42194-1*, Plenum Pr) Plenum.
Latorre, Robert, et al. Linear Simulation of Time Dependent Towing of Ocean Vehicles. (University of Michigan, Dept. of Naval Architecture & Marine Engineering, Report Ser.: No. 268). 82p. reprint ed. pap. 25.00 (*0-317-30469-0*, 2024825) Bks Demand.
LaTorre, Ronald A. Sexual Identity: Implications for Mental Health. LC 78-26442. 184p. 1979. 27.95 (*0-88229-360-5*) Nelson-Hall.
Latouche, C., jt. auth. see Jouanneau, J. M.
Latouche, Daniel, jt. auth. see Resnick, Philip.
LaTouche, Emmanuel. Peace in the World. (Illus.). 1991. 7.95 (*0-533-09190-X*) Vantage.
— With You! Poems, 1990. 1993. pap. 7.95 (*0-533-10393-2*) Vantage.
LaTouche, Marie B., jt. auth. see Trask, George G.
Latouche, P. Anarchy. 1976. lib. bdg. 250.00 (*0-8490-1423-9*) Gordon Pr.
Latouche, Serge. In the Wake of the Affluent Society: An Exploration of Post-Development. LC 93-13947. 224p. (C). 1993. text ed. 55.00 (*1-85649-171-4*, Pub. by Zed Books UK); pap. 19.95 (*1-85649-172-2*, Pub. by Zed Books UK) Humanities.
Latour, Alessandra. Louis I. Kahn: Writings, Lectures, Interviews. LC 90-50794. (Illus.). 240p. 1991. 50.00 (*0-8478-1331-2*); pap. 35.00 (*0-8478-1356-8*) Rizzoli Intl.
Latour, Bruno. The Pasteurization of France. Sheridan, Alan & Law, John, trs. LC 88-2670. (Illus.). 288p. 1988. 39.95 (*0-674-65760-8*) HUP.
— The Pasteurization of France. LC 88-2670. 288p. 1993. reprint ed. pap. 16.95 (*0-674-65761-6*) HUP.
— Science in Action: How to Follow Scientists & Engineers Through Society. 288p. 1988. reprint ed. pap. 16.50 (*0-674-79291-2*) HUP.
— We Have Never Been Modern. Porter, Catherine, tr. LC 93-15226. 168p. 1993. pap. 14.95 (*0-674-94839-4*) HUP.
— We Have Never Been Modern. Porter, Catherine, tr. LC 93-15226. 167p. 1993. 32.50 (*0-674-94838-6*) HUP.
Latour, Bruno & Woolgar, Steve. Laboratory Life: The Construction of Scientific Facts. LC 85-43378. 296p. 1986. pap. 15.95 (*0-691-02832-X*) Princeton U Pr.
Latour, Colette, ed. see Nahas, Gabriel G.
LaTour, Kathy. The Breast Cancer Companion. 512p. 1994. reprint ed. pap. 15.00 (*0-380-71996-7*) Avon.
— The Breast Cancer Companion: From Diagnosis, Through Treatment, to Recovery, Everything You Need to Know for Every Step along the Way. LC 93-7473. 1993. 22.00 (*0-688-11931-X*) Morrow.
Latourelle, Rene. Dictionnaire de la Theologie Fondamentale. (FRE.). 1993. pap. 195.00 (*0-7859-3020-5*) Fr & Eur.
— The Miracle of Jesus & the Theology of Miracles. 1988. pap. 14.95 (*0-8091-2997-3*) Paulist Pr.
— Theology of Revelation. LC 65-15734. 1966. pap. 17.95 (*0-8189-0401-1*) Alba.
Latourelle, Rene, ed. Vatican II: Assessment & Prespectives, Twenty-Five Years After (1962-1987), 2 vols., Vol. II. 1988. 25.00 (*0-8091-0413-X*) Paulist Pr.
— Vatican II: Assessment & Prespectives, Twenty-Five Years After (1962-1987), 2 vols., Vol. III. 1988. 25.00 (*0-8091-0414-8*) Paulist Pr.
***Latourelle, Rene & Fisichella, Rino.** Dictionary of Fundamental Theology. 1264p. 1992. lib. bdg. 200.00 (*0-85439-395-1*, Pub. by St Paul Pubns UK) St Mut.
Latourelle, Rene & Fisichella, Rino, eds. The Dictionary of Fundamental Theology. LC 93-42818. 1280p. 1994. 75.00 (*0-8245-1395-9*) Crossroad NY.
Latourette, Jane & Mathews. Daniel in the Lions' Den. (Arch Bks.: Set 3). 1966. 1.99 (*0-570-06018-4*, 59-1127) Concordia.
Latourette, Jane & Wind, Betty. Jon & the Little Lost Lamb. LC 65-15145. (Arch Bks.: Set 2). 1965. pap. 1.99 (*0-570-06008-7*, 59-1106) Concordia.
Latourette, Kenneth S. Christianity in a Revolutionary Age, 5 vols., 3. 1973. reprint ed. lib. bdg. 34.75 (*0-8371-5703-X*, LACK) Greenwood.
— Christianity in a Revolutionary Age, 5 vols., 4. 1973. reprint ed. lib. bdg. 34.75 (*0-8371-5704-8*, LACL) Greenwood.
— Christianity in a Revolutionary Age, 5 vols., 5. 1973. reprint ed. lib. bdg. 34.75 (*0-8371-5705-6*, LACM) Greenwood.
— Historia del Cristianismo, Tomo I. Quarles, Jaime C. & Quarles, Lemuel C., trs. Orig. Title: A History of the Expansion of Christianity. (SPA.). 819p. 1987. reprint ed. pap. 20.95 (*0-311-15010-1*) Casa Bautista.
— Historia del Cristianismo, Tomo II. Quarles, Jaime C. & Quarles, Lemuel C., trs. (Desde el Siglo XVI Hasta el Siglo XX). Orig. Title: A History of the Expansion of Christianity. 968p. 1987. reprint ed. pap. 21.95 (*0-311-15012-8*) Casa Bautista.
— A History of Christianity. rev. ed. Incl. Vol. 1. Beginnings to 1500. LC 74-25692. 758p. 1975. pap. text ed. 21.00 (*0-06-064952-6*, RD-93); Vol. 2. Reformation to the Present. LC 74-25692. 922p. 1975. pap. text ed. 20.00 (*0-06-064953-4*, RD-94); LC 74-25692. 1975. Set pap. write for info. (*0-318-52923-8*) Harper SF.
— The History of Early Relations Between the United States & China, 1784-1844. (Connecticut Academy of Arts & Sciences Ser., Trans.: Vol. 22). 1917. pap. 75.00 (*0-685-44362-0*) Elliots Bks.
— The History of Early Relations Between the United States & China, 1784-1844. LC 18-7805. (Transactions of the Connecticut Academy of Arts & Sciences Ser.: Vol. 22). 1990. reprint ed. 18.00 (*0-527-00391-3*) Periodicals Srv.
— Voyages of American Ships to China, 1784-1844. (Connecticut Academy of Arts & Sciences Ser., Trans.: Vol. 28). 1927. pap. 49.50 (*0-685-22810-X*) Elliots Bks.
Latourette, Kenneth S., ed. Gospel, the Church & the World. LC 76-134107. (Essay Index Reprint Ser.). 1977. 20.95 (*0-8369-1972-6*) Ayer.
Latourette, Victor A. From a Monastery Kitchen. 1989. pap. 14.00 (*0-06-250037-6*, PL) HarpC.
Latousek, Rob. Software Directory for the Classics. 95p. 1993. spiral bd. 10.00 (*0-939507-45-5*, W900) Amer Classical.
***Latow, Roberta.** Acts of Love. 400p. (Orig.). 1995. mass mkt. 5.50 (*0-380-77415-1*) Avon.
— Hungry Heart. 416p. (Orig.). 1994. mass mkt. 5.50 (*0-380-77414-3*) Avon.
— Those Wicked Pleasures. 1992. mass mkt. 5.99 (*0-449-14788-6*, GM) Fawcett.
— Three Rivers. 400p. 1990. mass mkt. 5.95 (*0-449-14690-1*, GM) Fawcett.
LaTrenta, Gregory S., jt. auth. see Rees, Thomas D.
Latrobe. The Engineering Drawings of Benjamin Henry Latrobe, Vol. 1. LC 78-15405. (Series II). 1980. text ed. 110.00 (*0-300-02227-1*) Yale U Pr.
Latrobe, Benjamin. The Virginia Journals of Benjamin Henry Latrobe, 1795-1798, Set. Carter, Edward C., ed. LC 77-76301. (Illus.). 1977. 125.00 (*0-300-02198-4*) Yale U Pr.
Latrobe, Benjamin H. The Correspondence & Miscellaneous Papers of Benjamin Henry Latrobe. Van Horne, John C. & Formwalt, Lee W., eds. LC 83-27423. (Series No. IV: Vol. I). (Illus.). 640p. 1985. text ed. 80.00 (*0-300-02901-2*) Yale U Pr.
— The Correspondence & Miscellaneous Papers of Benjamin Henry Latrobe, Vol. 3. LC 83-27423. 1024p. (C). 1988. text ed. 140.00 (*0-300-03521-7*) Yale U Pr.
— The Correspondence & Miscellaneous Papers of Benjamin Henry Latrobe: 1805-1810, Ser. IV, Vol. II. Van Horne, John C. et al, eds. LC 83-27423. (Papers of Benjamin Henry Latrobe). 1018p. 1987. text ed. 95.00 (*0-300-03229-3*) Yale U Pr.
— Latrobe's View of America 1795-1820: Selections from the Watercolors & Sketches. Carter, Edward C. et al, eds. LC 84-7580. (Papers of Benjamin Henry Latrobe: No. 3). (Illus.). 420p. 1985. 50.00 (*0-300-02949-7*) Yale U Pr.
Latrobe, Benjamin H., et al, eds. The Journals of Benjamin Henry Latrobe, 1799-1820: From Philadelphia to New Orleans. LC 79-19001. (Papers of Benjamin Henry Latrobe Ser. 1: Vol. 3). (Illus.). 432p. 1981. text ed. 90.00 (*0-300-02383-9*) Yale U Pr.
Latrobe, Kathy H., ed. Exploring the Great Lakes States Through Literature. LC 93-2486. (Exploring the United States Through Literature Ser.). 168p. (J). 1993. pap. 24.95 (*0-89774-731-3*) Oryx Pr.
Latrobe, Kathy H. & Laughlin, Mildred K. Readers Theatre for Young Adults: Scripts & Script Development. xi, 130p. 1989. pap. text ed. 20.00 (*0-87287-743-4*) Teacher Ideas Pr.
Latrobe, Kathy H., jt. auth. see Laughlin, Mildred K.
Latrobe, Kathy H., et al. Social Studies Readers Theatre for Young Adults. 150p. 1991. pap. text ed. 21.50 (*0-87287-864-3*) Teacher Ideas Pr.
Latron, Andre. La Vie Rurale en Syrie et au Liban: Etude d'economie sociale. LC 77-87618. reprint ed. 36.50 (*0-404-16439-0*) AMS Pr.
Latrouche, G., jt. ed. see Courtis, P. J.
Latruffe, N. & Bugaut, M., eds. Peroxisomes. 210p. 1994. Lab. manual. student ed 98.00 (*0-387-56860-3*) Spr-Verlag.
***Latsch, Marie-Luise.** Traditional Chinese Festivals. 103p. 1985. reprint ed. pap. 4.95 (*9971-947-80-3*) Heian Intl.
Latshaw. Veterinary Developmental Anatomy. (Illus.). 282p. (C). 1987. 33.00 (*0-941158-98-5*) Mosby Yr Bk.
Latson, W. R. Secrets of Mental Supremacy. 138p. 1968. reprint ed. spiral bd. 4.95 (*0-7873-1047-6*) Mokelumne.
— Secrets of Mental Supremacy: How to Cultivate Mind, Memory, Perspective, Imagination & Ideas. 1991. lib. bdg. 75.00 (*0-8490-4185-6*) Gordon Pr.
Latt, A. English Commercial Correspondence: Correspondencia Commercial Inglesa. 399p. (ENG & SPA.). 1985. 19.95 (*0-8288-1547-X*, S14171) Fr & Eur.
Latt, David J. & Monk, Samuel H. John Dryden: A Survey & Bibliography of Critical Studies, 1895-1974. LC 75-36033. 215p. reprint ed. pap. 61.30 (*0-8357-8928-4*, 2033267) Bks Demand.
Latt, Mimi L. Powers of Attorney. LC 93-16281. 512p. 1993. 23.00 (*0-671-78708-X*) S&S Trade.
— Powers of Attorney. Rubenstein, Julie, ed. 576p. 1994. reprint ed. mass mkt. 5.99 (*0-671-86916-7*) PB.
Latt, Samuel A. & Darlington, Gretchen J., eds. Methods in Cell Biology, Vol. 26: Prenatal Diagnosis: Cell Biological Approaches. 363p. 1982. text ed. 143.00 (*0-12-564126-5*) Acad Pr.
Latta, et al. Principles of Biology: Laboratory Investigations. 3rd ed. 198p. 1991. teacher ed, spiral bd. 18.95 (*0-88725-150-1*) Hunter Textbks.
Latta, A., jt. auth. see Turner, C.
Latta, Billy L., ed. Family History Is Fun. (Illus.). 1978. 24.95 (*0-932924-00-X*, Heritge Hse) Ye Olde Genealogie Shoppe.
— Family History Is Fun, Beginner Kit. 1992. 15.00 (*0-932924-04-2*, FH94, Heritge Hse) Ye Olde Genealogie Shoppe.
— Family History Is Fun, Deluxe Kit. 1992. 34.50 (*0-932924-01-8*, FH91, Heritge Hse) Ye Olde Genealogie Shoppe.
— Family History Is Fun, Instruction Booklet. 1992. 3.00 (*0-932924-10-7*, FH99, Heritge Hse) Ye Olde Genealogie Shoppe.

An Asterisk (*) at the beginning of an entry indicates that the title is appearing in BIP for the first time.

— Family History Is Fun, Master Kit. 1992. 39.50 (*0-932924-02-6*, FH92, Heritge Hse) Ye Olde Genealogie Shoppe.

Latta, Estelle. Controversial Mark Hopkins. 2nd rev. ed. (Illus.). 254p. 1963. 10.00 (*0-910740-23-2*) Holmes.

Latta, John. Rubbing Torsos. LC 79-465. 93p. 1979. 4.50 (*0-87886-101-7*, Greenfld Rev Pr) Greenfld Rev Lit.

Latta, L., jt. auth. see Sarmiento, Augusto.

Latta, Loren L., jt. auth. see Sarmiento, Augusto.

Latta, R. Sharon, jt. auth. see Taylor, John F.

Latta, Raymond F. & Downey, Carolyn J. Tools for Achieving TQE. (Total Quality Education for the World's Best Schools Ser.: Vol. 10). 160p. 1994. pap. 18.00 (*0-8039-6178-2*) Corwin Pr.

Latta, Rich. Dinosaur Mazes. 48p. (J). (gr. 2 up). 1990. bds. 2.95 (*0-8431-2822-4*) Price Stern.

— Twenty-Four Classics in Puzzle Form. 280p. (J). (gr. 4-8). 1993. pap. 19.95 (*0-913853-28-3*, 32542, Alleyside) Highsmith Pr.

Latta, Richard. Bible Easter Puzzles. (Bible Baffler Ser.). 48p. (J). (gr. 3 up). 1988. 7.95 (*0-86653-427-X*, SS885, Shining Star Pubns) Good Apple.

— Games for Travel. (Illus.). 48p. (J). (gr. 2 up). 1976. bds. 2.95 (*0-8431-0406-6*) Price Stern.

— More Dinosaur Mazes. (Illus.). 48p. (Orig.). (J). (gr. 2 up). 1992. bds. 2.95 (*0-8431-3420-8*) Price Stern.

— More Games for Travel. (Illus.). 48p. (Orig.). (J). (gr. 2 up). 1980. bds. 2.95 (*0-8431-0687-5*) Price Stern.

— This Little Pig Had a Riddle. Fay, Anne, ed. LC 83-26112. (Illus.). 32p. (J). (gr. 1-5). 1984. lib. bdg. 8.95 (*0-8075-7893-2*) A Whitman.

Lattal, Alice D., jt. auth. see Clark, Ralph W.

Latte, K. & Erbse, H. Lexica Graeca Minora. xvii, 372p. 1965. write for info. (*0-318-72039-6*, Pub. by Georg Olms GW) Lubrecht & Cramer.

Latter, J. H., ed. Volcanic Hazards: Assessment & Monitoring. (IAVECI Proceedings in Volcanology Ser.: Vol. 1). (Illus.). 625p. 1989. 115.00 (*0-387-19337-5*) Spr-Verlag.

Latter, Thomas. Grammar of the Language of Burma. 260p. (BUR & ENG.). 1991. 59.95 (*0-8288-8456-0*) Fr & Eur.

Latter, William B., jt. ed. see Cutri, Roc M.

Latterman, Harry. Celebration of Life: Your Guide Book To Prosperity. Hawkins, Mary E., ed. LC 85-62792. (Illus.). 136p. 1986. pap. 8.95 (*0-934739-02-1*) Pussywillow Pub.

Latterman, Terry. Little Joe, a Hopi Indian Boy, Learns a Hopi Indian Secret. Hawkins, Mary E., ed. LC 85-61836. (Illus.). 32p. (J). (gr. 4-12). 1985. 12.95 (*0-934739-01-3*) Pussywillow Pub.

— The Watermelon Treat. Hawkins, Mary E., ed. LC 85-63266. (Illus.). 48p. (J). (gr. 1-4). 1987. 8.95 (*0-934739-03-X*); pap. 5.95 (*0-934739-04-8*) Pussywillow Pub.

***Latterman, Terry & Perez, Maya.** Using the Power of the Psalms As Your Daily Guide. LC 94-61162. 127p. Date not set. pap. 6.95 (*1-55523-727-4*) Winston-Derek.

Latterman, Terry, jt. auth. see Perez, Maya.

Lattes, Raffaele. Atlas of Tumor Pathology: Tumors of the Soft Tissues. rev. ed. (Second Ser.: Fascicle 1). (Illus.). 282p. 1990. per., pap. 14.00 (*0-16-001828-5*, S/N 008-023-000) USGPO.

Lattes, Robert. Methods of Resolution for Selected Boundary Problems in Mathematical Physics. (Documents on Modern Physics Ser.). 200p. 1969. text ed. 169.00 (*0-677-30060-3*) Gordon & Breach.

— Quelques Methodes de Resolutions de Problemes aux Limites de la Physique Mathematiques. (Cours & Documents de Mathematiques & de Physique Ser.). 196p. (Orig.). 1967. text ed. 169.00 (*0-677-50060-2*); pap. text ed. 69.00 (*0-677-50065-3*) Gordon & Breach.

Lattimer, Pamela. A Family of Ginger Griffins. 112p. (C). 1988. 35.00 (*0-7212-0787-1*, Pub. by Regency Press) St Mut.

Lattimore. Frida's Story of Old California. (J). Date not set. 15.00 (*0-06-021026-5*, HarpT); 14.89 (*0-06-021027-3*, HarpT) HarpC.

Lattimore, Colin R. Erotic Bookplates. (Illus.). 64p. (C). 1989. text ed. 59.00 (*1-85183-022-7*, Silent Bks) St Mut.

— Introduction to Wrist Watches. 192p. (C). 1989. text ed. 90.00 (*1-85183-027-8*, Silent Bks) St Mut.

Lattimore, Dan & Terry, Art. Desktop Study Guide. (Illus.). 208p. (C). 1990. pap. text ed. 21.95x (*0-89582-209-1*) Morton Pub.

Lattimore, Dan & Windhauser, John. The Editorial Process. 2nd ed. 320p. (C). 1984. student ed 21.95x (*0-89582-115-X*) Morton Pub.

Lattimore, Dan, jt. auth. see Shook, Fred.

Lattimore, David, tr. The Harmony of the World: Chinese Poems. enl. rev. ed. 1980. pap. 4.50 (*0-914278-31-2*) Copper Beech.

Lattimore, Deborah. Digging into the Past. (BrainBooster Ser.). (Illus.). 32p. (J). (gr. 3 up). 1986. 5.95 (*0-88679-460-9*) Educ Insights.

***Lattimore, Deborah N.** Cinderhazel. LC 95-13089. (J). 1996. write for info. (*0-590-20232-4*); pap. write for info. (*0-590-20233-2*) Scholastic Inc.

— The Dragon's Robe. LC 89-34512. (Illus.). 32p. (J). (gr. 1-5). 1990. lib. bdg. 14.89 (*0-06-023723-6*) HarpC Child Bks.

— The Dragon's Robe. LC 89-34512. (Illus.). 32p. (J). (gr. 1-5). 1990. 15.00 (*0-06-023719-8*) HarpC Child Bks.

— Dragon's Robe. LC 89-34512. (Trophy Picture Bk.). (Illus.). 32p. (J). (gr. 1-5). 1993. pap. 4.95 (*0-06-443321-8*, Trophy) HarpC Child Bks.

— The Flame of Peace: A Tale of the Aztecs. LC 86-26934. (Illus.). 48p. (J). (gr. k-3). 1987. lib. bdg. 14.89 (*0-06-023709-0*) HarpC Child Bks.

— The Flame of Peace: A Tale of the Aztecs. LC 86-26934. (Trophy Picture Bk.). (Illus.). 48p. (J). (ps-3). 1991. pap. 5.95 (*0-06-443272-6*, Trophy) HarpC Child Bks.

— Frida Maria: A Story of the Old Southwest. LC 93-17250. (J). 1994. 14.95 (*0-15-276636-7*, Browndeer Pr) HarBrace.

— Lady with the Ship on Her Head. 28p. (J). (ps-3). 1990. 14.95 (*0-15-243525-5*) HarBrace.

— Lady with the Ship on Her Head. (J). (ps-3). 1992. pap. 4.95 (*0-15-243526-3*) HarBrace.

— The Prince & the Golden Ax: A Minoan Tale. LC 87-21193. (Illus.). 40p. (J). (gr. k-3). 1988. lib. bdg. 12.89 (*0-06-023716-3*) HarpC Child Bks.

— Punga: The Goddess of Ugly. LC 92-23191. 32p. (J). 1993. 14.95 (*0-15-292862-6*) HarBrace.

— The Sailor Who Captured the Sea. LC 89-26937. (Trophy Picture Bks.). (Illus.). 40p. (J). (gr. 2-5). 1993. pap. 5.95 (*0-06-443342-0*, Trophy) HarpC Child Bks.

— The Sailor Who Captured the Sea: A Story of the Book of Kells. LC 89-26937. (Illus.). 40p. (J). (gr. 2-5). 1991. lib. bdg. 15.89 (*0-06-023711-2*) HarpC Child Bks.

— Three Tales from The Arabian Nights. LC 94-9828. (Joanna Cotler Books). (Illus.). 64p. (J). (gr. 2 up). 1995. 16.95 (*0-06-024585-9*); lib. bdg. 16.89 (*0-06-024734-7*) HarpC Child Bks.

— Why There Is No Arguing in Heaven: A Mayan Myth. LC 87-35045. (Illus.). 40p. (J). (gr. 1-5). 1989. lib. bdg. 14.89 (*0-06-023718-X*) HarpC Child Bks.

— The Winged Cat: A Tale of Ancient Egypt. LC 90-38441. (Illus.). 40p. (J). (gr. 2-5). 1992. 15.00 (*0-06-023635-3*); lib. bdg. 14.89 (*0-06-023636-1*) HarpC Child Bks.

Lattimore, Eleanor, jt. auth. see Lattimore, Owen.

Lattimore, Eleanor F. Little Pear. D'Andrade, Diane, ed. (Odyssey Ser.). (Illus.). 106p. (J). (gr. 2-5). 1991. pap. 4.95 (*0-15-246685-1*, HB Juv Bks) HarBrace.

— Little Pear. (J). (gr. 1-4). 1992. 17.50 (*0-8446-6576-2*) Peter Smith.

— Little Pear. (Illus.). (J). 1992. reprint ed. lib. bdg. 14.95 (*0-89966-917-4*) Buccaneer Bks.

— Little Pear & His Friends. (Odyssey Ser.). (Illus.). 129p. (J). (gr. 2-5). 1991. pap. 4.95 (*0-15-246863-3*, HB Juv Bks) HarBrace.

— Little Pear & His Friends. (J). (gr. 1-4). 1992. 17.00 (*0-8446-6575-4*) Peter Smith.

Lattimore, Eleanor H. Turkestan Reunion. LC 72-4440. reprint ed. 24.75 (*0-404-10636-6*) AMS Pr.

— Turkestan Reunion. (Illus.). 320p. 1994. reprint ed. pap. 13.00 (*1-56836-053-3*) Kodansha.

Lattimore, Owen. China Memoirs. 1991. text ed. 34.50 (*0-86008-468-X*, Pub. by U of Tokyo JA) Col U Pr.

— The Desert Road to Turkestan. 384p. 1995. 15.00 (*1-56836-070-3*, Kodansha Globe) Kodansha.

— Desert Road to Turkestan. LC 70-112348. (Illus.). reprint ed. 27.50 (*0-404-03887-5*) AMS Pr.

— Gold Tribe Fishskin Tatars of the Lower Sungari. LC 34-3704. (American Anthropological Association Memoirs Ser.: No. 40). 1933. 15.00 (*0-527-00539-8*) Periodicals Srv.

— High Tartary. LC 72-4433. reprint ed. 30.00 (*0-404-10630-7*) AMS Pr.

— High Tartary. 384p. 1995. reprint ed. pap. 15.00 (*1-56836-054-1*) Kodansha.

— Inner Asian Frontiers of China. (Illus.). 610p. 1989. reprint ed. 32.50 (*0-19-582781-3*) OUP.

— Manchuria: Cradle of Conflict. rev. ed. LC 72-4435. reprint ed. 26.75 (*0-404-10632-3*) AMS Pr.

— Mongol Journeys. LC 72-4436. reprint ed. 27.50 (*0-404-10633-1*) AMS Pr.

— Pivot of Asia. LC 72-4438. reprint ed. 23.50 (*0-404-10634-X*) AMS Pr.

— Solution in Asia. LC 72-4439. reprint ed. 19.45 (*0-404-10635-8*) AMS Pr.

Lattimore, Owen & Lattimore, Eleanor. China: A Short History. LC 75-7663. reprint ed. 18.75 (*0-404-10646-3*) AMS Pr.

Lattimore, Ralston B. Fort Pulaski: National Monument, Georgia. (National Park Service Handbook Ser.: No. 18). (Illus.). 55p. 1984. reprint ed. pap. 2.25 (*0-16-003475-2*, S/N 024-005-00890-0) USGPO.

Lattimore, Richard. Poems from Three Decades. LC 80-39709. xiv, 274p. 1981. pap. text ed. 14.00 (*0-226-46946-8*) U Ch Pr.

Lattimore, Richmond, tr. Greek Lyrics. rev. ed. LC 60-51619. (Orig.). 1960. pap. 5.95 (*0-226-46944-1*, P48) U Ch Pr.

— The Odyssey of Homer. LC 90-55504. 384p. 1975. reprint ed. pap. 12.00 (*0-06-090479-8*, PL) HarpC.

Lattimore, Richmond, tr. see Aeschylus.

Lattimore, Richmond, tr. see Euripides.

Lattimore, Richmond, jt. ed. see Grene, David.

Lattimore, Richmond, tr. see Hesiod.

Lattimore, Richmond, tr. see Homer.

Lattimore, Richmond, tr. see Pindar.

***Lattimore, Richmond A.** Continuing Conclusions: New Poems & Translations. fac. ed. LC 83-727. 71p. 1983. reprint ed. pap. 25.00 (*0-7837-7743-4*, 2047499) Bks Demand.

Lattin. Corporations. 2nd ed. 1971. text ed. 27.00 (*0-88277-411-5*) Foundation Pr.

Lattin, A. W. & Petersson, C., eds. Rheumatoid Arthritis Surgery of the Shoulder. (Rheumatology, the Interdisciplinary Concept Ser.: Vol. 12). (Illus.). xiv, 138p. 1989. 112.00 (*3-8055-4804-4*) S Karger.

Lattin, Gerald W., et al. The Lodging & Food Service Industry. 3rd ed. Wood, Priscilla J., ed. LC 93-8630. (Illus.). 423p. 1993. text ed. 53.95 (*0-86612-071-8*) Educ Inst Am Hotel.

Lattin, Vernon E., ed. & intro. Contemporary Chicano Fiction: A Critical Survey. LC 85-71528. (Studies in the Language & Literature of United States Hispanos). 336p. (ENG & SPA.). (C). 1986. lib. bdg. 27.00 (*0-916950-56-5*); pap. text ed. 18.00 (*0-916950-57-3*) Biling Rev-Pr.

Lattin, Vernon E., et al, eds. Tomas Rivera, 1935-1984: The Man & His Work. LC 88-71440. (Illus.). xviii, 158p. 1988. pap. 16.00 (*0-916950-89-1*) Biling Rev-Pr.

Lattis, James M. Between Copernicus & Galileo: Christoph Clavius & the Collapse of Ptolemaic Cosmology. LC 94-8675. 1994. lib. bdg. 54.00 (*0-226-46927-1*); pap. text ed. 22.50 (*0-226-46929-8*) U Ch Pr.

Lattman, Eaton, jt. ed. see Love, Warner.

Lattman, Laurence H., jt. auth. see Zillman, Donald N.

Latto, L. P. & Rosen, Marcia. Difficulties in Tracheal Intubation. (Illus.). 183p. 1985. text ed. 51.95 (*0-7216-9996-0*, Bailliere-Tindall) Saunders.

Lattu, Kristan R., ed. History of Rocketry & Astronautics. LC 57-43769. (American Astronautical Society History Ser.: Vol. 8). (Illus.). 368p. 1989. lib. bdg. 50.00 (*0-87703-307-2*, Pub. by Am Astro Soc); pap. text ed. 35.00 (*0-87703-308-0*, Pub. by Am Astro Soc) Univelt Inc.

Latulippe, Laura D. Developing Academic Reading Skills. (Illus.). 224p. (C). 1986. pap. text ed. 21.00 (*0-13-204157-X*) P-H.

— Writing As a Personal Product. 2081p. (C). 1992. pap. text ed. 19.25 (*0-13-005869-6*) P-H.

Latus, Thomas, jt. ed. see Hehir, Thomas.

Latymer, Francis B. Ventures in Thought. LC 67-23238. (Essay Index Reprint Ser.). 1977. 20.95 (*0-8369-0610-1*) Ayer.

Latymer, Hugo. The Mediterranean Garden. 160p. 1990. 35.00 (*0-8120-6183-7*) Barron.

Latynin, Leonid. Sleeper at Harvest Time. Bromfield, Andrew, tr. (Illus.). 288p. 1994. 21.00 (*0-939010-36-4*); pap. 11.00 (*0-939010-37-2*) Zephyr Pr.

Latynski, Maya, ed. Reappraising the Munich Pact: Continental Perspectives. LC 91-45734. (Woodrow Wilson Center Press Ser.). 120p. 1992. text ed. 22.00 (*0-943875-38-2*); pap. text ed. 10.95 (*0-943875-39-0*) Johns Hopkins.

Latynski, Maya, tr. see Michnik, Adam.

***Latyon, David.** WW II: A Global Perspective. 304p. (C). 1994. per., pap. text ed. 28.76 (*0-7872-0421-8*) Kendall-Hunt.

Latypov, T., jt. auth. see Khrutsky, V.

Latyschev, Basilius, ed. Inscriptiones Antiquae Orae Septentrionalis Ponti Euxini Graecae et Latinae, Vols. I, II & IV. 1965. reprint ed. write for info. (*0-318-72101-5*, Pub. by Georg Olms GW) Lubrecht & Cramer.

Latyschev, Basillius. Inscriptiones Antiquae Orae Septentrionalis Ponti Euxini Graecae et Latinae, Vols. I, II & IV. xii, 1359p. (GER.). 1965. reprint ed. write for info. (*0-318-70445-5*, Pub. by Georg Olms GW) Lubrecht & Cramer.

Latysev, K. P., ed. see Steklov Institute of Mathematics, Academy of Sciences, U. S. S. R. Staff.

Latz, Gil. Agricultural Development in Japan: The Land Improvement District in Concept & Practice. (Research Papers Ser.: No. 225). (Illus.). 1989. pap. 12.00 (*0-89065-129-9*) U Chicago Comm Geo.

Latz, Gottlieb. The Secret of the Emerald Tablet of Hermes. Holmes, J. D., ed. Hauck, D. William, tr. 1993. pap. 9.95 (*1-55818-203-9*) Holmes Pub.

***Latzer, Barry.** State Constitutional Criminal Law. LC 94-69102. 1995. ring bd. 135.00 (*0-614-07299-9*) Clark Boardman Callaghan.

— State Constitutions & Criminal Justice, No. 65. LC 91-3249. (Contributions in Legal Studies). 232p. 1991. text ed. 55.00 (*0-313-26112-1*, LLF, Greenwood Pr) Greenwood.

***Latzke, Deborah.** When the Last Acorn Is Found. 64p. 1993. 12.95 (*0-9643956-1-4*) Legacy of Love.

Latzko, Adolf A. Men in War. LC 71-116961. (Short Story Index Reprint Ser.). 1977. 20.95 (*0-8369-3465-2*) Ayer.

Latzko, D. G., et al, eds. Post-Yield Fracture Mechanics. 2nd ed. (Illus.). 512p. 1985. 156.75 (*0-85334-276-8*, Pub. by Elsevier Applied Sci UK) Elsevier.

Latzko, William. Quality & Productivity for Bankers & Financial Managers. (Qualtiy & Reliability Ser.: Vol. 10). 224p. 1986. 59.75 (*0-8247-7682-8*) Dekker.

***Latzko, William J. & Saunders, David M.** Four Days with Dr. Deming: A Strategy for Modern Methods of Management. LC 94-29252. (Engineering Process Improvement Ser.). 256p. 1995. pap. 25.95 (*0-201-63366-3*) Addison-Wesley.

Latzky, Eric. Three Views from Vertical Cliffs. 1991. pap. 9.95 (*0-927200-11-2*) Amethyst NY.

***Lau & Tweddle, eds.** Topological Vector Spaces, Algebras & Related Areas. (Pitman Research Notes in Mathematics). 1995. pap. text ed. 79.95 (*0-470-23486-5*) Wiley.

***Lau, A. & Tweddle, I.** Topological Vector Spaces, Algebras, & Related Areas. (Pitman Research Notes in Mathematics Ser.). 1994. write for info. (*0-615-00302-8*) Wiley.

Lau, A., et al, eds. Time-Resolved Vibrational Spectroscopy VI: Proceedings of the Sixth International Conference on Time-Resolved Vibrational Spectroscopy, Berlin, Germany, May 23-28, 1993. LC 93-40610. (Proceedings in Physics Ser.: Vol. 74). 1994. 79.00 (*0-387-57573-1*) Spr-Verlag.

Lau, Alan C. Songs for Jadina. LC 80-66984. 94p. (Orig.). 1981. pap. 4.95 (*0-912678-46-1*, Greenfld Rev Pr) Greenfld Rev Lit.

Lau, Albert. The Malayan Union Controversy, 1942-1948. (South-East Asian Historical Monographs). 340p. 1991. 42.50 (*0-19-588964-9*) OUP.

Lau, Barbara, jt. auth. see Edwards, Ted L., Jr.

Lau, Benjamin. Garlic for Health. LC 88-80886. (Illus.). 78p. (Orig.). (C). 1988. pap. 3.95 (*0-941524-32-9*) Lotus Light.

Lau, Beth. Keats' Reading of the Romantic Poets. 224p. 1991. 37.50 (*0-472-09437-8*) U of Mich Pr.

Lau, Beth, jt. ed. see Hoeveler, Diane L.

Lau, Carolyn. Wode Shuofa: My Way of Speaking. 80p. (Orig.). 1988. pap. 6.00 (*0-940510-15-4*) Tooth of Time.

Lau, Charles & Glossbrenner, Alfred. The Art of Hitting Three Hundred. rev. ed. 1992. pap. 18.95 (*0-14-015335-7*, Penguin Bks) Viking Penguin.

— The Winning Hitter: How to Play Championship Baseball. LC 84-60203. (Illus.). 190p. 1984. pap. 7.95 (*0-688-03634-1*) Hearst Bks.

Lau, Christina. Object-Oriented Programming Using SOM & DSOM. LC 94-20906. 288p. 1995. pap. 39.95 (*0-442-01948-3*) Van Nos Reinhold.

Lau, Chu-Pak. Rate Adaptive Cardiac Pacing: Single & Dual Chamber. (Illus.). 488p. 1992. 80.00 (*0-87993-544-8*) Futura Pub.

Lau, Clifford. Neural Networks: Theoretical Foundations & Analysis. LC 91-39114. (Illus.). 336p. (C). 1992. text ed. 49.95 (*0-87942-280-7*, PC0279-0) Inst Electrical.

Lau, Clifford, jt. ed. see Sanchez-Sinencio, Edgar.

Lau, D. C., tr. Confucius: The Analects (Lun yu) 2nd ed. 288p. 1992. 67.50x (*962-201-527-1*, Pub. by Chinese Univ HK) Coronet Bks.

— Mencius. (Classics Ser.). 288p. 1970. pap. 9.95 (*0-14-044228-6*, Penguin Classics) Viking Penguin.

— Tao Te Ching. (Chinese Classics Ser.). 325p. 1982. 39.50 (*962-201-252-3*, Pub. by Chinese Univ HK) Coronet Bks.

Lau, D. C., tr. see Confucius.

Lau, Deborah, tr. see Adames, Jay.

Lau, Dicksen T. Engin Politism: A New Political Theory for Permanent World Peace. LC 83-62601. 396p. (Orig.). 1983. pap. 9.50 (*0-9612000-1-4*) Magnolia Bks.

— The New Religion & Relativity. LC 83-62038. 138p. (Orig.). 1983. pap. 5.95 (*0-9612000-0-6*) Magnolia Bks.

Lau, Edwin J. Performance Improvement of Virtual Memory Systems. LC 82-13393. (Computer Science: Systems Programming Ser.: No. 17). 228p. reprint ed. pap. 65.00 (*0-685-20845-1*, 2070073) Bks Demand.

Lau, Evelyn. Fresh Girls: And Other Stories. LC 94-7565. 128p. 1995. 17.95 (*0-7868-6058-8*) Hyperion.

— Other Women. LC 95-10686. 1996. write for info. (*0-7868-6107-X*) Hyperion.

Lau, Foo-Sun. A Dictionary of Nuclear Power & Waste Management with Abbreviations & Acronyms. LC 87-4288. 396p. 1987. text ed. 445.00 (*0-471-91517-3*) Wiley.

Lau, H. T. Algorithms on Graphs. 180p. 1989. 29.95 (*0-8306-3429-0*, TAB/TPR) TAB Bks.

— Algorithms on Graphs. 1991. 24.95 (*0-8306-5429-1*) TAB Bks.

— Chinese Chess. LC 84-52394. (Illus.). 248p. 1991. pap. 9.95 (*0-8048-1675-1*) C E Tuttle.

— Combinatorial Heuristic Algorithms with FORTRAN. (Lecture Notes in Economics & Mathematical Systems Ser.: Vol. 280). vii, 126p. 1986. pap. 29.60 (*0-387-17161-4*) Spr-Verlag.

— A Numerical Library in C for Scientists & Engineers. 816p. 1994. 69.95 (*0-8493-7376-X*, 7376) CRC Pr.

Lau, J. Chip on Board Technology. 1994. text ed. 64.95 (*0-442-01441-4*) Van Nos Reinhold.

Lau, James B. & Shani, A. B. Behavior in Organizations. 5th ed. 704p. (C). 1991. pap. text ed. 39.95 (*0-256-08701-6*, 08-1107-05) Irwin.

Lau, James B., jt. auth. see Shani, Abraham B.

Lau, Jesus, ed. see Muro, Ernest A.

***Lau, John H.** Ball Grid Array Technology. 1994. text ed. 75.00 (*0-07-036608-X*) McGraw.

Lau, John H., ed. Handbook of Fine Pitch Surface Mount Technology. LC 93-25289. 1994. text ed. 99.95 (*0-442-01258-6*) Van Nos Reinhold.

— Handbook of Tape Automated Bonding. (Illus.). 650p. 1992. text ed. 89.95 (*0-442-00427-3*) Van Nos Reinhold.

— Solder Joint Reliability: Theory & Applications. LC 90-12968. (Illus.). 576p. 1991. text ed. 84.95 (*0-442-00260-2*) Van Nos Reinhold.

— Thermal Stress & Strain in Microelectronics Packaging. LC 92-43285. 1993. text ed. 99.95 (*0-442-01058-3*) Van Nos Reinhold.

Lau, Joseph S., ed. The Unbroken Chain: An Anthology of Taiwan Fiction since 1926. LC 83-47904. 298p. 1984. 35.00 (*0-253-36162-1*); pap. 12.95 (*0-253-20489-5*, MB-489) Ind U Pr.

Lau, Joseph S. & Ross, Timothy A., eds. Chinese Stories from Taiwan, Nineteen Sixty to Nineteen Seventy. LC 75-4391. 359p. 1976. text ed. 50.00 (*0-231-04007-5*) Col U Pr.

Lau, Joseph S., jt. ed. see Ma, Y. W.

Lau, Joseph S., tr. see Ts'ao.

Lau, Joseph S., et al, eds. Modern Chinese Stories & Novellas, Nineteen Nineteen to Nineteen Forty-Nine. LC 80-27572. (Modern Asian Literature Ser.). 608p. (ENG.). 1981. pap. text ed. 25.00 (*0-231-04203-5*) Col U Pr.

***Lau, Joseph S. M. & Goldblatt, Howard, eds.** The Columbia Anthology of Modern Chinese Literature. LC 94-35304. (Modern Asian Literature Ser.). 726p. (CHI & ENG.). 1995. 39.00 (*0-231-08002-6*) Col U Pr.

Lau, Joy. Vegetables for the Home Gardener. 144p. 1987. pap. 16.95 (*0-85091-223-7*, Pub. by Lothian Pub AT) Intl Spec Bk.

Lau, Ka-Sing, jt. auth. see Ramachandran, B.

Lau, Kam. Cantonese Phrasebook. (Illus.). 180p. (Orig.). 1994. pap. 6.95 (*0-86442-217-2*) Lonely Planet.

— Cantonese Phrasebook. (Illus.). 224p. (Orig.). 1995. pap. 5.95 (*0-86442-340-3*) Lonely Planet.

— Japanese Phrasebook. 2nd ed. (Illus.). 224p. 1994. pap. 5.95 (*0-86442-230-X*) Lonely Planet.

An Asterisk (*) at the beginning of an entry indicates that the title is appearing in BIP for the first time.

Lau, Kung-Kiu & Clement, Tim P., eds. Logic Program Synthesis & Transformation: Proceedings of LOPSTR '92, International Workshop on Logic Program Synthesis & Transformation, University of Manchester, 2-3 July, 1992. LC 92-43296. (Workshops in Computing Ser.). 1993. 69.00 (0-387-19806-7) Spr-Verlag.

Lau, Kwan. Secrets of Chinese Astrology: A Handbook for Self-Discovery. (Illus.). 160p. (Orig.). 1994. pap. 9.95 (0-8348-0306-2, Tengu Bks) Weatherhill.

Lau, L. Wang. Elements of Nuclear Reactor Engineering. LC 77-156083. 256p. (C). 1974. text ed. 207.00 (0-677-02270-0) Gordon & Breach.

Lau, Laurence S. & DeCampo, John F. Notes on Radiological Diagnosis. 216p. 1985. pap. text ed. 39.50 (0-7216-1936-3) Saunders.

Lau, Lawrence J., ed. Models of Development: A Comparative Study of Economic Growth in South Korea & Taiwan. rev. ed. LC 89-32765. 217p. 1990. 24.95 (1-55815-102-8); pap. 12.95 (1-55815-005-6) ICS Pr.

Lau, Lawrence J., jt. auth. see Jamison, Dean T.

Lau, Lillian, ed. see American Micro Systems Staff.

Lau, Richard R. & Sears, David O., eds. Political Cognition: The 19th Annual Carnegie Mellon Symposium on Cognition. (Carnegie Symposium on Cognition Ser., 19th Annual). 424p. (C). 1986. text ed. 79.95 (0-89859-652-1) L Erlbaum Assocs.

Lau, Robert J. Old Babylonian Temple Records. (Columbia University. Oriental Studies: No. 3). reprint ed. 15.50 (0-404-50493-0) AMS Pr.

Lau, Siu-kai. Society & Politics in Hong Kong. x, 205p. 1982. text ed. 24.00 (962-201-336-8, Pub. by Chinese Univ HK) Coronet Bks.

Lau Siu-kai & Kuan Hsin-chi. The Ethos of the Hong Kong Chinese. 232p. (Orig.). 1989. pap. 24.00 (962-201-431-3, Pub. by Chinese Univ HK) Coronet Bks.

Lau, Theodora. Handbook of Chinese Horoscopes. rev. ed. 1988. pap. 13.00 (0-06-096290-9, PL) HarpC.

— The Handbook of Chinese Horoscopes. 3rd ed. (Illus.). 352p. (Orig.). 1995. pap. 13.00 (0-06-273370-2) HarpC.

Lau-Uhle, Margaret. Vox--Enciclopedia Cultural, Tomo 5: Continentes. 210p. (SPA.). 1977. 49.95 (0-8288-5549-8, S50504) Fr & Eur.

Lau, William W., ed. American University Programs in Computer Science: Their Resources, Facilities & Course Offerings. 2nd ed. LC 85-70986. 220p. 1986. 26.00 (0-915751-23-2) GGL Educ Press.

Lau, Wolfgang. Schriftgelehrte Prophetie in Jes 56-66: Eine Untersuchung zu den Literarischen Bezuegen in den Letzten Elf Kapiteln des Jesajabuches. (Beihefte zur Zeitschrift fuer die Alttestamentliche Wissenschaft Ser.: Vol. 225). ix, 357p. (GER.). (C). 1994. lib. bdg. 132.35 (3-11-014239-2) De Gruyter.

Lau, Yun-Fai, ed. Endocrine Genes: Analytical Methods, Experimental Approaches, & Selected Systems. 240p. 1988. 45.00 (0-19-504409-6) OUP.

Laub, A. J., jt. ed. see Denham, M. J.

Laub, Burton R. & Sell, W. Edward. Pennsylvania Keystone Lawyer's Desk Library of Practice, 8 vols., Set. 1995. ring bd. 425.00 (0-317-03817-6) Bisel Co.

Laub, Burton R., et al. Pennsylvania Manual of Penalties & Sentences: Civil & Criminal. LC 94-73046. 601p. 1994. pap. 89.50 (0-317-03819-2) Bisel Co.

Laub, Dori, jt. auth. see Felman, Shoshana.

Laub, Joan, jt. auth. see Cochran, Larry.

Laub, John H. Criminology in the Making: An Oral History. LC 83-8147. 287p. 1983. text ed. 32.50 (0-930350-46-4); pap. 12.95 (0-930350-53-7) NE U Pr.

Laub, John H., jt. ed. see McCord, Joan.

Laub, John H., jt. auth. see Sampson, Robert J.

Laub, Julian M. The College & Community Development: A Socioeconomic Analysis for Urban & Regional Growth. LC 75-166397. (Special Studies in U. S. Economic, Social & Political Issues). 1972. 39.50 (0-275-28207-4) Irvington.

Laub, Leonard. Data Compression: Applications in Communcations, Storage, Imaging, Audio, Video Multimedia. (Illus.). 256p. 1992. text ed. 39.95 (0-442-01393-0) Van Nos Reinhold.

Laub, Mark. How To Play Latin Organ. 1984. 12.95 (0-943748-04-6) Ekay Music.

Laub, Morris. Last Barrier to Freedom: Internment of Jewish Holocaust Survivors on Cyprus 1946-1949. LC 84-82475. (Illus.). (Orig.). 1985. pap. 8.95 (0-943376-25-4) Magnes Mus.

Laub, Richard S., et al, eds. Late Pleistocene & Early Holocene Paleoecology & Archaeology of the Eastern Great Lakes Region: Proceedings of the Smith Symposium, Held at the Buffalo Museum of Science, October 24-25, 1986. LC 88-6094. (Bulletin of the Buffalo Society of Natural Sciences Ser.: Vol. 33). 316p. (C). 1988. pap. 42.00 (0-944032-52-4) OR St U CSFA.

Laub, Rolf, illus. State Lines. LC 93-3512. 240p. (C). 1993. 29.50 (0-89096-557-9); pap. 14.95 (0-89096-562-5) Tex A&M Univ Pr.

Laub, Thomas. Laubster Tales. 1994. 12.95 (0-533-10860-8) Vantage.

Laubach, Don & Henckel, Mark. Deer Talk. (Illus.). 224p. (Orig.). 1992. pap. 12.95 (1-56044-149-6) Falcon Pr MT.

— The Elk Hunter: The Ultimate Source Book on Elk & Elk Hunting for the Beginner & Expert Alike. LC 89-83806. 248p. (Orig.). 1989. pap. 12.95 (0-937959-78-2) Falcon Pr MT.

— Elk Talk. LC 87-90834. (Illus.). 208p. 1987. pap. 12.95 (0-937959-22-7) Falcon Pr MT.

Laubach, Edwin G. Networking with Banyan Vines. (Applied Networking Ser.). (Illus.). 272p. 1990. pap. 21.95 (0-8306-3405-3, 3405, Windcrest) TAB Bks.

— Networking with Banyan VINES. 2nd ed. (Illus.). 448p. 1992. pap. 24.95 (0-8306-3747-8, 4088, Windcrest) TAB Bks.

Laubach, Frank, jt. auth. see Brother Lawrence.

Laubach, Mark E. The Well Connected Office. 250p. 1993. pap. 35.00 (0-13-950965-8) P-H.

Laubach, Rene. Guide to Natural Places: In the Berkshire Hills. 1992. pap. 9.95 (0-936399-25-2) Berkshire Hse.

Laubach, S. E. Fracture Analysis of the Travis Peak Formation, Western Flank of the Sabine Arch, East Texas. (Report of Investigations Ser.: RI 185). (Illus.). 55p. 1989. 4.00 (0-317-03120-1) Bur Econ Geology.

Laubach, S. E., jt. ed. see Nelson, P. P.

Laube, Clifford J., ed. Their Music Is Mary. 1961. 3.50 (0-910984-11-5) Montfort Pubns.

Laube, Gary, ed. see Newman-Swaney, Laura J.

Laube, James. California's Great Cabernets: The Wine Spectator's Guide for Consumers. 1989. 29.95 (0-918076-71-4, Wine Spectator) M Shanken Comm.

***Lauben, Philip.** Shall We Send Flowers? large type ed. (Mystery Library). 288p. 1995. pap. 14.95 (0-7089-7654-9, Linford) Ulverscroft.

— A Sort Tragedy. large type ed. (Linford Mystery Large Pr. Ser.). 1994. pap. 14.95 (0-7089-7639-5) Ulverscroft.

Laubenbacher, Reinhard C., tr. see Hilbert, David.

Laubenfels, Jean M. The Gifted Student: An Annotated Bibliography. LC 77-82696. (Contemporary Problems of Childhood Ser.: No. 1). 220p. 1977. text ed. 42.95 (0-8371-9760-0, LGC/, Greenwood Pr) Greenwood.

Laubenstein, Linda J., jt. ed. see Friedman-Kien, Alvin E.

Laubenstein, William J. This Is How It Was. (Illus.). vi, 132p. 1971. pap. 4.95 (0-913228-03-6) Dillon-Liederbach.

Laubenthal, Sanders A. The Gates of Wonder: Poetry of Places. 1966. pap. 3.95 (0-685-06843-9) Belmary.

— Interlude & Other Poems. 1969. pap. 3.95 (0-685-06844-7) Belmary.

— The Last Confederate. 1967. 6.95 (0-685-06845-5); pap. 4.95 (0-685-06846-3) Belmary.

Lauber. The Politics of Economic Policy. 366p. 1983. pap. text ed. 9.95 (0-275-91579-4, B1579, Praeger Pubs) Greenwood.

Lauber, Almon W. Indian Slavery in Colonial Times Within the Present Limits of the United States. LC 71-77994. (Columbia University. Studies in the Social Sciences: No. 134). reprint ed. 29.50 (0-404-51134-1) AMS Pr.

— Indian Slavery in Colonial Times Within the Present Limits of the United States. 352p. 1970. reprint ed. 25.00 (0-87928-008-5) Corner Hse.

Lauber, Daniel. The Government Job Finder. LC 90-92307. (Illus.). 336p. (Orig.). 1992. pap. 14.95 (0-9622019-1-X) Planning Comns.

— Government Job Finder. 2nd ed. LC 93-45780. (Illus.). 352p. 1994. 32.95 (1-884587-01-1); pap. 16.95 (0-9622019-7-9) Planning Comns.

— The Non-Profits' Job Finder. (Illus.). 320p. (Orig.). 1992. pap. 14.95 (0-9622019-4-4) Planning Comns.

— Non-Profits' Job Finder. 2nd ed. (Illus.). 320p. (Orig.). 1993. pap. 14.95 (0-9622019-5-2) Planning Comns.

— Non Profits' Job Finder. 3rd ed. LC 93-45781. (Illus.). 336p. 1994. 32.95 (1-884587-02-X); pap. 16.95 (0-9622019-8-7) Planning Comns.

— The Professional's Job Finder. LC 90-92306. (Illus.). 512p. (Orig.). 1992. pap. 15.95 (0-9622019-2-8) Planning Comns.

— Professional's Private Sector Job Finder. LC 93-45779. (Illus.). 536p. (Orig.). 1994. 36.95 (1-884587-00-3); pap. 18.95 (0-9622019-6-0) Planning Comns.

Lauber, John. Jane Austen. LC 93-3788. (English Authors Ser.: Vol. 498). 170p. 1993. text ed. 21.95 (0-8057-7014-3, Pub. by Royal Botanic Garden UK) Macmillan.

— The Making of Mark Twain. (Noonday Ser.). 1988. pap. 9.95 (0-374-52130-1) FS&G.

— Sir Walter Scott. rev. ed. (English Authors Ser.: No. 39). 184p. (C). 1989. text ed. 22.95 (0-8057-6964-1, TEAS 39, Pub. by Royal Botanic Garden UK) Macmillan.

Lauber, K. Chemie im Laboratorium. 4th ed. (Illus.). viii, 376p. 1983. pap. 62.50 (3-8055-3547-3) S Karger.

Lauber, Lynn. Twenty-One Sugar Street. 240p. 1994. pap. 10.00 (0-393-31235-6) Norton.

— White Girls. LC 91-50012. (Vintage Contemporaries Ser.). 192p. 1991. pap. 9.00 (0-679-73411-2, Vin) Random.

— White Girls. 1990. 17.95 (0-393-02717-1) Norton.

Lauber, Pat. Animals & Their Homes. LC 92-13129. (J). 1994. 16.95 (0-590-45071-9) Scholastic Inc.

— Dinosaurs Walked Here & Other Stories Fossils Tell. LC 91-40739. (Illus.). 64p. (J). (gr. 2-5). 1992. reprint ed. pap. 5.95 (0-689-71603-6, Aladdin Paperbacks) S&S Childrens.

Lauber, Patricia. Alligators: A Success Story. LC 93-3302. (Illus.). 64p. (J). (gr. 2-4). 1994. 14.95 (0-8050-1909-X, Bks Young Read) H Holt & Co.

— Be a Friend to Trees. LC 92-24082. (Let's-Read-&-Find-Out Science Bk.: Stage 2). (Illus.). 32p. (J). (gr. k-4). 1994. 15.00 (0-06-021528-3); lib. bdg. 14.89 (0-06-021529-1); pap. 4.95 (0-06-445120-8, Trophy) HarpC Child Bks.

— Dinosaurs Walked Here & Other Stories Fossils Tell. LC 86-8239. (Illus.). 64p. (J). (gr. 2-4). 1987. text ed. 16.95 (0-02-754510-5, Bradbury S&S) S&S Childrens.

— Earthquakes: New Scientific Ideas about How & Why the Earth Shakes. (Illus.). (J). (gr. 4-8). 1972. pap. 3.95 (0-394-82373-7) Random Bks Yng Read.

— Earthworms: Underground Farmers. LC 93-79784. (J). (ps-3). 1994. 14.95 (0-8050-1910-3) H Holt & Co.

— Get Ready for Robots. LC 85-48255. (Let's-Read-&-Find-Out Science Bk.). (Illus.). 32p. (J). (ps-3). 1987. lib. bdg. 13.89i (0-690-04578-6, Crowell Jr Bks) HarpC Child Bks.

— Great Whales: The Gentle Giants. (Redfeather Bks.). (Illus.). 64p. (J). (gr. 2-4). 1991. 14.95 (0-8050-1717-8, Redfeather BYR) H Holt & Co.

— Great Whales: The Gentle Giants. LC 91-692. (Illus.). 64p. (J). (gr. 2-4). 1993. pap. 4.95 (0-8050-2894-3, Bks Young Read) H Holt & Co.

— How Dinosaurs Came to Be. LC 94-6667. (J). 1995. text ed. 17.95 (0-02-754505-9, Bradbury S&S) S&S Childrens.

— How We Learned the Earth Is Round. LC 89-49650. (Let's-Read-&-Find-Out Science Bk.). (Illus.). 32p. (J). (gr. k-4). 1990. lib. bdg. 14.89 (0-690-04862-9) HarpC Child Bks.

— How We Learned the Earth Is Round. LC 89-49650. (Trophy Let's-Read-&-Find-Out Bk.). (Illus.). 32p. (J). (gr. k-4). 1992. pap. 4.95 (0-06-445109-7, Trophy) HarpC Child Bks.

— Journey to the Planets. rev. ed. LC 90-33102. (Illus.). (J). 1990. lib. bdg. 16.99 (0-517-58125-6) Crown Bks Yng Read.

— Journey to the Planets. 4th ed. LC 92-16094. 96p. (J). (gr. 4-9). 1993. 20.00 (0-517-59029-8) Crown Bks Yng Read.

— Living with Dinosaurs. LC 90-43265. (Illus.). 48p. (J). (gr. 1-5). 1991. text ed. 16.95 (0-02-754521-0, Bradbury S&S) S&S Childrens.

— Lost Star: The Story of Amelia Earhart. (J). (gr. 4-7). 1990. pap. 3.25 (0-590-41159-4) Scholastic Inc.

— The News about Dinosaurs. LC 88-24140. (Illus.). 48p. (J). (gr. 1-5). 1989. text ed. 16.95 (0-02-754520-2, Bradbury S&S) S&S Childrens.

— The News about Dinosaurs. LC 94-2373. (Illus.). 48p. (J). (gr. 1-5). 1994. pap. 6.95 (0-689-71870-5, Aladdin Paperbacks) S&S Childrens.

— An Octopus Is Amazing. LC 89-29300. (Let's-Read-&-Find-Out Science Bk.). (Illus.). 32p. (J). (ps-1). 1990. 15.00 (0-690-04801-7, Crowell Jr Bks); lib. bdg. 14.89 (0-690-04803-3, Crowell Jr Bks) HarpC Child Bks.

— Seeds: Pop Stick Glide. LC 80-14553. (Illus.). 64p. (J). (gr. 2-4). 1991. lib. bdg. 14.99 (0-517-58554-5) Crown Bks Yng Read.

— Seeing Earth from Space. LC 89-77523. (Illus.). 80p. (J). (gr. 5 up). 1990. 21.95 (0-531-05902-2); lib. bdg. 21.99 (0-531-08502-3) Orchard Bks Watts.

— Seeing Earth from Space. LC 89-77523. (Illus.). 80p. (YA). (gr. 5 up). 1994. pap. 9.95 (0-531-07057-3) Orchard Bks Watts.

— Snakes Are Hunters. LC 87-47695. (Let's-Read-&-Find-Out Science Bk.). (Illus.). 32p. (J). (ps-3). 1988. lib. bdg. 14.89 (0-690-04630-8, Crowell Jr Bks) HarpC Child Bks.

— Snakes Are Hunters. LC 87-47695. (Trophy Let's-Read-&-Find-Out Bk.). (Illus.). 32p. (J). (ps-4). 1989. pap. 4.95 (0-06-445091-0, Trophy) HarpC Child Bks.

— Summer of Fire: Yellowstone 1988. LC 90-23032. (Illus.). 64p. (J). (gr. 4 up). 1991. 19.95 (0-531-05943-X); lib. bdg. 19.99 (0-531-08543-0) Orchard Bks Watts.

— Tales Mummies Tell. LC 83-46172. (Illus.). 128p. (J). (gr. 5-9). 1985. lib. bdg. 15.89 (0-690-04389-9, Crowell Jr Bks) HarpC Child Bks.

— Volcano: The Eruption & Healing of Mount St. Helens. LC 85-22442. (Illus.). 64p. (J). (gr. 3-5). 1986. text ed. 16.95 (0-02-754500-8, Bradbury S&S) S&S Childrens.

— Volcano: The Eruption & Healing of Mount St. Helens. LC 92-23791. (Illus.). 64p. (J). (gr. 2-5). 1993. reprint ed. pap. 6.95 (0-689-71679-6, Aladdin Paperbacks) S&S Childrens.

— Volcanoes & Earthquakes. 80p. (J). (gr. 4-7). 1991. pap. 2.95 (0-590-42592-7) Scholastic Inc.

— Voyagers from Space: Meteors & Meteorites. LC 86-47745. (Illus.). 80p. (J). (gr. 5 up). 1989. lib. bdg. 15.89 (0-690-04634-0, Crowell Jr Bks) HarpC Child Bks.

— What Big Teeth You Have! LC 85-47902. (Illus.). 64p. (J). (gr. 2-6). 1986. lib. bdg. 13.89 (0-690-04507-7, Crowell Jr Bks) HarpC Child Bks.

— What Do You See? LC 93-2388. (Illus.). 48p. (J). (gr. 3-7). 1994. 17.00 (0-517-59390-4); lib. bdg. 17.99 (0-517-59391-2) Crown Bks Yng Read.

— Who Discovered America? Mysteries & Puzzles of the New World. LC 90-43604. (Illus.). 80p. (J). (gr. 2-6). 1992. lib. bdg. 15.89 (0-06-023729-5) HarpC Child Bks.

— Who Eats What? Food Chains & Food Webs. (Let's Read-&-Find-Out Science Bk.). (J). (ps-3). 1994. pap. 4.95 (0-06-445130-5) HarpC Child Bks.

— Who Eats What? Food Chains & Food Webs. LC 93-10609. (Let's-Read-&-Find-Out Science Bk.). (Illus.). 32p. (J). (gr. k-4). 1995. 15.00 (0-06-022981-0) HarpC Child Bks.

— Who Eats What? Food Chains & Food Webs. LC 93-10609. (Let's-Read-&-Find-Out Science Bk.). (Illus.). 32p. (J). (gr. k-4). 1995. lib. bdg. 14.89 (0-06-022982-9) HarpC Child Bks.

— You're Aboard Spaceship Earth. LC 94-18704. (Let's-Read-and-Find-Out Science Ser.: Stage 2). (Illus.). (J). (PS up). 1996. 15.00 (0-06-024407-0); lib. bdg. 14.89 (0-06-024408-9) HarpC.

Lauber, R., ed. see IFAC-IFIP-IFORS International Conference Staff.

Lauber, R., ed. see IFAC Symposium Staff.

Lauber, Timothy J. Furniture Associations in North America. LC 94-1179. 80p. (Orig.). 1994. pap. text ed. 280.00 (0-921577-41-9) AKTRIN.

— Furniture Exhibitions: Europe, Asia, Australia, Latin America. LC 94-29601. 112p. (Orig.). 1994. pap. text ed. 280.00x (0-921577-45-1) AKTRIN.

— Furniture Exhibitions: U. S. A.-Canada-Mexico. LC 94-45364. 90p. (Orig.). 1995. pap. text ed. 280.00 (0-921577-49-4) AKTRIN.

Lauber, William F., jt. ed. see Tucker, Allyson M.

Laubereau, A. & Seilmeier, A., eds. Ultrafast Processes in Spectroscopy 1991: Proceedings of the Seventh International Symposium, Bayreuth, 1991. (Illus.). 688p. 1992. 150.00 (0-7503-0198-8) IOP Pub.

***Laubersheimer, Sue.** South Dakota Changing, Changeless 1889-1989: A Selected Annotated Bibliography with Supplement & Index. 320p. (Orig.). 1985. pap. 9.00 (0-9632157-3-6) SD Human Fnd.

Laubheim, Charles, et al. Just Writing. 4th ed. 328p. (C). 1994. pap. text ed., spiral bd. 32.95 (0-8403-4517-8) Kendall-Hunt.

Laubich, Arnold & Spencer, Ray. Art Tatum: A Guide to His Recorded Music. LC 82-10752. (Studies in Jazz: No. 2). 359p. 1982. 35.00 (0-8108-1582-6) Scarecrow.

Laubier, Claire, ed. The Condition of Women in France: 1945 to the Present - A Documentary Anthology. (Illus.). 144p. 1991. pap. 29.95 (0-415-03091-9, A4635) Routledge.

Laubin, Gladys, jt. auth. see Laubin, Reginald.

Laubin, Reginald & Laubin, Gladys. American Indian Archery. LC 78-58108. (Civilization of the American Indian Ser.: Vol. 154). (Illus.). 192p. 1991. 27.95 (0-8061-1467-3); pap. 14.95 (0-8061-2387-7) U of Okla Pr.

— Indian Dances of North America: Their Importance to Indian Life. LC 76-40962. (Civilization of the American Indian Ser.: No.141). (Illus.). 576p. 1977. pap. 22.95 (0-8061-2172-6) U of Okla Pr.

Laubin, Reginald, et al. The Indian Tipi: Its History, Construction, & Use. 2nd ed. LC 77-23039. (Illus.). 384p. 1977. pap. 17.95 (0-8061-2236-6) U of Okla Pr.

Laubscher, B. J. Where Mystery Dwells: A Psychiatrist Studies Psychical Phenomena. 272p. 1972. 11.50 (0-227-67801-X) Attic Pr.

Laubscher, G. G. Syntactical Causes of Case Reduction in Old French. (Elliott Monographs: Vol. 7). 1921. 15.00 (0-527-02611-5) Periodicals Srv.

Laubscher, Michael R. Encounters with Difference: Student Perceptions of the Role of Out of Class Experiences in Education Abroad. LC 93-37505. (Contributions to the Study of Education Ser.: No. 105). 152p. 1994. text ed. 49.95 (0-313-28977-8, Greenwood Pr) Greenwood.

Laucella, Linda. Hormone Replacement Therapy: Conventional Medicine & Natural Alternates: Your Guide to Menopausal Health Care Choices. 204p. 1994. 22.95 (1-56565-154-5) Lowell Hse.

Lauchland, Henry. Touch Me Inside. LC 74-24548. 46p. (C). 1975. reprint ed. 9.95 (0-931820-00-6) High Q.

Lauchli, Andre & Bieleski, R. L., eds. Inorganic Plant Nutrition. (Encyclopedia of Plant Physiology Ser.: Vol. 15, Part A & B). (Illus.). 900p. 1983. 322.00 (0-387-12103-X) Spr-Verlag.

Lauchli, Andre, jt. ed. see Tinker, Bernard.

Lauchli, Andre, jt. ed. see Tinker, P. B.

Lauchman, Richard. Plain Style: Techniques for Simple, Concise, Emphatic Business Writing. LC 93-4324. 144p. 1993. 15.95 (0-8144-7852-2) AMACOM.

Lauck, Helen & Roybal, Mary A., eds. Downlink Directory 1985-1986, Vol. 1. 294p. (Orig.). 1985. pap. 125.00 (0-937007-01-3) V A Ostendorf.

Lauck, John H. Katyn Killings: In the Record. LC 88-80479. (Illus.). 335p. (C). 1988. 24.95 (0-940670-30-5) Kingston Pr.

Lauck, William J. & Sydenstricker, Edgar. Conditions of Labor in American Industries. LC 70-89746. (American Labor, from Conspiracy to Collective Bargaining Ser., No. 1). 404p. 1971. reprint ed. 26.95 (0-405-02134-8) Ayer.

Lauckner, Edie. Signs of Celebration. 1978. 3.95 (0-570-03770-0, 12-2706) Concordia.

Lauckner, Kurt F. & Lintner, Mildred D. Computers: Inside & Out. (Illus.). 400p. (C). 1991. pap. 31.95 (0-9624073-9-9) Pippin Publishing.

Lauckner, Nancy A., tr. see Gerber, Margy, et al, eds.

Laud, William. Articles Exhibited in Parliament Against William, Archbishop of Canterbury. LC 72-212. (English Experience Ser.: No. 333). 16p. 1971. reprint ed. 20.00 (90-221-0333-1) Walter J Johnson.

— A Speech Delivered in the Starr-Chamber, at the Censure of J. Bastwick. LC 79-171771. (English Experience Ser.: No. 396). 92p. 1971. reprint ed. 20.00 (90-221-0396-X) Walter J Johnson.

— The Works, 7 vols. in 5, Set. (Anglistica & Americana Ser.: No. 168). 1977. reprint ed. 518.70 (3-487-06277-1, Pub. by Georg Olms GW) Lubrecht & Cramer.

— The Works of the Most Reverend Father in God, William Laud, D. D., 9 Pts., Set. LC 74-5373. (Library of Anglo-Catholic Theology: No. 11). reprint ed. 805.00 (0-404-52120-7) AMS Pr.

Laudahr, W. R., et al. The Human & Divine Universe. 125p. 1989. 6.75 (0-913004-66-9, 353) Point Loma Pub.

Laudan, Larry. Progress & Its Problems: Towards a Theory of Scientific Growth. LC 76-24586. 1977. pap. 16.00 (0-520-03721-9) U CA Pr.

— Running Risks. LC 94-6762. 1994. pap. text ed. 12.95 (0-471-31034-4) Wiley.

— Science & Relativism: Some Key Controversies in the Philosophy of Science. LC 90-32112. (Science & Its Conceptual Foundations Ser.). 168p. 1990. pap. text ed. 13.95 (0-226-46949-2) U Ch Pr.

— Science & Relativism: Some Key Controversies in the Philosophy of Science. LC 90-32112. (Science & Its Conceptual Foundations Ser.). 168p. 1990. lib. bdg. 37.50 (0-226-46948-4) U Ch Pr.

— Science & Values: An Essay on the Aims of Science & Their Role in Scientific Debate. LC 84-249. (Pittsburgh Series in Philosophy & History of Science: No. 3). 160p. 1984. pap. 15.00 (0-520-05743-0) U CA Pr.

Laudan, Larry, ed. Mind & Medicine: Problems of Explanation & Evaluation in Psychiatry & the Biomedical Sciences. LC 82-40094. (Pittsburgh Series in Philosophy & History of Science: No. 1). (Illus.). 370p. 1982. 48.00 (0-520-04623-4) U CA Pr.

An Asterisk (*) at the beginning of an entry indicates that the title is appearing in BIP for the first time.

Laudan, Rachel. From Mineralogy to Geology: The Foundations of a Science, 1650-1830. LC 86-30783. (Science & Its Conceptual Foundations Ser.). (Illus.). xii, 278p. (C). 1987. 27.50 (*0-226-46950-6*) U Ch Pr.

— From Mineralogy to Geology: The Foundations of a Science, 1650-1830. (Science & Its Conceptual Foundations Ser.). (Illus.). xii, 278p. 1994. pap. text ed. 15.95 (*0-226-46947-6*) U Ch Pr.

Laude, Hubert & Vautherot, Jean-Francois, eds. Coronaviruses: Molecular Biology & Virus-Host Interactions. LC 93-46630. (Advances in Experimental Medicine & Biology Ser.: Vol. 342). (Illus.). 478p. 1993. 125.00 (*0-306-44599-9*, Plenum Pr) Plenum.

Laude, Jean. The Arts of Black Africa. Decock, Jean, tr. LC 71-125165. (African Studies Center, UCLA: No. 1). (Illus.). 1971. pap. 15.00 (*0-520-02358-7*) U CA Pr.

— The Beaches of Thule. Cloutier, David, tr. LC 84-48261. (Modern Poets in Translation Ser.: Vol. III). Orig. Title: Les Plages de Thule. ix, 57p. (Orig.). (C). 1985. 15.00 (*0-916426-09-2*); pap. 6.95 (*0-916426-10-6*) KOSMOS.

— Wavelength Division Multiplexing. 224p. 1993. 49.00 (*0-13-489865-6*) P-H.

Laude, L. D., ed. Laser-Assisted Processing II. 1990. 53.00 (*0-8194-0326-1*, VOL. 1279) SPIE.

Laude, L. D. & Letardi, T. Excimer Lasers & Applications III, Vol. 1503. 1991. 77.00 (*0-8194-0612-0*) SPIE.

Laude, L. D. & Rauscher, G., eds. Laser-Assisted Processing, Vol. 1022. 1989. 45.00 (*0-8194-0057-2*) SPIE.

Laude, Lucien D., ed. Cohesive Properties of Semi-Conductors under Laser Irradiation. 1983. lib. bdg. 186. 50 (*90-247-2857-6*) Kluwer Ac.

— Excimer Lasers: Proceedings of the NATO Advanced Study Institute on 'Excimer Lasers: The Tools, Fundamental Processes & Applications', Elounda, Crete, Greece, September 6-17, 1993. 512p. (C). 1994. lib. bdg. 220.00 (*0-7923-2819-1*) Kluwer Ac.

Laude, Lucien D., et al, eds. Interfaces under Laser Irradiation. (C). 1987. lib. bdg. 157.50 (*90-247-3569-6*) Kluwer Ac.

Laude, Patrick. L' Eden Entredit Vol. 2: Lecture de La Chanson D'Eve de Charles Van Lerberghe. LC 93-40235. (Belgian Francophone Library Ser.: Vol. 2). 150p. (FRE.). (C). 1994. text ed. 42.95 (*0-8204-2374-2*) P Lang Pubs.

***Laudelot, Marc.** Hommage a Ferdinand Celine. (Illus.). 1993. 450.00 (*0-914301-31-4*, Pub. by Marco GW) West-Art.

Lauder. On the Deutie of Kings. Hall, F., ed. (EETS, OS Ser.: Nos. 3, 41). 1974. reprint ed. 28.00 (*0-8115-3957-1*) Periodicals Srv.

Lauder, Evelyn. The Seasons Observed: Photographs. LC 94-8418. 1994. write for info. (*0-8109-4455-3*) Abrams.

Lauder, George V., jt. ed. see Feder, Martin E.

Lauder, Hugh & Brown, Phillip. Education: In Search of a Future. 270p. 1988. 65.00 (*1-85000-406-4*, Falmer Pr); pap. 33.00 (*1-85000-407-2*, Falmer Pr) Taylor & Francis.

Lauder, Hugh & Wylie. Towards Successful Schooling. 1990. 75.00 (*1-85000-722-5*, Falmer Pr); pap. 35.00 (*1-85000-723-3*, Falmer Pr) Taylor & Francis.

Lauder, Hugh, jt. ed. see Brown, Phillip.

Lauder, I. J., jt. auth. see Aitchison, J.

Lauder, Jean M., et al, eds. Molecular Aspects of Development & Aging of the Nervous System. LC 89-70995. (Advances in Experimental Medicine & Biology Ser.: Vol. 265). (Illus.). 335p. 1989. 85.00 (*0-306-43408-3*, Plenum Pr) Plenum.

Lauder, John. Historical Notices of Scottish Affairs, 2 Vols. LC 73-172303. (Bannatyne Club, Edinburgh. Publications: No. 87). reprint ed. 90.00 (*0-404-52828-7*) AMS Pr.

— Historical Observes of Memorable Occurents in Church & State. LC 77-172304. (Bannatyne Club, Edinburgh. Publications: No. 66). reprint ed. 34.50 (*0-404-52779-5*) AMS Pr.

***Lauder, Patricia.** Friendly Dolphins. (J). (ps-3). 1995. pap. 4.95 (*0-590-48134-7*) Scholastic Inc.

Lauder, Robert. Nothing but Love. (Spirit Life Ser.). 64p. (Orig.). 1993. pap. 3.95 (*1-878718-16-9*) Resurrection.

Lauder, Robert E. Becoming a Christian Person. 124p. (Orig.). 1984. pap. 6.95 (*0-914544-58-6*) Living Flame Pr.

— Loneliness Is for Loving. rev. ed. LC 88-80698. 114p. 1988. reprint ed. pap. 6.95 (*0-914544-72-1*) Living Flame Pr.

— The Love Explosion: Human Experience & the Christian Mystery. 154p. (Orig.). 1979. pap. 5.95 (*0-914544-22-5*) Living Flame Pr.

— Rediscovering Myself & Others in God: The Never-Ending Dialogue. LC 86-32171. 73p. (Orig.). 1987. pap. 4.95 (*0-8189-0517-4*) Alba.

Lauder, Robert S. Engraved Portrait of Thomas Thomson. (Bannatyne Club, Edinburgh. Publications: No. 95). reprint ed. 12.50 (*0-404-52839-2*) AMS Pr.

Lauder, Rosemary A., ed. Exmoor Travellers. LC 93-13524. 1993. 34.00 (*0-7509-0315-5*) A Sutton Pub.

Lauder, William. Essay on Milton's Use & Imitation of the Moderns in Paradise Lost. LC 74-172306. reprint ed. 40. 00 (*0-404-03888-3*) AMS Pr.

Lauder, William C. A Voyage Round the World in the Years 1785, 1786, 1787, & 1788. 150p. 1985. reprint ed. 14.95 (*0-87770-325-6*) Ye Galleon.

***Lauderbaugh, J. J.** Customer Service Management in a Telemarketing Environment: The Key to Corporate Survival. 160p. 1994. write for info. (*0-936840-15-3*) Tech Marketing.

Lauderbaugh, Richard A. American Steel Makers & the Coming of the Second World War. LC 80-39892. (Studies in American History & Culture: No. 20). 276p. reprint ed. pap. 78.70 (*0-8357-1150-1*, 2070101) Bks Demand.

Lauderdale, Beverly. The Long Wind. LC 87-91110. 1988. 16.95 (*0-87212-211-5*) Libra.

Lauderdale, Clifford M. The Color to Be. Hwayer, David, ed. (Poetry Ser.). (Illus.). 39p. (Orig.). 1994. pap. text ed. 8.00 (*1-882300-03-3*) Willo Trees.

***Lauderdale, David.** Alexander Brest Museum & Gallery: A Guide to the Collections. Sowder, Cheryl, ed. LC 94-78736. 112p. (Orig.). 1994. pap. write for info. (*0-9643165-0-1*) Jacksnvl Univ.

Lauderdale Graham, Sandra. House & Street: The Domestic World of Servants & Masters in Nineteenth-Century Rio de Janeiro. LC 92-26226. (Illus.). 224p. 1992. pap. 11.95 (*0-292-72757-7*) U of Tex Pr.

Lauderdale, James M. Inquiry into the Nature & Origin of Public Wealth & into the Means of Its Increase. 2nd ed. LC 66-24414. (Reprints of Economic Classics Ser.). 1969. reprint ed. 49.50 (*0-678-00208-8*) Kelley.

— Lauderdale's Notes on Adam Smith's Wealth of Nations. Sugiyama, Chuhei, ed. LC 95-11820. 1996. write for info. (*0-415-12284-8*) Routledge.

— Three Letters to the Duke of Wellington on the Fourth Report of the Select Committee of the House of Commons, Appointed in 1828 to Enquire into the Public Income & Expenditure of the United Kingdom. LC 64-7668. (Reprints of Economic Classics Ser.). 1965. reprint ed. 27.50 (*0-678-00089-1*) Kelley.

Lauderdale, Pat & Cruit, Michael. The Struggle for Control: A Study of Law, Disputes, & Deviance. LC 91-47942. (SUNY Series in Deviance & Social Control). 256p. 1993. 59.50 (*0-7914-1311-X*); pap. 19.95 (*0-7914-1312-8*) State U NY Pr.

Lauderdale, William B. Educational Reform: The Forgotten Half. LC 86-63882. (Fastback Ser.: No. 252). 50p. 1987. pap. 1.25 (*0-87367-252-6*) Phi Delta Kappa.

Laudermilk, Sharon & Hamlin, Teresa. The Regency Companion. LC 88-28203. 368p. 1989. 32.00 (*0-8240-2249-1*, H841) Garland.

***Laudet, Claire & Cox, Richard.** Le Peuple de France Aujourd'hui. (Illus.). 200p. 1995. text ed. 59.95 (*0-7190-4215-1*, Pub. by Manchester Univ Pr UK); text ed. 19.95 (*0-7190-4216-X*, Pub. by Manchester Univ Pr UK) St Martin.

***Laudet, Claire & Cox, Richard, eds.** La Vie Politique en France Aujourd'hui. LC 94-29770. (Readers in Contemporary French Civilisation Ser.). 1995. text ed. write for info. (*0-7190-4218-6*, Pub. by Manchester Univ Pr UK); text ed. write for info. (*0-7190-4217-8*) St Martin.

Laudicina, Paul. Applied Pathology for Radiographies. 308p. 1989. text ed. 44.50 (*0-7216-2143-0*) Saunders.

Laudicina, Paul & Wean, Douglas. Applied Angiography for Radiographers. LC 93-27002. 1994. text ed. 45.00 (*0-7216-3283-1*) Saunders.

Laudon, Jane P. & Laudon, Kenneth C. The Integrated Solution. (Illus.). 320p. (C). 1990. text ed. 39.00 (*0-03-031237-X*) Dryden Pr.

Laudon, Jane P., jt. auth. see Laudon, Kenneth C.

Laudon, Jane P., et al. Instructor's Manual with Transparency Masters to Accompany "Business Information Systems," Second Edition. 2nd ed. 283p. (C). 1993. pap. text ed. 14.75 (*0-03-097113-6*) Dryden Pr.

Laudon, Ken. Solve It! Management Problem Solving with PC Software, Version 2.0. (Illus.). 200p. 1988. pap. text ed. 14.00 (*0-945991-00-2*) Azimuth Corp.

— Solve It! Management Problem Solving with PC Software, Version 2.0. (Illus.). 250p. 1989. pap. text ed. 14.00 (*0-945991-02-9*) Azimuth Corp.

— Solve It! Management Problem Solving with PC Software, Version 2.0. (Illus.). 300p. (C). 1990. pap. text ed. 14.00 (*0-945991-03-7*) Azimuth Corp.

— Solve It! Management Problem Solving with PC Software, Version 2.0. (Illus.). 300p. (C). 1991. pap. text ed. 14.00 (*0-945991-04-5*) Azimuth Corp.

— Solve It! Management Problem Solving with PC Software, Version 2.0. (Illus.). (C). 1992. pap. text ed. 14.00 (*0-945991-05-3*) Azimuth Corp.

— Solve It! Management Problem Solving with PC Software, Version 2.0. (Illus.). (C). 1993. pap. text ed. 14.00 (*0-945991-06-1*) Azimuth Corp.

— Solve It! Management Problem Solving with PC Software, Version 2.0. (Illus.). 350p. (C). 1994. pap. text ed. 14.00 (*0-945991-08-8*) Azimuth Corp.

Laudon, Kenneth C. Dossier Society: Value Choices in the Design of National Information Systems. LC 85-29154. (Illus.). 400p. 1986. text ed. 63.00 (*0-231-06188-9*) Col U Pr.

— Tutorial Guide to Solving Classic Business Problems: An Introduction to Lotus 1-2-3, Release 2.3. 1992. pap. 23. 75 (*0-201-50695-5*) Addison-Wesley.

Laudon, Kenneth C. & Laudon, Jane P. Essentials of Management Information Systems: Organization & Technology. LC 94-9417. 640p. (C). 1994. write for info. (*0-02-368083-0*) Macmillan.

— Management Information Systems: A Contemporary Perspective. 3rd ed. (Illus.). 818p. (C). 1993. (*0-318-69911-7*) Macmillan.

— Management Information Systems: A Contemporary Perspective. 3rd ed. (Illus.). 818p. (C). 1994. text ed. write for info. (*0-02-368121-7*) Macmillan.

Laudon, Kenneth C. & Turner, Jon. Information Technology & Management Strategy. 224p. (C). 1989. pap. text ed. write for info. (*0-13-465022-0*) P-H.

Laudon, Kenneth C., jt. auth. see Laudon, Jane P.

***Laudon, Kenneth C., et al.** Information Technology: Concepts & Issues. LC 94-26935. 352p. 1994. pap. text ed. 30.95 (*0-534-24924-8*) Boyd & Fraser.

— Information Technology & Society. 600p. (C). 1994. pap. 38.95 (*0-534-19512-1*) Boyd & Fraser.

Laudon, Lowell R., jt. auth. see Moore, C. Raymond.

Laue, Alice. Cooking from Denim to Lace. (Illus.). 400p. 1989. ring bd. write for info. (*0-9624351-0-4*) A Laue.

Laue, James H. Direct Action & Desegregation, 1960-1962: Toward a Theory of the Rationalization of Protest. LC 89-9867. (Martin Luther King, Jr., & the Civil Rights Movement Ser.: Vol. 15). 440p. 1989. 90.00 (*0-926019-09-0*) Carlson Pub.

Laue, Kurt & Stenger, Helmut. Extrusion: Processes, Machinery, Tooling. Castle, A. F. & Lang, Gernot, trs. LC 80-23076. (Illus.). 471p. reprint ed. pap. 134.30 (*0-318-39652-1*, 2033057) Bks Demand.

Laue, Thomas M., jt. ed. see Schuster, Todd M.

Lauen, Roger. Community-managed Corrections & Other Solutions to America's Prison Crisis. 2nd ed. 156p. 1990. pap. 23.00 (*0-929310-41-1*, 379) Am Correctional.

Lauenroth, W. K. & Preston, E. M., eds. The Effects of SO2 on a Grassland: A Case Study in the Northern Great Plains of the United States. (Ecological Studies, Analysis & Synthesis: Vol. 45). (Illus.). 270p. 1984. 72.00 (*0-387-90943-5*) Spr-Verlag.

Lauenroth, W. K., et al. Analysis of Ecological Systems: State-of-the-Art in Ecological Modelling. (Developments in Environmental Modelling Ser.: Vol. 5). 1983. 182.00 (*0-444-42179-3*) Elsevier.

Lauenstein, Diether. Biblical Rhythms in Biography. 126p. 1990. pap. 8.95 (*0-86315-001-2*, 732, Pub. by Floris Books UK) Anthroposophic.

Lauer. Four Worlds of Writing. 3rd ed. (C). 1990. pap. text ed. 34.00 (*0-06-043860-6*) HarpCollege.

Lauer, jt. auth. see Delaney.

Lauer, Alphons, ed. see Gruen, Anselm.

Lauer, Alphonse, ed. see Colombas, Garcia M.

Lauer, Alphonse, ed. see Gruen, Anselm, et al.

Lauer, Alphonse, ed. see Gruen, Anselm.

Lauer, Alphonse, ed. see Stevens, Clifford J.

Lauer, Alphonse, ed. see Uebler, Leonard.

Lauer, Alphonse, ed. see Uhing, M. James.

Lauer, Alphonse M., ed. see Ruppert, Fidelis & Gruen, Anselm.

Lauer, Alponse, ed. see Gruen, Anselm & Dufner, Meinrad.

Lauer, Charles. Auto Body Repair. LC 85-702615. 1985. student ed 7.00 (*0-8064-0209-1*, 484); audio 239.00 (*0-8064-0210-5*) Bergwall.

Lauer, Charles D. Old West Adventures in Arizona. LC 88-24676. 176p. (Orig.). 1989. pap. 5.95 (*0-914846-39-6*) Golden West Pub.

— Tales of Arizona Territory. LC 90-3336. (Illus.). 160p. (Orig.). 1990. pap. 6.95 (*0-914846-47-7*) Golden West Pub.

Lauer, Charles S. Soar with the Eagles. LC 91-73259. 236p. 1991. 24.95 (*0-8163-1061-0*) CCI Bks WA.

— Soar with the Eagles: A Challenge to Excellence. LC 93-83849. 236p. 1993. pap. 11.95 (*1-881802-01-9*) CCI Bks WA.

Lauer, David, tr. see Vicens, Josefina.

Lauer, David A. Design Basics. 3rd ed. 260p. (C). 1990. pap. text ed. 41.25 (*0-03-030422-9*) HB Coll Pubs.

Lauer, Gary. Principles & Practices of the College-Based Radiography Program. Gardner, Alvin F., ed. (Allied Health Professions Monograph). 294p. (C). 1984. 37.50 (*0-87527-310-6*) Green.

***Lauer, Gerhard.** Die Verspaetete Revolution: Erich von Kahler Wissenschaftsgeschichte Zwischen Konservativer. (Revolution und Exil Philosophie und Wissenschaft Ser.: Bd. 6). 566p. (GER.). (C). 1994. pap. text ed. 58.00 (*3-11-014397-6*) De Gruyter.

Lauer, Hans E. Aggression & Repression in the Individual & Society. Castelliz, K. & Davies, Saunders, trs. 111p. 1981. pap. 9.95 (*0-85440-359-0*, Steinerbks) Anthroposophic.

Lauer, Janice M. & Asher, J. William. Composition Research: Empirical Designs. (Illus.). 336p. 1988. pap. 19.95 (*0-19-504171-2*); pap. text ed. 21.00 (*0-19-504172-0*) OUP.

Lauer, Jeanette C. & Lauer, Robert H. No Secrets? How Much Honesty Is Good for Your Marriage? LC 93-14383. 224p. 1993. pap. 9.99 (*0-310-37551-7*) Zondervan.

— Til Death Do Us Part: A Study & Guide to Long-Term Marriage. LC 86-22735. (Marriage & Family Review Ser.: Supp. No. 1). 192p. 1986. pap. text ed. 14.95 (*0-918393-32-9*) Harrington Pk.

— Til Death Do Us Part: How Couples Stay Together. LC 86-22735. (Supplement to Marriage & Family Review Ser.: No. 1). 192p. 1986. text ed. 39.95 (*0-86656-601-5*) Haworth Pr.

Lauer, Jeanette C., jt. auth. see Lauer, Robert H.

Lauer, Jeanette C., jt. auth. see Lauer, Robert.

Lauer, Kristin O., ed. see Wharton, Edith.

***Lauer, Mark T.** Buying & Selling a Business. Franco, Debra L., ed. 250p. (Orig.). 1995. pap. 24.95 (*1-880539-33-0*) Garrett FL.

Lauer, Mark T., ed. see Goldstein, Arnold S.

Lauer, Mark T., ed. see Hayes, Robert M.

Lauer, Mark T., ed. see Levinson, Robert E.

Lauer, N. V & Kolkhinskaya, A. Z., eds. The Oxygen Regime of the Organism & Its Regulation. 332p. reprint ed. text ed. 94.50 (*0-7065-0677-4*, Pub. by Keter Pub IS) Coronet Bks.

Lauer, O. Gary, et al. Evaluating Radiographic Quality: The Variables & Their Effects. (Illus.). 160p. (C). 1991. text ed. 48.00 (*0-916973-04-2*) Burnell Co.

Lauer, P. E., ed. Functional Programming, Concurrency, Simulation & Automated Reasoning: International Lecture Series 1991-1992, MacMaster University, Hamilton, Ontario, Canada. (Lecture Notes in Computer Science Ser.: Vol. 693). xi, 397p. 1993. pap. 60.00 (*0-387-56883-2*) Spr-Verlag.

Lauer, P. E., jt. auth. see Janicki, R.

Lauer, Paul E. Church & State in New England. LC 78-63809. (Johns Hopkins University. Studies in the Social Sciences. Thirtieth Ser. 1912: 2-3). reprint ed. 11.50 (*0-404-61072-2*) AMS Pr.

Lauer, Quentin. Essays in Hegelian Dialectic. LC 76-18465. viii, 208p. 1977. 35.00 (*0-8232-1021-9*); pap. 17.50 (*0-8232-1022-7*) Fordham.

— G. K. Chesterton: Philosopher Without a Portfolio. LC 88-80057. 191p. 1992. reprint ed. pap. 19.95 (*0-8232-1199-1*) Fordham.

— Hegel's Concept of God. LC 81-21452. 339p. (C). 1983. 64.50 (*0-87395-597-8*); pap. 21.95 (*0-87395-598-6*) State U NY Pr.

— Hegel's Idea of Philosophy. 2nd ed. LC 74-152244. xii, 159p. (C). 1983. pap. 14.00 (*0-8232-0927-X*) Fordham.

— Nature of Philosophical Inquiry. LC 88-64165. (Aquinas Lectures). 1989. text ed. 10.00 (*0-87462-156-9*, AQ-53) Marquette.

— A Reading of Hegel's Phenomenology of Spirit. rev. ed. LC 92-9891. (Illus.). 344p. 1993. 30.00 (*0-8232-1354-4*); pap. 17.50 (*0-8232-1355-2*) Fordham.

— The Triumph of Subjectivity: An Introduction to Transcendental Phenomenology. 2nd ed. LC 58-12363. xxiv, 182p. 1978. 30.00 (*0-8232-0336-0*) Fordham.

Lauer, Quentin, tr. see Husserl, Edmund.

Lauer, Reinhard. Langenscheidt Universal German-Serbocroatian, Serbocroatian-German Dictionary: Langenscheidt Serbokroatisch-Deutsch-Serbokroatisch Universal Woerterbuch. 7th ed. 448p. (GER & SER.). 1981. 14.95 (*0-8288-1051-6*, F19620) Fr & Eur.

Lauer, Robert. Social Problems & the Quality of Life. 6th ed. 672p. (C). 1995. pap. text ed. write for info. (*0-697-21352-8*) Brown & Benchmark.

Lauer, Robert & Lauer, Jeanette C. Marriage & Family: The Quest for Intimacy. 2nd ed. 560p. 1994. pap. write for info. (*0-697-12702-8*) Brown & Benchmark.

Lauer, Robert H. Perspectives on Social Change. 4th ed. 416p. 1991. text ed. 42.00 (*0-205-12575-1*, H25752) Allyn.

— Temporal Man: The Meaning & Uses of Social Time. LC 81-11917. 192p. 1981. text ed. 49.95 (*0-275-90666-3*, C0666, Praeger Pubs) Greenwood.

Lauer, Robert H, ed. Social Movements & Social Change. LC 76-18747. 320p. 1976. 10.00 (*0-8093-0771-5*) S Ill U Pr.

Lauer, Robert H. & Lauer, Jeanette C. For Better & Better: Building a Healthy Marriage for a Lifetime. LC 94-12861. 144p. (Orig.). 1995. pap. 9.00 (*0-687-23623-1*) Dimen for Liv.

— The Joy Ride: Everyday Ways to Lasting Happiness. LC 93-8153. 144p. (Orig.). 1994. pap. 9.00 (*0-687-13053-0*) Dimen for Liv.

— Watersheds: Mastering Life's Unpredictable Crises. 272p. 1988. 16.95 (*0-316-51629-5*) Little.

Lauer, Robert H., jt. auth. see Lauer, Jeanette C.

Lauer, Roger, jt. auth. see Ilfeld, Fred, Jr.

Lauer, Thomas, et al, eds. Questions & Information Systems. 376p. 1992. text ed. 69.95 (*0-8058-1018-8*); pap. 39.95 (*0-8058-1019-6*) L Erlbaum Assocs.

Lauer, Walter E. Battle Babies: The Story of the Ninety-Ninth Infantry Division. 28th ed. (Illus.). 353p. 1985. 29.95 (*0-89839-089-3*) Battery Pr.

Lauer, Wilhelm, ed. Natural Environment & Man in Tropical Ecosystems. (Illus.). 354p. (Orig.). 1985. pap. 147.50 (*3-515-04335-7*) Coronet Bks.

Lauer, Wilhelm, jt. ed. see Troll, Carl.

Lauerdure, Leo, et al. NAS Architecture Reference Manual: Networking & Data Communications Ser. (Illus.). 525p. 1993. pap. text ed. 34.95 (*1-55558-115-3*, EY-P941E-DP, Digital DEC) Buttrwrth-Heinemann.

***Lauerer, John A.** I Remember Fairbanks & Skibo. LC 94-61703. 96p. (Orig.). (YA). (gr. 9 up). 1994. pap. 8.95 (*0-9636894-1-X*) Estrn Itascan.

Lauersdorf, Lynn R., jt. ed. see Melander, John M.

Lauersdorf, Richard E. Hebrews. (People's Bible Commentary Ser.). 185p. (Orig.). 1992. pap. 8.99 (*0-570-04595-9*) Concordia.

— A Study Guide for Hebrews. Fischer, William E., ed. (Study Guide for People's Bible Ser.). 48p. (Orig.). 1986. pap. 1.95 (*0-938272-56-X*) WELS Board.

Lauersen, Niels, et al. It's Your Body: A Woman's Guide to Gynecology. rev. ed. LC 93-13395. 1993. pap. 18.95 (*0-399-51830-4*, Body Pr-Perigree) Berkley Pub.

Lauersen, Niels H. Childbirth with Love. 1985. pap. 9.95 (*0-425-07390-4*, Berkley Trade) Berkley Pub.

Lauersen, Niels H., ed. Modern Management of High-Risk Pregnancy. LC 83-11127. 530p. 1983. 105.00 (*0-306-41306-X*, Plenum Med Bk) Plenum.

Lauersen, Niels H. & Bouchez, Colette. Getting Pregnant: What Couples Need to Know Right Now. 368p. 1992. pap. 12.00 (*0-449-90667-1*, Columbine) Fawcett.

Lauersen, Niels H. & DeSwaan, Constance. The Endometriosis Answer Book: New Hope, New Help. 1989. pap. 12.00 (*0-449-90361-3*, Columbine) Fawcett.

Lauersen, Niels H. & Hendra, Judy. It's Your Pregnancy: Questions You Ask Yourself & Are Afraid to Ask Your Obstetrician. 192p. 1987. pap. 12.95 (*0-671-50211-5*, Fireside) S&S Trade.

Lauersen, Niels H. & Stukane, Eileen. Listen to Your Body: A Gynecologist Answers Women's Most Intimate Questions. 784p. (Orig.). 1987. pap. 6.99 (*0-425-10493-1*) Berkley Pub.

— PMS: Premenstrual Syndrome & You - Next Month Can Be Different. LC 83-11359. (Illus.). 224p. (Orig.). 1983. pap. 8.95 (*0-671-47242-9*, Fireside) S&S Trade.

— You're in Charge: A Teenage Girl's Guide to Sex & Her Body. (Illus.). 304p. (Orig.). 1993. pap. 8.50 (*0-449-90464-4*, Columbine) Fawcett.

Lauersen, Niels H. & Whitney, Steven. It's Your Body: A Woman's Guide to Gynecology. LC 80-80994. (Illus.). 576p. 1986. pap. 6.99 (*0-425-09917-2*) Berkley Pub.

An Asterisk (*) at the beginning of an entry indicates that the title is appearing in BIP for the first time.

Lauersen, Niels H., jt. ed. see Reyniak, J. Victor.

Lauf, Cornelia, ed. see Dwyer, Nancy.

Lauf, Robert J., jt. ed. see McCarthy, Gregory J.

Laufe, Abe, ed. see FitzGerald, Emily M.

Laufe, Leonard E. & Berkus, Michael. Assisted Vaginal Delivery: Obstetric Forceps & Vacuum Extraction Techniques. (Illus.). 160p. 1992. pap. text ed. 42.00 (0-07-105412-X) Hlth Prof Div.

***Laufenberg, Cindy, ed.** 1996 Songwriter's Market. 528p. 1995. 22.99 (0-89879-711-X) Writers Digest.

— Songwriter's Market 1995. 522p. 1994. 21.99 (0-89879-676-8) Writers Digest.

***Laufenberg, Frank.** Rock & Pop: Day by Day. 320p. 1994. 41.00x (0-8095-7619-8) Borgo Pr.

Laufenberg, T., et al, eds. Materials Interactions Relevant to Recycling of Wood-Based Materials. (Materials Research Society Symposium Proceedings Ser.: Vol. 266). 1992. text ed. 71.00 (1-55899-161-1) Materials Res.

Laufer, B. The Beginnings of Porcelain in China: Field Museum of Natural History, 3 vols. in 1. Bd. with The Diamond, a Study in Chinese & Hellenistic Folklore; Sino-Iranica. (Field Museum Monographs: Vol. 15). 1917. 45.00 (0-527-01875-9) Periodicals Srv.

— Notes on Turquois in the East: 1913-1914, Field Museum of Natural History. Bd. with Chinese Clay Figures. (Field Museum Monographs: Vol. 13). 1913. 45.00 (0-527-01873-2) Periodicals Srv.

— Sino Iranica: Chinese Contributions to the History of Civilization in Iran. 1976. lib. bdg. 59.95 (0-8490-2608-3) Gordon Pr.

Laufer, Berthold. The American Plant Migration, Vol.1: The Potato. (Field Museum of Natural History Ser.: Vol. 28). (Illus.). 1938. 15.00 (0-527-01888-0) Periodicals Srv.

— Chinese Baskets. LC 28-1443. (Illus.). 42p. 1925. ring bd. 50.00 (0-686-25961-0) Rare Oriental Bk Co.

— Chinese Grave: Sculptures of the Han Period. (Illus.). 45p. 1911. 65.00 (0-318-04695-4) Rare Oriental Bk Co.

— The Decorative Art of the Amur Tribes. LC 73-3524. (Jesup North Pacific Expedition. Publications: No. 4). reprint ed. 42.50 (0-404-58104-8) AMS Pr.

— Historical Jottings on Amber in Asia. LC 08-11467. (American Anthropological Association Memoirs Ser.). 1906. pap. 15.00 (0-527-00502-9) Periodicals Srv.

— Jade: A Study in Chinese Archaeology & Religion. (Field Museum of Natural History Ser.: Vol. 10). (Illus.). 1912. 45.00 (0-527-01870-8) Periodicals Srv.

— Reindeer & Its Domestication. LC 18-12075. (American Anthropological Association Memoirs Ser.). 1917. pap. 15.00 (0-527-00517-7) Periodicals Srv.

Laufer, Diana. Hide 'n' Seek Friends. (Illus.). 12p. (J). (ps-2). 1994. 10.95 (0-8431-3591-3) Price Stern.

— Peek-a-Boo Family: My First Photo Album. (Illus.). 12p. (J). (ps-1). 1993. 10.95 (0-8431-3386-4) Price Stern.

Laufer, Edward. Guide to the Study of Schenkerian Analysis. (Illus.). 1995. text ed. 49.95 (0-02-871325-7) Schirmer Bks.

Laufer, Geraldine A. Tussie Mussies. LC 92-50927. 1993. 22.95 (1-56305-106-0, 3106) Workman Pub.

Laufer, Hans & Downer, Roger G., eds. Endocrinology of Selected Invertebrate Types. 1988. text ed. 121.00 (0-471-61039-9) Wiley.

Laufer, Hans, jt. ed. see Downer, Roger G.

Laufer, Henry B. Normal Two-Dimensional Singularities. LC 78-160261. (Annals of Mathematics Studies: No. 71). 1971. 35.00 (0-691-08100-X) Princeton U Pr.

Laufer, Judy E. Where Did Papa Go: Looking at Death from a Young Child's Perspective. (Illus.). 32p. (Orig.). (J). (ps-2). 1991. pap. 9.95 (1-881669-00-9) Little Egg Pub.

Laufer, M. Egle, jt. auth. see Laufer, Moses.

***Laufer, Moses & Laufer, M. Egle.** Adolescence & Developmental Breakdown: A Psychoanalytic View. 224p. 1995. pap. 30.95 (1-85575-108-9) Brunner-Mazel.

— Developmental Breakdown & Psychoanalytic Treatment in Adolescence. LC 88-38741. 224p. (C). 1989. text ed. 32.00 (0-300-04437-2) Yale U Pr.

***Laufer, Peter.** Inside Talk Radio: America's Voice or Just Hot Air? (Illus.). 288p. 1995. 19.95 (1-55972-278-9, Birch Ln Pr) Carol Pub Group.

— Iron Curtain Rising: A Personal Journey Through the Changing Landscape of Eastern Europe. LC 91-11997. (Illus.). 215p. 1991. 19.50 (1-56279-015-3) Mercury Hse Inc.

— Nightmare Abroad: Stories of Americans Imprisoned in Foreign Lands. LC 92-15811. (Illus.). 208p. 1993. 20.00 (1-56279-028-5) Mercury Hse Inc.

— A Question of Consent: Innocence & Complicity in the Glen Ridge Rape Case. LC 93-42464. 208p. 1994. 19.95 (1-56279-059-5) Mercury Hse Inc.

Laufer, Peter, jt. auth. see Lester, Gene.

Laufer, Peter, jt. auth. see Swan, Sheila.

Laufer, Robert, jt. auth. see Frey-Wouters, Ellen.

Laufer, Romain & Paradeise, Catherine. Marketing Democracy: Public Opinion & Media Formation in Democratic Societies. 347p. 1989. 49.95 (0-88738-199-5) Transaction Pubs.

Laufer, William, jt. ed. see Day, James M.

Laufer, William S. & Adler, Freda, eds. Advances in Criminological Theory, Vol. 1. 256p. 1988. 39.95 (0-88738-182-0) Transaction Pubs.

— Advances in Criminological Theory, Vol. 2. 256p. 1990. 39.95 (0-88738-287-8) Transaction Pubs.

Laufer, William S., jt. ed. see Adler, Freda.

Laufer, William S., jt. ed. see Kagehiro, D.

Laufer, Y., jt. auth. see Chasseuil, G.

Lauffenburger, Douglas A. & Linderman, Jennifer J. Receptors: Models for Binding, Trafficking, & Signalling. LC 92-37216. (C). 1993. 69.95 (0-19-506466-6) OUP.

Lauffer, A. The Aim of the Game. LC 73-84873. 132p. 1974. 9.95 (0-88437-052-6) Psych Dimensions.

Lauffer, Armand. Assessment Tools: For Practitioners, Managers, & Trainers. LC 82-10552. (Sage Human Services Guides Ser.: No. 30). 192p. reprint ed. pap. 54. 80 (0-7837-6576-2, 2046141) Bks Demand.

— Careers, Colleagues, & Conflicts: Understanding Gender, Race, & Ethnicity in the Workplace. LC 85-14276. (Sage Human Services Guides Ser.: No. 43). 182p. reprint ed. pap. 51.90 (0-7837-6580-0, 2046145) Bks Demand.

— Grantsmanship. 2nd ed. (Human Services Guides Ser.: Vol. 1). 120p. 1983. pap. 17.95 (0-8039-2022-9) Sage.

— Strategic Marketing for Not-for-Profit Organizations: Program & Resource Development. LC 83-49509. 384p. (C). 1984. text ed. 35.00 (0-02-918260-3) Free Pr.

— Understanding Your Social Agency. 2nd ed. 168p. 1984. pap. 17.95 (0-8039-2349-X) Sage.

— Working in Social Work: Growing & Thriving in Human Services Practice. LC 86-29700. (Sage Sourcebooks for the Human Services Ser.: No. 6). 339p. reprint ed. pap. 96.70 (0-7837-6582-7, 2046147) Bks Demand.

Lauffer, Butch & Davie, Sandy. Soccer Coach's Guide to Practices, Drills & Skill Training. LC 91-19117. (Illus.). 160p. 1991. 17.95 (0-8069-8218-7) Sterling.

— Soccer Coach's Guide to Practices, Drills & Skill Training. LC 92-44087. (Illus.). 160p. (YA). (gr. 10-12). 1993. pap. 13.95 (0-8069-8219-5) Sterling.

***Lauffer, Lisa B., ed.** The Case of the Empty Tomb. (Real Life Bible Curriculum Ser.). (Illus.). 6p. 1995. pap. 2.99 (1-55945-527-6) Group Pub.

— Feeling Guilty: The Private Burden Kids Can't Shake. (Real Life Bible Curriculum Ser.). (Illus.). 6p. 1995. pap. 2.99 (1-55945-422-9) Group Pub.

— I Would Die for You: Why Kids Stay in Gangs. (Real Life Bible Curriculum Ser.). (Illus.). 6p. 1995. pap. 2.99 (1-55945-417-2) Group Pub.

— Listen Up: Learning to Hear God's Answers to Prayer. (Real Life Bible Curriculum Ser.). (Illus.). 6p. 1995. pap. 2.99 (1-55945-415-6) Group Pub.

— The Making of the Bible. (Real Life Bible Curriculum Ser.). (Illus.). 6p. 1995. pap. 2.99 (1-55945-419-9) Group Pub.

— Never Alone: God's Ultimate Answer to Loneliness. (Real Life Bible Curriculum Ser.). (Illus.). 6p. 1995. pap. 2.99 (1-55945-536-5) Group Pub.

— Personal Power. (Real Life Bible Curriculum Ser.). (Illus.). 6p. 1995. pap. 2.99 (1-55945-525-X) Group Pub.

— Too-Cool Kids: Survival Tactics of a Hurting Generation. (Real Life Bible Cirriculum Ser.). (Illus.). 6p. 1995. pap. 2.99 (1-55945-412-1) Group Pub.

— Why Do Bad Things Happen to Me? (Real Life Bible Curriculum Ser.). (Illus.). 6p. 1995. pap. 2.99 (1-55945-531-4) Group Pub.

Lauffer, Lisa B., jt. auth. see Parolini, Stephen.

Lauffer, Max A. Entropy-Driven Processes in Biology: Polymerization of Tobacco Mosaic Virus Protein & Similar Reactions. LC 74-18267. (Molecular Biology, Biochemistry & Biophysics Ser.: Vol. 20). (Illus.). x, 264p. 1975. 60.00 (0-387-06933-X) Spr-Verlag.

Lauffer, Max A. & Maramorosch, Karl, eds. Advances in Virus Research, Vol. 28. (Serial Publication Ser.). 1983. text ed. 151.00 (0-12-039828-1) Acad Pr.

Lauffer, Max A., ed. see Maramorosch, Karl, et al.

Lauffer, Randall B. Iron & Your Heart: The Newly Discovered Health Risks of Excess Iron - & How You Can Beat Them. LC 93-14712. 336p. 1993. pap. 13.95 (0-312-09469-8) St Martin.

— Iron Balance: The New "Iron-Lite" Health Plan That Restores Your Inner Vitality. (Illus.). 304p. 1991. 19.95 (0-312-06380-6) St Martin.

Lauffer, Randall B., ed. Iron & Human Disease. 534p. 1992. 228.00 (0-8493-6779-4, RC632) CRC Pr.

Lauffer, Rhod, jt. auth. see Mirocha, Paul.

Lauffer, Robert. Coaching Soccer. LC 89-37639. (Illus.). 160p. 1990. pap. 12.95 (0-8069-6923-7) Sterling.

— Coaching Soccer. 160p. 1994. lib. bdg. 33.00 (0-8095-7620-1) Borgo Pr.

Lauffer, Siegfried, ed. Diokletians Preisedikt. (Texte und Kommentare Ser.: Vol. 5). (C). 1971. 192.30 (3-11-002282-6) De Gruyter.

Lauffler, Max, jt. ed. see Smith, Kenneth M.

Laufman, Alan, ed. Organ Handbook, 1983. 136p. 1983. 5.00 (0-913499-50-1) Organ Hist Soc.

— Organ Handbook, 1984. 112p. 1984. 5.00 (0-913499-51-X) Organ Hist Soc.

— Organ Handbook, 1985. 100p. 1985. 5.00 (0-913499-52-8) Organ Hist Soc.

— Organ Handbook, 1987. (Illus.). 100p. (Orig.). 1987. pap. 5.00 (0-913499-54-4) Organ Hist Soc.

Laufman, Alan K. The Law of Medical Malpractice in Texas: A Primer for the Medical Community. LC 77-420. 136p. reprint ed. pap. 38.80 (0-8357-7750-2, 2036107) Bks Demand.

Laufman, Dudley. An Orchard & a Garden. 1974. pap. 3.95 (0-87233-026-5) Bauhan.

Laufman, Harold. Clio Chirugica: Veins. (Surgery Ser.). (Illus.). 280p. 1986. 65.00 (0-941432-18-1); pap. 35.00 (0-941432-19-X) R G Landes.

Laufman, Harold, jt. auth. see Banks, Sam W.

Laufs, Adolf. Rechtsentwicklungen in Deutschland. 3rd ed. (Lehrbuch der Allgemeinen Geographie Ser. Vol. 12). 1984. 32.35 (3-11-009758-3) De Gruyter.

Laugel, Auguste. United States During the Civil War. Nevins, A., ed. LC 61-13716. (Indiana University Civil War Centennial Ser.). 1968. reprint ed. 35.00 (0-527-55050-7) Periodicals Srv.

Lauger, Peter. Electrogenic Ion Pumps. LC 91-24382. (Illus.). 313p. 1992. text ed. 47.95x (0-87893-451-0) Sinauer Assocs.

Laugharne, P. Parliament & Specialist Advice. 1993. 75.00 (1-873534-03-5, Pub. by Manutius Pr UK) St Mut.

Laugher, Charles T. Thomas Bray's Grand Design: Libraries of the Church of England in America, 1695-1785. LC 73-16332. (ACRL Publications in Librarianship: No. 35). 125p. reprint ed. pap. 35.70 (0-317-29444-X, 2024224) Bks Demand.

Laughery, Kenneth R., Sr., et al, eds. Human Factors Perspectives on Warnings: Selections from Human Factors & Ergonomics Society Annual Meetings 1980-1993. 296p. 1994. pap. 50.00 (0-945289-02-2) Human Factors.

***Laughery, Kevin M., ed.** Faith Alive: A Study Companion to the Catechism. 1995. pap. 9.95 (2-242-14383-2) Liguori Pubns.

Laughingwand, Sparrow T. Queen of Shade. (Orig.). 1993. pap. 3.00 (0-929730-44-5) Zeitgeist Pr.

LaughingWand, Sparrow Thirteen. Seven Dollar Shoes. 20p. (Orig.). 1994. pap. 3.00 (0-916397-24-6) Manic D Pr.

Laughlin. Retirement Housing: Step by Step Guide for Investors, Developers, Accountants, & Other Professionals. (Real Estate For Professional Practitioners Ser.). 1989. text ed. 79.95 (0-471-63476-X) Wiley.

***Laughlin, Burgess.** The Aristotle Adventure: A Guide to the Greek, Arabic, & Latin Scholars Who Transmitted Aristotle's Logic to the Renaissance. LC 94-73795. (Illus.). 243p. (Orig.). 1995. pap. 19.95 (0-9644714-9-3) A Hale Pub.

— Job Opportunities in the Black Market. (Illus.). 80p. (Orig.). 1978. pap. text ed. 10.95 (1-55950-004-2) Loompanics.

Laughlin, Charles D., Jr. & Brady, Ivan A., eds. Extinction & Survival in Human Populations. LC 76-17596. 327p. 1978. text ed. 56.00 (0-231-04418-6) Col U Pr.

Laughlin, Charles D., Jr. & D'Aquili, Eugene G. Biogenetic Structuralism. LC 74-13245. (Illus.). 211p. 1974. text ed. 37.00 (0-231-03817-8) Col U Pr.

Laughlin, Charles D., Jr., et al. Brain, Symbol & Experience: Toward a Neurophenomenology of Human Consciousness. LC 92-22627. 424p. (Orig.). (C). 1993. pap. 20.00 (0-231-08139-1, Mrngside) Col U Pr.

Laughlin, Charlotte. Where's Baby Jesus? (J). 1992. 9.99 (0-8499-0902-3) Word Inc.

— Where's the Lost Sheep? (J). 1992. 9.99 (0-8499-0919-8) Word Inc.

Laughlin, Charlotte & Levack, Daniel J. De Camp: An L. Sprague de Camp Bibliography. 328p. 1983. text ed. 59. 95 (0-313-27677-3) Greenwood.

***Laughlin, Chuck.** Samurai Selling: The Ancient Art of Modern Service. 1994. pap. 8.95 (0-312-11885-6) St Martin.

Laughlin, Chuck, et al. Samurai Selling: The Ancient Art of Modern Service. LC 92-44201. 1993. 16.95 (0-312-08885-X) St Martin.

Laughlin, Clara E. Work-a-Day Girl: A Study of Some Present-Day Conditions. LC 74-3956. (Women in America Ser.). (Illus.). 320p. 1974. reprint ed. 26.95 (0-405-06105-6) Ayer.

Laughlin, Clarence J. Ghosts along The Mississippi: The Magic of Old Houses of Louisiana. 1988. 19.99 (0-517-00608-1) Random Hse Value.

Laughlin, D. E., jt. ed. see Chakrabarti, D. J.

Laughlin, Donna. Thorns & Angel Wings. LC 91-75212. 55p. 1992. pap. 6.95 (1-55523-462-3) Winston-Derek.

Laughlin, Florence. The Little Leftover Witch. 3rd ed. LC 92-41166. (Illus.). 96p. (J). (gr. 1-4). 1993. reprint ed. pap. 3.95 (0-689-71742-3, Aladdin Paperbacks) S&S Childrens.

Laughlin, Haller & Wheeler, Randy. Producing the Musical: A Guide for School, College & Community Theatres. LC 83-22704. (Illus.). 160p. 1984. text ed. 47.95 (0-313-24100-7, LPM/, Greenwood Pr) Greenwood.

Laughlin, J. Laurence, Jr. Industrial America. LC 72-1245. (Select Bibliographies Reprint Ser.). 1977. reprint ed. 23. 95 (0-8369-6832-8) Ayer.

Laughlin, J. Laurence, Jr. & Bruchey, Stuart, eds. Banking Reform. LC 80-1160. (Rise of Commercial Banking Ser.). 1981. reprint ed. lib. bdg. 38.95 (0-405-13667-6) Ayer.

Laughlin, James. The Bird of Endless Time. LC 88-63226. 128p. (Orig.). 1989. 15.00 (1-55659-020-2); pap. 9.00 (1-55659-021-0) Copper Canyon.

— Collected Poems of James Laughlin. (Illus.). 608p. 1995. 34.95 (1-55921-067-2) Moyer Bell.

— Collected Poems of James Laughlin. 608p. 1995. pap. 16. 95 (1-55921-128-8) Moyer Bell.

— The Country Road: New Poems. LC 94-33669. 160p. 1995. 22.95 (0-944072-46-1) Zoland Bks.

— James Laughlin: Selected Poems, 1935-1985. 208p. (Orig.). 1986. 25.95 (0-87286-180-5, Subterranean Co); pap. 9.95 (0-87286-179-1, Subterranean Co) City Lights.

— The Man in the Wall: Poems. LC 92-45790. 128p. 1993. 19.95 (0-8112-1236-X); pap. 9.95 (0-8112-1237-8, NDP759) New Directions.

— The Master of Those Who Know: Pound the Teacher. 40p. 1987. pap. 4.95 (0-87286-194-5) City Lights.

— The Owl of Minerva. LC 86-73198. 96p. (Orig.). 1987. 15.00 (1-55659-005-9); pap. 9.00 (1-55659-004-0) Copper Canyon.

— Phantoms: Poetry. LC 94-79649. (Illus.). 64p. 1995. 12.95 (0-89381-613-2) Aperture.

— Pound as Wuz: Essays & Lectures on Ezra Pound. LC 87-81376. (Illus.). 270p. (Orig.). 1987. 17.00 (1-55597-097-4); pap. 9.50 (1-55597-098-2) Graywolf.

— Random Essays. 302p. 1992. 18.95 (0-918825-86-5); pap. 9.95 (0-918825-87-3) Moyer Bell.

— Random Stories. 220p. 1990. 18.95 (1-55921-029-X) Moyer Bell.

— Remembering William Carlos Williams. LC 95-15719. 64p. (Orig.). 1995. pap. 7.95 (0-8112-1307-2) New Directions.

— Stolen & Contaminated Poems. 60p. 1985. text ed. 75.00 (0-918824-47-8) Turkey Pr.

Laughlin, James L. History of Bimetallism in the United States. LC 68-28639. 353p. 1968. reprint ed. text ed. 38. 50 (0-8371-0138-7, LAHB, Greenwood Pr) Greenwood.

Laughlin, Jeannine L. & Laughlin, Sherry, eds. Children's Authors Speak. (Illus.). 250p. 1993. lib. bdg. 25.00 (0-87287-921-6) Libs Unl.

Laughlin, Jeffrey A. PC Networking: The Successful Implementation of a Local Area Network. (Illus.). 256p. (Orig.). 1989. 29.95 (0-8306-9198-7, Windcrest); pap. 19.60 (0-8306-3198-4, Windcrest) TAB Bks.

Laughlin, Jerry N., ed. The Juvenile Court & Serious Offenders: Thirty-Eight Recommendations. 239p. 1985. 15.00 (0-318-21312-5) Natl Juv & Family Ct Judges.

Laughlin, Karen & Schuler, Catherine, eds. Theatre & Feminist Aesthetics. LC 94-20057. Date not set. write for info. (0-8386-3549-0) Fairleigh Dickinson.

***Laughlin, Kay, et al.** The Children's Song Index, 1978-1993. 200p. 1995. lib. bdg. 37.50 (1-56308-332-9) Libs Unl.

Laughlin, Keith. The Flow of Federal Funds, 1981-1988: A 359 Billon Dollar Imbalance. LC 90-6903. 350p. (Orig.). 1990. pap. text ed. 25.00 (1-882061-30-6) Northeast-Midwest.

Laughlin, Keith, jt. auth. see De Vaul, Diane.

Laughlin, Lizette M., jt. auth. see Marinelli, Patti J.

Laughlin, Margaret A., ed. see Sanders, Norris M.

Laughlin, Mark A. & Pomerantz, Roger J., eds. Retroviral Latency. (Medical Intelligence Unit Ser.). 115p. 1994. 89.95 (1-57059-034-6, LN9034) R G Landes.

Laughlin, Mary E. More Than Four: A Guide for Multiple Harness Weavers. 1992. pap. 12.95 (1-56659-048-5) Robin & Russ.

Laughlin, Mildred K. & Kardaleff, Patricia P. Literature-Based Social Studies: Children's Books & Activities to Enrich the K-5 Curriculum. 160p. 1990. pap. 27.50 (0-89774-605-8) Oryx Pr.

Laughlin, Mildred K. & Latrobe, Kathy H. Public Relations for School Library Media Centers. 145p. 1990. lib. bdg. 17.00 (0-87287-819-8) Libs Unl.

— Readers Theatre for Children: Scripts & Script Development. 125p. 1990. lib. bdg. 17.50 (0-87287-753-1) Teacher Ideas Pr.

Laughlin, Mildred K. & Street, Terri P., eds. Literature-Based Art & Music: Children's Books & Activities to Enrich the K-5 Curriculum. 168p. 1991. pap. 29.95 (0-89774-661-9) Oryx Pr.

Laughlin, Mildred K. & Swisher, Claudia L. Literature-Based Reading: Children's Books & Activities to Enrich the K-5 Curriculum. 168p. 1990. pap. 29.95 (0-89774-562-0) Oryx Pr.

Laughlin, Mildred K. & Watt, Letty S. Developing Learning Skills Through Children's Literature: An Idea Book for K-5 Classrooms & Libraries. LC 85-43470. 288p. 1986. pap. 30.00 (0-89774-258-3) Oryx Pr.

Laughlin, Mildred K., jt. auth. see Latrobe, Kathy H.

Laughlin, Mildred K., et al. Social Studies Readers Theatre for Children. 190p. 1991. pap. text ed. 22.50 (0-87287-865-1) Libs Unl.

Laughlin, Minnabell, jt. ed. see Burton, Susan S.

Laughlin, Paul. Lectionary Worship Aids, Series II, Cycle A. (Orig.). 1989. pap. 13.60 (1-55673-138-8, 9863) CSS OH.

Laughlin-Porter, Jeannine. Exploring the Southeast States Through Literature. (Exploring the United States Through Literature Ser.). 224p. 1994. pap. 24.95 (0-89774-770-4) Oryx Pr.

Laughlin, Robert. Continuing Chord Piano. (Illus.). (C). 1991. student ed, audio 75.00 (0-929983-16-5) New Schl Am Music.

Laughlin, Robert G. The Aqueous Phase Behavior of Surfactants. (Colloid Science Ser.). (Illus.). 558p. 1994. text ed. 105.00 (0-12-437745-9) Acad Pr.

Laughlin, Robert M. The Great Tzotzil Dictionary of San Lorenzo Zinacantan. LC 74-32060. (Smithsonian Contributions to Anthropology Ser.: No. 19). 624p. reprint ed. pap. 177.90 (0-317-28869-5, 2020310) Bks Demand.

— Of Cabbages & Kings: Tales from Zinacantan. LC 76-608180. (Smithsonian Contributions to Anthropology Ser.: No. 23). 437p. reprint ed. pap. 124.60 (0-317-28867-9, 2020311) Bks Demand.

Laughlin, Robert M. & Haviland, John B. The Great Tzotzil Dictionary of Santo Domingo Zinacantan: With Grammatical Analysis & Historical Commentary, 3 vols., Vol. 1: Tzotzil-English. LC 87-600364. (Smithsonian Contributions to Anthropology Ser.: No. 31). (Illus.). 370p. reprint ed. Vol. 1, Tzotzil-English, 370p. pap. 105. 50 (0-8357-8153-4, 2034080) Bks Demand.

— The Great Tzotzil Dictionary of Santo Domingo Zinacantan: With Grammatical Analysis & Historical Commentary, 3 vols., Vol. 2: English-Tzotzil. LC 87-600364. (Smithsonian Contributions to Anthropology Ser.: No. 31). (Illus.). 305p. reprint ed. Vol. 2, English-Tzotzil. pap. 87.00 (0-8357-8154-2, 2034080) Bks Demand.

— The Great Tzotzil Dictionary of Santo Domingo Zinacantan: With Grammatical Analysis & Historical Commentary, 3 vols., Vol. 3: Spanish-Tzotzil. LC 87-600364. (Smithsonian Contributions to Anthropology Ser.: No. 31). (Illus.). 472p. reprint ed. Vol. 3, Spanish-Tzotzil. pap. 134.60 (0-8357-8155-0, 2034080) Bks Demand.

Laughlin, Robert M., tr. see Karasik, Carol, ed.

Laughlin, Rosemary M. Trouble on the Shoshone. LC 88-50762. 94p. (J). (gr. 5-8). 1989. pap. 5.95 (1-55523-154-3) Winston-Derek.

Laughlin, Ruth. The Wind Leaves No Shadow. LC 48-10425. 1951. pap. 8.95 (0-87004-083-9) Caxton.

Laughlin, Sara, jt. ed. see Puckett, Katharyn E.

Laughlin, Sarah B. & Kibbe, Douglas P., eds. The Atlas of Breeding Birds of Vermont. LC 84-40589. (Illus.). 478p. 1985. text ed. 60.00 (0-87451-326-X) U Pr of New Eng.

Laughlin, Sherry, jt. ed. see Laughlin, Jeannine L.

Laughlin, T., jt. auth. see Coche, Andre G.

Laughlin, Wayne, jt. auth. see Atkin, Malcolm.

Laughlin, William S. Aleuts: Survivors of the Bering Land Bridge. 160p. (C). 1981. pap. text ed. 13.50 (0-03-081269-0) HB Coll Pubs.

Laughon, Helen & Laughon, Nel. August Edouart - A Quaker Album: American & English Duplicate Silhouettes 1827-1845. (Illus.). 144p. 1987. text ed. 29.95 (0-9616686-0-1) Cheswick Pr.

Laughon, Nel, jt. auth. see Laughon, Helen.

Laughrey, Christopher D. Petrology & Reservoir Characteristics of the Lower Silurian Medina Group Sandstones, Athens & Geneva Fields, Crawford County Pennsylvania. (Mineral Resource Report Ser.: No. 85). (Illus.). 126p. 1984. pap. 6.10 (0-8182-0054-5) Commonweal PA.

Laughridge, Eugene N. The Orient Out the Window: Places & Things Asian. 149p. (Orig.). 1993. pap. 7.95 (0-9639455-0-5) MLH Bks.

Laughridge, Pat. Let's Weave Color into Baskets. LC 85-63237. (Illus.). 58p. 1986. pap. 6.95 (0-88740-056-6) Schiffer.

Laughrin, M. Fidelia. Juan Pablo Forner As a Critic. LC 79-94173. (Catholic University of America. Studies in Romance Languages & Literatures: No. 26). reprint ed. 37.50 (0-404-50326-8) AMS Pr.

Laughter, John. Contemporary Saxophone. 56p. 1992. pap. text ed. 15.95 (0-931759-58-7) Centerstream Pub.

— Rock & Roll Saxophone. 64p. 1989. audio 17.95 (0-931759-36-6) Centerstream Pub.

Laughton, Bruce. The Drawings of Daumier & Millet. (Illus.). 256p. (C). 1991. text ed. 60.00 (0-300-04764-9) Yale U Pr.

— The Euston Road School: A Study in Objective. 384p. 1986. text ed. 118.95 (0-85967-694-3, Pub. by Scolar Pr UK) Ashgate Pub Co.

Laughton, Charles, tr. see Brecht, Bertolt.

Laughton, J. K., ed. State Papers Relating to the Defeat of the Spanish Armada Anno, 1588. 418p. 1987. text ed. 93.95 (0-566-05540-6, Pub. by Scolar Pr UK) Ashgate Pub Co.

Laughton, J. K. & Sulivan, J. Y. Journal of Rear-Admiral Bartholomew James, 1725-1828. (C). 1987. 100.00 (0-685-31900-8) St Mut.

Laughton, M. A., ed. Renewable Energy Sources: Watt Committee Report -- Published on Behalf of the Watt Committee on Energy, No. 22. 172p. 1990. 90.00 (1-85166-500-5) Elsevier.

Laughton, Robert, jt. auth. see Hayes, Cedric J.

Laughy, Linwood. Getting the Best Bite of the Apple: How to Take Control of Your Child's Education in the Public Schools. LC 93-77570. 165p. 1993. pap. 11.95 (0-945519-14-1) Mountn Meadw Pr.

— The Interactive Parent: How to Help Your Child Survive & Succeed in the Public Schools. LC 88-90511. (Orig.). 1988. pap. 11.95 (0-945519-07-9) Mountn Meadw Pr.

Laughy, Linwood, jt. auth. see Hendrickson, Borg.

Laugier, C., ed. Geometric Reasoning for Perception & Action: Proceedings of a Workshop, Grenoble, France, September 16-17, 1991. (Lecture Notes in Computer Science Ser.: Vol. 708). viii, 281p. 1993. pap. write for info. (3-540-57132-9) Spr-Verlag.

— Geometric Reasoning for Perception & Action: Selected Papers from the Workshop in Grenoble, France, September 16-17, 1991. (Lecture Notes in Computer Science Ser.: Vol. 708). viii, 281p. 1993. pap. 44.00 (0-387-57132-9) Spr-Verlag.

Laugier, Marc-Antoine. An Essay on Architecture. Herrmann, Wolfgang & Herrmann, Anni, trs. LC 75-28448. (Documents & Sources in Architecture Ser.: No. 1). 163p. 1985. reprint ed. pap. 12.95 (0-912158-92-1) Hennessey.

Lauglo, J. & Lillis, K., eds. Vocationalizing Education: An International Perspective. (Comparative & International Education Ser.: No. 6). (Illus.). 300p. 1988. text ed. 59.00 (0-08-035855-1, Pergamon Pr); pap. text ed. 29.00 (0-08-035856-X, Pergamon Pr) Elsevier.

***Lauing, Daniel A.** Manitou, Fountains of the Deep: The Crash of Flight 585, March 3, 1991, Widefield, Colorado. 1995. boxed 23.50 (0-9641269-1-5) Benchmark Books.

— Manitou, Fountains of the Deep: The Crash of Flight 585, March 3, 1991, Widefield, Colorado. 320p. 1995. 13.50 (0-9641269-0-7) Plumb Line CO.

Laulajainen, Risto. Spatial Strategies in Retailing. (C). 1987. lib. bdg. 107.00 (90-277-2595-0) Kluwer Ac.

***Laulajainen, Risto & Stafford, Howard A.** Corporate Geography: Business Location Principles & Cases. LC 94-42236. 1995. lib. bdg. 205.00 (0-7923-3326-8) Kluwer Ac.

Laulou, S., et al. Guideline for Survey Techniques in Evaluation of Research, EUR 14339. 72p. 1992. pap. 13.00 (92-826-4093-0, CG-NA-14339-EN-C, Pub. by Europ Com) UNIPUB.

Laumann, Edward O. Prestige & Association in an Urban Community: An Analysis of an Urban Stratification System. LC 66-29709. (Orig.). 1966. pap. 4.95 (0-672-60620-8, Bobbs) Macmillan.

Laumann, Edward O., ed. Social Stratification: Research & Theory for the 1970's. LC 77-135769. (Illus.). (Orig.). 1970. 8.50 (0-672-51402-8, Bobbs); pap. 6.95 (0-672-61195-3, Bobbs) Macmillan.

Laumann, Edward O. & Knoke, David. The Organizational State: Social Change in National Policy Domains. LC 87-40142. (Illus.). 592p. (C). 1988. text ed. 45.00 (0-299-11190-3) U of Wis Pr.

— Organizational State: Social Change in National Policy Domains. LC 87-40142. (Illus.). 592p. 1987. pap. text ed. 19.95 (0-299-11194-6) U of Wis Pr.

Laumann, Edward O., jt. auth. see Heinz, John P.

Laumann, Edward O., et al. The Social Organization of Sexuality: Sexual Practices in the United States. (Illus.). 672p. 1994. lib. bdg. 49.95 (0-226-46957-3) U Ch Pr.

Laumann, Maryta M. The Secret of Excellence in Ancient Chinese Silks: Factors Contributing to the Extraordinary Development of Textile Design & Technology Achieved in Ancient China. 1984. 35.00 (0-89986-357-4) Oriental Bk Store.

Laumark, Eleanor & Christianson, Victoria. Keeping Track: A Personal Medical Record System. large type ed. LC 80-22042. (Illus.). (Orig.). 1981. pap. 7.95 (0-912800-79-8) Woodbridge Pr.

Laumbach, Karl W., jt. ed. see Duran, Meliha S.

***Laumer, Frank.** Dade's Last Command. LC 94-26086. (Illus.). 312p. 1995. 29.95 (0-8130-1324-0) U Press Fla.

— Massacre! LC 68-9812. (Illus.). 1968. pap. 15.95 (0-8130-0479-9) U Press Fla.

Laumer, Keith. Alien Minds. 1991. mass mkt. 4.50 (0-671-72055-4) Baen Bks.

— Back to the Time Trap. 352p. (Orig.). 1992. mass mkt. 5.99 (0-671-72127-5) Baen Bks.

— The Breaking Earth. 288p. 1988. pap. 3.50 (0-8125-4387-4) Tor Bks.

— The Compleat Bolo. 320p. (Orig.). 1990. mass mkt. 4.99 (0-671-69879-6) Baen Bks.

— Earthblood. 1991. mass mkt. 4.50 (0-671-72060-0) Baen Bks.

— The Glory Game. 256p. (Orig.). 1985. pap. 2.95 (0-8125-4383-1) Tor Bks.

— Judsons Eden. 1991. mass mkt. 4.95 (0-671-72038-4) Baen Bks.

— The Other Sky & the House in November. 256p. 1985. pap. 2.95 (0-8125-4377-7) Tor Bks.

— Retief & the Rascals. 256p. (Orig.). 1993. mass mkt. 4.99 (0-671-72168-2) Baen Bks.

— The Return of Retief. 1984. pap. 2.95 (0-685-09411-1, Baen Bks) PB.

— The Return of Retief. (Retief Ser.). 224p. 1985. reprint ed. pap. 2.95 (0-671-55902-8) Baen Bks.

— Worlds of the Imperium. 288p. 1986. 2.95 (0-8125-4379-3) Tor Bks.

— Zone Yellow. (Orig.). 1990. mass mkt. 4.50 (0-671-72028-7) Baen Bks.

Laumer, Keith, creator. Bolos, Bk. 1: Honor of the Regiment. 320p. (Orig.). 1993. mass mkt. 4.99 (0-671-72184-4) Baen Bks.

— Bolos, Bk. 3. 1995. mass mkt. 5.99 (0-671-87683-X) Baen Bks.

— The Unconquerable Bolos, No. II. 336p. (Orig.). 1994. mass mkt. 5.99 (0-671-87629-5) Baen Bks.

***Laumon, Gerard.** Cohomology of Drinfeld Modular Varieties Part 1: Geometry, Counting of Points & Local Harmonic Analysis. (Cambridge Studies in Advanced Mathematics: 41). 350p. (C). 1995. write for info. (0-521-47060-9) Cambridge U Pr.

Laumond, J. P., jt. ed. see Boissonnat, L. D.

Laun, Charles. Handbook of Nature & Scientific Photography. 472p. 1994. lib. bdg. 17.95 (0-9640598-1-9); pap. 13.95 (0-9640598-0-0) Alsace Bks.

Laun, Hellmut. How I Met God: An Unusual Conversion. Smith, David, tr. 163p. 1983. 10.50 (0-8199-0871-1, Frncscn Herld) Franciscan Pr.

***Laun, Mary Ann, ed.** Vocational & Technical Resources for Community College Libraries: Selected Materials. LC 94-46648. 1995. pap. 85.00 (0-8389-7758-8) ALA.

Launay, A. J. Dictionary of Contemporaries, Famous People & Events. 1970. 25.00 (0-87556-145-4) Saifer.

Launay, Michel, ed. see Rousseau, Jean-Jacques.

Launay, Robert. Beyond the Stream: Islam & Society in a West African Town. (Comparative Studies on Muslim Societies: No. 15). (C). 1992. 38.00 (0-520-07718-0) U CA Pr.

Launchberry, Jane. At the Circus. 1988. 2.98 (0-671-09596-X) S&S Trade.

— In Nursery Rhyme Land. (J). 1988. 2.98 (0-671-09597-8) S&S Trade.

Launchbury, Jane. Witch Stories. 1991. 3.99 (0-517-06526-6) Random Hse Value.

Launchbury, John. Project Factorisations in Partial Evaluation. (Distinguished Dissertations in Computer Science Ser.: No. 1). 176p. (C). 1991. 44.95 (0-521-41497-0) Cambridge U Pr.

Launchbury, John & Sansom, Patrick, eds. Functional Programming, Glasgow 1992: Proceedings of the 1992 Glasgow Workshop on Functional Programming, Ayr, Scotland, 6-8 July 1992. LC 93-3308. 1993. 69.00 (0-387-19820-2) Spr-Verlag.

Launder, Elizabeth, jt. ed. see Legard, Hilary.

Launders, Michele & Spiegel, Penina. I Wish You Didn't Know My Name: The Story of Michele Launders & Her Daughter Lisa. 1990. 17.95 (0-446-51587-6) Warner Bks.

Laundon, Jack R. Lichens. 1989. pap. 25.00 (0-85263-811-6, Pub. by Shire UK) St Mut.

Laundrie, Amy C. Whinny of the Wild Horses. LC 88-21460. (Illus.). 128p. (J). (gr. 3-6). 1990. text ed. 13.95 (0-02-754542-3, Four Winds Pr) S&S Childrens.

Laundy, Philip. Parliaments in the Modern World. 250p. 1989. text ed. 57.95 (1-85521-042-8, Pub. by Dartmth Pub UK) Ashgate Pub Co.

Laune, Ferris F. Predicting Criminality: Forecasting Behavior on Parole. LC 73-10851. 163p. 1974. reprint ed. lib. bdg. 22.50 (0-8371-7041-9, LAPC, Greenwood Pr) Greenwood.

Laune, Seigniora R. Sand in My Eyes. LC 86-40089. (Illus.). 264p. 1986. reprint ed. pap. 9.95 (0-8061-2016-9) U of Okla Pr.

Launer, jt. auth. see DePriest.

***Launer, Donald.** A Cruising Guide to New Jersey Waters. LC 95-8590. (Illus.). 250p. (C). 1995. text ed. 25.95 (0-8135-2238-2) Rutgers U Pr.

Launer, Harold M. & Palenski, Joseph E., eds. Crime & the New Immigrants. 140p. (C). 1989. text ed. 38.95x (0-398-05520-3) C C Thomas.

— Crime & the New Immigrants. 140p. 1989. pap. 24.95 (0-398-06224-2) C C Thomas.

Launer, L. J., et al, eds. European Studies on the Incidence of Dementing Diseases: A Report of the EURODEM Research Group - Neuroepidemiology Journal, 1992, Vol. 11, Suppl. 1. (Illus.). vi, 122p. 1992. pap. 36.00 (3-8055-5593-8) S Karger.

Launer, Michael K., jt. auth. see Young, Marilyn J.

Laungan, Pittu. It Shouldn't Happen to a Patient: A Survivor's Guide to Fighting Life Threatening Illness. 192p. 1992. text ed. 29.95 (1-871177-14-6, Pub. by Whiting & Birch UK) Paul & Co Pubs.

Laungani, Pittu. It Shouldn't Happen to a Patient: A Survivor's Guide to Fighting Life-Threatening Illness. 192p. 1993. reprint ed. pap. 18.95 (1-871177-15-4, Pub. by Whiting & Birch UK) Paul & Co Pubs.

Launie, J. J., jt. auth. see Hollingsworth, E. P., Jr.

Launie, J. J., et al. Personal Insurance. 2nd ed. LC 90-86335. 321p. 1994. text ed. 25.00 (0-89462-061-4) IIA.

— Principles of Property & Liability Underwriting. 3rd ed. LC 77-80641. 497p. 1988. text ed. 26.00 (0-89462-030-4, AU61) IIA.

***Launius, Carl J.** It Seemed Like a Good Idea at the Time. LC 94-36003. 1995. write for info. (1-55728-337-0); pap. write for info. (1-55728-338-9) U of Ark Pr.

***Launius, Roger, ed.** History of Rocketry & Astronautics. LC 57-43769. (AAS History Ser.: 11). (Illus.). 236p. 1994. lib. bdg. 60.00x (0-87703-382-X, Pub. by Am Astro Soc) Univelt Inc.

— History of Rocketry & Astronautics. (AAS History Ser.: 11). (Illus.). 236p. 1994. pap. text ed. 40.00x (0-87703-383-8, Pub. by Am Astro Soc) Univelt Inc.

Launius, Roger D. Father Figure: Joseph Smith III & Creation of the Reorganized Church. 275p. 1990. pap. text ed. 20.00 (0-8309-0576-6) Herald Hse.

— Illustrated History of Kirtland Temple. (Illus.). 1986. pap. 7.00 (0-8309-0438-7) Herald Hse.

— Invisible Saints: A Study of Black Americans in the Reorganized Church. 1988. pap. 18.00 (0-8309-0508-1) Herald Hse.

— Joseph Smith III: Pragmatic Prophet. LC 87-35724. 424p. 1988. 24.95 (0-252-01514-2) U of Ill Pr.

— Joseph Smith III: Pragmatic Prophet. (Illus.). 424p. (C). 1995. pap. 15.95 (0-252-06515-8) U of Ill Pr.

— NASA: A History of the U. S. Civil Space Program. LC 93-35977. 286p. 1994. 16.50 (0-89464-878-0) Krieger.

— NASA: A History of the U. S. Civil Space Program. LC 93-35977. (Anvil Ser.). (C). 1994. pap. text ed. 12.50 (0-89464-727-X) Krieger.

— Zion's Camp: Expedition to Missouri, 1834. 1984. pap. 18.00 (0-8309-0384-4) Herald Hse.

***Launius, Roger D. & Hallwas, John E., eds.** Nauvoo in Mormon History: The Kingdom on the Mississippi Revisited. LC 95-14673. 1996. write for info. (0-252-02197-5); pap. write for info. (0-252-06494-1) U of Ill Pr.

Launius, Roger D. & Spillman, W. B., eds. Let Contention Cease: The Dynamics of Dissent in the Reorganized Church of Jesus Christ of Latter Day Saints. 304p. (Orig.). 1991. pap. text ed. 19.00 (0-8309-0592-8) Herald Hse.

Launius, Roger D. & Thatcher, Linda, eds. Differing Visions: Dissenters in Mormon History. LC 93-5463. 464p. 1994. 32.50 (0-252-02069-3) U of Ill Pr.

Launius, Roger D., jt. ed. see McKiernan, F. Mark.

Launo, R., jt. ed. see Koskiala, S.

Launois, Bernard & Jamieson, Glyn G. Modern Operative Techniques in Liver Surgery. LC 92-49203. 160p. 1993. 85.00 (0-443-04616-6) Churchill.

***Launsby, Robert G., et al.** Process Validation for Business Success. 150p. 1995. pap. text ed. 49.95 (0-9636093-4-3) Launsby Cnslting.

Launsby, Robert G. & Weese, Daniel L. Straight Talk on Designing Experiments. 150p. 1993. text ed. 39.95 (0-9636093-3-5) Launsby Cnslting.

Launsby, Robert G., jt. auth. see Schmidt, Stephen R.

Launsby, Robert G., jt. auth. see Schmidt, Stephen.

Laur, Timothy. Military Airlift Command. LC 92-56437. (Illus.). 325p. 1995. 29.95 (1-877853-15-1) Nautical & Aviation.

Laur, Timothy, jt. auth. see Polmar, Norman.

***Laur, Timothy M. & Llanso, Steven L.** Encyclopedia of Modern U. S. Military Weapons. Boyne, Walter J., ed. 544p. 1995. 49.95 (0-425-14781-9) Berkley Pub.

Laura, Judith. She Lives! The Return of Our Great Mother: Myths, Rituals, Meditations, & Music. 130p. (Orig.). 1989. pap. 8.95 (0-89594-332-8) Crossing Pr.

Laura, P. A., jt. auth. see Schinzinger, R.

***Laura, Ronald S.** Twelve Weeks to a Better Body for Men. 1994. pap. 9.95 (1-86373-482-1) IPG Chicago.

— Twelve Weeks to a Better Body for Women. 1994. pap. 9.95 (1-86373-483-X) IPG Chicago.

Laura, Ronald S. & Ashman, Adrian F., eds. Moral Issues in Mental Retardation. LC 84-29329. 224p. 1985. 35.00 (0-7099-1692-2, Pub. by Croom Helm UK) Routledge Chapman & Hall.

Laura, Ronald S. & Dutton, Kenneth R. The Matrix Principle: Drug-Free Training for Sport & Bodybuilding a Revolutionary Approach to Muscle Development. McDermott, Richard J. & Gardner, Gai, eds. LC 92-60316. (Illus.). 238p. (Orig.). 1992. pap. 19.95 (0-910944-02-4) Magee.

Laura, Ronald S. & Heaney, Sandra. The Philosophical Foundations of Health Education. (Philosophy of Education Research Library). 256p. 1990. 32.50 (0-415-90086-7, A2716, Routledge NY) Routledge.

Laura, Szabo-Cohen, jt. auth. see Karin, Kasdin.

Lauraitis, K. N., ed. Fatigue of Fibrous Composite Materials - STP 723. 311p. 1981. 30.00 (0-8031-0719-6, 04-723000-33) ASTM.

Laurance, Andrew. Other You: Develop Your Psychic Potential. 1987. pap. 6.95 (0-7137-1719-X, Pub. by Blandford Pr UK) Sterling.

Laurance, John D. Priest As Type of Christ: The Leader of the Eucharist in Salvation History According to Cyprian of Carthage. LC 84-47539. (American University Studies: Theology & Religion: Ser. VII, Vol. 5). 256p. (Orig.). (C). 1984. 37.25 (0-8204-0117-X) P Lang Pubs.

Laurance, Robert. Going Freelance: A Guide for Professionals. LC 87-28571. 218p. 1988. pap. text ed. 17.95 (0-471-63255-4) Wiley.

Laurant, Van, III. A Study of Relationships: Education; Employment; & Wealth. (Illus.). 242p. (Orig.). 1993. pap. 18.95 (0-9638420-3-X) Financial Info Syst.

Laure, Ettagale, jt. auth. see Laure, Jason.

Laure, Jason. Angola. LC 90-2143. (Enchantment of the World Ser.). (Illus.). 128p. (J). (gr. 5-9). 1990. lib. bdg. 20.55 (0-516-02721-2) Childrens.

— Bangladesh. LC 92-8891. (Enchantment of the World Ser.). (Illus.). 128p. (J). (gr. 5-9). 1992. lib. bdg. 20.55 (0-516-02609-7) Childrens.

— Botswana. LC 93-753. (Enchantment of the World Ser.). (Illus.). 128p. (J). (gr. 5-9). 1993. lib. bdg. 20.55 (0-516-02616-X) Childrens.

— Namibia. LC 92-39137. (Enchantment of the World Ser.). (Illus.). 128p. (J). (gr. 5-9). 1993. lib. bdg. 20.55 (0-516-02615-1) Childrens.

— Zambia. LC 89-34281. (Enchantment of the World Ser.). 128p. (J). (gr. 5-9). 1989. lib. bdg. 20.55 (0-516-02716-6) Childrens.

— Zimbabwe. LC 87-35426. (Enchantment of the World Ser.). (Illus.). 127p. (J). (gr. 4-8). 1988. lib. bdg. 20.55 (0-516-02704-2) Childrens.

***Laure, Jason & Blauer, Ettaglae.** Mozambique. LC 95-2690. (Enchantment of the World Ser.). (J). 1995. write for info. (0-516-02636-4) Childrens.

Laure, Jason & Laure, Ettagale. South Africa: Coming of Age under Apartheid. LC 79-23109. (Illus.). 192p. 1980. 15.95 (0-374-37146-6) FS&G.

Laure, Jason, jt. auth. see Blauer, Ettagale.

Laurel, Brenda. Art of Human Computer Interface. 1990. pap. 32.95 (0-201-51797-3) Addison-Wesley.

— Computers As Theatre. (Illus.). 320p. (C). 1991. text ed. 35.50 (0-201-51048-0) Addison-Wesley.

— Computers As Theatre. LC 93-17107. (Illus.). 227p. (C). 1993. pap. text ed. 19.50 (0-201-55060-1) Addison-Wesley.

Lauremberg, J. A. Description of Ancient Greece. (Illus.). 140p. 1969. Artificial Vellum. 52.50 (0-317-54451-9, Pub. by A M Hakkert SP) Coronet Bks.

Lauren. There Is a Rainbow in the Moon. 80p. 1985. 8.95 (0-911051-24-4) Plain View.

Lauren, Christer & Nordman, Marianne, eds. From Office to School: Special Language & Internalization. 164p. 1989. 99.00 (1-85359-038-X, Pub. by Multilingual Matters UK); pap. 39.95 (1-85359-037-1, Pub. by Multilingual Matters UK) Taylor & Francis.

— Special Language: From Human Thinking to Thinking Machines. 490p. 1989. 99.00 (1-85359-034-7, Pub. by Multilingual Matters UK); pap. 39.95 (1-85359-033-9, Pub. by Multilingual Matters UK) Taylor & Francis.

Lauren, Christer, jt. ed. see Herberts, Kjell.

Lauren, Covell K., jt. auth. see Covell, Stephen E.

Lauren, Jessica. She Died Twice. LC 91-105551. 192p. (Orig.). 1991. pap. 8.95 (0-934678-34-0) New Victoria Pubs.

***Lauren, Joan.** Portraits of Life, with Love. 1994. 30.00 (1-881649-43-1) Genl Pub Grp.

Lauren, Ricky A. My Island. 1994. 100.00 (0-679-43711-8) Random.

Lauren Rogers Museum of Art Staff. The Lauren Rogers Museum of Art: Handbook of the Collections. LC 89-5451. (Illus.). 198p. (Orig.). 1989. pap. 19.95 (0-685-45630-7) Lauren Rogers.

Laurence. Clinical Pharmacology. 7th ed. (Illus.). 704p. 1992. pap. text ed. 54.00 (0-443-04388-4) Churchill.

Laurence, jt. auth. see Hart.

Laurence, A., et al, eds. John Bunyan & His England, 1628-88. 204p. 1990. boxed 50.00 (1-85285-027-2) Hambledon Press.

Laurence, Anne. Parliamentary Army Chaplains, 1642-1651. (Royal Historical Society: Studies in History: No. 59). 224p. (C). 1990. 63.00 (0-86193-216-1) Boydell & Brewer.

— Remember When. (Superromance Ser.). 1993. mass mkt. 3.39 (0-373-70539-5, 1-70539-1) Harlequin Bks.

— Women in England, 1500-1760: A Social History. LC 94-7197. 1994. text ed. 39.95 (0-312-12207-1) St Martin.

Laurence, Berthe. Moments. (Orig.). 1980. pap. 2.50 (0-89083-565-9) Zebra.

Laurence, Dan H. A Portrait of the Author As a Bibliography. LC 83-600082. (Engelhard Lecture on the Book Ser.). 19p. 1983. 3.95 (0-8444-0426-8, 030-000-0241-5) Lib Congress.

— Shaw, Books & Libraries. LC 76-620048. (Bibliographical Monograph: No. 9). (Illus.). 1976. 8.00 (0-87959-022-X) U of Tex H Ransom Ctr.

Laurence, Dan H., comp. Shaw: An Exhibit. LC 76-620047. (Illus.). 1977. 20.00 (0-87959-081-5); pap. 15.00 (0-87959-082-3) U of Tex H Ransom Ctr.

Laurence, Dan H., ed. How to Become a Musical Critic. LC 77-26653. (Music Reprint Ser.: 1978). 1978. reprint ed. lib. bdg. 42.50 (0-306-77569-7) Da Capo.

— Selected Correspondence of Bernard Shaw: Theatrics, 1889-1950. 256p. 1995. 40.00 (0-8020-3000-9) U of Toronto Pr.

Laurence, Dan H., ed. see Shaw, Bernard.

Laurence, Dan H., ed. see Shaw, George Bernard.

Laurence, Desmond R., et al, eds. Safety Testing of New Drugs. 1984. text ed. 72.00 (0-12-438350-5) Acad Pr.

Laurence, Edward, Jr. The Duty & Office of a Land Steward: Represented Several Plain & Distinct Articles. Chandler, Alfred D., ed. LC 79-7549. (History of Management Thought & Practice Ser.). 1980. reprint ed. lib. bdg. 30.95 (0-405-12333-7) Ayer.

Laurence, Edward J., et al. Arms Watch: SIPRI Report on the First Year of the UN Register of Conventional Arms. LC 93-36596. (SIPRI Research Reports: Vol. 6). (Illus.). 160p. (C). 1994. 37.50 (0-19-829179-5); 24.00 (0-19-829177-9) OUP.

Laurence, Frank M. Hemingway & the Movies. LC 79-56697. (Illus.). 349p. reprint ed. pap. 99.50 (0-8357-4345-4, 2037148) Bks Demand.

— Hemingway & the Movies. (Quality Paperbacks Ser.). (Illus.). xix, 329p. (C). 1982. reprint ed. pap. 8.95 (0-306-80163-9) Da Capo.

Laurence, Janet. Death & the Epicure. 208p. 1993. 18.95 (0-312-10451-0, Pub. by Thomas Dunne Bks) St Martin.

— Hotel Morgue. large type ed. (Magna Mystery Ser.). 431p. 1992. 21.95 (0-7505-0298-3) Ulverscroft.

— Little Coffee Cookbook. (Illus.). 1992. 7.95 (0-8118-0256-6) Chronicle Bks.

— A Little French Cookbook. (Illus.). 60p. 1989. 6.95 (0-87701-642-9) Chronicle Bks.

— A Little Scandinavian Cookbook. 60p. 1990. 6.95 (0-87701-743-3) Chronicle Bks.

— Recipe for Death. large type ed. LC 93-20595. 1993. 17.95 (1-56054-794-4) Thorndike Pr.

— To Kill the Past. LC 94-36024. 1995. 19.95 (0-312-11906-2) St Martin.

Laurence, Janice H. & Ramsberger, Peter F. Low-Aptitude Men in the Military: Who Profits, Who Pays? LC 91-20081. 200p. 1991. text ed. 49.95 (0-275-94060-8, C4060, Praeger Pubs) Greenwood.

Laurence, Jean-Roch & Perry, Campbell. Hypnosis, Will & Memory: A Psycho-Legal History. LC 87-19672. (Guilford Clinical & Experimental Hypnosis Ser.). 432p. 1988. lib. bdg. 50.00 (0-89862-339-1); pap. text ed. 26.95 (0-89862-504-1) Guilford Pr.

Laurence, Jim, ed. Shoemaker & the Christmas Elves. (Illus.). (J). 1993. 6.99 (0-517-08488-0) Random Hse Value.

Laurence, John. The History of Capital Punishment. (Illus.). 230p. 1983. pap. 4.95 (0-8065-0840-X, Citadel Pr) Carol Pub Group.

Laurence, K. M., jt. ed. see Rocker, I.

Laurence, Leslie & Weinhouse, Beth. Outrageous Practices: The Alarming Truth about How Medicine Mistreats Women. LC 94-15950. 304p. 1994. 22.50 (0-449-90745-7, Columbine) Fawcett.

Laurence, Louise, jt. auth. see Brechling, Frank P.

Laurence, Margaret. A Bird in the House: Stories. (Phoenix Fiction Ser.). 208p. (C). 1993. pap. 9.95 (0-226-46934-4) U Ch Pr.

— The Diviners. (Phoenix Fiction Ser.). 392p. (C). 1993. pap. 12.95 (0-226-46935-2) U Ch Pr.

— Diviners, Notes. pap. 4.50 (0-8220-0398-8) Cliffs.

— The Fire-Dwellers. (Phoenix Fiction Ser.). viii, 308p. 1993. pap. 10.95 (0-226-46951-4) U Ch Pr.

— A Jest of God. LC 93-8034. (Phoenix Fiction Ser.). 218p. 1993. pap. 9.95 (0-226-46952-2) U Ch Pr.

— The Stone Angel. (Phoenix Fiction Ser.). 288p. (C). 1993. pap. 10.95 (0-226-46936-0) U Ch Pr.

— A Tree for Poverty. 160p. (C). 1993. pap. 16.00 (1-55022-177-9, Pub. by ECW Press CN) Genl Dist Srvs.

Laurence, Mary. All Kinds of Everything. 16p. 1986. pap. 23.00 (0-7223-2058-2, Pub. by A H S Ltd UK) St Mut.

Laurence, Mary S. Best Loved Poems to Read: Again & Again. (Second Ser.). 1989. 9.98 (0-88365-726-0) Galahad Bks.

— Best Loved Poems to Read Again & Again. 1989. 9.98 (0-88365-714-7) Galahad Bks.

— Best Loved Poems to Read Again & Again, 2 vols. 1990. boxed 19.98 (0-88365-760-0) Galahad Bks.

Laurence, Michael, et al. The Nineteen Eighty-Two Register. (Illus.). 124p. 1983. 30.00 (0-9610384-0-3) US Pict Res.

Laurence, Michael D., et al. Social Control of the Drinking Driver. (Studies in Crime & Justice). xxx, 452p. 1988. pap. text ed. 19.95 (0-226-46954-9) U Ch Pr.

Laurence, Murray. High Times in the Middle of Nowhere: The Misadventures of Murray Laurence, Compulsive Traveller. LC 86-11444. 317p. 1987. pap. 16.95 (0-7022-2013-2, Pub. by Univ Queensland Pr AT) Intl Spec Bk.

Laurence, Norman & Watts, Joanna. Handbook of Emergencies in General Practice. (Illus.). 608p. 1989. pap. 35.00 (0-19-261547-5) OUP.

Laurence, Patricia O. The Reading of Silence: Virginia Woolf in the English Tradition. LC 90-23636. 253p. 1991. 37.50 (0-8047-1831-8) Stanford U Pr.

— Reading of Silence: Virginia Woolf in the English Tradition. 253p. (C). 1993. pap. 12.95 (0-8047-2179-3) Stanford U Pr.

Laurence, R. V., ed. see Acton, John E.

Laurence, Rassophor-Monk, tr. Divine Liturgy of St. Gregory. 52p. (Orig.). 1993. pap. 3.50 (0-912927-22-4, D001) St John Kronstadt.

Laurence, Ray. Roman Pompeii: Space & Society. LC 93-42553. (Illus.). 176p. 1994. 45.00 (0-415-09502-6, B4672, Routledge NY) Routledge.

Laurence, Reginald V., ed. see Acton, John E.

***Laurence, Richard.** The Book of Enoch. LC 72-95273. (Secret Doctrine Reference Ser.). xlvii, 192p. 1995. reprint ed. pap. 11.00 (0-913510-67-X) Wizards.

— The Book of Enoch the Prophet. 2nd ed. LC 72-95273. (Secret Doctrine Reference Ser.). 220p. 1972. reprint ed. 14.00 (0-913510-01-7) Wizards.

Laurence, Richard H. Medals of Giovanni Cavino, the Paduan. 1981. reprint ed. pap. 6.00 (0-915262-56-8) S J Durst.

Laurence, Robert & Minzner, Pamela B. Student's Guide to Estates in Land & Future Interests: Text, Examples, Problems, & Answers. 2nd ed. (Student Guide Ser.). 1981. write for info. (0-8205-0351-7, 635); teacher ed write for info. (0-8205-0352-5) Bender.

— A Student's Guide to Estates in Land & Future Interests: Text, Examples, Problems, & Answers. 2nd ed. LC 93-14440. (Student Guide Ser.). 1993. write for info. (0-8205-0353-3) Bender.

Laurence, Theodor. The Parker Lifetime Treasury of Mystic & Occult Powers. 1986. 5.95 (0-13-650747-6, Reward) P-H.

Laurence Urdang Associates, Ltd. Staff. Longman Dictionary of English Idioms. (Illus.). 1979. 34.95 (0-582-55524-8, 74412) Longman.

— The Penguin Dictionary of Proverbs. Ferguson, Rosalind & Rosalind, eds. 256p. 1983. pap. 12.50 (0-14-051118-0, Penguin Bks) Viking Penguin.

Laurence, William L. Dawn over Zero: The Story of the Atomic Bomb. LC 71-153156. (Illus.). 289p. 1972. reprint ed. text ed. 35.00 (0-8371-6064-2, LADZ, Greenwood Pr) Greenwood.

Laurenceau, Jean. Speak to Us of Mary: Biblical Homilies As Aids to Prayer with the Blessed Virgin. (Orig.). 1987. pap. 3.95 (0-8199-0802-9, Frncscn Herld) Franciscan Pr.

Laurencena, Martha. Vacaciones: Vacations. (SPA.). 2.95 (84-7228-443-3, 220929, Pub. by Edit Clie SP) TSELF.

Laurencich, Laura, jt. auth. see Howe, Henry V.

Laurencin, Genevieve. Music! Bogard, Vicki, tr. LC 89-8892. (Young Discovery Library). (Illus.). (J). (gr. k-5). 1989. 5.95 (0-944589-25-1, 025) Young Discovery Lib.

***Laurencin, Michel.** Dictionnaire Biographique de Touraine. 1990. write for info. (0-7859-8654-5, 285443210X) Fr & Eur.

Laurencio, Angel A. Blas Hernandez y La Revolucion De 1933: La Campana En los Campos de Cuba. LC 93-73414. (Coleccion Cuba y Sus Jueces Ser.). (Illus.). 183p. (Orig.). (SPA.). 1994. pap. 19.95 (0-89729-706-7) Ediciones.

— Don Jose Maria Chacon y Calco en Su Correspondencia. 31p. (SPA.). 1987. pap. 5.00 (0-89729-452-1) Ediciones.

— Jose Antonio Saco Y la Cuba De Hoy. (Coleccion Cuba y Sus Jueces Ser.). 27p. (Orig.). (SPA.). 1989. pap. 5.00 (0-89729-558-7) Ediciones.

Laurendeau, Monique & Pinard, Adrien. Causal Thinking in the Child. LC 62-21895. 293p. 1963. text ed. 35.00 (0-8236-0680-5) Intl Univs Pr.

— Development of the Concept of Space in the Child. LC 77-125476. 465p. 1970. text ed. 57.50 (0-8236-1225-2) Intl Univs Pr.

Laurene, Ruth. Bellringer. LC 74-75851. (Illus.). 1974. 30.00 (0-933652-08-9) Domjan Studio.

Laurens County DAR Staff. The History of Laurens County, Georgia, 1942-1986. 992p. 1989. 45.00 (0-935265-13-9) Agee Pub.

Laurens, Henry. The Papers of Henry Laurens: Vol. X, December 12, 1774-January 4, 1776, Vol. X. Chesnutt, David R. et al, eds. LC 67-29381. (Papers of Henry Laurens Ser.). 736p. 1985. lib. bdg. 49.95 (0-87249-445-4) U of SC Pr.

— Papers of Henry Laurens: Vol. 1, September 11, 1746-October 31, 1755. Hamer, Philip M. & Rogers, George C., eds. LC 67-29381. (Papers of Henry Laurens Ser.). (Illus.). xlii, 408p. 1968. 49.95 (0-87249-128-5) U of SC Pr.

— Papers of Henry Laurens: Vol. 2, November 1, 1755-December 31, 1758. Hamer, Philip M. & Rogers, George C., Jr., eds. LC 67-29381. (Papers of Henry Laurens Ser.). (Illus.). xxviii, 582p. 1970. 49.95 (0-87249-141-2) U of SC Pr.

— The Papers of Henry Laurens: Vol. 3, January 1, 1759-August 31, 1763. Hamer, Philip M. & Rogers, George C., Jr., eds. LC 67-29381. (Papers of Henry Laurens Ser.). xxviii, 600p. 1972. lib. bdg. 49.95 (0-87249-228-1) U of SC Pr.

— The Papers of Henry Laurens: Vol. 4, September 1, 1763-August 31, 1765. Rogers, George C. & Chesnutt, David, eds. LC 67-29381. (Illus.). xxvi, 722p. 1974. 49.95 (0-87249-308-3) U of SC Pr.

— The Papers of Henry Laurens: Vol. 5, September 1, 1765-July 31, 1768. Rogers, George C., Jr. & Chesnutt, David R., eds. LC 67-29381. xxxii, 840p. 1976. 49.95 (0-87249-331-8) U of SC Pr.

— The Papers of Henry Laurens: Vol. 6, August 1, 1768-July 31, 1769. Rogers, George C., Jr. et al, eds. LC 67-29381. (Illus.). xxvi, 660p. 1978. lib. bdg. 49.95 (0-87249-356-3) U of SC Pr.

— Papers of Henry Laurens: Vol. 7, Aug. 1, 1769 to Oct. 9, 1771. Rogers, George C., Jr. et al, eds. LC 67-29381. xxx, 656p. 1979. 49.95 (0-87249-372-5) U of SC Pr.

— The Papers of Henry Laurens: Vol. 8, Oct 10, 1771 to April 19, 1773. Rogers, George C., Jr., ed. LC 67-29381. xxiv, 784p. 1980. lib. bdg. 49.95 (0-87249-385-7) U of SC Pr.

— The Papers of Henry Laurens, Vol. 9: April 19, 1773 to December 12, 1774. Rogers, George C., Jr. & Chesnutt, David R., eds. LC 67-29381. (Illus.). 770p. 1981. text ed. 49.95 (0-87249-399-7) U of SC Pr.

Laurens, Jeannine, jt. auth. see Stallaerts, Robert.

Laurens, John. Army Correspondence of Colonel John Laurens in the Years 1777-1778. Decker, Peter, ed. LC 78-77106. (Eyewitness Accounts of the American Revolution Ser., No. 1). 1969. reprint ed. 18.95 (0-405-01160-1) Ayer.

Laurens, Roy. Fully Alive. 252p. 1988. pap. 6.95 (0-933071-21-3) Saybrook Pub Co.

Laurens, Sidney. London's City: A Guide Through the Historic Square Mile. LC 94-75991. (Illus.). 344p. (Orig.). 1994. pap. 15.95 (0-9641263-0-3) Marmot Pubng.

Laurens, Stephanie. Four in Hand. large type ed. (Masquerade Historical Romance Ser.). 1993. 18.95 (0-263-13751-1, Pub. by Mills & Boon Ltd UK) Chivers N Amer.

— Impetuous Innocent. large type ed. 1994. 18.95 (0-263-14012-1, Pub. by Mills & Boon Ltd UK) Chivers N Amer.

— Tangled Reins. large type ed. (Masquerade Historical Romance Ser.). 1993. 18.95 (0-263-13545-4, Pub. by Mills & Boon Ltd UK) Chivers N Amer.

Laurenson, Robert M., ed. see American Society of Mechanical Engineers Staff.

***Laurent, Bertel.** Introduction to Spacetime. 200p. 1995. text ed. 32.00 (981-02-1929-6) World Scientific Pub.

Laurent, C., jt. ed. see Encrenaz, P.

Laurent, Francis W. The Business of a Trial Court: One Hundred Years of Cases; a Census of the Actions & Special Proceedings in the Circuit of Chippewa County, Wisconsin, 1855-1954. LC 59-5305. 348p. reprint ed. pap. 99.20 (0-8357-7498-8, 2021139) Bks Demand.

Laurent, G. Dizionario Italiano-Francese, Francese-Italiano. deluxe ed. 413p. (FRE & ITA.). 1979. 14.95 (0-8288-4731-2, M9173) Fr & Eur.

Laurent, Gilles, et al, eds. Research Traditions in Marketing. LC 93-14432. (International Series in Quantitative Marketing). 464p. (C). 1993. lib. bdg. 105.00 (0-7923-9388-0) Kluwer Ac.

Laurent, J., et al. Hypoglycaemic Tumors. 1971. 30.50 (90-219-2029-8, Excerpta Medica) Elsevier.

Laurent, J. P., ed. Coordination Chemistry-Twenty One: Twenty-First International Conference on Coordination Chemistry, Toulouse, France, 1980. (IUPAC Symposium Ser.). 200p. 1981. 88.00 (0-08-025300-8, Pub. by Pergamon Repr UK) Franklin.

Laurent, Jean-Pierre, jt. auth. see Ayel, Marc.

Laurent, John, ed. Tom Mann's Social & Economic Writings. 148p. 1988. 42.50 (0-85124-458-0, Pub. by Spokesman Bks UK) Coronet Bks.

Laurent, Monique. Rodin. LC 89-45937. (Illus.). 160p. 1990. 40.00 (0-8050-1252-4) H Holt & Co.

— Rodin. LC 89-45937. (Illus.). 160p. 1990. pap. 19.95 (0-8050-1363-6) H Holt & Co.

Laurent, P. J., et al. Curves & Surfaces in Geometric Design. Schumaker, Larry, ed. 500p. 1994. text ed. 69.95 (1-56881-039-3) AK Peters.

Laurent, P. J., et al, eds. Curves & Surfaces. (Illus.). 514p. 1991. text ed. 59.95 (0-12-438660-1) Acad Pr.

— Wavelets, Images & Surface Fitting. LC 94-11330. 544p. 1994. text ed. 69.95 (1-56881-040-7) AK Peters.

Laurent, Yves. Theorie de la Deuxieme Microlocalisation dans le Domaine Complex. (Progress in Mathematics Ser.: No. 53). 311p. (C). 1985. text ed. 52.00 (0-8176-3287-5) Birkhauser.

Laurenti, Joseph L. Bibliografia de la Literatura Picaresca: Desde Sus Origenes Hasta el Presente: A Bibliography of Picaresque Literature; from Its Origins to the Present. LC 79-6271. reprint ed. 32.50 (0-404-18019-1) AMS Pr.

— A Bibliography of Picaresque Literature: Supplement. LC 79-8635. 1981. 32.50 (0-404-18018-3) AMS Pr.

— A Catalog of Spanish Rare Books (1701-1974) in the Library of the University of Illinois & in Selected North American Libraries. LC 84-47693. (American University Studies: Romance Languages & Literature: Ser. II, Vol. 12). 215p. (Orig.). 1984. text ed. 23.40 (0-8204-0129-3) P Lang Pubs.

— Hispanic Rare Books of the Golden Age (1470-1699) in the Newberry Library of Chicago & in Selected North American Libraries. (American University Studies: Romance Languages & Literature: Ser. II, Vol. 111). 229p. (C). 1989. text ed. 29.95 (0-8204-1066-7) P Lang Pubs.

Laurenti, Luigi. Property Values & Race: Studies in Seven Cities. LC 76-5437. (Illus.). 256p. 1976. reprint ed. text ed. 65.00 (0-8371-8795-8, LAPV, Greenwood Pr) Greenwood.

Laurentin, Rene. Apparitions of Our Lady. 163p. (Orig.). 1990. pap. 13.95 (1-85390-054-0, Pub. by Veritas Publns IE) Ignatius Pr.

— An Appeal from Mary in Argentina: The Apparitions of San Nicolas. Faith Publishing Company Staff, ed. Gonzalez, Juan, Jr., tr. LC 90-85751. (Illus.). 160p. (Orig.). 1990. pap. 6.00 (0-9625975-5-4) Faith Pub OH.

— The Bible & the Fatima Message. 1992. 0.50 (1-56036-043-7) AMI Pr.

— The Cause of Liberation in U. S. S. R. Turner, Leslie S., tr. LC 93-83222. 208p. 1993. pap. 9.95 (1-882972-07-4) Queenship Pub.

— The Hail Mary: Its Meaning & Its Origin. Faith Publishing Company Staff, ed. Fackovec, William, tr. LC 91-71542. 96p. (Orig.). 1991. pap. 4.00 (0-9625975-7-0) Faith Pub OH.

— The Meaning of Consecration Today: A Marian Model for a Secularized Age. LC 91-77302. 208p. (Orig.). 1992. pap. 12.95 (0-89870-403-0) Ignatius Pr.

— Medjugorje - Thirteen Years Later. LC 94-73972. 144p. (Orig.). 1995. pap. 6.00 (1-877678-33-3) Riehle Found.

— Nine Years of Apparitions: Toward the Revelation of the Ten Secrets? Riehle Foundation Staff, ed. Gonzalez, Juan, Jr., tr. LC 91-65667. (Illus.). 224p. (Orig.). 1991. pap. 7.00 (1-877678-15-5) Riehle Found.

— Our Lady of Argentina. 1993. pap. text ed. 29.00 (0-85597-538-5) St Mut.

— Our Lord & Our Lady in Scottsdale: Fruitful Charisms in a Traditional American Parish. Faith Publishing Company Staff, ed. Laguette, Doris & Laguette, Ernesto V., trs. LC 92-71737. (Illus.). 176p. (Orig.). 1992. pap. 7.00 (1-880033-02-X) Faith Pub OH.

— Pilgrimages, Sanctuaries, Icons, Apparitions: An Historical & Biblical Account. LC 94-61409. 128p. (Orig.). 1994. pap. 3.50 (1-877678-30-9) Riehle Found.

— A Short Treatise on the Virgin Mary. 1991. 14.95 (1-56036-015-1) AMI Pr.

— Ten Years of Apparitions: New Growth & Recognition of the Pilgrimages. Faith Publishing Company Staff, ed. Gonzalez, Juan, Jr., tr. LC 91-77083. 168p. (Orig.). 1991. pap. 6.00 (1-880033-01-1) Faith Pub OH.

— The Truth of Christmas Beyond the Myths: The Gospel of the Infancy of Christ. LC 85-1402. (Studies in Scripture: Vol. III). 1986. pap. 21.95 (0-932506-34-8) St Bedes Pubns.

— The Way of the Cross in Santa Maria. LC 93-83641. 86p. 1993. pap. 5.95 (1-882972-03-1) Queenship Pub.

— Why Prayer? And How to Pray. Faith Publishing Company Staff, ed. Gonzalez, Juan, Jr., tr. LC 90-84579. 104p. (Orig.). 1990. pap. 4.00 (0-9625975-3-8) Faith Pub OH.

— A Year of Grace with Mary. 162p. 1989. pap. 22.00 (0-86217-797-9, Pub. by Veritas IE) St Mut.

— A Year of Grace with Mary: Rediscovering Her Presence. 161p. (Orig.). 1987. pap. 10.95 (0-86217-279-9) Ignatius Pr.

Laurents, Arthur. A Clearing in the Woods. 1960. pap. 4.75 (0-8222-0215-8) Dramatists Play.

— The Enclave. 1974. pap. 4.75 (0-8222-0359-6) Dramatists Play.

— Home of the Brave. 1949. pap. 4.75 (0-8222-0529-7) Dramatists Play.

— Invitation to a March. 1963. pap. 4.75 (0-8222-0575-0) Dramatists Play.

— The Way We Were. 20.95 (0-88411-446-5, Aeonian Pr) Amereon Ltd.

Laurents, Arthur & Sondheim, Stephen. Gypsy. LC 94-2588. 120p. 1994. pap. 9.95 (1-55936-086-0) Theatre Comm.

***Laurents, David, ed.** The Badboy Book of Erotic Poetry. Date not set. mass mkt., pap. 5.95 (1-56333-382-1) Masquerade.

— Wanderlust: Homoerotic Tales of Travel. (Orig.). 1996. mass mkt., pap. 5.95 (1-56333-395-3) Masquerade.

Laurenzi, Elise & Levinson, Gerald B. Portraits of Garden Bedfellows: The Gardeners Guide to Plants that Go - & Grow - Well Together. LC 86-92069. (Illus.). 24p. 1987. pap. 5.95 (0-9617942-0-8) Corydalis Pr.

Laurenzo, Peter V. College Financial Aid: How to Get Your Fair Share. 80p. 1991. pap. 10.95 (0-9629961-0-6) Hudson Fin.

— College Financial Aid: How to Get Your Fair Share. rev. ed. (Illus.). 1993. pap. text ed. 9.95 (0-9629961-1-4) Hudson Fin.

Laures, John. Catholic Church in Japan: A Short History. LC 73-100165. 252p. 1970. reprint ed. text ed. 38.50 (0-8371-2974-5, LACC, Greenwood Pr) Greenwood.

Lauret, A., jt. auth. see Ginguay, Michel.

Lauret, Maria. Liberating Literature: Feminist Fiction in America. LC 93-48839. 256p. 1994. 59.95x (0-415-06515-1, A7971, Routledge NY); pap. 16.95 (0-415-06516-X, A7975, Routledge NY) Routledge.

Laurgaard, Rachel K. Patty Reed's Doll: The Story of the Donner Party. LC 89-51264. (Illus.). 144p. (J). (gr. 3-6). 1989. reprint ed. pap. 7.95 (0-9617357-2-4) Tomato Enter.

Laurgeau, Claude, jt. auth. see Parent, Michel.

Lauria, A. & Gandolfi, F., eds. Embryonic Development & Manipulation in Animal Production: Trends in Research & Applications. (Proceedings Ser.: Vol. 2). 282p. 1992. 115.00 (1-85578-033-X, Pub. by Portland Pr Ltd UK) Ashgate Pub Co.

Lauria, Frank. Blue Limbo. 352p. (Orig.). 1991. pap. 3.95 (0-380-76164-5) Avon.

Lauria, Peter. New York's Strongest. 181p. 1992. pap. 3.50 (0-9635713-0-3) Longshot Prod.

— Shedding Light. 135p. 1992. pap. write for info. (0-9635713-1-1) Longshot Prod.

Lauria, Vince. Learn to Burn on Rock Guitar. 1993. 6.95 (0-87166-765-7, 94136); audio 9.98 (1-56222-627-4, 94136); audio 15.95 (0-685-74548-1, 94136) Mel Bay.

Laurian. An End to Innocence. 1992. 17.95 (0-533-10198-0) Vantage.

Laurian, C., jt. auth. see George, B.

Lauriat, Peter M. Massachusetts Deposition Practice Manual. LC 92-64380. 482p. 1992. ring bd. 95.00 (0-944490-42-5) Mass CLE.

Lauridsen, David. The Token Economy System. Langdon, Danny G., ed. LC 77-25897. (Instructional Design Library). (Illus.). 96p. 1978. 23.95 (0-87778-123-0) Educ Tech Pubns.

Lauridsen, I. & Dalgaard, P. The Beat Generation & the Russian New Wave. 1991. 21.95 (0-87501-034-2) Ardis Pubs.

Lauridsen, Peter. Vitus Bering. LC 70-94274. (Select Bibliographies Reprint Ser.). 1977. 23.95 (0-8369-5048-8) Ayer.

Laurie, Alex, et al. Commercial Flower Forcing. 8th ed. (Illus.). 1979. text ed. write for info. (0-07-036633-0) McGraw.

Laurie, Arthur P. Painter's Methods & Materials. (Illus.). 1967. reprint ed. pap. 8.95 (0-486-21868-6) Dover.

Laurie, Bruce. Artisans into Workers: Labor in Nineteenth-Century America. 1989. pap. 9.95 (0-374-52153-0) FS&G.

An Asterisk (*) at the beginning of an entry indicates that the title is appearing in BIP for the first time.

— The Life of Richard Kane: Britain's First Lieutenant-Governor of Minorca. LC 92-54650. 1994. write for info. (*0-8386-3501-6*) Fairleigh Dickinson.

Laurie, David. Reminiscences of a Fiddle Dealer. (Illus.). 1977. reprint ed. text ed. 22.00 (*0-918624-01-0*) Virtuoso.

Laurie, David R., jt. auth. see Corbin, Charles B.

Laurie, Dirk P. Numerical Solution of Partial Differential Equations. (International Series of Numerical Mathematics: Vol. 66). 334p. (C). 1983. text ed. 54.95 (*3-7643-1561-X*) Birkhauser.

Laurie, Doug, jt. auth. see Cape, Dave.

***Laurie, Erynn R.** A Circle of Stones: Journeys & Meditations for Modern Celts. 112p. 1995. 9.95 (*1-57353-106-5*, Eschaton Bks) Eschaton Prods.

Laurie, G. & Raymond, J., eds. Proceedings of G. I. N. I.'s Third International Polio & Independent Living Conference, May 10-12, 1985, St. Louis, Missouri. 68p. (Orig.). 1986. pap. 15.00 (*0-931301-02-5*) Gazette Intl.

— Proceedings of Rehabilitation Gazette's Second International Post-Polio Conference & Symposium on Living Independently with Severe Disability. 74p. (Orig.). 1984. pap. 15.00 (*0-931301-01-7*) Gazette Intl.

Laurie, G., et al, eds. Handbook on the Late Effects of Poliomyelitis for Physicians & Survivors. 48p. (Orig.). 1984. pap. 5.00 (*0-931301-00-9*) Gazette Intl.

Laurie, Greg. Discipleship: Giving God Your Best. LC 92-20897. 1993. pap. 3.99 (*1-56507-039-9*) Harvest Hse.

— Every Day with Jesus. LC 93-19334. 1993. 17.99 (*1-56507-058-5*) Harvest Hse.

— God's Design for Christian Dating. 2nd ed. LC 82-83836. 96p. (YA). (gr. 10-12). 1983. mass mkt. 2.99 (*0-89081-373-6*) Harvest Hse.

— New Believers Growth Book. 1994. pap. 5.99 (*0-8499-3587-3*) Word Inc.

— On Fire! LC 92-12396. 1993. pap. 7.99 (*0-89081-946-7*) Harvest Hse.

Laurie, Hilary, ed. see Moore, George E.

Laurie, Ian C., ed. Nature in Cities: The Natural Environment in the Design & Development of Urban Green Space. LC 77-20987. 448p. reprint ed. pap. 127.70 (*0-317-30322-8*, 2024803) Bks Demand.

Laurie, J. R., jt. ed. see Webby, B. D.

Laurie, Jessica. The Mistress of Harrowgate. 1981. pap. 2.25 (*0-89083-772-4*) Zebra.

Laurie, Joe, Jr., jt. auth. see Green, Abel.

Laurie, John C. The Science of Numerology Through the Law of Vibration. 75p. 1959. reprint ed. spiral bd. 7.15 (*0-7873-0537-5*) Mokelumne.

Laurie, Lucy. A Day in the Country. (J). 1990. 29.00 (*0-85439-374-9*, Pub. by St Paul Pubns UK) St Mut.

— A Way of Living. 109p. (C). 1990. text ed. 29.00 (*0-85439-348-X*, Pub. by St Paul Pubns UK) St Mut.

Laurie, Marjorie, tr. see De Maupassant, Guy.

Laurie, Michael. Introduction to Landscape Architecture. 2nd ed. xii, 248p. 1985. 41.00 (*0-444-00970-1*) P-H.

Laurie, Peter. Databases: How to Manage Information on Your Micro. (Illus.). 200p. (Orig.). 1985. pap. 19.95 (*0-412-26380-7*, NO. 9317) Chapman & Hall.

Laurie, Robertson-Lorant. Biography of Herman Melville. 1995. 35.00 (*0-517-59314-9*) Crown Pub Group.

***Laurie, Ron.** Auditioning: A Practical Guide for the Would-Be Actor & Drama Student. 64p. (Orig.). (YA). 1994. pap. 5.00 (*0-85343-585-5*, Pub. by J G Miller Ltd UK) Empire Pub Srvs.

Laurie, S. S. Studies in the History of Educational Opinion from the Renaissance. 261p. 1968. reprint ed. 30.00 (*0-7146-1447-5*, Pub. by F Cass Pubs UK) Intl Spec Bk.

Laurie, Sanders G. & Tucker, Melvin J. Centering: A Guide to Inner Growth. 2nd ed. LC 92-44726. 224p. 1993. pap. 9.95 (*0-89281-420-9*, Destiny Bks) Inner Tradit.

Laurie, Simon S. Historical Survey of Pre-Christian Education. 1977. lib. bdg. 59.95 (*0-8490-1954-0*) Gordon Pr.

— Historical Survey of Pre-Christian Education. 2nd rev. ed. LC 79-124596. reprint ed. 55.00 (*0-404-03889-1*) AMS Pr.

— Historical Survey of Pre-Christian Education. LC 76-108504. 1970. reprint ed. 25.00 (*0-403-00214-1*) Scholarly.

— Studies in the History of Educational Opinion from the Renaissance. LC 72-93272. vi, 261p. 1969. reprint ed. 35.00 (*0-678-05086-4*) Kelley.

Laurie, Williams, ed. see Williams, John J.

Laurier. Catharsis: Poems by Laurier. 65p. (Orig.). Date not set. pap. 9.95 (*1-55605-231-6*) Wyndhall Pr.

Lauriere, J. Problem Solving & Artificial Intelligence. 1990. pap. text ed. 29.80 (*0-13-711748-5*) P-H.

Laurikainen, K. V. & Montonen, C. Foundations of Modern Physics, 1992: Proceedings of the Symposium. 460p. 1993. text ed. 116.00 (*981-02-1324-7*) World Scientific Pub.

Laurila, J. & Hattari, A. Paper Container Dictionary, English, Finnish, Russian, Swedish, French, Spanish: Paperi-Ja Kartonkisanakirja Englanti-Suomi-Ruotsi-Saksa-Ranska-Espanja. 839p. (ENG, FIN, FRE, GER, SPA & SWE.). 1986. 295.00 (*0-8288-0334-X*, F23020) Fr & Eur.

Laurila, Simo H. Electronic Surveying in Practice. LC 82-20127. 401p. reprint ed. pap. 114.30 (*0-7837-2817-4*, 2057655) Bks Demand.

Laurillard, Diana. Re-Thinking University Teaching: A Framework for the Effective Use of Educational Technology. LC 93-20258. 272p. 1993. 59.95 (*0-415-09288-4*, B2541, Routledge NY); pap. 16.95 (*0-415-09289-2*, B2545, Routledge NY) Routledge.

Laurin. Atlas of Orthopedic Surgery, Set. (Illus.). 1992. 249.00 (*0-8151-5347-3*, Yr Bk Med Pubs) Mosby Yr Bk.

— Atlas of Orthopedic Surgery, Vol. 1: General. 1989. 99.50 (*0-8151-5344-9*, Yr Bk Med Pubs) Mosby Yr Bk.

Laurin, Anne. Perfect Crane. LC 80-7912. (Illus.). 32p. (J). (gr. 1-4). 1981. lib. bdg. 14.89 (*0-06-023744-9*) HarpC Child Bks.

— Perfect Crane. LC 80-7912. (Trophy Picture Bk.). (Illus.). 32p. (J). (gr. 1-4). 1987. pap. 4.95 (*0-06-443154-1*, Trophy) HarpC Child Bks.

Laurin, C. A., et al. Atlas of Orthopedic Surgery, Vol. II: Upper Extremity. (Illus.). 456p. 1990. 99.50 (*0-8151-5343-0*, Yr Bk Med Pubs) Mosby Yr Bk.

Laurin, Carl, et al. Scandinavian Art. LC 69-13242. (Illus.). 1972. reprint ed. 52.95 (*0-405-08735-7*) Ayer.

Laurin, Riley & Roy, Camille. Atlas of Orthopedic Surgery, Vol. 3: Lower Extremity. (Illus.). 751p. 1992. 95.00 (*0-8151-5345-7*) Mosby Yr Bk.

Laurin, Robert B. The Layperson's Introduction to the Old Testament. rev. ed. 1990. pap. 10.00 (*0-8170-1163-3*) Judson.

Laurin, Roy L. Acts of the Apostles: Life in Action. LC 85-8158. 408p. 1985. pap. 12.99 (*0-8254-3127-1*) Kregel.

— Colossians: Where Life Is Established. LC 88-12129. 192p. (C). reprint ed. pap. 8.99 (*0-8254-3135-2*) Kregel.

— Designed for Conquest: Biblical Models for Overcoming Life's Struggles. LC 90-36540. Orig. Title: Meet Yourself in the Bible. 189p. 1990. reprint ed. pap. 7.99 (*0-8254-3139-5*) Kregel.

— First Corinthians: Where Life Matures. LC 86-7163. 332p. 1987. reprint ed. pap. 10.99 (*0-8254-3132-8*) Kregel.

— First John: Life at its Best. LC 86-27394. 196p. (C). 1987. reprint ed. pap. 8.99 (*0-8254-3136-0*) Kregel.

— Philippians: Where Life Advances. LC 86-7177. 208p. 1987. reprint ed. pap. 8.99 (*0-8254-3134-4*) Kregel.

— Romans: Where Life Begins. LC 88-12130. 540p. pap. 15.99 (*0-8254-3130-1*) Kregel.

— Second Corinthians: Where Life Endures. LC 85-8154. 248p. 1985. pap. 10.99 (*0-8254-3129-8*) Kregel.

Lauring, Palle. History of Denmark. (Reprints Ser.). (Illus.). 274p. 1991. 24.95 (*0-88029-608-9*) Dorset Pr.

Laurini, Robert & Thompson, Derek. Fundamentals of Spatial Information Systems. (APIC Ser.). (Illus.). 704p. 1992. text ed. 49.95 (*0-12-438380-7*) Acad Pr.

Lauriston, Andy. Bilingual Dictionary of International Telecommunications, Vol. 2: Transmission Equipment. 506p. (ENG & FRE.). 1985. 225.00 (*0-8288-9449-3*) Fr & Eur.

— Bilingual Dictionary of International Telecommunications, Vol. 3: Switching Equipment. 544p. (ENG & FRE.). 1988. 225.00 (*0-8288-9450-7*) Fr & Eur.

— Bilingual Dictionary of International Telecommunications, Vol. 4: Telecommunications Services. 547p. (ENG & FRE.). 225.00 (*0-8288-9451-5*) Fr & Eur.

Laurita, Raymond E. Building Word Power Through Spelling Mastery: Questions & Answers about Words & Their Origins. 64p. (Orig.). (YA). (gr. 6-12). 1991. pap. text ed. 9.50 (*0-914051-25-3*) Leonardo Pr.

— The Complete & Simplified Spelling Book of Verbs. 87p. (Orig.). 1984. pap. 9.95 (*0-914051-02-4*) Leonardo Pr.

— The Complete How to Book: One Hundred One Lessons about Language. 400p. (Orig.). (J). (gr. 1-12). 1995. pap. text ed. 21.95 (*0-914051-34-2*) Leonardo Pr.

— The Day-by-Day Way to Spelling Mastery. 103p. (Orig.). 1993. pap. 10.50 (*0-914051-33-4*) Leonardo Pr.

— Greek Roots & Their Modern English Spelling: A Dictionary of Roots Transliterated from Ancient Greek with Their Modern English Spellings. LC 89-63327. 296p. (Orig.). (C). 1989. pap. text ed. 18.95 (*0-914051-10-5*) Leonardo Pr.

— A Handy Guide to Greek Derived Affixes. 70p. (Orig.). 1994. pap. text ed. 12.95x (*0-914051-35-0*) Leonardo Pr.

— The How to Books, Vol. IV, Bks. 19-24. 145p. (Orig.). 1989. pap. 15.00 (*0-914051-16-4*) Leonardo Pr.

— Lessons from the Spelling Doctor: Essays on the Way Words Work. 117p. (Orig.). 1991. pap. 12.50 (*0-914051-19-9*) Leonardo Pr.

— One Thousand & One Affixes & Their Meanings: A Dictionary of Prefixes, Suffixes & Inflections. rev. ed. 154p. 1990. pap. 14.95 (*0-914051-18-0*) Leonardo Pr.

— One Thousand & One Homonyms & Their Meanings: A Dictionary of Homonyms with Defining Sentences. 160p. (Orig.). 1992. pap. 13.95 (*0-914051-29-6*) Leonardo Pr.

— Reading, Writing & Creativity. LC 72-75225. 253p. (Orig.). 1973. pap. text ed. 9.95 (*0-914051-15-6*) Leonardo Pr.

— The Spelling Doctor Says..., Pt. 1: (Roots 1-10) 87p. (Orig.). (J). 1991. pap. text ed. 11.00 (*0-914051-20-2*) Leonardo Pr.

— Spelling Keys to Five Hundred One Words from 12 Old-Middle English Roots. 63p. (Orig.). 1992. pap. text ed. 9.50 (*0-914051-31-8*) Leonardo Pr.

— Spelling Keys to One Thousand One Words from Ten Greek Based Roots. 80p. (Orig.). (YA). (gr. 8-12). 1991. pap. text ed. 11.50 (*0-914051-26-1*) Leonardo Pr.

— Spelling Keys to One Thousand Words from 10 Latin Based Roots. 64p. (Orig.). 1991. pap. text ed. 9.50 (*0-914051-24-5*) Leonardo Pr.

— Spelling Keys to Two Thousand One Words from 10 Indo-European Roots. 140p. (Orig.). 1992. pap. text ed. 14.95 (*0-914051-30-X*) Leonardo Pr.

— The Vowel Category Individual Spelling Set, Pt. 1. 112p. (Orig.). (J). (gr. 1-6). 1980. pap. 28.95 (*0-914051-08-3*) Leonardo Pr.

— The Vowel Category Individual Spelling Set, Pt. 2. 305p. (Orig.). (J). (gr. 6 up). 1982. pap. 34.95 (*0-914051-09-1*) Leonardo Pr.

— The Vowel Category Resource Lists, Pt. 1. 112p. (Orig.). (J). (ps-8). 1980. pap. 13.95 (*0-914051-04-0*) Leonardo Pr.

— The Vowel Category Resource Lists, Pt. 1 (Lessons 1-15) 112p. (Orig.). (J). (ps-8). 1980. Stages 1-15. student ed, pap. 8.50 (*0-914051-05-9*) Leonardo Pr.

— The Vowel Category Resource Lists, Pt. 1 (Lessons 16-30) 112p. (Orig.). (J). (ps-8). 1980. Stages 16-30. student ed, pap. 8.50 (*0-914051-14-8*) Leonardo Pr.

— The Vowel Category Resource Lists, Pt. II. 305p. (Orig.). (J). (gr. 6 up). 1989. pap. 17.95 (*0-914051-06-7*) Leonardo Pr.

— The Vowel Category Resource Lists, Pt. 2 (Lessons 1-15) 305p. (Orig.). (J). (gr. 6 up). 1989. Stages 1-15. student ed, pap. 8.50 (*0-914051-07-5*) Leonardo Pr.

— The Vowel Category Resource Lists, Pt. 2 (Lessons 16-30) 305p. (Orig.). (J). (gr. 6 up). 1989. Stages 16-30. student ed, pap. 8.50 (*0-914051-17-2*) Leonardo Pr.

Lauritis, K. N., jt. ed. see Reifsnider, K. L.

Lauritsen, John. The AIDS War: Propaganda, Profiteering & Genocide from the Medical-Industrial Complex. (Illus.). 480p. (Orig.). 1993. pap. 20.00 (*0-943742-08-0*, Asklepios) Pagan Pr.

— A Freethinker's Primer on Male Love. LC 86-60441. (Illus.). 96p. (Orig.). 1996. pap. text ed. write for info. (*0-943742-04-8*) Pagan Pr.

— Poison by Prescription: The AZT Story. LC 90-81328. (Illus.). 192p. (Orig.). 1990. pap. 12.00 (*0-943742-06-4*, Asklepios) Pagan Pr.

Lauritsen, John & Thorstad, David. Early Homosexual Rights Movement (1864-1935) LC 74-79104. (Illus.). 96p. (Orig.). (C). 1974. 10.95 (*0-87810-527-1*) Times Change.

Lauritsen, John, ed. see Thomson, Michael M.

Lauritzen, jt. auth. see Cecil.

Lauritzen, C., ed. see Estrogens in the Post-Menopause Workshop Staff.

Lauritzen, Cyndi. Create & Write. (Learning Works Creative Writing Ser.). 48p. (J). (gr. 4-6). 1982. 5.95 (*0-88160-052-0*, LW 238) Learning Wks.

Lauritzen, Hal, jt. auth. see Ashley, Beth.

Lauritzen, Paul. Pursuing Parenthood: Ethical Issues in Assisted Reproduction. LC 92-16511. (Medical Ethics Ser.). 192p. 1992. 19.95 (*0-253-33261-3*) Ind U Pr.

— Religious Belief & Emotional Transformation: A Light in the Heart. LC 91-55509. 128p. 1992. 29.50 (*0-8387-5217-9*) Bucknell U Pr.

Lauritzen, Peter, tr. see Fernandez, Dominique.

Lauritzen, S. L. Extremal Families & Systems of Sufficient Statistics. (Lecture Notes in Statistics Ser.: Vol. 49). (Illus.). xv, 268p. 1988. pap. 39.00 (*0-387-96872-5*) Spr-Verlag.

Laurmann, J. A., jt. auth. see Robinson, Abraham.

Lauro, Al Di, jt. auth. see Rabkin, G.

***Lauro, N. C., et al.** Evaluation of Doses Programme Development of Statistical Expert Systems (1989-1993) No. 57. (Research Evaluation Report Ser.: No. Eur 15328). 121p. 1993. pap. 20.00 (*92-826-6736-7*, CGNA15328ENC, Pub. by Europ Com) UNIPUB.

Lauro, Shirley. The Coal Diamond. 1979. pap. 2.75 (*0-8222-0223-9*) Dramatists Play.

***Laursen, Brett, ed.** Close Friendships in Adolescence. LC 85-644581. (New Directions for Child Development Ser.: No. 60). 110p. (Orig.). 1993. pap. 17.95 (*1-55542-689-1*) Jossey-Bass.

Laursen, Byron, jt. auth. see Jack, Wolfman.

Laursen, Byron, jt. auth. see Wolfman Jack.

Laursen, Dan. Quarternary Shells Collected by the Fifth Thule Expedition 1921-24. LC 76-21342. (Thule Expedition, 5th, 1921-1924 Ser.: Vol. 1, No. 7). (Illus.). reprint ed. 28.00 (*0-404-58307-5*) AMS Pr.

Laursen, Finn. Small Powers at Sea: Scandinavia & the New International Marine Order. LC 93-10952. 336p. (C). 1993. lib. bdg. 119.00 (*0-7923-2341-6*) Kluwer Ac.

— Superpower at Sea: U. S. Ocean Policy. LC 83-21222. 224p. 1983. text ed. 55.00 (*0-275-91033-4*, C1033, Praeger Pubs) Greenwood.

— Toward a New International Marine Order. 1982. lib. bdg. 94.00 (*90-247-2597-6*) Kluwer Ac.

***Laursen, Finn & Vanhoonacker, Sophie, eds.** The Ratification of the Maastricht Treaty: Issues, Debates & Future Implications. LC 94-34814. 1994. lib. bdg. 152.00 (*0-7923-3125-7*) Kluwer Ac.

Laursen, Gary A. & Ammirati, Joseph F. Arctic & Alpine Mycology: The First International Symposium on Arcto-Alpine Mycology. LC 81-51281. 502p. 1981. 60.00 (*0-295-95856-1*) U of Wash Pr.

Laursen, Gary A., jt. auth. see Petrini, Orlando.

Laursen, Gary A., et al, eds. Arctic & Alpine Mycology II. LC 87-7814. (Environmental Science Research Ser.: Vol. 34). 374p. 1987. 120.00 (*0-306-42558-0*, Plenum Pr) Plenum.

Laursen, Harold I. Structural Analysis. 3rd ed. 512p. (C). 1988. text ed. write for info. (*0-07-036645-4*) McGraw.

Laursen, John, ed. see Chalmers, Wilma G.

Laursen, John, ed. see Edwards, G. Thomas.

Laursen, John C. The Politics of Skepticism in the Ancients, Montaigne, Hume, & Kant. LC 92-28512. (Brill's Studies in Intellectual History: Vol. 35). 253p. 1992. 71.50 (*90-04-09459-8*) E J Brill.

***Laursen, John C., ed.** New Essays on the Political Thought of the Huguenots of the Refuge. LC 94-24939. (Brill's Studies in Intellectual History: Vol. 60). 1994. 57.25 (*90-04-09986-7*) E J Brill.

Laursen, Per M. Description of Various Leafcasters, 1956-1982: Translation of Selected Passages in Beschreibung verschiedener Anfaserungsgerate, 1983. McCrady, Ellen R., ed. Tonnies, Moya, tr. (Monograph to Abbey Newsletter: Suppl. 2). (Illus.). v, 23p. (Orig.). 1992. pap. 30.00 (*0-9622071-1-X*) Abbey Pubns.

Laury, Jean R. The Creative Woman's Getting It All Together at Home Handbook. 2nd ed. (Illus.). reprint ed. pap. 8.95 (*0-9614804-0-8*) Hot Fudge Pr.

— Fourteen Thousand, Two Hundred Eighty-Seven Pieces of Fabric & Other Poems. Townsend, Louise O. & Lytle, Joyce E., eds. LC 93-34220. (Illus.). 48p. 1994. 17.95 (*0-914881-75-2*) C & T Pub.

— Imagery on Fabric. Nadel, Harold, ed. LC 92-538028. (Illus.). 128p. 1992. pap. 24.95 (*0-914881-56-6*) C & T Pub.

— Incredible Quilts for Kids of All Ages. LC 93-8358. 160p. 1993. pap. 21.95 (*0-913327-40-9*) Quilt Digest Pr.

— Keeping It All Together: The Not-Just-for-Quiltmakers Coping Book. 50p. (Orig.). 1983. pap. 5.95 (*0-9602970-5-7*) Leman Pubns.

— No Dragons On My Quilt. (J). (gr. k up). 1990. 12.95 (*0-89145-967-7*) Collector Bks.

— Sunbonnet Sue Gets It All Together at Home. (Adventures of Sunbonnet Sue Ser.). (Illus.). 24p. (Orig.). 1987. pap. 4.95 (*0-8442-2611-4*) Quilt Digest Pr.

— Sunbonnet Sue Goes to the Quilt Show. (Adventures of Sunbonnet Sue). (Illus.). 24p. (Orig.). 1987. pap. text ed. 4.95 (*0-8442-2610-6*) Quilt Digest Pr.

— Sunbonnet Sue Makes Her First Quilt. (Adventures of Sunbonnet Sue Ser.). (Illus.). 24p. (Orig.). 1987. pap. 4.95 (*0-8442-2609-2*) Quilt Digest Pr.

Laury, Samuel S. Elsa Von Eltz. 1993. 14.95 (*0-533-10377-0*) Vantage.

Laus, Universa. Growing in Church Music. 1985. 4.50 (*0-9602378-1-X*) Pastoral Pr.

Lausanne Committee Staff. Proclaim Christ until He Comes. 1990. pap. 16.95 (*0-89066-190-1*) World Wide Pubs.

Lausch, David, Graphics Staff, illus. U. S. Virgins Swimsuit Calendar, 1990. 8p. 1989. 9.95 (*0-927400-00-6*) Deaner Pub.

Lause, David B., jt. auth. see Colborn, Gene L.

Lause, Mark. Some Degree of Power: From Hired Hand to Union Craftsman in the Preindustrial American Printing Trade, 1778-1815. 224p. 1991. 28.00 (*1-55728-185-8*) U of Ark Pr.

Lause, Mary, ed. see Hill, Wanda J., et al.

***Laushey, David M.** A Primer for American History. LC 95-77375. (Illus.). 240p. (Orig.). (C). 1995. pap. text ed. write for info. (*0-15-502081-1*) HB Coll Pubs.

Laussat, Anthony, Jr. An Essay on Equity in Pennsylvania. LC 76-37981. (American Law Ser.: The Formative Years). 164p. 1972. reprint ed. 16.95 (*0-405-04024-5*) Ayer.

Laustsen, S., et al. Exploring the Southern Sky: A Pictorial Atlas from the European Southern Observatory. (Illus.). 274p. 1987. 59.00 (*0-387-17735-3*) Spr-Verlag.

Laut, Agnes C. Pathfinders of the West. LC 74-90651. (Essay Index Reprint Ser.). 1977. 30.95 (*0-8369-1220-9*) Ayer.

— The Romance of the Rails, 2 vols., Set. LC 75-37891. (Select Bibliographies Reprint Ser.). 1977. reprint ed. 48.95 (*0-8369-6728-3*) Ayer.

Laut, Phil. Money Is My Friend. 160p. 1990. mass mkt. 5.99 (*0-8041-0534-0*) Ivy Books.

— Money Is My Friend. rev. ed. LC 79-51206. 150p. 1989. pap. 7.95 (*0-9610132-2-2*) Vivation Pub.

Laut, Phil, jt. auth. see Leonard, Jim.

Lautenbach, E. Zahn - Mund - Kiefer: Rezepte und Therapien. (Illus.). vi, 1266p. 1990. 130.50 (*3-8055-5098-7*) S Karger.

Lauter, Estella. Women As Mythmakers: Poetry & Visual Art by Twentieth-Century Women. LC 83-48636. (Illus.). 288p. 1984. 35.00 (*0-253-36606-2*); pap. 14.95 (*0-253-20325-2*, MB-325) Ind U Pr.

Lauter, Estella & Rupprecht, Carol S., eds. Feminist Archetypal Theory: Interdisciplinary Re-visions of Jungian Thought. LC 84-12007. 304p. 1985. text ed. 32.00x (*0-87049-447-3*) U of Tenn Pr.

— Feminist Archetypal Theory: Interdisciplinary Re-Visions of Jungian Thought. LC 84-12007. (Illus.). Date not set. reprint ed. pap. 86.10 (*0-7837-9508-4*, 2060258) Bks Demand.

Lauter, Fred, ed. see Green, Coppie, et al.

Lauter, G. Peter, jt. auth. see Chikara Higashi.

Lauter, H. J., jt. ed. see Fedorov, V.

Lauter, H. J., jt. ed. see Wyatt, A. F.

Lauter, Ken. Before the Light. LC 87-70810. (Target Midwest Poetry Ser.). 64p. 1987. 8.95 (*0-933532-66-0*) BkMk.

Lauter-Klatell, Nancy. Readings in Child Development. LC 90-46200. 178p. (C). 1991. pap. text ed. 20.95 (*0-87484-942-X*) Mayfield Pub.

Lauter, Paul. Canons & Context. 320p. 1991. pap. 19.95 (*0-19-506832-7*) OUP.

Lauter, Paul, ed. Reconstructing American Literature: Courses, Syllabi, Issues. LC 83-20730. 288p. 1983. pap. 12.95 (*0-935312-14-5*) Feminist Pr.

***Lauter, Paul & Yarborough, Richard, eds.** The Heath Anthology of American Literature, 2 vols., Vol. 2. 2nd ed. 3156p. (C). 1994. pap. text ed. write for info. (*0-669-32973-8*) Heath.

Lauter, Paul, et al, eds. The Heath Anthology of American Literature, 2 vols. (C). 1990. pap. text ed. 19.50 (*0-685-74209-1*); Instr.'s guide, 752 p. teacher ed 2.00 (*0-669-12066-9*); Suppl. to Vol. 2, Selections from Whitman & Dickinson, 212 p. write for info. (*0-669-24998-X*) Heath.

— The Heath Anthology of American Literature, 2 vols., Vol. 1. 2935p. (C). 1990. pap. text ed. 19.50 (*0-669-12064-2*) Heath.

— The Heath Anthology of American Literature, 2 vols., Vol. 1. 2nd ed. 2965p. (C). 1994. pap. text ed. write for info. (*0-669-32972-X*) Heath.

— The Heath Anthology of American Literature, 2 vols., Vol. 2. 2615p. (C). 1990. pap. text ed. 19.50 (*0-669-12065-0*) Heath.

Lauterbach & Salisbury, E., trs. Soviet Psychotherapy. (Illus.). 255p. 1984. 109.00 (*0-08-024291-X*, Pub. by Pergamon Repr UK) Franklin.

Lauterbach, Ann. And, for Example: Poems. LC 94-5814. (Poets Ser.). 1994. 25.95 (*0-670-85883-8*, Penguin Classics); pap. 14.95 (*0-14-058715-2*, Penguin Classics) Viking Penguin.

— Before Recollection. 80p. 1987. text ed. 21.95 (0-691-06698-1); pap. text ed. 9.95 (0-691-01437-X) Princeton U Pr.

— Clamor. 96p. 1992. pap. 11.00 (0-14-058673-3, Penguin Bks) Viking Penguin.

Lauterbach, C. A., jt. auth. see Schumann, K. M.

***Lauterbach, Christiane.** Atlanta Restaurant Guide. 1995. pap. 9.95 (1-56554-031-X) Pelican.

Lauterbach, Christiane, jt. auth. see Cutler, William.

Lauterbach, Eva, ed. Eurythmy: Essays & Anecdotes in Art, Education & Therapy. LC 80-22938. (Illus.). 256p. (Orig.). 1981. pap. 15.95 (0-935690-01-8) Schaumburg Pubns.

Lauterbach, F., jt. ed. see Kramer, M.

Lauterbach, Jacob Z. Rabbinic Essays. LC 52-18170. 586p. reprint ed. pap. 167.10 (0-317-42031-3, 2025693) Bks Demand.

Lauterbach, Jeffery R., jt. auth. see Gourgues, Harold W., Jr.

Lauterbach, William A. Prayers for the Sickroom. 64p. 1953. pap. 1.95 (0-570-03524-4, 14-1236) Concordia.

Lauterback, Ruth A. Intruder in the House. (Illus.). 75p. 1987. 10.95 (0-9618709-0-7) Leander Pub.

***Lauterborn, W., et al.** Coherent Optics. 1995. 49.00 (0-387-58372-6) Spr-Verlag.

Lauterborn, W., ed. Cavitation & Inhomogeneities in Underwater Acoustics: Proceedings. (Electrophysics Ser.: Vol. 4). (Illus.). 319p. 1980. 46.00 (0-387-09939-5) Spr-Verlag.

***Lauterborn, W., et al.** Coherent Optics: Fundamentals & Applications. LC 95-9942. 1995. 49.00 (3-540-58372-6) Spr-Verlag.

Lauterer, Jock. Hogwild. (Illus.). (Orig.). 1993. pap. text ed. 12.95 (0-913239-69-0) Appalach Consortium.

— Runnin' on Rims: Appalachian Profiles. (Illus.). 284p. 1986. 24.95 (0-912697-33-4) Algonquin Bks.

— Wouldn't Take Nothin' for My Journey Now. LC 80-13425. (Illus.). 186p. reprint ed. pap. 53.10 (0-8357-3888-4, 2036620) Bks Demand.

Lauterjung, Helmut & Schmidt, Gangolf. Planning of Intake Structures. Deutsches Zentrum fur Entwicklungs-technologien-GATE, ed. (GATE Ser.). (Illus.). 122p. 1989. pap. 22.00 (3-528-02042-3, Pub. by Vieweg & Sohn GW) Ballen Bkslr.

Lautermilch, Steven. Grass Script. Sherman, Alana & DeGennaro, Lorraine, eds. 16p. (Orig.). 1991. pap. 4.95 (0-939689-14-6) Alms Hse Pr.

Lauterpacht, E. Aspects of the Administration of International Justice. 200p. (C). 1991. 140.00 (0-949009-90-3, Pub. by Grotius Pubns UK) St Mut.

Lauterpacht, E., comp. The United Nations Emergency Force: Basic Documents. (International & Comparative Law Quarterly Supplement Publication Ser.: No. 3). 1974. reprint ed. pap. 15.00 (0-8115-3194-5) Periodicals Srv.

Lauterpacht, E. & Greenwood, C. J. International Law Reports, 80 vols. (C). 1989. text ed. 11,800.00 (0-7855-0123-1, Pub. by Grotius Pubns UK) St Mut.

— International Law Reports, 88 vols. (C). 1993. text ed. 320.00 (0-318-70314-9, Pub. by Grotius Pubns UK) St Mut.

— International Law Reports, 80 vols., 80. (C). 1989. text ed. 270.00 (0-685-63529-5, Pub. by Grotius Pubns UK) St Mut.

— International Law Reports, 88 vols., Set. (C). 1993. text ed. 18,134.00x (0-318-70313-0, Pub. by Grotius Pubns UK) St Mut.

— International Law Reports, 80 vols., Vols. 1-50. (C). 1989. text ed. 140.00 (0-318-70033-6, Pub. by Grotius Pubns UK) St Mut.

— International Law Reports, 80 vols., Vols. 51-74. (C). 1989. text ed. 234.00 (0-318-70034-4, Pub. by Grotius Pubns UK) St Mut.

— International Law Reports, 80 vols., Vols. 75-79. (C). 1989. text ed. 254.00 (0-318-70035-2, Pub. by Grotius Pubns UK) St Mut.

***Lauterpacht, E. & Greenwood, C. J., eds.** International Law Reports, Vol. 100. 650p. (C). 1995. 135.00 (0-521-49647-0) Cambridge U Pr.

— International Law Reports, Vol. 101. 650p. (C). 1995. 135.00 (0-521-49648-9) Cambridge U Pr.

Lauterpacht, E., jt. ed. see Bethlehem, D. L.

Lauterpacht, E., ed. see Lauterpacht, Hersch.

Lauterpacht, E., ed. see Lauterpacht, Hersh.

Lauterpacht, E., jt. ed. see Weller, Marc.

Lauterpacht, E., et al. The Kuwait Crisis: Basic Documents. 330p. (C). 1991. pap. 140.00 (0-949009-86-5, Pub. by Grotius Pubns UK) St Mut.

Lauterpacht, Hersch. The Development of International Law by the International Court. 427p. (C). 1982. 150.00 (0-906496-30-6, Pub. by Grotius Pubns UK) St Mut.

— International Law: The Law of Peace, 4 vols. Lauterpacht, E., ed. Incl. Vol. 1. LC 70-92250. 500p. 1970. 140.00 (0-521-07643-9); LC 70-92250. write for info. (0-318-51283-1) Cambridge U Pr.

Lauterpacht, Hersh. International Law Vol. 2, Pt. 1: The Law of Peace: International Law in General. Lauterpacht, E., ed. LC 70-92250. 612p. reprint ed. Vol. 2, Pt. 1, The Law of Peace: International Law in General. pap. 174.50 (0-685-20556-8, 2030603) Bks Demand.

— Recognition in International Law. LC 76-29419. reprint ed. 31.00 (0-404-15338-0) AMS Pr.

Lauth, Thomas P., jt. auth. see Abney, Glenn.

Lauth, Thomas P., jt. ed. see Clynch, Edward J.

Lauther, Howard. Punctuation Thesaurus of the English Language. 360p. 1991. 19.95 (0-8283-1945-6) Branden Pub Co.

— The Resume Reference Book. LC 89-43711. (Illus.). 151p. 1990. pap. 19.95 (0-89950-498-1) McFarland & Co.

Lautier, Jack. Fenway Voices: From Smoky Joe to Rocket Roger. (Illus.). 208p. (Orig.). 1990. pap. 10.95 (0-89909-324-8, 80-551-4) Yankee Bks.

Lautman, Kay P. & Goldstein, Henry, eds. Dear Friend: Mastering the Art of Direct-Mail Fund Raising. 2nd ed. 378p. 1991. 70.00 (0-930807-18-9, 600301) Fund Raising.

Lautman, Victoria. The New Tattoo. LC 94-5033. (Illus.). 1994. 40.00 (1-55859-785-9) Abbeville Pr.

Lautner, Peter, tr. see Simplicius.

Lautreamont. Oeuvres Completes: Les Chants de Maldoror; Lettres; Poesies. (Poesie Ser.). 512p. (FRE.). 1973. pap. 12.95 (2-07-032000-6) Schoenhof.

Lautreamont, Comte. Oeuvres Completes. deluxe ed. (Pleiade Ser.). (FRE.). 77.95 (2-07-010304-8) Schoenhof.

Lautreamont, Comte D., pseud. Maldoror. Wernham, Guy, tr. LC 66-12289. 1947. pap. 11.95 (0-8112-0082-5, NDP207) New Directions.

Lautreamont, Comte D. Maldoror & Poems. Knight, Paul, tr. 288p. 1988. mass mkt. 10.95 (0-14-044342-8, Penguin Classics) Viking Penguin.

Lautreamont, Isidore de. Oeuvres Completes. 428p. 1970. 19.95 (0-686-54284-3) Fr & Eur.

Lautreamont-Nouveau. Oeuvres Completes. Walzer, Gerard, ed. 1488p. (FRE.). 1970. lib. bdg. 110.00 (0-7859-3763-3, 2070103048) Fr & Eur.

Lautrup, B., jt. auth. see Brunak, S.

Lautt, W. Wayne, ed. Hepatic Circulation in Health & Disease. 392p. 1981. text ed. 101.50 (0-89004-617-4) Raven.

Lauture, Denize. Father & Son. (Illus.). 32p. (J). (ps-3). 1993. 14.95 (0-399-21867-X, Philomel Bks) Putnam Pub Group.

Lautzenheiser, Tim. The Art of Successful Teaching: A Blend of Content & Context. LC 91-77572. 240p. 1992. 19.95 (0-941050-29-7, G-3722) GIA Pubns.

— The Joy of Inspired Teaching. LC 93-3985. 176p. 1993. 19.95 (0-941050-50-5, G-4041) GIA Pubns.

Lauvand, Rhona P., tr. see Bilheux, Ronald & Escoffier, Alain.

Lauvas, Per, jt. auth. see Handal, Gunnar.

Lauve, Richard, ed. Physician Payment Reform: Its Impact on Payers & Providers. LC 92-81837. (Orig.). (C). 1992. pap. text ed. 25.95 (0-924674-15-6) Am Coll Phys Execs.

Lauver, jt. auth. see Fogel.

Lauwerier, Hans. Fractals: Endlessly Repeated Geometrical Figures. Gill-Hoffstadt, Sophia, tr. (Illus.). 168p. 1990. 55.00 (0-691-08551-X); pap. 14.95 (0-691-02445-6) Princeton U Pr.

Lauwers, Susan, et al. All about Houseplants. rev. ed. Lipanovich, Marianne, ed. LC 93-86235. (Illus.). 112p. 1994. pap. 9.95 (0-89721-264-9, UPC 05223A) Ortho Info.

Lauwerys, Joseph A., jt. ed. see Bereday, George Z.

Lauwerys, Robert R. Industrial Chemical Exposure: Guidelines for Biological Monitoring. LC 82-70668. 162p. reprint ed. pap. 46.20 (0-8357-7861-4, 2036278) Bks Demand.

Lauwerys, Robert T. & Hoet, Perrine, eds. Industrial Chemical Exposure: Guidelines for Biological Monitoring. 2nd ed. 1993. 69.95 (0-87371-650-7, RA1223) Lewis Pubs.

***Laux, Constance.** Earthly Delights. 384p. 1995. mass mkt. 4.99 (0-8217-4866-1) Zebra.

— Moonlight Whispers. 336p. (Orig.). 1993. mass mkt. 4.99 (1-55773-844-0) Diamond.

Laux, Dorianne. Awake. (New Poets of America Ser.: No. 12). 62p. 1990. pap. 10.00 (0-918526-77-9) BOA Edns.

— What We Carry. (American Poets Continuum Ser.). 80p. 1994. pap. 12.50 (1-880238-07-1) BOA Edns.

Laux, H. E., jt. auth. see Enderle, M.

Laux, James M. The European Automobile Industry. 250p. (C). 1992. text ed. 26.95 (0-8057-3800-2, Pub. by Royal Botanic Garden UK); pap. 14.95 (0-8057-3801-0, Pub. by Royal Botanic Garden UK) Macmillan.

— European Automobile Industry. (International Business History Ser.). 1991. pap. 12.95 (0-685-54772-8) Macmillan.

Laux, James M., tr. see Bardou, Jean P., et al.

Laux, James M., jt. auth. see Kafker, Frank A.

Laux, James M., jt. ed. see Kafker, Frank A.

Laux, Jeanne K. & Molot, Maureen A. State Capitalism: Public Enterprise in Canada. LC 86-47600. (Cornell Studies in Political Economy). (Illus.). 272p. (C). 1988. 45.00 (0-935782-65-6); pap. 14.95 (0-8014-9469-9) Cornell U Pr.

Laux, John. Catholic Apologetics: God, Christianity & the Church. LC 90-70439. (Course in Religion for Catholic High Schools & Academies Ser.: Bk. IV). (Illus.). 134p. 1990. reprint ed. pap. text ed. 8.00 (0-89555-394-5) TAN Bks Pubs.

— Catholic Morality: Sin, Virtue, Conscience, Duties to God, Neighbor, Etc. LC 90-70439. (Course in Religion for Catholic High Schools & Academies Ser.: Bk. III). (Illus.). 164p. 1990. reprint ed. pap. text ed. 8.00 (0-89555-393-7) TAN Bks Pubs.

— Chief Truths of the Faith: Creation, Original Sin, Christ, Faith, Grace, Eternal Life, Etc. LC 90-70439. (Course in Religion for Catholic High Schools & Academies Ser.: Bk. I). (Illus.). 179p. 1990. reprint ed. pap. text ed. 8.00 (0-89555-391-0) TAN Bks Pubs.

— Introduction to the Bible: The Nature, History, Authorship & Content of the Holy Bible with Selections from & Commentaries on the Various Books. LC 90-70241. (Illus.). 315p. 1990. reprint ed. pap. text ed. 13.00 (0-89555-396-1) TAN Bks Pubs.

— Mass & the Sacraments: The Mass, Seven Sacraments, Indulgences, Sacramentals. LC 90-70439. (Course in Religion for Catholic High Schools & Academies Ser.: Bk. II). (Illus.). 199p. 1990. reprint ed. pap. text ed. 8.00 (0-89555-392-9) TAN Bks Pubs.

Laux, John J. Church History: A Complete History of the Catholic Church to the Present Day - For High School, College & Adult Reading. LC 88-51074. (Illus.). 659p. 1989. reprint ed. pap. text ed. 20.00 (0-89555-349-X) TAN Bks Pubs.

Laux, Keith R. The World's Greatest Paper Airplane & Toy Book. (Illus.). 1987. pap. text ed. 7.95 (0-07-155079-8) McGraw.

— The World's Greatest Paper Airplane & Toy Book. (Illus.). 120p. 1987. pap. 7.95 (0-8306-2846-0) TAB Bks.

Laux, Lothar, jt. ed. see Krohne, Heinz W.

Laux, Patricia, ed. Decision Driving Handbook. rev. ed. (Illus.). 200p. (Orig.). 1991. pap. 7.50 (0-934674-59-0, 24H) J J Keller.

Lauxtermann, P. F. Constantin Frantz: Romantik und Realismus im Werk eines Politischen Aussenseiters. (Historische Studies: Bk. XXXV). vi, 217p. (Orig.). 1978. pap. 21.00 (90-01-39021-8) Benjamins North Am.

Lauzen, Elizabeth, ed. see Madison, Kathy.

Lauzen, Sara, jt. auth. see Armstrong, Missy.

Lauzon, Russell. Smarick, Scourge of the Land. abr. ed. 240p. 1995. pap. 8.95 (1-56901-463-9) NW Pub.

Lava, Horacio C. Levels of Living in the Ilocos Region. LC 75-30066. (Institute of Pacific Relations Ser.). reprint ed. 29.50 (0-404-59538-3) AMS Pr.

***LaVaate, Cynthia.** His Hand Holding Mine. 1995. 12.95 (0-8062-5319-3) Carlton.

Lavabre, M. Aromaterapia: Libro de Trabajo. pap. 12.95 (0-89281-464-0) Inner Tradit.

Lavabre, Marcel. Aromatherapy Workbook. (Illus.). 192p. 1990. pap. 12.95 (0-89281-346-6, Heal Arts VT) Inner Tradit.

Lavacek, Joseph, Jr. In Time for the Way Station. 125p. 1994. pap. 8.00 (1-56002-237-X, Univ Edtns) Aegina Pr.

Lavach & Giddings. Veterinary Ophthalmology, Vol. I: Large Animal Ophthalmology. (Illus.). 408p. 1989. pap. 49.00 (0-8016-2773-7) Mosby Yr Bk.

— Veterinary Ophthalmology, Vol. II: Small Animal Ophthalmology. 475p. 1991. 41.95 (0-8016-2774-5) Mosby Yr Bk.

Lavachery, Henri A. Les Petroglyphes de l'Ile de Paques: Ouvrage publie avec le concours de la Fondation Universitaire de Belgique. LC 75-35198. reprint ed. 16.50 (0-404-14226-5) AMS Pr.

***Lavacic, Rosalind.** Local Management of Schools: Analysis & Practice. LC 95-5855. 1995. write for info. (0-335-19376-5, Open Univ Pr) Taylor & Francis.

Lavagnino. Guatemala. 3578p. 1986. reprint ed. pap. 3.75 (0-913129-15-1) La Tienda.

Lavagno, Luciano & Sangiovanni-Vincentelli, Alberto L. Algorithms for Synthesis & Testing of Asynchronous Circuits. LC 93-19510. (International Series in Engineering & Computer Science, VLSI, Computer Architecture, & Digital Screen Processing). 360p. (C). 1993. lib. bdg. 97.50 (0-7923-9364-3) Kluwer Ac.

Lavakare, P. J. & Waardenburg, J. G., eds. Science Policies in International Perspective: The Experience of India & the Netherlands. 280p. 1992. text ed. 49.00 (0-86187-826-4, Pub. by Pinter Pubs UK) St Martin.

Lavakare, P. J., et al, eds. Scientific Cooperation for Development: Search for New Directions. 216p. 1980. text ed. 20.00 (0-7069-0955-0, Pub. by Vikas II) S Asia.

Laval, J., jt. ed. see Lambert, M. W.

Laval, Pierre. The Diary of Pierre Laval. LC 72-6725. reprint ed. 22.50 (0-404-10644-7) AMS Pr.

LaVal, Richard K. & Fitch, Henry S. Structure, Movements & Reproduction in Three Costa Rican Bat Communities. (Occasional Papers: No. 69). 28p. 1977. pap. 1.00 (0-317-04875-9) U of KS Mus Nat Hist.

Laval Staff. Dictionnaire Biographique du Canada, Vol. 1: 1000-1700. 800p. (FRE.). 1966. 95.00 (0-8288-9452-3) Fr & Eur.

— Dictionnaire Biographique du Canada, Vol. 10: 1871-1880. 926p. (FRE.). 1972. 95.00 (0-8288-9460-4, 2763766382) Fr & Eur.

— Dictionnaire Biographique du Canada, Vol. 11: 1881-1890. 1212p. (FRE.). 1982. 95.00 (0-8288-9461-2) Fr & Eur.

— Dictionnaire Biographique du Canada, Vol. 2: 1701-1740. 834p. (FRE.). 1969. 95.00 (0-8288-9453-1) Fr & Eur.

— Dictionnaire Biographique du Canada, Vol. 3: 1741-1770. 888p. (FRE.). 1974. 95.00 (0-8288-9454-X) Fr & Eur.

— Dictionnaire Biographique du Canada, Vol. 4: 1771-1800. 1044p. (FRE.). 1980. 95.00 (0-8288-9455-8) Fr & Eur.

— Dictionnaire Biographique du Canada, Vol. 5: 1801-1820. 1168p. (FRE.). 1983. 95.00 (0-8288-9456-6) Fr & Eur.

— Dictionnaire Biographique du Canada, Vol. 6: 1821-1835. 1243p. (FRE.). 1987. 95.00 (0-8288-9457-4, 2763770983) Fr & Eur.

— Dictionnaire Biographique du Canada, Vol. 8: 1851-1860. 1243p. (FRE.). 1985. 95.00 (0-8288-9458-2, 276377069X) Fr & Eur.

— Dictionnaire Biographique du Canada, Vol. 9: 1861-1870. 1060p. (FRE.). 1977. 95.00 (0-8288-9459-0) Fr & Eur.

Lavalette, Antoine M. Memoirs of Count Lavallette. 1977. 41.95 (0-8369-7145-0, 7978) Ayer.

Lavalette, Michael. Child Employment in the Capitalist Labour Market. 318p. 1994. 54.95 (1-85628-600-2, Pub. by Avebury Pub UK) Ashgate Pub Co.

Lavalla, et al. Blueprint for Community Emergency Management: Managing Emergency Operations. (Illus.). 600p. 35.00 (0-913724-33-5) Emerg Response Inst.

— Disaster Exercise Planning & Evaluation. 186p. 1991. ring bd. 25.00 (0-913724-43-2) Emerg Response Inst.

— Managing Field Operations: An Introduction to Incident Management. (Illus.). 80p. 1989. ring bd. 15.00 (0-913724-42-4) Emerg Response Inst.

— School Disaster Planning. (Illus.). 178p. 1991. ring bd. 25.00 (0-913724-44-0) Emerg Response Inst.

Lavalla, Patrick. Handbook: Living Life's Emergencies. (Illus.). 72p. 1981. pap. 4.00 (0-913724-25-4) Emerg Response Inst.

Lavalla, Patrick, et al. Search Is an Emergency: Text for Managing Search Operations. (Illus.). 480p. 30.00 (0-913724-28-9); teacher ed 40.00 (0-913724-29-7) Emerg Response Inst.

Lavalla, Patrick & Stoffel, Robert. Instructor Guide for Managing Emergency Operations. 600p. 1992. ring bd. 40.00 (0-913724-38-6) Emerg Response Inst.

— National Emergency Training & Information Guide. (Illus.). 350p. 1992. ring bd. 30.00 (0-913724-35-1) Emerg Response Inst.

— Personnel Safety in Helicopter Operations: Helirescue Manual. (Illus.). 124p. 1988. ring bd. 8.50 (0-913724-36-X) Emerg Response Inst.

Lavalla, Patrick, jt. auth. see Stoffel, R. C.

Lavalla, Patrick, et al. Community Emergency Management: Development & Strategies. (Illus.). 1987. ring bd. 25.00 (0-913724-39-4) Emerg Response Inst.

— Disaster Planning Manual: How to Write a Community Disaster Coordination Plan. (Illus.). 300p. 1988. ring bd. 25.00 (0-913724-41-6) Emerg Response Inst.

— Search & Rescue Fundamentals. (Illus.). 396p. per. 30.00 (0-913724-37-8) Emerg Response Inst.

— Search Is an Emergency: Field Coordinator's Handbook. (Illus.). 154p. pap. 9.00 (0-913724-30-0) Emerg Response Inst.

LaValle, David E. A Glimpse of Reality: Sorties into the Truth Beyond Conditioning. 1992. 13.95 (0-533-10208-1) Vantage.

— Of Sex & Other Mythologies. 1994. 13.95 (0-533-11051-3) Vantage.

***LaValle, Deanna.** International Directory of Business & Management Scholars & Research, 2 vols. 2720p. 1995. 495.00 (0-87584-517-7) Harvard Busn.

LaValle, John, jt. auth. see Bandler, Richard.

LaValle, Maria T., tr. see Robertson, Jenny.

LaValle, Patrick, jt. auth. see Stoffel, Robert.

LaValle, Teresa, tr. see Ralph, Margaret.

***Lavallee, Barbara, illus.** Barbara Lavallee's Painted Ladies: And Other Celebrations. 80p. 1995. 34.95 (0-945397-36-4) Epicenter Pr.

— Barbara Lavallee's Painted Ladies: And Other Celebrations. 80p. 1995. pap. 22.95 (0-945397-37-2) Epicenter Pr.

Lavallee, Barbara & Shtainmets, Leon, illus. The Snow Child. 32p. (J). (gr. 2-5). 1989. pap. 2.50 (0-590-42141-7) Scholastic Inc.

Lavallee, David K. The Chemistry & Biochemistry of N-Substituted Porphyrins. LC 87-23206. 313p. 1988. lib. bdg. 55.00 (0-89573-147-9) VCH Pubs.

Lavallee, Louis. La Prairie en Nouvelle-France, 1647-1760: Etude d'Histoire Sociale. 304p. (FRE.). 1993. 49.95 (0-7735-0933-X, Pub. by McGill CN); pap. 29.95 (0-7735-1108-3, Pub. by McGill CN) U of Toronto Pr.

Lavallee, Omer. Van Horne's Road: Construction & Early Operation of the Canadian Pacific Railway. (Illus.). 304p. 45.00 (0-317-06118-6, Pub. by Boston Mills Pr CN) Genl Dist Srvs.

Lavallee, Omer, ed. Canadian Pacific Diagrams & Data: Steam Locomotives. (Illus.). 10.00 (0-317-06120-8, Pub. by Boston Mills Pr CN) Genl Dist Srvs.

Lavallee, Ronald. Tchipayuk: or The Way of the Wolf. Claxton, Patricia, tr. 400p. 1994. pap. 16.95 (0-88922-338-6, Pub. by Talonbooks CN) InBook.

Lavallet, Martha, jt. auth. see Varnum, Ann.

Lavalley, Al, ed. Invasion of the Body Snatchers. LC 89-30374. (Films in Print Ser.). (Illus.). 250p. (C). 1989. text ed. 35.00 (0-8135-1460-6); pap. text ed. 15.00 (0-8135-1461-4) Rutgers U Pr.

LaValley, Albert J., ed. Mildred Pierce. LC 80-5107. (Warner Bros. Screenplay Ser.). (Illus.). 264p. 1980. 19.95 (0-299-08370-5); pap. 9.95 (0-299-08374-8) U of Wis Pr.

Lavalley, Jack, et al. Mysteries from the Finger Lakes: Short Stories from In-Between Magazine. (Illus.). 128p. 1989. pap. 8.95 (0-685-29418-8) Six Lakes Arts.

Lavan, George, ed. see Cannon, James P.

Lavan, S. A. & Fletcher, B. G. Student Guide to Structural Design. (Illus.). 105p. 1989. pap. text ed. 36.95 (0-408-02171-3) Buttrwrth-Heinemann.

Lavan, Spencer. Unitarians & India: A Study in Encounter & Response. 3rd ed. LC 90-86029. (Illus.). 217p. 1991. reprint ed. pap. 18.95 (0-913552-46-1) Exploration Pr.

Lavanda, Violet, jt. auth. see Finocchiaro, Mary.

Lavandier, Odile, jt. auth. see Howard, Janet L.

Lavanger, Denis P., jt. ed. see Hermann, Richard K.

***Lavania, Shipra.** Juvenile Delinquency. (C). 1993. 18.00x (81-7033-207-9, Pub. by Rawat II) S Asia.

Lavaroni, Charles. California: Roots. 144p. (J). (gr. 4-6). 1984. reprint ed. pap. text ed. 11.45 (0-911981-04-7) Cloud Pub.

***Lavas, Ray.** Tracking & Locating Systems. Berkel, Bob, ed. (CCS SecuritySource Library: Vol. X). (Illus.). 720p. 1995. 300.00 (1-884674-10-0) CCS Security.

Lavash, Donald R. A Journey Through New Mexico History. rev. ed. LC 92-27191. (J). 1993. 24.95 (0-86534-194-X) Sunstone Pr.

LaVash, Donald R. Sheriff William Brady: Tragic Hero of the Lincoln County War. LC 85-8025. (Illus.). 128p. (Orig.). 1986. pap. 10.95 (0-86534-064-1) Sunstone Pr.

Lavash, Donald R. Wilson & the Kid. LC 90-34762. (Illus.). 171p. 1990. 21.95 (0-932702-49-X) Creative Texas.

Lavasik, Lawrence. Mary My Hope. rev. ed. (Illus.). 1977. 4.95 (0-89942-365-5, 365/00) Catholic Bk Pub.

LaVasque, Jeanne. Musings from the Menopause. LC 90-91722. (Illus.). 61p. (Orig.). 1990. pap. 9.95 (0-9628454-0-X) Polliwog Pr.

Lavater, J. C. Aphorisms on Man. LC 79-23298. 1980. reprint ed. 50.00 (0-8201-1336-0) Schol Facsimiles.

*Lavauzelle Staff. Dictionnaire des Communes. 1787p. (FRE.). 1984. 125.00 (0-7859-7915-8, 2702500757) Fr & Eur.

Lavay, Barry. Special Physical Education: A Resource Guide for Professors & Students. 224p. (C). 1992. pap. text ed. 16.95 (0-8403-7510-7) Kendall-Hunt.

Lavay, Barry, jt. ed. see French, Ron.

Lavay, Barry W., jt. auth. see Eichstaedt, Carl B.

Lavazzi, Thomas. Crossing-Borders. LC 93-6536. 64p. 1993. pap. 12.95 (0-7734-2784-8, Mellen Poetry Pr) E Mellen.

Lave, Charles, ed. Automobile Choice & Its Energy Implications. (Illus.). 137p. 1981. pap. write for info. (0-08-027397-1, Pergamon Pr) Elsevier.

Lave, Charles A., ed. Urban Transit: The Private Challenge to Public Transportation. LC 84-21529. (Illus.). 372p. 1985. 29.95 (0-936488-62-X); pap. 14.95 (0-936488-63-8) PRIPP.

Lave, Charles A. & March, James G. An Introduction to Models in the Social Sciences. 432p. (C). 1991. reprint ed. pap. 29.50 (0-8191-8381-4) U Pr of Amer.

Lave, Jean. Cognition in Practice: Mind, Mathematics & Culture. (Illus.). 264p. 1988. pap. 18.95 (0-521-35734-9) Cambridge U Pr.

— Cognition in Practice: Mind, Mathematics & Culture. (Illus.). 264p. 1988. 64.95 (0-521-35015-8) Cambridge U Pr.

Lave, Jean & Wenger, Etienne. Situated Learning: Legitimate Peripheral Participation. (Learning in Doing: Social, Cognitive & Computational Perspectives Ser.). 100p. (C). 1991. 34.95 (0-521-41308-7); pap. 12.95 (0-521-42374-0) Cambridge U Pr.

Lave, Jean, jt. ed. see Chaiklin, Seth.

Lave, Jean, jt. ed. see Rogoff, Barbara.

Lave, Lester, et al. Congestion Charges for Inland Waterways: A Means to Increase Both Equity & Efficiency. 21p. (Orig.). 1982. pap. 2.50 (0-911415-02-5) Natl Taxpayers Union Found.

Lave, Lester B. The Strategy of Social Regulation: Decision Frameworks for Policy. LC 81-7685. (Studies in the Regulation of Economic Activity). 166p. 1981. 31.95 (0-8157-5162-1); pap. 11.95 (0-8157-5161-3) Brookings.

Lave, Lester B., ed. Quantitative Risk Assessment in Regulation. LC 82-22603. (Studies in the Regulation of Economic Activity). 264p. 1983. 34.95 (0-8157-5164-8); pap. 14.95 (0-8157-5163-X) Brookings.

— Risk Assessment & Management. LC 87-21288. (Advances in Risk Analysis Ser.: Vol. 5). (Illus.). 752p. 1987. 145.00 (0-306-42683-8, Plenum Pr) Plenum.

Lave, Lester B. & Covello, Vincent T., eds. Uncertainty in Risk Assessment, Risk Management & Decision Making. (Advances in Risk Analysis Ser.: Vol. 4). 538p. 1987. 120.00 (0-306-42557-2, Plenum Pr) Plenum.

Lave, Lester B. & Omenn, Gilbert S. Clearing the Air: Reforming the Clean Air Act. LC 81-70469. (Studies in the Regulation of Economic Activity). 51p. 1981. pap. 7.95 (0-8157-5159-1) Brookings.

Lave, Lester B. & Seskin, Eugene. Air Pollution & Human Health. LC 74-6830. 388p. reprint ed. pap. 110.60 (0-8357-5282-8, 2030740) Bks Demand.

Lave, Lester B. & Upton, Arthur C., eds. Toxic Chemicals, Health & the Environment. LC 86-46276. (Johns Hopkins Series in Environmental Toxicology). 336p. 1987. pap. text ed. 18.95 (0-8018-3474-0) Johns Hopkins.

Lave, Lester B., jt. ed. see Crandall, Robert W.

Lavean, Gilbert E. & Schmidt, William G., eds. Communication Satellite Developments: Systems. LC 75-45244. (PAAS Ser.: Vol. 41). (Illus.). 333p. 1976. 34.95 (0-915928-05-1) AIAA.

— Communications Satellite Developments: Technology. LC 75-45243. (PAAS Ser.: Vol. 42). (Illus.). 419p. 1976. 54.95 (0-915928-06-X) AIAA.

LaVeck, James J. Collage: A Shattered Story. Stein, Jenny, ed. LC 93-10083. (Illus.). 150p. (Orig.). 1993. pap. 9.00 (1-882979-07-9) What the Heck.

*Laveissiere, Sylvain. Dictionnaire des Artistes et Ouvriers d'Art de Bourgogne Vol. 1: A-K. 290p. (FRE.). 1980. pap. 145.00 (0-7859-8066-0, 2851890069) Fr & Eur.

*LaVel, Sandra D. My Little Indiscretion. 24p. 1994. 7.00 (0-8059-3613-0) Dorrance.

Laveleye, Emile. On the Causes of War. 1972. 59.95 (0-8490-0763-1) Gordon Pr.

Lavelle, Brian M. The Sorrow & the Pity: A Prolegomenon to a History of Athens under the Peisistratids, 560-510 B.C. 200p. (Orig.). 1993. pap. 57.50 (3-515-06318-8) Coronet Bks.

Lavelle, C. L. Applied Oral Physiology. 2nd ed. (Illus.). 304p. 1988. 69.95 (0-7236-0818-0, Pub. by John Wright UK) Buttrwrth-Heinemann.

Lavelle, D. Discotheque Dancing. (Ballroom Dance Ser.). 1986. lib. bdg. 69.95 (0-8490-3257-1) Gordon Pr.

— Discotheque Dancing. (Ballroom Dance Ser.). 1985. lib. bdg. 72.00 (0-87700-849-3) Revisionist Pr.

Lavelle, Des. Skellig: Island of Europe. 112p. 1987. pap. 16.95 (0-86278-139-6, Pub. by OBrien Pr IE) Dufour.

— The Skellig Story: Ancient Monastic Outpost. (Illus.). 105p. 1994. pap. 19.95 (0-86278-295-3, Pub. by OBrien Pr IE) Dufour.

Lavelle, Doris. Latin & American Dances. (Ballroom Dance Ser.). 1984. lib. bdg. 79.95 (0-87700-512-5) Revisionist Pr.

*Lavelle, Geoffrey. Closing Arguments. LC 94-41938. 1995. 7.95 (0-943512-49-2) Linwood Pub.

— An Expatriate's Sketchbook. limited ed. Date not set. 7.00 (1-884185-05-3) O Zone.

Lavelle, Louis. The Dilemma of Narcissus. Gairdner, William T., tr. 230p. 1993. reprint ed. 22.95 (0-943914-61-2); reprint ed. pap. 15.95 (0-943914-62-0) Larson Pubns.

Lavelle, Robert, jt. ed. see Blackside, Inc. Staff.

Lavelle, S. M., jt. ed. see Beneken, J. E.

Lavelle, Sheila. The Disappearing Granny. (Banana Bks.). (Illus.). 42p. (J). (gr. 2-4). 1989. 3.95 (0-8120-6134-9) Barron.

LaVelle, Steven. Just Passing Through. (Illus.). 32p. (Orig.). (J). (gr. k-3). 1980. pap. 4.95 (0-87516-402-1) DeVorss.

Lavely, Carolyn, et al. At-Risk Students & Their Families. 1993. 15.95 (1-55691-103-3, 033) Learning Pubns.

Laven, Edward E. The Nez Perce National Forest Story. rev. ed. Zabinski, Mary & Moore, Shirley, eds. (Illus.). 57p. 1991. pap. 4.95 (0-914019-30-9) NW Interpretive.

Lavenberg, George N. Ceramic Tile Manual. 3rd ed. Jaffe, Sam, ed. (Illus.). 416p. 1988. text ed. 49.95 (0-07-036651-9) McGraw.

Lavenberg, Robert J., jt. auth. see Fitch, John E.

Lavenberg, Robert J., jt. auth. see Grove, Jack S.

Lavenberg, Stephen, ed. Computer Performance Modeling Handbook. (Notes & Reports in Computer Science & Applied Mathematics Ser.: No. 3). 1983. text ed. 91.00 (0-12-438720-9) Acad Pr.

Lavenda, Beranrd H. Statistical Physics: A Probabilistic Approach. 384p. 1991. text ed. 98.00 (0-471-54607-0) Wiley.

Lavenda, Bernard H. Nonequilibrium Statistical Thermodynamics. LC 84-26992. 213p. reprint ed. pap. 60.80 (0-7837-4010-7, 2043840) Bks Demand.

— Thermodynamics of Irreversible Processes. LC 93-3190. 182p. 1993. reprint ed. pap. 7.95 (0-486-67576-9) Dover.

Lavenda, Robert, jt. auth. see Schultz, Emily.

Lavenda, Robert H., jt. auth. see Schultz, Emily A.

Lavender, Abraham D. French Huguenots: From Mediterranean Catholics to White Anglo-Saxon Protestants. LC 89-12341. (American University Studies: History: Ser. IX, Vol. 80). 264p. 1990. text ed. 42.50 (0-8204-1136-1) P Lang Pubs.

Lavender, Abraham D., ed. A Coat of Many Colors: Jewish Subcommunities in the United States. LC 77-71865. (Contributions in Family Studies: No. 1). 324p. 1977. text ed. 59.95 (0-8371-9539-X, LCM/, Greenwood Pr) Greenwood.

*Lavender, Abraham D. & Steinberg, Clarence. Jewish Farmers of the Catskills: A Century of Survival. (Illus.). 288p. 1995. lib. bdg. 39.95 (0-8130-1343-7) U Press Fla.

Lavender, Cheryl. Making Each Minute Count: Time-Savers, Tips, & Kid-Tested Strategies for the Music Class. Crocker, Emily, ed. 200p. (Orig.). 1990. pap. 19.95 (0-7935-0348-5, HL44223055) Jenson Pubns.

— Moans, Groans & Skeleton Boans: Fun Songs & Activities for Kids. (MusicTivity Ser.). (Illus.). 32p. (Orig.). (J). 1993. cd-rom, pap. text ed. 12.95 (0-7935-2371-0, HL00330604) H Leonard.

— Moans, Groans & Skeleton Bones: Fun Songs & Activities for Kids. (MusicTivity Ser.). (Illus.). 32p. (Orig.). (J). 1993. audio, pap. text ed. 9.95 (0-7935-2372-9, HL00330605) H Leonard.

Lavender, David. Bent's Fort. 11.00 (0-8446-1279-0) Peter Smith.

— Bent's Fort. LC 54-7322. (Illus.). 479p. 1972. reprint ed. pap. 12.95 (0-8032-5753-8, Bison Books) U of Nebr Pr.

— California: Land of New Beginnings. LC 86-30929. x, 480p. 1987. reprint ed. 33.00 (0-8032-2874-0); reprint ed. pap. 17.95 (0-8032-7924-8) U of Nebr Pr.

— DeSoto, Coronado, Cabrillo: Explorers of the Northern Mystery. LC 91-47633. (Handbook Ser.: No. 144). (Illus.). 112p. (Orig.). 1992. pap. 4.00 (0-685-62342-4, 024-005-01102-1) Natl Park Serv.

— Fort Laramie & the Changing Frontier. LC 82-600401. (Handbook Ser.: No. 118). (Illus.). 160p. (Orig.). 1984. pap. 7.50 (0-912627-20-4) Natl Park Serv.

— The Great West. LC 85-13476. (American Heritage Library). (Illus.). 400p. 1985. pap. 8.95 (0-8281-0481-6) HM.

— One Man's West. LC 76-45450. (Illus.). iv, 316p. 1977. pap. 10.95 (0-8032-5855-0) U of Nebr Pr.

— Pipe Spring & the Arizona Strip. 64p. 1984. pap. 2.95 (0-915630-20-6) Zion.

— River Runners of the Grand Canyon. LC 85-70524. (Illus.). 134p. 1995. pap. 19.95 (0-938216-23-6, 30163) GCNHA.

— The Southwest. LC 83-19740. 362p. 1984. pap. 16.95 (0-8263-0736-1) U of NM Pr.

— The Telluride Story. 68p. (Orig.). 1987. pap. 19.95 (0-9608764-6-4) Wayfinder Pr.

— The Trail to Santa Fe. rev. ed. LC 58-9634. (Illus.). 112p. (J). (gr. 4-8). 1988. reprint ed. pap. 8.95 (0-939729-15-6) Trails West Pub.

— The Way to the Western Sea: Lewis & Clark Across the Continent. 1990. pap. 12.95 (0-385-41155-3, Anchor NY) Doubleday.

— Westward Vision: The Story of the Oregon Trail. LC 84-20815. (Illus.). xx, 425p. 1985. reprint ed. pap. 12.95 (0-8032-7915-9) U of Nebr Pr.

— Winner Take All: A History of the Trans-Canada Canoe Trail. LC 77-4864. 385p. (Orig.). 1985. pap. 13.95 (0-89301-104-5) U of Idaho Pr.

Lavender, David S. The Santa Fe Trail. LC 94-16638. (Illus.). 64p. (J). (gr. 3-7). 1995. lib. bdg. 15.95 (0-8234-1153-2) Holiday.

Lavender, Jane C., et al, illus. Heritage of Words: Written Memorabilia of the Suttle, Clements & Allied Families. 206p. (Orig.). 1988. pap. 18.00 (1-882063-02-7) Cottage Pr MA.

Lavender, Kenneth & Stockton, Scott. Book Repair: A How-to-Do-It Manual for School & Public Librarians. (How-to-Do-It Ser.). 128p. 1992. 39.95 (1-55570-103-5) Neal-Schuman.

Lavender, Lucille. Los Pastores Tambien Lloran. Smith, Josie H., tr. 136p. (Orig.). 1991. reprint ed. pap. 4.95 (0-311-42075-3) Casa Bautista.

Lavender, P., ed. see Gilbert & Sullivan.

Lavender, Peter. Songs & Dances of Ireland. (Illus.). 80p. 1982. pap. 9.95 (0-7119-0099-X, AM31402) Music Sales.

— Start Playing Keyboard. (Illus.). 48p. 1987. pap. 4.95 (0-8256-1113-X, AM36906) Music Sales.

— Start Playing Keyboard, Bk. 2. (Illus.). 48p. 1987. pap. 4.95 (0-8256-1186-5, AM65749) Music Sales.

— Start Playing Keyboard: Collection One. (Illus.). 48p. 1988. pap. 7.95 (0-7119-1623-3, AM72216) Music Sales.

— Start Playing Keyboard: Collection Three. (Illus.). 48p. 1988. pap. 7.95 (0-7119-1625-X, AM72232) Music Sales.

— Start Playing Keyboard: Collection Two. (Illus.). 48p. 1988. pap. 7.95 (0-7119-1624-1, AM72224) Music Sales.

— Start Playing Keyboard: Omnibus Edition, 2 bks. in 1. (Illus.). 96p. 1987. pap. 9.95 (0-8256-1187-3, AM67588) Music Sales.

Lavender, Sharline. Lone Star Time Machine: Game & Activity Workbook for Texas History Students. (Illus.). 37p. 1986. pap. 6.95 (0-937460-22-2) Hendrick-Long.

Lavenia, Joe & Terwilliger, Mark. House Painting. Fox, Jill, ed. LC 92-70584. (Illus.). 112p. (Orig.). 1992. pap. 9.95 (0-89721-246-0, UPC 05972) Ortho Info.

Laventhol & Horwath. Hotel-Motel Development. 212p. 1984. 64.95 (0-87420-629-4) Urban Land.

Laventhol & Horwath Staff. Uniform System of Accounts for Restaurants. 160p. 1990. pap. 36.00 (0-317-57883-9, MG936) Natl Restaurant Assn.

*Laver, Erik. The Missing Piece to the Weight Loss Puzzle. 224p. 1995. 2.50 (0-9642290-4-8) Bedford-Kennington.

Laver, James. Costume & Fashion. LC 84-51360. (World of Art Ser.). (Illus.). 288p. 1985. pap. 12.95 (0-500-20190-0) Thames Hudson.

— Costume & Fashion: A Concise History. rev. ed. LC 94-61062. (World of Art Ser.). (Illus.). 296p. 1995. pap. 14.95 (0-500-20266-4) Thames Hudson.

Laver, James, jt. auth. see Sheringham, George.

Laver, John. The Gift of Speech: Papers in the Analysis of Speech & Voice. (Illus.). 224p. 1992. 42.50 (0-7486-0313-1, Pub. by Edinburgh U Pr UK) Col U Pr.

— Principles of Phonetics. LC 93-18183. (Textbooks in Linguistics Ser.). (Illus.). 744p. (C). 1994. 89.95 (0-521-45031-4); pap. 29.95 (0-521-45655-X) Cambridge U Pr.

— Voice Quality: A Classified Research Bibliography. (Library & Information Sources in Linguistics: No. 5). viii, 225p. 1979. 52.00x (90-272-0996-0) Benjamins North Am.

Laver, John, jt. ed. see Jack, Mervyn.

Laver, Lance, et al. Process in Architecture: A Documentation in Six Examples. LC 79-88539. (Illus.). 144p. (Orig.). 1979. pap. 4.00 (0-938437-00-3) MIT List Visual Arts.

Laver, Michael. Invitation to Politics. (Invitation Ser.). 272p. 1984. pap. 15.95 (0-631-15138-9) Blackwell Pubs.

Laver, Michael, jt. ed. see Shepsle, Kenneth A.

Laver, Michael J. & Hunt, Ben. Policy & Party Competition. 288p. 1992. 45.00 (0-415-90219-3, A3976, Routledge NY) Routledge.

Laver, Michael J. & Schofield, Norman. Multiparty Government: The Politics of Coalition in Europe. (Comparative European Politics Ser.). (Illus.). 328p. 1990. 64.00 (0-19-827292-8) OUP.

— Multiparty Government: The Politics of Coalition in Europe. (Comparative European Politics Ser.). (Illus.). 328p. 1991. reprint ed. pap. 19.95 (0-19-827293-6) OUP.

Laver, Murray. Information Technology: Agent of Change. (Illus.). 208p. (C). 1989. 49.95 (0-521-35035-2); pap. 19.95 (0-521-35925-2) Cambridge U Pr.

— Planning Successful Computing. 52p. (C). 1986. 70.00 (0-86236-004-8, Pub. by Granary UK) St Mut.

Laver, W. G. & Air, Gillian, eds. Use of X-Ray Crystallography in the Design of Antiviral Agents. 360p. 1990. text ed. 116.00 (0-12-438745-4) Acad Pr.

Laver, W. G. & Bachmayer, H., eds. The Influenza Virus Haemagglutinin. LC 77-17581. (Topics in Infectious Diseases Ser.: Vol. 3). (Illus.). 1978. pap. 43.00 (0-387-81459-0) Spr-Verlag.

Laver, W. Graeme & Air, Gillian M., eds. Immune Recognition of Protein Antigens. (Current Communications in Molecular Biology Ser.). 197p. (Orig.). 1985. pap. 30.00 (0-87969-185-9) Cold Spring Harbor.

Laverack, M. S., ed. Physiological Adaptations of Marine Animals. (Society for Experimental Biology Symposia Ser.: No. 39). 540p. 1985. text ed. 60.00 (0-948601-00-0) Portland NC.

Laverack, M. S. & Kerkut, G. A. Physiology of Earthworms. (International Series of Monographs on Pure & Applied Mathematics: Vol. 15). 1963. 92.00 (0-08-009812-6, Pub. by Pergamon Repr UK) Franklin.

Laverdiere & Casgrain, eds. Le Journal des Jesuites. (French-Canadian Civilization Ser.). (FRE.). reprint ed. lib. bdg. 46.00 (0-697-00050-8) Irvington.

LaVerdiere, Eugene. Luke. LC 80-65618. (New Testament Message Ser.: Vol. 5). 296p. 1980. pap. 14.95 (0-8146-5128-3) Liturgical Pr.

LaVerdiere, Eugene A. Dining in the Kingdom of God: The Origins of the Eucharist According to Luke. LC 94-2940. 227p. (Orig.). 1994. pap. 11.95 (1-56854-022-1, DINING) Liturgy Tr Pubns.

*LaVere, Bill. Reclaiming Power: How to Take Back Our Government from Career Politicians. 215p. (Orig.). 1994. pap. 14.95 (1-886335-02-8) Bydand.

*LaVere, William R. Social Security Disability: A Comprehensive & Practical Guide to the Effective Representation of Claimants. 1995. write for info. (1-877663-01-8) Bydand.

— Social Security Disability: A Comprehensive & Practical Guide to the Effective Representation of Claimants. 3rd ed. 357p. 1994. ring bd. 125.00 (1-886335-00-1) Bydand.

Laverentz, Liana. Ashton's Secret. 224p. (Orig.). 1993. pap. 2.95 (1-56597-047-0, Kismet) Meteor Pub.

Laverghetta, Thomas S. Analog Communications for Technology. 600p. (C). 1991. text ed. 51.00 (0-03-029403-7) SCP.

— Handbook of Microwave Testing. LC 81-67941. (Illus.). 536p. reprint ed. pap. 152.80 (0-8357-3935-X, 2036670) Bks Demand.

— Microwave Materials & Fabrication Techniques. 2nd ed. (Artech House Microwave Library). 300p. 1991. 59.00 (0-89006-414-8, C1414) Artech Hse.

— Microwave Materials & Fabrication Techniques. LC 84-71819. (Artech House Microwave Library). (Illus.). 237p. reprint ed. pap. 67.60 (0-318-39751-X, 2033125) Bks Demand.

— Microwave Measurements & Techniques. LC 75-31383. (Illus.). 411p. reprint ed. pap. 117.20 (0-8357-4233-4, 2037020) Bks Demand.

— Modern Microwave Measurements & Techniques. (Microwave Library). 300p. 1988. text ed. 79.00 (0-89006-307-9) Artech Hse.

— Solid State Microwave Devices. LC 87-19319. (Artech House Microwave Library). (Illus.). 208p. reprint ed. pap. 59.30 (0-8357-3938-4, 2036673) Bks Demand.

Lavergne, Connie H. Self-Defense. 84p. (C). 1989. pap. text ed. 6.95 (0-89641-180-X) American Pr.

Lavergne, Michel. Seismic Methods. (C). 1989. lib. bdg. 83.00 (1-85333-224-0, Pub. by Graham & Trotman UK) Kluwer Ac.

— Seismic Methods. (Illus.). 192p. (C). 1988. text ed. 75.00 (2-7108-0552-9) Technip.

Laverick, Jack. Royalty & Their Jewels. Laverick, Mark, ed. LC 93-84490. (Illus.). 120p. (Orig.). 1993. per. 18.95 (1-884054-99-4) Printers Shopper.

Laverick, Mark, ed. see Laverick, Jack.

Laverne, Andy. Handbook of Chord Substitutions. 1992. pap. 12.95 (0-943748-51-8) Ekay Music.

Lavernia, E. J. & Gungor, M. N., eds. Microstructural Design by Solidification Processing. (Illus.). 251p. 1993. 86.00 (0-87339-193-4, 457) Minerals Metals.

Lavernia, E. J., jt. ed. see Srivatsan, T. S.

Lavernia, E. J., et al, eds. Synthesis & Analysis in Materials Processing: Characterization & Diagnostics of Ceramics & Metal Particulate Processing. LC 89-61036. (Illus.). 104p. 1989. 51.00 (0-87339-106-3, 363) Minerals Metals.

Laverov, N. Concise Terminological Dictionary of Fossil Energy Resources. 224p. (C). 1985. 60.00 (0-685-54132-0, Pub. by Collets) St Mut.

Lavers, Annette. Roland Barthes: Structuralism & After. LC 81-13447. 310p. 1982. 37.50 (0-674-77721-2) HUP.

Lavers, Annette, tr. see Barthes, Roland.

Lavers, Norman. The Northwest Passage. LC 83-27484. 137p. 1984. 15.95 (0-914590-86-3); pap. 7.95 (0-914590-87-1) Fiction Coll.

— Pop Culture into Art: The Novels of Manuel Puig. LC 88-4807. 80p. 1988. pap. 9.95 (0-8262-0685-9) U of Mo Pr.

Laverty, J. R., ed. see Laverty, R. V.

Laverty, Maura. Full & Plenty: Breads & Cakes, Vol. 1. (Illus.). 160p. (Orig.). 1985. reprint ed. pap. 7.95 (0-900068-99-X, Pub. by Anvil Bks Ltd IE) Irish Bks Media.

— Full & Plenty: Fish & Meat, No. 2. (Full & Plenty). (Illus.). 160p. (Orig.). 1986. pap. 9.95 (0-947962-13-1, Pub. by Anvil Bks Ltd IE) Irish Bks Media.

— Never No More. (Virago Modern Classic Ser.). 284p. 1992. pap. 10.95 (0-86068-484-9, Pub. by Virago Pr UK) Trafalgar.

*Laverty, Mike. Plug Fishing for Steelhead. 64p. 1994. pap. 12.95 (1-878175-92-0) F Amato Pubns.

Laverty, R. V. Railroad Law Digest. 2nd ed. Laverty, J. R., ed. lib. bdg. 47.00 (0-318-04011-5) J R Laverty.

Lavery. Modeling & Simulation on Microcomputers, 1985. 174p. 1985. 28.00 (0-317-60940-8, MSM85) Soc Computer Sim.

Lavery, jt. ed. see Beveridge.

Lavery, Brian. The Arming & Fitting of English Ships of War, 1600-1815. LC 87-62011. (Illus.). 288p. 1988. 59.95 (0-87021-009-2) Naval Inst Pr.

— Building the Wooden Walls: Design & Construction of the 74 Gun Ship Valiant. (Illus.). 224p. 1991. 41.95 (1-55750-078-9) Naval Inst Pr.

— Nelson's Navy: Its Ships, Men & Organization, 1793 to 1815. LC 89-62380. (Illus.). 352p. 1990. 45.95 (0-87021-258-3) Naval Inst Pr.

— The Seventy-Four Gun Ship Bellona. LC 85-72568. (Anatomy of the Ship Ser.). (Illus.). 120p. 1986. 36.95 (0-87021-148-X) Naval Inst Pr.

— The Susan Constant, 1607. LC 88-61602. (Anatomy of the Ship Ser.). (Illus.). 120p. 1988. 36.95 (0-87021-583-3) Naval Inst Pr.

Lavery, Brian, intro. Marine Architecture: Directions for Carrying on a Ship (1739) LC 93-13766. (Scholars' Facsimiles & Reprints, Maritime History Ser.: Vol. 481). 1993. 75.00 (0-8201-1481-2) Schol Facsimiles.

Lavery, Brian & Gardiner, Robert, eds. The Line of Battle: The Sailing Warship, 1650-1840. (Conway's History of the Ship Ser.). (Illus.). 192p. 1992. 44.95 (1-55750-501-2) Naval Inst Pr.

Lavery, Bryony. Her Aching Heart, Wicked, Two Marias. (Methuen New Theatrescripts Ser.). 150p. (Orig.). 1991. pap. 11.95 (0-413-66060-5, AO615, Pub. by Methuen UK) Heinemann.

An Asterisk (*) at the beginning of an entry indicates that the title is appearing in BIP for the first time.

Lavery, David. Late for the Sky: The Mentality of the Space Age. LC 91-24128. 272p. (C). 1992. 24.95 (0-8093-1767-2) S Ill U Pr.

Lavery, David, ed. Full of Secrets: Critical Approaches to Twin Peaks. LC 94-17604. (Contemporary Film & Television Ser.). 292p. (Orig.). 1994. pap. text ed. 18.95 (0-8143-2506-8) Wayne St U Pr.

Lavery, Dennis S. & Jordan, Mark H. Iron Brigade General: John Gibbon, a Rebel in Blue. LC 92-36516. 232p. 1993. text ed. 52.95 (0-313-28576-4, LIB, Greenwood Pr) Greenwood.

Lavery, Donald S., tr. see Lewin, Leif.

Lavery, H. I. Shipboard Operations. 2nd ed. 296p. 1990. pap. 39.95 (0-434-91091-0) Buttrwrth-Heinemann.

Lavery, Hugh. Reflections on the Creed. (C). 1988. 39.00 (0-85439-213-0, Pub. by St Paul Pubns UK) St Mut.

Lavery, Hugh, ed. The Kangaroo Keepers. (Illus.). 211p. 1986. 39.95 (0-7022-1875-8, Pub. by Univ Queensland Pr AT) Intl Spec Bk.

Lavery, J. P. & Sanfilippo, Joseph S., eds. Pediatric & Adolescent Obstetrics & Gynecology. (Clinical Perspectives in Obstetrics & Gynecology Ser.). (Illus.). 350p. 1985. 81.00 (0-387-96073-2) Spr-Verlag.

Lavery, P., jt. ed. see Pompl, W.

Lavery, Richard, et al, eds. Advances in Biomolecular Simulations. LC 91-58106. (Conference Proceeding Ser.: No. 239). (Illus.). 392p. 1992. lib. bdg. 85.00 (0-88318-940-2) Am Inst Physics.

Lavery, Vincent J., ed. see Dewazien, Karl.

Laves, W. H. & Thomson, C. A. UNESCO: Purpose, Progress, Prospects. LC 57-10728. 1968. reprint ed. 39.00 (0-527-55300-X) Periodicals Srv.

Laves, Walter H., jt. auth. see Thomson, Charles A.

Laves, Walter Herman. German Governmental Influence on Foreign Investment, 1871-1914. Wilkins, Mira, ed. LC 76-29742. (European Business Ser.). 1977. reprint ed. lib. bdg. 21.95 (0-405-09759-X) Ayer.

Lavett, Diane K. Student Companion with Complete Solutions for an Introduction to Genetic Analysis. 4th ed. 295p. 1989. teacher ed write for info. (0-318-67005-4) W H Freeman.

Lavett, Diane K., jt. auth. see Manheim, Carol J.

Lavetta, Gary. Civil War Angel. 128p. (Orig.). 1987. pap. 4.95 (0-9618951-0-1) Memory Ln Bks.

— Home in the Hills. LC 88-90882. (Illus.). 143p. (Orig.). 1988. pap. 4.95 (0-9618951-1-X) Memory Ln Bks.

— The Lily Trail. 144p. (YA). (gr. 7-12). 1990. pap. 4.95 (0-9618951-2-8) Memory Ln Bks.

LaVey, Anton S. The Devil's Notebook. 1992. pap. 10.95 (0-922915-11-3) Feral Hse.

— The Satanic Rituals. 1976. mass mkt. 6.50 (0-380-01392-4) Avon.

— The Satanic Rituals. (Illus.). 300p. 1991. reprint ed. lib. bdg. 23.95 (0-89966-827-5) Buccaneer Bks.

Lavey, Kathleen, ed. see Galbraith, James D. & Galbraith, Susan S.

Lavi, A. Ocean Thermal Energy Conversion. 80p. 1981. pap. 36.00 (0-08-026705-X, Pergamon Pr) Elsevier.

Lavi, Abrahim, ed. see Recent Advances in Optimization Techniques Symposium Staff.

Lavi, Zvi, ed. Kibbutz Members Study Kibbutz Children. LC 89-25872. (Kibbutz Study Ser.: No. 1). 256p. 1990. text ed. 55.00 (0-313-27387-1, LKB/, Greenwood Pr) Greenwood.

Lavia, L. A., ed. Cellular Signals Controlling Uterine Function. (Illus.). 184p. 1991. 75.00 (0-306-43822-4, Plenum Pr) Plenum.

Laviana & Cormier. Basic Computer Numerical Control Programming. 176p. (C). 1990. pap. write for info. (0-675-21298-7, Merrill Pub Co) Macmillan.

Laviana, Ken. Quick Cost Estimating Manual. Cormier, E. D., ed. 120p. (Orig.). 1985. pap. 35.00 (0-912227-03-6) C E Pub.

Laviana, Kenneth J. Basic C. N. C. Programming. Cormier, E. D., ed. 115p. (C). 1983. pap. text ed. 19.95 (0-912227-00-1) C E Pub.

Lavicka, William L., intro. Masonry, Carpentry, Joinery. LC 80-18621. (Illus.). 280p. 1991. reprint ed. pap. 15.00 (0-914090-92-5) Chicago Review.

Lavie, Arie & Kuhn, Robert L. Industrial Research & Development in Israel: Patterns & Portents. LC 87-32787. 160p. 1988. text ed. 45.00 (0-275-92967-1, C2967, Praeger Pubs) Greenwood.

Lavie, Arlette. Half a World Away. LC 90-49096. (J). (ps-3). 1990. 7.95 (0-85953-335-2); pap. 3.95 (0-85953-334-4) Childs Play.

— Tower. (J). (ps-3). 1990. 11.95 (0-85953-392-1); pap. 5.95 (0-85953-393-X) Childs Play.

Lavie, Smadar. The Poetics of Military Occupation: Mzeina Allegories of Bedouin Identity under Israeli & Egyptian Rule. 1990. 30.00 (0-520-06880-7) U CA Pr.

— The Poetics of Military Occupation: Mzeina Allegories of Bedouin Identity under Israeli & Egyptian Rule. (Illus.). 309p. 1991. reprint ed. pap. 15.00 (0-520-07552-8) U CA Pr.

Lavie, Smadar, et al, eds. Creativity - Anthropology. LC 92-52765. (Anthropology of Contemporary Issues Ser.). (Illus.). 368p. 1993. 43.50 (0-8014-2255-8); pap. 15.95 (0-8014-9542-3) Cornell U Pr.

Laviera, Tato. La Carreta Made a U-Turn. 2nd ed. LC 92-38421. 74p. (Orig.). 1992. pap. 7.00 (1-55885-064-3) Arte Publico.

— Enclave. LC 81-68067. 88p. (Orig.). 1981. pap. 7.00 (0-934770-11-5) Arte Publico.

— Mainstream Ethics. LC 88-6377. 64p. (Orig.). 1988. pap. 7.00 (0-934770-90-5) Arte Publico.

Laviera, Tato & Binder, Wolfgang, intros. Am-e-rican. LC 83-72577. 80p. (Orig.). (C). 1984. pap. 7.00 (0-934770-31-X) Arte Publico.

Lavies, Bianca. The Atlantic Salmon. LC 91-27990. (Illus.). 32p. (J). (gr. 2-5). 1992. 14.50 (0-525-44860-8, DCB) Dutton Child Bks.

— Backyard Hunter: The Praying Mantis. LC 89-37485. (Illus.). 32p. (J). (gr. 2-5). 1990. 13.95 (0-525-44547-1, DCB) Dutton Child Bks.

— Backyard Hunter: The Praying Mantis. (Illus.). 32p. (J). (gr. 2-5). 1995. pap. 4.99 (0-14-055494-7, Puff Unicorn) Puffin Bks.

— Compost Critters. LC 92-35651. (Illus.). 32p. (J). (gr. 2-6). 1993. 14.99 (0-525-44763-6, DCB) Dutton Child Bks.

— A Gathering of Garter Snakes. (Illus.). 32p. (J). (gr. 3 up). 1993. 15.99 (0-525-45099-8, DCB) Dutton Child Bks.

— It's an Armadillo! LC 89-31821. (Illus.). 32p. (J). (ps-2). 1989. 13.95 (0-525-44523-4, DCB) Dutton Child Bks.

— It's an Armadillo! (Illus.). 32p. (J). (ps-2). 1994. pap. 4.99 (0-14-050312-9, Puff Unicorn) Puffin Bks.

— Killer Bees. (Illus.). 32p. (J). (gr. 3-6). 1994. 15.99 (0-525-45243-5) Dutton Child Bks.

— Lily Pad Pond. LC 88-31697. (Illus.). 32p. (J). (ps-2). 1989. 14.00 (0-525-44483-1, DCB) Dutton Child Bks.

— Lily Pad Pond. (Illus.). 32p. (J). (ps-2). 1993. pap. 4.99 (0-14-054836-X) Puffin Bks.

— Mangrove Wilderness: Nature's Nursery. (Illus.). 32p. (J). (gr. 4 up). 1994. 15.99 (0-525-45186-2, DCB) Dutton Child Bks.

— Monarch Butterflies, Mysterious Travelers. (Illus.). 32p. (J). (gr. 3-6). 1993. 15.99 (0-525-44905-1, DCB) Dutton Child Bks.

— Secretive Timber Rattlesnake. LC 90-31964. (Illus.). 32p. (J). (gr. 3-6). 1990. 13.95 (0-525-44572-2, DCB) Dutton Child Bks.

— Tree Trunk Traffic. (Illus.). 32p. (J). (ps-2). 1993. pap. 4.99 (0-14-054837-8) Puffin Bks.

— Tundra Swans. (Illus.). 32p. (J). (gr. 2-5). 1994. 15.99 (0-525-45273-7) Dutton Child Bks.

— Wasps at Home. LC 90-27338. (Illus.). 32p. (J). (gr. 2-5). 1991. 13.95 (0-525-44704-0, DCB) Dutton Child Bks.

LaVigna, Gary W. & Donnellan-Walsh, Anne. Alternatives to Punishment: Non-Aversive Strategies for Solving Behavior Problems. 220p. 1986. text ed. 27.50 (0-8290-1245-1) Irvington.

LaVigna, Gary W., et al. The Periodic Service Review: A Total Quality Assurance System for Human Services & Education. LC 93-39241. 256p. 1994. spiral bd. 35.00 (1-55766-142-1) P H Brookes.

Lavignac, A. Music Dramas of Richard Wagner & His Musical Theatre in Bayreuth. LC 68-25293. (Studies in Music: No. 42). 1969. reprint ed. lib. bdg. 75.00 (0-8383-0284-X) M S G Haskell Hse.

Lavignac, Albert. Music Dramas of Richard Wagner. Singleton, Esther, tr. LC 77-121292. 1977. reprint ed. 22.75 (0-404-03890-5) AMS Pr.

— The Music Dramas of Richard Wagner & His Festival Theatre in Bayreuth. 515p. 1990. reprint ed. lib. bdg. 99.00 (0-7812-9157-7) Rprt Serv.

LaVigne, Duncan L. The Wine Inventory Book. 90p. 1990. 59.95 (0-9625723-0-6) Wine Bk Co.

LaVigne, James & Wechsler, Charles. Minnesota: State of Beauty. 2nd ed. (Illus.). 96p. 1992. pap. 6.98 (0-931714-12-5) Nodin Pr.

LaVigne, Jeanne M., jt. auth. see Sawner, Kathryn A.

Lavigne, John R. Instrumentation Applications for the Pulp & Paper Industry. LC 77-93837. (Illus.). 320p. 1979. 45.00 (0-87930-074-4) Miller Freeman.

— An Introduction to Paper Industry Instrumentation. rev. ed. LC 77-89603. (Pulp & Paper Book Ser.). (Illus.). 1977. 47.50 (0-87930-069-8) Miller Freeman.

— Pulp & Paper Dictionary. 480p. 1986. 75.00 (0-8288-1428-7, M15398) Fr & Eur.

— Pulp & Paper Dictionary. 2nd ed. Patrick, Kenneth L., ed. 370p. 1993. 65.00 (0-87930-303-4) Miller Freeman.

***Lavigne, Marie.** The Economics of Transition: From Socialist Economy to Market Economy. 1995. write for info. (0-312-12720-0); pap. write for info. (0-312-12721-9) St Martin.

— Financing the Transition in the U. S. S. R. The Shatalin Plan & the Soviet Union. 35p. (C). 1991. pap. text ed. 9.85 (0-8133-8279-3) Westview.

— International Political Economy & Socialism. Lambert, David, tr. (Illus.). 320p. (C). 1991. 74.95 (0-521-33427-6); pap. 19.95 (0-521-33663-5) Cambridge U Pr.

Lavigne, Marie, ed. The Soviet Union & Eastern Europe in the Global Economy. (International Council for Soviet & East European Studies). 224p. (C). 1992. 59.95 (0-521-41417-2) Cambridge U Pr.

Lavigne, Michel, jt. auth. see Brown, George.

***LaVigne, Michelle.** The Alien Abduction Survival Guide: How to Cope with Your ET Experience. Owen, Amy E. & Davenport, Marc, eds. 106p. (Orig.). 1995. pap. 12.95 (0-926524-27-5, Wild Flower Pr) Blue Wtr Pubng.

LaVigne, Ruth A. The Life of St. Claude de la Colombiere: Spiritual Director of St. Margaret Mary Alacoque. rev. ed. 127p. 1992. pap. 7.95 (0-8198-4467-5) Pauline Bks.

Lavigne, Shelly. Boy or Girl? Fifty Fun Ways to Find Out. (Illus.). (Orig.). 1992. mass mkt. 5.99 (0-440-50459-7, Dell Trade Pbks) Dell.

Lavigne, Yves. Good Guy, Bad Guy. 1993. mass mkt. 5.99 (0-345-39794-0) Ballantine.

— Hell's Angels: Three Can Keep a Secret If Two Are Dead. (Illus.). 344p. reprint ed. pap. 9.95 (0-8184-0514-7) Carol Pub Group.

LaVilla-Havelin, James. Simon's Masterpiece. 1983. pap. 6.00 (0-934834-40-7) White Pine.

LaVilla-Havelin, Lucia. The New Basket: A Vessel for the Future. (Illus.). 36p. 1984. pap. 10.00 (0-942746-06-6) SUNYP R Gibson.

***Lavin.** Meditations for Health. Date not set. pap. 8.99 (0-517-12415-7) Random.

— Meditations for Success. Date not set. 8.99 (0-517-12416-5) Random.

— Meditations on Joy. Date not set. 8.99 (0-517-12414-9) Random.

— Meditations on Love. Date not set. pap. 10.99 (0-517-12417-3) Random.

Lavin, jt. auth. see Bagley.

Lavin, jt. auth. see Rothman.

Lavin, Audrey A. Aspects of the Novelist: E. M. Forster's Pattern & Rhythm. LC 93-12338. (AUS IV: Vol. 151). 168p. (C). 1995. text ed. 35.95 (0-8204-1966-4) P Lang Pubs.

Lavin, Bebe, jt. auth. see Haug, Marie R.

Lavin Camacho, Enrique. Diccionario de Verbos Ingleses con Particula. 240p. (ENG & SPA.). 1989. pap. 32.95 (0-7859-5714-6, 8420516724) Fr & Eur.

Lavin, David E., et al. Right Versus Privilege: The Open Admissions Experiment at the City University of New York. LC 80-69571. (Illus.). 1981. 35.00 (0-02-918080-5) Free Pr.

Lavin, Edward. Life Meditations. 1993. 12.99 (0-517-09374-X) Random Hse Value.

Lavin, Hank & Freeman, Priscilla. How to Get - & Keep! - a Profitable Rep Agency by Effective Marketing. (Illus.). 216p. 1991. text ed. 33.95 (0-941890-06-6) Lavin Assocs.

Lavin, Henry. How to Get-& Keep-Good Industrial Customers Through Effective Direct Mail. LC 80-65947. (Illus.). 255p. 1980. 19.50 (0-685-45450-9) Lavin Assocs.

— How to Get & Keep Good Industrial Representatives. 3rd ed. (Illus.). 252p. 1995. 85.00 (0-941890-02-3) Lavin Assocs.

— How to Get & Keep Good Product Lines. 2nd ed. (Illus.). 95p. 1990. 29.95 (0-941890-03-1) Lavin Assocs.

Lavin, Irving. Past-Present: Essays on Historicism in Art from Donatello to Picasso. (Una's Lectures: No. 6). (C). 1992. 65.00 (0-520-06816-5) U CA Pr.

Lavin, Irving, ed. Gianlorenzo Bernini: New Aspects of His Art & Thought. LC 84-43087. (College Art Association Monograph Ser.: Vol. 37). (Illus.). 234p. 1985. 39.50 (0-271-00387-1) Pa St U Pr.

— World Art: Themes of Unity in Diversity, Acts of the XXVIth International Congress of the History of Art, 3 vols. 906p. 1989. 95.00 (0-271-00607-2) Pa St U Pr.

Lavin, Irving, ed. see Panofsky, Erwin.

Lavin, J. A., ed. see Goldsmith, Oliver.

Lavin, J. A., ed. see Sheridan, Richard B.

Lavin, James D., jt. auth. see Gusler, Wallace B.

Lavin, Lisa M. Radiography in Veterinary Technology. LC 93-26133. 1994. text ed. 36.95 (0-7216-6686-8) Saunders.

Lavin, Marilyn A. Piero Della Francesca. (Masters of Art Ser.). (Illus.). 128p. 1992. 22.95 (0-8109-3210-5) Abrams.

— Piero della Francesca: San Francesco, Arezzo. (Great Fresco Cycles of the Renaissance Ser.). 104p. 1994. 23.50 (0-8076-1317-7) Braziller.

— Piero Della Francesca: The Flagellation. (Illus.). 112p. 1990. pap. 12.95 (0-226-46958-1) U Ch Pr.

— The Place of Narrative: Mural Decoration in Italian Churches, 431-1600. (Illus.). xx, 406p. 1994. pap. text ed. 49.95 (0-226-46960-3) U Ch Pr.

— William Bostwick: Connecticut Yankee in Antebellum Georgia. LC 77-14787. (Dissertations in American Economic History Ser.). 1978. 37.95 (0-405-11044-8) Ayer.

Lavin, Marilyn A., ed. IL 60: Essays Honoring Irving Lavin on His Sixtieth Birthday. LC 89-85336. (Illus.). 303p. 1990. 45.00 (0-934977-18-6) Italica Pr.

— Piero Della Francesca & His Legacy. (Studies in the History of Art: No. 48). (Illus.). 328p. 1995. 60.00 (0-89468-203-2) U Pr of New Eng.

Lavin, Martin & Watters, Dianne, eds. Programmed Cell Death: The Cellular & Molecular Biology of Apoptosis. LC 93-27865. 331p. 1993. text ed. 96.00 (3-7186-5461-X) Gordon & Breach.

Lavin, Mary. The Story of the Widow's Son. (Short Stories Ser.). (J). (gr. 5 up). 1992. lib. bdg. 13.95 (0-88682-500-8) Creative Ed.

Lavin, Mary F., tr. see Bialas, Martin.

Lavin, Matt. Biogeography & Systematics of Poitea (Leguminosae) Anderson, Christiane, ed. (Systematic Botany Monographs: Vol. 37). (Illus.). 87p. 1993. pap. 11.00 (0-912861-37-1) Am Soc Plant.

— Systematics of Coursetia (Leguminosae-Papilionoideae) Anderson, Christiane, ed. (Systematic Botany Monographs: Vol. 21). (Illus.). 167p. 1988. pap. 20.00 (0-912861-21-5) Am Soc Plant.

Lavin, Maud. Cut with the Kitchen Knife: The Weimar Photomontages of Hannah Hoch. (Illus.). 280p. 1994. pap. 22.50 (0-300-06164-1) Yale U Pr.

— Cut with the Kitchen Knife: The Weimer Photomontages of Hannah Hoch. LC 92-14332. (Illus.). 256p. (C). 1993. text ed. 45.00x (0-300-04766-5) Yale U Pr.

Lavin, Michael R. Business Information: How to Find It, How to Use It. 2nd ed. 512p. 1992. 49.95 (0-89774-556-6); pap. 38.50 (0-89774-643-0) Oryx Pr.

— Understanding the Census: A Guide for Marketers, Planners, Grant Writers & Other Data Users. LC 92-74697. (Illus.). 200p. (Orig.). Date not set. pap. 49.95 (0-9629586-1-1) Epoch Bks.

Lavin, Norman. Manual of Endocrinology & Metabolism. 770p. 1986. pap. text ed. 21.00 (0-316-51651-1) Little.

Lavin, Norman, ed. Manual of Endocrinology & Metabolism. 2nd ed. LC 93-874. (Illus.). 688p. 1993. 35.95 (0-316-51657-0) Little.

Lavin, Paul. Parenting the Overactive Child: Alternatives to Drug Therapy. LC 89-2613. (Illus.). 160p. (Orig.). (C). 1989. 21.95 (0-8191-7297-9); pap. 10.95 (0-8191-7315-0) Madison Bks UPA.

***Lavin, Ronald J.** The Great I Am. 1995. pap. write for info. (0-7880-0576-6) CSS OH.

— Previews of Coming Attractions. 1991. pap. 8.25 (1-55673-317-8, 9138) CSS OH.

— You Can Grow in a Small Group. 144p. 1976. pap. 6.00 (0-89536-273-2, 2500) CSS OH.

Lavin, S. R. Let Myself Shine. 7.00 (0-686-65484-6); pap. 3.50 (0-686-65485-4) Kulchur Foun.

— The Stonecutters at War with the Cliffdwellers: 9 Poems. (Illus.). 1971. 95.00 (0-685-47825-4) Heron Pr.

— The Stonecutters at War with the Cliffdwellers: 9 Poems. deluxe ed. (Illus.). 1971. boxed 200.00 (0-685-47826-2) Heron Pr.

Lavin, Sylvia. Quatremere de Quincy & the Invention of a Modern Language of Architecture. (Illus.). 352p. 1992. 45.00 (0-262-12166-2) MIT Pr.

Lavina, Pedro T., jt. auth. see Jimenez-Lopez, Vicente.

Lavine, A. S., et al, eds. General Papers in Heat Transfer & Heat Transfer in Hazardous Waste Processing. (HTD Ser.: Vol. 212). 176p. 1992. 50.00 (0-7918-1052-6, G00696) ASME.

Lavine, Alan. Getting Started in Mutual Funds. text ed. write for info. (0-471-57696-4) Wiley.

— Getting Started in Mutual Funds. 1994. pap. text ed. 14.95 (0-471-57694-8) Wiley.

— Your Life Insurance Options. LC 92-14939. (ICFP Personal Wealth Building Guides Ser.). 224p. 1993. text ed. 45.00 (0-471-54918-5); pap. text ed. 12.95 (0-471-54919-3) Wiley.

Lavine, Alan, jt. auth. see Liberman, Gail.

Lavine, Alan, jt. auth. see Perritt, Gerald.

Lavine, Eileen, ed. Directory of Pathology Training Programs, 1988-89. 20th ed. (Illus.). 518p. 1987. pap. 50.00 (0-937888-04-4) Intersoc Comm Path Info.

— Directory of Pathology Training Programs, 1989-90. 21th rev. ed. (Illus.). 550p. (Orig.). 1988. pap. 55.00 (0-937888-05-2) Intersoc Comm Path Info.

Lavine, Eileen, jt. ed. see Intersociety Committee on Pathology Information Staff.

Lavine, Emanuel H. The Third Degree: A Detailed Account of Police Brutality. LC 74-676. (Civil Liberties in American History Ser.). 248p. 1974. reprint ed. lib. bdg. 32.50 (0-306-70601-6) Da Capo.

Lavine, Harold & Wechsler, James. War Propaganda & the U. S. 1972. 59.95 (0-8490-1277-5) Gordon Pr.

Lavine, Harold & Wechsler, James A. War Propaganda & the United States. LC 72-4668. (International Propaganda & Communications Ser.). (Illus.). 389p. 1972. reprint ed. 21.95 (0-405-04753-3) Ayer.

Lavine, Jane, ed. see Zagat, Eugene H., Jr. & Zagat, Nina S.

Lavine, John M. & Wackman, Daniel B. Managing Media Organizations. (Illus.). 454p. (C). 1988. pap. text ed. 39.95 (0-582-28634-4, 71658) Longman.

Lavine, Lance. Five Degrees of Conservation: A Graphic Analysis of Energy Alternatives for a Northern Climate. (Illus.). 65p. 1982. 19.50 (0-943352-00-2); pap. 10.95 (0-943352-01-0) Univ Minn Sch.

Lavine, Lance, et al. Five Degrees of Conservation: A Graphic Analysis of Energy Alternatives for a Northern Climate. LC 83-620711. 72p. reprint ed. pap. 25.00 (0-7837-2939-1, 2057515) Bks Demand.

Lavine, Ronald M. Introduction to Apple II BASIC. 1984. pap. 19.20 (0-395-35600-8) HM.

— Introduction to Apple II BASIC. 1984. teacher ed, pap. 127.20 (0-395-35601-6) HM.

Lavine, Shaughan. Understanding the Infinite. LC 93-49697. (Illus.). 376p. 1994. text ed. 39.95 (0-674-92096-1) HUP.

Lavine, Steven D., jt. ed. see Karp, Ivan.

Lavine, Thelma Z. From Socrates to Sartre. 432p. 1985. mass mkt. 6.99 (0-553-25161-9) Bantam.

Lavine, Thelma Z., jt. ed. see Tejera, V.

Lavington, Frederick. English Capital Market. LC 67-30469. (Reprints of Economic Classics Ser.). ix, 297p. 1968. reprint ed. 39.50 (0-678-00345-9) Kelley.

Lavington, Simon, jt. ed. see Abdelguerfi, Mahdi.

Lavinia, Alice S. Endocrinology: Index of New Information with Authors, Subjects & References. 150p. 1994. 49.50 (1-55914-718-0); pap. 39.50 (1-55914-719-9) ABBE Pubs Assn.

Lavinthal, Hy. Defense Strategy in Bridge. Coffin, George, ed. 192p. 1974. reprint ed. pap. 4.50 (0-486-23010-4) Dover.

LaViolette, Alyce D., jt. auth. see Barnett, Ola W.

LaViolette, Forrest E. Americans of Japanese Ancestry. Daniels, Roger, ed. LC 78-54822. (Asian Experience in North America Ser.). 1979. reprint ed. lib. bdg. 18.95 (0-405-11278-5) Ayer.

— The Canadian Japanese & World War II. LC 48-11190. 332p. reprint ed. pap. 94.70 (0-317-09537-4, 2055473) Bks Demand.

— The Struggle for Survival: Indian Cultures & the Protestant Ethic in British Columbia. rev. ed. LC 73-84433. 215p. reprint ed. pap. 61.30 (0-317-27022-2, 2023643) Bks Demand.

LaViolette, Paul. Beyond the Big Bang: Ancient Myth & the Science of Continuous Creation. (Illus.). 288p. 1995. 29.95 (0-89281-457-8) Inner Tradit.

***LaViolette, Paul A.** Subquantum Kinetics: The Alchemy of Creation. (Illus.). 208p. (Orig.). (C). 1994. pap. 15.00 (0-9642025-0-6) Starburst Pubns.

***LaViolette, Paul E., ed.** Seasonal & Interannual Variability of the Western Mediterranean Sea. LC 94-34453. (Coastal & Estuarine Studies: Vol. 46). 370p. 1994. 57.00 (0-87590-260-X) Am Geophysical.

LaViolette, Wesley. Love & Live. 1969. 5.95 (0-87516-038-7) DeVorss.

— Wings Unfolding. LC 70-140225. 1971. 5.95 (0-87516-040-9) DeVorss.

L

*Lavisse, Emile C. Field Equipment of the European Foot Soldier, 1900-1914. Lawton, Edward P., tr. (Reference Ser.: No. 2). (Illus.). 256p. 1994. reprint ed. 39.95 (0-89839-208-X) Battery Pr.

Lavisse, Ernest. Youth of Frederick the Great. LC 71-172308. reprint ed. 45.00 (0-404-03891-3) AMS Pr.

Lavisse, Ernest, ed. Histoire de France, Depuis les Origines Jusqu'a la Revolution, 18 pts. in 9 vols., Set. LC 73-89549. (Illus.). reprint ed. 720.00 (0-404-03900-6) AMS Pr.

LaVita, J. A., ed. see NATO Advanced Study Institute Staff.

Lavitt, Edward & McDowell, Robert. In the Beginning Creation Stories. 156p. (J). (gr. 6-12). 1973. 18.95 (0-89388-096-5) Okpaku Communications.

— Nihancan's Feast of Beaver: Animal Tales of the North American Indians. (Illus.). 112p. 1990. pap. 12.95 (0-89013-211-9) Museum NM Pr.

Lavitt, Edward, ed. see Goodall, Jane.

Lavitt, Edward, ed. see Krantz, Judith.

Lavitt, Edward, jt. ed. see McDowell, Robert E.

Lavitt, Mike, ed. see Gesar, A.

Lavitt, Wayne. Lotus Datalens in the Client Server Environment. 1994. pap. 36.95 (0-442-01514-3) Van Nos Reinhold.

Lavitt, Wendy, jt. auth. see Goddu, Krystyna P.

Lavitt, Wendy, jt. auth. see Weissman, Judith R.

Lavlin. Moments: Poems. 80p. 1992. 10.00 (0-7069-5892-6, Pub. by Vikas II) S Asia.

Lavo, Carl. Back from the Deep: The Strange Story of the Sister Subs, Squalus & Sculpin. LC 94-25853. (Illus.). 244p. 1994. 27.95 (1-55750-507-1) Naval Inst Pr.

Lavocat, Rene, jt. ed. see George, Wilma.

*Lavoie, Alphee. Lose This Book...& Find It Through Horary: A Practical Guide to Finding Lost Articles Through Horary Astrology. (Illus.). 134p. (Orig.). 1995. pap. 11.95 (0-9645621-0-3) AIR Soft.

Lavoie, Claire, tr. see Salmon, Pierre.

Lavoie, D. L., jt. ed. see Rezak, R.

Lavoie, Don, ed. Economics & Hermeneutics. 320p. 1991. 62.50 (0-415-05950-X, A5542) Routledge.

— Expectations & the Meaning of Institutions: Essays in Economics by Ludwig Lachmann. LC 93-29051. 1994. write for info. (0-415-10712-1, Routledge NY) Routledge.

Lavoie, Don C., ed. Solidarnosc z Wolnoscia: Solidarity with Liberty. 233p. (POL.). 1983. pap. 9.95 (0-932790-33-X) Cato Inst.

*Lavoie, Francine, et al, eds. Self-Help & Mutual Aid Groups: International & Multicultural Perspectives. LC 94-44762. (Prevention in Human Services Ser.). 175p. 1995. 49.95 (1-56024-716-9) Haworth Pr.

Lavoie, Kathleen H., ed. Cave Research Foundation Annual Report, 1983. (Illus.). 42p. (Orig.). 1984. pap. 5.00 (0-939748-15-0) Cave Bks MO.

Lavoie, Kathleen H., jt. auth. see Palmer, Arthur N.

Lavoie, Marc. Foundations of Post-Keynesian Economic Analysis. (New Directions in Modern Economics Ser.). (Illus.). 480p. 1994. pap. 29.95 (1-85278-816-X, Pub. by E Elgar Pub UK) Ashgate Pub Co.

Lavoie, Marc, ed. Foundations of Post-Keynesian Economic Analysis. (New Directions in Modern Economics Ser.). 512p. 1992. 99.95 (1-85278-322-2, Pub. by E Elgar Pub UK) Ashgate Pub Co.

Lavoie, Richard D. Lavoie Audio Workshop - Integrating Learning Disabled Students. 1992. audio 49.95 (1-55999-219-0) LinguiSystems.

Lavoie, Richard H. Discovering Mathematics. LC 92-30662. 640p. 1993. text ed. 55.95 (0-534-93340-8) PWS Pubs.

LaVoie, Roland. Greenberg's Model Railroading with Lionel Trains, Vol. I. 144p. (Orig.). (YA). (gr. 9-12). 1989. pap. 19.95 (0-89778-054-X, 10-6745); pap. text ed. 28.95 (0-685-67522-X, 10-6745LE) Greenberg Bks.

Lavoie, Roland E. Greenberg's Guide to Lionel Trains, 1970-1991, Vol. I: Motive Power & Rolling Stock. 3rd ed. Solly, Michael A., ed. (Illus.). 336p. 1991. 45.95 (0-89778-194-5, 10-7535HB); pap. 35.95 (0-89778-189-9, 10-7535) Greenberg Bks.

LaVoie, Steven. Erosion Surface. (Morning Coffee Chapbook Ser.). (Illus.). 40p. (Orig.). 1984. pap. 5.00 (0-915124-98-X) Coffee Hse.

Lavoine, J. L., jt. auth. see Misra, O. P.

Lavoisier & Hermann. Dictionnaire D'Informatique: English-French with French-English Dictonary. 680p. (FRE.). 1991. 175.00 (0-7859-0501-4, 2852067587) Fr & Eur.

Lavoisier, A. L. & Laplace, P. S. Memoir on Heat. Guerlac, Henry, ed. 1981. 14.95 (0-88202-195-8) Watson Pub Intl.

Lavoisier, Antoine. Elements of Chemistry. 539p. 1984. reprint ed. pap. 14.95 (0-486-64624-6) Dover.

— Essays, Physical & Chemical. Thomas, H., tr. 511p. 1970. reprint ed. 45.00 (0-7146-1604-4, Pub. by F Cass Pubs UK) Intl Spec Bk.

Lavon, Yaakov, tr. see Adler, Binyamin.

LaVopa, Anthony J. Prussian Schoolteachers: Profession & Office, 1763-1848. LC 79-24873. 230p. reprint ed. pap. 65.60 (0-7837-0312-0, 2040634) Bks Demand.

LaVor, Marty. No Borders. (Illus.). 1992. 35.00 (0-9632680-0-7) LaVor Grp.

Lavoy, Peter, tr. see Levesque, Jacques.

Lavrac, Nada & Dzeroski, Saso. Inductive Logic Programming: Techniques & Applications. LC 92-34371. (Ellis Horwood Series in Artificial Intelligence). 1993. 35.00 (0-13-457870-8, Tavistock-E Horwood) Routledge Chapman & Hall.

Lavrac, Nada, jt. ed. see Bratko, Ivan.

Lavrac, Nada, ed. see European Conference on Machine Learning Staff.

Lavrack, Kevin R. & Newell, Patricia J. Elementary Algebra: A Laboratory Workbook. 2nd ed. 112p. 1992. per. 9.95 (0-8403-7734-7) Kendall-Hunt.

— Pre-Algebra: A Laboratory Workbook. 2nd ed. 128p. 1992. per. 7.95 (0-8403-7733-9) Kendall-Hunt.

Lavrack, Kevin R. & Robinson, Rosalind. Basic Mathematics: A Laboratory Workbook. 60p. 1993. per. 4.45 (0-8403-8800-4) Kendall-Hunt.

Lavrakas, Paul. The Princess & the Pea. (Orig.). (J). 1993. pap. 5.00 (0-87602-321-9) Anchorage.

Lavrakas, Paul J. Telephone Survey Methods: Sampling, Selection & Supervision. 2nd ed. (Applied Social Research Methods Ser.). (Illus.). 160p. 1993. 37.00 (0-8039-5306-2); pap. 16.95 (0-8039-5307-0) Sage.

Lavrakas, Paul J. & Holley, Jack K., eds. Polling & Presidential Election Coverage. (Focus Editions Ser.: Vol. 127). (Illus.). 264p. (C). 1990. text ed. 49.95 (0-8039-4073-4); pap. text ed. 24.95 (0-8039-4074-2) Sage.

Lavranos, Destini & Ritchie, Sheri. The Magical Tree. (Illus.). 2p. (J). (ps-00). 1993. 14.95 (0-9638393-0-6) Bedtime Bks.

Lavranos, Destini, jt. auth. see Ritchie, Sheri.

Lavrenev, Boris A. The Forty-First. Wettlin, M. & Joche, N., trs. LC 75-39003. (Soviet Literature in English Translation Ser.). 190p. 1977. reprint ed. 17.60 (0-88355-406-2) Hyperion Conn.

Lavrenko, V. A., jt. auth. see Gogotsi, Yu.

Lavrent'ev, M., et al. One-Dimensional Inverse Problems of Mathematical Physics. LC 86-7917. (AMS Translations Ser.: Vol. 130, No. 2). 70p. 1992. text ed. 47.00 (0-8218-3099-6, TRANS 2-130) Am Math.

Lavrentev, M. A. Variational Methods for Boundary Value Problems (etc.) 1990. pap. 4.95 (0-486-66170-9) Dover.

Lavrent'ev, M. A., ed. Problems of Hydrodynamics & Continuum Mechanics. (Miscellaneous Bks.: No. 5). xi, 815p. 1969. text ed. 69.75 (0-89871-039-1) Soc Indus-Appl Math.

*Lavrent'ev, M. M., ed. International Symposium on Computerized Tomography (CT-93) 396p. 1994. 215.00 (90-6764-187-1, Pub. by VSP NE) Coronet Bks.

Lavrent'ev, M. M., et al. Ill-Posed Problems of Mathematical Physics & Analysis. LC 86-3642. (Translations of Mathematical Monographs: Vol. 64). 290p. 1986. text ed. 124.00 (0-8218-4517-9, MMONO-64) Am Math.

Lavrentev, V. V., jt. auth. see Bartenev, G. M.

Lavrentiev, Aleksander. Vavara Stepanova: The Complete Works. (Illus.). 1991. pap. 19.95 (0-262-62082-0) MIT Pr.

*Lavrentiev, Alexander, intro. Alexander Rodchenko Museum Series Portfolio. (Museum Series Portfolio: No. 1). 24p. 1994. write for info. (1-882277-03-1) Schickler-Lafaille.

Lavrentiev, Alexander, jt. ed. see Elliot, David.

Lavrent'sev, M. M., et al, eds. Conditionally Well-Posed Problems. 366p. 1994. 210.00x (90-6764-160-X) Coronet Bks.

Lavrik, O. I. Physicochemical Biology Reviews: Mechanisms of Enzyme Action, Vol. 9. Skulachev, V. P., ed. (Soviet Scientific Reviews Ser.: Vol. 9, Pt. 1). ii, 92p. 1989. text ed. 54.00 (3-7186-4918-7) Gordon & Breach.

*Lavrin, Asuncion. Women, Feminism & Social Change in Argentina, Chile & Uruguay. (Engendering Latin America Ser.). 725p. 1995. text ed. 34.50 (0-8032-2897-X) U of Nebr Pr.

Lavrin, Asuncion, ed. Latin American Women: Historical Perspectives. LC 77-94758. (Contributions in Women's Studies: No. 3). 343p. 1978. text ed. 55.00 (0-313-20309-1, LLA/, Greenwood Pr) Greenwood.

— Sexuality & Marriage in Colonial Latin America. LC 88-33980. (Latin American Studies). (Illus.). x, 349p. 1989. reprint ed. 35.00 (0-8032-2885-6); reprint ed. pap. 16.95x (0-8032-7940-X) U of Nebr Pr.

Lavrin, Janko. Aspects of Modernism, from Wilde to Pirandello. LC 68-22107. (Essay Index Reprint Ser.). 1977. reprint ed. 18.95 (0-8369-0611-X) Ayer.

— From Pushkin to Mayakovsky: A Study in the Evolution of a Literature. LC 72-114540. 308p. 1971. reprint ed. text ed. 59.75 (0-8371-4741-7, LAPM, Greenwood Pr) Greenwood.

— Gogol. LC 72-2123. (Studies in European Literature: No. 56). 1972. reprint ed. lib. bdg. 75.00 (0-8383-1473-2) M S G Haskell Hse.

— Ibsen & His Creation. LC 72-2140. (Studies in Scandinavian Life & Literature: No. 18). 1972. reprint ed. lib. bdg. 75.00 (0-8383-1484-8) M S G Haskell Hse.

— Nietzsche & Modern Consciousness. LC 72-2094. (Studies in German Literature: No. 13). 1972. reprint ed. lib. bdg. 75.00 (0-8383-1481-3) M S G Haskell Hse.

Lavrin, Janko, ed. A First Series of Representative Russian Stories, Pushkin to Gorky. LC 74-114539. (Illus.). 239p. 1975. reprint ed. text ed. 55.00 (0-8371-4740-9, LARS, Greenwood Pr) Greenwood.

Lavroff, Ellen C., et al, eds. Mas Cuentos y Juegos. 2nd rev. ed. (Illus.). (C). 1982. pap. text ed. 5.95 (0-393-95108-1) Norton.

Lavroff, Nic. Behind the Scenes at Sega: The Making of a Video Game. 1994. pap. 14.95 (1-55958-525-0) Prima Pub.

*Lavroff, Nicholas. Sega 32X Power Players Guide. (Illus.). (Orig.). 1995. pap. 13.95 (1-57280-050-X) IFTW Bks.

— Virtual Reality Playhouse: Explore Computer Generated Artificial Worlds on Your PC Including 3D Glasses. (Illus.). 128p. (Orig.). 1991. disk, pap. 23.95 (1-878739-19-0) Waite Group Pr.

Lavrov, S. & Sdasyuk, G., eds. Concepts of Regional Development. 268p. (C). 1988. 70.00 (0-685-31588-6) St Mut.

Lavrov, V. V. Deformation & Strength of Ice. 170p. 1971. text ed. 46.50 (0-7065-1098-4, Pub. by Keter Pub IS) Coronet Bks.

Lavrova, Elisaveta, tr. see Chekhov, Anton.

Lavry, M. Sh'ma B'ni. (BJE Choral Ser.). 6p. (HEB.). 0.65 (0-318-13634-1, 44-604) Board Jewish Educ.

Lavy, Victor. Investment in Human Capital: Schooling Supply Constraints in Rural Ghana. LC 92-41656. (Living Standards Measurement Study Working Paper Ser.: No. 93). 47p. 1992. 6.95 (0-8213-2321-0, 12321) World Bank.

Lavy, Victor & Germain, Jean-Marc. Quality & Cost in Health Care Choice in Developing Countries. LC 94-12590. (LSMS Working Papers: No. 105). 1994. write for info. (0-8213-2854-9) World Bank.

Lavy, Victor & Sheffer, Eliezer. Foreign Aid & Economic Development in the Middle East: Egypt, Syria & Jordan. LC 90-27796. 184p. 1991. text ed. 45.00 (0-275-93827-1, C3827, Praeger Pubs) Greenwood.

Lavy, Victor, jt. auth. see Behrman, Jere R.

Lavy, Victor, jt. auth. see Hanushek, Eric A.

*Lavy, Victor, et al. Changing Patterns of Illiteracy in Morocco: Assessment Methods Compared. LC 95-12294. (LSMS Working Paper Ser.: No. 115). 1995. write for info. (0-8213-3192-2) World Bank.

— The Impact of the Quality of Health Care on Children's Nutrition & Survival in Ghana. LC 94-41226. (LSMS Working Paper Ser.: No. 106). 1994. write for info. (0-8213-2997-9) World Bank.

*Law. Early Identification of Language Impairment. 1992. 42.50 (1-56593-026-6, 0270) Singular Publishing.

Law, jt. auth. see Adamczyk.

Law & Business Inc. Staff. Advising Corporations on Merger, Acquisition, & Takeover Situations. LC 85-242505. (Illus.). iv, 442p. 40.00 (0-685-13426-1) HarBrace.

Law & Business Inc. Staff, ed. The Lawyer's Almanac 1985: An Encyclopedia of Information About Law, Lawyers, & the Profession. 1018p. 1985. 60.00 (0-317-29466-0, #H4383X) HarBrace.

Law & Business Inc. Staff & Annas. American Health Law. 1990. 51.00 (0-316-04309-5) Little.

Law, A. G. & Wang, C. L., eds. Approximation, Optimization & Computing: Theory & Applications. 442p. 1990. 95.00 (0-444-88693-1, North Holland) Elsevier.

Law, Alexander, ed. Robert Fergusson: Scots Poems. 70p. 1986. 20.00 (0-85411-022-4, Pub. by Saltire Soc) St Mut.

*Law, Alma & Gordon, Mel. Meyerhold, Eisenstein & Biomechanics: Actor Training in Revolutionary Russia. 320p. 1995. lib. bdg. 42.50 (0-7864-0098-6) McFarland & Co.

Law, Alma H., tr. see Vampilov, Aleksandr.

Law, Averill M. & Kelton, W. David. Simulation Modeling & Analysis. 2nd ed. (Industrial Engineering & Management Ser.). 784p. 1991. pap. text ed. write for info. (0-07-036698-5) McGraw.

Law, B. C. A History of Pali Literature, 2 vols. 1972. lib. bdg. 600.00 (0-87968-535-2) Krishna Pr.

Law, B. C., tr. The Debates Commentary. (C). 1940. 12.00 (0-86013-019-3, Pub. by Pali Text) Wisdom MA.

— Designation of Human Types. (C). 1922. 16.00 (0-86013-009-6, Pub. by Pali Text) Wisdom MA.

— The Legend of the Topes. (C). 1986. 13.50 (81-7069-000-5, Pub. by Munshiram Manoharial II) S Asia.

Law, B. E. & Rice, D. D., eds. Hydrocarbons from Coal. (Studies in Geology: No. 38). (Illus.). viii, 400p. (Orig.). 1993. pap. 115.00 (0-89181-046-3) AAPG.

Law, B. W. & Law, R. G. From Reason to Romanticism. LC 72-4541. (Studies in French Literature: No. 45). 1972. reprint ed. lib. bdg. 49.95 (0-8383-1595-X) M S G Haskell Hse.

Law, Barbara & Eckes, Mary. The More Than Just Surviving Handbook: ESL for Every Classroom Teacher. (Illus.). 224p. (Orig.). (gr. k-12). 1990. teacher ed, pap. 17.95 (0-920541-98-4) Peguis Pubs Ltd.

Law, Bill. The Pre-Vocational Franchise: Organising Community-Linked Education for Adult & Working Life. 224p. (C). 1986. pap. 36.00 (0-06-318354-4, Pub. by P Chapman Pub UK) St Mut.

Law, Bill, ed. Uses & Abuses of Profiling: A Handbook on Reviewing & Recording Student Experience & Achievement. 192p. (C). 1984. 50.00 (0-06-318300-5, Pub. by P Chapman Pub UK) St Mut.

Law, Bimala C. The Buddhist Conception of Spirits. 2nd enl. rev. ed. LC 78-72462. reprint ed. 21.50 (0-404-17334-9) AMS Pr.

— Geography of Early Buddhism. 1979. reprint ed. 12.75 (0-685-46199-8, Pub. by Munshiram Manoharial II) S Asia.

— Some Ksatriya Tribes of Ancient India. LC 78-72468. reprint ed. 42.00 (0-404-17338-1) AMS Pr.

Law, Bimala C., ed. Buddhistic Studies. LC 78-72463. reprint ed. 74.50 (0-404-17335-7) AMS Pr.

— Geography of Early Buddhism. LC 78-72464. reprint ed. 21.00 (0-404-17336-5) AMS Pr.

— Historical Gleanings. LC 78-72466. reprint ed. 20.00 (0-404-17337-3) AMS Pr.

— A History of Pali Literature, 2 vols. LC 78-72467. reprint ed. 75.00 (0-404-17650-X) AMS Pr.

— A Study of the Mahavastu. LC 78-72469. reprint ed. 26.50 (0-404-17339-X) AMS Pr.

Law, Bimala C., tr. see Dhamma-Kitti.

Law, Bimala Churn. Historical Geography of Ancient India. 354p. reprint ed. text ed. 30.00 (0-685-14328-7) Coronet Bks.

Law, Bimla C. Concepts of Buddhism. (C). 1986. 9.00 (0-8364-2830-7, Pub. by Gian Publng Hse II) S Asia.

Law Bimla Churn. Concept of Buddhism. 142p. 1986. 22.95 (0-318-37011-5) Asia Bk Corp.

Law, Carolyn L., jt. ed. see Dews, C. L.

Law, Charles J. Tech Prep Education: A Total Quality Approach. LC 93-60982. 250p. 1993. pap. text ed. 39.00 (1-56676-086-0) Technomic.

Law, Christopher, et al, eds. The Uncertain Future of the Urban Core. 272p. 1988. lib. bdg. 55.00 (0-415-00464-0) Routledge.

Law, Christopher M., ed. Restructuring the Global Automobile Industry: Global, National & Regional Impacts. 304p. 1991. 69.95 (0-415-04712-9, A5889) Routledge.

Law, Clarence G., Jr. & Pollard, Richard, eds. Processing of Electronic Materials. LC 87-81560. 488p. 1987. 70.00 (0-8169-0427-8, P-50) Am Inst Chem Eng.

Law, Daniel, tr. see Stibbs, Alan N.

Law, David, jt. auth. see Gill, Stephen.

Law, David A. From Samaria to Samarkand: The Ten Lost Tribes of Israel. 228p. (C). 1992. lib. bdg. 38.50 (0-8191-8409-8) U Pr of Amer.

— Russian Civilization. (Illus.). 490p. (C). 1975. 39.50 (0-8422-5232-0); pap. text ed. 12.50 (0-8422-0529-2) Irvington.

Law, David R. The Hiddenness of God: Negative Theology in the Pseudonymous Works of Kierkegaard. LC 92-24777. (Oxford Theological Monographs). (C). 1993. 49.95 (0-19-826336-8, Clarendon Pr) OUP.

Law, David R., tr. see Thielicke, Helmut.

Law, Deborah. Growing Fuchsias. 2nd ed. (Growing Ser.). (Illus.). 96p. (Orig.). 1993. reprint ed. pap. 11.95 (0-86417-297-4, Pub. by Kangaroo Pr AT) Seven Hills Bk.

Law, Debra T. Expecting: Quick Reference Guide to Childbirth. rev. ed. (Illus.). 122p. (C). 1989. student ed write for info. (0-318-66610-3); pap. text ed. write for info. (0-318-66609-X) Imprint Commns.

Law, Dennis L. Mind-Land Rehabilitation. 198p. (C). 1984. text ed. 39.95 (0-442-25987-5) Krieger.

Law, Derek, jt. ed. see Howarth, Stephen.

Law, Donald E. Intimacy & the Black Man: Face to Face with the Truth about Black Men. 72p. (Orig.). 1994. pap. 10.00 (0-9641537-4-2) D E Law.

Law, Donald F., jt. auth. see Hinkle, Joseph D.

Law, Donald F., jt. auth. see Hukle, Joseph D.

Law, Elizabeth. Double Deception. 224p. 1987. 16.95 (0-8027-0950-8) Walker & Co.

— Double Deception. 1989. pap. 2.95 (0-8217-2825-3) Zebra.

— Regency Morning. 224p. 1988. 17.95 (0-8027-1043-3) Walker & Co.

— Regency Morning. 1990. pap. 2.95 (0-8217-3152-1) Zebra.

— Scent of Lilac. 224p. 1991. pap. 3.50 (0-8217-3324-9) Zebra.

— The Sealed Knot. 224p. 1989. 18.95 (0-8027-1085-9) Walker & Co.

Law, Elwin. The Beer Drinker's Dream Diet. (Illus.). 90p. 1991. pap. text ed. 7.95 (0-9631321-4-8) Winnstead Pub.

Law, Emma, jt. auth. see DeBolt, Margaret W.

Law, Eric H. F. The Wolf Shall Dwell with the Lamb: A Spirituality for Leadership in a Multicultural Community. LC 93-9205. 152p. (Orig.). 1993. pap. 13.99 (0-8272-4231-X) Chalice Pr.

Law Firm of Gage & Tucker Staff. Environmental Due Diligence Handbook. 2nd ed. 300p. 1991. 79.00 (0-86587-245-7) Gov Insts.

Law Firm of Schmeltzer, Aptaker & Sheppard Staff, ed. see Nolan, John J.

Law Firm of Sutherland, Asbill & Brennan. Georgia Environmental Law Handbook. (State Environmental Law Ser.). 152p. 1990. pap. text ed. 69.00 (0-86587-235-X) Gov Insts.

Law, Frederick H. Modern Great Americans. LC 72-99706. (Essay Index Reprint Ser.). 1977. 26.95 (0-8369-1417-1) Ayer.

Law, Frederick H., ed. Modern Plays, Short & Long. (Play Anthology Reprint Ser.). 1977. reprint ed. 29.95 (0-8369-8250-9) Ayer.

Law, Gordon T., Jr. & Reilly, Michael E. A Guide to Information on Closely Held Corporations. LC 86-32812. (Orig.). 1986. pap. text ed. 4.00 (0-9615917-1-4) NY Ind Labor.

Law, Graham, ed. The Evil Genius: Wilkie Collins. 280p. 1994. pap. 12.95 (1-55111-017-2) Broadview Pr.

Law, Hamish, jt. auth. see Lamb, Douglas W.

Law, Harry D. The Organic Chemistry of Peptides. LC 75-126888. 243p. reprint ed. pap. 69.30 (0-317-29324-9, 2024015) Bks Demand.

Law, Helen M., tr. see De Paul, Vincent.

Law, Henry. El Evangelio en el Exodo: The Gospel in Exodus. (SPA.). 5.50 (84-7645-096-6, 223151, Pub. by Edit Clie SP) TSELF.

— The Gospel in Genesis. 188p. 1993. reprint ed. pap. text ed. 5.95 (0-85151-038-8) Banner of Truth.

Law, Henry G., et al, eds. Research Methods for Multi-Mode Data Analysis. 272p. 1984. text ed. 95.00 (0-275-91210-8, C1210, Praeger Pubs) Greenwood.

Law, Hugh T. How to Trace Your Ancestors to Europe: 117 Stories, Procedures, Sources to Use for 24 countries, Vol. 1. (Illus.). 422p. (Orig.). 1987. 19.00 (0-935775-01-3) Cottonwood Bks.

Law, I. H. & Suckling, M. H. Handling When Children are Profoundly Handicapped. (C). 1989. 140.00 (1-85098-332-1, Pub. by Jordanhill College UK) St Mut.

Law in the Service of Man, Al Haq Staff. Punishing a Nation: Israeli Human Rights Violations During the Palestinian Uprising. 352p. (Orig.). (C). 1990. 40.00 (0-89608-379-9); pap. 16.00 (0-89608-378-0) South End Pr.

Law, Ivan. Gears & Gear Cutting. (Workshop Practice Ser.: No. 17). (Illus.). 136p. (Orig.). 1987. pap. 18.50x (0-85242-911-8, Pub. by Argus Books UK) Trans-Atl Phila.

An Asterisk (*) at the beginning of an entry indicates that the title is appearing in BIP for the first time.

— Measuring & Marking Metals. (Workshop Practice Ser.: No. 6). (Illus.). (Orig.). 1985. pap. 18.50x (0-85242-841-3, Pub. by Argus Books UK) Trans-Atl Phila.

Law, Jack, et al. Pictures of Practice, Vol. 1: Community Social Work in Scotland. Smale, Gerald, ed. (C). 1988. 40.00 (0-685-31909-1, Pub. by Natl Inst Soc Work) St Mut.

— Pictures of Practice, Vol. 1: Community Social Work in Scotland. Smale, G. & Bennett, W., eds. (C). 1989. 49.00 (0-685-46666-3, Pub. by Natl Inst Soc Work) St Mut.

***Law, James & Elias, Jane.** Trouble Talking: A Guide for Parents of Children with Difficulties Communicating. 200p. 1995. pap. text ed. 24.95x (1-85302-253-5) Taylor & Francis.

Law, Jane M., ed. Religious Reflections on the Human Body. LC 94-4436. 1994. 29.95 (0-253-33263-X); pap. 12.95 (0-253-20902-1) Ind U Pr.

— Waiting for the Dawn: Mircea Eliade in Perspective. (Illus.). 176p. 1991. pap. 14.95 (0-87081-239-4) Univ Pr Colo.

Law, Janice. Backfire. (Anna Peters Mystery Ser.). 208p. 1994. 18.95 (0-312-11474-5) St Martin.

— Infected Be the Air. 208p. 1991. 18.95 (0-8027-5799-5) Walker & Co.

— A Safe Place to Die. 1995. mass mkt. 3.99 (0-373-26179-9, 1-26179-1) Harlequin Bks.

— A Safe Place to Die. 208p. 1993. 17.95 (0-312-09300-4) St Martin.

— Time Lapse: An Anna Peters Mystery. 199p. 1992. 19.95 (0-8027-3221-6) Walker & Co.

Law, Joe, jt. ed. see Murphy, Christina.

Law, John. Money & Trade Considered: With a Proposal for Supplying the Nation with Money. LC 65-19649. (Library of Money & Banking History). 120p. 1966. reprint ed. 27.50 (0-678-00187-1) Kelley.

— Organizing Modernity. (Illus.). 320p. 1994. 49.95 (0-631-18512-7); pap. 21.95 (0-631-18513-5) Blackwell Pubs.

Law, John, pseud. Out of Work. (Radical Fiction Ser.). 304p. 1990. reprint ed. lib. bdg. 25.00 (0-929587-39-1) I R Dee.

Law, John, jt. ed. see Bijker, Wiebe E.

Law, John, jt. auth. see Hay, Denys.

Law, John, tr. see Latour, Bruno.

Law, Joy. The Midi: Languedoc & Roussillon. (Illus.). 308p. 1992. 39.95 (0-7195-4807-1, Pub. by John Murray UK) Trafalgar.

Law, Jules D. The Rhetoric of Empiricism: Language & Perception, from Locke to I. A. Richards. LC 92-44276. 280p. (C). 1993. 36.50 (0-8014-2706-1) Cornell U Pr.

Law, K. K., jt. auth. see Duncan, J. P.

Law, K. T., jt. auth. see Wang, J. G.

Law, Katheryn. Salish Folk Tales. (Indian Culture Ser.). (J). (gr. 2-8). 1972. 1.50 (0-89992-028-4) Coun India Ed.

Law, Kevin J. Canada. (Let's Visit Places & Peoples of the World Ser.). (Illus.). (J). (gr. 5 up). 1988. 14.95 (0-222-00912-8) Chelsea Hse.

— Canada. (Places & Peoples of the World Ser.). (Illus.). 128p. (YA). (gr. 5 up). 1990. lib. bdg. 14.95 (0-7910-1101-1) Chelsea Hse.

— The Environmental Protection Agency. (Know Your Government Ser.). (Illus.). 96p. (J). (gr. 5 up). 1988. lib. bdg. 14.95 (1-55546-105-0) Chelsea Hse.

— Millard Fillmore: Thirteenth President of the United States. Young, Richard G., ed. LC 89-25651. (Presidents of the United States Ser.). (Illus.). 128p. (J). (gr. 5-9). 1990. lib. bdg. 17.26 (0-944483-61-5) Garrett Ed Corp.

Law, L. GCSE Geography Coursework Assessment Evaluation Pack. (C). 1989. 150.00 (0-09-175862-9, Pub. by S Thornes Pubs UK) St Mut.

Law, L. & Smith, S. Decision Making Geography. (C). 1987. 100.00 (0-09-167981-8, Pub. by S Thornes Pubs UK) St Mut.

Law, L. Bradley. Tracks of Gypsy Angels. LC 86-70545. 50p. (Orig.). 1986. pap. 6.95 (0-933865-03-1) Doris Pubns.

Law Librarians' Society of the District of Columbia Staff, comp. Union List of Legislative Histories: 47th Congress, 1881-101st Congress, 1990. 6th ed. LC 91-31271. xxix, 605p. ring bd. 95.00 (0-8377-2705-7) Rothman.

Law, Margaret H., jt. auth. see Rosen, Bruce K.

Law, Marilyn, ed. see ICP Staff & Welke, Larry A.

Law, Marilyn, ed. see International Computer Programs, Inc. Staff.

***Law, Merry E.** A Guide to International Measurements. (Illus.). 65p. (Orig.). 1994. pap. 19.95 (0-9644773-0-0) WorldView Pubns.

Law, N., et al. GCSE Geography Coursework Assessment. (C). 1989. 160.00 (0-09-172957-2, Pub. by S Thornes Pubs UK) St Mut.

Law, N., et al, eds. GCSE Geography Coursework Assessment Worksheet Masters. (C). 1989. 250.00 (0-09-173098-8, Pub. by S Thornes Pubs UK) St Mut.

Law, Narendra N. Studies in Indian History & Culture. 1990. reprint ed. 17.50 (0-8364-2516-2, Pub. by Low Price II) S Asia.

Law, Norman & Smith, David. Decision-Making Geography: In-Depth Case Studies Worldwide. 2nd ed. (Illus.). 240p. 1991. pap. 33.50 (0-7487-1111-2, Pub. by Stanley Thornes UK) Trans-Atl Phila.

— Problem-Solving Geography: Analysis in a Changing World. (Illus.). 240p. (Orig.). 1993. pap. 36.50 (0-7487-1355-7, Pub. by Stanley Thornes UK) Trans-Atl Phila.

Law, Nova. African-American Genealogy Workbook: Finding Your Roots. 3rd ed. (Illus.). 118p. 1992. student ed 17.95 (1-882804-03-1) Legacy Pub AL.

Law, P. J., jt. auth. see Ireland, N. J.

Law, Peter K. Myoblast Transfer: The Therapy for Muscular Dystrophy. (Medical Intelligence Unit Ser.). 115p. 1993. 89.95 (1-879702-76-2, R) R G Landes.

***Law, Phillp.** The Antarctic Voyage of HMAS Wyatt Earp. (Illus.). 158p. 1995. pap. 29.95 (1-86373-803-7) Paul & Co Pubs.

Law, Preston E. Shipboard Antennas. 2nd ed. LC 86-70448. (Artech House Antenna Library). (Illus.). 566p. reprint ed. pap. 161.40 (0-7837-4725-X, 2044290) Bks Demand.

— Shipboard Antennas. LC 82-72892. (Illus.). 561p. reprint ed. pap. 159.90 (0-318-39756-0, 2033130) Bks Demand.

— Shipboard Electromagnetics. LC 87-19293. (Artech House Antenna Library). (Illus.). 278p. reprint ed. pap. 79.30 (0-8357-7926-2, 2036352) Bks Demand.

Law, R., et al, eds. The Exploitation of Evolving Resources: Proceedings of an International Conference Held at Julich, Germany, September 3-5, 1991. LC 93-32081. (Lecture Notes in Biomathematics Ser.: Vol. 99). 1993. 50.00 (3-540-57242-2) Spr-Verlag.

Law, R. G., jt. auth. see Law, B. W.

Law, R. J., ed. see Owen, John.

Law, Rachel N. & Taylor, Cynthia W. Appalachian White Oak Basketmaking: Handing down the Basket. LC 90-12043. 328p. 1990. 4.00 (0-87049-668-9); pap. 18.95 (0-87049-672-7) U of Tenn Pr.

***Law Reform Commission of Canada Staff.** Trial Within a Reasonable Time: Working Paper Prepared for the Law Reform Commission of Canada. 122p. (Orig.). 1994. pap. 38.95x (0-660-59103-0, Pub. by Canada Commun Grp CN) Accents Pubns.

Law, Robin. The Horse in West African History: The Role of the Horse in the Societies of Pre-Colonial West Africa. LC 81-129421. (Illus.). 239p. reprint ed. pap. 70.70 (0-8357-3012-3, 2057098) Bks Demand.

— The Oyo Empire c. 1600-c. 1836: A West African Imperialism in the Era of the Atlantic. (Modern Revivals in History Ser.). 354p. 1992. 61.95 (0-7512-0006-9, Pub. by Gregg Revivals UK) Ashgate Pub Co.

— The Slave Coast of West Africa, 1550-1750: The Impact of the Atlantic Slave Trade on an African Society. (Oxford Studies in African Affairs). (Illus.). 392p. 1991. 89.00 (0-19-820228-8) OUP.

Law, Robin, ed. Correspondence of the Royal African Company's Chief Merchants at Cabo Corso Castle with William's Fort, Whydah, & the Little Popo Factory, 1727-1728: An Annotated Transcription of Ms. Francklin 1055-1 in the Bedfordshire County Record Office. LC 91-15880. (African Primary Texts Ser.: No. 3). 53p. (Orig.). 1991. pap. 15.00 (0-942615-08-5) U Wis African Stud.

— From Slave Trade to 'Legitimate' Commerce: The Commercial Transition in Nineteenth-Century West Africa. (African Studies Ser.: No. 86). 288p. (C). 1995. write for info. (0-521-48127-9) Cambridge U Pr.

— Further Correspondence of the Royal African Company of England Relating to the 'Slave Coast', 1681-1699: Selected Documents from Ms. Rawlinson c.745-747 in the Bodleian Library, Oxford. LC 92-11701. (African Primary Texts Ser.: No. 5). 100p. (Orig.). 1992. 15.00 (0-942615-13-1) U Wis African Stud.

Law, Rod. Rod, Write On: Pts. I-VIII, 1970-80. (Orig.). (C). text ed. 19.95 (0-9601730-2-1); pap. text ed. 12.50 (0-9601730-3-X) Rod Law.

Law, Ruth. Dim Sum: Fast & Festive Chinese Cooking. Crossman, Nancy, ed. LC 82-45410. (Illus.). 256p. 1985. reprint ed. pap. 9.95 (0-9614250-9-1) Whats Cooking.

— Indian Light Cooking: Delicious & Healthy Food from One of the World's Great Cuisines. LC 93-72588. 464p. 1994. 25.00 (1-55611-389-7) D I Fine.

— The Southeast Asia Cookbook. (Illus.). 1990. 28.00 (1-55611-214-9) D I Fine.

— The Southeast Asia Cookbook. (Illus.). 464p. 1995. pap. 16.95 (1-55611-469-9, Primus) D I Fine.

***Law, S. K. & Reid, K. B.** Complement: In Focus. (In Focus Ser.). (Illus.). 88p. 1995. pap. text ed. 17.50 (0-19-963356-8, IRL Pr) OUP.

***Law School Admissions Council Staff.** Official Guide to U. S. Law Schools, 1996. 1995. pap. 19.95 (0-385-31489-2, Kaplan Source Bks) Doubleday.

Law, Scott, jt. auth. see Nelsen, John.

Law, Shirley, jt. auth. see Law, Terry.

Law Society of Upper Canada Staff. Ontario Reports (Second Series) Consolidated Index, 3 vols., Set, Vols. 1-75. 2268p. 1991. Set. 195.00 (0-409-90572-0) Butterworth Legal Pubs.

Law Student Division Members, jt. auth. see ABA, Economics of Law Practice Section Staff.

Law Student Division Members Staff. Energy Methods: Keeping Fresh Under the Pressure of Law Practice. LC 80-81336. 42p. 1981. 2.75 (0-685-14377-5, 213-0001) Amer Bar Assn.

Law, Susan. Traitorous Hearts. 1994. mass mkt. 4.50 (0-06-108183-3, Harp PBks) HarpC.

Law, Susan K. Journey Home. 1993. mass mkt. 4.50 (0-06-108146-9, Harp PBks) HarpC.

— Reckless Angel. 1994. pap. 4.99 (0-06-108306-2, Harp PBks) HarpC.

Law, Susan K. & Reid, K. B. Complement. (In Focus Ser.). 82p. 1988. pap. 13.95 (1-85221-061-3, IRL Pr) OUP.

Law, Sylvia A. Blue Cross: What Went Wrong? LC 76-11427. 1976. 40.00 (0-300-02053-8) Yale U Pr.

Law, Terry. The Power of Praise & Worship. (Illus.). 256p. (Orig.). 1985. pap. 8.95 (0-932081-01-0) Victory Hse.

— Praise Releases Faith. 252p. (Orig.). 1987. pap. 8.95 (0-932081-15-0) Victory Hse.

— The Truth about Angels. 1994. pap. 9.99 (0-88419-368-3, Creation Hse) Strang Comms Co.

— Your Spiritual Weapons. (Illus.). 48p. 1985. reprint ed. pap. 2.25 (0-932081-00-2) Victory Hse.

— Your Spiritual Weapons & How to Use Them. (Orig.). 1983. pap. write for info. (0-88144-028-0, CPS028) Christian Pub.

Law, Terry & Law, Shirley. Yet Will I Praise Him. LC 87-9836. (Illus.). 256p. (Orig.). 1987. pap. 8.99 (0-8007-9106-1) Chosen Bks.

Law, Travis. Sleepwalker. 1992. 16.95 (0-533-10004-6) Vantage.

Law, Vivien. The Insular Latin Grammarians. (Studies in Celtic History: No. III). 131p. (C). 1987. 70.00 (0-85115-147-7) Boydell & Brewer.

— Wisdom, Authority & Grammar in the Seventh Century: Decoding Virgilius Maro Grammaticus. 200p. (C). 1995. 49.95 (0-521-47113-3) Cambridge U Pr.

Law, Vivien, ed. History of Linguistic Thought in the Early Middle Ages. LC 93-5696. (Studies in the History of the Language Sciences: No. 71). viii, 243p. 1993. 59.00 (1-55619-366-1) Benjamins North Am.

Law, William. 'SDaily Readings with William Law. Llewelyn, Robert, ed. (Daily Readings Ser.). 96p. 1987. pap. 4.95 (0-87243-153-3) Templegate.

— Extracts from the Writings of William Law. 60p. 1992. pap. 12.95 (1-56459-121-2) Kessinger Pub.

— Freedom from a Self-Centered Life. Murray, Andrew, ed. LC 77-71426. 144p. 1977. pap. 4.99 (0-87123-104-2) Bethany Hse.

— Power of the Spirit. Hunt, D., ed. 1993. pap. 4.95 (0-87508-247-5) Chr Lit.

— A Serious Call to a Devout & Holy Life. LC 82-80470. (Treasures from the Spiritual Classics Ser.). 64p. 1982. reprint ed. pap. 2.95 (0-8192-1306-3) Morehouse Pub.

— A Serious Call to a Devout & Holy Life. Meister, John et al, eds. LC 55-5330. 156p. 1968. reprint ed. pap. 9.99 (0-664-24833-0, Westminster) Westminster John Knox.

— Wholly for God. Murray, Andrew, ed. LC 76-6622. 336p. 1976. reprint ed. pap. 7.99 (0-87123-602-8) Bethany Hse.

— William Law: Selections on the Interior Life. Morrison, Mary, ed. LC 62-15272. (Orig.). 1962. pap. 3.00 (0-87574-120-7) Pendle Hill.

— William Law & Eighteenth-Century Quakerism. Hobhouse, Stephen, ed. LC 77-175870. (Illus.). 1972. reprint ed. 26.95 (0-405-08736-5) Ayer.

— The Works, 9 vols. in 3, Set. (Anglistica & Americana Ser.: No. 146). 1974. reprint ed. 323.70 (3-487-05100-1, Pub. by Georg Olms GW) Lubrecht & Cramer.

Law, William, tr. The Key of Jacob Boehme. LC 90-47418. (Magnum Opus Hermetic Sourceworks Ser.: No. 9). (Illus.). 86p. (Orig.). 1991. 27.00 (0-933999-93-3); pap. 12.50 (0-933999-94-1) Phanes Pr.

Law, William, tr. see Boehme, Jacob.

Law, William, et al. OS 2 V2 C Plus Plus Class Library: Power GUI Programming with C Set. LC 93-34417. (Illus.). 800p. 1995. pap. 36.95 (0-442-01795-2) Van Nos Reinhold.

Law-Yone, Wendy. Irrawaddy Tango: A Novel. LC 92-45863. 1994. 23.00 (0-679-42192-0) Knopf.

Lawaetz, Gudie, ed. Spanish Short Stories Two. 216p. 1993. pap. 9.95 (0-14-003378-5, Penguin Bks) Viking Penguin.

***Lawal, Ibironke O., ed.** Metalworking in Africa South of the Sahara: An Annotated Bibliography. LC 95-7485. (African Special Bibliographic Ser.: No. 19). 304p. 1995. text ed. 79.50 (0-313-29324-4, Greenwood Pr) Greenwood.

Lawall, David B., ed. John Barber, 1893-1965: Selections from the Archive. (Illus.). 198p. (C). 1992. text ed. 40.00 (0-8139-1395-0) U Pr of Va.

Lawall, G. & Lawall, S. Euripides: Hippolytus. 166p. 1986. 13.75 (0-86292-212-7, Pub. by Brstl Class Pr UK) Focus Info Gr.

Lawall, Gilbert. Carmina Catulli I-XI. (J). (gr. 10-12). 1983. pap. 5.95 (0-88334-166-2) Longman.

— The Romans Speak for Themselves. 1989. teacher ed 7.50 (0-8013-0269-2, 78040) Longman.

— The Romans Speak for Themselves, Bk. I. 1988. pap. text ed. 7.80 (0-8013-0267-6, 75919) Longman.

— The Romans Speak for Themselves, Bk. II. 1987. pap. text ed. 7.80 (0-8013-0268-4, 78041) Longman.

***Lawall, Gilbert, ed.** Petronius: Selections from the Satiricon. (Textbook Ser.). (Illus.). 260p. (Orig.). 1995. pap. text ed. 13.00 (0-86516-284-0) Bolchazy-Carducci.

— Plautus' Aulularia: The Pot of Gold; An Adaptation for Production by High School Latin Students. 35p. (Orig.). (LAT.). 1992. spiral bd. 2.55 (0-939507-30-7, B724) Amer Classical.

— Teacher's Handbook to the Longman Latin Readers. 1988. pap. text ed. 13.95 (0-582-36770-0, 72542) Longman.

Lawall, Gilbert & Kindel, Gerde. The Phaedra of Seneca. 238p. pap. text ed. 13.00 (0-86516-016-3) Bolchazy-Carducci.

Lawall, Gilbert & Quinn, Betty N. The Aulularia of Plautus. 1988. pap. text ed. 14.88 (0-582-36753-0, 72529) Longman.

Lawall, Gilbert & Quinn, Betty N., eds. Plautus' Menaechmi. (Textbook Ser.). (Illus.). 200p. (Orig.). 1981. pap. 13.00 (0-86516-007-4) Bolchazy-Carducci.

Lawall, Gilbert & Tafe, David M. Ecce Romani, Bk. 2. 1990. teacher ed, pap. text ed. 10.44 (0-8013-0445-8, 78255) Longman.

Lawall, Gilbert, jt. auth. see Balme, Maurice G.

Lawall, Gilbert, jt. auth. see Davis, Sally.

Lawall, Gilbert, et al. Ecce Romani, Bk. 1. 1984. teacher ed, pap. text ed. 8.28 (0-582-36730-1, 72519); student ed, pap. text ed. 7.29 (0-582-36664-X, 72458) Longman.

— Ecce Romani, Bk. 1. 1986. student ed, pap. text ed. 6.04 (0-582-36654-2, 72448) Longman.

— Ecce Romani, Bk. 1. 1990. teacher ed, pap. text ed. 10.44 (0-8013-0444-X, 78254) Longman.

— Ecce Romani, Bk. 2. 1984. teacher ed, pap. text ed. 8.28 (0-582-36731-X, 72520); pap. text ed. 7.29 (0-582-36665-8, 72459) Longman.

— Ecce Romani, Bk. 2. 1986. student ed, pap. text ed. 4.53 (0-582-36655-0, 72449) Longman.

— Ecce Romani, Bk. 3. 1984. teacher ed, pap. text ed. 8.28 (0-582-36732-8, 72521); student ed, pap. text ed. 4.53 (0-582-36656-9, 72450); student ed, pap. text ed. 7.29 (0-582-36666-6, 72460) Longman.

— Ecce Romani, Bk. 3. 1990. teacher ed, pap. text ed. 10.44 (0-8013-0446-6, 78256) Longman.

— Ecce Romani, Bk. 4. 1984. teacher ed, pap. text ed. 8.28 (0-582-36733-6, 72522); student ed, pap. text ed. 4.53 (0-582-36657-7, 72451); student ed, pap. text ed. 7.29 (0-582-36667-4, 72461) Longman.

— Ecce Romani, Bk. 4. 1990. teacher ed, pap. text ed. 10.44 (0-8013-0447-4, 78257) Longman.

— Ecce Romani, Bk. 5. 1984. teacher ed, pap. text ed. 8.28 (0-582-36734-4, 72523); student ed, pap. text ed. 4.53 (0-582-36658-5, 72452) Longman.

— Ecce Romani, Bk. 5. 1990. teacher ed, pap. text ed. 10.44 (0-8013-0448-2, 78258); student ed, pap. text ed. 7.29 (0-8013-0559-4, 78463) Longman.

— Ecce Romani, Set, Vol. I, Bks. 1-3. 1990. Set. pap. text ed. 31.08 (0-8013-0646-9, 78588) Longman.

— Ecce Romani, Set, Vol. II, Bks. 3-4. 1990. Set. student ed, text ed. 24.96 (0-8013-0440-7, 78250) Longman.

— Ecce Romani, Set, Vol. II, Bks. 4-5. 1990. Set. pap. text ed. 23.31 (0-582-99857-3, 78587) Longman.

— Ecce Romani, Test 1. 1988. pap. text ed. 23.25 (0-8013-0241-2, 75897) Longman.

— Ecce Romani, Test 2. 1988. 23.25 (0-8013-0242-0, 75898) Longman.

— Ecce Romani, Test 3. 1991. pap. 24.20 (0-8013-0538-1, 78415) Longman.

Lawall, Robert, et al. Ecce Romani, Set, Vol. I, Bks. 1-2. 1990. Set. text ed. 24.96 (0-8013-0439-3, 78249) Longman.

Lawall, S., jt. auth. see Lawall, G.

Lawall, Sarah, ed. & intro. Reading World Literature: Theory, History, Practice. LC 94-4041. (Illus.). 376p. (C). 1994. text ed. 50.00x (0-292-74679-2) U of Tex Pr.

Lawall, Sarah N. Critics of Consciousness: The Existential Structures of Literature. LC 68-25614. 295p. reprint ed. pap. 84.10 (0-7837-1519-6, 2041796) Bks Demand.

Lawania, Vinod K. Rural Development in India. (C). 1992. 15.00 (81-7024-468-4, Pub. by Ashish II) S Asia.

Lawatsch, Anne & Storey, Judy. Hors d'Oeuvres & Desserts. (Illus.). 96p. 1988. pap. 8.95 (0-89709-167-1) Liberty Pub.

***Lawatsch-Boomgaarden, Barbara & Ijsewijn, Jozef, eds.** Relatio Itineris in Marilandiam: Narrative of a Voyage to Maryland, 1633. Ijsewijn, Jozef, tr. 1995. 50.00 (0-86516-279-4); pap. 25.00 (0-86516-280-8) Bolchazy-Carducci.

Lawden, D. F. Elliptic Functions & Applications. (Applied Mathematical Sciences Ser.: Vol. 80). (Illus.). xiv, 334p. 1989. 59.00 (0-387-96965-9, 2664) Spr-Verlag.

— Principles of Thermodynamics & Statistical Mechanics. LC 86-13324. 154p. 1987. text ed. 59.95 (0-471-91172-0) Wiley.

Lawder, Donald. The Wild Bird & Other Poems. Warren, Shirley, ed. 40p. (Orig.). 1992. pap. 5.00 (1-877801-20-8) Still Waters.

Lawenik, Libby. Anything Can Happen. 1993. 12.95 (1-56871-017-8) Targum Pr.

Lawerence, Paul R. Unsportsmanlike Conduct: The National Collegiate Athletic Association & the Business of College Football. LC 87-12496. 200p. 1987. text ed. 45.00 (0-275-92725-3, C2725, Praeger Pubs) Greenwood.

Lawerys. Industrial Chemical Exposure. 2nd ed. 1989. 20.00 (0-88416-716-X, Yr Bk Med Pubs) Mosby Yr Bk.

Lawes, D. A. & Thomas, H., eds. The Second International Oat Conference - Proceedings: World Corps, Production, Utilization & Description. 1986. lib. bdg. 92.50 (90-247-3335-9) Kluwer Ac.

Lawes, Diane N. Bahamas 1985. Fisher, Robert C., ed. (Fisher Annotated Travel Guides Ser.). 258p. 1984. 11.95 (0-8116-0070-X) NAL-Dutton.

Lawes, Grahame. Scanning Electron Microscopy & X-Ray Microanalysis. (Analytical Chemistry by Open Learning Ser.). 1987. pap. text ed. 49.95 (0-471-91391-X) Wiley.

Lawes, Lewis E. Man's Judgment of Death: An Analysis of the Operation & Effect of Capital Punishment Based on Facts, Not On Sentiment. LC 69-14938. (Criminology, Law Enforcement, & Social Problems Ser.: No. 62). 1969. reprint ed. 18.00 (0-87585-062-6) Patterson Smith.

— Twenty Thousand Years in Sing Sing. LC 74-3830. (Criminal Justice in America Ser.). 1974. reprint ed. 37.95 (0-405-06150-1) Ayer.

Lawes, Roy A. Living Stoically: Selections from Marcus Aurelius. 1985. 30.00 (0-7223-1848-0, Pub. by A H S Ltd UK) St Mut.

Lawes, William G. Grammar & Vocabulary of Language Spoken by Motu Tribe (New Guinea) 3rd enl. ed. LC 75-35132. 1976. reprint ed. 39.50 (0-404-14148-X) AMS Pr.

Lawesson, J. E., jt. ed. see Poulsen, E.

Lawfer, Norwood P., et al. A Workbook for Science in the Elementary School. 100p. (C). 1994. student ed 15.61 (1-884768-01-6) Charming Forge.

Lawford, Lady M. Mother Bitch: Lady Lawford Exposes the Kennedys, the Royal Family & Her Own Son, Peter Lawford. 1992. pap. 4.99 (1-56171-152-7) Sure Sellers.

Lawford, Mary S. & Galon, Beauregard B. Bitch: The Autobiography of Lady Lawford. (Illus.). 178p. 17.95 (0-8283-1995-2) Branden Pub Co.

*Lawford, Richard G., et al, eds. High Altitude Rain Forests & Associated Ecosystems of the West Coast of the Americans: Climate, Hydrology, Ecology, & Conservation. LC 95-5547. (Ecological Studies: Vol. 116). 1995. write for info. (3-7879-4487-7) Spr-Verlag.

Lawhead, Alice & Lawhead, Steve. The Ultimate College Student Handbook. rev. ed. (Illus.). 240p. (C). 1989. reprint ed. pap. 9.99 (0-87788-864-7) Shaw Pubs.

Lawhead, Alice S. Doing the Right Thing: Eleven Exercises for Your Ethical Mind. 192p. (Orig.). 1991. pap. 7.99 (0-87788-183-9) Shaw Pubs.

Lawhead, Stephen. The Endless Knot. LC 92-44645. (Song of Albion Trilogy Ser.). 450p. 1993. 19.95 (0-7459-2231-7) Lion USA.

— Endless Knot. 1994. pap. 11.95 (0-7459-2240-6) Lion USA.

— The Paradise War. (Song of Albion Ser.). 450p. 1991. 19.95 (0-7459-1850-6) Lion USA.

— The Paradise War. (Song of Albion Ser.). 420p. 1992. pap. 11.95 (0-7459-2242-2) Lion USA.

— The Search for Fierra. 2nd ed. (Empyrion Ser.: Vol. I). 448p. 1994. pap. 10.99 (0-89107-751-0) Crossway Bks.

— The Siege of Dome. 2nd ed. (Empyrion Ser.: Vol. II). 464p. 1994. pap. 10.99 (0-89107-752-9) Crossway Bks.

— Silver Hand. (Song of Albion Ser.: Bk. 2). 450p. 1992. 19.95 (0-7459-2230-9) Lion USA.

— The Silver Hand. (Song of Albion Ser.). 450p. 1993. pap. 11.95 (0-7459-2245-7) Lion USA.

Lawhead, Stephen R. Arthur. LC 89-50337. (Pendragon Cycle Ser.). 445p. 1989. pap. 11.99 (0-89107-475-9) Crossway Bks.

— Arthur. (Pendragon Cycle Ser.: Bk. 3). 448p. 1995. reprint ed. mass mkt. 5.99 (0-380-70890-6, AvoNova) Avon.

— Dragon King Trilogy, Bk. 1: In the Hall of the Dragon King. 1992. mass mkt. 4.99 (0-380-71629-1, AvoNova) Avon.

— The Dragon King Trilogy, Bk. 2: The Warlords of Nin. 416p. 1992. mass mkt. 4.99 (0-380-71630-5, AvoNova) Avon.

— The Dragon King Trilogy, Bk. 3: The Sword & the Flame. 384p. 1992. mass mkt. 4.99 (0-380-71631-3, AvoNova) Avon.

— Dream Thief. LC 83-71241. 450p. (Orig.). 1983. pap. 10.99 (0-89107-266-7) Crossway Bks.

— In the Hall of the Dragon King. (Dragon King Trilogy Ser.). (YA). (gr. 7-12). 1990. pap. 9.99 (0-89107-563-1) Crossway Bks.

— Merlin. LC 88-70498. (Pendragon Cycle Ser.: Bk. II). 448p. 1988. pap. 11.99 (0-89107-436-8) Crossway Bks.

— Merlin, No. 2. (Pendragon Cycle Ser.: Bk. 2). 448p. 1995. reprint ed. mass mkt. 5.99 (0-380-70889-2, AvoNova) Avon.

— The Pendragon. (Pendragon Cycle Ser.: Bk. 4). 448p. 1995. reprint ed. mass mkt. 5.99 (0-380-71757-3, AvoNova) Avon.

— Pendragon Cycle, Set. 1989. Boxed set. pap. 35.97 (0-89107-540-2) Crossway Bks.

— Riverbank Stories: The Tale of Anabelle Hedgehog. (Riverbank Stories Ser.: Bk. 3). 112p. (J). 1994. pap. 3.50 (0-380-72200-3, Camelot) Avon.

— Riverbank Stories: The Tale of Jeremy Vole. 112p. (J). (gr. 4). 1993. pap. 3.50 (0-380-72198-8, Camelot) Avon.

— Riverbank Stories: The Tale of Timothy Mallard. 112p. (J). (gr. 4). 1993. pap. 3.50 (0-380-72199-6, Camelot) Avon.

— Song of Albion, Bk. 1: The Paradise War. 432p. 1993. mass mkt. 4.99 (0-380-71646-1, AvoNova) Avon.

— Song of Albion, Bk. 2: The Silver Hand. 400p. 1993. mass mkt. 4.99 (0-380-71647-X, AvoNova) Avon.

— Song of Albion, Bk. 3: The Endless Knot. (Song of Albion Ser.). 416p. 1994. mass mkt. 4.99 (0-380-71648-8, AvoNova) Avon.

— Sword & the Flame. (Dragon King Trilogy Ser.). (YA). (gr. 7-12). 1990. pap. 9.99 (0-89107-565-8) Crossway Bks.

— The Tale of Anabelle Hedgehog. (Riverbank Stories Ser.). (Illus.). 128p. (J). (gr. 4-8). 1990. 9.99 (0-7459-1924-3) Lion USA.

— Tale of Jeremy Vole. (Riverbank Stories Ser.). (Illus.). 128p. (J). (ps-3). 1990. 9.99 (0-7459-1653-8) Lion USA.

— Taliesin. LC 86-72056. (Pendragon Cycle Ser.). 464p. (Orig.). 1987. pap. 11.99 (0-89107-407-4) Crossway Bks.

— Taliesin. (Pendragon Cycle Ser.: Bk. 1). 496p. (Orig.). 1995. reprint ed. mass mkt. 5.99 (0-380-70613-X, AvoNova) Avon.

— Warlords of Nin, Bk. 2. (Dragon King Trilogy Ser.). (YA). (gr. 7-12). 1990. pap. 9.99 (0-89107-564-X) Crossway Bks.

Lawhead, Steve, ed. After You Graduate: Answers to Twenty-Seven Most Frequently Asked Questions. rev. ed. 160p. 1991. pap. 12.99 (0-310-71211-4) Zondervan.

Lawhead, Steve, jt. auth. see Lawhead, Alice.

Lawhead, Steve, jt. auth. see Slaikeu, Karl.

Lawhead, Steven R. Pendragon. LC 94-19258. 1994. 23.00 (0-688-13714-8, AvoNova) Avon.

Lawhead, Terry, jt. auth. see Gibson, Robert M.

Lawhon, Catherine D., jt. auth. see Lawhon, John F.

*Lawhon, John F. The Selling Bible: For People in the Business of Selling. 496p. 1995. 36.95 (1-57178-007-6) Coun Oak Bks.

— Selling Retail: All the Secrets of Many of the Highest Paid Retail Salespeople in America. (Illus.). 373p. 1992. French ed. 24.95 (0-685-48511-0) J Franklin.

—Selling Retail: All the Secrets of Many of the Highest Paid Retail Salespeople in America. (Illus.). 360p. 1992. English ed. 29.95 (0-9616736-0-5) J Franklin. SELLING RETAIL by John F. Lawhon is now in its 11th printing. The book is used in over 15,000 companies as the basis of sales education. A primer for salespeople, SELLING RETAIL includes Book I (everything you need to know before you start to sell) & Book II (selling skills). Includes psychology of selling "revelations". Auxiliary support & aides available from publisher. Currently not available in bookstores except by special order from the publisher. Mr. Lawhon's May 1995 book, THE SELLING BIBLE FOR PEOPLE IN THE BUSINESS OF SELLING is distributed nationwide to bookstores through Council Oak Books. SELLING RETAIL is a "how-to" succeed at the profession of retail selling book & includes the secrets of successful professionals revealed through the author's research & over 35 years of experience. A step-by-step, learn-as-you-work instructional text for anyone who would like to be a professional salesperson & succeed--both professionally & monetarily in his/her field. The book is divided into two volumes. First tells novice all the steps to take to prepare to sell. Second is specific advice on how to sell. Laced with personal anecdotes; includes "revelations" of selling which pertain to the psychology of selling. Available only through publisher: 1-800-234-9384.
Publisher Provided Annotation.

Lawhon, John F. & Lawhon, Catherine D. La Vente Au Detail: Tous les Secrets Des Vendeurs Au Detail les Mieux Remuneres. (Illus.). 395p. (FRE.). (C). 1990. 23.95 (0-9616736-2-1) J Franklin.

Lawhon, M. L., jt. auth. see Smith, Dane F.

Lawhorn, Geraldine. On Different Roads: An Autobiography by Geraldine Lawhorn. 1991. 14.95 (0-533-08824-0) Vantage.

Lawhorne, Clifton O. & Long, Howard R. The Supreme Court & Libel. LC 80-21161. (New Horizons in Journalism Ser.). 176p. 1981. 19.95 (0-8093-0998-X) S Ill U Pr.

Lawin, P., et al, eds. Hydroxyethyl Starch: A Current Overview. Ladak, Alan & Van Ackern, K., trs. LC 92-445. 1992. write for info. (0-86577-448-X) Thieme Med Pubs.

Lawler & Rubin, Theodor I. Anti-Semitism: A Disease of the Mind. 144p. 1993. reprint ed. 10.95 (0-8245-1238-3) Crossroad NY.

Lawler, Andrew & Vedda, James. Space Station Directory. 184p. (Orig.). 1988. pap. text ed. 205.00 (0-935453-16-4) Pasha Pubns.

Lawler, Brian. Complete Trapping Guide. 1994. pap. 19.95 (1-56830-098-0) Hayden.

Lawler, Donald L. Approaches to Science Fiction. LC 77-77995. (Illus.). (C). 1978. pap. 35.96 (0-395-25496-5) HM.

Lawler, Donald L., ed. see Wilde, Oscar.

Lawler, E. L., et al. The Traveling Salesman Problem. LC 85-3158. (Discrete Mathematics Ser.). 1985. text ed. 145.00 (0-471-90413-9) Wiley.

*Lawler, Edmund. Underdog Marketing: Successful Strategies for Out Marketing the Leader. 1995. 19.95 (1-57101-053-X) MasterMedia Ltd.

Lawler, Edmund O. Copy Chasers on Creating Business-to-Business Ads. LC 93-4045. 220p. 1994. 39.95 (0-8442-3470-2, NTC Busn Bks) NTC Pub Grp.

Lawler, Edmund O., jt. auth. see Walden, Gene.

Lawler, Edward E., III. Employee Involvement & Total Quality Management: Practices & Results in Fortune 1000 Companies. LC 92-2557. (Management Ser.). 179p. 1992. 65.00 (1-55542-434-1) Jossey-Bass.

— High-Involvement Management: Participative Strategies for Improving Organizational Performance. LC 85-45909. (Management Ser.). 269p. 1986. 31.95 (0-87589-686-3) Jossey-Bass.

— High-Involvement Management: Participative Strategies for Improving Organizational Performance. LC 85-45909. (Management-Social & Behavioral Science Ser.). 272p. 1991. reprint ed. pap. 19.00 (1-55542-330-2) Jossey-Bass.

— Strategic Pay: Aligning Organizational Strategies & Pay Systems. LC 90-37168. (Management Ser.). 328p. 1990. 30.95 (1-55542-262-4) Jossey-Bass.

— The Ultimate Advantage: Creating the High-Involvement Organization. LC 91-41095. (Management Ser.). 392p. 1992. 29.95 (1-55542-414-7) Jossey-Bass.

Lawler, Edward E., 3rd & Lawler, Edward E., 3rd. Motivation in Work Organizations. LC 93-50161. (Management Ser.). 1994. pap. 25.00 (1-55542-661-1) Jossey-Bass.

Lawler, Edward E., 3rd, jt. auth. see Lawler, Edward E., 3rd.

Lawler, Edward E., 3rd, jt. auth. see McMahan, Gary C.

*Lawler, Edward E., 3rd, et al. Creating High Performance Organizations: Survey of Practices & Results of Employee Envolvement & TQM in Fortune 1000 Companies. (Management Ser.). 1995. pap. 65.00 (0-7879-0171-7) Jossey-Bass.

Lawler, Edward E., III, et al. Doing Research That Is Useful for Theory & Practice. LC 84-43092. (Management-Social & Behavioral Science Ser.). 394p. 1985. 40.95 (0-87589-649-9) Jossey-Bass.

Lawler, Edward J. Advances in Group Processes, Vol. 1. 73.25 (0-89232-369-8) Jai Pr.

Lawler, Edward J., ed. Advances in Group Processes, Vol. 2. 1985. 73.25 (0-89232-524-0) Jai Pr.

— Advances in Group Processes, Vol. 3. 1986. 73.25 (0-89232-572-0) Jai Pr.

— Advances in Group Processes, Vol. 5. 1988. 73.25 (0-89232-893-2) Jai Pr.

Lawler, Edward J. & Markovsky, Barry, eds. Social Psychology of Groups: A Reader. LC 93-41124. 1993. write for info. (1-55938-754-8) Jai Pr.

Lawler, Edward J., jt. auth. see Bacharach, Samuel B.

Lawler, Edward J., jt. ed. see Bacharach, Samuel.

Lawler, Edward J., jt. ed. see Foschi, Martha.

Lawler, Edward J., ed. see Markovsky, Barry.

Lawler, Edwina, tr. see Schlegel, Dorothea M.

Lawler, Edwina, tr. see Schlegel, Dorothea.

Lawler, Edwina, tr. see Schleiermacher, Friedrich.

Lawler, Edwina, jt. tr. see Tice, Terrence N.

Lawler, Eugene S. A Technique for Computing the Amount of New Aid Required for State Equalization Programs. LC 77-176981. (Columbia University. Teachers College. Contributions to Education Ser.: No. 547). reprint ed. 37.50 (0-404-55547-0) AMS Pr.

Lawler, G. Quantitative Skills for Health Science. 1995. 24.50 (0-8273-5968-3) Delmar.

Lawler, G. F. Intersections of Random Walks: Probability & Its Applications. x, 209p. 1991. 49.50 (0-8176-3557-2) Spr-Verlag.

*Lawler, Gregory F. Introduction to Stochastic Processes. 1995. write for info. (0-412-99511-5) Chapman & Hall.

Lawler, Howard E. Discover Deserts. (Discover Ser.). (Illus.). 48p. (J). (gr. 3-6). 1992. lib. bdg. 14.95 (1-56674-029-0, HTS Bks) Forest Hse.

Lawler, James. The Existentialist Marxism of Jean-Paul Sartre. (Philosophical Currents Ser.: No. 18). x, 291p. 1976. pap. 35.00 (90-6032-039-5, Pub. by Gruner NE) Benjamins North Am.

Lawler, James M. IQ, Heritability & Racism. LC 78-14264. 204p. reprint ed. pap. 58.20 (0-685-20527-4, 2029989) Bks Demand.

Lawler, James R. Rene Char: The Myth & the Poem. LC 77-85547. (Essays in Literature Ser.). 1978. 29.95x (0-691-06355-9) Princeton U Pr.

— Rene Char: The Myth & the Poem. LC 77-85547. (Princeton Essays in Literature Ser.). reprint ed. pap. 38.50 (0-7837-9369-3, 2060112) Bks Demand.

— Rimbaud's Theatre of the Self. 245p. (C). 1992. 42.50 (0-674-77075-7) HUP.

Lawler, James R., ed. Paul Valery. LC 76-3026. (Anthology Ser). 1976. 55.00 (0-691-09928-6); pap. 13.95 (0-691-01814-6) Princeton U Pr.

Lawler, Jocalyn. Behind the Screens: Nursing Somology & the Problem of the Body. 264p. 1991. pap. text ed. 24.00 (0-443-04444-9) Churchill.

— Behind the Screens: Nursing, Somology, & the Problem of the Body. LC 93-9933. 1993. write for info. (0-8053-4070-X) Benjamin-Cummings.

— Behind the Screens: Nursing, Somology, & the Problem of the Body. LC 93-9933. (C). 1993. pap. text ed. 22.75 (0-8053-4090-4) Benjamin-Cummings.

Lawler, John J. Unionization & Deunionization: Strategy, Tactics, & Outcomes. (Studies in Industrial Relations). 300p. (C). 1990. text ed. 34.95 (0-87249-662-7) U of SC Pr.

Lawler, Joy, jt. auth. see Hambrick, Charles.

Lawler, Justus. Speak That We May Know: A Spirituality for Uttering the Inner You. LC 88-42726. 96p. (Orig.). 1988. 7.95 (0-940989-41-7) Meyer Stone Bks.

Lawler, Justus G. Celestial Pantomime: Poetic Structures of Transcendence. rev. ed. 320p. (C). 1994. pap. text ed. 19.95 (0-8264-0679-3) Continuum.

— Continuum 1994 Annual of Hermeneutics & Social Concern. 324p. 1994. pap. text ed. 19.95 (0-8264-4605-1) Continuum.

Lawler, K. A. The Firm & Industrial Analysis. 1986. 79.00 (0-946796-03-3) St Mut.

Lawler, K. A. & Seddighi, H. A. Economic Theory & Modelling: An Integrated Approach. 1986. 110.00 (0-946796-05-X) St Mut.

— Problems & Solutions in Economic Theory. 1986. 100.00 (0-317-61989-6) St Mut.

Lawler-Kenet, Patricia, jt. auth. see Kenet, Barney.

*Lawler, Lillian B. The Dance in Ancient Greece. fac. ed. LC 65-13203. (Dance Ser.: No. 657). (Illus.). 160p. 1984. reprint ed. pap. 45.60 (0-7837-8196-2, 2047901) Bks Demand.

— The Dance on the Ancient Greek Theatre. LC 64-65259. (University of Iowa Monographs). 143p. reprint ed. pap. 40.80 (0-317-42125-5, 2025942) Bks Demand.

— Latin Club. 12th ed. 73p. (YA). (gr. 9-12). 4.95 (0-939507-08-0, B905) Amer Classical.

Lawler, Louise. Untitled, Red - Blue, 2 vols, 1. LC 78-59796. (Illus.). 1978. write for info. (0-931706-01-7) L Lawler.

— Untitled, Red - Blue, 2 vols, 2. LC 78-59796. (Illus.). 1978. write for info. (0-931706-02-5) L Lawler.

— Untitled, Red - Blue, 2 vols, Set. LC 78-59796. (Illus.). 1978. pap. text ed. 7.95 (0-931706-00-9) L Lawler.

Lawler, Martin J. Professionals: A Matter of Degree. 2nd ed. 475p. 1993. pap. text ed. 79.00 (1-878677-55-1) Amer Immi Law Assn.

Lawler, Mary. Marcus Garvey. (Black Americans of Achievement Ser.). (Illus.). 112p. (Orig.). (YA). (gr. 5 up). 1988. 17.95 (1-55546-587-0); pap. 9.95 (0-7910-0203-9) Chelsea Hse.

— Marcus Garvey. (Orig.). 1990. pap. 3.95 (0-87067-568-0, Melrose Sq) Holloway.

Lawler, Michael. Faith Trails: Uncommon Prayers for Skiers. (Illus.). 48p. 1989. pap. 7.95 (0-89622-402-3) Twenty-Third.

— Secular Marriage, Christian Sacrament. LC 85-51085. 192p. (Orig.). 1985. pap. text ed. 8.95 (0-89622-273-X) Twenty-Third.

— Theology of Ministry. LC 89-61929. 144p. (Orig.). 1990. pap. 10.95 (1-55612-310-8) Sheed & Ward MO.

Lawler, Michael G. Ecumenical Marriage & Remarriage: Gifts & Challenges to the Churches. LC 90-70353. 112p. (Orig.). 1990. pap. 8.95 (0-89622-441-4) Twenty-Third.

— Marriage & Sacrament: A Theology of Christian Marriage. LC 93-22619. 134p. (Orig.). 1993. pap. text ed. 9.95 (0-8146-5051-1, M Glazier) Liturgical Pr.

— Symbol & Sacrament: A Contemporary Sacramental Theology. rev. ed. 500p. (C). 1994. reprint ed. pap. 19.95 (1-881871-10-X) Creighton U Pr.

— Symbol & Sacrament: A Contemporary Sacramental Theology. 2nd rev. ed. 500p. (C). 1994. reprint ed. 29.95 (1-881871-11-8) Creighton U Pr.

*Lawler, Michael G. & Shanahan, Thomas J. Church: A Spirited Communion. LC 94-41758. (Theology & Life Ser.: Vol. 40). (Orig.). 1995. pap. text ed. 12.95 (0-8146-5821-0) Liturgical Pr.

Lawler, Moira, jt. auth. see Lankshear, Colin.

Lawler, Nan. Closing the Gap: The Coast Line & Its Bridges in Ventura & Santa Barbara Counties. (Illus.). 19p. (Orig.). 1984. reprint ed. pap. 2.00 (0-911773-03-7) Inst Am Res.

Lawler, Nancy E. Soldiers of Misfortune: Invoirien Tirailleurs of World War II. LC 91-24369. (Illus.). 273p. (C). 1992. text ed. 35.00 (0-8214-1012-1) Ohio U Pr.

Lawler, Patricia A. The Keys to Adult Learning: Theory & Practical Strategies. 61p. 1991. pap. 19.95 (1-56602-037-9) Research Better.

Lawler, Patrick. A Drowning Man is Never Tall Enough. LC 89-4823. (Contemporary Poetry Ser.). 104p. 1990. pap. 7.95 (0-8203-1158-8) U of Ga Pr.

Lawler, Peter. American Political Rhetoric: A Reader. 2nd ed. 180p. 1990. pap. text ed. 14.95 (0-8476-7642-0) Rowman.

— A Question of Values: Johan Galtung's Peace Research. LC 94-8624. (Critical Perspectives on World Politics Ser.). 280p. 1994. lib. bdg. 47.00 (1-55587-507-6) Lynne Rienner.

Lawler, Peter A. The Restless Mind: Alexis de Tocqueville on the Origin & Perpetuation of Human Liberty. 210p. (Orig.). (C). 1993. lib. bdg. 52.50 (0-8476-7823-7); pap. text ed. 21.95 (0-8476-7824-5) Rowman.

— Under God with Liberty: The Religious Dimension of American Liberty. LC 93-38666. 300p. 1994. text ed. 35.00 (0-89341-686-X, Longwood Academic) Hollowbrook.

Lawler, Peter A., ed. Tocqueville's Political Science, Vol. 1: Classic Essays. LC 91-35663. 442p. 1992. 63.00 (0-8153-0050-6, H1491) Garland.

Lawler, Peter A. & Alulis, Joseph, eds. Tocqueville's Defense of Human Liberty: Current Essays. LC 92-22994. 384p. 1992. 57.00 (0-8153-0051-4, 1492) Garland.

Lawler, Peter A. & Schaefer, Robert M., eds. The American Experiment: The Theory & Practice of Liberty. 420p. (C). 1994. lib. bdg. 58.50 (0-8476-7903-9); pap. text ed. 24.95 (0-8476-7904-7) Rowman.

— American Political Rhetoric: A Reader. 3rd ed. 320p. (C). 1995. pap. text ed. 19.95 (0-8476-8047-9) Rowman.

Lawler, Philip. Operation Rescue: A Challenge to the Nation's Conscience. (Illus.). (Orig.). 1992. pap. 5.95 (0-87973-506-6, 506) Our Sunday Visitor.

Lawler, Philip F. The Alternative Influence: The Impact of Investigative Reporting Groups on America's Media. LC 84-15274. 100p. (Orig.). 1985. pap. text ed. 13.50 (0-8191-4234-4, Media Institute) U Pr of Amer.

Lawler, R. & May, W. Perspectives in Bioethics. Lescoe, F. & Liptak, D., eds. (Pope John Paul II Lecture Series in Bioethics: Vol. I). 66p. (Orig.). 1983. pap. 3.75 (0-910919-00-3) Mariel Pubns.

Lawler, Rick. How to Write to World Leaders. 160p. (Orig.). 1992. pap. 7.00 (0-380-76538-1) Avon.

— How to Write World Leaders: Names & Addresses. LC 90-351003. 96p. (Orig.). 1990. pap. 6.95 (0-9624394-0-1) MinRef Pr.

— Myth: The Extinction Factor. 176p. (Orig.). 1994. pap. 8.50 (0-9624394-2-8) MinRef Pr.

Lawler, Rick, ed. Abortion Stories: Fiction on Fire. LC 92-61240. 248p. (Orig.). 1992. pap. 11.00 (0-9624394-1-X) MinRef Pr.

Lawler, Robert W. Computer Experience & Cognitive Development: A Child's Learning in a Computer Culture. LC 85-5534. (Cognitive Science Ser.). 275p. 1985. text ed. 61.95 (0-470-20193-2) P-H.

*Lawler, Robert W. & Carley, Kathleen. Advanced Qualitative Methods in the Study of Human Behavior: Computer-Supported Analysis of Case Studies. 1995. write for info. (1-56750-132-X); pap. write for info. (1-56750-133-8) Ablex Pub.

Lawler, Robert W. & Yazdani, Masoud. Artificial Intelligence & Education: Learning Environments & Tutoring Systems, Vol. 1. LC 87-956. 448p. (C). 1987. text ed. 65.00 (0-89391-438-X); pap. text ed. 27.50 (0-89391-439-8) Ablex Pub.

Lawler, Robert W., jt. auth. see Yazdani, Masoud.

Lawler, Ronald. Light from Light: What Catholics Believe about Jesus. 240p. (Orig.). Date not set. pap. 7.50 (0-87973-547-3, 547) Our Sunday Visitor.

Lawler, Ronald & Lescoe, Francis J., eds. Excellence in Seminary Education. 139p. (Orig.). 1988. pap. 10.00 (0-945810-00-8) Vincentian Fathers Erie.

An Asterisk (*) at the beginning of an entry indicates that the title is appearing in BIP for the first time.

Lawler, Ronald, et al. Catholic Sexual Ethics. LC 84-62225. 360p. (Orig.). 1985. pap. text ed. 7.95 (*0-87973-805-7*, 805) Our Sunday Visitor.
— The Teaching of Christ: A Catholic Catechism for Adults. 3rd rev. ed. LC 75-34852. 600p. 1991. pap. 12.95 (*0-87973-850-2*, 850) Our Sunday Visitor.
Lawler, Ronald, et al, eds. The Catholic Catechism. LC 85-63061. 200p. (Orig.). 1986. pap. 6.50 (*0-87973-802-2*, 802) Our Sunday Visitor.
Lawler, Ronald D. Divine Faith, Private Revelation, Popular Devotion. 1989. 0.50 (*0-911988-78-5*) AMI Pr.
Lawler, S. Dianne. Parent-Teacher Conferencing in Early Childhood Education. 112p. 1991. 11.95 (*0-8106-0356-X*) NEA.
Lawler, T. C., jt. ed. see Burghardt, W. J.
Lawler, T. Josephine. Good News for Your Autumn Years: Leader's Guide. 48p. (Orig.). 1994. teacher ed, pap. 7.95 (*0-89390-305-1*) Resource Pubns.
— Good News for Your Autumn Years: Reflections on the Gospel of Luke. LC 94-21114. 160p. (Orig.). 1994. pap. 10.95 (*0-89390-303-5*) Resource Pubns.
Lawler, Thomas, tr. see Augustine.
Lawler, Thomas A. Iowa Legal Forms: Probate, 1984-1993. (Iowa Legal Forms Ser.). 250p. disk, ring bd. 85.00 (*0-685-49483-7*) Butterworth Legal Pubs.
— Iowa Legal Forms: Probate, 1984-1993. (Iowa Legal Forms Ser.). 250p. 1993. disk, ring bd. 60.00 (*0-86678-326-1*) Butterworth Legal Pubs.
— Iowa Legal Forms: Probate, 1984-1993. suppl. ed. (Iowa Legal Forms Ser.). 250p. 37.50 (*0-86678-043-2*) Butterworth Legal Pubs.
Lawler, Thomas C. & Burghart, Johannes, eds. The Octavius of Marcus Minucius Felix. Clarke, G. W., tr. (Ancient Christian Writers Ser.: No. 39). 1974. 26.95 (*0-8091-0189-0*) Paulist Pr.
Lawler, Vinita. Tantalizing Thai Cuisine. 208p. (Orig.). 1993. pap. 12.95 (*1-878044-10-9*) Mayhaven Pub.
Lawless. Encyclopaedia of Essential Oils. 1992. pap. 14.95 (*1-85230-311-5*) Element MA.
Lawless, Agnes C. & Lawless, John W. The Drift into Heresy. 192p. 1995. pap. 10.99 (*0-8254-3163-8*) Kregel.
Lawless, Donald I. A Flying Skull: The Chronicle of a Fighter Pilot Who Fought in Southern Europe During the Second World War. Dreinhofer, D. L., ed. 230p. 1993. write for info. (*0-9638453-0-6*) D I Lawless.
Lawless, Edward W. & Smith, Ivan C. Inorganic High-Energy Oxidizers: Synthesis, Structure, & Properties. LC 68-56023. 314p. reprint ed. pap. 89.50 (*0-317-08379-1*, 2055046) Bks Demand.
Lawless, Elaine J. God's Peculiar People: Women's Voices & Folk Tradition in a Pentecostal Church. LC 88-4236. 152p. 1988. 16.00 (*0-8131-1628-7*) U Pr of Ky.
— Handmaidens of the Lord: Pentecostal Women & Traditional Religion. LC 88-4838. (Publications of the American Folklore Society, Bibliographical & Special Ser.). (Illus.). 294p. (Orig.). (C). 1988. text ed. 48.95 (*0-8122-8100-4*); pap. 19.95 (*0-8122-1265-7*) U of Pa Pr.
— Holy Women, Wholly Women: Sharing Ministries Through Life Stories & Reciprocal Ethnography. (Publications of the American Folklore Society, Bibliographical & Special Ser.). 256p. (Orig.). (C). 1993. text ed. 42.95 (*0-8122-8240-X*); pap. text ed. 16.95 (*0-8122-1444-7*) U of Pa Pr.
Lawless, Elinor R., jt. auth. see Ringer, Benjamin B.
Lawless, Gary. First Sight of Land. 120p. (Orig.). 1990. pap. 7.50 (*92-64-13396-8*) Blackberry ME.
— Sitka Spring. (Illus.). 32p. (Orig.). 1991. pap. 5.00 (*0-942396-63-4*) Blackberry ME.
— Wolf Driving Sled: Sel Poems 1970-1980. 1981. pap. 3.50 (*0-942396-28-6*) Blackberry ME.
***Lawless, Gary, ed.** Poems for the Wild Earth. 96p. (Orig.). 1995. pap. 10.00 (*0-942396-72-3*) Blackberry ME.
Lawless, Gary & Fox, S. Dark Moon-White Pine. 4.00 (*0-686-15298-0*) Great Raven Pr.
Lawless, Gary & Petrof, Stephen. Ice Tattoo. (Illus.). 32p. (Orig.). 1982. pap. 3.00 (*0-942396-30-8*) Blackberry ME.
Lawless, Harry T. & Klein, Barbara P., eds. Sensory Science Theory & Applications in Foods. (IFT Basic Symposium Ser.: Vol. 6). 456p. 1991. 79.75 (*0-8247-8537-1*) Dekker.
Lawless, J. F. Statistical Models & Methods for Lifetime Data. LC 81-11446. (Probability & Mathematical Statistics Ser.). 580p. 1982. text ed. 99.95 (*0-471-08544-8*, Wiley-Interscience) Wiley.
Lawless, James. The Lawless Theory Course: Complete Answers Book for the New Theory Series. 1993. 6.95 (*0-685-64727-7*, 94642) Mel Bay.
— The Lawless Theory Course: Preliminary Rudiments. 1993. 9.95 (*0-685-64724-2*, 94655) Mel Bay.
— The Lawless Theory Course, Level 1: Theory. 1993. 9.95 (*0-685-64725-0*, 94656) Mel Bay.
— The Lawless Theory Course, Level 2: Theory. 1993. 9.95 (*0-685-64726-9*, 94657) Mel Bay.
Lawless, Jo & Miller, Molly. Understanding CLOS. (Artificial Intelligence Ser.). (Illus.). 192p. 1991. pap. text ed. 26.95 (*1-55558-064-5*, EY-F591E-DP, Digital DEC) Buttrwrth-Heinemann.
Lawless, Joann A. Mysteries of the Mind. LC 77-10726. (Great Unsolved Mysteries Ser.). (Illus.). 48p. (J). (gr. 4 up). 1983. reprint ed. lib. bdg. 21.36 (*0-8172-1066-0*) Raintree Steck-V.
— Strange Stories of Life. LC 77-10866. (Great Unsolved Mysteries Ser.). (Illus.). 48p. (J). (gr. 4 up). 1983. reprint ed. lib. bdg. 21.36 (*0-8172-1062-8*) Raintree Steck-V.
Lawless, John W., jt. auth. see Lawless, Agnes C.
Lawless, Joseph F., Jr. Prosecutorial Misconduct: Law, Procedure, Forms. 812p. 1985. 80.00 (*0-930273-06-0*) Michie Butterworth.
— Prosecutorial Misconduct: Law, Procedure, Forms. suppl. ed. 812p. 1990. 45.00 (*0-930273-94-X*) Michie Butterworth.
***Lawless, Julia.** Illustrated Encyclopedia of Essential Oils. 1995. pap. 18.95 (*1-85230-721-8*) Element MA.
***Lawless, Ken & Lawless, Nan.** Bluff Your Way in New York. (Bluffers Ser.). 78p. (Orig.). 1993. pap. 3.95 (*1-57143-028-8*) RDR Bks.
Lawless, Michael W., jt. auth. see Goodman, Richard A.
Lawless, Nan, jt. auth. see Lawless, Ken.
Lawless, Paul. Britain's Inner Cities: Problems & Policies. 304p. (C). 1982. pap. 50.00 (*0-06-318185-1*, Pub. by P Chapman Pub UK) St Mut.
Lawless, Paul & Brown, Frank. Urban Growth & Change in Britain: An Introduction. 256p. (C). 1986. pap. 36.00 (*0-06-318336-6*, Pub. by P Chapman Pub UK) St Mut.
Lawless, Paul & Raban, Colin, eds. The Contemporary British City. 192p. (C). 1986. pap. 45.00 (*0-06-318340-4*, Pub. by P Chapman Pub UK) St Mut.
Lawless, Paul, jt. auth. see Chandler, J. A.
Lawless, R. I., jt. ed. see Blake, G. H.
Lawless, Ray M. Folksingers & Folksongs in America: A Handbook of Biography, Bibliography & Discography. LC 81-6398. (Illus.). xviii, 750p. 1981. reprint ed. text ed. 75.00 (*0-313-23104-4*, LAFO, Greenwood Pr) Greenwood.
Lawless, Richard. The Arab Israeli Conflict, 1947-1967. (Living Through History Ser.). (Illus.). 64p. 1990. 19.95 (*0-7134-5990-5*, Pub. by Batsford UK) Trafalgar.
Lawless, Richard, ed. The Middle Eastern Village. 320p. 1987. lib. bdg. 59.00 (*0-7099-1695-7*, Pub. by Croom Helm UK) Routledge Chapman & Hall.
Lawless, Richard I. Algeria. 2nd rev. ed. (World Bibliographical Ser.: No. 19). 215p. 1995. lib. bdg. 75.00 (*1-85109-130-0*) ABC-CLIO.
Lawless, Robert. Haiti's Bad Press. 261p. (Orig.). (C). 1992. 25.95 (*0-87047-060-4*); pap. 14.95 (*0-87047-061-2*) Schenkman Bks Inc.
Lawless, Robert, et al, eds. Fieldwork: The Human Experience. (Library of Anthropology). 218p. 1983. text ed. 55.00 (*0-677-16460-2*); pap. text ed. 36.00 (*0-677-16465-3*) Gordon & Breach.
Lawless, W. N. International Symposium on Applications of Ferroelectrics (ISAF) Gaithersburg, Maryland, U. S. A., June 1-3, 1983, 3 vols., Set. (Special Issue of the Journal Ferroelectrics & Related Materials). 892p. 1983. text ed. 567.00 (*0-677-16515-3*) Gordon & Breach.
Lawley, Alan. Atomization: The Production of Metal Powders. LC 92-13307. (Monographs in P-M Ser.: No. 1). (Illus.). 1992. pap. 60.00 (*1-878954-15-6*) Metal Powder.
Lawley, Alan & Swanson, Armour, eds. Advances in Powder Metallurgy & Particulate Materials - 1993, Set. (Illus.). 1953p. 1993. text ed. 385.00 (*1-878954-34-2*) Metal Powder.
***Lawley, Alan, et al, eds.** Reviews in Particulate Materials, Vol. 2. 320p. 1994. 75.00 (*0-614-04919-9*) Am Powder Metal.
***Lawley, David.** A Nature & Hiking Guide to Cape Breton's Cabot Trail. (Illus.). 164p. 1995. pap. 14.95 (*1-55109-105-4*, Pub. by Nimbus Publishing Ltd CN) Chelsea Green Pub.
Lawley, Elizabeth L. & Summerhill, Craig. An Internet Primer for Information Professionals: A Basic Guide to Internet Networking Technology. 175p. 1993. pap. 29.95 (*0-88736-831-X*) Mecklermedia.
Lawley, Francis E. The Growth of Collective Economy, 2 vols. LC 80-20904. (Studies in International Economics: No. 1). 1040p. 1981. reprint ed. lib. bdg. 95.00 (*0-87991-850-0*) Porcupine Pr.
Lawley, K. P. Molecular Scattering: Physical & Chemical Applications. LC 74-23667. (Advances in Chemical Physics Ser.: Vol. 30). 549p. reprint ed. pap. 156.50 (*0-317-29408-3*, 2024012) Bks Demand.
Lawley, K. P., ed. Ab Initio Methods in Quantum Chemistry, Pt. 1. LC 86-9168. (Advances in Chemical Physics Ser.: No. 67). (Illus.). 566p. 1987. reprint ed. pap. 161.40 (*0-8357-4619-4*, 2037551) Bks Demand.
— Dynamics of the Excited State. (Advances in Chemical Physics Ser.: No. 50). (Illus.). 675p. reprint ed. pap. 180.00 (*0-8357-3078-6*, 2039335) Bks Demand.
— Potential Energy Surfaces. LC 81-466015. 618p. reprint ed. pap. 176.20 (*0-317-26346-3*, 2025196) Bks Demand.
Lawley, Kenneth P., ed. Molecule Surface Interactions. (Advances in Chemical Physics Ser.). 1989. pap. text ed. 298.00 (*0-471-91782-6*) Wiley.
— Photodissociation & Photoionisation. LC 84-17333. (Advances in Chemical Physics Ser.). 1985. text ed. 489.00 (*0-471-90211-X*) Wiley.
— Potential Energy Surfaces, Vol. 42. (Advances in Chemical Energy Physics Ser.). 610p. 1980. text ed. 260.00 (*0-471-27633-2*, Wiley-Interscience) Wiley.
Lawley, Lisa. World of Elephants. 1994. pap. 11.95 (*1-56799-069-X*, Friedman-Fairfax) M Friedman Pub Grp Inc.
Lawley, Lisa, jt. auth. see Vitale, Gioietta.
Lawlis, Frank, jt. auth. see Achterberg, Jeanne.
Lawlis, G. Frank. The Cure: Caregiver's Guide. LC 93-29825. 56p. (Orig.). (C). 1994. pap. 9.95 (*0-89390-274-8*) Resource Pubns.
— The Cure: The Hero's Journey with Cancer. LC 93-29828. (Illus.). 104p. (Orig.). (C). 1994. pap. text ed. 9.95 (*0-89390-273-X*) Resource Pubns.
Lawlis, G. Frank & Chatfield, Douglas. Multivariate Approaches for the Behavioral Sciences: A Brief Text. (Illus.). 153p. (Orig.). 1974. pap. text ed. 5.00 (*0-89672-051-9*) Tex Tech Univ Pr.
Lawlis, G. Frank, jt. auth. see Achterberg, Jeanne.
Lawlis, Merritt E., ed. see Deloney, Thomas.
***Lawliss, Charles.** And God Cried. 175p. 1994. write for info. (*1-57215-036-X*) World Pubns.
— Jacqueline Kennedy Onassis. 128p. 1994. write for info. (*1-57215-040-8*) World Pubns.
Lawliss, Chuck. Civil War Sourcebook: A Traveler's Guide. (Illus.). 320p. 1991. 20.00 (*0-517-57767-4*, Harmony) Crown Pub Group.
— The Marine Book. 1990. pap. 15.99 (*0-517-05538-4*) Random Hse Value.
— The Marine Book: A Portrait of America's Military Elite. LC 91-67311. (Illus.). 192p. 1992. pap. 19.95 (*0-500-27665-X*) Thames Hudson.
— New York Theatre Sourcebook. 1990. pap. 12.95 (*0-671-69970-9*) S&S Trade.
— The Old West Sourcebook: A Traveler's Guide. LC 92-40763. 1994. pap. 20.00 (*0-517-88032-6*, Harmony) Crown Pub Group.
Lawlor, Alan. Productivity Improvement Manual. LC 85-12194. (Illus.). xviii, 306p. 1986. text ed. 59.95 (*0-89930-148-7*, LPY/, Quorum Bks) Greenwood.
Lawlor, Anthony. The Temple in the House: Finding the Sacred in Everyday Architecture. LC 94-6985. (Illus.). 256p. 1994. 17.95 (*0-87477-777-1*, J P T-Putnam) Putnam Pub Group.
***Lawlor, Brenda C.** If Laughter's the Best Medicine, I Can't Be Sick. 44p. 1994. pap. 5.95 (*1-884778-06-2*) Old Mountain.
***Lawlor, Brian A.** Behavioral Complications in Alzheimer's Disease. (Clinical Practice Ser.: No. 31). 272p. 1995. boxed 35.00 (*0-88048-477-2*, 8477) Am Psychiatric.
Lawlor, David W. Photosynthesis: Molecular, Physiological & Environmental Processes. 2nd ed. 318p. 1993. pap. text ed. 57.95 (*0-470-22077-5*) Halsted Pr.
Lawlor, David W., tr. see Mohr, Hans & Schopfer, Peter.
Lawlor, David W., jt. ed. see Porter, J. R.
Lawlor, Deborah, tr. see Schwaller De Lubicz, R. A.
Lawlor, Deborah, tr. see Schwaller De Lubicz, R. A.
Lawlor, Dorothy. Troubles & Other Poems. (J). 1993. 8.95 (*0-533-10522-6*) Vantage.
Lawlor, Edward, jt. auth. see Testa, Mark.
Lawlor, Edward E., III. Pay & Organization Development. 230p. (C). 1981. pap. text ed. 26.95 (*0-201-03990-7*) Addison-Wesley.
***Lawlor, Elizabeth P.** Discover Nature at Sundown: Things to Know & Things to Do. (Illus.). 224p. (J). 1995. pap. 14.95 (*0-8117-2527-8*) Stackpole.
— Discover Nature at the Seashore: Things to Know & Things to Do. LC 91-17260. (Discover Nature Ser.). (Illus.). 224p. (J). 1992. pap. 12.95 (*0-8117-3079-4*) Stackpole.
— Discover Nature Close to Home: Things to Know & Things to Do. (Discover Nature Ser.). (Illus.). 224p. (Orig.). (YA). (gr. 8 up). 1993. pap. 14.95 (*0-8117-3077-8*) Stackpole.
— Research in Science Education, 1953-1957. LC 69-12581. (Reviews of Research in Science Education Ser.). 120p. reprint ed. pap. 34.20 (*0-317-41897-1*, 2026040) Bks Demand.
Lawlor, Eric. In Bolivia. LC 88-40387. (Departures Ser.). 288p. 1989. pap. 11.00 (*0-394-75836-6*, Vin) Random.
— Looking for Osman: One Man's Travels Through the Paradox of Modern Turkey. LC 92-50090. (Departures Ser.). 1993. pap. 11.00 (*0-679-73822-3*, Vin) Random.
Lawlor, Florine. Mohave Desert OHV Trails. (Illus.). 1989. 4.50 (*0-910856-76-1*) La Siesta.
— Out from Las Vegas. (Illus.). 1970. 2.50 (*0-910856-36-2*) La Siesta.
Lawlor, G. A Sufficient Criterion for a Cone to Be Area-Minimizing. LC 91-8060. (MEMO Ser.: Vol. 91/446). 111p. 1991. 22.00 (*0-8218-2512-7*, MEMO 91/446) Am Math.
Lawlor, Glenn J., Jr. Manual of Immunology Asia, No. 2. 1987. 10.95 (*0-316-51669-4*) Little.
— Manual of Immunology ISE, No. 2. 1987. 15.95 (*0-316-51667-8*) Little.
***Lawlor, Glenn J., Jr., et al, eds.** Manual of Allergy & Immunology. 3rd ed. LC 94-26782. 1994. 32.95 (*0-316-51681-3*) Little.
Lawlor, Gudron, tr. see Mohr, Hans & Schopfer, Peter.
Lawlor, Hugh, jt. ed. see Brock, Colin.
Lawlor, Jacques. Beauty Is an Inside Job: A Hair & Skin Care Alternative to Beauty Industry Bondage. LC 89-82692. (Illus.). 95p. (Orig.). 1990. pap. 8.95 (*1-878398-02-4*) Blue Note Pubns.
Lawlor, John. Auto Math Handbook. 1991. pap. 14.95 (*1-55788-020-4*, HP Books) Berkley Pub.
***Lawlor, Julie.** The Real Johnny Appleseed. LC 94-22010. (Illus.). (J). (gr. 1-8). 1994. write for info. (*0-8075-6909-7*) A Whitman.
Lawlor, Laurie. Addie Across the Prairie. LC 85-15548. (Illus.). 128p. (J). (gr. 3-6). 1986. 11.95 (*0-8075-0165-4*) A Whitman.
— Addie Across the Prairie. MacDonald, Patricia, ed. (Illus.). 128p. (J). 1991. reprint ed. mass mkt. 3.99 (*0-671-70147-9*, Minstrel Bks) PB.
— Addie's Dakota Winter. Tucker, Kathy, ed. Gowing, Toby, tr. LC 89-5564. (Illus.). 160p. (J). (gr. 2-6). 1989. lib. bdg. 11.95 (*0-8075-0171-9*) A Whitman.
— Addie's Dakota Winter. MacDonald, Patricia, ed. 160p. (J). 1991. reprint ed. pap. 2.99 (*0-671-70148-7*, Minstrel Bks) PB.
— Addie's Long Summer. Tucker, Kathleen, ed. LC 91-34877. (Illus.). 176p. (J). (gr. 3-6). 1992. lib. bdg. 11.95 (*0-8075-0167-0*) A Whitman.
— Addie's Long Summer. (Illus.). (J). (gr. 3-6). 1995. reprint ed. pap. 3.50 (*0-671-52607-3*, Minstrel Bks) PB.
— Daniel Boone. Tucker, Kathleen, ed. LC 87-27373. (Illus.). 160p. (J). (gr. 4-8). 1989. lib. bdg. 12.95 (*0-8075-1462-4*) A Whitman.
— George on His Own. Tucker, Kathleen, ed. (Illus.). 144p. (J). (gr. 3-7). 1993. 11.95 (*0-8075-2823-4*) A Whitman.
— Gold in the Hills. 196p. (J). (gr. 4-8). 1995. 15.95 (*0-8027-8371-6*) Walker & Co.
— How To Survive Third Grade. Levine, Abby, ed. LC 87-25430. (Illus.). 72p. (J). (gr. 2-5). 1988. lib. bdg. 9.95 (*0-8075-3433-1*) A Whitman.
— How to Survive Third Grade. (Illus.). (J). (gr. 2-4). 1991. reprint ed. pap. 3.50 (*0-671-67713-6*, Minstrel Bks) PB.
— Little Women. (YA). 1994. mass mkt. 3.99 (*0-671-51902-6*, Minstrel Bks) PB.
— Second-Grade Dog. Levine, Abby, ed. LC 84-22700. (Illus.). 40p. (J). (gr. k-3). 1990. 13.95 (*0-8075-7280-2*) A Whitman.
— Shadow Catcher: The Life & Work of Edward Sherriff Curtis. LC 93-40272. (YA). 1994. 19.95 (*0-8027-8288-4*); lib. bdg. 20.85 (*0-8027-8289-2*) Walker & Co.
— The Worm Club. Clancy, Lisa, ed. 128p. (Orig.). (J). 1994. pap. 2.99 (*0-671-78900-7*, Minstrel Bks) PB.
Lawlor, Laurie, jt. auth. see Swicord, Robin.
Lawlor, Leonard. Imagination & Chance: The Difference Between the Thought of Ricoeur & Derrida. LC 92-13359. (SUNY Series, Intersections: Philosophy & Critical Theory). 203p. 1993. 59.50 (*0-7914-1217-2*); pap. 19.95 (*0-7914-1218-0*) State U NY Pr.
Lawlor, Mary A., jt. auth. see Foran, James.
Lawlor, Michael. Lawlor's Radio Values. (Orig.). 1991. pap. 12.50 (*0-9629640-0-X*) Bare Bones.
— Negotiating with Insight. (C). 1992. audio 36.00x (*0-85171-089-1*, Pub. by IPM Hse UK) St Mut.
Lawlor, Patricia M. La Fonctionnement de la Metaphore dans les Chants de Maldoror. LC 83-26991. (Romance Monographs: No. 44). 174p. (FRE.). 1984. 23.00 (*84-499-7154-3*) Romance.
Lawlor, Patrick T., comp. Thomas Merton: The Poet & the Contemplative Life. 64p. 1990. pap. 12.50 (*0-9607862-2-8*) Columbia U Libs.
***Lawlor, Peter.** Windsocks & Lyrica. LC 94-90586. 55p. 1994. pap. write for info. (*0-9644104-0-0*) Full Moon CA.
Lawlor, Robert. Earth Honoring: The New Male Sexuality. 256p. 1989. 16.95 (*0-89281-254-0*, Destiny Bks) Inner Tradit.
— Earth Honoring: The New Male Sexuality. 224p. 1991. reprint ed. pap. 12.95 (*0-89281-428-4*, Park St Pr) Inner Tradit.
— Sacred Geometry: Philosophy & Practice. LC 88-51328. (Art & Imagination Ser.). (Illus.). 112p. 1989. reprint ed. pap. 15.95 (*0-500-81030-3*) Thames Hudson.
— Voices of the First Day: Awakening in the Aboriginal Dreamtime. (Illus.). 352p. (Orig.). 1991. pap. 24.95 (*0-89281-355-5*) Inner Tradit.
Lawlor, Robert, tr. see Schwaller De Lubicz, R. A.
Lawlor, Robert, tr. see Schwaller De Lubicz, R. A.
Lawlor, Robert, tr. see Theon Of Smyrna.
Lawlor, Sheila. Churchill & the Politics of War, 1940-1941. LC 93-28733. 308p. (C). 1994. 69.95 (*0-521-44545-0*); pap. 22.95 (*0-521-46685-7*) Cambridge U Pr.
Lawlor, Steven C. ANSI C Programming. LC 94-189251. 550p. 1995. pap. text ed. 46.50 (*0-314-02830-7*) West Pub.
— Computer Information Systems. 316p. (C). 1990. pap. text ed. 37.25 (*0-15-512653-9*) HB Coll Pubs.
— Computer Information Systems. 2nd ed. 500p. (C). 1992. pap. text ed. 37.25 (*0-15-512679-2*) Dryden Pr.
— Computer Information Systems. 3rd ed. LC 93-72826. 508p. (C). 1993. pap. text ed. 37.75 (*0-03-098191-3*) Dryden Pr.
— Computer Information Systems. 3rd ed. LC 93-72826. (C). 1994. disk 21.50 (*0-03-098197-2*); disk 21.50 (*0-03-098199-9*) Dryden Pr.
— Introducing BASIC: A Structured Approach. 176p. (C). 1990. pap. text ed. 13.50 (*0-15-512658-X*) Dryden Pr.
Lawlor, Timothy E. Handbook to the Families & Orders of Living Mammals. 2nd ed. (Illus.). 327p. (C). 1979. pap. 19.95 (*0-916422-16-X*) Mad River.
Lawlor, Tom, jt. ed. see Erwitt, Jennifer.
***Lawlor, Veronica, illus. & sel.** I Was Dreaming to Come to America: Memories from the Ellis Island Oral History Project. 40p. (J). 1995. 14.99 (*0-670-86164-2*) Viking Child Bks.
Lawlor, William R. Cross-Border Transactions Between Related Companies: A Summary of Tax Rules. 322p. 1985. lib. bdg. 50.00 (*90-6544-232-4*) Kluwer Ac.
Lawman. Brut. Allen, Rosamund, tr. & intro. by. 528p. 1993. pap. 12.95 (*0-460-87021-1*, Everyman's Classic Lib) C E Tuttle.
— Brut. Allen, Rosamund, tr. & intro. by. LC 92-16866. 1992. text ed. 45.00 (*0-312-08576-1*) St Martin.
Lawn, Beverly. The Short Story: Thirty Masterpieces. 2nd ed. LC 90-71633. 512p. (C). 1992. pap. text ed. 8.50 (*0-312-04835-1*) St Martin.
— Throat of Feathers. 1979. 6.00 (*0-918870-07-0*); pap. 3.00 (*0-918870-08-9*) Pleasure Dome.
Lawn, Brian. Fracture of Brittle Solids. 2nd ed. (Solid State Science Ser.). (Illus.). 350p. (C). 1993. pap. 37.95 (*0-521-40972-1*) Cambridge U Pr.
— Fracture of Brittle Solids. 2nd ed. (Solid State Science Ser.). (Illus.). 350p. (C). 1993. 89.95 (*0-521-40176-3*) Cambridge U Pr.
— The Rise & Decline of the Scholastic Quaestio Disputata: With Special Emphasis on Its Use in the Teaching of Medicine & Science. LC 92-42729. (Education & Society in the Middle Ages & Renaissance Ser.: No. 2). 176p. 1993. 51.50 (*90-04-09740-6*) E J Brill.
Lawn, Brian R., jt. ed. see Blau, Peter J.
Lawn, Martin. Servants of the State: The Contested Control of Teaching 1900-1930. 180p. 1987. 60.00 (*1-85000-257-6*, Falmer Pr); pap. 30.00 (*1-85000-258-4*, Falmer Pr) Taylor & Francis.
Lawn, Martin & Grace, G., eds. Teachers: The Culture & Politics of Work. 225p. 1987. 60.00 (*1-85000-216-9*, Falmer Pr); pap. 33.00 (*1-85000-217-7*, Falmer Pr) Taylor & Francis.

Lawn, Martin, jt. ed. see Grace, Gerald.

Lawn, Richard J. & Hellmer, Jeffrey L. Jazz Theory & Practice. 303p. (C). 1993. pap. 37.95 (*0-534-19596-2*) Intl Thomson.

Lawn, Sand, jt. auth. see Kinzey, Allen.

Lawne, Christopher. Brownisme Turned the In-Side Out-Ward. LC 76-6282. (English Experience Ser.: No. 74). 40p. 1968. reprint ed. 7.00 (*90-221-0074-X*) Walter J Johnson.

Lawner, Ruth, ed. see Tomko, George P.

Lawrance, Alan. Mao Zedong: A Bibliography. LC 91-8424. (Bibliographies of World Leaders Ser.: No. 3). 232p. 1991. text ed. 65.00 (*0-313-28222-6*, LMZ/, Greenwood Pr) Greenwood.

***Lawrance, Alan & Dodd, Peter.** Anthony Eden, 1897-1977: A Bibliography. LC 95-7480. (Bibliographies of British Statesmen Ser.). 240p. 1995. text ed. 75.00 (*0-313-28286-2*, Greenwood Pr) Greenwood.

Lawrance, Jeremy, tr. see Vitoria, Francisco.

Lawren, Bill, jt. auth. see Sears, Barry.

Lawrence. Advances in Chiropractic, Vol. 1. 1994. 59.95 (*0-8151-5306-6*, Yr Bk Med Pubs) Mosby Yr Bk.

— Advances in Chiropractic, Vol. 2. 1995. 59.95 (*0-8151-5307-4*, Yr Bk Med Pubs) Mosby Yr Bk.

— Advances in Chiropractic, Vol. 3. 1996. 59.95 (*0-8151-5308-2*, Yr Bk Med Pubs) Mosby Yr Bk.

— Advances in Chiropractic, Vol. 4. 1997. 59.95 (*0-8151-5309-0*, Yr Bk Med Pubs) Mosby Yr Bk.

— Advances in Chiropractic, Vol. 5. 1998. 59.95 (*0-8151-5310-4*, Yr Bk Med Pubs) Mosby Yr Bk.

— Archaelogical Findings on the Ark of the Covenant. Date not set. write for info. (*0-614-07375-8*, Red River Pr) Archival Servs.

— Breastfeeding: A Guide for the Medical Profession. 650p. 1994. 46.95 (*0-8016-6858-1*) Mosby Yr Bk.

— Breastfeeding: A Guide for the Medical Profession. 3rd ed. (Illus.). 672p. 1989. 44.95 (*0-8016-2803-2*) Mosby Yr Bk.

— Color Atlas of Physical Signs in Dermatology. 192p. 1993. 75.00 (*0-8151-5333-3*, Yr Bk Med Pubs) Mosby Yr Bk.

— Falsecards. Date not set. 9.95 (*0-910791-47-3*, 0636) Devyn Pr.

— Food Constituents & Food Residues: Their Chromographic Determination. (Food Science & Technology Ser.: Vol. 11). 632p. 1984. 195.00 (*0-8247-7076-5*) Dekker.

— Holographic Dollhouse Pt. 2: The Merrywell Trilogy. 432p. 1995. pap. text ed. 5.99 (*1-56718-413-8*) Llewellyn Pubns.

— Introduction to BASIC Astronomy with a PC. 1989. 19. 95 (*0-943396-23-9*) Willmann-Bell.

— Kodar's Travels. 256p. 1996. pap. 19.95 (*0-614-07371-5*, 81-022, Red River Pr) Archival Servs.

— Muscle Art. Date not set. per. 35.00 (*0-85449-198-8*, Pub. by Gay Mens Pr UK) InBook.

— Partnership Understandings. Date not set. 3.95 (*0-910791-08-2*, 0634) Devyn Pr.

— Photography for the Archivist. (Collegiate Guide to Archival Science Ser.: No. 5). 56p. (Orig.). (C). 1995. 7.95 (*0-910653-10-0*, 80-013, Red River Pr) Archival Servs.

— Play Bridge with Mike Lawrence. Date not set. 11.95 (*0-910791-09-0*, 0635) Devyn Pr.

— Practicando la Presencia de Dios. LC 82-50949. 72p. (Orig.). (SPA.). 1983. pap. 1.35 (*0-8358-0456-9*) Upper Room Bks.

— Religious Archives, the Complete Technical Look for the Layperson. rev. ed. 96p. 1995. 10.95 (*0-614-07373-1*, 80-011, Red River Pr) Archival Servs.

— Unlock Your Psychic Powers. 1995. mass mkt. 4.99 (*0-312-95412-3*) St Martin.

— Vicki! The True - Life Adventures of Miss Fireball. 1995. 23.00 (*0-671-89204-5*) S&S Trade.

Lawrence & Arthur. Robust Regression: Analysis & Applications. (Statistics Ser.: Vol. 108). 312p. 1990. 110. 00 (*0-8247-8129-5*) Dekker.

***Lawrence & Eaton.** Great American Decorating Ideas. (Illus.). 96p. 1995. 12.98 (*0-8317-4057-4*) Smithmark.

Lawrence, jt. ed. see Case.

Lawrence, jt. auth. see McGovern.

Lawrence, jt. auth. see Rhead.

***Lawrence, et al.** Special Edition Using Turbo C Plus Plus for Windows. (Illus.). 800p. (Orig.). 1995. pap. 39.99 (*0-614-07261-1*) Que.

***Lawrence, et al, eds.** Oral History Textbook. rev. ed. 56p. 1995. 7.95 (*0-614-07374-X*, 82-001, Red River Pr) Archival Servs.

Lawrence & Penny, ed. see Effinger, Marta.

Lawrence & Wishart Ltd. Staff, ed. Documents of the First Council of the International Working Men's Association: 1864-1872, 5 vols. 705p. 1974. 115.00 (*0-8464-0340-4*) Beekman Pubs.

Lawrence, A. Who's Who among Living Authors of Older Nations. 1973. 59.95 (*0-8490-1297-X*) Gordon Pr.

Lawrence, A. B. & Rushen, J., eds. Stereotypic Animal Behaviour: Fundamentals & Applications to Welfare. 212p. 1993. 71.25 (*0-85198-824-5*) CAB Intl.

Lawrence, A. W., ed. T. E. Lawrence by His Friends. 576p. 1980. reprint ed. 75.00 (*0-87752-196-4*) Gordian.

Lawrence, A. W. & Young, Jean, eds. Narratives of the Discovery of America. xiii, 300p. 1987. reprint ed. pap. 17.50 (*1-55613-086-4*) Heritage Bk.

Lawrence, Alexander. Pocket Examiner in Medicine. LC 94-14558. (Orig.). 1994. write for info. (*0-443-04720-0*) Churchill.

Lawrence, Alexander A. Tongue in Cheek. LC 79-54272. 104p. 1979. bds. 13.95 (*0-87797-047-5*) Cherokee.

Lawrence, Allan. Running & Racing after Thirty-Five. 1990. pap. 12.95 (*0-316-51675-9*) Little.

Lawrence, Allan & Scheid, Mark. The Self-Coached Runner II: Cross-Country & the Shorter Distances. 1987. pap. 12.95 (*0-316-77302-6*) Little.

***Lawrence, Allen.** Huna: Ancient Miracle Healing Practices & the Future of Medicine. 1994. pap. 14.95 (*0-935016-14-7*, Hanover Hse) Excelsior Music Pub Co.

***Lawrence, Allen & Lawrence, Lisa R.** Healing with Huna. 70p. (Orig.). 1994. pap. 5.95 (*0-9641367-2-4*) ALLME Pubng.

— Stress Related Disorders: Illness: an Intelligent Act of the Body. 76p. (Orig.). 1994. pap. 8.95 (*0-9641367-0-8*) ALLME Pubng.

— When Your Body Talks, Listen! 160p. (Orig.). 1994. pap. 13.95 (*0-9641367-1-6*) ALLME Pubng.

Lawrence, Allen L. & Lawrence, Lisa. Special Report: A Doctor's Proven Nutritional Program for Conquering PMS. LC 93-10532. 1993. 24.95 (*0-13-772450-0*, Parker Publishing Co) P-H.

Lawrence, Althea. Unity Without Uniformity: History of the Rhinebeck, N. Y. Church Community, 1718-1918. LC 91-33508. 184p. 1992. 30.00 (*0-912526-54-8*) Lib Res.

Lawrence, Amy. Echo & Narcissus: Women's Voices in Classical Hollywood Cinema. LC 90-50903. (Illus.). 218p. 1991. 45.00 (*0-520-07071-2*); pap. 16.00 (*0-520-07082-8*) U CA Pr.

Lawrence, Anita. Acoustics & the Built Environment. 242p. 1989. 77.50 (*1-85166-308-8*) Elsevier.

— Architectural Acoustics. (Illus.). xiii, 235p. 1970. 63.00 (*0-444-20059-2*, Pub. by Elsevier Applied Sci UK) Elsevier.

Lawrence, Anita, ed. Comets to Cosmology. (Lecture Notes in Physics Ser.: Vol. 297). x, 415p. 1988. 53.00 (*0-387-19052-X*) Spr-Verlag.

— Inter-Noise, '91: Proceedings Held in Sydney, Australia on 1991 December 2-4, 2 vols. 1991. Vol. 1, xviii, 746p. write for info. (*0-318-69271-6*); Vol. 2, xvi, 543p. write for info. (*0-318-69272-4*) Noise Control.

— Inter-Noise, '91: Proceedings Held in Sydney, Australia on 1991 December 2-4, 2 vols., Set. (Inter-Noise Ser.). 1991. 130.00 (*0-909882-12-6*) Noise Control.

Lawrence, Ann. Merlin the Wizard. (Legends & Folktales Ser.). (Illus.). 32p. (J). (gr. 2-5). 1986. lib. bdg. 19.97 (*0-8172-2628-1*) Raintree Steck-V.

Lawrence, Ann T., jt. auth. see Schattinger, Joan M.

***Lawrence, Anthony.** The Fragrant Chinese: A Portrait of Hong Kong & Its People. (Illus.). 233p. 1993. 47.50x (*962-201-572-7*) Coronet Bks.

— Modern Inertial Technology: Navigation, Guidance, & Control. LC 92-16602. (Instrumentation & Systems Ser.). (Illus.). 328p. 1993. 59.00 (*0-387-97868-2*) Spr-Verlag.

— The Taipan Traders. (Illus.). 96p. 1994. 40.00 (*962-7283-07-X*) Weatherhill.

Lawrence, Anthony, ed. The Psalm Locator. 2nd ed. (Orig.). 1986. pap. 10.95 (*0-89390-085-0*) Resource Pubns.

Lawrence, Anthony G. Pricing & Planning in the U. S. Natural Gas Industry: An Econometric & Programming Study. Bruchey, Stuart, ed. LC 78-22693. (Energy in the American Economy Ser.). (Illus.). 1979. lib. bdg. 19.95 (*0-405-11996-8*) Ayer.

Lawrence, Ardi, jt. auth. see Lawrence, H. Lea.

***Lawrence, Ardis.** How to Eat an Elephant: One Bite at a Time. 60p. (Orig.). 1994. pap. 9.00 (*0-9644370-1-5*) Dryden Publ.

Lawrence, Arthur. The Management of Trade Marketing. 200p. 1983. text ed. 75.00 (*0-566-02395-4*) Ashgate Pub Co.

— Sir Arthur Sullivan. LC 79-27876. (Music Reprint Ser.: 1980). (Illus.). 340p. 1980. reprint ed. lib. bdg. 39.50 (*0-306-76029-0*) Da Capo.

— Sir Arthur Sullivan. LC 72-3244. (English Biography Ser.: No. 31). 1972. reprint ed. lib. bdg. 66.95 (*0-8383-1522-4*) M S G Haskell Hse.

Lawrence, B. M., et al, eds. Flavors & Fragrances - a World Perspective: Proceedings of the 10th International Congress of Essential Oils, Fragrances, & Flavors, Washington, DC, 16-20 Nov., 1986. (Developments in Food Science Ser.: No. 16). 1108p. 1988. 295.00 (*0-444-42964-6*) Elsevier.

Lawrence, Barbara. Mammals Found at the Awatovi Site. (HU PMP Ser.: Vol. 35, No. 3). (Illus.). 1951. pap. 15.00 (*0-527-01290-4*) Periodicals Srv.

Lawrence, Barbara & Branz, Nedra, eds. The Flagg Correspondence: Selected Letters, 1816-1854. LC 85-27774. 289p. 1986. text ed. 29.95 (*0-8093-1242-5*) S Ill U Pr.

Lawrence, Berta. Discovering the Quantocks. 1989. pap. 25. 00 (*0-85263-660-1*, Pub. by Shire UK) St Mut.

Lawrence, Beverly H. Reviving the Spirit: A Generation of African Americans Goes Home to Church. 288p. 1996. 21.00 (*0-8021-1562-4*) Grove-Atltic.

Lawrence, Bill. Early American Wilderness. 1994. 23.95 (*1-56924-870-2*) Marlowe & Co.

— Using Netware 3.X: Special Edition. 1994. pap. 39.99 (*1-56529-627-3*) Que.

— Using Novell NetWare 3. 2nd ed. (Using Ser.). 700p. 1991. pap. 29.95 (*0-88022-756-7*) Que.

Lawrence, Bill & Hansen, M. Using Novell NetWare 4: Special Edition. (Using Ser.). (Illus.). 1100p. (Orig.). 1993. pap. 35.00 (*1-56529-069-0*) Que.

***Lawrence, Bill, et al.** Special Edition Using NetWare 4.X. (Illus.). 1200p. (Orig.). 1995. pap. 39.99 (*1-56529-894-2*) Que.

***Lawrence, Bob.** A Guide to College Resource & Financial Management. LC 95-7250. (Managing Colleges Effectively Ser.: Vol. 1). 1995. write for info. (*0-7507-0445-4*, Falmer Pr); pap. write for info. (*0-7507-0446-2*, Falmer Pr) Taylor & Francis.

Lawrence, Bobbi & Taylor-Young, Olivia. The Child Snatchers. 200p. 1982. 12.95 (*0-89182-050-7*) Charles River Bks.

Lawrence, Bonnie M. The Credit Repair Handbook. rev. ed. Harris, Deborah F., ed. 60p. 1989. 29.95 (*0-685-29184-7*); pap. 19.95 (*0-9624059-0-6*) MoneyTree Enterprises.

Lawrence, Brooke. Brooke Lawrence's Permanent Weight: I Lost 40 Pounds, You Can Too! Davies, Dave, ed. 37p. (Orig.). 1989. pap. 29.95 (*1-56610-002-X*) Data Comms Grp.

Lawrence, Brother. Practica de la Presencia de Dios: Practice the Presence of God. (SPA.). 2.95 (*84-7228-825-0*; 222365, Pub. by Edit Clie SP) TSELF.

— The Practice of the Presence of God. Helms, Hal H., ed. LC 84-61019. (Living Library). 158p. 1984. pap. 7.95 (*0-941478-29-7*) Paraclete MA.

— Practice of the Presence of God. Attwater, Donald, tr. 1981. 8.95 (*0-87243-104-5*) Templegate.

— The Practice of the Presence of God. large type ed. LC 85-61019. 144p. 1985. reprint ed. pap. 7.95 (*0-8027-2510-4*) Walker & Co.

— The Practice of the Presence of God. 114p. 1990. reprint ed. 9.95 (*0-910261-12-1*, Pub. by Samata Bks II) Lotus Light.

— The Practice of the Presence of God. 96p. 1982. reprint ed. pap. 3.99 (*0-88368-105-6*) Whitaker Hse.

Lawrence, Bruce, intro. The Rose & the Rock: Mystical & Rational Elements in the Intellectual History of South Asian Islam. LC 78-61754. 200p. (C). 1979. 12.00 (*0-89089-995-9*) Ctr Intl Stud Duke.

Lawrence, Bruce B., ed. & tr. Nizam Ad-Din Awliya: Morals for the Heart. (Classics of Western Spirituality Ser.). 1991. 26.95 (*0-8091-0451-2*); pap. 18.95 (*0-8091-3280-X*) Paulist Pr.

Lawrence, C., jt. auth. see McDaniel, E.

Lawrence, C. A. & Chen, K. Z. Rotor Spinning, Vol. 13, No. 4. 78p. (C). 1984. pap. text ed. 70.00 (*0-900739-68-1*, Pub. by Textile Institue UK) St Mut.

***Lawrence, C. Edward.** How to Handle Staff Misconduct: A Step-by-Step Guide. (Illus.). 144p. 1994. pap. 29.95 (*0-8039-6185-5*) Corwin Pr.

Lawrence, C. Edward, et al. The Marginal Teacher: A Step-by-Step Guide to Fair Procedures for Identification & Dismissal. 192p. 1993. student ed, pap. 29.95 (*0-8039-6048-4*) Corwin Pr.

Lawrence, C. H. The Friars: The Impact of the Early Mendicant Movement on Western Society. LC 93-25750. (Medieval World Ser.). 320p. (C). 1994. text ed. 58.95 (*0-582-05633-0*, Pub. by Longman UK); pap. text ed. 25.50 (*0-582-05632-2*, Pub. by Longman UK) Longman.

— Medieval Monasticism: Forms of Religious Life in Western Europe in the Middle Ages. 2nd ed. (Illus.). 321p. (C). 1989. pap. text ed. 25.50 (*0-582-01727-0*, 78188) Longman.

Lawrence, C. J., et al. Terrain Evaluation Manual. (TRL State of the Art Review Ser.: No. 7). 300p. 1993. 85.00 (*0-11-551109-1*, HM11091, Pub. by HMSO UK) UNIPUB.

Lawrence, C. M., ed. see Witte, Karl.

***Lawrence, Candida.** Change of Circumstance. LC 94-41983. 200p. (Orig.). 1995. pap. 16.95 (*1-878448-63-3*) MacMurray & Beck.

— Reeling & Writhing. LC 93-80395. 425p. 1994. 22.95 (*1-878448-60-9*) MacMurray & Beck.

Lawrence, Carl. The Broken Letter. 130p. 1993. 9.95 (*0-685-68151-3*); pap. 6.95 (*0-9638575-0-9*) Shannon Pubs.

Lawrence, Charles. History of the Philadelphia Almshouses & Hospitals from the Beginning of the Eighteenth to the Ending of the Nineteenth Centuries, Covering a Period of Nearly Two Hundred Years. LC 75-17231. (Social Problems & Social Policy Ser.). (Illus.). 1976. reprint ed. 35.95 (*0-405-07500-6*) Ayer.

Lawrence, Charles G., ed. The New Jersey Political Almanac: The Constitutional Officers, the Senate, the Assembly, the U. S. Congressional Delegation, 1994 Edition. rev. ed. 289p. 1994. 40.00 (*0-926766-10-4*) Ctr Leader Stu.

Lawrence, Charlotte. The Rag Bone Man. LC 94-26188. (Psi-Fi Ser.). 336p. 1994. pap. 4.99 (*1-56718-412-X*) Llewellyn Pubns.

Lawrence, Christopher. Medicine in the Making of Modern Britain: 1700-1920. LC 93-33387. (Historical Connections Ser.). 120p. (Orig.). 1994. pap. 12.95x (*0-415-09168-3*, B3713, Routledge NY) Routledge.

Lawrence, Christopher, ed. Medical Theory, Surgical Practice: Studies in the History of Surgery. LC 91-32852. (Wellcome Institute Series in the History of Medicine). 300p. 1992. 85.00 (*0-415-00046-7*, A5969) Routledge.

Lawrence, Christopher J., jt. auth. see Fox, Daniel M.

Lawrence, Clifford H., ed. The English Church & the Papacy in the Middle Ages. LC 65-12529. 275p. reprint ed. pap. 78.40 (*0-7837-5610-0*, 2045516) Bks Demand.

Lawrence, Conrad. The Council to Save the Planet. Ingram, tr. 364p. (Orig.). 1994. pap. 9.95 (*1-56901-189-3*) NW Pub.

Lawrence, Cynthia. Take-Out City. 208p. 1993. 18.95 (*0-88184-942-1*) Carroll & Graf.

Lawrence, D. Baloti. Tarot: Twenty-Two Steps to a Higher Path. (Illus.). 128p. (Orig.). 1992. pap. 7.95 (*0-681-41414-6*) Longmeadow Pr.

Lawrence, D. G, jt. auth. see Shultz, G. D.

Lawrence, D. H. Aaron's Rod. Kalnins, Mara, ed. (Cambridge Edition of the Works of D. H. Lawrence). 400p. 1988. 94.95 (*0-521-25250-4*); pap. 32.95 (*0-521-27246-7*) Cambridge U Pr.

— Aaron's Rod. large type ed. (Classics Ser.). 480p. 1982. 23.95 (*0-7089-8068-6*, Charnwood) Ulverscroft.

— Apocalypse. 1976. 16.95 (*0-8488-0558-5*) Amereon Ltd.

— Apocalypse. 1977. mass mkt. 5.95 (*0-14-003856-6*, Penguin Bks) Viking Penguin.

— Apocalypse. 160p. 1990. pap. 8.95 (*0-14-018197-0*, Penguin Classics) Viking Penguin.

— Apropos of Lady Chatterley's Lover. LC 73-8959. (English Literature Ser.: No. 33). 1973. reprint ed. lib. bdg. 75.00 (*0-8383-1702-2*) M S G Haskell Hse.

— Assorted Articles. LC 68-29223. (Essay Index Reprint Ser.). 1977. reprint ed. 21.95 (*0-8369-0612-8*) Ayer.

— The Best Short Stories of D. H. Lawrence. (Longman Simplified English Ser.). 91p. Date not set. pap. text ed. 5.95 (*0-582-52646-9*) Addison-Wesley.

— Birds, Beasts & Flowers. LC 92-701. 213p. (Orig.). 1992. 20.00 (*0-87685-867-1*); pap. 13.00 (*0-87685-866-3*) Black Sparrow.

— Birds, Beasts & Flowers. deluxe ed. LC 92-701. 213p. (Orig.). 1992. 30.00 (*0-87685-868-X*) Black Sparrow.

— Birds, Beasts, & Flowers: Poems. LC 74-7102. (Studies in D. H. Lawrence: No. 20). 1974. lib. bdg. 75.00 (*0-8383-1966-1*) M S G Haskell Hse.

— The Boy in the Bush. Eggert, Paul, ed. (Cambridge Edition of the Works of D. H. Lawrence). 560p. (C). 1990. 94.95 (*0-521-30704-X*) Cambridge U Pr.

— The Boy in the Bush. 400p. 1992. 9.95 (*0-14-018446-5*, Penguin Classics) Viking Penguin.

— The Centaur Letters. Roberts, F. W., ed. LC 75-110977. 1970. 25.00 (*0-87959-060-2*) U of Tex H Ransom Ctr.

— Collected Stories: D. H. Lawrence. 1994. 25.00 (*0-679-43135-7*, Everymans Lib) Knopf.

— Complete Poems. Roberts, F. Warren, ed. & intro. by. 1088p. 1994. pap. 19.95 (*0-14-018657-3*, Penguin Classics) Viking Penguin.

— Complete Short Stories of D. H. Lawrence, 3 Vols, 1. 1976. mass mkt. 8.00 (*0-14-004382-9*, Penguin Bks) Viking Penguin.

— Complete Short Stories of D. H. Lawrence, 3 Vols, 2. 1976. pap. 8.00 (*0-14-004255-5*, Penguin Bks) Viking Penguin.

— Complete Short Stories of D. H. Lawrence, 3 Vols, 3. 1977. mass mkt. 8.00 (*0-14-004383-7*, Penguin Bks) Viking Penguin.

— D. H. Lawrence & Italy. (Nonfiction Ser.). 512p. 1985. pap. 13.99 (*0-14-009520-9*, Penguin Bks) Viking Penguin.

— David: A Play. LC 74-6380. (Studies in D. H. Lawrence: No. 20). (C). 1974. lib. bdg. 75.00 (*0-8383-1960-2*) M S G Haskell Hse.

— England, My England. 192p. 1982. mass mkt. 4.95 (*0-14-001482-9*, Penguin Bks) Viking Penguin.

— England, My England. LC 72-3279. (Short Story Index Reprint Ser.). 1980. reprint ed. 21.95 (*0-8369-4153-5*) Ayer.

— England, My England & Other Stories. Steele, Bruce, ed. (Cambridge Edition of the Works of D. H. Lawrence). (C). 1990. 89.95 (*0-521-35267-3*); pap. 32.95 (*0-521-35814-0*) Cambridge U Pr.

— Fantasia & Psychoanalysis & the Unconscious. 1978. pap. 7.95 (*0-14-003303-3*, Penguin Bks) Viking Penguin.

— Fantasia of the Unconscious: Psychoanalysis & the Unconscious. 256p. 1991. pap. 9.95 (*0-14-018199-7*, Penguin Classics) Viking Penguin.

— Four Short Novels. 1976. 30.95 (*0-8488-1074-0*) Amereon Ltd.

— Four Short Novels. 1976. pap. 9.95 (*0-14-003726-8*, Penguin Bks) Viking Penguin.

— The Fox, the Captain's Doll, the Ladybird. Mehl, Dieter, ed. (Cambridge Edition of the Works of D. H. Lawrence). (Illus.). 356p. (C). 1992. 94.95 (*0-521-35266-5*) Cambridge U Pr.

— John Thomas & Lady Jane. 1989. pap. 9.95 (*0-14-018200-4*, 459, Penguin Classics) Viking Penguin.

— John Thomas & Lady Jane: The Hitherto Unpublished Second Version of Lady Chatterley's Lover. LC 70-18528. 1977. mass mkt. 4.95 (*0-14-003732-2*, Penguin Bks) Viking Penguin.

— Kangaroo. 24.95 (*0-89190-613-4*, Am Repr) Amereon Ltd.

— Kangaroo. Steele, Bruce, ed. LC 93-31877. (Letters & Works of D. H. Lawrence). (Illus.). 434p. (C). 1994. 89. 95 (*0-521-38455-9*) Cambridge U Pr.

— Kangaroo. 1980. mass mkt. 5.95 (*0-14-000751-2*, Penguin Bks) Viking Penguin.

— Kangaroo. 400p. 1992. 9.95 (*0-14-018201-2*, Penguin Classics) Viking Penguin.

— Kangaroo: The Corrected Edition. 418p. 1993. pap. 12.00 (*0-207-17173-4*, Pub. by Angus & Robertson AT) HarpC.

— Lady Chatterley's Lover. 1976. 18.95 (*0-8488-0559-3*) Amereon Ltd.

— Lady Chatterley's Lover. Durrell, Lawrence, ed. (Bantam Classics Ser.). 360p. 1983. 3.50 (*0-553-21262-1*) Bantam.

— Lady Chatterley's Lover. LC 92-39247. 1993. 9.95 (*0-8021-3334-7*) Grove-Atltic.

— Lady Chatterley's Lover. 1959. pap. 4.95 (*0-451-52498-5*, CE1787, Sig Classics) NAL-Dutton.

— Lady Chatterley's Lover. LC 93-15337. 1993. 16.50 (*0-679-60065-5*, Modern Library Prakashan) Random.

— Lady Chatterley's Lover. large type ed. LC 92-38687. (General Ser.). 474p. 1993. 19.95 (*0-8161-5651-4*) G K Hall.

— Lady Chatterley's Lover. 1981. reprint ed. lib. bdg. 23.95 (*0-89966-375-3*) Buccaneer Bks.

— Lady Chatterley's Lover & a Propos of "Lady Chatterley's Lover" Squires, Michael, ed. (Cambridge Edition of the Works of D. H. Lawrence). 528p. (C). 1993. 95.00 (*0-521-22266-4*) Cambridge U Pr.

— Last Poems. LC 74-6449. (Studies in D. H. Lawrence: No. 20). 1974. lib. bdg. 75.00 (*0-8383-1954-8*) M S G Haskell Hse.

— Last Poems. 1971. reprint ed. 49.00 (*0-403-01066-7*) Scholarly.

An Asterisk (*) at the beginning of an entry indicates that the title is appearing in BIP for the first time.

L

— The Letters of D. H. Lawrence, 7 vols., Vol. 1: 1901-1913. Boulton, James T., ed. LC 78-7531. (Cambridge Edition of the Works of D. H. Lawrence). (Illus.). 1979. 94.95 (*0-521-22147-1*) Cambridge U Pr.
— The Letters of D. H. Lawrence, 7 vols., Vol. 2: 1913-1916. Boulton, James T., ed. LC 78-7531. (Cambridge Edition of the Works of D. H. Lawrence). (Illus.). 1982. 94.95 (*0-521-23111-6*) Cambridge U Pr.
— The Letters of D. H. Lawrence, 7 vols., Vol. 3: 1916-1921. Boulton, James T., ed. LC 78-7531. (Cambridge Edition of the Works of D. H. Lawrence). (Illus.). 1994. 44.50 (*0-685-42031-0*) Cambridge U Pr.
— The Letters of D. H. Lawrence, 7 vols., Vol. 4: 1921-1924. Boulton, James T., ed. LC 78-7531. (Cambridge Edition of the Works of D. H. Lawrence). (Illus.). 1987. 94.95 (*0-521-23113-2*) Cambridge U Pr.
— The Letters of D. H. Lawrence, 7 vols., Vol. 5: March 1924-March 1927. Boulton, James T., ed. LC 78-7531. (Cambridge Edition of the Works of D. H. Lawrence). (Illus.). 1989. 94.95 (*0-521-23114-0*) Cambridge U Pr.
— The Letters of D. H. Lawrence, 7 vols., Vol. 6: March 1927-Nov. 1928. Boulton, James T., ed. LC 78-7531. (Cambridge Edition of the Works of D. H. Lawrence). (Illus.). 1991. Vol. 6; March 1927-Nov. 1928. 94.95 (*0-521-23115-9*) Cambridge U Pr.
— The Letters of D. H. Lawrence, 7 vols., Vol. 7: Nov. 1928-Feb. 1930. Boulton, James T., ed. LC 78-7531. (Cambridge Edition of the Works of D. H. Lawrence). (Illus.). 1994. 94.95 (*0-521-23116-7*) Cambridge U Pr.
— Letters to Thomas & Adele Seltzer. Lacy, Gerald M., ed. LC 76-10782. (Illus.). 283p. (Orig.). 1976. pap. 9.00 (*0-87685-224-X*) Black Sparrow.
— The Lost Girl. 24.95 (*0-89190-611-8*, Am Repr) Amereon Ltd.
— The Lost Girl. Worthen, John, ed. LC 80-40457. (Cambridge Edition of the Works of D. H. Lawrence). (Illus.). 1981. pap. 32.95 (*0-521-29423-1*) Cambridge U Pr.
— Lost Girl. 1978. mass mkt. 5.95 (*0-14-000752-0*, Penguin Bks) Viking Penguin.
— Love among the Haystacks. (J). (gr. 5-6). reprint ed. lib. bdg. 18.95 (*0-88411-676-X*, Aeonian Pr) Amereon Ltd.
— Love among the Haystacks, & Other Pieces. (Select Bibliographies Reprint Ser.). 1977. reprint ed. 18.95 (*0-518-19074-9*) Ayer.
— Love among the Haystacks & Other Stories. 176p. 1991. pap. 8.95 (*0-14-018203-9*, Penguin Classics) Viking Penguin.
— Lovely Lady. LC 77-38721. (Short Story Index Reprint Ser.). 1977. reprint ed. 15.95 (*0-8369-4134-9*) Ayer.
— Memoir of Maurice Magnus. Cushman, Keith, ed. LC 87-22671. (Illus.). 158p. 1987. 30.00 (*0-87685-716-0*) Black Sparrow.
— Modern Lover. LC 70-38722. (Short Story Index Reprint Ser.). 1977. reprint ed. 17.95 (*0-8369-4135-7*) Ayer.
— Movements in European History. Crumpton, Philip, ed. (Cambridge Edition of the Works of D. H. Lawrence). (Illus.). 450p. (C). 1990. 89.95 (*0-521-26201-1*) Cambridge U Pr.
— Mr. Noon. 384p. 1987. pap. 8.95 (*0-14-008341-3*, Penguin Bks) Viking Penguin.
— New Poems. LC 74-6450. (Studies in D. H. Lawrence: No. 20). (C). 1974. lib. bdg. 75.00 (*0-8383-1967-X*) M S G Haskell Hse.
— Odour of Chrysanthemums. LC 92-44054. Date not set. 13.95 (*0-88682-586-5*) Creative Ed.
— Plumed Serpent. 1955. pap. 10.00 (*0-394-70023-6*, Vin) Random.
— The Plumed Serpent. Clark, L. D., ed. (Cambridge Edition of the Works of D. H. Lawrence). 624p. 1987. 115.00 (*0-521-22262-1*) Cambridge U Pr.
— The Plumed Serpent. 1992. pap. 12.00 (*0-679-73493-7*) McKay.
— Portable D. H. Lawrence. Trilling, Diana, ed. (Portable Library: No. 28). 1977. pap. 12.50 (*0-14-015028-5*, P28, Penguin Bks) Viking Penguin.
— The Prussian Officer. (Creative's Classics Ser.). 64p. (J). (gr. 6 up). 1982. lib. bdg. 13.95 (*0-87191-892-7*) Creative Ed.
— The Prussian Officer. Worthen, John, ed. (Classics Ser.). 1995. pap. 10.95 (*0-14-018780-4*, Penguin Bks) Viking Penguin.
— The Prussian Officer & Other Stories. Atkins, Antony, ed. (World's Classics Ser.). 240p. 1995. pap. 8.95 (*0-19-283181-X*) OUP.
— The Prussian Officer, & Other Stories. LC 72-160939. (Short Story Index Reprint Ser.). 1977. reprint ed. 23.95 (*0-8369-3918-2*) Ayer.
— Quetzalcoatl. (Illus.). 333p. 1995. 30.00 (*0-933806-60-4*) Black Swan CT.
— The Rainbow. LC 93-1860. 1993. 20.00 (*0-679-42305-2*, Everymans Lib) Knopf.
— The Rainbow. Kinkead-Weekes, Mark, ed. (Cambridge Edition of the Works of D. H. Lawrence). (Illus.). (C). 1989. 120.00 (*0-521-22869-7*) Cambridge U Pr.
— The Rainbow. 544p. 1991. pap. 4.95 (*0-451-52529-9*, Sig Classics) NAL-Dutton.
— The Rainbow. 1989. mass mkt. 7.95 (*0-14-018218-7*, 461, Penguin Classics) Viking Penguin.
— Rainbow. 1991. mass mkt. 4.95 (*0-553-21390-3*) Bantam.
— The Rainbow. Kinkead-Weekes, Mark, ed. (Twentieth Century Classics Ser.). 1995. pap. 8.95 (*0-14-018813-4*, Penguin Bks) Viking Penguin.
— The Rainbow. large type ed. (Large Print Ser.). 800p. 1993. reprint ed. lib. bdg. 24.00 (*0-939495-44-9*) North Bks.
— The Rainbow. 576p. 1989. reprint ed. lib. bdg. 35.95 (*0-89966-644-2*) Buccaneer Bks.
— Reflections on the Death of a Porcupine & Other Essays. Herbert, Michael, ed. (Cambridge Edition of the Works of D. H. Lawrence). 400p. 1988. 110.00 (*0-521-26622-X*); pap. 34.95 (*0-521-35847-7*) Cambridge U Pr.
— The Rocking Horse Winner. (Creative's Classics Ser.). 40p. (J). (gr. 6 up). 1982. lib. bdg. 13.95 (*0-87191-893-5*) Creative Ed.
— Selected Poems. (Poets Ser.). 1980. pap. 3.95 (*0-14-042281-1*, Penguin Bks) Viking Penguin.
— Selected Poems. 272p. 1989. mass mkt. 9.00 (*0-14-058540-0*, Penguin Bks) Viking Penguin.
— Selected Short Stories. 128p. 1993. reprint ed. pap. text ed. 1.00 (*0-486-27794-1*) Dover.
— Selected Works. LC 93-44691. 1994. 12.99 (*0-517-10124-6*) Random Hse Value.
— Sex, Literature & Censorship. 122p. 1953. 19.50 (*0-8290-0206-5*); pap. text ed. 8.95 (*0-8290-2394-1*) Irvington.
— Sketches of Etruscan Places. De Filippis, Simonetta, ed. (Cambridge Edition of the Works of D. H. Lawrence). 462p. (C). 1992. 125.00 (*0-521-25253-9*) Cambridge U Pr.
— Sons & Lovers. (Longman Simplified English Ser.). 124p. Date not set. pap. text ed. 5.95 (*0-582-52634-5*) Addison-Wesley.
— Sons & Lovers. 432p. 1991. 17.00 (*0-679-40572-0*, Everymans Lib) Knopf.
— Sons & Lovers. 1976. 21.95 (*0-8488-0561-5*) Amereon Ltd.
— Sons & Lovers. (Classics Ser.). 432p. 1985. 4.95 (*0-553-21192-7*) Bantam.
— Sons & Lovers. Baron, Helen & Baron, Carl, eds. (Cambridge Edition of the Works of D. H. Lawrence). 760p. (C). 1992. 110.00 (*0-521-24276-2*); 29.95 (*0-521-43221-9*) Cambridge U Pr.
— Sons & Lovers. (Study Texts Ser.). 1988. pap. text ed. 5.95 (*0-582-33166-8*, 72062) Longman.
— Sons & Lovers. 1985. pap. 4.95 (*0-451-51882-9*, Sig Classics) NAL-Dutton.
— Sons & Lovers. Trotter, David, ed. LC 94-11777. (World's Classics Ser.). 528p. 1995. pap. 7.95 (*0-19-283107-0*) OUP.
— Sons & Lovers. LC 63-1407. 1978. 8.95 (*0-394-60452-0*, Modern Lib) Random.
— Sons & Lovers. 1982. mass mkt. 4.95 (*0-14-043154-3*, Penguin Bks) Viking Penguin.
— Sons & Lovers. 1989. mass mkt. 8.95 (*0-14-018215-2*, 462, Penguin Classics) Viking Penguin.
— Sons & Lovers. large type ed. (Classics Ser.). 1988. 16.95 (*0-7089-8008-2*, Charnwood) Ulverscroft.
— Sons & Lovers. 1982. reprint ed. lib. bdg. 28.95 (*0-89966-400-8*) Buccaneer Bks.
— Sons & Lovers: Text & Criticism. Moynahan, Julian, ed. (Critical Library: No. 4). 1977. pap. text ed. 13.95 (*0-14-015504-X*, Viking) Viking Penguin.
— St. Mawr & the Man Who Died. 1976. 19.95 (*0-8488-0560-7*) Amereon Ltd.
— Studies in Classic American Literature. 1976. 22.95 (*0-8488-1075-9*) Amereon Ltd.
— Studies in Classic American Literature. 1977. mass mkt. 6.95 (*0-14-003300-9*, Penguin Bks) Viking Penguin.
— Study of Thomas Hardy & Other Essays. Steele, Bruce, ed. (Cambridge Edition of the Works of D. H. Lawrence). 400p. 1985. 89.95 (*0-521-25252-0*) Cambridge U Pr.
— Symbolic Meaning, Uncollected Versions of 'Studies in Classic American Literature' Arnold, Armin, ed. 264p. 1962. 35.00 (*0-87556-147-0*) Saifer.
— Ten Paintings. (Illus.). 64p. 1981. 25.00 (*0-933806-13-2*) Black Swan CT.
— The Trespasser. Mansfield, Elizabeth, ed. LC 80-41663. (Cambridge Edition of the Works of D. H. Lawrence). 350p. 1982. pap. 29.95 (*0-521-29424-X*) Cambridge U Pr.
— The Trespasser. (Classics Ser.). 224p. 1990. mass mkt. 6.95 (*0-14-018210-1*, Penguin Classics) Viking Penguin.
— The Trespasser. 350p. 1989. reprint ed. lib. bdg. 29.95 (*0-89966-645-0*) Buccaneer Bks.
— Trespasser. 1988. reprint ed. lib. bdg. 49.00 (*0-7812-0179-9*) Rprt Serv.
— Trespasser. 1971. reprint ed. 49.00 (*0-403-01067-5*) Scholarly.
— Twilight in Italy. 1990. 27.50 (*0-517-58239-2*, C P Pubs) Crown Pub Group.
— Twilight in Italy & Other Essays. Eggert, Paul, ed. LC 93-31879. (Cambridge Edition of the Works of D. H. Lawrence). 1988. pap. 6.95 (*0-521-36888-X*) Cambridge U Pr.
— Twilight in Italy & Other Essays. Eggert, Paul, ed. (Cambridge Edition of the Works of D. H. Lawrence). (Illus.). 400p. (C). 1994. 79.95 (*0-521-26888-5*) Cambridge U Pr.
— The Virgin & the Gipsy. LC 84-50303. 128p. 1984. pap. 8.00 (*0-394-72666-9*, Vin) Random.
— Virgin & the Gipsy. 1992. pap. 10.00 (*0-679-74077-5*, Vin) Random.
— We Need One Another. LC 74-1421. (Studies in D. H. Lawrence: No. 20). 1974. lib. bdg. 75.00 (*0-8383-2031-7*) M S G Haskell Hse.
— The White Peacock. 432p. 1990. pap. 9.95 (*0-14-018219-5*, Penguin Classics) Viking Penguin.
— The White Peacock. Robertson, Andrew, ed. (Twentieth Century Classics Ser.). 1995. pap. 10.95 (*0-14-018778-2*, Penguin Bks) Viking Penguin.
— The Woman Who Rode Away: And Other Stories. 256p. 1993. 9.95 (*0-14-018212-8*, Penguin Classics) Viking Penguin.
— The Woman Who Rode Away & Other Stories. Mehl, Dieter & Jansohn, Christa, eds. (Cambridge Edition of the Works of D. H. Lawrence). 554p. (C). Date not set. 89.95 (*0-521-22270-2*) Cambridge U Pr.
— Women in Love. 1992. 20.00 (*0-679-41326-X*, Everymans Lib); 20.00 (*0-679-40995-5*) Knopf.
— Women in Love. 28.95 (*0-89190-612-6*, Am Repr) Amereon Ltd.
— Women in Love. 480p. 1995. 4.95 (*0-451-52591-4*, Sig) NAL-Dutton.
— Women in Love. 1976. mass mkt. 7.95 (*0-14-004260-1*, Penguin Bks) Viking Penguin.
— Women in Love. Ross, Charles L., ed. (English Library). 512p. 1982. mass mkt. 4.95 (*0-14-043156-X*, Penguin Classics) Viking Penguin.
— Women in Love. 1990. mass mkt. 8.95 (*0-14-018221-7*, Penguin Bks) Viking Penguin.
— Women in Love. large type ed. 769p. 1982. 23.95 (*0-7089-8049-X*, Trail West Pubs) Ulverscroft.
— Women in Love. 421p. 1984. reprint ed. lib. bdg. 27.95 (*0-89966-496-2*) Buccaneer Bks.
— You Touched Me. (Creative's Classics Ser.). 48p. (J). (gr. 6 up). 1982. lib. bdg. 13.95 (*0-87191-894-3*) Creative Ed.
Lawrence, D. H., tr. see Gascar, Pierre.
Lawrence, D. H., tr. see Verga, Giovanni.
Lawrence, Dana, ed. see Beideman, Ronald P.
Lawrence, Dana, ed. see Gaucher-Peslherbe, Pierre-Louis.
Lawrence, Dana J. Fundamentals of Chiropractic Diagnosis & Management. (Illus.). 608p. 1991. 89.00 (*0-683-04902-X*) Williams & Wilkins.
Lawrence, Daniel. Black Migrants: White Natives. (Modern Revivals in Sociology Ser.). 272p. 1992. 54.95 (*0-7512-0057-3*, Pub. by Gregg Pub UK) Ashgate Pub Co.
***Lawrence, David.** California: The Politics of Diversity. LC 94-35221. 250p. 1994. pap. text ed. 23.25 (*0-314-04600-3*) West Pub.
— The Complete Guide to Barber Dimes. 124p. 1991. 40.95 (*1-880731-02-9*); pap. 23.95 (*1-880731-03-7*) DLRC Pr.
— The Complete Guide to Barber Halves. 120p. 1991. 40.95 (*1-880731-04-5*); pap. 24.95 (*1-880731-05-3*) DLRC Pr.
— The Complete Guide to Barber Quarters. 101p. 1989. 3.95 (*1-880731-00-2*); pap. 21.95 (*1-880731-01-0*) DLRC Pr.
— Ex-Mutants Graphic Novel: The Saga Begins, Vol. 1. (Illus.). 88p. (YA). 1988. pap. 6.95 (*0-944735-03-7*) Malibu Graphics.
— Ex-Mutants Graphic Novel, Vol. 2: Gods or Men. (Illus.). 100p. (YA). 1988. pap. 7.95 (*0-944735-05-3*) Malibu Graphics.
— Stripping & Polishing Furniture. 1985. 39.00 (*0-685-12460-6*, Pub. by Bishopsgate Pr Ltd UK); pap. 21.00 (*0-685-12461-4*, Pub. by Bishopsgte Pr UK) St Mut.
— Stripping & Polishing Furniture: A Practical Guide. (Illus.). 95p. 1987. pap. 11.95 (*0-900873-55-8*, Pub. by Bishopsgte Pr UK) Intl Spec Bk.
Lawrence, David, jt. auth. see Laibstain, Harry.
Lawrence, David B. Handbook of Consumer Lending. LC 92-10981. 1992. write for info. (*0-13-372772-6*) P-H.
Lawrence, David E. The Natural Lean. 80p. 1974. 7.50 (*0-87881-011-0*) Mojave Bks.
Lawrence, David H. The Man Who Died: A Story. LC 93-39307. 1994. 22.00 (*0-88001-353-2*) Ecco Pr.
— St. Mawr. Bd. with Man Who Died. 1959. Set pap. 7.00 (*0-394-70071-6*, Vin) Random.
Lawrence, David M. Financing Capital Projects in North Carolina. 98p. 1979. 5.50 (*1-56011-061-9*) Institute Government.
— Financing Capital Projects in North Carolina. 2nd ed. (C). 1994. pap. text ed. 12.50 (*1-56011-273-5*, 94.05) Institute Government.
— Financing Capital Projects in North Carolina. 2nd ed. 176p. (C). 1994. text ed. 15.00 (*1-56011-234-4*, 94.05HB) Institute Government.
— Interpreting North Carolina's Public Record Laws. 45p. 1987. Incl. 1991 bulletin update. pap. 8.50 (*1-56011-088-0*) Institute Government.
— The Local Government Budget & Fiscal Control Act. 3rd ed. 31p. 1988. pap. 5.00 (*1-56011-098-8*) Institute Government.
— Local Government Finance in North Carolina. rev. ed. 323p. (C). 1990. pap. text ed. 11.00 (*1-56011-099-6*) Institute Government.
— Local Government Property Transactions in North Carolina. 124p. (Orig.). (C). 1987. pap. text ed. 8.00 (*1-56011-100-3*, 87.13) Institute Government.
— Local Government's Role in Economic Development: Legal & Financial Aspects. 25p. 1982. pap. 6.00 (*1-56011-101-1*) Institute Government.
— 1995-1996 Finance Calendar of Duties for City & County Officials. (Orig.). (C). 1995. pap. text ed. write for info. (*1-56011-246-8*, 95.15) Institute Government.
— 1994-95 Finance Calendar of Duties for City & County Officials. (Orig.). (C). 1994. pap. text ed. 5.00 (*1-56011-225-5*, 94.11) Institute Government.
— Open Meetings & Local Governments in North Carolina: Some Questions & Answers. rev. ed. 48p. (C). 1992. pap. text ed. 5.00 (*1-56011-197-6*, 91.13) Institute Government.
— Open Meetings & Local Governments in North Carolina: Some Questions & Answers. 4th ed. (C). 1994. pap. text ed. 6.50 (*1-56011-231-X*) Institute Government.
— Property Interests in North Carolina City Streets. LC 86-621832. 59p. (C). 1986. 6.00 (*1-56011-131-3*) Institute Government.
***Lawrence, David M., comp.** Form of Government of North Carolina Cities. (C). 1995. pap. text ed. write for info. (*1-56011-233-6*, 94.21) Institute Government.
Lawrence, David M., jt. auth. see Campbell, William A.
Lawrence, David M., jt. auth. see Wicker, Warren J.
Lawrence, David P. The Graphing Calculator: Modeling & Applications. (Illus.). 92p. (C). 1994. spiral bd. 22.95 (*1-881641-12-0*) Pencil Point.
***Lawrence, Dean S.** Travels with Peppy: A Motorcycle Adventure Across the Country. LC 94-90172. 250p. 1994. pap. 12.95 (*0-9641348-0-2*) Triad Pubng.
***Lawrence, Debbi & Lawrence, Don.** Walk Log: Diary & Guide for the Exercise Walker. (Illus.). 176p. 1994. pap. 9.95 (*0-9624232-9-7*) Sports Log Pubs.
Lawrence, Denis. Enhancing Self-Esteem in the Classroom. 100p. (C). 1988. 55.00 (*1-85396-000-4*, Pub. by P Chapman Pub UK) St Mut.
Lawrence, Don. Cathy. (Illus.). 45p. 1991. pap. 9.95 (*1-56398-020-7*) Malibu Graphics.
Lawrence, Don, jt. auth. see Lawrence, Debbi.
Lawrence, Douglas H. & Festinger, Leon. Deterrents & Reinforcement: The Psychology of Insufficient Reward. vi, 180p. 1962. 27.50 (*0-8047-0117-2*) Stanford U Pr.
Lawrence, Drew, tr. The Way of Kings: Ancient Wisdom from the Sanskrit Vedas. 112p. 1991. pap. 8.95 (*0-399-51675-1*, Perigee Bks) Berkley Pub.
Lawrence, E. Spiritualism among Civilized & Savage Races. 1972. lib. bdg. 79.95 (*0-87968-536-0*) Krishna Pr.
Lawrence, Eddie. Fifty-Seven Original Auditions for Actors. Zapel, A., ed. LC 83-62157. 104p. (Orig.). 1983. pap. text ed. 8.95 (*0-916260-25-9*, B-181) Meriwether Pub.
Lawrence, Edgar D. El Lenguaje Por Senas Simplificado. LC 91-39463. (Illus.). 240p. 1992. text ed. 13.95 (*0-88243-300-8*, 02-0300) Gospel Pub.
— Sign Language Made Simple. LC 79-10417. (Illus.). 240p. (J). (gr. k up). 1975. text ed. 15.95 (*0-88243-604-X*, 02-0604) Gospel Pub.
Lawrence, Edith. The Wayfaring Princes: A Tale of Questing & Adventure. (Illus.). 136p. (Orig.). (J). (gr. 4-7). 1987. pap. 8.00 (*0-936132-86-8*) Merc Pr NY.
Lawrence, Edith C., jt. auth. see Waters, David B.
***Lawrence, Edward.** Complete Antique Shop Directory for Eastern Michigan, 1994-95. (Illus.). 260p. (Orig.). Date not set. pap. 10.95 (*0-9634597-2-4*) Complete Antique.
— Complete Antique Shop Directory for Indiana, 1994. (Illus.). 272p. (Orig.). 1993. pap. text ed. 5.00 (*0-9634597-1-6*) Complete Antique.
— Complete Antique Shop Directory for Western Michigan, 1993. (Illus.). 163p. (Orig.). 1992. pap. 5.00 (*0-9634597-0-8*) Complete Antique.
— Complete Antique Shop Directory for Western Michigan, 1995. rev. ed. (Illus.). 224p. 1994. pap. 10.95 (*0-9634597-3-2*) Complete Antique.
— Spiritualism among Civilised & Savage Races: A Study in Anthropology. 1977. 19.95 (*0-8369-5848-9*, 6912) Ayer.
Lawrence, Eleanor. Introduction to Modern Biology: Genetics, Cells & Systems. 1989. pap. text ed. 44.95 (*0-470-21401-5*) Halsted Pr.
Lawrence, Eleanor, ed. Henderson's Dictionary of Biological Terms. 10th ed. 1989. text ed. 67.95 (*0-470-21446-5*) Halsted Pr.
Lawrence, Elizabeth. The Complete Caterer: A Practical Guide to the Craft & Business of Catering. rev. ed. 1992. pap. 15.00 (*0-385-23480-5*) Doubleday.
— The Complete Restaurateur: A Practical Guide to the Craft & Business of Restaurant Ownership. 240p. (Orig.). 1992. pap. 11.95 (*0-452-26752-8*, Plume) NAL-Dutton.
— Gardening for Love: The Market Bulletins. Lacy, Allen, ed. LC 86-32896. (Illus.). ix, 238p. (Orig.). 1987. 26.95 (*0-8223-0715-4*); pap. text ed. 14.95 (*0-8223-0887-8*) Duke.
— Gardens in Winter. 1973. 15.95 (*0-685-00419-8*) Claitors.
— Gender & Trade Unions. LC 93-48358. (Gender & Society Ser.). 208p. 1994. 75.00 (*0-7484-0146-6*); pap. 25.00 (*0-7484-0147-4*) Taylor & Francis.
— Great Gift Wrapping. (Illus.). 80p. 1992. pap. 9.00 (*0-517-57769-0*, Crown) Crown Pub Group.
— The Little Bulbs: A Tale of Two Gardens. LC 57-6248. xiii, 261p. (Orig.). 1986. reprint ed. 31.95 (*0-8223-0671-9*); reprint ed. pap. 13.95 (*0-8223-0739-1*) Duke.
— A Rock Garden in the South. Goodwin, Nancy & Lacy, Allen, eds. LC 89-49426. 239p. 1990. 21.95 (*0-8223-0986-6*) Duke.
— A Southern Garden: Fiftieth Anniversary Edition. rev. ed. LC 90-44658. (Illus.). xxxvi, 252p. (C). 1991. reprint ed. pap. 16.95 (*0-8078-4355-5*) U of NC Pr.
— A Southern Garden: Fiftieth Anniversary Edition. 4th rev. ed. LC 90-44658. (Illus.). xxxvi, 252p. (C). 1991. reprint ed. 24.95 (*0-8078-1962-X*) U of NC Pr.
— Through the Garden Gate. Neal, Bill, ed. LC 89-27890. xiv, 256p. (C). 1990. 22.50 (*0-8078-1907-7*) U of NC Pr.
— Through the Garden Gate. Neal, Bill, ed. LC 89-27890. (Chapel Hill Bks. Ser.). 256p. 1995. pap. 14.95 (*0-8078-4519-1*) U of NC Pr.
Lawrence, Elizabeth A. His Very Silence Speaks: Comanche, the Horse Who Survived Custer's Last Stand. LC 89-5612. (Illus.). 351p. (C). 1989. 39.95 (*0-8143-2196-8*); pap. 16.95 (*0-8143-2197-6*) Wayne St U Pr.
— Hoofbeats & Society: Studies of Human-Horse Interactions. LC 84-48296. (Illus.). 224p. 1985. 29.95 (*0-253-32843-8*) Ind U Pr.
— Rodeo: An Anthropologist Looks at the Wild & the Tame. LC 83-18176. (Illus.). xvi, 288p. (C). 1984. reprint ed. pap. text ed. 12.95 (*0-226-46955-7*) U Ch Pr.
— Rodeo, an Anthropologist Looks at the Wild & the Tame. LC 81-3330. (Illus.). 304p. reprint ed. pap. 86.70 (*0-8357-8604-8*, 2035001) Bks Demand.
Lawrence, Ellen & Kliot, Kaethe. Bobbin Lace: Designs & Instruction. Kliot, Jules, ed. 1979. pap. 7.00 (*0-916896-14-5*) Lacis Pubns.

Lawrence, Elwood P., et al. George & Democracy in the British Isles: The American Social Philosopher Helped Form Britain's Social Conscience, Inspired the People's Struggle That Overthrew the Lords' Political Power & Launched Ireland's March Toward Freedom. Lissner, Will & Lissner, Dorothy B., eds. LC 92-56462. (George Studies Program Ser.: Vol. 2). 368p. (Orig.). 1993. 16.00 (*0-911312-88-9*); pap. 10.00 (*0-911312-87-0*) Schalkenbach.

Lawrence, Emeric. Believe the Good News: Daily Meditations on the Lenten Masses. LC 82-97. 144p. 1982. pap. 5.75 (*0-8146-1256-3*) Liturgical Pr.

— The Holy Way: Sunday & Weekday Meditations on the Masses for Ordinary Time. 464p. 1990. pap. 14.95 (*0-8146-1821-9*) Liturgical Pr.

Lawrence, Emeric A. Make Us Grow in Love: A Monk's Meditations for the Seasons. LC 90-60642. 132p. (Orig.). 1990. pap. 6.95 (*0-87973-442-6*, 442) Our Sunday Visitor.

— The Ministry of Believers. 28p. (Orig.). 1982. pap. text ed. 1.95 (*0-8146-1276-8*) Liturgical Pr.

Lawrence, Ernest O. Centennial of the Sheffield Scientific School. Baitsell, George A., ed. LC 70-107681. (Essay Index Reprint Ser.). 1977. 23.95 (*0-8369-1544-5*) Ayer.

— Science in Progress, First Series. Baitsell, George A., ed. LC 78-37534. (Essay Index Reprint Ser.). 1977. reprint ed. 39.95 (*0-8369-2526-2*) Ayer.

Lawrence, Eugene. The Science of Palmistry. 138p. 1973. reprint ed. spiral bd. 7.70 (*0-7873-0538-3*) Mokelumne.

Lawrence, F. L. Moliere: The Comedy of Unreason, Vol. 2. 119p. 1968. pap. 7.00 (*0-912788-01-1*) Tulane Romance Lang.

Lawrence, Florence, ed. see Wirths, Wallace R.

*__Lawrence, Francine.__ Country Decorator. 1994. 19.99 (*0-517-08795-2*) Random Hse Value.

Lawrence, Frederick G., tr. see Gadamer, Hans-Georg.

Lawrence, Frederick G., tr. see Habermas, Jurgen.

Lawrence, Frederick G., tr. see Habermas, Jurgen, ed.

Lawrence, G. Allen, jt. auth. see Harley, Randall K.

Lawrence, G. H. The Hunt Botanical Library: A Decennial Report. (Illus.). 45p. 1970. 4.00 (*0-913196-36-3*); pap. 3.00 (*0-685-57978-6*) Hunt Inst Botanical.

Lawrence, G. H., comp. Catalogue of the 2nd International Exhibition of Botanical Art & Illustration. (Illus.). 267p. 1968. 7.00 (*0-913196-11-8*) Hunt Inst Botanical.

Lawrence, G. H., ed. Adanson: The Bicentennial of Michel Adanson's "Familles des Plantes", 2 vols., 1. (Illus.). 392p. 1964. 19.00 (*0-913196-23-1*); pap. 17.00 (*0-913196-25-8*) Hunt Inst Botanical.

— Adanson: The Bicentennial of Michel Adanson's "Familles des Plantes", 2 vols., 2. (Illus.). 243p. 1964. 15.00 (*0-913196-24-X*); pap. 13.00 (*0-913196-26-6*) Hunt Inst Botanical.

Lawrence, G. R., jt. auth. see Gresswell, R. Kay.

Lawrence, G. R., ed. see Gresswell, R. Kay.

Lawrence, Gale. The Beginning Naturalist. LC 79-89171. (Illus.). xii, 209p. (Orig.). 1979. pap. 9.95 (*0-933050-02-X*) New Eng Pr VT.

— Vermont Life's Guide to Fall Foliage. LC 84-11890. (Illus.). 64p. 1984. pap. 3.95 (*0-936896-03-5*) VT Life Mag.

— Vermont Life's Guide to Fall Foliage. 2nd ed. 1993. pap. 4.95 (*0-936896-25-6*) VT Life Mag.

*__Lawrence, Gary M.__ Due Diligence in Business Transactions. LC 94-43241. 1994. write for info. (*0-615-00435-0*) Law Journal.

Lawrence, George, jt. auth. see Brown, Vinson.

Lawrence, George, tr. see De Tocqueville, Alexis.

Lawrence, George A. Guy Livingston; or, 'Thorough.' LC 79-8148. reprint ed. 44.50 (*0-404-61960-6*) AMS Pr.

*__Lawrence, Gerda & Hunter, Madeline.__ Parent-Teacher Conferencing. LC 95-12896. 1995. pap. text ed. write for info. (*0-8039-6327-0*) Corwin Pr.

Lawrence, Gerda & Hunter, Madeline C. Parent-Teacher Conferencing. 103p. (Orig.). (C). 1978. pap. 8.50 (*0-935567-08-9*) Corwin Pr.

Lawrence, Glenwood. A Broom to Fly: New Ways of Solving the Age-Old Problems of Self-Management. rev. ed. (Illus.). 112p. 1990. pap. text ed. 4.95 (*0-9624719-4-1*) Growth Pubs.

Lawrence, Glenwood A. Hurt: The Human Saga. (Illus.). 160p. (Orig.). 1989. pap. write for info. (*0-318-65941-7*) Growth Pubs.

Lawrence, Gordon. People Types & Tiger Stripes. 3rd ed. 244p. 1993. 11.00 (*0-935652-16-7*) Ctr Applications Psych.

Lawrence, Gordon D., jt. auth. see George, Paul S.

Lawrence, Greg, jt. auth. see Kirkland, Gelsey.

Lawrence, H. Lea. The Archer's & Bowhunter's Bible. LC 93-16901. 1993. 12.00 (*0-385-42221-0*) Doubleday.

Lawrence, H. Lea & Lawrence, Ardi. Natural Wonders of Tennessee. LC 94-20920. (Natural Wonders Ser.). 1994. pap. 9.95 (*1-56626-110-4*) Country Rds.

Lawrence, H. S. Addition: No Regrouping. (Puzzles & Practice Ser.). (Illus.). 30p. (Orig.). (ENG & SPA.). (J). (gr. 1-6). 1992. student ed, pap. 3.95 (*0-931993-49-0*, GP-049) Garlic Pr OR.

— Addition & Subtraction: No Regrouping. (Puzzles & Practice Ser.). (Illus.). 30p. (Orig.). (ENG & SPA.). (J). (gr. 1-6). 1992. student ed, pap. 3.95 (*0-931993-51-2*, GP-051) Garlic Pr OR.

— Multiplication: Factors 1-12. (Puzzles & Practice Ser.). (Illus.). 30p. (Orig.). (ENG & SPA.). (J). (gr. 3-6). 1992. student ed, pap. 3.95 (*0-931993-52-0*, GP-052) Garlic Pr OR.

— Subtraction: No Regrouping. (Puzzles & Practice Ser.). (Illus.). 30p. (Orig.). (ENG & SPA.). (J). (gr. 1-6). 1992. student ed, pap. 3.95 (*0-931993-50-4*, GP-050) Garlic Pr OR.

*__Lawrence, Hanson.__ Have I Got a Story for You. 1988. pap. 7.95 (*0-910791-15-5*) Devyn Pr.

*__Lawrence, Harold A.__ Asbury's South Carolina Visits. 115p. 1995. reprint ed. pap. 10.00 (*0-9644858-2-6*) Boyd Pub Co.

— Memory Hill. LC 94-12838. (Illus.). 160p. (Orig.). 1994. pap. 12.95 (*0-87797-263-X*) Cherokee.

— Southland: Poems of the South. (Illus.). 256p. (Orig.). 1992. pap. 14.95 (*0-87797-251-6*) Cherokee.

*__Lawrence, Harold A., ed.__ Methodist Preachers in Georgia 1783-1900 Supplement. 224p. 1995. 20.00 (*0-9644858-0-X*) Boyd Pub Co.

*__Lawrence, Harold A. & Culberson, Nancy, eds.__ Darien Baptist Church Records 1794-1863. 200p. 1995. 20.00 (*0-9644858-1-8*) Boyd Pub Co.

Lawrence, Heather, jt. auth. see Evans, Ifor M.

*__Lawrence, Helen.__ Career Search: A Personal Process. (Illus.). 140p. (C). 1993. pap. text ed. write for info. (*1-884155-05-7*) Day & Nite Pub.

— Taking Chances, Making Choices. 148p. (C). 1993. pap. text ed. write for info. (*1-884155-04-9*) Day & Nite Pub.

Lawrence, Helen, tr. see Pugnetti, Gino.

Lawrence, Henry W. Not Quite Puritans: Some Genial Follies & Peculiar Frailities of Our Revered New England Ancestors. (Illus.). 246p. 1995. reprint ed. 40.00 (*1-55888-198-0*) Omnigraphics Inc.

Lawrence, Hoe R. & Hufeland, Otto. Valentine's Manuals: A General Index to the Manuals of the Corporation of the City of New York, 1841-1870. LC 81-6437. 1981. 15.00 (*0-916346-42-0*) NY Bound.

*__Lawrence, Iain.__ Far-Away Places: 50 Anchorages on the Northwest Coast. (Illus.). 192p. (Orig.). 1995. pap. 14.95 (*1-55143-033-9*) Orca Bk Pubs.

Lawrence, Ian. Power & Politics at the Department of Education & Science. Sayer, John, ed. (Education Management Ser.). 192p. 1992. text ed. 60.00 (*0-304-32624-0*); pap. text ed. 24.95 (*0-304-32607-0*) Cassell.

Lawrence, Ian, ed. Education Tomorrow. (Education Management Ser.). 224p. 1994. 39.95 (*0-304-32927-4*) Cassell.

Lawrence, Irene. Linguistics & Theology: The Significance of Noam Chomsky for Theological Construction. LC 80-24210. (American Theological Library Association Monograph: No. 16). 214p. 1980. 22.50 (*0-8108-1347-5*) Scarecrow.

— Love Is Like That. large type ed. (Linford Romance Library). 288p. 1987. pap. 11.95 (*0-7089-6442-7*, Linford) Ulverscroft.

— Love's Last Barrier. large type ed. 1990. pap. 12.95 (*0-7089-6881-3*, Linford) Ulverscroft.

— No Escape from Love. large type ed. (Linford Romance Library). 1991. pap. 13.95 (*0-7089-7099-0*) Ulverscroft.

— Switch on to Love. large type ed. (Linford Romance Library). 224p. 1993. pap. 14.95 (*0-7089-7470-8*, Trailtree Bookshop) Ulverscroft.

— World Without Love. large type ed. LC 93-11379. 1993. 18.95 (*0-7927-1773-2*, Curley Lrg Print); pap. 17.95 (*0-7927-1772-4*, Curley Lrg Print) Chivers N Amer.

Lawrence, J. The Genealogy of the Family of John Lawrence of Wisset in Suffolk, England, & of Watertown & Groton, Mass. 332p. reprint ed. lib. bdg. 58.00 (*0-8328-0753-2*); reprint ed. pap. 50.00 (*0-8328-0754-0*) Higginson Bk Co.

Lawrence, J., jt. ed. see Boundy, Ray H.

Lawrence, J., jt. auth. see Crabb, Jr.

*__Lawrence, J. A.__ Mudd's Enterprise. 1994. mass mkt. 4.99 (*0-553-56982-1*) Bantam.

Lawrence, J. C., jt. auth. see Hilders, J. H.

Lawrence, J. Dennis. Catalog of Special Plane Curves. LC 72-80280. (Illus.). 218p. 1972. pap. text ed. 8.95 (*0-486-60288-5*) Dover.

Lawrence, J. F. & Frei, R. W. Chemical Derivatization in Liquid Chromatography. (Journal of Chromatography Library: Vol. 7). 214p. 1976. 92.50 (*0-444-41429-0*) Elsevier.

Lawrence, J. F., jt. ed. see Frei, R. W.

Lawrence, J. H., et al. Radioisotopes & Radiation: Recent Advances in Medicine, Agriculture, & Industry. (Illus.). 12.00 (*0-8446-0765-7*) Peter Smith.

Lawrence, J. M., jt. ed. see Jangoux, M.

Lawrence, J. R. & Hunter, J. D., eds. MCQs in General Medicine. 216p. (Orig.). 1986. pap. text ed. 26.00 (*0-443-03425-7*) Churchill.

Lawrence, Jacob. The Great Migration: An American Story. LC 93-16788. (Illus.). 48p. (J). (gr. 3-7). 1993. 23.50 (*0-06-023037-1*); lib. bdg. 23.89 (*0-06-023038-X*) HarpC Child Bks.

— The Great Migration: An American Story. (Illus.). 48p. (J). (gr. 3-7). 1993. 22.00 (*0-943044-20-0*); pap. write for info. (*0-943044-21-9*) Phillips Coll.

— Harriet & the Promised Land. LC 92-33740. (J). 1993. pap. 15.00 (*0-671-86673-7*, S&S Bks Young Read) S&S Childrens.

Lawrence, James & Martin, Rux. The Sweet Maple: Life, Lore & Recipes from the Sugarbush. LC 93-24090. 224p. 1993. 29.95 (*1-881527-00-X*); pap. 19.95 (*1-881527-01-8*) Chapters Pub.

Lawrence, James A. Whiskey, Guns, & Cows. 152p. 1992. 19.95 (*1-56044-182-8*) Falcon Pr MT.

Lawrence, James F. Organic Trace Analysis by Liquid Chromatography. LC 81-3464. 1981. text ed. 88.00 (*0-12-439150-8*) Acad Pr.

— Trace Analysis, Vol. 1. 1981. text ed. 103.00 (*0-12-682101-1*) Acad Pr.

— Trace Analysis, Vol. 2. (Serial Publication Ser.). 1982. text ed. 84.00 (*0-12-682102-X*) Acad Pr.

— Trace Analysis, Vol. 4. 1985. text ed. 138.00 (*0-12-682104-6*) Acad Pr.

Lawrence, James F., ed. Liquid Chromatography in Environmental Analysis. LC 83-10711. (Contemporary Instrumentation & Analysis Ser.). 392p. 1984. 89.50 (*0-89603-045-8*) Humana.

— Trace Analysis, Vol. 3. (Serial Publication Ser.). 1984. text ed. 106.00 (*0-12-682103-8*) Acad Pr.

Lawrence, James F., ed. see Borges, J. L., et al.

Lawrence, James F., ed. see Swedenborg, Emanuel.

Lawrence, James H. Empire of the Nairs: Or, the Rights of Women, 4 vols. in 1. LC 76-21346. 1050p. 1976. reprint ed. 90.00 (*0-8201-1270-4*) Schol Facsimiles.

Lawrence, James K., jt. auth. see Atherton, M. A.

Lawrence, Jan & Raskin, Linda. The Timeless Travels of J. J. & Kelly: The London Adventure. 78p. (Orig.). (J). (gr. 6-9). 1994. lib. bdg. 15.00 (*0-88092-086-6*); pap. 5.00 (*0-88092-085-8*) Royal Fireworks.

Lawrence, Janet. A Tasty Way to Die. large type ed. 464p. 1992. 21.95 (*0-7089-2613-4*) Ulverscroft.

Lawrence, Janet H., jt. auth. see Blackburn, Robert T.

Lawrence, Jean, et al. Disruptive Children: Disruptive Schools? 288p. 1984. 35.95 (*0-89397-200-2*) Nichols Pub.

Lawrence, Jeanette H., ed. see Salazar, Raul A.

Lawrence, Jeannette. Introduction to Neural Networks. 5th ed. (Illus.). 324p. (C). 1993. pap. text ed. 30.00 (*1-883157-00-5*) Calif Sci Sftware.

*__Lawrence, Jennie.__ Finding a Canine Companion: A Lifetime of Love. 102p. Date not set. pap. 10.95 (*0-9646463-0-7*) Heritage Concepts.

Lawrence, Jerome. Actor - the Life & Times of Paul Muni. 380p. 1982. reprint ed. 9.45 (*0-573-69034-0*) French.

— A Golden Circle: A Tale of the Stage & the Screen & Music of Yesterday & Now & Tomorrow & Maybe the Day after Tomorrow. 172p. 1993. 19.95 (*1-55713-086-8*) Sun & Moon CA.

— Inherit the Wind. 1982. mass mkt. 4.50 (*0-553-26915-1*) Bantam.

— Live Spelled Backwards. 1970. pap. 2.75 (*0-8222-0681-1*) Dramatists Play.

Lawrence, Jerome & Lee, Robert E. The Croccodile Smile. 1972. pap. 4.75 (*0-8222-0253-0*) Dramatists Play.

— The Gang's All Here. LC 60-11223. (Illus.). 129p. 1960. 14.95 (*0-910278-33-4*) Boulevard.

— The Incomparable Max. 1972. pap. 4.75 (*0-8222-0566-1*) Dramatists Play.

— Inherit the Wind. 1963. pap. 4.75 (*0-8222-0570-X*) Dramatists Play.

— The Night Thoreau Spent in Jail. 128p. (YA). (gr. 8-12). 1983. mass mkt. 4.99 (*0-553-27838-X*) Bantam.

— Sparks Fly Upward. 1967. pap. 4.75 (*0-8222-1064-9*) Dramatists Play.

Lawrence, Jill T. AS - 400 Architecture & Application: The Database Machine. 1993. pap. text ed. 39.95 (*0-471-58141-0*) Wiley.

— AS-400 Architecture & Application: The Database Machine. 1992. pap. 34.95 (*0-89435-434-5*) Wiley.

Lawrence, Joan. The House on the Cliff. LC 89-81666. (Illus.). 160p. 1990. 28.00 (*0-7206-0763-9*, Pub. by P Owen Ltd UK) Dufour.

— Scapegoat: A Novel on the Life of Moses. 188p. 1988. 26.00 (*0-7206-0708-6*, Pub. by P Owen Ltd UK) Dufour.

Lawrence, Joe, Jr. & Brucker, Roger W. The Caves Beyond: The Story of the Floyd Collins' Crystal Cave Exploration. LC 75-34060. (Illus.). 320p. 1975. reprint ed. pap. 8.95 (*0-914264-18-4*) Cave Bks MO.

Lawrence, John. Freemasonry: A Religion? Are Freemasonry & Christianity Compatible? (Orig.). 1987. pap. 24.50 (*0-86065-951-8*) Trans-Atl Phila.

— A Functional Biology of Echinoderms. LC 87-2843. 352p. 1987. text ed. 65.00 (*0-8018-3547-X*) Johns Hopkins.

Lawrence, John, illus. A New Treasury of Poetry. LC 89-49089. 256p. 1990. 25.00 (*1-55670-145-4*) Stewart Tabori & Chang.

— The Twelve Days of Christmas. (Miniature Editions Ser.). 88p. 1994. 4.95 (*1-56138-420-8*) Running Pr.

Lawrence, John, photos. Faulkner's Rowan Oak. LC 93-10719. (Illus.). 72p. (Orig.). (C). 1993. 25.00 (*0-87805-679-3*); pap. 14.95 (*0-87805-662-9*) U Pr of Miss.

Lawrence, John & Lynch, P. J., illus. The Candlewick Book of Fairy Tales. LC 92-54961. 96p. (J). (ps up). 1993. 16.95 (*1-56402-260-9*) Candlewick Pr.

Lawrence, John, ed. see Hubbard, B. F.

Lawrence, John C. The Cook's Book of Useful Information. LC 88-20572. 176p. (Orig.). 1988. pap. 5.00 (*0-914846-38-8*) Golden West Pub.

Lawrence, John F. & Britton, E. B. Australian Beetles. (Illus.). 184p. Date not set. 39.95 (*0-522-84519-3*) Intl Spec Bk.

Lawrence, John H. Preservation Guide 2: Photographs. LC 84-106237. (Illus.). ii, 14p. 1983. pap. 3.95 (*0-917860-17-9*) Historic New Orleans.

Lawrence, John H., intro. Guide to the Photographic Collections at the Historic New Orleans Collection. LC 89-81507. (Illus.). 24p. (Orig.). 1989. pap. 3.95 (*0-917860-29-2*) Historic New Orleans.

Lawrence, John H., ed. see Crawford, Ralston.

Lawrence, John H., ed. see Winchell, H. Saul.

Lawrence, John M. Echinoderms: Proceedings of the International Echinoderms Conference, Tampa Bay, 14-17 September 1981. 552p. (C). 1982. text ed. 180.00 (*90-6191-228-8*, Pub. by A A Balkema NE) Ashgate Pub Co.

Lawrence, John M., jt. ed. see Jangoux, M.

Lawrence, John M., jt. ed. see Jangoux, Michel.

Lawrence, John S. The Electronic Scholar. Voigt, Melvin J., ed. LC 84-16952. (Communication & Information Science Ser.). 192p. (Orig.). 1985. text ed. 45.00 (*0-89391-298-0*); pap. text ed. 24.50 (*0-89391-299-9*) Ablex Pub.

Lawrence, John S., et al, eds. Fair Use & Free Inquiry: Copyright Law & the New Media. 2nd ed. LC 89-213. (Communication & Information Science Ser.). 440p. (C). 1989. text ed. 65.00 (*0-89391-484-3*) Ablex Pub.

Lawrence, John T. A Dictionary of Musical Biography. 1976. lib. bdg. 75.00 (*0-8490-1720-3*) Gordon Pr.

— A History of Russia. rev. ed. 1978. pap. 13.00 (*0-452-00973-1*, Mer) NAL-Dutton.

— A History of Russia. 7th rev. ed. 382p. 1993. pap. 15.00 (*0-452-01084-5*, Mer) NAL-Dutton.

— The Slavery Question. 1977. 18.95 (*0-8369-9168-0*, 9043) Ayer.

*__Lawrence, John W.__ Las Siete Leyes de la Cosecha. 128p. (SPA.). 1995. pap. 6.99 (*0-8254-1444-X*) Kregel.

— The Seven Laws of the Harvest. 128p. 1995. pap. 7.99 (*0-8254-3151-4*) Kregel.

Lawrence, Johnny & White, James. They Seek Me Early. 42p. 1993. pap. 5.00 (*0-916092-18-6*) Tex Ctr Writers.

Lawrence, Joseph D. Fighting Soldier: The AEF in 1918. Ferrell, Robert H., ed. LC 85-72233. 1986. 17.50 (*0-87081-158-4*) Univ Pr Colo.

Lawrence, Josephine. The Sound of Running Feet. LC 74-22791. reprint ed. 22.50 (*0-404-58445-4*) AMS Pr.

Lawrence, Joy E., jt. auth. see Anderson, William M.

Lawrence, Judy. The Budget Kit. 97p. 1992. pap. 15.95 (*0-7931-0495-5*, 560874) Dearborn Finan.

— Common Cents: The Complete Money Management Workbook. 84p. (Orig.). 1989. 10.95 (*0-9607096-6-5*) Lawrence & Co Pubs.

— The Family Memory Book: Highlights of Our Times Together. 2nd ed. Spadaccini, Vic & Schreifels, Susan, eds. (Illus.). 96p. 1992. 14.95 (*0-911493-13-1*) Blue Sky.

— Our Family Memories: Highlights of Our Times Together. Spadaccini, Vic & Schreifels, Susan, eds. 96p. 1995. 14.95 (*0-911493-14-X*) Blue Sky.

Lawrence, Judy & Yurick, Clotilde. Sew Smart with Ultra Suede Fabric & Other Luxury Suedes. (Illus.). 106p. (C). 1981. pap. 5.95 (*0-9605860-0-8*) Sewing Knits.

Lawrence, Judy M. The Family Chronicle: The Complete Family Memory Book. 96p. (Orig.). 1987. pap. 12.95 (*0-9607096-5-7*) Lawrence & Co Pubs.

Lawrence, K. J. Zebra Finches. (Colorguide Ser.). 1982. pap. 6.95 (*0-940842-12-2*) South Group.

Lawrence, K. O. A Question of Labour: Indentured Immigration into Trinidad & British Guiana, 1875-1917. LC 94-1159. 1994. text ed. 49.95 (*0-312-12172-5*) St Martin.

Lawrence, Karen, et al. The McGraw-Hill Guide to English Literature, Vol. 2. 448p. 1985. pap. text ed. 9.95 (*0-07-036705-1*) McGraw.

Lawrence, Karen. Springs of Living Water. 256p. 1991. mass mkt. 4.95 (*0-345-34827-3*) Ballantine.

Lawrence, Karen, et al, eds. The McGraw-Hill Guide to English Literature: Beowulf to Jane Austen, Vol. 1. 1985. pap. text ed. 9.95 (*0-07-036704-3*) McGraw.

Lawrence, Karen R. Penelope Voyages: Women & Travel in the British Literary Tradition. (Reading Women Writing Ser.). 288p. 1994. 38.95 (*0-8014-2610-3*); pap. 15.95 (*0-8014-9913-5*) Cornell U Pr.

Lawrence, Karen R., ed. Decolonizing Tradition: New Views of Twentieth-Century "British" Literary Canons. 304p. 1991. 42.50 (*0-252-01821-4*); pap. 15.95 (*0-252-06193-4*) U of Ill Pr.

Lawrence, Kathleen R. Boys I Didn't Kiss. 1990. 17.95 (*0-945167-34-2*) British Amer Pub.

— Maud Gone. 1987. pap. 4.50 (*0-451-40180-8*, Onyx) NAL-Dutton.

Lawrence, Kathy. Tin Angel. 352p. (Orig.). 1989. pap. 3.95 (*0-380-75735-4*) Avon.

Lawrence, Kenneth. Introduction to Archival Science. 2nd rev. ed. Sibley, J. A., Jr., ed. (Archival Science Ser.: No. 1). 80p. 1992. pap. (*0-910653-23-2*, 8001F, Red River Pr) Archival Servs.

— Kodar's Travels: The Saga of an Israelite Family. (Illus.). 256p. (Orig.). (YA). 1993. pap. 15.00 (*0-910653-20-8*, Red River Pr) Archival Servs.

Lawrence, Kenneth, ed. Classic Themes of Disciples Theology: Rethinking the Traditional Affirmations of the Christian Church (Disciples of Christ) LC 85-50712. 150p. 1986. text ed. 20.00 (*0-87565-024-4*) Tex Christian.

Lawrence, Kenneth D., et al, eds. Advances in Mathematical Programming & Financial Planning, Vol. 1. 1987. 73.25 (*0-89232-582-8*) Jai Pr.

— Advances in Mathematical Programming & Financial Planning, Vol. 2. 1988. 73.25 (*0-89232-815-0*) Jai Pr.

— Advances in Mathematical Programming & Financial Planning, Vol. 3. 1991. 73.25 (*1-55938-251-1*) Jai Pr.

Lawrence, Kenneth E. & Painter, Sandra J., eds. Women's Health Patient Education Resource Manual. LC 93-33562. 1994. 179.00 (*0-8342-0547-5*) Aspen Pub.

Lawrence, Kenneth E., ed. see Aspen Reference Group Staff.

Lawrence, Kenneth E., jt. auth. see Aspen Reference Group Staff.

Lawrence, Kenneth E., ed. see Aspen Reference Group Staff.

Lawrence, Kenneth E., ed. see Aspen Reference Group.

Lawrence, Kevin, et al. Introduction to Body Sculpting. (Sports & Fitness Library). (Illus.). 40p. (Orig.). 1988. pap. 2.95 (*0-87983-481-1*) Keats.

Lawrence, L. J., tr. see Strauss, Richard.

Lawrence, Lady, pseud. Indian Embers. LC 91-18463. 406p. 1991. reprint ed. 22.95 (*1-879434-03-2*); reprint ed. pap. 13.95 (*1-879434-02-4*) Trackless Sands Pr.

Lawrence, Laurie. Sink or Swim. 64p. (C). 1990. pap. 30.00 (*0-86439-092-0*, Pub. by Boolarong Pubns AT) St Mut.

Lawrence, Lea. The Small-Game & Varmint Hunter's Bible. LC 94-1637. 1994. 12.00 (*0-385-46836-9*) Doubleday.

Lawrence, Lee E. The Wisconsin Ice Trade. (Wisconsin Stories Ser.). 12p. pap. 1.25 (*0-87020-197-2*) State Hist Soc Wis.

Lawrence, Les. Prophesy to the Land. 238p. (Orig.). 1994. pap. 8.99 (*1-56043-802-9*) Destiny Image.

An Asterisk (*) at the beginning of an entry indicates that the title is appearing in BIP for the first time.

*Lawrence-Lightfoot, Sara. Balm in Gilead: Journey of a Healer. (Illus.). 368p. 1995. 13.95 (0-14-024967-2, Penguin Bks) Viking Penguin.

— I've Know Rivers: Lives of Loss & Liberation. 672p. 1995. 14.95 (0-14-024970-2, Penguin Bks) Viking Penguin.

— I've Known Rivers: Lives of Loss & Liberation. 1994. 24.00 (0-201-58120-5) Addison-Wesley.

Lawrence, Linda & Thorne, Kate. Adventures in Arizona: An Illustrated History. Caillou, Aliza, ed. LC 91-65779. (Illus.). 48p. (Orig.). (J). (gr. 4 up). 1991. pap. 6.95 (0-9628329-3-6) Thorne Enterprises.

Lawrence, Lisa, jt. auth. see Lawrence, Allen L.

Lawrence, Lisa R., jt. auth. see Lawrence, Allen.

Lawrence, Lorna, jt. auth. see Taylor, Arlene.

***Lawrence, Lorrie.** Growing Flowers for Picking. Patrick, John, ed. (Lothian Australian Garden Ser.). (Illus.). 64p. (Orig.). 1995. pap. 9.95 (0-85091-607-0, Pub. by Lothian Pub AT) Seven Hills Bk.

Lawrence, Louis, jt. auth. see Schaefer, Jean.

Lawrence, Louise. Andra. LC 90-38595. 240p. (YA). (gr. 7 up). 1991. lib. bdg. 14.89 (0-06-023705-8) HarpC Child Bks.

— Calling B for Butterfly. LC 81-48648. (Trophy Starwanderer Bk.). 224p. (YA). (gr. 7 up). 1988. pap. 3.95 (0-06-447036-9, Trophy) HarpC Child Bks.

— Extinction Is Forever & Other Stories. LC 92-35464. (J). 1993. 15.00 (0-06-022913-6, HarpT); lib. bdg. 14.89 (0-06-022914-4, HarpT) HarpC.

— Keeper of the Universe. LC 92-2452. 240p. (J). (gr. 7 up). 1993. 13.95 (0-395-64340-6, Clarion Bks) HM.

— The Patchwork People. LC 93-40830. (J). 1994. 14.95 (0-395-67892-7, Clarion Bks) HM.

Lawrence, Lucy G., ed. see Medvedev, Zhores.

Lawrence, M. Hand Analysis. 1972. pap. 5.95 (0-13-372466-2, Reward) P-H.

— The Power House Within You. 1980. reprint ed. pap. 3.95 (0-937816-11-6) Tech Data.

Lawrence, M. & Pritchard, L., eds. General Practitioner Education: U. K. & Nordic Perspectives. 192p. 1992. pap. 19.00 (0-387-19741-9) Spr-Verlag.

Lawrence, M., jt. auth. see Wever, Glen.

Lawrence, M. F. Photochemistry & Photoelectrochemistry of Organic Thin Films, Vol. 1436. 1991. 42.00 (0-8194-0526-4) SPIE.

Lawrence, M. L. & Lombard, G. L. Murray - Conwell: Genealogy & Allied Families. (Illus.). 115p. 1992. reprint ed. lib. bdg. 29.50 (0-8328-2696-0); reprint ed. pap. 19.50 (0-8328-2697-9) Higginson Bk Co.

Lawrence, Maggie, et al. Christmas Plays for Young Audiences: 'Twas the Night Before Columbus Day...I Mean Christmas; The Angels' Greatest Message; How Santa Claus Discovered Christmas. (Illus.). 52p. (YA). (gr. 6-12). 1994. pap. 4.00 (0-88680-391-8) I E Clark.

Lawrence, Marc. Long Time No See: Confessions of a Movie Gangster. (Illus.). 199p. (Orig.). (C). 1993. pap. text ed. 19.95 (0-9636700-0-X) Ursus Pr CA.

Lawrence, Marcia. How to Take the SAT. 336p. 1979. pap. 7.95 (0-452-25781-6, Z5466, Plume) NAL-Dutton.

— How to Take the SAT. 336p. (YA). (gr. 9-12). 1979. pap. 10.00 (0-452-26296-8, Plume) NAL-Dutton.

Lawrence, Marcia & Piemonte, Charles. Acing the New SAT: Scholastic Assessment Test. LC 94-14769. 400p. 1994. pap. 12.95 (0-452-27233-5, Plume) NAL-Dutton.

Lawrence, Marjorie. Interrupted Melody: The Story of My Life: Music Book Index. 307p. 1993. reprint ed. lib. bdg. 89.00 (0-7812-9632-3) Rprt Serv.

— What? Me Teach Music? A Classroom Teacher's Guide to Music in Early Childhood. 140p. (Orig.). 1982. pap. text ed. 18.95 (0-88284-213-7, 2075) Alfred Pub.

Lawrence, Mark. The Bear & the Eagle. 48p. (Orig.). 1986. pap. 2.50 (0-9616610-0-3) M A Lawrence.

Lawrence, Mark A. Lawrence's Poetic Poetry. 27p. (Orig.). 1986. pap. 1.75 (0-9616610-1-1) M A Lawrence.

Lawrence, Martha. Lightship Baskets of Nantucket. Schiffer, Nancy N., ed. (Illus.). 120p. (Orig.). 1990. pap. text ed. 24.95 (0-88740-256-9) Schiffer.

— Scrimshaw, the Whaler's Legacy. (Illus.). 240p. 1993. 69.95 (0-88740-455-3) Schiffer.

Lawrence, Martin. The Yachtsman's Pilot to the West Coast of Scotland: Castle Bay to Cape Wrath. (Illus.). 190p. (C). 1990. 41.95 (0-85288-144-4, Pub. by Laurie Norie & Wilson Ltd UK) Bluewater Bks.

— The Yachtsman's Pilot to the West Coast of Scotland: Clyde to Colonsay. (Illus.). 152p. (C). 1993. pap. 36.95x (0-85288-132-0, Pub. by Imray Laurie Norie & Wilson UK) Bluewater Bks.

— The Yachtsman's Pilot to the West Coast of Scotland: Crinan to Canna. (Illus.). 164p. 1994. pap. 36.95 (0-85288-250-5, Pub. by Imray Laurie Norie & Wilson UK) Bluewater Bks.

— The Yachtsman's Pilot to the West Coast of Scotland: Crinan to Canna. 170p. (C). 1987. 110.00 (0-85288-107-X, Pub. by Imray Laurie Norie & Wilson UK) St Mut.

— You So Crazy. (Illus.). 128p. 1994. pap. 7.95 (0-7868-8083-X) Hyperion.

Lawrence, Martin, jt. ed. see Grol, Richard.

Lawrence, Martin S. & Schofield, Theo, eds. Medical Audit in Primary Health Care. LC 92-48416. (Oxford Medical Pubns.). 272p. 1993. 31.50 (0-19-262267-6) OUP.

Lawrence, Marty. Vests to Dye For. (Illus.). 8p. 1990. pap. 4.95 (0-944588-14-X) K Wood Pub.

Lawrence, Mary. The Creative Book of Pressed Flowers. (Creative Book Ser.). (Illus.). 124p. 1989. pap. 9.95 (0-937769-12-6) Mark Inc CA.

— Little Book of Potpourri. 1994. 4.98 (1-55521-989-6) Bk Sales Inc.

Lawrence, Mary C. The Captain's Best Mate: The Journal of Mary Chipman Lawrence on the Whaler Addison, 1856-1860. Garner, Stanton, ed. LC 83-40018. (Illus.). 335p. 1986. pap. 16.95 (0-87451-366-9) U Pr of New Eng.

Lawrence, Mary S. Reading, Thinking, Writing: A Text for Students of English As a Second Language. (C). 1975. 14.95 (0-472-08548-4); teacher ed 2.00 (0-472-08549-2) U of Mich Pr.

— Writing As a Thinking Process. LC 78-185153. (Illus.). (C). 1972. Net. teacher ed 2.95 (0-472-08551-4); pap. text ed. 14.95 (0-472-08550-6) U of Mich Pr.

Lawrence, Melinda. My Life, Melinda's Story. 15p. 1987. pap. 4.95 (0-317-61838-5) Child Hospice VA.

Lawrence, Merle, jt. auth. see Wever, Ernest G.

Lawrence, Merloyd, tr. see Flaubert, Gustave.

Lawrence, Michael. The Complete Book on Takeout Doubles. (Doubles Ser.). 256p. 1994. pap. text ed. 12.95 (0-9637533-1-2) Magnus Bks.

— Major Suit Raises. 86p. (Orig.). 1987. pap. 4.95 (0-9628297-1-4) C & T Bridge.

Lawrence, Michael D. & Ryan, Joan S. Essentials of Accounting. 8th ed. LC 94-3885. 1995. text ed. 29.95 (0-538-83213-4) S-W Pub.

Lawrence, Michael D., jt. auth. see Dansby, Robert L.

Lawrence, Micheal J., jt. auth. see Jeffery, D. Ross.

Lawrence, Mike. A-Z of Sports Cars since 1945. (Illus.). 256p. 1991. 39.95 (1-870979-23-0) Motorbooks Intl.

— Bathrooms. 1989. 7.98 (1-85368-004-4, Pub. by New Holland Pubs UK) St Mut.

— Bidding Quizzes, Vol. 1: The Uncontested Auction. LC 90-91520. 288p. (Orig.). 1990. pap. 13.95 (1-877908-02-9) Lawrence & Leong Pub.

— Complete Book of Home Decorating: A Step-by-Step Guide. 1994. 19.98 (0-8317-6508-9) Smithmark.

— The Complete Book on Balancing in Contract Bridge. LC 84-223527. 209p. 1981. 14.95 (0-939460-14-9); pap. 11.95 (0-939460-13-0) Devyn Pr.

— The Complete Book on Hand Evaluation in Contract Bridge. LC 84-223827. 194p. 1983. pap. 11.95 (0-939460-27-0) Devyn Pr.

— The Complete Book on Overcalls in Contract Bridge. LC 80-123383. 202p. 1979. 14.95 (0-939460-08-4); pap. 11.95 (0-939460-07-6) Devyn Pr.

— The Complete Decorating & Home Improvement Book: A Step-by-Step Guide. 256p. Date not set. 19.98 (0-8317-2739-X) Smithmark.

— The Complete Guide to Contested Auctions. LC 92-90023. 368p. (Orig.). 1992. text ed. 14.95 (1-877908-04-5) Lawrence & Leong Pub.

— The Complete Guide to Passed Hand Bidding. LC 89-80899. 224p. 1989. pap. 12.95 (1-877908-01-0) Lawrence & Leong Pub.

— Dynamic Defense. 228p. 1991. pap. 11.95 (0-910791-01-5) Devyn Pr.

— Essential Austin Healey 100 & 3000. (Essential Ser.). (Illus.). 80p. 1994. pap. 12.95 (1-870979-49-4, Pub. by Bay View Bks UK) Motorbooks Intl.

— Essential Jaguar XK, XK120, 140, 150: The Cars & Their Story 1949-61. (Essential Ser.). (Illus.). 80p. 1995. pap. 12.95 (1-870979-61-3, Pub. by Bay View Bks UK) Motorbooks Intl.

— How to Play Card Combinations at Bridge: Unlocking the Secrets. 1989. pap. 11.95 (0-910791-63-5) Devyn Pr.

— How to Read Your Opponent's Cards: The Bridge Experts' Way to Locate Missing High Cards. 175p. 1991. pap. 9.95 (0-910791-48-1) Devyn Pr.

— Judgement at Bridge. LC 80-123381. 151p. 1976. pap. 9.95 (0-939460-02-5) Devyn Pr.

— Kitchens. 1989. 7.98 (1-85368-008-7, Pub. by New Holland Pubs UK) St Mut.

— Play a Swiss Teams of Four with Mike Lawrence. LC 84-223798. 99p. 1982. pap. 7.95 (0-939460-19-X) Devyn Pr.

— Practical Home Improvement. 128p. 1995. 14.98 (0-8317-6958-0) Smithmark.

— Step-by-Step Outdoor Woodwork. 1994. 9.99 (0-517-10257-9) Random Hse Value.

— The Story of March-Four. (Illus.). 256p. 1989. 29.95 (0-946627-24-X, Pub. by Aston Pubns UK) Motorbooks Intl.

Lawrence, Mike, ed. Backyard Brickwork: How to Build Walls, Paths, Patios, & Barbecues. LC 89-45218. (Illus.). 96p. 1989. pap. 14.95 (0-88266-562-6, Garden Way Pub) Storey Comm Inc.

— Garden Brickwork: How to Build Walls, Paths, Patios & Barbecues. 96p. (C). 1988. 80.00 (1-85368-006-0, Pub. by New Holland Pubs UK) St Mut.

— Step-by-Step Outdoor Stonework: Over Twenty Easy-to-Build Projects for Your Patio & Garden. LC 94-23205. 1995. pap. 18.95 (0-88266-891-9, Garden Way Pub) Storey Comm Inc.

Lawrence, Mike & Bradford, Derek, eds. The Complete Home Renovation Manual. LC 92-32002. (Illus.). 224p. 1993. 19.98 (0-8317-1588-X) Smithmark.

Lawrence, Milo. The Next Dominant Species. LC 93-74163. 403p. 1994. 19.95 (*0-9639372-5-1*) Altos Pubng. It is the compelling story of a team of computer scientists & teachers struggling to create & educate an intelligent robot. "Congratulations on writing what I think could be called 'Son of HAL'! It's a convincing & exciting anticipation of the problems & promise of artificial intelligence, & you put both sides of the argument very fairly."--ARTHUR C. CLARKE. "The action riddled plot makes one hang in there until the last page"--THE VOICE. "Provocative thesis...it succeeds."--RAPPORT. "Suspenseful first novel."--BOOKLIST. "THE NEXT DOMINANT SPECIES packs in everything from romance & intrigue to high technology, while it may be argued that almost too many angles & factors are pushed into the story of the creation of an intelligent machine, the complexity ultimately serves to create a sophisticated, probing account which includes strong characterization & the spicy lure of high technology. Librarians & general interest audiences will find this a thrilling & involving read with many unexpected twists & turns."--THE MIDWEST BOOK REVIEW. Available from: Baker & Taylor, Brodart & Altos Publishing, 12303 Hidden Meadows Circle, Auburn, CA 95603. (916) 888-7235. ***Publisher Provided Annotation.***

Lawrence, Nancy. Delightful Deception. 1990. pap. 2.95 (0-8217-3053-3) Zebra.

Lawrence, Nathaniel. Alfred North Whitehead: A Primer of His Philosophy. 192p. 1974. 59.50 (0-685-63209-1) Elliots Bks.

— Whitehead's Philosophical Development. LC 68-23306. 370p. 1968. reprint ed. text ed. 35.00 (0-8371-0139-5, LAWD, Greenwood Pr) Greenwood.

Lawrence, Nathaniel M., jt. auth. see Brumbaugh, Robert S.

Lawrence, Neal H. Shining Moments: Tanka Poems in English. (Illus.). 140p. 1993. 12.00 (0-944676-39-1) AHA Bks.

Lawrence, P. Management in the Land of Israel. (C). 1990. 280.00 (0-7487-0401-9, Pub. by S Thornes Pubs UK) St Mut.

Lawrence, P. & Mauch, K. Real-Time Microcomputer System Design: An Introduction. (Electrical Engineering Ser.). 592p. 1987. text ed. write for info. (0-07-036731-0) McGraw.

Lawrence, P., jt. auth. see Barsoux, J. L.

Lawrence, P. A. & Lee, R. Alton. Insight into Management. 2nd ed. (Illus.). 248p. 1989. 60.00 (0-19-856227-6); pap. 24.95 (0-19-856226-8) OUP.

Lawrence, Pat. Beyond the Hype: Illusion & Reality in Real Estate Sales, Why 95 Percent of the Agents are Doomed to Failure & How the Successful Ones Destroy Their Lives. 284p. (Orig.). 1991. pap. 19.95 (0-9630082-0-X) Hazelhurst.

Lawrence, Patricia, jt. auth. see Amyx, D. A.

Lawrence, Patricia A. In the Wind's Eye. (Orig.). 1991. pap. 6.00 (1-879533-07-3) Poetic Page.

Lawrence, Paul R. The Changing of Organizational Behavior Patterns: A Case Study of Decentralization. 256p. (C). 1991. pap. 19.95 (0-88738-894-9) Transaction Pubs.

Lawrence, Paul R. & Dyer, Davis. Renewing American Industry. LC 82-72096. 400p. (C). 1983. 24.95 (0-02-918170-4) Free Pr.

— Renewing American Industry. LC 82-72096. 400p. (C). 1984. pap. 14.95 (0-02-918220-4) Free Pr.

Lawrence, Paul R. & Lorch, Jay W. Organization & Environment: Managing Differentiation & Integration. 1986. pap. text ed. 14.95 (0-07-103246-0) McGraw.

Lawrence, Paul R. & Lorsch, Jay W. Developing Organizations: Diagnosis & Action. LC 78-93985. (Organization Development Ser.). (Orig.). (C). 1969. pap. text ed. 26.95 (0-201-04204-5) Addison-Wesley.

— Organization & Environment: Managing Differentiation & Integration. (Harvard Business School Publications). 295p. (C). 1967. 19.50 (0-87584-064-7) HUP.

Lawrence, Paul R. & Vlachoutsicos, Charalambos A., eds. Behind the Factory Walls: Decision Making in Soviet & U. S. Enterprises. 1990. text ed. 29.95 (0-07-103247-9) McGraw.

Lawrence, Paul R., jt. ed. see Cash, James I., Jr.

Lawrence, Paul R., jt. ed. see Cash, James I.

Lawrence, Paul R., jt. ed. see Etzioni, Amitai.

Lawrence, Paul R., jt. ed. see Walton, Richard E.

Lawrence, Peter. Management in the Netherlands. 200p. 1991. 48.00 (0-19-828684-8) OUP.

— Road Belong Cargo: A Study of the Cargo Movement in the Southern Madang District New Guinea. (Illus.). 293p. (C). 1989. reprint ed. pap. text ed. 11.50x (0-88133-458-8) Waveland Pr.

Lawrence, Peter, jt. ed. see Berndt, Ronald M.

Lawrence, Peter, jt. ed. see Calori, Roland.

Lawrence, Peter, jt. auth. see Cason, Jeff.

Lawrence, Peter, ed. see Cason, Jeffrey.

Lawrence, Peter, jt. auth. see Edwards, Vincent.

Lawrence, Peter, jt. auth. see Whitman, Neal A.

Lawrence, Peter A. The Making of a Fly: The Genetics of Animal Design. (Illus.). 242p. 1992. pap. 34.95 (0-632-03048-8) Blackwell Sci.

Lawrence, Peter F. & Goldman, Mitchell H. Essentials of General Surgery: Oral Examinations. 2nd ed. (Illus.). 112p. 1992. pap. 35.00 (0-683-04870-8) Williams & Wilkins.

Lawrence, Peter F. & Goldman, Mitchell H., eds. Oral Exams for Surgical Specialties. LC 92-48675. 96p. 1993. 10.00 (0-683-04865-1) Williams & Wilkins.

Lawrence, Peter F., et al. Essentials of General Surgery. 2nd ed. (Illus.). 454p. 1992. pap. 35.00 (0-683-04869-4) Williams & Wilkins.

Lawrence, Peter F., et al, eds. Essentials of Surgical Specialties. LC 92-21071. (Illus.). 448p. 1993. 35.00 (0-683-04871-6) Williams & Wilkins.

Lawrence, Philip K. Democracy & the Liberal State. 213p. 1989. text ed. 55.95 (1-85521-019-3, Pub. by Dartmth Pub UK) Ashgate Pub Co.

— Preparing for Armageddon: A Critique of Western Strategy. LC 87-32333. 204p. 1988. text ed. 39.95 (0-312-01893-2) St Martin.

Lawrence, Priscilla O. Before Disaster Strikes: Prevention, Planning, & Recovery: Caring for Your Personal Collections in the Event of Disaster. LC 92-37511. 1992. pap. 6.95 (0-917860-32-2) Historic New Orleans.

Lawrence, R. The Descendants of Major Samuel Lawrence of Groton, Mass., with Some Mention of Allied Family. (Illus.). 355p. reprint ed. lib. bdg. 54.00 (0-8328-0755-9); reprint ed. pap. 44.00 (0-8328-0756-7) Higginson Bk Co.

Lawrence, R., jt. auth. see Nair, P. K.

Lawrence, R. D. Cry Wild. 224p. 1992. mass mkt. 3.99 (1-55817-636-5, Pinnacle NY) Windsor NY.

— The Green Trees Beyond: A Memoir. LC 93-11961. 1994. 25.00 (0-8050-1297-4) H Holt & Co.

— In Praise of Wolves. 1988. mass mkt. 4.95 (0-345-34916-4) Ballantine.

— Secret Go the Wolves. 240p. 1985. mass mkt. 5.99 (0-345-33200-8) Ballantine.

— Shark! Nature's Masterpiece. (Curious Naturalist Ser.). (Illus.). 192p. 1994. reprint ed. pap. 12.95 (1-881527-57-3) Chapters Pub.

— The Study of Life: A Naturalist's View. (Illus.). 43p. (gr. 7-12). 1980. pap. 1.50 (0-913098-37-X) Myrin Institute.

— Trail of the Wolf. LC 92-44404. (Illus.). 160p. 1993. 35.00 (0-87596-594-6) Rodale Pr Inc.

— White Puma. 1991. mass mkt. 4.95 (1-55817-532-6, Pinnacle NY) Windsor NY.

— Wolves. (Sierra Club Wildlife Library). 64p. (J). (gr. 3-6). 1990. 15.95 (0-316-51676-7) Little.

Lawrence, R. D., ed. see Grace, Eric S.

Lawrence, R. F. The Centipedes & Millipedes of Southern Africa: A Guide. 168p. (C). 1984. text ed. 70.00 (0-86961-142-9, Pub. by A A Balkema NE) Ashgate Pub Co.

Lawrence, R. S., jt. ed. see Goldbloom, R. B.

Lawrence, R. W., et al, eds. Fundamental & Applied Biohydrometallurgy: Proceedings of the Sixth International Conference on Biohydrometallurgy, Vancouver, BC, Canada, Aug., 21-24, 1985. 502p. 1986. 161.75 (0-444-42658-2) Elsevier.

Lawrence, Raymond J., Jr. The Poisoning of Eros: Sexual Values in Conflict. LC 89-92038. 281p. (C). 1989. 19.95 (0-9623310-0-7) Augustine Moore.

***Lawrence, Rebecca L., ed.** Drawing Your Own Conclusions: 30 Years of Public Support for the Arts in New Hampshire, 1965-1995. 40p. 1995. ring bd. write for info. (0-9621915-1-5) NH SCA.

Lawrence, Rebecca L. & Sylvester, Audrey V., eds. Art in Unexpected Places. LC 88-64115. (Illus.). 96p. (Orig.). 1989. pap. 10.00 (0-9621915-0-7) NH SCA.

Lawrence, Richard, tr. The Book of Enoch. LC 80-65736. 96p. 1980. reprint ed. pap. 5.00 (0-934666-06-7) Artisan Sales.

Lawrence, Richard D. & Record, Jeffrey. United States Force Structure in NATO: an Alternative: A Staff Paper. LC 74-1436. (Studies in Defense Policy). (Illus.). 148p. reprint ed. pap. 42.20 (0-685-23673-0, 2027968) Bks Demand.

Lawrence, Richard H. The Paduans, Medals by Giovanni Cavino. (Illus.). 1980. pap. 5.00 (0-916710-74-2) Obol Intl.

Lawrence, Rick. Evil & the Occult. (Active Bible Curriculum Ser.). 48p. (Orig.). 1990. pap. 9.99 (1-55945-102-5) Group Pub.

Lawrence, Robb. Heathcliffs Night Before Christmas. 1989. pap. 1.95 (0-8167-1559-9) Troll Assocs.

Lawrence, Robert. The Impact of Trade on OECD Markets. (Orig.). 1993. pap. text ed. write for info. (1-56708-041-3) Grp of Thirty.

— The World of Opera. LC 77-2268. (Illus.). 208p. 1977. reprint ed. text ed. 55.00 (0-8371-9551-9, LAWO, Greenwood Pr) Greenwood.

Lawrence, Robert, ed. Energy Policy Issues. (C). 1978. pap. 12.00 (0-918592-28-3) Pol Studies.

— New Dimensions to Energy Policy. (Organization Ser.). 233p. 1979. 12.00 (0-317-35630-5) Pol Studies.

Lawrence, Robert, jt. ed. see Case, Deborah.

Lawrence, Robert C. International Tax & Estate Planning: A Practical Guide for Multinational Investors. 850p. 1989. text ed. 95.00 (0-685-46013-4, J6-1470) PLI.

— The State of Robeson County, North Carolina. 279p. 1994. reprint ed. lib. bdg. 32.50 (0-8328-4154-4) Higginson Bk Co.

Lawrence, Robert C., III, ed. International Personal Tax Planning Encyclopedia, 2 vols. suppl. ed. 1994. ring bd. 69.00 (0-318-72491-X) Butterworth Legal Pubs.

— International Personal Tax Planning Encyclopedia, 2 vols., Set. 1000p. 1994. ring bd. 175.00 (0-406-51200-0) Michie Butterworth.

Lawrence, Robert D. Burba, Burbee, Burby: Descendants of Peter Burbee, Sr. & Others Who Share These Surnames. LC 94-77401. 500p. 1994. 45.00 (0-9617907-4-1) Lawrence KS.

— The Graying of My Guardian Angel. 112p. (Orig.). 1991. pap. 3.00 (0-9617907-3-3) Lawrence KS.

— The Many Generations of Davis Dimock Cheever, 1851-1920, Lest We Forget. (Illus.). 64p. 1983. pap. text ed. 5.00 (0-9617907-0-9) Lawrence KS.

Lawrence, Robert M. The Magic of the Horseshoe & Other Folk-Lore Notes. 1976. lib. bdg. 59.95 (0-8490-2195-2) Gordon Pr.

An Asterisk (*) at the beginning of an entry indicates that the title is appearing in BIP for the first time.

Lawrence, Robert M. & Larus, Joel, eds. Nuclear Proliferation: Phase II. LC 74-11724. viii, 256p. (Orig.). (C). 1974. pap. 12.95 (*0-7006-0128-7*) U Pr of KS.

Lawrence, Robert Z. Can America Compete? LC 84-9401. 156p. 1984. 28.95 (*0-8157-5176-1*); pap. 10.95 (*0-8157-5175-3*) Brookings.

— Regionalism, Multilateralism & Deeper Integration. (Integrating National Economies: Promise & Pitfalls Ser.). 1995. 28.95 (*0-8157-5182-6*); pap. 10.95 (*0-8157-5181-8*) Brookings.

Lawrence, Robert Z. & Litan, Robert E. Saving Free Trade: A Pragmatic Approach. LC 86-14705. 132p. 1986. 28.95 (*0-8157-5178-8*); pap. 10.95 (*0-8157-5177-X*) Brookings.

Lawrence, Robert Z. & Schultze, Charles L., eds. American Trade Strategy: Options for the 1990's. 234p. 1990. pap. 12.95 (*0-8157-5179-6*) Brookings.

— Barriers to European Growth: A Transatlantic View. LC 87-26900. 619p. 1987. 39.95 (*0-8157-7770-1*); pap. 19.95 (*0-8157-7769-8*) Brookings.

Lawrence, Robert Z., jt. auth. see Bosworth, Barry P.

Lawrence, Robert Z., jt. ed. see Litan, Robert E.

***Lawrence, Robert Z., et al.** A Vision for the World Economy: Openness, Diversity, & Cohesion. (Integrating National Economies Ser.). 150p. (C). 1995. 28.95x (*0-8157-5184-2*); pap. 10.95x (*0-8157-5183-4*) Brookings.

Lawrence, Ronald M. Goodbye Pain! LC 88-28001. (Illus.). 112p. (Orig.). 1988. pap. 5.95 (*0-88007-169-9*) Woodbridge Pr.

Lawrence, Rosemary, jt. auth. see Mason, John.

Lawrence, Roy. How to Pray When Life Hurts: Experiencing the Power of Healing Prayer. LC 92-35136. (Quest, Adventure, Survival Ser.). (Illus.). 129p. (Orig.). 1993. pap. 7.99 (*0-8308-1384-5*, 1384, Saltshaker Bk) InterVarsity.

— Motive & Intention: An Essay in the Appreciation of Action. LC 72-186548. (Publications in Analytical Philosophy). 146p. reprint ed. 41.70 (*0-8357-9465-2*, 2015301) Bks Demand.

Lawrence, Ruth A., jt. auth. see Jones, Carl.

***Lawrence, Ruth A., et al.** Breastfeeding Care: Setting the Environment, Supporting the Process. LC 94-29660. 1994. write for info. (*0-86525-058-8*) March of Dimes.

***Lawrence, Sandra.** Rapture's Voyage. (Bedroom Adventures Ser.). 1993. write for info. (*1-884057-00-4*) Trivial Development Corp.

Lawrence, Shirley B. Behind Numerology: Complete Details on the Hidden Meaning of Letters & Numbers. 1990. pap. 14.95 (*0-87877-145-X*) Newcastle Pub.

— Numerology & the English Cabalah: Translating Numbers into Words & Words into Numbers. Lammey, William L. & Misiroglu, Gina, eds. (Illus.). 224p. (Orig.). 1994. pap. 18.95 (*0-87877-188-3*) Newcastle Pub.

Lawrence, Sidney. Roger Brown. (Illus.). 120p. 1987. pap. 17.95 (*0-8076-1179-4*) Braziller.

Lawrence, Stephen S., jt. auth. see Hulan, Richard.

Lawrence, Steven C. Bullet Welcome. 1992. 14.95 (*0-7451-4547-7*, Gunsmoke) Chivers N Amer.

— Day of the Comancheros. large type ed. (Linford Western Library). 272p. 1985. pap. 11.95 (*0-7089-6080-4*, Trailtree Bookshop) Ulverscroft.

— Edge of the Land. 1995. 15.95 (*0-7451-4633-3*) Chivers N Amer.

— Gun Blast. large type ed. 1990. pap. 16.95 (*0-7927-0381-2*, C0416, Curley Lrg Print) Chivers N Amer.

— The Iron Marshal. large type ed. 1990. pap. 16.95 (*0-7927-0593-9*, Curley Lrg Print) Chivers N Amer.

— Night of the Gunmen. 1993. 14.95 (*0-7451-4575-2*, Gunsmoke) Chivers N Amer.

— Trial for Tennihan. 1993. 14.95 (*0-7451-4585-X*, Gunsmoke) Chivers N Amer.

Lawrence, Stewart, jt. auth. see Hilsman, Roger.

Lawrence, Sue. Entertaining at Home in Scotland. (Illus.). 124p. 1993. 29.95 (*1-85158-409-9*, Pub. by Mnstream UK) Trafalgar.

— Food with Flair. (Illus.). 208p. 1994. 34.95 (*1-85158-559-1*, Pub. by Mnstream UK) Trafalgar.

Lawrence, Susan E. Law & Politics in the Supreme Court: Cases & Reading. 224p. (C). 1993. per. 24.95 (*0-8403-8659-1*) Kendall-Hunt.

— The Poor in Court: The Legal Services Program & Supreme Court Decision Making. 201p. 1990. text ed. 32.50 (*0-691-07855-6*) Princeton U Pr.

Lawrence, Sylvia. Angels & Cupids. LC 93-85149. (Illus.). 1993. 12.95 (*0-8478-1774-1*) Rizzoli Intl.

Lawrence, T. E. Crusader Castles. (Insider's Guides Ser.). 1992. pap. 16.95 (*0-7818-0038-2*) Hippocrene Bks.

— Crusader Castles. 224p. (C). 1990. 150.00 (*0-907151-68-X*, Pub. by IMMEL Pubng UK); pap. 125.00 (*0-907151-67-1*, Pub. by IMMEL Pubng UK) St Mut.

— Crusader Castles. 2nd ed. (Illus.). 224p. 1992. pap. 24.95 (*0-87052-290-6*) Hippocrene Bks.

— The Diary Kept by T. E. Lawrence: While Traveling in Arabia During 1911. 86p. 1993. 45.00 (*1-873938-24-1*, Pub. by Ithaca UK) Paul & Co Pubs.

— The Essential T. E. Lawrence. Garnett, David, ed. 334p. 1992. pap. 14.95 (*0-19-282962-9*) OUP.

— Lawrence of Arabia, Strange Man of Letters: The Literary Criticism of T. E. Lawrence. Orlans, Harold, ed. LC 92-53456. 1993. 47.50 (*0-8386-3508-3*) Fairleigh Dickinson.

— Revolt in the Desert. large type ed. 438p. 1990. 22.95 (*1-85089-401-9*, Pub. by ISIS UK) Transaction Pubs.

— Seven Pillars of Wisdom. 1976. 34.95 (*0-8488-0562-3*) Amereon Ltd.

— Seven Pillars of Wisdom. (Reprints Ser.). (Illus.). 672p. 1989. 29.95 (*0-88029-258-X*) Dorset Pr.

— Seven Pillars of Wisdom: A Triumph. 1991. pap. 15.00 (*0-385-41895-7*) Doubleday.

Lawrence, T. E., tr. see Homer.

Lawrence, T. J. Essays on Some Disputed Questions in Modern International Law. 2nd rev. ed. xiii, 313p. 1990. reprint ed. lib. bdg. 35.00 (*0-8377-2412-0*) Rothman.

— The Principles of International Law. xxi, 645p. 1987. reprint ed. lib. bdg. 57.50 (*0-8377-2405-8*) Rothman.

***Lawrence, Terry.** A Man's Man. (Loveswept Ser.: No. 718). 1994. pap. 3.50 (*0-553-44461-1*, Loveswept) Bantam.

— Turning Wooden Toys. (Illus.). 176p. 1994. pap. 17.95 (*0-946819-61-0*, Pub. by Guild Mstr Craftsman UK) Sterling.

Lawrence, Thea. Unity Without Uniformity: The Story of Rhinebeck Churches. (Illus.). (Orig.). (C). 1990. pap. write for info. (*0-318-65920-4*) Dawn Treader.

Lawrence, Theodor. Sexual Key to the Tarot. (Illus.). 1971. 5.95 (*0-8065-0242-8*, Citadel Pr) Carol Pub Group.

Lawrence, Thomas & Sheppeck, Michael A. The Game Called Industry. LC 93-73954. 96p. (C). 1993. pap. 6.95 (*0-9639245-0-8*) Black Collegiate.

Lawrence, Thomas E. Afstand In der Wuste. (Illus.). 402p. 1988. reprint ed. write for info. (*3-487-08300-0*, Pub. by Georg Olms GW) Lubrecht & Cramer.

— Selected Letters. Garnett, David, ed. LC 78-20478. 1988. reprint ed. 34.50 (*0-88355-856-4*) Hyperion Conn.

Lawrence-Tree Company Staff. Tree I. D. Kit. 48p. 1992. 16.50 (*0-9635744-0-X*) Lawrence-Tree.

Lawrence, V. J. Nine Plays for African American Youth: Children's Window to Africa. 45p. (YA). (gr. 1-12). 1993. pap. 8.95 (*0-929917-06-5*) Magnolia PA.

Lawrence, V. L., jt. auth. see Gould, W. J.

Lawrence, Valerie. Southern Skies Cry... LC 88-61291. 60p. 1988. pap. 8.95 (*0-929917-03-0*) Magnolia PA.

— What's Yr Hair Like after U Wash It? Natural Poems by Valerie Lawrence. LC 90-6188. 100p. (J). (gr. 6 up). 1990. 10.95 (*0-929917-01-4*) Magnolia PA.

Lawrence, Valerie, jt. ed. see Penny, Rob.

***Lawrence, Vera B.** Strong on Music: The New York Music Scene in the Days of George Templeton Strong. 736p. 1994. lib. bdg. 85.00 (*0-226-47010-5*); pap. text ed. 27.50 (*0-226-47011-3*) U Ch Pr.

— Strong on Music - The New York Music Scene in the Days of George Templeton Strong, 1836-1850 Vol. 1: Resonances, 1836-1850. LC 94-205956. 1995. pap. text ed. 27.50 (*0-226-47009-1*) U Ch Pr.

— Wa-Wan Press, 1901-1911, 5 vols. LC 74-97068. (American Music Ser.). 1970. reprint ed. 245.00 (*0-405-02407-X*) Ayer.

Lawrence, Vera B., ed. see Joplin, Scott.

***Lawrence, Vicki & Eliot, Marc.** Vicki! The True - Life Adventures of Miss Fireball. LC 94-46710. 1995. 23.00 (*0-684-80286-4*) S&S Trade.

Lawrence, Victor J. Easy Steps to Playing Guitar, Vol. I. 1946. 5.95 (*0-913650-27-7*) CPP Belwin.

— Elementary Guitar Method. 1943. 5.95 (*0-913650-30-7*) CPP Belwin.

Lawrence, W., Jr., et al. Manual of Soft-Tissue Tumor Surgery. (Comprehensive Manuals of Surgical Specialties Ser.). (Illus.). 214p. 1983. 146.00 (*0-387-90843-9*) Spr-Verlag.

Lawrence, W. G., jt. auth. see Tichane, Robert.

Lawrence, W. Gordon, ed. Exploring Individual & Organizational Boundaries: A Tavistock Open Systems Approach. LC 78-8603. (Wiley Series on Individuals, Groups & Organizations). 274p. reprint ed. pap. 78.10 (*0-685-15407-6*, 2026675) Bks Demand.

Lawrence, W. J. Shakespeare's Workshop. 161p. (C). 1966. text ed. 75.00 (*0-8383-0580-6*) M S G Haskell Hse.

— Those Nut-Cracking Elizabethans. LC 74-98684. (Studies in Drama: No. 39). 1970. reprint ed. lib. bdg. 49.95 (*0-8383-0988-7*) M S G Haskell Hse.

Lawrence, William. Beyond the Bottom Line. 1994. pap. 9.99 (*0-8024-1082-0*) Moody.

***Lawrence, William B.** Painting Light & Shadow in Watercolor. LC 94-21078. (Illus.). 144p. 1995. 27.99 (*0-89134-577-9*) North Light Bks.

Lawrence, William H. Commercial Paper & Check Collection. 650p. 1990. pap. 40.00 (*0-88063-740-4*) Michie Butterworth.

— Commercial Paper & Payment Systems, 2 vols., Set. 880p. 1990. ring bd. 150.00 (*0-88063-325-5*) Michie Butterworth.

Lawrence, William H. & Minan, John H. The Law of Commercial Leasing. 1993. text ed. 145.00 (*0-685-69639-1*, LCL) Warren Gorham & Lamont.

Lawrence, William J. Life of Amos A. Lawrence. LC 70-154158. (Select Bibliographies Reprint Ser.). 1977. reprint ed. 23.95 (*0-8369-5774-1*) Ayer.

— Old Theatre Days & Ways. LC 68-20236. 1972. reprint ed. 20.95 (*0-405-08737-3*, Pub. by Blom Pubns UK) Ayer.

— Pre-Restoration Stage Studies. LC 67-23857. 1972. reprint ed. 30.95 (*0-405-08738-1*, Pub. by Blom Pubns UK) Ayer.

— Shakespeare's Workshop. (BCL1-PR English Literature Ser.). 161p. 1992. reprint ed. lib. bdg. 69.00 (*0-7812-7296-3*) Rprt Serv.

— Speeding up Shakespeare. LC 68-20235. 1972. reprint ed. 20.95 (*0-405-08739-X*) Ayer.

Lawrence, William J. & Leeds, Stephen. An Inventory of Federal Income Transfer Programs, Fiscal Year 1977. LC 77-92998. 219p. 1978. 12.00 (*0-915312-07-7*) Inst Socioecon.

— An Inventory of State & Local Income Transfer Programs: Fiscal Year 1977. LC 80-82153. 301p. 1980. 12.00 (*0-915312-09-3*) Inst Socioecon.

***Lawrenson, Derek.** Dream Ryder Cup: The Best All-Time Players from America & Europe at the Home of Golf. (Illus.). 208p. 1995. 24.95 (*0-7137-2525-7*, Pub. by Blandford Pr UK) Sterling.

Lawrenson, P. J., jt. auth. see Binns, K. J.

Lawrenson, Thomas E. The French Stage & Playhouse in the Seventeenth Century. 2nd rev. ed. LC 79-3697. (Studies in the Seventeenth Century: No. 1). 1986. 47.50 (*0-404-61721-2*) AMS Pr.

***Lawrenz, Mel & Green, Daniel.** Light at the End of the Tunnel: Getting Through Loss & Trauma. (Strategic Christian Living Ser.). 144p. (Orig.). 1995. pap. 13.99 (*0-8010-5268-8*) Baker Bk.

— Overcoming Grief & Trauma. (Strategic Pastoral Counseling Resources Ser.). 192p. 1995. text ed. 17.99 (*0-8010-1056-X*) Baker Bk.

Lawrenz, Mel, jt. auth. see Green, Daniel R.

Lawrenz, Mel, jt. auth. see Green, Daniel.

Lawrey, James D. & Hale, Mason E., Jr. Biology of Lichenized Fungi. LC 84-9908. 416p. 1984. text ed. 42.95 (*0-275-91211-6*, C1211, Praeger Pubs) Greenwood.

Lawrie & Morris. Coronary Artery Bypass Surgery. 1991. 45.00 (*0-8151-5334-1*, Yr Bk Med Pubs) Mosby Yr Bk.

Lawrie, A., et al. Glimmer of Cold Brine: A Scottish Sea Anthology. (Illus.). 250p. 1988. pap. 18.00 (*0-08-036579-5*, Pergamon Pr) Elsevier.

***Lawrie, Christine.** Ask about Animals. LC 94-28180. (Read All about It Ser.). (Illus.). (J). 1995. lib. bdg. write for info. (*0-8114-5729-X*) Raintree Steck-V.

Lawrie, James. The Premarital Workshop. 1991. pap. 8.50 (*1-55673-293-7*, 9126) CSS OH.

Lawrie, R. A. Developments in Meat Science, 2 vols., 2. (Illus.). 1981. 90.00 (*0-85334-986-X*, Pub. by Elsevier Applied Sci UK) Elsevier.

— Meat Science. (C). 1985. text ed. 74.00 (*0-08-030790-6*, Pergamon Pr); pap. text ed. 42.00 (*0-08-030789-2*, Pergamon Pr) Elsevier.

— Meat Science. 5th ed. (Food Science Ser.). (Illus.). 300p. (C). 1991. text ed. 81.00 (*0-08-040824-9*, Pergamon Pr); pap. text ed. 47.00 (*0-08-040825-7*, Pergamon Pr) Elsevier.

Lawrie, R. A., ed. Development in Meat Science, Vol. 4. 366p. 1989. 93.75 (*1-85166-198-0*) Elsevier.

— Developments in Meat Science, Vol. 5. 254p. 1991. 120.00 (*1-85166-534-X*) Elsevier.

— Developments in Meat Science 3. 240p. 1985. 72.00 (*0-85334-361-6*, Pub. by Elsevier Applied Sci UK) Elsevier.

Lawrie, R. A., ed. see Easter School in Agricultural Science (21st: 1974: University of Nottingham) Staff.

Lawrie, R. A., ed. see Easter School in Agricultural Science (16th: 1969: University of Nottingham) Staff.

Lawrie, Richard A., jt. auth. see Heins, Conrad P.

Lawrie, Robert J. Electric Motor Manual. (Illus.). 128p. 1987. text ed. 43.00 (*0-07-036730-2*) McGraw.

Lawrie, Robin, illus. Fantasy Stories. LC 94-2338. 256p. (J). (gr. 5-10). 1994. pap. 6.95 (*1-85697-982-2*, Kingfisher LKC) LKC.

Lawrie, Robin, ed. see Lewis, C. S.

Lawrie, T. D., jt. ed. see Macfarlane, Peter W.

Lawrinowicz, Julian, ed. Deformations of Mathematical Structures II: Hurwitz-Type Structures & Applications to Surface Physics: Selected Papers from the Seminar on Deformations, Lodz'-Malinka 1988-92. LC 93-33466. 480p. (C). 1994. lib. bdg. 199.00 (*0-7923-2576-1*) Kluwer Ac.

Lawriwsky, Michael. Corporate Structure & Performance: The Role of Owners, Managers & Markets. LC 83-24748. 304p. 1984. text ed. 39.95 (*0-312-17001-7*) St Martin.

Lawry. College 101: A Freshman Reader. 316p. 1992. text ed. write for info. (*0-07-036733-7*) McGraw.

Lawry, Antje, tr. see Von Balthasar, Hans U.

Lawry, John D. Guide to the History of Psychology. 128p. (C). 1990. reprint ed. pap. text ed. 17.50 (*0-8191-7851-9*) U Pr of Amer.

— How to Succeed at School. LC 88-60047. 144p. (Orig.). 1988. pap. 6.95 (*1-55612-116-4*) Sheed & Ward MO.

Lawry, Mark H. I-DEAS Student Guide. 650p. (C). 1993. pap. text ed. 19.50 (*0-9638178-0-9*) Structrl Dynmcs.

— I-DEAS Student Guide: Master Series 2.0. 500p. (C). Date not set. pap. text ed. 25.00 (*0-9638178-1-7*) Structrl Dynmcs.

Lawry, Robert P., jt. ed. see Clarke, Robert W.

Lawry, Robert P., jt. auth. see Davies, Jack.

Lawry, Walt. Classic Guitar Solos in First & Second Position. 1993. 4.95 (*0-685-64357-3*, 93770) Mel Bay.

— Classical Guitar Position Studies. 1993. 9.95 (*1-56222-177-9*, 93864) Mel Bay.

— Teaching Pieces for Classic Guitar. 1993. 9.95 (*1-56222-304-6*, 94703) Mel Bay.

Lawrynowicz, Julian, ed. Deformations of Mathematical Structures: Complex Analysis with Physical Applications. (C). 1988. lib. bdg. 157.50 (*0-7923-0023-8*) Kluwer Ac.

— Seminar on Deformations. (Lecture Notes in Mathematics Ser.: Vol. 1165). ix, 331p. 1985. pap. 42.30 (*0-387-16050-7*) Spr-Verlag.

Lawrynowicz, Julian & Lodz, J., eds. Analytic Functions, Blazejewko 1982. (Lecture Notes in Mathematics Ser.: Vol. 1039). 494p. (ENG & FRE.). 1984. pap. 52.60 (*0-387-12712-7*) Spr-Verlag.

Laws, Anna C. Author Notation in the Library of Congress. 1976. lib. bdg. 59.95 (*0-8490-1463-8*) Gordon Pr.

Laws, Bill. Old English Farmhouses. 160p. 1992. 29.95 (*1-55859-407-8*) Abbeville Pr.

— Perfect Country Cottage. (Illus.). 144p. 1994. 30.00 (*1-55859-784-0*) Abbeville Pr.

— Traditional Houses of Rural France. (Illus.). 160p. 1991. 27.50 (*1-55859-229-6*) Abbeville Pr.

Laws, D. Richard, ed. Relapse Prevention with Sex Offenders. LC 88-36840. 338p. 1989. lib. bdg. 40.00 (*0-89862-381-2*) Guilford Pr.

Laws, Diane M., ed. see Laws, James E.

Laws, E. R., jt. ed. see Karim, A. B.

Laws, Edward A. Aquatic Pollution. (Illus.). 496p. (C). reprint ed. text ed. 60.00 (*1-878907-09-3*, RAN) TechBooks.

Laws, Edward R., Jr., ed. Diagnosis & Management of Orbital Tumors. (Illus.). 336p. 1988. 55.00 (*0-87993-304-6*) Futura Pub.

Laws, Edward R., Jr. & Fox, William L. Dandy of Johns Hopkins. (Illus.). 291p. 1984. lib. bdg. 21.00 (*0-683-04903-8*) Williams & Wilkins.

Laws, Edward R., Jr., jt. ed. see Hayes, Wayland J., Jr.

Laws, Edward R., jt. ed. see Kaye, Andrew H.

Laws, Edward S. Aquatic Pollution: An Introductory Text. 2nd ed. LC 92-26501. (Environmental Science & Technology: A Wiley-Interscience Series of Texts & Monographs). 611p. 1993. pap. text ed. 64.95 (*0-471-58883-0*, Wiley-Interscience) Wiley.

Laws, Eric. Tourism Marketing: Service & Quality Management Perspectives. 288p. (Orig.). 1991. pap. 47.50 (*0-7487-0428-0*, Pub. by Stanley Thornes UK) Trans-Atl Phila.

— Tourism Marketing Service & Quality Management Perspectives. 288p. (C). 1991. 75.00 (*0-7478-0428-1*, Pub. by S Thornes Pubs UK) St Mut.

— Tourist Destination Management: Issues, Analysis & Policies. LC 94-32453. (Topics in Tourism Ser.). 176p. 1995. pap. 16.95 (*0-415-10591-9*, C0385) Routledge.

***Laws, James E.** Let the Ancestors Speak: Removing the Veil of Mysticism from Medu Netcher. Laws, Diane M. & Grimball, Gilberta D., eds. (Illus.). 288p. (Orig.). 1995. pap. text ed. 19.95 (*0-9640661-1-4*) J E Laws.

Laws, Jay B. Steam. 398p. (Orig.). 1991. pap. 9.95 (*1-55583-184-2*) Alyson Pubns.

— The Unfinished. 283p. (Orig.). 1993. pap. 9.95 (*1-55583-217-2*) Alyson Pubns.

Laws, Jim, ed. The Book of Mark: Jesus - The Servant of Jehovah Fourteenth Annual Spiritual Sword Lectureship. 457p. 1989. 20.00 (*0-9615751-5-8*) Getwell Church.

— God's Amazing Grace: The Twentieth Annual Spiritual Sword Lectureship. 1995. 24.00 (*1-886220-01-8*) Getwell Church.

— The Restoration: The Winds of Change - Eighteenth Annual Spiritual Sword Lectureship. 1993. write for info. (*0-9615751-9-0*) Getwell Church.

— The Scheme of Redemption: Fifteenth Annual Spiritual Sword Lectureship. 618p. 1990. 24.00 (*0-9615751-7-4*) Getwell Church.

— There Was a Man Named Job: Sixteenth Annual Spiritual Sword Lectureship. (Illus.). 416p. 1991. 24.00 (*0-9615751-6-6*) Getwell Church.

— Women to the Glory of God: The Nineteenth Annual Spiritual Sword Lectureship. 475p. 1994. 24.00 (*1-886220-00-X*) Getwell Church.

Laws, Judi. High & Why: A Flow of Consciousness on Addictions. 100p. (Orig.). 1991. pap. 9.95 (*0-912865-01-6*) Amethyst.

Laws, Kenneth. The Physics of Dance. (Illus.). 160p. 1986. pap. 16.95 (*0-02-873360-6*) Schirmer Bks.

Laws, Kenneth & Harvey, Cynthia. Physics, Dance, & the Pas de Deux. (Illus.). 227p. 1994. Professional book - includes videotape. text ed. 50.00 (*0-02-871329-X*) Schirmer Bks.

— Physics, Dance & the Pas de Deux: Text Only. 1994. text ed. 22.00 (*0-02-871326-5*) Schirmer Bks.

Laws, Lynda, ed. see Brown, John F.

Laws, Richard. Antarctica the Last Frontier. 192p. (C). 1990. 60.00 (*1-85283-247-9*, Pub. by Boxtree Ltd UK) St Mut.

Laws, Richard M. Antarctic Seals: Research Methods & Techniques. LC 92-47467. (Illus.). 350p. (C). 1993. 84.95 (*0-521-44302-4*) Cambridge U Pr.

Laws, Richard M., ed. Antarctic Ecology, 1. 1984. text ed. 137.00 (*0-12-439501-5*) Acad Pr.

Laws, Richard M., jt. ed. see Le Boeuf, Burney J.

***Laws, Robert A.** Dance of the Hanging Men: The Story of Francois Villon, Killer, Thief & Poet. 105p. 1993. lib. bdg. 31.00 (*0-8095-6774-1*); pap. 21.00 (*0-946650-50-0*) Borgo Pr.

Laws, Sophie. Issues of Blood. 288p. 1990. 40.00 (*0-8147-5056-7*) NYU Pr.

Lawson. Teaching of Classical Ballet. 1985. 19.95 (*0-87830-143-7*) Routledge Chapman & Hall.

— Yagi Antenna Design. 1986. 15.00 (*0-87259-041-0*) Am Radio.

Lawson & Mirzai. Wave Digital Filters. 300p. 1990. boxed write for info. (*0-13-946997-4*) P-H.

Lawson & Skip. Sexo y Mas (Sex & That) (SPA.). Date not set. 3.50 (*0-8423-6521-4*, 490249) Editorial Unilit.

Lawson, jt. auth. see Evans.

***Lawson, et al.** Essentials of Chemical Dependency Counseling. 2nd ed. 227p. 1995. 38.00 (*0-8342-0683-8*) Aspen Pub.

Lawson, A. California Earthquake of April 18, 1906: Report of the State Earthquake Commission. (Illus.). 721p. 1970. reprint ed. 35.00 (*0-87279-086-X*, 87) Carnegie Inst.

— Star Baby. (J). 1992. 15.95 (*0-15-200905-1*, HB Juv Bks) HarBrace.

Lawson, A. M., jt. auth. see Chalmers, R. A.

***Lawson, A. M., et al, eds.** Clinical Biochemistry: Principles - Methods - Applications Vol. 1: Mass Spectrometry. (Illus.). xx, 745p. (C). 1989. 253.85 (*3-11-007751-5*) De Gruyter.

— Clinical Biochemistry: Principles - Methods - Applications, Vol. 1: Mass Spectrometry. (Illus.). xx, 745p. (C). 1989. Series. 253.85 (*0-89925-581-7*); Single volume. 210.70 (*0-89925-488-8*) De Gruyter.

Lawson, Alan. Michael Douglas. large type ed. 347p. 1994. 19.95 (*0-7505-0596-6*, Pub. by Magna Print Bks) Ulverscroft.

Lawson, Alan, ed. see Baynton, Barbara.

Lawson, Alan, jt. ed. see Tiffin, Chris.

An Asterisk (*) at the beginning of an entry indicates that the title is appearing in BIP for the first time.

Lawson, Alexander, ed. see James First King of Scotland.

Lawson, Alexander S. Anatomy of a Typeface. LC 81-47326. (Illus.). 420p. 1989. 40.00 (*0-87923-332-X*) Godine.

— Anatomy of a Typeface. 1990. pap. 24.95 (*0-87923-333-8*) Godine.

— Printing Types: An Introduction. rev. ed. LC 70-136232. 160p. 1974. pap. 14.00 (*0-8070-6661-3*, BP474) Beacon Pr.

Lawson, Andrew J. Cave Art. 1989. pap. 25.00 (*0-7478-0120-7*, Pub. by Shire UK) St Mut.

***Lawson, Anita.** Girl! Serenity Courage & Wisdom. 74p. 1995. pap. text ed. 13.95 (*0-9647410-3-2*) Lawson & Collins.

— Irvin S. Cobb. LC 83-73108. 1984. 25.95 (*0-87972-275-4*); pap. 13.95 (*0-87972-300-9*) Bowling Green Univ.

Lawson, Ann. Kids & Gangs: What Parents & Educators Need to Know. LC 93-48373. 60p. 1994. pap. 4.95 (*1-56246-091-9*, P322) Johnsn Inst.

Lawson, Ann W., jt. auth. see Lawson, Gary W.

Lawson, Annette, jt. ed. see Rhode, Deborah L.

Lawson, Anton E. Science Teaching & the Development of Thinking. LC 94-6339. 593p. 1995. text ed. 42.95 (*0-534-23994-3*) Intl Thomson.

— Studying for Biology. LC 94-20073. (C). 1995. 12.50 (*0-06-500650-X*) HarpCollege.

Lawson, B. How Designers Think. 2nd ed. (Illus.). 243p. 1990. pap. text ed. 27.95 (*0-7506-0268-6*) Buttrwrth-Heinemann.

Lawson, Barbara, jt. auth. see Harman, Thomas L.

Lawson, Barbara, jt. auth. see Harmon, Thomas L.

Lawson, Benjamin S. Joaquin Miller. LC 80-69014. (Western Writers Ser.: No. 43). (Illus.). 52p. (Orig.). 1980. pap. 3.95 (*0-88430-067-6*) Boise St U W Writ Ser.

Lawson, Betty. Shelling San Sal. (Illus.). 63p. (Orig.). 1993. pap. text ed. 12.00 (*0-935909-44-3*) Bahamian.

Lawson, Bill E., ed. The Underclass Question. 350p. (C). 1992. 39.95 (*0-87722-922-8*) Temple U Pr.

Lawson, Bill E. & Wilson, William J., intros. The Underclass Question. 232p. 1993. pap. 18.95 (*1-56639-062-1*) Temple U Pr.

Lawson, Bill E., jt. auth. see McGary, Howard, Jr.

Lawson, Bryan. Design in Mind. LC 93-50198. (Illus.). 160p. 1994. pap. 34.95 (*0-7506-1211-8*, Butterwrth Archit) Buttrwrth-Heinemann.

Lawson, Byran. How Designers Think. (Illus.). 212p. 20.00 (*0-89860-047-2*) Eastview.

***Lawson, Carol S., ed.** Gold from Aspirin: Spiritual Views on Chaos & Order. (Chrysalis Reader Ser.: Vol. 1). xv, 192p. 1995. pap. 12.95 (*0-87785-225-1*) Swedenborg.

Lawson, Cathie, ed. see Roman, Beverly D.

Lawson, Cathie, ed. see Williams, Brent.

Lawson, Cathleen, ed. see Roman, Beverly D.

Lawson, Charles E. Surveying Your Land: A Common-Sense Guide to Surveys, Deeds, & Title Searches. rev. ed. LC 90-1998. (Illus.). 144p. 1990. pap. 10.00 (*0-88150-180-8*) Countryman.

Lawson, Cheryl A., jt. auth. see Goodman, George J.

Lawson, Christine. Wanted Sister. large type ed. (Linford Romance Library). 304p. 1988. pap. 11.95 (*0-7089-6586-5*, Linford) Ulverscroft.

— With All My Heart. large type ed. (Linford Romance Library). 288p. 1985. pap. 11.95 (*0-7089-6152-5*, Trailtree Bookshop) Ulverscroft.

***Lawson, Colin.** The Cambridge Companion to the Clarinet. (Cambridge Companions to Music Ser.). (Illus.). 300p. (C). 1995. write for info. (*0-521-47066-8*); pap. write for info. (*0-521-47668-2*) Cambridge U Pr.

Lawson, Colin J. The Chalumeau in Eighteenth-Century Music. LC 81-15961. (Studies in British Musicology: No. 6). (Illus.). 218p. reprint ed. pap. 62.20 (*0-8357-1246-X*, 2070221) Bks Demand.

Lawson, Dave, jt. auth. see Hitzges, Norm.

Lawson, David. Wellness: Safety & Accident Prevention. 128p. 1992. 13.50 (*0-87967-864-X*) Dushkin Pub.

***Lawson, David & Griffiths, Jennifer.** Star Healing: Your Sun Sign, Your Health & Your Success. 340p. 1995. pap. 11.95 (*0-340-60646-0*, Pub. by Hodder & Stoughton Ltd UK) Trafalgar.

Lawson, David A., ed. Current Medicine Three. (Illus.). 300p. (Orig.). 1991. pap. text ed. 36.00 (*0-443-04598-4*) Churchill.

Lawson, Dawn, tr. see Oshima, Nagisa.

Lawson, Dominic. End Game. 1994. 22.50 (*0-517-59810-8*) Crown Pub Group.

***Lawson, Dominic, ed.** The Spectator Annual. (Illus.). 256p. 1995. 45.00 (*0-7195-5704-6*, Pub. by John Murray UK) Trafalgar.

Lawson, Don. America Held Hostage: From the Teheran Embassy Takeover to the Iran-Contra Affair. LC 90-20515. (Twentieth Century American History Ser.). (Illus.). 144p. (YA). (gr. 9-12). 1991. lib. bdg. 14.77 (*0-531-11009-5*) Watts.

— Famous Presidential Scandals. LC 89-35874. (Illus.). 128p. (gr. 6 up). 1990. lib. bdg. 17.95 (*0-89490-247-4*) Enslow Pubs.

Lawson, Don & Barish, Wendy. The French Resistance. (Spyshelf Ser.). 192p. (J). (gr. 3-7). 1984. lib. bdg. 8.79 (*0-685-07808-6*) S&S Trade.

Lawson, Douglas M. Give to Live: How Giving Can Change Your Life. LC 91-72216. 200p. 1991. 18.95 (*0-9625399-3-7*); pap. 11.95 (*0-9625399-9-6*) ALTI Pub.

Lawson, E. Leroy. Matthew. (Bible Studies). 352p. 1986. pap. 12.99 (*0-87403-161-3*, 40101) Standard Pub.

— Very Sure of God: Religious Language in the Poetry of Robert Browning. LC 73-21617. xiii, 168p. 1974. 12.95 (*0-8265-1195-3*) Vanderbilt U Pr.

Lawson, E. Thomas & McCauley, Robert N. Rethinking Religion: Connecting Cognition & Culture. (Illus.). 203p. (C). 1993. pap. 18.95 (*0-521-43806-3*) Cambridge U Pr.

Lawson, Earl. Cincinnati Seasons: My Thirty-Four Years with the Reds. LC 87-15743. 218p. 1987. 16.95 (*0-912083-24-7*) Diamond Communications.

— Cincinnati Seasons: My Thirty-Four Years with the Reds. LC 87-15943. 218p. 1990. pap. 9.95 (*0-912083-36-0*) Diamond Communications.

***Lawson, Ed J., ed.** The Billiard Industry Source Book. 256p. 1995. 150.00 (*0-945071-54-X*) Lawco.

Lawson, Edward H. Encyclopedia of Human Rights. 2080p. 1991. 295.00 (*0-8002-8003-2*, Pub. by Tay Francis Ltd UK) Taylor & Francis.

Lawson, Edwin D., comp. Personal Names & Naming: An Annotated Bibliography. LC 86-31789. (Bibliographies & Indexes in Anthropology Ser.: No. 3). 198p. 1987. text ed. 55.00 (*0-313-23817-0*, LNN/, Greenwood Pr) Greenwood.

Lawson, Ellen N. The Three Sarahs: Documents of Antebellum Black College Women. LC 84-18914. (Studies in Women & Religion: Vol. 13). (Illus.). 350p. 1984. lib. bdg. 99.95 (*0-88946-536-3*) E Mellen.

Lawson, Eugene K. The Sino-Vietnamese Conflict. LC 84-8329. 336p. 1984. text ed. 55.00 (*0-275-91212-4*, C1212, Praeger Pubs) Greenwood.

Lawson, Eugene K., ed. U. S. - China Trade: Problems & Prospects. LC 88-3214. 352p. 1988. text ed. 69.50 (*0-275-92494-7*, C2494, Praeger Pubs) Greenwood.

Lawson, Evald B., jt. auth. see Olson, Ernest W.

Lawson, Evald R. Two Primary Sources for a Study of the Life of Jonas Swensson. (Augustana Historical Society Publication Ser.: Vol. 17). 39p. 1957. pap. 3.00 (*0-910184-17-8*) Augustana.

Lawson, F. H. A Common Lawyer Looks at the Civil Law. LC 88-61807. (Michigan Legal Publications). xvii, 238p. 1988. reprint ed. lib. bdg. 39.00 (*0-89941-661-6*, 305680) W S Hein.

— The Rational Strength of English Law. viii, 147p. 1988. reprint ed. lib. bdg. 27.50 (*0-8377-2410-4*) Rothman.

***Lawson, Fred.** Hotel & Resorts: Planning, Design & Refurbishment. (Illus.). 168p. 1995. 59.95 (*0-7506-1861-2*, Butterwrth Archit) Buttrwrth-Heinemann.

— Restaurants, Clubs & Bars: Planning, Design & Investment. rev. ed. (Illus.). 338p. 1995. pap. 59.95 (*0-7506-2076-5*, Butterwrth Archit) Buttrwrth-Heinemann.

Lawson, Fred H. Opposition Movements & U. S. Policy Toward the Arab Gulf States. (Critical Issues 1992 Ser.: No. 9). 44p. 1992. pap. 4.95 (*0-87609-140-0*) Coun Foreign.

Lawson, Frederick H. Bahrain: The Modernization of Autocracy. (Profiles - Nations of Contemporary Middle East Ser.: No. 39). 146p. 1989. text ed. 55.50 (*0-8133-0123-8*) Westview.

— A Common Lawyer Looks at the Civil Law: Five Lectures Delivered at the University of Michigan, November 16, 17, 18, 19, & 20, 1953. LC 77-23760. (Thomas M. Cooley Lecture Ser.: No. 5). 238p. 1977. reprint ed. text ed. 35.00 (*0-8371-9778-3*, LACO) Greenwood.

— The Comparison: Selected Essays, Vol. 2. (European Studies in Law Ser.: Vol. 5). 386p. 1978. 77.00 (*0-7204-0760-5*, North Holland) Elsevier.

— Selected Essays, 2 vols., Set. (European Studies in Law Ser.). 1978. 125.75 (*0-7204-0816-4*, North Holland) Elsevier.

— Selected Essays, 2 vols., Vol. 1. (European Studies in Law Ser.). 1978. 66.75 (*0-7204-0759-1*, North Holland) Elsevier.

— Selected Essays, 2 vols., Vol. 2. 1978. write for info. (*0-318-56966-3*, North Holland) Elsevier.

— The Social Origins of Egyptian Expansionism During the Muhammad Ali Period. 224p. 1992. text ed. 40.00 (*0-231-07632-0*) Col U Pr.

Lawson, Frederick H. & Markesinis, Basil S. Tortious Liability for Unintentional Harm in the Common Law & the Civil Law, 2 vols. LC 81-102302. (Cambridge Studies in International & Comparative Law). 1982. pap. 39.95 (*0-521-27209-2*); pap. 39.95 (*0-521-27210-6*) Cambridge U Pr.

— Tortious Liability for Unintentional Harm in the Common Law & the Civil Law, 2 vols., Vol. 1: Texts. LC 81-102302. (Cambridge Studies in International & Comparative Law). 1982. 69.95 (*0-521-23585-5*) Cambridge U Pr.

Lawson, G. & John, D. M. The Marine Algae & Coastal Environment of Tropical West Africa. 2nd ed. (Nova Hedwigia Beiheft Ser.: No. 93). (Illus.). 416p. 1987. pap. 155.00 (*3-443-51015-9*) Lubrecht & Cramer.

Lawson, G. H., ed. Studies in Cash Flow Accounting & Analysis: Aspects of Interface Between Managerial Planning, Reporting & Control & External Performance Measurement. LC 92-5927. (New Works in Accounting History). 328p. 1992. 63.00 (*0-8153-0687-3*) Garland.

Lawson, G. W. Plant Ecology in West Africa. LC 84-17347. 357p. 1986. text ed. 225.00 (*0-471-90364-7*) Wiley.

Lawson, Gary M. The Perfect Paradox. LC 93-30580. (Lewiston Poetry Ser.: Vol. 20). 64p. 1993. pap. 12.95 (*0-7734-2789-9*, Mellen Poetry Pr) E Mellen.

Lawson, Gary W. Lawson's Guide to Health Care Business Development & Marketing. LC 93-43473. 1994. write for info. (*0-939644-94-0*, Midgrd Press) Media Pub.

Lawson, Gary W. & Cooperrider, Craig C. Clinical Psychopharmacology: A Practical Reference for Nonmedical Psychotherapists. LC 87-33480. 375p. (C). 1988. 65.00 (*0-87189-751-2*) Aspen Pub.

Lawson, Gary W. & Lawson, Ann W. Adolescent Substance Abuse: Etiology, Treatment & Prevention. LC 92-11363. 576p. 1992. pap. 41.00 (*0-8342-0254-9*) Aspen Pub.

— Alcoholism & Substance Abuse in Special Populations. LC 88-7600. 370p. (C). 1989. 58.00 (*0-8342-0007-4*) Aspen Pub.

Lawson, Gary W., et al. Alcoholism & the Family: A Guide to Treatment & Prevention. LC 82-24352. 296p. (C). 1983. 38.00 (*0-87189-606-0*) Aspen Pub.

— Essentials of Chemical Dependency Counseling. LC 83-26573. 227p. (C). 1984. 36.00 (*0-89443-583-3*) Aspen Pub.

Lawson, George. Commentary on Proverbs, 2 vols. in 1. LC 80-8070. 572p. 1993. pap. 19.99 (*0-8254-3123-9*) Kregel.

— Commentary on Proverbs, 2 vols. in 1. deluxe ed. LC 80-8070. 572p. 1993. 26.99 (*0-8254-3149-2*) Kregel.

— The Life of Joseph. 576p. 1989. 25.95 (*0-85151-161-9*) Banner of Truth.

— Politica Sacra et Civilis. Condren, Conal, ed. (Cambridge Texts in the History of Political Thought Ser.). 352p. (C). 1993. 19.95 (*0-521-39248-9*) Cambridge U Pr.

Lawson, Glenn. BayKeeper. 340p. (Orig.). 1993. pap. 12.95 (*0-9620439-5-8*) ZAK Bks.

— DuckMaker. 340p. (Orig.). 1994. pap. 12.95 (*0-9620439-6-6*) ZAK Bks.

— Last Waterman. 240p. 1994. 15.95 (*0-9620439-1-5*) ZAK Bks.

— The Last Waterman. 211p. (Orig.). 1988. reprint ed. pap. 9.95 (*0-9620439-0-7*) ZAK Bks.

— The Story of Lem Ward As Told by Ida Ward to Glenn Lawson. LC 84-72621. (Illus.). 128p. 1984. 35.00 (*0-88740-028-0*) Schiffer.

Lawson, Gloria. Caring Kitchen Recipes. LC 93-61485. 229p. (Orig.). ring bd. 12.95 (*0-945383-63-0*) Teach Servs.

Lawson, Gordon, jt. auth. see Liljestrand, Walter.

Lawson, Greg. Hawaii. LC 83-81363. (Illus.). 72p. 1990. pap. 11.95 (*0-916251-41-1*) Sunbelt Pubns.

— Palm Springs Oasis. LC 89-85067. 1990. 17.95 (*0-916251-40-3*) Sunbelt Pubns.

— San Diego. rev. ed. LC 82-71547. (Illus.). 72p. 1989. 11.95 (*0-916251-38-1*); pap. 10.95 (*0-685-74117-6*) Sunbelt Pubns.

— San Diego-County. LC 86-81144. (Illus.). 128p. 1986. 34.95 (*0-916251-29-2*) Sunbelt Pubns.

Lawson, Greg, ed. & photos. Oh . . . California. LC 89-83997. (Illus.). 160p. 1990. 39.95 (*0-916251-34-9*) Sunbelt Pubns.

Lawson, Greg, illus. California. rev. ed. LC 82-90775. (ENG, FRE, GER, JPN & SPA.). 1989. pap. 11.95 (*0-916251-33-0*) Sunbelt Pubns.

Lawson, Greg C. Race, Racism & Rhyme. (Illus.). (Orig.). 1990. 8.00 (*0-685-27231-1*) SunLaw Pubns.

***Lawson, H. Blaine.** The Quantitative Theory of Foliations. LC 76-51339. (Regional Conference Series in Mathematics: Vol. 27). (Illus.). 78p. 1977. reprint ed. pap. 25.00 (*0-7837-8856-8*, 2049566) Bks Demand.

Lawson, H. Blaine, Jr. The Quantitative Theory of Foliations. LC 76-51339. (CBMS Regional Conference Series in Mathematics: No. 27). 65p. 1990. reprint ed. pap. 22.00 (*0-8218-1677-2*, CBMS27) Am Math.

— The Theory of Gauge Fields in Four Dimensions. LC 85-441. (CBMS Regional Conference Series in Mathematics: No. 58). 101p. 1987. pap. text ed. 24.00 (*0-8218-0708-0*, CBMS-58) Am Math.

Lawson, H. Blaine, Jr. & Michelsohn, Marie-Louise. Spin Geometry. 450p. 1990. text ed. 69.50 (*0-691-08542-0*) Princeton U Pr.

***Lawson, H. H.** Corrosion Testing Made Easy Vol. 4: Atmospheric Corrosion Test Methods. (Illus.). 80p. 1994. 80.00 (*1-877914-82-7*) NACE Intl.

Lawson, H. M. History & Genealogy of the Descendants of Clement Corbin of Muddy River (Brookline), Mass. & Woodstock, Conn., with Other Lines of Corbins. (Illus.). 378p. 1989. reprint ed. lib. bdg. 64.50 (*0-8328-0422-3*); reprint ed. pap. 56.50 (*0-8328-0423-1*) Higginson Bk Co.

Lawson, H. W., et al. Large Scale Integration: Technology, Applications, & Impacts. 380p. 1979. 82.00 (*0-444-85249-2*, North Holland) Elsevier.

Lawson, Hal A. Invitation to Physical Education. 264p. 1984. pap. 19.00x (*0-87322-934-7*, BLAW0934) Human Kinetics.

Lawson, Hal A., ed. Undergraduate Physical Education Programs: Issues & Approaches. 112p. reprint ed. pap. 32.00 (*0-685-15769-5*, 2026622) Bks Demand.

***Lawson-Hall, Toni & Rotheva, Brian.** Hydrangeas: A Gardener's Guide. (Illus.). 160p. 1995. 34.95 (*0-88192-327-3*) Timber.

Lawson, Harold. Parallel Processing in Industrial Real-Time Applications. 1992. text ed. 59.00 (*0-13-654518-1*) P-H.

Lawson, Harry. Food Oils & Fats: Technology, Utilization, & Nutrition. LC 94-17775. 1994. write for info. (*0-412-98841-0*) Chapman & Hall.

Lawson, Harry D. Dynamic Muscular Relaxation. LC 86-17410. (Illus.). 1989. 150.00 (*0-87949-270-8*) Ashley Bks.

Lawson, Harry H. College-Bound Blacks: How to Succeed in College. LC 83-194830. (Illus.). 65p. (Orig.). 1983. pap. 4.95 (*0-9611668-0-0*) Lawsons Psych.

Lawson, Harry O. & Gletne, Barbara J. Workload Measures in the Court. 202p. 1980. pap. 2.50 (*0-89656-043-0*, R-051) Natl Ctr St Courts.

Lawson, Harry W. The L. J. Minor Foodservice Standards Series, Vol. 5: Standards for Fats & Oils. (Illus.). 1985. text ed. 39.95 (*0-87055-467-0*) AVI.

— Standards for Fats & Oils. 2nd ed. 1992. text ed. write for info. (*0-442-01053-2*) Chapman & Hall.

Lawson, Harvey & Blazucki, Joan. Bench-Top Orthodontics. (Illus.). 140p. 1990. pap. text ed. 38.00 (*0-86715-233-8*) Quint Pub Co.

Lawson, Herbert H., jt. ed. see Kirk, W. W.

Lawson, Hilary. Reflexivity. LC 85-18757. 129p. 1986. pap. 12.95 (*0-8126-9011-7*) Open Court.

Lawson, J. D., jt. ed. see Boucot, A. J.

Lawson, J. H. A Synopsis of Fevers & Their Treatment. 12th ed. 1977. pap. 15.95 (*0-8151-5335-X*, Yr Bk Med Pubs) Mosby Yr Bk.

Lawson, J. Richard. The Language of Success: How to Join the Inner Circle. 256p. (Orig.). 1989. pap. 19.95 (*0-945071-10-8*) Lawco.

Lawson, J. W. & Smith, B. How to Develop a Personnel Policy Manual. 5th ed. 509p. 1990. ring bd. 91.50 (*0-85013-167-7*) Dartnell Corp.

Lawson, Jack. Andro, This Is Crazy. 96p. (Orig.). (J). 1991. pap. 2.95 (*0-380-76234-X*, Camelot) Avon.

Lawson, Jacqueline. Cerrillos: Yesterday, Today & Tomorrow. LC 88-34578. (Illus.). 96p. (Orig.). 1989. pap. 8.95 (*0-86534-130-3*) Sunstone Pr.

Lawson, Jacqueline E. Domestic Misconduct in the Novels of Defoe, Richardson, & Fielding. LC 93-26975. 200p. 1993. text ed. 79.95 (*0-7734-9978-4*) E Mellen.

***Lawson, James & Rotem, A.** Planning & Organizing Modern Hospitals & Health. (Illus.). 256p. Date not set. text ed. write for info. (*0-07-470153-3*) Hlth Prof Div.

Lawson, James, jt. auth. see Saint, Steven.

Lawson, James B., tr. see Frischmuth, Barbara.

Lawson, James G. The Book of Dogs: An Illustrated Guide & Photos of All Breeds. 1991. lib. bdg. 88.00 (*0-8490-5222-X*) Gordon Pr.

— Deeper Experiences of Famous Christians. 1981. pap. 4.95 (*0-87162-069-3*, D3349) Warner Pr.

Lawson, James R. The Advanced Pool Player's Handbook. Thompson, Bill, ed. 124p. (Orig.). 1994. pap. 18.95 (*0-945071-91-4*) Lawco.

Lawson, James R., ed. Billiard Industry Source Book. 128p. 1992. 90.00 (*0-945071-75-2*) Lawco.

— Billiard Market Place: BMP, 2 vols., Set. (Orig.). 1994. pap. 1,200.00 (*0-945071-61-2*) Lawco.

— Pocket Billiard Guidebook for Pool Players, TournamentDirectors & Spectators. 192p. (Orig.). 1994. pap. 39.95 (*0-945071-55-8*) Lawco.

— Pool Player's National Pocket Billiard Directory: Commercial Edition, 1992. 288p. 1992. pap. 150.00 (*0-945071-76-0*) Lawco.

— The Pool Player's National Pocket Billiard Directory: 1992 Edition. 288p. (Orig.). 1992. pap. 29.95 (*0-945071-51-5*) Lawco.

— The Pool Player's National Pocket Billiards Directory. (YA). 1991. pap. 19.95 (*0-945071-50-7*) Lawco.

— The Pool Player's Road Atlas. 200p. (Orig.). 1994. pap. 34.95 (*0-945071-80-9*) Lawco.

Lawson, James S. Public Health in Australia: An Introduction. (Illus.). 225p. 1991. pap. 24.00 (*0-07-452913-7*) Hlth Prof Div.

Lawson, Jennifer. Hands-on Science: Early Childhood. (Illus.). 121p. (gr. k). 1991. teacher ed 85.00 (*1-895411-02-5*) Peguis Pubs Ltd.

— Hands-on Science: Level Four. (Illus.). 239p. (gr. 4). 1991. teacher ed 85.00 (*1-895411-10-6*) Peguis Pubs Ltd.

— Hands-on Science: Level One. (Illus.). 215p. (gr. 1). 1991. teacher ed 85.00 (*1-895411-04-1*) Peguis Pubs Ltd.

— Hands-on Science: Level Three. (Illus.). 237p. (gr. 3). 1991. teacher ed 85.00 (*1-895411-08-4*) Peguis Pubs Ltd.

— Hands-on Science: Level Two. (Illus.). 199p. (gr. 2). 1991. teacher ed 85.00 (*1-895411-06-8*) Peguis Pubs Ltd.

Lawson, Jim C. Washington Ethnic Bakery Book. 118p. 1991. pap. 9.95 (*0-9623888-2-3*) Ardmore Pubns.

— Washington Ethnic Food Store Guide. 2nd ed. 157p. 1992. pap. 9.95 (*0-9623888-7-4*) Ardmore Pubns.

Lawson, Jimmie D. The Physics of Charged-Particle Beams. 2nd ed. (International Series of Monographs on Physics: No. 75). (Illus.). 472p. 1988. 125.00 (*0-19-851719-X*) OUP.

Lawson, Joan. Ballet Class. (Illus.). 126p. 1988. pap. 18.95 (*0-87830-989-6*, A2130, Theatre Arts Bks) Routledge Chapman & Hall.

— A Balletmaker's Handbook. (Illus.). 112p. 1991. pap. 18.95 (*0-87830-017-1*, A6219, Theatre Arts Bks) Routledge Chapman & Hall.

— Beginning Ballet: From the Classroom to the Stage. 2nd ed. (Illus.). 1994. pap. 16.95 (*0-87830-056-2*, B4551) Routledge.

— European Folk Dance. LC 79-7773. (Dance Ser.). 1980. reprint ed. lib. bdg. 42.95 (*0-8369-9300-4*) Ayer.

— The Teaching of Classical Ballet. LC 73-83997. (Illus.). 1974. 19.95 (*0-87830-583-1*, Theatre Arts Bks) Routledge Chapman & Hall.

— Teaching Young Dancers: Muscular Coordination in Classical Ballet. LC 75-15369. (Illus.). 1975. 19.95 (*0-87830-144-5*, Theatre Arts Bks) Routledge Chapman & Hall.

Lawson, Joanne & Carter, Louise. The Three-Year Gardener's Journal. (Illus.). 208p. 1989. 27.95 (*0-912347-36-8*) Fulcrum Pub.

Lawson, John. The Affirmation of Life: A Reichian Energetic Perspective. LC 91-75113. 128p. 1991. pap. 7.95 (*0-9630338-1-6*) Ardengrove.

— The High Hills. LC 80-53537. (Illus.). 220p. (Orig.). 1981. pap. 4.95 (*0-938658-01-8*) West SW Pub Co.

— The Law of Presumptive Evidence, Including Presumptions Both of Law & Fact, & the Burden of Proof Both in Civil & Crimminal Cases, Reduced to Rules. lxxxix, 648p. 1982. reprint ed. lib. bdg. 45.00 (*0-8377-0812-5*) Rothman.

— Lectures Concerning Oratory. Claussen, E. Neal & Wallace, Karl R., eds. LC 78-156792. (Landmarks in Rhetoric & Public Address Ser.). 530p. 1972. 15.00 (*0-8093-0519-4*) S Ill U Pr.

— A New Voyage to Carolina. Lefler, Hugh T., ed. LC 67-23498. liv, 305p. 1984. pap. 14.95 (*0-8078-4126-9*) U of NC Pr.

Lawson, John D. The Law of Expert & Opinion Evidence Reduced to Rules: With Illustrations from Adjudged Cases. lxxii, 595p. 1982. reprint ed. lib. bdg. 42.50 (*0-8377-0813-3*) Rothman.

— Leading Cases Simplified: A Collection of the Leading Cases of the Common Law. (Illus.). xxvi, 327p. 1987. reprint ed. lib. bdg. 35.00 (*0-8377-2406-6*) Rothman.

— Redding & Shasta County: Gateway to the Cascades. LC 86-22375. (Illus.). 184p. 1986. 27.95 (0-89781-187-9) Preferred Mktg.

— When You Preside. 5th ed. 1980. 19.95 (0-8134-2036-9, 2036) Interstate.

Lawson, John D., ed. American State Trials: Sixteen Fifty-Nine to Nineteen Twenty, 17 vols., Set. LC 74-182150. 1972. reprint ed. lib. bdg. 400.00 (0-8420-0510-2) Scholarly Res Inc.

Lawson, John H. Film in the Battle of Ideas. LC 53-13277. 126p. 1982. reprint ed. lib. bdg. 33.00x (0-89370-715-5) Borgo Pr.

— Hidden Heritage. 1968. reprint ed. pap. 4.95 (0-8065-0129-4, Citadel Pr) Carol Pub Group.

Lawson, Jonathan N., ed. see Bloomfield, Robert.

Lawson, Joseph W., II. The Employer's Guide to Understanding & Complying with the Americans with Disabilities Act. 480p. 1992. ring bd. 129.00 (0-85013-214-2) Dartnell Corp.

Lawson, Joseph W. How to Develop a Personnel Policy Manual. 5th ed. 1991. pap. 39.95 (0-85013-179-0) Dartnell Corp.

— How to Develop an Employee Handbook. 368p. 1991. ring bd. 91.50 (0-685-65963-1) Dartnell Corp.

— How to Develop an Employee Handbook. 368p. 1991. pap. 34.95 (0-85013-180-4) Dartnell Corp.

Lawson, Julie. The Dragon's Pearl. (Illus.). 32p. (J). (gr. k-3). 1993. 15.95 (0-395-63623-X, Clarion Bks) HM.

— Kate's Castle. (J). (ps-3). 1994. pap. 6.95 (0-19-541001-7) OUP.

— A Morning to Polish & Keep. (Illus.). 32p. (J). 1995. 12.95 (0-88995-082-2, Pub. by Red Deer CN) BookWorld Dist.

***Lawson, Julie & McKenzie, Ray, eds.** Photography 1900. (Illus.). 112p. 1992. pap. text ed. 35.00 (0-903598-45-0, Pub. by Natl Mus Scotland UK) A Schwartz & Co.

Lawson, K. H. Analysis & Ideology: Conceptual Essays on the Education of Adults. 100p. (C). 1983. text ed. 75.00 (0-685-22156-3, Pub. by Univ Nottingham UK) St Mut.

— Philosophical Concepts & Values in Adult Education. 128p. 1979. pap. 32.00 (0-335-00254-4, Open Univ Pr) Taylor & Francis.

Lawson, Karen, jt. auth. see Silberman, Mel.

Lawson, Kate, ed. see Heller, Ann.

Lawson, Kay. The Human Polity: An Introduction to Political Science. 2nd ed. 1988. teacher ed write for info. (0-318-63319-1) HM.

Lawson, Kay, ed. How Political Parties Work: Perspectives from Within. LC 93-23674. 336p. 1994. text ed. 59.95 (0-275-94393-3, Praeger Pubs) Greenwood.

— Political Parties & Linkage: A Comparative Perspective. LC 79-26751. 416p. reprint ed. pap. 118.60 (0-7837-4532-X, 2080216) Bks Demand.

Lawson, Kay & Merkl, Peter H., eds. When Parties Fail: Emerging Alternative Organizations. (Illus.). 568p. 1988. text ed. 87.50 (0-691-07758-4); pap. text ed. 24.95 (0-691-10242-2) Princeton U Pr.

Lawson, Ken, jt. auth. see Matthew, Stewart.

Lawson, Ken, jt. auth. see Matthews, Stewart.

Lawson, Kenneth. Analysis & Ideology. (C). 1982. 90.00 (0-902031-77-5, Pub. by Univ Nottingham UK) St Mut.

Lawson, Kristan. The Rules of Speed Chess. LC 92-73541. (Illus.). 56p. (Orig.). 1992. pap. 5.95 (0-9634205-7-7) J Roger Pr.

Lawson, L. & Hardy, H. The Town They Called the World Charters Towers. Roderick, Don, ed. 64p. (C). 1990. 69.00 (0-908175-94-9, Pub. by Boolarong Pubns AT) St Mut.

Lawson, L., jt. auth. see Redmond, R.

Lawson, L. L. & Rushforth, S. R. The Diatom Flora of the Provo River, Utah (U. S. A.) 1975. 30.00 (3-7682-0955-5) Lubrecht & Cramer.

Lawson, Laura. Lamb Problems: Detecting, Diagnosing, Treating. LC 92-7300. (Illus.). 352p. (Orig.). 1992. pap. 29.95 (0-9633923-0-1) LDF Pubns.

— Managing Your Ewe: And Her Newborn Lambs. LC 93-79480. (Illus.). 352p. (Orig.). 1993. pap. text ed. 29.95 (0-9633923-1-X) LDF Pubns.

— Showing Sheep: Select, Feed, Fit & Show. LC 94-78838. (Illus.). 224p. (Orig.). 1994. pap. 12.95 (0-9633923-2-8) LDF Pubns.

Lawson, LeRoy. Come to the Party! Celebrate Jesus. LC 93-28842. 192p. (Orig.). 1994. pap. 5.99 (0-7847-0144-X) Standard Pub.

— Guidelines for Growing Christians. rev. ed. 160p. 1989. pap. 5.99 (0-87403-520-1, 39950) Standard Pub.

— Questions for God. 146p. (C). 1990. text ed. 6.99 (0-89900-414-8) College Pr Pub.

— Ten Commandments, Touchstone for Morality. 161p. (Orig.). 1991. 12.99 (0-89900-403-2) College Pr Pub.

Lawson, Leslie G., et al. Lead On! The Complete Handbook for Group Leaders. LC 82-15553. 168p. (Orig.). 1982. pap. 8.95 (0-915166-27-5) Impact Pubs CA.

Lawson, Lewis A. Another Generation: Southern Fiction since World War II. LC 83-16738. 158p. 1984. pap. 11.95 (0-87805-196-1) U Pr of Miss.

— Following Percy: Essays on Walker Percy's Work. LC 87-61269. 177p. 1988. 18.50 (0-87875-345-1) Whitston Pub.

— Still Following Percy. 256p. 1995. text ed. 37.50 (0-87805-826-5) U Pr of Miss.

Lawson, Lewis A. & Kramer, Victor A., eds. Conversations with Walker Percy. LC 84-40715. (Literary Conversations Ser.). 240p. 1985. pap. 15.95 (0-87805-252-6) U Pr of Miss.

— More Conservations with Walker Percy. (Literary Conversations Ser.). 288p. 1993. text ed. 37.50 (0-87805-623-8); pap. 15.95 (0-87805-624-6) U Pr of Miss.

Lawson, Lewis A. & Oleksy, Elzbieta, eds. Walker Percy's Feminine Characters. 150p. 1994. write for info. (0-87875-456-3) Whitston Pub.

Lawson, Linda. Truth in Publishing: Federal Regulation of the Press's Business Practices, 1880-1920. LC 92-34828. 224p. (C). 1993. 29.95 (0-8093-1829-6) S Ill U Pr.

Lawson, Lynn. Staying Well in a Toxic World: Understanding Environmental Illness, Multiple Chemical Sensitivities, Chemical Injuries, & Sick Building Syndrome. (Orig.). 1994. pap. 15.95 (1-879360-33-0) Noble Pr.

Lawson, Lynne N., jt. auth. see McKinnon, Lawrence W.

Lawson, M. K. Cnut: The Danes in England in the Early Eleventh Century. LC 92-12808. (Medieval World Ser.). 1994. text ed. 53.75 (0-582-05969-0, 79461) Longman.

— Cnut: The Danes in England in the Early Eleventh Century. LC 92-12808. (Medieval World Ser.). (C). 1994. pap. text ed. 17.95 (0-582-05970-4, 79460) Longman.

***Lawson, Mandi.** Haven in Winter. LC 94-80062. 120p. (Orig.). 1995. 8.95 (1-884570-23-2) Research Triangle.

Lawson, Margaret & Monte, Tom. The Naturally Healthy Gourmet: Secrets of Quick, Tasty, & Wholesome Cooking. Ruggles, Laurel, ed. LC 94-76116. 232p. (Orig.). 1994. pap. 14.95 (0-918860-53-9) G Ohsawa.

Lawson, Mattie. From Colored Water till Now. 176p. (Orig.). 1994. pap. 3.95 (0-87067-394-7) Holloway.

Lawson, Mel. Eighth Notes. limited ed. Wensrich, Margaret, ed. (Illus.). 96p. 1987. Limited. 13.95 (0-943787-00-9) Hibiscus Pr.

— The Parables a Poetic Version. 1991. write for info. (0-943787-02-5) Hibiscus Pr.

Lawson, Melanie & Hochgesang, Jim, illus. Hiking & Biking in Lake County, Illinois. 128p. 1994. pap. 10.95 (1-884721-00-1) Roots & Wings.

Lawson, Merlin P. & Baker, Maurice E., eds. The Great Plains: Perspectives & Prospects. LC 80-70962. 294p. reprint ed. pap. 83.80 (0-8357-3805-1, 2036533) Bks Demand.

Lawson, Merlin P., jt. ed. see Blouet, Brian W.

***Lawson, Michael.** Dammed Indians: The Pick-Sloan Plan & the Missouri River Sioux, 1944-1980. LC 81-19721. (Illus.). 300p. (Orig.). 1994. pap. 14.95 (0-8061-2672-8) U of Okla Pr.

— Dealing with Conflict: Healing Our Hurts. LC 90-71752. 152p. (Orig.). 1991. pap. 8.95 (0-89622-468-6) Twenty-Third.

— Facing Depression: Toward Healing the Mind, Body, & Spirit. LC 90-70269. 160p. (Orig.). 1990. pap. 7.95 (0-89622-431-7) Twenty-Third.

***Lawson, Michael & Choun, Robert.** Christian Education for the 21st Century. 416p. 1995. pap. 13.99 (0-8254-2348-1) Kregel.

Lawson, Michael & Skipp, David. Sexo y Mas: Guia Para la Juventud. (Illus.). 110p. (Orig.). (SPA.). (YA). (gr. 10-12). 1988. pap. 2.95 (0-945792-02-6) Editorial Unilit.

Lawson, Michael S. & Choun, Robert J., Jr. Directing Christian Education: The Changing Role of the Christian Education Specialist. 1992. pap. 17.99 (0-8024-1702-7) Moody.

***Lawson, Mindy A.** God Revealed to Me. 1995. 14.95 (0-533-11145-5) Vantage.

***Lawson, Myldred.** Big Black Buzzard & Little Rabbit. Rowden, Thomas, tr. (Illus.). 32p. (Orig.). (J). (ps-5). 1994. per., pap. text ed. 5.95 (0-9642481-1-5) NE Texas Pub.

Lawson, N. V., intro. Australasian Port & Harbour Conference, 4th, 1992: Shaping the Port of the Future. (Illus.). 315p. (Orig.). 1992. pap. 72.00 (0-85825-555-3) Accents Pubns.

Lawson, Nigel. Autumn Statement, 1990. 57p. 1990. pap. 22.00 (0-10-113112-7, HM7112) UNIPUB.

— Autumn Statement, 1992. 57p. 1992. pap. 25.00 (0-10-120962-2, HMO9622, Pub. by HMSO UK) UNIPUB.

Lawson, P. The Tangled Garden. large type ed. 608p. 1986. 23.95 (0-7089-8357-X, Trail West Pubs) Ulverscroft.

Lawson, P. V. Fleming Family & Allied Lines: Baird, Blair, Butler, Cook, Childs, Clark, Cole, Crane, et al. 304p. 1992. reprint ed. lib. bdg. 56.50 (0-8328-2315-5); reprint ed. pap. 46.50 (0-8328-2316-3) Higginson Bk Co.

Lawson, Pate, jt. auth. see Lawson, Tony.

Lawson, Paul E. Solving Somebody Else's Blues: A Study of Police Mediation Activities. LC 81-40881. (Illus.). 246p. (Orig.). 1982. pap. text ed. 23.00 (0-8191-2174-6) U Pr of Amer.

Lawson-Peebles, R., jt. ed. see Gidley, M.

Lawson-Peebles, Robert. Landscape & Written Expression in Revolutionary America: The World Turned Upside Down. (Cambridge Studies in American Literature & Culture: No. 28). (Illus.). 392p. 1988. 69.95 (0-521-34647-9) Cambridge U Pr.

Lawson-Peebles, Robert, jt. ed. see Gidley, Mick.

***Lawson, Peter, illus.** The Sooty Little Mouse. 16p. (J). (ps). 1994. 10.98 (1-881445-30-5) Sandvik Pub.

Lawson, Philip. The East India Company: A History. LC 92-44920. (Studies in Modern History). (C). 1993. text ed. 54.50 (0-582-07386-3, 79776, Pub. by Longman UK) Longman.

— The East India Company: A History. LC 92-44920. (Studies in Modern History). (C). 1994. pap. text ed. 21.95 (0-582-07385-5, 79775, Pub. by Longman UK) Longman.

— George Grenville: A Political Life. (Illus.). 309p. 1984. 59.00 (0-19-822755-8) OUP.

— The Imperial Challenge: Quebec & Britain in the Age of the American Revolution. 196p. (C). 1989. text ed. 44.95 (0-7735-0698-5, Pub. by McGill CN) U of Toronto Pr.

— The Imperial Challenge: Quebec & Britain in the Age of the American Revolution. 208p. (C). 1994. pap. text ed. 17.95 (0-7735-1205-5, Pub. by McGill CN) U of Toronto Pr.

Lawson, Philip J. Lawson Perspective Charts. rev. ed. 1940. text ed. 34.95 (0-442-13053-8) Van Nos Reinhold.

Lawson, Polly, tr. see Berger, Thomas.

Lawson, Polly, tr. see Glockler, Michaela & Goebel, Wolfgang.

Lawson, Polly, tr. see Leeuwen, M. & Moeskops, J.

Lawson, Polly, tr. see Lesch, Christiane.

Lawson, R. Exclusion Clauses. (C). 1983. 230.00 (0-685-32821-X, Pub. by Witherby & Co UK) St Mut.

Lawson, R. D. Theory of the Nuclear Shell Model. (OSNP). (Illus.). (C). 1980. text ed. 98.00 (0-19-851516-2) OUP.

Lawson, R. G. & Smith, D. Business Law. 2nd ed. 208p. 1992. pap. 29.95 (0-7506-0375-5) Buttrwrth-Heinemann.

Lawson, Richard A. & Mavigliano, George J. Fred E. Myers, Wood-Carver. LC 80-14243. (Illus.). 167p. 1980. 15.00 (0-8093-0974-2) S Ill U Pr.

Lawson, Richard A., jt. auth. see Mavigliano, George J.

Lawson, Richard H. Understanding Elias Canetti. Hardin, James N., ed. LC 91-13888. (Understanding Modern European & Latin American Literature Ser.). 123p. 1991. text ed. 34.95 (0-87249-768-2) U of SC Pr.

***Lawson, Richard H., ed.** Seven Contemporary Austrian Plays. LC 95-14086. (Studies in Austrian Literature, Culture & Thought; Translation Ser.). 400p. 1995. pap. 28.50 (1-57241-017-5) Ariadne CA.

***Lawson, Richard H., tr. & intro.** Brother Hermann's "Life of the Countess Yolanda of Vianden" (Leben Der Graefin Iolande von Vianden. (MEDVL). 130p. 1995. 55.95 (1-57113-050-0) Camden Hse.

Lawson, Richard H., jt. ed. see Berlin, Jeffrey B.

***Lawson, Rick, ed.** The Dynamics of the Protection of Human Rights in Europe: Essays in Honour of Henry G. Schermers, Vol. III. 440p. (C). 1994. lib. bdg. 169.50 (0-7923-3161-3, Pub. by M Nijhoff) Kluwer Ac.

Lawson, Robert. Ben & Me. (Illus.). 1939p. (J). (gr. 7-10). 1939. 15.95 (0-316-51732-1) Little.

— Ben & Me. (Illus.). 1939p. (J). (gr. 7-10). 1988. mass mkt. 5.95 (0-316-51730-5) Little.

— Captain Kidd's Cat. (Illus.). (J). (gr. 2-4). 1984. mass mkt. 7.95 (0-316-51735-6) Little.

— The Fabulous Flight. (Illus.). 152p. (J). (gr. 4-8). 1984. mass mkt. 5.95 (0-316-51731-3) Little.

— The Great Wheel. (Illus.). 180p. (J). 1993. pap. 7.95 (0-8027-7392-3) Walker & Co.

— I Discover Columbus. (Illus.). (J). (gr. 3-6). 1991. mass mkt. 4.95 (0-316-51760-7) Little.

— I Discover Columbus. (J). 1994. 18.00 (0-8446-6766-8) Peter Smith.

— Mr. Revere & I. (Illus.). (J). (gr. 7-10). 1953. 16.95 (0-316-51739-9) Little.

— Mr. Revere & I. (Illus.). 152p. (J). (gr. 3-6). 1988. mass mkt. 5.95 (0-316-51729-1) Little.

— Rabbit Hill. (Illus.). (J). (gr. 1-3). 1977. pap. 3.99 (0-14-031010-X, Puffin) Puffin Bks.

— Rabbit Hill. (Illus.). (J). (gr. 4-6). 1944. pap. 14.00 (0-670-58675-7) Viking Child Bks.

— They Were Strong & Good. (Illus.). (J). (gr. 4-6). 1940. pap. 14.99 (0-670-69949-7) Viking Child Bks.

— The Tough Winter. (J). (gr. 2-6). 1992. 16.75 (0-8446-6565-7) Peter Smith.

— Upton-on-Severn Words & Phrases. (English Dialect Society Publications Ser.: No. 42). 1974. reprint ed. pap. 15.00 (0-8115-0468-9) Periodicals Srv.

Lawson, Robert & Murphy, Gene. The Black Pursuit Study Guide. LC 85-73098. 281p. 1985. pap. 19.95 (0-935979-00-X) Prof Dynamics.

— Yes We Can! Black Achievement. 320p. 1995. 17.50 (0-7872-0575-3) Kendall-Hunt.

Lawson, Robert, ed. see Buckman, Repha.

Lawson, Robert F., et al, eds. Education & Social Concern: An Approach to Social Foundations. LC 86-63415. 354p. (Orig.). 1987. pap. 25.00 (0-911168-66-4) Prakken.

Lawson, Robert G. The Kentucky Evidence Law Handbook. 3rd ed. (Kluwer Litigation Library). 744p. 1993. 95.00 (1-55834-009-2) Michie Butterworth.

— The Kentucky Evidence Law Handbook: With 1989 Supplement. 2nd suppl. ed. (State Practice Publications Ser.). 470p. 1984. 65.00 (0-87215-747-4); 25.00 (0-87473-476-2) Michie Butterworth.

Lawson, Robert L. Destined for Greatness: Getting the Results You Desire from Yourself & Others. 160p. (Orig.). 1994. per., pap. text ed. 16.95 (0-8403-9339-3) Kendall-Hunt.

— Destined for Greatness: Getting the Results You Desire from Yourself & Others. 160p. (Orig.). reprint ed. pap. text ed. 9.95 (0-935979-01-8) Prof Dynamics.

Lawson, Robert N., ed. see Sadowski, Larry R., et al.

Lawson, Robert N., ed. see Takahashi, Tetsuro.

Lawson, Robert W. Job Hunter's Guide to Vermont. LC 92-83726. 228p. (Orig.). 1993. pap. 19.95 (1-881535-00-2) New Eng Pr VT.

— Teletraffic Concepts in Corporate Communications. (Traffic Ser.). (Illus.). 220p. 1989. pap. 39.95 (1-56016-042-X) ABC TeleTraining.

***Lawson, Robert W. & Walton, Richard K.** Backyard Bird Song: Eastern & Central North America. 32p. 1991. 19.95 (0-395-58416-7) HM.

— Birding by Ear: Western North America. 1994. 35.00 (0-395-71257-2) HM.

Lawson, Robert W., tr. see Einstein, Albert.

Lawson, Robert W., jt. auth. see Walton, Richard K.

Lawson, Robyn, jt. ed. see Taylor-Gooby, Peter.

Lawson, Ronald, jt. auth. see Harry, Mike.

Lawson, Rowena. Adair County Kentucky 1810-1840: Censuses. iv, 69p. (Orig.). 1986. pap. 10.50 (0-917890-84-1) Heritage Bk.

— Allen County, Kentucky, Censuses, 1820-1840. iii, 51p. (Orig.). 1987. pap. 8.00 (1-55613-031-7) Heritage Bk.

— Bath County Kentucky: 1820-1840 Censuses. iv, 67p. (Orig.). 1986. pap. 10.00 (0-917890-88-4) Heritage Bk.

— Boone County Kentucky: 1810-1840 Censuses. iv, 68p. (Orig.). 1986. pap. 10.00 (0-917890-79-5) Heritage Bk.

— Boone County Kentucky: 1850 Census. iv, 93p. (Orig.). 1986. pap. 12.50 (0-917890-80-9) Heritage Bk.

— Economics of Fisheries Development. LC 84-15074. 296p. 1984. text ed. 49.95 (0-275-91213-2, C1213, Praeger Pubs) Greenwood.

— Franklin County, Kentucky, 1810-1840 Censuses. 73p. (Orig.). 1986. pap. 11.50 (1-55613-016-3) Heritage Bk.

— Montgomery Co Kentucky 1810-1840: Censuses. 63p. (Orig.). 1985. pap. 9.50 (0-917890-62-0) Heritage Bk.

— Montgomery County, Kentucky 1850 Census. iii, 70p. (Orig.). 1986. pap. 10.00 (0-917890-68-X) Heritage Bk.

— Morgan County, Kentucky: 1830-1850 Censuses. iv, 90p. (Orig.). 1987. pap. 12.50 (0-685-43813-9) Heritage Bk.

— Nelson County, Kentucky 1850 Census. iv, 88p. (Orig.). 1985. pap. 12.50 (0-917890-60-4) Heritage Bk.

— Nicholas County Kentucky: 1810-1840 Censuses. iv, 55p. (Orig.). 1984. pap. 9.00 (0-917890-39-6) Heritage Bk.

— Nicholas County Kentucky: 1850 Census. iv, 92p. (Orig.). 1983. pap. 12.50 (0-917890-34-5) Heritage Bk.

— Ohio County Kentucky: 1810-1840 Censuses. (Orig.). 1984. pap. 7.00 (0-917890-44-2) Heritage Bk.

— Ohio County Kentucky 1850 Census. iv, 87p. (Orig.). 1984. pap. 12.50 (0-917890-40-X) Heritage Bk.

— Washington County, Kentucky, 1810-1840 Censuses. 112p. (Orig.). 1987. pap. 13.50 (1-55613-027-9) Heritage Bk.

Lawson, Rowena, jt. auth. see Crutchfield, James A.

Lawson, Rowena M. The Changing Economy of the Lower Volta, 1954-1967: A Study in the Dynamics of Rural Economic Growth. LC 72-177589. 139p. reprint ed. pap. 39.70 (0-8357-3013-1, 2057099) Bks Demand.

Lawson, Russell K., jt. ed. see Lepor, Herbert.

Lawson, Ruth C., comp. Homelessness - A Journey Down Homeless Avenue. 66p. 1991. pap. write for info. (0-9632210-0-0) R C Lawson.

Lawson, Sandra M., comp. Generations Past: A Selected List of Sources for Afro-American Genealogical Research. LC 88-600100. 101p. 1988. 4.50 (0-8444-0604-X, 030-001-00129-6) Lib Congress.

Lawson, Sarah, tr. see De Pizan, Christine.

Lawson, Simpson, et al. Courthouse Design: The First International Conference. LC 93-28652. (Illus.). 100p. 1993. pap. 20.00 (1-55835-118-3) AIA Press.

Lawson, Stephanie. The Failure of Democratic Politics in Fiji. (Illus.). 328p. 1991. 69.00 (0-19-827322-3) OUP.

Lawson, Stephen P. Daddy, Why Are You Going to Jail? The True Story of a Father's Descent into White-Collar Crime & His Amazing Restoration. LC 92-23261. 1992. 8.99 (0-87788-161-8) Shaw Pubs.

***Lawson, Steve.** When All Heaven Breaks Loose. 240p. 1995. 16.00 (0-614-01635-5, NavPr) NavPress.

Lawson, Steven F. Black Ballots: Voting Rights in the South 1944-1969. LC 76-18886. (Contemporary American History Ser.). 474p. 1976. pap. text ed. 23.50 (0-231-08352-1) Col U Pr.

— In Pursuit of Power: Southern Blacks & Electoral Politics 1965-1982. LC 84-17036. (Contemporary American History Ser.). 391p. 1987. pap. text ed. 16.00 (0-231-04627-8) Col U Pr.

— Running for Freedom: Civil Rights & Black Politics in America. 1991. pap. text ed. write for info. (0-07-556975-2) McGraw.

— Running for Freedom: Civil Rights & Black Politics in America, 1941-1988. (Illus.). 320p. (C). 1990. 39.95 (0-87722-792-6) Temple U Pr.

***Lawson, Steven J.** Faith Under Fire: Standing Strong When Satan Attacks. 224p. 1995. 17.99 (0-89107-847-9) Crossway Bks.

— Final Call: It's Time for the Church to Wake up & Answer the Call! LC 94-7174. 224p. 1994. 15.99 (0-89107-796-0) Crossway Bks.

— Men Who Win: Pursuing the Ultimate Prize. LC 92-60187. 222p. 1992. pap. 15.00 (0-89109-664-7) NavPress.

— When All Hell Breaks Loose...You May Be Doing Something Right! LC 93-24957. 256p. 1993. 17.00 (0-89109-732-5) NavPress.

***Lawson, Steven L.** Heaven Help Us! Truths about Eternity that will Help You Live Today--Insights from the Book of Revelation. LC 95-8616. 1995. write for info. (0-89109-912-3, NavPr) NavPress.

Lawson, Suzy. Amish Patchwork: Full-Size Patterns for 46 Authentic Designs. (Illus.). 144p. 1988. reprint ed. pap. 5.95 (0-486-25701-0) Dover.

Lawson, T. V. Wind Effects on Buildings, Vol. 1: Design Applications. (Illus.). 1980. 88.25 (0-85334-887-1, Pub. by Elsevier Applied Sci UK) Elsevier.

— Wind Effects on Buildings, Vol. 2: Statistics & Meteorology. (Illus.). 1980. 54.00 (0-85334-893-6, Pub. by Elsevier Applied Sci UK) Elsevier.

Lawson-Tancred, Hugh, tr. see Aristotle.

Lawson, Ted. Understanding Alcoholism: A Starting Point for Families. LC 90-64269. 64p. (Orig.). 1991. pap. 1.95 (0-89243-341-8) Liguori Pubns.

Lawson, Ted W. Thirty Seconds over Tokyo. 290p. 1992. reprint ed. lib. bdg. 25.95x (0-89966-886-0) Buccaneer Bks.

Lawson, Thomas. Claes Oldenburg: Multiples in Retrospect, 1964-1990. LC 90-50799. (Illus.). 1991. 65.00 (0-8478-1335-5) Rizzoli Intl.

Lawson, Thomas, jt. auth. see McCollum, Allan.

Lawson, Thomas B. Fundamentals of Aquacultural Engineering. LC 93-38073. 1994. 59.95 (0-442-23772-3) Chapman & Hall.

An Asterisk (*) at the beginning of an entry indicates that the title is appearing in BIP for the first time.

Lawson, Thomas E. Religions of Africa. LC 84-47729. (Religious Traditions of the World Ser.). (Illus.). 128p. (Orig.). 1985. pap. 9.00 (*0-06-065211-X*) Harper SF.

Lawson, Thomas L., jt. ed. see Middleton, William D.

Lawson, Thomas L., jt. auth. see Wagner, Marvin.

Lawson, Thomas L., et al. Diagnostic Ultrasonography Test & Syllabus. LC 94-16701. (Professional Self-Evaluation Program Ser.: Vol. 38). (Illus.). 940p. 1994. 200.00 (*1-55903-038-0*) Am Coll Radiology.

Lawson, Tom, ed. see Rotherham, J. B., et al.

Lawson, Tom E. Formative Instructional Product Evaluation: Instruments & Strategies. LC 73-22336. 132p. 1974. pap. 24.95 (*0-87778-068-4*) Educ Tech Pubns.

Lawson, Tony. The Cat Lovers Cookbook: Recipes. LC 93-46033. 1994. 6.99 (*0-517-10110-6*, Pub. by Wings Bks) Random Hse Value.

Lawson, Tony & Lawson, Pate. The Cat-Lovers' Cookbook. LC 86-45042. (Illus.). 112p. (Orig.). 1986. pap. 7.95 (*0-88266-426-3*, Storey Pub) Storey Comm Inc.

Lawson, Tony, et al, eds. Kaldor's Political Economy. 283p. 1989. text ed. 40.00 (*0-12-439640-2*) Acad Pr.

Lawson, V. Paul Lawrence Dunbar Critically Examined. 1972. 59.95 (*0-8490-0808-5*) Gordon Pr.

Lawson, V. K. Thinking Is a Basic Skill: Creating Humanities Materials for the Adult New Reader. 55p. 1988. pap. text ed. 5.00 (*0-930713-33-8*) Lit Vol Am.

Lawson, V. K. Read On! Two. 60p. 1987. Introductory Set. pap. text ed. 10.00 (*0-930713-01-X*); teacher ed, pap. text ed. 5.50 (*0-930713-20-6*); teacher ed, pap. text ed. 2.00 (*0-930713-21-4*) Lit Vol Am.

— Read On! Two, Set. 60p. 1987. pap. text ed. 45.00 (*0-930713-00-1*); 50.00 (*0-930713-46-X*) Lit Vol Am.

— READ Trainer's Kit. 1982. Cassette tape, script & guide. 20.00 (*0-930713-40-0*) Lit Vol Am.

Lawson, V. K. & MacDonald, Barbara J., eds. Core Library for Literacy - Conversational English Programs: A Bibliography. 34p. 1984. pap. text ed. 5.00 (*0-930713-35-4*) Lit Vol Am.

Lawson, V. K., ed. see Colvin, Ruth J. & Root, Jane.

Lawson, V. K., ed. see Coville, Bruce & Lee, Artis.

Lawson, V. K., ed. see Elmore, Fred & Lee, Artis.

Lawson, V. K., ed. see Lee, Artis, et al.

Lawson, V. K., ed. see Lee, Artis.

Lawson, V. K., ed. see Literacy Volunteers Computer Task Force Staff.

Lawson, V. K., ed. see LVA Basic Reading Task Force Staff.

Lawson, V. K., ed. see Price, Margaret, et al.

Lawson, V. K., ed. see Simmons, Judy D. & Lee, Artis.

Lawson, V. K., ed. see Trabert, Judith A. & McKallip, Jonathan.

Lawson, V. K., ed. see Williams, Margaret, et al.

Lawson, V. K., et al. Read All About It - Tutor Adults with Daily Newspaper: Tutor Handbook. 95p. 1984. pap. text ed. 4.00 (*0-930713-31-1*) Lit Vol Am.

Lawson, W., jt. auth. see Zak, F. G.

Lawson, Will. Pacific Steamers. (C). 1987. 96.00 (*0-85174-245-9*, Pub. by Brwn Son Ferg) St Mut.

Lawson, William. Zeppelin Coming Down. Young, Al, ed. LC 76-9412. 1976. pap. 5.50 (*0-918412-02-1*) Yardbird Wing.

Lawter, William C., Jr. Smokey Bear 20252: A Biography. LC 94-5997. 1994. write for info. (*0-9640017-0-5*) L Smith Pubs.

Lawther, Gail. The Book of Cross-Stitch. (Illus.). 128p. 1994. 22.50 (*0-8230-0517-8*, Watsn-Guptill) Watsn-Guptill.

— Christmas Craft Source Book: Over Two-Hundred Ideas & Motifs for the Festive Season. (Illus.). 144p. 1995. 24.95 (*1-57076-019-5*, Trafalgar Sq Pub) Trafalgar.

— Patterns & Borders: Needlecraft Source Book. (Illus.). 144p. Date not set. 29.95 (*0-943955-71-8*, Trafalgar Sq Pub) Trafalgar.

***Lawton, Alan & McKevitt, David, eds.** Case Studies in Public Services Management. (Illus.). 200p. (Orig.). (C). 1996. pap. write for info. (*0-631-19579-3*) Blackwell Pubs.

Lawton, Alan & Rose, Aidan. Organisation & Management in the Public Sector. 2nd ed. 288p. (Orig.). 1994. pap. 47.50 (*0-273-60191-1*, Pub. by Pitman Pub Ltd UK) Trans-Atl Phila.

Lawton, Alan, jt. ed. see McKevitt, David.

Lawton, Anna. Kinoglasnost: Soviet Cinema in Our Time. (Cambridge Soviet Paperbacks Ser.: No. 9). (Illus.). 296p. (C). 1992. pap. 17.95 (*0-521-38814-7*) Cambridge U Pr.

— Kinoglasnost: Soviet Cinema in Our Time. (Cambridge Soviet Paperbacks Ser.: No. 9). (Illus.). 296p. (C). 1993. 59.95 (*0-521-38117-7*) Cambridge U Pr.

Lawton, Anna, ed. The Red Screen: Politics, Society, Art in Soviet Cinema. LC 91-33268. 352p. 1992. 67.50 (*0-415-07818-0*, A8196); pap. 22.50 (*0-415-07819-9*, A8197) Routledge.

Lawton, Anna & Eagle, Herbert, eds. Russian Futurism Through Its Manifestos, 1912-1928. Eagle, Herbert, tr. LC 88-47733. 320p. 1988. 49.95 (*0-8014-1883-6*); pap. 16.95 (*0-8014-9492-3*) Cornell U Pr.

Lawton, B. W. Desperado, No. 1. 176p. (Orig.). 1993. pap. 3.99 (*0-515-11077-9*) Jove Pubns.

— Desperado, No. 2: Edge of the Law. 176p. (Orig.). 1993. pap. 3.99 (*0-515-11133-3*) Jove Pubns.

— Desperado, No. 3: Hard Justice. 1993. pap. 3.99 (*0-515-11213-5*) Jove Pubns.

Lawton, Barbara P. Improving Your Garden Soil. Braasch, Barbara J., ed. LC 92-70587. (Illus.). 112p. (Orig.). 1992. pap. 9.95 (*0-89721-244-4*, UPC 05311) Ortho Info.

— Seasonal Guide to the Natural Year: A Month by Month Guide to Natural Events-Illinois, Missouri & Arkansas. (Illus.). 320p. (Orig.). 1994. pap. 15.95 (*1-55591-156-0*) Fulcrum Pub.

Lawton, Barbara P. & Van Patten, George F. Organic Gardener's Basics. Daniels, Stevie O., ed. (Organic Gardener's Ser.). (Illus.). 208p. (Orig.). 1993. 19.95 (*1-878823-14-0*); pap. 12.95 (*1-878823-01-9*) Van Patten Pub.

Lawton, Ben, tr. see Pasolini, Pier P.

Lawton, Carl W., ed. see American Society of Mechanical Engineers Staff.

***Lawton, Carol L.** Attic Document Reliefs: Art & Politics in Ancient Athens. (Oxford Monographs on Classical Archaeology). (Illus.). 256p. 1995. 96.00 (*0-19-814955-7*) OUP.

Lawton, David. Blasphemy. LC 93-19145. 228p. (Orig.). (C). 1993. text ed. 39.95 (*0-8122-3219-4*); pap. 16.95 (*0-8122-1503-6*) U of Pa Pr.

— Chaucer's Narrators. (Chaucer Studies: XIII). 208p. (C). 1985. 79.00 (*0-85991-217-5*) Boydell & Brewer.

— Faith, Text & History: The Bible in English. (C). 1991. text ed. 35.00 (*0-8139-1325-X*); pap. 12.95 (*0-8139-1326-8*) U Pr of Va.

— A Lovely Country: A Novel. 288p. 1995. 22.00 (*0-15-100171-5*) HarBrace.

— A Lovely Country: A Novel of Vietnam. LC 94-33535. 1995. write for info. (*0-15-100118-9*) HarBrace.

Lawton, David, ed. see Verdi, Giuseppe.

Lawton, Denis. Education & Politics for the Nineteen Nineties: Conflict or Consensus? LC 92-13828. 224p. 1992. 75.00 (*0-7507-0078-5*, Falmer Pr); pap. 29.00 (*0-7507-0079-3*, Falmer Pr) Taylor & Francis.

— Education & Social Justice. LC 74-31568. (Sage Studies in Social & Educational Change: Vol. 7). 206p. reprint ed. pap. 58.80 (*0-317-07913-1*, 2021921) Bks Demand.

— The Tory Mind on Education. LC 94-28780. 168p. 1994. 75.00x (*0-7507-0350-4*, Falmer Pr); pap. 24.95x (*0-7507-0351-2*, Falmer Pr) Taylor & Francis.

Lawton, E. P. The South & the Nation. LC 63-16251. 1963. pap. 6.95 (*0-87208-003-X*) Island Pr Pubs.

Lawton, Edward M., Jr. The Seventy-Year Challenge, 1920-1990: A Private Schoolmaster Reviews His Responses to Some Challenges of Life. (Illus.). 226p. (Orig.). 1992. pap. text ed. 22.00 (*1-880836-00-9*) Pine Isl Pr.

Lawton, Edward P. A Saga of the South. LC 65-19041. (Illus.). 1974. 15.00 (*0-87208-005-6*) Island Pr Pubs.

Lawton, Edward P., tr. see Lavisse, Emile C.

Lawton, Elise T. Swimming: Gift for Life, Vol. I. (Illus.). 64p. 1986. pap. text ed. 3.00 (*0-9617193-0-3*) Lawton E T.

Lawton, George. Practical Guide to Genetic Algorithms in C. 1994. pap. 34.95 (*0-471-30306-2*) Wiley.

— A Practical Guide to Genetic Algorithms in C. Date not set. pap. text ed. 49.95 (*0-471-30307-0*) Wiley.

Lawton, George, ed. New Goals for Old Age. LC 76-169390. (Family in America Ser.). 230p. 1972. reprint ed. 17.95 (*0-405-03868-2*) Ayer.

Lawton, George, jt. auth. see Schneider, Herbert.

Lawton, H. W., ed. see Bellay, Joachim Du.

Lawton, Harry. Head on the Tracks. 32p. write for info. (*0-938631-31-4*) Pennywhistle Pr.

— Willie Boy: A Desert Manhunt. (Illus.). xii, 224p. (C). 1993. reprint ed. lib. bdg. 27.00x (*0-8095-6207-3*) Borgo Pr.

Lawton, Harry, tr. see Marotti, Giorgio.

Lawton, Harry W., jt. auth. see Bean, L. John.

Lawton, Helen. The Diary of Helen Lawton: 1909-1911. Shurtleff, William R., ed. 59p. (Orig.). 1987. Spiral bound. spiral bd. 19.95 (*0-942515-00-5*) Pine Hill CA.

— Moggy the Mouser. LC 93-6571. (Voyages Ser.). (Illus.). (J). 1994. write for info. (*0-383-03702-6*) SRA Schl Grp.

Lawton, Henry. The Psychohistorian's Handbook. 240p. 1988. 25.95 (*0-914434-27-6*) Psychohistory Pr.

Lawton, James, ed. Shop Talk: Papers on Historical Business & Commercial Records of New England. 1975. 3.00 (*0-89073-003-2*) Boston Public Lib.

Lawton, James, ed. see Singer, Jonathan M. & Deitch, Samuel L.

Lawton, James M. Family Names of Huguenot Refugees to America. LC 73-1574. 20p. 1991. reprint ed. pap. 4.00 (*0-8063-0208-9*) Genealog Pub.

***Lawton, John.** Black Out. LC 95-1264. 1995. 22.95 (*0-670-85767-X*, Viking) Viking Penguin.

— Nineteen Sixty-Three Five Hundred Days. (Illus.). 407p. 1993. 45.00 (*0-340-50846-9*, Pub. by Headline UK) Trafalgar.

— Samarkand & Bukhara. (Travel to Landmarks Ser.). 1992. 24.95 (*1-85043-178-7*, Pub. by I B Tauris UK) St Martin.

***Lawton, John H. & May, Robert M., eds.** Extinction Rates. (Illus.). 248p. 1995. pap. text ed. 27.95 (*0-19-854829-X*) OUP.

Lawton, John T., jt. ed. see Jones, Clive G.

Lawton, Jorge A., ed. Privatizing Amidst Poverty: Contemporary Challenges in Latin American Political Economy. 300p. (C). 1993. pap. 21.95 (*1-56000-709-5*, U Miami North-South Ctr) Transaction Pubs.

Lawton, Joseph T. Introduction to Child Care & Early Childhood Education. (C). 1988. text ed. 31.75 (*0-673-39735-1*) HarpCollege.

Lawton, Lewis S. Integrated Digital Networks. 404p. (Orig.). 1993. pap. 72.50 (*1-85058-181-9*, Pub. by Sigma Press UK) Coronet Bks.

Lawton, Lynna. Glory's Mistress. 480p. (Orig.). 1985. pap. 3.95 (*0-8439-2804-2*) Dorchester Pub Co.

— Under Crimson Sails. 352p. 1987. reprint ed. pap. 3.75 (*0-8439-2515-9*) Dorchester Pub Co.

Lawton, M., jt. auth. see Maguire, M.

Lawton, M. P. & Herzog, A. R., eds. Special Research Methods for Gerontology. (Society & Aging Ser.: Vol. 2). 257p. 1989. text ed. 34.95x (*0-89503-061-6*); pap. text ed. 26.25 (*0-89503-053-5*) Baywood Pub.

Lawton, M. Powell. Environment & Aging. 2nd ed. LC 86-9665. 1986. 14.95 (*0-937829-00-5*) Ctr Study Aging.

Lawton, M. Powell, ed. Annual Review of Gerontology & Geriatrics, Vol. 9, 1989. 416p. 1989. 43.00 (*0-8261-6491-9*) Springer Pub.

Lawton, M. Powell & Hoover, Sally L., eds. Community Housing Choices for Older Americans. 336p. 1981. 33.95 (*0-8261-3640-0*) Springer Pub.

Lawton, M. Powell & Maddox, George L. Annual Review of Gerontology & Geriatrics, Vol. 5. 352p. 1985. 39.00 (*0-8261-3084-4*) Springer Pub.

***Lawton, M. Powell & Teresi, Jeanne, eds.** The Annual Review of Gerontology & Geriatrics Vol. 14. (Illus.). 416p. 1994. 54.00 (*0-8261-6496-X*) Springer Pub.

Lawton, M. Powell, jt. ed. see Maddox, George L.

Lawton, M. Powell, et al. Respite for Caregivers of Alzheimer's Patients: Research & Practice. 176p. 1991. 24.95 (*0-8261-6610-5*) Springer Pub.

Lawton, Manny. Some Survived. 280p. 1984. 16.95 (*0-912697-13-X*) Algonquin Bks.

***Lawton, Marcia J. & Jackim, Linda W.** Prevention Today: Strategies That Win or Lose. 21p. 1994. pap. 19.95 (*1-884937-13-6*) Manisses Communs.

Lawton, Mary. A Lifetime with Mark Twain. LC 72-3627. (American Literature Ser.: No. 49). (Illus.). 1972. reprint ed. lib. bdg. 53.95 (*0-8383-1562-3*) M S G Haskell Hse.

— Schumann-Heink: The Last of the Titans. Farkas, Andrew, ed. LC 76-29945. (Opera Biographies Ser.). (Illus.). 1977. reprint ed. lib. bdg. 41.95 (*0-405-09687-9*) Ayer.

Lawton, Mary, jt. auth. see Paderewski, Jan I.

Lawton, Mary S. Hsieh Shih-ch'en: A Ming Dynasty Painter Reinterprets the Past. LC 77-18637. (Illus.). 55p. (Orig.). 1977. pap. 3.00 (*0-935573-04-6*) D & A Smart Museum.

Lawton, Mortimer P. Planning & Managing Housing for the Elderly. LC 74-28099. (Illus.). 350p. reprint ed. pap. 99.80 (*0-317-09607-9*, 2022488) Bks Demand.

Lawton, Moyra F. Before the Face of the Sun. large type ed. 368p. 1994. 21.95 (*0-7089-3096-4*) Ulverscroft.

Lawton, Philip. The Kernel of Truth in Freud. 154p. (Orig.). (C). 1991. lib. bdg. 32.50 (*0-8191-8034-3*); pap. text ed. 18.50 (*0-8191-8035-1*) U Pr of Amer.

Lawton, R., jt. ed. see Gould, W. T.

Lawton, Richard, ed. Census & Social Structure: An Interpretative Guide to Nineteenth-Century Censuses for England & Wales. 330p. 1978. 35.00 (*0-7146-2965-0*, Pub. by F Cass Pubs UK) Intl Spec Bk.

— The Rise & Fall of Great Cities. (Illus.). 197p. 1992. pap. text ed. 19.50 (*1-85293-235-X*, Pub. by Pinter Publishers UK) Wiley.

— The Rise & Fall of Great Cities: Aspects of Urbanization in the Western World. 1993. text ed. 49.95 (*0-471-94704-0*) Wiley.

— The Rise & Fall of the Great Cities: Aspects of Urbanization in the Western World. 185p. 1992. text ed. 43.95 (*0-470-21896-7*) Halsted Pr.

Lawton, Richard & Pooley, Colin G. Britain 1740-1950: An Historical Geography. (Illus.). 288p. (Orig.). 1992. pap. 22.50 (*0-7131-6550-2*, A6105, Pub. by E Arnold UK) Routledge Chapman & Hall.

Lawton, Robin L. Creating a Customer-Centered Culture: Leadership in Quality, Innovation, & Speed. LC 93-15572. 180p. 1993. 21.95 (*0-87389-151-1*) ASQC Qual Pr.

Lawton, Samuel. Municipal Legal Forms: 1964-1992, 10 vols. LC 76-49998. 900.00 (*0-685-09237-2*) Clark Boardman Callaghan.

Lawton, Steve, ed. see Stedt, Jim.

Lawton, Thomas. Chinese Art of the Warring States Period: Change & Continuity, 480-222 B.C. LC 82-600184. (Illus.). 204p. (Orig.). 1982. 35.00 (*0-934686-39-4*); pap. 20.00 (*0-934686-50-5*) Freer.

Lawton, Thomas, ed. New Perspectives on Chu Culture During the Eastern Zhou Period. (Illus.). 230p. 1991. text ed. 45.00 (*0-691-04095-8*); pap. text ed. 19.95 (*0-691-00290-8*) Princeton U Pr.

Lawton, Thomas & Merrill, Linda. Freer: A Legacy of Art. LC 92-19399. (Illus.). 272p. 1993. 49.50 (*0-8109-3315-2*) Abrams.

Lawton, W. C. Successors of Homer. LC 69-17001. reprint ed. 57.00 (*0-8154-0276-7*) Cooper Sq.

Lawton, William C. New England Poets: A Study of Emerson, Hawthorne, Longfellow, Whittier, Lowell, Holmes. LC 72-6941. (Essay Index Reprint Ser.). 1977. reprint ed. 23.95 (*0-8369-7245-7*) Ayer.

Lawton, William J. The Better Time to Be: Utopian Attitudes to Society among Sydney Anglicans, 1885 to 1914. 220p. 1990. pap. 24.95 (*0-86840-068-8*, Pub. by New South Wales Univ Pr AT) Intl Spec Bk.

Lawvere, F. W. & Schanuel, S. H., eds. Categories in Continuum Physics. (Lecture Notes in Mathematics Ser.: Vol. 1174). v, 126p. 1986. pap. 23.00 (*0-387-16096-5*) Spr-Verlag.

Lawvere, F. William & Schanuel, Stephen. Conceptual Mathematics: A First Introduction to Categories. rev. ed. (Illus.). 353p. 1993. pap. text ed. 28.00 (*0-9631805-1-7*) Buffalo Wksp.

Lawwill, Theodore. ERG, VER & Psychophysics. (Documenta Ophthalmologica Proceedings Ser.: Vol. 13). 1977. lib. bdg. 126.50 (*90-6193-153-3*) Kluwer Ac.

Lawwill, Theodore, jt. ed. see Heckenlively, John R.

Lawyer, John, jt. auth. see Meyers, J. Gordon.

Lawyer, John W., jt. auth. see Katz, Neil.

Lawyer, Verne, jt. auth. see Cone, Al J.

Lawyers & Judges Publishing Staff. About Divorce: Eighty-Three Questions & Answers. rev. ed. 1984. pap. 1.80 (*0-88450-052-7*, 6110) Lawyers & Judges.

— About Your Deposition: Ninety-Five Questions & Answers. rev. ed. 1984. pap. 1.80 (*0-88450-051-9*, 6109) Lawyers & Judges.

Lawyers Alliance for N. Y. Staff. Getting Organized: Incorporation & Tax Exemption for Non-Profit Organizations in New York. 336p. 1989. 70.00 (*0-918825-89-X*) Moyer Bell.

Lawyer's Association of G. D. R. Staff. Law & Legislation in the German Democratic Republic, 1959-1989, 11 vols., Set. 1982. reprint ed. lib. bdg. 649.00 (*0-89941-281-5*, 108410) W S Hein.

Lawyers Club of San Francisco. When Disaster Strikes: How to Handle Law Office Emergencies. 41p. 1988. pap. 16.95 (*0-89707-321-5*, 511-0245) Amer Bar Assn.

Lawyers Co-Operative Publishing Company Staff. ALR Medical Malpractice, 12 vols. LC 70-1405. 1987. 824.00 (*0-686-14517-8*) Lawyers Cooperative.

— ALR Medical Malpractice, 12 vols. suppl. ed. LC 70-1405. 1993. Suppl. 1993. 75.00 (*0-317-03150-3*) Lawyers Cooperative.

— Decisions of the United States Supreme Court: 1963-64, 1964-65, 1965-66, 1966-67, 1967-68, 1968-69, 1969-70, 1970-71, 1971-72, 1972-73, 1973-74, 1974-75, 1975-76, 1976-77, 1977-78, 1978-79, 1979-80, 1980-81, 1981-82, 1982-83, 1983-84, 1984-85, 1985-86, 1986-87, 1987-88, 1988-89, 1989-90, 1990-91, 29 vols. 1,100.00 (*0-317-00149-3*) Lawyers Cooperative.

— Decisions of the United States Supreme Court: 1963-64, 1964-65, 1965-66, 1966-67, 1967-68, 1968-69, 1969-70, 1970-71, 1971-72, 1972-73, 1973-74, 1974-75, 1975-76, 1976-77, 1977-78, 1978-79, 1979-80, 1980-81, 1981-82, 1982-83, 1983-84, 1984-85, 1985-86, 1986-87, 1987-88, 1988-89, 1989-90, 1990-91, 29 vols., Set. 1,426.50 (*0-317-00147-7*) Lawyers Cooperative.

Lawyers Co-operative Publishing Staff. Georgia Code Research Guide. 1988. 85.00 (*0-318-43159-9*) Lawyers Cooperative.

— Georgia Code Research Guide. suppl. ed. 1991. Suppl. 1991. 32.50 (*0-317-03345-X*) Lawyers Cooperative.

— Louisiana Code Research Guide. 1988. write for info. (*0-318-43161-0*) Lawyers Cooperative.

— Michigan Research Guide, 2 vols. 1991. 87.50 (*0-318-43162-9*) Lawyers Cooperative.

— Michigan Research Guide, 2 vols. suppl. ed. 1993. Suppl. 1993. 40.00 (*0-317-03347-6*) Lawyers Cooperative.

Lawyers Co-Operative Publishing Staff & Bancroft-Whitney Company. ALR Index: Covering ALR 2d, ALR3d, ALR 4th, ALR Fed. suppl. ed. 1993. Suppl. 1993. write for info. (*0-318-62121-5*) Lawyers Cooperative.

Lawyers Committee for Human Rights. Critique: Review of the U. S. Department of State's Country Reports on Human Rights Practices for 1991. Armstrong, Patricia, ed. 460p. (Orig.). 1992. pap. text ed. 19.95 (*0-934143-55-2*) Lawyers Comm Human.

— In Defense of Rights: Attacks on Judges & Lawyers in 1991. Masih, Jeneen, ed. (Illus.). 200p. (Orig.). 1992. pap. text ed. 19.95 (*0-934143-50-1*, U of Pa Pr) Lawyers Comm Human.

— Liberia: A Promise Betrayed. 1986. pap. 10.00 (*0-934143-13-7*) Lawyers Comm Human.

— Seeking Shelter: Cambodian Refugees in Thailand. (Orig.). 1986. pap. 7.00 (*0-934143-14-5*) Lawyers Comm Human.

— Sixteen Unresolved Cases: El Salvador. (Orig.). pap. 8.00 (*0-934143-12-9*) Lawyers Comm Human.

— The War Against Children: South Africa's Youngest Victims. 94p. (Orig.). 1986. pap. 10.00 (*0-934143-00-5*) Lawyers Comm Human.

Lawyers Committee for Human Rights, jt. auth. see Americas Watch Staff.

Lawyers Committee for Human Rights, jt. auth. see Helsinki Watch Staff.

Lawyers Committee for Human Rights & the Washington Office on Latin America Staff, jt. auth. see Americas Watch Staff.

Lawyers Committee for Human Rights Staff. Abandoning the Victims: The U.N. Advisory Service Program in Guatemala. 101p. 1990. lib. bdg. 8.00 (*0-934143-31-5*); pap. text ed. 10.00 (*0-685-37748-2*) Lawyers Comm Human.

— A Childhood Abducted: Children Cutting Sugar Cane in the Dominican Republic. 110p. (Orig.). 1991. pap. 10.00 (*0-934143-42-0*) Lawyers Comm Human.

— Cleaning the Face of Morocco: Human Rights Abuses & Recent Developments. 51p. 1990. pap. 8.00 (*0-934143-36-6*) Lawyers Comm Human.

— Critique: Review of the Department of State's Country Reports on Human Rights Practice for 1989. 267p. 1990. pap. text ed. 15.00 (*0-934143-34-X*) Lawyers Comm Human.

— Critique: Review of the Department of State's Country Reports on Human Rights Practice for 1989. 335p. 1991. pap. 15.00 (*0-934143-43-9*) Lawyers Comm Human.

— Human Rights & U. S. Foreign Policy Reports & Recommendations, 1992. 86p. (Orig.). 1992. pap. 10.00 (*0-934143-51-X*) Lawyers Comm Human.

— Impunity: Prosecutions of Human Rights Violations in the Philippines. 175p. 1991. pap. 12.00 (*0-934143-44-7*) Lawyers Comm Human.

— In Defense of Rights: Attacks on Judges & Lawyers in 1992. (Illus.). 210p. (Orig.). 1993. pap. text ed. 19.95 (*0-934143-61-7*, U of Pa Pr) Lawyers Comm Human.

— In Defense of Rights: Attacks on Lawyers & Judges in 1989. 118p. 1990. lib. bdg. 8.00 (*0-934143-33-1*); pap. text ed. 10.00 (*0-685-37745-8*) Lawyers Comm Human.

— In Defense of Rights: Attacks on Lawyers & Judges in 1990. 174p. (Orig.). 1991. pap. 12.00 (*0-934143-40-4*) Lawyers Comm Human.

— Kampuchea: After the Worst. 161p. 1990. reprint ed. 10.00 (*0-934143-29-3*); reprint ed. lib. bdg. 8.00 (*0-685-37743-1*); reprint ed. pap. 10.00 (*0-685-37744-X*) Lawyers Comm Human.

— Kuwait Building the Rule of Law. 53p. (Orig.). 1992. pap. 10.00 (*0-934143-49-8*) Lawyers Comm Human.

— Out of Control: Militia Abuses in the Philippines. 149p. (Orig.). 1990. pap. 8.00 (*0-934143-37-4*) Lawyers Comm Human.
— Refugee Refoulement: The Forced Return of Haitians under the U. S. - Haitian Interdiction Agreement. 64p. 1990. lib. bdg. 8.00 (*0-934143-30-7*); pap. 10.00 (*0-685-37746-6*); pap. text ed. 10.00 (*0-685-37747-4*) Lawyers Comm Human.
— Summary Injustice: Military Tribunals in Burma. 63p. (Orig.). 1991. pap. 10.00 (*0-934143-41-2*) Lawyers Comm Human.
— Uncertain Haven: Refugee Protection on the 40th Anniversary of the 1951 United Nations Refugee Convention. 243p. (Orig.). 1991. pap. 12.00 (*0-934143-45-5*) Lawyers Comm Human.
— The UNHCR at Forty: Refugee Protection at the Crossroads. 156p. (Orig.). 1991. pap. 12.00 (*0-934143-39-0*) Lawyers Comm Human.
— Zaire: Repression as Policy. 230p. 1990. pap. text ed. 12.00 (*0-934143-35-8*) Lawyers Comm Human.
Lawyers Committee for Human Rights Staff & O'Neill, William G. Paper Laws Steel Bayonets: Breakdown of the Rule of Law in Haiti. 215p. (Orig.). 1990. pap. 12.00 (*0-934143-38-2*) Lawyers Comm Human.
Lawyers Committee for Human Rights Staff, ed. see Biel, Eric & Walter, Sheryl L.
Lawyers Committee for Human Rights Staff, jt. auth. see Human Rights Watch Staff.
Lawyers Committee for Human Rights Staff, ed. see Turnbull, Bruce H. & Naftalin, Ethan S.
Lawyers Committee for Human Rights Staff, et al. Human Rights & U. S. Foreign Policy: Report & Recommendations. Waldman, Roger et al, eds. 70p. (Orig.). 1988. 5.00 (*0-934143-18-8*) Lawyers Comm Human.
Lawyers Committee for International Human Rights, ed. see Americas Watch Committee (U. S.).
Lawyers Cooperative Publishing Editorial Staff, ed. Federal Rules of Evidence: Annotations from the ALR System. LC 90-63684. (Critical Issues Ser.). 1990. 90.00 (*0-317-03034-5*) Lawyers Cooperative.
— Trademarks: Annotations from the ALR System. LC 90-63738. (Critical Issues Ser.). 1991. ring bd. 105.00 (*0-317-03033-7*) Lawyers Cooperative.
Lawyers Cooperative Publishing Staff. Americans with Disabilities Decisions. 1993. 370.00 (*0-317-05365-5*) Lawyers Cooperative.
— Employee Dismissal - Critical Issues & Proofs, 3 vols., Set. 1993. ring bd. 300.00 (*0-317-05361-2*) Lawyers Cooperative.
— Florida Uniform Commercial Code, 4 vols., Set. 1992. ring bd. 290.00 (*0-317-05368-X*) Lawyers Cooperative.
— Handling Sexual Harassment Cases: Practice Guide. 1993. ring bd. 105.00 (*0-317-05380-9*) Lawyers Cooperative.
— Hedonic Damages: Critical Issues & Proofs Regarding Damages for Loss of Enjoyment of Life, 2 vols., Set. 1992. ring bd. 150.00 (*0-317-05362-0*) Lawyers Cooperative.
— New York Litigation Checklists, 2 vols., Set. 1992. ring bd. 150.00 (*0-317-05372-8*) Lawyers Cooperative.
— New York Uniform Commercial Code, 4 vols., Set. 1993. ring bd. 290.00 (*0-317-05379-5*) Lawyers Cooperative.
— Ohio Uniform Commercial Code, 4 vols., Set. 1992. ring bd. 290.00 (*0-317-05369-8*) Lawyers Cooperative.
— Pre-Natal Injuries & Wrongful Life: Practice Guide. 1993. ring bd. 105.00 (*0-317-05381-7*) Lawyers Cooperative.
— United States District Court for the Northern District of Ohio Rules. 1993. ring bd. 39.50 (*0-317-05383-3*) Lawyers Cooperative.
Lawyer's Cooperative Publishing Staff, ed. Age Discrimination: Critical Issues & Proofs. 1992. ring bd. 105.00 (*0-317-05359-0*) Lawyers Cooperative.
— Age Discrimination: Critical Issues & Proofs. suppl. ed. 1993. Suppl. 1993. 40.00 (*0-317-05707-3*) Lawyers Cooperative.
Lawyers Cooperative Staff. Federal Trial Handbook. 3rd ed. LC 84-81649. 1993. 175.00 (*0-318-04258-4*) Lawyers Cooperative.
Lax, Anneli. Modern Algebra & Discrete Structures. (C). 1990. pap. text ed. 66.50 (*0-06-043878-9*) HarpCollege.
Lax, David A. & Sebenius, James K. The Manager As Negotiator: Bargaining for Cooperation & Competitive Gain. 304p. 1987. 32.95 (*0-02-918770-2*) Free Pr.
Lax, Edward S. Summit: Treaty of Peace. 90p. (C). 1988. lib. bdg. 30.00 (*0-9620530-0-7*) Hist Bks Ltd.
Lax, Eric. Woody Allen. 1991. 23.50 (*0-394-58349-3*) Knopf.
— Woody Allen: A Biography. 1992. pap. 13.00 (*0-679-73847-9*, Vin) Random.
Lax, Howard L. Political Risk in the International Oil & Gas Industry. LC 82-83329. (Illus.). 195p. 1983. lib. bdg. 36.00 (*0-934634-20-3*) Intl Human Res.
— States & Companies: Political Risks in the International Oil Industry. LC 88-15227. (Illus.). 209p. 1988. text ed. 55.00 (*0-275-93074-2*, C3074, Praeger Pubs) Greenwood.
Lax, M., et al, eds. Frontiers in Condensed Matter Theory: Proceedings of a U. S. - U. S. S. R. Conference Held in New York City, December 4-8 1989. (Conference Proceeding Ser.: No. 213). 220p. 1990. 70.00 (*0-88318-771-X*); pap. 30.00 (*0-88318-772-8*) Am Inst Physics.
Lax, Marc D. Selected Strategic Minerals: The Impending Crisis. 356p. (C). 1991. lib. bdg. 51.00 (*0-8191-8300-8*) U Pr of Amer.
Lax, Michael J., ed. The Inaugural Addresses of the Presidents of the United States, 1789 to 1985. 192p. 1985. 24.95 (*0-932037-00-3*) Am Inheritance Pr.
— The Inaugural Addresses of the Presidents of the United States, 1789 to 1985. 192p. 1985. 29.95 (*0-685-09756-0*) Am Inheritance Pr.
— The Inaugural Addresses of the Presidents of the United States, 1789 to 1985. deluxe limited ed. 192p. 1985. 115.00 (*0-685-09757-9*) Am Inheritance Pr.
Lax, P. D. Hyperbolic Systems of Conservation Laws & the Mathematical Theory of Shock Waves. (CBMS-NSF Regional Conference Ser.: No. 11). v, 48p. 1973. reprint ed. pap. text ed. 14.50 (*0-89871-177-0*) Soc Indus-Appl Math.
Lax, Peter D., ed. Mathematical Aspects of Production & Distribution of Energy. LC 77-7174. (Proceedings of Symposia in Applied Mathematics Ser.: No. 21). 137p. 1979. reprint ed. pap. 26.00 (*0-8218-0121-X*, PSAPM-21) Am Math.
Lax, Peter D. & Phillips, Ralph S. Scattering Theory for Automorphic Functions. LC 76-3028. (Annals of Mathematics Studies: No. 87). 260p. 1976. 49.50x (*0-691-08179-4*) Princeton U Pr.
Lax, Peter D. & Phillips, Ralph S., eds. Scattering Theory. rev. ed. (Pure & Applied Mathematics Ser.: Vol. 26). 309p. 1990. text ed. 73.00 (*0-12-440051-5*) Acad Pr.
Lax, Peter D., jt. auth. see Glimm, James.
Lax, Peter D., et al. Calculus with Applications & Computing, Vol. 1. (Illus.). 600p. 1983. 51.00 (*0-387-90179-5*) Spr-Verlag.
Lax, Robert. Thirty-Three Poems. Kellein, Thomas, ed. 203p. 1988. pap. 12.95 (*0-8112-1085-5*) New Directions.
Lax, Robert, jt. auth. see Merton, Thomas.
Lax, Roger & Smith, Frederick. The Great Song Thesaurus. 2nd enl. rev. ed. 792p. 1989. 85.00 (*0-19-505408-3*) OUP.
Lax, Ruth F., ed. Essential Papers on Character Neurosis & Treatment. (Essential Papers in Psychoanalysis). 384p. 1989. 75.00x (*0-8147-5041-9*); pap. 25.00 (*0-8147-5042-7*) NYU Pr.
Lax, Ruth F., et al, eds. Rapprochment: The Critical Subphase of Separation-Individuation. LC 80-66351. 528p. 1994. pap. 40.00x (*1-56821-103-1*) Aronson.
— Self & Object Constancy: Clinical & Theoretical Perspectives. LC 85-27365. (Guilford Psychiatry Ser.). 355p. 1985. lib. bdg. 45.00 (*0-89862-226-3*) Guilford Pr.
Laxalt, Robert. The Basque Hotel. LC 89-4953. (Basque Ser.). 136p. 1993. pap. 15.00 (*0-87417-216-0*) U of Nev Pr.
— Child of the Holy Ghost. LC 92-7216. (Basque Ser.). 168p. (C). 1992. 20.00 (*0-87417-196-2*) U of Nev Pr.
— Cup of Tea in Pamplona. LC 85-16371. (Basque Ser.). (Illus.). 96p. (C). 1993. pap. 12.00 (*0-87417-192-X*) U of Nev Pr.
— The Governor's Mansion. LC 94-4858. (Basque Book Ser.). 240p. 1994. 23.00 (*0-87417-251-9*) U of Nev Pr.
— In a Hundred Graves: A Basque Portrait. LC 72-86404. (Basque Ser.). 156p. 1972. 16.95 (*0-87417-035-4*) U of Nev Pr.
— A Lean Year: And Other Stories. LC 93-33529. (Western Literature Ser.). 208p. 1994. 21.00 (*0-87417-241-1*) U of Nev Pr.
— A Man in the Wheatfield. LC 87-10774. 192p. 1987. reprint ed. 18.00 (*0-87417-130-X*) U of Nev Pr.
— Nevada: A Bicentennial History. LC 91-31281. (Illus.). 164p. 1991. reprint ed. pap. 14.95 (*0-87417-179-2*) U of Nev Pr.
— Sweet Promised Land. limited ed. (Basque Ser.). (Illus.). 200p. 1986. 125.00 (*0-87417-118-0*) U of Nev Pr.
— Sweet Promised Land. (Basque Ser.). (Illus.). 200p. 1986. reprint ed. 18.95 (*0-87417-114-8*) U of Nev Pr.
— Sweet Promised Land. (Basque Ser.). (Illus.). 200p. 1988. reprint ed. pap. 11.95 (*0-87417-137-7*) U of Nev Pr.
Laxer, Mark E. Take Me for a Ride: Coming of Age in a Destructive Cult. 200p. 1993. pap. 14.00 (*0-9638108-3-9*) Outer Rim Pr.
Laxmanan, V., et al, eds. Materials Processing in Space. (Materials Science Forum Ser.). 450p. 1989. text ed. 88.00 (*0-87849-592-4*, Pub. by Trans Tech GW) LPS Dist Ctr.
Laxness, Halldor. Atom Station. 1976. 18.95 (*0-8488-0177-6*) Amereon Ltd.
— The Atom Station. LC 81-85725. 206p. (C). 1982. reprint ed. pap. 16.95 (*0-933256-31-0*) Second Chance.
Laxson, Ruth. HO Plus GO (Squared) Equals It. 1986. 30.00 (*0-932526-10-1*) Nexus Pr.
Lay, jt. auth. see Bartlett.
Lay, Arthur H. Brief Sketch of the History of Political Parties in Japan. Bd. with Political Ideas of Modern Japan: An Interpretation Studies in Japanese Law & Government. LC 78-78387. 461p. 1979. reprint ed. Set text ed. 65.00 (*0-313-26997-1*, U6997, Greenwood Pr) Greenwood.
Lay, Artie K. & Runnels, Gayle S. Amigo, the Friendly Gray Whale. LC 91-65227. (Blubber Buddy Adventure Ser.). (Illus.). 140p. (J). (gr. 2-6). 1991. audio 24.95 (*0-9628626-0-6*) Blubber Budd.
Lay, Beirne, Jr. & Bartlett, Sy. Twelve O'Clock High! Gilbert, James B., ed. LC 79-7278. (Flight: Its First Seventy-Five Years Ser.). (Illus.). 1980. reprint ed. lib. bdg. 25.95 (*0-405-12187-3*) Ayer.
Lay, Benjamin. All Slave-Keepers That Keep the Innocent in Bondage, Apostates Pretending to Lay Claim to the Pure & Holy Christian Religion. LC 72-82203. (Anti-Slavery Crusade in America Ser.). 1970. reprint ed. 15.95 (*0-405-00642-X*) Ayer.
*__Lay, Carol & Brown, M. K.__ Twisted Sisters Vol. 2: Drawing the Line. Noomin, Diane & Amara, Phil, eds. (Illus.). 176p. 1995. write for info. (*0-87816-344-1*); write for info. (*0-87816-345-X*) Kitchen Sink.
*__Lay, Carol, et al.__ Twisted Sisters Vol. 2: Drawing the Line. Noomin, Diane & Amara, Phil, eds. (Illus.). 176p. 1995. pap. 15.95 (*0-87816-339-5*) Kitchen Sink.
Lay Commission on Catholic Social Teaching & the U. S. Economy. Toward the Future: Catholic Social Thought & the U. S. Economy, a Lay Letter. 120p. 1985. reprint ed. pap. text ed. 15.00 (*0-8191-4860-1*) U Pr of Amer.
Lay, Daniel W., jt. auth. see Truett, Joe C.
Lay, David C. Getting Your Job in the Middle East. 200p. 1992. pap. 19.95 (*0-9631540-0-1*) DCL Pub.
— Linear Algebra & Its Applications. (Illus.). 592p. (C). 1994. text ed. 60.25 (*0-201-52031-1*) Addison-Wesley.
*__Lay, David C. & Leerburger, Benedict A.__ Jobs Worldwide. 200p. (Orig.). 1995. pap. 15.95 (*1-57023-019-6*) Impact VA.
Lay, David C., jt. auth. see Taylor, Angus E.
Lay-Dopyera, Margaret. Becoming a Teacher of Young Children. 3rd ed. 416p. (C). 1989. text ed. 31.95 (*0-07-555547-6*) McGraw.
Lay-Dopyera, Margaret & Dopyera, John. Becoming a Teacher of Young Children. 4th ed. 1990. teacher ed 10.95 (*0-07-036776-0*); text ed. write for info. (*0-07-036775-2*) McGraw.
— Becoming a Teacher of Young Children. 5th ed. LC 92-14951. 1992. text ed. write for info. (*0-07-036777-9*) McGraw.
Lay, Eldonna, ed. see Schorsch, Harry.
Lay, Graeme. Motu Tapu: Short Stories of the South Pacific. 172p. (C). 1990. pap. text ed. 19.95 (*0-908597-06-1*, Pub. by Polynesian Pr) UH Pr.
Lay, J. E., ed. see Midwestern Mechanics Conference Staff.
Lay, Joachim E. Statistical Mechanics & Thermodynamics. 672p. (C). 1990. text ed. 76.00 (*0-06-043884-3*) HarpCollege.
Lay, K. W., ed. see AIME, Metallurgical Society Staff.
Lay, Kathryn. The Sports-a-Thon. 18p. (J). (ps-2). 1993. 10.95 (*1-879680-17-3*) About You.
Lay, Kathryn & Peck, Jan. The First Christmas. 18p. (J). (ps-2). 1992. 10.95 (*1-879680-13-0*) About You.
Lay, M. G. Handbook of Road Technology, 1. (Transportation Studies: Vol. 8). 712p. 1986. text ed. 90.00 (*2-88124-159-X*) Gordon & Breach.
— Handbook of Road Technology, 2. (Transportation Studies: Vol. 8). 712p. 1986. text ed. 90.00 (*2-88124-160-3*) Gordon & Breach.
— Handbook of Road Technology, 2 vols., Set. (Transportation Studies: Vol. 8). 712p. 1986. text ed. 145.00 (*2-88124-161-1*) Gordon & Breach.
Lay, Ma M. Not Out of Hate: A Novel of Burma. Frederick, William, ed. Aung-Thwin, Margaret, tr. LC 90-28553. (Monographs in International Studies, Southeast Asia Ser.: No. 88). 260p. (Orig.). 1991. pap. text ed. 20.00 (*0-89680-167-5*) Ohio U Pr.
Lay, Marilyn, ed. see International Oil Scouts.
*__Lay, Mary M.__ Technical Communication. LC 94-29205. 784p. (C). 1994. 49.95 (*0-256-11985-6*) Irwin.
Lay, Mary M. & Karis, William M., eds. Collaborative Writing in Industry: Investigations in Theory & Practice. (Technical Communications Ser.). 284p. 1991. text ed. 29.95 (*0-89503-071-3*); pap. text ed. 22.50 (*0-89503-070-5*) Baywood Pub.
Lay, Maxwell G. Ways of the World: A History of the World's Roads & of the Vehicles That Used Them. LC 91-23148. (Illus.). 500p. (C). 1992. text ed. 50.00 (*0-8135-1758-3*) Rutgers U Pr.
Lay, Nancy. Making the Most of English: An Intermediate Reading-Writing Text for ESL Students. (C). 1983. pap. text ed. 19.50 (*0-03-058283-0*) HB Coll Pubs.
— No Film in the Camera. (Orig.). 1992. pap. 8.00 (*0-912449-21-7*) Floating Island.
Lay, Nancy D. Say It in Chinese. (Say It Ser.). (Orig.). 1980. pap. 3.50 (*0-486-23325-1*) Dover.
Lay, Peter W. Zyzyskqa's War & Other Stories. 69p. (Orig.). 1992. pap. 6.75 (*971-10-0491-7*, Pub. by New Day Pub PH) Cellar.
Lay, Richard, ed. see Schorsch, Harry.
Lay, Richard A. Measuring the Metric Way. (Illus.). 76p. 1975. pap. text ed. 2.50 (*0-88323-123-9*, 211) Pendergrass Pub.
Lay, Robert S. & Endo, Jean J., eds. Designing & Using Market Research. LC 85-645339. (New Directions for Institutional Research Ser.: No. IR 54). 1987. 16.95 (*1-55542-965-3*) Jossey-Bass.
*__Lay, Shawn.__ Hooded Knights on the Niagara: The Ku Klux Klan in Buffalo, New York. LC 95-4285. 1995. write for info. (*0-8147-5092-3*) NYU Pr.
— Hooded Knights on the Niagara: The Ku Klux Klan in Buffalo, New York. 208p. 1995. 45.00 (*0-8147-5101-6*); pap. 15.95 (*0-8147-5102-4*) NYU Pr.
— War, Revolution & the Ku Klux Klan: A Study of Intolerance in a Border City. LC 85-90937. 224p. 1985. 20.00 (*0-87404-094-9*) Tex Western.
Lay, Shawn, ed. The Invisible Empire in the West: Toward a New Historical Appraisal of the Ku Klux Klan of the 1920s. (Illus.). 240p. 1992. 32.50 (*0-252-01832-X*) U of Ill Pr.
Lay, Steven R. Analysis with an Introduction to Proof. 2nd ed. 304p. (C). 1990. Casebound. text ed. write for info. (*0-13-033267-4*) P-H.
— Convex Sets & Their Applications. rev. ed. LC 90-49488. 262p. (C). 1992. reprint ed. 49.95 (*0-89464-537-4*) Krieger.
*__Lay, Thorne & Wallace, Terry C.__ Modern Global Seismology. (International Geophysics Ser.: Vol. 58). (Illus.). 498p. 1995. text ed. 54.95 (*0-12-732870-X*) Acad Pr.
Layachi, Azzedine. The United States & North Africa: A Cognitive Approach to Foreign Policy. LC 89-22962. 217p. 1990. text ed. 55.00 (*0-275-93365-2*, C3365, Greenwood Pr) Greenwood.
Layachi, Larbi. The Jealous Lover. 140p. (Orig.). 1986. 13.95 (*0-939180-41-3*); pap. 7.50 (*0-939180-30-8*) Tombouctou.
— Yesterday & Today. LC 85-3912. 189p. (Orig.). 1985. 14.00 (*0-87685-632-6*); pap. 8.50 (*0-87685-631-8*) Black Sparrow.
— Yesterday & Today, signed ed. deluxe ed. LC 85-3912. 189p. (Orig.). 1985. 25.00 (*0-87685-633-4*) Black Sparrow.
Layamon. Layamon's Brut: Selections. (BCL1-PR English Literature Ser.). 150p. 1992. reprint ed. lib. bdg. 69.00 (*0-7812-7184-3*) Rprt Serv.
— Layamons Brut, or Chronicle of Britain, 3 Vols, 1. Madden, Frederic, tr. LC 72-137262. reprint ed. 65.00 (*0-404-03911-1*) AMS Pr.
— Layamons Brut, or Chronicle of Britain, 3 Vols, 2. Madden, Frederic, tr. LC 72-137262. reprint ed. 65.00 (*0-404-03912-X*) AMS Pr.
— Layamons Brut, or Chronicle of Britain, 3 Vols, 3. Madden, Frederic, tr. LC 72-137262. reprint ed. 65.00 (*0-404-03913-8*) AMS Pr.
— Layamons Brut, or Chronicle of Britain, 3 Vols, Set. Madden, Frederic, tr. LC 72-137262. reprint ed. 195.00 (*0-404-03910-3*) AMS Pr.
Layard, G. S., jt. auth. see Spielmann, M. H.
Layard, Henry, ed. Despatches of Michele Suriand & Marc'Antonio Barbaro, Venetian Ambassadors at the Court of France, 1560-1563. Bd. with Registers of the French Conformed Churches of St. Patrick & St. Mary, Dublin. (Huguenot Society of London Publications Ser.: Vol. 6 & 7). 1972. reprint ed. (*0-8115-1645-8*) Periodicals Srv.
Layard, John. A Celtic Quest: Sexuality & Soul in Individuation. LC 87-34569. (Seminar Ser.: No. 10). (Illus.). 264p. (Orig.). 1975. reprint ed. pap. 17.00 (*0-88214-110-4*) Spring Pubns.
Layard, John W. The Lady of the Hare, Being a Study in the Healing Power of Dreams. LC 75-35133. reprint ed. 29.00 (*0-404-14149-8*) AMS Pr.
Layard, P., jt. ed. see Ashenfelter, Orley C.
Layard, Richard. How to Beat Unemployment. (Illus.). 192p. 1986. 32.50 (*0-19-877265-3*) OUP.
Layard, Richard & Calmfors, Lars, eds. The Fight Against Unemployment: Macroeconomic Analysis from the Centre for European Policy Studies. (CEPS Annual Ser.: No. 2). 240p. 1987. 32.50 (*0-262-12122-0*) MIT Pr.
Layard, Richard & Glaister, Stephen, eds. Cost Benefit Analysis. LC 93-37740. (Illus.). 500p. (C). 1994. pap. 22.95 (*0-521-46674-1*) Cambridge U Pr.
— Cost Benefit Analysis. 2nd ed. LC 93-37740. (Illus.). 500p. (C). 1994. 59.95 (*0-521-46128-6*) Cambridge U Pr.
Layard, Richard, jt. ed. see Aslund, Anders.
Layard, Richard, jt. ed. see Dornbusch, Rudiger.
Layard, Richard, et al. East - West Migration: The Alternatives. 104p. 1994. pap. 11.00x (*0-262-62092-8*) MIT Pr.
— East-West Migration: The Alternatives. (Illus.). 76p. 1992. 21.00 (*0-262-12168-9*) MIT Pr.
— Microeconomic Theory. (Illus.). 1978. text ed. write for info. (*0-07-036786-8*) McGraw.
— Unemployment: Macroeconomic Performance & the Labour Market. Jackman, Richard, ed. (Illus.). 640p. 1991. pap. text ed. 32.50 (*0-19-828434-9*) OUP.
— The Unemployment Crisis. 160p. 1994. 29.95 (*0-19-877395-1*); pap. 13.95 (*0-19-877394-3*) OUP.
Layard, Richard, et al, eds. Britain's Training Deficit: A Centre for Economic Performance Report. 352p. 1994. 59.95 (*1-85628-878-1*, Pub. by Avebury Pub UK) Ashgate Pub Co.
Laybourn, Carole A., jt. auth. see Laybourn, Richard T.
Laybourn, Keith. Britain on the Breadline: A Social & Political History of Britain Between the Wars. (Illus.). 240p. (C). 1990. 35.00 (*0-86299-490-X*) A Sutton Pub.
— British Trade Unionism, 1770-1990: A Reader in History. (C). 1991. pap. text ed. 15.00 (*0-86299-784-4*) A Sutton Pub.
— The General Strike of 1926. LC 93-28180. (New Frontiers in History Ser.). 1993. text ed. 49.95 (*0-7190-3864-2*, Pub. by Manchester Univ Pr UK) St Martin.
— The General Strike of 1926. LC 93-28180. (New Frontiers in History Ser.). 1993. text ed. 16.93 (*0-7190-3865-0*, Pub. by Manchester Univ Pr UK) St Martin.
— The Guild of Help & the Changing Face of Edwardian Philanthropy: The Guild of Help, Voluntary Work & the State, 1904-1919. LC 93-51035. 236p. 1994. text ed. 89.95 (*0-7734-9144-9*) E Mellen.
— The History of British Trade Unionism c. 1770-1990. (Illus.). 256p. 1992. 48.00 (*0-86299-785-2*) A Sutton Pub.
— Philip Snowden: A Biography. 150p. 1988. text ed. 57.95 (*0-566-07017-0*, Pub. by Dartmth Pub UK) Ashgate Pub Co.
— Rise of Labour: The British Labour Party 1890-1979. 192p. 1991. 34.95 (*0-7131-6600-2*, A3045, Pub. by E Arnold UK) Routledge Chapman & Hall.
Laybourn-Parry, Johanna. A Functional Biology of Free-Living Protozoa. LC 84-2569. (Functional Biology Ser.). (Illus.). 224p. 1978. 45.00 (*0-520-05339-7*); pap. 28.00 (*0-520-05340-0*) U CA Pr.
— Protozoan Plankton Ecology. (Illus.). 248p. (C). 1992. text ed. 99.00 (*0-412-34440-8*, A3306) Chapman & Hall.
*__Laybourn, Richard T. & Laybourn, Carole A.__ The Original Gourmet Doggie Treat Cook Book. (Illus.). 32p. 1994. pap. 9.95 (*0-9645100-7-3*) Vis Impct.
— The Original Gourmet Doggie Treat Cook Book: With Bone Shaped Cookie Cutter. 32p. 1994. pap. 10.95 (*0-9645100-5-7*) Vis Impct.
Laybourne, Gerry B., jt. auth. see Gaffney, Maureen.
Laybourne, Kit. The Animation Book. 1988. pap. 20.00 (*0-517-52946-7*, Crown) Crown Pub Group.
Laycock. Supplement Modern America '89. 1989. 9.95 (*0-316-51757-7*) Little.
— Supplement Modern America '91. 1991. 12.95 (*0-316-51761-5*) Little.

An Asterisk (*) at the beginning of an entry indicates that the title is appearing in BIP for the first time.

Laycock, David. Populism & Democratic Thought in the Canadian Prairies, 1910-1945. (State & Economic Life Ser.). 369p. 1990. 45.00 (0-8020-2637-0); pap. 19.95 (0-8020-6681-X) U of Toronto Pr.

Laycock, Don, tr. see Beier, Ulli, ed.

Laycock, Donald C. The Complete Enochian Dictionary: A Dictionary of the Angelic Language As Revealed to John Dee & Edward Kelley. (Illus.). 272p. (Orig.). 1994. pap. 16.95 (0-87728-817-8) Weiser.

Laycock, Douglas. The Death of the Irreparable Injury Rule. 382p. 1991. 48.00 (0-19-506356-2) OUP.

— Modern American Remedies: Cases & Materials. LC 84-82267. (C). 1985. 46.00 (0-316-51749-6) Little.

Laycock, Frank. Gifted Children. (C). 1979. pap. text ed. 14.25 (0-673-15142-5) HarpCollege.

Laycock, George. Birdwatcher's Bible. rev. ed. LC 93-32541. 1994. pap. 12.00 (0-385-46835-0) Doubleday.

— Deer Hunter's Bible. LC 85-29215. (Illus.). 176p. 1986. pap. 12.00 (0-385-19985-6, Outdoor Bible) Doubleday.

— John Ruthven, in the Audobon Tradition. (Illus.). 196p. Date not set. text ed. 75.00 (1-882151-01-1) Cinc Mus Nat Hist.

Laycock, Mary. Base Ten Mathematics. (J). (gr. 1-9). 1976. pap. 7.95 (0-918932-03-3) Activity Resources.

— Bucky for Beginners. (Illus.). 64p. (Orig.). (J). (gr. 4-12). 1984. pap. text ed. 7.95 (0-918932-82-3) Activity Resources.

Laycock, Mary & Dominques, Manuel. Discover It! 32p. (Orig.). (J). (gr. 5-10). 1986. pap. 7.50 (0-918932-87-4) Activity Resources.

Laycock, Mary & Johnson, Connie. The Tapestry of Mathematics. (Illus.). 1978. pap. text ed. 18.50 (0-918932-51-3) Activity Resources.

Laycock, Mary & McLean, Peggy. Skateboard Practice: Multiplication & Division. (Illus.). (gr. 3-6). 1979. pap. text ed. 7.95 (0-918932-65-3) Activity Resources.

Laycock, Mary & Schadler, Reuben. Algebra in Concrete. (J). (gr. 6-10). 1973. pap. 7.95 (0-918932-00-9) Activity Resources.

Laycock, Mary & Smaer, Margaret. Hands-on Math for Secondary Teachers. (Illus.). 64p. (Orig.). 1984. pap. 7.95 (0-918932-83-1) Activity Resources.

Laycock, Mary & Smart, Margaret. Solid Sense of Mathematics, 3 vols. (Illus.). 64p. (Orig.). (J). (gr. 4-9). 1981. pap. text ed. 7.95 (0-918932-74-2) Activity Resources.

Laycock, Mary & Watson, Gene. The Fabric of Mathematics: A Resource Book for Teachers. (Illus.). 1975. 18.50 (0-918932-11-4) Activity Resources.

Laycock, Mary, ed. see Brandes, Louis G.

Laycock, Mary, ed. see Bureloff, Morris.

Laycock, Mary, ed. see Bureloff, Morris, et al.

Laycock, Mary, ed. see Jenkins, Lee & McLean, Peggy.

Laycock, Mary, ed. see Jenkins, Lee.

Laycock, Mary, ed. see Lund, Charles.

Laycock, Mary, jt. auth. see Smart, Margaret A.

Laycock, Mary, ed. see Smart, Margaret.

Laycock, Mary, ed. see Stonerod, David.

Laycock, Mary, et al. Geoblocks & Geojackets: Metric Version. 2nd rev. ed. (Illus.). 96p. (Orig.). (J). (gr. 3-10). 1988. pap. 8.95 (0-918932-91-2) Activity Resources.

— Skateboard Practice: Addition & Subtraction. (Illus.). (J). (gr. 1-2). 1978. pap. text ed. 7.95 (0-918932-55-6) Activity Resources.

Laycock, Mike, jt. ed. see Stephenson, John.

Laycock, Steven W. Foundations for a Phenomenological Theology. LC 87-37233. (Problems in Contemporary Philosophy Ser.: Vol. 8). 258p. 1988. lib. bdg. 89.95 (0-88946-335-2) E Mellen.

— Mind As Mirror & the Mirroring of Mind: Buddhist Reflections on Western Phenomenology. LC 93-41539. 337p. (C). 1994. 64.50 (0-7914-1997-5); pap. 21.95 (0-7914-1998-3) State U NY Pr.

Laycock, Steven W. & Hart, James G., eds. Essays in Phenomenological Theology. LC 85-14674. 219p. (C). 1986. 64.50 (0-88706-164-8); pap. 21.95 (0-88706-165-6) State U NY Pr.

Laycock, T., tr. see Prochaska, Georg.

Laycock, Thomas. Mind & Brain: Or, the Correlations of Consciousness & Organization with Their Applications to Philosophy, Zoology, Physiology, Mental Pathology & the Practice of Medicine, 2 vols. in 1. LC 75-16715. (Classics in Psychiatry Ser.). (Illus.). 1976. reprint ed. 75.95 (0-405-07443-3) Ayer.

Laycook, Mary & McLean, Peggy. Weaving Your Way from Arithmetic to Mathematics with Manipulatives. Smart, Margaret, ed. & illus. by. 128p. 1993. pap. text ed. 18.95 (1-882293-00-2) Activity Resources.

***Layden, Joe.** The Great American Baseball Strike. LC 95-14292. (Headliners Ser.). (Illus.). 64p. (J). (gr. 5-8). 1995. 15.90 (1-56294-930-6) Millbrook Pr.

Layden, Joe, jt. auth. see Wood, Ernie.

***Layden, John J.** Through the Eyes of a Poet: A Collection of Philosophical Poems. 70p. (Orig.). (YA). (gr. 9-12). 1995. pap. write for info. (1-57502-028-9) Morris Pub.

Layden, Mary A., et al. Cognitive Theory of Borderline Personality Disorder. 256p. Date not set. write for info. (0-318-71704-2) Allyn.

— Cognitive Therapy of Borderline Personality Disorder. LC 93-16298. (Practitioner Guidebook Ser.). 218p. 1993. 29.95 (0-205-14807-7, Longwood Div) Allyn.

Layder, Derek. New Strategies in Social Research: An Introduction & Guide. LC 92-30551. 1993. 39.95 (0-7456-0880-9); pap. 19.95 (0-7456-0881-7) Blackwell Pubs.

— The Realist Image in Social Science. LC 89-34396. 256p. 1990. text ed. 49.95 (0-312-03532-2) St Martin.

— Understanding Social Theory. 240p. (C). 1994. text ed. 65.00 (0-8039-8448-0); pap. text ed. 19.95 (0-8039-8449-9) Sage.

Layder, Derek & Davidson, Julia O. Methods, Sex & Madness. LC 94-5596. 240p. 1994. 59.95x (0-415-09763-0, B4622); pap. 17.95 (0-415-09764-9, B4626) Routledge.

Laye, Camara. Dramouss. (FRE.). 1991. pap. 8.95 (0-7859-3236-4, 2266040243) Fr & Eur.

— L' Enfant Noir. (FRE.). 1976. pap. 9.95 (0-7859-3219-4, 2266023128) Fr & Eur.

— Le Maitre de la Parole - Kouma Lafolo Kouma. (FRE.). 1980. pap. 11.95 (0-7859-3231-3, 2266033891) Fr & Eur.

— Radiance of the King. (International Ser.). 1989. pap. 12.00 (0-679-72200-9, Vin) Random.

— Le Regard du Roi. (FRE.). 1975. pap. 8.95 (0-7859-3251-8, 2266046705) Fr & Eur.

Laye, Patricia. Miss Blum's Dilemma. 304p. 1994. mass mkt. 3.99 (0-8217-4505-0) Zebra.

— The Perilous Castle. (Orig.). 1981. pap. 1.75 (0-8439-8027-3) Dorchester Pub Co.

— Touch of Venus. 1990. pap. 3.95 (0-8217-3153-X) Zebra.

Layer, Harold A. ZByte High Tech Playing Cards. (Illus.). 32p. 1992. boxed write for info. (1-882569-00-8) ZByte Play Card.

Layers, Ralph, jt. auth. see Grant, Joan M.

Layfer, Lawrence F., et al. Rheumatology Disorders. (Illus.). 208p. 1988. pap. text ed. 42.95 (0-7216-2385-9) Saunders.

Layfield, Eleanor N., jt. auth. see Newman, Gerald.

Layish, Aharon. Divorce in the Libyan Family. (Studies in Near Eastern Civilization: No. 15). 368p. 1991. text ed. 45.00 (0-8147-5053-2) NYU Pr.

— Women & Islamic Law in a Non-Muslim State. 352p. 1975. boxed 34.95x (0-87855-170-0) Transaction Pubs.

***Layland.** LAN Internetworking: Building the Corporate Network for the 90's. 1996. 39.75 (0-201-63360-4) Addison-Wesley.

LaymaBruccoli, Mary, et al. Dictionary of Literary Biography, Vol. 136. 1994. 128.00 (0-8103-5395-4, 007471) Gale.

Layman, C. H., ed. Man of Letters. 1991. text ed. 45.00 (0-7486-0164-3, Pub. by Edinburgh U Pr UK) Col U Pr.

— Man of Letters: The Early Life & Love-Letters of Robert Chambers. (Illus.). 204p. 1993. pap. 16.50 (0-7486-0193-7, Pub. by Edinburgh U Pr UK) Col U Pr.

Layman, C. Stephen. The Shape of the Good: Christian Reflections on the Foundation of Ethics. LC 90-50977. (Library of Religious Philosophy: Vol. 7). (C). 1994. reprint ed. pap. text ed. 12.95 (0-268-01752-2) U of Notre Dame Pr.

Layman, Carol S. Growing up Rich in Vernon, Indiana: A Celebration of American Small-Town Life in the 1940s & '50s. LC 92-80229. (Illus.). 288p. 1992. 19.95 (0-9631855-7-8) Still Waters Pr.

Layman, Dale P. The Medical Language: A Programmed, Body-Systems Approach. LC 93-37629. 513p. 1994. pap. text ed. 32.95 (0-8273-5612-9) Delmar.

Layman, Donald K., ed. Nutrition & Aerobic Exercise. LC 85-26872. (ACS Symposium Ser.: No. 294). 160p. reprint ed. pap. 45.60 (0-7837-1967-1, 2052445) Bks Demand.

Layman, Gary. Touchstone Art Magic. 153p. 1985. pap. 19.95 (0-9616550-0-3) Touch Art Magic.

Layman, George. Military Remington Rolling Block Rifle. 1992. 21.00 (1-879356-12-0) Wolfe Pub Co.

Layman, George & Powers, Jack. Dental Office Planning: Conception to Occupancy. 144p. 1982. 31.95 (0-87814-183-9, D4202) PennWell Bks.

Layman, George, jt. auth. see Powers, Jack.

Layman, Katie. Microsoft Word 5.0 Made Easy: Applications & Procedures. 260p. (C). 1990. pap. text ed. write for info. (0-13-582388-9) P-H.

— Microsoft Word 5.5 Made Easy. 352p. 1991. pap. text ed. 34.60 (0-13-587478-5) P-H.

— WordPerfect for Windows Comprehensive. 1995. pap. text ed. write for info. (0-13-034653-5) P-H.

— WordPerfect for Windows Made Easy: Covers Version 5.2. LC 92-46728. 320p. 1993. pap. text ed. 35.60 (0-13-950981-X) P-H Gen Ref & Trav.

— WordPerfect 5.0 Made Easy: Applications & Procedures. 256p. (C). 1989. pap. text ed. write for info. (0-13-964727-9) P-H.

— WordPerfect 5.1 Made Easy. 320p. (C). 1991. pap. text ed. write for info. (0-13-963125-9) P-H.

— WordPerfect 6.0 Comprehensive Edition. 550p. (C). 1994. pap. text ed. write for info. (0-13-013103-2) P-H.

— WordPerfect 6.0 Made Easy. 320p. (C). 1993. pap. text ed. write for info. (0-13-953829-1) P-H.

Layman, Katie & Hart, Lavaughn. Microsoft Word for Windows 2.0 Made Easy. 352p. (C). 1992. pap. text ed. 24.00 (0-13-952474-6) P-H.

— Microsoft Word 6.0 for Windows. LC 95-12903. 1995. pap. text ed. write for info. (0-13-124868-5) P-H.

Layman, Katie & Hart, LaVaughn. WordPerfect 6.0 for Windows Made Easy. LC 94-12097. 1994. pap. text ed. 37.33 (0-13-142986-8) P-H.

Layman, Katie & Renner, Adrienne G. Learn Apple Writer IIe the Easy Way. 1986. 17.95 (0-13-527060-X) S&S Trade.

Layman, Kim F. Poems for Everyday People. 57p. (Orig.). 1993. pap. 9.95 (0-9639836-0-1) K F Layman.

Layman, Layman A. Feel Terrific! A New Health System Starting with the Common Cold. 220p. (Orig.). 1988. pap. 9.95 (0-9621303-7-0) Volunteer Pr.

Layman, N. Kathryn & Renner, Adrienne G. Word Processing Exercises for Word Processors, Microcomputers, & Electronic Typewriters. 2nd ed. (Illus.). 272p. (C). 1988. pap. text ed. write for info. (0-13-963588-2) P-H.

Layman, Nancy S. Sexual Harassment in American Secondary Schools: A Legal Guide for Administrators, Teachers, & Students. LC 93-11323. 207p. 1993. pap. 18.95 (0-935061-52-5) Contemp Res.

— Sexual Harassment in American Secondary Schools: A Legal Guide for Administrators, Teachers, & Students. 207p. 1994. 50.00 (0-935061-57-6) Contemp Res.

Layman, R. D. To Ascend from a Floating Base: Shipboard Aeronautics & Aviation, 1783-1914. LC 77-89782. (Illus.). 272p. 1979. 35.00 (0-8386-2078-7) Fairleigh Dickinson.

Layman, R. D. & McLaughlin, Stephen. The Hybrid Warship: The Amalgamation of Big Guns & Aircraft. LC 90-62897. (Illus.). 192p. 1991. 42.95 (1-55750-374-5) Naval Inst Pr.

Layman, Richard. Current Issues: Child Abuse, Vol. 1. 122p. 1990. lib. bdg. 45.00 (1-55888-271-5) Omnigraphics Inc.

— Dashiell Hammett: A Descriptive Bibliography. LC 78-53600. (Series in Bibliography). (Illus.). 200p. 1979. 100.00 (0-8229-3394-2) U of Pittsburgh Pr.

— Shadow Man: The Life of Dashiell Hammett. LC 83-16645. 312p. 1984. pap. 7.95 (0-15-681400-5, Harvest Bks) HarBrace.

Layman, Richard, ed. Afterglow & Other Undergraduate Writings of John Dos Passos. (Archive of Literary Documents Ser.). xviii, 277p. 1990. lib. bdg. 125.00 (1-55888-265-0) Omnigraphics Inc.

Layman, Richard, jt. ed. see Bruccoli, Mary.

Layman, Richard, jt. auth. see Bruccoli, Matthew J.

Layman, Richard, jt. ed. see Bruccoli, Matthew J.

Layman, Richard, ed. see Lardner, Ring, Jr.

Layman, Richard P., et al. U. S. - U. K. Integrated Tax Planning: Estates, Gifts, & Trusts. LC 92-11398. 1992. write for info. (1-55871-274-7) Tax Mgmt.

Layman, Sue, jt. auth. see Porter, Gail.

Layman, Teresa & Morgenroth, Barbara. Gingerbread: Things to Make & Bake. (Illus.). 144p. 1992. 29.95 (0-8109-3367-5) Abrams.

Layman, Thomas A., jt. auth. see Dickie, Robert B.

Laymon, Charles M., ed. Interpreter's One-Volume Commentary on the Bible. (Illus.). 1971. 34.95 (0-687-19299-4); 39.95 (0-687-19300-1) Abingdon.

Laymon, Heather & Yasenchack, Mark. Nothing but theworldtheworldtheworld & Family Practice. 44p. (Orig.). 1989. pap. text ed. 30.00 (0-9623107-0-0) Mybrothers Pr.

Laymon, Lynn. Underwater Videographers Handbook. 1992. pap. 19.95 (0-936262-18-4) Amherst Media.

Laymon, Richard. Alarms. 1986. 25.00 (0-929480-72-4) Mark Ziesing.

— Alarms. limited ed. 1986. 60.00 (0-929480-71-6) Mark Ziesing.

— A Good, Secret Place: Short Fiction by Richard Laymon. (Illus.). 224p. 1992. 35.00 (0-9631367-4-7) Deadline Pr.

— Midnight's Lair. LC 92-33850. 1992. 18.95 (0-312-08845-0, Pub. by Thomas Dunne Bks) St Martin.

— Midnight's Lair. 304p. 1994. mass mkt. 4.50 (0-8217-4684-7) Zebra.

— The Quake. 400p. 1995. 22.95 (0-312-13150-X, Pub. by Thomas Dunne Bks) St Martin.

— Savage. 352p. 1993. 21.95 (0-312-10537-1, Pub. by Thomas Dunne Bks) St Martin.

— Stake. 1991. 19.95 (0-312-06016-5) St Martin.

— The Stake. 512p. 1995. mass mkt. 4.99 (0-8217-4897-1) Zebra.

Layne, C. E. ST(P) Caribbean Mathematics, Vol. I. (C). 1987. text ed. 40.00 (0-85950-762-9, Pub. by S Thornes Pubs UK) St Mut.

— ST(P) Caribbean Mathematics, Vol. II. (C). 1987. text ed. 50.00 (0-85950-763-7, Pub. by S Thornes Pubs UK) St Mut.

— ST(P) Caribbean Mathematics, Vol. III. (C). 1988. text ed. 55.00 (0-85950-764-5, Pub. by S Thornes Pubs UK) St Mut.

Layne, C. E. & Lowe, C. Practice Questions - CXC Mathematics General Profic - Paper 11. (C). 1990. text ed. 35.00 (0-7487-0026-9, Pub. by S Thornes Pubs UK) St Mut.

Layne, C. E., jt. auth. see Greer, A.

Layne, Carol, ed. see Reichler, Arny.

Layne, F. B. Lane: Layne - Lain - Lane Genealogy, Being a Compilation of Names & Historical Information of Male Descendants of 16 Branches of the Layne - Lain - Lane Family in the U. S. 336p. 1992. reprint ed. lib. bdg. 62.00 (0-8328-2319-8); reprint ed. pap. 52.00 (0-8328-2320-1) Higginson Bk Co.

— Layne Genealogy. (Illus.). 251p. 1993. reprint ed. lib. bdg. 49.00 (0-8328-2806-8); reprint ed. pap. 39.00 (0-8328-2807-6) Higginson Bk Co.

— Layne Genealogy. (Illus.). 251p. 1993. reprint ed. lib. bdg. 49.00 (0-8328-3693-1); reprint ed. pap. 39.00 (0-8328-3694-X) Higginson Bk Co.

Layne, Gwendolyn, tr. see Banabhatta.

Layne, James N., jt. ed. see Kirkland, Gordon L., Jr.

Layne, Ken. Automotive Engine Performance: Tune-Up, Testing & Service. LC 85-22599. (Illus.). 487p. 1986. pap. text ed. 29.95 (0-471-82992-7); Practice Manual. teacher ed, pap. text ed. 29.95 (0-471-82991-9) P-H.

— Automotive Engine Performance: Tuneup, Testing, & Service. 2nd ed. 1993. write for info. (0-318-69518-9) P-H.

— Automotive Engine Performance, Vol. I: Tuneup, Testing & Service. 2nd ed. 528p. 1992. pap. text ed. 45.00 (0-13-059775-9) P-H.

— Automotive Engine Performance, Vol. II: Tuneup, Testing, & Service, Practice Manual. 2nd ed. 544p. 1992. pap. text ed. 45.00 (0-13-061177-8) P-H.

Layne, Kendall, jt. auth. see McClure, Joy.

Layne, Leah, jt. auth. see Dey, Dena.

Layne, Linda L. Home & Homeland: The Dialogics of Tribal & National Identities in Jordan. LC 93-23878. 158p. 1994. text ed. 29.95 (0-691-09478-0) Princeton U Pr.

Layne, Ron L., jt. auth. see Wall, Allie P.

Layoun, Mary N. Travels of a Genre: The Modern Novel & Ideology. 318p. 1990. text ed. 35.00 (0-691-06834-8) Princeton U Pr.

Layrock, George. An Eye on Nature: A Photographer's Introduction to Familiar Wildlife. (Illus.). 160p. 1986. 19.95 (0-668-06536-2) P-H.

Layson, June, jt. ed. see Abshead-Landsdale, Janet.

Laythorpe, Mark. The Penny Pincher's Profit Portfolio: How to Make Dollars in Cents. (Illus.). 80p. 1981. pap. 19.95 (0-939230-00-3) SNOWCO.

Laytin, Peter. Photography: Creative Camera Control. (Illus.). 128p. 1993. pap. 7.95 (0-240-80135-0, Focal) Buttrwrth-Heinemann.

Laytner, Anson. Arguing with God: A Jewish Tradition. LC 89-28654. 336p. 1990. 27.50 (0-87668-817-2) Aronson.

***Layton.** Gnostic Scriptures: A New Translation with Introduction & Notes. 1995. pap. (0-385-47843-7) Doubleday.

— A True Lady. 1995. mass mkt. 5.99 (0-671-88301-1) PB.

Layton-Anderson, Laurie. The Art of William Alexander & Lowell Speers, Ser. 1. (Illus.). 76p. 1987. pap. text ed. write for info. (1-883576-00-8) Alexander Art.

— The Art of William Alexander & Lowell Speers, Series 2. (Illus.). 80p. 1987. pap. text ed. write for info. (1-883576-01-6) Alexander Art.

***Layton, Arthur.** Maine: Cruising the Coast by Car. (Illus.). 140p. (Orig.). 1994. pap. 9.95 (1-56626-087-6) Country Rds.

— The Navy War. LC 91-77858. (Illus.). 150p. (Orig.). 1992. pap. 14.95 (0-9630646-9-X) Country Rds.

— Relocation Tax Advisor. 34p. 1993. pap. 7.00 (0-9636296-5-4) Hessel Group.

Layton, B. Cooking for One Cookbook. (Illus.). 212p. 1994. 11.95 (1-57166-011-9) Quixote Pr IA.

— Off-to-College Cookbook. (Illus.). 176p. 1994. 5.95 (1-57166-013-5) Quixote Pr IA.

— Super Simple Cooking. (Illus.). 192p. 1994. 5.95 (1-57166-012-7) Quixote Pr IA.

Layton, Barry, ed. see Hurnard, Hannah.

Layton, Bentley. The Gnostic Scriptures: A New Translation with Annotations. LC 85-25234. (Illus.). 800p. 1987. pap. 35.00 (0-385-17447-0) Doubleday.

Layton, Bob. Hercules: Full Circle. 80p. 1988. 6.95 (0-87135-397-0) Marvel Entmnt.

— Hercules: Prince of Power. 96p. 1988. pap. 5.95 (0-87135-365-2) Marvel Entmnt.

***Layton, Boschka.** The Prodigal Sun: Poems, Stories & Drawings. 80p. 1995. 20.00 (0-8095-4578-0) Borgo Pr.

Layton, C. D. Hansen's Improved Ex-Meridian Tables. (C). 1987. 36.00 (0-85174-093-6, Pub. by Brwn Son Ferg) St Mut.

***Layton, C. W.** Dictionary of Nautical Words & Terms. 4th ed. 395p. 1994. text ed. 45.00x (0-85174-618-7) Sheridan.

Layton, Daphne, ed. Integrated Planning for Campus Information Systems. (Library, Information, & Computer Science Ser.: No. 12). (Illus.). 130p. (Orig.). 1989. pap. 13.00 (1-55653-071-4) OCLC Online Comp.

Layton, Daphne N. Philanthropy & Voluntarism: An Annotated Bibliography. LC 87-12032. 308p. 1987. 18.50 (0-87954-198-9) Foundation Ctr.

Layton, David. German Shorthaired Pointers Today. LC 93-39078. (Illus.). 1994. 25.95 (0-87605-181-6) Howell Bk.

— Science for the People: The Origins of the School Science Curriculum in England. 222p. 1974. text ed. 17.00 (0-88202-028-5, Sci Hist) Watson Pub Intl.

— Technology's Challenge to Science Education: Cathedral, Quarry, or Company Store? LC 92-30287. (Developing Science & Technology Education Ser.). 1993. 82.00 (0-335-09959-9, Open Univ Pr); pap. 25.00 (0-335-09958-0, Open Univ Pr) Taylor & Francis.

***Layton, Dian.** Mommy, Why Can't I Watch That TV Show? (Mommy, Why...Ser.). (Illus.). 24p. (Orig.). 1995. pap. 2.99 (1-56043-148-2) Destiny Image.

— Mommy, Why Did Jesus Have to Die? (Mommy, Why... Ser.). (Illus.). 24p. 1995. pap. 2.99 (1-56043-146-6) Destiny Image.

— Soldiers with Little Feet. 182p. (Orig.). 1992. pap. 7.99 (0-914903-86-1) Destiny Image.

Layton, Dian, ed. see Hurnard, Hannah.

Layton, Diane C. Marrying Down. 1992. 8.95 (0-533-08301-X) Vantage.

Layton, Donald. Aircraft Performance. 224p. 1988. 39.95 (0-916460-40-1) Weber Systems.

— System Safety: Including Department of Defense Standards. 200p. 1989. text ed. 39.95 (0-938862-64-2) Weber Systems.

Layton, Donald H. & Scribner, Jay D., eds. Teaching Educational Politics & Policy. 102p. 1989. 4.50 (0-922971-04-8) Univ Council Educ Admin.

Layton, Donald H., jt. auth. see Campbell, Roald F.

Layton, Donald H., jt. ed. see Scribner, Jay D.

Layton, Donald H., jt. auth. see Sroufe, Gerald E.

Layton, Donald M. Helicopter Performance. 170p. 1984. 49.95 (0-916460-39-8, Matrix Pubs Inc) Weber Systems.

Layton, E. T., et al, eds. The Dynamics of Science & Technology. (Sociology of the Sciences Yearbook Ser.: No. 2). 1978. lib. bdg. 80.00 (90-277-0880-0); pap. text ed. 44.50 (90-277-0881-9) Kluwer Ac.

Layton, Edith. The Disdainful Marquess. 1983. pap. 3.99 (0-451-15880-6, Sig) NAL-Dutton.

— False Angel. (Signet Regency Romance Ser.). 224p. 1985. mass mkt., pap. 3.99 (0-451-13856-2, Sig) NAL-Dutton.

— The Indian Maiden. (Regency Romance Ser.). 1986. pap. 3.99 (0-451-14301-9, Sig) NAL-Dutton.

— A Lady of Spirit. 224p. 1986. pap. 3.99 (0-451-14517-8, Sig) NAL-Dutton.

— A Love for All Seasons: Five Stories. (Super Regency Ser.). 352p. (Orig.). 1992. pap. 4.99 (0-451-17232-9, Sig) NAL-Dutton.

— Love in Disguise. 384p. 1987. pap. 4.50 (0-451-14923-8, Sig) NAL-Dutton.

Layton, Edith, et al. A Regency Valentine, No. 2. 352p. 1992. pap. 4.50 (0-451-17167-5, Sig) NAL-Dutton.

Layton, Edwin T., et al. And I Was There: Pearl Harbor & Midway--Breaking the Secrets. LC 86-21199. (Illus.). 596p. 1987. reprint ed. pap. 15.00 (0-688-06968-1, Quill) Morrow.

Layton, Edwin T., Jr. The Revolt of the Engineers: Social Responsibility & the American Engineering Profession. LC 85-23981. 312p. (Orig.). 1986. reprint ed. text ed. 37.50 (0-8018-3286-1); reprint ed. pap. text ed. 14.95 (0-8018-3287-X) Johns Hopkins.

Layton, Eunice & Layton, Felix. Life Your Great Adventure: A Theosophical View. rev. ed. LC 88-40136. Orig. Title: Theosophy: Key to Understanding. 194p. (Orig.). 1988. reprint ed. pap. 7.25 (0-8356-0635-X, Quest) Theos Pub Hse.

Layton, Felix, jt. auth. see Layton, Eunice.

Layton-Henry, Zig. The Politics of Immigration: Immigration, Race, & Race Relations in Post-War Britain. LC 92-11076. (Making Contemporary Britain Ser.). 280p. 1993. 39.95 (0-631-16743-9); 19.95 (0-631-16744-7) Blackwell Pubs.

Layton-Henry, Zig, ed. Conservative Politics in Western Europe. LC 81-710. 320p. 1982. text ed. 32.50 (0-312-16418-1) St Martin.

— The Political Rights of Migrant Workers in Western Europe. (Modern Politics Ser.: Vol. 25). 256p. (C). 1990. text ed. 45.00 (0-8039-8271-2) Sage.

***Layton, Irving.** Final Reckoning: Poems 1982-1986. 84p. 1995. lib. bdg. 27.00 (0-8095-4543-8) Borgo Pr.

— Fornalutx: Selected Poems, 1928-1990. 192p. 1992. 34.95 (0-7735-0952-6, Pub. by McGill CN); pap. 15.95 (0-7735-0963-1, Pub. by McGill CN) U of Toronto Pr.

— The Selected Poems of Irving Layton. LC 76-54704. 1977. 8.50 (0-8112-0641-6); pap. 2.25 (0-8112-0642-4, NDP431) New Directions.

Layton, Irving & Creeley, Robert. Irving Layton & Robert Creeley: The Complete Correspondence, 1953-1978. Faas, Ekbert & Reed, Sabrina, eds. (Illus.). 288p. (C). 1990. 44.95 (0-7735-0657-8, Pub. by McGill CN) U of Toronto Pr.

***Layton, Jeffrey.** Blowout. 400p. (Orig.). 1995. mass mkt. 4.99 (0-380-78066-6) Avon.

Layton, John M. Multivariable Control Theory. LC 77-360712. (IEE Control Engineering Ser.: Vol. 1). (Illus.). 246p. reprint ed. pap. 70.20 (0-685-23327-8, 2032252) Bks Demand.

Layton, Karen & Layton, Ron. Bible Word Fun. (Bible Baffler Ser.). 48p. (J). (gr. 3 up). 1986. student ed 7.95 (0-86653-367-2, SS 882, Shining Star Pubns) Good Apple.

— Bible Word Play. (Bible Baffler Ser.). (Illus.). 48p. (J). (gr. 3 up). 1989. 7.95 (0-86653-472-5, SS888, Shining Star Pubns) Good Apple.

***Layton, L. & Steinwall, R.** Butterworths Annotated Acts: Trade Practices Act. 550p. 1994. pap. 30.00 (0-409-30968-0, Austral) Butterworth Legal Pubs.

Layton, Lesley. Singapore. LC 89-25465. (Cultures of the World Ser.: Group 1: Asia). (Illus.). 128p. (YA). (gr. 5-9). 1991. lib. bdg. 21.95 (1-85435-295-4) Marshall Cavendish.

— Songbirds in Singapore: The Growth of a Pastime. (Images of Asia Ser.). (Illus.). 120p. 1991. 19.95 (0-19-588999-1) OUP.

Layton, Marcia. Successful Fine Art Marketing. 256p. 1993. 39.95 (0-913069-45-0); pap. 19.95 (0-913069-39-6) Consultant Pr.

Layton, Marcia, jt. auth. see Paulson, Ed.

Layton, Marilyn S. Choosing to Emerge As Readers & Writers: A Multicultural Reader. LC 92-25113. (C). 1992. text ed. 26.00 (0-06-500727-1) HarpCollege.

— Intercultural Journeys Through Reading & Writing. (C). 1990. pap. text ed. 28.00 (0-06-046437-2) HarpCollege.

Layton, Marilyn S., jt. auth. see Handlin, Mimi.

***Layton, Max.** Objects in Mirror Are Closer Than They Appear. 200p. 1995. lib. bdg. 37.00 (0-8095-4828-3) Borgo Pr.

— Some Kind of Hero. 253p. 1995. 29.00 (0-8095-4584-5) Borgo Pr.

Layton, Miriam, et al. The I'd-Rather-Be-Quilting Cookbook. LC 82-7152. (Connecting Threads Series on the Fiber Arts). (Illus.). 120p. (Orig.). 1982. pap. 6.95 (0-914842-86-2) Madrona Pubs.

Layton, Monique, tr. see Levi-Strauss, Claude.

***Layton, R., ed.** Conflict in the Archaeology of Living Traditions. (One World Archaeology Ser.). 272p. 1994. pap. 22.95 (0-415-09559-X, B4610) Routledge.

— Who Needs the Past? Indigenous Values in Archaeology. (One World Archaeology Ser.). 240p. 1994. pap. 19.95 (0-415-09558-1, B4706) Routledge.

Layton, R. B. The Purple Martin. LC 71-92883. (Illus.). 192p. 1969. reprint ed. pap. 9.95 (0-912542-01-2) Nature Bks Pubs.

Layton, R. B., illus. Thirty Birds That Will Build in Bird Houses. LC 77-81805. 1977. pap. 10.95 (0-912542-05-5) Nature Bks Pubs.

Layton, Robert. The Anthropology of Art. 2nd ed. (Illus.). 264p. (C). 1991. 64.95 (0-521-36367-5); pap. 17.95 (0-521-36894-4) Cambridge U Pr.

— Australian Rock Art: A New Synthesis. (Illus.). 256p. (C). 1992. 69.95 (0-521-34666-5) Cambridge U Pr.

— Sibelius. (Master Musicians Ser.). (Illus.). 247p. 1993. text ed. 30.00 (0-02-871322-2) Schirmer Bks.

Layton, Robert, ed. A Companion to the Concerto. 369p. 1989. text ed. 40.00 (0-02-871961-1) Schirmer Bks.

— A Guide to the Symphony. (Illus.). 572p. 1995. pap. 19.95 (0-19-288005-5) OUP.

— Who Needs the Past? Indigenous Values & Archaeology. (One World Archaeology Ser.: No. 5). 256p. 1988. 55.00 (0-04-445020-6) Routledge Chapman & Hall.

Layton, Robert, jt. ed. see Greenfield, Edward.

Layton, Ron, jt. auth. see Layton, Karen.

***Layton, Sarah, et al.** Competitive Strategy: Planning Your Organizations Success. Gerould, Philip, ed. LC 95-67038. (50-Minute Ser.). (Illus.). 103p. (Orig.). 1995. pap. 9.95 (1-56052-350-6) Crisp Pubns.

Layton, Scott C. Archaic Features of the Cannanite Personal Names in the Hebrew Bible. (Harvard Semitic Monographs). 314p. 1990. 29.95 (1-55540-513-4, 04 00 47) Scholars Pr GA.

Layton, Stanford J. To No Privileged Class: The Rationalization of Homesteading & Rural Life in the Early Twentieth-Century American West. LC 87-14299. 105p. 1988. pap. 6.95 (0-941214-59-1) Signature Bks.

Layton, Susan. Russian Literature & Empire: The Conquest of the Caucasus from Pushkin to Tolstoy. LC 93-47121. (Studies in Russian Literature). 280p. (C). 1995. 59.95 (0-521-44443-8) Cambridge U Pr.

Layton, T. A. The Cheese Handbook: A Guide to the World's Best Cheeses. rev. ed. 160p. 1973. reprint ed. pap. 4.50 (0-486-22955-6) Dover.

Layton, Thomas N. Western Pomo Prehistory: Excavations at Albion Head, Nightbirds' Retreat, & Three Chop Village, Mendocino County, California. LC 89-71653. (Monograph: No. 32). (Illus.). 229p. (Orig.). 1990. pap. text ed. 19.00 (0-917956-67-2) UCLA Arch.

Layton, W. T., rev. Harbord's Glossary of Navigation. rev. ed. (C). 1987. 68.00 (0-85174-277-7, Pub. by Brwn Son Ferg) St Mut.

Layton, William I. College Arithmetic. 2nd ed. LC 73-155121. 244p. reprint ed. pap. 69.60 (0-317-08545-X, 2055108) Bks Demand.

***Laywine, Alison.** Kant's Early Metaphysics & the Origins of the Critical Philosophy. (North American Kant Society Studies in Philosophy: Vol. 3). ix, 178p. (Orig.). 1994. lib. bdg. 39.00 (0-924922-70-2); pap. text ed. 20.00 (0-924922-20-6) Ridgeview.

Layzell, A. D., jt. auth. see Bailey, J. M.

Layzell, Daniel T. & Lyddon, Jan W., eds. Budgeting for Higher Education at the State Level: Enigma, Paradox, & Ritual. LC 90-63845. (ASHE-ERIC Higher Education Report Ser.: No. 4). 110p. 1990. pap. 17.00 (1-878380-01-X) GWU Schl E&HD.

Layzell, Paul, jt. auth. see Spurr, Kathy.

Layzell, Paul, jt. ed. see Spurr, Kathy.

Layzer, David. Cosmogenesis: The Growth of Order in the Universe. (Illus.). 336p. 1990. 27.95 (0-19-505528-4) OUP.

— Cosmogenesis: The Growth of Order in the Universe. (Illus.). 336p. 1991. reprint ed. pap. 13.95 (0-19-506908-0) OUP.

Layzer, David, jt. ed. see Dalgarno, A.

Layzer, Robert B. Neuromuscular Manifestations of Systemic Disease. LC 84-10096. (Contemporary Neurology Ser.: No. 25). (Illus.). 434p. 1985. text ed. 68.00 (0-8036-5521-5) Davis Co.

Laz, Bob. Epic of Wonderland Park: So We Build a Resort. (Illus.). 370p. (Orig.). 1989. pap. text ed. 16.70 (0-9625861-0-2) R & L Enterprise.

Laz, Medard. Helps for the Separated & Divorced. 64p. 1981. pap. 3.95 (0-89243-147-4) Liguori Pubns.

— Helps for the Widowed. 64p. 1983. pap. 3.95 (0-89243-176-8) Liguori Pubns.

Lazakis, Christopher T. America, Greece & Pasok: The Politics of Dependence & Independence. LC 89-61079. 110p. (Orig.). (C). 1989. pap. text ed. 14.95 (0-9622952-0-5) Ciel Trappe Bks.

Lazalier, James H., ed. see Taylor, Bayard.

Lazamon. Lazamon's Arthur: The Arthurian Section of Lazamon's Brut. Barron, W. R. & Weinberg, S. C., eds. 340p. 1989. text ed. 45.00 (0-292-74660-1) U of Tex Pr.

Lazan, B. Damping of Materials & Members in Structural Mechanics. LC 66-27370. 1968. 134.00 (0-08-013221-9, Pub. by Pergamon Repr UK) Franklin.

Lazan, Marian B., jt. auth. see Perl, Lila.

Lazar, jt. auth. see Schoen.

Lazar, A. L. & Taylor, D. C. Multipliers of Pedersen's Ideal. LC 75-44302. (Memoirs Ser.: No. 5/169). 111p. 1976. pap. 22.00 (0-8218-1869-4, MEMO 5/169) Am Math.

Lazar, Arthur. Intimate Landscapes. LC 93-80036. (Illus.). 96p. 1994. 60.00 (0-9638189-5-3) Lke Forest Coll.

Lazar, Chaim. Despite It All. Wachsman, Goldie, tr. LC 84-50677. (Illus.). 208p. 1985. 13.95 (0-88400-106-7) Shengold.

— Destruction & Resistance. LC 84-52354. (Illus.). 240p. 1985. pap. 15.95 (0-88400-113-X) Shengold.

Lazar, Clifford. Ten Minutes to MS-DOS Word Perfect, WordStar, Lotus BASIC. (Illus.). 210p. 1989. teacher ed 24.95 (0-685-30761-1, TM01); lib. bdg. 29.95 (0-9624618-0-6, TM01); pap. 24.95 (0-685-30759-X, TM01); pap. text ed. 24.95 (0-685-30760-3, TM01) Systems Express.

Lazar, Clifford W. Ten Minutes to MS-DOS, WordPerfect, WordStar, Lotus, BASIC. (Illus.). 210p. 1989. lib. bdg. 24.95 (0-685-29336-X, TM01); pap. 24.95 (0-685-29337-8, TM01); pap. text ed. 24.95 (0-685-29338-6, TM01) Systems Express.

***Lazar-Curatolo, Linda.** Are You Green Yet? 72p. (YA). (gr. 7-12). 1992. pap. write for info. (1-57515-013-1) PPI Pubng.

Lazar, David, ed. Conversations with M. F. K. Fisher. LC 92-28485. (Literary Conversations Ser.). 184p. 1993. 37.50 (0-87805-595-9); pap. 15.95 (0-87805-596-7) U Pr of Miss.

***Lazar, Ed.** Tibet: The Issue Is Independence. 1994. pap. 9.50 (0-938077-75-9) Parallax Pr.

Lazar, Edward. Thoughts: Reflections in a Search for Meaning. Banwarth, Francine & Lembeck, Michael, eds. LC 89-91041. (Illus.). 138p. (Orig.). 1989. pap. 6.00 (0-9622548-0-0) JZ Redman Pubs.

— Thoughts: Reflections in the Search for Meaning. Tobin, Sheilah & Banwarth, Francine, eds. 144p. 1989. write for info. (0-318-64896-2) JZ Redman Pubs.

Lazar, Elysa. Museum Shop Report: A Guide to Museum Shop Catalogs. 1992. pap. 14.95 (1-881642-02-X) Lazar Comms.

— Outlet Report. 1992. pap. 9.95 (1-881642-01-1) Lazar Comms.

— Shop-by-Mail: The Mail Order Bible. 1992. pap. 9.95 (1-881642-00-3) Lazar Comms.

Lazar, Elysa & Miceli, Eve. Elysa Lazar's Smart Shopping: An Amateur's Guide to Shopping Like a Pro. (Illus.). 320p. (Orig.). 1993. pap. 14.95 (1-881642-03-8) Lazar Comms.

— Lazar's Museum Shop Treasures: The Exclusive Guide to Museum Catalog Shopping. 2nd ed. (Illus.). 300p. 1994. pap. 14.95 (1-881642-05-4) Lazar Comms.

— Lazar's Outlet Shopper's Guide: A Field Guide to Factory Outlet Shopping. 2nd ed. 250p. 1994. pap. 12.95 (1-881642-06-2) Lazar Comms.

— Lazar's Shop by Mail: A Field Guide to Shopping by Mail. 2nd ed. (Illus.). 350p. 1993. pap. 14.95 (1-881642-04-6) Lazar Comms.

Lazar, Gillian. Using Literature in Language Teaching: A Guide for Teachers & Trainers. LC 92-8942. (Teacher Training & Development Ser.). 228p. (C). 1993. 44.95 (0-521-40480-0); pap. 16.95 (0-521-40651-X) Cambridge U Pr.

Lazar, H. P., jt. auth. see Van Der Reis, L.

Lazar, Harold L., ed. Current Therapy for Acute Coronary Ischemia. LC 93-14925. (Illus.). 320p. 1993. 65.00 (0-87993-555-3) Futura Pub.

Lazar, I. Hungary. (Illus.). 143p. (C). 1988. pap. 100.00 (0-685-37537-4, Pub. by Collets) St Mut.

— Hungary: Budapest Istvan Sziklai, 1988. (Illus.). 143p. (C). 1988. 100.00 (0-685-32391-9, Pub. by Collets UK) Pro-Am Music.

— Hungary: A View from the Air. (C). 1991. 68.00 (0-89771-851-8, Pub. by Collets) St Mut.

***Lazar, Irving & Tapert, Annette.** Swifty: My Life & Good Times. LC 94-47215. 1995. 24.00 (0-684-80418-2) S&S Trade.

***Lazar, Jerry.** Red Cloud: North American Indians of Achievement. LC 94-22728. (North American Indians of Achievement Ser.). (J). (gr. 1-8). Date not set. write for info. (0-7910-1718-4); pap. write for info. (0-7910-2044-4) Chelsea Hse.

***Lazar, John.** Outpouring of the Spirit. 1995. 11.95 (0-8062-5261-8) Carlton.

Lazar, John I., jt. auth. see Loeb, Ben F., Jr.

Lazar, Joseph. Due Process in Disciplinary Hearings: Decisions of the National Railroad Adjustment Board. (Monograph & Research Ser.: No. 25). 459p. 1980. 10.50 (0-89215-108-0) U Cal LA Indus Rel.

***Lazar, Larry, ed.** New Jersey's Distinguished Restaurants 1995. 160p. 1994. pap. 9.95 (0-9634765-3-X) Qual Restaurants.

Lazar, Leonard. Transnational Economic & Monetary Law: Transactions & Contracts, 10 binders. LC 77-8398. 1977. 100.00 (0-379-10220-X) Oceana.

— Transnational Economic & Monetary Law: Transactions & Contracts, 10 binders. annuals LC 77-8398. 1977. Annual release. ring bd. 850.00 (0-379-10215-3) Oceana.

Lazar, Milan, et al. Free Radicals in Chemistry & Biology. (Illus.). 304p. 1989. 191.00 (0-8493-5387-4, QD471) CRC Pr.

Lazar, Moche & Dilligan, Robert, eds. The Ladino Mahzor of Ferrara (1553) Lazar, Moshe, tr. LC 93-77908. (Sephardic Classical Library). 320p. (HEB & LAD.). 1993. text ed. 55.00 (0-911437-60-6) Labyrinthos.

Lazar, Moshe, ed. The Anxious Subject: Nightmares & Daymares in Literature & Film. LC 82-70791. (Interplay Ser.: Vol. 2). 208p. 1983. pap. 20.50 (0-89003-116-9) Undena Pubns.

— The Dream & the Play: Ionesco's Theatrical Quest. LC 81-71734. (Interplay Ser.: Vol. 1). 184p. (Orig.). 1982. pap. 20.50 (0-89003-108-8) Undena Pubns.

— Play Durrenmatt. (Interplay Ser.: Vol. 3). 219p. (C). 1983. pap. text ed. 21.75 (0-89003-129-0, 82-50986) Undena Pubns.

— Text & Concordance of Biblioteca Nacional, Madrid, MS10289: Moses Maimonides, Mostrador e Ensennador de los Turbados. Toledo, Pedro, tr. 8p. (SPA.). 1987. 10.00 (0-942260-84-8) Hispanic Seminary.

Lazar, Moshe, tr. & intro. The Ladino Bible of Ferrara (1553) The Sephardic Classical Library. LC 92-70756. 766p. (LAD.). 1992. 100.00 (0-911437-56-8) Labyrinthos.

— Ladino Pentateuch: (Constantinople, 1547) LC 88-82628. (Sephardic Classical Library). (Illus.). 560p. (HEB & LAD.). 1988. lib. bdg. 90.00 (0-911437-46-0) Labyrinthos.

Lazar, Moshe & Dilligan, Robert, eds. The Ladino Five Scrolls: Abraham Asa's Versions of the Hebrew & Aramaic Texts. LC 92-73523. (Sephardic Classical Library). 304p. (HEB & LAD.). 1992. text ed. 65.00 (0-911437-58-4) Labyrinthos.

— Libro de las Generaciones & The Book of Yashar. LC 89-85090. (Sephardic Classical Library: No. 3). 515p. (C). 1990. lib. bdg. 90.00x (0-911437-51-7) Labyrinthos.

— Sefer Tesubah: Book on Repentance. LC 93-85953. (Sephardic Classical Library). 304p. (LAD.). (C). 1993. text ed. 65.00 (0-911437-62-2) Labyrinthos.

Lazar, Moshe & Gottesman, Ronald, eds. The Dove & the Mole: Kafka's Journey into Darkness & Creativity. (Interplay Ser.: Vol. 5). 256p. (Orig.). 1987. 31.25 (0-89003-251-3); pap. 23.00 (0-89003-250-5) Undena Pubns.

Lazar, Moshe, tr. see Dilligan, Robert, ed.

Lazar, Moshe, ed. see Halevi, Yehuda.

Lazar, Moshe, ed. see Halevi, Yehudah.

Lazar, Moshe, tr. see Lazar, Moche & Dilligan, Robert, eds.

Lazar, Moshe, ed. see Maimonides.

Lazar, Paul. Films on Africa. LC 81-71700. 50p. (Orig.). 1982. pap. text ed. 5.00 (0-941934-38-1) Indiana Africa.

Lazar, Paul, jt. ed. see Drill, Victor A.

Lazar, Shelley F. Oriental Collection: Twenty Original Needlepoint Designs. (Illus.). 96p. 1993. 24.95 (0-8048-1849-5) C E Tuttle.

— Pictures in Needlework: Twenty Miniature Designs for All Occasions. (Illus.). 96p. 1990. text ed. 15.95 (0-02-569510-X) Macmillan.

***Lazar, Swifty.** Swifty: The Autobiography of Irving Lazar. 1995. 24.00 (0-671-52505-0) S&S Trade.

Lazar, Walter. The Combination Book for Lottery Games with Six Winning Numbers Jackpots, Vol. 1. 1991. pap. 10.00 (0-533-08585-3) Vantage.

Lazaraton. Research Manual for ESL: Comp. Supp. 1990. pap. 10.00 (0-8384-2674-3) Heinle & Heinle.

Lazaravich, Gordana, ed. Livietta e Tracollo: (La Contadina Astuta) Intermezzi. LC 85-753856. (Complete Works of Pergolesi: No. 2, Vol. 6). (Illus.). 132p. 1991. lib. bdg. 112.00 (0-918728-45-2) Pendragon NY.

Lazard, Gilbert. Dictionnaire Persan-Francais. LC 90-40583. xvii, 482p. (FRE & PER.). 1990. 114.50 (90-04-08549-1) E J Brill.

— Grammar of Contemporary Persian. Lyon, Shirley A., tr. (Persian Studies: No. 14). 310p. (C). 1992. lib. bdg. 35.00 (0-939214-85-7); pap. 19.95 (0-939214-11-3) Mazda Pubs.

Lazard, Naomi. The Moonlit Upper Deckerina. LC 76-57519. 65p. 1977. 11.95 (0-8180-1536-5); pap. 7.95 (0-8180-1540-3) Sheep Meadow.

— Ordinances. (Poetry Chapbook Ser.). 58p. (Orig.). 1984. pap. 5.00 (0-937669-11-3) Owl Creek Pr.

— The True Subject: Selected Poems of Faiz Ahmed Faiz. 110p. 1987. text ed. 35.00 (0-691-06704-X); pap. text ed. 12.95 (0-691-01438-8) Princeton U Pr.

Lazardfeld, Paul & Reitz, Jeffery G. An Introduction to Applied Sociology. LC 75-8274. 196p. 1981. text ed. 25.00 (0-444-99006-2, LAP/) Greenwood.

Lazare, Aaron. Outpatient Psychiatry. 2nd ed. (Illus.). 752p. 1988. lib. bdg. 79.00 (0-683-04851-1) Williams & Wilkins.

Lazare, Bernard. Anti-Semitism: Its History & Causes. 1982. lib. bdg. 300.00 (0-87700-426-9) Revisionist Pr.

— Antisemitism, Its History & Causes. 208p. 1995. pap. 10.00 (0-8032-7954-X, Bison Books) U of Nebr Pr.

Lazare, S., jt. ed. see Fogarassy, E.

Lazareski, Vladimir, tr. see Spiridovich, Alexander I.

Lazareth, William H. & Rasolondraibe, Peri. Lutheran Identity & Mission: Evangelical & Evangelistic? LC 94-9257. 1994. 15.00 (0-8006-2837-3, Fortress Pr) Augsburg Fortress.

Lazareth, William H., jt. ed. see Forell, George W.

Lazarev, Nikolai I. Dyshormonal Tumors: The Theory of Prophylaxis & Treatment. Haigh, Basil, tr. LC 65-27347. 146p. reprint ed. pap. 41.70 (0-317-07808-9, 2020671) Bks Demand.

Lazarev, P. I., ed. Molecular Electronics: Materials & Methods. (C). 1991. lib. bdg. 125.50 (0-7923-1196-5) Kluwer Ac.

Lazarev, V. Novgorodian Icon-Painting. (Illus.). 210p. (C). 1976. text ed. 180.00 (0-569-08320-6, Pub. by Collets) St Mut.

Lazarev, V. N. Pages from the History of Novgorodian Painting. 1983. 74.00 (0-317-61340-5, Pub. by Collets UK) Pro-Am Music.

— Russian Icon Painting: Russkaia Ikonopis'. Ot Istokov Do Nachala XVI Veka. 538p. (ENG & RUS.). 1984. 305.00 (0-317-57449-3, Pub. by Collets UK) St Mut.

Lazarevich, Gordana. The Musical World of Frances James & Murray Adaskin. 331p. 1988. 40.00 (0-8020-5738-1) U of Toronto Pr.

Lazarides, G. & Shafi, Q., eds. Particles & the Universe. 296p. 1986. 54.00 (0-444-87005-9, North Holland) Elsevier.

Lazarides, M. The Tropical Grasses of Southeast Asia: Excluding Bamboos. 350p. 1980. lib. bdg. 50.00 (3-7682-1255-6) Lubrecht & Cramer.

Lazarkiewi, S. & Troskolanski, A. T. Impeller Pumps. LC 65-14226. 1965. 320.00 (0-08-011172-6, Pub. by Pergamon Repr UK) Franklin.

Lazarnick, George. Netsuke & Inro Artists, & How to Read Their Signatures, 2 vols. deluxe ed. LC 81-51945. (Illus.). 1376p. 1982. 950.00 (0-686-79507-5) Reed Pubs.

— Netsuke & Inro Artists, & How to Read Their Signatures, 2 vols., Set. LC 81-51945. (Illus.). 1376p. 1982. 475.00 (0-917064-02-X) Reed Pubs.

— The Signature Book of Netsuke, Inro & Ojime Artists in Photographs. LC 76-9504. (Illus.). 1976. 85.00 (0-917064-01-1) Reed Pubs.

Lazaro Carreter, Fernando, jt. auth. see Garcia Lorca, Federico.

Lazaro, Iciaro. Diccionario de Quimica. 130p. 1988. 32.95 (0-7859-6030-9, 8439712693) Fr & Eur.

Lazaro, Jose M. El Pensar Logico. 321p. 1985. 6.50 (0-8477-2825-0) U of PR Pr.

Lazaro, Roberto & Waterman, Floyd. A Comparison of the Corporate Structures & Delivery of City Services in Omaha & Manila. 104p. (Orig.). 1984. pap. 6.50 (1-55719-075-5) U NE CPAR.

An Asterisk (*) at the beginning of an entry indicates that the title is appearing in BIP for the first time.

Lazaro, Timothy. Urban Hydrology. rev. ed. LC 89-51913. 260p. 1989. 42.50 (*0-87762-547-6*) Technomic.

Lazaroff, David W. Sabino Canyon: The Life of a Southwestern Oasis. LC 92-18057. (Illus.). 119p. (Orig.). 1993. pap. 16.95 (*0-8165-1344-9*) U of Ariz Pr.

— The Secret Lives of Hummingbirds. (Illus.). 24p. (Orig.). 1995. pap. 4.95 (*1-886679-00-2*) Ariz-Sonora Des Mus.

Lazaron, Hilda. Gabriel Marcel the Dramatist. 186p. 1978. 30.00 (*0-901072-77-X*, Pub. by Colin Smythe Ltd UK) Dufour.

Lazarov, Conner & Wasserman, Arthur. Complex Actions of Lie Groups. LC 73-18039. (Memoirs Ser.: No. 1/137). 82p. 1973. pap. 17.00 (*0-8218-1837-6*, MEMO 1/137) Am Math.

Lazarowich, N. Michael. Granny Flats As Housing for the Elderly: International Perspectives. (Journal of Housing for the Elderly: Vol. 7 No. 2). (Illus.). 82p. 1991. text ed. 19.95 (*1-56024-124-1*) Haworth Pr.

Lazarowitz, Arlene. Years in Exile: The Liberal Democrats, 1950-1959. LC 88-25978. (Modern American History Ser.). 200p. 1988. 25.00 (*0-8240-4333-2*) Garland.

Lazarre, Jacob. Beating Sea & Changeless Bar. LC 79-86149. (Short Story Index Reprint Ser.). 1977. 17.95 (*0-8369-3053-3*) Ayer.

Lazarre, Jane. The Mother Knot. LC 85-47944. 210p. 1986. reprint ed. pap. 11.95 (*0-8070-6725-3*, BP710) Beacon Pr.

Lazarro-Carreter, Fernando. Diccionario de Terminos Filologicos. 3rd ed. 444p. 1990. pap. 29.95 (*0-7859-5787-1*) Fr & Eur.

Lazarsfeld & Van de Ven, eds. Topics in the Geometry of Projective Space: Recent Work of F. L. Zak. (DMV Seminar Ser.: No. 4). 52p. 1985. pap. 24.50 (*0-8176-1660-8*) Birkhauser.

Lazarsfeld, Patricia K., ed. The Varied Sociology of Paul Lazarsfeld. LC 81-24205. 400p. 1982. text ed. 63.00 (*0-231-05122-0*); pap. text ed. 23.50 (*0-231-05123-9*) Col U Pr.

Lazarsfeld, Paul F. On Social Research & Its Language. LC 93-12748. (Heritage of Sociology Ser.). (Illus.). 328p. 1993. lib. bdg. 49.95 (*0-226-46961-1*); pap. text ed. 19.95 (*0-226-46963-8*) U Ch Pr.

— Radio & the Printed Page: An Introduction to the Study of Radio & Its Role in the Communication of Ideas. LC 70-161161. (History of Broadcasting: Radio to Television Ser.). 1976. reprint ed. 28.95 (*0-405-03575-6*) Ayer.

Lazarsfeld, Paul F. & Kendall, Patricia L. Radio Listening in America: The People Look at Radio-Again. Coser, Lewis A. & Powell, Walter W., eds. LC 79-7002. (Perennial Works in Sociology Ser.). (Illus.). 1980. reprint ed. lib. bdg. 18.95 (*0-405-12100-8*) Ayer.

Lazarsfeld, Paul F. & Reitz, Jeffrey G. An Introduction to Applied Sociology. LC 75-8274. 203p. reprint ed. pap. 57.90 (*0-685-15318-5*, 2056099) Bks Demand.

Lazarsfeld, Paul F. & Thielens, Wagner P., Jr. The Academic Mind: Social Scientists in Time of Crisis. Metzger, Walter P., ed. LC 76-55178. (Academic Profession Ser.). (Illus.). 1977. reprint ed. 39.95 (*0-405-10006-X*) Ayer.

Lazarsfeld, Paul F., jt. ed. see Merton, Robert K.

Lazarsfeld, Paul F., jt. auth. see Stouffer, Samuel A.

Lazarsfeld, Paul F., et al. Jugend und Beruf: Youth & Job. LC 74-25762. (European Sociology Ser.). 206p. 1975. reprint ed. 24.95 (*0-405-06516-7*) Ayer.

— The People's Choice: How the Voter Makes up His Mind in a Presidential Campaign. 3rd ed. LC 68-20443. 224p. reprint ed. pap. 63.90 (*0-685-20795-1*, 2030109) Bks Demand.

Lazarsfeld, Paul F., et al, eds. Communications Research, Nineteen Forty-Eight to Nineteen Forty-Nine. LC 79-7005. (Perennial Works in Sociology Ser.). (Illus.). 1980. reprint ed. lib. bdg. 29.95 (*0-405-12103-2*) Ayer.

— Radio Research, Nineteen Hundred Forty-One. LC 79-7003. (Perennial Works in Sociology Ser.). (Illus.). 1980. reprint ed. lib. bdg. 29.95 (*0-405-12101-6*) Ayer.

— Radio Research, Nineteen Hundred Forty-Two to Nineteen Hundred Forty-Three. LC 79-7004. (Perennial Works in Sociology Ser.). (Illus.). 1980. reprint ed. lib. bdg. 49.95 (*0-405-12102-4*) Ayer.

Lazarton, jt. auth. see Hatch.

Lazarus. Country Is My Music! (J). Date not set. 15.00 (*0-671-86773-3*, S&S Bks Young Read) S&S Childrens.

— Parole aux Jeunes. 1992. pap. 29.95 (*0-8384-3688-9*) Heinle & Heinle.

Lazarus, tr. see Berainchaniov, Ignatius.

Lazarus, A., jt. auth. see Wolpe, Joseph.

Lazarus, A. L. Some Light: New & Selected Verse. Wazbinski, Louise A., ed. 80p. 1988. 12.50 (*0-934958-05-X*) Bellflower.

Lazarus, A. L., ed. The Best of George Ade. LC 84-43170. (Illus.). 280p. 1985. 17.95 (*0-253-10609-5*) Ind U Pr.

— A George Jean Nathan Reader. LC 88-45873. (Illus.). 408p. 1990. 45.00 (*0-8386-3369-2*) Fairleigh Dickinson.

Lazarus, Alan, jt. auth. see Funes, Marilyn.

Lazarus, Arnold & Fay, Allen. I Can If I Want To. LC 92-5966. 1992. pap. 8.00 (*0-688-11612-4*, Quill) Morrow.

Lazarus, Arnold A. In the Mind's Eye: The Power of Imagery for Personal Enrichment. LC 84-9016. 208p. 1984. reprint ed. pap. text ed. 15.95 (*0-89862-641-2*) Guilford Pr.

— Marital Myths: Two Dozen Mistaken Beliefs That Can Ruin a Marriage (Or Make a Bad One Worse) LC 85-14362. 176p. (Orig.). 1985. pap. 7.95 (*0-915166-51-8*) Impact Pubs CA.

— The Practice of Multimodal Therapy: Systematic, Comprehensive, & Effective Psychotherapy. LC 88-46076. 288p. 1989. reprint ed. pap. text ed. 15.95 (*0-8018-3811-8*) Johns Hopkins.

Lazarus, Arnold A., ed. Casebook of Multimodal Therapy. LC 84-19835. 212p. 1985. lib. bdg. 30.00 (*0-89862-647-1*) Guilford Pr.

Lazarus, Arnold A., et al. Don't Believe It for a Minute: Forty Toxic Ideas That Are Driving You Crazy. LC 93-4934. 192p. (Orig.). 1993. pap. 9.95 (*0-915166-80-1*) Impact Pubs CA.

Lazarus, Arnold L., ed. The Indiana Experience: An Anthology. LC 76-50528. 442p. reprint ed. pap. 126.00 (*0-7837-6103-1*, 2059149) Bks Demand.

Lazarus, Arthur, et al. The Neuroleptic Malignant Syndrome & Related Conditions: Clinical Practice, No. 6. LC 88-24242. 268p. 1989. text ed. 25.00 (*0-88048-134-X*) Am Psychiatric.

Lazarus, Bernice N., jt. auth. see Lazarus, Richard S.

Lazarus-Black, Mindie. Legitimate Acts & Illegal Encounters: A Historical Enthnography of Life & Law in Antigua & Barbuda. LC 93-11005. (Ethnographic Inquiry Ser.). 424p. (C). 1994. text ed. 49.00 (*1-56098-327-2*); pap. text ed. 24.95 (*1-56098-326-4*) Smithsonian.

Lazarus-Black, Mindie & Hirsch, Susan F., eds. Contested States: Law, Hegemony, & Resistance. LC 93-47569. (After the Law Ser.). 1994. write for info. (*0-415-90779-9*); pap. write for info. (*0-415-90780-2*) Routledge.

***Lazarus, C. & Berman, J.** Glorafilia: The Miniature Needle Point Collection. 1994. 22.50 (*0-517-79986-3*, Crown) Crown Pub Group.

Lazarus, Carole. Glorafilia: The Impressionists in Needlepoint. 1993. 12.25 (*0-517-59223-1*, Crown) Crown Pub Group.

***Lazarus, Carole & Berman, Jennifer.** Glorafilia: the Venice Collection: 25 Original Projects in Needlepoint & Embroidery. (Illus.). 160p. 1995. pap. 24.95 (*1-85029-623-5*, Pub. by Conran Octopus UK) Trafalgar.

Lazarus, Carole, jt. auth. see Berman, Jennifer.

Lazarus, David & Raether, Manfred. Practical Physics: How Things Work. (Illus.). 1984. pap. text ed. 15.80 (*0-87563-167-3*) Stipes.

Lazarus, Edward. Black Hills - White Justice: The Sioux Nation vs. the United States, 1775 to the Present. LC 90-56383. 1992. pap. 15.00 (*0-06-092207-9*, PL) HarpC.

Lazarus, Emma. Admetus. LC 77-104508. reprint ed. lib. bdg. 36.00 (*0-8398-1152-7*) Irvington.

— An Epistle to the Hebrews. LC 87-2912. (Illus.). 1987. pap. 10.00 (*0-916790-02-9*) Jewish Hist.

— Letters to Emma Lazarus in the Columbia University Library. Rusk, Ralph L., ed. LC 39-14112. 1984. reprint ed. 20.00 (*0-404-05459-5*) AMS Pr.

Lazarus, George & Wexler, Bruce. Marketing Immunity: Breaking Through Customer Resistance. 200p. 1987. text ed. 30.00 (*0-87094-949-7*) Irwin Prof Pubng.

Lazarus, H. Method for Clarinet, 2 pts., Pt. 1. Bellison, Simeon, ed. (Illus.). 140p. 1946. pap. 15.95 (*0-8258-0206-7*, 0-327) Fischer Inc NY.

— Method for Clarinet, 2 pts., Pt. 2. Bellison, Simeon, ed. (Illus.). 142p. 1946. pap. 12.95 (*0-8258-0207-5*, 0-328) Fischer Inc NY.

Lazarus, J. H., jt. auth. see Wheeler, M. H.

Lazarus, J. Michael & Brenner, Barry M. Acute Renal Failure. 3rd ed. (Illus.). 632p. 1993. text ed. 119.95 (*0-443-08792-X*) Churchill.

Lazarus, J. Michael, jt. auth. see Brenner, Barry M.

Lazarus, J. Michael, jt. ed. see Brenner, Barry M.

Lazarus, John, jt. auth. see Cockburn, Andrew.

Lazarus, John H. Endocrine & Metabolic Effects of Lithium. LC 85-28308. 220p. 1986. 59.50 (*0-306-42057-0*, Plenum Med Bk) Plenum.

Lazarus, Joseph. In Praise of the King Without a Face. LC 77-82728. (Scene Award Ser.). 80p. (Orig.). 1978. pap. 5.00 (*0-912292-45-8*) The Smith.

Lazarus, Josephine. Spirit of Judaism. LC 77-38031. (Essay Index Reprint Ser.). 1977. reprint ed. 18.95 (*0-8369-2602-1*) Ayer.

Lazarus, Lawrence W., et al, eds. Essentials of Geriatric Psychiatry: A Guide for Health Professionals. 272p. 1988. 35.95 (*0-8261-5990-7*) Springer Pub.

Lazarus, M., et al. Die Ethnik des Judenthums, 2 vols., Set. LC 79-7146. (Jewish Philosophy, Mysticism & History of Ideas Ser.). 1980. reprint ed. lib. bdg. 88.95 (*0-405-12276-4*) Ayer.

Lazarus, Neil. Resistance in Postcolonial African Fiction. LC 89-38349. 288p. (C). 1990. text ed. 32.00 (*0-300-04553-0*) Yale U Pr.

***Lazarus, Pat.** Healing the Mind the Natural Way: Nutritional Solutions to Psychological Problems. LC 95-11787. 1995. write for info. (*0-87477-752-6*, Putnam) Putnam Pub Group.

— Keep Your Pet Healthy the Natural Way. LC 82-17846. 228p. 1983. write for info. (*0-672-52726-X*) Macmillan.

— Keep Your Pet Healthy the Natural Way. 1985. 12.95 (*0-02-569550-9*) Macmillan.

— Keep Your Pet Healthy the Natural Way. LC 86-7323. (Pivot Original Health Bks.). 198p. 1986. reprint ed. 5.95 (*0-87983-388-2*) Keats.

Lazarus, Paul N., III. The Film Producer. (Illus.). 224p. 1992. pap. 12.95 (*0-312-06969-3*) St Martin.

— Working in Film: The Marketplace in the '90s. LC 93-677. 224p. (Orig.). 1993. pap. 14.95 (*0-312-09418-3*) St Martin.

Lazarus, Rachel M. The Education of the Heart: The Correspondence of Rachel Mordecai Lazarus & Maria Edgeworth. MacDonald, Edgar E., ed. LC 76-29062. 364p. reprint ed. pap. 103.80 (*0-8357-3880-9*, 2036612) Bks Demand.

Lazarus, Richard. A Journey into Mystery. LC 91-67742. 148p. 1993. pap. 7.95 (*1-56002-158-6*, Univ Edtns) Aegina Pr.

Lazarus, Richard S. Emotion & Adaptation. (Illus.). 512p. 1991. 49.95 (*0-19-506994-3*) OUP.

— Emotion & Adaptation. (Illus.). 576p. 1994. reprint ed. pap. 24.95 (*0-19-509266-X*) OUP.

— Patterns of Adjustment. 3rd ed. (Illus.). 448p. (C). 1976. text ed. write for info. (*0-07-036802-3*); Instr's. ed. teacher ed, pap. text ed. write for info. (*0-07-036803-1*) McGraw.

— Patterns of Adjustment & Human Effectiveness. (Psychology Ser.). 1968. text ed. write for info. (*0-07-036795-7*) McGraw.

Lazarus, Richard S. & Folkman, Susan. Stress, Appraisal, & Coping. 464p. (C). 1984. pap. 37.95 (*0-8261-4191-9*) Springer Pub.

Lazarus, Richard S. & Lazarus, Bernice N. The Emotional Mind: Making Sense of Our Emotions. LC 94-9320. 320p. 1994. 25.00 (*0-19-508757-7*) OUP.

Lazarus, Richard S., jt. auth. see Monat, Alan.

Lazarus, S. The Parenthood Handbook. 1980. pap. write for info. (*0-201-04370-X*) Addison-Wesley.

Lazarus-Yafeh, Hava. Intertwined Worlds: Medieval Islam & Bible Criticism. 200p. 1992. text ed. 32.50 (*0-691-07398-8*) Princeton U Pr.

Lazary, Betsy. Work with Me! How to Make of Office Support Staff. 1990. pap. 9.95 (*0-942361-23-7*) MasterMedia Ltd.

Lazear, David. Seven Pathways to Learning: Teaching Students & Parents about Multiple Intelligences. LC 93-33054. 256p. 1994. 30.00 (*0-913705-92-6*) Zephyr Pr AZ.

— Seven Ways of Knowing: Teaching for Multiple Intelligences. 2nd ed. LC 91-67598. (Illus.). 256p. (Orig.). 1991. pap. text ed. 36.00 (*0-932935-39-7*) IRI-Skylght.

— Seven Ways of Teaching: The Artistry of Teaching with Multiple Intelligences. LC 91-65666. (Illus.). 192p. (Orig.). 1991. pap. text ed. 27.95 (*0-932935-32-X*) IRI-Skylght.

Lazear, David G. Multiple Intelligence Approaches to Assessment: Solving the Assessment Conundrum. LC 94-216. 1994. write for info. (*0-913705-95-0*) Zephyr Pr AZ.

***Lazear, Edward P.** Personnel Economics. (Wicksell Lectures). (Illus.). 160p. 1995. 27.50 (*0-262-12188-3*) MIT Pr.

***Lazear, Edward P., ed.** Economic Transition Eastern Europe & Russia: Realities of Reform. 448p. (C). 1995. 42.95 (*0-8179-9331-2*) Hoover Inst Pr.

— Economic Transition Eastern Europe & Russia: Realities of Reform. 448p. (C). 1995. pap. 24.95 (*0-8179-9332-0*) Hoover Inst Pr.

Lazear, Edward P. & Michael, Robert T. Allocation of Income Within the Household. (Illus.). 200p. 1988. 34.95 (*0-226-46966-2*) U Ch Pr.

Lazear, Edward P., jt. ed. see Krauss, Melvyn B.

Lazear, Edward P., jt. ed. see Ricardo-Campbell, Rita.

Lazear, Jonathon. Meditations for Men Who Do Too Much. LC 92-20030. (Fireside - Parkside Recovery Book Ser.). 1992. pap. 9.00 (*0-671-75908-6*, Fireside) S&S Trade.

— Remembrance of Father: Words to Heal the Heart. LC 94-48791. 1995. pap. 10.00 (*0-684-80201-5*, Fireside) S&S Trade.

— Remembrance of Mother. 1994. pap. 10.00 (*0-671-88696-7*, Fireside) S&S Trade.

Lazear, Jonathon & Lazear, Wendy. Meditations for Parents Who Do Too Much. LC 93-12432. (Meditation Book Ser.). 384p. (Orig.). 1993. pap. 9.00 (*0-671-79635-6*, Fireside) S&S Trade.

Lazear, Roberto. Parabolas de Platero. 191p. 1990. pap. 5.25 (*0-685-50565-0*) Edit Caribe.

Lazear, Wendy, jt. auth. see Lazear, Jonathon.

Lazega, Emmanuel. The Micropolitics of Knowledge: Communication & Indirect Control in Workgroups. (Communication & Social Order Ser.). 156p. 1992. lib. bdg. 41.95 (*0-202-30426-4*); pap. text ed. 18.95 (*0-202-30427-2*) Aldine de Gruyter.

***Lazell, Barry.** Bob Marley: The Illustrated Legend. (Reed Illustrated Bks.). (Illus.). 80p. (Orig.). 1995. pap. text ed. 14.95 (*0-7935-4034-8*, HL00330008) H Leonard.

Lazell, James D., Jr. Wildlife of the Florida Keys: A Natural History. LC 89-1780. (Illus.). 250p. (Orig.). 1989. 19.95 (*0-933280-98-X*); pap. 19.95 (*0-933280-97-1*) Island Pr.

Lazell, James D., Jr., jt. auth. see Alexander, John R.

Lazell, T. S. Nathaniel Whiting of Dedham MA, 1641, & Five Generations of His Descendants. 80p. 1990. reprint ed. lib. bdg. 24.00 (*0-8328-1560-8*); reprint ed. pap. 16.00 (*0-8328-1561-6*) Higginson Bk Co.

Lazenby. The Defence of Greece 490-479 B.C. pap. write for info. (*0-85668-591-7*, Pub. by Aris & Phillips UK) David Brown.

— Hannibal's War. reprint ed. 39.95 (*0-85668-080-X*, Pub. by Aris & Phillips UK) David Brown.

Lazenby, A., jt. auth. see Jones, M. B.

Lazenby, Nat. Singing Lead. large type ed. (Linford Western Library). 240p. 1989. pap. 11.95 (*0-7089-6678-0*, Linford) Ulverscroft.

Lazenby, Norman. Gunplay over Laredo. large type ed. (Linford Western Library). 1991. pap. 13.95 (*0-7089-7091-5*) Ulverscroft.

Lazenby, Norman A. Dead Sinners. large type ed. (Linford Mystery Library). 256p. 1993. pap. 14.95 (*0-7089-7422-8*, Trailtree Bookshop) Ulverscroft.

— Death in the Stars. large type ed. (Linford Mystery Library). 224p. 1993. pap. 14.95 (*0-7089-7419-8*, Trailtree Bookshop) Ulverscroft.

— A Fightin' Hombre. large type ed. (Linford Western Library). 1990. pap. 12.95 (*0-7089-6810-4*, Trailtree Bookshop) Ulverscroft.

— I Never Killed. large type ed. (Linford Mystery Library). 240p. 1992. pap. 14.95 (*0-7089-7220-9*, Trailtree Bookshop) Ulverscroft.

— Texas Frontier. large type ed. 184p. 1993. pap. 16.95 (*1-85389-371-4*, Medcom-Trainex) Ulverscroft.

— We the Condemned. large type ed. (Linford Mystery Library). 272p. 1992. pap. 14.95 (*0-7089-7229-2*, Trailtree Bookshop) Ulverscroft.

***Lazenby, Roland.** And Now, Your Chicago Bulls: A 30-Year Celebration. 240p. 1995. 39.95 (*0-87833-113-1*) Taylor Pub.

— And Now, Your Chicago Bulls: A 30-Year Celebration. limited ed. 1995. 75.00 (*0-87833-114-X*) Taylor Pub.

— Boston Celtics, 1991-92. 1991. 17.95 (*0-87833-032-1*) Taylor Pub.

— Championship Basketball: Top Coaches Present Their Winning Strategies, Tips, & Techniques for Players & Coaches. (Illus.). 192p. (Orig.). 1986. pap. 11.95 (*0-8092-4874-3*) Contemp Bks.

— Georgetown, the Championships & Thompson. (Illus.). 128p. (J). (gr. 4-12). 1985. 19.95 (*0-913767-08-5*) Full Court VA.

— The Lakers. (Illus.). 304p. 1993. 22.95 (*0-312-09840-5*) St Martin.

— The Lakers: A Basketball Journey. rev. ed. (Illus.). 320p. 1995. reprint ed. pap. 14.95 (*1-57028-062-2*) Masters Pr IN.

— One Hundred Greatest Quarterbacks. 1988. 4.99 (*0-517-65840-2*) Random Hse Value.

— Sampson: A Life above the Rim. (Illus.). 235p. 1983. 14.95 (*0-913767-00-X*); teacher ed 12.70 (*0-685-42768-4*); pap. 8.95 (*0-913767-01-8*) Full Court VA.

— The Second Season: Virginia's Rise to the Final Four. 1984. pap. 9.95 (*0-913767-02-6*) Full Court VA.

***Lazenby, Roland & Doughty, Doug.** Hoos 'n Hokies, the Rivalry: 100 Years of Virginia Tech-Virginia Football. 192p. 1995. 29.95 (*0-87833-116-6*) Taylor Pub.

— Hoos 'n Hokies, the Rivalry: 100 Years of Virginia Tech-Virginia Football. limited ed. 1995. 75.00 (*0-87833-117-4*) Taylor Pub.

Lazenby, Sita. The Elegant Prison. (Illus.). 258p. (Orig.). pap. 7.95 (*0-9601054-9-2*) Cleaning Cons.

Lazer, Hank. Doublespace. LC 91-66723. 192p. (Orig.). 1992. pap. 12.00 (*0-937804-44-4*) Segue NYC.

— Inter (ir) ruptions. (Chapbook Ser.). 22p. 1992. 4.00 (*0-945112-14-9*) Generator Pr.

— What Is a Poet? LC 86-19234. 296p. 1987. 32.50 (*0-8173-0325-1*); pap. 21.50 (*0-8173-0326-X*) U of Ala Pr.

Lazer, Hank, ed. On Louis Simpson: Depths Beyond Happiness. (Under Discussion Ser.). (Orig.). 1988. 39.50 (*0-472-09382-7*); pap. 15.95 (*0-472-06382-0*) U of Mich Pr.

Lazer, Harriet L., jt. auth. see Walker, James W.

Lazer, Lou. Effie's Bytes. 52p. 1987. pap. 10.00 (*0-937953-04-0*) Tiptoe Lit Serv.

***Lazer, William.** Handbook of Demographics for Marketing & Advertising: New Trends in the American Marketplace. 1994. pap. 45.00 (*0-02-918175-5*) Macmillan.

— Handbook of Demographics for Marketing & Advertising: Sources & Trends on the U. S. Consumer. 240p. 1987. text ed. 45.00 (*0-669-16013-X*) Free Pr.

— Marketing Management: A Systems Perspective. LC 74-136717. (Wiley Marketing Ser.). (Illus.). 736p. reprint ed. pap. 180.00 (*0-317-09246-4*, 2011875) Bks Demand.

— Marketing 2000 & Beyond: Future Perspecitves in Marketing. LC 89-29851. 293p. 1990. 29.95 (*0-87757-204-6*) Am Mktg.

Lazer, William, ed. see Academy of Marketing Science Staff.

Lazer, William, jt. auth. see Kelley, Eugene J.

Lazer, Williams & Kelley, Eugene J. Social Marketing: Perspectives & Viewpoints. LC 72-92419. (Illus.). 523p. reprint ed. pap. 149.10 (*0-317-09632-X*, 2055674) Bks Demand.

Lazere, Cathy, jt. auth. see Shasha, Dennis E.

Lazere, Donald, ed. American Media & Mass Culture: Left Perspectives. (Illus.). 560p. 1988. pap. 18.00 (*0-520-04496-7*) U CA Pr.

— American Media & Mass Culture: Left Perspectives. LC 87-22182. (Illus.). 630p. reprint ed. pap. 179.60 (*0-7837-4819-1*, 2044466) Bks Demand.

Lazere, Monroe R., ed. Commercial Financing. LC 67-30356. 317p. reprint ed. pap. 90.40 (*0-317-28646-3*, 2055107) Bks Demand.

***Lazerow, Jama.** Religion & the Working Class in Antebellum America. LC 95-8600. 1995. write for info. (*1-56098-544-5*) Smithsonian.

Lazerowitz, M. & Ambrose, A. Philosophical Theories. 1976. text ed. 42.35 (*90-279-7501-9*) Mouton.

Lazerowitz, Morris. The Language of Philosophy. LC 77-23068. (Boston Studies in the Philosophy of Science: No. 55). 1977. lib. bdg. 65.50 (*90-277-0826-6*); pap. text ed. 44.50 (*90-277-0862-2*) Kluwer Ac.

Lazerowitz, Morris & Ambrose, Alice. Essays in the Unknown Wittgenstein. LC 83-62923. 233p. 1984. 38.95x (*0-87975-234-3*) Prometheus Bks.

— Necessity & Language. LC 85-22201. 272p. 1986. text ed. 39.95 (*0-312-56259-4*) St Martin.

Lazerowitz, Morris, jt. ed. see Hanly, Charles.

Lazerson, Arlyne, jt. auth. see Bloom, Floyd E.

Lazerson, Arlyne, jt. auth. see Fischer, Kurt.

Lazerson, Arlyne, jt. auth. see Hayes, Floyd.

Lazerson, David B. Skullcaps n Switchblades. (Illus.). 204p. (C). 1988. 14.95 (*0-935063-30-7*, Bristol Rhein) CIS Comm.

Lazerson, Joshua. Against the Tide: Whites in the Struggle Against Apartheid. 1994. text ed. 39.95 (*0-8133-8487-7*) Westview.

L

L

Lazerson, Marvin. Origins of the Urban School: Public Education in Massachusetts, 1870-1915. LC 77-168433. (Joint Center for Urban Studies Publications). 302p. reprint ed. 86.10 (*0-685-07747-0*, 2017686) Bks Demand.

Lazerson, Marvin, ed. American Education in the Twentieth Century: A Documentary History. (Classics in Education Ser.). 224p. (C). 1987. pap. text ed. 6.00 (*0-8077-2851-9*) Tchrs Coll.

***Lazerson, Marvin & Grubb, W. Norton, eds.** American Education & Vocationalism: A Documentary History, 1870-1970. LC 73-87511. (Classics in Education Ser.: Vol. 48). 189p. 1974. pap. 53.90 (*0-7837-8951-3*, 2049663) Bks Demand.

Lazerson, Marvin, jt. auth. see Grubb, W. Norton.

Lazerson, Marvin, et al. An Education of Value: The Purposes & Practices of Schools. 175p. 1985. pap. 16.95 (*0-521-31515-8*) Cambridge U Pr.

Lazewnik, Baruch. Handwriting Analysis: A Guide to Understanding Personalities. LC 90-70970. 208p. 1991. pap. 12.95 (*0-924608-06-4*, Whitford Pr) Schiffer.

Lazewnik, Libby. Absolutely Shira. 190p. (J). (gr. 6-9). 1993. 12.95 (*1-56871-032-1*) Targum Pr.

— Baker's Dozen: The Inside Story, No. 5. (J). 1992. pap. 7.95 (*0-944070-93-0*) Targum Pr.

— Bakers Dozen, No. 1: On Our Own. 144p. 1991. 7.95 (*0-944070-34-5*) Targum Pr.

— Baker's Dozen, No. 1: On Our Own. (J). 1993. pap. 7.95 (*0-685-65302-1*) Feldheim.

— Baker's Dozen, No. 5: The Inside Story. (J). 1993. pap. 7.95 (*0-685-65306-4*) Feldheim.

— Between the Thorns. (Illus.). 526p. 1994. 21.95 (*1-56871-057-7*) Targum Pr.

— The Search for Miri. 273p. 1991. 15.95 (*0-944070-35-3*); pap. 12.95 (*0-944070-36-1*) Targum Pr.

— Shira's New Start. (J). (gr. 6-9). 1988. 12.95 (*0-87306-471-2*); pap. 9.95 (*0-685-21963-1*) Feldheim.

— Shira's Summer. (YA). (gr. 6-9). 1988. 12.95 (*0-87306-467-4*); pap. 9.95 (*0-87306-468-2*) Feldheim.

— Top Secret: A Shraga Morgenstern-Pinny Katz Mystery Trilogy. (Little Black Box Ser.: Pt. 1). 165p. (J). (gr. 5-9). 1995. 11.95 (*1-56871-078-X*) Targum Pr.

Lazewnik, Libby, jt. ed. see Zukon, Miriam.

Lazewnik, Libby, et al. Baker's Dozen, No. 6: Trapped. (J). 1993. pap. 7.95 (*0-685-65307-2*) Feldheim.

Lazich, Robert S., jt. ed. see Reddy, Marlita A.

Lazicki, Ted. Do You Mean Me Lord? (Illus.). 120p. (Orig.). 1993. pap. 7.95 (*0-943167-24-8*) Faith & Fellowship Pr.

— Something for the Kids. Zapel, Arthur L., ed. LC 85-62468. 96p. (Orig.). 1985. pap. 8.95 (*0-916260-34-8*, B-192) Meriwether Pub.

— Where Does God Live? Fifty Eight More "Something for the Kids" Children's Sermons for Worship. Zapel, Arthur L. & Wray, Rhonda, eds. LC 91-8734. (Illus.). 144p. (Orig.). (J). (ps-5). 1991. pap. 8.95 (*0-916260-77-1*, B189) Meriwether Pub.

Lazier, jt. auth. see Mann.

Lazier, Christine. Seashore Life. Bogard, Vicki, tr. LC 90-50781. (Young Discovery Library). (Illus.). 38p. (J). (gr. k-5). 1991. 5.95 (*0-944589-39-1*, 391) Young Discovery Lib.

Lazier, William C., jt. auth. see Collins, James C.

Lazin, Fred, et al, eds. Developing Areas, Universities, & Public Policy. 184p. (Orig.). 1986. pap. 12.00 (*0-918592-86-0*) Pol Studies.

— The Policy Impact of Universities in Developing Countries. LC 88-1387. (Policy Studies Organization). 256p. 1988. text ed. 49.95 (*0-312-01698-0*) St Martin.

Lazin, Frederick A. Policy Implementation & Social Welfare in the 1980s: Israel & the United States. 145p. (Orig.). 1986. 32.95 (*0-88738-084-0*); pap. 12.95 (*0-88738-629-6*) Transaction Pubs.

— Politics & Policy Implementation: Project Renewal in Israel. LC 92-40308. (SUNY Series in Israeli Studies). 201p. (C). 1993. 49.50 (*0-7914-1691-7*); pap. 19.95 (*0-7914-1692-5*) State U NY Pr.

Lazinger, Susan S. & Shoval, Peretz. Prototyping a Microcomputer-Based Online Library Catalog. (Occasional Papers: No. 177). 1985. pap. 2.50 (*0-317-59035-9*) U of Ill Lib Info Sci.

Lazitch, Branko & Drachkovitch, Milorad M. Biographical Dictionary of the Comintern. rev. ed. (Publication Ser.: No. 340). 550p. (C). 1986. text ed. 44.95 (*0-8179-8401-1*) Hoover Inst Pr.

Lazlo, Gyula. The Art of the Migration Period. Balogh, Barna, tr. LC 70-171454. (Illus.). 158p. 1973. 15.95 (*0-87024-222-9*) U of Miami Pr.

Lazlo, P., ed. Comprehensive Biochemistry, Vol. 34A: The Recognition of Molecular Correlate of Biological Concepts. 1986. 152.00 (*0-685-01556-4*) Elsevier.

Laznicka, M. Physics of Solid Surfaces. (Studies in Surface Science & Catalysts: Vol. 9). 282p. 1982. pap. 95.00 (*0-444-99716-4*) Elsevier.

Laznicka, P. Breccias & Coarse Fragmentites: Petrology, Environments, Associations, Ores. (Developments in Economic Geology Ser.: Vol. 25). 842p. 1988. 164.00 (*0-444-42938-7*) Elsevier.

— Empirical Metallogeny: Depositional Environments, Lithologic Associations & Metallic Ores, Vol. 1: Phanerozoic Environments, Associations & Deposits, 2 vols., Set. (Developments in Economic Geology Ser.: No. 19). 1758p. 1986. 256.50 (*0-444-42554-3*) Elsevier.

— Precambrian Empirical Metallogeny: Precambrian Lithologic Associations & Metallic Ores. (Developments in Economic Geology Ser.: Vol. 29). 1640p. 1993. 331.50 (*0-444-89953-7*) Elsevier.

Laznow, J. Air Pollution Permitting Reference & Workbook. 1992. text ed. write for info. (*0-442-01446-5*) Van Nos Reinhold.

Lazo, et al. Review for USMLE: United States Medical Licensing Examination, Step 1. 21th ed. (Illus.). 137p. 1994. 29.95 (*0-683-06209-3*) Williams & Wilkins.

Lazo, Caroline. Eleanor Roosevelt. LC 93-6610. (Peacemakers Ser.). (Illus.). 64p. (J). (gr. 4 up). 1993. text ed. 13.95 (*0-87518-594-0*, Dillon Silver Burdett) Silver Burdett Pr.

— Elie Wiesel. LC 93-44473. (J). 1994. text ed. 13.95 (*0-87518-636-X*, Dillon Silver Burdett) Silver Burdett Pr.

— Mahatma Gandhi. LC 92-14314. (Peacemakers Ser.). (Illus.). 64p. (J). (gr. 4 up). 1993. text ed. 13.95 (*0-87518-526-6*, Dillon Silver Burdett) Silver Burdett Pr.

— Martin Luther King, Jr. LC 93-9069. (Peacemakers Ser.). (Illus.). 64p. (J). (gr. 4 up). 1994. text ed. 13.95 (*0-87518-618-1*, Dillon Silver Burdett) Silver Burdett Pr.

— Mother Teresa. LC 92-23765. (Peacemakers Ser.). (Illus.). 64p. (J). (gr. 4 up). 1993. text ed. 13.95 (*0-87518-559-2*, Dillon Silver Burdett) Silver Burdett Pr.

— Rigoberta Menchu. LC 93-8381. (Peacemakers Ser.). (Illus.). 64p. (J). (gr. 4 up). 1994. text ed. 13.95 (*0-87518-619-X*, Dillon Silver Burdett) Silver Burdett Pr.

— The Terra Cotta Army of Emperor Qin. LC 92-26189. (Illus.). 80p. (YA). (gr. 6 up). 1993. lib. bdg. 14.95 (*0-02-754631-4*, Mac Bks Young Read) S&S Childrens.

— Wilma Mankiller. LC 94-1229. (Peacemakers Ser.). (J). (gr. 4 up). 1994. text ed. 13.95 (*0-87518-635-1*, Dillon Silver Burdett) Silver Burdett Pr.

Lazo, Caroline E. Divorce. LC 89-2156. (Facts About Ser.). (Illus.). 48p. (J). (gr. 5-6). 1989. text ed. 12.95 (*0-89686-436-7*, Crstwood Hse) Silver Burdett Pr.

— Endangered Species. LC 90-35494. (Earth Alert Ser.). (Illus.). 48p. (J). (gr. 6). 1990. text ed. 12.95 (*0-89686-545-2*, Crstwood Hse) Silver Burdett Pr.

— Lech Walesa. LC 92-39959. (Peacemakers Ser.). (Illus.). 64p. (J). (gr. 4 up). 1993. text ed. 13.95 (*0-87518-525-8*, Dillon Silver Burdett) Silver Burdett Pr.

— Missing Treasure. (Incredible Histories Ser.). (Illus.). 48p. (J). (gr. 5-6). 1990. text ed. 11.95 (*0-89686-510-X*, Crstwood Hse) Silver Burdett Pr.

Lazo, Donald M. If You Care...Let Your Alcoholic Suffer! A Battle Plan for Families of Alcoholics. Fair, Erik, ed. (Illus.). 128p. (Orig.). 1996. pap. 11.95 (*0-913581-12-7*) Publitec.

Lazo, John, jt. ed. see Hacker, Miles.

Lazo, John A., ed. Directory of the APA, 1993. 1952p. 1993. 70.00 (*1-55798-210-4*) Am Psychol.

Lazo, John S., jt. ed. see Huber, Brian E.

Lazo, John S., et al. Review for USMLE: United States Medical Licensing Examination, Step 1. LC 93-41661. (National Medical Series for Independent Study). (Illus.). 300p. 1994. 29.95 (*0-683-06265-4*) Williams & Wilkins.

Lazo, Julia A., tr. see Rice, Wayne & Yaconelli, Mike.

Lazo, William. Augustine's Trick. (Augustine Detective Ser.). 64p. (Orig.). (C). 1991. pap. 4.00 (*1-880046-05-9*) Baculite Pub.

Lazo, William J. The Ching Poems. (Minority Poet Ser.). 38p. (ENG & SPA.). 1990. pap. 5.00 (*1-880046-02-4*) Baculite Pub.

Lazofsky, Saul L. Everyone's Guide to Credit. (Illus.). 330p. (Orig.). 1991. pap. 21.95 (*0-9627797-0-9*) Everyones Guide to Credit.

Lazonick, William. Business Organization & the Myth of the Market Economy. (Illus.). 350p. (C). 1992. 49.95 (*0-521-39419-8*) Cambridge U Pr.

— Business Organization & the Myth of the Market Economy. (Illus.). 396p. (C). 1993. pap. 16.95 (*0-521-44788-7*) Cambridge U Pr.

— Competitive Advantage on the Shop Floor. LC 90-32203. (Illus.). 419p. 1990. 46.50 (*0-674-15416-9*) HUP.

— Organization & Technology in Capitalist Development. LC 92-2430. (Economists of the Twentieth Century Ser.). 320p. 1992. 69.95 (*1-85278-742-2*, Pub. by E Elgar Pub UK) Ashgate Pub Co.

***Lazonick, William & Mass, William, eds.** Organizational Capability & Competitive Advantage. LC 94-44343. (International Library of Critical Writings in Business History: Reference Collection: Vol. 11). 704p. 1995. 199.95 (*1-85278-776-7*, Pub. by E Elgar Pub UK) Ashgate Pub Co.

Lazor-Bahr, Beverly, illus. Fievel Saves the Day. LC 90-85174. (American Tail: Fievel Goes West Ser.). 14p. (J). (ps). 1991. 5.95 (*0-448-41075-3*, G&D) Putnam Pub Group.

Lazor, Paul, tr. see Uspensky, Nicholas.

Lazorthes, Yves & Upton, Adrian R., eds. Neurostimulation: An Overview. (Illus.). 372p. 1985. 55.00 (*0-87993-261-9*) Futura Pub.

Lazou, Christopher. Supercomputers & Their Use. rev. ed. (Illus.). 276p. 1988. pap. 27.50 (*0-19-853759-X*) OUP.

Lazow, Alfred & Nelson, Pearl A. The ABCs of Herbs. (Illus.). 1977. 3.95 (*0-914634-48-8*, 7718) DOK Pubs.

Lazowska, Edward. PPOPP, '90: Second SIGPLAN Symposium on Principles & Practice of Parallel Programming, Held in Seattle, WA, March 14-16, 1990. (Sigplan Notices Ser.: Vol. 23, No. 3). (Illus.). viii, 206p. 1990. pap. text ed. 21.00 (*0-89791-350-7*, 551900) Assn Compu Machinery.

Lazowska, Edward D., et al. Quantitative System Performance: Computer System Analysis Using Queueing Network Models. LC 83-13791. (Illus.). 417p. (C). 1983. text ed. 89.00 (*0-13-746975-6*) P-H.

Lazreg, Marnia. The Eloquence of Silence: Algerian Women in Question. LC 94-6193. 1994. 55.00 (*0-415-90730-6*); pap. 16.95 (*0-415-90731-4*) Routledge.

***Lazur, Carole & Riegel, Lynn.** The Night Thoughts Dream Guide. Robertson, Jon, ed. 160p. (YA). 1995. 19.95 (*0-87604-343-0*) ARE Pr.

Lazure, Noel. Dictionnaire d'Intelligence Artificielle, Anglais-Francais. 216p. 1993. pap. 115.00 (*0-7859-5617-4*, 2225840288) Fr & Eur.

Lazurus, John, ed. The Opera Handbook. (Monograph Ser.). 242p. 1990. text ed. 25.00 (*0-8161-9094-1*, Hall Reference); pap. 15.95 (*0-8161-1827-2*, Hall Reference) Macmillan.

Lazutkin, Vladimir F. KAM Theory & Semiclassical Approximations to Eigenfunctions. LC 93-17491. (Ergebnisse der Mathematik und Ihrer Grenzgebiete Ser.: Vol. 24). (Illus.). ix, 389p. 1993. 139.00 (*0-387-53389-3*) Spr-Verlag.

Lazutkin, Y. Socialism & Wealth: The Creation & Distribution of Socialist Wealth. 217p. 1975. 22.95 (*0-8464-0859-7*) Beekman Pubs.

Lazzara, Judy, jt. auth. see Olson, Beverly.

Lazzara, Ralph, jt. ed. see Aliot, Etienne.

Lazzari, Andrea & Peters, Patricia. HELP Elementary (Handbook of Exercising for Language Processing) 1993. student ed, spiral bd. 27.95 (*1-55999-259-X*) LinguiSystems.

Lazzari, Andrea & Peters, Patricia M. HELP 1 & 2 Language Game Instruction Manual: Handbook of Exercises for Language Processing. 1990. 34.95 (*1-55999-104-6*) LinguiSystems.

— HELP 1 (Handbook of Exercises for Language Processing) 2nd ed. 1987. spiral bd. 27.95 (*1-55999-045-7*) LinguiSystems.

— HELP 2 (Handbook of Exercises for Language Processing) 2nd ed. 1987. spiral bd. 27.95 (*1-55999-046-5*) LinguiSystems.

— HELP 3 & 4 Language Game Instruction Manual: Handbook of Exercises for Language Processing. 1990. 34.95 (*1-55999-105-4*) LinguiSystems.

— HELP 3 (Handbook of Exercises for Language Processing) 1988. spiral bd. 27.95 (*1-55999-047-3*) LinguiSystems.

Lazzari, Andrea, et al. Best of Auditory Skills. 1993. 19.95 (*1-55999-390-1*) LinguiSystems.

— Best of General Information. 1993. 19.95 (*1-55999-391-X*) LinguiSystems.

— Best of Problem Solving. 1993. 19.95 (*1-55999-393-6*) LinguiSystems.

— Best of Word Finding. 1993. 19.95 (*1-55999-392-8*) LinguiSystems.

Lazzari, Andrea M. Just for Adults: An Adult Handbook for Language Rehabilitation. (Illus.). 190p. 1990. student ed, spiral bd. 31.95 (*1-55999-116-X*) LinguiSystems.

Lazzari, Andrea M. & Peters, Patricia M. HELP 4 (Handbook of Exercises for Language Processing) 1989. student ed, spiral bd. 27.95 (*1-55999-048-1*) LinguiSystems.

— HELP 5: Handbook of Exercises for Language Processing. (Illus.). 190p. 1991. spiral bd. 27.95 (*1-55999-181-X*) LinguiSystems.

Lazzari, Eugene P., ed. CRC Handbook of Experimental Aspects of Oral Biochemistry. 384p. 1983. 145.00 (*0-8493-3162-5*, QP146, CRC Reprint) Franklin.

Lazzari, Margaret R. Art & Design Fundamentals. 1990. pap. 34.95 (*0-442-31943-6*) Van Nos Reinhold.

***Lazzari, Marie.** Nineteenth Century Literary Criticism: Excerpts from Criticism of the Works of Novelists, Poets, Playwrights, Short Story Writers, Philosophers & Other Creative Writers Who Died Between 1800 & 1899, from the First Published Critical Appraisals to Current Evaluations, Vol. 48. (Nineteenth Century Literary Criticism Ser.: Vol. 48 Topics). 460p. 1995. text ed. 122.00 (*0-8103-8939-8*) Gale.

Lazzari, Marie, ed. Environmental Viewpoints 2. 2nd ed. 430p. (C). 1993. 60.00 (*0-8103-8932-0*, 101632) Gale.

— Nineteenth Century Literary Criticism: Excerpts from Criticism of the Works of Novelists, Poets, Playwrights, Short Story Writers, Philosophers & Other Creative Writers Who Died Between 1800 & 1899, from the First Published Critical Appraisals to Current Evaluations, Vol. 47. (Nineteenth Century Literary Criticism Ser.: Vol. 47). 460p. 1995. text ed. 122.00 (*0-8103-8938-X*) Gale.

— Twentieth Century Criticism Vol. 55 & Index: Excerpts from Criticism of the Works of Novelists, Poets, Playwrights, Short Story Writers & Other Creative Writers who Lived Between 1900 & 1960, from the First Published Critical Appraisals to Current Evaluations. 532p. 1994. text ed. 119.00 (*0-8103-2435-0*) Gale.

— Twentieth-Century Literary Criticism Vol. 55: Excerpts from Criticism of the Works of Novelists, Poets, Playwrights, Short Story Writers, & Other Creative Writers Who Lived Between 1900 & 1960, from the First Published Critical Appraisals to Current Evaluations. 532p. 1994. text ed. 119.00 (*0-8103-2436-9*) Gale.

Lazzari, Marie, jt. ed. see Cerrito, Joann.

Lazzarino, Graziana. Prego. 554p. (ITA.). (C). 1985. 12.95 (*0-07-554573-X*) McGraw.

***Lazzarino, Graziana, et al.** Prego! An Invitation to Italian. 4th ed. LC 94-42536. 1995. text ed. write for info. (*0-07-037722-7*) McGraw.

Lazzarino, Graziana. Prego! An Invitation to Italian. 1990. student ed write for info. (*0-07-557432-2*); student ed write for info. (*0-07-909486-4*); write for info. (*0-07-557171-4*); write for info. (*0-07-540865-1*) McGraw.

— Prego! An Invitation to Italian. 3rd ed. 1990. text ed. write for info. (*0-07-557426-8*) McGraw.

— Prego! An Invitation to Italian. 3rd ed. 1990. student ed, pap. text ed. 13.03 (*0-07-557428-4*); student ed, pap. text ed. 15.00 (*0-07-557476-4*) McGraw.

— Prego! An Invitation to Italian. 3rd ed. 1990. student ed, pap. text ed. 13.03 (*0-07-557430-6*); write for info. (*0-07-540866-X*) McGraw.

***Lazzarino, Graziana & Moneti, Annamaria.** Da Capo. 4th ed. (C). Date not set. pap. write for info. (*0-03-009522-0*) HR&W Schl Div.

— Da Capo: An Italian Review Grammar. 3rd ed. 404p. (ITA.). (C). 1990. 173.75 (*0-03-053792-4*) HB Coll Pubs.

— Da Capo: An Italian Review Grammar. 3rd ed. 404p. (ITA.). (C). 1991. pap. text ed. 29.50 (*0-03-072232-2*); pap. text ed. 17.00 (*0-03-053898-X*) HB Coll Pubs.

— Da Capo: An Italian Review Grammar. 3rd ed. 404p. (ITA.). (C). 1992. pap. text ed. 21.75 (*0-03-072234-9*); audio 28.50 (*0-03-072312-4*); 28.50 (*0-03-072233-0*) HB Coll Pubs.

— Da Capo: An Italian Review Grammar, Level II. 3rd ed. 404p. (ITA.). (C). 1991. write for info. (*0-318-69164-7*) HB Coll Pubs.

Lazzaro, Bea, jt. auth. see Mendelsohn, Lotte.

Lazzaro-Bruno, C., jt. auth. see Sopher, M. S.

Lazzaro-Bruno, Claudia, jt. auth. see Sopher, Marcus S.

Lazzaro, Claudia. The Italian Renaissance Garden: From the Conventions of Planting, Design & Ornament to the Grand Gardens of Sixteenth-Century Italy. (Illus.). 352p. (C). 1990. 55.00 (*0-300-04765-7*) Yale U Pr.

Lazzaro, Joseph J. Adaptive Technologies for Learning & Work Environments. LC 92-46993. (Illus.). 250p. 1993. pap. 35.00 (*0-8389-0615-X*) ALA.

Lazzaro-Weis, Carol M. Confused Epiphanies: L'Abbe Prevost & the Romance Tradition. LC 90-24446. (American University Studies: Romance Languages & Literature: Ser. II, Vol. 161). 195p. (C). 1991. text ed. 34.95 (*0-8204-1459-X*) P Lang Pubs.

— From Margins to Mainstream: Feminism & Fictional Modes in Italian Women's Writing, 1968-1990. LC 93-10867. 240p. (Orig.). (C). 1993. text ed. 34.95 (*0-8122-3195-3*); pap. text ed. 16.95 (*0-8122-1438-2*) U of Pa Pr.

Lazzati, Santiago. Diccionario del Verbo Castellano: Dictionary of Castilian Verbs. 438p. (SPA.). 1977. pap. 24.95 (*0-8288-5332-0*, S12049) Fr & Eur.

Lazzell, K. M., jt. auth. see Redick, S. S.

Lazzerini, Beatrice & Lopriore, Lanfranco. Program Debugging Environments: Design & Utilization. 170p. 1992. text ed. 56.00 (*0-13-721838-9*) P-H.

Lazzerini, Edward J., jt. auth. see Yang, Richard.

LBJ Library Staff. Lyndon B. Johnson: A Bibliography. LC 83-23264. 272p. 1984. text ed. 25.00 (*0-292-74017-4*) U of Tex Pr.

LBJ Space Center Staff & NASA Space Center Staff. Journal of the Geochemical Society & Meteoritical Society: Supplement 4, 3 vols., Set. LC 73-15974. 1973. 1,378.00 (*0-08-017909-6*, Pub. by Pergamon Repr UK) Franklin.

L.B.K.C. Staff. Recent Nepal: An Analysis of Recent Democratic Upsurge & Its Aftermath. (C). 1993. 71.00 (*0-7855-0212-2*, Pub. by Ratna Pustak Bhandar) St Mut.

LC Marc Tapes Staff & New York Public Library Staff. Bibliographic Guide to Microform Publications: 1990. (Bibliographic Guides Ser.). 600p. (C). 1991. lib. bdg. 250.00 (*0-8161-7144-0*) G K Hall.

LC Marc Tapes Staff & Oriental Division of the New York Public Library Staff. Bibliographic Guide to East Asian Studies, 1990. (Bibliographic Guides Ser.). 350p. (C). 1991. lib. bdg. 165.00 (*0-8161-7137-8*) G K Hall.

Lcakey, Mercedes. Winds of Change. (Mage Winds Ser.: Bk. 2). 480p. 1993. mass mkt. 5.99 (*0-88677-563-9*) DAW Bks.

***LCC-ST Staff.** Directory of Certified Surgical Technologists & Certified First Assistants, 1995. Davis, Nadine A., ed. 1995. pap. text ed. write for info. (*0-9622332-5-0*) Liaison Coun.

***LCE, Inc. Staff.** Finding Legal Help: An Older Person's Guide. 25p. 1995. pap. text ed. 3.00 (*0-933945-12-4*) Legal Coun Elderly.

Ldekker, John W. Faithful Mohawks. 312p. 1993. reprint ed. lib. bdg. 89.00 (*0-7812-5159-1*) Rprt Serv.

LDI Productions Staff. All That Jazz & More... 2nd ed. 160p. 1994. per., pap. text ed. 21.95 (*0-8403-9020-3*) Kendall-Hunt.

***Le.** Filipino American Lives. (C). 1995. pap. text ed. 16.95 (*1-56639-317-5*) Temple U Pr.

— Good Wood Bear. 1995. pap. 4.99 (*0-440-40974-8*) Dell.

Le, ed. Fundamentals of Biostatistical Inference. (Statistics: Vol. 124). 272p. 1991. 55.00 (*0-8247-8674-2*) Dekker.

Le-Ba-Khanh & Le-Ba-Kong. Vietnamese-English-Vietnamese Dictionary. 9th ed. 501p. (ENG & VIE.). 1980. 69.95 (*0-8288-1085-0*, M 9502) Fr & Eur.

Le-Ba-Kong, jt. auth. see Le-Ba-Khanh.

***Le Bailly, Pamela.** Pressed Flowers. 1994. 18.95 (*1-870586-14-X*, Pub. by D Porteous Edits UK) Seven Hills Bk.

Le Baron Stockwell, M. Descendants of Francis LeBaron of Plymouth, Mass. (Illus.). 521p. reprint ed. lib. bdg. 91.50 (*0-8328-0757-5*); reprint ed. pap. 81.50 (*0-8328-0758-3*) Higginson Bk Co.

Le Bas, Elizabeth, tr. see Le Febvre, Henri.

***Le Bas, M. J., ed.** Milestones in Geology. (Geological Society Memoir Ser.: No. 16). 272p. 1995. 49.00 (*1-897799-24-1*, Pub. by Geol Soc Pub Hse UK) AAPG.

Le Bas, Michael J. Carbonatite-Nephelinite Volcanism: An African Case History. LC 76-21090. (Illus.). 401p. reprint ed. pap. 114.30 (*0-685-24171-8*, 2033049) Bks Demand.

Le Bas, Philippe & Waddington, William H. Inscriptions Grecques et Latines Recueillies en Grece et Asie Mineure, 2 vols., Set. (Subsidia Epigraphica Ser.: Vols. I-II). xi, 884p. (GER.). 1972. reprint ed. write for info. (*3-487-04396-3*, Pub. by Georg Olms GW) Lubrecht & Cramer.

— Inscriptions Grecques et Latines Recueillies en Grece et Asie Mineure, Vol. I: Textes en Majuscules. xi, 884p. (GER.). 1972. reprint ed. write for info. (*0-318-71362-4*, Pub. by Georg Olms GW) Lubrecht & Cramer.

An Asterisk (*) at the beginning of an entry indicates that the title is appearing in BIP for the first time.

— Inscriptions Grecques et Latines Recueillies en Grece et Asie Mineure, Vol. II: Textes en Minuscules et Explications. xi, 884p. (GER.). 1972. reprint ed. write for info. (0-318-71363-2, Pub. by Georg Olms GW) Lubrecht & Cramer.

Le Beau, Bryan F. Frederic Henry Hedge: Nineteenth Century American Transcendentalist: Intellectually Radical, Ecclesiastically Conservative. LC 85-570. (Pittsburgh Theological Monographs, New Ser.: No. 16). (Orig.). 1985. pap. 10.00 (0-915138-71-9) Pickwick.

Le Beau, Claude. Avantures Du Sr. C. Le Beau, Avocat En Parlement, Ou Voyage Curieux et Nouveau Parmi les Sauvages De L'amerique Septentrionale, 2 vols., Set. (Canadiana Avant 1867 Ser.: No. 16). 1966. 83.10 (3-10-800086-1) Mouton.

***Le Bel, Pauline.** The Song Spinner. (Illus.). 72p. (J). 1995. pap. 7.95 (0-88995-120-9, Pub. by Red Deer CN) BookWorld Dist.

Le Bellac, Michel. Quantum & Statistical Field Theory. Barton, Gabriel, tr. 640p. 1992. pap. 42.50 (0-19-853964-9) OUP.

Le Beouf. Elephant Seals. 1985. pap. 4.50 (0-910286-98-1) Boxwood.

Le Berre, Francois. The New Chameleons Handbook. 160p. (Orig.). 1994. pap. 8.95 (0-8120-1805-2) Barron.

Le Bert, Joseph J. CICS Essentials for Application Developers & Programmers. LC 92-25967. 384p. 1993. text ed. 45.00 (0-07-035869-9) McGraw.

Le Bidois. Syntaxe du Francais Moderne, 2 tomes, Set. 35. 90 (0-685-36655-3); 60.95 (0-8288-7865-X, F135480) Fr & Eur.

***Le Bihan, Denis, ed.** Diffusion & Perfusion Magnetic Resonance Imaging. LC 94-24643. 408p. 1995. 149.00 (0-7817-0244-5) Raven.

Le Blanc, Charles. Huai-nan Tzu: Philosophical Synthesis in Early Han Thought. 268p. 1985. 57.50x (962-209-179-2, Pub. by Hong Kong Univ Pr HK) Coronet Bks.

— Huai-nan Tzu: Philosophical Synthesis in Early Han Thought. 268p. (C). 1985. text ed. 90.00 (0-685-65776-0, Pub. by Hong Kong U Pr HK); pap. text ed. 69.00 (962-209-169-5, Pub. by Hong Kong U Pr HK) St Mut.

Le Blanc, Charles & Blader, Susan, eds. Chinese Ideas about Nature & Society. 360p. 1987. 57.50 (962-209-189-X, Pub. by Hong Kong Univ Pr HK) Coronet Bks.

— Chinese Ideas about Nature & Society Studies in Honour of Derk Bodde. 360p. (C). 1987. text ed. 132.00 (0-685-65777-9, Pub. by Hong Kong U Pr HK); pap. text ed. 110.00 (962-209-188-1, Pub. by Hong Kong U Pr HK) St Mut.

Le Blanc, Daird, ed. see Calvet, Koala.

Le Blanc, H., jt. auth. see Wyatt, J.

Le Blanc, L. Little Frog Learns to Sing. LC 68-16394. (Illus.). 32p. (J). (ps-2). 1967. lib. bdg. 9.95 (0-87783-022-3); audio 7.94 (0-87783-191-2) Oddo.

Le Blanc, Marcel & Frechette, M. Male Criminal Activity from Childhood Through Youth. (Research in Criminology Ser.). (Illus.). xi, 228p. 1989. 102.00 (0-387-96859-8) Spr-Verlag.

Le Blanc, Paul. Lenin & the Revolutionary Party. LC 88-18067. 456p. (C). 1990. text ed. 60.00 (0-391-03604-1) Humanities.

— Lenin & the Revolutionary Party. LC 88-18067. 456p. (C). 1993. pap. 25.00 (0-391-03742-0) Humanities.

Le Blanc, Paul, jt. ed. see McLemee, Scott.

***Le Blanc, Pierre.** Teacher Not Preacher. 160p. 1994. per. 18.50 (0-945383-65-7) Teach Servs.

Le Blanc, Rufus J. & Breeding, Julia G., eds. Regional Aspects of Carbonate Deposition: A Symposium. LC 57-2837. (Society of Economic Paleontologists & Mineralogists, Special Publication Ser.: No. 5). 215p. reprint ed. pap. 61.30 (0-317-27104-0, 2024732) Bks Demand.

Le Blanc, Sydney. Whitney Guide to Twentieth Century American Architecture. LC 92-46410. (Illus.). 224p. 1993. pap. 18.95 (0-8230-2174-2, Whitney Lib) Watsn-Guptill.

Le Blant, Edmont F. Inscriptions Chretiennes de la Gaule Anterieure au Huitieme Siecle, 2 vols. clvi, 1142p. reprint ed. write for info. (0-318-71364-0, Pub. by Georg Olms GW) Lubrecht & Cramer.

— Inscriptions Chretiennes de la Gaule Anterieure au VIIIe Siecle, 2 vols. reprint ed. write for info. (0-318-72102-3, Pub. by Georg Olms GW) Lubrecht & Cramer.

Le Boeuf, Burney J. & Laws, Richard M., eds. Elephant Seals: Population Ecology, Behavior, & Physiology. LC 93-38142. 1994. 58.00 (0-520-08364-4) U CA Pr.

Le Boeuf, Michael. How to Win Customers & Keep Them for Life. 1989. pap. 11.00 (0-425-11468-6, Berkley Trade) Berkley Pub.

Le Bohec, Yann. The Imperial Roman Army. (Illus.). 400p. 1994. 35.00 (0-7818-0259-8) Hippocrene Bks.

Le Bon, Daniel, tr. see Jackins, Harvey.

***Le Bon, Gustav.** The Crowd. rev. ed. 224p. (C). 1994. pap. 19.95 (1-56000-788-5) Transaction Pubs.

Le Bon, Gustave. The Evolution of Forces. 1991. lib. bdg. 75.95 (0-8490-4812-5) Gordon Pr.

— The Evolution of Matter. 1991. lib. bdg. 79.95 (0-8490-4809-5) Gordon Pr.

— The Psychology of Peoples. LC 73-14164. (Perspectives in Social Inquiry Ser.). 252p. 1979. reprint ed. 19.95 (0-405-05509-9) Ayer.

— The Psychology of Revolution. LC 68-29699. 1968. reprint ed. 18.00 (0-87034-026-3) Fraser Pub Co.

Le Bon, Leo. Where Mountains Live: Twelve Great Treks of the World. (Illus.). 144p. 1988. 40.00 (0-89381-242-0) Aperture.

Le Bon, S., ed. see Sartre, Jean-Paul.

Le Bossu, Adam. Jeu de la Feuille. 181p. (FRE.). 1970. 19. 95 (0-8288-7471-9) Fr & Eur.

— Jeu de Robin et Marion. 91p. (FRE.). 1968. 9.95 (0-8288-7494-8) Fr & Eur.

Le Bossu, Rene. Traite du Poeme Epique, 2 vols. 646p. reprint ed. write for info. (0-318-71365-9, Pub. by Georg Olms GW) Lubrecht & Cramer.

***Le Bot, Marc.** Michelangelo. Agueros, Marie-Helene, tr. LC 94-45574. (Art Library). (Illus.). 1995. pap. 12.00 (0-517-88375-9, Crown) Crown Pub Group.

— Rembrandt. (CAL Art Ser.). (Illus.). 96p. 1991. 18.00 (0-517-58535-9, Crown) Crown Pub Group.

— Rembrandt. (CAL Art Ser.). 1991. 18.00 (0-517-58348-8, Crown) Crown Pub Group.

Le Bourdais, Donat M. Stefansson: Ambassador of the North. LC 63-17243. (Emulation Bks.). 206p. reprint ed. pap. 58.80 (0-317-28425-8, 2022307) Bks Demand.

Le Bourgeois, Helen, ed. see Ward, Ola M.

Le Boursicaud, Henri. Rags to Riches: The Story of the Companions of Emmaus. 144p. 1989. pap. 22.00 (1-85390-053-2, Pub. by Veritas IE) St Mut.

Le Bras, Gabriel. Etudes De Sociologie Religieuse: Studies in Religious Sociology, 2 vols. in one. LC 74-25763. (European Sociology Ser.). 824p. 1975. reprint ed. 65.95 (0-405-06517-5) Ayer.

Le Braz, Anatole. Dealings with the Dead: Narratives from "La Legende de la mort en Basse Bretagne" Whitehead, E. A., tr. LC 77-87695. reprint ed. 18.50 (0-404-16491-9) AMS Pr.

— The Night of Fires & Other Breton Studies. Gostling, Frances M., tr. LC 77-87696. (Illus.). reprint ed. 24.50 (0-404-16492-7) AMS Pr.

Le Breton, Anna L. Memoir of Mrs. Barbauld, Including Letters & Notices of Her Family & Friends. LC 73-172311. reprint ed. 39.50 (0-404-07397-2) AMS Pr.

Le Breton, Binka. Voices from the Amazon. LC 93-16349. (Books for a World That Works). (Illus.). xiv, 165p. 1993. pap. 14.95 (1-56549-021-5) Kumarian Pr.

Le Breton, Kenny. Lovebirds As a Hobby. (TT Ser.). (Illus.). 98p. 1992. pap. 7.95 (0-86622-411-4, TT011) TFH Pubns.

***Le Bris, Annie.** Phraseological Dictionary of Economics & & Business Terms French-Italian--Italian-French. (FRE & ITA.). Date not set. 125.00 (0-7859-8864-5) Fr & Eur.

***Le Bris, Pierre & Prost, Andre.** Dictionnaire Bobo-Francais. 1981. write for info. (0-7859-8653-7, 285297102X) Fr & Eur.

Le Brizault, Jean-Louis. Dictionnaires des Sigles Anglais Utilises en Electronique et en Informatique. 240p. (FRE.). 1990. pap. 125.00 (0-8288-2587-4, 2852065835) Fr & Eur.

Le Brocquy, Sybil. Swift's Most Valuable Friend. LC 68-26028. 1968. 11.95 (0-8023-1165-2) Dufour.

Le Brun, Annie. Sade: A Sudden Abyss. Naish, Camille, tr. 232p. (Orig.). 1991. pap. 12.95 (0-87286-250-X) City Lights.

Le Brun, Charles. A Method to Learn to Design the Passions, Proposed in a Conference on Their General & Particular Expression. Williams, John, tr. LC 92-24907. (Augustan Reprints Ser.: Nos. 200-201 (1980)). reprint ed. 18.50 (0-404-70200-7, NC825) AMS Pr.

— Methode Pour Apprendre A Dessiner les Passions. vi, 63p. 1982. reprint ed. write for info. (3-487-06717-X, Pub. by Georg Olms GW) Lubrecht & Cramer.

***Le Brun, Marlene & Johnstone, Richard.** The Quiet (R) evolution: Improving Student Learning in Law. 350p. 1994. pap. 65.00 (0-455-21279-1, Pub. by Law Bk Co) W W Gaunt.

Le Bruyn, Lieven, jt. ed. see Van Oystaeyen, Freddy.

Le Bruyn, Lieven, et al. Graded Orders. 250p. 1988. 32.50 (0-8176-3360-X) Birkhauser.

Le Cain, Errol, jt. auth. see Barber, Antonia.

Le Cain, Errol, jt. auth. see Price, M.

Le Cain, George, jt. auth. see Donaldson, Cyril.

Le Cam, Lucien M. Asymptotic Methods in Statistical Decision Theory. (Series in Statistics). 770p. 1986. 49.95 (0-387-96307-3) Spr-Verlag.

Le Cam, Lucien M. & Lo Yang, G. Asymptotics in Statistics: Some Basic Concepts. Berger, J. O. et al, eds. (Series in Statistics). (Illus.). viii, 180p. 1990. 32.00 (0-387-97372-9) Spr-Verlag.

Le Cam, Lucien M. & Neyman, J., eds. Probability Models & Cancer: Proceedings of an Interdisciplinary Cancer Study Conference. 310p. 1983. 87.25 (0-444-86514-4, North Holland) Elsevier.

Le Cam, Lucien M. & Olshen, Richard A., eds. Proceedings of the Berkeley Conference in Honor of Jerzy Neyman & Jack Keifer, 2 vols., Vol. 1. LC 85-13750. 500p. (C). 1985. 57.95 (0-534-03312-1) Chapman & Hall.

— Proceedings of the Berkeley Conference in Honor of Jerzy Neyman & Jack Keifer, 2 vols., Vol. 2. LC 85-13750. 500p. (C). 1985. 57.95 (0-534-03357-1) Chapman & Hall.

Le Camus de Mezieres, Nicolas. The Genius of Architecture: or The Analogy of That Art with Our Sensations. Britt, David, tr. LC 92-875. (Texts & Documents Ser.). (Illus.). 224p. 1992. 29.95 (0-89236-234-0); pap. 19.95 (0-89236-235-9) J P Getty Trust.

Le Carre, John. The Honourable Schoolboy. LC 77-75001. 1977. 24.95 (0-394-41645-7) Knopf.

— Honourable Schoolboy. 1985. mass mkt. 6.99 (0-553-27437-6) Bantam.

— The Little Drummer Girl. LC 82-48733. 430p. 1983. 24. 95 (0-394-53015-2) Knopf.

— The Little Drummer Girl. 528p. 1984. mass mkt. 6.99 (0-553-26757-4) Bantam.

— Looking Glass War. 1992. mass mkt. 5.99 (0-345-37736-2) Ballantine.

— The Night Manager. LC 92-55070. 1993. 24.00 (0-679-42513-6) Knopf.

— The Night Manager. 1994. mass mkt. 6.99 (0-345-38576-4) Ballantine.

— The Night Manager. large type ed. 1993. pap. 22.00 (0-679-74728-1) Random.

— Our Game. 1995. 24.00 (0-679-44189-1) Knopf.

— Our Game. large type ed. 1995. pap. 23.00 (0-679-76227-2) Knopf.

— A Perfect Spy. LC 85-45587. 479p. 1986. 18.95 (0-394-55141-9) Knopf.

— A Perfect Spy. 536p. 1990. mass mkt. 6.99 (0-553-26456-7) Bantam.

— The Quest for Karla. LC 82-47961. 1982. 13.95 (0-394-52848-4) Knopf.

— The Russia House. 1989. 19.95 (0-394-57789-2) Knopf.

— Russia House. 1990. mass mkt. 6.99 (0-553-28534-3) Bantam.

— The Russia House. large type ed. (General Ser.). 560p. 1990. 14.95 (0-8161-4884-8, Large Print Bks) Hall.

— The Secret Pilgrim. 1990. 21.95 (0-394-58842-8) Knopf.

— The Secret Pilgrim. 1992. mass mkt. 5.99 (0-345-37476-2) Ballantine.

— Smiley's People. LC 79-2299. 1979. 25.00 (0-394-50843-2) Knopf.

— Smiley's People. 400p. 1985. mass mkt. 6.99 (0-553-26487-7) Bantam.

— Spy Who Came In From the Cold. 1992. mass mkt. 5.99 (0-345-37737-0) Ballantine.

— Tinker, Tailor, Soldier, Spy. 1974. 24.50 (0-394-49219-6) Knopf.

— Tinker, Tailor, Soldier, Spy. 384p. 1985. mass mkt. 6.99 (0-553-26778-7) Bantam.

Le Cato, Nathaniel J. The Curse of Caste. LC 75-39092. (Black Heritage Library Collection). 1977. reprint ed. 24. 95 (0-8369-9030-7) Ayer.

***Le, Chap T.** Health & Numbers: Basic Biostatistical Methods. LC 94-25553. 1994. pap. text ed. 34.95 (0-471-01248-3) Wiley.

***Le Charlier, B., ed.** Static Analysis: Proceedings of the First International Static Analysis Symposium, SAS '94, Namur, Belgium, September 28-30, 1994. (Lecture Notes in Computer Science: Vol. 864). xii, 465p. 1994. 62.00 (3-540-58485-4) Spr-Verlag.

Le Charlier, Baudouin, ed. see SAS Staff.

Le Chenadec, Philippe. Canonical Forms in Finitely Presented Algebras. 216p. (C). 1986. pap. text ed. 180. 00 (0-685-40851-5, Pub. by Pitman Pubng UK) St Mut.

Le Chevalier, T., jt. ed. see Arriagada, R.

Le Clair, Charles. The Art of Watercolor. rev. ed. LC 93-38097. (Illus.). 144p. 1994. 29.95 (0-8230-0291-8, Watsn-Guptill) Watsn-Guptill.

— Color in Contemporary Painting: Integrating Practice & Theory. (Illus.). 192p. 1991. 32.50 (0-8230-0738-3, Watsn-Guptill) Watsn-Guptill.

Le Clair, Kim & Rousseau, David. Environmental by Design: A Sourcebook of Environmentally Conscious Choices for Homeowners, Builders & Designers, Bk. 1: Finishes & Furnishings. (Illus.). 200p. 1992. pap. 14.95 (0-88179-085-0) Hartley & Marks.

Le Clair, Mary & Fortune, Peter. A Lazy Man's Guide to Public Speaking. 139p. (C). 1986. text ed. 60.00 (0-9588155-0-X, Pub. by Peter Fortune AT) St Mut.

Le Clair, Robert C. Three American Travellers in England. (BCL1-PS American Literature Ser.). 223p. 1993. reprint ed. lib. bdg. 79.00 (0-7812-6571-1) Rprt Serv.

— Three American Travellers in England: James Russell Lowell, Henry Adams, Henry James. LC 77-19341. 222p. 1978. reprint ed. text ed. 55.00 (0-313-20190-0, LETA, Greenwood Pr) Greenwood.

— Young Henry James 1813-1876. LC 77-153337. reprint ed. 39.50 (0-404-03897-2) AMS Pr.

Le Clair, Robert C., ed. see James, William & Flournoy, Theodore.

Le Clerc, D. Histoire de la Medecine, 2 vols. in 1, Set. 858p. reprint ed. lib. bdg. 92.50 (90-6078-019-1, Pub. by B M Israel NE) Coronet Bks.

Le Clerc, Guillaume. Fergus of Galloway: Knight of King Arthur. Owen, D. D., tr. & intro. by. 192p. 1991. pap. 7.95 (0-460-87025-4, Everyman's Classic Lib) C E Tuttle.

Le Clercq, Chretien. First Establishment of the Faith in New France, 2 vols., 1. LC 77-172312. reprint ed. write for info. (0-404-03915-4) AMS Pr.

— First Establishment of the Faith in New France, 2 vols., 2. LC 77-172312. reprint ed. write for info. (0-404-03916-2) AMS Pr.

— First Establishment of the Faith in New France, 2 vols., Set. LC 77-172312. reprint ed. 87.50 (0-404-03914-6) AMS Pr.

— New Relation of Gaspesia: With the Customs & Religion of the Gaspesian Indian, Vol. 5. Ganong, William F., ed. LC 68-28600. 452p. 1969. reprint ed. text ed. 75.00 (0-8371-5044-2, LERG, Greenwood Pr) Greenwood.

Le Clercq, Jacques, tr. see Goncourt, Edmond L.

Le Clerq, Jacques, tr. see Reyles, Carlos.

Le Clezio, Alexandrina. Effective Team Management. 120p. 1993. 26.00 (1-85431-209-X, Pub. by Blackstone Pr UK) W W Gaunt.

Le Clezio, J. M. Celui Qui N'Avait Jamais vu la Mer. (Folio - Junior Ser.: No. 492). (Illus.). 107p. (FRE.). (J). (gr. 5-10). 1988. pap. 6.95 (2-07-033492-9) Schoenhof.

— Chercheir D'or. (Folio Ser.: No. 2000). (FRE.). pap. 10.95 (2-07-038082-3) Schoenhof.

— Le Chercheur d'Or. (FRE.). 1988. pap. 13.95 (0-8288-3706-6) Fr & Eur.

— Desert. (FRE.). 1985. pap. 13.95 (0-7859-0646-0, F113320) Fr & Eur.

— Desert. (Folio Ser.: No. 1670). (FRE.). pap. 10.95 (2-07-037670-2) Schoenhof.

— L' Extase Materielle. (FRE.). 1971. pap. 10.95 (0-7859-2838-3) Fr & Eur.

— Fievre. (Imaginaire Ser.). (FRE.). pap. 13.95 (2-07-072257-0) Schoenhof.

— La Fievre. (FRE.). 1991. pap. 16.95 (0-7859-2946-0) Fr & Eur.

— Guerre. (Imaginaire Ser.). (FRE.). 1992. pap. 12.95 (2-07-072546-4) Schoenhof.

— La Guerre. (FRE.). 1992. pap. 15.95 (0-7859-2952-5) Fr & Eur.

— Livre des Fuites. (Imaginaire Ser.). (FRE.). 1990. pap. 13. 95 (2-07-071820-4) Schoenhof.

— Le Livre des Fuites. (FRE.). 1989. pap. 16.95 (0-7859-2941-X, 2070718204) Fr & Eur.

— Lullaby. (Folio - Junior Ser.: No. 448). (Illus.). (FRE.). (J). (gr. 5-10). 1995. pap. 6.95 (2-07-033448-1) Schoenhof.

— The Mexican Dream: or The Interrupted Thought of Amerindian Civilizations. Fagan, Teresa L., tr. (Illus.). 240p. 1993. 22.50 (0-226-11002-8) U Ch Pr.

— Mondo et Autres Histoires. (FRE.). 1982. pap. 11.95 (0-8288-3704-X, M1262) Fr & Eur.

— Mondo et Autres Histoires. (Folio Ser.: No. 1365). (FRE.). pap. 9.95 (2-07-037365-7) Schoenhof.

— Onitsha. (Folio Ser.: No. 2472). (FRE.). 1991. pap. 29.95 (2-07-038726-7) Schoenhof.

— Printemps et Autres Saisons. (Folio Ser.: No. 2264). (FRE.). pap. 8.95 (0-685-65407-9) Schoenhof.

— Le Proces Verbal. (FRE.). 1973. pap. 11.95 (0-8288-3707-4) Fr & Eur.

— Proces-Verbal. (Folio Ser.: No. 353). (FRE.). pap. 9.95 (2-07-036353-8) Schoenhof.

— Reve Mexicain. (Folio Essais Ser.: No. 178). (FRE.). pap. 11.95 (2-07-032680-2) Schoenhof.

— La Ronde et Autres Faits Divers. (FRE.). 1990. pap. 10. 95 (0-8288-3708-2) Fr & Eur.

— Ronde et Autres Faits Divers. (Folio Ser.: No. 2148). (FRE.). pap. 8.95 (2-07-038237-0) Schoenhof.

— Villa Aurore. (Folio - Junior Ser.: No. 603). (Illus.). 112p. (FRE.). (J). (gr. 5-10). 1990. pap. 7.95 (2-07-033603-4) Schoenhof.

— Voyage au Pays des Arbres. (Folio - Cadet Rouge Ser.: No. 187). (Illus.). 48p. (FRE.). (J). (gr. 3-7). 1990. pap. 8.95 (2-07-031187-2) Schoenhof.

Le Coeur, C. Le Culte de la Generation et l'Evolution Religieuse et Sociale en Guinee. (B. E. Ser.: No. 150). (FRE.). 1932. 18.00 (0-8115-3070-1) Periodicals Srv.

Le Comte, Edward. Carnal Sin. 1994. 15.95 (0-8313-5002-4) Lantern.

— Milton Re-Viewed: Ten Essays. LC 91-1083. 160p. 1991. 23.00 (0-8153-0306-8, 1446) Garland.

Le Comte, Edward S. Dictionary of Puns in Milton's English Poetry. LC 80-15500. 240p. 1981. text ed. 50.00 (0-231-05102-6) Col U Pr.

Le Conte, John E. Le Conte's Report of East Florida. LC 77-9286. (FTU Monograph Ser.: No. 1). 90p. reprint ed. pap. 25.70 (0-7837-5025-0, 2044693) Bks Demand.

Le Conte, Joseph. Race Problem in the South. LC 78-81123. (Black Heritage Library Collection). 1977. 11.95 (0-8369-8619-9) Ayer.

— Religion & Science. LC 75-3239. reprint ed. 21.50 (0-404-59231-7) AMS Pr.

Le Coq, John L., photos. Cowboy Tales: Classic Stories by American Masters. (Illus.). 96p. 1990. pap. 12.95 (0-670-83193-X, Viking Studio) Studio Bks.

Le Corbeiller, Clare. Eighteenth-Century Italian Porcelain. (Illus.). 32p. 1985. pap. 1.95 (0-87099-421-2) Metro Mus Art.

— Gold Boxes: The Wrightsman Collection. LC 77-23592. (Illus.). 1977. pap. 1.00 (0-87099-166-3) Metro Mus Art.

Le Corbeiller, Philippe. Dimensional Analysis. (C). 1966. pap. text ed. 16.95 (0-89197-126-2) Irvington.

Le Corbusier. Appartement de Beistegni, Cite Universitaire: Pavillion Suisse, Ville Radieuse, & Other Buildings & Projects, 1930, Vol. VIII. Brooks, H. Allen, ed. LC 82-15492. (Le Corbusier Archive Ser.). 576p. 1982. lib. bdg. 260.00 (0-8240-5057-6) Garland.

— Armee du Salut: Cite de Refuge, Vol. VI. Brooks, H. Allen, ed. LC 83-9075. (Le Corbusier Archive Ser.). 440p. 1983. lib. bdg. 260.00 (0-8240-5055-X) Garland.

— Buildings & Projects: 1933-1937, Vol. XII. Brooks, H. Allen, ed. LC 82-24246. (Le Corbusier Archive Ser.). 632p. 1983. lib. bdg. 260.00 (0-8240-5061-4) Garland.

— The City of Tomorrow & Its Planning. 352p. 1987. reprint ed. pap. 8.95 (0-486-25332-5) Dover.

— Le Corbusier: Les Voyages D'Allemagne, Carnets, 5 vols., Set. Gresleri, Giuliano, ed. Dau, Mila, tr. (Illus.). 1995. boxed 250.00 (1-885254-15-6) Monacelli Pr.

— Early Buildings & Projects, 1912-1923, Vol. 1. Brooks, H. Allen, ed. LC 82-3098. (Le Corbusier Archive Ser.). 728p. 1982. lib. bdg. 260.00 (0-8240-5050-9) Garland.

— Etude Sur Le Mouvement D'art Decoratif En Allemagne. LC 68-26652. (Architecture & Decorative Art Ser.). 1968. reprint ed. lib. bdg. 27.50 (0-306-71147-8) Da Capo.

— Immeuble, Twenty Four Rue Nungesser-et-Coli & Other Buildings & Projects, 1933, Vol. XI. Brooks, H. Allen, ed. LC 82-18379. (Le Corbusier Archive Ser.). 536p. 1982. lib. bdg. 260.00 (0-8240-5060-6) Garland.

— Palais de la Societe des Nations, Villa les Tarrasses, & Other Buildings & Projects, 1926-1927, Vol. III. Brooks, H. Allen, ed. LC 82-12058. (Le Corbusier Archive Ser.). 592p. 1982. lib. bdg. 260.00 (0-8240-5052-5) Garland.

— Palais des Soviets & Other Buildings & Projects, 1930, Vol. IX. Brooks, H. Allen, ed. LC 82-15647. (Le Corbusier Archive Ser.). 560p. 1982. lib. bdg. 260.00 (0-8240-5058-4) Garland.

— Towards a New Architecture. 1970. 36.95 (0-85139-652-6) Buttrwrth-Heinemann.

— Towards a New Architecture. 320p. 1986. reprint ed. pap. 8.95 (0-486-25023-7) Dover.

— Unite d'Habitation, Vol. II. Brooks, H. Allen, ed. LC 83-1579. (Le Corbusier Archive Ser.: Vol. XVII). 592p. 1983. lib. bdg. 260.00 (0-8240-5066-5) Garland.

Le Corbusier, jt. ed. see Ozenfant, Amadee.

An Asterisk (*) at the beginning of an entry indicates that the title is appearing in BIP for the first time.

Le Corbusier Staff. The Decorative Art of Today. Dunnett, James, tr. (Illus.). 256p. (Orig.). 1987. 32.00 (*0-262-12118-2*); pap. 13.95x (*0-262-62055-3*) MIT Pr.

— Journey to the East. Zaknic, Ivan, ed. & tr. by. Pertuiset, Nicole, tr. (Illus.). 296p. 1987. 29.95x (*0-262-12091-7*); pap. 17.95x (*0-262-62068-5*) MIT Pr.

— The Modulor & Modulor 2. (Illus.). 240p. 1980. pap. 16.95 (*0-674-58102-4*) HUP.

— Oeuvres Completes, 9 tomes. Incl. 1910-192995.00 (*0-685-35993-X*); 1929-193495.00 (*0-685-35994-8*); 1934-193895.00 (*0-685-35995-6*); 1938-194695.00 (*0-685-35996-4*); 1947-195195.00 (*0-685-35997-2*); 1952-195795.00 (*0-685-35998-0*); 1957-196595.00 (*0-685-35999-9*); Tome Recapitulatif (1910-1965) 95.00 (*0-685-36000-8*); Dernieres Oeuvres. 95.00 (*0-685-36001-6*); write for info. (*0-318-52163-6*) Fr & Eur.

Le Cossec, Clement. Verdades Biblicas Tomo 1: Christian Truths, Vol. 1. (SPA.). 3.50 (*84-7645-506-2*, 223600, Pub. by Edit Clie SP) TSELF.

Le Count, Cynthia G. Andean Folk Knitting. 2nd ed. LC 87-72565. 1990. pap. 29.95 (*0-685-66216-0*) Dos Tejedoras.

Le Cren, E. D. & Lowe-McConnell, R. H., eds. The Functioning of Freshwater Ecosystems. LC 79-50504. (International Biological Programme Ser.: No. 22). (Illus.). 1980. 155.00 (*0-521-22507-8*) Cambridge U Pr.

Le Cuff-Renourard, Madeleine & Ditner, Dolores. Enjeux Debats Expression: Contemporary Issues & Essay Writing in French. 311p. (C). 1989. 69.00 (*0-946139-12-1*, Pub. by Elm Pubns UK) St Mut.

Le Dantec, ed. see Baudelaire, Charles.

Le Dantec, ed. see Verlaine, Paul.

Le Dantec, Denise & Le Dantec, Jean-Pierre. Reading French Gardens: Story & History. Levine, Jessica, tr. (Illus.). 288p. (C). 1993. pap. 13.95 (*0-262-62087-1*) MIT Pr.

Le Dantec, Denise, jt. auth. see Le Dantec, Jean-Pierre.

Le Dantec, Jean-Pierre & Le Dantec, Denise. Paris in Bloom. 300p. 1991. 24.98 (*2-08-013518-X*, Pub. by Flammarion) Abbeville Pr.

Le Dantec, Jean-Pierre, jt. auth. see Le Dantec, Denise.

Le Dentu, Jose. Bridge: Triumphs & Disasters. Reese, Terence, tr. 144p. 1991. pap. 13.95 (*0-575-04806-9*, Pub. by V Gollancz UK) Trafalgar.

Le Dimet, F. X. & Navon, I. M. Variational Methods in Atmospheric Sciences. 450p. 1994. text ed. 68.00 (*981-02-0890-1*) World Scientific Pub.

***Le Dimet, Francois-Xavier.** High Performance Computing in the Geosciences: Proceedings of the Workshop Held at the Centre de Physique, Les Houches, Frances, 21-25 June 1993. LC 95-12569. (NATO ASI Ser.: Series C, Mathematical & Physical Sciences: No. 462). 1995. write for info. (*0-7923-3488-4*) Kluwer Ac.

***Le Docte, E.** Legal Dictionary in Four Languages: French - Dutch - English - German. 800p. 1988. 150.00 (*90-6215-163-9*, Pub. by Maklu Uitgevers BE) W W Gaunt.

Le Docte, Edgard. Diccionario de Terminos Juridicos en Cuatro Idiomas. 760p. 1987. 295.00 (*0-7859-6220-4*, 8473984692) Fr & Eur.

— Legal Dictionary in Four Languages. 3rd ed. 758p. (DUT, ENG, FRE & GER.). 1982. 195.00 (*0-8288-1532-1*, M6349) Fr & Eur.

— Legal Dictionary in Four Languages. 4th ed. 822p. (DUT, ENG, FRE & GER.). 1987. 295.00 (*0-8288-0412-5*, M15088) Fr & Eur.

— Quadralingual Legal Dictionary. 822p. (ENG, FRE, GER & SPA.). 1992. 295.00 (*0-8288-9433-7*) Fr & Eur.

Le Doeuff, Michele. The Philosophical Imaginary. Gordon, Colin, tr. LC 88-63325. 222p. 1990. 32.50 (*0-8047-1619-6*) Stanford U Pr.

Le Doeuff, R. & Robert, J. Modelling & Control of Electrical Machines: New Trends. 1991. 111.50 (*0-444-88732-6*) Elsevier.

***Le Doran, Serge.** Dictionnaire San-Antonio. 638p. (FRE.). 1993. text ed. 65.00 (*0-7859-7871-2*, 2265049646) Fr & Eur.

Le Douarin, Nicole & McLaren, Anne, eds. Chimaeras in Development Biology. 1984. text ed. 176.00 (*0-12-440580-0*) Acad Pr.

Le Douarin, Nicole & Monroy, A., eds. Cell Lineage, Stem Cells & Cell Determination. (INSERM Symposium Ser.: Vol. 10). 378p. 1979. 88.75 (*0-7204-0673-0*, North Holland) Elsevier.

Le Doux, Joan. Come Sing, Jimmy Jo: A Study Guide. (Novel-Ties Ser.). (gr. 7-10). 1988. student ed., teacher ed 15.95 (*0-88122-109-0*) Lrn Links.

Le Drean, Laura T., jt. auth. see Fellag, Linda R.

Le, Duan. The Vietnamese Revolution: Fundamental Problems & Essential Tasks. LC 71-171528. 159p. reprint ed. pap. 45.40 (*0-317-28060-0*, 2025549) Bks Demand.

Le Duc, Don R., jt. auth. see Teeter, Dwight L., Jr.

Le Duc, Thomas. Piety & Intellect at Amherst College, 1865-1912. LC 77-89196. (American Education: Its Men, Institutions & Ideas, Ser. 1). 1977. reprint ed. 17.95 (*0-405-01434-1*) Ayer.

***Le Espiritu, Yen.** Filipino American Lives. (Asian American History & Culture Ser.). (Illus.). 256p. (Orig.). (C). 1995. pap. text ed. 18.95 (*1-56639-771-5*) Temple U Pr.

***Le-Falle-Collins, Lizzetta.** Betye Saar: Personal Icons. Gladsky, Kristen, ed. 28p. (Orig.). (C). 1995. 10.00 (*1-882603-01-X*) Mid Am Arts.

Le Fanu, J. Sheridan. Best Ghost Stories. Bleiler, E. F., ed. (Illus.). (Orig.). pap. 8.95 (*0-486-20415-4*) Dover.

— Ghost Stories & Mysteries. Bleiler, E. F., ed. LC 74-75845. 480p. 1975. pap. 7.95 (*0-486-20715-3*) Dover.

— Uncle Silas. 1966. reprint ed. pap. 8.95 (*0-486-21715-9*) Dover.

Le Fanu, Joseph S. All in the Dark, 2 vols., 1. Varma, Devendra P., ed. LC 76-4046. (Collected Works). 1977. reprint ed. 26.95 (*0-405-09192-3*) Ayer.

— All in the Dark, 2 vols., 2. Varma, Devendra P., ed. LC 76-4046. (Collected Works). 1977. reprint ed. 26.95 (*0-405-09193-1*) Ayer.

— All in the Dark, 2 vols., Set. Varma, Devendra P., ed. LC 76-4046. (Collected Works). 1977. reprint ed. 53.95 (*0-405-09191-5*) Ayer.

— Checkmate, 3 vols., 1. Varma, Devendra P., ed. LC 76-4184. (Collected Works). 1977. reprint ed. 30.95 (*0-405-09195-8*) Ayer.

— Checkmate, 3 vols., 2. Varma, Devendra P., ed. LC 76-4184. (Collected Works). 1977. reprint ed. 30.95 (*0-405-09196-6*) Ayer.

— Checkmate, 3 vols., 3. Varma, Devendra P., ed. LC 76-4184. (Collected Works). 1977. reprint ed. 30.95 (*0-405-09197-4*) Ayer.

— Checkmate, 3 vols., Set. Varma, Devendra P., ed. LC 76-4184. (Collected Works). 1977. reprint ed. 90.95 (*0-405-09194-X*) Ayer.

— Chronicles of Golden Friars, 3 vols., 1. Varma, Devendra P., ed. LC 76-4178. (Collected Works). 1977. reprint ed. 29.95 (*0-405-09199-0*) Ayer.

— Chronicles of Golden Friars, 3 vols., 2. Varma, Devendra P., ed. LC 76-4178. (Collected Works). 1977. reprint ed. 29.95 (*0-405-09200-8*) Ayer.

— Chronicles of Golden Friars, 3 vols., 3. Varma, Devendra P., ed. LC 76-4178. (Collected Works). 1977. reprint ed. 29.95 (*0-405-09201-6*) Ayer.

— Chronicles of Golden Friars, 3 vols., Set. Varma, Devendra P., ed. LC 76-4178. (Collected Works). 1977. reprint ed. 87.95 (*0-405-09198-2*) Ayer.

— The Cock & Anchor: Being a Chronicle of Old Dublin City, 3 vols., 1. Varma, Devendra P., ed. LC 76-4606. (Collected Works). 1977. reprint ed. 30.95 (*0-405-09203-2*) Ayer.

— The Cock & Anchor: Being a Chronicle of Old Dublin City, 3 vols., 2. Varma, Devendra P., ed. LC 76-4606. (Collected Works). 1977. reprint ed. 30.95 (*0-405-09204-0*) Ayer.

— The Cock & Anchor: Being a Chronicle of Old Dublin City, 3 vols., 3. Varma, Devendra P., ed. LC 76-4606. (Collected Works). 1977. reprint ed. 30.95 (*0-405-09205-9*) Ayer.

— The Cock & Anchor: Being a Chronicle of Old Dublin City, 3 vols., Set. Varma, Devendra P., ed. LC 76-4606. (Collected Works). 1977. reprint ed. 90.95 (*0-405-09202-4*) Ayer.

— The Collected Works of Joseph Sheridan Le Fanu. Varma, Devendra P., ed. (Illus.). 1977. 1,327.50 (*0-405-09190-7*) Ayer.

— The Evil Guest. Varma, Devendra P., ed. LC 76-4605. (Collected Works). (Illus.). 1977. reprint ed. lib. bdg. 25.95 (*0-405-09206-7*) Ayer.

— The Fortunes of Colonial Torlogh O'Brien: A Tale of the Wars of King James. Varma, Devendra P., ed. LC 76-4603. (Collected Works). (Illus.). 1977. reprint ed. 39.95 (*0-405-09207-5*) Ayer.

— Ghost Stories & Tales of Mystery. Varma, Devendra P., ed. LC 76-6013. (Collected Works). (Illus.). 1977. reprint ed. 27.95 (*0-405-09254-7*) Ayer.

— Guy Deverell, 3 vols., 1. Varma, Devendra P., ed. LC 76-6015. (Collected Works). 1977. reprint ed. 25.95 (*0-405-09256-3*) Ayer.

— Guy Deverell, 3 vols., 2. Varma, Devendra P., ed. LC 76-6015. (Collected Works). 1977. reprint ed. 26.95 (*0-405-09257-1*) Ayer.

— Guy Deverell, 3 vols., 3. Varma, Devendra P., ed. LC 76-6015. (Collected Works). 1977. reprint ed. 26.95 (*0-405-09258-X*) Ayer.

— Guy Deverell, 3 vols., Set. Varma, Devendra P., ed. LC 76-6015. (Collected Works). 1977. reprint ed. 78.95 (*0-405-09255-5*) Ayer.

— Haunted Lives: A Novel, 3 vols., 1. Varma, Devendra P., ed. LC 76-5268. (Collected Works). 1977. reprint ed. 26.95 (*0-405-09209-1*) Ayer.

— Haunted Lives: A Novel, 3 vols., 2. Varma, Devendra P., ed. LC 76-5268. (Collected Works). 1977. reprint ed. 26.95 (*0-405-09210-5*) Ayer.

— Haunted Lives: A Novel, 3 vols., 3. Varma, Devendra P., ed. LC 76-5268. (Collected Works). 1977. reprint ed. 26.95 (*0-405-09211-3*) Ayer.

— Haunted Lives: A Novel, 3 vols., Set. Varma, Devendra P., ed. LC 76-5268. (Collected Works). 1977. reprint ed. 80.95 (*0-405-09208-3*) Ayer.

— The House by the Church-Yard, 3 vols. in 1. LC 74-148811. reprint ed. 57.50 (*0-404-08877-5*) AMS Pr.

— The House by the Church-Yard, 3 vols., 1. Varma, Devendra P., ed. LC 76-5270. (Collected Works). 1977. reprint ed. 29.95 (*0-405-09213-X*) Ayer.

— The House by the Church-Yard, 3 vols., 2. Varma, Devendra P., ed. LC 76-5270. (Collected Works). 1977. reprint ed. 29.95 (*0-405-09214-8*) Ayer.

— The House by the Church-Yard, 3 vols., 3. Varma, Devendra P., ed. LC 76-5270. (Collected Works). 1977. reprint ed. 29.95 (*0-405-09215-6*) Ayer.

— The House by the Church-Yard, 3 vols., Set. Varma, Devendra P., ed. LC 76-5270. (Collected Works). 1977. reprint ed. 87.95 (*0-405-09212-1*) Ayer.

— In a Glass Darkly. LC 92-18158. (World's Classics Ser.). 384p. 1993. 9.95 (*0-19-282805-3*) OUP.

— In a Glass Darkly, 3 vols., 1. Varma, Devendra P., ed. LC 76-5271. (Collected Works). 1977. reprint ed. 26.95 (*0-405-09217-2*) Ayer.

— In a Glass Darkly, 3 vols., 2. Varma, Devendra P., ed. LC 76-5271. (Collected Works). 1977. reprint ed. 26.95 (*0-405-09218-0*) Ayer.

— In a Glass Darkly, 3 vols., 3. Varma, Devendra P., ed. LC 76-5271. (Collected Works). 1977. reprint ed. 26.95 (*0-405-09219-9*) Ayer.

— In a Glass Darkly, 3 vols., Set. Varma, Devendra P., ed. LC 76-5271. (Collected Works). 1977. reprint ed. 80.95 (*0-405-09216-4*) Ayer.

— A Lost Name, 3 vols, 1. Varma, Devendra P., ed. LC 76-5272. (Collected Works). (Illus.). 1977. reprint ed. 29.95 (*0-405-09221-0*) Ayer.

— A Lost Name, 3 vols, 2. Varma, Devendra P., ed. LC 76-5272. (Collected Works). (Illus.). 1977. reprint ed. 29.95 (*0-405-09222-9*) Ayer.

— A Lost Name, 3 vols, 3. Varma, Devendra P., ed. LC 76-5272. (Collected Works). (Illus.). 1977. reprint ed. 29.95 (*0-405-09223-7*) Ayer.

— A Lost Name, 3 vols, Set. Varma, Devendra P., ed. LC 76-5272. (Collected Works). (Illus.). 1977. reprint ed. 87.95 (*0-405-09220-2*) Ayer.

— Madame Crowl's Ghost, & Other Tales of Mystery. James, Montague R., ed. LC 72-167459. (Short Story Index Reprint Ser.). 1977. reprint ed. 18.95 (*0-8369-3985-9*) Ayer.

— The Poems of Joseph Sheridan Le Fanu. LC 78-148812. reprint ed. 32.50 (*0-404-08878-3*) AMS Pr.

— The Poems of Joseph Sheridan Le Fanu. Varma, Devendra P., ed. LC 76-5273. (Collected Works). 1977. reprint ed. 23.95 (*0-405-09224-5*) Ayer.

— The Purcell Papers. LC 75-2524. 1975. 8.95 (*0-87054-072-6*) Arkham.

— The Purcell Papers, 3 vols. LC 71-148813. reprint ed. 145.00 (*0-404-08880-5*) AMS Pr.

— The Purcell Papers: With a Memoir by Alfred Perceval Graves, 3 vols., 1. Varma, Devendra P., ed. LC 76-5274. (Collected Works). 1977. reprint ed. 25.95 (*0-405-09226-1*) Ayer.

— The Purcell Papers: With a Memoir by Alfred Perceval Graves, 3 vols., 2. Varma, Devendra P., ed. LC 76-5274. (Collected Works). 1977. reprint ed. 25.95 (*0-405-09227-X*) Ayer.

— The Purcell Papers: With a Memoir by Alfred Perceval Graves, 3 vols., 3. Varma, Devendra P., ed. LC 76-5274. (Collected Works). 1977. reprint ed. 25.95 (*0-405-09228-8*) Ayer.

— The Purcell Papers: With a Memoir by Alfred Perceval Graves, 3 vols., Set. Varma, Devendra P., ed. LC 76-5274. (Collected Works). 1977. reprint ed. 76.95 (*0-405-09225-3*) Ayer.

— The Rose & the Key, 3 vols, 1. Varma, Devendra P., ed. LC 76-5275. (Collected Works). 1977. reprint ed. 29.95 (*0-405-09230-X*) Ayer.

— The Rose & the Key, 3 vols, 2. Varma, Devendra P., ed. LC 76-5275. (Collected Works). 1977. reprint ed. 29.95 (*0-405-09231-8*) Ayer.

— The Rose & the Key, 3 vols, 3. Varma, Devendra P., ed. LC 76-5275. (Collected Works). 1977. reprint ed. 29.95 (*0-405-09232-6*) Ayer.

— The Rose & the Key, 3 vols, Set. Varma, Devendra P., ed. LC 76-5275. (Collected Works). 1977. reprint ed. 87.95 (*0-405-09229-6*) Ayer.

— A Stable for Nightmares or Weird Tales: Anthology. LC 75-46286. (Supernatural & Occult Fiction Ser.). (Illus.). 1976. reprint ed. lib. bdg. 23.95 (*0-405-08147-2*) Ayer.

— The Tenants of Malory: A Novel, 3 vols, 1. Varma, Devendra P., ed. LC 76-5276. (Collected Works). 1977. reprint ed. 25.95 (*0-405-09234-2*) Ayer.

— The Tenants of Malory: A Novel, 3 vols, 2. Varma, Devendra P., ed. LC 76-5276. (Collected Works). 1977. reprint ed. 25.95 (*0-405-09235-0*) Ayer.

— The Tenants of Malory: A Novel, 3 vols, 3. Varma, Devendra P., ed. LC 76-5276. (Collected Works). 1977. reprint ed. 25.95 (*0-405-09236-9*) Ayer.

— The Tenants of Malory: A Novel, 3 vols, Set. Varma, Devendra P., ed. LC 76-5276. (Collected Works). 1977. reprint ed. 76.95 (*0-405-09233-4*) Ayer.

— Uncle Silas. McCormack, W. J., ed. (World's Classics Ser.). 1982. pap. 9.95 (*0-19-281541-5*) OUP.

— Uncle Silas: A Tale of Bartram-Haugh, 3 vols, 1. Varma, Devendra P., ed. LC 76-5278. (Collected Works). 1977. reprint ed. 30.95 (*0-405-09238-5*) Ayer.

— Uncle Silas: A Tale of Bartram-Haugh, 3 vols, 2. Varma, Devendra P., ed. LC 76-5278. (Collected Works). 1977. reprint ed. 30.95 (*0-405-09239-3*) Ayer.

— Uncle Silas: A Tale of Bartram-Haugh, 3 vols, 3. Varma, Devendra P., ed. LC 76-5278. (Collected Works). 1977. reprint ed. 30.95 (*0-405-09240-7*) Ayer.

— Uncle Silas: A Tale of Bartram-Haugh, 3 vols, Set. Varma, Devendra P., ed. LC 76-5278. (Collected Works). 1977. reprint ed. 90.95 (*0-405-09237-7*) Ayer.

— The Watcher & Other Weird Stories. Varma, Devendra P., ed. LC 76-5279. (Collected Works). (Illus.). 1977. reprint ed. 26.95 (*0-405-09241-5*) Ayer.

— Willing to Die, 3 vols., 1. Varma, Devendra P., ed. LC 76-5280. (Collected Works). 1977. reprint ed. 29.95 (*0-405-09243-1*) Ayer.

— Willing to Die, 3 vols., 2. Varma, Devendra P., ed. LC 76-5280. (Collected Works). 1977. reprint ed. 29.95 (*0-405-09244-X*) Ayer.

— Willing to Die, 3 vols., 3. Varma, Devendra P., ed. LC 76-5280. (Collected Works). 1977. reprint ed. 29.95 (*0-405-09245-8*) Ayer.

— Willing to Die, 3 vols., Set. Varma, Devendra P., ed. LC 76-5280. (Collected Works). 1977. reprint ed. 87.95 (*0-405-09242-3*) Ayer.

— Wylder's Hand: A Novel, 3 vols., 1. Varma, Devendra P., ed. LC 76-5281. (Collected Works). 1977. reprint ed. 29.95 (*0-405-09247-4*) Ayer.

— Wylder's Hand: A Novel, 3 vols., 2. Varma, Devendra P., ed. LC 76-5281. (Collected Works). 1977. reprint ed. 29.95 (*0-405-09248-2*) Ayer.

— Wylder's Hand: A Novel, 3 vols., 3. Varma, Devendra P., ed. LC 76-5281. (Collected Works). 1977. reprint ed. 29.95 (*0-405-09249-0*) Ayer.

— Wylder's Hand: A Novel, 3 vols., Set. Varma, Devendra P., ed. LC 76-5281. (Collected Works). 1977. reprint ed. 87.95 (*0-405-09246-6*) Ayer.

— The Wyvern Mystery: A Novel, 3 vols., 1. Varma, Devendra P., ed. LC 76-5282. (Collected Works). 1977. reprint ed. 25.95 (*0-405-09251-2*) Ayer.

— The Wyvern Mystery: A Novel, 3 vols., 2. Varma, Devendra P., ed. LC 76-5282. (Collected Works). 1977. reprint ed. 25.95 (*0-405-09252-0*) Ayer.

— The Wyvern Mystery: A Novel, 3 vols., 3. Varma, Devendra P., ed. LC 76-5282. (Collected Works). 1977. reprint ed. 25.95 (*0-405-09253-9*) Ayer.

— The Wyvern Mystery: A Novel, 3 vols., Set. Varma, Devendra P., ed. LC 76-5282. (Collected Works). 1977. reprint ed. 76.95 (*0-405-09250-4*) Ayer.

Le Fanu, Mark. The Cinema of Andrei Tarkovsky. 156p. 1987. 39.95 (*0-85170-193-0*, Pub. by British Film Inst UK); pap. 16.95 (*0-85170-194-9*, Pub. by British Film Inst UK) Ind U Pr.

Le Fanu, Sheridan. Uncle Silas. large type ed. (Large-Print Ser.). 678p. 1992. reprint ed. lib. bdg. 22.00 (*0-939495-37-6*) North Bks.

Le Fanu, Sheridan, et al. Three Short Novels of Mystery & Suspense. large type ed. (Large-Print Ser.). 542p. 1992. reprint ed. lib. bdg. 22.00 (*0-939495-41-4*) North Bks.

Le Fanu, Thomas P., ed.

Le Fanu, William R. Seventy Years of Irish Life: Being Anecdotes & Reminiscences. LC 75-28821. reprint ed. 27.00 (*0-404-13813-6*) AMS Pr.

Le Faye, Deirdre. Jane Austen: A Family Record. (Reference Guides to Literature Ser.). 332p. 1989. text ed. 40.00 (*0-8161-9092-5*, Hall Reference) Macmillan.

Le Faye, Deirdre, jt. auth. see Black, Maggie.

Le Faye, Dierdre, ed. see Austen, Jane.

***Le Febvre, Henri.** Writings on Cities. Kofman, Eleonore & Le Bas, Elizabeth, trs. 272p. 1995. write for info. (*0-631-19187-9*); pap. write for info. (*0-631-19188-7*) Blackwell Pubs.

Le Fevers, Stephen & Marshall, Loren. Prehospital Care for the EMT-Intermediate: Assessment & Intervention. 288p. 1983. pap. 18.95 (*0-317-58949-0*) P-H.

Le Fleming, L. S., ed. see Chekhov.

Le Fleming, Svetlana & Kay, Susan. Colloquial Russian. LC 93-16782. (Colloquial Ser.). 306p. 1993. pap. 16.95 (*0-415-05784-1*, B2374); audio 17.95 (*0-415-05785-X*, B2366) Routledge.

— Colloquial Russian, Set. LC 93-16782. (Colloquial Ser.). 306p. 1993. Incl. cassette. audio 35.00 (*0-415-05786-8*, B2370) Routledge.

Le Gac, Y., ed. Les Inscriptions d'Assur-Nasir-Aplu III, roi d'Assyrie. LC 78-72728. (Ancient Mesopotamian Texts & Studies). reprint ed. 37.50 (*0-404-18164-3*) AMS Pr.

Le Gai Eaton, Charles. Islam & the Destiny of Man. LC 85-14877. (SUNY Series in Islam). 242p. 1985. 49.50 (*0-88706-161-3*); pap. 16.95 (*0-88706-163-X*) State U NY Pr.

Le Gal, M. Recherches Sur les Ornementations Sporales Des Discomycetes Opercules. 1970. reprint ed. 24.00 (*3-7682-0694-7*) Lubrecht & Cramer.

Le Gall, J. F., jt. auth. see Freidlin, M. I.

***Le Gall, Robert.** Dictionnaire de Liturgie. 279p. (FRE.). 1987. pap. 38.95 (*0-7859-8089-X*, 2854431359) Fr & Eur.

Le Gallez, Paula. The Rhys Woman: An Examination of Character in the Work of Jean Rhys. LC 89-38381. 170p. 1990. text ed. 39.95 (*0-312-03702-3*) St Martin.

Le Gallienne, Eva. The Mystic in the Theatre: Eleonora Duse. LC 72-11975. (Arcturus Books Paperbacks). 189p. 1973. pap. 12.95 (*0-8093-0631-X*) S Ill U Pr.

Le Gallienne, Eva, tr. see Andersen, Hans Christian.

Le Gallienne, Eva, tr. see Ibsen, Henrik.

Le Gallienne, Richard. Attitudes & Avowals with Some Retrospective Reviews. LC 71-99640. (Essay Index Reprint Ser.). 1977. 28.95 (*0-8369-1418-X*) Ayer.

— Little Dinners with the Sphinx, & Other Prose Fancies. LC 72-11932. (Short Story Index Reprint Ser.). 1977. reprint ed. 26.95 (*0-8369-4239-6*) Ayer.

— Maker of Rainbows, & Other Fairy-Tales & Fables. LC 77-167460. (Short Story Index Reprint Ser.). (Illus.). 1977. reprint ed. 18.95 (*0-8369-3986-7*) Ayer.

— Painted Shadows. LC 77-94738. (Short Story Index Reprint Ser.). 1977. 21.95 (*0-8369-3118-1*) Ayer.

— Romances of Old France. LC 75-81271. (Short Story Index Reprint Ser.). 1977. 20.95 (*0-8369-3023-1*) Ayer.

Le Gallienne, Richard, ed. see Hallam, Arthur H.

Le Garsmeur, Alain, photos. James Joyce: Reflections of Ireland. LC 93-21770. (Illus.). 160p. 1993. text ed. 35.00 (*0-02-559895-3*) Macmillan.

Le Gassick, Trevor, ed. Critical Perspectives on Naguib Mahfouz. LC 90-48890. 192p. 1991. 25.00 (*0-89410-659-7*); pap. 15.00 (*0-89410-660-0*) Three Continents.

Le Gassick, Trevor, tr. see Barakat, Halim I.

Le Gassick, Trevor, tr. see Habiby, Emile.

Le Gear, Clara E., ed. United States Atlases. LC 71-154058. (Library of Congress Publications in Reprint). 1971. reprint ed. 23.95 (*0-405-03424-5*) Ayer.

***Le Glay, Marcel, et al.** A History of Rome. Nevill, Antonia, tr. (Illus.). 484p. (C). 1996. write for info. (*0-631-19457-6*) Blackwell Pubs.

— A History of Rome. Nevill, Antonia, tr. (Illus.). 484p. 1996. pap. write for info. (*0-631-19458-4*) Blackwell Pubs.

***Le Gleau, Rene.** Dictionnaire Classique Francais-Breton Vol. 2: C-Debla. 352p. (BRE & FRE.). 1984. pap. 45.00 (*0-7859-7999-9*, 2736800087) Fr & Eur.

— Dictionnaire Classique Francais-Breton Vol. 3: Deblo-Embeg. 352p. (BRE & FRE.). 1986. pap. 45.00 (*0-7859-8000-8*, 2736800141) Fr & Eur.

An Asterisk (*) at the beginning of an entry indicates that the title is appearing in BIP for the first time.

— Dictionnaire Classique Francais-Breton Vol. 6. 384p. (BRE & FRE.). 1987. pap. 55.00 (*0-7859-8001-6*, 2736800184) Fr & Eur.

— Dictionnaire Classique Francais-Breton Vol. 6. 384p. (BRE & FRE.). 1988. pap. 45.00 (*0-7859-8002-4*, 2736800206) Fr & Eur.

— Dictionnaire Classique Francais-Breton Vol. 6. 348p. (BRE & FRE.). 1989. pap. 45.00 (*0-7859-8003-2*, 2736800265) Fr & Eur.

Le Goff, Claude. French for Business: Le Francais des Affaires. 27p. 1987. teacher ed 5.95 (*0-318-24035-1*, U0975) Hatier Pub.

— French for Business: Le Francais des Affaires. 160p. 1989. pap. 32.95 (*2-218-02469-1*) Schoenhof.

Le Goff, Denise-Claude. Peter Neagoe: l'Homme et l'Oeuvre. (American University Studies: General Literature: Ser. XIX, Vol. 16). 423p. (C). 1988. text ed. 51.50 (*0-8204-0658-9*) P Lang Pubs.

Le Goff, Jacques. The Birth of Purgatory. Goldhammer, Arthur, tr. LC 83-1108. (Illus.). 448p. 1986. pap. text ed. 17.95 (*0-226-47083-0*) U Ch Pr.

— History & Memory. Rendall, Stephen & Claman, Elizabeth, trs. (European Perspectives Ser.). 320p. (C). 1992. text ed. 29.50 (*0-231-07590-1*) Col U Pr.

— Intellectuals in the Middle Ages. Fagan, Teresa L., tr. (Illus.). 256p. 1992. 44.95 (*0-631-17078-2*); pap. 18.95 (*0-631-18519-4*) Blackwell Pubs.

— Medieval Callings. Cochrane, Lydia G., tr. xiii, 392p. 1995. pap. 16.95 (*0-226-47087-3*) U Ch Pr.

— Medieval Civilization, 400-1500. Barrow, Julia, tr. 1990. pap. 17.95 (*0-631-17566-0*) Blackwell Pubs.

— The Medieval Imagination. Goldhammer, Arthur, tr. 296p. 1988. 29.95 (*0-226-47084-9*) U Ch Pr.

— The Medieval Imagination. Goldhammer, Arthur, tr. LC 88-4787. 304p. 1992. pap. text ed. 13.95 (*0-226-47085-7*) U Ch Pr.

— Time, Work, & Culture in the Middle Ages. Goldhammer, Arthur, tr. LC 79-25400. xvi, 384p. (C). 1982. pap. 22.50 (*0-226-47081-4*) U Ch Pr.

— Your Money or Your Life: Economy & Religion in the Middle Ages. Ranum, Patricia, tr. LC 87-25248. 116p. 1988. 24.95 (*0-942299-14-0*); pap. 10.95 (*0-942299-15-9*) Zone Bks.

Le Goff, Jacques, ed. Medieval Callings. Cochrane, Lydia G., tr. x, 350p. 1990. 39.95 (*0-226-47086-5*) U Ch Pr.

Le Goff, Jacques, ed. see Benevolo, Leonardo.

Le Goff, Tim J. State & Society in France, 1661-1789. 288p. 1993. pap. 18.95 (*0-7131-6527-8*, A9527, Pub. by E Arnold UK) Routledge Chapman & Hall.

*__Le Golvan, Yves.__ Dictionnaire Marketing. 1988. write for info. (*0-7859-7704-X*, 2040169962) Fr & Eur.

Le Grand, H. E. Drifting Continents & Shifting Theories: The Modern Revolution in Geology & Scientific Change. (Illus.). 250p. 1989. pap. 24.95 (*0-521-31105-5*) Cambridge U Pr.

Le Grand, H. E., ed. Experimental Inquiries: Historical, Philosophical & Social Studies of Experimentation in Science. (C). 1990. lib. bdg. 95.00 (*0-7923-0790-9*) Kluwer Ac.

Le Grand, Julia, jt. auth. see Robinson, Ray.

Le Grand, Julian. Equity & Choice: An Essay in Economics & Applied Philosophy. 256p. 1991. 44.95 (*0-04-350065-X*, A8165); pap. 19.95 (*0-04-350066-8*, A8166) Routledge Chapman & Hall.

Le Grand, Julian & Estrin, Saul, eds. Market Socialism. (Illus.). 232p. 1989. 55.00 (*0-19-827701-6*); pap. 22.00 (*0-19-827700-8*) OUP.

Le Grand, Julian & Robinson, Ray, eds. Privatisation & the Welfare State. 256p. (C). 1984. pap. text ed. 17.95 (*0-04-336080-7*) Routledge Chapman & Hall.

Le Grand, Scott M., jt. ed. see Merz, Kenneth M., Jr.

Le Gray, Gustave, jt. auth. see Croucher, J. H.

*__Le Grice, Lyn.__ The Stenciled House. (Illus.). 176p. 1995. pap. 14.95 (*0-7894-0014-6*) Dorling Kindersley.

Le Grice, Lynn. Art of Stencilling. (Illus.). 1990. pap. 17.95 (*0-517-58016-0*, C P Pubs) Crown Pub Group.

— The Stenciled House: Innovative Ideas for Creative Home Design. (Illus.). 176p. 1991. pap. 16.95 (*0-671-73192-0*, Fireside) S&S Trade.

Le Gros, Clark F. & Dunne, Agnes C. Ageing in Industry: An Inquiry, Based on Figures Derived from Census Reports. LC 75-136890. (Illus.). 146p. 1971. reprint ed. text ed. 49.75 (*0-8371-5332-8*, CLAI, Greenwood Pr) Greenwood.

Le Guerer, Annick. Scent: The Mysterious & Essential Powers of Smell. Turner, Philip, ed. Miller, Richard, tr. 272p. 1994. pap. 13.00 (*1-56836-024-X*) Kodansha.

— Scent: The Mysterious & Essential Powers of Smell. 1992. 20.00 (*0-394-58526-7*) Random.

Le Guillou, J. C. & Zinn-Justin, J., eds. Large Order Behaviour of Perturbation Theory. (Current Physics Sources & Comments Ser.: Vol. 7). 560p. 1990. 102.50 (*0-685-45103-8*, North Holland); pap. 48.75 (*0-444-88597-8*, North Holland) Elsevier.

Le Guilloux, Isabelle, jt. auth. see Beeching, Kate.

Le Guin, Charles A., ed. A Home-Concealed Woman: The Diaries of Magnolia Wynn Le Guin, 1901-1913. LC 90-34163. (Illus.). 416p. 1990. 24.95 (*0-8203-1236-3*) U of Ga Pr.

*__Le Guin, Ursula.__ Searoad. 1994. pap. 4.99 (*0-06-105400-3*, Prism Bks) P-H.

Le Guin, Ursula K. The Altered I: Ursula K. Le Guin's Science Fiction Writing Workshop. Harding, Lee, ed. 1978. pap. 7.50 (*0-425-03849-1*) Ultramarine Pub.

— Beginning Place. 1991. mass mkt. 4.50 (*0-06-100148-1*, Harp PBks) HarpC.

— Buffalo Gals & Other Animal Presences. 222p. 1994. pap. 8.95 (*0-451-45434-0*, ROC) NAL-Dutton.

— Buffalo Gals, Won't You Come Out Tonight. LC 94-18443. (Illus.). 80p. 1994. 16.95 (*0-87654-071-X*) Pomegranate Calif.

— Catwings. LC 87-33104. (Illus.). 48p. (J). (gr. 2-5). 1988. 11.95 (*0-531-05759-3*); lib. bdg. 11.99 (*0-531-08359-4*) Orchard Bks Watts.

— Catwings. 1990. pap. 2.95 (*0-590-42833-0*) Scholastic Inc.

— Catwings Return. LC 88-17902. (Illus.). 56p. (J). (gr. 2-5). 1989. 11.95 (*0-531-05803-4*); lib. bdg. 11.99 (*0-531-08403-5*) Orchard Bks Watts.

— Catwing's Return. (J). (ps-3). 1991. pap. 2.95 (*0-590-42832-2*) Scholastic Inc.

— Compass Rose. 1991. mass mkt. 4.50 (*0-06-100181-3*, Harp PBks) HarpC.

— Dancing at the Edge of the World: Thoughts on Words, Women, Places. 1990. pap. 12.00 (*0-06-097289-0*, PL) HarpC.

— The Dispossessed: An Ambiguous Utopia. 1976. pap. 3.95 (*0-380-00382-1*) Avon.

— Eye of the Heron. 1991. mass mkt. 4.50 (*0-06-100138-4*, Harp PBks) HarpC.

— The Farthest Shore. 208p. (gr. 6 up). 1984. mass mkt. 5.50 (*0-553-26847-3*) Bantam.

— The Farthest Shore. rev. ed. LC 72-75273. (Illus.). 240p. (YA). (gr. 6 up). 1990. text ed. 16.95 (*0-689-31683-6*, Atheneum Bks Young) S&S Childrens.

— Fire & Stone. LC 88-16799. (Illus.). 32p. (J). (gr. 1-3). 1989. text ed. 13.95 (*0-689-31408-6*, Atheneum Bks Young) S&S Childrens.

— Fish Soup. LC 91-29740. (Illus.). 40p. (J). (gr. 2-4). 1992. text ed. 13.95 (*0-689-31733-6*, Atheneum Bks Young) S&S Childrens.

— Fisherman of the Inland Sea: Science Fiction Stories. LC 94-5397. 1994. 19.99 (*0-06-105200-0*) HarpC.

— Four Ways to Forgiveness. LC 95-11459. 1995. 5.50 (*0-06-105234-5*, HarpT) HarpC.

— Going Out with Peacocks & Other Poems. 96p. (Orig.). 1994. pap. 12.00 (*0-06-095057-9*, PL) HarpC.

— Gwilan's Harp. deluxe limited ed. 1981. 35.00 (*0-935716-11-4*) Lord John.

— In the Red Zone. deluxe limited ed. (Illus.). 50p. 1983. 75.00 (*0-935716-21-1*) Lord John.

— King Dog: A Screenplay. Bd. with Dostoevsky: A Screenplay. LC 85-7872. LC 85-7872. (Back-to-Back Bks.). 208p. (Orig.). 1985. Set pap. 9.50 (*0-88496-236-9*) Capra Pr.

— The Language of the Night. Wood, Susan, ed. LC 78-24350. 270p. 1979. 25.00 (*0-399-12325-3*) Ultramarine Pub.

— The Language of the Night: Essays on Fantasy & Science Fiction. LC 91-58377. 256p. 1993. pap. 10.00 (*0-06-092412-8*, PL) HarpC.

— The Lathe of Heaven. 176p. 1976. mass mkt. 4.99 (*0-380-01320-7*) Avon.

— The Lathe of Heaven. LC 81-18093. 192p. 1982. reprint ed. 14.00 (*0-8376-0464-8*) Bentley.

— The Left Hand of Darkness. 320p. 1983. mass mkt. 5.50 (*0-441-47812-3*) Ace Bks.

— The Left Hand of Darkness. LC 94-27147. 1994. 27.50 (*0-8027-1302-5*) Walker & Co.

— The Ones Who Walk Away from Omelas. (Short Stories Ser.). (J). (gr. 5 up). 1992. lib. bdg. 13.95 (*0-88682-501-6*) Creative Ed.

— Orsinian Tales. 1991. mass mkt. 4.50 (*0-06-100182-1*, Harp PBks) HarpC.

— Orsinian Tales. LC 76-5545. 1976. 25.00 (*0-06-012561-6*) Ultramarine Pub.

— A Ride on the Red Mare's Back. LC 91-21677. (Illus.). 48p. (J). (gr. 1-4). 1992. 16.95 (*0-531-05991-X*); lib. bdg. 16.99 (*0-531-08591-0*) Orchard Bks Watts.

— Rocannon's World. LC 76-47250. 136p. 1977. 25.00 (*0-06-012568-3*) Ultramarine Pub.

— Searoad: Chronicles of Klatsand. 1992. reprint ed. pap. 9.00 (*0-06-092329-6*, PL) HarpC.

— Solomon Leviathan's Nine Hundred Thirty-First Trip Around the World. (Adventures in Kroy Ser.: No. 2). (Illus.). 40p. (YA). (gr. 7 up). 1983. 70.00 (*0-941826-03-1*) Cheap St.

— Tehanu. 1991. mass mkt. 5.50 (*0-553-28873-3*, Spectra) Bantam.

— Tehanu: The Last Book of Earthsea. LC 89-32780. (Earthsea Quartet Ser.). 240p. (J). (ps up). 1990. lib. bdg. 16.95 (*0-689-31595-3*, Atheneum Bks Young) S&S Childrens.

— The Tombs of Atuan. 160p. 1984. mass mkt. 5.50 (*0-553-27331-0*, Bantam Classics) Bantam.

— The Tombs of Atuan. LC 70-154753. (Illus.). 176p. (J). (gr. 6-9). 1990. lib. bdg. 16.95 (*0-689-31684-4*, Atheneum Bks Young) S&S Childrens.

— Very Far Away from Anywhere Else. LC 76-4472. 96p. (J). (gr. 5-9). 1976. text ed. 13.95 (*0-689-30525-7*, Atheneum Bks Young) S&S Childrens.

— The Visionary: The Life Story of Flicker of the Serpentine. Bd. with Wonders Hidden: Audubon's Early Years. LC 84-7656. LC 84-7656. (Back-to-Back Ser.). 128p. (Orig.). 1984. Set pap. 7.50 (*0-88496-219-9*) Capra Pr.

— A Visit from Dr. Katz. LC 87-1783. (Illus.). 32p. (J). (gr. k-3). 1988. text ed. 13.95 (*0-689-31332-2*, Atheneum Bks Young) S&S Childrens.

— Wind's Twelve Quarters. 1991. mass mkt. 4.50 (*0-06-100162-7*, Harp PBks) HarpC.

— The Wizard of Earthsea. 192p. (gr. 9-12). 1984. mass mkt. 5.50 (*0-553-26250-5*) Bantam.

— A Wizard of Earthsea. LC 68-21992. 208p. (J). 1991. text ed. 16.95 (*0-689-31720-4*, Atheneum Bks Young) S&S Childrens.

— Wonderful Alexander & the Catwings. LC 93-49397. (Illus.). 48p. (J). (gr. k-3). 1994. 12.95 (*0-531-06851-X*); lib. bdg. 12.99 (*0-531-08701-8*) Orchard Bks Watts.

Le Guin, Ursula K. & Attebery, Brian, eds. The Norton Book of Science Fiction. LC 93-16130. 1993. 27.50 (*0-393-03546-8*) Norton.

Le Guin, Ursula K. & Dorband, Roger. Blue Moon over Thurman Street. 1993. pap. 16.95 (*0-939165-22-8*) NewSage Press.

Le Guin, Ursula K. & Sanders, Scott R. The Visionary; Wonders Hidden. (Capra Back-to-Back Ser.: No. 1). 133p. (C). 1988. reprint ed. lib. bdg. 25.00x (*0-8095-4100-9*) Borgo Pr.

Le Heron, Richard. Globalized Agriculture: Political Choice. LC 93-20539. 1993. 88.00 (*0-08-040804-4*, Pergamon Pr); pap. 32.00 (*0-08-040803-6*, Pergamon Pr) Elsevier.

Le Heron, Richard, jt. ed. see van der Knaap, Bert.

Le Hir, Marie-Pierre. Le Romantisme Aux Encheres: Ducange, Pixerecourt, Hugo. LC 92-3694. (Purdue University Monographs in Romance Languages: Vol. 42). viii, 225p. 1992. 65.00x (*1-55619-312-2*); pap. 27.95x (*1-55619-313-0*) Benjamins North Am.

Le Hir, Yves. Analyses Stylistiques. 302p. 1965. 9.95 (*0-8288-7489-1*) Fr & Eur.

Le Hir, Yves, ed. see De LaClos, Pierre-Ambroise F.

*__Le, Ho P.__ Angels from the Heart. 64p. 1995. 14.95 (*0-87588-431-8*, 4828) Hobby Hse.

*__Le, Ho Phi.__ Forget Me Not: Teddy Bears, Dolls, & Memories. 64p. 1994. 14.95 (*0-87588-425-3*, 4740) Hobby Hse.

— Romance of Dolls & Teddy Bears. (Illus.). 176p. 1992. 39.95 (*0-87588-390-7*) Hobby Hse.

Le Houerou, H. N. The Grazing Land Ecosystems of the African Sahel. (Ecological Studies: Vol. 75). (Illus.). 290p. 1989. 117.00 (*0-387-50791-4*) Spr-Verlag.

*__Le Houerou, Philippe H.__ Investment Policy in Russia. (Studies of Economies in Transformation). 1995. write for info. (*0-8213-3202-3*) World Bank.

Le Huray, Peter. Music & the Reformation in England: 1549-1660. LC 77-87383. (Cambridge Studies in Music). 484p. reprint ed. pap. 138.00 (*0-685-15583-8*, 2026344) Bks Demand.

Le Huray, Peter, et al. Anthems for Men's Voices, 2 vols. Incl. Vol. 1. Altos, Tenors & Basses. 1985. 21.95 (*0-19-353234-4*); 1965. write for info. (*0-318-54806-2*) OUP.

Le Janu, Richard, tr. see Gouverneur, Jacques.

Le Joly, Edward. A Woman in Love...Mother Teresa. LC 92-75249. (Illus.). 192p. (Orig.). 1993. pap. 7.95 (*0-87793-496-7*) Ave Maria.

Le Juez, Brigitte, jt. ed. see Gratton, Johnnie.

Le Kernec, Bill. Alaskan Malamutes. (Illus.). 128p. 1991. 11.95 (*0-87666-711-6*, KW-094) TFH Pubns.

Le Lay, G., et al. Semiconductor Interfaces: Formation & Properties. (Proceedings in Physics Ser.: Vol. 22). (Illus.). 420p. 1987. 75.00 (*0-387-18328-0*) Spr-Verlag.

Le Letty, L., ed. see IFAC Symposium Staff & Babary, J. P.

Le Lionnais, Francois. Dictionary of Mathematics. 3rd ed. 848p. (ENG & FRE.). 1992. 150.00 (*0-7859-4704-3*, F70764) Fr & Eur.

Le Lionnais, Francois & Maget, E. Dictionnaire des Echecs. 2nd ed. (FRE.). 1984. 115.00 (*0-8288-2341-3*, F60500) Fr & Eur.

Le Luc, Don R. Beyond Broadcasting: Patterns in Policy & Law. LC 87-2654. 1987. text ed. 39.16 (*0-582-29039-2*, 71737) Longman.

Le Magnen, Jacques. Hunger. (Problems in the Behavioural Sciences Ser.: No. 3). (Illus.). 176p. 1986. 49.95 (*0-521-26450-2*) Cambridge U Pr.

— Neurobiology of Feeding & Nutrition. (Illus.). 385p. 1991. text ed. 99.00 (*0-12-443340-5*) Acad Pr.

Le Maguer, M., ed. see International Congress on Engineering & Food Staff.

Le Maingre, Jean. Le Livre des Faicts du Bon Messire Jean le Maingre. LC 79-8367. reprint ed. 27.50 (*0-404-18351-4*) AMS Pr.

Le Maire De Belges, Jean. Oeuvres, 4 vols., Set. 1790p. 1972. reprint ed. write for info. (*3-487-04348-3*, Pub. by Georg Olms GW) Lubrecht & Cramer.

Le Maire, M., et al. Laboratory Guide to Biochemistry, Enzymology, & Protein Physical Chemistry: A Study of Aspartate Transcarbamylase. (Illus.). 155p. 1991. 34.50 (*0-306-43639-6*, Plenum Pr) Plenum.

Le Maistre. Dictionnaire Jersais-Francais, 2 tomes, Set. (FRE.). 150.00 (*0-685-57713-9*, F136580) Fr & Eur.

Le Maistre, Christopher & El-Sawy, Ahmed. Computer Integrated Manufacturing: A Systems Approach. (Illus.). 160p. 1987. pap. 19.95 (*0-527-91624-2*, 916242) Qual Resc.

Le Maitre, J. F., jt. auth. see Paquet, J. G.

Le Maitre, R. W. Numerical Petrology. (Developments in Petrology Ser.: No. 8). 282p. 1982. 84.75 (*0-444-42098-3*, I-038-84) Elsevier.

Le Marchant, C. M., jt. auth. see Johns, Richard A.

Le Mare, Karina. Great Danes: An Owner's Companion. (Illus.). 224p. 1993. 39.95 (*1-85223-316-8*, Pub. by Crowood Pr UK) Trafalgar.

*__Le Marechal, J. F. & Soulie, L.__ Dictionnaire Pratique de la Chimie. 158p. (FRE.). 1984. pap. 16.95 (*0-7859-7790-2*, 2218056070) Fr & Eur.

Le Marque, Tina. Warrior Woman: A Journal of My Life As an Artist. LC 91-73200. 168p. 1991. pap. 18.95 (*0-9630131-0-6*) Artists & Writers.

Le Massena, Clarence E. Galli-Curci's Life of Song. LC 76-46603. 1978. 14.95 (*0-917734-00-9*) Monitor Bk.

Le Massena, Robert A. & Yanosey, Robert J. Union Pacific Official Color Photography. (Illus.). 128p. 1993. 49.95 (*1-878887-25-4*) Morning NJ.

Le Master, Dennis C. & Towell, William E., frwds. Decade of Change: The Remaking of Forest Service Statutory Authority During the 1970s. LC 83-22641. (Contributions in Political Science Ser.: No. 113). (Illus.). xv, 290p. 1984. text ed. 37.50 (*0-313-24341-7*, LDC/) Greenwood.

Le May, Alan. The Unforgiven. 304p. 1985. pap. 4.50 (*0-425-07680-6*) Berkley Pub.

*__Le May, G. H.__ The Afrikaners: A Political History. (Illus.). 320p. (C). 1995. write for info. (*0-631-18204-7*) Blackwell Pubs.

Le May, I., ed. Advances in Materials Technology in the Americas, 2 vols. Incl. Vol. 1. Materials Recovery & Utilization: Bk. No. H00161, MD1. 168p. 1980. (*0-318-50918-0*); Vol. 2. Materials Processing & Performance: Bk. No. H00162, MD2. 220p. 1980. (*0-318-50919-9*); 1980. Set. 30.00 (*0-686-70426-6*) ASME.

Le May, Iain, ed. see Interamerican Conference on Materials Technology Staff.

Le May, Malcolm M., jt. ed. see Hillman, Jeffrey S.

Le May, Reginald S. An Asian Arcady: The Land & Peoples of Northern Siam. LC 77-87041. reprint ed. 27.00 (*0-404-16833-7*) AMS Pr.

— The Culture of South-East Asia: The Heritage of India. LC 77-87065. reprint ed. 30.00 (*0-404-16834-5*) AMS Pr.

Le Meal, Joselyne. English-French Dictionary of Fibre-Optic Cables: Dictionnaire Anglais-Francais de Cables a Fibres Optiques. (ENG & FRE.). 1984. 39.95 (*0-8288-2232-8*, F107570) Fr & Eur.

*__Le Mee, Katharine.__ Chant: The Origins, Form, Practice, & Healing Power of Gregorian Chant. 1995. 15.00 (*0-517-70037-9*, Crown) Crown Pub Group.

Le Mee, Katherine W. A Metrical Study of Five Lais of Marie de France. (De Proprietatibus Litterarum, Ser. Practica: No. 85). 1978. pap. text ed. 50.00 (*0-685-03441-0*) Mouton.

*__Le Mehaute, Bernard & Wang, Shen.__ Water Waves Generated by Underwater Explosion. LC 94-45506. (Advanced Series in Ocean Engineering). 400p. 1995. text ed. 74.00 (*981-02-2083-9*) World Scientific Pub.

— Water Waves Generated by Underwater Explosion. LC 94-45506. (Advanced Series in Ocean Engineering). 400p. 1995. pap. text ed. 43.00 (*981-02-2132-0*) World Scientific Pub.

*__Le Messurier, Brian.__ Devon. (Visitor's Guides Ser.). (Illus.). 256p. 1990. reprint ed. pap. 13.95 (*0-86190-512-1*) Hunter NJ.

— South West Coast Path: Exmouth to Poole. (National Trail Guides Ser.). (Illus.). 168p. Date not set. pap. 19.95 (*1-85410-097-1*, London Bridge) Genl Dist Srvs.

Le Moignan, Luke. Jersey on the Move: A Glimpse at Luke le Moignans Historic Photographs. (Jersey Heritage Editions Ser.). 1991. write for info. (*0-86120-022-5*, Pub. by Aris & Phillips UK) David Brown.

*__Le Moigne, Guy, ed.__ A Guide to the Formulation of Water Resources Strategy. LC 94-37850. (Technical Papers: No. 263). 1994. write for info. (*0-8213-3038-1*) World Bank.

Le Moigne, Guy, jt. auth. see Barghouti, Shawki.

Le Moigne, Guy, et al, eds. Country Experiences with Water Resources Management: Economic, Institutional, Technological, & Environmental Issues. LC 92-18831. (Technical Paper Ser.: No. 175). 223p. 1992. 11.95 (*0-8213-2159-5*, 12159) World Bank.

— Developing & Improving Irrigation & Drainage Systems: Selected Papers from World Bank Seminars. LC 92-17888. (Technical Paper Ser.: No. 178). 177p. 1992. 10.95 (*0-8213-2165-X*, 12165) World Bank.

— Technological & Institutional Innovation in Irrigation. (Technical Paper Ser.: No. 94). 150p. 1989. 9.95 (*0-614-02855-8*, 11185) World Bank.

— Water Policy & Water Markets: Selected Papers & Proceedings from the World Bank's Ninth Annual Irrigation & Drainage Seminar Held in Annapolis, Maryland, December 8-10, 1992. LC 94-18954. (Technical Papers Ser.: Vol. 249). 1994. write for info. (*0-8213-2861-1*) World Bank.

Le Moigne, Guy J., et al, eds. Dam Safety & the Environment. (Technical Paper Ser.: No. 115). 196p. 1990. 11.95 (*0-8213-1438-6*, 11438) World Bank.

— Technological & Institutional Innovation in Irrigation. (Technical Paper Ser.: No. 94). 94p. 1989. 7.95 (*0-8213-1185-9*, BK1185) World Bank.

Le Mouel, J. L., et al, eds. Dynamics of Earth's Deep Interior & Earth Rotation. LC 93-7784. (Geophysical Monograph Ser.: No. 72). 1993. 30.00 (*0-87590-463-7*) Am Geophysical.

Le Nard, M., jt. ed. see De Hertogh, A.

Le Neindre, B., jt. auth. see Vodar, B.

Le Nevelon, Jean. Venjance Alixandre. Ham, E. B., ed. (Elliott Monographs: Vol. 27). 1931. 20.00 (*0-527-02630-1*) Periodicals Srv.

Le-Ngoc, Tho, jt. auth. see Jamali, S. Hamidreza.

*__Le Ninan, Claude.__ Le Francais des Affaires Par la Video. 190p. 1993. pap. text ed. 23.95 (*2-278-04272-6*) Hatier Pub.

— Le Francais des Affaires Par la Video, 2 vols., Set. 1993. vhs 172.95 (*0-87774-002-X*) Hatier Pub.

Le Noble, W. J., ed. Organic High Pressure Chemistry. (Studies in Organic Chemistry: No. 37). 500p. 1988. 164.00 (*0-444-43023-7*) Elsevier.

Le Noble, William J. Highlights of Organic Chemistry: An Advanced Textbook. (Studies in Organic Chemistry: Vol. 3). 1000p. 1974. 140.00 (*0-8247-6210-X*) Dekker.

Le Noire, Rosetta, jt. auth. see Mitchell, Loften.

Le Page, Bill. The Turning of the Key: Meher Baba in Australia. (Illus.). 460p. (Orig.). 1993. pap. 12.00 (*0-913078-70-0*) Sheriar Pr.

Le Page, Jane W. Women Composers, Conductors & Musicians of the Twenieth Century: Selected Biographies, Vol. II. LC 80-12162. (Illus.). 388p. 1983. lib. bdg. 35.00 (*0-8108-1597-4*) Scarecrow.

Le Page, Jean-Francois. Applied Heterogeneous Catalysis: Design, Manufacture & Use of Solid Catalysts. (Illus.). 516p. 1988. 175.00 (*0-87201-146-1*) Gulf Pub.

An Asterisk (*) at the beginning of an entry indicates that the title is appearing in BIP for the first time.

Le Page, Jean-Francois & Chatila, Sami G. Resid & Heavy Oil Processing, Vol. 1. Davison, Michel, ed. 192p. (C). 1992. text ed. 320.00 (*2-7108-0621-5*) Technip.

***Le Page, Jean-Franois.** Applied Heterogeneous Catalysis: Design, Manufacture, Use of Solid Catalysts. (Illus.). 552p. (C). 1987. text ed. 192.00 (*2-7108-0531-6*) Technip.

Le Page, R. B., jt. ed. see Casidy, Frederic G.

Le Page, R. B., jt. auth. see O'Dwyer, R.

Le Patourel, John. Feudal Empires: Norman & Plantagenet. 385p. (C). 1984. text ed. 55.00 (*0-907628-22-2*) Hambledon Press.

Le Peau, Phyllis J. Acts: Seeing God's Power in Action. (LifeGuide Bible Studies). 112p. (Orig.). 1992. pap. 4.99 (*0-8308-1007-2*) InterVarsity.

— Caring for Emotional Needs. (Caring People Bible Studies). 96p. (Orig.). 1991. pap. 4.99 (*0-8308-1195-8*, 1195) InterVarsity.

— Caring for People in Conflict. (Caring People Bible Studies). 96p. (Orig.). 1991. pap. 4.99 (*0-8308-1192-3*, 1192) InterVarsity.

— Caring for People in Grief. (Caring People Bible Studies). 96p. (Orig.). 1991. pap. 4.99 (*0-8308-1193-1*, 1193) InterVarsity.

— Caring for Physical Needs. (Caring People Bible Studies). 96p. (Orig.). 1991. pap. 4.99 (*0-8308-1196-6*, 1196) InterVarsity.

— Caring for Spiritual Needs. (Caring People Bible Studies). 96p. (Orig.). 1991. pap. 4.99 (*0-8308-1194-X*, 1194) InterVarsity.

— The Character of Caring People. (Caring People Bible Studies). 96p. (Orig.). 1991. pap. 4.99 (*0-8308-1197-4*, 1197) InterVarsity.

— Resources for Caring People. (Caring People Bible Studies). 64p. (Orig.). 1991. pap. 4.99 (*0-8308-1191-5*, 1191) InterVarsity.

Le Peau, Phyllis J. & Miller, Bonnie J. Handbook for Caring People. (Caring People Bible Studies). 96p. (Orig.). 1991. pap. 4.99 (*0-8308-1198-2*, 1198) InterVarsity.

Le Pelletier, Louis. Etymological Dictionary of the Breton Language: Dictionnaire Etymologique de la Langue Bretonne. 1716p. (BRE & FRE.). 1973. reprint ed. pap. write for info. (*0-7859-4912-7*) Fr & Eur.

***Le Penven, Yves.** Dictionnaire des Signes et des Symptomes en Homeopathie et des Remedes Correspondent. 412p. (FRE.). 1986. 95.00 (*0-7859-7818-6*, 2224011733) Fr & Eur.

Le Pera, George, ed. Stray. (Illus.). 66p. (Orig.). 1989. pap. text ed. 7.95 (*0-9624466-0-2*) United Action.

Le Petit, Jean Francois. The Low Country Commonwealth. Grimeston, E., tr. LC 72-25634. (English Experience Ser.: No. 208). 1969. reprint ed. 45.00 (*90-221-0208-4*) Walter J Johnson.

Le Petit, Jules. Bibliographie Des Principales Editions Originales D'Ecrivains Francaise Du Fifteenth Au Eighteenth Siecle. viii, 583p. 1969. reprint ed. write for info. (*3-487-04174-X*, Pub. by Georg Olms GW) Lubrecht & Cramer.

Le Play, Frederick. La Reforme Sociale En France Deduite De L'observation Comparee Des Peuples Europeens: Social Reform in France Deduced from the Comparative Observation of the European Peoples, 2 vols. in one. LC 74-25766. (European Sociology Ser.). 936p. 1975. reprint ed. 74.95 (*0-405-06520-5*) Ayer.

Le Plongeon, Alice D. Queen Moo's Talisman: The Fall of the Maya Empire. 90p. 1994. reprint ed. pap. 15.95 (*1-56459-426-2*) Kessinger Pub.

Le Plongeon, Augustus. Origin of the Egyptians. 1985. 17.50 (*0-89314-418-5*) Philos Res.

— Queen Moo & the Egyptian Sphinx. 2nd ed. 277p. 1972. reprint ed. spiral bd. 20.35 (*0-7873-0539-1*) Mokelumne.

Le Poidevin, Robin. Change, Cause & Contradiction: A Defence of the Tenseless Theory of Time. LC 90-19925. 186p. 1991. text ed. 55.00 (*0-312-05786-5*) St Martin.

Le Poidevin, Robin, ed. see MacBeath, Murray.

Le Poitier, Joseph, jt. ed. see Verdier, Jean-Louis.

Le Poncin-Lafitte, M. & Rapin, J. R., eds. Deoxyglucose Uptake & Oxygen Consumption: A Metabolic Approach to Cerebral Function. (Journal: European Neurology: Vol. 20, No. 3). (Illus.). 170p. 1981. pap. 40.00 (*3-8055-3412-4*) S Karger.

Le Poncin Lafitte, M., et al, eds. Functions of the Ageing Brain from Physiological Ageing to Dementia. (Journal: Gerontology: Vol. 32, Suppl. 1, 1986). (Illus.). iv, 128p. 1986. pap. 38.50 (*3-8055-4386-7*) S Karger.

Le Poullioun, Maria-Luisa. Lexi-Tourisme Espagnol-Francais. 144p. 1993. pap. 22.95 (*0-7859-5636-0*, 2713512433) Fr & Eur.

Le Prade, R. Debs & the Poets. 1972. 34.95 (*0-8490-0012-2*) Gordon Pr.

Le Prestre, Philippe. The World Bank & the Environmental Challenge. LC 88-42825. 264p. 1989. 40.00 (*0-941664-98-8*) Susquehanna U Pr.

Le Quesne, A. L., et al. Victorian Thinkers: Carlyle, Ruskin, Arnold, Morris. LC 92-30091. 1993. 14.95 (*0-19-283104-6*) OUP.

Le Quesne, P. W., jt. ed. see Atta-ur-Rahman.

Le Queue, Jake the Rake. The Mind's Eye. (Illus.). 112p. (Orig.). 1993. pap. write for info. (*1-56167-122-3*) Am Literary Pr.

Le Queux, William T. The Eye of Istar: A Romance of the Land of No Return. Reginald, R. & Melville, Douglas, eds. LC 77-84247. (Lost Race & Adult Fantasy Ser.). (Illus.). 1978. reprint ed. lib. bdg. 36.95 (*0-405-10993-8*) Ayer.

— The Great White Queen: A Tale of Treasure & Treason. LC 74-16505. (Science Fiction Ser.). (Illus.). 322p. 1975. reprint ed. 26.95 (*0-405-06303-2*) Ayer.

Le Quin, Ursula, contrib. Wynn Bullock: The Enchanted Landscape, Photographs 1940-1975. 120p. 1993. 50.00 (*0-89381-546-2*) Aperture.

***Le Riche, William H.** A Chemical Feast. LC 82-2442. 216p. 1982. reprint ed. pap. 61.60 (*0-7837-8155-5*, 2047860) Bks Demand.

Le Rider, Jacques. Modernity & Crises of Identity. 352p. (C). 1993. 34.95 (*0-8264-0631-9*) Continuum.

Le Riverend Brusone, Pablo. Homenaje a Eduardo Le Riverend Brusone. LC 83-50312. (Senda de Estudios y Ensayos Ser.). (Illus.). 55p. 1983. pap. 4.95 (*0-918454-37-9*) Senda Nueva.

Le Roith, Derek, jt. ed. see Draznin, Boris.

***Le Rond D'Alembert, Jean.** Preliminary Discourse to the Encyclopedia of Diderot. Schwab, Richard N., tr. 226p. 1995. pap. text ed. 10.95 (*0-226-13476-8*) U Ch Pr.

Le Rossignol, James E. Backgrounds to Communist Thought. 1979. 8.75 (*0-8446-2454-3*) Peter Smith.

Le Rougetel, Hazel. A Heritage of Roses. (Illus.). 176p. 1988. 29.95 (*0-88045-110-6*) Stemmer Hse.

— The Little Book of Old Roses. LC 92-17184. (Illus.). 60p. 1992. 7.95 (*0-399-13787-4*, Putnam) Putnam Pub Group.

Le Roux de Lincy, Antoine J. Recherches Sur Jean Grolier, Sur Sa Vie et Sa Bibliotheque. (In Zusammenarbeit Mit Dem Verlag B. de Graaf, Nieuwkoop Ser.). lix, 491p. 1971. reprint ed. write for info. (*3-487-04035-2*, Pub. by Georg Olms GW) Lubrecht & Cramer.

Le-Roux De Lincy, M., ed. see Philippe De Remi.

***Le Roux, Pak & Van Niekerk, Andre.** South African Law of Unfair Dismissal. 380p. 1994. pap. 52.00 (*0-7021-3162-8*, Pub. by Juta SA) W W Gaunt.

Le Rouzic, Pierre. Compatibility of Names: A Companion to the Name Book. 1989. pap. 7.95 (*0-9622069-1-1*) Topos Pr.

— The Name Book. rev. ed. Charles, Rodney, ed. LC 94-67155. (Illus.). 646p. 1995. pap. 15.95 (*0-9638502-1-0*) Sunstar Pubng.

— The Name Book: A Name for a Lifetime. rev. ed. LC 89-50198. 570p. reprint ed. pap. text ed. 14.95 (*0-9622069-0-3*) Topos Pr.

Le Roy, Bruce, ed. see Chittenden, Hiram Martin.

Le Roy, Gaylord C. Perplexed Prophets: Six Nineteenth Century British Authors. LC 78-147220. 205p. 1971. reprint ed. text ed. 55.00 (*0-8371-5985-7*, LEPR, Greenwood Pr) Greenwood.

Le Roy, James A. Americans in the Philippines, 2 Vols. LC 73-126681. reprint ed. 125.00 (*0-404-03974-X*) AMS Pr.

Le Roy-Ladurie, Emmanuel. The Mind & Method of the Historian. Reynolds, Sian & Reynolds, Ben, trs. LC 81-449. 224p. (C). 1981. lib. bdg. 26.00 (*0-226-47326-0*) U Ch Pr.

— Montaillou, Village Occitan de 1294 a 1324. (Folio-Histoire Ser.: No. 9). 640p. (FRE.). 1982. pap. 14.95 (*2-07-032328-5*) Schoenhof.

Le Roy Ladurie, Emmanuel. The Royal French State, 1460-1610: Louis XI-Henri IV, 1460-1610. Vale, Juliet, tr. (History of France Ser.). (Illus.). 384p. 1994. 49.95 (*0-631-17027-8*) Blackwell Pubs.

Le Roy-Ladurie, Emmanuel, tr. see Cottret, B. J.

Le Sage, Alain R. The Devil on Two Sticks. LC 75-46287. (Supernatural & Occult Fiction Ser.). (Illus.). 1976. reprint ed. lib. bdg. 25.95 (*0-405-08148-0*) Ayer.

Le Saux, Francoise. Layamon's Brut: The Poem & Its Sources. (Arthurian Studies). 352p. (C). 1989. 79.00 (*0-85991-282-5*) Boydell & Brewer.

Le Saux, Henri. The Eyes of Light. 1983. pap. 12.95 (*0-87193-202-4*) Dimension Bks.

Le Scrope, Richard. De Controversia in Curia Militari inter Ricardum le Scrope et Robertum Grosvenor Milites, 2 vols., Set. LC 78-63514. reprint ed. 115.00 (*0-404-17220-2*) AMS Pr.

Le Sieg, Theodore. Eye Book. (Bright & Early Bks.). (Illus.). (J). (ps-1). 1968. 6.95 (*0-394-81094-5*, BE2); lib. bdg. 7.99 (*0-394-91094-X*, BE2) Random Bks Yng Read.

— In a People House. (Bright & Early Bks.: No. 12). (Illus.). (J). (ps-1). 1972. 7.99 (*0-394-82395-8*); lib. bdg. 9.99 (*0-394-92395-2*) Random Bks Yng Read.

— Maybe You Should Fly a Jet! Maybe You Should Be a Vet. LC 80-5084. (Beginner Bks.: No. 67). (Illus.). 48p. (J). (ps-3). 1980. lib. bdg. 9.99 (*0-394-94448-8*) Beginner.

— Please Try to Remember the First of October. LC 77-4504. (Illus.). 48p. (J). (gr. 1-4). 1977. lib. bdg. 7.99 (*0-394-93563-2*) Beginner.

— Ten Apples up on Top. LC 61-7068. (Illus.). 72p. (J). (gr. 1-2). 1961. 7.99 (*0-394-80019-2*); lib. bdg. 7.99 (*0-394-90019-7*) Beginner.

— The Tooth Book. LC 80-28320. (Bright & Early Bks.: No. 25). (Illus.). 48p. (J). (ps-1). 1981. 7.99 (*0-394-84825-X*, XBYR); lib. bdg. 9.99 (*0-394-94825-4*) Random Bks Yng Read.

— Wacky Wednesday. LC 74-5520. (Illus.). 48p. (J). (gr. k-4). 1974. 6.95 (*0-394-82912-3*); lib. bdg. 7.99 (*0-394-92912-8*) Beginner.

Le Sourd, Howard M. The University Work of the United Lutheran Church in America: A Study of the Work among Lutheran Students at Non-Lutheran Institutions. LC 70-176990. (Columbia University. Teachers College. Contributions to Education Ser.: No. 377). reprint ed. 37.50 (*0-404-55377-X*) AMS Pr.

Le Sourd, Leonard, jt. auth. see Marshall, Catherine.

Le Strange, Guy. Don Juan of Persia. LC 73-6288. (Middle East Ser.). 1973. reprint ed. 28.95 (*0-405-05333-9*) Ayer.

— The Lands of the Eastern Caliphate. LC 77-180355. (Cambridge Geographical Ser.). reprint ed. 41.50 (*0-404-56287-6*) AMS Pr.

***Le Strange, Guy, ed. & tr.** Don Juan of Persia: A Shi'ah Catholic (1560-1604) (Curzon Travellers Ser.). 360p. (C). 1995. text ed. 70.00 (*0-7007-0347-0*, Pub. by Curzon Pr UK) Humanities.

Le Strange, Guy, tr. Palestine under the Moslems. LC 70-180356. reprint ed. 47.50 (*0-404-56288-4*) AMS Pr.

Le Sueur, Jean-Francois & Dercy, Palat dit. La Caverne. Mongredien, Jean, ed. LC 85-750828. (French Opera in the 17th & 18th Centuries Ser.: No. 2, Vol. LXXIV). (Illus.). 1985. lib. bdg. 94.00 (*0-918728-33-9*) Pendragon NY.

Le Sueur, Meridel. Chanticleer of Wilderness Road: A Story of Davy Crockett. LC 88-45372. (Meridel Le Sueur Wilderness Bk.). (Illus.). 160p. 1990. reprint ed. 13.95 (*0-930100-35-2*) Holy Cow.

— Crusaders: The Radical Legacy of Marian & Arthur Lesueur. LC 84-14696. (Illus.). 109p. 1984. reprint ed. 11.95 (*0-87351-174-3*, Borealis Book); reprint ed. pap. 6.95 (*0-87351-178-6*, Borealis Book) Minn Hist.

— The Dread Road. (Illus.). 65p. (Orig.). 1991. pap. 11.95 (*0-931122-63-5*) West End.

— The Girl. LC 82-20021. 159p. 1982. 14.95 (*0-930656-27-X*); pap. 4.50 (*0-930656-28-8*) MEP Pubns.

— The Girl. 158p. 1990. pap. 10.95 (*0-931122-56-2*) West End.

— Harvest Song: Collected Stories & Essays, 1926-58. rev. ed. 244p. 1990. pap. 12.95 (*0-931122-60-0*) West End.

— I Hear Men Talking & Other Stories. 243p. (Orig.). 1984. pap. 5.95 (*0-931122-37-6*) West End.

— Little Brother of the Wilderness: The Story of Johnny Appleseed. LC 87-80574. (Illus.). 68p. (J). (gr. 5 up). 1987. reprint ed. 9.95 (*0-930100-21-2*) Holy Cow.

— Nancy Hanks of Wilderness Road: A Story of Abraham Lincoln's Mother. (Illus.). 88p. 1990. reprint ed. 10.95 (*0-930100-36-0*) Holy Cow.

— Ripening: Selected Work. 2nd ed. Hedges, Elaine, ed. LC 86-18308. (Illus.). 312p. (C). 1990. pap. 10.95 (*0-935312-41-2*) Feminist Pr.

— River Road: A Story of Abraham Lincoln. 1991. 14.95 (*0-930100-37-9*) Holy Cow.

— Salute to Spring. LC 75-38588. 192p. (Orig.). 1989. pap. 3.95 (*0-7178-0463-1*) Intl Pubs Co.

— Sparrow Hawk. LC 87-80573. (Illus.). 176p. (YA). (gr. 7 up). 1987. reprint ed. 13.95 (*0-930100-22-0*) Holy Cow.

— Women on the Breadlines. LC 78-108080. (Worker Writer Ser.). (Illus.). 1978. pap. text ed. 2.00 (*0-931122-34-1*) West End.

— Word Is Movement: Journal Notes from Atlanta to Tulsa to Wounded Knee. 74p. 1984. pap. 6.00 (*0-943594-07-3*) Cardinal Pr.

— Worker Writers. (Worker Writer Ser.: No. 4). 32p. (Orig.). 1982. pap. 3.00 (*0-931122-07-4*) West End.

Le Tallec, P. V. Numerical Analysis of Viscoelastic Problems. Ciarlet, P. G. & Lions, J. L., eds. (Recherches en Mathematiques Appliquees Ser.: Vol. 15). iv, 136p. 1990. pap. 30.00 (*0-387-52450-9*) Spr-Verlag.

Le Tallec, Patrick, jt. auth. see Glowinski, Roland.

Le Targat, Francois. Chagall. LC 85-42875. (Illus.). 128p. 1985. 24.95 (*0-8478-0624-3*) Rizzoli Intl.

— Kandinsky. LC 86-43201. (Illus.). 128p. 1987. 24.95 (*0-8478-0810-6*) Rizzoli Intl.

Le Targat, P. Kandinsky. (C). 1990. 200.00 (*0-685-34364-2*, Pub. by Collets) St Mut.

Le Targat, P., ed. Chagall. (C). 1990. 100.00 (*0-685-34373-1*, Pub. by Collets) St Mut.

***Le Target, Francois.** Toulouse-Lautrec. (Grandes Monografias). (Illus.). 200p. (SPA.). 1993. 200.00 (*84-343-0541-0*) Elliots Bks.

***Le Tirant, P., ed.** Offshore Pile Design: Design Guides for Offshore Structures. (Design Guides for Offshore Structures: Vol. 1). (Illus.). 324p. (C). 1992. text ed. 98.00 (*2-7108-0614-2*) Technip.

***Le Tirant, P. & Nauroy, J. F., eds.** Foundations in Carbonate Soils: Design Guides for Offshore Structures, Vol. 5. (Illus.). 232p. (C). 1994. pap. text ed. 66.00 (*2-7108-0665-7*) Technip.

***Le Tirant, P. & Perol, C., eds.** Stability & Operation of Jackups: Design Guides for Offshore Structures. (Design Guides for Offshore Structures: Vol. 4). (Illus.). 350p. (C). 1993. pap. text ed. 108.00 (*2-7108-0636-3*) Technip.

Le Tissier, Jeckie. Food Combining for Vegetarians. 1992. pap. 12.00 (*0-7225-2543-5*) Thorsons SF.

***Le Tissier, Tony.** Zukov At the Oder: The Decisive Battle for Berlin. LC 95-10099. 1995. text ed. write for info. (*0-275-95230-4*, Praeger Pubs) Greenwood.

Le, Tony, jt. auth. see Brown, G. S.

Le Tord, Bijou. Elephant Moon. LC 92-28234. (J). 1993. 14.95 (*0-385-30623-7*) Doubleday.

— Little Hills of Nazareth. 1994. mass mkt. 5.99 (*0-440-40997-7*) Dell.

— Little Shepherd: The Twenty-Third Psalm. (J). 1991. 13.00 (*0-385-30417-X*) Delacorte.

— Peace on Earth: A Book of Prayers from Around the World. LC 91-39913. (Illus.). 80p. (J). 1992. 18.00 (*0-385-30692-X*) Doubleday.

— Rabbit Seeds. (J). (ps-3). 1993. mass mkt. 3.99 (*0-440-40767-2*) Dell.

— The River & the Rain: The Lord's Prayer. LC 93-20730. (J). 1994. 15.95 (*0-385-32034-5*) Doubleday.

Le Tourneau, Roger. Fes avant le Protectorat: Etude economique et sociale d'une fille de l'occident musulman. LC 74-15063. (Illus.). reprint ed. 95.00 (*0-404-12104-7*) AMS Pr.

Le Treut. Mammography. 216p. 1991. 89.00 (*0-8151-5315-5*, Yr Bk Med Pubs) Mosby Yr Bk.

Le, Trong Cuc & Rambo, A. Terry, eds. Too Many People, Too Little Land: The Human Ecology of a Wet Rice-Growing Village in the Red River Delta of Vietnam. LC 93-23834. (Occasional Paper Ser.: Vol. 15). 1993. write for info. (*0-86638-157-0*) EW Ctr HI.

Le Trosne, Guillaume F. De l'Ordre Social. (Economistes Francais du XVIIIe Siecle Ser.). 1990. reprint ed. pap. 70.00 (*3-601-00155-1*) Periodicals Srv.

Le Van, Gerald. Getting to Win-Win in Family Business. LC 93-60388. 160p. (Orig.). 1993. pap. 23.00 (*1-56664-047-4*) WorldComm.

Le Van, Leon C. Poems from Swedenborg. LC 87-60469. 178p. 1987. pap. 5.95 (*0-87785-134-4*) Swedenborg.

***Le Vasseur, Guillaume & De Beauplan, Sieur.** A Description of Ukraine. Pernal, Andrew B. & Essar, Dennis F., trs. LC 92-54347. (Harvard Series in Ukrainian Studies). (Illus.). 256p. (UKR.). 1990. write for info. (*0-916458-40-7*) Harvard Ukrainian.

— A Description of Ukraine. fac. ed. Pernal, Andrew B. & Essar, Dennis F., trs. LC 92-54347. (Harvard Series in Ukrainian Studies). (Illus.). 112p. 1990. write for info. (*0-916458-39-3*) Harvard Ukrainian.

— A Description of Ukraine: Guillaume le Vasseur & Sieur de Beauplan. Pernal, Andrew B. & Essar, Dennis F., trs. LC 92-54347. (Harvard Series in Ukrainian Studies). (Illus.). cxiv, 243p. (C). 1993. 75.00 (*0-916458-44-X*) Harvard Ukrainian.

Le Vay, D. The History of Orthopaedics. (History of Medicine Ser.). (Illus.). 694p. 1990. 125.00 (*1-85070-145-8*) Prthnon Pub.

Le Vay, David. Teach Yourself Human Anatomy & Physiology. (Teach Yourself Ser.). 1978. pap. 10.95 (*0-679-10399-6*) McKay.

Le Vay, David, tr. see LeBlanc, Andre.

Le Vay, David, tr. see Roth, Joseph.

Le Vay, David, tr. see Wittig, Monique.

Le Vay, Simon. The Sexual Brain. LC 92-44691. (Illus.). 220p. 1993. 25.00 (*0-262-12178-6*, Bradford Bks) MIT Pr.

Le Veque, R. J. Numerical Methods for Conservations Laws. 2nd ed. (Lectures in Mathematics ETH Zurich). 232p. 1994. pap. 28.50 (*0-8176-2723-5*) Birkhauser.

Le Vert, Suzanne. Huey Long: The Kingfish of Louisiana. LC 94-19439. (Makers of America Ser.). 128p. (J). (gr. 5-12). 1995. 17.95x (*0-8160-2880-X*) Facts on File.

Le Vey, David, tr. see Colette, Sidonie-Gabrielle.

Le Vine, Robert, et al, eds. Parental Behavior in Diverse Societies. LC 85-644581. (New Directions for Child Development Ser.: No. CD 40). 1988. 17.95 (*1-55542-915-7*) Jossey-Bass.

***Le Vitus, Bob.** Magic Cap for Road Warriors: How to Master Mobile Reality Without Even Trying, Set. (Illus.). 400p. 1995. disk, pap. write for info. (*0-12-445570-0*) Acad Pr.

Le Yaouanc, A., et al. Hadron Transitions of the Quark Model. 322p. 1987. text ed. 164.00 (*2-88124-214-6*) Gordon & Breach.

Lea & Foster. Perspectives on Mental Handicap in South Africa. 1990. pap. text ed. 36.95 (*0-409-10919-3*) Buttrwrth-Heinemann.

Lea, ed. see Pilling.

***Lea, Ani.** Altura: Fusion of the Soul. 64p. (Orig.). 1995. pap. text ed. 7.95 (*0-9645725-2-4*) Numina.

Lea, C. A. On Trek in Kordofan: The Diaries of a British District Officer in the Sudan, 1931-1933. Daly, Martin W., ed. (Oriental & African Archives New Ser.: No. 2). (Illus.). 332p. 1994. 45.00 (*0-19-726128-0*) OUP.

Lea, Carole A. Guess What, Mrs. Lea? 58p. (Orig.). 1990. pap. 10.00 (*0-9625906-0-6*) C A Lea.

Lea, Christine. The Oxford Paperback Spanish Dictionary: Spanish-English, English-Spanish - Espanol-Ingles, Ingles-Espanol. LC 93-30406. (Oxford Paperback Reference Ser.). 512p. (ENG & SPA.). 1994. pap. 5.95 (*0-19-280013-2*) OUP.

— The Oxford Spanish Minidictionary: Spanish English, English Spanish. LC 92-44892. 660p. (ENG & SPA.). 1993. 5.95 (*0-19-864156-7*) OUP.

***Lea, Christine, ed.** Oxford Colour Spanish Dictionary. 512p. (SPA.). 1995. 8.95 (*0-19-864540-6*) OUP.

Lea, David A. & Chaudhri, D. P., eds. Rural Development & the State: Contradictions & Dilemmas in Developing Countries. 338p. 1984. pap. 22.50 (*0-416-31320-5*, NO. 3955) Routledge Chapman & Hall.

Lea, F. Shelley & the Romantic Revolution. LC 71-164028. (Studies in Shelley: No. 25). 1971. reprint ed. lib. bdg. 52.95 (*0-8383-1328-0*) M S G Haskell Hse.

Lea, F. A. The Tragic Philosopher: Friedrich Nietzsche. LC 93-9875. 354p. (C). 1993. reprint ed. pap. 29.95 (*0-485-12095-X*, Pub. by Athlone Pr UK) Humanities.

Lea, F. M. Chemistry of Cement & Concrete. 1971. 80.00 (*0-8206-0212-4*) Chem Pub.

Lea, Fannie H. Jaconetta Stories. LC 76-130061. (Short Story Index Reprint Ser.). (Illus.). 1977. 17.95 (*0-8369-3647-7*) Ayer.

Lea, H. Thomas Hardy's Wessex. 1972. 35.00 (*0-8490-1201-5*) Gordon Pr.

***Lea, H. Daniel & Leibowitz, Zandy B.** Adult Career Development: Concepts, Issues, & Practices. 1992. pap. text ed. 36.00 (*1-55620-095-1*) Am Coun Assn.

Lea, Henry. Moriscos of Spain, Their Conversion & Expulsion. LC 68-26358. (Studies in Spanish Literature: No. 36). 1969. reprint ed. lib. bdg. 75.00 (*0-8383-0266-1*) M S G Haskell Hse.

Lea, Henry C. Chapters from the Religious History of Spain Connected with the Inquisition. LC 83-48778. 1988. reprint ed. 54.00 (*0-404-19156-8*) AMS Pr.

— History of Auricular Confession & Indulgences in the Latin Church, 3 Vols. LC 68-19287. 1968. reprint ed. text ed. 67.25 (*0-8371-0140-9*, LEHC, Greenwood Pr) Greenwood.

— History of Sacerdotal Celibacy in the Christian Church. LC 83-48779. 1988. reprint ed. 84.50 (*0-318-36187-6*) AMS Pr.

— History of Sacerdotal Celibacy in the Christian Church. LC 83-48779. 1988. reprint ed. 84.50 (*0-404-19115-0*) AMS Pr.

— History of the Inquisition of Spain, 4 vols., 1. LC 83-45968. 1988. reprint ed. write for info. (*0-404-03921-9*) AMS Pr.

An Asterisk (*) at the beginning of an entry indicates that the title is appearing in BIP for the first time.

— History of the Inquisition of Spain, 4 vols., 2. LC 83-45968. 1988. reprint ed. write for info. (0-404-03922-7) AMS Pr.
— History of the Inquisition of Spain, 4 vols., 3. LC 83-45968. 1988. reprint ed. write for info. (0-404-03923-5) AMS Pr.
— History of the Inquisition of Spain, 4 vols., 4. LC 83-45968. 1988. reprint ed. write for info. (0-404-03924-3) AMS Pr.
— History of the Inquisition of Spain, 4 vols., Set. LC 83-45968. 1988. reprint ed. 275.00 (0-404-03920-0) AMS Pr.
— A History of the Inquisition of the Middle Ages. LC 83-48776. 1988. reprint ed. 97.50 (0-404-19157-6) AMS Pr.
— The Inquisition in the Spanish Dependencies. LC 83-48777. 1988. reprint ed. 57.50 (0-404-19158-4) AMS Pr.
— Moriscos of Spain: Their Conversion & Expulsion. LC 68-19286. 463p. 1968. reprint ed. text ed. 65.00 (0-8371-0141-7, LEMS, Greenwood Pr) Greenwood.
— Studies in Church History. LC 83-48780. 1988. reprint ed. 57.50 (0-404-19154-1) AMS Pr.
— Superstition & Force. LC 79-148823. (World History Ser.: No. 48). 1971. reprint ed. lib. bdg. 75.00 (0-8383-1228-4) M S G Haskell Hse.
— Translations & Other Rhymes. 1973. 59.95 (0-8490-1226-0) Gordon Pr.

Lea, Henry C. & Burr, George L., eds. Materials Toward a History of Witchcraft, 3 vols. LC 79-8109. reprint ed. 265.00 (0-404-18420-0) AMS Pr.

Lea, Homer. Homer Lea: Prophet of the West. 1991. lib. bdg. 65.95 (0-8490-4434-0) Gordon Pr.

Lea, J., tr. An Answer to the Untruthes Published in Spaine, in Glorie of Their Supposed Victorie Against Our English Navie. LC 72-25756. (English Experience Ser.: No. 189). 56p. 1969. reprint ed. 20.00 (90-221-0189-4) Walter J Johnson.

Lea, J. H. & Hutchinson, J. R. Lincoln: The Ancestry of Abraham Lincoln. (Illus.). 310p. 1991. reprint ed. lib. bdg. 50.00 (0-8328-1818-6); reprint ed. pap. 40.00 (0-8328-1819-4) Higginson Bk Co.

Lea, James F. Political Consciousness & American Democracy. LC 81-13133. 218p. 1982. pap. 16.95 (0-87805-151-1) U Pr of Miss.

Lea, James W. Keeping It in the Family: Successful Succession of the Family Business. 224p. 1991. text ed. 29.95 (0-471-53913-9) Wiley.

***Lea, John.** Capitalism & Organized Crime: Towards a Marxist History of the Mafia. 1996. pap. 16.50 (1-899438-10-6, Pub. by Porcupine Bks UK) Humanities.

Lea, John & Young, Jock. What Is to Be Done about Law & Order: Crisis in the Nineties. (C). 1993. text ed. 65.00 (0-7453-0735-3, Pub. by Pluto Pr UK) Westview.

Lea, John, tr. see Pitch, Tamar.

Lea, John P. Tourism & Development in the Third World. (Introductions to Development Ser.). 80p. 1988. pap. text ed. 9.95 (0-415-00671-6) Routledge.

Lea, John P. & Young, Jock. What Is to Be Done about Law & Order? Crisis in the Nineties. 2nd ed. 284p. (C). 1993. pap. text ed. 20.95 (0-7453-0398-6, Pub. by Pluto Pr UK) Westview.

Lea, John P., jt. auth. see Murison, Hamish S.

Lea, Judy, ed. see McCann, Yvette B.

Lea, Katherine, ed. see Segal, Audrey.

Lea, L. J., ed. Compendium of the Scriptures. 1951. pap. 13.50 (0-8309-0253-8) Herald Hse.

Lea, Larry. Armas Para la Lucha Espiritual. 240p. (SPA.). 1990. 4.95 (0-8297-0366-7) Life Pubs Intl.
— Hearing Ear: Learning to Listen to God. 1990. pap. 7.99 (0-88419-278-4, Creation Hse) Strang Comms Co.
— Llamdo Supremo. (SPA.). Date not set. pap. 6.99 (0-88113-105-9) Edit Betania.
— Ni Tan Solo Una Hora. 176p. (Orig.). (SPA.). 1990. pap. 4.95 (0-88113-053-2) Edit Betania.

Lea, M. Sheridan, jt. auth. see Anderson, James M.

Lea, Michael, ed. Tax Policy & Housing. (Contemporary Studies in Economic & Financial Analysis: Vol. 54). 1989. 73.25 (0-89232-602-6) Jai Pr.

Lea, P. D., jt. ed. see Clark, P. U.

***Lea, P. J. & Leegood, R. C.** Plant Biochemistry & Molecular Biology. 1993. text ed. 132.95 (0-471-93895-5) Wiley.

Lea, Peter J., ed. The Genetic Manipulation of Plants & Its Application to Agriculture. (Annual Proceedings of the Phytochemical Society of Europe: Vol. 23). 350p. 1985. 30.00 (0-19-854152-X) OUP.

Lea, Peter J, ed. Methods in Plant Biochemistry, Vol. 9: Enzymes of Secondary Metabolism. (Illus.). 478p. 1993. text ed. 115.00 (0-12-461019-6) Acad Pr.

Lea, Peter J. & Leegood, Richard, eds. Plant Biochemistry & Molecular Biology. LC 92-22064. 312p. (Orig.). 1993. pap. text ed. 54.95 (0-471-93313-9, Wiley-Liss) Wiley.

Lea, Peter J., ed. see Van Sumere, C. F.

Lea, Peter J., et al, eds. Methods in Plant Biochemistry, Vol. 3: Enzymes of Primary Metabolism. 414p. 1990. text ed. 110.00 (0-12-461013-7) Acad Pr.

Lea, R. M., ed. Wafer-Scale Integration: Proceedings of the 2nd IFIP WG10.5 Workshop, Egham, Surrey, UK, 23-25 Sept., 1987, Vol. II. 250p. 1988. 64.00 (0-444-70535-X, North Holland) Elsevier.

Lea, Richard. Job Title Index to SIC (Standard Industrial Classification) Codes. LC 87-43167. 94p. 1988. lib. bdg. 21.95x (0-89950-311-X) McFarland & Co.

Lea, Rob. Display Pilot. (Color Library). (Illus.). 128p. 1994. pap. 15.95 (1-85532-445-8, Pub. by Osprey Pubng Ltd UK) Motorbooks Intl.

Lea, Robert N., jt. auth. see Miller, Daniel J.

Lea, Sidney. No Sign. LC 86-19160. (Contemporary Poetry Ser.). 112p. 1987. 15.00 (0-8203-0916-8); pap. 7.95 (0-8203-0917-6) U of Ga Pr.

Lea, Sidney, ed. The Burdens of Formality: Essays on the Poetry of Anthony Hecht. LC 88-17519. 232p. 1989. 30.00 (0-8203-1091-3) U of Ga Pr.

Lea, Sperry & Webley, Simon. Multinational Corporations in Developed Countries: A Review of Recent Research & Policy Thinking. LC 73-77813. (British-North American Committee Ser.). 88p. 1973. 2.00 (0-902594-07-9) Natl Planning.

Lea, Stephen. Instinct, Environment & Behavior. Herriot, Peter, ed. LC 83-17308. (New Essential Psychology Ser.). 160p. 1984. pap. 8.95 (0-416-33640-X, NO. 4042) Routledge Chapman & Hall.

Lea, Stephen E., et al. New Directions in Economic Psychology: Theory, Experiment & Application. 287p. 1992. text ed. 64.95 (1-85278-462-8, Pub. by E Elgar Pub UK) Ashgate Pub Co.

Lea, Sydney. The Blainsville Testament. 94p. 1992. pap. 11.95 (0-934257-80-9) Story Line.
— Hunting the Whole Way Home. LC 94-20491. 211p. 1994. 19.95 (0-87451-689-7) U Pr of New Eng.
— Searching the Drowned Man: Poems. fac. ed. LC 79-26565. 84p. 1980. reprint ed. pap. 25.00 (0-7837-8075-3, 2047828) Bks Demand.

Lea, Sydney, et al, eds. Richard Eberhart: A Celebration. 76p. (Orig.). (C). 1980. pap. 6.00 (0-917241-00-2) Kenyon Hill.

Lea, Sydney L. Gothic to Fantastic: Readings in Supernatural Fiction. Varma, Devendra P., ed. LC 79-8463. (Gothic Studies & Dissertations). 1980. lib. bdg. 28.95 (0-405-12653-0) Ayer.

Lea, Thomas D. A Student's Introduction to the New Testament. LC 93-46945. 1995. 19.99 (0-8054-1078-3) Broadman.

Lea, Thomas D. & Griffin, Hayne P. The New American Commentary, Vol. 34: One, Two Timothy, Titus. 1992. 24.99 (0-8054-0134-2) Broadman.

Lea, Thomas D. & Latham, Bill. Sigueme 3. Martinez, Mario, tr. 128p. (Orig.). (SPA.). (J). (gr. 5 up). 1989. pap. 3.75 (0-311-13847-0) Casa Bautista.

Lea, Tom. The Art of Tom Lea. LC 88-23425. (Illus.). 272p. 1989. 50.00 (0-89096-366-5) Tex A&M Univ Pr.
— Battle Stations: A Grizzly from the Coral Sea (1944) & Peleliu Landing (1945) deluxe ed. LC 88-19176. (Illus.). 88p. 1988. 30.00 (0-933841-07-8) Still Point TX.
— The King Ranch, 2 vols., Set. (Illus.). 1957. boxed 125.00 (0-316-51745-3) Little.
— A Portfolio of Six Paintings. (Illus.). 1953. 50.00 (0-292-73680-0) U of Tex Pr.

Lea, Wayne A. Selecting, Designing, & Using Speech Recognizers. (Speech Technology Ser.). (Illus.). 400p. 1982. 74.00 (0-686-37644-7); student ed 49.00 (0-686-37645-5) Speech Science.

Leab, Daniel & Leab, Katharine, eds. American Book Prices Current, Vol. 97. 1100p. 1991. 129.95 (0-914022-25-3) Bancroft Parkman.

Leab, Daniel J. & Mason, Philip P., eds. Labor History Archives in the United States. LC 91-38550. 286p. 1992. pap. 15.95 (0-8143-2389-8) Wayne St U Pr.

Leab, Daniel J. & Morris, Richard B., eds. Labor History Reader. (Working Class in American History Ser.). 496p. 1985. 39.95 (0-252-01197-X); pap. 17.95 (0-252-01198-8) U of Ill Pr.

Leab, Daniel J., jt. auth. see Leab, Katharine K.

Leab, Daniel J., jt. ed. see Leab, Katharine K.

Leab, Katharine, jt. ed. see Leab, Daniel.

Leab, Katharine K. & Leab, Daniel J. American Book Prices Current. 1050p. 1989. 116.95 (0-914022-23-7) Bancroft Parkman.

Leab, Katharine K. & Leab, Daniel J., eds. American Book Prices Current, Vol. 98. 1100p. 1993. 129.95 (0-914022-27-X) Bancroft Parkman.
— American Book Prices Current, Vol. 99. 1100p. 1994. 129.95 (0-914022-37-7) Bancroft Parkman.
— American Book Prices Current, Vol. 100. 1000p. 1995. 129.95 (0-914022-29-6) Bancroft Parkman.
— American Book Prices Current, Index 1987-1991, 2 vols. 2300p. 1992. Set. 495.00 (0-914022-26-1) Bancroft Parkman.

Leabeater, C. W. The Perfume of Egypt & Other Stories. 270p. 1993. pap. 16.95 (1-56459-381-9) Kessinger Pub.

Leabhart, et al. Canadian Post-Modern Performance. Leabhart, Thomas, ed. (Mime Journal Ser.). (Illus.). 91p. (Orig.). 1986. pap. 12.00 (0-9611066-4-6) Pomona Coll.
— Words on Decroux. Leabhart, Thomas, ed. (Mime Journal Ser.). (Illus.). 229p. (Orig.). 1993. pap. 12.00 (0-685-67820-2) Pomona Coll.

Leabhart, Sally, tr. see DeCroux, Etienne.

Leabhart, Thomas, ed. see Abdoh, et al.

Leabhart, Thomas, ed. see Bu, Peter.

Leabhart, Thomas, ed. see DeCroux, Etienne.

Leabhart, Thomas, ed. see Decroux, Etienne.

Leabhart, Thomas, ed. see Leabhart, et al.

Leabhart, Thomas, ed. see Moore, Jim, et al.

Leabhart, Thomas, ed. see Shank.

Leabhart, Thomas, ed. see Teele, et al.

***Leabo, Karen.** Beach Baby. (Desire Ser.). 1995. mass mkt. 3.25 (0-373-05922-1, 1-05922-9) Silhouette.
— A Changed Man. large type ed. 224p. 1993. reprint ed. lib. bdg. 13.95 (1-56054-612-3) Thorndike Pr.
— Feathers & Lace. (Silhouette Desire Ser.). 1993. mass mkt. 2.99 (0-373-05824-1, 5-05824-3) Silhouette.
— Into Thin Air. (Intimate Moments Ser.). 1995. mass mkt. 3.75 (0-373-07619-3, 1-07619-9) Silhouette.
— Lindy & the Law. large type ed. (Silhouette Desire Ser.). 1994. 17.95 (0-373-58859-3, Silhouette Lrg Print) Chivers N Amer.
— Le Magicien des Bayous. (Rouge Passion Ser.). (FRE.). 1994. pap. 3.50 (0-373-37292-2, 1-37292-9) Harlequin Bks.
— Man Overboard. (Desire Ser.). 1995. mass mkt. 3.25 (0-373-05946-9, 1-05946-8) Silhouette.
— Megan's Miracle. (Desire Ser.). 1994. mass mkt. 2.99 (0-373-05880-2, 1-05880-9) Silhouette.
— Twilight Man. (Silhouette Desire Ser.). 1994. mass mkt. 2.99 (0-373-05838-1, 5-05838-3) Silhouette.

Leabo, Karl, ed. Tragical Comedy or Comical Tragedy of Punch & Judy. LC 83-70096. (Illus.). 1983. pap. 2.50 (0-87830-582-3, Theatre Arts Bks) Routledge Chapman & Hall.

Leacacos, John P. Fires in the In-Basket: The ABC's of the State Department. LC 75-36097. 1977. reprint ed. text ed. 79.50 (0-8371-8623-4, LEFI, Greenwood Pr) Greenwood.

***Leach.** AutoCad Instructor. 1995. pap. 55.00 (0-7863-0462-6) Irwin Prof Pubng.
— Intergovernmental Relations in the 1980's. (Annals of Public Administration Ser.: Vol. 4). 120p. 1983. 65.00 (0-8247-1742-2) Dekker.

Leach & Logan. Future Interests & Estate Planning. 1961. text ed. 29.00 (0-88277-512-X) Foundation Pr.
— Nineteen Sixty-Two Supplement to Future Interests & Estate Planning. 1962. pap. text ed. 5.75 (0-88277-389-5) Foundation Pr.

Leach, A. F. Schools of Medieval England. LC 68-56478. (Illus.). 1972. reprint ed. 23.95 (0-405-08740-3) Ayer.

***Leach, Ann.** PostScripts from Prairie Switch. 225p. (Orig.). 1994. pap. write for info. (1-885591-30-6) Morris Pubng.

***Leach, Anne, ed.** Marketing Your Indexing Services. LC 94-46408. 1995. 15.00 (0-936547-28-6) Am Soc Index.

Leach, Arthur F. Educational Charters & Documents, 598-1909. LC 76-137263. reprint ed. 54.00 (0-404-03893-X) AMS Pr.
— The School of Medieval England. 1976. lib. bdg. 59.95 (0-8490-2570-2) Gordon Pr.

***Leach, Bernadette.** Anna Who? (Bright Sparks Ser.). 144p. (Orig.). (YA). 1994. pap. 9.99 (1-85594-092-2, Pub. by Attic IE) InBook.
— I'm a Vegetarian. (Bright Sparks Ser.). 144p. (Orig.). (YA). 1992. pap. 7.99 (1-85594-040-X, Pub. by Attic IE) InBook.
— Summer Without Mum. (Bright Sparks Ser.). (Orig.). (YA). 1993. pap. 9.99 (1-85594-074-4, Pub. by Attic IE) InBook.
— Vanessa. (Bright Sparks Ser.). 144p. (Orig.). 1994. pap. 9.99 (1-85594-093-0, Pub. by Attic IE) InBook.

Leach, Bernard. Bernard Leach. 1966. boxed 300.00 (0-685-45126-7) R S Barnes.
— An Exhibition of the Art of Bernard Leach: His Masterpieces Loaned by British Museums & Collectors. (Illus.). 192p. 1980. pap. 100.00 (0-685-45125-9) R S Barnes.
— My Faith. (Illus.). 1966. pap. 40.00 (0-685-45124-0) R S Barnes.
— Potter's Book. (J). 1946. pap. 14.00 (0-693-01157-2) Transatl Arts.

Leach, Catherine S., tr. see Lem, Stanislaw.

Leach, Catherine S., tr. see Milosz, Czeslaw.

Leach, Catherine S., ed. see Pasek, Jan C.

Leach, Charles. The Primordial Field. 24p. 1974. reprint ed. spiral bd. 8.25 (0-7873-0540-5) Mokelumne.

Leach, Charles R. In Tornado's Wake, a History of the 8th Armored Division. (Division Ser.: No. 42). (Illus.). 240p. reprint ed. 39.95 (0-89839-176-8) Battery Pr.

Leach, Chris. Introduction to Statistics: A Nonparametric Approach for the Social Sciences. LC 78-10194. (Illus.). 363p. reprint ed. pap. 103.50 (0-8357-4320-9, 2037119) Bks Demand.

Leach, Cliff. Alpha: A Strategic Review. LC 93-45758. 250p. 1994. pap. text ed. 40.00 (0-13-327925-1) P-H.
— NT: A Strategic Review. 400p. 1993. pap. text ed. 49.00 (0-13-045261-0) P-H.

Leach, Colin, tr. see Euripides.

Leach, D. Genetic Recombination. 1994. pap. write for info. (0-632-03861-6) Blackwell Sci.

Leach, D. & Schamhardt, H. C., eds. Animal Locomotion. (Journal: Acta Anatomica: Vol. 146, No. 2-3, 1993). (Illus.). 124p. 1993. pap. 197.00 (3-8055-5777-9) S Karger.

Leach, David A. Genesis: The Book of Beginnings. 96p. 1984. pap. 7.00 (0-8170-1047-5) Judson.

***Leach, Diana & Mertzlufft, Nancy.** Now & Forever: The Responsibilities of Sex. 252p. 1994. student ed, pap. 22.95x (1-55959-064-5); teacher ed, pap. 13.95x (1-55959-065-3) Accel Devel.

Leach, Donald P. Discrete & Integrated Circuit Electronics. 790p. (C). 1992. text ed. 55.00 (0-03-020844-0) SCP.
— Experiments in Digital Principles. 3rd ed. 224p. 1986. pap. text ed. 23.95 (0-07-036918-6); Lab manual. student ed write for info. (0-07-036928-3) McGraw.
— Mathematics for Electronics. 2nd ed. (Illus.). 448p. (C). 1987. text ed. write for info. (0-318-61354-9) P-H.

Leach, Donald P. & Malvino, Albert P. Digital Principles & Applications. LC 93-29589. 1993. write for info. (0-02-801821-4) Glencoe.

Leach, Donald P., jt. auth. see Malvino, Albert P.

Leach, Donn. What the Bible Says about Jesus. LC 88-63248. 444p. 1989. 13.99 (0-89900-091-6) College Pr Pub.

Leach, Douglas E. Flintlock & Tomahawk: New England in King Philip's War. LC 58-5467. 320p. (YA). 1992. reprint ed. pap. 12.50 (0-940160-55-2) Parnassus Imprints.
— Now Hear This: The Memoir of a Junior Naval Officer in the Great Pacific War. fac. ed. LC 87-3905. (Illus.). 202p. 1994. pap. 57.60 (0-7837-7630-6, 2047382) Bks Demand.
— Roots of Conflict: British Armed Forces & Colonial Americans, 1677-1763. LC 85-24492. xv, 232p. (C). 1989. reprint ed. 32.50 (0-8078-1688-4); reprint ed. pap. 14.95 (0-8078-4258-3) U of NC Pr.

Leach, Edmund. Pul Eliya, A Village in Ceylon: A Study of Land Tenure & Kinship. LC 61-1517. 375p. reprint ed. pap. 106.90 (0-317-20602-8, 2024486) Bks Demand.

Leach, Edmund R. Aspects of Caste in South India, Ceylon & North West Pakistan. (Cambridge Papers in Social Anthropology: No. 2). (Illus.). 1971. pap. 16.95 (0-521-09664-2) Cambridge U Pr.
— Claude Levi-Strauss. 160p. 1989. pap. 9.95 (0-226-46968-9) U Ch Pr.
— Culture & Communication. LC 75-30439. (Themes in the Social Sciences Ser.). (Illus.). 120p. 1976. pap. 15.95 (0-521-29052-X) Cambridge U Pr.
— Political Systems of Highlands Burma: A Study of Kachin Social Structure. 4th ed. (Monographs on Social Anthropology: No.44). (Illus.). 324p. (C). 1954. pap. 25.00 (0-485-19644-1, Pub. by Athlone Pr UK) Humanities.
— Rethinking Anthropology. 5th ed. (London School of Economics Monographs on Social Anthropology: No. 22). 146p. (C). 1961. pap. 18.50 (0-485-19622-0, Pub. by Athlone Pr UK) Humanities.

Leach, Edmund R., ed. Structural Study of Myth & Totemism. (Orig.). 1968. pap. 13.95 (0-422-72530-7, NO.2287, Pub. by Tavistock UK) Routledge Chapman & Hall.

Leach, Eleanor. The Rhetoric of Space: Literary & Artistic Representations of Landscape in Republican & Augustan Rome. (Illus.). 552p. 1988. 79.50 (0-691-04237-3) Princeton U Pr.

Leach, Eleanor W. Vergil's Eclogues: Landscapes of Experience. LC 73-17699. 288p. 1974. 39.95 (0-8014-0820-2) Cornell U Pr.

Leach, Elizabeth, jt. auth. see Klinkersberg, Marty.

Leach, Frank A. Recollections of a Newspaperman: (A Record Life & Events in California) (American Biography Ser.). 146p. 1991. reprint ed. lib. bdg. 59.00 (0-7812-8239-X) Rprt Serv.

Leach, Frank A. & Bowers, David Q. Recollections of a Mint Director. (Illus.). 136p. (Orig.). 1987. pap. 9.95 (0-943161-01-0) Bowers & Merena.

Leach, G. Household Energy in South Asia. 112p. 1987. 38.00 (1-85166-125-5, Pub. by Elsevier Applied Sci UK) Elsevier.

Leach, Garry, ed. see Moore, Alan & Parkhouse, Steve.

Leach, George. UNIX: Self Teaching Guide. 272p. 1992. pap. text ed. 19.95 (0-471-57924-6) Wiley.

***Leach, George W. & Topham, Douglas W.** UNIX: Self-Teaching Guide & Portable UNIX, 2 vols., Set. 1993. pap. text ed. 34.90 (0-471-59678-7) Wiley.

Leach, Gerald & Gowen, Marcia. Household Energy Handbook: An Interim Guide & Reference Manual. (Technical Paper Ser.: No. 67). 1987. 12.95 (0-8213-0937-4, BK0937) World Bank.

Leach, Graham. South Africa: No Easy Path to Peace. (Illus.). 312p. 1987. pap. 8.95 (0-413-15330-4, A0168) Routledge.

Leach, Hamish A. The Founding of Fort Amherstburg (Malden) along the Detroit Frontier-1796: A Political, Military, & Legal Frontier Study, with Computer Applications. LC 74-20147. (Veldt Protea International Study, An Official American Bicentennial Heritage Project, Registered As Part of the Nederland-Amerika Bicentennial). (Illus.). xxxii, 593p. 1984. 32.50 (0-917538-01-3); lib. bdg. 43.50 (0-685-09640-8) Veldt Protea Inst.

Leach, Henry. Endure No Makeshifts: Some Naval Recollections by the Admiral of the Fleet. (Illus.). 274p. 1993. 52.50 (0-85052-370-2, Pub. by L Cooper Bks UK) Trans-Atl Phila.

Leach, Henry G., ed. Pageant of Old Scandinavia. LC 68-57061. (Granger Index Reprint Ser.). 1977. 21.95 (0-8369-6025-4) Ayer.

Leach, J. G. Bringhurst: History of the Bringhurst Family with Notes on the Clarkson, de Peyster & Boude Families. (Illus.). 152p. 1992. reprint ed. lib. bdg. 34.00 (0-8328-2645-6); reprint ed. pap. 24.00 (0-8328-2646-4) Higginson Bk Co.

Leach, J. G., ed. see Carter, C. M.

Leach, J. J., et al, eds. Science, Decision & Value. LC 72-77877. (Western Ontario Ser.: Vol. 1). 213p. 1973. lib. bdg. 64.00 (90-277-0239-X) Kluwer Ac.
— Science, Decision & Value. LC 72-77877. (Western Ontario Ser.: Vol. 1). 213p. 1973. pap. text ed. 33.00 (90-277-0327-2) Kluwer Ac.

Leach, James & McKenzie, William P., eds. A Newer World: The Progressive Republican Vision of America. LC 88-21529. 172p. 1988. 16.95 (0-8191-6827-0) Madison Bks UPA.

***Leach, James A.** AutoCAD Companion. LC 94-48563. (Graphics Ser.). 1995. write for info. (0-256-16137-2) Irwin.
— AutoCAD Instructor. LC 94-29190. 968p. (C). 1994. 43.95 (0-256-17144-0) Irwin.
— Problems in Engineering Graphics Fundamentals, Series A. (Illus.). 50p. (C). 1984. pap. text ed. 17.95 (0-89892-055-8) Contemp Pub Co of Raleigh.
— Problems in Engineering Graphics Fundamentals: Series B. (Illus.). 46p. (C). 1985. pap. text ed. 17.95 (0-89892-058-2) Contemp Pub Co of Raleigh.

Leach, Jennifer, ed. see Fontoura, Marco.

Leach, Jim. A Possible Cinema: The Films of Alain Tanner. LC 84-10610. 220p. 1984. 22.00 (0-8108-1714-4) Scarecrow.

***Leach, Joel.** Earthquake Prepared: Securing Your Home, Protecting Your Family. 2nd ed. (Illus.). 102p. (Orig.). 1995. pap. 10.95 (1-882349-42-3) Studio Four Prods.

Leach, John. Pompey the Great. (Classical Lives Ser.). 256p. (Orig.). 1986. reprint ed. pap. 14.95 (0-7099-4127-7, Pub. by Croom Helm UK) Routledge Chapman & Hall.
— Running Applied Psychology Experiments. (Open Guides to Psychology Ser.). 160p. 1991. pap. 29.00 (0-335-09482-1, Open Univ Pr) Taylor & Francis.

An Asterisk (*) at the beginning of an entry indicates that the title is appearing in BIP for the first time.

— Survival Psychology. 232p. 1994. 45.00 (*0-8147-5090-7*) NYU Pr.

Leach, Joseph. Bright Particular Star: The Life & Times of Charlotte Cushman. LC 76-99829. 469p. reprint ed. pap. 133.70 (*0-8357-8048-1*, 2033798) Bks Demand.

— Sun Country Banker: The Life & the Bank of Samuel Doak Young. LC 88-90911. (Illus.). 300p. 1989. 19.95 (*0-930208-26-9*) Mangan Books TX.

Leach, Josiah G. History of the Bringhurst Family: With Notes on the Clarkson, De Peyster & Boude Families. With a Partial Listing of 20th Century Bringhurst Descendents by Robert Taylor. 2nd ed. LC 89-85223. (Illus.). 200p. 1989. reprint ed. lib. bdg. 24.75 (*0-944419-11-9*) Everett Cos Pub.

***Leach, Joy.** A Practical Guide to Working with Diversity: The Process, the Tools, the Resources. LC 94-44293. 320p. 1995. pap. 55.00 (*0-8144-0244-5*) AMACOM.

Leach, L. York. Indian Miniature Paintings & Drawings, Pt. One. LC 85-7740. (Illus.). 334p. 1986. 50.00 (*0-910386-78-1*) Cleveland Mus Art.

Leach, Leonora. Phonics the African Way: With Its Aid to Helpers Brochure. 80p. 1993. Incl. helper brochure. student ed, text ed. 10.95 (*0-9636440-0-9*) Leach Assocs.

Leach, MacEdward & Glassie, Henry. A Guide for Collectors of Oral Traditions & Folk Cultural Material in Pennsylvania. LC 72-650605. (Illus.). 70p. (Orig.). (C). 1973. pap. 3.95 (*0-911124-60-8*) Pa Hist & Mus.

Leach, Maria & Fried, Jerome, eds. Funk & Wagnall's Standard Dictionary of Folklore, Mythology, & Legend. 1984. pap. 40.00 (*0-06-250511-4*) Harper SF.

Leach, Marianne, comp. Newspaper Holdings of the California State Library. 396p. 1986. pap. 40.00 (*0-929722-09-4*) CA State Library Fndtn.

Leach, Marjorie. A Guide to the Gods: A Dictionary of the Functions & Aspects of Deities. (Mythology & Religion Ser.). 995p. 1991. lib. bdg. 150.00 (*0-87436-591-0*) ABC-CLIO.

Leach, Mark, jt. ed. see Bellini, Paolo.

Leach, Mark C & Morse, Peter, eds. Illustrated Bartsch, Vol. 2: Netherlandish Artists. LC 79-50679. 1978. 140.00 (*0-89835-002-6*) Abaris Bks.

***Leach, Mark R., contrib.** Structure & Surface: Beads in Contemporary American Art. (Illus.). 48p. 1990. pap. 15.95 (*0-932718-28-0*) Kohler Arts.

***Leach, Mark R., text.** Inside Out, Contemporary Japanese Photography. (Illus.). 57p. 1995. pap. 20.00 (*0-9642772-0-4*) Light Factory.

Leach, Mary M. Cottonwood Collection: A History of Sinclair Island. (Illus.). 160p. (Orig.). 1988. pap. write for info. (*0-318-63124-5*) M M Leach.

Leach, Maureen, jt. auth. see Schreck, Nancy.

Leach, Melissa. Rainforest Relations: Gender & Resource Use among the Mende of Gola, Sierra Leone. (Illus.). 296p. (C). 1994. text ed. 49.00 (*1-56098-500-3*) Smithsonian.

Leach, Michael. The Complete Owl. (Illus.). 160p. 1993. pap. 22.95 (*0-7011-3786-X*, Pub. by Chatto & Windus UK) Trafalgar.

— Exploring Rural Italy. (Exploring Rural Europe Ser.). 208p. 1988. pap. 12.95 (*0-8442-9461-6*, Passport Bks) NTC Pub Grp.

— Mice of the British Isles. 1989. pap. 25.00 (*0-7478-0056-1*, Pub. by Shire UK) St Mut.

— The Secret Life of Snowdonia. (Illus.). 128p. 1992. 39.95 (*0-7011-3686-3*, Pub. by Chatto & Windus UK) Trafalgar.

Leach, Mortimer. Lettering for Advertising. LC 56-10596. 244p. reprint ed. pap. 69.60 (*0-317-10495-0*, 2005789) Bks Demand.

***Leach, Nicky.** Bryce Canyon National Park: A Visual Interpretation. Houk, Rose & Nicholas, Jeff, eds. (Wish You Were Here Ser.). (Illus.). 48p. (Orig.). 1995. pap. 7.95 (*0-939365-42-1*) Sierra Pr CA.

— Zion: A Visual Interpretation. Houck, Rose, ed. (Wish You Were Here Ser.). 64p. (Orig.). 1994. pap. 9.95 (*0-939365-36-7*) Sierra Pr CA.

Leach, Nicky, ed. Hawaiian National Parks: The Site-by-Site Guide. (Illus.). 48p. 1989. pap. 5.95 (*0-917859-11-1*) Sunrise SBCA.

Leach, Nicky, ed. see Aitchison, Stewart & Yazzie, Susie.

Leach, Nicky, ed. see Gilmore, Jackie.

Leach, Nicky, ed. see Lister, Florence & Wilson, Lynn.

Leach, Nicky, ed. see Nicholas, Jeff.

Leach, Nicky, ed. see Robinson, George.

Leach, Nicky, ed. see Wilson, Lynn, et al.

Leach, Nicky, ed. see Wuerthner, George.

Leach, Nicky J. The Guide to National Parks of the Southwest. Houk, Rose et al, eds. LC 91-68245. (Illus.). 80p. 1992. pap. 9.95 (*1-877856-14-2*) SW Pks Mnmts.

Leach, Noel J. Modern Wood Finishing Techniques. LC 92-37402. (Illus.). 226p. 1993. pap. 29.95 (*0-941936-24-4*) Linden Pub Fresno.

Leach, Norman. My Wicked Stepmother. LC 92-19674. (Illus.). 32p. (J). (ps-3). 1993. text ed. 13.95 (*0-02-754700-0*, Mac Bks Young Read) S&S Childrens.

***Leach, Patricia E.** Because I Love You. 193p. 1994. 19.95 (*0-9642323-0-8*) Garnet Hse Pub.

Leach, Penelope. Babyhood. enl. rev. ed. LC 82-48881. 1983. pap. 16.00 (*0-394-71436-9*) Knopf.

— Children First. 1995. pap. 12.00 (*0-679-75466-0*) Random.

— Children First: What Our Society Must Do--& Is Doing--for Our Children Today. 1994. 22.00 (*0-679-42133-5*) Random.

— Your Baby & Child. enl. rev. ed. (Illus.). 1989. 29.95 (*0-394-57951-8*); pap. 19.95 (*0-679-72425-7*) Knopf.

— Your Growing Child: From Babyhood Through Adolescence. 1986. pap. 19.95 (*0-394-71066-5*) Knopf.

Leach, Peter. James Paine. Harris, John & Laing, Alastair, eds. LC 87-50752. (Studies in Architecture). (Illus.). 240p. 1988. 95.00 (*0-302-00602-8*, Pub. by Zwemmer Bks UK) Sothebys Pubns.

Leach, R. H., et al, eds. The Printing Ink Manual. 5th ed. LC 93-34099. 1993. write for info. (*0-948905-81-6*, Chap & Hall NY) Chapman & Hall.

Leach, R. J. International Schools & Their Role in the Field of International Education. (C). 1969. 121.00 (*0-08-013037-2*, Pub. by Pergamon Repr UK) Franklin.

Leach, R. M., jt. auth. see Jeffrey, Hugh C.

Leach, Richard H., ed. Contemporary Canada. LC 68-17411. (Duke University Commonwealth Studies Center: No. 32). 340p. reprint ed. 96.90 (*0-685-07743-8*, 2017909) Bks Demand.

Leach, Richard H., jt. auth. see Connery, R. H.

Leach, Richard M. & Utera, Catherine. Gadabouts Cookbook & Travel Guide: Hanover - New London - Killington - Woodstock - Quechee. 288p. 1992. pap. 19.95 (*0-9633069-3-6*) Garlic NH.

— Gadabouts Cookbook & Travel Guide: Woodstock - Quechee - Killington - Hanover - New London. 288p. 1992. pap. 19.95 (*0-9633069-2-8*) Garlic NH.

***Leach, Robert.** Changing Party Allegiance by British Politicians: Turncoats. (Illus.). 300p. 1995. text ed. 59.95 (*1-85521-617-5*) Ashgate Pub Co.

— Political Ideologies: An Australian Introduction. 2nd ed. 260p. 1994. 64.95 (*0-7329-2002-7*, Pub. by Macmill Educ AT); pap. 32.95 (*0-7329-2001-9*, Pub. by Macmill Educ AT) Paul & Co Pubs.

— Revolutionary Theatre. LC 93-35722. (Illus.). 256p. 1994. 59.95x (*0-415-03223-7*, B3719, Routledge NY) Routledge.

— Vsevolod Meyerhold. (Directors in Perspective Ser.). (Illus.). 240p. (C). 1993. pap. 21.95 (*0-521-31843-2*) Cambridge U Pr.

Leach, Robert A. Chiropractic Theories. 2nd ed. (Illus.). 252p. (C). 1985. text ed. 42.00 (*0-683-04906-2*) Williams & Wilkins.

— The Chiropractic Theories. 3rd ed. LC 93-17891. (Illus.). 288p. 1994. 49.00 (*0-683-04904-6*) Williams & Wilkins.

Leach, Robert E. Alpine Skiing. 2nd ed. LC 93-26993. (Handbook of Sports Medicine & Science Ser.). (Illus.). 144p. (Orig.). 1994. pap. text ed. write for info. (*0-632-03033-X*) Blackwell Sci.

Leach, Robert J. Women Ministers: A Quaker Contribution. Blattenberger, Ruth, ed. LC 79-84922. 1979. pap. 3.00 (*0-87574-227-0*) Pendle Hill.

Leach, Robert J., ed. see Penington, Isaac.

Leach, Robert P., Jr. Riggers Bible Handbook of Heavy Rigging. 1983. reprint ed. 39.95 (*0-9600992-1-2*) Riggers Bible.

Leach, Robin. The Lifestyles of the Rich & Famous Cookbook: Recipes & Entertaining Secrets from the Most Extraordinary People in the World. LC 91-45173. (Illus.). 256p. 1992. 24.95 (*0-670-84245-1*, Viking Studio) Studio Bks.

— Lifestyles of the Rich & Famous Cookbook: Recipes & Entertaining Secrets from the Most Extraordinary People in the World. (Illus.). 288p. 1994. 16.95 (*0-14-023800-X*, Viking Studio) Studio Bks.

***Leach, Robin & Regan, Mardee H.** Robin Leach's Healthy Lifestyles Cookbook: Menus & Recipes from the Rich, Famous & Fascinating. (Illus.). 250p. 1995. 27.95 (*0-670-85730-0*, Viking Studio) Studio Bks.

Leach, Ronald. Using C in Software Design. (Illus.). 416p. 1993. disk, pap. 39.95 (*0-12-440210-0*, AP Prof) Acad Pr.

Leach, Ronald J. Advanced Topics in UNIX. LC 94-10834. 1994. disk, pap. 49.95 (*0-471-03685-4*); pap. text ed. 34.95 (*0-471-03663-3*) Wiley.

— Object Oriented Design & Programming with C++ (Illus.). 400p. 1995. disk, pap. text ed. 34.95 (*0-12-440215-1*) Acad Pr.

Leach, Sally. The Scholar at Work: An Exhibit. 53p. 1975. 12.00 (*0-87959-119-6*); pap. 6.00 (*0-87959-120-X*) U of Tex H Ransom Ctr.

Leach, Sally, comp. Lord Byron: A Sesquicentennial Exhibition Catalogue. (Illus.). 40p. 1975. pap. 7.00 (*0-87959-017-3*) U of Tex H Ransom Ctr.

Leach, Sally, jt. ed. see Henderson, Cathy.

Leach, Sid D. Photographic Perspective Drawing Techniques. (Illus.). 256p. 1990. text ed. 39.95 (*0-07-036814-7*) McGraw.

Leach, Susan & Harrison, Frank F. Shakespeare in the Classroom: What's the Matter? 160p. 1992. pap. 27.00 (*0-335-09674-3*, Open Univ Pr) Taylor & Francis.

Leach, Susan, ed. see Shakespeare, William.

Leach, T. M., jt. auth. see Mitchell, A. H.

Leach, Thomas. How to Prepare, Stage, & Deliver Winning Presentations. LC 81-69351. (Illus.). 425p. reprint ed. pap. 121.20 (*0-7837-4236-3*, 2043925) Bks Demand.

Leach, Virgil. Attitudes I. 1979. pap. 5.50 (*0-89137-803-0*) Quality Pubns.

— Attitudes II. 1981. pap. 5.50 (*0-89137-804-9*) Quality Pubns.

— Get Behind Me Satan. 1977. 9.95 (*0-89137-521-X*); pap. 7.50 (*0-89137-520-1*) Quality Pubns.

Leach, W. Barton. Perpetuities in a Nutshell & The Nutshell Revisited, 2 vols., Set. 1983. reprint ed. pap. 5.00 (*0-686-89066-3*) Michie Butterworth.

Leach, W. Barton & Logan, James K. Future Interests & Estate Planning, Teacher's Manual to Accompany Cases & Text On. 272p. 1992. reprint ed. pap. text ed. write for info. (*0-88277-511-1*) Foundation Pr.

Leach, W. Barton, jt. auth. see Casner, A. James.

Leach, William. Edith Wharton. (American Women of Achievement Ser.). (Illus.). 112p. (J). (gr. 5 up). 1987. lib. bdg. 17.95 (*1-55546-682-6*) Chelsea Hse.

— A Green Sound: Nature Writing from the Living Tradition of Unitarian Universalism. LC 92-20332. 1992. pap. 6.00 (*1-55896-301-4*, Skinner Hse Bks) Unitarian Univ.

— Land of Desire: Merchants, Power, & the Rise of a New America. LC 92-50785. 1993. 30.00 (*0-394-54350-5*) Pantheon.

— Land of Desire: Merchants, Power & the Rise of a New American Culture. 1994. pap. 15.00 (*0-679-75411-3*, Vin) Random.

— True Love & Perfect Union: The Feminist Reform of Sex & Society. 2nd ed. LC 89-35791. 474p. 1989. pap. 22.95 (*0-8195-6227-0*, Wesleyan Univ Pr) U Pr of New Eng.

Leach, William R., ed. see Baum, L. Frank.

Leachman. Coronary & Peripheral Angiography & Angioplasty. (Illus.). 200p. 1989. text ed. 37.50 (*0-397-58311-7*) Lippincott.

Leachman, Robert B. & Althoff, Philip, eds. Preventing Nuclear Theft: Guidelines for Industry & Government. LC 72-76452. (Special Studies in U. S. Economic, Social & Political Issues). 1972. 49.50 (*0-275-28618-5*) Irvington.

Leachman, Robert C., jt. auth. see Ciriani, Tito A.

Leachman, Robert C., jt. ed. see Ciriani, Tito A.

Leacock, E. G., ed. see Morgan, L. H.

Leacock, Eleanor B. Myths of Male Dominance: Collected Articles on Women Cross-Culturally. LC 79-3870. 352p. reprint ed. pap. 100.40 (*0-7837-6993-8*, 2046805) Bks Demand.

Leacock, Eleanor B. & Lee, Richard B., eds. Politics & History in Band Societies. (Illus.). 368p. 1982. pap. 32.95 (*0-521-28412-0*) Cambridge U Pr.

Leacock, Eleanor B. & Lurie, Nancy O., eds. North American Indians in Historical Perspective. (Illus.). 498p. (C). 1988. reprint ed. pap. text ed. 18.95 (*0-88133-377-8*) Waveland Pr.

Leacock, Eleanor B. & Rothschild, Nan A., eds. Labrador Winter: The Ethnographic Journals of William Duncan Strong, 1927-1928. LC 93-34521. (Illus.). 320p. (C). 1994. text ed. 45.00 (*1-56098-345-0*) Smithsonian.

Leacock, Eleanor B. & Safa, Helen I. Women's Work: Development & the Division of Labor by Gender. LC 85-26674. 320p. 1986. text ed. 55.00 (*0-89789-035-3*, Bergin & Garvey) Greenwood.

— Women's Work: Development & the Division of Labor by Gender. LC 85-26674. 320p. 1988. pap. text ed. 19.95 (*0-89789-036-1*, Bergin & Garvey) Greenwood.

Leacock, Eleanor B., ed. see Engels, Frederick.

Leacock, Eleanor B., jt. ed. see Etienne, Mona.

Leacock, John. The First Book of the American Chronicles of the Times, 1774-1775. LC 86-40594. 128p. 1988. 28.50 (*0-87413-305-X*) U Delaware Pr.

Leacock, Robert J., jt. ed. see Eichhorn, Heinrich K.

Leacock, Ruth. Requiem for Revolution: The United States & Brazil, 1961-1969. LC 89-20054. (American Diplomatic History Ser.: No. 3). 329p. 1990. 30.00 (*0-87338-401-6*); pap. 19.00x (*0-87338-402-4*) Kent St U Pr.

Leacock, Stephen. Cuentecitos Risuenos. Ventura, Liliana, tr. (Illus.). 46p. (SPA.). 1987. pap. text ed. 5.00 (*0-9619890-0-9*) L Ventura.

— Mark Twain. LC 73-21633. (Mark Twain Ser.: No. 76). 1974. lib. bdg. 75.00 (*0-8383-1789-8*) M S G Haskell Hse.

— Social Criticism: The Unsolved Riddle of Social Justice & Other Essays. Bowker, Alan, ed. 208p. (C). 1995. reprint ed. pap. 14.95 (*0-8020-7799-4*) U of Toronto Pr.

— The Social Criticism of Stephen Leacock: The Unsolved Riddle of Social Justice & Other Essays. LC 73-79860. (Social History of Canada Ser.). 193p. reprint ed. pap. 55.10 (*0-8357-3766-7*, 2036495) Bks Demand.

Leacock, Stephen B. Frenzied Fiction. LC 78-125227. (Short Story Index Reprint Ser.). 1977. 30.95 (*0-8369-3594-2*) Ayer.

— Here Are My Lectures & Stories. LC 72-14188. (Essay Index Reprint Ser.). 1977. reprint ed. 20.95 (*0-518-10017-0*) Ayer.

— Literary Lapses. LC 70-122728. (Short Story Index Reprint Ser.). 1980. 18.95 (*0-8369-3561-6*) Ayer.

— Model Memoirs: And Other Sketches from Simple to Serious. LC 77-156678. (Essay Index Reprint Ser.). 1977. reprint ed. 32.95 (*0-8369-2434-7*) Ayer.

— Sunshine Sketches of a Little Town. LC 71-125228. (Short Story Index Reprint Ser.). 1980. 24.95 (*0-8369-3595-0*) Ayer.

— Winsome Winnie, & Other New Nonsense Novels. LC 74-140333. (Short Story Index Reprint Ser.). 1977. 16.95 (*0-8369-3725-2*) Ayer.

Leacroft, Richard. The Development of the English Playhouse. 368p. 1988. 49.95 (*0-413-60600-7*, A0075) Heinemann.

Lead Developmental Association Staff & Hughes, A. Lead Sixty-Five Edited Proceedings 2nd International Conference on Lead Arnhem. LC 66-18688. 1967. 140.00 (*0-08-011425-3*, Pub. by Pergamon Repr UK) Franklin.

Leadabrand. California Ghost Town Trails. LC 85-71228. (Illus.). 128p. 1985. pap. 6.95 (*0-935182-21-7*) Gem Guides Bk.

Leadam, I. S. History of England from the Accession of Anne to the Death of George Second: Seventeen Hundred Two to Seventeen Sixty. (Political History of England Ser.). reprint ed. 39.00 (*0-685-02854-2*, Lodestar Bks) Dutton Child Bks.

Leadam, Issac S. History of England from the Accession of Anne to the Death of George the Second. LC 76-5628. (Political History of England Ser.: No. 9). reprint ed. 45.00 (*0-404-50779-4*) AMS Pr.

***Leadbeater.** Hidden Side of Things. 1994. 14.50 (*0-8356-7007-4*, Quest); 14.50 (*81-7059-176-7*, Quest) Theos Pub Hse.

Leadbeater, B. S., jt. ed. see Green, J. C.

Leadbeater, Barry S. & Riding, Robvert, eds. Biomineralization in Lower Plants & Animals. (Illus.). 400p. 1986. 80.00 (*0-19-857702-8*) OUP.

Leadbeater, C. W. The Astral Plane. 100p. 1972. reprint ed. spiral bd. 4.95 (*0-7873-1122-7*) Mokelumne.

— The Christian Creed: Its Origin & Signification. 172p. 1992. pap. 16.95 (*1-56459-238-3*) Kessinger Pub.

— The Christian Creed, Its Origin & Signification. 109p. 1976. reprint ed. spiral bd. 3.85 (*0-7873-0541-3*) Mokelumne.

— Clairvoyance. 61p. 1959. reprint ed. spiral bd. 4.40 (*0-7873-1244-4*) Mokelumne.

— The Devachanic Plane. 102p. 1972. reprint ed. spiral bd. 4.40 (*0-7873-1247-9*) Mokelumne.

— Dreams. 4th ed. 32p. 1959. reprint ed. spiral bd. 2.75 (*0-7873-1248-7*) Mokelumne.

— Glimpses of Masonic History. 380p. 1974. reprint ed. spiral bd. 19.25 (*0-7873-0543-X*) Mokelumne.

— Hidden Life in Freemasonry. 375p. 1992. pap. 24.95 (*1-56459-026-7*) Kessinger Pub.

— The Hidden Life in Freemasonry. 3rd ed. 374p. 1973. reprint ed. spiral bd. 19.25 (*0-7873-0544-8*) Mokelumne.

— The Inner Life. 265p. 1976. reprint ed. spiral bd. 9.90 (*0-7873-0542-1*) Mokelumne.

— Invisible Helpers. 45p. 1960. reprint ed. spiral bd. 3.30 (*0-7873-1190-1*) Mokelumne.

— Life after Death: And How Theosophy Unveils It. 58p. 1975. reprint ed. spiral bd. 3.30 (*0-7873-1246-0*) Mokelumne.

— The Life After Death & How Theosophy Unveils It. 73p. 1992. pap. 9.95 (*1-56459-156-5*) Kessinger Pub.

— The Masters & the Path. 354p. 1985. reprint ed. spiral bd. 22.00 (*0-7873-0545-6*) Mokelumne.

— The Perfume of Egypt & Other Weird Stories. 306p. 1971. reprint ed. spiral bd. 11.00 (*0-7873-1070-0*) Mokelumne.

— The Soul & Its Vestures. 24p. 1983. pap. 1.50 (*0-918980-12-7*) St Alban Pr.

— Starlight: Seven Address Given for Love of the Star. 104p. 1985. reprint ed. spiral bd. 7.15 (*0-7873-1245-2*) Mokelumne.

— Starlight: Seven Addresses Given for Love of the Star. 104p. 1992. pap. 9.95 (*1-56459-244-8*) Kessinger Pub.

— Vegetarianism & Occultism. 1995. pap. 7.95 (*1-56459-490-4*) Kessinger Pub.

Leadbeater, C. W., jt. auth. see Besant, Annie.

Leadbeater, Charles W. Ancient Mystic Rites. LC 86-40125. Orig. Title: Glimpses of Masonic History. (Illus.). 270p. 1986. reprint ed. pap. 9.75 (*0-8356-0609-0*, Quest) Theos Pub Hse.

— Astral Plane. 1973. 7.95 (*81-7059-067-1*) Theos Pub Hse.

— Chakras. LC 73-147976. (Illus.). 148p. 1972. pap. 10.95 (*0-8356-0422-5*, Quest) Theos Pub Hse.

— Clairvoyance. 10th ed. 1968. 8.95 (*81-7059-142-2*) Theos Pub Hse.

— Devachanic Plane. 1984. 7.50 (*0-8356-7075-9*) Theos Pub Hse.

— Dreams. 1989. pap. 4.25 (*81-7059-095-7*) Theos Pub Hse.

— The Inner Life. LC 77-17044. 1978. reprint ed. pap. 12.00 (*0-8356-0502-7*, Quest) Theos Pub Hse.

— Invisible Helpers. 1986. 11.50 (*0-8356-7160-7*) Theos Pub Hse.

— Life after Death. 1986. 6.95 (*81-7059-196-1*) Theos Pub Hse.

— Man Visible & Invisible. rev. ed. (Illus.). 1969. pap. 13.00 (*0-8356-0311-3*, Quest) Theos Pub Hse.

— Monad. 1988. 7.95 (*0-8356-0102-1*) Theos Pub Hse.

— Outline of Theosophy. 1987. 5.50 (*0-8356-7185-2*) Theos Pub Hse.

— Saved by a Ghost. LC 79-9981. 1979. reprint ed. pap. 5.50 (*0-8356-0526-4*, Quest) Theos Pub Hse.

— Science of the Sacraments. 1988. 39.95 (*81-7059-181-3*) Theos Pub Hse.

— Textbook of Theosophy. 1912. 8.25 (*0-8356-7110-0*) Theos Pub Hse.

***Leadbeater, Charles W. & Besant, Annie.** Talks on the Path of Occultism Vol. 1: At the Feet of the Master. 1980. 19.95 (*81-7059-160-0*) Theos Pub Hse.

— Talks on the Path of Occultism Vol. 2: Voice of the Silence. 1980. 17.95 (*81-7059-162-7*) Theos Pub Hse.

— Talks on the Path of Occultism, Vol. 1: At the Feet of the Master. 1980. 13.50 (*0-8356-7047-3*) Theos Pub Hse.

— Talks on the Path of Occultism, Vol. 3: Light on the Path. 1981. 17.95 (*0-8356-7068-6*) Theos Pub Hse.

Leadbeater, Charles W., jt. auth. see Besant, Annie.

Leadbeater, Eliza. Handspinning. 1976. 18.00 (*0-8231-5048-8*) Robin & Russ.

— Spinning & Spinning Wheels. 1989. pap. 25.00 (*0-85263-469-2*, Pub. by Shire UK) St Mut.

Leadbeater, Simon R. The Politics of Textiles: The Indian Cotton-Mill Industry & the Legacy of Swadeshi, 1900-1985. LC 92-17600. (Illus.). 312p. (C). 1993. text ed. 36.00 (*0-8039-9440-0*) Sage.

Leadbetter, David. David Leadbetter's Faults & Fixes: How to Correct the 80 Most Common Mistakes Golfers Make. LC 92-56202. (Illus.). 144p. 1993. 25.00 (*0-06-016977-X*, HarpT) HarpC.

Leadbetter, David & Huggan, John. The Golf Swing. (Illus.). 144p. 1990. 29.95 (*0-8289-0800-1*) Viking Penguin.

Leadbetter, Edward R. & Poindexter, Jeanne S., eds. Bacteria in Nature, Vol. 1: Bacterial Activities in Perspective. LC 85-3433. 282p. 1985. 75.00 (*0-306-41944-0*, Plenum Pr) Plenum.

Leadbetter, Edward R., jt. ed. see Poindexter, Jeanne S.

Leadbetter, Jane & Leadbetter, Peter. Special Children: Meeting the Challenge in the Primary School. Solity, Jonathan, ed. LC 92-38452. (Introduction to Education Ser.). 160p. 1993. 75.00 (*0-304-32522-8*); pap. 25.00 (*0-304-32524-4*) Weidner & Sons.

An Asterisk (*) at the beginning of an entry indicates that the title is appearing in BIP for the first time.

Leadbetter, Laurie & Barrows, William, eds. Women in Development: Status, Issues, Information: APLIC Proceedings of the 23rd Annual Conference. 86p. (Orig.). 1991. pap. text ed. 20.00 (*0-933438-17-6*) APLIC Intl.

Leadbetter, M. R., et al. Extremes & Related Properties of Random Sequences & Processes. (Series in Statistics). (Illus.). 368p. 1983. 49.80 (*0-387-90731-9*) Spr-Verlag.

Leadbetter, Peter, jt. auth. see Leadbetter, Jane.

Leadbetter, Wayne B., et al, eds. Sports-Induced Inflammation: Clinical & Basic Science Concepts. LC 90-1055. 799p. 1990. 95.00 (*0-89203-037-2*) Amer Acad Ortho Surg.

***Leadbitter, Mike, et al, comps.** Blues Records: 1943-1970, Vol. 2 (L-2) 810p. 1995. 115.00 (*0-907872-25-5*) Big Nickel.

***Leadem, Christopher.** Highland Ballad. LC 94-74988. 184p. (Orig.). 1995. pap. 7.95 (*0-88100-086-8*) Natl Writ Pr.

Leadem, Paul J. Christopher's Light. LC 86-60839. 100p. (Orig.). 1986. pap. 7.95 (*0-88100-053-1*) Natl Writ Pr.

Leadenham, Carol A., comp. Guide to the Collections in the Hoover Institution Archives Relating to Imperial Russia, the Russian Revolutions & Civil War, & the First Emigration. (Bibliographical Ser.: No. 68). 208p. (C). 1986. 18.95 (*0-8179-2681-X*) Hoover Inst Pr.

Leader, Damian R. A History of the University of Cambridge, Vol. 1: The University to 1546. (Illus.). 400p. 1989. 74.95 (*0-521-32882-9*) Cambridge U Pr.

Leader, Daniel & Blahnik, Judith. Bread Alone: Bold Fresh Loaves from Your Own Hands. LC 92-47236. 1993. 25.00 (*0-688-09261-6*) Morrow.

Leader, Edward R. Understanding Malcolm X: His Controversial Philosophical Changes. 1992. 18.95 (*0-533-09520-4*) Vantage.

***Leader, Elliot & Predazzi, Enrico.** An Introduction to Gauge Theories & Modern Particle Physics Vol. 1: Electroweak Interactions, the "New Particles" & the Parton Model. (Cambridge Monographs on Particle Physics, Nuclear Physics & Cosmology: No. 3). (Illus.). 800p. (C). 1994. write for info. (*0-521-46468-4*) Cambridge U Pr.

— An Introduction to Gauge Theories & Modern Particle Physics Vol. 1: Electroweak Interactions, the "New Particles" & the Parton Model. (Cambridge Monographs on Particle Physics, Nuclear Physics & Cosmology: No. 3). (Illus.). 800p. (C). 1995. pap. write for info. (*0-521-46840-X*) Cambridge U Pr.

— An Introduction to Gauge Theories & Modern Particle Physics Vol. 2: CP-Violation, QCD & Hard Processes. (Cambridge Monographs on Particle Physics, Nuclear Physics & Cosmology: No. 3). (Illus.). 440p. (C). 1995. write for info. (*0-521-49617-9*); pap. write for info. (*0-521-49951-8*) Cambridge U Pr.

Leader, Janice, ed. see Weber, Rosalind.

Leader, John P., jt. ed. see Macknight, Anthony D.

Leader, L. Lecturing at Your Best. (C). 1989. 40.00 (*0-85297-214-8*, Pub. by Inst Bankers UK) St Mut.

Leader, L. & Kyritsis, K. Fundamentals of Marketing. (C). 1989. 150.00 (*0-09-172943-2*, Pub. by S Thornes Pubs UK) St Mut.

Leader, Laurie E. Employment Law: Wage-Hour Law & Practice. 1990. write for info. (*0-8205-1629-5*, 629) Bender.

Leader, Lawrence. Drafting Employment & Termination Agreements. LC 93-15610. 1993. write for info. (*0-8205-1274-5*) Bender.

Leader, Leonard J. Los Angeles & the Great Depression. LC 91-25485. (Modern American History: New Studies & Outstanding Dissertations). 344p. 1991. 74.00 (*0-8240-1903-2*) Garland.

Leader, Mary. Salem's Children. 368p. 1981. reprint ed. pap. 2.75 (*0-8439-0982-X*) Dorchester Pub Co.

Leader, Miriam. Second Chance to Dance. (Illus.). 50p. (Orig.). 1991. pap. text ed. 10.00 (*0-9620092-6-1*) Pine Isl Pr.

Leader-Post Carrier Foundation Inc. Staff. Money & Time Saving Household Hints. LC 92-73856. (Illus.). 128p. (Orig.). 1992. pap. 6.95 (*0-911493-15-8*) Blue Sky.

Leader, R. L. Faithful Soldiers. (J). (gr. 7 up). 1989. 12.95 (*0-944070-12-4*) Targum Pr.

Leader, Ray. Colors & Markings Vol. 7: Special Purpose, C-130 Hercules. (Illus.). 64p. (Orig.). 1987. pap. 12.95 (*0-8306-8531-6*, 24531) TAB Bks.

Leader, Ray, jt. auth. see Kinzey, Bert.

Leader, Sheldon. Freedom of Association: A Study in Labor Law & Political Theory. 336p. (C). 1992. text ed. 35.00 (*0-300-05137-9*) Yale U Pr.

Leader, W. G. How to Pass Exams. (C). 1984. 50.00 (*0-7121-0823-8*, Pub. by S Thornes Pubs UK) St Mut.

— How to Pass Exams. 2nd ed. 128p. (C). 1990. pap. 21.00x (*0-7487-0235-0*, Pub. by S Thornes Pubs UK) St Mut.

Leader-Williams, N. Reindeer on South Georgia: The Ecology of an Introduced Population. (Studies in Polar Research). (Illus.). 275p. 1988. 64.95 (*0-521-24271-1*) Cambridge U Pr.

Leader, Zachary. Writer's Block. LC 90-4744. 272p. 1991. 42.50x (*0-8018-4032-5*) Johns Hopkins.

Leading Edge Group Staff. The U. S. Chemotherapy Market. 325p. 1987. 1,950.00 (*0-317-63102-0*) Busn Trend.

***Leading Guides Ltd. Staff.** Egon Ronay's Cellnet Guide, 1995: Hotels & Restaurants. 1995. pap. 19.95 (*0-312-11781-7*) St Martin.

***Leadingham, Everett.** I Believe, Now Tell Me Why. 1994. pap. 4.95 (*0-8341-1518-2*) Beacon Hill.

— I Believe, Now Tell Me Why: Leader's Guide. 1994. pap. 3.95 (*0-8341-1517-4*) Beacon Hill.

Leadley, Robert, jt. auth. see Johns, Helen.

Leaf, Alexander & Cotran, Ramzi. Renal Pathophysiology. 3rd ed. (Illus.). 1985. pap. text ed. 26.95 (*0-19-503488-0*) OUP.

Leaf, Alexander & Weber, Peter C. Prevention & Noninvasive Therapy of Atherosclerosis. (Atherosclerosis Reviews Ser.: Vol. 21). 224p. 1990. 80.50 (*0-88167-684-5*) Raven.

Leaf, Alexander, jt. auth. see Weber, Peter C.

Leaf, Alexander, jt. ed. see Weber, Peter c.

***Leaf, Alexander, et al, eds.** Renal Pathophysiology: Recent Advances. fac. ed. LC 79-63038. (Illus.). 299p. Date not set. pap. 85.30 (*0-7837-7290-4*, 2047016) Bks Demand.

Leaf, Alexandra. The Impressionists' Table: Gastronomy & Recipes of 19th-Century France. LC 94-10790. 160p. 1994. 27.50 (*0-8478-1837-3*) Rizzoli Intl.

Leaf, David A. Exercise & Nutrition in Preventative Cardiology. 296p. (C). 1991. pap. text ed. write for info. (*0-697-14839-4*) Brown & Benchmark.

Leaf, Edwin B. Ship Modeling from Scratch: Tips & Techniques for Building Without Kits. 1993. pap. 17.95 (*0-87742-389-X*) Intl Marine.

— Ship Modeling from Scratch: Tips & Techniques for Building Without Kits. 1994. pap. text ed. 17.95 (*0-07-036817-1*) McGraw.

Leaf, G. A. Practical Statistics for the Textile Industry (Mott), Pt. 2. 95p. (C). 1987. pap. text ed. 130.00 (*0-900739-52-5*, Pub. by Textile Institue UK) St Mut.

Leaf, Hayim, jt. auth. see Ben-Asher, Naomi.

***Leaf, June.** People. (Illus.). 62p. 1994. pap. 19.95 (*1-879886-36-7*) Addison Gallery.

Leaf, Margaret. Eyes of the Dragon. LC 85-11670. (Illus.). 32p. (J). (ps-2). 1987. 18.00 (*0-688-06155-9*); lib. bdg. 16.93 (*0-688-06156-7*) Lothrop.

Leaf, Munro. El Cuento de Ferdinando. Belpre, Pura, tr. (Illus.). 72p. (SPA.). (J). (ps-3). 1962. pap. 13.99 (*0-670-25065-1*) Viking Child Bks.

— El Cuento De Ferdinando. (Illus.). (SPA.). (J). (gr. k-3). 1990. audio 22.95 (*0-87499-217-6*); audio, pap. 14.95 (*0-87499-216-8*) Live Oak Media.

— El Cuento De Ferdinando, 4 bks., Set. (Illus.). (J). (gr. k-3). 1990. audio, pap. 31.95 (*0-87499-218-4*) Live Oak Media.

— El Cuento de Ferdinando: (The Story of Ferdinand) Belpre, Pura, tr. (SPA.). (J). (gr. k-3). 1990. pap. 27.95 (*0-87499-191-9*) Live Oak Media.

— El Cuento de Ferdinando: The Story of Ferdinand. Belpre, Pura, tr. (Illus.). 72p. (SPA.). (J). (ps-3). 1990. pap. 4.99 (*0-14-054253-1*, Puffin) Puffin Bks.

— Manners Can Be Fun. 2nd rev. ed. LC 84-48459. (Trophy Picture Bk.). (Illus.). 48p. (J). (gr. k-3). 1985. pap. 4.95 (*0-06-443053-7*, Trophy) HarpC Child Bks.

— The Story of Ferdinand. (Illus.). (J). (ps-3). 1988. pap. 9.95 (*0-14-095075-3*, Puffin); audio 6.95 (*0-318-37106-5*, Puffin); 9.95 (*0-318-37105-7*, Puffin) Puffin Bks.

— The Story of Ferdinand. (Illus.). (J). 1993. audio 6.99 (*0-14-095115-6*, Puffin) Puffin Bks.

— The Story of Ferdinand. LC 36-19452. (Illus.). (J). (gr. k-3). 1936. pap. 13.99 (*0-670-67424-9*) Viking Child Bks.

— The Story of Ferdinand. (Illus.). 72p. 1989. reprint ed. lib. bdg. 17.95 (*0-89966-590-X*) Buccaneer Bks.

Leaf, Munro, jt. auth. see Kimmel, Eric A.

Leaf, Murray J. Man, Mind, & Science: A History of Anthropology. LC 78-27724. 400p. 1983. pap. text ed. 19.50 (*0-231-04619-7*) Col U Pr.

Leaf, Reuben. Hebrew Alphabets: 400 B.C.E. to Our Times. LC 87-15820. 125p. 1987. 35.00 (*0-8197-0518-7*); spiral bd. 17.95 (*0-685-17377-1*) Bloch.

Leaf, Ruth. Etching, Engraving & Other Intaglio Printmaking Techniques. 240p. 1984. pap. 10.95 (*0-486-24721-X*) Dover.

***Leaf, Vadonna J.** Father for Jason: The Story of God's Love for a Child Without a Father. LC 94-78746. (J). (ps-3). 1994. pap. 5.99 (*0-8066-2733-6*, Augsburg) Augsburg Fortress.

Leaf, Walter. Troy: a Study in Homeric Geography. LC 70-150191. (Select Bibliographies Reprint Ser.). 1977. reprint ed. 39.95 (*0-8369-5704-0*) Ayer.

Leaf, Walter, tr. see Solovyoff, Vsevolod S.

Leafe, David, ed. The Film & Television Handbook 1990. (Illus.). 272p. 1990. 22.50 (*0-85170-246-5*, Pub. by British Film Inst UK) Ind U Pr.

— Film & Television Handbook 1991. (Illus.). 304p. 1991. pap. 28.95 (*0-85170-277-5*, Pub. by British Film Inst UK) Ind U Pr.

— Film & Television Handbook, 1992. (Illus.). 332p. 1992. pap. 28.95 (*0-85170-317-8*, Pub. by British Film Inst UK) Ind U Pr.

— Film & Television Handbook 1993. (Illus.). 328p. (C). 1993. pap. 28.95 (*0-85170-344-5*, Pub. by British Film Inst UK) Ind U Pr.

— Film & Television Handbook, 1994. (Illus.). 328p. 1994. pap. 28.95 (*0-85170-411-5*, Pub. by British Film Inst UK) Ind U Pr.

Leafe, G. Harry. Running to Win! A Positive Biblical Approach to Rewards & Inheritance. 108p. (Orig.). 1992. pap. 5.00 (*0-9635128-0-3*) Scriptel Pubs.

Leaffer. Understanding Copyright Law. 1989. write for info. (*0-8205-0556-0*, 839) Bender.

***Leaffer, Marshall A.** Understanding Copyright Law. 2nd ed. LC 94-39940. (Legal Text Ser.). 1995. pap. write for info. (*0-256-16448-7*) Bender.

Leaffer, Marshall A., ed. International Treaties on Intellectual Property. LC 90-46683. 646p. 1990. pap. text ed. 66.00 (*0-87179-659-7*, 0659) BNA.

Leafgren, Fred, ed. see Moore, Dwight.

***Leaflet Missal Company Staff.** A Holy Card Prayer Book I & II: A Compilation of Saints & Holy People. (Illus.). 230p. 1994. 29.95 (*1-885845-02-2*) Leaflet Missal.

— A Holy Card Prayer Book II: A Compilation of Saints & Holy People. (Illus.). 115p. 1994. 19.95 (*1-885845-01-4*) Leaflet Missal.

Leagans, J. Paul, et al. Selected Concepts from Educational Psychology & Adult Education for Extension & Continuing Educators. LC 74-171881. (Notes & Essays Ser.: No. 71). 1971. pap. text ed. 3.50 (*0-87060-046-X*, NES 71) Syracuse U Cont Ed.

Leage, R. W. Roman Private Law: Founded on the "Institutes" of Gaius & Justinian. 2nd ed. LC 93-79712. 476p. 1994. reprint ed. 105.00 (*1-56169-070-8*) W W Gaunt.

— Roman Private Law: Founded on the Institutes of Gaius & Justinian. LC 93-79711. 450p. 1994. reprint ed. 95.00 (*1-56169-069-4*, Pub. by Juta SA) W W Gaunt.

Leagjeld, Ted. Voyageur the Moose. (Illus.). (Orig.). (J). (gr. 4-8). Date not set. pap. write for info. (*0-9616127-0-3*) T Leagjeld.

League of Nations, Economic, Financial & Transit Department Staff. The Course & Control of Inflation. Wilkins, Mira, ed. LC 78-3928. (International Finance Ser.). (Illus.). 1979. reprint ed. lib. bdg. 18.95 (*0-405-11231-9*) Ayer.

League of Nations, Financial Committee, Gold Delegation. Report & Interim Report, 2 vols. in 1. Wilkins, Mira, ed. LC 78-3929. (International Finance Ser.). 1979. reprint ed. lib. bdg. 23.95 (*0-405-11232-7*) Ayer.

League of Nations, Secretariat, Economic, Financial & Transit Department Staff. International Currency Experience, Lessons of the Inter-War Period. Wilkins, Mira, ed. LC 78-3932. (International Finance Ser.). 1979. reprint ed. lib. bdg. 24.95 (*0-405-11235-1*) Ayer.

League of Nations, Secretariat Staff. Memorandum on Currency & Central Banks: 1913-1924, 2 vols. in 1. Wilkins, Mira, ed. LC 78-3931. (International Finance Ser.). (Illus.). 1979. reprint ed. lib. bdg. 53.95 (*0-405-11234-3*) Ayer.

— Memorandum on Currency & Central Banks: 1913-1925, 2 vols. in 1. Wilkins, Mira, ed. LC 78-3930. (International Finance Ser.). (Illus.). 1979. reprint ed. lib. bdg. 34.95 (*0-405-11233-5*) Ayer.

League of Nations Staff. European Conference on Rural Life, 29 parts in 3 vols., Set. LC 77-87670. reprint ed. 134.00 (*0-404-16550-8*) AMS Pr.

***League of Saint Gerard Staff.** Gerard Majella: The Mother's Saint. 16p. (Orig.). 1994. pap. 2.95 (*0-89243-706-5*) Liguori Pubns.

League of Vermont Writers Members. Vermont Voices: An Anthology. 288p. 1991. pap. 13.95 (*0-9630872-0-7*) League VT Writs.

***League of Women Voters.** Targeting Tomorrow: Washington's Economy Adjusts to the '90s. 42p. 1991. pap. text ed. 4.95 (*1-878170-02-3*) LWV WA.

League of Women Voters Education Fund Staff. America's Growing Dilemma: Pesticides in Food & Water. 20p. 1989. 4.95 (*0-89959-414-X*, 887) LWVUS.

— Coping with Conflict: Reproductive Choices & Community Controversy. 36p. (Orig.). 1986. pap. 2.50 (*0-89959-367-4*, 802) LWVUS.

— Crosscurrents: The Water We Drink. 17p. 1989. 4.95 (*0-89959-413-1*, 880) LWVUS.

— Fighting Hunger: A Guide for Development of Community Action Projects. 16p. 1990. 5.00 (*0-89959-416-6*, 893) LWVUS.

— Going to Court in the Public Interest. 1983. 0.85 (*0-89959-339-9*, 244) LWVUS.

— Groundwater: A Citizen's Guide. 24p. (Orig.). 1986. 1.75 (*0-89959-369-0*, 803) LWVUS.

— Know Your Community. 48p. 1972. pap. 1.75 (*0-89959-056-X*, 288) LWVUS.

— Nuclear Waste Primer: A Handbook for Citizens. rev. ed. (Illus.). 176p. 1993. pap. 10.95 (*1-55821-226-4*, 448) * LWVUS.

— Plastic Waste Primer: A Handbook for Citizens. (Illus.). 137p. 1993. 10.95 (*1-55821-229-9*, 954) LWVUS.

— Protect Your Groundwater: Educating for Action. 64p. 1994. 6.95 (*0-89959-384-4*, 980) LWVUS.

— Recycling Is More Than Collections: Questions & Concerns from the Ground Up. 1992. 5.95 (*0-89959-421-2*, 926) LWVUS.

— Safety on Tap: A Citizen's Drinking Water Handbook. 68p. 1987. pap. 7.95 (*0-89959-402-6*, 840) LWVUS.

— Seeds of Tomorrow: Issues in Agricultural Research & Technology. 16p. 1992. 4.95 (*0-89959-422-0*, 927) LWVUS.

— Tell It to Washington. 87p. 1995. 2.75 (*0-89959-309-7*) LWVUS.

— Thinking Globally...Acting Locally. 87p. 1988. pap. 5.00 (*0-89959-406-9*, 849) LWVUS.

— U. S. Farm Policy: Who Benefits? Who Pays? Who Decides? 24p. 1990. 4.95 (*0-89959-418-2*, 904) LWVUS.

— Unmet Needs: The Growing Crisis in America. 71p. 1988. pap. 5.00 (*0-89959-409-3*, 853) LWVUS.

— You & Your National Government. rev. ed. (Illus.). 32p. 1985. pap. 1.75 (*0-89959-027-6*, 273) LWVUS.

League of Women Voters of California Staff, ed. Guide to California Government. rev. ed. 197p. 1992. pap. 8.95 (*0-9632465-0-X*) Leag Women Voters.

League of Women Voters of Cleveland Educational Fund, Inc. Staff. From Ordinance to Constitution: Government of & by the People. 73p. (YA). (gr. 9-12). 1987. pap. text ed. 10.00 (*1-880746-05-0*) LOWV Cleve Educ.

— New Voter's Guide to Practical Politics. 61p. (YA). (gr. 7-12). 1982. reprint ed. pap. 2.00 (*1-880746-02-6*) LOWV Cleve Educ.

— Ohio: From Territory to Statehood - From Ordinance to Constitution. 99p. (J). (gr. 7-8). 1987. pap. text ed. 10.00 (*1-880746-04-2*) LOWV Cleve Educ.

— Ohio: From Wilderness to Territory - The Law of the Land. (J). (gr. 3-6). 1987. pap. text ed. 10.00 (*1-880746-03-4*) LOWV Cleve Educ.

— One Man, One Vote: The History of the African-American Vote in the United States. 56p. 1991. pap. 10.50 (*1-880746-00-X*) LOWV Cleve Educ.

— Seven Making History: A Mayoral Retrospective. 51p. 1990. pap. 10.00 (*1-880746-01-8*) LOWV Cleve Educ.

League of Women Voters of Minnesota Education Fund Staff. Citizens in Action. rev. ed. (Illus.). 78p. 1985. pap. text ed. 6.50 (*0-939816-03-2*) LWV MN.

— Facts & Issues - How Should We Pay for Our Schools: Financing Education in Minnesota. 1991. 3.00 (*1-877889-01-6*) LWV MN.

— Facts & Issues - How We Pay for Our Schools: Financing Education in Minnesota. 1990. 3.00 (*1-877889-00-8*) LWV MN.

— Facts & Issues-Minnesota's Liquid Asset: Water Use & Policy Options. (Illus.). 12p. (Orig.). 1984. pap. 2.00 (*0-9613566-0-X*) League Wmn Voters MN.

— How to Make a Difference: A Citizens Guide to State Government. rev. ed. (Illus.). 100p. 1993. pap. text ed. 10.00 (*1-877889-05-9*) League Wmn Voters MN.

— How Will We Pay for Our Schools? Financing Public Education in Minnesota (K-12) (Illus.). 59p. (Orig.). 1982. pap. text ed. 5.00 (*0-939816-02-4*) LWV MN.

— Minnesota Judiciary: Structures & Procedures. 2nd ed. (Illus.). 64p. (C). 1981. pap. text ed. 2.00 (*0-939816-00-8*) LWV MN.

— Monitoring Mental Health Services at the County Level: A Workbook. Flanigan, Barbara, ed. 168p. 1989. 15.00 (*0-9613566-8-5*) LWV MN.

— Pay Equity: A Monitoring Guidebook. 16p. (Orig.). 1984. pap. 2.00 (*0-9613566-1-8*) League Wmn Voters MN.

— The People's Choice Cookbook. (Illus.). 192p. (Orig.). 1983. pap. text ed. 8.95 (*0-939816-04-0*) LWV MN.

— Protecting Minnesota's Children: Public Issues. (Illus.). 29p. 1986. pap. 2.50 (*0-9613566-2-6*) League Wmn Voters MN.

League of Women Voters of Minnesota Staff. Citizens in Action. 1991. 7.50 (*1-877889-02-4*) LWV MN.

League of Women Voters of New York State Education Fund Staff. New York State: A Citizen's Handbook. Richman, Jeanne, ed. LC 79-24095. (Illus.). 119p. (Orig.). 1979. pap. 2.95 (*0-938588-03-6*) LWV NYS.

League of Women Voters of New York State Staff, jt. ed. see Fairbanks, Mary J.

League of Women Voters of Newtown Staff. Newtown, Connecticut: Directions & Images. Telfair, Carol & Greene, Carolyn, eds. (Illus.). 1989. text ed. 30.00 (*0-9623444-0-0*) LWV Newtown.

League of Women Voters of Pennsylvania Education Fund Staff. Key to the Keystone State: Pennsylvania. Brandt, Susan E. & Piccoli, Terese S., eds. LC 87-43184. 1988. pap. 12.95 (*0-271-00635-8*) Pa St U Pr.

League of Women Voters Staff. Choosing the President, 1992. 160p. 1992. pap. 9.95 (*1-55821-169-1*) Lyons & Burford.

— The Garbage Primer: A Handbook for Citizens. 190p. 1993. 10.95 (*1-55821-250-7*) LWVUS.

— The State We're In: Washington: A Citizen's Guide to Washington State Government. 3rd ed. Bakke, Jean, ed. (Illus.). (YA). (gr. 9-12). 1990. pap. text ed. 5.50 (*1-878170-00-7*) LWV WA.

League, Richard. Psycholinguistic Matrices Investigation into Osgood & Morris. (Approaches to Semiotics Ser.: Vol. 47). (Illus.). 1977. 32.75 (*90-279-3116-X*) Mouton.

Leah. Celebrated Songs, Vol. 1. Date not set. pap. 9.95 (*0-685-68986-7*, Chester Music) Music Sales.

— Celebrated Songs, Vol. 2. Date not set. pap. 9.95 (*0-685-68987-5*, Chester Music) Music Sales.

— Celebrated Songs, Vol. 3. Date not set. pap. 9.95 (*0-685-68988-3*, Chester Music) Music Sales.

Leah, Devora, ed. Lost Erev Shabbos in the Zoo. rev. ed. (Illus.). 32p. (J). (gr. k-3). 1986. 9.95 (*0-910818-56-8*) Judaica Pr.

Leah, Devorah, ed. Lost Erev Shabbos in the Zoo. rev. ed. (Illus.). 32p. (J). (gr. k-3). 1986. pap. 7.95 (*0-910818-57-6*) Judaica Pr.

Leah Komaiko & Kids. A Million Moms & Mine. (Illus.). 28p. (J). 1992. 11.95 (*0-9634893-0-5*); pap. 5.95 (*0-9634893-1-3*) L Claiborne.

Leahey, Grace E., jt. auth. see Leahey, Thomas H.

Leahey, Maureen, jt. auth. see Wright, Lorraine M.

Leahey, Maureen M., jt. ed. see Wright, Lorraine M.

Leahey, Thomas H. A History of Modern Psychology. 2nd ed. LC 93-34463. 1993. text ed. write for info. (*0-13-501271-6*) P-H.

— A History of Psychology: Main Currents in Psychological Thought. 3rd ed. 512p. 1992. text ed. 46.67 (*0-13-387945-3*) P-H.

Leahey, Thomas H. & Harris, Richard J. Learning & Cognition. 3rd ed. 496p. 1992. text ed. write for info. (*0-13-446550-4*) P-H.

Leahey, Thomas H. & Leahey, Grace E. Psychology's Occult Doubles: Psychology & the Problem of Pseudoscience. LC 82-24635. 296p. 1983. lib. bdg. 29.95 (*0-88229-717-1*) Nelson-Hall.

Leahigh, David, jt. auth. see Reilly, Frank K.

Leahy. The Development of the Worcester Police Department. pap. 6.00 (*0-914206-13-3*) Clark U Pr.

— Excavations at Malkata & the Birket Habu 1971-1974: The Inscriptions. (Egyptology Today Ser.: Vol. 4). 1978. pap. 35.00 (*0-85668-121-0*, Pub. by Aris & Phillips UK) David Brown.

***Leahy, A.** The Insect Workbook. (Illus.). 80p. (J). 1994. pap. 4.95 (*0-938522-51-5*) Entomol Soc.

Leahy, Alice M. The Measurement of Urban Home Environments: Validation & Standardization of the Minnesota Home Status Index, Vol. 11. LC 79-142314. (Monograph Ser.: No. 11). (Illus.). 70p. 1975. reprint ed. text ed. 45.00 (*0-8371-5902-4*, CWLM) Greenwood.

Leahy, Anthony. Libya & Egypt in the First Millennium BC. 224p. 1988. lib. bdg. 39.95 (*0-415-00478-0*) Routledge.

An Asterisk (*) at the beginning of an entry indicates that the title is appearing in BIP for the first time.

Leahy, Barbara H. Marijuana: A Dangerous "High" Way. rev. ed. Farrell, Lee et al, eds. LC 82-62440. (Illus.). 173p. (Orig.). (J). (gr. 4-9). 1983. pap. 6.95 (*0-9610312-1-2*) B Leahy.

Leahy, Christopher. Peterson First Guide To Insects. (Illus.). 128p. (Orig.). 1987. pap. 4.95 (*0-395-35640-7*) HM.

Leahy, D. G. Foundation: Matter the Body Itself. 320p. (C). 1995. 89.50x (*0-7914-2021-3*); pap. 29.95x (*0-7914-2022-1*) State U NY Pr.

— Novitas Mundi: Perception of the History of Being. LC 79-20388. 1980. 50.00x (*0-8147-4993-3*) NYU Pr.

Leahy, David G. Novitas Mundi: Perception of the History of Being. LC 93-45673. 422p. (C). 1994. 59.50x (*0-7914-2137-6*); pap. 19.95x (*0-7914-2138-4*) State U NY Pr.

Leahy, Frederick S. Satan Cast Out. 200p. 1990. reprint ed. pap. 7.95 (*0-85151-234-8*) Banner of Truth.

Leahy, James E. The First Amendment, 1791-1991: Two Hundred Years of Freedom. LC 90-53502. 320p. 1991. lib. bdg. 31.50 (*0-89950-573-2*) McFarland & Co.

— Liberty, Justice & Equality: How These Constitutional Guarantees Have Been Shaped by United States Supreme Court Decisions since 1789. LC 92-50308. 224p. 1992. lib. bdg. 31.50x (*0-89950-742-5*) McFarland & Co.

Leahy, John A. Eagle's Chase: The Agony of Success. LC 85-21644. (Illus.). 192p. 1986. 19.95 (*0-88280-114-7*) ETC Pubns.

Leahy, John J., jt. auth. see Kristiansen, Rolf H.

Leahy, Kathleen M., et al. Community Health Nursing. 4th ed. 432p. 1982. text ed. 26.95 (*0-07-036834-1*) McGraw.

Leahy, Leo. Lumber Men: Non Traditional Statistical Measurements of the Batting Careers of over 900 Major League Regulars from 1876 to 1992. LC 93-40431. (Illus.). 551p. 1994. lib. bdg. 35.00 (*0-89950-925-8*) McFarland & Co.

Leahy, Linda R. The All-Natural Sugar-Free Dessert Cookbook. 1992. mass mkt. 4.99 (*0-440-21100-X*) Dell.

Leahy, Linda R. & Maguire, Jack. The Universal Peanut Butter Cookbook. LC 93-18222. 1994. 12.00 (*0-679-74659-5*, Villard Bks) Random.

***Leahy, Margaret, ed.** Disorders of Communication: The Science of Intervention. 2nd ed. (Illus.). 346p. (C). 1995. pap. text ed. 37.50 (*1-56593-515-2*, 1188) Singular Publishing.

Leahy, Margaret M., jt. ed. see Rouseff, Russell L.

Leahy, Michael. Against Liberation: Putting Animals in Perspective. 272p. 1991. 59.95 (*0-415-03584-8*, A5672) Routledge.

— Privileged Class: Senior Year at Beverly Hills High School. 320p. 1988. 17.95 (*0-316-51815-8*) Little.

Leahy, Michael J. Explorations into Highland New Guinea, 1930-1935. Jones, Douglas E., ed. 272p. 1991. pap. 22.50 (*0-8173-0446-0*) U of Ala Pr.

Leahy, Michael P. How to Overcome Your Fears. 1978. pap. 3.00 (*0-87980-062-3*) Wilshire.

Leahy, Noreen M. Quick Reference to Neurological Critical Care Nursing. LC 89-18022. 248p. (C). 1990. 52.00 (*0-8342-0127-5*, 20127) Aspen Pub.

Leahy, P. Patrick, et al, eds. National Water Quality Assessment Program. (Monograph Ser.: No. 19). (Illus.). 184p. (Orig.). 1993. pap. 6.00 (*1-882132-27-0*) Am Water Resources.

Leahy, Philippa. Spain. LC 93-2663. (Discovering Our Universe Ser.). (Illus.). 32p. (J). (gr. 5). 1993. text ed. 13.95 (*0-89686-772-2*, Crstwood Hse) Silver Burdett Pr.

***Leahy, Rita B. & Von Quintus, Harold.** Validation of Relationships Between Specification Properties & Performance. (SHRP Ser.: A-409). (Illus.). 104p. (Orig.). (C). 1994. pap. text ed. 15.00 (*0-309-05813-9*) Natl Res Coun.

Leahy, Robert J., ed. The Development Self. (Developmental Psychology Ser.). 1985. text ed. 59.00 (*0-12-439870-7*) Acad Pr.

Leahy, Robert L., ed. The Child's Construction of Social Inequality. LC 82-24287. (Developmental Psychology Ser.). 1983. text ed. 84.00 (*0-12-439880-4*) Acad Pr.

Leahy, Syrell R. A Book of Ruth. 384p. 1988. pap. 3.95 (*0-8217-2483-5*) Zebra.

— Family Truths. large type ed. 496p. 1986. 23.95 (*0-7089-8345-6*, Charnwood) Ulverscroft.

— Love Affair. large type ed. 464p. 1987. 23.95 (*0-7089-8406-1*, Charnwood) Ulverscroft.

— Only Yesterday. 1990. mass mkt. 4.50 (*1-55817-410-9*, Pinnacle NY) Windsor NY.

— Only Yesterday. large type ed. 1991. 21.95 (*0-7089-2448-4*) Ulverscroft.

Leahy, W. H., et al. Urban Economics. LC 75-88859. 1970. pap. text ed. 10.95 (*0-685-01683-8*) Free Pr.

Leahy, William & Wallenfeldt, Jeffrey W., eds. The Motion Picture Guide Annual 1991 (the Films of 1990) (Illus.). 700p. 1991. Dist. by R.R. Bowker to libraries only. 134.95 (*0-685-60083-1*, CineBooks) Baseline Bks.

— Motion Picture Guide, 1991 Annual: The Films of 1990. 461p. 1991. 134.95 (*0-918432-92-8*) Bowker.

— The Motion Picture Guide, 1992 Annual: The Films of 1991. (Illus.). 593p. 1993. 148.00 (*0-918432-93-6*) Bowker.

Leahy, William D. I Was There. Kohn, Richard H., ed. LC 78-22382. (American Military Experience Ser.). (Illus.). 1980. reprint ed. lib. bdg. 42.95 (*0-405-11859-7*) Ayer.

Leahy, William P. Adapting to America: Catholics, Jesuits, & Higher Education in the Twentieth Century. LC 90-40505. 210p. 1991. pap. 25.95 (*0-87840-504-6*) Georgetown U Pr.

Leaird, Tom. Scuba Lifesaving & Accident Management. 80p. 1988. pap. text ed. 12.00 (*0-87322-132-X*, 4929, YMCA USA) Human Kinetics.

Leak, Andrew N. The Perverted Consciousness: Sexuality & Sartre. 192p. 1989. text ed. 45.00 (*0-312-03231-5*) St Martin.

Leake, Brenda, jt. ed. see Strahan, David.

Leake, C. D. The Old Egyptian Medical Papyri: The Hearst Papyrus. 108p. (C). 1994. pap. text ed. 15.00 (*0-89005-271-9*) Ares.

Leake, Chauncey D. Some Founders of Physiology: Contributors to the Growth of Functional Biology. LC 58-622. 132p. pap. 37.70 (*0-685-15953-1*, 2026395) Bks Demand.

Leake, Chauncey D., tr. see Harvey, William.

Leake, Chauncey D., ed. see Percival, Thomas.

Leake County Chamber of Commerce Staff, jt. auth. see Leake County Historical Society.

Leake County Historical Society & Leake County Chamber of Commerce Staff. The History of Leake County, Mississippi. (Illus.). 363p. 1985. 50.00 (*0-88107-027-0*) Curtis Media.

Leake, David, Jr. Brunei: The Modern Southeast-Asian Islamic Sultanate. LC 89-42730. 190p. 1989. lib. bdg. 27.50x (*0-89950-434-5*) McFarland & Co.

Leake, David. Evaluating Explanations: A Content Theory. (Roger Schank's Artificial Intelligence Ser.). 280p. 1992. text ed. 49.95 (*0-8058-1064-1*) L Erlbaum Assocs.

Leake, David, ed. Case-Based Reasoning: Papers from the 1993 Workshop. (Technical Reports). (Illus.). 130p. (Orig.). 1993. spiral bd. 25.00 (*0-929280-48-2*) Amer Artificial.

Leake, David B., jt. ed. see Ram, Ashwin.

Leake, Dorothy, jt. auth. see Leake, Henderson.

Leake, Dorothy V., et al. Desert & Mountain Plants of the Southwest. LC 92-50716. (Illus.). 1993. pap. 18.95 (*0-8061-2489-X*) U of Okla Pr.

***Leake, Earnie & Stanley, John L.** Benchmarking for Facility Management Workbook. 108p. (Orig.). 1994. pap. 150.00 (*1-883176-05-0*, 146050) Intl Facility Mgmt Assn.

Leake, Henderson & Leake, Dorothy. Wildflowers of the Ozarks. LC 81-50400. (Illus.). vi, 170p. (Orig.). 1981. pap. 9.95 (*0-912456-04-3*) Ozark Soc Bks.

Leake, I. Q. Memoir of the Life & Times of General John Lamb. LC 72-152230. (Era of the American Revolution Ser.). 1971. reprint ed. lib. bdg. 59.50 (*0-306-70122-7*) Da Capo.

Leake, Percy D. Commercial Goodwill: Its History, Value & Treatment in Accounts. Brief, Richard P., ed. LC 80-1507. (Dimensions of Accounting Theory & Practice Ser.). 1980. reprint ed. lib. bdg. 30.95 (*0-405-13532-7*) Ayer.

— Depreciation & Wasting Assets & Their Treatment in Assessing Annual Profit & Loss. LC 75-18474. (History of Accounting Ser.). (Illus.). 1979. 20.95 (*0-405-07556-1*) Ayer.

Leake, William M. Journal of a Tour in Asia Minor with Comparative Remarks on the Ancient & Modern Geography of That Country. xxvii, 362p. (GER.). 1976. reprint ed. lib. bdg. 44.20 (*3-487-06055-8*, Pub. by Georg Olms GW) Lubrecht & Cramer.

Leakey, F. W. Baudelaire: "Les Fleurs du Mal" (Landmarks of World Literature Ser.). 128p. (C). 1992. 29.95 (*0-521-36116-8*); pap. 10.95 (*0-521-36937-1*) Cambridge U Pr.

— Baudelaire: Collected Essays, 1953-1988. (Cambridge Studies in French: No. 30). (Illus.). 320p. (C). 1990. 69.95 (*0-521-32335-5*) Cambridge U Pr.

Leakey, John & Yost, Nellie S. The West That Was: From Texas to Montana. LC 58-14110. (Illus.). xii, 287p. 1965. pap. 9.95 (*0-8032-5117-3*, Bison Books) U of Nebr Pr.

Leakey, L. S., et al, eds. Adam or Ape: A Sourcebook of Discoveries about Early Man. 450p. 1982. 24.95 (*0-87073-700-7*); pap. text ed. 16.95 (*0-87073-701-5*) Schenkman Bks Inc.

Leakey, Lewin. Origins Reconsidered. 1993. pap. 14.95 (*0-385-46792-3*, Anchor NY) Doubleday.

Leakey, Louis S. Defeating Mau Mau. LC 74-15061. reprint ed. 27.50 (*0-404-12102-0*) AMS Pr.

Leakey, M. D. & Harris, J. M., eds. Laetoli: A Pliocene Site in Northern Tanzania. (Illus.). 584p. 1987. 150.00 (*0-19-854441-3*) OUP.

Leakey, Mary. Olduvai Gorge Vol. 5: Excavations in Beds III, IV & the Masek Beds. (Illus.). 341p. (C). 1995. 175.00 (*0-521-33403-9*) Cambridge U Pr.

Leakey, Meave G. & Leakey, Richard E., eds. Koobi Fora: Research Projects, Vol. 1. (Illus.). 1977. text ed. 115.00 (*0-19-857392-8*) OUP.

***Leakey, Richard.** The Origin of Humankind. LC 94-3617. (Science Masters Ser.). 171p. 1994. 20.00 (*0-465-03135-8*) Basic.

Leakey, Richard E. & Lewin, Roger. Origins: What New Discoveries Reveal About the Emergence of Our Species & Its Possible Future. (C). 1991. pap. 11.95 (*0-14-015336-5*, Penguin Bks) Viking Penguin.

— People of the Lake. 272p. 1979. mass mkt. 4.95 (*0-380-45575-7*, Discus) Avon.

Leakey, Richard E. & Slikkerveer, L. Jan, eds. Origins & Development of Agriculture in East Africa: The Ethnosystems Approach to the Study of Early Food Production in Kenya. (Studies in Technology & Social Change: No. 19). (Illus.). 302p. (Orig.). (C). 1991. pap. 20.00 (*0-945271-28-X*) ISU-TSCP.

Leakey, Richard E., jt. ed. see Leakey, Meave G.

Leakey, Richard E., jt. ed. see Walker, Alan.

***Leal, Brigitte.** Picasso: Les Demoiselles de Avignon - Album de Dibujos. (Ediciones Especiales y de Bibliofilo Ser.). (Illus.). 116p. (SPA.). 1993. 375.00 (*84-343-0533-X*) Elliots Bks.

Leal, David M., jt. auth. see Gritczek, Laura J.

Leal, Donald E., jt. ed. see Baden, John A.

Leal, Donald R., jt. auth. see Anderson, Terry L.

Leal-Khouri, Susana, jt. auth. see Mallory, Susan B.

Leal, L. Gary. Laminar Flow & Convective Transport Processes: Scaling Principles & Asymptotic Analysis. (Illus.). 607p. 1992. 79.00 (*0-7506-9117-4*) Buttrwrth-Heinemann.

Leal, Luis. Aztlan y Mexico: Perfiles Literarios e Historicos. LC 83-71984. 260p. (SPA.). 1985. lib. bdg. 24.00 (*0-916950-46-8*) Biling Rev-Pr.

— Mexico: Civilizaciones y Culturas, 2 Vols. rev. ed. (Illus.). (C). 1971. pap. 24.36 (*0-395-12744-0*) HM.

— Spanish-English, English-Spanish Naval Dictionary. 3rd enl. rev. ed. 232p. 1987. pap. 23.00 (*84-283-1089-0*) IBD Ltd.

Leal, Luis L. Diccionario Naval: Ingles-Espanol, Espanol-Ingles. 4th ed. 232p. (ENG & SPA.). 1987. pap. 39.95 (*0-7859-3679-3*, S38405) Fr & Eur.

Leal, Maria T., tr. see Veiga, Jose C., et al.

Leal-McBride, Maria-Odilia. Narrativas e narradores em A Pedra do Reino: Estruturas e perspectivas Cambiantes. (American University Studies: Romance Languages & Literature: Ser. II, Vol. 110). 199p. (C). 1989. text ed. 36.50 (*0-8204-1049-7*) P Lang Pubs.

Leal, Victor N. Coronelismo: The Municipality & Representative Government in Brazil. LC 76-46044. (Cambridge Latin American Studies: No. 28). 254p. reprint ed. pap. 72.40 (*0-317-28406-1*, 2022459) Bks Demand.

Leale, Judy. Three-Minute Bible Stories. (Illus.). 32p. (J). 1992. 9.95 (*1-56156-152-5*) Kidsbks.

Leaman, Christine, ed. see Yates, Elizabeth.

Leaman, Frank, jt. auth. see Puippe, Jean-Claude.

Leaman, James R. Faith Roots: Learning from & Sharing Witness with Jewish People. Johns, Helen, ed. LC 92-75500. (Illus.). (Orig.). (C). 1993. pap. 8.95 (*0-916035-57-3*) Evangel Indiana.

Leaman, Jeremy. The Political Economy of West Germany, 1945-1985: An Introduction. 256p. 1988. text ed. 45.00 (*0-312-00541-5*) St Martin.

Leaman, Jeremy, jt. ed. see Hargreaves, Alec G.

Leaman, Oliver. Averroes & His Philosophy. (Illus.). 224p. 1988. 55.00 (*0-19-826540-9*) OUP.

— Death & Loss: Compassionate Approaches in the Classroom. (Cassell Studies in Pastoral Care & PSE). (Illus.). 160p. 1995. 60.00 (*0-304-33087-6*); pap. 19.95 (*0-304-33089-2*) Cassell.

— Evil & Suffering in Jewish Philosophy. (Cambridge Studies in Religious Traditions: No. 6). 289p. (C). 1992. 59.95 (*0-521-41724-4*) Cambridge U Pr.

— An Introduction to Medieval Islamic Philosophy. 224p. 1985. pap. 21.95 (*0-521-28911-4*) Cambridge U Pr.

— Moses Maimonides. 1990. 49.95 (*0-415-03481-7*); pap. 15.95 (*0-415-03608-9*) Routledge.

***Leaman, Oliver, ed.** Friendship East & West: Philosophical Perspectives. (Curzon Studies in Asian Philosophy: No. 2). 260p. (C). 1995. text ed. 70.00 (*0-7007-0358-6*, Pub. by Curzon Pr UK) Humanities.

Leaman, Oliver, jt. ed. see Nasr, Seyyed H.

Leaman, T. L. Healing the Anxiety Diseases. (Illus.). 275p. 1992. 23.95 (*0-306-44128-4*, Plenum Pr) Plenum.

Leaman, T. L. & Saxton, J. W. Preventing Malpractice: The Co-Active Solution. (Illus.). 205p. (C). 1994. 35.00 (*0-306-44441-0*, Plenum Med Bk) Plenum.

***Leamer, Edward E.** The Heckscher-Ohlin Model in Theory & Practice. LC 94-49591. (Studies in International Finance: No. 77). 1995. 11.00 (*0-88165-249-0*) Princeton U Int Finan Econ.

— Specification Searches: Ad Hoc Inference with Nonexperimental Data. LC 77-26855. 383p. reprint ed. pap. 109.20 (*0-7837-2816-6*, 2057656) Bks Demand.

— Sturdy Econometrics. LC 94-4208. (Economists of the Twentieth Century Ser.). 392p. 1994. 74.95 (*1-85278-802-X*, Pub. by E Elgar Pub UK) Ashgate Pub Co.

Leamer, Laurence. As Time Goes By: The Life of Ingrid Bergman. 1987. pap. 4.95 (*0-451-40022-4*, Onyx) NAL-Dutton.

— The Kennedy Women. 1995. mass mkt. 7.99 (*0-8041-1361-0*) Ivy Books.

— The Kennedy Women. 1994. 27.50 (*0-679-42860-7*) Random.

— King of the Night: The Life of Johnny Carson. 1990. mass mkt. 5.95 (*0-312-92256-6*) St Martin.

Leaming, Barbara. Bette Davis: A Biography. 1993. mass mkt. 5.99 (*0-345-38272-2*) Ballantine.

— If This Was Happiness: A Biography of Rita Hayworth. 384p. 1990. mass mkt. 5.95 (*0-345-36931-9*) Ballantine.

— Katharine Hepburn. 1995. 27.50 (*0-517-59284-3*, Crown) Crown Pub Group.

— Orson Welles: A Biography. 1995. pap. 18.95 (*0-614-06772-3*) Limelight Edns.

— Orson Welles: A Biography. 1986. mass mkt. 4.95 (*0-14-009620-5*) Viking Penguin.

— Orson Welles: A Biography. (Illus.). 592p. 1995. reprint ed. pap. write for info. (*0-87910-199-7*) Limelight Edns.

— Rita Hayworth: Her Story. write for info. (*0-318-62112-6*) Viking Penguin.

Leaming, Chris, jt. auth. see Leaming, Stan.

***Leaming, Hugo P.** Hidden Americans: Maroons of Virginia & the Carolinas. rev. ed. LC 94-34177. (Studies in African American History & Culture). 505p. 1994. 87.00 (*0-8153-1543-0*) Garland.

Leaming, Stan & Leaming, Chris. Western Rocks & Minerals. (Illus.). 33p. (Orig.). 1980. pap. 4.95 (*0-88839-053-X*) Hancock House.

Leaming, Thomas. A Philadelphia Lawyer in the London Courts. (Illus.). xiii, 199p. 1987. reprint ed. lib. bdg. 30.00 (*0-8377-2408-2*) Rothman.

***Leamnson, Robert N.** Learning Your Way Through College. LC 94-24778. 121p. 1995. pap. 17.95 (*0-534-24504-8*) Intl Thomson.

***Leamon, James S.** Revolution Downeast: The War for American Independence in Maine. LC 92-17757. (Illus.). 320p. (Orig.). 1995. pap. 16.95 (*0-87023-959-7*) U of Mass Pr.

Leamon, Warren. Harry Mathews. LC 93-929. (United States Authors Ser.: No. 628). 144p. 1993. text ed. 22.95 (*0-8057-4008-2*, Pub. by Royal Botanic Garden UK) Macmillan.

Leamy, Edmund. Fairy Minstrel of Glenmalure & Other Stories for Children. LC 76-9901. (Children's Literature Reprint Ser.). (Illus.). (J). (gr. 4-6). 1976. reprint ed. 15.00 (*0-8486-0210-2*) Roth Pub Inc.

— Golden Spears & Other Fairy Tales. LC 76-9902. (Children's Literature Reprint Ser.). (Illus.). (J). (gr. 4-6). 1976. reprint ed. 15.00 (*0-8486-0211-0*) Roth Pub Inc.

— Irish Fairy Stories for Children. (Illus.). 86p. (J). (gr. 2 up). 1992. pap. 9.95 (*1-85635-008-8*, Pub. by Mercier Pr IE) Dufour.

— Irish Fairy Tales. 1991. reprint ed. pap. 10.95 (*0-85342-917-0*, Pub. by Mercier Pr IE) Dufour.

Lean, Arthur E. And Merely Teach: Irreverent Essays on the Mythology of Education. 2nd ed. LC 75-42233. (Illus.). 143p. 1976. 8.95 (*0-8093-0744-8*); pap. 4.95 (*0-8093-0745-6*) S Ill U Pr.

Lean, Arthur E. & Eaton, William E. Education or Catastrophe? LC 89-37671. 125p. (Orig.). (C). 1989. 25.00 (*0-89341-588-X*, Longwood Academic); pap. 14.95 (*0-89341-589-8*, Longwood Academic) Hollowbrook.

Lean, David, jt. auth. see Kemp, Richard.

Lean, Garth. Cast Out Your Nets: Sharing Your Faith with Others. 144p. (Orig.). 1990. pap. 7.95 (*1-85239-010-7*, Pub. by Linden Hall UK) Grosvenor USA.

— God's Politician: William Wilberforce's Struggle. LC 87-23705. 200p. (Orig.). (C). 1988. pap. 12.95 (*0-939443-03-1*) Helmers Howard Pub.

— Good God, It Works! 1989. 2.95 (*0-7137-0719-4*) Grosvenor USA.

— On the Tail of a Comet: The Life of Frank Buchman. LC 87-32740. (Illus.). 632p. 1988. 36.95 (*0-939443-06-6*); pap. 19.95 (*0-939443-07-4*) Helmers Howard Pub.

***Lean, Geoffrey.** Atlas of Environment. Date not set. write for info. (*0-09-177433-0*) Random.

— Rich World, Poor World. 1979. pap. 13.50 (*0-04-309012-5*) Routledge Chapman & Hall.

Lean, Geoffrey & Hinrichsen, Don. Atlas of the Environment. 192p. 1994. lib. bdg. 39.50 (*0-87436-768-9*) ABC-CLIO.

— World Wildlife Federation Atlas of the Environment. 2nd ed. (Illus.). 192p. (Orig.). 1994. pap. 20.00 (*0-06-273314-1*, Harper Ref) HarpC.

***Lean, Mary.** Bread, Bricks, & Belief: Communities in Charge of Their Future. LC 95-14670. (Kumarian Press Books for a World That Works). (Illus.). 192p. 1995. pap. 15.95 (*1-56549-046-0*) Kumarian Pr.

Lean, Vincent S. Lean's Collectanea. 1973. 59.95 (*0-8490-0493-4*) Gordon Pr.

— Lean's Collecteana, 5 vols., Set. 1969. reprint ed. 210.00 (*1-55888-181-6*) Omnigraphics Inc.

Leana, Carrie R. Coping with Job Loss: How Individuals, Corporations, Unions & Communities Respond to a Layoff. 1992. text ed. 24.95 (*0-669-16569-7*) Free Pr.

Leana, Frank. Getting into College: A Guide for Students & Parents. 1990. pap. 9.95 (*0-374-52242-1*, Noonday) FS&G.

Leander, O. & Tuft, Candy. The Absolutely, Positively Perfect Book of Basic Gardening. LC 94-19210. (Illus.). 1994. pap. write for info. (*0-89865-903-5*) Donning Co.

Leaney, Alfred R. Jewish & Christian World. 1984. pap. 27.95 (*0-521-28557-7*) Cambridge U Pr.

— Letters of Peter & Jude. (Cambridge Bible Commentary on the New English Bible, New Testament Ser.). (Orig.). (C). 1966. 16.95 (*0-521-04216-X*) Cambridge U Pr.

Leannah, Michael. Waiting for Dinner or Death. abr. ed. 140p. 1995. pap. 7.95 (*1-56901-491-4*) NW Pub.

Leante, Cesar. Calembour. 189p. (Orig.). (SPA.). 1988. pap. 9.95 (*84-86214-41-6*) Ediciones.

Leanza, Frank. How to Get Started with the Baritone Horn. (Illus.). 32p. (YA). 1993. pap. 5.95 (*0-934687-15-3*) Crystal Pubs.

— How to Get Started with the Baritone Horn. (Illus.). 32p. 1994. text ed. 9.95 (*0-934687-32-3*) Crystal Pubs.

— How to Get Started with the Baritone Horn. rev. ed. (Illus.). 32p. (YA). Date not set. pap. 5.95 (*0-614-03676-3*) Crystal Pubs.

— How to Get Started with the Bassoon. (Illus.). 24p. 1994. text ed. 9.95 (*0-934687-27-7*) Crystal Pubs.

— How to Get Started with the Bassoon. rev. ed. (Illus.). 24p. (YA). 1993. pap. 5.95 (*0-934687-10-2*) Crystal Pubs.

— How to Get Started with the 'Cello. (Illus.). 24p. 1994. text ed. 9.95 (*0-934687-38-2*) Crystal Pubs.

— How to Get Started with the Cello. rev. ed. (Illus.). 24p. (YA). 1993. pap. 5.95 (*0-934687-21-8*) Crystal Pubs.

— How to Get Started with the Clarinet. (Illus.). 24p. (YA). 1993. pap. 5.95 (*0-934687-09-9*) Crystal Pubs.

— How to Get Started with the Clarinet. (Illus.). 24p. 1994. text ed. 9.95 (*0-934687-26-9*) Crystal Pubs.

— How to Get Started with the Drums. (Illus.). 28p. 1994. text ed. 9.95 (*0-934687-35-8*) Crystal Pubs.

— How to Get Started with the Drums. rev. ed. (Illus.). 28p. (YA). 1993. pap. 5.95 (*0-934687-18-8*) Crystal Pubs.

— How to Get Started with the Flute. (Illus.). 24p. 1994. text ed. 9.95 (*0-934687-24-2*) Crystal Pubs.

— How to Get Started with the Flute. rev. ed. (Illus.). 24p. (YA). 1993. pap. 5.95 (*0-934865-07-2*) Crystal Pubs.

— How to Get Started with the French Horn. (Illus.). 36p. 1994. text ed. 9.95 (*0-934687-31-5*) Crystal Pubs.

— How to Get Started with the French Horn. rev. ed. (Illus.). 36p. (YA). 1993. pap. 5.95 (*0-934687-14-5*) Crystal Pubs.

— How to Get Started with the Guitar. (Illus.). 32p. 1994. text ed. 9.95 (*0-934687-33-1*) Crystal Pubs.
— How to Get Started with the Guitar. rev. ed. (Illus.). 34p. (YA). 1993. pap. 5.95 (*0-934687-17-X*) Crystal Pubs.
— How to Get Started with the Oboe. (Illus.). 28p. 1994. text ed. 9.95 (*0-934687-25-0*) Crystal Pubs.
— How to Get Started with the Oboe. rev. ed. (Illus.). 28p. (YA). 1993. pap. 5.95 (*0-934687-08-0*) Crystal Pubs.
— How to Get Started with the Piano. (Illus.). 24p. 1994. text ed. 9.95 (*0-934687-40-4*) Crystal Pubs.
— How to Get Started with the Piano. rev. ed. (Illus.). 24p. (YA). 1993. pap. 5.95 (*0-934687-23-4*) Crystal Pubs.
— How to Get Started with the Saxophone. (Illus.). 24p. 1994. text ed. 9.95 (*0-934687-28-5*) Crystal Pubs.
— How to Get Started with the Saxophone. rev. ed. (Illus.). 24p. (YA). 1993. pap. 5.95 (*0-934687-11-0*) Crystal Pubs.
— How to Get Started with the String Bass. (Illus.). 24p. 1994. text ed. 9.95 (*0-934687-39-0*) Crystal Pubs.
— How to Get Started with the String Bass. rev. ed. (Illus.). 24p. (YA). 1993. pap. 5.95 (*0-934687-22-6*) Crystal Pubs.
— How to Get Started with the Trombone. (Illus.). 28p. 1994. text ed. 9.95 (*0-934687-30-7*) Crystal Pubs.
— How to Get Started with the Trombone. rev. ed. (Illus.). 28p. (YA). 1993. pap. 5.95 (*0-934687-13-7*) Crystal Pubs.
— How to Get Started with the Trumpet. (Illus.). 32p. 1994. text ed. 9.95 (*0-934687-29-3*) Crystal Pubs.
— How to Get Started with the Trumpet. rev. ed. (Illus.). 32p. (YA). 1993. pap. 5.95 (*0-934687-12-9*) Crystal Pubs.
— How to Get Started with the Tuba. rev. ed. (Illus.). 28p. (YA). 1993. pap. 5.95 (*0-934687-16-1*) Crystal Pubs.
— How to Get Started with the Viola. (Illus.). 24p. 1994. text ed. 9.95 (*0-934687-37-4*) Crystal Pubs.
— How to Get Started with the Viola. rev. ed. (Illus.). 24p. (YA). 1993. pap. 5.95 (*0-934687-20-X*) Crystal Pubs.
— How to Get Started with the Violin. (Illus.). 24p. 1994. text ed. 9.95 (*0-934687-36-6*) Crystal Pubs.
— How to Get Started with the Violin. rev. ed. (Illus.). 24p. (YA). 1993. pap. 5.95 (*0-934687-19-6*) Crystal Pubs.
— Music Book for Kids of Any Age, Bk. 1. rev. ed. (Illus.). 32p. (J). (gr. 1-4). 1988. pap. 3.45 (*0-934687-02-1*) Crystal Pubs.
— Music Book for Kids of Any Age, Bk. 2. rev. ed. (Illus.). 60p. (J). (gr. 1-4). 1988. pap. 3.45 (*0-934687-03-X*) Crystal Pubs.
— Music Book for Kids of Any Age, Bk. 3. rev. ed. LC 88-71395. (Illus.). 32p. (Orig.). (J). (gr. 1-4). 1988. pap. 3.45 (*0-934687-04-8*) Crystal Pubs.
— The Technique of Modern Jazz Theory. (Illus.). 94p. (C). 1993. pap. 17.95 (*0-934687-06-4*) Crystal Pubs.

Leanza, Frank & Gallo, Leonard. Music Theory for Everyone. LC 85-71876. (Illus.). 224p. (Orig.). (C). 1985. teacher ed 12.95 (*0-934687-01-3*); pap. 19.95 (*0-934687-00-5*) Crystal Pubs.

Leanza, Umberto, jt. ed. see Pharand, Donat.

Leanza, Umberto, et al. The Future of International Telecommunications: The Legal Regime of Telecommunications by Geostationary-Orbit Satellite, 4 vols., Set. 2890p. 1993. lib. bdg. 350.00 (*0-379-20158-5*) Oceana.
— The Mediterranean Continental Shelf: Deliminations & Regimes: International & National Legal Sources II University of Rome, University of Naples, 2 vols. in 4 bks., Set. LC 87-37217. 2003p. (ENG, FRE, ITA & SPA.). 1988. lib. bdg. 250.00 (*0-379-20784-2*) Oceana.

Leap, Nicky & Hunter, Billie. The Midwife's Tale: An Oral History from Handywoman to Professional Midwife. (Illus.). 238p. 1993. pap. 20.95 (*1-85727-041-X*, Pub. by Scarlet Pr UK) InBook.
— The Midwife's Tale: An Oral History from Handywoman to Professional Midwife. (Illus.). 238p. 1993. 55.95 (*1-85727-036-3*, Pub. by Scarlet Pr UK) InBook.

Leap, Terry L. Collective Bargaining & Labor Relations. 768p. (C). 1991. write for info. (*0-02-369070-4*) Macmillan.
— Collective Bargaining & Labor Relations. 2nd ed. LC 94-19444. 1994. text ed. 63.00 (*0-02-369101-8*) P-H.
— Health & Job Retention: The Arbitrator's Perspective. (Key Issues Ser.: No. 26). 60p. 1984. pap. 6.00 (*0-87546-107-7*) ILR Pr.
— Tenure, Discrimination, & the Courts. 224p. 1993. 34.00 (*0-87546-313-4*); pap. 16.95 (*0-87546-314-2*) ILR Pr.

Leap, Terry L. & Crino, Michael D. Personnel-Human Resource Management. 2nd ed. LC 92-20064. 752p. (C). 1993. write for info. (*0-02-368521-2*) Macmillan.

Leap, William L. American Indian English. 352p. 1993. 37.50 (*0-87480-416-7*) U of Utah Pr.

Leap, William L., jt. ed. see St. Clair, Robert N.

Leapard, Dave. Making a Dream Come True. (C). 1993. student ed 14.00 (*1-881592-33-2*) Hayden-McNeil.

Leape, Jonathan, et al, eds. Business in the Shadow of Apartheid: U. S. Firms in South Africa. LC 84-47741. 288p. 1984. text ed. 35.00 (*0-669-08404-2*) Free Pr.

Leape, Lucian L. Pediatric Care in Pediatric Surgery. 448p. (Orig.). 1987. 52.95 (*0-316-51821-2*, Little Med Div) Little.

Leape, Lucian L., et al. Coronary Angiography: Ratings of Appropriateness & Necessity by a Canadian Panel. LC 93-34519. 1993. write for info. (*0-8330-1453-6*, MR-129-CWF) Rand Corp.

Leape, Martha P. & Vacca, Susan M. The Harvard Guide to Careers. 3rd ed. 222p. (C). 1991. pap. 12.95 (*0-674-37565-3*) HUP.

***Leaper, Campbell, ed.** Childhood Gender Segregation: Causes & Consequences. LC 85-644751. (New Directions for Student Services Ser.: No. 65). 104p. (Orig.). 1994. pap. 16.95 (*0-7879-9985-7*) Jossey-Bass.

Leaper, D. J., ed. Selected Papers & Discussion from the Second Annual Meeting of the SISE June 2-3, 1989, Geneva, Switzerland. (Surgical Research Communications Ser.). ii, 138p. 1990. pap. text ed. 80.00 (*3-7186-5023-1*) Gordon & Breach.
— Selected Papers from the First Meeting of the SISE. (Surgical Research Communications Ser.). 90p. 1989. pap. text ed. 45.00 (*3-7186-4894-6*) Gordon & Breach.

Leaper, David J. & Branicki, Frank J., eds. International Surgical Practice. (Illus.). 432p. 1992. 125.00 (*0-19-261999-3*); pap. 59.00 (*0-19-262252-8*) OUP.

Leaper, Mary J., ed. see Mills, Kenneth G.

***Leaphart, C. Mark & Leaphart, J. Kirk, Jr.** The Seventy Percent Factor: Accumulating Savings Through Residential Real Estate Buying. 2nd ed. 233p. (Orig.). 1994. pap. write for info. (*0-9644909-0-0*); pap. write for info. (*0-9644909-1-9*) VCI Invest.

Leaphart, J. Kirk, Jr., jt. auth. see Leaphart, C. Mark.

Leapman, Michael. Arrogant Aussie: The Rupert Murdoch Story. LC 84-24093. (Illus.). 288p. 1985. 14.95 (*0-8184-0370-5*) Carol Pub Group.
— Companion Guide to New York. (Companion Guide Ser.). (Illus.). 350p. 1991. pap. 18.95 (*0-685-48925-6*, Harper Ref) HarpC.
— London. LC 92-53470. (Eyewitness Travel Guides Ser.). (Illus.). 432p. 1993. 24.95 (*1-56458-183-7*) Dorling Kindersley.
— Treacherous Estate: The Press after Fleet Street. 320p. 1993. 39.95 (*0-340-57742-8*, Pub. by H & S UK) Trafalgar.

Lear. The Owl & the Pussycat. (J). Date not set. 15.00 (*0-06-205010-9*, HarpT); lib. bdg. 14.89 (*0-06-205011-7*, HarpT) HarpC.
— The Pelican Chorus: And Other Nonsense. LC 94-78570. (J). 1995. lib. bdg. 14.89 (*0-06-205063-X*) HarpC.
— Play Helps. 2nd ed. (Illus.). 186p. 1986. pap. text ed. 32.95 (*0-433-19086-8*) Buttrwrth-Heinemann.

Lear, jt. auth. see Fisher.

Lear, jt. auth. see Sowerby.

Lear, Adam J. It's Your Turn to Get Rich! rev. ed. (Illus.). 164p. (Orig.). 1986. pap. 4.95 (*0-915451-05-0*) New Start Pubns.

Lear, Amy C., jt. auth. see Bane, Adele F.

Lear, Edward. A Book of Learned Nonsense. Haining, Peter, ed. (Pocket Classic Ser.). (Illus.). 192p. 1992. reprint ed. pap. 6.00 (*0-7509-0087-3*) A Sutton Pub.
— A Book of Nonsense. LC 92-53176. (Everyman's Library of Children's Classics). (Illus.). 240p. (J). 1992. 12.95 (*0-679-41798-2*, Evrymans Lib Childs) Knopf.
— Collected Works. 1973. 59.95 (*0-87968-892-0*) Gordon Pr.
— Complete Nonsense Book of Edward Lear. 1994. 8.98 (*0-7858-0168-5*) Bk Sales Inc.
— The Complete Nonsense of Edward Lear. 22.95 (*0-89190-090-X*, Am Repr) Amereon Ltd.
— The Complete Nonsense of Edward Lear. (Illus.). xxix, 287p. (J). (gr. 4-6). pap. 5.95 (*0-486-20167-8*) Dover.
— The Complete Nonsense of Edward Lear. Jackson, Holdrook, ed. (Illus.). 18.50 (*0-8446-0722-3*) Peter Smith.
— Daffy Down Dillies: Silly Limericks. LC 91-72986. (Illus.). 32p. (J). 1992. 14.95 (*1-56397-007-4*) Boyds Mills Pr.
— The Dong with a Luminous Nose. LC 86-1143. (Illus.). 1986. 6.95 (*0-915361-46-9*) Modan-Adama Bks.
— An Edward Lear Alphabet. LC 82-10037. (Illus.). 32p. (J). (gr. k-3). 1983. lib. bdg. 11.88 (*0-688-00965-4*) Lothrop.
— An Edward Lear Alphabet. LC 82-10037. (Illus.). 32p. (J). (ps up). 1986. 4.95 (*0-688-06523-6*, Mulberry) Morrow.
— Edward Lear's Nonsense Coloring Book. (Illus.). (J). (gr. 4-7). 1990. pap. 2.95 (*0-486-22744-8*) Dover.
— How Pleasant to Know Mr. Lear: Nonsense Poems. LC 94-4389. (Poetry for Young People Ser.). (Illus.). 64p. (J). (gr. 1 up). 1994. 14.95 (*0-88045-126-2*) Stemmer Hse.
— The Jumblies. LC 86-1147. (Illus.). 1986. 6.95 (*0-915361-34-5*) Modan-Adama Bks.
— Later Letters of Edward Lear. Strachey, Lady, ed. LC 75-175702. (Select Bibliographies Reprint Ser.). 1977. reprint ed. 27.95 (*0-8369-6617-1*) Ayer.
— Letters of Edward Lear, 2 vols., Set. 1976. lib. bdg. 200.00 (*0-8490-2151-0*) Gordon Pr.
— Letters of Edward Lear to Chichester Fortescue & Frances Countess Waldegrave. LC 70-107812. (Select Bibliographies Reprint Ser.). 1977. 27.95 (*0-8369-5208-1*) Ayer.
— A Little Book of Nonsense. Cott, Jonathan, ed. LC 93-24485. (Little Barefoot Bks.). (Illus.). 168p. (J). 1994. 6.00 (*1-56957-910-5*) Barefoot Bks.
— The New Vestments. LC 94-16713. (Illus.). (J). (ps-4). 1995. 16.00 (*0-671-50089-9*) S&S Trade.
— Nonsense Books, 4 vols. in 1. (BCL1-PR English Literature Ser.). 1992. reprint ed. lib. bdg. 139.00 (*0-7812-7589-X*) Rprt Serv.
— Nonsense Poems. LC 93-39193. (Illus.). 96p. (Orig.). (J). 1994. reprint ed. pap. 1.00 (*0-486-28031-4*) Dover.
— Nonsense Poems of Edward Lear. (Illus.). 128p. (J). 1991. 18.95 (*0-395-57001-8*, Clarion Bks) HM.
— The Owl & the Pussy-Cat. LC 90-39673. (Illus.). 32p. (J). (ps up). 1991. 13.95 (*0-688-09536-4*); lib. bdg. 13.88 (*0-688-09537-2*) Lothrop.
— The Owl & the Pussy Cat. (Illus.). 32p. (J). 1992. 15.95 (*0-575-04709-7*, Pub. by V Gollancz UK) Trafalgar.
— The Owl & the Pussy-Cat, & Other Nonsense Poems. LC 95-13076. (Illus.). (J). 1995. write for info. (*1-55858-467-6*); lib. bdg. write for info. (*1-55858-468-4*) North-South Bks NYC.
— The Owl & the Pussycat. (Illus.). 16p. (J). (ps-2). 1993. 12.95 (*0-8249-8571-0*, Ideals Child) Hambleton-Hill.
— The Owl & the Pussycat. LC 86-46115. (Poetry Pop-up Bk.). (Illus.). 14p. (J). (ps-3). 1987. 6.95 (*0-694-00193-7*) HarpC Child Bks.
— The Owl & the Pussycat. (J). (ps-1). 1989. pap. 5.95 (*0-89919-854-6*, Clarion Bks) HM.
— The Pelican Chorus: And Other Nonsense. LC 94-78570. (Illus.). 40p. (J). (gr. k up). 1995. 14.95 (*0-06-205062-1*, HarpT) HarpC.
— The Quangle Wangle's Hat. (Illus.). 32p. (J). (ps-3). 1988. 12.95 (*0-15-264450-4*) HarBrace.
— There Was an Old Man: A Gallery of Nonsense Rhythms. LC 93-46492. (Illus.). 80p. (J). 1994. 15.00 (*0-688-10788-5*) Morrow Jr Bks.
— There Was an Old Man: A Gallery of Nonsense Rhythms, a Selection of Limericks. LC 93-46492. (Illus.). 80p. (J). 1994. lib. bdg. 14.93 (*0-688-10789-3*) Morrow Jr Bks.

Lear, Edward & Allen, Jonathan. Nonsense Songs. (Illus.). 208p. (J). (gr. 4-8). 1993. 14.95 (*0-8050-2774-2*, Bks Young Read) H Holt & Co.

Lear, Edward & Carroll, Lewis. Owls & Pussycats: Nonsense Verse. LC 93-2714. (Illus.). 64p. (J). (gr. 3 up). 1993. 18.95 (*0-87226-366-5*) P Bedrick Bks.

Lear, Edward & De Paola, Tomie. Bonjour, Mister Satie. (Illus.). (J). (ps-3). 1991. 15.95 (*0-399-21782-7*, Putnam) Putnam Pub Group.

Lear, Edward, jt. auth. see Brett, Jan.

Lear, Floyd S., jt. ed. see Drew, Katherine F.

***Lear, Frances.** Second Seduction. 1994. pap. 3.98 (*0-517-13069-6*) Random Hse Value.

Lear, G. M. Abramos la Biblia. Orig. Title: Let's Open the Bible. 200p. (SPA.). 1989. pap. 4.99 (*0-8254-1438-5*) Kregel.

Lear, Gilberto. Discursos Sobre el Libro De: Lectures on Revelation. (SPA.). 5.50 (*84-7228-957-5*, 223017, Pub. by Edit Clie SP) TSELF.

Lear, John. Skilful Weight Lifting. (Skilful Ser.). (Illus.). 96p. 1991. pap. 14.95 (*0-7136-3396-4*, Pub. by A&C Black UK) Talman.

Lear, John, jt. auth. see Collins, Joseph.

Lear, Jonathan. Aristotle: The Desire to Understand. 350p. 1988. 54.95 (*0-521-34523-5*); pap. 19.95 (*0-521-34762-9*) Cambridge U Pr.
— Aristotle & Logical Theory. (Illus.). 136p. 1986. pap. 16.95 (*0-521-31178-0*) Cambridge U Pr.
— Love & Its Place in Nature: A Philosophical Interpretation of Freudian Psychoanalysis. 243p. 1991. pap. 10.00 (*0-374-52320-7*, Noonday) FS&G.

Lear, Linda J., jt. auth. see Fisher, Perry G.

Lear, Pat. The New Carbohydrate Diet Counter. 64p. 1982. pap. 2.00 (*0-941990-00-1*) Lear.

Lear, Peter. Computer Play. (E. G. Let's Look At Ser.). (Illus.). 48p. (J). (gr. 1-5). 1985. pap. 4.95 (*0-88625-087-0*) Durkin Hayes Pub.
— Computers. (E. G. Let's Look At Ser.). (Illus.). 32p. (J). (gr. 1-5). 1985. pap. 4.95 (*0-88625-083-8*) Durkin Hayes Pub.

Lear, Robert W. On Balance: The Three Stages of a CEO's Career. Foltz-Gray, Dorothy, ed. LC 92-61351. (Chief Executive Press Ser.). (Illus.). 96p. 1992. 13.95 (*1-879736-10-1*) Whittle Comns.

Lear, Roma. More Play Helps: Play Ideas for Profoundly Handicapped Children. (Illus.). 212p. 1990. 30.00 (*0-433-00106-2*) Buttrwrth-Heinemann.
— Play Helps. 3rd ed. LC 92-33203. (Illus.). 1993. pap. 30.00 (*0-7506-0572-3*) Buttrwrth-Heinemann.

Leard, A. Morocco & the Moors. 416p. 1985. 280.00 (*1-85077-026-3*, Darf Pubs Ltd) St Mut.

Leardi, Lois. The Red Shirt. 137p. 1991. 19.00 (*1-883285-07-0*) Delphinium.

Leardl, Lois. Red Shirt. 1994. pap. 9.95 (*1-883285-12-7*) Delphinium.

Learmont, David, ed. Flight. LC 92-7670. (Eyewitness Visual Dictionaries Ser.). (Illus.). 64p. 1993. 14.95 (*1-56458-101-2*) Dorling Kindersley.

Learmonth, A. T., jt. auth. see Spate, O. H.

Learmonth, Andrew. Disease Ecology: An Introduction to Ecological Medical Geography. (Illus.). 352p. 1988. pap. 34.95 (*0-631-15799-9*) Blackwell Pubs.

Learmonth, Andrew, ed. The Geography of Health. (Social Science & Medicine Ser.: No. 15). (Illus.). 268p. 1981. 32.00 (*0-08-027434-X*, Pergamon Pr) Elsevier.

Learmonth, Bob, jt. auth. see Cluett, D.

Learmonth, Bob, et al. The First Croydon Airport Nineteen Fifteen to Nineteen Twenty-Eight. (Illus.). 1985. pap. 35.00 (*0-9503224-3-1*, Pub. by Sutton Libs & Arts) St Mut.

Learmouth, John. Soccer Fundamentals. LC 94-12571. 1994. pap. 6.95 (*0-312-11532-6*) St Martin.

LEARN Incorporated Staff. High Efficiency Meetings: The Key to Leadership. 64p. 1989. pap. text ed. 60.00 (*1-55678-010-9*) Learn Inc.
— Speed Learning; Science-Engineering Edition. 39p. 1990. student ed 25.00 (*1-55678-035-4*) Learn Inc.

Learn, PC. Learn PC WordPerfect 6.0 for Dos. 1994. pap. text ed. 15.00 (*0-13-101981-3*) P-H.

Learn-PC Staff. Computer Literacy. 96p. (C). 1991. pap. text ed. write for info. (*0-13-159575-X*) P-H.
— DBASE Four. 400p. (C). 1991. pap. text ed. write for info. (*0-13-203142-6*) P-H.
— DBase Three Plus. 96p. (C). 1991. pap. text ed. write for info. (*0-13-203159-0*) P-H.

Learn PC Staff. Harvard Graphics. LC 93-32096. 1993. pap. text ed. 16.00 (*0-13-083163-8*) P-H.

Learn-PC Staff. Learn PC Computer Literacy. 2nd ed. 200p. (C). 1993. pap. text ed. write for info. (*0-13-010844-8*) P-H.
— Learn PC DOS 5. (C). 1993. pap. text ed. write for info. (*0-13-010877-4*) P-H.
— Learn PC Lotus 1-2-3 Release 2.3. 500p. (C). 1993. pap. text ed. write for info. (*0-13-010927-4*) P-H.
— Learn PC Microsoft Windows 3.1. 400p. (C). 1993. pap. text ed. write for info. (*0-13-011024-8*) P-H.
— Learn-PC Video Series Sampler. 32p. 1991. write for info. (*0-13-529157-7*) P-H.
— Learn PC WordPerfect 5.1 for Windows. 500p. (C). 1993. pap. text ed. write for info. (*0-13-011123-6*) P-H.
— Lotus 1-2-3 Release 2.2: Beginning Through Advanced Skills. 352p. (C). 1991. pap. text ed. write for info. (*0-13-515776-5*) P-H.
— Microcomputer Applications. 848p. 1992. pap. text ed. write for info. (*0-13-584814-8*) P-H.
— WordPerfect 5.1: Beginning Through Advanced Skills. 576p. (C). 1991. pap. text ed. write for info. (*0-13-952730-3*) P-H.

Learned, E. Old Portuguese Vocalic Finals, Phonology & Orthography of Accented -Ou, -Eu, Iu, & -Ao, Eo, -Io. (LD Ser.: No. 44). 1950. pap. 16.00 (*0-527-00790-0*) Periodicals Srv.

Learned, J. G., jt. auth. see Learned, W. L.

Learned, M. D. America Germanica. 1972. 59.95 (*0-87968-593-X*) Gordon Pr.

Learned, M. D., ed. Guide to Manuscript Materials Relating to American History in the German State Archives. (Carnegie Institute Ser.: Vol. 11). 1912. 35.00 (*0-527-00691-2*) Periodicals Srv.

Learned, Marion D. Life of Francis Daniel Pastorius. 1993. reprint ed. lib. bdg. 89.00 (*0-7812-5480-9*) Rprt Serv.
— The Saga of Walther of Aquitaine. (BCL1-PR English Literature Ser.). 208p. 1992. reprint ed. lib. bdg. 79.00 (*0-7812-7165-7*) Rprt Serv.

Learned, Marion D., ed. Saga of Walther of Aquitaine. LC 76-98848. 225p. 1970. reprint ed. text ed. 55.00 (*0-8371-3903-1*, LEWA, Greenwood Pr) Greenwood.

Learned, W. L. & Learned, J. G. Learned Family (Learned, Larned, Learnard, Lannard & Lerned), Being Descendants of William Learned Who Was of Charlestown, Mass., in 1632. 2nd ed. (Illus.). 510p. 1989. reprint ed. lib. bdg. 83.00 (*0-8328-0759-1*); reprint ed. pap. 75.00 (*0-8328-0760-5*) Higginson Bk Co.

Learned, Walter. Treasury of American Verse. LC 74-86799. (Granger Index Reprint Ser.). 1977. 29.95 (*0-8369-6081-5*) Ayer.

Learned, Walter, ed. see Coppee, Francois.

Learned, William S. Quality of the Educational Process in the United States & Europe. LC 75-165740. (American Education Ser, No. 2). 1972. reprint ed. 13.95 (*0-405-03610-8*) Ayer.

Learner, Marsha. Meeting Strangers. LC 91-91842. 185p. 1991. pap. 12.95 (*0-9628968-0-2*) M Brandsdorfer.

Learner, Paul, ed. The Soviet Union, Nineteen Eighty-Eight: Essays from the Harriman Institute Forum. 128p. (C). 1989. pap. text ed. 44.00 (*0-8448-1611-6*, Crane Russak) Taylor & Francis.

Learning Achievement Corporation Staff. Decimals, Percent & Money: Measurement & Transportation. Zak, Therese A., ed. (MATCH Ser.: Bk. 4). (Illus.). 144p. 1981. text ed. 13.96 (*0-07-037114-8*) McGraw.
— Fractions & Food: Fractions, Decimals & Electronic Communications. Zak, Therese A., ed. (MATCH Ser.: Bk. 3). (Illus.). 144p. 1981. text ed. 13.96 (*0-07-037113-X*) McGraw.
— Geometry & Design & Maintenance: Ratio, Proportion, Reading Graphs & Data. Zak, Therese A., ed. (MATCH Ser.: Bk. 5). (Illus.). 128p. 1981. text ed. 13.96 (*0-07-037115-6*) McGraw.
— Learning Achievements: Proofamatics Instructors Guide Binder. 1983. disk 145.00 (*0-685-07154-5*); 40.00 (*0-07-054530-8*) McGraw.
— Multiplication & Energy & Construction: Division & Medicine. Zak, Therese A., ed. (MATCH Ser.: Bk. 2). (Illus.). 144p. 1981. text ed. 13.96 (*0-07-037112-1*) McGraw.
— Number Systems, Addition & Personal Communication; Subtraction & Recreation. (MATCH Ser.: Bk. 1). (Illus.). 128p. 1981. text ed. 13.96 (*0-07-037111-3*) McGraw.

***Learning, Barbara.** Katharine Hepburn. Date not set. write for info. (*0-517-70111-1*) Random.

Learning Community Staff. A Journey to the Heart: Capturing the Spirit of Global Education. 136p. (Orig.). 1991. pap. 9.95 (*0-9615210-1-5*) Rainbow Bdg.

Learning Disabilities Council, Inc. Staff. Understanding Learning Disabilities: A Parent Guide & Workbook. 181p. 1991. pap. 19.95 (*0-9636305-0-4*) Lrning Disabil Coun.

Learning Exchange Staff. Free & Inexpensive Teaching Tools to Make & Use. 112p. (J). (gr. 2-6). 1986. student ed 10.95 (*0-86653-388-5*, GA 1004) Good Apple.
— Seasonal Learning Activities. 112p. (J). (gr. 2-6). 1988. student ed 10.95 (*0-86653-435-0*, GA1045) Good Apple.

Learning Forum Staff. Communications & Motivation Personal Growth Set. (YA). (gr. 8-12). 1988. 45.00 (*0-945525-14-1*) Supercamp.
— Study Skills Set. (Success Products Ser.). (YA). (gr. 8-12). 1989. 130.00 (*0-945525-13-3*) Supercamp.
— Success Through Math Mastery. (SuperCamp Success Ser.). (YA). (gr. 8-12). 1989. 24.95 (*0-945525-11-7*) Supercamp.

Learning Lab Students at Deephaven Elementary School Staff, jt. auth. see Holen-Dineen, Margo.

Learning Odyssey Staff, ed. Junior Drafter Operations Manual. (Illus.). 552p. 1986. write for info. (*0-934869-02-2*) Cad-Cam Pub.

Learning Systems Ltd. Staff. Discounted Cash Flow, a Method of Investment Appraisal. 1967. 45.00 (*0-08-014026-2*, Pub. by Pergamon Repr UK) Franklin.

Learning Systems Ltd., Staff, ed. Elements of Injection Moulding of Thermoplastics. (Illus.). (Orig.). (gr. 10 up). 1969. pap. text ed. 7.95 (*0-85334-043-9*) Transatl Arts.

Learning the Art of Pyrography, jt. auth. see Chapman, Al.

Learning Works Staff. Solution Sleuth. (Critical Thinking Ser.). (J). (gr. 4-8). 1989. 7.95 (0-88160-170-5, LW 278) Learning Wks.
— Travel Pack, No. 1: Doodle One. (Just for Fun Ser.). (J). (gr. k-6). 1989. 8.95 (0-88160-175-6, LW 290) Learning Wks.
— Travel Pack, No. 2: Doodle Two. (Just for Fun Ser.). (J). (gr. k-6). 1989. 8.95 (0-88160-176-4, LW 291) Learning Wks.
— Travel Pack, No. 3: Games. (Just for Fun Ser.). (J). (gr. k-6). 1989. 14.95 (0-88160-177-2, LW 292) Learning Wks.
— Travel Pack, No. 4: Dinosaurs. (Just for Fun Ser.). (J). (gr. k-6). 1989. 8.95 (0-88160-178-0, LW 293) Learning Wks.
Lears, T. Fables of Abundance: A Cultural History of Advertising in America. LC 94-12749. 1994. 30.00 (0-465-09076-1) Basic.
Lears, T. J., jt. ed. see Fox, Richard W.
Lears, T. J. Jackson. No Place of Grace: Antimodernism & the Transformation of American Culture, 1880-1920. LC 93-39767. 1994. pap. text ed. 16.95 (0-226-46970-0) U Ch Pr.
Learsi, Rufus. Prince of Judah & Other Stories of a Great Journey. 1,962th ed. LC 62-21985. (Illus.). (J). (gr. 6-10). 11.95 (0-88400-031-1) Shengold.
Learsi, Rufus, tr. see Asch, Sholem.
LeArta, Moulton. Nature's Medicine Chest, 6 bks., Set. 1990. 41.70 (0-935596-10-0) Nat Med Chest.
— Nature's Medicine Chest, Set 1. 96p. 1974. 7.50 (0-935596-04-6) Nat Med Chest.
— Nature's Medicine Chest, Set 2. 96p. 1975. 7.50 (0-935596-05-4) Nat Med Chest.
— Nature's Medicine Chest, Set 3. 96p. 1976. 7.50 (0-935596-06-2) Nat Med Chest.
— Nature's Medicine Chest, Set 5. 96p. 1976. 7.50 (0-935596-08-9) Nat Med Chest.
— Nature's Medicine Chest, Set 6. 96p. 1977. 7.50 (0-935596-09-7) Nat Med Chest.
Leary. Motive & Method in the Cantos of Ezra Pound. 1961. pap. text ed. 15.00 (0-231-08520-6) Col U Pr.
Leary, Anna A. AndeLear Nail Care. LC 86-73045. (Illus.). 78p. 1987. 9.95 (0-9617600-0-1) AndeLear Pub.
Leary, Brian. Reengineering Handbook. 2nd rev. ed. Carlisle, Patti, ed. (AT&T Quality Library). 146p. 1992. pap. 29.95 (0-932764-36-3, 500-449) AT&T Customer Info.
Leary, Brian & MacDorman, John. Quality Manager's Handbook. 2nd rev. ed. Carlisle, Patti, ed. (AT&T Quality Library). 146p. 1992. reprint ed. pap. 29.95 (0-932764-35-5, 500-442) AT&T Customer Info.
Leary, Daniel J. Shaw's Plays in Performance. LC 83-2188. (Annual of Bernard Shaw Studies: Vol. 3). 268p. 1983. 35.00 (0-271-00346-4) Pa St U Pr.
Leary, Daniel J., ed. see Shaw, Bernard.
Leary, Daniel J., ed. see Shaw, George Bernard.
Leary, David E., ed. Metaphors in the History of Psychology. (Studies in the History of Psychology). (Illus.). 416p. (C). 1990. 69.95 (0-521-37166-X) Cambridge U Pr.
— Metaphors in the History of Psychology. (Cambridge Studies in the History of Psychology). (Illus.). 416p. (C). 1994. pap. 17.95 (0-521-42152-7) Cambridge U Pr.
Leary, David E., jt. ed. see Koch, Sigmund.
Leary, Elizabeth D. Space Dreams. LC 84-80867. 168p. (Orig.). 1984. pap. 7.95 (0-937884-08-1, Bennington Bks) Hystry Mystry.
Leary, Emmeline, jt. auth. see Fairclough, Oliver.
Leary, James F. Hear, O Israel: A Guide to the Old Testament. LC 80-80627. 144p. 1986. reprint ed. pap. 5.95 (0-88479-029-0) Chr Classics.
— A Light to the Nations: A Guide to the New Testament. LC 80-80627. 144p. 1986. reprint ed. pap. 5.95 (0-88479-036-3) Chr Classics.
Leary, James J., jt. auth. see Skoog, Douglas A.
Leary, James P. Midwestern Folk Humor. (American Folklore Ser.: No. 13). 264p. 1988. 24.95 (0-87483-108-3); pap. 11.95 (0-87483-107-5) August Hse.
Leary, James R., et al. Cross-Cultural Studies of Factors Related to Differential Food Consumption. (Cross-Cultural Research Ser.). 1984. 22.00 (0-317-37054-5) HRAFP.
***Leary, John.** Violence & the Dream People: The Orang Asli in the Malayan Emergency, 1948-1960. (Monographs in International Studies Southeast Asia: No. 95). (Illus.). 275p. (Orig.). (C). 1995. pap. 22.00x (0-89680-186-1) Ohio U Pr.
Leary, John, jt. auth. see Boisen, Anton T.
Leary, John E., Jr. Francis Bacon & the Politics of Science. LC 93-31898. (History of Science & Technology Reprint Ser.). 240p. (C). 1994. text ed. 34.95 (0-8138-1407-3) Iowa St U Pr.
Leary, Katherine, tr. see Lejeune, Philippe.
Leary, L., ed. see Chopin, K.
Leary, Lewis. The Book-Peddling Parson: An Account of the Life & Works of Mason Locke Weems. (Illus.). 176p. 1984. 15.95 (0-912697-09-1) Algonquin Bks.
— John Lathop, Jr. The Quiet Poet of Federalist Boston. 51p. 1981. pap. 6.00 (0-912296-51-8) Am Antiquarian.
— Literary Career of Nathaniel Tucker. LC 78-115998. (Duke University. Trinity College Historical Society. Historical Papers: No. 29). 1970. reprint ed. 30.00 (0-404-51779-X) AMS Pr.
— Mark Twain's Letters to Mary. 1963. pap. text ed. 17.00 (0-231-08545-1) Col U Pr.
— Norman Douglas. LC 68-19753. (Columbia Essays on Modern Writers Ser.: No. 32). 48p. (Orig.). 1968. pap. text ed. 7.50 (0-231-02874-1) Col U Pr.
Leary, Lewis, ed. Contemporary Literary Scholarship: A Critical Review. LC 58-6939. 1958. 49.50 (0-89197-107-6) Irvington.
Leary, Lewis, ed. see Brackenridge, Hugh H.
Leary, Lewis, jt. auth. see Freneau, Philip M.
Leary, Lewis, ed. see Thoreau, Henry David.
Leary, Lewis, ed. see Twain, Mark.
Leary, Lory B. An Alaskan Child's Garden of Verse. (Illus.). 40p. (Orig.). (J). (gr. 6 up). 1989. pap. 6.95 (0-924663-02-2) Alaskan Viewpoint.
Leary, Lory B., ed. Alaska Women: Yesterday, Today & Tomorrow. (Illus.). 60p. (Orig.). 1990. pap. 6.95 (0-924663-10-3) Alaskan Viewpoint.
Leary, Mark. Self-Presentation: Impression Management & Interpersonal Behavior. 264p. (C). 1994. pap. text ed. write for info. (0-697-14796-7) Brown & Benchmark.
Leary, Mark, ed. see Hartford Courant Staff, et al.
Leary, Mark R. Introduction to Behavioral Research Methods. 360p. (C). 1990. text ed. 50.95 (0-534-13818-7) Brooks-Cole.
— Introduction to Behavioral Research Methods. 2nd ed. LC 94-32272. 384p. 1995. text ed. 52.95 (0-534-20490-2) Brooks-Cole.
— The State of Social Psychology: Issues, Themes, & Controversies. 152p. (C). 1989. text ed. 36.00 (0-8039-3621-4); pap. text ed. 16.95 (0-8039-3622-2) Sage.
— Understanding Social Anxiety: Social, Personality & Clinical Perspectives. LC 83-17722. (Sage Library of Social Research: No. 153). 224p. reprint ed. pap. 63.90 (0-8357-4818-9, 2037755) Bks Demand.
Leary, Mark R. & Miller, R. S. Social Psychology & Dysfunctional Behavior. (Social Psychology Ser.). (Illus.). 250p. 1986. 59.00 (0-387-96325-1) Spr-Verlag.
Leary, Martha, jt. auth. see Hill, David.
Leary, Martha R., jt. auth. see Donnellan, Anne M.
Leary, Mary B., jt. ed. see Ellis, John S.
Leary, Michael E. Photography: From Theory to Practice. 2nd ed. (Illus.). 176p. (C). 1988. pap. 29.95 (0-89863-124-6) Star Pub CA.
Leary, Patty, et al. Nurse Aide Test Study Guide. Balkema, Sandra et al, eds. (Illus.). 200p. (Orig.). 1989. pap. 10.00 (0-685-44697-2) Matthew Scott.
Leary, Paul M., ed. Virgin Islands of the United States Major Political Documents, 1666-1991. 450p. (Orig.). (C). 1992. pap. text ed. 19.95 (0-9628909-2-8) U VI CES.
Leary, Penn. The Second Cryptographic Shakespeare. rev. ed. (Illus.). 313p. 1990. pap. 15.00 (0-9617917-1-3) Westchester Hse.
Leary, Richard L. Early Pennsylvanian Geology & Paleobotany of the Rock Island County, Illinois Area. (Reports of Investigations Ser.: No. 37). (Illus.). 100p. 1981. pap. 3.50 (0-89792-089-9) Ill St Museum.
Leary, Rolfe A. Interaction Theory in Forest Ecology & Management. LC 85-18146. (Forestry Sciences Ser.). 1985. lib. bdg. 97.50 (90-247-3220-4) Kluwer Ac.
Leary, Thomas E. & Sholes, Elizabeth C. From Fire to Rust: Business, Technology & Work at the Lackawana Steel Plant, 1899-1983. (Illus.). 134p. 1987. pap. 17.75 (0-939032-00-9) Buffalo Erie.
Leary, Thomas J., et al. DOS. 1991. pap. text ed. write for info. (0-07-048805-3) McGraw.
***Leary, Timothy.** Chaos & Cyber Culture. 1994. pap. 19.95 (0-614-00335-0) Ronin Pub.
— Flashbacks: A Personal & Cultural History of an Era. rev. ed. (Illus.). 432p. 1990. pap. 15.95 (0-87477-497-7) J P Tarcher.
— Game of Life. LC 79-2283. (Illus.). 300p. (Orig.). 1993. pap. 14.95 (1-56184-050-5) New Falcon Pubns.
— Game of Life: Theory of Genetic Enlightment. 1989. pap. 9.95 (0-941404-64-1) New Falcon Pubns.
— High Priest. 1976. 32.95 (0-8488-1408-8) Amereon Ltd.
— High Priest. (Illus.). 352p. 1995. pap. 14.95 (0-914171-80-1) Ronin Pub.
— High Priest. 500p. 1991. reprint ed. lib. bdg. 33.95 (0-89966-801-1) Buccaneer Bks.
— Info-Psychology: A Revision of Exo-Psychology. 2nd ed. LC 76-56056. (Future History Ser.). (Illus.). 180p. 1987. reprint ed. pap. 12.95 (1-56184-105-6) New Falcon Pubns.
— Intelligence Agents. 200p. (Orig.). 1994. pap. 14.95 (1-56184-038-6) New Falcon Pubns.
— Neuropolitique. rev. ed. LC 88-81431. 200p. 1991. pap. 12.95 (1-56184-012-2) New Falcon Pubns.
— Politics of Ecstasy. 384p. 1990. 12.95 (0-914171-33-X) Ronin Pub.
— Surfing the Consciousness Net: The Adventures of Dani Mellon Du Pont. 1995. pap. 12.95 (0-86719-410-3) Last Gasp.
— What Does Woman Want. rev. ed. LC 87-83574. (Future History Ser.). (Illus.). 275p. 1987. reprint ed. 17.95 (0-941404-76-5); reprint ed. pap. 9.95 (0-941404-62-5) New Falcon Pubns.
Leary, Timothy & Metzner, Ralph. The Psychedelic Experience: A Manual Based on the Tibetan Book of the Dead. 1976. pap. 5.95 (0-8065-0552-4, Citadel Pr) Carol Pub Group.
***Leary, Timothy, et al.** The Psychedelic Experience: A Manual Based on the Tibetan Book of the Dead. 160p. 1995. pap. 9.95 (0-8065-1652-6, Citadel Pr) Carol Pub Group.
Leary, Timothy, et al, eds. The Psychedelic Reader: Classic Selections from the Psychedelic Review, the Revolutionary 1960s Forum of Psychopharmacological Substances. (Illus.). 272p. 1993. pap. 12.95 (0-8065-1451-5, Citadel Pr) Carol Pub Group.
Leary, Virginia A. Ethnic Conflict & Violence in Sri Lanka. (International Commission of Jurists). 87p. 1981. pap. 3.50 (0-89192-360-8) Interbk Inc.
— Ethnic Conflict & Violence in Sri Lanka: Report of a Mission to Sri Lanka in July-August 1981 on Behalf of the International Commission of Jurists: with a Supplement by the ICJ Staff for the Period 1981-1983. LC 84-172852. 92p. reprint ed. pap. 26.30 (0-685-23720-6, 2032708) Bks Demand.
— International Labour & National Law. 1982. lib. bdg. 112.50 (90-247-2551-8) Kluwer Ac.
Leary, William. Methodism in the Town of Boston. (C). 1989. text ed. 35.00 (0-902662-55-4, Pub. by R K Pubns UK); pap. text ed. 21.00 (0-685-65763-9, Pub. by R K Pubns UK) St Mut.
Leary, William M. Aerial Pioneers: The U. S. Air Mail Service, 1918-1927. LC 85-600033. (Illus.). 310p. 1986. 29.95 (0-87474-610-8, LEAP) Smithsonian.
— Perilous Missions: Civil Air Transport & CIA Covert Operations in Asia. LC 83-3554. (Illus.). 291p. 1984. 27.50 (0-8173-0164-X) U of Ala Pr.
Leary, William M., Jr. The Progressive Era & the Great War: 1896-1920. 2nd ed. LC 78-70030. (Goldentree Bibliographies Series in American History). (C). 1978. text ed. write for info. (0-88295-574-8); pap. text ed. write for info. (0-88295-575-6) Harlan Davidson.
Leary, William M., ed. The Airline Industry. (Encyclopedia of American Business History & Biography Ser.). (Illus.). 352p. 1992. lib. bdg. 85.00 (0-8160-2675-0) Facts on File.
— Aviation's Golden Age: Portraits from the 1920s & 1930s. LC 89-4753. (Illus.). 232p. 1989. 28.95x (0-87745-242-3) U of Iowa Pr.
— The Central Intelligence Agency: History & Documents. LC 83-17896. 200p. 1984. pap. 12.95 (0-8173-0219-0) U of Ala Pr.
— From Airships to Airbus: The History of Civil & Commercial Aviation Vol. 1: Infrastructure & Environment. LC 94-26006. (Proceeding of the International Conference on the History of Civil Commercial Aviation: Vol. 1-2). 1995. write for info. (1-56098-467-8) Smithsonian.
— Pilots' Directions: The Transcontinental Airway & Its History. LC 89-20479. (American Land & Life Ser.). (Illus.). 112p. 1990. reprint ed. 19.95 (0-87745-278-4) U of Iowa Pr.
— We Shall Return! MacArthur's Commanders & the Defeat of Japan, 1942-1945. LC 88-2731. 320p. 1988. 32.00 (0-8131-1654-6) U Pr of Ky.
Leary, William P., jt. ed. see Reyes, Ariel J.
Leas, Allan. Abolition of the Slave Trade. (Living Through History Ser.). (Illus.). 72p. (YA). (gr. 7-10). 1989. 19.95 (0-7134-5668-X, Pub. by Batsford UK) Trafalgar.
— South Africa. (Questions of Today Ser.). (Illus.). 72p. (YA). (gr. 7-12). 1992. 22.95 (0-7134-6499-2, Pub. by Batsford UK) Trafalgar.
Leas, Speed, jt. auth. see Kittlaus, Paul.
Leas, Speed B. Leadership & Conflict. (Creative Leadership Ser.). 128p. (Orig.). 1982. pap. 9.95 (0-687-21264-2) Abingdon.
— Moving Your Church Through Conflict. 84p. (Orig.). 1985. pap. 12.95 (1-56699-012-2, AL82) Alban Inst.
Leas, Speed B., jt. auth. see Oswald, Roy M.
Leas, Speed B., jt. auth. see Parsons, George D.
Lease, Benjamin. Emily Dickinson's Readings of Men & Books: Sacred Soundings. (Illus.). 170p. 1990. text ed. 45.00 (0-312-03650-7) St Martin.
— That Wild Fellow John Neal & the American Literary Revolution. LC 72-81630. 255p. reprint ed. pap. 72.70 (0-317-26518-0, 2024054) Bks Demand.
Lease, David. Play the Game: Field Athletics. rev. ed. (Illus.). 80p. 1994. pap. 7.95 (0-7137-2450-1, Pub. by Blandford Pr UK) Sterling.
***Lease, Gary.** Odd Fellows in the Politics of Religion: Modernism, National Socialism, & German Judaism. LC 94-23869. (Religion & Society Ser.: No. 35). 325p. (C). 1994. lib. bdg. 109.00 (3-11-014323-2) Mouton.
Lease, Gary, jt. ed. see Soule, Michael.
Lease, John R. Cecil. Core, Graham, ed. LC 92-61877. (Illus.). 47p. 1992. 16.95 (1-880439-01-8) PERQ Pubns.
Lease, Joseph. The Room. LC 94-71039. (Series of Poetry & Verse Translation). 48p. 1994. pap. 12.00 (1-882509-01-3) Alef Bks.
Leaseurope Staff & Andersen, Arthur. Leasing in Europe. 1992. write for info. (0-318-69540-5) McGraw.
Leash, Moroni. Death Notification: A Practical Guide to the Process. (Orig.). 1994. pap. 19.95 (0-942679-08-3) Upper Access.
Leasher, Evelyn, comp. Oregon Women: A Bio-Bibliography. (Bibliographic Ser.: No. 18). 64p. 1981. pap. 8.95 (0-87071-138-5) Oreg St U Pr.
Leasher, Evelyn, ed. see Bailey, Margaret J.
Leashore, Bogart R., jt. ed. see Everett, Joyce E., et al.
Leask, Harold G. Irish Castles. (Illus.). 1977. reprint ed. 27.00 (0-85221-010-8) Dufour.
— Irish Churches & Monastic Buildings, 2 vols., Vol. I: First Phases & Romanesque. 173p. 1987. 45.00 (0-85221-016-7) Dufour.
— Irish Churches & Monastic Buildings, 2 vols., Vol. II: Gothic to A.D. 1400. 162p. 1987. 45.00 (0-85221-011-6) Dufour.
— Irish Churches & Monastic Buildings, 2 vols., Vol. III: Medieval Gothic, the Last Phases. 190p. 1987. Vol. III: Medieval Gothic, The Last Phases, 190p. 45.00 (0-85221-012-4) Dufour.
Leask, Ian G. The Wounded: And Other Stories about Sons & Fathers. LC 91-61264. 232p. 1992. pap. 9.95 (0-89823-139-6) New Rivers Pr.
Leask, Marilyn & Goddard, Del. The Search for Quality: Planning for Improvement & Managing Change. 160p. 1992. pap. 37.50 (1-85396-190-6, Pub. by P Chapman UK) Taylor & Francis.
Leask, Nigel. British Romantic Writers & the East: Anxieties of Empire. LC 92-11690. (Cambridge Studies in Romanticism: No. 12). (Illus.). 276p. (C). 1993. 59.95 (0-521-41168-8) Cambridge U Pr.
— The Politics of Imagination in Coleridge's Critical Thought. LC 88-3265. 220p. 1988. text ed. 39.95 (0-312-02041-4) St Martin.
Leask, R. A., jt. ed. see Kocurek, M. J.
Leaska, Mitchell A., ed. A Passionate Apprentice: The Early Journals, 1897-1909. 1992. pap. 14.95 (0-15-671160-5, Harvest Bks) HarBrace.
Leaska, Mitchell A. & Phillips, John, eds. Violet to Vita: The Letters of Violet Trefusis to Vita Sackville-West. (Illus.). 320p. 1991. reprint ed. pap. 10.95 (0-14-015796-4, Penguin Bks) Viking Penguin.
Leaska, Mitchell A., ed. see Woolf, Virginia.
Leason, Barney. Grand Illusions. 1989. pap. 3.95 (1-55817-234-3, Pinnacle NY) Windsor NY.
— Passions. 1990. mass mkt. 4.95 (1-55817-456-7, Pinnacle NY) Windsor NY.
— Rodeo Drive. 416p. 1988. pap. 3.95 (1-55817-093-6, Pinnacle NY) Windsor NY.
***Leasor, James.** Boarding Party: The Last Action of the Calcutta Light Horse. (Bluejacket Bks.). (Illus.). 224p. 1995. pap. 13.95 (1-55750-512-8) Naval Inst Pr.
— Follow the Drum. large type ed. 632p. 1982. 23.95 (0-7089-8033-3, Trail West Pubs) Ulverscroft.
— Frozen Assets. braille ed. 497p. 1992. vinyl bd. 39.76 (1-56956-059-5, BR8769) W A T Braille.
— Love Down Under. large type ed. (Adventure Suspense Ser.). 512p. 1993. 21.95 (0-7089-2969-9) Ulverscroft.
— Open Secret. large type ed. 480p. 1983. 23.95 (0-7089-8141-0, Charnwood) Ulverscroft.
— Passport for a Pilgrim. large type ed. 381p. 1982. 21.95 (0-7089-0837-3) Ulverscroft.
— Passport to Oblivion. 1,964th ed. (Spies & Intrigues Ser.: No. 5). 220p. pap. 5.95 (0-918172-18-7) Leetes Isl.
— Passport to Peril. large type ed. 1980. 12.00 (0-7089-0428-9) Ulverscroft.
— Passport to Peril. (Spies & Intrigues Ser.: No. 6). 240p. reprint ed. pap. 5.95 (0-918172-19-5) Leetes Isl.
— Tank of Serpents. large type ed. 528p. 1987. 16.95 (0-7089-1712-7) Ulverscroft.
Least Heat Moon, William. Blue Highways. 1986. mass mkt. 5.95 (0-449-21109-6) Fawcett.
Leasure, Paula, ed. see Siembieda, Kevin.
Leat, Mike, jt. auth. see Hollinshead, Graham.
Leatham, A., et al. Lecture Notes on Cardiology. 3rd ed. 1991. pap. 34.95 (0-632-01944-1) Blackwell Sci.
Leatham, Gary, ed. Frontiers in Industrial Mycology. (Illus.). 228p. 1992. 75.00 (0-412-03461-1, A6800, Chapman & Hall) Chapman & Hall.
Leatham, Gary F. & Himmel, Michael E., eds. Enzymes in Biomass Conversion. LC 91-11798. (ACS Symposium Ser.: No. 460). (Illus.). 536p. 1991. 99.95 (0-8412-1995-8) Am Chemical.
Leatham-Jones, Barry. Introduction to Computer Numerical Control. 256p. (C). 1986. pap. text ed. 120.00 (0-273-02402-7, Pub. by Pitman Pubng UK) St Mut.
Leatham-Jones, Barry, ed. Elements of Industrial Robotics. 240p. (C). 1987. pap. text ed. 125.00 (0-273-02592-9, Pub. by Pitman Pubng UK) St Mut.
Leatham, Victoria. In My Father's House: Life at Burghley. LC 92-10739. 1992. 40.00 (0-316-51846-8) Little.
Leathard, Audrey, ed. Going Inter-Professional: Working Together for Health & Welfare. LC 93-44328. 216p. 1994. 65.00x (0-415-09285-X, B4173, Routledge NY); pap. 19.95 (0-415-09286-8, B4177, Routledge NY) Routledge.
Leathem, Diana. They Built on Rock: The Story of the Celtic Christian Church. 1977. lib. bdg. 59.95 (0-8490-2743-8) Gordon Pr.
Leather, Bob, jt. auth. see Martin, Tony.
Leather, J., jt. ed. see James, A.
Leather, John. Apritsails & Lugsails. (Illus.). 392p. 1989. text ed. 45.00 (0-87742-998-7) Intl Marine.
— Clinker Boatbuilding. (Illus.). 224p. 1987. pap. 19.95 (0-229-11818-6, Adlard Coles) Sheridan.
— The North-Seamen: The Story of the Fishermen, Yachtsmen & Shipbuilders of the Colne & Blackwater Rivers. 336p. 1994. 45.00 (0-900963-22-0, Pub. by T Dalton UK) St Mut.
— Sail & Oar. LC 82-48098. (Illus.). 144p. 1982. 27.00 (0-87742-161-7) Intl Marine.
— The Salty Shore: The Story of the River Blackwater. 216p. 1994. 36.00 (0-900963-52-2, Pub. by T Dalton UK) St Mut.
— Smacks & Bawleys. 160p. (C). 1989. 50.00 (0-86138-079-7, Pub. by T Dalton UK) St Mut.
Leather, Margaret, ed. Saltwater Village. 140p. 1994. pap. 21.00 (0-86138-022-3, Pub. by T Dalton UK) St Mut.
Leather, S., jt. auth. see Burdon, J.
Leather, Simon R. & Hardie, Jim. Insect Reproduction. 288p. 1995. 189.95 (0-8493-6695-X, 6695, CRC Reprint) CRC Pr.
Leather, Simon R., et al. The Ecology of Insect Overwintering. (Illus.). 300p. (C). 1993. 64.95 (0-521-41758-9) Cambridge U Pr.
Leather, Simon R., et al, eds. Insect Overwintering. (Illus.). 400p. 1991. 49.95 (0-7131-2940-9, A2932, Pub. by E Arnold UK) Routledge Chapman & Hall.
Leather, Stephen. The Chinaman. Grose, Bill, ed. 368p. 1993. mass mkt. 5.99 (0-671-74302-3) PB.
— Hungry Ghost. 384p. (Orig.). 1993. mass mkt. 5.50 (0-671-75300-2) PB.
— The Vets. Grose, Bill, ed. 512p. 1994. reprint ed. mass mkt. 5.99 (0-671-74304-X) PB.

An Asterisk (*) at the beginning of an entry indicates that the title is appearing in BIP for the first time.

Leatherbarrow, David. The Roots of Architectural Invention: Site, Enclosure, Materials. LC 92-38508. (RES Monographs on Anthropology & Aesthetics). (Illus.). 272p. (C). 1993. 65.00 (*0-521-44265-6*) Cambridge U Pr.

Leatherbarrow, David, jt. auth. see Mostafavi, Mohsen.

Leatherbarrow, Margaret. Gold in the Grass. Bargyla & Rateaver, Gylver, eds. LC 75-23179. (Conservation Gardening & Farming Ser.: Ser. C). (C). 1975. reprint ed. pap. 20.00 (*0-9600698-8-7*) Rateavers.

***Leatherbarrow, W. J., ed.** Dostoevskii & Britain. LC 94-32406. 1995. 54.95 (*0-85496-784-2*) Berg Pubs.

Leatherbarrow, W. J., ed. see Dostoevsky, Fyodor.

Leatherbarrow, William J. Dostoyevsky: "The Brothers Karamazov" (Landmarks of World Literature Ser.). (Illus.). 128p. (C). 1992. 29.95 (*0-521-38424-9*); pap. 10.95 (*0-521-38601-2*) Cambridge U Pr.

— Feodor Dostoevsky. (World Authors Ser.: No. 636). 192p. 1981. text ed. 22.95 (*0-8057-6480-1*, Pub. by Royal Botanic Garden UK) Macmillan.

— Feodor Dostoevsky: A Reference Guide. (Reference Guides to Literature Ser.). 429p. (C). 1990. text ed. 40.00 (*0-8161-8941-2*, Hall Reference) Macmillan.

Leatherbarrow, William J. & Offord, D. C., eds. A Documentary of Russian Thought: From the Enlightenment to Marxism. 316p. (RUS.). 1987. pap. 18.95 (*0-87501-019-9*) Ardis Pubs.

Leatherbarrow, William J., ed. see Dostoyevsky, Fyodor.

Leatherberry, Donna, jt. auth. see Leatherberry, Keith.

***Leatherberry, Keith & Leatherberry, Donna.** UFOs Exposed in Scripture. 120p. 1995. pap. 7.95 (*1-56901-538-4*) NW Pub.

Leatherbury, Leven C., ed. see Dean, Wayne.

Leatherdale, Clive. Britain & Saudi Arabia 1925-1939: The Imperial Oasis. 414p. 1983. text ed. 42.00 (*0-7146-3220-1*, Pub. by F Cass Pubs UK) Intl Spec Bk.

***Leatherdale, Frank & Leatherdale, Paul.** Successful Pistol Shooting. (Illus.). 160p. 1995. 35.00 (*1-85223-883-6*, Pub. by Crowood Pr UK) Trafalgar.

Leatherdale, Paul, jt. auth. see Leatherdale, Frank.

Leatherman. Old Man & the Dog. 1991. 16.95 (*1-879034-01-8*) MS River Pub.

Leatherman, Dick. Quality Leadership Through Empowerment: Standards of Leadership Behavior. 408p. (Orig.). 1992. pap. 24.95 (*0-87425-171-0*) Human Res Dev Pr.

— The Training Trilogy: Assessing Needs. 72p. 1990. 10.00 (*0-87425-141-9*) Human Res Dev Pr.

— The Training Trilogy: Designing Programs. 136p. 1990. 15.00 (*0-87425-142-7*) Human Res Dev Pr.

— The Training Trilogy: Facilitation Skills. 96p. 1990. 10.00 (*0-87425-143-5*) Human Res Dev Pr.

Leatherman, K. D. & Dickson, R. A. The Management of Spinal Deformities. (Illus.). 468p. 1988. 250.00 (*0-7236-0740-0*, Pub. by John Wright UK) Buttrwrth-Heinemann.

Leatherman, Lyndell. Contemporary Praise for Organ. 1988. 8.95 (*0-8341-9043-5*, MB-599) Lillenas.

— Exalt Him Worship Services. 1984. (*0-318-72216-X*, MB-540) Lillenas.

Leatherman, Richard W. The Supervisor's Complete Guide to Leadership Behavior. rev. ed. (Illus.). 102p. 1981. 17.50 (*0-9603702-1-8*) Intl Training.

Leatherman, Robin R. Rhymes of a Bluejacket: Verses of a World War II Navy Vet. LC 86-82065. (Illus.). 112p. (Orig.). 1986. pap. 6.95 (*0-939127-00-8*) Gulf Coast Pub.

Leatherman, Stephen P., ed. Barrier Islands: From the Gulf of St. Lawrence to the Gulf of Mexico. LC 79-15954. 1979. text ed. 75.00 (*0-12-440260-7*) Acad Pr.

Leathers, Dale G. Successful Nonverbal Communications. 2nd ed. (Illus.). 432p. (C). 1991. pap. write for info. (*0-02-369025-9*) Macmillan.

Leathers, Noel L. The Japanese in America. LC 67-15684. (In America Bks.). (Illus.). 72p. (J). (gr. 5 up). 1991. pap. 5.95 (*0-8225-1014-6*, Lerner Publctns) Lerner Group.

— The Japanese in America. LC 67-15684. (In America Bks.). (Illus.). 72p. (YA). (gr. 5 up). 1991. lib. bdg. 17.50 (*0-8225-0241-0*, Lerner Publctns) Lerner Group.

— Japanese in America. (YA). (gr. 5 up). 1991. pap. 5.95 (*0-8225-1042-1*, Lerner Publctns) Lerner Group.

Leathers, Park & Ritts, Blaine. A Guide for Evaluating Energy Management. (Illus.). 177p. 1983. pap. text ed. 47.00 (*0-89413-100-1*, 516) Inst Inter Aud.

Leatherwood, Stephen & Reeves, Randall R. The Sierra Club Handbook of Whales & Dolphins. LC 83-388. (Illus.). 320p. 1983. 25.00 (*0-87156-341-X*); pap. 18.00 (*0-87156-340-1*) Sierra.

Leatherwood, Stephen, et al. Whales, Dolphins, & Porpoises of the Eastern North Pacific & Adjacent Arctic Waters: A Guide to Their Identification. (Illus.). 256p. 1988. reprint ed. pap. 12.95 (*0-486-25651-0*) Dover.

Leatherwood, Stephen P. & Reeves, Randall R. The Sea World Book of Dolphins. LC 86-46212. 111p. (J). (gr. 4-7). 1987. pap. 9.95 (*0-15-271957-1*, Voyager Bks) HarBrace.

Leatherwood, Stephen P. & Reeves, Randall R., eds. The Bottlenose Dolphin: Tursiops Truncatus. 653p. 1989. text ed. 121.00 (*0-12-440280-1*) Acad Pr.

***Leathwood, J., et al, eds.** Light Foods: An Assessment of Their Psychological, Sociocultural, Physiological, Nutritional, & Safety Aspects. LC 95-75553. (Illus.). 98p. 1995. pap. 22.50 (*0-944398-44-8*) ILSI.

Leathwood, Peter, et al, eds. For a Better Nutrition in the Twenty-First Century. LC 92-49782. (Nestle Nutrition Workshop Ser.: Vol. 27). 272p. 1993. 63.00 (*0-88167-964-X*) Raven.

Leaton, Gwen, jt. auth. see Kinney, Jean.

Leatt, James, et al, eds. Contending Ideologies in South Africa. LC 86-531. 328p. (Orig.). reprint ed. pap. 93.50 (*0-685-23458-4*, 2032736) Bks Demand.

Leatz, Christine A. & Stolar, Mark W. Career Success - Personal Stress: How to Stay Healthy in a High-Stress Environment. 1992. text ed. 29.95 (*0-07-036966-6*) McGraw.

— Career Success - Personal Stress: How to Stay Healthy in a High-Stress Environment. 1992. pap. text ed. 14.95 (*0-07-036977-1*) McGraw.

Leau, Leopold, jt. auth. see Couturat, Louis.

Leautaud, Paul. Amours. (FRE.). 1973. pap. 8.95 (*0-7859-4019-7*) Fr & Eur.

— A Child of Montmartre. 1995. 13.50 (*0-679-60158-9*) Random.

— Journal Litteraire. Pia & Guyot-Clement, Christine, eds. 65.00 (*0-685-34264-6*) Fr & Eur.

— Moments of Love. Wainhouse, Austryn, tr. LC 83-60468. Orig. Title: Amours. 96p. (Orig.). 1983. pap. 6.95 (*0-910395-06-3*) Marlboro Pr.

Leautey, Eugene & Guilbaut, Adolfe. La Science des Conptes Mise a la Portee de Tous: The Science of Accounting Put Within Reach of Us All. Brief, Richard P., ed. LC 80-1508. (Dimensions of Accounting Theory & Practice Ser.). (FRE.). 1980. reprint ed. lib. bdg. 50.95 (*0-405-13533-5*) Ayer.

Leavell, Jo A. Joy in the Journey. LC 93-47619. 224p. 1994. 15.95 (*1-56554-021-2*) Pelican.

Leavell, Jo Ann P. Don't Miss the Blessing. LC 89-38308. 216p. 1990. 15.95 (*0-88289-747-0*) Pelican.

Leavell, L. P., jt. auth. see Bunyan, Juan.

Leavell, Landrum P. Angels, Angels, Angels. LC 73-75627. 96p. 1973. pap. 6.99 (*0-8054-2222-6*) Broadman.

Leavell, Landrum P. & Bryson, Harold. Evangelism: Christ's Imperative Commission. rev. ed. LC 78-59983. 1991. 12.99 (*0-8054-2534-9*) Broadman.

***Leavell, Linda.** Marianne Moore & the Visual Arts: Prismatic Color. (Illus.). 232p. 1995. text ed. 30.00 (*0-8071-1986-5*) La State U Pr.

Leavell, Lorraine. Family Fishing Holes. (Illus.). 116p. (Orig.). 1991. per., pap. text ed. 11.95 (*0-9628581-0-2*) Baylake Pubns.

— Family Fishing Holes: Within One Hundred Twenty Miles of Downtown Houston. 2nd ed. (Illus.). 120p. 1993. per., pap. 11.95 (*0-9628581-1-0*) Baylake Pubns.

Leavell, Perry. Harry S. Truman. (World Leaders - Past & Present Ser.). (Illus.). 112p. (J). (gr. 5 up). 1988. lib. bdg. 17.95 (*0-87754-558-8*) Chelsea Hse.

— James Madison. (World Leaders - Past & Present Ser.). (Illus.). 112p. (J). (gr. 5 up). 1988. 17.95 (*1-55546-815-2*) Chelsea Hse.

— Woodrow Wilson. (World Leaders - Past & Present Ser.). (Illus.). 112p. (YA). (gr. 5 up). 1987. lib. bdg. 17.95 (*0-87754-557-X*) Chelsea Hse.

***Leavell, Robert N., et al.** Equitable Remedies, Restitution & Damages. 5th ed. (American Casebook Ser.). 190p. (C). 1994. teacher ed, pap. text ed. write for info. (*0-314-04838-3*) West Pub.

— Equitable Remedies, Restitution & Damages: Cases & Materials On. (American Casebook Ser.). 207p. 1992. teacher ed, pap. text ed. write for info. (*0-314-59184-2*) West Pub.

— Equitable Remedies, Restitution & Damages: Cases & Materials On. 4th ed. (American Casebook Ser.). 1111p. 1992. reprint ed. text ed. 46.00 (*0-314-99368-1*) West Pub.

— Equitable Remedies, Restitution & Damages, Cases & Materials on. 5th ed. (American Casebook Ser.). 1216p. 1994. text ed. 52.00 (*0-314-03719-5*) West Pub.

Leavell, Ronald P., jt. auth. see Girard, James A.

Leavell, Ronald Q. Mateo: El Rey Y el Reino. Quezada, Alfredo, tr. 160p. (SPA.). 1988. pap. 3.95 (*0-311-04363-1*) Casa Bautista.

***Leavengood, Betty.** Tucson ABC Coloring & Activity Book. (Illus.). 32p. (J). (gr. 1-3). 1995. pap. 4.95 (*0-9645487-0-4*) MP Pub AZ.

— Tucson Hiking Guide. LC 91-13851. 198p. (Orig.). 1991. pap. 13.95 (*0-87108-810-X*) Pruett.

Leavengood, Betty & Liebert, Mike. Hiker's Guide to the Santa Rita Mountains. (Illus.). 192p. (Orig.). 1995. pap. 17.50 (*0-87108-846-0*) Pruett.

Leavens, Alex. Moving into Windows NT Programming. 1993. disk, pap. 39.95 (*0-672-30295-0*) Sams.

— Visual C Plus Plus: A Developer's Guide. 1993. pap. 39.95 (*1-55851-339-6*) M&T Bks.

— Visual C Plus Plus 2.0: A Developer's Guide. 1995. disk, pap. 39.95 (*1-55851-416-3*) M&T Bks.

— Windows Programmer's Guide to Resources. (Illus.). (Orig.). 1992. pap. 34.95 (*0-672-30097-4*) Sams.

Leavens, C. R. & Taylor, R., eds. Interfaces, Quantum Wells, & Superlattices. LC 88-19476. (NATO ASI Series B, Physics: Vol. 179). (Illus.). 412p. 1988. 95.00 (*0-306-42983-7*, Plenum Pr) Plenum.

Leavens, Donald C., jt. auth. see Murray, Helen.

Leavens, Ileana B. & Bruce, Chris. No! Contemporary American Dada, 2 Vols., Vols. 1 & 2. LC 85-81311. (Illus.). (Orig.). 1986. Vol. 1, 64p. Vol. 2, 52p. pap. 35.00 (*0-935558-17-9*) Henry Art.

Leavens, John M. Catboat Book. 160p. 1991. pap. 17.95 (*0-87742-314-8*) Intl Marine.

Leavens, John M., ed. The Catboat Book. 1992. pap. text ed. 17.95 (*0-07-010442-5*) McGraw.

Leavenworth, E. W. A Genealogy of the Leavenworth Family in the United States. (Illus.). 376p. 1989. reprint ed. lib. bdg. 64.50 (*0-8328-0761-3*); reprint ed. pap. 56.50 (*0-8328-0762-1*) Higginson Bk Co.

Leavenworth, Geoffrey. Historic Galveston. Barnhill, Stephen, ed. (Illus.). 102p. 1985. 49.95 (*0-917001-02-8*) Herring Pr.

Leavenworth, Richard S., jt. auth. see Grant, Eugene L.

Leavenworth, Russ, jt. auth. see Brengelman, Fred.

Leaver, Darren, jt. auth. see Weaver, Gregory.

Leaver, K. D., et al. Thin Films. LC 75-153871. (Wykeham Science Ser.: No. 17). 120p. (C). 1971. 18.00 (*0-8448-1119-X*, Crane Russak) Taylor & Francis.

— Thin Films. (Wykeham Science Ser.: No.17). 120p. 1971. pap. 18.00 (*0-85109-230-6*) Taylor & Francis.

Leaver, Mike & Sanghera, Hardev. The IBM RISC System - 6000 User Guide. LC 92-38718. (IBM McGraw-Hill Ser.). 1993. pap. text ed. 34.95 (*0-07-707687-7*) McGraw.

Leaver, Richard & Richardson, Jim. Post Cold War Order. 192p. 1994. pap. 24.95 (*1-86373-399-X*, Pub. by Allen Unwin AT) Paul & Co Pubs.

Leaver, Richard L., jt. ed. see Richardson, James L.

Leaver, Robin. Goostly Psalmes & Spirituall Songes: English & Dutch Metrical Psalms from Coverdale to Utenhove, 1535-1566. (Oxford Studies in British Church Music). (Illus.). 380p. 1991. 89.00 (*0-19-816168-9*) OUP.

Leaver, Robin A. J. S. Bach As Preacher: His Passions & Music in Worship. (Illus.). 56p. (Orig.). 1985. pap. 5.25 (*0-570-01332-1*, 99-1262) Concordia.

— Music in the Service of the Church: The Funeral Sermon for Heinrich Schuetz. 68p. (Orig.). 1985. pap. 6.75 (*0-570-01331-3*, 99-1261) Concordia.

Leaver, Robin A., jt. ed. see Brouwer, Frans.

Leaver, Robin A., ed. see Micklem, Caryl, et al.

Leaver, Robin A., ed. see Stiller, Gunther.

Leavers, V. F. Shape Detection in Computer Vision Using the Hough Transform. LC 92-23019. xiv, 201p. 1992. pap. 49.00 (*0-387-19723-0*) Spr-Verlag.

Leaverton, Paul E. Environmental Epidemiology. Masse, Louis et al, eds. LC 82-5335. 192p. 1982. text ed. 55.00 (*0-275-91369-4*, C1369, Praeger Pubs) Greenwood.

— A Review of Biostatistics. 3rd ed. 128p. 1986. pap. 16.50 (*0-316-51853-0*) Little.

— A Review of Biostatistics: A Program for Self-Instruction. LC 94-22888. 1994. 22.95 (*0-316-51883-2*) Little.

— A Review of Biostatistics: A Program for Self-Instruction. 3rd ed. 1986. spiral bd. 12.00 (*0-316-51852-2*, Little Med Div) Little.

Leaverton, Paul E. & Masse, Louis, eds. Health Information Systems. LC 84-3480. 220p. 1984. text ed. 45.00 (*0-275-91440-2*, C1440, Praeger Pubs) Greenwood.

Leavey, Carmel, et al. Sponsoring Faith in Adolescence. 1992. pap. 19.95 (*0-85574-005-1*, Pub. by E J Dwyer AT) Morehouse Pub.

Leavey, John P., Jr. Glassary. LC 85-30902. iv, 320p. 1986. 55.00 (*0-8032-2871-6*) U of Nebr Pr.

Leavey, John P., Jr., tr. see Derrida, Jacques.

Leavis, Frank R. D. H. Lawrence. LC 72-3172. (Studies in D. H. Lawrence: No. 20). 1972. reprint ed. lib. bdg. 75.00 (*0-8383-1541-0*) M S G Haskell Hse.

— Determinations: Critical Essays. LC 70-119085. (English Literature Ser.: No. 33). 1970. reprint ed. lib. bdg. 75.00 (*0-8383-1081-8*) M S G Haskell Hse.

— For Continuity. LC 68-54355. (Essay Index Reprint Ser.). 1977. 23.95 (*0-8369-0613-6*) Ayer.

— New Bearings in English Poetry: A Study of the Contemporary Situation. LC 75-30032. reprint ed. 32.50 (*0-404-14035-1*) AMS Pr.

— Revaluation: Tradition & Development in English Poetry. LC 75-17192. 275p. 1975. reprint ed. text ed. 59.75 (*0-8371-8297-2*, LEREV, Greenwood Pr) Greenwood.

— Valuation in Criticism & Other Essays. Singh, G., ed. (Cambridge Paperback Library). 280p. 1986. 74.95 (*0-521-30966-2*) Cambridge U Pr.

***Leavis, Frank R. & Leavis, Q. D.** Dickens, the Novelest. LC 77-135367. 391p. Date not set. reprint ed. pap. 111.50 (*0-7837-9211-5*, 2049961) Bks Demand.

— Dickens the Novelist. (C). 1979. reprint ed. pap. 15.00 (*0-8135-0881-9*) Rutgers U Pr.

Leavis, Frank R. & Thompson, Denys. Culture & Environment: The Training of Critical Awareness. LC 77-23346. 150p. 1977. reprint ed. text ed. 52.50 (*0-8371-9696-5*, LECU, Greenwood Pr) Greenwood.

Leavis, Q. D. Collected Essays Vol. 2: The American Novel & Reflections on the European Novel. Singh, G., ed. 312p. 1985. 74.95 (*0-521-26702-1*) Cambridge U Pr.

— Collected Essays Vol. 3: The Novel of Religious Controversy. Singh, G., ed. 280p. (C). 1989. 74.95 (*0-521-26703-X*) Cambridge U Pr.

Leavis, Q. D., jt. auth. see Leavis, Frank R.

Leavitt, Alan J. Shame the Devil. LC 86-82113. 222p. 1987. 17.95 (*1-55611-006-5*) D I Fine.

Leavitt, Alga W., ed. Stories & Poems from the Old North State. LC 71-163039. (Short Story Index Reprint Ser.). (Illus.). 1977. reprint ed. 23.95 (*0-8369-3953-0*) Ayer.

Leavitt, Caroline. Into Thin Air. (Fresh Voices Ser.). Date not set. pap. write for info. (*0-446-36542-4*) Warner Bks.

— Living Other Lives. 336p. 1995. 21.95 (*0-446-51705-4*) Warner Bks.

— Meeting Rozzy Halfway. 256p. 1982. pap. 2.75 (*0-345-29797-0*) Ballantine.

Leavitt, Charles. Monarch Notes on Twain's a Connecticut Yankee in King Arthur's Court & Other Works. (Orig.). (C). pap. 3.95 (*0-671-00879-X*, Arco Test) P-H Gen Ref & Trav.

Leavitt, Christine & McCarron, Robert J. Solid Waste Management in Minnesota: Economic Status & Outlook. (Illus.). 101p. (Orig.). (C). 1994. pap. text ed. 55.00 (*0-7881-0222-2*) Diane Pub.

Leavitt, David. Equal Affections. 1990. pap. 12.00 (*0-06-097287-4*, PL) HarpC.

— Family Dancing. LC 84-47679. 200p. 1984. 13.95 (*0-394-53872-2*) Knopf.

— Family Dancing. 224p. 1985. mass mkt. 4.99 (*0-446-32845-6*) Warner Bks.

— The Lost Language of Cranes. LC 87-47561. 336p. 1987. pap. 10.00 (*0-553-34465-X*, Windstone) Bantam.

— Penguin Book of Gay Short Fiction. LC 93-1390. 1994. pap. write for info. (*0-670-84337-7*, Viking) Viking Penguin.

— A Place I've Never Been: Stories. (Contemporary American Fiction Ser.). 224p. 1991. reprint ed. pap. 10.95 (*0-14-010959-5*, Penguin Bks) Viking Penguin.

— While England Sleeps. LC 92-45878. (Illus.). 320p. 1993. 22.00 (*0-670-83349-5*, Viking) Viking Penguin.

Leavitt, David & Mitchell, Mark, eds. The Penguin Book of Gay Short Stories. 688p. 1994. reprint ed. pap. 13.95 (*0-14-024249-X*, Penguin Bks) Viking Penguin.

Leavitt, Edward D., jt. auth. see Cummings, O. R.

Leavitt, Emily W. The Blair Family of New England. 197p. 1988. reprint ed. lib. bdg. 50.00 (*0-8328-0260-3*); reprint ed. pap. 40.00 (*0-8328-0261-1*) Higginson Bk Co.

Leavitt, Emily W., jt. auth. see Morse, J. H.

***Leavitt, Fred.** Drugs & Behavior. 3rd ed. 424p. 1994. 55.00 (*0-8039-4783-6*); pap. 26.95 (*0-8039-4784-4*) Sage.

— Unloosing Monsters: Plunging to the Depths of Human Wisdom. LC 84-90338. 1984. 10.00 (*0-87212-179-8*) Libra.

Leavitt, Harold J. & Bahrami, Homa. Managerial Psychology: Managing Behavior in Organizations. 5th ed. (Illus.). 368p. 1988. 29.95 (*0-226-46973-5*) U Ch Pr.

Leavitt, Harold J. & Pondy, Louis R. Readings in Managerial Psychology. 3rd ed. LC 79-21587. xii, 732p. 1980. lib. bdg. 30.00 (*0-226-46986-7*) U Ch Pr.

Leavitt, Harold J., et al. Readings in Managerial Psychology. (Illus.). 784p. 1988. pap. text ed. 25.00 (*0-226-46992-1*) U Ch Pr.

— Readings in Managerial Psychology. 4th ed. (Illus.). 784p. 1988. lib. bdg. 60.00 (*0-226-46991-3*) U Ch Pr.

Leavitt, Howard B., ed. Issues & Problems in Teacher Education: An International Handbook. LC 91-33503. 312p. 1992. text ed. 69.50 (*0-313-25991-7*, LTC, Greenwood Pr) Greenwood.

***Leavitt, Howard S.** Looking for Angels & Answers. LC 94-38175. 1995. 12.95 (*1-883911-04-4*) Brandylane.

***Leavitt, Jacqueline.** Defining Cultural Differences in Space: Public Housing As a Microcosm. (Urban Studies & Planning Monograph Ser.: No. 11). 84p. 1994. pap. 7.50 (*0-913749-21-4*) U MD Urban Stud.

Leavitt, Jacqueline & Saegert, Susan. From Abandonment to Hope: Community-Households in Harlem. (History of Urban Life Ser.). 800p. 1989. text ed. 40.00 (*0-231-06846-8*) Col U Pr.

Leavitt, Jeffrey S. Total Quality Through Project Management. 1994. text ed. 49.00 (*0-07-036980-1*) McGraw.

Leavitt, Jerome E. Easy Carpentry Projects for Children. Orig. Title: Carpentry for Children. 96p. (J). (gr. 2 up). 1986. reprint ed. pap. 3.95 (*0-486-25057-1*) Dover.

Leavitt, Jerome E., ed. Child Abuse & Neglect: Research & Innovation. 1983. lib. bdg. 107.50 (*90-247-2862-2*) Kluwer Ac.

Leavitt, John F. The Charles W. Morgan. (Illus.). xvi, 131p. 1973. pap. 14.95 (*0-913372-10-2*) Mystic Seaport.

— Wake of the Coasters. rev. ed. LC 75-120265. (American Maritime Library: Vol. 2). (Illus.). xvii, 201p. 1984. pap. 21.95 (*0-913372-34-X*) Mystic Seaport.

Leavitt, Joy. Adventures of Huckleberry Finn: A Study Guide. (Novel-Ties Ser.). (YA). (gr. 10-12). 1983. 15.95 (*0-88122-020-5*) Lrn Links.

— Adventures of Tom Sawyer: A Study Guide. (Novel-Ties Ser.). (YA). (gr. 7-12). 1984. 15.95 (*0-88122-103-1*) Lrn Links.

— All Quiet on the Western Front: A Study Guide. (Novel-Ties Ser.). (J). 1983. student ed, teacher ed 15.95 (*0-88122-035-3*) Lrn Links.

— Catcher in the Rye: A Study Guide. (Novel-Ties Ser.). (gr. 7-12). 1985. student ed, teacher ed 15.95 (*0-88122-107-4*) Lrn Links.

— Death of a Salesman: A Study Guide. (Novel-Ties Ser.). (YA). (gr. 10-12). 1984. student ed, teacher ed 15.95 (*0-88122-113-9*) Lrn Links.

— The Red Pony: A Study Guide. (Novel-Ties Ser.). 1985. student ed, teacher ed 15.95 (*0-88122-125-2*) Lrn Links.

Leavitt, Judith A. American Women Managers & Administrators: A Selective Biographical Dictionary of Twentieth Century Leaders in Business, Education, & Government. LC 84-12814. xv, 317p. 1985. text ed. 69.50 (*0-313-23748-4*, LAO/, Greenwood Pr) Greenwood.

Leavitt, Judith A. & Wasserman, Paul. Women in Administration & Management: An Information Sourcebook. (Sourcebook Series in Business & Management: No. 7). 240p. 1988. 43.50 (*0-89774-379-2*) Oryx Pr.

Leavitt, Judith W. Brought to Bed: Childbearing in America, 1750-1950. (Illus.). 304p. 1988. pap. 11.95 (*0-19-505690-6*) OUP.

— The Healthiest City: Milwaukee & the Politics of Health Reform. LC 81-47932. (Illus.). 280p. 1982. 47.50 (*0-691-08298-7*) Princeton U Pr.

Leavitt, Judith W., ed. Women & Health in America. LC 83-40267. (Wisconsin Publications in the History of Science & Medicine: No. 4). (Illus.). 540p. 1984. text ed. 32.50 (*0-299-09640-8*); pap. 16.95 (*0-299-09644-0*) U of Wis Pr.

Leavitt, Judith W. & Numbers, Ronald L., eds. Sickness & Health in America: Readings in the History of Medicine & Public Health. LC 78-53288. (Illus.). 464p. 1978. 35.00 (*0-299-07620-2*); pap. 13.50 (*0-299-07624-5*) U of Wis Pr.

— Sickness & Health in America: Readings in the History of Medicine & Public Health. 2nd rev. ed. LC 85-40370. (Illus.). 560p. 1985. pap. text ed. 16.95 (*0-299-10274-2*) U of Wis Pr.

— Sickness & Health in America: Readings in the History of Medicine & Public Health. 2nd rev. ed. LC 85-40370. (Illus.). 548p. 1986. text ed. 32.50 (*0-299-10270-X*) U of Wis Pr.

Leavitt, Judith W., jt. auth. see Numbers, Ronald L.

Leavitt, June. The Flight to Seven Swan Bay. 1985. 10.95 (*0-87306-381-3*); pap. 8.95 (*0-87306-387-2*) Feldheim.

L

Leavitt, Lewis A. & Fox, Nathan A., eds. Psychological Effects of War & Violence on Children. 392p. 1993. text ed. 89.95 (*0-8058-1171-0*); pap. 34.50 (*0-8058-1172-9*) L Erlbaum Assocs.

Leavitt, Mel. Great Characters of New Orleans. LC 83-49199. (Illus.). 96p. (Orig.). 1984. pap. 9.95 (*0-938530-31-3*) Lexikos.

***Leavitt, Melvin.** Grena & the Magic Pomegranate. (Carolrhoda Picture Bks.). (Illus.). 32p. (J). (ps-3). 1994. lib. bdg. 18.95 (*0-87614-760-0*, First Ave Edns) Lerner Group.

***Leavitt, Melvin J.** A Snow Story. LC 94-21532. (Illus.). 1995. write for info. (*0-02-754633-0*, S&S Bks Young Read) S&S Childrens.

Leavitt, Michelle. Tarot of the Cloisters. 24p. 1993. 24.95 (*0-88079-665-0*) US Games Syst.

Leavitt, Mort, ed. see Giusi, Nadya.

Leavitt, Moses A. Handicapped Wage Earners As Studied by A Family Welfare Agency. Phillips, William R. & Rosenberg, Janet, eds. LC 79-6913. (Physically Handicapped in Society Ser.). 1980. reprint ed. lib. bdg. 15.95 (*0-405-13122-4*) Ayer.

Leavitt, Robert M., ed. see Chute, Robert M.

Leavitt, Robin L. Power & Emotion in Infant-Toddler Day Care. LC 93-28222. (Series in Early Childhood Education: Inquiry & Insights). 140p. (C). 1994. 49.50x (*0-7914-1885-5*); pap. 16.95x (*0-7914-1886-3*) State U NY Pr.

Leavitt, Robin L. & Eheart, Brenda K. Toddler Day Care: A Guide to Responsive Caregiving. 192p. (C). 1985. text ed. 19.95 (*0-669-09981-3*) Free Pr.

Leavitt, Ronnie L. Disability & Rehabilitation in Rural Jamaica: An Ethnographic Study. LC 90-56172. (Illus.). 256p. 1992. 39.50 (*0-685-54895-3*) Fairleigh Dickinson.

Leavitt, Ruby R. The Puerto Ricans: Culture Change & Language Deviance. LC 73-90914. (Viking Fund Publications in Anthropology: No. 51). 268p. 1974. pap. 11.95 (*0-8165-0457-1*) U of Ariz Pr.

Leavitt, Shelley E. Active Parenting: A Trainer's Manual. 150p. (Orig.). 1982. pap. 6.95 (*0-938510-02-9*, 81-001) Boys Town Pr.

Leavitt, Susan, ed. see Morgan, Ffiona.

Leavitt, Thomas D., jt. auth. see Schulz, James H.

Leavitt, W. W., ed. Cell & Molecular Biology of the Uterus. LC 88-5793. (Advances in Experimental Medicine & Biology Ser.: Vol. 230). (Illus.). 254p. 1988. 75.00 (*0-306-42836-9*, Plenum Pr) Plenum.

***Leavy, Barbara F.** In Search of the Swan Maiden: A Narrative on Folklore & Gender. 374p. 1995. pap. 18.95 (*0-8147-5100-8*) NYU Pr.

— To Blight with Plague: Studies in a Literary Theme. 300p. 1992. text ed. 50.00 (*0-8147-5059-1*); pap. text ed. 18.50 (*0-8147-5083-4*) NYU Pr.

Leavy, Brain & Wilson, David. Strategy & Leadership. LC 93-23853. 1993. write for info. (*0-415-07091-0*); pap. write for info. (*0-415-07092-9*) Routledge.

Leavy, John. MicroStation Reference Guide 5.X. 3rd ed. 290p. 1993. pap. 18.95 (*0-934605-95-5*, OnWord Pr) High Mtn.

Leavy, Margaret R. Looking for the Armenians: Eli Smith's Missionary Adventure, 1830-1831. (Transactions Ser.: Vol. 50, Pt. 4). (Illus.). 84p. 1992. pap. 16.00 (*1-878508-07-5*) CT Acad Arts & Sciences.

Leavy, Stanley A. In the Image of God: A Psychoanalyst's View. LC 87-36770. (C). 1988. 20.00 (*0-300-04130-6*) Yale U Pr.

— The Psychoanalytic Dialogue. LC 79-21796. 141p. 1987. pap. 12.00 (*0-300-04037-7*, Y-683) Yale U Pr.

Leavy, Una. Harry's Stormy Night. LC 94-12772. (Illus.). (J). (gr. 3 up). 1995. text ed. 15.95 (*0-689-50625-2*, McElderry) S&S Childrens.

Leax, John. Grace Is Where I Live: Writing As a Christian Vocation. (Raven's Ridge Imprint Ser.). 160p. 1993. 12.99 (*0-8010-5685-3*) Baker Bk.

— 120 Significant Things Men Should Know...but Never Ask About. (Fingertip Books). 96p. (Orig.). 1995. mass mkt. 4.99 (*0-8010-5694-2*) Baker Bk.

***Leazer, Gary.** Fundamentalism & Freemasonry: The Southern Baptist Investigation of the Fraternal Order. LC 94-49038. 1995. 19.95 (*0-87131-775-3*) M Evans.

Leazes, Francis J., Jr. Accountability & the Business State: The Structure of Federal Corporation. LC 86-25244. 160p. 1987. text ed. 55.00 (*0-275-92495-5*, C2495, Praeger Pubs) Greenwood.

Leb, G., ed. see Passath, A. & Hoefler, H.

Leba, John K., et al. The Vietnamese Entrepreneurs in the U. S. A. The First Decade. 276p. 1985. 14.50 (*0-936675-00-4*) Zieleks Co.

Lebacqz, Karen. Six Theories of Justice: Perspectives from Philosophical & Theological Ethics. LC 86-26457. 160p. (Orig.). (C). 1986. pap. 14.99 (*0-8066-2245-8*, 10-5820, Augsburg) Augsburg Fortress.

Lebacqz, Karen & Barton, Ronald. Sex in the Parish. 256p. (Orig.). 1991. pap. 14.99 (*0-664-25087-4*) Westminster John Knox.

Lebaigue, Charles. Dictionnaire Latin-Francais. 1382p. (FRE & LAT.). 59.95 (*0-7859-0744-0*, M-6340) Fr & Eur.

Leban, Roy. FullWrite Professional Advanced Text. 1989. pap. 24.95 (*0-13-331919-9*) P-H.

Lebano, Edoardo A. Italian: A Self-Teaching Guide. LC 87-17311. 282p. 1988. pap. text ed. 14.95 (*0-471-01143-6*); audio 12.95 (*0-471-63838-2*) Wiley.

Lebano, Edoardo A. & Baldini, Pier R. Buon Giorno a Tutti: First Year Italian. 2nd ed. 1989. Net. student ed write for info. (*0-471-63128-0*); Net. text ed. write for info. (*0-471-63129-9*); Net. audio write for info. (*0-471-50250-2*) Wiley.

LeBar, Frank M., ed. Ethnic Groups of Insular Southeast Asia Vol. 1: Indonesia. LC 72-90940. (Area & Country Surveys Ser.). 244p. 1972. 30.00x (*0-87536-403-9*) HRAFP.

— Ethnic Groups of Insular Southeast Asia Vol. 2: Philippines & Formosa. LC 74-19513. (Area & Country Surveys Ser.). 200p. 1975. 30.00x (*0-87536-405-5*) HRAFP.

LeBar, Frank M. & Suddard, Adrienne, eds. Laos. LC 60-7381. (Area & Country Surveys Ser.). 312p. 1967. 20.00x (*0-87536-915-4*) HRAFP.

LeBar, Frank M., et al. Ethnic Groups of Mainland Southeast Asia. LC 64-25414. 302p. reprint ed. 86.10 (*0-685-07748-9*, 2019258) Bks Demand.

LeBar, James J. Cults, Sects, & the New Age. LC 88-63530. (Orig.). 1989. pap. 7.95 (*0-87973-431-0*, 431) Our Sunday Visitor.

LeBar, John, jt. auth. see Eddy, Ruth.

Lebar, Lois & Berg, Miguel. Llamados a Ensenar. Blanch, Jose M., tr. LC 77-5183. (Illus.). 160p. (SPA.). 1970. pap. 4.95 (*0-89922-006-1*) Edit Caribe.

***LeBar, Lois E. & Plueddemann, James E.** Education That Is Christian. 324p. (Orig.). (C). 1995. pap. 13.99 (*1-56476-412-5*, Victor Books) SP Pubns.

LeBard, Meredith, jt. auth. see Friedman, George.

LeBaron, Anthony. Chamber Music. (Illus.). 48p. 1988. 9.95 (*0-921254-04-0*, Pub. by Penumbra Pr CN) U of Toronto Pr.

LeBaron, E. Dale. All Are Alike unto God. 9.95 (*0-88494-738-6*) Bookcraft Inc.

LeBaron, Gaye & Mitchell, Joann. Santa Rosa, a Twentieth Century Town, Vol. II. LC 93-79227. (Illus.). 352p. 1993. 59.95 (*0-9615010-2-2*) Historia Ltd.

LeBaron, Gaye, et al. Santa Rosa, a Nineteenth Century Town. LC 86-109023. (Illus.). 224p. 1992. reprint ed. pap. 24.95 (*0-9615010-1-4*) Historia Ltd.

LeBaron, Homer M., et al, eds. Biotechnology in Agricultural Chemistry. LC 87-1803. (Symposium Ser.: No. 334). (Illus.). xxii, 354p. 1987. 71.95 (*0-8412-1019-5*) Am Chemical.

***LeBaron, Jeff.** Shed Antler Records of North American Big Game: A Record Book for the Recognition of North America's Big Game Shed Antlers. Falck, Sandi, ed. 210p. 1994. text ed. 29.95 (*0-9644514-4-1*) NAm Shed Hunt.

LeBaron, John. Making Television: A Video Production Guide for Teachers. LC 81-703. (Illus.). 352p. (Orig.). reprint ed. pap. 100.40 (*0-7837-0989-7*, 2041295) Bks Demand.

LeBaron, Melvin J. Workable Workplace: Excellence at Work for You. LC 87-83597. 200p. (C). 1988. text ed. 18.95 (*0-944329-01-2*) Et Cetera.

LeBaron, Melvin J., jt. auth. see Graham, Morris A.

LeBaron, Samuel, jt. auth. see Hilgard, Josephine R.

LeBarz, P. & Hervier, Y., eds. Enumerative Geometry & Classical Algebra. (Progress in Mathematics Ser.: Vol. 24). 246p. 1982. text ed. 42.00 (*0-8176-3106-2*) Birkhauser.

Lebas, Elizabeth, jt. ed. see Harloe, Michael.

Lebauer, Roni S. Learn to Listen; Listen to Learn. (Illus.). 256p. (C). 1988. pap. text ed. 19.95 (*0-13-527128-2*) P-H.

Lebauer, Roni S. & Scarcella, Robin. Reactions: Multi-Cultural Reading Based Writing Modules. 384p. 1992. pap. text ed. 18.95 (*0-13-756214-4*) P-H.

Lebay, Charles, jt. auth. see Gnann, Pearl R.

Lebbad, M. J. The Intelligent Buyer's Guide to New & Used Vehicles. (Illus.). 64p. (Orig.). 1990. pap. 1.25 (*0-9627718-0-5*) M J Lebbad.

Lebeau, Andre, jt. auth. see Salomon, Jean-Jacques.

Lebeau, Caroline. Fabrics. LC 94-2604. 1994. 55.00 (*0-517-57434-9*, C P Pubs) Crown Pub Group.

LeBeau, Charles & Lucas, David W. Technical Traders Guide to Computer Analysis of the Futures Market. 312p. 1991. text ed. 70.00 (*1-55623-468-6*) Irwin Prof Pubng.

LeBeau, Chris. The Healthy Heart Cookbook. LC 90-71663. (Illus.). xii, 310p. (Orig.). 1991. 19.95 (*0-934955-19-0*) Watercress Pr.

Lebeau, Michael, jt. auth. see Cameron-Bandler, Leslie.

LeBeau, Roy. Bolt Action-Trigger Guard, 2 vols. in 1. (Double Buckskin Ser.). 400p. 1989. pap. 3.95 (*0-8439-2872-7*) Dorchester Pub Co.

— Buckskin No. 10: Bolt-Action. 208p. (Orig.). 1986. pap. 2.50 (*0-8439-2315-6*) Dorchester Pub Co.

— Buckskin No. 11: Trigger Guard. 192p. 1986. pap. 2.50 (*0-8439-2336-9*) Dorchester Pub Co.

— Buckskin No. 6: Trigger Spring. 240p. (Orig.). 1985. pap. 2.50 (*0-8439-2229-X*) Dorchester Pub Co.

— Buckskin No. 7: Cartridge Coast. 240p. (Orig.). 1985. pap. 2.50 (*0-8439-2252-4*) Dorchester Pub Co.

— Buckskin No. 8: Hangfire Hill. 208p. (Orig.). 1985. pap. 2.50 (*0-8439-2271-0*) Dorchester Pub Co.

— Colt Creek. (Buckskin Ser.: No. 4). 240p. (Orig.). 1984. pap. 2.75 (*0-8439-2168-4*) Dorchester Pub Co.

— Gunsight Gap. (Buckskin Ser.: No. 5). 240p. (Orig.). 1985. pap. 2.75 (*0-8439-2189-7*) Dorchester Pub Co.

— Gunstock. (Buckskin Ser.). 240p. 1984. pap. 2.50 (*0-8439-2088-2*) Dorchester Pub Co.

— Pistoltown. (Buckskin Ser.: No. 3). 240p. (Orig.). 1984. pap. 2.75 (*0-8439-2126-9*) Dorchester Pub Co.

— Recoil. (Buckskin Ser.: No. 12). 208p. (Orig.). 1986. pap. 2.50 (*0-8439-2355-5*) Dorchester Pub Co.

— Rifle River. (Buckskin Ser.: No. 1). 240p. (Orig.). 1984. pap. 2.50 (*0-8439-2066-1*) Dorchester Pub Co.

Lebeau, T. K. The Crystal Skull: Destiny's Courier. (Orig.). 1988. pap. 8.95 (*0-945680-00-7*) Harmony AZ.

— The Crystal Tunnel. 188p. (Orig.). 1989. pap. 9.95 (*0-945680-01-5*) Harmony AZ.

Lebeau, Vicky. Lost Angels: Psychoanalysis & Cinema. LC 94-11706. 168p. 1994. 49.95x (*0-415-10720-2*, B4791, Routledge NY) Routledge.

— Lost Angels: Psychoanalysis & Cinema. 1995. pap. write for info. (*0-415-10721-0*, B4795) Routledge.

***Lebeaupin, R. V.** Photographies. 1995. pap. 34.95 (*3-86187-024-X*) InBook.

Lebeaux, Charles N., jt. auth. see Wilensky, Harold L.

Lebeaux, M. O., jt. auth. see Jambu, Michel.

Lebeaux, Richard. Thoreau's Seasons. LC 83-17982. 432p. 1984. 37.50 (*0-87023-401-3*); pap. 18.95 (*0-87023-686-5*) U of Mass Pr.

— Young Man Thoreau. LC 76-44851. 272p. (C). 1989. reprint ed. pap. text ed. 16.95 (*0-87023-687-3*) U of Mass Pr.

Lebeck, A. O., jt. auth. see Brown, Franklin L.

Lebeck, Alan O. Principles & Design of Mechanical Face Seals. 800p. 1991. text ed. 165.00 (*0-471-51533-7*) Wiley.

Lebedeff, Herasim. A Grammar of the Pure & Mixed East Indian Dialects. (C). 1988. 21.00 (*0-8364-2373-9*, Pub. by Firma KLM) S Asia.

Lebedev, A. Soviet Painting in the Tretyakov Gallery. 136p. 1976. 50.00 (*0-569-08318-4*, Pub. by Collets UK) St Mut.

Lebedev, A. N., ed. The Climate of Africa: Air Temperature & Precipitation. 488p. 1970. text ed. 110.00 (*0-7065-0733-9*, Pub. by Keter Pub IS) Coronet Bks.

Lebedev, A. V. & Antonevich, A. B. Functional Differential Equations: C - Theory. LC 92-26873. (Pitman Monographs & Surveys in Pure & Applied Mathematics). 1993. write for info. (*0-582-07251-4*) Longman.

Lebedev, Andrei, jt. auth. see Antonevich, Anatolij.

Lebedev, K. A. Russian-Pashto-Dari Dictionary. 768p. (PUS & RUS.). 1983. 59.95 (*0-8288-1738-3*, F 47690) Fr & Eur.

Lebedev, K. A., et al. Immunology Reviews: Immune Monitoring: Its Principles & Application in Natural & Model Clinical Systems, Vol. 2. Petrov, R. V., ed. (Soviet Medical Reviews Ser.: Vol. 2, Pt. 1). x, 124p. 1989. pap. text ed. 95.00 (*3-7186-4922-5*) Gordon & Breach.

Lebedev, N. N. Special Functions & Their Applications. rev. ed. Silverman, Richard A., tr. LC 72-86228. 320p. 1972. reprint ed. pap. 7.95 (*0-486-60624-4*) Dover.

Lebedev, N. N., et al. Worked Problems in Applied Mathematics. LC 78-67857. 1979. pap. text ed. 8.50 (*0-486-63730-1*) Dover.

Lebedev, P. N. & Skalskaya, I. Problems in Mathematical Physics. LC 65-14785. (International Series Mono on Pure & Applied Mathematics: Vol. 84). 1966. 170.00 (*0-08-011134-3*, Pub. by Pergamon Repr UK) Franklin.

Lebedev, P. N., jt. ed. see Feinberg, E. L.

Lebedev, P. N., jt. auth. see Ginzburg, V. L.

Lebedev, V. I., jt. auth. see Marchuk, Gurii I.

Lebedev, V. L. Random Processes in Electrical & Mechanical Systems. 128p. 1961. text ed. 34.50 (*0-7065-0121-7*, Pub. by Keter Pub IS) Coronet Bks.

Lebedev, V. V., jt. auth. see Kats, Efim I.

Lebedeva, V. Boris Kustodiev. (Illus.). 212p. (C). 1981. text ed. 150.00 (*0-685-40275-4*, Pub. by Collets) St Mut.

— Kustodiev, Boris. 212p. (C). 1981. 133.00 (*0-685-34437-1*, Pub. by Collets) St Mut.

Lebedeva, Victoria. Boris Kustodiev: The Artist & His Work. (Illus.). 212p. 1981. 132.00 (*0-317-57292-X*, Pub. by Collets UK) St Mut.

Lebel, Gerard, jt. auth. see Falcrest, Thomas J.

Lebel, Gerard, jt. auth. see Laforest, Thomas J.

Lebel, Marc, tr. see Bessette, Gerard.

LeBel, Paul A. John Barleycorn Must Pay: Compensating the Victims of Drinking Drivers. 360p. 1992. 39.95 (*0-252-01792-7*) U of Ill Pr.

LeBel, Phillip. Economic Choices for Sustainable Agriculture in Africa. 97p. 1988. pap. 7.00 (*0-944572-01-4*) MSU Ctr Econ Res Africa.

— Energy Economics & Technology. LC 82-15183. 576p. (C). 1982. pap. text ed. 22.95 (*0-8018-2773-6*) Johns Hopkins.

— Promoting Human Resource Development in Africa. (Illus.). 104p. (Orig.). 1993. pap. 9.50 (*0-944572-06-5*) MSU Ctr Econ Res Africa.

LeBel, Phillip, ed. Europe, Africa, & the U. S. Nineteen Ninety-Two. 110p. (Orig.). 1990. pap. 8.50 (*0-944572-03-0*) MSU Ctr Econ Res Africa.

LeBel, Phillip, ed. & intro. Managing Africa's Economic Recovery. 72p. 1987. pap. 7.00 (*0-944572-00-6*) MSU Ctr Econ Res Africa.

LeBel, Phillip, ed. New Initiatives for Africa's Debt. 104p. (Orig.). 1989. pap. 9.00 (*0-944572-02-2*) MSU Ctr Econ Res Africa.

— Privatization Strategies in Africa. 108p. (Orig.). 1992. pap. 9.00 (*0-944572-05-7*) MSU Ctr Econ Res Africa.

LeBel, Phillip, intro. Environmental Policies for Sustainable Growth in Africa. 101p. (Orig.). 1991. pap. 9.00 (*0-944572-04-9*) MSU Ctr Econ Res Africa.

LeBell, Gene. Grappling Master: Combat for Street Defense & Competition. Pimenta, Wendy, ed. LC 91-90363. (Illus.). 160p. (Orig.). 1992. pap. 14.95 (*0-9615126-2-8*) Pro Action Pub.

LeBell, Judo G. Pro-Wrestling Finishing Holds. LC 85-61959. (Illus.). 160p. (Orig.). 1985. pap. 10.95 (*0-9615126-0-1*) Pro Action Pub.

Lebell, Sharon, ed. see Epictetus.

Lebelson, Harry & Rush, Bette. Ovni, Toda la Verdad: Coleccion Almanaque Mundial. Roman, Carlos, ed. Quintana, Francisco, tr. (Illus.). 224p. (SPA.). 1993. pap. 3.95 (*1-56259-027-8*) Editorial Amer.

Leben, Joe, jt. auth. see Martin, James.

Leben, Ulrich. Ebeniste, Bernard Molitor: The Ancient Regime to the Bourbon Restoration, with a Complete Catalog of the Furniture. (Illus.). 352p. 1992. 145.00 (*0-85667-407-9*) Sothebys Pubns.

Leben, William R., jt. auth. see Denning, Keith.

Leben, William R., et al. Hausar yau Da Kullum: Intermediate & Advanced Lessons in Hausa Language & Culture. LC 91-3933. (Illus.). 153p. (Orig.). (C). 1991. student ed 7.50 (*0-937073-69-5*); pap. text ed. 19.95 (*0-937073-68-7*) Ctr Study Language.

Lebensart, Charlotte, tr. see Pelikan, Wilhelm.

Lebenson, Richard & Creighton, Kathleen. RSVP: The Directory of Illustration & Design. (Illus.). 320p. (Orig.). 1992. pap. 21.00 (*1-878118-01-3*) RSVP NY.

Lebenson, Richard & Creighton, Kathleen, eds. RSVP, No. 19: The Directory of Illustration & Design. (Illus.). 304p. 1994. pap. 21.00 (*1-878118-03-X*) RSVP NY.

— RSVP Twenty: The Directory of Illustration & Design. 320p. 1995. pap. 24.00 (*1-878118-04-8*) RSVP NY.

— RSVP16: The Directory of Illustration & Design. (Illus.). 320p. (Orig.). 1991. pap. 20.00 (*1-878118-00-5*) RSVP NY.

— RSVP18: The Directory of Illustration & Design. (Directory of Illustration & Design Ser.). (Illus.). 304p. 1993. pap. 21.00 (*1-878118-02-1*) RSVP NY.

***Lebensztejn, Jean-Claude.** Recent American Art. LC 94-42314. Date not set. lib. bdg. 40.00 (*0-226-46996-4*); pap. text ed. 17.95 (*0-226-46997-2*) U Ch Pr.

Lebenthal, Emanuel. Human Gastrointestinal Development. 841p. 1989. 165.50 (*0-88167-521-0*) Raven.

— Textbook of Gastroenterology & Nutrition in Infancy. 2nd ed. 1406p. 1989. 199.00 (*0-88167-522-9*) Raven.

Lebenthal, Emanuel, ed. Total Parenteral Nutrition: Indications, Utilization, Complications, & Pathophysiological Considerations. (Illus.). 528p. 1986. text ed. 142.50 (*0-88167-136-3*) Raven.

Lebenthal, Emanuel & Duffey, Michael E. Textbook of Secretory Diarrhea. 464p. 1990. 129.00 (*0-88167-666-7*, 2125) Raven.

Lebeque, A., jt. auth. see Kaibel, G.

Leber, et al. Handbook of Over-the-Counter Drugs. 464p. (Orig.). 1994. pap. 14.95 (*0-89087-734-3*) Celestial Arts.

— Handbook of Over-the-Counter Drugs & Pharmacy Products. 1992. 22.95 (*1-878060-01-5*) Mosby Yr Bk.

Leber, Annedore. Conscience in Revolt: Sixty-Four Stories of Resistance in Germany, 1933-1945. (C). 1994. reprint ed. pap. text ed. 26.50 (*0-8133-2185-9*) Westview.

Leber, Manfred. Vom Modernen Roman zur Antiken Tragodie: Interpretation von Max Frischs "HomoFaber" (Quellen und Forschungen zur Sprach und Kulturgeschichte der Germanischen Voelker Ser.). xii, 201p. (C). 1990. lib. bdg. 80.00 (*3-11-012240-5*) De Gruyter.

***Leber, Michael & Sandling, Judy.** L. S. Lowry. (Illus.). 144p. (C). 1995. pap. 19.95 (*0-7148-3244-8*, Pub. by Phaidon Press UK) Chronicle Bks.

Leber, William R., jt. ed. see Beckham, Edward E.

Leberge, Albert. Bitter Bread. Dion, Conrad, tr. LC 78-305999. (French Writers of Canada Ser.). 128p. reprint ed. pap. 36.50 (*0-8357-7281-0*, 2026119) Bks Demand.

Lebergott, Stanley. The American Economy: Income, Wealth, & Want. LC 75-4661. 364p. 1975. 60.00x (*0-691-04210-1*) Princeton U Pr.

— The American Economy: Income, Wealth, & Want. LC 75-4461. reprint ed. pap. 111.50 (*0-7837-9371-5*, 2060115) Bks Demand.

— The Americans: An Economic Record. 526p. (C). 1984. pap. text ed. 14.95 (*0-393-95311-4*) Norton.

— Consumer Expenditures: New Measures & Old Motives. LC 95-2852. 1995. write for info. (*0-691-04321-3*) Princeton U Pr.

— Pursuing Happiness: American Consumers in the Twentieth Century. LC 92-40491. 1993. 26.95 (*0-691-04322-1*) Princeton U Pr.

— Wealth & Want. LC 75-4460. 188p. 1975. 39.50x (*0-691-04211-X*) Princeton U Pr.

— Wealth & Want. LC 75-4460. 229p. reprint ed. pap. 65.30 (*0-7837-6773-0*, 2046603) Bks Demand.

Leberl, Franz W. Radargrammetric Image Processing. (Remote Sensing Library). (Illus.). 595p. 1989. text ed. 88.00 (*0-89006-273-0*) Artech Hse.

Leberman, Robert C. The Birds of the Ligonier Valley. (Special Publication CMNH Ser.: No. 3). (Illus.). 77p. (Orig.). 1976. pap. 6.00 (*0-911239-07-3*) Carnegie Mus.

— Birds of Western Pennsylvania & Adjacent Regions. (Special Publication CMNH Ser.: No. 13). 52p. 1988. pap. 6.00 (*0-911239-29-4*) Carnegie Mus.

LeBert, Joseph J. CICS for Microcomputers. 384p. 1989. pap. text ed. 32.95 (*0-07-036968-2*) McGraw.

***LeBert, Margo A.** Life in Christ. (Breaking Open the Catechism of the Catholic Church for Small Groups Ser.). 48p. (C). 1995. pap. 3.95 (*0-8091-9445-7*) Paulist Pr.

Lebesgue, Henri. Lecons sur L'integration et la Recherche des Fonctions Primitives. 3rd ed. LC 73-921. 340p. (FRE.). (gr. 12 up). 1973. text ed. 24.95 (*0-8284-0267-1*) Chelsea Pub.

Lebet, Philip E. & Perry, David J. Vocabula Et Sermones - Basic Vocabulary & Sample Conversations. 25p. (LAT.). (YA). (gr. 6-12). 1991. spiral bd. 1.70 (*0-939507-19-6*, B4) Amer Classical.

***Lebeyka, Jan, illus.** Elmo under the Sea. (Magic Window Bks.). 9p. (J). (ps). 1995. 6.99 (*0-679-85313-8*) Random Bks Yng Read.

LeBihan, Jill, jt. auth. see Green, Keith.

Leblanc. The OAS & the Promotion & Protection of Human Rights. 1977. pap. text ed. 65.50 (*90-247-1943-7*) Kluwer Ac.

Leblanc, A. Anatomy & Imaging of the Cranial Nerves: Investigative Technique for the Imaging by Magnetic Resonance Imaging (MRI) & Computed Tomography (CT) (Illus.). xv, 277p. 1992. 248.00 (*0-387-18240-3*) Spr-Verlag.

An Asterisk (*) at the beginning of an entry indicates that the title is appearing in BIP for the first time.

***LeBlanc, Andre.** The Cranial Nerves: Anatomy, Imaging, Vascularisation. 2nd enl. rev. ed. Le Vay, David, tr. LC 95-8410. Orig. Title: Anatomy & Imaging of the Cranial Nerves. (Illus.). 1995. write for info. (0-387-58702-0) Spr-Verlag.

***LeBlanc, D.** The Acadian Miracle. 1966. 13.95 (0-614-06315-9) Claitors.

***LeBlanc, Dee-Ann & LeBlanc, Robert.** Using Eudora. (Illus.). 384p. (Orig.). 1995. pap. text ed. 19.99 (0-7897-0178-2) Que.

Leblanc, Donna. You Can't Quit Until You Know What's Eating You: Overcoming Compulsive Eating. 1990. pap. 7.95 (1-55874-103-8) Health Comm.

LeBlanc, Elaine P., jt. auth. see Fredericks, Anthony D.

Leblanc, Georgette. Souvenirs, Eighteen Ninety-Five to Nineteen Eighteen: My Life with Maeterlinck. Flanner, Janet, tr. LC 76-22154. (Music Reprint Ser.). 352p. 1976. reprint ed. lib. bdg. 39.50 (0-306-70841-8) Da Capo.

Leblanc, Gerald, tr. see Villemaire, Yolande.

Leblanc, Hugues & Wisdom, William. Deductive Logic. 3rd ed. LC 92-26701. 480p. 1993. text ed. write for info. (0-13-203852-8) P-H.

LeBlanc, Hugues, et al. Essays in Epistemology & Semantics. LC 83-83298. (Language, Logic & Linguistics Ser.). 300p. 1983. pap. 24.00 (0-930586-16-6) Haven Pubns.

LeBlanc, J. Dudley. The Acadian Miracle. 1966. write for info. (0-685-27202-8) Claitors.

LeBlanc, J. G. & Williams, W. G. The Operative & Post-Operative Management of Congenital Heart Defects. LC 92-14879. (Illus.). 448p. 1993. 97.00 (0-87993-535-9) Futura Pub.

LeBlanc, Jerry. Java & Bali. (Insider's Guides Ser.). (Illus.). 200p. (Orig.). 1992. pap. 14.95 (0-7818-0037-4) Hippocrene Bks.

Leblanc, John F., et al. Mathematics-Methods Program: Graphs, the Picturing of Information. (Mathematics Ser.). (Illus.). 160p. (C). 1976. pap. text ed. write for info. (0-201-14622-3); write for info. (0-201-14623-1) Addison-Wesley.

— Mathematics-Methods Program: Number Theory. (Mathematics Ser.). (Illus.). 128p. (C). 1976. pap. text ed. write for info. (0-201-14624-X) Addison-Wesley.

LeBlanc, John F., et al. Mathematics Methods Program: Rational Numbers with Integers & Reals. (Mathematics Ser.). (Illus.). 240p. 1976. pap. text ed. write for info. (0-201-14612-6); write for info. (0-201-14613-4) Addison-Wesley.

LeBlanc, Joyce Y. Pelican Guide to Gardens of Louisiana. 2nd ed. (Pelican Guide Ser.). (Illus.). 80p. 1989. reprint ed. pap. 7.95 (0-88289-729-2) Pelican.

LeBlanc, Judy, ed. see Shazryl, Eskay & Hanks, Jarrod.

LeBlanc, Judy A. Things My Father Never Taught Me. 1994. 12.95 (0-533-10817-9) Vantage.

LeBlanc, Kathleen B. & De Gale, Sylvia R. Career Development Workbook. 96p. 1991. per. 11.95 (0-8403-7188-8) Kendall-Hunt.

LeBlanc, Lawrence J. The Convention on the Rights of the Child. LC 94-11887. (Human Rights in International Perspective Ser.: Vol. 3). xvi, 338p. 1995. text ed. 45.00 (0-8032-2909-7) U of Nebr Pr.

— The United States & the Genocide Convention. LC 90-45572. 303p. 1991. text ed. 41.95 (0-8223-1109-7) Duke.

LeBlanc, Leslie, jt. auth. see Moscato, Michael.

Leblanc, Liz. Cheap Entertainment. 1986. pap. 5.00 (0-941240-04-5) Ommation Pr.

LeBlanc, Liz. No Mean Feet. (Dialogues on Dance Ser.: No. 4). 13p. 1985. pap. 4.00 (0-941240-01-0) Ommation Pr.

***Leblanc, Louise.** Maddie Goes to Paris. (First Novels Ser.). (Illus.). 64p. (J). (gr. 1-4). 1995. pap. 4.95 (0-88780-278-8); bds. 14.95 (0-88780-279-6) Formac Dist Ltd.

— Maddie in Danger. (First Novels Ser.). (Illus.). 64p. (J). (gr. 1-4). 1995. pap. 4.95 (0-88780-306-7); bds. 14.95 (0-88780-307-5) Formac Dist Ltd.

— Maddie in Goal. (First Novels Ser.). (Illus.). 64p. (J). (gr. 1-4). 1995. pap. 4.95 (0-88780-202-8); bds. 14.95 (0-88780-203-6) Formac Dist Ltd.

— Maddie Wants Music. (First Novels Ser.). (Illus.). 64p. (J). (gr. 1-4). 1995. pap. 4.95 (0-88780-219-2); bds. 14.95 (0-88780-220-6) Formac Dist Ltd.

— That's Enough, Maddie! (First Novels Ser.). (Illus.). 64p. (J). (gr. 1-4). 1995. pap. 4.95 (0-88780-090-4); bds. 14.95 (0-88780-091-2) Formac Dist Ltd.

— Ya Basta, Sofia. (Illus.). 60p. (SPA.). (YA). (gr. 5 up). 1994. pap. 5.95 (958-07-0080-X) Firefly Bks Ltd.

LeBlanc, Maurice. The Confessions of Arsene Lupin. 327p. 1980. reprint ed. lib. bdg. 15.50 (0-89968-202-2, Lghtyr Pr) Buccaneer Bks.

— The Crystal Stopper. 287p. 1980. reprint ed. lib. bdg. 14.25 (0-89968-201-4, Lghtyr Pr) Buccaneer Bks.

Leblanc, Maurice. The Exploits of Arsene Lupin. De Mattos, Alexander T., tr. LC 75-32758. (Literature of Mystery & Detection Ser.). 1976. reprint ed. 26.95 (0-405-07881-1) Ayer.

LeBlanc, Maurice. The Extraordinary Adventures of Arsene Lupin: Gentleman Burglar. 16.95 (0-89190-091-8, Am Repr) Amereon Ltd.

Leblanc, Maurice. The Extraordinary Adventures of Arsene Lupin, Gentleman-Burglar. LC 77-74106. 1977. reprint ed. pap. 4.95 (0-486-23508-4) Dover.

— Extraordinary Adventures of Arsene Lupin, Gentleman-Burgler. Morehead, George, tr. LC 76-163040. (Short Story Index Reprint Ser.). 1977. reprint ed. 19.95 (0-8369-3954-9) Ayer.

LeBlanc, Maurice. The Hollow Needle. 325p. 1980. reprint ed. lib. bdg. 15.50 (0-89968-203-0, Lghtyr Pr) Buccaneer Bks.

— Teeth of the Tiger. 490p. 1980. reprint ed. lib. bdg. 17.95 (0-89968-204-9, Lghtyr Pr) Buccaneer Bks.

LeBlanc, Paul, jt. ed. see Hawisher, Gail.

LeBlanc, Paul J. Writing Teachers Writing Software: Creating Our Place in the Electronic Age. (Advances in Computer & Composition Studies). (Illus.). 188p. 1993. pap. 24.95 (0-8141-5911-7) NCTE.

Leblanc, R. Gold Leaf Techniques. 3rd ed. LC 85-63630. (Illus.). 162p. 1992. reprint ed. 32.95 (0-911380-71-X) ST Pubns.

LeBlanc, Richard, jt. auth. see Fischer, Charles.

LeBlanc, Robert, jt. auth. see LeBlanc, Dee-Ann.

LeBlanc, Ronald D. The Russianization of Gil Blas: A Study in Literary Appropriation. 292p. (Orig.). 1986. pap. 18.95 (0-89357-159-8) Slavica.

LeBlanc, Steven, jt. auth. see Folger, H.

LeBlanc, Steven, jt. auth. see Watson, Patty J.

LeBlanc, Sydney, jt. auth. see Fahy, Charles L.

LeBlanc, Thomas. The General Radio-Telephone Operator's License Study Guide. 2nd ed. (Illus.). 230p. 1990. 23.95 (0-8306-9518-4, 3118); pap. 16.95 (0-8306-3118-6, 3118) TAB Bks.

— General Radiotelephone Operator's License Study Guide. 3rd ed. 344p. 1992. 27.95 (0-8306-3555-6, 4075); pap. 17.95 (0-8306-3554-8, 4075) TAB Bks.

— General Radiotelephone Operator's License Study Guide. 4th ed. LC 94-37458. 1995. text ed. 29.95 (0-07-036936-4); pap. text ed. 18.95 (0-07-036937-2) TAB Bks.

***LeBlanc, Yvonne.** Va Lettre Va: The French Verse Epistle (1400-1550) LC 94-74076. 268p. 1995. lib. bdg. 41.95 (1-883479-04-5) Summa Pubns.

Leblang, Bonnie T. & Hayes, Joanne L. Rice: Eighty-Five Irrestible Recipes from Risotto to Rifsstafel. 128p. 1991. 14.00 (0-517-57694-5, Harmony) Crown Pub Group.

Leblang, Bonnie T., jt. auth. see Hayes, Joanne L.

LeBlang, Theodore R., et al. Law of Medical Practice in Illinois. LC 86-83023. 1986. 110.00 (0-317-03805-2) Lawyers Cooperative.

— Law of Medical Practice in Illinois. suppl. ed. LC 86-83023. 1993. Suppl. 1993. 59.95 (0-317-03806-0) Lawyers Cooperative.

Leble, S. B. Nonlinear Waves in Waveguides: With Stratification. (Research Reports in Physics). (Illus.). ix, 163p. 1991. pap. 69.00 (0-387-52149-6) Spr-Verlag.

Leblebici, Yusuf & Kang, Sung-Mo. Hot-Carrier Reliability of MOS VLSI Circuits. LC 93-15447. (International Series in Engineering & Computer Science, VLSI, Computer Architecture, & Digital Screen Processing: Vol. 227). 240p. (C). 1993. lib. bdg. 99.50 (0-7923-9352-X) Kluwer Ac.

Lebleu, Bernard, jt. ed. see Crooke, Stanley T.

Lebling, Robert W., Jr., ed. Gas Daily's Natural Gas Marketing Pipeline Guide. 900p. 1990. reprint ed. 567.00 (0-935453-35-0) Pasha Pubns.

Leblon, Jean M., ed. see Perec, Georges.

Leblon, Jean M., tr. see Zola, Emile.

LeBlond, Bill, ed. see Ashley, Beth & Lauritzen, Hal.

LeBlond, Bill, ed. see Cabarga, Leslie.

LeBlond, Bill, ed. see Croce, Julia Della.

LeBlond, Bill, ed. see Della Croce, Julia.

LeBlond, Bill, ed. see Erbe, Maureen, et al.

LeBlond, Bill, ed. see Hosler, Ray.

LeBlond, Bill, ed. see Kagel, Katherine.

LeBlond, Bill, ed. see Marks, Copeland & Kim, Manjo.

LeBlond, Bill, ed. see Martin, Don & Martin, Betty.

LeBlond, Bill, ed. see Pappas, Lou S.

LeBlond, Bill, ed. see Perry, Sara.

Leblond, C. P., jt. auth. see Begg, R. W.

LeBlond, Donald E. Thousand Year Gamble, the World Awaits. LC 89-81711. 1991. pap. 8.95 (0-8158-0457-1) Chris Mass.

LeBlond, Geoffrey T. Using Unix System V Release 3. 1990. pap. text ed. 27.95 (0-07-881556-8) Osborne-McGraw.

Leblond, Geoffrey T. Windows 3.1 Power Tools. 2nd ed. 1992. pap. 49.95 (0-679-79075-6) Random.

Leblond, Gerard F. The Hip-Pocket Guide to Basic Drum Beats. LC 82-70339. 60p. 1982. pap. 4.95 (0-942836-00-6) West Gate Pr.

LeBlond Group. PC Magazine Guide to Using Quattro Pro 3.0. (Guide to...Ser.). (Illus.). 1040p. (Orig.). 1991. pap. 27.95 (1-56276-003-3) Ziff-Davis.

Leblond Group Staff. Friendly DOS. 1993. pap. 5.99 (0-679-79186-8) Random.

LeBlond Group Staff. Friendly DOS 6.0. 1993. pap. 6.99 (0-679-79190-6) Random.

Leblond Group Staff. Friendly Quicken for Windows. 1993. pap. 5.99 (0-679-79188-4) Random.

— PC Magazine Guide to Quattro Pro for Windows. (Guide to...Ser.). (Illus.). 1221p. (Orig.). 1992. pap. 27.95 (1-56276-044-0) Ziff-Davis.

— PC Magazine Guide to Using Quattro Pro 3.0-4.0. (Guide to...Ser.). 1064p. (Orig.). 1992. pap. 27.95 (1-56276-071-8) Ziff-Davis.

— Windows NT Power Tools. 1994. pap. 50.00 (0-679-79142-6) Random.

Leblond, Richard E. & Madden, Meg. From Chaos to Fragility. 208p. 1988. per. 23.95 (0-8403-5013-9) Kendall-Hunt.

LeBlond, William, ed. see Kobayashi, Tsukasa.

***Lebo.** Truth About Sinusitis. 1995. 12.95 (1-880688-01-8) New Life Opt.

Lebo, Fern. Mastering the Diversity Challenge: Easy On-the-Job Applications for Measuring Results. 200p. 1995. 39.95 (1-884015-35-2) St Lucie Pr.

Lebo, Laurie & Sanders, Lydia, comps. Art Lover's Book of Days. LC 86-62498. 176p. 1986. 12.95 (0-87846-275-9) Mus Fine Arts Boston.

LeBoeuf, Burney & Kaza, Stephanie, eds. The Natural History of Ano Nuevo. (Illus.). (Orig.). 1985. reprint ed. pap. 12.95 (0-910286-77-9) Boxwood.

Leboeuf, Michael. Fast Forward: How to Do a Lot More Business in a Lot Less Time4. LC 93-30862. 224p. 1994. 21.95 (0-399-13884-6, Putnam) Putnam Pub Group.

— Fast Forward: How to Win a Lot More Business in a Lot Less Time. 224p. (Orig.). 1995. pap. 12.00 (0-425-14613-8, Berkley Trade) Berkley Pub.

— Getting Results! The Secret of Motivating Yourself & Others. 176p. 1986. pap. 10.00 (0-425-08776-X, Berkley Trade) Berkley Pub.

LeBoeuf, Michael. The Greatest Management Principle in the World. 1989. mass mkt. 5.50 (0-425-11397-3) Berkley Pub.

Leboeuf, Michael. Imagineering: How to Profit from Your Creative Powers. 1990. mass mkt. 4.99 (0-425-12626-9) Berkley Pub.

LeBoeuf, Michael. Working Smart: How to Accomplish More in Half the Time. 272p. 1988. mass mkt. 5.50 (0-446-35356-6) Warner Bks.

LeBoeuff, Randall, Jr. Some Notes on the Life of Robert Fulton. (Illus.). 1971. 0.50 (0-913344-11-7) South St Sea Mus.

***LeBoit, Joseph & Capponi, Attilio, eds.** Treating Borderline Patients: The Major Clinical Explorers. LC 95-4050. 538p. 1995. pap. 40.00 (1-56821-525-8) Aronson.

Lebolt, Gladys. D. H. Lawrence: The True Redeemers? 1985. 7.50 (0-916620-63-8) Portals Pr.

Lebon, G., jt. ed. see Vazquez, J. C.

LeBon, Gustav, jt. auth. see Mackay, Charles.

LeBon, Gustave. The Crowd. LC 82-14042. 240p. 1982. reprint ed. pap. 12.95 (0-87797-168-4) Cherokee.

— The French Revolution & the Psychology of Revolution. LC 78-62691. (Social Science Classics Ser.). 337p. 1980. 37.95x (0-87855-310-X); pap. 21.95 (0-87855-697-4) Transaction Pubs.

— Gustave Lebon: The Man & His Works. 1991. lib. bdg. 74.95 (0-8490-4435-9) Gordon Pr.

— The Psychology of Socialism. LC 64-25423. 1965. reprint ed. 20.00 (0-87034-025-5) Fraser Pub Co.

— Psychology of Socialism. LC 81-1973. 415p. (C). 1982. reprint ed. pap. 21.95 (0-87855-703-2) Transaction Pubs.

Lebon, Jean. How to Understand the Liturgy. (How-to Ser.). (Illus.). 164p. (Orig.). (C). 1988. pap. 11.95 (0-8245-0867-X) Crossroad NY.

Lebon, Joseph. Le Monophysisme severien: Etude historique, litteraire et theologique sur la resistance monophysite au Concile de Chalcedoine jusqu'a la constitution de l'eglise jacobite. LC 77-84704. reprint ed. 72.50 (0-404-16111-1) AMS Pr.

LeBond, P. H. & Mysak, L. A. Waves in the Ocean. (Oceanography Ser.: Vol. 20). 602p. 1981. pap. 84.00 (0-444-41926-8) Elsevier.

LeBorg, Reginald. The Films of Reginald LeBorg: Interviews, Essays, & Filmography. Dixon, Wheeler W., ed. LC 92-14668. (Filmmakers Ser.: No. 31). (Illus.). 203p. 1992. 25.00 (0-8108-2550-3) Scarecrow.

***LeBorgne, Leon J.** The Bull's-Eye of Life. 76p. (Orig.). (YA). 1995. pap. text ed. 4.95 (1-886707-01-4) L & L Enter.

— Study Guide for the Bull's-Eye of Life. 76p. (YA). 1995. pap. text ed. 4.95 (1-886707-02-2) L & L Enter.

— You Can't Legislate Attitudes. 68p. (Orig.). 1995. pap. text ed. 4.95 (1-886707-00-6) L & L Enter.

Lebot, Vincent, et al. Kava: The Pacific Drug. LC 92-13444. (Psychoactive Plants of the World Ser.). (Illus.). 256p. (C). 1993. text ed. 47.00 (0-300-05213-8) Yale U Pr.

Lebour, M. V. The Planktonic Diatoms of Northern Seas. (Ray Society Publication Ser.: No. 116). (Illus.). 244p. 1978. reprint ed. lib. bdg. 59.00 (3-87429-147-2) Koeltz Sci Bks.

LeBoutiller, Megan. Little Miss Perfect. 192p. 1990. mass mkt. 4.95 (0-345-36283-7) Ballantine.

Leboutillier, John. Coming to Terms with Vietnam: The Case for Normalizing Relations with Hanoi. LC 89-3670. 134p. 1989. text ed. 29.95 (0-275-93278-8, C3278, Praeger Pubs) Greenwood.

LeBoutillier, Megan. Little Miss Perfect. 140p. (Orig.). 1987. pap. 8.95 (0-910223-10-6) MAC Pub.

— No Is a Complete Sentence: Learning the Sacredness of Personal Boundaries. (Orig.). 1995. mass mkt. 5.99 (0-345-37647-1) Ballantine.

LeBouton. Molecular & Cell Biology of the Liver. 1993. 198.00 (0-8493-8891-0, QP185) CRC Pr.

Lebov, Myrna. Practical Tools & Techniques for Managing Time. 1981. pap. 5.95 (0-917386-38-8) Exec Ent Pubns.

Lebov, Myrna, jt. auth. see Morrow, Jodie B.

Lebovic, James H. Deadly Dilemmas: Deterrence in U. S. Nuclear Strategy. 248p. 1990. text ed. 38.00 (0-231-06844-1) Col U Pr.

Lebovici, Serge & Widlocher, K., eds. Psychoanalysis in France. Diamanti, J., tr. LC 79-2483. 620p. 1980. text ed. 65.00 (0-8236-5210-6) Intl Univs Pr.

Lebovici, Serge, jt. auth. see Buckle, D.

Lebovici, Serge, ed. see Esman, Aaron H.

Lebovici, Serge, jt. auth. see McDougall, Joyce.

Lebovics, Adel. What Will the World Be Like? (Illus.). 32p. (J). (ps-1). 1993. 8.95 (0-922613-56-7); Russian translation. 8.95 (0-922613-58-3); Italian translation. 8.95 (0-922613-59-1); pap. 6.95 (0-922613-57-5) Hachai Pubns.

Lebovics, Herman. Alliance of Iron & Wheat in the Third French Republic, 1860-1914: Origins of the New Conservatism. LC 87-21386. 240p. 1988. text ed. 32.50 (0-8071-1350-6) La State U Pr.

— True France: The Wars over Cultural Identity, 1900-1945. LC 91-44697. (Wilder House Ser.). (Illus.). 248p. 1992. 32.50 (0-8014-2687-1) Cornell U Pr.

— True France: The Wars over Cultural Identity, 1900-1945. (Wilder House Series in Politics, History, & Culture). (Illus.). 248p. 1994. pap. 13.95 (0-8014-8193-7) Cornell U Pr.

Lebovitch, William L. Design for Dignity: Accessible Environments for People with Disabilities. LC 93-3310. 250p. 1993. text ed. 59.95 (0-471-56910-0) Wiley.

***Lebovits, Allen H., et al.** Exposure to Hazardous Substances: Psychological Parameters. fac. ed. LC 85-31163. (Advances in Environmental Psychology Ser.: No. 6). (Illus.). 151p. 1986. reprint ed. pap. 43.10 (0-7837-7831-7, 2047587) Bks Demand.

Lebovits, Yehudah. Shidduchim & Zivugim: The Torah Perspective on Finding Your Mate. 1988. 11.95 (0-317-68131-1) Feldheim.

— Shidduchim & Zivugim: The Torah's Perspective on Choosing Your Mate. 176p. (Orig.). 1988. 10.95 (0-944070-01-9) Targum Pr.

Lebovitz, J. L. & Montroll, E. W., eds. Nonequilibrium Phenomena: The Boltzmann Equation, No. 1. (Studies in Statistical Mechanics: Vol. 10). 251p. 1983. 45.00 (0-444-86519-5, North Holland) Elsevier.

Lebovitz, Norman, ed. Fluid Dynamics in Astrophysics & Geophysics. LC 83-2705. (Lectures in Applied Mathematics: Vol. 20). 269p. 1983. text ed. 70.00 (0-8218-1120-7, LAM-20) Am Math.

Lebovitz, Norman, et al. Theoretical Principles in Astrophysics & Relativity. Reid, William H. & Vandervoort, Peter O., eds. LC 76-25636. 272p. 1981. pap. text ed. 8.50 (0-226-46990-5) U Ch Pr.

Lebow. Adult Obesity Therapy. (Practitioner Guidebook Ser.). (C). 1989. pap. 25.95 (0-205-14404-7, H4404, Longwood Div) Allyn.

***Lebow, Barbara.** The Keepers. 1995. pap. 4.75 (0-8222-1459-8) Dramatists Play.

— Little Joe Monaghan. 1995. pap. 4.75 (0-8222-1414-8) Dramatists Play.

— A Shayna Maidel. 1988. pap. 4.75 (0-8222-1019-3) Dramatists Play.

— Tiny Tim Is Dead. 1993. 4.75 (0-8222-1363-X) Dramatists Play.

***Lebow, Edward.** Kenneth Ferguson Ceramics Retrospective: From the Nelson-Atkins Museum of Art. (Illus.). 120p. 1995. pap. text ed. 29.95 (0-942614-23-2) Nelson-Atkins.

Lebow, Eileen F. Cal Rodgers & the Vin Fiz: The First Transcontinental Flight. (Illus.). 264p. 1989. 29.95 (0-87474-704-X) Smithsonian.

Lebow, Fred. New York Road Runners Club Complete Book of Running. 1994. pap. 16.00 (0-679-74861-X) Random.

Lebow, Fred, et al. The New York Road Runners Club Complete Guide to Running. Averbuch, Gloria, ed. LC 92-16254. 1992. 19.50 (0-679-40980-7, Random Ref) Random.

Lebow, Guy. Are We on the Air: The Hilarious, Scandalous Confessions of a TV Pioneer. 1991. 18.95 (1-56171-049-0) Sure Sellers.

— Watch Your Cleavage, Check Your Zipper! 1994. pap. 5.99 (1-56171-284-1, S P I Bks) Sure Sellers.

Lebow, Irwin. The Digital Connection: A Layman's Guide to the Information Age. 256p. 1995. pap. text ed. 15.95 (0-7167-8203-0) W H Freeman.

— Information Highways & Byways: From the Telegraph to the Twentieth Century. LC 94-45457. 1995. write for info. (0-7803-1073-X) Inst Electrical.

Lebow, Jeanne. The Outlaw James Copeland & the Champion-Belted Empress. LC 90-36868. (Contemporary Poetry Ser.). 72p. 1991. 18.00 (0-8203-1280-0); pap. 8.95 (0-8203-1281-9) U of Ga Pr.

LeBow, M. D. Overweight Children: Helping Your Child Achieve Lifetime Weight Control. (Illus.). 230p. 1991. 22.95 (0-306-43961-1, Plenum Insight) Plenum.

***LeBow, Michael.** Overweight Teenagers: Don't Bear the Burden Alone. 250p. 1995. 23.95 (0-306-45047-X, Plenum Pr) Plenum.

LeBow, Michael D. The Thin Plan. LC 87-35282. (Illus.). 184p. (Orig.). 1988. pap. 11.95 (0-87322-927-4, PLEB0350) Human Kinetics.

— Weight Control: The Behavioural Strategies. LC 79-41728. (Illus.). 358p. reprint ed. pap. 102.10 (0-685-20593-2, 2030527) Bks Demand.

Lebow, Ned & Strauss, Barry S., eds. Hegemonic Rivalry: From Thucydides to the Nuclear Age. 295p. (C). 1991. pap. text ed. 53.50 (0-8133-7744-7) Westview.

Lebow, Richard N. Between Peace & War: The Nature of International Crisis. LC 80-21982. 368p. 1984. pap. 14.95 (0-8018-3247-0) Johns Hopkins.

— Nuclear Crisis Management: A Dangerous Illusion. LC 86-16767. (Cornell Studies in Security Affairs). 232p. 1987. 32.50 (0-8014-1989-1); pap. 13.95 (0-8014-9531-8) Cornell U Pr.

***Lebow, Richard N. & Risse-Kappen, Thomas.** International Relations Theory & the End of the Cold War. LC 94-42569. 1995. write for info. (0-231-10194-5); pap. write for info. (0-231-10195-3) Col U Pr.

Lebow, Richard N. & Stein, Janice G. We All Lost the Cold War. (Studies in International History & Politics). 552p. 1994. text ed. 35.00 (0-691-03308-0) Princeton U Pr.

***Lebow, Rob.** Journey into the Heroic Environment: Eight Principles That Lead to Greater Productivity. 1995. pap. 10.95 (1-55958-688-5) Prima Pub.

— A Journey into the Heroic Environment: Eight Principles That Lead to Greater Productivity, Quality, Job Satisfaction & Profits. 140p. 1990. 16.95 (1-55958-047-X) Prima Pub.

Lebowitz, Albert. Matter of Days. Stories. LC 88-22054. 113p. 1989. 15.95 (0-8071-1417-0) La State U Pr.

Lebowitz, Arieh & Malmgreen, Gail, eds. Robert F. Wagner Labor Archives, New York University: The Papers of the Jewish Labor Committee. LC 89-16915. (Archives of the Holocaust Ser.: Vol. 14). 528p. 1993. 125.00 (0-8240-5496-2) Garland.

Lebowitz, Barry, jt. ed. see Light, Enid.

Lebowitz, Barry D., ed. Alzheimer's Disease Treatment & Family Stress: Directions for Research. LC 89-600727. (Illus.). 498p. 1989. per., pap. 14.00 (*0-16-002499-4*, S/N 017-024-013) USGPO.

Lebowitz, Barry D., jt. ed. see Salzman, Carl.

Lebowitz, Clara. Tuvia & the Tiny Teacher. (Illus.). 100p. (J). (gr. 3-4). 1991. 8.95 (*1-56062-105-2*) CIS Comm.

Lebowitz, Fran. Exterior Signs: Health. Date not set. mass mkt. write for info. (*0-8041-1264-9*) Ivy Books.

— The Fran Lebowitz Reader. 1994. pap. 13.00 (*0-679-76180-2*) Knopf.

— Metropolitan Life. 1982. pap. 3.95 (*0-449-20089-2*) Fawcett.

— Metropolitan Life. 1988. pap. 7.95 (*0-452-26069-8*, Plume) NAL-Dutton.

— Mr. Chas & Lisa Sue Meet the Pandas. LC 94-1132. (Illus.). 72p. (J). (gr. 2-7). 1994. 15.00 (*0-679-86052-5*) Knopf Bks Yng Read.

Lebowitz, Gary N. Autovisor: The Ultimate Log Book & Maintenance Guide. (Illus.). 64p. (Orig.). 1995. pap. 6.95 (*0-9638788-3-2*) Autoviser.

Lebowitz Greenspan, Amy, ed. New York Employer's Guide, 1992-1994: A Handbook of Employment Laws & Regulations. LC 92-13997. 350p. 1994. ring bd. 89.50 (*0-9625969-7-3*) Summers Pr.

Lebowitz, Harvey M. Bankruptcy Deskbook. 2nd ed. 836p. 1990. text ed. 80.00 (*0-87224-004-5*, A1-1411) PLI.

Lebowitz, Joel L., ed. Fifth International Conference on Collective Phenomena, Vol. 410. 70.00 (*0-89766-213-X*); pap. 70.00 (*0-89766-214-8*) NY Acad Sci.

— Simple Models of Equilibrium & Nonequilibrium Phenomena. (Studies in Statistical Mechanics: Vol. 13). 272p. 1987. 89.75 (*0-444-87039-3*, North Holland) Elsevier.

Lebowitz, Joel L. & Montroll, E. W., eds. Nonequilibrium Phenomena II: From Stochastics to Hydrodynamics. (Studies in Statistical Mechanics: Vol. 11). 308p. 1984. 47.75 (*0-444-86806-2*) Elsevier.

Lebowitz, Joel L., jt. ed. see Chernyak, Yuri B.

Lebowitz, Joel L., jt. ed. see Domb, Cyril M.

Lebowitz, Joel L., jt. auth. see Fischer-Hjalmars, Inga.

Lebowitz, Joel L., jt. ed. see Montroll, E. W.

Lebowitz, Joel L., et al, eds. International Conference on Collective Phenomena, 3rd. LC 80-17323. (Annals Ser.: Vol. 337). 41.00 (*0-89766-074-9*); pap. 41.00 (*0-89766-075-7*) NY Acad Sci.

Lebowitz, Marcia, ed. Children's Divorce Center Reading Guide: 1992 Edition. 1991. 24.95 (*0-935769-08-0*) CDC Pr.

Lebowitz, Marcia L. I Think Divorce Stinks. 16p. (Orig.). (YA). (gr. 7-10). 1989. pap. 4.95 (*0-935769-05-6*) CDC Pr.

Lebowitz, Michael A. Beyond Capital: Marx's Political Economy of the Working Class. LC 91-2248. 200p. (C). 1992. text ed. 49.95 (*0-312-06184-6*); pap. 16.95 (*0-312-06186-2*) St Martin.

***Lebowitz, Michael D., et al, eds.** Measuring, Understanding, & Predicting Exposures in the 21st Century. (Journal of Exposure Analysis & Environmental Epidemiology Ser.: Vol. 2, Suppl. 1). (Illus.). 244p. 1994. 50.00 (*0-911131-84-1*) Princeton Sci Pubs.

— Measuring, Understanding, & Predicting Exposures in the 21st Century. (Journal of Exposure Analysis & Environmental Epidemiology Ser.: Vol. 2, Suppl. 2). (Illus.). 220p. 1994. 50.00 (*0-614-03985-1*) Princeton Sci Pubs.

Lebowitz, Milton M., ed. Practice Issues in Social Welfare Administration, Policy & Planning. LC 82-6269. (Administration in Social Work Ser.: Vol. 6, Nos. 2 & 3). 157p. 1982. text ed. 39.95 (*0-86656-142-0*, B142); pap. text ed. 17.95 (*0-86656-166-8*) Haworth Pr.

Lebowitz, Naomi. Ibsen & the Great World. LC 89-12988. 272p. 1990. text ed. 37.50 (*0-8071-1543-6*) La State U Pr.

— The Imagination of Loving: Henry James's Legacy to the Novel. LC 65-14595. 184p. reprint ed. pap. 52.50 (*0-7837-3807-2*, 2043627) Bks Demand.

— Kierkegaard: A Life of Allegory. LC 84-12618. 242p. 1985. text ed. 35.00 (*0-8071-1186-4*) La State U Pr.

— The Philosophy of Literary Amateurism. 152p. 1994. 29.95 (*0-8262-0970-X*) U of Mo Pr.

Lebowitz, Naomi, jt. auth. see Newton, Ruth.

Lebowitz, Robert. Plant Biotechnology: A Laboratory Course. 160p. (C). 1994. spiral bd. write for info. (*0-697-15119-0*) Wm C Brown Pubs.

Lebowitz, Sally E. Friend of the Family: A Hospice Volunteer's Experience. 128p. (Orig.). 1989. pap. 12.95 (*0-9619155-1-X*) Laurel & Herbert.

Leboyer, Frederick. Birth Without Violence. 1975. 18.95 (*0-394-49581-0*) Knopf.

— Birth Without Violence. 1995. pap. 12.95 (*1-85230-632-7*) Element MA.

— Birth Without Violence: The Book that Revolutionized the Way We Bring Our Children into the World. LC 95-13382. (Illus.). 128p. 1995. 14.95 (*0-89281-545-0*, Heal Arts VT) Inner Tradit.

— Loving Hands: The Traditional Indian Art of Baby Massaging. 1976. 24.95 (*0-394-40469-6*) Knopf.

Lebra-Chapman, Joyce. Japanese-Trained Armies in Southeast Asia: Independence & Volunteer Forces in World War II. LC 75-16116. 226p. 1977. text ed. 42.00 (*0-231-03995-6*) Col U Pr.

— The Rani of Jhansi: A Study of Female Heroism in India. LC 85-20677. (Illus.). 216p. 1986. 25.00 (*0-8248-0984-X*) UH Pr.

Lebra, Joyce. Women's Voices in Hawaii. (C). 1993. pap. 17.50 (*0-87081-299-8*) Univ Pr Colo.

Lebra, Joyce C. Women's Voices in Hawaii. (Illus.). 320p. 1991. 24.95 (*0-87081-238-6*) Univ Pr Colo.

***Lebra, Takie S.** Above the Clouds: Status Culture of the Modern Japanese Nobility. 1992. pap. 16.00 (*0-520-07602-8*) U CA Pr.

— Above the Clouds: Status Culture of the Modern Japanese Nobility. (C). 1992. 45.00 (*0-520-07600-1*) U CA Pr.

— Japanese Patterns of Behavior. LC 76-110392. 312p. (C). 1976. pap. text ed. 11.95 (*0-8248-0460-0*, Eastwest Ctr Pr) UH Pr.

— Japanese Women: Constraint & Fulfillment. LC 83-18029. 360p. (C). 1985. pap. text ed. 9.50 (*0-8248-1025-2*) UH Pr.

Lebra, Takie S., ed. Japanese Social Organization. LC 92-3835. 304p. (C). 1992. text ed. 34.00 (*0-8248-1386-3*); pap. text ed. 14.95 (*0-8248-1420-7*) UH Pr.

Lebra, Takie S. & Lebra, William P., eds. Japanese Culture & Behavior: Selected Readings. rev. ed. LC 86-4367. 458p. 1986. pap. text ed. 12.95 (*0-8248-1055-4*) UH Pr.

Lebra, William P. Okinawan Religion: Belief, Ritual, & Social Structure. LC 66-16506. 256p. 1985. reprint ed. pap. text ed. 8.95 (*0-87022-450-6*) UH Pr.

Lebra, William P., ed. see Conference on Culture & Mental Health Research in Asia & the Pacific Staff.

Lebra, William P., jt. ed. see Lebra, Takie S.

Lebrat, Jean, jt. auth. see Biasini, Emile.

Lebrecht, Elbie. Sugar-Free Cakes & Biscuits. 2nd ed. 144p. 1989. pap. 8.95 (*0-571-15418-2*) Faber & Faber.

— Sugar-Free Cooking. (Illus.). 224p. 1994. pap. 12.00 (*0-7225-2857-4*) Thorsons SF.

— Sugar Free Desserts, Drinks & Ices. 180p. (Orig.). 1993. pap. 10.95 (*0-571-16645-8*) Faber & Faber.

LeBrecht, James, jt. auth. see Kaye, Deena.

Lebrecht, Norman. The Book of Musical Anecdotes: Hundreds of Classic & Little-Known Stories about the World's Greatest Composers & Performers. LC 85-16809. 480p. 1985. 24.95 (*0-02-918710-9*) Free Pr.

— A Companion to Twentieth-Century Music. (Illus.). 288p. 1993. 30.00 (*0-671-66654-1*) S&S Trade.

— Maestro Myth: Great Conductors in Pursuit of Power. (Illus.). 384p. 1993. pap. 14.95 (*0-8065-1450-7*, Citadel Pr) Carol Pub Group.

— The Maestro Myth: Great Conductors in the Pursuit of Power. (Illus.). 384p. 1992. 22.50 (*1-55972-108-1*, Birch Ln Pr) Carol Pub Group.

Lebrecht, Norman, ed. Mahler Remembered. (Illus.). 1988. 25.00 (*0-393-02572-1*) Norton.

Lebredo, Raquel, jt. auth. see Jarvis, Ana C.

Lebreton, G. J. Optics for Computers, Vol. 1505: Architectures & Technologies. 1991. 58.00 (*0-8194-0614-7*) SPIE.

LeBreton, J. The White Magic Book: The Correct Answers to Your Problems. 1991. lib. bdg. 79.95 (*0-8490-4553-3*) Gordon Pr.

Lebreton, J. D. & North, Ph. M., eds. Marked Individuals in the Study of Bird Population. LC 93-3400. (Advances in Life Sciences Ser.). xviii, 397p. 1993. 92.00 (*0-8176-2780-4*, Pub. by Birkhauser Vlg SZ) Birkhauser.

LeBreton, John. The White Magic Book. 100p. 1970. reprint ed. spiral bd. 5.50 (*0-7873-0546-4*) Mokelumne.

Lebreton, Jules. Etudes sur la Langue et la Grammaire de Ciceron. xxvii, 471p. 1979. reprint ed. write for info. (*3-487-00994-3*, Pub. by Georg Olms GW) Lubrecht & Cramer.

Lebreton, Jules & Zeiller, Jacques. History of the Primitive Church. 1973. 80.00 (*0-8490-0361-X*) Gordon Pr.

LeBreton, Mariettta M. Northwestern State University of Louisiana, 1884-1948: A History. LC 85-61932. (Illus.). 320p. 1985. 30.00 (*0-917898-10-9*) NSU Pr LA.

LeBrie, Isolde. Joyous Feasts: A Cookbook for Easy Entertaining. LC 93-71135. (Illus.). 254p. 1993. 14.95 (*0-9637567-0-2*) Daniels OH.

Lebris, P. Dictionnaire Bobo-Francais. 416p. (FRE.). 1981. 69.95 (*0-8288-1599-2*, F37450) Fr & Eur.

***Lebrun.** Mutism. 1990. 65.00 (*1-56593-539-X*, 0042) Singular Publishing.

***Lebrun, Claude.** Being Sick. LC 95-1138. (Little Brown Bear Bks.). (Illus.). (J). 1995. write for info. (*0-516-07821-6*) Childrens.

— Learning to Share. LC 95-1136. (Little Brown Bear Bks.). (Illus.). (J). 1995. write for info. (*0-516-07822-4*) Childrens.

— Little Brown Bear Does Not Want to Eat. LC 95-1134. (Little Brown Bear Bks.). (Illus.). (J). 1995. write for info. (*0-516-07823-2*) Childrens.

— Little Brown Bear Goes Collecting & Exploring. LC 95-1135. (Little Brown Bear Bks.). (Illus.). (J). 1995. write for info. (*0-516-07824-0*) Childrens.

— Little Brown Bear is Afraid of the Dark. LC 95-1133. (Little Brown Bear Bks.). (Illus.). (J). 1995. write for info. (*0-516-07825-9*) Childrens.

— Little Brown Bear Is Ill. (Little Brown Bear Ser.). (Illus.). 14p. (J). (gr. k-3). 1982. 4.95 (*0-8120-5499-7*) Barron.

— Little Brown Bear Learns All Uses of a Chair. LC 95-1132. (Little Brown Bear Bks.). (Illus.). (J). 1995. write for info. (*0-516-07826-7*) Childrens.

— Little Brown Bear Learns the Value of Money. LC 95-5731. (Little Brown Bear Bks.). (Illus.). (J). 1995. write for info. (*0-516-07827-5*) Childrens.

— Little Brown Bear Obstinately Says "No" to Everything. LC 95-5732. (Little Brown Bear Bks.). (Illus.). 1995. write for info. (*0-516-07828-3*) Childrens.

— Little Brown Bear Wants to Be Read To. LC 95-5733. (Little Brown Bear Bks.). (Illus.). (J). 1995. write for info. (*0-516-07829-1*) Childrens.

— Little Brown Bear Wants to Go to School. LC 95-5734. (Little Brown Bear Bks.). (Illus.). (J). 1995. write for info. (*0-516-07830-5*) Childrens.

— Sharing Mama's Love with Daddy. LC 95-5736. (Little Brown Bear Bks.). (Illus.). (J). 1995. write for info. (*0-516-07831-3*) Childrens.

— Things Little Brown Bear Can Do by Himself. LC 95-5735. (Little Brown Bear Bks.). (Illus.). (J). 1995. write for info. (*0-516-07832-1*) Childrens.

Lebrun, Elisabeth V. Memoirs of Madame Vigee Lebrun. Strachey, Lionel, tr. LC 88-38757. (Illus.). 233p. (C). 1989. 24.95 (*0-8076-1221-9*) Braziller.

Lebrun, Francesca & Bayon, Mlle. Keyboard Sonatas: Six Sonatas for Harpsichord or Pianoforte with Accompaniment for Violin; Six Sonatas pour le Clavecin ou le Piano Forte dont 3 avec Accompagnement de Violon Oblige. Hayes, Deborah, ed. (Women Composers Ser.: No. 23). 90p. 1990. reprint ed. lib. bdg. 39.50 (*0-306-76285-4*) Da Capo.

LeBrun, J. Dictionnaire des Services Publics Relevant de l'Etat: Dictionary of Public Services Related to Government. 1020p. (FRE.). 1978. 175.00 (*0-8288-5187-5*, M6341) Fr & Eur.

LeBrun, Ken. The Earthly Life of Jesus. LC 91-65760. 277p. (Orig.). 1991. boxed 14.95 (*0-945383-24-X*, 945-5814) Teach Servs.

— The Earthly Life of Jesus. LC 91-65760. 277p. (Orig.). 1991. pap. 9.95 (*0-945383-25-8*, 945-5815) Teach Servs.

Lebrun, Richard, ed. see De Maistre, Joseph.

Lebrun, Richard, tr. see Maistre, Joseph.

Lebrun, Richard A. Joseph de Maistre: An Intellectual Militant. 400p. (C). 1988. text ed. 49.95 (*0-7735-0645-4*, Pub. by McGill CN) U of Toronto Pr.

Lebrun, Richard A., ed. & tr. Maistre Studies. LC 88-26147. 318p. (C). 1988. lib. bdg. 49.00 (*0-8191-7201-4*) U Pr of Amer.

Lebrun, Y. The Artificial Larynx. (Neurolinguistics Ser.: Vol. 1). 90p. 1973. 18.50 (*90-265-0173-0*, Pub. by Swets Pub Serv NE) Taylor & Francis.

Lebrun, Y. & Hoops, R. Intelligence & Aphasia. (Neurolinguistics Ser.: Vol. 2). 140p. 1974. 18.50 (*90-265-0182-X*, Pub. by Swets Pub Serv NE) Taylor & Francis.

Lebrun, Y. & Hoops, R., eds. The Management of Aphasia. (Neurolinguistics Ser.: Vol. 8). 124p. 1978. 31.00 (*90-265-0280-X*, Pub. by Swets Pub Serv NE) Taylor & Francis.

— Problems of Aphasia. (Neurolinguistics Ser.: Vol. 9). 198p. 1979. 42.75 (*90-265-0309-1*, Pub. by Swets Pub Serv NE) Taylor & Francis.

— Recovery in Aphasics. (Neurolinguistics Ser.: Vol. 4). 270p. 1976. 41.50 (*90-265-0228-1*, Pub. by Swets Pub Serv NE) Taylor & Francis.

Lebrun, Y. & Zangwill, O., eds. Lateralisation of Language in the Child. (Neurolinguistics Ser.: Vol. 10). 175p. 1982. 37.25 (*90-265-0337-7*, Pub. by Swets Pub Serv NE) Taylor & Francis.

Lebrun, Y., ed. see International Symposium on Stuttering Staff.

Lebrun, Y., jt. ed. see Paradis, M.

LeBruyn, Lieven. Trace Rings of Generic Two by Two Matrices. LC 87-1810. (Memoirs of the American Mathematical Society Ser.: Vol. 363). 100p. 1987. 18.00 (*0-8218-2425-2*, MEMO/66/363C) Am Math.

Lebsock, Suzanne. The Free Women of Petersburg: Status & Culture in a Southern Town, 1784-1860. (Illus.). 320p. 1985. reprint ed. pap. 12.95 (*0-393-95264-9*) Norton.

Lebsock, Suzanne, jt. ed. see Hewitt, Nancy A.

Lebsock, Suzanne, jt. auth. see Scott, Anne F.

LeBuff, Charles R., Jr. The Loggerhead Turtle in the Eastern Gulf of Mexico. LC 89-81763. (Illus.). 1990. 24.95 (*0-9625013-0-1*) R Curtis Pubng.

Leburton, Jean-Pierre, et al, eds. Phonons in Semiconductor Nanostructures. LC 93-17083. (NATO Advanced Study Institutes Series E, Applied Sciences: Vol. 236). 1993. lib. bdg. 181.00 (*0-7923-2277-0*) Kluwer Ac.

Lebwohl, Mark, ed. Difficult Diagnoses in Dermatology. LC 87-25675. (Illus.). 466p. reprint ed. pap. 132.90 (*0-7837-6226-7*, 2045940) Bks Demand.

Lebwohl, Mark G. The Skin & Systemic Disease. (Illus.). 1995. text ed. write for info. (*0-443-08739-3*) Churchill.

Lebzelter, Gisela C. Political Anti-Semitism in England 1918-1939. LC 78-16795. 222p. 1979. 49.50 (*0-8419-0426-X*) Holmes & Meier.

Leca, Jean, jt. ed. see Birnbaum, Pierre.

Lecaillon, J., jt. auth. see Lafary, J. D.

Lecaillon, J., et al. Income Distribution & Economic Development: An Analytical Survey. (WEP Study Ser.). ix, 211p. 1986. 32.00 (*92-2-103559-X*); pap. 24.00 (*92-2-103366-X*) Intl Labour Office.

LeCain, Errol. Twelve Dancing Princesses. 32p. (J). (ps-00). 1981. pap. 3.95 (*0-14-050322-6*, Puffin) Puffin Bks.

LeCam, Lucien M. Convergence in Distribution of Stochastic Processes. LC 57-9424. (University of California Publications in Social Welfare: Vol. 2, No. 11). 32p. reprint ed. pap. 25.00 (*0-317-08319-8*, 2021183) Bks Demand.

***Lecanuet, Jean-Pierre, et al, eds.** Fetal Development: A Psychobiological Perspective. LC 94-44324. 496p. 1995. text ed. 99.95 (*0-8058-1485-X*) L Erlbaum Assocs.

Lecar, Harold, jt. ed. see Marton, Claire.

Lecar, Harold, jt. auth. see Nossal, Ralph.

Lecar, M., ed. see International Astronomical Union Staff.

Lecar, M., jt. auth. see Vilcu, R.

Lecarme, Olivier & Pellissier-Gart, M. Software Portability. 256p. 1986. text ed. 35.00 (*0-07-036948-8*) McGraw.

LeCarre, John. The Naive & Sentimental Lover. large type ed. 1992. 21.95 (*0-7927-1005-3*, E0028, Eagle Lrg Print) Chivers N Amer.

— The Naive & Sentimental Lover. large type ed. 1992. pap. 17.95 (*0-7927-1006-1*, Paragon Lrg Print) Chivers N Amer.

— A Small Town in Germany. large type ed. LC 92-12648. (Eagle Large Print Ser.). 1992. 19.95 (*0-7927-1361-3*, Eagle Lrg Print) Chivers N Amer.

— A Small Town in Germany. large type ed. 1993. pap. 17.95 (*0-7927-1360-5*, Paragon Lrg Print) Chivers N Amer.

Lecca, Pedro J. & McNeill, John S., eds. Interdisciplinary Team Practice: Issues & Trends. LC 85-3612. 256p. 1985. text ed. 55.00 (*0-275-90134-3*, C0134, Praeger Pubs) Greenwood.

Lecca, Pedro J. & Watts, Thomas D. Pathways for Minorities into the Health Professions. 98p. 1989. 33.00 (*0-8191-7552-8*) U Pr of Amer.

— Preschoolers & Substance Abuse: Strategies for Prevention & Intervention. LC 91-35921. 118p. 1993. lib. bdg. 29.95 (*1-56024-234-5*) Haworth Pr.

— Preschoolers & Substance Abuse: Strategies for Prevention & Intervention. LC 91-35921. 112p. 1993. pap. 14.95 (*1-56024-235-3*) Haworth Pr.

Lecca, Pedro J., jt. ed. see Callicutt, James W.

Leccabue, F. & Llamazares, J. L., eds. Magnetism, Magnetic Materials & Their Applications: Proceedings of the International Workshop, La Habana, Cuba, 21-29 May 1991. (Illus.). 356p. 1992. 103.00 (*0-7503-0189-9*) IOP Pub.

Leccese, Arthur P. Drugs & Society: Behavioral Medicines & Abusable Drugs. 1990. text ed. 30.00 (*0-13-221623-X*, 670111) P-H.

Leccese, Michael. Short Bike Rides in & Around Washington, D. C. 2nd ed. LC 92-27089. (East Woods Book Ser.). 176p. (Orig.). 1993. pap. 9.95 (*1-56440-146-4*) Globe Pequot.

***Leccesse, Michael.** Short Bike Rides in Colorado. (Short Bike Rides Ser.). (Illus.). 224p. (Orig.). 1995. pap. 9.95 (*1-56440-640-7*) Globe Pequot.

Lecercle, Jean-Jacques. Philosophy of Nonsense: The Intuitions of Victorian Nonsense Literature. LC 93-5384. 1994. write for info. (*0-415-07652-8*); pap. write for info. (*0-415-07653-6*) Routledge.

— Violence of Language. 320p. 1990. 69.95 (*0-415-03430-2*, A4963); pap. 18.95 (*0-415-03431-0*, A4967) Routledge.

Lech, Mike, jt. auth. see Godish, Don.

Lechaczynski, Jean & Lechaczynski, Serge. Verre Contemporain. 154p. (FRE.). 1993. lib. bdg. 150.00 (*0-7859-3649-1*, 2859171320); lib. bdg. 150.00 (*0-7859-3650-5*, 2859171339) Fr & Eur.

Lechaczynski, Serge, jt. auth. see Lechaczynski, Jean.

Lechan, Jan. American Transformations. 1959. 3.00 (*0-940962-00-4*) Polish Inst Art & Sci.

— Aut Caesar Aut Nihil. 46p. (LAT.). 1955. 4.00 (*0-940962-01-2*) Polish Inst Art & Sci.

Lechat, Lagier. Dictionary of Principal Medications: Dictionnaire des Medicaments Principaux. 528p. 1982. 110.00 (*0-8288-1815-0*, M15386) Fr & Eur.

Lechat, P. Local Anesthetics. 1971. 165.00 (*0-08-015836-6*, Pub. by Pergamon Repr UK) Franklin.

Lechat, P., et al, eds. Aminopyridines & Similarly Acting Drugs: Effects on Nerves, Muscles & Synapses. LC 82-533. (Advances in the Biosciences Ser.: Vol. 35). (Illus.). 352p. 1982. 151.00 (*0-08-028000-5*, Pub. by Pergamon Repr UK) Franklin.

Leche League International Staff. The Womanly Art of Breastfeeding. LC 83-61753. (Illus.). 384p. 1983. pap. 8.95 (*0-452-26212-7*, Plume) NAL-Dutton.

Lechene, Maxine T. Across the Gap: From War to Peace. 1994. 9.95 (*0-8062-4864-5*) Carlton.

Lecher, Doris. Angelita's Magic Yarn. (Illus.). 32p. (J). (ps-3). 1992. 14.00 (*0-374-30332-0*) FS&G.

Lecher, Wolfgang, ed. Trade Unions in the European Union: A Handbook. 288p. (C). 1994. pap. 29.95 (*0-85315-766-9*, Pub. by Lawrence & Wishart UK) Humanities.

Lechevalier, H., jt. auth. see Laskin, A.

Lechevalier, Hubert, jt. ed. see Laskin, Allan I.

Lechevalier, Hubert, jt. auth. see Laskin, Allen I.

Lechevalier, Hubert, jt. ed. see Laskin, Allen I.

LeChevalier, Patricia, ed. Atlantean Press Review, 1992. (Illus.). 230p. 1992. pap. 12.00 (*0-9626854-4-5*) Atlantean Pr.

LeChevalier, Patricia, ed. see Hugo, Victor.

***Lechevallier-Chevignard, Edmond.** European Costumes of the Sixteenth through Eighteenth Centuries: In Full Color. LC 95-5988. 1995. write for info. (*0-486-28519-7*) Dover.

Lechevallier, Y., jt. ed. see Diday, E.

Lechford, Thomas. Note-Book Kept by Thomas Lechford, Esq., in Boston, Massachusetts Bay, from June 27, 1638, to July 29, 1641. rev. ed. Hale, Edward E., Jr. et al, eds. LC 88-30732. 512p. 1989. reprint ed. 49.50 (*0-929539-06-0*) Picton Pr.

— Plain Dealings: Or, News from New England. 1972. reprint ed. lib. bdg. 17.50 (*0-8422-8140-1*) Irvington.

Lechich, Whitney, ed. see Lee, Soon C.

LeChien, Paul. The Tattooed Loverboy & Other Drawings. (Illus.). 62p. (Orig.). 1999. pap. 25.00 (*1-873741-03-0*, Pub. by Millvres Bks UK) InBook.

Lechin, Fuad & Van der Dijs, Bertha, eds. Neurochemistry & Clinical Disorders: Circuitry of Some Psychiatric & Psychosomatic Syndromes. 208p. 1988. 161.00 (*0-8493-6595-3*, RC483) CRC Pr.

Lechler, Doris. French & German Dolls, Dishes & Accessories. (Illus.). 184p. (Orig.). 1991. 37.95 (*0-915410-71-0*, 3076); pap. 29.95 (*0-915410-70-2*, 3075) Antique Pubns.

Lechler, Doris A. Children's Glass Dishes, China & Furniture. 2nd ed. 208p. 1990. 19.95 (*0-89145-303-2*, 1627) Collector Bks.

— English Toy China. (Illus.). 216p. 1990. 32.95 (*0-915410-60-5*, 3042); pap. 24.95 (*0-915410-61-3*, 3041) Antique Pubns.

— Toy Glass. (Illus.). 264p. 1989. pap. 24.95 (*0-915410-58-3*) Antique Pubns.

Lechler, Gotthard V. John Wycliffe & His English Precursors. LC 78-63197. (Heresies of the Early Christian & Medieval Era Ser.: Second Ser.). reprint ed. 49.50 (*0-404-16235-5*) AMS Pr.

An Asterisk (*) at the beginning of an entry indicates that the title is appearing in BIP for the first time.

Lechler, Robert. HLA & Disease. (Illus.). 320p. 1994. text ed. 59.95 (0-12-440320-4) Acad Pr.

Lechlitner, Laurie. Love Is... 80p. 1988. pap. 3.95 (0-88144-125-2) Christian Pub.

Lechner, Doris E., jt. ed. see Cayne, Bernard S.

Lechner, Doris E., ed. see Williams, Bill.

Lechner, G., jt. ed. see Pokierser, Herbert.

Lechner, George & Hopkins, Terri. Scott Sonniksen Paintings 1972-1982. (Illus.). 1983. pap. 2.00 (0-914435-02-7) Marylhurst Art.

Lechner, H., ed. Importance of Haemorheologic Aspects in the Diagnosis & Treatment of Ischaemic Cerebrovascular Disease. (Journal: European Neurology: Vol. 22, Suppl. 1). (Illus.). iv, 132p. 1983. pap. 31.25 (3-8055-3731-X) S Karger.

Lechner, H., ed. see Agnoli, A., et al.

Lechner, H., et al, eds. Cerebrovascular Disease: Research & Clinical Management, Vol. 1. 350p. 1986. 153.00 (0-444-80782-9) Elsevier.

— Progress in Cerebrovascular Disease: Papers Presented at the XIVth World Congress of Neurology, New Delhi, 22-27 Oct., 1989. 152p. 1991. 103.75 (0-444-81421-3) Elsevier.

*Lechner, H. (Graz). Epilepsy State of the Art, 1993. Scollo-Lavizzari, G., ed. (Journal: European Neurology: Vol. 34, Suppl. 1, 1994). (Illus.). iv, 90p. 1994. pap. 37.75 (3-8055-6038-9) S Karger.

Lechner, Jack, comp. Film Producers, Studios, Agents & Casting Directors Guide. 4th ed. 1994. 45.00 (0-943728-62-2) Lone Eagle Pub.

Lechner, Joan M. Renaissance Concepts of the Commonplaces. LC 74-6153. 268p. 1974. reprint ed. text ed. 87.50 (0-8371-7491-0, LERC, Greenwood Pr) Greenwood.

*Lechner, Judith. Struggling Toward Civil Rights. Friedland, J. & Kessler, R., eds. (Novel-Ties Ser.). (YA). (gr. 6-10). 1993. student ed, pap. text ed. 20.95 (1-56982-024-4) Lrn Links.

Lechner, K., jt. ed. see Gadner, H.

*Lechner, M. D. Ultracentrifugation, 94. Kremer, F. et al, eds. (Progress in Colloid & Polymer Science/Ser.). 120p. 1994. 63.00 (0-387-91483-8) Spr-Verlag.

Lechner, Mildred. World of Salt Shakers. 2nd ed. 1991. 24.95 (0-89145-467-5) Collector Bks.

Lechner, Norbert. Heating, Cooling & Lighting: Design Methods for Architects. 1991. text ed. 79.95 (0-471-62887-5) Wiley.

Lechner, Susan, jt. auth. see Altman, Susan.

Lechner, Sybille K., jt. auth. see MacGregory, Alastair R.

Lechner, Tammy. In the Cal: Pastime Goes Primetime in California's Minor League. LC 94-96164. (Illus.). 114p. (Orig.). 1994. pap. 20.00 (0-9641987-0-3) Still Prods.

Lechner, Viola M. & Creedon, Michael. Managing Work & Family Life: The U. S. Response. (Springer Series on Social Work). (Illus.). 200p. 1994. 34.95 (0-8261-8470-7) Springer Pub.

Lechner, W. Europaworterbucher Business & Law: 1991. (DUT, ENG, FRE, GER & SPA.). 1991. lib. bdg. 195.00 (0-8288-3898-4, F63838) Fr & Eur.

Lecht, Leonard A. Experience Under Railway Labor Legislation. LC 68-59260. (Columbia University. Studies in the Social Sciences: No. 587). reprint ed. 31.00 (0-404-51587-8) AMS Pr.

— Priorities for Planning in Vocational Education: Alternatives for the 1970s. LC 75-37419. 68p. 1975. 3.00 (0-89068-006-X) Natl Planning.

Lechte, John. Fifty Key Contemporary Thinkers: From Structuralism to Postmodernity. LC 94-996. 192p. 1994. 45.00x (0-415-05727-2, B4147); pap. 15.95 (0-415-07408-8, B4722) Routledge.

— Julia Kristeva. 256p. 1990. 55.00 (0-415-00809-3, A4178); pap. 15.95 (0-415-00834-4, A4182) Routledge.

Lechtenberg. Handbook of Cerebellar Diseases. (Neurological Disease & Therapy Ser.: Vol. 16). 592p. 1993. 199.00 (0-8247-8776-5) Dekker.

Lechtenberg, Richard. Epilepsy & the Family. (Illus.). 240p. 1984. 25.00 (0-674-25888-6) HUP.

— Epilepsy & the Family. (Illus.). 240p. 1986. pap. text ed. 10.95 (0-674-25889-4) HUP.

— Multiple Sclerosis Fact Book. 2nd ed. (Illus.). 235p. (C). 1995. pap. text ed. 19.95 (0-8036-0074-7) Davis Co.

— Neurology: Pretest Self-Assessment & Review. 2nd ed. LC 94-4587. (Clinical Sciences PreTest Ser.). 236p. 1995. pap. text ed. 16.95 (0-07-052025-9) Hlth Prof Div.

— Seizure Recognition & Treatment. (Illus.). 204p. 1990. text ed. 59.95 (0-443-08701-6) Churchill.

— Synopsis of Neurology. LC 90-6387. (Illus.). 173p. 1990. text ed. 24.00 (0-8121-1356-X) Williams & Wilkins.

Lechtenberg, Richard & Ohl, Dana A. Sexual Dysfunction: Neurologic, Urologic & Gynecologic Aspects. LC 94-450. 1994. 69.50 (0-8121-1496-5) Williams & Wilkins.

Lechtenberg, Richard & Sher, Joan H. AIDS in the Nervous System. (Illus.). 136p. 1988. text ed. 55.95 (0-443-08616-8) Churchill.

Lechter, Michael & Musberger, R., eds. Six O'Clock High: Making Television News. (Communication Ser.). 1993. vhs 40.00 (1-56321-106-8); vhs write for info. (1-56321-105-X) LEA S&AM.

*Lechter, Michael A. Intellectual Property Handbook. LC 94-61489. 164p. 1994. pap. text ed. 19.95 (0-9643856-0-0) TechPress.

*Lechter, Michael A., ed. Successful Patents & Patenting for Engineers & Scientists. LC 94-46193. 1995. write for info. (0-7803-1086-1) Inst Electrical.

Lechter, Owen. Big Game Hunting in North-Eastern Rhodesia. (Illus.). 272p. 1987. 15.95 (0-312-00107-X) St Martin.

Lechtman, Heather, et al. Seven Matched Hollow Gold Jaguars from Peru's Early Horizon. LC 75-21192. (Studies in Pre-Columbian Art & Archaeology: No. 16). (Illus.). 49p. 1975. pap. 6.00 (0-88402-060-6) Dumbarton Oaks.

Lechtman, Max D., et al. The Games Cells Play. 160p. (C). 1993. per. 14.95 (0-8403-8382-7) Kendall-Hunt.

*Lechtman, Michael. Lost Tribe of Eden. 360p. 1995. pap. 9.95 (1-56901-816-2) NW Pub.

Lechuga, Armando. No Dejes para Manana: Don't Leave for Tomorrow. (SPA.). 3.95 (84-7645-483-X, 223573, Pub. by Edit Clie SP) TSELF.

— Recluta de Jesus: Soldier for Jesus. (SPA.). 3.25 (84-7645-273-X, 223334, Pub. by Edit Clie SP) TSELF.

*Lechuga, Carlos. In the Eye of the Storm: Castro, Khrushchev, Kennedy & the Missile Crisis. (Illus.). 215p. 1995. 15.95 (1-875284-87-7, Pub. by Ocean Pr AT) Talman.

*Lechuga, Ruth D. & Sayer, Chloe. Mask Arts of Mexico. 1995. pap. 17.95 (0-8118-0811-4) Chronicle Bks.

*Leck, Charles. Birds of New Jersey. 1975. pap. 9.95 (0-8135-0838-X) Rutgers U Pr.

Leck, Charles F. The Status & Distribution of New Jersey's Birds. LC 83-17655. 210p. 1984. text ed. 30.00 (0-8135-1033-3) Rutgers U Pr.

Leck, Charles F., jt. auth. see Norton, Robert L.

Leck, Mary A., et al. Ecology of Soil Seed Banks. 462p. 1989. text ed. 97.00 (0-12-440405-7) Acad Pr.

Leck, Mary A., et al, eds. Ecology of Soil Seed Banks. (Illus.). 462p. 1993. pap. text ed. 39.95 (0-12-440406-5) Acad Pr.

Leckenby, John D., ed. Proceedings of the 1988 Conference of the American Academy of Advertising. 1988. pap. 25.00 (0-931030-11-0) Am Acad Advert.

*Lecker, Michael. Muslims, Jews, & Pagans: Studies on Early Islamic Medina. LC 95-9833. (Islamic History & Civilization: Studies & Text: Vol. 13). 1995. write for info. (90-04-10247-7) E J Brill.

Lecker, Robert. On the Line. 130p. (C). 1982. pap. text ed. 8.95 (0-920802-31-1, Pub. by ECW Press CN) Genl Dist Srvs.

— An Other I: The Fictions of Clark Blaise. 246p. (C). 1988. text ed. 28.00 (1-55022-083-7, Pub. by ECW Press CN); pap. text ed. 16.00 (1-55022-082-9, Pub. by ECW Press CN) Genl Dist Srvs.

Lecker, Robert, ed. Canadian Canons: Essays in Literary Value. 288p. 1992. 35.00 (0-8020-5826-4); pap. 16.95 (0-8020-6700-X) U of Toronto Pr.

Lecker, Robert & Brown, Kathleen R., eds. An Anthology of Maine Literature. 260p. 1982. pap. 13.95 (0-89101-050-5) U Maine Pr.

Lecker, Robert & David, Jack. Introduction to Literature: British American-Canadian. 1065p. (C). 1990. pap. text ed. 23.50 (0-06-043891-6) HarpCollege.

Lecker, Robert & David, Jack, eds. The Annotated Bibliography of Canada's Major Authors, Vol. I. 263p. (C). 1979. text ed. 45.00 (0-920802-02-8) Genl Dist Srvs.

— The Annotated Bibliography of Canada's Major Authors, Vol. 2. 277p. (C). 1980. text ed. 45.00 (0-920802-38-9); pap. text ed. 28.00 (0-920802-40-0) Genl Dist Srvs.

— The Annotated Bibliography of Canada's Major Authors, Vol. 3. 395p. (C). 1981. text ed. 45.00 (0-920802-23-0) Genl Dist Srvs.

— The Annotated Bibliography of Canada's Major Authors, Vol. 4. 370p. (C). 1983. text ed. 45.00 (0-920802-52-4); pap. text ed. 28.00 (0-920802-54-0) Genl Dist Srvs.

— The Annotated Bibliography of Canada's Major Authors, Vol. 5. 480p. (C). 1984. text ed. 45.00 (0-920802-68-0) Genl Dist Srvs.

— The Annotated Bibliography of Canada's Major Authors, Vol. 6. 448p. (C). 1985. text ed. 45.00 (0-920802-93-1); pap. text ed. 28.00 (0-920802-95-8) Genl Dist Srvs.

— The Annotated Bibliography of Canada's Major Authors, Vol. 7. 477p. (C). 1987. text ed. 45.00 (0-920763-11-1); pap. text ed. 28.00 (0-920763-12-X) Genl Dist Srvs.

— The Annotated Bibliography of Canada's Major Authors, Vol. 8. (C). 1993. pap. text ed. 28.00 (1-55022-043-8) Genl Dist Srvs.

— The Annotated Bibliography of Canada's Major Authors: Marian Engel, Anne Hebert, Robert Kroetsch, Stephen Leacock & Thomas Raddall, Vol. 7. (G. K. Hall Reference Bks.). 450p. 1988. text ed. 50.00 (0-8161-8796-7, Hall Reference) Macmillan.

— The Annotated Bibliography of Canada's Major Authors Vol. 8, Vol. 8. (C). 1993. text ed. 50.00 (1-55022-044-6, Pub. by ECW Press CN) Genl Dist Srvs.

Lecker, Robert, ed. see Artibise, A.

Lecker, Robert, jt. ed. see David, Jack.

Lecker, Robert, ed. see Donovan, Josephine.

Lecker, Robert, ed. see Lyons, Charles R.

Lecker, Robert, ed. see Matthews, John T.

Lecker, Robert, ed. see Page, Norman.

Lecker, Robert, ed. see Seidel, Michael.

Lecker, Robert, ed. see Vivante, Paolo.

Lecker, Robert, et al, eds. Canadian Writers & Their Works, Vol. 1: Fiction. (Illus.). 256p. (C). 1983. text ed. 45.00 (0-920802-45-1, Pub. by ECW Press CN) Genl Dist Srvs.

— Canadian Writers & Their Works, Vol. 1: Poetry. (Illus.). 250p. (C). 1988. text ed. 45.00 (0-920763-69-3, Pub. by ECW Press CN) Genl Dist Srvs.

— Canadian Writers & Their Works, Vol. 10: Fiction. (Illus.). 294p. (C). 1989. text ed. 45.00 (0-920763-85-5, Pub. by ECW Press CN) Genl Dist Srvs.

— Canadian Writers & Their Works, Vol. 10: Poetry. (Illus.). 395p. (C). 1992. text ed. 45.00 (1-55022-069-1, Pub. by ECW Press CN) Genl Dist Srvs.

— Canadian Writers & Their Works, Vol. 2: Fiction. (Illus.). 270p. (C). 1989. text ed. 45.00 (1-55022-046-2, Pub. by ECW Press CN) Genl Dist Srvs.

— Canadian Writers & Their Works, Vol. 2: Poetry. (Illus.). 289p. (C). 1983. text ed. 45.00 (0-920802-46-X, Pub. by ECW Press CN) Genl Dist Srvs.

— Canadian Writers & Their Works, Vol. 3: Poetry. (Illus.). 200p. (C). 1987. text ed. 45.00 (0-920763-19-7, Pub. by ECW Press CN) Genl Dist Srvs.

— Canadian Writers & Their Works, Vol. 4: Fiction. (Illus.). 298p. (C). 1991. text ed. 45.00 (1-55022-052-7, Pub. by ECW Press CN) Genl Dist Srvs.

— Canadian Writers & Their Works, Vol. 4: Poetry. (Illus.). 286p. (C). 1990. text ed. 45.00 (1-55022-021-7, Pub. by ECW Press CN) Genl Dist Srvs.

— Canadian Writers & Their Works, Vol. 5: Fiction. (Illus.). 257p. (C). 1990. text ed. 45.00 (1-55022-027-6, Pub. by ECW Press CN) Genl Dist Srvs.

— Canadian Writers & Their Works, Vol. 5: Poetry. (Illus.). 329p. (C). 1985. text ed. 45.00 (0-920802-90-7, Pub. by ECW Press CN) Genl Dist Srvs.

— Canadian Writers & Their Works, Vol. 6: Fiction. (Illus.). 272p. (C). 1985. text ed. 45.00 (0-920802-86-9, Pub. by ECW Press CN) Genl Dist Srvs.

— Canadian Writers & Their Works, Vol. 6: Poetry. (Illus.). 316p. (C). 1989. text ed. 45.00 (1-55022-007-1, Pub. by ECW Press CN) Genl Dist Srvs.

— Canadian Writers & Their Works, Vol. 7: Fiction. (Illus.). 310p. (C). 1985. text ed. 45.00 (0-920802-88-5, Pub. by ECW Press CN) Genl Dist Srvs.

— Canadian Writers & Their Works, Vol. 7: Poetry. (Illus.). 316p. (C). 1990. text ed. 45.00 (1-55022-057-8, Pub. by ECW Press CN) Genl Dist Srvs.

— Canadian Writers & Their Works, Vol. 8: Fiction. (Illus.). 283p. (C). 1989. text ed. 45.00 (1-55022-032-2, Pub. by ECW Press CN) Genl Dist Srvs.

— Canadian Writers & Their Works, Vol. 8: Poetry. (Illus.). 412p. (C). 1992. text ed. 45.00 (1-55022-063-2, Pub. by ECW Press CN) Genl Dist Srvs.

— Canadian Writers & Their Works, Vol. 9: Fiction. (Illus.). 373p. (C). 1987. text ed. 45.00 (0-920763-79-0, Pub. by ECW Press CN) Genl Dist Srvs.

— Canadian Writers & Their Works, Vol. 9: Poetry. (Illus.). 271p. (C). 1985. text ed. 45.00 (0-920802-47-8, Pub. by ECW Press CN) Genl Dist Srvs.

— Canadian Writers & Thier Works, Vol. 3: Fiction. (Illus.). 276p. (C). 1988. text ed. 45.00 (0-920763-74-X, Pub. by ECW Press CN) Genl Dist Srvs.

Lecker, Seymour. Deadly Brew: Advanced Improvised Explosives. (Illus.). 64p. 1987. pap. 10.00 (0-87364-418-2) Paladin Pr.

— Explosive Dusts: Advanced Improvised Explosives. (Illus.). 60p. 1991. pap. 10.00 (0-87364-587-1) Paladin Pr.

— Homemade Semtex: C-4's Ugly Sister. (Illus.). 40p. 1991. pap. 12.00 (0-87364-617-7) Paladin Pr.

— Improvised Explosives: How to Make Your Own. (Illus.). 80p. 1985. pap. 12.00 (0-87364-320-8) Paladin Pr.

— Incendiaries: Advanced Improvised Explosives. (Illus.). 64p. 1988. pap. 10.00 (0-87364-483-2) Paladin Pr.

— Professional Booby Traps. (Illus.). 128p. 1993. pap. 15.00 (0-87364-699-1) Paladin Pr.

Lecker, Sidney. The Success Factor. LC 85-16135. 111p. reprint ed. pap. 31.70 (0-8357-4245-8, 2037033) Bks Demand.

— Who Are You? 1979. 4.95 (0-686-66206-7, Fireside) S&S Trade.

Leckey, Andrew. The Twenty Hottest Investments for the 21st Century. 288p. 1994. 19.95 (0-8092-3558-7) Contemp Bks.

Leckey, Dave. Trading Western Softwood Lumber: The Basics. 192p. (Orig.). 1989. pap. 24.95 (0-9621022-0-2) Highland Oregon.

Leckey, Dolores. Winter Music: A Life of Jessica Powers: Poet, Nun, Woman of the 20th Century. LC 92-27486. 182p. (Orig.). 1992. pap. 12.95 (1-55612-559-3, LL1559) Sheed & Ward MO.

— Women & Creativity. (Madeleva Lectures, 1991). 1991. pap. 3.95 (0-8091-3259-1) Paulist Pr.

Leckey, Dolores R., intro. One Body - Different Gifts, Many Roles: Reflections on the American Catholic Laity. 64p. (Orig.). 1987. pap. 3.95 (1-55586-162-8) US Catholic.

Leckey, Hugo. Set for Edwin Honig. (First Edition Ser.: Vol. 2, No. 3). (Illus.). (Orig.). 1973. pap. 1.50 (0-916912-07-8) Hellcoal Pr.

Leckie, Dale A., jt. ed. see MacQueen, Roger W.

Leckie, George G., ed. see Korschelt, O.

Leckie, George G., tr. see Korschelt, O.

Leckie, James O., jt. ed. see Kavanaugh, Michael.

Leckie, R. From Sea to Shining Sea. 1994. pap. 15.00 (0-06-092254-0) HarpC.

Leckie, Robert. Delivered from Evil: The Saga of World War II - The First Complete One-Volume History. LC 86-46305. 1024p. 1988. reprint ed. pap. 18.00 (0-06-091535-8, PL 1535, PL) HarpC.

— From Sea to Shining Sea: From the War of 1812 to the Mexican War, the Saga of America's Expansion. LC 92-56243. (Illus.). 704p. 1993. 30.00 (0-06-016802-1, HarpT) HarpC.

— George Washington's War: The Saga of the American Revolution. LC 92-52607. (Illus.). 672p. 1993. reprint ed. pap. 15.00 (0-06-092215-X, PL) HarpC.

— None Died in Vain: The Saga of the American Civil War. LC 89-45832. 640p. 1991. reprint ed. pap. 17.00 (0-06-092116-1, PL) HarpC.

— The Wars of America: From 1600 to 1900, Vol. 1. LC 92-54863. (Illus.). 640p. 1993. pap. 16.00 (0-06-092409-8, PL) HarpC.

— The Wars of America: From 1900 to 1992, Vol. 2. LC 92-54863. (Illus.). 672p. 1993. pap. 16.00 (0-06-092410-1, PL) HarpC.

*Leckie, Robert, narr. Okinawa: Okinawa, Final Battle of WW II. LC 94-39145. 1995. 24.95 (0-670-84716-X, Viking) Viking Penguin.

Leckie, Shirley A. Elizabeth Bacon Custer & the Making of a Myth. LC 92-50717. 1993. 26.95 (0-8061-2501-2) U of Okla Pr.

Leckie, Shirley A., jt. auth. see Leckie, William H.

*Leckie-Tarry, Helen. Language & Context: A Functional Linguistic Theory of Register. Birch, David, ed. LC 95-3907. 1995. pap. write for info. (1-85567-272-3, Pub. by Pinter Pubs UK) St Martin.

Leckie, William H. The Buffalo Soldiers: A Narrative of the Negro Cavalry in the West. LC 67-15571. (Illus.). 1975. pap. 13.95 (0-8061-1244-1) U of Okla Pr.

— The Military Conquest of the Southern Plains. LC 63-17160. (Illus.). 295p. reprint ed. 84.10 (0-8357-9736-8, 2016236) Bks Demand.

Leckie, William H. & Leckie, Shirley A. Unlikely Warriors: General Benjamin H. Grierson & His Family. LC 84-40275. (Illus.). 384p. 1984. 27.95 (0-8061-1912-8) U of Okla Pr.

Lecklider, G. Robert & Lund, John W. Road Design Handbook. 3rd ed. (Illus.). 151p. (C). 1976. pap. text ed. 12.00 (0-9619389-0-0) J W Lund.

Leckrone, Michael. Popular Music in the U. S. 2nd ed. 128p. 1991. pap. 15.95 (0-945483-19-8) E Bowers Pub.

Lecky, Prescott. Self-Consistency: A Theory of Personality. LC 82-82238. 144p. 1982. pap. 6.95 (0-87208-221-0) Island Pr Pubs.

— Self-Consistency: A Theory of Personality. rev. ed. LC 93-81260. 176p. (C). 1994. pap. 12.95 (0-87208-310-1) Island Pr Pubs.

Lecky, William E. Democracy & Liberty, Set. LC 80-82371. 1981. reprint ed. 20.00 (0-913966-80-0); reprint ed. pap. 10.00 (0-913966-81-9) Liberty Fund.

— Democracy & Liberty, Vol. I. LC 80-82371. 520p. 1981. reprint ed. 10.00 (0-913966-82-7) Liberty Fund.

— Democracy & Liberty, Vol. II. 528p. 1981. reprint ed. write for info. (0-913966-83-5) Liberty Fund.

— Historical & Political Essays. LC 76-99707. (Essay Index Reprint Ser.). 1977. 23.95 (0-8369-1973-4) Ayer.

— History of England in the Eighteenth Century, 7 Vols, Set. rev. ed. LC 68-57226. reprint ed. 540.00 (0-404-03930-8) AMS Pr.

— History of European Morals from Augustus to Charlemagne, 2vols. in one. 3rd ed. LC 74-25764. (European Sociology Ser.). 912p. 1975. reprint ed. 59.95 (0-405-06518-3) Ayer.

— A History of Ireland in the Eighteenth Century. LC 78-184286. (Classics of British Historical Literature Ser.). 565p. reprint ed. pap. 161.10 (0-8357-8907-1, 2056772) Bks Demand.

— History of Ireland in the Eighteenth Century, 5 Vols, 1. LC 70-77896. reprint ed. write for info. (0-404-03941-3) AMS Pr.

— History of Ireland in the Eighteenth Century, 5 Vols, 2. LC 70-77896. reprint ed. write for info. (0-404-03942-1) AMS Pr.

— History of Ireland in the Eighteenth Century, 5 Vols, 3. LC 70-77896. reprint ed. write for info. (0-404-03943-X) AMS Pr.

— History of Ireland in the Eighteenth Century, 5 Vols, 4. LC 70-77896. reprint ed. write for info. (0-404-03944-8) AMS Pr.

— History of Ireland in the Eighteenth Century, 5 Vols, 5. LC 70-77896. reprint ed. write for info. (0-404-03945-6) AMS Pr.

— History of Ireland in the Eighteenth Century, 5 Vols, Set. LC 70-77896. reprint ed. 385.00 (0-404-03940-5) AMS Pr.

— A History of Ireland in the Eighteenth Century, 5 vols., Set. 1972. reprint ed. 55.00 (0-403-03601-1) Scholarly.

— A History of Ireland in the 18th Century, 5 vols. 1972. 500.00 (0-8490-0331-8) Gordon Pr.

— Leaders of Public Opinion in Ireland, 2 vols, Set. LC 76-159800. (Europe 1815-1945 Ser.). 720p. 1973. reprint ed. lib. bdg. 79.50 (0-306-70574-5) Da Capo.

Leclair, jt. auth. see Baldwin.

Leclair, Normand. Chicken Expressions. 1991. pap. 9.95 (0-9620331-0-3) Normand Pub.

— Chicken Expressions. (Illus.). 68p. 1992. spiral bd. 11.00 (0-317-89539-7) Normand Pub.

Leclair, Normand J. Seafood Expressions. (Illus.). 312p. (Orig.). 1991. pap. 12.95 (0-9620331-2-X) Normand Pub.

*LeClair, Pete & Congdon-Martin, Douglas. Carving Caricature Hands & Faces: 33 Caricatures with Step-by-Step Carving Instructions. LC 95-15653. (Illus.). 1995. write for info. (0-88740-784-6) Schiffer.

LeClair, Tom. The Art of Excess: Mastery in Contemporary American Fiction. LC 88-31582. 256p. 1989. pap. 15.95 (0-252-06102-0) U of Ill Pr.

— In the Loop: Don DeLillo & the Systems Novel. LC 87-10783. 260p. 1988. 27.50 (0-252-01483-9) U of Ill Pr.

*LeClair, W. Pete. Carving Caricature Heads & Faces. LC 95-15653. (Illus.). 64p. (Orig.). 1995. pap. 12.95 (0-614-06658-1) Schiffer.

LeClaire, Anne. Sideshow. 336p. 1994. 20.95 (0-670-84328-8, Viking) Viking Penguin.

LeClaire, Anne D. Grace Point. 352p. 1993. pap. 5.99 (0-451-40395-9, Sig) NAL-Dutton.

LeClaire, Cynthia. Homage to the Light. (New Poets Ser.: No. 1). 96p. 1985. pap. 6.00 (0-933806-42-6) Black Swan CT.

Leclaire, Day. In the Market. (Romance Ser.: No. 183). 1992. pap. 2.89 (0-373-03183-1, 1-03183-0) Harlequin Bks.

— Mail-Order Bridegroom. (Romance Ser.). 1995. pap. 2.99 (0-373-03361-3, 1-03361-2) Harlequin Bks.

An Asterisk (*) at the beginning of an entry indicates that the title is appearing in BIP for the first time.

L

— Once a Cowboy... Back to the Ranch. (Romance Ser.). 1994. mass mkt. 2.99 (*0-373-03301-X*, 1-03301-8) Harlequin Bks.

— To Catch a Ghost. (Romance Ser.). 1993. mass mkt. 2.99 (*0-373-03285-4*, 1-03285-3) Harlequin Bks.

— A Wholesale Arrangement. large type ed. LC 93-20048. 247p. 1993. reprint ed. Alk. paper. lib. bdg. 13.95 (*1-56054-681-6*) Thorndike Pr.

— Who's Holding the Baby? 1994. mass mkt. 2.99 (*0-373-03338-9*, 1-03338-0) Harlequin Bks.

Leclant, J. & Clerc, G. Inventaire Bibliographique des Isiaca (IBIS), Vol. 4, R-Z. LC 72-340099. (Etudes Preliminaires aux Religions Orientales dans l'Empire Romain Ser.: Vol. 18). ix, 374p. (FRE.). 1990. 103.00 (*90-04-09247-1*) E J Brill.

Leclerc, Annette, et al. Dictionnaire D'Epidemiologie. 143p. (FRE.). 1990. write for info. (*0-7859-0506-5*, 2876710382) Fr & Eur.

Leclerc, Denise, ed. The Crisis of Abstraction in Canada: The 1950s. (Illus.). 272p. 1993. pap. 39.95 (*0-88884-624-X*, Pub. by Natl Gallery CN) U Ch Pr.

Leclerc, Eloi. People of God in the Night. Lachance, Paul & Schwartz, Paul, trs. (Tau Ser.). 1979. 2.95 (*0-8199-0768-5*, Frncscn Herld) Frncscn Pr.

— The Wisdom of the Poor One of Assisi. Johnson, Marie-Louise, tr. LC 91-27207. 118p. 1992. reprint ed. lib. bdg. 13.95 (*0-932727-47-6*); reprint ed. pap. 8.95 (*0-932727-45-X*) Hope Pub Hse.

— The Wisdom of the Poverello. Johnson, Marie-Louise, tr. 126p. 1989. reprint ed. pap. 6.95 (*0-8199-0147-4*, Frncscn Herld) Franciscan Pr.

Leclerc, Felix. The Madman, the Kite & the Island. 153p. 1983. pap. 3.95 (*0-7736-7054-8*, Pub. by Stoddart Pubng CN) Genl Dist Srvs.

Leclerc, Georges-Louis. Three Hundred Sixty-Eight Animal Illustrations from Buffon's "Natural History" LC 93-3708. (Pictorial Archive Ser.). (Illus.). 1993. write for info. (*0-486-27703-8*) Dover.

Leclerc, Ivor. The Nature of Physical Existence. 382p. 1986. reprint ed. text ed. 25.50 (*0-8191-4853-9*) U Pr of Amer.

— The Philosophy of Nature. LC 85-9607. (Studies in Philosophy & the History of Philosophy: Vol. 14). 232p. 1986. 31.95 (*0-8132-0613-8*) Cath U Pr.

— The Philosophy of Nature. LC 85-9607. (Studies in Philosophy & the History of Philosophy: No. 14). reprint ed. pap. 66.70 (*0-7837-9112-7*, 2049914) Bks Demand.

Leclerc, J. C. & Cornu, A. Neutron Activation Analysis Tables: Analyses Per Activation. LC 74-77710. 72p. reprint ed. pap. 25.00 (*0-317-29323-0*, 2024014) Bks Demand.

LeClerc, Jacinthe, tr. see Manara, Milo.

LeClerc, Jacinthe, tr. see Pichard, Georges & Masoch, Count.

Leclerc, Jacques R. Venous Thromboembolic Disorders. LC 90-5923. (Illus.). 448p. 1991. text ed. 79.50 (*0-8121-1308-X*) Williams & Wilkins.

Leclercq, D. & Bruno, J., eds. Item Banking: Interactive Testing & Self-Assessment. (NATO ASI Series F: Computer & Systems Sciences, Special Programme AET: Vol. 112). viii, 263p. 1993. 69.00 (*0-387-56653-8*) Spr-Verlag.

Leclercq, Dom H. & Marron, Henri. Dictionnaire d'Archeologie Chretienne et de Liturgie, 28 vols., Set. (FRE.). 1903. 2,995.00 (*0-8288-6892-1*, M-6342) Fr & Eur.

Leclercq, Jacques, tr. see Verlaine, Paul M.

Leclercq, Jean. Love of Learning & Desire for God: A Study of Monastic Culture. 3rd ed. LC 60-53004. x, 282p. 1985. pap. 14.00 (*0-8232-0407-3*) Fordham.

— A Second Look at Saint Bernard. Said, Marie-Bernard, tr. (Cistercian Studies: No. 105). 150p. 1991. 35.95 (*0-87907-605-4*); pap. 19.95 (*0-87907-405-1*) Cistercian Pubns.

— St. Bernard on Women. 1989. 8.95 (*0-318-41660-3*); pap. 19.95 (*0-318-41661-1*) Cistercian Pubns.

— Women & St. Bernard of Clairvaux. Said, Marie B., tr. (Cistercian Studies: No. 104). 171p. 1990. 34.95 (*0-87907-604-6*); pap. 16.95 (*0-87907-404-3*) Cistercian Pubns.

Leclercq, Jean, intro. Thomas Merton on St. Bernard. (Cistercian Studies: No. 9). 1980. 13.95 (*0-87907-809-X*); pap. 4.95 (*0-87907-909-6*) Cistercian Pubns.

Leclercq, Jean, tr. see Bernard Of Clairvaux.

***LeClercq, Terri.** Expert Legal Writing. LC 95-6449. 1995. write for info. (*0-292-74687-3*); pap. write for info. (*0-292-27468-8*) U of Tex Pr.

Leclere, Adhemard. Le Buddhisme au Cambodge. LC 76-179215. reprint ed. 72.00 (*0-404-54843-1*) AMS Pr.

— Cambodge: Fetes Civiles et Religieuses. LC 77-87040. reprint ed. 47.50 (*0-404-16832-9*) AMS Pr.

— Contes Laotiens et Contes Cambodgiens: Recueillis, Traduits et Annotes. LC 70-179216. reprint ed. 49.50 (*0-404-54844-X*) AMS Pr.

— Histoire du Cambodge Depuis le Premier Siecle De Notre Ere. LC 73-179217. (FRE.). reprint ed. 82.50 (*0-404-54845-8*) AMS Pr.

LeClere, Christian, jt. ed. see Labelle, Jacques.

LeClere, Felicia B., jt. ed. see Hendershot, Gerry E.

LeClerq, B., ed. Feeding of Non-Ruminant Livestock. 214p. 1987. text ed. 125.00 (*0-407-00460-2*) Buttrwrth-Heinemann.

Leclerq, B. & Whitehead, C. C. Leanness in Domestic Birds: Genetic Metabolic & Hormonal Aspects. (Illus.). 405p. 1988. text ed. 185.00 (*0-408-01036-3*) Buttrwrth-Heinemann.

Leclerq, D., et al. New Information Technology in Education: Belgium. 72p. 1993. pap. 30.00 (*92-826-4678-5*, CY-03-92-002-EN-C, Pub. by Europ Com) UNIPUB.

Leclerq, Patricia R., tr. see Berlandier, Jean L.

LeClezio, J. M. The Prospector. Marshall, Carol, tr. 320p. 1993. 22.95 (*0-87923-976-X*) Godine.

LeCocque, Andre, intro. Commitment & Commemoration: Jews, Christians, Muslims in Dialogue. LC 93-72787. 151p. 1994. text ed. 25.95 (*0-913552-54-2*) Exploration Pr.

LeCoff, Albert. Lathe-Turned Objects: An International Exhibition. Field, Carol & Silver, Eileen J., eds. LC 88-20688. (Illus.). 168p. 1988. text ed. 40.00 (*0-685-47238-8*); boxed 40.00 (*0-685-37565-X*) Wood Turn Ctr.

LeCoff, Albert, ed. International Lathe-Turning: New Perspectives. Date not set. write for info. (*0-9624385-6-1*); pap. write for info. (*0-9624385-5-3*) Wood Turn Ctr.

— Lathe-Turned Objects: An International Exhibition. 168p. 1988. pap. 29.95 (*0-9624385-2-9*) Wood Turn Ctr.

LeCoff, Albert B. International Lathe-Turned Objects: Challenge IV. Silver, Eileen et al, eds. (Illus.). 68p. (Orig.). 1991. pap. text ed. 16.00 (*0-9624385-3-7*) Wood Turn Ctr.

— Revolving Techniques: Clay - Glass - Metal - Wood. LeCoff, Tina C. et al, eds. (Illus.). 24p. (Orig.). 1992. pap. 6.00 (*0-9624385-4-5*) Wood Turn Ctr.

LeCoff, Albert B., ed. Challenge V: International Lathe-Turned Objects. (Illus.). 74p. (Orig.). 1994. pap. 20.00 (*0-9624385-7-X*) Wood Turn Ctr.

LeCoff, Tina C., ed. see LeCoff, Albert B.

Lecointe, Jean. Dictionnaire des Synonymes et des Equivalences. 354p. 1993. pap. 19.95 (*0-7859-5625-5*, 2253061417) Fr & Eur.

LeCompte, Fay P. Copper Pieces. LC 86-72349. 100p. 1987. 10.00 (*0-934943-08-7*) Thirteen Colonies Pr.

LeCompte, I. C., ed. Roman des Romans. (Elliott Monographs: Vol. 14). 1974. reprint ed. 15.00 (*0-527-02617-4*) Periodicals Srv.

Lecompte, Janet. Pueblo, Hardscrabble, Greenhorn: Society on the High Plains, 1832-1856. LC 77-18616. (Illus.). 368p. 1981. reprint ed. pap. 15.95 (*0-8061-1723-0*) U of Okla Pr.

Lecompte, Janet, ed. see French, Emily.

LeCompte, Margaret D. & Preissle, Judith. Ethnography & Qualitative Design in Educational Research. 2nd ed. (Illus.). 425p. 1993. text ed. 49.95 (*0-12-440575-4*) Acad Pr.

LeCompte, Margaret D., jt. auth. see Bennett, Kathleen P.

LeCompte, Margaret D., jt. auth. see DeMarrais, Kathleen B.

LeCompte, Margaret D., et al. Giving up on School: Student Dropouts & Teacher Burnouts. 312p. 1991. text ed. 42.00 (*0-8039-3490-4*, D1478); pap. text ed. 21.00 (*0-8039-3491-2*, D1478) Corwin Pr.

LeCompte, Margaret D., et al, eds. The Handbook of Qualitative Research in Education. (Illus.). 881p. 1992. text ed. 55.95 (*0-12-440570-3*) Acad Pr.

LeCompte, Mary L. Cowgirls of the Rodeo: Pioneer Professional Athletes. LC 92-42635. (Sport & Society Ser.). (Illus.). 200p. 1993. 22.50 (*0-252-02029-4*) U of Ill Pr.

Lecompte, Stuart, tr. see Roy, Jean-Louis.

***Lecomte, Barbara J.** Aphasia: What Is It? 16p. 1995. 14.95 (*0-614-07072-4*, 1550) Speech Bin.

Lecomte, Bernard, jt. auth. see Lesourne, Jacques.

LeComte, Edward. Milton & Sex. LC 77-1081. 154p. 1978. text ed. 31.00 (*0-231-04340-6*) Col U Pr.

Lecomte, Eva. Paula, la Pequena Valdense. 200p. 1987. 2.25 (*0-317-02030-7*) Rod & Staff.

— Paula, the Waldensian. Strong, W. M., tr. (J). (gr. 3-7). 1942. pap. 5.99 (*0-87213-511-X*) Loizeaux.

Lecomte, Serge. Crimson Rice. limited ed. 14.95 (*0-685-40173-1*) Librado Pr.

— Laruen at Two: Poems. LC 92-24464. (Illus.). 88p. 1992. pap. 12.95 (*0-7734-9612-2*) E Mellen.

— What Shall I Tell You, Nikos? LC 93-28610. 64p. 1993. pap. 9.95 (*0-7734-2773-2*, Mellen Poetry Pr) E Mellen.

Lecomte, Serge, tr. see Khlebnikov, Kirill T.

Leconte De Lisle, Charles-Rene-Marie. Poemes Barbares. (Poesie Ser.). (FRE.). pap. 16.95 (*2-07-032326-9*) Schoenhof.

LeConte, Emma. When the World Ended: The Diary of Emma LeConte. Miers, Earl S., ed. LC 87-5937. xxxii, 124p. 1987. reprint ed. pap. 6.95 (*0-8032-8151-X*, Bison Books) U of Nebr Pr.

LeConte, John L. & Horn, George H. Classification of the Coleoptera of North America: Smithsonian Miscellaneous Collections, No. 507. Sterling, Keir B., ed. LC 77-81103. (Biologists & Their World Ser.). 1978. reprint ed. lib. bdg. 51.95 (*0-405-10689-0*) Ayer.

Leconte, John L., ed. see Say, Thomas.

LeConte, Joseph. A Journal of Ramblings Through the High Sierras of California by the "University Excursion Party" LC 93-43686. (High Sierra Classics Ser.). (Illus.). 1994. 7.95 (*0-939666-70-7*) Yosemite Assn.

Lecorche, P. P., jt. ed. see Dallmeyer, R. D.

Lecorne, Martin. Uptown Downtown Growing Up. 1987. pap. 12.50 (*0-940984-32-6*) U of SW LA Ctr LA Studies.

Lecot, K., jt. comp. see Balbin, I.

LeCount, Albert L. Black Bear Field Guide: A Manager's Manual. (Orig.). 1986. pap. write for info. (*0-917563-04-2*) AZ Game & Fish.

Lecours, Andre R., et al. Aphasiology. (Illus.). 464p. 1983. text ed. 60.95 (*0-7020-1014-6*, Bailliere-Tindall) Saunders.

Lecourt, Nancy. Abracadabra to Zigzag. (Illus.). (J). (ps-3). 1991. 13.95 (*0-688-09481-3*); lib. bdg. 13.88 (*0-688-09482-1*) Lothrop.

— Abracadabra to Zigzag: An Alphabet Book. LC 92-12503. (Illus.). 32p. (J). (ps-3). 1992. pap. 4.99 (*0-14-054470-4*) Puffin Bks.

Lecourt, Nancy H. Teddy the Better-Than-New Bear. (Sunshine Ser.). 32p. (J). 1993. pap. 5.95 (*0-8163-1116-1*) Pacific Pr Pub Assn.

Lecourtier, J. & Cartalos, M. V. Cementing Technology & Procedures. (Illus.). 128p. (C). 1993. 115.00 (*2-7108-0649-5*, Pub. by Edits Technip FR) St Mut.

Lecourtier, J., jt. ed. see Toulhoat, H.

***Lecouteux, Claude.** Petit Dictionnaire de Mythologie Allemande. 286p. (FRE.). 1991. pap. 49.95 (*0-7859-7971-9*, 2726601014) Fr & Eur.

Lecrompe, Rene, ed. Caesar: De Bello Gallico - Index Verborum. Vol. XI. xvi, 373p. 1968. write for info. (*0-318-71972-X*, Pub. by Georg Olms GW) Lubrecht & Cramer.

— Caesar - De Bello Gallico - Index Verborum. Bd. XI. xvi, 373p. 1968. write for info. (*0-318-71084-6*, Pub. by Georg Olms GW) Lubrecht & Cramer.

— Caesar - De Bello Gallico. Index Verborum. Bd. XI. xvi, 373p. 1968. write for info. (*0-318-70657-1*, Pub. by Georg Olms GW) Lubrecht & Cramer.

— Vergilius: Virgile, Bucoliques, Index Verborum, Releves Statistiques. Vol. XXIV. 148p. 1970. write for info. (*0-318-71977-0*, Pub. by Georg Olms GW) Lubrecht & Cramer.

— Vergilius - Virgile, Bucoliques. Index Verborum, Releves Statistiques. Bd. XXIV. 148p. 1970. write for info. (*0-318-70662-8*, Pub. by Georg Olms GW) Lubrecht & Cramer.

Lecrompe, Rene, ed. see Vergil.

Lecrompe, Rene, ed. see Vergilius.

LeCron, Leslie & Bordeaux, Jean. Hypnotism Today. 1976. pap. 5.00 (*0-87980-081-X*) Wilshire.

LeCron, Leslie M. Self Hypnotism: The Technique & Its Use in Daily Living. 1970. pap. 4.99 (*0-451-15984-5*, Sig) NAL-Dutton.

Lecron, Leslie M. Self-Hypnotism: The Technique & Its Use in Daily Living. pap. 4.95 (*0-13-803486-9*, Reward) P-H.

— Self-Hypnotism: The Technique & Its Use in Daily Living. 224p. 1988. pap. text ed. 8.95 (*0-13-803339-0*) P-H.

LeCroy, Barbara & Holder, Bonnie. Bookwebs: A Brainstorm of Ideas for the Primary Classroom. (Illus.). 175p. 1994. pap. 21.00 (*1-56308-109-1*) Teacher Ideas Pr.

LeCroy, Craig. Handbook of Child & Adolescent Treatment Manuals. LC 93-40136. 432p. 1994. text ed. 40.00 (*0-02-918485-1*) Macmillan.

LeCroy, Craig W. Case Studies in Social Work Practice. 296p. (C). 1992. pap. 31.95 (*0-534-15138-8*) Brooks-Cole.

LeCroy, Craig W., ed. Social Skills Training for Children & Youth. LC 83-228. (Child & Youth Services Ser.: Vol. 5, Nos. 3 & 4). 152p. 1983. text ed. 39.95 (*0-86656-184-6*) Haworth Pr.

Lectorium Rosicrucianum Staff, tr. see De Petri, Catharose.

Lectorium Rosicrucianum Staff, ed. see De Petri, Catharose.

Lectorium Rosicrucianum Staff, tr. see Van Rijckenborgh, Jan.

LeCuyer, Annette W., jt. auth. see Libeskind, Daniel.

LeCuyer, E. J. College Mathematics with a Programming Language. (Undergraduate Texts in Mathematics Ser.). 1978. 35.00 (*0-387-90280-5*) Spr-Verlag.

LeCuyer, James M. A Brick for Offissa Pupp. (Orig.). 1989. pap. 8.00 (*0-912449-31-4*) Floating Island.

Lecuyer, Raymond. Historie de la Photographie. Bunnell, Peter C. & Sobieszek, Robert A., eds. LC 76-23050. (Sources of Modern Photography Ser.). (Illus.). (FRE.). 1979. reprint ed. lib. bdg. 40.00 (*0-405-09609-7*) Ayer.

LeDantec, Jean-Pierre, jt. auth. see LeDentec, Denise.

Ledbetter, Calvin R., Jr. The Carpenter from Conway: George Washington Donaghey As Governor of Arkansas, 1909-1913. LC 92-29038. (Illus.). 320p. 1993. pap. 12.00 (*1-55728-374-5*) U of Ark Pr.

Ledbetter, Cathy, jt. auth. see Dickler, Howard.

Ledbetter, Cynthia E. & Jones, Richard C. John Muir. LC 92-46763. (Biographies: Pioneers Ser.). (J). 1993. 19.93 (*0-86625-494-3*); 14.95 (*0-685-67774-5*) Rourke Pubns.

Ledbetter, Cynthia E., jt. auth. see Fifer, Fred L.

Ledbetter, Dale. From Mother, with Love: Reflections on Achieving Sales Success. Gage, Randy, ed. (Sales Mastery Ser.). (Orig.). 1994. pap. 11.95 (*1-884667-01-5*) Gage Res & Develop.

— Success Yearbook: Three Hundred Sixty-Five Days to Mastery. (Sales Mastery Ser.). 425p. 1994. pap. 15.95 (*1-884667-00-7*) Gage Res & Develop.

— The Ultimate Sales Professional. Gaye, Randy, ed. (Sales Mastery Ser.). (Orig.). 1994. pap. 11.95 (*1-884667-02-3*) Gage Res & Develop.

Ledbetter, Darriel, jt. auth. see Graham, Leland.

Ledbetter, David. Continuo Playing According to Handel. (Early Music Ser.: No. 12). (Illus.). 112p. 1990. 55.00 (*0-19-318434-6*); pap. 29.95 (*0-19-318433-8*) OUP.

— Harpsichord & Lute Music in Seventeenth Century France. LC 87-17041. (Illus.). 214p. 1988. 39.95 (*0-253-32707-5*) Ind U Pr.

Ledbetter, Frances M., jt. auth. see Melton, Dana D.

Ledbetter, H. & Lomax, John A. Buenas Noches, Irene. Pike, D., ed. Pichardo, Hector, tr. (Illus.). (SPA.). (J). (ps-2). 1993. pap. text ed. 15.00 (*0-922053-27-8*) N Edge Res.

— Goodnight Irene Big Book. Pike, D., ed. (Illus.). (J). (ps-2). 1988. pap. text ed. 14.00 (*0-922053-08-1*) N Edge Res.

Ledbetter, Jim. First-Class Cricket: A Complete Record 1937. 251p. 1993. pap. 59.00 (*1-874524-04-1*, Pub. by Limlow Bks UK) St Mut.

Ledbetter, Jim & Wynne-Thomas, Peter. First-Class Cricket: A Complete Record 1939. 252p. 1992. 59.00 (*1-874524-00-9*, Pub. by Limlow Bks UK) St Mut.

Ledbetter, Joe O. Air Pollution, Part 1: Analysis. LC 77-160112. (Environmental Health Engineering Textbooks Ser.: Vol. 2). (Illus.). 440p. reprint ed. pap. 125.40 (*0-8357-5284-4*, 2029001) Bks Demand.

— Air Pollution, Part 2: Prevention & Control. LC 77-160112. (Environmental Health Engineering Textbooks Ser.: Vol. 2). 304p. pap. 86.70 (*0-7837-0024-5*, 2029001) Bks Demand.

Ledbetter, Joe O., jt. auth. see Gloyna, Earnest F.

***Ledbetter, Ken.** Not Enough Women. 220p. 1995. lib. bdg. 27.00 (*0-8095-4570-5*) Borgo Pr.

Ledbetter, Kenneth W., jt. auth. see Wall, Stephen D.

Ledbetter, M. L. General Biology. 81p. (C). 1993. teacher ed 11.23 (*1-56870-056-3*) RonJon Pub.

Ledbetter, Marie, jt. auth. see Thiel, Linda.

Ledbetter, Mark. Virtuous Intentions: The Religious Dimension of Narrative. 100p. 1989. 20.95 (*1-55540-394-8*, 01 01 66); pap. 13.95 (*1-55540-395-6*, 01 01 66) Scholars Pr GA.

***Ledbetter, Mark & Jasper, David, eds.** In Good Company: Essays in Honor of Robert Detweiler. LC 94-33428. (AAR Studies in Religion: 71). 478p. 1994. pap. 44.95 (*0-7885-0039-2*, 010071) Scholars Pr GA.

Ledbetter, Mary L. Cell Biology. 98p. (C). 1993. 11.23 (*1-56870-042-3*) RonJon Pub.

Ledbetter, Steven, ed. see Marenzio, Luca.

***Ledbetter, Suzann.** I Have Everything I Had Twenty Years Ago: Except Now It's All Lower. 1995. 17.00 (*0-517-59979-1*, Crown) Crown Pub Group.

— Nellie Cashman Prospector & Trailblazer. LC 92-62201. (Southwestern Studies: No. 98). 1993. pap. 12.50 (*0-87404-194-5*) Tex Western.

Ledbetter, William B. & Lemer, Andrew C., eds. Inspection & Other Strategies for Assuring Quality in Government Construction. 84p. 1991. pap. 19.00 (*0-309-04547-9*) Natl Acad Pr.

Ledbetter, William B., jt. auth. see Collier, Courtland.

Ledbetter, William B., jt. auth. see Peurifoy, Robert L.

Ledd, Paul. Shelter: Apache Trail, No. 9. (Orig.). 1982. pap. 2.25 (*0-89083-956-5*) Zebra.

— Shelter: Bang-Up Showdown, No. 29. 224p. 1987. pap. 2.50 (*0-8217-2240-9*) Zebra.

— Shelter: Chain Gang Kill, No. 3. 256p. (Orig.). 1980. pap. 1.95 (*0-89083-658-2*) Zebra.

— Shelter: China Doll, No. 4. 1980. pap. 1.95 (*0-89083-682-5*) Zebra.

— Shelter: Circus of Death, No. 6. (Orig.). 1981. pap. 1.95 (*0-89083-723-6*) Zebra.

— Shelter: Comanchero Blood, No. 13. (Orig.). 1983. pap. 2.25 (*0-8217-1208-X*) Zebra.

— Shelter: Fast-Draw Filly, No. 22. 1985. pap. 2.25 (*0-8217-1612-3*) Zebra.

— Shelter: Hanging Moon, No. 2. 256p. (Orig.). 1980. pap. 1.95 (*0-89083-637-X*) Zebra.

— Shelter: Heavenly Hands, No. 27. 224p. 1987. pap. 2.25 (*0-8217-2023-6*) Zebra.

— Shelter: Hot & Spicy, No. 31. 224p. 1988. pap. 2.95 (*0-8217-2519-X*) Zebra.

— Shelter: Lookout Mountain, No. 7. 1981. pap. 1.95 (*0-89083-756-2*) Zebra.

— Shelter: Massacre Mountain, No. 10. (Orig.). 1982. pap. 2.25 (*0-89083-972-7*) Zebra.

— Shelter: Prisoner of Revenge, No. 1. 224p. (Orig.). 1980. pap. 1.95 (*0-89083-598-5*) Zebra.

— Shelter: Rio Rampage, No. 11. 1983. pap. 2.25 (*0-8217-1141-5*) Zebra.

— Shelter: Savage Night, No. 15. 1983. pap. 2.25 (*0-685-07875-2*) Zebra.

— Shelter: Shotgun Sugar, No. 21. 192p. 1987. pap. 2.25 (*0-8217-1547-X*) Zebra.

— Shelter: Taboo Territory, No. 18. 1984. pap. 2.25 (*0-8217-1379-5*) Zebra.

— Shelter: Tattle-Tail, No. 32. 224p. 1989. pap. 2.95 (*0-8217-2565-3*) Zebra.

— Shelter: The Bandit Queen, No. 8. (Orig.). 1981. pap. 2.25 (*0-89083-869-0*) Zebra.

— Shelter: The Golden Shaft, Vol. 14. 1983. pap. 2.25 (*0-8217-1235-7*) Zebra.

— Shelter: The Hard Men, No, 19. 192p. 1984. pap. 2.25 (*0-8217-1428-7*) Zebra.

— Shelter: The Lazarus Guns, No. 5. 256p. (Orig.). 1980. pap. 1.95 (*0-89083-694-9*) Zebra.

— Shelter: The Naked Outpost, No. 17. 1984. pap. 2.25 (*0-8217-1330-2*) Zebra.

— Shelter: The Slave Queen, No. 25. 192p. 1986. pap. 2.25 (*0-8217-1869-X*) Zebra.

— Shelter: Treasure Chest, No. 26. 208p. 1986. pap. 2.25 (*0-8217-1955-6*) Zebra.

— Shelter: Wyoming Wench, No. 33. 1989. pap. 2.95 (*0-8217-2608-0*) Zebra.

— Shelter, No. 12: Blood Mesa. 1983. pap. 3.50 (*0-8217-1181-4*) Zebra.

— Ute Revenge. 224p. 1986. pap. 2.50 (*0-8217-1957-2*) Zebra.

Leddick, George R., jt. auth. see Borders, L. D.

Leddy. Conceptual Bases of Professional Nursing. 3rd ed. (Illus.). 1993. text ed. 27.95 (*0-397-54932-6*) Lippincott.

Leddy, jt. auth. see Roach.

Leddy, Mary J. Reweaving Religious Life: Beyond the Liberal Model. 208p. (Orig.). (C). 1990. pap. 9.95 (*0-89622-440-6*) Twenty-Third.

Leddy, Tracy. Allison's Shadow. LC 82-61020. 124p. (Orig.). 1982. pap. 12.00 (*0-89142-040-1*) Sant Bani Ash.

***Lede, Naomi W.** Mary Allen College: Its Rich History, Pioneering Spirit, & Continuing Tradition. 104p. (YA). 1995. 24.95 (*0-9646839-0-3*) NAAMAC.

— Precious Memories of a Black Socialite: A Narrative of the Life & Times of Constance Houston Thompson. LC 91-65957. 300p. (Orig.). 1991. 24.95 (*0-9630007-0-5*) Lede Consult.

An Asterisk (*) at the beginning of an entry indicates that the title is appearing in BIP for the first time.

— Samuel W. Houston & His Contemporaries: A Documentary History of Education. 348p. (Orig.). 1991. pap. 16.00 (*0-9630007-1-3*) Lede Consult.

Ledebour, K. F. Icones Plantarum Novarum Vel Imperfecte Cognitarm Floram Rossicam. (C). 1988. text ed. 1,200.00 (*0-685-22101-6*, Scientific) St Mut.

— Icones Plantarum Novarum Vel Imperfecte Cognitarum Floram Rossicam, 5 Vols. in 1. 1968. 495.00 (*3-7682-0567-3*) Lubrecht & Cramer.

***Ledec, George & Goodland, Robert.** Wildlands: Their Protection & Management in Economic Development. 312p. 1988. 17.95 (*0-614-02881-7*, 11154) World Bank.

Ledeen, Michael. Superpower Dilemmas: The U. S. & U. S. S. R. at Century's End. 264p. (C). 1991. pap. 21.95 (*0-88738-891-4*) Transaction Pubs.

— Universal Fascism: The Theory & Practice of the Fascist International, 1928-1936. LC 70-185794. xxi, 200p. 1995. reprint ed. lib. bdg. 35.00 (*0-86527-202-6*) Fertig.

Ledeen, Michael A. The First Duce: D'Annunzio at Fiume. LC 76-47376. 240p. reprint ed. pap. 68.40 (*0-8357-6746-9*, 2035401) Bks Demand.

— West European Communism & American Foreign Policy. 310p. 1987. 34.95 (*0-88738-140-5*) Transaction Pubs.

Ledeen, Robert W., et al, eds. New Trends in Ganglioside Research: Neurochemical & Neuroregenerative Aspects. (FIDIA Research Ser.: Vol. 14). xiv, 660p. 1988. 141.00 (*0-387-96797-4*) Spr-Verlag.

Ledell, Marjorie & Arnsparger, Arleen. How to Deal with Community Criticism of School Change. LC 93-22715. 39p. (Orig.). 1993. pap. 6.95 (*0-87120-205-0*) Assn Supervision.

LeDentec, Denise & LeDantec, Jean-Pierre. Reading the French Gardens: Story & History. Levine, Jessica, tr. (Illus.). 296p. 1990. 27.50 (*0-262-12144-1*) MIT Pr.

Leder, Arie C. Conozca Su Iglesia. (SPA.). 1984. 4.50 (*1-55955-057-0*) CITE MI.

— Los Diez Mandamientos. (SPA.). 1985. 3.10 (*1-55955-059-7*) CITE MI.

— Exodo. (SPA.). 1986. 2.90 (*1-55955-082-1*) CITE MI.

— Genesis. (SPA.). 1985. 2.80 (*1-55955-083-X*) CITE MI.

— Introduccion al Hebreo Biblico. (SPA.). 1983. 12.00 (*1-55955-092-9*) CITE MI.

Leder, Dora, illus. Bedtime Bear's Book of Bedtime Poems. (Care Bear Bks.). 40p. (J). (ps-3). 1983. lib. bdg. 4.99 (*0-394-95956-6*) Random Bks Yng Read.

— Let's Peek in Santa's Pack. LC 89-61375. (Peek-a-Boo Board Bks.). 14p. (J). (ps). 1990. bds. 3.99 (*0-679-80277-0*) Random Bks Yng Read.

Leder, Drew. The Absent Body. 224p. 1990. lib. bdg. 34.95 (*0-226-46999-9*); pap. text ed. 14.95 (*0-226-47000-8*) U Ch Pr.

Leder, Drew, ed. The Body in Medical Thought & Practice. (Philosophy & Medicine Ser.). 272p. (C). 1992. lib. bdg. 109.50 (*0-7923-1657-6*) Kluwer Ac.

Leder, Gilah, ed. Assessment & Learning of Mathematics. (C). 1990. 75.00 (*0-86431-122-2*, Pub. by Aust Council Educ Res AT) St Mut.

Leder, Gilah, jt. ed. see Fennema, Elizabeth.

Leder, Gilah C., jt. auth. see Gunstone, Richard.

Leder, Hans H. Cultural Persistence in a Portuguese-American Community. Cordasco, Francesco, ed. LC 80-874. (American Ethnic Groups Ser.). 1981. lib. bdg. 20.95 (*0-405-13435-5*) Ayer.

Leder, Jan. Women in Jazz: A Discography of Instrumental Music, Nineteen Thirteen to Nineteen Sixty-eight. LC 85-17657. (Discographies Ser.: No. 19). xv, 311p. 1985. text ed. 45.00 (*0-313-24790-0*, LMI/, Greenwood Pr) Greenwood.

Leder, Jane. Amelia Earhart: Opposing Viewpoints. LC 89-12028. (Great Mysteries Ser.). (Illus.). 112p. (J). (gr. 5-8). 1989. lib. bdg. 16.95 (*0-89908-070-7*) Greenhaven.

Leder, Jane M. Brothers & Sisters. 1994. mass mkt. 5.99 (*0-345-37995-0*) Ballantine.

— Brothers & Sisters: How They Shape Our Lives. 304p. 1991. 19.95 (*0-312-06312-1*) St Martin.

— Dead Serious: A Book for Teenagers about Teenage Suicide. 160p. (YA). (gr. 7 up). 1989. pap. 3.50 (*0-380-70661-X*, Flare) Avon.

— Dead Serious: A Book for Teenagers about Teenage Suicide. LC 86-25880. 160p. (YA). (gr. 7 up). 1987. text ed. 14.95 (*0-689-31262-8*, Atheneum Bks Young) S&S Childrens.

— Exotic Cars. LC 87-15572. (Super-Charged Ser.). (Illus.). 48p. (J). (gr. 5-6). 1987. lib. bdg. 11.95 (*0-89686-351-4*, Crstwood Hse) Silver Burdett Pr.

— Learning How: Gymnastics. James, Jody, ed. (Learning How Sports Ser.). (Illus.). 48p. (J). (gr. 4-7). 1992. lib. bdg. 14.95 (*0-944280-35-8*); pap. 5.95 (*0-944280-40-4*) Bancroft-Sage.

— Learning How: Karate. James, Jody, ed. (Learning How Sports Ser.). (Illus.). 48p. (J). (gr. 4-7). 1992. lib. bdg. 14.95 (*0-944280-34-X*); pap. 5.95 (*0-944280-39-0*) Bancroft-Sage.

— Learning How: Skateboarding. James, Jody, ed. (Learning How Sports Ser.). (Illus.). 48p. (J). (gr. 4-7). 1992. lib. bdg. 14.95 (*0-944280-33-1*); pap. 5.95 (*0-944280-42-0*) Bancroft-Sage.

— Learning How: Soccer. James, Jody, ed. (Learning How Sports Ser.). (Illus.). 48p. (J). (gr. 4-7). 1992. lib. bdg. 14.95 (*0-944280-32-3*); pap. 5.95 (*0-944280-38-2*) Bancroft-Sage.

— Marcus Allen. LC 84-11375. (Sports Close-Ups 2 Ser.). (Illus.). 48p. (J). (gr. 5-6). 1985. text ed. 11.95 (*0-89686-251-8*, Crstwood Hse) Silver Burdett Pr.

— Martina Navratilova. LC 89-99550. (Sports Close-Ups 2 Ser.). (Illus.). 48p. (J). (gr. 5-6). 1985. text ed. 11.95 (*0-89686-252-6*, Crstwood Hse) Silver Burdett Pr.

— Wayne Gretzky. LC 84-14980. (Sports Close-Ups 2 Ser.). (Illus.). 48p. (J). (gr. 5-6). 1985. text ed. 11.95 (*0-89686-255-0*, Crstwood Hse) Silver Burdett Pr.

Leder, Lawrence H., ed. The Livingston Indian Records, Sixteen Sixty-Six to Seventeen Twenty-Three. (American Indians at Law Ser.). 1980. reprint ed. text ed. 25.00 (*0-930576-33-0*) E M Coleman Ent.

Leder, Sharon & Abbott, Andrea. The Language of Exclusion: The Poetry of Emily Dickinson & Christina Rossetti. LC 87-7519. (Contributions in Women's Studies: No. 83). (Illus.). 250p. 1987. text ed. 55.00 (*0-313-25629-2*, LLE/, Greenwood Pr) Greenwood.

Leder, Sharon, jt. ed. see Teichman, Milton.

Lederach, John, jt. auth. see Lederach, Naomi.

***Lederach, John P.** Preparing for Peace: Conflict Transformation Across Cultures. (Studies on Peace & Conflict Resolution). 160p. 1995. text ed. 24.95x (*0-8156-2656-8*) Syracuse U Pr.

Lederach, Naomi & Lederach, John. Recovery of Hope. LC 91-74057. 169p. 1991. pap. 11.95 (*1-56148-046-0*) Good Bks PA.

Lederach, Paul M. Daniel. (Believers Church Bible Commentary Ser.: No. 6). 328p. (Orig.). (C). 1995. pap. 17.95 (*0-8361-3663-2*) Herald Pr.

— Teaching in the Congregation. LC 79-83594. (Mennonite Faith Ser.: No. 7). 72p. 1979. pap. 2.95 (*0-8361-1886-3*) Herald Pr.

— A Third Way. LC 80-18041. 160p. 1980. pap. 7.95 (*0-8361-1934-7*) Herald Pr.

Lederberg, Joshua, comp. & intro. The Excitement & Fascination of Science, Set. (Illus.). 1990. 90.00 (*0-8243-2603-2*) Annual Reviews.

Lederberg, Joshua, ed. Encyclopedia of Microbiology, 1. (Illus.). 2650p. 1992. text ed. 199.00 (*0-12-226891-1*) Acad Pr.

— Encyclopedia of Microbiology, 2. (Illus.). 2650p. 1992. text ed. 199.00 (*0-12-226892-X*) Acad Pr.

— Encyclopedia of Microbiology, 3. (Illus.). 2650p. 1992. text ed. 199.00 (*0-12-226893-8*) Acad Pr.

— Encyclopedia of Microbiology, 4. (Illus.). 2650p. 1992. text ed. 199.00 (*0-12-226894-6*) Acad Pr.

— Encyclopedia of Microbiology, Vols. 1-4. (Illus.). 2650p. 1992. text ed. 695.00 (*0-12-226890-3*) Acad Pr.

Lederer & Posey Staff & Kelley, Gibbs & Reynolds Staff. Basic Virginia Law for Non-Lawyers: Legal Survival in the Commonwealth of Virginia. Lederer, Fredric, ed. 96p. 1993. pap. 8.95 (*0-9615670-3-1*, King & Queen Pr) Soc Alu Wm.

Lederer, C. Michael & Shirley, Virginia S., eds. Table of Isotopes. 7th ed. LC 78-14938. 1600p. 1978. pap. text ed. 220.00 (*0-471-04180-7*) Wiley.

Lederer, Dolores P. The "Perfectionist's" How To: "Custom Draperies" 3rd ed. LC 88-91302. ("Perfectionist's" How To Bks.: Bk. 1). (Illus.). 104p. (Orig.). 1982. reprint ed. pap. text ed. 35.00 (*0-9608040-0-5*) Lederer Enterprises.

— The "Perfectionist's" How To: "Drapery Top Treatments" ("Perfectionist's" How To Books Ser.: Bk. II). (Illus.). 108p. (Orig.). 1983. reprint ed. pap. text ed. 35.00 (*0-9608040-1-3*) Lederer Enterprises.

— The "Perfectionist's" How To: "Window Specialties" (" Perfectionist's" How To Books Ser.: Bk. III). (Illus.). 112p. (Orig.). 1985. reprint ed. pap. text ed. 35.00 (*0-9608040-2-1*) Lederer Enterprises.

—The "Perfectionist's" How to Books, 3 vols., Set. (Illus.). (Orig.). 1992. reprint ed. pap. text ed. 90.00 (*0-9608040-3-X*) Lederer Enterprises.
THE "PERFECTIONIST'S" HOW TO DRAPERY BOOKS, written by Dee Lederer, are the most detailed & complete instruction manuals ever written. There are three books in the series, each with easy to follow instructions & numerous step-by-step photos & illustrations showing every minute detail of fabrication & tips on installing. BOOK I: "CUSTOM DRAPERIES" is complete with instructions for measuring; calculating the yardage; fabricating both pleated & shirred draperies (including arched & slanted tops); customizing (pleating without premarking); working with prints (so the same pattern is showing on both sides of the window when the draperies are open). BOOK II: "DRAPERY TOP TREATMENTS" has instructions for calculating the yardage & fabricating, many styles of pleated valances (French, double, reverse, cartridge, box, etc.); Cornices; Lambrequins; Austrian Swags; Empire Style Swags; Jabots; Queen Anne Style Swags; Cascades; Original Style Swags. BOOK III: "WINDOW SPECIALTIES" has instructions for calculating the yardage & fabricating many styles of vertically operated window coverings: Romans (Flat, Tucked, Prefolded); Austrians; Balloons (Pleated, Shirred); Pouffs; Opera Drapery. Shows how to adapt some of the styles to shaped windows (arched) & to one piece bay window treatments.
Publisher Provided Annotation.

Lederer, Emil. Die Privatangestellten in der Modernen Wirtschaftsentwicklung: White Collar Workers in Modern Economic Development. LC 74-25765. (European Sociology Ser.). 300p. 1975. reprint ed. 28.95 (*0-405-06519-1*) Ayer.

Lederer, Eric M., ed. Calculus One Exam File. (Exam File Ser.). 250p. (Orig.). 1986. pap. 12.50 (*0-910554-61-7*) Engineering.

— College Algebra Exam File. LC 89-17085. (Exam File Ser.). 410p. (Orig.). 1990. pap. 15.50 (*0-910554-77-3*) Engineering.

— Linear Algebra Exam File. LC 88-23498. (Exam File Ser.). 442p. (Orig.). (C). 1989. pap. 16.50 (*0-910554-69-2*) Engineering.

Lederer, Florence, tr. see Shabistari, Mahmud.

Lederer, Florence, ed. see Shabistari, Sa'd Ud Din Mahmud.

Lederer, Frederic, jt. auth. see Moliterno, James E.

Lederer, Fredric, ed. see Lederer & Posey Staff & Kelley, Gibbs & Reynolds Staff.

Lederer, Fredric I., jt. auth. see Gilligan, Francis A.

Lederer, Herbert. Handbook of East German Drama 1945-1985: DDR Drama Handbuch. (DDR-Studien - East German Studies: Vol. 1). 280p. (C). 1987. text ed. 39.95 (*0-8204-0367-9*) P Lang Pubs.

— Reference Grammar of German. 1981. 22.50 (*0-684-41329-9*, Scribners) S&S Trade.

— A Reference Grammar of the German Language. (C). 1969. pap. text ed. write for info. (*0-13-033713-7*) P-H.

Lederer, Herbert, et al, eds. A Reference Grammar of the German Language. LC 69-17352. 709p. (C). 1969. pap. text ed. write for info. (*0-13-033705-6*) P-H.

Lederer, Ivo. Russian Foreign Policy: Essays in Historical Perspective. 1962. 97.50 (*0-685-26675-3*) Elliots Bks.

Lederer, Ivo, ed. Western Approaches to Eastern Europe. LC 92-16998. 112p. 1992. pap. 14.95 (*0-87609-130-3*) Coun Foreign.

Lederer, Ivo J., jt. ed. see Sugar, Peter F.

Lederer, Janet R. Care Planning Pocket Guide. 3rd ed. 1990. spiral bd. 13.56 (*0-201-58298-8*) Addison-Wesley.

— Care Planning Pocket Guide: A Nursing Diagnosis Approach. 4th ed. 288p. (C). 1991. spiral bd. 21.50 (*0-8053-4103-X*) Addison-Wesley.

— Care Planning Pocket Guide: A Nursing Diagnosis Approach. 22th ed. LC 87-28987. 1988. pap. 17.50 (*0-201-16399-3*) Addison-Wesley.

Lederer, Janet R., jt. auth. see Wilkinson, Judith M.

Lederer, Janet R., et al. Care Planning Pocket Guide: A Nursing Diagnosis Approach. 5th ed. LC 92-48222. (C). 1993. spiral bd. 26.95 (*0-8053-4104-8*) Benjamin-Cummings.

Lederer, Jean. Encyclopedia Moderne de l'Hygiene Alimentaire, Vol. 1: Exigences Alimentaires de l'Homme Normal. 198p. (FRE.). 1978. pap. write for info. (*0-7859-5076-1*) Fr & Eur.

— Encyclopedie Modern De L'hygiene Alimentaire, 4 vols. (FRE.). 95.00 (*0-686-57003-0*, M-6344) Fr & Eur.

— Encyclopedie Moderne de l'Hygiene Alimentaire: Vol. 2, Hygiene des Aliments. 282p. (FRE.). 1977. 55.00 (*0-8288-5421-1*, M6346) Fr & Eur.

— Encyclopedie Moderne de l'Hygiene Alimentaire, Vol. 4: Les Intoxications Alimentaire. 164p. (FRE.). 1978. pap. write for info. (*0-7859-5078-8*) Fr & Eur.

— Encyclopedie Moderne de l'Hygiene Alimentaire, Vol. 3: Technologie et Hygiene Alimentaire. 138p. (FRE.). 1978. pap. write for info. (*0-7859-5077-X*) Fr & Eur.

Lederer, Katherine. Lillian Hellman. (United States Authors Ser.: No. 338). 176p. 1979. text ed. 21.95 (*0-8057-7275-8*, Twayne) Macmillan.

***Lederer, Laura.** Price We Pay the Case Against Racist Speech, Hate Propaganda, & Pornography. 1995. 30.00 (*0-8090-7883-X*); pap. 15.00 (*0-8090-1577-3*) Hill & Wang.

Lederer, Laura, ed. Take Back the Night: Women on Pornography. LC 80-23701. 352p. 1980. pap. 11.00 (*0-688-08728-0*, Quill) Morrow.

Lederer, Michael. Advanced Thin-Layer Chromatography. 1971. 21.50 (*0-317-17781-8*) Elsevier.

— Chromatography for Organic Chemistry. LC 93-31657. 1994. text ed. 49.95 (*0-471-94285-5*) Wiley.

— The Periodic Table for Chromatographers. 175p. 1992. text ed. 185.00 (*0-471-93149-7*) Wiley.

Lederer, Michael, ed. Chromatographic Reviews. 1963. pap. 51.50 (*0-444-40365-5*) Elsevier.

Lederer, Mira. Adriatic Formula. 1980. pap. 1.95 (*0-8439-0829-7*) Dorchester Pub Co.

— Tell Me No Lies. 304p. 1988. pap. 3.95 (*0-8217-2435-5*) Zebra.

Lederer, Paul J. Cheyenne Dreams. (Indian Heritage Ser.: No. 4). 1989. pap. 3.50 (*0-451-13651-9*) NAL-Dutton.

— Way of Wind. (Indian Heritage Ser.: No. 5). 1989. pap. 3.50 (*0-451-14038-9*) NAL-Dutton.

Lederer, Richard. Adventures of a Verbivore. LC 93-32287. 1994. 21.00 (*0-671-70941-0*) PB.

— Adventures of a Verbivore. Rosenman, Jane, ed. 288p. 1995. pap. 10.00 (*0-671-70942-9*) PB.

— Anguished English. 1989. mass mkt. 5.99 (*0-440-20352-X*, LFL) Dell.

— Anguished English: An Anthology of Accidental Assaults upon Our Language. LC 87-40532. (Illus.). 128p. 1987. pap. 7.95 (*0-941711-04-8*) Wyrick & Co.

— Crazy English. Pfefferblit, Elaine, ed. 1990. reprint ed. mass mkt. 5.99 (*0-671-68907-X*) PB.

— Get Thee to a Punnery. 1990. mass mkt. 5.95 (*0-440-20499-2*) Dell.

— Get Thee to a Punnery. (Illus.). 160p. 1988. pap. 7.95 (*0-941711-08-0*) Wyrick & Co.

— Literary Trivia: Fun & Games for Book Lovers. 1994. pap. 10.00 (*0-679-75380-X*, Vin) Random.

— The Miracle of Language. Rosenman, Jane, ed. 272p. 1992. reprint ed. mass mkt. 5.99 (*0-671-70940-2*) PB.

— More Anguished English. LC 93-3000. (Illus.). 1993. 17.95 (*0-385-31017-X*) Delacorte.

— More Anguished English. 1994. pap. 5.99 (*0-440-21577-3*) Dell.

— Nothing Risque, Nothing Gained: Ribald Riddles, Lascivious Limericks, Carnal Corn, & Other Good, Clean, Dirty Fun. LC 95-12959. (Illus.). 1995. write for info. (*1-55652-243-6*) Chicago Review.

— Nothing Risque, Nothing Gained: Ribald Riddles, Lascivious Limericks, Carnal Corn, & Other Good, Clean Dirty Fun. LC 95-12959. (Illus.). 312p. (Orig.). 1995. pap. text ed. 12.00 (*0-614-07074-0*) Chicago Review.

— The Play of Words. Pfefferblit, Elaine, ed. 288p. 1991. reprint ed. pap. 10.00 (*0-671-68909-6*) PB.

Lederer, Richard, jt. auth. see Burnham, Phillip.

Lederer, Richard, jt. auth. see Fisher, Arnold.

Lederer, Richard M., Jr. Colonial American English: A Glossary. LC 85-50954. 1985. 24.95 (*0-930454-19-7*) Verbatim Bks.

Lederer, Roger J. Bird Finder: A Guide to Common Birds of Eastern North America. (Illus.). 60p. 1990. pap. 2.50 (*0-912550-18-X*, T) Nature Study.

— Ecology & Field Biology. (C). 1984. text ed. 41.95 (*0-8053-5718-1*) Benjamin-Cummings.

— Pacific Coast Bird Finder: A Manual for Identifying 61 Common Birds of Pacific Coast. (Illus.). 62p. 1977. pap. 2.50 (*0-912550-04-X*) Nature Study.

Lederer, Susan E. Subjected to Science: Human Experimentation in America Before the Second World War. (Henry E. Siegrist Series in the History of Medicine). 192p. 1995. text ed. 32.95x (*0-8018-4820-2*) Johns Hopkins.

Lederer, William H., jt. auth. see Keleti, Georg.

Lederer, William J. Creating a Good Relationship. 272p. 1984. reprint ed. pap. 8.95 (*0-393-30155-9*) Norton.

— New, Complete Book of Cross Country Skiing. 1983. pap. 9.95 (*0-393-30152-4*) Norton.

— Our Own Worst Enemy. LC 68-13847. 1968. 4.95 (*0-393-05357-1*) Norton.

— Ugly American. 1987. mass mkt. 5.95 (*0-449-21526-1*) Fawcett.

Lederer, William J. & Burdick, Eugene. Ugly American. (J). (gr. 9 up). 1965. pap. 10.95 (*0-393-00305-1*) Norton.

— The Ugly American. large type ed. LC 93-40483. 1994. write for info. (*0-8161-5938-6*, Large Print Bks) G K Hall.

Lederer, William J. & Jackson, Don D. Mirages of Marriage. LC 67-16608. 1968. 21.95 (*0-393-08400-0*) Norton.

— The Mirages of Marriage. 1990. pap. 11.00 (*0-393-30632-1*) Norton.

Lederer, Wolfgang. Dragons, Delinquents & Destiny: An Essay on Positive Superego Functions. LC 64-23955. (Psychological Issues Monograph: No. 15, Vol. 4, No. 3). 83p. (Orig.). 1964. text ed. 25.00 (*0-8236-1420-4*) Intl Univs Pr.

— The Kiss of the Snow Queen: Hans Christian Andersen & Man's Redemption by Woman. 275p. 1986. pap. 13.00 (*0-520-07190-5*) U CA Pr.

— The Kiss of the Snow Queen: Hans Christian Andersen & Man's Redemption by Woman. Dundes, Alan, ed. 1986. 35.00 (*0-520-05774-0*) U CA Pr.

Lederer, Zdenek. Ghetto Theresienstadt. Weisskopf, K., tr. LC 81-12615. 275p. 1983. reprint ed. lib. bdg. 40.00 (*0-86527-341-3*) Fertig.

Lederhandler, Sarah, tr. see Shulman, Eliezer.

Lederhendlender, Eli. Jewish Response to Modernity: New Voices in America & Eastern Europe. LC 94-2486. (Illus.). 250p. 1994. 40.00 (*0-8147-5084-2*) NYU Pr.

Lederhendler, Eli. The Road to Modern Jewish Politics: Political Tradition & Political Reconstruction in the Jewish Community of Tsarist Russia. (Studies in Jewish History). 256p. 1989. 39.95 (*0-19-505891-7*) OUP.

Lederis, K. & Veale, W. L., eds. Current Studies of Hypothalamic Function 1978. Incl. Part I: Hormones. 1978. 78.50 (*3-8055-2860-4*); Part II: Metabolism & Behaviour. 1978. 78.50 (*3-8055-2861-2*); (Illus.). 1978. 141.00 (*3-8055-2969-4*) S Karger.

Lederis, K., ed. see Symposium, Calgary, Alberta Staff.

Lederle, Henry I. Interpretations of "Spirit-Baptism" in the Charismatic Renewal Movement: Treasures Old & New. 368p. 1987. pap. 14.95 (*0-913573-75-2*) Hendrickson MA.

Lederleitner, Joseph. Faces of Perfection. 1992. 8.95 (*0-8062-4287-6*) Carlton.

Lederleitner, Joseph B. Essence of Being. 1994. 9.95 (*0-8062-4877-7*) Carlton.

— The Essence of Transcendence. 96p. 1991. 9.95 (*0-8062-4008-3*) Carlton.

Lederman, Audrey W. & Lederman, Jan C. Mission: Serendipity! An Adventure in Creative Problem Solving. (Illus.). 144p. (gr. k-12). 1983. pap. 12.95 (*0-88047-028-3*, 8311) DOK Pubs.

Lederman, David. Multiple Choice Questions in Preparation for the AP Calculus (AB) Examination. 90p. 1991. student ed 15.95 (*1-878621-01-7*) D & S Mktg Syst.

— Multiple Choice Questions in Preparation for the AP Calculus (AB) Examination. 5th ed. 127p. 1991. student ed 15.95 (*1-878621-00-9*) D & S Mktg Syst.

— Multiple Choice Questions in Preparation for the AP Calculus (BC) Examination. 90p. 1991. student ed 15.95 (*1-878621-03-3*) D & S Mktg Syst.

— Multiple Choice Questions in Preparation for the AP Calculus (BC) Examination. 4th ed. 121p. 1991. student ed 15.95 (*1-878621-02-5*) D & S Mktg Syst.

***Lederman, Diana.** Make-Me-a-Match - Chabat. (Illus.). (FRE.). 1994. spiral bd. 4.95 (*965-229-115-3*, Pub. by Gefen Pub Hse IS) Gefen Bks.

— Make-Me-a-Match - 'Hanouka. (FRE.). 1994. spiral bd. 4.95 (*965-229-118-8*, Pub. by Gefen Pub Hse IS) Gefen Bks.
— Make-Me-a-Match - Israel. (Illus.). (FRE.). 1994. spiral bd. 4.95 (*965-229-120-X*, Pub. by Gefen Pub Hse IS) Gefen Bks.
— Make-Me-a-Match - Les Fetes des Tishri. (Illus.). (FRE.). 1994. spiral bd. 4.95 (*965-229-119-6*, Pub. by Gefen Pub Hse IS) Gefen Bks.
— Make-Me-a-Match - Pessa'h. (Illus.). (FRE.). 1994. spiral bd. 4.95 (*965-229-116-1*, Pub. by Gefen Pub Hse IS) Gefen Bks.
— Make-Me-a-Match - Pourim. (Illus.). (FRE.). 1994. spiral bd. 4.95 (*965-229-117-X*, Pub. by Gefen Pub Hse IS) Gefen Bks.
Lederman, Diana, illus. Make-Me-a-Match. (FRE.). (J). 1992. spiral bd. 4.95 (*965-229-025-4*, Pub. by Gefen Pub Hse IS) Gefen Bks.
Lederman, Dov B., tr. see Soloukhin, R. I., ed.
Lederman, Dov B., tr. see Styrikovich, M. A., et al.
Lederman, Dov B., tr. see Suris, A. L.
Lederman, Dov B., tr. see Sychev, V. V., et al, eds.
Lederman, Dov B., tr. see Vilemas, J., et al.
Lederman, Dov B., tr. see Zukauskas, A. A., et al.
Lederman, Ellen. The Best Places to Meet Good Men. 352p. (Orig.). 1991. pap. 12.95 (*1-55958-106-9*) Prima Pub.
— College Majors: A Complete Guide from Accounting to Zoology. LC 89-29540. 140p. 1990. lib. bdg. 20.95x (*0-89950-462-0*) McFarland & Co.
— Health Care Planning: A Realistic Guide. 224p. 1988. 35. 95 (*0-89885-397-4*, Plenum Insight); pap. 18.95 (*0-89885-401-6*, Plenum Insight) Human Sci Pr.
— Making Life More Livable. 1994. pap. 14.00 (*0-671-87531-0*, Fireside) S&S Trade.
Lederman, I. English-Portuguese Dictionary of Electronics: Brazilian. 130p. 1986. pap. 39.00 (*0-88431-043-4*) IBD Ltd.
Lederman, Jan C., jt. auth. see Lederman, Audrey W.
Lederman, Jess. Adjustable Rate Mortgages & Mortgage Backed Securities: The Complete Reference Guide for Originators, Issuers, & Investors. 500p. 1991. text ed. 95.00 (*1-55623-232-2*) Irwin Prof Pubng.
— Global Asset Allocation: Techniques for Optimizing Portfolio Management. 1994. text ed. 60.00 (*0-471-59373-7*) Wiley.
— The Secondary Mortgage Market: Strategies for Surviving & Thriving in Today's Challenging Markets. rev. ed. 675p. 1992. 69.95 (*1-55738-288-3*) Probus Pub Co.
— Virtual Trading: How Any Trader with a PC Can Use the Power of Neural Nets & Expert Systems. 1994. 45.00 (*1-55738-812-1*) Probus Pub Co.
Lederman, Jess, ed. Commercial Loan Resale Market: A Banker's Guide to Selling Commercial, Industrial & LBO Debt. 1991. 60.00 (*1-55738-158-5*) Probus Pub Co.
— The Handbook of Asset-Backed Securities. 1990. 64.95 (*0-13-372301-1*) NY Inst Finance.
— The Handbook of Mortgage Banking: Trends, Opportunities & Strategies. rev. ed. 600p. 1993. 75.00 (*1-55738-494-0*) Probus Pub Co.
***Lederman, Jess, ed. & intro.** Handbook of Mortgage Lending. (Mortgage Lending Handbook Ser.). 300p. Date not set. 75.00 (*0-945359-43-8*) Mortgage Bankers.
Lederman, Jess, ed. Housing America: Mobilizing Bankers, Builders & Communities to Solve the Nation's Affordable-Housing Crisis. 400p. 1993. 32.50 (*1-55738-435-5*) Probus Pub Co.
Lederman, Jess & Klein, Richard A. Small Cap Stocks: Investment & Portfolio Strategies for the Institutional Investor. 1993. 65.00 (*1-55738-518-1*) Probus Pub Co.
***Lederman, Jess & Klein, Robert.** Hedge Funds: Investment & Portfolio Strategies for the Institutional Investor. 250p. 1995. 60.00 (*1-55738-861-X*) Probus Pub Co.
***Lederman, Jess & Klein, Robert, eds.** Financial Engineering with Derivatives: Cutting-Edge Innovations & Real-World Applications. 300p. 1995. 60.00 (*1-55738-854-7*) Probus Pub Co.
***Lederman, Jess & Klein, Robert A.** Equity Style Management: Evaluating & Selecting Investment Styles. 250p. 1995. 60.00 (*1-55738-860-1*) Probus Pub Co.
Lederman, Jess & Park, Keith, eds. Global Bond Markets: State-of-the-Art Research, Analysis & Investment Strategies. (Guide to World Markets Ser.). 1990. 70.00 (*1-55738-153-4*) Probus Pub Co.
— The Global Equity Markets: State-of-the-Art Research, Analysis & Investment Strategies. (Guide to World Markets Ser.). 1990. 70.00 (*1-55738-152-6*) Probus Pub Co.
Lederman, Jess & Sullivan, Michael P., eds. The New High-Yield Bond Market: Investment Opportunities. 400p. 1993. 55.00 (*1-55738-436-3*) Probus Pub Co.
***Lederman, Jess & Swoyer, G. Benjamin, eds.** Handbook of Commercial Real Estate Finance. (Mortgage Lending Handbook Ser.). 450p. 1995. 85.00 (*0-945359-42-X*) Mortgage Bankers.
Lederman, Jess, jt. auth. see Klein, Robert A.
Lederman, Jess, et al. Handbook of Municipal Bonds. 1994. 85.00 (*1-55738-577-7*) Probus Pub Co.
Lederman, L., jt. ed. see Weneser, J.
Lederman, Lawrence. Tombstones: A Lawyer's Tales from the Takeover Decades. 342p. 1992. 24.00 (*0-374-27845-8*) FS&G.
Lederman, Leon. God Particle: If the Universe Is the Answer, What's the Question. 1994. pap. 12.95 (*0-385-31211-3*, Delta) Dell.
Lederman, Leon & Schramm, David. From Quarks to Cosmos: Tools of Discovery. 256p. 1995. text ed. write for info. (*0-7167-5052-X*) W H Freeman.
Lederman, Linda C. & Dervin, Brenda, eds. Communication Pedagogy: Approaches to Teaching Undergraduate Courses in Communication. (Communication & Information Science Ser.). 352p. (C). 1992. text ed. 59. 50 (*0-89391-848-2*); pap. text ed. 27.50 (*0-89391-893-8*) Ablex Pub.
Lederman, Martin. The Slim Gourmet's Soup Book: A Complete Book of Soups. 1974. lib. bdg. 69.95 (*0-685-51364-5*) Revisionist Pr.
Lederman, Minna. The Life & Death of a Small Magazine (Modern Music, 1924-1946) LC 83-80057. (I.S.A.M. Monographs: No. 18). (Illus.). 211p. (Orig.). 1983. pap. 20.00 (*0-914678-20-5*) Inst Am Music.
Lederman, Minna, ed. Stravinsky in the Theatre. LC 74-34377. (Music Reprint Ser.). (Illus.). 228p. 1975. reprint ed. lib. bdg. 32.50 (*0-306-70665-2*); reprint ed. pap. 9.95 (*0-306-80022-5*) Da Capo.
Lederman, Norman, jt. auth. see Spector, Barbara S.
Lederman, Raizel, jt. auth. see Teitelbaum, Chaya S.
***Lederman, S. & Scheiderman, P.** Smoking Cessation: HP 609 Study Guide. 15p. (C). 1989. student ed, spiral bd. write for info. (*0-931657-18-0*) Learning Proc Ctr.
Lederman, Stan & Scheiderman, Patricia. If You Smoke, Please Try...Quitting. (Illus.). 100p. (Orig.). 1986. pap. text ed. 18.00 (*0-931657-02-4*) Learning Proc Ctr.
Ledermann, E. K. Philosophy & Medicine. (Avebury Series in the Philosophy of Science). 196p. 1986. text ed. 68.95 (*0-566-05062-5*, Pub. by Avebury Pub UK) Ashgate Pub Co.
— Your Health Is in Your Hands: A Case for Natural Medicine. 172p. (Orig.). 1991. pap. 9.95 (*1-870098-12-9*, Pub. by Green Bks UK) Seven Hills Bk.
Ledermann, Isaac. Dicionario Tecnico de Electronica Ingles - Portugues. (ENG & POR.). 1986. pap. 39.95 (*0-8288-3966-2*, F92230) Fr & Eur.
Ledermann, Walter. Introduction to Group Characters. 2nd ed. 240p. 1987. pap. 21.95 (*0-521-33781-X*) Cambridge U Pr.
***Ledesma, L., jt. auth. see Chavez, Lettie.**
Ledesma, Ron. Solaris for X86 Hardware Configuration Guide. 352p. 1994. pap. text ed. 40.00 (*0-13-124678-X*) P-H.
Ledet, David A. Oboe Reed Styles: Theory & Practice. LC 80-8152. (Illus.). 224p. 1981. 35.00 (*0-253-37891-5*) Ind U Pr.
Ledford. Reviewing Your Writing Skills. 192p. 1985. per. 16. 95 (*0-8403-3842-2*) Kendall-Hunt.
Ledford, Cathleen, jt. auth. see Mikuleky, Maureen P.
Ledford, Cawood, jt. auth. see Cameron, Chris.
Ledford, Dan. Cash in a Flash!, Vol. 1: How to Make a Fortune in Photography. 150p. (Orig.). 1990. 19.95 (*1-879497-00-X*) Natl Crdt Ctr.
Ledford, Ibbie. Hill Country Cookin' & Memoirs. LC 91-12217. (Illus.). 208p. 1991. 15.95 (*0-88289-848-5*) Pelican.
— Y'all Come Back, Now: Recipes & Memories. LC 93-6074. (Illus.). 224p. 1994. 15.95 (*1-56554-015-8*) Pelican.
Ledford, Jan R., jt. auth. see Gayton, Johnny L.
Ledford, Janice. Exercises in Refractometry. LC 89-42920. 151p. 1990. pap. 37.00 (*1-55642-120-6*) SLACK Inc.
— In-Office Training Program & Series Review. Benes, Susan C., ed. (Ophthalmic Technical Skills Ser.: Vol. II). 152p. 1991. pap. text ed. 40.00 (*1-55642-175-3*) SLACK Inc.
Ledgard, Henry. ADA: An Introduction. 2nd ed. (Illus.). 135p. 1987. pap. text ed. 30.00 (*0-387-90814-5*) Spr-Verlag.
— ANSI-IEEE Pascal Standard: The American Pascal Standard. 1984. 39.00 (*0-387-91248-7*) Spr-Verlag.
— Professional Software: Programming Practice, Vol. 2. (C). 1987. pap. text ed. 18.36 (*0-201-12232-4*) Addison-Wesley.
— Professional Software: Software Engineering Concepts, Vol. 1. LC 87-1760. (C). 1987. pap. text ed. 24.75 (*0-201-12231-6*) Addison-Wesley.
Ledgard, Henry & Singer, Andrew. Pascal for the Macintosh. LC 84-24503. 456p. (C). 1986. teacher ed write for info. (*0-201-11773-8*) Addison-Wesley.
Ledgard, Henry, jt. auth. see Marcotty, M. W.
Ledgard, Henry, et al. Directions in Human Factors for Interactive Systems. (Lecture Notes in Computer Science Ser.: Vol. 103). 190p. 1984. pap. 32.00 (*0-387-10574-3*) Spr-Verlag.
Ledger, jt. auth. see Marx.
Ledger, Allison C. Sex & Psychosexual Development: Index of New Information with Authors, Subjects & Bibliography. 180p. 1993. 49.50 (*1-55914-824-1*); pap. 39.50 (*1-55914-825-X*) ABBE Pubs Assn.
Ledger, David. Shifting Sands: The British in South Arabia. 232p. (C). 1990. 150.00 (*0-907151-08-6*, Pub. by IMMEL Pubng UK) St Mut.
Ledger, Frank & Sallis, Howard. Crisis Management in the Power Industry: An Inside Story. LC 94-12501. (Illus.). 360p. 1995. 65.00x (*0-415-11876-X*, C0109) Routledge.
Ledger, G. R. Re-Counting Plato: A Computer Analysis of Plato's Style. (Illus.). 272p. 1990. 78.00 (*0-19-814681-7*) OUP.
Ledger, Marshall A., jt. auth. see Cooper, David Y.
Ledger, Marshall A., jt. auth. see Ledger, Martha.
Ledger, Martha & Ledger, Marshall A. Dear Old Penn in Postcards: The University of Pennsylvania, 1900-1923. (Illus.). 60p. (Orig.). 1989. pap. write for info. (*0-318-65907-7*) M & M Ledger.
Ledger, Philip, ed. Anthems for Choirs Three: Twenty-Four Anthems for Sopranos & Altos, Three or More Parts. 1974. pap. text ed. 16.95 (*0-19-353242-5*) OUP.
— Anthems for Choirs Two: Twenty-Four Anthems for Sopranos & Altos, Unison & Two-Part. 1974. pap. text ed. 16.95 (*0-19-353240-9*) OUP.
— The Oxford Book of English Madrigals. 1979. pap. 16.95 (*0-19-343664-7*) OUP.
***Ledger, Sally & McCracken, Scott, eds.** Cultural Politics at the 'Fin de Siecle' (Illus.). 316p. (C). 1995. 59.95 (*0-521-44385-7*) Cambridge U Pr.
Ledger, Sally, ed. see Kee Yong Lim & Long, John.
Ledger, William J. Antibiotics in Obstetrics & Gynecology: Developments in Perinatal Medicine, No. 2. 320p. 1982. lib. bdg. 112.50 (*90-247-2529-1*) Kluwer Ac.
Ledgerwood, Byron K., ed. Control Engineering Conference: Proceedings of the First Annual Control Engineering Conference. 239p. 1982. 75.00 (*0-914331-50-7*, Control Engrng) Cahners Des Plaines.
— Control Engineering Conference: Proceedings of the Second Annual Control Engineering Conference. 347p. 1983. 75.00 (*0-914331-51-5*, Control Engrng) Cahners Des Plaines.
— Control Engineering Conference: Proceedings of the Third Annual Control Engineering Conference. 486p. 1984. 85.00 (*0-914331-52-3*, Control Engrng) Cahners Des Plaines.
Ledgerwood, Byron K., ed. & intro. Proceedings of the Fifth Annual Control Engineering Conference. (Control Engineering Conference Ser.). 478p. 1986. 85.00 (*0-914331-55-8*, Control Engrng) Cahners Des Plaines.
Ledgerwood, Byron K., ed. Proceedings of the Fourth Annual Control Engineering Conference. 528p. 1985. 85.00 (*0-914331-54-X*, Control Engrng) Cahners Des Plaines.
Ledgerwood, Byron K., ed. & intro. Proceedings of the Sixth Annual Control Engineering Conference-1987. (Control Engineering Conference Ser.). 703p. 1987. pap. 100.00 (*0-914331-56-6*, Control Engrng) Cahners Des Plaines.
Ledgerwood, Byron K., intro. Proceeding of the Eighth Annual Control Engineering Conference: Held As Part of the Control Engineering Conference & Exposition, O'Hare Exposition Center, Rosemont, IL, May 23-25, 1989. (Illus.). (Orig.). 1989. pap. 105.00 (*0-914331-58-2*, Control Engrng) Cahners Des Plaines.
— Proceedings of the Seventh Annual Control Engineering Conference: Held as Part of the Control Engineering Conference & Exposition Center, Rosemont, IL June 7-9, 1988. (Illus.). (Orig.). (C). 1988. pap. 100.00 (*0-914331-57-4*, Control Engrng) Cahners Des Plaines.
Ledgerwood, Graham V. Keys to Higher Consciousness: How to Contact Your Inner Self. Kubis, Pat, ed. (Illus.). 512p. 1989. 24.95 (*0-9623840-0-3*) Everest Costa.
Ledgerwood, Grant. Implementing an Environmental Audit: How to Gain a Competitive Advantage Using Quality & Environmental Responsibility. 228p. 1994. text ed. 45.00 (*0-7863-0142-2*) Irwin Prof Pubng.
Ledgerwood, Grant, et al, eds. The Environmental Audit & Business Strategy: A Total Quality Approach. (Financial Times Management Ser.). 256p. 1992. 111.00x (*0-273-03850-8*, Pub. by Pitman Pub Ltd UK) Trans-Atl Phila.
Ledgerwood, Judy, jt. ed. see Heder, Steve.
Ledingham, Iain M. & Mackay, Colin, eds. Jamieson's & Kay's Textbook of Surgical Physiology. 4th ed. (Illus.). 512p. 1988. text ed. 156.00 (*0-443-02640-8*) Churchill.
Ledingham, J. G., ed. see Advanced Medicine Symposia Staff & Royal College of Physicians Staff.
Leditschke, Anna. Tiny Timothy Turtle. (Illus.). 32p. (J). (ps-2). 1991. lib. bdg. 18.60 (*0-8368-0667-0*) Gareth Stevens Inc.
Ledkovsky, Boris. Great Vespers. (Music Ser.). 218p. 1976. pap. 15.00 (*0-913836-26-5*) St Vladimirs.
Ledkovsky, Marina, intro. Russia According to Women. LC 91-11292. (Illus.). 172p. (Orig.). (C). 1991. pap. text ed. 9.50 (*1-55779-023-X*) Hermitage.
Ledkovsky, Marina, et al, eds. Dictionary of Russian Women Writers. LC 93-13012. 960p. 1994. text ed. 145. 00 (*0-313-26265-9*, ASV/, Greenwood Pr) Greenwood.
Ledl, Arthur. Studien Zur Alteren Athenischen Verfassungsgeschichte. LC 72-7898. (Greek History Ser.). (GER.). 1973. reprint ed. 31.95 (*0-405-04797-5*) Ayer.
***Ledlie, Georgina.** How to Recreate Your Own Antique Bears & Dolls. (Illus.). 136p. 1994. 24.95 (*0-86417-634-1*) Seven Hills Bk.
Ledlie, James C., tr. see Sohm, Rudolph.
Ledney, Douglas. My Hero! (J). 1994. 7.95 (*0-8062-4865-3*) Carlton.
Ledney, G. D., jt. ed. see Baum, S. J.
Lednicer, Daniel, ed. Chronicles of Drug Discovery, Vol. 3. LC 81-11471. (Illus.). 350p. 1993. 84.95 (*0-8412-2523-0*); pap. 34.95 (*0-8412-2733-0*) Am Chemical.
— Contraception: The Chemical Control of Fertility. LC 79-99957. (Illus.). 285p. reprint ed. pap. 81.30 (*0-7837-0957-9*, 2041262) Bks Demand.
Lednicer, Daniel & Mitscher, Lester A. Organic Chemistry of Drug Synthesis, 4 vols., Set. LC 76-28387. 1990. text ed. 220.00 (*0-471-53176-6*) Wiley.
— Organic Chemistry of Drug Synthesis, 4 vols., Vol. 1. LC 76-28387. 471p. 1977. text ed. 94.95 (*0-471-52141-8*) Wiley.
— Organic Chemistry of Drug Synthesis, 4 vols., Vol. 2. LC 76-28387. 526p. 1980. text ed. 94.95 (*0-471-04392-3*) Wiley.
— Organic Chemistry of Drug Synthesis, 4 vols., Vol. 3. LC 76-28387. 284p. 1984. text ed. 79.95 (*0-471-09250-9*) Wiley.
— Organic Chemistry of Drug Synthesis, 4 vols., Vol. 4. LC 76-28387. 1990. text ed. 79.95 (*0-471-85548-0*) Wiley.
— The Organic Chemistry of Drug Synthesis, Vol. 5. 1994. text ed. 69.95 (*0-471-58959-4*) Wiley.
Lednicki, Waclaw. Pushkin's Bronze Horseman: The Story of a Masterpiece. LC 78-5547. (Univ. of California Publications Slavis Studies: Vol. 1). 163p. 1978. text ed. 35.00 (*0-313-20482-9*, LEPB, Greenwood Pr) Greenwood.
— Reminiscences: The Adventures of a Modern Gil Glas During the Last War. LC 68-23199. (Slavistic Printings & Reprintings Ser.). 278p. 1971. text ed. 50.75 (*90-279-1947-X*) Mouton.
Lednicki, Waclaw, ed. Zygmunt Krasinski, Romantic Universalist: An International Tribute. 227p. 1964. 6.00 (*0-940962-47-0*) Polish Inst Art & Sci.
LeDocte, E. Legal Dictionary in Four Languages. 822p. (ENG, FRE, GER & SPA.). 1987. 220.00 (*3-7890-1872-4*) IBD Ltd.
Ledolter, Johannes, jt. auth. see Abraham, Bovas.
Ledolter, Johannes, jt. auth. see Hogg, Robert V.
LeDonne, John. Ruling Russia. LC 84-2168. (Illus.). 368p. 1984. text ed. 65.00 (*0-691-05425-8*) Princeton U Pr.
LeDonne, John P. Absolutism & Ruling Class: The Formation of the Russian Political Order, 1700-1825. 400p. 1991. 55.00 (*0-19-506805-X*) OUP.
Ledoux, Claude N. L' Architecture Consideree sous le Rapport de l'Art, des Moeurs et de la Legislation. 250p. 1980. reprint ed. write for info. (*3-487-07010-3*, Pub. by Georg Olms GW) Lubrecht & Cramer.
— C. N. Ledoux: L'Architecture. (Illus.). 328p. 1982. 65.00 (*0-910413-03-7*) Princeton Arch.
Ledoux, Denis. Mountain Dance & Other Stories. 1990. pap. write for info. (*0-9626857-0-4*) Coastwise Pr.
— Turning Memories into Memories: A Handbook for Writing Lifestories. (Illus.). 208p. (Orig.). (C). 1993. pap. text ed. 17.95 (*0-9619373-2-7*) Soleil Pr.
— What Became of Them & Other Stories from Franco-America. 104p. (Orig.). 1988. pap. 8.95 (*0-9619373-0-0*) Soleil Pr.
Ledoux, Denis, intro. Lives in Translation: An Anthology of Contemporary Franco-American Writings. 144p. (Orig.). 1990. pap. 12.95 (*0-9619373-1-9*) Soleil Pr.
LeDoux, Joseph E. & Hirst, William, eds. Mind & Brain: Dialogues Between Cognitive Psychology & Neuroscience. (Illus.). 528p. 1986. 84.95 (*0-521-26756-0*) Cambridge U Pr.
— Mind & Brain: Dialogues Between Cognitive Psychology & Neuroscience. (Illus.). 528p. 1986. pap. 29.95 (*0-521-31853-X*) Cambridge U Pr.
LeDoux, Joseph E., jt. auth. see Gazzaniga, Michael S.
Ledoux-Lebard, Denise. Dictionary of French Furniture Makers of the 19th Century - Dictionnaire Des Ebenistes et Des Menuisiers. (Illus.). 736p. 250.00 (*1-55660-195-6*) A Wofsy Fine Arts.
— Mobilier Francais de XVIIIe Siecle: Dictionnaire des Ebenistes et des Menusiers. 736p. (FRE.). 1991. 450.00 (*0-8288-7315-1*, 285917088X) Fr & Eur.
— Versailles, le Petit Trianon: Le Mobilier des Inventaires de 1807-1810. 248p. (FRE.). 1993. lib. bdg. 225.00 (*0-7859-3646-7*, 2859170863) Fr & Eur.
Ledoux, Louis V., jt. ed. see Henderson, Harold G.
Ledoux, M. & Talagrand, M. Probability in Banach Spaces: Isoperimetry & Processes. (Ergebnisse der Mathematik und Ihrer Grenzgebiete Ser.: Vol. 23). (Illus.). 490p. 1991. 129.00 (*0-387-52013-9*) Spr-Verlag.
Ledoux, P., ed. see International Astronomical Union Staff.
Ledoux, Stephen F. About Behaviorology: An Introduction to the Incompatible Paradigms & Historical & Philosophical Developments among Disciplines Addressing the Behavior of Individuals. LC 92-94322. 96p. (C). 1993. pap. text ed. 18.00 (*1-882508-03-3*) ABCs.
Ledoux, Stephen F. & Fraley, Lawrence E. The Origins, Status, & Mission: Emergence of the Discipline of Behaviorology. LC 92-97400. 230p. 1992. student ed 23. 00 (*1-882508-00-9*) ABCs.
— The Origins, Status, & Mission: Emergence of the Discipline of Behaviorology. LC 92-97400. 230p. 1992. reprint ed. 38.00 (*1-882508-02-5*); reprint ed. pap. 26.00 (*1-882508-01-7*) ABCs.
***Ledoux, Steve.** How to Win Lotteries, Sweepstakes, & Contests. 224p. (Orig.). 1995. pap. 12.95 (*0-9639946-1-1*) Snta Monica.
Ledray, Linda. Recovering from Rape. 2nd ed. 1994. pap. 12.95 (*0-8050-2928-1*) H Holt & Co.
Ledray, Linda E. Recovering from Rape. LC 84-9138. 272p. 1989. pap. 9.95 (*0-8050-1253-2*, Owl) H Holt & Co.
Ledrew, Ellsworth, ed. Canadian Sea Ice Atlas from Microwave Remotely Sensed Imagery, July 1987-June 1990. (Climatological Studies: No. 41). (Illus.). 80p. (Orig.). 1993. pap. 32.45 (*0-660-57966-9*, Pub. by Canada Commun Grp CN) Accents Pubns.
Ledson, Sidney. Raising Brighter Children. (Illus.). 256p. 1987. 17.95 (*0-8027-0924-9*); pap. 9.95 (*0-8027-7299-4*) Walker & Co.
LeDuc, Don R., jt. auth. see Tetter, Dwight L., Jr.
Leduc, G. Les Prix et Leur Formation. 1964. write for info. (*0-318-58838-2*) Periodicals Srv.
***Leduc, Herman.** Dictionnaire d'Homeopathie Pediatrique a l'Usage des Familles et des Medecins de Famille. 494p. (FRE.). 1990. pap. 79.95 (*0-7859-7910-7*, 2700211057) Fr & Eur.
***Leduc, Jean-Pierre.** Digital Moving Pictures: Coding & Transmission on ATM Networks. LC 94-27698. 1994. 168.50 (*0-444-81786-7*) Elsevier.
***Leduc, Joanne, ed.** Overland from Canada to British Columbia: By Mr. Thomas McMicking of Queenston, Canada West. 169p. 1981. pap. 15.95 (*0-7748-0393-2*) U of Wash Pr.
Leduc, Lucien. Motivating Correctional Staff, 3 bks., Set. Geiman, Diane et al, eds. (Orig.). 1992. pap. 65.00 (*0-929310-67-5*, 174) Am Correctional.

An Asterisk (*) at the beginning of an entry indicates that the title is appearing in BIP for the first time.

***Leduc, Steven A.** Differential Equations Quick Review. (Cliffs Quick Reviews Ser.). (Illus.). 188p. (Orig.). (C). 1995. pap. text ed. 9.95 (*0-8220-5320-9*) Cliffs.
Leduc, Sylva, jt. auth. see Smith, Nancy J.
Leduc, Violette. La Batarde. (FRE.). 1964. pap. 49.95 (*0-7859-3960-1*) Fr & Eur.
— La Femme au Petit Renard. (FRE.). 1976. pap. 8.95 (*0-7859-4052-9*) Fr & Eur.
— Tresors a Prendre. (FRE.). 1978. pap. 10.95 (*0-7859-4101-0*) Fr & Eur.
Ledvinka, James & Scarpello, Vida G. Federal Regulation of Personnel & Human Resource Management. 2nd ed. 343p. (C). 1991. pap. 20.95 (*0-534-87206-9*) Intl Thomson.
Ledvinka, James, jt. auth. see Scarpello, Vida G.
Ledward, R. S., et al. Drug Treatment in Obstetrics: A Handbook of Prescribing. 2nd rev. ed. 275p. 1991. pap. 30.95 (*0-442-31312-8*) Chapman & Hall.
Ledwards, D. A., jt. ed. see Mitchell, J. R.
Ledwidge, Asher. The Black Family: Towards More Self-Love. (Orig.). 1993. pap. 8.00 (*0-9636109-0-2*) Nuf-Love Pub.
Ledwith, A., jt. ed. see Jenkins, A. D.
Ledwith, A., jt. ed. see Moss, S. J.
Ledwith, Irene. The Dog Bite. 1988. pap. 10.00 (*0-932526-20-9*) Nexus Pr.
— R. B. Schueller. (Illus.). 48p. (Orig.). 1992. pap. 12.00 (*0-89822-101-3*) Visual Studies.
Ledwith, Nettie H. A Rorschach Study of Child Development. LC 75-26632. 336p. 1975. reprint ed. text ed. 59.75 (*0-8371-8365-0*, LERS, Greenwood Pr) Greenwood.
Ledwith, Stuart. Mary Magdalene: The Disciple Jesus Loved. J, Kathlyn, ed. LC 90-91795. (Illus.). 122p. (Orig.). 1990. pap. 6.95 (*0-9627250-0-5*) Soul Works Intl.
Ledwith, Tim, ed. see Hayes, Roger, et al.
***Ledwoch, Janusz.** Messerschmitt Bf 110 Aircraft Monograph. (Illus.). 56p. 1995. pap. 14.95 (*83-86208-12-0*, Pub. by Bks Intl UK) Motorbooks Intl.
Ledyard, Gleason H. Eskimos: Now the World. (Illus.). 256p. 1958. pap. text ed. 6.00 (*0-913201-26-X*) Christian Lit.
— His Life. (Illus.). 224p. 1991. pap. text ed. 6.00 (*0-913201-22-7*) Christian Lit.
— Teacher's Manual: Companion to Gleason H. Ledyard's Topical Study Outlines. 80p. 1975. pap. text ed. 5.00 (*0-913201-18-9*) Christian Lit.
— Topical Study Outlines. 160p. 1970. pap. text ed. 5.00 (*0-913201-34-0*) Christian Lit.
— Topical Study Outlines Workbook. 112p. 1988. 3.00 (*0-913201-35-9*) Christian Lit.
Ledyard, Gleason H., tr. Precious Moments Children's Bible: Easy-to-Read, New Life Version. LC 90-36671. (Illus.). 1424p. (J). 1991. 24.99 (*0-8010-5664-0*); pap. 19.99 (*0-8010-5684-5*) Baker Bk.
Ledyard, John. Journey Through Russia & Siberia, 1787-1788: The Journals & Selected Letters. LC 66-22855. (Illus.). 316p. reprint ed. pap. 90.10 (*0-317-09556-0*, 2010974) Bks Demand.
***Ledyard, John O., ed.** The Economics of Informational Decentralization: Complexity, Efficiency, & Stability : Essays in Honor of Stanley Reiter. LC 94-32947. 1995. lib. bdg. write for info. (*0-7923-9502-6*) Kluwer Ac.
Lee. Advances in Fingerprint Technology. 1991. 50.00 (*0-685-66704-9*, HV6074) CRC Pr.
— Advances in Forensic Science, Vol. 4. 1990. 69.95 (*0-8151-5393-7*, Yr Bk Med Pubs) Mosby Yr Bk.
— Animal Rights. (Troubled Society Ser.: Set II). (J). 1991. 12.95 (*0-86593-112-7*) Rourke Corp.
— Bellydancer. (NFS Canada Ser.). Date not set. pap. 14.95 (*0-88974-039-9*, Pub. by Press Gang CN) InBook.
— Company Financial Reporting U. K. 2nd ed. 1982. pap. 46.95 (*0-442-30707-1*) Chapman & Hall.
— Computer-Aided Analysis & Design of Switch-Mode Power Suppies. (Electrical Engineering & Electronics Ser.: Vol. 81). 648p. 1993. 140.00 (*0-8247-8803-6*) Dekker.
— Concise Inorganic Chemistry U. K. 3rd ed. pap. 28.95 (*0-685-19092-7*) Chapman & Hall.
— Contract Programming for DP. 1987. pap. 19.95 (*0-9611810-8-7*) CCD Online Syst.
— Current Obstetric Medicine, Vol. 2. 380p. 1993. 64.95 (*0-8151-5550-6*, Yr Bk Med Pubs) Mosby Yr Bk.
— Current Obstetric Medicine, Vol. 3. 380p. 1995. 64.95 (*0-8151-5551-4*, Yr Bk Med Pubs) Mosby Yr Bk.
— Current Obstetric Medicine, Vol. 4. 270p. 1997. 64.95 (*0-8151-5552-2*, Yr Bk Med Pubs) Mosby Yr Bk.
— Current Obstetric Medicine, Vol. 5. 270p. 1999. 64.95 (*0-8151-5553-0*, Yr Bk Med Pubs) Mosby Yr Bk.
— Current Obstetrics Medicine. 380p. 1991. 59.95 (*0-8151-5647-2*, Yr Bk Med Pubs) Mosby Yr Bk.
— Dads & Daughters, Fathers & Sons. 1994. pap. text ed. 16.95 (*1-879323-12-5*) Sound Horizons AV.
— Data & Algorithms. (Math-Computers Ser.). (C). 1992. boxed 38.75 (*0-86720-219-X*) Jones & Bartlett.
— Discrimination. (Troubled Society Ser.: Set II). (J). 1991. 12.95 (*0-86593-113-5*) Rourke Corp.
— Eating Dog: Travel Stories. 200p. 1994. pap. 16.95 (*0-7022-2184-8*, Pub. by Univ Queensland Pr AT) Intl Spec Bk.
— Flight Nursing: Principles & Practice. (Illus.). 728p. 1990. 59.95 (*0-8016-6138-2*) Mosby Yr Bk.
— Great Graphing. 1995. pap. (*0-590-49470-8*) Scholastic Inc.
— Handbook of Epoxy Resins. 400p. 1982. 90.00 (*0-318-37718-7*) T-C Pubns CA.
— IMS-VS DL 1 Programming with Cobol Examples. 1985. pap. 34.95 (*0-9611810-4-4*) CCD Online Syst.
— Income & Value Measurement. 3rd ed. 1986. pap. 27.95 (*0-442-30615-6*) Chapman & Hall.
— Introduction to the Design & Analysis of Algorithms. 1991. pap. 53.33 (*0-13-480773-1*) P-H.
— Last Princess Manchuria. 1994. 3.99 (*0-517-13445-4*) Random Hse Value.
— Liver Pathology. 768p. 1993. 115.00 (*0-8016-2805-9*) Mosby Yr Bk.
— Men in Balance. 1995. 16.95 (*1-879323-13-3*) Sound Horizons AV.
— Nim. write for info. (*0-679-97622-1*) Random.
— Occasional Paper No. 1, Historical Perspectives on Urban Design: Washington, D.C. 1890-1910. 1983. 4.00 (*0-318-21782-1*) G Washington Univ.
— Official Book of the Scottish Terrier. 1995. 29.95 (*0-7938-0078-1*) TFH Pubns.
— Operator Methods for Optimal Control Problems. (Lecture Notes in Pure & Applied Mathematics Ser.: Vol. 108). 344p. 1987. 125.00 (*0-8247-7811-1*) Dekker.
— Peptide & Protein Drug Delivery. (Advances in Parenteral Sciences Ser.: Vol. 4). 832p. 1990. 199.00 (*0-8247-7896-0*) Dekker.
— Regulation of Banks & Other Depository Institutions in Malaysia - A Study in Monetary, Prudential & Other Controls. 1992. 137.00 (*0-409-99601-7*) Butterworth Legal Pubs.
— Stardust. 1994. pap. 12.99 (*0-517-13406-3*) Random.
— Telecourse Study Guide II: Executive, Legislative & Judicial. 3rd ed. 320p. 1993. spiral bd. 15.95 (*0-8403-8687-7*) Kendall-Hunt.
— Telecourse Study Guide II: Executive, Legislative & Judicial. 3rd ed. 320p. (C). 1993. per. 17.95 (*0-8403-8442-4*) Kendall-Hunt.
— Telecourse Study Guide to Government by Consent: A National Perspective. 3rd ed. 320p. 1993. per. 17.95 (*0-8403-8439-4*) Kendall-Hunt.
— U-Statistics: Theory & Practice. (Statistics: Vol. 110). 320p. 1990. 99.75 (*0-8247-8253-4*) Dekker.
— Ultrasonographic Diagnosis of Diseases of the Prostate. 1991. 99.95 (*0-8151-5518-2*, Yr Bk Med Pubs) Mosby Yr Bk.
— The Underground Blue Book: A Guide to Buying & Selling New & Used Cars, Trucks & R. V.'s. 136p. (Orig.). 1987. pap. 9.95 (*0-9617946-0-7*) Diamond S Pub.
Lee, ed. Blood Vessel Changes in Hypertension, I. 1989. 132.00 (*0-8493-4883-8*, RC685) CRC Pr.
— Blood Vessel Changes in Hypertension, II. 1989. 132.00 (*0-8493-4884-6*, RC685) CRC Pr.
— Computer-Generated Holography, No. II. 1988. 45.00 (*0-89252-919-9*, 884) SPIE.
— Ion. 1994. write for info. (*0-85668-244-6*, Pub. by Aris & Phillips UK); pap. write for info. (*0-85668-245-4*, Pub. by Aris & Phillips UK) David Brown.
— Oil Shale Technology. 1990. 205.00 (*0-8493-4615-0*, TP699) CRC Pr.
— Remote Sensing in Exploration Geology. (IGC Field Trip Guidebooks Ser.). 64p. 1989. 21.00 (*0-87590-564-1*, T182) Am Geophysical.
Lee & Nolan. Surgery of Inflammatory Bowel Disorders: Vol. 14, CSI. (Illus.). 1987. pap. 15.00 (*0-443-03439-7*) Churchill.
Lee & Progris. I Want to Play Alto Recorder. 1990. 3.95 (*0-685-32168-1*, N234) Hansen Ed Mus.
— I Want to Play Alto Saxophone. 1990. 3.95 (*0-685-32217-3*, N228) Hansen Ed Mus.
— I Want to Play Clarinet. 1990. 3.95 (*0-685-32202-5*, N230) Hansen Ed Mus.
— I Want to Play Flute. 1990. 3.95 (*0-685-32114-2*, N225) Hansen Ed Mus.
— I Want to Play Harmonica. 1990. 3.95 (*0-685-32196-7*, N235) Hansen Ed Mus.
— I Want to Play Soprano Recorder. 1990. 3.95 (*0-685-32167-3*, N233) Hansen Ed Mus.
— I Want to Play Tenor Saxophone. 1990. 3.95 (*0-685-32218-1*, N229) Hansen Ed Mus.
— I Want to Play Trombone. 1990. 3.95 (*0-685-32234-3*, N227) Hansen Ed Mus.
— I Want to Play Trumpet. 1990. 3.95 (*0-685-32184-3*, N226) Hansen Ed Mus.
— Top Score Solo Songbook. 1990. 1.95 (*0-685-32120-7*, N245); 1.95 (*0-685-32198-3*, N258); 1.95 (*0-685-47133-0*, N250); 1.95 (*0-685-47134-9*, N247) Hansen Ed Mus.
— Top Score Solo Songbook: Alto Saxophone. 1990. 1.95 (*0-685-32212-2*, N248) Hansen Ed Mus.
***Lee & Turner.** Introduction to World Agriscience & Technology. 1994. teacher ed 12.95 (*0-8134-2960-9*); student ed 14.95 (*0-8134-2961-7*); teacher ed 14.95 (*0-8134-2974-9*); text ed. 36.95 (*0-614-01832-3*) Interstate.
Lee & Wood, L. J. Adjustment in the Urban System: The Tasman Bridge Collapse & Its Effects on Metropolitan Hobart. (Progress in Planning Ser.: Vol. 15, Pt. 2). 85p. 1981. pap. 16.25 (*0-08-026810-2*) Elsevier.
Lee, jt. auth. see Balch.
Lee, jt. ed. see Lanier.
Lee, jt. auth. see Newell.
Lee, jt. auth. see Robinson.
Lee, jt. ed. see VanPatten, Bill.
Lee, et al. Captain America. (Marvel Masterworks Ser.: Vol. 14). 232p. 1990. 34.95 (*0-87135-630-9*) Marvel Entmnt.
— The Earth & AgriScience. 1994. teacher ed 9.95 (*0-8134-3016-X*); text ed. 35.95 (*0-614-01831-5*) Interstate.
— Guided Weapons. (Brassey's Battlefield Weapons Systems & Technology Ser.: Vol. 8). 160p. 1983. text ed. 33.00 (*0-08-028336-5*, Pergamon Pr); pap. text ed. 14.25 (*0-08-028337-3*, Pergamon Pr) Elsevier.
— Marvel Masterworks, Vol. 16: Spider-Man. 244p. 1991. 34.95 (*0-87135-730-5*) Marvel Entmnt.
— Marvel Masterworks, Vol. 19: Silver Surfer. 328p. 1991. 44.95 (*0-87135-808-5*) Marvel Entmnt.
— The Spinal Cord Injured Patient: Comprehensive Management. (Illus.). 400p. 1991. text ed. 85.95 (*0-7216-5699-4*) Saunders.
***Lee & Turner Staff.** Introduction to World Agriscience & Technology. 1994. 49.25 (*0-8134-2959-5*) Interstate.
Lee, A. Collingwood. Decameron: Its Sources & Analogues. LC 68-814. (Studies in Comparative Literature: No. 35). 1909. lib. bdg. 75.00 (*0-8383-0581-4*) M S G Haskell Hse.
Lee, A. D. Information & Frontiers: Roman Foreign Relations in Late Antiquity. LC 92-34199. 225p. (C). 1993. 59.95 (*0-521-39256-X*) Cambridge U Pr.
Lee, A. G., ed. Ovid - Metamorphoses, Bk. 1. 1985. 13.00 (*0-86516-040-6*) Bolchazy-Carducci.
Lee, A. G., ed. see Ovid.
***Lee, A. J.** Guia Hacia una Temprana Recuperation: A Guide to Early Recovery. 40p. 1993. pap. 2.99 (*0-9638101-1-1*) Lee Counsel Srvs.
— A Guide to Early Recovery. 40p. 1993. pap. 2.99 (*0-9638101-0-3*) Lee Counsel Srvs.
Lee, A. J., ed. see European Conference on Biomaterials Staff.
Lee, A. K. & Cockburn, Andrew. Evolutionary Ecology of Marsupials. (Monographs on Marsupial Biology). (Illus.). 300p. 1985. 79.95 (*0-521-25292-X*) Cambridge U Pr.
Lee, A. K., et al, eds. Biology of the Koala. 346p. (C). 1991. text ed. 125.00 (*0-949324-34-5*, Pub. by Surrey Beatty & Sons AT) St Mut.
Lee, A. Robert. James Baldwin: Climbing to the Light. (Critical Studies). 224p. 1991. write for info. (*0-312-03573-X*) St Martin.
— A Permanent Etcetera: Cross-cultural Perspectives on Post-War America. LC 93-24953. 199p. (C). 1994. text ed. 73.50 (*0-7453-0640-3*, Pub. by Pluto Pr UK); pap. text ed. 19.95 (*0-7453-0641-1*, Pub. by Pluto Pr UK) Westview.
Lee, A. Robert, ed. First Person Singular: Studies in American Autobiography. LC 87-15504. (Critical Studies). 256p. 1988. text ed. 39.95 (*0-312-02425-8*) St Martin.
— Herman Melville: Reassessments. LC 83-22340. 222p. 1984. 44.00 (*0-389-20376-9*, 07248); pap. 16.00 (*0-389-20471-4*, 08033) B&N Imports.
— The Modern American Novella. LC 89-5876. 224p. 1989. text ed. 39.95 (*0-312-02424-X*) St Martin.
— The Nineteenth-Century American Short Story. LC 85-15707. (Critical Studies). 224p. 1986. 56.50 (*0-389-20593-1*, N8151) B&N Imports.
— William Faulkner: The Yoknapatawpha Fiction. (Critical Studies of Key Texts). 224p. 1990. text ed. 39.95 (*0-312-03571-3*) St Martin.
Lee, A. Robert, ed. see Melville, Herman.
Lee, A. Y., jt. auth. see Reghbati, H.
Lee, Adrianne. Endless Fear. 320p. 1992. mass mkt. 4.50 (*0-8217-3852-6*) Zebra.
— Night Terror. 320p. 1993. mass mkt. 4.50 (*0-8217-4162-4*) Zebra.
Lee, Adrienne. Something Borrowed, Something Blue. 1994. mass mkt. 2.99 (*0-373-22296-3*, 1-22296-7) Harlequin Bks.
***Lee, Alan.** Lord Ted: The Dexter Enigma. (Illus.). 256p. 1995. 39.95 (*0-85493-245-3*, Pub. by Withrby UK) Trafalgar.
Lee, Alan, et al. Tolkien's Dragons & Monsters: A Book of Twenty Postcards. 1994. pap. 8.00 (*0-261-10301-6*, Haas Ent NH) HarpC.
Lee, Alan J., jt. ed. see Harris, Michael.
Lee, Albert. Thrilling Escapes by Night. 296p. 1968. 8.75 (*0-686-05596-9*) Rod & Staff.
— Weather Wisdom: Facts & Folklore of Weather Forecasting. rev. ed. (Illus.). 192p. 1990. reprint ed. pap. 7.95 (*0-86553-212-5*) Congdon & Weed.
***Lee, Alex.** Force Recon Command: A Special Marine Unit in Vietnam, 1969-1970. Gatlin, Mark, ed. LC 95-15533. (Naval Institute Special Warfare Ser.). (Illus.). 308p. 1995. 29.95 (*1-55750-513-6*) Naval Inst Pr.
Lee, Alfred M. Sociology for People: A Caring Profession. LC 88-9672. 259p. 1988. text ed. 39.95x (*0-8156-2442-5*) Syracuse U Pr.
— Sociology for People: Toward a Caring Profession. 228p. (C). 1990. pap. text ed. 14.95 (*0-8156-2510-3*) Syracuse U Pr.
— Sociology for Whom. 2nd ed. LC 85-26134. 280p. 1986. pap. text ed. 14.95x (*0-8156-2355-0*) Syracuse U Pr.
— Terrorism in Northern Ireland. LC 83-80158. 253p. 1983. lib. bdg. 34.95 (*0-930390-51-2*); pap. text ed. 17.95 (*0-930390-50-4*) Gen Hall.
Lee, Alfred M., ed. see Bowers, Raymond.
Lee, Alice, jt. auth. see Lee, Fred.
Lee, Alison. Realism & Power: Postmodern British Fiction. 176p. 1990. 45.00 (*0-415-04452-9*, A4022); pap. 15.95 (*0-415-04103-1*, A4026) Routledge.
Lee, Allan. American Transportation: History & Museums. 1993. pap. 17.95 (*0-943231-57-4*) Howell Pr VA.
Lee, Allan E., jt. auth. see Lee, Hilde G.
Lee, Allison. A Handbook of Creative Dance & Drama: Ideas for Teachers. LC 91-4980. 106p. 1992. pap. text ed. 16.00 (*0-435-08702-9*, 08702) Heinemann.
Lee, Alton, comp. Dwight David Eisenhower: A Bibliography of His Times & Presidency. LC 90-23694. (Twentieth-Century Presidential Bibliography Ser.). 240p. 1991. 70.00 (*0-8420-2288-0*) Scholarly Res Inc.
Lee, Alton R. Dwight D. Eisenhower: Soldier & Statesman. LC 81-519. (Illus.). 384p. (C). 1981. text ed. 29.95 (*0-88229-626-4*) Nelson-Hall.
Lee, Alvin A. The Guest-Hall of Eden: Four Essays on the Design of Old English Poetry. LC 76-151581. 254p. reprint ed. pap. 72.40 (*0-317-29269-2*, 2022012) Bks Demand.
***Lee, Alvin A. & Denham, Robert D., eds.** The Legacy of Northrop Frye. 354p. 1994. 55.00 (*0-8020-0632-9*) U of Toronto Pr.
— The Legacy of Northrop Frye. 354p. 1994. pap. 24.95 (*0-8020-7588-6*) U of Toronto Pr.
Lee, Alyssa. Sweet Jasmine. (Homespun Ser.). 352p. (Orig.). 1992. mass mkt. 4.99 (*1-55773-810-6*) Diamond.
Lee, Amy F. & Lowman, Al, intros. Watercolor, Wax & Wool: The Art of Janet Shook LaCoste. LC 80-82780. (Illus.). 96p. (Orig.). 1980. pap. 1.58 (*0-933164-81-5*) U of Tex Inst Tex Culture.
Lee, Amy K., ed. see Okimoto, Daniel I. & Yoshikawa, Aki.
Lee, Andrea. Russian Journal. LC 81-40214. 1981. 13.00 (*0-394-51891-8*) Random.
— Russian Journal. 1984. pap. 7.95 (*0-394-71127-0*, Vin) Random.
— Sarah Phillips. (Northeastern Library of Black Literature). 144p. 1993. reprint ed. pap. 10.95 (*1-55553-158-X*) NE U Pr.
Lee, Andrew. Lincoln. (Reputations Ser.). (Illus.). 64p. (YA). (gr. 6-9). 1989. 19.95 (*0-7134-5662-0*, Pub. by Batsford UK) Trafalgar.
— Workshop of the World. (How It Was Ser.). (Illus.). 48p. (YA). (gr. 7-10). Date not set. 19.95 (*0-7134-6353-8*, Pub. by Batsford UK) Trafalgar.
Lee, Andy. Backyard Market Gardening: The Entrepreneur's Guide to Selling What You Grow. LC 90-84585. (Illus.). 352p. (Orig.). 1995. pap. 19.95 (*0-9624648-0-5*) Good Earth Pubns.
— Chicken Tractor: The Gardener's Guide to Happy Hens & Healthy Soil. LC 92-76194. (Illus.). 232p. 1995. pap. 15.95 (*0-9624648-2-1*) Good Earth Pubns.
Lee, Anita. Knowledge-Based Flexible Manufacturing Systems (FMS) Scheduling. LC 93-43003. (Studies on Industrial Productivity). 136p. 1994. 36.00 (*0-8153-1627-5*) Garland.
Lee, Anita J. Keys to Understanding Securities. (Business Keys Ser.). 160p. 1989. pap. 4.95 (*0-8120-4229-8*) Barron.
Lee, Anna. Modeling & You! (Illus.). 117p. (Orig.). (YA). (gr. 6-12). 1991. pap. 12.95 (*0-9629647-0-0*) CUE Pubns.
***Lee, Anna C.** From the Editor's Desk. 107p. (CHI.). 1989. pap. 4.00 (*1-56582-089-4*) Christ Renew Min.
Lee, Anna C., tr. see Schaeffer, Francis A.
Lee, Anne F. Hawaii State Constitution: A Reference Guide. LC 92-35920. (Reference Guides to the State Constitutions of the United States Ser.: No. 14). 272p. 1993. text ed. 65.00 (*0-313-27950-0*, LHI/) Greenwood.
***Lee, Anne M. & Wisdom, Elaine.** Stories, Symbols, Songs & Skits for Lively Children's Liturgies. LC 94-61925. 88p. (Orig.). 1995. pap. 9.95 (*0-89622-640-9*) Twenty-Third.
Lee, Anthony & Martin, Roger. The Koala: A Natural History. 1988. pap. 19.95 (*0-86840-354-7*, Pub. by New South Wales Univ Pr AT) Intl Spec Bk.
Lee, Anthony A. The Cornerstone: A Story About 'Abdu'l-Baha in America. (Stories About 'Abdu'l-Baha Ser.). (Illus.). 24p. (Orig.). (J). (gr. k-5). 1979. pap. 3.00 (*0-933770-01-4*) Kalimat.
— The Scottish Visitors: A Story about 'Abdu'l-Baha in Britain. (Stories About 'Abdu'l-Baha Ser.). (Illus.). 24p. (Orig.). (J). (gr. k-5). 1981. pap. 3.00 (*0-933770-04-9*) Kalimat.
— The Unfriendly Governor. (Stories About 'Abdu'l-Baha Ser.). (Illus.). 24p. (J). (gr. k-5). 1980. pap. 3.00 (*0-933770-02-2*) Kalimat.
Lee, Anthony A., ed. Circle of Peace: Reflections on the Baha'i Teachings. (Orig.). 1986. 11.95 (*0-933770-48-0*) Kalimat.
— Circle of Unity: Baha'i Approaches to Current Social Issues. 268p. (Orig.). 1984. pap. 11.95 (*0-933770-28-6*) Kalimat.
Lee, Antoinette J. Past Meets Future: Saving America's Historic Environments. (Illus.). 384p. 1992. 25.95 (*0-89133-198-0*) Preservation Pr.
Lee, Antoinette J., ed. Historical Perspectives on Urban Design Vol. O1: Washington, D. C. 1890-1910. 1983. 4.00 (*0-317-01830-2*) GWU CWAS.
Lee, Antoinette J., jt. auth. see Scott, Pamela.
Lee, Antoinette J., jt. ed. see Stipe, Robert E.
***Lee, Arlee.** Lafayette County War Book. (Illus.). 382p. 1990. 34.95 (*0-88107-154-4*) Curtis Media.
Lee, Art. Leftover Lefse. (Illus.). 224p. (Orig.). 1987. pap. 7.95 (*0-934860-48-3*) Adventure Pubns.
— Leftover Lutefisk. 1984. 7.95 (*0-934860-32-7*) Adventure Pubns.
Lee, Art, ed. The Lutefisk Ghetto. 1978. 7.95 (*0-934860-02-5*) Adventure Pubns.
Lee, Arthur B. The Microtomist's Vade-Mecum. (History of Microscopy Ser.). 448p. 1987. reprint ed. 65.60 (*0-940095-04-1*) Sci Heritage Ltd.
Lee, Arthur T. & Thomas, W. Stephen. Fort Davis & the Texas Frontier: Paintings by Captain Arthur T. Lee, Eighth U. S. Infantry. LC 75-40896. (Illus.). 122p. 1976. 12.95 (*0-89096-012-7*) Tex A&M Univ Pr.
Lee, Artis. Read On! Two, Bk. 5. Lawson, V. K., ed. (Illus.). 78p. 1987. pap. text ed. 3.75 (*0-930713-06-0*); audio 10.00 (*0-318-41218-7*) Lit Vol Am.
— Read On! Two, Wkbk. 5. Lawson, V. K., ed. (Illus.). 84p. 1987. Workbook 5, 84p. pap. text ed. 2.75 (*0-930713-15-X*) Lit Vol Am.
Lee, Artis, jt. auth. see Coville, Bruce.
Lee, Artis, jt. auth. see Elmore, Fred.
Lee, Artis, jt. auth. see Simmons, Judy D.
Lee, Artis, et al. Read On! Two, Bk. 1. Lawson, V. K., ed. 68p. 1987. pap. 3.75 (*0-930713-02-8*, Large Print Bks); digital audio 8.00 (*0-930713-08-7*, Large Print Bks) Lit Vol Am.

L

— Read On! Two, Wkbk. 1. Lawson, V. K., ed. 68p. 1987. Workbook 1, 68p. 2.75 (0-930713-11-7, Large Print Bks) Lit Vol Am.
Lee, Asher, ed. The Soviet Air & Rocket Forces. LC 75-27682. (Illus.). 311p. 1976. reprint ed. text ed. 65.00 (0-8371-8456-8, LESAR, Greenwood Pr) Greenwood.
***Lee, Ashley.** Relationships: How to Have Relationships, God's Way. 96p. 1995. pap. 7.95 (0-9643797-0-8) Ashley Lee.
Lee, B. Chiral Dynamics. 130p. (C). 1972. pap. text ed. 121.00 (0-677-01385-X) Gordon & Breach.
— Music Made Easy, Pt. 1. (Made Easy Ser.). 1990. 5.95 (0-685-32064-2, 8413) Hansen Ed Mus.
Lee, B. B., jt. ed. see Valberg, A.
Lee, B. L., jt. auth. see Cleghorn, J. M.
Lee, Bang W. & Sheu, Bing J. Hardware Annealing in Analog VLSI Neurocomputing. (International Series in Engineering & Computer Science, VLSI, Computer Architecture, & Digital Screen Processing). 256p. 1990. lib. bdg. 69.00 (0-7923-9132-2) Kluwer Ac.
***Lee, Barbara.** Death in Still Waters: A Chesapeake Bay Murder Mystery. 240p. 1995. 20.95 (0-312-13048-1, Pub. by Thomas Dunne Bks) St Martin.
***Lee, Barbara & Nellis, John.** Enterprise Reform & Privitization in Socialist Economies. (Discussion Paper Ser.: No. 104). 34p. 1990. 6.95 (0-614-02777-2, 11666) World Bank.
Lee, Barbara, ed. see Roberson, William H.
Lee, Barbara A. Reasonable Accommodation under the Americans with Disabilities Act. (ADA Practice Ser.). 47p. 1994. pap. 16.00 (0-934753 92-X) LRP Pubns.
Lee, Barbara A., jt. auth. see Hendrickson, Robert M.
Lee, Barbara A., jt. auth. see Kaplan, William A.
Lee, Barbara A., jt. auth. see LaNoue, George R.
Lee, Barbara A., jt. auth. see Olswang, Steven G.
Lee, Barbara W. Productivity & Employee Ownership: The Case of Sweden. (Studia Oeconomiae Upsaliensia: No. 16). 110p. (Orig.). 1989. pap. 36.00x (91-554-2424-4, Pub. by Umea U Bibl SW) Coronet Bks.
Lee, Barry, illus. A Clear & Present Danger to Society. 24p. 1981. pap. 4.00 (0-939622-10-6) Four Zoas Night Ltd.
Lee, Ben, jt. auth. see Jolliffe, Norm.
Lee, Benjamin. Psychosocial Theories of the Self. (PATH in Psychology Ser.). 230p. 1982. 55.00 (0-306-41117-2, Plenum Pr) Plenum.
Lee, Benjamin & Urban, Greg, eds. Semiotics, Self & Society. (Approaches to Semiotics Ser.: No. 84). xviii, 311p. (C). 1989. lib. bdg. 95.40 (0-89925-560-4) Mouton.
Lee-Benner. Physicians' Guide to Free Radicals, Immunity & Aging. 1986. lib. bdg. 125.00 (0-944213-00-6) World Hlth Found.
— Turning Back the Aging Clock: Dr. Lee-Benners' Scientifically Designed & Medically Based Longevity Program. (Illus.). 230p. (Orig.). 1991. pap. 25.00 (0-944213-05-7) World Hlth Found.
Lee-Benner, Lord. Physician's Guide to Free Radicals, Immunity & Aging. deluxe ed. LC 90-71564. (Illus.). 301p. (C). 1991. write for info. (0-944213-27-8) World Hlth Found.
— Physician's Guide to Free Radicals, Immunity & Aging. rev. ed. LC 90-71564. (Illus.). 301p. (C). 1991. lib. bdg. 150.00 (0-944213-26-X) World Hlth Found.
— Physician's Guide to Free Radicals, Immunity & Aging. 2nd rev. ed. LC 90-71564. (Illus.). 301p. (C). 1991. 125.00 (0-944213-25-1) World Hlth Found.
Lee, Bennett & Wong-Chu, Jim, eds. Many Mouthed Birds: Contemporary Writings by Chinese Canadians. LC 91-19664. 250p. 1991. 26.95 (0-295-97149-5) U of Wash Pr.
Lee, Bennett, tr. see Jiang, Yang.
Lee, Bernard. Jesus & the Metaphors of God, Vol. 2: Conversation on the Road Not Taken. LC 93-14256. (Stimulus Book Ser.). 224p. (Orig.). 1993. pap. 10.95 (0-8091-3429-2) Paulist Pr.
Lee, Bernard J. The Galilean Jewishness of Jesus: Retrieving the Jewish Origins of Christianity. 1988. pap. 9.95 (0-8091-3021-1) Paulist Pr.
Lee, Bernard J. & Cowan, Michael. Dangerous Memories: House Churches & Our American Story. LC 86-62123. 208p. (Orig.). 1986. pap. 9.95 (0-934134-70-7) Sheed & Ward MO.
Lee, Bernie. Murder at Musket Beach. 1990. 17.95 (1-55611-171-1) D I Fine.
— Murder Takes Two. LC 91-58656. 240p. 1992. 18.95 (1-55611-280-7) D I Fine.
— Murder Takes Two. 1993. mass mkt. 3.99 (0-373-26127-6, 1-26127-0) Harlequin Bks.
— Murder Without Reservation. 1991. 18.95 (1-55611-184-3) D I Fine.
— Murder Without Reservation. (Worldwide Library Mystery: No. 96). 1992. mass mkt. 3.99 (0-373-26096-2, 1-26096-7) Harlequin Bks.
Lee, Bertram T., ed. see Carvajal, Gaspar de.
Lee, Betsy. Judy Blume's Story. LC 81-12494. (Illus.). 112p. (J). (gr. 5 up). 1981. text ed. 11.95 (0-87518-209-7, Dillon Silver Burdett) Silver Burdett Pr.
Lee, Betsy, ed. see Peeples, Mary G. & Peeples, Sam L., Jr.
Lee, Betty. Dancing: All the Latest Steps. (Ballroom Dance Ser.). 1986. lib. bdg. 79.95 (0-8490-3329-2) Gordon Pr.
Lee, Bibbi, tr. see Nedreaas, Torborg.
Lee, Bill. Bi-Ranchers, Bi-Mates. 176p. (Orig.). 1991. pap. 9.95 (1-879194-02-3) GLB Pubs.
— Leather Rogues. (Rogues Ser.: No. 2). 168p. (Orig.). 1991. pap. 10.95 (1-879194-01-5) GLB Pubs.
— People in Jazz. 1984. 19.95 (0-89898-358-4) CPP Belwin.
— Rogues to Remember. (Rogues Ser.: No. 1). 168p. (Orig.). 1991. pap. 10.95 (1-879194-00-7) GLB Pubs.
***Lee, Bill, ed.** Country Rogues: Short Story Anthology. (Rogues Ser.: No. 4). 211p. 1995. pap. 12.95 (1-879194-19-8) GLB Pubs.
— Rogues of San Francisco. (Rogues Ser.: No. 3). 230p. (Orig.). 1993. pap. 11.95 (1-879194-15-5) GLB Pubs.
Lee, Bill, jt. auth. see Legum, Colin.
Lee, Billi. Get Savvy: Thirty Days to a Different Perspective. (Illus.). 71p. (Orig.). 1992. pap. 10.00 (1-883330-69-6); pap. 45.00 (1-883330-68-8); pap. 300.00 (1-883330-67-X) Alliance CO.
Lee, Billie. Til Death Do Us Part: A Widow's Story. 88p. 1993. 19.95 (0-8059-3433-2) Dorrance.
Lee, Billie W. Rainshine & Sundrops: Language Fun for Young Children. (Illus.). 40p. (Orig.). (J). 1987. 6.95 (0-9619675-0-1) P&M Bear Pubns.
***Lee, Bob.** Back to the Future: Tokheim. (Gas Pump Ser.: No. 5). (Illus.). 172p. 1993. text ed. 44.95 (0-9638220-0-4) Bob Lee.
Lee, Bob, jt. auth. see Wallington, Peter.
Lee, Bob, jt. ed. see Wallington, Peter.
Lee, Boon C. The Economics of International Debt Renegotiation: The Role of Bargaining & Information. 141p. (C). 1993. pap. text ed. 41.00 (0-8133-1766-5) Westview.
Lee Bowen, Donna & Early, Evelyn A., eds. Everyday Life in the Muslim Middle East. LC 92-40710. (Indiana Series in Arab & Islamic Studies). 1993. 39.95 (0-253-31253-1); pap. 16.95 (0-253-20779-7) Ind U Pr.
Lee, Bradford A. Britain & the Sino-Japanese War, 1937-1939: A Study in the Dilemmas of British Decline. LC 77-190526. xiv, 320p. 1973. 42.50 (0-8047-0799-5) Stanford U Pr.
Lee, Brian. American Fiction, 1865-1940. (Literature in English Ser.). 288p. (Orig.). (C). 1987. text ed. 41.95 (0-582-49317-X, 73574); pap. text ed. 24.95 (0-582-49316-1, 73574) Longman.
— Poetry & the System. (C). 1989. 30.00 (0-907839-05-3, Pub. by Brynmill Pr Ltd UK) St Mut.
Lee, Brian, ed. The Bookplate Designs of Claude Lovat Fraser. (Illus.). 85p. 1988. 80.00 (0-685-26974-4) H Berliner.
— Byron: Don Juan (Eighteen Nineteen) 2nd ed. (Annotated Student Texts Ser.). 192p. (Orig.). 1988. pap. text ed. 20.00 (1-85373-015-7, Pub. by Northcote House UK) Trans-Atl Phila.
Lee, Brian N. British Royal Bookplates: And Ex-Libris of Related Families. 280p. 1991. text ed. 120.00 (0-85967-883-0, Pub. by Scolar Pr UK) Ashgate Pub Co.
— Early Printed Book Labels. (Illus.). 207p. 1976. 28.00 (0-900002-72-7, Pub. by Priv Lib Assn UK) Oak Knoll.
Lee, Briant H. Theatre Primer: A Manual for Success in Early College or University Theatre Courses. 192p. (C). 1991. pap. text ed. 11.95 (0-8403-6910-7) Kendall-Hunt.
Lee, Briant H. & Wedwick, Daryl M. Corrugated Cardboard Scenery. 2nd ed. LC 93-15777. (Illus.). 176p. 1993. pap. 20.00 (0-88734-628-6) Players Pr.
— Corrugated Scenery. LC 82-81244. (Illus.). 96p. 1982. pap. 9.00 (0-88127-004-0) Oracle Pr LA.
Lee, Bruce. Bruce Lee's One & Three Inch Power Punch. 1989. pap. 3.95 (0-86568-112-0) Unique Pubns.
— Chinese Gung Fu. LC 86-43242. (Specialties Ser.: No. 451). 112p. 1987. reprint ed. pap. 8.50 (0-89750-112-8) Ohara Pubns.
— Marching Orders: The Untold Story of World War II. 1995. 30.00 (0-517-57576-0, Crown) Crown Pub Group.
— Tao of Jeet Kune Do. LC 75-13803. (Specialties Ser.). (Illus.). 1975. pap. 12.50 (0-89750-048-2, 401, Wehman) Ohara Pubns.
Lee, Bruce & Uyehara, Mitoshi. Bruce Lee's Fighting Method: Advanced Techniques, Vol. 4, No. 405. LC 77-92737. (Specialties Ser.). (Illus.). 1977. pap. 8.95 (0-89750-053-9) Ohara Pubns.
— Bruce Lee's Fighting Method: Basic Training, Vol. II, No. 403. Shelrud, Doris, ed. LC 77-79057. (Specialties Ser.). (Illus.). 1977. pap. text ed. 8.95 (0-89750-051-2, Wehman) Ohara Pubns.
— Bruce Lee's Fighting Method: Self-Defense Techniques, Vol. 1, No. 402. LC 76-51476. (Specialties Ser.). (Illus.). 1976. pap. text ed. 8.95 (0-89750-050-4, Wehman) Ohara Pubns.
— Bruce Lee's Fighting Method: Skill in Techniques, Vol. 3, No. 404. LC 77-81831. (Specialties Ser.). (Illus.). 1977. pap. 8.95 (0-89750-052-0, Wehman) Ohara Pubns.
Lee, Bruce, ed. see Parrish, Thomas.
Lee, Burtrand I. & Pope, Edward J., eds. Chemical Processing of Ceramics. LC 94-25396. (Engineering Materials Ser.: Vol. 8). 560p. 1994. 165.00 (0-8247-9244-0) Dekker.
Lee, Butch & Rover, Red. Night-Vision: Illuminating War & Class on the Neo-Colonial Terrain. 188p. (Orig.). 1993. pap. 14.95 (1-883780-00-4) Vagabond NY.
Lee, Byeong G. Scrambling Techniques for Digital Transmission. 1994. 59.00 (0-387-19863-6) Spr-Verlag.
Lee, Byeong G. & Kang, Minho. Broadband Telecommunications Technology. (Telecommunications Ser.). 600p. 1993. text ed. 84.00 (0-89006-653-1) Artech Hse.
Lee, Byung Ik, jt. auth. see Edmister, Wayne C.
***Lee, C. Allyson & Silvera, Makeda, eds.** Pearls of Passion. 1994. pap. 12.95 (0-920813-99-2) InBook.
Lee, C. C. Environmental Engineering Dictionary. 2nd ed. 630p. 1992. text ed. 88.00 (0-86587-328-3); pap. text ed. 68.00 (0-86587-298-8) Gov Insts.
— Environmental Law Index to Chemicals. 250p. 1993. pap. text ed. 55.00 (0-86587-338-0) Gov Insts.
— Environmental Law Index to Chemicals, 1995 Edition. 250p. 1995. pap. text ed. 75.00 (0-86587-461-1) Gov Insts.
— Medical Waste Incineration Handbook. 270p. 1990. pap. text ed. 79.00 (0-86587-223-6) Gov Insts.
Lee, C. C., jt. auth. see Buncel, E.
Lee, C. C., jt. ed. see Buncel, E.
Lee, C. F. Statistics for Business & Financial Economics. 864p. (C). 1993. text ed. write for info. (0-669-24598-4); Study guide. student ed write for info. (0-669-24599-2); Minitab manual. student ed write for info. (0-669-32684-4); Instr.'s manual & test bank. teacher ed write for info. (0-669-24600-X) Heath.
Lee, C. F., et al. Security Analysis & Portfolio Management. (C). 1990. text ed. 76.00 (0-673-38635-X) HarpCollege.
Lee, C. J. Caldwell Lee: The Poet to Be: The Forthright Omnipotence Era. 56p. 1994. pap. 7.95 (0-8059-3526-6) Dorrance.
Lee, C. K., ed. Developments in Food Carbohydrates, Vol. 2. (Illus.). 219p. 1980. 117.00 (0-85334-857-X, Pub. by Elsevier Applied Sci UK) Elsevier.
— Developments in Food Carbohydrates, Vol. 3. (Illus.). xii, 216p. 1982. 84.75 (0-85334-996-7, Pub. by Elsevier Applied Sci UK) Elsevier.
Lee, C. M., ed. Child Abuse: A Reader & Source-Book. 312p. 1978. pap. 32.00 (0-335-00230-7, Open Univ Pr) Taylor & Francis.
Lee, C. M. & Inglis, J. K. Science for Hairdressing Students. 3rd ed. (Illus.). 200p. 1983. text ed. 109.00 (0-08-027440-4, Pub. by Pergamon Repr UK) Franklin.
Lee, C. P., ed. Current Topics in Bioenergetics, Vol. 16. (Illus.). 407p. 1991. text ed. 127.00 (0-12-152516-3) Acad Pr.
— Current Topics in Bioenergetics, Vol. 17: Molecular Aspects of Mitochondrial Pathology. (Illus.). 254p. 1994. text ed. 99.00 (0-12-152517-1) Acad Pr.
— Current Topics in Bioenergetics, Volume 15: Structure, Biogenesis & Assembly of Energy Transducing Enzyme Systems. 389p. 1987. text ed. 137.00 (0-12-152515-5) Acad Pr.
Lee, C. S., ed. Sensor-Based Robots: Algorithms & Architectures. (NATO ASI Series F: Computer & Systems Sciences, Special Programme AET: Vol. 66). x, 285p. 1991. 77.00 (0-387-52298-0) Spr-Verlag.
Lee, Cara. West Rock to the Barndoor Hills: The Traprock Ridges of Connecticut. (Illus.). 60p. 1985. pap. 5.00 (0-942081-00-5) CT DEP CGNHS.
Lee, Carol. The Blind Side of Eden: The Sexes in Perspective. 224p. 1991. pap. 13.95 (0-7475-0572-1, Pub. by Bloomsbury Pub Ltd UK) Trafalgar.
— Good Grief: Experiencing Loss. 256p. 1995. pap. 19.95 (1-85702-184-3, Pub. by Fourth Estate UK) Trafalgar.
— Legacy of the Land: Two Hundred Fifty Years of Agriculture in Carroll County, Maryland. LC 82-83567. (Illus.). 177p. 1982. 6.00 (0-685-33351-5) Hist Soc Carroll.
— The Ostrich Position. pap. 5.95 (0-86316-057-3) Writers & Readers.
Lee, Carol & Edwards, Fay. Fifty Games to Play in the Library & Classroom. 124p. 1988. spiral bd. 9.95 (0-913853-06-2, 32514, Alleyside) Highsmith Pr.
Lee, Carol D. Signifying As a Scaffold for Literary Interpretation: The Pedagogical Implications of an African American Discourse Genre. (Research Report Ser.). (Illus.). 200p. (Orig.). 1993. pap. 22.95 (0-8141-4471-3) NCTE.
Lee, Carol M., jt. auth. see Olk, R. Joseph.
Lee, Carol W. Blue Garter Club: Ties That Bind Fourteen Christian Women for 40 Years. Hermanson, Renee, ed. LC 92-4563. (Illus.). 260p. (Orig.). 1992. pap. 11.95 (1-880292-20-3) LangMarc.
***Lee, Carole A.** Banner's Bonus. 400p. (Orig.). 1995. mass mkt., pap. text ed. 4.99 (0-505-52027-3) Dorchester Pub Co.
Lee, Carvel. Thirty-Six One-Day Discovery Tours: Fun Places to Drive Within & from Minneapolis & St. Paul. rev. ed. (Illus.). 1994. 11.95 (0-931714-40-0) Nodin Pr.
Lee, Catherine T., jt. auth. see Lee, Warren F.
Lee, Cathy & Uhlmann, Chris. Worship Dramas for Children & Adults. LC 88-31755. (Illus.). 192p. (C). 1988. pap. 12.95 (0-89390-130-X) Resource Pubns.
Lee, Cathy H., ed. see Mailer, Stan.
Lee, Cathy H., ed. see Nelsen, John & Law, Scott.
Lee, Cazenove G. Lee Chronicle: Studies of the Early Generations of the Lees of Virginia. Parker, Dorothy M., ed. LC 56-10782. 468p. reprint ed. pap. 133.40 (0-317-09109-3, 2050258) Bks Demand.
Lee, Celeste. Understanding the Body Organs: And the Eight Laws of Health. LC 94-60068. 128p. (YA). 1994. reprint ed. pap. 7.95 (0-945383-44-4) Teach Servs.
Lee, Chae-Jin. China & Japan: New Economic Diplomacy. LC 84-6602. (Publication Ser.: No. 297). (Illus.). xviii, 174p. (C). 1984. lib. bdg. 19.95 (0-8179-7971-9); pap. 9.95 (0-8179-7972-7) Hoover Inst Pr.
— Japan Faces China: Political & Economic Relations in the Postwar Era. LC 75-40408. (Illus.). 256p. 1976. 36.00 (0-8018-1738-2) Johns Hopkins.
— Zhou Enlai: The Early Years. LC 93-33525. 1994. 35.00 (0-8047-2302-8) Stanford U Pr.
Lee, Chae-Jin, ed. The United States & Japan: Changing Relations. (Occasional Papers, Keck Center, Claremont McKenna College: No. 2). 96p. 1992. pap. 10.95 (0-930607-13-9) Regina Bks.
Lee, Chae-Jin & Sato, Hideo, eds. U. S. - Japan Partnership in Conflict Management: The Case of Korea. LC 93-34391. 1993. 7.00 (0-930607-16-3) Keck Ctr.
Lee, Chae-Jin, jt. ed. see Speakman, Jay.
Lee, Chae-Jin, jt. ed. see Suh, Dae-Sook.
***Lee, Chang-Rae.** Native Speaker. 1995. 21.95 (1-57322-001-9) Riverhead Bks.
Lee, Changsoo & DeVos, George. Koreans in Japan: Ethnic Conflict & Accommodation. LC 80-6053. (Illus.). 448p. 1981. 55.00 (0-520-04258-1) U CA Pr.
Lee, Charles. The Hidden Public: The Story of the Book-of-the-Month Club. LC 73-724. 236p. 1973. reprint ed. text ed. 55.00 (0-8371-6785-X, LEHI, Greenwood Pr) Greenwood.
— Love, Life, & Laughter. Harris, Paul N., ed. 180p. 1990. 12.50 (0-915180-32-4) Harrowood Bks.
— Love, Life, & Laughter. Harris, Paul N., ed. 180p. 1991. pap. 9.95 (0-915180-34-0) Harrowood Bks.
— Ten Sevens. LC 82-15771. 80p. 1983. 12.50 (0-915180-23-5) Harrowood Bks.
Lee, Charles, ed. The Vale of Lanherne. (C). 1989. 30.00 (0-907566-45-6, Pub. by Dyllansow Truran UK) St Mut.
Lee, Charles, jt. ed. see Kerr, Mary L.
Lee, Charles, jt. ed. see Lewis, Dominic B.
Lee, Charles A. & Dalman, G. Conrad. Microwave Devices, Circuits & Their Interaction. LC 93-10605. (Microwave & Optical Engineering Ser.). 368p. 1994. text ed. 59.95 (0-471-55216-X) Wiley.
Lee, Charles E., jt. auth. see Richardson, Katherine H.
Lee, Charles R., Jr. The Confederate Constitutions. LC 73-16628. 225p. 1974. reprint ed. text ed. 52.50 (0-8371-7201-2, LECC, Greenwood Pr) Greenwood.
Lee, Charlotte A. In Touch with the Infinite. 2nd ed. 145p. 1972. 4.50 (0-87516-169-3) DeVorss.
Lee, Charlotte I. & Gura, Timothy. Oral Interpretation, 8 Vols. 8th ed. (C). 1991. text ed. 51.56 (0-395-59329-8) HM.
Lee, Charmaine, tr. see Orlando, Francesco.
Lee, Chas. Totally Trusting. (Illus.). 222p. (J). (gr. 4-10). 1992. 19.95 (1-878044-09-5) Mayhaven Pub.
Lee, Chauncey. The American Accountant. LC 82-48375. (Accountancy in Transition Ser.). 318p. 1982. lib. bdg. 15.00 (0-8240-5324-9) Garland.
Lee, Chaur-Shyan. Production & Marketing of Milkfish in Taiwan: An Economic Analysis. (ICLARM Technical Reports: No. 6). (Illus.). 41p. (Orig.). 1983. pap. text ed. 9.50 (0-89955-390-7, Pub. by ICLARM PH) Intl Spec Bk.
Lee, Cheng F., ed. Advances in Financial Planning & Forecasting, Vol. 1. 1985. 73.25 (0-89232-355-8) Jai Pr.
— Advances in Financial Planning & Forecasting, Vol. 2. 1987. 73.25 (0-89232-624-7) Jai Pr.
— Advances in Financial Planning & Forecasting, Vol. 3. 1987. 73.25 (0-89232-651-4) Jai Pr.
Lee, Cheng F. & Finnerty, Joseph E. Corporate Finance: Theory, Method & Applications. 765p. (C). 1989. text ed. 50.00 (0-15-514085-X) Dryden Pr.
Lee, Cheng-Sheng & Liao, I-Chiu, eds. Reproduction & Culture of Milkfish. (Illus.). 226p. (Orig.). 1985. pap. write for info. (0-9617016-1-7) Oceanic Inst.
Lee, Cheng-Sheng, et al. Aquaculture of Milkfish Chanos Chanos: State of the Art. (Illus.). 284p. (Orig.). 1986. pap. write for info. (0-9617016-0-9) Oceanic Inst.
Lee, Chester M., ed. Apollo Soyuz Mission Report. LC 57-43769. (Advances in the Astronautical Sciences Ser.: Vol. 34). (Illus.). 1977. lib. bdg. 35.00 (0-87703-089-8, Univelt Inc) Univelt Inc.
Lee, Chi H., ed. Picosecond Optoelectronic Devices. LC 84-3016. 1984. text ed. 121.00 (0-12-440880-X) Acad Pr.
Lee, Chi-Jen. Development - Evaluation - Drugs: From Laboratory Through Licensure to Market. 1993. 79.95 (0-8493-4447-6, RM301) CRC Pr.
Lee, Chi-Ming, tr. see Kraft, Charles H.
Lee, Chin-Chuan. China's Media, Media's China. LC 94-949. (C). 1994. text ed. 59.95 (0-8133-8800-7) Westview.
Lee, Chin-Hwa. Digital System Design Using VHDL. LC 92-75589. (Illus.). 304p. (C). 1993. text ed. 29.00 (1-882819-00-4) CorralTek.
— Digital System Design Using VHDL Examples Diskette. (C). Date not set. 3.5 hd 15.00 (1-882819-01-2) CorralTek.
Lee, Chong. Advanced Explosive Kicks. LC 78-61152. (Specialties Ser.). (Illus.). 1978. pap. 14.95 (0-89750-060-1, 133) Ohara Pubns.
— Dynamic Kicks: Essentials for Free Fighting. Johnson, Gilbert, ed. LC 75-36052. (Specialties Ser.). (Illus.). 1975. pap. text ed. 11.95 (0-89750-017-2, 122) Ohara Pubns.
— Super Dynamic Kicks. LC 80-84496. (Korean Arts Ser.). (Illus.). 1980. pap. 9.95 (0-89750-072-5, 409) Ohara Pubns.
Lee, Chong-Sik. Japan & Korea: The Political Dimension. LC 85-5455. (Publication Ser.: No. 318). (Illus.). xiv, 234p. 1985. lib. bdg. 24.95 (0-8179-8181-0) Hoover Inst Pr.
— Korean Workers' Party: A Short History. Staar, Richard F., ed. LC 77-2427. (Publication Series: Histories of Ruling Communist Parties: No. 185). (Illus.). 1978. pap. 7.95 (0-8179-6852-0) Hoover Inst Pr.
Lee, Chong-Sik & Yoo, Se-Hee, eds. North Korea in Transition. LC 90-85946. (Korea Research Monographs: No. 16). xx, 156p. (Orig.). 1991. pap. 12.00 (1-55729-024-5) IEAS.
Lee, Chong-Won. Vibration Analysis of Rotors. LC 93-15585. (Solid Mechanics & Its Applications Ser.: Vol. 21). 328p. (C). 1993. lib. bdg. 114.00 (0-7923-2300-9) Kluwer Ac.
Lee, Christopher & Jackson, Rosemary F. Faking It: A Look into the Mind of a Creative Learner. 181p. 1992. pap. 14.95 (0-86709-296-3, 0296) Boynton Cook Pubs.
Lee, Chun-Jean, jt. ed. see Yang, Wen-Jei.
Lee, Chung H. & Naya, Seiji, eds. Trade & Investment in Services in the Asia-Pacific Region. (Monographs of the Center for International Studies, Inha University). (Illus.). 216p. (C). 1989. pap. text ed. 31.00 (0-8133-0585-3) Westview.
Lee, Chung H., jt. auth. see Haggard, Stephan.
Lee, Chung-Nim & Wasserman, Arthur G. On the Groups JO(G) (Memoirs Ser.: No. 2/159). 62p. 1975. pap. 17.00 (0-8218-1859-7, MEMO 2/159) Am Math.
Lee, Chwen J. & Hand, Thomas G. A Taste of Water. 195p. 1990. pap. 11.95 (0-8091-3149-8) Paulist Pr.

*Lee, Clive. Scotland & the United Kingdom: The Economy & the Union in the Twentieth Century. LC 95-5482. (Insights from Economic History Ser.). 1995. text ed. write for info. (*0-7190-4100-7*, Pub. by Manchester Univ Pr UK); text ed. write for info. (*0-7190-4101-5*, Pub. by Manchester Univ Pr UK) St Martin.

Lee, Colin, jt. ed. see Gilroy, Andrea.

Lee, Courtland C., ed. Counseling for Diversity: A Guide for School Counselors & Related Professionals. 1994. 32.95 (*0-205-15321-6*, Longwood Div) Allyn.

Lee, Courtland C. & Richardson, Bernard, eds. Multicultural Issues in Counseling: New Approaches to Diversity. 1991. 35.95 (*1-55620-082-X*) Am Coun Assn.

Lee, Cyrus A. Soldat: The WW II German Army Combat Uniform Collector's Handbook, Equipping the German Army Foot Soldier in Europe 1943, Vol. 2. LC 88-90959. (Illus.). 88p. 1988. pap. 7.95 (*0-929521-01-3*) Pictorial Hist.

— Soldat: the World War II German Army Combat Uniform: Collections Handbook 1939-1942, Vol. 1. LC 92-61981. (Illus.). 232p. (Orig.). 1992. pap. 12.95 (*0-929521-59-5*) Pictorial Hist.

— Soldat, Vol. III: Equipping the German Foot Soldier in Europe 1944-1945. LC 90-64461. (Illus.). 196p. 1991. pap. 10.95 (*0-929521-46-3*) Pictorial Hist.

— Soldat, Vol. 5: The WW Two German Army Combat Uniform Collector's Handbook. LC 88-90959. (Illus.). 226p. 1993. pap. 12.95 (*0-929521-76-5*) Pictorial Hist.

Lee, D. C. I. I. Marine Law, No. 180M/063. (C). 1986. 230.00 (*0-685-33751-0*, Pub. by Witherby & Co UK) St Mut.

Lee, D. & McDaniel, S. T. Ocean Acoustic Propagation by Finite Difference Methods. (International Series in Modern Applied Mathematics & Computer Science: No. 15). 127p. 1988. 36.00 (*0-08-034871-8*, Pergamon Pr) Elsevier.

Lee, D., tr. see Scholz, Erhard.

Lee, D., et al. Theoretical & Computational Acoustics, 2 Vols. 1024p. 1994. text ed. 213.00 (*981-02-1695-5*) World Scientific Pub.

Lee, D., et al, eds. Computational Acoustics. 856p. 1988. Vol. 1, Wave Propagation. 95.00 (*0-444-70349-7*, North Holland); Vol. 2, Algorithms & Applications. 95.00 (*0-444-70350-0*, North Holland) Elsevier.

— Computational Acoustics, Set. 856p. 1988. 151.50 (*0-444-70351-9*, North Holland) Elsevier.

— Computational Acoustics: Proceedings of the 2nd IMACS Symposium Princeton, NJ, 15-17 March, 1989, 3 vols. 276p. 1990. Vol. 1, Ocean-Acoustic Models & Supercomputing, 276p. 61.75 (*0-444-88720-2*, North Holland); Vol. 2, Scattering, Gaussian Beams, & Aeroacoustics, 322p. 77.00 (*0-444-88721-0*, North Holland); Vol. 3, Seismo-Ocean Acoustics & Modeling, 344p. 82.00 (*0-444-88722-9*, North Holland) Elsevier.

— Computational Acoustics: Proceedings of the 2nd IMACS Symposium Princeton, NJ, 15-17 March, 1989, 3 vols., Set. 1990. 205.25 (*0-444-88723-7*, North Holland) Elsevier.

Lee, D. B., ed. Intestinal Absorption of Minerals: Experimental & Clinical. (Journal: Mineral & Electrolyte Metabolism: Vol. 16, Nos. 2-3, 1990). (Illus.). 100p. 1990. pap. 144.00 (*3-8055-5212-2*) S Karger.

Lee, D. E., jt. auth. see Amrhein, J. E.

Lee, D. John, ed. Life & Story: Autobiographies for a Narrative Psychology. LC 93-19093. 304p. 1993. text ed. 59.95 (*0-275-94095-0*, C4095, Praeger Pubs) Greenwood.

— Storying Ourselves: A Narrative Perspective on Christians in Psychology. LC 93-1889. (Christian Explorations in Psychology Ser.). 1993. pap. 16.99 (*0-8010-5683-7*) Baker Bk.

Lee, D. John & Stronks, Gloria G., eds. Assessment in Christian Higher Education: Rhetoric & Reality. (Calvin College Ser.: Vol. II). 270p. (Orig.). Date not set. lib. bdg. 53.00 (*0-8191-9408-5*); pap. text ed. 24.50 (*0-8191-9409-3*) U Pr of Amer.

Lee, D. S., et al. Atlas of North American Freshwater Fishes. LC 80-620039. (Illus.). 867p. 1980. 25.00 (*0-917134-03-6*) NC Natl Sci.

— Atlas of North American Freshwater Fishes: 1983 Supplement. (Occasional Papers of the North Carolina Biological Survey: 1983-6). (Illus.). 67p. 1991. reprint ed. 10.00 (*0-917134-06-0*) NC Natl Sci.

Lee, D. T., jt. auth. see Sarrafzadeh, M.

Lee, D. Y. & Shah, S. P., eds. New Horizons in Construction Materials. (Session Proceedings Ser.). 96p. 1988. 16.00 (*0-87262-677-6*) Am Soc Civil Eng.

Lee, Dalton S. The Basis of Management in Public Organizations. LC 89-13360. (American University Studies: Political Science: Ser. X, Vol. 24). 240p. 1990. text ed. 47.95 (*0-8204-1111-6*) P Lang Pubs.

Lee, Dalton S. & Cayer, N. Joseph. Supervision for Success in Government: A Practical Guide for First Line Managers. (Public Administration Ser.). 225p. 1994. 26.95 (*0-685-71219-2*) Jossey-Bass.

Lee, Dan. On the Porch & on the Trail. LC 90-70315. 81p. (Orig.). 1990. pap. 5.95 (*1-55523-332-5*) Winston-Derek.

Lee, Daniel & Frost, Joseph H. Ten Years in Oregon. LC 72-9457. (Far Western Frontier Ser.). (Illus.). 348p. 1973. reprint ed. 26.95 (*0-405-04985-4*) Ayer.

— Ten Years in Oregon. 344p. 1968. reprint ed. 19.95 (*0-87770-017-6*) Ye Galleon.

Lee, Daniel E. Hope Is Where We Least Expect to Find It. 100p. (Orig.). (C). 1993. lib. bdg. 36.50 (*0-8191-9055-1*); pap. text ed. 16.95 (*0-8191-9056-X*) U Pr of Amer.

Lee, Daniel O. & Wickins, John F. Crustacean Farming. 392p. 1992. text ed. 95.00 (*0-470-21850-9*) Halsted Pr.

Lee, Danny, ed. see Sumeria Staff.

Lee, David. Competing Discourses: Perspective & Ideology in Language. (Real Language Ser.). 216p. (C). 1992. pap. text ed. 24.95 (*0-582-07850-4*) Longman.

— Day's Work. LC 89-81836. 144p. (Orig.). 1990. pap. 10.00 (*1-55659-027-X*) Copper Canyon.

— Language, Children, & Society: An Introduction to Linguistic & Language Development. 248p. 1988. pap. 18.50 (*0-8147-5040-0*) NYU Pr.

— My Town. 132p. (Orig.). 1995. pap. 12.00 (*1-55659-074-1*) Copper Canyon.

— The Porcine Canticles. LC 84-71252. 120p. (Orig.). 1984. pap. 10.00 (*0-914742-83-3*) Copper Canyon.

Lee, David & Newby, Howard. The Problem of Sociology: An Introduction to the Discipline. 379p. (C). 1990. pap. text ed. 21.95 (*0-04-445641-7*) Routledge Chapman & Hall.

Lee, David, jt. auth. see Evans, Arthur S.

Lee, David, jt. ed. see Goebel, Ulrich.

Lee, David, et al. Scheming for Youth: A Study of the YTS in the Enterprise Culture. 208p. 1990. 90.00 (*0-335-15193-0*); pap. 34.00 (*0-335-15192-2*) Taylor & Francis.

Lee, David A., jt. auth. see Dyer, John A.

Lee, David A., jt. ed. see Higginbitham, Eve J.

Lee, David C. Gravity Golf: The Evolution & Revolution of Golf Instruction. (Illus.). 184p. 1995. 18.75 (*0-9645478-7-2*) Gravty Sports. PGA & Senior PGA Tour guru David Lee has recently released his fascinating new book GRAVITY GOLF. The product of 17 years of research, this book contains never before revealed truths about swing mechanics which give insights to how our effortless swings occur & how we can experience them more often. The research, based in fundamental physics & efficient motion, has produced the first physics pure analysis of the swing in the history of golf. The book is written in an easy, flowing, &, at times, funny style which makes for easy reading while flooding the reader with original, logical information about the swing & how humans learn to swing. The experience of soaking in this book leads the reader to the conclusion that they've finally found "THE SECRET." Truly the most enlightening information in years, & free of any teaching aids required by so many of the current swing training methods, Lee's concepts were originally endorsed by Jack Nicklaus in 1977, & have gained acclaim from others such as Chi Chi Rodriguez, Rocky Thompson, numerous members of the medical & scientific community & countless amateurs at all levels. DAVID LEE HAS BEEN FEATURED IN GOLF MAGAZINE & GOLF DIGEST, WITH THE LATTER LISTING HIM AS ONE OF THE TOP TEACHERS IN THE COUNTRY REPEATEDLY. Order directly from Gravity Sports Concepts, Inc., 11778 West Waterway, Homosassa, FL 34448. (904) 628-6314, or your local distributor.** ***Publisher Provided Annotation.

— The People's Universities of the U. S. S. R. LC 88-15486. (Contributions to the Study of Education Ser.: No. 29). (Illus.). 279p. 1988. text ed. 55.00 (*0-313-26344-2*, LPU/, Greenwood Pr) Greenwood.

Lee, David D. Sergeant York: An American Hero. LC 84-10465. (Illus.). 184p. 1985. 20.00 (*0-8131-1517-5*) U Pr of Ky.

Lee, David E. The Motivating Administrator. LC 80-29157. 112p. 1981. 9.95 (*0-88289-255-X*) Pelican.

Lee, David J. Bridge Bearings & Expansion Joints. LC 93-32192. 1994. write for info. (*0-419-14570-2*, E & FN Spon) Routledge Chapman & Hall.

Lee, David M., ed. Liability in Construction Management. 89p. 1983. pap. 17.00 (*0-87262-383-1*) Am Soc Civil Eng.

Lee, David S. & Parnell, James F. Endangered, Threatened, & Rare Fauna of North Carolina, Pt. 3: A Re-evaluation of the Birds. (Occasional Papers of the North Carolina Biological Survey). 52p. (Orig.). 1990. pap. 8.00 (*0-917134-19-2*) NC Natl Sci.

Lee, David S. & Socci, Mary C. Potential Effects of Oil Spills on Seabirds & Selected Other Oceanic Vertebrates Off the North Carolina Coast. (Occasional Papers of the North Carolina Biological Survey). (Illus.). 64p. (Orig.). 1989. pap. text ed. 8.00 (*0-917134-18-4*) NC Natl Sci.

Lee, David S., et al. A Distributional Survey of North Carolina Mammals. (Occasional Papers of the North Carolina Biological Survey: 1982-10). (Illus.). 70p. 1982. 5.00 (*0-917134-04-4*) NC Natl Sci.

***Lee, David T. & Pfaltzgraff, Robert L., Jr., eds.** Taiwan in a Transformed Global Setting. (Institute for Foreign Policy Analysis Ser.). 147p. 1995. pap. 11.95x (*0-02-881138-0*) Brasseys Inc.

Lee de Munoz-Marin, Muna. Sea-Change. 1977. lib. bdg. 59.95 (*0-8490-2580-X*) Gordon Pr.

Lee, Deborah. Exploring Nature's Uncultivated Garden. rev. ed. (Illus.). 195p. 1989. reprint ed. 12.50 (*0-925909-00-9*) Havelin Comns.

Lee, Debra. Heartbeat. LC 87-31823. 1989. pap. 13.95 (*0-87949-274-0*) Ashley Bks.

Lee, Deemer. Esther's Town. LC 89-24440. (Iowa Heritage Collection). (Illus.). 276p. 1989. reprint ed. pap. 7.95 (*0-8138-0459-0*) Iowa St U Pr.

Lee, Delene W. & Lee, Jasper S. Agribusiness Procedures & Practices. (Career Preparation for Agriculture-Agribusiness Ser.). (Illus.). 1980. text ed. 16.96 (*0-07-036737-X*) McGraw.

Lee, Dennis. Civil Elegies & Other Poems. 59p. (Orig.). 1972. 7.95 (*0-88784-123-6*, Pub. by Hse of Anansi Pr CN); pap. 7.95 (*0-88784-023-X*, Pub. by Hse of Anansi Pr CN) Genl Dist Srvs.

— The Ice Cream Store. (Illus.). (J). (ps). 1992. 14.95 (*0-590-45861-2*, 002, Scholastic Hardcover) Scholastic Inc.

— Lord Lyndhurst: The Flexible Tory. (Illus.). 288p. 1994. 29.95 (*0-87081-358-7*) Univ Pr Colo.

— Savage Fields: An Essay in Literature & Cosmology. 125p. 1977. 14.95 (*0-88784-059-0*, Pub. by Hse of Anansi Pr CN) Genl Dist Srvs.

***Lee, Dennis M.** The Alternative. (Illus.). 360p. (Orig.). 1994. pap. 19.95 (*0-9644068-0-2*) Better Wrld Tech.

Lee, Diane. The Pelvic Girdle. (Illus.). 149p. 1989. text ed. 49.95 (*0-443-03795-7*) Churchill.

***Lee, Don & Daniel, David, eds.** Regrets Only. (Ploughshares Ser.). 230p. (Orig.). (C). 1994. pap. text ed. 8.95 (*0-933277-12-1*) Ploughshares.

Lee, Don, ed. see Aung Chin Win Aung.

Lee, Don, ed. see Eann.

***Lee, Don, et al, eds.** An Annotated Bibliography on South Asia: Research. LC 94-78180. 200p. (C). 1995. 57.00x (*0-939758-29-6*) Eastern Pr.

Lee, Don L. Think Black. 3rd ed. LC 70-882333. (YA). (gr. 12 up). 1969. pap. 3.00 (*0-910296-03-0*) Broadside Pr.

— We Walk the Way of the New World. LC 70-121885. (YA). (gr. 12 up). 1970. 6.00 (*0-910296-26-X*); pap. 1.50 (*0-685-00872-X*) Broadside Pr.

Lee, Don L., see Haki R. Madhubuti, pseud..

Lee, Don Y. An Annotated Archaeological Bibliography of Selected Works on Northern & Central Asia. LC 83-81570. 94p. (C). 1983. 33.00 (*0-939758-05-9*) Eastern Pr.

— An Annotated Bibliography of Selected Works on China. LC 81-67771. 270p. (C). 1990. reprint ed. 46.50 (*0-939758-02-4*) Eastern Pr.

— An Annotated Bibliography on Inner Asia. LC 83-80529. 183p. (C). 1983. 45.50 (*0-939758-04-0*) Eastern Pr.

— An Annotated Prehistoric Bibliography on South Asia. 170p. (C). 1995. 47.50 (*0-939758-32-6*) Eastern Pr.

— Arabic Verb Frequency: Analytic & Synthetic Observations. (C). 1991. text ed. 49.00 (*0-939758-22-9*) Eastern Pr.

— Art in Korea: Historical. (C). 1990. 59.00 (*0-939758-20-2*) Eastern Pr.

— Chinese Eulogy & the Textual Variation. LC 83-82652. 96p. (C). 1983. 32.50 (*0-939758-06-7*) Eastern Pr.

— East Asian Languages & Linguistics. LC 85-81335. (C). 1986. 47.00 (*0-939758-13-X*) Eastern Pr.

— The History of Early Relations Between China & Tibet. LC 81-147860. 267p. (C). 1981. 43.50 (*0-939758-00-8*) Eastern Pr.

— An Introduction to East Asian & Tibetan Linguistics & Cultures. LC 81-67770. 339p. (C). 1981. 43.50 (*0-939758-01-6*) Eastern Pr.

— Learning Standard Arabic: Root & Pattern Reference. LC 86-82210. (C). 1988. 69.00 (*0-939758-15-6*) Eastern Pr.

— Light Literature & Philosophy of East Asia. LC 82-90698. 220p. (C). 1982. 36.50 (*0-939758-03-2*) Eastern Pr.

— An Outline of Confucianism. LC 85-80477. 113p. (C). 1984. 29.50 (*0-939758-10-5*) Eastern Pr.

— An Outline of Confucianism. rev. ed. LC 85-80477. (C). 1988. 33.50 (*0-939758-16-4*) Eastern Pr.

— Traditional Chinese Thought: The Four Schools. (C). 1990. 43.50 (*0-939758-17-2*) Eastern Pr.

— Western Asia: An Annotated Historical Bibliography. LC 84-70884. 213p. (C). 1984. 43.50 (*0-939758-07-5*) Eastern Pr.

— Written & Spoken Arabic: Based on Modern Standard Arabic. (ARA & ENG.). (C). 1993. text ed. 57.50 (*0-939758-26-1*) Eastern Pr.

Lee, Don Y., ed. The Poet As Mythmaker: A Study of Edwin Muir. 124p. (C). 1990. 34.50 (*0-939758-21-0*) Eastern Pr.

Lee, Don Y., tr. & intro. Korean Literature: Sijo. abr. ed. 200p. (C). 1994. 43.50x (*0-939758-27-X*) Eastern Pr.

Lee, Don Y., ed. see Bernett, Donna L.

Lee, Don Y., ed. see Fields, Brian A.

Lee, Don Y., ed. see Goehlert, Robert.

Lee, Don Y., ed. see Notzon, Mark.

Lee, Don Y., ed. see Payne, David C.

Lee, Don Y., ed. see Traylor, Kenneth L.

Lee, Don Y., ed. see Young, Margaret H.

Lee, Donald C. Toward a Sound World Order: A Multidimensional, Hierarchical Ethical Theory. LC 91-40942. (Contributions in Philosophy Ser.: No. 49). 240p. 1992. text ed. 45.00 (*0-313-27903-9*, LTA, Greenwood Pr) Greenwood.

Lee, Donald G., jt. auth. see Way, Robert F.

Lee, Donald J. Polyarchy: The Political Theory of Robert A. Dahl. LC 91-32764. (Political Theory & Political Philosophy Ser.). 224p. 1991. 20.00 (*0-8153-0202-9*) Garland.

Lee, Donald L. Electromagnetic Principles of Integrated Optics. 348p. 1986. 58.50 (*0-471-87978-9*) Krieger.

Lee, Donald Lewis & Atkinson, H. J. Physiology of Nematodes. 2nd ed. LC 77-1232. (Illus.). 215p. 1977. text ed. 51.50 (*0-231-04358-9*) Col U Pr.

Lee, Donald W. Harbrace Vocabulary Guide. 2nd ed. 184p. (Orig.). (C). 1970. pap. text ed. 16.75 (*0-15-534471-4*); pap. text ed. 1.00 (*0-15-534472-2*) HB Coll Pubs.

— HarBrace Vocabulary Guide. 3rd ed. 1993. pap. 18.75 (*0-15-500855-2*) HarBrace.

Lee, Donna & Ivey, Jean M. Facts & Fancy: Acadia Mount Desert Island. 1993. pap. 9.95 (*0-9639078-0-8*) Facts & Fancy.

Lee, Donna, jt. ed. see Carlson, Linda.

Lee, Donna S. Springtime Romance. 1993. 7.95 (*0-533-09574-3*) Vantage.

Lee, Dorothy. Freedom & Culture. 179p. (C). 1987. reprint ed. pap. text ed. 9.95 (*0-88133-303-4*) Waveland Pr.

— Valuing the Self: What We Can Learn from Other Cultures. (Illus.). 1986. reprint ed. pap. text ed. 7.95 (*0-88133-229-1*) Waveland Pr.

Lee, Dorothy E., Jr. & Brower, Walter A. Secretarial Office Procedures. 2nd ed. (Illus.). 416p. 1981. text ed. 29.95 (*0-07-037037-0*) McGraw.

Lee, Dorothy E., et al. Secretarial Office Procedures. (Illus.). 400p. 1988. pap. text ed. 23.00 (*0-07-037050-8*) McGraw.

Lee, Dorothy S. Native North American Music & Oral Data: A Catalogue of Sound Recordings, 1893-1976. LC 78-20337. 480p. 1979. 25.00 (*0-253-18877-6*) Ind U Pr.

Lee, Dorris. The Reader's Edge. 1992. write for info. (*0-318-69207-4*) Momentum Assocs.

Lee, Dorris M. The Importance of Reading for Achieving in Grades Four, Five, & Six. LC 75-176978. (No. 556). reprint ed. 37.50 (*0-404-55556-X*) AMS Pr.

— Rapidreader! Manual. (Illus.). 160p. (Orig.). 1988. vhs 99.95 (*0-317-89789-6*) Norman Leslie.

Lee, Douglas. T'ai Chi Ch'uan the Philosophy of Yin & Yang & Its Applications. Lucas, Charles, ed. LC 76-6249. (Chinese Arts Ser.). (Illus.). 1976. pap. text ed. 10.95 (*0-89750-044-X*, 317, Wehman) Ohara Pubns.

Lee, Douglas B., et al. Stage for a Nation: The Story of the National Theatre. LC 85-22761. (Illus.). 152p. (C). 1986. 30.75 (*0-8191-5021-5*, National Theatre) U Pr of Amer.

Lee, Douglas H. Climate & Economic Development in the Tropics. LC 76-56184. 182p. 1977. reprint ed. text ed. 49.75 (*0-8371-9410-5*, LECE, Greenwood Pr) Greenwood.

Lee, Douglas H., jt. auth. see Selikoff, Irving J.

Lee, Douglas H., et al, eds. Handbook of Physiology: Section 9, Reactions to Environmental Agents. (American Physiological Society Book). (Illus.). 667p. 1988. 100.00 (*0-19-520684-3*) OUP.

Lee, Dwight. The Next Environmental Battleground: Indoor Air. 1992. pap. 10.00 (*0-943802-78-4*, 174) Natl Ctr Pol.

Lee, Dwight & McKenzie, Richard. Failure & Progress: The Bright Side of the Dismal Science. 1993. 19.95 (*1-882577-03-5*); pap. 10.95 (*1-882577-02-7*) Cato Inst.

Lee, Dwight, jt. auth. see Doti, James.

Lee, Dwight, jt. auth. see McKenzie, Richard.

Lee, Dwight E. Europe's Crucial Years: The Diplomatic Background of World War I, 1902-1914. LC 73-91315. (Illus.). 496p. reprint ed. pap. 141.40 (*0-685-44068-0*, 2030031) Bks Demand.

— Great Britain & the Cyprus Convention Policy of 1878. LC 35-2422. (Historical Studies: No. 38). (Illus.). 240p. 1934. 16.50 (*0-674-36100-8*) HUP.

— The Outbreak of the First World War. 4th ed. (Problems in European Civilization Ser.). 168p. (C). 1975. pap. text ed. 8.50 (*0-669-94706-7*) Heath.

Lee, Dwight R. The Inflationary Impact of Labor Unions. 24p. 1979. 1.00 (*0-86599-006-9*) PERC.

Lee, Dwight R., ed. Taxation & the Deficit Economy: Fiscal Policy & Capital Formation in the United States. LC 85-63549. (Illus.). 554p. (C). 1986. 34.95 (*0-936488-13-1*); pap. 15.95 (*0-936488-03-4*) PRIPP.

Lee, Dwight R. & McKenzie, Richard B. Regulating Government: The Positive-Sum Solution. 208p. 1986. text ed. 27.95 (*0-669-13443-0*) Free Pr.

Lee, Dwight R., jt. auth. see McKenzie, Richard B.

Lee, E., et al. Starstruck. 85p. (Orig.). 1985. pap. 9.95 (*0-88145-023-5*) Broadway Play.

Lee, E. H. & Symonds, P. S., eds. Plasticity: Proceedings, Symposium on Naval Structural Mechanics, 2nd, Brown University, 1960. 1960. 260.00 (*0-08-009459-7*, Pub. by Pergamon Repr UK) Franklin.

Lee, E. H., ed. see Joint National & Western Applied Mechanics Conference Staff.

Lee, E. Lawrence. New Hanover County: A Brief History. (Illus.). xiv, 124p. 1984. pap. 5.00 (*0-86526-128-8*) NC Archives.

Lee, E. M. An Introduction to Pension Schemes. (C). 1986. 250.00 (*0-685-32759-0*, Pub. by Witherby & Co UK) St Mut.

— The Story of Symphony. 1972. 59.95 (*0-8490-1138-8*) Gordon Pr.

Lee, E. W. Magnetism: An Introductory Survey. 281p. 1984. reprint ed. pap. 6.95 (*0-486-24689-2*) Dover.

Lee, E. W., ed. Light-Weight Alloys for Aerospace Applications, No. II. (Illus.). 612p. 1991. 165.00 (*0-87339-135-7*, 430) Minerals Metals.

Lee, E. W., et al, eds. Light-Weight Alloys for Aerospace Applications. LC 89-60375. (Illus.). 515p. 1989. 165.00 (*0-87339-094-6*, 364) Minerals Metals.

— Recent Advances in Insulin Therapy: Proceedings of the 5th Korea-Japan Symposium on Diabetes Mellitus, Chejudo, Korea, 27-28 April, 1989. (International Congress Ser.: Vol. 867). 400p. 1990. 118.00 (*0-444-81131-1*, Excerpta Medica) Elsevier.

***Lee, Earl.** Drakulya. Date not set. 21.95 (*1-884365-01-9*) See Sharp Pr.

— Drakulya: The Lost Journal of Mircea Drakulya, Lord of the Undead. 224p. (Orig.). 1994. pap. 10.95 (*1-884365-02-7*) See Sharp Pr.

Lee, Earl & Lee, Hazel. Committed to Grace. 79p. (Orig.). 1993. pap. 5.95 (*0-8341-1500-X*, 55705) Beacon Hill.

An Asterisk (*) at the beginning of an entry indicates that the title is appearing in BIP for the first time.

Lee, Earl G. El Ciclo De la Vida Victoriosa: Recyled for Living. (SPA.). 3.25 (*84-7228-333-X*, 220153, Pub. by Edit Clie SP) TSELF.

Lee, Edward. The Chosen. 384p. 1993. mass mkt. 4.50 (*0-8217-4372-4*) Zebra.

— Creekers. 416p. 1994. mass mkt. 4.50 (*0-8217-4568-9*) Zebra.

Lee, Edward A. Digital Communication. 2nd ed. LC 93-26197. 912p. (C). 1993. lib. bdg. 120.00 (*0-7923-9391-0*) Kluwer Ac.

— Digital Communication: Solutions Manual. 2nd ed. 112p. (C). 1993. pap. text ed. 20.00 (*0-7923-9405-4*) Kluwer Ac.

Lee, Edward A. & Messerschmitt, David G. Digital Communication. 736p. (C). 1988. lib. bdg. 82.50 (*0-89838-274-2*) Kluwer Ac.

Lee, Edward G. & Nelson, W. M. Soldiers' National Cemetery - Gettysburg: Revised Report of the Select Committee Relative to the Soldiers' National Cemetery. Slack, Alfred, ed. (Illus.). 212p. (C). 1988. reprint ed. pap. 11.95 (*0-939631-08-3*) Thomas Publications.

Lee, Edward L., III, jt. auth. see Harvey, Gordon E.

Lee, Elain & Kaluta, Mike. Starstruck. 80p. (Orig.). 1984. 6.95 (*0-87135-001-7*) Marvel Entmnt.

***Lee, Elaine.** Vamps. Kahan, B., ed. (Illus.). 160p. Date not set. pap. write for info. (*1-56389-220-0*) DC Comics.

Lee, Elaine & Sherman, James. Trans. of Ike Garuda, No. 1. 48p. 1991. 3.95 (*0-87135-775-5*) Marvel Entmnt.

— Trans. of Ike Garuda, No. 2. 48p. 1992. 3.95 (*0-87135-776-3*) Marvel Entmnt.

***Lee, Elaine, et al.** Skin Tight Orbit. 52p. 1995. pap. 9.95x (*1-56163-118-3*, Amerotica) NBM.

— Skin Tight Orbit. deluxe ed. 52p. 1995. 45.00x (*1-56163-119-1*, Amerotica) NBM.

— Skin Tight Orbit, 2. 52p. 1995. pap. 9.95 (*1-56163-132-9*, Amerotica) NBM.

— Skin Tight Orbit, Vol. 2. 52p. 1995. 50.00 (*1-56163-137-X*, Amerotica) NBM.

Lee, Elisa T. Statistical Methods for Survival Data Analysis. 2nd ed. (Probability & Mathematical Statistics: Applied Probability & Statistics Section Ser.). 496p. 1992. text ed. 74.95 (*0-471-61592-7*) Wiley.

Lee, Elizabeth, jt. auth. see Carty, Winthrop P.

Lee, Elizabeth, tr. see Jusserand, Jean J.

Lee, Elizabeth M. He Wears Orchids & Other Latin American Stories. LC 76-117327. (Biography Index Reprint Ser.). 1977. 21.95 (*0-8369-8019-0*) Ayer.

***Lee, Elizabeth N.** King George County, Virginia, Death Records 1853-1896. 425p. (Orig.). 1995. pap. text ed. 50.50 (*0-614-05250-5*) Heritage Bk.

Lee, Ellen W. Seurat at Gravelines: The Last Landscapes. LC 90-83128. (Illus.). 80p. 1991. 29.95 (*0-936260-56-4*); pap. 19.95 (*0-936260-55-6*) Ind Mus Art.

Lee, Ellis. Finding the Career That Fits You: The Companion Workbook to Your Career in Changing Times. 1993. pap. 19.99 (*0-8024-1668-3*) Moody.

Lee, Elly, ed. see Blackman, Jackson F.

Lee, Elsie. Barrow Sinister. 1989. pap. 2.95 (*0-8217-2634-X*) Zebra.

— The Curse of Carranca. 224p. 1989. pap. 2.95 (*0-8217-2564-5*) Zebra.

— Dark Moon, Lost Lady. 224p. 1986. pap. 2.95 (*0-8217-1918-1*) Zebra.

— The Diplomatic Lover. 256p. 1987. pap. 2.95 (*0-8217-2234-4*) Zebra.

— The Drifting Sands. 272p. 1986. pap. 2.95 (*0-8217-1917-3*) Zebra.

— Mansion of Golden Windows. 224p. 1988. pap. 2.95 (*0-8217-2386-3*) Zebra.

— Season of Evil. 224p. 1987. pap. 2.95 (*0-8217-1970-X*) Zebra.

— Silence Is Golden. 272p. 1987. pap. 2.95 (*0-8217-2045-7*) Zebra.

— Sinister Abbey. 288p. 1988. pap. 2.95 (*0-8217-2464-9*) Zebra.

— The Spy at Villa Miranda. 272p. 1987. pap. 2.95 (*0-8217-2096-1*) Zebra.

Lee, Eric. Saigon to Jerusalem: Conversations with U. S. Veterans of the Vietnam War Who Emigrated to Israel. LC 92-53501. 208p. 1992. pap. 24.95x (*0-89950-727-1*) McFarland & Co.

Lee, Eric M. Common Objects: Money a Vehicle of Values. (Illus.). 62p. (Orig.). 1986. pap. 3.00 (*0-9615526-0-3*) Mtn Light Pubns.

— Translations: Turner & Printmaking. LC 93-60992. (Illus.). 48p. (Orig.). 1993. pap. 8.95 (*0-930606-71-X*) Yale Ctr Brit Art.

Lee, Ernest M. Brahms, the Man & His Music. LC 74-24138. (Illus.). reprint ed. 37.50 (*0-404-13001-1*) AMS Pr.

— The Story of Opera. 1972. 59.95 (*0-8490-1136-1*) Gordon Pr.

Lee, Essie E. Breaking the Connection: How Young People Achieve Drug-Free Lives. LC 87-18586. (Illus.). 160p. (YA). (gr. 7 up). 1988. pap. 5.95 (*0-671-67059-X*, Julian Messner) Silver Burdett Pr.

***Lee, Etrulia R.** Phonics Is My Way Series, 21 bks. Incl. Red Beans & Rice. (Illus.). 32p. (J). (gr. k-2). 1994. pap. text ed. (*1-884876-20-X*); I Can Jump. (Illus.). 16p. (J). (ps-2). 1994. pap. text ed. (*1-884876-01-3*); Dill. (Illus.). 20p. (J). (ps-2). 1995. pap. text ed. (*1-884876-03-X*); Jam, Ham, & Yams. (Illus.). 20p. (J). (ps-2). 1994. pap. text ed. (*1-884876-02-1*); Wake up Time. (Illus.). 20p. (J). (ps-2). 1994. pap. text ed. (*0-614-04415-4*); Tiff & His Bone. (Illus.). 28p. (J). (ps-2). 1994. pap. text ed. (*1-884876-04-8*); Mel. (Illus.). 20p. (J). (ps-2). 1994. pap. text ed. (*1-884876-07-2*); Team. (Illus.). 24p. (J). (ps-2). 1994. pap. text ed. (*1-884876-08-0*); Blake the Duck. (Illus.). 24p. (J). (ps-2). 1994. pap. text ed. (*1-884876-09-9*); I Like to Dream. (Illus.). 32p. (J). (gr. k-2). 1994. pap. text ed. (*1-884876-11-0*); Skates & Grapes. (Illus.). 24p. (J). (gr. k-2). 1994. pap. text ed. (*1-884876-12-9*); Train Ride. (Illus.). 20p. (J). (ps-2). 1994. pap. text ed. (*1-884876-10-2*); Mel Is Back. (Illus.). 32p. (J). (gr. k-2). 1994. pap. text ed. (*1-884876-13-7*); What Would You Say? (Illus.). 24p. (J). (gr. k-2). 1994. pap. text ed. (*1-884876-14-5*); Horse on a Porch. (Illus.). 36p. (J). (gr. k-2). 1994. pap. text ed. (*1-884876-15-3*); Zip-a-Zap Zing. (Illus.). 32p. (J). (gr. k-2). 1994. pap. text ed. (*1-884876-16-1*); Stuff. (Illus.). 20p. (J). (gr. k-2). 1994. pap. text ed. (*1-884876-17-X*); Space Trip. (Illus.). 24p. (J). (gr. k-2). 1994. pap. text ed. (*1-884876-18-8*); Footprints in the Sand. (Illus.). 32p. (J). (gr. k-2). 1994. pap. text ed. (*1-884876-19-6*); Mel's Store. (Illus.). 36p. (J). (gr. k-2). 1994. pap. text ed. (*1-884876-21-8*); 149.95 (*1-884876-00-5*) Chamike Pubs.

Lee, Eugene C. Managing Multicampus Systems: Effective Administration in an Unsteady State: A Report for the Carnegie Council on Policy Studies in Higher Education. LC 75-24012. (Carnegie Council Ser.). 192p. reprint ed. pap. 54.80 (*0-317-41800-9*, 2025661) Bks Demand.

— The Origins of the Chancellorship: The Buried Report of 1948. LC 94-24409. (Chapters in the History of the University of California Ser.). 77p. (Orig.). 1995. pap. 10.00 (*0-87772-360-5*) UCB IGS.

***Lee, Eui W. & Kim, Nack J., eds.** Light-Weight Alloys for Aerospace Applications No. 2: Proceedings of a Symposium Sponsored by the TMS Nonferrous Metals Committee, Held During the 1991 TMS Annual Meeting, New Orleans, Louisiana, February 17-21, 1991. LC 91-62555. 516p. Date not set. reprint ed. pap. 147.10 (*0-7837-9127-5*, 2049927) Bks Demand.

Lee, Eun S., jt. auth. see Forthofer, Ronald N.

Lee, Eun S., et al. Analyzing Complex Survey Data. (Quantitative Applications in the Social Sciences Ser.: Vol. 71). 80p. (C). 1989. pap. text ed. 9.95 (*0-8039-3014-3*) Sage.

Lee, Eva, jt. auth. see Teo, Kenneth.

Lee, Evelyn. Ten Principles on Raising Chinese-American Teens. (Illus.). 69p. (Orig.). 1988. student ed. pap. 10.65 (*0-9621298-0-1*); 7.50 (*0-9621298-1-X*) Chinatown Youth Ctr.

Lee, Everett S. & Goldsmith, Harold F., eds. Population Estimates: Methods for Small Area Analysis. LC 82-648. 248p. reprint ed. pap. 70.70 (*0-8357-8446-0*, 2034710) Bks Demand.

Lee, F. & Dyke, C. Surgical Attending Rounds. 450p. 1992. pap. 29.50 (*0-8121-1470-1*) Williams & Wilkins.

Lee, Fitzhugh. General Lee. (Illus.). 433p. 1989. reprint ed. 30.00 (*0-916107-91-4*) Broadfoot.

— General Lee: A Biography of Robert E. Lee. LC 94-11564. (Illus.). 478p. 1994. reprint ed. pap. 15.95 (*0-306-80589-8*) Da Capo.

Lee, Fitzhugh & Wheeler, Joseph. Cuba's Struggle Against Spain. 1976. lib. bdg. 75.95 (*0-8490-1692-4*) Gordon Pr.

Lee, Florence. Ten Lessons in Chinese Cooking. 1989. 14.95 (*0-930878-62-0*) Hollym Intl.

Lee, Florence C. Facts about Ginseng: The Elixir of Life. (Illus.). 104p. (C). 1993. 22.50 (*0-930878-83-3*) Hollym Intl.

Lee, Florence C. & Lee, Helen C. Kimchi: A Natural Health Food. (Illus.). 64p. 1988. 14.50 (*0-930878-59-0*) Hollym Intl.

***Lee Fook Hong.** Company Secretarial Practice Manual. 396p. 1993. boxed 115.00 (*0-409-99649-1*, SI) Butterworth Legal Pubs.

Lee, Francis G. Neither Conservative nor Liberal: The Burger Court on Civil Rights & Civil Liberties. LC 82-120. 144p. (Orig.). (C). 1983. pap. 9.50 (*0-89874-425-3*) Krieger.

— Wall of Controversy. LC 85-19697. 132p. 1986. pap. 9.50 (*0-89874-828-3*) Krieger.

***Lee, Francis G., ed.** All Imaginable Liberty: The Religious Liberty Clauses & the First Amendment. 191p. (C). 1990. pap. text ed. 24.50 (*0-8191-9886-2*) U Pr of Amer.

— All Imaginable Liberty - The Religious Liberty Clauses of the First Amendment. 191p. 1990. write for info. (*0-916191-08-7*) St Joseph.

Lee, Frank. My Bedtime Book of the Saints. rev. ed. (Illus.). 64p. (J). 1993. pap. 3.95 (*0-89243-585-2*) Liguori Pubns.

Lee, Frank A. Basic Food Chemistry. 2nd ed. (Illus.). (C). 1983. text ed. 58.95 (*0-87055-416-6*) AVI.

Lee, Frank E. Central Office Plant. 2nd ed. LC 73-85629. (ABC of the Telephone Ser.: Vol. 3). (Illus.). 68p. (C). 1985. pap. text ed. 13.95 (*1-56016-002-0*) ABC TeleTraining.

— Outside Plant. rev. ed. Leonard, E. J., ed. LC 73-85629. (ABC of the Telephone Ser.: Vol. 4). (Illus.). 132p. (C). 1987. pap. text ed. 16.95 (*1-56016-003-9*) ABC TeleTraining.

— Station Installation & Maintenance. rev. ed. LC 73-85629. (ABC of the Telephone Ser.: Vol. 2). (Illus.). 104p. (C). 1986. pap. text ed. 16.95 (*1-56016-001-2*) ABC TeleTraining.

— Telephone Theory, Principles & Practice. rev. ed. LC 73-85629. (ABC of the Telephone Ser.: Vol. 1). (Illus.). 148p. (C). 1988. pap. text ed. 16.95 (*1-56016-000-4*) ABC TeleTraining.

Lee, Frank F. Negro & White in a Connecticut Town: A Study in Race Relations. 1961. pap. 15.95x (*0-8084-0404-0*) NCUP.

Lee, Franklyn E. Maxwell Macmillan Preparing the 1040 Return. 1991. pap. 19.50 (*0-02-081143-8*) Macmillan.

Lee, Franklyn E. & Berkowitz, Lawrence B. Preparing the 1040 Return, 1992. 650p. 1992. 54.95 (*0-7811-0001-1*, Maxwell Macmillan) Macmillan.

— Preparing the 1040 Return, 1993. rev. ed. LC 78-71966. (Professional Tax Advisor's Guide Ser.). (Illus.). 650p. 1992. pap. text ed. 56.00 (*0-7811-0058-5*) Res Inst Am.

Lee, Fred. The Computer Book. LC 78-17450. 381p. reprint ed. pap. 108.60 (*0-317-27667-0*, 2025058) Bks Demand.

Lee, Fred & Lee, Alice. The Fifty Best Retirement Communities in America. (Illus.). 304p. (Orig.). 1994. pap. 14.95 (*0-312-10926-1*) St Martin.

Lee, Fred J. Casey Jones: The True Story of John Luther "Casey" Jones. 312p. 1994. 22.95 (*1-55793-038-4*) Guild Bindery Pr.

Lee, Frederic S. & Samuels, Warren J., eds. The Heterodox Economics of Gardiner C. Means: A Collection. LC 90-8836. (Studies in Institutional Economics Ser.). 432p. 1991. 67.95 (*0-87332-717-9*) M E Sharpe.

Lee, Frederic S., ed. see Means, Gardiner C.

Lee, Frederic S., jt. ed. see Samuels, Warren J.

Lee, Frederick S. & Earl, Peter, eds. The Economics of Competitive Enterprise: Selected Essays of P. W. S. Andrews. (Economists of the Twentieth Century Ser.). 464p. 1993. 74.95 (*1-85278-891-7*, Pub. by E Elgar Pub UK) Ashgate Pub Co.

Lee, G. A. Ebony Sun. (Illus.). 52p. (Orig.). 1989. pap. 5.00 (*0-685-27008-4*) Phoenix NJ.

Lee, G. Avery. Affirmations of a Skeptical Believer. (C). 1993. pap. 14.95 (*0-86554-395-X*) Mercer Univ Pr.

— Living in the Meantime. 188p. 1993. pap. 10.95 (*1-880837-39-0*) Smyth & Helwys.

Lee, G. Enell. Quick Emergency Care Reference. 60p. 1991. spiral bd. 8.95 (*0-8016-6584-1*) Mosby Yr Bk.

Lee, G. K., ed. Computer Applications in Design Simulation & Analysis. (Conference Proceedings Ser.). 250p. (C). 1992. write for info. (*1-880843-00-5*) Int Soc Comp App.

— Software & Hardware Applications of Microcomputers: Proceedings IASTED Symposium, Fort Collins, U. S. A., February 4-6, 1987. 127p. 1987. 58.00 (*0-88986-102-1*, 108) Acta Pr.

Lee, G. K., jt. ed. see Hamza, M. H.

Lee, G. L., et al. The Sampling & Analysis of Compressed Air to Be Used for Breathing Purposes. (C). 1985. 45.00 (*0-905927-17-6*, Pub. by H&H Sci Cnslts UK) St Mut.

Lee, G. Richard, et al. Wintrobe's Clinical Hematology. 9th ed. LC 90-6194. (Illus.). 2320p. 1992. 169.50 (*0-8121-1188-5*) Williams & Wilkins.

Lee, Gary. Wok. LC 79-19094. (Illus.). 192p. (Orig.). 1970. pap. 7.95 (*0-911954-06-6*) Bristol Pub Ent CA.

— Wok Appetizers & Light Snacks. (Illus.). 182p. (Orig.). 1982. pap. 6.95 (*0-911954-67-8*) Bristol Pub Ent CA.

Lee, Gary, jt. auth. see Coward, Raymond.

Lee, Gary C., jt. auth. see Wong, Alice K.

Lee, Gary R., jt. auth. see Reiss, Ira L.

Lee, Gary T. Family Structure & Interaction: A Comparative Analysis. 2nd ed. LC 82-4844. 349p. 1982. text ed. 19.95 (*0-8166-1091-6*) U of Minn Pr.

***Lee, Gentry.** Bright Messengers. LC 95-977. 1995. pap. 21.95 (*0-553-09006-2*) Bantam.

Lee, Gentry, jt. auth. see Clarke, Arthur C.

Lee, Gentry, jt. auth. see Clarke, Lee.

Lee, Gentry, jt. auth. see Sagan, Carl.

Lee, Geoff. Object Oriented GUI Application Development. LC 93-4104. 250p. 1993. pap. text ed. 36.00 (*0-13-363086-2*) P-H.

Lee, Geoffrey, ed. see Grace, Charles C.

Lee, George L. Inspiring African Americans: Black History Makers in the United States, 1750-1980. LC 90-53503. (Illus.). 144p. 1991. lib. bdg. 18.95x (*0-89950-576-7*) McFarland & Co.

— Interesting Athletes: A Newspaper Artist's Look at Blacks in Sports. LC 89-29306. (Illus.). 176p. 1990. pap. 18.95x (*0-89950-482-5*) McFarland & Co.

— Interesting Athletes: African-American Sports Heroes. 176p. 1993. mass mkt. 5.99 (*0-345-38220-X*, One World) Ballantine.

— Interesting People: Black American History Makers. LC 88-43542. 224p. 1992. mass mkt. 5.99 (*0-345-37677-3*, Ballantine Trade) Ballantine.

— Interesting People: Black American History Makers. LC 88-43542. (Illus.). 224p. 1989. lib. bdg. 20.95x (*0-89950-403-5*) McFarland & Co.

— Worldwide Interesting People: One Hundred Sixty-Two History Makers of African Descent. LC 91-50939. (Illus.). 144p. (J). 1992. lib. bdg. 21.95 (*0-89950-670-4*) McFarland & Co.

Lee, George W. River George. LC 73-18590. reprint ed. 36.00 (*0-404-11401-6*) AMS Pr.

Lee, Georgia. Rock Art & Cultural Resource Management. LC 91-33681. (Illus.). 72p. (Orig.). (C). 1991. pap. text ed. 6.95 (*0-937523-04-6*) Wormwood Pr.

— The Rock Art of Easter Island: Symbols of Power, Prayers to the Gods. LC 92-47034. (Monumenta Archaeologica Ser.: No. 17). (Illus.). 256p. (C). 1992. 35.00 (*0-917956-74-5*) UCLA Arch.

— An Uncommon Guide to Easter Island: Exploring Archaeological Mysteries of Rapa Nui. (Illus.). 128p. 1989. 18.95 (*0-937480-17-7*) Intl Resources.

Lee, Georgia, ed. see Drake, Alan.

Lee, Gerald. True Love & How to Get It. (Paperbacks Ser.). 204p. 1985. pap. 14.95 (*0-7022-1778-6*, Pub. by Univ Queensland Pr AT) Intl Spec Bk.

Lee, Gerald J. Dancing at Ground Zero. 48p. 1985. pap. 5.95 (*0-917658-21-3*) BPW & P.

Lee, Gerard. Troppo Man. 1990. pap. 14.95 (*0-7022-2299-2*, Pub. by Univ Queensland Pr AT) Intl Spec Bk.

Lee, Gerard & Campion, Jane. Sweetie: The Screenplay. 1991. pap. 12.95 (*0-7022-2371-9*, Pub. by Univ Queensland Pr AT) Intl Spec Bk.

Lee, Gim, jt. auth. see Lim Ching San.

Lee, Gim, jt. auth. see San, Lim-Ching.

Lee, Glenda. One Hundred One Bright Bulletin Board Ideas. 1991. pap. 7.25 (*0-89137-626-7*) Quality Pubns.

— One Hundred-Two Bright Bulletin Board Ideas. 1992. pap. 7.25 (*0-89137-627-5*) Quality Pubns.

Lee, Gloria. Why We Are Here. 183p. 1974. reprint ed. spiral bd. 9.35 (*0-7873-0547-2*) Mokelumne.

Lee, Gloria L., jt. ed. see Smith, Chris.

Lee, Gordon C. The Struggle for Federal Aid, First Phase: A History of the Attempts to Obtain Federal Aid for the Common Schools. LC 79-176979. (Columbia University. Teachers College. Contributions to Education Ser.: No. 957). reprint ed. 37.50 (*0-404-55957-3*) AMS Pr.

Lee, Grace L. The Huguenot Settlements in Ireland. 281p. 1993. reprint ed. pap. 25.00 (*0-685-69972-2*, 9208) Clearfield Co.

Lee, Grant S. Talkstory: Linking the Stories of Jesus with Our Individual & Collective Stories. Mau, Rennie, ed. 125p. (Orig.). 1989. student ed write for info. (*0-318-66302-3*); pap. write for info. (*0-318-66301-5*); audio write for info. (*0-318-66303-1*) Media Bridge.

Lee, Greg. Jim Abbott, Pitcher. LC 92-43251. (Reaching Your Goal Bks.). (J). 1993. 14.60 (*0-86593-258-1*); 10.95 (*0-685-66274-8*) Rourke Corp.

— Money. LC 92-44074. (J). 1993. 12.67 (*0-86593-268-9*); 9.50 (*0-685-66360-4*) Rourke Corp.

— School. LC 92-44073. (J). (gr. 3 up). 1993. 12.67 (*0-86593-269-7*); 9.50 (*0-685-66359-0*) Rourke Corp.

— Vacation. LC 92-45692. (Little Jokester Ser.). (J). 1993. 12.67 (*0-86593-270-0*); 9.50 (*0-685-66420-1*) Rourke Corp.

Lee, Greg, comp. Food: Wacky Words. LC 92-41730. (Little Jokester Ser.). (J). (gr. 3 up). 1993. 12.67 (*0-86593-265-4*); 9.50 (*0-685-66289-6*) Rourke Corp.

— Outer Space: Wacky Words. LC 92-43965. (Little Jokester Ser.). (J). (gr. 3 up). 1993. 12.67 (*0-86593-267-0*); 9.50 (*0-685-66292-6*) Rourke Corp.

— Pets: Wacky Words. LC 92-43964. (Little Jokester Ser.). (J). (gr. 3 up). 1993. 12.67 (*0-86593-266-2*); 9.50 (*0-685-66291-8*) Rourke Corp.

Lee, Greglon & Campbell, Sid. Dragon & Tiger: The Oakland Years. (Illus.). 300p. 1983. write for info. (*0-318-57559-0*) Gong Prods.

Lee, Greglon, ed. see Demura, Fumio.

Lee, Greglon, ed. see Lee, James Y.

Lee, Gregory. The Best of Orange County, California: A Guide to Scenic, Recreational & Historical Attractions. LC 93-24671. (Illus.). 304p. (Orig.). 1993. pap. 12.95 (*1-881409-05-8*) Jhnstn Assocs.

— California Traveler Missions of California: A Guide to the State's Spanish Heritage. (American Traveler Ser.). (Illus.). 48p. (Orig.). 1992. pap. 4.95 (*1-55838-122-8*) R H Pub.

— California Traveler Whale Watching & Tidal Pools: A Guide to California Marine Life. (American Traveler Ser.). (Illus.). 48p. (Orig.). 1992. pap. 4.95 (*1-55838-123-6*) R H Pub.

— Chris Burke: He Overcame Down Syndrome. LC 93-18213. (Reaching Your Goal Bks.). (J). 1993. 14.60 (*0-86593-263-8*); 10.95 (*0-685-66611-5*) Rourke Corp.

— Dai Wangshu: The Life & Poetry of a Chinese Modernist. (Illus.). 362p. 1989. 67.50 (*962-201-408-9*, Pub. by Chinese Univ HK) Coronet Bks.

— Physical Geography Study Guide. 144p. (C). 1993. per. 9.95 (*0-8403-8950-7*) Kendall-Hunt.

***Lee, Gregory B.** Troubadours, Trumpeters & Troubled Makers: Lyricism, Nationalism & Hybridity in China & Its Others. LC 95-5193. 1995. write for info. (*0-8223-1671-4*) Duke.

***Lee, Gregroy B.** Troubadours, Trumpeters & Troubled Makers: Lyricism, Nationalism & Hybridity in China & Its Others. LC 95-5193. (Asia-Pacific, Culture, Politics & Society Ser.). 1995. write for info. (*0-8223-1659-5*) Duke.

Lee, Gus. China Boy. LC 93-27236. 336p. 1994. pap. 10.95 (*0-452-27158-4*, Plume) NAL-Dutton.

— Honor & Duty. LC 92-42711. 1994. 24.00 (*0-679-41258-1*) Knopf.

— Honor & Duty. 1995. mass mkt. 6.99 (*0-8041-1004-2*) Ivy Books.

Lee, Guy, tr. see Catullus, Gaius V.

Lee, Guy, tr. see Propertius, Sextus.

Lee, Guy, tr. see Virgil.

Lee, Guy C. Historical Jurisprudence: An Introduction to the Systematic Study of the Development of Law. LC 90-55181. xv, 517p. 1990. reprint ed. lib. bdg. 66.00 (*0-912004-81-9*) W W Gaunt.

Lee, Gypsy Rose. The G-String Murders. 22.95 (*0-89190-147-7*, Am Repr) Amereon Ltd.

Lee, H. & Wade, G., eds. Acoustical Imaging, Vol. 18. (Illus.). 536p. 1991. 125.00 (*0-306-43900-X*, Plenum Pr) Plenum.

Lee, H. A. & Raman, G. Venkat. Handbook of Parenteral Nutrition: Hospital & Home Applications. 180p. 1990. pap. 25.50 (*0-412-28030-2*, A4435) Chapman & Hall.

Lee, H. C. An Introduction to Kaluza-Klein Theories: Proceedings of the Workshop on Kaluza-Klein Theories, Chalk River, Canada, Aug. 11-16, 1983. 380p. (C). 1984. 67.00 (*9971-966-19-0*); pap. 33.00 (*9971-966-20-4*) World Scientific Pub.

An Asterisk (*) at the beginning of an entry indicates that the title is appearing in BIP for the first time.

Lee, H. C. & Gaensslen, R. E., eds. Advanced Fingerprint Technology. (Series in Forensic & Police Science). (Illus.). 401p. 1991. 44.95 (*0-444-01579-5*, CRC Reprint) Franklin.

Lee, H. D., tr. see Plato.

***Lee, H. P.** Constitutional Conflicts in Contemporary Malaysia. 200p. 1995. 45.00 (*967-65-3095-6*) OUP.

Lee, H. P. & Winterton, George, eds. Australian Constitutional Perspectives. 347p. 1992. 82.00 (*0-455-21084-5*, Pub. by Law Bk Co); pap. 63.00 (*0-455-21085-3*, Pub. by Law Bk Co) W W Gaunt.

***Lee, Haeduck & Bobadilla, Jose-Luis.** The Americas: Health Statistics. LC 94-36261. (Technical Paper Ser.: No. 262). 64p. 1994. 6.95 (*0-8213-3037-3*, 13037) World Bank.

Lee, Hai-In, tr. see Stokes, Penelope J.

Lee, Hak C., jt. ed. see Chung, Kae H.

***Lee, Hannah F.** The Huguenots in France & America, 2 vols., Set. 638p. 1994. pap. 45.00 (*0-614-00926-X*, 3320) Clearfield Co.

Lee, Hannah S. Memoir of Pierre Toussaint: Born a Slave in St. Domingo. LC 91-68114. (Illus.). 93p. (Orig.). 1992. reprint ed. pap. 9.95 (*1-881008-02-9*) Am Soc Defense TFP.

Lee, Hans & Munsell, Paul. The Design & Implementation of Programs in FORTRAN 77. 448p. 1990. pap. text ed. 35.00 (*0-13-199993-1*) P-H.

Lee, Hansol H. Korean Grammar. (Illus.). 232p. 1989. 65.00 (*0-19-713606-0*) OUP.

Lee, Harold. Roswell Garst: A Biography. LC 83-26452. (Henry A. Wallace Series on Agricultrual History & Rural Studies). (Illus.). 351p. reprint ed. pap. 100.10 (*0-8357-6756-6*, 2035413) Bks Demand.

Lee, Harold, ed. see Garst, Roswell.

Lee, Harper. To Kill a Mockingbird. 288p. 1988. mass mkt. 4.99 (*0-446-31078-6*) Warner Bks.

— To Kill a Mockingbird. aniversary ed. 1995. 16.00 (*0-06-017322-X*, HarpT) HarpC.

— To Kill a Mockingbird. braille ed. 561p. 1993. vinyl bd. 44.88 (*1-56956-442-6*, BR9237) W A T Braille.

— To Kill a Mockingbird. large type ed. (General Ser.). 430p. 1992. pap. 16.95 (*0-8161-5241-1*) G K Hall.

— To Kill a Mockingbird. 300p. 1991. reprint ed. lib. bdg. 22.95 (*0-89966-858-5*) Buccaneer Bks.

— To Kill a Mockingbird - 1-Act. 1990. 3.95 (*0-87129-457-5*, T59) Dramatic Pub.

Lee, Harris W. Effective Church Leadership: A Practical Sourcebook. LC 89-6486. 224p. (Orig.). 1989. pap. 13.99 (*0-8066-2423-X*, 9-2423) Augsburg Fortress.

Lee, Harry O. & LaForester, Wilford A. Review & Reduction of Real Property Assessments in New York: 1992 Supplement. 3rd ed. Nagy, Jill, ed. LC 92-54177. 50p. 1992. pap. 35.00 (*0-942954-50-5*, 4A1223) NYS Bar.

***Lee, Harry O. & Nagy, Jill.** Review & Reduction of Real Property Assessments in New York-1994 Supplement. 68p. 1994. pap. text ed. 25.00 (*0-942954-70-X*) NYS Bar.

Lee, Harry O., et al. Review & Reduction of Real Property Assessments in New York. 3rd ed. Nagy, Jill, ed. LC 88-43298. 600p. 1988. 70.00 (*0-942954-22-X*, 4A1264) NYS Bar.

Lee, Hazel, jt. auth. see Lee, Earl.

Lee, Helen, jt. auth. see Clarke, Ian.

Lee, Helen C., jt. auth. see Lee, Florence C.

Lee, Helen E. The Serpent's Gift. 384p. 1994. text ed. 21.00 (*0-689-12193-8*, Pub. by Ctrl Bur voor Schimmel NE) Macmillan.

— The Serpent's Gift. 1995. pap. 12.00 (*0-684-80160-4*, Scribners) S&S Trade.

Lee, Henry. Anti-Scepticism: or Notes upon Each Chapter of Mr. Lock's Essay Concerning Human Understanding. (Anglistica & Americana Ser.: No. 115). xxx, 342p. 1973. reprint ed. 115.70 (*3-487-04753-5*, Pub. by Georg Olms GW) Lubrecht & Cramer.

— Cyanoacrylate Resins: The Instant Adhesives. 245p. (C). 1991. reprint ed. 52.00 (*0-938648-27-6*) T-C Pubns CA.

— Memoirs of the War in the Southern Department of the United States. Decker, Peter, ed. LC 75-76561. (Eyewitness Accounts of the American Revolution Ser., No. 1). 1969. reprint ed. 36.95 (*0-405-01161-X*) Ayer.

Lee, Henry, ed. Shaping National Responses to Climate Change: A Post-Rio Policy Guide. 352p. 1995. text ed. 48.00 (*1-55963-343-3*); pap. text ed. 24.95 (*1-55963-344-1*) Island Pr.

Lee, Henry & Neville, Kris. Handbook of Epoxy Resins. LC 65-26165. (Illus.). 922p. reprint ed. pap. 180.00 (*0-317-10839-5*, 2051838) Bks Demand.

Lee, Henry, jt. auth. see Forbes, H. A.

Lee, Henry C. DNA & Other Polymorphisms in Forensic Sciences. (Advances in Forensic Sciences Ser.: Vol. III). 320p. 1990. 105.00 (*0-8151-5348-1*, Yr Bk Med Pubs) Mosby Yr Bk.

Lee, Henry C., ed. Physics, Geometry, & Topology. (NATO ASI Series B, Physics: Vol. 232). (Illus.). 670p. 1990. 139.50 (*0-306-43693-0*, Plenum Pr) Plenum.

Lee, Henry C. & Gaesslen, R. E., eds. Advances in Fingerprint Technology. LC 93-46614. (CRC Series in Forensic & Police Science). 1994. write for info. (*0-8493-9513-5*) CRC Pr.

Lee, Henry C., et al, eds. Super Field Theories. LC 87-14159. (NATO ASI Series B, Physics: Vol. 160). (Illus.). 608p. 1987. 135.00 (*0-306-42660-9*, Plenum Pr) Plenum.

Lee, Hermione. The Novels of Virginia Woolf. LC 77-4981. 237p. 1977. 19.50 (*0-8419-0314-X*) Holmes & Meier.

— Willa Cather: Double Lives. LC 91-50018. (Illus.). 432p. 1991. pap. 15.00 (*0-679-73649-2*, Vin) Random.

Lee, Hermione, ed. The Secret Self: Short Stories by Women. 384p. 1993. pap. 6.95 (*0-460-87348-2*, Everyman's Classic Lib) C E Tuttle.

Lee, Hermione, ed. see Trollope, Anthony.

Lee, Hian K., ed. Fourth Symposium on Our Environment. (C). 1992. lib. bdg. 190.00 (*0-7923-1562-6*) Kluwer Ac.

Lee, Hilde G. Serve with Champagne. 288p. 1988. 21.95 (*0-89815-262-3*); pap. 17.95 (*0-89815-274-7*) Ten Speed Pr.

— Taste of the States: A Food History of America. 1992. 45.00 (*0-943231-56-6*) Howell Pr VA.

Lee, Hilde G. & Lee, Allan E. Virginia Wine Country Revisited. (Illus.). 256p. (Orig.). 1993. pap. 14.95 (*0-9639605-0-4*) Hildesigns Pr.

Lee, Hong H. Heterogeneous Reactor Design. (Illus.). 624p. 1984. 72.95 (*0-409-95073-4*) Buttrwrth-Heinemann.

Lee, Hong Y. The Politics of the Chinese Cultural Revolution: A Case Study. LC 76-19993. (Center for Chinese Studies, UC Berkeley: No. 17). 1978. pap. 16.00 (*0-520-04065-1*) U CA Pr.

Lee, Hong Y., ed. Korean Options in a Changing International Order. LC 93-28487. (Korea Research Monographs: No. 18). 1993. 17.00 (*1-55729-040-7*) IEAS.

Lee, Hongkoo, jt. ed. see Scalapino, Robert A.

Lee, Howard, jt. auth. see Comrey, Andrew.

Lee, Howard B. Bloodletting in Appalachia. 8th ed. (Illus.). 224p. 1988. reprint ed. pap. 8.00 (*0-87012-041-7*) McClain.

— The Burning Springs & Other Tales of the Little Kanawha. 3rd ed. 160p. 1991. reprint ed. pap. 8.00 (*0-87012-016-6*) McClain.

Lee, Howard B., jt. auth. see Comrey, Andrew L.

Lee, Hua & Wade, Glen, eds. Imaging Technology. (IEEE Selected Reprints Ser.). 544p. 1985. 49.95 (*0-87942-199-1*, PC01925) Inst Electrical.

Lee, Hua, jt. auth. see Schilling, Robert J.

Lee, Hugh, ed. A Cezanne in the Hedge & Other Memories of Charleston & Bloomsbury. LC 92-7268. (Illus.). 1992. 24.95 (*0-226-47003-2*) U Ch Pr.

— A Cezanne in the Hedge & Other Memories of Charleston & Bloomsbury. LC 92-7268. 192p. 1993. pap. 11.95 (*0-226-47004-0*) U Ch Pr.

Lee, Huy-Voun. At the Beach. LC 93-25462. (Illus.). 32p. (J). 1994. 14.95 (*0-8050-2768-8*) H Holt & Co.

***Lee, Huy Voun.** In the Snow. LC 94-48807. (J). 1995. 15.95 (*0-8050-3172-3*) H Holt & Co.

Lee Hwa Lin, ed. Favorite Chinese Dishes. 96p. (CHI & ENG.). 1992. pap. 15.95 (*0-941676-27-7*) Wei-Chuan Pub.

Lee, Hwa-Wei & Hunt, Gary A. Fundraising for the Nineteen Nineties: The Challenge Ahead. vi, 177p. (Orig.). 1992. pap. 39.95 (*0-943970-08-3*) Genaway.

Lee, Ian, jt. ed. see Barnett, Lynn.

***Lee, Ida J.** Lancaster County, Virginia, Marriage Bonds, 1652-1850. 71p. 1994. pap. 9.00 (*0-614-00905-7*, 3335) Clearfield Co.

Lee, Irving. Language Habits in Human Affairs: An Introduction to General Semantics. LC 78-31179. (Illus.). 278p. 1979. reprint ed. text ed. 76.50 (*0-313-20962-6*, LELH, Greenwood Pr) Greenwood.

Lee, Irving, ed. Language of Wisdom & Folly. 3rd ed. LC 67-30831. 361p. 1977. reprint ed. pap. text ed. 14.00 (*0-918970-00-8*) Intl Gen Semantics.

Lee, Irving J. How to Talk with People. LC 52-5459. 176p. pap. text ed. 9.00 (*0-918970-30-X*) Intl Gen Semantics.

— Language Habits in Human Affairs: An Introduction to General Semantics. 2nd ed. Berman, Sanford I., ed. LC 94-36138. 1994. 17.00 (*0-918970-41-5*) Intl Gen Semantics.

Lee, Iva H. Data Entry for Microcomputers & Terminals: With Business Applications. LC 86-5562. 203p. (C). 1986. pap. text ed. 28.95 (*0-471-82052-0*) P-H.

— Data Entry for Microcomputers & Terminals with Business Applications. 2nd ed. 336p. (C). 1991. pap. text ed. 12.00 (*0-13-201138-7*, 250101) P-H.

— DOS-VSE & VSE-Power Job Control Language & Concepts. 175p. 1989. pap. text ed. 45.00 (*0-13-218629-2*) P-H.

Lee, Ivy & Maykovich, Minako. Statistics: A Tool for Understanding Society. LC 94-4804. 1994. text ed. write for info. (*0-205-13961-2*) Allyn.

Lee, J., ed. Robots in Inspection. 170p. 1987. 28.00 (*0-87263-286-5*) SME.

Lee, J., jt. ed. see Jerome H. Holland Laboratory Staff.

Lee, J. A. A Lexical Study of the Septuagint Version of the Pentateuch. LC 82-5460. (Septuagint & Cognate Studies). 186p. (C). 1983. pap. 18.95 (*0-89130-576-9*, 06 04 14) Scholars Pr GA.

Lee, J. A. & Bryce-Smith, R., eds. Practical Regional Analgesia. (Monographs in Anesthesiology: Vol. 5). 1976. 85.25 (*0-444-16718-8*, Excerpta Medica) Elsevier.

Lee, J. A., et al, eds. Nitrogen As an Ecological Factor. (Illus.). 480p. 1983. text ed. 86.95 (*0-632-01074-6*) Blackwell Sci.

Lee, J. D., ed. Simulation Software for Robotics. (Robotics & Computer Integrated Manufacturing Ser.). 80p. 1989. 40.00 (*0-08-037196-5*, Pergamon Pr) Elsevier.

Lee, J. D. & Lindahl, Barry A. Modern Tort Law, 4 vols. rev. ed. LC 88-2910. 1988. ring bd. 500.00 (*0-685-34582-3*) Clark Boardman Callaghan.

Lee, J. H. & Cheung, Y. K., eds. Environmental Hydraulics: Proceedings of the International Symposium on, Hong Kong, 16-18 December 1991, 2 vols., Set. (Illus.). 1500p. (C). 1991. text ed. 190.00 (*90-5410-038-9*, Pub. by A A Balkema NE) Ashgate Pub Co.

Lee, J. J. Ireland, Nineteen Twelve to Nineteen Eighty-Five: Politics & Society. (Illus.). (C). 1990. pap. 37.95 (*0-521-37741-2*) Cambridge U Pr.

***Lee, J. P. & Grinstein, G. G., eds.** Database Issues for Data Visualization: Proceedings of the IEEE Visualization '93 Workshop, San Jose, California, USA, October 26, 1993. (Lecture Notes in Computer Science: Vol. 871). xiv, 229p. 1994. 37.00 (*3-540-58519-2*) Spr-Verlag.

Lee, J. S. Abstraction & Aging: A Social Psychological Analysis. (Recent Research in Psychology Ser.). (Illus.). 136p. 1990. pap. 48.00 (*0-387-97433-4*) Spr-Verlag.

— Introduction to Geomechanics. 2nd ed. 234p. 1984. text ed. 154.00 (*0-677-31070-6*) Gordon & Breach.

Lee, J. S. & Newman, M. E. Aquaculture: An Introduction. (Illus.). 464p. 1992. 39.95 (*0-8134-2911-0*); teacher ed 6.95 (*0-8134-2912-9*); pap. 29.95 (*0-685-38488-8*) Interstate.

Lee, J. S. & Skalak, T. C., eds. Microvascular Mechanics. (Illus.). xv, 222p. 1989. 89.00 (*0-387-97038-X*) Spr-Verlag.

Lee, J. S., jt. ed. see Sancaktar, E.

Lee, J. S., et al, eds. Mechanics of Electromagnetic Materials & Structures. LC 93-71575. (AMD Series, Vol. 161; MD: Vol. 42). 209p. 1993. pap. 50.00 (*0-7918-1140-9*, G00784) ASME.

Lee, J. W., jt. ed. see Pollak, J. K.

Lee, J. Yimm. Wing Chun Kung-Fu. LC 72-87863. (Chinese Arts Ser.). (Illus.). 1972. pap. 12.95 (*0-89750-037-7*, 309, Wehman) Ohara Pubns.

***Lee, Jackson F., Jr. & Pruitt, K. Wayne.** Providing for Individual Differences in Student Learning: A Mastery Learning Approach. (Illus.). 130p. 1984. pap. 16.95 (*0-398-06225-0*) C C Thomas.

— Providing for Individual Differences in Student Learning: A Mastery Learning Approach. (Illus.). 130p. (C). 1984. 31.95x (*0-398-05028-7*) C C Thomas.

Lee, Jackson F., jt. auth. see Rinehart, James R.

Lee, Jae H. The Exploration of the Inner Wounds - Han. LC 94-2375. (AAR Academy Ser.: Vol. 86). 198p. 1994. 29.95 (*1-55540-961-X*, 010186); pap. 19.95 (*1-55540-962-8*, 010186) Scholars Pr GA.

Lee, Jae K., jt. auth. see Liang, Ting-Peng.

Lee, Jae K., jt. auth. see Trippi, Robert R.

Lee, Jae Num. Swift & Scatological Satire. LC 76-129807. 158p. 1976. text ed. 29.95 (*0-8263-0196-7*) Irvington.

Lee, James. Career. LC 57-13380. 175p. 1957. 16.95 (*0-910278-34-2*) Boulevard.

— Electronics for the Radio Amateur. Stone, Jack L., ed. (Illus.). 1989. write for info. (*0-318-65728-7*) Franklin-Belle.

Lee, James, ed. see Anderson, Elaine.

Lee, James A. The Environment, Public Health, & Human Ecology: Considerations for Economic Development. LC 85-6574. 300p. 1986. pap. text ed. 16.95 (*0-8018-2911-9*) Johns Hopkins.

— The Gold & the Garbage in Management Theories & Prescriptions. LC 80-12758. (Illus.). x, 480p. 1980. 34.95 (*0-8214-0436-9*); pap. 19.95 (*0-8214-0578-0*) Ohio U Pr.

Lee, James A. & Martin, Philip L. Contemporary Labor Relations. 196p. (C). 1990. pap. text ed. 19.95 (*0-929655-95-8*) CT Pub.

Lee, James F., et al. Ideas: Estrategias, Lecturas, Actividades & Composiciones. 1994. write for info. (*0-318-72333-6*) McGraw.

***Lee, James F. & Vanpatten, Bill.** Directions for Language Learning & Teaching, Vol. 1. (Foreign Language Professional Ser.). 1995. write for info. (*0-07-037693-X*) McGraw.

Lee, James L. & Pulvino, Charles J. Self-Exploration Inventories: Sixteen Reproducible Self-Scoring Instruments. 2nd ed. 32p. 1993. pap. text ed. 12.95 (*0-932796-58-5*) Ed Media Corp.

***Lee, James L., et al.** Dynamic Counseling. 3rd ed. LC 94-72559. 288p. (C). 1994. pap. text ed. 21.95x (*0-932796-66-4*) Ed Media Corp.

— Structured Activities for Dynamic Counseling. LC 94-72560. 248p. (Orig.). (C). 1994. pap. text ed. 21.95x (*0-932796-67-2*) Ed Media Corp.

Lee, James M. The Content of Religious Instruction: A Social Science Approach. LC 84-18255. 815p. (Orig.). 1985. pap. 15.95 (*0-89135-050-0*) Religious Educ.

— The Flow of Religious Instruction: A Social-Science Approach. LC 74-29824. (Illus.). 379p. (Orig.). 1975. reprint ed. lib. bdg. 15.95 (*0-89135-001-2*); reprint ed. pap. 15.95 (*0-89135-003-9*) Religious Educ.

— The Shape of Religious Instruction: A Social-Science Approach. LC 74-29823. 330p. (Orig.). 1971. reprint ed. lib. bdg. 15.95 (*0-89135-000-4*); reprint ed. pap. 15.95 (*0-89135-002-0*) Religious Educ.

Lee, James M., ed. Handbook of Faith. LC 90-31685. 328p. 1990. 25.95 (*0-89135-075-6*) Religious Educ.

— The Spirituality of the Religious Educator. LC 85-2250. 209p. (Orig.). 1985. pap. 14.95 (*0-89135-045-4*) Religious Educ.

Lee, James R. Contact Lens Handbook. (Illus.). 161p. 1986. text ed. 30.50 (*0-7216-1585-6*) Saunders.

Lee, James R., ed. The Theory & Practice of International Relations. 9th ed. LC 92-45698. 1993. pap. text ed. 22.50 (*0-13-669029-7*) P-H Gen Ref & Trav.

Lee, James W. Classics of Texas Fiction. 200p. (Orig.). (C). 1987. 15.95 (*0-935014-09-8*); pap. 9.95 (*0-935014-10-1*) E-Heart Pr.

— John Braine. LC 67-25191. (Twayne's English Authors Ser.). (C). 1968. lib. bdg. 17.95 (*0-8057-1056-6*) Irvington.

— Texas My Texas. LC 92-38219. 112p. 1993. pap. 9.95 (*0-929398-54-8*) UNTX Pr.

Lee, James W., ed. Nineteen Forty-One: Texas Goes to War. LC 91-36090. (Illus.). 244p. (J). 1991. pap. 19.95 (*0-929398-29-7*) UNTX Pr.

Lee, James W., ed. see Clayton, Lawrence.

Lee, James W., jt. ed. see McGuire, Kathryn S.

Lee, James Y. Modern Kung-Fu Karate: Iron Poison Hand Training. 2nd ed. Lee, Greglon, ed. (Illus.). 116p. 1990. reprint ed. pap. 11.95 (*0-317-02839-1*) Gong Prods.

***Lee, Jane.** Derain, to Accompany the Exhibition Derain: The Late Work. 144p. 1993. pap. 100.00 (*0-7148-2649-9*, Pub. by Museum Modern Art UK) St Mut.

Lee, Janet, ed. With Special Distinction: A Collection of Recipes from the Mississippi College Family. LC 93-77090. (Illus.). 384p. 1993. 19.95 (*0-685-65593-8*) MS Coll Ckbk.

Lee, Janet, jt. auth. see Malecki, Joseph.

Lee, Jasper S. Agricultural Education: Review & Synthesis of the Research. 4th ed. 38p. 1985. text ed. 4.75 (*0-318-20330-8*, IN298) Ctr Educ Trng Employ.

— Commercial Catfish Farming. 3rd ed. (Illus.). 338p. 1991. text ed. 31.95 (*0-8134-2905-6*); text ed. 23.95 (*0-685-47576-X*) Interstate.

— Working in Agricultural Industry. (Illus.). (J). (gr. 9-10). 1978. text ed. 17.96 (*0-07-000831-0*) McGraw.

Lee, Jasper S., ed. see Brown, Ronald & Oren, John W.

Lee, Jasper S., jt. auth. see Lee, Delene W.

Lee, Jasper S., ed. see Long, Don L., et al.

Lee, Jasper S., jt. auth. see McGuire, James E.

Lee, Jasper S., ed. see Miller, Larry.

Lee, Jean B. The Price of Nationhood: The American Revolution in Charles County. LC 93-42536. 1994. write for info. (*0-393-36958-7*) Norton.

— The Price of Nationhood: The American Revolution in Charles County. 1994. 29.95 (*0-393-03658-8*) Norton.

Lee, Jeanette. The Ibsen Secret. LC 75-30877. (Studies in Scandinavian Life & Literature: No. 18). 1975. lib. bdg. 75.00 (*0-8383-2092-9*) M S G Haskell Hse.

Lee, Jeanne. Silent Lotus. (Illus.). 32p. (J). (gr. k-3). 1991. 14.95 (*0-374-36911-9*) FS&G.

Lee, Jeanne M. Legend of the Milky Way. LC 81-6906. (Illus.). 32p. (J). (ps-2). 1990. pap. 5.95 (*0-8050-1361-X*, Owlet BYR) H Holt & Co.

— Silent Lotus. (J). (ps-3). 1994. pap. 4.95 (*0-374-46646-7*, Sunburst Bks) FS&G.

Lee, Jeanne M., illus. & ret. Toad Is the Uncle of Heaven: A Vietnamese Folk Tale. LC 85-5639. 32p. (J). (ps-2). 1989. pap. 5.95 (*0-8050-1147-1*, Owlet BYR) H Holt & Co.

Lee, Jenni. Come Feel the Sea. (Illus.). 1991. pap. text ed. write for info. (*0-318-68544-2*) Jennilee-Angel.

Lee, Jennifer. Talking Germany. (C). 1990. pap. text ed. 32.00 (*0-948032-78-2*, Pub. by Rosters Ltd) St Mut.

— Tarnished Angel. 1993. mass mkt. 5.50 (*0-06-100559-2*, Harp PBks) HarpC.

Lee, Jennifer M., ed. Aids to Physiotherapy. 2nd ed. (Illus.). 216p. 1989. pap. text ed. 15.00 (*0-443-03438-9*) Churchill.

Lee, Jenny. Meanjin: New Critical Essays, Fiction & Poetry. 846p. (C). 1990. 50.00 (*0-685-52916-9*, Pub. by Pascoe Pub AT) St Mut.

Lee, Jesse. Live...From Golgotha. 20p. (Orig.). 1987. pap. 3.00 (*0-88680-272-5*) I E Clark.

Lee, Jesse & Thrift, Minton. Memoir of the Reverend Jesse Lee, with Extracts from His Journals. LC 72-83428. (Religion in America, Ser. 1). 1977. reprint ed. 21.95 (*0-405-00253-X*) Ayer.

Lee, Jik-Joen. Development, Delivery, & Utilization of Services under the Older Americans Act: A Perspective of Asian-American Elderly. LC 91-40937. (Studies on Elderly in America). 199p. 1992. 57.00 (*0-8153-0527-3*) Garland.

***Lee, Jim, ed. & pref.** Fast Forward: A Focus on the Rapidly Changing Media from Your Hometown Paper to Hands-on TV. (Southern Exposure Ser.). (Illus.). 64p. (Orig.). (C). 1992. 5.00 (*0-943810-55-8*) Inst Southern Studies.

***Lee, Jim & Choi, Brandon.** Gen 13 TPB. 2nd ed. Kaplan, Bill, ed. (Illus.). 144p. Date not set. pap. 12.95 (*1-887279-05-9*) Image Comics.

Lee, Jim, jt. auth. see Potts, Carl.

Lee, Jim, et al. Explorations in Macroeconomics. 4th ed. 1992. pap. 31.50 (*1-56226-112-6*) CT Pub.

— Explorations in Microeconomics. 3rd ed. 276p. (C). 1991. pap. text ed. 30.40 (*1-56226-047-2*) CT Pub.

Lee, Jimmy. Behind Our Sunday Smiles: Helping Those with Life-Controlling Problems. 176p. (Orig.). 1991. pap. 9.99 (*0-8010-5667-5*) Baker Bk.

***Lee, Jimmy R.** Committed Couples: God's Plan for Marriage & the Family. 168p. (Orig.). 1995. pap. 9.99 (*0-8010-5693-4*) Baker Bk.

— Living Free! A Christ-Centered Twelve-Step Program. 128p. 1993. pap. 9.99 (*0-8010-5680-2*) Baker Bk.

Lee, Jin-Woo. Politische Philosophie des Nihilismus: Neitzsches Neubestimmung des Verhaeltnisses von Politik & Metaphysik. (Monographien und Texte zur Nietzscge-Forschung Ser.: Bd. 26). xi, 441p. (GER.). (C). 1992. lib. bdg. 166.15 (*3-11-012908-6*) De Gruyter.

Lee, Jo A. Proofreading for Word Processing. 2nd ed. LC 93-43962. 248p. (C). 1994. pap. text ed. 20.50 (*0-03-098011-9*) Dryden Pr.

— Proofreading for Word Processing. 2nd ed. LC 93-43962. 68p. (C). 1994. teacher ed, pap. text ed. 28.50 (*0-03-098012-7*) Dryden Pr.

— Proofreading for Wordprocessing. 184p. (C). 1988. pap. text ed. 17.75 (*0-15-572260-3*); teacher ed, pap. text ed. 2.00 (*0-15-572261-1*) Dryden Pr.

Lee, Jo Ann. Online Searching: The Basics, Settings, & Management. 2nd ed. Tenopir, Carol, ed. (Database Searching Ser.). 230p. 1989. lib. bdg. 33.00 (*0-87287-738-8*) Libs Unl.

***Lee, Jo Ann & Satterwhite, Marilyn L.** The Irwin Law Office Reference Manual. LC 95-12105. 1995. write for info. (*0-256-18747-9*) Irwin.

— Irwin Office Reference Manual. 440p. (C). 1993. 17.50 (*0-256-15639-5*) Irwin.

Lee, Jo Anne. First Hunger. LC 73-76638. (Hip-Pocket Ser.: No. 2). 1973. pap. 2.50 (*0-87922-017-1*) Christophers Bks.

Lee, Joann F. Asian American Experiences in the United States: Oral Histories of First to Fourth Generation Americans from China, the Philippines, Japan, India, the Pacific Islands, Vietnam & Cambodia. LC 90-53504. (Illus.). 240p. 1991. lib. bdg. 27.50x (*0-89950-585-6*) McFarland & Co.

— Asian Americans: Oral Histories of First to Fourth Generation Americans from China, Korea, the Philippines, Japan, India, the Pacific Islands, Vietnam, & Cambodia. LC 92-53730. (Illus.). 256p. 1992. pap. 11.95 (*1-56584-023-2*) New Press NY.

Lee, Joanna. I Want to Keep My Baby! 176p. (Orig.). (YA). (gr. 9-12). 1977. pap. 3.50 (*0-451-15733-8*, Sig) NAL-Dutton.

Lee, Joanna & Cook, T. S. Mary Jane Harper Cried Last Night. (Illus.). (Orig.). 1978. pap. 2.95 (*0-451-13980-1*, E9692, Sig) NAL-Dutton.

Lee, Jocely, ed. see Zagat, Eugene H., Jr. & Zagat, Nina S.

Lee, Joe. Bankruptcy Practice Systems PSL. LC 79-92367. 1993. ring bd. 112.00 (*0-685-59823-3*) Clark Boardman Callaghan.

Lee, Joe W., tr. see Urabe, Kuniyoshi.

Lee, Joel M. & Hamilton, Beth A., eds. As Much to Learn As to Teach: Essays in Honor of Lester Asheim. LC 78-11313. 239p. 1979. 59.50 (*0-208-01751-8*) Elliots Bks.

Lee, John. The Flying Boy: Healing the Wounded Man. (Orig.). 1989. pap. 7.95 (*1-55874-006-6*) Health Comm.

— The Flying Boy, Bk. Two: The Journey Continues. Orig. Title: I Don't Want to be Alone. 140p. (Orig.). 1991. pap. text ed. 8.95 (*1-55874-180-1*) Health Comm.

— Generic Volunteer Orientation Manual: Your Guide to Developing an Orientation Manual for Volunteers. 74p. 1995. 25.00 (*1-887555-00-5*) Essential Pr.

— Standard Catalog of Chrysler 1924-1990. LC 90-60577. (Illus.). 480p. (Orig.). 1990. pap. 19.95 (*0-87341-142-0*, AY01) Krause Pubns.

— The Unicorn Dilemma. (Unicorn Ser.: No. 2). 384p. 1992. mass mkt. 4.99 (*0-8125-2092-0*) Tor Bks.

— Unicorn Peace. 352p. 1993. mass mkt. 4.99 (*0-8125-1981-7*) Tor Bks.

— Unicorn Quest. (Unicorn Ser.: No. 1). 1992. mass mkt. 3.99 (*0-8125-2055-6*) Tor Bks.

— Unicorn Solution. 1991. pap. 3.95 (*0-8125-0346-5*) Tor Bks.

— Unicorn War. 352p. 1995. 22.95 (*0-312-85913-9*) Tor Bks.

— Well Testing. 150p. 1982. 40.00 (*0-89520-317-0*) Soc Petrol Engineers.

Lee, John & Button, Graham. Talk & Social Organization. 290p. 1987. 99.00 (*0-905028-75-9*, Pub. by Multilingual Matters UK); pap. 39.95 (*0-905028-74-0*, Pub. by Multilingual Matters UK) Taylor & Francis.

Lee, John & Miller-Kritsberg, Ceci. Writing from the Body. 160p. 1994. pap. 9.95 (*0-312-11536-9*) St Martin.

Lee, John & Stott, Bill. Facing the Fire: Experiencing and Expressing Anger Appropriately. LC 92-46216. 1993. pap. 10.95 (*0-553-37240-8*) Bantam.

Lee, John, jt. auth. see Armitage, Katie.

Lee, John, jt. auth. see Friedlander, Edward J.

Lee, John, jt. auth. see Payne-Jackson, Arvilla.

Lee, John, ed. see Robertson, George & Charteris, Henry.

*__Lee, John A.__ Computer Pioneers (2-95) 800p. 1995. text ed. 54.00 (*0-8186-6357-X*, BP06357) IEEE Comp Soc.

— Gay Midlife & Maturity. LC 90-5285. (Journal of Homosexuality). 246p. 1990. text ed. 32.95 (*1-56024-028-8*); pap. text ed. 14.95 (*0-918393-80-9*) Haworth Pr.

Lee, John A. & Allen, David G., eds. Modulation of Cardiac Calcium Sensitivity: A New Approach to Increasing the Strength of the Heart. LC 92-43149. (Illus.). 368p. (C). 1993. 65.00 (*0-19-262347-8*) OUP.

Lee, John B. & Merisotis, Jamie P., eds. Proprietary Schools: Programs, Policies, & Prospects. LC 91-60263. (ASHE-ERIC Higher Education Report Ser.: No. 5). 90p. 1990. pap. 17.00 (*1-878380-02-8*) GWU Schl E&HD.

Lee, John C., jt. auth. see Snider, Ray S.

Lee, John D. Concise Inorganic Chemistry. 4th enl. rev. ed. (Illus.). 950p. 1991. pap. 39.95 (*0-412-40290-4*, A5898) Chapman & Hall.

— Journals of John D. Lee, 1846-47 & 1859. Kelly, Charles, ed. LC 84-234912. 292p. reprint ed. pap. 83.30 (*0-8357-3270-3*, 2039491) Bks Demand.

— A Mormon Chronicle: The Diaries of John D. Lee, 1848-1876, Vol. 2. LC 55-11914. 486p. 1983. reprint ed. pap. 138.60 (*0-7837-8568-2*, 2049383) Bks Demand.

— Wordstar & CP-M Made Easy. LC 83-5939. (Illus.). 235p. reprint ed. pap. 67.00 (*0-8357-4600-3*, 2037533) Bks Demand.

*__Lee, John D. & Brooks, Juanita.__ A Mormon Chronicle: The Diaries of John D. Lee, 1848-1876, Vol. 1. Brooks, Juanita, ed. 376p. 1983. pap. 107.20 (*0-7837-8567-4*, 2049383) Bks Demand.

Lee, John E., tr. see Keller, Ferdinand.

Lee, John F. Last Lap. (Illus.). 132p. (Orig.). 1990. pap. 11.95 (*1-877603-08-2*) Pecan Grove.

Lee, John H., Jr. Management: A Study of Industrial Organization. Chandler, Alfred D., ed. LC 79-7550. (History of Management Thought & Practice Ser.). 1980. reprint ed. lib. bdg. 15.95 (*0-405-12334-5*) Ayer.

Lee, John H. The Origin & Progress of the American Party in Politics: Embracing a Complete History of the Philadelphia Riots in May & July of 1844. LC 79-117881. (Select Bibliographies Reprint Ser.). 1977. reprint ed. 26.95 (*0-8369-5334-7*) Ayer.

Lee, John H., Jr. & Chandler, Alfred D., eds. Pitman's Dictionary of Industrial Administration: A Comprehensive Encyclopedia of the Organization, Administration, & Management of Modern Industry, 2 vols., 1. LC 79-7552. (History of Management Thought & Practice Ser.). 1980. reprint ed. lib. bdg. 79.95 (*0-405-12337-X*) Ayer.

— Pitman's Dictionary of Industrial Administration: A Comprehensive Encyclopedia of the Organization, Administration, & Management of Modern Industry, 2 vols., 2. LC 79-7552. (History of Management Thought & Practice Ser.). 1980. reprint ed. lib. bdg. 79.95 (*0-405-12338-8*) Ayer.

— Pitman's Dictionary of Industrial Administration: A Comprehensive Encyclopedia of the Organization, Administration, & Management of Modern Industry, 2 vols., Set. LC 79-7552. (History of Management Thought & Practice Ser.). 1980. reprint ed. lib. bdg. 158.95 (*0-405-12336-1*) Ayer.

Lee, John J. & Anderson, O. Roger, eds. Biology of Foraminifera. (Illus.). 368p. 1991. text ed. 132.00 (*0-12-440670-X*) Acad Pr.

Lee, John J. & Fredrick, Jerome F., eds. Endocytobiology III. (Annals Ser.: Vol. 503). (Illus.). 590p. 1987. 149.00 (*0-89766-402-7*) NY Acad Sci.

Lee, John J., et al, eds. Illustrated Guide to the Protozoa. (Illus.). 629p. 1985. 80.00 (*0-914023-25-X*) Allen Pr.

Lee, John M. Counter-Clockwise. LC 73-18591. reprint ed. 29.50 (*0-404-11402-4*) AMS Pr.

— Custom Auto Upholstery. (Illus.). 160p. 1988. pap. 16.95 (*0-87938-323-2*) Motorbooks Intl.

— How to Restore Auto Upholstery. (Illus.). 160p. 1994. pap. 17.95 (*0-87938-948-6*) Motorbooks Intl.

Lee, John M., et al. To Unite Our Strength: Enhancing United Nations Peace & Security. LC 92-26899. 180p. (Orig.). (C). 1992. lib. bdg. 46.50 (*0-8191-8865-4*); pap. text ed. 18.50 (*0-8191-8866-2*) U Pr of Amer.

*__Lee, John N., ed.__ Design Issues in Optical Processing. (Cambridge Studies in Modern Optics: 16). (Illus.). 265p. (C). 1995. 59.95 (*0-521-43048-8*) Cambridge U Pr.

Lee, John N., jt. ed. see Berg, Norman J.

Lee, John P. Childhood Stories & Letters from Mama. 116p. 1991. pap. 10.00 (*0-9638295-0-5*) Xanthus Pr.

— A Mixed Marriage. 61p. 1993. pap. 8.00 (*0-9638295-2-1*) Xanthus Pr.

— On the Square. 88p. 1994. pap. 8.00 (*0-9638295-4-8*) Xanthus Pr.

*__Lee, John P. & Grinstein, Georges G., eds.__ Database Issues for Data Visualization: Proceedings of the IEEE Visualization '93 Workshop, San Jose, California, USA, October 26, 1993. LC 94-34257. (Lecture Notes in Computer Science: Vol. 871). 1994. write for info. (*0-387-58519-2*) Spr-Verlag.

*__Lee, John R. & Hopkins, Virginia.__ Hormone Balance & Progesteronene: What Your Doctor May Not Tell You about Your Menopause Needs. (Orig.). 1996. pap. write for info. (*0-446-67144-4*) Warner Bks.

Lee, John W., jt. auth. see Guenther, Ronald B.

Lee, John Y. Managerial Accounting Changes for the 1990s. 96p. (Orig.). 1987. pap. text ed. 9.95 (*0-9617977-0-3*) McKay Busn Systs.

Lee, Johnny K. Pa Kua Chang - The Dragon Way. 136p. 1992. pap. 29.95 (*0-9635087-0-9*) On-Line Pub.

— Wu Style Tai Chi Chuan: The Thirteen Golden Postures. (Illus.). 42p. (Orig.). 1992. pap. 15.00 (*0-9635087-1-7*) On-Line Pub.

Lee, Jonathan A. & Mykkanen, Donald L. Metal & Polymer Matrix Composites. LC 86-31202. (Illus.). 205p. 1987. 36.00 (*0-8155-1111-6*) Noyes.

Lee, Jonathan S. Jacques Lacan. (Twayne's World Authors Ser.: No. 817). 272p. (C). 1990. text ed. 26.95 (*0-8057-8256-7*, Pub. by Royal Botanic Garden UK) Macmillan.

— Jacques Lacan. LC 90-21076. 264p. 1991. pap. 16.95x (*0-87023-737-3*) U of Mass Pr.

Lee, Jonathan S., jt. ed. see Hord, Fred L., pseud.

Lee, Joseph. The Modernization of Irish Society. 2nd ed. 181p. (C). 1989. reprint ed. pap. 15.95 (*0-7171-0567-9*, Pub. by Gill & MacMill IE) Irish Bks Media.

Lee, Joseph J., ed. Europe in Transition: Political, Economic, & Security Prospects for the 1990s. (Tom Slick World Peace Ser.). 339p. 1991. 15.00 (*0-89940-425-1*) LBJ Sch Pub Aff.

Lee, Joseph K., et al, eds. Computed Body Tomography: With MRI Correlation. 2nd ed. (Illus.). 1184p. 1989. 194.50 (*0-88167-331-5*) Raven.

Lee, Joy E. Further Collective Thoughts. 32p. 1986. pap. 22.00 (*0-7223-2027-2*, Pub. by A H S Ltd UK) St Mut.

Lee, Juanita E., jt. auth. see Shortridge, Lillie M.

Lee, Judith A. Group Work with the Poor & Oppressed. LC 88-32009. (Social Work with Groups Ser.: Vol. 11, No. 4). (Illus.). 138p. 1989. text ed. 29.95 (*0-86656-884-0*) Haworth Pr.

Lee, Judith A. B. The Empowerment Approach to Social Work Practice. LC 94-16601. 352p. 1994. 35.00 (*0-231-08026-3*) Col U Pr.

— The Empowerment Approach to Social Work Practice. 95p. 1994. write for info. (*0-231-09997-5*) Col U Pr.

*__Lee, Judith L.__ Look at Me. LC 94-61955. (Illus.). 64p. (Orig.). 1995. pap. 6.95 (*1-878893-50-5*) Telcraft Bks.

Lee, Judith Y. Garrison Keillor: A Voice of America. LC 90-24702. 1991. 35.00 (*0-87805-457-X*); pap. 15.95 (*0-87805-473-1*) U Pr of Miss.

Lee, Judith Y., jt. ed. see Slade, Joseph W.

*__Lee, Julian C.__ The Amphibians & Reptiles of the Yucatan Peninsula. (Comstock Book Ser.). (Illus.). 512p. 1996. 175.00 (*0-8014-2450-X*) Cornell U Pr.

Lee, Jung Y. Death & Beyond in the Eastern Perspective. LC 73-85065. 112p. 1974. text ed. 62.00 (*0-677-05010-0*) Gordon & Breach.

— Embracing Change: Postmodern Interpretations on the I Ching from a Christain Perspective. LC 92-85296. 1994. write for info. (*0-940866-23-4*) U Scranton Pr.

— The I Ching & Modern Man. LC 74-28541. 1975. 8.95 (*0-8216-0253-5*, Univ Bks) Carol Pub Group.

— Korean Shamanistic Rituals. (Religion & Society Ser.: No. 12). 250p. 1980. 57.50 (*90-279-3378-2*) Mouton.

— Marginality: The Key to Multicultural Theology. LC 94-31475. 1995. pap. 16.00 (*0-8006-2810-1*, Fortress Pr) Augsburg Fortress.

— Patterns of Inner Process. 226p. 1977. pap. 5.95 (*0-8065-0528-1*, Citadel Pr) Carol Pub Group.

— The Theology of Change: A Christian Concept of God in an Eastern Perspective. LC 78-16745. 160p. reprint ed. pap. 45.60 (*0-8357-7054-0*, 2033547) Bks Demand.

Lee, Jung Y., ed. Ancestor Worship & Christianity in Korea. LC 88-39988. (Studies in Asian Thought & Religion). 112p. 1989. lib. bdg. 59.95 (*0-88946-059-0*) E Mellen.

Lee, K., jt. ed. see Vidyadhar, I.

Lee, K. C. Diplomacy of a Tiny State. 2nd ed. 364p. 1993. pap. text ed. 29.00 (*981-02-1219-4*) World Scientific Pub.

Lee, K. C., et al, eds. Optical Properties of Solids. 350p. (C). 1991. text ed. 104.00 (*981-02-0596-1*) World Scientific Pub.

Lee, K. H., jt. ed. see Chun, Daphne.

Lee, K. H., jt. auth. see Teoh, S. H.

Lee, K. J. Essential Otolaryngology: Head & Neck Surgery. 1000p. 1991. 69.50 (*0-8385-2267-X*, A2267-1) Appleton & Lange.

— Essential Otolaryngology: Head & Neck Surgery. 6th ed. LC 94-34211. 1994. pap. text ed. 70.00 (*0-8385-2214-9*, A2214-3) Appleton & Lange.

Lee, K. J. & Stewart, Carol. Ambulatory Surgery & Office Procedures in Head & Neck Surgery. 352p. 1986. text ed. 125.00 (*0-8089-1803-6*, 792599, Grune) Saunders.

Lee, K. K., ed. Lectures on Dynamical Systems, Structural Stability & Their Application. 420p. (C). 1992. text ed. 74.00 (*9971-5-0965-2*) World Scientific Pub.

Lee, K. R., et al. Semiconductor Device Modeling for VLSI. 450p. 1993. text ed. 58.00 (*0-13-805656-0*) P-H.

Lee, K. S., ed. EMP Interaction: Principles, Techniques, & Reference Data. rev. ed. LC 66-55005. 744p. 1986. 99.50 (*0-89116-581-9*) Hemisp Pub.

Lee, K. S., jt. auth. see Whelan, A.

Lee, K. S., jt. ed. see Whelan, A.

Lee, K. T., ed. Atherosclerosis. (Annals Ser.: Vol. 454). 327p. 1985. text ed. 75.00 (*0-89766-303-9*); pap. text ed. 75.00 (*0-89766-304-7*) NY Acad Sci.

Lee, K. Y. & Takahashi, H., eds. Fracture & Strength, '90. 576p. 1991. text ed. 200.00 (*0-87849-618-1*, Pub. by Trans Tech GW) LPS Dist Ctr.

Lee, Kai. Computers in Nuclear Medicine: A Practical Approach. LC 91-4859. (Illus.). 290p. (Orig.). 1991. pap. text ed. 45.00 (*0-932004-36-9*) Soc Nuclear Med.

Lee, Kai F. Principles of Antenna Theory. LC 83-7042. 338p. reprint ed. pap. 96.40 (*0-8357-7879-7*, 2036297) Bks Demand.

Lee, Kai-Fu. Automatic Speech Recognition: The Development of the SPHINX Recognition System. (International Series in Engineering & Computer Science, VLSI, Computer Architecture, & Digital Screen Processing). 224p. (C). 1988. lib. bdg. 85.50 (*0-89838-296-3*) Kluwer Ac.

Lee, Kai N. Compass & Gyroscope: Integrating Science & Politics for the Environment. LC 92-38824. (Illus.). 290p. 1993. 29.95 (*1-55963-197-X*) Island Pr.

— Compass & Gyroscope: Integrating Science & Politics for the Environment. LC 92-38824. 243p. (C). 1994. reprint ed. pap. text ed. 16.95 (*1-55963-198-8*) Island Pr.

Lee, Kaiman. Air Pollution: Its Effect on the Urban Man & His Adaptive Strategies. LC 74-182905. 52p. 1974. 12.00 (*0-915250-13-6*) Environ Design.

— Comparison of Doctoral Programs in Architecture - U. S. A. 1976. 30.00 (*0-915250-22-5*) Environ Design.

— Computer Aided Architectural Design: 16 ARK-2 Articles. LC 74-160961. 1973. 30.00 (*0-915250-04-7*) Environ Design.

— Computer-Aided Building Code Checking: A Demonstration. 2nd ed. LC 74-308127. 34p. 1974. 12.00 (*0-915250-08-X*) Environ Design.

— Computer Aided Space Planning. LC 76-366704. 1976. 30.00 (*0-915250-20-9*) Environ Design.

— The Computer As an Architectural Design Tool: An Exploration into Certain Multi-Story Building Plan Layouts. 190p. 1979. 25.00 (*0-915250-00-4*) Environ Design.

— Computer Programs in Environmental Design, 5 vols., Set. LC 74-169212. (Illus.). 1308p. 1974. 210.00 (*0-915250-05-5*) Environ Design.

— Encyclopedia of Energy-Efficient Building Design: 391 Practical Case Studies, 2 vols., Set. LC 77-150686. 1977. 150.00 (*0-915250-18-7*) Environ Design.

— Evaluation of Computer Graphic Terminals. 2nd ed. LC 74-184824. 92p. 1975. 12.00 (*0-915250-11-X*) Environ Design.

— Evaluation, Syntheses & Development of an Interactive Approach to Space Allocation. 2nd ed. LC 74-187884. 50p. 1975. 15.00 (*0-915250-10-1*) Environ Design.

— Federal Environmental Impact Statements Related to Buildings. LC 75-323048. 102p. 1975. 30.00 (*0-915250-16-0*) Environ Design.

— Inevitability: Strategic Basis for Investing. LC 82-125420. 93p. 1982. 14.95 (*0-915250-39-X*) Environ Design.

— Integrated Municipal Information System. LC 74-184835. 52p. 1974. 12.00 (*0-915250-12-8*) Environ Design.

— Interactive Computer Aided Architectural Design: Four Applications. 1976. pap. 12.00 (*0-915250-26-8*) Environ Design.

— Interactive Computer Graphics in Architecture. LC 76-366950. 100p. 1976. 30.00 (*0-915250-21-7*) Environ Design.

— Performance Specification of Computer Aided Environmental Design, 2 vols. LC 75-309149. (Illus.). 554p. 1975. 150.00 (*0-915250-15-2*) Environ Design.

— State of the Art of Computer Aided Environmental Design. LC 76-358975. (Illus.). 309p. 1975. 50.00 (*0-915250-14-4*) Environ Design.

Lee, Kaiman, ed. Bibliography of the Computer in Environmental Design, 3 Vols., Set. 2nd ed. LC 73-158197. 650p. 1973. 110.00 (*0-915250-03-9*) Environ Design.

— Energy Film List. 1977. pap. text ed. 4.50 (*0-915250-25-X*) Environ Design.

Lee, Kaiman & Donnelly, Linda. Solar Failure. LC 80-130467. (Illus.). 1980. 30.00 (*0-915250-36-5*) Environ Design.

Lee, Kaiman & Koumjian, Lauren. Environmental Court Cases Related to Buildings. LC 79-105955. 1979. 30.00 (*0-915250-28-4*) Environ Design.

— Environmental Impact Statement: A Reference Manual for the Architect Planner. 2nd ed. 1978. 30.00 (*0-915250-27-6*) Environ Design.

Lee, Kaiman & Masloff, Jacqueline. Energy-Oriented Computer Programs for the Design & Monitoring of Buildings, 2 vols., Set. LC 79-104533. (Illus.). 400p. 1979. 150.00 (*0-915250-29-2*) Environ Design.

— Kaiman's Encyclopedia of Energy Topics, 2 vols., Set. LC 79-104541. (Illus.). 1979. 150.00 (*0-915250-31-4*) Environ Design.

Lee, Kaiman & Moberg, John. Environmental Design Evaluation: A Matrix Method. LC 75-330795. 190p. 1975. 30.00 (*0-915250-17-9*) Environ Design.

Lee, Kaiman & Rehr, Stuart. Energy Conservation & Building Codes: The Legislative & Planning Processes. LC 77-362518. 1977. 30.00 (*0-915250-23-3*) Environ Design.

Lee, Kaiman & Silverstein, Michael. The Buyer's Book of Solar Water Heaters. 4th ed. LC 79-104450. (Illus.). 1979. 50.00 (*0-915250-30-6*) Environ Design.

Lee, Kaiman & Yang, Rita. Encyclopedia of Financial & Personal Survival: Six Hundred Fifty Coping Strategies. LC 80-130472. 1980. 210.00 (*0-915250-34-9*) Environ Design.

Lee, Kam H., jt. ed. see Kaynak, Erdener.

*__Lee Kam Hing.__ The Sultanate of Aceh: Relations with the British 1760-1824. (South-East Asian Historical Monographs). 270p. 1995. 59.00 (*967-65-3055-7*) OUP.

*__Lee, Karen.__ Karen Lee's Personal Healthcare Plan for Women in Their Second Forty Years Vol. 1, Vol. 1. (Illus.). 80p. (Orig.). 1994. vhs 49.95 (*0-9642935-0-1*) WTW.

Lee, Karen & Porter, Diana. The Occasional Vegetarian: More Than 200 Robust Dishes to Satisfy Both Full & Part-time Vegetarians. 272p. 1995. 24.95 (*0-446-51792-5*) Warner Bks.

Lee, Karen K., jt. auth. see Lee, Ronald.

Lee, Kate. Tender Heart: An Incest Survivor's Story in Poetry. 83p. 1991. pap. 12.95 (*0-9626031-5-5*) Children Light Pubns.

Lee, Katharine C., jt. sel. see Wood, James N.

Lee, Kathleen. American Origins: Tracing Our Chinese Roots. LC 93-35616. (American Origins Ser.). (Illus.). 48p. (J). (gr. 4-7). 1994. 12.95 (*1-56261-159-3*) John Muir.

— Tracing Our Italian Roots. (American Origins Ser.). (Illus.). 48p. (J). (gr. 4-7). 1993. text ed. 12.95 (*1-56261-149-6*) John Muir.

Lee, Kathleen, tr. see Kappeler, Max.

Lee, Kathy S. & Thomas, Debra J. Selecting Access Systems for Individuals with Physical Disabilities. 310p. 1990. pap. 50.00 (*0-8020-6695-X*) U of Toronto Pr.

Lee, Katie. Ten Thousand Goddam Cattle: A History of the American Cowboy in Song, Story & Verse. limited rev. ed. (Illus.). 257p. 1985. reprint ed. pap. 12.95 (*0-934573-68-9*) Katyd Bks & Music.

— Visit to Galapagos. 1994. pap. 16.95 (*0-8109-2597-4*) Abrams.

Lee, Kay, tr. see Kappeler, Max.

Lee, Kee-Dong. Kusaiean-English Dictionary. (PALI Language Texts, Micronesia Ser.). 330p. 1976. pap. text ed. 22.00 (*0-8248-0413-9*) UH Pr.

— Kusaiean Reference Grammar. LC 75-6863. (PALI Language Texts, Micronesia Ser.). 444p. 1975. pap. text ed. 14.50 (*0-8248-0355-8*) UH Pr.

Lee, Keekok. The Legal-Rational State: A Comparison of Hobbes, Bentham & Kelsen. (Avebury Series in Philosophy). 264p. 1990. text ed. 59.95 (*1-85628-095-0*, Pub. by Avebury Pub UK) Ashgate Pub Co.

— A New Basis for Moral Philosophy. (International Library of Philosophy). 288p. 1985. 42.50 (*0-7102-0445-0*, RKP) Routledge.

— The Positivist Science of Law. 224p. 1989. text ed. 68.95 (*0-566-07032-4*, Pub. by Avebury Pub UK) Ashgate Pub Co.

Lee, Keenan & Fetter, Charles W., Jr. Laboratory Manual in Hydrogeology. 128p. (C). 1994. pap. write for info. (*0-02-369201-4*) Macmillan.

Lee, Kenneth & Mills, Anne, eds. The Economics of Health in Developing Countries. (Illus.). 1983. 39.95 (*0-19-261385-5*) OUP.

Lee, Kenneth, jt. ed. see Barnard, Keith.

Lee, Kenneth, jt. ed. see Mills, Anne.

Lee, Kent D., tr. see Arbatov, Alexei G.

Lee, Kent D., tr. see Svechin, Aleksandr A.

Lee, Kent D., ed. see Svechin, Aleksandr.

Lee, Keun. Chinese Firms & the State in Transition: Property Rights & Agency Problems in the Reform Era. LC 91-2075. (Studies on Contemporary China Ser.). 224p. 1992. 57.95 (*0-87332-850-7*) M E Sharpe.

An Asterisk (*) at the beginning of an entry indicates that the title is appearing in BIP for the first time.

— New East Asian Economic Development: Interacting Capitalism & Socialism. LC 93-19555. 224p. (C). 1993. text ed. 62.95 (*1-56324-218-4*, East Gate Bk); pap. text ed. 23.95 (*1-56324-219-2*, East Gate Bk) M E Sharpe.

Lee, Kevin, jt. auth. see Edwards, Lois.

Lee, Kevin D. & Cohen, Yosef. Fractal Attraction: A Fractal Design System for the Macintosh. (Illus.). 67p. 1991. pap. text ed. 49.95 (*0-12-440740-4*) Acad Pr.

Lee, Ki-baik. A New History of Korea. Wagner, Edward W. & Schultz, Edward J., trs. LC 83-246. (Harvard-Yenching Institute Ser.). (Illus.). 472p. 1985. 25.00x (*0-674-61575-1*) HUP.

— A New History of Korea. Wagner, Edward W. & Schultz, Edward J., trs. LC 83-246. (Harvard-Yenching Institute Publications). (Illus.). 518p. 1988. reprint ed. pap. 14.95 (*0-674-61576-X*) HUP.

Lee, Knute. Survivor. LC 84-81767. 224p. 1984. pap. 9.95 (*0-8187-0057-2*) Harlo Press.

***Lee, Kou L.** The Owl & Mrs. Wren: Correct Behavior. 36p. (Orig.). (ENG & LAO.). (J). 1995. pap. text ed. 10.95 (*0-9645686-1-6*) NKL Multicult Educ.

Lee, Kristina, et al. Songs of the Season. (Sound Forth Ser.). (Illus.). 80p. (Orig.). (YA). 1991. pap. 7.95 (*0-89084-555-7*) Bob Jones Univ Pr.

Lee, Kuen H. College Algebra: A Step-by-Step Approach. (Illus.). 658p. 1992. 38.90 (*0-9618665-3-5*) Edmund Pub.

— Elementary Algebra: A Step-by-Step Approach. 2nd ed. (Illus.). 346p. (C). 1988. reprint ed. 32.50 (*0-9618665-2-7*) Edmund Pub.

— Elementary Algebra: A Step-by-Step Approach. 3rd expanded ed. 524p. Date not set. 36.50 (*0-9618665-4-3*) Edmund Pub.

Lee, Kwan-Jo. Search for Nirvana: Korean Monks' Life. (Illus.). 128p. 1984. 24.00 (*0-8048-1417-1*, Pub. by Seoul Intl Tourist KO) C E Tuttle.

Lee, Kyu S. The Location of Jobs in a Developing Metropolis: Patterns of Growth in Bogota and Cali, Colombia. (World Bank Research Publications Ser.). (Illus.). 192p. 1989. 18.95 (*0-19-520786-6*) OUP.

Lee, Kyung M., jt. auth. see Chung, Kuk H.

Lee, Kyung-Shik, tr. see Han, Woo-Keun.

Lee, L. Basic Systems Analysis. (C). 1989. 100.00 (*0-09-154091-7*, Pub. by S Thornes Pubs UK) St Mut.

Lee, L. & Lee, S. F. Lee: John Lee of Farmington, Hartford County, CT, & His Descendants, 1634-1897. (Illus.). 572p. 1993. reprint ed. lib. bdg. 97.00 (*0-8328-3697-4*); reprint ed. pap. 87.00 (*0-8328-3698-2*) Higginson Bk Co.

Lee, L., et al. Purchasing & Materials Management. Burt, B., ed. 796p. (C). 1984. 515.00 (*0-685-39935-4*, Inst Pur & Supply); student ed 165.00 (*0-685-39936-2*, Inst Pur & Supply) St Mut.

Lee, L. H., ed. Adhesion & Adsorption of Polymers, 2 vols., Set. Incl. Pt. A. LC 80-262. 504p. 1980. 89.50 (*0-306-40427-3*); Pt. B. LC 80-262. 456p. 1980. 89.50 (*0-306-40428-1*); LC 80-262. (Polymer Science & Technology Ser.: Vols. 12A & B). 1980. 145.00 (*0-685-04067-4*, Plenum Pr) Plenum.

— Adhesive Bonding. (Illus.). 510p. 1991. 115.00 (*0-306-43471-7*, Plenum Pr) Plenum.

— Adhesives, Sealants, & Coatings for Space & Harsh Environments. LC 88-21002. (Polymer Science & Technology Ser.: Vol. 37). (Illus.). 550p. 1988. 125.00 (*0-306-42989-6*, Plenum Pr) Plenum.

— Fundamentals of Adhesion. (Illus.). 430p. 1991. 89.50 (*0-306-43470-9*, Plenum Pr) Plenum.

— New Trends in Physics & Physical Chemistry of Polymers. LC 89-22965. (Illus.). 672p. 1989. 145.00 (*0-306-43383-4*, Plenum Pr) Plenum.

Lee, L. L. Vladimar Nabokov. Bowman, Sylvia E., ed. LC 76-128. (Twayne's United States Authors Ser.). 166p. (C). 1976. lib. bdg. 17.95 (*0-8057-7166-2*) Irvington.

— Walter Van Tilburg Clark. LC 73-8337. (Western Writers Ser.: No. 8). 50p. 1973. pap. 3.95 (*0-88430-007-2*) Boise St U W Writ Ser.

Lee, L. L. & Johnson, Ellwood. A Directory of Scholarly Journals in English Language & Literature. 250p. 1990. 25.00 (*0-87875-401-6*) Whitston Pub.

Lee, L. L. & Lee, Sylvia. Virginia Sorensen. LC 78-52559. (Western Writers Ser.: No. 31). 50p. 1978. pap. 3.95 (*0-88430-055-2*) Boise St U W Writ Ser.

Lee, L. L., jt. ed. see Lewis, Merrill.

Lee, Lai T. The Reunification of China: Pro-Taiwan Relations in Flux. LC 90-44388. 200p. 1991. text ed. 49.95 (*0-275-93772-0*, C3772, Praeger Pubs) Greenwood.

Lee, Lance. Wrestling with the Angel. 92p. 1990. pap. 9.95 (*0-912292-86-5*) The Smith.

Lee, Lance, jt. auth. see Brady, Ben.

Lee, Lance, jt. auth. see Cook, Kaye.

Lee, Larry. American Eagle: The Story of a Navajo Vietnam Veteran. (C). 1977. pap. text ed. 6.00 (*0-686-12227-5*) Packrat Pr.

Lee, Laura. Dial-a-Porn: Verbal Intercourse or Mass Corruption? (Orig.). 1993. pap. 16.95 (*0-9634724-0-2*) Bench Pr CA.

***Lee, Lauren.** Japanese Americans. (Cultures of America Ser.). 80p. (J). (gr. 3-5). 1995. lib. bdg. write for info. (*0-7614-0162-8*, Benchmark NY) Marshall Cavendish.

— Korean Americans. (Cultures of America Ser.). 80p. (J). (gr. 3-5). 1995. lib. bdg. 19.95 (*0-7614-0151-2*) Marshall Cavendish.

— Stella: On the Edge of Popularity. LC 93-43917. (J). 1994. 10.95 (*1-879965-08-9*) Polychrome Pub.

Lee, Lauren K. & Hoyle, Gary D., eds. Elementary School Library Collection: A Guide to Books & Other Media. 18th ed. 1992. 99.95 (*0-87272-095-0*) Brodart.

Lee, Lauren K., et al, eds. The Elementary School Library Collection: A Guide to Books & Other Media, Phases 1-2-3. 19th ed. LC 93-24494. 1994. 99.95 (*0-87272-096-9*) Brodart.

Lee, Laurie. Cider with Rosie. (Chatto Pocket Library). 388p. 1994. 17.95 (*0-7011-4973-6*, Pub. by Chatto & Windus UK) Trafalgar.

— A Moment of War: A Memoir of the Spanish Civil War. LC 92-50840. (Illus.). 192p. 1993. 17.95 (*1-56584-060-7*) New Press NY.

— A Moment of War: A Memoir of the Spanish Civil War. 192p. 1994. pap. 9.95 (*1-56584-173-5*) New Press NY.

— Selected Poems. 68p. 1984. pap. 11.95 (*0-233-97503-9*, Pub. by A Deutsch UK) Trafalgar.

Lee, Lawrence. Cockcrow at Night, the Heroic Journey, & 18 Other Stories. (Illus.). 250p. (Orig.). 1973. 6.00 (*0-910286-35-3*) Boxwood.

Lee, Lawrence, jt. auth. see Gifford, Barry.

Lee, Lawrence B. Kansas & the Homestead Act: Eighteen Sixty-Two to Nineteen Five, 2 vols. in one. Bruchey, Stuart, ed. LC 78-36703. (Management of Public Lands in the U. S. Ser.). (Illus.). 1979. lib. bdg. 50.95 (*0-405-11341-2*) Ayer.

Lee, Lawrence D., tr. see Oldman, Oliver S., et al.

Lee, Lawrence L. & Lewis, Merrill E., eds. Women, Women Writers & the West. LC 78-69805. 252p. 1978. 15.00 (*0-87875-146-7*) Whitston Pub.

Lee, Leo O. The Romantic Generation of Modern Chinese Writers. LC 73-75058. (Harvard East Asian Ser.: No. 71). (Illus.). 379p. reprint ed. pap. 109.20 (*0-7837-4166-9*, 2059014) Bks Demand.

— Voices from the Iron House: A Study of Lu Xun. LC 85-46049. (Studies in Chinese Literature & Society). 266p. 1987. 34.95 (*0-253-36263-6*) Ind U Pr.

Lee, Leo O., jt. ed. see Arkush, R. David.

Lee, Leonard. The Complete Guide to Sharpening. 245p. 1995. pap. 34.95 (*1-56158-067-8*) Taunton.

— Day the Phones Stopped. 1992. pap. 12.95 (*1-55611-286-6*, Primus Lib Contemp) D I Fine.

Lee, Les. The Michael Jackson Scrapbook. (Illus.). 200p. 1992. pap. 15.95 (*0-8065-1375-6*, Citadel Pr) Carol Pub Group.

Lee, Leslie. Backcountry Ranger: In Glacier National Park 1910-1913 the Diaries & Photographs of Norton Pearl. LC 94-75921. (Illus.). 264p. (Orig.). 1994. write for info. (*0-9641250-0-5*); text ed. write for info. (*0-9641250-2-1*); lib. bdg. write for info. (*0-9641250-1-3*); pap. write for info. (*0-9641250-3-X*); pap. text ed. write for info. (*0-9641250-4-8*) L Lee Pub.

Lee, Leslie & Comte, Robert. Management Procedures. LC 74-18677. (Allied Health Ser.). 1975. pap. 6.35 (*0-672-61397-2*, Bobbs) Macmillan.

Lee, Levi, jt. auth. see Larson, Larry.

Lee, Levi, et al. Tent Meeting. 1987. pap. 4.75 (*0-8222-1121-1*) Dramatists Play.

Lee, Lewis E. & Davidson, J. Scott. Managing Intellectual Property Rights: Understanding, Analyzing & Managing Your Company's Intellectual Property Rights. LC 93-9881. (Business Practice Library). 328p. (Orig.). 1993. pap. text ed. 83.00 (*0-471-59728-7*) Wiley.

Lee, Li-Young. The City in Which I Love You. (American Poets Continuum Ser.: No. 20). 80p. 1991. 18.00 (*0-918526-82-5*); pap. 10.00 (*0-918526-83-3*) BOA Edns.

— Rose. 71p. 1986. pap. 10.00 (*0-918526-53-1*) BOA Edns.

— Winged Seed. 1995. 19.00 (*0-671-70708-6*) S&S Trade.

Lee, Lieng-Huang. Adhesion Science & Technology. Incl. Pt. A. LC 75-35744. 470p. 1975. (*0-306-36493-X*); Pt. B. LC 75-35744. 456p. 1975. (*0-306-36494-8*); LC 75-35744. (Polymer Science & Technology Ser.: Vols. 9A & 9B). 1975. write for info. (*0-318-55304-X*, Plenum Pr) Plenum.

Lee, Lieng-Huang, ed. Recent Advances in Adhesion. LC 73-86915. 568p. 1973. text ed. 342.00 (*0-677-12190-3*) Gordon & Breach.

Lee, Lilian. Farewell My Concubine. 1994. pap. 9.00 (*0-06-097644-6*) HarpC.

— Last Princess of Manchuria: A Novel. 1992. 15.00 (*0-688-10834-2*) Morrow.

Lee, Lillian. Farewell to My Concubine. LC 93-16777. (CHI & ENG.). 1993. 18.00 (*0-688-12020-2*) Morrow.

Lee, Lily. The Virtue of Yin: Essays on Chinese Women. 128p. (C). 1994. pap. text ed. 13.95 (*0-646-14925-3*, Pub. by Wild Peony Pty AT) UH Pr.

Lee, Linda. The Bruce Lee Story. Vaughan, Jack, ed. LC 88-63487. 192p. 1988. pap. text ed. 19.95 (*0-89750-121-7*, 460) Ohara Pubns.

— English Connections: Book 2. LC 93-22804. 1994. pap. 9.66 (*0-8092-4206-0*) Contemp Bks.

— How to Write & Sell Romance Novels: A Step-by-Step Guide. LC 88-81232. 164p. (Orig.). 1988. pap. 9.95 (*0-929195-00-0*) Heartsong Pr.

— Mastering Reading: TRB Office Work. 1991. teacher ed 10.00 (*0-8273-4539-9*) Delmar.

Lee, Linda, jt. auth. see Blanton, Linda L.

Lee, Linda, ed. see Rodin, Cuia & Rodin, Tibor S.

Lee, Linda D. Right-to-Know for Hospital Workers. (Illus.). 116p. (Orig.). 1991. pap. 50.00 (*0-87258-571-9*, 057006) Am Hospital.

— Safety Management for Health Care Facilities. (Management & Compliance Ser.: Vol. 5). (Illus.). 275p. 1989. ring bd. 110.00 (*0-87258-512-3*, 055204) Am Hospital.

— Waste Management for Health Care Facilities. rev. ed. (Management & Compliance Ser.: Vol. 1). (Illus.). 300p. 1992. ring bd. 110.00 (*0-87258-585-9*, 055401) Am Hospital.

Lee, Linda F. Texas Angel. 336p. (Orig.). 1994. mass mkt. 4.99 (*0-7865-0007-7*) Diamond.

— The Wallflower. 272p. (Orig.). 1995. pap. text ed. 4.99 (*0-515-11683-1*) Jove Pubns.

— Wild Hearts. 272p. (Orig.). 1994. pap. text ed. 4.99 (*0-7865-0062-X*) Diamond.

Lee, Linda S. Mastering Reading: Skills for Success: Office Work, 4 bks., Bk. 3. 1991. pap. text ed. 10.95 (*0-8273-4540-2*) Delmar.

Lee, Lissa, tr. see Hannah, Valerie.

Lee, Lita. Radiation Protection Manual. 3rd rev. ed. (Illus.). 150p. 1991. pap. 6.95 (*1-880358-00-X*) Lita Lee.

Lee, Liz. How to Have a Radical Attitude! Toward God (& Really Believe It) 208p. (J). (gr. 5-7). 1994. pap. 7.99 (*0-8054-4009-7*, 4240-09) Broadman.

Lee, Liz, jt. auth. see Nally, Susan.

Lee, Lloyd E. The Politics of Harmony: Civil Service, & Social Reform in Baden, 1800-1850. LC 77-92569. 272p. 1980. 38.50 (*0-87413-143-X*) U Delaware Pr.

— The War Years: A Global History of the Second World War. 496p. 1989. 55.00 (*0-04-445266-7*); pap. 21.95 (*0-04-445265-9*) Routledge Chapman & Hall.

Lee, Lois B. Rhymes for Talking Time. 1973. text ed. 2.50 (*0-686-09389-5*) Expression.

Lee, Lorraine. The Magic Dulcimer. LC 83-17125. (Illus.). 130p. 1983. pap. 12.95 (*0-938756-09-5*) Yellow Moon.

Lee, Loyd E., ed. World War II: Crucible of the Contemporary World Commentary & Readings. LC 90-25544. 448p. (C). 1991. 57.95 (*0-87332-731-4*); pap. text ed. 20.95 (*0-87332-732-2*) M E Sharpe.

Lee, Luke T. Consular Law & Practice. 2nd ed. 776p. 1991. 165.00 (*0-19-825601-9*) OUP.

Lee, Luther. Slavery Examined in the Light of the Bible. 1988. reprint ed. lib. bdg. 75.00 (*0-7812-0277-9*) Rprt Serv.

— Slavery Examined in the Light of the Bible. LC 76-92434. 185p. 1855. reprint ed. 39.00 (*0-403-00166-8*) Scholarly.

Lee, Lyle. Words of the Metis Poet. 1977. 2.00 (*0-686-75955-9*) Luna Bisonte.

Lee, Lynn, jt. auth. see Lee, William H.

Lee, M. A., jt. ed. see Koch-Miramond, L.

***Lee, M. Evelyn.** A Potpourri of Poems. 104p. (Orig.). 1994. pap. write for info. (*0-89716-553-5*) P B Pubng.

Lee, M. J., jt. auth. see Bunting, G. R.

Lee, M. Owen. Death & Rebirth in Virgil's Arcadia. LC 88-24824. (Classical Studies). 140p. (C). 1989. 59.50 (*0-7914-0016-6*); pap. 19.95 (*0-7914-0017-4*) State U NY Pr.

— Fathers & Sons in Virgil's Aeneid: Tum Genitor Natum. LC 79-15157. 200p. 1982. 59.50 (*0-87395-402-5*); pap. 19.95 (*0-87395-451-3*) State U NY Pr.

— First Intermissions: Twenty-One Great Operas Explored, Explained & Brought to Life from the Met. (Illus.). 224p. 1995. 23.00 (*0-19-509255-4*) OUP.

— Virgil As Orpheus: A Study of the Georgics. (Classical Studies). 160p. (C). 1996. text ed. 44.50x (*0-7914-2783-8*); pap. text ed. 14.95x (*0-7914-2784-6*) State U NY Pr.

— Wagner's Ring: Turning the Sky Around. LC 94-29968. 120p. 1994. reprint ed. pap. 10.00 (*0-87910-186-5*) Limelight Edns.

Lee, Mabel & Syrokomla-Stefanowska, A. D., eds. Modernization of the Chinese Past. (University of Sydney School of Asian Studies Ser.: No. 1). 195p. (C). 1993. pap. text ed. 20.00 (*0-86758-658-3*, Pub. by Wild Peony Pty AT) UH Pr.

Lee, Mabel & Wagner, Miriam M. Fundamentals of Body Mechanics & Conditioning: An Illustrated Teaching Manual. LC 75-91765. 377p. 1969. reprint ed. text ed. 65.00 (*0-8371-2417-4*, LEBM, Greenwood Pr) Greenwood.

Lee, Mabel & Zhang Wu-Ai. Putonghua: A Practical Course in Spoken Chinese. 110p. 1984. pap. text ed. 12.50 (*0-9590735-0-7*) UH Pr.

Lee, Mabel, jt. auth. see Syrokomla-Stefanowska, A. D.

Lee, Mabel, tr. see Yang, Lian.

Lee, Mabel B. Cripple Creek Days. LC 84-5204. xviii, 286p. 1984. reprint ed. pap. 8.95 (*0-8032-7912-4*, Bison Books) U of Nebr Pr.

Lee, Mabel P. Economic History of China. LC 70-78006. (Columbia University. Studies in the Social Sciences: No. 225). reprint ed. 32.50 (*0-404-51225-9*) AMS Pr.

— The Economic History of China with Special Reference to Agriculture. 1976. lib. bdg. 59.95 (*0-8490-1746-7*) Gordon Pr.

Lee, Man-Gap. Sociology & Social Change in Korea. 342p. 1982. text ed. 18.00 (*0-8248-0937-8*) UH Pr.

Lee, Manwoo. The Odyssey of Korean Democracy: Korean Politics, 1987-1990. LC 90-7393. 184p. 1990. text ed. 49.95 (*0-275-93660-0*, C3660, Praeger Pubs) Greenwood.

Lee, Manwoo & Mansbach, Richard W. The Changing Order in Northeast Asia & the Korean Peninsula. LC 93-23226. 290p. (C). 1993. pap. text ed. 42.00 (*0-8133-8795-7*) Westview.

Lee, Margaret, tr. see Maisel, John.

Lee, Margaret C. Resource Guide to Information on Southern Africa. LC 88-50831. 54p. 1988. student ed 3.95 (*1-55523-163-2*) Winston-Derek.

— SADCC Political Economy of Development in Southern Africa. LC 88-50765. 242p. 1989. pap. 16.95 (*1-55523-156-X*) Winston-Derek.

Lee, Margaret E. Memories of Nauvoo: Walker County, Alabama. (Illus.). 272p. 1992. 35.00 (*0-9634326-1-3*); pap. 25.00 (*0-9634326-0-5*) Treasured Mem.

***Lee, Marie.** The Curious Cape Cod Skull. LC 94-96731. 213p. 1995. 17.95 (*0-8034-9109-3*) Avalon Bks.

Lee, Marie G. Finding My Voice. 1994. mass mkt. 3.99 (*0-440-21896-9*) Dell.

— Finding My Voice. LC 92-2947. 176p. (YA). (gr. 6 up). 1992. 13.95 (*0-395-62134-8*) HM.

— If It Hadn't Been for Yoon Jun. LC 92-9557. 144p. (J). (gr. 3-7). 1993. 13.95 (*0-395-62941-1*) HM.

— If It Hadn't Been for Yoon Jun. 144p. (J). 1995. pap. 3.50 (*0-380-72347-6*, Camelot) Avon.

— Saying Goodbye. LC 93-26092. (J). 1994. 14.95 (*0-395-67066-7*) HM.

***Lee, Mark.** Finishing Well. 208p. 1995. pap. 9.99 (*0-87509-585-2*) Chr Pubns.

— Rebel Armies Deep into Chad. 1989. pap. 4.75 (*0-8222-0934-9*) Dramatists Play.

Lee, Mark R. Antitrust Law & Local Government. LC 84-23722. (Illus.). xi, 220p. 1985. text ed. 49.95 (*0-89930-090-1*, LNL/, Quorum Bks) Greenwood.

Lee, Marshall, ed. Bookmaking: The Illustrated Guide to Design, Production, Editing. enl. rev. ed. LC 79-65014. 485p. 1980. 49.95 (*0-8352-1097-9*) Bowker.

Lee, Marshall, ed. see Erte.

Lee, Marshall, ed. see Howard, Richard.

Lee, Marshall M. & Michalka, Wolfgang. German Foreign Policy Nineteen Seventeen to Nineteen Thirty-Three: Continuity or Break? LC 85-22833. 180p. 1987. 52.00 (*0-907582-52-4*) Berg Pubs.

***Lee, Martha F.** Earth First! Environmental Apocalypse. (Illus.). 200p. 1995. 34.95 (*0-8156-2677-0*); pap. 16.95 (*0-8156-0365-7*) Syracuse U Pr.

Lee, Martha J., jt. auth. see Bates, Craig D.

Lee, Martin. Clear & Simple Basic Algebra. 1986. pap. 9.00 (*0-671-54555-8*) S&S Trade.

— Clear & Simple Intermediate Algebra. 1986. 6.95 (*0-685-43080-4*) S&S Trade.

— The Seminoles. LC 89-8900. (First Bks.). (Illus.). 64p. (J). (gr. 4-7). 1989. lib. bdg. 13.93 (*0-531-10752-3*) Watts.

— The Seminoles. (First Bks.). (Illus.). 64p. (J). (gr. 5-8). 1991. pap. 5.95 (*0-531-15604-4*) Watts.

Lee, Martin, ed. Coaching Children in Sport: Principles & Practice. LC 93-18009. 1993. write for info. (*0-419-18250-0*, E & FN Spon) Routledge Chapman & Hall.

Lee, Martin & Shlain, Bruce. Acid Dreams: The CIA, LSD, & the Sixties Rebellion. 384p. (Orig.). 1987. pap. 13.95 (*0-8021-3062-3*) Grove-Atltic.

Lee, Martin, jt. auth. see Miller, Marcia.

Lee, Martin A. Unreliable Sources: A Guide to Detecting Bias in News Media. 320p. 1990. 19.95 (*0-8184-0521-X*) Carol Pub Group.

Lee, Martin A. & Solomon, Norman. Unreliable Sources: A Guide to Detecting Bias in News Media. 448p. 1991. reprint ed. pap. text ed. 12.95 (*0-8184-0561-9*, Citadel Pr) Carol Pub Group.

***Lee, Marty.** Estimation Investigations. (J). (gr. 4-6). 1995. pap. 9.95 (*0-590-49602-6*) Scholastic Inc.

Lee, Martyn J. Consumer Culture Reborn: The Cultural Politics of Consumption. LC 92-34903. 208p. 1993. 59.95 (*0-415-08413-X*, B2272); pap. 16.95 (*0-415-08414-8*, B2276) Routledge.

***Lee, Mary.** AIDS is a Woman's Nightmare. King, Barbara, ed. (Orig.). (YA). Date not set. pap. text ed. write for info. (*1-881242-00-5*) Pyramid Educ Inc.

Lee, Mary, ed. see Petersen, Phil.

Lee, Mary, et al. The Handbook of Technical Writing: Form & Style. 487p. (C). 1990. pap. text ed. 18.75 (*0-15-530985-4*) HB Coll Pubs.

Lee, Mary A. I Love You to Death. (Orig.). 1989. pap. write for info. (*0-318-65730-9*) Franklin-Belle.

— Twinkle, Twinkle - You're a Star. 40p. 1994. pap. 8.95 (*0-8059-3555-X*) Dorrance.

Lee, Mary D. & Hackman, J. Richard. Redesigning Work: A Strategy for Change. (Studies in Productivity: Vol. 9). 43p. 1979. pap. 55.00 (*0-08-029490-1*) Work in Amer.

Lee, Mary P. Coping with Money. Rosen, Ruth, ed. (Coping Ser.). (YA). (gr. 7 up). 1988. lib. bdg. 15.95 (*0-8239-0783-X*) Rosen Group.

— Quiet Odyssey: A Pioneer Korean Woman in America. LC 89-28077. (Samuel & Althea Stroum Book Ser.). (Illus.). 264p. (Orig.). 1990. pap. 14.95 (*0-295-96969-5*) U of Wash Pr.

Lee, Mary P. & Lee, Richard. Careers in the Restaurant Industry. rev. ed. Rosen, R., ed. (Careers in Depth Ser.). (Illus.). 160p. (YA). (gr. 7-12). 1990. 14.95 (*0-8239-1142-X*) Rosen Group.

Lee, Mary P. & Lee, Richard S. Careers in Firefighting. Rosen, Ruth, ed. (Careers in Depth Ser.). (YA). (gr. 7-12). 1993. lib. bdg. 14.95 (*0-8239-1515-8*); pap. 9.95 (*0-8239-1724-X*) Rosen Group.

— Drugs & Codependency. LC 94-35234. (The Drug Abuse Prevention Library). (J). 1995. write for info. (*0-8239-2065-8*) Rosen Group.

— Last Names First ..& Some First Names too. LC 84-20860. (Illus.). 119p. (J). (gr. 5-9). 1985. 12.00 (*0-664-32719-2*, Westminster) Westminster John Knox.

— Opportunities in Animal & Pet Care. (Illus.). 160p. 1987. 13.95 (*0-8442-6244-7*, VGM Career Bks); pap. 10.95 (*0-8442-6245-5*, VGM Career Bks) NTC Pub Grp.

Lee, Mary P., jt. auth. see Lee, Richard S.

Lee, Mary Price & Lee, Richard S. Opportunities in Animal & Pet Care Careers. LC 93-17661. 1994. 13.95 (*0-8442-4079-6*, VGM Career Bks); pap. 10.95 (*0-8442-4081-8*) NTC Pub Grp.

Lee, Mathew, pref. Rehabilitation, Music & Human Well-Being. (Illus.). 282p. (Orig.). 1989. pap. 29.95 (*0-918812-59-3*, ST 190) MMB Music.

Lee, Maurice, Jr. Great Britain's Solomon: King James VI & I in His Three Kingdoms. (Illus.). 352p. 1990. 32.50 (*0-252-01686-6*) U of Ill Pr.

— James I & Henri IV: An Essay in English Foreign Policy, 1603-1610. LC 74-100377. (Illus.). 192p. 1970. 24.95 (*0-252-00084-6*) U of Ill Pr.

— James Stewart, Earl of Moray: A Political Study of the Reformation in Scotland. LC 73-104251. 320p. 1971. reprint ed. text ed. 38.50 (*0-8371-3975-9*, LEJS, Greenwood Pr) Greenwood.

— John Maitland of Thirlestane & the Foundation of Stewart Despotism in Scotland. (Studies in History: Vol. 11). (Illus.). 1959. 55.00 (*0-691-05129-1*) Princeton U Pr.

— The Road to Revolution: Scotland under Charles I, 1625-37. LC 84-8750. 276p. 1985. 29.95 (*0-252-01136-8*) U of Ill Pr.

Lee, Maurice D., III & Hurt, Martha R. Lifetime & Testamentary Estate Planning: Pennsylvania Supplement. 10th ed. LC 90-55618. 48p. 1990. pap. 30.00 (*0-8318-0493-9*, B493) Am Law Inst.

Lee, Maurice D., III, jt. auth. see David, Edward M.

Lee, Melicent H. Indians of the Oaks. rev. ed. (Illus.). 1978. reprint ed. pap. 10.95 (*0-916552-17-9*) Acoma Bks.

Lee, Melinda & Lane, Chris. Kitchen Notes. Date not set. 15.95 (*1-56015-209-5*) Penton Overseas.

Lee, Melvin, et al. Diagnosis & Treatment of Prevalent Diseases of North American Indian Populations. (American Indian Health Ser.: Vol. 1). 302p. 1974. text ed. 27.50 (*0-8422-7215-1*) Irvington.

Lee, Michael, jt. auth. see Cotts, David G.

Lee, Michele. Teenage Sexuality. LC 93-47225. (Life Issues Ser.). (YA). 1994. 14.95 (*1-85435-616-X*) Marshall Cavendish.

Lee, Michelle. Estes Park Souvenir Coloring Book. 48p. (J). (ps-8). 1993. 4.50 (*0-9637687-0-0*) Vacation Color.

Lee, Mickey & Williams, Maryann, eds. Tennessee Statistical Abstract, 1977. (Illus.). 737p. (C). 1977. pap. text ed. 15.00 (*0-940191-03-2*) Univ TN Ctr Bus Econ.

Lee, Mike, ed. see Black Belt Magazine Editors.

Lee, Mike, ed. see Bryne, Richard.

Lee, Mike, ed. see Cheung, William.

Lee, Mike, ed. see Cheung, William & Wong, Ted.

Lee, Mike, ed. see Chung, George & Rothrock, Cynthia.

Lee, Mike, ed. see Gwon, Pu G.

Lee, Mike, ed. see Hayes, Stephen.

Lee, Mike, ed. see Ho'o, Marshall.

Lee, Mike, ed. see Jay, Wally.

Lee, Mike, ed. see Kirby, George.

Lee, Mike, ed. see Lowry, Dave.

Lee, Mike, jt. auth. see Lowry, Dave.

Lee, Mike, ed. see McCarthy, Pat.

Lee, Mike, ed. see Yamashita, Tadashi.

Lee, Miles E. Near Misses in Cardiac Surgery: Great Saves. 1992. pap. 29.95 (*0-7506-9391-6*) Buttrwrth-Heinemann.

Lee-Milne, Avide & Moore, Derry. The Englishman's Room. 1986. write for info. (*0-318-61628-9*) Viking Penguin.

Lee, Milton L., et al. Open Tubular Column Gas Chromatography: Theory & Practice. LC 83-14780. 445p. 1984. text ed. 114.00 (*0-471-88024-8*, Wiley-Interscience) Wiley.

Lee, Min, jt. auth. see Dudley, Walter C.

Lee, Miranda. Asking for Trouble. 1993. mass mkt. 2.99 (*0-373-11614-4*, 1-11614-4) Harlequin Bks.

— Beth & the Barbarian: Presents Plus. (Presents Ser.). 1995. pap. 2.99 (*0-373-11711-6*, 1-11711-8) Harlequin Bks.

— A Daring Proposition. (Presents Ser.). 1994. mass mkt. 2.99 (*0-373-11664-0*, 1-11664-9) Harlequin Bks.

— A Date with Destiny. 1994. 2.99 (*0-373-11651-9*) Harlequin Bks.

— A Date with Destiny. large type ed. 1992. lib. bdg. 18.95 (*0-263-13125-4*, Pub. by Mills & Boon UK) Thorndike Pr.

— A Daughter's Dilemma. large type ed. 1993. 17.95 (*0-263-13316-8*, Pub. by Mills & Boon Ltd UK) Chivers N Amer.

— Desire & Deception. (Presents Ser.). 1995. mass mkt. 3.25 (*0-373-11760-4*, 1-11760-5) Harlequin Bks.

— Fantasies & the Future. 1995. mass mkt. 3.25 (*0-373-11772-8*, 1-11772-0) Harlequin Bks.

— Heart-Throb for Hire. large type ed. (Harlequin Romance Ser.). 1994. 18.95 (*0-263-13821-6*) Thorndike Pr.

— Knight to the Rescue. 1994. mass mkt. 2.99 (*0-373-11702-7*, 1-11702-7) Harlequin Bks.

— Marriage & Miracles. 1995. pap. 3.25 (*0-373-11784-1*, 1-11784-5) Harlequin Bks.

— Marriage in Jeopardy. large type ed. (Harlequin Ser.). 1994. bds. 18.95 (*0-263-13714-7*) Thorndike Pr.

— Marriage in Jeopardy: (Presents Plus) (Presents Ser.). 1995. pap. 3.25 (*0-373-11728-0*, 1-11728-2) Harlequin Bks.

— Outback Man. (Presents Ser.). 1993. mass mkt. 2.99 (*0-373-11562-8*, 1-11562-5) Harlequin Bks.

— An Outrageous Proposal. (Presents Ser.). 1995. mass mkt. 3.25 (*0-373-11737-X*, 1-11737-3) Harlequin Bks.

— An Outrageous Proposal. large type ed. 1993. 17.95 (*0-263-13411-3*, Pub. by Mills & Boon Ltd UK) Chivers N Amer.

— Scandalous Seduction. (Presents Ser.). 1993. mass mkt. 2.99 (*0-373-11589-X*, 1-11589-8) Harlequin Bks.

— Scandals & Secrets (Hearts of Fire) 1995. mass mkt. 3.25 (*0-373-11778-7*) Harlequin Bks.

— Seduction & Sacrifice. (Presents Ser.). 1995. mass mkt. 3.25 (*0-373-11754-X*, 1-11754-8) Harlequin Bks.

— Simply Irresistible. large type ed. (Harlequin Ser.). 1994. 18.95 (*0-263-13651-5*) Thorndike Pr.

Lee, Miriam. Insights of a Senior Acupuncturist: One Combination of Points Can Treat Many Diseases. Flaws, Bob, ed. LC 92-70742. 140p. (Orig.). 1992. pap. 15.95 (*0-936185-33-3*) Blue Poppy.

Lee, Miriam, tr. & comment. Master Tong's Acupuncture: An Ancient Alternative Style in Modern Clinical Practice. LC 92-73391. (Illus.). 240p. 1992. pap. 19.95 (*0-936185-37-6*) Blue Poppy.

***Lee, Molly & Woodward, Kesler.** Lockwood de Forest: Alaska Oil Sketches. (Illus.). 46p. (YA). 1988. pap. text ed. write for info. (*0-614-00853-0*) AK State Musms.

Lee, Monica. Facsimile Transmission of Court Documents: A Feasibility Study - Fifty State Survey of FAX Use by State Courts. 87p. 1990. 5.50 (*0-685-38107-2*, WRO-116) Natl Ctr St Courts.

Lee, Monica, jt. auth. see Henderson, Larry.

Lee, Monica, jt. auth. see Russillo, Frederick.

Lee, Monica, et al. Study of the Appointment of Indigent Defense Council in the State of Alaska. 126p. 1992. 7.50 (*0-685-55329-9*, WRO135) Natl Ctr St Courts.

Lee, Moon H. Purchasing Power Parity. LC 76-22815. (Business Economics & Finance Ser.: No. 9). 144p. reprint ed. pap. 41.10 (*0-7837-0965-X*, 2041270) Bks Demand.

Lee, Motoko, ed. Needs of Foreign Students from Developing Nations at U. S. College & Universities. 180p. 1981. 12.00 (*0-912207-27-2*) NAFSA Washington.

Lee, Motoko, jt. auth. see Oulman, Charles S.

Lee, Muna, ed. Art in Review: Puerto Rico. (Puerto Rico Ser.). 1979. lib. bdg. 59.95 (*0-8490-2868-X*) Gordon Pr.

Lee, Muriel P. The Dog Breeders' Organizer. LC 83-62667. (Illus.). 1984. pap. 5.95 (*0-9612546-1-0*) Plantin Pr.

— The Whelping & Rearing of Puppies: A Complete & Practical Guide. 4th ed. LC 84-60962. (Illus.). 126p. 1984. pap. 11.95 (*0-9612546-0-2*) Plantin Pr.

Lee, Myrtle M. Branches of Poetry. 64p. 1993. pap. 9.95 (*1-57087-009-8*) Prof Pr NC.

Lee, Myung W., jt. auth. see Balch, A. H.

Lee, Nanci & Kelley, Jane. Accounting: An Introduction, Pt. I. 960p. (C). 1988. student ed, pap. text ed. 18.50 (*0-15-500439-5*) Dryden Pr.

— Accounting: An Introduction, Pt. I. 960p. (C). 1989. student ed 7.00 (*0-15-500449-2*) Dryden Pr.

— Accounting: An Introduction, Pt. II. 960p. (C). 1989. write for info. (*0-318-67134-4*) Dryden Pr.

— Accounting: An Introduction, Pts. I & II. 960p. (C). 1989. trans. write for info. (*0-318-67135-2*) Dryden Pr.

Lee, Nancy. My Turn. (Illus.). 150p. 1982. pap. 10.95 (*0-933704-23-2*) Dawn Pr.

Lee, Nancy & Oldham, Linda. Hands on Heritage. LC 78-52312. 320p. 1978. 14.95 (*0-931178-01-0*) Hands on Pubns.

— Tacos, Tempura & Teem Gok. LC 78-75120. 80p. (J). (ps-8). 1979. 3.95 (*0-931178-02-9*) Hands on Pubns.

Lee, Nathaniel. Lucius Junius Brutus. Loftis, John, ed. LC 67-12644. xxiv, 107p. 1967. pap. 6.95 (*0-8032-5362-1*) U of Nebr Pr.

— The Rival Queens. Vernon, P. F., ed. xxviii, 112p. 1970. pap. 6.95 (*0-8032-5374-5*) U of Nebr Pr.

Lee, Neil M. Patriot above Profit. LC 88-12032. 704p. 1988. 29.95 (*0-934395-68-3*) Rutledge Hill Pr.

Lee, Nelson. Three Years among the Comanches: The Narrative of Nelson Lee, the Texas Ranger. LC 57-11197. (Western Frontier Library: Vol. 9). 200p. 1991. pap. 9.95 (*0-8061-2339-7*) U of Okla Pr.

Lee, Newton S. The Nightmares of a Journalist. (Orig.). 1991. pap. 4.79 (*0-9627016-1-0*) VTLS.

Lee, Norman, jt. ed. see Artis, Michael.

Lee, O-Young. The Compact Culture: The Japanese Tradition of Smaller is Better. Huey, Robert N., tr. (Illus.). 192p. 1992. reprint ed. pap. text ed. 6.95 (*4-7700-1643-3*) Kodansha.

Lee, Owen. The Skin Diver's Bible. rev. ed. LC 85-45522. (Illus.). 192p. 1986. pap. 12.00 (*0-385-13543-2*, Outdoor Bible) Doubleday.

Lee, P. A., ed. Optical & Electrical Properties. (Physics & Chemistry of Materials with Layered Structures Ser.: No. 4). 1976. lib. bdg. 140.00 (*90-277-0676-X*) Kluwer Ac.

Lee, P. A., et al, eds. Theories of Heavy-Electron Systems. (Journal Comments on Condensed Matter Physics). 65p. 1986. pap. text ed. 35.00 (*0-677-21460-X*) Gordon & Breach.

Lee, P. N. Environmental Tobacco Smoke & Mortality: A Detailed Review of Epidemiological Evidence Relating Environmental Tobacco Smoke to the Risk of Cancer, Heart Disease & Other Causes of Death in Adults Who Have Never Smoked. (Illus.). xx, 224p. 1992. 142.50 (*3-8055-5529-6*) S Karger.

Lee, P. Y. Lanzhou Lectures on Henstork Integration. (Series in Real Analysis: Vol. 2). 192p. (C). 1989. text ed. 61.00 (*9971-5-0891-5*); pap. text ed. 28.00 (*9971-5-0892-3*) World Scientific Pub.

Lee, Pamela. Introduction to Art. 192p. (C). 1991. spiral bd. 19.95 (*0-8403-6657-4*) Kendall-Hunt.

Lee, Pao-Chen. Read about China. 1953. 8.95 (*0-88710-061-9*); audio write for info. (*0-88710-062-7*) Yale Far Eastern Pubns.

Lee, Pat, illus. I Live Here Too. LC 77-82740. 112p. 1977. pap. 8.95 (*0-89334-013-8*) Humanics Ltd.

Lee, Patricia. The Complete Guide to Job Sharing. 192p. 1983. 13.95 (*0-8027-0740-8*); pap. 6.95 (*0-8027-7213-7*) Walker & Co.

Lee, Patricia, jt. ed. see Lee, Ronald S.

Lee, Patricia, et al. The Patient Care Technician Manual. 315p. 1991. pap. 45.00 (*1-56488-004-4*) Dialyrn.

Lee, Patrick, tr. see Iotti, Paolo.

Lee, Paul. My Heart a Hiding Place. 1986. pap. 7.95 (*0-87508-316-1*) Chr Lit.

Lee, Paul A. Florence the Goose: A True Story for Children of All Ages. (Illus.). 47p. (J). 1992. 14.95 (*0-937011-51-7*) Platonic Acad Pr.

— The Quality of Mercy: Homelessness in Santa Cruz 1985-1992. 141p. 1992. pap. 7.95 (*0-937011-50-9*) Platonic Acad Pr.

Lee, Paul P., et al. Cataract Surgery: A Literature Review & Ratings of Appropriateness & Cruciality. LC 93-25076. 1993. write for info. (*0-8330-1405-6*, JRA-06) Rand Corp.

— Estimating Eye Care Provider Supply & Workforce Requirements. LC 95-18056. 164p. 1995. pap. text ed. 9.00 (*0-8330-1652-0*, MR-516-AAO) Rand Corp.

Lee, Paul S. A Computerized Demonstration of the Central Limit Theorem in Statistics. 37p. (Orig.). 1978. pap. 3.00 (*1-55719-041-0*) U NE CPAR.

Lee, Paul S. & Chen, Yeshen. A Study of Boat Ownership in the Omaha-Council Bluffs Metropolitan Area. 26p. (Orig.). 1978. pap. 2.50 (*1-55719-079-8*) U NE CPAR.

***Lee, Paula M.** Emerald's Desire. (YA). 1994. pap. 3.99 (*0-06-106242-1*) HarpC Child Bks.

Lee, Paula M., ed. see Massie, Brigid M. & Waters, John.

Lee, Peggy. Miss Peggy Lee: An Autobiography. (Illus.). 1988. 18.95 (*1-55611-112-6*) D I Fine.

Lee, Peng. The Soul of the Orient: A Personal View of the Life & Thought of the Orient. LC 88-90252. (Illus.). 122p. (Orig.). 1988. pap. text ed. 9.95 (*0-9621445-0-9*) Lee Pubs.

Lee Peng Yee, tr. see Orlicz, W.

Lee, Peter. Realistic Compiler Generation. (Foundations of Computing Ser.). 225p. 1989. 32.50 (*0-262-12141-7*) MIT Pr.

— Topics in Advanced Language Implementation. 350p. 1990. 42.00 (*0-262-12151-4*) MIT Pr.

Lee, Peter A. Straight Talk about Sex. LC 89-33414. 1989. 9.99 (*0-8007-1622-1*) Revell.

Lee, Peter A., jt. ed. see Banatre, Michel.

Lee, Peter H. Celebration of Continuity: Themes in Classic East Asian Poetry. LC 78-26145. 276p. reprint ed. pap. 78.70 (*0-7837-1520-X*, 2041797) Bks Demand.

— Korean Literature: Topics & Themes. LC 64-19167. (Association for Asian Studies, Monographs & Papers: No. 16). 151p. reprint ed. pap. 43.10 (*0-317-10017-3*, 2003443) Bks Demand.

— Songs of Flying Dragons. LC 73-92866. (Harvard-Yenching Institute Monograph: No. 22). 352p. 1975. 22.50 (*0-674-82075-4*) HUP.

Lee, Peter H., ed. Anthology of Korean Literature: From Early Times to the Nineteenth Century. LC 81-69567. 342p. 1981. pap. text ed. 12.95 (*0-8248-0756-1*) UH Pr.

— Modern Korean Literature: An Anthology. LC 90-41824. 464p. 1990. text ed. 40.00 (*0-8248-1255-7*); pap. text ed. 18.95 (*0-8248-1321-9*) UH Pr.

— Pine River & Lone Peak: An Anthology of Three Choson Dynasty Poets. LC 90-44433. 208p. 1991. text ed. 24.00 (*0-8248-1298-0*) UH Pr.

— The Silence of Love: Twentieth-Century Korean Poetry. LC 80-21999. 367p. 1980. pap. 8.95 (*0-8248-0732-4*) UH Pr.

Lee, Peter H., tr. see Kakhun.

Lee, Peter H., tr. see P'aegwan Chapki of O Sukkwon Staff.

Lee, Peter H., et al, eds. Sources of Korean Tradition. (Introduction to Asian Civilizations Ser.: Vol. I). 640p. 1993. text ed. 49.50 (*0-231-07912-5*) Col U Pr.

Lee, Peter K., ed. Confucian-Christian Encounters in Historical & Contemporary Perspective. LC 91-40387. (Religions in Dialogue Ser.: Vol. 5). 500p. 1992. lib. bdg. 109.95 (*0-88946-521-5*) E Mellen.

Lee, Peter L. Nonlinear Process Control: Applications of Generic Model Control. LC 93-21311. (Advances in Industrial Control Ser.). 1993. 59.00 (*0-387-19856-3*) Spr-Verlag.

Lee, Peter M. Bayesian Statistics: An Introduction. 294p. 1992. pap. text ed. 34.95 (*0-470-21961-0*) Halsted Pr.

Lee, Peter W. & Corbonars, Robert S., eds. Rapidly Solidified Materials: Proceedings of an International Conference, San Diego, CA, U. S. A., 3-5 February 1985 i.e. 1986. LC 85-73692. (Illus.). 446p. reprint ed. pap. 127.20 (*0-318-39722-6*, 2033078) Bks Demand.

Lee, Phil & Raban, Colin. Welfare Theory & Social Policy: Reform or Revolution? 224p. (C). 1988. text ed. 45.00 (*0-8039-8130-9*); pap. text ed. 22.00 (*0-8039-8131-7*) Sage.

Lee, Phil, jt. auth. see Jepson, Tim.

Lee, Phil, jt. ed. see Langan, Mary.

Lee, Philip. Public Procurement. 1991. pap. 170.00 (*0-406-04557-7*, U.K.) Butterworth Legal Pubs.

Lee, Philip J. Against the Protestant Gnostics. 368p. 1993. reprint ed. pap. 19.95 (*0-19-508436-5*) OUP.

Lee, Philip R. & Estes, Carroll L. The Nation's Health. 3rd ed. 576p. 1990. pap. 37.50 (*0-86720-428-1*) Jones & Bartlett.

Lee, Philip R. & Estes, Carroll L., eds. The Nation's Health. 4th ed. LC 93-41200. 416p. 1994. pap. 40.00 (*0-86720-840-6*) Jones & Bartlett.

Lee, Philip R., jt. auth. see Lipton, Helene L.

Lee, Phyllis C., jt. ed. see Else, James G.

Lee, Ping, jt. auth. see Robinson, Allan R.

Lee, Ping I. & Good, William R. Controlled-Release Technology: Pharmaceutical Applications. LC 87-17447. (ACS Symposium Ser.: No. 348). (Illus.). 376p. 1987. 76.95 (*0-8412-1413-1*) Am Chemical.

Lee, Pong K. & Ryu, Chi S. Let's Talk in Korean. LC 78-72953. 312p. 1982. pap. 12.50 (*0-930878-10-8*) Hollym Intl.

Lee, Pong K. & Ryu, Chi Sik. Easy Way to Korean Conversation. 3rd rev. ed. (Illus.). 78p. 1984. audio, pap. 18.50x (*0-930878-17-5*) Hollym Intl.

Lee, Pongsoon & Um, Young A. Libraries & Librarianship in Korea. LC 93-47094. (Guides to Asian Librarianship Ser.). 192p. 1994. text ed. 55.00 (*0-313-28743-0*, Greenwood Pr) Greenwood.

Lee-Potter, Charlie, jt. auth. see Probert, Christina.

Lee, Preston. Research in Corporate Social Performance & Policy, Vol. 6. 73.25 (*0-89232-499-6*) Jai Pr.

***Lee, Quarterman.** Facility & Workplace Design. (Engineers in Business Ser.: Vol. 3). (Illus.). Date not set. pap. text ed. 25.00 (*0-89806-147-4*) Ind Eng Mgmt Pr.

Lee, Quarterman, jt. ed. see Wrenall, William.

Lee, R. SWOT Constitutional & Administrative Law. (C). 1991. 59.00 (*1-85431-155-7*, Pub. by Blackstone Pr UK) W W Gaunt.

— Victory at Guadalcanal. Date not set. 7.98 (*0-89141-105-4*) Presidio Pr.

Lee, R., jt. auth. see Almenas, K.

Lee, R. Alton. Eisenhower & Landrum-Griffin: A Study in Labor-Management Politics. LC 89-35961. 216p. 1990. text ed. 24.00 (*0-8131-1683-X*) U Pr of Ky.

— Truman & Taft-Hartley: A Question of Mandate. LC 80-17251. viii, 254p. 1980. reprint ed. text ed. 45.00 (*0-313-22618-0*, LETT, Greenwood Pr) Greenwood.

Lee, R. Alton, jt. auth. see Lawrence, P. A.

Lee, R. C., jt. ed. see Hsu, W. L.

Lee, R. C., et al, eds. Electrical Trauma: The Pathophysiology, Manifestations, & Clinical Management. (Illus.). 380p. (C). 1992. 125.00 (*0-521-38345-5*) Cambridge U Pr.

Lee, R. E. Extending Science, No. 16: The Chemical Industry. 96p. (C). 1989. 30.00 (*0-85950-821-8*, Pub. by S Thornes Pubs UK) St Mut.

— Extending Science, No. 9: Nuclear Power. 90p. (C). 1986. 50.00 (*0-85950-554-5*, Pub. by S Thornes Pubs UK) St Mut.

Lee, R. E., ed. Extending Science, No. 6: Land & Soil. 72p. (C). 1985. 39.00 (*0-85950-189-2*, Pub. by S Thornes Pubs UK) St Mut.

Lee, R. E., jt. auth. see Ramsden, E. N.

Lee, R. G. Community & Forestry. 315p. 1990. 98.00 (*81-7089-430-1*, Pub. by Intl Bk Distr II) St Mut.

— Community & Forestry. 315p. (C). 1990. 295.00 (*0-685-61468-9*, Pub. by Intl Bk Distr II); text ed. 300.00 (*81-7089-130-2*, Pub. by Intl Bk Distr II) St Mut.

— An Introduction to Battlefield Weapons Systems & Technology. (Illus.). 160p. 1981. text ed. 29.50 (*0-08-027043-3*, Pergamon Pr); pap. text ed. 15.00 (*0-08-027044-1*, Pergamon Pr) Elsevier.

— Introduction to Battlefield Weapons Systems & Technology. (Battlefield Weapons Systems & Technology Ser.: No. 12). (Illus.). 276p. 1985. 28.00 (*0-08-031199-7*, Pergamon Pr); pap. text ed. 24.00 (*0-08-031198-9*, Pergamon Pr) Elsevier.

Lee, R. G., ed. Battlefield Weapons Systems & Technology Series, 12 vols., Set. 2540p. 1985. text ed. 350.00 (*0-08-030003-0*, Pergamon Pr); pap. text ed. 187.00 (*0-08-030526-1*, Pergamon Pr) Elsevier.

— Defence Terminology. 200p. 1991. 39.00 (*0-08-041320-X*, Pub. by Brasseys UK); pap. 18.00 (*0-08-041334-X*, Pub. by Brasseys UK) Brasseys Inc.

— Guided Weapons. (Battlefield Weapons Systems & Technology Ser.: Vol. 1). 200p. 1988. 40.00 (*0-08-035828-4*, Pub. by Brasseys UK); 25.00 (*0-08-035827-6*, Pub. by Brasseys UK) Brasseys Inc.

Lee, R. G., ed. see Bailey, A. & Murray, S. G.

Lee, R. G., ed. see Courtney-Green, P. R.

Lee, R. G., ed. see Everett-Heath, E. J., et al.

Lee, R. G., ed. see Hall, P. S., et al.

Lee, R. G., ed. see International Workshop on Nitric Acid-Based Fertilizers & the Environment Staff.

Lee, R. G., ed. see Rice, M. A. & Sammes, A. J.

Lee, R. M. & McCosh, A. M., eds. Organizational Decision Support Systems: Proceeding of the IFIP WG8.2 Working Conference Lake Como, Italy, 20-22. 334p. 1988. 82.00 (*0-444-70444-2*, North Holland) Elsevier.

Lee, R. R. Pocket Guide to Electrical Equipment & Instrumentation. 2nd ed. (Illus.). 340p. (Orig.). 1991. pap. 26.00 (*0-87201-234-4*) Gulf Pub.

— Pocket Guide to Flanges, Fittings, & Piping Data. 2nd ed. (Illus.). 176p. (Orig.). 1992. pap. 24.00 (*0-88415-023-2*, 5023) Gulf Pub.

Lee, R. S., et al, eds. Aerothermodynamics in Combustors: IUTAM Symposium, Taipei, Taiwan, 1991. LC 92-13620. (International Union of Theoretical & Applied Mechanics Symposia Ser.). ix, 353p. 1992. 125.00 (*0-387-55404-1*) Spr-Verlag.

Lee, R. W., ed. see Macdonell, John.

Lee, R. Wayne. Federal Prisons: Fact & Fiction. 1987. pap. text ed. 34.95 (*0-685-20105-8*) Cambridge Law.

— Federal Prisons: Fact & Fiction, 1987. LC 87-90764. 219p. (Orig.). (C). 1987. pap. text ed. 34.95 (*0-685-54307-2*, Chicago Law Bk) Cambridge Law.

***Lee, Rachel.** Cowboy Cop. (Montana Mavericks Ser.). 1995. pap. 3.99 (*0-373-50176-5*, 1-50176-6) Harlequin Bks.

— Ironheart. (Silhouette Intimate Moments Ser.). 1993. mass mkt. 3.39 (*0-373-07494-8*, 5-07494-3) Silhouette.

— Lost Warriors: American Hero, Conard County. (Silhouette Intimate Moments Ser.). 1993. mass mkt. 3.50 (*0-373-07535-9*, 5-07535-3) Silhouette.

— Miss Emmaline & the Archangel. (Silhouette Intimate Moments Ser.). 1993. mass mkt. 3.39 (*0-373-07482-4*, 5-07482-8) Silhouette.

— Point of No Return. 1994. 3.50 (*0-373-07566-9*) Silhouette.

— A Question of Justice. (Intimate Moments Ser.). 1995. pap. 3.50 (*0-373-07613-4*, 1-07613-2) Silhouette.

Lee, Ralph E. Nine Ways to Buy a House. 100p. (Orig.). 1981. pap. 6.95 (*0-9606268-0-8*) ProPress Pub.

Lee, Rance P., ed. Corruption & Its Control in Hong Kong. viii, 221p. 1981. text ed. 34.50x (*962-201-251-5*, Pub. by Chinese Univ HK) Coronet Bks.

Lee, Randall B., ed. Model Railroading's Guide to Modeling & Detailing Diesels, Vol. I. (Illus.). 88p. 1991. pap. 9.95 (*0-9612692-4-3*) Rocky Mntn Pub Co.

— Model Railroading's Guide to Modeling & Detailing Diesels, Vol. II. (Illus.). 128p. 1993. pap. 14.95 (*0-9612692-7-8*) Rocky Mntn Pub Co.

Lee, Randall B., ed. see Nall, Bruce N.

Lee, Raphael C., et al, eds. Electrical Injury: A Multidisciplinary Approach to Therapy, Prevention, & Rehabilitation. LC 94-9282. (Annals Ser.: Vol. 720). 1994. write for info. (*0-89766-864-2*); pap. 95.00 (*0-89766-865-0*) NY Acad Sci.

Lee, Rawdon. Modern Dogs: Sporting Division, Hound Breeds & the Great Dane. 1991. lib. bdg. 88.00 (*0-8490-5216-5*) Gordon Pr.

Lee, Raymond A. Atlas of Gynecologic Surgery. (Illus.). 367p. 1992. text ed. 88.50 (*0-7216-3358-7*) Saunders.

Lee, Raymond L. & Palmer, Dorothy A. Government by the People: Basic. 12th ed. 160p. (C). 1985. pap. text ed. write for info. (*0-13-361395-X*) P-H.

— Guide to Government by the People: National. 12th ed. 208p. (C). 1984. student ed 8.95 (*0-685-08771-9*) P-H.

Lee, Raymond L., jt. auth. see Ackerman, Susan E.

Lee, Raymond L., jt. auth. see Krislov, Samuel.

An Asterisk (*) at the beginning of an entry indicates that the title is appearing in BIP for the first time.

***Lee, Raymond M.** Dangerous Fieldwork. (Qualitative Research Methods Ser.: Vol. 34). 96p. 1994. 21.50 (*0-8039-5660-6*); pap. 9.50 (*0-8039-5661-4*) Sage.

— Doing Research on Sensitive Topics. (Illus.). 240p. 1993. 55.00 (*0-8039-8860-5*); pap. 18.95 (*0-8039-8861-3*) Sage.

— Mixed & Matched: Interreligious Courtship & Marriage in Northern Ireland. (Class, Ethnicity, Gender, & the Democratic Nation Ser.: Vol. 2). 154p. (C). 1992. lib. bdg. 31.50 (*0-8191-8480-2*) U Pr of Amer.

***Lee, Raymond M., ed.** Information Technology for the Social Scientist. LC 94-39456. (Social Research Today Ser.: Vol. 7). 1995. 65.00 (*1-85728-280-9*, Pub. by UCL Pr UK); pap. text ed. 27.50 (*1-85728-281-7*, Pub. by UCL Pr UK) Taylor & Francis.

— Redundancy, Layoffs & Plant Closures: Their Nature & Social Impact. 352p. 1986. 59.95 (*0-7099-4129-3*, Pub. by Croom Helm UK) Routledge Chapman & Hall.

Lee, Raymond M., jt. ed. see Fielding, Nigel G.

Lee, Raymond M., jt. auth. see Renzetti, Claire M.

Lee, Rebecca, jt. auth. see Benbury, Karen.

Lee, Rebecca H. Golden Chances. (Homespun Ser.). 352p. (Orig.). 1992. mass mkt. 4.99 (*1-55773-750-9*) Diamond.

— Harvest Moon. 336p. (Orig.). 1993. mass mkt. 4.99 (*1-55773-914-5*) Diamond.

— Something Borrowed. 288p. (Orig.). 1995. pap. 4.99 (*0-7865-0073-5*) Diamond.

— Taking Chances. (Town Called Harmony Ser.). 288p. (Orig.). 1994. pap. 4.99 (*0-7865-0022-0*) Diamond.

Lee, Rebecca H., et al. A Homespun Mother's Day. 336p. (Orig.). 1994. mass mkt. 4.99 (*0-7865-0008-5*) Diamond.

Lee, Rebecca S. Mary Austin Holley: A Biography. (Elma Dill Russell Spencer Foundation Ser.: No. 2). (Illus.). 480p. 1987. reprint ed. pap. 14.95 (*0-292-75098-6*) U of Tex Pr.

Lee, Regina. Burial-Cremation Consumer Guide: A Self-Help Reference Guide for Learning How to Reduce the Cost of Dying. LC 92-74963. (Illus.). (Orig.). 1993. pap. text ed. 21.95 (*0-9634812-7-4*) Funeral Store.

Lee, Reiko T., jt. ed. see Lee, Y. C.

Lee, Rensselaer W. Names on Trees: Ariosto into Art. (Essays on the Arts Ser.). 1976. 35.00 (*0-691-03914-3*) Princeton U Pr.

— The White Labyrinth: Cocaine & Political Power. 256p. 1989. 32.95 (*0-88738-285-1*) Transaction Pubs.

Lee, Rensselaer W., III. The White Labyrinth: Cocaine & Political Power. 262p. (C). 1991. pap. text ed. 19.95 (*1-56000-565-3*) Transaction Pubs.

Lee, Reuben, et al. Electronic Transformers & Circuits. 3rd ed. LC 87-34062. 480p. 1988. text ed. 110.00 (*0-471-81976-X*) Wiley.

Lee, Rex E. The Case for Federalism: Grace A. Tanner Lecture in Human Values. 1985. 8.00 (*0-685-60165-X*) E T Woolf.

— What Do Mormons Believe? LC 92-36087. vii, 118p. 1992. 9.95 (*0-87579-639-7*) Deseret Bk.

Lee, Ricardo. Salome: Filmscript by Ricardo Lee. Brion, Rofel, tr. LC 92-72850. (Illus.). (Orig.). (C). 1992. lib. bdg. 27.95 (*1-881261-31-X*); pap. text ed. 8.95 (*1-881261-32-8*) U Wisc Ctr SE Asian.

Lee, Richard. Forest Hydrology. LC 79-19542. 349p. 1980. text ed. 56.50 (*0-231-04718-5*) Col U Pr.

— Forest Microclimatology. LC 77-21961. (Illus.). 276p. 1978. text ed. 54.00 (*0-231-04156-X*) Col U Pr.

— There's Hope for the Hurting. LC 94-15731. 1994. pap. 8.99 (*1-56507-164-6*) Harvest Hse.

— You Can Tell Your Kid Will Grow up to Be a Librarian When: Cartoons about the Profession. LC 92-50309. 128p. 1992. pap. 20.95x (*0-89950-743-3*) McFarland & Co.

Lee, Richard & Hindson, Ed. Angels of Deceit: The Dangerous Deception of False Religions. 1993. 8.99 (*1-56507-163-8*) Harvest Hse.

— No Greater Savior. LC 94-29308. 1995. 16.99 (*1-56507-265-0*) Harvest Hse.

Lee, Richard, jt. auth. see Lee, Mary P.

Lee, Richard, ed. see Rubin, Rhea J. & Suvak, Daniel.

Lee, Richard B. The Dobe Ju-'hoansi. (Case Studies in Cultural Anthropology). (Illus.). 224p. (C). Date not set. pap. text ed. write for info. (*0-03-032284-7*) HB Coll Pubs.

— The Dobe! Kung. LC 83-12916. (Case Studies in Cultural Anthropology). 173p. (C). 1984. pap. text ed. 13.50 (*0-03-063803-8*) HB Coll Pubs.

— The Kung San: Men, Women, & Work in a Foraging Society. (Illus.). 550p. (C). 1979. pap. 24.95 (*0-521-29561-0*) Cambridge U Pr.

Lee, Richard B. & DeVore, Irven, eds. Kalahari Hunter-Gatherers: Studies of the Kung San & Their Neighbors. 390p. 1976. pap. 17.50 (*0-674-49985-9*) HUP.

— Man the Hunter. LC 67-17603. 431p. 1968. pap. 29.95 (*0-202-33032-X*) Aldine de Gruyter.

Lee, Richard B., jt. ed. see Leacock, Eleanor B.

Lee, Richard C., jt. auth. see Chang, Chin-Liang.

Lee, Richard E., Jr. & Denlinger, David L., eds. Insects at Low Temperatures. (Illus.). 600p. 1990. 99.50 (*0-412-02801-8*, A4787, Chap & Hall NY) Chapman & Hall.

***Lee, Richard E., Jr., et al, eds.** Biological Ice Nucleation & Its Applications. LC 95-75812. (Illus.). ix, 370p. 1995. 75.00 (*0-89054-172-8*) Am Phytopathol Soc.

Lee, Richard H. Life of Arthur Lee, 2 vols., Set. LC 69-18528. (Select Bibliographies Reprint Ser.). 1977. 54.95 (*0-8369-5010-0*) Ayer.

Lee, Richard M. General Lee's City: An Illustrated Guide to the Historic Sites of Confederate Richmond. LC 87-643. (Illus.). 184p. (Orig.). 1987. pap. 16.95 (*0-914440-99-3*) EPM Pubns.

— Mr. Lincoln's City: An Illustrated Guide to the Civil War Sites of Washington. LC 81-3267. 176p. 1981. pap. 17. 95 (*0-914440-48-9*) EPM Pubns.

Lee, Richard S. A Birder's Guide to the Atlin Valley. (Illus.). 120p. (Orig.). 1989. pap. text ed. 14.95 (*0-317-93502-X*) Moose Mtn Pubns.

Lee, Richard S. & Lee, Mary P. Caffeine & Nicotine. LC 94-2279. (Drug Abuse Prevention Library). (J). (gr. 7 up). 1994. 15.95 (*0-8239-1701-0*) Rosen Group.

— Careers for Women in Politics. Rosen, Ruth, ed. (YA). (gr. 7-12). 1989. lib. bdg. 14.95 (*0-8239-0966-2*) Rosen Group.

— Drugs & the Media. LC 93-21099. (Drug Abuse Prevention Library). (J). 1994. 15.95 (*0-8239-1537-9*) Rosen Group.

— Everything You Need to Know about Natural Disasters & Post-Traumatic Stress Disorder. LC 95-13665. (Need to Know Library). (J). 1995. write for info. (*0-8239-2053-4*) Rosen Group.

Lee, Richard S., jt. auth. see Lee, Mary P.

Lee, Richard S., jt. auth. see Lee, Mary Price.

Lee, Richard T., et al. Overview of Cardiac Surgery for the Cardiologist. (Illus.). 190p. 1993. write for info. (*3-540-94066-9*) Spr-Verlag.

Lee, Richard T., et al, eds. Overview of Cardiac Surgery for the Cardiologist. LC 93-3832. 1993. 59.00 (*0-387-94066-9*) Spr-Verlag.

Lee, Robert. China Journal: Glimpses of a Nation in Transition. LC 80-52783. (Illus.). (Orig.). 1980. 9.25 (*0-934788-00-6*); pap. 5.25 (*0-686-96708-9*) E-W Pub Co.

— Fort Meade & the Black Hills. LC 91-4362. (Illus.). xii, 321p. 1991. 40.00 (*0-8032-2896-1*) U of Nebr Pr.

— Getting Ahead: Taking Charge of Your Finances. JAD Staff, ed. (Illus.). 65p. (C). 1989. 6.95 (*0-685-30076-5*, HC3291) JAD Enterprises.

— Guide to Chinese American Philanthropy & Charitable Giving Patterns. 165p. (Orig.). 1990. pap. 25.00 (*0-9627474-0-8*) Pathway CA.

— How to Fail: The One Minute Success Tape for People Who Fail. JAD Staff, ed. 120p. (C). 1989. 6.95 (*0-685-30077-3*) JAD Enterprises.

— Keep It in Your Pocket: The Car Buyers Strategy. JAD Staff, ed. 1989. audio 8.95 (*0-685-30075-7*, CB3675) JAD Enterprises.

— Outline Studies in Acts. LC 87-3083. 128p. (Orig.). 1987. reprint ed. pap. 4.99 (*0-8254-3141-7*) Kregel.

— Outline Studies in Galatians. LC 87-3096. 128p. (Orig.). 1987. reprint ed. pap. 4.99 (*0-8254-3143-3*) Kregel.

— Outline Studies in John. LC 87-3623. 144p. (Orig.). 1987. reprint ed. pap. 4.99 (*0-8254-3140-9*) Kregel.

— Outline Studies in Romans. LC 87-3094. 128p. (Orig.). 1987. reprint ed. pap. 4.99 (*0-8254-3142-5*) Kregel.

— Persistent Seraching for the True Light: Life & Spiritual Journal of a Taiwanese Immigrant. 103p. 1993. pap. write for info. (*0-9631789-4-6*) Evan Formosan.

— SWOT Constitutional & Administrative Law. 204p. (C). 1990. 80.00 (*1-85431-030-5*, Pub. by Blackstone Pr UK) St Mut.

— Turner Journals. 1994. 19.95 (*0-8027-3234-8*) Walker & Co.

— The Turner Journals. 1996. write for info. (*0-8027-3260-7*) Walker & Co.

Lee, Robert, ed. Landlord & Tenant. (C). 1991. text ed. 22. 00 (*1-85431-137-9*, Pub. by Blackstone Pr UK) W W Gaunt.

Lee, Robert & Misiorowski, Robert. Script Models: A Handbook for the Media Writer. 1978. pap. 10.00 (*0-8038-6754-9*) Hastings.

Lee, Robert & Morgan, Derek, eds. Birthrights: Law & the Beginnings of Life. 236p. 1990. pap. 17.50 (*0-415-01065-9*, A4683) Routledge.

— Death Rites: Law & Ethics at the End of Life. LC 93-6982. (Illus.). 352p. 1993. 59.95 (*0-415-06260-8*, B2279, Routledge NY) Routledge.

Lee, Robert, jt. auth. see Katz, Donald.

Lee, Robert A. Alistair MacLean: The Key Is Fear. LC 76-29047. (Milford Series: Popular Writers of Today: Vol. 2). 60p. 1976. lib. bdg. 20.00 (*0-89370-103-3*); pap. 10. 00 (*0-89370-203-X*) Borgo Pr.

— First Impressions: Presenting an Inviting Church Facility. Miller, Herb, ed. LC 93-12891. (Effective Church Ser.). 144p. (Orig.). 1993. pap. 11.95 (*0-687-07855-5*) Abingdon.

Lee, Robert C. Summer of the Green Star. LC 80-27427. (Junior Literary Guild Selection Ser.). 128p. (J). (gr. 5-9). 1981. 11.00 (*0-664-32681-1*, Westminster) Westminster John Knox.

Lee, Robert D. Keeper. 224p. 1993. mass mkt. 4.50 (*1-55817-722-1*, Pinnacle NY) Windsor NY.

Lee, Robert D., Jr. Public Personnel Systems. 3rd ed. 450p. 1993. 52.00 (*0-8342-0392-8*, 20392) Aspen Pub.

Lee, Robert D. & Johnson, Ronald W. Public Budgeting Systems. 5th ed. LC 94-9164. 1994. 49.00 (*0-8342-0601-3*) Aspen Pub.

Lee, Robert E. AIDS in America: Our Chances, Our Choices (A Survival Guide for the Individual & Society) LC 87-51105. 200p. 1987. 18.50 (*0-87875-355-9*); pap. 9.95 (*0-87875-357-5*) Whitston Pub.

— Blackbeard the Pirate: A Reappraisal of His Life & Times. LC 74-75752. 264p. 1984. pap. 8.95 (*0-89587-032-0*) Blair.

— Colonel Noah Lee of Salisbury, Conn. & Castleton, Vt. & His Descendants: A 1990 Supplement to the 1897 Edition of John Lee of Farmington, Conn., & His Descendants - Thomas Branch. (Illus.). 171p. (Orig.). 1990. per., pap. 20.00 (*0-9625530-0-X*) R E Lee.

— The Dialogues of Lewis & Clark: A Narrative Poem. LC 78-67631. (Illus.). 87p. reprint ed. pap. 25.00 (*0-8357-5504-5*, 2035119) Bks Demand.

— The Library Sponsored Discussion Group. LC 57-4833. 87p. reprint ed. pap. 25.00 (*0-317-26837-6*, 2024210) Bks Demand.

— North Carolina Family Law with 1991 Cumulative Supplements, 4 vols. 4th suppl. ed. 1991. 85.00 (*0-87473-865-2*) Michie Butterworth.

— Phycology. 2nd ed. (Illus.). (C). 1989. 79.95 (*0-521-36502-3*); pap. 37.95 (*0-521-36744-1*) Cambridge U Pr.

— The Recollections & Letters of Robert E. Lee. (Civil War Ser.). 471p. 1993. 12.95 (*0-914427-66-0*) W S Konecky Assocs.

— Scanning Electron Microscopy & X-Ray Microanalysis. 464p. 1992. text ed. 89.00 (*0-13-813759-5*) P-H.

— Victory at Guadalcanal. (World-at-War Ser.). 1983. pap. 3.50 (*0-8217-1198-9*) Zebra.

Lee, Robert E., ed. see Dennis, Patrick.

Lee, Robert E., jt. auth. see Lawrence, Jerome.

Lee, Robert E., et al. North Carolina Family Law with 1991 Cumulative Supplements, 4 vols., Set. 4th ed. 1987. 210. 00x (*0-87215-473-4*) Michie Butterworth.

Lee, Robert F. Conrad's Colonialism. LC 68-30868. (Studies in English Literature: No. 54). 1969. text ed. 52.35 (*3-11-000273-6*) Mouton.

***Lee, Robert G.** Broken Trust, Broken Land: Freeing Ourselves from the War over the Environment. 220p. (Orig.). 1994. pap. 14.95 (*1-885221-02-9*) BookPartners.

— Como Conducir un Alma a Cristo: How to Win a Soul to Christ. (SPA.). 2.95 (*84-7228-187-6*, 220162, Pub. by Edit Clie SP) TSELF.

Lee, Robert G., jt. ed. see Morgan, Derek.

Lee, Robert G., jt. auth. see Wallington, Peter.

Lee, Robert J. & Freedman, Arthur M., eds. Consultation Skills Readings. 148p. (Orig.). 1984. pap. 18.00 (*0-9610392-1-3*) NTL Inst.

Lee, Robert L. Fever Saga. (Illus.). 160p. (Orig.). 1985. pap. 6.95 (*0-9615377-0-1*) Heirloom Pr.

Lee, Robert M. Death & Deliverance: The True Story of an Airplane Crash at the North Pole. LC 92-54763. (Illus.). 288p. (Orig.). 1993. pap. 12.95 (*1-55591-140-4*) Fulcrum Pub.

Lee, Robert S. France & the Exploitation of China: A Study in Economic Imperialism, 1885-1901. (Illus.). 372p. 1990. 29.95 (*0-19-582708-2*) OUP.

Lee, Robyn. Directions: Quality Assurance Manual for Physician Office Laboratories. (C). 1991. 121.00 (*0-933948-39-5*, 2891) Ctr Res Ambulatory.

Lee, Roger D. Heavenly Hosts. 40p. (Orig.). 1991. pap. 4.59 (*0-685-48294-4*) Dayspring Pr.

— Love & Divorce. 33p. (Orig.). 1991. pap. 3.98 (*0-685-48295-2*) Dayspring Pr.

— Love Notes. 67p. (Orig.). 1991. pap. 7.64 (*0-685-48296-0*) Dayspring Pr.

Lee, Roger L. The Baton. LC 59-17691. (Illus.). 98p. 1949. pap. 4.25 (*0-913932-14-0*) Boosey & Hawkes.

Lee, Rohama, ed. Film News Index, 1939-1981. 749p. 1992. pap. text ed. 59.00 (*0-917846-10-9*, 95510) Highsmith Pr.

Lee, Roland, ed. Commercial Real Estate Loan Administration. 171p. (Orig.). 1993. pap. 60.00 (*0-945359-20-9*) Mortgage Bankers.

Lee, Ron R., ed. Marriage Ain't for Wimps: The Best Cartoons from Marriage Partnership. LC 93-39831. 1994. 8.99 (*0-310-40521-1*) Zondervan.

Lee, Ronald. Goddamn Gypsy. (Illus.). 248p. 1971. pap. 5.95 (*0-88776-159-3*) Tundra Bks.

Lee, Ronald & Lee, Karen K. Arguing Persuasively. 432p. (C). 1989. text ed. 32.25 (*0-582-28670-0*, 71686) Longman.

Lee, Ronald, jt. auth. see Hicks, Richard.

Lee, Ronald D. Econometric Studies of Topics in Demographic History. LC 77-14749. (Dissertations in American Economic History Ser.). 1978. 30.95 (*0-405-11045-6*) Ayer.

— Working with Sidekick. 150p. (Orig.). 1988. pap. 14.95 (*0-938862-82-0*) Weber Systems.

Lee, Ronald D., jt. ed. see Johnson, D. Gale.

Lee, Ronald D., et al. Economics of Changing Age Distributions in Developed Countries. (International Studies in Demography). (Illus.). 192p. 1995. reprint ed. pap. 17.95 (*0-19-828887-5*) OUP.

Lee, Ronald D., et al, eds. Population, Food & Rural Development. (International Studies in Demography). (Illus.). 224p. 1992. pap. 19.95 (*0-19-828391-1*) OUP.

Lee, Ronald R. & Martin, J. Colby. Psychotherapy after Kohut: A Textbook. 376p. 1991. 39.95 (*0-88163-129-9*) Analytic Pr.

Lee, Ronald S. & Lee, Patricia, eds. Stubs: London Edition of All the London (West End) & Select Regional Theatres, 1981 Edition. (Illus.). 1981. pap. 6.95 (*0-911458-03-4*) Stubs.

— Stubs: The Seating Plan Guide for New York Theaters, Music Halls & Sports Stadia, 1986 Edition. (Illus.). 1986. pap. 6.95 (*0-911458-06-9*, MNYE9) Stubs.

Lee, Ronny. Jazz Guitar Method, Vol. 1. 1993. 5.95 (*0-7866-0036-5*, 93240) Mel Bay.

— Jazz Guitar Method, Vol. 2. 1993. 5.95 (*0-685-64273-9*, 93241) Mel Bay.

— Learn to Sing Step by Step. 144p. (J). 1984. pap. 12.95 (*0-934401-00-4*) Sunrise Pub NY.

Lee, Rose H. The Growth & Decline of Chinese Communities in the Rocky Mountain Region. Daniels, Roger, ed. LC 78-54823. (Asian Experience in North America Ser.). (Illus.). 1979. lib. bdg. 25.95 (*0-405-11279-3*) Ayer.

Lee, Rowena. The Catalyst. large type ed. 1975. 15.95 (*0-85456-335-0*) Ulverscroft.

— The Rhino Stayed for Breakfast. large type ed. 1975. 15. 95 (*0-85456-371-7*) Ulverscroft.

Lee, Roy F. Setting for Black Business Development: A Study in Sociology & Political Economy. LC 72-619630. 272p. 1973. 1.00 (*0-87546-275-8*) ILR Pr.

Lee, Roy S., jt. ed. see Jasentuliyana, Nandasiri.

***Lee, Ruben.** What Is an Exchange? Automation & the Regulation of Trading Markets. 400p. 1995. 60.00 (*0-19-828840-9*) OUP.

Lee-Ruff, Edward, et al, eds. Strained Organic Molecules. 128p. (Orig.). 1991. pap. text ed. 35.00 (*1-56081-509-4*) VCH Pubs.

Lee, Russell. Coming Home. 1994. reprint ed. pap. 4.95 (*1-55673-448-4*, 7907) CSS OH.

Lee, Russell, et al. Far from Main Street: Three Photographers in Depression-Era New Mexico. (Illus.). 88p. (Orig.). 1994. pap. 27.50 (*0-89013-259-3*) Museum NM Pr.

Lee, Ruth. Double-Bed Machine Knitting: For All Double-Bed Machines or Single-Bed Machines with Ribber Attachment. (Illus.). 128p. 1994. pap. 34.95 (*0-7134-6817-3*, Pub. by Batsford UK) Trafalgar.

— Pattern on the Knitting Machine. (Illus.). 144p. 1993. pap. 29.95 (*0-7134-7230-8*, Pub. by Batsford UK) Trafalgar.

Lee, Ruth M. Orientation to Health Services. LC 77-15094. 1978. teacher ed write for info. (*0-672-61435-9*); pap. write for info. (*0-672-61434-0*) Macmillan.

Lee, Ruthie, ed. see Grennell, Jim, et al.

Lee, S. The Travels of Ibn Batuta. 264p. 1985. 210.00 (*1-85077-035-2*, Darf Pubs Ltd) St Mut.

Lee, S., jt. ed. see Cindrich, I. N.

Lee, S. E. Recollections of Country Joe. LC 75-31650. (Illus.). 104p. 1976. 10.95 (*0-88289-040-9*) Pelican.

Lee, S. F., jt. auth. see Lee, L.

Lee, S. H., jt. ed. see Cindrich, I. N.

Lee, S. Howard, et al. Cranial MRI & CT. 3rd ed. (Illus.). 880p. 1992. text ed. 169.00 (*0-07-037508-9*) Hlth Prof Div.

Lee, S. L., ed. Charlemagne Romances, Nos. 7 & 8, Pts. 1-2. Bourchier, John, tr. (EETS, ES Ser.: Nos. 40-41). 1972. reprint ed. 65.00 (*0-527-00249-6*) Periodicals Srv.

— Durability of Building Materials & Components: Proceedings of the International Conference, 4-6 November 1987, 2 vols., Set. 1048p. 1987. pap. 436.00 (*0-08-035914-0*, Pub. by Pergamon Repr UK) Franklin.

Lee, S. M., et al. Network Analysis for Management Decisions. (International Series in Management Science-Operations Research). 1981. lib. bdg. 49.50 (*0-89838-077-4*) Kluwer Ac.

Lee S. Sproull & Assoc. Staff, et al. Technology & Organizations. LC 89-26993. (Management Ser.). 303p. 1990. 31.95 (*1-55542-209-8*) Jossey-Bass.

Lee, S. W., jt. ed. see Lo, Y. T.

Lee, S. Y. & Jao, Y. C. Financial Structures & Monetary Policies in Southeast Asia. 1982. text ed. 39.95 (*0-312-28973-1*) St Martin.

Lee, Sally. Hurricanes. LC 92-27367. (First Bks.). (Illus.). 64p. (J). (gr. 5-8). 1993. lib. bdg. 13.98 (*0-531-20152-X*); pap. 5.95 (*0-531-15665-6*) Watts.

— Pesticides. LC 90-46839. (Impact Ser.). (Illus.). 144p. (YA). (gr. 7-12). 1991. lib. bdg. 14.98 (*0-531-13017-7*) Watts.

— San Antonio. LC 91-34303. (Downtown America Ser.). (Illus.). 60p. (J). (gr. 4 up). 1992. text ed. 13.95 (*0-87518-510-X*, Dillon Silver Burdett) Silver Burdett Pr.

Lee, Sam. The Perfect War. 2nd ed. Valentine, Margaret, ed. 186p. 1990. 15.95 (*0-9621667-1-5*) Chengalera Pr.

Lee, Samantha, ret. Dr. Jekyll & Mr. Hyde. (Fleshcreepers Ser.). 160p. (J). (gr. 6 up). 1988. pap. 2.95 (*0-8120-4072-4*) Barron.

Lee, Sander H., ed. Inquiries into Values: The Inaugural Session of the International Society for Value Inquiry. LC 91-40171. (Problems in Contemporary Philosophy Ser.: Vol. 11). 776p. 1991. reprint ed. lib. bdg. 139.95 (*0-88946-338-7*) E Mellen.

Lee, Sandra. Bald Eagles. (Nature Books Ser.). 32p. (J). (gr. 2-6). 1991. lib. bdg. 22.79 (*0-89565-706-6*) Childs World.

— Coyotes. (Nature Books Ser.). (J). (gr. 2-6). 1992. lib. bdg. 22.79 (*0-89565-843-7*) Childs World.

— Giant Pandas. LC 92-35066. (Naturebooks Ser.). (J). (gr. 2-6). 1993. lib. bdg. 22.79 (*1-56766-009-6*) Childs World.

— Koalas. LC 92-38807. (Naturebooks Ser.). 32p. (J). (gr. 2-6). 1993. lib. bdg. 22.79 (*1-56766-013-4*) Childs World.

— Lions. (Nature Books Ser.). 32p. (J). 1991. 22.79 (*0-89565-707-4*) Childs World.

— Rattlesnakes. (Nature Books Ser.). (J). (gr. 2-6). 1992. lib. bdg. 22.79 (*0-89565-842-9*) Childs World.

Lee Sands, Audrey. Soltera y Satisfecha: Single & Satisfied. (SPA.). 4.25 (*84-7228-340-2*, 220849, Pub. by Edit Clie SP) TSELF.

***Lee, Sang-Bok.** A Comparative Study Between Minjung Theology & Reformed Theology from a Missiological Perspective. (Asian Thought & Culture Ser.: Vol. 22). 1995. write for info. (*0-8204-2702-0*) P Lang Pubs.

Lee, Sang H. The End of Communism. 459p. (C). 1985. 25. 00 (*0-9606480-1-1*); pap. text ed. 18.00 (*0-9606480-2-X*) Unificat Thght.

— Explaining Unification Thought. 357p. (Orig.). (C). 1981. pap. text ed. 15.00 (*0-9606480-0-3*) Unificat Thght.

Lee, Sang M. Introduction to Management Science. 2nd ed. (Illus.). 802p. (C). 1988. pap. text ed. 19.00 (*0-03-008894-1*) Dryden Pr.

— Japanese Management: Cultural & Environmental. Schwendiman, Gary, ed. LC 82-106116. 318p. 1982. text ed. 65.00 (*0-275-91709-6*, C1709, Praeger Pubs) Greenwood.

— Management by Japanese Systems. Schwendiman, Gary, ed. LC 82-7612. 576p. 1982. text ed. 105.00 (*0-275-91710-X*, C1710, Praeger Pubs) Greenwood.

Lee, Sang M. & Shim, Jung P. Micro Management Science: Microcomputer Applications of Management Science. 2nd ed. 500p. 1990. text ed. 74.00 (*0-205-12260-4*, H22601) Allyn.

L

Lee, Sang M. & Van Horn, James C. Academic Administration: Planning, Budgeting, & Decision Making with Multiple Objectives. LC 81-24061. (Illus.). 266p. reprint ed. pap. 75.90 (0-8357-4102-8, 2036868) Bks Demand.

Lee, Sang M., ed. see Thorp, Cary.

Lee, Sang M., et al. Management Science. 3rd ed. 900p. 1989. text ed. 59.00 (0-205-12145-4, H21454); write for info. (0-318-66337-6, H21462); write for info. (0-318-66338-4, H21470) Allyn.

***Lee, Sara, et al, eds.** A Congregation of Learners: Transforming the Synagogue into a Learning Community. 1995. pap. text ed. 12.95 (0-8074-0538-8, 243873) UAHC.

Lee, Sarah H., jt. auth. see Velvel, Lawrence R.

Lee, Scout. The Excellence Principle. rev. ed. (Skill Builder Ser.). (Illus.). 272p. 1989. pap. 16.95 (1-55552-003-0) Metamorphous Pr.

Lee, Scout & Summers, Jan. Basic Terminology for Therapeutic Recreation & Other Action Therapies. 1990. pap. text ed. 6.80 (0-87563-350-1) Stipes.

Lee, Scout, et al. Challenge of Excellence: Learning the Ropes of Change. rev. ed. (Skill Builder Ser.). (Illus.). 192p. 1990. pap. 16.95 (1-55552-004-9) Metamorphous Pr.

***Lee, Scout C.** Circle Is Sacred: A Medicine Book for Women. LC 94-37045. 272p. (Orig.). 1994. pap. 17.95 (0-933031-97-1) Coun Oak Bks.

Lee Sesquicentennial Committee Staff. Lee County, Arkansas. (Illus.). 384p. 1987. 55.00 (0-88107-101-3) Curtis Media.

Lee, Seung-Chong, jt. auth. see Garver, Newton.

***Lee, Sharice A.** The Survivor's Guide: A Guide for Teenage Girls Who Are Survivors of Sexual Abuse. LC 94-45028. 1995. 25.00 (0-8039-5780-7); pap. text ed. 12.95 (0-8039-5781-5) Sage.

Lee, Sharon. Glory Time for the Family Advent: Christmas Devotions & Activities. 96p. 1987. pap. 7.95 (0-570-03995-9, 12-3023) Concordia.
— Jack & the Beanstalk. (Mini-Storybooks Ser.). (Illus.). 24p. (Orig.). (J). (ps-00). 1993. pap. 1.50 (0-679-84794-4) Random Bks Yng Read.

Lee, Sharon, jt. auth. see Stopsky, Fred.

Lee, Shelley A., jt. auth. see Anderson, Lester W.

***Lee, Sherman & Cunningham, Michael R.** One Thousand Years of Japanese Art (650-1650) (Illus.). 86p. 1995. pap. 20.00 (0-913304-12-3, 123X) Japan Soc.

Lee, Sherman E. Asian Art: Selections from the Collection of Mr. & Mrs. John D. Rockefeller, 3rd. (Illus.). 1970. pap. text ed. 35.00 (0-89192-278-4); 25.00 (0-685-02525-X) Interbk Inc.
— The Colors of Ink: Chinese Paintings & Related Ceramics from the Cleveland Museum of Art. LC 74-27415. (Asia Society Ser.). (Illus.). 1976. reprint ed. lib. bdg. 33.95 (0-405-06564-7) Ayer.
— The Genius of Japanese Design. LC 79-66246. (Illus.). 1981. 70.00 (0-87011-395-X) Kodansha.
— A History of Far Eastern Art. 5th ed. Richard, Naomi N., ed. LC 93-7267. 1993. text ed. 60.95 (0-13-393398-9) P-H.
— History of Far Eastern Art. 5th ed. 1994. 60.00 (0-8109-3414-0) Abrams.
— The Sketchbooks of Hiroshige, 2 vols. LC 84-14590. (Illus.). 200p. 1984. boxed 60.00 (0-8076-1105-0) Braziller.
— Tea Taste in Japanese Art. LC 74-27416. (Asia Society Ser.). (Illus.). 1976. reprint ed. lib. bdg. 31.95 (0-405-06565-5) Ayer.

Lee, Sherman E., ed. On Understanding Art Museums. 1975. pap. 2.95 (0-13-936278-9) Am Assembly.

Lee, Sherman E. & Ho, Wai-Kam. Chinese Art under the Mongols: The Yuan Dynasty 1279-1368. LC 68-9276. (Illus.). 415p. reprint ed. pap. 118.30 (0-317-10189-7, 2005108) Bks Demand.

Lee, Sherman E. & Indiana University Press. Reflections of Reality in Japanese Art. LC 82-45940. (Illus.). 304p. 1983. 35.00 (0-910386-70-6) Cleveland Mus Art.

Lee, Sherman E., jt. auth. see Rogers, Howard.

Lee, Sherman E., et al, eds. Eight Dynasties of Chinese Painting: The Collections of the Nelson Gallery-Atkins Museum, Kansas City, & The Cleveland Museum of Art. LC 80-66110. (Illus.). 472p. 1981. 30.00 (0-910386-53-6) Cleveland Mus Art.

Lee, Sidney. Elizabethan & Other Essays. Boas, Frederick S., ed. LC 68-22108. (Essay Index Reprint Ser.). 1977. 23.95 (0-8369-0614-4) Ayer.
— Elizabethan & Other Essays. Boas, F. S., ed. LC 78-133811. reprint ed. 29.50 (0-404-03928-6) AMS Pr.
— The French Renaissance in England: An Account of the Literary Relations of England & France in the Sixteenth Century. (BCL1-PR English Literature Ser.). 494p. 1992. reprint ed. lib. bdg. 99.00 (0-7812-7025-1) Rprt Serv.
— Great Englishmen of the Sixteenth Century. LC 77-128269. (Essay Index Reprint Ser.). 1977. 23.95 (0-8369-1885-1) Ayer.
— Life of William Shakespeare. LC 70-145137. (Illus.). 1971. reprint ed. 59.00 (0-403-01069-1) Scholarly.
— A Life of William Shakespeare. (BCL1-PR English Literature Ser.). 476p. 1992. reprint ed. lib. bdg. 99.00 (0-7812-7282-3) Rprt Serv.
— Shakespeare & the Modern Stage. LC 74-172042. reprint ed. 29.50 (0-404-03929-4) AMS Pr.
— Stratford-On-Avon from the Earliest Times to the Death of Shakespeare. LC 71-109654. (Select Bibliographies Reprint Ser.). 1977. 26.95 (0-8369-5263-4) Ayer.
— Stratford-on-Avon from the Earliest Times to the Death of Shakespeare. (BCL1-PR English Literature Ser.). 327p. 1992. reprint ed. lib. bdg. 89.00 (0-7812-7286-6) Rprt Serv.

Lee, Sidney, ed. see Smith, George.

Lee, Simon. Law & Morals: Warnock, Gillick, & Beyond. 1986. pap. 15.95 (0-19-283052-X) OUP.
— Tennis. rev. ed. (Play the Game Ser.). (Illus.). 80p. 1994. pap. 7.95 (0-7137-2413-7, Pub. by Blandford Pr UK) Sterling.

Lee, Simon, ed. French Short Stories Two. 256p. 1993. pap. 8.00 (0-14-003414-5, Penguin Bks) Viking Penguin.

Lee, Simon & Fox, Marie. Learning Legal Skills. 224p. (C). 1991. text ed. 24.00 (1-85431-112-3, Pub. by Blackstone Pr UK) W W Gaunt.
— Learning Legal Skills, Vol. 1. 2nd ed. 307p. 1994. pap. text ed. 24.00 (1-85431-333-9, Blckstone AT) W W Gaunt.

Lee, Simon & Ricks, David, eds. The New Penguin French Reader. 224p. 1993. pap. 10.00 (0-14-013339-9, Penguin Bks) Viking Penguin.

Lee, Sin H., jt. ed. see Pertschuk, Louis.

Lee, Sing H., ed. Diffractive & Miniaturized Optics: Proceedings of a Conference Held 12-13 July 1993, San Diego, California. LC 93-47390. (Critical Reviews of Optical Science & Technology Ser.: Vol. CR49). 1993. 91.00 (0-8194-1292-9); 76.00 (0-8194-1291-0) SPIE.

Lee, Sing H., jt. ed. see Jahns, Jurgen.

Lee, Siu-Lam, jt. auth. see Lyon, John F.

Lee, Sky. Disappearing Moon Cafe. LC 91-22580. 1991. 18.95 (1-878067-11-7) Seal Pr Feminist.
— Disappearing Moon Cafe. LC 91-22580. 237p. reprint ed. pap. 10.95 (1-878067-12-5) Seal Pr Feminist.

***Lee, Soon C.** The Fifth Wheel. Lechich, Whitney, ed. 80p. (YA). 1994. 24.00 (1-884740-01-4) Whys World Pubns.

Lee, Sophia. Recess, or, a Tale of Other Times, 3 vols., Set. LC 77-131325. (Gothic Novels Ser.). 1979. reprint ed. 54.95 (0-405-00806-6) Ayer.

Lee, Sophia, ed. Canterbury Tales, 2 Vols, 1. rev. ed. LC 71-162886. (Illus.). reprint ed. write for info. (0-404-54412-6) AMS Pr.
— Canterbury Tales, 2 Vols, 2. rev. ed. LC 71-162886. (Illus.). reprint ed. write for info. (0-404-54413-4) AMS Pr.
— Canterbury Tales, 2 Vols, Set. rev. ed. LC 71-162886. (Illus.). reprint ed. 90.00 (0-404-54550-5) AMS Pr.

Lee, Spike. Inside Guerrilla Filmmaking. 1987. pap. write for info. (0-318-62087-1, Fireside) S&S Trade.
— She's Gotta Have It. 1987. pap. write for info. (0-318-62086-3, Fireside) S&S Trade.

Lee, Stan. The Amazing Spider-Man. 128p. (Orig.). 1992. pap. 3.99 (0-8125-1019-4) Tor Bks.
— Best of the World's Worst. 1994. pap. 9.99 (1-881649-46-6) Genl Pub Grp.
— The Incredible Hulk: A Man-Brute Berserk. (Illus.). 128p. 1991. pap. 3.50 (0-8125-1172-7) Tor Bks.
— Marvels Greatest Super Battles. 1994. pap. 15.95 (0-7851-0031-8) Marvel Entmnt.

Lee, Stan, et al. Silver Surfer: The Enslavers. 80p. 1990. 16.95 (0-87135-617-1) Marvel Entmnt.

***Lee, Stan.** Spider-Man. (Masterworks Ser.). 1994. 34.95 (0-7851-0051-2) Marvel Entmnt.
— Spider-Man Wedding. 144p. 1991. pap. 12.95 (0-87135-770-4) Marvel Entmnt.
— The Ultimate Spiderman. 352p. (Orig.). 1994. pap. 12.00 (0-425-14610-3, Berkley Trade) Berkley Pub.
— Uncanny X-Men Masterworks. (Illus.). 1993. pap. 12.95 (0-87135-964-2) Marvel Entmnt.
— Very Best of Spider-Man. 176p. 1994. pap. 15.95 (0-7851-0045-8) Marvel Entmnt.
— X-Men. (Masterworks Ser.). 1994. pap. 34.95 (0-7851-0052-0) Marvel Entmnt.

Lee, Stan & Buscema, John. How to Draw Comics the Marvel Way. (Illus.). 1984. pap. 13.00 (0-671-53077-1) S&S Trade.
— Silver Surfer. (Marvel Masterworks Ser.: Vol. 15). 206p. 1990. 34.95 (0-87135-631-7) Marvel Entmnt.
— Silver Surfer: Judgement Day. 64p. 1988. 14.95 (0-87135-427-6) Marvel Entmnt.
— Silver Surfer: Judgment Day. 64p. 1990. reprint ed. pap. 10.95 (0-87135-663-5) Marvel Entmnt.

Lee, Stan & Ditko, Steve. Amazing Spider-Man. (Marvel Masterworks Ser.: Vol. 10). 264p. 1989. 29.95 (0-87135-596-5) Marvel Entmnt.
— Spider-Man. (Marvel Masterworks Ser.: Vol. 5). 232p. 1988. 34.95 (0-87135-480-2) Marvel Entmnt.
— Spider-Man Masterworks. 144p. 1992. pap. 12.95 (0-87135-902-2) Marvel Entmnt.

Lee, Stan & Kirby, Jack. Avengers. (Marvel Masterworks Ser.: Vol. 4). 232p. 1988. 34.95 (0-87135-479-9) Marvel Entmnt.
— Incredible Hulk. (Marvel Masterworks Ser.: Vol. 8). 150p. 1989. 34.95 (0-87135-594-9) Marvel Entmnt.
— Marvel Masterworks, Vol. 13: Fantastic Four. 280p. 1990. 34.95 (0-87135-629-5) Marvel Entmnt.
— Marvel Masterworks, Vol. 2: Fantastic Four. 248p. 1987. 34.95 (0-87135-307-5) Marvel Entmnt.
— Marvel Masterworks, Vol. 6: Fantastic Four. 232p. 1988. 34.95 (0-87135-481-0) Marvel Entmnt.
— X-Men. (Marvel Masterworks Ser.: Vol. 3). (Illus.). 232p. 1987. 34.95 (0-87135-308-3) Marvel Entmnt.
— X-Men. (Marvel Masterworks Ser.: Vol. 7). 232p. 1988. 34.95 (0-87135-482-9) Marvel Entmnt.

Lee, Stan & Moebius. Silver Surfer: Parable. (Illus.) 72p. 1988. 19.95 (0-87135-491-8) Marvel Entmnt.

***Lee, Stan & Robinson, Graham.** Process Development: Fine Chemicals from Grams to Kilograms. (Oxford Chemistry Primers Ser.: No. 30). 96p. (C). 1995. pap. text ed. 9.95 (0-19-855824-4) OUP.

Lee, Stan & Wood, Wally. Marvel Masterworks, Vol. 17: Daredevil. 248p. 1991. 34.95 (0-87135-806-9) Marvel Entmnt.

Lee, Stan, et al. Avengers. (Marvel Masterworks Ser.: Vol. 9). 210p. 1989. 29.95 (0-87135-595-7) Marvel Entmnt.
— Marvel Masterworks, Vol. 18: Thor. 262p. 1991. 34.95 (0-87135-807-7) Marvel Entmnt.
— Night Cat. 48p. 1991. 3.95 (0-87135-755-0) Marvel Entmnt.

Lee, Stellasue, jt. auth. see Widup, Dave.

Lee, Stephen. The Andes. (Illus.). 144p. 1992. 39.95 (0-7134-6595-6, Pub. by Batsford UK) Trafalgar.

Lee, Stephen C., jt. auth. see Hu, Jerome P.

Lee, Stephen J. Aspects of British Political History, 1815-1914. LC 94-432. (Aspects of History Ser.). (Illus.). 368p. 1994. 59.95x (0-415-09006-7, B3977); pap. 16.95 (0-415-09007-5, B3981) Routledge.
— Aspects of European History 1494-1789. 2nd ed. 336p. 1984. pap. 14.95 (0-416-37490-5, NO. 9079) Routledge Chapman & Hall.
— The European Dictatorships, 1918-1945. 352p. 1987. pap. 15.95 (0-416-42280-2) Routledge Chapman & Hall.
— Peter the Great. LC 92-44016. (Lancaster Pamphlets Ser.). 96p. 1993. pap. 9.95 (0-415-09279-5, B2385, Routledge NY) Routledge.
— The Thirty Years War. LC 91-16159. (Lancaster Pamphlets Ser.). 80p. 1991. pap. 8.95 (0-415-06027-3, A6684) Routledge.

Lee, Steve A., jt. auth. see Stagner, Lloyd E.

Lee, Steven, jt. ed. see Cohen, Avner.

Lee, Steven P. Morality, Prudence, & Nuclear Weapons. LC 92-30904. (Cambridge Studies in Philosophy & Public Policy). 448p. (C). 1993. 69.95 (0-521-38272-6) Cambridge U Pr.

Lee, Stuart. Dictionary of Composite Materials Technology. LC 89-50813. 171p. 1989. 49.00 (0-87762-600-6) Technomic.

Lee, Stuart, ed. Advances in Biomaterials I. LC 86-72347. 292p. 1987. 29.00 (0-87762-504-2) Technomic.
— International Encyclopedia of Composites, Set. LC 89-24893. (Encyclopedia of Composites Ser.). 524p. 1990. write for info. (0-89573-290-4) VCH Pubs.
— International Encyclopedia of Composites, Vol. 2. LC 89-24893. (Encyclopedia of Composites Ser.). 524p. 1990. text ed. 275.00 (0-89573-732-9); 235.00 (0-685-56104-6) VCH Pubs.
— International Encyclopedia of Composites, Vol. 3. LC 89-24893. (Encyclopedia of Composites Ser.). 526p. 1990. text ed. 275.00 (0-89573-733-7); 235.00 (0-685-62693-8) VCH Pubs.
— International Encyclopedia of Composites, Vol. 5. LC 89-24893. (Encyclopedia of Composites Ser.). 548p. 1991. text ed. 275.00 (0-685-62694-6); 235.00 (0-685-62695-4) VCH Pubs.
— International Encyclopedia of Composites, Vol. 6. LC 89-24893. (Encyclopedia of Composites Ser.). 600p. 1992. text ed. 275.00 (0-89573-736-1); 235.00 (0-685-62696-2) VCH Pubs.

Lee, Stuart M. Quality Assurance & Quality Control to Thermophysical Properties. (International Encyclopedia of Composites Ser.: Vol. 5). 548p. 1991. lib. bdg. 2,160.00 (0-89573-735-3); 215.00 (0-685-54385-4) VCH Pubs.
— Reference Book for Composite Technology, Vol. 1. LC 89-50073. 334p. 1989. 39.00 (0-87762-564-6) Technomic.
— Reference Book for Composite Technology, Vol. 2. LC 89-50073. 203p. 1989. 29.00 (0-87762-565-4) Technomic.

Lee, Stuart M., ed. Handbook of Composite Reinforcements. LC 92-38661. 715p. 1992. 145.00 (1-56081-632-5) VCH Pubs.
— The International Encyclopedia of Composites, Vol. 1. LC 89-24893. (Illus.). 563p. 1990. text ed. 275.00 (0-89573-731-0); 235.00 (0-685-56122-4) VCH Pubs.
— The International Encyclopedia of Composites, Vol. 4: Natural Composites, Fiber Modification to Protective Coatings Space Environs. (Illus.). 532p. 1991. lib. bdg. 275.00 (0-89573-734-5); 235.00 (0-685-54261-0) VCH Pubs.

Lee, Sukhan, jt. ed. see Homen De Mello, Luiz S.

Lee, Sul H. Acquisitions, Budgets & Material Costs: Issues & Approaches. LC 87-29867. (Journal of Library Administration & Supplement: No. 2). (Illus.). 165p. 1988. 39.95 (0-86656-690-2) Haworth Pr.

***Lee, Sul H., ed.** Access, Ownership & Resource Sharing. LC 95-4208. 1995. write for info. (1-56024-727-4) Haworth Pr.
— Access to Scholarly Information: Issues & Strategies. LC 85-60595. (Library Management Ser.: No. 9). 1985. 30.00 (0-87650-189-7) Pierian.
— Budgets for Acquisitions: Strategies for Serials, Monographs, & Electronic Formats. LC 91-12603. (Journal of Library Administration). (Illus.). 133p. 1991. lib. bdg. 29.95 (1-56024-158-6) Haworth Pr.
— A Challenge for Academic Libraries: How to Motivate Students to Use the Library. LC 73-78295. (Library Orientation Ser.: No. 2). 1973. 25.00 (0-87650-039-4) Pierian.
— Emerging Trends in Library Organization: What Influences Change. LC 78-56102. (Library Management Ser.: No. 4). 1978. 24.50 (0-87650-093-9) Pierian.
— Issues in Acquisitions: Programs & Evaluation. LC 84-61226. (Library Management Ser.: No. 8). 1984. 30.00 (0-87650-188-9) Pierian.
— Library Budgeting: Critical Challenges for the Future. LC 77-85231. (Library Management Ser.: No. 3). 1977. 24.50 (0-87650-083-1) Pierian.
— Library Materials Costs & Access to Information. LC 91-12604. (Journal of Library Administration). (Illus.). 114p. 1991. lib. bdg. 29.95 (1-56024-146-2) Haworth Pr.
— Planning-Programming-Budgeting System (PPBS) Implications for Library Management. LC 73-78314. (Library Management Ser.: No. 1). 1973. 24.50 (0-87650-040-8) Pierian.
— Pricing & Costs of Monographs & Serials: National & International Issues. LC 86-33653. (Journal of Library Administration Supplement: No. 1). 109p. 1987. text ed. 29.95 (0-86656-620-1) Haworth Pr.
— Reference Service: A Perspective. LC 83-60917. (Library Management Ser.: No. 6). 1983. 30.00 (0-87650-150-1) Pierian.
— Serials Collection Development: Choices & Strategies. LC 81-84645. (Library Management Ser.: No. 5). 1981. 30.00 (0-87650-136-6) Pierian.

Lee, Sul H., intro. Collection Assessment & Acquisitions Budgets. LC 92-28676. (Journal of Library Administration: Vol. 17, No. 2). (Illus.). 229p. 1993. 29.95 (1-56024-390-2) Haworth Pr.
— Declining Acquisitions Budgets: Allocation, Collection Development & Impact Communication. LC 93-39258. (Illus.). 160p. 1994. lib. bdg. 39.95 (1-56024-613-8) Haworth Pr.
— Declining Acquisitions Budgets: Allocation, Collection Development & Impact Communication. LC 93-39258. (Illus.). 160p. 1994. pap. text ed. 19.95 (1-56024-614-6) Haworth Pr.
— The Impact of Rising Costs of Serials & Monographs on Library Services & Programs. LC 88-36774. (Journal of Library Administration: Vol. 10, No. 1). (Illus.). 125p. 1989. text ed. 29.95 (0-86656-885-9) Haworth Pr.
— The Role & Future of Special Collections in Research Libraries: British & American Perspectives. LC 93-30716. (Journal of Library Administration: Vol. 19, No. 1). 110p. 1993. lib. bdg. 29.95 (1-56024-479-8) Haworth Pr.
— Vendor Evaluation & Acquisition Budgets. LC 92-10146. (Journal of Library Administration). (Illus.). 142p. 1992. text ed. 29.95 (1-56024-253-1) Haworth Pr.

Lee, Sul H., jt. ed. see Woodrum, Pat.

Lee, Sun. Color Atlas of Microsurgery. 385p. 1993. 145.00 (0-318-72976-8, D7066) PennWell Bks.

Lee, Sun, ed. Manual of Microsurgery. (Illus.). 160p. 1985. 102.95 (0-8493-0726-0, RD33, CRC Reprint) Franklin.

Lee, Sun, et al. Color Atlas of Microsurgery. Hacke, Gregory, ed. LC 92-56746. (Illus.). 388p. 1993. text ed. 145.00 (0-912791-64-0); pap. 120.00 (0-685-70856-X) Ishiyaku Euro.

Lee, Sun O. & Heyman, Alan. Zen Dance: Meditation in Movement. (Illus.). 108p. 1985. 24.00 (0-8048-1428-7, Pub. by Seoul Intl Tourist KO) C E Tuttle.

Lee, Sunggyu & Iredell, Robert. Methanol Synthesis Technology. 240p. 1989. 179.00 (0-8493-4610-X, TP594) CRC Pr.

Lee, Sungkee, jt. auth. see Bhanu, Bir.

Lee, Susan. The Dancer: One Woman's Journey from Tragedy to Triumph. 128p. (Orig.). 1991. pap. 7.99 (0-8010-5671-3) Baker Bk.

Lee, Susan & Libana, Susanaha. You Said, Why This Interest in Goddesses. (Fastbook 1985 Ser.). 20p. 1985. 6.00 (0-911051-17-1) Plain View.

Lee, Susan D., ed. Ohio Records & Pioneer Families, Vol. 33. 1992. 9.00 (0-935057-69-2) OH Genealogical.
— Ohio Records & Pioneer Families, Vol. 34. 1993. 18.00 (0-935057-72-2) OH Genealogical.
— Ohio Records & Pioneer Families, Vol. 34. 1994. 18.00 (0-935057-75-7) OH Genealogical.
— Ohio Records & Pioneer Families: Surname Index, Vol. 27. 1986. 15.00 (0-935057-44-7) OH Genealogical.
— Ohio Records & Pioneer Families: Topical Index, Vols. I-XXV. 1986. 1.00 (0-935057-43-9) OH Genealogical.

Lee, Susan P. The Westward Movement of the Cotton Economy, 1840-1860: Perceived Interests & Economic Realities. Bruchey, Stuart, ed. LC 76-39832. (Nineteen Seventy-Seven Dissertations Ser.). (Illus.). 1977. lib. bdg. 24.95 (0-405-09912-6) Ayer.

Lee, Susan P. & Passell, Peter. A New Economic View of American History. (Illus.). (C). 1979. pap. text ed. 18.95 (0-393-95067-0) Norton.

Lee, Susan P., et al. A New Economic View of American History. 2nd ed. (C). 1994. pap. text ed. 24.95 (0-393-96315-2) Norton.

***Lee, Susan R.** Lee's New School History of the United States. (Johnson Ser.). (Illus.). 422p. Date not set. pap. 17.95 (0-9627989-0-8) Grapevine ID.

Lee, Suzanne. Bicycling Japan: A Touring Handbook. LC 90-83529. (Illus.). 168p. (Orig.). 1991. pap. 6.95 (0-9627458-0-4) Zievid Pr.

Lee, Sylvain A. The Practice of Hypnotic Suggestion. 160p. 1973. reprint ed. spiral bd. 6.05 (0-7873-0548-0) Mokelumne.

Lee, Sylvia, ed. The Holy Spirit in Christian Education. LC 88-80549. (Sunday School Staff Training Ser.). 144p. (Orig.). (J). (gr. k up). 1988. teacher ed, pap. 2.95 (0-88243-854-9, 02-0854) Gospel Pub.

Lee, Sylvia, jt. auth. see Lee, L. L.

Lee, T. Advanced Industrial Hygiene. 1990. text ed. write for info. (0-442-23532-1) Van Nos Reinhold.

Lee, T., et al. Revisiting the Americas: Teaching & Learning the Geography of the Western Hemisphere. Martinson, T. L. & Brooker-Gross, Susan, eds. (Pathways in Geography Ser.: No. 4). (Illus.). 260p. (Orig.). 1992. pap. text ed. 25.00 (0-9627379-2-5) NCFGE.

Lee, T. A. & Tweedie, D. P. Shareholder Use & Understanding Financial Information. (Accounting History & Thought Ser.). 400p. 1990. reprint ed. 80.00 (0-8240-3321-3) Garland.

Lee, T. C. The Wu Style of Tai Chi Chuan. LC 81-50511. (Illus.). 120p. (Orig.). 1981. pap. 9.95 (0-86568-022-1, 211) Unique Pubns.

Lee, T. D. Lee: Selected Papers, 1. Feinberg, Gerald, ed. (Contemporary Physicists Ser.). 1986. lib. bdg. 90.00 (0-8176-3341-3) Birkhauser.
— Lee: Selected Papers, 2. Feinberg, Gerald, ed. (Contemporary Physicists Ser.). 1986. lib. bdg. 90.00 (0-8176-3342-1) Birkhauser.
— Lee: Selected Papers, 3. Feinberg, Gerald, ed. (Contemporary Physicists Ser.). 1986. lib. bdg. 90.00 (0-8176-3343-X) Birkhauser.

An Asterisk (*) at the beginning of an entry indicates that the title is appearing in BIP for the first time.

— Lee: Selected Papers, Set. Feinberg, Gerald, ed. (Contemporary Physicists Ser.). 1986. lib. bdg. 225.00 (0-8176-3344-8) Birkhauser.

— Symmetries, Asymmetries & the World of Particles. (Illus.). 80p. 1987. 15.00 (0-295-96519-3) U of Wash Pr.

Lee, T. D., ed. Particle Physics & Introduction to Field Theory. (Contemporary Concepts in Physics Ser.: Vol. 1). 886p. 1981. text ed. 142.00 (3-7186-0032-3); pap. text ed. 41.00 (3-7186-0033-1) Gordon & Breach.

Lee, T. H., et al, eds. The Methane Age. (C). 1988. lib. bdg. 100.50 (90-277-2745-7) Kluwer Ac.

Lee, T. J., ed. Neurohumoral Control of Blood Vessel Tone: Springfield Blood Vessel Symposium. (Journal: Blood Vessels: Vol. 24, No. 3). (Illus.). 80p. 1987. pap. 39.25 (3-8055-4604-1) S Karger.

Lee, T. P. Current Trends in Integrated Optoelectronics. (Current Topics in Electronics & Systems). 200p. 1994. text ed. 61.00 (981-02-1862-1) World Scientific Pub.

Lee, T. R., jt. auth. see Allen, P. T.

Lee, T. S., jt. ed. see Dean, Sheldon W.

Lee, T. S., jt. ed. see Francis, P. E.

Lee, Ta-Ling & Copper, John F. Reform in Reverse: Human Rights in the People's Republic of China, No. 6. 150p. 1987. 8.00 (0-942182-86-3, 83) Occasional Papers.

Lee, Ta-ling, jt. auth. see Cooper, John F.

Lee, Tammie. Leather & Lace, No. 8: Texas Wildflower. 1983. pap. 2.50 (0-8217-1178-4) Zebra.

Lee, Tanith. Black Unicorn. LC 91-15646. (Dragonflight Ser.). (Illus.). 144p. (YA). (gr. 7 up). 1991. text ed. 14.95 (0-689-31575-9, Atheneum Bks Young) S&S Childrens.

— Black Unicorn. 192p. 1993. mass mkt. 3.99 (0-8125-2459-4) Tor Bks.

— The Book of the Beast: The Secret Books of Paradys Two. 240p. 1991. 19.95 (0-87951-417-5) Overlook Pr.

— The Book of the Damned: The Secret Books of Paradys-I. 240p. 1990. 19.95 (0-87951-408-6) Overlook Pr.

— The Book of the Dead: The Secret Books of Paradys III. 196p. 1991. 19.95 (0-87951-440-X) Overlook Pr.

— The Book of the Mad: The Secret Books of Paradys IV. LC 92-36788. 1993. 19.95 (0-87951-481-7) Overlook Pr.

— Gold Unicorn. (J). 1994. 14.95 (0-689-31814-6, Atheneum Bks Young) S&S Childrens.

— Gold Unicorn. 1996. pap. write for info. (0-614-05526-1) Tor Bks.

— Heart-Beast. 1993. mass mkt. 4.99 (0-440-21455-6, Dell Trade Pbks) Dell.

— Personal Darkness. 1994. mass mkt. 4.99 (0-440-21470-X) Dell.

— Unsilent Night. LC 81-80331. (Boskone Bks.). 1981. 10.00 (0-915368-18-8) New Eng SF Assoc.

Lee, Teri, ed. see Lackey, Mercedes.

Lee, Terri. Aquacises: Terri Lee's Water Workout Book. 256p. 1984. spiral bd. 22.50 (0-8359-0152-1, Reston) P-H.

— Aquacises: Terri Lee's Water Workout Book. (Illus.). 240p. 1990. reprint ed. pap. text ed. 22.50 (0-9627703-0-2) Lee Pub AZ.
600 illustrated water exercises for muscular strength, flexibility, endurance & cardio-respiratory fitness. Full color, plastic-coated cover. Publishers Weekly --"Terri Lee's Aquacises & the benefits of exercising in the water are convincing...a complete shape-up plan which can be pursued modestly or energetically depending on one's initial fitness level...appropriate for beginning & advanced athletes, young - ages 12 & up - or old ...intelligent & worthwhile book." Booklist --"Recommended for most fitness collections." Karl G. Stoedefalke Ph.D., Fellow American College of Sports Medicine --"Aquacises is literally a pharmacopoeia of body movements to be performed in the water. Components of physical or motor fitness such as flexibility, muscle strength, or coordination are identified with each exercise. Exercises are applicable to children & adults with medically defined disabilities & can also be used by fitness-oriented swimmers in their routines...a text for everyone. Only a lifetime of teaching & experimentation could have produced this text. Terri Lee's enthusiasm for aquatics is visible throughout. Her penchant for detail is commendable, & I recommend this text as the bridge between the science & art of aquatic exercise." *Publisher Provided Annotation.*

Lee, Thomas, ed. see Maple Summer Workshop & Symposium.

Lee, Thomas A. Stalking the Wild Golf Ball: A Guide to Finding, & Not Losing, Golf Balls. 128p. 1994. pap. 16.95 (0-9638807-4-8) Fairway Pubng.

Lee, Thomas A., ed. Cash Flow Reporting: A Recent History of an Accounting Practice. LC 93-607. (New Works in Accounting History). 424p. 1993. reprint ed. 90.00 (0-8153-1217-2) Garland.

Lee, Thomas F. Gene Future: The Promise & Perils of the New Biology. 300p. 1993. 24.95 (0-306-44509-3, Plenum Pr) Plenum.

— The Human Genome Project: Cracking the Genetic Code of Life. (Illus.). 332p. 1991. 24.50 (0-306-43965-4, Plenum Pr) Plenum.

Lee, Thomas H., Jr. Cardiology Problems in Primary Care. 320p. 1989. 39.95 (0-87489-463-8) Med Economics.

Lee, Thomas H. Government Education & Examinations in Sung China. (Institute of Chinese Studies Monograph Ser.: No. 7). 327p. 1985. 57.50 (962-201-302-3, Pub. by Chinese Univ HK) Coronet Bks.

Lee, Thomas H., comp. A Guide to East Asian Collections in North America. LC 91-46698. (Bibliographies & Indexes in World History Ser.: No. 25). 184p. 1992. text ed. 49.95 (0-313-27397-9, LGA, Greenwood Pr) Greenwood.

Lee, Thomas H., ed. China & Europe: Images & Influences in 16th-18th Centuries. (Illus.). 356p. 1991. 87.50x (962-201-465-8, Pub. by Chinese Univ HK) Coronet Bks.

Lee, Thomas H., ed. see National Academy of Engineering, Committee on Engineering as an International Enterprise Staff.

Lee, Thomas H., et al. Energy Aftermath. 1990. text ed. 24.95 (0-07-103248-7) McGraw.

Lee, Thomas R. Studies in the Form of Sirach 44-50. LC 85-26179. (Society of Biblical Literature Dissertation Ser.). 284p. (C). 1986. 25.95 (0-89130-834-2, 06-01-75); pap. 16.95 (0-89130-835-0) Scholars Pr GA.

— Turbines Westward. 1975. 16.95 (0-686-00363-2) AG Pr.

Lee, Thomas W. & Pabbisetty, Seshu V., eds. Microelectronic Failure Analysis: Desk Reference. 3rd ed. LC 93-7792. 350p. 1993. 131.00 (0-87170-479-X) ASM.

*Lee-Thorp, Karen. Ever Wonder What the Bible Is All About? The Story of Stories. LC 91-61423. 352p. 1995. per., pap. 10.00 (0-89109-670-1, NavPr) NavPress.

— Exploring the Essentials. (Thinking Through Discipleship Ser.). 80p. (Orig.). 1993. pap. 5.00 (0-89109-736-8) NavPress.

— Who's in Control? Thinking Through the Authority of Christ, the Thinking Through Discipleship. (Thinking Through Discipleship Ser.). 80p. (Orig.). 1993. pap. 5.00 (0-89109-739-2) NavPress.

Lee-Thorp, Karen, ed. see Navigators Staff.

Lee, Timothy-James, jt. auth. see Hudspeth, Lee.

*Lee, Ting W. Call to Ministry - from Dream to Reality. 137p. (CHI.). 1989. pap. 5.00 (1-56582-023-1) Christ Renew Min.

— Equipping the Saints No. 1: Teacher's Hand Book. 75p. (CHI.). 1992. pap. 8.00 (1-56582-046-0) Christ Renew Min.

— Equipping the Saints No. 2: Teacher's Hand Book. (CHI.). Date not set. write for info. (1-56582-047-9) Christ Renew Min.

— Kingdom & Little People. Kam, May-Chun, tr. 169p. (CHI.). 1989. pap. 5.00 (1-56582-022-3) Christ Renew Min.

Lee, Ting W., tr. see Dawson, David.

Lee, Tisha. My Image Is My Choice: How to Create the Perfect Haircut for Your Lifestyle. (Illus.). 260p. (Orig.). 1988. pap. text ed. write for info. (0-9620833-0-5) Tisha Lees.

*Lee, Todd. The Snoring Log Mystery: Wilderness Adventures of a Young Naturalist. (Illus.). 96p. (Orig.). (J). (gr. 4-8). 1993. pap. 8.95 (0-919591-76-0, Pub. by Polestar Bk Pubs CN) Orca Bk Pubs.

— The Twilight Marsh & Other Wilderness Adventures. (Illus.). (Orig.). Date not set. pap. 8.95 (1-896095-07-0) Orca Bk Pubs.

Lee, Tom. Corporate Audit Theory. LC 92-36202. 1993. write for info. (0-412-45220-0) Chapman & Hall.

Lee, Tom, jt. auth. see Vickers, Roderic.

Lee, Tom L. Lawyer Advertising: Consumer Attitudes, Response Patterns & Motivation Factors. LC 85-11699. 207p. (Orig.). 1985. pap. 325.00 (0-934547-00-9) CRI-Comm Res.

— Lawyers Direct Mail Advertising Handbook. 1989. write for info. (0-934547-06-8) CRI-Comm Res.

— Lawyers Publicity Handbook. 145p. 1986. ring bd. 68.00 (0-934547-02-5) CRI-Comm Res.

Lee Tsao Yuan. Growth Triangle: The Johor-Singapore-Riau Experience. 132p. 1991. 23.95 (981-3016-11-6, Pub. by Inst SE Asian Studies SI) Ashgate Pub Co.

Lee, Tunney, jt. auth. see Hollister, Robert.

Lee, Tyrone, jt. ed. see Sen, Amartya K.

Lee, Umphrey. Historical Backgrounds of Early Methodist Enthusiasm. LC 31-18047. (Columbia University. Studies in the Social Sciences: No. 339). reprint ed. 20.00 (0-404-51339-5) AMS Pr.

Lee, V. J., ed. English Literature in Schools. (Exploring Curriculum Ser.). 356p. 1987. 90.00 (0-335-15246-5, Open Univ Pr); pap. 32.00 (0-335-15245-7, Open Univ Pr) Taylor & Francis.

Lee, Valerie. Dysfunctional Families. (Family Ser.). (Illus.). 64p. (YA). (gr. 7 up). 1990. lib. bdg. 15.93 (0-86593-077-5); lib. bdg. 12.95 (0-685-36296-5) Rourke Corp.

— National Assessment of Educational Progress Reading Proficiency, 1983-84: Catholic School Results & National Averages Final Report 1985. 36p. 6.75 (0-317-65727-5) Natl Cath Educ.

— National Assessment of Educational Progress Writing Profiency, 1983-84: Catholic School Results & National Averages Final Report. 1987. 6.75 (0-317-60235-7) Natl Cath Educ.

— Pregnancy in the Executive Suite. LC 87-61045. 224p. (C). 1988. 19.95 (0-944315-00-3) Success Pubns.

Lee, Valerie & Stewart, Carolee. National Assessment of Educational Progress Proficiency in Mathematics & Science, 1985-86, Catholic & Public Schools Compared Final Report, 1989. 66p. (Orig.). 1989. pap. 6.60 (1-55833-025-9) Natl Cath Educ.

Lee, Valerie, jt. auth. see Littleford, John C.

Lee, Valeska. The Colors of Passion. 150p. 1996. pap. 3.79 (0-9634431-1-9) C Y Pub Grp.

Lee, Vera. Love & Strategy in the Eighteenth Century French Novel. 150p. (Orig.). 1986. text ed. 18.95 (0-87047-018-3); pap. 11.25 (0-87047-019-1) Schenkman Bks Inc.

— Quest for a Public: French Popular Theatre Since 1945. 200p. 1976. text ed. 18.95 (0-87073-180-7) Schenkman Bks Inc.

— Reign of Women in Eighteenth Century France. (Illus.). 140p. 1976. 18.95 (0-87073-990-5); pap. 11.95 (0-87073-991-3) Schenkman Bks Inc.

— Secrets of Venus: A Lover's Guide to Charms, Potions & Aphrodisiacs. 1995. pap. 14.95 (0-9635257-6-X) Mt Ivy Pr.

— Something Old, Something New: The Wedding Ceremonies, Rituals, Customs & Traditions that Join Us Together. LC 94-235. 1994. 14.95 (1-57071-002-3) Sourcebks.

Lee, Vernell, ed. see Gall-Clayton, Nancy.

Lee, Vernon. Gospels of Anarchy. 1976. lib. bdg. 59.95 (0-8490-1896-X) Gordon Pr.

— The Handling of Words & Other Studies in Literary Psychology. LC 92-38266. 1993. reprint ed. text ed. write for info. (0-7734-9174-0) E Mellen.

— Studies of the Eighteenth Century in Italy. LC 77-17466. (Music Reprint Ser.: 1978). 1978. reprint ed. lib. bdg. 37.50 (0-306-77517-4) Da Capo.

— Supernatural Tales: Excursions into Fantasy. LC 87-60976. 222p. 1987. 27.00 (0-7206-0680-2, Pub. by P Owen Ltd UK) Dufour.

Lee, Vicki L. Beyond Behaviorism. 216p. 1988. 39.95 (0-8058-0115-4) L Erlbaum Assocs.

*Lee, Victor & Das Gupta, Prajna, eds. Children's Cognitive & Language Development. (Child Development Ser.). (Illus.). 344p. (C). 1995. pap. 21.95 (0-631-19428-2) Blackwell Pubs.

*Lee, Victor & Gupta, Prajna D., eds. Children's Cognitive & Language Development. (Child Guidance Mental Health Ser.). (Illus.). 344p. (C). 1995. 54.95 (0-631-19427-4) Blackwell Pubs.

Lee, Virginia. Affairs of the Heart: Women & Men Reveal the Truth about Extramarital Affairs. 200p. 1993. 10.95 (0-89594-621-1) Crossing Pr.

Lee, Virginia, jt. auth. see Claiborne, Craig.

Lee, Virginia, jt. auth. see Elliot, Elaine.

Lee, Virginia, jt. auth. see Pogue, Pamela.

Lee, Vivian W., jt. auth. see Sing, Rachel N.

Lee, W. John Lee of Aganam (Ipswich), Mass., 1634-1671, & His Descendants of the Name of Lee. (Illus.). 506p. 1989. reprint ed. lib. bdg. 83.00 (0-8328-0763-X); reprint ed. pap. 75.00 (0-8328-0764-8) Higginson Bk Co.

Lee, W. A. Manual of Queensland Succession Law. 3rd ed. xlviii, 295p. 1991. pap. 49.00 (0-455-21034-9, Pub. by Law Bk Co) W W Gaunt.

Lee, W. A., jt. auth. see Ford, H. A.

Lee, W. B., ed. Advances in Engineering Plasticity & Its Applications: Proceedings of the Asia-Pacific Symposium (AEPA '92), Hong Kong, 15-17 December, 1992. LC 93-10542. xviii, 1136p. 1993. 468.75 (0-444-89991-X) Elsevier.

Lee, W. Dean. Beyond the Uniform: A Career & Family Transition Guide for Veterans & Federal Employees. 224p. 1991. pap. text ed. 14.95 (0-471-54620-8) Wiley.

*Lee, W. E. & Bell, A., eds. Electroceramics: Production, Properties & Microstructures. (British Ceramics Proceedings Ser.: No. 52). 320p. 1994. 150.00 (0-901716-42-1, Pub. by Inst Materials UK) Ashgate Pub Co.

*Lee, W. H. & Dodge, D. A., eds. A Course on PC-Based Seismic Networks. (Illus.). 535p. (Orig.). (C). 1994. pap. text ed. 145.00x (0-7881-1247-3) Diane Pub.

Lee, W. H. & Steward, S. W. Advances in Geophysics, Supplement 2: Principles & Applications of Microearthquake Networks. LC 80-70588. 1981. text ed. 96.00 (0-12-018862-7) Acad Pr.

Lee, W. H., et al, eds. Historical Seismograms & Earthquakes of the World. 513p. 1988. text ed. 79.00 (0-12-440870-2) Acad Pr.

Lee, W. Melville. History of Police in England. LC 70-108236. (Criminology, Law Enforcement, & Social Problems Ser.: No. 119). 1970. reprint ed. 24.00 (0-87585-119-3) Patterson Smith.

Lee, W. O. Social Change & Educational Problems in Japan, Singapore & Hong Kong. LC 90-44166. 304p. 1991. text ed. 49.95 (0-312-05371-1) St Martin.

Lee, W. R. Ophthalmic Histopathology. (Illus.). 352p. 1993. 250.00 (0-387-19686-2) Spr-Verlag.

— Population Growth, Economic Development & Social Change in Bavaria: 1750-1850. Bruchey, Stuart, ed. LC 77-77194. (Dissertations in European Economic History Ser.). (Illus.). 1978. lib. bdg. 47.95 (0-405-10806-0) Ayer.

Lee, W. R., ed. German Industry & German Industrialisation: Essays in German Economic & Business History in the Nineteenth & Twentieth Centuries. 336p. 1991. 74.50 (0-415-02155-3, A3436) Routledge.

Lee, W. R. & Lee, Z. Teach Yourself Czech. (Teach Yourself Ser.). 1979. 10.95 (0-679-10211-6) McKay.

Lee, W. Robert, jt. ed. see Evans, Richard J.

*Lee, W. W. Cannon's Revenge. LC 94-22437. 171p. 1995. 19.95 (0-8027-4147-9) Walker & Co.

— Outlaw's Fortune. LC 92-44495. 154p. 1993. 19.95 (0-8027-1270-3) Walker & Co.

— Outlaw's Fortune. large type ed. LC 93-47267. 1994. 15.95 (0-7862-0161-4) Thorndike Pr.

— Rancher's Blood. 192p. 1991. 18.95 (0-8027-4120-7) Walker & Co.

— Robber's Trail. 150p. 1992. 18.95 (0-8027-4133-9) Walker & Co.

— Rogue's Gold. 192p. 1989. 17.95 (0-8027-4096-0) Walker & Co.

— Rustler's Venom. 192p. 1990. 18.95 (0-8027-4112-6) Walker & Co.

Lee, Walt, ed. Reference Guide to Fantastic Films, Science Fiction, Fantasy, & Horror, 3 vols., Set. LC 72-88775. (Illus.). 742p. (Orig.). 1974. pap. 100.00 (0-913974-04-8) Chelsea-Lee Bks.

— Reference Guide to Fantastic Films, Science Fiction, Fantasy, & Horror, Vol. 1: A-F. LC 72-88775. (Illus.). 230p. (Orig.). 1972. pap. 59.95 (0-913974-01-3) Chelsea-Lee Bks.

— Reference Guide to Fantastic Films, Science Fiction, Fantasy, & Horror, Vol. 2: G-O. LC 72-88775. (Illus.). 242p. (Orig.). 1973. pap. 24.95 (0-913974-02-1) Chelsea-Lee Bks.

— Reference Guide to Fantastic Films, Science Fiction, Fantasy, & Horror, Vol. 3: P-Z. LC 72-88775. (Illus.). 270p. (Orig.). 1974. pap. 24.95 (0-913974-03-X) Chelsea-Lee Bks.

*Lee, Walter. AH. (Illus.). 200p. 1995. write for info. (0-615-00661-2) Faun Pub Co.

— Ah. 200p. 1995. write for info. (1-887409-01-7); pap. write for info. (1-887409-00-9) Faun Pub Co.

— Poems & Prayers. 1995. pap. write for info. (1-887409-06-8) Faun Pub Co.

— Radiation in Our Environment. 200p. 1995. write for info. (1-887409-04-1); pap. write for info. (1-887409-03-3) Faun Pub Co.

— Radiation in Our Environment. 200p. 1995. write for info. (1-887409-04-1) pap. write for info. (1-887409-03-3) Faun Pub Co.
There is a big concern about radiation, because of its biological effects on our daily lives, & because the amount of environmental radiation is constantly increasing. RADIATION IN OUR ENVIRONMENT gives conceptual understandings & insights into the nature & impact of radiation. These far reaching influences deserve our attention & basic understanding. Numerous illustrations are included to make understanding a breeze, & NO MATH IS REQUIRED for the reader to use or understand. RADIATION IN OUR ENVIRONMENT is divided into two parts. Part one is a description of radiation concepts, & a distinction between sensed & non-sensed radiation. Part two gives examples of the effects of radiation on living things (of various species) & radiation in the environment (the earth, our homes & workplaces). The book also explains environmental terms, like: radiation contamination, ozone & the greenhouse effect. A short conclusion follows. Each one of us may be affected by radiation. Our controls include understanding what it is, & guarding our health by limiting our exposure to it. EVERYBODY SHOULD KNOW ABOUT RADIATION! This is an ideal hand-ready reference for many of the health & environmental topics that are in the news & general discussions. Under 200 pages. *Publisher Provided Annotation.*

Lee, Wanda. Angels in the Trees: A Poetry Collection. (Spiritual Growth & Awareness Ser.). 96p. (Orig.). Date not set. pap. 7.95 (1-883855-03-9) St Georges Pr.

Lee, Warner. Night Sounds. Tobias, Eric, ed. 288p. (Orig.). 1992. mass mkt. 4.99 (0-671-70426-5) PB.

Lee-Warren, Annabelle. Blueprint for Health. 1994. 18.95 (0-8329-0509-7) New Win Pub.

*Lee-Warren, Annabelle & Willard, Jo. A Blueprint for Health. LC 95-14339. 1995. pap. write for info. (0-8329-0512-7) New Win Pub.

Lee, Warren F. Down along the Old Bel-Del: The History of the Belvidere Delaware Railroad Company. LC 86-61285. (Illus.). 350p. 1987. 34.95 (0-9616893-0-7) Bel-Del Ent.

Lee, Warren F. & Lee, Catherine T. A Chronology of the Belvidere Delaware Railroad & the Region Through Which It Operated. (Illus.). 325p. (Orig.). 1988. pap. 19.95 (0-9616893-1-5) Bel-Del Ent.

Lee, Warren F., et al. Agricultural Finance. 8th rev. ed. LC 87-31081. 480p. (C). 1988. text ed. 36.95 (0-8138-0051-X) Iowa St U Pr.

Lee, Warren W. A Dream for South Central: The Autobiography of an Afro-Americanized Korean Christian Minister. LC 93-80837. 114p. (Orig.). 1993. pap. 6.95 (0-9639920-0-7) W W Lee.

Lee, Wayne C. Bad Men & Bad Towns. LC 92-17951. (Orig.). 1993. pap. 14.95 (0-87004-349-8) Caxton.

— Devil Wire. large type ed. LC 92-41945. 1993. 19.95 (0-7927-1552-7, Curley Lrg Print) Chivers N Amer.

L

— Ghost of a Gunfighter. (Orig.). 1979. pap. 1.95 (*0-89083-559-4*) Zebra.

— Shadow of the Gun. 1981. pap. 1.95 (*0-89083-758-9*) Zebra.

— Trails of the Smoky Hill. LC 79-67199. (Illus.). 235p. (Orig.). 1980. pap. 12.95 (*0-87004-276-9*) Caxton.

— Wild Towns of Nebraska. (Illus.). 147p. (Orig.). 1988. pap. 14.95 (*0-87004-325-0*) Caxton.

Lee, Wei-Chin, ed. Taiwan. annot. ed. (World Bibliographical Ser.: No. 113). 250p. 1990. lib. bdg. 69.00 (*1-85109-091-6*) ABC-CLIO.

Lee, Welton L., ed. see Light, William J.

Lee, Welton L., ed. see Lindberg, David R.

Lee, Welton L., et al, eds. Guidelines to Acquisition & Management of Biological Specimens. 44p. 1982. pap. 5.00 (*0-942924-02-9*) Assn Syst Coll.

Lee, Wendi. The Good Daughter. 224p. 1994. 19.95 (*0-312-11259-9*) St Martin.

Lee-Whiting, Brenda. Harvest of Stones: The German Settlement in Renfrew County. 336p. 1985. 27.50 (*0-8020-2562-5*) U of Toronto Pr.

Lee, Wilford D. Control of Children Through Love & Counseling. 128p. (Orig.). 1975. pap. 2.95 (*0-89036-047-2*) Hawkes Pub Inc.

Lee, William. Belwin Dictionary of Music. Bullock, Jack, ed. (Illus.). 152p. (YA). Date not set. pap. text ed. 9.95 (*0-89898-818-7*) CPP Belwin.

— Belwin Dictionary of Music. rev. ed. Bullock, Jack, ed. (Illus.). 152p. (C). 1994. disk, pap. text ed. 14.95 (*0-89898-919-1*) CPP Belwin.

— Belwin Dictionary of Music. rev. ed. Bullock, Jack, ed. (Illus.). 152p. (C). 1994. disk, pap. text ed. 14.95 (*0-89898-920-5*) CPP Belwin.

— Belwin Pocket Dictionary of Music. Bullock, Jack, ed. (Illus.). 250p. (Orig.). (YA). Date not set. pap. text ed. 4.95 (*0-89898-817-9*) CPP Belwin.

— Daniel Defoe: His Life, & Recently Discovered Writings: Extending from 1716 to 1729, 3 vols., Set. 1968. reprint ed. 219.70 (*0-685-66489-9*, 05101846, Pub. by Georg Olms GW) Lubrecht & Cramer.

— Herbs & Herbal Medicine. Passwater, Richard A. & Mindell, Earl, eds. (Good Health Guide Ser.). 1982. pap. 2.50 (*0-87983-294-0*) Keats.

— A History of the World's Safest Banks. Scott, Gary & Scott, Merri, eds. 221p. 1990. reprint ed. lib. bdg. 99.00 (*1-884875-04-1*) Adams Carter.

— Letters of William Lee, 1766-1783, 3 vols. in 1, Set. Ford, Worthington, ed. LC 70-140863. (Eyewitness Accounts of the American Revolution Ser., No. 1). (Illus.). 1971. reprint ed. 69.95 (*0-405-01254-3*) Ayer.

— Music in the 21st Century: The New Language. Bullock, Jack, ed. 84p. (Orig.). (C). 1994. disk 14.95 (*0-910957-63-0*); disk 14.95 (*0-910957-62-2*); pap. text ed. 9.95 (*0-910957-64-9*); pap. text ed. 4.95 (*0-910957-65-7*) CPP Belwin.

— Music in the 21st Century: The New Language. Bullock, Jack, ed. 84p. (Orig.). 1994. disk 14.95 (*0-7604-0067-9*); disk 14.95 (*0-7604-0068-7*) CPP Belwin.

— Music in the 21st Century: The New Language. Bullock, Jack, ed. 84p. (Orig.). (C). 1994. pap. text ed. 9.95 (*0-7604-0066-0*); pap. text ed. 4.95 (*0-7604-0065-2*) CPP Belwin.

— Raw Fruit & Vegetable Juices & Drinks. LC 82-82323. 32p. (Orig.). 1982. pap. 4.50 (*0-87983-306-8*) Keats.

Lee, William, ed. see Somerville, Thomas.

Lee, William B. & Steinberg, Earle. Service Parts Management: Principles & Practices. LC 84-70976. 129p. 1984. pap. 25.00 (*0-935406-47-6*) Am Prod & Inventory.

Lee, William C. Digital Cellular Systems. (Series in Telecommunications). 1994. text ed. write for info. (*0-471-52430-1*) Wiley.

— Mobile Cellular Telecommunications Systems. 464p. 1989. text ed. 69.00 (*0-07-037030-3*) McGraw.

— Mobile Cellular Telecommunications Systems. 2nd ed. 1995. text ed. 60.00 (*0-07-038089-9*) McGraw.

— Mobile Communications Design Fundamentals. 2nd ed. (Series in Telecommunications). 372p. 1993. text ed. 69.95 (*0-471-57446-5*) Wiley.

Lee, William H. Coenzyme Q-10. Passwater, Richard & Mindell, Earl, eds. (Good Health Guide Ser.). 32p. (Orig.). 1987. pap. 2.50 (*0-87983-427-7*) Keats.

— Friendly Bacteria. (Good Health Guide Ser.). 32p. (Orig.). 1988. pap. 2.50 (*0-87983-491-9*) Keats.

— Getting the Best Out of Your Juicer. 1992. pap. 8.95 (*0-87983-586-9*) Keats.

— Herbal Love Potions: The Magic & Ritual Use of Aphrodisiac Herbs. 160p. (Orig.). 1990. pap. 9.95 (*0-87983-544-3*) Keats.

— New Power to Love: Concentrated Virility Foods. (Illus.). 176p. 1987. 29.98 (*0-941683-00-1*) Instant Improve.

— Orotates & Other Mineral Transporters. (Good Health Guide Ser.). (Orig.). 1985. pap. 1.95 (*0-87983-337-8*) Keats.

Lee, William H. & Lee, Lynn. Book of Practical Aromatherapy. 160p. (Orig.). 1990. pap. 4.95 (*0-87983-539-7*) Keats.

— Concentrated Youth-Restoring Foods. LC 93-50191. 315p. 1994. 29.98 (*0-941683-10-9*) Instant Improve.

— The Encyclopedia of Concentrated Aphrodisiacs. 300p. 1994. 29.98 (*0-941683-29-X*) Instant Improve.

Lee, William H. & Rosenbaum, Michael. Chlorella. (Good Health Guide Ser.). 32p. (Orig.). 1987. pap. 2.50 (*0-87983-464-1*) Keats.

Lee, William O., comp. Personal & Historical Sketches & Facial History of & by Members of the Seventh Regiment Michigan Volunteer Cavalry, 1862-1865. LC 89-83404. (Illus.). 313p. 1990. reprint ed. 25.00 (*0-914905-50-3*) Detroit Bk Pr.

Lee, William R. Kelp, Dulse & Other Supplements from the Sea. (Good Health Guide Ser.). 1983. pap. text ed. 2.50 (*0-87983-313-0*) Keats.

— Language Teaching Games & Contests. 2nd ed. 1979. pap. text ed. 11.95 (*0-19-432716-7*) OUP.

Lee, William R., jt. auth. see James, C. Vaughan.

***Lee, William S. & Brown, Derrick C.** Advances in Telecommunications Networks. LC 94-44499. 1995. write for info. (*0-89006-606-X*) Artech Hse.

Lee, William W. Barkhamsted, Connecticut & Its Centennial, 1879. 178p. 1994. reprint ed. lib. bdg. 29.50 (*0-8328-4260-5*) Higginson Bk Co.

***Lee, William W. & Mamone, Robert A.** The Computer Based Training Handbook: Assessment, Design, Development, Evaluation. LC 94-46482. 283p. 1995. pap. 37.95 (*0-87778-286-5*) Educ Tech Pubns.

Lee, Winnie, jt. auth. see Lewis, Daniel I.

Lee, Wo-Yen, jt. auth. see Geping, Qu.

Lee, Y. C. Evolution, Learning & Cognition. 600p. (Orig.). (C). 1989. pap. 48.00 (*9971-5-0530-4*) World Scientific Pub.

Lee, Y. C. & Bennett, T. J., eds. Manufacturing Aspects in Electronic Packaging. (EEP Series, Vol. 2: PED: Vol. 60). 220p. 1992. 57.50 (*0-7918-1112-3*, G00756) ASME.

Lee, Y. C. & Lee, Reiko T., eds. Neoglycoconjugates: Preparation & Applications. (Illus.). 549p. 1994. text ed. 120.00 (*0-12-440585-1*) Acad Pr.

Lee, Y. C., et al, eds. Manufacturing Aspects in Electronic Packaging 1993. LC 93-73267. 125p. Date not set. pap. 40.00 (*0-7918-1032-1*) ASME.

— Methods in Enzymology Vol. 247: Neoglycoconjugates Biomedical Applications, Pt. B. (Illus.). 450p. 1994. text ed. 80.00 (*0-12-182148-X*) Acad Pr.

— Methods in Enzymology, Vol. 242: Neoglycoconjugates. (Illus.). 328p. 1994. boxed 70.00 (*0-12-182143-9*) Acad Pr.

Lee, Y. H. & Krishna, C. M. Real-Time Systems (Readings In) LC 92-14542. 256p. 1993. text ed. 45.00 (*0-8186-2997-5*, 2997) IEEE Comp Soc.

Lee, Y. K., jt. ed. see Nga, B. H.

***Lee, Y. T.** Interviews & Speeches. 244p. 1994. pap. text ed. 12.00 (*1-879771-12-8*) Global Pub NJ.

Lee Yao, Esther S. Chinese Women: Past & Present. (Woman in History Ser.: Vol. 82). (Illus.). 271p. (Orig.). 1983. lib. bdg. 30.00 (*0-86663-099-6*); pap. text ed. 15.00 (*0-86663-098-8*) Ide Hse.

Lee, Yeong H. Vertical Integration & Technological Innovation: A Transaction Cost Approach. LC 93-38432. (Studies on Industrial Productivity). 144p. 1994. 39.00 (*0-8153-1569-4*) Garland.

Lee, Yong S. Public Personnel Administration & Constitutional Values. LC 92-8404. 184p. 1992. text ed. 49.95 (*0-89930-610-1*, LCS, Quorum Bks) Greenwood.

***Lee, Yong S., ed.** Technology Transfer & Public Policy: Preparing for the Twenty-First Century. 236p. (Orig.). 1994. pap. 12.00 (*0-944285-38-4*) Pol Studies.

Lee, Young C., et al. Across the Pacific: Contemporary Korean & Korean American Art. Kim, Su G. & Kang, Myung Y., trs. (Illus.). 102p. (Orig.). (C). 1993. pap. text ed. 26.00 (*0-9604514-4-7*) Queens Mus.

Lee, Young-Sook C., jt. auth. see Martin, Samuel E.

***Lee, Yueh-Ting, et al, eds.** Stereotype Accuracy: Toward Appreciating Group Differences. 200p. 1995. text ed. 40.00 (*1-55798-307-0*) Am Psychol.

Lee, Yur-Bok. West Goes East: Paul Georg von Mollendorff & Great Power Imperialism in Late Yi Korea. LC 88-20640. (Illus.). 288p. 1988. text ed. 29.00 (*0-8248-1150-X*) UH Pr.

Lee, Z., jt. auth. see Lee, W. R.

Lee, Z., jt. auth. see Rand, W.

LeeAnn. Put Your Best Foot Forward. 135p. (J). (ps). 1995. teacher ed, text ed. 12.95 (*1-881907-07-4*) Two Bytes Pub.

Leeb, Johannes, jt. auth. see Heydecker, Joe.

Leeb, Linda, tr. see Caicedo, Andes.

Leeb-Lundberg, Kristina. Mathematics is More Than Counting. LC 85-5967. 23p. 1985. 5.00 (*0-87173-110-X*) ACEI.

Leeb, Olli. Ausgewaehlte Desserts. (Illus.). 197p. (GER.). 1985. 20.50 (*3-921799-84-8*, Pub. by Olli Leeb GW) Lubrecht & Cramer.

— Bavarian Cooking. Assembled by O. L. (Illus.). 171p. 1992. 20.50 (*3-921799-85-6*, Pub. by Olli Leeb GW) Lubrecht & Cramer.

— Bayerische Leibspeisen. Zusammengetragen von O. L. (Illus.). 171p. (GER.). 1991. 20.50 (*3-921799-80-5*, Pub. by Olli Leeb GW) Lubrecht & Cramer.

— Eva Kocht Fuer Adam, Natuerlich Collwertig - Adam Kocht Fuer Eva. (Illus.). 180p. (GER.). 1989. 20.50 (*3-921799-78-3*, Pub. by Olli Leeb GW) Lubrecht & Cramer.

— Die Feinsten Plaetzchen Rezepte: Gesammel von E. L. (Illus.). 189p. (GER.). 1991. 20.50 (*3-921799-98-8*, Pub. by Olli Leeb GW) Lubrecht & Cramer.

— Der Fleck Muss Weg. Pflege, Waesche und Reinigung Edler Textilien & Leder. (Illus.). 83p. (GER.). 1986. 17.25 (*3-921799-86-4*, Pub. by Olli Leeb GW) Lubrecht & Cramer.

— Garment Care - Stain Removal Made Easy - Laundering & Cleaning of Exclusive Fabrics & Leather. (Illus.). 84p. 1988. 17.95 (*3-921799-83-X*, Pub. by Olli Leeb GW) Lubrecht & Cramer.

— Koestlich Frische Salate. (Illus.). 192p. (GER.). 1984. 20.50 (*3-921799-88-0*, Pub. by Olli Leeb GW) Lubrecht & Cramer.

— Kuchen (Cakes) (Illus.). 155p. (GER.). 1992. 22.95 (*3-921799-70-8*, Pub. by Olli Leeb GW) Lubrecht & Cramer.

— My Favorite Cookies from the Old Country: Loved Recipes Assembled by... (Illus.). 189p. 1985. 20.50 (*3-921799-97-X*, Pub. by Olli Leeb GW) Lubrecht & Cramer.

— Schnell was Feines, Natuerlich Frisch Fuer Dich und Mich. (Illus.). 209p. (GER.). 1989. 20.50 (*3-921799-81-3*, Pub. by Olli Leeb GW) Lubrecht & Cramer.

— Von Frueh an Fit Mit Nico's Kinderkueche. 2nd ed. (Illus.). 77p. (GER.). (J). 1990. 17.25 (*3-921799-87-2*, Pub. by Olli Leeb GW) Lubrecht & Cramer.

Leeb, Olli, jt. auth. see Windisch, W. W.

Leeb, Rudolph. Konstantin und Christus: Die Verchristlichung der Imperialen Repraesentations Unter Konstantin Dem Grossen Als Spiegel Seiner Kirchenpolitik und Seines Selbstverstaendnisses Als Christlicher Kaiser. (Arbeiten zur Kirchengeschichte Ser.: Bd. 58). xiv, 225p. (GER.). (C). 1992. lib. bdg. 110.80 (*3-11-013544-2*) De Gruyter.

Leeb, Stephen & Conrad, Roger S. Market Timing for the Nineties: The Five Key Signals for When to Buy, Hold, & Sell. LC 92-5433. 208p. 1994. reprint ed. pap. 12.00 (*0-88730-689-6*) Harper Busn.

***Leebaert, Derek, ed.** The Future of Software. (Illus.). 300p. 1994. 24.95 (*0-262-12184-0*) MIT Pr.

— Soviet Military Thinking. 304p. (C). 1981. pap. text ed. 16.95 (*0-04-355016-9*) Routledge Chapman & Hall.

— Technology 2001: The Future of Computing & Communications. (Illus.). 416p. 1992. reprint ed. pap. 17.95 (*0-262-62084-7*) MIT Pr.

Leebaert, Derek & Dickinson, Timothy, eds. Soviet Strategy & the New Military Thinking. 320p. (C). 1992. pap. 19.95 (*0-521-40769-9*) Cambridge U Pr.

— Soviet Strategy & the New Military Thinking. 320p. (C). 1992. 59.95 (*0-521-40429-0*) Cambridge U Pr.

Leebaert, Derek, jt. ed. see Zeckhauser, Richard F.

Leebov, Wendy. Customer Service in Health Care. 32p. 1990. 24.95 (*0-318-69719-X*, 049254) AHPI.

— Effective Complaint Handling in Health Care. 32p. 1990. 24.95 (*0-318-69720-3*, 049256); Lot of 10 24.95. write for info. (*0-318-69721-1*) AHPI.

— Job Satisfaction Strategies for Health Care Professionals. 32p. 1991. 24.95 (*0-318-69722-X*, 049257) AHPI.

— Positive Co-Worker Relationships in Health Care. 32p. 1990. 24.95 (*0-318-69723-8*, 049255) AHPI.

— Practical Assertiveness for Health Care Professionals. (Orig.). 1991. Lot of 10 24.95. write for info. (*0-318-68382-2*, 049258) AHPI.

— The Quality Quest: A Briefing for Health Care Professionals. LC 91-26800. 43p. (Orig.). 1991. pap. 43.50 (*1-55648-076-8*, 049160); Pkg. of 10 24.95. write for info. (*0-318-68743-7*, 049260) AHPI.

— Stress: Controlling It Before It Controls You. 32p. (Orig.). 1990. Pkg. of 10 24.95. write for info. (*0-318-68808-5*, 070293) AHPI.

— Telephone Tactics for Health Care Professionals. 32p. (Orig.). 1990. Pkg. of 10 24.95. write for info. (*0-318-68807-7*, 049253) AHPI.

Leebov, Wendy & Ersoz, Clara J. The Health Care Manager's Guide to Continuous Quality Improvement. LC 91-31600. 233p. (Orig.). 1991. 49.95 (*1-55648-078-4*, 169103) AHPI.

Leebov, Wendy & Scott, Gail. Health Care Managers in Transition: Shifting Roles & Changing Organizations. LC 90-38789. (Health-Management Ser.). 228p. 1990. 30.95 (*1-55542-248-9*) Jossey-Bass.

— Service Quality Improvement: The Customer Satisfaction Strategy for Health Care. LC 93-32889. 378p. 1993. 52.00 (*1-55648-110-1*, 136107) AHPI.

Leebov, Wendy, et al. Patient Satisfaction: A Guide to Practice Enhancement. 415p. 1989. 49.95 (*0-87489-546-4*) Med Economics.

Leeburg, Verlene & Larsen, Gwynne. Using WordPerfect for Windows. 532p. 1993. pap. text ed. write for info. (*0-07-037586-0*) McGraw.

Leeburg, Verlene & Purvis, Peggy. First Look at WordPerfect 6.0 for DOS. 1994. pap. text ed. write for info. (*0-07-037599-2*) McGraw.

— Lotus 1-2-3 for Accounting: A Beginner's Supplement. 1994. pap. text ed. write for info. (*0-07-037598-4*) McGraw.

— Using WordPerfect 6.0 for DOS. 1994. pap. text ed. write for info. (*0-07-037625-5*) McGraw.

Leeburg, Verlene, jt. auth. see Larsen, Gwynne.

Leech & Brumback. Current Critical Concepts of Hydrocephalus, Vol. 1. 224p. 1991. 59.00 (*0-8151-5555-7*, Yr Bk Med Pubs) Mosby Yr Bk.

Leech, Anthony R., jt. auth. see Newsholme, Eric A.

Leech, Bryan J. John Jeremy Colton. LC 93-2472. (Illus.). 32p. (J). (ps-3). 1994. 14.95 (*1-56282-650-6*); lib. bdg. 14.89 (*1-56282-651-4*) Hyprn Child.

Leech, Bryan J., jt. ed. see Bock, Fred.

Leech, Clifford. Christopher Marlowe: Poet for the Stage. Lancashire, Anne, ed. LC 83-45278. (Studies in the Renaissance: No. 11). 1986. 39.50 (*0-404-62281-X*) AMS Pr.

— John Webster. 1972. 59.95 (*0-8490-0459-4*) Gordon Pr.

— John Webster. LC 78-143481. (English Biography Ser.: No. 31). 1969. reprint ed. lib. bdg. 75.00 (*0-8383-0690-X*) M S G Haskell Hse.

— Shakespeare's Tragedies & Other Studies in Seventeenth Century Drama. LC 75-16846. 232p. 1975. reprint ed. text ed. 49.75 (*0-8371-8266-2*, LESTO, Greenwood Pr) Greenwood.

— Tragedy. (Critical Idiom Ser.: Vol. 1). (C). 1969. pap. 8.50 (*0-416-15720-3*, NO. 2291) Routledge Chapman & Hall.

Leech, Clifford, ed. see Fane, Mildmay.

Leech, Clifford, ed. see Shakespeare, William.

Leech, D. Project Management for Profit. 1991. 69.50 (*0-13-721887-7*, 140106) P-H.

Leech, Daniel D. The Post Office Department of the United States of America. LC 75-22825. (America in Two Centuries Ser.). 1976. reprint ed. 18.95 (*0-405-07696-7*) Ayer.

Leech, F. B. & Sellers, K. C. Statistical Epidemiology in Veterinary Science. 1979. 30.00 (*0-85264-211-3*) Lubrecht & Cramer.

Leech, Geoffrey & Svartvik, Jan. A Communicative Grammar of English. 2nd ed. LC 93-45811. 1994. pap. write for info. (*0-582-08573-X*, Pub. by Longman UK); boxed write for info. (*0-582-23827-7*, Pub. by Longman UK) Longman.

Leech, Geoffrey N. Meaning & the English Verb. 2nd ed. 160p. 1987. pap. text ed. 17.95 (*0-582-30531-4*, 71922) Longman.

— Principles of Pragmatics. LC 82-22850. (Linguistics Library). (C). 1983. pap. text ed. 18.95 (*0-582-55110-2*, 74320) Longman.

Leech, Geoffrey N. & Candlin, Christopher N., eds. Computers in English Language Teaching & Research. (Applied Linguistics & Language Study Ser.). 320p. (Orig.). (C). 1986. pap. text ed. 27.95 (*0-582-55069-6*, 74300) Longman.

Leech, Geoffrey N. & Short, M. H. Style in Fiction. (English Language Ser.). 384p. (C). 1981. pap. text ed. 25.50 (*0-582-29103-8*, 71741) Longman.

Leech, Geoffrey N. & Svartvik, Jan. A Communicative Grammar of English. (Illus.). 368p. (C). 1975. pap. text ed. 23.75 (*0-582-55238-9*, 74338) Longman.

***Leech, Geoffrey N., et al, eds.** Spoken English on Computer: Transcription, Mark-up & Application. LC 94-41504. 1995. pap. write for info. (*0-582-25021-8*, Pub. by Longman UK) Longman.

Leech, Harper & Carroll, John C. Armour & His Times. LC 79-179528. (Select Bibliographies Reprint Ser.). 1977. reprint ed. 29.95 (*0-8369-6657-0*) Ayer.

Leech, J. The Comic English Grammar. 1903. 12.00 (*0-8196-5097-8*) Biblo.

— Computational Problems in Abstract Algebra. 1970. 172.00 (*0-08-012975-7*, Pub. by Pergamon Repr UK) Franklin.

— Two Papers: Eta-Coextensions of Monoids & the Structure of a Band of Groups. (Memoirs Ser.: No. 2/157). 95p. 1975. 18.00 (*0-8218-1857-0*, MEMO 2/157) Am Math.

Leech, James H., et al, eds. Parasitic Infections. (Contemporary Issues in Infectious Diseases Ser.: Vol. 7). (Illus.). 364p. 1988. text ed. 62.00 (*0-443-08561-7*) Churchill.

Leech, John. Halt! Who Goes Where? The Future of NATO in the New Europe. (Illus.). 156p. 1991. 19.95 (*0-08-040978-4*, Pub. by Brasseys UK) Brasseys Inc.

Leech, Kenneth. Soul Friend: An Invitation to Spiritual Direction. LC 91-58136. 272p. 1992. reprint ed. pap. 13.00 (*0-06-065214-4*) Harper SF.

— Spirituality & Pastoral Care. LC 89-22141. 149p. 1989. pap. 10.95 (*0-936384-84-0*) Cowley Pubns.

— True Prayer: An Invitation to Christian Spirituality. LC 80-8358. 208p. 1986. pap. 13.00 (*0-06-065232-2*) Harper SF.

— True Prayer: An Invitation to Christian Spirituality. 208p. Date not set. reprint ed. pap. 12.95 (*0-8192-1646-1*) Morehouse Pub.

— We Preach Christ Crucified: Cowley's Lent Book for 1995. 105p. 1995. pap. 9.95 (*1-56101-105-3*) Cowley Pubns.

Leech, Kenneth, jt. auth. see Gatta, Julia.

Leech, Margaret. Reveille in Washington, 1860-1865. 496p. 1991. pap. 12.95 (*0-88184-732-1*) Carroll & Graf.

***Leech, Mark.** The Prisoners' Handbook. 448p. 1995. 49.95 (*0-19-825960-3*) OUP.

Leech, Michael T., jt. auth. see Holloway, William J.

Leech, Noyes E., et al. International Legal System, Documentary Supplement: Cases & Materials. 3rd ed. (University Casebook Ser.). 574p. 1991. reprint ed. pap. text ed. 15.95 (*0-88277-674-6*) Foundation Pr.

Leech, R. Milton, ed. U.T. El Paso 2001: A Diamond Jubilee Commission Report. 1990. 10.00 (*0-87404-217-8*) Tex Western.

Leech, Richard, jt. auth. see Brumback, Roger A.

Leech, Richard W., jt. auth. see Brumback, Roger A.

Leech, Thomas. How to Prepare, Stage, & Deliver Winning Presentations. LC 92-29518. 400p. 1993. pap. 27.95 (*0-8144-7813-1*) AMACOM.

Leech-Wilkinson, Daniel. Machaut's Mass: An Introduction. 224p. 1992. reprint ed. pap. text ed. 16.95 (*0-19-816306-1*) OUP.

Leech, Wolfgang. Die Deutschen Archivare 1500 to 1945, Vol. 2: Biographisches Lexikon. 737p. (GER.). 1992. lib. bdg. 28.50 (*3-598-10605-X*) K G Saur.

Leecraft, Jodie, ed. The Auxiliaries. 2nd ed. (Rotary Drilling Ser.: Unit I, Lesson 9). (Illus.). 35p. 1981. pap. text ed. 12.00 (*0-88698-013-5*, 2.10920) PETEX.

— The Auxiliaries: Canadian Metric Edition. 2nd ed. (Rotary Drilling Ser.: Unit I, Lesson 9). (Illus.). 35p. 1981. pap. text ed. 12.00 (*0-88698-025-9*, 2.10921) PETEX.

— The Bit: Canadian Metric Edition. 3rd ed. (Rotary Drilling Ser.: Unit I, Lesson 2). (Illus.). 55p. 1980. pap. text ed. 14.00 (*0-88698-018-6*, 2.10231) PETEX.

— The Blocks & Drilling Line. Albornoz, Fernando, tr. (Rotary Drilling Ser.: Unit I, Lesson 5). (Illus.). 67p. (Orig.). (SPA.). 1982. pap. text ed. 14.00 (*0-88698-033-X*, 2.10522) PETEX.

— The Blocks & Drilling Line: Canadian Metric Edition. 2nd ed. (Rotary Drilling Ser.: Unit I, Lesson 5). (Illus.). 50p. 1980. pap. text ed. 14.00 (*0-88698-021-6*, 2.10521) PETEX.

— Circulating Systems. 3rd rev. ed. (Rotary Drilling Ser.: Unit I, Lesson 8). (Illus.). 47p. 1981. pap. text ed. 14.00 (*0-88698-012-7*, 2.10830) PETEX.

An Asterisk (*) at the beginning of an entry indicates that the title is appearing in BIP for the first time.

— Circulating Systems: Canadian Metric Edition. 3rd rev. ed. (Rotary Drilling Ser.: Unit I, Lesson 8). (Illus.). 47p. 1981. pap. text ed. 14.00 (*0-88698-024-0*, 2.10831) PETEX.
— Diesel Engines & Electric Power. 2nd rev. ed. (Rotary Drilling Ser.: Unit I, Lesson 11). (Illus.). 102p. 1982. pap. text ed. 12.00 (*0-88698-015-1*, 2.11120) PETEX.
— Diesel Engines & Electric Power: Canadian Metric Edition. 2nd rev. ed. (Rotary Drilling Ser.: Unit I, Lesson 11). (Illus.). 102p. 1982. pap. text ed. 12.00 (*0-88698-027-5*, 2.11121) PETEX.
— The Drill Stem: Canadian Metric Edition. 2nd rev. ed. (Rotary Drilling Ser.: Unit I, Lesson 3). (Illus.). 52p. 1981. pap. text ed. 14.00 (*0-88698-019-4*, 2.10321) PETEX.
— Field Handling of Natural Gas. 4th rev. ed. (Illus.). 177p. 1987. pap. text ed. 30.00 (*0-88698-127-1*, 3.10040) PETEX.
— The Hoist: Canadian Metric Edition. 2nd rev. ed. (Rotary Drilling Ser.: Unit I, Lesson 6). (Illus.). 48p. 1982. pap. text ed. 14.00 (*0-88698-022-4*, 2.10621) PETEX.
— Mud Pumps & Conditioning Equipment. 2nd rev. ed. (Rotary Drilling Ser.: Unit I, Lesson 12). (Illus.). 63p. 1982. pap. text ed. 14.00 (*0-88698-016-X*, 2.11220) PETEX.
— Mud Pumps & Conditioning Equipment: Canadian Metric Edition. 2nd rev. ed. (Rotary Drilling Ser.: Unit I, Lesson 12). (Illus.). 63p. 1982. pap. text ed. 14.00 (*0-88698-028-3*, 2.11221) PETEX.
— Power & Power Transmission. 2nd ed. (Rotary Drilling Ser.: Unit I, Lesson 7). (Illus.). 68p. 1983. pap. text ed. 14.00 (*0-88698-011-9*, 2.10720) PETEX.
— Power & Power Transmission: Canadian Metric Edition. 2nd ed. (Rotary Drilling Ser.: Unit I, Lesson 7). (Illus.). 68p. 1983. pap. text ed. 14.00 (*0-88698-023-2*, 2.10721) PETEX.
— Rotary, Kelly & Swivel: Canadian Metric Edition. 2nd ed. (Rotary Drilling Ser.: Unit I, Lesson 4). (Illus.). 68p. 1981. pap. text ed. 14.00 (*0-88698-020-8*, 2.10421) PETEX.
— Safety on the Rig. 3rd ed. (Rotary Drilling Ser.: Unit I, Lesson 10). (Illus.). 76p. 1981. pap. text ed. 14.00 (*0-88698-014-3*, 2.11030) PETEX.
Leecraft, Jodie & Greenlaw, Martha, eds. Safety on the Rig: Canadian Metric Version. 3rd ed. (Rotary Drilling Ser.: Unit I, Lesson 10). (Illus.). 76p. 1980. pap. text ed. 14.00 (*0-88698-026-7*, 2.11031) PETEX.
Leecraft, Jodie, ed. see Donnelly, Richard W.
Leecraft, Jodie, ed. see Eubank, Judith.
Leecraft, Jodie, ed. see Hall, Lewis W.
Leecraft, Jodie, ed. see Longley, Mark.
Leecraft, Jodie, ed. see Morris, Jeff, et al.
Leed, Eric J. The Mind of the Traveler: From Gilgamesh to Global Tourism. LC 90-55590. (Illus.). 352p. 1992. reprint ed. pap. 15.00 (*0-465-04619-3*) Basic.
Leed, Gretel & Goodman, L. M., eds. New York Crafts: A Historical Survey Seventeen Hundred to Eighteen Seventy-Five. (Illus.). 54p. 1972. pap. 3.00 (*0-87282-083-1*) Am Life Foun.
Leed, Richard L. Beginning Russian: Teacher's Manual. 2nd rev. ed. 78p. (C). 1991. pap. text ed. 5.95 (*0-89357-222-5*) Slavica.
Leed, Richard L. & Paperno, Slava. Five Thousand Russian Words with All Their Inflected Forms: A Russian-English Dictionary. xiv, 322p. (Orig.). (C). 1987. pap. text ed. 19.95 (*0-89357-170-9*) Slavica.
Leed, Richard L., jt. auth. see Nakhimovsky, Alexander D.
Leed, Richard L., ed. see Zhitkov, Boris.
Leed, Richard L., et al. Beginning Russian. 2nd rev. ed. (Illus.). xii, 283p. (Orig.). (C). 1991. pap. text ed. 19.95 (*0-89357-221-7*) Slavica.
Leed, Theodore W., jt. auth. see German, Gene A.
Leedale, Mark. Intervention & the East London Clothing Industry. (C). 1988. 29.00 (*0-685-30246-6*, Pub. by Oxford Polytechnic UK) St Mut.
Leeder, Elaine. The Gentle General: Rose Pesotta, Anarchist & Labor Organizer. LC 92-43028. (SUNY Series in American Labor History). 212p. (C). 1993. 59.50 (*0-7914-1671-2*); pap. 19.95 (*0-7914-1672-0*) State U NY Pr.
— Treating Abuse in Families: A Feminist & Community Approach. 232p. 1994. 41.95 (*0-8261-8530-4*) Springer Pub.
Leeder, Ellen L. El Desarraigo En las Novelas De Angel Maria De Lera. LC 77-82359. 1978. pap. 8.00 (*0-89729-176-X*) Ediciones.
— Justo Sierra y el Mar. LC 78-58669. (Coleccion Polymita Ser.). 83p. (Orig.). (SPA.). 1979. pap. 7.00 (*0-89729-202-2*) Ediciones.
Leeder, Karen, tr. see Munsterer, Hans O.
Leeder, M. R. Sedimentology: Process & Product. (Illus.). 528p. (C). 1982. pap. text ed. 34.95 (*0-04-551054-7*) Routledge Chapman & Hall.
Leeder, Ninon A. Hungarian Classical Ballads & Their Folklore. LC 67-11526. 379p. reprint ed. pap. 108.10 (*0-317-09666-4*, 2022460) Bks Demand.
Leeder, S. H. Modern Sons of the Pharaohs. LC 73-6288. (Middle East Ser.). 1973. reprint ed. 31.95 (*0-405-05346-0*) Ayer.
Leedham, G., jt. auth. see Plamondon, R.
Leedham-Green, E. S. Books in Cambridge Inventories: Book-Lists from Vice-Chancellor's Court Probate Inventories in the Tudor & Stuart Periods, 2 vols. 1987. Catalogue, Vol. II, 867pp. 165.00 (*0-521-30888-7*) Cambridge U Pr.
— Books in Cambridge Inventories: Book-Lists from Vice-Chancellor's Court Probate Inventories in the Tudor & Stuart Periods, 2 vols., Vol. I: The Inventories. 682p. 1987. The Inventories, Vol. I, 682pp. 165.00 (*0-521-30873-9*) Cambridge U Pr.
— Guide to the Archives of the Cambridge University Press 1696-1902. (Archives of British & American Publishers Ser.). 36p. (Orig.). 1973. pap. 15.00 (*0-85964-001-9*) Chadwyck-Healey.
Leedham-Green, E. S., jt. ed. see Fehrenbach, R. J.
Leedom-Ackerman, Joanne. No Marble Angels. LC 86-27897. 146p. 1987. pap. 7.95 (*0-933071-12-4*) Saybrook Pub Co.
— No Marble Angels. 1985. 13.95 (*0-916092-10-0*) Tex Ctr Writers.
***Leedom, John H.** The Group & You. 250p. 1994. 17.95 (*1-884363-05-9*) Odenwald Pr.
Leedom, Tim C., ed. see Allen, Steve, et al.
Leeds, Anthony. Cities, Classes, & the Social Order. Sanjek, Roger, ed. (Anthropology of Contemporary Issues Ser.). (Illus.). 288p. 1994. 39.95 (*0-8014-2957-9*); pap. 16.95 (*0-8014-8168-6*) Cornell U Pr.
Leeds, Barbara. Fairy Tale Rap: "Jack & the Beanstalk" & Other Stories. 32p. (Orig.). (J). (gr. k-8). 1990. pap. 5.95 (*0-9624932-0-1*); audio, pap. 12.95 (*0-9624932-2-8*); audio 8.95 (*0-9624932-1-X*) Miramonte Pr.
— Fairy Tale Rap, No. 2: The Fisherman & His Wife & Other Stories. (Illus.). 40p. (Orig.). (J). (ps-6). 1992. pap. 6.95 (*0-9624932-4-4*); audio, pap. 13.95 (*0-9624932-6-0*); audio 8.95 (*0-9624932-5-2*) Miramonte Pr.
— Give an Artichoke a Break. (Illus.). 12p. (Orig.). 1990. pap. 2.95 (*0-9624932-3-6*) Miramonte Pr.
Leeds, Bruce. Prompts: Readings for ESL Composition. (Illus.). 78p. (Orig.). (C). 1990. pap. text ed. 8.95 (*0-916177-68-8*) Am Eng Pubns.
Leeds, C. Peace & War: A First Sourcebook. (C). 1987. 50.00 (*0-685-47492-5*, Pub. by S Thornes Pubs UK) St Mut.
Leeds, Chris. Peace & War: A First Sourcebook. (Illus.). 212p. (YA). 1987. pap. 17.95 (*0-85950-526-X*, Pub. by S Thornes UK) Dufour.
— Peace & War: A First Sourcebook. 224p. (C). 1987. 47.00 (*0-685-33837-1*, Pub. by S Thornes Pubs UK) St Mut.
Leeds, D. Smart Questions on Child Education. 1994. pap. 8.99 (*0-06-104240-4*, PL) HarpC.
Leeds, David J., ed. see Brandow, Gregg.
Leeds, Dorothy. Marketing Yourself: The Ultimate Job Seeker's Guide. LC 89-46543. 320p. 1992. reprint ed. pap. 12.00 (*0-06-098418-X*, PL) HarpC.
— Powerspeak. 1991. pap. 5.50 (*0-425-12489-4*) Berkley Pub.
— Smart Questions. 1988. mass mkt. 5.99 (*0-425-11132-6*) Berkley Pub.
— Smart Questions for Savvy Shoppers. 1994. pap. 8.99 (*0-06-104313-3*, Harp PBks) HarpC.
— Smart Questions to Ask Your Insurance Agent. 1992. pap. 8.99 (*0-06-104134-3*, Harp PBks) HarpC.
— Smart Questions to Ask Your Stockbroker. 1993. pap. 8.99 (*0-06-104241-2*, PL) HarpC.
Leeds, Dorothy & Schilling, Sue B. Smart Questions to Ask Your Lawyer. 1992. pap. 8.99 (*0-06-104132-7*, Harp PBks) HarpC.
Leeds, Dorothy & Strauss, Jon M. Smart Questions to Ask Your Doctor. 1992. pap. 8.99 (*0-06-104086-X*, Harp PBks) HarpC.
Leeds, Edward T. Early Anglo-Saxon Art & Archaeology. LC 77-109764. (Illus.). xii, 130p. 1971. reprint ed. text ed. 55.00 (*0-8371-4254-7*, LEEA, Greenwood Pr) Greenwood.
Leeds, Frank. Building Backbones: Designing LAN WAN Infrastructure. 1994. pap. 29.95 (*1-55851-337-X*) M&T Bks.
Leeds-Hurwitz, Wendy. Communication in Everyday Life: A Social Interpretation. Thayer, Lee, ed. LC 89-282. (Communication: The Human Context Ser.: Vol. 3). 224p. (C). 1989. text ed. 42.50 (*0-89391-524-6*); pap. text ed. 19.95 (*0-89391-812-1*) Ablex Pub.
— Semiotics & Communication: Signs, Codes, & Cultures. (Communication Ser.). 232p. (C). 1993. text ed. 49.95 (*0-8058-1139-7*); pap. 22.50 (*0-8058-1140-0*) L Erlbaum Assocs.
Leeds, Lewis W. Lectures on Ventilation. (Library of Victorian Culture). (Illus.). 1976. reprint ed. pap. text ed. 5.00 (*0-89257-015-6*) Am Life Foun.
Leeds, Marc. The Vonnegut Encyclopedia: An Authorized Compendium with Selected Concordance. LC 94-16122. 693p. 1994. text ed. 75.00 (*0-313-29230-2*, Greenwood Pr) Greenwood.
Leeds, Marc, jt. ed. see Reed, Peter.
***Leeds, Michelle S.** Perchloroethylene (Carbon Dichloride, Tetrachloroethylene, Drycleaner, Fumigant) - Effects on Health & Work: Index of New Information. 91p. 1995. 21.95 (*0-7883-0352-X*); pap. 17.50 (*0-7883-0353-8*) ABBE Pubs Assn.
Leeds, Mike. Passports Guide to Ethnic New York. (Illus.). 1991. pap. 14.95 (*0-8442-9542-6*, Passport Bks) NTC Pub Grp.
Leeds, Morton. Ben Myer's Tales. (Illus.). 136p. (Orig.). 1988. pap. 4.95 (*0-317-90584-8*) Lone Oak Pr.
— The Devil's Disciple's Dictionary & Monodialogues. (Illus.). 136p. (Orig.). 1988. pap. text ed. 4.95 (*0-317-91132-5*) Lone Oak Pr.
Leeds, Norman E., jt. auth. see Burrows, Edmund H.
Leeds, Rachel L., et al. What to Say When: A Guide to More Effective Communication. 2nd ed. 192p. (C). 1994. per. 12.76 (*0-8403-9315-6*) Kendall-Hunt.
Leeds, Richard J., jt. ed. see Acson, Veneeta.
Leeds, Robert S. & Thompson, Gale. Mexican Debt Negotiations, 1982: Response to a Financial Crisis. 56p. (Orig.). (C). 1987. pap. text ed. write for info. (*0-318-63151-2*) JH FPI SAIS.
— The Nineteen Eighty-Two Mexican Debt Negotiations: Response to a Financial Crisis. 56p. (Orig.). (C). 1987. pap. text ed. 13.25 (*0-941700-07-0*) JH FPI SAIS.
Leeds, Roger S. & Thompson, Gale. The Nineteen Eighty-Two Mexican Debt Negotiations. (Pew Case Studies in International Affairs). 50p. (C). 1993. pap. text ed. 2.50 (*1-56927-201-8*) Geo U Inst Dplmcy.
Leeds, Salvatore L. Hernia-Simple & Complex: Index of New Information & Medical Research Bible. 150p. 1994. 44.50 (*0-7883-0136-5*); pap. 39.50 (*0-7883-0137-3*) ABBE Pubs Assn.
Leeds, Stephen, jt. auth. see Lawrence, William J.
Leeds, Valerie A. Hidden Treasures: American Paintings from Florida Private Collections. 80p. 1992. pap. write for info. (*1-880699-00-1*) Orlando Mus Art.
Leeds, Valerie A., et al. My People: The Portraits of Robert Henri. 2nd ed. Schwartz, Sheila, ed. LC 94-27381. (Illus.). 120p. Date not set. pap. 25.00 (*1-880699-03-6*) Orlando Mus Art.
Leeds, Wendy. The Child Sellers. 1981. pap. 2.25 (*0-8439-0889-0*) Dorchester Pub Co.
Leeds, William M., jt. auth. see Masser, Barry Z.
Leedskalnin, Edward. Magnetic Current. 26p. 1988. reprint ed. spiral bd. 5.50 (*0-7873-0549-9*) Mokelumne.
Leedy, Daniel L., jt. ed. see Adams, Lowell W.
Leedy, Daniel L., et al. Compatibility of Fish, Wildlife, & Floral Resources with Electric Power Facilities & Lands: An Industry Survey Analysis. 130p. 1980. write for info. (*0-318-60025-0*) Natl Inst Urban Wildlife.
Leedy, G. Frank. Check List for Marriage. LC 72-181367. 1971. 10.00 (*0-87212-023-6*) Libra.
Leedy, Jack J. & Wynbrandt, James. Executive Retirement Management: A Manager's Guide to the Planning & Implementation of a Successful Retirement. LC 86-24010. 272p. reprint ed. pap. 77.60 (*0-8357-4244-X*, 2037032) Bks Demand.
Leedy, Loreen. Blast off to Earth! A Look at Geography. LC 92-2567. (Illus.). 32p. (J). (ps-3). 1992. lib. bdg. 14.95 (*0-8234-0973-2*) Holiday.
— The Bunny Play. LC 87-17793. (Illus.). 32p. (J). (ps-3). 1988. lib. bdg. 12.95 (*0-8234-0679-2*) Holiday.
— The Dragon ABC Hunt. LC 85-21907. (Illus.). 36p. (J). (ps-1). 1986. lib. bdg. 14.95 (*0-8234-0596-6*) Holiday.
— A Dragon Christmas: Things to Make & Do. LC 88-4635. (Illus.). 32p. (J). (ps-3). 1988. lib. bdg. 13.95 (*0-8234-0716-0*) Holiday.
— The Dragon Halloween Party. LC 86-286. (Illus.). 32p. (J). (ps-3). 1986. lib. bdg. 14.95 (*0-8234-0611-3*); pap. 5.95 (*0-8234-0765-9*) Holiday.
— The Dragon Thanksgiving Feast: Things to Make & Do. LC 90-55110. (Illus.). 32p. (J). (ps-3). 1990. lib. bdg. 14.95 (*0-8234-0828-0*) Holiday.
— The Edible Pyramid. LC 94-2122. (Illus.). 32p. (J). (ps-3). 1994. lib. bdg. 15.95 (*0-8234-1126-5*) Holiday.
— Fraction Action. LC 93-22800. (Illus.). 32p. (J). (ps-3). 1994. lib. bdg. 15.95 (*0-8234-1109-5*) Holiday.
— The Furry News: How to Make a Newspaper. LC 89-20094. (Illus.). 32p. (J). (ps-3). 1990. lib. bdg. 14.95 (*0-8234-0793-4*) Holiday.
— The Furry News - How to Make a Newspaper: A Reading Rainbow Feature Book. (Illus.). (J). (ps-3). 1993. reprint ed. pap. 5.95 (*0-8234-1026-9*) Holiday.
— The Great Trash Bash. LC 90-46554. (Illus.). 32p. (J). (ps-3). 1991. lib. bdg. 14.95 (*0-8234-0869-8*) Holiday.
— Messages in the Mailbox: How to Write a Letter. LC 91-8718. (Illus.). 32p. (J). (ps-3). 1991. lib. bdg. 15.95 (*0-8234-0889-2*) Holiday.
— Messages in the Mailbox: How to Write a Letter. (Illus.). (J). 1994. pap. 5.95 (*0-8234-1079-X*) Holiday.
— The Monster Money Book. LC 91-18168. (Illus.). 32p. (J). (ps-3). 1992. lib. bdg. 14.95 (*0-8234-0922-8*) Holiday.
— A Number of Dragons. LC 85-730. (Illus.). 32p. (J). (ps-1). 1985. lib. bdg. 14.95 (*0-8234-0568-0*) Holiday.
— Pingo the Plaid Panda. LC 88-17005. (Illus.). 32p. (J). (ps-3). 1989. lib. bdg. 13.95 (*0-8234-0727-6*) Holiday.
— Postcards from Pluto: A Tour of the Solar System. LC 92-32658. (Illus.). 32p. (J). (ps-3). 1993. lib. bdg. 15.95 (*0-8234-1000-5*) Holiday.
— The Potato Party & Other Troll Tales. LC 89-1746. (Illus.). 32p. (J). (ps-3). 1989. lib. bdg. 14.95 (*0-8234-0761-6*) Holiday.
— Tracks in the Sand. LC 92-3405. (J). (ps-3). 1993. 15.00 (*0-385-30658-X*) Doubleday.
— 2 X 2 = BOO! A Set of Spooky Multiplication Stories. LC 94-46711. (Illus.). 32p. (J). 1995. lib. bdg. 15.95 (*0-8234-1190-7*) Holiday.
— Who's Who in My Family. LC 94-16611. (Illus.). 32p. (J). (ps-3). 1995. lib. bdg. 15.95 (*0-8234-1151-6*) Holiday.
Leedy, Paul D. Practical Research: Planning & Design. 5th ed. (Illus.). 368p. (C). 1993. pap. write for info. (*0-02-369242-1*) Macmillan.
Leedy, Walter, Jr. Fan Vaults: A Study of Form, Technology & Meaning. LC 79-56250. (Illus.). 1980. pap. 16.95 (*0-931228-03-4*) Arts & Arch.
Leedy, Walter C., Jr. Cleveland Builds an Art Museum: Patronage, Politics, & Architecture, 1884-1916. LC 91-3424. (Illus.). 104p. 1991. pap. 14.50 (*0-940717-09-3*) Cleveland Mus Art.
Leefeldt, Christine, jt. auth. see Callenbach, Ernest.
Leefeldt, Ed. In Search of the Paper Children. 1982. 6.00 (*0-943136-00-8*) Ctr Analysis Public Issues.
Leeflang, P. S. Mathematical Models in Marketing. lib. bdg. 24.00 (*0-685-02820-8*) Kluwer Ac.
Leeflang, P. S., jt. auth. see Naert, P. A.
***Leeftink, Bertholt.** The Desirability of Currency Unification Theory & Some Evidence. (Tinbergen Institute Research Ser.: No. 92). 227p. 1995. pap. 26.50 (*90-5170-328-7*, Pub. by Thesis Pubs NE) IBD Ltd.
Leege, David C. & Kellstedt, Lyman A. Rediscovering the Religious Factor in American Politics. LC 92-34293. 320p. (C). 1993. 49.95 (*1-56324-133-1*); pap. text ed. 19.95 (*1-56324-134-X*) M E Sharpe.
Leegood, R. C., jt. auth. see Lea, P. J.
Leegood, Richard, jt. ed. see Lea, Peter J.
Leehan, James. Defiant Hope: Spirituality for Survivors of Family Abuse. 176p. (Orig.). 1993. pap. 11.99 (*0-664-25463-2*) Westminster John Knox.
— Pastoral Care for Survivors of Family Abuse. 156p. (Orig.). 1989. pap. 12.99 (*0-664-25025-4*) Westminster John Knox.
Leehey, Kevin. Teens at Risk: How to Recognize & Prevent Adolescent Suicide. 144p. (Orig.). 1991. pap. 8.95 (*0-929162-25-0*) PIA Pr.
Leek. Human Remains from the Tomb of Tutankhamun, Vol. 5: Tutankhamun's Tomb. 1972. 34.00 (*0-900416-02-5*, Pub. by Aris & Phillips UK) David Brown.
Leek, James C., et al, eds. Principles of Physical Medicine & Rehabilitation in the Musculoskeletal Diseases. 544p. 1986. text ed. 110.00 (*0-8089-1773-0*, 792502, Grune) Saunders.
Leek, Janet, et al. Made in Africa: Learning from Carpentry Hand Tool Projects. 86p. (Orig.). 1993. pap. 9.50 (*1-85339-214-6*, Pub. by Intermed Tech UK) Women Ink.
Leek, Leslie. Heart of a Western Woman. 2nd ed. 72p. 1993. pap. 10.00 (*0-937179-09-4*) Blue Scarab.
Leek, Matthew. CD-ROM Slide Show. 118p. 1993. sl. 175.00 (*0-89258-263-4*, V124) Assn Inform & Image Mgmt.
Leek, Michael. Art of Nautical Illustration. 1991. 29.98 (*1-55521-737-0*) Bk Sales Inc.
***Leek, Michael E.** The Encyclopedia of Airbrush Techniques. (Illus.). 176p. 1995. 24.95 (*1-56138-353-8*) Running Pr.
Leek, Sybil. Astrological Guide to Successful Everyday Living. 288p. 1988. 6.99 (*0-517-67664-8*) Random Hse Value.
— The Complete Art of Witchcraft. (Illus.). 208p. 1973. pap. 4.99 (*0-451-16421-0*, Sig) NAL-Dutton.
— The Complete Art of Witchcraft. 1989. pap. 3.95 (*0-451-15344-8*) NAL-Dutton.
— How to Be Your Own Astrologer. 1980. pap. 4.95 (*0-451-16546-2*, E9426, Sig) NAL-Dutton.
Leeka, M. C. The Doll's Tea Party. (Storytime Bks.). (Illus.). 24p. (J). (ps-2). 1993. pap. text ed. 0.99 (*1-56293-343-4*) McClanahan Bk.
— Just Like Mommy, Just Like Daddy. (Storytime Bks.). (Illus.). 24p. (J). (ps-2). 1993. pap. text ed. 0.99 (*1-56293-345-0*) McClanahan Bk.
Leeka, Melinda. Andy Goes to the Zoo. LC 89-51092. 44p. (J). (gr. k-3). 1990. 5.95 (*1-55523-247-7*) Winston-Derek.
— Let's Count with Baby Lamb Chop. (Little Look-In Ser.). (Illus.). 20p. (J). 1994. write for info. (*0-307-16708-9*) Western Pub.
Leeke, Jim. Sudden Ice. LC 87-26771. (Illus.). 188p. (Orig.). 1988. pap. 8.95 (*0-89407-073-8*) Strawberry Hill.
Leeke, John, jt. auth. see Ball, John E.
Leekley, Dorothy & Noyes, Robert. Archaeological Excavations in Southern Greece. LC 76-17378. 150p. 1977. 15.00 (*0-8155-5048-0*, NP) Noyes.
Leekley, John, ed. see Catton, Bruce.
Leelakrishnan, P. Law & Environment. (C). 1992. 130.00 (*0-89771-782-1*, Pub. by Eastern Book II) St Mut.
Leelakrishnan, P., ed. Consumer Protection & Legal Control, Essays & Papers. (C). 1989. 75.00 (*0-89771-762-7*, Pub. by Eastern Book II) St Mut.
Leelanau Historical Museum Staff. Hans W. Anderson: His Life & Art. (Illus.). 80p. 1988. 20.00 (*0-930095-10-3*) Signal Bks.
***Leeland, Jeff.** One Small Sparrow: The Remarkable, Real-Life Drama of One Community's Compassionate Response. 1995. 14.99 (*0-88070-723-2*) Questar Pubs.
Leeler, Aric, jt. auth. see Van Halsema, Thea B.
Leeman, A. D. Orationis Ratio: The Stylistic Theories & Practice of the Roman Orators, Historians, & Philosophers, 2 vols. in 1. 558p. 1986. reprint ed. lib. bdg. 82.50 (*0-317-54484-5*, Pub. by A M Hakkert SP) Coronet Bks.
Leeman, Bob, jt. auth. see Stewart, Dick.
Leeman, I., jt. ed. see Taitz, J.
Leeman, Leonard. In a Nutshell: Reflections by Leonard Leeman. LC 84-90418. (Illus.). 76p. (Orig.). 1984. pap. 5.95 (*0-9613628-0-4*) G Leeman.
Leeman, Richard W. Do Everything Reform: The Reform Oratory of Frances E. Willard. LC 91-35714. (Great American Orators: Critical Studies, Speeches & Sources: No. 15). 232p. 1992. text ed. 55.00 (*0-313-27487-8*, LEE/, Greenwood Pr) Greenwood.
— The Rhetoric of Terrorism & Counterterrorism. LC 90-47522. (Contributions to the Study of Mass Media & Communications Ser.: No. 29). 232p. 1991. text ed. 55.00 (*0-313-27587-4*, LRT/, Greenwood Pr) Greenwood.
Leeman, Susan E., et al, eds. Substance P & Related Peptides: Cellular & Molecular Physiology. LC 91-27332. (Annals Ser.: Vol. 632). 497p. 1992. pap. 135.00 (*0-89766-664-X*, QP552) NY Acad Sci.
***Leemann, Sergio.** Robert Wise on His Films: From Editing Room to Director's Chair. (Illus.). 224p. (Orig.). 1995. pap. 24.95 (*1-879505-24-X*) Silman James Pr.
Leemans, Rik, et al, eds. Theory & Models in Vegetation Science: Abstracts. (Illus.). 112p. (Orig.). 1985. pap. text ed. 33.00x (*91-7210-816-9*, Pub. by Almqv & Wiksell SW) Coronet Bks.
***Leemans, W. F.** Ishtar of Lagaba & Her Dress. vi, 41p. 1952. pap. text ed. 11.75 (*0-614-04001-9*, Pub. by Netherlands Inst NE) Eisenbrauns.
— Legal & Administrative Documents of the Time of Hammurabi & the Samsuiluna (Mainly from Lagaba) vi, 120p. 1960. pap. text ed. 23.25 (*0-614-04002-7*, Pub. by Netherlands Inst NE) Eisenbrauns.
— Legal & Economic Records from the Kingdom of Larsa. viii, 103p. 1954. pap. text ed. 23.25 (*0-614-03986-X*, Pub. by Netherlands Inst NE) Eisenbrauns.

An Asterisk (*) at the beginning of an entry indicates that the title is appearing in BIP for the first time.

L

Leemhuis, F., et al. The Arabic Text of the Apocalypse of Baruch: Edited & Translated with a Parallel Translation of the Syriac Text. viii, 154p. 1986. 43.50 (*90-04-07608-5*) E J Brill.

***Leeming, Bruce.** An Anger Bequeathed. 288p. (C). 1994. pap. 32.00 (*1-874640-70-X*, Pub. by Argyll Pubng UK) St Mut.

Leeming, D. & Hartley, R. Heavy Vehicle Technology. 2nd ed. (Illus.). 260p. 1981. pap. 38.00x (*0-7487-0275-X*, Pub. by S Thornes Pubs UK) St Mut.

Leeming, D. W., jt. auth. see Farrar, C. L.

***Leeming, David.** James Baldwin: A Biography. LC 94-43198. 1995. pap. 15.95 (*0-8050-3835-3*) H Holt & Co.

— James Baldwin: Prophet on the Threshing Door. LC 93-30847. 1994. 25.00 (*0-394-57708-6*) Knopf.

Leeming, David & Page, Jake. Goddess: Myths of the Feminine Divine. (Illus.). 240p. 1994. 22.00 (*0-19-508639-2*) OUP.

Leeming, David A. ABC-CLIO Literary Companion to the Encyclopedia of Allegory. 250p. 1996. lib. bdg. 65.00 (*0-87436-781-6*) ABC-CLIO.

— Encyclopedia of Creation Myths. 256p. 1994. lib. bdg. 60.00 (*0-87436-739-5*) ABC-CLIO.

— Mythology: The Voyage of the Hero. 2nd ed. (Illus.). 370p. (C). 1990. pap. text ed. 31.50 (*0-06-043942-4*) HarpCollege.

— The World of Myth: An Anthology. (Illus.). 384p. 1991. 24.95 (*0-19-505601-9*) OUP.

— The World of Myth: An Anthology. 384p. 1992. pap. 13.95 (*0-19-507475-0*) OUP.

***Leeming, David A. & Leeming, Margaret A.** A Dictionary of Creation Myths. (Illus.). 344p. 1996. pap. 15.95 (*0-19-510275-4*) OUP.

Leeming, Donald, jt. auth. see Tidy, Michael.

Leeming, E. Janice & Tripp, Cynthia F. Segmenting the Women's Market: Using Niche Marketing to Understand & Meet the Divers Needs. 1994. 32.50 (*1-55738-561-0*) Probus Pub Co.

Leeming, Frank. The Changing Geography of China. LC 92-14969. (IBG Studies in Geography). 208p. 1993. 44.95 (*0-631-17675-6*); pap. 19.95 (*0-631-18137-7*) Blackwell Pubs.

Leeming, Glenda. Christopher Fry. (Twayne's English Authors Ser.: No. 479). 200p. (C). 1990. text ed. 22.95 (*0-8057-6998-6*, Twayne) Macmillan.

— Wesker the Playwright. 224p. 1988. pap. 11.95 (*0-413-49240-0*, A0315, Pub. by Methuen UK) Heinemann.

Leeming, Glenda, jt. comp. see Trussler, Simon.

Leeming, H., jt. ed. see Grad, A.

Leeming, Joseph. Brave Ships of England & America. LC 68-58801. (Essay Index Reprint Ser.). 1977. 24.95 (*0-8369-0024-3*) Ayer.

— Fun with String. LC 74-75260. (Illus.). 192p. 1974. reprint ed. pap. 3.95 (*0-486-23063-5*) Dover.

— Games & Fun with Playing Cards. (Illus.). 188p. 1980. reprint ed. pap. 3.95 (*0-486-23977-2*) Dover.

Leeming, Margaret. A History of Food: From Manna to Microwave. (Illus.). 184p. 1992. 26.95 (*0-563-36126-3*, BBC-Parkwest) Parkwest Pubns.

Leeming, Margaret A., jt. auth. see Leeming, David A.

***Leemis, Lawrence.** Reliability: Probabalistic Models & Statistical Methods. 1994. text ed. 71.00 (*0-13-720517-1*) P-H.

Leemis, Ralph. Mister Momboo's Hat. LC 90-34397. (Illus.). 24p. (J). (ps-00). 1991. 11.95 (*0-525-65045-8*, Cobblehill Bks) Dutton Child Bks.

— Smart Dog. (Illus.). 32p. (J). (ps-3). 1993. 14.95 (*1-56397-109-7*) Boyds Mills Pr.

***Leemon, Sheldon.** CD-ROM a Beginner's Guide. 1995. 19.99 (*0-7821-1710-4*) Sybex.

Leen. Strength Training for Beauty. 1983. 7.95 (*0-02-499810-9*) Macmillan.

Leen, Daniel. The Freighthopper's Manual for North America: Hoboing in the 21st Century. 112p. (C). 1992. pap. 7.95 (*0-9632912-7-0*) Ecodesigns NW.

Leen, Edie. Complete Women's Weight Training Guide. LC 78-64384. (Illus.). 160p. 1980. pap. 6.95 (*0-89037-161-X*) Anderson World.

— Strength Training for Beauty. 160p. 1983. pap. 7.95 (*0-89037-266-7*) Anderson World.

Leen, Edie & Bertling, Ed. The Bodybuilder's Training Diary. 160p. 1983. spiral bd. 7.95 (*0-89037-258-6*) Anderson World.

Leen, Jason. The Death of the Prophet. rev. ed. LC 88-32021. 1988. reprint ed. pap. 7.95 (*0-935699-02-3*) Illum Arts.

— Peace at Last: The After-Death Experiences of John Lennon. Thompson, John M. et al, eds. (Illus.). 172p. 1989. pap. 11.95 (*0-935699-00-7*) Illum Arts.

Leen, Jeff, jt. auth. see Gugliotta, Guy.

Leen, Nina. Images of Sound. (Illus.). 1977. pap. 3.95 (*0-393-08800-6*) Norton.

Leenaars, Antoon. Suicide Notes: Predictive Clues & Patterns. 272p. 1988. 42.95 (*0-89885-399-0*) Human Sci Pr.

Leenaars, Antoon, ed. Life Span Perspectives of Suicide: Time-Lines in the Suicide Process. (Illus.). 320p. 1991. 45.00 (*0-306-43620-5*, Plenum Pr) Plenum.

Leenaars, Antoon & Wenkstern. Suicide Prevention in Schools. 1990. 63.00 (*0-89116-954-7*); pap. 35.00 (*1-56032-081-8*) Hemisp Pub.

Leenaars, Antoon, et al, eds. Suicide & the Older Adult. 160p. 1992. lib. bdg. 25.00 (*0-89862-587-4*) Guilford Pr.

Leenaars, Antoon A., ed. Suicidology: Essays in Honor of Edwin Shneidman. LC 93-12028. 440p. 1993. 45.00 (*0-87668-571-8*) Aronson.

Leenaars, Antoon A., et al, eds. Treatment of Suicidal People. 240p. 1994. 49.50 (*1-56032-287-X*) Hemisp Pub.

***Leenaars, Ellie.** Prevention & Early Detection of Sexually Transmitted Diseases. 213p. 1994. pap. 26.50 (*90-5170-267-1*, Pub. by Thesis Pubs NE) IBD Ltd.

Leenders, Michael, jt. auth. see England, Wilbur.

Leenders, Michael R. & Blenkhorn, David L. Reverse Marketing. 1987. text ed. 40.00 (*0-02-918381-2*) Free Pr.

Leenders, Michael R. & Fearon, Harold E. Purchasing & Materials Management. 10th ed. LC 92-20079. 704p. (C). 1992. text ed. 68.95 (*0-256-10334-8*) Irwin.

Leenders, Michael R., et al. Purchasing & Materials Management. 9th ed. 672p. (C). 1989. text ed. 61.95 (*0-256-06984-0*) Irwin.

***Leenders, Michiel R. & Flynn, Anna E.** Value-Driven Purchasing: Managing the Key Steps in the Acquisition Process. LC 94-21172. (NAPM Professional Development Ser.: 13). 264p. 1994. 45.00 (*0-7863-0236-4*) Irwin.

Leene, Jentina E., ed. Textile Conservation. LC 74-179287. (Illus.). 285p. reprint ed. pap. 81.30 (*0-317-10509-4*, 2004628) Bks Demand.

Leenen, Frans H. & Haynes, R. Brian, eds. Controlling High Blood Pressure. 200p. 1989. reprint ed. 15.95 (*0-914629-87-5*) Prima Pub.

Leenen, Frans H., et al, eds. Controlling High Blood Pressure. 200p. 1991. reprint ed. pap. 8.95 (*1-55958-087-9*) Prima Pub.

Leenen, H. J., et al. The Rights of Patients in Europe: A Comparative Study. LC 92-37647. 1992. 55.00 (*90-6544-671-0*) Kluwer Law Tax Pubs.

Leenhardt, Maurice. Do Kamo: La Personne et le Mythe Dans le Monde Melanesien. Bolle, Kees W., ed. LC 77-79137. (Mythology Ser.). (FRE.). 1978. reprint ed. lib. bdg. 26.95 (*0-405-10547-9*) Ayer.

Leenhouts, H. P., jt. auth. see Chadwick, K. H.

Leenhouts, P. W. Genus Canarium in the Pacific. (BMB Ser.: No. 216). 1969. reprint ed. pap. 15.00 (*0-527-02324-8*) Periodicals Srv.

Leeper, Alexander W. A History of Medieval Austria. Seton-Watson, R. W., ed. LC 76-29416. reprint ed. 57.50 (*0-404-15347-X*) AMS Pr.

Leeper, Doris, et al. The First Decade: Atlantic Center for the Arts. 82p. (Orig.). (C). 1987. pap. 12.00 (*1-882070-00-3*) Atlantic Ctr Arts.

Leeper, Fran. Journey of the Sparrows. (J). (gr. 4-7). 1993. pap. 3.50 (*0-440-40785-0*) Dell.

Leeper, G. W. Managing the Heavy Metals. (Pollution Engineering & Technology Ser.: Vol. 6). 144p. 1978. 89.75 (*0-8247-6661-X*) Dekker.

— Soil Science: An Introduction. (Illus.). 300p. (Orig.). 1993. pap. 29.95 (*0-522-84464-2*) Intl Spec Bk.

Leeper, G. W., jt. auth. see Attiwill, P. M.

***Leeper, Gillian & Barker, Christine.** Picture It in Counted Beadwork. (Illus.). 128p. 1995. 24.95 (*0-7153-0170-5*, Pub. by D & C Pub UK) Sterling.

Leeper, John H. & Tomassoni, Mark, eds. Coal Exports & Port Development. 2nd ed. LC 81-71245. (Illus.). 116p. 1982. pap. text ed. 10.00 (*0-87033-286-4*) Cornell Maritime.

Leeper, Merton D. Colorado Trout Fishing Methods & Techniques. 2nd ed. (Illus.). 91p. (Orig.). 1989. pap. 8.95 (*0-9617325-2-0*) ML Pubns.

— Colorado Trout Fishing, Pt. 2: Prime Fishing Locations - Find Out Where 10 Percent of the Fishermen Catch 90 Percent of the Fish. (Illus.). 100p. (Orig.). 1988. per., pap. text ed. 9.95 (*0-9617325-1-2*) ML Pubns.

— Rocky Mountain Trout Fishing. (Illus.). (Orig.). 1991. pap. text ed. 9.95 (*0-9617325-3-9*) ML Pubns.

Leeper, Robert. The Brindle Mule. LC 83-15521. 1983. 11.95 (*0-913239-09-7*); pap. 7.95 (*0-913239-08-9*) Appalach Consortium.

Leeper, Sarah H., et al. Good Schools for Young Children. 5th ed. 608p. (C). 1984. text ed. write for info. (*0-02-369380-0*) Macmillan.

Leeper, Steven L., tr. see Nasu, Masamoto.

Leeper, Wayne D. Star of Jacob: Insights into the Birth of Jesus of Nazareth. 164p. 1988. pap. 8.99 (*0-89225-345-2*) Gospel Advocate.

Leer, Jeff, jt. auth. see Nyman, Elizabeth.

Leer, Norman. I Dream My Father in a Song: Poems. LC 93-15647. (Illus.). 52p. 1993. reprint ed. pap. 12.95 (*0-7734-9453-7*) E Mellen.

Leerburger, Benedict A. Marketing the Library. LC 81-18132. (Professional Librarian Ser.). 124p. 1982. pap. 26.50 (*0-914236-89-X*, Hall Reference) Macmillan.

— Promoting & Marketing the Library. rev. ed. (Professional Librarian Ser.). 300p. 1989. text ed. 38.50 (*0-8161-1926-0*, Hall Reference); pap. 26.50 (*0-8161-1895-7*, Hall Reference) Macmillan.

Leerburger, Benedict A., jt. auth. see Lay, David C.

Leerhsen, Charles, jt. auth. see Trump, Donald J.

Leerhsen, Charles, jt. auth. see Yeager, Chuck.

Leermakers, Rene. The Functional Treatment of Parsing. LC 93-22799. 176p. (C). 1993. lib. bdg. 79.95 (*0-7923-9376-7*) Kluwer Ac.

Leers, Bernadino, jt. auth. see Moser, Antonio.

Leerssen, Joseph T. Mere Irish & Fior-Ghael: Studies in the Idea of Irish Nationality, Its Development & Literary Expression Prior to the Nineteenth Century. LC 86-6879. (Utrecht Publications in General & Comparative Literature: Vol. 22). xv, 543p. 1986. 124.00 (*90-272-2198-7*) Benjamins North Am.

***Lees.** Children with Acquired Aphasia. 1993. 36.50 (*1-56593-252-8*, 0545) Singular Publishing.

— Children with Language Disorders. 254p. 1990. pap. 62.25 (*1-56593-540-3*, 0043) Singular Publishing.

Lees & Karel. Omega-Three Fatty Acids in Health & Disease. (Food Science & Technology Ser.: Vol. 37). 328p. 1990. 130.00 (*0-8247-8292-5*) Dekker.

Lees, Alfred & Heyn, Ernest V. Popular Science Decks & Sun Spaces. LC 90-10380. (Illus.). 256p. 1991. pap. 17.95 (*0-8069-7448-6*) Sterling.

Lees, Andrew & Lees, Lynn H. The Urbanization of European Society in the Nineteenth Century. (Problems in European Civilization Ser.). 237p. (C). 1976. pap. text ed. 8.50 (*0-669-95992-8*) Heath.

Lees, Bill. Is it a Sacrifice. 1987. pap. 4.95 (*9971-972-53-0*) OMF Bks.

Lees, Clare A., ed. Medieval Masculinities: Regarding Men in the Middle Ages. LC 93-37311. 1994. text ed. 44.95 (*0-8166-2425-9*); pap. text ed. 17.95 (*0-8166-2426-7*) U of Minn Pr.

Lees, D. R. & Edwards, D., eds. Evolutionary Patterns & Processes. (Linnean Society Symposium Ser.: No. 14). (Illus.). 325p. 1993. text ed. 75.00 (*0-12-440895-8*) Acad Pr.

Lees, David H. & Singer, Albert. Color Atlas of Gynecological Surgery Vol. 3: Operations for Malignant Diseases. (Illus.). 1979. 117.00 (*0-8151-5353-8*, Yr Bk Med Pubs) Mosby Yr Bk.

— Color Atlas of Gynecological Surgery Vol. 4: Surgery of Vulva & Lower Genital Tract. (Illus.). 1980. 116.50 (*0-8151-5354-6*, Yr Bk Med Pubs) Mosby Yr Bk.

— Color Atlas of Gynecological Surgery Vol. 6: Surgical Conditions Complicating Pregnancy. (Illus.). 1983. 117.00 (*0-8151-5356-2*, Yr Bk Med Pubs) Mosby Yr Bk.

Lees, F. P. & Ang, M. L. Safety Cases. 363p. 1990. text ed. 155.00 (*0-408-02708-8*) Buttrwrth-Heinemann.

Lees, Francis A., jt. auth. see Gordon, Sara L.

Lees, Francis A., et al. Global Finance. 1992. text ed. write for info. (*0-07-037069-9*) McGraw.

Lees, Frank P. Loss Prevention in Process Industries, 2 Vols. (C). 1980. 1,160.00 (*0-685-32739-6*, Pub. by Witherby & Co UK) St Mut.

— Loss Prevention in the Process Industry, 2 vols. 1980. 375.00 (*0-7506-1529-X*) Buttrwrth-Heinemann.

Lees, G. D. & Williamson, W. G. Handbook for Marine Radio Communication. 1993. 30.00 (*1-85044-472-2*) Lloyds London Pr.

Lees, Gene. Cats of Any Color: Jazz, Black & White. LC 94-8058. 288p. 1994. 25.00 (*0-19-508448-9*) OUP.

— Cats of Any Color: Jazz Black & White. 256p. 1995. reprint ed. pap. 11.95 (*0-19-510287-8*) OUP.

— Jazz Lives. (Illus.). 240p. 1992. pap. 24.95 (*1-895246-40-7*) Firefly Bks Ltd.

— Jazz Lives. (Illus.). 240p. 1992. text ed. 39.95 (*1-895565-12-X*) Firefly Bks Ltd.

— Leader of the Band: The Life of Woody Herman. (Illus.). 384p. 1995. 25.00 (*0-19-505671-X*) OUP.

— Meet Me at Jim & Andy's: Jazz Musicians & Their World. 288p. 1988. 24.95 (*0-19-504611-0*) OUP.

— Meet Me at Jim & Andy's: Jazz Musicians & Their World. braille ed. 547p. 1992. Braille. vinyl bd. 43.76 (*1-56956-280-6*, BR8449) W A T Braille.

— Meet Me at Jim & Andy's: Jazz Musicians & Their World. 288p. 1990. reprint ed. pap. 10.95 (*0-19-506580-8*) OUP.

— The Modern Rhyming Dictionary. 364p. (Orig.). (YA). (gr. 8 up). 1986. 19.95 (*0-89524-129-3*, 8649); pap. 14.95 (*0-89524-317-2*) Cherry Lane.

— Oscar Peterson: The Will to Swing. (Illus.). 304p. 1991. pap. 12.95 (*1-55958-111-5*) Prima Pub.

— Singers & the Song. 272p. 1987. 24.95 (*0-19-504293-X*) OUP.

— Singers & the Song. 272p. 1989. pap. 9.95 (*0-19-506087-3*) OUP.

— Waiting for Dizzy. 272p. 1991. 22.95 (*0-19-505670-1*) OUP.

— Waiting for Dizzy. 272p. 1992. pap. 10.95 (*0-19-507908-6*) OUP.

Lees-Haley, Cheryl E. Quality Control Circles: An Important Tool for Productivity. (Illus.). 1982. pap. text ed. 6.95 (*0-317-03935-0*) Rubicon.

Lees-Haley, Paul R. The Questionnaire Design Handbook. LC 80-82969. 150p. (Orig.). 1980. pap. 20.00 (*0-938124-00-5*) Rubicon.

— U. S. Army Tradoc Evaluation Methodology. 257p. 1983. 395.00 (*0-938124-03-X*) Rubicon.

Lees, J. D., et al. American Politics Today. LC 85-23145. 208p. (Orig.). 1988. text ed. 9.95 (*0-7190-1838-2*, Pub. by Manchester Univ Pr UK) St Martin.

Lees, James. The Masting & Rigging of English Ships of War, 1625-1860. 2nd ed. (Illus.). 212p. 1984. 59.95 (*0-87021-948-0*) Naval Inst Pr.

***Lees, Janet.** Pediatric Oral Skills Package: POSP. 80p. 1994. spiral bd. 300.00 (*0-614-00857-3*, 0762) Singular Publishing.

Lees, Janet & Urwin, Shelagh. Children with Language Disorders. 208p. 1990. 56.00 (*0-85066-496-9*); pap. 28.00 (*0-85066-497-7*) Singular Publishing.

Lees, John & Rosenhaum, Stephanie. A Programmer's Guide to C. write for info. (*0-318-58252-X*) P-H.

Lees, Lynn H. Exiles of Erin: Irish Migrants in Victorian London. LC 78-11046. 264p. 1979. 36.50 (*0-8014-1176-9*) Cornell U Pr.

Lees, Lynn H., jt. auth. see Hohenberg, Paul M.

Lees, Lynn H., jt. auth. see Lees, Andrew.

Lees, Lynne S., tr. see Duncker, Karl.

Lees, Marguerite. Still Waters. large type ed. 1977. 12.00 (*0-7089-0045-3*) Ulverscroft.

Lees, Mark. Milady's Skin Care Reference Guide. LC 93-28236. 384p. 1994. pap. text ed. 28.50 (*1-56253-071-2*) Milady Pub.

Lees, Michael. Rape of Serbia. 1990. 29.95 (*0-15-195910-2*) HarBrace.

Lees-Milne. Venetian Evenings. LC 92-8549. 1995. 14.95 (*1-56131-012-3*) New Amsterdam Bks.

Lees-Milne, Alvilde & Verey, Rosemary. The New Englishwoman's Garden. (Illus.). 152p. 1992. pap. 22.95 (*0-7011-3492-5*, Pub. by Chatto & Windus UK) Trafalgar.

Lees-Milne, James. The Age of Adam. 1988. reprint ed. lib. bdg. 59.00 (*0-7812-0146-2*) Rprt Serv.

— English Country Houses - Baroque 1685-1715. (Illus.). 304p. 1986. reprint ed. 59.50 (*1-85149-043-4*) Antique Collect.

— A Mingled Measure: Diaries, 1953-1972. 256p. 1995. 39.95 (*0-7195-5362-8*, Pub. by John Murray UK) Trafalgar.

— Roman Mornings. 148p. (Orig.). 1992. pap. 14.95 (*1-56131-011-5*) New Amsterdam Bks.

Lees, Robert B. English for Turks. (English for Foreigners Ser.). 353p. (ENG & TUR.). 1980. digital audio 100.00 (*0-87950-615-6*) Spoken Lang Serv.

— English for Turks. (English for Foreigners Ser.). 353p. (ENG & TUR.). 1980. student ed, pap. 20.00 (*0-87950-309-2*); audio 80.00 (*0-87950-614-8*) Spoken Lang Serv.

Lees, Ron. Design Construction & Refurbishment of Laboratories, Vol. 2. 256p. 1993. pap. 46.00 (*0-13-034463-X*) P-H.

— Perfect Your Legering. (Illus.). 128p. 1994. 29.95 (*1-85223-749-X*, Pub. by Crowood Pr UK) Trafalgar.

Lees, Stella, ed. A Track to Unknown Water: Proceedings of the Second Pacific Rim Conference on Children's Literature. LC 87-12852. (Illus.). 420p. 1987. reprint ed. 37.50 (*0-8108-2006-4*) Scarecrow.

Lees, Stella & Macintyre, Pamela. The Oxford Companion to Australian Children's Literature. (Illus.). 496p. 1994. 49.95 (*0-19-553284-8*) OUP.

Lees, Sue. Sugar & Spice: Sexuality & Adolescent Girls. 368p. (Orig.). 1993. pap. 12.95 (*0-14-016874-5*, Penguin Bks) Viking Penguin.

Lees, Susan, jt. ed. see Ortiz, Sutti.

Lees, T. P., jt. auth. see Jull, S. P.

Lees, Thomas. A Glossary of the Dialect of Almondbury & Huddersfield. (English Dialect Society Publications Ser.: No. 39). 1969. reprint ed. pap. 20.00 (*0-8115-0464-6*) Periodicals Srv.

Lees, W. A. Adhesives in Engineering Design. 156p. (C). 1984. text ed. 110.00 (*0-85072-150-4*) St Mut.

Leesch, Wolfgang. Die Deutschen Archivare 1500 to 1945,, Vol. 1 & 2. rev. ed. 1005p. (GER.). 1992. lib. bdg. 58.00 (*3-598-10606-8*) K G Saur.

— Die Deutschen Archivare 1500 to 1945, vol. 1: Verzeichnis nach ihren Wirkungsstatten. 268p. (GER.). 1985. lib. bdg. 28.50 (*3-598-10530-4*) K G Saur.

Leesch, Wolfgang, jt. auth. see Brenneke, Adolf.

Leese, ed. see Beman, Lynn S.

Leese, A. Agriculture & the Banking System. 1991. lib. bdg. 61.75 (*0-8490-4442-1*) Gordon Pr.

Leese, Brenda, jt. auth. see Bosanquet, Nick.

Leese, C. Leonard, tr. see Bobillier, Marie.

Leese, Charles. Leese: The Lawrence Leese Family: Two Centuries in America (1741-1941) (Illus.). 214p. 1993. reprint ed. lib. bdg. 44.00 (*0-8328-3361-4*); reprint ed. pap. 34.00 (*0-8328-3362-2*) Higginson Bk Co.

Leese, Elizabeth. Costume Design in the Movies: An Illustrated Guide to the Work of 158 Great Designers. 1990. pap. 13.95 (*0-486-26548-X*) Dover.

Leeser, Isaac. The Holy Scriptures Holy Bible Commentary. 32.50 (*0-87559-196-5*) Shalom.

Leeser, M. & Brown, G., eds. Hardware Specification, Verification & Synthesis: Mathematical Aspects. (Lecture Notes in Computer Science Ser.: Vol. 408). (Illus.). vi, 402p. 1990. pap. 39.00 (*0-387-97226-9*) Spr-Verlag.

Leesley, Michael E., ed. Computer-Aided Process Plant Design. LC 81-20335. 1400p. 1982. 50.00 (*0-87201-130-5*) Gulf Pub.

Leeson, Alan, tr. Manual of Sheep Production in the Humid Tropics of Africa. 250p. (Orig.). 1992. pap. 28.50 (*0-85198-795-8*) CAB Intl.

Leeson, C. Roland, et al. Text-Atlas of Histology. (Illus.). 768p. 1988. text ed. 67.50 (*0-7216-2386-7*) Saunders.

— Text-Atlas of Histology Slide Set. 1989. 350.00 (*0-7216-2824-9*) Saunders.

Leeson, Edward, ed. The New Golden Treasury of English Verse. 506p. (Orig.). 1994. pap. 32.50 (*0-333-61649-9*, Pub. by Papermac UK) Trans-Atl Phila.

Leeson, Francis L. A Directory of British Peerages from the Earliest Times to the Present Day. LC 85-70013. 174p. 1986. pap. 12.50 (*0-8063-1121-5*) Genealog Pub.

Leeson, George, tr. see Martin-Santos, Luis.

Leeson, Kenneth W. International Communications: Blue Print for Policy. LC 84-1603. (Information Research & Resource Reports Ser.: Vol. 4). 1984. 59.00 (*0-444-86877-1*, I-084-84, North Holland) Elsevier.

Leeson, Kenneth W., jt. auth. see Machlup, Fritz.

Leeson, M. A. Documents & Biography Pertaining to the Settlement & Progress of Stark County, Containing an Authentic Summary of Records, Documents, Historical Works & Newspapers. (Illus.). 708p. 1989. reprint ed. lib. bdg. write for info. (*0-8328-0559-9*) Higginson Bk Co.

Leeson, Muriel. Journey to Freedom. (Illus.). 128p. (Orig.). (J). (gr. 4-8). 1989. pap. 4.95 (*0-8361-3498-2*) Herald Pr.

Leeson, P. F. & Minogue, M. M., eds. Perspectives on Development: Cross-Disciplinary Themes in Development. LC 87-31386. (Contemporary Issues in Development Studies). 272p. 1988. text ed. 16.95 (*0-7190-2243-6*, Pub. by Manchester Univ Pr UK) St Martin.

Leeson, Pat & Leeson, Tom. Olympic Peninsula. (Illus.). 96p. 1988. 19.95 (*1-55652-041-7*) Chicago Review.

Leeson, Pat, jt. auth. see Leeson, Tom.

Leeson, Pat, jt. photos see Leeson, Tom.

An Asterisk (*) at the beginning of an entry indicates that the title is appearing in BIP for the first time.

Leeson, Richard. Voyage a Paris. (Illus.). 1971. pap. text ed. 5.25 (*0-582-36036-6*); audio 12.50 (*0-582-37175-9*) Longman.

Leeson, Richard M. William Inge: A Research & Production Sourcebook. LC 93-46360. (Modern Dramatists Research & Production Sourcebooks Ser.: Vol. 5). 240p. 1994. text ed. 65.00 (*0-313-27407-X*, Greenwood Pr) Greenwood.

Leeson, Robert. The Demon Bike Rider. large type ed. (Illus.). (J). (gr. 1-8). 1994. 16.95 (*0-7451-2226-4*, Galaxy Child Lrg Print) Chivers N Amer.

Leeson, Susan M. & Foster, James C. Constitutional Law: Cases in Context. LC 90-63560. 912p. (C). 1992. pap. text ed. 41.00 (*0-312-02512-2*) St Martin.

Leeson, Susan M. & Johnston, Bryan M. Ending It: Dispute Resolution in America. 164p. 1988. pap. 24.00 (*0-87084-404-0*) Anderson Pub Co.

Leeson, Ted. The Habit of Rivers. 240p. 1994. 22.95 (*1-55821-300-7*) Lyons & Burford.

— The Habit of Rivers: Reflections on Trout Streams & Fly Fishing. 192p. 1995. 10.95 (*0-14-024260-0*, Penguin Bks) Viking Penguin.

Leeson, Tom & Leeson, Pat. The American Eagle. Black, Cynthia, ed. (Earthsong Collection Ser.). (Illus.). 128p. (C). 1990. 39.95 (*0-941831-30-2*); pap. 22.95 (*0-941831-51-5*) Beyond Words Pub.

Leeson, Tom & Leeson, Pat, photos. The Wonder of Bald Eagles. LC 92-16943. (Animal Wonders Ser.). (Illus.). (J). 1992. lib. bdg. 18.60 (*0-8368-0854-1*) Gareth Stevens Inc.

Leeson, Tom, jt. auth. see Leeson, Pat.

Leestama, Sanford, jt. auth. see Nyhoff, Larry.

Leestma, Jan E. Forensic Neuropathology. Kirkpatrick, Joel B., ed. (Illus.). 464p. 1988. text ed. 215.50 (*0-88167-338-2*) Raven.

Leestma, Robert & Walberg, Herbert J., eds. Japanese Educational Productivity. LC 91-32032. (Michigan Papers in Japanese Studies: No. 22). xi, 425p. (Orig.). 1992. pap. 24.95 (*0-939512-55-6*) U MI Japan.

***Leestma, Sanford.** Turbo C Plus Plus: Programming & Problem Solving. 1996. pap. 40.00 (*0-02-369725-3*) Macmillan.

Leestma, Sanford & Nyhoff, Larry. Pascal Programming & Problem Solving. 4th ed. (Illus.). 800p. (C). 1993. pap. write for info. (*0-02-388731-1*) Macmillan.

— Programming & Problem-Solving in Modula-2. 873p. (C). 1989. pap. write for info. (*0-02-369691-5*) Macmillan.

— Turbo Pascal: Programming & Problem Solving. 2nd ed. (Illus.). 1008p. (C). 1993. pap. write for info. (*0-02-388701-X*) Macmillan.

Leestma, Sanford, jt. auth. see Nyhoff, Larry.

Leet, Don R. Population Pressure & Human Fertility Response: Ohio, 1810-1860. LC 77-14754. (Dissertations in American Economic History Ser.). 1978. 33.95 (*0-405-11046-4*) Ayer.

Leet, Don R. & Driggers, Joann. Economic Decisions for Consumers. 2nd ed. (Illus.). 1143p. (C). 1990. text ed. write for info. (*0-02-369491-2*) Macmillan.

Leet, Frank R. When Santa Was Late. (Illus.). 24p. (J). (ps-2). 1990. pap. 3.95 (*0-8249-8483-8*, Ideals Child) Hambleton-Hill.

Leet, Judith. Pleasure Seeker's Guide. (New Poetry Ser.). 1976. 6.95 (*0-395-24313-0*) HM.

Leet, Judith, ed. Good Sports: A Large Print Anthology of Great Sports Writing, Vol. 1: Baseball, Boxing, Fishing & Football. large type ed. 400p. 1990. lib. bdg. 19.95 (*0-8161-4735-3*) G K Hall.

Leet, Judith & Shur, Renee, eds. The Family: A Large Print Anthology Ser. large type ed. LC 93-30646. 1993. 21.95 (*0-8161-5643-3*) Hall.

Leet, Judith, jt. auth. see Flemming, Laraine M.

Leet, Judith, jt. ed. see Shur, Renee.

Leet, Kenneth M. Reinforced Concrete Design. (Illus.). 544p. (C). 1982. 36.00 (*0-07-037024-9*) McGraw.

— Reinforced Concrete Design. 2nd ed. 1991. text ed. write for info. (*0-07-037052-4*) McGraw.

Leet, Kenneth M. & Roesset, Jose. Fundamentals of Structural Analysis. 592p. (C). 1988. text ed. write for info. (*0-02-369480-7*) Macmillan.

Leet, Lewis D. Vibrations from Blasting Rock. LC 60-10037. 150p. reprint ed. 42.80 (*0-8357-9183-1*, 2017747) Bks Demand.

Leet, Richard E. Bil Baird...He Pulled Lots of Strings. LC 88-61658. (Illus.). 72p. (Orig.). 1988. pap. 12.50 (*0-685-49318-0*) C H MacNider Mus.

— Twenty-Five Selections American Art: Charles H. MacNider Museum. LC 91-70433. (Illus.). 72p. (Orig.). 1991. pap. 12.50 (*0-9628930-0-5*) C H MacNider Mus.

Leet, Stephen, ed. Franco Albini: Architecture & Design. LC 90-9002. (Illus.). 138p. (Orig.). 1990. pap. 9.95 (*0-910413-79-7*) Princeton Arch.

Leetch, Beverly & Grundlehner, Philip. Que Pasa? 200p. (C). 1984. pap. text ed. 24.00 (*0-03-060558-X*) HB Coll Pubs.

Leete. Learning French the Fast & Fun Way. (Fun Way Ser.). 128p. 1985. pap. 14.95 (*0-8120-2852-X*) Barron.

Leete, Burt A. & Fox, Karla H. Business Law & the Legal Environment. 3rd ed. 1216p. 1989. teacher ed write for info. (*0-318-63874-6*, H1842-9); trans. write for info. (*0-318-63877-0*, H88008); write for info. (*0-318-63875-4*, H18658); write for info. (*0-318-63876-2*, H1843-7); write for info. (*0-318-63878-9*, H88016) Allyn.

Leete, E. Leete: The Family of William Leete. (Illus.). 168p. 1990. reprint ed. lib. bdg. 34.00 (*0-8328-1486-5*); reprint ed. pap. 26.00 (*0-8328-1487-3*) Higginson Bk Co.

Leete, Richard & Alam, Iqbal, eds. The Revolution in Asian Fertility: Dimensions, Causes, & Implications. LC 92-30010. (International Studies in Demography). 1994. 55.00 (*0-19-828791-7*, Clarendon Pr) OUP.

Leeth, John. A Short Biography of John Leeth: With an Account of His Life among the Indians. (American Biography Ser.). 90p. 1991. reprint ed. lib. bdg. 59.00 (*0-7812-8240-3*) Rprt Serv.

Leeth, John D., jt. ed. see Kniesner, Thomas J.

Leetham, Helen. Sir Percy & the Dragon. (Illus.). 32p. (J). (ps-1). 1994. 17.95 (*0-86264-273-6*, Pub. by Andersen Pr UK) Trafalgar.

Leetz, Thomas. Snakes As a Hobby. (Illus.). 99p. 1991. pap. 7.95 (*0-86622-415-7*, TT001) TFH Pubns.

Leeuw, Frans L., et al, eds. Can Governments Learn? Comparative Perspectives on Evaluation & Organizational Learning. 270p. (C). 1994. text ed. 34.95 (*1-56000-130-5*) Transaction Pubs.

***Leeuwen, Jean Van.** A Fourth of July on the Plains. LC 94-33172. 1996. write for info. (*0-8037-1771-7*) Dial Bks Young.

— A Fourth of July on the Plains. LC 94-33172. 1996. lib. bdg. write for info. (*0-8037-1772-5*) Dial Bks Young.

Leeuwen, M. & Moeskops, J. The Nature Corner: Celebrating the Year's Cycle with a Seasonal Tableau. Lawson, Polly, tr. (Illus.). 88p. (DUT.). (J). (ps-3). 1990. reprint ed. pap. 12.95 (*0-86315-111-6*, Pub. by Floris Bks UK) Gryphon Hse.

Leeuwenberg, A. J. Medicinal & Poisonous Plants of the Tropics. 152p. 1988. 95.00 (*81-7089-098-5*, Pub. by Intl Bk Distr II) St Mut.

Leeuwenberg, E. L. & Buffart, H. F., eds. Formal Theories of Visual Perception. LC 77-12441. (Illus.). 357p. reprint ed. pap. 101.80 (*0-8357-3109-X*, 2039365) Bks Demand.

Leeuwenburg, Charles. Captain Boz & the Rusty Bicycle. (J). 1994. 7.95 (*0-533-10818-7*) Vantage.

Leeves, Juliet. Library Systems: A Buyer's Guide. 2nd ed. (Illus.). 230p. 1989. text ed. 89.95 (*0-566-05751-4*, Pub. by Gower UK) Ashgate Pub Co.

Leevy. Liver Diseases. 1991. write for info. (*0-8151-5364-3*, Yr Bk Med Pubs) Mosby Yr Bk.

Leevy, C. M., ed. see International Association for the Study of the Liver Staff.

Leevy, Carroll M., et al. Diseases of the Liver & Biliary Tract: Standardization of Nomenclature, Diagnostic Criteria, & Prognosis. LC 94-2183. 224p. 1995. 40.00 (*0-7817-0211-9*) Raven.

Lefafa Sedek. The Bandlet of Righteousness, an Ethiopian Book of the Dead. Budge, E. A., tr. LC 77-87667. (Luzac's Semitic Text & Translation Ser.: No. 19). reprint ed. 27.50 (*0-404-11349-4*) AMS Pr.

Lefaivre, Liane, jt. auth. see Tzonis, Alexander.

LeFanu, J. Sheridan. The House by the Church-Yard. 500p. 1992. reprint ed. lib. bdg. 43.95 (*0-89968-312-6*, Lghtyr Pr) Buccaneer Bks.

— Uncle Silas. 400p. 1992. reprint ed. lib. bdg. 34.95 (*0-89968-311-8*, Lghtyr Pr) Buccaneer Bks.

Lefanu, J. Sheridan. Wylder's Hand. LC 77-84059. 1978. reprint ed. pap. 8.95 (*0-486-23570-X*) Dover.

LeFanu, Joseph. Green Tea & Other Ghost Stories. LC 93-11037. (Thrift Editions Ser.). 96p. 1993. pap. 1.00 (*0-486-27795-X*) Dover.

Lefanu, Sarah. Feminism & Science Fiction. LC 88-8555. (Illus.). 272p. 1989. 29.95 (*0-253-33287-7*); pap. 9.95 (*0-253-23100-0*) Ind U Pr.

LeFanu, Sheridan & Donaldson, Norman. The Rose & the Key. (Mystery Ser.). 448p. 1983. reprint ed. pap. 7.95 (*0-486-24377-X*) Dover.

***LeFanu, William.** Nehemiah Grew: A Study & Bibliography of His Writings. 199p. 1990. 36.00 (*0-614-07331-6*) Oak Knoll Pr.

LeFanu, William R. Notable Medical Books: From the Lilly Library Indiana University. Waife, S. O. et al, eds. (Illus.). 275p. (C). 1976. 20.00 (*0-685-20051-5*) IN Univ Lilly Library.

LeFar, Mable F. & Wilson, Caroline P. Abstract of Wills Catham County, Georgia, 1773-1817. 160p. 1985. 7.50 (*0-915156-06-7*, SP 6) Natl Genealogical.

Lefave, Linda. Mammography: Pretest Self-Assessment & Review. LC 93-3913. (Pretest Specialty Level Ser.). 160p. 1994. pap. 22.00 (*0-07-052017-8*) Hlth Prof Div.

— Medical Radiography: PreTest Self-Assessment & Review. (Specialty Level PreTest Ser.). (Illus.). 304p. 6995. pap. text ed. 28.00 (*0-07-052078-X*) Hlth Prof Div.

Lefavi, Bruce. Bulletproof Financial Future. 1994. pap. 12.00 (*0-671-76980-4*) S&S Trade.

Lefavor, Marshall. Locals Only. 64p. 1993. pap. 4.95 (*1-880365-51-0*) Prof Pr NC.

LeFay, Dee. Love Is Forever. 1993. 8.95 (*0-533-10455-6*) Vantage.

Lefco, Helene. Dance Therapy: Narrative Case Histories of Therapy Sessions with Six Patients. LC 73-88511. 158p. 1974. 28.95 (*0-911012-93-1*) Nelson-Hall.

Lefcoe, George, ed. Urban Land Policy for the 1980s: The Message for State & Local Government. LC 82-48492. (Lincoln Institute of Land Policy Book Ser.). 233p. reprint ed. pap. 66.50 (*0-7837-3269-4*, 2043288) Bks Demand.

Lefcoe, George, ed. see Conference on Local Governments' Decisions & the Local Tax Base Staff.

Lefcoe, George, jt. ed. see Noothoven van Goor, J. M.

Lefcourt, Carol H. Women & the Law. LC 84-11150. (Civil Rights Ser.). 1984. ring bd. 140.00 (*0-87632-441-3*) Clark Boardman Callaghan.

Lefcourt, H. M. Humor & Life Stress. (Illus.). 168p. 1986. 50.00 (*0-387-96249-2*) Spr-Verlag.

Lefcourt, Herbert M. Locus of Control: Current Trends in Theory & Research. 2nd ed. 288p. (C). 1982. text ed. 49.95 (*0-89859-222-4*) L Erlbaum Assocs.

Lefcourt, Herbert M., ed. Research with the Locus of Control Construct: Assessment Methods, Vol. I. LC 81-7876. 1981. text ed. 85.00 (*0-12-443201-8*) Acad Pr.

— Research with the Locus of Control Construct: Developments & Social Problems, Vol. 2. 1983. text ed. 85.00 (*0-12-443202-6*) Acad Pr.

— Research with the Locus of Control Construct, Vol. 3: Extensions & Limitations. 1984. text ed. 85.00 (*0-12-443203-4*) Acad Pr.

Lefcourt, Peter. The Deal. 1991. 18.50 (*0-679-40152-0*) Random.

— The Deal: A Novel of Hollywood. LC 92-54927. 304p. 1993. pap. 12.00 (*0-06-097560-1*, PL) HarpC.

— Di & I. LC 93-38837. 1994. 20.00 (*0-679-42583-7*) Random.

— Di & I: A Novel. 1995. pap. 12.00 (*0-06-097668-3*, PL) HarpC.

— The Dreyfus Affair: A Love Story. LC 92-54926. 304p. 1993. pap. 12.00 (*0-06-097559-8*, PL) HarpC.

Lefcowitz, Allan B., jt. auth. see Jason, Philip K.

Lefcowitz, Barbara. The Queen of Lost Baggage. LC 85-52078. (Series Ten). 72p. (Orig.). 1986. pap. 7.00 (*0-931846-29-3*) Wash Writers Pub.

Lefcowitz, Barbara F. Red Lies & White Lies. LC 93-85470. 270p. (Orig.). 1994. pap. 9.00 (*0-9637290-0-4*) East Coast Bks.

— Shadows & Goatbones. LC 92-51111. (SCOP Ser.: No. 18). 64p. 1992. pap. 9.95 (*0-930526-17-1*) SCOP Pubns.

Lefcowitz, Eric. Buy American: Buy This Book. LC 92-18554. 96p. 1992. pap. 5.95 (*0-89815-495-2*) Ten Speed Pr.

— Monkees Tale. rev. ed. 1990. pap. 11.95 (*0-86719-378-6*) Last Gasp.

— Tomorrow Never Knows: The Beatles' Last Concert. Sethi, Anita, ed. LC 87-80730. (Illus.). 104p. (Orig.). 1987. pap. 12.95 (*0-943249-02-3*) Terra Firma Bks.

— Tomorrow Never Knows: The Beatles' Last Concert. 2nd ed. (Illus.). 104p. (Orig.). 1991. 24.95 (*0-943249-04-X*) Terra Firma Bks.

— The United States Immigration History Timeline. (Illus.). 1990. 5.95 (*0-943249-03-1*) Terra Firma Bks.

Lefeber, Louis, et al. Regional Development: Experiences & Prospects in South & Southeast Asia. LC 72-152080. (Regional Planning Ser.: No. 1). 278p. 1971. text ed. 33.85 (*90-279-6914-0*) Mouton.

Lefeber, Rene, ed. The Changing Political Structure of Europe: Aspects of International Law. 298p. (C). 1991. lib. bdg. 100.00 (*0-7923-1379-8*) Kluwer Ac.

Lefeber, Rosalind, tr. see Goldman, Robert P., ed.

Lefebure, Leo D. The Buddha & the Christ: Explorations in Buddhist & Christian Dialogue. LC 93-7972. (Faith Meets Faith Ser.). 250p. (Orig.). 1993. pap. 18.95 (*0-88344-924-2*) Orbis Bks.

— Life Transformed: Meditations on the Christian Scriptures in Light of Buddhist Perspectives. (Illus.). 192p. (Orig.). 1989. pap. 9.95 (*0-914070-61-4*, 115) ACTA Pubns.

— Toward a Contemporary Wisdom Christology: A Study of Karl Rahner & Norman Pittenger. LC 88-22798. 298p. (Orig.). (C). 1988. lib. bdg. 45.00 (*0-8191-7151-4*); pap. text ed. 25.00 (*0-8191-7152-2*) U Pr of Amer.

Lefebure, Marcus & Schauder, Hans. Conversations on Counselling: Between a Doctor & a Priest. 3rd ed. 288p. 1990. pap. 25.95 (*0-567-29164-2*, Pub. by T & T Clark UK) Bks Intl VA.

Lefebure, Molly. Blitz! braille ed. 728p. 1992. vinyl bd. 58.24 (*1-56956-197-4*, BR8325) W A T Braille.

— Thunder in the Sky. 352p. 1993. 24.95 (*0-575-04807-7*, Pub. by V Gollancz UK) Trafalgar.

Lefebure, Molly, jt. ed. see Gravil, Richard.

Lefebvre. Glossaire de la Finance. 284p. (ENG & FRE.). 1976. 39.95 (*0-8288-5699-0*, M6350) Fr & Eur.

***Lefebvre, Andre.** Dictionnaire Pratique des Collectivites Territoriales. 1988. write for info. (*0-7859-8176-4*, 2-87603-010-1) Fr & Eur.

Lefebvre, Anny, tr. see Beaud, Michel.

Lefebvre, Arthur H. Atomization & Sprays. (Combustion: An International Ser.). 433p. 1988. 99.50 (*0-89116-603-3*) Hemisp Pub.

Lefebvre, Arthur H., ed. Gas Turbine Combustion. LC 79-22350. 431p. 1983. pap. 68.00 (*0-89116-896-6*) Hemisp Pub.

Lefebvre-Brion, Helene & Field, Robert W. Perturbations in the Spectrum of Diatomic Molecues. 1986. text ed. 68.00 (*0-12-442690-5*); pap. text ed. 68.00 (*0-12-442691-3*) Acad Pr.

Lefebvre, Christian. European Financial Reporting: Belgium. LC 93-34971. (Illus.). 240p. 1994. 110.00x (*0-415-06776-6*, B0272) Routledge.

Lefebvre, Claire, ed. Serial Verbs: Grammatical, Comparative & Cognitive Approaches. LC 91-7128. (Studies in the Sciences of Language: No. 8). viii, 210p. 1991. pap. 50.00 (*1-55619-384-X*) Benjamins North Am.

Lefebvre, Claire & Muysken, Pieter. Mixed Categories. (C). 1988. lib. bdg. 100.50 (*1-55608-050-6*); pap. text ed. 38.00 (*1-55608-051-4*) Kluwer Ac.

Lefebvre, Dom G. God Present. 1979. pap. 3.95 (*0-03-053436-4*) Harper SF.

Lefebvre, G., ed. Inscriptiones Graecae Aegypti, No. 5: Christian Inscriptions. xii, 173p. 1978. 30.00 (*0-89005-248-4*) Ares.

Lefebvre, G., jt. ed. see Pedrizet, P.

LeFebvre, George, jt. auth. see Bloom, Anthony.

Lefebvre, Georges. Coming of the French Revolution. Palmer, Robert R., tr. 256p. 1989. 45.00 (*0-691-05112-7*); pap. 9.95 (*0-691-00751-9*) Princeton U Pr.

— Napoleon, 2 vols., Set. Stockhold, Henry F. & Anderson, J. E., trs. 776p. 1990. pap. text ed. 32.50 (*0-231-07387-9*) Col U Pr.

— Napoleon, 2 vols., Vol. 1: From 18 Brumaire to Tilsit, 1799-1807. Stockhold, Henry F. & Anderson, J. E., trs. 776p. 1990. pap. text ed. 14.50 (*0-231-07389-5*) Col U Pr.

— Napoleon, 2 vols., Vol. 2: From Tilsit to Waterloo, 1807-1815. Stockhold, Henry F. & Anderson, J. E., trs. 776p. 1990. pap. text ed. 19.50 (*0-231-07391-7*) Col U Pr.

— Napoleon, Vol. 1: From Eighteen Brumaire to Tilsit, 1799-1807. Stockhold, Henry F., tr. LC 68-29160. 337p. 1969. text ed. 52.50 (*0-231-02558-0*) Col U Pr.

— Napoleon, Vol. 2: From Tilsit to Waterloo, 1807-1815. Anderson, J. E., tr. LC 74-79193. 414p. 1969. text ed. 53.00 (*0-231-03313-3*) Col U Pr.

Lefebvre, Gilles, jt. auth. see Chauvel, Alain.

Lefebvre, Henri. Critique of Everyday Life. 1991. 39.95 (*0-86091-340-6*, Pub. by Verso UK) Routledge Chapman & Hall.

— Critique of Everyday Life, Vol. 1. Moore, John, tr. 336p. 1991. 39.95 (*0-86091-331-7*, A6393, Pub. by Verso UK) Routledge Chapman & Hall.

— Critique of Everyday Life, Vol. 1. Moore, John, tr. 312p. 1992. pap. 18.95 (*0-86091-587-5*, A9726, Pub. by Verso UK) Routledge Chapman & Hall.

— Everyday Life in the Modern World. Rabinovitch, Sacha, tr. 226p. 1994. pap. 21.95 (*0-87855-972-8*) Transaction Pubs.

— The Explosion: Marxism & the French Revolution. LC 69-19790. 157p. reprint ed. pap. 44.80 (*0-317-27734-0*, 2019475) Bks Demand.

— Introduction to Modernity. Moore, John, tr. 400p. 1995. 64.95x (*1-85984-961-X*, C0498, Pub. by Verso UK); pap. 22.95 (*1-85984-056-6*, C0499, Pub. by Verso UK) Routledge Chapman & Hall.

— The Production of Space. Nicholson-Smith, Donald, tr. 500p. 1991. pap. text ed. 21.95 (*0-631-18177-6*) Blackwell Pubs.

— The Sociology of Marx. LC 82-9539. (Morningside Bk.). 218p. 1982. text ed. 47.50 (*0-231-05580-3*); pap. text ed. 15.50 (*0-231-05581-1*) Col U Pr.

Lefebvre, Jeffrey. Arms for the Horn: U. S. Security Policy in Ethiopia & Somalia, 1953-1991. LC 90-28360. (Policy & Institutional Studies). 360p. (C). 1991. text ed. 49.95 (*0-8229-3680-1*) U of Pittsburgh Pr.

Lefebvre, M. N., jt. auth. see Ginns, J.

***Lefebvre, Marcel.** Commentaries on the Acts of the Magisterium. Angelus Press Staff, ed. SSPX Staff, tr. 384p. (Orig.). 1995. pap. 8.95 (*0-935952-28-4*) Angelus Pr.

— Open Letter to Confused Catholics. 3rd ed. Society of St. Pius X Staff, tr. 163p. 1992. reprint ed. pap. 8.95 (*0-935952-13-6*) Angelus Pr.

— Pastoral Letters. Society of St. Pius X Staff, tr. 148p. (Orig.). 1992. pap. text ed. 8.95 (*0-935952-99-3*) Angelus Pr.

— Spiritual Journey. Society of St. Pius X Staff, tr. 73p. (Orig.). 1991. pap. text ed. 5.95 (*0-935952-16-0*) Angelus Pr.

— They Have Uncrowned Him. 3rd ed. Society of St. Pius X Staff, tr. 261p. 1992. reprint ed. pap. text ed. 9.95 (*0-935952-05-5*) Angelus Pr.

Lefebvre, P. J. & Standl, E., eds. New Aspects in Diabetes: Treatment Strategies with Alphaglucosidase Inhibitors. (Illus.). xii, 306p. (C). 1993. lib. bdg. 98.50 (*3-11-013469-1*) De Gruyter.

Lefebvre, Philip, jt. auth. see Miller, Susan J.

Lefebvre, Pierre J., ed. Glucagon I. (Handbook of Experimental Pharmacology Ser.: Vol. 66, I). (Illus.). 535p. 1983. 287.00 (*0-387-12068-8*) Spr-Verlag.

Lefebvre, Pierre J. & Unger, R. Glucagon: Molecular Physiology Clinical & Therapeutic Implications. LC 72-75311. 1972. 160.00 (*0-08-016851-5*, Pub. by Pergamon Repr UK) Franklin.

Lefebvre, Pierre J., jt. ed. see Creutzfeldt, W.

Lefebvre, Pierre J., jt. ed. see Serrano-Rios, M.

Lefebvre, R. & Mukamel, S., eds. Stochasticity & Intramolecular Redistribution of Energy. (C). 1987. lib. bdg. 114.00 (*90-277-2462-8*) Kluwer Ac.

Lefebvre, Sue. Hermosillo from A to Z. LC 82-60112. (Illus.). 193p. (ENG & SPA.). (gr. 5-12). 1982. pap. 13.50 (*0-9608702-0-2*) Shared Care.

Lefebvre, Vladimir A. Algebra of Conscience. 1982. lib. bdg. 84.00 (*90-277-1301-4*) Kluwer Ac.

— A Psychological Theory of Bipolarity & Reflexivity. LC 92-21158. 120p. 1992. text ed. 59.95 (*0-7734-9226-7*) E Mellen.

Lefer, Diane. The Circles I Move In: Short Stories. LC 94-14562. (Illus.). 192p. 1994. 19.95 (*0-944072-41-0*) Zoland Bks.

— Emma Lazarus. (American Women of Achievement Ser.). (Illus.). 112p. (YA). (gr. 5 up). 1988. lib. bdg. 17.95 (*1-55546-664-8*) Chelsea Hse.

Lefeuvre, Amy. Hijos Prodigos: Prodigal Children. (SPA.). 3.25 (*84-7228-295-3*, 220460, Pub. by Edit Clie SP) TSELF.

Lefever, Alan J. Fighting the Good Fight: The Life & Work of Benajah Harvey Carroll. LC 93-44797. 200p. 1994. 19.95 (*0-89015-943-2*) Sunbelt Media.

Lefever, Ernest W. Nairobi to Vancouver: The World Council of Churches & the World, 1975-87. LC 87-30302. 166p. (Orig.). (C). 1988. lib. bdg. 31.50 (*0-89633-117-2*); pap. text ed. 12.75 (*0-89633-118-0*) Ethics & Public Policy.

— Nuclear Arms in the Third World: U. S. Policy Dilemma. LC 78-24810. 168p. reprint ed. pap. 47.90 (*0-317-26734-5*, 2025388) Bks Demand.

— Uncertain Mandate: Politics of the U. N. Congo Operation. LC 67-22890. 270p. reprint ed. pap. 77.00 (*0-317-28789-3*, 2020540) Bks Demand.

Lefever, Ernest W., ed. Morality & Foreign Policy: A Symposium on President Carter's Stance. LC 77-92745. 82p. 1977. pap. 12.25 (*0-89633-005-2*) Ethics & Public Policy.

— Reinvigorating Our Schools: A Challenge to Parents, Teachers, & Policymakers. 56p. 1985. pap. 10.50 (*0-89633-094-X*) Ethics & Public Policy.

An Asterisk (*) at the beginning of an entry indicates that the title is appearing in BIP for the first time.

Lefever, Ernest W. & Kalb, Marvin. Ethics & United States Foreign Policy. 236p. 1986. reprint ed. pap. text ed. 22. 00 (0-8191-5168-8) U Pr of Amer.

Lefever, Ernest W. & Vander Lugt, Robert D., eds. Perestroika: How New Is Gorbachev's New Thinking? LC 88-21855. 259p. 1989. 29.95 (0-89633-133-4); pap. 12.95 (0-89633-134-2) Ethics & Public Policy.

Lefever, Ernest W., ed. see Niebuhr, Reinhold.

Lefever, Ernest W., et al. Scholars, Dollars & Public Policy: New Frontiers in Corporate Giving. LC 82-25126. 62p. 1983. pap. 13.50 (0-89633-065-6) Ethics & Public Policy.

Lefever, Ernest W., et al, eds. Ethics & World Politics: Four Perspectives. LC 88-3832. 116p. (C). reprint ed. pap. text ed. 15.50 (0-89633-132-6) Ethics & Public Policy.

Lefever, Harry G. Turtle Bogue: Afro-Caribbean Life & Culture in a Costa Rican Village. LC 90-50792. (Illus.). 256p. 1992. 39.50 (0-945636-23-7) Susquehanna U Pr.

LeFever, Marlene. Creative Hospitality. 1980. 9.99 (0-8423-0489-4) Tyndale.

— 50 Days to Welcome Jesus to My Church: Children's Journal for the 50-Day Adventure Series. (1991 50-Day Spiritual Adventure Ser.). (Illus.). 64p. (Orig.). (J). (gr. 3-6). 1990. student ed, pap. text ed. 3.95 (1-879050-02-1) Chapel of Air.

— God's Special Creation--Me! (Bible Discovery Guide for Junior Campers Ser.). (Illus.). 48p. (Orig.). (J). (gr. 4-6). 1987. Camper Ed. student ed, pap. 1.50 (0-87788-313-0); Counselor Ed. teacher ed, pap. 3.50 (0-87788-314-9) Shaw Pubs.

— Survival Kit for Growing Christians. (Bible Discovery Guide Ser.). 32p. (J). (gr. 4-6). 1988. 1.50 (0-87788-796-9); 3.50 (0-87788-797-7) Shaw Pubs.

LeFever, Marlene D. Creative Teaching Methods: Helps You Be a Better Teacher. 320p. 1985. 21.95 (0-89191-760-8, 25254) Cook.

***Lefever, Michael.** Hospitality Review. 560p. (C). 1995. pap. text ed. 59.95 (0-7872-0251-7) Kendall-Hunt.

Lefever, Michael, jt. auth. see Brymer, Robert A.

Lefever, Michael M. Restaurant Reality: A Manager's Guide. (Illus.). 304p. (Orig.). (C). 1989. pap. 29.95 (0-442-25938-7) Van Nos Reinhold.

Lefever, R., jt. auth. see Horsthemke, W.

Lefever, Robert A., ed. Preparation & Properties of Solid State Materials: Aspects of Crystal Growth, Vol. 1. LC 78-155744. (Illus.). 292p. reprint ed. pap. 83.30 (0-317-08022-9, 2017856) Bks Demand.

Lefever, Robert A., jt. ed. see Wilcox, William R.

Lefevere, Andre. Translating Literature: Translational Practice, Literary Theory, Comparative Literature. LC 92-20469. 170p. (C). 1992. text ed. 37.50 (0-87352-393-8, S760C); pap. text ed. 15.50 (0-87352-394-6, S760P) Modern Lang.

Lefevere, Andre, tr. see Jaccottet, Phillipe.

Lefevere, Andre, tr. see Streuvels, Stijn.

Lefevere, Andre, tr. see Verdeyen, Paul.

Lefevere, Andre, ed. see Von Eschenbach, Wolfram.

Lefevere, Andre, tr. see Vuyk, Beb & Friedericy, H. J.

LeFevour, Edward. Western Enterprise in Late Ch'ing China: A Selective Survey of Jardine, Matheson & Company's Operations, 1842-1895. LC 73-386. (East Asian Monographs: No. 26). 222p. 1968. pap. 11.00 (0-674-95010-0) HUP.

Lefevre, jt. auth. see Schrock.

Lefevre, Andre. Translation, Rewriting & the Manipulation of Literary Fame. LC 92-7608. (Translation Studies). 208p. 1992. 59.95 (0-415-07699-4, A9566); pap. 15.95 (0-415-07700-1, A9570) Routledge.

Lefevre, Andre, ed. Translation - History - Culture: A Sourcebook. LC 92-6010. (Translation Studies). 256p. 1992. 69.95 (0-415-07697-8, A9617); pap. 15.95 (0-415-07698-6, A9621) Routledge.

Lefevre, Andre, jt. ed. see Bassnett, Susan.

Lefevre, Carl A. & Lefevre, Helen E. Reading Power & Study Skills for College Work. 2nd ed. 356p. (C). 1984. pap. text ed. 18.75 (0-15-575759-8) HB Coll Pubs.

LeFevre, Carol & LeFevre, Perry, eds. Aging & the Human Spirit: A Reader in Religion & Gerontology. 2nd ed. LC 84-72932. 367p. (C). 1985. text ed. 31.95 (0-913552-27-5) Exploration Pr.

LeFevre, Dale N. New Games for the Whole Family. 160p. 1988. pap. 9.95 (0-399-51448-1, Perigree Bks) Berkley Pub.

Lefevre, Edwin. The Golden Flood. LC 90-81218. 199p. 1990. reprint ed. pap. 14.00 (0-87034-096-4) Fraser Pub Co.

— The Making of a Stockbroker. LC 75-2645. (Wall Street & the Security Market Ser.). 1975. reprint ed. 28.95 (0-405-06970-7) Ayer.

— The Plunderers. LC 83-80981. (Illus.). 344p. 1983. reprint ed. pap. 18.00 (0-87034-067-0) Fraser Pub Co.

— The Plunderers: A Novel. LC 75-152945. (Short Story Index Reprint Ser.). 1977. reprint ed. 23.95 (0-8369-3804-6) Ayer.

— Reminiscence of a Stock Operator. 1994. text ed. 37.95 (0-471-05968-4); pap. text ed. 16.95 (0-471-05970-6) Wiley.

— Reminiscences of a Stock Operator. 248p. 1987. reprint ed. lib. bdg. 25.95 (0-89966-605-1) Buccaneer Bks.

— Sampson Rock of Wall Street. LC 85-70939. 400p. 1985. reprint ed. pap. 20.00 (0-87034-076-X) Fraser Pub Co.

— Wall Street Stories. LC 75-150478. (Short Story Index Reprint Ser.). 1977. reprint ed. 19.95 (0-8369-3819-4) Ayer.

Lefevre, Frances, tr. see Moro, Cesar.

Lefevre, George, Jr., jt. auth. see Oppenheimer, Steven B.

Lefevre, Gustave, ed. see Piccinni, Niccolo.

Lefevre, Gustave, ed. see Salieri, Antonio.

Lefevre, Helen E., jt. auth. see Lefevre, Carl A.

Lefevre, Henry L. Quality Service Pays: Six Keys to Success. (Illus.). 375p. 1989. 32.95 (0-527-91629-3, 916293) Qual Resc.

Lefevre, Henry L., ed. Government Quality & Productivity: Success Stories. LC 92-12927. 344p. 1992. 25.95 (0-87389-150-3) ASQC Qual Pr.

Lefevre, Herve C. The Fiber-Optic Gyroscope. LC 92-28194. (Optoelectronics Ser.). 300p. 1992. text ed. 85.00 (0-89006-537-3) Artech Hse.

Lefevre, J. P., jt. auth. see Pfleger, S.

Lefevre, Jean-Francois, jt. auth. see Lafaurie, Andre-Jean.

Lefevre, Julie, ed. see Jacobsen, Jay.

LeFevre, Karen B. Invention As a Social Act. LC 86-15437. (Studies in Writing & Rhetoric). 187p. (Orig.). 1986. pap. text ed. 12.95 (0-8093-1328-6) S Ill U Pr.

Lefevre, Ken, ed. see Parnau, Jeffery R.

LeFevre, Perry. Radical Prayer: Contemporary Interpretations. LC 82-72097. 94p. 1982. text ed. 16.95 (0-913552-18-6); pap. text ed. 8.95 (0-913552-19-4) Exploration Pr.

LeFevre, Perry & Schroeder, W. Widick, eds. Creative Ministries in Contemporary Christianity. LC 90-86031. (Studies in Ministry & Parish Life). 280p. 1991. 31.95 (0-913552-44-5) Exploration Pr.

— Pastoral Care & Liberation Praxis: Studies in Personal & Social Transformation. (Studies in Ministry & Parish Life). 112p. 1986. text ed. 19.95 (0-913552-31-3); pap. text ed. 12.95x (0-913552-32-1) Exploration Pr.

Lefevre, Perry & Schroeder, W. Widick, eds. Spiritual Nurture & Congregational Development. (Studies in Ministry & Parish Life). 186p. 1984. text ed. 21.95 (0-913552-20-8) Exploration Pr.

LeFevre, Perry, jt. ed. see LeFevre, Carol.

LeFevre, Perry, ed. see Tillich, Paul.

LeFevre, Perry, ed. see Williams, Daniel D.

***LeFevre, Perry D.** Modern Theologies of Prayer. LC 95-60692. 376p. 1995. text ed. 32.95 (0-913552-56-9); pap. text ed. 19.95 (0-913552-57-7) Exploration Pr.

LeFevre, Perry D., ed. Conflict in a Voluntary Association: A Case Study of a Classic Suburban Church Fight. LC 75-12388. (Studies in Ministry & Parish Life). 1975. pap. 9.95 (0-913552-09-7) Exploration Pr.

— Prayers of Kierkegaard. LC 56-11000. (Midway Reprint Ser.). 1978. pap. text ed. 17.00 (0-226-47059-8) U Ch Pr.

Lefevre, Pierre. One Hundred Stories to Change Your Life. 150p. (C). 1990. 50.00 (0-85439-382-X, Pub. by St Paul Pubns UK) St Mut.

Lefevre-Pontalis, P. Chansons et fetes du Laos. LC 78-20131. (Collection de contes et de chansons populaires: Vol. 22). reprint ed. 21.50 (0-404-60372-6) AMS Pr.

LeFevre, R. James. Redirecting Boards: A New Vision of Governance for Planned Parenthood. LC 92-46519. 134p. 1993. 11.95 (0-934586-73-X) Plan Parent.

Lefevre, Ralph. History of New Paltz, New York, & Its Old Families from 1678 to 1820: Including the Huguenot Pioneers & Others Who Settled in New Paltz Previous to the Revolution. (Illus.). 593p. reprint ed. pap. 35.50 (1-55613-629-3) Heritage Bk.

Lefevre, Raoul. The Recuyell of the Historyes of Troye, 2 vols. in 1. Caxton, William, tr. LC 70-178542. reprint ed. 115.00 (0-404-56624-3) AMS Pr.

LeFevre, Robert. The Fundamentals of Liberty. (Illus.). 487p. (C). 1988. 24.95 (0-9620480-0-3) Rampart Inst.

— Nature of Man & His Government. LC 59-5901. 1959. pap. 4.95 (0-87004-086-3) Caxton.

Lefevre, Yves, ed. see Cambrensis, Giraldus.

Leff, Alan R. & Schumacker, Paul T. Respiratory Physiology: Basics & Applications. (Illus.). 224p. 1993. pap. text ed. 23.00 (0-7216-3952-6) Saunders.

Leff, Carol S. National Conflict in Czechoslovakia: The Making & Remaking of the State, 1918-1987. 304p. 1988. text ed. 47.50 (0-691-07768-1) Princeton U Pr.

Leff, Edward, jt. auth. see Emanuel, Pericles J.

Leff, Enrique. Ecology & Capital. LC 94-10841. (Democracy & Ecology Ser.). 174p. 1995. lib. bdg. 36.95 (0-89862-411-8, C2411); pap. text ed. 16.95 (0-89862-410-X, C2410) Guilford Pr.

Leff, Harvey V. & Rex, Andrew F., eds. Maxwell's Demon: Entropy, Information, Computing. (Physics Ser.). 368p. 1990. text ed. 80.00 (0-691-08726-1); pap. text ed. 26. 95x (0-691-08727-X) Princeton U Pr.

Leff, Herb & Nevin, Ann. Turning Learning Inside Out: A Guide to Using Any Subject to Enrich Life & Creativity. LC 94-11062. 1994. write for info. (1-56976-000-4) Zephyr Pr AZ.

Leff, Herbert L. Playful Perception: Choosing How to Experience Your World. LC 83-19876. (Illus.). 172p. (Orig.). 1984. 15.95 (0-914525-01-8); pap. 9.95 (0-914525-00-X) Waterfront Bks.

Leff, J. & Isaacs, A. Psychiatric Examination in Clinical Practice. 3rd ed. 1990. pap. 36.95 (0-632-02878-5) Blackwell Sci.

Leff, Jay C. Near Eastern & Far Eastern Art. 1966. pap. 4.50 (0-8079-0092-3) October.

Leff, Jonathan, jt. auth. see Consumer Reports Books Editors.

Leff, Julian & Vaughn, Christine. Expressed Emotion in Families: Its Significance for Mental Illness. LC 84-549. 241p. 1985. lib. bdg. 32.95 (0-89862-058-9) Guilford Pr.

Leff, Julian P. Psychiatry Around the Globe: A Transcultural View. LC 89-43755. (Gaskell Psychiatry Ser.). 240p. reprint ed. pap. 68.40 (0-7837-6211-9, 2045935) Bks Demand.

Leff, Julian P., jt. auth. see Bhugra, Dinesh.

Leff, Larry. The Power of Pascal. 1986. text ed. 39.95 (0-13-687450-9, Busn) P-H.

***Leff, Lawrence S.** College Algebra. LC 94-26836. (C). 1995. write for info. (0-8120-1940-7) Barron.

— Geometry the Easy Way. 2nd ed. (Easy Way Ser.). 336p. 1990. pap. 9.95 (0-8120-4287-5) Barron.

— Let's Review: Sequential Mathematics, Course I. 2nd ed. LC 95-2341. (Review Course Ser.). 1995. write for info. (0-8120-9036-5) Barron.

— Let's Review: Sequential Mathematics, Course III. 440p. 1992. pap. 7.95 (0-8120-4767-2) Barron.

— Let's Review: Sequential Mathematics Course, No. 1. 1988. pap. 9.95 (0-8120-3843-6) Barron.

— Let's Review: Sequential Mathematics Course Two. 480p. 1989. pap. 9.95 (0-8120-4047-3) Barron.

Leff, Leonard J. Film Plots: Scene-by-Scene Narrative Outlines for Feature Film Study, Vol. 1. LC 83-60916. 1983. 65.00 (0-87650-149-8) Pierian.

— Film Plots: Scene-by-Scene Narrative Outlines for Feature Film Study, Vol. 2. LC 83-60916. 483p. 1988. 65.00 (0-87650-241-9) Pierian.

Leff, Michael, jt. ed. see Horner, Winifred B.

Leff, Michael C. & Kauffeld, Fred J., eds. Texts in Context: Critical Dialogues on Significant Episodes in American Political Rhetoric: With Newly-Edited Speeches by Anna E. Dickinson & by Martin Luther King, Jr. x, 327p. (Orig.). (C). 1989. text ed. 20.50 (0-9611800-5-6); pap. text ed. 14.95 (0-9611800-4-8) Hermagoras Pr.

Leff, Nathaniel H. Brazilian Capital Goods Industry, Nineteen Twenty-Nine to Nineteen Sixty-Four. LC 68-21976. (Center for International Affairs Ser.). 198p. 1968. 22.00 (0-674-08090-4) HUP.

Leff, Richard D. & Roberts, Robert J. Practical Aspects of Intravenous Drug Administration: Principles for Nurses, Pharmacists, & Physicians. 64p. (C). 1992. pap. text ed. 15.00 (1-879907-23-2) Am Soc Hlth-Syst.

Leff, Walli F. & Haft, Marilyn G. Time Without Work: People Who Are Not Working Tell Their Stories, How They Feel, What They Do, How They Survive. LC 83-61477. 403p. 1983. 35.00 (0-89608-186-9); pap. 9.00 (0-89608-185-0) South End Pr.

Leff, Z. Outlooks & Insights. 1993. 13.95 (0-89906-531-7) Mesorah Pubns.

— Outlooks & Insights. 1993. 16.95 (0-89906-530-9) Mesorah Pubns.

Leffel, John C., ed. History of Posey County, Indiana. (Illus.). 401p. 1992. reprint ed. lib. bdg. 41.00 (0-8328-2569-7) Higginson Bk Co.

Leffel, Katherine & Bouchard, Denis. Views on Phrase Structure. (Studies in Natural Language & Linguistic Theory). 240p. (C). 1991. lib. bdg. 97.00 (0-7923-1295-3) Kluwer Ac.

Leffelaar, P. A., ed. On Systems Analysis & Simulation of Ecological Processes with Examples in CSMP & FORTRAN. (Current Issues in Production Ecology Ser.). 308p. (C). 1993. lib. bdg. 113.00 (0-7923-2434-X); pap. text ed. 46.00 (0-7923-2435-8) Kluwer Ac.

Leffert, Robert. Brachial Plexus Injuries. LC 85-13319. (Illus.). 235p. 1986. text ed. 72.00 (0-443-08026-7) Churchill.

Lefferts, Amy, jt. ed. see Hollander, Joe.

Lefferts, Amy, ed. see Petersons Guides Staff.

Lefferts, H. Leedon, Jr., jt. auth. see Gittinger, Mattiebelle.

Lefferts, Peter. The Motet in England in the Fourteenth Century. LC 86-6900. (Studies in Musicology: No. 94). (Illus.). 391p. reprint ed. pap. 111.50 (0-8357-1722-4, 2070594) Bks Demand.

Lefferts, Peter M., ed. see Handlo, Robertus D. & Hanboys, Johannes.

Leffin, Walter, et al. Introduction to Technical Mathematics: With Problem Solving. 2nd ed. (Illus.). 438p. (C). 1993. pap. text ed. 24.95 (0-88133-698-X) Waveland Pr.

Leffingwell, Albert. Illegitimacy & the Influence of Seasons Upon Conduct: Two Studies in Demography. LC 75-38134. (Demography Ser.). (Illus.). 1976. reprint ed. 19. 95 (0-405-07987-7) Ayer.

***Leffingwell, Edward.** Earthly Paradise. (Illus.). 1994. 40.00 (0-9642964-0-3) Earthly Paradise.

— Earthly Paradise. (Illus.). 128p. 1994. 40.00 (1-885203-04-7) Jrny Editions.

Leffingwell, Edward, ed. Yamagata: The Car Series. (Illus.). 96p. (Orig.). 1993. pap. 25.95 (1-882299-02-7) Dirs Gallery BAP.

Leffingwell, Edward, jt. auth. see Johnstone, Mark.

Leffingwell, Georgia W. Social & Private Life at Rome in the Time of Plautus & Terence. LC 18-17902. (Columbia University. Studies in the Social Sciences: No. 188). reprint ed. 20.00 (0-404-51188-0) AMS Pr.

Leffingwell, Rand. Classic John Deere Tractors. (Enthusiast Color Ser.). (Illus.). 96p. 1994. pap. 12.95 (0-87938-865-X) Motorbooks Intl.

Leffingwell, Randy. The American Farm Tractor. (Illus.). 176p. 1991. 29.95 (0-87938-532-4) Motorbooks Intl.

— American Muscle: Muscle Cars from the Otis Chandler Collection. (Illus.). 192p. 1994. reprint ed. 29.95 (0-87938-465-4) Motorbooks Intl.

— Caterpillar. (Illus.). 192p. 1994. 29.95 (0-87938-921-4) Motorbooks Intl.

— Classic Farm Tractors. LC 92-1774. 1993. 19.98 (0-87938-813-7) Motorbooks Intl.

— Farm Tractors: A Living History. LC 95-5976. 256p. 1995. 24.98 (0-7603-0030-5) Motorbooks Intl.

— Harley-Davidson. (Illus.). 192p. 1995. 19.98 (0-7603-0031-3) Motorbooks Intl.

— John Deere Farm Tractors. LC 93-1158. 1993. 29.95 (0-87938-755-6) Motorbooks Intl.

— Mustang. (Illus.). 192p. 1995. 29.95 (0-7603-0048-8) Motorbooks Intl.

— Porsche. (Enthusiast Color Ser.). (Illus.). 96p. 1995. pap. 12.95 (0-87938-992-3) Motorbooks Intl.

— Porsche: Inside History of the Legendary Cars. LC 92-35443. (MBI Ser.). (Illus.). 192p. 1993. 29.95 (0-87938-710-6) Motorbooks Intl.

Leffingwell, Russell C., jt. auth. see Bogart, Ernest L.

Leffkowitz, M. & Steinitz, H., eds. Life Assurance Medicine Congress, 9th, Tel Aviv, March 1967: Proceedings. vi, 368p. 1968. pap. 91.25 (3-8055-0910-3) S Karger.

Leffland, Ella. Last Courtesies & Other Stories. LC 84-73374. (Short Fiction Ser.). 235p. 1985. reprint ed. pap. 8.50 (0-915308-71-1) Graywolf.

— Mrs. Munck. LC 84-73373. 284p. 1985. reprint ed. pap. 12.00 (0-915308-70-3) Graywolf.

— Rumors of Peace. LC 78-20209. 400p. 1985. pap. 13.00 (0-06-091301-0, PL 1301, PL) HarpC.

Leffler, Adrianne K. California Traveler Wine Country: Discover the Essence of California. (American Traveler Ser.). (Illus.). 48p. (Orig.). 1992. pap. 4.95 (1-55838-125-2) R H Pub.

Leffler, Holley G. Letters to My Friends. unabridged ed. LC 92-73017. 104p. (Orig.). 1992. pap. 9.95 (0-9633801-1-7); audio 10.95 (0-9633801-0-9) In Lite Ten.

Leffler, John E. An Introduction to Free Radicals. 304p. 1993. text ed. 69.95 (0-471-59406-7) Wiley.

Leffler, Keith B. Explanations in Search of Facts, a Critique of "A Study of Physicians' Fees" (LEC Occasional Paper). 1978. pap. text ed. 2.50 (0-916770-08-7) Law & Econ U Miami.

Leffler, Maryann C. My A B C's at Home. (Wee Pudgy Board Bks.). (Illus.). 24p. (J). (ps). 1990. bds. 2.50 (0-448-02257-5, G&D) Putnam Pub Group.

Leffler, Melvyn P. The Elusive Guest: America's Pursuit of European Stability & French Security, 1919-1933. LC 78-9782. 426p. reprint ed. pap. 121.50 (0-8357-3890-6, 2036622) Bks Demand.

— A Preponderance of Power: National Security, the Truman Administration, & the Cold War. (Nuclear Age Ser.). (Illus.). 711p. 1992. 55.00 (0-8047-1924-1) Stanford U Pr.

— A Preponderance of Power: National Security, the Truman Administration, & the Cold War. (Illus.). 711p. (C). 1993. pap. 19.95 (0-8047-2218-8) Stanford U Pr.

— The Specter of Communisms: The United States & the Origins of the Cold War, 1917-1953. Foner, Eric, ed. LC 94-13419. 1994. 20.00 (0-8090-8791-X); pap. 7.95 (0-8090-1574-9) Hill & Wang.

Leffler, Melvyn P. & Painter, David S., eds. Origins of the Cold War: An International History. LC 93-23298. 1994. write for info. (0-415-09693-6, Routledge NY); pap. write for info. (0-415-09694-4, Routledge NY) Routledge.

Leffler, Merrill. Partly Pandemonium, Partly Love. LC 82-70051. 64p. 1982. pap. 7.95 (0-931848-50-4) Dryad Pr.

Leffler, Merrill, ed. see Neiditz, Minerva H.

Leffler, Phyllis K. & Brent, Joseph, III. Public & Academic History: Philosophy & Pardism. LC 89-2628. 108p. (Orig.). (C). 1990. 16.00 (0-89464-298-7); pap. 12.50 (0-89464-299-5) Krieger.

— Public History Readings: A Book Of Readings. 552p. (C). 1992. 44.50 (0-89464-433-5) Krieger.

Leffler, Richard, ed. & intro. The Response to the Federalist: Contemporary Commentaries on a Political Masterwork, 1787-1788. (Constitutional Heritage Ser.: Vol. 3). 200p. 1996. write for info. (0-945612-03-6) Madison Hse.

Leffler, Richard, jt. ed. see Kaminski, John P.

Leffler, Richard E. Where Are All the Angels? Heavenly Host Handbook. (Illus.). 192p. 1994. pap. 8.95 (0-9640465-1-2) Del King Pubng.

Leffler, Samuel J., et al. The Design & Implementation of 4.3 BSD Unix Operation System Answer Book. (Illus.). 64p. (C). 1991. pap. text ed. 10.75 (0-201-54629-9) Addison-Wesley.

Leffler, William L. Petroleum Refining for the NonTechnical Person. 2nd ed. 184p. 1985. 59.95 (0-87814-280-0, P4360) PennWell Bks.

Leffler, William L. & Burdick, Donald L. Petrochemicals in Nontechnical Language. 2nd ed. 360p. 1990. 59.95 (0-87814-344-0, P4463) PennWell Bks.

Lefft, Elizabeth, jt. auth. see Gethers, Judith.

Lefgren & Jackson. Power Tools for Teaching. pap. 5.95 (0-88494-660-6) Bookcraft Inc.

Lefgren, Beth & Jackson, Jennifer. More Power Tools for Teaching. 1991. pap. 5.95 (0-88494-780-7) Bookcraft Inc.

— Sharing Time, Family Time, Anytime. 1992. pap. 7.95 (0-88494-846-3) Bookcraft Inc.

— Sharing Time, Family Time, Anytime Bk. 2. 1994. pap. 7.95 (0-88494-941-9) Bookcraft Inc.

Lefield, Walter. Como Predicar Expositivamente. 192p. (SPA.). 1990. 8.95 (0-8297-1218-6) Life Pubs Intl.

Lefko, Linda C. & Knickerbocker, Barbara. The Art of Theorem Painting: A History & Complete Instruction Manual. (Illus.). 112p. 1992. 30.00 (0-525-93532-0, Dutton Studio); pap. 20.00 (0-525-48596-1, Dutton Studio) Studio Bks.

Lefkof, Amy, jt. auth. see Schorr, Kenneth L.

Lefkoff, Gerald. Analyzed Examples of Four-Part Harmony: For the Study of Harmonic Dictation, Part Singing & Keyboard Reading. LC 79-92507. 140p. 1980. pap. text ed. 29.95 (0-935964-00-2) Glyphic Pr.

— The Elements of Tonal Harmony. LC 84-81074. 150p. (C). 1984. pap. text ed. 35.95 (0-935964-02-9) Glyphic Pr.

— Reading & Writing Intervals: A Self-Instruction Book. 130p. 1980. pap. text ed. 21.95 (0-935964-01-0) Glyphic Pr.

Lefkoff, Gerald, ed. Computer Application in Music. LC 67-24519. 105p. 1967. 17.50 (0-318-36153-1) West Va U Pr.

Lefkoff, Gerald, jt. auth. see Horacek, Leo.

***Lefkovitch, L. P.** Optimal Set Covering for Biological Classification: Theory of Conditional Clustering & Its Use in Biological Classification & Identification. 454p. (Orig.). 1993. pap. 32.50x (0-660-14821-8, Pub. by Canada Commun Grp CN) Accents Pubns.

An Asterisk (*) at the beginning of an entry indicates that the title is appearing in BIP for the first time.

Lefkovits, Henry C. IBM's Repository Manager - MVS: Concepts, Facilities, & Capabilities. 1991. 49.95 (*0-89435-349-7*) Wiley.

— IBM's Repository Manager - MVS Concepts, Facilities, & Capabilities. 345p. 1993. text ed. 54.95 (*0-471-58156-9*) Wiley.

Lefkovits, Ivan & Pernis, Benvenuto, eds. Immunological Methods, Vol. 1. LC 78-3342. 1979. text ed. 95.00 (*0-12-442750-2*) Acad Pr.

— Immunological Methods, Vol. 3. 1985. text ed. 116.00 (*0-12-442703-0*) Acad Pr.

— Immunological Methods, Vol. 4. 338p. 1990. text ed. 88. 00 (*0-12-442704-9*) Acad Pr.

Lefkovits, Ivan, jt. ed. see Steinberg, C. M.

Lefkowitch, Jay H. Histopathology of Disease. (Illus.). 234p. 1989. pap. text ed. 45.00 (*0-443-08566-8*) Churchill.

Lefkowith, Christie M. The Art of Perfume: Discovering & Collecting Perfume Bottles. LC 94-60270. (Illus.). 208p. 1994. 60.00 (*0-500-23686-0*) Thames Hudson.

Lefkowitz, et al. International Symposium on Phase Transitions in Polymers: Proceedings, Ohio, 1980. 326p. 1984. pap. text ed. 447.00 (*0-677-40325-9*) Gordon & Breach.

Lefkowitz, Bernard. Tough Changes: Growing up on Your Own in America. 1987. text ed. 29.95 (*0-02-918490-8*) Free Pr.

Lefkowitz, Elliot B. A Passion for Life: The Story of Herman & Maurice Spertus. 70p. 1994. pap. 8.95 (*0-935982-48-5*) Spertus Coll.

Lefkowitz, Eric. Monkees Tale. 1986. pap. 9.95 (*0-86719-338-7*) Last Gasp.

***Lefkowitz, Frances.** Marilyn Monroe. (Pop Culture Legends Ser.). (J). 1995. 18.95 (*0-7910-2342-7*); pap. write for info. (*0-7910-2367-2*) Chelsea Hse.

***Lefkowitz, Howard N. & Akselrad, Ira.** New York Limited Liability Company Forms & Practice Manual. 520p. 1995. ring bd. 149.95 (*0-9637468-7-1*) Data Trace Legal.

Lefkowitz, I. The Fourth European Meeting on Ferroelectricity: Proceedings, Portoroz, Yugoslavia, Sept. 1979, 3 vols., Set. 864p. 1980. pap. 775.00 (*0-677-16225-1*) Gordon & Breach.

Lefkowitz, I. & Sakr, M. F., eds. Computer Applications in Industry: Proceedings of IASTED Symposium, Cairo, Egypt, February 1-3, 1988. 156p. 1988. 50.00 (*0-88986-095-5*, 139) Acta Pr.

Lefkowitz, I. & Taylor, G. Proceedings of the Fifth International Meeting on Ferroelectricity, 5 pts. 1370p. 1981. 814.00 (*0-685-27100-5*) Gordon & Breach.

Lefkowitz, I. & Taylor, G., eds. Proceedings of the Nineteen Seventy-Five IEEE Symposium on Applications of Ferroelectrics (Albuquerque), 2 Vols. 428p. 1976. text ed. 646.00 (*0-677-40195-7*) Gordon & Breach.

— The Third European Meeting on Ferroelectricity (Zurich, 1975) Special Issue of Journal Ferroelectrics, 3 Vols. 762p. 1976. pap. 589.00 (*0-677-40205-8*) Gordon & Breach.

— The Third International Meeting on Ferroelectricity, (Edinburgh, 1973) Special Issue of Journal Ferroelectrics, 2 Vols. 620p. 1974. 355.00 (*0-677-40215-5*) Gordon & Breach.

Lefkowitz, I., ed. see Semiconducting Ferroelectrics Symposium Staff, et al.

Lefkowitz, I., et al. IEEE International Symposium on Applications of Ferroelectricity: Proceedings, Minnesota, 1979, 2 pt. 430p. 1980. text ed. 920.00 (*0-677-40315-1*) Gordon & Breach.

— International Conference on Low Lying Lattice Vibrational Modes & Their Relationship to Superconductivity & Ferroelectricity: Proceedings, Puerto Rico, 1975, 2 vols., Set. 472p. 1977. pap. 387.00 (*0-677-15535-2*) Gordon & Breach.

Lefkowitz, Irene, tr. see Prichard, Elizabeth R., et al, eds.

Lefkowitz, Jerome. Public Employee Unionism in Israel. LC 78-634400. (Comparative Studies in Public Employment Labor Relations Ser.). 1971. 10.00 (*0-87736-017-0*); pap. 5.00 (*0-87736-018-9*) U of Mich Inst Labor.

— Public Sector Labor & Employment Law. LC 87-62965. 1100p. 1987. text ed. 70.00 (*0-942954-18-1*) NYS Bar.

Lefkowitz, Jerome, ed. Evolving Process - Collective Negotiations in Public Employment. LC 85-80621. 553p. 1985. 35.00 (*0-934753-00-8*) LRP Pubns.

Lefkowitz, Lester, jt. auth. see Eastman Kodak Company Staff.

Lefkowitz, M. M., et al. Growing up to Be Violent: A Longitudinal Study of the Development of Aggression. 1977. 104.00 (*0-08-019515-6*, Pub. by Pergamon Repr UK) Franklin.

Lefkowitz, Mary R. First-Person Fictions: Pindar's Poetic "I" 240p. 1991. 65.00 (*0-19-814686-8*) OUP.

— The Victory Ode: An Introduction. LC 76-11650. 186p. 1977. 18.00 (*0-8155-5045-6*, NP) Noyes.

— Women in Greek Myth. LC 86-7146. 160p. 1990. reprint ed. pap. text ed. 12.95x (*0-8018-4108-9*) Johns Hopkins.

Lefkowitz, Mary R. & Fant, Maureen B., eds. Women's Life in Greece & Rome: A Source Book in Translation. rev. ed. 376p. 1992. pap. text ed. 14.95 (*0-8018-4475-4*) Johns Hopkins.

— Women's Life in Greece & Rome: A Source Book in Translation. 2nd rev. ed. 376p. 1992. text ed. 38.50 (*0-8018-4474-6*) Johns Hopkins.

***Lefkowitz, Mary R. & Rogers, Guy M., eds.** Black Athena Revisited. LC 95-8903. 1996. write for info. (*0-8078-2246-9*); pap. write for info. (*0-8078-4555-8*) U of NC Pr.

Lefkowitz, Natalie & Hedgecock, John. Impressions Personnelles. 240p. (C). 1990. pap. text ed. 21.50 (*0-03-021518-8*) HB Coll Pubs.

Lefkowitz, Patricia S. & Zimmer, Joy S. New York Part-Ease. 1982. pap. 7.95 (*0-9607664-0-5*) Part-Ease.

Lefkowitz, Rochelle & Withorn, Ann, eds. For Crying Out Loud. LC 86-9302. 408p. (Orig.). 1986. pap. 16.95 (*0-8298-0581-8*) Pilgrim OH.

Leflar, Robert A. One Life in the Law: A Sixty Year Review. LC 84-28017. 300p. 1985. pap. 10.00 (*0-938626-99-X*) U of Ark Pr.

Leflar, Robert A., et al. American Conflicts Law: Cases & Materials. 2nd ed. (Contemporary Legal Education Ser.). 672p. 1989. 40.00 (*0-87473-446-0*) Michie Butterworth.

LeFlemming, Svetlana, jt. auth. see Harrison, W.

Lefler, Hugh T. & Newsome, Albert R. North Carolina: The History of a Southern State. LC 72-81330. (Illus.). 825p. reprint ed. pap. 180.00 (*0-8357-3869-8*, 2036601) Bks Demand.

Lefler, Hugh T. & Powell, William S. Colonial North Carolina: A History. LC 73-5188. (History of the American Colonies Ser.). 318p. 1973. lib. bdg. 35.00 (*0-527-18718-6*) Kraus Intl.

Lefler, Hugh T., jt. auth. see Barck, Oscar T., Jr.

Lefler, Hugh T., ed. see Clark, Walter.

Lefler, Hugh T., ed. see Lawson, John.

Lefley, Harriet P. & Johnson, Dale L., eds. Families as Allies in Treatment of the Mentally Ill: New Directions for Mental Health Professionals. LC 89-17778. 400p. 1990. text ed. 38.50 (*0-88048-298-2*) Am Psychiatric.

Lefley, Harriet P. & Pedersen, Paul B., eds. Cross-Cultural Training for Mental Health Professionals. (Illus.). 360p. (C). 1986. 53.95 (*0-398-05257-3*) C C Thomas.

— Cross-Cultural Training for Mental Health Professionals. (Illus.). 360p. 1986. pap. 32.95 (*0-398-06226-9*) C C Thomas.

Lefley, Harriet P., jt. auth. see Hatfield, Agnes B.

Lefley, Harriet P., jt. ed. see Hatfield, Agnes B.

Leflon, Jean. Eugene de Mazenod: Bishop of Marseilles, Founder of the Oblates of Mary Immaculate, 1782-1861, Vol. 1. LC 61-13025. 537p. reprint ed. pap. 145.00 (*0-7837-5710-7*, 2045375) Bks Demand.

— Eugene de Mazenod: Bishop of Marseilles, Founder of the Oblates of Mary Immaculate, 1782-1861, Vol. 2. LC 61-13025. 716p. reprint ed. pap. 180.00 (*0-7837-5711-5*) Bks Demand.

— De Mazenod: 1782-1864, Founder of the Oblates of Mary Immaculate. Flanagan, Francis D., tr. LC 94-11821. 394p. (Orig.). 1994. 45.00 (*1-56518-061-5*); pap. 17.50 (*1-56518-062-3*) Coun Res Values.

Lefohn, A. S. Surface-Level Ozone Exposures & Their Effects on Vegetation. 400p. 1991. 85.00 (*0-87371-169-6*, QK751) Lewis Pubs.

Lefond, Stanley J., ed. Industrial Minerals & Rocks, 2 vols., Set. 5th ed. LC 82-71993. (Illus.). 1508p. 1983. 80.00 (*0-89520-402-9*, 402-9) SMM&E Inc.

— Industrial Minerals & Rocks: (Nonmetallics Other Than Fuels) 4th rev. ed. LC 73-85689. (Seeley W. Mudd Ser.). 1372p. reprint ed. pap. 180.00 (*0-317-29747-3*, 2017421) Bks Demand.

— Industrial Minerals & Rocks (Nonmetallics Other Than Fuels), Vol. 1. 5th ed. (Illus.). 763p. reprint ed. pap. 180. 00 (*0-7837-9168-2*, 2049869) Bks Demand.

— Industrial Minerals & Rocks (Nonmetallics Other Than Fuels), Vol. 2. 5th ed. (Illus.). 764p. reprint ed. pap. 180. 00 (*0-7837-9169-0*, 2049869) Bks Demand.

Lefond, Stanley J., jt. ed. see Barker, James M.

LeFontaine, Joseph R. The Collector's Bookshelf: A Comprehensive Listing of Authors, Their Pseudonyms, & Their Books. 333p. (C). 1990. 73.95 (*0-87975-605-5*) Prometheus Bks.

— The Collector's Bookshelf Value Guide. 113p. (Orig.). (C). 1990. pap. 19.95 (*0-87975-606-3*) Prometheus Bks.

— A Handbook for Booklovers. 612p. 1988. 55.95 (*0-87975-491-5*) Prometheus Bks.

Lefor, Alan T., jt. auth. see Gomella, Leonard G.

LeForge, P. V. The Principle of Interchange & Other Stories. LC 89-92412. 179p. (Orig.). 1990. pap. 7.95 (*0-9624878-0-5*) Paperback Rack Bks.

— The Secret Life of Moles. LC 91-78124. 72p. (Orig.). (C). 1992. pap. 8.00 (*0-938078-35-6*) Anhinga Pr.

Leforge, Thomas H. Memoirs of a White Crow Indian. LC 74-6222. xxiv, 356p. 1974. reprint ed. pap. 10.95 (*0-8032-5800-3*) U of Nebr Pr.

LeFors, Rufe. Facts As I Remember Them: The Autobiography of Rufe LeFors. Peterson, John A., ed. (M. K. Brown Range Life Ser.: No. 16). (Illus.). 192p. 1986. text ed. 20.95 (*0-292-70379-1*); pap. 10.95 (*0-292-72457-8*) U of Tex Pr.

Lefort, Claude. Democracy & Political Theory. Macey, David, tr. LC 88-22034. 304p. (Orig.). 1989. text ed. 44. 95 (*0-8166-1754-6*); pap. text ed. 17.95 (*0-8166-1755-4*) U of Minn Pr.

— The Political Forms of Modern Society Bureaucracy: Democracy, Totalitarianism. Thompson, John B., ed. 352p. (Orig.). 1986. pap. 17.00 (*0-262-62054-5*) MIT Pr.

Lefort, Claude, ed. see Merleau-Ponty, Maurice.

Lefort, Rosine. Birth of the Other. Du Ry, Marc et al, trs. LC 93-40386. 344p. (C). 1994. 49.95 (*0-252-01900-8*); pap. 18.95 (*0-252-06393-7*) U of Ill Pr.

Lefrak, Babs, jt. auth. see Mark, Libby.

***LeFrak, Samuel J., et al.** A Passion for Art: The LeFrak Family Collection. (Illus.). 120p. Date not set. text ed. write for info. (*0-9620593-1-5*) Lefrak Organization.

Lefranc, Abel. Under the Mask of William Shakespeare. Cragg, Cecil, tr. (C). 1989. 45.00 (*0-86303-352-0*, Pub. by Merlin Bks UK) St Mut.

LeFranc, Elsie, jt. ed. see Blustain, Harvey.

LeFranc, G., jt. auth. see LeFranc, Marie-Paule.

LeFranc, George B. A Jewelled Universe. 1991. 7.95 (*0-533-09396-1*) Vantage.

LeFranc, Marie-Paule & LeFranc, G. Restriction Fragment Length Polymorphism. (Experimental & Clinical Immunogenetics Journal: Vol. 7, No. 1, 1990). (Illus.). 88p. 1989. pap. 37.75 (*3-8055-5113-4*) S Karger.

Lefrancois, Guy R. The Lifespan. 4th ed. 739p. (C). 1993. text ed. 48.95 (*0-534-17778-6*) Intl Thomson.

— Of Children: An Introduction to Child Development. 7th ed. 762p. (C). 1992. student ed, pap. 15.95 (*0-534-16825-6*) Intl Thomson.

— Of Children: An Introduction to Child Development. 7th ed. 762p. (C). 1992. text ed. 48.95 (*0-534-16824-8*) Intl Thomson.

— Of Children: An Introduction to Child Development. 8th ed. LC 94-30151. (Illus.). 688p. 1995. text ed. 48.95 (*0-534-21936-5*) Intl Thomson.

— Psychological Theories of Human Learning. 2nd ed. LC 81-15511. (Psychology Ser.). 348p. (C). 1982. boxed 39. 95 (*0-8185-0501-X*) Brooks-Cole.

— Psychological Theories of Learning. 3rd ed. LC 94-30411. 380p. 1995. text ed. 53.95 (*0-534-23202-7*) Brooks-Cole.

— Psychology for Teaching: A Bear Faces the Future. 8th ed. 443p. 1994. text ed. 47.95 (*0-534-20550-X*) Intl Thomson.

— Psychology for Teaching: A Bear Will Not Commit Himself Just Now. 7th ed. 448p. (C). 1991. pap. 45.95 (*0-534-14412-8*) Intl Thomson.

LeFree, Betty. Santa Clara Pottery Today. LC 73-92996. (School of American Research Monograph: No. 29). (Illus.). 125p. 1975. pap. 11.95 (*0-8263-0322-6*) U of NM Pr.

Lefrox, A. H., tr. see Girard, Paul F.

Lefroy, Augustus H., tr. see Girard, Paul F.

Lefroy, H. Maxwell. Indian Insect Pest. 2nd ed. xii, 318p. 1990. reprint ed. 25.00 (*1-55528-214-8*, Messers Today & Tomorrow) Scholarly Pubns.

Lefroy, William. Church Leaders in Primitive Times. 1977. lib. bdg. 69.95 (*0-8490-1628-2*) Gordon Pr.

Lefschetz, Solomon. Algebraic Topology. LC 41-6147. (Colloquium Publications: Vol. 27). 389p. 1986. reprint ed. pap. 57.00 (*0-8218-1027-8*, COLL-27) Am Math.

— Contributions to the Theory of Nonlinear Oscillations, Vols. 1, 1950. (Annals of Mathematics Studies). 1972. Vol. 1, No. 20,. 26.00 (*0-527-02736-7*); Vol. 2, No. 29 of Annals,. 15.00 (*0-527-02745-6*); Vol. 3, No. 36 of Annals, 1956. 23.00 (*0-527-02753-7*); Vol. 5, No. 45 of Annals, 1960. 23.00 (*0-527-02761-8*) Periodicals Srv.

— Differential Equations: Geometric Theory. 1977. reprint ed. pap. text ed. 8.95 (*0-486-63463-9*) Dover.

— Selected Papers. LC 73-113137. 639p. (C). 1990. text ed. 59.50 (*0-8284-0234-5*, 234) Chelsea Pub.

— Topology. 2nd rev. ed. LC 56-11513. (Illus.). 410p. (C). 1990. text ed. 23.95 (*0-8284-0116-0*, 116) Chelsea Pub.

Lefter, James & Bergin, Thomas J. A Microcomputer Based Primer on Structural Behavior. (Illus.). 448p. (C). 1986. disk (*0-318-60165-6*) P-H.

Leftheris, B. & Brebbia, C. A., eds. STREMA '95--Structural Studies, Repair & Maintenance of Historical Buildings IV: Proceedings of the Fourth International Conference. (STREMA Ser.: Vol. 4). 750p. 1995. 295.00 (*1-56252-238-8*) Computational Mech MA.

***Leftin, Howard I.** The Family Contract: A Blueprint for Successful Parenting. 144p. 1994. pap. 10.95 (*1-56838-025-9*) Hazelden.

— The Family Contract: A Blueprint for Successful Parenting. 144p. 1990. pap. 7.95 (*0-929162-17-X*) PIA Pr.

Lefton, Lester A. Psychology. 5th ed. LC 93-27969. 1993. text ed. write for info. (*0-205-15248-1*) Allyn.

Lefton, Lester A. & Valvatine, Laura. Mastering Psychology. 3rd ed. 680p. (C). 1988. pap. text ed. 34.00 (*0-205-10626-9*, H0626-5) Allyn.

Lefton, Philip. Barron's Regents Exams & Answers Global Studies. 160p. 1992. pap. 5.95 (*0-8120-4344-8*) Barron.

Lefton, Phillip, jt. auth. see Midgley, David A.

Lefton, Robert E., et al. Improving Productivity Through People Skills: Dimensional Management Strategies. LC 80-21691. 498p. 1991. reprint ed. text ed. 25.00 (*0-9630421-1-4*) Psy Assocs.

Leftow, Brian. Time & Eternity. LC 90-55890. (Cornell Studies in the Philosophy of Religion). 352p. 1991. 45. 95 (*0-8014-2459-3*) Cornell U Pr.

Leftschatz, William. The Death of Tutankhamen. 220p. (Orig.). 1989. pap. 10.95 (*0-933753-07-1*) Canterbury.

Leftwich. Redefining Politics. 1986. 32.00 (*0-416-68150-6*) Routledge Chapman & Hall.

Leftwich, A. W. A Dictionary of Entomology. LC 75-27143. 368p. pap. 104.90 (*0-318-34739-3*, 2031996) Bks Demand.

Leftwich, Adrian, ed. New Developments in Political Science: An International Review of Achievements & Prospects. (Illus.). 256p. 1990. text ed. 59.95 (*1-85278-107-6*, Pub. by E Elgar Pub UK) Ashgate Pub Co.

Leftwich, Howard, et al. The Executive Simulation. 172p. (C). 1994. per. 20.95 (*0-8403-9462-4*) Kendall-Hunt.

***Leftwich, Jim.** Dirt. 14p. (Orig.). 1995. pap. 4.00 (*0-935350-56-X*) Luna Bisonte.

Leftwich, Joseph. Years at the Ending. LC 83-45131. 72p. 1984. 11.95 (*0-8453-4767-5*, Cornwall Bks) Assoc Univ Prs.

Leftwich, Joseph, ed. An Anthology of Modern Yiddish Literature. LC 74-82386. (Anthology Ser: No. 1). 346p. (C). 1974. pap. text ed. 26.15 (*90-279-3496-7*) Mouton.

Leftwich, Joseph & Chertoff, Mordecai S., eds. Why Do the Jews Need a Land of Their Own? LC 83-45297. 242p. 1984. 19.95 (*0-8453-4774-8*, Cornwall Bks) Assoc Univ Prs.

Leftwich, Joseph, tr. see Lewin, Samuel.

Leftwich, Richard H. & Gay, David. A Basic Framework for Economics. 3rd ed. 408p. (C). 1987. pap. 28.50 (*0-256-03702-7*) Irwin.

Leftwich, Richard H., jt. auth. see Eckert, Ross D.

Leftwich, Rodney L. Arts & Crafts of the Cherokee. 160p. 1986. reprint ed. pap. 8.95 (*0-935741-11-9*) Cherokee Pubns.

Leftwich, Samuel E., intro. Proceedings of the National Communications Forum: 1990, Vol. XXXXIV. (Illus.). 1042p. 1990. 139.00 (*0-933217-06-4*) Prof Educ Intl.

Lega, Leonor, jt. ed. see Dimattia, Dominic.

Lega Navale Italiana. Dizionario Enciclopedico Marinaresco. (ITA.). 1991. 195.00 (*0-8288-8457-9*) Fr & Eur.

Legacy, James, et al. Microcomputing in Agriculture. (C). 1984. teacher ed write for info. (*0-8359-4355-0*, Reston) P-H.

Legal Assistance Foundation of Chicago. Authorization Agreements for Legal Services Clients. 52p. 1987. pap. 5.00 (*0-685-23156-9*, 42,246) NCLS Inc.

Legal Center Staff. The Prentice Hall ADA Compliance Advisor. LC 93-28762. 1993. 69.95 (*0-13-031204-5*) P-H.

Legal Counsel for the Elderly Staff. Decisionmaking, Incapacity, & the Elderly 1987 (1990 Supplement) 186p. 1987. pap. 44.95 (*0-933945-00-0*) Legal Coun Elderly.

— Life Changes & Their Effects on Public Benefits. 728p. 1990. pap. 80.00 (*0-933945-03-5*) Legal Coun Elderly.

— Medicare Practice Manual. 314p. 1990. pap. 49.95 (*0-933945-05-1*) Legal Coun Elderly.

— Organizing Your Future: A Guide to Decisionmaking in Your Later Years. 102p. 1990. pap. 10.00 (*0-933945-04-3*) Legal Coun Elderly.

— A Practical Guide to Nursing Home Advocacy. 245p. 1990. pap. 39.95 (*0-933945-02-7*) Legal Coun Elderly.

***Legal Research Network Staff.** Rules of the Road for the Information Superhighway: Electronic Communications & the Law. 738p. (C). 1995. pap. text ed. write for info. (*0-314-06663-2*) West Pub.

Legal Services Corporation Staff. Final Evaluation Report Demonstration: Computer Assisted Legal Research & Technological Improvements. (Illus.). 223p. (Orig.). 1981. pap. 5.00 (*0-941077-13-6*, 32,789) NCLS Inc.

Legal Star Communications Staff, jt. auth. see Nolo Press Staff.

LeGall, Jean, jt. ed. see Peck, Harry D., Jr.

LeGallienne, Eva. With a Quiet Heart: An Autobiography. LC 74-3745. (Illus.). 311p. 1974. reprint ed. text ed. 59. 75 (*0-8371-7470-8*, LEQH, Greenwood Pr) Greenwood.

LeGallienne, Richard. Rudyard Kipling. LC 73-21739. (English Literature Ser.: No. 33). 1974. lib. bdg. 49.95 (*0-8383-1838-X*) M S G Haskell Hse.

Legally, M. C., ed. Kinetics of Ordering & Growth at Surfaces. (NATO ASI Series B, Physics: Vol. 239). (Illus.). 510p. 1990. 135.00 (*0-306-43702-3*, Plenum Pr) Plenum.

Legany, Oezso. Liszt & His Country, 1874-1886. Smith-Csicsery-Ronay, Elizabeth, tr. (Illus.). 331p. 1992. 39.50 (*0-911050-66-3*) Occidental.

Legard, Hilary & Launder, Elizabeth, eds. Understanding the Chambon. 88p. (C). 1990. 21.00 (*0-85131-439-2*, Pub. by J A Allen & Co UK) St Mut.

Legarde, Lisa. Paris. LC 93-6988. (Frommer's Walking Tours Ser.). 1993. 12.00 (*0-671-79764-6*, P-H Travel) P-H Gen Ref & Trav.

— San Francisco. (Frommer's Walking Tours Ser.). (Illus.). 176p. 1993. pap. 12.00 (*0-671-79766-2*, P-H Travel) P-H Gen Ref & Trav.

Legare, H. S. Writings of Hugh Swinton Legare. Bullen, Mary S. L., ed. LC 70-107413. (American Public Figures Ser.). 1970. reprint ed. lib. bdg. 145.00 (*0-306-71885-5*) Da Capo.

Legare, Romain, jt. auth. see Dupuis, Hector.

Legarreta, Dorothy. The Guernica Generation: Basque Refugee Children of the Spanish Civil War. LC 84-13136. (Basque Ser.). (Illus.). 416p. 1985. 24.95 (*0-87417-088-5*) U of Nev Pr.

LeGassick, Trevor, tr. see Khalifeh, Sahar.

Legat, Michael. The Cast Iron Man. large type ed. 560p. 1988. 15.95 (*0-7089-1881-6*) Ulverscroft.

— Mario's Vineyard. large type ed. 752p. 1983. 23.95 (*0-7089-8099-6*, Charnwood) Ulverscroft.

— Putting on a Play. LC 84-13242. 208p. 1984. 12.95 (*0-685-08886-3*) St Martin.

— The Shapiro Diamond. large type ed. 448p. 1984. 23.95 (*0-7089-8213-1*, Trail West Pubs) Ulverscroft.

— The Silver Fountain. large type ed. 608p. 1984. 23.95 (*0-7089-8189-5*, Trail West Pubs) Ulverscroft.

Legates. Genetics of Dairy Cattle. 1995. write for info. (*0-8493-8755-8*) CRC Pr.

Legates, J. E. & Warwick, E. J. Breeding & Improvement of Farm Animals. 8th ed. 1990. text ed. write for info. (*0-07-068376-X*) McGraw.

Legates, J. E., jt. auth. see Warwick, E. J.

LeGates, Richard T., jt. auth. see Phillips, E. Barbara.

Legato, Marianne J. Female Heart: The Truth about Women & Coronary Artery Disease. 1991. pap. 19.95 (*0-13-321811-2*) P-H.

Legato, Marianne J., ed. The Developing Heart. 1984. lib. bdg. 94.50 (*0-89838-672-1*) Kluwer Ac.

— The Stressed Heart. (Developments in Cardiovascular Medicine Ser.). 1987. lib. bdg. 116.00 (*0-89838-849-X*) Kluwer Ac.

Legato, Marianne J. & Colman, Carol. The Female Heart: The Truth about Women & Coronary Artery Disease. (Illus.). 272p. 1992. pap. 21.00 (*0-671-76110-2*) S&S Trade.

— The Female Heart: The Truth about Women & Heart Disease. 272p. 1993. reprint ed. pap. 10.00 (*0-380-72003-5*) Avon.

Legator & Hollaender. Occupational Monitoring for Genetic Hazards, Vol. 269. 1975. 14.00 (*0-89072-023-1*) NY Acad Sci.

Legator, Marvin S. & Strawn, Sabrina F., eds. Chemical Alert! A Community Action Handbook. rev. ed. LC 92-25304. Orig. Title: The Health Detective's Handbook. 254p. (C). 1993. text ed. 35.00 (*0-292-74675-X*); pap. text ed. 14.95 (*0-292-74676-8*) U of Tex Pr.

Legator, Marvin S., et al, eds. The Health Detective's Handbook: A Guide to the Investigation of Environmental Health Hazards by Nonprofessionals. LC 84-20105. (Illus.). 272p. reprint ed. pap. 77.60 (*0-8357-6138-X*, 2034147) Bks Demand.

Legatos, Stephanie, ed. see Sweeney, Patricia M. & Gagnon, Donna.

Legault, Albert & Fortmann, Michel. A Diplomacy of Hope: Canada & Disarmament, 1945-1988. 632p. 1992. 75.00 (*0-7735-0920-8*, Pub. by McGill CN); pap. 29.95 (*0-7735-0955-0*, Pub. by McGill CN) U of Toronto Pr.

Legault, Albert & Lindsey, George R. The Dynamics of Nuclear Balance. rev. ed. LC 75-36367. 288p. 1976. 35.00 (*0-8014-1007-X*) Cornell U Pr.

Legault, Albert, et al. The State of the United Nations: 1992. (Reports & Papers). 92p. (C). 1992. pap. text ed. 10.00 (*1-880660-04-0*) Acad Coun UN Syst.

Legault, Jim. Resume II: Artists, Galleries & Craftspersons of the Door Penisula. (Illus.). 64p. (Orig.). 1982. 12.75 (*0-933072-02-3*); pap. 6.50 (*0-933072-03-1*) Golden Glow.

Legault, R., jt. auth. see Biberman, L. M.

***Legay, Gilbert.** Atlas of North American Indians. LC 95-13019. (Illus.). 1995. write for info. (*0-8120-6515-8*) Barron.

LeGaye, Rocky. Authentic Civil War Battle Sites. 82p. 1991. pap. 15.95 (*0-941620-42-5*) Carson Ent.

— Gold! the ABC's of Panning. (Illus.). 96p. 1987. pap. 8.95 (*0-941620-04-2*) Carson Ent.

LeGear, Clara E. A List of Geographical Atlases in the Library of Congress: Vol. 9: Comprehensive Author List. LC 90-35009. 290p. 1992. 19.00 (*0-8444-0117-X*, 030-000-00233-4) Lib Congress.

Legel, Debra, jt. auth. see Kennedy, Carol.

Legendi, T., et al, eds. Parallel Processing by Cellular Automata & Arrays: Parcella '86: Proceedings of the Third International Workshop, Berlin, GDR, September 9-11, 1986. 275p. 1987. 79.50 (*0-444-70149-4*, North Holland) Elsevier.

Legendre, A. F. Modern Chinese Civilization. Jones, Elsie M., tr. LC 72-7076. (Select Bibliographies Reprint Ser.). 1977. reprint ed. 23.95 (*0-8369-6946-4*) Ayer.

Legendre, Geraldine. Topics in French Syntax. rev. ed. Hankamer, Jorge, ed. LC 93-46502. (Outstanding Dissertations in Linguistics Ser.). (Illus.). 346p. 1994. 75.00 (*0-8153-1689-5*) Garland.

Legendre, Gertrude S. The Time of My Life. LC 87-50640. (Illus.). 235p. 1994. 18.95 (*0-941711-02-1*) Wyrick & Co.

Legendre, L., jt. ed. see Legendre, P.

Legendre, P. & Legendre, L., eds. Developments in Numerical Ecology. (NATO ASI Series G: Vol. 14). 600p. 1987. 245.00 (*0-387-16086-8*) Spr-Verlag.

Legendre, Pierre. Ecrits Juridiques du Moyen Age Occidental. (Collected Studies: No. CS280). 280p. (C). 1988. reprint ed. text ed. 89.95 (*0-86078-228-X*, Pub. by Variorum UK) Ashgate Pub Co.

Legendre, Renald. Dictionnaire Actuel de l'Education. 2nd ed. 679p. (ENG & FRE.). 1993. 79.95 (*0-8288-1387-6*, M 520) Fr & Eur.

Legenhausen, Gary, ed. see Taleqani, Mahmud, et al.

Legenhausen, Gary, tr. see Taleqani, Mahmud, et al.

***Legent, F., ed.** Use of Ciprofloxacin in the Treatment of Chronic Otitis & Sinusitis & Malignant External Otitis. (Journal: Chemotherapy: Vol. 40, Suppl. 1, 1994). (Illus.). iv, 42p. 1994. pap. 13.00 (*3-8055-6071-0*) S Karger.

Leger. Biological Foundations of Behavior. (C). 1991. text ed. 54.50 (*0-06-043894-0*) HarpCollege.

Leger, A., et al, eds. Polycyclic Aromatic Hydrocarbons & Astrophysics. 1986. lib. bdg. 121.50 (*90-277-2361-3*) Kluwer Ac.

Leger, Daniel W., ed. Nebraska Symposium on Motivation, 1987: Comparative Perspectives in Modern Psychology. LC 53-11655. (Nebraska Symposium on Motivation Ser.: Vol. 35). xvi, 327p. 1988. 33.95 (*0-8032-2880-5*); pap. 18.95 (*0-8032-7926-4*) U of Nebr Pr.

***Leger, Diane.** Maxine's Tree. (Illus.). 32p. (Orig.). (J). (gr. 1-4). 1990. pap. 5.95 (*0-920501-38-9*) Orca Bk Pubs.

— Rosette & the Muddy River. (Illus.). 32p. (Orig.). (J). (gr. 1-4). 1991. pap. 6.95 (*0-920501-65-6*) Orca Bk Pubs.

Leger, E., et al. Second Career Vocations. O'Hara, F. & Lescoe, F., trs. 20p. (C). 1986. pap. 1.50 (*0-910919-02-X*) Mariel Pubns.

Leger, Eugene. Complete Building Construction. 4th ed. 736p. 1994. pap. 30.00 (*0-02-517882-2*) Macmillan.

Leger, Jacques N. Haiti: Her History & Her Detractors. 1976. lib. bdg. 59.95 (*0-8490-1926-5*) Gordon Pr.

— Haiti, Her History & Her Detractors. LC 78-107482. 372p. 1970. reprint ed. text ed. 35.00 (*0-8371-3784-5*, LEH&, Negro U Pr) Greenwood.

Leger, L. Recueil de contes populaires slaves. LC 78-20114. (Collection de contes et de chansons populaires: Vol. 5). reprint ed. 21.50 (*0-404-60355-6*) AMS Pr.

Leger, Mary C. The Catholic Indian Missions in Maine (1611-1820) LC 73-3563. (Catholic University of America. Studies in Romance Languages & Literatures: No. 8). reprint ed. 39.50 (*0-404-57758-X*) AMS Pr.

Leger-Orine, Monique, jt. ed. see Schneider, Jean.

Leger, Sivard R. World Energy Survey. 1981. 5.00 (*0-918281-02-4*) World Prior.

***Legere, Kersten.** Woerterbuch Deutsch-Swahili. 267p. (GER & SWA.). 1990. 65.00 (*0-7859-8311-2*, 3324005051) Fr & Eur.

LeGeros, R. Z. Calcium Phosphates in Oral Biology & Medicine. (Monographs in Oral Science: Vol. 15). (Illus.). x, 200p. 1991. 158.50 (*3-8055-5236-X*) S Karger.

LeGette, Bernard. LeGettes Calorie Encyclopedia. 448p. 1988. mass mkt. 5.99 (*0-446-35679-4*) Warner Bks.

— LeGette's Cholesterol Encyclopedia. 256p. (Orig.). 1989. mass mkt. 3.95 (*0-446-35092-3*) Warner Bks.

Legey, Francoise. The Folklore of Morocco. Hotz, Lucy, tr. LC 77-87639. reprint ed. 23.50 (*0-404-16428-5*) AMS Pr.

Legeza, Laszlo. Tao Magic: The Secret Language of Diagrams & Calligraphy. LC 86-51463. (Illus.). 167p. 1987. pap. 10.95 (*0-500-27062-7*) Thames Hudson.

Legeza, Laszlo, jt. auth. see Rawson, Philip.

***Legg.** Blood at Fort Bridger. 1995. mass mkt. 4.99 (*0-312-95447-6*) St Martin.

— Modern Greece. (Nations of the Modern World: Europe Ser.). 1996. text ed. 36.95 (*0-8133-1655-3*) Westview.

— Winter of the Heart. 1986. 16.95 (*0-915463-37-7*) Green Hill.

Legg, A., et al. What Guitar. 2nd ed. (Illus.). 118p. 1990. pap. 12.95 (*0-933224-49-4*, Pub. by Track Record UK) Bold Strummer Ltd.

Legg, A. K. Haynes Audi 4000 Owners Workshop Manual, No. 165: '80-'87. 16.95 (*1-85010-242-2*) Haynes Pubns.

— Haynes Nissan Pulsar Owners Workshop Manual, No. 876: 1983 thru 1986. rev. ed. (Illus.). 301p. 1987. pap. 16.95 (*1-85010-322-4*) Haynes Pubns.

— Haynes Saab 99 Owners Workshop Manual, No. 247: 1969-1980. 1990. 16.95 (*0-85696-844-7*) Haynes Pubns.

— Haynes VW Rabbit, Jetta, Scirocco & Pick-Up Owners Workshop Manual, No. 884: 1975-1991. 1982. 16.95 (*1-56392-016-6*) Haynes Pubns.

— Haynes Weber Carburetors, No. 393. (Illus.). 196p. pap. 16.95 (*1-85010-020-9*) Haynes Pubns.

Legg, A. K. & Haynes, J. H. Haynes BMW 528i Owners Workshop Manual: 1975-1980, No. 632. 16.95 (*0-85696-632-0*) Haynes Pubns.

Legg, A. K., jt. auth. see Haynes, J. H.

Legg, Adrian. Customising Your Electric Guitar. (Illus.). 64p. 1983. pap. 9.95 (*0-8256-2262-X*, AM40973) Music Sales.

Legg, Alicia. Painting & Sculpture in the Museum of Modern Art. 1990. pap. 12.50 (*0-8109-6060-5*) Abrams.

Legg, Alicia & Smalley, Mary B., eds. Painting & Sculpture in the Museum of Modern Art: Catalog of the Collection, 1987. rev. ed. 136p. 1989. pap. 12.50 (*0-87070-572-5*, 0-8109-6060-5) Mus of Modern Art.

Legg, C. R. Issues in Psychobiology. 256p. 1989. 47.50 (*0-415-01405-0*, 1091); pap. 17.95 (*0-415-01406-9*, A3367) Routledge.

Legg, Charles R. & Booth, David A., eds. Appetite: Neural & Behavioural Bases. LC 94-11806. (The European Brain & Behavior Ser.). (Illus.). 352p. 1995. text ed. 58.95 (*0-19-854787-0*) OUP.

Legg, Christopher. Remote Sensing & Geographic Information Systems: Geological Mapping, Mineral Exploration & Mining. LC 92-21708. (Ellis Horwood Library of Space Science & Space Technology). 256p. 1993. 59.95 (*0-13-772336-9*, Tavistock-E Horwood) Routledge Chapman & Hall.

Legg, Gerald. Amazing Animals. LC 93-36703. (X-Ray Picture Bks.). (Illus.). 48p. (J). (gr. 5-8). 1994. lib. bdg. 14.98 (*0-531-14285-X*); pap. 8.95 (*0-531-15708-3*) Watts.

— Amazing Tropical Birds. LC 91-6515. (Eyewitness Juniors Ser.). (Illus.). 32p. (Orig.). (J). (gr. 1-5). 1991. pap. 6.95 (*0-679-81520-1*) Knopf Bks Yng Read.

— Amazing Tropical Birds. LC 91-6515. (Eyewitness Juniors Ser.). (Illus.). 32p. (Orig.). (J). (gr. 1-5). 1991. lib. bdg. 9.99 (*0-679-91520-6*) Knopf Bks Yng Read.

— Incredible Creatures. LC 94-26901. (X-Ray Picture Bks.). (Illus.). 48p. (J). 1995. lib. bdg. 14.98 (*0-531-14346-5*) Watts.

— Incredible Creatures. LC 94-26901. (X-Ray Picture Bks.). (Illus.). 48p. (J). (ps-3). 1995. pap. 8.95 (*0-531-15730-X*) Orchard Bks Watts.

Legg, Jackie, ed. William & Mary Cookbook: A Treasury of Recipes & Memories of Good Eating at the College of William & Mary in Virginia Collected by Alumni & Friends. 276p. 1993. pap. 16.93 (*0-9615670-5-8*) Soc Alu Wm.

Legg, Joe, jt. auth. see L'Annunziata, Michael F.

Legg, Joe, jt. ed. see L'Annunziata, Michael F.

Legg, John. Apache Coffin. 1991. pap. 3.50 (*0-8217-3476-8*) Zebra.

— Blood in the Snow. 304p. 1993. pap. 3.50 (*0-8217-4136-5*) Zebra.

— Buckskins & Blood. 1994. mass mkt. 3.50 (*0-06-100749-8*) HarpC.

— Collecting Shane Stevens a.k.a. J. W. Rider. 88p. 1995. pap. 24.95 (*0-9644069-0-X*) Black Diamond.

— The Footsteps of God: Christian Biographies. 1986. pap. 9.99 (*0-85234-227-6*, Pub. by Evangel Pr UK) Presby & Reformed.

— Frontiersman. 1994. pap. 3.99 (*0-06-100801-X*, Harp PBks) HarpC.

— Mountain Country: Southwest Thunder; Masters of Survival, Freetrappers by Trade. 1993. mass mkt. 3.99 (*0-06-100629-7*, Harp PBks) HarpC.

— Mountain Country 2. (Mountain Country Ser.: No. 2). 1994. mass mkt. 3.99 (*0-06-100630-0*, Harp PBks) HarpC.

— Mountain Thunder. 1994. mass mkt. 3.99 (*0-06-100631-9*, Harp PBks) HarpC.

— Sheriff's Blood. 288p. 1994. pap. 3.50 (*0-8217-4440-2*) Zebra.

— Shoshoni Vengeance. 304p. 1993. pap. 3.50 (*0-8217-4334-1*) Zebra.

— Siege at Fort Defiance Vol. 1. 1994. pap. 4.99 (*0-312-95307-0*) St Martin.

— Treaty at Fort Laramie. (Forts of Freedom Ser.). 304p. 1994. mass mkt. 4.99 (*0-312-95128-0*) St Martin.

— Vigilante Coffin. 304p. 1993. pap. 3.50 (*0-8217-4228-0*) Zebra.

— War at Bent's Fort: 1832-1869. 1994. mass mkt. 4.99 (*0-312-95053-5*) St Martin.

— When We Don't Understand. 1992. pap. 6.99 (*0-85234-291-8*, Pub. by Evangel Pr UK) Presby & Reformed.

Legg, John D. Dear Tom: Letters to an Enquiring Christian. 1990. pap. 3.99 (*0-85234-275-6*, Pub. by Evangel Pr UK) Presby & Reformed.

Legg, John P. Arizona Coffin. 1989. pap. 2.95 (*0-8217-2605-6*) Zebra.

— Cheyenne Lance - Medicine Wagon, 2 vols. in 1. 464p. 1990. pap. 3.95 (*0-8439-2994-4*) Dorchester Pub Co.

— Gunfight in Mescalito. 1991. pap. 3.50 (*0-8217-3601-9*) Zebra.

— Guns of Apache Springs. 256p. 1988. pap. 2.95 (*0-8217-2492-4*) Zebra.

— Guns of Arizona. 1992. pap. 3.50 (*0-8217-3753-8*) Zebra.

— High Country Showdown. 256p. 1991. pap. 3.50 (*0-8217-3375-3*) Zebra.

— Shinin' Trails: A Possibles Bag of Fur Trade Trivia. Smith, Monte, ed. (Illus.). 112p. 1988. per. 7.95 (*0-943604-20-6*) Eagles View.

— Showdown at Six-Gun Mine. 1989. pap. 2.95 (*0-8217-2660-9*) Zebra.

— Trouble in Tall Pine. 1990. pap. 2.95 (*0-8217-3047-9*) Zebra.

Legg, Keith R. Patrons, Clients, & Politicians: New Perspectives on Political Clientelism. (Working Papers on Development Ser.: No. 3). 60p. 1975. pap. 2.00 (*0-87725-403-6*) U of Cal IAS.

— Politics in Modern Greece. LC 69-18495. xii, 367p. 1969. 45.00 (*0-8047-0705-7*) Stanford U Pr.

Legg, Merle A. & Reid, Lynne M. Pulmonary Pathology: Proceedings of the 46th Annual Anatomic Pathology Slide Seminar. LC 86-7992. 156p. 1986. pap. text ed. 35.00 (*0-89189-178-1*) Am Soc Clinical.

Legg, Michael, ed. Research Monograph, 1988, No. 17. 70p. 1988. pap. 7.50 (*1-879931-00-1*) Natl Assoc Interp.

Legg, Phillip R. Oliver Cowdery: The Elusive Second Elder of the Restoration. (Illus.). 190p. 1989. pap. 15.00 (*0-8309-0536-7*) Herald Hse.

Legg, Phyllida, jt. auth. see Harrold, Robert.

Legg, Rodney, et al. Ghosts of Dorset, Devon & Somerset. 117p. 1986. 30.00 (*0-686-75656-8*) Dorset Pr.

Legg, Stuart. Barbarians of Asia: The Peoples of the Steppes from 1600 B.C. (Dorset Press Reprints Ser.). (Illus.). 350p. 1990. reprint ed. 19.95 (*0-88029-534-1*) Dorset Pr.

Legg, Stuart, jt. auth. see Klingender, F. D.

Legg, Sue M., et al, eds. Cognitive Assessment of Language & Math Outcomes. LC 90-36747. (Advances in Discourse Processes Ser.: Vol. 36). 304p. (C). 1990. text ed. 65.00 (*0-89391-541-6*); pap. text ed. 39.50 (*0-89391-542-4*) Ablex Pub.

Legg, W. Dorr, ed. Homophile Studies in Theory & Practice. 464p. (Orig.). 1994. 27.95 (*1-879194-16-3*); pap. 14.95 (*1-879194-17-1*) GLB Pubs.

Leggat, Bonnie-Alise. Punt, Pass & Point! Thatch, Nancy R., ed. LC 92-17598. (Books for Students by Students Ser.). (Illus.). 26p. (J). (gr. 3-5). 1992. lib. bdg. 14.95 (*0-933849-39-7*) Landmark Edns.

Leggat, Gillian. The Artist & the Bully. (Junior African Writers Ser.). (Illus.). (J). (gr. 5-6). 1992. pap. 3.95 (*0-7910-2913-1*) Chelsea Hse.

***Leggat, Ian.** How to Travel Without Losing Your Shirt, Your Socks or Your Soapbag. 1995. 9.95 (*0-8062-5262-6*) Carlton.

Leggatt, Alexander. English Drama: Shakespeare to Restoration 1590-1660. (Literature in English Ser.). 312p. (C). 1988. pap. text ed. 25.95 (*0-582-49311-0*, 73571) Longman.

— Jacobean Public Theatre. LC 91-47105. (Theatre Production Ser.). (Illus.). 208p. 1992. 49.95 (*0-415-01048-9*, A7708) Routledge.

— King Lear. LC 88-18052. (Twayne's New Critical Introduction to Shakespeare Ser.: No. 6). 192p. 1988. lib. bdg. 20.95 (*0-8057-8707-0*, TNIS NO. 6, Twayne); pap. 13.95 (*0-8057-8711-9*, Twayne) Macmillan.

— King Lear. (Shakespeare in Performance Ser.). (Illus.). 160p. 1991. text ed. 14.95 (*0-7190-2748-9*, Pub. by Manchester Univ Pr UK) St Martin.

— Shakespeare's Political Drama: The History Plays & the Roman Plays. 288p. 1989. pap. 15.95 (*0-415-03888-X*) Routledge.

Leggatt, D. V., jt. auth. see Leggatt, P. O.

Leggatt, Jeremy, tr. see Carriere, Jean-Claude.

Leggatt, Jeremy, tr. see Gerber, Alain.

Leggatt, Jeremy, tr. see Raspail, Jean.

Leggatt, P. O. & Leggatt, D. V. The Healing Wells: Cornish Cults & Customs. (C). 1989. 45.00 (*1-85022-033-6*, Pub. by Dyllansow Truran UK) St Mut.

Legge, tr. A Record of Buddhistic Kingdoms. (C). 1991. 23.50 (*0-685-50018-7*, Pub. by Munshiram Manoharial II) S Asia.

Legge, Allan H., jt. ed. see Krupa, Sagar V.

***Legge, David.** Bamboozled. LC 94-18647. (J). 1995. 14.95 (*0-590-47989-X*) Scholastic Inc.

Legge, David, jt. auth. see Barber, Paul J.

Legge, David R., jt. auth. see McCormack, John.

Legge, Derek. The Education of Adults in Britain. 256p. 1982. 85.00 (*0-335-00267-6*, Open Univ Pr) Taylor & Francis.

Legge, Elizabeth M. Max Ernst: The Psychoanalytic Sources. Foster, Stephen, ed. LC 89-31850. (Studies in the Fine Arts: The Avant-Garde: No. 67). 246p. reprint ed. 69.90 (*0-8357-1964-2*, 2070731) Bks Demand.

Legge, Francis. Forerunners & Rivals of Christianity, 2 vols. in 1. 19.00 (*0-8446-1280-4*) Peter Smith.

Legge, Gordon E. & Campbell, Fergus W. Vision of Color & Pattern. Head, J. J., ed. LC 84-45835. (Carolina Biology Readers Ser.: No. 165). (Illus.). 16p. (Orig.). (YA). (gr. 10 up). 1987. pap. text ed. 2.75 (*0-89278-365-6*, 45-9765) Carolina Biological.

Legge, J. D. Intellectuals & Nationalism in Indonesia: The Following Recruited by Sutan Sjahrir in Occupation Jakarta. (Monograph Ser.: No. 68). 168p. (Orig.). (C). 1988. pap. text ed. 8.00 (*0-87763-034-8*) Cornell Mod Indo.

Legge, J. E. Rhyme & Revolution in Germany. 1973. 59.95 (*0-8490-0954-5*) Gordon Pr.

Legge, James. Chanticleer: A Study of the French Muse. 1972. 59.95 (*0-87968-835-1*) Gordon Pr.

— I Ching: Book of Changes. 449p. 1983. pap. 9.95 (*0-8065-0458-7*, Citadel Pr) Carol Pub Group.

— The Sacred Books of China, 6 vols, Set. 1975. 1,800.00 (*0-317-00108-6*) Krishna Pr.

Legge, James, tr. The Chinese Classics, 4 vols. (CHI & ENG.). 1991. reprint ed. Vol. I, Four Books of Chinese Classics: Confucian Analects; Great Learning: Doctrine of the Mean; Wo. 35.00 (*0-318-63251-9*); reprint ed. Vol. II, Sho King, or the Book of Historical Documents. 35.00 (*0-318-63252-7*) Oriental Bk Store.

— Chinese Classics, 4 vols., Set. (CHI & ENG.). 1991. 135.00 (*0-685-65145-2*, Pub. by SMC Pub CC) Oriental Bk Store.

— The Chinese Classics, 4 vols., Set. (CHI & ENG.). 1991. reprint ed. 135.00 (*957-638-038-3*, Pub. by SMC Pub CC) Oriental Bk Store.

— The Chinese Classics, 4 vols., Vol. III: She King, or the Book of Poetry. (CHI & ENG.). 1991. reprint ed. Vol. III, She King, or the Book of Poetry. 35.00 (*0-318-63253-5*) Oriental Bk Store.

— The Chinese Classics, 4 vols., Vol. IV: Ch'un Ts'ew with the Tso Chuen. (CHI & ENG.). 1991. reprint ed. Vol. IV, Ch'un Ts'ew with the Tso Chuen. 35.00 (*0-318-63254-3*) Oriental Bk Store.

— The Chinese Classics: With a Translation, Critical & Exegetical Notes, Prolegomena, & Copious Indexes, 5 vols., Set. 3852p. (C). 1982. text ed. 600.00 (*962-209-102-4*, Pub. by Hong Kong U Pr HK) St Mut.

— The Ch'un Ts'ew with the Tso Chuen, Vol. IV. (CHI & ENG.). 1991. 35.00 (*957-638-042-1*, Pub. by SMC Pub CC) Oriental Bk Store.

— Four Books of the Chinese Classics: Confucian Analects; Great Learning; Doctrine of the Mean, Works of Mencius, 4 vols., Set. (CHI & ENG.). 1991. 130.00 (*0-318-69419-0*) Oriental Bk Store.

— Four Books of the Chinese Classics: Confucian Analects; Great Learning; Doctrine of the Mean, Works of Mencius, 4 vols., Vol. I. (CHI & ENG.). 1991. 35.00 (*957-638-039-1*, Pub. by SMC Pub CC) Oriental Bk Store.

— I Ching. rev. ed. 470p. 1990. pap. 19.95 (*9971-4-9200-8*) Heian Intl.

— I Ching. 2nd ed. 1899. pap. 7.95 (*0-486-21062-6*) Dover.

— The She King, or the Book of Poetry, Vol. III. (CHI & ENG.). 1991. 35.00 (*957-638-041-3*, Pub. by SMC Pub CC) Oriental Bk Store.

— The Shoo King, or the Book of Historical Documents, Vol. II. (CHI & ENG.). 1991. 35.00 (*957-638-040-5*, Pub. by SMC Pub CC) Oriental Bk Store.

Legge, James, tr. see Muller, F. Max, ed.

Legge, James, tr. see Streep, Peg, ed.

Legge, James G. Rhyme & Revolution in Germany: A Study in German History, Life, Literature & Character. LC 72-126646. reprint ed. 33.45 (*0-404-03947-2*) AMS Pr.

Legge, Jerome S., Jr. Abortion Policy: An Evaluation of the Consequences for Maternal & Infant Health. LC 84-16356. 182p. 1985. 64.50 (*0-87395-958-2*); pap. 21.95 (*0-87395-959-0*) State U NY Pr.

— Traffic Safety Reform in the United States & Great Britain. LC 90-49091. (Series in Policy & Institutional Studies). 198p. (C). 1991. 49.95 (*0-8229-3662-3*) U of Pittsburgh Pr.

Legge, K. & Mumford, E. Designing Organizations for Satisfaction & Efficiency. 160p. 1978. text ed. 52.95 (*0-566-02102-1*) Ashgate Pub Co.

Legge, Karen. Evaluating Planned Organizational Change. (Organizational & Occupational Psychology Ser.). 1984. text ed. 76.00 (*0-12-440980-6*) Acad Pr.

Legge, Marilyn J. The Grace of Difference: A Canadian Feminist Theological Ethic. LC 92-16229. (American Academy of Religion Academy Ser.: Vol. 80). 312p. 1992. 29.95 (*1-55540-736-6*, 010180); pap. 19.95 (*1-55540-737-4*) Scholars Pr GA.

Legge, Mary D. Anglo-Norman Literature & Its Background. LC 78-17093. 389p. 1978. reprint ed. text ed. 35.00 (*0-313-20588-4*, LEAL, Greenwood Pr) Greenwood.

Legge, Norman R., et al. Thermoplastic Elastometers: A Comprehensive Review. 575p. (C). 1987. text ed. 125.00 (*1-56990-053-1*) Hanser-Gardner.

Legge, Ronald. Find Your Ancestors. 32p. 1987. pap. 25.00 (*0-85937-129-8*, Pub. by K Mason Pubns Ltd UK) St Mut.

Legge, Rupert. Fashionable Circles. 448p. 1992. pap. 11.95 (*0-7472-3716-6*, Pub. by Headline UK) Trafalgar.

Leggeri, A., et al. Intraoperative Choledochoscopy. 116p. 1983. text ed. 48.00 (*1-57235-041-5*) Piccin NY.

Legget, Gerene C. Bouvier des Flandres. (Illus.). 192p. 1989. lib. bdg. 11.95 (*0-86622-691-5*, KW-168) TFH Pubns.

Legget, Robert F. The Ottawa River Canals & the Defence of British North America. (Illus.). 308p. 1988. 35.00 (*0-8020-5794-2*) U of Toronto Pr.

— Ottawa Waterway: Gateway to a Continent. LC 75-6780. (Illus.). 303p. reprint ed. pap. 86.40 (*0-8357-8258-1*, 2034050) Bks Demand.

— Rideau Waterway. rev. ed. LC 72-197084. 279p. reprint ed. pap. 79.60 (*0-317-27021-4*, 2023644) Bks Demand.

— Rideau Waterway. 2nd ed. (Illus.). 320p. 1986. 32.50 (*0-8020-2573-0*); pap. 17.95 (*0-8020-6591-0*) U of Toronto Pr.

— Rideau Waterway. LC 72-197084. 279p. reprint ed. pap. 79.60 (*0-318-34715-6*, 2031916) Bks Demand.

An Asterisk (*) at the beginning of an entry indicates that the title is appearing in BIP for the first time.

Legget, Robert F., ed. Geology under Cities. LC 82-20991. (Reviews in Engineering Geology Ser.: No. 5). (Illus.). 141p. reprint ed. pap. 40.20 (*0-7837-1848-9*, 2042048) Bks Demand.

Legget, Robert F., ed. see Geological Society of America Staff.

Legget, Trevor. Fingers & Moons. 200p. 1995. pap. 10.95 (*0-946672-07-5*, Pub. by Buddhist Pubng UK) Atrium Pubs.

Leggett, Abraham. Narrative of Major Abraham Leggett. LC 70-140871. (Eyewitness Accounts of the American Revolution Ser., No. 1). 1971. reprint ed. 16.95 (*0-405-01215-2*) Ayer.

Leggett, Anthony J., jt. ed. see Kagan, Yu A.

Leggett, Anthony J., tr. see Migdal, A. B.

Leggett, B. J. Early Stevens: The Nietzschean Intertext. LC 91-34864. 285p. 1992. text ed. 36.95 (*0-8223-1201-8*) Duke.

Leggett, B. J., jt. ed. see Serio, John N.

Leggett, Bobby J. Houseman's Land of Lost Content: A Critical Study of a Shropshire Lad. LC 71-100407. 172p. reprint ed. pap. 49.10 (*0-8357-8605-6*, 2035002) Bks Demand.

— The Poetic Art of A. E. Housman: Theory & Practice. LC 77-15792. 173p. reprint ed. pap. 49.40 (*0-7837-6032-9*, 2045845) Bks Demand.

Leggett, Chris, jt. auth. see Teachout, Woden.

Leggett, Conway, & Co. Staff. The History of Marion County, Ohio. (Illus.). 915p. 1992. reprint ed. pap. 50.00 (*1-55613-549-1*) Heritage Bk.

— History of Wyandot Co., OH Vol. 2: A History of Its Townships. (Illus.). 627p. 1994. pap. 37.00 (*0-7884-0079-7*) Heritage Bk.

***Leggett, Conway, & Co. Staff, ed.** The History of Wyandot County, OH Vol. 1: A General History of the County. (Illus.). 297p. 1994. pap. text ed. 22.00 (*0-7884-0061-4*) Heritage Bk.

Leggett, David J., ed. Computational Methods for the Determination of Formation Constants. LC 85-16991. (Modern Inorganic Chemistry Ser.). 494p. 1985. 125.00 (*0-306-41957-2*, Plenum Pr) Plenum.

Leggett, Dennis. People Trap. LC 90-46400. (Operation Earth Ser.). (Illus.). 48p. (J). (gr. 5-9). 1991. lib. bdg. 12.95 (*1-85435-378-0*) Marshall Cavendish.

— Troubled Waters. LC 90-46572. (Operation Earth Ser.). (Illus.). 48p. (J). (gr. 5-9). 1991. lib. bdg. 12.95 (*1-85435-275-X*) Marshall Cavendish.

Leggett, Dennis, jt. auth. see Leggett, Jeremy.

Leggett, Donald A. Loving God & Disturbing Men: Preaching from the Prophets. LC 90-32753. 224p. 1990. pap. 12.99 (*0-8010-5660-8*) Baker Bk.

Leggett, Gary. Letters to Timothy. LC 80-82830. (Radiant Life Ser.). 128p. (Orig.). 1981. 2.95 (*0-88243-877-8*, 02-0877); teacher ed 4.50 (*0-88243-189-7*, 32-0189) Gospel Pub.

Leggett, Glen, et al. Prentice Hall Handbook for Writers. 11th ed. 608p. (C). 1990. text ed. write for info. (*0-13-716093-3*) P-H.

Leggett, J. K., ed. Marine Clastic Sedimentology. (C). 1987. lib. bdg. 105.00 (*0-86010-897-X*, Pub. by Graham & Trotman UK) Kluwer Ac.

Leggett, Jeremy. Air Scare. LC 90-46420. (Operation Earth Ser.). (Illus.). 48p. (J). (gr. 5-9). 1991. lib. bdg. 12.95 (*1-85435-274-1*) Marshall Cavendish.

— Dying Forests. LC 90-46574. (Operation Earth Ser.). (Illus.). 48p. (J). (gr. 5-9). 1991. lib. bdg. 12.95 (*1-85435-276-8*) Marshall Cavendish.

— Energy Gap. LC 90-46431. (Operation Earth Ser.). (Illus.). 48p. (J). (gr. 5-9). 1991. lib. bdg. 12.95 (*1-85435-377-2*) Marshall Cavendish.

— Waste War. LC 90-46573. (Operation Earth Ser.). (Illus.). 48p. (J). (gr. 5-9). 1991. lib. bdg. 12.95 (*1-85435-277-6*) Marshall Cavendish.

Leggett, Jeremy, ed. Global Warming: The Greenpeace Report. (Illus.). 576p. 1990. 10.95 (*0-19-286119-0*) OUP.

Leggett, Jeremy & Leggett, Dennis. Operation Earth Series, 6 vols. (Illus.). (J). (gr. 5-9). 1991. lib. bdg. 77.70 (*1-85435-273-3*) Marshall Cavendish.

Leggett, Jeremy, tr. see Fleutiaux, Pierrette.

Leggett, John. Race, Class & Political Consciousness. 243p. 1972. pap. 11.95 (*0-87073-257-9*) Schenkman Bks Inc.

— Race, Class, & Political Consciousness. 243p. 1972. boxed 32.95 (*0-87073-256-0*) Transaction Pubs.

Leggett, John C. Mining the Fields: Farmworkers Fight Back. (Illus.). 133p. (Orig.). (C). 1991. text ed. 34.95 (*0-9625270-0-9*); pap. text ed. 24.95 (*0-9625270-1-7*) Raritan Inst.

Leggett, Linda R. & Andrews, Linda G. The Rose-Colored Glasses: Melanie Adjusts to Poor Vision. LC 79-12501. (Illus.). 32p. (J). (gr. 3 up). 1979. 16.95 (*0-87705-408-8*) Human Sci Pr.

Leggett, M. D., ed. Subject-Matter Index of Patents for Inventions Issued by the United States Patent Office from 1790 to 1873, Inclusive, 3 vols., 1. LC 75-24110. (America in Two Centuries Ser.). 1976. reprint ed. 58.95 (*0-405-07738-6*) Ayer.

— Subject-Matter Index of Patents for Inventions Issued by the United States Patent Office from 1790 to 1873, Inclusive, 3 vols., 2. LC 75-24110. (America in Two Centuries Ser.). 1976. reprint ed. 58.95 (*0-405-07739-4*) Ayer.

— Subject-Matter Index of Patents for Inventions Issued by the United States Patent Office from 1790 to 1873, Inclusive, 3 vols., 3. LC 75-24110. (America in Two Centuries Ser.). 1976. reprint ed. 58.95 (*0-405-07740-8*) Ayer.

— Subject-Matter Index of Patents for Inventions Issued by the United States Patent Office from 1790 to 1873, Inclusive, 3 vols., Set. LC 75-24110. (America in Two Centuries Ser.). 1976. reprint ed. 173.95 (*0-405-07737-8*) Ayer.

Leggett, Marshall. Genuine Ministers. LC 89-43012. 112p. (Orig.). 1989. pap. 5.99 (*0-89900-342-7*) College Pr Pub.

— Introduction to the Restoration Ideal. 240p. 1986. pap. text ed. 8.99 (*0-87403-067-6*, 3175) Standard Pub.

— Workbook for the Restoration Ideal. 96p. 1986. student ed, pap. 2.99 (*0-87403-068-4*, 3176) Standard Pub.

Leggett, Mike, photos & text. Rio Grande: The People & Politics of One of America's Greatest Rivers. LC 93-81146. (Illus.). 128p. 1994. 20.00 (*1-56352-139-3*) Longstreet Pr Inc.

Leggett, Penny, ed. see Bailey, Becky.

***Leggett, Peter & Bricker, Linda.** Johnny Long Tail. LC 93-94306. (Illus.). 64p. (Orig.). (J). 1994. pap. 9.00 (*1-56002-423-2*, Univ Edtns) Aegina Pr.

Leggett, Stanton, jt. auth. see Bunce, Roy.

Leggett, Trevor. Encounters in Yoga & Zen: Meetings of Cloth & Stone. (Illus.). 112p. 1993. pap. 9.95 (*0-8048-1909-2*) C E Tuttle.

— From the Lotus Lake & the Dragon Pool. (Illus.). 200p. (Orig.). 1994. pap. 12.95 (*0-8048-1932-7*) C E Tuttle.

— Shogi: Japan's Game of Strategy. 100p. 1993. pap. 14.95 (*0-8048-1903-3*) C E Tuttle.

— Three Ages of Zen: Samurai, Feudal & Modern. 192p. 1993. pap. 12.95 (*0-8048-1898-3*) C E Tuttle.

Leggett, Trevor P. First Zen Reader. LC 60-12739. (Illus.). 236p. 1960. pap. 12.95 (*0-8048-0180-0*) C E Tuttle.

— Sankara on the Yoga-Sutras: The Vivarana Sub-Commentary to Vyasa-Bhasya on the Yoga-Sultras of Pantanjali. 600p. 1981. text ed. 30.00 (*0-7103-0277-0*, Pub. by Kegan Paul Intl UK) Routledge Chapman & Hall.

— Second Zen Reader: The Tiger's Cave & Translations of other Zen Writings. LC 87-50163. (Illus.). 196p. (Orig.). 1988. pap. 9.95 (*0-8048-1525-9*) C E Tuttle.

— Zen & the Ways. LC 87-50165. (Illus.). 258p. 1987. pap. 12.95 (*0-8048-1524-0*) C E Tuttle.

Leggett, Trevor P., tr. Sankara on the Yoga-Sutras: The Vivarana Sub-Commentary to Vyasa-Bhasya, 2 vols., 1. 220p. 1983. 30.00 (*0-7100-0826-0*, RKP) Routledge.

— Sankara on the Yoga-Sutras: The Vivarana Sub-Commentary to Vyasa-Bhasya, 2 vols., 2. 220p. 1983. 30.00 (*0-7100-9539-2*, RKP) Routledge.

Leggett, William. Collection of the Political Writings of William Leggett. LC 76-125702. (American Journalists Ser.). 1971. reprint ed. 30.95 (*0-405-01681-6*) Ayer.

— Democratick Editorials: Essays in Jacksonian Political Economy. White, Lawrence H., ed. LC 83-24893. 432p. (C). 1984. 12.00 (*0-86597-036-X*); pap. 6.00 (*0-86597-037-8*) Liberty Fund.

Leggewie, Robert. Anthologie de la Litterature Francaise, Tome 1: Des Origines a la fin du Dix-Huitieme Siecle. 3rd ed. (Illus.). 464p. (C). 1990. pap. text ed. 29.95 (*0-19-506276-0*) OUP.

— Anthologie de la Litterature Francaise, Tome 2: Dix-Neuvieme et Vinqtieme Siecles. 3rd ed. (Illus.). 480p. (C). 1990. pap. text ed. 29.95 (*0-19-506277-9*) OUP.

Leggewie, Robert, ed. Anthologie de la Litterature Francaise Tome I: Des Origines a la Fin du Dix-Huitieme Siecle. 4th ed. (Illus.). 432p. (C). Date not set. pap. text ed. 27.95 (*0-19-508585-X*) OUP.

— Anthologie de la Litterature Francaise Tome II: Dix-Neuvieme et Vingtieme Siecles. 4th ed. (Illus.). 480p. (C). Date not set. pap. 27.95 (*0-19-508586-8*) OUP.

Leggitt, Hunter, jt. auth. see Myers, Lonny.

Leggitt, W. E., ed. see Iron & Steel Society of AIME Staff.

Leggon, Cheryl B., jt. ed. see Marett, Cora B.

Leggon, Cheryl B., jt. auth. see Marrett, Cora B.

Leggon, Cheryl B., jt. ed. see Marrett, Cora B.

Leggott, Michele J. Reading Zukofsky's "80 Flowers" LC 88-6769. 464p. 1989. text ed. 52.50x (*0-8018-3368-X*) Johns Hopkins.

***Leghorn, Lindsay.** Proud of Our Feelings. (Illus.). 32p. (J). (ps-3). 1995. 11.95 (*0-945354-68-1*) Magination Pr.

Legingham, J. G., jt. auth. see Gardiner, P.

Legis Administration Staff. Dictionary of Agri-Business: Dictionnaire Permanent Entreprise Agricole. 1722p. (FRE.). 1983. 195.00 (*0-8288-1173-3*, M15326) Fr & Eur.

Legislative Administrative Staff. Permanent Fiscal Dictionary: Dictionnaire Permanent Fiscal, 2 vols. 5000p. (FRE.). 1989. 495.00 (*0-7859-4928-3*) Fr & Eur.

Legislative Drafting Research Fund of Columbia University Staff. Index Digest of State Constitutions. vii, 1546p. 1993. reprint ed. lib. bdg. 115.00 (*0-8377-2177-6*) Rothman.

Legislative Guidebooks Editors. Guidebook to New Jersey Legislators 1994. 520p. 1994. pap. 197.00 (*0-9635376-3-6*) Legis Guidebks.

— Guidebook to New York Legislators 1993-1994. 650p. 1993. pap. 197.00 (*0-9635376-2-8*) Legis Guidebks.

— Guidebook to Pennsylvania Legislators 1993-1994. 790p. 1993. pap. 197.00 (*0-9635376-1-X*) Legis Guidebks.

— Guidebook to Virginia Legislators 1994. 520p. 1993. pap. 197.00 (*0-9635376-4-4*) Legis Guidebks.

Legislative Reference Bureau Staff. Laws of Pennsylvania. 1982, Vol. 2. 818p. 1983. text ed. 7.45 (*0-8182-0015-4*) Commonweal PA.

— Pennsylvania Consolidated Statutes, Constitution: 1984 Permanent Edition. (Orig.). (C). 1984. pap. 4.00 (*0-8182-0046-4*) Commonweal PA.

— Pennsylvania Consolidated Statutes, Title 13: Commercial Code, 1982 Edition. 310p. (C). 1992. pap. 8.50 (*0-8182-0006-5*) Commonweal PA.

— Pennsylvania Consolidated Statutes, Title 18: Crime & Offence, 1990 Edition. rev. ed. 302p. (C). 1990. pap. text ed. 6.55 (*0-8182-0007-3*) Commonweal PA.

— Pennsylvania Consolidated Statutes, Title 20 , Decedents, Estates & Fiduciaries: 1992 Edition. 278p. (C). 1992. pap. 7.50 (*0-8182-0008-1*) Commonweal PA.

— Pennsylvania Consolidated Statutes, Title 24, Education: 1984 Permanent Edition. (Orig.). (C). 1984. pap. 3.00 (*0-8182-0043-X*) Commonweal PA.

— Pennsylvania Consolidated Statutes, Title 30, Fish: 1989 Permanent Edition. (Orig.). (C). 1989. pap. 3.90 (*0-8182-0044-8*) Commonweal PA.

— Pennsylvania Consolidated Statutes, Title 42, Judiciary & Judicial Procedure: 1990 Edition. rev. ed. 554p. (C). 1990. pap. text ed. 8.50 (*0-8182-0010-3*) Commonweal PA.

— Pennsylvania Consolidated Statutes, Title 71, State Government: 1984 Permanent Edition. (Orig.). (C). 1984. pap. 3.00 (*0-8182-0045-6*) Commonweal PA.

Legislative Reference Bureau Staff, intro. Pennsylvania Consolidated Statutes Title: Names 1982 Special Edition. rev. ed. 29p. 1992. pap. text ed. 3.55 (*0-8182-0011-1*) Commonweal PA.

Legislative Reference Bureau Staff, ed. see Commonwealth of Pennsylvania Staff.

Legl, Elisabeth. The Japanese Chin. (Breed Bks.). (Illus.). 1995. write for info. (*0-87714-131-2*) Denlingers.

***Legler, Gretchen.** All the Powerful Invisible Things: A Sportswoman's Notebook. 180p. (Orig.). 1995. text ed. 20.95 (*1-878067-70-2*); pap. text ed. 12.95 (*1-878067-69-9*) Seal Pr Feminist.

Legler, Henry E. Walt Whitman: Yesterday & Today. LC 76-2434. (Studies in Whitman: No. 28). 1976. lib. bdg. 32.95 (*0-8383-2118-6*) M S G Haskell Hse.

Legler, John B. Regional Distribution of Federal Receipts & Expenditures in the 19th Century: A Quantitative Study. Bruchey, Stuart, ed. LC 76-39833. (Nineteen Seventy-Seven Dissertations Ser.). (Illus.). 1977. lib. bdg. 23.95 (*0-405-09913-4*) Ayer.

Legman, G. The Fake Revolt. 1974. 250.00 (*0-685-26308-8*) Revisionist Pr.

— The Limerick. 592p. 1991. reprint ed. 12.99 (*0-517-06505-3*) Random Hse Value.

— No Laughing Matter: An Analysis of Sexual Humor, 2 vols. Incl. Vol. 1. LC 81-48469. 816p. 1982. 37.50 (*0-253-34775-0*); LC 81-48469. 1982. reprint ed. 75.00 (*0-253-34777-7*) Ind U Pr.

Legman, G., ed. see Randolph, Vance.

Legman, G., ed. see Twain, Mark.

Legman, Gershon. Horn Book: Studies in Erotic Folklore & Bibliography. 1963. 12.50 (*0-8216-0091-5*, Univ Bks) Carol Pub Group.

— Love & Death: A Study in Censorship. pap. 1.75 (*0-87817-012-X*) Hacker.

Legmann, P., jt. auth. see Burstein, M.

Legner, E. F., jt. auth. see Moore, Ian.

Lego, Suzanne. Fear & AIDS HIV: Empathy & Communication. LC 93-30743. (Real Nursing Ser.). 136p. 1994. pap. text ed. 19.95 (*0-8273-6155-6*) Delmar.

LeGoff, Jacques, ed. see Tilly, Charles.

LeGoffe, Claude. French for Business. Le Francais des Affaires. Livret du Professeur. 2nd ed. (Hatier Ser.). 29p. (FRE.). 1989. pap. 12.95 (*2-218-02522-1*) Schoenhof.

Legomsky, Stephen H. Immigration & the Judiciary: Law & Politics in Britain & America. LC 86-23798. 384p. 1987. 79.00 (*0-19-825561-6*) OUP.

— Immigration Law & Policy. (University Casebook Ser.). 1111p. (C). 1991. text ed. 45.25 (*0-88277-943-5*) Foundation Pr.

— Immigration Law & Policy: Teacher's Manual. (University Casebook Ser.). 416p. 1991. pap. text ed. write for info. (*0-88277-973-7*) Foundation Pr.

— Immigration Law & Policy: 1994 Supplement. (University Casebook Ser.). 100p. 1994. pap. text ed. 7.95 (*1-56662-205-0*) Foundation Pr.

— Specialized Justice: Courts, Administrative Tribunals, & a Cross-National Theory of Specialization. 144p. 1990. 49.95 (*0-19-825429-6*) OUP.

Legon, Ronald P. Megara: The Political History of a Greek City-State to 336 B. C. LC 80-69828. (Illus.). 344p. 1981. 44.95 (*0-8014-1370-2*) Cornell U Pr.

Legouis, Emile. The Early Life of William Wordsworth, 1770-1798. Mathews, J. W., tr. 494p. 1992. reprint ed. text ed. 60.00 (*1-870352-30-0*, Pub. by Libris UK); reprint ed. pap. text ed. 25.00 (*1-870352-01-7*, Pub. by Libris UK) Paul & Co Pubs.

— Early Life of William Wordsworth, 1770-1798: A Study of the Prelude. Matthews, T. W., tr. LC 74-145138. 1971. reprint ed. 49.00 (*0-403-01070-5*) Scholarly.

— Edmund Spenser. LC 71-172044. reprint ed. 27.50 (*0-404-03948-0*) AMS Pr.

Legowis, Emile H. William Wordsworth & Annette Vallon. (BCL1-PR English Literature Ser.). 146p. 1992. reprint ed. lib. bdg. 69.00 (*0-7812-7680-2*) Rprt Serv.

LeGrady, George. Stockfootage. (Illus.). 12p. 1984. pap. 10.00 (*0-939784-07-6*) CEPA Gall.

Legrain, L. Terra-Cottas from Nippur. (Publications of the Babylonian Section). (Illus.). 52p. 1930. 60.00 (*0-686-11926-6*) U PA Mus Pubns.

Legrain, M. Nephrology. 400p. 1987. pap. text ed. 17.00 (*0-89352-230-9*, Yr Bk Med Pubs) Mosby Yr Bk.

Legrain, M., jt. auth. see Keen, Harry.

Legrand, et al. The Nature & Future of Episcopal Conferences. LC 88-28555. 410p. 1988. pap. 19.95 (*0-8132-0703-7*) Cath U Pr.

Legrand, A. P. & Flandrois, S., eds. Chemical Physics of Intercalation. LC 88-24688. (NATO ASI Series B, Physics: Vol. 172). 530p. 1988. 135.00 (*0-306-42831-8*, Plenum Pr) Plenum.

Legrand, B. APL, Management Problems with Answers & "Kit of Tools" Matthews, Julian G., tr. LC 83-25908. 167p. reprint ed. pap. 47.60 (*0-8357-5656-4*, 2032660) Bks Demand.

— Learning & Applying APL. Matthews, Julian G., tr. LC 83-10620. 414p. reprint ed. pap. 118.00 (*0-685-23423-1*, 2032659) Bks Demand.

LeGrand, Catherine. Frontier Expansion & Peasant Protest in Colombia, 1850-1936. LC 85-24244. 320p. reprint ed. pap. 91.20 (*0-7837-5870-7*, 2045589) Bks Demand.

Legrand, E., tr. Recueil de contes populaires grecs. LC 78-20108. (Collection de contes et de chansons populaires: Vol. 1). reprint ed. 21.50 (*0-404-60351-3*) AMS Pr.

LeGrand, Harry. A Standardized System for Evaluating Waste Disposal Sites. 42p. 1983. 15.00 (*1-56034-043-6*, T005) Natl Water Well.

LeGrand, Jacques & Suk-Hbaatar, Tsegmidijn. Dictionnaire Mongol-Francais. 288p. (FRE & MON.). 1992. 49.95 (*0-7859-1018-2*, 2901795498) Fr & Eur.

LeGrand, Julian & Robinson, Ray. The Economics of Social Problems. 200p. (C). 1980. pap. text ed. 17.50 (*0-15-518910-7*) HB Coll Pubs.

LeGrand, Julian, jt. auth. see Goodin, Robert E.

LeGrand, Louis, see Orville J. Victor, pseud..

Legrand, Lucien. Unity & Plurality: Mission in the Bible. LC 90-38940. 1990. pap. 19.95 (*0-88344-692-8*) Orbis Bks.

Legrand, M., ed. Cities & Subsurface Use: Proceedings of an International Conference, Bordeaux, 21-23 October 1987. 480p. (C). 1987. text ed. 155.00 (*90-6191-715-8*, Pub. by A A Balkema NE) Ashgate Pub Co.

— Tunneling in Soft & Water-Bearing Grounds: Proceedings of an International Symposium, Lyon, 27-29 November 1984. 286p. (C). 1985. text ed. 155.00 (*90-6191-590-2*, Pub. by A A Balkema NE) Ashgate Pub Co.

— Underground Crossing for Europe: Proceedings of an International Conference, Lille, 16 - 18 October 1990. (Illus.). 372p. (C). 1990. text ed. 125.00 (*90-6191-157-5*, Pub. by A A Balkema NE) Ashgate Pub Co.

Legrand, Pierre. Dictionary of Lille Patois: Dictionnaire du Patois de Lille. 174p. (FRE.). 1990. pap. write for info. (*0-7859-4858-9*) Fr & Eur.

— Dictionnaire du Patois de Lille. fac. ed. 180p. (FRE.). 1987. pap. 79.95 (*0-7859-8229-9*, 2904951288) Fr & Eur.

LeGrand, Y. & El Hage, S. G. Physiological Optics. (Optical Sciences Ser.: Vol. 13). (Illus.). 350p. 1980. pap. 67.00 (*0-387-09919-0*) Spr-Verlag.

LeGrande, William. Christian Persecution & Genocide. 1982. lib. bdg. 59.95 (*0-87700-392-0*) Revisionist Pr.

Legrez, Didier, tr. see International Conference on Private Aeronautical Law Staff.

***Legris, Renee.** Dictionnaire des Auteurs du Radio-Feuilleton Quebecois. 200p. (FRE.). 1981. pap. 29.95 (*0-7859-8026-1*, 2762110904) Fr & Eur.

***Legro, Jeffrey W.** Cooperation under Fire: Anglo-German Restraint During World War II. LC 94-35482. (Studies in Security Affairs). 272p. 1995. 35.00x (*0-8014-2938-2*) Cornell U Pr.

Legros, J. C., jt. ed. see Kaldis, E.

Legros, J. C., jt. auth. see Platten, J. K.

Legros, J. J., jt. ed. see Enjalbert, A.

LeGros, Lucy C. Activities & Games. rev. ed. (Illus.). 75p. (Orig.). (J). (gr. k-2). 1989. pap. 7.95 (*0-318-41419-8*) Creat Res NC.

— Instant Centers: Numbers. (Illus.). 48p. (Orig.). (J). (gr. k-2). 1984. pap. 5.95 (*0-937306-05-3*) Creat Res NC.

— Instant Centers - Colors. (Illus.). 40p. (Orig.). (J). (gr. k-2). 1984. pap. 5.95 (*0-937306-03-7*) Creat Res NC.

— Instant Centers - Holidays. (Illus.). 45p. (Orig.). (J). (gr. k-2). 1985. 5.95 (*0-937306-06-1*) Creat Res NC.

— Instant Centers - Holidays. rev. ed. 51p. (Orig.). (J). (gr. k-2). 1988. teacher ed 5.95 (*0-317-65724-0*) Creat Res NC.

— Instant Centers - Letters. (Illus.). 46p. (Orig.). (J). (gr. k-2). 1984. pap. 5.95 (*0-937306-04-5*) Creat Res NC.

— Instant Centers - Numbers 10-20. 33p. (J). (gr. k-2). 1988. teacher ed 5.95 (*0-937306-07-X*) Creat Res NC.

— Reading Success for School & Home. rev. ed. (Illus.). 230p. (Orig.). (J). 1989. pap. 10.95 (*0-318-41420-1*) Creat Res NC.

— Square One. 41p. (J). (gr. k-2). 1988. teacher ed 4.95 (*0-937306-08-8*); 16.95 (*0-937306-09-6*) Creat Res NC.

LeGrys, Vicky A. The Laboratory Diagnosis of Selected Inborn Errors of Metabolism. LC 83-22941. (Methods in Laboratory Medicine Ser.: Vol. 4). 208p. 1984. text ed. 45.00 (*0-275-91441-0*, C1441, Praeger Pubs) Greenwood.

Legters, Lyman H., ed. Eastern Europe - Transformation & Revolution, 1945-1991: Documents & Analyses. (Sources in Modern History Ser.). 665p. (C). 1992. pap. text ed. write for info. (*0-669-24994-7*) Heath.

Legters, Lyman H. & Lyden, Fremont J., eds. American Indian Policy: Self-Governance & Economic Development. LC 93-9319. (Contributions in Political Science Ser.: No. 329). 240p. 1993. text ed. 55.00 (*0-313-28992-1*, G8892, Greenwood Pr) Greenwood.

Legters, Lyman H., jt. ed. see Lyden, Fremont J.

Legters, Lyman H., jt. ed. see Lyden, Fremont.

Legters, Lyman H., et al, eds. Critical Perspectives on Democracy. 188p. (C). 1994. pap. text ed. 23.95 (*0-8476-7889-X*) Rowman.

Leguillo, J. C., jt. auth. see Zinn-Justin, J.

Leguillon, D. & Sanchez-Palencia, E. Computation of Singular Solutions in Elliptic Problems & Elasticity. 1987. pap. text ed. 69.95 (*0-471-91757-5*) Wiley.

LeGuin, Ursula K. Catwings. (Illus.). 64p. (J). (gr. 2-5). 1992. pap. 2.95 (*0-590-46072-2*) Scholastic Inc.

Leguin, Ursula K. The Visionary, 2 vols. in 1. Bd. with Wonders Hidden. (Back-to-Back Ser.: Vol. 1). (YA). 7.50 (*0-685-10479-6*) McGraw.

Leguizamo, John. Mambo Mouth: A Savage Comedy. LC 93-9783. 1993. pap. 9.95 (*0-553-37087-1*) Bantam.

Leguizamon, Martha, tr. see Tobin, William J.

Legum, Colin. Africa Contemporary Record, Vol. 12:1979-80. LC 70-7957. 1294p. 1981. 345.00 (*0-8419-0550-9*, Africana) Holmes & Meier.

An Asterisk (*) at the beginning of an entry indicates that the title is appearing in BIP for the first time.

— Africa Contemporary Record: Annual Survey & Documents 1986-1987, Vol. XIX. LC 70-7957. 1000p. 1988. lib. bdg. 345.00 (*0-8419-0557-6*, Africana) Holmes & Meier.
— The Battlefronts of Southern Africa. LC 87-25481. 1988. 49.50 (*0-8419-1135-5*); pap. 34.50 (*0-8419-1144-4*) Holmes & Meier.
— Pan-Africanism: A Short Political Guide. LC 75-25492. (Illus.). 296p. 1976. reprint ed. text ed. 35.00 (*0-8371-8420-7*, LEPA, Greenwood Pr) Greenwood.
— Southern Africa: Year of the Whirlwind. LC 77-6264. (Current Affairs Ser.). 72p. 1977. pap. 8.50 (*0-8419-0318-2*, Africana) Holmes & Meier.
— Western Crisis Over Southern Africa. LC 79-9723. (Current Affairs Ser.). (Illus.). (C). 1979. 24.50 (*0-8419-0492-8*, Africana); pap. 17.95 (*0-8419-0496-0*, Africana) Holmes & Meier.
Legum, Colin, ed. Africa Contemporary Record, Vol. 8:1975-76. LC 70-7957. (Illus.). 1220p. 1976. 345.00 (*0-8419-0157-0*, Africana) Holmes & Meier.
— Africa Contemporary Record, Vol. 10:1977-78. LC 70-7957. 1472p. 1979. 345.00 (*0-8419-0159-7*, Africana) Holmes & Meier.
— Africa Contemporary Record, Vol. 11:1978-79. LC 70-7957. 1354p. 1980. 345.00 (*0-8419-0160-0*, Africana) Holmes & Meier.
— Africa Contemporary Record, Vol. 13:1980-81. LC 70-7957. 1300p. 1982. 345.00 (*0-8419-0551-7*, Africana) Holmes & Meier.
— Africa Contemporary Record: Annual Survey & Documents, 1985-1986, Volume XVIII. 1392p. 1987. 345.00 (*0-8419-0556-8*, Africana) Holmes & Meier.
— Africa Contemporary Record Annual Survey & Documents: Volume XVII: 1984-85. 1100p. 1986. 345.00 (*0-8419-0555-X*, Africana) Holmes & Meier.
— Africa Contemporary Record Annual Survey & Documents, Vol. I, 1968-69. 1970. 345.00 (*0-8419-0150-3*, Africana) Holmes & Meier.
— Africa Contemporary Record Annual Survey & Documents, Vol. III, 1970-71. 1972. 345.00 (*0-8419-0152-X*, Africana) Holmes & Meier.
— Africa Contemporary Record Annual Survey & Documents, Vol. IV, 1971-72. 1973. 345.00 (*0-8419-0153-8*, Africana) Holmes & Meier.
— Africa Contemporary Record Annual Survey & Documents, Vol. IX, 1976-77. LC 70-7957. (Illus.). 1293p. 1978. 345.00 (*0-8419-0158-9*, Africana) Holmes & Meier.
— Africa Contemporary Record Annual Survey & Documents, Vol. V, 1972-73. 1974. 345.00 (*0-8419-0154-6*, Africana) Holmes & Meier.
— Africa Contemporary Record Annual Survey & Documents, Vol. VII, 1974-75. LC 70-7957. (Illus.). 1185p. 1975. 345.00 (*0-8419-0156-2*, Africana) Holmes & Meier.
— Africa Contemporary Record, Vol. 14: 1981-82. 1280p. 1983. 345.00 (*0-8419-0552-5*, Africana) Holmes & Meier.
— Africa Contemporary Record, Vol. 15: 1982-1983. 1216p. 1984. 345.00 (*0-8419-0553-3*, Africana) Holmes & Meier.
— Africa Contemporary Record, Vol. 16: 1983-84. (Illus.). 1344p. 1985. 345.00 (*0-8419-0554-1*, Africana) Holmes & Meier.
— Africa Contemporary Record, Vol. 6: 1973-74. LC 70-7957. (Illus.). 1255p. 1974. 345.00 (*0-8419-0155-4*, Africana) Holmes & Meier.
— Middle East Contemporary Survey, Vol. 1: 1976-1977. (Illus.). 684p. 1978. 245.00 (*0-8419-0323-9*) Holmes & Meier.
Legum, Colin & Doro, Marion, eds. Africa Contemporary Record Annual Survey & Documents, Vol. XX, 1987-88. 1182p. 1990. 359.00 (*0-8419-0558-4*, Africana) Holmes & Meier.
Legum, Colin & Hodges, Tony. After Angola: The War over Southern Africa. LC 76-17076. (Current Affairs Ser.). (C). 1976. pap. 6.95 (*0-8419-0279-8*, Africana) Holmes & Meier.
Legum, Colin & Lee, Bill. Conflict in the Horn of Africa. LC 77-18152. (Current Affairs Ser.). 95p. 1978. pap. 9.50 (*0-8419-0358-1*, Africana) Holmes & Meier.
***Legum, Colin & Mmari, Geoffrey, eds.** Mwalimu: The Influence of Nyerere. LC 95-3926. 1995. write for info. (*0-86543-478-6*); pap. write for info. (*0-86543-479-4*) Africa World.
Legum, Colin & Shaked, Haim, eds. Arab Relations in the Middle East: The Road to Realignment. LC 78-20888. (Middle East Affairs Ser.: No. 1). 104p. (C). 1979. pap. 12.50 (*0-8419-0447-2*) Holmes & Meier.
— Middle East Contemporary Survey, Vol. 2: 1977-1978. LC 78-648245. (Illus.). 824p. 1979. 245.00 (*0-8419-0398-0*) Holmes & Meier.
— Middle East Contemporary Survey, Vol. 3: 1978-1979. 1980. 245.00 (*0-8419-0514-2*) Holmes & Meier.
— Middle East Contemporary Survey, Vol. 4: 1979-1980. LC 78-648245. (Illus.). 890p. 1982. 245.00 (*0-8419-0609-2*) Holmes & Meier.
Legum, Colin, et al. Horn of Africa in Continuing Crisis. LC 79-873. (Current Affairs Ser.). (Illus.). 184p. (C). 1979. pap. 13.75 (*0-8419-0491-X*, Africana) Holmes & Meier.
Legum, Colin, et al, eds. Crisis & Conflict in the Middle East: The Changing Strategy, from Iran to Afghanistan. LC 81-84135. 600p. (Orig.). (C). 1982. pap. 14.50 (*0-8419-0784-6*) Holmes & Meier.
— Middle East Contemporary Survey, Vol. 5: 1980-1981. 896p. 1983. 245.00 (*0-8419-0825-7*) Holmes & Meier.
— Middle East Contemporary Survey, Vol. 6: 1981-1982. 957p. 1984. 245.00 (*0-8419-0878-8*) Holmes & Meier.
— Middle East Contemporary Survey, Vol. 7: 1982-1983. (Illus.). 950p. 1985. 245.00 (*0-8419-1014-6*) Holmes & Meier.
Legutke, Michael & Thomas, Howard. Process & Experience in the Language Classroom. (Applied Linguistics & Language Ser.). 332p. (C). 1991. pap. text ed. 26.95 (*0-582-01654-1*) Longman.
Legvold, Robert, jt. auth. see Task Force on Soviet New Thinking.
Legvold, Robert H. Soviet Policy in West Africa. LC 79-115477. 386p. 1970. 34.50 (*0-674-82775-9*) HUP.
Legvold, Robert H., jt. ed. see Colton, Timothy J.
LeGwin, J. Hardy. The Complete Guide to the Home Remodeling & Construction Process. 1990. pap. 29.95 (*0-685-47694-4*) J H LeGwin Assocs.
— Construction Estimating System. Bicknell, Susan J., ed. 1991. ring bd. 24.95 (*1-878088-16-5*) J H LeGwin Assocs.
— Construction Inspection Checklist. 20p. 1994. pap. 15.00 (*1-878088-03-3*) J H LeGwin Assocs.
— Easyspec Construction Specifications. 1990. ring bd. 129.00 (*1-878088-13-0*) J H LeGwin Assocs.
— Easyspec Construction Specifications: PC Version for IBM. 300p. 1993. ring bd. 199.00 (*1-878088-14-9*) J H LeGwin Assocs.
— Easyspec Construction Specifications: PC Version for Mac. 300p. 1993. 199.00 (*1-878088-15-7*) J H LeGwin Assocs.
— Minispec Residential Construction Specifications. 150p. 1991. ring bd. 59.00 (*1-878088-21-1*) J H LeGwin Assocs.
— Minispec Residential Construction Specifications: PC Version for IBM. 150p. 1991. ring bd. 89.00 (*1-878088-23-8*) J H LeGwin Assocs.
— Minispec Residential Construction Specifications: PC Version for Mac. 150p. 1991. 89.00 (*1-878088-24-6*) J H LeGwin Assocs.
— Project Checklist. 10p. 1991. pap. 12.00 (*0-614-04563-0*) J H LeGwin Assocs.
— Project Notebook: Basic Edition. 1990. 29.95 (*1-878088-12-2*) J H LeGwin Assocs.
— Project Notebook: Professional Edition. Bicknell, Susan J., ed. 1991. ring bd. 59.95 (*1-878088-18-1*) J H LeGwin Assocs.
Legwold, Gary. Last Word on Lefse. 1991. 9.95 (*0-934860-78-5*) Adventure Pubns.
Legzdins, Peter & Richter-Addo, George B. Metal Nitrosyls. (Illus.). 384p. 1992. 59.95 (*0-19-506793-2*) OUP.
***Leham.** Making War. Date not set. 5.98 (*0-517-13510-8*) Random Hse Value.
Lehan, Daniel. Crocodile Snaps - Kangaroo Jumps. LC 92-50842. (Illus.). 32p. (J). (ps-k). 1993. 13.95 (*0-531-05484-5*) Orchard Bks Watts.
Lehan, Edward A. Simplified Governmental Budgeting. LC 81-82463. (Illus.). 86p. 1981. 30.00 (*0-686-84272-3*); student ed 15.00 (*0-686-84273-1*) Municipal.
Lehan, Richard. The Great Gatsby: The Limits of Wonder. (Masterwork Studies). 128p. 1989. text ed. 21.95 (*0-8057-7960-4*, MWS-36, Pub. by Royal Botanic Garden UK); pap. 12.95 (*0-8057-8013-0*, Pub. by Royal Botanic Garden UK) Macmillan.
Lehan, Richard, ed. see Dreiser, Theodore.
Lehane, Brendan. The Quest of Three Abbots: The Golden Age of Celtic Christianity. 256p. 1994. reprint ed. pap. 16.95 (*0-940262-65-7*) Lindisfarne Pr.
— Wild Ireland. LC 94-34011. (Orig.). 1995. pap. 16.00 (*0-87156-427-0*) Sierra.
Lehane, Dennis. A Drink Before the War. LC 94-12274. 1994. write for info. (*0-15-100093-X*) HarBrace.
Lehane, Mike. Biology of Blood-Sucking Insects. 256p. (C). 1991. text ed. 99.95 (*0-04-445409-0*, A8243); pap. text ed. 29.95 (*0-04-445410-4*, A8244) Routledge Chapman & Hall.
Lehane, Stephen. Your Personally Tailored Diet. (Illus.). 1984. 15.95 (*0-13-980541-9*, Busn); pap. 5.95 (*0-13-980525-7*, Busn) P-H.
Lehane, Stephen, ed. see Goldman, Richard, et al.
Lehar, Franz. The Merry Widow: Complete Score for Piano & Voice. (Music Ser.). 224p. 1983. reprint ed. pap. 9.95 (*0-486-24514-4*) Dover.
***Lehar, Steven M., et al.** Architecture, Vol. 5. Omidvar, Omid M. & Wilson, Charles L., eds. (Progress in Neural Networks Ser.). 256p. 1995. write for info. (*1-56750-045-5*) Ablex Pub.
Lehbrink, Hartmut. World Sports Cars, 1945-1980. (Illus.). 463p. (C). 1993. reprint ed. 39.95 (*3-927258-19-9*) Gingko Press.
Leheny, James, ed. see Addison, Joseph.
LeHeron, Richard, jt. ed. see Park, Sam O.
***Lehey, Greg.** The UNIX Porting Guide. 600p. 1995. 29.95 (*1-56592-126-7*) OReilly & Assocs.
Lehigh, David S. Restaurants - Conditions & Syndromes: Index of Actions & Reports. LC 90-56273. 160p. 1991. 44.50 (*1-55914-328-2*); pap. 39.50 (*1-55914-329-0*) ABBE Pubs Assn.
Lehigh University Staff. Study of the 'Clock' Reaction on Copper Surfaces. 87p. 1983. write for info. (*0-318-60086-2*, 333A) Intl Copper.
Lehiste, Ilse. Consonant Quantity & Phonological Units in Estonian. LC 66-63013. (Uralic & Altaic Ser.: Vol. 65). 73p. 1966. pap. text ed. 8.00 (*0-87750-022-3*) Res Inst Inner Asian Studies.
Lehmacher, W. & Hoermann, A., eds. Statistik-Software Three: Konferenz Ueber die Wissenschaftliche Anwendung von Statistik-Software, 1985. 393p. (GER.). 1986. pap. 37.70 (*3-437-40170-X*) Lubrecht & Cramer.
Lehman. Chordate Development. 3rd ed. 342p. 1987. pap. text ed. 32.95 (*0-88725-083-1*) Hunter Textbks.
— Facts & Circumstances. 1994. pap. 3.99 (*0-517-13430-6*) Random.
— Operational Organic Chemistry: A Laboratory Course. 2nd ed. 730p. (C). 1988. text ed. write for info. (*0-205-11255-2*, H12552) P-H.
— Running Scared: Masculinity & the Representation of the Male Body. (C). 1995. pap. text ed. 16.95 (*1-56639-222-5*) Temple U Pr.
Lehman, jt. auth. see Anthony.
Lehman, jt. auth. see Lites, Emily.
Lehman, Anita J. Writing for Industry: An Instruction Manual. 224p. (C). 1984. pap. text ed. 20.00 (*0-03-061963-7*) HB Coll Pubs.
Lehman, Anthony, jt. auth. see Bernheim, Kayla F.
Lehman, B. H. Carlyle's Theory of the Hero. LC 76-181944. reprint ed. 24.50 (*0-404-03949-9*) AMS Pr.
Lehman, Banjamin H. Carlyle's Theory of the Hero. (BCL1-PR English Literature Ser.). 212p. 1992. reprint ed. lib. bdg. 79.00 (*0-7812-7491-5*) Rprt Serv.
Lehman, Barbara, jt. ed. see Sorensen, Marilou.
Lehman, Bob & Lehman, Elaine. Petey the Peacock Breaks a Leg. LC 93-60914. (Illus.). 44p. (J). (gr. k-3). 1994. 7.95 (*1-55523-649-9*) Winston-Derek.
Lehman, Carol M., jt. auth. see Lehman, Mark W.
Lehman, Carol M., et al. The AppleWriter Word Processing Book: Applications for the Apple II & IIe. 1985. teacher ed write for info. (*0-8359-9229-2*, Reston); text ed. 26.00 (*0-8359-9228-4*, Reston) P-H.
— Business Communications. 11th ed. LC 95-12251. 1996. pap. 53.95 (*0-538-84778-6*) S-W Pub.
— TRS-80 Word Processing Applications Using SuperScripsit. 1984. teacher ed write for info. (*0-8359-7880-X*, Reston) P-H.
***Lehman, Celia.** The History of Kidron. (Illus.). 32p. (J). (gr. 1 up). 1994. pap. 4.95 (*1-878893-48-3*) Telcraft Bks.
Lehman, Celia, jt. auth. see Davis, Irma.
Lehman, Celia, jt. auth. see Shepard, Eva.
***Lehman, Charles.** Ancient Images of the Sign Who Is Christ. (Illus.). (Orig.). 1995. pap. 24.95 (*1-55612-822-3*) Sheed & Ward MO.
Lehman, Charles, jt. auth. see Gunderson, William.
Lehman, Charles A. Desert Survival Handbook. Fessler, Diane M., ed. (Illus.). 96p. 1993. pap. 5.00 (*0-935810-34-X*) Primer Pubs.
Lehman, Cheryl, et al, eds. Advances in Public Interest Accounting, Vol. 4. 1991. 73.25 (*1-55938-254-6*) Jai Pr.
Lehman, Cheryl R. Accounting's Changing Role in Social Conflict. LC 91-47864. (Critical Accounting Research Ser.). 186p. (C). 1995. 39.95 (*1-55876-030-X*) Wiener Pubs Inc.
— Accounting's Changing Role in Social Conflict. LC 91-47864. (Critical Accounting Research Ser.). 186p. (C). 1995. pap. text ed. 24.95x (*1-55876-101-2*) Wiener Pubs Inc.
Lehman, Cheryl R. & Moore, Russell M., eds. Multinational Culture: Social Impacts of a Global Economy. LC 91-27. (Contributions in Economics & Economic History Ser.: No. 122). 360p. 1992. text ed. 55.00 (*0-313-27822-9*, LMB, Greenwood Pr) Greenwood.
Lehman, Chester K. Biblical Theology, 2 vols., Vol. 1: Old Testament. LC 74-141829. reprint ed. Vol. 1 Old Testament. pap. 120.00 (*0-8357-3603-2*, 2029245) Bks Demand.
— Biblical Theology, 2 vols., Vol. 2: New Testament. LC 74-141829. 567p. reprint ed. Vol. 2 New Testament. pap. 161.60 (*0-8357-7165-2*) Bks Demand.
Lehman, Danny. Bring 'Em Back Alive. 176p. (Orig.). 1992. pap. 4.99 (*0-88368-199-4*) Whitaker Hse.
Lehman, David. An Alternative to Speech. (Contemporary Poets Ser.). 88p. 1986. text ed. 21.95 (*0-691-06684-1*); pap. text ed. 9.95 (*0-691-01432-9*) Princeton U Pr.
— Best American Poetry, 1989. 272p. 1989. pap. 9.95 (*0-02-044182-7*) Macmillan.
— The Big Question. LC 95-5493. (Poets on Poetry Ser.). 1995. 39.50 (*0-472-09583-8*); pap. text ed. 13.95 (*0-472-06583-1*) U of Mich Pr.
— The Line Forms Here. (Poets on Poetry Ser.). (Illus.). 240p. (C). 1992. text ed. 39.50 (*0-472-09483-1*); pap. 13.95 (*0-472-06483-5*) U of Mich Pr.
— Operation Memory. 60p. (Orig.). 1990. text ed. 17.50 (*0-691-06848-8*); pap. 9.95 (*0-691-01482-5*) Princeton U Pr.
— Twenty Questions. (Illus.). 10p. (Orig.). 1988. pap. 10.00 (*0-918273-49-8*) Coffee Hse.
Lehman, David, ed. Beyond Amazement: New Essays on John Ashbery. LC 79-6850. 312p. 1980. 42.50 (*0-8014-1235-8*); pap. 17.95 (*0-8014-9183-5*) Cornell U Pr.
Lehman, David & Berger, Charles, eds. James Merrill: Essays in Criticism. 352p. 1982. 42.50 (*0-8014-1404-0*) Cornell U Pr.
Lehman, David & Gluck, Louise. The Best American Poetry, 1993. 288p. 1993. pap. 13.00 (*0-02-069846-1*, Scribners) S&S Trade.
Lehman, David, jt. ed. see Simic, Charles.
Lehman, Dennis D., jt. auth. see Sackheim, George I.
Lehman, Donald R. & Winer, Russell S. Product Management. LC 93-10645. 464p. (C). 1993. text ed. 66.95 (*0-256-11623-7*) Irwin.
Lehman, Donna. What on Earth Can You Do? Making Your Church a Creation Awareness Center. 192p. (Orig.). 1993. pap. 9.95 (*0-8361-3632-2*) Herald Pr.
Lehman, Edward C., Jr. Gender & Work: The Case of the Clergy. LC 92-30543. (SUNY Series in Religion, Culture, & Society). 230p. (C). 1993. 59.50 (*0-7914-1591-0*); pap. 19.95 (*0-7914-1592-9*) State U NY Pr.
— Women Clergy: Breaking Through Gender Barriers. 300p. 1985. 34.95 (*0-88738-071-9*) Transaction Pubs.
— Women Clergy in England: Sexism, Modern Consciousness, & Church Viability. LC 86-28547. (Studies in Religion & Society: Vol. 16). 232p. 1987. lib. bdg. 89.95 (*0-88946-858-3*) E Mellen.
Lehman, Edward R. Profits, Profitability, & the Oil Industry. Bruchey, Stuart, ed. LC 78-22694. (Energy in the American Economy Ser.). (Illus.). 1979. lib. bdg. 25.95 (*0-405-11997-6*) Ayer.
Lehman, Edward W. Political Society: A Macrosociology of Politics. LC 77-23887. 247p. 1977. text ed. 43.00 (*0-231-04003-2*) Col U Pr.
— The Viable Polity. LC 92-9854. 296p. (C). 1992. 39.95 (*0-87722-994-5*) Temple U Pr.
Lehman, Elaine, jt. auth. see Lehman, Bob.
***Lehman, Eleanor R. & Grabowski, Barbara L.** Constructivism: Its Foundations & Applications: A Selected Bibliography. LC 95-3903. (Selected Bibliography Ser.: Vol. 14). 1995. 19.95 (*0-87778-288-1*) Educ Tech Pubns.
Lehman, Elsie E. God Sends His Son Activity Book. (Story Bible Activity Ser.: No. 8). 80p. (Orig.). (J). (gr. 3-9). 1987. pap. 3.00 (*0-8361-3429-X*) Herald Pr.
— God's Wisdom & Power Activity Book. (Story Bible Activity Ser.). 80p. (J). (ps-1). 1985. pap. 3.00 (*0-8361-3391-9*) Herald Pr.
Lehman, Emil. Israel: Idea & Reality. (Illus.). (J). (gr. 8 up). 3.95 (*0-8381-0205-0*, 10-205) United Syn Bk.
Lehman, Eric G. Quaspeck: A Novel. LC 92-42343. 352p. 1993. 20.00 (*1-56279-036-6*) Mercury Hse Inc.
Lehman, Ernest. Farewell Performance. 1989. pap. 3.95 (*1-55817-299-8*, Pinnacle NY) Windsor NY.
— North by Northwest: The Screenplay. 1976. 16.95 (*0-8488-0178-4*) Amereon Ltd.
— Sweet Smell of Success. 17.95 (*0-88411-447-3*, Aeonian Pr) Amereon Ltd.
Lehman, Fred, jt. auth. see Robinson, Keith.
Lehman, G. J. & Coleman, C. F. Taxation Law in Australia. 2nd ed. 1134p. 1991. Australia. 132.00 (*0-409-30343-7*); Australia. pap. 87.00 (*0-409-30342-9*) Butterworth Legal Pubs.
Lehman, Gail, ed. see Shapiro, Michele.
Lehman, Gail, ed. see Shinpoch, Jan, et al.
Lehman, Gaylord L. Sunday Words for a Monday World. 75p. (Orig.). 1986. pap. 6.95 (*0-938828-03-7*) Falls Tar.
Lehman, George & Hunt, David. Carving Twenty Realistic Game & Songbirds: Complete Patterns & Instructions. (Woodcarvers' Favorite Patterns Ser.: Bk. 1). 100p. 1991. spiral bd., pap. 19.95 (*1-56523-004-3*) Fox Chapel Pub.
— Carving Wildlife in Wood: Complete Patterns & Instructions for 20 Exciting Projects. (Woodcarvers' Favorite Patterns Ser.: Bk. 4). 100p. 1991. spiral bd., pap. 19.95 (*1-56523-007-8*) Fox Chapel Pub.
— Nature in Wood: Great Patterns for Carving 21 Birds & 18 Wild Animals. (Woodcarvers' Favorite Patterns Ser.: Bk. 3). 128p. 1991. pap. 16.95 (*1-56523-006-X*) Fox Chapel Pub.
— Realism in Wood: Carving Twenty-Two Different Birds & Animals. (Woodcarvers' Favorite Patterns Ser.: Bk. 2). 100p. 1991. spiral bd. 19.95 (*1-56523-005-1*) Fox Chapel Pub.
Lehman, Glenn. Johnny Godshall: A Pilgrim's Process. 216p. (Orig.). 1992. pap. 8.95 (*0-8361-3597-0*) Herald Pr.
— You Can Lead Singing: A Song Leader's Manual. (Illus.). 96p. (Orig.). 1994. pap. 6.95 (*1-56148-117-3*) Good Bks PA.
Lehman, Godfrey D. The Ordeal of Edward Bushell. 276p. (Orig.). 1988. pap. 14.95 (*1-879563-04-5*) Lexicon CA.
Lehman, H. Peter & Catrou, Paul G. Conversion: A Program for Medical SI Unit Conversion. 1987. disk 47.00 (*0-685-54501-6*); write for info. (*0-89189-250-8*, 68-9-022-20(IBM)); write for info. (*0-89189-249-4*) Am Soc Clinical.
Lehman, Harvey C. Age & Achievement. LC 52-13159. (American Philosophical Society, Philadelphia. Memoirs Ser.: Vol. 33). 373p. reprint ed. pap. 106.40 (*0-8357-5249-6*, 2006396) Bks Demand.
Lehman, Harvey C. & Witty, Paul A. Psychology of Play Activities. LC 75-35074. (Studies in Play & Games). (Illus.). 1976. reprint ed. 23.95 (*0-405-07924-9*) Ayer.
***Lehman-Haupt, Christopher.** Crooked Man. 351p. 1995. 23.00 (*0-671-73444-X*) S&S Trade.
Lehman, Helmut T., jt. ed. see Bergendoff, Conrad.
Lehman, Howard P. Indebted Development: Strategic Bargaining & Economic Adjustment in the Third World. LC 92-47353. (International Political Economy Ser.). 240p. 1993. text ed. 49.95 (*0-312-09635-6*) St Martin.
***Lehman, Hugh.** Rationality & Ethics in Agriculture. 1995. pap. 24.95 (*0-89301-179-7*) U of Idaho Pr.
Lehman, Hugh, jt. ed. see Pimental, David.
Lehman, J. Lee. The Book of Rulerships: Keywords from Classical Astrology. LC 92-60607. 352p. (Orig.). 1992. pap. 18.95 (*0-924608-13-7*, Whitford Pr) Schiffer.
— Essential Dignities. LC 89-51940. 256p. 1989. pap. 14.95 (*0-924608-03-X*, Whitford Pr) Schiffer.
— The Ultimate Asteroid Book. LC 88-50479. (Illus.). 250p. (Orig.). 1988. pap. 18.95 (*0-914918-78-8*, Whitford Pr) Schiffer.
Lehman, James. Invendex, Inventors Index, Sparks the Flash of Genius. (Creator, the Inspirator with All of the Books Now Named Invendex Ser.). (Orig.). (YA). (gr. 8 up). 1993. pap. 7.95 (*0-9637633-0-X*) WLC Pub.
Lehman, James H. The Old Brethren. LC 76-20274. (Illus.). 1976. pap. 2.45 (*0-87178-650-8*) Brethren.
— The Owl & the Tuba. LC 91-73880. (Illus.). 32p. (J). 1991. 13.95 (*1-878925-02-4*) Brotherstone Pubs.
— The Saga of Shakespeare Pintlewood & the Great Silver Fountain Pen. LC 90-82303. (Illus.). 32p. (J). (gr. k-3). 1990. lib. bdg. 13.95 (*1-878925-00-8*) Brotherstone Pubs.
Lehman, Jane, jt. auth. see Kolzow, Lee V.
Lehman, Jeffrey S., jt. auth. see Kahn, Douglas A.
Lehman, Jerry D. Tracing Life's Footprints. LC 88-91214. 1989. 10.00 (*0-87212-218-2*) Libra.

An Asterisk (*) at the beginning of an entry indicates that the title is appearing in BIP for the first time.

Lehman, Jill F. Adaptive Parsing: Self-Extending Natural Language Interfaces. (C). 1991. lib. bdg. 69.50 (*0-7923-9183-7*) Kluwer Ac.

Lehman, Jill F., jt. ed. see Moore, Johanna D.

Lehman, Joanne. Traces of Treasure: Quest for God in the Commonplace. 160p. (Orig.). 1994. pap. 7.95 (*0-8361-3655-1*) Herald Pr.

Lehman, John. Facts & Circumstances. 219p. 1993. 19.95 (*0-8027-1230-4*) Walker & Co.

— Making War: The President & Congress from Barbary to Baghdad. 320p. 1992. text ed. 24.00 (*0-684-19239-X*, Scribners) S&S Trade.

Lehman, John, jt. ed. see Day-Lewis, Cecil.

Lehman, John A. Systems Design in the Fourth Generation Object-Based Development Using dBASE 3.0 & dBASE 4.0. 1991. Net. pap. text ed. write for info. (*0-471-52752-1*) Wiley.

Lehman, John F. Naval Power after Cold War Victory. (Chester W. Nimitz Memorial Lectures in National Security Affairs: No. 6). 89p. (Orig.). 1992. pap. 7.95 (*0-87725-606-3*) U of Cal IAS.

Lehman, John F. & Weiss, Seymour. Beyond the Salt II Failure. LC 81-2874. 224p. 1981. text ed. 49.95 (*0-275-90667-1*, C0667, Praeger Pubs) Greenwood.

Lehman, June, ed. see Burroughs, Eugene B.

Lehman, June, ed. see Tingstad, Phyllis F.

Lehman, June M., ed. see McGinn, Daniel F.

Lehman, Karl. Samothrace, a Guide to the Excavation & the Museum. 5th ed. LC 55-8563. pap. 8.50 (*0-685-73230-4*) J J Augustin.

Lehman, Karl, jt. auth. see Lehmann, Phyllis W.

Lehman, Katey & Lehman, Ross. Open House. (Illus.). 1989. 19.50 (*0-685-29451-X*) Bingham Bks.

Lehman, Kathleen, jt. auth. see Hatcher, Dale.

Lehman, L. Latin-American Dances. (Ballroom Dance Ser.). 1986. lib. bdg. 79.95 (*0-8490-3278-4*) Gordon Pr.

— Latin-American Dances. (Ballroom Dance Ser.). 1985. lib. bdg. 79.00 (*0-87700-823-X*) Revisionist Pr.

Lehman, Lilli. My Path Through Life. Farkas, Andrew, ed. Seligman, Alice B., tr. LC 76-29947. (Opera Biographies Ser.). (Illus.). 1977. reprint ed. lib. bdg. 53.95 (*0-405-09689-5*) Ayer.

Lehman, M. M. & Belady, L. A. Program Evolution: Processes of Software Change. (APIC Studies in Data Processing). 1985. text ed. 108.00 (*0-12-442440-6*); pap. text ed. 53.00 (*0-12-442441-4*) Acad Pr.

Lehman, Mark L. Seventeen Haunted Houses. (Illus.). 64p. 1979. 20.00 (*0-88014-011-9*) Mosaic Pr OH.

Lehman, Mark W. & Lehman, Carol M. Using the Microcomputer in Financial Accounting: Lotus 1-2-3 Edition. (Illus.). 308p. (Orig.). (C). 1986. pap. text ed. 32.75 (*0-314-98514-X*) West Pub.

Lehman, Mark W., et al. Using Microcomputers in Managerial Accounting. 406p. (C). 1987. spiral bd. 32.75 (*0-314-98515-8*) West Pub.

Lehman, Martin E. & Lehmann, Helmut T., eds. Luther's Works: Word & Sacrament Vol. IV, Vol. 38. LC 55-9893. 1971. 25.00 (*0-8006-0338-9*, 1-338, Fortress Pr) Augsburg Fortress.

Lehman, Matt. McGee's Alaska. (Illus.). 80p. (Orig.). Date not set. pap. text ed. 9.95 (*0-9638896-9-9*) Kikuchi Intl.

Lehman, Maxwell, ed. Communication Technologies & Information Flow. (Policy Studies on Science & Technology). (Illus.). 175p. 1981. 48.00 (*0-08-027169-3*, Pergamon Pr); pap. 25.00 (*0-08-027528-1*, Pergamon Pr) Elsevier.

Lehman, Maxwell, jt. auth. see Costikyan, Edward N.

Lehman, Melanie, jt. auth. see Hayes, Dympna.

Lehman, Milton. Robert H. Goddard: Pioneer of Space Research. (Quality Paperbacks Ser.). (Illus.). 488p. 1988. reprint ed. pap. 12.95 (*0-306-80331-3*) Da Capo.

Lehman, Paul E. Action at the Bitterroot. large type ed. LC 92-37076. 1993. 19.95 (*0-7927-1447-4*, Curley Lrg Print); pap. 17.95 (*0-7927-1446-6*, Curley Lrg Print) Chivers N Amer.

— Blood on the Range. large type ed. 1991. pap. 15.95 (*1-55504-818-8*, 98, Curley Lrg Print) Chivers N Amer.

— The Cougar of Canyon Caballo. Bd. with Devil's Doorstep. (Double Western Ser.). 1979. reprint ed. Set pap. 2.25 (*0-8439-0688-X*) Dorchester Pub Co.

— Double-Barrel Western: The Tough Texan & Bandit in Black. 272p. 1989. pap. 3.95 (*0-8439-2821-2*) Dorchester Pub Co.

— Hot Triggers. 1993. 14.95 (*0-7451-4558-2*, Gunsmoke) Chivers N Amer.

— Hot Triggers. 1979. reprint ed. pap. 1.75 (*0-8439-0661-8*) Dorchester Pub Co.

— Law of the Gun. large type ed. 1992. pap. 17.95 (*0-7927-0756-7*, Curley Lrg Print) Chivers N Amer.

— Montana Man. 1979. reprint ed. pap. 1.25 (*0-8439-0672-3*) Dorchester Pub Co.

— Only the Brave. 1993. 14.95 (*0-7451-4578-7*, Gunsmoke) Chivers N Amer.

— Pistol Law. large type ed. (Linford Western Library). 280p. 1985. pap. 11.95 (*0-7089-6088-X*) Ulverscroft.

— The Tough Texan. 1992. 13.95 (*0-7451-4530-2*, Gunsmoke) Chivers N Amer.

— Tough Texan. 1979. reprint ed. pap. 1.25 (*0-8439-0635-9*) Dorchester Pub Co.

— Troubled Range. (Gunsmoke Western Ser.). 172p. 1989. text ed. 12.95 (*0-86220-920-X*, Gunsmoke) Chivers N Amer.

— The Valley of the Hunted Men: Calamity Range. (Double Western Ser.). 1979. reprint ed. pap. 2.25 (*0-8439-0679-0*) Dorchester Pub Co.

— Vultures on Horseback. 1979. reprint ed. pap. 1.25 (*0-8439-0645-6*) Dorchester Pub Co.

Lehman, Paula D. Journey with Justice. Hull, Eddy & Shelly, Maynard, eds. LC 90-81509. (Illus.). 100p. (Orig.). (YA). 1990. pap. 7.95 (*0-87303-139-3*) Faith & Life.

Lehman, Peter. Running Scared. (C). 1992. pap. 12.95 (*0-691-00612-1*) Princeton U Pr.

— Running Scared: Masculinity & the Representation of the Male Body. LC 92-46733. (Illus.). 256p. 1993. 29.95 (*1-56639-099-0*) Temple U Pr.

— Running Scared: Masculinity & the Representation of the Male Body. LC 92-46733. (Illus.). 256p. 1995. pap. write for info. (*0-614-03054-4*) Temple U Pr.

Lehman, Peter, ed. Close Viewings: An Anthology of Film Criticism. 464p. 1990. 49.95 (*0-8130-0967-7*); pap. 22.95 (*0-8130-0991-X*) U Press Fla.

Lehman, Peter & Luhr, William. Blake Edwards. LC 80-28440. (Illus.). 302p. 1981. 21.95 (*0-8214-0605-1*) Ohio U Pr.

Lehman, Peter, jt. auth. see Luhr, William.

Lehman, Phyllis W. & Frazer, Alfred, eds. Samothrace, Vol. 10: The Propylon of Ptolemy II. (Bollingen Ser.: Vol. 60, No. 10). (Illus.). 224p. (C). 1990. text ed. 130.00 (*0-691-09922-7*) Princeton U Pr.

Lehman, Richard S. Computer Simulation & Modeling: An Introduction. 424p. (C). 1977. text ed. 89.95 (*0-89859-133-3*) L Erlbaum Assocs.

— Statistics & Research Design in the Behavioral Sciences. 571p. (C). 1991. text ed. 50.95 (*0-534-13878-0*) Brooks-Cole.

— Statistics in the Behavioral Sciences: A Conceptual Introduction. LC 94-22175. 464p. 1995. text ed. 52.95 (*0-534-25320-2*) Brooks-Cole.

Lehman, Richard S., ed. Programming for the Social Sciences: Algorithms & FORTRAN 77 Coding. 592p. (C). 1986. text ed. 99.95 (*0-89859-588-6*); pap. 36.00 (*0-89859-978-4*) L Erlbaum Assocs.

Lehman, Ross, jt. auth. see Lehman, Katey.

Lehman, S. C. Nutrition & Food Preparation & Preventive Care & Maintenance. (Lifeworks Ser.). 1981. text ed. 13. 96 (*0-07-037094-X*) McGraw.

Lehman, Sarah, ed. see Lewitter, Sidney R.

Lehman, Sherry & Brook, Micki. It Was Better in the Backseat: How to Recharge Your Sex Life. 1994. pap. 8.95 (*1-55850-359-5*) Adams Pubng.

***Lehman, Tim.** Public Values, Private Lands: Farmland Preservation Policy. LC 94-19636. xiv, 240p. 1995. lib. bdg. 39.95x (*0-8078-2177-2*); pap. text ed. 16.95x (*0-8078-4491-8*) U of NC Pr.

— Seeking the Wilderness: A Spiritual Journey. LC 93-71663. 240p. (Orig.). 1993. pap. 12.95 (*0-87303-205-5*) Faith & Life.

Lehman, Urich, et al. Fossil Invertebrates. Lettau, J., tr. LC 82-9419. (Cambridge Earth Science Ser.). (Illus.). 240p. 1983. pap. 29.95 (*0-521-27028-6*) Cambridge U Pr.

Lehman, Vivian. Homo Sapiens Modern: Our Archaic State, Vols. 1, 2, 3. 128p. 1994. pap. 15.95 (*0-8059-3502-9*) Dorrance.

Lehman, Wallace B., et al. Operating Room Guide to Cross Sectional Anatomy of the Extremities & Pelvis. (Illus.). 26p. 1989. ring bd. 254.00 (*0-88167-562-8*, 2024) Raven.

Lehman-Wilzig, Sam. Wildfire: Grassroots Revolts in Israel in the Post-Socialist Era. LC 90-26930. (SUNY Series in Israeli Studies). 198p. (C). 1992. 49.50 (*0-7914-0871-X*); pap. 16.95 (*0-7914-0872-8*) State U NY Pr.

Lehman-Wilzig, Sam N. Stiff-Necked People, Bottle-Necked System: The Evolution & Roots of Israeli Public Protest, 1949-1986. LC 89-45858. (Jewish Political & Social Studies). 224p. 1990. 25.00 (*0-253-33293-1*) Ind U Pr.

Lehman, Yvette K. Know & Tell: A Work Book for Parents & Children. Myles, Glenn, ed. 50p. (J). (ps-3). 1991. pap. write for info. (*0-318-68734-8*) Artmans Pr.

— Know & Tell: A Workbook for Parents & Children on How to Prevent Child Abuse. 2nd ed. 46p. (CHI, ENG & SPA.). (J). (ps-4). 1992. student ed 9.00 (*0-9638555-0-6*) Y K Lehman.

— Know & Tell: A Workbook for Parents & Children on How to Prevent Child Abuse. 2nd ed. Naeb, Yuli, tr. (Illus.). 46p. (J). (ps-4). 1993. 9.00 (*0-9638555-2-2*) Y K Lehman.

— Saber y Decir: El Manual Para Padres e Hijos Sobre Como Prevenir el Abuso a los Ninos. 2nd ed. Chavez, Vivian & Costas, Gloria, trs. (Illus.). 46p. (J). (ps-4). 1993. student ed 9.00 (*0-9638555-1-4*) Y K Lehman.

Lehman, Yvonne. In Shady Groves. LC 83-7431. 1989. 6.99 (*0-8007-9143-6*) Chosen Bks.

***Lehmann.** In the Purely Pagan Sense. Date not set. per. 10. 95 (*0-85449-125-2*, Pub. by Gay Mens Pr UK) InBook.

— Testing Statistical Hypotheses. 2nd ed. 624p. (C). 1991. text ed. 54.75 (*0-534-15984-2*) Chapman & Hall.

— Theory of Point Estimation. (Wadsworth & Brooks-Cole Advanced Books & Software). 528p. (C). 1991. text ed. 54.75 (*0-534-15978-8*) Chapman & Hall.

Lehmann & Shapiro. Personal Career Consultant: A Step-by-Step Guide to Finding a Successful & Satisfying Career. (Education & Guidance Ser.). 256p. 1988. pap. 8.95 (*0-13-973041-9*, Arco Test) P-H Gen Ref & Trav.

Lehmann, jt. auth. see Kottke, Frederic J.

Lehmann, jt. auth. see Krug.

Lehmann, jt. ed. see Wentz, Abdel R.

Lehmann, A. Church Musicians Enchiridion. 1979. 3.25 (*0-8100-0111-X*, 15N0369) Northwest Pub.

Lehmann, Ann, jt. ed. see Sall, John.

Lehmann, Armin D. Travel & Tourism: An Introduction to Travel Agency Operations. LC 77-12589. 1978. pap. write for info. (*0-672-97090-2*) Macmillan.

Lehmann, Arnold O. Lehmann's Little Dictionary of Liturgical Terms. 1980. 3.75 (*0-8100-0127-6*, 15N0371) Northwest Pub.

Lehmann, Arthur C. & Myers, James E., eds. Magic, Witchcraft, & Religion: An Anthropological Study of the Supernatural. 3rd ed. LC 92-20473. 474p. 1993. pap. text ed. 39.95 (*1-55934-170-X*) Mayfield Pub.

Lehmann, Asher. Young Moses, Crown Prince of Egypt. Hirschler, Gertrude, tr. 150p. (YA). (gr. 9-12). 1987. pap. 7.95 (*0-685-18059-X*) Judaica Pr.

— Young Moses, Crown Prince of Egypt. Hirschler, Gertrude, tr. 150p. (YA). (gr. 9-12). 1987. 10.95 (*0-910818-64-9*) Judaica Pr.

Lehmann, B. Metallogeny of Tin. Bhattacharji, S. et al, eds. (Lecture Notes in Earth Sciences Ser.: Vol. 32). (Illus.). viii, 211p. 1990. pap. 31.00 (*0-387-52806-7*) Spr-Verlag.

Lehmann, B., et al. Transmission & Reflection Tomographic Inversion of Offset VSP Data & the Use, EUR 14040. 127p. 1992. pap. 19.00 (*92-826-3979-7*, CD-NA-14040-EN-C, Pub. by Europ Com) UNIPUB.

Lehmann, Brian, jt. auth. see Gennadi, Elfimov.

Lehmann, Charles H. College Algebra. LC 62-8778. 444p. reprint ed. pap. 126.60 (*0-317-09369-X*, 2055102) Bks Demand.

Lehmann, Danny. Before You Hit the Wall: Spiritual Discipline in Your Daily Life, Discipleship. 124p. 1991. pap. 7.99 (*0-927545-13-6*) YWAM Pub.

Lehmann, David. Democracy & Development in Latin America: Economics, Politics & Religion in the Postwar Period. 1990. 49.95 (*0-87722-723-3*) Temple U Pr.

— Democracy & Development in Latin America: Economics, Politics & Religion in the Postwar Period. (C). 1992. pap. 22.95 (*1-56639-011-7*) Temple U Pr.

Lehmann, David, ed. Peasants, Landlords & Governments: Agrarian Reform in the Third World. LC 74-6091. 344p. (C). 1974. 34.95 (*0-8419-0162-7*); pap. 17.95 (*0-8419-0163-5*) Holmes & Meier.

Lehmann, Donald R. Marketing Research & Analysis. 3rd ed. 879p. (C). 1988. text ed. 61.95 (*0-256-07038-5*) Irwin.

Lehmann, Donald R. & Winer, Russell S. Analysis for Marketing Planning. 3rd ed. LC 93-12894. 208p. (C). 1993. text ed. 33.95 (*0-256-12276-8*) Irwin.

Lehmann, Douglas K. The Postal History of Christmas Seals. (Illus.). 40p. (Orig.). 1990. pap. 5.00 (*1-878770-00-4*) Paragon VA.

Lehmann, E., jt. auth. see Hodges, J. L., Jr.

Lehmann, E. L. Nonparametrics: Statistical Methods Based on Ranks. LC 72-93538. 1975. text ed. 49.95 (*0-8162-4994-6*) Holden-Day.

Lehmann, Edward J., ed. Catalog of Government Inventions Available for Licensing, 1987. LC 88-101951. (Orig.). 1988. pap. 36.00 (*0-934213-09-7*) Natl Tech Info.

Lehmann, Edward J., ed. & intro. Catalog of Government Inventions Available for Licensing, 1992. (Orig.). 1993. pap. text ed. 59.00 (*0-934213-38-0*, PB93-128205) Natl Tech Info.

Lehmann, Edward J., ed. Catalog of Government Patents: Inventions Available for Licensing to U.S. Businesses, 1985. LC 86-116175. (Orig.). 1986. pap. 29.00 (*0-934213-01-1*) Natl Tech Info.

— Catalog of Governments Patents: Inventions Available for Licensing to U. S. Businesses, 1986. LC 87-125670. 274p. (Orig.). 1987. pap. 33.00 (*0-934213-06-2*) Natl Tech Info.

— Federal Technology Catalog: A Guide to New & Practical Technologies, 1985. LC 86-116167. 300p. (Orig.). 1986. pap. 25.00 (*0-934213-02-X*) Natl Tech Info.

— Federal Technology Catalog: A Guide to New & Practical Technologies, 1986. LC 87-125688. 276p. (Orig.). 1987. pap. 27.00 (*0-934213-05-4*) Natl Tech Info.

Lehmann, Edward J., intro. Catalog of Government Inventions Available for Licensing, 1988. LC 89-111140. (Orig.). 1989. pap. text ed. 45.00 (*0-934213-16-X*) Natl Tech Info.

— Catalog of Government Inventions Available for Licensing, 1990. (Orig.). 1991. pap. text ed. 54.00 (*0-934213-30-5*, PB91-100206) Natl Tech Info.

Lehmann, Edward J., intro. & pref. Catalog of Government Inventions Available for Licensing, 1989. (Orig.). 1990. pap. text ed. 48.00 (*0-934213-22-4*, PB90-104472) Natl Tech Info.

— Catalog of Government Inventions Available for Licensing, 1991. (Orig.). 1992. pap. text ed. 59.00 (*0-934213-35-6*, PB92-100171) Natl Tech Info.

— Directory of Federal Laboratory & Technology Resources: A Guide to Services, Facilities, & Expertise. 5th ed. 1993. pap. 65.00 (*0-934213-40-2*, PB93-100097) Natl Tech Info.

Lehmann, Edward J., intro. Federal Technology Catalog: A Guide to New & Practical Technologies, 1987. LC 88-101969. 300p. (Orig.). 1988. pap. text ed. 33.00 (*0-934213-11-9*) Natl Tech Info.

— Federal Technology Catalog: A Guide to New & Practical Technologies, 1988. LC 89-111132. 300p. (Orig.). 1989. pap. text ed. 36.00 (*0-934213-15-1*) Natl Tech Info.

Lehmann, Elmar. Ordnung und Chaos das Englische Restaurationsdrama, 1660-1685. (Beihefte zu Poetica Ser.: Vol. 19). 194p. (GER.). 1988. 56.00x (*90-6032-307-6*, Pub. by B R Gruener NE) Benjamins North Am.

Lehmann, Elmar & Lenz, Bernd, eds. Telling Stories: Studies in Honour of Ulrich Broich on the Occasion of His 60th Birthday. LC 92-12496. 1992. 76.00x (*90-6032-334-3*) Benjamins North Am.

Lehmann, F. G., ed. Carcino-Embryonic Proteins: Chemistry, Biology, Clinical Application, 2 vols., Set. 1979. 236.00 (*0-444-80097-2*, North Holland) Elsevier.

Lehmann, G. Danger on the Sunita. 1987. pap. 4.95 (*0-87508-438-9*) Chr Lit.

— On the Trail of a Spy. 1987. pap. 4.95 (*0-87508-437-0*) Chr Lit.

— Red Gang. 1988. pap. 4.95 (*0-87508-439-7*) Chr Lit.

Lehmann, G. & Ziesche, P. Electronic Properties of Metals. (Materials Science Monographs: No. 64). 192p. 1991. 100.00 (*0-444-98838-6*) Elsevier.

Lehmann, G. D. The Curse of the Amulet. (Asha's Adventures Ser.). 164p. (J). (gr. 4-8). 1992. pap. 4.95 (*0-87508-443-5*) Chr Lit.

— Saved by Fire. (Asha's Adventures Ser.). (Illus.). 125p. (J). (gr. 4-8). 1992. pap. 4.95 (*0-87508-441-9*) Chr Lit.

Lehmann, Geoffrey. Spring Forest. 192p. (Orig.). 1994. pap. 10.95 (*0-571-17246-6*) Faber & Faber.

Lehmann, Gerhard. Beitraege zur Geschichte und Interpretation der Philosophie Kants. (C). 1969. 107.70 (*3-11-002561-2*) De Gruyter.

Lehmann-Grube, F., ed. Lymphocytic Choriomeningitis. LC 70-167276. (Virology Monographs: Vol. 10). 1972. 45.00 (*0-387-81017-X*) Spr-Verlag.

Lehmann, H. & Weitenberg, J. J., eds. Armenian Texts, Tasks & Tools: How to Assess Variant Readings in Armenian Manuscripts. (Acta Jutlandica LXIX: 1, Humanities Ser.: No. 68). (Illus.). 130p. (Orig.). 1993. pap. 47.50 (*87-7288-111-9*, Pub. by Aarhus Univ Pr DK) Coronet Bks.

Lehmann, H. E., ed. Non-Trycyclic & Non-Monamine Oxydase Inhibitors. (Modern Problems of Pharmacopsychiatry Ser.: Vol. 18). (Illus.). viii, 212p. 1982. 92.00 (*3-8055-3428-0*) S Karger.

Lehmann, H. E., jt. ed. see Ghadirian, A. M.

Lehmann, H. L., jt. ed. see Exwood, Maurice.

Lehmann, H. L., tr. see Exwood, Maurice & Lehmann, H. L., eds.

Lehmann, H. L., jt. ed. see Exwood, Maurice.

Lehmann, H. Peter, jt. ed. see Ban, T. A.

Lehmann, Hans & Lehmann, Thelma. Out of the Dustbin: Sentimental Musings on Art & Music in Seattle from 1936 to 1992. 112p. 1992. pap. 12.95 (*0-9635567-0-3*) H Lehmann.

***Lehmann, Hartmut & Roth, Guenther, eds.** Weber's Protestant Ethic: Origins, Evidence, Contexts. (Publications of the German Historical Institute, Washington, D.C.). 416p. (C). Date not set. pap. 18.95 (*0-521-55829-8*) Cambridge U Pr.

— Weber's Protestant Ethic: Origins, Evidence, Contexts. (Publications of the German Historical Institute, Washington, D.C.). 300p. (C). 1993. 54.95 (*0-521-44062-9*) Cambridge U Pr.

Lehmann, Hartmut & Sheehan, James J., eds. An Interrupted Past: German-Speaking Refugee Historians in the United States after 1933. (Publications of the German Historical Institute, Washington, D.C.). 272p. (C). 1991. 47.95 (*0-521-40326-X*) Cambridge U Pr.

Lehmann, Hartmut & Van Horn Melton, James, eds. Paths of Continuity: Central European Historiography from the 1930s Through the 1950s. (Publications of the German Historical Institute, Washington, D.C.). 416p. (C). 1994. 64.95 (*0-521-45199-X*) Cambridge U Pr.

Lehmann, Hartmut, jt. ed. see Hutchison, William R.

Lehmann, Hartmut, jt. ed. see Po-Chia Hsia, R.

Lehmann-Haupt, Carl-Friedrich. Armenien Einst und Jetzt, 3 vols., Set. xliv, 1714p. (GER.). 1988. reprint ed. write for info. (*3-487-09027-9*, Pub. by Georg Olms GW) Lubrecht & Cramer.

Lehmann-Haupt, Hellmut. The Book of Trades in the Iconography of Social Typology. 1976. 3.00 (*0-89073-010-5*) Boston Public Lib.

— An Introduction to the Woodcut of the Seventeenth Century. LC 77-86220. 1978. 49.50 (*0-913870-49-8*) Abaris Bks.

— The Life of the Book. LC 75-17193. (Illus.). 240p. 1975. reprint ed. text ed. 59.75 (*0-8371-8293-X*, LELB, Greenwood Pr) Greenwood.

— One Hundred Books about Bookmaking. LC 75-34148. 87p. 1976. reprint ed. text ed. 55.00 (*0-8371-8546-7*, LEOB, Greenwood Pr) Greenwood.

Lehmann, Helmut & Kleiner, John, trs. The Correspondence of Heinrich Melchior Muhlenberg, Vol. 1: 1740-1748. LC 93-86108. 750p. 1993. 59.50 (*0-89725-096-6*) Picton Pr.

Lehmann, Helmut T. & Atkinson, James, eds. Luther's Works: The Christian in Society Vol. I, Vol. 44. LC 55-9893. 1966. 25.00 (*0-8006-0344-3*, 1-344, Fortress Pr) Augsburg Fortress.

Lehmann, Helmut T. & Doberstein, John W., eds. Luther's Works: Sermons I, Vol. 51. Doberstein, John W., tr. LC 55-9893. 1959. 25.00 (*0-8006-0351-6*, 1-351, Fortress Pr) Augsburg Fortress.

Lehmann, Helmut T. & Gritsch, Eric W., eds. Luther's Works: Church & Ministry III, Vol. 41. LC 55-9893. 1966. 25.00 (*0-8006-0341-9*, 1-341, Fortress Pr) Augsburg Fortress.

Lehmann, Helmut T., jt. ed. see Bachmann, Theodore.

Lehmann, Helmut T., jt. ed. see Brandt, Walter I.

Lehmann, Helmut T., jt. ed. see Dietrich, Martin O.

Lehmann, Helmut T., jt. ed. see Fischer, Robert H.

Lehmann, Helmut T., jt. ed. see Forell, George W.

Lehmann, Helmut T., jt. ed. see Grimm, Harold J.

Lehmann, Helmut T., jt. ed. see Gritsch, Eric W.

Lehmann, Helmut T., jt. ed. see Hillerbrand, Hans J.

Lehmann, Helmut T., jt. ed. see Krodel, Gottfried G.

Lehmann, Helmut T., jt. ed. see Lehman, Martin E.

Lehmann, Helmut T., jt. ed. see Leupold, Ulrich S.

Lehmann, Helmut T., tr. see Muhlenburg, Heinrich M.

Lehmann, Helmut T., jt. ed. see Schultz, Robert C.

Lehmann, Helmut T., jt. ed. see Sherman, Franklin.

Lehmann, Helmut T., jt. ed. see Spitz, Lewis W.

Lehmann, Helmut T., jt. ed. see Tappert, Theodore G.

Lehmann, Helmut T., jt. ed. see Watson, Philip S.

Lehmann, Helmut T., jt. ed. see Wiencke, Gustav K.

L

Lehmann, Herman. Nine Years among the Indians, 1870-1970: The Story of the Captivity & Life of a Texan among the Indians. Hunter, J. Marvin, ed. LC 93-3032. (Illus.). 260p. 1993. pap. 15.95 (*0-8263-1417-1*) U of NM Pr.

Lehmann, Irvin J., jt. auth. see Mehrens, William A.

Lehmann, J. H. A Time Out of Joint: Living Through Two World Wars. (Illus.). 240p. (Orig.). 1990. pap. 9.95 (*0-910303-15-0*) Writers Pub Serv.

Lehmann, Jane, jt. auth. see Vogel, Lee.

Lehmann, Jean-Pierre, jt. ed. see Henny, Sue.

***Lehmann, Jennifer M.** Deconstructing Durkheim. 288p. 1995. pap. 17.95 (*0-415-12374-7*, C0393) Routledge.

— Deconstructing Durkheim: A Post-Post Structuralist Critique. LC 92-28815. 1993. write for info. (*0-415-07039-2*, Routledge NY) Routledge.

— Durkheim & Women. LC 93-29360. x, 175p. 1994. text ed. 30.00 (*0-8032-2907-0*) U of Nebr Pr.

Lehmann, Jerry. We Walked to Moscow. Harvey, Arthur, ed. 100p. (Orig.). 1966. pap. 7.50 (*0-934676-07-0*) Greenlf Bks.

Lehmann, John. The Craft of Letters in England. LC 74-2588. 248p. 1974. reprint ed. text ed. 55.00 (*0-8371-7410-4*, LECL, Greenwood Pr) Greenwood.

— Open Night. LC 72-142654. (Essay Index Reprint Ser.). 1977. reprint ed. 18.95 (*0-8369-2407-X*) Ayer.

— Virginia Woolf & Her World. LC 76-46232. (Illus.). 128p. 1977. pap. 4.95 (*0-15-693581-3*, Harvest Bks) HarBrace.

Lehmann, John, ed. New Writing: Spring 1938. LC 72-178450. (Short Story Index Reprint Ser.). 1977. reprint ed. 19.95 (*0-8369-4051-2*) Ayer.

Lehmann, John, jt. ed. see Day-Lewis, Cecil.

Lehmann, John, ed. see London Magazine Editors.

Lehmann, Joseph H. Sex, War & Fancies. 208p. 1984. 65.00 (*0-7212-0659-X*, Pub. by Regency Press) St Mut.

Lehmann, Justus F. Therapeutic Heat & Cold. 4th ed. (Rehabilitation Medicine Library). (Illus.). 752p. 1990. lib. bdg. 76.00 (*0-683-04908-9*) Williams & Wilkins.

Lehmann, K. A. & Zech, D., eds. Transdermal Fentanyl. (Illus.). 192p. 1991. pap. 59.00 (*0-387-54440-2*) Spr-Verlag.

Lehmann, Karl. Thomas Jefferson, American Humanist. LC 85-13479. xviii, 273p. 1985. reprint ed. pap. 14.95 (*0-8139-1078-1*) U Pr of Va.

Lehmann, Karl & Lehmann, Phyllis W., eds. Samothrace - the Rotunda of Arisinoe, Vol. 7: Excavations Conducted by the Institute of Fine Arts, New York University. (Bollingen Ser.: Vol. LX, Pt. 7). (Illus.). 416p. 1992. text ed. 250.00 (*0-691-09919-7*) Princeton U Pr.

Lehmann, Karl, ed. see Rahner, Karl.

Lehmann, Lilli. How to Sing. rev. ed. Aldrich, Richard, tr. LC 92-43865. (Illus.). 128p. 1993. reprint ed. pap. 5.95 (*0-486-27501-9*) Dover.

— How to Sing. (Music Book Index Ser.). 303p. 1992. reprint ed. lib. bdg. 89.00 (*0-7812-9508-4*) Rprt Serv.

— My Path Through Life. Seligman, Alice B., tr. LC 80-2286. (Illus.). reprint ed. 54.50 (*0-404-18855-9*) AMS Pr.

Lehmann, Linwood, tr. see Jefferson, Thomas.

Lehmann, Liza. The Life of Liza Lehmann. LC 79-25647. (Music Reprint Ser.). (Illus.). 1980. reprint ed. lib. bdg. 29.50 (*0-306-76010-X*) Da Capo.

Lehmann, Lotte. Five Operas & Richard Strauss. Pawel, Ernst, tr. LC 81-22198. (Music Reprint Ser.). (Illus.). ix, 209p. 1982. reprint ed. lib. bdg. 29.50 (*0-306-76150-5*) Da Capo.

— Midway in My Song: The Autobiography of Lotte Lehmann. (American Biography Ser.). 250p. 1991. reprint ed. lib. bdg. 69.00 (*0-7812-8241-1*) Rprt Serv.

— Midway in My Song, the Autobiography of Lotte Lehmann. LC 73-107813. (Select Bibliographies Reprint Ser.). 1977. 26.95 (*0-8369-5186-7*) Ayer.

— More Than Singing. Holden, Frances, tr. LC 75-8688. 192p. 1975. reprint ed. text ed. 49.75 (*0-8371-8116-X*, LEMT, Greenwood Pr) Greenwood.

— More Than Singing: The Interpretation of Songs. (Music Bks.). 192p. 1985. reprint ed. pap. 4.95 (*0-486-24831-3*) Dover.

— More Than Singing, the Interpretation of Songs: Music Book Index. 192p. 1993. reprint ed. lib. bdg. 69.00 (*0-7812-9675-7*) Rprt Serv.

— My Many Lives. Holden, Frances, tr. LC 74-3689. (Illus.). 262p. 1975. reprint ed. text ed. 38.50 (*0-8371-7361-2*, LEML, Greenwood Pr) Greenwood.

— My Many Lives. (American Autobiography Ser.). 262p. 1995. reprint ed. lib. bdg. 79.00 (*0-7812-8576-3*) Rprt Serv.

— My Many Lives: Music Book Index. 262p. 1993. reprint ed. lib. bdg. 79.00 (*0-7812-9633-1*) Rprt Serv.

Lehmann, Marcus. Family y Aguilar. (J). (gr. 7 up). 9.95 (*0-87306-122-5*) Feldheim.

— Just in Time: A Novel about Medieval Jewish Community. 1982. pap. 8.95 (*0-87306-257-4*) Feldheim.

— Royal Resident. 1981. 7.95 (*0-686-76251-7*) Feldheim.

Lehmann, Marcus & Prins, Eliezer. Lehmann-Prins Pirkei Avos. 1992. 23.95 (*0-87306-589-1*) Feldheim.

Lehmann, Marlys. All I Could Do Was Love You. 240p. 1989. pap. 3.95 (*0-8439-2839-5*) Dorchester Pub Co.

***Lehmann, Michael.** Real World Economic Applications: The Wall Street Journal. 2nd ed. 276p. (C). 1991. text ed. 33.95 (*0-256-09102-1*) Irwin.

Lehmann, Michael, jt. ed. see Tapper, Colin.

Lehmann, Michael B. The Business One Irwin Guide to Using the Wall Street Journal. 4th rev. ed. LC 92-39045. (Illus.). 416p. 1992. write for info. (*1-55623-840-1*) Irwin Prof Pubng.

— Irwin Guide to Using the Wall Street Journal. 4th ed. 375p. 1992. text ed. 28.00 (*1-55623-700-6*) Irwin Prof Pubng.

— Real World Economic Applications: The Wall Street Journal Workbook. 3rd ed. 300p. (C). 1994. pap. text ed. 33.95 (*0-256-13152-X*) Irwin.

— Real World Economic Applications: The Wall Street Journal Workbook. 4th ed. 272p. (C). 1995. pap. 33.95 (*0-256-13729-3*) Irwin.

Lehmann, Millianne. Exploring Calculus Mathematica. (C). 1992. pap. text ed. 10.75 (*0-201-55572-7*) Addison-Wesley.

Lehmann, O. J. Multiple Choice Questions in Ophthalmic & Neuroanatomy. 144p. 1994. pap. 30.00 (*0-7506-0988-5*) Buttrwrth-Heinemann.

Lehmann, Oskar. Die Tachygraphischen Abkurzungen der Griechischen Handschriften. vi, 111p. 1965. reprint ed. write for info. (*0-318-70957-0*, Pub. by Georg Olms GW) Lubrecht & Cramer.

Lehmann, P. Samothrace Excavations: Conducted by the Institute of Fine Arts of New York University, 5 vols. Incl. Vol. 3. Hieron. 1969. 140.00 (*0-691-09823-9*); (Bollingen Ser.: Vol. 60). write for info. (*0-318-55369-4*) Princeton U Pr.

***Lehmann, Paul L.** The Decalogue & a Human Future: The Meaning of the Commandments for Making & Keeping Human Life Human. 240p. 1995. pap. 17.99 (*0-8028-0835-2*) Eerdmans.

— Ethics in a Christian Context. LC 78-31749. 384p. 1979. reprint ed. text ed. 38.50 (*0-313-20971-5*, LEEC, Greenwood Pr) Greenwood.

Lehmann, Peggy & Pettus, Dania. Oh No... Not Another Summer. 224p. (Orig.). 1984. pap. 4.95 (*0-9613376-0-5*) P & L Res.

Lehmann, Phyllis W. Cyriacus of Angona's Egyptian Visit & its Reflections in Gentili: Bellini & Hieronymus Bosch. LC 77-88599. (Flexner Lectures at Bryn Hawr College Ser.). 1978. 12.00 (*0-686-92652-8*) J J Augustin.

— The Pedimental Sculptures of the Hieron in Samothrace. LC 62-19124. (Illus.). 4.00 (*0-685-71751-8*) J J Augustin.

Lehmann, Phyllis W. & Lehman, Karl. Samothracian Reflections: Aspects of the Revival of the Antique. LC 71-163867. (Bollingen Ser.: No. 92). 216p. 1973. 75.00x (*0-691-09909-X*) Princeton U Pr.

Lehmann, Phyllis W. & Spittle, Denys. Samothrace: The Temenos, Vol. 5. 1990. 200.00 (*0-691-09917-0*) Princeton U Pr.

Lehmann, Phyllis W., jt. ed. see Lehmann, Karl.

Lehmann, R., ed. see Dickens, Charles.

Lehmann, R., tr. see Michlin, S. G. & Prossdorf, S.

Lehmann, R. C. The Complete Oarsman. 1977. lib. bdg. 250.00 (*0-8490-1656-8*) Gordon Pr.

Lehmann, R. P. & Lehmann, W. P. An Introduction to Old Irish. (Introductions to Older Languages Ser.: No. 1). xv, 201p. 1975. 19.75 (*0-87352-289-3*, Z100) Modern Lang.

Lehmann, Ronald, ed. Plant, Technology, & Safety Management (Monograph, 1985) Managing Hazardous Wastes & Materials. 64p. 1986. pap. 30.00 (*0-86688-097-6*) Joint Comm Hlthcare.

Lehmann, Ronald R. & Winer, Russell S. Analysis for Marketing Planning. 2nd ed. 200p. (C). 1990. text ed. 33.95 (*0-256-08681-8*) Irwin.

Lehmann, Rosamond. A Note in Music. (Virago Modern Classic Ser.). 318p. 1992. pap. 10.95 (*0-86068-248-X*, Pub. by Virago Pr UK) Trafalgar.

— The Weather in the Streets. (Virago Modern Classic Ser.). 383p. 1992. pap. 10.95 (*0-86068-203-X*, Pub. by Virago Pr UK) Trafalgar.

Lehmann, Rosamond, tr. see Cocteau, Jean.

Lehmann, Rosamond, ed. see Lady Sandys.

Lehmann, Rosamond, jt. auth. see Pole, Wellesley T.

Lehmann, Rudolf. The Leibstandarte, Vol. 1. Olcott, Nick, tr. (Illus.). 400p. 1987. 30.00 (*0-921991-01-0*) J J Fedorowicz.

Lehmann, Ruth P., ed. & tr. Early Irish Verse. LC 81-11669. 144p. 1982. text ed. 22.50 (*0-292-72032-7*) U of Tex Pr.

Lehmann, Ruth P., tr. Beowulf: An Imitative Translation. LC 88-10306. (Illus.). 127p. 1988. pap. 6.95 (*0-292-70771-1*) U of Tex Pr.

***Lehmann, Scott.** Privatizing Public Lands. (Environmental Ethics & Science Policy Ser.). (Illus.). 240p. 1995. text ed. 45.00 (*0-19-508972-3*) OUP.

Lehmann, Stephen & Sartori, Eva, eds. Women's Studies in Western Europe: A Resource Guide. 129p. 1986. pap. text ed. 19.95 (*0-8389-7037-0*); pap. text ed. 16.50 (*0-685-67540-8*) Assn Coll & Res Libs.

Lehmann, Stephen, tr. see Nietzsche, Friedrich.

Lehmann, Terry & Nobisso, Joi. How to Fill an Empty Lap. (Illus.). 32p. (Orig.). (J). (ps). 1980. pap. text ed. 3.00 (*0-940112-00-0*) Little Feat.

Lehmann, Thelma, jt. auth. see Lehmann, Hans.

Lehmann, Ulrich. Paleantologisches Woerterbuch. 3rd ed. 739p. (GER.). 1985. pap. 45.00 (*0-8288-5506-4*, M7577) Fr & Eur.

Lehmann, Val W. Bobwhites in the Rio Grande Plain of Texas. LC 83-40495. (Illus.). 394p. 1985. 40.00 (*0-89096-186-7*) Tex A&M Univ Pr.

Lehmann, W. P. & Hewitt, H. J., eds. Language Typology 1988: Typological Models in the Service of Reconstruction. LC 91-12542. (Current Issues in Linguistic Theory Ser.: Vol. 81). vi, 182p. 1991. 50.00 (*1-55619-136-7*) Benjamins North Am.

Lehmann, W. P., jt. auth. see Heffner, Roe-Merrill S.

Lehmann, W. P., jt. ed. see Heffner, Roe-Merrill S.

Lehmann, W. P., jt. auth. see Lehmann, R. P.

Lehmann, Walter. The Art of Old Peru. LC 72-87767. (Illus.). 1975. reprint ed. 60.00 (*0-87817-119-3*) Hacker.

***Lehmann, William.** How to Be a Great First-Time Father. LC 94-23748. 1995. 7.99 (*0-570-04692-0*) Concordia.

Lehmann, William C. John Millar of Glascow: 1735-1801. Mayer, J. P., ed. LC 78-67364. (European Political Thought Ser.). 1980. reprint ed. lib. bdg. 35.95 (*0-405-11712-4*) Ayer.

Lehmann, Winfred P. Development of Germanic Verse Form. LC 70-131252. 217p. 1971. reprint ed. 50.00 (*0-87752-014-3*) Gordian.

— A Gothic Etymological Dictionary Based on the Third Edition of Vergleichendes Worterbuch der Gotischen Sprache by Sigmund Feist. xx, 712p. 1986. 83.00 (*90-04-08176-3*) E J Brill.

— Historical Linguistics. 3rd ed. LC 92-45655. 288p. 1992. 69.95 (*0-415-07242-5*, A9573); pap. 17.95 (*0-415-07243-3*, A9577) Routledge.

— Language: An Introduction. 241p. (C). 1983. pap. text ed. write for info. (*0-07-554251-X*) McGraw.

— Language Typology Nineteen Eighty-Five: Papers from the Linguistic Typology Symposium, Moscow, 9-13 Dec. 1985. LC 86-26341. (Current Issues in Linguistic Theory Ser.: No. 47). viii, 200p. 1986. 52.00x (*90-272-3541-4*) Benjamins North Am.

— Proto-Indo-European Phonology. 147p. (C). 1980. reprint ed. text ed. 17.50 (*0-292-73341-0*) U of Tex Pr.

— Theoretical Bases of Indo-European Linguistics. LC 92-6898. 288p. 1993. 77.50 (*0-415-08201-3*, A7836) Routledge.

Lehmann, Winfred P., ed. Language & Linguistics in the People's Republic of China. LC 75-3572. 178p. 1975. 15.00 (*0-292-74615-6*); pap. 6.95 (*0-292-74616-4*) U of Tex Pr.

— Language Typology 1987 - Systemic Balance in Language: Papers from the Linguistic Typology Symposium, Berkeley, 1-3, December 1987. LC 90-30. (Current Issues in Linguistic Theory Ser.: Vol. 67). x, 212p. 1990. 52.00x (*90-272-3564-3*) Benjamins North Am.

— Syntactic Typology: Studies in the Phenomenology of Language. LC 78-56377. 477p. 1978. 22.50 (*0-292-77545-8*) U of Tex Pr.

Lehmann, Winfred P. & Malkiel, Yakov. Perspectives on Historical Linguistics. (Current Issues in Linguistic Theory Ser.: No. 24). xii, 379p. 1982. 78.00x (*90-272-3516-3*) Benjamins North Am.

Lehmann, Winfred P., ed. see Bennett, William H.

Lehmann, Winfred P., et al. Biblical Hebrew: An Analytical Introduction. LC 94-15418. (Berkeley Models of Grammars Ser.: Vol. 3). 1994. write for info. (*0-8204-2283-5*) P Lang Pubs.

***Lehmberg, Stanford E.** Cathedrals under Siege: Cathedrals in English Society, 1600-1700. LC 95-7502. 1996. write for info. (*0-271-01494-6*) Pa St U Pr.

— The Peoples of the British Isles, Vol. 1: A New History from Prehistoric Times to 1688. 366p. (C). 1992. pap. 19.95 (*0-534-15078-0*) Intl Thomson.

— The Reformation of Cathedrals: Cathedrals in English Society, 1485-1603. (Illus.). 352p. 1989. 65.00 (*0-691-05539-4*) Princeton U Pr.

***Lehmen, Celia.** Our Swiss Heritage. (Illus.). 32p. (J). (gr. 1 up). 1994. pap. 4.95 (*1-878893-47-5*) Telcraft Bks.

Lehmer. Keyboard Harmony. 1977. 11.95 (*0-935058-00-1*) Donato Music.

Lehmer, Emna, tr. see Delone, Boris N. & Faddeev, D. K.

Lehmkuhl, Dennis, et al. Aquatic Insects. (Pictured Key Nature Ser.). 180p. (C). 1979. spiral bd. write for info. (*0-697-04767-9*) Wm C Brown Pubs.

***Lehmkuhl, Don, ed.** Brain Injury Glossary. 45p. 1992. pap. 9.50 (*1-882855-06-X*) HDI Pubs.

Lehmkuhl, L. Don & Smith, Laura K., revs. Brunnstrom's Clinical Kinesiology. 4th ed. LC 82-25249. (Illus.). 453p. (C). 1983. text ed. 29.95 (*0-8036-5529-0*) Davis Co.

Lehmkuhl, Nonna. FORTRAN 77. 576p. (C). 1983. pap. write for info. (*0-02-369390-8*) Macmillan.

— An Introduction to VAX Assembly Language Programming. LC 86-24708. (Illus.). 486p. (C). 1987. text ed. 63.25 (*0-314-93194-5*); teacher ed, pap. text ed. write for info. (*0-314-35222-8*) West Pub.

Lehmkul, Dorothy. Organizing for the Creative Person: How to Find the Organizing Style that Works for You. 1993. pap. 14.00 (*0-517-88164-0*, Crown) Crown Pub Group.

Lehmstedt, Mark. Ich Bin Nicht Gewohnt, Mit Kunstlern Zu Dingen. 46p. 1989. write for info. (*0-318-71837-5*, Pub. by Georg Olms GW) Lubrecht & Cramer.

Lehn, Cornelia. God Keeps His Promise: A Bible Story Book for Young Children. LC 76-90377. (Illus.). (J). (gr. k-4). 1970. 12.95 (*0-87303-291-8*) Faith & Life.

— I Heard Good News Today. LC 83-80401. (Illus.). 148p. (J). (gr. 1-6). 1983. 12.95 (*0-87303-073-7*) Faith & Life.

— Peace Be with You. LC 80-70190. (Illus.). 126p. (J). (gr. k-5). 1981. 12.95 (*0-87303-061-3*) Faith & Life.

— The Sun & the Wind. (Illus.). 32p. (J). (gr. k-5). 1983. 7.95 (*0-87303-072-9*) Faith & Life.

Lehn, J. M., ed. see Simon, J. & Andre, J. J.

***Lehn, Jean-Marie.** Supermolecular Chemistry: Concepts & Perspectives: A Personal Account Built upon the George Fisher Baker Non-Resident Lectureship in Chemistry at Cornell University & the Lezione Lincee, Accademia Nazionaleei (i.e., Nazaionale Dei), Lincei, Roma. LC 95-13502. 1995. pap. write for info. (*3-527-29311-6*, Pub. by Vlg Chemie) VCH Pubs.

— Supermolecular Chemistry: Concepts & Perspectives: A Personal Account Built upon the George Fisher Baker Non-Resident Lectureship in Chemistry at Cornell University & the Lezione Lincee, Accademia Nazionaleei (i.e., Nazaionale Dei), Lincei, Roma. LC 95-13502. 1995. write for info. (*3-527-29312-4*, Pub. by Vlg Chemie) VCH Pubs.

Lehn, Kenneth & Kamphuis, Robert W., Jr., eds. Modernizing U.S. Securities Regulations: Economic & Legal Perspectives. 608p. 1993. text ed. 75.00 (*1-55623-777-4*) Irwin Prof Pubng.

Lehn, Walter. The Development of Palestinian Resistance. (Information Papers: No. 14). 47p. (Orig.). (C). 1974. pap. 2.75 (*0-937694-30-4*) Assn Arab-Amer U Grads.

Lehn, Walter & Davies, Uri. The Jewish National Fund. 374p. 1987. 65.00 (*0-7103-0053-0*, Pub. by Kegan Paul Intl UK) Routledge Chapman & Hall.

Lehnartz, Klaus. New York in the Sixties. LC 78-53190. (Illus.). 1978. pap. 7.95 (*0-486-23674-9*) Dover.

***Lehne, Judith L.** Coyote Girl. (J). 1995. 15.00 (*0-689-51156-6*, S&S Bks Young Read) S&S Childrens.

— The Never-Be-Bored Book: Quick Things to Make When There's Nothing to Do. LC 92-16529. (Illus.). 128p. (J). 1992. 17.95 (*0-8069-1254-5*) Sterling.

— The Never-Be-Bored Book: Quick Things to Make When There's Nothing to Do. (Illus.). 128p. 1994. pap. 6.95 (*0-8069-1255-3*) Sterling.

Lehne, Richard. Casino Policy. 288p. 1986. lib. bdg. 40.00 (*0-8135-1153-4*) Rutgers U Pr.

— Industry & Politics: United States in Comparative Perspective. 304p. 1992. pap. text ed. write for info. (*0-13-359118-2*) P-H.

Lehne, Richard A., et al. Pharmacology for Nursing Care. 2nd ed. LC 93-26136. 1994. text ed. 52.50 (*0-7216-5166-6*) Saunders.

Lehner, Christine. Expecting. LC 82-8120. 192p. 1982. 12.95 (*0-8112-0848-6*); pap. 6.95 (*0-8112-0898-2*, NDP573) New Directions.

Lehner, Devony. Tinker's Journey Home. Maloney, P. Dennis, ed. (Illus.). 34p. (J). (ps-6). 12.95 (*0-940305-00-3*) P D Maloney.

***Lehner, Eleanor.** Crosses, Domes & Crescents: From Byzantium to Victorian. (Illus.). 168p. Date not set. per. 15.00 (*0-934616-43-4*) Valkyrie Pub Hse.

Lehner, Ernst. Alphabets & Ornaments. (Pictorial Archive Ser.). (Illus.). 1968. pap. 8.95 (*0-486-21905-4*) Dover.

— Symbols, Signs & Signets. (Illus.). 1950. pap. 7.95 (*0-486-22241-1*) Dover.

— Symbols, Signs & Signets. (Illus.). 21.00 (*0-8446-0771-1*) Peter Smith.

Lehner, Ernst & Lehner, Johanna. Folklore & Symbolism of Flowers, Plants & Trees. (Illus.). 128p. 1990. reprint ed. lib. bdg. 55.00 (*1-55888-886-1*) Omnigraphics Inc.

— Picture Book of Devils, Demons, & Witchcraft. LC 72-137002. 1972. pap. 7.95 (*0-486-22751-0*) Dover.

Lehner, F. International Scientific Cooperation: Consolidated Report of Activities, EUR 13970. 199p. 1992. pap. 60.00 (*92-826-3812-X*, CD-NA-13970-EN-C, Pub. by Europ Com) UNIPUB.

Lehner, J. Authentic Art Nouveau Lettering & Design in Full Color. 1989. pap. 11.95 (*0-486-25981-1*) Dover.

Lehner, Johanna, jt. auth. see Lehner, Ernst.

Lehner, Joseph. Discontinuous Groups & Automorphic Functions. LC 63-11987. (Mathematical Surveys Ser.: Vol. 8). 425p. 1990. reprint ed. pap. 49.00 (*0-8218-1508-3*, SURV-8) Am Math.

Lehner, Lois. Lehner's Encyclopedia of U. S. Marks on Pottery, Porcelain & Clay. (Illus.). 636p. 1988. 24.95 (*0-89145-365-2*, 1845) Collector Bks.

Lehner, Paul E. Artificial Intelligence & National Defense: Opportunity & Challenge. (Applications in Artificial Intelligence Ser.). (Illus.). xxxx, 240p. 1988. 34.95 (*0-89433-286-4*) Petrocelli.

— Artificial Intelligence & National Defense: Opportunity & Challenge. (Illus.). 240p. 1989. 36.95 (*0-8306-3235-2*, TAB/TPR) TAB Bks.

Lehner, T. Immunology of Oral Diseases. 3rd ed. (Illus.). 200p. 1992. pap. 46.95 (*0-632-01984-0*) Blackwell Sci.

Lehner, T., et al, eds. Injection in Process Metallurgy. (Illus.). 325p. 1991. 105.00 (*0-87339-163-2*, 407) Minerals Metals.

— Injection in Process Metallurgy, No. II. (Illus.). 120p. 1991. 46.00 (*0-87339-127-6*, 416) Minerals Metals.

Lehnert, Frederick, tr. see Schutz, Alfred.

Lehnert, G., jt. ed. see Henschler, D.

Lehnert, Hendrik, et al, eds. Endocrine & Nutritional Control of Basic Biological Functions. LC 91-35313. (Neuronal Control of Bodily Function Ser.: Vol. 7). (Illus.). 560p. 1993. text ed. 138.00 (*0-88937-076-1*) Hogrefe & Huber Pubs.

Lehnert, Martin. Altenglisches Elementarbuch: Einfuehrung, Grammatik, Text mit Uebersetzung und Woerterbuch. 9th rev. ed. (Sammlung Goeschen Ser.: No. 2210). (GER.). (C). 1978. 9.85 (*3-11-007643-8*) De Gruyter.

— Altenglisches Elementarbuch: Einfuhrung, Grammatik, Woerterbuch. 10th ed. 179p. (ENG & GER.). 1990. 29.95 (*0-7859-8274-4*, 3110124718) Fr & Eur.

Lehnert, Wendy G. & Ringle, Martin H., eds. Strategies for Natural Language Processing. (Illus.). 560p. 1982. pap. text ed. 69.95 (*0-89859-266-6*) L Erlbaum Assocs.

Lehnhoff, Nora, ed. see Brooks, Robert E.

Lehnig, Beverly. Your Silky Terrier. LC 77-187774. (Your Dog Bk.). (Illus.). 128p. 1972. 13.95 (*0-87714-002-2*) Denlingers.

Lehnigk, S. H. The Generalized Feller Equation & Related Topics. (Pitman Monographs & Surveys in Pure & Applied Mathematics: No. 68). 292p. 1993. text ed. 159.00 (*0-470-22171-2*) Halsted Pr.

***Lehning, James R.** Peasant & French: Cultural Contact in Rural France During the Nineteenth Century. (Illus.). 256p. (C). 1995. 54.95 (*0-521-46210-X*); pap. 18.95 (*0-521-46770-5*) Cambridge U Pr.

— The Peasants of Marlhes: Economic Development & Family Organization in Nineteenth-Century France. LC 79-18707. ix, 218p. 1980. 27.50 (*0-8078-1411-3*) U of NC Pr.

— The Peasants of Marlhes: Economic Development & Family Organization in Nineteenth-Century France. LC 79-18707. 232p. reprint ed. pap. 66.20 (*0-7837-3760-2*, 2043577) Bks Demand.

Lehninger, Albert L. Biochemistry: The Molecular Basis of Cell Structure & Function. 2nd ed. LC 75-11082. 1975. text ed. 69.95x (*0-87901-047-9*) Worth.

— A Short Course in Biochemistry. LC 72-93199. (Illus.). 452p. (C). 1973. text ed. 59.95x (*0-87901-024-X*) Worth.

An Asterisk (*) at the beginning of an entry indicates that the title is appearing in BIP for the first time.

Lehninger, Albert L., et al. Principles of Biochemistry. 2nd ed. (Illus.). 1013p. (C). 1993. text ed. 67.95 (*0-87901-500-4*) Worth.

— Principles of Biochemistry. 2nd ed. (Illus.). 1036p. (C). 1993. text ed. 72.95x (*0-87901-711-2*) Worth.

Lehnus, Donald J. Angels to Zeppelins: A Guide to the Persons, Objects, Topics, & Themes on United States Postage Stamps, 1847-1980. LC 82-918. xiii, 279p. 1982. text ed. 59.95 (*0-313-23475-2*, LPS, Greenwood Pr) Greenwood.

— Enchiridion of Form & Procedure for Typewritten Catalog Cards According to the International Standards of Bibliographic Description of Separately Published Monographs, Manual 2. (Serie Bibliotecologica). 28p. 1975. pap. 1.50 (*0-8477-0902-7*) U of PR Pr.

— Signaturas Libristicas: Normas para Su Aplicacion en Bibliotecas de Habla. (Serie Bibliotecologica). 35p. 1975. pap. text ed. 1.50 (*0-8477-0903-5*) U of PR Pr.

Lehodey, Domitry V. The Ways of Mental Prayer. LC 82-50584. 408p. 1982. reprint ed. pap. 11.00 (*0-89555-178-0*) TAN Bks Pubs.

***Leholzky, Sandor & Rusczyk, Richard.** The Art of Problem Solving: The Basics & Beyond, Text & Solutions, 4 vols., Set. 1136p. (YA). (gr. 7-12). 1994. pap. text ed. 60.00 (*1-885875-04-5*) Greater Testing.

— The Art of Problem Solving: The Basics & Beyond, Texts, 2 vols., Set. 749p. (YA). (gr. 7-12). 1994. pap. text ed. 47.00 (*1-885875-05-3*) Greater Testing.

— The Art of Problem Solving Vol. 1: The Basics, Solutions. 176p. (YA). (gr. 7-12). 1993. pap. text ed. 7.00 (*1-885875-01-0*) Greater Testing.

— The Art of Problem Solving Vol. 1: The Basics, Text. 360p. (YA). (gr. 7-12). 1993. pap. text ed. 25.00 (*0-614-00586-8*) Greater Testing.

— The Art of Problem Solving Vol. 2: And Beyond, Solutions. 211p. (YA). (gr. 7-12). 1994. pap. text ed. 8.00 (*1-885875-02-9*) Greater Testing.

— The Art of Problem Solving Vol. 2: And Beyond, Text. 389p. (YA). (gr. 7-12). 1994. pap. text ed. 27.00 (*1-885875-03-7*) Greater Testing.

Lehotay, Denis C., ed. The Relationship of Man & Nature in the Modern Age: Dominion over the Earth. LC 93-10128. (Illus.). 284p. 1993. 89.95 (*0-7734-9273-9*) E Mellen.

Lehr. Battling Dragons: Issues & Controversy in Children's Literature. LC 94-31973. (Illus.). 350p. 1995. pap. text ed. 22.50 (*0-435-08828-9*) Heinemann.

Lehr & Swanson. Fit, Firm & Fifty: A Fitness Guide for Men-Women over 50. 1990. 19.95 (*0-87371-399-0*, GV481) Lewis Pubs.

Lehr, Claire J., jt. auth. see Spirson, Leslie L.

Lehr, Dick, jt. auth. see O'Neill, Gerard.

Lehr, Elizabeth D. King Lehr & the Gilded Age. (American Biography Ser.). 332p. 1991. reprint ed. lib. bdg. 79.00 (*0-7812-8242-X*) Rprt Serv.

— King Lehr & the Gilded Age: With Extracts from the Locked Diary of Harry Lehr. LC 75-1852. (Leisure Class in America Ser.). (Illus.). 1975. reprint ed. 29.95 (*0-405-06918-9*) Ayer.

Lehr, Ellen, et al. Psychological Management of Traumatic Brain Injuries in Children & Adolescents. LC 89-17550. (Rehabilitation Institute of Chicago Ser.). 248p. (C). 1989. 54.00 (*0-8342-0095-3*) Aspen Pub.

Lehr, Fran. People of Gumption & Other Stories. 90p. 1987. 7.95 (*0-935153-03-9*) Stormline Pr.

Lehr, Fran & Osborn, Jean, eds. Reading, Language, & Literacy: Reading Instruction for the Twenty-First Century. 312p. 1992. text ed. 59.95 (*0-8058-1166-4*) L Erlbaum Assocs.

Lehr, Genevieve. Come & I Will Sing You: A Newfoundland Songbook. 234p. 1985. 27.50 (*0-8020-2567-6*); pap. 12.50 (*0-8020-6586-4*) U of Toronto Pr.

Lehr, Helene. The Passionate Rebel. 400p. (Orig.). 1993. pap. 4.99 (*0-505-51918-6*, Love Spell) Dorchester Pub Co.

— White Heather. 448p. (Orig.). 1995. mass mkt., pap. text ed. 4.99 (*0-8439-3795-5*) Dorchester Pub Co.

Lehr, J. Harry. A Catalogue of the Flora of Arizona. 1978. 4.75 (*0-9605656-0-4*) Desert Botanical.

Lehr, Jane, jt. auth. see Collins, Tim.

Lehr, Jay, ed. Rational Readings on Environmental Concerns. (Environmental Engineering Ser.). (Illus.). 900p. 1992. text ed. 49.95 (*0-442-01146-6*) Van Nos Reinhold.

Lehr, Jay H. World's Ground Water According to Lehr. 104p. 1988. 7.50 (*1-56034-071-1*, T471) Natl Water Well.

Lehr, Jay H. & Stanley, A. Editorially Speaking about Ground Water (Its First Quarter Century) 319p. 1988. 16.75 (*1-56034-046-0*, T434) Natl Water Well.

Lehr, Jay H., jt. auth. see Warner, Don L.

Lehr, Judy B. & Harris, Hazel W. At-Risk: Low-Achieving Students in the Classroom. 104p. 1988. 9.95 (*0-8106-3338-8*) NEA.

***Lehr, Judy B. & Martin, Craig.** Schools Without Fear: Group Activities for Building Community. LC 94-72561. (Illus.). 192p. (Orig.). (C). 1994. pap. text ed. 19.95x (*0-932796-68-0*) Ed Media Corp.

Lehr, Lauralee. The Princess & the Dragon. (Illus.). 32p. (J). 1994. 5.95 (*0-8059-3565-7*) Dorrance.

Lehr, Louis A., Jr. Premises Liability from Complaint to Verdict. LC 93-12899. (Trial Practice Ser.). 900p. 1993. text ed. 125.00 (*0-07-172371-4*) Shepards-McGraw.

Lehr, Norma. The Secret of the Floating Phantom. LC 94-3004. 192p. (J). (gr. 3-6). 1994. lib. bdg. 17.50 (*0-8225-0736-6*, Lerner Publctns) Lerner Group.

— The Shimmering Ghost of Riversend. (Fiction Ser.). 160p. (J). (gr. 3-6). 1991. lib. bdg. 17.50 (*0-8225-0732-3*, Lerner Publctns) Lerner Group.

— Shimmering Ghost of Riversend. (J). (gr. 4-7). 1991. pap. 3.95 (*0-8225-9589-3*, Lerner Publctns) Lerner Group.

Lehr, Paul E., et al. Weather. rev. ed. (Golden Guide Ser.). (Illus.). 160p. 1987. reprint ed. pap. write for info. (*0-307-24051-7*, Golden Bks) Western Pub.

***Lehr, Richard.** New Union Tactics for Organizing Your Company. 1994. pap. text ed. 29.95 (*0-471-11283-6*) Wiley.

Lehr, Richard, et al. How to Avoid Charges of Age Discrimination. pap. 29.95 (*1-55840-211-X*) Exec Ent Pubns.

Lehr, Richard I. & Middlebrooks, David J. New Union Tactics for Organizing Your Company. 1990. pap. 29.95 (*1-55840-210-1*) Exec Ent Pubns.

Lehr, Susan S. The Child's Developing Sense of Theme: A Response to Literature. (Language & Literacy Ser.: No. 3). 208p. (C). 1991. text ed. 38.95 (*0-8077-3106-4*); pap. text ed. 17.95 (*0-8077-3105-6*) Tchrs Coll.

Lehr, Thomas A., ed. Industrial Energy Management: A Cost Cutting Approach. LC 82-62406. (Manufacturing Update Ser.). (Illus.). 270p. reprint ed. pap. 77.00 (*0-7837-6276-3*, 2045991) Bks Demand.

Lehr, William, ed. Quality & Reliability of Telecommunications Infrastructure. (Telecommunications Ser.). 264p. 1995. text ed. 49.95 (*0-8058-1610-0*) L Erlbaum Assocs.

Lehr, William, jt. auth. see Kantor, David.

Lehr, William D. Powder Coating Systems. 288p. 1991. text ed. 55.00 (*0-07-037072-9*) McGraw.

Lehrack, Otto J. No Shining Armor: The Marines at War in Vietnam. LC 91-39414. (Modern War Studies). (Illus.). 400p. 1992. 35.00 (*0-7006-0533-9*); pap. 14.95 (*0-7006-0534-7*) U Pr of KS.

Lehrberger, John. Functor Analysis of Natural Language. LC 74-82387. (Janua Linguarum, Ser. Minor: No. 197). 155p. (C). 1974. pap. text ed. 103.10 (*90-279-3342-1*) Mouton.

Lehrberger, John & Bourbeau, Laurent. Machine Translation: Linguistic Characteristics of MT Systems & General Methodology of Evaluation. LC 87-17441. (Lingvisticae Investigationes Supplementa Ser.: Vol. 15). viii, 240p. (C). 1988. 44.00x (*90-272-3124-9*) Benjamins North Am.

Lehrberger, John, jt. ed. see Kittredge, Richard.

Lehrenbaum, Burton, jt. auth. see Witkin, Mildred H.

Lehrer, Adrienne. Wine & Conversation. LC 82-48538. 256p. 1983. 35.00 (*0-253-36550-3*); pap. 17.95 (*0-253-20308-2*, MB-308) Ind U Pr.

Lehrer, Adrienne & Kittay, Eva F., eds. Frames, Fields, & Contrasts: New Essays in Semantic & Lexical Organization. 480p. 1992. text ed. 99.95 (*0-8058-1088-9*); pap. 49.95 (*0-8058-1089-7*) L Erlbaum Assocs.

Lehrer, Brian. The Korean Americans. (Peoples of North America Ser.). (Illus.). 112p. (J). (gr. 5 up). 1988. lib. bdg. 17.95 (*0-87754-888-9*) Chelsea Hse.

— The Korean Americans. rev. ed. LC 94-40428. (The Immigrant Experience Ser.). 1995. pap. text ed. write for info. (*0-7910-3374-0*) Chelsea Hse.

— The Korean Americans. rev. ed. LC 94-40428. (Immigrant Experience Ser). (J). 1995. write for info. (*0-7910-3352-X*) Chelsea Hse.

Lehrer, Jim. Blue Hearts. LC 92-37167. 224p. 1993. 20.00 (*0-679-42216-1*) Random.

— Blue Hearts. large type ed. LC 93-39162. 1994. pap. 18.95 (*0-7862-0112-6*) Thorndike Pr.

— A Bus of My Own. LC 92-7526. (Illus.). 256p. 1992. 24.95 (*0-399-13765-3*, Putnam) Putnam Pub Group.

— Fine Lines. large type ed. LC 94-13010. 249p. 1994. 20.95 (*0-7862-0248-3*) Thorndike Pr.

— Fine Lines: A Novel. LC 93-36848. 1994. 20.00 (*0-679-42823-2*) Random.

— Last Debate. 1995. 23.00 (*0-679-44159-X*) Random.

— Lost & Found. large type ed. LC 91-13716. 249p. 1991. reprint ed. bds. 20.95 (*1-56054-180-6*) Thorndike Pr.

— Short List. large type ed. LC 92-6487. 303p. 1992. reprint ed. lib. bdg. 20.95 (*1-56054-397-3*) Thorndike Pr.

— The Sooner Spy. large type ed. LC 90-45972. 290p. 1990. reprint ed. lib. bdg. 19.95 (*1-56054-067-2*) Thorndike Pr.

Lehrer, John. World of Turtles. (Illus.). 160p. 1993. 24.95 (*1-56465-116-9*, 16089) Tetra Pr.

Lehrer, Kate. When They Took Away the Man in the Moon. 1993. 20.00 (*0-517-59441-2*, CPT Corp) Crown Pub Group.

— When They Took Away the Man in the Moon. large type ed. LC 93-30904. 1993. 17.95 (*0-7862-0042-1*) Thorndike Pr.

Lehrer, Keith. Theory of Knowledge. 212p. (C). 1990. pap. text ed. 20.95 (*0-8133-0571-3*) Westview.

— Thomas Reid. 400p. 1989. 49.95 (*0-415-03886-3*, A3536) Routledge.

— Thomas Reid. 324p. 1991. pap. 22.50 (*0-415-06390-6*, A5714) Routledge.

Lehrer, Keith, ed. Analysis & Metaphysics: Essays in Honor of R. M. Chisholm. LC 75-5500. (Philosophical Studies: No. 4). 316p. 1975. lib. bdg. 117.00 (*90-277-0571-2*) Kluwer Ac.

Lehrer, Keith & Sosa, Ernest, eds. The Opened Curtain: A U.S.-Soviet Philosophy Summit. 308p. (C). 1991. pap. text ed. 54.00 (*0-8133-1234-5*) Westview.

Lehrer, Keith & Wagner, Carl. Rational Consensus in Science & Society: A Philosophical & Mathematical Study. 160p. 1981. lib. bdg. 56.50 (*90-277-1306-5*) Kluwer Ac.

Lehrer, Keith, ed. see Reid, Thomas.

Lehrer, Marc, jt. auth. see Kopelman, Orion M.

Lehrer, Marc, jt. auth. see Van De Carr, Rene.

Lehrer, Mark. Intellektuelle Aporte und Literarische Originalitat: Wissenschaftgeschichtliche Studien zum Deutschen Realismus: Keller, Raabe und Fontane. LC 90-24409. (North American Studies in Nineteenth-Century German Literature: Vol. 8). 169p. (C). 1991. text ed. 36.95 (*0-8204-1476-X*) P Lang Pubs.

Lehrer, Melinda. Classical Myth & the "Polifemo" of Gongora. 130p. 1990. 39.50 (*0-916379-60-4*) Scripta.

Lehrer, Milton G. Transylvania: History & Reality. Martin, David, ed. & frwd. by. LC 86-25861. 320p. 1987. 18.95 (*0-910155-04-6*) Bartleby Pr.

Lehrer, Paul M. & Woolfolk, Robert L., eds. Principles & Practices of Stress Management. 2nd ed. LC 92-49253. 621p. 1993. lib. bdg. 65.00 (*0-89862-766-4*) Guilford Pr.

— Principles & Practices of Stress Management. 2nd ed. LC 92-49253. 621p. 1993. pap. text ed. 35.00 (*0-89862-162-3*) Guilford Pr.

Lehrer, Paul M., jt. ed. see Woolfolk, Robert L.

Lehrer, Robert, et al. Immunologic Aspects of Infectious Diseases. Steigbigel, Roy, ed. (C). Date not set. pap. text ed. write for info. (*1-878294-06-7*) Health Dimensions.

Lehrer, Ronald. Nietzsche's Presence in Freud's Life & Thought: On the Origins of a Psychology of Dynamic Unconscious Mental Functioning. LC 94-571. 370p. (C). 1994. 69.50 (*0-7914-2145-7*); pap. 23.95 (*0-7914-2146-5*) State U NY Pr.

Lehrer, Stanley, jt. ed. see Brickman, William W.

Lehrer, Stanley, jt. auth. see Ehrensperger, Harold A.

Lehrer, Stephen M. Cooking with the Chicken Breast: Delicious Main Dishes Starring the Delectable Skinless & Boneless White Meat. LC 89-91671. (Illus.). 224p. (Orig.). 1990. pap. 11.95 (*0-9623104-8-4*) Madeira-Hudson Pub.

Lehrer, Steven. Understanding Lung Sounds. 2nd ed. 144p. 1993. pap. text ed. 39.95 (*0-7216-4902-5*) Saunders.

Lehrer, Susan. Origins of Protective Labor Legislation for Women, 1905-1925. LC 87-6485. (SUNY Series on Women & Work). 318p. 1987. 64.50 (*0-88706-506-6*); pap. 21.95 (*0-88706-505-8*) State U NY Pr.

Lehrer, Tom. Song Book. 14.95 (*0-89190-092-6*, Am Repr) Amereon Ltd.

— Too Many Songs by Tom Lehrer with Not Enough Pictures by Ronald Searle. (Illus.). 1981. pap. 15.00 (*0-394-74930-8*) Pantheon.

***Lehrer, Warren.** Brother Blue: A Narrative Portrait of Dr. Hugh Morgan Hill, aka Brother Blue. LC 95-5813. (Portrait Ser.). (Illus.). (Orig.). 1995. pap. 12.95 (*0-941920-36-4*) Bay Pr.

— Charlie: A Narrative Portrait of Charlie Lang. LC 95-9933. (Portrait Ser.). (Illus.). 208p. (Orig.). 1995. pap. 12.95 (*0-941920-34-8*) Bay Pr.

— Claude: A Narrative Portrait of Claude Debs. LC 95-5812. (Portrait Ser.). (Illus.). 264p. (Orig.). 1995. pap. 12.95 (*0-941920-35-6*) Bay Pr.

— GRRRHHHH: A Study of Social Patterns. 462p. 1987. 100.00 (*0-9613871-1-4*) Ear Say.

— I Mean You Know. (Illus.). 156p. 1983. 25.00 (*0-89822-035-1*) Ear Say.

— Nicky D. from L. I. C. A Narrative Portrait of Nicholas DeTommaso. LC 95-5814. (Portrait Ser.). (Illus.). 268p. (Orig.). 1995. pap. 12.95 (*0-941920-37-2*) Bay Pr.

Lehrling, George. Machinist: Basic Skill Development. LC 77-73238. 256p. reprint ed. pap. 73.00 (*0-317-11103-5*, 2011575) Bks Demand.

Lehrman, Alexander, tr. see Apresjan, Yuri D.

Lehrman, Edgar. A Handbook to the Russian Text of Crime & Punishment. 1977. 103.10 (*90-279-3327-8*) Mouton.

Lehrman, Edgar, tr. see Gorchakov, Nikolai A.

Lehrman, Edgar H. A Handbook to Eighty-Six of Chekhov's Stories in Russia. 327p. (Orig.). 1985. pap. text ed. 18.95 (*0-89357-151-2*) Slavica.

Lehrman, Fredric. Loving the Earth. (Illus.). 48p. (YA). (gr. 6-12). 1990. 14.95 (*0-89087-603-7*) Celestial Arts.

— The Sacred Landscape. (Illus.). 128p. 1989. pap. 29.95 (*0-89087-542-1*) Celestial Arts.

— The Sacred Landscape. deluxe ed. (Illus.). 128p. 1989. boxed 100.00 (*0-89087-549-9*) Celestial Arts.

Lehrman, Jane A. Around Douglas & Beyond: A Collection of Columns about the People of Douglas County. Lehrman, Sally, ed. (Illus.). 123p. (Orig.). 1990. lib. bdg. 27.50 (*0-685-46926-3*); pap. text ed. 24.50 (*0-922082-01-4*) Desk Top Pubs Inc.

Lehrman, Lew. Being an Artist. (Illus.). 144p. 1992. 29.95 (*0-89134-429-2*, 30409) North Light Bks.

Lehrman, Lew B. Freshen Your Paintings with New Ideas. (Elements of Painting Ser.). (Illus.). 144p. 1995. 27.99 (*0-89134-566-3*) North Light Bks.

Lehrman, Lewis. Dining Room Service. LC 70-142510. 1971. text ed. write for info. (*0-672-96065-6*) Macmillan.

Lehrman, Lewis B. Energize Your Paintings with Color. (Elements of Painting Ser.). (Illus.). 144p. 1993. 27.95 (*0-89134-476-4*, 30522) North Light Bks.

Lehrman, Lewis E. Real Money: The Case for the Gold Standard. 13.50 (*0-394-51904-3*) Random.

Lehrman, Neil. Perdut. LC 78-20558. 1979. pap. 6.95 (*0-931848-23-7*) Dryad Pr.

— Perdut. deluxe limited ed. LC 78-20558. 1979. 15.00 (*0-931848-22-9*) Dryad Pr.

Lehrman, Philip R., ed. see Freud, Anna & Burlingham, Dorothy T.

Lehrman, Robert. The Store That Mama Built. LC 91-39983. 128p. (J). (gr. 3-7). 1992. text ed. 13.95 (*0-02-754632-2*, Mac Bks Young Read) S&S Childrens.

Lehrman, Robert L. Physics the Easy Way. 2nd ed. 432p. 1990. pap. 10.95 (*0-8120-4390-1*) Barron.

Lehrman, S. M. The Jewish Design for Living. LC 76-24242. 1976. 15.95 (*0-88400-003-6*) Shengold.

Lehrman, S. M., tr. see Kahana, S. Z.

Lehrman, Sally, ed. see Lehrman, Jane A.

Lehrmann, Charles C. Jewish Influences on European Thought. Klin, George & Carpenter, Victor, trs. LC 72-3264. 323p. 1975. 27.50 (*0-8386-7908-0*) Fairleigh Dickinson.

Lehrmann, Paul & Tully, Tim. MIDI for the Professional. (Illus.). 240p. 1993. pap. 19.95 (*0-685-70429-7*) Music Sales.

Lehrs, Ernst. Spiritual Science, Electricity & Michael Faraday. 30p. 1975. pap. 5.00 (*0-85440-296-9*, Steinerbks) Anthroposophic.

Lehrs, Karl. De Aristarchi Studiis Homericis. x, 506p. 1964. reprint ed. write for info. (*0-318-70958-9*, Pub. by Georg Olms GW) Lubrecht & Cramer.

— Kleine Schriften. viii, 582p. 1979. reprint ed. write for info. (*3-487-06756-0*, Pub. by Georg Olms GW) Lubrecht & Cramer.

— Quaestiones Epicae. viii, 339p. 1977. reprint ed. write for info. (*3-487-06235-6*, Pub. by Georg Olms GW) Lubrecht & Cramer.

Lehrs, Max. Geschichte & Kritscher Katalog des Deutschen, Niederlandischen & Franzosischen Kupferstichs im XV Jahrhundert, 9 Vols. (Illus.). 1969. 1,100.00 (*0-8115-0044-6*) Periodicals Srv.

Lehtcmaa, Linda R., jt. auth. see McVey, Mary A.

Lehtinen, Ritva. Grandchildren of the Incas. (J). (gr. 3-6). 1992. pap. 6.95 (*0-87614-566-7*, Carolrhoda) Lerner Group.

Lehtipuu, Markus & Makela, Virpi. Finland: A Travel Survival Kit. (Illus.). 380p. (Orig.). 1993. pap. 15.95 (*0-86442-156-7*) Lonely Planet.

Lehto, Mark R. & Miller, James M. Warnings, Vol. 1: Fundamentals, Design & Evaluation Methodologies. LC 86-22866. (Illus.). 287p. 1986. 55.00 (*0-940537-00-1*) Fuller Tech.

Lehto, O. Univalent Functions & Teichmuller Spaces. (Graduate Texts in Mathematics Ser.: Vol. 109). (Illus.). 270p. 1986. 49.90 (*0-387-96310-3*) Spr-Verlag.

Lehto, O., ed. International Congress of Mathematicians: Proceedings, Helsinki, 1980, 2 vols., Set. 1022p. 1980. 80.00 (*951-41-0352-1*, PICM-78) Am Math.

Lehtonen, Risto & Pahkinen, Erkki J. Practical Methods for Design & Analysis of Complex Surveys. LC 94-20917. (Statistics in Practice Ser.). 1994. text ed. 55.95 (*0-471-93934-X*) Wiley.

Lei. Role of Copper in Lipid Metabolism. 1990. 190.00 (*0-8493-5564-8*, QR186) CRC Pr.

***Lei, Donise.** Ancient China: Its History & Culture from 2250 B.C. to A.D. 250 (A Learning Unit) LC 91-91297. (Illus.). 42p. (Orig.). (YA). (gr. 6 up). 1992. pap. text ed. 7.95 (*1-879600-01-3*) Pac Asia Pr.

***Lei, Lei.** User Participation & the Success of Information System Development: An Integrated Model of User-Specialist Relationships. (Tinbergen Research Institute Research Ser.: No. 73, Series B). 257p. 1994. pap. 28.00 (*90-5170-285-X*, Pub. by Thesis Pubs NE) IBD Ltd.

Leib, Franklin. Fire Arrow. 1989. mass mkt. 4.95 (*0-8041-0421-2*) Ivy Books.

Leib, G., tr. see Krasilshchikova, E. A.

Leibbrand, Kurt. Stadt und Verkehr: Theorie und Praxis der Stadtischen Verkehrsplanung. 404p. (GER.). 1980. 97.00 (*0-8176-1072-3*) Birkhauser.

Leibbrandt, G. Noncovariant Gauges: Quantization of Yang-Mills. 220p. 1994. text ed. 48.00 (*981-02-1384-0*) World Scientific Pub.

Leibecq, C., ed. Compendium of Biochemical Nomenclature & Related Documents. 2nd ed. 350p. 1992. pap. 36.00 (*1-85578-005-4*, Pub. by Portland Pr Ltd UK) Ashgate Pub Co.

Leibenluft, Ellen, et al, eds. Less Time to Do More: Psychotherapy on the Short-Term Inpatient Unit. LC 93-20081. 336p. 1993. text ed. 42.50 (*0-88048-512-4*) Am Psychiatric.

Leibenstein, Dov. Chumash & Rashi Curriculum. (Orig.). 1990. Looseleaf Binder. ring bd. 28.00 (*0-914131-94-X*, C030) Torah Umesorah.

Leibenstein, Harvey. Beyond Economic Man: A New Approach to Micro-Economic Theory. (Illus.). 302p. 1980. pap. 14.50 (*0-674-06892-0*) HUP.

— Inflation, Income Distribution & X-Efficiency Theory: A Study Prepared for the International Labour Office Within the Framework of the World Employment Programme. 122p. 1980. 45.00 (*0-06-494169-8*, 06556) B&N Imports.

— Inside the Firm: The Inefficiencies of Hierarchy. LC 87-8426. (Illus.). 304p. 1987. 37.00 (*0-674-45515-0*) HUP.

Leibenstein, Margaret. The Edible Mushroom. 1986. 14.95 (*0-449-90204-8*, Columbine) Fawcett.

— The Edible Mushroom. (Illus.). 224p. 1989. pap. 7.95 (*0-449-90454-7*, Columbine) Fawcett.

— The Edible Mushroom: A Gourmet Cook's Guide. rev. ed. LC 92-41571. (Illus.). 224p. 1993. reprint ed. pap. 8.95 (*1-56440-172-3*) Globe Pequot.

Leiber, Fritz. The Big Time. 1976. reprint ed. lib. bdg. 18.95 (*0-88411-931-9*, Aeonian Pr) Amereon Ltd.

— The Big Time. 1990. reprint ed. lib. bdg. 16.95 (*0-89968-537-4*) Buccaneer Bks.

— The Big Time. (Collier Nucleus Science Fiction Ser.). 192p. 1991. reprint ed. mass mkt., pap. 4.95 (*0-02-069841-0*, Collier S&S) S&S Trade.

— Conjure Wife. 1993. reprint ed. lib. bdg. 18.95x (*0-89968-435-1*, Lghtyr Pr) Buccaneer Bks.

— Conjure Wife & Our Lady of Darkness. 352p. 1991. mass mkt. 4.99 (*0-8125-1296-0*) Tor Bks.

— Gather, Darkness! 224p. 1992. pap. 9.00 (*0-02-022348-X*, Pub. by Gebrueder Borntraeger GW) Macmillan.

— Green Millenium. 1976. 19.95 (*0-8488-1076-7*) Amereon Ltd.

— The Green Millenium. 1993. reprint ed. lib. bdg. 18.95 (*0-89968-348-7*, Lghtyr Pr) Buccaneer Bks.

— The Green Millennium. 192p. 1992. reprint ed. pap. 4.95 (*0-02-022346-3*, Pub. by Gebrueder Borntraeger GW) Macmillan.

— The Green Millennium. LC 80-22108. 256p. 1980. reprint ed. 25.00 (*0-8398-2641-9*) Ultramarine Pub.

— Gummitch & Friends. (Illus.). 224p. 1992. 30.00 (*1-880418-18-5*); 60.00 (*1-880418-17-7*) D M Grant.

— Heroes & Horrors. Schiff, Stuart D., ed. LC 78-64600. (Illus.). 1978. 12.00 (*0-918372-03-8*) Whispers.

— Heroes & Horrors. deluxe ed. Schiff, Stuart D., ed. LC 78-64600. (Illus.). 1978. boxed 25.00 (*0-918372-02-X*) Whispers.
— Night's Black Agent. 1976. reprint ed. lib. bdg. 19.95 (*0-88411-932-7*, Aeonian Pr) Amereon Ltd.
— Night's Black Agent. 1990. reprint ed. lib. bdg. 17.95 (*0-89968-538-2*) Buccaneer Bks.
— Our Lady of Darkness. 1993. reprint ed. lib. bdg. 18.95x (*0-89968-436-X*, Lghtyr Pr) Buccaneer Bks.
— Pail of Air. 1976. reprint ed. lib. bdg. 18.95 (*0-88411-933-5*, Aeonian Pr) Amereon Ltd.
— Rime Isle. (Illus.). 1977. 10.00 (*0-918372-01-1*) Whispers.
— A Specter Is Haunting Texas. 256p. 1992. pap. 9.00 (*0-02-022347-1*, Pub. by Gebrueder Borntraeger GW) Macmillan.
— Swords' Masters, 3 vols. in 1. (Illus.). 544p. Date not set. 12.98 (*1-56865-046-9*, GuildAmerica) Dblday Bk Music.
— Two Sought Adventure. 1993. reprint ed. lib. bdg. 18.95 (*0-89968-405-X*, Lghtyr Pr) Buccaneer Bks.
— The Wanderer. braille ed. 675p. (Orig.). 1992. vinyl bd. 54.00 (*1-56956-101-X*, BR8641) W A T Braille.
— The Wanderer. (Orig.). 1993. reprint ed. lib. bdg. 18.95 (*0-89968-349-5*, Lghtyr Pr) Buccaneer Bks.
— You're All Alone. 245p. 1990. pap. 3.95 (*0-88184-679-1*) Carroll & Graf.

Leiber, Justin. Can Animals & Machines Be Persons? A Dialogue. LC 85-21888. 88p. (C). 1985. lib. bdg. 21.50 (*0-87220-003-5*); pap. 3.95 (*0-87220-002-7*) Hackett Pub.
— An Invitation to Cognitive Science. 192p. 1991. pap. 18.95 (*0-631-17005-7*) Blackwell Pubs.
— Paradoxes. 96p. 1993. pap. 9.95 (*0-7156-2426-1*, Pub. by Duckworth UK) Focus Info Gr.

***Leiber, Vivian.** Baby Makes Nine. (American Romance Ser.). 1995. pap. 3.50 (*0-373-16576-5*, 1-16576-0) Harlequin Bks.
— Goody Two-Shoes. large type ed. 256p. 1992. reprint ed. lib. bdg. 13.95 (*1-56054-539-9*) Thorndike Pr.
— Safety of His Arms. (Sil Romance Ser.). 1995. pap. 2.99 (*0-373-19070-0*, 1-19070-1) Silhouette.

Leiberman, Louis, jt. auth. see Westheimer, Ruth.

Leiberman, Marcia & Leiberman, Philip. Walking the Alpine Parks of France & Northwest Italy. (Illus.). 240p. 1994. pap. 14.95 (*0-89886-398-8*) Mountaineers.

Leiberman, Norman P. Process Design for Reliable Operations. 2nd ed. LC 88-1463. 254p. 1988. 55.00 (*0-87201-683-8*) Gulf Pub.

Leiberman, Philip, jt. auth. see Leiberman, Marcia.

Leibfried, Kathleen H., jt. auth. see McNair, C. J.

Leibfried, Stephan. The Bureaucracy of the "Statist Reserve" The Case of the U. S. A. (Western Societies Papers). 117p. 1979. 11.95 (*0-8014-9634-9*) Cornell U Pr.

Leibfried, Stephan, ed. see Pierson, Paul.

***Leibholz-Bonhoeffer, Sabine.** The Bonhoeffers: Portrait of a Family. (Orig.). 1994. pap. 12.95 (*0-910452-78-4*) Covenant.

Leibig, Michael T. & Kahn, Wendy L. Public Employee Organizing & the Law. 258p. 1987. pap. 34.00 (*0-87179-499-3*, 0499) BNA.
— Public Employee Organizing & the Law. LC 87-18398. 258p. reprint ed. pap. 73.60 (*0-7837-4604-0*, 2044323) Bks Demand.

Leibing, Edward. NetWare User's Guide: Versions 3.11 & 3.12. LC 93-4987. 1993. pap. 29.95 (*1-55851-318-3*) M&T Bks.

***Leibler, John.** Frog Counts to Ten. (J). (ps-3). 1994. 9.95 (*1-56294-739-7*) Millbrook Pr.

Leiblich, J. H., ed. see Powers Management Consultants Staff.

Leiblum, Sandra R. & Rosen, Raymond C., eds. Principles & Practice of Sex Therapy: Update for the 1990's. 2nd ed. LC 89-7458. 413p. 1989. lib. bdg. 38.95 (*0-89862-389-8*) Guilford Pr.
— Sexual Desire Disorders. LC 87-21192. 470p. 1988. lib. bdg. 45.00 (*0-89862-714-1*) Guilford Pr.
— Sexual Desire Disorders. LC 87-21192. 470p. 1992. reprint ed. pap. text ed. 24.95 (*0-89862-153-4*) Guilford Pr.

***Leibman, Nina C.** Living Room Lectures: The Fifties Family in Film & Television. LC 94-36606. (Texas Film Studies). (Illus.). 384p. 1995. text ed. 45.00x (*0-292-74683-0*); pap. 18.95x (*0-292-74684-9*) U of Tex Pr.

Leibniz & Lexicon. A Dual Concordance to Leibniz's Philosophische Schriften. Hunter, Graeme et al, eds. vii, 419p. 1988. write for info. (*3-487-09094-5*, Pub. by Georg Olms GW); fiche write for info. (*0-318-71367-5*, Pub. by Georg Olms GW) Lubrecht & Cramer.

Leibniz, G. W. Discourse on Metaphysics & Other Essays. Garber, Daniel, ed. Ariew, Roger & Garber, Daniel, trs. (HPC Classics Ser.). 96p. (C). 1991. lib. bdg. 24.50 (*0-87220-133-3*); pap. text ed. 4.95 (*0-87220-132-5*) Hackett Pub.

Leibniz, Gottfried W. Der Briefwechsel von Gottfried Wilhelm Leibniz Mit Mathematikern. xxviii, 760p. 1987. reprint ed. write for info. (*3-487-00343-0*, Pub. by Georg Olms GW) Lubrecht & Cramer.
— Briefwechsel Zwischen Leibniz und Christian Wolff. 188p. 1971. reprint ed. write for info. (*0-318-71366-7*, Pub. by Georg Olms GW) Lubrecht & Cramer.
— Catalogue Critique Des Manuscrits De Leibniz, Vol. Two: Mars 1672-Novembre 1676. xiv, 257p. 1986. reprint ed. write for info. (*3-487-07797-3*, Pub. by Georg Olms GW) Lubrecht & Cramer.
— De Summe-Rerum: Metaphysical Papers, 1675-1676. Parkinson, G. H., tr. (Leibniz Ser.). 208p. (C). 1992. text ed. 40.00 (*0-300-05187-5*) Yale U Pr.
— Discourse on Metaphysics & the Monadology. (Great Books in Philosophy). 123p. 1992. pap. 6.95 (*0-87975-775-2*) Prometheus Bks.
— G. W. Leibniz: Discourse on Metaphysics & Related Writings. Martin, R. Niall & Brown, Stuart, eds. 182p. 1989. text ed. 18.95 (*0-7190-1702-5*) St Martin.
— General Investigations Concerning the Analysis of Concepts & Truths: A Translations & an Evaluation. O'Briant, Walter H., tr. LC 68-54890. (Georgia University Monographs: No. 17). 129p. reprint ed. pap. 36.80 (*0-317-08968-4*, 2002853) Bks Demand.
— Leibniz & Ludolf on Things Linguistic: Excerpts from Their Correspondence, 1688-1703. Waterman, John T., ed. & tr. by. LC 77-83104. (University of California Publications in Social Welfare: No. 88). 101p. reprint ed. pap. 28.80 (*0-317-55482-4*, 2029593) Bks Demand.
— Lettres de Leibniz a Arnauld D'Apres un Manuscrit Inedit. LC 84-48423. (Philosophy of Leibniz Ser.). 111p. 1985. lib. bdg. 15.00 (*0-8240-6536-0*) Garland.
— Lettres et Opuscules Inedits. cxii, 336p. 1975. reprint ed. write for info. (*3-487-05321-7*, Pub. by Georg Olms GW) Lubrecht & Cramer.
— Mathematische Schriften, 7 vols., Set. xxviii, 3401p. 1971. reprint ed. write for info. (*0-318-71368-3*, Pub. by Georg Olms GW); reprint ed. pap. write for info. (*0-318-71369-1*, Pub. by Georg Olms GW) Lubrecht & Cramer.

Leibniz, Gottfried W., et al. Monadology & Other Philosophical Essays. LC 65-26531. 208p. (Orig.). (C). 1965. pap. write for info. (*0-02-406970-1*, LLA188) Macmillan.

Leibniz, Gottfried W. New Essays on Human Understanding. Remnant, Peter & Bennett, Jonathan, eds. 610p. 1981. 125.00 (*0-521-23147-7*); pap. 37.95 (*0-521-29836-9*) Cambridge U Pr.
— New Essays on Human Understanding. abr. ed. Remnant, Peter & Bennett, Jonathan, eds. LC 82-1334. 280p. 1982. pap. 24.95 (*0-521-28539-9*) Cambridge U Pr.
— Nouvelles Lettres et Opuscules Inedits De Leibniz. ccxix, 440p. 1971. reprint ed. write for info. (*3-487-04179-0*, Pub. by Georg Olms GW) Lubrecht & Cramer.
— Oeuvres, 7 vols., Set. ccliv, 3472p. 1969. reprint ed. write for info. (*0-318-71370-5*, Pub. by Georg Olms GW) Lubrecht & Cramer.
— Opuscules et Fragments Inedits. xiv, 682p. 1988. reprint ed. write for info. (*3-487-01197-2*, Pub. by Georg Olms GW); reprint ed. pap. write for info. (*3-487-00099-7*, Pub. by Georg Olms GW) Lubrecht & Cramer.
— Philosophical Essays. Ariew, Roger & Garber, Daniel, eds. Garber, Daniel, tr. LC 88-38259. (HPC Classics Ser.). 386p. (C). 1989. 37.50 (*0-87220-063-9*); pap. 10.95 (*0-87220-062-0*) Hackett Pub.
— Philosophical Writings. rev. ed. Parkinson, G. H., ed. 296p. 1995. pap. 7.50 (*0-460-87546-9*, Everyman's Classic Lib) C E Tuttle.
— Die Philosophischen Schriften, 7 vols., Set. 4040p. 1978. reprint ed. write for info. (*3-487-00064-4*, Pub. by Georg Olms GW); reprint ed. pap. write for info. (*3-487-00926-9*, Pub. by Georg Olms GW) Lubrecht & Cramer.
— Political Writings. Riley, Patrick, ed. (Cambridge Texts in the History of Political Thought Ser.). 214p. 1988. 59.95 (*0-521-35380-7*) Cambridge U Pr.
— Political Writings. Riley, Patrick, ed. (Cambridge Texts in the History of Political Thought Ser.). 214p. 1988. pap. 18.95 (*0-521-35899-X*) Cambridge U Pr.
— The Preface to Leibniz' Novissima Sinice. Lach, Donald F., tr. LC 57-14876. 116p. reprint ed. pap. 33.10 (*0-317-08437-2*, 2001168) Bks Demand.
— Theodicy. LC 85-8833. 400p. (C). 1985. pap. 12.00 (*0-87548-437-9*) Open Court.
— Writings on China. Cook, Daniel J. & Rosemont, Henry, eds. 173p. 1994. 32.95 (*0-8126-9250-0*); pap. 16.95 (*0-8126-9251-9*) Open Court.

Leibo, Steven A. Transferring Technology to China: Prosper Giquel & the Self-Strengthening Movement. LC 85-60380. (China Research Monographs: No. 28). 175p. 1985. pap. 7.50 (*0-912966-76-9*) IEAS.

***Leibold.** Treasure Hunt: A Super Eye Adventure. (J). 1995. pap. 3.99 (*0-553-48320-X*) Bantam.

Leibold, Cheryl, jt. ed. see Danly, Susan.

Leibold, Cheryl, jt. ed. see Foster, Kathleen A.

Leibold, Jay. The Lost Ninja. (Choose Your Own Adventure Ser.: No. 113). (YA). 1991. pap. 3.50 (*0-553-28960-8*) Bantam.
— Ninja Cyborg. (Choose Your Own Adventure Ser.: No. 155). (YA). 1995. pap. 3.50 (*0-553-56395-5*) Bantam.
— Return of the Ninja. (Choose Your Own Adventure Ser.: No. 92). (J). 1989. pap. 3.25 (*0-553-27968-8*) Bantam.
— Return of the Ninja. large type ed. LC 94-44201. (Choose Your Own Adventure Ser.: No. 92). (Illus.). 128p. (J). 1995. lib. bdg. 15.93 (*0-8368-1313-8*) Gareth Stevens Inc.
— The Search for Aladdin's Lamp. (Choose Your Own Adventure Ser.: No. 117). (YA). 1991. pap. 3.25 (*0-553-29185-8*) Bantam.
— The Search for Aladdin's Lamp. large type ed. (Choose Your Own Adventure Ser.: No. 117). (Illus.). 128p. (J). 1995. lib. bdg. 15.93 (*0-8368-1311-1*) Gareth Stevens Inc.
— Surf Monkeys. (Choose Your Own Adventure Ser.: No. 131). (J). (gr. 4-7). 1993. pap. 3.25 (*0-553-29301-X*) Bantam.
— You Are a Millionaire. large type ed. (Choose Your Own Adventure Ser.: No. 100). (Illus.). 128p. (J). 1995. lib. bdg. 15.93 (*0-614-01255-4*) Gareth Stevens Inc.
— You Are a Millionaire, No. 98. 1990. pap. 3.50 (*0-553-28351-0*) Bantam.

Leibovic, K. N., ed. Science of Vision. (Illus.). 472p. 1990. 54.00 (*0-387-97270-6*) Spr-Verlag.

***Leibovich, Anna F.** The Russian Concept of Work: Suffering, Drama, & Tradition in Pre & Post Revolutionary Russia. LC 95-3869. 184p. 1995. text ed. 49.95 (*0-275-95135-9*, Praeger Pubs) Greenwood.

Leibovitch, Evan. Using Electronic Mail & News. 1993. pap. write for info. (*0-13-016791-6*) P-H.

Leibovitch, K. A., tr. see Neuhaus, Heinrich.

Leibovitz, Annie. Photographs. LC 83-2385. (Illus.). 144p. 1984. pap. 35.00 (*0-394-72597-2*) Pantheon.

Leibovitz, Annie, photos. Photographs: Annie Leibovitz, 1970-1990. LC 90-56384. (Illus.). 1992. pap. 35.00 (*0-06-092346-6*, PL) HarpC.

***Leibovitz, Maury.** Legacies: Stories of Courage, Humor, & Resilience, of Love, Loss, & Life-Changing... 1994. pap. 13.00 (*0-06-092559-0*, HarpT) HarpC.

Leibovitz, Maury, ed. The Prints of LeRoy Neiman: A Catalogue Raisonne of Serigraphs, Lithographs & Etchings. (Illus.). 359p. 100.00 (*0-937608-00-9*) Knoedler.

Leibovitz, Maury & Lynch, Richard, eds. The Prints of LeRoy Neiman: A Catalogue Raisonne of Serigraphs & Etchings, 1980-1990. (Illus.). 212p. 1991. 150.00 (*0-685-40168-5*) Knoedler.

Leibovitz, Shirley. The Enduring Spirit: The Inspiring True Story of a Holocaust Survivor. 320p. 1993. pap. 14.95 (*0-9635993-0-5*) Gildith Pr.

***Leibowitch, Michele, et al.** An Atlas of Vulval Diseases: A Combined Dermatological, Gynecological & Venereological Approach. 1995. 65.00 (*1-85317-127-1*) Scovill Paterson.

Leibowitt, S. David. Wit & Whimsy. (Illus.). 87p. (Orig.). 1989. pap. 5.95 (*0-9625362-0-2*) S D Leibowitt.

Leibowitz, A. H. Chochmas Hamussar. (Annual Fryer Memorial Lecture Ser.). 1.00 (*0-914131-11-7*, B150) Torah Umesorah.

Leibowitz, Alan. The Record Collector's Record Books. Adler, Roger & Adler, Andrew, eds. 1979. pap. 5.95 (*0-916844-07-2*) Turtle Pr.

Leibowitz, H. Majesty of Man. 1992. 18.95 (*0-89906-542-2*); pap. 15.95 (*0-89906-543-0*) Mesorah Pubns.

Leibowitz, Herbert. Fabricating Lives: Explorations in American Autobiography. LC 90-21152. (Illus.). 416p. 1991. reprint ed. pap. 14.95 (*0-8112-1168-1*, NDP715) New Directions.

***Leibowitz, Herbert, ed.** Parnassus: Twenty Years of Poetry in Review. 400p. 1994. pap. 16.95 (*0-472-06577-7*) U of Mich Pr.
— Parnassus: Twenty Years of Poetry in Review. 400p. 1994. text ed. 39.50 (*0-472-09577-3*) U of Mich Pr.

Leibowitz, Howard M. Corneal Disorders: Clinical Diagnosis & Management. (Illus.). 550p. 1984. text ed. 185.00 (*0-7216-5727-3*) Saunders.

Leibowitz, Jane, jt. ed. see Cuthbertson, Ian M.

Leibowitz, Jeff, jt. auth. see Park, Y. H.

***Leibowitz, Joan.** Yellow Ware. (Illus.). 119p. (Orig.). 1993. pap. 19.95 (*0-614-04425-1*) Schiffer.
— Yellow Ware. rev. ed. LC 85-61524. (Illus.). 119p. (Orig.). 1993. pap. 19.95 (*0-88740-041-8*) Schiffer.

Leibowitz, Judith. Narrative Purpose in the Novella. (De Proprietatibus Litterarum, Ser. Minor: No. 10). 139p. 1974. pap. text ed. 32.35 (*90-279-3007-4*) Mouton.

Leibowitz, Judith & Connington, Bill. The Alexander Technique. LC 89-46084. (Illus.). 208p. 1991. reprint ed. pap. 14.00 (*0-06-092085-8*, PL) HarpC.

Leibowitz, Rene. Schoenberg & His School: The Contemporary Stage of the Language of Music. Newlin, Dika, tr. LC 75-115338. (Music Ser.). 1970. reprint ed. lib. bdg. 37.50 (*0-306-71930-4*) Da Capo.
— Schoenberg & His School: The Contemporary Stage of the Language of Music. LC 75-14128. (Quality Paperbacks Ser.). 1975. reprint ed. pap. 5.95 (*0-306-80020-9*) Da Capo.

Leibowitz, Robert. The Defender: The Life & Career of Samuel Leibowitz. LC 81-5948. (Illus.). 255p. 1981. 15.00 (*0-685-03822-X*) P-H.

Leibowitz, Ronald D., jt. auth. see Churchill, Robert R.

Leibowitz, Yeshaiahu. The Faith of Maimonides. 228p. (Orig.). 1987. pap. 9.95 (*0-915361-93-0*) Modan-Adama Bks.
— Faith of Maimonides. 90p. 1989. pap. 12.00 (*965-05-0466-4*, Pub. by Israel Ministry Def IS) Gefen Bks.

Leibowitz, Yeshayahu. Judaism, Human Values, & the Jewish State. Goldman, Eliezer, ed. & tr. by. Navon, Yoram et al, trs. 291p. (Orig.). (C). 1992. text ed. 45.00 (*0-674-48775-3*) HUP.
— Judaism, Human Values, & the Jewish State. 328p. (Orig.). (C). 1995. pap. 16.95 (*0-674-48776-1*) HUP.

Leibowitz, Zandy B., jt. auth. see Forrer, Stephen E.

Leibowitz, Zandy B., jt. auth. see Lea, H. Daniel.

Leibowitz, Zandy B., et al. Designing Career Development Systems. LC 86-45623. (Management Ser.). 341p. 1986. 34.95 (*1-55542-024-9*) Jossey-Bass.

Leibrecht, Walter. Religion & Culture: Essays in Honor of Paul Tillich. LC 78-167376. (Essay Index Reprint Ser.). 1977. reprint ed. 26.95 (*0-8369-2558-0*) Ayer.

Leibrock, Cynthia A. Beautiful Barrier Free: A Visual Guide to Accessibility. 1993. text ed. 59.95 (*0-442-00882-1*) Van Nos Reinhold.

***Leiby, Adrian C.** The Buildings of South Church, Bergenfield, New Jersey. (Illus.). 72p. 1992. pap. 9.95 (*1-881576-10-8*) Providence Hse.
— The Revolutionary War in the Hackensack Valley: The Jersey Dutch & Neutral Ground, 1775 - 1783. 329p. 1980. reprint ed. pap. 14.95 (*0-8135-0898-3*) Rutgers U Pr.

Leiby, Bruce R. Gordon MacRae: A Bio-Bibliography. LC 90-29291. (Bio-Bibliographies in the Performing Arts Ser.: No. 17). 248p. 1991. text ed. 42.95 (*0-313-26633-6*, LGM, Greenwood Pr) Greenwood.

Leiby, James R. Carroll Wright & Labor Reform: The Origin of Labor Statistics. LC 60-15240. (Historical Monographs: No. 46). 251p. 1960. 15.00 (*0-674-09800-5*) HUP.
— A History of Social Welfare & Social Work in the United States, 1815-1972. LC 78-3774. 426p. 1978. text ed. 35.50 (*0-231-03352-4*) Col U Pr.

Leiby, John S. Colonial Bureaucrats & the Mexican Economy: The Growth of a Patrimonial State, 1763-1821. (American University Studies: History: Ser. IX, Vol. 13). 252p. 1986. text ed. 32.00 (*0-8204-0239-7*) P Lang Pubs.
— Report to the King: Colonel Juan Camargo y Cavallero's Account of New Spain, 1815. (American University Studies: History: Ser. IX, Vol. 3). 227p. (Orig.). 1984. pap. text ed. 22.70 (*0-8204-0050-5*) P Lang Pubs.

Leiby, Larry R. Florida Construction Law Manual. LC 81-5723. (Construction Law: Land Use-Environmental Publications). 500p. 1981. text ed. 105.00 (*0-07-037076-1*) Shepards-McGraw.
— Florida Construction Law Manual. 2nd ed. 626p. 1988. text ed. 110.00 (*0-07-172157-6*) Shepards-McGraw.
— Florida Construction Law Manual. 3rd ed. LC 94-32266. (Construction Law Ser.). 1994. write for info. (*0-07-172531-8*) Shepards-McGraw.
— Florida Construction Law Manual. 3rd ed. LC 95-8142. (Construction Law Ser.). 1995. pap. text ed. write for info. (*0-07-172670-5*) Shepards-McGraw.

Leicester, Charles. Bloodstock Breeding. 536p. 1990. 100.00 (*0-85131-349-3*, Pub. by J A Allen & Co UK) St Mut.
— Bloodstock Breeding: Theory & Practice. (Illus.). 1983. 40.00 (*0-87556-148-9*) Saifer.

Leicester, H. Marshall, Jr. The Disenchanted Self: Representing the Subject in the Canterbury Tales. 1990. 60.00 (*0-520-06760-6*); pap. 18.00 (*0-520-06833-5*) U CA Pr.

Leicester, Henry M. Historical Background of Chemistry. LC 79-166426. (Illus.). 1971. reprint ed. pap. text ed. 6.95 (*0-486-61053-5*) Dover.
— Source Book in Chemistry, Nineteen Hundred to Nineteen Fifty. (Source Books in the History of the Sciences). 432p. 1968. 32.00 (*0-674-82231-5*) HUP.

Leicester, Henry M., tr. see Lomonosov, Mikhail V.

Leicester, J. H. & Farndale, W. A., eds. Trends in the Services for Youth. 1967. 276.00 (*0-08-011604-3*, Pub. by Pergamon Repr UK) Franklin.

Leicester, Mal. Race for a Change in Continuing & Higher Education. LC 93-1895. (Cutting Edge Ser.). 1993. 79.00 (*0-335-09768-5*, Open Univ Pr); pap. 29.00 (*0-335-09767-7*, Open Univ Pr) Taylor & Francis.

Leicester, Mal, jt. auth. see Taylor, Monica.

Leicester, Robert D. Correspondence of Robert Dudley, Earl of Leycester. Bruce, John, ed. LC 17-1209. (Camden Society, London. Publications, First Ser.: No. 27). reprint ed. 125.00 (*0-404-50127-3*) AMS Pr.

Leich, Marian N. Digest of United States Practice in International Law: Cumulative Index, 1973-1980. 371p. 1989. boxed 17.00 (*0-16-021551-X*, S/N 044-000-02282-6) USGPO.

Leichentritt, Hugo. Serge Koussevitsky, the Boston Symphony Orchestra & the New American Music: Music Book Index. 199p. 1993. reprint ed. lib. bdg. 69.00 (*0-7812-9636-6*) Rprt Serv.

***Leicher, Eberhard.** Woerterbuch der Arabischen Wirtschaftssprache und Rechtssprache: Arabisch-Deutsch. 609p. 1992. 225.00 (*0-7859-8473-9*, 3789027774) Fr & Eur.

Leichester Polytechnic University Library Staff, comp. Designers International Index, 3 vols., Set. 1700p. 1991. 640.00 (*0-86291-770-0*) U Pubns Amer.

***Leichman, Laurence.** 90% Off! How & Where to Get the Lowest Possible Price on Absolutely Anything. 1995. pap. 14.95 (*0-9636867-5-5*) Leichman Assocs.
— The Real Estate Tycoon's Handbook! Secrets & Essentials of Today's Sharpest Property Magnates. 1995. pap. 14.95 (*0-9636867-1-2*) Leichman Assocs.
— Sell-Publish Your Own Best Seller! Complete Production & Marketing for Success & Profits. 1995. pap. 14.95 (*0-9636867-2-0*) Leichman Assocs.
— Steal These Homes! As Well As Vacation Houses, Retirement & Investment Real Estate & Commercial Property. 1995. pap. 14.95 (*0-9636867-4-7*) Leichman Assocs.

Leichman, Laurence, ed. see Investor Action Group Staff.

***Leichner, Greg.** Citizens for a Poodle-Free Montana. limited ed. Trusky, Tom, ed. (Hemingway Western Studies Ser.). (Illus.). 17p. (Orig.). 1995. 7.95 (*0-932129-22-6*) Heming W Studies.

Leichner, Jeannine T. Called to His Supper. (Illus.). 64p. (Orig.). (J). (gr. 1-3). 1990. pap. 3.95 (*0-87973-138-9*, 138) Our Sunday Visitor.
— Joy Joy, the Mass: Our Family Celebration. (Illus.). (J). (gr. k-3). 1978. Spanish Edition. 2.95 (*0-87973-348-9*, 348); pap. 2.95 (*0-87973-350-0*) Our Sunday Visitor.
— Making Things Right: The Sacrament of Reconciliation. (Illus.). 62p. (Orig.). (J). (gr. 2-4). 1980. Spanish Edition. 3.95 (*0-87973-349-7*, 349); pap. 3.95 (*0-87973-351-9*, 351) Our Sunday Visitor.

Leichner, Stephanie, jt. auth. see Appelbe, William F.

Leicht, S. & Karotemprel, eds. Early History of the Catholic Missions in North-East India. (C). 1989. 26.00 (*0-8364-2446-8*, Pub. by Firma KLM) S Asia.

Leicht, T., et al, eds. PCB Assembly Systems, 1989. (Illus.). 200p. 1989. pap. 119.00 (*0-387-50938-0*) Spr-Verlag.

Leichtentritt, Hugo. Music, History, & Ideas. LC 38-17551. 320p. reprint ed. pap. 91.20 (*0-685-20530-4*, 2029992) Bks Demand.
— Musical Form. LC 51-11139. 479p. reprint ed. pap. 136.60 (*0-7837-2292-3*, 2057380) Bks Demand.
— Serge Koussevitsky, the Boston Symphony Orchestra & the New American Music. LC 75-41172. reprint ed. 16.45 (*0-404-14680-5*) AMS Pr.

Leichter, H. M., Jr. & Rodgers, Harrell R. American Public Policy in a Comparative Context. 1984. text ed. write for info. (*0-07-037067-2*) McGraw.

An Asterisk (*) at the beginning of an entry indicates that the title is appearing in BIP for the first time.

Leichter, Hope J. & Mitchell, William E. Kinship & Casework. LC 66-24898. 344p. 1967. 39.95 (0-87154-522-5) Russell Sage.

Leichter, Howard M. Free to Be Foolish: Politics & Health Promotion in the United States & Great Britain. (Illus.). 294p. 1991. text ed. 39.50 (0-691-07867-X) Princeton U Pr.

Leichter, Howard M., ed. Health Policy Reform in America: Innovations from the States. LC 92-22293. 240p. 1992. 46.95 (1-56324-053-X); pap. text ed. 20.95 (1-56324-054-8) M E Sharpe.

Leichter, Larry R. Epidemic! 1989. pap. 3.95 (0-8217-2601-3) Zebra.

— State Games. LC 89-62823. 1990. 20.00 (0-87212-232-8); pap. 15.00 (0-87212-247-6) Libra.

Leichtman, Caron, ed. see St. Laurent, Jonathan & Neave, Charles.

Leichtman, Ellen C., jt. auth. see Brandel, Rose.

Leichtman, Harry M. Helping Work Environments Work Manual & Workbook. 1994. student ed 9.95 (0-87868-575-8); text ed. 22.95 (0-87868-549-9) Child Welfare.

Leichtman, Kerry, ed. see St. Laurent, Jonathan & Neave, Charles.

***Leichtman, Martin.** The Rorschach: A Developmental Perspective. 1995. write for info. (0-88163-138-8) Analytic Pr.

Leichtman, Robert R. Cheiro Returns. (From Heaven to Earth Ser.). (Illus.). 80p. (Orig.). 1979. pap. 3.50 (0-89804-053-1) Ariel GA.

— Churchill Returns. LC 81-66847. (From Heaven to Earth Ser.). (Illus.). 96p. (Orig.). 1981. pap. 3.50 (0-89804-065-5) Ariel GA.

— Destiny of America. (From Heaven to Earth Ser.). 1996. pap. 11.95 (0-89804-086-8) Ariel GA.

— Dynamics of Creativity. (From Heaven to Earth Ser.). 256p. 1995. pap. 11.95 (0-89804-085-X) Ariel GA.

— Edgar Cayce Returns. (From Heaven to Earth Ser.). (Illus.). 112p. (Orig.). 1978. pap. 3.50 (0-89804-052-3) Ariel GA.

— Eileen Garrett Returns. (From Heaven to Earth Ser.). (Illus.). 96p. (Orig.). 1980. pap. 3.50 (0-89804-061-2) Ariel GA.

— Einstein Returns. LC 81-69184. (From Heaven to Earth Ser.). (Illus.). 112p. (Orig.). 1982. pap. 3.50 (0-89804-068-X) Ariel GA.

— The Hidden Side of Science. (From Heaven to Earth Ser.). 256p. 1992. pap. 11.95 (0-89804-083-3) Ariel GA.

— The Inner Side of Life. (From Heaven to Earth Ser.). 1990. pap. 11.95 (0-89804-082-5) Ariel GA.

— Jefferson Returns. (From Heaven to Earth Ser.). (Illus.). 64p. (Orig.). 1979. pap. 3.50 (0-89804-057-4) Ariel GA.

— Leadbeater Returns. (From Heaven to Earth Ser.). (Illus.). 96p. (Orig.). 1979. pap. 3.50 (0-89804-055-8) Ariel GA.

— Priests of God. (From Heaven to Earth Ser.). 1995. pap. 11.95 (0-89804-084-1) Ariel GA.

— The Psychic Perspective. (From Heaven to Earth Ser.). 1991. pap. 11.95 (0-89804-081-7) Ariel GA.

— Rembrandt Returns. (From Heaven to Earth Ser.). (Illus.). 96p. (Orig.). 1981. pap. 3.50 (0-89804-064-7) Ariel GA.

— Schweitzer Returns. (From Heaven to Earth Ser.). (Illus.). 104p. (Orig.). 1980. pap. 3.50 (0-89804-063-9) Ariel GA.

— Shakespeare Returns. (From Heaven to Earth Ser.). (Illus.). 70p. (Orig.). 1978. pap. 3.50 (0-89804-051-5) Ariel GA.

— Stewart White Returns. (From Heaven to Earth Ser.). (Illus.). 96p. (Orig.). 1980. pap. 3.50 (0-89804-062-0) Ariel GA.

— Yogananda Returns. (From Heaven to Earth Ser.). 104p. (Orig.). 1981. pap. 3.50 (0-89804-066-3) Ariel GA.

Leichtman, Robert R. & Japikse, Carl. Act of Meditation. 96p. 1995. pap. 7.95 (0-89804-830-3, Enthea Pr) Ariel GA.

— Active Meditation. 1990. pap. 19.95 (0-89804-041-8) Ariel GA.

— The Art of Living, Vol. I. LC 70-76900. (Essay Index Reprint Ser.). 256p. 1979. pap. 9.95 (0-89804-076-0) Ariel GA.

— The Art of Living, Vol. I. 256p. 1979. pap. 9.95 (0-89804-032-9) Ariel GA.

— The Art of Living, Vol. II. (Illus.). 264p. 1980. pap. 7.95 (0-89804-033-7) Ariel GA.

— The Art of Living, Vol. III. LC 81-69186. (Illus.). 264p. 1982. pap. 7.95 (0-89804-034-5) Ariel GA.

— The Art of Living, Vol. IV. LC 83-703086. (Illus.). 280p. 1984. pap. 7.95 (0-89804-035-3) Ariel GA.

— The Art of Living, Vol. V. (Illus.). 240p. 1986. pap. 7.95 (0-89804-036-1) Ariel GA.

— Celebrating Life. 90p. 1993. pap. 7.95 (0-89804-806-0, Enthea Pr) Ariel GA.

— Changing Lines. 1993. pap. 7.95 (0-89804-093-0) Ariel GA.

— Connecting Lines. 160p. 1992. pap. 7.95 (0-89804-092-2) Ariel GA.

— The Destiny of America. LC 83-70303. (From Heaven to Earth Ser.). 128p. 1984. 7.95 (0-89804-075-2); pap. 3.50 (0-89804-074-4) Ariel GA.

— Forces of the Zodiac: Companions of the Soul. LC 85-70204. 456p. 1985. 21.50 (0-89804-038-8) Ariel GA.

— Healing Emotional Wounds. 144p. 1995. pap. 9.95 (0-89804-829-X, Enthea Pr) Ariel GA.

— Healing Lines. 1989. pap. 7.95 (0-89804-090-6) Ariel GA.

— Life of Spirit, Vol. I. (Illus.). 216p. (Orig.). 1986. pap. 8.95 (0-89804-132-5) Ariel GA.

— Life of Spirit, Vol. II. 275p. (Orig.). 1987. pap. 8.95 (0-89804-133-3) Ariel GA.

— Life of Spirit, Vol. III. 200p. (Orig.). 1988. pap. 8.95 (0-89804-134-1) Ariel GA.

— Life of Spirit, Vol. IV. (Orig.). 1995. pap. 8.95 (0-89804-135-X) Ariel GA.

— Making Prayer Work. 144p. 1995. pap. 9.95 (0-89804-828-1, Enthea Pr) Ariel GA.

— Mark Twain Returns. LC 81-69185. (From Heaven to Earth Ser.). 80p. (Orig.). 1982. pap. 3.50 (0-89804-067-1) Ariel GA.

— Ruling Lines. 1990. pap. 7.95 (0-89804-091-4) Ariel GA.

— The Way to Health. 128p. 1994. pap. 9.95 (0-89804-805-2, Enthea Pr) Ariel GA.

Leichtman, Robert R. & Japikse, Carl, eds. Books of Light. (Illus.). 160p. (Orig.). 1986. pap. 4.95 (0-89804-155-4) Ariel GA.

Leichtman, Robert R., jt. auth. see Japikse, Carl.

Leichty, E. V. The Series Summa Izbu. LC 66-25697. 24.00 (0-685-71732-1) J J Augustin.

Leichty, Erle, et al, eds. A Scientific Humanist: Studies in Memory of Abraham Sachs. (Occasional Publications of the Samuel Noah Kramer Fund: No. 9). xvi, 378p. 1988. 50.00 (0-934718-90-3) U PA Mus Pubns.

Leick, Alfred. GPS Satellite Surveying. LC 89-34212. 1990. text ed. 79.95 (0-471-81990-5) Wiley.

Leick, Gwendolyn. A Dictionary of Ancient Near Eastern Architecture. 272p. 1988. text ed. 52.50 (0-415-00240-0) Routledge.

— A Dictionary of Ancient Near Eastern Mythology. (Illus.). 240p. 1991. 55.00 (0-415-00762-3, A5254) Routledge.

— Sex & Eroticism in Mesopotamian Literature. LC 93-49776. (Illus.). 336p. 1994. 55.00x (0-415-06534-8, B4367) Routledge.

Leick, Nini & Davidsen-Nielsen, Marianne. Healing Pain: Attachment, Loss & Grief Therapy. 224p. 1991. 74.50 (0-415-06087-7, A5770); pap. 18.95 (0-415-04795-1, A5419) Routledge.

Leidecker, Kurt F. Scientific German by the Method of Discovery. 1947. 10.95 (0-913298-67-0) S F Vanni.

Leidecker, Kurt F., ed. The Record Book of the St. Louis Philosophical Society, Founded February, 1866. LC 89-37669. (Studies in the History of Philosophy: Vol. 14). (Illus.). 136p. 1990. lib. bdg. 69.95 (0-88946-289-5) E Mellen.

Leider, Anna. Don't Miss Out: The Ambition Student's Guide to Financial Aid. 19th ed. 1994. pap. 7.00 (0-945981-84-8, TN7672) Octameron Assocs.

— I Am Somebody. 6th ed. 96p. (Orig.). 1994. pap. 6.00 (0-945981-94-5, TN7730-06) Octameron Assocs.

— Loans & Grants from Uncle Sam: Am I Eligible & for How Much? 2nd ed. 1994. 5.00 (0-945981-86-4) Octameron Assocs.

Leider, Anna, jt. auth. see Leider, Robert.

Leider, Emily W. California's Daughter: Gertrude Atherton & Her Times. LC 90-32410. 425p. 1991. 35.00 (0-8047-1820-2) Stanford U Pr.

— California's Daughter: Gertrude Atherton & Her Times. (Illus.). 425p. (C). 1993. pap. 14.95 (0-8047-2219-6) Stanford U Pr.

Leider, Frida. Playing My Part. Osborne, Charles, tr. LC 77-26171. (Music Reprint Ser.: 1978). (Illus.). 1978. reprint ed. lib. bdg. 32.50 (0-306-77535-2) Da Capo.

Leider, Richard J. Life Skills: Taking Charge of Your Personal & Professional Growth. 196p. 1993. pap. 17.95 (0-89384-230-3) Pfeiffer & Co.

***Leider, Richard J. & Shapiro, David A.** Repacking Your Bags: Lighten Your Load for the Rest of Your Life. LC 94-37974. 250p. 1995. 21.95 (1-881052-67-2) Berrett-Koehler.

Leider, Robert. Lovejoy's Guide to Financial Aid. LC 84-62593. 1985. pap. 9.95 (0-671-49714-6) S&S Trade.

Leider, Robert & Leider, Anna. Leider's Lecture: A Complete Course in Understanding Financial Aid. 40p. 1994. 15.00 (0-945981-95-3) Octameron Assocs.

Leiderman, Leonardo. Inflation & Disinflation: The Israeli Experiment. LC 92-37436. (Illus.). 296p. (C). 1993. 45.00 (0-226-47110-1) U Ch Pr.

Leiderman, Leonardo & Razin, Assaf, eds. Capital Mobility: The Impact on Consumption, Investment & Growth. (Illus.). 275p. (C). 1994. 54.95 (0-521-45438-7) Cambridge U Pr.

Leiderman, Marcos, et al, eds. Roots & New Frontiers in Social Group Work. LC 88-529. (Social Work with Groups Supplement Ser.: No. 3). 252p. 1989. text ed. 49.95 (0-86656-727-5) Haworth Pr.

Leiderman, P. Herbert & Shapiro, David, eds. Psychobiological Approaches to Social Behavior. xv, 203p. 1964. 27.50 (0-8047-0202-0) Stanford U Pr.

— Psychobiological Approaches to Social Behavior. fac. ed. LC 64-170178. (Illus.). 111p. 1964. pap. 30.00 (0-7837-7913-5, 2047669) Bks Demand.

Leiderman, P. Herbert, et al, eds. Culture & Infancy: Variations in the Human Experience. (Child Psychology Ser.). 1977. text ed. 79.00 (0-12-442050-8) Acad Pr.

Leidersdorf, Craig B., jt. ed. see Chen, Andrie T.

Leidheiser, H., Jr., ed. Corrosion Control by Organic Coatings. LC 81-84733. (Illus.). 300p. 1981. 53.00 (0-915567-93-8) NACE Intl.

Leidheiser, Henry, Jr. The Corrosion of Copper, Tin, & Their Alloys. LC 78-12566. (Illus.). 426p. 1979. reprint ed. lib. bdg. 42.50 (0-88275-752-0) Krieger.

Leidholdt, Dorchen & Raymond, Janice G. The Sexual Liberals & the Attack on Feminism. (Athene Ser.). 256p. 1990. text ed. 35.00 (0-08-037458-1, Pergamon Pr); pap. text ed. 16.95 (0-08-037457-3, Pergamon Pr) Elsevier.

Leidholdt, Dorchen & Raymond, Janice G., eds. The Sexual Liberals & the Attack on Feminism. (Athene Ser.). 256p. (C). text ed. 35.00 (0-8077-6239-3); pap. text ed. 17.95 (0-685-53794-3) Tchrs Coll.

Leidig, jt. auth. see Pratt.

Leidig, Guido, jt. auth. see Weimar, Robert.

Leidlich, Mercedes. Feel Well Again: Three Hundred Fifty Questions & Answers about Depression & Anxiety. 127p. (Orig.). 1991. pap. 9.95 (0-929895-06-1) Maupin Hse.

Leidner, Alan C. The Impatient Muse: Germany & the Sturm & Drang. LC 93-36492. (Germanic Languages & Literatures Ser.: No. 115). xii, 156p. (C). 1994. 37.50 (0-8078-8115-5) U of NC Pr.

Leidner, Alan C. & Madland, Helga S., eds. Space to Act: The Theater of J. M. R. Lenz. LC 93-4998. (Studies in German Literature, Linguistics & Culture). 193p. 1993. 59.50 (1-879751-62-3) Camden Hse.

Leidner, Alan C., ed. see Schiller, Friedrich, et al.

Leidner, Jacob. Plastics Waste: Recovery of Economic Value. LC 81-2752. (Plastics Engineering Ser.: No. 1). 327p. reprint ed. pap. 93.20 (0-7837-5885-5, 2045605) Bks Demand.

***Leidner, Larry H.** The Northern Rockies: A Touring Guide. (Touring Guide Ser.). (Illus.). 184p. (Orig.). 1995. pap. 11.95 (1-55650-684-8) Hunter NJ.

Leidner, Robin. Fast Food, Fast Talk: Service Work & the Routinization of Everyday Life. LC 92-38004. 1993. 40.00 (0-520-08169-2); pap. 15.00 (0-520-08500-0) U CA Pr.

Leidy, Denise P. Treasures of Asian Art: The Asia Society's Mr. & Mrs. John D Rockefeller 3rd Collection. LC 94-9437. 1994. 65.00 (1-55859-863-4) Abbeville Pr.

Leidy, Denise P., jt. auth. see Chutiwongs, Nandana.

Leidy, Denise P., jt. auth. see Desai, Vishakha N.

Leidy, Joseph. The Extinct Mammalian Fauna of Dakota & Nebraska, & a Account of Some Allied Forms from Other Localities: Synopsis of the Mammalian Remains of North America. 2nd ed. LC 73-17828. (Natural Sciences in America Ser.: Vol. 3). (Illus.). 536p. 1974. reprint ed. 41.95 (0-405-05746-6) Ayer.

Leidy, W. Philip. A Popular Guide to Government Publications. 4th ed. LC 76-17803. 440p. 1976. text ed. 63.00 (0-231-04019-9) Col U Pr.

Leier, Carl V., ed. Cardiotonic Drugs: A Clinical Review. 2nd rev. ed. (Fundamental & Clinical Cardiology Ser.: Vol. 2). 384p. 1991. 140.00 (0-8247-8471-5) Dekker.

Leier, Carl V. & Boudoulas, Harisios. CardioRenal Disorders & Diseases. 2nd rev. ed. (Illus.). 608p. 1992. 96.00 (0-87993-517-0) Futura Pub.

***Leier, Mark.** Red Flags & Red Tape: The Making of a Labour Bureaucracy. (Illus.). 248p. (C). 1995. 50.00 (0-8020-0661-2); pap. 17.95 (0-8020-7615-7) U of Toronto Pr.

Leies, John A., jt. ed. see McCarthy, Donald G.

Leies, John A., et al, eds. Handbook on Critical Life Issues. 6th rev. ed. 220p. 1989. pap. 9.95 (0-935372-24-5) Pope John Ctr.

Leif Fjellestad Family. Miner County History. 53p. 1981. pap. 3.00 (0-931170-14-1) Ctr Western Studies.

Leif, Irving P. Larry Eigner: A Bibliography of His Works. LC 88-27017. (Author Bibliographies Ser.: No. 84). (Illus.). 251p. 1989. 27.50 (0-8108-2210-5) Scarecrow.

Leif, Irving P. & Clark, Terry N. Community Power & Decision-Making. (Current Sociology - la Sociologie Contemporaine Ser.: Vol. 20, No. 2). 138p. 1973. pap. text ed. 19.25 (90-279-7941-3) Mouton.

Leif, Norway. Sister City & Other Tales. (Illus.). 22p. (Orig.). 1971. pap. 2.50 (0-932264-18-2) Trask Hse Bks.

Leifchild, J. R. Cornwall: Its Mines & Miners. 304p. 1968. reprint ed. 35.00 (0-7146-1402-5, Pub. by F Cass Pubs UK) Intl Spec Bk.

— Our Coal & Coal-Pits. (Illus.). 243p. 1968. reprint ed. 30.00 (0-7146-1401-7, Pub. by F Cass Pubs UK) Intl Spec Bk.

Leifchild, John R. Our Coal & Our Coal-Pits: The People in Them, & the Scenes Around Them, by a Traveller Underground. 2nd ed. LC 68-58856. (Reprints of Economic Classics Ser.). (Illus.). 243p. 1968. reprint ed. 35.00 (0-678-05065-1) Kelley.

Leifeld, Wendy. Mothers of the Saints: Portraits of Ten Mothers of the Saints & Three Saints who were Mothers. 230p. (Orig.). 1991. pap. 8.99 (0-89283-678-4) Servant.

Leifer, Asa. The Kinetics of Environmental Aquatic Photochemistry: Theory & Practice. LC 88-16718. (Illus.). xxx, 304p. 1988. 64.95 (0-8412-1464-6) Am Chemical.

***Leifer, Eric M.** Making the Majors: The Transformation of Team Sports in America. LC 95-13469. (Illus.). 400p. (C). 1995. 39.95 (0-674-54322-X) HUP.

Leifer, Jacqueline C. & Glomb, Michael B. The Legal Obligations of Nonprofit Boards: A Guidebook for Board Members. (Nonprofit Governance Ser.: No. 39). 57p. (Orig.). (C). 1993. reprint ed. pap. text ed. 26.00 (0-925299-21-9) Natl Ctr Nonprofit.

Leifer, Michael. ASEAN & the Security of South-East Asia. 224p. (C). 1989. lib. bdg. 57.50 (0-415-01008-X, A2503) Routledge.

— Indonesia's Foreign Policy. (Royal Institute of International Affairs Ser.). 224p. 1983. text ed. 49.95 (0-04-327069-7) Routledge Chapman & Hall.

Leifer, Michael, ed. Dictionary of the Modern Politics of South-East Asia. (Dictionaries of Contemporary Politics Ser.). (Illus.). 384p. 1995. 75.00 (0-415-04219-4, A9989) Routledge.

Leifer, Myra. Psychological Effects of Motherhood: A Study of First Pregnancy. LC 79-26179. 304p. 1980. text ed. 14.95 (0-275-91691-X, C1691, Praeger Pubs) Greenwood.

Leifer, Neil & Morrow, Lance. Safari: Experiencing the Wild. LC 92-25587. (Illus.). 168p. 1992. 25.00 (0-89577-458-5) RD Assn.

Leifermann, Henry. Compass American Guide: South Carolina. (Compass American Guides Ser.). 1994. 24.95 (1-878867-67-9); pap. 16.95 (1-878867-66-0, Compass Amrcn) Fodors Travel.

Leifman, Lev J. Functional Analysis, Optimization, & Mathematical Economics: A Collection of Papers Dedicated to the Memory of Leonid Vital'evick Kantorovitch. (Illus.). 360p. 1990. 79.00 (0-19-505729-5) OUP.

Leifman, Lev J., ed. Twelve Papers in Algebra. LC 82-24434. (Translations Ser.: No. 2, Vol. 119). 139p. 1983. 45.00 (0-8218-3074-0, TRANS 2-119) Am Math.

Leiggi, Patrick & May, Peter J., eds. Vertebrate Paleontological Techniques Vol. 1: Methods of Obtaining & Preparing Vertebrate Fossils. (Illus.). 380p. (C). 1995. 69.95 (0-521-44357-1) Cambridge U Pr.

Leigh, A. W. Real Time Software for Small Systems. 250p. 1988. pap. text ed. 43.95 (0-470-20980-1) Wiley.

Leigh, Ana. Angel Hunter. 448p. (Orig.). 1992. pap. 4.99 (0-8439-3365-8) Dorchester Pub Co.

— Forever, My Love. 384p. (Orig.). 1995. mass mkt. 4.99 (0-380-77351-1) Avon.

— The Golden Spike. 448p. (Orig.). 1994. pap. 4.99 (0-8439-3616-9) Dorchester Pub Co.

— A Kindled Flame. 480p. (Orig.). 1991. pap. 4.50 (0-8439-3126-4) Dorchester Pub Co.

— Love's Long Journey. 1981. pap. 2.25 (0-8439-0884-X) Dorchester Pub Co.

— Oh, Promised Destiny. 432p. 1990. reprint ed. pap. 3.95 (0-8439-3065-9) Dorchester Pub Co.

— Paradise Redeemed. 448p. (Orig.). 1989. pap. 3.95 (0-8439-2876-X) Dorchester Pub Co.

— Proud Pillars Rising. 448p. (Orig.). 1991. pap. 4.99 (0-8439-3184-1) Dorchester Pub Co.

— A Question of Honor. (Kirkland Chronicles Ser.: Vol. II). 432p. (Orig.). 1986. pap. 3.95 (0-8439-2787-9) Dorchester Pub Co.

— Sweet Enemy Mine. 448p. (Orig.). 1991. pap. 4.50 (0-8439-3114-0) Dorchester Pub Co.

— Tender Is the Touch. 384p. (Orig.). 1994. mass mkt. 4.50 (0-380-77350-3) Avon.

— These Hallowed Hills. 480p. 1991. reprint ed. pap. 4.50 (0-8439-3146-9) Dorchester Pub Co.

Leigh, Andrew. Decisions, Decisions! A Practical Guide to Problem Solving & Decision Making. 224p. (C). 1983. 63.00 (0-85292-315-5) St Mut.

— Effective Change: Twenty Ways to Make It Happen. 256p. (C). 1988. 54.00 (0-85292-412-7) St Mut.

— Understanding Management Software. 288p. (C). 1985. 69.00 (0-333-40946-9) St Mut.

Leigh, Andrew, ed. Twenty Ways to Manage Better. 192p. (C). 1984. 60.00 (0-85292-334-1) St Mut.

Leigh, Andrew & Maynard, Michael. ACE Teams. 280p. 1993. 49.50 (0-7506-0664-9) Buttrwrth-Heinemann.

— ACE Teams: Creating Star Performance in Business. 280p. 1994. pap. 15.95 (0-7506-1883-3) Buttrwrth-Heinemann.

***Leigh-Austen, Joan.** Visit to Highbury: Another View of Emma. 1995. 18.95 (0-312-11860-0) St Martin.

Leigh, Avra, ed. see Kaslow, Florence R.

***Leigh, Barbara.** For Love Alone. (Historical Ser.). 1995. pap. 3.99 (0-373-28854-9, 1-28854-7) Harlequin Bks.

— For Love of Rory. 1995. pap. 4.50 (0-373-28897-2, 1-28897-6) Harlequin Bks.

— Web of Loving Lies. (Historical Ser.). 1993. mass mkt. 3.99 (0-373-28777-1, 1-28777-0) Harlequin Bks.

Leigh, Benedicta. The Catch of Hands: An Autobiography. 144p. 1992. pap. 13.95 (1-85381-191-2, Pub. by Virago Pr UK) Trafalgar.

Leigh-Bennett, Ernest. Handbook of Early Christian Fathers. 1973. 59.95 (0-8490-0276-1) Gordon Pr.

— Handbook of the Early Church Fathers. 1980. lib. bdg. 75.00 (0-8490-3107-9) Gordon Pr.

Leigh, Bob, et al. Automatic, Manual Transmissions, Transaxles, & Drive Trains. rev. ed. Fennema, Roger L. & Lahue, Kalton C., eds. (Automobile Mechanics Refresher Course Ser.: Bk. 5). (Illus.). 84p. 1981. student ed, pap. 9.95 (0-88098-066-4, H M Gousha); audio 13.90 (0-88098-072-9, H M Gousha) P-H Gen Ref & Trav.

— Brakes, Steering, Front Suspension, Wheels & Tires. rev. ed. Fennema, Roger L. & Shewan, Paul B., eds. (Automobile Mechanics Refresher Course Ser.: Bk. 4). (Illus.). 79p. 1981. student ed, pap. 9.95 (0-88098-065-6, H M Gousha); audio 13.90 (0-88098-071-0, H M Gousha) P-H Gen Ref & Trav.

— Complete Automobile Mechanics Refresher Course. (Illus.). 441p. 1981. student ed 79.95 (0-88098-067-2, H M Gousha) P-H Gen Ref & Trav.

— Complete Automobile Mechanics Refresher Course, 5 cass., Set. rev. ed. (Illus.). 441p. 1981. audio 70.00 (0-88098-073-7, H M Gousha) P-H Gen Ref & Trav.

— Electrical Systems, Heating, & Air Conditioning. rev. ed. Fenneman, Roger L. & Dark, Harris E., eds. (Automobile Mechanics Refresher Course Ser.: Bk. 3). (Illus.). 94p. 1981. student ed, pap. 9.95 (0-88098-064-8, H M Gousha); audio 13.90 (0-88098-070-2, H M Gousha) P-H Gen Ref & Trav.

— Engines, Lubricating & Coding Systems. Fennema, Roger L. & Wiseman, Leslie A., eds. (Automobile Mechanics Refresher Course Ser.: Bk. 2). (Illus.). 80p. 1981. student ed, pap. 9.95 (0-88098-063-X, H M Gousha) P-H Gen Ref & Trav.

— Engines, Lubricating & Coding Systems. rev. ed. Fennema, Roger L. & Wiseman, Leslie A., eds. (Automobile Mechanics Refresher Course Ser.: Bk. 2). (Illus.). 80p. 1981. audio 13.90 (0-88098-069-9, H M Gousha) P-H Gen Ref & Trav.

— Tune-up Ignition & Fuel Induction Systems. Fennema, Roger L. et al, eds. (Automobile Mechanics Refresher Course Ser.: Bk. 1). (Illus.). 104p. 1981. student ed, pap. 9.95 (0-88098-062-1, H M Gousha) P-H Gen Ref & Trav.

— Tune-up Ignition & Fuel Induction Systems. rev. ed. Fennema, Roger L. et al, eds. (Automobile Mechanics Refresher Course Ser.: Bk. 1). (Illus.). 104p. 1981. audio 13.90 (*0-88098-068-0*, H M Gousha) P-H Gen Ref & Trav.

***Leigh Brown, Alison.** Fear, Truth, Writing: From Paper Village to Electronic Community. (SUNY Series in Postmodern Culture). 160p. (C). 1995. text ed. 44.50x (*0-7914-2531-2*); pap. text ed. 14.95x (*0-7914-2532-0*) State U NY Pr.

Leigh, Carol. California Gardens: A Nature Lover's Guide: Highlights of Public Gardens from San Diego to Arcata. LC 92-45277. (Illus.). 160p. (Orig.). 1993. pap. 12.95 (*0-88496-337-3*) Capra Pr.

— California Gardens: A Nature Lover's Guide: Highlights of Public Gardens from San Diego to Arcata. LC 92-45277. (Illus.). 224p. (Orig.). (C). 1993. reprint ed. lib. bdg. 33.00x (*0-8095-4114-9*) Borgo Pr.

Leigh, Carole. What You Always Wanted to Know about Football but Were Afraid to Ask: The Beginner's Guide. Berg, Kristi K., ed. (Illus.). 65p. (Orig.). 1994. pap. 6.90 (*0-9638943-1-5*) Leigh Enter.

Leigh, Colin H., jt. auth. see Aiken, S. Robert.

Leigh, D. Historical Development of British Psychiatry, Vol. 1: Eighteenth & Nineteenth Century. LC 61-14243. 1961. 120.00 (*0-08-009537-2*, Pub. by Pergamon Repr UK) Franklin.

Leigh, D. & Marley, E. Bronchial Asthma: Genetic Population & Psychiatric Study. LC 67-14544. 1967. 89.00 (*0-08-012167-5*, Pub. by Pergamon Repr UK) Franklin.

Leigh, David. The Frontiers of Secrecy: Closed Government in Britain. LC 82-6757. 291p. 1980. text ed. 45.00 (*0-313-27093-7*, U7093, Greenwood Pr) Greenwood.

Leigh, Duane E. Assisting Displaced Workers: Do the States Have a Better Idea? LC 89-5844. 172p. 1989. text ed. 22.00 (*0-88099-073-2*); pap. text ed. 12.00 (*0-88099-074-0*) W E Upjohn.

— Assisting Workers Displaced by Structural Change. 220p. 1995. text ed. 25.00 (*0-88099-154-2*); pap. text ed. 15.00 (*0-88099-153-4*) W E Upjohn.

— Does Training Work for Displaced Workers? A Survey of Existing Evidence. LC 90-38433. 120p. 1990. text ed. 21.00 (*0-88099-093-7*); pap. text ed. 11.00 (*0-88099-094-5*) W E Upjohn.

Leigh, Edward. Critica Sacra. reprint ed. write for info. (*0-318-72037-X*, Pub. by Georg Olms GW) Lubrecht & Cramer.

Leigh, Egbert G., Jr., et al, eds. The Ecology of a Tropical Forest: Seasonal Rhythms & Long-Term Changes. LC 82-600181. (Illus.). 468p. 1983. pap. text ed. 29.95 (*0-87474-601-9*, LEETP) Smithsonian.

Leigh, Elizabeth. Counterfeit Caress. 1991. mass mkt. 4.25 (*0-8217-3585-3*) Zebra.

— Creole Caress. 1989. pap. 3.95 (*0-8217-2784-2*) Zebra.

— Fiery Virginia Jewel. 1991. mass mkt. 4.25 (*0-8217-3282-X*) Zebra.

— Louisiana Passion. 384p. 1992. mass mkt. 4.25 (*0-8217-3915-8*) Zebra.

— Prairie Ecstasy. 384p. 1993. mass mkt. 4.25 (*0-8217-4172-1*) Zebra.

— Prairie Paradise. 416p. 1994. mass mkt. 4.50 (*0-8217-4636-7*) Zebra.

Leigh, Frances A., jt. auth. see Kemble, Frances A.

***Leigh, Frances B.** Ten Years on a Georgia Plantation since the War (1866-1876) 141p. 1992. 30.00 (*0-88322-010-5*) Beehive GA.

— Ten Years on a Georgian Plantation. 1973. reprint ed. lib. bdg. 59.95 (*0-8490-1185-X*) Gordon Pr.

Leigh, Gillian. All about Twins. 1985. pap. 8.95 (*0-7100-9888-X*, RKP) Routledge.

— All about Twins: A Handbook for Parents. (Illus.). 253p. (Orig.). 1984. pap. 14.95 (*0-415-04287-9*, 9888-X) Routledge.

Leigh, H., ed. Behavioral Medicine, Biofeedback, & Behavioral Approaches in Psychosomatic Medicine. (Journal: Psychotherapy & Psychosomatics: Vol. 36, No. 3-4, 1981). (Illus.). 122p. 1982. pap. 48.00 (*3-8055-3521-X*) S Karger.

— Consultation-Liaison Psychiatry: Nineteen Ninety & Beyond. (Illus.). 175p. (C). 1994. text ed. 65.00 (*0-306-44725-8*, Plenum Pr) Plenum.

Leigh, Heather. Comprende Usted? 1991. pap. text ed. 10.00 (*0-582-22344-X*) Longman.

Leigh, Heather & Ortiz-Carboneres, Salvador. Conversaciones, Situaciones. 1984. pap. text ed. 8.55 (*0-582-22178-1*, 70890); audio 22.61 (*0-582-24270-3*, 70971) Longman.

Leigh, Helena. The Grapes of Paradise. large type ed. 416p. 1986. 23.95 (*0-7089-8326-X*, Charnwood) Ulverscroft.

— Kingdoms of the Vine. large type ed. 352p. 1986. 23.95 (*0-7089-8350-2*, Trail West Pubs) Ulverscroft.

— Wild Vines. large type ed. 448p. 1986. 23.95 (*0-7089-8340-5*, Trail West Pubs) Ulverscroft.

Leigh, Hoyle & Reiser, Morton F. The Patient: Biological, Psychological, & Social Dimensions of Medical Practice. 3rd ed. (Illus.). 496p. 1992. 42.50 (*0-306-44142-X*, Plenum Med Bk) Plenum.

Leigh, I. M., ed. Keratinocyte Methods. (Illus.). 150p. (C). 1995. pap. 54.95 (*0-521-45013-6*) Cambridge U Pr.

Leigh, Ian, jt. auth. see Lustgarten, Laurence.

Leigh, Irene, jt. ed. see McKay, Ian.

Leigh, Irene M. & Watt, Fiona M., eds. Keratinocyte: Methods. LC 93-42614. Date not set. write for info. (*0-521-45103-5*) Cambridge U Pr.

Leigh, Irene M., et al, eds. The Keratinocyte Handbook. LC 93-21304. (Illus.). 425p. (C). 1995. 180.00 (*0-521-43416-5*) Cambridge U Pr.

Leigh, Ivan E., jt. ed. see Pesek, Joseph J.

Leigh, J. H. The Timber Trade: An Introduction to Commercial Aspects. LC 79-42776. 115p. 1980. 58.00 (*0-08-024917-5*, Pub. by Pergamon Repr UK) Franklin.

***Leigh, J. Paul.** Causes of Death in the Workplace. LC 94-36796. 328p. 1995. text ed. 59.95 (*0-89930-951-8*, Quorum Bks) Greenwood.

Leigh, J. R. Applied Control Theory. rev. ed. (IEE Control Engineering Ser.: No. 18). 220p. 1988. pap. 39.00 (*0-86341-089-8*, CER18) Inst Elect Eng.

— Control Theory: A Guided Tour. (Control Engineering Ser.: No. 45). xii, 186p. 1992. 72.00 (*0-86341-241-6*, Pub. by Peregrinus UK); pap. 37.00 (*0-86341-284-X*, Pub. by Peregrinus UK) Inst Elect Eng.

— Essentials of Non-Linear Control Theory. (Topics in Control Ser.: No. 2). 104p. 1983. pap. 39.00 (*0-906048-96-6*, SP006) Inst Elect Eng.

— Functional Analysis & Linear Control Theory. (Mathematics in Science & Engineering Ser.). 1981. text ed. 109.00 (*0-12-441880-5*) Acad Pr.

— Modelling & Control of Fermentation Processes. (Control Engineering Ser.: No. 31). 328p. 1987. 99.00 (*0-86341-104-5*, CE031) Inst Elect Eng.

— Modelling & Simulation. (Topics in Control Ser.: No. 1). 110p. 1983. pap. 39.00 (*0-906048-95-8*, SP009) Inst Elect Eng.

— Temperature Measurement & Control. (Control Engineering Ser.: No. 33). 208p. 1988. 77.00 (*0-86341-111-8*, CE033) Inst Elect Eng.

Leigh, Jack. Nets & Doors. (Illus.). 96p. 1989. 45.00 (*0-941711-12-9*) Wyrick & Co.

Leigh, Jack, illus. Oystering: A Way of Life. LC 83-71934. 1983. 25.00 (*0-910326-17-7*) Carolina Art.

— Oystering: A Way of Life. deluxe limited ed. LC 83-71934. 1983. boxed 150.00 (*0-685-07649-0*) Carolina Art.

***Leigh, Janet.** House of Destiny. (Orig.). 1995. 19.95 (*1-55166-125-X*, Mira Bks) Harlequin Bks.

***Leigh, Janet & Nickens, C.** Psycho: Behind the Scenes of the Classic Thriller. 224p. 1995. 22.00 (*0-517-70112-X*, Harmony) Crown Pub Group.

Leigh, Janice. Consumer Living Trust Guide: The Future & You. 248p. 1992. pap. 19.95 (*1-881306-00-3*) Media Mstr.

***Leigh, Jo.** Hunted. (Intimate Moments Ser.). 1995. mass mkt. 3.75 (*0-373-07659-2*, 1-07659-5) Silhouette.

— Special Effects. 224p. (Orig.). 1992. pap. 2.95 (*1-56597-009-8*, Kismet) Meteor Pub.

— Suspect. 1994. 3.50 (*0-373-07569-3*) Silhouette.

— Wild Beauty. 224p. (Orig.). 1993. pap. 2.95 (*1-56597-092-6*, Kismet) Meteor Pub.

Leigh, John, ed. see Leigh, R. A.

Leigh, Julianne. My Beastiary. Mycue, Edward, ed. (Took Modern Poetry in English Ser.: No. 11). (Illus.). 28p. (Orig.). 1993. pap. 3.00 (*1-879457-05-9*) Norton Coker Pr.

Leigh, Keri. Stevie Ray: Soul to Soul. LC 93-24011. (Illus.). 200p. 1993. pap. 18.95 (*0-87833-838-1*) Taylor Pub.

Leigh, L. H., et al. Introduction to Company Law. 4th ed. 1987. pap. 44.00 (*0-406-63107-7*, U.K.) Butterworth Legal Pubs.

Leigh, L. H. Leigh: Police Powers in England & Wales. 2nd ed. 1985. pap. 46.00 (*0-406-84542-5*) Butterworth Legal Pubs.

Leigh-Loohuizen, Ria, tr. see Morrien, Adrian.

Leigh, Lora. The Club. LC 90-70467. 170p. (Orig.). 1992. pap. 8.00 (*1-56002-124-1*) Aegina Pr.

Leigh, M., jt. auth. see O'Callaghan, A. J.

Leigh, Mark & Lepine, Mike. How to Be a Superhero. 176p. 1992. pap. 7.95 (*1-56163-051-9*) NBM.

Leigh, Maxwell. Touring Southern Africa. (Illus.). 1990. pap. 20.00 (*0-87556-731-2*) Saifer.

Leigh, Meredith. An Elegant Education. 1987. 16.95 (*0-8027-0974-5*) Walker & Co.

Leigh, Micah. Texas Dreams. 512p. 1986. pap. 3.95 (*0-8217-1875-4*) Zebra.

Leigh, Michael. Checklist of Holdings on Borneo in the Cornell University Libraries. LC 67-63728. (Cornell University, Southeast Asia Program, Data Paper Ser.: No. 62). 78p. reprint ed. pap. 25.00 (*0-317-29895-X*, 2021840) Bks Demand.

— Mobilizing Consent: Public Opinion & American Foreign Policy, 1937-1947. LC 75-44656. 256p. 1976. text ed. 45.00 (*0-8371-8772-9*, LMC/, Greenwood Pr) Greenwood.

***Leigh, Michelle D.** Inner Peace, Outer Beauty: Natural Japanese Health & Beauty Secrets Revealed. (Illus.). 224p. 1995. pap. 14.95 (*0-8065-1628-3*, Citadel Pr) Carol Pub Group.

— The Japanese Way of Beauty: Natural Beauty & Health Secrets. (Illus.). 208p. 1992. 22.50 (*1-55972-065-4*, Birch Ln Pr) Carol Pub Group.

— The New Beauty. Calogeras, Meagan, ed. (Illus.). 240p. 1995. pap. 15.00 (*4-7700-1869-X*) Kodansha.

***Leigh, Mike.** Naked & Other Screenplays. 272p. (Orig.). 1995. pap. 18.95 (*0-571-17386-1*) Faber & Faber.

Leigh, Mitch & Darion, Joe. Man of La Mancha: Complete Vocal Score. (Illus.). 150p. pap. 40.00 (*0-89524-265-6*, 3709) Cherry Lane.

— The Man of La Mancha: Complete Vocal Selection. (Illus.). 31p. 1965. pap. 9.95 (*0-89524-091-2*) Cherry Lane.

— Man of La Mancha: Vocal Score. Flato, Ludwig, ed. (Illus.). 150p. (Orig.). 1990. pap. text ed. 40.95 (*0-89524-558-2*) Cherry Lane.

Leigh, Nancey G. Stemming Middle-Class Decline: The Challenges to Economic Development Planning. LC 94-18279. 236p. (C). 1994. pap. text ed. 14.95 (*0-88285-149-7*) Ctr Urban Pol Res.

Leigh, Nigel. Radical Fictions & the Novels of Norman Mailer. LC 89-4564. 280p. 1990. text ed. 39.95 (*0-312-03464-4*) St Martin.

Leigh, Nila K. Learning to Swim in Swaziland: A Child's Eye-View of a Southern African Country. LC 92-13223. (Illus.). 48p. (J). (gr. k-3). 1993. 15.95 (*0-590-45938-4*) Scholastic Inc.

Leigh, Oretta. Aloysius Sebastian Mozart Mouse. (Illus.). 32p. (J). (gr. k-2). 1984. 6.95 (*0-685-09671-8*, Julian Messner) Silver Burdett Pr.

Leigh, P. N. & Swash, Michael, eds. Motor Neuron Disease. LC 94-14875. 1995. 135.00 (*0-387-19685-4*) Spr-Verlag.

***Leigh-Phippard, Helen.** Congress & U. S. Military Aid to Britain: Interdependence & Dependence, 1949-56. LC 94-35564. 1995. write for info. (*0-312-12516-X*) St Martin.

***Leigh, R. & Johnston, A. E., eds.** Long-Term Experiments in Agricultural & Ecological Sciences. 460p. 1994. 95.00x (*0-85198-933-0*) CAB Intl.

Leigh, R. A. Unsolved Problems in the Bibliography of J. J. Rousseau. Leigh, John, ed. (Sandars Lectures in Bibliography). (Illus.). 164p. (C). 1990. 79.95 (*0-521-38481-8*) Cambridge U Pr.

Leigh, R. John & Zee, David S. The Neurology of Eye Movements. 2nd ed. LC 90-14134. (Contemporary Neurology Ser.: No. 35). (Illus.). 561p. 1991. 80.00 (*0-8036-5528-2*) Davis Co.

Leigh, R. W. Dental Morphology & Pathology of Prehistoric Guam. (BMB Ser.). (Orig.). 1929. reprint ed. pap. 15.00 (*0-527-01668-3*) Periodicals Srv.

Leigh, Randy, jt. auth. see Hearn, David.

Leigh, Rhoda. Autumn Love. large type ed. (Linford Romance Library). 208p. 1993. pap. 14.95 (*0-7089-7318-3*, Linford) Ulverscroft.

Leigh, Richard. The Copie of a Letter Sent out of England to Don B. Mendoza. LC 72-6010. (English Experience Ser.: No. 536). 1973. reprint ed. 6.00 (*90-221-0536-9*) Walter J Johnson.

Leigh, Richard, jt. auth. see Baigent, Michael.

Leigh, Robert, comp. Index to Song Books. LC 72-8344. (Music Ser.). 242p. 1973. reprint ed. lib. bdg. 29.50 (*0-306-70553-2*) Da Capo.

Leigh, Robert D. A Free & Responsible Press, a General Report on Mass Communication: Newspapers, Radio, Motion Pictures, Magazines & Books. Commission on Freedom of the Press, ed. LC 46-13. (Midway Reprint Ser.). 139p. 1974. reprint ed. pap. text ed. 10.00 (*0-226-47135-7*) U Ch Pr.

Leigh, Robert D., jt. auth. see White, Llewellyn.

Leigh, Roberta. Bachelor at Heart. (Presents Ser.). 1993. mass mkt. 2.99 (*0-373-11568-7*, 1-11568-2) Harlequin Bks.

— Bachelor at Heart. large type ed. (Harlequin Ser.). 1993. 18.95 (*0-263-13355-9*, Pub. by Mills & Boon UK) Thorndike Pr.

— Flower of the Desert. 1979. pap. 1.75 (*0-449-14150-0*, GM) Fawcett.

— Give a Man a Bad Name. 1994. 2.99 (*0-373-11647-0*) Harlequin Bks.

— Give a Man a Bad Name. large type ed. (Harlequin Ser.). 1994. 18.95 (*0-263-13660-4*) Thorndike Pr.

— Night of Love. 1979. pap. 1.75 (*0-449-14071-7*, GM) Fawcett.

— Not His Kind of Woman. large type ed. 1992. reprint ed. lib. bdg. 18.95 (*0-263-13097-5*, Pub. by Mills & Boon UK) Thorndike Pr.

— One Girl at a Time. large type ed. 1991. reprint ed. lib. bdg. 18.95 (*0-263-12512-2*, Pub. by Mills & Boon UK) Thorndike Pr.

— The Savage Aristocrat. 1980. pap. 1.75 (*0-449-14246-9*, GM) Fawcett.

— Two-Faced Woman. (Presents Ser.). 1993. pap. 2.89 (*0-373-11541-5*, 1-11541-9) Harlequin Bks.

— Two-Timing Man. 1993. mass mkt. 2.99 (*0-373-11609-8*, 1-11609-4) Harlequin Bks.

***Leigh, Roberta & Wentworth, Sally.** The Wrong Kind of Wife. (Presents Ser.). 1995. pap. 3.25 (*0-373-11725-6*, 1-11725-8) Harlequin Bks.

Leigh, Robin. The Hawk & the Heather. 400p. (Orig.). 1992. mass mkt. 4.50 (*0-380-76319-2*) Avon.

Leigh, Ron. Applied Digital Control. 2nd ed. 480p. 1992. pap. text ed. 48.00 (*0-13-044249-6*) P-H.

Leigh, Ronald W., jt. auth. see Elliot, Steven.

Leigh, S. The Haunted Tower. (Puzzle Adventures Ser.). (Illus.). 48p. (J). 1989. lib. bdg. 11.96 (*0-88110-367-5*, Usborne) EDC.

— Journey to the Lost Temple. (Puzzle Adventures Ser.). (Illus.). 48p. (J). 1989. lib. bdg. 11.96 (*0-88110-406-X*); pap. 4.95 (*0-7460-0308-0*) EDC.

— Puzzle Castle. (Young Puzzles Ser.). (Illus.). 32p. (J). (ps up). 1993. lib. bdg. 13.96 (*0-88110-624-0*); pap. 5.95 (*0-7460-1284-5*) EDC.

— Puzzle Dungeon. (Young Puzzles Ser.). (Illus.). 32p. (J). (ps up). 1995. lib. bdg. 13.96 (*0-88110-753-0*, Usborne); pap. 5.95 (*0-7460-1679-4*, Usborne) EDC.

— Puzzle Farm. (Young Puzzles Ser.). (Illus.). 32p. (J). (ps up). 1992. lib. bdg. 13.96 (*0-88110-555-4*, Usborne); pap. 5.95 (*0-7460-0712-4*, Usborne) EDC.

— Puzzle Island. (Young Puzzles Ser.). (Illus.). 32p. (J). (ps up). 1991. lib. bdg. 13.96 (*0-88110-558-9*, Usborne); pap. 5.95 (*0-7460-0596-2*, Usborne) EDC.

— Puzzle Town. (Young Puzzles Ser.). (Illus.). 32p. (J). (ps up). 1991. lib. bdg. 13.96 (*0-88110-554-6*, Usborne); pap. 5.95 (*0-7460-0681-0*, Usborne) EDC.

— Puzzle World (B - U) (Young Puzzles Ser.). (Illus.). 96p. (J). (ps up). 1992. pap. 9.95 (*0-7460-0731-0*) EDC.

— Uncle Pete the Pirate. (Young Puzzle Adventure Ser.). (Illus.). 32p. (J). (ps). 1994. lib. bdg. 12.96 (*0-88110-713-1*, Usborne); pap. 4.95 (*0-7460-1529-1*, Usborne) EDC.

Leigh, Stephen. Ray Bradbury Presents: Dinosaur Warriors. 327p. (Orig.). 1994. mass mkt. 4.99 (*0-380-76280-3*, AvoNova) Avon.

— Ray Bradbury Presents Dinosaur Planet. 304p. (Orig.). 1993. mass mkt. 4.99 (*0-380-76278-1*, AvoNova) Avon.

— Ray Bradbury Presents Dinosaur World. 304p. (Orig.). 1992. mass mkt. 4.99 (*0-380-76277-3*, AvoNova) Avon.

***Leigh, Stephen & Miller, John J.** Ray Bradbury Presents: Dinosaur Empire. (Ray Bradbury Presents Ser.). 256p. (Orig.). 1995. mass mkt. 4.99 (*0-380-76282-X*, AvoNova) Avon.

— Ray Bradbury Presents: Dinosaur Samurai. 256p. (Orig.). 1993. mass mkt. 4.99 (*0-380-76279-X*, AvoNova) Avon.

Leigh, Sue, ed. see Burke, Peter.

Leigh, Sue, ed. see Egmond, Florike.

Leigh, Sue, ed. see Eyerman, Ron.

Leigh, Sue, ed. see Hall, John.

Leigh, Sue, ed. see Moscovici, Serge.

Leigh, Sue, ed. see Nolan, Bryan.

Leigh, Susannah. Dawn of Fire. 384p. 1992. 4.99 (*0-451-40311-8*, Onyx) NAL-Dutton.

— Dawn Shadows. 384p. (Orig.). 1994. pap. 4.99 (*0-451-40510-2*, Topaz) NAL-Dutton.

— Jade Dawn. 384p. 1993. pap. 4.99 (*0-451-40398-3*, Topaz) NAL-Dutton.

— Moonwind. 512p. 1988. pap. 3.95 (*0-317-66162-0*, Sig) NAL-Dutton.

— Puzzle Jungle. (Young Puzzles Ser.). (Illus.). 32p. (J). (ps up). 1995. lib. bdg. 13.96 (*0-88110-767-0*, Usborne); pap. 5.95 (*0-7460-1707-3*, Usborne) EDC.

— Puzzle Planet. (Young Puzzles Ser.). (Illus.). 32p. (J). (gr. k-5). 1993. lib. bdg. 13.96 (*0-88110-646-1*, Usborne); pap. 5.95 (*0-7460-1286-1*, Usborne) EDC.

Leigh, Susannah & Haw, Brenda. Complete Puzzle World. (Young Puzzles Ser.). (Illus.). 1192p. (J). (gr. 2 up). 1994. pap. 18.95 (*0-7460-1859-2*, Usborne) EDC.

— Puzzle Mountain. (Young Puzzles Ser.). (Illus.). 32p. (J). (gr. 2 up). 1994. lib. bdg. 13.96 (*0-88110-665-8*, Usborne); pap. 5.95 (*0-7460-1288-8*, Usborne) EDC.

***Leigh, Tamara.** Pagan Bride. 1995. pap. 5.50 (*0-553-56535-4*) Bantam.

— Virgin Bride. 1994. mass mkt. 5.50 (*0-553-56536-2*) Bantam.

— Warrior Bride. 1994. mass mkt. 5.50 (*0-553-56533-8*) Bantam.

Leigh, Tom, illus. The Sesame Street Word Book. (Golden Bestsellers Ser.). 72p. (J). (ps). 1983. write for info. (*0-307-15549-8*, 15818, Golden Bks) Western Pub.

Leigh, Valentine. A Most Profitable Science of Surveying. LC 72-171772. (English Experience Ser.: No. 397). 128p. 1971. reprint ed. 45.00 (*90-221-0397-8*) Walter J Johnson.

***Leigh, Victoria.** Blackthorne's Woman. (Loveswept Ser.: No. 712). 1994. pap. 3.50 (*0-553-44446-8*, Loveswept) Bantam.

— Sizzling Southwest Cuisine. 48p. 1993. pap. 4.95 (*0-9642805-0-7*) Victoria Leigh.

— Stalking the Giant. (Loveswept Ser.: No. 729). 1995. pap. 3.50 (*0-553-44449-2*, Loveswept) Bantam.

Leigh, Wendy. Liza: Born a Star. large type ed. 1993. 23.95 (*1-56895-010-1*) Wheeler Pub.

— Liza: Born a Star. (Illus.). 344p. 1993. reprint ed. pap. 5.99 (*0-451-40406-8*, Sig) NAL-Dutton.

— Prince Charming: The John F. Kennedy, Jr. Story. 352p. 1994. pap. 5.99 (*0-451-17838-6*) NAL-Dutton.

Leigh, Wilhelmina A. Shelter Affordability for Blacks: Crisis or Clamor? 90p. (Orig.). 1982. pap. 11.95 (*0-87855-901-9*) Transaction Pubs.

Leigh, Wilhelmina A. & Stewart, James B., eds. The Housing Status of Black Americans. 250p. (C). 1991. pap. text ed. 19.95 (*1-56000-579-3*) Transaction Pubs.

Leigh, William E. Business Analysis & Decision Making with Spreadsheet Software. 1991. pap. 14.95 (*0-89600-017-6*) IE Pasadena.

— FORTRAN: The Engineers' & Science Language. 384p. (Orig.). (C). 1987. pap. text ed. 28.95 (*0-938188-67-4*) Mitchell Pub.

— PROLOG to Expert Systems. 288p. (Orig.). (C). 1987. pap. text ed. write for info. (*0-07-555362-7*) McGraw.

Leighfield, M. LRTA (Leisure, Recreation, & Tourism Abstracts) A User Handbook. 125p. (Orig.). 1990. pap. text ed. 30.50 (*0-85198-676-5*) CAB Intl.

Leighland, James & Rappaport, Stephen, eds. The Handbook of Municipal Bonds & Public Finance. LC 92-26109. 1992. write for info. (*0-13-373960-0*) P-H.

Leighland, James, jt. auth. see Hausker, Arthur J.

Leighninger, Leslie. Social Work: Search for Identity. LC 86-12155. (Studies in Social Welfare Policies & Programs: No. 4). 262p. 1987. text ed. 55.00 (*0-313-24775-7*, LSW/, Greenwood Pr) Greenwood.

Leighninger, Leslie, jt. auth. see Popple, Philip R.

Leight, Lynn. Raising Sexually Healthy Children. 304p. 1990. pap. 10.00 (*0-380-70857-4*) Avon.

Leight, Samuel. The Futility of Reformism: A Case for Peaceful Democratic Social Revolution. (Illus.). 229p. 1984. pap. 8.95 (*0-9613654-0-4*) WWW Pubs.

— World Without Wages (Money, Poverty & War!) 229p. 1981. pap. text ed. 8.95 (*0-9613654-1-2*) WWW Pubs.

Leight, Wes. Indoor Soccer Tactics & Skills: The Player's, Coach's, & Fan's Guide to the Secrets of the Indoor Game. (Illus.). 139p. (Orig.). 1987. pap. 13.95 (*0-9619872-0-0*) Green Forest Prods.

Leighten, Patricia. Re-Ordering the Universe: Picasso & Anarchism, 1897-1914. (Illus.). 216p. (C). 1990. text ed. 55.00 (*0-691-04059-1*); pap. text ed. 19.95 (*0-691-00284-3*) Princeton U Pr.

***Leighton.** Window of Time. 1995. 15.95 (*0-9636335-1-1*) Nadja Pub.

Leighton, Alan, tr. see Manchen-Helfen, Otto J.

Leighton, Alexander H. & Leighton, Dorothea C. Lucky the Navajo Singer. Griffen, Joyce J., ed. LC 92-9027. 266p. 1992. 29.95x (*0-8263-1374-4*) U of NM Pr.

An Asterisk (*) at the beginning of an entry indicates that the title is appearing in BIP for the first time.

Leighton, Angela. Victorian Women Poets: Writing Against the Heart. (Victorian Literature & Culture Ser.). 336p. (C). 1992. text ed. 45.00 (0-8139-1426-4); pap. text ed. 14.95 (0-8139-1427-2) U Pr of Va.

***Leighton, Angela, ed.** Victorian Women Poets: A Critical Reader. (Blackwell Critical Readers in Literature Ser.). 272p. (C). 1996. write for info. (0-631-19756-7); pap. write for info. (0-631-19757-5) Blackwell Pubs.

***Leighton, Angela & Reynolds, Margaret, eds.** Victorian Women Poets: An Anthology. (Anthologies Ser.). 800p. 1995. write for info. (0-631-17608-X, Pub. by Polity Pr UK) Blackwell Pubs.

— Victorian Women Poets: An Anthology. (Anthologies Ser.). 800p. 1995. pap. write for info. (0-631-17609-8, Pub. by Polity Pr UK) Blackwell Pubs.

Leighton, Ann. American Gardens in the Eighteenth Century: "For Use or for Delight" LC 86-6975. (Illus.). 544p. 1986. reprint ed. pap. 20.95 (0-87023-531-1) U of Mass Pr.

— American Gardens of the Nineteenth Century: "For Comfort & Affluence" LC 86-11330. (Illus.). 424p. 1987. 37.50 (0-87023-532-X); pap. 18.95 (0-87023-533-8) U of Mass Pr.

— Early American Gardens: "For Meate or Medicine" LC 86-6980. (Illus.). 464p. 1986. pap. 18.95 (0-87023-530-3) U of Mass Pr.

Leighton, B. C., jt. auth. see Bhatia, S. N.

Leighton, Beach. Mr. Dutch: The Arkansas Traveler. LC 91-60004. (Illus.). 263p. 1991. 19.95 (0-915611-44-9) Sagamore Pub.

***Leighton, Betty.** Indiana Album. 200p. Date not set. 7.95 (0-7610-0358-4) NW Pub.

Leighton, C. D. Catholicism in a Protestant Kingdom: A Study of the Irish Ancient "Regime" LC 93-5866. (Studies in Modern History). 250p. 1994. text ed. 65.00 (0-312-10301-8) St Martin.

Leighton, Caroline. Life at Puget Sound. (Illus.). 139p. 1980. 19.95 (0-87770-209-8) Ye Galleon.

***Leighton, Caroline C.** West Coast Journeys, 1865-1879: The Travelogue of a Remarkable Woman. LC 95-12198. 176p. 1995. 14.95 (1-57061-012-6) Sasquatch Bks.

— West Coast Journeys, 1865-1879: The Travelogue of a Remarkable Woman. 176p. 1995. reprint ed. pap. 14.95 (0-614-06286-1) Sasquatch Bks.

Leighton, Clare. The Farmer's Year. (Illus.). 56p. 1993. 50.00 (0-7125-5288-X, Pub. by Sumach UK) Trafalgar.

— Give Us This Day. LC 76-152187. (Essay Index Reprint Ser.). 1977. reprint ed. 19.95 (0-8369-2513-0) Ayer.

— Tempestuous Petticoat: The Story of an Invincible Edwardian. 272p. 1984. reprint ed. pap. 10.00 (0-89733-099-4) Academy Chi Pubs.

— Where Land Meets Sea: The Enduring Cape Cod. LC 54-7922. (Illus.). 208p. 1973. reprint ed. pap. 9.95 (0-85699-056-6) Chatham Pr.

Leighton, Clarence F. Leighton: Memorials of the Leightons of Ulishaven, Forfarshire, & Other Scottish Families of the Name, A. D. 1260-1518 (with Added Pedigress Through 1920's) 126p. 1993. reprint ed. lib. bdg. 37.00 (0-8328-3363-0); reprint ed. pap. 27.00 (0-8328-3364-9) Higginson Bk Co.

Leighton, David, jt. auth. see Stevens, Anne.

Leighton, Dorothea C. & Adair, John. People of the Middle Place: A Study of the Zuni Indians. LC 65-28463. (Monographs). 189p. 1966. pap. 20.00x (0-87536-320-2) HRAFP.

Leighton, Dorothea C., jt. auth. see Kluckhohn, Clyde.

Leighton, Dorothea C., jt. auth. see Leighton, Alexander H.

Leighton, F. Thomson. Introduction to Parallel Algorithms & Architectures: Arrays, Trees & Hypercubes. 500p. 1991. 64.95 (1-55860-117-1) Morgan Kaufmann.

Leighton, F. W., jt. auth. see Hardy, H. R.

Leighton, Frances H. A Basis for Building a Course in Economics of the Home. LC 74-176983. (Columbia University. Teachers College. Contributions to Education Ser.: No. 459). reprint ed. 37.50 (0-404-55459-8) AMS Pr.

Leighton, Frances S., jt. auth. see Collier, Oscar.

Leighton, Frederick W., jt. auth. see Hardy, H. Reginald.

Leighton, George R. Five Cities: The Story of Their Youth & Old Age. 408p. 1974. reprint ed. 24.95 (0-405-02802-4) Ayer.

Leighton, George R., jt. auth. see Brenner, Anita.

Leighton, George R., jt. auth. see Brown, Earl L.

Leighton, Hal. How to Play the Harmonica for Fun & Profit. (Orig.). 1978. 6.50 (0-87505-084-0); pap. 3.00 (0-87505-291-6) Borden.

Leighton-Hardman, A. C. Stallion Management. 1975. pap. 5.00 (0-87980-297-9) Wilshire.

Leighton, Jean. Simone de Beauvoir on Women. LC 74-3615. 230p. 1975. 35.00 (0-8386-1504-X) Fairleigh Dickinson.

Leighton, Lauren G. The Esoteric Tradition in Russian Romantic Literature: Decembrism & Freemasonry. LC 93-13983. Date not set. pap. write for info. (0-271-01025-8) Pa St U Pr.

— The Esoteric Tradition in Russian Romantic Literature: Decembrism & Freemasonry. LC 93-13983. 1994. 39.50 (0-271-01024-X) Pa St U Pr.

— Two Worlds, One Art: Literary Translation in Russia & America. LC 90-28531. 292p. 1991. lib. bdg. 35.00 (0-87580-160-9) N Ill U Pr.

Leighton, Lauren G., ed. Russian Romantic Criticism: An Anthology. LC 86-29605. (Contributions to the Study of World Literature Ser.: No. 18). 227p. 1987. text ed. 49.95 (0-313-25584-9, LRU/, Greenwood Pr) Greenwood.

— Studies in Honor of Xenia Gasiorowska. (Illus.). 191p. (Orig.). 1983. pap. 17.95 (0-89357-102-4) Slavica.

Leighton, Lauren G., ed. see Chukovsky, Kornei.

Leighton, Lauren G., jt. ed. see Gutsche, George J.

Leighton, Lee. Cassidy. 1980. pap. 1.75 (0-345-29120-4) Ballantine.

— Law Man. 1995. 15.95 (0-7451-4621-X, Gunsmoke) Chivers N Amer.

Leighton, Marian. The Deceptive Lure of Detente. 500p. 1989. text ed. 39.95 (0-312-02801-6) St Martin.

— Soviet Propaganda As a Foreign Policy Tool. 198p. (C). 1991. 19.95 (0-932088-51-1) Freedom Hse.

— The Soviet Threat in NATO's Northern Flank. 95p. 1979. pap. 11.95 (0-87855-803-9) Transaction Pubs.

Leighton, Marie C. & Leighton, Robert. Michael Dred, Detective: The Unravelling of a Mystery of Twenty Years. LC 75-32761. (Literature of Mystery & Detection Ser.). (Illus.). 1976. reprint ed. 28.95 (0-405-07882-X) Ayer.

Leighton, Maxinne R. An Ellis Island Christmas. (Illus.). 32p. (J). (ps-3). 1994. pap. 4.99 (0-14-055344-4) Puffin Bks.

— An Ellis Island Christmas. (Illus.). 32p. (J). (gr. 1-4). 1992. 15.00 (0-670-83182-4) Viking Child Bks.

Leighton, Patricia. Schools & Employment Law. Sayer, John, ed. (Education Management Ser.). 192p. 1992. pap. text ed. 29.95 (0-304-32445-0) Cassell.

Leighton, Patricia & Syrett, Michel. New Work Patterns: Putting Policy into Practice. 320p. 1989. 46.50x (0-273-02864-2, Pub. by Pitman Pub Ltd UK) Trans-Atl Phila.

Leighton, Perly, comp. A Leighton Genealogy: Dscendants of Thomas Leighton of Dover New Hampshire, 2 vols. 1054p. 1989. 60.00 (0-88082-023-3, S3-33650) New Eng Hist.

Leighton, Peter. Variable Force Technique. LC 87-63607. (Illus.). 199p. 1988. ring bd. 39.95 (0-945817-01-0) Origin Bks.

Leighton, Ralph. Tuva or Bust! Richard Feynman's Last Journey. (Illus.). 256p. 1992. pap. 11.00 (0-14-015614-3, Penguin Bks) Viking Penguin.

Leighton, Richard J. & Regnery, Alfred S. U. S. Direct Marketing Law: The Complete Handbook for Managers. LC 93-26620. 302p. 1993. 70.00 (1-882222-02-4) Libey Pub.

Leighton, Robert. The Complete Book of the Dog. 1992. lib. bdg. 88.00 (0-8490-5225-4) Gordon Pr.

— Morgantina Studies, Vol. IV: The Protohistoric Settlement on the Cittadella. (Illus.). 265p. 1993. text ed. 80.00 (0-691-04015-X) Princeton U Pr.

Leighton, Robert, jt. auth. see Leighton, Marie C.

Leighton, Robert L., ed. Some Techniques & Procedures in Small Animal Surgery. 3rd ed. 264p. 1982. text ed. 15.00 (0-935078-21-5) Veterinary Med.

Leighton, Robert L. & Jones, Kathy. A Compendium of Small Animal Surgery. (Venture Series in Veterinary Medicine). (Illus.). 282p. (C). 1983. pap. text ed. 36.95 (0-8138-0366-7) Iowa St U Pr.

Leighton, Robert L., jt. auth. see Morgan, Joe P.

***Leighton, S.** Search for Manhood. 1994. pap. 2.99 (0-517-13389-X) Random.

***Leighton, Taigen D., ed. & tr.** Dogen's Pure Standards for the Zen Community: A Translation of Eihei Shingi. Okumura, Shohaku, tr. (Buddhist Studies Ser.). 258p. (C). 1995. text ed. 59.50x (0-7914-2709-9) State U NY Pr.

— Dogen's Pure Standards for the Zen Community: A Translation of Eihei Shingi. Okumura, Shohaku, tr. (Buddhist Studies Ser.). 258p. (C). 1995. pap. text ed. 19.95x (0-7914-2710-2) State U NY Pr.

Leighton, Taigen D. & Wu, Yi, trs. Cultivating the Empty Field: The Silent Illumination of Zen Master Hongzhi. (Illus.). 128p. 1991. 24.95 (0-86547-474-5, North Pt Pr); pap. 11.95 (0-86547-475-3, North Pt Pr) FS&G.

***Leighton, Thomson F. & Maggs, Bruce.** Introduction to Parallel Algorithms & Architectures Vol. 2: Algorithms & VLSI. 1997. 59.95 (1-55860-118-X) Morgan Kaufmann.

Leighton, Timothy G. The Acoustic Bubble. (Illus.). 640p. 1994. text ed. 150.00 (0-12-441920-8) Acad Pr.

Leighton, Tom, tr. see Baciliero, Paolo.

Leighton, Tom, tr. see Bilal, Enki.

Leighton, Tom, tr. see Cadelo, Silvio.

Leighton, Tom, tr. see Christin, Pierre.

Leighton, Tom, tr. see Giardino, Vittorio.

Leighton, Tom, tr. see Magnus, pseud.

Leighton, Tom, tr. see Magnus.

Leighton, Tom, tr. see Manara, Milo.

Leighton, Tom, tr. see Mattioli, Massimo.

Leighton, Tom, tr. see Mattotti, Lorenzo.

Leighton, Tom, tr. see Schultheiss, Matthias.

Leighton, Tom, tr. see Serpieri, Paolo E.

Leighton, Tom, tr. see Tamburini, Stefano, et al.

Leighton, Walter L. French Philosophers - New England Transcendentalism. LC 68-19289. 105p. 1970. reprint ed. text ed. 45.00 (0-8371-0143-3, LEPT, Greenwood Pr) Greenwood.

Leighton, William, tr. see Sachs, Hans.

Leighton, Willie E. Texas: The Way It Was. (Illus.). 272p. 1990. 19.95 (0-9626069-0-1) Insite Pub.

***Leighwood, Kenneth & Aitken, Robert.** Making Schools Smarter: A System for Monitoring School & District Progress. (Illus.). 192p. 1995. pap. 29.95 (0-8039-6292-4) Corwin Pr.

Leigland, Sam, ed. Radical Behaviorism: Willard Day on Psychology & Philosophy. 208p. (Orig.). (C). 1992. text ed. 49.95 (1-878978-08-X); pap. text ed. 29.95 (1-878978-02-0) Context Pr.

Leih, janet, ed. see Bakkum, Maria.

Leih, Janet, ed. see Bogue, Lois.

Leih, Janet, ed. see Dickerson, Stella M.

Leih, Janet, ed. see Eikamp, Helen.

Leih, Janet, ed. see Farmer, Carol P.

Leih, Janet, ed. see Forelle, Helen.

Leih, Janet, ed. see Johnson, Gertrude.

Leih, Janet, ed. see Ovesen, Ellis.

Leih, Janet, ed. see Todd, Wanda.

Leih, Janet, ed. see Winklepleck-Stuefen, Fern E.

Leih, Virginia K. Enjoy! 133p. 1983. pap. 5.95 (0-8341-0814-3) Beacon Hill.

Leijnse. Mathematical Tools - Changing Spatial Scales. 1993. 39.95 (0-8493-8934-8) CRC Pr.

Leijonhufvud. Going Against the Tide: A Study of Dissent in China. (C). 1990. pap. 29.95 (0-7007-0222-9, Pub. by Curzon Pr UK) Humanities.

***Leijonhufvud, Axel & Heymann, Daniel.** High Inflation: The Arne Ryde Memorial Lectures. (Illus.). 238p. 1995. text ed. 39.95 (0-19-828844-1) OUP.

Leik, Robert K. Methods, Logic, & Research of Sociology. LC 72-85667. (Studies in Sociology). (C). 1972. pap. write for info. (0-672-61242-9, Bobbs) Macmillan.

***Leiken, Robert S., ed.** A New Moment in the Americas. LC 94-47503. 1995. write for info. (1-56000-811-3) Transaction Pubs.

Leiken, Robert S., jt. auth. see Carnegie Endowment for International Peace Staff.

Leikin, Ezekiel. The Beilis Transcripts: The Anti-Semitic Trial That Shook the World. LC 92-39643. 280p. 1993. 25.00 (0-87668-179-8) Aronson.

Leikin, Jerrold B., et al. Poisoning & Toxicology Handbook 1995-96. (Clinical Reference Library). 1523p. 1994. pap. 32.50 (0-916589-08-0) Lexi-Comp.

Leikin, Molly-Ann. How to Write a Hit Song: The Complete Guide to Writing & Marketing Chart-Topping Lyrics & Music. 112p. 1989. reprint ed. pap. 9.95 (0-88188-881-8, 00330006) H Leonard.

***Leikola, J. & Contreras, M., eds.** Blood Transfusion Services for the Developing World. (Journal Ser.: Vol. 67, Supplement 5, 1994). (Illus.). iv, 66p. 1994. pap. 28.00 (3-8055-6094-X) S Karger.

Leiman, Arnold L., jt. auth. see Rosenzweig, Mark R.

Leiman, J., ed. see Freedman, Carleton H.

Leiman, Mel. The Political Economy of Racism: A History. LC 92-8518. 421p. (C). 1993. text ed. 63.00 (0-7453-0488-5, Pub. by Pluto Pr UK); pap. text ed. 18.95 (0-7453-0487-7, Pub. by Pluto Pr UK) Westview.

Leiman, Sid Z. The Canonization of Hebrew Scripture: The Talmudic & Midrashic Evidence. 2nd ed. LC 91-72569. (Transactions Ser.: Vol. 47). 242p. 1991. pap. 24.50 (1-878508-04-0) CT Acad Arts & Sciences.

Leiman, Sondra. America: The Jewish Experience. Sarna, Jonathan, ed. (Illus.). (Orig.). (J). (gr. 4-6). 1994. teacher ed 15.00 (0-8074-0501-9, 208034); pap. text ed. 12.00 (0-8074-0500-0, 123938) UAHC.

Leiman, Y., tr. see Oshry, Ephraim.

***Leimann, Dan & Smithson, Kimberly, eds.** The Achievers. 133p. 1994. 34.95 (0-9642203-0-X) Hgh Impact Pr.

***Leimbach, Judy & Vydra, Joan.** Imagination Celebration: Creativity Exercises. Draze, Dianne & Conroy, Sonsie, eds. (Illus.). 64p. (J). (gr. 4-7). 1994. teacher ed 8.95 (1-883055-05-9, 97) Dandy Lion.

Leimbacher, Ed, ed. see Duncan, Don.

Leimberg. Federal Income Tax Law Annual. LC 87-50708. 85.00 (0-685-56162-3) Warren Gorham & Lamont.

Leimberg, Stephan. Tools & Techniques of Life Insurance. Date not set. 37.50 (0-87218-483-8) Natl Underwriter.

Leimberg, Stephan, et al. The Corporate Buy-Sell Handbook: An Essential Guide to Business Succession Planning. 333p. (Orig.). 1992. pap. 32.95 (0-7931-0405-X, 2402-34) Dearborn Finan.

Leimberg, Stephan R. Tools & Techniques of Employee Benefits & Retirement Planning. 2nd ed. LC 90-61466. 453p. (C). 1990. pap. 32.50 (0-87218-474-9) Natl Underwriter.

— Tools & Techniques of Life Insurance. LC 85-62523. 1992. pap. 37.50 (0-87218-438-2) Natl Underwriter.

Leimberg, Stephan R. & Feldman, Linda I. The Deferred Compensation Handbook: A Complete Guide to Non-Qualified Plans. 240p. 1989. 32.95 (0-88462-834-5, 2402-31) Dearborn Finan.

Leimberg, Stephan R., jt. auth. see Plotnick, Charles K.

Leimberg, Stephan R., et al. Stanley & Kilcullen's Federal Income Tax Law. LC 84-50708. 1991. pap. 78.00 (0-7913-0971-1, SK) Warren Gorham & Lamont.

— The Tools & Techniques of Estate Planning. 9th ed. LC 92-61608. 672p. 1992. pap. 37.50 (0-87218-101-4) Natl Underwriter.

— The Tools & Techniques of Financial Planning. 3rd ed. LC 88-62296. 580p. (C). 1989. pap. text ed. 35.00 (0-87218-459-5) Natl Underwriter.

Leimberg, Stephen, jt. auth. see Zaritsky, Howard.

Leimberg, Stephen F., jt. auth. see Zaritsky, Howard M.

Leimbigler, Peter. Dutch, Fast-Track Course. 344p. 1993. 16.95 (0-88432-686-1, FTDU91); audio 125.00 (0-88432-685-3, FTDU20) Audio-Forum.

— German: Fast-Track Course. 340p. 1985. audio 125.00 (0-88432-123-1, FTG100); 15.95 (0-318-58125-6, FTG099) Audio-Forum.

— Japanese: Fast-Track Course. 367p. 1985. 11.95 (0-88432-801-5, FTJ099) Audio-Forum.

— Japanese: Fast-Track Course, Set 6. 367p. 1985. audio 125.00x (0-88432-121-5, FTJ210) Audio-Forum.

— Mandarin: Fast-Track Course. 269p. 1986. audio 125.00x (0-88432-122-3, FTM520); 23.95 (0-88432-802-3, FTM099) Audio-Forum.

Leimenstoll, Jo R. Turkey, Vol. IV. (Historic Preservation in Other Countries Ser.). (Illus.). 54p. (Orig.). (C). 1990. pap. text ed. 15.00 (0-911697-06-3) US ICOMOS.

Leimer, Karl, jt. auth. see Gieseking, Walter.

Leimert, Karen M. Goodnight Blessings. LC 93-41583. (J). (ps-3). 1994. pap. 10.99 (0-8499-1134-6) Word Pub.

Leimone & Earl. Dental Assisting: Basic & Dental Sciences. (Illus.). 384p. 1987. pap. text ed. 33.95 (0-8016-2942-X) Mosby Yr Bk.

Leims, Thomas F. Die Entstehung des Kabuki: Transkulturation Europa-Japan im 16. und 17. Jahrhundert. (Japanese Studies Library: Vol. 2). (Illus.). xviii, 364p. (GER.). 1990. 85.75 (90-04-08988-8) E J Brill.

Lein, Alla Yu, jt. ed. see Brimblecombe, Peter.

***Lein, Clayton D., ed.** British Prose Writers of the Early Seventeenth Century, Vol. 151. LC 95-5786. (Dictionary of Literary Biography Ser.: Vol. 151). 1995. 128.00 (0-8103-5712-7) Gale.

Lein, Laura, ed. Child Care, Higher Education, & Pension System in Japan & the United States. (Special Project Report Ser.). 84p. 1983. 9.00 (0-89940-901-6) LBJ Sch Pub Aff.

Lein, Laura & Rickards, Robert. Property Crime Victims: An Analysis of Needs & Services in Texas. (Special Project Report Ser.). 65p. (Orig.). 1992. pap. text ed. 9.00 (0-89940-872-9) LBJ Sch Pub Aff.

— Services for Crime Victims. (Policy Research Project Report Ser.: No. 92). 76p. 1991. 9.00 (0-89940-700-5) LBJ Sch Pub Aff.

Lein, Laura & Sussman, Marvin B., eds. The Ties That Bind: Men's & Women's Social Networks. LC 82-23230. (Marriage & Family Review Ser.: Vol. 5, No. 4). 111p. 1983. text ed. 29.95 (0-86656-161-7) Haworth Pr.

Lein, Laura, jt. contrib. see Richards, Robert C.

Lein, Laura, jt. auth. see Rickards, Robert.

Leinbach, L. Carl. Calculus Laboratories Using DERIVE. 147p. (C). 1991. pap. 27.95 (0-534-15480-8) PWS Pubs.

Leinbach, L. Carl, et al, eds. The Laboratory Approach to Teaching Calculus. rev. ed. LC 91-62171. (MAA Notes Ser.). 290p. 1991. pap. 24.00 (0-88385-074-5) Math Assn.

Leinbach, Philip E., ed. Personnel Administration in an Automated Environment. LC 90-39450. (Journal of Library Administration: Vol. 13, Nos. 1-2). 207p. 1990. text ed. 39.95 (1-56024-032-6) Haworth Pr.

Leinbach, T., jt. auth. see Brunn, S.

Leinbach, Thomas R. & Chai Lin Sien. South-East Asian Transport: Issues in Development. (East Asian Social Science Monographs). (Illus.). 286p. 1989. 35.00 (0-19-588895-2) OUP.

***Leinberger, Christopher B.** Strategy for Real Estate Companies: Marketing, Finance, Organization. 136p. 1993. pap. text ed. 41.95 (0-87420-742-8, S43) Urban Land.

***Leindler, L.** Strong Approximation by Fourier Series. 209p. (C). 1985. 69.00x (963-05-4044-4, Pub. by Akad Kiado HU) St Mut.

Leindler, Laszlo. Strong Approximation by Fourier Series. 210p. (C). 1985. 157.00 (0-685-46648-5, Pub. by Collets) St Mut.

Leinecker, Richard. Making Noise: Creating Sounds on Your PC. 1994. disk, pap. 24.95 (1-55851-386-8) M&T Bks.

Leinecker, Rick. Developing Dinosaurs & Ancient Worlds. 1994. disk, pap. 34.95 (0-672-30482-1) Sams.

***Leinecker, Rick & Nye, Jamie.** Visual C Plus Plus Power Toolkit: Cutting-Edge Tools & Techniques for Programmers. (Illus.). 1995. audio 49.95 (1-56604-191-0) Ventana Pr.

Leinen, Margaret & Sarnthein, Michael, eds. Paleoclimatology & Paleometeorology: Modern & Past Patterns of Global Atmospheric Transport. (C). 1989. lib. bdg. 246.50 (0-7923-0341-5) Kluwer Ac.

Leinen, Patricia. Arthritis & Ulcer Disease: New Directions & Controversies. (Audioconference Workbook Ser.). (Illus.). 12p. (Orig.). 1994. write for info. (0-944036-98-8) Medicine Grp USA.

— Arthritis & Ulcer Disease: New Directions & Controversies. (Audioconference Manual Ser.). (Illus.). 28p. (Orig.). 1994. (0-944036-96-1) Medicine Grp USA.

Leinen, Patricia, ed. Arthritis & Ulcer Disease: New Directions & Controversies NSAIDS in Arthritis. (Slide Resource Ser.: Pt. 1). (Illus.). (Orig.). 1994. write for info. (1-57130-001-5) Medicine Grp USA.

— Arthritis & Ulcer Disease New Directions & Controversies: Approaches for the Prevention of NSAID-Induced GI Damage & Complications. (Slide Resource Ser.: Pt. 4). (Illus.). (Orig.). 1994. write for info. (1-57130-004-X) Medicine Grp USA.

— Arthritis & Ulcer Disease New Directions & Controversies: Epidemiology of NSAID-Induced GI Damage. (Slide Resource Ser.: Pt. 3). (Illus.). (Orig.). 1994. write for info. (1-57130-003-1) Medicine Grp USA.

— Arthritis & Ulcer Disease New Directions & Controversies: Pathophysiology of GI Injury: NSAIDS & H. Pylori. (Slide Resource Ser.: Pt. 2). (Illus.). (Orig.). 1994. write for info. (1-57130-002-3) Medicine Grp USA.

***Leinen, Patty, ed.** Dornase Alfa in Cystic Fibrosis: Clinical Use & Pharmaeconomic Issues. (Illus.). 1994. write for info. (1-57130-010-4) Medicine Grp USA.

Leinen, Stephen. Gay Cops. LC 93-9216. 320p. (C). 1993. 22.95 (0-8135-2000-2) Rutgers U Pr.

Leinen, Stephen H. Black Police, White Society. LC 83-23622. 250p. 1985. 45.00x (0-8147-5008-7); pap. 17.50x (0-8147-5017-6) NYU Pr.

Leinenweber, John, sel. Letters of Saint Augustine. LC 91-28845. 256p. 1992. pap. 9.95 (0-89243-502-X, Triumph Books) Liguori Pubns.

Leiner, jt. ed. see Rees.

***Leiner, Katherine.** First Children. LC 95-2250. (Illus.). 1995. write for info. (0-615-00510-1, Tambourine Bks) Morrow.

— Halloween. LC 92-39343. (Illus.). 48p. (J). (gr. 2-6). 1993. text ed. 15.95 (0-689-31769-7, Atheneum Bks Young) S&S Childrens.

An Asterisk (*) at the beginning of an entry indicates that the title is appearing in BIP for the first time.

Leiner, Marvin. Sexual Politics in Cuba: Machismo, Homosexuality, & AIDS. LC 93-29166. (Series in Political Economy & Economic Development in Latin America). 184p. 1993. text ed. 50.00 (*0-8133-8654-3*) Westview.

— Sexual Politics in Cuba: Machismo, Homosexuality, & AIDS. (C). 1994. pap. text ed. 18.95 (*0-8133-2122-0*) Westview.

Leinert, Christoph, jt. ed. see Bowyer, Stuart.

Leinfelder, Karl F. & Taylor, Duane F. Laboratory & Clinical Dental Materials. 3rd ed. Moor, Douglas V., ed. (Dental Laboratory Technology Manuals Ser.). xiii, 202p. (C). 1982. pap. 25.00 (*0-8078-7906-1*) U of NC Pr.

Leinfelder, Karl F., et al. Dental Materials & Technical Application. 3rd ed. (Dental Assisting Manuals Ser.: No. 6). ix, 145p. (C). 1980. pap. 18.00 (*0-8078-1380-X*) U of NC Pr.

Leinfellner, Werner & Koehler, E. Developments in the Methodology of Social Science. LC 74-83003. (Theory & Decision Library: No. 6). 400p. 1974. lib. bdg. 140.00 (*90-277-0493-7*); pap. text ed. 90.00 (*90-277-0539-9*) Kluwer Ac.

Leinfellner, Werner, jt. auth. see Gottinger, Hans W.

Leinhardt, Gaea & Beck, Isabel L., eds. Teaching & Learning in History. 280p. 1994. text ed. 59.95 (*0-8058-1245-8*) L Erlbaum Assocs.

Leinhardt, Gaea, et al. Analysis of Arithmetic for Mathematics Teaching. 464p. 1991. text ed. 89.95 (*0-8058-0929-5*) L Erlbaum Assocs.

Leinhardt, Samuel, ed. Sociological Methodology, 1982. LC 68-54940. (Jossey-Bass Social & Behavioral Science Ser.). (Illus.). 406p. reprint ed. pap. 115.80 (*0-8357-4901-0*, 2037831) Bks Demand.

— Sociological Methodology, 1983-1984. LC 68-54940. (Jossey-Bass Social & Behavioral Science Ser.). 383p. reprint ed. pap. 109.20 (*0-8357-4902-9*, 2037832) Bks Demand.

Leinhardt, Samuel, jt. ed. see Holland, Paul W.

Leinhauser, Jean & Weiss, Rita. Seven-Day Afghans. LC 89-22038. (Illus.). 144p. 1990. pap. 12.95 (*0-8069-5709-3*) Sterling.

— Weekend Afghans. (Illus.). 144p. (C). 1990. reprint ed. lib. bdg. 33.00x (*0-8095-7561-2*) Borgo Pr.

Leinieks, Valdis. The Plays of Sophokles. vi, 215p. (Orig.). (C). 1982. pap. 35.00 (*90-6032-226-6*, Pub. by B R Gruener NE) Benjamins North Am.

Leinieks, Valdis, ed. The Structure of Latin: An Introductory Text Based on Caesar & Cicero. 423p. (LAT.). 1975. text ed. 39.50 (*0-8422-5236-3*); pap. text ed. 19.95 (*0-8290-0461-0*) Irvington.

***Leining, Catherine R.** Pollution Prevention: A Guide for Local Government. (Special Report Ser.). (Illus.). 107p. 1994. pap. 28.00 (*0-87326-073-2*) Intl City-Cnty Mgt.

***Leininger.** AIX - 6000 Developer's Tool Kit. 1995. cd-rom, pap. text ed. 49.95 (*0-07-911993-X*) McGraw.

***Leininger, et al.** Mosaic & the New Internet. 1995. cd-rom, pap. text ed. 39.95 (*0-07-912097-0*) McGraw.

Leininger, Anita. Consulting & Independent Contracting. 80p. Date not set. pap. text ed. 25.00 (*0-914548-77-8*) Soc Tech Comm.

Leininger, G. G., jt. auth. see IFAC Symposium Staff.

***Leininger, Kevin E.** Solaris Developer's Tool Kit. LC 94-34427. (J. Ranade Workstation Ser.). 1995. text ed. 70.00 (*0-07-911851-8*); pap. text ed. 49.95 (*0-07-911852-6*) McGraw.

— UNIX Developer's Tool Kit. LC 93-44068. (J. Ranade Workstation Ser.). 1994. text ed. 65.00 (*0-07-911836-4*); pap. text ed. 49.95 (*0-685-70129-8*) McGraw.

***Leininger, Madeleine.** Nursing & Anthropology: Two Worlds to Blend. 180p. (C). 1994. pap. text ed. 17.95 (*1-57074-113-1*) Greyden Pr.

— Transcultural Nursing: Concepts, Theories, & Practices. 532p. 1994. pap. text ed. 25.95 (*1-57074-121-2*) Greyden Pr.

Leininger, Madeleine, ed. Culture Care Diversity & Universality: A Theory of Nursing. LC 15-2402. (Illus.). 448p. (Orig.). (C). 1991. pap. text ed. 34.95 (*0-88737-519-7*) Natl League Nurse.

Leininger, Madeleine & Watson, Jean, eds. The Caring Imperative in Education. 316p. 1990. 22.95 (*0-88737-470-0*) Natl League Nurse.

Leininger, Madeleine, jt. ed. see Gaut, Delores.

Leininger, Madeleine, jt. auth. see Reynolds, Cheryl L.

Leininger, Madeleine M., ed. Care: Discovery & Uses in Clinical & Community Nursing. LC 88-10804. (Human Care & Health Ser.). 202p. 1988. pap. 19.95 (*0-8143-1997-1*) Wayne St U Pr.

— Care: The Essence of Nursing & Health. LC 87-30043. (Human Care & Health Ser.). 276p. (C). 1988. reprint ed. pap. 19.95 (*0-8143-1995-5*) Wayne St U Pr.

— Caring: An Essential Human Need: Proceedings of the Three National Caring Conferences. LC 87-29577. (Human Care & Health Ser.). 177p. (C). 1988. reprint ed. pap. 19.95 (*0-8143-1993-9*) Wayne St U Pr.

— Ethical & Moral Dimensions of Care. LC 90-38404. (Human Care & Health Ser.). 116p. (C). 1990. pap. text ed. 19.95 (*0-8143-2332-4*) Wayne St U Pr.

— Qualitative Research Methods in Nursing. 384p. 1985. text ed. 54.50 (*0-8089-1676-9*, 792508, Grune) Saunders.

Leininger, Phillip, ed. see Hart, James D.

Leininger, Robert. Black Sun. 320p. (Orig.). 1991. mass mkt. 4.50 (*0-380-76012-6*) Avon.

Leininger, Wayne E., jt. auth. see Hicks, James O., Jr.

Leininger, Wayne E., jt. auth. see Killough, Larry N.

Leino, Lily, tr. see Tuominen, Arvo.

Leinonen, George, jt. auth. see Filer, Robert F.

Leins, P., et al, eds. Aspects of Floral Development: Proceedings of the Double Symposium "Floral Development; Evolutionary Aspects & Special Topics" Held at the XIVth International Botanical Congress Berlin, 1987. (Illus.). 239p. 1988. pap. 85.00 (*3-443-50011-0*) Lubrecht & Cramer.

Leinster-Mackay, Donald & Sarfaty, Elizabeth. Education & the Times: An Index of Letters to 1910. 800p. 1995. text ed. 190.00 (*0-7201-2101-9*, Mansell Pub) Cassell.

Leinster, Murray. Forgotten Planet. 209p. 1990. pap. 3.95 (*0-88184-616-3*) Carroll & Graf.

— The Forgotten Planet. 1993. reprint ed. lib. bdg. 18.95 (*0-89968-350-9*, Lghtyr Pr) Buccaneer Bks.

— Quarantine World. 272p. 1992. pap. 4.50 (*0-88184-844-1*) Carroll & Graf.

Leinster, P. & Mitchell, E. Review of Indoor Air Quality & Its Impact on Health & Well-Being of Office Workers, EUR 14029. 118p. 1992. pap. 17.00 (*92-826-4279-8*, CE-NA-14029-EN-C, Pub. by Europ Com) UNIPUB.

***Leinwand, Allan & Conroy, Karen F.** Network Management: A Practical Perspective. 2nd ed. 352p. (C). 1995. pap. text ed. 39.75x (*0-201-60999-1*) Addison-Wesley.

Leinwand, Allan & Fang, Karen. A Practical Approach to Network Management. (Illus.). 256p. (C). 1993. text ed. 40.95 (*0-201-52771-5*) Addison-Wesley.

***Leinwand, Gerald.** American Immigration: Should the Open Door Be Closed? (Impact Bks.). (Illus.). 154p. (YA). (gr. 9-12). 1995. lib. bdg. 14.56 (*0-531-13038-X*) Watts.

— Do We Need a New Constitution? LC 93-31847. (Democracy in Action Ser.). (Illus.). 136p. (YA). (gr. 9-12). 1994. lib. bdg. 14.21 (*0-531-11127-X*) Watts.

— The Environment. (American Issues Ser.). 128p. (YA). (gr. 7-12). 1990. 16.95 (*0-8160-2099-X*) Facts on File.

— Freedom of Speech. (American Issues Ser.). 128p. 1990. 16.95 (*0-8160-2101-5*) Facts on File.

— Public Education. (American Issues Ser.). 128p. (YA). (gr. 7-12). 1992. lib. bdg. 16.95 (*0-8160-2100-7*) Facts on File.

— Teaching of World History. LC 77-95099. (National Council for the Social Studies Bulletin: No. 54). 96p. reprint ed. pap. 27.40 (*0-685-16452-7*, 2052194) Bks Demand.

— Transplants: Today's Medical Miracles. rev. ed. LC 92-17087. (Impact Bks.). (Illus.). (YA). (gr. 9-12). 1992. lib. bdg. 14.42 (*0-531-13026-6*) Watts.

Leinwand, Gerald, ed. see LeVert, Marianne.

Leinwand, Theodore B. The City Staged: Jacobean Comedy, 1603-1613. LC 86-1683. 240p. 1986. text ed. 27.50 (*0-299-10670-5*) U of Wis Pr.

Leinwoll. Low Cholesterol Low Calorie Desserts. 1986. pap. 6.95 (*0-684-13380-6*, Scribners) S&S Trade.

Leipart, Charles. Deep Sleepers. 1989. pap. 4.75 (*0-8222-0297-2*) Dramatists Play.

— The Undefeated Rhumba Champ. 1982. pap. 2.75 (*0-8222-1193-9*) Dramatists Play.

Leiper, jt. auth. see Harris.

Leiper, Brian. Gerbils & Jirds. (C). 1989. 35.00 (*0-946873-94-1*, Pub. by Basset Pubns UK) St Mut.

Leiper, Esther. Stone Country. Mitchell, Carolynn, ed. (Collection of Poetry Ser.). (Illus.). 84p. (Orig.). 1993. pap. text ed. 8.95 (*1-882362-04-7*) Caro-Lynn Pubn.

Leiper, Esther M. Flatlanders Guide to North Country Cooking. Moore, Eugenia, ed. (Illus.). 32p. 1988. pap. 3.95 (*0-9617284-5-0*) Sand & Silk.

— Home from the War. Dermen, Elizabeth & Moore, Eugenia, eds. (Illus.). 32p. (Orig.). 1989. pap. 3.95 (*0-9617284-6-9*) Sand & Silk.

— Tamar's Son & Other Christmas Sonnets. 28p. 1987. pap. 3.95 (*0-9617284-2-6*) Sand & Silk.

Leiper, Esther M., ed. see Lindow, Sandra.

Leiper, Esther M., ed. see Moore, Eugenia.

Leiper, Rob & Field, Vida, eds. Counting for Something: Effective User Feedback in Mental Health Services. 160p. 1993. 54.95 (*1-85628-477-8*, Pub. by Avebury Pub UK) Ashgate Pub Co.

Leipert, Jack. The Master's Plan: How the Church Can Keep You Sane in a Crazy World. LC 93-83259. 112p. (Orig.). 1993. pap. 6.95 (*0-87973-549-X*, 549) Our Sunday Visitor.

— Read the Fine Print Before You Say "I Do" LC 94-5156. 96p. (Orig.). 1994. pap. 5.95 (*0-8091-3464-0*) Paulist Pr.

Leipert, Jack, jt. auth. see Rabior, William.

Leipholz, Horst. Stability of Elastic Systems. (Mechanics of Elastic Stability Ser.: No. 7). 492p. 1980. lib. bdg. 159.50 (*90-286-0050-7*) Kluwer Ac.

— Stability Theory: An Introduction to the Stability of Dynamic Systems & Rigid Bodies. 2nd ed. 1987. text ed. 110.00 (*0-471-91181-X*) Wiley.

Leipholz, Horst, ed. Structural Control. (C). 1987. lib. bdg. 267.50 (*90-247-3429-0*) Kluwer Ac.

Leipholz, Horst & Abdel-Rohman, M. Control of Structures. 1986. lib. bdg. 173.00 (*90-247-3321-9*) Kluwer Ac.

Leipman, Flora. The Long Journey Home: The Memoirs of Flora Leipman. large type ed. (Illus.). 464p. 1988. 15.95 (*0-7089-1801-8*) Ulverscroft.

***Leipnitz, W.** Dictionary of Coal Chemistry & Petrochemistry. (ENG, FRE, GER & RUS.). 1992. 158.00 (*0-7859-8833-5*) Fr & Eur.

Leipnitz, Walter. Dictionary of Coal Chemistry & Petrochemistry: English-German-French-Russian. rev. ed. 340p. (ENG, FRE, GER & RUS.). 1992. 158.00 (*3-86117-039-6*, Pub. by A Hatier GW) IBD Ltd.

— Woerterbuch Erdoelverarbeitung-Petrolchemie: Dictionary of Petroleum-Processing. (ENG, FRE, GER & RUS.). 1977. 125.00 (*0-8288-5568-4*, M6925) Fr & Eur.

Leipold, Alessandro, et al. International Capital Markets: Developments & Prospects. (World Economic & Financial Surveys Ser.). vii, 136p. 1991. pap. 20.00 (*1-55775-218-4*) Intl Monetary.

Leipold, Dieter. Beweismass und Beweislast im Zivilprozess. (Schriftenreihe der Juristischen Gesellschaft zu Berlin Ser.: Heft 93). 26p. (GER.). 1985. pap. 13.85 (*3-11-010580-2*) De Gruyter.

Leipoldt, Gabriele. Zur Biologie des Phytopathogenen Pilzes: Gerlachia nivalis (Erreger des Schneeschimmels) Molekularbiologische Untersuchungen an verschiedenen Feldisolaten. (Bibliotheca Mycologica Ser.: Vol. 109). (Illus.). 164p. (GER.). (C). 1987. pap. text ed. 56.95 (*3-443-59010-1*) Lubrecht & Cramer.

Leipp, Emile. The Violin: History, Aesthetics, Manufacture, & Acoustics. Parry, Hildegarde W., tr. LC 79-414278. (Illus.). 126p. reprint ed. pap. 36.00 (*0-317-09906-X*, 2014298) Bks Demand.

Leippe, Michael R., jt. auth. see Zimbardo, Philip G.

Leipunskii, O. I., et al. The Propagation of Gamma Quanta in Matter. 1965. 85.00 (*0-08-010553-X*, Pub. by Pergamon Repr UK); pap. 101.00 (*0-08-013564-1*, Pub. by Pergamon Repr UK) Franklin.

***Leipzig, Arthur.** Growing Up in New York. (Imago Mundi Ser.). 132p. 1995. 40.00 (*1-56792-051-9*) Godine.

— Sarah's Daughters: A Celebration of Jewish Women. Gould, Nathan & Vitiello, Jane K., eds. (Illus.). 94p. 1988. 25.00 (*0-685-26588-9*) Womens Am ORT.

Leipzig, Marwayne. Beginner's Guide to Easy Horo Const. 1978. 6.00 (*0-86690-211-2*, L1273-014) Am Fed Astrologers.

Leipziger, Danny M. & Petri, Peter A. Korean Industrial Policy: Legacies of the Past & Directions for the Future. LC 93-7329. (Discussion Paper, East Asia & Pacific Region Ser.: Vol. 197). 52p. 1993. 6.95 (*0-8213-2414-4*, 12414) World Bank.

Leipziger, Danny M. & Thomas, Vinod. The Lessons of East Asia: An Overview of Country Experience - Experiencia de Asia Oriental. 48p. (SPA.). 1993. 6.95 (*0-8213-2743-7*, 12743) World Bank.

Leipziger, Danny M. & Thomas, Vinrod. The Lessons of East Asia: An Overview of Country Experience - Experiencia de Asia Oriental. 48p. 1993. 6.95 (*0-8213-2607-4*, 12607) World Bank.

Leipziger, Danny M., jt. auth. see Kim, Kihwan.

Leipziger, Danny M., et al. The Distribution of Income & Wealth in Korea. LC 92-14468. (EDI Development Studies). 135p. 1992. 9.95 (*0-8213-2124-2*, 12124) World Bank.

Leira, Arnlaug. Welfare States & Working Mothers: The Scandinavian Experience. (Illus.). 192p. (C). 1992. 54.95 (*0-521-41720-1*) Cambridge U Pr.

Leiren, Terje I. & Lovoll, Odd S. Marcus Thrane: A Norwegian Radical in America. (Biographical Series: Special Publications). (Illus.). 167p. 1987. 12.00 (*0-87732-073-X*) Norwegian-Am Hist Assn.

***Leiren, William.** Shakespeare's Coloring Book. 50p. (YA). 1993. pap. 4.95 (*1-56850-032-7*) Chicago Plays.

Leiris, M., ed. see Miro, Joan.

Leiris, Michael. Aurora. Warby, Anna, tr. 1991. pap. 12.50 (*0-947757-25-2*) Serpents Tail.

Leiris, Michel. L' Afrique Fantome. (FRE.). 1988. pap. 38.95 (*0-7859-2938-X*, 2070711889) Fr & Eur.

— Age d'Homme. (Folio Ser.: No. 435). (FRE.). pap. 8.95 (*2-07-036435-6*) Schoenhof.

— Aurora. (Imaginaire Ser.). 193p. (FRE.). 1977. pap. 11.95 (*2-07-029647-4*) Schoenhof.

— Biffures. (Imaginaire Ser.). (FRE.). 1975. pap. 13.95 (*2-07-072348-8*) Schoenhof.

— Brisees. (FRE.). 1992. pap. 19.95 (*0-7859-2826-X*, 2070326837) Fr & Eur.

— Contacts de Civilisations en Martinique et en Guadeloupe. 191p. (Orig.). (FRE.). 1986. pap. text ed. 16.00 (*92-3-200422-4*, UFP17) UNIPUB.

— Fourbis. (Imaginaire Ser.). (FRE.). 1991. pap. 12.95 (*2-07-072347-X*) Schoenhof.

— Haut Mal. Autres Lancers. (Poesie Ser.). 256p. (FRE.). 1969. pap. 9.95 (*2-07-030166-4*) Schoenhof.

— Langage, Tangage Ou Ce Que les Mots Me Disent. (Gallimard Ser.). 188p. (FRE.). 1985. pap. 25.95 (*2-07-070442-4*) Schoenhof.

— Manhood: A Journey from Childhood into the Fierce Order of Virility. Howard, Richard, tr. LC 84-60687. 184p. (Orig.). 1992. pap. 12.95 (*0-226-47141-1*) U Ch Pr.

— Nights as Day, Days as Night. Sieburth, Richard, tr. LC 87-83301. 169p. 1988. 22.00 (*0-941419-06-1*, Eridanos Library); pap. 13.00 (*0-941419-07-X*, Eridanos Library) Marsilio Pubs.

— La Regle du Jeu, Vol. 1: Biffures. (FRE.). 1991. pap. 16.95 (*0-7859-2947-9*) Fr & Eur.

— La Regle du Jeu, Vol. 2: Fourbis. (FRE.). 1991. pap. 15.95 (*0-7859-3395-6*) Fr & Eur.

— La Regle du Jeu, Vol. 3: Fibrilles. (FRE.). 1991. pap. 16.95 (*0-7859-2953-3*) Fr & Eur.

— La Regle du Jeu, Vol. 4: Frele Bruit. (FRE.). 1991. pap. 19.95 (*0-7859-2954-1*) Fr & Eur.

— Ruban au Cou d'Olympia. (Imaginaire Ser.). (FRE.). pap. 14.95 (*2-07-071702-X*) Schoenhof.

— Zebrage. (FRE.). 1992. pap. 17.95 (*0-7859-2828-6*) Fr & Eur.

Leiris, Michel, ed. see Miro, Joan.

Leirman, Walter. Four Cultures of Education: Engineer, Expert, Communicator, Prophet. LC 94-1338. 1994. write for info. (*3-631-47097-5*) P Lang Pubs.

Leirman, Walter & Kulich, Jindra, eds. Adult Education & the Challenges of the 1990's. 224p. 1987. lib. bdg. 47.50 (*0-7099-4169-2*, Pub. by Croom Helm UK) Routledge Chapman & Hall.

***Leirner, Jac, text.** Leirner, Jac. (Illus.). 1991. pap. 21.00 (*0-905836-74-X*, Pub. by Museum Modern Art UK) St Mut.

Leis, Brian N. Environmentally Assisted Cracking: Science & Engineering, STP 1049. Lisagore, W. Barry & Crooker, Thomas W., eds. LC 89-18581. (Special Technical Publication (STP) Ser.). (Illus.). 555p. 1990. text ed. 112.00 (*0-8031-1276-9*, 04-010490-30) ASTM.

Leis, Brian N., jt. ed. see Crooker, T. W.

Leis, J. M., et al. The Larvae of Indo-Pacific Shorefishes. (Illus.). 375p. 1989. text ed. 32.00 (*0-8248-1265-4*) UH Pr.

Leis, Philip E. Enculturation & Socialization in an Ijaw Village. Spindler, George & Spindler, Louise, eds. (Case Studies in Cultural Anthropology). 128p. 1983. reprint ed. pap. text ed. 6.95 (*0-8290-0306-1*) Irvington.

Leis, Philip E., jt. auth. see Hollos, Marida.

Leis, R. Initial Value Boundary Problems in Mathematical Physics. LC 85-12473. 266p. 1986. text ed. 180.00 (*0-471-90863-0*) Wiley.

Leis, R., jt. ed. see Hildebrandt, S.

Leisch, Juanita. An Introduction to Civil War Civilians. (Illus.). 86p. (C). 1994. pap. text ed. 7.95 (*0-939631-70-9*) Thomas Publications.

Leisegang, Hans. Einfuehrung in die Philosophie. 8th ed. (Sammlung Goeschen Ser.: Vol. 4281). 148p. (C). 1973. pap. 12.95 (*3-11-004626-1*) De Gruyter.

— Pneuma Hagion. Nr. 4. vi, 150p. 1970. reprint ed. write for info. (*0-318-70959-7*, Pub. by Georg Olms GW) Lubrecht & Cramer.

Leisenring, A. C. Mathematical Logic & Hilbert's E-Symbol. 152p. 1969. text ed. 154.00 (*0-677-61790-9*) Gordon & Breach.

***Leiser.** Orvis Guide Beginning Fly Tying. 1995. pap. text ed. 9.95 (*1-55821-372-4*) Lyons & Burford.

Leiser, Andrew T., jt. auth. see Gray, Donald H.

Leiser, Andrew T., jt. auth. see McClintock, Elizabeth.

Leiser, Burton M. Liberty, Justice & Morals: Contemporary Value Conflicts. 3rd ed. 579p. (C). 1986. pap. write for info. (*0-02-369530-7*) Macmillan.

Leiser, Clara. Jean De Reszke & the Great Days of Opera. LC 77-107814. (Select Bibliographies Reprint Ser.). 1977. 30.95 (*0-8369-5187-5*) Ayer.

Leiser, D. & Gillieron, C. Cognitive Science & Genetic Epistemology: A Case Study of Understanding. LC 89-22970. (PATH in Psychology Ser.). (Illus.). 216p. 1990. 45.00 (*0-306-43193-9*, Plenum Pr) Plenum.

Leiser, Eric. Book of Fly Patterns. LC 87-45102. 496p. 1987. 49.50 (*0-394-54394-7*) Knopf.

— The Complete Book of Fly Tying. LC 77-74975. 1977. 27.50 (*0-394-40047-X*) Knopf.

— The Dettes - A Catskill Legend: Their Story & Their Techniques. 264p. 1992. 35.00 (*0-9632705-0-8*) Willowkill Pr.

Leiser, Eric & Boyle, Robert H. Stoneflies for the Angler. LC 90-9576. (Illus.). 192p. 1990. reprint ed. pap. 14.95 (*0-8117-2401-8*) Stackpole.

Leiser, Gary, ed. & tr. A History of the Seljuks: Ibrahim Kafesoglu's Interpretation & the Resulting Controversy. LC 87-26377. 219p. 1988. text ed. 40.00 (*0-8093-1414-2*) S Ill U Pr.

Leiser, Gary, ed. see Koprulu, M. Fuad.

Leiser, Gary, ed. see Koprulu, Mehmed F.

Leiser, Gary, ed. see Olcen, Mehmet A.

Leiser, Joseph. American Judaism: The Religion & Religious Institutions of the Jewish People in the United States. LC 78-26230. 1979. reprint ed. text ed. 69.50 (*0-313-20879-4*, LEAJ, Greenwood Pr) Greenwood.

Leiserson, Avery. Administrative Regulation: A Study in Representation of Interests. rev. ed. LC 74-12761. 292p. 1975. reprint ed. lib. bdg. 22.50 (*0-8371-7744-8*, LEAR, Greenwood Pr) Greenwood.

Leiserson, Avery, et al. Political Research & Political Theory. Garceau, Oliver, ed. LC 68-28693. (Illus.). 268p. reprint ed. pap. 76.40 (*0-7837-4470-6*, 2044178) Bks Demand.

Leiserson, Charles E. Area-Efficient VLSI Computation. (Association for Computing Machinery Doctoral Dissertation Award Ser.). (Illus.). 152p. 1983. pap. 32.50x (*0-262-12102-6*) MIT Pr.

Leiserson, Mark W. Wages & Economic Control in Norway, 1945-1957. LC 59-5565. (Wertheim Publications in Industrial Relations). 190p. 1959. 12.50 (*0-674-94470-4*) HUP.

Leiserson, William M. American Trade Union Democracy. LC 75-40926. 354p. 1976. reprint ed. text ed. 65.00 (*0-8371-8688-9*, LEAT, Greenwood Pr) Greenwood.

Leisher, Gary, tr. see Koprulu, Mehmed F.

Leisher, William & Amt, Richard. Required Photographic Documentation & Equipment. 1980. 4.50 (*0-318-18701-9*) Am Inst Conser Hist.

Leishman, J. B., tr. see Rilke, Rainer Maria.

Leishman, Robert K., ed. see Marshburn, Tom.

Leisi, Ernst & Schlesinger, Eilhard. Der Zeuge im Attischen Recht & die Griechische Asylie, 2 vols. in one. Vlastos, Gregory, ed. LC 78-14608. (Morals & Law in Ancient Greece Ser.). 1979. reprint ed. lib. bdg. 23.95 (*0-405-11584-9*) Ayer.

Leising, Marlene. Everyday & Gourmet Microwave Cookbook. 196p. 1980. pap. 8.95 (*0-9606096-0-1*) Micro Magic.

Leisinger, Klaus. All Our People: Population Policy with a Human Face. LC 93-50647. 350p. 1994. text ed. 45.00 (*1-55963-292-5*); pap. text ed. 24.95 (*1-55963-293-3*) Island Pr.

Leisinger, T., et al, eds. Microbial Degradation of Xenobiotics & Recalcitrant Compounds. LC 81-67908. 1982. text ed. 157.00 (*0-12-442920-3*) Acad Pr.

Leisink, Peter, jt. ed. see Coenen, Harry.

An Asterisk (*) at the beginning of an entry indicates that the title is appearing in BIP for the first time.

Leisner, Marcia. Literary Neighborhoods of New York. LC 88-34870. (Literary Cities Ser.). (Illus.). 72p. (Orig.). 1989. pap. 8.95 (*0-913515-40-X*, Starrhill) Elliott & Clark.

Leiss, Elisabeth. Die Verbalkategorien des Deutschen: Ein Beitrang Zur Theorie der Sprachlichen Kategorisierung. (Studia Linguistica Germanica: No. 31). vi, 334p. (GER.). (C). 1992. lib. bdg. 107.70 (*3-11-012746-6*) De Gruyter.

***Leiss, Ernst L.** Parallel & Vector Computing: A Practical Introduction. LC 94-41072. (Computer Engineering Ser.). 1995. text ed. 55.00 (*0-07-037692-1*) McGraw.

— Principles of Data Security. LC 82-22272. (Foundations of Computer Science Ser.). 238p. 1982. 45.00 (*0-306-41098-2*, Plenum Pr) Plenum.

Leiss, William. C. B. Macpherson: Dilemmas of Liberalism & Socialism. 192p. 1988. text ed. 29.95 (*0-312-02475-4*) St Martin.

— The Domination of Nature. LC 94-900223. 272p. (C). 1994. pap. text ed. 19.95 (*0-7735-1198-9*, Pub. by McGill CN) U of Toronto Pr.

— Ecology Versus Politics in Canada. 1979. pap. 13.95 (*0-8020-6332-2*) U of Toronto Pr.

— The Limits to Satisfaction: An Essay on the Problem of Needs & Commodities. 184p. (C). 1988. reprint ed. pap. 22.95 (*0-7735-0688-8*, Pub. by McGill CN) U of Toronto Pr.

— Under Technology's Thumb. 184p. (C). 1990. pap. text ed. 19.95 (*0-7735-0748-5*, Pub. by McGill CN) U of Toronto Pr.

Leiss, William & Chociolko, Christina. Risk & Responsibility. 424p. 1994. 55.00 (*0-7735-1177-6*, Pub. by McGill CN); pap. 22.95 (*0-7735-1194-6*, Pub. by McGill CN) U of Toronto Pr.

Leiss, William, et al. Social Communication in Advertising: Persons, Products & Images of Well-Being. (Illus.). 327p. 1986. pap. 14.95 (*0-415-90084-0*, 9685, Routledge NY) Routledge.

— Social Communication in Advertising: Persons, Products & Images of Well-Being. 2nd ed. 1990. pap. 14.95 (*0-415-90354-8*, A4785, Routledge NY) Routledge.

Leister, Jack, et al. California Politics & Government, 1970-1983: A Selected Bibliography. LC 84-23492. (Occasional Bibliographies Ser.: No. 3). 86p. reprint ed. pap. 25.00 (*0-7837-2135-8*, 2042417) Bks Demand.

Leister, Mary. Seasons of Heron Pond: Wildings of Air, Earth, & Water. LC 81-9408. (Illus.). 192p. 1981. 10.95 (*0-916144-84-4*) Stemmer Hse.

— Wee Green Witch. LC 78-12380. (Illus.). 44p. (J). (ps up). 1978. 12.95 (*0-916144-30-5*) Stemmer Hse.

— Wildlings. LC 76-2063. (Illus.). 192p. 1976. 14.95 (*0-916144-06-2*) Stemmer Hse.

Leistico, Agnes. I Learn Better by Teaching Myself. 2nd ed. Hegener, Helen, ed. 152p. 1990. pap. 9.75 (*0-945097-10-7*) Home Educ Pr.

— Still Teaching Ourselves. LC 95-10137. 1995. write for info. (*0-945097-27-1*) Home Educ Pr.

Leistner, G. Abbreviations Guide to French Forms in Justice & Administration. 2nd ed. 101p. (ENG, FRE & GER.). 1975. 49.95 (*0-8288-5785-7*) Fr & Eur.

Leistritz, F. Larry & Hamm, Rita R., eds. Economic Development, 1975-1993: An Annotated Bibliography. LC 94-6778. (Bibliographies & Indexes in Economics & Economic History Ser.: No. 16). 320p. 1994. text ed. 65.00 (*0-313-29159-4*, Greenwood Pr) Greenwood.

Leistritz, F. Larry, jt. auth. see Murdock, Steve H.

***Leisure Arts Staff.** The Cookie Jar. 1995. 19.95 (*0-942237-50-1*) Leisure AR.

— Easy Does It. 1994. 8.95 (*0-942237-39-0*) Leisure AR.

— In the Nick of Time. LC 94-75390. 1994. 19.95 (*0-942237-38-2*) Leisure AR.

— Quilt Book I. 1994. 24.95 (*0-942237-43-9*) Leisure AR.

— Seasons Remembered. 1995. 24.95 (*0-942237-40-4*) Leisure AR.

— Spirit of Christmas, Bk. 8. LC 93-80809. 1994. 24.95 (*0-942237-36-6*) Leisure AR.

Leisure, Jerry, jt. auth. see Block, Jonathan.

Leitao, Vitor. Boundary Elements in Non Linear Fracture Mechanics. LC 94-72219. (Topics in Engineering Ser.: No. 21). 288p. 1994. text ed. 119.00 (*1-56252-259-0*) Computational Mech MA.

Leitch, A. R., et al. In Situ Hybridization. (Microscopy Handbook Ser.: No. 27). (Illus.). 128p. (Orig.). 1994. pap. 39.50 (*1-872748-48-1*, Pub. by Bios Scientific UK) Coronet Bks.

Leitch, Alexander. A Princeton Companion. LC 78-51178. 1978. 49.50 (*0-691-04654-9*) Princeton U Pr.

Leitch, Barbara, et al. A Concise Dictionary of Indian Tribes of North American. 2nd rev. ed. Irvine, Keith, ed. write for info. (*0-917256-48-4*) Ref Pubns.

Leitch, Carol, jt. auth. see Clack, Alice.

Leitch, Carol, jt. auth. see Clark, Alice.

Leitch, E. C. & Scheibner, E., eds. Terrane Accretion & Orogenic Belts. (Geodynamics Ser.: Vol. 19). (Illus.). 343p. 1987. 38.00 (*0-87590-516-1*) Am Geophysical.

Leitch, Gordon, Jr. From Dollar to Counterfeit: The Path of American Government Dishonesty. LC 80-71064. (Illus.). 168p. (Orig.). (gr. 9-12). 1981. pap. 8.00 (*0-9605734-1-0*) Bicent Era.

— The Monetary Errors & Deceptions of the Supreme Court. LC 78-57901. 166p. (YA). (gr. 9-12). 1978. pap. 5.00 (*0-9605734-0-2*) Bicent Era.

— U. S. Government & IRS Tax Cheating. 7p. 1992. 1.00 (*0-9605734-2-9*) Bicent Era.

Leitch, J. M., ed. see International Congress of Food & Science Technology Staff.

Leitch, James W., tr. see Conzelmann, Hans.

Leitch, James W., tr. see Ebeling, Gerhard.

Leitch, James W., tr. see Moltmann, Jurgen.

Leitch, Jay A. & Ekstrom, Brenda L. Wetland Economics & Assessment: An Annotated Bibliography. LC 88-30977. 208p. 1989. 29.00 (*0-8240-3648-4*, SS508) Garland.

***Leitch, Jay A. & Ludwig, Herbert R.** Wetland Economics, 1989-1993: A Selected Annotated Bibliography. LC 94-39564. (Bibliographies & Indexes in Economics & Economic History Ser.: Vol. 17). 152p. 1995. text ed. 65.00 (*0-313-29286-8*, Greenwood Pr) Greenwood.

Leitch, Mary. Seven Years in Ceylon: Stories of Mission Life. 1993. reprint ed. 24.00 (*81-7013-105-7*, Pub. by Navrang) S Asia.

Leitch, Mary, jt. auth. see Escalona, Sybelle K.

Leitch, R. D. BASIC Reliability Engineering Analysis. (Illus.). 168p. 1988. pap. text ed. 24.95 (*0-408-01830-5*) Buttrwrth-Heinemann.

Leitch, R. R., jt. auth. see Tokhi, M. O.

***Leitch, Richard D., et al.** Japan's Role in the Post Cold War World. LC 95-9875. (Contributions in Political Science Ser.: Vol. 361). 1995. text ed. write for info. (*0-313-29731-2*, Greenwood Pr) Greenwood.

Leitch, Robert A. & Davis, Roscoe K. Accounting Information Systems: Theory & Practice. 2nd ed. 768p. (C). 1992. text ed. write for info. (*0-13-006032-1*) P-H.

Leitch, Robert A., jt. auth. see McKeown, Patrick G.

***Leitch, Roger D.** Reliability Analysis for Engineers: An Introduction. (Illus.). 248p. 1995. 70.00 (*0-19-856372-8*); pap. 28.00 (*0-19-856371-X*) OUP.

Leitch, Thomas M. Find the Director & Other Hitchcock Games. LC 90-45353. 296p. 1991. pap. 15.00 (*0-8203-1341-6*) U of Ga Pr.

— Lionel Trilling: An Annotated Bibliography. LC 92-23192. (Bibliographies of Modern Critics & Critical Schools Ser.: Vol. 19). 672p. 1992. 99.00 (*0-8240-7128-X*, H1303) Garland.

— What Stories Are: Narrative Theory & Interpretation. LC 85-43559. 232p. 1986. 20.00 (*0-271-00431-2*) Pa St U Pr.

Leitch, Vincent B. American Literary Criticism from the Thirties to the Eighties. 480p. 1989. text ed. 67.00 (*0-231-06426-8*); pap. text ed. 18.00 (*0-231-06427-6*) Col U Pr.

— Cultural Criticism, Literary Theory, Poststructuralism. 192p. 1992. 29.50 (*0-231-07970-2*) Col U Pr.

— Cultural Criticism, Literary Theory, Poststructuralism. 192p. 1992. pap. 15.50 (*0-231-07971-0*) Col U Pr.

— Deconstructive Criticism: An Advanced Introduction & Survey. LC 82-1120. 256p. 1982. text ed. 50.50 (*0-231-05472-6*); pap. text ed. 18.50 (*0-231-05473-4*) Col U Pr.

Leitch, William. South America's National Parks: A Visitor's Guide. LC 90-35389. (Illus.). 336p. (Orig.). 1990. 25.00 (*0-89886-259-0*); pap. 16.95 (*0-89886-248-5*) Mountaineers.

Leitch, William C. Argentine Trout Fishing: A Fly Fisherman's Guide to Patagonia. (Illus.). 192p. 1991. 34.95 (*1-878175-07-6*); pap. 24.95 (*1-878175-06-8*) F Amato Pubns.

Leite, E. B., jt. ed. see Cunha-Vaz, J. G.

Leite, Evelyn. Mending Family Relationships. 44p. (Orig.). 1987. pap. 3.95 (*0-9613416-7-X*) Comm Intervention.

— Newcomers to Al-Anon. 22p. (Orig.). 1979. pap. 1.55 (*0-89486-075-5*, 1285B) Hazelden.

— Saving Face Through Surrender & Grace: A First Step Guide for Codependents. 24p. (Orig.). 1988. pap. 3.95 (*0-945485-03-4*) Comm Intervention.

Leite, Evelyn & Espeland, Pamela. Different Like Me: A Book for Teens Who Worry about Their Parents' Use of Alcohol - Drugs. (Illus.). 120p. (Orig.). 1987. pap. text ed. 8.95 (*0-935908-34-X*, P097) Johnsn Inst.

Leite, George & Porter, Bern, eds. Circle (Ten Issues), 2 vols., 1. (Avant-Garde Magazines Ser.). 890p. 1974. reprint ed. 30.95 (*0-405-01760-X*) Ayer.

— Circle (Ten Issues), 2 vols., 2. (Avant-Garde Magazines Ser.). 890p. 1974. reprint ed. 30.95 (*0-405-01761-8*) Ayer.

— Circle (Ten Issues), 2 vols., Set. (Avant-Garde Magazines Ser.). 890p. 1974. reprint ed. 60.95 (*0-405-01756-1*) Ayer.

Leite, J. R., et al, eds. Semiconductor Physics: Proceedings of the 5th Brazilian School. 450p. (C). 1992. text ed. 127.00 (*981-02-0613-5*) World Scientific Pub.

Leiten, Georges K. Colonialism, Class & Nation: The Confrontation in Bombay 1930. 1985. 22.50 (*0-8364-1274-5*, Pub. by KP Bagchi IA) S Asia.

Leitenberg, Harold, ed. Handbook of Social & Evaluation Anxiety. LC 90-6853. (Illus.). 570p. 1990. 85.00 (*0-306-43438-5*, Plenum Med Bk) Plenum.

Leitenberg, Milton. Soviet Submarine Operations in Swedish Waters 1980-1986. LC 87-13216. (Washington Papers: No. 128). 208p. 1987. text ed. 45.00 (*0-275-92841-1*, C2841, Praeger Pubs); pap. text ed. 11.95 (*0-275-92842-X*, B2842, Praeger Pubs) Greenwood.

Leiter, Elliot, intro. The Second International Congress on Ethics in Medicine, 1987: Proceedings. 224p. 1988. 30.00 (*0-685-22943-2*) BIMC.

Leiter, Jeffrey, et al, eds. Hanging by a Thread: Social Change in Southern Textiles. 256p. (Orig.). 1991. 32.00 (*0-87546-173-5*); pap. 14.95 (*0-87546-174-3*) ILR Pr.

Leiter, John S. Successful Parenting: A Common Sense Guide to Raising Your Teenagers. 1991. pap. 11.95 (*1-55874-156-9*) Health Comm.

***Leiter, Lawrence A., ed.** The Endocrine Society Forty-Sixth Annual Postgraduate Assembly Syllabus, 1994. (Illus.). 350p. (C). 1994. pap. text ed. 45.00 (*1-879225-15-8*) Endocrine Soc.

Leiter, Louis H., jt. auth. see Clerc, Charles.

Leiter, Michael P. & Webb, Mark. Developing Human Service Networks: Community & Organizatonal Relations. LC 83-4352. 279p. 1983. text ed. 29.50 (*0-8290-1262-1*) Irvington.

Leiter, Richard A. National Survey of State Laws 1992, Vol. 1. 1993. 55.00 (*0-8103-8406-X*) Gale.

— New Frontiers in Forensic & Demonstrative Evidence: A Bibliography. (Legal Bibliography Ser.: No. 29). 27p. (Orig.). 1985. pap. 15.00 (*0-935630-12-0*) U of Tex Tarlton Law Lib.

Leiter, Richard A., ed. The Spirit of Law Librarianship: A Reader. LC 91-19305. ix, 264p. 1991. 37.50 (*0-8377-0865-6*) Rothman.

Leiter, Robert D. Foreman in Industrial Relations. LC 68-58600. (Columbia University. Studies in the Social Sciences: No. 542). reprint ed. 20.00 (*0-404-51542-8*) AMS Pr.

Leiter, Robert D., jt. ed. see Galatin, Malcolm.

Leiter, Samuel L. The Encyclopedia of the New York Stage, 1930-1940. LC 88-5688. 1339p. 1989. text ed. 195.00 (*0-313-25509-1*, LNY/, Greenwood Pr) Greenwood.

— The Encyclopedia of the New York Stage, 1940-1950. LC 92-7397. 1000p. 1992. text ed. 195.00 (*0-313-27510-6*, LEY, Greenwood Pr) Greenwood.

— From Belasco to Brook. 1990. 18.95 (*0-525-24594-4*, 01840-550, Dutton) NAL-Dutton.

— From Belasco to Brook: Representative Directors of the English-Speaking Stage. LC 90-45350. (Contributions in Drama & Theatre Studies: No. 33). 320p. 1991. text ed. 59.95 (*0-313-27662-5*, LBB, Greenwood Pr) Greenwood.

— From Stanislavsky to Barrault. LC 90-45612. (Contributions in Drama & Theatre Studies: No. 34). 264p. 1991. text ed. 49.95 (*0-313-27661-7*, LSE, Greenwood Pr) Greenwood.

— The Great Stage Directors: One Hundred Distinguished Careers of the Theater. LC 93-33380. (Illus.). 352p. 1994. 35.00 (*0-8160-2602-5*) Facts on File.

— Kabuki Encyclopedia: An English-Language Adaptation of Kabuki Jiten. LC 78-73801. (Illus.). 572p. 1980. text ed. 55.00 (*0-313-20654-6*, LKE/, Greenwood Pr) Greenwood.

— Ten Seasons: New York Theatre in the Seventies. LC 86-369. (Contributions in Drama & Theatre Studies). 257p. 1986. text ed. 55.00 (*0-313-24994-6*, LTS/, Greenwood Pr) Greenwood.

Leiter, Samuel L., ed. Shakespeare Around the Globe: A Guide to Notable Postwar Revivals. LC 85-27124. 987p. 1986. text ed. 145.00 (*0-313-23756-5*, LES/, Greenwood Pr) Greenwood.

Leiter, Samuel L. & Hill, Holly, eds. The Encyclopedia of the New York Stage, 1920-1930, 2 vols., 1. LC 84-6558. xxxiii, 1331p. 1985. text ed. 195.00 (*0-313-25037-5*, LEN/01) Greenwood.

— The Encyclopedia of the New York Stage, 1920-1930, 2 vols., Set. LC 84-6558. xxxiii, 1331p. 1985. text ed. 195.00 (*0-313-23615-1*, LEN/) Greenwood.

— The Encyclopedia of the New York Stage, 1920-1930, 2 vols., Vol. 2. LC 84-6558. xxxiii, 1331p. 1985. text ed. 195.00 (*0-313-25038-3*, LEN/02) Greenwood.

Leiter, Yechiel. Crisis in Israel: A Peace Plan to Resist. 1994. pap. 4.99 (*1-56171-338-4*) Sure Sellers.

Leiterer, Jurgen, jt. auth. see Henkin, Gennadi M.

Leites, D. A., tr. see Fomenko, A. T.

Leites, D. A., tr. see Leznov, A. N. & Saveliev, M. V.

Leites, D. A., tr. see Prasolov, V. V.

Leites, Edmund, ed. Conscience & Casuistry in Early Modern Europe. (Ideas in Context Ser.). 270p. 1988. 59.95 (*0-521-30113-0*) Cambridge U Pr.

Leites, Nathan C. The Rules of the Game in Paris. Coltman, Derek, tr. LC 69-19276. 365p. reprint ed. pap. 104.10 (*0-317-26519-9*, 2024055) Bks Demand.

Leitgeb, Grete, tr. see Saint-Exupery, Antoine de.

Leitgeb, H. Untersuchungen ueber die Lebermoose. 1970. 120.00 (*3-7682-7187-0*) Lubrecht & Cramer.

***Leitgeb, Hanna.** Der Ausgezeichnete Autor: Staeditsche Literaturpreise und Kulturpolitik in Deutschland 1926-1971. (European Cultures Ser.: No. 4). 436p. (GER.). (C). 1994. lib. bdg. 124.65 (*3-11-014402-6*) De Gruyter.

Leitgeb, Josef, tr. see Saint-Exupery, Antoine de.

Leitgeber, Boleslaw. East & West in Man's Perennial Quest. (Writers Workshop Greybird Ser.). 157p. 1978. 16.00 (*0-86578-055-2*); 8.00 (*0-86578-054-4*) Ind-US Inc.

Leith, Dick. A Social History of English. (Language & Society Ser.). 224p. 1983. pap. 14.95 (*0-7100-9261-X*, RKP) Routledge.

Leith, Dick & Myerson, George. The Power of Address: Explorations in Rhetoric. 320p. 1990. 49.95 (*0-415-03932-0*, A4126); pap. 14.95 (*0-415-02938-4*, A4130) Routledge.

Leith, J. Clark. Ghana. LC 74-77690. (Foreign Trade Regimes & Economic Development Ser.: No. 2). 238p. reprint ed. pap. 67.90 (*0-8357-7575-5*, 2056896) Bks Demand.

— Ghana. (Special Conference Series on Foreign Trade Regimes & Economic Development: No. 2). 238p. 1974. reprint ed. 61.90 (*0-87014-502-9*) Natl Bur Econ Res.

— Ghana, Structural Adjustment Experience. LC 94-42551. (Country Studies: No. 13). 1995. write for info. (*1-55815-431-0*) ICS Pr.

Leith, James A. The Idea of Art As Propaganda in France, 1750-1799: A Study in the History of Ideas. LC 65-1875. (University of Toronto Romance Ser.: No. 8). 196p. reprint ed. pap. 55.90 (*0-685-15275-8*, 2026468) Bks Demand.

— Space & Revolution: Projects for Monuments, Squares, & Public Buildings in France, 1789-1799. (Illus.). 1991. 70.00 (*0-7735-0757-4*, Pub. by McGill CN) U of Toronto Pr.

— Symbols in Life & Art. 224p. 1987. 49.95 (*0-7735-0616-0*, Pub. by McGill CN) U of Toronto Pr.

***Leith, James A., et al, eds.** Planet Earth: Problems & Prospects. 192p. 1995. 44.95 (*0-7735-1292-6*) U of Toronto Pr.

— Planet Earth: Problems & Prospects. 192p. 1995. pap. 19.95 (*0-7735-1312-4*) U of Toronto Pr.

Leith, Jennifer, tr. see Fraisse, Paul.

Leith, John H. Basic Christian Doctrine: A Summary of Christian Faith - Catholic, Protestant, & Reformed. 368p. (Orig.). 1993. pap. 19.99 (*0-664-25192-7*) Westminster John Knox.

— The Church, a Believing Fellowship. LC 80-82192. 192p. 1981. pap. 7.99 (*0-8042-0518-3*, John Knox) Westminster John Knox.

— From Generation to Generation: The Renewal of the Church According to Its Own Theology & Practice. 252p. (Orig.). 1990. pap. 14.99 (*0-664-25122-6*) Westminster John Knox.

— Introduction to the Reformed Tradition: A Way of Being the Christian Community. rev. ed. LC 81-5968. (Illus.). 253p. (C). 1981. pap. 14.99 (*0-8042-0479-9*, John Knox) Westminster John Knox.

— John Calvin's Doctrine of the Christian Life. LC 88-28058. 232p. 1989. 17.00 (*0-664-21330-8*) Westminster John Knox.

— The Reformed Imperative: What the Church Has To Say That No One Else Can Say. 168p. 1987. pap. 12.99 (*0-664-25023-8*, Westminster) Westminster John Knox.

Leith, John H., ed. Creeds of the Churches: A Reader in Christian Doctrine from the Bible to the Present. 3rd ed. LC 82-48029. 1982. pap. 18.99 (*0-8042-0526-4*, John Knox) Westminster John Knox.

Leith, John H., jt. ed. see Johnson, William S.

Leith, John T. & Dexter, Daniel L., eds. Mammalian Tumor Cell Heterogeneity. 160p. 1986. 119.00 (*0-8493-6162-1*, RC267, CRC Reprint) Franklin.

Leith, Larry M. Coaches Guide to Sport Administration. LC 89-39169. (ACEP Level Two Ser.). (Illus.). 96p. 1990. student ed 26.00 (*0-88011-382-0*, ACEP0206); pap. text ed. 18.00 (*0-88011-379-0*, PLEI0379) Human Kinetics.

— Foundations of Exercise & Mental Health. LC 94-72237. 254p. (C). 1994. text ed. 36.00 (*0-9627926-6-7*) Fit Info Tech.

Leith, Linda. Introducing Hugh MacLennan's Two Solitudes. (Canadian Fiction Studies: No. 10). 92p. (C). 1990. text ed. 18.95 (*1-55022-018-7*, Pub. by ECW Press CN) Genl Dist Srvs.

Leith, Philip. The Computerised Lawyer: A Guide to the Use of Computers in the Legal Profession. Morgan, G. G., ed. (Applications of Advanced Computing Techniques Ser.). (Illus.). 256p. 1991. pap. text ed. 39.00 (*0-387-19658-7*) Spr-Verlag.

Leith, Philip, jt. auth. see Morison, John.

Leith, Prue. The Cook's Handbook. (Illus.). 224p. 1989. reprint ed. pap. 10.95 (*0-912608-73-0*) Mid Atlantic.

Leith, Rod. The Prostitute Murders. (Illus.). 256p. 1983. 14.95 (*0-8184-0345-4*) Carol Pub Group.

Leith, Ron. Torso Killer: Shocking True Crimes. 1991. mass mkt. 4.50 (*1-55817-518-0*, Pinnacle NY) Windsor NY.

Leith-Ross, Prudence. The John Tradescants: Gardeners to the Rose & Lily Queen. 320p. 1984. 39.00 (*0-317-61300-6*, Pub. by P Owen Ltd UK) Dufour.

Leith-Ross, Prudence, ed. The John Tradescants: Gardeners to the Rose & Lily Queen. 320p. 1984. 40.00 (*0-7206-0612-8*, Pub. by P Owen Ltd UK) Dufour.

Leith-Ross, Sylvia. African Women. LC 74-15062. (Illus.). reprint ed. 32.50 (*0-404-12103-9*) AMS Pr.

— Stepping Stones: Memoirs of Colonial Nigeria, 1907-1960. 191p. 1983. 30.00 (*0-7206-0600-4*, Pub. by P Owen Ltd UK) Dufour.

Leith, William R. Clinical Methods in Communication Disorders. 2nd ed. LC 92-17022. 288p. 1993. pap. text ed. 27.00 (*0-89079-568-1*, 4047) PRO-ED.

Leith, William R., et al. Handbook of Supervision: A Cognitive Behavioral System. LC 90-8749. 125p. (Orig.). (C). 1989. pap. text ed. 24.00 (*0-89079-399-9*, 1723) PRO-ED.

Leithart, Peter, jt. auth. see DeMar, Gary.

Leithart, Peter J. Daddy, Why Was I Excommunicated? An Examination of Leonard J. Coppes, "Daddy, May I Take Communion?" 81p. 1992. pap. 7.00 (*1-883690-00-5*) Transfig Pr.

— The Kingdom & the Power: Rediscovering the Centrality of the Church. 270p. (Orig.). 1993. pap. 11.99 (*0-87552-300-5*) Presby & Reformed.

Leithart, Peter J., jt. auth. see DeMar, Gary.

***Leithauser.** Seaward. 1994. 4.99 (*0-517-13632-5*) Random Hse Value.

Leithauser, Brad. Cats of the Temple. LC 85-40228. (Poetry Ser.). 80p. 1986. 14.95 (*0-394-54806-X*) Knopf.

— Penchants & Places: Essays & Criticism. LC 94-28629. 1995. 25.00 (*0-679-42998-0*) Knopf.

— Seaward. LC 92-31047. 1993. 25.00 (*0-685-61666-5*); 23.00 (*0-394-58587-9*) Knopf.

Leithauser, Brad, ed. The Norton Book of Ghost Stories. LC 94-17383. 1994. 25.00 (*0-393-03564-6*) Norton.

Leithauser, David. Exploring Natural Language. 1991. Incl. 5.25" disk. disk 24.95 (*0-8306-6668-0*); Incl. 3.5" disk. disk 24.95 (*0-8306-6669-9*) TAB Bks.

— QBASIC Games & More! (Illus.). 320p. (Orig.). 1993. disk 29.95 (*1-56529-231-6*) Que.

Leithauser, Gladys, jt. auth. see Breitmeyer, Lois.

Leithauser, Gladys G. & Bell, Marilyn P. The World of Science: An Anthology for Writers. 408p. (C). 1987. pap. text ed. 19.50 (*0-03-006117-2*) HB Coll Pubs.

Leithe. Japanese Hand Guns. LC 67-29814. 1968. 18.00 (*0-87505-103-0*) Borden.

Leithe-Jasper, Manfred. Renaissance Master Bronzes from the Kunsthistorisches Museum, Vienna. (Illus.). 304p. 1986. lib. bdg. 35.00 (*0-935748-69-5*) Scala Books.

Leithe, W. Analysis of Air Pollutants. 304p. 1970. text ed. 77.50 (*0-317-46403-5*, Pub. by Keter Pub IS) Coronet Bks.

An Asterisk (*) at the beginning of an entry indicates that the title is appearing in BIP for the first time.

Leitherer, Claus, et al, eds. Massive Stars in Starbursts: Proceedings of the Massive Stars in Starbursts Meeting, Baltimore, 1990 May 15-17. (Space Telescope Science Institute Symposium Ser.: 5). 1991. 59.95 (0-521-40465-7) Cambridge U Pr.

Leithold, Louis. Before Calculus: Functions, Graphs, & Analytic Geometry. 3rd ed. LC 93-34084. (C). 1994. 42.00 (0-673-46911-5) HarpCollege.

— Calculus Single Variable with Analytic Geometry. 6th ed. 900p. (C). 1990. text ed. 74.50 (0-06-043930-0) HarpCollege.

— Calculus with Analytic Geometry, 2 vols. 3rd ed. (C). 1976. (0-06-363953-X); write for info. (0-06-363954-8) HarpCollege.

— Calculus with Analytic Geometry, 2 vols. 4th ed. (C). 1981. write for info. (0-06-363958-0); Set, 2 vols. in 1. text ed. 34.00 (0-06-043935-1) HarpCollege.

— Calculus with Analytic Geometry. 6th ed. 1400p. (C). 1990. text ed. 81.50 (0-06-044107-0) HarpCollege.

— College Algebra. (Illus.). 482p. (C). 1989. text ed. 50.50 (0-201-17051-5) Addison-Wesley.

— College Algebra. 2nd ed. (Illus.). (C). 1980. text ed. write for info. (0-02-369580-3) Macmillan.

— College Algebra & Trigonometry. (Illus.). 702p. (C). 1989. teacher ed 12.95 (0-201-15731-4); student ed 18.25 (0-201-15732-2); teacher ed 12.95 (0-201-15733-0); text ed. 50.50 (0-201-15730-6); teacher ed, disk 12.95 (0-201-15700-4) Addison-Wesley.

— Plane Trigonometry. (Illus.). (C). 1989. text ed. 48.50 (0-201-17056-6); student ed 18.25 (0-201-17058-2); 12.95 (0-201-17072-8); 12.95 (0-201-17059-0); 12.95 (0-201-17057-4) Addison-Wesley.

Leithold, Louis, jt. auth. see Hayman, D'Arcy.

Leithwood, Kenneth, ed. Effective School District Leadership: Transforming Politics into Education. (SUNY Series, Educational Leadership). 320p. (C). 1995. text ed. 59.50 (0-7914-2253-4); pap. 19.95 (0-7914-2254-2) State U NY Pr.

Leithwood, Kenneth & Steinbach, Rosanne, eds. Expert Problem Solving: Evidence from School & District Leaders. LC 93-42686. (SUNY Series, Educational Leadership). 366p. (C). 1994. text ed. 64.50 (0-7914-2107-4); pap. text ed. 21.95 (0-7914-2108-2) State U NY Pr.

Leithwood, Kenneth A. & Musella, Donald, eds. Understanding School System Administration: Studies of the Contemporary Chief Education Officer. 250p. 1991. 55.00 (1-85000-869-8, Falmer Pr); pap. 27.00 (1-85000-870-1, Falmer Pr) Taylor & Francis.

Leithwood, Kenneth A., et al. Developing Leaders for Future Schools. 240p. 1992. 85.00 (1-85000-743-8, Falmer Pr) Taylor & Francis.

Leithwood, Kenneth A., et al, eds. Preparing School Leaders for Educational Improvement. (Education Management Ser.). 224p. 1987. 45.00 (0-7099-4123-4, Pub. by Croom Helm UK) Routledge Chapman & Hall.

Leitinger, Ilse A., ed. & tr. The Costa Rican Women's Movement: A Reader. (Pitt Latin American Ser.). (Illus.). 384p. (C). 1995. 49.95 (0-8229-3862-6); pap. 19.95 (0-8229-5543-1) U of Pittsburgh Pr.

Leitman, Allan. Science for Deaf Children. LC 68-58037. 1968. pap. text ed. 7.95 (0-88200-109-4, D2668) Alexander Graham.

Leitman, M. Manual for Eye Examination & Diagnosis. 4th ed. 1993. pap. 29.95 (0-86542-339-3) Blackwell Sci.

Leitman, Mark W. Manual for Eye Examination & Diagnosis. 3rd ed. 90p. 1987. pap. 24.95 (0-87489-441-7) Med Economics.

Leitmann, George. The Calculus of Variations & Optimal Control. LC 81-4582. (Mathematical Concepts & Methods in Science & Engineering Ser.: Vol. 24). 328p. 1981. 69.50 (0-306-40707-8, Plenum Pr) Plenum.

Leitmann, Josef. Rapid Urban Environmental Assessment: Lessons from Cities in the Developing World. LC 94-10848. (Urban Management & the Environment Ser.: Vol. 14). 1994. write for info. (0-8213-2790-9) World Bank.

— Rapid Urban Environmental Assessment: Lessons from Cities in the Developing World. LC 94-9395. (Urban Management Programme Ser.: No. 15). 156p. 1994. write for info. (0-8213-2791-7) World Bank.

Leitner, Gerhard, ed. English Traditional Grammars: An International Perspective. LC 91-24951. (Studies in the History of the Language Sciences: Vol. 62). x, 392p. 1991. 89.00x (1-55619-357-2) Benjamins North Am.

— New Directions in English Language Corpora: Methdology, Results, Software Developments. LC 92-26798. (Topics in English Linguistics Ser.: Vol. 9). (Illus.). ix, 368p. 1992. lib. bdg. 136.95 (3-11-013201-X) Mouton.

***Leitner, Gloria J.** A Fairy's Tale. 154p. 1991. 8.00 (0-9617633-2-9) Little Wing Pub.

— Full Moon, Silver Glimpses. 203p. (Orig.). 1986. pap. 7.50 (0-9617633-1-0) Little Wing Pub.

Leitner, Helga, jt. ed. see Nijkamp, Peter.

Leitner, Irving, jt. auth. see Leitner, Isabella.

Leitner, Irving A., jt. auth. see Leitner, Isabella.

***Leitner, Isabella.** Big Lie: A True Story. (J). (gr. 4-7). 1994. pap. 2.95 (0-590-45570-2) Scholastic Inc.

Leitner, Isabella & Leitner, Irving. The Big Lie: A True Story. (J). 1992. 13.95 (0-590-45569-9, 025, Scholastic Hardcover) Scholastic Inc.

Leitner, Isabella & Leitner, Irving A. Isabella: From Auschwitz to Freedom. LC 93-47892. 1994. 12.95 (0-385-47318-4, Anchor NY) Doubleday.

Leitner, L. M. & Dunnett, N. G., eds. Critical Issues in Personal Construct Psychotherapy. 330p. (C). 1993. 35.00 (0-89464-519-6) Krieger.

Leitner, L. M., jt. auth. see Faidley, A. J.

Leitner, Michael J. & Leitner, Sara. How to Improve Your Life Through Leisure. 248p. 1994. pap. 8.95 (1-56901-361-6) NW Pub.

Leitner, Michael J. & Leitner, Sara F. Leisure in Later Life: A Sourcebook for the Provision of Recreation Services for Elders. LC 85-17635. (Activities, Adaptation & Aging Ser.: Vol. 7, Nos. 3-4). 341p. 1986. text ed. 49.95 (0-86656-452-7); pap. text ed. 24.95 (0-86656-476-4) Haworth Pr.

Leitner, Patricia, jt. auth. see Bach, Daniel J.

Leitner, Sara, jt. auth. see Leitner, Michael J.

Leitner, Sara F., ed. Leisure Enhancement. LC 89-15549. (Illus.). 412p. 1989. text ed. 49.95 (0-86656-892-1); pap. text ed. 24.95 (0-86656-847-6) Haworth Pr.

Leitner, Sara F., jt. auth. see Leitner, Michael J.

Leitritz, Earl & Lewis, Robert C. Trout & Salmon Culture (Hatchery Methods) (Illus.). 197p. 1980. reprint ed. pap. 6.50 (0-931876-36-2, 4100) ANR Pubns CA.

Leitz, David E. The Fly Fishing Corpse. 160p. 1994. 19.95 (1-882418-15-8); pap. 12.95 (1-882418-13-1) Centenn Pubns.

Leitz (KRMA-TV) Staff. The Earth Explored Study Guide. 144p. (C). 1985. per., pap. text ed. 10.95 (0-8403-3495-8) Kendall-Hunt.

Leitz, Pierr M., jt. auth. see Edge, Nellie.

Leitz, Robert C., III, jt. ed. see London, Jack.

Leitz, Robert C., III, jt. auth. see Price, Kenneth M.

***Leitzel, James & Tucker, Alan.** Assessing Calculus Reform Efforts: A Report to the Community. LC 94-72962. 100p. (C). 1994. pap. text ed. 15.00 (0-88385-093-1, NTE37CAT) Math Assn.

Leitzel, James R., ed. A Call for Change: Recommendations for the Mathematical Preparation of Teachers. 60p. 1991. pap. 11.00 (0-88385-072-9) Math Assn.

***Leitzel, Jim.** Russian Economic Reform. LC 94-24768. 208p. 1995. 59.95x (0-415-12510-3, C0437); pap. 18.95 (0-415-12511-1, C0438) Routledge.

Leitzel, Jim, ed. Economics & National Security. (Pew Studies in Economics & Security). 134p. (C). 1993. text ed. 45.00 (0-8133-8553-9) Westview.

Leitzel, Jim & Tirole, Jean, eds. Incentives in Procurement Contracting. (Pew Studies in Economics & Security). 161p. (C). 1993. text ed. 50.00 (0-8133-8566-0) Westview.

Leitzell, Terry L. Extinction, Evolution, & Environmental Management. (Working Papers on the Preservation of Species). 1988. 2.50 (0-318-33311-2, PS2) IPPP.

Leitzmann, C. Worterbuch der Ernahrungswissenschaft. 298p. (ENG, FRE, GER, ITA & SPA.). 1988. lib. bdg. 115.00 (0-8288-3592-6, F113450) Fr & Eur.

Leiva, Erasmo, tr. see Von Balthasar, Hans U.

Leiva, Manuel R. Relacion Hospedante-Parasito Mecanismo De Patogenicidad De los Microorganismos. (Serie de Biologia: No. 14). 91p. (C). 1981. pap. 3.50 (0-8270-1322-1) OAS.

Leiva-Merikakis, Erasmo. The Blossoming Thorn: Georg Trakl's Poetry of Atonement. LC 85-43246. 192p. 1987. 36.50 (0-8387-5102-4) Bucknell U Pr.

Leiva-Merikakis, Erasmo & Waniek, Erdmann, eds. Memoriae Vis: Essays in Celebration of Arthur R. Evans. LC 93-3343. (Homage Ser.). 400p. 1993. 59.95 (1-55540-851-6) Scholars Pr GA.

Leiva-Merikakis, Erasmo, tr. see Auer, Johann.

Leiva-Merikakis, Erasmo, tr. see Von Balthasar, Hans U.

Leiva-Merikakis, Erasmo, tr. see Von Speyr, Adrienne.

Leiva, Miriam, ed. see Burton, Grace, et al.

Leiva, Miriam A., ed. see Burton, Grace, et al.

Leive, Loretta, ed. Bacterial Membranes & Walls. LC 73-82622. (Microbiology Ser.: No. 1). (Illus.). 515p. reprint ed. pap. 146.80 (0-7837-0905-6, 2041210) Bks Demand.

Leiviska, K., ed. CIM in Process & Manufacturing Industries: IFAC Workshop, Espoo, Finland, 23-25 November 1992. LC 93-17913. (IFAC Pre-Print Ser.). 1993. pap. 91.00 (0-08-042182-2, Pergamon Pr) Elsevier.

Leiz, Juliet P. Barcelona Design Guide. (Illus.). 120p. (ENG & SPA.). 1992. pap. 18.95 (84-252-1446-7) Rizzoli Intl.

Leja, Jan. Surface Chemistry of Froth Flotation. 744p. 1981. 135.00 (0-306-40588-1, Plenum Pr) Plenum.

Leja, Michael. Narration. (Illus.). 1978. 2.00 (0-910663-17-3) ICA Inc.

— Reframing Abstract Expressionism: Subjectivity & Painting in the 1940s. LC 92-32992. (Illus.). 448p. (C). 1993. text ed. 50.00 (0-300-04461-5) Yale U Pr.

Lejbowicz, Agnes. Omraam Mikhael Aivanhov: Master of the Great Universal White Brotherhood. (Testimonials Ser.). 115p. (Orig.). 1982. pap. 6.95 (2-85566-191-9, Pub. by Prosveta FR) Prosveta USA.

LeJeune, A., jt. auth. see Perdang, J. M.

Lejeune, Abbe P. An Introduction to the Mystical Life. 1977. lib. bdg. 59.95 (0-8490-2070-0) Gordon Pr.

Lejeune, Albert. L' Optique de Claude Ptolemee. 2nd ed. LC 89-9858. (Collection de Travaux de l'Academie Internationale d'Histoire des Sciences: Vol. 31). 371p. (FRE & LAT.). 1989. reprint ed. text ed. 188.75 (90-04-09126-2) E J Brill.

Lejeune, Anthony, ed. see Lejeune, C. A.

***Lejeune, C. A.** The C. A. Lejeune Film Reader. Lejeune, Anthony, ed. (Film Reader Ser.). 366p. 1995. 39.95 (1-55783-207-2) Applause Theatre Bk Pubs.

— Cinema. 1972. 69.95 (0-87968-871-8) Gordon Pr.

Lejeune-Dirichlet, P. G. Werke, 2 Vols. in 1. Kronecker, L., ed. LC 68-54716. 1969. reprint ed. 75.00 (0-8284-0225-6) Chelsea Pub.

Lejeune, F. & Bunjes, Werner E. Dictionary for Physicians. 2nd ed. 459p. (ENG & GER.). 1968. 175.00 (0-7859-0829-3, M-7106) Fr & Eur.

— Woerterbuch fuer Aerzte: Dictionary for Physicians. 2nd ed. (GER.). 1968. pap. 55.00 (0-685-01779-6, M-6924) Fr & Eur.

Lejeune, F. & Stiennon. La Legende de Roland dans l'Art du Moyen Age. 125.00 (0-685-34014-7) Fr & Eur.

Lejeune, Ferdy J., et al. Malignant Melanoma: Medical & Surgical Management. (Illus.). 400p. 1994. text ed. 110.00 (0-07-105421-9) Hlth Prof Div.

Lejeune, H., jt. ed. see Blackman, D. E.

Lejeune, H., jt. auth. see Richelle, M.

***Lejeune, Jean-Francois, ed.** Modern Cities. (New City Ser.: Vol. 3). (Illus.). 160p. (Orig.). 1995. pap. 25.00 (1-56898-058-2) Princeton Arch.

Lejeune, Jean-Francois, jt. ed. see Culot, Maurice.

Lejeune, Jerome. The Concentration Can: When Does Human Life Begin? An Eminent Geneticist Testifies. LC 91-77302. 228p. (Orig.). 1992. pap. 13.95 (0-89870-394-8) Ignatius Pr.

Lejeune, John A. The Reminiscences of a Marine. Kohn, Richard H., ed. LC 78-22384. (American Military Experience Ser.). (Illus.). 1980. reprint ed. lib. bdg. 37.95 (0-405-11860-0) Ayer.

— The Reminiscences of a Marine. (Illus.). 488p. Date not set. reprint ed. 8.95 (0-686-30999-5) Marine Corps.

Lejeune, Philippe. On Autobiography. Eakin, Paul J., ed. Leary, Katherine, tr. (Theory & History of Literature Ser.: Vol. 52). 1989. text ed. 49.95 (0-8166-1631-0); pap. text ed. 16.95 (0-8166-1632-9) U of Minn Pr.

Lejeune, R. Christoph Blumhardt & His Message. LC 63-15816. 240p. 1963. 9.00 (0-87486-200-0) Plough.

LeJeune, Shonda. God Is. (Illus.). 32p. (Orig.). (J). (gr. 3-8). 1993. pap. 8.95 (0-87516-659-8) DeVorss.

LeJeune, Steele. Introduction to Personal Computers: Beginner's Guide. rev. ed. LC 90-61076. (Basic Computer: No. 1). (Illus.). 96p. 1990. reprint ed. pap. 9.95 (0-9625447-1-X) Myriad & Then Some.

***Lejeune, Urban.** Mosaic & Web Explorer. 1995. cd-rom, pap. 34.99 (1-883577-16-0) Coriolis Grp.

Lejins, Atis, jt. ed. see Huldt, Bo.

Lejour, Madeline. Vertical Mammaplasty & Liposuction. LC 93-11760. 1994. 245.00 (0-942219-55-4) Quality Med Pub.

LeJuene, jt. auth. see Duntemann.

Lekachman. Capitalism for Beginners. (Documentary Comic Bks.). (Illus.). 1986. 6.95 (0-317-03094-9) Writers & Readers.

Lekachman, Robert. Varieties of Economics: Documents, Examples & Manifestoes, Vol. 1. 11.50 (0-8446-2449-7) Peter Smith.

Lekai, Louis J. The Cistercians: Ideals & Reality. LC 77-3692. (Illus.). 534p. 1977. 35.00 (0-87338-201-3) Kent St U Pr.

— Nicolas Cotheret's Annals of Citeaux, Outlined from the Original French. (Cistercian Studies: 57). 1983. pap. 13.95 (0-87907-857-X) Cistercian Pubns.

Lekas, Danny. Complete Works, Vol. 1. LC 84-90478. (Orig.). 1984. pap. 2.00 (0-930759-00-1) D Lekas.

— Complete Works, Vol. 2. LC 84-90478. (Orig.). 1985. pap. 2.00 (0-930759-01-X) D Lekas.

— P M. LC 84-91446. 1985. pap. 2.00 (0-930759-05-2) D Lekas.

Lekas, Padelis. Marx on Classical Antiquity: Problems of Historical Methodology. LC 88-192. 256p. 1988. text ed. 39.95 (0-312-02023-6) St Martin.

Lekatsas, Barbara. Persephone. Barkan, Stanley H., ed. Anghelaki-Rooke, Katerina, tr. (Review Woman Writers Chapbook Ser.: No. 1). 20p. (ENG & GRE.). 1986. 15.00 (0-89304-400-8, CCC160); 15.00 (0-89304-402-4); pap. 5.00 (0-89304-401-6); pap. 5.00 (0-89304-403-2) Cross-Cultrl NY.

Lekatsas, Barbara, comp. The Howard L. & Muriel Weingrow Collection of Avant-Garde Art & Literature at Hofstra University: An Annotated Bibliography. LC 85-12659. (Illus.). xxv, 322p. 1985. text ed. 195.00 (0-313-25090-1, LWC/, Greenwood Pr) Greenwood.

Lekatsos, Anthony, tr. see Makrakis, Apostolos.

LeKemp, pseud. A Boat Buyer's Guide: Answers to Questions You Have about Boating but Don't Know Who to Ask. rev. ed. Orig. Title: A Boat Buyer's Handbook. (Illus.). 1991. reprint ed. pap. 7.00 (0-9627438-2-8) L E Kemppainen.

Leker, Andrew, jt. auth. see Coleman, Joseph S.

***Leker, Andrew, et al.** Skyrealms of Jorune: The Role Playing Game. 3rd ed. (Illus.). 216p. (YA). 1992. pap. text ed. 20.00 (1-883240-00-X) Chessex.

Lekeux, Martial. The Art of Prayer. Oligny, Paul J., tr. LC 59-14706. 314p. reprint ed. pap. 89.50 (0-8357-5764-1, 2022570) Bks Demand.

Lekhnitskii, S. G. Anisotropic Plates. 2nd ed. 550p. 1968. text ed. 210.00 (0-677-20670-4) Gordon & Breach.

Lekhtman, I., jt. auth. see Ginzburg, S.

***Lekhwani, Kanhaiyalal.** Intensive Course in Sindhi. 882p. 1995. 28.95 (0-7818-0389-6) Hippocrene Bks.

***Leki, Ilona.** Academic Writing: Exploring Processes & Strategies. 2nd ed. 336p. (C). 1995. pap. text ed. 24.61 (0-312-09214-8) St Martin.

— Understanding ESL Writers: A Guide for Teachers. 151p. 1992. pap. text ed. 19.50 (0-86709-303-X, 0303) Boynton Cook Pubs.

Leki, Ilona, jt. ed. see Carson, Joan.

Lekic, Anita. The Poetry of Vasko Popa. LC 92-7285. (Balkan Studies: Vol. 2). 178p. (C). 1993. text ed. 44.95 (0-8204-1777-7) P Lang Pubs.

Lekic, Maria, jt. auth. see Robin, Richard.

Lekic, Maria D. Ogonyok: Advanced. 160p. (RUS.). (YA). 1994. teacher ed 10.60 (0-685-62844-2, F4276-4, Natl Textbk); pap. 23.95 (0-8442-4275-6, F4275-6, Natl Textbk) NTC Pub Grp.

— Russian Listening Comprehension I, Pt. B: "The Courier" (Illus.). 173p. (RUS.). (C). 1992. student ed, pap. 7.50 (0-87415-179-1, 72); teacher ed, audio 35.00 (0-87415-180-5); audio 5.00 (0-87415-181-3, 72B); 3.50 (0-87415-172-4, 72C) OSU Foreign Lang.

***Lekic, Maria D., et al.** What Do You Think about That? (C). 1994. pap. text ed. 29.90 (0-9643332-0-1) ACTR.

Lekisch, Barbara. Tahoe Place Names. Browning, Peter, ed. LC 88-80574. (Illus.). 192p. (Orig.). (C). 1988. pap. 11.95 (0-944220-01-0) Great West Bks.

Lekkerkerker, C., jt. auth. see Gruber, P. M.

Lekson, Stephen, et al. Chaco Canyon: A Center & Its World. (Illus.). 124p. 1994. 35.00 (0-89013-260-7) Museum NM Pr.

Lekson, Stephen H. Mimbres Archaeology of the Upper Gila, New Mexico. LC 89-20538. (Anthropological Papers: No. 53). 116p. (Orig.). 1990. pap. 32.50 (0-8165-1164-0) U of Ariz Pr.

— Nana's Raid. LC 86-51206. (Southwestern Studies: No. 81). (Illus.). 56p. 1987. pap. 10.00 (0-87404-159-7) Tex Western.

Lekson, Stephen H. & Swentzel, Rina. Ancient Land, Ancestral Places: Paul Logsdon in th Pueblo Southwest. 1994. pap. 29.95 (0-89013-246-1) Museum NM Pr.

Lekson, Stephen H. & Swentzel, Rine. Ancient Land Ancestral Places: Paul Logsdon in the Pueblo Southwest. 1993. 39.95 (0-89013-245-3) Museum NM Pr.

Lekson, Stephen H. & Swentzell, Rina. Ancient Land, Ancestral Places: Paul Logsdon in the Pueblo Southwest. (Illus.). 168p. 1994. pap. 29.95 (0-685-70793-8) Museum NM Pr.

***LeLaCheur, Dan.** Generational Legacy: Breaking a Curse - Starting a Blessing. 187p. (YA). 1994. pap. 8.99 (0-9642286-0-2) Family Survival.

Lelah, Michael D. & Cooper, Stuart L. Polyurethanes in Medicine. 256p. 1986. 128.00 (0-8493-6307-1, R857, CRC Reprint) Franklin.

Leland, Abby P. The Educational Theory & Practice of T. H. Green. LC 78-176984. (Columbia University. Teachers College. Contributions to Education Ser.: No. 46). reprint ed. 37.50 (0-404-55046-0) AMS Pr.

Leland, Abigail T. Way Back Yonder. Perkins, Priscilla L., ed. (Illus.). 64p. (Orig.). 1993. pap. 10.00 (1-881459-11-X) Eagle Pr SC.

Leland, Allan & Cohn, Joanne. Four Stages of Teacher Development. 176p. 1991. per. 24.95 (0-8403-6668-X) Kendall-Hunt.

Leland, Bruce. Connections: Reading & Writing. 368p. (C). 1992. pap. text ed. 19.96 (0-8403-7769-X) Kendall-Hunt.

— Discovery: Writing to Learn. 304p. (C). 1992. per. 20.95 (0-8403-8230-8) Kendall-Hunt.

Leland, C. G. Kuloskap the Master & Other Algonquin Poems. 1977. lib. bdg. 59.95 (0-8490-2120-0) Gordon Pr.

Leland, Carole A., jt. auth. see Astin, Helen S.

Leland, Caryn. The Art Law Primer. 32p. 1981. pap. 5.00 (0-933032-03-X) Foun Commun Artists.

— Licensing Art & Design. LC 89-80743. 112p. 1990. pap. 12.95 (0-927629-04-6, 30207) Allworth Pr.

— Licensing Art & Design. rev. ed. LC 95-75288. (Illus.). 144p. 1995. pap. 16.95 (1-880559-27-7) Allworth Pr.

Leland, Charles. Gypsy Sorcery. (Illus.). 288p. reprint ed. text ed. 35.00 (1-872736-10-6, Pub. by Mandrake Pr UK) Holmes Pub.

Leland, Charles G. The Algonquin Legends of New England. (Illus.). 416p. 1992. reprint ed. pap. 10.95 (0-486-26944-2) Dover.

— Aradia: Gospel of the Witches. 135p. 1989. pap. 5.95 (0-919345-10-7) Phoenix WA.

— Aradia or the Gospel of the Witches. White, Nelson & White, Anne, eds. LC 85-52307. 100p. (Orig.). 1986. pap. 10.00 (0-939856-54-9) Tech Group.

— Etruscan Roman Remains in Popular Tradition. LC 77-87718. reprint ed. 28.50 (0-404-16515-X) AMS Pr.

— Fusang or the Discovery of America by Chinese Buddhist Priests. 212p. 1981. pap. 18.00 (0-89540-094-4, SB-094) Sun Pub.

— The Gypsies. LC 75-3460. reprint ed. 27.00 (0-404-16891-4) AMS Pr.

— Gypsy Sorcery & Fortune Telling. 1990. pap. 12.95 (0-8065-1198-2, Citadel Pr) Carol Pub Group.

— Hans Breitmann's Ballads. 260p. 1914. pap. 2.95 (0-486-21444-3) Dover.

— Legends of Florence. 1976. lib. bdg. 59.95 (0-8490-2146-4) Gordon Pr.

— Meister Karl's Sketch-Book. LC 75-104510. reprint ed. lib. bdg. 19.50 (0-8398-1154-3) Irvington.

Leland, Charles G., pseud. Memoirs. (American Biography Ser.). 439p. 1991. reprint ed. lib. bdg. 89.00 (0-7812-8243-8) Rprt Serv.

Leland, Charles G. The Mystic Will. 1976. reprint ed. 9.00 (0-911662-58-8) Yoga.

— Pidgin-English Sing-Song. LC 74-166796. 1971. reprint ed. 25.00 (0-403-01418-2) Scholarly.

Leland, Charles G., tr. see Heine, Heinrich.

Leland, Charles G., et al. English-Gypsy Songs: In Romany, with Metrical English Translations. LC 75-3459. reprint ed. 22.50 (0-404-16890-6) AMS Pr.

Leland, Christopher. The Last Happy Men: The Generation of 1922, Fiction, & the Argentine Reality. (Illus.). 232p. 1986. text ed. 35.00x (0-8156-2376-3) Syracuse U Pr.

Leland, Christopher T. The Professor of Aesthetics. LC 93-38225. 160p. 1994. 18.95 (0-944072-37-2) Zoland Bks.

Leland, Dorothy, ed. Husserl, Heidegger, Sartre, Merleau-Ponty: Phenomenology & the Problem of Intentionality. 512p. (Orig.). (C). 1994. lib. bdg. 45.00 (0-87220-005-1); pap. text ed. 18.95 (0-87220-004-3) Hackett Pub.

Leland, Dorothy K. A Short History of Sacramento. (Illus.). 150p. (Orig.). 1988. pap. 9.95 (0-938530-40-2) Lexikos.

Leland, Elizabeth. The Vanishing Coast. LC 92-6498. (Illus.). 141p. 1992. 21.95 (0-89587-092-4) Blair.

Leland, G. Waldo & Mereness, Newton D. Introduction to the American Official Sources for the Economic & Social History of the World War. LC 74-75248. (United States in World War I Ser.). xlvii, 532p. 1974. reprint ed. lib. bdg. 59.95 (0-89198-109-8) Ozer.

***Leland, Irene.** The Maze Comes to Life. (Illus.). 199p. 1995. 19.95 (0-9646386-1-4) Uplifting Pr.

— On the Right Course. 26p. (J). 1993. pap. text ed. 11.95 (0-9646386-0-6) Uplifting Pr.

Leland, Isabella G. Charleston, S. C. Crossroads of History. 1980. 17.95 (0-89781-008-2, 3286) Preferred Mktg.

Leland, Jeremy. Last Sandcastle. 123p. 1983. pap. 7.95 (0-86278-051-9, Pub. by OBrien Pr IE) Dufour.

Leland, John. A Guide to Hemingway's Paris. (Illus.). 1989. pap. 8.95 (0-945575-23-8) Algonquin Bks.

— The Labouryouse Journey & Serche of Johan Leylande for Englandes Antiquitees. LC 74-28871. (English Experience Ser.: No. 750). 1975. reprint ed. 25.00 (90-221-0750-7) Walter J Johnson.

— A Voice from South Carolina. LC 72-37310. (Black Heritage Library Collection). 1977. reprint ed. 20.95 (0-8369-8947-3) Ayer.

— Writings of the Late Elder John Leland, Including Some Events of His Life. Greene, L. F., ed. LC 73-83420. (Religion in America, Ser. 1). 1977. reprint ed. 60.95 (0-405-00245-9) Ayer.

Leland, Joy H. Firewater Myths: North American Indian Drinking & Alcohol Addiction. LC 75-620113. (Monograph Ser.: No. 11). 1976. 6.00 (0-911290-43-5) Rutgers Ctr Alcohol.

Leland, Lorrin, ed. The Kansas Experience in Poetry. rev. ed. LC 80-621211. (Kansas Studies). 150p. (Orig.). 1986. reprint ed. pap. text ed. 6.00 (0-936352-01-9, B929) U of KS Cont Ed.

Leland, Louis S., Jr. A Personal Kiwi-Yankee Dictionary. 1, 983th ed. LC 83-22092. 115p. pap. 6.50 (0-88289-414-5) Pelican.

Leland, Nita. Creative Artist. (Illus.). 160p. 1993. pap. 22.95 (0-89134-465-9, 30479) North Light Bks.

— Exploring Color. (Illus.). 192p. 1991. pap. 24.99 (0-89134-363-6, 30233) North Light Bks.

Leland, Nita & Williams, Virginia L. Creative Collage Techniques. 144p. 1994. 27.95 (0-89134-563-9) North Light Bks.

Leland, R. P. Stochastic Models for Laser Propagation in Atmospheric Turbulence. (Lecture Notes in Control & Information Sciences Ser.: Vol. 133). (Illus.). xii, 145p. 1989. pap. 35.00 (0-387-51538-0) Spr-Verlag.

Leland, Sophia, tr. see Abess Thaisia of Leushino.

Leland, Thomas. Longsword, Earl of Salisbury: An Historical Romance, 2 vols., Set. LC 73-22765. 420p. 1975. reprint ed. 87.95 (0-405-06016-5) Ayer.

Leland, Thomas, tr. see Demosthenes.

Leland, W. G. Guide to Materials for American History in the Libraries & Archives of Paris, 2 Vols, Set. (Carnegie Institute Ser.: Vol. 12). 1969. reprint ed. 100.00 (0-527-00692-0) Periodicals Srv.

— Steam Turbines. 1984. reprint ed. pap. 8.95 (0-917914-20-1) Lindsay Pubns.

Leland, W. G., jt. auth. see Van Tyne, C. H.

Lelande, A. Technical & Critical Vocabulary of Philosophy: Vocabulaire Technique et Critique de la Philosophie. 13th ed. 1323p. (FRE.). 1980. 150.00 (0-8288-2274-3, F18440) Fr & Eur.

Lelchuk, Alan. On Home Ground. LC 87-8496. (Illus.). 72p. (J). (gr. 5 up). 1987. 9.95 (0-15-200560-9, Gulliver Bks) HarBrace.

— Playing the Game. 365p. 1995. 23.00 (1-880909-32-4) Baskerville.

Lele, J. K. & Singh, R. Language & Society: Steps Towards an Integrated Theory. LC 88-24107. (Monographs & Theoretical Studies in Sociology & Anthropology in Honour of Nels Anderson: No. 27). xix, 146p. (Orig.). 1989. pap. text ed. 35.50 (90-04-08789-3) E J Brill.

Lele, Jayant. Elite Pluralism & Class Rule: Political Development in Maharashtra, India. LC 78-12267. 301p. reprint ed. pap. 85.80 (0-685-15254-5, 2026467) Bks Demand.

Lele, Jayant & Vora, Rajendra, eds. Boeings & Bullock Carts Vol. 5: State & Society in India. 1990. 54.00 (81-7001-067-5, Pub. by Chanakya II) S Asia.

Lele, Milind M. Creating Strategic Leverage: Matching Company Strengths with Market Opportunities. 352p. 1991. text ed. 34.95 (0-471-63142-6) Wiley.

Lele, Milind M. & Sheth, Jagdish N. The Customer Is Key: Gaining an Unbeaten Advantage Through Customer Satisfaction. LC 87-21549. 260p. 1987. text ed. 24.95 (0-471-82859-9) Wiley.

— The Customer Is Key: Gaining an Unbeaten Advantage Through Customer Satisfaction. LC 87-21549. 260p. 1991. pap. text ed. 14.95 (0-471-54917-7) Wiley.

Lele, Uma. Agricultural Growth & Assistance to Africa: Lessons of a Quarter Century. LC 89-48873. 106p. 1990. pap. 9.95 (1-55815-063-3) ICS Pr.

— The Design of Rural Development: Lessons from Africa. LC 75-10896. (World Bank Research Publication Ser.). (Illus.). 260p. 1975. pap. 11.95 (0-8018-1769-2) Johns Hopkins.

Lele, Uma, ed. Aid to African Agriculture: Lessons from Two Decades of Donors' Experience. 648p. 1992. text ed. 52.95 (0-8018-4366-9, 44366) Johns Hopkins.

Lele, Uma & Christiansen, Robert E. Markets, Marketing Boards, & Cooperatives in Africa: Issues in Adjustment Policy. (Managing Agricultural Development in Africa Discussion Paper Ser.: No. 11). 32p. 1990. 6.95 (0-8213-1327-4, 11327) World Bank.

Lele, Uma & Nabi, Ijaz, eds. Transitions in Development: The Role of Aid & Commercial Flows. LC 89-26922. 535p. 1990. 34.95 (1-55815-078-1); pap. 14.95 (1-55815-093-5) ICS Pr.

Lele, Uma & Stone, Steven W. Population Pressure, the Environment, & Agricultural Intensification: Variations on the Boserup Hypothesis. (MADIA Discussion Paper Ser.: No. 4). 79p. 1990. 7.95 (0-8213-1320-7, 11320) World Bank.

***Leledakis, Kanakis.** Society & Psyche: Social Theory & the Unconscious Dimension of the Social. 256p. 1995. 49.95 (1-85973-062-0); pap. 19.95 (1-85973-067-1) Berg Pubs.

Lelek, A. The Freshwater Fishes of Europe, Vol. 9: Threatened Fishes of Europe. (Illus.). 343p. 1987. 180.00 (3-89104-048-2, Pub. by AULA Verlag) Koeltz Sci Bks.

Lelen, J. M. Pray the Rosary. (Illus.). 1980. 0.60 (0-89942-040-0, 40/05) Catholic Bk Pub.

Lelend, Charles G. Fusang, or the Discovery of America by Chinese Buddhist Priests in the 15th Century. 1977. lib. bdg. 59.95 (0-8490-1874-9) Gordon Pr.

Leler, William. Constraint Programming Languages: Their Specification & Generation. LC 87-1236. (Computer Science Ser.). 145p. (C). 1988. pap. text ed. 31.25 (0-201-06243-7) Addison-Wesley.

Lelevkin, V. M., et al. Physics of Non-Equilibrium Plasmas. LC 92-44398. 1992. write for info. (0-444-89533-7, North Holland) Elsevier.

Lelewer, Nancy. Something's Not Right: One Family's Struggle with Learning Disabilities. LC 94-60521. 184p. 1994. 21.95 (0-9641089-0-9); pap. 14.95 (0-9641089-1-7) VanderWyk & Burnham.

Leliard, J. D. Judicial Terminology. 4th rev. ed. 413p. (DUT & FRE.). 1992. 95.00 (0-8288-9436-1) Fr & Eur.

Lelie, HErman, jt. auth. see Bateson, Maggie.

Lelievre, Eva, jt. auth. see Courgeau, Daniel.

Lelievre, Mateo. Juan Wesley - Su Vida y Su Obra: The Life & Work of John Wesley. (SPA.). 11.50 (84-7645-295-0, 223338, Pub. by Edit Clie SP) TSELF.

***Leliveld, A.** Social Security in Developing Countries: Operation & Dynamics of Social Security Mechanisms in Rural Swaziland. (Tinbergen Institute Research Ser.: No. 85). 442p. 1994. pap. 33.00 (90-5170-305-8, Pub. by Thesis Pubs NE) IBD Ltd.

Leliwa-Kopystynski, J. & Teisseyre, R. Constitution of the Earth's Interior. (Physics & Evolution of the Earth's Interior Ser.: Vol. 1). 1984. 113.00 (0-444-99646-X, I-344-83) Elsevier.

Lellenberg, Jon L. Nova 57 Minor: The Waxing & Waning of the Sixty-First Adventure of Sherlock Holmes. LC 89-80834. (Illus.). 109p. 1990. 19.00 (0-934468-26-5) Gaslight.

Lellenberg, Jon L., ed. Irregular Records of the Early Forties. LC 91-76681. (Baker Street Irregular's Archival Ser.: Vol. 3). (Illus.). 160p. 1992. pap. 18.95 (0-8232-1356-0) Fordham.

— The Quest for Sir Arthur Conan Doyle: Thirteen Biographers in Search of a Life. LC 87-9529. 236p. 1987. text ed. 29.95 (0-8093-1384-7) S Ill U Pr.

Lelley, Jan. Pilzanbau: Biotechnologie der Kulturspeisepilze. 2nd ed. (Illus.). 404p. (GER.). 1991. lib. bdg. 87.50 (3-8001-5131-6, Pub. by Ulmer Verlog GW) Lubrecht & Cramer.

Lellie, Herman & Bateson, Margaret. A Victorian Dollhouse. (Illus.). 4p. (J). 1991. bds. 19.95 (0-312-06228-1) St Martin.

Lellinger, D. B. Flora of the Guianas, Series B: Ferns & Fern Allies. Fascicle 3 Hymenophyllaceae. 100p. 1994. pap. 89.00 (1-878762-53-2) Koeltz Sci Bks.

Lellinger, David B. The Ferns & Fern-Allies of Costa Rica, Panama, & the Choco, Pt. 1: Psilotaceae Through Dicksoniaceae. LC 89-6461. (Pteridolgia Ser.: No. 2A). (Illus.). 364p. 1989. pap. 32.00 (0-933500-01-7) Am Fern Soc.

— A Field Manual of the Ferns & Fern-Allies of the United States & Canada. LC 84-22216. (Illus.). 446p. 1985. pap. 29.95 (0-87474-603-5, LEFNP) Smithsonian.

Lellis, George P. Bertolt Brecht, "Cahiers du Cinema", & Contemporary Film Theory. Kirkpatrick, Diane, ed. LC 82-2051. (Studies in Cinema: No. 13). 208p. reprint ed. 59.30 (0-8357-1300-8, 2070332) Bks Demand.

Lello, J. Official View on Education. LC 63-19251. 1964. 67.00 (0-08-010354-5, Pub. by Pergamon Repr UK) Franklin.

Lello, John. Accountability in Practice. Sayer, John, ed. (Education Ser.). 128p. 1994. 70.00 (0-304-32748-4); pap. 22.50 (0-304-32740-9) Cassell.

LeLoeuff, Jean. La Aventura de la Vida (The Adventure of Life) Puebla, Luis M., tr. (Explorer Ser.). (Illus.). 96p. (SPA.). (J). (gr. 4 up). 1992. lib. bdg. 15.90 (1-56294-177-1) Millbrook Pr.

Leloir, Michel. Dictionnaire du Costume. 400p. (FRE.). 1992. 295.00 (0-8288-9477-9) Fr & Eur.

Lelong, Guy, jt. auth. see Soleil, Jean-Jacques.

Lelong, P. Fonctions Plurisousharmoniques et Formes Differentielles Positives. (Cours & Documents de Mathematiques & de Physique Ser.). 90p. 1968. text ed. 87.00 (0-677-50220-6) Gordon & Breach.

— Plurisubharmonic Functions & Positive Differential Forms. (Notes on Mathematics & Its Applications Ser.). 88p. 1969. text ed. 87.00 (0-677-30220-7) Gordon & Breach.

Lelong, P., et al, eds. Seminaire d'Analyse. (Lecture Notes in Mathematics Ser.: Vol. 1198). x, 260p. 1986. pap. 34.80 (0-387-16762-5) Spr-Verlag.

Lelong, P. & Gruman, L. Entire Functions of Several Complex Variables. (Grundlehren der Mathematischen Wissenschaften Ser.: Vol. 282). 285p. 1986. 79.00 (0-387-15296-2) Spr-Verlag.

LeLoo, Mary, ed. Through the Fire: Personal Recovery Stories. 260p. (Orig.). 1992. pap. 10.95 (0-89594-527-4) Crossing Pr.

LeLoo, Mary, jt. auth. see Calof, David L.

LeLoup, Lance T. The Fiscal Congress: Legislative Control of the Budget. LC 79-6823. (Contributions in Political Science Ser.: No. 47). (Illus.). xii, 227p. 1980. text ed. 55.00 (0-313-22009-3, LFC/, Greenwood Pr) Greenwood.

— Politics in America: The Ability to Govern. 3rd ed. Schiller, ed. 593p. (C). 1991. text ed. 54.75 (0-314-79502-2) West Pub.

LeLoup, Lance T. & Shull, Steven A. Congress & the President: The Policy Connection. 274p. (C). 1993. pap. 19.95 (0-534-15876-5) Intl Thomson.

Leloup, Roger. The Three Suns of Vina. Decker, Dwight, tr. (Adventures of Yoko, Vic & Paul Ser.). (Illus.). 49p. 1989. pap. 6.95 (0-87416-076-6, Comcat Comics) Catalan Communs.

— Vulcan's Forge. Surbeck, Jean-Jacques, tr. (Adventures of Yoko, Vic & Paul Ser.). (Illus.). 49p. (Orig.). (YA). (gr. 12 up). 1989. pap. 6.95 (0-87416-065-0, Comcat Comics) Catalan Communs.

Lely, G., ed. see De Sade, Marquis.

Lely, Gilbert. Vie du Marquis de Sade. 24.40 (0-685-34061-9) Fr & Eur.

Lely, James A. Aquarius. (Sun Sign Ser.). 40p. (J). (gr. 4). 1989. lib. bdg. 13.95 (0-88682-258-0) Creative Ed.

— Libra. (Sun Sign Ser.). 40p. (J). (gr. 4). 1989. lib. bdg. 13.95 (0-88682-262-9) Creative Ed.

— Virgo. (Sun Sign Ser.). 40p. (J). (gr. 4). 1989. lib. bdg. 13.95 (0-88682-259-9) Creative Ed.

***Lelyveld, Arthur.** The Steadfast Stream: An Introduction to Jewish Social Values. 120p. 1995. pap. 10.95 (0-8298-1023-4) Pilgrim OH.

Lelyveld, David. Aligarh's First Generation: Muslim Solidarity in British India. LC 77-71990. 406p. reprint ed. pap. 115.80 (0-8357-3299-1, 2039522) Bks Demand.

Lelyveld, I., jt. auth. see Hutzinger, O.

Lelyveld, Joseph. Move Your Shadow: South Africa, Black & White. 402p. 1986. pap. 11.00 (0-14-009326-5, Penguin Bks) Viking Penguin.

Lem, Carol. The Hermit's Journey: Tarot Poems for Meditation. 53p. 1992. pap. 9.95 (1-882868-00-5) Peddler Pr.

Lem, Dean P. Graphics Master 5: A Workbook of Planning Aids, Reference Guides & Graphic Tools for the Design, Estimating, Preparation & Production of Typography, Electronic Prepress Imaging, Printing, Print Advertising & Desktop Publishing. (Illus.). 154p. (C). 1993. 74.50 (0-914218-08-5); pap. text ed. 54.50 (0-914218-09-3) D Lem Assocs.

Lem, Kenneth W., intro. Handbook of Nonprescription Drugs: Case Studies Workbook. 10th ed. 160p. (C). 1993. 30.00 (0-917330-64-1) Am Pharm Assn.

Lem, Stanislaw. Chain of Chance. LC 83-22620. 182p. 1984. pap. 7.95 (0-15-616500-7, Harvest Bks) HarBrace.

— The Cyberiad: Fables for the Cybernetic Age. Kandel, Michael, tr. LC 84-22589. (Illus.). 302p. 1985. pap. 8.95 (0-15-623550-1, Harvest Bks) HarBrace.

— Eden. Heine, Marc E., tr. 1989. 19.95 (0-15-127580-7) HarBrace.

— Eden. 1991. pap. 10.95 (0-15-627806-5, Harvest Bks) HarBrace.

— Fiasco. Kandel, Michael, tr. (Helen & Kurt Wolff Bk.). 1987. 17.95 (0-15-130640-0) HarBrace.

— Fiasco. 336p. 1988. pap. 8.95 (0-15-630630-1) HarBrace.

— The Futurological Congress. Kandel, Michael, tr. LC 85-5500. 154p. 1985. reprint ed. pap. 7.95 (0-15-634040-2, Harvest Bks) HarBrace.

— Highcastle: A Remembrance. Kandel, Michael, tr. LC 95-7882. 1995. 22.00 (0-15-140218-3) HarBrace.

— His Master's Voice. LC 83-18467. 210p. 1984. pap. 6.95 (0-15-640300-5, Harvest Bks) HarBrace.

— Hospital of the Transfiguration. 1991. pap. 9.95 (0-15-642176-3, Harvest Bks) HarBrace.

— Imaginary Magnitude. Heine, Marc E., tr. LC 83-18624. (Helen & Kurt Wolff Bk.). 176p. 1985. reprint ed. pap. 9.00 (0-15-644180-2, Harvest Bks) HarBrace.

— The Investigation. Mich, Adele, tr. LC 85-24841. 224p. 1986. pap. 8.00 (0-15-645158-1, Harvest Bks) HarBrace.

— Memoirs Found in a Bathtub. Kandel, Adele, tr. LC 85-14867. 192p. 1986. pap. 7.95 (0-15-658585-5, Harvest Bks) HarBrace.

— Memoirs of a Space Traveler: Further Reminiscences of Ijon Tichy. Stern, Joel & Swiecicka-Ziemianek, Maria, trs. LC 81-47310. (Helen & Kurt Wolff Bk.). 156p. 1983. pap. 6.00 (0-15-658635-5, Harvest Bks) HarBrace.

— Microworlds: Writings on Science Fiction & Fantasy. Rottensteiner, Franz, ed. 252p. 1986. pap. 6.95 (0-15-659443-9, Harvest Bks) HarBrace.

— More Tales of Pirx the Pilot. Iribarne, Louis et al, trs. LC 82-47668. (Helen & Kurt Wolff Bk.). 230p. 1983. reprint ed. pap. 8.00 (0-15-662143-6, Harvest Bks) HarBrace.

— Mortal Engines. 1992. pap. 8.95 (0-15-662161-4, Harvest Bks) HarBrace.

— One Human Minute. Leach, Catherine S., tr. 140p. 1986. pap. 5.00 (0-15-668795-X, Harvest Bks) HarBrace.

— Peace On Earth. 1994. 19.95 (0-15-171554-8) HarBrace.

— A Perfect Vacuum. Kandel, Michael, tr. LC 78-14076. (Helen & Kurt Wolff Bk.). 240p. 1983. pap. 6.95 (0-15-671686-0, Harvest Bks) HarBrace.

— Return from the Stars. 1989. pap. 7.95 (0-15-676593-4) HarBrace.

— Solaris. 1987. pap. 9.00 (0-15-683750-1, Harvest Bks) HarBrace.

— Solaris. 1993. reprint ed. lib. bdg. 18.95 (0-89968-351-7, Lghtyr Pr) Buccaneer Bks.

— The Star Diaries. Kandel, Michael, tr. LC 83-26385. (Illus.). 286p. 1985. pap. 8.95 (0-15-684905-4, Harvest Bks) HarBrace.

— Tales of Pirx the Pilot. Iribarne, Louis, tr. 216p. 1990. pap. 7.95 (0-15-688150-0, Harvest Bks) HarBrace.

Lema-Patino, Jorge. Uncommon Words Often Used in Print Journalism. 1991. 13.95 (0-533-09142-X) Vantage.

Lemagny, Jean-Claude, intro. Visionary Architects: Boullee, Ledoux, Lequeu. (Illus.). 240p. 1968. pap. 24.95 (0-914412-21-3) Inst for the Arts.

LeMahieu, D. L. A Culture for Democracy: Mass Communication & the Cultivated Mind in Britain Between the Wars. (Illus.). 408p. 1988. 79.00 (0-19-820137-0) OUP.

— The Mind of William Paley: A Philosopher & His Age. LC 75-22547. 229p. reprint ed. pap. 65.30 (0-7837-6172-4, 2045894) Bks Demand.

Lemaine, G., et al. Strategies et Choix dans la Recherche. (Maison des Sciences de l'Homme, Paris, Publications: No. 5). 1977. pap. 33.85 (90-279-7674-0) Mouton.

Lemaine, Gerard. Perspectives on the Emergence of Scientific Disciplines. 1977. text ed. 38.50 (90-279-7743-7) Mouton.

Lemaine, Gerard & Lemaine, Jean-Marie. Psychologie Sociale et Experimentation. (Textes de Sciences Sociales Ser.: No. 2). 1969. pap. 26.95 (90-279-6308-8) Mouton.

Lemaine, Jean-Marie, jt. auth. see Lemaine, Gerard.

LeMair, Henriette. Child's Garden of Verses. (Illus.). 112p. (J). (gr. k up). 1991. 15.95 (0-399-21818-1, Philomel Bks) Putnam Pub Group.

Lemaire, Anika. Jacques Lacan. Macey, David, tr. 1979. reprint ed. pap. 14.95 (0-7100-0350-1, RKP) Routledge.

Lemaire, F., ed. Mechanical Ventilation. xii, 198p. 1991 pap. 63.00 (0-387-53322-2) Spr-Verlag.

LeMaire, Francois, jt. ed. see Zapol, Warren M.

LeMaire, H. Paul. Personal Decisions. LC 81-43668. 220p. (Orig.). 1982. pap. text ed. 21.50 (0-8191-2330-7) U Pr of Amer.

Lemaire, Jean. Automobile Insurance: Actuarial Models. (S. S. Huebner International Ser.). 1985. lib. bdg. 63.00 (0-89838-166-5) Huebner Foun Insur.

— Automobile Insurance: Actuarial Models. (C). 1985. 335.00 (0-685-33794-4, Pub. by Witherby & Co UK) St Mut.

***Lemaire, Jean, ed.** Bonus-Malus Systems in Automobile Insurance. LC 94-41825. (Huebner International Series on Risk, Insurance & Economic Security: Vol. 19). 312p. (C). 1995. lib. bdg. 85.00 (0-7923-9545-X) Kluwer Ac.

Lemaire, Luc, jt. auth. see Eells, James.

Lemaire, P. G. Les Ondelettes en, Nineteen Eighty-Nine: Seminaire d'Analyse Harmonique Universite de Paris-Sud, Orsay. Dold, A. et al, eds. (Lecture Notes in Mathematics Ser.: Vol. 1438). v, 212p. 1990. pap. 30.00 (0-387-52932-2) Spr-Verlag.

***LeMaistre, JoAnn.** After the Diagnosis. 214p. (Orig.). 1995. pap. 12.95 (1-56975-046-7) Ulysses Pr.

— Beyond Rage: Mastering Unavoidable Health Changes. rev. ed. LC 93-36467. 208p. 1993. 24.95 (0-931712-11-4); audio 12.95 (0-931712-12-2) Alpine Guild.

***Lemaitre, Alain J. & Lessing, Erich.** Florence & the Renaissance. (Illus.). 224p. 1995. pap. 24.95 (2-87939-068-0) Stewart Tabori & Chang.

Lemaitre, Georges E. From Cubism to Surrealism in French Literature. LC 77-18121. (Illus.). 256p. 1978. reprint ed. text ed. 59.75 (0-313-20112-9, LEFC, Greenwood Pr) Greenwood.

***Lemaitre, Henri.** Dictionnaire Bordas de Litterature Francaise. 1994. write for info. (0-7859-8614-6, 204019682X) Fr & Eur.

— Le Litterature Francaise, 5 tomes. Incl. Tome I. Du Moyen Age a L'age Baroque. 29.95 (0-685-36710-X); Tome II. Des Classiques aux Philosophes. 29.95 (0-685-36711-8); Tome III. Evolutions du Dix-Neuvieme Siecle. 29.95 (0-685-36712-6); Tome IV. Metamorphoses du Vingtieme Siecle. 29.95 (0-685-36713-4); Tome V. Litterature Aujourd'hui. 17.50 (0-685-36714-2); (Bibliotheque des Connaissances Essentielles Ser.). write for info. (0-318-52038-9) Fr & Eur.

— Poesie Depuis Baudelaire. 368p. 1965. 39.95 (0-8288-7422-0) Fr & Eur.

Lemaitre, Henri, ed. Litterature Francaise, 5 tomes, Vol. 1. write for info. (0-8288-7870-6, FA104) Fr & Eur.

Lemaitre, Henri, ed. see Baudelaire, Charles P.

***Lemaitre, Jean & Chaboche, Jean-Louis.** Mechanics of Solid Materials. (Illus.). 577p. (C). 1994. pap. 34.95 (0-521-47758-1) Cambridge U Pr.

Lemaitre, Jean P. A Course on Damage Mechanics. (Illus.). 250p. 1992. 89.00 (0-387-53609-4) Spr-Verlag.

Lemaitre, Jean P. & Chaboche, Jean-Louis. Mechanics of Solid Materials. 500p. 1990. 150.00 (0-521-32853-5) Cambridge U Pr.

Lemaitre, Jean P., jt. ed. see Krajcinovic, D.

Lemaitre, Joseph. French: How to Speak & Write It. (Illus.). 1962. pap. 6.95 (0-486-20268-2) Dover.

LeMaitre, Jules. On the Margins of Old Books. Stratton, Clarence, tr. LC 70-163041. (Short Story Index Reprint Ser.). 1977. reprint ed. 23.95 (0-8369-3955-7) Ayer.

Lemaitre, Jules & Cavaignac, Godegroy. En Marge des Vieux Livres: Contes, 2 vols. LC 75-41173. (FRE.). reprint ed. 72.50 (0-404-15020-9) AMS Pr.

***Lemaitre, Nicole, et al.** Dictionnaire Culturel du Christianisme. 332p. 1994. 59.95 (0-7859-7723-6, 2091800813) Fr & Eur.

Lemaitre, Pascal. Emily the Giraffe. LC 92-85508. (Illus.). 32p. (J). (ps-2). 1993. 13.95 (1-56282-403-1); lib. bdg. 13.89 (1-56282-404-X) Hyprn Child.

— Zelda's Secret. LC 93-28448. (Illus.). (J). (ps-3). 1993. lib. bdg. 13.95 (0-8167-3309-0); pap. 3.95 (0-8167-3310-4) BrdgeWater.

***Lemaitre, Rafael.** A Review of the Hermit Crabs of the Genus Xylopagurus A. Milne Edwards, 1880 (Crustacea, Decapoda, Paguridae), Including Descriptions of Two New Species. (Contributions to Zoology Ser.: No. 570). 1995. write for info. (0-615-00310-9) Smithsonian.

LeMaitre, Roger, comp. A Classification of Igneous Rocks & Glossary of Terms. (Illus.). 206p. (C). 1989. text ed. 55.00 (0-632-02593-X) Blackwell Sci.

Lemaitre, Solange. Ramakrishna & the Vitality of Hinduism. Markmann, Charles L., tr. LC 68-54059. (Spiritual Masters Ser.). (Illus.). 224p. 1986. 18.95 (0-87951-194-X); pap. 9.95 (0-87951-241-5) Overlook Pr.

Lemak, N. A., jt. auth. see Gehan, E. A.

Lemak, Noreen A., jt. auth. see Fields, William S.

Lemak, Noreen A., jt. auth. see Freireich, Emil J.

Leman, jt. auth. see Byram, Michael.

An Asterisk (*) at the beginning of an entry indicates that the title is appearing in BIP for the first time.

Leman, A. D., et al, eds. Diseases of Swine. 7th ed. LC 91-35402. (Illus.). 1038p. (C). 1992. text ed. 114.95 (*0-8138-0442-6*) Iowa St U Pr.

Leman, Bonnie & Martin, Judy. Log Cabin Quilts. 36p. 1980. pap. 5.95 (*0-9602970-1-4*) Leman Pubns.

— Taking the Math Out of Making Patchwork Quilts. (Illus.). (Orig.). 1981. pap. 4.95 (*0-9602970-3-0*) Leman Pubns.

***Leman, Bonnie & Quilter's Newsletter Magazine Editors.** Choice Scrap Quilts. (Illus.). 120p. (Orig.). 1994. pap. 19.95 (*0-943721-14-8*) Leman Pubns.

Leman, Bonnie & Townsend, Louise O. How to Make a Quilt: Twenty-Five Easy Lessons for Beginners. 2nd rev. ed. (Illus.). 44p. reprint ed. pap. 7.95 (*0-9602970-4-9*) Leman Pubns.

Leman, Bonnie, jt. auth. see Quilter's Newsletter Magazine Editors.

Leman, Chris, jt. auth. see Leman, Laurie.

Leman, Chris, jt. ed. see Leman, Laurie.

Leman, Jill. Sleepy Kittens. LC 93-24232. (Illus.). 32p. (J). 1994. 14.00 (*0-688-13288-X*, Tambourine Bks); lib. bdg. 13.93 (*0-688-13289-8*, Tambourine Bks) Morrow.

Leman, Jill, jt. auth. see Leman, Martin.

Leman, K. Sexo y Comunicacion-Matrimonio (Sex & Communication in Marriage) (SPA.). Date not set. 1.79 (*1-56063-260-7*, 497416) Editorial Unilit.

Leman, Kevin. El Amor Comienza en la Cocina. Farias, Monica R., tr. 144p. (SPA.). 1986. pap. 3.95 (*0-88113-013-3*) Edit Betania.

— The Birth Order Book. 192p. 1985. pap. 4.99 (*0-8007-8596-7*) Revell.

— Birth Order Book. 1992. mass mkt. 9.95 (*0-440-50471-6*, Dell Trade Pbks) Dell.

— Bonkers: Why Women Get Stressed Out & What They Can Do about It. pap. 3.99 (*0-8007-8612-2*) Revell.

— Bringing up Kids Without Tearing Them Down. 1994. 15.99 (*1-56179-276-4*) Focus Family.

— Getting the Best Out of Your Kids: Before They Get the Best of You. 224p. 1992. 14.99 (*0-89081-963-7*) Harvest Hse.

— Growing up Firstborn. 1990. reprint ed. mass mkt. 4.99 (*0-440-20743-6*) Dell.

— Keeping Your Family Together When the World Is Falling Apart. LC 93-5068. 1993. reprint ed. write for info. (*1-56179-180-6*) Focus Family.

— Making Children Mind. 1987. mass mkt. 8.95 (*0-440-55184-6*) Dell.

— Making Children Mind Without Losing Yours. 192p. 1983. pap. 8.99 (*0-8007-5256-2*) Revell.

— Measuring Up. pap. 4.99 (*0-8007-8598-3*) Revell.

— The Pleasers: Woman Who Can't Say No - & the Men Who Control Them. pap. 4.99 (*0-8007-8597-5*) Revell.

— The Pleasers: Women Who Can't Say No & the Men Who Control Them. 1992. mass mkt. 4.99 (*0-440-20169-1*) Dell.

— Sex Begins in the Kitchen. LC 80-54004. 1983. pap. 6.99 (*0-8307-0920-7*) Regal.

— Smart Girls Don't & Guys Don't Either. 1982. 8.95 (*0-8307-0824-3*) Regal.

Leman, Kevin & Carlson, Randy. Unlocking the Secrets of Your Childhood Memories. 288p. 1990. mass mkt. 5.99 (*0-671-70317-X*) PB.

Leman, Laurie & Leman, Chris. Mountain Biker's Guide to Pacific NW. (Dennis Coello's America by Mountain Bike Ser.). (Illus.). 300p. (Orig.). 1994. pap. 14.95 (*1-56044-288-3*) Falcon Pr MT.

Leman, Laurie & Leman, Chris, eds. The Mountain Biker's Guide to Southern California. (America by Mountain Bike Ser.). (Illus.). 184p. (Orig.). 1993. pap. 12.95 (*1-56044-197-6*) Falcon Pr MT.

Leman, Martin. The Little Cats ABC Book. LC 93-26272. (J). 1994. 13.00 (*0-671-88612-6*) S&S Trade.

Leman, Martin & Leman, Jill. Martin Leman's Teddy Bears. LC 89-60796. (Illus.). 48p. 1989. 9.95 (*0-7207-1885-6*) Viking Penguin.

Leman-Stefanovic, I. The Event of Death: A Phenomenological Enquiry. (C). 1986. lib. bdg. 107.00 (*90-247-3414-2*) Kluwer Ac.

Leman, Walter M. Memoirs of an Old Actor. LC 78-91905. 1972. 26.95 (*0-405-08741-1*) Ayer.

— Memories of an Old Actor. (American Biography Ser.). 406p. 1991. reprint ed. lib. bdg. 89.00 (*0-7812-8244-6*) Rprt Serv.

— Memories of an Old Actor. LC 70-106905. 1970. reprint ed. 16.00 (*0-403-00199-4*) Scholarly.

***Lemann, Bernard, et al, eds.** Talk about Architecture: A Century of Architectural Education at Tulane. LC 93-60383. (Illus.). 247p. 1993. 40.00 (*0-9637302-0-7*) Tulane U Archit.

Lemann, Nancy. Lives of the Saints. 156p. 1986. pap. 7.95 (*0-452-25886-3*, Plume) NAL-Dutton.

Lemann, Nicholas. The Promised Land. 1992. pap. 14.00 (*0-679-73347-7*) McKay.

— The Promised Land: The Great Black Migrants & How It Changed America. 1992. pap. 13.00 (*0-685-57357-5*, Vin) Random.

— Promised Land: The Great Black Migration & How It Changed America. 1991. 24.95 (*0-394-56004-3*) Knopf.

— Promised Land: The Great Black Migration & How It Changed America. 1995. pap. 14.00 (*0-394-26967-5*, Vin) Random.

Lemans, Martin. Curiouser Cats. (Illus.). 32p. (J). (ps-2). 1993. 16.95 (*0-575-04707-0*, Pub. by V Gollancz UK) Trafalgar.

Lemaout, B. General System of Botany: Descriptive & Analytical, 2 pts. 1968p. 1985. reprint ed. 750.00 (*81-7089-029-2*, Pub. by Intl Bk Distr II) St Mut.

Lemar, J. & Mast, Lois A. A Journey Through Europe. 20p. 1992. pap. 4.00 (*1-883294-06-1*) Olde Sprgfld.

Lemarchand-Beraud, T. & Fossati, P., eds. Androgens: Pathophysiological & Behavioural Aspects. (Journal: Hormone Research: Vol. 18, No. 1-3). (Illus.). 152p. 1983. pap. 65.75 (*3-8055-3728-X*) S Karger.

Lemarchand-Beraud, T. & Vanhaelst, L., eds. Actual Trends in Thyroid Physiopathology. (Journal: Hormone Research: Vol. 26, No. 1-4, 1987). ii, 230p. 1987. 155.25 (*3-8055-4582-7*) S Karger.

Lemarchand, Elizabeth. The Affacombe Affair. large type ed. 1979. 12.00 (*0-7089-0280-4*) Ulverscroft.

— Buried in the Past. large type ed. 1976. 12.00 (*0-85456-431-4*) Ulverscroft.

— Cyanide with Compliments. (Black Dagger Crime Ser.). 184p. 1992. reprint ed. 16.50 (*0-86220-829-7*, Black Dagger) Chivers N Amer.

— Death of an Old Girl. 264p. 1993. 16.50 (*0-7451-8623-8*, Black Dagger) Chivers N Amer.

— Death on Doomsday. large type ed. 1973. 12.00 (*0-85456-173-0*) Ulverscroft.

— The Glade Manor Murder. large type ed. (Mystery Ser.). 304p. 1992. 21.95 (*0-7089-2647-9*) Ulverscroft.

— The Glade Manor Murders. 192p. 1989. 17.95 (*0-8027-5741-3*) Walker & Co.

— Let or Hindrance. large type ed. 1979. 12.00 (*0-7089-0303-7*) Ulverscroft.

— Light Through Glass. large type ed. 288p. 1986. 15.95 (*0-7089-1505-1*) Ulverscroft.

— Light Through the Glass. 192p. 1986. 15.95 (*0-8027-5649-2*) Walker & Co.

— Troubled Waters. large type ed. 352p. 1984. 21.95 (*0-7089-1130-7*) Ulverscroft.

— Unhappy Returns. large type ed. 1980. 12.00 (*0-7089-0407-6*) Ulverscroft.

— Who Goes Home? 192p. 1987. 15.95 (*0-8027-5675-1*) Walker & Co.

— Who Goes Home? large type ed. 304p. 1987. 16.95 (*0-7089-1599-X*) Ulverscroft.

Lemarchand, Rene. Burundi: Ethnocide As Discourse & Practice. (Woodrow Wilson Center Press Ser.). 200p. (C). 1994. 54.95 (*0-521-45176-0*) Cambridge U Pr.

— The World Bank in Rwanda: The Case of the Office de Valorisation Agricole et Pastorale du Mutara. LC 82-70681. 78p. 1982. pap. text ed. 5.00 (*0-941934-39-X*) Indiana Africa.

Lemarchand, Rene, ed. African Kingships in Perspective: Political Change & Modernization in Monarchical Settings. 325p. 1977. 37.50 (*0-7146-3027-6*, Pub. by F Cass Pubs UK) Intl Spec Bk.

— American Policy in Southern Africa: The Stakes & the Stance. 2nd ed. LC 80-6222. 513p. (C). 1981. lib. bdg. 57.00 (*0-8191-1436-7*) U Pr of Amer.

— The Green & the Black: Qadhafi's Policies in Africa. LC 87-46088. (Indiana Series in Arab & Islamic Studies). (Illus.). 198p. 1988. 29.95 (*0-253-32678-8*) Ind U Pr.

Lemarchand, Rene, jt. ed. see Eisenstadt, S. N.

Lemarchand, Rene, et al. Political Awakening in the Belgian Congo. LC 82-2986. (Illus.). xii, 357p. 1982. reprint ed. text ed. 69.50 (*0-313-23415-9*, LEPOL, Greenwood Pr) Greenwood.

Lemard, Joseph A. History of Olmsted County, Minnesota. (Illus.). 674p. 1994. reprint ed. lib. bdg. 67.50 (*0-8328-3617-6*) Higginson Bk Co.

Lemare, Edwin H. Organs I Have Met. (Illus.). 137p. 1992. 25.00 (*0-913746-32-0*) Organ Lit.

Lemarechal, Claude, jt. auth. see Hiriart-Urruty, Jean-Baptiste.

Lemarechale, C & Mifflin, R., eds. Nonsmooth Optimization: Proceedings of an IIASA Workshop, 28 March-8 April 1977. 1978. 86.00 (*0-08-023428-3*, Pub. by Pergamon Repr UK) Franklin.

LeMarr, John. America's Best Hoax: How Doctors Get Fat on Fitness. LC 93-77223. (Illus.). 160p. (Orig.). 1993. pap. 12.95 (*0-9632923-7-4*) HealthMasters.

***LeMassena, Robert.** America's Workhorse Locomotive: The 2-8-2. 1993. pap. 14.95 (*0-915276-54-2*) Quadrant Pr.

LeMassena, Robert A. American Steam Vol. 1: The Photos of Ben F. Cutler. (Illus.). 256p. 1987. 29.00 (*0-913582-19-0*) Sundance.

— American Steam Vol. 2: Locomotives of the Northeast. (Illus.). 256p. 1989. 29.00 (*0-913582-05-0*) Sundance.

— Articulated Steam Locomotives of North America: A Catalogue of "Giant Steam" (Illus.). 416p. 1979. 55.00 (*0-913582-26-3*) Sundance.

— Rio Grande... to the Pacific! (Illus.). 416p. 1974. 45.00 (*0-913582-10-7*) Sundance.

LeMaster, Carolyn G. A Corner of the Tapestry: A History of the Jewish Experience in Arkansas, 1820s - 1990s. LC 93-48940. 622p. 1994. 60.00 (*1-55728-304-4*) U of Ark Pr.

LeMaster, Dennis C., ed. Community Stability in Forest-Based Economies. LC 88-24831. 1989. text ed. 34.95 (*0-88192-129-7*) Timber.

LeMaster, J. R. Journey to Beijing: Poems. LC 92-6726. 100p. 1992. pap. 12.95 (*0-7734-0030-3*) E Mellen.

LeMaster, J. R., ed. Jesse Stuart on Education. LC 91-24688. 176p. 1991. text ed. 19.00 (*0-8131-1765-8*) U Pr of Ky.

— The World of Jesse Stuart: Selected Poems. 303p. 1975. 40.00 (*0-07-062212-4*) McGraw.

***LeMaster, J. R. & Clarke, Mary W., eds.** Jesse Stuart, Essays on His Work. fac. ed. LC 76-46032. 173p. 1994. pap. 49.40 (*0-7837-7594-6*, 2047347) Bks Demand.

LeMaster, J. R. & Wilson, James D., eds. The Mark Twain Encyclopedia. LC 92-45662. 888p. 1993. 95.00 (*0-8240-7212-X*, H1249) Garland.

Lemaster, James A., ed. see Grubbs, Robert L. & Ober, B. Scott.

LeMaster, Leslie J. Bacteria & Viruses. LC 84-27414. (New True Bks.). (Illus.). 48p. (J). (gr. k-4). 1985. lib. bdg. 12.90 (*0-516-01937-6*) Childrens.

— Cells & Tissues. LC 85-6695. (New True Bks.). (Illus.). 45p. (J). (gr. k-3). 1985. lib. bdg. 12.90 (*0-516-01266-5*) Childrens.

— Nutrition. LC 85-7728. (New True Bks.). (Illus.). 45p. (J). (gr. k-3). 1985. lib. bdg. 12.90 (*0-516-01271-1*) Childrens.

— Your Brain & Nervous System. LC 84-7635. (New True Bks.). (Illus.). 48p. (J). (gr. k-4). 1984. lib. bdg. 12.90 (*0-516-01931-7*); pap. 4.95 (*0-516-41931-5*) Childrens.

— Your Heart & Blood. LC 84-7604. (New True Bks.). (Illus.). 48p. (J). (gr. k-4). 1984. lib. bdg. 12.90 (*0-516-01933-3*); pap. 4.95 (*0-516-41933-1*) Childrens.

Lemaster, Melanie M. Starting College on the Right Foot. 96p. (C). 1992. per. 11.95 (*0-8403-7903-X*) Kendall-Hunt.

***LeMaster, Richard.** The Great Gallery of Ducks & Other Waterfowl. LC 94-28557. 1995. 49.95 (*0-8117-0706-7*) Stackpole.

LeMasters, E. E. Blue Collar Aristocrats: Life Styles at a Working-Class Tavern. LC 74-27309. 228p. 1975. 25.00 (*0-299-06550-2*) U of Wis Pr.

— Blue Collar Aristocrats: Life Styles at a Working-Class Tavern. LC 74-27309. 228p. 1976. pap. 13.95 (*0-299-06554-5*) U of Wis Pr.

Lemasters, J. J., et al, eds. Integration of Mitochondrial Function. LC 88-22444. (Illus.). 678p. 1988. 135.00 (*0-306-42999-3*, Plenum Pr) Plenum.

LeMasters, J. R. Jesse Stuart: Selected Criticism. LC 76-584. 140p. 1978. 10.00 (*0-912760-21-4*) Valkyrie Pub Hse.

Lemasters, John J., jt. ed. see Herman, Brian.

LeMasters, Philip. Discipleship for All Believers: Christian Ethics & the Kingdom of God. 160p. (Orig.). 1992. pap. 14.95 (*0-8361-3579-2*) Herald Pr.

— The Import of Eschatology in John Howard Yoder's Critique of Constantinianism. LC 91-44635. 264p. 1992. lib. bdg. 89.95 (*0-7734-9808-7*) E Mellen.

LeMasurier, W. E. & Thomson, J. W., eds. Volcanoes of the Antarctic Plate & Southern Oceans. (Antarctic Research Ser.: Vol. 48). 512p. 1990. 55.00 (*0-87590-172-7*) Am Geophysical.

***Lemay.** Introduction to DOS & Windows. (C). 1995. pap. text ed. write for info. (*0-8053-6372-6*) Benjamin-Cummings.

Lemay, Alan. By Dim & Flaring Lamps. 272p. 1994. mass mkt. 4.99 (*0-425-14254-X*) Berkley Pub.

Lemay, Allan. The Searchers. reprint ed. lib. bdg. 21.95 (*0-88411-179-2*, Aeonian Pr) Amereon Ltd.

Lemay, Anne. Dog Days & Winter Ways: Skits to Promote Reading All Year Long. LC 94-7904. 56p. (J). (gr. k-6). 1994. pap. 9.95 (*0-917846-40-0*, 33899, Alleyside) Highsmith Pr.

LeMay, Brian W., ed. Science, Ethics, & Food: Papers & Proceedings of a Colloquium Organized by the Smithsonian Institution. LC 88-18399. (Illus.). 144p. (Orig.). 1988. pap. 14.95 (*0-87474-605-1*) Smithsonian.

***Lemay, Edna H.** Dictionnaire des Constituants 1789-91, 2 vols. (FRE.). 1991. 395.00 (*0-7859-8019-9*, 2740000030) Fr & Eur.

Lemay, Eric C. Heidegger for Beginners. 1994. pap. 9.95 (*0-86316-172-3*) Writers & Readers.

Lemay, Gerald J. C for Pascal & Fortran Programmers. 114p. (C). 1993. student ed 15.00 (*1-883496-02-0*); pap. text ed. 25.00 (*1-883496-01-2*) P S Melvil Pr.

LeMay, H. Eugene, Jr., ed. see Nelson, John H. & Kemp, Kenneth C.

Lemay, Harding. Inside, Looking Out. 320p. (Orig.). 1982. pap. 3.25 (*0-8439-1086-0*) Dorchester Pub Co.

Lemay, Helen R. Women's Secrets: A Translation of Pseudo-Albertus Magnus' De Secretis Mulierum with Commentaries. LC 91-30690. (SUNY Series in Medieval Studies). 200p. (C). 1992. 57.50 (*0-7914-1143-5*); pap. 18.95 (*0-7914-1144-3*) State U NY Pr.

LeMay, Iain & Schetky, McDonald, eds. Copper in Iron & Steel. LC 82-17615. 446p. 1982. 59.50 (*0-471-05913-7*) Wiley.

Lemay, J. A. The American Dream of Captain John Smith. 1991. text ed. 32.50 (*0-8139-1321-7*) U Pr of Va.

— The Canon of Benjamin Franklin, 1722-1776: New Attributions & Reconsiderations. LC 85-40530. 160p. 1986. 28.50 (*0-87413-290-8*) U Delaware Pr.

— Did Pocahontas Save Captain John Smith? LC 92-791. (Illus.). 144p. 1992. 22.50 (*0-8203-1461-7*) U of Ga Pr.

— New England's Annoyances: America's First Folk Song. LC 84-40414. (Illus.). 160p. 1985. 29.50 (*0-87413-278-9*) U Delaware Pr.

Lemay, J. A., ed. Deism, Masonry, & the Enlightenment: Essays Honoring Alfred Owen Aldrige. LC 86-40585. (Illus.). 216p. 1987. 32.50 (*0-87413-317-3*) U Delaware Pr.

— Reappraising Benjamin Franklin: A Bicentennial Perspective. LC 91-50237. (Illus.). 504p. (C). 1993. 39.50 (*0-87413-448-X*) U Delaware Pr.

— Robert Bolling Woos Anne Miller: Courtship & Love in Colonial Virginia, 1760. (Illus.). 208p. 1990. lib. bdg. 25.00x (*0-8139-1259-8*) U Pr of Va.

Lemay, J. A., ed. see Franklin, Benjamin.

Lemay, J. Leo. A Calendar of American Poetry in the Colonial Newspapers & Magazines & in the Major English Magazines Through 1765. LC 70-26435. 353p. 1972. 20.00 (*0-912296-01-1*, U Pr of Va) Am Antiquarian.

— The Frontiersman from Lout to Hero: Notes on the Significance of the Comparative Method & the Stage Theory in Early American Literature & Culture. 1979. pap. 3.50 (*0-912296-39-9*) Am Antiquarian.

***Lemay, Laura.** Teach Yourself Web Publishing with HTML in a Week. (Illus.). 400p. (Orig.). 1995. pap. 25.00 (*0-672-30667-0*) Sams.

LeMay, Michael C. Anatomy of a Public Policy: The Reform of Contemporary American Immigration Law. LC 94-6376. 224p. 1994. text ed. 55.00 (*0-275-94902-8*, Praeger Pubs) Greenwood.

— From Open Door to Dutch Door: An Analysis of U. S. Immigration Policy since 1820. LC 87-2368. 200p. 1987. pap. text ed. 12.95 (*0-275-92628-1*, B2628) Greenwood.

— From Open Door to Dutch Door: An Analysis of U. S. Immigration Policy since 1820. LC 87-2368. 200p. 1987. text ed. 55.00 (*0-275-92492-0*, C2492, Praeger Pubs) Greenwood.

Lemay, Michael C., ed. The Gatekeepers: Comparative Immigration Policy. LC 88-17993. 240p. 1989. text ed. 55.00 (*0-275-93079-3*, C3079, Praeger Pubs) Greenwood.

***Lemay, Michele H. & Hale, Lynne Z.** Coastal Resources Management: A Guide to Public Education Programs & Materials. fac. ed. LC 89-27274. (Kumarian Press Library of Management for Development). 62p. 1994. pap. 25.00 (*0-7837-7571-7*, 2047324) Bks Demand.

Lemay, Nita K., jt. auth. see Newman, Matt.

Lembark, Connie W. The Prints of Sam Francis: A Catalogue Raisonne, 1960-1990, 2 vols., Set. LC 91-58633. (Illus.). 612p. 1992. boxed 125.00 (*1-55595-062-0*) Hudson Hills.

Lembcke, Jerry. Capitalist Development & Class Capacities: Marxist Theory & Union Organization. LC 87-37546. (Contributions in Labor Studies: No. 25). 213p. 1988. text ed. 55.00 (*0-313-26209-8*, LCD/, Greenwood Pr) Greenwood.

Lembcke, Jerry & Tattam, William. One Union in Wood. LC 84-15808. 210p. 1984. pap. 7.95 (*0-7178-0619-7*) Intl Pubs Co.

Lembeck, Fred. Science Alternative Animal Experiments. 1990. boxed write for info. (*0-318-68271-0*) P-H.

Lembeck, Fred, ed. Scientific Alternatives to Animal Experiments. Welch, Jacqui, tr. (Ellis Horwood Series in Biochemistry & Biotechnology). 300p. 1990. 69.95 (*0-412-02771-2*, A4476, Chap & Hall NY) Chapman & Hall.

***Lembeck, Frederick.** Beat the House: Sixteen Ways to Win at Blackjack, Craps, Roulette, Baccarat & Other Table Games. 224p. 1995. pap. 12.95 (*0-8065-1607-0*, Citadel Pr) Carol Pub Group.

Lembeck, Karl-Heinz. Gegenstand Geschichte. 1988. lib. bdg. 117.50 (*90-247-3635-8*) Kluwer Ac.

Lembeck, Michael, ed. see Lazar, Edward.

Lembeke, Jerry, jt. ed. see Levine, Rhonda F.

Lember, Barbara H., photos & text. Book of Fruit. LC 94-4067. (Illus.). 32p. (J). (ps-2). 1994. lib. bdg. 14.95 (*0-395-66989-8*) Ticknor & Flds Bks Yng Read.

Lemberg, Alexis, jt. auth. see Lemberg, Ray.

Lemberg, H. L., jt. auth. see Hutcheson, L. D.

Lemberg, Lauri. St. Croix Avenue. Eldridge, Miriam, tr. 424p. 1992. pap. 14.95 (*0-9633780-0-7*) Tyomies Soc.

Lemberg, R., jt. auth. see Falk, J.

Lemberg, Ray & Lemberg, Alexis. Daddy, Me & the Adventures of Growing Up. 32p. (Orig.). (J). (gr. k-4). 1988. pap. 6.45 (*0-9619208-5-8*) Small Hands Pr.

Lemberg, Raymond, ed. Controlling Eating Disorders with Facts, Advice, & Resources. (Illus.). 240p. 1992. pap. 29.50 (*0-89774-691-0*) Oryx Pr.

Lemberg, Sally, jt. auth. see Griffith, Ernest R.

Lemberg, Stephen. Scaredy Dog. LC 92-24440. (Illus.). 40p. (J). (ps-3). 1994. 8.99 (*0-679-83175-4*) Knopf Bks Yng Read.

— Scaredy Dog. LC 92-24440. (Illus.). 40p. (J). (ps-3). 1994. lib. bdg. 9.99 (*0-679-93175-9*) Knopf Bks Yng Read.

Lemberg, Stephen H. Alphabet Town. (Illus.). (J). (ps). 1993. Incl. cass. 7.95 (*1-882500-02-4*) SmartSong.

— Learning Land. (Illus.). (J). (ps). 1993. Incl. cass. audio 7.95 (*1-882500-00-8*) SmartSong.

— Numberville. (Illus.). (J). (ps). 1993. Incl. cass. audio 7.95 (*1-882500-03-2*) SmartSong.

— Rainbow Village. (Illus.). (J). (ps). 1993. Incl. cass. 7.95 (*1-882500-01-6*) SmartSong.

Lemberger, L. & Reidenberg, M. M., eds. Proceedings of the Second World Conference on Clinical Pharmacology & Therapeutics. (Illus.). 996p. (Orig.). 1984. pap. 50.00 (*0-9609094-1-9*) Am Phar & Ex.

Lemberger, LeAnn. Dear Leigh Michaels... A Novelist Answers the Most-Asked Questions about Getting Published. 84p. (Orig.). 1994. pap. 9.95 (*0-9641275-0-4*) PBL Ltd.

Lemberger, Mark. Crime of Magnitude: The Murder of Little Annie. LC 93-6866. (Illus.). 320p. 1993. 23.95 (*1-879483-12-2*); pap. 14.95 (*1-879483-13-0*) Prairie Oak Pr.

Lembi, Carole A. & Waaland, J. Robert, eds. Algae & Human Affairs. (Illus.). 585p. 1989. 84.95 (*0-521-32115-8*) Cambridge U Pr.

Lembi, Carole A., et al. Green Algae, II: Cytology. LC 73-10108. 216p. (C). 1973. 26.00 (*0-8422-7161-9*) Irvington.

Lembke, Janet. Dangerous Birds. 192p. 1992. 21.95 (*1-55821-190-X*) Lyons & Burford.

— Looking for Eagles: Reflections of a Classical Naturalist. 1990. 19.95 (*1-55821-077-6*) Lyons & Burford.

— River Time. 192p. 1989. 16.95 (*1-55821-035-0*) Lyons & Burford.

— Skinny-Dipping: And Other Immersions in Water, Myth & Being Human. LC 94-15378. 192p. 1994. 21.95 (*1-55821-274-4*) Lyons & Burford.

Lembke, Janet, tr. see Aeschylus.

Lembke, Janet, tr. see Euripides.

Lembke, Ruth C. Calico's Country Cats. LC 82-80861. (Illus.). 64p. 1982. 5.95 (*0-686-39811-4*) R C Lembke.

Lembo, Anne & Surkiewicz, Joe. Short Bike Rides in & Around Philadelphia. LC 93-48965. (East Woods Book Ser.). (Illus.). 128p. 1994. pap. 9.95 (*1-56440-073-5*) Globe Pequot.

An Asterisk (*) at the beginning of an entry indicates that the title is appearing in BIP for the first time.

Lembo, Diana L., jt. auth. see Gillespie, John T.

Lembo, J. Lawrence, ed. see Whitman, Walt.

Lembo, John M. The Counseling Process: A Cognitive-Behavioral Approach. LC 76-4232. 1976. 10.95 (*0-87212-060-0*) Libra.

— How to Cope with Your Fears & Frustrations. LC 76-52139. 1977. 10.95 (*0-87212-091-0*) Libra.

Lemche, Niels P. Early Israel: Anthropological & Historical Studies on the Israelite Society before the Monarchy. (Supplements to Vetus Testamentum Ser.: No. 37). (Illus.). xv, 496p. 1986. 96.00 (*90-04-07853-3*) E J Brill.

Lemcio, Eugene E. The Past of Jesus in the Gospels. (Society for New Testament Studies Monographs: No. 68). 200p. (C). 1991. 54.95 (*0-521-40113-5*) Cambridge U Pr.

Lemcio, Eugene E., jt. auth. see Wall, Robert W.

***Lemcke.** Primary Care of Women. (Illus.). 624p. (C). 1995. pap. text ed. 34.95 (*0-8385-9813-7*) Appleton & Lange.

Lemcke, Doris. Passion's Secret. 416p. 1993. mass mkt. 4.25 (*0-8217-4277-9*) Zebra.

Lemco, Gary. Nietzsche As Educator. LC 92-4107. 160p. 1992. lib. bdg. 69.95 (*0-7734-9962-8*) E Mellen.

Lemco, Jonathan. Canada & the Crisis in Central America. LC 90-43134. 208p. 1991. text ed. 49.95 (*0-275-93718-6*, C3718, Praeger Pubs) Greenwood.

— Political Stability in Federal Governments. LC 91-6777. 224p. 1991. text ed. 55.00 (*0-275-93854-9*, C3854, Praeger Pubs) Greenwood.

— Turmoil in the Peacable Kingdom: The Quebec Sovereignty Movement & Its Implications for Canada & the U. S. (Illus.). 266p. 1994. 50.00 (*0-8020-0532-2*); pap. 17.95 (*0-8020-6970-3*) U of Toronto Pr.

Lemco, Jonathan, ed. The Canada - United States Relationship: The Politics of Energy & Environmental Coordination. LC 91-34774. 240p. 1992. text ed. 47.95 (*0-275-94239-2*, C4239, Praeger Pubs) Greenwood.

— National Health Care: Lessons for the United States & Canada. 286p. 1994. text ed. 47.50x (*0-472-10440-3*) U of Mich Pr.

— Tensions at the Border: Energy & Environmental Concerns in Canada & the United States. LC 91-34775. 216p. 1992. text ed. 49.95 (*0-275-94001-2*, C4001, Praeger Pubs) Greenwood.

***Lemco, Jonathan & Robson, William B., eds.** Ties Beyond Trade: Labor & Environmental Issues under the NAFTA. 162p. (Orig.). 1993. pap. text ed. 14.95 (*0-89068-120-1*, CAC 61(NPA 265)) Natl Planning.

Lemco, Jonathan, jt. ed. see Belous, Richard S.

Leme, ed. Hormones & Inflammation. 1988. 143.00 (*0-8493-5928-7*, RB131, CRC Reprint) Franklin.

Leme, J. Garcia, jt. auth. see Rocha E Silva, M.

Leme, R. A. Dictionary of Geotechnical Engineering. 159p. (ENG & POR.). 1980. pap. 39.95 (*0-8288-0958-5*, M6073) Fr & Eur.

***Lemeh, Eva M.** For the Love of Money. 180p. Date not set. pap. 7.95 (*0-7610-0256-1*) NW Pub.

Lemehaute, Bernard & Hanes, Daniel M. The Sea, Vol. 9: Ocean Engineering Science, 2 vols., Set. 1990. text ed. 300.00 (*0-471-63393-3*) Wiley.

Lemelin, Maurice. The Public Service Alliance of Canada: A Look at a Union in the Public Sector. (Monograph & Research Ser.: No. 21). 1978. 6.50 (*0-89215-085-8*) U Cal LA Indus Rel.

Lemelle, Anthony J. Black Male Deviance. LC 94-25040. 208p. 1994. text ed. 52.95 (*0-275-95004-2*, Praeger Pubs) Greenwood.

Lemelle, Sid. Pan-Africanism for Beginners. LC 91-50561. (Writers & Readers Documentary Comic Bks.). (Illus.). 176p. (Orig.). (C). 1992. pap. 9.95 (*0-86316-148-0*) Writers & Readers.

***Lemelle, Sidney.** Imagining Home: Class, Culture & Nationalism in the African Diaspora. 1994. 64.95 (*0-86091-386-4*, Pub. by Verso UK); pap. 18.95 (*0-86091-585-9*, Pub. by Verso UK) Routledge Chapman & Hall.

Lemelman, Martin. Chanukah Is... (Illus.). 10p. (J). (ps-00). 1988. bds. 4.95 (*0-8074-0424-1*) UAHC.

— My Jewish Home. (Illus.). 10p. (J). (ps). 1988. bds., pap. 3.95 (*0-8074-0415-2*, 102002) UAHC.

— My Jewish Home: Simchah Ba'ambatyah - Fun in the Bathtub. (Illus.). 10p. (J). (ps). 1987. vinyl bd. 3.95 (*0-8074-0327-X*, 102001) UAHC.

Lemelman, Martin, illus. Jewish Holiday Book. 10p. (J). 1989. bds. 4.95 (*0-8074-0431-4*, 102004) UAHC.

LeMenager, Charles R. Julian City & Cuyamaca Country: A History & Guide to the Past & Present. (Illus.). 256p. 1992. 19.95 (*0-9611102-5-2*); pap. 12.95 (*0-9611102-4-4*) Eagle Peak Pub.

— Off the Main Road: San Vicente & Barona. (Illus.). 188p. (Orig.). 1983. per., pap. 7.95 (*0-9611102-0-1*) Eagle Peak Pub.

— Off the Main Road: San Vicente & Barona. 2nd rev. ed. (Illus.). 206p. (Orig.). 1990. per., pap. 9.95 (*0-9611102-3-6*) Eagle Peak Pub.

— Ramona & Round About: A History of San Diego County's Little Known Back Country. (Illus.). 252p. 1989. 18.95 (*0-9611102-1-X*); pap. 11.95 (*0-9611102-2-8*) Eagle Peak Pub.

Lemer, Andrew C., jt. ed. see Gould, James P.

Lemer, Andrew C., jt. ed. see Grant, Albert T.

Lemer, Andrew C., jt. ed. see Ledbetter, William B.

Lemer, Andrew C., ed. see National Research Council, Committee on Vision Staff.

Lemer, Paule. Astrological Key to Mahabharata. (C). 1989. 21.00 (*81-208-0453-8*, Pub. by Motilal Banarsidass II) S Asia.

Lemerand, Pamela. SAFE, Student Assistance & Family Education Program: A Dynamic Program for Elementary Schools. LC 92-40065. 208p. 1993. pap. 29.95 (*1-56246-053-6*, P236) Johnsn Inst.

Lemercier-Quelquejay, Chantal, jt. auth. see Bennigsen, Alexandre.

Lemerise, Bruce. Sheldon's Lunch. LC 94-11355. 1994. lib. bdg. 14.60 (*0-8368-0991-2*) Gareth Stevens Inc.

— Sheldon's Lunch. LC 80-10449. (Illus.). (J). (ps-3). 1980. 5.95 (*0-8193-1025-5*) Parents.

Lemers, Andrew C., jt. ed. see McDowell, Bruce D.

***Lemert, Charles.** Sociology after the Crisis. LC 95-15689. 1995. write for info. (*0-8133-2543-9*) Westview.

— Sociology after the Crisis. LC 95-15689. 1995. pap. 14.95 (*0-8133-2544-7*) Westview.

Lemert, Charles, ed. see Denzin, Norman K.

Lemert, Charles C. Sociology & the Twilight of Man: Homocentrism & Discourse in Sociological Theory. LC 78-17146. 276p. 1980. pap. 9.95 (*0-8093-0975-0*) S Ill U Pr.

Lemert, Charles C., ed. French Sociology: Rupture & Renewal Since 1968. LC 80-25714. 528p. 1981. text ed. 63.00 (*0-231-04698-7*) Col U Pr.

— Intellectuals & Politics: Social Theory Beyond the Academy. (Key Issues in Sociological Theory Ser.: Vol. 5). (Illus.). 224p. (C). 1990. text ed. 48.00 (*0-8039-3731-8*); pap. text ed. 22.95 (*0-8039-3732-6*) Sage.

— Social Theory: Multicultural & Classic Readings. LC 93-1043. 672p. (C). 1993. text ed. 68.50 (*0-8133-1583-2*); pap. text ed. 23.95 (*0-8133-1584-0*) Westview.

Lemert, Charles C. & Gillan, Garth. Michel Foucault: Social Theory & Transgression. LC 82-4276. 187p. reprint ed. pap. 53.30 (*0-8357-7782-0*, 2036142) Bks Demand.

Lemert, James B. Criticizing the Media: Empirical Approaches. (CommText Ser.: Vol. 21). 160p. (C). 1989. text ed. 37.00 (*0-8039-2636-7*); pap. text ed. 16.95 (*0-8039-2637-5*) Sage.

— Does Mass Communication Change Public Opinion After All? A New Approach to Effects Analysis. LC 80-23826. 260p. (C). 1981. text ed. 31.95 (*0-88229-474-1*) Nelson-Hall.

Lemert, James B., et al. News Verdicts, the Debates, & Presidential Campaigns. LC 91-8749. 312p. 1991. text ed. 55.00 (*0-275-93758-5*, C3758, Praeger Pubs) Greenwood.

Lemeshow, Stanley, jt. auth. see Hosmer, David W.

Lemeshow, Stanley, jt. auth. see Levy, Paul S.

Lemeshow, Stanley, et al. Adequacy of Sample Size in Health Studies. 1989. text ed. 64.95 (*0-471-92517-9*) Wiley.

Lemesurier. Heart of Religion. 1990. pap. 22.50 (*1-85230-014-0*, HERELP) Element MA.

Lemesurier, Peter. The Armageddon Script: Prophecy in Action. (Illus.). 270p. 1993. write for info. (*0-906540-19-4*); pap. 15.95 (*0-906540-37-2*) Element MA.

— Beyond All Belief: Science, Religion & Reality. (Illus.). 222p. 1990. 19.95 (*0-906540-41-0*) Element MA.

— Gospel of the Stars: The Mystery of the Cycle of the Ages. (Illus.). 144p. 1990. pap. 12.95 (*1-85230-148-1*) Element MA.

— Great Pyramid Decoded. 1993. pap. 17.95 (*1-85230-088-4*) Element MA.

— Great Pyramid Your Person. 1991. pap. 17.95 (*1-85230-016-7*) Element MA.

— The Healing of the Gods: The Magic of Symbols & the Practice of Theotherapy. 208p. 1993. pap. 12.95 (*1-85230-033-7*, Pub. by Element Bks UK) Element MA.

— Nostradamus: The Next Fifty Years. 304p. 1994. pap. 11.00 (*0-425-14433-X*, Berkley Trade) Berkley Pub.

Lemeunier. Dictionnaire Juridique. (FRE.). 1988. pap. 75.00 (*0-7859-3914-8*) Fr & Eur.

LeMeunier. French Dictionary of Legal Terms: Dic. Juridique. 305p. 1988. pap. 35.00 (*2-85608-028-6*) IBD Ltd.

Lemic, Jesse. Quitting in Time: How to Stop Smoking on Your Own. (Illus.). 39p. (Orig.). 1987. write for info. (*0-944566-00-6*) Start Today.

***LeMieux, A. C.** Do Angels Sing the Blues. LC 94-26411. (J). (gr. 1-8). Date not set. write for info. (*0-688-13725-3*, Tambourine Bks) Morrow.

— Fruit Flies, Fish & Fortune Cookies. LC 93-29606. (Illus.). (J). 1994. write for info. (*0-688-13299-5*, Tambourine Bks) Morrow.

— The TV Guidance Counselor. 192p. (YA). 1994. pap. 3.50 (*0-380-72050-7*, Flare) Avon.

— The TV Guidance Counselor. LC 92-33664. 240p. (YA). (gr. 7 up). 1993. 13.00 (*0-688-12402-X*, Tambourine Bks) Morrow.

***Lemieux, Andre.** Canadian Mines: Perspective: Production, Reserves, Development, Exploration-1991. (Mineral Bulletin Ser.: No. 233). 42p. (Orig.). 1993. pap. 24.65x (*0-660-58966-4*, Pub. by Canada Commun Grp CN) Accents Pubns.

***LeMieux, Anne.** Fruit Flies, Fish & Fortune Cookies. (Illus.). 192p. (J). (gr. 5-6). 1995. reprint ed. pap. 3.99 (*0-380-72291-7*, Camelot) Avon.

— Super Snoop Sam Snout & the Case of the Missing Marble. 64p. (Orig.). (J). (ps-3). 1994. pap. 3.50 (*0-380-77460-7*, Camelot Young) Avon.

— Super Snoop Sam Snout & the Case of the Stolen Snowman. 64p. (Orig.). (J). (ps-3). 1994. pap. 3.50 (*0-380-77459-3*, Camelot Young) Avon.

— Super Snoop Sam Snout & the Case of the Yogurt-Poker. 64p. (Orig.). (J). (ps-3). 1994. pap. 3.50 (*0-380-77462-3*, Camelot Young) Avon.

Lemieux, Christina M. Coping with the Loss of a Pet: A Gentle Guide for All Who Love a Pet. rev. ed. (Illus.). 60p. (Orig.). 1989. 14.95 (*0-9622158-0-5*); pap. 9.95 (*0-9622158-1-3*) W R Clark Co.

This gentle & caring guide was written to assist & comfort those who have experienced the loss of a cherished pet. COPING WITH THE LOSS OF A PET is a "how to" book & contains specific strategies to assist the bereaved pet owner & those supportive friends who are attempting to comfort one who has lost a pet. The death of a beloved pet can be a devastating emotional experience & is an experience faced by all who love & cherish a pet. Unlike other areas where loss & death occur, the grief & pain felt at the loss of a beloved pet is little understood & only slight guidance or comfort has been available. Authored by thanatologist & cultural anthropologist Christina M. Lemieux, COPING WITH THE LOSS OF A PET helps us understand the dimensions & effects of bereavement with regard to ourselves & those whom we care about. By drawing on her own background of compassion, experience, & practical wisdom, Dr. Lemieux is able to combine encouragement with insight as she provides help & counsel while accompanying us through the experience of aloneness, grieving, & ultimately the process of healing. Dr. Lemieux has devoted much of her professional career to the subject of death & dying. She is an Associate Professor of Anthropology at Kutztown University of Pennsylvania & maintains an extensive involvement in fieldwork, classroom instruction, educational programs for health care professionals, & involvement in hospice training programs. ***Publisher Provided Annotation.***

LeMieux, David. The Ancient Tarot & Its Symbolism: A Guide to the Secret Keys of the Tarot Cards. LC 84-4318. (Illus.). 208p. 1985. 25.00 (*0-8453-4714-4*, Cornwall Bks) Assoc Univ Prs.

LeMieux, Dotty. Let Us Not Blame Foolish Women. (Desert Island Chapbook Ser.). 32p. 1983. pap. text ed. 3.50 (*0-939180-26-X*) Tombouctou.

Lemieux, G., ed. see Symposium, Montreal Staff.

Lemieux, Margo. Full Worm Moon. LC 93-14728. (Illus.). 32p. (J). 1994. 15.00 (*0-688-12105-5*, Tambourine Bks); lib. bdg. 14.93 (*0-688-12106-3*, Tambourine Bks) Morrow.

— Paul & the Wolf. LC 95-9686. (Illus.). (J). 1995. write for info. (*0-382-39099-7*); pap. write for info. (*0-382-39100-4*) Silver Burdett Pr.

Lemieux, Michele. The Pied Piper of Hamelin. LC 92-21338. (Illus.). 32p. (J). 1993. 15.00 (*0-688-09848-7*); lib. bdg. 14.93 (*0-688-09849-5*) Morrow Jr Bks.

— What's That Noise? LC 84-16631. (Illus.). 32p. (J). (ps-1). 1985. 11.95 (*0-688-04139-6*); lib. bdg. 11.88 (*0-688-04140-X*) Morrow Jr Bks.

Lemieux, Michele, illus. & ret. Peter & the Wolf. LC 90-6486. 32p. 1991. 13.95 (*0-688-09846-0*); lib. bdg. 13.88 (*0-688-09847-9*) Morrow Jr Bks.

***Lemieux, P.** Chaos & Society. LC 94-74250. 1995. 75.00 (*90-5199-214-9*) IOS Press.

Lemieux, R. N., et al. Customer-Satisfaction Audit: A Management Perspective. Holman, Richard, ed. (IIA Monograph). (Illus.). 61p. 1985. pap. text ed. 15.00 (*0-89413-142-7*) Inst Inter Aud.

Lemieux, Victoria L., jt. auth. see Leonard, David W.

Lemin, Marion, et al, eds. Value Strategies for Classroom Teachers. 200p. 1995. pap. 26.95 (*0-86431-111-7*, Pub. by Aust Coun Educ Res AT) Paul & Co Pubs.

Leming, Charles. Computer Problems for Classical Dynamics: An Integrated Approach. 3rd ed. 128p. (C). 1988. pap. text ed. 17.00 (*0-15-507635-3*) HB Coll Pubs.

— Computer Problems in Modern Physics. 128p. (C). 1990. pap. text ed. 13.50 (*0-03-046207-X*) SCP.

Leming, James S., comp. Foundations of Moral Education: An Annotated Bibliography. LC 83-12834. xv, 325p. 1983. text ed. 69.50 (*0-313-24165-1*, LME/, Greenwood Pr) Greenwood.

Leming, Michael & Dickinson, George. Understanding Dying, Death, & Bereavement. 552p. (C). Date not set. pap. text ed. 36.25 (*0-15-500632-0*) HB Coll Pubs.

Leming, Michael R. & Dickinson, George E. Understanding Dying, Death & Bereavement. 2nd ed. LC 89-29924. (Illus.). 500p. (C). 1990. text ed. 33.25 (*0-03-028377-9*) HB Coll Pubs.

Leming, Michael R., jt. auth. see Dickinson, George E.

***Lemire, Maurice.** Dictionnaires des Oeuvres Litteraires du Quebec Vol. 1: Origines a 1900. rev. ed. 998p. (FRE.). 1980. 250.00 (*0-7859-5221-7*) Fr & Eur.

Lemire, Ronald J., et al. Anencephaly. LC 77-83688. (Illus.). 281p. reprint ed. pap. 80.10 (*0-7837-7116-9*, 2046945) Bks Demand.

Lemisch, Jesse. Jack Tar in the Streets: Merchant Seamen in the Politics of Revolutionary America. (Irvington Reprint Series in American History). (C). 1991. reprint ed. pap. text ed. 2.90 (*0-8290-2613-4*, H-431) Irvington.

***Lemish, Michael.** War Dogs: Canines in Combat. (Illus.). 256p. 1995. pap. 23.95 (*1-57488-017-9*) Brasseys Inc.

Lemius, J. B. Catechism of Modernism. LC 81-52536. 160p. 1981. reprint ed. pap. 4.00 (*0-89555-167-5*) TAN Bks Pubs.

Lemke, A. B., tr. see Schweitzer, Albert.

Lemke, Bob & Grace, Sally. SCD Sportscard Counterfeit Detector. 2nd ed. LC 91-77563. (Illus.). 256p. 1993. pap. 16.95 (*0-87341-252-4*) Krause Pubns.

Lemke, Bradley N. & Della Rocca, Robert C. Surgery of the Eyelids & Orbit: An Anatomical Approach. (Illus.). 1989. boxed 170.00 (*0-8385-7500-5*, A7500-0) Appleton & Lange.

Lemke, C. E., ed. see Society for Industrial & Applied Mathematics Staff & American Mathematical Society Staff.

Lemke, Christiane & Marks, Gary, eds. The Crisis of Socialism in Europe. LC 91-14680. 264p. 1991. lib. bdg. 41.95 (*0-8223-1180-1*); pap. text ed. 16.95 (*0-8223-1197-6*) Duke.

Lemke, Christiane, jt. ed. see Rueschemeyer, Marilyn.

Lemke, H. U., et al, eds. Computer Assisted Radiology - Computergestutze Radiologie: Proceedings of the International Symposium. (Illus.). xxxv, 836p. 1993. 180.00 (*0-387-56595-7*) Spr-Verlag.

— Computer Assisted Radiology Computergestutzte Radiologie: Proceedings of the International Symposium Vortrage des Internationalen Symposiums, CAR '91 Computer Assisted Radiology. (Illus.). 944p. 1991. 168.00 (*0-387-54143-8*) Spr-Verlag.

— Computer Assisted Radiology-Computergestutzte Radiologie CAR '87. (Illus.). 900p. 1987. 99.00 (*0-387-17812-0*) Spr-Verlag.

— Computer Assisted Radiology-Computergestutzte Radiologie CAR' 89. (Illus.). xxxiii, 860p. 1989. 126.00 (*0-387-50890-2*, 2903) Spr-Verlag.

Lemke, Horst, illus. Places & Faces. LC 78-160446. 32p. (J). (ps-00). 8.95 (*0-87592-041-1*) Scroll Pr.

Lemke, Ian & Tinney, Mike. The Apocalypse. (Mind's Eye Theatre Ser.). 128p. per., pap. 15.00 (*1-56504-121-6*, 5300) White Wolf.

Lemke, Ian, jt. auth. see Brooks, Deirdre.

***Lemke, J.** Textual Politics: Discourse & Social Dynamics. (Critical Perspectives on Literacy & Education Ser.). 240p. 1995. 80.00x (*0-7484-0215-2*); pap. 26.00x (*0-7484-0216-0*) Taylor & Francis.

Lemke, Jay L. Talking Science: Language, Learning & Values. Green, Judith, ed. (Language & Educational Processes Ser.: Vol. 1). 288p. (C). 1990. text ed. 47.50 (*0-89391-565-3*); pap. text ed. 24.95 (*0-89391-566-1*) Ablex Pub.

— Using Language in the Classroom. (Language Education Ser.). 60p. 1989. pap. text ed. 7.95 (*0-19-437157-3*) OUP.

— Using Language in the Classroom. (C). 1985. pap. 38.00x (*0-7300-0308-6*, ECS805, Pub. by Deakin Univ AT) St Mut.

Lemke, Jeffrey J., jt. auth. see Thompson, J. Mark.

Lemke, Jurgen. Gay Voices from East Germany. Borneman, John, ed. LC 90-43690. 208p. 1991. 35.00 (*0-253-33319-9*); pap. 12.95 (*0-253-20630-8*, MB-630) Ind U Pr.

Lemke, Kenneth W., jt. ed. see Sterling, Robert R.

Lemke, Nancy. Cabrillo. (Illus.). 128p. (Orig.). 1991. pap. 8.95 (*0-945092-19-9*) EZ Nature.

Lemke, P. A., jt. ed. see Esser, K.

Lemke, P. A., ed. see Melton, A. C.

Lemke, Raymond L. Yes You Can! An Innovative Approach to Happiness. Wilcox, Lucie, ed. LC 88-61002. (Illus.). 192p. (Orig.). 1988. pap. 6.95 (*0-929099-00-1*) Omaha Pr Pub.

Lemke, Robert, jt. auth. see Krause, Chester.

Lemke, Sonne, jt. auth. see Moos, Rudolf H.

Lemke, Stefan. Gran Atlas del Mundo Para Ninos. 14p. 1991. pap. 24.95 (*0-8477-0079-8*) U of PR Pr.

Lemke, Stefan & Pricken, Marie-Luise L. Making Toys & Gifts. LC 91-3880. (Craft Bks.). (Illus.). 64p. (J). 1991. lib. bdg. 15.45 (*0-516-09259-6*); pap. 8.95 (*0-516-49259-4*) Childrens.

Lemke, Thomas. Review of Organic Functional Group: Introduction to Medicinal Organic Chemistry. 3rd ed. LC 91-4855. (Illus.). 142p. 1991. pap. 25.95 (*0-8121-1428-0*) Williams & Wilkins.

***Lemke, Thomas & Lins, Gerald T.** Regulation of Investment Advisers, 1995. (Securities Law Ser.). 1991. pap. 137.50 (*0-614-07306-5*) Clark Boardman Callaghan.

Lemke, Thomas L., et al. Science of Drug Action: Course Outline. 4th ed. 208p. 1992. spiral bd. 12.76 (*0-8403-8318-5*) Kendall-Hunt.

***Lemke, Thomas P., et al.** Regulation of Investment Companies. LC 95-11825. 1995. ring bd. write for info. (*0-8205-1022-X*) Bender.

Lemke, William. Wild, Wild East. 188p. 1994. reprint ed. pap. 10.95 (*1-56626-116-3*) Country Rds.

Lemkey, F. D., et al, eds. High-Temperature - High-Performance Composites. (Symposium Proceedings Ser.: Vol. 120). 1988. text ed. 40.00 (*0-931837-90-1*) Materials Res.

***Lemkhin, Mikhail.** Missing Frames. LC 95-1321. 1995. write for info. (*1-55779-083-3*) Hermitage.

Lemkhin, Mikhail, photos. Russkie Razgovory: Antologiia Sovremennoi Prozy. LC 92-17803. (Illus.). 200p. (Orig.). (RUS.). (C). 1992. pap. 10.00 (*1-55779-049-3*) Hermitage.

Lemkin, Johnathan, jt. auth. see Walters, Daniel.

***Lemkow, Anna F.** The Wholeness Principle: Dynamics of Unity Within Science, Religion & Society. 2nd ed. LC 94-34924. 355p. 1995. pap. 14.00 (*0-8356-0715-1*, Quest) Theos Pub Hse.

Lemkowitz, Florence. Mexico, 1985. Fisher, Robert C., ed. (Fisher Annotated Travel Guides Ser.). 448p. 1984. 13.95 (*0-8116-0068-8*) NAL-Dutton.

Lemkowitz, S. M., jt. auth. see De Zeeuw, M. A.

An Asterisk (*) at the beginning of an entry indicates that the title is appearing in BIP for the first time.

Lemlech, Johanna K. Classroom Management: Methods & Techniques for Elementary & Secondary Teachers. 2nd ed. (Illus.). 339p. (C). 1991. reprint ed. pap. text ed. 19.95x (*0-88133-620-3*) Waveland Pr.
— Curriculum & Instructional Methods for the Elementary & Middle School. 3rd rev. ed. LC 93-14778. (Illus.). 464p. (C). 1994. text ed. write for info. (*0-02-369742-3*) Macmillan.
***Lemlech, Johanna K., ed. & intro.** Becoming a Professional Leader: Becoming a Professional Leader. LC 94-29653. (Leadership Policy Reseach Ser.). (Illus.). 240p. (C). 1995. 24.95x (*0-590-49334-5*) Scholastic Inc.
Lemler, Kathleen. Transformation Through Flowers: Spiritual & Physical Healing. (Illus.). 128p. (Orig.). 1993. pap. 5.95 (*0-9635987-0-8*) Express of Nature.
Lemley, Amy, jt. auth. see Berent, Jonathan.
Lemley, Brad, jt. auth. see Mitchell, W.
Lemley, Jo, jt. auth. see Lemley, Virg.
Lemley, Virg & Lemley, Jo. Children's Cookery, Naturally. (Illus.). 57p. (J). (gr. 1-10). 1980. pap. 4.25 (*0-931798-05-1*) Wilderness Hse.
— Soybean Cookery. 1975. pap. 4.25 (*0-931798-04-3*) Wilderness Hse.
Lemlich, Jeffrey M. Savage Lost: Florida Garage Bands - The '60s & Beyond. LC 91-15241. (Illus.). 424p. 1992. pap. 19.95 (*0-942963-12-1*) Distinctive Pub.
Lemlin, Jeanne. Quick Vegetarian Pleasures: Fast, Delicious, & Healthy Meatless Recipes. LC 91-50515. (Illus.). 288p. 1992. pap. 16.00 (*0-06-096911-3*, PL) HarpC.
— Vegetarian Pleasures: A Menu Cookbook. (Illus.). 320p. 1986. pap. 19.00 (*0-394-74302-4*) Knopf.
— Vegetarian Pleasures: One Hundred Twenty-Five Delicious Meatless Entrees. 1995. pap. 15.00 (*0-06-095022-6*) HarpC.
Lemm, W., ed. The Reference Materials of the European Communities: Results of Hemocompatibility Tests. LC 92-30458. 272p. (C). 1992. lib. bdg. 112.50 (*0-7923-2002-6*) Kluwer Ac.
Lemm, W., jt. ed. see Missirlis, Y. F.
Lemma, Aklilu, et al. Phytolacca Dodecandra (Endod) 332p. 1984. text ed. 60.00 (*0-907567-84-3*, Tycooly Pub); pap. 40.00 (*0-907567-85-1*, Tycooly Pub) Weidner & Sons.
***Lemma-Wright, Alessandra.** Invitation to Psychodynamic Psychology. 220p. 1995. pap. 25.00 (*1-56821-629-7*) Aronson.
— Invitation to Psychodynamic Psychology. 150p. 1995. pap. 24.95 (*1-56593-500-4*, 1158) Singular Publishing.
***Lemme, Barbara H.** Development in Adulthood. LC 94-34465. 1994. text ed. write for info. (*0-205-14165-X*) Allyn.
Lemme, Margaret L., ed. Clinical Aphasiology, Vol. 21. LC 86-647891. 364p. (C). 1992. text ed. 49.00 (*0-89079-564-9*, 1808) PRO-ED.
Lemme, Philip. American Streamline: A Handbook of Neon Advertising Design. LC 87-37650. (Illus.). 160p. 1988. reprint ed. pap. 12.95 (*0-911380-80-9*) ST Pubns.
Lemmens, Frans & De Rooi, Allard. Algerian Sahara. (Illus.). 102p. 1993. 50.00 (*90-72216-37-7*, Pub. by Focus NE); pap. 35.00 (*90-72216-08-3*, Pub. by Focus NE) Dist Art Pubs.
Lemmens, P. & Raes, S., eds. Civil Procedure. 1991. ring bd. write for info. (*0-318-68488-8*) Kluwer Law Tax Pubs.
Lemmer. Chronopharmacology: Cellular & Biomedical Interactions. (Cellular Clocks Ser.: Vol. 3). 744p. 1989. 215.00 (*0-8247-8103-1*) Dekker.
Lemmer, B. & Huller, H., eds. Clinical Chronopharmacology. (Clinical Pharmacology Ser.: Vol. 6). (Illus.). 208p. 1990. text ed. 48.00 (*3-88603-374-0*, Pub. by W Zuckschwerdt GW) Scholium Intl.
Lemmer, Bill & Smits, Martin. Facilitating Change in Mental Health. 236p. 1990. pap. 25.50 (*0-412-33010-5*, A4458) Chapman & Hall.
Lemmer, J. F. & Kanal, L. N., eds. Uncertainty in Artificial Intelligence, Vol. 2. (Machine Intelligence & Pattern Recognition Ser.: No. 2). 484p. 1988. 102.75 (*0-444-70396-9*, North Holland) Elsevier.
Lemmer, J. F., jt. ed. see Kanal, L. N.
Lemmer, R. H. Multistep Direct Reactions. 236p. 1992. text ed. 81.00 (*981-02-1171-6*) World Scientific Pub.
Lemmerz, A. H. Basiswissen-Ekg-Registrierung: 2., Erweiterte Auflage. (Illus.). viii, 96p. 1975. 15.25 (*3-8055-2298-3*) S Karger.
— Examples Illustrating the Use of Frank Leads. (Illus.). 48p. 1972. pap. 9.75 (*3-8055-1294-5*) S Karger.
Lemmerz, A. H. & Schmidt, R. R. Auswertung und Deutung des EKG. 12th ed. (Illus.). xii, 260p. 1981. pap. 38.50 (*3-8055-1932-X*) S Karger.
Lemming, J. Siddles. 1981. pap. 3.50 (*0-449-12811-3*) Fawcett.
Lemmings, David. Gentlemen & Barristers: The Inns of Court & the English Bar 1680-1730. (Oxford Historical Monographs). (Illus.). 344p. 1990. 74.00 (*0-19-822155-X*) OUP.
Lemmo, Peter S., ed. see Schoendorf, Robert.
Lemmon, Alfred E. La Musica de Guatemala en el Siglo XVIII: Music from Eighteenth Century Guatemala. LC 85-63627. (Illus.). 174p. (Orig.). (ENG & SPA.). 1986. pap. 10.50 (*0-910443-03-3*) CIRMA.
Lemmon, David. The Benson & Hedges British Theatre Yearbook, 1992. (Illus.). 376p. 1993. pap. 34.95 (*0-233-98780-0*, Pub. by A Deutsch UK) Trafalgar.
Lemmon, David, ed. British Theatre Yearbook, 1989. 360p. 1989. text ed. 39.95 (*0-312-03198-X*) St Martin.
— British Theatre Yearbook, 1990. 384p. 1990. text ed. 45.00 (*0-312-04531-X*) St Martin.
Lemmon, E. J. Beginning Logic. LC 78-51926. 235p. (C). 1978. pap. text ed. 14.95 (*0-915144-50-6*) Hackett Pub.
Lemmon, Ed. Boss Cowman: The Recollections of Ed Lemmon, 1857-1946. LC 69-10313. (Pioneer Heritage Ser.: No. 6). 341p. reprint ed. pap. 97.20 (*0-7837-6464-2*, 2046468) Bks Demand.
Lemmon, Jim. The Log of Rowing at the University of California Berkeley, 1870-1987. LC 88-33945. (Western Heritage Book Ser.). (Illus.). 160p. 1989. 35.00 (*0-9621956-0-X*) Wstrn Heritage.
Lemmon, John A. Family Mediation Practice. 244p. 1985. text ed. 27.95 (*0-02-918550-5*) Free Pr.
Lemmon, John A., jt. auth. see Brieland, Donald.
Lemmon, M., jt. ed. see Goin, J.
Lemmon, Michael. Competitively Inhibited Neural Networks for Adaptive Parameter Estimation. (C). 1990. lib. bdg. 61.00 (*0-7923-9086-5*) Kluwer Ac.
Lemmon, Nadine, jt. ed. see Druckrey, Timothy.
***Lemmon, Richard.** The Shuttle Conspiracy. 260p. 1995. pap. 8.95 (*1-56901-834-0*) NW Pub.
Lemmon, Sarah M. North Carolina & the War of 1812. (Illus.). iv, 54p. 1984. pap. 4.00 (*0-86526-087-7*) NC Archives.
— North Carolina's Role in the First World War. (Illus.). viii, 91p. 1975. pap. 4.00 (*0-86526-094-X*) NC Archives.
— North Carolina's Role in World War II. (Illus.). viii, 69p. 1985. reprint ed. pap. 4.00 (*0-86526-095-8*) NC Archives.
Lemmon, Sarah M., ed. Pettigrew Papers, Vol. 1, 1685-1818. (Illus.). xl, 699p. 1971. 15.00 (*0-86526-068-0*) NC Archives.
Lemmon, Sarah M., ed. & intro. The Pettigrew Papers, Vol. 2, 1819-1843. (Pettigrew Papers Ser.). (Illus.). xlv, 631p. 1988. 45.00 (*0-86526-069-9*) NC Archives.
Lemmon, Sarah M., jt. ed. see London, Lawrence F.
Lemmon, Tess. Apes. LC 92-37693. (Illus.). 32p. (J). (gr. 2-4). 1993. 15.95 (*0-395-66901-4*) Ticknor & Flds Bks Yng Read.
Lemmons, jt. auth. see Mirza.
Lemmons, Cherilynn. Randolph's Wonderful Adventure. (Illus.). 48p. (J). (gr. 1-6). 1992. 6.95 (*0-8059-3289-5*) Dorrance.
Lemmons, Phillip. A Buyer's Guide to Software for the IBM Personal Computer. 1983. pap. 18.95 (*0-07-037150-4*, BYTE Bks) McGraw.
Lemmons, Reuel, et al. Unto Us a Child is Born. 126p. (Orig.). 1982. pap. 2.95 (*0-88027-109-4*) Firm Foun Pub.
Lemmons, Russel G. Goebbels & der Angriff. LC 93-33405. 184p. (C). 1993. 22.00 (*0-8131-1848-4*) U Pr of Ky.
Lemmons, Thom. Daniel: The Man Who Saw Tomorrow. 320p. (Orig.). 1993. pap. 9.99 (*0-945564-83-X*, Multnomah Bks) Questar Pubs.
— Destiny by Choice. 192p. (Orig.). 1989. pap. 7.99 (*0-945564-13-9*, Multnomah Bks) Questar Pubs.
— Jeremiah: He Who Wept. 320p. 1993. pap. 9.99 (*0-88070-596-5*, Multnomah Bks) Questar Pubs.
— Once upon a Cross. 314p. 1992. pap. 9.99 (*0-945564-47-3*, Multnomah Bks) Questar Pubs.
Lemoff, Theodore C., ed. Liquefied Petroleum Gases Handbook. 3rd ed. LC 89-60576. (Illus.). 450p. 1992. 67.25 (*0-87765-382-8*, NFPA 58HB92) Natl Fire Prot.
Lemoine, A., et al. ESVITAF: Vitamin Status in Three Groups of French Adults: Control, Obese Subjects, Alcohol Drinkers. (Journal: Annals of Nutrition & Metabolism: Vol. 30, Suppl. 1, 1986). (Illus.). 96p. (ENG & FRE.). 1986. pap. 23.25 (*3-8055-4244-5*) S Karger.
LeMoine, Ann, jt. ed. see Buxman, Karen.
Lemoine, Charles A. Louisiana's Cypress Bayou Elves: Pontain the Trapper. (Illus.). 40p. (Orig.). (J). (gr. 1-12). 1986. pap. 5.00 (*0-941327-01-9*) Charles A Lemoine.
— Santa Clawfish. (Christmas Story & Coloring Book Ser.). (Illus.). 32p. (Orig.). (J). 1986. pap. 3.20 (*0-941327-00-0*) Charles A Lemoine.
LeMoine, Fannie & Kleinhenz, Christopher, eds. Saint Augustine the Bishop: A Book of Essays. LC 94-7258. (Medieval Casebook Ser.: Vol. 9). (Illus.). 232p. 1994. 34.00 (*0-8153-1639-9*, H1830) Garland.
Lemoine, Francoise, jt. auth. see Sokoloff, Georges.
Lemoine, Georges, illus. The Christmas Story According to St. Luke. (Creative's Christmas Stories Ser.). 32p. (J). 1978. lib. bdg. 13.95 (*0-87191-957-5*) Creative Ed.
— Pied. (Gallimard - Mes Premieres Decouvertes Ser.: No. 9). (FRE.). (J). (ps-1). 1989. 12.95 (*2-07-035701-5*) Schoenhof.
***Lemoine, H.** Dictionnaire des Communes Vol. 1: Departement de la Meuse. fac. ed. (FRE.). 1991. pap. 185.00 (*0-7859-8250-7*, 2909112047) Fr & Eur.
— Etudes Enfantines for Piano, Op. 37. (Carl Fischer Music Library: No. 323). 52p. (J). 1904. pap. 7.00 (*0-8258-0106-0*, L 323) Fischer Inc NY.
***Lemoine, Jacques.** The International Civil Servant: An Endangered Species. LC 95-11895. 1995. write for info. (*0-7923-3444-2*) Kluwer Ac.
Lemoine, Jo. Rita, Saint of the Impossible - Rita, la Sainte Des Impossibles. Audette, Florestine, tr. LC 92-34919. 128p. (Orig.). 1992. pap. 5.95 (*0-8198-6422-6*) Pauline Bks.
Lemoine, N. & Wright, N. A., eds. The Molecular Pathology of Cancer. (Cancer Surveys Ser.: Vol. 16). (Illus.). 235p. (C). 1993. text ed. 69.00 (*0-87969-389-4*) Cold Spring Harbor.
Lemoine, Nicholas R. & Epenetos, Agamemnon A., eds. Mutant Oncogenes: Targets for Therapy. LC 92-48907. 1992. write for info. (*0-412-48110-3*) Chapman & Hall.
Lemoine, Roy E. The Anagogic Theory of Wittgenstein's Tractatus. LC 74-80541. (Janua Linguarum, Series Minor: No. 214). 215p. (Orig.). 1975. pap. text ed. 44.65 (*90-279-3393-6*) Mouton.
Lemoisne, Paul-Andre. Degas et son Oeuvre, 4 Vols. LC 83-48625. (Illus.). 1500p. 1984. 473.00 (*0-8240-5526-8*) Garland.
Lemon. Collected Practical Problems. (C). 1959. 110.00 (*0-685-36030-X*, Pub. by British Textile Tech UK) St Mut.
— Physical Geology. 608p. 1995. 37.95 (*0-8016-2571-8*) Mosby Yr Bk.
— Physical Geology SG. 192p. 1994. pap. 16.95 (*0-8016-2556-4*) Mosby Yr Bk.
— The Third Planet: An Introduction to Earth Science. 608p. 1994. 39.95 (*0-8016-7470-0*) Mosby Yr Bk.
Lemon, Andrew. The Young Man from Home: James Balfour Eighteen Thirty to Nineteen Thirteen. (Illus.). 194p. 1983. 24.95 (*0-522-84238-0*) Intl Spec Bk.
***Lemon, Anthony, ed.** The Geography of Change in South Africa. LC 94-21402. 1995. text ed. 64.95 (*0-471-94938-8*) Wiley.
— Homes Apart: South Africa's Segregated Cities. (Illus.). 252p. 1991. 35.00 (*0-253-33321-0*) Ind U Pr.
Lemon, Anthony & Pollock, Norman. Studies in Overseas Settlement & Population. LC 79-42738. 133p. reprint ed. pap. 38.00 (*0-317-30106-3*, 2025274) Bks Demand.
Lemon, Dean. Guide to the Outdoor Exhibits at the Borax Museum. (Illus.). 20p. (Orig.). (C). 1992. pap. 1.00 (*1-878900-25-0*) DVNH Assn.
Lemon, Fresh, pseud. Fresh Lemonade. 125p. (Orig.). 1990. pap. 5.95 (*0-9626578-1-6*) Savage Pubns.
Lemon, H. How to Find Out about the Wool Textile Industry. 1968. 93.00 (*0-08-012984-6*, Pub. by Pergamon Repr UK) Franklin.
Lemon, Harvey B. From Galileo to the Nuclear Age: An Introduction to Physics. (Phoenix Science Ser.). 480p. reprint ed. pap. 136.80 (*0-317-08845-9*, 2020104) Bks Demand.
Lemon, Lee T. Portraits of the Artist in Contemporary Fiction. LC 84-22005. xx, 261p. 1985. 25.00 (*0-8032-2868-6*) U of Nebr Pr.
Lemon, Lee T. & Reis, Marion J., trs. Russian Formalist Criticism: Four Essays. LC 65-21899. (Regents Critics Ser.). xviii, 143p. 1965. pap. 7.00 (*0-8032-5460-1*) U of Nebr Pr.
***Lemon, M. C.** The Discipline of History & the History of Thought. LC 94-41276. 1995. write for info. (*0-415-12346-1*) Routledge.
***Lemon, Nancy K., ed. & intro.** Domestic Violence Law: A Comprehensive Overview of Cases & Sources. 428p. (C). 1995. text ed. 69.95 (*1-57292-023-8*); pap. text ed. 49.95 (*1-57292-022-X*) Austin & Winfield.
Lemon, R., ed. Collected Practical Problems. 1959. 80.00 (*0-317-43607-4*) St Mut.
Lemon, Roger. Methods for Neuronal Recording in Conscious Animals. LC 83-10483. (IBRO Handbook Ser.: Methods in the Neurosciences: No. 1-569). 162p. 1984. pap. text ed. 82.95 (*0-471-90237-3*, Wiley-Interscience) Wiley.
Lemon, Roger, jt. auth. see Porter, Robert.
Lemon, Roy R. Principles of Stratigraphy. 640p. (C). 1990. write for info. (*0-675-20537-9*, Merrill Pub Co) Macmillan.
— Vanished Worlds: An Introduction to Historical Geology. 496p. (C). 1992. pap. text ed. write for info. (*0-697-11249-7*) Wm C Brown Pubs.
Lemon, Sandra E. From Captivity to Comeback. LC 90-85375. 328p. (Orig.). 1991. pap. 17.95 (*0-935132-20-1*) C H Fairfax.
LeMoncheck, Linda. Dehumanizing Women: Treating Persons As Sex Objects. (New Feminist Perspectives Ser.). 180p. 1985. 45.00 (*0-8476-7331-6*) Rowman.
— Dehumanizing Women: Treating Persons As Sex Objects. (New Feminist Perspectives Ser.). 184p. 1985. pap. 16.00 (*0-8476-7386-3*) Rowman.
Lemond, Greg & Gordis, Kent. Greg LeMond's Complete Book of Bicycling. (Illus.). 352p. 1990. pap. 12.00 (*0-399-51594-1*, Perigree Bks) Berkley Pub.
LeMone, Charles S. A Dance in the Street. 256p. (Orig.). 1993. mass mkt. 3.99 (*0-380-76713-9*) Avon.
Lemone, Karen A. Assembly Language & Computer Organization for the Eighty-Six Family Computers. LC 92-25646. (C). 1992. 53.00 (*0-06-500747-6*) HarpCollege.
— Assembly Language & Systems for the IBM PC. 1985. 19.95 (*0-316-52069-1*) Little.
— Design of Compilers: Techniques of Programming Language Translation. 1992. 52.00 (*0-8493-7342-5*, QA76) CRC Pr.
— Fundamentals of Compilers: An Introduction to Computer Language Translation. (Illus.). 600p. 1991. 49.95 (*0-8493-7341-7*, TP308) CRC Pr.
Lemonick, Michael D. The Light at the Edge of the Universe: Astronomers on the Front Lines of the Cosmological Revolution. LC 92-35058. 1993. 24.00 (*0-679-41304-9*, Villard Bks) Random.
— The Light at the Edge of the Universe: Dispatches from the Front Lines of Cosmology. LC 94-39324. 1995. write for info. (*0-691-00158-8*) Princeton U Pr.
Lemonnier, Pierre. Elements for an Anthropology of Technology. LC 92-19485. (Anthropological Papers: No. 88). 1992. pap. 15.00 (*0-915703-30-0*) U Mich Mus Anthro.
Lemonnier, Pierre, ed. Technological Choices: Arbitraries in Technology from the Neolithic to Modern High Technology. LC 92-23310. (Material Cultures Ser.). (Illus.). 320p. 1993. 74.50 (*0-415-07331-6*, B0311) Routledge.
Lemons, C. Dale. Education & Training for a Technological World. 42p. 1984. 4.25 (*0-318-22084-9*, IN267) Ctr Educ Trng Employ.
Lemons, J. Stanley. The Woman Citizen: Social Feminism in the 1920s. 288p. 1990. reprint ed. pap. text ed. 10.95 (*0-8139-1302-0*) U Pr of Va.
Lemons, Jack, ed. Quantitative Characterization & Performance of Porous Implants for Hard Tissue Applications. LC 87-33430. (Special Technical Publication Ser.: No. 953). 420p. 1988. text ed. 75.00 (*0-8031-0965-2*, 04-053000-54) ASTM.
Lemons, Jack, jt. ed. see Ducheyne, Paul.
***Lemons, John & Brown, Donald A., eds.** Sustainable Development: Science, Ethics & Public Policy. LC 95-10769. (Environmental Science & Technology Library). 1995. write for info. (*0-7923-3500-7*) Kluwer Ac.
Lemons, Rhonda K., ed. see Woytowich, Andy.
Lemons, T. M., jt. ed. see Chang, B. J.
Lemont, Harvey, jt. auth. see Witkowski, Joseph A.
***Lemont, Levi P.** Historical Dates of the Town & City of Bath, ME, & Town of Georgetown, from 1604 to 1874. 104p. 1995. reprint ed. pap. 15.00 (*0-8328-4462-4*) Higginson Bk Co.
Lemos, M. C., et al, eds. Wave Breaking: A Numerical Study. (Lecture Notes in Engineering Ser.: Vol. 71). (Illus.). viii, 196p. 1992. pap. 54.00 (*0-387-54942-0*) Spr-Verlag.
Lemos, Noah M. Intrinsic Value: Concept & Warrant. LC 93-48142. (Cambridge Studies in Philosophy). 256p. (C). 1994. 49.95 (*0-521-46207-X*) Cambridge U Pr.
Lemos, Ramon M. Metaphysical Investigations. LC 86-46324. 288p. 1988. 38.50 (*0-8386-3307-2*) Fairleigh Dickinson.
— The Nature of Value: Axiological Investigations. LC 95-1079. 240p. 1995. lib. bdg. 34.95 (*0-8130-1366-6*) U Press Fla.
— Rights, Goods & Democracy. LC 85-47801. 208p. 1986. 38.50 (*0-87413-312-2*) U Delaware Pr.

Lemos, William. LorcaLines: Combinations Inspired by Federico Garcia Lorca. (Illus.). 60p. (Orig.). 1994. pap. 12.95 (*0-9642125-1-X*) Daylight Ducks. LORCALINES is a delightful poetry journal set in motion by the words of the Spanish poet Federico Garcia Lorca. The author, William Lemos, & the illustrator, Jim Bertram, showcase their arts in this fine example of collaboration. The poetry is in the surrealism mode of Lorca; the art that mirrors each page of writing is the psychic language that has made Mr. Bertram's work, which has been compared to the Zen-Tao, famous worldwide. Karin Faulkner, poet & board member of California Poets in the Schools, states, "Lemos' poems are bright & alight with the unexpected image in ways which are always perfectly congruent & angelicly askew. Together these two artists do 'this pencil dance with reason,' 'dressed in the language of feathers.' The book is a marvelous word-ride of sense & other-sense. It is where we find the fine echoes of Garcia Lorca brought forward in 'liquid thought' & 'tiny marigold shoes.'" This book is sure to please. The ideas are original; the art work, provocative. It is a fine example of how art & poetry can be combined to form new inspirations & meditations on elements of the surreal. To order: Daylight Ducks Publishing Company, P.O. Box 168, Mendocino, CA 95460.
Publisher Provided Annotation.

Lemp, Helena B. Manual for the Organization of Scientific Congresses. 1978. pap. 26.50 (*3-8055-2962-7*) S Karger.
Lemp, M. A. & Marquardt, R., eds. The Dry Eye: A Comprehensive Guide. (Illus.). 256p. 1992. 98.00 (*0-387-53308-7*) Spr-Verlag.
Lemp, Michael, jt. ed. see Snell, Richard.
Lempereur, Agnes, jt. auth. see Thines, Georges.
Lemperle, G. & Nievergelt, J. Plastic & Reconstructive Breast Surgery. (Illus.). x, 192p. 1991. 193.00 (*0-387-52868-7*) Spr-Verlag.
***Lempert, David H.** Escape from the Ivory Tower: Student Adventures in Democratic Experiential Education. (Higher & Adult Education Ser.). 1995. 28.95 (*0-7879-0136-9*) Jossey-Bass.
***Lempert, David H., et al.** A Model Development Plan: New Strategies & Perspectives. LC 95-2225. 312p. 1995. text ed. 55.00 (*0-275-95068-9*) Greenwood.
Lempert, Leo. Industrialisation of Developing Countries. 363p. 1973. 24.00 (*0-8464-1471-6*) Beekman Pubs.
— Millionaires & Managers: Structure of U. S. Financial Oligarchy. (Illus.). 1969. 22.00 (*0-8464-0632-2*) Beekman Pubs.
Lempert, Richard & Sanders, Joseph. An Invitation to Law & Social Science. LC 85-12899. (Law in Social Context Ser.). 541p. 1989. pap. text ed. 18.95 (*0-8122-1329-7*) U of Pa Pr.
Lempert, Richard O. & Saltzburg, Stephen A. Modern Approach to Evidence: Teacher's Manual. 2nd ed. (American Casebook Ser.). 553p. (C). 1983. pap. text ed. write for info. (*0-314-76113-6*) West Pub.
— A Modern Approach to Evidence: Text, Problems, Transcripts, & Cases. 2nd ed. LC 82-13578. (American Casebook Ser.). 1232p. (C). 1990. reprint ed. text ed. 49.00 (*0-314-67594-9*) West Pub.
Lempert, Robert J. & Schwabe, William L. Transition to Sustainable Waste Management: A Simulation Gaming Approach. LC 93-14765. 1993. 13.00 (*0-8330-1339-4*, MR-183) Rand Corp.
Lempert, Todd E., jt. auth. see Truwit, Charles L.

An Asterisk (*) at the beginning of an entry indicates that the title is appearing in BIP for the first time.

Lempfrit, Honore-Timothee. His Oregon Trail Journal & Letters from the Pacific Northwest 1848-1853. Meyer, Patricia & Levesque, Catou, eds. 1985. 16.95 (*0-87770-347-7*) Ye Galleon.

Lempinen, M., ed. see European Society for Surgical Research Staff.

Lemprecht, Sandra J. California: A Bibliography of Theses & Dissertations in Geography, No. 753. 1975. 5.50 (*0-686-20344-5*) CPL Biblios.

Lempriere, John A. A Classical Dictionary, 2 vols, Set. 1973. lib. bdg. 600.00 (*0-87968-878-5*) Gordon Pr.

Lems-Dworkin, Carol. Africa in Scott Joplin's Music. (Illus.). 27p. (Orig.). 1991. pap. 11.00 (*0-9637048-0-X*) C Lems-Dworkin Pubs.

— African Music: A Pan-African Annotated Bibliography. 400p. 1991. 96.00 (*0-905450-91-4*, Pub. by H Zell Pubs UK) Bowker-Saur.

Lemsine, Aicha. Beneath a Sky of Porphyry. Blair, Dorothy, tr. 224p. 1990. 19.95 (*0-7043-2695-7*, Pub. by Quartet UK); pap. 11.95 (*0-7043-0161-X*, Pub. by Quartet UK) Interlink Pub.

— The Chrysalis. Blair, Dorothy S., tr. 189p. 1993. 19.95 (*0-7043-7034-4*, Pub. by Quartet UK) Interlink Pub.

Lemstra, P. J., ed. Integration of Fundamental Polymer Science & Technology. 404p. 1989. 99.00 (*1-85166-340-1*) Elsevier.

— Integration of Fundamental Polymer Science & Technology: Proceedings of the International Meeting, Rolduc Polymer Meeting - 2, Rolduc Abbey, Limburg, the Netherlands, 26-30 April 1987. 436p. 1991. 136.00 (*1-85166-587-0*) Elsevier.

— Integration of Fundamental Polymer Science & Technology, No. 4: Proceedings of the International Meeting on Polymer Science & Technology, Rolduc Polymer Meeting, Rolduc Abbey Limburg, The Netherlands, 23-27 April 1989. 416p. 1990. 104.50 (*1-85166-489-0*) Elsevier.

Lemstra, P. J. & Kleintjens, L. A., eds. Integration of Fundamental Polymer Science & Technology: Proceedings of the International Meeting, Rolduc Polymer Meeting - 2, Rolduc Abbey, Limburg, the Netherlands, 26-30 April 1987. 614p. 1988. 128.00 (*1-85166-208-1*) Elsevier.

Lemstra, P. J., jt. auth. see Kleintjens, L. A.

Lemstra, Tjitske, jt. auth. see Doornenbal, Baukje.

Lemstra, W., ed. Telecommunication Access Networks: Technology & Service Trends: Proceedings of the IX International Symposium on Subscriber Loops & Services (ISSLS 91), Amsterdam, the Netherlands, 22-26 April 1991. 440p. 1991. 128.50 (*0-444-89050-5*, North Holland) Elsevier.

Lemu, Ahmed. A Book of Fasting. Lemu, Bridget, ed. 86p. (Orig.). (C). 1993. pap. 4.00 (*1-881963-01-2*) Al-Saadawi Pubns.

Lemu, Aisha & Heeren, Fatima. Women in Islam. 51p. (Orig.). 1978. pap. 3.50 (*0-86037-004-6*, Pub. by Islamic Fnd UK) New Era Publns MI.

Lemu, Bridget. The Ideal Muslim Husband. 22p. (Orig.). 1993. pap. 1.75 (*1-881963-03-9*) Al-Saadawi Pubns.

— Islam & Alcohol. 18p. (Orig.). 1993. pap. 1.75 (*1-881963-02-0*) Al-Saadawi Pubns.

Lemu, Bridget, ed. see Lemu, Ahmed.

Lemus, B. V. Pushkin: Ekaterinskii Dvorets-muzei, Parki Goroda Pushkina, Pushkinskie Mesta. 1982. 39.00 (*0-317-14280-1*, Pub. by Collets UK) Pro-Am Music.

Lemus, V. Pushkin, Palaces & Parks. (Illus.). 170p. (C). 1984. 250.00 (*0-685-47203-5*, Pub. by Collets) St Mut.

Lemus, Vera. The Palaces & Parks of Pushkin. 1986. 175.00 (*0-317-61344-8*, Pub. by Collets UK) Pro-Am Music.

Lemut, Enrica, et al, eds. Cognitive Models & Intelligent Environments for Learning Programming. LC 93-25348. (NATO ASI Series F: Computer & Systems Sciences, Special Programme AET: Vol. 111). 315p. 1993. 69.00 (*0-387-56580-9*) Spr-Verlag.

Len Sen, George A., tr. see Bolkhovitinov, Nikolai.

Lena, Dan. Defend: Preventing Date Rape & Other Sexual Assaults. 1992. pap. 4.95 (*1-56171-077-6*) Sure Sellers.

***Lena, Dan & Lena, Marie.** I Am Special & You Are Special Too! (Illus.). 35p. (Orig.). (J). (gr. k-4). 1995. pap. write for info. (*0-9645027-1-2*) S-Team Unltd.

— My Power Book. (Self Help Motivation Ser.). (Illus.). 60p. (YA). 1991. student ed 10.00 (*0-9617032-0-2*) D & M Lena.

Lena, Daniel S. & Howard, Marie. Hands off . . . I'm Special! How to Tell Your Boyfriend No. Bartimole, John, ed. (Illus.). 96p. (Orig.). (YA). (gr. 7 up). 1988. pap. 6.95 (*0-936320-30-3*) Compact Books.

Lena, Hugh. Primis Reader in Sociology. 1992. pap. text ed. write for info. (*0-07-037581-X*) McGraw.

Lena, Hugh, et al. Contemporary Issues in Society. 576p. 1992. text ed. write for info. (*0-07-027965-9*) McGraw.

Lena, Marie, jt. auth. see Lena, Dan.

Lena, P. Observational Astrophysics. (Astronomy & Astrophysics Library). (Illus.). 340p. 1988. 64.50 (*0-387-18433-3*) Spr-Verlag.

Lena, Willie, jt. auth. see Howard, James H.

Lenaerts, Vincent M. & Gurny, Robert, eds. Bioadhesive Drug Delivery Systems. 272p. 1989. 191.00 (*0-8493-5367-X*, RS201) CRC Pr.

Lenaghan, John, tr. see Baily, Samuel L. & Ramella, Franco, eds.

Lenahan, Shelia, ed. see Toy, Gerald.

***Lenahan, Thomas W. & Blanchfield, Thomas A.** New York Security Officer Training Manual. 120p. Date not set. pap. 8.95 (*0-614-06128-8*) Gould.

Lenanton, John. The Home Gardener. 2nd ed. (Illus.). 291p. (C). 1980. pap. 29.95 (*0-943281-00-8*) Matrix Grp.

Lenarcic, J., jt. ed. see Stifter, S.

Lenarcic, Jadran & Ravani, Bahram, eds. Advances in Robot Kinematics & Computational Geometry. LC 94-21074. (Diversity & Direction in Children's Literature Ser.). 520p. (C). 1994. lib. bdg. 216.00 (*0-7923-2983-X*) Kluwer Ac.

Lenard. L' Art de la Conversation. 2nd ed. 1985. pap. 30.95 (*0-8384-3702-8*) Heinle & Heinle.

— Parole et Pensee. 5th ed. 1987. text ed. 49.95 (*0-8384-3689-7*); student ed. pap. 29.95 (*0-8384-3693-5*) Heinle & Heinle.

Lenard, Alexander, tr. see Milne, A. A.

Lenard, J. G., ed. Modelling Hot Deformation of Steels. (Illus.). viii, 145p. 1989. 69.00 (*0-387-50754-X*) Spr-Verlag.

Lenard, J. G., jt. auth. see Pietrzyk, M.

Lenard, Lane, jt. auth. see Block, Will.

Lenard, Philipp E. Great Men of Science. Hatfield, H. Stafford, tr. LC 74-105026. (Essay Index Reprint Ser.). 1977. 27.95 (*0-8369-1614-X*) Ayer.

Lenardon, Robert, jt. auth. see Morford, Mark.

Lenardon, Robert J., jt. auth. see Morford, Mark P.

Lenart, Silvo. Shaping Political Attitudes: The Impact of Interpersonal Communication & Mass Media. LC 94-15533. 192p. 1994. 38.95 (*0-8039-5708-4*); pap. 17.95 (*0-8039-5709-2*) Sage.

Lenau, H., jt. ed. see Volkmar, Tilsner.

Lenaz, Giorgio, et al, eds. Highlights in Ubiquinone Research. 328p. 1990. 99.00 (*0-85066-848-4*, Taylor & Francis) Taylor & Francis.

Lenburg, Jeff. Baseball's All-Star Game: A Game-by-Game Guide. LC 86-2708. 223p. 1986. lib. bdg. 27.50x (*0-89950-231-8*) McFarland & Co.

— The Encyclopedia of Animated Cartoon Series. LC 82-23638. (Quality Paperbacks Ser.). (Illus.). 192p. 1983. reprint ed. pap. 14.95 (*0-306-80191-4*) Da Capo.

— The Encyclopedia of Animated Cartoons. rev. ed. (Illus.). 400p. 1991. 40.00 (*0-8160-2252-6*) Facts on File.

— The Great Cartoon Directors. LC 82-23923. (Illus.). 190p. 1983. lib. bdg. 28.50x (*0-89950-036-6*) McFarland & Co.

— The Great Cartoon Directors. rev. ed. LC 93-2928. (Illus.). 272p. 1993. reprint ed. pap. 14.95 (*0-306-80521-9*) Da Capo.

Lenburg, Jeff, et al. The Three Stooges Scrapbook. 256p. 1982. 18.95 (*0-8065-0803-5*, Citadel Pr) Carol Pub Group.

— Three Stooges Scrapbook: The Three Stooges Collection. (Illus.). 1991. 21.95 (*0-8065-9975-8*, Citadel Pr) Carol Pub Group.

Lence, Ross M., ed. see Calhoun, John C.

Lencek, Lena. The Antic Alphabet. LC 93-31010. (Illus.). 36p. (J). 1994. 11.95 (*0-8118-0480-1*) Chronicle Bks.

Lencek, Lena, jt. auth. see Bosker, Gideon.

Lencek, Rado L. & Cooper, Henry R., Jr., eds. To Honor Jernej Kopitar: Paper in Slavic Philology, No. 2. 1982. pap. 10.00 (*0-930042-46-8*) Mich Slavic Pubns.

Lencek, Rado L., et al, eds. SSS Newsletter, 11 vols. 238p. 1978. write for info. (*0-318-60013-7*) Soc Slovene Studies.

Lencheck, Tom, et al. The Energy Conserving House: A Guide to Super-Efficient Design & Construction. (Illus.). 224p. 1992. 19.95 (*0-88179-109-1*) Hartley & Marks.

Lenchek, Allen M. Physics of Pulsars. (Topics in Astrophysics & Space Physics Ser.). 184p. (C). 1972. text ed. 156.00 (*0-677-14290-0*); pap. text ed. 117.00 (*0-677-14295-1*) Gordon & Breach.

Lenchner, George. Mathematical Olympiad Contest Problems for Children (Also for Teachers, Parents, & Other Adults) LC 90-83825. (Illus.). 176p. (Orig.). (J). (gr. 3-8). 1990. pap. 18.95 (*0-9626662-0-3*) Glenwood Pubns.

Lenchner, George, jt. auth. see Broadwin, Judith.

Lenci, Francesco, jt. ed. see Colombetti, Giuliano.

Lenci, Francesco, et al, eds. Biophysics of Photoreceptors & Photomovements in Microorganisms. (NATO ASI Series A, Life Sciences: Vol. 211). (Illus.). 364p. 1991. 115.00 (*0-306-44022-9*, Plenum Pr) Plenum.

Lenczewski, Romuald, jt. ed. see Gruber, Bruno.

Lenczner, D. Elements of Loadbearing Brickwork. 125p. (C). 1972. 56.00 (*0-08-016814-0*, Pub. by Pergamon Repr UK) Franklin.

Lenczowski, George. American Presidents & the Middle East. LC 89-17056. 368p. (C). 1989. lib. bdg. 42.00 (*0-8223-0963-7*); pap. text ed. 21.95 (*0-8223-0972-6*) Duke.

— Oil & State in the Middle East. (Illus.). 398p. 1960. 41.95 (*0-8014-0256-5*) Cornell U Pr.

— Russia & the West in Iran, 1918-1948: A Study in Big Power Rivalry. LC 68-23307. (Illus.). 383p. 1968. reprint ed. text ed. 69.50 (*0-8371-0144-1*, LERW, Greenwood Pr) Greenwood.

Lenczowski, George, ed. Political Elites in the Middle East. LC 75-10898. (Foreign Affairs Study Ser.: No. 19). 235p. reprint ed. pap. 67.00 (*0-8357-4522-8*, 2037383) Bks Demand.

Lenczowski, John. The Sources of Soviet Perestroika. (Essay Ser.: No. 2). 60p. (Orig.). (C). 1990. pap. text ed. 3.00 (*1-878802-01-1*) J M Ashbrook Ctr Pub Affairs.

— Soviet Perceptions of U. S. Foreign Policy. LC 81-70713. 312p. 1982. 42.50 (*0-8014-1451-2*) Cornell U Pr.

Lenczycki, Donna M., jt. auth. see Zeilenga, Donald G.

Lender, Mark E. Dictionary of American Temperance Biography: From Temperance Reform to Alcohol Research, the 1600s to the 1980s. LC 83-12589. xv, 572p. 1984. text ed. 105.00 (*0-313-22335-1*, LAT/, Greenwood Pr) Greenwood.

— The Middlesex Water Company: A Business History. 235p. 1994. 20.00 (*0-9642916-0-6*) Upland Press.

Lender, Mark E. & Martin, James K. Drinking in America. rev. ed. 222p. 1987. pap. 14.95 (*0-02-918570-X*) Free Pr.

Lender, Mark E., jt. auth. see Martin, James K.

Lender, T. Dictionary of Biology: Diccionario de Biologia. 2nd ed. 208p. (SPA.). 1985. write for info. (*0-7859-4915-1*) Fr & Eur.

Lender, T., jt. ed. see Wolff, E.

***Lender, Theodore.** Dictionnaire de Biologie. 2nd ed. 448p. (FRE.). 1992. 275.00 (*0-7859-7747-3*, 2130447031) Fr & Eur.

Lenderink, R. S. & Siebrand, J. C. A Disequilibrium Analysis of the Labour Market. 126p. 1975. text ed. 58.00 (*90-237-2277-9*) Ashgate Pub Co.

***Lenderman, Teddy.** The Complete Idiot's Guide to the Perfect Wedding. 350p. 1995. 16.99 (*1-56761-532-5*) Alpha Bks IN.

***Lenders, Edward, frwd.** The Best Nature Writing of Joseph Wood Krutch. (Illus.). 392p. 1995. pap. 17.95 (*0-87480-480-9*) U of Utah Pr.

Lendhoff, Janet. The Noontime Walker's Guide to Downtown Los Angeles. (Illus.). 16p. 1994. 5.95 (*1-883897-04-1*) River Rock CA.

Lendi, K., jt. auth. see Alicki, R.

Lendl, Ivan & Mendoza, George. Hitting Hot: Ivan Lendl's Fourteen Day Tennis Clinic. (Illus.). 192p. 1986. 14.95 (*0-394-55407-8*) Random.

Lendl, Ivan & Scott, Eugene L. Ivan Lendl's Tennis Technique Book. 1983. 8.95 (*0-686-44921-5*, Fireside) S&S Trade.

Lendler, Marc. Just the Working Life: Opposition & Accommodation in Daily Industrial Life. LC 89-70267. 224p. 1990. 51.95 (*0-87332-608-3*) M E Sharpe.

Lendrum, Susan & Syme, Gabrielle. Gift of Tears: A Practical Approach to Loss & Bereavement Counselling. LC 91-43922. 1992. 59.95 (*0-415-08120-3*, A7645, Pub. by Tavistock UK); pap. 15.95 (*0-415-07349-9*, A7649, Pub. by Tavistock UK) Routledge Chapman & Hall.

Lendrum, Susan, jt. auth. see Tolan, Janet.

Lendt, David L. Ding: The Life of Jay Norwood Darling. LC 89-7432. (Iowa Heritage Collection). (Illus.). 216p. 1989. reprint ed. pap. 10.95 (*0-8138-0406-X*) Iowa St U Pr.

Lendvai, Erno. Bela Bartok: An Analysis of His Music. 1991. 16.95 (*0-912483-33-4*) Pro-Am Music.

— Verdi & Wagner. Palos, Monika & Pokoly, Judit, trs. 504p. 36.50 (*0-685-30700-X*, Pub. by Intl Hse HU) Pro-Am Music.

Lendvai, J., jt. ed. see Kovacs, I.

Lendvai, Paul. Hungary: The Art of Survival. 160p. 1990. text ed. 59.50 (*1-85043-118-3*, Pub. by I B Tauris UK) St Martin.

Lendvay, E., ed. Epitaxial Crystal Growth. 1000p. 1991. text ed. 252.00 (*0-87849-616-5*, Pub. by Trans Tech GW) LPS Dist Ctr.

— Gallium Arsenide. 374p. 1987. text ed. 85.00 (*0-87849-555-X*, Pub. by Trans Tech GW) LPS Dist Ctr.

Leneaux, Grant F., tr. see Duhem, Pierre M.

Lenehan, Arthur F., ed. The Best of Bits & Pieces. 300p. Date not set. 29.95 (*0-910187-08-8*) Economics Pr.

Lenehan, William & Myers, Andrew B., eds. The Alhambra: A Series of Tales & Sketches of the Moors & Spaniards (1982) The Complete Works of Washington Irving. (Complete Works of Washington Irving Ser.). 1983. text ed. 50.00 (*0-8057-8512-4*, Twayne) Macmillan.

Lenel, Fritz V. Powder Metallurgy: Principles & Applications. LC 80-81890. (Illus.). 602p. reprint ed. pap. 171.60 (*0-7837-1562-5*, 2041854) Bks Demand.

Leneman. The Tofu Cookbook. 1992. pap. 11.00 (*0-7225-2587-7*) Thorsons SF.

Leneman, Helen, ed. Bar - Bat Mitzvah Education: A Sourcebook. LC 93-70473. 370p. (Orig.). 1993. pap. text ed. 45.00 (*0-86705-031-4*) A R E Pub.

Leneman, Leah. Fit for Heroes? Land Settlement in Scotland after World War I. (Illus.). 1989. text ed. 35.00 (*0-08-037720-3*, Pergamon Pr) Elsevier.

— International Tofu Cookery Book. 1986. pap. 8.50 (*0-7102-0702-6*, RKP) Routledge.

— Into the Foreground: A Century of Scottish Women in Photographs. (Illus.). 132p. 1993. 32.50 (*0-7509-0444-5*) A Sutton Pub.

— Living in Atholl, 1685-1785. 200p. 1985. 30.00 (*0-85224-507-6*, Pub. by Edinburgh U Pr UK) Col U Pr.

— Perspectives in Scottish Social History: Essays in Honour of Rosalind Mitchison. 200p. 1988. pap. text ed. 29.95 (*0-08-036574-4*, Pub. by Aberdeen U Pr) Macmillan.

— The Single Vegan: Simple, Convenient & Appetizing Meals for One. (Illus.). 128p. 1989. pap. 8.95 (*0-7225-1454-9*) Thorsons SF.

— Slim the Vegetarian Way. rev. ed. 144p. 1988. pap. 8.00 (*0-7225-2807-8*) Thorsons SF.

— Slimming the Vegetarian Way. 128p. 1988. pap. 6.95 (*0-7225-1587-1*) Thorsons SF.

— Women's Suffrage Movement in Scotland: A Guid Cause. (SWSS Ser.). (Illus.). 192p. 1991. pap. text ed. 23.90 (*0-08-041201-7*, Pub. by Aberdeen U Pr) Macmillan.

Leneman, Leah, jt. auth. see Mitchison, Rosalind.

Lenero, Vicente. The Gospel of Lucas Gavilan. Mowry, Robert G., tr. 272p. (Orig.). (C). 1991. lib. bdg. 45.00 (*0-8191-7958-2*); pap. text ed. 29.00 (*0-8191-7959-0*) U Pr of Amer.

Lenett, Robin, et al. Sometimes It's O. K. to Tell Secrets! 128p. (Orig.). (J). 1986. pap. 3.95 (*0-8125-9454-1*) Tor Bks.

Leney, David & Burney, Allan. From the Flightdeck: Concorde. (Illus.). 80p. 1991. pap. text ed. 11.95 (*0-7110-1896-0*, Ian Allan) Motorbooks Intl.

Leney, Terttu. Teach Yourself Finnish. (ENG & FIN.). 1993. pap. 29.95 (*0-7859-1053-0*, 0-340-561734) Fr & Eur.

Lenf, John D. Handbook of Simplified Solid State Circuit Design. 2nd ed. LC 77-23555. (Illus.). 1977. 16.95 (*0-13-381707-5*) P-H.

— Handbook of Simplified Solid State Circuit Design. 2nd ed. LC 77-23555. (Illus.). 1979. text ed. 41.00 (*0-13-381715-6*) P-H.

Lenfant, C., et al, eds. Growth Factors of the Vascular & Nervous Systems: Functional Characterization & Biotechnology. (Illus.). viii, 132p. 1992. 99.25 (*3-8055-5475-3*) S Karger.

Lenfant, C. L., jt. auth. see Wood.

Lenfant, C. L., jt. ed. see Yamori, Y.

Lenfant, Claude, et al. Biotechnology of Dyslipoproteinemias: Applications in Diagnosis & Control. (Atherosclerosis Reviews Ser.: Vol. 20). 352p. 1990. 104.50 (*0-88167-616-0*) Raven.

Lenfestey, Thompson. Facts on File Dictionary of Nautical Terms. (Dictionaries Ser.). (Illus.). 432p. 1993. lib. bdg. 40.00 (*0-8160-2087-6*) Facts on File.

Lenfestey, Tom. Gunkholer's Cruising Guide to Florida's West Coast. 9th rev. ed. (Illus.). 156p. 1994. pap. 17.95 (*0-8200-0131-7*) Great Outdoors.

***Leng, Flavia.** Daphne Du Maurier: A Daughter's Memoir. (Illus.). 206p. 1995. pap. 15.95 (*1-85158-720-9*, Pub. by Mnstream UK) Trafalgar.

Leng, Gareth, ed. Pulsatility in Neuroendocrine Systems. 272p. 1988. 155.00 (*0-8493-4944-3*, QP356, CRC Reprint) Franklin.

Leng, Gareth, jt. auth. see Cross, B. A.

Leng, Lee Y. The Razor's Edge: Boundaries & Boundary Disputes in Southeast Asia. 29p. (Orig.). 1980. pap. text ed. 13.95 (*9971-902-05-2*, Pub. by Inst SE Asian Studies SI) Ashgate Pub Co.

***Leng, Marguerite L., et al.** Agrochemical Environmental Fate Studies: State of the Art. LC 94-38029. 416p. 1995. 75.00 (*1-56670-034-5*, L1034) Lewis Pubs.

Leng, P. & Charlton, C. Principles of Computer Organisation: A First Course Using the 68000 Processor. 1990. pap. text ed. write for info. (*0-07-707217-0*) McGraw.

Leng-Peschlow, Elke, ed. Senna & Its Rational Use. (Journal: Pharmacology: Vol. 44, Suppl. 1, 1992). (Illus.). iv, 52p. 1992. pap. 16.00 (*3-8055-5574-1*) S Karger.

Leng, Roger. Right to Silence in Police Interrogation: Study of Some Issues Underlying Debate. (Research Study Ser.: No. 10). 86p. 1993. pap. 20.00 (*0-11-341063-8*, HM10638, Pub. by HMSO UK) UNIPUB.

Leng, Roger & Manchester, Colin. A Guide to the Criminal Justice Act 1991. 424p. 1991. 90.00 (*1-85190-152-3*, Pub. by Tolley Pubng UK) St Mut.

Leng, Russell J. Interstate Crisis Behavior, 1816-1980: Realism vs. Reciprocity. LC 92-32370. (Studies in International Relations: Vol. 28). (Illus.). 272p. (C). 1993. 59.95 (*0-521-39141-5*) Cambridge U Pr.

Leng, Shao-Chuan. Japan & Communist China. LC 75-11893. 166p. 1975. reprint ed. text ed. 35.00 (*0-8371-8134-8*, LEJC, Greenwood Pr) Greenwood.

Leng, Shao-Chuan, ed. Chiang Ching-Kuo's Leadership in the Development of the Republic of China on Taiwan, Vol. III. LC 92-31103. (Miller Center Series on Asian Political Leadership). 230p. (Orig.). (C). 1993. lib. bdg. 52.00 (*0-8191-8903-0*, Pub. by White Miller Center); pap. text ed. 21.50 (*0-8191-8904-9*, Pub. by White Miller Center) U Pr of Amer.

— Coping with Crises: How Governments Deal with Emergencies, Vol. II. LC 89-16734. (Miller Center Series on Asian Political Leadership). 242p. (Orig.). (C). 1990. lib. bdg. 47.00 (*0-8191-7584-6*, Pub. by White Miller Center); pap. text ed. 24.00 (*0-8191-7585-4*, Pub. by White Miller Center) U Pr of Amer.

— Post-Mao China & U. S.-China Trade. LC 77-20811. 168p. reprint ed. pap. 47.90 (*0-8357-2713-0*, 2039827) Bks Demand.

— Reform & Development in Deng's China. LC 94-4725. (Miller Center Series on Asian Political Leadership: Vol. 4). 214p. (C). Date not set. lib. bdg. 54.50 (*0-8191-9503-0*); pap. text ed. 23.50 (*0-8191-9504-9*) U Pr of Amer.

Leng, Shao-Chuan, jt. ed. see Chiu, Hungdah.

Leng, Vikki. A Vegetarian Feast: Over Seven Hundred Fifty Simple & Delicious Recipes for Everyday Meals & Special Occasions. (Illus.). 352p. 1994. 32.00 (*0-207-18443-7*) Thorsons SF.

Leng, Virginia. Training the Event Horse. (Illus.). 224p. 1991. 24.95 (*0-943955-38-6*, Trafalgar Sq Pub) Trafalgar.

Lengauer, Thomas. Combinatorial Algorithms for Integrated Circuit Layout. (Teubner Series in Computer Science). 1990. text ed. 70.00 (*0-471-92838-0*) Wiley.

Lengauer, Thomas, ed. Algorithms - ESA '93: First Annual European Symposium, Bad Honnef, Germany, September 30-October 2, 1993 Proceedings. LC 93-34004. (Lecture Notes in Computer Science Ser.: Vol. 726). 1993. 60.00 (*0-387-57273-2*) Spr-Verlag.

Lengauer, Thomas, jt. ed. see Choffrut, C.

Lengefeld, Uelaine. Study Skills Strategies. rev. ed. Gerould, W. Philip, ed. LC 93-72976. (Fifty-Minute Ser.). (Illus.). 100p. (Orig.). 1994. pap. 9.95 (*1-56052-260-7*) Crisp Pubns.

***Lengel, Darlene.** Effective Conversations. (Illus.). 120p. (J). (gr. 1-8). 1994. 18.95 (*0-937857-52-1*, 1483) Speech Bin.

Lengel, J., jt. auth. see Kendall, D.

Lengel, Olga. Five Chimneys: The Story of Auschwitz. Coch, Clifford, tr. LC 81-20260. 213p. 1983. reprint ed. 35.00 (*0-86527-343-X*) Fertig.

Lengeler, B., et al. Formation of Semiconductor Interfaces: Proceedings of the 4th International Conference. 816p. 1994. text ed. 178.00 (*981-02-1559-2*) World Scientific Pub.

Lengenfelder, Helga, ed. Libraries, Information Centers & Databases in Science & Technology: A World Guide. 2nd ed. 696p. 1988. lib. bdg. 225.00 (*3-598-10757-9*) K G Saur.

***Lengenfelder, Helga, et al, eds.** Handbuch der Universitaten und Fachhochschulen Bundesrepublik Deutschland, Osterreich, Schweiz. 6th ed. 546p. (GER.). 1993. lib. bdg. 160.00 (*3-598-11155-X*) K G Saur.

Lengenfelder, Jack W. A Picture Postcard History of U. S. Aviation. LC 88-36433. (Illus.). 128p. (Orig.). 1989. pap. 12.95 (*0-930256-19-0*) Almar.

Lengermann, Patricia M. & Wallace, Ruth A. Gender in America: Social Control & Social Change. (Illus.). 384p. (C). 1985. pap. text ed. write for info. (*0-13-347493-3*) P-H.

Lengerova, Alena, ed. see Symposium, Liblice Prague Staff.

Lenges, J. J., jt. ed. see Morton, I. D.

Lengjak, Laura S., ed. United States Export Policy on Technology Transfer. (Wisconsin International Law Journal, 1982 Ser.: Vol. 1983). 228p. (Orig.). 1984. pap. 8.00 (*0-933431-01-5*) U Wisc Law Madison.

Lengle, James I. Representation & Presidential Primaries: The Democratic Party in the Post-Reform Era. LC 80-1791. (Contributions in Political Science Ser.: No. 57). (Illus.). xv, 133p. 1981. text ed. 45.00 (*0-313-22482-X*, LEP/, Greenwood Pr) Greenwood.

L'Engle, Madeleine. An Acceptable Time. (YA). (gr. 7 up). 1989. 18.00 (*0-374-30027-5*) FS&G.

— An Acceptable Time. 1990. reprint ed. mass mkt. 3.99 (*0-440-20814-9*, LFL) Dell.

— And Both Were Young. (Young Love Romance Ser.). (Orig.). (YA). (gr. 7 up). 1983. mass mkt. 3.99 (*0-440-90229-0*, LFL) Dell.

— And It Was Good: Reflections on Beginnings. LC 83-8518. (Wheaton Literary Ser.). 219p. 1983. 14.99 (*0-87788-046-8*) Shaw Pubs.

— Anytime Prayers. LC 93-46429. (Illus.). 64p. (J). (gr. 1-6). 1994. 14.99 (*0-87788-055-7*) Shaw Pubs.

— The Arm of the Starfish. 240p. (YA). (gr. 7 up). 1980. mass mkt. 3.99 (*0-440-90183-9*, LFL) Dell.

— The Arm of the Starfish. LC 65-10919. 256p. (J). (gr. 7 up). 1965. 18.00 (*0-374-30396-7*) FS&G.

— Camila. Barbadillo, Pedro, tr. 197p. (SPA.). (YA). (gr. 9-12). 1992. pap. write for info. (*84-204-4555-X*) Santillana.

— Camilla. (Young Love Romance Ser.). 288p. (YA). (gr. 7 up). 1982. pap. 3.99 (*0-440-91171-0*, LFL) Dell.

— Camilla. 1995. 17.25 (*0-8446-6833-8*) Peter Smith.

— Certain Women. 1992. 21.00 (*0-374-12025-0*) FS&G.

— Certain Women. LC 92-56136. 368p. 1993. Alk. paper. pap. 12.00 (*0-06-065207-1*) Harper SF.

— A Circle of Quiet. 246p. 1971. 20.00 (*0-374-12374-8*) FS&G.

— Circle of Quiet. 1984. pap. 12.00 (*0-06-254503-5*, PL) HarpC.

— A Circle of Quiet, 3 vols., Set. (Crosswicks Journal Trilogy Ser.). 246p. 1977. 19.95 (*0-685-06341-0*) Harper SF.

— A Cry Like a Bell. LC 87-26940. (Wheaton Literary Ser.). 128p. (Orig.). 1987. pap. 8.99 (*0-87788-148-0*) Shaw Pubs.

— Dance in the Desert. LC 68-29465. (Illus.). 64p. (J). (ps up). 1969. 14.95 (*0-374-31684-8*) FS&G.

— Dance in the Desert. (Sunburst Ser.). (Illus.). 56p. (J). (ps up). 1988. pap. 6.95 (*0-374-41684-2*) FS&G.

— Dragons in the Waters. 288p. (J). (gr. 7 up). 1982. mass mkt. 4.50 (*0-440-91719-0*, LFL) Dell.

— Dragons in the Waters. LC 76-2477. 304p. (J). (gr. 7 up). 1976. 17.00 (*0-374-31868-9*) FS&G.

— The Glorious Impossible. (Illus.). 64p. (J). (gr. 3 up). 1990. pap. 19.95 (*0-671-68690-9*, Litl Simon S&S) S&S Childrens.

— A House Like a Lotus. (J). (gr. 6-12). 1985. mass mkt. 3.99 (*0-440-93685-3*, LFL) Dell.

— A House Like a Lotus. LC 84-48471. 307p. (J). (gr. 7 up). 1984. 17.00 (*0-374-33385-8*) FS&G.

— The Irrational Season. (Crosswicks Journal Trilogy Ser.). 224p. 1983. pap. 7.95 (*0-8164-2261-3*) Harper SF.

— The Irrational Season. large type ed. 430p. 1985. reprint ed. pap. 13.95 (*0-8027-2476-0*) Walker & Co.

— The Irrational Season. 215p. 1987. reprint ed. 17.95 (*0-374-17733-3*) FS&G.

— The Journey with Jonah. (J). (ps up). 1991. pap. 5.95 (*0-374-43858-7*) FS&G.

— Ladder of Angels. 1988. pap. 15.00 (*0-06-255619-3*, PL) HarpC.

Lengle, Madeleine. Madeleine l'Engle's Time Quartet, 4 Vols., Set. 1991. Boxed set. boxed 15.96 (*0-440-36037-4*) Dell.

L'Engle, Madeleine. Many Waters. (J). (gr. 4-7). 1987. mass mkt. 4.50 (*0-440-40548-3*) Dell.

— Many Waters. LC 86-14911. 310p. (J). (gr. 4 up). 1986. 17.00 (*0-374-34796-4*) FS&G.

— Meet the Austins. 192p. (YA). (gr. 5-9). 1981. mass mkt. 3.99 (*0-440-95777-X*, LE) Dell.

— The Moon by Night. 256p. (YA). (gr. 6 up). 1981. mass mkt. 3.99 (*0-440-95776-1*, LE) Dell.

— The Moon by Night. LC 63-9072. 224p. (J). (gr. 7 up). 1963. 16.00 (*0-374-35049-3*) FS&G.

— The Other Side of the Sun. large type ed. LC 93-35731. 1993. 19.93 (*0-7862-0089-8*, Large Print Bks) Thorndike Pr.

— A Ring of Endless Light. 336p. (YA). (gr. 9 up). 1981. mass mkt. 4.50 (*0-440-97232-9*, LE) Dell.

— The Rock That Is Higher: Story As Truth. LC 92-24204. 296p. 1993. 17.99 (*0-87788-726-8*) Shaw Pubs.

— A Severed Wasp. 388p. 1983. pap. 13.00 (*0-374-51783-5*) FS&G.

— The Small Rain: A Novel. LC 84-47839. 371p. (J). (gr. 7 up). 1984. 14.95 (*0-374-26637-9*) FS&G.

— Small Rain: A Novel. LC 84-47839. 371p. (J). (gr. 7 up). 1985. pap. 10.00 (*0-374-51912-9*) FS&G.

— Sold Into Egypt: Joseph's Journey into Human Being. LC 89-32030. (Wheaton Literary Ser.). 208p. 1989. 14.99 (*0-87788-766-7*) Shaw Pubs.

— Spirit & Light Essays in History. 1985. 8.95 (*0-8164-0310-4*) Harper SF.

— A Stone for a Pillow. LC 86-6487. (Wheaton Literary Ser.). 240p. 1986. 14.99 (*0-87788-789-6*) Shaw Pubs.

— The Summer of the Great Grandmother. (Crosswicks Journal Trilogy Ser.). 245p. 1980. pap. 7.95 (*0-8164-2259-1*) Harper SF.

— The Summer of the Great-Grandmother. 245p. 1974. 25.00 (*0-374-27174-7*) FS&G.

— Summer of the Great-Grandmother. 1984. pap. 12.00 (*0-06-254506-X*, PL) HarpC.

— A Swiftly Tilting Planet. (YA). (gr. 7 up). 1979. mass mkt. 4.50 (*0-440-90158-8*, LFL) Dell.

— A Swiftly Tilting Planet. LC 78-9648. 288p. (J). (gr. 5 up). 1978. 17.00 (*0-374-37362-0*) FS&G.

— Swiftly Tilting Planet. (J). (gr. 4-7). 1981. mass mkt. 4.50 (*0-440-40158-5*) Dell.

— A Swiftly Tilting Planet. 317p. 1993. lib. bdg. 15.95 (*1-56054-701-4*) Thorndike Pr.

— A Swiftly Tilting Planet. large type ed. LC 93-21812. (J). 1993. Alk. paper. lib. bdg. 15.95 (*1-56054-710-3*) Thorndike Pr.

— The Time Trilogy: A Wrinkle in Time; A Wind in the Door; A Swiftly Tilting Planet, 3 vols., Set. 710p. (J). (gr. 5 up). 1979. boxed 47.85 (*0-374-37592-5*) FS&G.

— Troubling a Star. LC 93-50956. (J). 1994. 16.00 (*0-374-37783-9*) FS&G.

— The Twenty-Four Days Before Christmas. (J). (gr. k-6). 1987. pap. 3.50 (*0-440-40105-4*, YB) Dell.

— The Twenty-Four Days Before Christmas: An Austin Family Story. LC 84-5540. (Illus.). 48p. 1984. 11.99 (*0-87788-843-4*) Shaw Pubs.

— Two-Part Invention. 64p. 1993. pap. 5.00 (*0-06-250638-2*) Harper SF.

— Two-Part Invention: The Story of a Marriage. 224p. 1988. 18.95 (*0-374-28020-7*) FS&G.

— Two-Part Invention: The Story of a Marriage. 1989. pap. 11.00 (*0-06-250501-7*) Harper SF.

— Two-Part Invention: The Story of a Marriage. large type ed. (Large Print Christian Classics Ser.). 1991. reprint ed. pap. 12.95 (*0-8027-2652-6*) Walker & Co.

— Walking on Water: Reflections on Faith & Art. 198p. (Orig.). 1995. pap. 10.00 (*0-86547-487-7*, North Pt Pr) FS&G.

— Walking on Water: Reflections on Faith & Art. LC 80-21066. (Wheaton Literary Ser.). 198p. (Orig.). 1980. pap. 9.99 (*0-87788-919-8*) Shaw Pubs.

— The Weather of the Heart. LC 78-62202. (Wheaton Literary Ser.). 96p. 1978. pap. 9.99 (*0-87788-931-7*) Shaw Pubs.

— A Wind in the Door. 224p. (J). (gr. 5-9). 1974. mass mkt. 3.99 (*0-440-48761-7*, YB) Dell.

— A Wind in the Door. 224p. (YA). (gr. 5-9). 1976. mass mkt. 3.99 (*0-440-98761-X*, LFL) Dell.

— A Wind in the Door. LC 73-75176. 224p. (J). (gr. 7 up). 1973. 17.00 (*0-374-38443-6*) FS&G.

— A Wind in the Door. large type ed. 270p. (J). 1993. reprint ed. lib. bdg. 15.95 (*1-56054-615-8*) Thorndike Pr.

— A Wrinkle in Time. 224p. (J). (gr. 5-9). 1973. mass mkt. 4.50 (*0-440-49805-8*, YB) Dell.

— A Wrinkle in Time. 224p. (J). (gr. 5-9). 1976. mass mkt. 4.50 (*0-440-99805-0*, LFL) Dell.

— A Wrinkle in Time. LC 62-7203. 224p. (J). (gr. 7 up). 1962. 17.00 (*0-374-38613-7*) FS&G.

— A Wrinkle in Time: (Una Arruga en el Tiempo) (J). (gr. 1-6). 15.95 (*84-204-4074-4*) Santillana.

— The Young Unicorns. 224p. (YA). (gr. 8 up). 1989. mass mkt. 3.99 (*0-440-99919-7*, LFL) Dell.

— The Young Unicorns. LC 68-13682. 256p. (J). (gr. 7 up). 1968. 16.95 (*0-374-38778-8*) FS&G.

Lengnick-Hall, Cynthia A. & Lengnick-Hall, Mark L. Interactive Human Resource Management & Strategic Planning. LC 90-8959. 200p. 1990. text ed. 49.95 (*0-89930-502-4*, LHA/, Quorum Bks) Greenwood.

Lengnick-Hall, Mark L., jt. auth. see Bereman, Nancy A.

Lengnick-Hall, Mark L., jt. auth. see Lengnick-Hall, Cynthia A.

Lenguage, Inc., Translation Services Staff, tr. see Walls, James, III, ed.

Lengwin, Ron. Praying the Rosary. large type ed. LC 92-410. 96p. 1995. pap. 6.95 (*0-8027-2671-2*) Walker & Co.

Lengy, J. I., tr. see Nikol'skii, G. V.

Lengyel. Atom Clock. pap. 1.00 (*0-686-00466-3*) Fantasy Pub Co.

Lengyel, A. & Radan, G. T., eds. The Archaeology of Roman Pannonia. LC 81-51021. (Illus.). 674p. 1981. 55.00 (*0-8131-1370-9*) U Pr of Ky.

Lengyel, Alfonz. Archaeology for Museologists. (Museum Study Ser.: No. 2). (Illus.). 158p. (Orig.). 1993. pap. 15.00 (*0-9626500-1-3*) Fudan Mus Fndtn.

— Chinese Chronological History: From Prehistory Through 1950. (Museum Study Ser.: No. 4). 108p. (Orig.). 1993. pap. 10.00 (*0-9626500-3-X*) Fudan Mus Fndtn.

Lengyel, Alfonz & Liu-Lengyel, Hongying. Ray Leight & Shanghai Cartoonists' Views of Columbus. (Museum Study Ser.: No. 3). (Illus.). 17p. (Orig.). (C). 1992. pap. 3.00 (*0-9626500-2-1*) Fudan Mus Fndtn.

Lengyel, Cornel. The Case of Benedict Arnold. LC 79-56427. (New Poetic Drama Ser.: No. 2). 1982. pap. 3.50 (*0-934218-20-X*) Dragons Teeth.

— Four Dozen Songs. 80p. 1976. pap. 10.00 (*0-912950-29-3*) Blue Oak.

— Four Dozen Songs. LC 72-96887. (Living Poets' Library Ser.). pap. 2.50 (*0-686-02577-6*) Dragons Teeth.

— Late News from Adam's Acres. (Living Poets' Library Ser.). 1983. pap. 3.50 (*0-934218-25-0*) Dragons Teeth.

— The Lookout's Letter. LC 75-148857. (Living Poets' Library Ser.). pap. 2.50 (*0-686-05006-1*) Dragons Teeth.

— The Master Plan. (Living Playwright's Ser.). 1978. pap. 2.50 (*0-686-00548-1*) Dragons Teeth.

Lengyel, Cornel, ed. History of Music in San Francisco, 7 vols., Set. reprint ed. 364.50 (*0-404-07240-2*) AMS Pr.

Lengyel, Emil. Americans from Hungary. (History - United States Ser.). 319p. 1993. reprint ed. lib. bdg. 89.00 (*0-7812-4868-X*) Rprt Serv.

Lengyel, Eva, tr. see Agoston, Vilmos, ed.

Lengyel, Gyorgy, ed. Hungarian Economy & Society During World War II. (Atlantic Studies on Society & Change: No. 74). 240p. (C). 1993. text ed. 34.00 (*0-88033-259-X*, 362) Col U Pr.

***Lengyel, I.** Palaeoserology: Blood Typing with Fluorescent Antibody Method. 240p. (C). 1975. 45.00x (*963-05-0355-7*, Pub. by Akad Kiado HU) St Mut.

Lengyel, I. A. Palaeoserology: (Blood Typing with the Fluorescent Antibody Method) 240p. 1975. 75.00 (*0-569-08236-6*, Pub. by Collets UK) Pro-Am Music.

Lengyel, Jozsef. From Beginning to End. 175p. 1964. 22.00 (*0-8464-1466-X*) Beekman Pubs.

— The Judge's Chair. 19.95 (*0-8464-0539-3*) Beekman Pubs.

— Prenn Drifting. 293p. 1966. 19.95 (*0-8464-0747-7*) Beekman Pubs.

Lengyel, Olga. Five Chimneys. 1992. pap. 10.00 (*0-89733-376-4*) Academy Chi Pubs.

Lengyel, Peter. Cobblestone: A Detective Novel. Batki, John, tr. 528p. (Orig.). (C). 1993. pap. 14.95 (*0-930523-86-5*) Readers Intl.

— International Social Science: The UNESCO Experience. 145p. 1986. 34.95 (*0-685-65258-0*); pap. 21.95 (*0-685-65259-9*) Transaction Pubs.

Lengyel, Peter, jt. ed. see Bornschier, Volker.

Lengyel, V. I., et al. Resonance Phenomena in Electron-Atom Collisions. (Atoms & Plasmas Ser.: Vol. 11). (Illus.). 200p. 1992. 84.00 (*0-387-54093-8*) Spr-Verlag.

Lenhardt, Christian, tr. see Habermas, Jurgen.

Lenhart, Gary. Light Heart. 1991. 15.00 (*0-914610-92-9*); pap. 9.00 (*0-914610-91-0*) Hanging Loose.

Lenhart, John N. Gershom Carmichael on Samuel Pufendor's de Officio Hominis et Civis Juxta Legem Naturalem Libro Duo. Reeves, Charles H., tr. LC 85-80343. (Illus.). 64p. (Orig.). 1985. pap. 4.00 (*0-9615380-0-7*) Lenhart.

Lenhart, Maria, jt. auth. see Rapoport, Roger.

Lenhart, Michael. Newspaper Capers. (Learning Works Reading Ser.). 48p. (gr. 4-6). 1986. 5.95 (*0-88160-135-7*, LW.259) Learning Wks.

Lenhart, Sharyn A., jt. auth. see Bernstein, Anne E.

Lenhoff, Arthur. Comments, Cases & Other Materials on Legislation. xxxvii, 1046p. 1954. reprint ed. lib. bdg. 40.00 (*0-89941-603-9*, 501960) W S Hein.

Lenhoff, Gail. The Martyred Princes Boris & Gleb: A Social-Cultural Study of the Cult & the Texts. (UCLA Slavic Studies: Vol. 19). 168p. 1989. 18.95 (*0-89357-204-7*) Slavica.

Lenhoff, Howard M. Conception to Birth: Human Reproduction, Genetics, & Development. 352p. 1990. per. 26.95 (*0-8403-6156-4*) Kendall-Hunt.

— Conception to Birth: Human Reproduction, Genetics & Development. rev. ed. 400p. (C). 1994. per. 27.95 (*0-8403-9213-3*) Kendall-Hunt.

Lenhoff, Howard M., ed. Experimental Coelenterate Biology. LC 73-127331. 291p. reprint ed. pap. 83.00 (*0-685-17123-X*, 2027028) Bks Demand.

— Hydra: Research Methods. LC 82-24648. 496p. 1983. 110.00 (*0-306-41086-9*, Plenum Pr) Plenum.

Lenhoff, Howard M. & Loomis, W. Farnsworth, eds. Biology of Hydra & of Some Other Coelenterates. LC 61-18157. 1961. 15.95 (*0-87024-010-2*) U of Miami Pr.

Lenhoff, Howard M., jt. ed. see Hessinger, David A.

Lenhoff, Howard M., jt. ed. see Ngo, T. T.

Lenhoff, Howard M., tr. see Trembley, Abraham.

Lenhoff, Sylvia, tr. see Trembley, Abraham.

Lenia, jt. ed. see Cichon, Michael.

Leniashin, O. Soviet Art, 1920's-1930's. (C). 1990. 170.00 (*0-685-34343-X*, Pub. by Collets) St Mut.

Leniashin, Vladimir A. The Soviet Character: Painting by Soviet Artists 1960s-1980s. (C). 1986. 300.00 (*0-317-61393-6*, Pub. by Collets UK) Pro-Am Music.

Leniashin, Vladimir A., comp. The Russian Museum, Leningrad. (C). 1987. 195.00 (*0-685-22621-2*, Pub. by Collets) St Mut.

Lenica, Jan, jt. auth. see Kamyszew, Christopher D.

Lenier, Minnette & Maker, Janet. College Reading, Bk. 1. 3rd ed. 375p. (C). 1991. pap. 24.95 (*0-534-15390-9*) Intl Thomson.

— Keys to a Powerful Vocabulary: Level II. 3rd ed. LC 93-10923. 1993. pap. text ed. 27.67 (*0-13-668955-8*) P-H Gen Ref & Trav.

— Keys to College Success. 3rd ed. 400p. (C). 1989. pap. text ed. write for info. (*0-13-514811-1*) P-H.

Lenier, Minnette, jt. auth. see Maker-Inmon, Janet.

Lenier, Minnette, jt. auth. see Maker, Janet.

Lenier, Susan J. Rain Following: Poems. (Modern Poets Ser.: Vol. 13). 64p. 1984. 15.00 (*0-906672-19-8*); pap. 8.95 (*0-906672-20-1*) Oleander Pr.

— Swansongs: Poems. (Modern Poets Ser.: Vol. 12). (Illus.). (Orig.). 1982. 15.00 (*0-906672-04-X*); pap. 8.95 (*0-906672-03-1*) Oleander Pr.

Lenihan, Dan. Greenhouse Blues. 56p. (Orig.). 1993. pap. 4.00 (*0-935390-18-9*) Wormwood Bks & Mag.

— The Weaning of Baby Roy. 48p. (Orig.). 1989. pap. 4.00 (*0-935390-14-6*) Wormwood Bks & Mag.

Lenihan, Daniel F. Shipwrecks of Isle Royale National Park. 1994. pap. 34.95 (*0-942235-18-5*) LSPC Inc.

***Lenihan, Donald G., et al.** Canada: Reclaiming the Middle Ground. 162p. 1994. pap. 16.95 (*0-88645-167-1*) Ashgate Pub Co.

Lenihan, Edmund. Ferocious Irish Women. 1991. pap. 12.95 (*0-85342-977-4*) Dufour.

— Fionn MacCumhail & the Baking Hags. 128p. (J). 1994. pap. 9.95 (*1-85635-071-1*, Pub. by Mercier Pr IE) Dufour.

— In Search of Biddy Early. 1987. pap. 9.95 (*0-85342-820-4*) Dufour.

— In the Tracks of the West Clare Railway. 225p. 1990. pap. 19.95 (*0-85342-909-X*, Pub. by Mercier Pr IE) Dufour.

— Long Ago by Shannon Side. 1982. pap. 7.95 (*0-85342-671-6*) Dufour.

— Stories of Old Ireland for Children. (J). 1990. pap. 9.95 (*0-85342-777-1*) Dufour.

— Strange Irish Tales for Children. (Illus.). 128p. (J). (ps-8). 1992. reprint ed. pap. 9.95 (*0-85342-833-6*, Pub. by Mercier Pr IE) Dufour.

Lenihan, J. The Crumbs of Creation: Trace Elements in History, Medicine, Industry, Crime & Folklore. (Illus.). 176p. 1988. 30.00 (*0-85274-390-4*) IOP Pub.

Lenihan, John. The Good News about Radiation. LC 93-27500. (Focus on Science Ser.). 75p. (Orig.). 1993. pap. text ed. 9.00 (*0-944838-34-0*, Cogito Bks) Med Physics Pub.

— How the Body Works. LC 94-42774. 1994. write for info. (*0-944838-48-0*) Med Physics Pub.

— How the Body Works. 1995. pap. text ed. 15.00 (*0-614-03717-4*) Med Physics Pub.

— Human Engineering: The Body Re-Examined. LC 74-25318. 212p. 1975. 7.95 (*0-8076-0782-7*) Braziller.

— Science in Action. (Illus.). 236p. 1990. pap. 23.90 (*0-85274-285-1*) IOP Pub.

— Well Its Not My Fault! About the San Andreas Fault & Other Things. (Illus.). 223p. (gr. 12 up). 1988. pap. 10.00 (*0-944838-00-6*) Med Physics Pub.

Lenihan, John H. Showdown: Confronting Modern America in the Western Film. LC 79-25271. (Illus.). 224p. 1985. 11.95 (*0-252-01254-2*) U of Ill Pr.

Lenin. Imperialism, the Highest Stage of Capitalism. 1975. reprint ed. 3.95 (*0-8351-0113-4*) China Bks.

— Lenin: Against Imperialist War. 1978. 24.95 (*0-8464-0554-7*) Beekman Pubs.

— Lenin: Against Liquidationism. 1978. 24.95 (*0-8464-0553-9*) Beekman Pubs.

— Lenin: On Utopian & Scientific Socialism. 1978. 24.95 (*0-8464-0558-X*) Beekman Pubs.

***Lenin, V. I.** Collection Works, 45 Vols. Plus 2 Vol. Index. 4th ed. Date not set. lib. bdg. 500.00 (*0-8285-1588-3*) Pathfinder NY.

— Imperialism: The Highest Stage of Capitalism. 124p. Date not set. pap. 3.95 (*0-614-04205-4*) Pathfinder NY.

— Lenin's Final Fight: Writings & Speeches, 1922-1923. Fyson, George, ed. 320p. 1995. pap. 19.95 (*0-87348-807-5*) Pathfinder NY.

— Lenin's Final Fight: Writings & Speeches, 1922-1923. Fyson, George, ed. 320p. 1995. lib. bdg. 50.00 (*0-87348-808-3*) Pathfinder NY.

— On the Emancipation of Women. 136p. Date not set. pap. 4.95 (*0-614-04207-0*) Pathfinder NY.

— On Trade Unions: A Collection of Articles & Speeches. 540p. Date not set. lib. bdg. 17.95 (*0-614-04208-9*) Pathfinder NY.

— The Right of Nations to Self-Determination. 79p. Date not set. pap. 4.00 (*0-614-04206-2*) Pathfinder NY.

— Selected Works of V. I. Lenin, 3 vols., Set. 2458p. Date not set. lib. bdg. 50.00 (*0-614-04211-9*) Pathfinder NY.

— What Is to Be Done? 207p. Date not set. pap. 6.95 (*0-614-04210-0*) Pathfinder NY.

Lenin, Vladimir I. British Labour & British Imperialism. 316p. 1969. 25.00 (*0-8464-0214-9*) Beekman Pubs.

— The Emancipation of Women. 136p. 1970. pap. text ed. 2.75 (*0-7178-0290-6*) Intl Pubs Co.

— Essential Works of Lenin: "What Is to Be Done?" & Other Writings. Christman, Henry, ed. 372p. 1987. reprint ed. pap. 9.95 (*0-486-25333-3*) Dover.

— Imperialism: The Highest Stage of Capitalism. 128p. (C). 1969. pap. text ed. 2.95 (*0-7178-0098-9*) Intl Pubs Co.

— Introduction to Marx, Engels & Marxism. Smith, Betty, ed. LC 86-21012. 108p. 1987. pap. text ed. 2.95 (*0-7178-0647-2*) Intl Pubs Co.

— Left-Wing Communism, An Infantile Disorder. 95p. 1940. pap. text ed. 2.50 (*0-7178-0107-1*) Intl Pubs Co.

— Lenin on War & Peace. 1966. pap. 1.95 (*0-8351-0130-4*) China Bks.

— Letter to American Workers. 1970. pap. 0.45 (*0-87898-047-4*) New Outlook.

— New Data for Lenin's "Imperialism..." Varga, E. & Mendelsohn, L., eds. LC 71-121288. reprint ed. 22.75 (*0-404-03965-0*) AMS Pr.

— The Right of Nations to Self Determination: Selected Writings. LC 77-22314. 128p. 1977. reprint ed. text ed. 38.50 (*0-8371-9731-7*, LERN, Greenwood Pr) Greenwood.

— State & Revolution. 1965. pap. 3.95 (*0-8351-0372-2*) China Bks.

— State & Revolution. 103p. (C). 1932. pap. text ed. 2.75 (*0-7178-0196-9*) Intl Pubs Co.

— The State & Revolution. Service, Robert, tr. & intro. by. 192p. 1993. 11.95 (*0-14-018435-X*, Penguin Classics) Viking Penguin.

— State & Revolution: Marxist Teachings about the Theory of the State & the Tasks of the Proletariat in the Revolution. LC 78-2228. 104p. 1978. reprint ed. text ed. 35.00 (*0-313-20351-2*, LESTR, Greenwood Pr) Greenwood.

— Two Tactics of Social Democracy in the Democratic Revolution. Trachtenberg, Alexander, tr. xxx, 128p. 1989. reprint ed. pap. text ed. 3.25 (*0-7178-0206-X*) Intl Pubs Co.

— What Is to Be Done? 1990. pap. 9.95 (*0-14-018126-1*, 468, Penguin Classics) Viking Penguin.

— What Is to Be Done? Burning Questions of Our Movement. Allen, James S., ed. LC 69-18884. 200p. (C). 1969. pap. text ed. 5.75 (*0-7178-0218-3*) Intl Pubs Co.

An Asterisk (*) at the beginning of an entry indicates that the title is appearing in BIP for the first time.

Lenin, Vladimir I. & Trotsky, L. Kronstadt. Mutnick, Barbara, ed. Wright, John G. et al, trs. LC 78-65893. 1979. lib. bdg. 45.00 (*0-913460-73-7*); pap. 15.95 (*0-913460-74-5*) Pathfinder NY.

Leniston, Florence. Popular Irish Songs. 1991. pap. 9.95 (*0-486-26755-5*) Dover.

***Lenk.** Simplified Design Micropower. 1995. write for info. (*0-7506-9510-2*, Focal) Buttrwrth-Heinemann.

Lenk, Hans. Social Philosophy of Athletics. 1979. pap. text ed. 9.60 (*0-87563-165-7*) Stipes.

Lenk, Hans & Paul, Gregor, eds. Epistemological Issues in Classical Chinese Philosophy. LC 92-17185. (SUNY Series in Chinese Philosophy & Culture). 194p. (C). 1993. 59.50 (*0-7914-1449-3*); pap. 19.95 (*0-7914-1450-7*) State U NY Pr.

Lenk, John D. Complete Guide to Digital Television Troubleshooting & Repair. 240p. 1988. text ed. 46.00 (*0-13-160094-X*) P-H.

— Complete Guide to Modern VCR Troubleshooting & Repair. (Illus.). 288p. (C). 1985. text ed. 68.00 (*0-13-160359-0*) P-H.

— Complete Guide to Stereo Television (MIS-MCS) Troubleshooting & Repair. (Illus.). 160p. (C). 1988. text ed. 44.00 (*0-13-160839-8*) P-H.

— Handbook of Basic Electronic Troubleshooting. (Illus.). 1979. 18.95 (*0-13-372482-4*); 15.50 (*0-13-372474-3*) P-H.

— Handbook of Digital Electronics. (Illus.). 384p. 1981. pap. text ed. 39.00 (*0-13-377184-9*) P-H.

— Handbook of Microcomputer Based Instrumentation & Controls. (Illus.). 384p. (C). 1983. text ed. 53.00 (*0-13-380519-0*) P-H.

— Handbook of Microprocessors, Microcomputers & Minicomputers. (Illus.). 1979. text ed. 39.00 (*0-13-380378-3*) P-H.

— Handbook of Modern Solid State Amplifiers. (Illus.). 400p. 1974. pap. text ed. 39.00 (*0-13-380394-5*) P-H.

— Handbook of Oscilloscopes: Theory & Application. enl. rev. ed. (Illus.). 320p. (C). 1982. text ed. 44.00 (*0-13-380576-X*) P-H.

— Handbook of Practical CB Service. (Illus.). 1978. 15.50 (*0-13-380550-6*); pap. text ed. 39.00 (*0-13-380568-9*) P-H.

— Handbook of Practical Electronic Circuits. (Illus.). 352p. 1982. pap. text ed. 39.00 (*0-13-380741-X*) P-H.

— Handbook of Simplified Electrical Wiring Design. (Illus.). 416p. 1978. 19.50 (*0-13-381681-8*) P-H.

— Handbook of Simplified Television Service. (Illus.). 1986. 18.50 (*0-13-381780-6*) P-H.

— A Hobbyist's Guide to Computer Experimentation. (Illus.). 288p. (C). 1985. pap. text ed. 39.00 (*0-13-392473-4*) P-H.

— Lenk's Audio Handbook: Operation & Troubleshooting. 320p. 1991. text ed. 39.50 (*0-07-037503-8*) McGraw.

— Lenk's Audio Handbook: Operation & Troubleshooting. 1992. pap. text ed. 22.95 (*0-07-004276-4*) McGraw.

— Lenk's Audio Handbook: Operation & Troubleshooting. 304p. 1992. pap. 22.95 (*0-8306-4276-5*, 4309) TAB Bks.

— Lenk's Digital Handbook: Design & Troubleshooting. 1992. text ed. 39.50 (*0-07-037516-X*) McGraw.

— Lenk's Laser Handbook: Featuring CD, CDV, & CR-Rom Technology. 1993. pap. 22.95 (*0-8306-4429-6*) TAB Bks.

— Lenk's Laser Handbook: Featuring Cd, Dv & CD-ROM Technologies. 1992. text ed. 39.50 (*0-07-037505-4*) McGraw.

— Lenk's Laser Handbook: Featuring Cd, Dv, & CD-ROM Technology. 1993. pap. text ed. 22.95 (*0-07-037608-5*) McGraw.

— Lenk's Reference Handbook: Operation & Troubleshooting. 1993. pap. text ed. 22.95 (*0-8306-4560-8*) TAB Bks.

— Lenk's RF Handbook: Operation & Troubleshooting. 1992. text ed. 39.50 (*0-07-037504-6*) McGraw.

— Lenk's RF Handbook: Operation & Troubleshooting. 1993. pap. text ed. 22.95 (*0-07-037618-2*) McGraw.

— Lenk's Television Handbook: Operation & Troubleshooting. 1993. text ed. 39.50 (*0-07-037517-8*) McGraw.

— Lenk's Video Handbook. 2nd ed. 1996. text ed. 39.50 (*0-07-037616-6*); pap. text ed. 22.95 (*0-07-037617-4*) McGraw.

— Lenk's Video Handbook: Operation & Troubleshooting. 1992. pap. text ed. 22.95 (*0-07-037573-9*) McGraw.

— Lenk's Video Handbook: Operation & Troubleshooting. 384p. 1992. pap. 22.95 (*0-8306-4072-X*) TAB Bks.

— McGraw-Hill Circuit Encyclopedia & Troubleshooting Guide. LC 92-33275. 1993. text ed. 59.50 (*0-07-037603-4*) McGraw.

— McGraw-Hill Circuit Encyclopedia, & Troubleshooting Guide, Vol. 2. 1994. text ed. 59.50 (*0-07-037610-7*) McGraw.

— McGraw-Hill Electric Testing Handbook: Procedures & Techniques. 1993. text ed. 42.95 (*0-07-037602-6*) McGraw.

— McGraw-Hill Electronic Troubleshooting Handbook. 1995. text ed. 39.50 (*0-07-037658-1*) McGraw.

— Practical Guide to Electronic Amplifiers. 1991. boxed 36.00 (*0-13-690843-8*) P-H.

— Simplified Design of Linear Power Supplies. LC 94-16077. 218p. 1994. 29.95 (*0-7506-9506-4*) Buttrwrth-Heinemann.

— Simplified Design of Switching Power Supplies. LC 94-32727. 221p. 1995. 39.95 (*0-7506-9507-2*) Buttrwrth-Heinemann.

— Simplified Electrical Wiring Design Handbook. LC 92-11463. 336p. 1992. text ed. 48.00 (*0-13-814047-2*) P-H.

Lenk, John D., jt. auth. see Marcus, Abraham.

Lenk, R. S. Fluctuations, Diffusion & Spin Relaxation. (Studies in Physical & Theoretical Chemistry: No. 43). 280p. 1986. 100.00 (*0-444-42718-X*) Elsevier.

— Polymer Rheology. (Illus.). 375p. 1978. 110.00 (*0-85334-765-4*, Pub. by Elsevier Applied Sci UK) Elsevier.

Lenke, Leif. Alcohol & Criminal Violence: Time Series Analyses in a Comparative Perspective. 187p. (Orig.). 1990. pap. 47.50x (*91-22-01415-2*, Pub. by Almqv & Wiksell SW) Coronet Bks.

Lenker, John N., ed. see Luther, Martin.

Lenker, L. T., jt. ed. see Deats, S. M.

Lenker, Lagretta T., jt. ed. see Deats, Sara M.

Lenker, Lagretta T., jt. auth. see Moxley, Joseph M.

Len'kov, V. D., et al. The Komandorskii Camp of the Bering Expedition: An Experiment in Complex Study. Arndt, Katherine L., tr. (Illus.). 176p. (Orig.). 1992. pap. 12.00 (*0-940521-00-8*) AK Hist Soc.

Lenkowsky, Leslie. Politics, Economics & Welfare Reform: The Failure of the Negative Income Tax in Britain & the United States. LC 85-29456. 216p. (Orig.). 1986. pap. text ed. 20.00 (*0-8191-5216-1*) U Pr of Amer.

Lenman, Bruce. Integration, Enlightenment, & Industrialization: Scotland, 1746-1832. LC 81-193623. (New History of Scotland Ser.: No. 6). 192p. reprint ed. pap. 54.80 (*0-685-15810-1*, 2026369) Bks Demand.

— Larousse Dictionary of World History. 1008p. 1994. 40.00 (*0-7523-5001-3*, Chambers LKC) LKC.

***Lenman, Bruce, ed.** Larousse Dictionary of British History. 336p. 1995. pap. 8.95 (*0-7523-0004-0*, Larousse LKC) LKC.

— Larousse Dictionary of North American History. 320p. 1995. pap. 8.95 (*0-7523-0005-9*, Larousse LKC) LKC.

— Larousse Dictionary of Twentieth Century History. 784p. 1995. pap. 12.95 (*0-7523-0003-2*, Larousse LKC) LKC.

— Larousse Dictionary of World History. 1008p. 1995. pap. 18.95 (*0-7523-5008-0*, Chambers LKC) LKC.

Lenman, Bruce P. The Eclipse of Parliament: British Government & Politics since 1914. 256p. 1992. pap. 17.95 (*0-340-49492-1*, A9514, Pub. by E Arnold UK) Routledge Chapman & Hall.

— Integration & Enlightenment: Scotland, 1746-1832. (New History of Scotland Ser.). 200p. 1993. pap. 20.00 (*0-7486-0385-9*, Pub. by Edinburgh U Pr UK) Col U Pr.

Lenman, J. A., jt. auth. see Davidson, D. L.

Lenman, Karin, ed. see Radha, Sivananda.

Lenn, Dorothy, tr. see Steiner, Rudolf.

Lenn, Peter D. Active Learning: A Parent's Guide to Helping Your Teen Make the Grade in School. LC 92-34814. 224p. 1993. pap. 10.00 (*0-14-017653-5*, Penguin Bks) Viking Penguin.

Lenna, Harry R., jt. auth. see Woodman, Natalie J.

***Lennan, Richard.** The Ecclesiology of Karl Rahner. 256p. 1995. 55.00 (*0-19-826358-9*) OUP.

Lennander, Jean. Crafty Recycling: Wallpaper Craft from Throw-Aways. LC 93-86374. (Illus.). 192p. (Orig.). 1994. pap. 12.95 (*0-9639009-1-9*) Tassel Pr.

Lennard, Erica. Classic Gardens. LC 83-80908. (Illus.). 128p. 1982. 27.95 (*0-912810-38-6*) Lustrum Pr.

Lennard, Henry L. & Gralnick, Alexander, eds. The Psychiatric Hospital: Context, Values & Therapeutic Process. 221p. 1986. 35.95 (*0-89885-297-8*) Human Sci Pr.

Lennard, Henry L. & Lennard, Suzanne H., eds. Ethics of Health Care: Dilemmas of Technology & Techniques in Health Care & Psychotherapy. LC 79-57022. 174p. (Orig.). 1979. pap. 16.00 (*0-935824-01-4*) Gondolier.

Lennard, Henry L., jt. auth. see Crowhurst-Lennard, Suzanne H.

Lennard, Henry L., jt. auth. see Lennard, Suzanne H.

Lennard, John. But I Digress: The Exploitation of Parentheses in English Printed Verse. (Illus.). 344p. 1992. 69.00 (*0-19-811247-5*) OUP.

Lennard-Jones, John E., jt. ed. see Kamm, Michael A.

Lennard, Reginald V. Rural England, Ten Eighty-Six to Eleven Thirty-Five: A Study of Social & Agrarian Conditions. LC 80-2222. reprint ed. 49.50 (*0-404-18767-6*) AMS Pr.

Lennard, Suzanne H. & Lennard, Henry L. Livable Cities: People & Places, Social & Design Principles for the Future of the City. LC 87-83357. 166p. (Orig.). 1987. pap. 30.00 (*0-935824-04-9*) Gondolier.

— Livable Cities Observed: A Source Book of Images & Ideas. (Illus.). 272p. (Orig.). 1995. 38.00 (*0-935824-05-7*); pap. 33.00 (*0-935824-06-5*) Gondolier.

Lennard, Suzanne H., jt. ed. see Lennard, Henry L.

Lennard, Ted A., ed. Psychiatric Procedures in Clinical Practice. (Illus.). 400p. 1995. text ed. 69.00 (*1-56053-069-3*) Hanley & Belfus.

Lenne, Gerard. Sex on the Screen: Eroticism in Film. (Illus.). 352p. 1985. pap. 15.95 (*0-312-71335-5*) St Martin.

Lenne, J. M. Phytopathological Paper, No. 31: World List of Fungal Diseases of Tropical Pasture Species, No. 31. 192p. (Orig.). (C). 1990. pap. text ed. 34.50 (*0-85198-674-9*) CAB Intl.

***Lenne, J. M. & Trutmann, P., eds.** Diseases of Tropical Pasture Plants. 400p. 1994. 108.00x (*0-85198-917-9*) CAB Intl.

Lenne, Peter J. Peter Joseph Lenne: The Drawings. (Illus.). 460p. 1993. 95.00 (*3-8030-2805-1*, Pub. by Ernst Wasmuth GW) Dist Art Pubs.

Lenneberg, Elizabeth, jt. ed. see Miller, George A.

Lenneberg, Hans. Witness & Scholars: Studies in Musical Biography. (Monographs on Musicology: Vol. 5). 223p. 1988. text ed. 68.00 (*2-88124-210-3*, ML3797.L46) Gordon & Breach.

Lenneberg, Hans, tr. & comment. Breitkoph & Hartel in Paris (1833-1844) The Letters of Heinrich Probst. LC 90-7036. (Musical Life in Nineteenth-Century France Ser.: No. 5). (Illus.). 200p. (GER.). 1990. lib. bdg. 47.00 (*0-918728-64-9*) Pendragon NY.

Lennerstrand, G. & Bach-Y-Rita, Paul, eds. Basic Mechanisms of Ocular Motility & Their Clinical Implications. 1975. 234.00 (*0-08-018885-0*, Pub. by Pergamon Repr UK) Franklin.

Lennerstrand, G. & Keller, E. L., eds. Functional Basis of Ocular Motility Disorders: Proceedings of a Wenner-Gren Center & Smith-Kettlewell Eye Research Foundation International Symposium, Held in the Wenner-Gren Center, Stockholm, August 31 to September 3, 1981. (Wenner-Gren Center International Symposium Ser.: Vol. 37). (Illus.). 624p. 1982. 254.00 (*0-08-029772-2*, Pub. by Pergamon Repr UK) Franklin.

Lennerstrand, G., et al, eds. Strabismus & Amblyopia: Experimental Basis for Advances in Clinical Management. (Wenner-Gren International Symposia Ser.: Vol. 49). (Illus.). 452p. 1988. 110.00 (*0-306-42943-8*, Plenum Pr) Plenum.

***Lennerstrand, Gunnar & American Association for Pediatric Ophthalmology & Strabismus Staff, eds.** Update on Strabismus & Pediatric Ophthalmology: Proceedings of the June, 1994 Joint ISA & AAPO&S Meeting, Vancouver, Canada. LC 94-46587. 752p. 1995. 189.95 (*0-8493-8961-5*, 8961) CRC Pr.

Lennerstrand, Gunnar, jt. auth. see Ygge, J.

Lennert, K. & Feller, A. C. Histopathology of Non-Hodgkin's Lymphomas: Based on the Updated Kiel Classification. 2nd rev. ed. (Illus.). xiv, 312p. 1994. 160.00 (*0-387-51270-5*) Spr-Verlag.

Lennert, K. & Hubner, K., eds. Pathology of the Bone Marrow. (Illus.). 426p. 1984. lib. bdg. 115.00 (*0-89574-195-4*, Pub. by Gustav Fischer Verlag) VCH Pubs.

Lennette, ed. Laboratory Diagnosis of Viral Infections. 2nd expanded rev. ed. 800p. 1992. 195.00 (*0-8247-8585-1*) Dekker.

Lennette, Edwin H., ed. see American Society for Microbiology Staff, et al.

Lennette, Edwin H., et al, eds. Laboratory Diagnosis of Infectious Diseases: Principles & Practice, Vol. 2. (Illus.). 825p. 1988. 239.00 (*0-387-96756-7*) Spr-Verlag.

Lenning, Janet, ed. see Hoffman, Mark, et al.

Lenning, Lorene. More Than Money, K-Grade Three. 90p. 1989. pap. 7.95 (*0-673-38556-6*) GdYrBks.

Lenninger, Jack. Time Heals No Wounds. (Orig.). 1993. mass mkt. 4.99 (*0-8041-0916-8*) Ivy Books.

Lennon. Another's Fandango. Date not set. 5.95 (*0-685-75000-0*, 93987) Mel Bay.

— Sagebrush Bohemian. 1994. pap. 10.95 (*1-56924-946-6*) Marlowe & Co.

Lennon, Alexander T., jt. ed. see Mazarr, Michael J.

Lennon, Andy & Rutan, Burt, frwds. Canard: A Revolution in Flight. LC 84-71364. (AV Bk.: No. 8). (Illus.). 200p. 1984. pap. 19.95 (*0-938716-18-2*) Markowski Intl.

Lennon, Biddy W. Biddy White Lennon's Eating at Home Cookbook. 180p. (Orig.). 1990. pap. 10.95 (*1-85371-096-2*, Pub. by Poolbeg Pr IE) Dufour.

— The Poolbeg Book of Traditional Irish Cooking. 186p. 1990. pap. 9.95 (*1-85371-092-X*, Pub. by Poolbeg Pr IE) Dufour.

Lennon, Cheryl, ed. see Frederickson, Jeanette A. & Holton, Court C.

Lennon, Colm. The Lords of Dublin in the Age of Reformation. 320p. 1989. 45.00 (*0-7165-2419-8*, Pub. by Irish Acad Pr IE) Intl Spec Bk.

— Sixteenth Century Ireland: The Incomplete Conquest. LC 94-32460. 1995. write for info. (*0-312-12462-7*) St Martin.

Lennon, Dianne, et al. Same Song-Separate Voices: The Collective Memoirs of the Lennon Sisters. LC 84-60761. (Illus.). 368p. 1985. 17.95 (*0-915677-10-5*) Roundtable Pub.

Lennon, Donald R., jt. auth. see Bennett, Charles E.

Lennon, Edith, ed. see Grant, Doug.

Lennon, Florence B. Victoria Through the Looking Glass: The Life of Lewis Carroll. 25.95 (*0-89190-991-5*, Am Repr) Amereon Ltd.

Lennon, Gerard P., ed. Symposium on Ground Water. LC 91-21956. 320p. 1991. pap. text ed. 35.00 (*0-87262-817-5*) Am Soc Civil Eng.

Lennon, J. Michael, ed. Conversations with Norman Mailer. LC 87-34316. (Literary Conversations Ser.). 396p. 1988. 37.50 (*0-87805-351-4*); pap. 15.95 (*0-87805-352-2*) U Pr of Miss.

Lennon, Jane. Happier in the Country. LC 87-61162. (Illus.). (Orig.). 1987. 12.95 (*0-941526-04-6*) Prospect Hill.

Lennon, Jodi, jt. auth. see Sullivan, Margaret.

Lennon, John. Ai: Japan Through John Lennon's Eyes: A Personal Sketchbook. Horibuchi, Seiji, ed. Fujii, Satoru, tr. (Illus.). 194p. (Orig.). 1992. pap. 21.95 (*0-929279-78-6*, Cadence Bks) Viz Commns Inc.

— Imagine. 1990. 13.95 (*1-55972-038-7*, Birch Ln Pr) Carol Pub Group.

— In His Own Write. 1993. reprint ed. lib. bdg. 25.95 (*1-56849-147-6*) Buccaneer Bks.

— In His Own Write & A Spaniard in the Works. 1967. pap. 4.50 (*0-451-15697-8*, Sig) NAL-Dutton.

— Misadventures of Sherlock Holmes. 1991. 16.95 (*0-8065-1245-8*, Citadel); pap. 10.95 (*0-8065-1235-0*, Citadel) Carol Pub Group.

— Skywriting by Word of Mouth, & Other Writings, Including the Ballad of John & Yoko. 200p. 1991. reprint ed. lib. bdg. 23.00x (*0-8095-9075-1*) Borgo Pr.

— A Spaniard in the Works. 1994. reprint ed. lib. bdg. 27.95 (*1-56849-299-5*) Buccaneer Bks.

Lennon, John & McCartney, Paul. Yellow Submarine. (Sing-a-Song Storybooks Ser.). (Illus.). 24p. (J). 1993. 9.95 (*0-7935-1859-8*, 00183013) H Leonard.

Lennon, Kathleen. Explaining Human Action. 176p. (C). 1990. 35.95 (*0-8126-9134-2*); pap. 15.95 (*0-8126-9135-0*) Open Court.

Lennon, Kathleen, jt. ed. see Whitford, Margaret.

Lennon, Kethleen, jt. ed. see Charles, David.

Lennon, Mary B. & Walthall, Barbara, eds. Sourcebook for Science, Mathematics & Technology Education 1992. 218p. 1991. 12.95 (*0-87168-429-2*, 91-38S) AAAS.

Lennon, Nigey. Alfred Jarry: The Man with the Axe. 1991. pap. 9.95 (*0-86719-382-4*) Last Gasp.

— Alfred Jarry: The Man with the Axe. (Illus.). 120p. 1984. 15.95 (*0-915572-74-5*); pap. 6.95 (*0-915572-73-7*) Panjandrum.

— Being Frank: My Time with Frank Zappa. (Illus.). 160p. (Orig.). 1995. pap. 14.95 (*1-879395-55-X*) CA Classics Bks.

Lennon, Nigey, jt. auth. see Rolfe, Lionel.

Lennon, Patricia & Moore, Douglas. Te Toca a Ti. (Aiming for Proficiency Ser.). (Illus.). 160p. (Orig.). (SPA.). 1990. student ed 14.95 (*1-879279-04-5*, TX 3-018-188) Proficiency Pr.

Lennon, Patricia, et al. The Foreign Language Teacher's Handbook: Aiming for Proficiency in Spanish. (Illus.). 200p. (Orig.). (SPA.). 1989. teacher ed 28.95 (*1-879279-01-0*, TX 2-670-457) Proficiency Pr.

Lennon, Rebecca D. Keyboard Capers: Music Theory for Children. 143p. (J). 1993. pap. text ed. 18.95 (*1-884098-01-0*) Elijah Co.

Lennon, Rosemarie. David Letterman: On Stage & 320p. 1994. pap. 4.99 (*0-7860-0084-8*, Pinnacle NY) Windsor NY.

***Lennon, Sharron J., et al.** Social Science Aspects of Dress: New Directions. (ITAA Special Publication: No. 5). 211p. (C). 1993. pap. text ed. 35.00 (*1-885715-01-3*) Intl Textile.

Lennon, Sheila, jt. ed. see Riddoch, Jane.

Lennon, Thomas M. The Battle of the Gods & Giants: The Legacies of Descartes & Gassendi, 1655-1715. LC 92-26088. (Studies in Intellectual History & the History of Philosophy). 456p. 1993. 62.50 (*0-691-07400-3*) Princeton U Pr.

Lennon, Thomas M., tr. see Malebranch, Nicolas.

Lennon, Thomas M., tr. see Malebranche, Nicolas.

Lennon, Thomas M., et al, eds. Problems of Cartesianism. (Studies in the History of Ideas). 272p. 1982. 49.95 (*0-7735-1000-1*, Pub. by McGill CN) U of Toronto Pr.

Lennon, Todd M. Statistics on Social Work Education in the U. S. 1993. 131p. (Orig.). (C). 1994. pap. text ed. 13.00 (*0-87293-041-6*) Coun Soc Wk Ed.

Lennor, Linda A., jt. auth. see Miller, Ruth M.

Lennox. Heinemann Medical Dictionary, 1988. 624p. 1988. pap. text ed. 45.00 (*0-433-19156-2*) Buttrwrth-Heinemann.

Lennox-Boyd, Christopher, et al. George Stubbs. (Illus.). 432p. 1990. 290.00 (*0-85667-375-7*, Pub. by P Wilson Pubs) Sothebys Pubns.

Lennox, C. Shakespeare Illustrated, 3 Vols, Set. LC 72-172047. reprint ed. 135.00 (*0-404-03970-7*) AMS Pr.

Lennox, C. M., jt. auth. see McLatchie, G. R.

Lennox, Charlotte. Euphemia. LC 88-38442. 1989. 50.00 (*0-8201-1435-9*) Schol Facsimiles.

— The Female Quixote: Or, The Adventures of Arabella. Dalziel, Margaret, ed. (World's Classics Ser.). (Illus.). 466p. 1989. pap. 9.95 (*0-19-281765-5*) OUP.

— The Female Quixote, or the Adventures of Arabella, 2 vols. in one. LC 79-104511. 603p. reprint ed. lib. bdg. 74.50 (*0-8398-1155-1*) Irvington.

— The Life of Harriot Stuart, Written by Herself. Kubica, Susan, ed. & intro. by. LC 94-29387. 328p. 1995. 45.00 (*0-8386-3579-2*) Fairleigh Dickinson.

Lennox, Daphne. See Me after School: Identifying & Helping Children with Emotional & Behavioral Problems. 144p. (Orig.). 1991. pap. 34.95 (*0-8464-1496-1*) Beekman Pubs.

— See Me after School: Identifying & Helping Children with Emotional & Behavioral Problems. 144p. (Orig.). 1991. pap. 29.95 (*1-85346-163-6*, Pub. by D Fulton UK) Taylor & Francis.

Lennox, Duncan, ed. Jane's Air-Launched Weapons, 95-96. (Illus.). 260p. 470.00x (*0-7106-0866-7*) Janes Info Group.

— Jane's Strategic Weapon Systems. (Illus.). 250p. ring bd. 470.00x (*0-7106-0880-2*) Janes Info Group.

Lennox, E. R. The Wizard's Dressing-Gown. (Illus.). 32p. (J). (gr. 2-4). 1991. 14.95 (*0-237-51100-2*, Pub. by Evans Bros Ltd UK) Trafalgar.

Lennox, E. S., jt. auth. see Birch, J. R.

Lennox, Elsie, jt. auth. see Cohen, Daniel.

Lennox, Gladys R. Mists & Megaliths of Michael in the Mount. 1986. 39.00 (*0-7223-2036-1*, Pub. by A H S Ltd UK); pap. 25.00 (*0-7223-2091-4*, Pub. by A H S Ltd UK) St Mut.

Lennox, James G., jt. ed. see Gill, Mary L.

Lennox, John. Ralph Connor & His Works. (Canadian Author Studies). 60p. (C). 1988. pap. text ed. 9.95 (*0-920763-78-2*, Pub. by ECW Press CN) Genl Dist Srvs.

Lennox, John & Lacombe, Michele, eds. Dear Bill: The Correspondence of William Arthur Deacon. 400p. 1988. 40.00 (*0-8020-2624-9*) U of Toronto Pr.

Lennox, John & Paterson, Janet M., eds. Challenges, Projects, Texts: Canadian Editing: Papers Given at the Conference on Editorial Problems, University of Toronto, 17-18, November, 1989. LC 91-12400. (Conference on Editorial Problems Ser.: No. 25). Orig. Title: Defis, Projets et Textes dans l'Edition Critique au Canada. 120p. 1993. 37.50 (*0-404-63675-6*) AMS Pr.

Lennox, John, jt. auth. see Thomas, Clara.

Lennox, John C. & Stonehewer, Stewart. Subnormal Subgroups of Groups. (Oxford Mathematical Monographs). (Illus.). 268p. 1987. 69.00 (*0-19-853552-X*) OUP.

Lennox, John C., tr. see Adian, S. I.

Lennox, Judith. The Glittering Strand. 480p. 1994. 24.95 (*0-312-10469-3*) St Martin.
— The Italian Garden. 480p. 1993. 24.95 (*0-312-09810-3*) St Martin.
— The Secret Years. 608p. 1995. 25.95 (*0-312-13166-6*) St Martin.

Lennox-Kerr, Peter. Flexible Textile Composites. 161p. (C). 1973. pap. text ed. 90.00 (*0-685-36088-1*, Pub. by Textile Institue UK) St Mut.
— Needle Felted Fabrics. 140p. (C). 1972. pap. text ed. 75.00 (*0-685-46402-4*, Pub. by Textile Institue UK) St Mut.
— Nonwovens '71. 394p. (C). 1971. pap. text ed. 110.00 (*0-685-46400-8*, Pub. by Textile Institue UK) St Mut.

Lennox, M. S. & Ackroyd, J. S. Illustrated Handbook of General Surgery. 792p. 1991. text ed. 65.00 (*0-471-91457-6*, Wiley-Liss) Wiley.

Lennox, Marion. Wings of Healing. large type ed. 1992. 16.95 (*0-263-13152-1*, MB079, Pub. by Mills & Boon Ltd UK) Chivers N Amer.

Leno, Jay. Jay Leno's Headlines. 1992. 9.99 (*0-517-08238-1*) Random Hse Value.
— Jay Leno's Police Blotter: Real-Life Crime Headlines from "The Tonight Show with Jay Leno" 1994. pap. 6.95 (*0-8362-1751-9*) Andrews & McMeel.
— More Headlines. 1990. mass mkt. 6.95 (*0-446-39236-7*) Warner Bks.

Leno, Jay, comp. Headlines IV: The Generation. (Illus.). 192p. (Orig.). 1992. mass mkt. 6.99 (*0-446-39417-3*) Warner Bks.
— Headlines III: Not the Movie, Still the Book. 1991. mass mkt. 6.99 (*0-446-39374-6*) Warner Bks.

Lenoble, Jacqueline. Atmospheric Radiative Transfer. LC 93-12711. (Illus.). 500p. 1993. 94.00 (*0-937194-21-2*) A Deepak Pub.

Lenoble, Jacqueline, ed. Radiative Transfer in Scattering & Absorbing Atmospheres: Standard Computational Procedures. LC 85-31116. 300p. 1985. 71.00 (*0-937194-05-0*) A Deepak Pub.

Lenoble, Jacqueline & Geleyn, J. F., eds. IRS '88: Current Problems in Atmospheric Radiation. LC 89-33588. (Illus.). 653p. 1989. 82.00 (*0-937194-16-6*) A Deepak Pub.

***Lenoir, Robert.** The Language of Business: Dictionnaire Commercial et Economique Bilingue: French-English, English-French. 920p. (ENG & FRE.). 1989. pap. 105.00 (*0-7859-7954-9*, 2717817182) Fr & Eur.

Lenoir, Timothy. The Strategy of Life: Teleology & Mechanics in Nineteenth Century German Biology. (Illus.). 326p. 1989. pap. text ed. 14.95 (*0-226-47183-7*) U Ch Pr.

Lenoir, William B. History of Sweetwater Valley, Tennessee: With a New Index. 419p. 1994. reprint ed. pap. 34.00 (*0-685-75133-3*, 3355) Clearfield Co.

Lenon, Lance, jt. auth. see Kern, Marc F.

Lenora. A Black Entrepreneur's Prayer & Other Motivational Poems. 36p. 1994. pap. 5.00 (*0-9642175-0-3*) N Williams Commun.

***Lenore, Buth, illus.** How to Talk Confidently with Your Children About Sex. (Sex Education Ser.). 144p. 1988. pap. 7.99 (*0-570-08486-5*, 14-1626) Concordia.

Lenormand, Rene & Carner, Mosco. A Study of Twentieth-Century Harmony: Harmony in France to 1914 & Contemporary Harmony, 2 vols. in 1. LC 76-40058. (Music Reprint Ser.). 1975. reprint ed. lib. bdg. 32.50 (*0-306-70717-9*) Da Capo.

***Lenormant, Francois.** Chaldean Magic Its Origin & Development. 449p. 1994. pap. 27.00 (*1-56459-468-8*) Kessinger Pub.
— Essai sur L'organisation Politique et economique de la monnaie dans l'antiquite. 192p. (Orig.). (FRE.). (C). 1970. reprint ed. pap. 33.00 (*90-70265-22-2*, Pub. by Gieben NE) Benjamins North Am.

***Lenoski, Dan & Weber, Wolf-Dietrich.** Scaleable Shared Memory Multiprocessing. 1995. 54.95 (*1-55860-315-8*) Morgan Kaufmann.

Lenotre, Gaston. The Best of Lenotre: Glorious Desserts from France's Finest Pastry Maker. Hyman, Philip & Hyman, Mary, trs. 1983. pap. 14.95 (*0-8120-2450-8*) Barron.

***Lenover, Kathleen.** How to Win the Money Game: Going for the Gold, Silver & Assorted Loose Change. Date not set. audio 29.95 (*0-9642745-0-7*) KTL Finan Grp.

Lenowitz, Harris. Origins: Creation Texts from the Ancient Mediterranean. Doria, Charles, ed. LC 74-18844. 1976. lib. bdg. 32.50 (*0-404-14849-2*) AMS Pr.

Lenowitz, Harris, ed. Exiled in the Word: Poems & Other Visions of the Jews from Tribal Times to Present. rev. ed. LC 89-61458. (Illus.). 280p. (Orig.). 1989. reprint ed. pap. 12.00 (*1-55659-026-1*) Copper Canyon.

Lenowitz, Harris, jt. auth. see Rothenberg, Jerome.

Lenox, Edward H. Overland to Oregon. LC 93-13113. Orig. Title: Overland to Oregon in the Tracks of Lewis & Clarke. 1993. 14.95 (*0-87770-520-8*); pap. 9.95 (*0-685-71895-6*) Ye Galleon.

Lenox Hill Hospital Staff. Lenox Hill Hospital Book of Symptoms & Solutions. 1994. 24.00 (*0-679-42333-8*, Random Ref) Random.

***Lenox, John G.** Fire-Specks. Ingram, tr. 270p. 1996. pap. 8.95 (*0-7610-0483-1*) NW Pub.

Lenrott, Katherine F., jt. auth. see Lundberg, Emma O.

Lens, Willy, jt. ed. see D'Ydewalle, Gery.

Lensberg, Terje, jt. auth. see Thomson, William.

Lenschou, Donald H., ed. Probing the Atmospheric Boundary Layer. (Illus.). 269p. 1986. 45.00 (*0-933876-63-7*) Am Meteorological.

Lense, Esther. Light Triumphant. 1978. pap. 3.40 (*0-89536-301-1*, 1253) CSS OH.

Lenselaer, A. Swahili-French Dictionary: Dictionnaire Swahili-Francais. 646p. (FRE & SWA.). 1983. 175.00 (*0-8288-1100-8*, F60950) Fr & Eur.

Lensen, George A. The Damned Inheritance: The Soviet Union & the Manchurian Crises, 1924-1935. LC 74-186318. (Illus.). 533p. 1974. 19.80 (*0-910512-17-5*) Diplomatic IN.
— Japanese Recognition of the U. S. S. R. Soviet-Japanese Relations, 1921-1930. LC 77-186316. 419p. 1970. 15.00 (*0-910512-09-4*) Diplomatic IN.
— Report from Hokkaido: The Remains of Russian Culture in Northern Japan. LC 73-2878. (Illus.). 216p. 1974. reprint ed. text ed. 49.75 (*0-8371-6818-X*, LERH, Greenwood Pr) Greenwood.
— Russia's Japan Expedition of Eighteen Eighty-Five. LC 82-9156. (Illus.). xxviii, 208p. 1982. reprint ed. text ed. 55.00 (*0-313-23621-6*, LERJ, Greenwood Pr) Greenwood.
— The Strange Neutrality: Soviet - Japanese Relations During the Second World War, 1941-1945. LC 72-178091. (Illus.). 332p. 1972. 15.00 (*0-910512-14-0*) Diplomatic IN.

Lensen, George A., comp. Japanese Diplomatic & Consular Officials in Russia: A Handbook of Japanese Representatives in Russia from 1874 to 1968. LC 68-26392. 230p. 1968. 15.00 (*0-910512-05-1*) Diplomatic IN.

Lensen, George A., ed. Russian Diplomatic & Consular Officials in East Asia. LC 68-26393. (Monuments Nipponica Monograph). 294p. 1968. 15.00 (*0-910512-06-X*) Diplomatic IN.

Lensen, George A., ed. see Abrikossow, Dmitrii I.

Lensen, George A., ed. see Poutiatine, Olga.

Lensing, George S. Wallace Stevens: A Poet's Growth. LC 86-7280. xii, 313p. 1986. pap. text ed. 12.95 (*0-8071-1671-8*) La State U Pr.

***Lensing, George S. & Moran, Ronald.** Four Poets & the Emotive Imagination - Robert Bly, James Wright, Louis Simpson & William Stafford. fac. ed. LC 75-5348. 240p. 1976. reprint ed. pap. 68.40 (*0-7837-7803-1*, 2047559) Bks Demand.

Lensing, Leo A., ed. see Fassbinder, Rainer W.

Lensink, Judy N. A Secret to Be Burried: The Diary & Life of Emily Hawley Gillespie, 1858-1888. LC 88-38514. (Bur Oak Original Ser.). (Illus.). 472p. 1989. text ed. 42.95x (*0-87745-229-6*); pap. 16.95 (*0-87745-237-7*) U of Iowa Pr.

Lenski, Gerhard, et al. Human Societies: An Introduction to Macrosociology. 6th ed. 1991. text ed. write for info. (*0-07-037242-X*) McGraw.
— Human Societies: An Introduction to Macrosociology. 6th ed. 1991. pap. text ed. write for info. (*0-07-037273-X*) McGraw.
— Human Societies: An Introduction to Macrosociology. 7th ed. LC 94-15796. 1994. text ed. 33.50 (*0-07-037631-X*) McGraw.

Lenski, Gerhard E. Power & Privilege: A Theory of Social Stratification. LC 83-26049. 512p. 1984. reprint ed. pap. 13.95 (*0-8078-4119-6*) U of NC Pr.
— The Religious Factor: A Sociological Study of Religion's Impact on Politics, Economics, & Family Life. LC 77-1275. 381p. 1977. reprint ed. text ed. 38.50 (*0-8371-9506-3*, LERF, Greenwood Pr) Greenwood.
— Status Crystallization: A Non-Vertical Dimension of Social Status. (Reprint Series in Social Sciences). (C). 1993. reprint ed. pap. text ed. 1.00 (*0-8290-3968-6*, S-168) Irvington.

Lenski, Jean. Genesis. 176p. (Orig.). 1993. pap. 9.95 (*1-879934-25-6*) St Andrews NC.

Lenski, Lois. Adventures in Understanding. 1968. 4.95 (*0-9607778-1-4*) Friends Fla St.
— Adventures in Understanding. deluxe ed. 1968. 12.50 (*0-9607778-2-2*) Friends Fla St.
— Bayou Suzette. 1976. 18.95 (*0-8488-4049-6*) Amereon Ltd.
— Bayou Suzette. 250p. 1991. reprint ed. lib. bdg. 19.95 (*0-89966-852-6*) Buccaneer Bks.
— Big Book of Mr. Small. (Illus.). (J). (ps-3). 1980. pap. 9.95 (*0-8098-6026-0*) McKay.
— Bound Girl of Cobble Hill. 21.95 (*0-89190-632-0*, Am Repr) Amereon Ltd.
— Cowboy Small. LC 60-12094. (Mr. Small Bks.). (Illus.). (J). (gr. k-3). 1980. 5.25 (*0-8098-1021-2*) McKay.
— Indian Captive: The Story of Mary Jemison. LC 41-51956. (Illus.). 272p. (J). (gr. 7-9). 1990. 16.00 (*0-397-30072-7*, Lipp Jr Bks); lib. bdg. 15.89 (*0-397-30076-X*, Lipp Jr Bks) HarpC Child Bks.
— Little Airplane. LC 59-12487. (Mr. Small Bks.). (Illus.). (J). (gr. k-3). 1980. 5.25 (*0-8098-1004-2*) McKay.
— Little Auto. LC 58-14239. (Mr. Small Bks.). (Illus.). (J). (gr. k-3). 1980. 5.25 (*0-8098-1001-8*) McKay.
— Little Farm. LC 58-12902. (Mr. Small Bks.). (Illus.). (J). (gr. k-3). 1980. 5.25 (*0-8098-1009-3*) McKay.
— Little Sailboat. 1980. 5.25 (*0-8098-1002-6*) McKay.
— Lois Lenski's Big Big Book of Mr. Small. (Illus.). 300p. (J). (ps-1). 1985. 5.98 (*0-517-46307-5*) Random Hse Value.
— Mr. & Mrs. Noah. LC 48-5989. (Illus.). 48p. (J). (ps-1). 1962. lib. bdg. 12.89 (*0-690-54562-2*, Crowell Jr Bks) HarpC Child Bks.
— More Mr. Small. (J). (ps-3). 1980. 9.95 (*0-8098-6300-6*) McKay.
— Sing a Song of People. (J). (ps-3). 1987. pap. 15.95 (*0-316-52074-8*) Little.
— Sing for Peace. (Christian Peace Shelf Ser.). 16p. (J). (ps-2). 1985. pap. 1.50 (*0-8361-3396-X*) Herald Pr.
— Strawberry Girl. 1976. 18.95 (*0-8488-1410-X*) Amereon Ltd.
— Strawberry Girl. LC 45-7609. (Illus.). 192p. (J). (gr. 4-6). 1945. 16.00 (*0-397-30109-X*, Lipp Jr Bks); lib. bdg. 15.89 (*0-397-30110-3*, Lipp Jr Bks) HarpC Child Bks.
— Strawberry Girl. LC 45-7609. (Illus.). 192p. (J). (gr. 4-6). 1995. pap. 3.95 (*0-06-440585-0*, Trophy) HarpC Child Bks.
— Strawberry Girl. 250p. 1991. reprint ed. lib. bdg. 19.95 (*0-89966-851-8*) Buccaneer Bks.

***Lenski, Lois, illus.** Indian Captive: The Story of Mary Jemison. LC 41-51956. (Trophy Nonfiction Bk.). 320p. (YA). (gr. 5 up). 1995. pap. 4.95 (*0-06-446162-9*, Trophy) HarpC Child Bks.

Lenski, Richard C. Interpretation of Acts. 1934. 32.99 (*0-8066-9009-7*, 10-3365, Augsburg) Augsburg Fortress.
— Interpretation of Colossians, Thessalonians First & Second, Timothy First & Second, Titus, & Philemon. 1937. 32.99 (*0-8066-9006-2*, 10-3369, Augsburg) Augsburg Fortress.
— Interpretation of First & Second Corinthians. 1935. 32.99 (*0-8066-9008-9*, 10-3367, Augsburg) Augsburg Fortress.
— Interpretation of First & Second Peter, First, Second & Third John, Jude. 1938. 32.99 (*0-8066-9011-9*, 10-3371, Augsburg) Augsburg Fortress.
— Interpretation of Galatians, Ephesians, & Philippians. 1937. 32.99 (*0-8066-9007-0*, 10-3368, Augsburg) Augsburg Fortress.
— Interpretation of Hebrews & James. 1938. 32.99 (*0-8066-9010-0*, 10-3370, Augsburg) Augsburg Fortress.
— Interpretation of Romans. 1936. 32.99 (*0-8066-9005-4*, 10-3366, Augsburg) Augsburg Fortress.
— Interpretation of St. John's Gospel. 1942. 32.99 (*0-8066-9000-3*, 10-3364, Augsburg) Augsburg Fortress.
— Interpretation of St. John's Revelation. 676p. 1935. 32.99 (*0-8066-9001-1*, 10-3372, Augsburg) Augsburg Fortress.
— Interpretation of St. Luke's Gospel. 1216p. 1934. 32.99 (*0-8066-9002-X*, 10-3363, Augsburg) Augsburg Fortress.
— Interpretation of St. Mark's Gospel. 776p. 1946. 32.99 (*0-8066-9003-8*, 0-3362, Augsburg) Augsburg Fortress.
— Interpretation of St. Matthew's Gospel. 1182p. 1932. 32.99 (*0-8066-9004-6*, 10-3361, Augsburg) Augsburg Fortress.
— Interpretation of the New Testament, 12 Vols, Set. 1946. 355.00 (*0-8066-9012-7*, 10-3360, Augsburg) Augsburg Fortress.

Lenskii, V. S., jt. auth. see Ilyushin, A. A.

Lensmire, Timothy J. When Children Write: Critical Re-Visions of the Writing Workshop. LC 93-44983. 192p. (C). 1994. text ed. 38.00 (*0-8077-3329-6*); pap. text ed. 17.95 (*0-8077-3328-8*) Tchrs Coll.

Lensmith, Lawrence E. Persuasive Resume! A Guide to Writing, Formatting & Finishing. 1991. pap. text ed. 7.95 (*1-880381-00-1*); 22.95 (*1-880381-01-X*) Desktop Impress.

Lenson, David. The Birth of Tragedy: A Commentary. (Twayne's Masterwork Studies). 152p. 1987. text ed. 21.95 (*0-8057-7968-X*, Twayne); pap. 12.95 (*0-8057-8008-4*, Twayne) Macmillan.
— The Gambler. LC 76-55929. 57p. 1978. pap. 7.00 (*0-89924-013-5*) Lynx Hse.
— On Drugs. 256p. 1995. 21.95 (*0-8166-2710-X*) U of Minn Pr.
— Ride the Shadow. LC 78-78115. 53p. 1979. pap. 3.75 (*0-934332-13-4*) LEpervier Pr.

Lenson, Eileen S. Succeeding in Private Practice: A Business Guide for Psychotherapists. (Illus.). 296p. (C). 1993. text ed. 52.00 (*0-8039-4957-X*); pap. text ed. 24.95 (*0-8039-4958-8*) Sage.

Lenssen, Ann. A Rainbow Balloon: A Book of Concepts. LC 91-31830. (Illus.). 32p. (J). (ps-3). 1992. 13.50 (*0-525-65093-8*, Cobblehill Bks) Dutton Child Bks.

Lenssen, Nicholas. Empowering Development: The New Energy Equation. 70p. (Orig.). 1992. pap. 5.00 (*1-878071-12-2*) Worldwatch Inst.
— Nuclear Waste: The Problem That Won't Go Away. 70p. (Orig.). 1991. pap. 5.00 (*1-878071-07-6*) Worldwatch Inst.

***Lenssen, Nicholas & Roodman, David.** A Building Revolution: How Ecology & Health Concerns Are Transforming Construction. 70p. (Orig.). 1995. pap. 5.00 (*1-878071-25-4*) Worldwatch Inst.

Lenssen, Nicholas, jt. auth. see Flavin, Christopher.

Lenssen, Polly, jt. auth. see Aker, Saundra N.

Lenstra, A. K. & Lenstra, H. W., Jr. The Development of the Number Field Sieve. LC 93-5229. (Lecture Notes in Mathematics Ser.: Vol. 1554). 1994. 23.00 (*0-387-57013-6*) Spr-Verlag.

Lenstra, Daan, jt. ed. see Van Haeringen, Willem.

Lenstra, H. W., Jr., ed. The Number Field Sieve. (Lecture Notes in Mathematics Ser.: Vol. 1554). (Illus.). vii, 132p. 1993. pap. write for info. (*3-540-57013-6*) Spr-Verlag.

Lenstra, H. W., Jr., jt. auth. see Lenstra, A. K.

Lenstra, J. K., et al. History of Mathematical Programming. 1991. 63.75 (*0-444-88818-7*) Elsevier.

***Lent, Anne F.** The Ultimate Desktop Publishing Starter Kit. LC 95-891. 1995. pap. 29.95 (*0-201-41032-X*) Addison-Wesley.

Lent, Anne F. & Miastkowski, Stan. Practical Applications Circuits Handbook. 350p. 1989. text ed. 68.00 (*0-12-443775-3*) Acad Pr.

Lent, Blair. Bayberry Bluff. (Illus.). 32p. (J). (gr. k-3). 1992. pap. 4.95 (*0-395-62984-5*, Sandpiper) HM.
— Molasses Flood. LC 92-1125. (Illus.). 32p. (J). (ps-3). 1992. 14.95 (*0-395-45314-3*) HM.

Lent, Blair, illus. Tikki Tikki Tembo. LC 68-11839. 48p. (J). (ps-2). 1989. pap. 5.95 (*0-8050-1166-8*, Bks Young Read) H Holt & Co.

Lent, Blair, jt. auth. see Small, Ernest.

Lent, Bogdan. Dataflow Architecture for Machine Control. 1989. text ed. 124.00 (*0-471-92473-3*) Wiley.

Lent, Deane. Analysis & Design of Mechanisms. 2nd ed. (Technology Ser.). (C). 1970. text ed. 51.00 (*0-13-032797-2*) P-H.
— Analysis & Design of Mechanisms. 2nd ed. (Illus.). 423p. (C). 1992. reprint ed. text ed. 46.95 (*1-879215-14-4*) Sheffield WI.

Lent, George E. Impact of the Undistributed Profits Tax, 1936-37. LC 68-58601. (Columbia University. Studies in the Social Sciences: No. 539). reprint ed. 20.00 (*0-404-51539-8*) AMS Pr.
— The Ownership of Tax-Exempt Securities, 1913-1953. (Occasional Papers: No. 47). 150p. 1955. reprint ed. 39.00 (*0-87014-361-1*); reprint ed. mic. film 20.00 (*0-685-61302-X*) Natl Bur Econ Res.

Lent, James, jt. auth. see Horner, Don R.

Lent, James, et al. Using Cream Antiseptic, Set. (Taking Care of Simple Injuries Ser.). (Illus.). 32p. (Orig.). 1978. pap. text ed. 149.00 (*0-685-05766-6*) PRO-ED.

Lent, John, ed. Animation, Caricature & Gag & Political Cartoons in the United States: An International Bibliography. LC 94-14433. (Bibliographies & Indexes in Popular Culture Ser.: No. 3). 440p. 1994. text ed. 75.00 (*0-313-28681-7*, Greenwood Pr) Greenwood.

Lent, John A. The Asian Film Industry. (Film Studies). (Illus.). 320p. 1990. text ed. 32.50 (*0-292-70421-6*); pap. 17.95 (*0-292-70422-4*) U of Tex Pr.
— Asian Popular Culture. LC 94-45530. (International Communication & Popular Culture Ser.). (C). 1995. pap. text ed. 19.95 (*0-8133-2049-6*) Westview.
— Bibliographic Guide to Caribbean Mass Communication. LC 92-19373. (Bibliographies & Indexes in Mass Media & Communications Ser.: No. 5). 320p. 1992. text ed. 65.00 (*0-313-28210-2*, LBM, Greenwood Pr) Greenwood.
— Bibliography of Cuban Mass Communications. LC 92-24462. (Bibliographies & Indexes in Mass Media & Communications Ser.: No. 6). 384p. 1992. text ed. 69.50 (*0-313-28455-5*, LBN, Greenwood Pr) Greenwood.
— Global Guide to Media & Communications. 160p. 1986. 49.50 (*0-914746-49-9*); write for info. (*0-317-39334-0*) G Kurian.
— Mass Communications in the Caribbean. LC 90-33583. (Illus.). 412p. (C). 1990. text ed. 36.95 (*0-8138-1182-1*) Iowa St U Pr.
— Third World Mass Media & Their Search for Modernity: The Case of Commonwealth Caribbean, 1717-1976. LC 75-39110. 405p. 1978. 45.00 (*0-8387-1896-5*) Bucknell U Pr.

Lent, John A., comp. Women & Mass Communications: An International Annotated Bibliography. LC 90-23780. (Bibliographies & Indexes in Women's Studies Ser.: No. 11). 512p. 1991. text ed. 89.50 (*0-313-26579-8*, LWM/, Greenwood Pr) Greenwood.

***Lent, John A., ed.** Asian Popular Culture. LC 94-45530. (International Communication & Popular Culture Ser.). 1995. text ed. 69.95 (*0-8133-2048-8*) Westview.
— Caribbean Popular Culture. LC 90-83084. (Illus.). 156p. (C). 1990. text ed. 26.95 (*0-87972-499-4*); pap. text ed. 13.95 (*0-87972-500-1*) Bowling Green Univ.
— Comic Art of Europe: An International, Comprehensive Bibliography. LC 94-14432. (Bibliographies & Indexes in Popular Culture Ser.: No. 5). 688p. 1994. text ed. 95.00 (*0-313-28212-9*, Greenwood Pr) Greenwood.
— Comic Books & Comic Strips in the United States: An International Bibliography. LC 94-10852. (Bibliographies & Indexes in Popular Culture Ser.: No. 4). 624p. 1994. text ed. 85.00 (*0-313-28211-0*, Greenwood Pr) Greenwood.
— Global Guide to Media & Communications. (Communication Research & Broadcasting Ser.). xii, 145p. 1987. lib. bdg. 70.00 (*3-598-10746-3*) K G Saur.

Lent, John A. & Mulliner, Kent, eds. Malaysian Studies: Archaeology, Historiography, Geography, & Bibliography. (Occasional Paper Ser.: No. 11). 235p. 1985. 16.00 (*0-685-62384-X*) North Ill U Ctr SE Asian.

Lent, John A., jt. auth. see Sussman, Gerald.

Lent, John A., jt. ed. see Sussman, Gerald.

Lent, Joseph M., ed. The Home Vegetable Garden. (Plants & Gardens Ser.). (Illus.). 1972. pap. 3.95 (*0-686-21161-8*) Bklyn Botanic.

***Lent, Joy.** Houston's Heritage: Using Antique Postcards. (Illus.). Date not set. per., pap. 12.95 (*0-9643284-0-2*) Clem Interests.

***Lent, Max.** Government Online. 1995. pap. 15.00 (*0-06-273301-X*, Harper Ref) HarpC.

***Lent, Penny.** Young Writer's Contest Manual: Competitions for Students Work. 2nd rev. ed. LC 94-79466. (Young Writer's Ser.). 68p. (J). (gr. k up). 1994. per., pap. 7.95 (*1-885371-05-5*) Kldoscope Pr.
— Young Writer's Manuscript Manual: A Guide on How to Send Writing for Publication. rev. ed. LC 94-76618. (Young Writers Ser.). (Illus.). 84p. 1994. pap. 7.95 (*1-885371-01-2*) Kldoscope Pr.
— Young Writer's Market Manual: Publications Seeking Student Work. 2nd rev. ed. LC 94-76617. (Young Writers Ser.). 80p. 1994. pap. 7.95 (*1-885371-02-0*) Kldoscope Pr.

***Lent, Penny, ed.** Meeker Mansion Mysteries: A Fiction Anthology. LC 94-76615. (Illus.). 84p. (Orig.). 1994. pap. 5.95 (*1-885371-03-9*) Kldoscope Pr.

Lent, Penny, ed. see Amos, Chuck & Amos, Sheila.

Lent, Penny, ed. see Bird, Tia.

Lent, Penny, ed. see Etchison, Birdie.

Lent, Penny, ed. see Rabe, Sheila & Schneider, Eric.

Lent, Penny, ed. see Reece, Colleen L.

Lent, Robert, jt. ed. see Savickas, Mark.

Lent, Robert W., jt. auth. see Brown, Steven D.

Lent, Roberto, ed. The Visual System from Genesis to Maturity. LC 92-21738. xii, 285p. 1992. 105.00 (*0-8176-3598-X*) Birkhauser.

***Lenten, Roelie.** Cooking under the Volcanoes: Communal Kitchens in the Southern Peruvian City of Arequipa. (CEDLA Latin America Studies (CLAS): No. 68). 232p. 1993. pap. 23.50 (*90-70280-15-9*, Pub. by Thesis Pubs NE) IBD Ltd.

Lenters, William R. The Church Cares. 77p. (Orig.). (YA). (gr. 7-8). 1987. teacher ed 8.95 (*0-930265-33-5*); pap. text ed. 7.25 (*0-930265-32-7*) CRC Pubns.

An Asterisk (*) at the beginning of an entry indicates that the title is appearing in BIP for the first time.

Lentfoehr, Therese. Words & Silence: On the Poetry of Thomas Merton. LC 78-21475. 1979. 12.50 (*0-8112-0712-9*) New Directions.

Lenth, Charles S., ed. Using National Data Bases. LC 85-645339. (New Directions for Institutional Research Ser.: No. IR 69). 1991. 16.95 (*1-55542-791-X*) Jossey-Bass.

Lenthall, Lisa-Theresa. My Clothes. (Illus.). (J). (ps). 1994. pap. 5.99 (*0-553-09658-3*) Bantam.

— My Family & Friends. (J). (ps). 1994. mass mkt. 5.99 (*0-553-09657-5*) Bantam.

— My Food. (Illus.). (J). (ps). 1994. 5.99 (*0-553-09659-1*) Bantam.

Lenti, Paul, tr. see De La Colina, Jose & Turrent, Tomas P.

Lenti, Paul, tr. see De la Colina, Jose & Turrent, Tomas P.

Lentin, A., ed. Voltaire & Catherine the Great: Selected Correspondence. (Illus.). 196p. 1974. 16.00 (*0-89250-099-9*) Orient Res Partners.

Lentin, Ronit. Night Train to Mother. 224p. (Orig.). (C). 1989. pap. 11.95 (*0-946211-72-8*, Pub. by Attic IE) InBook.

— Night Train to Mother. 220p. (Orig.). 1990. reprint ed. 24.95 (*0-939416-32-8*); reprint ed. pap. 9.95 (*0-939416-33-6*) Cleis Pr.

Lentin, Ronit, et al. Triad: Modern Irish Fiction. 176p. 1986. 18.95 (*0-86327-056-5*, Pub. by Wolfhound Pr IE); pap. 7.95 (*0-86327-057-3*, Pub. by Wolfhound Pr IE) Dufour.

***Lentini, Peter, ed.** Elections & Political Order in Russia: The Implications of the 1993 Elections to the Federal Assembly. (Central European University Press Book Ser.). (Illus.). 240p. 1995. 59.00 (*1-85866-017-3*); pap. 19.95 (*1-85866-018-1*) OUP.

Lentner, Howard H. State Formation in Central America: The Struggle for Autonomy, Development, & Democracy. LC 93-12603. (Contributions in Latin American Studies: No. 2). 264p. 1993. text ed. 55.00 (*0-313-28921-2*, GM8921) Greenwood.

Lentner, Marvin & Bishop, Thomas. Experimental Design & Analysis. (Illus.). xi, 565p. (C). 1986. text ed. 32.75 (*0-9616255-0-3*) Valley Bk.

Lentner, Timothy H., jt. ed. see Cooper, Saul.

Lento, Robert. Woodworking: Tools, Fabrication, Design, & Manufacturing. (Illus.). 1979. student ed 24.95 (*0-685-03911-0*) P-H.

Lento, Takako, tr. see Makoto, Ooka.

Lento, Thomas, tr. see Makoto, Ooka.

Lentricchia, Frank. After the New Criticism. LC 79-23715. 1981. 21.00 (*0-226-47197-7*); pap. text ed. 18.95 (*0-226-47198-5*) U Ch Pr.

— Ariel & the Police: Michel Foucault, William James, Wallace Stevens. LC 87-18885. 208p. (C). 1987. text ed. 27.50 (*0-299-11540-2*) U of Wis Pr.

— Ariel & the Police: Michel Foucault, William James, Wallace Stevens. LC 87-18885. 208p. 1989. pap. text ed. 14.95 (*0-299-11544-5*) U of Wis Pr.

— Criticism & Social Change. LC 83-9299. viii, 176p. 1984. 15.00 (*0-226-47199-3*) U Ch Pr.

— Criticism & Social Change. LC 83-9299. viii, 176p. 1985. pap. text ed. 12.95 (*0-226-47200-0*) U Ch Pr.

— Edge of Night: A Confession. LC 93-25410. 1994. 21.00 (*0-679-43072-5*) Random.

— Modernist Quartet. 320p. (C). 1994. pap. 16.95 (*0-521-46975-9*) Cambridge U Pr.

— Modernist Quartet. 320p. (C). 1994. 54.95 (*0-521-47004-8*) Cambridge U Pr.

Lentricchia, Frank, ed. Introducing Don DeLillo. LC 90-15567. 221p. 1991. lib. bdg. 31.95 (*0-8223-1135-6*); pap. text ed. 12.95 (*0-8223-1144-5*) Duke.

— New Essays on "White Noise" (American Novel Ser.). 130p. (C). 1991. pap. 11.95 (*0-521-39893-2*) Cambridge U Pr.

— New Essays on "White Noise" (American Novel Ser.). 130p. (C). 1991. 27.95 (*0-521-39291-8*) Cambridge U Pr.

Lentricchia, Frank & McLaughlin, Thomas, eds. Critical Terms for Literary Study. LC 89-4910. 384p. 1989. lib. bdg. 45.00 (*0-226-47201-9*); pap. text ed. 16.95 (*0-226-47202-7*) U Ch Pr.

— Critical Terms for Literary Study. 2nd ed. (Literary Studies). 480p. 1995. lib. bdg. 47.50 (*0-226-47204-3*); pap. 17.95 (*0-226-47203-5*) U Ch Pr.

Lentricchia, Frank, jt. auth. see McLaughlin, Thomas.

Lents, Don G., jt. auth. see Hansen, Charles.

Lentz, et al. Teaching Through Adventure: A Practical Approach. 97p. 1976. pap. 8.50 (*0-934387-03-6*) Project Advent.

Lentz, Andrea D. A Guide to the Manuscripts at the Ohio Historical Society. 281p. 1972. pap. 5.00 (*0-318-00848-3*) Ohio Hist Soc.

— The Warren G. Harding Papers: An Inventory to the Microfilm Edition. 283p. 1970. 4.00 (*0-318-03212-0*) Ohio Hist Soc.

***Lentz, Bernard F. & Laband, David N.** Sex Discrimination in the Legal Profession. LC 95-3777. 256p. 1995. text ed. 49.95 (*0-89930-928-3*, Quorum Bks) Greenwood.

Lentz, Bernard F., jt. auth. see Laband, David N.

Lentz, Donald A. The Gamelan Music of Java & Bali: An Artistic Anomaly Complementary to Primary Tonal Theoretical Systems. LC 65-10545. 78p. reprint ed. pap. 25.00 (*0-317-26623-3*, 2025428) Bks Demand.

Lentz, Eleanor, jt. auth. see Lentz, Harold.

Lentz, Florence K. Centennial Snapshots: Historic Places Around King County from the First Twenty-Five Years of Statehood. (Illus.). 119p. (Orig.). 1991. pap. text ed. 8.95 (*0-914019-28-7*) NW Interpretive.

— Kent: Valley of Opportunity. 1990. 24.95 (*0-89781-356-1*) Preferred Mktg.

Lentz, Harold & Lentz, Eleanor. Twenty-Two Who Changed the World. Sherer, Michael L., ed. 1988. pap. 6.00 (*1-55673-038-1*, 8822) CSS OH.

Lentz, Harold B. The Pop-Up Mother Goose. LC 94-71382. (Illus.). 24p. (J). (ps-3). 1994. 14.95 (*1-55709-237-0*) Applewood.

Lentz, Harris M., III. Assassinations & Executions: An Encyclopedia of Political Violence, 1865-1986. LC 87-46383. 296p. 1988. lib. bdg. 38.50x (*0-89950-312-8*) McFarland & Co.

— Heads of States & Governments: A Worldwide Encyclopedia of 2,300 Leaders, 1945-1992. 924p. 1994. lib. bdg. 95.00 (*0-89950-926-6*) McFarland & Co.

— Science Fiction, Horror & Fantasy Film & Television Credits, 2 Vols, 1. LC 82-23956. 1400p. 1983. lib. bdg. 55.00x (*0-89950-069-2*) McFarland & Co.

— Science Fiction, Horror & Fantasy Film & Television Credits, 2 Vols, 2. LC 82-23956. 1400p. 1983. lib. bdg. 55.00x (*0-89950-070-6*) McFarland & Co.

— Science Fiction, Horror & Fantasy Film & Television Credits, 2 Vols, Set. LC 82-23956. 1400p. 1983. lib. bdg. 105.00x (*0-89950-071-4*) McFarland & Co.

— Science Fiction, Horror & Fantasy Film & Television Credits, Suppl. 2: Through 1993. LC 93-33878. 864p. 1994. lib. bdg. 85.00 (*0-89950-927-4*) McFarland & Co.

— Science Fiction, Horror & Fantasy Film & Television Credits Supplement I: Through 1987. LC 88-42646. 936p. 1989. lib. bdg. 82.00x (*0-89950-364-0*) McFarland & Co.

Lentz, John C., Jr. Luke's Portrait of Paul. LC 92-15802. (Society for New Testament Studies Monographs: No. 77). 224p. (C). 1993. 54.95 (*0-521-43316-9*) Cambridge U Pr.

***Lentz, John D.** Effective Handling of Manipulative Persons. (Illus.). 112p. 1989. pap. 18.95 (*0-398-06227-7*) C C Thomas.

— Effective Handling of Manipulative Persons. (Illus.). 112p. (C). 1989. text ed. 33.95x (*0-398-05555-6*) C C Thomas.

Lentz, K. Design of Automatic Machinery. 1992. text ed. write for info. (*0-442-01222-5*) Chapman & Hall.

Lentz, Lloyd C., III. Guthrie: A History of the Capital City, 1889-1910. LC 90-62164. (Illus.). 165p. 1990. pap. 20.00 (*0-9603564-2-8*) Logan Cnty Hist Soc.

Lentz, Pam. My Camera. (J). (ps). 1993. 3.99 (*0-307-15903-5*, Golden Pr) Western Pub.

— My Flightbag. (J). (ps). 1993. 3.99 (*0-307-15902-7*, Golden Pr) Western Pub.

— My Purse. (J). (ps). 1993. 3.99 (*0-307-15901-9*, Golden Pr) Western Pub.

— My Schoolbag. (J). (ps). 1993. 3.99 (*0-307-15900-0*, Golden Pr) Western Pub.

Lentz, Perry. The Falling Hills: A Novel of the Civil War. LC 93-24496. 470p. (C). 1994. reprint ed. pap. 14.95 (*0-87249-988-X*) U of SC Pr.

Lentz, Richard. Symbols, the News Magazines & Martin Luther King. LC 89-12852. 384p. 1989. text ed. 35.00 (*0-8071-1523-1*) La State U Pr.

Lentz, Robert J., jt. auth. see Paul, Gordon L.

Lentz, Theodore F. An Experimental Method for the Discovery & Development of Tests of Character. LC 71-176985. (Columbia University. Teachers College. Contributions to Education Ser.: No. 180). reprint ed. 37.50 (*0-404-55180-7*) AMS Pr.

— Towards a Science of Peace. 1955. 4.00 (*0-318-03980-X*) Lentz Peace Res.

— Towards a Technology of Peace. 1972. pap. 3.00 (*0-933061-11-0*) Lentz Peace Res.

Lentz, Theodore F., ed. Humatriotism. 1976. 6.00 (*0-933061-07-2*) Lentz Peace Res.

Lentz, Theodore F., jt. auth. see Eckhardt, William.

Lentz, Thomas L. Primitive Nervous Systems. LC 68-27760. 160p. reprint ed. pap. 45.60 (*0-8357-8283-2*, 2033799) Bks Demand.

Lentz, Thomas W. & Lowry, Glenn D. Timur & the Princely Vision: Persian Art & Culture in the Fifteenth Century. LC 88-27337. (Illus.). 400p. (C). 1989. 79.95 (*0-87474-706-6*) Smithsonian.

Lentz, Thomas W., jt. auth. see De Angelis, Michele A.

Lentz, Thomas W., jt. auth. see Runk, Wesley T.

Lentz, Tony M. Orality & Literacy in Hellenic Greece. LC 88-14152. 232p. (C). 1988. text ed. 24.95 (*0-8093-1359-6*) S Ill U Pr.

Lentze, M., ed. see Falk Symposium Staff.

Lenz. Flexible Manufacturing: Benefits for the Low-Inventory Factory. (Manufacturing Engineering & Materials Processing Ser.: Vol. 27). 336p. 1989. 99.75 (*0-8247-7683-6*) Dekker.

Lenz, Allen J. Beyond Blue Economic Horizons: U. S. Trade Performance & International Competitiveness in the 1990s. LC 90-7625. 288p. 1990. text ed. 49.95 (*0-275-93624-4*, C3624, Praeger Pubs) Greenwood.

— Narrowing the United States Current Account Deficit: A Sectoral Assessment. LC 92-8778. reprint ed. pap. 178.70 (*0-7837-9049-X*, 2049800) Bks Demand.

***Lenz, B. Keith, et al.** Strategic Instruction for Adolescents with Learning Disabilities. LC 94-41597. 1995. write for info. (*0-89079-650-5*) PRO-ED.

Lenz, Bernd, jt. ed. see Lehmann, Elmar.

Lenz, Carolyn R., et al, eds. The Woman's Part: Feminist Criticism of Shakespeare. LC 79-26896. 360p. 1983. pap. 13.95 (*0-252-01016-7*) U of Ill Pr.

Lenz, Christian. The Neue Pinakothek, Munich. (Illus.). 132p. 1989. 25.00 (*1-870248-19-8*) Scala Books.

Lenz, E. E. Lenz Family: History of the American Branch Established at Stone Arabia, N.Y., in 1854, by Friedrich Konrad Lenz of Werdorf, Germany. (Illus.). 187p. 1993. reprint ed. lib. bdg. 41.00 (*0-8328-3699-0*); reprint ed. pap. 31.00 (*0-8328-3700-8*) Higginson Bk Co.

Lenz, Elinor. Rights of Passage: How Women Can Find a New Freedom in Their Midyears. 224p. 1992. 21.95 (*0-929923-50-2*) Lowell Hse.

— Rights of Passage: How Women Can Find a New Freedom in Their Midyears. 224p. 1993. pap. 14.95 (*1-56565-076-X*, Woman-Woman) Lowell Hse.

Lenz, Elinor, jt. auth. see Adams, Linda.

Lenz, F. W. Ovid's Metamorphoses - Prolegomena to a Revision of Hugo Magnus' Edition. iv, 104p. 1967. write for info. (*3-296-14180-4*, Pub. by Georg Olms GW) Lubrecht & Cramer.

Lenz, Frederick. Lifetimes: True Accounts of Reincarnation. 224p. 1985. mass mkt. 4.95 (*0-449-20908-3*, Crest) Fawcett.

Lenz, G. & Pakesch, G., eds. The Polydiagnostic Approach in Psychiatry. (Journal: Psychopathology: Vol. 19, No. 5, 1986). (Illus.). 76p. 1987. pap. 38.50 (*3-8055-4540-1*) S Karger.

Lenz, Gary L. Fixed Asset Accounting & Reporting. (Illus.). 432p. 1980. pap. 27.50 (*0-686-84265-0*); pap. 25.00 (*0-686-84266-9*) Municipal.

Lenz, Gunter H., et al, eds. Reconstructing American Literary & Historical Studies. LC 90-32645. 435p. 1990. text ed. 49.95 (*0-312-04661-8*) St Martin.

Lenz, H. J., et al, eds. Frontiers in Statistical Quality Control 3. x, 265p. 1987. pap. 89.00 (*0-387-91315-7*) Spr-Verlag.

— Frontiers in Statistical Quality Control 4. (Illus.). x, 266p. 1992. pap. 88.00 (*0-387-91434-X*) Spr-Verlag.

Lenz, H. P. Mixture Formation for Spark Ignition Engines. 400p. 1992. 99.00 (*1-56091-188-3*, R-113) Soc Auto Engineers.

Lenz, Heinz & Murray, John L. Fit for Life: The Annapolis Way. (Illus.). 352p. (C). 1985. pap. text ed. 16.95 (*0-88011-032-5*, PLEN0032) Human Kinetics.

Lenz, J. E., ed. Simulation in Manufacturing. 260p. 1986. 133.00 (*0-387-16329-8*) Spr-Verlag.

Lenz, John W., ed. see Hume, David.

Lenz, K. & Laggner, A. N., eds. Patient Data Management in Intensive Care. (Illus.). 157p. 1993. pap. 31.00 (*0-387-82513-4*) Spr-Verlag.

Lenz, Lee W. An Annotated Catalogue of the Plants of Baja California Sur, Mexico. 128p. 1993. pap. 16.50 (*0-9634595-0-3*) Cape Pr.

— Marcus Jones: Western Geologist, Mining Engineer & Botanist. LC 85-61956. (Illus.). xv, 486p. 1986. 28.00 (*0-9605808-2-4*) Rancho Santa Ana.

Lenz, Lee W. & Dourley, John. California Native Trees & Shrubs for Garden & Environmental Use in Southern California & Adjacent Areas. LC 81-50257. (Illus.). xiii, 232p. (C). 1981. kivar 23.50 (*0-9605808-1-6*) Rancho Santa Ana.

Lenz, Leslie, ed. see Shelton, Connie.

Lenz, Mark J. Study Guide for Leviticus. (People's Bible Ser.). 62p. (Orig.). 1989. pap. text ed. 2.25 (*0-938272-68-3*) WELS Board.

Lenz, Martin. Computed Tomography & Magnetic Resonance Imaging of Head & Neck Tumors: Methods, Guidelines, Differential Diagnoses, & Clinical Results. Bergman, Clifford, tr. LC 93-28314. 206p. 1993. 105.00 (*0-86577-504-4*) Thieme Med Pubs.

Lenz, Millicent & Meachem, Mary. Young Adult Literature & Nonprint Materials: Resources for Selection. LC 94-13774. 1994. 37.50 (*0-8108-2906-1*) Scarecrow.

Lenz, R. W. & Ciardelli, I., eds. Advances in the Preparation & Properties of Stereo-Regular Polymers. (NATO Advanced Study Institutes Series C, Mathematical & Physical Sciences: No. 51). 1979. lib. bdg. 94.00 (*90-277-1055-4*) Kluwer Ac.

***Lenz, Robert R.** Explosives & Bomb Disposal Guide. (Illus.). 320p. 1976. pap. 32.95 (*0-398-06228-5*) C C Thomas.

— Explosives & Bomb Disposal Guide. fac. ed. (Illus.). 320p. 1976. 54.95x (*0-398-01097-8*) C C Thomas.

Lenz, Sidney. Your Money & Your Home: A Step-by-Step Guide to Financing or Refinancing Your Home. (Orig.). 1992. pap. 12.95 (*1-882180-00-3*) Griffin CA.

Lenz, Siegfried. The German Lesson. Kaiser, Ernst & Wilkins, Eithne, trs. LC 77-163567. (Revived Modern Classics Ser.). 480p. 1986. reprint ed. pap. 15.95 (*0-8112-0982-2*, NDP618) New Directions.

— The Selected Stories. Mitchell, Breon, ed. & tr. by. LC 89-13120. 1989. 19.95 (*0-8112-1105-3*) New Directions.

Lenz, William E. Fast Talk & Flush Times: The Confidence Man As a Literary Convention. LC 84-2200. (Illus.). 248p. 1985. text ed. 26.00 (*0-8262-0450-3*) U of Mo Pr.

— The Poetics of the Antarctic: A Study in Nineteenth-Century American Cultural Perceptions. LC 94-27300. (Reference Library of the Humanities, Vol. 785, Studies in Nineteenth Century American Literature: Vol. 5). (Illus.). 248p. 1995. 37.00 (*0-8153-1473-6*, H1785) Garland.

Lenzen, Charlotte. Reading Step-by-Step: A Winning Formula. (Illus.). 286p. 1989. ring bd. 89.95 (*0-9623658-3-1*) Chalen Edu Systs.

Lenzen, Dieter, jt. auth. see Benner, Dietrich.

Lenzen, Donald L. Ancient Metrology. (Illus.). 108p. 1989. 14.95 (*0-9625309-0-5*) D L Lenzen.

Lenzen, V. F. Benjamin Peirce & the U. S. Coast Survey. (Illus.). 1968. 5.00 (*0-911302-06-9*) San Francisco Pr.

Lenzen, Wolfgang. Das System der Leibnizschen Logik. (Foundations of Communication & Cognition Ser.). xvi, 235p. (C). 1990. lib. bdg. 83.10 (*3-11-012353-3*) De Gruyter.

***Lenzenweger, Mark F. & Haugaard, Jeffery J., eds.** Frontiers of Developmental Psychopathology. (Illus.). 224p. 1995. text ed. 35.00 (*0-19-509001-2*) OUP.

Lenzerini, Maurizio, et al, eds. Inheritance Hierarchies in Knowledge Representation & Programming Languages. 1991. text ed. 64.95 (*0-471-92741-4*) Wiley.

Lenzi, G. L., jt. ed. see Orgogozo, J. M.

Lenzi, Gian L., jt. ed. see Fieschi, Cesare.

Lenzi, Paul, jt. auth. see Snyder, Geraldine A.

Lenzi, S. & Descovich, G. C., eds. Atherosclerosis & Cardiovascular Disease. (C). 1987. lib. bdg. 191.00 (*0-85200-836-8*) Kluwer Ac.

Lenzi, S. & Descovich, G. C., eds. Atherosclerosis & Cardiovascular Disease. 1984. lib. bdg. 148.00 (*0-85200-793-0*) Kluwer Ac.

Lenzi, S., jt. ed. see Descovich, G.

Lenzing, H., jt. auth. see Jensen, C. U.

Lenzing, Helmut, jt. ed. see Dlab, Vlastimil.

Lenzke, James T. & Buttolph, Ken, eds. Standard Guide to Cars & Prices, 1994. 6th ed. LC 89-80091. (Illus.). 608p. 1993. pap. 15.95 (*0-87341-265-6*) Krause Pubns.

Lenzke, Jim & Butolph, Ken. Standard Guide to Cars & Prices: 1995 Edition. (Illus.). 608p. 1994. pap. 15.95 (*0-87341-314-8*) Krause Pubns.

Lenzkes, Susan. Crossing the Bridge Between You & Me. 1994. pap. 7.99 (*0-929239-83-0*) Discovery Hse Pubs.

— Everybody's Breaking Pieces off of Me: Stress Relieving Devotions for Women. 128p. (Orig.). 1992. pap. 7.99 (*0-929239-58-X*) Discovery Hse Pubs.

— No Rain, No Gain: Growing Through Life's Storms. (Orig.). 1995. pap. 7.99 (*0-929239-93-8*) Discovery Hse Pubs.

— When Life Takes What Matters. LC 92-31268. 1993. 7.99 (*0-929239-70-9*) Discovery Hse Pubs.

***Lenzo, Fran.** Angel Messages from Above: Stories, Poems, Essays & Loving Words from John, My Guardian Angel. Lenzo, Jerry, ed. (Illus.). 224p. (Orig.). 1995. pap. 14.95 (*0-9644821-0-X*) Angel Guidance.

Lenzo, Jerry, ed. see Lenzo, Fran.

Leo. The Practice of Humility. O'Connor, John F., tr. 1976. lib. bdg. 59.95 (*0-8490-2462-5*) Gordon Pr.

— The Practice of Humility. O'Connor, John F., tr. 1980. lib. bdg. 59.95 (*0-8490-3177-X*) Gordon Pr.

Leo, A. Practical Astrology. 228p. 1988. 10.95 (*0-318-36378-X*) Asia Bk Corp.

Leo, Alan. The Art of Synthesis. (Astrologer's Library). 318p. 1989. pap. 12.95 (*0-89281-178-1*) Inner Tradit.

— Astrology for All. (Astrologer's Library). 348p. 1989. pap. 12.95 (*0-89281-175-7*) Inner Tradit.

— Astrology for All. 336p. 1973. reprint ed. spiral bd. 8.80 (*0-7873-0553-7*) Mokelumne.

— Casting the Horoscope. (Astrologer's Library). 384p. 1989. pap. 12.95 (*0-89281-176-5*) Inner Tradit.

— The Complete Dictionary of Astrology. (Astrologer's Library). 216p. 1989. pap. 12.95 (*0-89281-182-X*) Inner Tradit.

— Esoteric Astrology. (Astrologer's Library). 320p. 1989. pap. 16.95 (*0-89281-181-1*, Destiny Bks) Inner Tradit.

— How to Judge a Nativity. (Astrologer's Library). 358p. 1989. pap. 12.95 (*0-89281-177-3*, Destiny Bks) Inner Tradit.

— The Key to Your Own Nativity. (Astrologer's Library). 144p. 1989. pap. 12.95 (*0-89281-179-X*) Inner Tradit.

— Mars: The War Lord. 99p. 1993. reprint ed. spiral bd. 5.50 (*0-7873-0550-2*) Mokelumne.

— Thousand & One Notable Nativities: Astrologer's "Who's Who" 4th ed. 130p. 1978. reprint ed. spiral bd. 6.60 (*0-7873-0551-0*) Mokelumne.

Leo, Alan & Robson, Vivian E. Alan Leo's Dictionary of Astrology. 224p. 1981. pap. 12.00 (*0-89540-101-0*, SB-101, Sun Bks) Sun Pub.

Leo Baeck Institut Staff, ed. see Wassermann, Henry.

Leo Burnett Company Staff. The Leo Burnett Worldwide Advertising Media Factbook: The International Sourcebook of Media Conditions, Facts & Statistics. (Illus.). 700p. 1994. text ed. 250.00 (*1-880141-57-4*) Triumph Bks.

Leo, Carl & Zavin, Benjamin. The Family Man. 1956. pap. 4.75 (*0-8222-0383-9*) Dramatists Play.

Leo, Christopher. Land & Class in Kenya. (Political Economy of World Poverty Ser.: No. 3). 256p. 1984. 30.00 (*0-8020-2532-3*); pap. 13.95 (*0-8020-6547-3*) U of Toronto Pr.

Leo, Eleanor. Powerful Reading, Efficient Learning. LC 93-886. 336p. (C). 1994. pap. write for info. (*0-02-369762-8*) Macmillan.

Leo, F. Damian & Amador, Antonio A. Corporate Taxation in the Netherlands Antilles 1978. 95p. pap. 18.00 (*0-686-41010-6*) Kluwer Ac.

Leo, Friedrich. Geschichte der Romischen Literatur, Band I: Die Archaische Literatur. iv, 496p. (GER.). 1967. write for info. (*3-296-14200-2*, Pub. by Georg Olms GW) Lubrecht & Cramer.

— Die Griechisch-Romische Biographie Nach Ihrer Literarischen Form. x, 330p. (GER.). 1991. reprint ed. write for info. (*3-487-00986-2*, Pub. by Georg Olms GW) Lubrecht & Cramer.

— Plutinische Forschungen Zur Kritik und Geschichte der Komodie. vii, 375p. (GER.). 1973. write for info. (*3-296-14210-X*, Pub. by Georg Olms GW) Lubrecht & Cramer.

Leo, Friedrich & Kiessling, Adolf. Philologische Untersuchungen, Heft 2: Zu Augusteischen Dichtern. 122p. write for info. (*0-318-70816-7*, Pub. by Georg Olms GW) Lubrecht & Cramer.

Leo, Friedrich, ed. see Plautus.

Leo, Friedrich, ed. see Seneca.

Leo, Johannes. A Geographical Historie of Africa. Pory, John, tr. LC 72-213. (English Experience Ser.: No. 133). 420p. 1969. reprint ed. 125.00 (*90-221-0133-9*) Walter J Johnson.

Leo, John. Two Steps Ahead of the Thought. 1994. 22.00 (*0-671-88698-3*) S&S Trade.

Leo, John R. Guide to Poetry Explication: American Poetry, Vol. 2. (Poetry Explication Ser.). 450p. 1989. text ed. 50.00 (*0-8161-8918-8*, Hall Reference) Macmillan.

Leo, K. J. Company Accounting in Australia PPR. 1984. pap. 33.25 (*0-471-33393-X*) Wiley.

Leo, K. R., ed. see Blain, Alexander.

Leo, Kathleen R. The Circle Is Assembled. 14p. 1994. pap. 7.00 (*0-941543-08-0*) Sun Dog Pr.

— Inner Timbres. LC 81-90254. (Illus.). 60p. (Orig.). 1981. pap. 4.95 (*0-9606678-0-6*) Sylvan Pubns.

— The Old Ways. Berlinski, Allen, ed. 12p. (Orig.). 1990. pap. 4.95 (*0-941543-01-3*) Sun Dog Pr.

Leo, Kathleen R., et al, eds. Waiting for the Apples. LC 82-62746. (Illus.). 100p. (Orig.). (J). (gr. k up). 1983. pap. 6.50 (*0-9606678-2-2*) Sylvan Pubns.

Leo, Leonard, jt. ed. see Clegg, Roger.

Leo, Punana. Pai Ka Leo. (Illus.). 40p. (Orig.). (J). (ps-6). 1989. pap. 4.95 (*0-935848-63-0*) Bess Pr.

Leo, Richard. Edges of the Earth. 384p. 1993. mass mkt. 5.99 (*0-8217-4122-5*) Zebra.

Leo, Roger J. Business Contracts & the Sale of Goods. Schneider, Alan L., ed. (Business Law Ser.). 69p. (Orig.). 1987. pap. 25.75 (*0-685-28082-9*) BLI Inc.

Leo, Roger J. & Schneider, Alan L. Understanding Commercial Leases. (Business Law Ser.). 76p. (Orig.). 1987. pap. 25.75 (*0-685-28079-9*) BLI Inc.

Leo The Great. Letters. LC 63-18826. (Fathers of the Church Ser.: Vol. 34). 312p. 1957. 15.95 (*0-8132-0034-2*) Cath U Pr.

***Leo, Veronica & Daknewa, Tashi.** The Three Silver Coins: A Story from Tibet. Aberg, Nina, tr. LC 94-39648. (Illus.). (J). 1995. pap. 12.95 (*1-55939-040-9*) Snow Lion Pubns.

***Leo, Vince, ed.** Heads up: A Guide to Youth Arts Activities in the Twin Cities. (Illus.). 140p. (Orig.). 1995. pap. 7.95 (*0-9645862-0-7*) United Arts.

Leo, William R. Techniques for Nuclear & Particle Physics Experiments: A How-to Approach. LC 92-7633. 1992. write for info. (*3-540-17386-2*) Spr-Verlag.

— Techniques for Nuclear & Particle Physics Experiments: A How-To Approach. 2nd rev. ed. LC 93-38494. 1994. 49.50 (*0-387-57280-5*) Spr-Verlag.

— Techniques for Nuclear & Particle Physics Experiments: A How-To Approach. (Illus.). xvi, 368p. 1992. reprint ed. pap. 49.50 (*0-387-17386-2*) Spr-Verlag.

Leocha, Charles. Myths, Legends & Tales of Europe for Travellers. 360p. (Orig.). Date not set. pap. 14.95 (*0-915009-15-3*) World Leis Corp.

— Ski Europe. 9th ed. Scholfield, Diane S., ed. 400p. (Orig.). 1993. pap. 16.95 (*0-915009-26-9*) World Leis Corp.

— Ski Europe. 10th ed. Scholfield, Diane, ed. (Illus.). 428p. (Orig.). 1995. pap. 17.95 (*0-915009-41-2*) World Leis Corp.

— Skiing America, 1995. 7th ed. Scholfield, Diane S., ed. (Illus.). 480p. 1994. pap. 17.95 (*0-915009-34-X*) World Leis Corp.

— Skiing America, 1996. 8th ed. Scholfield, Diane, ed. (Illus.). 512p. (Orig.). 1995. pap. 18.95 (*0-915009-40-4*) World Leis Corp.

— Travel Rights. 196p. (Orig.). 1994. pap. 9.95 (*0-915009-28-5*) World Leis Corp.

— Travel Rights. 160p. (Orig.). 1994. 95.40 (*0-915009-29-3*) World Leis Corp.

— Travel Rights. 2nd ed. 194p. (Orig.). 1995. pap. 6.95 (*0-915009-37-4*) World Leis Corp.

Leocha, Charles, jt. auth. see McSweeney, Jeanne.

Leocha, Charles A. Eastern Germany. (Illus.). 322p. (Orig.). 1992. pap. 14.95 (*0-915009-20-X*) World Leis Corp.

Leodas, Gus. The Forgotten Mission. (Orig.). 1982. pap. 2.95 (*0-89083-970-0*) Zebra.

Leoff, Eve. Monarch Notes on Shakespeare's A Midsummer Night's Dream. (Orig.). (C). pap. 3.95 (*0-671-00638-X*, Arco Test) P-H Gen Ref & Trav.

LeoGrande, William M. Cuba's Policy in Africa, Nineteen Fifty-Nine to Nineteen Eighty. LC 80-52088. (Policy Papers in International Affairs Ser.: No. 13). vi, 80p. 1980. pap. 6.50 (*0-87725-513-X*) U of Cal IAS.

LeoGrande, William M., jt. auth. see Washington Office on Latin America Staff.

Leoin, Larry. Telecommunications for Information Specialties. (Library, Information, & Computer Science Ser.: No. 11). (Illus.). 180p. (Orig.). 1989. pap. 15.00 (*1-55653-075-7*) OCLC Online Comp.

***Leok, Goh C. & Nee, Tham S.** Color Atlas of Skin Diseases. (Illus.). 300p. 1995. pap. text ed. write for info. (*0-07-113839-0*) Hlth Prof Div.

Leokum, Arkady. Neighbors. 1972. pap. 2.75 (*0-8222-0809-1*) Dramatists Play.

Leon & Holmes. Studies on Archaeology of Michoacan Mexico. 33p. reprint ed. pap. 3.95 (*0-8466-4012-0*, 112) Shorey.

Leon & Mintz. Intravascular Ultrasound. 250p. 1994. 95.00 (*0-8016-7246-5*) Mosby Yr Bk.

Leon, A. K. Haynes Mazda 626 Owners Workshop Manual, No. 648: 1979-1982. 16.95 (*0-85696-996-6*) Haynes Pubns.

Leon, Abram. The Jewish Question: A Marxist Interpretation. LC 76-108721. 270p. 1993. reprint ed. lib. bdg. 50.00 (*0-87348-133-X*); reprint ed. pap. 17.95 (*0-87348-134-8*) Pathfinder NY.

Leon, Adolfo, jt. auth. see Christophersen, Merrill G.

***Leon, Adriano G.** Viejo. 1995. pap. 14.95 (*0-679-76337-6*, Vin) Random.

Leon, Arnoldo De. The Mexican Image in Nineteenth Century Texas. (Texas History Ser.). (Illus.). 45p. 1983. pap. text ed. 3.95x (*0-89641-106-0*) American Pr.

Leon, Arthur S., jt. auth. see Smith, Timothy W.

Leon, Burke & Leon, Stephanie. The Insider's Guide to Buying a New or Used Car: Hundreds of Tips in Easy to Use Checklist Format from a Veteran Insider. 192p. (Orig.). 1993. pap. 9.99 (*1-55870-284-9*) Betterway Bks.

Leon County Genealogical Society Staff. History of Leon County, Texas. (Illus.). 924p. 1986. 60.00 (*0-88107-050-5*) Curtis Media.

Leon, D. Kibbutz: New Way of Life. 1969. 87.00 (*0-08-013357-6*, Pub. by Pergamon Repr UK) Franklin.

Leon, Daniel, jt. auth. see Santano, Daniel.

***Leon, Donna.** Death & Judgement. 1995. 20.00 (*0-06-017796-9*) HarpC.

— Death at la Fenice. 1994. pap. 4.50 (*0-06-104337-0*, Harp PBks) HarpC.

— Dressed for Death. LC 93-47279. 256p. 1994. 20.00 (*0-06-017795-0*, HarpT) HarpC.

Leon-Dufour, Xavier. Diccionario del Nuevo Testamento: Dictionary of the New Testament. 480p. (SPA.). 1977. 29.95 (*0-8288-5329-0*, S50103) Fr & Eur.

— Larousse des Grands Peintres, Vol. 1. 2nd ed. 576p. (FRE.). 1978. pap. write for info. (*0-7859-4829-5*) Fr & Eur.

— Woerterbuch Zum Neuen Testament. 469p. (GER.). 1977. 39.95 (*0-7859-8384-8*, 3466202191) Fr & Eur.

— Woerterbuch Zur Biblischen Botschaft. 2nd ed. 826p. (GER.). 1981. 95.00 (*0-7859-8373-2*, 3451141779) Fr & Eur.

***Leon-Dufour, Xavier, ed.** Dictionary of Biblical Theology. 2nd ed. Cahill, P. Joseph & Stewart, E. M., trs. 744p. (FRE.). 1995. pap. 29.95 (*0-932085-09-1*) Word Among Us.

Leon-Dufour, Xavier & Viola, G. Dictionary of Biblical Theology: Dizionario di Teologia Biblica. 1424p. (ITA.). 1980. 110.00 (*0-8288-2314-6*, M7691) Fr & Eur.

Leon, Edel, ed. see James, Henry.

Leon, Eli. Arbie Williams Transforms the Britches Quilt: Contemporary Britches Quilts in the African-American Tradition. (Illus.). (Orig.). (C). 1993. pap. text ed. 8.00 (*0-939982-19-6*) Sesnon Art Gall.

Leon, Felix, jt. auth. see DaSilva, Howard.

Leon, Fray L. de. De Los Nombres de Cristo. Sanchez Zamarreno, Antonio, ed. (Nueva Austral Ser.: Vol. 190). (SPA.). 1991. pap. text ed. 32.95x (*84-239-1990-0*) Elliots Bks.

Leon-Garcia, Alberto. Probability & Random Processes for Electrical Engineering. (Electrical & Computer Engineering Ser.). (Illus.). 488p. (C). 1989. text ed. 62.50 (*0-201-12906-X*) Addison-Wesley.

— Probability & Random Processes for Electrical Engineering. 2nd ed. (Illus.). 596p. (C). 1994. text ed. 62.50 (*0-201-50037-X*) Addison-Wesley.

Leon, George B. The Greek Socialist Movement & the First World War. (East European Monographs: No. 18). 204p. 1976. text ed. 42.00 (*0-914710-11-7*) East Eur Quarterly.

Leon, George D. Electronics Projects for Young Scientists. LC 91-17823. (Projects for Young Scientists Ser.). (Illus.). 128p. (YA). (gr. 9-12). 1991. lib. bdg. 14.77 (*0-531-11071-0*) Watts.

— Explorers of the Americas Before Columbus. LC 88-38064. (Illus.). 64p. (J). (gr. 7-9). 1990. 13.72 (*0-531-10667-5*) Watts.

— How to Make Simple, Sturdy, Attractive, Inexpensive Furniture from Cardboard. (Illus.). 96p. 1994. pap. 12.95 (*0-8117-2548-0*) Stackpole.

— The Story of Communications: From Fire to Fax. (Illus.). 128p. (Orig.). 1993. pap. text ed. 6.95 (*0-486-27353-9*) Dover.

— The Story of Electricity: With Twenty Easy-to-Perform Experiments. (Illus.). 112p. 1988. reprint ed. pap. 4.95 (*0-486-25581-6*) Dover.

Leon, Gloria R. Case Histories of Psychopathology. 4th ed. 368p. 1989. pap. text ed. 25.00 (*0-205-12085-7*, H20852) Allyn.

***Leon, Harry J.** The Jews of Ancient Rome. rev. ed. Osiek, Carolyn, ed. & frwd. by. (Illus.). 432p. 1995. 24.95 (*1-56563-076-9*) Hendrickson MA.

Leon, Irving G. When a Baby Dies: Psychotherapy for Pregnancy & Newborn Loss. LC 89-22706. 248p. (C). 1990. 14.00 (*0-300-04575-1*) Yale U Pr.

— When a Baby Dies: Psychotherapy for Pregnancy & Newborn Loss. 248p. (C). 1992. reprint ed. pap. text ed. 13.00 (*0-300-05230-8*) Yale U Pr.

Leon, J. K. How to Test & Buy a Used Car. (Illus.). 29p. (Orig.). 1984. pap. 4.95 (*0-932675-00-X*) Used Car Pubns.

Leon, J. Mustrede, jt. ed. see Barthes, M.

Leon, Jane E. Becoming Best Friends. 1993. mass mkt. 4.99 (*0-425-13956-5*) Berkley Pub.

— Becoming Best Friends: Building a Loving Relationship Between Your Pet & Your Child. 1991. pap. 8.95 (*0-9625043-2-7*) Pecos Pr.

— Cat for All Seasons: Keeping Your Cat Healthy & Happy Throughout the Year. 1991. pap. 8.95 (*0-9625043-4-3*) Pecos Pr.

— Dog for All Seasons: Keeping Your Dog Healthy & Happy Throughout the Year. 1991. pap. 8.95 (*0-9625043-3-5*) Pecos Pr.

Leon, Jane F. Your Older Cat: Loving Care for the Golden Years. 1992. pap. 9.95 (*0-9625043-6-X*) Pecos Pr.

— Your Older Dog: Loving Care for the Golden Years. 1992. pap. 9.95 (*0-9625043-5-1*) Pecos Pr.

Leon, John P., jt. auth. see Arcudi, John.

Leon, Jorge A. Cada Muchacho Necesita un Modelo Vivo. 96p. (SPA.). 1988. reprint ed. pap. 4.25 (*0-311-46087-9*) Casa Bautista.

— Problematica Sicologica de los Solteros. 144p. (Orig.). (SPA.). 1981. pap. 4.95 (*0-89922-219-6*) Edit Caribe.

— Psicologia Pastoral de la Iglesia. LC 77-43121. 192p. (Orig.). (SPA.). 1978. pap. 6.25 (*0-89922-113-0*) Edit Caribe.

— Psicologia Pastoral para Todos los Cristianos. LC 76-43121. 181p. (Orig.). (SPA.). 1976. reprint ed. pap. 6.25 (*0-89922-020-7*) Edit Caribe.

Leon, Joseph J., jt. ed. see Cretser, Gary A.

Leon, Joseph M. Worldly Philosophers Notes. 1974. pap. 3.95 (*0-8220-1385-1*) Cliffs.

Leon, Lu S., jt. auth. see Wick, Calhoun W.

Leon, Luis A. Reflexiones Sobre Cuba y Su Futuro. 2nd ed. LC 90-85538. (Coleccion Cuba y Sus Jueces Ser.). 192p. (Orig.). (SPA.). 1992. pap. 16.00 (*0-89729-647-8*) Ediciones.

Leon, M. Particle Physics: An Introduction. 1973. text ed. 77.00 (*0-12-443850-4*) Acad Pr.

Leon, Margaret. Barnaby Bear. (Illus.). 32p. (J). (ps-8). 1983. 7.95 (*0-920806-42-2*, Pub. by Penumbra Pr CN) U of Toronto Pr.

Leon, Mariette, tr. see Grousset, Rene.

***Leon, Mark.** Mind-Surfer. 272p. (Orig.). 1995. mass mkt. 4.99 (*0-380-77582-4*, AvoNova) Avon.

Leon, Marynel, jt. auth. see Noel, Leon.

Leon, Monique. Exercises Systematique. 183p. (FRE.). 1991. 24.95 (*0-8288-7483-2*) Fr & Eur.

— Exercises Systematiques de Prononciation Francaise. 55p. (FRE.). 1969. pap. write for info. (*0-7859-4634-9*) Fr & Eur.

— Prononciation du Francais Standard. (Coll. Linguistique Appliquee). 16.50 (*0-685-36699-5*); 39.95 (*0-8288-7873-0*, F139430); audio 59.95 (*0-685-36700-2*) Fr & Eur.

Leon, N. H. Chemical Reactivity & Modification of Keratin Fibres. 81p. 1975. 95.00 (*0-686-63750-X*) St Mut.

— Chemical Reactivity & Modifications of Keratin Fibres, Vol. 7, No. 1. 81p. (C). 1975. pap. text ed. 70.00 (*0-685-46410-5*, Pub. by Textile Institue UK) St Mut.

Leon Nunez, Victor. Diccionario de Argot Espanol. 9th ed. 160p. (SPA.). 1991. pap. 8.95 (*0-7859-5720-0*, 8420617660) Fr & Eur.

Leon-Portilla, Miguel. Aztec Image of Self & Society: An Introduction to Nahua Culture. LC 90-53559. (Illus.). 264p. (C). 1992. lib. bdg. 27.50 (*0-87480-360-8*) U of Utah Pr.

— Aztec Thought & Culture: A Study of the Ancient Nahuatl Mind. Davis, Jack E., tr. LC 63-11019. (Civilization of the American Indian Ser.: Vol. 67). (Illus.). 272p. 1990. reprint ed. pap. 15.95 (*0-8061-2295-1*) U of Okla Pr.

— Endangered Cultures. Goodson-Lawes, Julie, tr. LC 90-52658. (Illus.). 276p. 1990. pap. text ed. 14.95x (*0-87074-311-2*) SMU Press.

— Fifteen Poets of the Aztec World. LC 92-7108. (Illus.). 328p. 1992. 26.95 (*0-8061-2441-5*) U of Okla Pr.

— Pre-Columbian Literatures of Mexico. Lobanov, Grace, tr. LC 79-32551. (Civilization of the American Indian Ser.: Vol. 92). (Illus.). 256p. (Orig.). 1986. pap. 12.95 (*0-8061-1974-8*) U of Okla Pr.

— Time & Reality in the Thought of the Maya. 2nd ed. Boiles, Charles L. & Horcasitas, Fernando, trs. LC 88-40207. (Civilization of the American Indian Ser.: Vol. 190). (Illus.). 256p. 1990. pap. 15.95 (*0-8061-2308-7*) U of Okla Pr.

Leon-Portilla, Miguel, ed. Native Mesoamerican Spirituality. Anderson, Arthur J. et al, trs. LC 80-80821. (Classics of Western Spirituality Ser.). 320p. 1980. pap. 17.95 (*0-8091-2231-6*) Paulist Pr.

Leon-Portilla, Miguel, intro. The Broken Spears: The Aztec Account of the Conquest of Mexico. LC 91-35657. (Illus.). 224p. 1992. pap. 14.00 (*0-8070-5501-8*) Beacon Pr.

Leon-Portilla, Miguel, jt. ed. see Gossen, Gary H.

Leon, Robert. Democracy (B. Nineteen Eighty-Four) 1993. 18.95 (*0-533-10586-2*) Vantage.

Leon, Ruth. Applause: New York's Guide to the Performing Arts. (Companion Ser.). (Illus.). 528p. 1992. pap. 15.95 (*1-55783-096-7*) Applause Theatre Bk Pubns.

Leon, Sharon, jt. auth. see Hitzeroth, Deborah.

***Leon, Silvia. Songs for Little Ones - Canciones Para Pequenos: Teacher's Guide - Guia de Maestros. (Illus.). 61p. (Orig.). 1995. pap. text ed. 8.95 (*0-9643490-0-0*) Smarty Kat.**

Is there a better way for young children to develop primary or secondary language than through songs & rhymes? There is no better way! SONGS FOR LITTLE ONES/CANCIONES PARA PEQUENOS is a teacher's guide that helps educators offer children a stress-free, enjoyable & natural way to acquire new words in a meaningful context. The guide contains the following: nine familiar early childhood songs or rhymes in both English & Spanish, lesson plans, follow-up activities, autoharp keys & a reference of related literature. A cassette accompanies the book with one side in English & the other in Spanish. Furthermore, vibrant & beautifully illustrated characters have been printed on nine thick, quality pieces of felt material that bring each song or rhyme visually alive for young children on the flannel board. The illustrations to one of the songs, Ten Little Children/Diez Ninitos, features multi-ethnic & physically challenged youngsters counting in American sign language from one to ten. This easy-to-read teacher's guide, delightful cassette & colorful felt characters are essential assets to any early childhood program, especially those with latino preschool or kindergarten children. While the book is available separately, the full kit (book, cassette & felt characters) retails for $89.95. To order, call: 213-567-4731 or write to Smarty Kat Designs, 7621 Firestone Blvd., MSC A1, Downey, CA 90241. ***Publisher Provided Annotation.***

Leon, Stephanie, jt. auth. see Leon, Burke.

Leon, Steven J. Linear Algebra with Applications. 4th ed. 528p. (C). 1994. text ed. write for info. (*0-02-369831-4*) Macmillan.

Leon, V. Slang Dictionary of Spanish: Diccionario del Argot Espanol. 157p. (SPA.). 1983. pap. 9.95 (*0-8288-2050-3*, S33020) Fr & Eur.

Leon, Vicki. Hearst Castle Photo Tour Guide. 2nd ed. (Illus.). 32p. 1983. pap. 6.95 (*0-918303-04-4*) Blake Pub.

— Monterey Peninsula. (Illus.). 56p. (Orig.). 1985. pap. 7.95 (*0-918303-03-6*) Blake Pub.

— Parrots, Macaws & Cockatoos. LC 94-30908. (Close up: A Focus on Nature Ser.). (Illus.). 40p. (YA). (gr. 5 up). 1994. lib. bdg. 14.95 (*0-382-24898-8*); pap. 7.95 (*0-382-24899-6*) Silver Burdett Pr.

— A Pod of Killer Whales: The Mysterious & Beautiful Life of the Orca. LC 94-30906. (Close up Ser.). (Illus.). 40p. (YA). (gr. 5 up). 1994. lib. bdg. 14.95 (*0-382-24900-3*); pap. 7.95 (*0-382-24901-1*) Silver Burdett Pr.

— San Luis Obispo County Coast & Castle. (Illus.). 72p. (Orig.). 1986. pap. 9.95 (*0-918303-11-7*) Blake Pub.

— Scenic Highway One: Monterey to Morro Bay. rev. ed. (Illus.). 64p. (Orig.). 1984. pap. 8.95 (*0-918303-02-8*) Blake Pub.

— Seals & Sea Lions: An Affectionate Portrait. LC 94-31827. (Close Up Ser.). (Illus.). 40p. (YA). (gr. 5 up). 1994. lib. bdg. 14.95 (*0-382-24889-9*); pap. 7.95 (*0-382-24890-2*) Silver Burdett Pr.

— Uppity Women of Ancient Times. (Illus.). 256p. 1995. pap. 12.95 (*1-57324-010-9*) Conari Press.

***Leon, Vicki, ed.** A Raft of Sea Otters: An Affectionate Portrait. rev. ed. LC 94-31826. (Close up Ser.). (Illus.). 48p. (YA). (gr. 5 up). 1994. lib. bdg. 14.95 (*0-382-24885-6*); pap. 7.95 (*0-382-24886-4*) Silver Burdett Pr.

Leon, Vicki, jt. auth. see Barnhart, Diana.

Leon, Vicki, ed. see Berger, Bruce.

Leon, Vicki, ed. see Brody, Jean.

Leon, Vicki, ed. see Fourie, Denise K.

Leon, Vicki, ed. see Gohier, Francois.

Leon, Vicki, ed. see Hall, Howard.

Leon, Vicki, ed. see Hamilton, Jean.

Leon, Vicki, ed. see Holing, Dwight, et al.

Leon, Vicki, ed. see Hunt, Joni P.

Leon, Vicki, ed. see Wilson, Barbara.

Leon, Warren & Rosenzweig, Roy, eds. History Museums in the United States: A Critical Assessment. LC 88-27883. (Illus.). 360p. 1989. pap. 14.95 (*0-252-06064-4*) U of Ill Pr.

Leonaites, Joseph. New Genesis & the Technoid Movement. (Illus.). 1977. pap. write for info. (*0-9601272-1-6*) Leonaitis.

Leonard. Air Quality Permitting. 1995. write for info. (*0-87371-790-2*) Lewis Pubs.

— Barnaby & the Gorilla. (J). 1994. pap. 4.99 (*0-517-13486-1*) Random Hse Value.

— Kitten for Christmas. 1988. 2.95 (*0-8167-1489-4*) Troll Assocs.

— Mouses Christmas. 1988. 2.95 (*0-8167-1494-0*) Troll Assocs.

— Packaging: Specifications, Purchasing, & Quality Control. 3rd ed. (Packaging & Converting Technology Ser.: Vol. 1). 240p. 1987. 85.00 (*0-8247-7729-8*) Dekker.

— Pine Cones & Holly. 1988. 2.95 (*0-8167-1493-2*) Troll Assocs.

— Waiting for Christmas. 1988. 2.95 (*0-8167-1490-8*) Troll Assocs.

— Wish on a Star. 1988. 2.95 (*0-8167-1491-6*) Troll Assocs.

***Leonard, A., et al.** AIDS Law & Policy. 2nd ed. LC 94-72965. 562p. 1995. write for info. (*0-916081-35-4*) J Marshall Pub Co.

Leonard, A. B., jt. auth. see Murray, Harold D.

Leonard, Alain. Barnaby & the Big Gorilla. LC 91-25414. (Illus.). 32p. (J). (ps-3). 1992. 15.00 (*0-688-11291-9*, Tambourine Bks); lib. bdg. 14.93 (*0-688-11292-7*, Tambourine Bks) Morrow.

— Theodore's Superheroes. Tambourine Books Staff, tr. LC 92-82140. (Illus.). 32p. (J). (ps up). 1993. 15.00 (*0-688-12766-5*, Tambourine Bks); lib. bdg. 14.93 (*0-688-12767-3*, Tambourine Bks) Morrow.

Leonard, Alan, jt. auth. see Baker, Rodney.

Leonard, Albert, Jr. The Jordan Valley Survey, 1953: Some Unpublished Soundings Conducted by James Mellaart. LC 91-36535. (Annual of the American Schools of Oriental Research Ser.: Vol. 50). (Illus.). vii, 199p. 1992. text ed. 32.50 (*0-685-57082-7*) Eisenbrauns.

— The Jordan Valley Survey, 1953: Some Unpublished Soundings Conducted by James Mellaart. (Annual of the American Schools of Oriental Research Ser.: No. 50). (Illus.). vii, 199p. 1992. text ed. 40.00 (*0-931464-72-2*) Eisenbrauns.

Leonard, Albert, Jr. & Williams, Bruce B., eds. Essays in Ancient Civilization Presented to Helen J. Kantor. LC 89-60852. (Studies in Ancient Oriental Civilization: No. 47). (Illus.). xxxix, 393p. 1989. pap. 54.00 (*0-918986-57-5*) Orientl Inst Pr IT.

Leonard, Alice M. Judging Inequality: The Effectiveness of the Tribunal System in Sex. (C). 1988. 49.00 (*0-900137-28-2*, Pub. by NCCL UK) St Mut.

Leonard, Alice M., jt. auth. see Gaylord, Catherine L.

Leonard, Allenna, jt. ed. see Harnden, Roger.

***Leonard, Andrea.** A Crocker Genealogy. 311p. (Orig.). 1995. pap. text ed. 23.00 (*0-7884-0197-1*) Heritage Bk.

Leonard, Angela M., ed. Antislavery Materials at Bowdoin College: A Finding Aid. LC 92-70213. (Illus.). 100p. (Orig.). 1992. pap. 7.95 (*0-916606-22-8*) Bowdoin Coll.

An Asterisk (*) at the beginning of an entry indicates that the title is appearing in BIP for the first time.

Leonard, Ann, ed. Proceedings of the Fifteenth Annual Conference. LC 76-643241. iii, 79p. (Orig.). 1983. pap. 10.00 (*0-933438-07-9*) APLIC Intl.
— Seeds: Supporting Women's Work in the Third World. LC 89-23329. (Illus.). 256p. 1989. 35.00 (*0-935312-92-7*); pap. 12.95 (*0-935312-93-5*) Feminist Pr.
— Seeds 2. 200p. (Orig.). 1995. lib. bdg. 35.00 (*1-55861-107-X*) Feminist Pr.
— Seeds 2. 200p. (Orig.). 1995. pap. 12.95 (*1-55861-106-1*) Feminist Pr.
Leonard, Anne. Homes of Their Own: A Community Care Initiative for Children with Learning Difficulties. (Studies in Cash & Care). 161p. 1991. text ed. 55.95 (*1-85628-156-6*, Pub. by Avebury Pub UK) Ashgate Pub Co.
Leonard, Arthur G. Lower Niger & Its Tribes. 564p. 1968. reprint ed. 45.00 (*0-7146-1687-7*, Pub. by F Cass Pubs UK) Intl Spec Bk.
Leonard, Arthur S., comp. AIDS Legal Bibliography. (Legal Bibliography Ser.: No. 33). 25p. 1989. 40.00 (*0-935630-28-7*) U of Tex Tarlton Law Lib.
— AIDS Legal Bibliography. 2nd ed. (Tarlton Law Library Legal Bibliography Ser.: No. 37). 97p. 1993. 40.00 (*0-935630-39-2*) U of Tex Tarlton Law Lib.
Leonard, Arthur S., ed. Sexuality & the Law: An Encyclopedia of Major Legal Cases, Vol. 3. LC 92-45133. 736p. 1993. 95.00 (*0-8240-3421-X*, H1272) Garland.
***Leonard, B. & Miller, K., eds.** Stress, the Immune System & Psychiatry. 1995. text ed. 54.95 (*0-471-95258-3*) Wiley.
Leonard, B. E., ed. Fundamentals of Psychopharmacology. 267p. 1992. pap. text ed. 34.95 (*0-471-93388-0*) Wiley.
***Leonard-Barton, Dorothy.** Wellsprings of Knowledge: Building & Sustaining Core Technological Capabilities. LC 95-14582. 1995. write for info. (*0-87584-612-2*) Harvard Busn.
***Leonard, Benjamin F. & Rosentreter, Roger.** Dating a Twentieth-Century Fault, Elk Summit Talus Apron, Big Creek Area, Valley County, Idaho. Vol. 2101. 1995. write for info. (*0-615-00057-6*) US Geol Survey.
Leonard, Bill J. God's Last & Only Hope: The Fragmentation of the Southern Baptist Convention. 200p. (Orig.). 1990. pap. 12.99 (*0-8028-0498-5*) Eerdmans.
— La Naturaleza de la Iglesia - Nature of the Church. Clark, Stanley, Jr., tr. 156p. (Orig.). (SPA.). 1989. pap. 5.25 (*0-311-09122-9*) Casa Bautista.
Leonard, Bill J., ed. Becoming Christian. 252p. (Orig.). 1990. pap. 16.99 (*0-664-25119-6*) Westminster John Knox.
— Dictionary of Baptists in America. LC 94-31573. 298p. (Orig.). 1994. pap. 16.99 (*0-8308-1447-7*, 1447) InterVarsity.
***Leonard, Bruce.** A Tradition of Integrity: The Story of Quantas Engineering & Maintenance. 232p. Date not set. pap. 19.95 (*0-86840-110-2*, Pub. by New South Wales Univ Pr AT) Intl Spec Bk.
Leonard, Buck. Buck Leonard: In His Own Words. 1976. 29.95 (*0-8488-1544-0*) Amereon Ltd.
Leonard, Buck & Riley, James. Buck Leonard: the Black Lou Gehrig: The Hall of Famers's Story in His Own Words. 304p. 1995. 20.00 (*0-7867-0119-6*) Carroll & Graf.
Leonard, C. Henri & Christy, Thomas. Dictionary of Materia Medica & Therapeutics. 1980. lib. bdg. 75.00 (*0-8490-3120-6*) Gordon Pr.
Leonard, Calista V. Guess Who. 36p. (J). (ps-6). 1992. lib. bdg. write for info. (*0-9634165-0-2*) Vistoso Bks.
Leonard, Carol S. Reform & Regicide: The Reign of Peter III of Russia. LC 92-5176. (Indiana-Michigan Series in Russian & East European Studies). 320p. 1992. 35.00 (*0-253-33322-9*) Ind U Pr.
Leonard, Carolyn & Colclasure, Marian. Print Shop Graphics for Libraries, Vol. 5 - States & Politics. iii, 36p. 1988. Apple version. disk 26.50 (*0-87287-726-4*); IBM version. disk 27.25 (*0-87287-888-0*) Libs Unl.
— Print Shop Graphics for Libraries, Vol. 6 - American Heritage. 40p. 1989. Apple version. disk 27.50 (*0-87287-746-9*); IBM version. disk 27.75 (*0-87287-889-9*) Libs Unl.
— Print Shop Graphics for Libraries, Vol. 7: World Nations & History. (Illus.). 40p. 1990. Apple version. disk 28.00 (*0-87287-748-5*); IBM version. disk 28.50 (*0-87287-890-2*) Libs Unl.
Leonard, Carolyn, ed. see Waugh, Meredith.
Leonard, Carolyn, et al. Print Shop Graphics for Libraries, Vol. II. 20p. 1987. Apple version. disk 24.00 (*0-87287-606-3*); IBM version. disk 24.00 (*0-87287-688-8*) Libs Unl.
— Print Shop Graphics for Libraries: Books & Fonts, Vol. 3. 1988. Apple version. disk 23.50 (*0-87287-659-4*); IBM version. disk 23.75 (*0-87287-886-4*) Libs Unl.
Leonard, Charles, ed. see Chekhov, Michael.
Leonard, Charles, jt. auth. see Warner, David.
Leonard, Charles R., jt. auth. see Bruce, Roy W.
Leonard, Charlotte. Tied Together: Topics & Thoughts for Introducing Children's Books. LC 80-11135. 261p. 1980. lib. bdg. 25.00 (*0-8108-1293-2*) Scarecrow.
Leonard, Chien-Fu-Wu, jt. ed. see Box, G. E.
Leonard Clayton Gallery Staff, jt. auth. see Royal Cortissoz.
***Leonard, Curtis & Kappele, William.** Contemporary Wire Wrapped Jewelry. LC 95-75187. (Illus.). 144p. (Orig.). 1995. pap. text ed. 14.95 (*0-935182-71-3*) Gem Guides Bk.
Leonard, Cynthia M., comp. The General Assembly of Virginia, July 30, 1619-January 11, 1978: A Bicentennial Register of Members. xxxi, 884p. 1978. 29.95 (*0-88490-008-8*) VA State Lib.
Leonard, Daniel. Massachusettensis. LC 72-10246. (American Revolutionary Ser.). 1979. reprint ed. lib. bdg. 19.50 (*0-8398-1180-2*) Irvington.
Leonard, Daniel & Long, Ngo V. Optimal Control Theory & Static Optimization in Economics. (Illus.). 384p. (C). 1992. 69.95 (*0-521-33158-7*); pap. 34.95 (*0-521-33746-1*) Cambridge U Pr.
***Leonard, David C. & Dillon, Patrick M.** Multimedia Technology from A to Z. LC 94-37853. 192p. 1994. pap. 19.95 (*0-89774-892-1*) Oryx Pr.
Leonard, David K. African Successes: Four Public Managers of Kenyan Rural Development. LC 90-11089. (Illus.). 390p. 1991. 55.00 (*0-520-07075-5*); pap. 19.00 (*0-520-07076-3*) U CA Pr.
Leonard, David K. & Marshall, Dale R., eds. Institutions of Rural Development for the Poor: Decentralization & Organizational Linkages. LC 82-15651. (Research Ser.: No. 49). xii, 237p. 1982. pap. 12.95 (*0-87725-149-5*) U of Cal IAS.
***Leonard, David W. & Lemieux, Victoria L.** The Lure of the Peace River Country: A Fostered Dream. (Illus.). 195p. 1992. 29.95 (*1-55059-044-8*) Temeron Bks.
Leonard, Dennis. Overcoming Depression. 1991. pap. 4.95 (*1-880809-01-X*) D Leonard Pubns.
— You Can Forgive Yourself: If God Can Forgive You...You Can Forgive Yourself. 1991. pap. 4.95 (*1-880809-00-1*) D Leonard Pubns.
Leonard, Diana & Allen, Sheila, eds. Sexual Divisions Revisited. LC 90-8802. 208p. 1991. text ed. 45.00 (*0-312-05210-3*) St Martin.
Leonard, Diana, ed. see Delphy, Christine.
Leonard, Diana, jt. auth. see Delphy, Christine.
Leonard, Dick. Elections in Britain: A Guide to Voters & Students. 2nd rev. ed. 176p. 1991. text ed. 39.95 (*0-312-01186-5*) St Martin.
Leonard, Don, jt. auth. see Waters, Max L.
Leonard, Donald E. A Pragmatic Guide to Advertising. 336p. (C). 1992. pap. text ed. 35.95 (*0-8403-7429-1*) Kendall-Hunt.
— A Pragmatic Guide to Consumer Behavior. 308p. 1993. per. 32.95 (*0-8403-8256-1*) Kendall-Hunt.
— A Pragmatic Guide to Marketing. 272p. (C). 1990. per. 28.95 (*0-8403-6371-0*) Kendall-Hunt.
Leonard, Donald J. & Shurter, Robert L. Effective Letters in Business. 3rd ed. 252p. 1984. pap. text ed. 9.95 (*0-07-057485-5*) McGraw.
Leonard, Donald J., jt. ed. see Holland, G. Pepper.
Leonard, Donald J., jt. auth. see Smeltzer, Larry R.
Leonard, E. Bruce & Besant, Christopher W., eds. Current Issues in Cross-Border Insolvency & Reorganizations. LC 94-7617. (International Bar Association Ser.). 432p. (C). 1994. lib. bdg. 140.00 (*1-85333-958-X*, Pub. by Graham & Trotman UK) Kluwer Ac.
Leonard, E. G. Histoire Universelle: De la Reforme a nos Jours, Vol. 3. 2340p. write for info. (*0-318-52027-3*) Fr & Eur.
— Histoire Universelle, Vol. 3: De la Reforme a Nos Jours. 1340p. (FRE.). 1958. 135.00 (*0-7859-4547-4*) Fr & Eur.
Leonard, E. G., jt. auth. see Grousset, R.
Leonard, E. J., ed. see Lee, Frank E.
Leonard, Edson. Feather in the Breeze. (Illus.). 1974. 7.95 (*0-88395-026-X*) Freshet Pr.
Leonard, Edward A. Rails at the Pass of the North. (Southwestern Studies: No. 63). 1981. pap. 10.00 (*0-87404-122-8*) Tex Western.
Leonard, Edward F., jt. ed. see Vroman, Leo.
Leonard, Edward F., et al, eds. Blood in Contact with Natural & Artificial Surfaces. (Annals Ser.: Vol. 516). 688p. 1987. 172.00 (*0-89766-427-2*) NY Acad Sci.
Leonard, Edwin C., jt. auth. see Hilgert, Raymond L.
Leonard, Eileen B., et al, eds. In Search of Community: Essays in Memory of Werner Stark, 1905-1985. LC 91-30219. 272p. 1993. 40.00 (*0-8232-1352-8*) Fordham.
Leonard, Eliot. Operating a Bookstore: Practical Details for Improving Profit. 120p. (Orig.). 1992. pap. 12.95 (*1-879923-04-1*) Booksellers Pub.
Leonard, Elizabeth. Painting Flowers. (Illus.). 144p. 1991. pap. 18.95 (*0-8230-3630-8*, Watsn-Guptill) Watsn-Guptill.
Leonard, Elizabeth D. Yankee Women: Gender Battles in the Civil War. LC 93-48813. (Illus.). 1994. 23.00 (*0-393-03666-9*) Norton.
— Yankee Women: Gender Battles in the Civil War. (Illus.). 336p. 1995. pap. 12.95 (*0-393-31372-7*, Norton Paperbks) Norton.
Leonard, Elizabeth L. Friendly Rebel: A Personal & Social History of Eduard C. Lindeman. 1991. 25.00 (*0-912362-11-1*) Adamant Pr.
Leonard, Ellen. Unresting Transformation: The Theology & Spirituality of Maude Petre. 256p. (Orig.). (C). 1991. lib. bdg. 51.00 (*0-8191-8220-6*); pap. text ed. 29.00 (*0-8191-8221-4*) U Pr of Amer.
Leonard, Elmore. Bandits. 384p. 1988. mass mkt. 5.99 (*0-446-30130-2*, Mysterious Paperbk) Warner Bks.
— Bandits. large type ed. 382p. 1987. lib. bdg. 18.95 (*0-8161-4297-1*) G K Hall.
— Bounty Hunters. 1993. mass mkt. 3.99 (*0-440-21306-1*) Dell.
— Cat Chaser. 288p. 1995. pap. 4.99 (*0-380-64642-0*) Avon.
— City Primeval: High Noon in Detroit. 224p. 1982. pap. 3.95 (*0-380-56952-3*) Avon.
— Elmore Leonard: Three Complete Novels. 576p. 1992. 11.99 (*0-517-06492-8*, Pub. by Wings Bks) Random Hse Value.
— Escape from Five Shadows. (Orig.). 1994. mass mkt. 4.50 (*0-440-21333-9*) Dell.
— Fifty-Two Pick-Up. 192p. 1995. pap. 4.99 (*0-380-65490-3*) Avon.
— Freaky Deaky. 1989. mass mkt. 5.95 (*0-446-35039-7*) Warner Bks.
— Get Shorty. 1991. mass mkt. 5.99 (*0-440-20980-3*) Dell.
— Get Shorty. large type ed. 1990. pap. 21.95 (*0-385-30150-2*, Delacorte LT) BDD LT Grp.
— Get Shorty. large type ed. LC 93-1992. 1993. pap. 17.95 (*0-8161-5809-6*) Hall.
— Glitz. 368p. 1987. mass mkt. 5.99 (*0-446-34343-9*) Warner Bks.
— Gold Coast. (Orig.). 1990. mass mkt. 5.99 (*0-440-20832-7*) Dell.
— Hombre. limited ed. LC 89-18329. 192p. 1990. reprint ed. Limited edition. 75.00 (*0-922890-15-3*) Armchair Detective.
— Hombre. LC 89-18329. 192p. 1990. reprint ed. 17.95 (*0-922890-04-8*); reprint ed. Collector edition. 25.00 (*0-922890-08-0*) Armchair Detective.
— The Hunted. 240p. 1986. mass mkt. 3.95 (*0-445-40204-0*, Mysterious Paperbk) Warner Bks.
— Killshot. large type ed. (General Ser.). 432p. 1990. reprint ed. 20.95 (*0-8161-4865-1*, Large Print Bks) G K Hall.
— Killshot. 352p. 1990. reprint ed. mass mkt. 5.95 (*0-446-35041-9*) Warner Bks.
— LaBrava. 256p. 1995. mass mkt. 4.99 (*0-380-69237-6*) Avon.
— Last Stand At Saber River. 1994. mass mkt. 4.50 (*0-440-21336-3*) Dell.
— Last Stand at Saber River. 1994. reprint ed. lib. bdg. 29.95 (*1-56849-301-0*) Buccaneer Bks.
— Law at Randado. (Orig.). 1994. mass mkt. 3.99 (*0-440-21308-8*) Dell.
— Maximum Bob. 1992. mass mkt. 5.99 (*0-440-21218-9*) Dell.
— Maximum Bob. large type ed. 416p. 1991. pap. 23.50 (*0-385-30456-0*, Delacorte LT) BDD LT Grp.
— Maximum Bob. large type ed. LC 93-40532. 1994. write for info. (*0-8161-5808-8*) G K Hall.
— Maximum Bob. limited ed. 304p. 1991. 100.00 (*0-385-30493-5*) Delacorte.
— The Moonshine War. 1985. mass mkt. 4.99 (*0-440-15807-9*) Dell.
— Mr. Majestyk. 192p. 1986. mass mkt. 4.99 (*0-445-40228-8*, Mysterious Paperbk) Warner Bks.
— Notebooks. deluxe ed. 60p. 1990. 50.00 (*0-935716-52-1*) Lord John.
— Pronto. LC 93-2999. 1993. 21.95 (*0-385-30846-9*) Delacorte.
— Pronto. 1995. mass mkt. 5.99 (*0-440-21443-2*) Dell.
— Pronto. large type ed. 1993. 27.95 (*0-385-31087-0*) Delacorte.
— Riding the Rap. LC 94-38211. 294p. 1995. 21.95 (*0-385-30847-7*) Delacorte.
— Riding the Rap. large type ed. 1995. 26.95 (*1-56895-224-4*) Wheeler Pub.
— Rum Punch. 1992. 21.00 (*0-385-30143-X*) Delacorte.
— Rum Punch. 1993. mass mkt. 6.50 (*0-440-21415-7*) Dell.
— Rum Punch. large type ed. 1992. 25.00 (*0-385-30765-9*, Delacorte LT) BDD LT Grp.
— Rum Punch. large type ed. LC 93-35521. (General Ser.). 1994. pap. 17.95 (*0-8161-5807-X*, Large Print Bks) Hall.
— Split Images. 288p. 1983. mass mkt. 4.95 (*0-380-63107-5*) Avon.
— Stick. 304p. 1995. mass mkt. 4.99 (*0-380-67652-4*) Avon.
— Swag. 1984. mass mkt. 4.99 (*0-440-18424-X*) Dell.
— Switch. 1990. mass mkt. 4.99 (*0-440-20831-9*) Dell.
— The Switch. large type ed. LC 93-24852. 258p. 1993. pap. 16.95 (*0-8161-5653-0*) Hall.
— Touch. 240p. 1988. mass mkt. 4.50 (*0-380-70386-6*) Avon.
— Unknown Man, No. 89. 272p. 1984. pap. 3.95 (*0-380-67041-0*) Avon.
— Unknown Man, No. 89. limited ed. 276p. 1993. reprint ed. 75.00 (*1-56287-049-1*) Armchair Detective.
— Unknown Man, No. 89. 276p. 1993. reprint ed. 20.00 (*1-56287-050-5*) Armchair Detective.
— Unknown Man Number 89. large type ed. LC 92-35897. (General Ser.). 379p. 1993. pap. 16.95 (*0-8161-5696-4*, Large Print Bks) Hall.
— Valdez Is Coming. 1993. reprint ed. lib. bdg. 21.95 (*1-56849-176-X*) Buccaneer Bks.
— Valdez Is Coming. 1994. reprint ed. lib. bdg. 27.95 (*1-56849-300-2*) Buccaneer Bks.
Leonard, Elmore, intro. The Big Bounce. LC 88-38210. 208p. 1989. reprint ed. 25.00 (*0-922890-00-5*); reprint ed. 18.95 (*0-922890-05-6*) Armchair Detective.
Leonard, Eugenie. Concerning Our Girls & What They Tell Us: A Study of Some Phases of the Confidential Relationship of Mothers & Adolescent Daughters. LC 75-176986. (Columbia University. Teachers College. Contributions to Education Ser.: No. 430). reprint ed. 37.50 (*0-404-55430-X*) AMS Pr.
Leonard, Eva, jt. auth. see Downton, Joseph.
Leonard, Fannie A., jt. auth. see Leonard, Justin W.
Leonard, Frances. Money & the Mature Woman: How to Hold on to Your Income, Keep Your Home, Plan Your Estate. LC 92-34822. 1993. 19.18 (*0-201-60897-9*) Addison-Wesley.
— Time Is Money: Use Your Youth to Make a Million. 1995. pap. write for info. (*0-201-40962-3*) Addison-Wesley.
— Women & Money at 40: The Independent Woman's Guide to Financial Security for Life. 1991. pap. 12.45 (*0-201-55097-0*) Addison-Wesley.
Leonard, Frances M. Laughter in the Courts of Love: Comedy in Allegory, from Chaucer to Spencer. LC 81-10676. 184p. 1981. 18.95 (*0-937664-54-5*) Pilgrim Bks OK.
Leonard, Francis. Money & the Mature Woman: How to Hold on to Your Income, Keep Your Home, Plan Your Estate. (Illus.). 288p. 1994. pap. 11.49 (*0-201-62700-0*) Addison-Wesley.
Leonard, Garry. Reading Dubliners Again: A Lacanian Perspective. (Irish Studies). 260p. 1993. text ed. 45.00 (*0-8156-2574-X*) Syracuse U Pr.
Leonard, Garry M. Reading Dubliners Again: A Lacanian Perspective. LC 92-33860. (Irish Studies). 384p. (C). 1993. pap. text ed. 18.95 (*0-8156-2600-2*) Syracuse U Pr.
Leonard, Gary. Eucalypts: A Bushwalker's Guide. pap. 17.95 (*0-86840-340-7*, Pub. by New South Wales Univ Pr AT) Intl Spec Bk.
Leonard, George. Education & Ecstasy: With the Great School Reform Hoax. rev. ed. 288p. 1987. text ed. 25.00 (*1-55643-007-8*); pap. 12.95 (*1-55643-005-1*) North Atlantic.
— Mastery: The Keys to Long-Term Success & Fulfillment. 192p. 1992. reprint ed. pap. 9.00 (*0-452-26756-0*, Plume) NAL-Dutton.
— The Ultimate Athlete: Revisioning Sports, Physical Education & the Body. 280p. 1990. reprint ed. pap. 12.95 (*1-55643-076-0*) North Atlantic.
***Leonard, George & Murphy, Michael.** The Life We Are Given: A Comprehensive Program for Altering Your Body & Transforming Your Life Through Disciplined Practice. LC 95-8623. 1995. write for info. (*0-87477-792-5*) J P Tarcher.
Leonard, George B. The Transformation: A Guide to the Inevitable Changes in Humankind. LC 80-53151. 288p. 1987. pap. 8.95 (*0-87477-169-2*) J P Tarcher.
Leonard, George J. Into the Light of Things: The Art of the Commonplace from Wordsworth to John Cage. LC 93-24555. (C). 1994. 24.95 (*0-226-47252-3*) U Ch Pr.
— Into the Light of Things: The Art of the Commonplace from Wordsworth to John Cage. (Literary Studies Art Philosophy). 250p. 1995. pap. text ed. 15.95 (*0-226-47253-1*) U Ch Pr.
Leonard, Gladys O. My Life in Two Worlds. LC 92-26512. (Collector's Library of the Unknown). (Illus.). 300p. 1992. reprint ed. write for info. (*0-8094-8116-2*); reprint ed. lib. bdg. write for info. (*0-8094-8117-0*) Time-Life.
Leonard, Glen M., jt. auth. see Allen, James B.
Leonard, Grant. Harley Davidson. 1993. 6.98 (*1-55521-862-8*) Bk Sales Inc.
Leonard, H. Jeffrey. Pollution & the Struggle for the World Product: Multinational Corporations, Environment, & International Comparative Advantage. (Illus.). 1988. 69.95 (*0-521-34042-X*) Cambridge U Pr.
Leonard, H. Jeffrey, ed. Divesting Nature's Capital: The Political Economy of Environmental Abuse in the Third World. LC 83-18534. 350p. 1985. 59.50 (*0-8419-0897-4*) Holmes & Meier.
Leonard, H. Jeffrey, et al. Environment & the Poor: Development Strategies for a Common Agenda. Feinberg, Richard E. & Kallab, Valeriana, eds. (U. S. Third World Policy Perspective Ser.: No. 11). 192p. 1989. 32.95 (*0-88738-282-7*); pap. 17.95 (*0-88738-786-1*) Transaction Pubs.
Leonard, Hal. The Best Songs Ever. rev. ed. (Best Ever Ser.). 264p. (Orig.). 1995. pap. 19.95 (*0-7935-0445-7*, HL00359224) H Leonard.
— Birth of Rock N' Roll: From Rhythm & Blues to Rockabilly, From the Roots of Rock to Elvis. (Piano-Vocal-Guitar History of Rock Ser.). 136p. (Orig.). 1991. pap. 12.95 (*0-88188-995-4*, HL00490216) H Leonard.
— The Christmas Card Songbook: Featuring Designs from the Hallmark Collection. (Illus.). 224p. 1991. 24.95 (*0-7935-0383-3*, 00183000); pap. 19.95 (*0-7935-0384-1*, 00183001) H Leonard.
— Disney Babies Songbook. Date not set. pap. 12.95 (*0-7935-0746-4*, HL00311512) H Leonard.
— Disney Children's Favorites Songbook. (Illus.). 112p. (J). 1991. pap. 12.95 (*0-7935-0090-7*, 00490496) H Leonard.
— Disney Children's Songbook. 1993. pap. 12.95 (*0-7935-0084-2*, HL00490489) H Leonard.
— Disney Family Fun Activity Book. (Illus.). 80p. (J). 1991. pap. 12.95 (*0-7935-0755-3*, 00290344) H Leonard.
— History of Rock: Early 60s. (Piano-Vocal-Guitar Ser.). 184p. 1991. pap. 14.95 (*0-7935-0020-6*, HL00490322) H Leonard.
— History of Rock: Late 50s. 1991. pap. 14.95 (*0-7935-0019-2*, HL00490321) H Leonard.
— New Age Piano Solos. 48p. 1992. pap. 6.95 (*0-7935-1078-3*, 00221008) H Leonard.
— Rodgers & Hammerstein Rediscovered. 40p. 1990. pap. 7.95 (*0-7935-0010-9*, 00490286) H Leonard.
— Songs of the 80's. (Decade Ser.). 1990. pap. 14.95 (*0-88188-875-3*, HL00490275) H Leonard.
Leonard, Hal, Publishing Staff. Buddy Holly Golden Anniversary Songbook. 1991. 14.95 (*0-88188-557-6*, HL00383750) H Leonard.
— Great Songs of Madison Avenue. 1991. 14.95 (*0-88188-238-0*, HL00657060) H Leonard.
— New Kids on the Block - Step by Step. 1991. pap. 14.95 (*0-7935-0077-X*, HL00490443) H Leonard.
Leonard, Harry, ed. J. N. Andrews: The Man & the Mission. LC 85-71649. 368p. (Orig.). 1985. pap. 16.99 (*0-943872-91-X*) Andrews Univ Pr.
Leonard, Henry B. The Open Gates: The Protest Against the Movement to Restrict European Immigration, 1896-1924. Cordasco, Francesco, ed. LC 80-875. (American Ethnic Groups Ser.). 1981. lib. bdg. 35.95 (*0-405-13437-1*) Ayer.
Leonard, Herman. The Eye of Jazz: The Jazz Photographs of Herman Leonard. LC 88-51495. (Illus.). 160p. 1990. 35.00 (*0-670-82771-1*, Viking) Viking Penguin.
— History of the Oregon Territory from its First Discovery up to the Present Time. 88p. 1980. 12.00 (*0-87770-230-6*) Ye Galleon.
Leonard, Herman B. By Choice or By Chance? Tracking the Values in Massachusetts' Public Spending. (Pioneer Paper Ser.: No. 6). 168p. (Orig.). 1992. pap. 10.00 (*0-929930-08-8*) Pioneer Inst.
Leonard, Hugh. Out after Dark. 192p. 1991. 24.95 (*0-233-98474-7*, Pub. by A Deutsch UK) Trafalgar.

— Parnell & the Englishwoman. 256p. 1991. text ed. 19.95 (*0-689-12127-X*, Atheneum S&S) S&S Trade.

— Selected Plays of Hugh Leonard. LC 91-25924. (Irish Drama Selections Ser.). 464p. 1992. text ed. 49.95 (*0-8132-0759-2*); pap. 14.95 (*0-8132-0760-6*) Cath U Pr.

Leonard, Ira M. & Parmet, Robert D. American Nativism, Eighteen Thirty to Eighteen Sixty. LC 71-156750. (Anvil Ser.). 192p. 1971. pap. 10.50 (*0-88275-901-9*) Krieger.

Leonard, Irving. Portraits & Essays: Historical & Literary Sketches of Early Spanish America. Lathrop, Thomas et al, eds. 157p. 1986. pap. 10.50 (*0-936388-34-X*) Juan de la Cuesta.

Leonard, Irving, ed. Colonial Travelers in Latin America. 236p. 1986. 15.00 (*0-936388-29-3*); pap. 10.50 (*0-936388-30-7*) Juan de la Cuesta.

Leonard, Irving A. Baroque Times in Old Mexico: Seventeenth-Century Persons, Places, & Practices. (Illus.). 1959. pap. 16.95 (*0-472-06110-0*, 110, Ann Arbor Bks) U of Mich Pr.

— Baroque Times in Old Mexico: Seventeenth-Century Persons, Places, & Practices. LC 80-29256. (Illus.). xi, 260p. 1981. reprint ed. text ed. 59.75 (*0-313-22826-4*, LEBT, Greenwood Pr) Greenwood.

— Books of the Brave: Being an Account of Books & of Men in the Spanish Conquest & Settlement of the Sixteenth-Century New World. (C). 1992. 45.00 (*0-520-07990-6*); pap. 16.00 (*0-520-07816-0*) U CA Pr.

— The Florida Adventures of Kirk Munroe. LC 75-21373. (Illus.). 213p. 1975. 11.75 (*0-913122-07-6*) Mickler Hse.

— Mercurio Volante of Don Carlos De Siguenza Y Gongora. LC 67-24715. (Quivira Society Publications, Vol. 3). 1967. reprint ed. 19.95 (*0-405-00073-1*) Ayer.

Leonard, Irving A., ed. Spanish Approach to Pensacola 1689-1693. LC 67-24720. (Quivira Society Publications: Vol. 9). 1967. reprint ed. 19.95 (*0-405-00083-9*) Ayer.

Leonard, Irving A., ed. see De Bibar, Geronimo.

Leonard, Irving A., tr. see Picon-Salas, Mariano.

Leonard, Isabel A., tr. see Maurette, Michel.

Leonard, Isabel A., tr. see Olomucki, Martin.

Leonard, J. A., jt. ed. see Mintzer, Irving.

Leonard, J. E. Come Out of Her, My People: A Study of the Revelation to John. 208p. 1991. pap. 9.75 (*1-884454-00-3*) Laudemont Pr.

— Heritage from the Lord: The Place of Children in Worship. 48p. 1993. pap. 4.95 (*1-884454-02-X*) Laudemont Pr.

— I Will Be Their God: Understanding the Covenant. 160p. 1992. pap. 7.95 (*1-884454-01-1*) Laudemont Pr.

— Processions of God: The Significance of Ceremony. 28p. 1992. pap. 3.95 (*1-884454-03-8*) Laudemont Pr.

Leonard, J. W., III, ed. Coal Preparation. 5th ed. LC 91-61678. (Illus.). 1131p. (C). 1991. 83.50 (*0-87335-104-5*) SMM&E Inc.

Leonard, Jack & Shapira, Sid. The Time of My Life. (Illus.). 189p. 1993. 14.95 (*0-9639900-0-4*) Drumalee.

Leonard, James S., ed. Author-ity & Textuality: Current Views of Collaborative Writing. LC 94-15111. (Locust Hill Literary Studies: No. 14). (Illus.). 254p. (C). 1994. lib. bdg. 30.00 (*0-933951-57-4*) Locust Hill Pr.

Leonard, James S., et al, eds. Satire or Evasion? Black Perspectives on Huckleberry Finn. LC 91-14315. 288p. 1991. lib. bdg. 45.00 (*0-8223-1163-1*); pap. text ed. 19.95 (*0-8223-1174-7*) Duke.

Leonard, James V., jt. auth. see Zobrist, George W.

Leonard, Jane K. Controlling from Afar: The Daoguahg Emperor's Management of the Grand Canal Crisis, 1824-1826. (Michigan Monographs in Chinese Studies: No. 69). 1994. write for info. (*0-89264-114-2*); pap. write for info. (*0-89264-115-0*) Ctr Chinese Studies.

— Wei Yuan & China's Rediscovery of the Maritime World. (East Asian Monographs: No. 111). (Illus.). 300p. 1984. 30.00 (*0-674-94855-6*) HUP.

— Wei Yuan & China's Rediscovery of the Maritime World. (Harvard East Asian Monographs: No. 111). (Illus.). 300p. 1983. 20.00 (*0-317-01568-0*) Harvard E Asian.

Leonard, Jane K. & Watt, John, eds. To Achieve Security & Wealth: The Qing Imperial State & the Economy, 1644-1911. (Cornell East Asia Ser.: No. 56). (Illus.). 206p. (Orig.). (C). 1993. pap. 10.00 (*0-939657-56-2*) Cornell East Asia Pgm.

Leonard, Jason A., jt. ed. see Glenwick, David S.

Leonard, Jerry D., ed. Legal Studies As Cultural Studies: A Reader in (Post) Modern Critical Theory. LC 94-9240. 392p. (C). 1995. 59.50 (*0-7914-2295-X*); pap. 19.95 (*0-7914-2296-8*) State U NY Pr.

Leonard, Jim, Jr. And They Dance Real Slow in Jackson. 91p. 1986. pap. 4.75 (*0-8222-0045-7*) Dramatists Play.

Leonard, Jim & Laut, Phil. Vivation: The Science of Enjoying All of Your Life. Orig. Title: Rebirthing: The Science of Enjoying all of Your Life. 320p. 1991. pap. 12.95 (*0-9610132-4-9*) Vivation Pub.

Leonard, JoAnn K. A Wedding Planner for Brides: Questions You Need to Ask When Planning the Perfect Wedding. 190p. 1991. pap. 24.95 (*0-9629412-5-5*) Garnet Rose.

Leonard, Joe, Jr., jt. auth. see Olson, Richard P.

Leonard, John. The Last Innocent White Man in America & Other Writings. LC 92-50838. 320p. 1993. 21.95 (*1-56584-072-0*) New Press NY.

— Naming in Paradise: Milton & the Language of Adam & Eve. 318p. 1990. 69.00 (*0-19-812958-0*) OUP.

— Science of Coaching Swimming. LC 91-12705. (Science of Coaching Ser.). (Illus.). 168p. (Orig.). 1992. text ed. 19.95 (*0-88011-450-9*, PLEO0450) Human Kinetics.

Leonard, John, jt. auth. see American Sport Education Program Staff.

Leonard, John, jt. auth. see Frumkin, Lyn.

Leonard, John, jt. auth. see Mitchell, Nathan D.

Leonard, John J. Directed Sonar Sensing for Mobile Robot Navigation. (International Series in Engineering & Computer Science, VLSI, Computer Architecture, & Digital Screen Processing). 208p. (C). 1992. lib. bdg. 75.50 (*0-7923-9242-6*) Kluwer Ac.

***Leonard, John L.** Yum! Irresistible, Fun-to-Create, Reliable Recipes. LC 95-94321. (Illus.). 394p. 1995. 17.95 (*0-9646465-5-2*) Heron Hill Pr.

Leonard, John M., jt. auth. see Frumkin, Lyn R.

Leonard, John W. Tension Structures: Behavior & Analysis. LC 87-3950. 416p. 1988. text ed. 60.00 (*0-07-037226-8*) McGraw.

Leonard, Jonathan N. Crusaders of Chemistry. LC 72-8533. (Essay Index Reprint Ser.). 1977. reprint ed. 26.95 (*0-8369-7320-8*) Ayer.

Leonard, Joseph A. History of Olmsted County, Minnesota. (Illus.). 674p. 1994. reprint ed. lib. bdg. 67.50 (*0-8328-3836-5*) Higginson Bk Co.

Leonard, Joseph M. Pocket Power, No. 1: Medical. 48p. (Orig.). 1988. pap. 2.95 (*0-945893-00-0*) Pocket Power.

Leonard, Joseph M., jt. auth. see Augustine, John L.

Leonard, Joseph M., jt. auth. see Brannon, Wayne A.

Leonard, Joseph M., ed. see Burnette, Allyson C.

Leonard, Joseph M., ed. see Leonard, Lois L.

Leonard, Joseph M., ed. see Stoodt, Douglas A.

Leonard, Joseph W., jt. ed. see Humphreys, Kenneth K.

Leonard, Justin W. & Leonard, Fannie A. Mayflies of Michigan Trout Streams. LC 62-9726. (Bulletin Ser.: No. 43). 139p. 1962. pap. 8.50 (*0-87737-020-6*) Cranbrook.

Leonard, Karen I. Making Ethnic Choices: California's Punjabi Mexican Americans. (Asian American History & Culture Ser.). 368p. (C). 1994. 49.95 (*0-87722-890-6*); pap. 18.95 (*1-56639-202-0*) Temple U Pr.

— Social History of an Indian Caste: The Kayasths of Hyderabad. (C). 1995. 16.00x (*81-250-0032-1*, Pub. by UBS Pubs Dist II) S Asia.

— Social History of an Indian Caste: The Kayasths of Hyderabad. LC 76-52031. (Illus.). 371p. reprint ed. pap. 105.80 (*0-7837-4846-9*, 2044493) Bks Demand.

Leonard, Kay. How to Read a Painting: Lessons in Proportion, Balance & Symmetry. (Illus.). 102p. 1988. student ed 8.95 (*0-685-26429-7*) Eye Cue.

— Paper Kaleidoscopes. (Illus.). 40p. (J). (gr. k-12). 1989. pap. 5.95 (*0-685-26430-0*) Eye Cue.

Leonard, Kenneth E., jt. ed. see Blane, Howard T.

***Leonard, Kimberly K., et al, eds.** Minorities in Juvenile Justice. 232p. (C). 1995. 45.00 (*0-8039-7264-4*); pap. 21.95 (*0-8039-7265-2*) Sage.

Leonard, Larry. Far Walker. LC 88-12290. (Illus.). 120p. (J). (gr. 1 up). 1988. 12.95 (*0-932576-60-5*) Breitenbush Bks.

— Fishing the Lower Columbia: The Greatest Salmon Hole in the World. (Illus.). 64p. 1993. pap. 8.95 (*1-878175-53-X*) F Amato Pubns.

— The Meanest Fish on Earth. (Illus.). 102p. (Orig.). 1984. pap. 5.95 (*0-936608-29-3*) F Amato Pubns.

— Sturgeon Fishing. (Illus.). 1987. pap. 8.95 (*0-936608-57-9*) F Amato Pubns.

Leonard, Larry & McCormick, Jack, comps. Youth Program Hour Idea Book. 144p. 1985. pap. 7.95 (*0-8341-0949-2*) Beacon Hill.

Leonard, Laura. Finding Papa. LC 90-23742. 192p. (J). (gr. 3-7). 1991. text ed. 14.95 (*0-689-31526-0*, Atheneum Bks Young) S&S Childrens.

Leonard, Laura L. Energy-Generating Resources: Index of New Information. 150p. 1994. 44.50 (*0-7883-0026-1*); pap. 39.50 (*0-7883-0027-X*) ABBE Pubs Assn.

Leonard, Leah W. Jewish Cookery. (International Cookbook Ser.). 1949. 15.00 (*0-517-09758-3*, Crown) Crown Pub Group.

Leonard, Linda S. Meeting the Madwoman. 1994. pap. 12.95 (*0-553-37318-8*) Bantam.

— On the Way to the Wedding: Transforming the Love Relationship. LC 85-27888. 261p. 1987. pap. 11.00 (*0-87773-402-X*) Shambhala Pubns.

— Witness to the Fire: Creativity & the Veil of Addiction. LC 89-42634. 390p. 1990. pap. 20.00 (*0-87773-588-3*) Shambhala Pubns.

— The Wounded Woman: Healing the Father-Daughter Relationship. LC 83-42801. 179p. 1983. pap. 12.00 (*0-394-72183-7*) Shambhala Pubns.

— The Wounded Woman: Healing the Father-Daughter Relationship. LC 82-6289. xx, 186p. 1982. 24.95 (*0-8040-0397-1*) Swallow.

Leonard, Lois L. Pocket Power, No. 2: Taxes. Leonard, Joseph M., ed. 48p. (Orig.). 1988. pap. text ed. 2.95 (*0-945893-01-9*) Pocket Power.

Leonard, M. Leonard Memorial: Genealogy, History, & Biography of Solomon Leonard; 1637, of Duxbury & Bridgewater, Mass., & Some of His Descendants. (Illus.). 454p. 1989. reprint ed. lib. bdg. 76.00 (*0-8328-0765-6*); reprint ed. pap. 68.00 (*0-8328-0766-4*) Higginson Bk Co.

Leonard, M. C., ed. The Illustrated Guide to the Florida West Coast. (Illus.). 64p. (Orig.). 1992. pap. text ed. 3.95 (*0-9634223-0-8*) Purple Islands.

Leonard, Mack. Another Front: A Novel of World War II. 165p. 1976. 8.95 (*0-87881-036-6*); pap. 3.95 (*0-87881-037-4*) Mojave Bks.

— From Love to Love. 140p. 1975. 6.95 (*0-87881-023-4*) Mojave Bks.

Leonard, Madeleine. Informal Economic Activity in Belfast. 224p. 1994. 555.95 (*1-85628-478-6*, Pub. by Avebury Pub UK) Ashgate Pub Co.

Leonard, Marcia. Alphabet Bandits: An ABC Book. LC 89-4933. (Illus.). 24p. (J). (gr. k-2). 1990. lib. bdg. 9.59 (*0-8167-1718-4*); pap. text ed. 2.50 (*0-8167-1719-2*) Troll Assocs.

— Bear's Busy Year: A Book about Seasons. LC 89-4946. (Illus.). 24p. (J). (gr. k-2). 1990. lib. bdg. 9.59 (*0-8167-1720-6*); pap. text ed. 2.50 (*0-8167-1721-4*) Troll Assocs.

— Best Snowman Ever. 10p. (J). (ps). 1989. Bk. & ornament. pap. 2.95 (*0-8167-1488-6*) Troll Assocs.

— Birthday in a Bathtub. Brook, Bonnie, ed. (What Next Ser.). (Illus.). 24p. (J). (ps-1). 1989. 4.95 (*0-671-68592-9*); lib. bdg. 6.95 (*0-671-68588-0*) Silver Pr.

— Counting Kangaroos, A Book about Numbers. LC 89-4960. (Illus.). 24p. (J). (gr. k-2). 1990. lib. bdg. 9.59 (*0-8167-1722-2*); pap. text ed. 2.50 (*0-8167-1723-0*) Troll Assocs.

— The Elves & the Shoemaker. Brook, Bonnie, ed. (What's Missing? Ser.). (Illus.). 24p. (J). (ps-1). 1990. 4.95 (*0-671-69351-4*); lib. bdg. 6.95 (*0-671-69347-6*) Silver Pr.

— The Giant Baby & Other Giant Tales. LC 93-6225. (Hello Reader! Ser.: Level 4). (Illus.). (J). 1994. pap. 3.50 (*0-590-46892-8*) Scholastic Inc.

— Goldilocks & the Three Bears. Brook, Bonnie, ed. (What's Missing? Ser.). (Illus.). 24p. (J). (ps-1). 1990. 4.95 (*0-671-69350-6*); lib. bdg. 6.95 (*0-671-69346-8*) Silver Pr.

— Gregory & Mr. Grump. Brook, Bonnie, ed. (How Did That Happen? Ser.). (Illus.). 24p. (J). (ps-1). 1990. 4.95 (*0-671-70406-0*); lib. bdg. 6.95 (*0-671-70402-8*) Silver Pr.

— Hannah the Hamster Hunter. Brook, Bonnie, ed. (How Did That Happen? Ser.). (Illus.). 24p. (J). (ps-1). 1990. 4.95 (*0-671-70404-4*); lib. bdg. 6.95 (*0-671-70399-4*) Silver Pr.

— Haunted House. (J). 1989. bds. 2.95 (*0-8167-1889-X*) Troll Assocs.

— How Did That Happen? Series, 4 vols., Set. (Illus.). 96p. (J). (ps-1). 1990. 19.80 (*0-671-31235-9*); lib. bdg. 27.80 (*0-671-31234-0*) Silver Pr.

— Is That You, Amy? (Here Come the Brownies, Brownie Girl Scout Bks.: No. 8). (Illus.). 64p. (J). (gr. 1-4). 1994. lib. bdg. 7.99 (*0-448-40840-6*, G&D); pap. 3.95 (*0-448-40839-2*, G&D) Putnam Pub Group.

— Jeffrey Lee, Future Fireman. Brook, Bonnie, ed. LC 90-31299. (How Did That Happen? Ser.). (Illus.). 24p. (J). (ps-1). 1990. 4.95 (*0-671-70407-9*); lib. bdg. 6.95 (*0-671-70403-6*) Silver Pr.

— King Lionheart's Castle. (What Belongs? Ser.). (Illus.). 24p. (J). (ps-1). 1992. 5.95 (*0-382-72974-9*); lib. bdg. 9.98 (*0-382-72973-0*) Silver.

— The Kitten Twins: A Book about Opposites. LC 89-4945. (Illus.). 24p. (J). (gr. k-2). 1990. lib. bdg. 9.59 (*0-8167-1724-9*); pap. text ed. 2.50 (*0-8167-1725-7*) Troll Assocs.

— Laura Jean the Yard Sale Queen. Brook, Bonnie, ed. LC 89-70304. (How Did That Happen? Ser.). (Illus.). 24p. (J). (ps-1). 1990. 4.95 (*0-671-70405-2*); lib. bdg. 6.95 (*0-671-70401-X*) Silver Pr.

— Marsha's Unbearable Day. LC 95-2652. (Here Come the Brownies Ser.: Vol. 10). (Illus.). 1995. write for info. (*0-448-40843-0*, G&D); lib. bdg. write for info. (*0-448-40844-9*, G&D) Putnam Pub Group.

— Midnight Cat. (J). 1989. bds. 2.95 (*0-8167-1887-3*) Troll Assocs.

— Noisy Neighbors: A Book about Animal Sounds. LC 89-4959. (Illus.). 24p. (J). (gr. k-2). 1990. lib. bdg. 9.59 (*0-8167-1726-5*); pap. text ed. 2.50 (*0-8167-1727-3*) Troll Assocs.

— Paintbox Penguins, A Book about Colors. LC 89-4979. (Illus.). 24p. (J). (gr. k-2). 1990. lib. bdg. 9.59 (*0-8167-1716-8*); pap. text ed. 2.50 (*0-8167-1717-6*) Troll Assocs.

— Pumpkin Magic. (J). 1989. bds. 2.95 (*0-8167-1888-1*) Troll Assocs.

— Rainboots for Breakfast. Brook, Bonnie, ed. (What Next Ser.). (Illus.). 24p. (J). (ps-1). 1989. 4.95 (*0-671-68591-0*); lib. bdg. 6.95 (*0-671-68587-2*) Silver Pr.

— Rumplestiltskin. Brook, Bonnie, ed. (What's Missing? Ser.). (Illus.). 24p. (J). (ps-1). 1990. 4.95 (*0-671-69352-2*); lib. bdg. 6.95 (*0-671-69348-4*) Silver Pr.

— Santa Bear. 1988. 2.95 (*0-8167-1495-9*) Troll Assocs.

— Shopping for Snowflakes. Brook, Bonnie, ed. (What Next Ser.). (Illus.). 24p. (J). (ps-1). 1989. 4.95 (*0-671-68594-5*); lib. bdg. 6.95 (*0-671-68590-2*) Silver Pr.

— Swimming in the Sand. Brook, Bonnie, ed. (What Next Ser.). (Illus.). 24p. (J). (ps-1). 1989. 4.95 (*0-671-68593-7*); lib. bdg. 6.95 (*0-671-68589-9*) Silver Pr.

— Take a Bow, Krissy! (Here Come the Brownies, Brownie Girl Scout Bks.: No. 7). (Illus.). 64p. (J). (gr. 1-4). 1994. lib. bdg. 7.99 (*0-448-40838-4*, G&D); pap. 3.95 (*0-448-40837-6*, G&D) Putnam Pub Group.

— The Three Little Pigs. Brook, Bonnie, ed. (What's Missing? Ser.). (Illus.). 24p. (J). (ps-1). 1990. 4.95 (*0-671-69349-2*); lib. bdg. 6.95 (*0-671-69345-X*) Silver Pr.

— Violet & the Pirates. (What Belongs? Ser.). (Illus.). 24p. (J). (ps-1). 1992. 4.95 (*0-671-72976-4*); lib. bdg. 6.95 (*0-671-72975-6*) Silver Pr.

— What Next?, 4 bks., Set. (Illus.). (J). (ps-1). 1990. 19.80 (*0-671-94102-X*, Julian Messner); lib. bdg. 39.92 (*0-671-94101-1*, Julian Messner) Silver Burdett Pr.

— What's Missing? Ser., 4 vols., Set. (Illus.). 96p. (J). (ps-1). 1990. 19.80 (*0-671-94433-9*); lib. bdg. 27.80 (*0-671-94432-0*) Silver Pr.

— Witches Brew. 1989. 2.95 (*0-8167-1886-5*) Troll Assocs.

Leonard, Margaret. Headgear for the Future. 1987. pap. 3.50 (*0-942396-43-X*) Blackberry ME.

Leonard, Mark, jt. auth. see Carr, Dawson.

Leonard, Mary K. Art for the Classroom Teacher. Cooper, William H., ed. LC 82-73585. (Illus.). 100p. (Orig.). (J). (gr. k-6). 1982. pap. text ed. 10.95 (*0-914127-00-4*) Univ Class.

Leonard, Maurice. Mae West: Empress of Sex. (Illus.). 424p. 1992. 22.50 (*1-55972-151-0*, Birch Ln Pr) Carol Pub Group.

Leonard, Michael. Badman. 1993. 16.95 (*0-533-10640-0*) Vantage.

Leonard, Michael E. Bible Puzzle Fun, 4 bks. (Illus.). 1989. pap. write for info. (*0-87403-528-7*, 2738); pap. write for info. (*0-87403-529-5*, 2739); pap. write for info. (*0-87403-530-9*, 2740); pap. write for info. (*0-87403-531-7*, 2741) Standard Pub.

— Bible Puzzle Fun, 4 bks., Set. (Illus.). 48p. 1989. pap. 3.99 (*0-318-43184-X*) Standard Pub.

***Leonard, Naomi E.** Using Metlab to Analyze & Design Control Systems. 2nd ed. (C). 1995. pap. text ed. 18.95 (*0-8053-2193-4*) Benjamin-Cummings.

Leonard, Neil. Jazz & the White Americans: The Acceptance of a New Art Form. LC 62-19626. 225p. reprint ed. pap. 64.20 (*0-685-15767-9*, 2026780) Bks Demand.

— Wellington's Army: Recreated in Color Photographs. (Illus.). 96p. 1994. pap. 19.95 (*1-872004-79-2*, Pub. by Windrow & Green UK) Motorbooks Intl.

Leonard, P. & Rommel, J. Lens Implantation. 1982. lib. bdg. 224.50 (*90-6193-804-X*) Kluwer Ac.

Leonard, Pamela & Hoffmann, Walter. Effective Global Environmental Protection: World Federalist Proposals to Strengthen the Role of the U. N. 42p. 1990. pap. 5.00 (*1-880533-00-6*) Wrld Federal.

Leonard, Pat. Damned If You Do. LC 93-90854. 260p. 1994. lib. bdg. 20.00 (*0-9632933-2-X*) Leonard Pubns.

— Proceed with Caution. LC 92-93411. 254p. 1992. lib. bdg. 19.95 (*0-9632933-0-3*) Leonard Pubns.

***Leonard, Paul.** Dancing the Code. (Dr. Who Ser.). (Illus.). Date not set. pap. 5.95 (*0-426-20441-7*, London Bridge) Genl Dist Srvs.

— Venusian Lullaby. (Dr. Who Ser.). (Illus.). Date not set. pap. 5.95 (*0-426-20424-7*, London Bridge) Genl Dist Srvs.

Leonard, Paul A. Commercial Bank Underwriting of Municipal Revenue Bonds. LC 82-4753. (Research for Business Decisions Ser.: No. 48). 107p. reprint ed. pap. 30.50 (*0-685-20848-6*, 2070080) Bks Demand.

Leonard, Paul H., jt. auth. see Boone, J. Allen.

Leonard, Peggy C. Building a Medical Vocabulary. 3rd ed. (Illus.). 560p. 1992. pap. text ed. 27.95 (*0-7216-4690-5*) Saunders.

— Quick & Easy Medical Terminology. 2nd ed. 352p. 1995. pap. text ed. 26.00 (*0-7216-5686-2*) Saunders.

Leonard, Peter. Records of a Voyage to the Western Coast of Africa in His Majesty's Ship Dryad & of Service on That Station for the Suppression of the Slave Trade in the Years 1830, 1831 & 1832. (B. E. Ser.: No. 154). 1833. 26.00 (*0-8115-3072-8*) Periodicals Srv.

— Saigon Guidebook. (Illus.). 96p. (Orig.). 1995. pap. 9.95 (*0-9645457-9-9*) VietnAm Trading.

Leonard, Peter, jt. ed. see McLaren, Peter.

Leonard, Phyllis. Choose, Use, Enjoy, Share: Library Media Skills for the Gifted Child. Montgomery, Paula K., ed. LC 85-4532. (Teaching Library Media Research & Information Skills Ser.). 153p. 1985. lib. bdg. 23.50 (*0-87287-417-6*) Libs Unl.

Leonard, R. Interpretation of English Noun Sequences on the Computer. (Linguistic Ser.: Vol. 51). 436p. 1984. 92.50 (*0-444-87658-8*, North Holland) Elsevier.

Leonard, R. C., jt. auth. see Roulston, J. E.

Leonard, R. E., et al. Backcountry Facilities: Design & Maintenance. (Illus.). 224p. 1980. pap. 9.95 (*0-910146-31-4*) AMC Books.

Leonard, R. F., jt. auth. see Bhasin, K. B.

Leonard, R. L. & Glassgold, C. A., eds. Modern American Design: By the American Union of Decorative Artists & Craftsmen. LC 92-74043. (Twentieth Century: Landmarks in Design Ser.: Vol. 2). (Illus.). 208p. 1993. reprint ed. 70.00 (*0-926494-01-5*) Acanthus Pr.

Leonard, R. M., ed. A Book of Light Verse. LC 71-168784. (Granger Index Reprint Ser.). 1977. reprint ed. 24.95 (*0-8369-6304-0*) Ayer.

Leonard, R. V., ed. see Gotliffe, Harvey L.

Leonard, Rebecca. The First Year Experience. 2nd ed. 92p. 1992. per. 9.95 (*0-8403-7905-6*) Kendall-Hunt.

Leonard, Richard. Apartheid Whitewash: South Africa Propaganda in the United States. 64p. 1989. pap. 5.00 (*0-685-39026-8*) Africa Fund.

— With Unveiled Face: Charismatic Christians & Fulfilled Eschatology. 44p. 1993. pap. 4.95 (*1-884454-04-6*) Laudemont Pr.

Leonard, Richard & Hill, Lawrence. South Africa at War: White Power & the Crisis in Southern Africa. 280p. (Orig.). 1983. 8.95 (*0-317-36642-4*) Africa Fund.

Leonard, Richard, jt. auth. see Zandl, Irma.

Leonard, Richard A. A History of Russian Music. LC 77-6760. 395p. 1977. reprint ed. text ed. 75.00 (*0-8371-9658-2*, LERM, Greenwood Pr) Greenwood.

— The Stream of Music: Music Book Index. 454p. 1993. reprint ed. lib. bdg. 99.00 (*0-7812-9581-5*) Rprt Serv.

Leonard, Robert. Swahili Phrasebook. 104p. (Orig.). 1988. pap. 2.95 (*0-86442-025-0*) Lonely Planet.

Leonard, Robert D. Anasazi Faunal Exploitation: Prehistoric Subsistence on Northern Black Mesa, Arizona. LC 88-70300. (Center for Archaeological Investigations Research Paper Ser.: No. 13). (Illus.). xiv, 218p. (Orig.). 1989. pap. 20.00 (*0-88104-069-X*) Center Archaeo.

Leonard, Robert D., jt. ed. see Wills, W. H.

Leonard, Robert E., jt. auth. see Mundis, Jerrold J.

***Leonard, Robert J.** Human Gross Anatomy: An Outline Text. 400p. 1995. pap. 24.95 (*0-19-509003-9*) OUP.

— Stupid Stories: Nonstop Nonsense for Children of All Ages. (Illus.). 108p. (Orig.). (J). (gr. 5-10). 1989. pap. 5.95 (*0-930753-05-4*) Spect Ln Pr.

An Asterisk (*) at the beginning of an entry indicates that the title is appearing in BIP for the first time.

Leonard, Robert T. & Hepler, Peter K., eds. Calcium in Plant Growth: Thirteenth Annual Symposium in Plant Physiology. LC 89-82676. (Current Topics in Plant Physiology: an American Society of Plant Physiologists Ser.: Vol. IV). (Illus.). 275p. (Orig.). 1990. pap. 25.00 (0-943088-18-6) Am Soc of Plant.

***Leonard, Robin.** Chapter 13 Bankruptcy: Repay Your Debts. 400p. 1995. pap. 29.95 (0-614-02567-2) Nolo Pr.

— Money Troubles: Legal Strategies to Cope with Your Debts. 3rd ed. LC 94-36930. (Illus.). 360p. 1995. pap. 18.95 (0-87337-286-7) Nolo Pr.

— Nolo's Law Form Kit: Rebuild Your Credit. 1993. pap. 14.95 (0-87337-205-0) Nolo Pr.

Leonard, Robin, ed. see Ihara, Toni & Warner, Ralph.

Leonard, Robin D. & Elias, Stephen R. Nolo's Pocket Guide to Family Law. 3rd ed. (Illus.). 255p. 1994. pap. 14.95 (0-87337-217-4) Nolo Pr.

Leonard, Roger K. Triptychos by Thrice by Thrice. 76p. 1993. write for info. (0-9637851-0-9) R K Leonard.

Leonard, Rosa M., ed. see Deans, Mary L.

Leonard, S. J. Thirty Years after the War. LC 92-61970. 104p. (Orig.). 1994. pap. 9.00 (1-56002-217-5, Univ Edtns) Aegina Pr.

Leonard, Sam. Mediation: the Book: A Step-by-Step Guide for Dispute Resolvers. (Illus.). 208p. (Orig.). 1994. pap. 19.95 (1-879260-25-5) Evanston Pub.

Leonard, Scott, jt. ed. see Knowles, Sebastian.

Leonard, Sheldon. And the Show Goes On: Broadway & Hollywood Adventures. LC 94-40934. (Illus.). 256p. 1995. 25.00 (0-87910-184-9) Limelight Edns.

Leonard, Stephen J. Trials & Triumphs: A Colorado Portrait of the Great Depression, with FSA Photographs. (Illus.). 272p. 1993. 29.95 (0-87081-311-0) Univ Pr Colo.

Leonard, Stephen J. & Noel, Thomas J. Denver: From Mining Camp to Metropolis. (Illus.). 512p. 1990. 39.95 (0-87081-185-1) Univ Pr Colo.

— Denver: Mining Camp to Metropolis. (Illus.). 560p. 1991. pap. 19.95 (0-87081-240-8) Univ Pr Colo.

Leonard, Stephen T. Critical Theory in Political Practice. 318p. 1990. text ed. 42.50 (0-691-07840-8) Princeton U Pr.

Leonard, Susan & Munde, Gail. At the Movies with Bad Dog: Using Nontraditional Film & Video with Children. (Illus.). xii, 160p. (Orig.). (C). 1989. 15.95 (0-87520-001-X) AFVA.

***Leonard, Tara.** 50 Ways to Resist the Urge to Smoke. (Illus.). 6p. 1995. write for info. (1-56885-061-1) Journeyworks Pub.

— The Tobacco Quiz. (Illus.). 6p. 1995. write for info. (1-56885-060-3) Journeyworks Pub.

— Truth or Lies? Young Women & Smoking. (Illus.). 6p. 1995. write for info. (1-56885-063-8) Journeyworks Pub.

Leonard, Ted. Neath the Midnight Sun. abr. ed. 192p. 1995. pap. 7.95 (1-56901-407-8) NW Pub.

Leonard, Ted H. Now! We're Having Fun: Humorous Anecdotes of Life on the Last Frontier. 160p. 1994. pap. 9.50 (0-9641553-0-3) Alaska Wrdwrks.

Leonard, Thom. The Bread Book: A Natural, Whole-Grain Seed-to-Loaf Approach to Real Bread. 128p. 1990. pap. 8.95 (0-936184-09-4) E W-Nat Hlth Bks.

Leonard, Thomas, et al. Day by Day: The Seventies, 2 vols., Set. (Day by Day Ser.). (Illus.). 1328p. 1988. 195.00 (0-8160-1020-X) Facts on File.

Leonard, Thomas C. News at the Hearth: A Drama of Reading in Nineteenth-Century America. 1993. pap. 7.00 (0-944026-42-7) Am Antiquarian.

— News for All: America's Coming-of-Age with the Press. (Illus.). 320p. 1995. 30.00 (0-19-506454-2) OUP.

— The Power of the Press: The Birth of American Political Reporting. (Illus.). 288p. 1987. pap. 9.95 (0-19-505184-X) OUP.

Leonard, Thomas M. Central America & the United States: The Search for Stability. LC 90-24818. (United States & the Americas Ser.). 256p. 1991. 35.00 (0-8203-1320-3); pap. 15.00 (0-8203-1321-1) U of Ga Pr.

— Day by Day: The Forties. (Day by Day Ser). (Illus.). 1072p. 1977. lib. bdg. 125.00 (0-87196-375-2) Facts on File.

— A Guide to Central American Collections in the United States. LC 94-10359. (Reference Guides to Archival & Manuscript Sources in World History Ser.: No. 3). 200p. 1994. text ed. 65.00 (0-313-28689-2, Greenwood Pr) Greenwood.

— Panama, the Canal, & the United States: A Guide to Issues & References. LC 93-26255. (Guides to Contemporary Issues Ser.: No. 9). 1993. 21.95 (0-941690-55-5); pap. 11.95 (0-941690-56-3) Regina Bks.

— The United States & Central America, 1944-1949: Perceptions of Political Dynamics. LC 83-5032. (Illus.). xii, 227p. 1984. 26.50 (0-8173-0190-9) U of Ala Pr.

Leonard, Timothy. Geno: A Biography of Eugene Walsh, SS. 1988. pap. 12.95 (0-318-41386-8) Pastoral Pr.

Leonard, Tom. On the Mass Bombing of Kuwait, Commonly Known As the "Gulf War" 24p. (Orig.). 1992. pap. 4.00 (1-873176-25-2, AK Pr San Fran) AK Pr Dist.

Leonard, V. A. & More, Harry W. Police Organization & Management. 7th ed. (Police Science Ser.). 568p. (C). 1986. text ed. 28.95 (0-88277-344-5) Foundation Pr.

— Police Organization & Management. 8th ed. (Police Science Ser.). 650p. (C). 1993. text ed. 34.95 (1-56662-049-X) Foundation Pr.

Leonard, Vincent F., Jr. Analog Circuit Design. Fry, Jim, ed. LC 84-21727. (Circuit Design Ser.). (Illus.). 750p. 1984. ring bd. 69.95 (0-87119-102-4, EE-1003) Heathkit-Zenith Ed.

— Passive Circuit Design. (Engineering Design Ser.). (Illus.). 583p. (C). 1983. pap. text ed. 17.95 (0-87119-020-6); ring bd. 10.95 (0-87119-021-4); 9.95 (0-87119-022-2); 49.95 (0-87119-019-2, EE-1001) Heathkit-Zenith Ed.

— Transistor Circuit Design. (Engineering Design Ser.). (Illus.). 583p. (C). 1983. teacher ed 9.95 (0-87119-018-4); student ed 10.95 (0-87119-017-6); pap. text ed. 19.95 (0-87119-016-8); ring bd. 59.95 (0-87119-015-X, EE-1002) Heathkit-Zenith Ed.

Leonard, Virginia. Politicians, Pupils, & Priests: Argentino Education since 1743. (American University Studies: Ser. XXII, Vol. 2). 456p. (C). 1989. text ed. 59.95 (0-8204-0748-8) P Lang Pubs.

Leonard, W. A. Stephen Banks Leonard of Owego, Tioga Co., N. Y. (Illus.). 342p. 1990. reprint ed. lib. bdg. 60.00 (0-8328-1490-3); reprint ed. pap. 52.00 (0-8328-1491-1) Higginson Bk Co.

Leonard, Walter B., jt. auth. see Consumer Reports Editors.

***Leonard, Wilbert M., II.** Basic Social Statistics. 458p. (C). 1994. pap. text ed. 29.95 (0-87563-509-1) Stipes.

— A Sociological Perspective of Sport. 4th ed. LC 92-28102. 512p. (C). 1993. pap. write for info. (0-02-369871-3) Macmillan.

Leonard, Willard. Horse Sense. (Illus.). 144p. 1984. pap. 15.95 (0-87595-115-5); pap. 9.95 (0-87595-116-3) Oregon Hist.

Leonard, William, jt. auth. see Barba, James.

Leonard, William A. No Upper Limits. (Illus.). 122p. 1977. teacher ed, pap. text ed. 8.95 (1-878669-28-1, 4425) Crea Tea Assocs.

Leonard, William E. Byron & Byronism in America. LC 64-23597. 126p. (C). 1964. text ed. 75.00 (0-8383-0582-2) M S G Haskell Hse.

— Byron & Byronism in America. LC 65-24997. 126p. 1965. reprint ed. 40.00 (0-87752-062-3) Gordian.

Leonard, William E., ed. see Lucretius.

Leonard, William F. & Martin, Thomas L. Electronic Structure & Transport Properties of Crystals. LC 79-13471. 720p. (Orig.). 1980. lib. bdg. 72.00 (0-88275-986-8) Krieger.

Leonard, William J. The Letter Carrier: Autobiography of William J. Leonard, S.J. LC 93-18887. 384p. (Orig.). 1993. 29.95 (1-55612-651-4); pap. 15.95 (1-55612-671-9) Sheed & Ward MO.

— Where Thousands Fell. (Orig.). 1995. write for info. (1-55612-755-3); pap. 15.95 (1-55612-756-1) Sheed & Ward MO.

***Leonard, William L.** Radiography Examination Review. (Illus.). 174p. (C). 1994. pap. 26.95x (0-9644624-0-0) JLW Pub.

— Radiography Examination Review. 7th ed. 260p. 1991. pap. 24.00 (0-8385-8241-9, A8241-0) Appleton & Lange.

— Self-Study Exercises in Radiography. LC 94-40511. 272p. 1994. pap. 17.40 (0-13-011651-3) P-H.

Leonard, William N. Railroad Consolidation under the Transportation Act of 1920. LC 68-58602. (Columbia University. Studies in the Social Sciences: No. 522). reprint ed. 24.50 (0-404-51522-3) AMS Pr.

Leonard, William R., et al. U. N. Developmet Aid: Criteria & Methods of Evaluation. LC 75-140126. (UNITAR Studies). 1971. 23.95 (0-405-02235-2) Ayer.

Leonard, William T. Masquerade in Black. LC 86-6597. (Illus.). 443p. 1986. 45.00 (0-8108-1895-7) Scarecrow.

— Theatre: Stage to Screen to Television, 2 vols. 1812p. 1981. Vol. I: A-L. write for info. (0-318-55640-5); Vol. II: M-Z. write for info. (0-318-55641-3) Scarecrow.

— Theatre: Stage to Screen to Television, 2 vols., Set. LC 80-22987. 1812p. 1981. 92.50 (0-8108-1374-2) Scarecrow.

Leonard, Zenas. Adventures of a Mountain Man: The Narrative of Zenas Leonard. Quaife, Milo M., ed. LC 78-17427. (Illus.). xx, 274p. 1978. reprint ed. 25.00 (0-8032-2853-8); reprint ed. pap. 9.95 (0-8032-7903-5) U of Nebr Pr.

Leonardelli, Carol A. The Milwaukee Evaluation of Daily Living Skills: Evaluation in Long-Term Psychiatric Care. LC 88-42542. 136p. 1988. pap. 25.00 (1-55642-039-0) SLACK Inc.

Leonardi, Dell. The Reincarnation of John Wilkes Booth. LC 74-27952. 1975. 18.95 (0-8159-6716-0) Devin.

— The Reincarnation of John Wilkes Booth: A Study in Hypnotic Regression. LC 74-27952. 180p. reprint ed. pap. 51.30 (0-317-08182-9, 2022710) Bks Demand.

Leonardi, Leonardo & Ribolini, Gabriele. Pocket Watches: L'Orologio da Tasca. LC 93-48527. (Bella Cosa Ser.). (Illus.). 144p. 1994. pap. 12.95 (0-8118-0753-3) Chronicle Bks.

Leonardi Leone, Norma. A Mother's Guide to Computers. Koenemann, Jean, ed. LC 85-46037. (Illus.). 102p. (Orig.). 1986. pap. 5.95 (0-936635-03-7) Lion Pr & Vid.

Leonardi, Paolo & Santambrogio, Marco, eds. On Quine: New Essays. (Illus.). 384p. (C). 1995. 64.95 (0-521-47091-9) Cambridge U Pr.

***Leonardi, Robert.** Convergence, Cohesion & Intergration in the European Union. LC 94-31779. 1995. write for info. (0-312-12384-1) St Martin.

— Italian Politics, Vol. 1. 204p. 1987. text ed. 40.00 (0-86187-691-1, Pub. by Pinter Pubs UK) St Martin.

Leonardi, Robert, ed. The Regions & the European Community: The Regional Response to the Single Market in the Underdeveloped Areas. LC 92-28756. 1992. 30.00 (0-7146-3460-3, Pub. by F Cass Pubs UK) Intl Spec Bk.

Leonardi, Robert & Anderlini, Fausto, eds. Italian Politics, Vol. 6: A Review. 250p. 1992. text ed. 59.00 (1-85567-047-X, Pub. by Pinter Pubs UK) St Martin.

Leonardi, Robert & Corbetta, Piergiorgio, eds. Italian Politics, Vol. 4: A Review. 250p. 1990. text ed. 47.50 (0-86187-852-3, Pub. by Pinter Pubs UK) St Martin.

Leonardi, Robert & Nanetti, Rafaella Y., eds. Regional Development in a Modern European Economy: The Case of Tuscany. 256p. 1994. 49.00 (1-85567-155-7, Pub. by Pinter Pubs UK) St Martin.

Leonardi, Robert & Wertman, Douglas A. Italian Christian Democracy: The Politics of Dominance. LC 89-30613. 304p. 1989. text ed. 49.95 (0-312-03114-9) St Martin.

Leonardi, Robert, jt. ed. see Nanetti, Rafaella Y.

Leonardi, Susan J. Dangerous by Degrees: Women at Oxford & the Somerville College Novelists. (Illus.). 260p. 1989. text ed. 45.00 (0-8135-1365-0); pap. text ed. 12.95 (0-8135-1366-9) Rutgers U Pr.

***Leonardi, Tom.** Secrets of Sensual Lovemaking: How to Give Her the Ultimate Pleasure. LC 94-47136. 1995. 15.95 (0-525-93983-0, Dutton) NAL-Dutton.

Leonardo, Bianca, ed. see Conwell, Russell H.

Leonardo, Bianca, jt. auth. see Gregory, Scott J.

Leonardo, Bianca, ed. see Gregory, Scott J.

Leonardo, Bianca, ed. see Notovitch, Nicolas.

Leonardo, Bianca, jt. auth. see Welsh, Philip J.

Leonberger, F. J., et al, eds. Picosecond Electronics & Optoelectronics II. (Electronics & Photonics Ser.: Vol. 24). (Illus.). 280p. 1987. 69.00 (0-387-18329-9) Spr-Verlag.

Leoncini, Mauro, jt. auth. see Codenotti, B.

Leoncini, Mauro, jt. auth. see Codenotti, Bruno.

Leoncker, Tracy, ed. Computing in Civil Engineering. LC 86-25911. (Proceedings of the Fourth Conference Ser.). 1018p. 1986. pap. 84.00 (0-87262-569-9) Am Soc Civil Eng.

Leondar, Barbara, jt. ed. see Perkins, David.

Leondes, Cornelius T. Control & Dynamic Systems: Advances in Theory & Applications, Vol. 21. (Serial Publication Ser.). 1984. text ed. 112.00 (0-12-012721-0) Acad Pr.

— Control & Dynamic Systems, Vol. 36: Advances in Large Scale Systems Dynamics. 410p. 1990. text ed. 99.00 (0-12-012736-9) Acad Pr.

Leondes, Cornelius T., ed. Advances in Control & Dynamic Systems, Vol. 19. (Serial Publication Ser.). 1983. text ed. 112.00 (0-12-012719-9) Acad Pr.

— Control & Dynamic Systems, Vol. 23. (Serial Publication Ser.). 336p. 1986. text ed. 112.00 (0-12-012723-7) Acad Pr.

— Control & Dynamic Systems, Vol. 24. (Serial Publication Ser.). 384p. 1986. text ed. 112.00 (0-12-012724-5) Acad Pr.

— Control & Dynamic Systems, Vol. 26. (Serial Publication Ser.). 339p. 1987. text ed. 112.00 (0-12-012726-1) Acad Pr.

— Control & Dynamic Systems, Vol. 30. (Serial Publication Ser.). 257p. 1989. text ed. 104.00 (0-12-012730-X) Acad Pr.

— Control & Dynamic Systems: Advances in Aerospace Systems Dynamics & Control Systems, Vol. 31. (Advances in Theory & Applications Ser.). 264p. 1989. text ed. 126.00 (0-12-012731-8) Acad Pr.

— Control & Dynamic Systems: Advances in Aerospace Systems Dynamics & Control Systems, Vol. 33. (Advances in Theory & Applications Ser.). 305p. 1990. text ed. 132.00 (0-12-012733-4) Acad Pr.

— Control & Dynamic Systems: Advances in Aerospace Systems Dynamics & Control Systems; Advances in Theory & Applications, Vol. 32. 280p. 1990. text ed. 126.00 (0-12-012732-6) Acad Pr.

— Control & Dynamic Systems: Advances in Algorithm & Computational Techniques in Dynamic Systems Control, Vol. 29. (Advances in Theory & Applications Ser.). 393p. 1988. text ed. 112.00 (0-12-012729-6) Acad Pr.

— Control & Dynamic Systems: Advances in Control Mechanics, Vol. 34. 333p. 1990. text ed. 92.00 (0-12-012734-2) Acad Pr.

— Control & Dynamic Systems: Advances in Theory & Applications, Set. Vol. 20. 1983. Pt. 2. write for info. (0-318-56829-2) Acad Pr.

— Control & Dynamic Systems: Advances in Theory & Applications, Vol. 20. (Serial Publication Ser.). 1983. text ed. 112.00 (0-12-012720-2) Acad Pr.

— Control & Dynamic Systems: Advances in Theory & Applications, Vol. 22. (Serial Publication Ser.). 1985. text ed. 112.00 (0-12-012722-9) Acad Pr.

— Control & Dynamic Systems: Advances in Theory & Applications, Vol. 25. (Serial Publication Ser.). 258p. 1987. text ed. 112.00 (0-12-012725-3) Acad Pr.

— Control & Dynamic Systems: Advances in Theory & Applications, 3 pts., Vol. 27. (System Identification & Adaptive Control Ser.: Pt. 3). 377p. 1988. text ed. 112.00 (0-12-012727-X) Acad Pr.

— Control & Dynamic Systems: Robust Control System Techniques & Applications, Pt. 2, Vol. 50. (Illus.). 467p. 1992. text ed. 85.00 (0-12-012750-4) Acad Pr.

— Control & Dynamic Systems: Robust Control System Techniques & Applications, Pt 2, Vol. 51. (Illus.). 478p. 1992. text ed. 85.00 (0-12-012751-2) Acad Pr.

— Control & Dynamic Systems Vol. 66: Discrete-Time Dynamic & Control System Techniques. (Illus.). 366p. 1994. text ed. 99.00 (0-12-012766-0) Acad Pr.

— Control & Dynamic Systems Vol. 68: Digital Signal Processing Systems Implementation Techniques. (Illus.). 424p. 1995. text ed. 99.00 (0-12-012768-7) Acad Pr.

— Control & Dynamic Systems Vol. 70: Digital Control Systems Implementation Techniques. (Illus.). 376p. 1995. boxed write for info. (0-12-012770-9) Acad Pr.

— Control & Dynamic Systems Vol. 71: Discrete-Time Control System Analysis & Design. (Illus.). 344p. 1995. boxed write for info. (0-12-012771-7) Acad Pr.

— Control & Dynamic Systems Vol. 72: Discrete-Time Control System Implementation Techniques. (Illus.). 346p. 1995. boxed write for info. (0-12-012772-5) Acad Pr.

— Control & Dynamic Systems, Vol. 35: Advances in Control Mechanics. 318p. 1990. text ed. 92.00 (0-12-012735-0) Acad Pr.

— Control & Dynamic Systems, Vol. 37: Advances in Industrial Systems. 425p. 1990. text ed. 99.00 (0-12-012737-7) Acad Pr.

— Control & Dynamic Systems, Vol. 38: Advances in Aeronautical Systems. (Illus.). 407p. 1990. text ed. 99.00 (0-12-012738-5) Acad Pr.

— Control & Dynamic Systems, Vol. 39: Advances in Robotic Systems, Pt. 1. (Illus.). 472p. 1991. text ed. 105.00 (0-12-012739-3) Acad Pr.

— Control & Dynamic Systems, Vol. 40: Advances in Robotic Systems, Pt. 2. (Illus.). 419p. 1991. text ed. 94.00 (0-12-012740-7) Acad Pr.

— Control & Dynamic Systems, Vol. 41: Analysis & Control System Techniques for Electric Power Systems, Pt. 1 of 4. (Illus.). 478p. 1991. text ed. 94.00 (0-12-012741-5) Acad Pr.

— Control & Dynamic Systems, Vol. 42: Analysis & Control System Techniques for Electric Power Systems, Pt. 2 of 4. (Illus.). 488p. 1991. text ed. 94.00 (0-12-012742-3) Acad Pr.

— Control & Dynamic Systems, Vol. 43: Analysis & Control System Techniques for Electric Power Systems, Pt. 3 of 4. (Illus.). 468p. 1991. text ed. 94.00 (0-12-012743-1) Acad Pr.

— Control & Dynamic Systems, Vol. 44: Analysis & Control System Techniques for Electric Power Systems, Pt. 4 of 4. (Illus.). 497p. 1991. text ed. 94.00 (0-12-012744-X) Acad Pr.

— Control & Dynamic Systems, Vol. 45: Advances in Manufacturing & Automation Systems. (Illus.). 353p. 1992. text ed. 79.00 (0-12-012745-8) Acad Pr.

— Control & Dynamic Systems, Vol. 46: Manufacturing & Automation Systems, Pt. 2. (Illus.). 421p. 1991. text ed. 94.00 (0-12-012746-6) Acad Pr.

— Control & Dynamic Systems, Vol. 47: Manufacturing & Automation Systems, Pt. 3. (Illus.). 431p. 1991. text ed. 94.00 (0-12-012747-4) Acad Pr.

— Control & Dynamic Systems, Vol. 48: Manufacturing & Automation Systems, Pt. 4. (Illus.). 447p. 1991. text ed. 94.00 (0-12-012748-2) Acad Pr.

— Control & Dynamic Systems, Vol. 49: Manufacturing & Automation Systems, Pt. 5. (Illus.). 424p. 1991. text ed. 94.00 (0-12-012749-0) Acad Pr.

— Control & Dynamic Systems, Vol. 52: Integrated Technology Methods & Applications in Aerospace Systems Design. (Illus.). 550p. 1992. text ed. 85.00 (0-12-012752-0) Acad Pr.

— Control & Dynamic Systems, Vol. 53: High Performance Systems Techniques & Applications. (Illus.). 527p. 1992. text ed. 95.00 (0-12-012753-9) Acad Pr.

— Control & Dynamic Systems, Vol. 54: System Performance Improvement & Optimization Techniques & Their Applications in Aerospace Systems. (Illus.). 521p. 1993. text ed. 99.00 (0-12-012754-7) Acad Pr.

— Control & Dynamic Systems, Vol. 55: Digital & Numeric Techniques & Their Applications in Control Systems, Pt. 1. (Illus.). 521p. 1993. text ed. 99.00 (0-12-012755-5) Acad Pr.

— Control & Dynamic Systems, Vol. 56: Digital & Numeric Techniques & Their Applications in Control Systems, Pt. 2. (Illus.). 574p. 1993. text ed. 99.00 (0-12-012756-3) Acad Pr.

— Control & Dynamic Systems, Vol. 57: Multidisciplinary Engineering Systems: Design & Optimization Techniques & Their Application. (Illus.). 493p. 1993. text ed. 99.00 (0-12-012757-1) Acad Pr.

— Control & Dynamic Systems, Vol. 58: Computer Aided Design-Engineering (CAD-CAE), Part 1 of 2, Techniques & Their Application. (Illus.). 349p. 1993. text ed. 99.00 (0-12-012758-X) Acad Pr.

— Control & Dynamic Systems, Vol. 59: Computer Aided Design-Engineering (CAD-CAE), Part 2 of 2, Techniques & Their Application. (Illus.). 329p. 1993. text ed. 99.00 (0-12-012759-8) Acad Pr.

— Control & Dynamic Systems, Vol. 60: CAM - CTM: Computer-Aided Manufacturing - Computer-Integrated Manufacturing, Pt. 1 of 2. (Illus.). 460p. 1993. text ed. 99.00 (0-12-012760-1) Acad Pr.

— Control & Dynamic Systems, Vol. 61: CAM - CTM: Computer-Aided Manufacturing - Computer-Integrated Manufacturing, Pt. 2 of 2. (Illus.). 414p. 1994. text ed. 99.00 (0-12-012761-X) Acad Pr.

— Control & Dynamic Systems, Vol. 62: Concurrent Engineering Techniques & Applications. (Illus.). 462p. 1994. text ed. 99.00 (0-12-012762-8) Acad Pr.

— Control & Dynamic Systems, Vol. 63: Analysis & Synthesis Techniques in Control & Dynamic Systems. (Illus.). 419p. 1994. text ed. 99.00 (0-12-012763-6) Acad Pr.

— Control & Dynamic Systems, Vol. 64, Pt. 1: Stochastic Techniques in Digital Processing Systems. (Illus.). 424p. 1994. text ed. 99.00 (0-12-012764-4) Acad Pr.

— Control & Dynamic Systems, Vol. 65, Pt. 2: Stochastic Techniques in Digital Processing Systems. (Illus.). 406p. 1994. text ed. 99.00 (0-12-012765-2) Acad Pr.

— Control & Dynamic Systems, Vol. 67: Digital Image Processing: Techniques & Applications. (Illus.). 386p. 1994. text ed. 99.00 (0-12-012767-9) Acad Pr.

— Control & Dynamic Sytems: Advances in Theory & Applications, 3 pts., Vol. 28. (Advances in Algorithms & Computational Techniques in Dynamic Systems Control Ser.: Pt. I). 278p. 1988. text ed. 112.00 (0-12-012728-8) Acad Pr.

Leondopoulos, Jordan. Still the Moving World: Intolerance, Modernism, & Heart of Darkness. LC 90-35558. (Literature & the Visual Arts: New Foundations Ser.: Vol. 7). 210p. (C). 1991. text ed. 40.95 (0-8204-1388-7) P Lang Pubs.

Leone. Ionizing Radiation & Immune Processes. 532p. 1962. text ed. 400.00 (0-677-10300-X) Gordon & Breach.

Leone, Anthony, jt. auth. see Turner Publishing Company Staff.

Leone, Bruno, ed. Capitalism: Opposing Viewpoints. rev. ed. LC 86-3079. (IMS Ser.). (Illus.). 150p. (Orig.). (YA). (gr. 9-12). 1986. pap. text ed. 11.55 (*0-89908-359-5*) Greenhaven.

— Communism: Opposing Viewpoints. 2nd rev. ed. LC 86-338. (Isms Ser.). (Illus.). 210p. (Orig.). (YA). (gr. 9-12). 1986. lib. bdg. 19.95 (*0-89908-385-4*); pap. text ed. 11.55 (*0-89908-360-9*) Greenhaven.

— Free Speech. LC 93-19855. (Current Controversies Ser.). (YA). 1994. lib. bdg. 17.95 (*1-56510-078-6*); pap. 9.95 (*1-56510-077-8*) Greenhaven.

— Internationalism: Opposing Viewpoints. 2nd rev. ed. LC 86-339. (Isms Ser.). (Illus.). 150p. (YA). (gr. 9-12). 1986. 19.95 (*0-89908-383-8*); pap. text ed. 11.55 (*0-89908-358-7*) Greenhaven.

— Nationalism. 2nd rev. ed. LC 86-324. (Isms Ser.). (Illus.). 150p. (YA). (gr. 9-12). 1986. lib. bdg. 19.95 (*0-89908-387-0*); pap. text ed. 11.55 (*0-89908-362-5*) Greenhaven.

— Racism: Opposing Viewpoints. rev. ed. LC 86-360. (Isms Ser.). (Illus.). 150p. (Orig.). (YA). (gr. 9-12). 1986. pap. 11.55 (*0-89908-357-9*) Greenhaven.

***Leone, Bruno & De Koster, Katie, eds.** Rape on Campus. LC 94-42400. (At Issue Ser.). 1995. lib. bdg. 11.95 (*1-56510-296-7*) Greenhaven.

Leone, Bruno, jt. ed. see DeKoster, Katie.

Leone, Dee. Bible Bulletin Boards for Holidays. (Bulletin Board Ser.). (Illus.). 96p. (J). (gr. k-5). 1994. 9.95 (*0-86653-777-5*, 3810, Shining Star Pubns) Good Apple.

— Christmas A-Z. (Bible Crafts Ser.). 96p. (J). (gr. 2-7). 1989. 10.95 (*0-86653-499-7*, SS1892, Shining Star Pubns) Good Apple.

— Make Your Own Worship Bulletins for Autumn & Winter. (Children's Bulletin Ser.). (Illus.). 112p. 1992. 11.95 (*0-86653-696-5*, SS2826, Shining Star Pubns) Good Apple.

— Making Worship Bulletins for Young Children for Spring & Summer. (Children's Bulletin Ser.). (Illus.). 112p. (J). (ps-1). 1994. 10.95 (*0-86653-769-4*, SS3802, Shining Star Pubns) Good Apple.

— The Miracles of Jesus. 48p. (J). (ps-1). 1990. 7.95 (*0-86653-554-3*, SS1874, Shining Star Pubns) Good Apple.

— The Stories of Noah & Joseph. (Bible-Time Puzzle Ser.). (Illus.). 48p. (J). (ps-1). 1992. 7.95 (*0-86653-645-0*, SS2811, Shining Star Pubns) Good Apple.

— Vacation Bible School Activities. (Teacher Helper Ser.). 96p. (J). (gr. 2-7). 1990. 10.95 (*0-86653-525-X*, SS1818, Shining Star Pubns) Good Apple.

— The World God Made. (Bible-Time Puzzle Ser.). 48p. (J). (ps-1). 1991. 7.95 (*0-86653-636-1*, SS1894, Shining Star Pubns) Good Apple.

Leone, Diana. Attic Windows - A Contemporary View. 64p. 1988. pap. 16.95 (*0-942786-09-2*) Leone Pubns.

— Diana's Watercolor Jacket. (Illus.). 32p. 1995. pap. text ed. 14.95 (*0-942786-37-8*) Leone Pubns.

— Fine Hand Quilting. (Illus.). 84p. 1986. pap. 12.95 (*0-942786-48-3*) Leone Pubns.

— Investments. 2nd ed. (Illus.). 104p. 1982. pap. 14.95 (*0-942786-02-5*) Leone Pubns.

— The New Sampler Quilt. rev. ed. LC 93-1914. Orig. Title: The Sampler Quilt. (Illus.). 144p. 1993. reprint ed. 19.95 (*0-942786-41-6*) Leone Pubns.

— The New Sampler Quilt. rev. ed. LC 93-1914. (Illus.). 144p. 1994. reprint ed. spiral bd. 24.95 (*0-942786-44-0*) Leone Pubns.

Leone, Edward. Seasons of Love. LC 92-7373. 80p. 1992. 9.95 (*0-87319-035-1*) Hallberg Pub Corp.

Leone, Francis. The Atom: Heart & Science & Technology. LC 86-81737. (Illus.). 177p. 1986. 24.95 (*0-914587-03-X*) Helix Pr.

— Genetics: The Mystery & the Promise. 1992. pap. text ed. 14.95 (*0-07-157645-2*) McGraw.

— Genetics: The Mystery & the Promise. 240p. 1991. 24.95 (*0-8306-3068-6*); pap. 14.95 (*0-8306-3067-8*) TAB Bks.

***Leone, Gene.** Mama Leone's Italian Cookbook. 1994. lib. bdg. 35.95x (*1-56849-509-9*) Buccaneer Bks.

Leone, Jay. Italian Without Words: An Illustrated Guide to Italian Hand Gestures. (Illus.). 136p. 1990. pap. 4.99 (*1-56171-026-1*) Sure Sellers.

Leone, Laura. Under the Voodoo Moon. (Silhouette Desire Ser.). 1994. mass mkt. 2.99 (*0-373-05834-9*, 5-05834-2) Silhouette.

Leone, Mark P. Roots of Modern Mormonism. LC 78-25965. 259p. 1979. 23.95 (*0-674-77970-3*) HUP.

Leone, Mark P., ed. Contemporary Archaeology: A Guide to Theory & Contributions. LC 79-156779. (Illus.). 476p. 1972. pap. 19.95 (*0-8093-0534-8*) S Ill U Pr.

Leone, Mark P. & Potter, Parker B., eds. The Recovery of Meaning: Historical Archaeology in the Eastern United States. LC 87-26499. (Anthropological Society of Washington Ser.). (Illus.). 506p. (C). 1988. 45.00 (*0-87474-616-7*) Smithsonian.

Leone, Mark P. & Potter, Parker B., Jr., eds. The Recovery of Meaning: Historical Archaeology in the Eastern United States. LC 87-26499. (Anthropological Society of Washington Ser.). (Illus.). 506p. (C). 1994. pap. text ed. 19.95 (*1-56098-460-0*) Smithsonian.

***Leone, Mark P. & Silberman, Neil A.** Invisible America: Unearthing Our Hidden History. (Illus.). 288p. 1995. 35.00 (*0-8050-3525-7*) H Holt & Co.

Leone, Mark P., jt. ed. see Zaretsky, Irving I.

Leone, Michele. L' Industria Nella Letteratura Italiana Contemporanea. (Stanford French & Italian Studies: No. 2). 156p. (ITA.). 1976. pap. 46.50 (*0-915838-30-3*) Anma Libri.

***Leone, Norma L.** Computers Made Really Easy for Beginners. LC 95-2941. 120p. (Orig.). 1995. pap. 8.95 (*0-936635-08-8*) Lion Pr & Vid.

Leone, Norma L., jt. auth. see O'Connell, Avice M.

Leone, Norma L., jt. auth. see Parkman, Elmerina L.

Leone, Peter E. Alcohol & Other Drugs: Use, Abuse, & Disabilities. (Exceptional Children at Risk Ser.). 33p. 1991. 8.90 (*0-86586-215-X*, P358) Coun Exc Child.

Leone, Peter E., ed. Understanding Troubled & Troubling Youth: Multiple Perspectives. (Focus Editions Ser.: Vol. 116). (Illus.). 320p. (C). 1990. 49.95 (*0-8039-3442-4*); pap. 23.95 (*0-8039-3443-2*) Sage.

Leone, Ray. Success Secrets of the Sales Funnel. 1992. 24.95 (*1-881196-25-9*) SSS Pub.

Leone, Roland, contrib. Joe Pass Live!! 1993. 9.95 (*0-87166-972-2*, 94380); audio 10.98 (*0-87166-973-0*, 94380) Mel Bay.

— Joe Pass Plays the Blues. 1993. 9.95 (*0-87166-885-8*, 94109); audio 10.98 (*1-56222-625-8*, 94109) Mel Bay.

Leone, Sierra. Conditions of Trust. 256p. (Orig.). 1995. pap. 3.95 (*1-877606-00-6*) R Romance.

— Love Express. 256p. (Orig.). 1995. pap. text ed. 0.95 (*1-877606-01-4*) R Romance.

— Southern Enchantment. 256p. (Orig.). 1995. pap. text ed. 3.95 (*1-877606-02-2*) R Romance.

***Leone, Susan.** Survivor. 130p. 1995. pap. 7.95 (*1-56901-895-2*) NW Pub.

***Leone, Ugo, ed.** The Death Penalty: A Bibliographic Research. 119p. (Orig.). (C). 1995. pap. text ed. 40.00x (*0-7881-1573-1*) Diane Pub.

Leone, William C. Production Automation & Numerical Control. LC 67-21679. (Illus.). 245p. reprint ed. pap. 69.90 (*0-317-11119-1*, 2012419) Bks Demand.

***Leonelli, Leslie.** A Guide to Alternative Health Care in New York. 1995. pap. 9.95 (*1-885492-15-4*) City & Co.

Leonenko, N. N., jt. auth. see Ivanov, A. V.

Leonessa, Anna. Journal Entries Acapulco 93. limited ed. (Codex Edition Ser.). (Illus.). 12p. 1993. 10.00 (*1-884185-01-0*) O Zone.

— The Last Poem. limited ed. (Illus.). Date not set. 5.00 (*1-884185-09-6*) O Zone.

Leonetti, Gastone & Cuspidi, Cesare, eds. Hypertension in the Elderly. LC 94-12005. (Developments in Cardiovascular Medicine Ser.: Vol. 157). 1994. lib. bdg. 69.00 (*0-7923-2852-3*) Kluwer Ac.

Leonetti, Michael E. Retire Worry-Free: Financial Strategies for Tomorrow's Independence. rev. ed. 264p. 1993. pap. 12.95 (*0-7931-0088-7*, 5608-4201) Dearborn Finan.

Leonetti, Mike, jt. auth. see Henderson, Paul.

Leong. Family Law in Singapore. 1990. 167.00 (*0-409-99583-5*) Butterworth Legal Pubs.

Leong, A. S., jt. auth. see Forbes, I. J.

Leong, Albert, ed. The Millenium: Christianity & Russia (AD 988-1988) LC 90-46791. 224p. 1990. pap. 13.95 (*0-88141-080-2*) St Vladimirs.

— Oregon Studies in Chinese & Russian Culture. LC 90-5520. (American University Studies: Slavic Languages & Literature: Ser. XII, Vol. 13). 376p. (C). 1990. text ed. 72.95 (*0-8204-1309-7*) P Lang Pubs.

— Proceedings of the Summer 1986 Intensive Workshop in Chinese & Russian. 1987. 15.00 (*0-87114-177-9*) U Oreg Russian Dept.

***Leong, Andrew P. & Kheong, Chin Yoong.** Cheshire, Fifoot & Furmston's Law of Contract: Singapore & Malaysian Edition. 1006p. 1994. pap. 186.00 (*0-409-99682-3*, SI) Butterworth Legal Pubs.

Leong, Carol. Serials Cataloging Handbook: An Illustrative Guide to the Use of AACR2 & L C Rule Interpretations. 320p. 1989. text ed. 55.00 (*0-8389-0501-3*) ALA.

Leong, Charles L., jt. auth. see Kan, Johnny.

Leong, Che K. Children with Specific Reading Disabilities. 360p. 1988. pap. 86.00 (*90-265-0291-5*, Pub. by Swets Pub Serv NE) Taylor & Francis.

***Leong, Che K., ed.** Developmental & Acquired Dyslexia: Neuropsychological & Neurolinguistic Perspectives. (Neuropsychology & Cognition Ser.). 300p. (C). 1995. lib. bdg. 112.00 (*0-7923-3166-4*) Kluwer Ac.

Leong, Che K. & Randhawa, Bikkar S., eds. Understanding Literacy & Cognition: Theory, Research & Application. LC 89-77899. (Illus.). 330p. 1989. 85.00 (*0-306-43489-X*, Plenum Pr) Plenum.

Leong, Che K., jt. ed. see Joshi, R. Malatesha.

Leong, Deborah, jt. auth. see McAfee, Oralie.

Leong, Frederick, ed. Career Development & Vocational Behavior of Racial & Ethnic Minorities. (Vocational Psychology Ser.). 304p. 1995. text ed. 59.95 (*0-8058-1303-9*) L Erlbaum Assocs.

Leong, Frederick T. & Whitfield, James R., eds. Asians in the United States: Abstracts of the Psychological & Behaviorial Literature, 1967-1991. LC 92-17379. (Bibliographies in Psychology Ser.: No. 11). 226p. 1992. pap. 27.50 (*1-55798-178-7*) Am Psychol.

Leong, Frederick T., ed. see Sekaran, Uma.

***Leong, Kenneth S.** The Zen Teachings of Jesus. 192p. (Orig.). 1995. pap. 14.95 (*0-8245-1481-5*) Crossroad NY.

Leong, Peng C. Nutrition Bibliography of Malaya. LC 52-40995. 32p. reprint ed. pap. 25.00 (*0-317-10449-7*, 2001359) Bks Demand.

Leong, Russell. The Country of Dreams & Dust. 71p. 1993. pap. 8.95 (*0-931122-76-7*) West End.

Leong, Russell, intro. Moving the Image: Independent Asian Pacific American Media Arts 1970-1990. LC 90-71789. (Illus.). 312p. (Orig.). 1992. pap. 19.95 (*0-934052-13-1*) UCLA Asian Am Studies Ctr.

Leong, Russell, jt. ed. see Chang, Edward T.

Leong, Russell, jt. ed. see Higa, Karin M.

Leong, Russell, ed. see Him Mark Lai.

Leong, S. P. Vaccine Therapy & Immunotherapy of Malignant Melanoma. (Medical Intelligence Unit Ser.). 1995. write for info. (*1-57059-161-X*) R G Landes.

Leong, Sally A. & Berka, Randy, eds. Molecular Industrial Mycology: Systems & Applications for Filamentous Fungi. (Mycology Ser.: Vol. 8). 304p. 1991. 115.00 (*0-8247-8392-1*) Dekker.

***Leong, Simon.** As I See the World Today. 1994. pap. 6.95 (*0-533-10937-X*) Vantage.

Leong, Stanley. Malignant Melanoma: Advances in Treatment. (Medical Intelligence Unit Ser.). 150p. 1992. 89.95 (*1-879702-26-6*) R G Landes.

Leong, Y. S. Silver: An Analysis of Factors Affecting Its Price. 2nd ed. (Brookings Institution Reprint Ser.). reprint ed. lib. bdg. 39.50 (*0-697-00162-8*) Irvington.

Leong, Yu K., jt. ed. see Cheng, Kai N.

Leonhard, Alan T. & Mercuro, Nicholas, eds. Neutrality: Changing Concepts & Practices. LC 88-21755. 164p. (Orig.). (C). 1988. pap. text ed. 18.00 (*0-8191-7141-7*) U Pr of Amer.

Leonhard, Charles. The Status of Arts Education in American Public Schools. 1992. 10.00 (*0-317-05162-8*) U IL Sch Music.

— The Status of Arts Education in American Public Schools: Summary & Conclusions. 1992. 3.00 (*0-317-05163-6*) U IL Sch Music.

Leonhard, Robert. The Art of Maneuver: Maneuver-Warfare Theory & AirLand Battle. 327p. 1995. 14.95 (*0-89141-532-7*) Presidio Pr.

Leonhard, Robert R. Art of Maneuver. 1992. 24.95 (*0-89141-403-7*) Presidio Pr.

— Fighting by Minutes: Time & the Art of War. LC 93-50685. 216p. 1994. text ed. 55.00 (*0-275-94736-X*, Praeger Pubs) Greenwood.

Leonhard, W. Control of Electrical Drives. (Electric Energy Systems & Engineering Ser.). 315p. 1991. 79.00 (*0-387-13650-9*) Spr-Verlag.

Leonhard, W., ed. see IFAC Symposium Staff.

Leonhard, Woody. CD-Mom: The Mother of All Windows Packages, Set. 1993. cd-rom 49.95 (*0-201-62708-6*) Addison-Wesley.

— Hacker's Guide to Word for Windows. 1992. pap. 39.95 (*0-201-63273-X*) Addison-Wesley.

— Hacker's Guide to Word for Windows, Set. 2nd ed. 1995. disk, pap. 39.95 (*0-201-40763-9*) Addison-Wesley.

— Mother of All Windows Books, Set. 1993. disk write for info. (*0-201-62475-3*) Addison-Wesley.

— Underground Guide to Word for Windows: Slightly Askew Advice from a Winword Wizard. 1994. pap. 19.95 (*0-201-40650-0*) Addison-Wesley.

— Windows Programming for Mere Mortals. 1992. pap. 36.95 (*0-201-60832-4*) Addison-Wesley.

***Leonhard, Woody & Simon, Barry.** PC Mom: The Mother of All PC Books. LC 94-34324. 1994. cd-rom 49.95 (*0-201-40681-0*) Addison-Wesley.

Leonhardt, Barbara A. & Berzoa, Morton, eds. Insect Pheromone Technology: Chemistry & Applications. LC 82-8714. (ACS Symposium Ser.: No. 190). 1982. 43.95 (*0-8412-0724-0*) Am Chemical.

Leonhardt, Gay. My Laundry & My Life: Or My Life in My Laundry. (Illus.). 32p. (Orig.). 1993. pap. 9.00 (*0-932430-06-6*) Boss Bks.

Leonhardt, H. Fundamentals of Electroacupuncture According to Voll. Sarkisyanz, Helga, tr. (Illus.). 284p. 1980. text ed. 85.00 (*3-88136-081-6*, Pub. by ML-Verlag GW) Medicina Bio.

Leonhardt, Helmut. Human Histology, Cytology & Microanatomy. 4th ed. (Illus.). 1977. pap. 20.95 (*0-8151-5375-9*, Yr Bk Med Pubs) Mosby Yr Bk.

Leonhardt, Kenneth. Sex Scells: Light Verses Celebrate the Way of All Flesh. 72p. (Orig.). 1994. pap. 8.95 (*1-56474-104-4*) Fithian Pr.

***Leonhardt-Lupa, Merete.** A Mother Is Born: Preparing for Motherhood During Pregnancy. LC 94-29716. 176p. 1995. text ed. 16.95 (*0-89789-353-0*, Bergin & Garvey) Greenwood.

***Leonhardt, Mary.** Keeping Kids Reading. Date not set. write for info. (*0-517-70114-6*) Random.

— Parents Who Love Reading, Kids Who Don't. LC 93-16655. 1993. 20.00 (*0-517-59164-2*, Crown) Crown Pub Group.

— Parents Who Love Reading, Kids Who Don't. 1995. pap. 12.00 (*0-517-88222-1*, Crown) Crown Pub Group.

— 75 Ways to End Reading. Date not set. write for info. (*0-517-88419-4*) Random.

Leonhardt, Thomas W., ed. Information Technology: It's for Everyone! 206p. 1992. pap. 22.00 (*0-8389-7634-4*, Z678) ALA.

Leonhardy, Frank C. Domebo: A Paleo-Indian Mammoth Kill in the Prairie-Plains. LC 65-26284. (Contributions of the Museum of the Great Plains Ser.: No. 1). 1966. 6.95 (*0-685-85506-6*) Mus Great Plains.

— Test Excavations in the Mangum Reservoir Area of Southwestern Oklahoma. (Contributions of the Museum of the Great Plains Ser.: No. 2). (Illus.). 1966. 4.00 (*0-685-85507-4*) Mus Great Plains.

Leoni, Bruno. Freedom & the Law. LC 91-3283. 274p. (C). 1991. text ed. 17.50 (*0-86597-096-3*); pap. 7.50 (*0-86597-097-1*) Liberty Fund.

Leoni, Edgar. Nostradamus & His Prophecies. LC 82-9479. 1988. 13.99 (*0-517-38809-X*) Random Hse Value.

Leonid, Sobolev. Romanoff. Freemantle, Alfred, tr. LC 74-10091. (Soviet Literature in English Translation Ser.). 311p. 1975. reprint ed. 21.45 (*0-88355-177-2*) Hyperion Conn.

Leonidov, Pavel. U Nikh V Michigane. LC 85-61782. 120p. (Orig.). 1987. pap. 12.50 (*0-89830-100-9*) Russica Pubs.

Leonidova. Russian-Bulgarian Dictionary. 463p. (BUL & RUS.). 1978. 14.95 (*0-8288-5269-3*, M9101) Fr & Eur.

Leonis, James. Filmed on Location: A Guide to Leasing Your Property As a Film Location. 1994. pap. 28.00 (*0-9639781-0-1*) Premiere Pub.

Leonor, M. D. & Richards, P. J., eds. Target Setting for Basic Needs: The Operation of Selected Government Services. vii, 130p. 1982. 20.00 (*92-2-102946-8*) Intl Labour Office.

Leonov, A. I. & Fomichev, K. J. Monopulse Radar. Barton, William F. & Barton, David K., trs. 320p. 1986. text ed. 29.00 (*0-89006-217-X*) Artech Hse.

Leonov, A. I. & Prokunin, A. N. Nonlinear Viscoelastic Effects in Flows of Polymer Melts & Concentrated Polymer Solutions. LC 92-39252. 1993. write for info. (*1-85166-847-0*) Elsevier.

Leonov, A. I. & Sokolov, A. Life Amongst the Stars. 160p. 1981. 50.00 (*0-317-39514-9*, Pub. by Collets UK) Pro-Am Music.

Leonov, George, ed. The Application of Drainage. 228p. text ed. 70.50 (*0-317-46401-9*, Pub. by Keter Pub IS) Coronet Bks.

Leonov, Leonid M. The Badgers. LC 72-14053. (Soviet Literature in English Translation Ser.). 336p. 1992. reprint ed. 31.50 (*0-88355-008-3*) Hyperion Conn.

— Skutarevsky. Brown, Alec, tr. LC 76-135250. 444p. 1971. reprint ed. text ed. 79.50 (*0-8371-5170-8*, LESK, Greenwood Pr) Greenwood.

— Soviet River. Montagu, Ivor & Nalbandov, Sergei, trs. LC 72-90298. (Soviet Literature in English Translation Ser.). 383p. 1981. reprint ed. 23.50 (*0-88355-009-1*) Hyperion Conn.

Leonov, Sergey A. & Barton, William F. Russian-English & English-Russion Dictionary of Radar & Electronics. LC 93-30104. (ENG & RUS.). 1993. 49.00 (*0-89006-705-8*) Artech Hse.

***Leonov, Viktor.** Blood on the Shores: Soviet SEALs in World War II. Gebhardt, James F., tr. (Orig.). 1994. mass mkt. 5.99 (*0-8041-0732-7*) Ivy Books.

Leonov, Viktor & Gebhardt, James. Blood on the Shores: Soviet Naval Commandos in World War II. LC 93-27869. 224p. 1993. 26.95 (*1-55750-506-3*) Naval Inst Pr.

***Leonov, Yu G. & Khain, V. E., eds.** Global Correlation of Tectonics Movements. fac. ed. LC 86-13361. (Illus.). 318p. 1994. pap. 90.70 (*0-7837-7656-X*, 2047409) Bks Demand.

Leonowens, Anna. The Romance of the Harem. (Victorian Literature & Culture Ser.). (Illus.). 368p. 1991. text ed. 35.00 (*0-8139-1327-6*); pap. 14.95 (*0-8139-1328-4*) U Pr of Va.

Leons, Madeline B. & Rothstein, Frances A., eds. New Directions in Political Economy: An Approach from Anthropology. LC 78-4290. (Contributions in Economics & Economic History Ser.: No. 22). xxviii, 350p. 1979. text ed. 65.00 (*0-313-20414-4*, LND/) Greenwood.

Leonsis, Ted, jt. auth. see Chposky, James.

Leontaritis, George B. Greece & the First World War: From Neutrality to Intervention, 1917-1918. (East European Monographs). 640p. 1990. text ed. 75.00 (*0-88033-181-X*) Col U Pr.

Leont'eva, G. K. Karl Briullov. 336p. (RUS.). 1983. 40.00 (*0-317-57278-4*, Pub. by Collets UK) St Mut.

— Karl Pavlovich Briullov. 196p. 1986. 123.00 (*0-317-61311-1*, Pub. by Collets UK) Pro-Am Music.

Leontiades, James C. Multinational Corporate Strategy: Planning for World Markets. LC 83-48686. 256p. 1984. pap. 16.95 (*0-685-09125-2*) Free Pr.

Leontidou, E., jt. ed. see Ammer, S.

Leontidou, Lila. The Mediterranean City in Transition: Social Change & Urban Development. (Cambridge Human Geography Ser.). (Illus.). (C). 1990. 74.95 (*0-521-34467-0*) Cambridge U Pr.

Leontief, Estelle. Sellie & Dee: A Friendship. LC 93-29920. (Crimson Edge Chapbook Ser.). 1993. 7.95 (*0-9619111-6-6*) Chicory Blue.

Leontief, Wassily W. Essays in Economics: Theories, Theorizing, Facts, & Policies. 423p. (C). 1985. pap. 22.95 (*0-87855-993-0*) Transaction Pubs.

— Essays in Economics, Vol. 1: Theories & Theorizing. LC 76-21999. 252p. 1976. reprint ed. 67.95 (*0-87332-091-3*) M E Sharpe.

— Essays in Economics, Vol. 2: Theories, Facts & Policies. LC 77-79062. 168p. 1978. 67.95 (*0-87332-092-1*) M E Sharpe.

— Input-Output Economics. 320p. 1986. pap. 29.95 (*0-19-503527-5*) OUP.

— The Structure of American Economy, Nineteen Nineteen to Nineteen Thirty-Nine: An Empirical Application of Equilibrium Analysis. 2nd enl. ed. LC 76-17415. 264p. 1977. reprint ed. 67.95 (*0-87332-087-5*) M E Sharpe.

— Studies in Structure of American Economy: Theoretical & Empirical Explorations in Input-Output Analysis. LC 76-16433. 562p. 1977. reprint ed. 67.95 (*0-87332-086-7*) M E Sharpe.

Leontief, Wassily W. & Duchin, Faye. The Future Impact of Automation on Workers. (Illus.). 184p. 1986. 42.00 (*0-19-503623-9*) OUP.

Leontiev, A. I., jt. auth. see Kutateladze, S. S.

***Leontis, Artemis.** Topographies of Hellenism: Mapping the Homeland. (Myth & Poetics Ser.). 240p. 1995. 29.95x (*0-8014-3057-7*) Cornell U Pr.

***Leontos, Carolyn & Palmer, Jeanne.** Chefs Creating Lean: A Nutrition Course for Food Professionals. LC 94-38126. 1994. ring bd. 95.00 (*0-88091-136-0*) Am Dietetic Assn.

Leontovich, M. A. English Russian Dictionary of Quantum Electronics & Holography. (ENG & RUS.). 1977. 49.95 (*0-8288-3960-3*, M8921) Fr & Eur.

— Plasma Physics Problem Controlled Thermonuclear Reactions, Vol. 1. LC 59-11208. 1961. 152.00 (*0-08-009277-2*, Pub. by Pergamon Repr UK) Franklin.

Leontovich, M. A., ed. Reviews of Plasma Physics, Vol. 4, 1966. Lashinsky, Herbert, tr. LC 64-23244. (Illus.). 249p. reprint ed. pap. 71.00 (*0-8357-4388-8*, 2037243) Bks Demand.

An Asterisk (*) at the beginning of an entry indicates that the title is appearing in BIP for the first time.

— Reviews of Plasma Physics, Vol. 9. Mikhailovskii, A. B. et al, trs. LC 64-23244. 352p. 1986. 89.50 (*0-306-10999-9*, Consultants) Plenum.

— Reviews of Plasma Physics, Vol. 10. Glebov, Oleg H., tr. LC 64-23244. 526p. 1986. 125.00 (*0-306-11000-8*, Consultants) Plenum.

— Reviews of Plasma Physics, Vol. 11. Hugill, J., tr. LC 64-23244. 316p. 1986. 89.50 (*0-306-11001-6*, Consultants) Plenum.

Leontovich, M. A., et al, eds. Reviews of Plasma Physics, Vol. 12. LC 64-23244. (Illus.). 364p. 1987. 95.00 (*0-306-11002-4*, Consultants) Plenum.

Leontovich, Mary. Close Encounters: Systems & Interactions. (Explore! Science Ser.). (Illus.). 48p. (J). (gr. 3-6). 1995. 12.95 (*0-673-36220-5*); pap. 4.95 (*0-673-36215-9*) GdYrBks.

— Force, of Course! Force & Motion. (Explore! Science Ser.). (Illus.). 48p. (J). (gr. 3-6). 1995. 12.95 (*0-673-36218-3*); pap. 4.95 (*0-673-36213-2*) GdYrBks.

Leontyev, A., jt. auth. see Kostomarov, V.

Leontyev, L. Political Economy: A Condensed Course. (Rus. Ser.). (Illus.). 248p. 1974. text ed. 19.95 (*0-8464-1268-3*) Beekman Pubs.

— Short Course of Political Economy. 19.95 (*0-8464-0844-9*) Beekman Pubs.

Leonzio, Claudio, ed. see Fossi, M. Cristina.

Leopard, Donald. World War II: A Concise History. 2nd ed. (Illus.). 202p. (C). 1992. pap. text ed. 11.50 (*0-88133-506-1*) Waveland Pr.

Leopard, John. Ships in Bottles: A Modeller's Guide. (Illus.). 96p. 1991. 24.95 (*0-7137-2138-3*, Pub. by Blandford Pr UK) Sterling.

Leopard Productions Inc., ed. see Troy, Gene.

Leopardi. Quarterly Review of Literature: The 1950s, Special Issue, Vol. VIII, No. 1. 1950. pap. 10.00 (*0-317-05297-7*) Quarterly Rev.

Leopardi, Giacomo. Concordanze Diacroniche Delle 'Operette Morali' Di Giacomo Leopardi. (Alpha-Omega, Series F, Italienische Autoren). xiii, 775p. 1988. write for info. (*3-487-07757-4*, Pub. by Georg Olms GW) Lubrecht & Cramer.

— Leopardi: Poems. 2nd ed. Vivante, Arturo, tr. & intro. by. 85p. 1994. pap. 12.00 (*0-9620305-0-3*) Delphinium Pr.

— Leopardi: Poems & Prose. Flores, Angel, ed. LC 86-29460. 153p. 1987. reprint ed. text ed. 75.00 (*0-313-25769-8*, FLLE, Greenwood Pr) Greenwood.

— A Leopardi Reader. fac. ed. Casale, Ottavio M., ed. & tr. by. LC 80-29068. 288p. 1994. pap. 82.10 (*0-7837-7611-X*, 2047363) Bks Demand.

— The Moral Essays. Creagh, Patrick, tr. LC 82-23473. Orig. Title: Operette Morali. 265p. 1985. pap. text ed. 16.50 (*0-231-05707-5*) Col U Pr.

— The Moral Essays: Operette Morali. Creagh, Patrick, tr. LC 82-23473. (Works of Giacomo Leopardi: Vol. 1). 265p. reprint ed. pap. 75.60 (*0-7837-0429-1*, 2040752) Bks Demand.

— Operette Morali: Essays & Dialogues. Del Cecchetti, Giovanni, tr. LC 82-2627. (Biblioteca Italiana Ser.: No. 3). 672p. 1982. pap. 13.00 (*0-520-04928-4*) U CA Pr.

— Zibaldone: A Selection by Giacomo Leopardi. King, Martha, ed. & intro. by. LC 91-43276. (Studies in Italian Culture: Literature in History: Vol. 8). 209p. (C). 1993. text ed. 46.95 (*0-8204-1723-8*) P Lang Pubs.

Leopardi, Linda. Policy for School Boards. (School Board Library Ser.). 68p. (Orig.). 1983. pap. 9.95 (*0-912337-03-6*) NJ Schl Bds.

Leopold, A. Carl, ed. Membranes, Metabolism & Dry Organisms. LC 86-47646. (Comstock Book Ser.). (Illus.). 352p. 1986. 52.50 (*0-8014-1979-4*) Cornell U Pr.

Leopold, A. Carl, jt. ed. see Nooden, L. D.

Leopold, A. Starker. The California Quail. LC 76-48003. (Illus.). 1978. pap. 15.00 (*0-520-05456-3*) U CA Pr.

Leopold, A. Starker, et al. Wild California: Vanishing Lands, Vanishing Wildlife. Dasmann, Raymond F., ed. 150p. 1985. 50.00 (*0-520-05293-5*); pap. 25.00 (*0-520-06024-5*) U CA Pr.

Leopold, Aldo. Game Management. LC 86-40055. 512p. 1986. reprint ed. pap. 14.00 (*0-299-10774-4*) U of Wis Pr.

— The River of the Mother of God & Other Essays by Aldo Leopold. Flader, Susan L. & Callicott, J. Baird, eds. LC 90-45491. 400p. 1991. 24.95 (*0-299-12760-5*) U of Wis Pr.

— The River of the Mother of God & Other Essays by Aldo Leopold. Flader, Susan L. & Callicott, J. Baird, eds. LC 90-45491. (Illus.). 400p. 1993. reprint ed. pap. 14.95 (*0-299-12764-8*) U of Wis Pr.

— A Sand County Almanac: And Sketches Here & There. (Illus.). 1968. pap. 8.95 (*0-19-500777-8*) OUP.

— A Sand County Almanac: And Sketches Here & There. (Illus.). 256p. 1989. pap. 8.95 (*0-19-505928-X*) OUP.

— A Sand County Almanac: With Essays on Conservation from Round River. (Ecological Main Event Ser.). 320p. 1986. mass mkt. 5.95 (*0-345-34505-3*) Ballantine.

— A Sand County Almanac & Sketches Here & There: Commemorative Edition. (Illus.). 272p. 1987. 25.00 (*0-19-505305-2*) OUP.

Leopold, Allison K. Cherished Objects: Living with & Collecting Victoriana. 1991. 35.00 (*0-517-57435-7*, C P Pubs) Crown Pub Group.

— Holiday Treats: Thirty Vintage Recipes for Festive Cookies, Confections, & Other Delights. LC 95-3198. 1995. 17.00 (*0-517-59144-8*, Clarkson Potter) Crown Bks Yng Read.

— Victorian Frozen Dainties: Ices, Ice Creams, & Refreshing, Thirst-Quenching Drinks. LC 92-30641. 1993. 12.00 (*0-517-59143-X*, C P Pubs) Crown Pub Group.

— Victorian Garden Primer: A Treasury of 19th-Century Garden Lore. LC 94-37318. (J). 1995. 35.00 (*0-517-58660-6*, Clarkson Potter) Crown Bks Yng Read.

— Victorian Preserves, Pickles, & Relishes. (Illus.). 64p. 1992. 10.00 (*0-517-58315-1*, C P Pubs) Crown Pub Group.

Leopold, Dennette C., jt. auth. see Michaels, Carolyn.

***Leopold, Donald A.** Nose & Paranasal Sinuses: Allergy. Anon, Jack B., tr. (Current Opinion in Otolaryngology & Head & Neck Surgery Ser.). (Illus.). 72p. (Orig.). 1995. pap. text ed. 34.95 (*1-85922-736-8*) Current Science.

— Nose & Paranasal Sinuses: Laryngology & Bonchoesophagology. Kashima, Haskins K., ed. (Current Opinion in Otolaryngology & Head & Neck Surgery Ser.). (Illus.). 88p. 1994. pap. text ed. write for info. (*1-85922-630-2*) Current Science.

Leopold, Ellen, jt. auth. see Fine, Ben.

Leopold, George, ed. Ultrasound in Breast & Endocrine Disease. (Clinics in Diagnostic Ultrasound Ser.: Vol. 12). (Illus.). 198p. 1984. text ed. 37.00 (*0-443-08234-0*) Churchill.

***Leopold, George R.** Ultrasound in Breast & Endocrine Disease. fac. ed. LC 83-21054. (Clinics in Diagnostic Ultrasound Ser.: No. 12). (Illus.). 210p. 1984. reprint ed. pap. 59.90 (*0-7837-7878-3*, 2047635) Bks Demand.

Leopold, Jay, jt. auth. see McMahon, Bob.

***Leopold, Joan.** Contributions to Comparative Indo-European, African, & Chinese Linguistics. LC 94-27056. (Prix Volney Essay Ser.: Vol. 3). 1994. lib. bdg. write for info. (*0-7923-2507-9*) Kluwer Ac.

— The Letter Liveth: The Life Work & Library of August Friedrick Pott (1802-1887) (Library & Information Sources in Linguistics: 9). clii, 438p. 1983. 130.00x (*90-272-3733-6*) Benjamins North Am.

***Leopold, Joan, ed.** The Prix Volney: Its History & Significance for the Development of Linguistic Research, 1. LC 94-27057. (Prix Volney Essay Ser.). 1994. lib. bdg. write for info. (*0-7923-2505-2*) Kluwer Ac.

Leopold, Joan, ed. see Swiggers, Pierre & Boewe, Charles.

Leopold, John A. Alfred Hugenberg: The Radical Nationalist Campaign Against the Weimar Republic. LC 77-4026. (Illus.). 314p. reprint ed. pap. 89.50 (*0-8357-5303-4*, 2032135) Bks Demand.

Leopold, Kathleen & Orians, Thomas, eds. Theological Pastoral Resources: A Collection of Articles on Homosexuality from a Pastoral Perspective. rev. ed. LC 81-69476. 81p. 1985. pap. 4.00 (*0-940680-01-7*) Dignity Inc.

Leopold, Ladyvienna, see Antara-An, Astara V., pseud..

Leopold, Luna B. A View of the River. LC 93-34698. 312p. 1994. 39.95 (*0-674-93732-5*) HUP.

Leopold, Luna B., ed. Round River: From the Journals of Aldo Leopold. (Illus.). (C). 1972. reprint ed. pap. 9.95 (*0-19-501563-0*) OUP.

Leopold, Luna B., jt. auth. see Dunne, Thomas.

***Leopold, Luna B., et al.** Fluvial Processes in Geomorphology. (Illus.). xxiii, 522p. 1995. pap. text ed. 16.95 (*0-486-68588-8*) Dover.

Leopold, Nathan F., Jr. Life Plus Ninety-Nine Years. LC 73-16644. 381p. 1974. reprint ed. text ed. 69.50 (*0-8371-7207-1*, LELP, Greenwood Pr) Greenwood.

Leopold, Nikia C. Sandcastle Seahorses. LC 87-35978. 45p. (Orig.). (J). 1988. pap. 5.95 (*0-913123-17-X*) Galileo.

Leopold, Robert L., jt. ed. see Duhl, Leonard J.

Leopold, Silke. Monteverdi: Music in Transition. Smith, Anne, tr. (Illus.). 288p. 1991. 75.00 (*0-19-315248-7*) OUP.

Leopold, Simon R. Spiritual Aspects of Indian Music. 1985. 22.50 (*0-8364-1258-3*, Pub. by Sundeep II) S Asia.

Leopold, Sy, ed. see Zachary, John.

Leopold, Vincent, illus. The Alliance & Labor Songster. LC 74-30660. (American Farmers & the Rise of Agribusiness Ser.). 1975. reprint ed. 16.95 (*0-405-06837-9*) Ayer.

Leopold, Werner F. Bibliography of Child Language. LC 71-128944. (Northwestern Humanities Ser.: No. 28). reprint ed. 27.50 (*0-404-50728-X*) AMS Pr.

— Speech Development of a Bilingual Child, 4 vols, Set. Incl. Vol. 6. Vocabulary Growth in the First Two Years. reprint ed. 38.75 (*0-404-50706-9*); Vol. 11. Sound-Learning in the First Two Years. reprint ed. 38.75 (*0-404-50711-5*); Vol. 18. Grammar & General Problems in the First Two Years. reprint ed. 38.75 (*0-404-50718-2*); Vol. 19. Diary from Age Two. reprint ed. 38.75 (*0-404-50719-0*); (Northwestern University. Humanities Ser.). 155.00 (*0-404-50749-2*) AMS Pr.

Leopold-Wildburger, U., jt. auth. see Heuer, G. A.

Leopoldo, Solis M., jt. ed. see Norton, Roger D.

Leopoldt, Heinrich W., ed. see Hasse, Helmut.

Leopole, David, ed. see Stirner, Max.

Leos, Frances, tr. see Birdwell, Norman.

Leos, Nancy A., jt. auth. see Leos, Robert H.

Leos, Robert H. & Leos, Nancy A. The Low Fat Mexican Cookbook. LC 91-50690. 100p. 1992. pap. 6.95 (*0-88247-896-6*, 896) R & E Pubs.

Leos, Ruben. Twenty-Five Romantic Lines to Say to Your Lover in Spanish. 28p. (Orig.). 1987. pap. 1.50 (*0-945228-00-7*) Chico Bks.

— Twenty-Five Ways to Tell Someone off in Spanish. 28p. (Orig.). 1987. pap. 1.50 (*0-945228-01-5*) Chico Bks.

Leoter, John, jt. auth. see Richards, Karen K.

Leotta, G. G., jt. ed. see Brunelli, B.

Leoung & Mills. Opportunistic Infections in Patients with the Acquired Immunodeficiency Syndrome. (Infectious Disease & Therapy Ser.: Vol. 3). 476p. 1989. 125.00 (*0-8247-8080-9*) Dekker.

Lep, Annette. Crocheting Baby Blankets & Carriage Covers. (Illus.). 48p. (Orig.). 1983. pap. 2.95 (*0-486-24480-6*) Dover.

— Crocheting Fashion Sweaters for Women: Directions for 12 Cardigans, Pullovers & Vests. 48p. 1986. pap. 2.95 (*0-486-24957-3*) Dover.

— Crocheting Patchwork Patterns. 48p. (Orig.). 1981. pap. 3.50 (*0-486-23967-5*) Dover.

Lepa, E., tr. see Goldman, I. I. & Krivchenkov, V. D.

Lepa, Eugene, tr. see Maurin, Krzysztof.

Lepa, Eugene, jt. auth. see Rutkowski, J.

Lepa, Eugene, jt. auth. see Sadowski, W.

Lepa, Maria O., tr. see Nowak, Stefan.

LePage, Andy. Transforming Education: The New Three R's. LC 87-18534. 218p. (Orig.). 1987. pap. 14.95 (*0-941079-03-1*) Oakmore Hse.

LePage, Elaine B. Brain Surgery: What to Know & Ask. Hollingsworth, Anna, ed. (Illus.). 36p. (Orig.). 1994. pap. text ed. 4.65 (*0-939838-36-2*) Pritchett & Hull.

LePage, Jane W. Women Composers, Conductors, & Musicians of the Twentieth Century: Seclected Biographies, Vol. III. LC 80-12162. (Illus.). 333p. 1988. 35.00 (*0-8108-2082-X*) Scarecrow.

— Women Composers, Conductors & Musicians of the Twentieth Century: Selected Biographies, Vol. I. LC 80-12162. 388p. 1980. 32.50 (*0-8108-1298-3*) Scarecrow.

LePage, Raoul & Billard, Lynne. Exploring the Limits of Bootstrap. (Probability & Mathematical Statistics: Applied Probability & Statistics Section Ser.). 1992. text ed. 79.95 (*0-471-53631-8*) Wiley.

LePage, Wilbur R. Applied APL Programming. LC 78-6619. (Illus.). 1978. pap. text ed. write for info. (*0-13-040063-7*) P-H.

— Complex Variables & the Laplace Transform for Engineers. (Illus.). 1980. reprint ed. pap. text ed. 9.95 (*0-486-63926-6*) Dover.

Lepak, Anne F. The Frary Family in America: A Continuation. enl. ed. Frary, Robert Barnes, ed. (Illus.). 296p. 1985. 16.00 (*0-9616030-1-1*) Frary Family.

Lepak, Anne F., jt. auth. see Frary, Marty M.

Lepak, Keith J. Prelude to Solidarity: Poland & the Politics of the Gierek Regime. 320p. 1988. text ed. 47.00 (*0-231-06608-2*) Col U Pr.

***LePan, Don.** The Cognitive Revolution in Western Culture. 388p. 1989. pap. 19.95 (*1-55111-081-4*, Pub. by Macmillan UK) Broadview Pr.

LePan, Don, jt. auth. see Babington, Doug.

LePan, Don, jt. auth. see Boyne, Martin.

Lepape, Georges, et al. French Fashion Plates in Full Color from the Gazette Du Bon Ton (1912-1925) 58 Illustrations of Styles by Paul Poiret, Worth, Paquin & Others. LC 79-50347. (Illus.). 1979. pap. 8.95 (*0-486-23805-9*) Dover.

LePar, William A., et al. Life After Death: A New Revelation. (Illus.). 256p. (Orig.). 1994. pap. 14.95 (*1-885728-00-X*) Solar Press. An extraordinary view from "the other side" of humanity's journey to the other side - from the lower reaches of the Man-Made Heavenly Realm to the wondrous heights of the God-Made Heavenly Realm. Must reading for all who yearn to know where we go from here & why. Certain to stimulate & reassure. Meet deep trance psychic William Allen LePar & the Council, a union of 12 evolved souls communicating with humanity through LePar's Trances. An ongoing phenomenon for a quarter-century, the trances began involuntarily, shattering LePar's efforts to ignore his psychic abilities & lead a normal life. The trances have since been witnessed by hundreds & studied by journalists, educators, medical professionals, etc. More than 1.25 million words of dialogue with The Council exist - all meticulously preserved to provide unprecedented awareness of humanity's past, present, future. Co-authors Sherilyn Highben & David Ries are senior associates of the SOL Association for Research, the not-for-profit organization maintaining & disseminating the LePar Trance material. LIFE AFTER DEATH: A NEW REVELATION is a rewarding experience that gives readers not just food for thought, but a feast for thought. Order from Solar Press, Box 2276, North Canton, OH 44720.** ***Publisher Provided Annotation.

***LePard, Don.** Make My Day. (Illus.). 40p. (Orig.). 1995. pap. 4.00 (*1-56167-197-5*) Am Literary Pr.

Leparsky, E. & Nussel, F. E., eds. Protocol & Guidelines for Monotoring & Evaluation Procedures. xiii, 60p. 1987. pap. 32.70 (*0-387-18458-9*) Spr-Verlag.

Lepawsky, Albert, jt. auth. see Lepawsky, Rosalind.

Lepawsky, Rosalind & Lepawsky, Albert. Coalition & Coalescence: Berkeley Links Ecology & Ethnicity. (Environmental Studies: No. 1). 8p. 1972. 1.00 (*0-912102-46-2*) Cal Inst Public.

LePeau, Andrew T. & LePeau, Phyllis J. Ephesians. (LifeGuide Bible Studies). 60p. (Orig.). 1985. pap. 4.99 (*0-8308-1012-9*, 1012) InterVarsity.

— James: Faith That Works. (LifeGuide Bible Studies). 64p. (Orig.). 1987. pap. 4.99 (*0-8308-1018-8*, 1018) InterVarsity.

LePeau, Phyllis J. Caring People Bible Studies, 8 titles, Set. 1991. 39.92 (*0-8308-1190-7*, 1190) InterVarsity.

LePeau, Phyllis J., jt. auth. see LePeau, Andrew T.

Lepelletier, Edmond A. Paul Verlaine: His Life, His Work. Lang. E. M., tr. LC 71-128944. (Illus.). reprint ed. 55.00 (*0-404-03968-5*) AMS Pr.

***Lepelley, Rene.** Dictionnaire du Francais Regional de Normandie. 157p. (FRE.). 1993. 39.95 (*0-7859-8121-7*, 2862531502) Fr & Eur.

— Dictionnaire Etymologique des Noms de Communes de Normandie. 1993. write for info. (*0-7859-8096-2*, 2-85480-455-4) Fr & Eur.

Lepenies, Wolf. Between Literature & Science: The Rise of Sociology. Hollingdale, R. J., tr. (Cambridge Ideas in Context Ser.). 392p. 1988. pap. 22.95 (*0-521-33810-7*) Cambridge U Pr.

— Melancholy & Society. Gaines, Jeremy & Jones, Doris L., trs. 253p. (C). 1992. 45.00 (*0-674-56468-5*) HUP.

Lepeschkin, E., ed. see Body Surface Mapping of Cardiac Fields Symposium Staff.

Lepetit, Bernard. The Pre-Industrial Urban System: France, 1740-1840. Rogers, Godfrey, tr. LC 93-26676. (Themes in International Urban History Ser.: No. 2). (Illus.). 464p. (C). 1994. 79.95 (*0-521-41734-1*) Cambridge U Pr.

Lepetit, Charles. Poor in Spirit: Modern Parables of the Reign of God. LC 90-80672. 208p. (Orig.). 1990. pap. 5.95 (*0-87793-422-3*) Ave Maria.

Lepgold, Joseph. The Declining Hegemon: The United States & European Defense, 1960-1990. LC 90-3132. (Contributions in Military Studies: No. 103). 232p. 1990. text ed. 55.00 (*0-313-26373-6*, B3657, Greenwood Pr); pap. text ed. 15.95 (*0-275-93657-0*, LDH, Praeger Pubs) Greenwood.

Lepicier, A. M. Unseen World: Catholic Theology & Spiritualism. 1972. 69.95 (*0-8490-1251-1*) Gordon Pr.

Lepidus, Henry. The History of Mexican Journalism. 1976. 59.95 (*0-8490-1978-8*) Gordon Pr.

Lepik, E. E. Floral Evolution in Relation to Pollination Ecology. 164p. 1977. 35.00 (*0-685-59956-6*, Messers Today & Tomorrow) Scholarly Pubns.

Lepine, Christopher. God Without the Garbage: A Reasonable Approach to God. 64p. (Orig.). 1993. pap. 2.25 (*0-9634081-0-0*) Revelation CO.

***Lepine, David.** A Brotherhood of Canons Serving God: English Secular Cathedrals in the Later Middle Ages. (Studies in the History of Medieval Religion: No. 9). 256p. (C). 1995. text ed. 63.00 (*0-85115-620-7*) Boydell & Brewer.

Lepine, Mike, jt. auth. see Leigh, Mark.

Lepine, Pierre. Dictionnaire Francais-Anglais et Anglais-Francais des Termes Medicaux et Biologiques. 2nd ed. 896p. (ENG & FRE.). 1974. 175.00 (*0-8288-6027-0*, M4665) Fr & Eur.

— French-English - English-French Dictionary of Medical & Biological Terms. 2nd ed. (ENG & FRE.). 1991. 162.50 (*0-7859-8938-2*) Fr & Eur.

— French-English - English-French Dictionary of Medical & Biological Terms. 2nd ed. 876p. (ENG & FRE.). 1991. reprint ed. 162.50 (*2-257-10598-2*) IBD Ltd.

***Leping, A. A.** Russisch-Deutsches Woerterbuch. 34th ed. 514p. (GER & RUS.). 1992. 29.95 (*0-7859-8573-5*, 5200021472) Fr & Eur.

Lepingle, Dominique, jt. auth. see Bouleau, Nicolas.

Lepke, Helen S., ed. Shaping the Future: Challenges & Opportunities. (Reports of the Northeast Conference on the Teaching of Foreign Languages). 164p. 1989. pap. 10.95 (*0-915432-89-7*) NE Conf Teach Foreign.

Lepkyi, Bohdan. Opovidannia. (Ukrains'ka Kul'turna Skarbnytsia Ser.). (UKR.). 1975. 20.00 (*0-918884-26-8*) Slavia Lib.

Leplante, Phil. Easy PC Maintenance & Repair. 152p. 1992. 22.95 (*0-8306-3952-7*, 4143, Windcrest); pap. 14.95 (*0-8306-3953-5*, 4143, Windcrest) TAB Bks.

Lepley, Marvin, jt. auth. see Esch, Dortha.

Lepley, Mary M., jt. auth. see LaBaw, Jeanine L.

Lepley, William M.

***Leplin, Jarrett, ed.** The Creation of Ideas in Physics: Studies for a Methodology of Theory Construction. LC 95-13782. (University of Western Ontario Series in Phylosophy of Science: Vol. 55). 1995. write for info. (*0-7923-3461-2*) Kluwer Ac.

Leplin, Jarrett, jt. ed. see Fine, Arthur.

Leplongeon, A. D. Here & There in Yucatan. 1977. lib. bdg. 59.95 (*0-8490-1943-5*) Gordon Pr.

LePlongeon, Augustus. Queen Moo & the Egyptian Sphinx: Mayan & Egyptian Civilization, Influences. 1991. lib. bdg. 75.00 (*0-8490-5049-9*) Gordon Pr.

— Sacred Mysteries among the Mayas & Quiches: Their Relation to the Sacred Mysteries of Egypt, Greece, Chaldea & India. 1991. lib. bdg. 79.95 (*0-8490-4555-X*) Gordon Pr.

— Sacred Mysteries among the Mayas & the Quiches. 163p. 1976. reprint ed. spiral bd. 9.35 (*0-7873-0554-5*) Mokelumne.

LePlongeon, Augustus & Allen, Paul M. Maya-Atlantis: Queen Moo & the Egyptian Sphinx. LC 73-186768. (Illus.). 424p. 1991. reprint ed. pap. 16.00 (*0-89345-238-6*, Steinerbks) Garber Comm.

LePoer, Barbara L., ed. Thailand: A Country Study. 6th ed. LC 88-600485. (Area Handbook Ser.). (Illus.). 396p. 1989. text ed. 18.00 (*0-16-001732-7*, S/N 008-020-01184-3) USGPO.

LePoff, Arlene, jt. auth. see Prager, Janice.

Lepon, S. Holiday Rhymes & Riddles. 1994. 13.95 (*0-89906-820-0*); pap. 10.95 (*0-89906-821-9*) Mesorah Pubns.

— Torah Rhymes & Riddles. 1992. 13.95 (*0-89906-995-9*); pap. 10.95 (*0-89906-996-7*) Mesorah Pubns.

Lepon, Shoshana. Hanukkah Carousel. (J). (ps-1). 1993. 12.95 (*0-943706-11-4*) Pitspopany.

— Hillel Builds a House. LC 92-39383. (Illus.). (J). (ps-2). 1993. pap. 5.95 (*0-929371-42-9*) Kar Ben.

— No Greater Treasure: Stories of Extraordinary Women Drawn from the Talmud & Misdrash. 190p. 1990. 13.95 (*0-944070-62-0*) Targum Pr.

— Noah & the Rainbow. LC 92-26431. (J). (gr. k-4). 1993. 11.95 (*1-880582-04-X*); pap. 8.95 (*1-880582-05-8*) Judaica Pr.

— The Ten Plagues of Egypt. Goldstein-Alpern, Neva, ed. (Illus.). 32p. (J). (gr. k-4). 1988. 11.95 (*0-910818-77-0*); pap. 8.95 (*0-910818-76-2*) Judaica Pr.

— The Ten Tests of Abraham. (Judaica Bible Series for Young Children). (Illus.). 32p. (Orig.). (J). (gr. k-4). 1986. pap. 8.95 (*0-910818-67-3*) Judaica Pr.

Lepon, Shoshona. Joseph the Dreamer. (Bible Series for Young Children). 32p. (J). (gr. k-4). 1991. 11.95 (*0-910818-92-4*); pap. 8.95 (*0-910818-93-2*) Judaica Pr.

Lepor, Herbert & Lawson, Russell K., eds. Prostate Diseases. LC 92-49620. (Illus.). 512p. 1993. text ed. 99.95 (*0-7216-4545-3*) Saunders.

— Therapy for Genitourinary Cancer. (Cancer Treatment & Research Ser.). 176p. (C). 1992. lib. bdg. 99.00 (*0-7923-1412-3*) Kluwer Ac.

Lepor, Herbert & McGuire, William L., eds. Urologic Oncology. (Cancer Treatment & Research Ser.). (C). 1989. lib. bdg. 116.00 (*0-7923-0161-7*) Kluwer Ac.

Leporati, Ezio. The Assessment of Structural Safety: A Comparative Statistical Study of the Evolution & Use of Levels 1, 2, & 3. Grimoldi, Nicoletta, tr. LC 79-50708. (Series in Cement & Concrete Research: No. 1). (Illus.). 143p. reprint ed. pap. 40.80 (*0-8357-8808-3*, 2033344) Bks Demand.

Lepore, Bruce A. & Lepore, Chris N. The Employer's Back Injury Prevention Handbook. (Illus.). 164p. (C). 1984. pap. 24.95 (*0-9613365-0-1*) Bridgeview.

— Not Tonite Dear, My Back Is Killing Me! (Illus.). 52p. 1986. pap. 5.95 (*0-9613365-5-2*) Bridgeview.

Lepore, Chris N., jt. auth. see Lepore, Bruce A.

Lepore, Don. The Ultimate Healing System. 402p. 1987. pap. 19.95 (*0-913923-63-X*) Woodland UT.

LePore, Ernest. New Directions in Semantics. (Cognitive Science Ser.: No. 2). 512p. 1987. text ed. 119.00 (*0-12-444040-1*); pap. text ed. 58.00 (*0-12-444041-X*) Acad Pr.

Lepore, Ernest, ed. Truth & Interpretation: Perspectives on the Philosophy of Donald Davidson. 400p. 1989. pap. 26.95 (*0-631-16948-2*) Blackwell Pubs.

Lepore, Ernest & Van Gulick, Robert, eds. John Searle & His Critics. (Philosophers & Their Critics Ser.). 420p. 1993. pap. 24.95 (*0-631-18702-2*) Blackwell Pubs.

Lepore, Ernest, jt. auth. see Fodor, Jerry.

Lepovitz, Helena W. Images of Faith: Expressionism, Catholic Folk Art, & the Industrial Revolution. LC 90-33630. (Illus.). 280p. 1991. 40.00 (*0-8203-1256-8*) U of Ga Pr.

Lepow, Lauren. Enacting the Sacrament: Counter-Lollardy in the Towneley Cycle. LC 90-55003. 168p. 1991. 28.50 (*0-8386-3368-4*) Fairleigh Dickinson.

Lepowsky, James & Primc, M. Structure of the Standard Modules for the Affine Lie Algebra A - Sub 1. LC 85-15639. (Contemporary Mathematics Ser.: Vol. 46). 84p. 1985. pap. text ed. 21.00 (*0-8218-5048-2*, CONM-46) Am Math.

Lepowsky, James, jt. auth. see Dong, Chong-Ying.

Lepowsky, James, et al, eds. Vertex Operators in Mathematics & Physics. (Mathematical Sciences Research Institute Publications: Vol. 3). (Illus.). xiv, 482p. 1985. 49.00 (*0-387-96121-6*) Spr-Verlag.

Lepowsky, Maria A. Fruit of the Motherland: Gender in an Egalitarian Society. LC 93-8314. 383p. 1993. pap. 49.00 (*0-231-08120-0*) Col U Pr.

— Fruit of the Motherland: Gender in an Egalitarian Society. LC 93-8314. 383p. 1994. 49.00 (*0-685-71379-2*); pap. 17.50 (*0-231-08121-9*) Col U Pr.

***Lepp, George & Dickerson, Joe.** Magic Lantern Guide to Canon Lenses. (Magic Lantern Guide Ser.). (Illus.). 176p. (Orig.). (C). 1995. pap. 19.95 (*1-883403-16-2*, Silver Pixel Pr) Saunders Photo.

Lepp, George D. Beyond the Basics: Innovative Techniques for Nature Photography. 156p. 1993. pap. 32.95 (*0-9637313-0-0*) Lepp & Assocs.

— Vintage Automobile Racing. (Illus.). 128p. 1990. pap. 12.98 (*0-87938-422-0*) Motorbooks Intl.

Lepp, N. W., ed. Effect of Heavy Metal Pollution on Plants: Effects of Trace Metals on Plant Function, Vol. 1. (Pollution Monitoring Ser.). (Illus.). 352p. 1981. 93.75 (*0-85334-959-2*, Pub. by Elsevier Applied Sci UK) Elsevier.

— Effect of Heavy Metal Pollution on Plants: Metals in the Environment, Vol. 2. (Pollution Monitoring Ser.). (Illus.). 257p. 1981. 74.00 (*0-85334-923-1*, Pub. by Elsevier Applied Sci UK) Elsevier.

Leppa, Carol J. Women's Health Perspectives: An Annual Review, Vol. 2. 288p. 1989. 29.50 (*0-89774-526-4*) Oryx Pr.

— Women's Health Perspectives, Vol. 3: An Annual Review. 336p. 1990. 29.50 (*0-89774-597-3*) Oryx Pr.

Leppa, Carol J. & Miller, Connie, eds. Women's Health Perspectives: An Annual Review, Vol. I. LC 89-647163. 238p. 1989. reprint ed. pap. 14.95 (*0-91 2078-85-5*) Volcano Pr.

Leppakoski, Markku. The Transcendental How: Kant's Transcendental Deduction of Objective Cognition. (Stockholm Studies in Philosophy: No. 13). 280p. (Orig.). 1993. pap. 53.00x (*91-22-01560-4*, Pub. by Almqv & Wiksell SW) Coronet Bks.

Leppaluoto, Jean R., ed. Women on the Move: A Feminist Perspective. 306p. 1972. pap. 6.00 (*0-317-34800-0*, X050) Know Inc.

Leppanen, Pentti A., jt. ed. see Glisic, Savo G.

***Leppard, Barbara & Ashton, Richard.** Treatment in Dermatology. rev. ed. Wieder, Joshua & Lowe, Nicholas J., eds. LC 94-40427. 1995. 39.95 (*1-85775-135-3*, Radcliffe Med Pr); text ed. 115.00 (*1-85775-130-2*, Radcliffe Med Pr) Scovill Paterson.

— Treatment in Dermatology. 2nd ed. 1995. pap. 39.95 (*1-870905-52-0*) Scovill Paterson.

Leppard, Barbara, jt. auth. see Ashton, Richard.

Leppard, John & Molyneux, Liz. Auditing Your Customer Service: The Foundation for Success. LC 93-41814. (Marketing for Managers Ser.). 144p. 1994. pap. 13.95 (*0-415-09732-0*, B3937) Routledge.

Leppard, John, jt. auth. see McDonald, Malcolm H.

Leppard, John, jt. auth. see McDonald, Malcolm.

Leppard, John W., jt. auth. see Vyakarnam, Sheilendra.

***Leppard, Lois G.** Mandie & Her Missing Kin. (Mandie Ser.: Bk. 25). 144p. (J). 1995. mass mkt. 3.99 (*1-55661-511-6*) Bethany Hse.

— Mandie & Joe's Christmas Suprise. (Mandie Bks.). (J). Date not set. pap. write for info. (*1-55661-552-3*) Bethany Hse.

— Mandie & the Abandoned Mine, Bk. 8. LC 87-70883. (Mandie Bks.). 144p. (Orig.). (J). (gr. 5-8). 1987. pap. 3.99 (*0-87123-932-9*) Bethany Hse.

— Mandie & the Angel's Secret. (J). (gr. 4-7). 1993. pap. 3.99 (*1-55661-370-9*) Bethany Hse.

— Mandie & the Charleston Phantom, Bk. 7. LC 86-7098. 128p. (Orig.). (J). (gr. 4-7). 1986. pap. 3.99 (*0-87123-650-8*) Bethany Hse.

— Mandie & the Cherokee Legend, Bk. 2. LC 83-70894. (Mandie Bks.: No. 2). 144p. (Orig.). (J). (gr. 4-7). 1983. pap. 3.99 (*0-87123-321-5*) Bethany Hse.

— Mandie & the Dangerous Imposter. (J). (gr. 4-7). 1994. pap. 3.99 (*1-55661-459-4*) Bethany Hse.

— Mandie & the Fiery Rescue. (Mandie Bks.). 160p. (Orig.). (J). (gr. 3-7). 1993. pap. 3.99 (*1-55661-289-3*) Bethany Hse.

— Mandie & the Forbidden Attic, Bk. 4. LC 84-72710. 144p. (Orig.). (J). (gr. 4-7). 1985. pap. 3.99 (*0-87123-822-5*) Bethany Hse.

— Mandie & the Foreign Spies. (Mandie Bks.). 160p. (Orig.). (J). (gr. 3-8). 1990. pap. 3.99 (*1-55661-147-1*) Bethany Hse.

— Mandie & the Ghost Bandits, Bk. 3. LC 84-71151. (Mandie Bks.). 128p. (Orig.). (J). (gr. 5-7). 1984. pap. 3.99 (*0-87123-442-4*) Bethany Hse.

— Mandie & the Hidden Treasure, Bk. 9. LC 87-71606. (Mandie Bks.). 144p. (Orig.). (J). (gr. 5-8). 1987. pap. 3.99 (*0-87123-977-9*) Bethany Hse.

— Mandie & the Holiday Surprise, Bk. 11. LC 88-71502. 160p. (J). (gr. 3-6). 1988. pap. 3.99 (*1-55661-036-X*) Bethany Hse.

— Mandie & the Invisible Troublemaker. LC 94-25134. (Mandie Book Ser.: Bk. 24). 144p. (J). (gr. 4-7). 1995. mass mkt. 3.99 (*1-55661-510-8*) Bethany Hse.

— Mandie & the Jumping Juniper. (Mandie Bks.). 160p. (Orig.). (J). (gr. 3-7). 1991. 3.99 (*1-55661-200-1*) Bethany Hse.

— Mandie & the Medicine Man, Bk. 6. LC 85-73426. 150p. (Orig.). (J). (gr. 4-8). 1986. pap. 3.99 (*0-87123-891-8*) Bethany Hse.

— Mandie & the Midnight Journey. (Mandie Bks.: No. 13). 160p. (Orig.). (J). (gr. 1-6). 1989. pap. 3.99 (*1-55661-084-X*) Bethany Hse.

— Mandie & the Mysterious Bells, Bk. 10. LC 87-72792. (Mandie Bks.). 160p. (Orig.). (J). (gr. 4-8). 1988. pap. 3.99 (*1-55661-000-9*) Bethany Hse.

— Mandie & the Mysterious Fisherman. (J). (gr. 4-7). 1992. pap. 3.99 (*1-55661-235-4*) Bethany Hse.

— Mandie & the Secret Tunnel, Bk. 1. LC 82-74053. (Mandie Bks.: No. 1). 144p. (Orig.). (J). (gr. 4-7). 1983. pap. 3.99 (*0-87123-320-7*) Bethany Hse.

— Mandie & the Shipboard Mystery, Bk. 14. (Mandie Bks.). 160p. (Orig.). (J). (gr. 3-8). 1990. 3.99 (*1-55661-120-X*) Bethany Hse.

— Mandie & the Silent Catacombs. (Mandie Bks.). 160p. (J). (gr. 3-8). 1990. 3.99 (*1-55661-148-X*) Bethany Hse.

— Mandie & the Singing Chalet. (Mandie Bks.). 160p. (Orig.). (J). (ps-8). 1991. pap. 3.99 (*1-55661-198-6*) Bethany Hse.

— Mandie & the Trunk's Secret, Bk. 5. LC 85-71474. 144p. (Orig.). (J). (gr. 3-7). 1985. pap. 3.99 (*0-87123-839-X*) Bethany Hse.

— Mandie & the Washington Nightmare, Bk. 12. LC 88-63464. (Mandie Bks.). 160p. (Orig.). (J). (gr. 4-8). 1989. pap. 3.99 (*1-55661-065-3*) Bethany Hse.

— Mandie & the Windmill's Message. (Mandie Bks.). 160p. (Orig.). (J). (gr. 3-7). 1992. pap. 3.99 (*1-55661-288-5*) Bethany Hse.

— Mandie Books Eleven-Fifteen Giftset, 5 bks., Set. (Orig.). 1990. pap. 19.99 (*1-55661-758-5*) Bethany Hse.

— Mandie Books One-Five Giftset, 5 bks., Set. (Orig.). 1987. pap. 19.99 (*1-55661-750-X*) Bethany Hse.

— Mandie Books Six-Ten Giftset, 5 bks., Set. (Orig.). 1988. pap. 19.99 (*1-55661-752-6*) Bethany Hse.

— Mandie Books 16-20 Giftset. (Mandie Bks.). (Orig.). (J). 1992. 19.99 (*1-55661-769-0*) Bethany Hse.

— Mandie's Cookbook. (Mandie Bks.). 80p. (Orig.). (J). (gr. 3-7). 1991. spiral bd. 9.99 (*1-55661-224-9*) Bethany Hse.

— Secret Money: In the Lily Adventures, No. 1. (Lily Adventures Ser.). 224p. (Orig.). 1995. pap. 5.99 (*0-345-39576-X*, Moorings) Ballantine.

***Leppard, Lois Gladys.** Suspicious Identities. (Lily Adventures: 2). 192p. 1995. pap. 5.99 (*0-345-39575-1*, Moorings) Ballantine.

Leppard, Raymond. Authenticity in Music. 88p. (Orig.). 1988. pap. 8.50 (*0-931340-20-9*, Amadeus Pr) Timber.

— Raymond Leppard on Music: An Anthology of Critical & Personal Writings. Lewis, Thomas P., ed. (Illus.). 760p. 1993. 45.00 (*0-912483-96-2*) Pro-Am Music.

Leppelman, John. Blood on the Risers: An Airborne Soldier's Thirty-Five Months in Vietnam. (Orig.). 1991. mass mkt. 4.95 (*0-8041-0562-6*) Ivy Books.

***Lepper, Bradley T., ed.** Current Research in the Pleistocene. (Illus.). 140p. (Orig.). (C). 1994. pap. text ed. 20.00 (*0-614-00503-5*) Ctr Study First Am.

Lepper, F. A. Trajan's Parthian War. rev. ed. xv, 262p. (ENG & GRE.). (C). 1994. text ed. 30.00 (*0-89005-530-0*) Ares.

Lepper, F. A., jt. auth. see Ferre, S. S.

Lepper, Gary. Bibliographical Introduction to Seventy-Five Modern American Authors. 1975. 30.00 (*0-685-56280-8*) SPD-Small Pr Dist.

Lepper, J. D. Mediterranean Orchids. 86p. (C). 1990. pap. 35.00 (*0-7223-2450-2*, Pub. by A H S Ltd UK) St Mut.

— Orchids of Greece. 60p. 1982. 35.00 (*0-7223-1450-7*, Pub. by A H S Ltd UK) St Mut.

Leppert, Clara. Simple Times. (Folk Literature Ser.). 48p. 1993. pap. 5.95 (*1-878781-07-3*) Free River Pr.

Leppert, Mary, ed. see Oblander, Ruth.

Leppert, Paul. Doing Business with China. LC 94-9350. (Global Business Ser.). 128p. (Orig.). 1994. pap. 12.00 (*0-87573-045-0*) Jain Pub Co.

— Doing Business with Korea. LC 95-14750. (Global Business Ser.). Orig. Title: Doing Business with the Koreans. 144p. (Orig.). 1995. pap. 12.00 (*0-87573-043-4*) Jain Pub Co.

— Doing Business with Mexico. (Global Business Ser.). 144p. (Orig.). 1995. pap. 12.00 (*0-87573-046-9*) Jain Pub Co.

— Doing Business with Singapore. LC 95-14751. (Global Business Ser.). Orig. Title: Doing Business in Singapore. 144p. (Orig.). 1995. pap. 12.00 (*0-87573-042-6*) Jain Pub Co.

— Doing Business with Taiwan. LC 95-14753. (Global Business Ser.). Orig. Title: Doing Business with the Chinese. 144p. (Orig.). 1995. pap. 12.00 (*0-87573-041-8*) Jain Pub Co.

— Doing Business with Thailand. LC 95-14752. (Global Business Ser.). Orig. Title: Doing Business with the Thais. 144p. (Orig.). 1995. pap. 12.00 (*0-87573-044-2*) Jain Pub Co.

Leppert, Phyllis C. & Woessner, J. Frederick, eds. The Extracellular Matrix of the Uterus, Cervix & Fetal Membranes: Synthesis, Degradation & Hormonal Regulation. (Research in Perinatal Medicine Ser.: No. X). (Illus.). 296p. 1991. 110.00 (*0-916859-43-6*) Perinatology.

Leppert, Richard D. Arcadia at Versailles: Noble Amateur Musicians & Their Musettes & Hurdy-Gurdies at the French Court (C. 1660-1789), a Visual Study. 138p. 1978. pap. text ed. 39.50 (*90-265-0246-X*, Pub. by Swets Pub Serv NE) Swets North Am.

— Music & Image: Domesticity, Ideology & Socio-Cultural Formation in 18th Century England. (Illus.). 264p. (C). 1993. pap. 21.95 (*0-521-44854-9*) Cambridge U Pr.

— The Sight of Sound: Music, Representation, & the History of the Body. LC 92-39075. 1993. 45.00 (*0-520-08174-9*) U CA Pr.

— The Sight of Sound: Music, Representation, & the History of the Body. 1995. pap. 17.95 (*0-520-20342-9*) U CA Pr.

Leppert, Richard D. & McClary, Susan, eds. Music & Society: The Politics of Composition, Performance, & Reception. LC 86-31672. (Illus.). 250p. 1989. pap. 18.95 (*0-521-37977-6*) Cambridge U Pr.

***Leppik, Ilo E.** Contemporary Diagnosis & Management of the Patient with Epilepsy. 2nd ed. LC 93-79282. 1995. write for info. (*1-884065-02-3*) Assocs in Med.

Leppik, Ilo E., jt. ed. see Schmidt, D. A.

Leppmann, P., tr. see Hoermann, H.

Leppmann, Wolfgang. Rilke: A Life. Stockman, Russell M., tr. LC 84-6062. (Illus.). 421p. 1984. pap. 12.95 (*0-88064-015-4*) Fromm Intl Pub.

LePre, C. Gerard. God's Money-Back Guarantee: The Seven Steps to Financial Success. LC 93-40623. 248p. 1994. 21.95 (*1-56554-027-1*) Pelican.

Lepre, J. P. The Egyptian Pyramids: A Comprehensive, Illustrated Reference. LC 89-43623. 359p. 1990. lib. bdg. 55.00x (*0-89950-461-2*) McFarland & Co.

LePrestre, Philippe G., ed. French Security Policy in a Disarming World: Domestic Challenges & International Constraints. LC 88-21703. 152p. 1988. lib. bdg. 30.00 (*1-55587-132-1*) Lynne Rienner.

Leprince de Beaumont, Marie. Beauty & the Beast. Howard, Richard, tr. (Illus.). 48p. (J). (gr. 1-5). 1990. pap. 14.95 (*0-671-70720-5*, S&S Bks Young Read) S&S Childrens.

Leprince de Beaumont, Marie & Perrault, Charles. Beauty & the Beast & Other Fairy Tales. (Illus.). 96p. (Orig.). (J). (ps-3). 1994. pap. 1.00 (*0-486-28032-2*) Dover.

Leprince-Ringuet, Louis. Atoms & Men. Halperin, Elaine P., tr. LC 61-11292. 128p. reprint ed. pap. 36.50 (*0-8357-5859-1*, 2020200) Bks Demand.

Leps, Marie-Christine. Apprehending the Criminal: The Production of Deviance in Nineteenth-Century Discourse. LC 92-7451. (Post-Contemporary Interventions Ser.). (Illus.). 277p. 1992. lib. bdg. 45.00 (*0-8223-1255-7*); pap. text ed. 15.95 (*0-8223-1271-9*) Duke.

Lepschy, A., ed. Book Production & Letters in the Western European Renaissance: Essays for C. Fahy. (Publications of the Modern Humanities Research Association: Vol. 12). 1986. 86.00 (*0-317-02860-X*) Modern Humanities Res.

Lepschy, Anna L. & Lepschy, Guilio. The Italian Language Today. 2nd ed. LC 92-6700. 272p. 1989. pap. 19.95 (*0-415-07862-8*, A8529) Routledge.

Lepschy, Anne L. & Lepschy, Giulio C. The Italian Language Today. 2nd ed. LC 88-5320. 272p. (C). 1988. text ed. 25.00 (*0-941533-21-2*); pap. text ed. 16.95 (*0-941533-22-0*) New Amsterdam Bks.

***Lepschy, Giulio.** History of Linguistics Vol. 1. 1994. pap. 19.95 (*0-582-09489-5*, Pub. by Longman UK) Longman.

— History of Linguistics Vol. 2. 1994. pap. 23.75 (*0-582-09491-7*, Pub. by Longman UK) Longman.

Lepschy, Giulio, ed. History of Linguistics. LC 93-31169. 1994. write for info. (*0-582-09488-7*, Pub. by Longman UK) Longman.

Lepschy, Giulio C., jt. auth. see Lepschy, Anne L.

Lepschy, Guilio, jt. auth. see Lepschy, Anna L.

***Lepscky.** Einstein Albert. 1984. 9.95 (*0-8120-5464-4*) Barron.

— Leonardo Da Vinci. (Famous People Ser.). 24p. 1984. 9.95 (*0-8120-5512-8*) Barron.

— Pablo Picasso. LC 83-347. (Famous People Ser.). 24p. 1984. 9.95 (*0-8120-5511-X*) Barron.

Lepscky, Ibi. Albert Einstein. (Famous People Ser.). (Illus.). 24p. (J). (gr. k-3). 1992. pap. 4.95 (*0-8120-1452-9*) Barron.

— Amadeus Mozart. (Famous People Ser.). (Illus.). 24p. (J). (gr. k-3). 1992. pap. 4.95 (*0-8120-1493-6*) Barron.

— Leonardo da Vinci. (Famous People Ser.). (Illus.). 24p. (J). (gr. k-3). 1992. pap. 4.95 (*0-8120-1451-0*) Barron.

— Marie Curie. (Famous People Ser.). (Illus.). 24p. (J). (gr. k-3). 1993. 9.95 (*0-8120-6340-6*); pap. 4.95 (*0-8120-1558-4*) Barron.

— Pablo Picasso. (Famous People Ser.). (Illus.). 24p. (J). (gr. k-3). pap. 4.95 (*0-8120-1450-2*) Barron.

— William Shakespeare. (Famous People Ser.). (Illus.). 28p. (J). (gr. k-3). 1989. 7.95 (*0-8120-6106-3*) Barron.

Lepse, Signe D. Poems. 80p. (Orig.). 1993. 9.95 (*0-944266-15-0*) Maecenas Pr.

Lepsius, Richard. Standard Alphabet for Reducing Unwritten Languages & Foreign Graphic Systems to a Uniform Orthography in European Letters. 2nd ed. Kemp, J. Alan, ed. (Amsterdam Classics in Linguistics Ser.: Vol. 5). xvii, 336p. 1981. 87.00x (*90-272-0876-X*) Benjamins North Am.

Lepsky, Michele. Pathway to Promise. LC 93-19926. 250p. (Orig.). 1993. pap. 7.99 (*1-56722-008-8*) Word Aflame.

Lepson, Ruth. Dreaming in Color. LC 79-54882. 72p. 1980. pap. 9.95 (*0-914086-27-8*) Alicejamesbooks.

Lepthein, Emilie U. Peru. LC 92-4813. (Enchantment of the World Ser.). (Illus.). 128p. (J). (gr. 5-9). 1992. lib. bdg. 20.55 (*0-516-02610-0*) Childrens.

Lepthien, Emilie U. Australia. LC 82-4541. (Enchantment of the World Ser.). (Illus.). (J). (gr. 5-9). 1982. lib. bdg. 20.55 (*0-516-02751-4*) Childrens.

— Bald Eagles. LC 88-38055. (New True Bks.). (Illus.). 45p. (J). (gr. k-2). 1989. lib. bdg. 12.90 (*0-516-01160-X*); pap. 4.95 (*0-516-41160-8*) Childrens.

— Beavers. LC 92-14909. (New True Book Ser.). (Illus.). 48p. (J). (gr. k-4). 1992. lib. bdg. 12.90 (*0-516-01131-6*) Childrens.

— Beavers. (New True Bks.). (Illus.). 48p. (J). (gr. k-4). 1993. pap. 4.95 (*0-516-41131-4*) Childrens.

— Buffalo. LC 89-457. (New True Bks.). (Illus.). 48p. (J). (gr. k-4). 1989. lib. bdg. 12.90 (*0-516-01161-8*); pap. 4.95 (*0-516-41161-6*) Childrens.

— The Cherokee. LC 84-27476. (New True Bks.). (Illus.). 48p. (J). (gr. k-4). 1985. lib. bdg. 12.90 (*0-516-01938-4*); pap. 4.95 (*0-516-41938-2*) Childrens.

— The Choctaw. LC 87-14583. (New True Bks.). (Illus.). 48p. (J). (gr. k-4). 1987. lib. bdg. 12.90 (*0-516-01240-1*); pap. 4.95 (*0-516-41240-X*) Childrens.

— Coyotes. LC 92-35050. (New True Book Ser.). (Illus.). 48p. (J). (gr. k-4). 1993. lib. bdg. 12.90 (*0-516-01331-9*); pap. 4.95 (*0-516-41331-7*) Childrens.

— Ecuador. LC 85-26967. (Enchantment of the World Ser.). (Illus.). 128p. (J). (gr. 5-9). 1986. lib. bdg. 20.55 (*0-516-02760-3*) Childrens.

— Elk. LC 94-10469. (New True Book Ser.). (Illus.). 48p. (J). (gr. k-4). 1994. lib. bdg. 12.90 (*0-516-01063-8*); pap. 4.95 (*0-516-41063-6*) Childrens.

— Greenland. LC 88-37374. (Enchantment of the World Ser.). (Illus.). 128p. (J). (gr. 5-9). 1989. lib. bdg. 20.55 (*0-516-02710-7*) Childrens.

— Iceland. LC 86-29966. (Enchantment of the World Ser.). (Illus.). 128p. (J). (gr. 5-9). 1987. lib. bdg. 20.55 (*0-516-02775-1*) Childrens.

— Kangaroos. LC 94-36351. (New True Bks.). 48p. (J). (gr. k-4). 1995. lib. bdg. 12.90 (*0-516-01075-1*) Childrens.

— Koalas. LC 90-2219. (New True Bks.). (Illus.). 48p. (J). (gr. k-4). 1990. lib. bdg. 12.90 (*0-516-01108-1*); pap. 4.95 (*0-516-41108-X*) Childrens.

— Luxembourg. LC 89-34664. (Enchantment of the World Ser.). 128p. (J). (gr. 5-9). 1989. lib. bdg. 20.55 (*0-516-02714-X*) Childrens.

— Manatees. LC 90-21138. (New True Bks.). (Illus.). 48p. (J). (gr. k-4). 1991. lib. bdg. 12.90 (*0-516-01114-6*); pap. 4.95 (*0-516-41114-4*) Childrens.

— The Mandans. LC 89-22235. (New True Bks.). 48p. (J). (gr. k-4). 1989. lib. bdg. 12.90 (*0-516-01180-4*); pap. 4.95 (*0-516-41180-2*) Childrens.

— Monarch Butterflies. LC 89-456. (New True Bks.). (Illus.). 48p. (J). (gr. k-4). 1989. lib. bdg. 12.90 (*0-516-01165-0*); pap. 4.95 (*0-516-41165-9*) Childrens.

— Opossums. LC 93-33516. (New True Bks.). (Illus.). 48p. (J). (gr. k-4). 1994. lib. bdg. 12.90 (*0-516-01055-7*) Childrens.

— Opossums. (New True Bks.). (J). (ps-2). 1994. pap. 4.95 (*0-516-41055-5*) Childrens.

— Ostriches. LC 93-3407. (New True Bks.). (Illus.). 48p. (J). (gr. k-4). 1993. lib. bdg. 12.90 (*0-516-01193-6*); pap. 4.95 (*0-516-41193-4*) Childrens.

— Otters. LC 93-33515. (New True Bks.). (Illus.). 48p. (J). (gr. k-4). 1994. lib. bdg. 12.90 (*0-516-01056-5*) Childrens.

— Otters. (J). (ps-2). 1994. pap. 4.95 (*0-516-41056-3*) Childrens.

— Penguins. LC 82-17911. (New True Bks.). (Illus.). 48p. (J). (gr. k-4). 1983. lib. bdg. 12.90 (0-516-01683-0); pap. 4.95 (0-516-41683-9) Childrens.
— The Philippines. LC 83-23152. (Enchantment of the World Ser.). (Illus.). 128p. (J). (gr. 5-9). 1986. lib. bdg. 20.55 (0-516-02782-4) Childrens.
— The Philippines. LC 93-15017. (New True Bks.). (Illus.). 48p. (J). (gr. k-4). 1993. lib. bdg. 12.90 (0-516-01195-2); pap. 4.95 (0-516-41195-0) Childrens.
— Polar Bears. LC 91-8892. (New True Bks.). 48p. (J). (gr. k-4). 1991. lib. bdg. 12.90 (0-516-01127-8); pap. 4.95 (0-516-41127-6) Childrens.
— Rabbits & Hares. LC 93-33514. (New True Bks.). (Illus.). 48p. (J). (gr. k-4). 1994. lib. bdg. 12.90 (0-516-01058-1) Childrens.
— Rabbits & Hares. (J). (ps-2). 1994. pap. 4.95 (0-516-41058-X) Childrens.
— Reindeer. LC 93-33513. (New True Bks.). (Illus.). 48p. (J). (gr. k-4). 1994. lib. bdg. 12.90 (0-516-01059-X) Childrens.
— Reindeer. (J). (ps-2). 1994. pap. 4.95 (0-516-41059-8) Childrens.
— The Seminole. LC 84-23141. (New True Bks.). (Illus.). 45p. (J). (gr. 2-4). 1985. lib. bdg. 12.90 (0-516-01941-4); pap. 4.95 (0-516-41941-2) Childrens.
— Skunks. LC 93-3410. (New True Bks.). (Illus.). 48p. (J). (gr. k-4). 1993. lib. bdg. 12.90 (0-516-01197-9); pap. 4.95 (0-516-41197-7) Childrens.
— South Dakota. LC 90-21137. (America the Beautiful Ser.). 144p. (J). (gr. 4 up). 1991. lib. bdg. 20.55 (0-516-00487-5) Childrens.
— South Dakota. braille ed. 195p. (J). 1993. vinyl bd. 15.40 (1-56956-143-5) W A T Braille.
— Squirrels. LC 92-9207. (New True Bks.). (Illus.). 48p. (J). (gr. k-4). 1992. lib. bdg. 12.90 (0-516-01947-3) Childrens.
— Squirrels. LC 92-9207. (New True Bks.). (Illus.). 48p. (J). (gr. k-4). 1993. pap. 4.95 (0-516-41947-1) Childrens.
— Tropical Rainforests. LC 93-3408. (New True Bks.). (Illus.). 48p. (J). (gr. k-4). 1993. lib. bdg. 12.90 (0-516-01198-7); pap. 4.95 (0-516-41198-5) Childrens.
— Wolves. LC 91-3035. (New True Bks.). 48p. (J). (gr. k-4). 1991. lib. bdg. 12.90 (0-516-01129-4); pap. 4.95 (0-516-41129-2) Childrens.
— Woodchucks. LC 91-35276. (New True Bks.). (Illus.). 48p. (J). (gr. k-4). 1992. lib. bdg. 12.90 (0-516-01140-5); pap. 4.95 (0-516-41140-3) Childrens.
— Zebras. LC 94-10945. (New True Books Ser.). (Illus.). 48p. (J). (gr. k-4). 1994. lib. bdg. 12.90 (0-516-01072-7); pap. 4.95 (0-516-41072-5) Childrens.
Lepthien, Emilie U. & Kalbacken, Joan. Foxes. LC 93-3409. (New True Bks.). (Illus.). 48p. (J). (gr. k-4). 1993. lib. bdg. 12.90 (0-516-01191-X); pap. 4.95 (0-516-41191-8) Childrens.
— Recycling. LC 90-21275. (New True Bks.). (Illus.). 48p. (J). (gr. k-4). 1991. lib. bdg. 12.90 (0-516-01118-9); pap. 4.95 (0-516-41118-7) Childrens.
Lepthien, Emilie U. & Klabacken, Joan. Wetlands. LC 92-35051. (New True Book Ser.). (Illus.). 48p. (J). (gr. k-4). 1993. lib. bdg. 12.90 (0-516-01334-3); pap. 4.95 (0-516-41334-1) Childrens.
Leptich, Anne & Evans, Jacque. Calligraphy for Fun & Profit. 1982. pap. 7.00 (0-87980-385-1) Wilshire.
***Leptin, Horst & Ludwig, Jean.** Unitary Representation Theory of Exponential Lie Groups. LC 94-27983. (Expositions in Mathematics Ser.: Vol. 18). 210p. (C). 1994. lib. bdg. 98.95 (3-11-013938-5) De Gruyter.
Lepuil, Roger, jt. auth. see Guegan, Yannick.
Lequeux, James. Physique et Evolution Des Galaxies. LC 66-28070. (Cours & Documents de Mathematiques & de Physique Ser.). 240p. (Orig.). (FRE.). 1967. text ed. 207.00 (0-677-50110-2) Gordon & Breach.
— Structure & Evolution of Galaxies. (Documents on Modern Physics Ser.). 230p. 1969. text ed. 169.00 (0-677-30110-3); pap. text ed. 69.00 (0-677-30115-4) Gordon & Breach.
Lequin, Frank, ed. The Private Correspondence of Isaac Titsingh, Vol. 1: 1785-1811. (Japonica Neerlandica Ser.: Vol. 4). xlix, 534p. (DUT.). 1990. 85.00 (90-5063-052-9, Pub. by Gieben NE) Benjamins North Am.
Lerager, Jim. In the Shadow of the Cloud: Photographs & Histories of America's Atomic Veterans. LC 87-33682. (Illus.). 116p. 1988. 23.95 (1-55591-030-0) Fulcrum Pub.
***Lerangis, Peter.** Driver's Dead. (YA). 1994. pap. 3.50 (0-590-46677-1) Scholastic Inc.
— The Sultan's Secret. (G. I. Joe Ser.). (YA). (gr. 8 up). 1988. pap. 2.95 (0-345-35099-5) Ballantine.
— Yearbook. (YA). 1994. pap. 3.50 (0-590-46678-X) Scholastic Inc.
Leray, Jean. Lagrangian Analysis & Quantum Mechanics: A Mathematical Structure Related to Asymptotic Expansions & the Maslov Index. Schroeder, Carolyn, tr. 1982. 47.50 (0-262-12087-9) MIT Pr.
Lerbinger, Otto, ed. Who's Who in Public Relations. 6th ed. 762p. 1992. 50.00 (0-9632901-0-X) P R Pub Co.
Lerch, Gregory D. How to Sell Your Home When Homes Aren't Selling. (Illus.). 256p. (Orig.). 1991. pap. 16.95 (1-55870-182-6) Betterway Bks.
Lerch, Harold A. & Stopka, Christine. Developmental Motor Activities for All Children from Theory to Practice. 199p. (C). 1992. pap. text ed. write for info. (0-697-14479-8) Brown & Benchmark.
Lerch, Harold A., jt. auth. see Welch, Paula D.
Lerche, Charles O., Jr. America in World Affairs. LC 79-26759. (Foundations of American Government & Political Science Ser.). (Illus.). 118p. 1980. reprint ed. text ed. 49.75 (0-313-22315-7, LEAMW, Greenwood Pr) Greenwood.
Lerche, H. R. Boundary Crossing of Brownian Motion. (Lecture Notes in Statistics Ser.: Vol. 40). 142p. 1986. pap. 29.00 (0-387-96433-9) Spr-Verlag.
***Lerche, I. & Petersen, K.** Salt & Sediment Dynamics. LC 95-2515. 1995. write for info. (0-8493-7684-X) CRC Pr.
Lerche, Ian. Basin Analysis, Vol. 2: Quantitative Methods. (Geology Ser.: Academic Press). 570p. 1990. 115.00 (0-685-31084-1) Acad Pr.
— Oil Exploration: Basin Analysis & Economics. (Illus.). 178p. 1992. text ed. 65.00 (0-12-444175-0) Acad Pr.
Lerche, Ian, ed. Basin Analysis, Vol. 1: Quantitative Methods. 562p. 1989. text ed. 160.00 (0-12-444172-6) Acad Pr.
Lerche, Ian & O'Brien, J. J., eds. Dynamical Geology of Salt & Related Structures. 856p. 1987. text ed. 81.00 (0-12-444170-X) Acad Pr.
***Lerche, Ian & Petersen, Kenneth.** Salt & Sediment Dynamics. 320p. 1995. 169.95 (0-614-07249-2, 7684) CRC Pr.
***Lerche, Ian & Thomsen, Rene O.** Hydrodynamics of Oil & Gas. LC 94-48514. 325p. 1995. 75.00 (0-306-44872-6, Plenum Pr) Plenum.
Lerche, Mario R. Deutsch-Spanisches Glossarium Finanz und Wirtschaft: German - Spanish Glossary of Finance & Economics. 460p. (GER & SPA.). 1967. 75.00 (0-8288-6671-6, M8176) Fr & Eur.
Lerda, Alberto. Anyons: Quantum Mechanics of Particles with Fractional Statistics. LC 92-33779. (Lecture Notes in Physics, New Series, Monographs: Vol. 14). 1992. 42.00 (0-387-56105-6) Spr-Verlag.
Lerdahl, Herman & Cernick, Cliff. Skystruck: True Tales of an Alaska Bush Pilot. LC 89-33729. (Illus.). 192p. (Orig.). 1989. pap. 9.95 (0-88240-356-7) Alaska Northwest.
Lerdau, Enrique, tr. see Escarpenter, Claudio & Fargas.
Lerdau, Federico, tr. see Escarpenter, Claudio & Fargas.
Lere, John C. Managerial Accounting: A Planning-Operations-Control Framework. 1991. text ed. write for info. (0-471-60754-1); student ed. write for info. (0-471-54605-4); student ed write for info. (0-318-63042-7); write for info. (0-471-54707-7); write for info. (0-318-63043-5); write for info. (0-471-54606-2) Wiley.
Lereah, David A. Insurance Markets: Information Problems & Regulation. LC 84-26403. 192p. 1985. text ed. 55.00 (0-275-90135-1, C0135, Praeger Pubs) Greenwood.
— Insurance Markets: Information Problems & Regulations. (C). 1985. 320.00 (0-685-32774-4, Pub. by Witherby & Co UK) St Mut.
Lerebours, N. P. A Treatise on Photography. LC 72-9215. (Literature of Photography Ser.). 1973. reprint ed. 19.95 (0-405-04923-4) Ayer.
Leredo, P., et al. Research Networks Built by the - M H R 4 - Programme. (EUR Ser.: No. 14700). 280p. 1992. pap. 40.00 (92-826-4823-0, CG-NA-14700-EN-C, Pub. by Europ Com) UNIPUB.
Lerer, Bernard & Gershon, S., eds. New Directions in Affective Disorders. (Illus.). 625p. 1989. 182.00 (0-387-96769-9) Spr-Verlag.
Lerer, Bernard, et al, eds. ECT: Basic Mechanisms. LC 86-3507. 192p. 1986. reprint ed. pap. text ed. 22.00 (0-88048-237-0, 48-237-0) Am Psychiatric.
Lerer, Seth. Boethius & Dialogue: Literary Method in "The Consolation of Philosophy" LC 85-42937. 280p. 1985. text ed. 42.50 (0-691-06653-1) Princeton U Pr.
— Boethius & Dialogue: Literary Method in the Consolation of Philosophy. LC 85-42937. reprint ed. pap. 79.00 (0-7837-9372-3, 2060116) Bks Demand.
— Chaucer & His Readers: Imagining the Author in Late Medieval England. LC 92-33454. (Illus.). 320p. (C). 1993. text ed. 39.50 (0-691-06811-9) Princeton U Pr.
— Literacy & Power in Anglo-Saxon Literature. LC 90-40463. (Regents Studies in Medieval Culture). (Illus.). xii, 269p. 1991. 40.00 (0-8032-2895-3) U of Nebr Pr.
Lerer, Susan. African Metalwork & Ivory. (Illus.). 48p. (Orig.). (C). 1993. pap. text ed. 22.00 (0-9635857-0-3) Images of Cult.
Leresche, G. & Bovet, J., eds. Relations Between Psychopathological & Socio-Professional Factors in Out-Patient Department Psychiatry. (Journal: Psychopathology: Vol. 19, Suppl. 1, 1986). (Illus.). 260p. 1986. pap. 62.50 (3-8055-4332-8) S Karger.
Lergessner, J. White Specks on Dark Shores. 80p. (C). 1990. pap. 30.00 (0-86439-147-1, Pub. by Boolarong Pubns AT) St Mut.
Leridon, Henri. Human Fertility: The Basic Components. Helzner, Judith F., tr. LC 77-1913. 1977. lib. bdg. 21.00 (0-226-47297-3) U Ch Pr.
Leridon, Henri, jt. ed. see Gray, Ronald.
Lerille, Red, ed. see Billac, Pete.
Lerin, Alfredo, comp. Quinientas Ilustraciones. 324p. (SPA.). 1990. reprint ed. pap. 7.50 (0-311-42037-0) Casa Bautista.
Lerin, Alfredo, tr. see Brown, Raymond B.
Lerin, Alfredo, jt. auth. see Sloan, W. H.
Lerin, Alfredo, tr. see Summers, Ray.
Lerin, Olivia, tr. see Brown, Raymond B.
Lerin, S. D., tr. see Stowell, Gordon.
Lerin, S. D. de, tr. see Stowell, Gordon.
Leritz, Len. No-Fault Negotiating: A Practical Guide to the New Dealmaking Strategy That Lets Both Sides Win. 1990. pap. 12.95 (0-446-39104-2) Warner Bks.
Lerma, Olivia, tr. see Harmon, Ed & Jarmin, Marge.
Lermack, Paul. How to Get into the Right Law School. LC 92-14744. 1992. 14.95 (0-8442-4165-2, VGM Career Bks) NTC Pub Grp.
***Lerman.** Young Unwed Fathers: Changing Roles & Emerging Policies. (C). 1995. pap. text ed. 18.95 (1-56639-318-3) Temple U Pr.
Lerman & Tripathi. Ocular Toxicology. 410p. 1990. 140.00 (0-8247-8309-3) Dekker.
Lerman, A. Geochemical Processes Water & Sediment Environments. LC 87-3270. 496p. (C). 1987. reprint ed. text ed. 44.50 (0-89874-990-5) Krieger.
Lerman, A. & Meybeck, M., eds. Physical & Chemical Weathering in Geochemical Cycles. (C). 1988. lib. bdg. 133.00 (90-277-2821-6) Kluwer Ac.
***Lerman, Abraham, et al, eds.** Physics & Chemistry of Lakes. 2nd ed. LC 95-6098. 1995. write for info. (3-540-57891-9) Spr-Verlag.
Lerman, Alice. Birth Environments: Emerging Trends & Implications for Design. (Publications in Architecture & Urban Planning: No. R91-3). (Illus.). 110p. (C). 1991. 15.00 (0-938744-76-3) U of Wis Ctr Arch-Urban.
Lerman, Andrea. The Macrobiotic Community Cookbook: Favorite Recipes from America's Macrobiotic Leaders. LC 88-32260. 224p. (Orig.). 1989. pap. 12.95 (0-89529-396-X) Avery Pub.
Lerman, Dan & Linne, Eric B., eds. Hospital Home Care: Strategic Management for Integrated Care Delivery. LC 93-16411. 328p. 1993. 60.00 (1-55648-096-2, 079200) AHPI.
***Lerman, Dan & Tehan, Claire, eds.** Hospital-Hospice Mangement Models: Integration & Collaboration. LC 95-14333. 1995. pap. write for info. (1-55648-137-3) AHPI.
Lerman, Dan, jt. ed. see Nathanson, Susan N.
Lerman, Eleanor. Armed Love. LC 73-6013. (Wesleyan Poetry Program Ser.: Vol. 68). 64p. 1973. pap. 10.95 (0-8195-1068-8, Wesleyan Univ Pr) U Pr of New Eng.
— Come the Sweet By & By. LC 75-8449. 80p. 1975. 15.00 (0-87023-194-4); pap. 9.95 (0-87023-195-2) U of Mass Pr.
Lerman, G. & Rudolph, L. The Parallel Evolution of Parallel Processors. (Frontiers of Computer Science Ser.). 1993. 65.00 (0-306-44537-9, Plenum Pr) Plenum.
***Lerman-Golomb, Barbara.** AIDS. LC 94-30055. (Teen Hot Line Ser.). (YA). 1995. lib. bdg. write for info. (0-8114-3814-7) Raintree Steck-V.
Lerman, Hannah. A Mote in Freud's Eye: From Psychoanalysis to the Psychology of Women. 256p. (C). 1986. 28.95 (0-8261-5420-4) Springer Pub.
Lerman, Hannah & Porter, Natalie, eds. Feminist Ethics in Psychotherapy. LC 90-9625. 296p. 1990. 36.95 (0-8261-6290-8) Springer Pub.
Lerman, J. M., tr. see Kahana, S. Z.
Lerman, Katharine A. The Chancellor As Courtier: Bernhard von Bulow & the Governance of Germany, 1900-1909. 352p. (C). 1990. 64.95 (0-521-38155-X) Cambridge U Pr.
Lerman, Leonard S., ed. DNA Probes: Applications in Genetic & Infectious Disease & Cancer. LC 86-212410. (Current Communications in Molecular Biology Ser.). 198p. reprint ed. pap. 56.50 (0-8357-2755-6, 2039871) Bks Demand.
Lerman, M. Degrees of Unsolvability: Local & Global Theory. (Perspectives in Mathematical Logic Ser.). (Illus.). 307p. 1983. 103.00 (0-387-12155-2) Spr-Verlag.
Lerman, Matthew. Marine Biology: Environment, Diversity, & Ecology. (Illus.). 450p. (C). 1986. pap. text ed. 37.75 (0-8053-6402-1) Benjamin-Cummings.
***Lerman, Ora, et al.** Inside the Ark. 32p. 1995. pap. 10.00 (0-9645942-7-7) Lerman Studios.
Lerman, Rhoda. Animal Acts. 272p. 1994. 22.50 (0-8050-1418-7) H Holt & Co.
— The Book of the Night. 292p. 1993. pap. 5.95 (0-7043-3991-9, Pub. by Womens Pr UK) Interlink Pub.
Lerman, Robert A., jt. auth. see Kolk, W. Richard.
Lerman, Robert I. & Ooms, Theodora J., eds. Young Unwed Fathers: Changing Roles & Emerging Policies. LC 92-39617. 384p. 1993. 44.95 (1-56639-048-6) Temple U Pr.
— Young Unwed Fathers: Changing Roles & Emerging Policies. LC 92-39617. 384p. 1995. pap. write for info. (0-614-03055-2) Temple U Pr.
Lerman, Saf. Your Child from Six to Twelve: Saf Lerman Answers Questions about Those Middle Years. (Winston Family Handbooks Ser.). 96p. (Orig.). 1985. pap. 9.95 (0-86683-825-2) Harper SF.
Lerman, Stephen, ed. Cultural Perspectives on the Mathematics Classroom. (Mathematics Education Library: Vol. 14). 218p. (C). 1994. lib. bdg. 71.00 (0-7923-2931-7) Kluwer Ac.
Lerman, Steven, jt. auth. see Ben-Akiva, Moshe.
Lerman, Steven R. Problem Solving & Computation for Scientists & Engineers: An Introduction Using C. LC 92-24326. 544p. 1992. pap. text ed. 53.00 (0-13-482126-2) P-H.
Lerman, Z., ed. see Gorbatskii, Vitalii G.
Lerman, Zvi, jt. auth. see Brooks, Karen.
***Lerman, Zvi, et al.** Land Reform & Farm Restructuring in Ukraine. LC 94-43327. (Discussion Papers: Vol. 270). 1994. write for info. (0-8213-3149-3) World Bank.
***Lermontor, Mikhail.** A Hero of Our Time. Cornwell, Neil, ed. 208p. (Orig.). 1995. pap. 6.95 (0-460-87566-3, Everyman's Classic Lib) C E Tuttle.
Lermontov. Lermontov: A Hero of Our Time: Bela, Maxim Maximovich, Taman, Princess Mary, the Fatalist: Geroi Nashego Vremeni; Bela, Maksim Maksimych, Taman', Knyazhna Meri, Fatalist. Richards, D. J., ed. (C). reprint ed. pap. text ed. 17.95 (1-85399-314-X, Pub. by Brstl Class Pr UK) Focus Info Gr.
Lermontov, M. Iu. Demon. 142p. 1978. 22.00 (0-317-92447-8, Pub. by Collets UK) Pro-Am Music.
— Taman. 60p. (C). 1984. 30.00 (0-569-08083-5, Pub. by Collets UK) Pro-Am Music.
Lermontov, Michel. Un Heroes de Montre Temps, La Princess Ligovskoi. (FRE.). 1976. pap. 11.95 (0-7859-4031-6) Fr & Eur.
Lermontov, Mikhail. A Hero of Our Time. Foote, Paul, tr. (Classics Ser.). 1966. mass mkt. 9.95 (0-14-044176-X, Penguin Classics) Viking Penguin.
— Hero of Our Time. 1992. 15.00 (0-679-41327-8, Everymans Lib) Knopf.
— A Hero of Our Time. Nabokov, Vladimir & Nabokov, Dmitri, trs. 210p. 1988. reprint ed. pap. 12.95 (0-87501-049-0) Ardis Pubs.
— Major Poetical Works. Liberman, Anatoly, tr. LC 82-23798. (Minnesota Publications in the Humanities: Vol.3). (Illus.). 652p. 1984. text ed. 49.95 (0-8166-1124-6) U of Minn Pr.
***Lermontov, Mikhail, et al.** Eros Russe: Russkii Erot ne Dlia Dam. 3rd ed. (Illus.). 94p. (RUS.). 1995. reprint ed. pap. 8.95 (1-57201-004-5) Berkeley Slavic.
LERN Staff. Front-Line Staff Training Manual. 47p. Date not set. 24.95 (0-914951-68-8) LERN.
— Ratios for Success. 42p. Date not set. 39.95 (0-914951-69-6) LERN.
Lerner, ed. Application & Theory of Periodic Structures, Diffraction Gratings, & Moire Phenomena, No. III. 1987. 45.00 (0-89252-850-8, 815) SPIE.
Lerner, et al. New Words Dictionary. 1992. pap. 2.95 (0-345-80089-3) Ballantine.
Lerner, A. W. The Manipulators: Personality & Politics in Multiple Perspectives. 168p. (C). 1989. text ed. 29.95 (0-8058-0335-1) L Erlbaum Assocs.
Lerner, Abba P. Economics of Control: Principles of Welfare Economics. LC 75-107922. (Reprints of Economic Classics Ser.). (Illus.). xxii, 428p. 1970. reprint ed. 39.50 (0-678-00618-0) Kelley.
— Economics of Employment. LC 77-18756. (Economics Handbook Ser.). 397p. 1978. reprint ed. text ed. 38.50 (0-313-20181-1, LEEE, Greenwood Pr) Greenwood.
— Essays in Economic Analysis. LC 79-1585. 1988. reprint ed. 34.50 (0-88355-890-4) Hyperion Conn.
Lerner, Abe, ed. see Rathe, John F.
Lerner, Abe, ed. see Schmoller, Hans.
Lerner, Adam, jt. ed. see Ringrose, Marjorie.
Lerner, Alan C., ed. The Grants Register, 1989-1991. 11th ed. LC 77-12055. 1000p. 1988. 75.00 (0-312-02118-6) St Martin.
Lerner, Alan J. A Hymn to Him: The Lyrics of Alan Jay Lerner. Green, Benny, ed. (Illus.). 320p. 1987. 20.00 (0-87910-109-1) Limelight Edns.
— The Musical Theatre: A Celebration. (Quality Paperbacks Ser.). (Illus.). 256p. 1989. pap. 16.95 (0-306-80364-X) Da Capo.
— The Street Where I Live. (Illus.). 333p. 1994. reprint ed. pap. 13.95 (0-306-80602-9) Da Capo.
***Lerner, Alan J., ed.** The Little Black Book of Neurology: A Manual for Neurological House Officers. 3rd ed. LC 94-22738. 1994. write for info. (0-8151-5440-2, Yr Bk Med Pubs) Mosby Yr Bk.
Lerner, Alan J. & Loewe, Frederick. Camelot. 1961. 13.95 (0-394-40521-8) Random.
Lerner, Alan J., jt. auth. see Shaw, George Bernard.
Lerner, Alexander. Change of Heart. (Illus.). 1992. lib. bdg. write for info. (0-86689-030-0) Balaban Intl Sci Serv.
— Change of Heart. (Illus.). 237p. (J). (gr. 4-9). 1992. 18.95 (0-8225-0773-0, Lerner Publctns) Lerner Group.
Lerner, Allan W. & King, B. Kay. Continuing Higher Education: The Coming Wave. 176p. (C). 1992. text ed. 31.00 (0-8077-3197-8) Tchrs Coll.
Lerner, Allan W. & Wanat, John. Public Administration: Scenarios in Public Management. LC 92-16366. 192p. (C). 1993. pap. text ed. write for info. (0-13-739046-7) P-H.
Lerner, Andrea, ed. Dancing on the Rim of the World: An Anthology of Contemporary Northwest Native American Writing. LC 90-11006. (Sun Tracks Ser.: Vol. 19). (Illus.). 266p. (Orig.). 1990. lib. bdg. 37.50 (0-8165-1097-0); pap. 16.95 (0-8165-1215-9) U of Ariz Pr.
Lerner, Andrew. All-Star Mystery Athlete Puzzle Book. (J). (gr. 4-7). 1994. 3.50 (0-553-48163-0) Bantam.
Lerner, Andy. Halloween KidDoodles, No. 4. (KidDoodles Ser. Storytime Bks.). (Illus.). 64p. (J). (ps-2). 1992. pap. 0.99 (1-56293-262-4) McClanahan Bk.
***Lerner, Arthur.** Poetry in the Therapeutic Experience. (Illus.). 144p. (Orig.). (C). 1994. pap. 14.95 (0-918812-79-8) MMB Music.
— Words for All Seasons. (Illus.). 104p. (Orig.). 1983. pap. 6.95 (0-938292-06-4) Being Bks.
Lerner, Arthur & Mahlendorf, Ursula R. Life Guidance Through Literature. LC 91-27499. 236p. (C). 1992. text ed. 15.00 (0-8389-0580-3) ALA.
Lerner, B. Rosie & Netzhammer, Beverly S. Possum in the Pawpaw Tree: A Seasonal Guide to Midwestern Gardening. LC 94-12066. (Illus.). 324p. 1994. 24.95 (1-55753-053-X); pap. 14.95 (1-55753-054-8) Purdue U Pr.
Lerner, Barbara. Minimum Competence, Maximum Choice: Educational Vouchers for Children Who Need Them Most. (C). 1982. text ed. 19.50 (0-8290-0414-9) Irvington.
— Therapy in the Ghetto: Political Impotence & Personal Disintegration. LC 74-186606. 256p. 1972. 38.50x (0-8018-1373-5) Johns Hopkins.
Lerner, Barbara & Vining, Daniel R. Intelligence & National Achievement. Cattell, Raymond B., Jr., ed. (C). 1984. 40.00 (0-941694-14-3) Inst Study Man.
***Lerner, Carol.** Backyard Birds of Summer. (Illus.). 1996. write for info. (0-688-13600-1); lib. bdg. write for info. (0-688-13601-X) Morrow Jr Bks.
— Backyard Birds of Winter. LC 94-3036. (Illus.). 48p. (J). 1994. 16.00 (0-688-12819-X); lib. bdg. 15.93 (0-688-12820-3) Morrow Jr Bks.
— Cactus. LC 91-35678. (Illus.). 32p. (J). 1992. 15.00 (0-688-09636-0); lib. bdg. 14.93 (0-688-09637-9) Morrow Jr Bks.
— A Desert Year. LC 90-44643. (Illus.). 48p. (J). 1991. 13.95 (0-688-09382-5); lib. bdg. 13.88 (0-688-09383-3) Morrow Jr Bks.

An Asterisk (*) at the beginning of an entry indicates that the title is appearing in BIP for the first time.

— Dumb Cane & Daffodils: Poisonous Plants in the House & Garden. LC 89-33622. (Illus.). 32p. (J). 1990. lib. bdg. 13.88 (*0-688-08796-5*) Morrow Jr Bks.

— A Forest Year. LC 86-9741. (Illus.). 48p. (J). (ps up). 1987. 12.95 (*0-688-06413-2*); lib. bdg. 12.88 (*0-688-06414-0*) Morrow Jr Bks.

— Moonseed & Mistletoe: A Book of Poisonous Wild Plants. LC 87-13989. (Illus.). 32p. (J). (ps up). 1988. 12.95 (*0-688-07307-7*); lib. bdg. 12.88 (*0-688-07308-5*) Morrow Jr Bks.

— Plant Families. LC 88-26653. (Illus.). 32p. (J). (gr. 4 up). 1989. 15.00 (*0-688-07881-8*); lib. bdg. 14.93 (*0-688-07882-6*) Morrow Jr Bks.

— Plants That Make You Sniffle & Sneeze. LC 92-21561. (Illus.). 32p. (J). 1993. 15.00 (*0-688-11489-X*); lib. bdg. 14.93 (*0-688-11490-3*) Morrow Jr Bks.

Lerner, Christopher, jt. auth. see Brams, Robert S.

Lerner, D., et al. Sources & Movement of Chlorinated Solvents in Dual Porosity Rock Coventry Ground Soil & Groundwater Research Report IV, No. EUR 14379. 137p. 1993. pap. 19.00 (*92-826-5323-4*, CD-NA-14379-EN-C, Pub. by Europ Com) UNIPUB.

Lerner, Daniel, ed. Human Meaning of the Social Sciences. 11.25 (*0-8446-2281-8*) Peter Smith.

— Propaganda in War & Crisis. LC 72-4669. (International Propaganda & Communications Ser.). 516p. 1978. reprint ed. 30.95 (*0-405-04754-1*) Ayer.

Lerner, Daniel & Nelson, Lyle M., eds. Communication Research: A Half-Century Appraisal. LC 77-89616. 359p. reprint ed. pap. 102.40 (*0-7837-3976-1*, 2043806) Bks Demand.

Lerner, Daniel, jt. ed. see Lasswell, Harold D.

Lerner, Daniel, jt. ed. see Schramm, Wilbur.

Lerner, David. Pray Like the Hunted. 91p. (Orig.). 1992. pap. 6.00 (*0-929730-38-0*) Zeitgeist Pr.

— Why Rimbaud Went to Africa. 76p. (Orig.). 1990. pap. 5.95 (*0-929730-12-7*) Zeitgeist Pr.

Lerner, Deborah, jt. auth. see Pardini, Alan.

Lerner, Debra J. & Stone, Elliot M. Employee Health Benefits Survey & User's Manual. LC 90-81856. 53p. (Orig.). 1990. pap. 20.00 (*0-89154-405-4*) Intl Found Employ.

Lerner, E., ed. Methods for the Study of Personality in Young Children. (SRCD M: Vol. 6, No. 4). 1941. 23.00 (*0-527-01520-2*) Periodicals Srv.

Lerner, Edward M. Probe. 1991. mass mkt. 4.99 (*0-446-36081-3*) Warner Bks.

Lerner, Eric. The Big Bang Never Happened. 1992. 14.00 (*0-679-74049-X*, Vin) Random.

— The Big Bang Never Happened: A Startling Refutation of the Dominant Theory of the Origin of the Universe. 480p. 1991. 21.45 (*0-8129-1853-3*, Times Bks) Random.

Lerner, Ethan A. Comprendiendo el SIDA. (Coping with Modern Problems Ser.). (Illus.). 64p. (SPA.). (J). (gr. 4 up). 1988. 17.50 (*0-8225-2000-1*, Lerner Publctns) Lerner Group.

***Lerner, Fred.** A Bookman's Fantasy: How Science Fiction Became Respectable & Other Essays. LC 94-73980. iv, 97p. (Orig.). 1995. pap. 11.95 (*0-915368-65-X*) New Eng SF Assoc.

— A Silverlock Companion: The Life & Works of John Myers Myers. LC 89-861. 52p. (Orig.). (C). 1989. reprint ed. lib. bdg. 23.00x (*0-8095-6850-0*) Borgo Pr.

Lerner, Fred, ed. A Silverlock Companion: The Life & Works of John Myers Myers. (Illus.). 52p. (Orig.). 1988. pap. 7.95 (*0-910619-02-6*) Niekas Pubns.

Lerner, Frederick A. Modern Science Fiction & the American Literary Community. LC 85-1874. 343p. 1985. 29.50 (*0-8108-1794-2*) Scarecrow.

Lerner, G. E. & Klein, K. K., eds. Canadian Agricultural Trade: Disputes, Actions & Prospects. 300p. 1990. pap. 24.95 (*0-919813-90-9*, Pub. by Univ Calgary CN) Paul & Co Pubs.

***Lerner Geography Department Staff.** United States--in Pictures. LC 94-44841. (Visual Geography Ser.). (J). 1995. lib. bdg. write for info. (*0-8225-1896-1*) Lerner Group.

Lerner Geography Department Staff, ed. Algeria in Pictures. (Visual Geography Ser.). (Illus.). 64p. (YA). (gr. 5 up). 1992. lib. bdg. 18.95 (*0-8225-1901-1*, Lerner Publctns) Lerner Group.

— Armenia. (Then & Now Ser.). (Illus.). 64p. (YA). (gr. 5 up). 1993. lib. bdg. 21.50 (*0-8225-2806-1*, Lerner Publctns) Lerner Group.

— Azerbaijan. (Then & Now Ser.). (Illus.). 64p. (YA). (gr. 5 up). 1993. lib. bdg. 21.50 (*0-8225-2810-X*, Lerner Publctns) Lerner Group.

— Belarus. (Then & Now Ser.). (Illus.). 64p. (YA). (gr. 5 up). 1993. lib. bdg. 21.50 (*0-8225-2811-8*, Lerner Publctns) Lerner Group.

— Cyprus in Pictures. (Visual Geography Ser.). (Illus.). 64p. (J). (gr. 5-12). 1992. lib. bdg. 18.95 (*0-8225-1910-0*, Lerner Publctns) Lerner Group.

— Estonia. (Then & Now Ser.). (Illus.). 64p. (YA). (gr. 5 up). 1992. lib. bdg. 21.50 (*0-8225-2803-7*, Lerner Publctns) Lerner Group.

— Georgia. (Then & Now Ser.). (Illus.). 64p. (YA). (gr. 5 up). 1993. lib. bdg. 21.50 (*0-8225-2807-X*, Lerner Publctns) Lerner Group.

— Greece in Pictures. (Visual Geography Ser.). (Illus.). 64p. (YA). (gr. 5 up). 1991. lib. bdg. 18.95 (*0-8225-1882-1*, Lerner Publctns) Lerner Group.

— Kazakhstan. (Then & Now Ser.). (Illus.). 64p. (YA). (gr. 5 up). 1993. lib. bdg. 21.50 (*0-8225-2815-0*, Lerner Publctns) Lerner Group.

— Kirghyzstan. (Then & Now Ser.). (Illus.). 64p. (YA). (gr. 5 up). 1993. lib. bdg. 21.50 (*0-8225-2814-2*, Lerner Publctns) Lerner Group.

— Latvia. LC 92-7260. (Then & Now Ser.). (Illus.). 64p. (YA). (gr. 5 up). 1992. lib. bdg. 21.50 (*0-8225-2802-9*, Lerner Publctns) Lerner Group.

— Lithuania. LC 92-9698. (Then & Now Ser.). (Illus.). 64p. (YA). (gr. 5 up). 1992. lib. bdg. 21.50 (*0-8225-2804-5*, Lerner Publctns) Lerner Group.

— Moldova. (Then & Now Ser.). (Illus.). 64p. (YA). (gr. 5 up). 1993. lib. bdg. 21.50 (*0-8225-2809-6*, Lerner Publctns) Lerner Group.

— Russia. (Then & Now Ser.). (Illus.). 64p. (YA). (gr. 5 up). 1992. lib. bdg. 21.50 (*0-8225-2805-3*, Lerner Publctns) Lerner Group.

— Tadzhikistan. (Then & Now Ser.). (Illus.). 64p. (YA). (gr. 5 up). 1993. lib. bdg. 21.50 (*0-8225-2816-9*, Lerner Publctns) Lerner Group.

— Turkmenistan. (Then & Now Ser.). (Illus.). 64p. (YA). (gr. 5 up). 1993. lib. bdg. 21.50 (*0-8225-2813-4*, Lerner Publctns) Lerner Group.

— Uzbekistan. (Then & Now Ser.). (Illus.). 64p. (YA). (gr. 5 up). 1993. lib. bdg. 21.50 (*0-8225-2812-6*, Lerner Publctns) Lerner Group.

— Zaire in Pictures. (Visual Geography Ser.). (Illus.). 64p. (YA). (gr. 5 up). 1992. lib. bdg. 18.95 (*0-8225-1899-6*, Lerner Publctns) Lerner Group.

Lerner Geography Department Staff, ed. see Barysh, Ann, et al.

Lerner Geography Department Staff, ed. see Brown, Dottie.

Lerner Geography Department Staff, ed. see Fredeen, Charles.

Lerner Geography Department Staff, ed. see Gelman, Amy.

Lerner Geography Department Staff, ed. see LaDoux, Rita C.

Lerner Geography Department Staff, ed. see Porter, A. P.

Lerner Geography Department Staff, ed. see Sitvaitis, Karen.

Lerner Geography Department Staff, ed. see Swain, Gwenyth.

Lerner Geography Department Staff, ed. see Verba, Joan M.

Lerner Geography Dept. Staff, ed. Albania in Pictures. LC 94-10616. (Visual Geography Ser.). (Illus.). 64p. (YA). (gr. 5 up). 1995. lib. bdg. 18.95 (*0-8225-1902-X*, Lerner Publctns) Lerner Group.

— Denmark in Pictures. (Visual Geography Ser.). (Illus.). 64p. (YA). (gr. 5 up). 1991. reprint ed. lib. bdg. 18.95 (*0-8225-1880-5*, Lerner Publctns) Lerner Group.

— Finland in Pictures. (Visual Geography Ser.). (Illus.). 64p. (YA). (gr. 5 up). 1991. reprint ed. lib. bdg. 18.95 (*0-8225-1881-3*, Lerner Publctns) Lerner Group.

— Iceland in Pictures. (Visual Geography Ser.). (Illus.). 64p. (YA). (gr. 5 up). 1991. reprint ed. lib. bdg. 17.50 (*0-8225-1892-9*, Lerner Publctns) Lerner Group.

— Northern Ireland in Pictures. (Visual Geography Ser.). (Illus.). 64p. (YA). (gr. 5 up). 1991. reprint ed. lib. bdg. 18.95 (*0-8225-1898-8*, Lerner Publctns) Lerner Group.

— Portugal in Pictures. (Visual Geography Ser.). (Illus.). 64p. (J). 1991. reprint ed. lib. bdg. 18.95 (*0-8225-1886-4*, Lerner Publctns) Lerner Group.

Lerner, Gerda. Black Women in White America: A Documentary History. 1992. pap. 15.00 (*0-679-74314-6*, Vin) Random.

— The Creation of Feminist Consciousness: From the Middle Ages to 1870. 416p. 1994. reprint ed. pap. 11.95 (*0-19-509060-8*) OUP.

— The Creation of Patriarchy. LC 85-21578. (Women & History Ser.). (Illus.). 318p. 1986. reprint ed. 30.00 (*0-19-503996-3*) OUP.

— The Creation of Patriarchy. LC 85-21578. (Women & History Ser.). (Illus.). 318p. 1987. reprint ed. pap. 12.95 (*0-19-505185-8*) OUP.

— A Death of One's Own. LC 85-40371. 272p. 1985. reprint ed. pap. 12.95 (*0-299-10444-3*) U of Wis Pr.

— The Female Experience: An American Documentary. 560p. 1992. pap. 15.95 (*0-19-507258-8*) OUP.

— The Majority Finds Its Past: Placing Women in History. 1981. pap. 9.95 (*0-19-502899-6*) OUP.

— What Women Thought: The Creation of Feminist Consciousness, 700 A.D.-1870. LC 92-20411. (Women & History Ser.: Vol. 2). 320p. 1993. 30.00 (*0-19-506604-9*) OUP.

Lerner, Gerda, ed. Black Women in White America: A Documentary History. LC 72-8643. 672p. 1988. pap. 12.00 (*0-394-71880-1*, Vin) Random.

***Lerner Group Staff.** Create-a-Story Book. 1995. pap. text ed. (*0-8225-9998-8*) Lerner Group.

Lerner, Harriet G. Dance of Anger. 1989. pap. 13.00 (*0-06-091565-X*, PL) HarpC.

— The Dance of Deception: Pretending & Truth-Telling in Women's Lives. 272p. 1994. pap. 13.00 (*0-06-092463-2*, PL) HarpC.

— The Dance of Intimacy: A Woman's Guide to Courageous Acts of Change in Key Relationships. LC 88-45519. 272p. 1990. reprint ed. pap. 13.00 (*0-06-091646-X*, PL) HarpC.

— Women in Therapy. LC 88-45938. 320p. 1989. reprint ed. pap. 13.00 (*0-06-097228-9*, PL 7228, PL) HarpC.

— Women in Therapy. LC 87-19326. 320p. 1992. reprint ed. 40.00 (*0-87668-978-0*) Aronson.

Lerner, Harriet G. & Goldhor, Susan H. What's So Terrible about Swallowing an Appleseed. LC 94-2769. (Illus.). (J). Date not set. 15.00 (*0-06-024523-9*); lib. bdg. 14.89 (*0-06-024524-7*) HarpC.

Lerner, Helen. Take It Off & Keep It Off: Based on the Successful Methods of Overeaters Anonymous. 176p. (Orig.). 1989. pap. 8.95 (*0-8092-4493-4*) Contemp Bks.

Lerner, Helene & Elins, Roberta. Stress Breakers. LC 84-17506. (Illus.). 110p. 1985. pap. 8.95 (*0-89638-074-2*) Hazelden.

Lerner, Herbert J. & Antes, Richard S. Federal Income Taxation of Corporations Filing Consolidated Returns, 3 vols. 1975. Updates. ring bd. write for info. (*0-8205-1227-3*) Bender.

Lerner, Howard D. & Lerner, Paul M., eds. Primitive Mental States & the Rorschach Test. 1988. text ed. 70.00 (*0-8236-4295-X*) Intl Univs Pr.

Lerner, I. Michael, tr. see Medvedev, Zhores.

Lerner, Isha & Lerner, Mark. Inner Child Cards: A Journey into Fairy Tales, Myth & Nature. (Illus.). 336p. (Orig.). 1992. text ed. 34.95 (*0-939680-95-5*) Bear & Co.

Lerner, J. M. & McKinney, W. R. International Conference on the Application & Theory of Periodic Structures. 1992. 62.00 (*0-8194-0673-2*, 1545) SPIE.

Lerner, J. M. & McNamara, B. J. Optical Spectroscopic Instrumentation & Techniques for the 1990s, Vol. 1318: Applications in Astronomy, Chemistry, & Physics, June 1990, Las Cruces, NM. 260p. 1990. 62.00 (*0-8194-0373-3*) SPIE.

Lerner, Jacqueline V. Working Mothers & Their Families. (Family Studies Text Ser.: Vol. 13). (Illus.). 128p. (C). 1993. text ed. 37.00 (*0-8039-4209-5*); pap. text ed. 16.95 (*0-8039-4210-9*) Sage.

Lerner, Jacqueline V. & Galambos, Nancy L., eds. Employed Mothers & Their Children. LC 90-25897. (Reference Books on Family Issues: Vol. 17). 320p. 1991. 33.00 (*0-8240-6344-9*, 475) Garland.

Lerner, Jacqueline V. & Lerner, Richard M., eds. Temperament & Social Interaction in Infants & Children. LC 85-60824. (New Directions for Child Development Ser.: No. CD 31). (Orig.). 1986. pap. 17.95 (*0-87589-798-3*) Jossey-Bass.

Lerner, Janet, et al. Cases in Learning & Behavior Problems: A Guide to Individualized Education Programs. 354p. (C). 1992. reprint ed. student ed, pap. text ed. 23.95 (*1-879215-06-3*) Sheffield WI.

Lerner, Janet W. Learning Disabilities: Theories, Diagnosis, & Teaching Strategies. 4th ed. LC 84-82413. 640p. (C). 1984. student ed 14.76 (*0-685-10561-X*) HM.

— Learning Disabilities: Theories, Diagnosis, & Teaching Strategies. 5th ed. 1988. teacher ed write for info. (*0-318-63320-5*); student ed 13.96 (*0-318-36897-8*) HM.

Lerner, Janet W. & List, Lynne K. Reading & Learning Disabilities. 1980. 12.95 (*0-07-037270-5*) McGraw.

Lerner, Janet W., jt. ed. see Cruickshank, William M.

Lerner, Janet W., et al. Attention Deficit Disorders: Assessment & Teaching. LC 94-20274. (Special Education Ser.). 1995. pap. 18.95 (*0-534-25044-0*) Brooks-Cole.

— Special Education for the Early Childhood Years. 416p. 1981. text ed. write for info. (*0-13-826461-9*) P-H.

Lerner, Jeff R. The Complete Manual of Ice Dance Patterns. (Illus.). 402p. 1992. student ed 40.00 (*0-9696538-0-8*) Platoro Pr.

Lerner, Joel. Financial Planning for the Utterly Confused. 4th ed. 1994. text ed. 29.95 (*0-07-037646-8*); pap. text ed. 9.95 (*0-07-037647-6*) McGraw.

— Our Thought for the Day: The Best of Professor Joel Lerner's Lifetime Collection of Quotes. 366p. 1995. spiral bd., pap. 5.95 (*1-56245-182-0*) Great Quotations.

Lerner, Joel, tr. see Herczl, Moshe Y.

Lerner, Joel J. Schaum's Outline of Bookkeeping & Accounting. 2nd ed. 1988. pap. text ed. 12.95 (*0-07-037231-4*) McGraw.

— Schaum's Outline of Theory & Problems of Bookkeeping & Accounting. 3rd ed. LC 93-41304. 1994. pap. text ed. 12.95 (*0-07-037593-3*) McGraw.

Lerner, Joel J. & Cashin, James A. Schaum's Outline of Principles of Accounting II. 4th ed. LC 92-4387. (Schaum's Outline Ser.). 1993. pap. text ed. 12.95 (*0-07-037589-5*) McGraw.

— Schaum's Outline of Theory & Problems of Principles of Accounting I. 4th ed. LC 92-2432. 1993. pap. text ed. 12.95 (*0-07-037278-0*) McGraw.

Lerner, Joel J. & Zima, P. Schaum's Outline of Theory & Problems of Business Mathematics. 320p. 1985. pap. text ed. 12.95 (*0-07-037212-8*) McGraw.

Lerner, Joel M. The Complete Home Landscape Designer. (Illus.). 144p. (Orig.). 1991. pap. 19.95 (*0-312-06937-5*) St Martin.

— One Hundred & One Home Landscaping Ideas: For Every Size & Shape. Summerlin, Randy, ed. (Illus.). 136p. (Orig.). 1988. pap. 9.95 (*0-89586-721-4*, HP Books) Berkley Pub.

— One Hundred & One Townhouse Garden Designs. 1988. pap. 9.95 (*0-89586-545-9*, HP Books) Berkley Pub.

Lerner, Jonathan. Caught in a Still Place. 128p. (Orig.). 1990. pap. 9.95 (*1-85242-146-0*) Serpents Tail.

Lerner, Joseph. A Review of Amino Acid Transport Processes in Animal Cells & Tissues. LC 78-55683. 1978. text ed. 20.00 (*0-89101-036-X*) U Maine Pr.

Lerner, Laurence. A.R.T.H.U.R. The Life & Opinions of a Digital Computer. LC 74-21241. 66p. 1975. reprint ed. pap. 8.95 (*0-87023-181-2*) U of Mass Pr.

— The Frontiers of Literature. 256p. 1988. text ed. 39.95 (*0-631-14967-8*) Blackwell Pubs.

— Rembrandt's Mirror. LC 86-32526. 72p. 1987. pap. 9.95 (*0-8265-1223-2*) Vanderbilt U Pr.

Lerner, Laurence, ed. The Victorians. LC 78-15642. (Context of English Literature Ser.). 228p. 1978. 35.95 (*0-8419-0419-7*); pap. 19.95 (*0-8419-0420-0*) Holmes & Meier.

Lerner, Laurence, jt. ed. see Bell, Vereen.

***Lerner, Lawrence.** Physics: An Introduction for Engineers. (Physics Ser.). 1300p. 1995. 75.00 (*0-86720-479-6*) Jones & Bartlett.

Lerner, Lawrence S., ed. see Bruno, Giordano.

Lerner, Lawrence S., tr. see Bruno, Giordano.

Lerner, Leila, jt. ed. see Friedman, Robert M.

Lerner, Leon L. Being Human. 86p. 1982. pap. 5.95 (*0-9607964-0-1*) Galaxy Pr MD.

— Biography of a Century & Other Poems. 80p. 1976. pap. 8.95 (*0-9607964-1-X*) Galaxy Pr MD.

— In These Strange Times: Poetry As News. 189p. 1993. 21.99 (*0-9607964-2-8*); pap. 14.99 (*0-9607964-3-6*) Galaxy Pr MD.

Lerner, Lily & Stuart, S. L. The Silence. 1980. 10.95 (*0-8184-0306-3*) Carol Pub Group.

Lerner, Linda. City Girl. 32p. (Orig.). 1990. pap. text ed. 4.00 (*0-935839-09-7*) Vergin Pr.

Lerner, M. J. & Lerner, S. C., eds. The Justice Motive in Social Behavior: Adapting to Times of Scarcity & Change. LC 81-10605. (Critical Issues in Social Justice Ser.). 516p. 1981. 70.00 (*0-306-40675-6*, Plenum Pr) Plenum.

Lerner, M. J. & Mikula, G., eds. Entitlement & the Affectional Bond: Justice in Close Relations. (Critical Issues in Social Justice Ser.). (Illus.). 358p. (C). 1994. 49.50 (*0-306-44699-5*) Plenum.

Lerner, Marcia, jt. auth. see Princeton Review Staff.

Lerner, Mark. Mysteries of Venus. (Illus.). 208p. (Orig.). 1986. pap. 10.95 (*0-938559-00-1*) Great Bear Pr.

Lerner, Mark, jt. auth. see Lerner, Isha.

Lerner, Mark, tr. see Mitgutsch, Ali.

Lerner, Martin. The Flame & the Lotus: Indian & Southeast Asia Art from the Kronos Collections. (Illus.). 192p. 1984. pap. 8.95 (*0-87099-401-8*) Metro Mus Art.

Lerner, Martin & Kossak, Steven. Lotus Transcendent: Indian & Southeast Asian Sculpture from the Samuel Eilenberg Collection. (Illus.). 245p. 1991. 60.00 (*0-8109-6407-4*) Abrams.

Lerner, Martin, jt. auth. see Felten, Wolfgang.

Lerner, Max. America As a Civilization. 1987. pap. 19.95 (*0-8050-0355-X*) H Holt & Co.

— Articulation Between For-Profit Private Occupational Schools & Secondary Vocational Programs: Colleges & Universities. 39p. 1987. 5.25 (*0-318-23410-6*, IN315) Ctr Educ Trng Employ.

— Ideas Are Weapons: The History & Uses of Ideas. 585p. (C). 1990. 24.95 (*0-88738-364-5*) Transaction Pubs.

— Ideas for the Ice Age: Studies in a Revolutionary Era. 450p. (C). 1992. pap. 24.95 (*1-56000-595-5*) Transaction Pubs.

— It Is Later Than You Think. 278p. 1989. 34.95 (*0-88738-782-9*) Transaction Pubs.

— Magisterial Imagination: Six Masters of the Human Sciences. 212p. (C). 1994. 29.95 (*1-56000-168-2*) Transaction Pubs.

— Masters of the Human Sciences. LC 93-39856. 1994. pap. write for info. (*1-56000-728-1*) Transaction Pubs.

— Nine Scorpions in a Bottle: Great Judges & Cases of the Supreme Court. Cummings, Richard, ed. LC 93-24463. 352p. 1995. pap. 13.95 (*1-55970-291-5*) Arcade Pub Inc.

— Tocqueville & American Civilization. 136p. (C). 1993. reprint ed. pap. text ed. 17.95 (*1-56000-703-6*) Transaction Pubs.

— Wrestling with the Angel: A Memoir of My Triumph over Illness. 1990. 18.95 (*0-393-02846-1*) Norton.

Lerner, Max, intro. The Mind & Faith of Justice Holmes: His Speeches, Essays, Letters, & Judicial Opinions. 500p. 1989. pap. 21.95 (*0-88738-765-9*) Transaction Pubs.

Lerner, Melvin J. The Belief in a Just World: A Fundamental Delusion. LC 80-16359. (Perspectives in Social Psychology Ser.). (Illus.). 224p. 1980. 45.00 (*0-306-40495-8*, Plenum Pr) Plenum.

Lerner, Michael. Choice in Healing: Integrating the Best of Conventional & Alternative Approaches to Cancer. (Illus.). 500p. 1994. 24.95 (*0-262-12180-8*) MIT Pr.

— Jewish Renewal: A Path to Healing & Transformation. 480p. 1994. 24.95 (*0-399-13980-X*) Putnam Pub Group.

— Socialism of Fools: Anti-Semitism on the Left. (C). 1992. pap. 10.00 (*0-03-593305-4*) HB Coll Pubs.

— The Socialism of Fools: Anti-Semitism on the Left. 1992. pap. 10.00 (*0-935933-05-0*) Inst Labor & Mental.

— Surplus Powerlessness. LC 85-62314. 320p. 1986. 14.95 (*0-935933-01-8*); pap. 9.95 (*0-935933-02-6*) Inst Labor & Mental.

— Surplus Powerlessness: The Psychodynamics of Everyday Life & the Psychology of Individual & Social Transformation. LC 91-7279. 424p. (C). 1991. pap. 18.50 (*0-391-03706-4*) Humanities.

— Tikkun: To Heal, Repair & Transform the World. 1992. 39.95 (*0-935933-03-4*); pap. 16.95 (*0-935933-04-2*) Inst Labor & Mental.

Lerner, Michael, jt. auth. see O'Manique, John.

Lerner, Michael, jt. auth. see West, Cornel.

Lerner, Michael G. Pierre Loti. LC 73-2368. (Twayne's World Authors Ser.). 172p. (C). 1974. lib. bdg. 17.95 (*0-8057-2546-6*) Irvington.

Lerner, Morris W. The Analysis of Elemental Boron. LC 74-607964. (AEC Critical Review Ser.). 137p. 1970. pap. 11.25 (*0-87079-134-6*, TID-25190); fiche 9.00 (*0-87079-135-4*, TID-25190) DOE.

Lerner, Nancy, jt. auth. see Brownstein, Irv.

Lerner, Natan. Group Rights & Discrimination in International Law. (International Studies in Human Rights). (C). 1990. lib. bdg. 85.50 (*0-7923-0853-0*) Kluwer Ac.

— United Nations Convention on the Elimination of All Forms of Racial Discrimination. LC 80-51738. 278p. 1980. lib. bdg. 80.50 (*90-286-0160-0*) Kluwer Ac.

Lerner, Norbert, jt. auth. see Sobel, Max A.

Lerner, Norbert, jt. auth. see Sobel, Max.

Lerner, Paul M. Psychoanalytic Theory & the Rorschach. 2nd ed. 304p. 1990. text ed. 39.95 (*0-88163-122-1*) Analytic Pr.

Lerner, Paul M., ed. Handbook of Rorschach Research Scales. LC 73-7022. 523p. 1974. text ed. 62.50x (*0-8236-2305-X*) Intl Univs Pr.

Lerner, Paul M., jt. ed. see Lerner, Howard D.

***Lerner, Preston.** Fools on the Hill. 352p. (Orig.). 1995. mass mkt. 5.50 (*0-671-51048-7*) PB.

— Scarab. 1991. 39.95 (*0-87938-499-9*) Motorbooks Intl.

An Asterisk (*) at the beginning of an entry indicates that the title is appearing in BIP for the first time.

***Lerner Publications Company, Geography Department Staff.** Czech Republic--in Pictures. LC 94-37432. (Visual Geography Ser.). 1995. write for info. (*0-8225-1879-1*) Lerner Group.

— Germany - in Pictures. LC 93-40971. (Visual Geography Ser.). (Illus.). 64p. (J). (gr. 5 up). 1994. lib. bdg. 18.95 (*0-8225-1873-2*, Lerner Publctns) Lerner Group.

— Romania: In Pictures. LC 92-32861. (Visual Geography Ser.). (J). 1993. lib. bdg. 18.95 (*0-8225-1894-5*, Lerner Publctns) Lerner Group.

— Switzerland--in Pictures. LC 95-2807. (Visual Georgraphy Ser.: Vol. 27, No. 16). (Illus.). (J). 1996. lib. bdg. write for info. (*0-8225-1895-3*, Lerner Publctns) Lerner Group.

Lerner Publications Company Geography Department Staff, comp. Ukraine. LC 92-10284. (Then & Now Ser.). (Illus.). 64p. (YA). (gr. 5 up). 1993. lib. bdg. 21.50 (*0-8225-2808-8*, Lerner Publctns) Lerner Group.

Lerner Publications, Department of Geography Staff. Botswana in Pictures. (Visual Geography Ser.). (Illus.). 64p. (YA). (gr. 5 up). 1990. lib. bdg. 18.95 (*0-8225-1856-2*, Lerner Publctns) Lerner Group.

— Canada in Pictures. (Visual Geography Ser.). (Illus.). 64p. (YA). (gr. 5 up). 1989. lib. bdg. 18.95 (*0-8225-1870-8*, Lerner Publctns) Lerner Group.

— Costa Rica in Pictures. (Visual Geography Ser.). (Illus.). 64p. (YA). (gr. 5 up). 1987. lib. bdg. 18.95 (*0-8225-1805-8*, Lerner Publctns) Lerner Group.

— Ecuador in Pictures. (Visual Geography Ser.). (Illus.). 64p. (YA). (gr. 5 up). 1987. lib. bdg. 18.95 (*0-8225-1813-9*, Lerner Publctns) Lerner Group.

— Ghana in Pictures. (Visual Geography Ser.). (Illus.). 64p. (YA). (gr. 5 up). 1988. 18.95 (*0-8225-1829-5*, Lerner Publctns) Lerner Group.

— Guatemala in Pictures. (Visual Geography Ser.). (Illus.). 64p. (YA). (gr. 5 up). 1987. lib. bdg. 18.95 (*0-8225-1803-1*, Lerner Publctns) Lerner Group.

— Guyana in Pictures. (Visual Geography Ser.). (Illus.). 64p. (YA). (gr. 5 up). 1988. lib. bdg. 18.95 (*0-8225-1815-5*, Lerner Publctns) Lerner Group.

— Haiti in Pictures. (Visual Geography Ser.). (Illus.). 64p. (YA). (gr. 5 up). 1987. lib. bdg. 18.95 (*0-8225-1816-3*, Lerner Publctns) Lerner Group.

— Honduras in Pictures. (Visual Geography Ser.). (Illus.). 64p. (YA). (gr. 5 up). 1987. lib. bdg. 18.95 (*0-8225-1804-X*, Lerner Publctns) Lerner Group.

— Iraq in Pictures. (Visual Geography Ser.). (Illus.). 64p. (YA). (gr. 5 up). 1990. lib. bdg. 18.95 (*0-8225-1847-3*, Lerner Publctns) Lerner Group.

— Jamaica in Pictures. (Visual Geography Ser.). (Illus.). 64p. (YA). (gr. 5 up). 1987. lib. bdg. 18.95 (*0-8225-1814-7*, Lerner Publctns) Lerner Group.

— Japan in Pictures. (Visual Geography Ser.). (Illus.). 64p. (YA). (gr. 5 up). 1989. lib. bdg. 18.95 (*0-8225-1861-9*, Lerner Publctns) Lerner Group.

— Kenya in Pictures. (Visual Geography Ser.). (Illus.). 64p. (YA). (gr. 5 up). 1988. 18.95 (*0-8225-1830-9*, Lerner Publctns) Lerner Group.

— New Zealand in Pictures. (Visual Geography Ser.). (Illus.). 64p. (YA). (gr. 5 up). 1990. lib. bdg. 18.95 (*0-8225-1862-7*, Lerner Publctns) Lerner Group.

— Panama in Pictures. (Visual Geography Ser.). (Illus.). 64p. (YA). (gr. 5 up). 1987. lib. bdg. 18.95 (*0-8225-1818-X*, Lerner Publctns) Lerner Group.

— Peru in Pictures. (Visual Geography Ser.). (Illus.). 64p. (YA). (gr. 5 up). 1987. lib. bdg. 18.95 (*0-8225-1820-1*, Lerner Publctns) Lerner Group.

— Puerto Rico in Pictures. (Visual Geography Ser.). (Illus.). 64p. (YA). (gr. 5 up). 1987. lib. bdg. 18.95 (*0-8225-1821-X*, Lerner Publctns) Lerner Group.

— Syria in Pictures. (Visual Geography Ser.). (Illus.). 64p. (YA). (gr. 5 up). 1990. lib. bdg. 18.95 (*0-8225-1867-8*, Lerner Publctns) Lerner Group.

— Venezuela in Pictures. (Visual Geography Ser.). (Illus.). 64p. (YA). (gr. 5 up). 1987. lib. bdg. 18.95 (*0-8225-1824-4*, Lerner Publctns) Lerner Group.

Lerner Publications, Department of Geography Staff, ed. Afghanistan in Pictures. (Visual Geography Ser.). (Illus.). 64p. (YA). (gr. 5 up). 1989. 18.95 (*0-8225-1849-X*, Lerner Publctns) Lerner Group.

— Argentina in Pictures. (Visual Geography Ser.). (Illus.). 64p. (YA). (gr. 5 up). 1988. lib. bdg. 18.95 (*0-8225-1807-4*, Lerner Publctns) Lerner Group.

— Australia in Pictures. (Visual Geography Ser.). (Illus.). 64p. (YA). (gr. 5 up). 1990. lib. bdg. 18.95 (*0-8225-1855-4*, Lerner Publctns) Lerner Group.

— Bolivia in Pictures. (Visual Geography Ser.). (Illus.). 64p. (YA). (gr. 5 up). 1987. lib. bdg. 18.95 (*0-8225-1808-2*, Lerner Publctns) Lerner Group.

— Cameroon in Pictures. (Visual Geography Ser.). (Illus.). 64p. (YA). (gr. 5 up). 1989. lib. bdg. 18.95 (*0-8225-1857-0*, Lerner Publctns) Lerner Group.

— Central African Republic in Pictures. (Visual Geography Ser.). (Illus.). 64p. (YA). (gr. 5 up). 1989. 18.95 (*0-8225-1858-9*, Lerner Publctns) Lerner Group.

— Chile in Pictures. (Visual Geography Ser.). (Illus.). 64p. (YA). (gr. 5 up). 1988. lib. bdg. 18.95 (*0-8225-1809-0*, Lerner Publctns) Lerner Group.

— China in Pictures. (Visual Geography Ser.). (Illus.). 64p. (YA). (gr. 5 up). 1989. 18.95 (*0-8225-1859-7*, Lerner Publctns) Lerner Group.

— Colombia in Pictures. (Visual Geography Ser.). (Illus.). 64p. (YA). (gr. 5 up). 1987. lib. bdg. 18.95 (*0-8225-1810-4*, Lerner Publctns) Lerner Group.

— England in Pictures. (Visual Geography Ser.). (Illus.). 64p. (YA). (gr. 5 up). 1990. lib. bdg. 18.95 (*0-8225-1874-0*, Lerner Publctns) Lerner Group.

— India in Pictures. (Visual Geography Ser.). (Illus.). 64p. (YA). (gr. 5 up). 1989. 18.95 (*0-8225-1852-X*, Lerner Publctns) Lerner Group.

— Indonesia in Pictures. (Visual Geography Ser.). (Illus.). 64p. (YA). (gr. 5 up). 1990. lib. bdg. 18.95 (*0-8225-1860-0*, Lerner Publctns) Lerner Group.

— Iran in Pictures. (Visual Geography Ser.). (Illus.). 64p. (YA). (gr. 5 up). 1989. 18.95 (*0-8225-1848-1*, Lerner Publctns) Lerner Group.

— Ireland in Pictures. (Visual Geography Ser.). (Illus.). 64p. (YA). (gr. 5 up). 1990. lib. bdg. 18.95 (*0-8225-1878-3*, Lerner Publctns) Lerner Group.

— Kuwait in Pictures. (Visual Geography Ser.). (Illus.). 64p. (YA). (gr. 5 up). 1989. 18.95 (*0-8225-1846-5*, Lerner Publctns) Lerner Group.

— Lebanon in Pictures. (Visual Geography Ser.). (Illus.). 64p. (YA). (gr. 5 up). 1988. 18.95 (*0-8225-1832-5*, Lerner Publctns) Lerner Group.

— Malaysia in Pictures. (Visual Geography Ser.). (Illus.). 64p. (YA). (gr. 5 up). 1989. 18.95 (*0-8225-1854-6*, Lerner Publctns) Lerner Group.

— Mali in Pictures. (Visual Geography Ser.). (Illus.). 64p. (YA). (gr. 5 up). 1990. lib. bdg. 18.95 (*0-8225-1869-4*, Lerner Publctns) Lerner Group.

— Morocco in Pictures. (Visual Geography Ser.). (Illus.). 64p. (YA). (gr. 5 up). 1988. 18.95 (*0-8225-1843-0*, Lerner Publctns) Lerner Group.

— Nepal in Pictures. (Visual Geography Ser.). (Illus.). 64p. (YA). (gr. 5 up). 1989. 18.95 (*0-8225-1851-1*, Lerner Publctns) Lerner Group.

— Norway in Pictures. (Visual Geography Ser.). (Illus.). 64p. (YA). (gr. 5 up). 1990. lib. bdg. 18.95 (*0-8225-1871-6*, Lerner Publctns) Lerner Group.

— Pakistan in Pictures. (Visual Geography Ser.). (Illus.). 64p. (YA). (gr. 5 up). 1989. 18.95 (*0-8225-1850-3*, Lerner Publctns) Lerner Group.

— Phillipines in Pictures. (Visual Geography Ser.). (Illus.). 64p. (YA). (gr. 5 up). 1989. lib. bdg. 18.95 (*0-8225-1863-5*, Lerner Publctns) Lerner Group.

— Scotland in Pictures. (Visual Geography Ser.). (Illus.). 64p. (YA). (gr. 5 up). 1991. lib. bdg. 18.95 (*0-8225-1875-9*, Lerner Publctns) Lerner Group.

— South Korea in Pictures. (Visual Geography Ser.). (Illus.). 64p. (YA). (gr. 5 up). 1989. lib. bdg. 18.95 (*0-8225-1868-6*, Lerner Publctns) Lerner Group.

— Soviet Union in Pictures. (Visual Geography Ser.). (Illus.). 64p. (YA). (gr. 5 up). 1989. lib. bdg. 18.95 (*0-8225-1864-3*, Lerner Publctns) Lerner Group.

— Sri Lanka in Pictures. (Visual Geography Ser.). (Illus.). 64p. (YA). (gr. 5 up). 1988. 18.95 (*0-8225-1853-8*, Lerner Publctns) Lerner Group.

— Sweden in Pictures. (Visual Geography Ser.). (Illus.). 64p. (YA). (gr. 5 up). 1990. lib. bdg. 18.95 (*0-8225-1872-4*, Lerner Publctns) Lerner Group.

— Taiwan in Pictures. (Visual Geography Ser.). (Illus.). 64p. (YA). (gr. 5 up). 1989. lib. bdg. 18.95 (*0-8225-1865-1*, Lerner Publctns) Lerner Group.

— Thailand in Pictures. (Visual Geography Ser.). (Illus.). 64p. (YA). (gr. 5 up). 1989. lib. bdg. 18.95 (*0-8225-1866-X*, Lerner Publctns) Lerner Group.

— Tunisia in Pictures. (Visual Geography Ser.). (Illus.). 64p. (YA). (gr. 5 up). 1989. 18.95 (*0-8225-1844-9*, Lerner Publctns) Lerner Group.

— Wales in Pictures. (Visual Geography Ser.). (Illus.). 64p. (YA). (gr. 5 up). 1990. lib. bdg. 18.95 (*0-8225-1877-5*, Lerner Publctns) Lerner Group.

***Lerner Publications Geography Department Staff.** Slovakia in Pictures. LC 94-45803. (Visual Geography Ser.). (Illus.). (J). 1995. lib. bdg. write for info. (*0-8225-1912-7*) Lerner Group.

Lerner, Ralph. Revolutions Revisited: Two Faces of the Politics of Enlightenment. LC 93-36438. xvi, 136p. (C). 1994. 19.95 (*0-8078-2136-5*) U of NC Pr.

— The Thinking Revolutionary: Principle & Practice in the New Republic. LC 87-5287. 256p. (C). 1987. 34.50 (*0-8014-2007-5*); pap. 13.95 (*0-8014-9532-6*) Cornell U Pr.

Lerner, Ralph & Mahdi, Muhsin, eds. Medieval Political Philosophy: A Sourcebook. (Agora Paperback Editions Ser.). 544p. 1972. pap. 16.95 (*0-8014-9139-8*) Cornell U Pr.

Lerner, Ralph, jt. ed. see Kurland, Philip B.

Lerner, Ralph E. & Bresler, Judith. Art Law: The Guide for Collectors, Investors, Dealers, & Artists - 1992. 2nd ed. 478p. 1992. pap. 50.00 (*0-685-69381-3*) PLI.

***Lerner, Richard.** Hiking & Backpacking with Your Dog. (Nuts-n-Bolts Guides Ser.). (Illus.). 32p. (Orig.). 1994. pap. 4.95 (*0-89732-164-2*) Menasha Ridge.

Lerner, Richard A. Concepts & Theories of Human Development. 2nd ed. 512p. 1985. text ed. 29.95 (*0-89859-886-9*) L Erlbaum Assocs.

Lerner, Richard A., jt. ed. see Chanock, Robert M.

Lerner, Richard A., et al, eds. Vaccines Eighty-Nine: Modern Approaches to New Vaccines Including the Prevention of AIDS. (Illus.). 1989. pap. 100.00 (*0-87969-323-1*) Cold Spring Harbor.

— Vaccines 85: Molecular & Chemical Basis of Resistance to Parasitic, Bacterial & Viral Diseases. LC 84-29372. 407p. (Orig.). 1985. pap. 75.00 (*0-87969-181-6*) Cold Spring Harbor.

***Lerner, Richard M.** America's Children & Youth in Crisis: Challenges & Options for Programs & Policies. 160p. 1994. 39.95 (*0-8039-7068-4*); pap. 18.95 (*0-8039-7069-2*) Sage.

— Concepts & Theories of Human Development. LC 75-12098. (Illus.). (C). 1976. text ed. 22.00 (*0-394-34773-0*) Random.

— Concepts & Theories of Human Development. 2nd ed. 512p. 1986. text ed. write for info. (*0-07-554899-2*) McGraw.

— Final Solutions: Biology, Prejudice, & Genocide. (Illus.). 224p. 1992. text ed. 25.00 (*0-271-00793-1*) Pa St U Pr.

Lerner, Richard M., ed. Developmental Psychology: Historical & Philosophical Perspectives. 288p. (C). 1983. text ed. 49.95 (*0-89859-247-X*) L Erlbaum Assocs.

— Early Adolescence: Perspectives on Research, Policy, & Intervention. (Penn State Series on Child & Adolescent Development). 528p. 1992. text ed. 99.95 (*0-8058-1164-8*) L Erlbaum Assocs.

Lerner, Richard M. & Foch, Terryl, eds. Biological-Psychosocial Interactions in Early Adolescence: A Life-Span Perspective. (Child Psychology Ser.). 408p. 1987. text ed. 69.95 (*0-89859-787-0*) L Erlbaum Assocs.

Lerner, Richard M. & Galambos, Nancy L., eds. Experiencing Adolescents: A Sourcebook for Parents, Teachers, & Teens. LC 87-10129. 432p. reprint ed. pap. 123.20 (*0-7837-3886-2*, 2043734) Bks Demand.

Lerner, Richard M. & Spanier, Graham B., eds. Child Influences on Marital & Family Interaction: A Life-Span Perspectives. 1978. text ed. 59.00 (*0-12-444450-4*) Acad Pr.

Lerner, Richard M., jt. ed. see Fisher, Celia B.

Lerner, Richard M., jt. auth. see Ford, Donald H.

Lerner, Richard M., jt. ed. see Kreppner, Kurt.

Lerner, Richard M., jt. ed. see Lerner, Jacqueline V.

Lerner, Richard M., jt. ed. see Villaruel, Francisco A.

Lerner, Richard M., et al, eds. Encyclopedia of Adolescence, 2 vols., Set. LC 90-14033. 1248p. 1991. 150.00 (*0-8240-4378-2*, SS495) Garland.

Lerner, Rita G. & Trigg, George L., eds. Concise Encyclopedia of Solid State Physics. 300p. (C). 1983. text ed. 55.95 (*0-201-14204-X*, Adv Bk Prog); pap. text ed. 40.95 (*0-201-14205-8*, Adv Bk Prog) Addison-Wesley.

Lerner-Robbins, Helene. Creativity. LC 92-56433. 96p. 1993. pap. 7.00 (*0-06-255289-9*, Hazelden SF) Harper SF.

— Embrace Change: Trusting Intuition. (Meditation Ser.). 96p. (Orig.). 1992. pap. 4.95 (*0-89486-806-3*, 5470A) Hazelden.

— Finding Balance. LC 92-56419. 96p. 1993. pap. 7.00 (*0-06-255288-0*, Hazelden SF) Harper SF.

— My Timing Is Always Right: Trusting Intuition. (Meditation Ser.). 96p. (Orig.). 1992. pap. 4.95 (*0-89486-807-1*, 5471A) Hazelden.

***Lerner, Robert, et al.** Molding the Good Citizen: The Politics of High School History Texts. LC 94-32922. 200p. 1995. text ed. 55.00 (*0-275-94919-2*, Praeger Pubs); pap. text ed. 17.95 (*0-275-95100-6*) Greenwood.

Lerner, Robert E. The Heresy of the Free Spirit in the Later Middle Ages. LC 78-45790. (C). 1991. reprint ed. pap. text ed. 15.95 (*0-268-01094-3*) U of Notre Dame Pr.

Lerner, Robert E., et al. Western Civilizations, I. (Illus.). 1090p. (C). 1988. student ed, pap. text ed. 13.95 (*0-393-95660-1*) Norton.

— Western Civilizations, I. 11th ed. (Illus.). 1090p. (C). 1988. pap. text ed. 31.95 (*0-393-95659-8*) Norton.

— Western Civilizations, II. (Illus.). 1090p. (C). 1988. student ed, pap. text ed. 13.95 (*0-393-95662-8*) Norton.

Lerner, Rokelle. Affirmations for the Inner Child. 1989. pap. 6.95 (*1-55874-054-6*) Health Comm.

— Daily Affirmations. 372p. 1985. pap. text ed. 7.95 (*0-932194-27-3*, 4273) Health Comm.

— Life in the Comfort Zone: Creating Well-Being in Relationships. 150p. 1995. pap. 9.95 (*1-55874-370-7*, 3707) Health Comm.

Lerner, S. & Cable, J. Workshop Wage Determination. LC 70-91465. 1969. 126.00 (*0-08-006579-1*, Pub. by Pergamon Repr UK) Franklin.

Lerner, S. C., jt. ed. see Lerner, M. J.

Lerner, Sharon. Big Bird Says...A Game to Read & Play. LC 85-1959. 1985. 3.50 (*0-394-87499-4*) Random Bks Yng Read.

— Big Bird's Copycat Day: A Step 1 Book. LC 84-6869. (Step into Reading Bks.). (Illus.). 32p. (J). (ps-2). 1984. lib. bdg. 7.99 (*0-394-96912-X*); pap. 3.50 (*0-394-86912-5*) Random Bks Yng Read.

— Follow the Monsters. LC 84-18031. (Step into Reading Bks.). (Illus.). 32p. (J). (ps-1). 1985. pap. 3.50 (*0-394-87126-X*) Random Bks Yng Read.

Lerner, Sharon, ed. Noah's Ark. LC 77-92377. (Pictureback Ser.). (Illus.). (J). (ps-2). 1978. lib. bdg. 5.99 (*0-394-93861-5*); pap. 2.25 (*0-394-83861-0*) Random Bks Yng Read.

Lerner, Sharon, ed. see Berenstain, Stan & Berenstain, Janice.

Lerner, Sharon, ed. see Hill, Susan.

Lerner, Sharon, ed. see Jonsen, George.

Lerner, Sid, et al. The New New Words Dictionary. 1989p. 1988. pap. 2.95 (*0-345-35696-9*) Ballantine.

Lerner, Steve. Beyond the Earth Summit: Conversations with Advocates of Sustainable Development. 320p. 1992. pap. 12.50 (*0-943004-07-1*) Common Knowledge.

— Bodily Harm: The Pattern of Fear & Violence at the California Youth Authority. 72p. 1986. pap. 4.95 (*0-943004-03-9*) Common Knowledge.

— The CYA Report: Conditions of Life at the California Youth Authority. LC 82-4973. 176p. (Orig.). 1982. pap. 6.95 (*0-943004-00-4*) Common Knowledge.

— Earth Summit: Conversations with Architects of an Ecologically Sustainable Future. 288p. 1991. pap. 9.95 (*0-943004-06-3*) Common Knowledge.

— The Good News about Juvenile Justice: The Movement Away from Large Institutions & Toward Community-Based Services. 128p. 1990. pap. 5.95 (*0-943004-05-5*) Common Knowledge.

Lerner, Warren. A History of Socialism & Communism in Modern Times: Theorists, Activists, & Humanists. 2nd ed. LC 93-6680. 1993. pap. text ed. write for info. (*0-13-389552-1*) P-H.

— Karl Radek: The Last Internationalist. LC 70-97915. (Illus.). xiv, 242p. 1970. 32.50 (*0-8047-0722-7*) Stanford U Pr.

Lerner, William D. & Barr, Marjorie A. Handbook of Hospital Based Substance Abuse Treatment. (Illus.). 256p. 1990. 50.00 (*0-08-036077-7*, Pub. by PPI UK); pap. 25.00 (*0-08-036076-9*, Pub. by PPI UK) McGraw.

— Handbook of Hospital-Based Substance Abuse Treatment. 256p. 1990. text ed. 50.00 (*0-07-105338-7*); pap. text ed. 25.00 (*0-07-105292-5*) Hlth Prof Div.

Lernet-Holenia, Alexander. Baron Bagge & Count Luna. Winston, Richard et al, trs. LC 88-80805. 240p. 1988. 23.00 (*0-941419-20-7*, Eridanos Library); pap. 14.00 (*0-941419-21-5*, Eridanos Library) Marsilio Pubs.

— The Resurrection of Maltravers. Neugroschel, Joachim, tr. LC 88-80806. 223p. 1989. 23.00 (*0-941419-22-3*, Eridanos Library); pap. 14.00 (*0-941419-23-1*, Eridanos Library) Marsilio Pubs.

Lernmark, A., et al, eds. Molecular Mimicry in Health & Disease: Interactions of Biological with Neural, Endocrine & Immune Cells. (International Congress Ser.: No. 823). 412p. 1989. 120.50 (*0-444-81059-5*, Excerpta Medica) Elsevier.

Lernout, Geert. The French Joyce. 304p. (C). 1992. pap. text ed. 16.95 (*0-472-08180-2*) U of Mich Pr.

— The French Joyce. 156p. (C). 1990. reprint ed. text ed. 37.50 (*0-472-10195-1*) U of Mich Pr.

— The Poet as Thinker: Hoelderlin in France. (Studies in German Literature, Linguistics & Culture). xii, 138p. 1994. 59.95 (*1-879751-98-4*) Camden Hse.

Lernoux, Penny. Cry of the People: The Struggle for Human Rights in Latin America - The Catholic Church Conflict with U. S. Policy. 552p. 1982. pap. 9.95 (*0-14-006047-2*, Penguin Bks) Viking Penguin.

— Cry of the People: The Struggle for Human Rights in Latin America - The Catholic Church Conflict with U. S. Policy. 576p. 1991. pap. 9.95 (*0-14-015385-3*, Penguin Bks) Viking Penguin.

— Hearts on Fire, 1993: The Story of the Maryknoll Sisters. LC 93-36831. (Illus.). 325p. (Orig.). 1993. 22.95 (*0-88344-925-0*) Orbis Bks.

— Hearts on Fire, 1993: The Story of the Maryknoll Sisters. LC 93-36831. 328p. (Orig.). 1995. pap. 14.95 (*1-57075-019-X*) Orbis Bks.

— People of God: The Struggle for World Catholicism. 448p. 1990. pap. 9.95 (*0-14-009816-X*, Penguin Bks) Viking Penguin.

Leroe, Ellen. Ghost Dog. LC 92-72020. (Illus.). 64p. (J). (gr. 2-5). 1993. 12.95 (*1-56282-268-3*); lib. bdg. 12.89 (*1-56282-269-1*) Hyprn Child.

— Ghost Dog. LC 92-72020. (Illus.). 64p. (J). (gr. 2-5). 1994. pap. 2.95 (*0-7868-1003-3*) Hyprn Ppbks.

— H. O. W. L. High Goes Bats. MacDonald, Patricia, ed. 144p. (Orig.). (YA). 1993. pap. 2.99 (*0-671-79838-3*, Minstrel Bks) PB.

— Heebie Jeebies at H.O.W.L. High. MacDonald, Patricia, ed. 144p. (J). (gr. 3-6). 1992. pap. 2.99 (*0-671-75415-7*, Minstrel Bks) PB.

— H.O.W.L. High, No. 1. MacDonald, Patricia, ed. 144p. (J). (gr. 4-7). 1991. pap. 2.95 (*0-671-68568-6*, Minstrel Bks) PB.

— Monkey Business. Greenberg, Anne, ed. (Orig.). (J). 1994. mass mkt. 3.99 (*0-671-88740-8*, Minstrel Bks) PB.

— Single Bed Blues. Fitzgerald, Elisa B., ed. LC 81-23307. 72p. 1981. pap. 5.95 (*0-913024-12-0*) Tandem Pr.

Leroi, A. The Cell, the Human Organism & Cancer. 1973. lib. bdg. 79.95 (*0-87968-538-7*) Krishna Pr.

Leroi-Gourham, Andre. Gesture & Speech. Berger, Anna B., tr. (October Bks.). (Illus.). 360p. 1993. pap. 42.50 (*0-262-12173-5*) MIT Pr.

Leroi, Rita. An Anthroposophical Approach to Cancer. 45p. (Orig.). 1982. pap. 5.00 (*0-936132-21-3*) Merc Pr NY.

LeRoith, D. & Raizada, M. K., eds. Molecular & Cellular Biology of Insulin-Like Growth Factors. (Illus.). 524p. 1989. 120.00 (*0-306-43254-4*, Plenum Pr) Plenum.

LeRoith, D., jt. ed. see Raizada, M. K.

LeRoith, Derek. Insulin-Like Growth Factors: Molecular & Cellular Aspects. (Illus.). 305p. 1991. 205.00 (*0-8493-5712-8*, QP552) CRC Pr.

LeRoith, Derek, jt. ed. see Draznin, Boris.

LeRoith, Derek, jt. ed. see Raizada, Mohan K.

LeRoith, Derek, et al, eds. Purification of Fermentation Products: Applications to Large-Scale Processes. LC 84-24316. (ACS Symposium Ser.: No. 271). 198p. 1985. lib. bdg. 49.95 (*0-8412-0890-5*) Am Chemical.

— Purification of Fermentation Products: Applications to Large-Scale Processes - Based on a Symposium Sponsored by the Division of Microbial & Biochemical Technology. LC 84-24316. (ACS Symposium Ser.: No. 271). 208p. reprint ed. pap. 59.30 (*0-7837-1966-3*, 2052444) Bks Demand.

Leron, U., jt. auth. see Dubinsky, E.

Leron, Uri, jt. auth. see Dubinsky, Ed.

Lerond, A. Dictionnaire de la Prononciation: Pronounciation Dictionary. 589p. (FRE.). 1980. 45.00 (*0-8288-1943-2*, M9124) Fr & Eur.

LeRoque, Ellen E. A Tale of a Teddy Bear. (Illus.). 28p. (Orig.). (J). (ps-2). 1985. pap. 3.95 (*0-932967-03-5*) Pacific Shoreline.

LeRossignol, James E. The Habitant-Merchant. LC 70-167461. (Short Story Index Reprint Ser.). (Illus.). 1977. reprint ed. 23.95 (*0-8369-3987-5*) Ayer.

Lerot, Jacques. Analyse Grammaticale. 130p. (FRE.). lib. bdg. 24.95 (*0-8288-3324-9*, 2801106100) Fr & Eur.

LeRougetel, Hazel. The Chelsea Gardener: Philip Miller, 1691-1771. 2nd ed. (Illus.). 228p. 1990. 29.95 (*0-88192-176-9*) Timber.

LeRoux, David F. & Rudersdorf, Martha G. Paddle Washington. LC 84-61009. (Illus.). 163p. 1984. pap. 8.95 (*0-9613570-0-2*) Neah Bay Bks.

An Asterisk (*) at the beginning of an entry indicates that the title is appearing in BIP for the first time.

L

Leroux, Didier, intro. Industrial Robots, 12th Intl. Symposium. Bd. with Industrial Robot Technology, 6th International Conference, June 1982, Paris, France, Proceedings. (Illus.). 540p. 1982. Set text ed. write for info. (0-903608-24-3) Scholium Intl.

Leroux, Gaston. The Bride of the Sun. Reginald, R. & Melville, Douglas, eds. LC 77-84248. (Lost Race & Adult Fantasy Ser.). 1978. reprint ed. lib. bdg. 26.95 (0-405-10994-6) Ayer.

— Le Fantome De l'Opera. 1992. pap. 10.95 (0-8442-1233-4, Natl Textbk) NTC Pub Grp.

— The Mystery of the Yellow Room. 1992. lib. bdg. 25.95 (0-89966-141-6) Buccaneer Bks.

— The Perfume of the Lady in Black. 1975. lib. bdg. 16.70 (0-89966-138-6) Buccaneer Bks.

— The Phantom of the Opera. 1975. lib. bdg. 26.95 (0-89966-136-X) Buccaneer Bks.

— The Phantom of the Opera. 1987. pap. 4.50 (0-451-52432-2, Sig Classics) NAL-Dutton.

— The Phantom of the Opera. (Classics Ser.). 352p. (J). (gr. 5 up). 1994. pap. 3.99 (0-14-036813-2) Puffin Bks.

— The Phantom of the Opera. LC 88-34079. (Bullseye Chillers Ser.). (Illus.). 96p. (J). (gr. 3-7). 1989. pap. 3.50 (0-394-83847-5, Bullseye Bks) Random Bks Yng Read.

— The Phantom of the Opera. LC 88-34079. (Bullseye Chillers Ser.). (Illus.). 96p. (J). (gr. 3-7). 1993. lib. bdg. 5.99 (0-394-93847-X, Bullseye Bks) Random Bks Yng Read.

— The Phantom of the Opera. 272p. 1986. mass mkt. 5.50 (0-446-30120-5) Warner Bks.

— Phantom of the Opera. 1987. lib. bdg. 175.00 (0-8490-3905-3) Gordon Pr.

— Phantom of the Opera. 1990. mass mkt. 4.95 (0-553-21376-8) Bantam.

— Phantom of the Opera. (Reprints Ser.). 264p. 1989. 24.95 (0-88029-298-9) Dorset Pr.

— Phantom of the Opera. (Illus.). 208p. (YA). (gr. 7 up). 1988. 9.95 (0-88101-121-5) Unicorn Pub.

— Phantom of the Opera. (J). (gr. 4 up). 1988. 14.95 (0-88101-082-0) Unicorn Pub.

— The Phantom of the Opera. 269p. 1986. reprint ed. pap. 3.95 (0-88184-249-4) Carroll & Graf.

— The Phantom of the Opera: The Original Novel. LC 87-45635. 357p. 1987. reprint ed. mass mkt. 6.00 (0-06-080924-8, PL-7140, PL) HarpC.

— Phantom of the Opera: The Play. 1979. 4.95 (0-87129-363-3, P45) Dramatic Pub.

— The Secret of the Night. 1975. lib. bdg. 16.70 (0-89966-139-4) Buccaneer Bks.

Leroux, Odette, et al, eds. Inuit Women Artists: Voices from Cape Dorset. LC 94-11711. (Illus.). 256p. 1994. 45.00 (0-295-97389-7) U of Wash Pr.

LeRoux, Paul. Selling to a Group: Presentation Strategies. LC 84-47586. (Illus.). 176p. 1984. pap. 11.00 (0-06-463598-8, EH 598) HarpC.

***Leroux, Pierre.** Encyclopedie Nouvelle ou Dictionnaire Philosophique, Scientifique, Litteraire et Industriel, Offrant le Tableaux des Connaissances Humaines au XIXe Siecle, 6 vols. 5060p. (FRE.). 1991. pap. 3,850.00 (0-7859-7713-9, 2051011664) Fr & Eur.

Leroux, Pierre, jt. ed. see Labelle, G.

Leroy. Systemic Vasculitis: The Biological Basis. (Inflammatory Disease & Therapy Ser.: Vol. 11). 600p. 1992. 190.00 (0-8247-8650-5) Dekker.

Leroy, Andre L. David Hume. Mayer, J. P., ed. LC 78-67413. (European Political Thought Ser.). (FRE.). 1980. reprint ed. lib. bdg. 28.95 (0-405-11713-2) Ayer.

Leroy, Annick M., jt. auth. see Rousseeuw, Peter J.

Leroy, B. Community of Twelve & Drug Demand Comparative Study of Legislation, No. EUR 13447. 188p. 1991. pap. 19.00 (92-826-0594-9, CD-NA-13447-2A-C) UNIPUB.

Leroy, Beatrice. Le Royaume de Navarre a la Fin du Moyen Age: Gouvernement et Societe. (Collected Studies: No. CS 335). 320p. (FRE.). 1991. text ed. 89.95 (0-86078-284-0, Pub. by Variorum UK) Ashgate Pub Co.

Leroy-Beaulieu, Anatole. Empire of the Tsars & the Russians, 3 vols., Set. Ragozin, Zenaide A., tr. LC 70-86377. reprint ed. 265.00 (0-404-03990-1) AMS Pr.

— Israel among the Nations: A Study of the Jews & Antisemitism. Hellman, Frances, tr. LC 74-27996. (Modern Jewish Experience Ser.). (ENG.). 1975. reprint ed. 35.95 (0-405-06723-2) Ayer.

LeRoy, Bernard. Dictionnaire Encyclopedique des Sports, des Sportifs et des Performances. 864p. (FRE.). 1973. 135.00 (0-8288-6266-4, M-6353) Fr & Eur.

Leroy, Catherine, jt. auth. see Clifton, Tony.

LeRoy, Clarice, ed. see Schumacher, Claire W.

Leroy, Claude E., et al. Portugues Para Principiantes. (Illus.). xii, 422p. (POR.). (C). 1993. text ed. 18.00 (0-9636612-0-5) U WI Dept Span.

LeRoy, D. A., jt. auth. see LeRoy, L. W.

LeRoy, D. O., jt. ed. see LeRoy, L. W.

Leroy, F., ed. Blastocyst-Endometrium Relationships. (Progress in Reproductive Biology & Medicine Ser.: Vol. 7). (Illus.). 338p. 1980. 158.50 (3-8055-0988-X) S Karger.

LeRoy, Ford. Design for Teaching & Training: A Self-Study Guide to Lesson Planning. LC 77-87249. (Illus.). 1978. pap. 16.99 (0-8054-3422-4) Broadman.

***LeRoy, Gaylord C.** Toward a Reconstituted Left: A New Stage in Marxism. 1995. pap. 12.00 (0-9646521-0-2) G C LeRoy.

LeRoy, Gen. Taxi Cat & Huey. LC 90-27383. (Illus.). 144p. (J). (gr. 3-7). 1992. lib. bdg. 14.89 (0-06-021769-3) HarpC Child Bks.

Leroy, Gen, jt. auth. see Pump, Anna.

LeRoy, Gene, ed. see Schumacher, Claire W.

LeRoy, Greg. Pantex Plant: Practices, Policy, & the Environmental Impact of the Final Assembly Point. (Illus.). 35p. 1988. pap. text ed. 4.00 (0-945210-00-0) Public Search.

— Research Centers: The Pentagon Moves the High-Tech Battlefield on Campus. (Illus.). 22p. (Orig.). 1988. pap. text ed. 3.00 (0-945210-01-9) Public Search.

Leroy, Jackson, see J. L. Thomas, pseud..

Leroy, Jacques de, ed. see Sainte-Beuve, Charles-Augustin.

Leroy, Jacques L., jt. ed. see Pagel, Maurice.

Leroy, Jules, tr. see Cartan, Elie.

LeRoy, L. David. Biography of Gerald R. Ford. 1974. 4.75 (0-87948-036-X) Beatty.

LeRoy, L. W. & Finney, J. J. Fading Shadows. LC 73-620142. 182p. 1973. 5.00 (0-87108-900-9) Colo Sch Mines.

LeRoy, L. W. & LeRoy, D. A. Red Rocks Park: Geology & Flowers. LC 78-15784. 29p. 1978. pap. 3.00 (0-918062-02-0) Colo Sch Mines.

LeRoy, L. W. & LeRoy, D. O., eds. Subsurface Geology: Petroleum, Mining, Construction. 4th ed. LC 76-51265. 941p. 1977. 21.00 (0-918062-00-4) Colo Sch Mines.

Leroy, L. W. & Weimer, R. J. Professional Contributions, No. 7. 1984. pap. 2.00 (0-685-09169-4) Colo Sch Mines.

LeRoy, L. W., et al, eds. Subsurface Geology: Petroleum, Mining, Construction. 5th ed. LC 86-18806. (Illus.). 1081p. (C). 1987. 50.00 (0-918062-68-3) Colo Sch Mines.

Leroy, M. Population & World Politics. (Publications of the Netherlands Inter-University Demographic Institute & the Population & Family Study Centre Ser.: Vol. 4). 1978. pap. text ed. 41.50 (90-207-0744-2) Kluwer Ac.

Leroy, O. & Breazeale, M. A., eds. Physical Acoustics: Fundamentals & Applications. (Illus.). 724p. 1991. 139.50 (0-306-43883-6, Plenum Pr) Plenum.

Leroy-Terquem, Gerald & Parisot, Jean. Orchids: Care & Cultivation. (Illus.). 200p. 1991. 24.95 (0-7137-2184-7, Pub. by Blandford Pr UK) Sterling.

— Orchids: Care & Cultivation. (Illus.). 200p. 1993. pap. 17.95 (0-304-34329-3, Pub. by Cassell UK) Sterling.

LeRoy, Thomas, jt. auth. see Adams, William D.

Leroy, Thomas R., jt. auth. see Adams, William D.

Lerrick, Alison, jt. auth. see Mian, Q. Javed.

Lerrigo, Marion O. Health Problem Sources. LC 76-176989. (Columbia University. Teachers College. Contributions to Education Ser.: No. 224). reprint ed. 37.50 (0-404-55224-2) AMS Pr.

Lersch, Laurenz. Die Griechiscsh-Romische Biographie Nach Ihrer Literarischen Form, 3 vols. in 1. xxii, 701p. 1971. reprint ed. write for info. (0-318-70778-0, Pub. by Georg Olms GW) Lubrecht & Cramer.

***Lerski, George J.** Historical Dictionary of Poland, 963-1945. LC 94-46940. 1995. text ed. write for info. (0-313-26007-9, Greenwood Pr) Greenwood.

Lerski, George J., ed. Herbert Hoover & Poland: A Documentary History of a Friendship. LC 77-72051. (Publication Ser.: No. 174). (Illus.). 144p. 1977. 4.38 (0-8179-6741-9) Hoover Inst Pr.

Lerski, George J. & Lerski, Halina T., comps. Jewish-Polish Co-Existence, Seventeen Seventy-Two to Nineteen Thirty-Nine: A Topical Bibliography. LC 86-12119. (Bibliographies & Indexes in World History Ser.: No. 5). 244p. 1986. text ed. 49.95 (0-313-24758-7, LJP/) Greenwood.

Lerski, Halina T., jt. comp. see Lerski, George J.

Lerski, R. A., ed. Practical Ultrasound. (Practical Medicine Ser.). (Illus.). 256p. 1988. 59.95 (1-85221-068-0, IRL Pr); pap. 50.00 (1-85221-157-1, IRL Pr) OUP.

Lerstrom, Kirsten, jt. auth. see Bernsen, Jens.

Lertz, Laurie, ed. see De'Medici, Lorenza.

Lerud, Joan V., ed. see Geoscience Information Society Meeting Staff.

Lerude, Warren, jt. auth. see Merriman, Marion.

Lerup, Lars. Building the Unfinished: Architecture & Human Action. LC 77-12370. (Sage Library of Social Research: No. 53). (Illus.). 171p. reprint ed. pap. 48.80 (0-8357-8447-9, 2034711) Bks Demand.

— Planned Assaults: The No Family House, Love-House, Texas Zero. (Illus.). 112p. (Orig.). 1987. 35.00 (0-262-12123-9) MIT Pr.

Leruste, C., jt. auth. see Karoubi, M.

Lerwick, Alan. The Kilted Fiddler. 86p. 1985. pap. 8.95 (0-931759-00-5, 286) Centerstream Pub.

Lerzundi, Patricio C., ed. see Lihn, Enrique.

Les Folles Alliees Staff. Miss Autobody: A Play. Gaboriau, Linda, tr. (Illus.). 128p. (Orig.). 1993. pap. 9.95 (0-921881-25-8, Pub. by Gynergy-Ragweed CN) InBook.

Les Houches Summer School. Relativity, Groups & Topology, II: Proceedings of the Les Houches Summer School, Session XL, 27 June-4 August, 1983, Vol. 40, Pt. I. DeWitt, B. & Stora, R., eds. 380p. 1986. Pt. I, 380p. pap. 32.50 (0-444-87019-9, North Holland) Elsevier.

— Relativity, Groups & Topology, II: Proceedings of the Les Houches Summer School, Session XL, 27 June-4 August, 1983, Vol. 40, Pt. II. DeWitt, B. & Stora, R., eds. 406p. 1986. Pt. II, 406p. pap. 32.50 (0-444-87021-0, North Holland) Elsevier.

— Relativity, Groups & Topology, II: Proceedings of the Les Houches Summer School, Session XL, 27 June-4 August, 1983, Vol. 40, Pt. III. DeWitt, B. & Stora, R., eds. 538p. 1986. Pt. III, 538p. pap. 31.75 (0-317-55238-4, North Holland) Elsevier.

— Relativity, Groups & Topology, II: Proceedings of the Les Houches Summer School, Session XL, 27 June-4 August, 1983, Vol. 40, Set. DeWitt, B. & Stora, R., eds. 1986. Set. pap. 95.00 (0-444-87017-2, North Holland) Elsevier.

Les Strang, Jacques. Cargo Carriers of the Great Lakes. 3rd ed. (Illus.). 193p. 1985. reprint ed. pap. 10.50 (0-937360-06-6) Harbor Hse MI.

Lesage, Alain-Rene. Histoire de Gil Blas de Santillane, 2 tomes, Set. Bardon, ed. (Coll. Prestige). 99.95 (0-685-34040-6) Fr & Eur.

— Turcaret. pap. 4.95 (0-685-11607-7) Fr & Eur.

LeSage, Joan & Barhyte, Diana Y. Nursing Quality Assurance in Long-Term Care. 288p. 1989. 52.00 (0-8342-0066-X) Aspen Pub.

Lesage, Suzanne & Jackson, Richard E., eds. Groundwater Contamination & Analysis at Hazardous Waste Sites. LC 92-20758. (Environmental Science & Pollution Control Ser.: Vol. 4). 552p. 1992. 190.00 (0-8247-8720-X) Dekker.

LeSaux, Francoise, ed. Text & Tradition of Layamon's Brut. LC 94-10443. (Arthurian Studies: No. XXXIII). (Illus.). 288p. (C). (gr. 12 up). 1994. text ed. 53.00 (0-85991-412-7, DS Brewer) Boydell & Brewer.

***LeSaux, Francoise H., ed.** Cultural Intermediaries in Medieval Britain: Collected Essays. LC 94-37245. 212p. 1995. text ed. 89.95 (0-7734-9119-8) E Mellen.

Lesavoy, Malcolm A., jt. auth. see Meals, Roy A.

Lesbaupin, Ivo. Blessed Are the Persecuted: Christian Life in the Roman Empire, A.D. 64-313. Barr, Robert R., tr. LC 87-5746. 112p. (Orig.). reprint ed. pap. 32.00 (0-8357-2682-7, 2040218) Bks Demand.

Lesberg, Sandy, jt. auth. see Bernhardt, Sarah.

Lesbian & Gay Media Advocates Staff. Talk Back: The Gay Person's Guide to Media Action. 120p. (Orig.). 1982. pap. 3.95 (0-932870-10-4) Alyson Pubns.

Lescanne, P., ed. Rewriting Techniques & Applications. (Lecture Notes in Computer Science Ser.: Vol. 256). vi, 285p. 1987. pap. 36.00 (0-387-17220-3) Spr-Verlag.

Lescarbot, Marc. History of New France, 1. LC 68-28596. 331p. 1969. reprint ed. text ed. 65.00 (0-8371-5039-6, LHFA) Greenwood.

— History of New France, Vol. 7. LC 68-28596. 584p. 1969. reprint ed. text ed. 75.00 (0-8371-5040-X, LHFB) Greenwood.

— History of New France, Vol. 11. LC 68-28596. 555p. 1969. reprint ed. text ed. 75.00 (0-8371-5041-8, LHFC) Greenwood.

— Nova Francia, or the Description of That Part of New France, Which Is One Continent with Virginia. Erondelle, Pierre E., tr. LC 77-7415. (English Experience Ser.: No. 877). 1977. reprint ed. lib. bdg. 31.00 (90-221-0877-5) Walter J Johnson.

Lescarboura, Austin C. Behind the Motion-Picture Screen. LC 75-174878. (Illus.). 1972. reprint ed. 30.95 (0-405-08742-X, Pub. by Blom Pubns UK) Ayer.

Lesce, Tony. The Big House: How American Prisons Work. LC 91-62781. 192p. (Orig.). 1991. pap. 19.95 (1-55950-075-1, 40071) Loompanics.

— Escape from Controlled Custody. LC 90-61242. 144p. (Orig.). 1990. pap. 10.95 (1-55950-038-7, 40066) Loompanics.

— Espionage: Down & Dirty. LC 91-60972. 192p. (Orig.). (C). 1991. pap. write for info. (1-55950-068-9, 55083) Loompanics.

— Police Products Handbook. 480p. 1990. 59.95 (0-13-684739-0) P-H.

— The Privacy Poachers: How the Government & Big Corporations Gather, Use & Sell Information about You. LC 92-81233. (Illus.). 155p. (Orig.). 1992. pap. 16.95 (1-55950-086-7, 58080) Loompanics.

— Secrets of Successful Job Hunting: Surefire Tactics for Finding Hidden Jobs, Writing Effective Resumes, Handling Tough Interviews, & Beating Chemical & Psychological Tests. (Illus.). 104p. 1994. pap. 14.00 (0-87364-776-9) Paladin Pr.

— The Shotgun in Combat. (Illus.). 152p. 1984. pap. 10.00 (0-87364-314-3) Paladin Pr.

Lesce, Tony, jt. auth. see Cheek, John C.

Lesce, Tony, jt. auth. see Turner, Donald M.

Lescelius, Robert. Lordship Salvation: Some Crucial Questions & Answers. 1992. pap. 6.99 (1-56632-001-1) Revival Lit.

Lesch, Ann M. Political Perceptions of the Palestinians on the West Bank & the Gaza Strip. LC 80-81807. (Middle East Institute Special Study Ser.: No. 3). (Illus.). 119p. reprint ed. pap. 34.00 (0-317-09280-4, 2022763) Bks Demand.

— Transition to Palestinian Self-Government: Practical Steps Toward Israeli-Palestinian Peace. (Illus.). 160p. (C). 1993. 27.50 (0-253-33326-1, MB-794); pap. 10.95 (0-253-20794-0) Ind U Pr.

Lesch, Ann M. & Tessler, Mark A. Israel, Egypt, & the Palestinians: From Camp David to Intifada. LC 88-45448. (Illus.). 316p. 1989. 45.00 (0-253-33320-2) Ind U Pr.

Lesch, Christiane. A Farmyard Morning. Lawson, Polly, tr. (Illus.). 24p. (J). (ps-00). 1990. reprint ed. lib. bdg. 12.95 (0-86315-117-5) Gryphon Hse.

— In Bethlehem Long Ago. Lawson, Polly, tr. (Illus.). 28p. (J). (ps-2). reprint ed. 14.95 (0-86315-076-4, Pub. by Floris Bks UK) Gryphon Hse.

Lesch, David W. Syria & the United States: Eisenhower's Cold War in the Middle East. LC 92-25519. 234p. (C). 1992. pap. text ed. 52.00 (0-8133-8582-2) Westview.

Lesch, William C. & Rupert, David. New Product Screening: A Step-Wise Approach. LC 93-15579. (Illus.). 116p. 1994. lib. bdg. 29.95 (1-56024-404-6) Haworth Pr.

Leschak, Peter. The Bear Guardian. (Illus.). 184p. 1990. 9.95 (0-87839-061-8) North Star.

Leschak, Peter M. Bumming with the Furies: Out on the Trail of Experience. LC 93-7993. (Illus.). 1993. pap. 9.95 (0-87839-078-2) North Star.

— Hellroaring. (Illus.). 240p. 1994. 14.95 (0-87839-087-1) North Star.

— Letters from Side Lake: A Chronicle of Life in the North Woods. LC 92-8713. 208p. 1992. pap. 11.95 (0-8166-2243-4) U of Minn Pr.

— Seeing the Raven: A Narrative of Renewal. LC 93-27943. 1994. 16.95 (0-8166-2429-1) U of Minn Pr.

Leschber, R., et al, eds. Chemical Methods for Assessing Bio-Available Metals in Sludges & Soils: Proceedings of a CEC Seminar Held at the Josef-Konig Institute, Munster, West Germany, 11-13 April 1984. 104p. 1985. 47.00 (0-85334-359-4, Pub. by Elsevier Applied Sci UK) Elsevier.

***Lescher, Marianne L.** Portfolios: Assessing Learning in the Primary Grades. LC 95-4295. (What Research Says to the Teacher Ser.). 1995. write for info. (0-8106-1094-9) NEA.

Leschert, Dale F., jt. auth. see National Association of Baptist Professors of Religion.

Leschied, Alan W., et al, eds. Young Offenders Act Revolution: Changing the Face of Canadian Juvenile Justice. 256p. 1991. 60.00 (0-8020-2623-0); pap. 24.95 (0-8020-6714-X) U of Toronto Pr.

Leschmelle, Pierre. Montaigne, or the Anguished Soul. Beck, William J., tr. LC 93-46833. (Currents in Comparative Romance Languages & Literatures Ser.: Vol. 29). 222p. (C). 1994. text ed. 51.95 (0-8204-2476-5) P Lang Pubs.

Leschnitzer, Adolf. The Magic Background of Modern Anti-Semitism: An Analysis of the German-Jewish Relationship. LC 55-6501. 246p. reprint ed. pap. 70.20 (0-317-11194-9, 2010437) Bks Demand.

Leschonski, K. & Carter, F. L. Elseviers Dictionary of Particle Technology: English - German & German - English. 1991. 123.00 (0-685-50934-6) Elsevier.

Leschonski, K. & Carter, R. F., eds. Elseviers Dictionary of Particle Technology. 286p. (ENG & GER.). 1978. 105.25 (0-444-41746-X) Elsevier.

Leschziner, Michael. EUROVAL - A European Initiative on Validation of CFD Codes: Results of the EC-Brite-Euram Project EUROVAL, 1990-1992. Haase, Werner et al, eds. (Notes on Numerical Fluid Mechanics Ser.: Vol. 42). xiv, 531p. 1993. 104.00 (3-528-07642-9, Pub. by Vieweg & Sohn GW) Ballen Bkslr.

Lescoe, F., ed. see Dennehy, R. & Grisez, G.

Lescoe, F., ed. see Krapiec, M. A.

Lescoe, F., ed. see Krapiec, M.

Lescoe, F., ed. see Lawler, R. & May, W.

Lescoe, F., tr. see Leger, E., et al.

Lescoe, Francis J., jt. ed. see Lawler, Ronald.

Lescoe, M., tr. see Krapiec, M. A.

Lescoe, M., tr. see Krapiec, M.

Lescohier, Don D. Knights of St. Crispin, Eighteen Sixty-Seven to Eighteen Seventy-Four. LC 77-89748. (American Labor, from Conspiracy to Collective Bargaining Ser., No. 1). 101p. 1974. reprint ed. 17.95 (0-405-02136-4) Ayer.

Lescourret, Marie-Anne. Rubens: A Double Life. Powell, Elfreda, tr. (Illus.). 352p. 1993. 27.50 (1-56663-015-0) I R Dee.

Lescow, Theodor. Das Stufenschema: Unterschungen zur Struktur Alttestamentlicher Texte. (Beihefte zur Zeitschrift fuer die Alttestamentliche Wissenschaft Ser.: Bd. 211). x, 282p. (GER.). (C). 1992. lib. bdg. 98.50 (3-11-013768-2) De Gruyter.

Lescroart, John E., ed. Fieldston Coal Transportation Manual, 1986-1987. (Fieldston Coal Transportation Manual Ser.). 604p. 1986. 150.00 (0-9613656-1-7) Fieldston Co.

***Lescroart, John T.** A Certain Justice: A Novel. 448p. 1995. 22.95 (1-55611-445-1) D I Fine.

— Dead Irish. 1990. 18.95 (1-55611-159-2) D I Fine.

— Hard Evidence. LC 92-54457. 1993. 21.95 (1-55611-344-7) D I Fine.

— Hard Evidence. Date not set. pap. write for info. (0-449-22241-1) Fawcett.

— Hard Evidence. (Northern California Mysteries Ser.). 1994. mass mkt. 5.99 (0-8041-1275-4) Ivy Books.

— Rasputin's Revenge. LC 86-82179. 288p. 1987. 17.95 (1-55611-011-1) D I Fine.

— Rasputin's Revenge. 288p. 1988. reprint ed. pap. 3.50 (0-8439-2671-6) Dorchester Pub Co.

— Son of Holmes. LC 85-81872. 223p. 1986. 15.95 (0-917657-64-0) D I Fine.

— Son of Holmes. 240p. 1987. reprint ed. pap. 3.25 (0-8439-2461-6) Dorchester Pub Co.

— Son of Holmes & Rasputin's Revenge: The Early Works of John T. Lescroart. 544p. 1995. pap. 12.95 (1-55611-437-0) D I Fine.

— The Thirteenth Juror. LC 93-74487. 496p. 1994. 22.95 (1-55611-402-8) D I Fine.

— The Thirteenth Juror. large type ed. LC 94-32218. 803p. 1994. 23.95 (0-8161-7448-2) Hall.

— The Vig. 1991. 18.95 (1-55611-221-1) D I Fine.

***Lescroat, John, et al, eds.** Fieldston Coal Transportation Manual 1988-1989. 610p. Date not set. write for info. (0-9613656-2-5) Fieldston Co.

***Leseho, Johanna & Howard-Rose, Dawn.** Anger in the Classroom: A Practical Guide for Teachers. (Illus.). 96p. (Orig.). (C). 1994. pap. text ed. 14.95x (1-55059-080-4) Temeron Bks.

Lesel, R., ed. Microbiology in Poecilotherms: International Symposium on Microbiology in Poecilotherms, Paris, France, 10-12 July, 1989. 282p. 1990. 92.25 (0-444-81166-4) Elsevier.

Lesem, Jeanne. Preserving Today. 1992. 22.50 (0-394-58653-0) Knopf.

Lesemann, D. E., jt. ed. see Mendgen, K.

Lesemann, Frederic & Martin, Claude, eds. Home-Based Care, the Elderly, the Family & the Welfare State: An International Comparison. 277p. 1994. pap. 25.00 (0-7766-0369-8, Pub. by Univ Ottawa Pr CN) Paul & Co Pubs.

***Leser.** Diercke Woerterbuch Allgemeinisches Geographie: A-M, Vol. 1. (GER.). Date not set. 29.95 (0-614-00365-2) Fr & Eur.

An Asterisk (*) at the beginning of an entry indicates that the title is appearing in BIP for the first time.

— Diercke Woerterbuch Allgemeinisches Geographie: N-Z, Vol. 1. (GER.). Date not set. 29.95 (*0-614-00366-0*, 3423034181) Fr & Eur.

— Diercke Woerterbuch Umwel Oekologie Vol. 2. (GER.). Date not set. 29.95 (*0-614-00367-9*, 3423034203) Fr & Eur.

Leser, C. E. Econometric Techniques & Problems. 2nd ed. 1974. 17.95 (*0-85264-218-0*) Lubrecht & Cramer.

Leser, Esther H. Thomas Mann's Short Fiction: An Intellectual Biography. LC 87-45369. 352p. 1989. 47.50 (*0-8386-3319-6*) Fairleigh Dickinson.

Leserman, Lee, jt. auth. see Machy, Patrick.

***Lesesne, Tamara & Harrill, Helen.** I'm Special: A Program for Third & Fourth Graders. 2nd ed. (Illus.). 142p. (C). 1992. teacher ed 25.00 (*0-934337-04-7*) Drug Ed Ctr.

Lesesne, Tamara S. I'm Special: A Program for Third & Fourth Graders. rev. ed. Harrill, Helen S. et al, eds. LC 85-147179. (Illus.). 114p. 1986. pap. text ed. 10.00 (*0-934337-01-2*) Drug Ed Ctr.

***LeSeur, Geta.** Ten Is the Age of Darkness: The Black Bildungsroman. 224p. 1995. 34.95 (*0-8262-1011-2*) U of Mo Pr.

Lesgold, Alan & Glaser, Robert, eds. Foundations for a Psychology of Education. 328p. 1988. 69.95 (*0-8058-0296-7*) L Erlbaum Assocs.

Lesgold, Alan M. & Perfetti, Charles A., eds. Interactive Processes in Reading. LC 80-21048. 448p. 1981. text ed. 79.95 (*0-89859-079-5*) L Erlbaum Assocs.

Lesgold, Alan M., jt. ed. see Mandl, Heinz.

Lesgold, Alan M., et al, eds. Cognitive Psychology & Instruction. LC 77-27133. (NATO Conference Series III, Human Factors: Vol. 5). 540p. 1978. 75.00 (*0-306-32886-0*, Plenum Pr) Plenum.

Lesh, Donald. Treatise on Thoroughbred Selection. 80p. 1990. pap. 21.00 (*0-85131-296-9*, Pub. by J A Allen & Co UK) St Mut.

Lesh, Kay, jt. auth. see Golden, Bonnie J.

Lesh, O. E., jt. ed. see Tyndall, John W.

***Lesh, Richard & Lamon, Susan J., eds.** Assessment of Authentic Performance in School Mathematics. 456p. 1994. pap. 24.95 (*0-8058-1877-4*) L Erlbaum Assocs.

Lesh, Richard & Landau, Marsha, eds. Acquisitions of Mathematics Concepts & Processes. LC 83-2845. (Developmental Psychology Ser.). 1983. text ed. 79.00 (*0-12-444220-X*) Acad Pr.

Lesh, Richard A. & Lamon, Susan J., eds. Assessment of Authentic Performance in School Mathematics. LC 92-14967. 456p. 1992. pap. 39.95 (*0-87168-500-0*, 92-16S) AAAS.

LeShan, Eda. Grandparenting in a Changing World. LC 93-24988. 224p. 1993. 19.95 (*1-55704-175-X*) Newmarket.

— Grandparents: A Special Kind of Love. LC 84-5673. (Illus.). 128p. (J). (gr. 3-7). 1984. text ed. 13.95 (*0-02-756380-4*, Mac Bks Young Read) S&S Childrens.

— It's Better to Be over the Hill Than under It: Thoughts on Life over Sixty. LC 90-41274. 240p. 1991. 18.95 (*1-55704-071-0*); pap. 10.95 (*1-55704-102-4*) Newmarket.

— It's Better to Be over the Hill Than under It: Thoughts on Life over Sixty. braille ed. 245p. 1992. vinyl bd. 19.60 (*1-56956-064-1*, BR8610) W A T Braille.

— Learning to Say Good-Bye: When a Child's Parent Dies. 128p. 1978. pap. 8.00 (*0-380-40105-3*) Avon.

— Learning to Say Good-bye: When a Parent Dies. LC 76-15155. (Illus.). 96p. (J). (gr. 3 up). 1976. text ed. 13.95 (*0-02-756360-X*, Mac Bks Young Read) S&S Childrens.

— What Makes Me Feel This Way? Growing up with Human Emotions. LC 71-165573. (Illus.). 128p. (J). (gr. 3-6). 1974. pap. 4.95 (*0-02-044340-4*, Mac Bks Young Read) S&S Childrens.

— What Makes You So Special? LC 91-16925. 160p. (J). (gr. 3-7). 1992. 15.00 (*0-8037-1155-7*) Dial Bks Young.

— What's Going to Happen to Me? When Parents Separate or Divorce. LC 78-4340. (Illus.). 144p. (J). (gr. 3-7). 1984. text ed. 13.95 (*0-02-759230-8*, Four Winds Pr) S&S Childrens.

— What's Going to Happen to Me? When Parents Separate or Divorce. rev. ed. LC 86-10769. (Illus.). 144p. (J). (gr. 3-7). 1986. reprint ed. pap. 4.95 (*0-689-71093-3*, Aladdin Paperbacks) S&S Childrens.

— When Grownups Drive You Crazy. LC 87-22005. 128p. (J). (gr. 3-7). 1988. text ed. 13.95 (*0-02-756340-5*, Mac Bks Young Read) S&S Childrens.

Leshan, Eda. When Your Child Drives You Crazy. 1992. mass mkt. 5.99 (*0-312-92930-7*) St Martin.

***Leshan, Eda J.** I Want More of Everything. LC 94-22544. 240p. 1994. 20.00 (*1-55704-211-X*) Newmarket.

***LeShan, Lawrence.** Beyond Technique: An Individualized Approach to Psychotherapy. 1996. 30.00 (*1-56821-550-9*) Aronson.

— Cancer As a Turning Point: A Handbook for People with Cancer, Their Families & Health Professionals. 228p. 1990. pap. 10.00 (*0-452-26419-7*, Plume) NAL-Dutton.

— Cancer As a Turning Point: A Handbook for People with Cancer, Their Families & Health Professionals. rev. ed. 240p. 1994. pap. 10.95 (*0-452-27137-1*) NAL-Dutton.

— How to Meditate: A Guide to Self-Discovery. 176p. 1984. mass mkt. 4.99 (*0-553-24453-1*) Bantam.

— Meditating to Attain a Healthy Body Weight. LC 93-43320. 1994. 19.95 (*0-385-47285-4*) Doubleday.

— Meditating to Attain a Healthy Body Weight. 1995. pap. 9.95 (*0-553-37372-2*) Bantam.

— The Medium, the Mystic & the Physicist. 304p. 1982. pap. 3.95 (*0-345-30312-1*) Ballantine.

— The Medium, the Mystic & the Physicist: Toward a General Theory of the Paranormal. 320p. 1995. pap. 10.95 (*0-14-019499-1*, Arkana) Viking Penguin.

— The Psychology of War: Comprehending Its Mystique & Its Madness. LC 92-50438. 163p. 1992. 16.95 (*1-879360-20-9*) Noble Pr.

— Toward a General Theory of the Paranormal. 3rd ed. LC 73-80027. (Parapsychological Monograph Ser.: No. 9). 1969. pap. 7.00 (*0-912328-13-4*) Parapsych Foun.

— You Can Fight for Your Life: Emotional Factors in the Treatment of Cancer. LC 76-30464. 204p. 1976. pap. 6.95 (*0-87131-494-0*) M Evans.

LeShan, Lawrence & Margenau, Henry. Einstein's Space & Van Gogh's Sky: Physical Reality & Beyond. 288p. 1983. pap. 12.95 (*0-02-093180-8*, Pub. by Gebrueder Borntraeger GW) Macmillan.

Leshane, Patricia. Vegetarian Cooking for People with Diabetes. 144p. 1994. pap. 10.95 (*0-913990-22-1*) Book Pub Co.

Leshay, Jeff. How to Launch Your Career in TV News. 144p. 1993. pap. 14.95 (*0-8442-4138-5*, VGM Career Bks) NTC Pub Grp.

Leshchisky, D., jt. auth. see Tatsuoka, F.

Leshem, Ya'acov Y. The Molecular & Hormonal Basis of Plant Growth Regulation. LC 73-6802. 168p. 1973. 71.00 (*0-08-017649-6*, Pub. by Pergamon Repr UK) Franklin.

— Plant Membranes: A Biophysical Approach. 280p. (C). 1992. lib. bdg. 144.00 (*0-7923-1353-4*) Kluwer Ac.

Leshem, Ya'acov Y., et al, eds. Processes & Control of Plant Senescence. (Developments in Crop Science Ser.: Vol. 8). 1986. 97.50 (*0-444-42521-7*) Elsevier.

Lesher, Emerson L. The Muppie Manual. LC 85-80988. (Illus.). 96p. 1985. pap. 4.95 (*0-934672-31-8*) Good Bks PA.

Lesher, J. H., ed. Xenophanes of Colophon: Fragments - A Text & Translation with a Commentary. (Phoenix Supplementary Volumes Ser.: No. XXX: Pre-Socratics). 380p. 1992. 45.00 (*0-8020-5990-2*) U of Toronto Pr.

Lesher, James, jt. ed. see Marolda, Edward J.

Lesher, Stephan. George Wallace: American Populist. LC 93-40384. 1993. 28.95 (*0-201-62210-6*) Addison-Wesley.

— George Wallace: American Populist. 1995. pap. 14.42 (*0-201-40798-1*) Addison-Wesley.

***Leshin, Cynthia.** Internet Adventures: Step-By-Step Guide to Finding & Using Educational Resources. (Internet Adventures Ser.). (Illus.). 320p. (Orig.). (J). (gr. k up). 1995. pap. text ed. 24.95 (*0-9645588-0-7*) XPlora.

— Netscape Adventures: Step-by-Step Guide to Netscape Navigator & the World Wide Web. (Internet Adventures Ser.). (Illus.). 148p. (Orig.). 1995. pap. text ed. 22.95 (*0-9645588-1-5*) XPlora.

Leshin, Cynthia B., et al. Instructional Design Strategies & Tactics. LC 91-32884. (Illus.). 360p. (Orig.). 1992. pap. 34.95 (*0-87778-240-7*) Educ Tech Pubns.

Leshin, George. Speech for the Hearing-Impaired Child. 151p. 1975. pap. 14.95 (*0-8165-0540-3*) U of Ariz Pr.

Leshin, Geraldine. EEO Law: Impact on Fringe Benefits. Hinman, Faye, ed. (Policy & Practice Publication). 1993. reprint ed. 9.00 (*0-89215-102-1*) U Cal LA Indus Rel.

— The Prevailing Wage Concept in Public Sector Bargaining. (Policy & Practice Publication). 161p. 1977. 6.00 (*0-89215-078-5*) U Cal LA Indus Rel.

Leshin, Geraldine & Schwartz, Rosalind, eds. EEO for Practitioners, 1988. (Current Issues Ser.: No. 8). 52p. 1993. reprint ed. pap. 7.50 (*0-89215-146-3*) U Cal LA Indus Rel.

Leshin, Geraldine, jt. ed. see Schwartz, Rosalind.

Leshin, Michael. Compendium of Massachusetts Family Law. LC 90-63089. 300p. 1990. ring bd. 50.00 (*0-944490-28-X*) Mass CLE.

— Compendium of Massachusetts Family Law. LC 90-63089. 503p. 1990. ring bd. 50.00 (*0-944490-60-3*) Mass CLE.

Leshinskie, Matthew, jt. auth. see Gustafson, Bruce.

Leshko, Jaroslaw. Orbus Pictus: The Prints of Oskar Kokoschka, 1906-1976. LC 87-9853. (Illus.). 104p. 1987. pap. 20.00 (*0-295-96574-6*) U of Wash Pr.

Leshnik, Lawrence S. South Indian Megalithic Burials: The Pandukal Complex. (Illus.). 321p. 1974. text ed. 97.50 (*3-515-01955-3*) Coronet Bks.

Leshy, John D. Arizona State Constitution: A Reference Guide. LC 92-35922. (Reference Guides to the State Constitutions of the United States Ser.: No. 15). 456p. 1993. text ed. 85.00 (*0-313-27266-2*, LAH/, Greenwood Pr) Greenwood.

— The Mining Law: A Study in Perpetual Motion. LC 86-42610. 521p. 1987. 35.00 (*0-915707-26-8*) Resources Future.

Leshy, John D., ed. see Coggins, George C. & Wilkinson, Charles F.

Lesiak, Judi L., jt. auth. see Bradley-Johnson, Sharon.

Lesiak, Judi L., jt. auth. see Lesiak, Walter J.

Lesiak, Walter J. & Lesiak, Judi L. Developmental Tasks for Kindergarten Readiness II (DTKR II) Assessment of Prekindergarten Children to Determine Kindergarten Readiness. LC 93-41855. 72p. 1994. pap. 19.95 (*0-88422-095-8*) Clinical Psych.

***Lesic, Zdenko, ed.** Children of Atlantis: Voices from the Former Yugoslavia. (A Central European University Press Bk.). 208p. 1995. pap. 12.95 (*1-85866-041-6*) OUP.

Lesick, Lawrence T. The Lane Rebels: Evangelicalism & Antislavery in Antebellum America. LC 80-24123. (Studies in Evangelicalism: No. 2). 287p. 1980. 27.50 (*0-8108-1372-6*) Scarecrow.

LeSieg, Theo. I Can Write! A Book by Me, Myself. (Bright & Early Bks.). (Illus.). 32p. (J). (ps-1). 1993. pap. 2.99 (*0-679-84700-6*) Random Bks Yng Read.

— I Wish That I Had Duck Feet. LC 65-21211. (Beginner Bks.). (Illus.). 64p. (J). (ps-2). 1965. 7.99 (*0-394-80040-0*) Random Bks Yng Read.

— I Wish That I Had Duck Feet. LC 65-21211. (Beginner Bks.). (Illus.). 64p. (J). (ps-2). 1965. lib. bdg. 9.99 (*0-394-90040-5*) Random Bks Yng Read.

— I Wish That I Had Duck Feet. (Beginner Book & Cassette Library). (Illus.). 64p. (J). (ps-1). 1988. 6.95 (*0-394-89777-3*) Random Bks Yng Read.

— The Pop-up Mice of Mr. Brice. LC 89-60507. (Illus.). 20p. (J). (ps-3). 1989. 10.00 (*0-679-80132-4*) Random Bks Yng Read.

Lesieur, Frederick G., ed. Scanlon Plan: A Frontier in Labor-Management Cooperation. 1958. pap. 13.95 (*0-262-62008-1*) MIT Pr.

Lesieur, Henry. The Chase: The Compulsive Gambler. 352p. 1984. 29.95 (*0-87073-642-6*); pap. 15.95 (*0-87073-643-4*) Schenkman Bks Inc.

— Understanding Compulsive Gambling. 32p. 1994. pap. 2.55 (*0-89486-388-6*, 5497) Hazelden.

Lesieur, Marcel. Turbulence in Fluids. 2nd rev. ed. (C). 1990. lib. bdg. 129.00 (*0-7923-0645-7*) Kluwer Ac.

— Turbulence in Fluids: Stochastic & Numerical Modelling. 1987. lib. bdg. 114.00 (*90-247-3470-3*) Kluwer Ac.

***Lesikar, Raymond, et al.** Basic Business Communication. 6th ed. 136p. (C). 1994. student ed, text ed. 19.50 (*0-256-11059-X*) Irwin.

— Basic Business Communication, Canadian. 688p. (C). 1993. text ed. 43.75 (*0-256-11690-3*) Irwin.

Lesikar, Raymond V., Sr. Basic Business Communication. 5th ed. (Business Communication Ser.). (C). 1990. student ed 17.95 (*0-256-08614-1*); text ed. 54.95 (*0-256-08327-4*) Irwin.

— Basic Business Communication. 6th ed. LC 92-19974. 761p. (C). 1992. text ed. 59.95 (*0-256-10936-2*) Irwin.

***Lesikar, Raymond V. & Petit, John D., Jr.** Report Writing for Business. 9th ed. 1995. pap. write for info. (*0-256-18021-0*) Irwin.

Lesikar, Raymond V., Sr. & Pettit, John. Report Writing for Business. 8th ed. 480p. (C). 1990. text ed. 56.95 (*0-256-06948-4*, 12-0420-08) Irwin.

Lesikar, Raymond V. & Pettit, John D. Report Writing for Business. 9th ed. LC 94-12499. 480p. (C). 1994. 56.95 (*0-256-11565-6*) Irwin.

Lesina, D. Roberto. Software & Hardware Dictionary: Italian - English, English - Italian. (ENG & ITA.). 1991. 89.95 (*0-7859-3709-9*, 8808114880) Fr & Eur.

— Software & Hardware Dictionary: Italian-English - English-Italian. 416p. 1991. 102.00 (*88-08-11488-0*) IBD Ltd.

Lesk, Arthur M. Introduction to Physical Chemistry. (Illus.). ▼ 784p. (C). 1982. Solutions manual. write for info. (*0-13-492728-1*) P-H.

Lesk, Arthur M., ed. Computational Molecular Biology: Sources & Methods for Sequence Analysis. (Illus.). 272p. 1989. 55.00 (*0-19-854218-6*) OUP.

— Protein Architecture: A Practical Approach. (Practical Approach Ser.). (Illus.). 312p. 1991. pap. 39.00 (*0-19-963055-0*, IRL Pr) OUP.

***Lesk, Michael.** Image Formats for Preservation & Access: A Report of the Technology Assessment Advisory Committee. 10p. 1990. pap. text ed. 10.00 (*1-887334-39-4*) Comm Preserv & Access.

— Preservation of New Technology: A Report of the Technology Assessment Advisory Committee. 19p. 1992. pap. 5.00 (*1-887334-19-X*) Comm Preserv & Access.

Lesk, Sara M., ed. see Time-Life Editors.

Lesk, Sara M., ed. see Time Life Inc. Editors.

Leske, Steven. Sir Richard & the Dragon. 14p. (J). (gr. k-6). 1992. pap. text ed. 5.99 (*1-881617-01-7*) Teapot Tales.

— A Two Headed Tale. 16p. (J). (gr. k-6). 1992. pap. text ed. 5.99 (*1-881617-02-5*) Teapot Tales.

Lesker, G. A., ed. Three Late Medieval Morality Plays: Mankind, Everyman & Mundis et Infans. (New Mermaid Ser.). (C). 1984. pap. text ed. 7.95 (*0-393-90054-1*) Norton.

Leskes, Andrea, tr. see Bebel-Gisler, Dany.

Leskes, Andrea, tr. see Lopes, Henri.

Leski, Lenet. My Philosophy. LC 93-60355. 30p. 1994. 7.95 (*1-55523-619-7*) Winston-Derek.

Leskiewicz, H. J., ed. see IFAC Symposium Staff.

Leskiw, Donald M., jt. auth. see Miller, Kenneth S.

Lesko, Barbara S. Remarkable Women of Ancient Egypt. 2nd rev. ed. (Illus.). 1987. pap. 8.95 (*0-930548-09-4*) B C Scribe.

Lesko, Barbara S., ed. Women's Earliest Records: From Ancient Egypt & Western Asia. LC 89-4135. (Brown Judaic Studies). (Illus.). 350p. 1989. 69.95 (*1-55540-319-0*, 14 01 66) Scholars Pr GA.

Lesko, Diane. James Ensor: The Creative Years. LC 84-26452. (Illus.). 191p. reprint ed. pap. 54.50 (*0-8357-6552-0*, 2035916) Bks Demand.

Lesko, Diane, et al, eds. Catalogue of the Collection Museum of Fine Arts, St. Petersburg, Florida. LC 93-78274. (Illus.). 367p. (Orig.). (C). 1993. pap. 35.00 (*1-878390-02-3*) Mus St Pete.

***Lesko, John & Irish, Michael, eds.** Technology Exchange: A Guide to Successful Cooperative Research & Development Partnerships. 1995. 22.95 (*0-935470-86-7*) Battelle.

Lesko, Kathleen M., et al. Black Georgetown Remembered: A History of Its Black Community from the Founding of the "Town of George" in 1751 to the Present Day. LC 91-29357. (Illus.). 210p. 1991. reprint ed. pap. 25.00 (*0-87840-526-7*) Georgetown U Pr.

Lesko, Leonard H. Index of the Spells on Egyptian Middle Kingdom Coffins & Related Documents. LC 79-66500. (Orig.). 1979. pap. text ed. 6.00 (*0-930548-02-7*) B C Scribe.

— King Tut's Wine Cellar. LC 77-85654. (Illus.). 1977. pap. 3.95 (*0-930548-00-0*) B C Scribe.

Lesko, Leonard H., ed. Dictionary of Late Egyptian, Vol. 1 of 4 Vols. (EGY.). 1982. lib. bdg. 35.00 (*0-930548-03-5*); pap. text ed. 20.00 (*0-930548-04-3*) B C Scribe.

— Egyptological Studies in Honor of Richard A. Parker. LC 84-40590. (Illus.). 191p. 1986. text ed. 35.00 (*0-87451-321-9*) U Pr of New Eng.

— Pharaoh's Workers: The Villagers of Deir el Medina. (Illus.). 212p. 1994. 32.50 (*0-8014-2915-3*); pap. 13.95 (*0-8014-8143-0*) Cornell U Pr.

Lesko, Marian, ed. see Arnold, Marti.

Lesko, Matthew. Getting Yours: The Complete Guide to Government Money. LC 81-52256. 324p. 1982. mass mkt. 4.95 (*0-14-046510-3*) Viking Penguin.

— Getting Yours: The Complete Guide to Government Money. rev. ed. (Handbook Ser.). 352p. 1984. pap. 8.95 (*0-14-046652-5*, Penguin Bks) Viking Penguin.

— Getting Yours: The Complete Guide to Government Money. 3rd ed. LC 86-22688. 336p. 1987. pap. 11.95 (*0-14-046760-2*, Penguin Bks) Viking Penguin.

— Government Giveaways for Entrepreneurs II. rev. ed. Naprawa, Andrew, ed. 642p. 1993. pap. 37.95 (*1-878346-19-9*) Info USA.

— Information U. S. A. (Handbook Ser.). 1288p. 1986. pap. 25.00 (*0-14-046745-9*, Penguin Bks) Viking Penguin.

— Lesko's Info-Power, Vol. 2. 1994. pap. 29.95 (*0-8103-9485-5*) Visible Ink Pr.

— Lesko's Info-Power II. 2nd ed. 1600p. 1993. 59.00 (*0-8103-9642-4*, M89334-107152) Gale.

— Lesko's Info-Power II Sourcebook. 2nd ed. Naprawa, Andrew, ed. 1000p. 1994. pap. text ed. 39.95 (*1-878346-17-2*) Info USA.

— One Thousand One Free Goodies & Cheapies. 482p. (Orig.). 1995. pap. 19.95 (*1-878346-25-3*) Info USA.

— One Thousand One Freebies & Cheapies. 1994. pap. 19.95 (*1-878346-22-9*) Info USA.

***Lesko, Matthew & Martello, Mary Ann.** Free College Money, Term Papers, Sex (Ed) Hess, Martha, ed. 1051p. (Orig.). 1994. pap. 36.95 (*1-878346-24-5*) Info USA.

— What to Do When You Can't Afford Health Care. Naprawa, Andrew, ed. 769p. (Orig.). 1993. pap. 24.95 (*1-878346-16-4*) Info USA.

Lesko, Matthew & Naprawa, Andrew. Great American Gripe Book. 2nd ed. 367p. 1994. pap. 12.92 (*1-878346-18-0*) Info USA.

Lesko, Nancy. Symbolizing Society: Stories, Rites & Structure in a Catholic High School. (Education Policy Perspectives Ser.). 170p. 1988. 60.00 (*1-85000-302-5*, Falmer Pr); pap. 28.00 (*1-85000-307-6*, Falmer Pr) Taylor & Francis.

Lesko, Wayne A., ed. Readings in Social Psychology: General, Classical, & Contemporary Selections. 2nd ed. LC 93-22615. 1993. pap. text ed. 18.00 (*0-205-15207-4*) Allyn.

Lesko, Wendy S. No Kidding Around! America's Young Activists Are Changing Our World & You Can Too. (Illus.). 250p. (Orig.). 1992. pap. 18.95 (*1-878346-10-5*) Info USA.

Leskorsek, Valentin. Slovenia, Vol. 2: A Bibliography in Foreign Languages. 115p. 1991. 12.00 (*0-685-41046-3*) Studia Slovenica.

Leskov, Chtchedri, jt. auth. see Leskov, Saltykov.

Leskov, Nicolas. Lady Macbeth au Village, l'Ange Scelle, la Vagabond Enchante. (FRE.). 1982. pap. 17.95 (*0-7859-4174-6*) Fr & Eur.

Leskov, Nikolai. On the Edge of the World. Prokurat, Michael, tr. LC 92-31940. 136p. 1993. 7.95 (*0-88141-118-3*) St Vladimirs.

Leskov, Nikolai S. The Cathedral Folk. Hapgood, I., tr. LC 76-23885. (Classics of Russian Literature Ser.). 439p. 1986. reprint ed. pap. 22.00 (*0-88355-488-7*) Hyperion Conn.

— The Enchanted Pilgrim & Other Stories. Magarshack, David, tr. LC 76-23886. (Classics of Russian Literature Ser.). 1987. reprint ed. 25.00 (*0-88355-497-6*) Hyperion Conn.

— The Enchanted Wanderer. Paschkoff, A. G., tr. 251p. 1985. reprint ed. pap. 13.95 (*0-948166-04-5*, Pub. by Soho Bk Co UK) Dufour.

— Five Tales. Shotton, Michael, tr. 1984. 25.00 (*0-946162-12-3*); pap. 13.95 (*0-946162-13-1*) Dufour.

— The Jews in Russia. Schefski, Harold K., ed. & tr. by. LC 87-80844. 143p. 1986. 21.00 (*0-940670-29-1*) Kingston Pr.

— Lady Macbeth of the Mtsensk District & Other Stories. 424p. 1988. pap. 10.95 (*0-14-044491-2*, Penguin Classics) Viking Penguin.

— The Musk-Ox & Other Tales. Norman, R., tr. LC 76-23887. (Classics of Russian Literature Ser.). 1987. reprint ed. 18.00 (*0-88355-499-2*) Hyperion Conn.

— The Sealed Angel & Other Stories. Lantz, K. A., ed. LC 83-14547. 267p. reprint ed. pap. 76.10 (*0-7837-7080-4*, 2046892) Bks Demand.

— The Sentry & Other Tales. Chamot, A., tr. LC 76-23888. (Classics of Russian Literature Ser.). (Illus.). 1987. reprint ed. 22.50 (*0-88355-501-8*) Hyperion Conn.

Leskov, Saltykov & Leskov, Chtchedri. Oeuvres. Luneau, Andre, ed. 1676p. (FRE.). 1967. lib. bdg. 110.00 (*0-7859-3764-1*, 2070103102) Fr & Eur.

Leskov, Saltykov-Chtchedrine. Oeuvres. 1676p. 42.95 (*0-686-56534-7*) Fr & Eur.

Leskova, T. & Plisek, V. Czech-English Technical Textile Dictionary. 468p. (CZE & ENG.). 1980. 60.00 (*0-686-72090-3*, Pub. by Collets UK) St Mut.

Leskovsek, Valentin. Slovenia, Vol. 1: A Bibliography in Foreign Languages. 105p. 1990. 12.00 (*0-685-34712-5*) Studia Slovenica.

— Yugoslavia, Vol. 1: A Bibliography. LC 77-374918. 192p. 1974. 10.00 (*0-686-28383-X*) Studia Slovenica.

— Yugoslavia, Vol. 2: A Bibliography. LC 77-374918. 168p. 1978. 10.00 (*0-686-28386-4*) Studia Slovenica.

— Yugoslavia, Vol. 3: A Bibliography. LC 77-374918. 120p. 1980. pap. 10.00 (*0-686-26712-5*) Studia Slovenica.

— Yugoslavia, Vol. 4: A Bibliography. LC 77-374918. 153p. 1982. 10.00 (*0-938616-15-3*) Studia Slovenica.

Leskowitz, Sidney, jt. ed. see Benjamini, Eli.

Lesky, Albin. Greek Tragic Poetry. LC 82-1886. xii, 504p. 1983. text ed. 57.00 (*0-300-02647-1*) Yale U Pr.

— Historia de la Literatura Griega. 1004p. (SPA.). 1993. 200.00 (*84-249-3132-7*) Elliots Bks.

— Thalatta: Der Weg der Griechen Zum Meer. LC 72-7899. (Greek History Ser.). (GER.). 1980. reprint ed. 31.95 (*0-405-04798-3*) Ayer.

Lesky, Erna, ed. see Frank, Johann P.

***Leslau, Charlotte & Leslau, Wolf, eds.** African Love Poems & Proverbs. (Petites Ser.). (Illus.). 80p. 1995. 4.95 (*0-88088-791-5*) Peter Pauper.

Leslau, Wolf. Concise Amharic Dictionary. (AMH & ENG.). 95.00 (*0-8288-1153-9*, F 55180) Fr & Eur.

— Ethiopians Speak: Studies in Cultural Background, Vol. 2: Chana. LC 66-64912. (University of California Publications, Near Eastern Studies: Vol. 7). 225p. reprint ed. pap. 64.20 (*0-317-09934-5*, 2014803) Bks Demand.

— Ethiopians Speak: Studies in Cultural Background, Vol. 3: Soddo. LC 66-64912. (University of California Publications, Near Eastern Studies: Vol. 11). 246p. reprint ed. Vol. 3; Soddo. pap. 70.20 (*0-317-10200-1*, 2021378) Bks Demand.

— Etymological Dictionary of Gurage (Ethiopic), 3 vols., Set. 2950p. 1980. 495.00 (*0-8288-1775-8*, M15182) Fr & Eur.

— Gafat Documents: Records of a South-Ethiopic Language. (American Oriental Ser.: Vol. 28). 1945. pap. 5.00 (*0-940490-28-5*) Am Orient Soc.

Leslau, Wolf, jt. auth. see Courlander, Harold.

Leslau, Wolf, jt. ed. see Leslau, Charlotte.

Lesley, Alexander. McD. (Illus.). 1989. pap. 9.95 (*0-317-93841-X*) Palm Tree Words.

Lesley, Craig. Dreamers & Desperadoes: Contemporary Short Fiction of the American West. Stavrakis, Katheryn, ed. 1993. pap. 12.95 (*0-440-50517-8*, LE) Dell.

— The Sky Fisherman. LC 94-47493. 320p. 1995. 21.95 (*0-395-67724-6*, Marc Jaffe Bk) HM.

— Winterkill. 1990. pap. 9.95 (*0-385-31180-X*, Delta) Dell.

Lesley, Jason, jt. auth. see Wineka, Mark.

Lesley, Mary. A Day at the Farm. (Story Puzzle Book Ser.). 4p. (J). 1990. 9.95 (*0-88679-842-6*) Educ Insights.

— A Day at the Mountains. (Story Puzzle Book Ser.). 4p. (J). 1990. 9.95 (*0-88679-844-2*) Educ Insights.

Lesley, Millard. Adult Learners: Study Skills & Teaching Methods. (C). 1981. 35.00 (*0-685-50346-1*, Pub. by Univ Nottingham UK) St Mut.

Lesley, Robert W., et al. History of the Portland Cement Industry in the United States. LC 72-5061. (Technology & Society Ser.). (Illus.). 346p. 1972. reprint ed. 23.95 (*0-405-04712-6*) Ayer.

Lesley, Salley M. Cookbook Index Plus. 96p. (YA). 1979. pap. 5.95 (*0-918544-33-5*) Wimmer Bks.

***Lesley, Serena.** Menu: Portland & Vicinity: The Best Restaurants. Date not set. pap. 12.95 (*0-9628274-8-7*) D Thomas Pub.

Lesley, Susan I., jt. ed. see Tiffany, Nina M.

***Lesley, Ted.** Paramiracles. Minch, Stephen, ed. Palmer, Bill & Erens, Oliver, trs. (Illus.). 213p. 1994. 32.00 (*0-945296-12-6*) Hermetic Pr.

***Leslie.** Dying with AIDS-Living with AIDS. 1993. per. 19.95 (*0-919754-46-5*) InBook.

— Environmental Chemistry of Agriculture. 1995. write for info. (*0-87371-855-0*) Lewis Pubs.

— Integrated Pest Management. 1994. 75.00 (*0-87371-350-8*, SD608) Lewis Pubs.

— Integrated Pest Management for Environmentally Compatible Agricultural. 1992. 79.95 (*0-87371-502-0*, SB950) Lewis Pubs.

Leslie, et al. Land Use Regulation: A Handbook for the Eighties. 171p. 1984. 12.00 (*0-318-04412-9*) Stanford Enviro.

Leslie, A., et al, eds. A Tribute to Hermann Weigand. 144p. 1982. pap. 9.95 (*0-911173-00-5*) Dimension Pr.

Leslie, Alfred. Alfred Leslie: The Killing Cycle. (Illus.). 96p. 1992. pap. 29.95 (*0-89178-036-X*) Flynn Gallery.

Leslie, Amanda. Play Kitten Play: Ten Animal Fingerwiggles. LC 91-58752. (Illus.). 10p. (J). (ps up). 1992. 6.95 (*1-56402-088-6*) Candlewick Pr.

— Play Puppy Play: Ten Animal Fingerwiggles. LC 91-58753. (Illus.). 10p. (J). (ps up). 1992. 6.95 (*1-56402-087-8*) Candlewick Pr.

Leslie, Anne R., jt. ed. see Nash, Ralph G.

Leslie, Anne R., jt. ed. see Racke, Kenneth D.

Leslie, Benjamin C. Trinitaria Hermeneutics: The Hermeneutical Significance of Karl Barth's Doctrine of the Trinity. LC 91-17450. (American University Studies: Theology & Religion: Ser. VII, Vol. 66). 286p. (C). 1991. text ed. 47.95 (*0-8204-1461-1*) P Lang Pubs.

Leslie, Bennett, jt. auth. see Daley, Dennis.

Leslie, Bruce R. Ronsard's Successful Epic Venture: The Epyllion. LC 78-52838. (French Forum Monographs: No. 11). 137p. (Orig.). 1979. pap. 9.95 (*0-917058-10-0*) French Forum.

Leslie, C. R. Memoirs of the Life of John Constable. (Landmarks in Art History Ser.). (Illus.). 450p. 1980. pap. 16.95 (*0-8014-9190-8*) Cornell U Pr.

— Memoirs of the Life of John Constable. rev. ed. Mayne, Jonathan, ed. (Arts & Letters Ser.). (Illus.). 464p. (C). 1995. pap. 14.95 (*0-7148-3360-6*, Pub. by Phaidon Press UK) Chronicle Bks.

Leslie, Candace. From Forge & Anvil: Erich Riesel, Hill Country Iron Worker. LC 92-71227. (Illus.). 96p. 1992. 29.95 (*0-9626069-7-9*) Insite Pub.

— Hidden Florida Keys & Everglades: The Adventurer's Guide. 3rd ed. Henriques, Leslie, ed. LC 93-60476. (Hidden Travel Guide Ser.). (Illus.). 168p. 1993. pap. 9.95 (*0-915233-91-6*) Ulysses Pr.

— Hidden Florida Keys & Everglades: The Adventurer's Guide. 4th ed. LC 95-60711. (Hidden Travel Ser.). (Illus.). 180p. 1995. pap. 9.95 (*1-56975-041-6*) Ulysses Pr.

Leslie, Candace, jt. auth. see Ritz, Stacy.

Leslie, Charles & Young, Allan, eds. Paths to Asian Medical Knowledge. 306p. 1993. 39.50 (*81-215-0608-5*, Pub. by M Manoharial II) Coronet Bks.

Leslie, Charles M. Now We Are Civilized: A Study of the World View of the Zapotec Indians of Mitla, Oaxaca. LC 60-7651. 133p. reprint ed. pap. 38.00 (*0-7837-3686-X*, 2043560) Bks Demand.

— Now We Are Civilized: A Study of the World View of the Zapotec Indians of Mitla, Oaxaca. LC 81-14. (Illus.). xi, 108p. 1981. reprint ed. text ed. 49.75 (*0-313-22847-7*, LENW, Greenwood Pr) Greenwood.

Leslie, Charles M. & Young, Allan H., eds. Paths to Asian Medical Knowledge. LC 91-796. (Comparative Studies of Health Systems & Medical Care: Vol. 32). 296p. (C). 1992. pap. 15.00 (*0-520-07318-5*) U CA Pr.

— Paths to Asian Medical Knowledge. LC 91-796. (Comparative Studies of Health Systems & Medical Care: Vol. 32). 296p. (C). 1992. 40.00 (*0-520-07317-7*) U CA Pr.

Leslie, Charles M., ed. see Kunitz, Stephen J.

***Leslie, Clare W.** Field Sketching. 196p. (C). 1995. per., pap. text ed. 19.95 (*0-7872-0579-6*) Kendall-Hunt.

— Nature All Year Long. LC 90-47866. (Illus.). 56p. (J). (gr. 2 up). 1991. 16.95 (*0-688-09183-0*) Greenwillow.

— Nature Drawing. 208p. (C). 1995. per., pap. text ed. 19.95 (*0-7872-0580-X*) Kendall-Hunt.

Leslie, Darla G., jt. ed. see Summers, Joseph B.

Leslie, David W., jt. auth. see Gappa, Judith M.

Leslie, David W., et al. Part-Time Faculty in American Higher Education. LC 81-13773. 160p. 1982. text ed. 45.00 (*0-275-90846-1*, C0846, Praeger Pubs) Greenwood.

Leslie, Derek. Advanced Macroeconomics: Beyond IS-LM. LC 92-38140. 1993. 17.95 (*0-07-707724-5*) McGraw.

Leslie, Diane & Sandburg, Helga. Joel & the Wild Goose: Music. 36p. 1991. pap. 3.75 (*0-87129-118-5*, J02) Dramatic Pub.

Leslie, Donald, tr. see Hallyn, Fernand.

Leslie, Donna, illus. Alitji in Dreamland: Alitjinya Ngura Tjukurmankuntjala: An Aboriginal Version of Lewis Carroll's Alice's Adventures in Wonderland. LC 92-17640. 104p. (J). (gr. 6 up). 1992. 16.95 (*0-89815-478-2*) Ten Speed Pr.

Leslie, Doris. The Great Corinthian. large type ed. (Shadows of the Crown Ser.). 1974. 15.95 (*0-85456-597-3*) Ulverscroft.

— The Sceptre & the Rose. large type ed. (Shadows of the Crown Ser.). 1974. 15.95 (*0-85456-618-X*) Ulverscroft.

— That Enchantress. large type ed. (Shadows of the Crown Ser.). 1974. 15.95 (*0-85456-593-0*) Ulverscroft.

Leslie, Douglas L. Cases & Materials on Labor Law: Process & Policy. 2nd ed. 1247p. 1985. 42.00 (*0-316-52161-2*) Little.

— Labor Law in a Nutshell. 3rd ed. (Nutshell Ser.). 388p. (C). 1993. reprint ed. pap. text ed. 16.50 (*0-314-92205-9*) West Pub.

Leslie, Edward E. Desperate Journeys, Abandoned Souls: True Stories of Castaways & Other Survivors. LC 88-644. (Illus.). 448p. 1988. pap. 11.95 (*0-395-43608-7*) HM.

Leslie, Eliza. Directions for Cookery, in Its Various Branches. with Improvements, Supplementary Receipts, & a New Appendix. LC 72-9797. (Cookery Americana Ser.). 1973. reprint ed. 17.95 (*0-405-05050-X*) Ayer.

— Miss Leslie's Behaviour Book: A Guide & Manual for Ladies. LC 72-2611. (American Women Ser.: Images & Realities). 340p. 1974. reprint ed. 24.95 (*0-405-04465-8*) Ayer.

— Seventy-Five Receipts for Pastry, Cakes & Sweetmeats. 96p. 1988. reprint ed. pap. 7.95 (*1-55709-116-1*) Applewood.

Leslie, Elsie. Is Satan Real? (Illus.). (J). (gr. k-6). 1987. pap. 4.25 (*1-55976-153-9*) CEF Press.

Leslie, Emma. La Casa De Dona Constanza: The House of Mrs. Constanza. (SPA.). 3.25 (*84-7228-322-4*, 220140, Pub. by Edit Clie SP) TSELF.

— Glaucia, la Esclava Griega: Glaucia, the Greek Slave Girl. (SPA.). 4.95 (*0-317-04313-7*, 220427, Pub. by Edit Clie SP) TSELF.

Leslie, F. & Helmers, C. H. Project Planning & Income Distribution. (Studies in Development & Planning: Vol. 9). 1979. lib. bdg. 47.50 (*0-89838-010-3*) Kluwer Ac.

Leslie, F. Andrew. Boy with Green Hair. 1961. pap. 4.75 (*0-8222-0144-5*) Dramatists Play.

Leslie, Frank. Leslie's Illustrated Civil War. LC 92-8815. (Illus.). 275p. 1992. 50.00 (*0-87805-567-3*) U Pr of Miss.

Leslie, G. B. & Lunau, F. W., eds. Indoor Air Pollution: Problems & Priorities. (Illus.). 300p. (C). 1992. 84.95 (*0-521-38510-5*) Cambridge U Pr.

— Indoor Air Pollution: Problems & Priorities. (Illus.). 340p. (C). 1994. pap. 29.95 (*0-521-47794-8*) Cambridge U Pr.

Leslie, G. B., jt. auth. see Poole, A.

Leslie, Gay, ed. see Udell, Jon G.

Leslie, George D. The Inner Life of the Royal Academy, with an Account of Its Schools & Exhibitions, Principally in the Reign of Queen Victoria. 1972. 21.95 (*0-405-18181-7*, 1730) Ayer.

Leslie, Gerald R. & Korman, Sheila K. The Family in Social Context. 7th ed. (Illus.). 624p. (C). 1989. text ed. 35.00 (*0-19-504974-8*); Objective tests. write for info. (*0-19-505813-5*) OUP.

Leslie, Gerrie, ed. Immunoglobulin D: Structure & Function. (Annals Ser.: Vol. 399). 410p. 1982. lib. bdg. 80.00 (*0-89766-188-5*); pap. 80.00 (*0-89766-189-3*) NY Acad Sci.

Leslie-Hynan, Lauren, jt. auth. see Hynan, Michael T.

Leslie, J. D., ed. see Solar Energy Conversion Course, 5th, University of Waterloo, Ontario, August 6-19, 1978.

***Leslie, Jacques.** The Mark: A Memoir of Vietnam. LC 94-38062. 305p. 1995. 22.00 (*1-56858-024-X*) FWEW.

Leslie, James W. Land of Cypress & Pine: More Southeast Arkansas History. (Illus.). 216p. 1976. 19.95 (*0-914546-09-0*) J W Bell.

— Saracen's Country: Some Southeast Arkansas History. (Illus.). 216p. 1974. 19.95 (*0-914546-03-1*) J W Bell.

Leslie, Jean B., jt. auth. see Van Velsor, Ellen.

Leslie, John. Damaged Goods. Grad, Doug, ed. 320p. (Orig.). 1993. mass mkt. 5.50 (*0-671-72479-7*) PB.

— Havana Hustle. 1994. mass mkt. 5.50 (*0-671-78166-9*) PB.

— History of Scotland, from the Death of King James First in the Year 1436, to the Year 1561. LC 78-172315. (Bannatyne Club, Edinburgh. Publications: No. 38). reprint ed. 42.50 (*0-404-52744-2*) AMS Pr.

— Killing Me Softly. Grose, Bill, ed. 256p. (Orig.). 1995. mass mkt. 5.50 (*0-671-86421-1*) PB.

— Night & Day: A Gideon Lowry Mystery. Grose, William, ed. LC 94-22915. 256p. (Orig.). 1995. 20.00 (*0-671-86422-X*) PB.

— Physical Cosmology & Philosophy. Edwards, Paul, ed. (Philosophical Topics Ser.). 250p. (C). 1990. pap. write for info. (*0-02-370021-1*) Macmillan.

— Universes. 1990. 25.00 (*0-415-04144-9*, A4027) Routledge.

***Leslie, John F. & Frederiksen, Richard A., eds.** Disease Analysis Through Genetics & Biotechnology: Interdisciplinary Bridges to Improved Sorghum & Millet Crops. LC 94-46977. (Illus.). 372p. 1995. 32.95 (*0-8138-2125-8*) Iowa St U Pr.

Leslie, Julia, ed. Roles & Rituals for Hindu Women. LC 91-18883. 256p. 1991. 42.50 (*0-8386-3475-3*) Fairleigh Dickinson.

Leslie, Julie, ed. Myth & Mythmaking: Continuous Evolution in Indian Tradition. 256p. (C). 1995. text ed. 60.00 (*0-7007-0303-9*, Pub. by Curzon Pr UK) Humanities.

Leslie, K. H. Leslie: Historical Records of the Family of Leslie, 3 vols. 1991. reprint ed. lib. bdg. 144.50 (*0-8328-2158-6*); reprint ed. pap. 134.50 (*0-8328-2159-4*) Higginson Bk Co.

Leslie, Karen. Faith & Little Children: A Guide for Parents & Teachers. LC 89-51903. 128p. (Orig.). 1990. pap. 7.95 (*0-89622-404-X*) Twenty-Third.

Leslie, Kenneth D. Oil Pastel: Materials & Techniques for Today's Artist. (Illus.). 144p. 1990. 29.95 (*0-8230-3310-4*, Watson-Guptill) Watson-Guptill.

Leslie, Kent A. Woman of Color, Daughter of Privilege: Amanda America Dickson, 1849-1893. LC 94-17033. (Illus.). 240p. 1995. 29.95 (*0-8203-1688-1*) U of Ga Pr.

Leslie, Kim C., ed. Roots of America: A Anthology of Documents Relating to American History in the West Sussex Record Office. 114p. 1976. 75.00 (*0-686-75544-8*) St Mut.

Leslie, Larry L. & Brinkman, Paul T. The Economic Value of Higher Education. LC 93-4906. (American Council on Education-Oryx Press Series on Higher Education). 288p. 1988. 29.95 (*0-89774-828-X*) Oryx Pr.

Leslie, Larry L., jt. auth. see Anderson, Richard E.

Leslie, Lauren & Caldwell, JoAnne. Qualitative Reading Inventory. (C). 1989. pap. text ed. 28.50 (*0-673-18791-8*) HarpCollege.

— Qualitative Reading Inventory, II. rev. ed. LC 94-18636. (C). 1995. 23.50 (*0-673-99086-9*) HarpCollege.

Leslie, Leigh A., jt. ed. see Sollie, Donna L.

Leslie, Louis A., et al. Gregg Shorthand for Colleges, Transcription. 2nd ed. LC 79-11916. (Series 90). (Illus.). 448p. 1981. text ed. 41.50 (*0-07-037760-X*) McGraw.

Leslie, Louis A. Story of Gregg Shorthand. 1964. text ed. 16.65 (*0-07-037223-3*) McGraw.

— Twenty Thousand Words. 7th large type ed. 300p. (YA). (gr. 7 up). 1981. reprint ed. 75.50 (*0-317-01950-3*, 2-26190-00) Am Printing Hse.

Leslie, Louis A. & Coffin, Kenneth B. Handbook for the Legal Secretary: Diamond Jubilee Series. 1958. text ed. 39.00 (*0-07-037277-2*) McGraw.

Leslie, Louis A. & Zoubek, Charles E. Dictation BookShort Course: Letters & Memos. (Gregg Shorthand for Electronic Office Ser.: No. 90, Pt. 2). 1984. pap. text ed. 24.95 (*0-07-037920-3*) McGraw.

— Dictation for Mailable Transcripts. 1950. text ed. 30.25 (*0-07-037236-5*) McGraw.

— Dictation for Transcription. 2nd ed. (Diamond Jubilee Ser.). 1972. text ed. 29.95 (*0-07-037248-9*) McGraw.

— Gregg Shorthand: A Gregg Text-Kit in Continuing Education, 2 bks., Bk. 1. (Diamond Jubilee Ser.). 1966. 27.95 (*0-07-037225-X*) McGraw.

— Gregg Shorthand: A Gregg Text-Kit in Continuing Education, 2 bks., Bk. 2. (Diamond Jubilee Ser.). 1966. 28.10 (*0-07-037227-6*) McGraw.

— Gregg Shorthand for the Electronic Office, Pt. I. (Short Course Ser.: Series 90). 320p. 1984. text ed. 29.96 (*0-07-037914-9*) McGraw.

— Gregg Shorthand for the Electronic Office: Short Course, Pt. II. (Series 90). 320p. 1984. text ed. 29.96 (*0-07-037917-3*) McGraw.

— Gregg Shorthand Functional Method. 2nd ed. (Diamond Jubilee Ser.). 1971. text ed. 25.00 (*0-07-037255-1*) McGraw.

— Gregg Shorthand Theory Presentation Booklet. (Diamond Jubilee Ser.). 1971. pap. text ed. 11.95 (*0-07-037247-0*) McGraw.

— Gregg Transcription. 2nd ed. (Diamond Jubilee Ser.). 1971. text ed. 25.00 (*0-07-037262-4*) McGraw.

— Transcription Dictation. 1956. text ed. 32.75 (*0-07-037276-4*) McGraw.

Leslie, Louis A., et al. Gregg Dictation: Diamond Jubilee Series. 2nd ed. 1970. pap. text ed. 24.12 (*0-07-037257-8*) McGraw.

— Gregg Dictation & Transcription: Individual Progress Method. (Diamond Jubilee Ser.: Kit 2). 1974. text ed. 39.50 (*0-07-037249-7*) McGraw.

— Gregg Notehand. 2nd ed. 1968. text ed. 20.24 (*0-07-037331-0*) McGraw.

— Gregg Shorthand for Colleges, Vol. 1. (Series 90). 1980. text ed. 38.95 (*0-07-037749-9*) McGraw.

— Gregg Shorthand for Colleges, Vol. 1. 2nd ed. (Diamond Jubilee Ser.). (Illus.). 352p. (C). 1973. text ed. 39.50 (*0-07-037401-5*) McGraw.

— Gregg Shorthand for Colleges, Vol. 2. (Series 90). 1980. text ed. 38.95 (*0-07-037754-5*) McGraw.

— Gregg Shorthand for Colleges, Vol. 2. 2nd ed. (Diamond Jubilee Ser.). (Illus.). 448p. (C). 1973. text ed. 39.95 (*0-07-037406-6*) McGraw.

— Gregg Shorthand for Colleges, Transcription. (Diamond Jubilee Ser.). 1974. text ed. 39.95 (*0-07-037425-2*) McGraw.

— Gregg Shorthand, Individual Progress Method. (Diamond Jubilee Ser.: Kit 1). 1972. 38.95 (*0-07-037233-0*) McGraw.

— Gregg Shorthand One Series Ninety: A Gregg Text-Kit in Continuing Education. (Microcomputer Software Program Ser.). 1984. 27.25 (*0-07-037769-3*) McGraw.

— Gregg Shorthand Two: A Gregg Text-Kit in Continuing Education. (Series 90). 1984. 27.25 (*0-07-037770-7*) McGraw.

— Gregg Transcription. (Series 90). 1979. text ed. 24.56 (*0-07-037740-5*) McGraw.

Leslie, Lynn. Courage, My Love: Women Who Dare. (Superromance Ser.). 1993. mass mkt. 3.50 (*0-373-70566-2*, 1-70566-4) Harlequin Bks.

— Night of the Nile. (Intrigue Ser.). 1994. mass mkt. 2.99 (*0-373-22287-4*, 1-22287-6) Harlequin Bks.

— Singapore Fling. (Superromance Ser.). 1994. mass mkt. 3.50 (*0-373-70604-9*, 1-70604-3) Harlequin Bks.

Leslie, Marsha R., ed. The Single Mother's Companion: Essays & Stories by Women. 300p. (Orig.). 1994. pap. 12.95 (*1-878067-56-7*) Seal Pr Feminist.

Leslie, Mary E., et al, eds. American Women in Sport, Eighteen Eighty-Seven to Nineteen Eighty-Seven: A 100-Year Chronology. LC 89-6150. (Illus.). 173p. 1989. 25.00 (*0-8108-2205-9*) Scarecrow.

Leslie, Michael. Spenser's 'Fierce Warres & Faithful Loves' Martial & Chivalric Symbolism in 'The Faerie Queene' Martial & Chivalric Symbolism in 'The Faerie Queene' (Illus.). 216p. 1984. 79.00 (*0-85991-150-0*) Boydell & Brewer.

***Leslie, Michael & Raylor, Timothy, eds.** Culture & Cultivation in Early Modern England. 256p. 1994. pap. 19.95 (*0-7185-2148-X*) St Martin.

— Culture & Cultivation in Early Modern England: Writing & the Land. LC 92-8560. 1992. 59.00 (*0-7185-1399-1*) St Martin.

Leslie, Mike, ed. see Turner, David G. & Complo, Jennifer.

Leslie, Naton & Villani, Jim, eds. Third World. LC 88-60726. (Pig Iron Ser.: No. 15). (Illus.). 96p. (Orig.). 1988. pap. 8.95 (*0-917530-23-3*) Pig Iron Pr.

Leslie, Nicholas, jt. auth. see Lorenz, Christopher.

Leslie, Noel. Three Plays. LC 79-50026. (One-Act Plays in Reprint Ser.). 1980. reprint ed. 15.00 (*0-8486-2050-X*) Roth Pub Inc.

Leslie, Patty, jt. auth. see Cox, Paul W.

Leslie, Peter. No Deal in Diamonds. 224p. 1992. 19.00 (*0-7278-4371-0*) Severn Hse.

Leslie, Peter M. Federal State, National Economy. 213p. 1987. pap. 19.95 (*0-8020-6611-9*) U of Toronto Pr.

Leslie, R. D., ed. Cause of Diabetes: Genetic & Environmental Factors. LC 93-11222. 1993. text ed. 159.95 (*0-471-94040-2*) Wiley.

Leslie, R. D. & Robbins, David C., eds. Diabetes: Clinical Science in Practice. (Illus.). 550p. (C). 1995. 150.00 (*0-521-45029-2*) Cambridge U Pr.

Leslie, R. F. Reform & Insurrection in Russian Poland, 1856-1865. LC 72-91767. 272p. 1970. reprint ed. text ed. 35.00 (*0-8371-2415-8*, LERI, Greenwood Pr) Greenwood.

Leslie, Richard, ed. see Chalifoux, Paul R.

Leslie, Robert F. In the Shadow of a Rainbow: The True Story of a Friendship Between Man & Wolf. 192p. 1986. reprint ed. pap. 9.95 (*0-393-30392-6*) Norton.

Leslie, Roberts, et al, eds. Arbitration & Mediation. 1987. write for info. (*0-318-61746-3*) OR Bar CLE.

Leslie, Roderick, jt. auth. see Avery, Mark.

Leslie, Russell P. & Conway, Kathryn M. The Lighting Pattern Book for Homes. LC 93-80008. (Illus.). 232p. 1993. 50.00 (*1-883297-00-1*) RPI Lght Res.

Leslie, S. The Celt & the World: A Study of the Relation of Celt & Teuton in History. 1972. 59.95 (*0-87968-822-X*) Gordon Pr.

Leslie, Serge. A Bibliography of the Dance Collection of Doris Niles & Serge Leslie: A-Z, Pt. 4. 283p. 1981. 59.95 (*0-903102-56-0*, Pub. by Dance Bks UK) Princeton Bk Co.

— A Dancer's Scrapbook. (Illus.). 256p. 1987. 34.95 (*1-85273-001-3*) Princeton Bk Co.

Leslie, Shane. Men Were Different: Five Studies in Late Victorian Biography. LC 67-26754. (Essay Index Reprint Ser.). 1977. 20.95 (*0-8369-0615-2*) Ayer.

— Salutation to Five: Mrs. Fitzherbert, Edmund Warre, Sir William Butler, Leo Tolstoy, Sir Mark Sykes. LC 75-126231. (Biography Index Reprint Ser.). 1977. 19.95 (*0-8369-8027-1*) Ayer.

— The Skull of Swift. LC 79-169767. (Select Bibliographies Reprint Ser.). 1977. reprint ed. 26.95 (*0-8369-5987-6*) Ayer.

— Studies in Sublime Failure. LC 70-117817. (Essay Index Reprint Ser.). 1977. 23.95 (*0-8369-1670-0*) Ayer.

An Asterisk (*) at the beginning of an entry indicates that the title is appearing in BIP for the first time.

Leslie-Spinks, Tim. Treasures of Trinkamalee. (J). (gr. 4-7). 1993. lib. bdg. 15.95 (*1-55037-320-X*, Pub. by Annick CN) Firefly Bks Ltd.
— Treasures of Trinkamalee. (J). (gr. 4-7). 1993. pap. 5.95 (*1-55037-323-4*, Pub. by Annick CN) Firefly Bks Ltd.
Leslie, Stuart W. Boss Kettering. LC 82-17906. (Illus.). 382p. 1986. pap. text ed. 17.00 (*0-231-05601-X*) Col U Pr.
— The Cold War & American Science. 320p. 1993. text ed. 42.00 (*0-231-07958-3*) Col U Pr.
— Cold War & American Science. 1994. pap. 16.50 (*0-231-07959-1*) Col U Pr.
Leslie, Susan. The Happiness of God. (C). 1988. 39.00 (*0-85439-272-6*, Pub. by St Paul Pubns UK) St Mut.
— The Happiness of God: Holiness in Therese of Lisieux. LC 88-21658. 81p. 1988. pap. 4.95 (*0-8189-0540-9*) Alba.
Leslie, Tanya, tr. see Ernaux, Annie.
Leslie, Thomas, jt. auth. see Minch, John.
Leslie, Thomas E. Essays in Political Economy. 2nd ed. LC 69-20305. (Reprints of Economic Classics Ser.). xii, 437p. 1969. reprint ed. 45.00 (*0-678-00480-3*) Kelley.
— Land Systems & Industrial Economy of Ireland, England, & Continental Countries. LC 67-18570. (Reprints of Economic Classics Ser.). vi, 379p. 1968. reprint ed. 45.00 (*0-678-00346-7*) Kelley.
Leslie, Thomas E., tr. see De Laveleye, Emile.
Leslie, W. Bruce. Gentlemen & Scholars: College & Community in the "Age of the University" (Illus.). 320p. 1993. 45.00 (*0-271-00829-6*) Pa St U Pr.
Leslie, William C. Physical Metallurgy of Steels. (Illus.). 396p. (C). reprint ed. 45.00 (*0-685-50061-6*) TechBooks.
Leslie, Winsome J. Zaire: Continuity & Political Change in an Oppressive State. LC 92-46921. (Profiles Ser.). 204p. 1993. text ed. 49.50 (*0-86531-298-2*) Westview.
Lesly, Mark, jt. auth. see Shuttleworth, Charles.
Lesly, Philip. Bonanzas & Fool's Gold: Treasures & Dross from the Nuggetizing of Our Lives. 180p. 1987. 9.95 (*0-9602866-2-4*) Lesly Co.
— Lesly's Handbook of Public Relations & Communications. 4th ed. 850p. 1991. 79.95 (*0-8144-0108-2*) AMACOM.
— Overcoming Opposition: A Survival Manual for Executives. LC 83-24790. 212p. 1986. 15.95 (*0-13-646597-8*, Busn) P-H.
— Selections from Managing the Human Climate. 178p. (Orig.). 1979. pap. 9.00 (*0-9602866-0-8*) Lesly Co.
Lesman, Ann S., et al. Espanol para Hoy: En el Mundo y la Comunidad. 388p. (Orig.). (C). 1992. pap. text ed. 39.50 (*0-8191-8858-1*) U Pr of Amer.
Lesman, Helen. Friend to Friend. (Illus.). 366p. 1990. spiral bd. 6.50 (*1-879127-07-5*) Lighten Up Enter.
— Heart Delights. 366p. 1992. spiral bd. 6.50 (*1-879127-11-3*) Lighten Up Enter.
— Hugs for the Heart. 366p. 1992. spiral bd. 6.50 (*1-879127-12-1*) Lighten Up Enter.
Lesman, Helen & Cleaveland, Teta. Heart Delights for Mothers & Daughters. (Illus.). 366p. 1992. spiral bd. 6.50 (*1-879127-13-X*) Lighten Up Enter.
Lesman, Helen, jt. auth. see Estrem, Victoria L.
Lesmes, George R. & Hearst, Margo R. Intervention Information Systems: Smoking Cessation. (Illus.). 80p. (C). 1993. Participant handbk., 80p. student ed write for info. (*1-882953-03-7*); Assessment, 13p. write for info. (*1-882953-04-5*); audio write for info. (*1-882953-05-3*); write for info. (*1-882953-06-1*) Intervent Info.
— Intervention Information Systems: Smoking Cessation, Pt. I. (Illus.). 150p. (C). 1993. Part I Facilitator Manual, 150p. teacher ed write for info. (*1-882953-01-0*) Intervent Info.
— Intervention Information Systems: Smoking Cessation, Pt. II. (Illus.). 150p. (C). 1993. Part II Instructional Modules, 150p. write for info. (*1-882953-02-9*) Intervent Info.
— Intervention Information Systems: Smoking Cessation, Set. (Illus.). (C). 1993. write for info. (*1-882953-00-2*) Intervent Info.
Lesmian, Boselaw. Mythematics & Extropy: Selected Prose of Boselaw Lesmian. Chciuk-Celt, Alexandra, ed. & tr. by. LC 91-20519. (American University Studies: Slavic Languages & Literature: Ser. XII, Vol. 3). 160p. (C). 1992. text ed. 29.95 (*0-8204-1636-3*) P Lang Pubs.
Lesmueller, A. Thurn, ed. Iosephi Genesii Regum Libri Quattuor. (Corpus Fontium Historiae Byzantinae Ser.: Vol. XIV). (C). 1978. 119.25 (*3-11-006599-1*) De Gruyter.
Lesniak, James. Contemporary Authors New Revision, Vol. 44. Draper, James P. & Trosky, Susan M., eds. (Contemporary Authors Revised Ser.). 491p. 1994. 122.00 (*0-8103-1929-2*, 000084) Gale.
— Contemporary Authors New Revision Series, Vol. 4. 1994. write for info. (*0-8103-1928-4*, 101354) Gale.
— Contemporary Authors New Revision Series, Vol. 42. (Contemporary Authors Revised Ser.). 1993. 115.00 (*0-8103-1973-X*, 000082) Gale.
— Contemporary Authors New Revision Series & Contemporary Authors Index, Vol. 43. 1994. 119.00 (*0-8103-1974-8*, 000083) Gale.
Lesniak, James, ed. Contemporary Authors, Vol. 31. (New Revision Ser.). 500p. 1990. text ed. 122.00 (*0-8103-1985-3*) Gale.
— Contemporary Authors New Revision Series, Vol. 30. 500p. 1990. 115.00 (*0-8103-1984-5*) Gale.
Lesniak, James, ed. see Gale Research Inc. Staff.
Lesniak, James, jt. auth. see May, Hal.
Lesniak, James, jt. ed. see May, Hal.
Lesniak, James, jt. auth. see Trosky, Susan M.
Lesniak, Linda, jt. auth. see Chartrand, Gary.
Lesniak, Louis A. Human Psychology of the Single Person: Index of New Information with Authors, Subjects & Bibliography. 180p. 1993. 49.50 (*1-55914-802-0*); pap. 39.50 (*1-55914-803-9*) ABBE Pubs Assn.
Lesnick, Daniel R. Preaching in Medieval Florence: The Social World of Franciscan & Dominincan Spirituality. LC 88-4837. (Illus.). 312p. 1989. 40.00 (*0-8203-1047-6*) U of Ga Pr.
Lesnick, Howard. Becoming a Lawyer: Individual Choice & Responsibility in the Practice of Law, Teacher's Manual to Accompany. (American Casebook Ser.). 100p. (C). 1992. pap. text ed. write for info. (*0-314-01332-6*) West Pub.
— Being a Lawyer: Individual Choice & Responsibility in the Practice of Law. LC 92-16679. (American Casebook Ser.). 500p. (C). 1992. pap. text ed. 29.00 (*0-314-00916-7*) West Pub.
Lesnick, Irving, jt. auth. see Harnett, Bertram.
***Lesnick, Michael E.** Skilled Nursing Facility Management: Cost Reporting. 250p. 1995. 175.00 (*1-55738-637-4*) Probus Pub Co.
— Skilled Nursing Facility Management: Coverage Issues. 200p. 1995. 175.00 (*1-55738-638-2*) Probus Pub Co.
— Skilled Nursing Facility Management: New Directions in Long Term Care. 250p. 1995. 50.00 (*1-55738-639-0*) Probus Pub Co.
— Skilled Nursing Facility Management: Optimizing Reimbursement. 300p. 1995. 175.00 (*1-55738-636-6*) Probus Pub Co.
Lesnick, Michael T. & Crowfoot, James E. A Bibliography for the Study of Natural Resource & Environmental Conflict. (CPL Bibliographies Ser.: No. 64). 55p. 1981. 8.00 (*0-86602-064-0*) Coun Plan Librarians.
Lesniewicz, Paul. Bonsai: The Complete Guide to Art & Technique. (Illus.). 192p. 1984. 24.95 (*0-7137-1362-3*, Pub. by Blandford Pr UK) Sterling.
— Bonsai in Your Home: An Indoor Grower's Guide. LC 94-17466. (Illus.). 208p. 1994. 27.95 (*0-8069-0780-0*) Sterling.
— Indoor Bonsai. (Illus.). 208p. (Orig.). 1986. pap. 14.95 (*0-7137-1700-9*, Pub. by Blandford Pr UK) Sterling.
Lesniewski, John, jt. auth. see Lesniewski, Karen.
Lesniewski, Karen & Lesniewski, John. Kiss Collectibles: Identification & Price Guide. 200p. (Orig.). 1993. pap. 10.00 (*0-380-77166-7*, Confident Collect) Avon.
Lesniewski, Stanislaw. Collected Works, Set. Surma, S. J. et al, eds. (Nijhoff International Philosophy Ser.: No. 44). 620p. 1991. lib. bdg. 309.00 (*0-7923-1512-X*) Kluwer Ac.
Lesnik, Milton & Anderson, Bernice E. Nursing Practice & the Law. 2nd ed. LC 75-45453. 400p. 1976. reprint ed. text ed. 65.00 (*0-8371-8729-X*, LENP, Greenwood Pr) Greenwood.
Lesnik-Oberstein, Karin. Children's Literature: Criticism & the Fictional Child. LC 93-35484. 264p. 1994. 39.95 (*0-19-811998-4*) OUP.
Lesnikowski, Wojciech. The New French Architecture. LC 90-35057. (New Architecture Ser.). (Illus.). 224p. 1990. 50.00 (*0-8478-1224-3*); pap. 35.00 (*0-8478-1265-0*) Rizzoli Intl.
Lesnoff-Caravaglia, Gari. Handbook of Applied Gerontology. LC 86-20811. 460p. 1987. 54.95 (*0-89885-314-1*) Human Sci Pr.
— Realistic Expectations for Long Life, Vol. V. LC 86-27223. (Frontiers in Aging Ser.). 279p. 1987. 43.95 (*0-89885-343-5*) Human Sci Pr.
Lesnoff-Caravaglia, Gari, ed. Aging & the Human Condition, Vol. II. LC 81-6630. (Frontiers in Aging Ser.). 160p. 1982. 32.95 (*0-89885-029-0*) Human Sci Pr.
— Aging in a Technological Society, Vol. VI. (Frontiers in Aging Ser.). 264p. 1988. 43.95 (*0-89885-382-6*) Human Sci Pr.
— Health Care of the Elderly: Strategies for Prevention & Intervention. LC 79-19192. (Frontiers in Aging Ser.: Vol. I). 232p. 1980. 42.95 (*0-87705-417-7*) Human Sci Pr.
— Values, Ethics & Aging, Vol. IV. (Frontiers in Aging Ser.). (Illus.). 196p. 1985. 35.95 (*0-89885-162-9*) Human Sci Pr.
— The World of the Older Woman: Conflicts & Resolutions. (Frontiers in Aging Ser.: Vol. III). 176p. 1984. 35.95 (*0-89885-089-4*) Human Sci Pr.
Lesnoff-Caravaglia, Gari, tr. see Pitskhelauri, G. Z.
Lesobre, J., et al. French-English (American)-English (American)-French Dictionary of Risk Insurance & Reinsurance. 371p. (ENG & FRE.). 1993. pap. 130.00 (*2-902189-46-X*) IBD Ltd.
Lesobre, Jacques, et al. Risk Insurance Reinsurance Lexicon: Francais - English - American. 3rd ed. 375p. (ENG & FRE.). 1993. pap. 150.00 (*0-7859-1079-4*, 290218945X) Fr & Eur.
Lesoil, M. French-Norwegian Dictionary: Fransk-Norsk-Ordbok. 435p. (FRE & NOR.). 1986. 49.95 (*0-8288-1032-X*, M9457) Fr & Eur.
— Norsk-Fransk Ordbok: Norwegian-French Dictionary. 445p. (FRE.). 1978. 39.95 (*0-8288-5258-8*, M9463) Fr & Eur.
Lesoing, Jan. Forever Yesterday. 1988. pap. 3.95 (*0-517-00623-5*) Random Hse Value.
Leson, Nancy, jt. ed. see Irving, Stephanie.
***Lesourd, Jean-Baptiste, et al, eds.** Models for Energy Policy. LC 95-813. (New International Studies in Economic Modelling). 1995. write for info. (*0-415-12975-3*) Routledge.
LeSourd, Leonard, ed. see Marshall, Catherine.
LeSourd, Leonard E. Strong Men, Weak Men: Godly Strength & the Male Identity. LC 90-35761. 256p. 1994. reprint ed. pap. 8.99 (*0-8007-9211-4*) Revell.
***LeSourd, Leonard E., ed.** The Best of Catherine Marshall. large type ed. LC 94-42713. Date not set. pap. 14.95 (*0-8027-2687-9*) Walker & Co.
— The Best of Catherine Marshall: Her Intimate Life. 352p. 1995. reprint ed. pap. 9.00 (*0-380-72383-2*) Avon.
— Touching the Heart of God. LC 89-48161. 1990. pap. 9.99 (*0-8007-9159-2*) Chosen Bks.
LeSourd, Leonard E., ed. see Marshall, Catherine.
LeSourd, Philip S. Accent & Syllable Structure in Passamaquoddy. LC 92-36574. (Outstanding Dissertations in Linguistics Ser.). 496p. 1992. 105.00 (*0-8153-0213-4*) Garland.
LeSourd, Sandra S. The Compulsive Woman. LC 90-38108. 317p. 1987. pap. 9.99 (*0-8007-9171-1*) Chosen Bks.
— The Not-So-Compulsive Woman: Twenty Recovery Principles to Pull You Out of the Pit. 224p. 1992. 14.99 (*0-8007-9201-7*) Chosen Bks.
Lesourne, J., ed. see Anas, A.
Lesourne, J., ed. see Hahn, R. W.
Lesourne, J., ed. see Mokyr, J.
Lesourne, J., ed. see Pollard, S.
Lesourne, J., ed. see Vogelsang, I.
Lesourne, J., ed. see Weiss, A.
Lesourne, Jacques. Cost Benefit Analysis & Economic Theory. LC 74-84213. (Studies in Mathematical & Managerial Economics: Vol. 19). 521p. 1976. pap. 92.50 (*0-7204-3097-6*, North Holland) Elsevier.
— The Economics of Order & Disorder. 192p. 1992. 46.00 (*0-19-828739-9*) OUP.
— World Perspectives: A European Assessment. Romeo, Sharon L., tr. 360p. (FRE.). 1986. text ed. 49.00 (*2-88124-179-4*) Gordon & Breach.
Lesourne, Jacques & Lecomte, Bernard. After Communism; from the Atlantic to the Urals. 271p. 1991. text ed. 58.00 (*3-7186-5211-0*, HX) Gordon & Breach.
Lesourne, Jacques, ed. see Hartwick, John M.
L'Esperance. Ophthalmic Lasers. 3rd ed. (Illus.). 1120p. 1988. 185.00 (*0-8016-2965-9*) Mosby Yr Bk.
L'Esperance, Anne. Idioms: An Amusing Look at American Speech. (Illus.). 112p. (Orig.). 1990. pap. 5.95 (*0-9628506-0-8*) Cpstrano Pr.
Lesperance, Gary L. & Purvins, John J. Computers Simplified & Illustrated, Bk. 1: Learn the Easy Way. (Illus.). 80p. (Orig.). (C). 1985. pap. 5.95 (*0-932285-00-7*) Rockway Hse.
Lespes, Anthony. Les Semences de la Colere. (B. E. Ser.: No. 49). (FRE.). 1949. 27.00 (*0-318-36539-1*) Periodicals Srv.
LesPes, Claudine & Oluer-Zimmerman, Joelle. Dinou et Dina: Introductory French. 1993. write for info. (*0-8013-0811-9*) Longman.
Less, Menahem, et al. Evaluating Driving Potential of Persons With Physical Disabilities. LC 78-62052. (Illus.). 36p. 1978. 4.25 (*0-686-38803-8*) Human Res Ctr.
— Hand Controls & Assistive Devices for the Physically Disabled Driver. (Illus.). 60p. 1977. 5.00 (*0-686-38804-6*) Human Res Ctr.
Lessa, William A. Spearhead Governatore: Remembrances of the Campaign in Italy. LC 85-50821. (Illus.). 272p. 1985. 31.25 (*0-89003-163-0*) Undena Pubns.
— Ulithi: A Micronesian Design for Living. (Illus.). 118p. (C). 1986. reprint ed. pap. text ed. 8.50 (*0-88133-212-7*) Waveland Pr.
Lessa, William A. & Vogt, Evon Z. Reader in Comparative Religion: An Anthropological Approach. 4th ed. (C). 1990. pap. text ed. 53.50 (*0-06-043991-2*) HarpCollege.
Lessac, Arthur. The Use & Training of the Human Voice. LC 67-28352. 297p. (C). 1967. text ed. 31.95 (*0-87484-845-8*) Mayfield Pub.
Lessac, Frane. Caribbean Alphabet. LC 93-15833. (Illus.). 32p. (J). 1994. 15.00 (*0-688-12952-8*, Tambourine Bks); lib. bdg. 14.93 (*0-688-12953-6*, Tambourine Bks) Morrow.
— Caribbean Canvas. LC 93-61864. (Illus.). 32p. 1994. 15.95 (*1-56397-390-1*, Wordsong) Boyds Mills Pr.
— My Little Island. LC 84-48355. (Illus.). 48p. (J). (gr. 1-4). 1985. lib. bdg. 14.89 (*0-397-32115-5*, Lipp Jr Bks) HarpC Child Bks.
— My Little Island. LC 84-48355. (Trophy Picture Bk.). (Illus.). 48p. (J). (ps-3). 1987. reprint ed. pap. 4.95 (*0-06-443146-0*, Trophy) HarpC Child Bks.
Lessac, Frane, illus. The Fire Children: A West African Creation Tale. LC 92-34685. (J). (ps-3). 1993. 14.50 (*0-8037-1477-7*) Dial Bks Young.
***Lessard, Brady.** Your Guide to Slide: The Slacker's Guide to College. (Illus.). 96p. (Orig.). 1995. pap. 6.95 (*0-9640713-1-2*) Fine Print.
Lessard, Donald R. Financial Intermediation Beyond the Debt Crisis. LC 85-18092. (Policy Analysis in International Economics Ser.: No. 12). 118p. (Orig.). 1985. pap. 12.00 (*0-88132-021-8*) Inst Intl Eco.
Lessard, Donald R., ed. International Financial Management: Theory & Application. 2nd ed. LC 84-15378. 606p. reprint ed. pap. 172.80 (*0-7837-2378-4*, 2040064) Bks Demand.
Lessard, Donald R. & Williamson, John. Capital Flight: The Problem & Policy Responses. LC 87-17279. (Policy Analyses in International Economics Ser.: No. 23). 77p. reprint ed. pap. 25.00 (*0-7837-6407-3*, 2046387) Bks Demand.
— Capital Flight & Third World Debt. LC 87-17279. 271p. reprint ed. pap. 77.30 (*0-7837-4222-3*, 2043911) Bks Demand.
— Financial Intermediation Beyond the Debt Crisis. LC 85-18092. (Policy Analyses in International Economics Ser.: No. 12). 132p. (Orig.). 1985. pap. 37.70 (*0-7837-8494-5*, 2049301) Bks Demand.
Lessard, Gregory, jt. ed. see Hamm, Jean-Jaques.
Lessard, Gregory, ed. see Stendhal.
Lessard, Paul N. Sermons Alive! Fifty-Two Short Dramatic Sketches for Sunday Worship. Wray, Rhonda, ed. LC 92-44911. 208p. (Orig.). 1993. pap. 12.95 (*0-916260-95-X*, B132) Meriwether Pub.
Lessard, Paul N., jt. ed. see Nappa, Mike.
Lessard, R., ed. Photopolymer Device Physics, Chemistry, & Applications. 1990. 53.00 (*0-8194-0254-0*, VOL. 1213) SPIE.
Lessard, R. A. Photopolymer Device Physics, Chemistry, & Applications Two. 1992. 77.00 (*0-8194-0687-2*, 1559) SPIE.
Lessard, Richard L. The Circus. 32p. (J). 1993. pap. 4.95 (*1-883656-00-1*) Earth Bound.
Lessard, Sabin, ed. Mathematical & Statistical Developments of Evolutionary Theory: Proceedings of the NATO Advanced Study Institute Dordrecht, The Netherlands and Seminaire de Mathematiques Superleures Held in Montreal, Canada, August 3-21, 1987. (C). 1990. lib. bdg. 137.00 (*0-7923-0595-7*) Kluwer Ac.
Lessard, Sabin, jt. auth. see Karlin, Samuel.
Lessard, Victoria C., jt. auth. see Hall, Jack.
Lessard, W. O. The Complete Book of Bananas. Wilbur, Joan, ed. (Illus.). 120p. 1992. text ed. 35.00 (*0-9633161-0-9*) W O Lessard.
Lesse, Nicholas, tr. see Erasmus, Desiderius.
Lesse, Nicholas, tr. see Melanchthon, Philipp.
Lesse, Stanley, ed. Masked Depression. LC 73-17744. 394p. 1983. 50.00 (*0-87668-688-9*) Aronson.
Lessell. Current Neuro-Ophthalmology, Vol. 2. 432p. 1989. 89.95 (*0-8151-5389-9*, Yr Bk Med Pubs) Mosby Yr Bk.
Lessell, Simmons, ed. Current Neuro-Ophthalmology. 420p. 1991. 89.95 (*0-8151-5390-2*, Yr Bk Med Pubs) Mosby Yr Bk.
Lessels, Allen. Black Bear Baseball. 1987. pap. 8.95 (*0-930096-78-9*) G Gannett.
Lessels, Bruce. Whitewater Handbook. 3rd ed. LC 93-21066. 288p. 1994. 14.95 (*1-878239-01-5*) AMC Books.
Lessels, John, intro. Australia's Greenhouse Policy Seminar. (Illus.). 137p. (Orig.). 1992. pap. text ed. 36.00 (*0-85825-569-3*, Pub. by Inst Engrs Aust-EA Bks AT) Accents Pubns.
— Target Two Thousand: Defence Industry Spinoffs for the 21st Century. (Illus.). 253p. (Orig.). 1992. pap. 57.75 (*0-85825-572-3*) Accents Pubns.
— Wheels 'Ninety-Two. (Illus.). 259p. (Orig.). 1992. pap. 57.75 (*0-85825-584-7*, Pub. by Inst Engrs Aust-EA Bks AT) Accents Pubns.
Lessem, Don. Dinosaurs Rediscovered: New Discoveries That Are Revolutionizing Our Understanding of Dinosaurs. (Illus.). 320p. 1992. 25.00 (*0-671-73491-1*) S&S Trade.
— Dinosaurs Rediscovered: New Findings Which Are Revolutionizing Dinosaur Science. (Illus.). 368p. 1993. pap. 12.00 (*0-671-79715-8*, Touchstone Bks) S&S Trade.
— The Iceman. LC 93-31534. (Illus.). 32p. (J). (gr. 2-6). 1994. 14.00 (*0-517-59596-6*); lib. bdg. 14.99 (*0-517-59597-4*) Crown Bks Yng Read.
— Inside the Amazing Amazon. LC 94-43227. (Illus.). (J). 1995. 18.00 (*0-517-59490-0*, Crown) Crown Pub Group.
— John Horner Living with Dinosaurs. 48p. (J). (gr. 3-7). 1995. text ed. 14.95 (*0-7167-6546-2*, Sci Am Yng Rdrs); pap. text ed. 4.95 (*0-7167-6549-7*, Sci Am Yng Rdrs) W H Freeman.
— Ornithomimids, the Fastest Dinosaur. LC 93-10264. (Special Dinosaurs Ser.). (Illus.). (J). 1993. 19.95 (*0-87614-813-5*, Carolrhoda) Lerner Group.
— Raptors! The Nastiest Dinosaurs. LC 95-7110. (Illus.). (J). 1996. write for info. (*0-316-52119-1*) Little.
— Troodon, the Smartest Dinosaur. LC 92-44689. (Illus.). (J). 1993. 19.95 (*0-87614-798-8*, Carolrhoda) Lerner Group.
Lessem, Don, jt. auth. see Horner, Jack.
Lessem, Don, jt. auth. see Horner, John R.
Lessem, Don, jt. auth. see Horner, John.
Lessem, Ronnie. Business As a Learning Community. LC 92-44981. 1993. 19.95 (*0-07-707787-3*) McGraw.
— Developmental Management: Learning to Manage with Vision. (Illus.). 220p. 1990. text ed. 32.95 (*0-631-16844-3*) Blackwell Pubs.
— Enterprise Development. 200p. 1986. text ed. 49.95 (*0-566-02601-5*, Pub. by Gower UK) Ashgate Pub Co.
— Managing Corporate Culture. (Illus.). 240p. 1990. text ed. 49.95 (*0-566-02774-7*, Pub. by Gower UK) Ashgate Pub Co.
— Total Quality Learning. (Developmental Management Ser.). 300p. 1991. 39.95 (*0-631-16828-1*) Blackwell Pubs.
— Total Quality Learning. 1994. pap. 19.95 (*0-631-19306-5*) Blackwell Pubs.
Lessem, Ronnie & Neubauer, Fred. European Management Systems: Towards Unity Out of Cultural Diversity. LC 93-29857. 1993. write for info. (*0-07-707908-6*) McGraw.
Lessem, Ronnie, ed. see Jaques, Elliott & Clement, Stephen D.
Lessem, Ronnie, jt. auth. see Koopman, Albert.
Lessen, Don, jt. auth. see Horner, John R.
Lessen, Knots. The Adventures of Roundup & the Sacred Cow Cattle Drive. 145p. (Orig.). 1992. pap. 8.50 (*0-9632144-0-3*) Unidox Print.
***Lessen, Laurie S.** The Dance of the Carbon-Atom. LC 95-3921. 68p. 1995. pap. 12.95 (*0-7734-2723-6*, Mellen Poetry Pr) E Mellen.
***Lesser.** Linguistic Invest. Aphasia. 1989. 64.50 (*1-56593-541-1*, 0045) Singular Publishing.
Lesser, Alexander. Pawnee Ghost Dance Hand Game. LC 79-82340. (Columbia Univ. Contributions to Anthropology Ser.: Vol. 16). 1969. reprint ed. 37.00 (*0-404-50566-X*) AMS Pr.
— The Pawnee Ghost Dance Hand Game: A Study of Cultural Change. LC 79-82340. (Illus.). 368p. 1978. reprint ed. 22.50 (*0-299-07480-3*) U of Wis Pr.
Lesser, Allen. Israel's Impact, 1950-1951: A Personal Record. LC 84-12013. (Orig.). 1984. lib. bdg. 52.50 (*0-8191-4125-9*); pap. text ed. 29.00 (*0-8191-4126-7*) U Pr of Amer.

An Asterisk (*) at the beginning of an entry indicates that the title is appearing in BIP for the first time.

Lesser, Andrew J. Drive with Less Stress: A Motorist's Survival Guide for the 90's. Brown, Jane W., ed. LC 90-91498. (Illus.). 176p. (Orig.). 1990. pap. 5.95 (*0-945375-01-8*) Less Stress Pr.

Lesser, Barry, et al. National & International Information Policies. Cunningham, Ann M. & Schipper, Wendy, eds. (Report Series, 1991: No. 4). 170p. 1991. pap. text ed. 100.00 (*0-942308-31-X*) NFAIS.

***Lesser, Carolyn.** Dig Hole, Soft Mole. LC 95-11697. (Illus.). (J). 1996. write for info. (*0-15-223491-8*) HarBrace.

— Flamingo Knees. 3rd ed. 52p. (J). (gr. 5 up). 1991. pap. 10.00 (*0-9630604-0-6*) Oakwood MO.

— Flamingo Knees. 4th ed. (Illus.). 52p. (J). (gr. k up). 1993. 10.00 (*0-9630604-2-2*) Oakwood MO.

— The Goodnight Circle. LC 84-4501. (Illus.). 30p. (J). (ps-3). 1984. 14.95 (*0-15-232158-6*, HB Juv Bks) HarBrace.

— The Goodnight Circle. 30p. (J). (ps-3). 1991. pap. 4.95 (*0-15-232159-4*, HB Juv Bks) HarBrace.

— Great Crystal Bear. LC 95-12383. (Illus.). (J). 1996. write for info. (*0-15-200667-2*) HarBrace.

— The Knees Knock Again. 2nd ed. 56p. (J). 1991. pap. 10.00 (*0-9630604-1-4*) Oakwood MO.

— The Knees Knock Again. 3rd ed. (Illus.). 56p. (J). (gr. k up). 1993. pap. 10.00 (*0-9630604-3-0*) Oakwood MO.

— What a Wonderful Day to Be a Cow. LC 93-13211. (Illus.). 36p. (J). (ps-2). 1995. 15.00 (*0-679-82430-8*); lib. bdg. 15.99 (*0-679-92430-2*) Knopf Bks Yng Read.

Lesser, Charles H. Relic of the Lost Cause. Brimelow, Judith M., ed. (Illus.). 32p. 1990. write for info. (*1-880067-01-3*) SC Dept of Arch & Hist.

Lesser, Charles H., jt. ed. see White, J. Todd.

Lesser, Eugene. Drug Abuse in Marin County. 136p. (Orig.). 1985. pap. 8.95 (*0-912449-09-8*) Floating Island.

— A Palindrome Is a Pal Indeed. (Orig.). 1991. pap. 5.00 (*0-912449-38-1*) Floating Island.

— Sports Birthdays: The Fan's Daybook. LC 85-71054. 400p. pap. 9.95 (*0-916804-03-8*) Ed Buryn Pub.

Lesser, Gerald S., ed. see Conference on Contemporary Issues in Thematic Apperceptive Methods.

Lesser, Gerald S., jt. auth. see Kandel, Denise B.

Lesser, H., ed. Television & the Preschool Child: A Psychological Theory of Instruction & Curriculum Development. (Educational Psychology Ser.). 1977. text ed. 51.00 (*0-12-444250-1*) Acad Pr.

Lesser, Harry, jt. auth. see Loizou, Andros.

Lesser, Ian O. Bridge or Barrier? Turkey & the West after the Cold War. LC 92-17308. 1992. write for info. (*0-8330-1256-8*, R-4204-AF/A) Rand Corp.

— Resources & Strategy: Vital Materials in International Conflict, 1600-Present Day. 280p. 1989. text ed. 49.95 (*0-312-02372-3*) St Martin.

Lesser, Ian O., jt. auth. see Fuller, Graham E.

Lesser, Isaac. The Pentateuch-Haftaroth & Sabbath Prayers: Hebrew with English. 35.00 (*0-87559-197-3*) Shalom.

Lesser, Jeffrey. Welcoming the Undesirables: Brazil & the Jewish Question. LC 93-21199. 1994. 42.00 (*0-520-08412-8*); pap. 18.00 (*0-520-08413-6*) U CA Pr.

***Lesser, Joe & Youngblood, Pete.** Realistic Railroading with Toy Trains. (Illus.). 96p. 1995. per., pap. 17.95 (*0-89778-399-9*, 10-7975) Kalmbach.

Lesser, M. X. Jonathan Edwards. (United States Authors Ser.: No. 537). 152p. 1988. text ed. 26.95 (*0-8057-7519-6*, TUSAS 537, Pub. by Royal Botanic Garden UK) Macmillan.

— Jonathan Edwards: An Annotated Bibliography, 1979-1993. LC 94-31540. (Bibliographies & Indexes in Religious Studies). 232p. 1994. text ed. 65.00 (*0-313-29237-X*) Greenwood.

Lesser, Maximus. The Historical Development of the Jury System. 1976. lib. bdg. 34.95 (*0-8490-1957-5*) Gordon Pr.

Lesser, Maximus A. The Historical Development of the Jury System. LC 92-28982. 284p. 1992. 62.00 (*0-89941-816-3*, 307690) W S Hein.

Lesser, May H. An Artist in the University Medical Center: A Textile Technique from Laos. LC 89-51422. (Illus.). 192p. 1990. text ed. 35.00 (*0-295-97028-6*) U of Wash Pr.

Lesser, Mike, jt. auth. see Wuensche, Andrew.

Lesser, R. H. Indian Mosaic. (Writers Workshop Greybird Ser.). 41p. (C). 1975. 12.00 (*0-88253-564-1*); pap. text ed. 4.80 (*0-88253-563-3*) Ind-US Inc.

Lesser, R. P., jt. ed. see Luders, Hans.

***Lesser, Rika.** All We Need of Hell. 83p. 1995. 15.95 (*0-929398-85-8*); pap. 10.95 (*0-929398-92-0*) UNTX Pr.

Lesser, Rika, tr. see Andersson, Claes.

Lesser, Rika, tr. see Dahlback, Helena.

Lesser, Rika, tr. see Ekelof, Gunnar.

Lesser, Rika, tr. see Hesse, Hermann.

Lesser, Rika, tr. see Jersild, P. C.

Lesser, Rika, tr. see Rilke, Rainer Maria.

Lesser, Rika, tr. see Schami, Rafik.

Lesser, Rika, ed. see Sonnevi, Goran.

Lesser, Ronald, ed. Diagnosis & Management of Seizure Disorders. 162p. 1992. pap. 29.95 (*0-939957-31-0*) Demos Vermande.

Lesser, Ruth & Milroy, Lesley. Linguistics & Aphasia: Psycholinguistics & Pragmatic Aspects of Intervention. LC 92-11601. (Language in Social Life Ser.). 1993. 27.95 (*0-582-02221-5*, 79409) Longman.

Lesser, Simon O. The Whispered Meanings: Selected Essays of Simon O. Lesser. Sprich, Robert W. & Noland, Richard, eds. LC 77-73480. 248p. 1977. pap. 16.95x (*0-87023-244-4*) U of Mass Pr.

Lesser, Stephen, jt. ed. see Morsberger, Robert.

Lesser, T. H., jt. ed. see Williams, K. R.

***Lesser, Victor & Gasser, Les, eds.** Proceedings of the First International Conference on Multiagent Systems: June 12-14, 1995, San Francisco. (AAAI Press Ser.). (Illus.). 900p. (C). 1995. pap. 70.00x (*0-262-62102-9*) MIT Pr.

Lesser, W. Animal Patents. 380p. 1990. 100.00 (*0-935859-63-2*, Stockton Pr) Groves Dictionaries.

Lesser, Wendy. His Other Half: Men Looking at Women Through Art. LC 90-37165. (Illus.). 294p. 1991. text ed. 32.00 (*0-674-39210-8*, LESHIS) HUP.

— His Other Half: Men Looking at Women Through Art. (Illus.). 304p. 1992. pap. text ed. 12.95 (*0-674-39211-6*) HUP.

— The Life below the Ground: A Study of the Subterranean in Literature & History. 288p. 1987. 19.95 (*0-571-12954-4*) Faber & Faber.

— Pictures at an Execution. LC 93-7336. 284p. 1993. 24.95 (*0-674-66735-2*) HUP.

— Pictures at an Execution: An Inquiry into the Subject of Murder. (Illus.). 288p. (Orig.). (C). 1995. pap. 14.95 (*0-674-66736-0*) HUP.

Lesser, Wendy, intro. Hiding in Plain Sight: Essays in Criticism & Autobiography. LC 92-42345. 304p. 1993. 21.95 (*1-56279-037-4*) Mercury Hse Inc.

Lesser, William. Marketing Livestock & Meat. 471p. 1993. pap. 24.95 (*1-56022-017-1*) Haworth Jrnl Co-Edits.

— Marketing Livestock & Meat. LC 91-32989. (Illus.). 484p. 1993. lib. bdg. 69.95 (*1-56022-016-3*) Haworth Pr.

Lessin, Alexander. Great Relations: Do-It-Yourself Counseling for Couples. (Lessin's Lessons Ser.). (Illus.). (Orig.). 1988. pap. 12.00 (*0-945596-00-6*) Schl Counsel Psy.

Lessin, Barton M., ed. Off-Campus Library Services: Selected Readings from Central Michigan University's Conferences. LC 91-38119. 256p. 1991. 27.50 (*0-8108-2512-0*) Scarecrow.

Lessin, Roy. Como Criar Hijos Felices y Obedientes. 160p. 1981. 3.50 (*0-88113-037-0*) Edit Betania.

— Como Disciplinar a Tus Hijos. 96p. 1982. 2.95 (*0-88113-032-X*) Edit Betania.

— How to Be Parents of Happy Obedient Children. 1978. pap. 4.95 (*0-686-67298-4*) Omega Pubns OR.

— Knowing His Best...Walking in Rest. 96p. 1993. pap. 5.95 (*1-884009-03-4*) DaySpring.

— Never Forgotten, Always Loved. 96p. 1992. pap. 5.95 (*1-884009-00-X*) DaySpring.

— Receiving His Blessing, Giving His Love. 96p. 1993. pap. 5.95 (*1-884009-02-6*) DaySpring.

— Spanking: Why? When? How? LC 79-54028. 96p. 1979. pap. 4.99 (*0-87123-494-7*) Bethany Hse.

— Within His Hands, Without a Fear. 96p. 1993. pap. 5.95 (*1-884009-01-8*) DaySpring.

Lessing, Carl. Scriptorum Historiae Augustae Lexicon. iii, 747p. 1964. reprint ed. write for info. (*0-318-71160-5*, Pub. by Georg Olms GW); reprint ed. write for info. (*0-318-72038-8*, Pub. by Georg Olms GW) Lubrecht & Cramer.

Lessing, Doris. African Laughter: Four Visits to Zimbabwe. 464p. 1993. reprint ed. pap. 13.00 (*0-06-092433-0*, PL) HarpC.

— Briefing for a Descent into Hell. 1981. pap. 9.00 (*0-394-74662-7*) Knopf.

— Briefing for a Descent into Hell. LC 80-6142. 308p. 1981. pap. 3.95 (*0-685-04268-5*, V-662, Vin) Random.

— Canopus in Argos: Archives: Including Re-Colonised Planet 5: Shikasta; the Marriages Between. LC 91-5119. 1992. pap. 20.00 (*0-679-74184-4*, Vin) Random.

— Diaries of Jane Somers. 1984. pap. 12.00 (*0-394-72955-2*, Vin) Random.

— Documents Relating to the Sentimental Agents in the Volyen Empire. 1984. pap. 4.95 (*0-394-72386-4*, Vin) Random.

— The Doris Lessing Reader. 656p. 1989. 24.95 (*0-394-57307-2*) Knopf.

— The Fifth Child. LC 87-40487. 144p. 1988. 16.95 (*0-394-57105-3*) Knopf.

— Fifth Child. (International Ser.). 1989. pap. 9.00 (*0-679-72182-7*, Vin) Random.

— The Golden Notebook: A Novel. 576p. 1994. lib. bdg. 31.00 (*0-8095-9146-4*) Borgo Pr.

— The Golden Notebook: A Novel. 576p. 1994. reprint ed. pap. 12.00 (*0-06-097590-3*, PL) HarpC.

— The Good Terrorist. LC 86-40142. 400p. 1986. pap. 10.00 (*0-394-74629-5*, Vin) Random.

— The Grass Is Singing. 1976. pap. 7.95 (*0-452-25772-7*, Z5482, Plume); pap. 10.95 (*0-452-26119-8*) NAL-Dutton.

— Landlocked: A Complete Novel from Doris Lessing's Masterwork, Children of Violence. 1970. pap. 3.95 (*0-452-25138-9*, Z5138, Plume) NAL-Dutton.

— The Marriages Between Zones Three, Four, & Five. LC 81-40193. 256p. 1981. pap. 10.00 (*0-394-74978-2*, Vin) Random.

— Martha Quest. 1970. pap. 8.95 (*0-452-26124-4*) NAL-Dutton.

— Martha Quest. 256p. 1991. pap. 11.00 (*0-452-26576-2*, Plume) NAL-Dutton.

— Martha Quest: A Complete Novel from Doris Lessing's Masterwork, Children of Violence. 1970. mass mkt. 6.95 (*0-452-25968-1*, Plume) NAL-Dutton.

— The Memoirs of a Survivor. Freedgood, Anne, ed. LC 87-45951. 224p. 1988. reprint ed. pap. 10.00 (*0-394-75759-9*, Vin) Random.

— Particularly Cats...& Rufus. LC 90-53669. (Illus.). 144p. 1991. 19.50 (*0-394-58671-9*) Knopf.

— Playing the Game Graphic Novel. 1993. mass mkt. 6.99 (*0-06-105007-5*, PL) HarpC.

— Prisons We Choose to Live Inside. 80p. 1994. 25.00x (*0-8095-9157-X*) Borgo Pr.

— Prisons We Choose to Live Inside. LC 87-45064. 96p. 1987. pap. 9.00 (*0-06-039077-8*, HarpT) HarpC.

— Proper Marriage: A Complete Novel from Doris Lessing's Masterwork, Children of Violence. 1970. pap. 7.95 (*0-452-25789-1*, Z5093, Plume) NAL-Dutton.

— Re: Colonized Planet 5-Shikasta. LC 81-40194. 384p. 1981. pap. 8.95 (*0-394-74977-4*, Vin) Random.

— The Real Thing: Stories & Sketches. LC 91-59932. 224p. 1993. pap. 11.00 (*0-06-092417-9*, PL) HarpC.

— The Sirian Experiments. LC 81-52259. 400p. 1982. pap. 7.95 (*0-394-75195-7*, Vin) Random.

— Stories. LC 79-22320. 1980. pap. 24.00 (*0-394-74249-4*, Vin) Random.

— The Summer Before Dark. LC 82-40421. 256p. 1983. pap. 8.00 (*0-394-71095-9*, Vin) Random.

— Through the Tunnel. (Creative Short Stories Ser.). (YA). (gr. 4-12). 1989. 13.95 (*0-88682-346-3*, 97224-098) Creative Ed.

— Under My Skin. LC 94-20051. 1994. 25.00 (*0-06-017150-2*) HarpC.

Lessing, Erich, jt. auth. see Lemaitre, Alain J.

Lessing, Ferdinand D. Ritual & Symbol: Essays on Lamaism & Chinese Symbolism. (Asian Folklore & Social Life Monographs: No. 91). (ENG & GER.). 1976. 20.00 (*0-89986-305-1*) Oriental Bk Store.

Lessing, Gotthold E. Emilia Galotti: A Tragedy in Five Acts. Dvoretzky, Edward, tr. & pref. by. 82p. (C). 1992. pap. text ed. 5.95 (*0-917324-17-X*) M S Rosenberg.

— Lacoon. McCormick, Edward A., tr. 1962. pap. 5.50 (*0-672-60260-1*, Bobbs) Macmillan.

— Laocoon: An Essay on the Limits of Painting & Poetry. McCormick, Edward A., tr. LC 83-23880. 1984. pap. 14.95 (*0-8018-3139-3*) Johns Hopkins.

— Lessings Saemtliche Schriften, 23 vols., Set. 3rd ed. Lachmann, Karl, ed. (C). 1968. reprint ed. 1,523.10 (*3-11-005161-3*) De Gruyter.

— Lessing's Theological Writings: Selections in Translation. Chadwick, Henry, tr. 110p. 1957. reprint ed. pap. 9.95 (*0-8047-0335-3*) Stanford U Pr.

— Ubersetzungen aus dem Franzosischen Friedrichs des Grossen und Voltaires. Schmidt, Erich, ed. 1990. reprint ed. 44.00 (*3-262-01425-7*) Periodicals Srv.

Lessing, Lawrence P. Understanding Chemistry. LC 59-14418. 192p. reprint ed. pap. 54.80 (*0-317-08764-9*, 2007397) Bks Demand.

Lessing, Otto E. Masters in Modern German Literature. LC 67-23239. (Essay Index Reprint Ser.). 1977. 19.95 (*0-8369-0616-0*) Ayer.

Lessinger, Jack. The Crash of Suburbia: The Coming Boom of Small Towns. rev. ed. (Illus.). 1990. write for info. (*0-318-66598-0*) Socioeconomics.

— Penturbia: Where Real Estate Will Boom After the Crash of Suburbia. (Illus.). 1991. 22.95 (*0-9625182-5-5*) Socioeconomics.

Lessinger, Leon, jt. auth. see Burt, Samuel M.

Lessiter, Frank D. Horsepower. LC 76-45044. 1977. 11.98 (*0-89821-018-6*) Reiman Pubns.

Lessius, Leonard & Cornaro, Luigi. A Treatise of Health & Long Life with the Future Means of Attaining It. Kastenbaum, Robert, ed. Smith, Timothy, tr. LC 78-22206. (Aging & Old Age Ser.). 1979. reprint ed. lib. bdg. 17.95 (*0-405-11821-X*) Ayer.

Lessler, F. H., jt. auth. see Korepin, V. E.

Lessler, Judith T. & Kalsbeek, William D. Nonsampling Error in Surveys. (Probability & Mathematical Statistics: Applied Probability & Statistics Section Ser.). 1992. text ed. 91.95 (*0-471-86908-2*) Wiley.

Lessler, Richard S., jt. auth. see Wedding, C. Nugent.

Lessman, F., jt. auth. see Levy, H.

Lessmann, Heinrich. Aufgaben und Ziele der Vergleichenden Mythenforschung: Tasks & Goals of Comparative Mythology. Bolle, Kees W., ed. LC 77-79138. (Mythology Ser.). (GER.). 1978. reprint ed. lib. bdg. 19.95 (*0-405-10548-7*) Ayer.

Lessmann, Judith. Be a Natural Woman: Fitness for Teens. Kaste, Harry, ed. LC 81-80111. (Illus.). 184p. (Orig.). (gr. 7-12). 1981. pap. 5.95 (*0-939390-00-0*) Pizzazz Pr.

Lessmann, Sabine. The Future of Party Government, Vol. 4 - Budgetary Politics & Elections: An Investigation of Public Expenditures. Wildenmann, Rudolf, ed. (European University Institute, Series C (Political & Social Science): No. 5-4). xii, 212p. 1987. lib. bdg. 66.95 (*0-89925-189-7*) De Gruyter.

— The Future of Party Government, Vol. 4 - Budgetary Politics & Elections: An Investigation of Public Expenditures. Wildenmann, Rudolf, ed. (European University Institute, Series C (Political & Social Science): No. 5-4). xii, 212p. 1987. lib. bdg. 366.95 (*3-11-010943-3*) De Gruyter.

Lessner, Grace, ed. see Fitch, David A.

Lessner, Richard, ed. see Benson, Steve.

***Lessnick, David.** Ski Shape: How to Get Fit for Skiing, the Ultimate Illustrated Guide. 2nd ed. (Illus.). 1994. pap. 12.95 (*1-55698-342-5*) Movie Pubs Servs.

— Ski Shape: How to Get Fit for Skiing: The Ultimate Illustrated Guide. (Illus.). 1992. pap. 12.95 (*1-55698-351-4*) Movie Pubs Servs.

Lessnoff, M. Social Contract Theory. 330p. 1990. 45.00 (*0-8147-5054-0*); pap. 17.50 (*0-8147-5055-9*) NYU Pr.

Lessnoff, Michael H. The Spirit of Capitalism & the Protestant Ethic: An Enquiry into the Weber Thesis. 160p. 1994. 49.95 (*1-85278-875-5*, Pub. by E Elgar Pub UK) Ashgate Pub Co.

Lessof, M. H. Clinical Reactions to Food. LC 82-11101. 222p. 1983. text ed. 99.95 (*0-471-10436-1*, A R Liss) Wiley.

— Food Allergy & Other Adverse Reactions to Food. (Illus.). 22p. 1994. pap. text ed. 12.50 (*0-944395-19-8*) ILSI.

— Food Intolerance. (Food Safety Ser.: No. 2). 212p. 1993. 84.95 (*0-412-44850-5*) Chapman & Hall.

Lessof, Maurice H., ed. Immunology of Cardiovascular Disease. LC 81-15208. (Basic & Clinical Cardiology Ser.: No. 1). 447p. reprint ed. pap. 127.40 (*0-7837-3355-0*, 2043313) Bks Demand.

Lessoff, Alan. The Nation & Its City: Politics, Corruption, & Progress in Washington, D.C., 1861-1902. LC 93-17513. 1994. 45.00 (*0-8018-4464-9*) Johns Hopkins.

Lesson, Pierre A. Les Polynesiens: Leur Origine, Leurs Migrations, Leur Langage, 4 vols., Set. LC 75-35201. reprint ed. 162.50 (*0-404-14270-2*) AMS Pr.

Lesson, Rene P. Voyage Autour du Monde...Sur la Covette Tome 1: La Coquille. (Discovery of the Pacific & Australia Ser.). (Illus.). 518p. (FRE.). (C). 1989. reprint ed. 135.00 (*1-85297-006-5*, Pub. by Archival Facs UK) St Mut.

Lessow-Hurley, Judith. A Commonsense Guide to Bilingual Education. LC 91-21874. 84p. 1991. pap. 6.95 (*0-87120-183-6*, 611-91115) Assn Supervision.

— The Foundations of Dual Language Instruction. 208p. (Orig.). (C). 1990. pap. text ed. 27.50 (*0-8013-0131-9*, 75795) Longman.

***LesStrang, Barbara H.** AfterLoss: A Recovery Companion for Those Who Are Grieving. 240p. (Orig.). 1995. pap. 12.95 (*1-879560-36-4*) Harbor Hse West.

Lestarjette, Steve, jt. auth. see Palandro, Michael.

Lester. Look to the East. 15.95 (*0-685-22017-6*) Wehman.

Lester, ed. see Clark.

Lester, jt. auth. see Dente.

Lester, et al, eds. Quality Control for Profit. 3rd expanded rev. ed. (Quality & Reliability Ser.: Vol. 34). 592p. 1992. 89.75 (*0-8247-8658-0*) Dekker.

Lester, Alan. Merchant Ship Stability. (Marine Engineering Ser.). (Illus.). 328p. 1985. text ed. 42.95 (*0-408-01448-2*) Buttrwrth-Heinemann.

Lester, Albert. Project Planning & Control. 2nd ed. (Illus.). 256p. 1992. 67.95 (*0-7506-1100-6*) Buttrwrth-Heinemann.

Lester, Alison. Bibs & Boots. (Illus.). 16p. (J). (ps-00). 1989. 3.50 (*0-670-81988-3*) Viking Child Bks.

— Bumping & Bouncing. (Illus.). 16p. (J). (ps-00). 1989. pap. 3.50 (*0-670-81991-3*) Viking Child Bks.

— Clive Eats Alligators. (J). (ps). 1991. pap. 4.95 (*0-395-58408-6*) HM.

— Crashing & Splashing. (Illus.). 16p. (J). (ps-00). 1989. pap. 3.50 (*0-670-81989-1*) Viking Child Bks.

— Happy & Sad. (Illus.). 16p. (J). (ps-00). 1989. pap. 3.50 (*0-670-81990-5*) Viking Child Bks.

— I'm Green & I'm Grumpy. (Open-the-Door Bks.). 16p. (J). (ps-1). 1993. pap. 4.99 (*0-14-054478-X*, Puffin) Puffin Bks.

— Imagine. (Illus.). 32p. (J). (gr. k-3). 1990. 13.95 (*0-395-53753-3*) HM.

— Imagine. (J). (ps-3). 1993. pap. 6.95 (*0-395-66953-7*) HM.

— Isabella's Bed. LC 92-22935. (Illus.). 32p. (J). (gr. k-3). 1993. reprint ed. 14.95 (*0-395-65565-X*) HM.

— The Journey Home. LC 89-28355. (Illus.). 32p. (J). (gr. k-3). 1991. 14.95 (*0-395-53355-4*) HM.

— Magic Beach. (Illus.). 32p. (J). (ps-3). 1992. 13.95 (*0-316-52177-9*, Joy St Bks) Little.

— Monsters Are Knocking. (Open-the-Door Bks.). 16p. (J). (ps-1). 1993. pap. 4.99 (*0-14-054967-6*, Puffin) Puffin Bks.

— My Farm. LC 93-30894. (J). 1994. 14.95 (*0-395-68193-6*) HM.

— Rosie Sips Spiders. (Illus.). 32p. (J). (ps-00). 1989. 13.95 (*0-395-51526-2*) HM.

— Tessa Snaps Snakes. LC 91-2665. (Illus.). 32p. (J). (ps-00). 1991. pap. 13.95 (*0-685-52551-1*, Sandpiper) HM.

— Tessa Snaps Snakes. (Illus.). 32p. (J). (ps-00). 1991. 13.95 (*0-395-59505-3*) HM.

Lester, Andrew D. Coping with Your Anger: A Christian Guide. LC 82-24730. 114p. 1983. pap. 8.99 (*0-664-24471-8*, Westminster) Westminster John Knox.

— Hope in Pastoral Care & Counseling. LC 94-36895. 176p. (Orig.). 1995. pap. 16.99 (*0-664-25588-4*) Westminster John Knox.

— It Hurts So Bad, Lord: Ya No Pueda Mas, Senor! Robleto, Adolfo, tr. 138p. (Orig.). (SPA.). 1989. pap. 4.75 (*0-311-46120-4*) Casa Bautista.

— Pastoral Care with Children in Crisis. LC 84-21901. 144p. (Orig.). (C). 1985. pap. 11.99 (*0-664-24598-6*, Westminster) Westminster John Knox.

Lester, Andrew D., ed. Cuando los Ninos Sufren - When Children Suffer. Morales, Edgar O., tr. 240p. (Orig.). (SPA.). 1992. pap. 6.95 (*0-311-11061-4*, Edit Mundo) Casa Bautista.

— When Children Suffer: A Sourcebook for Ministry with Children in Crisis. LC 87-8165. 210p. (C). 1987. 16.00 (*0-664-21327-8*, Westminster) Westminster John Knox.

Lester, Andrew D. & Lester, Judith L. Understanding Aging Parents. LC 80-17832. (Christian Care Bks.: No. 8). 120p. reprint ed. pap. 34.20 (*0-7837-2636-8*, 2042987) Bks Demand.

Lester, Andrew D., ed. see Reed, John P.

Lester, Barry M. & Boukydis, C. F., eds. Infant Crying: Theoretical & Research Perspectives. LC 84-26414. 400p. 1985. 75.00 (*0-306-41775-8*, Plenum Pr) Plenum.

Lester, Bonnie. Women & AIDS: A Practical Guide for Those Who Help Others. 144p. 1989. 15.95 (*0-8245-1348-7*) Crossroad NY.

Lester, Bruce P. The Art of Parallel Programming. 464p. 1993. text ed. 62.00 (*0-13-045923-2*) P-H.

Lester, C. B. Hydraulics for Pipeliners. 2nd ed. 256p. 1994. write for info. (*0-318-71719-0*) Gulf Pub.

— Hydraulics for Pipeliners, Vol. 1. 2nd ed. 300p. 1994. 85.00 (*0-88415-400-9*) Gulf Pub.

Lester, Charles E. Artists of America: A Series of Biographical Sketches of American Artists. LC 68-8689. (American Art Ser.). (Illus.). 1969. reprint ed. lib. bdg. 39.50 (*0-306-71169-9*) Da Capo.

An Asterisk (*) at the beginning of an entry indicates that the title is appearing in BIP for the first time.

— The Life of Sam Houston: The Only Authentic Memoir of Him Ever Published. LC 70-38360. (Select Bibliographies Reprint Ser.). 1977. reprint ed. 25.95 (0-8369-6777-1) Ayer.

Lester, Cheryl, tr. see Lacoue-Labarthe, Philippe & Nancy, Jean-Luc.

***Lester, David.** The Biochemical Basis of Suicide. (Illus.). 150p. 1988. pap. 24.95 (0-398-06229-3) C C Thomas.

— The Biochemical Basis of Suicide. (Illus.). 150p. (C). 1988. text ed. 37.95x (0-398-05443-6) C C Thomas.

— Can We Prevent Suicide? LC 87-47813. (Studies in Modern Society: Political & Social Issues: No. 20). 1987. 34.50 (0-404-61627-5) AMS Pr.

— The Cruelest Death: The Enigma of Adolescent Suicide. LC 92-34448. 178p. (Orig.). 1993. pap. 16.95 (0-914783-64-5) Charles.

— The Death Penalty: Issues & Answers. 102p. 1987. 31.95x (0-398-05305-7) C C Thomas.

— Gun Control: Issues & Answers. 146p. 1984. spiral bd. 24.95x (0-398-04880-0) C C Thomas.

— The Murderer & His Murder: A Review of Research. LC 85-48007. (Studies in Modern Society: Political & Social Issues: No. 19). 1986. 32.50 (0-404-61626-7) AMS Pr.

— Patterns of Suicide & Homocide in America. 143p. (C). 1994. lib. bdg. 59.00 (1-56072-148-0) Nova Sci Pubs.

— The Psychological Basis of Handwriting Analysis: The Relationship of Handwriting to Personality & Psychopathology. LC 79-23957. 192p. (C). 1981. text ed. 24.95 (0-88229-533-0) Nelson-Hall.

— Psychotherapy for Suicidal Clients. (Illus.). 150p. 1991. pap. 19.95 (0-398-06231-5) C C Thomas.

— Psychotherapy for Suicidal Clients. (Illus.). 150p. (C). 1991. text ed. 34.95x (0-398-05738-9) C C Thomas.

— Questions & Answers about Murder. LC 91-23439. 192p. (Orig.). 1991. pap. 11.95 (0-914783-46-7) Charles.

— Questions & Answers about Suicide. LC 89-60683. 176p. (Orig.). (C). 1989. pap. 10.95 (0-914783-31-9) Charles.

— Suicide As a Learned Behavior. (Illus.). 144p. 1987. 35.95x (0-398-05340-5) C C Thomas.

— Suicide As a Learned Behavior. (Illus.). 144p. 1987. pap. 19.95 (0-398-06232-3) C C Thomas.

— Suicide from a Psychological Perspective. 142p. (C). 1988. text ed. 37.95x (0-398-05489-4) C C Thomas.

— Suicide from a Psychological Perspective. 142p. 1989. pap. 22.95 (0-398-06233-1) C C Thomas.

— Suicide from a Sociological Perspective. 138p. 1989. 36.95 (0-398-05595-5) C C Thomas.

— Suicide from a Sociological Perspective. 138p. 1989. pap. 19.95 (0-398-06234-X) C C Thomas.

— Suicide in Creative Women. 189p. (C). 1994. lib. bdg. 59.00 (1-56072-150-2) Nova Sci Pubs.

— Theories of Personality. 200p. 1995. 59.50x (1-56032-350-7); pap. 29.50x (1-56032-351-5) Taylor & Francis.

— Understanding & Preventing Suicide: New Perspectives. (Illus.). 134p. 1990. pap. 18.95 (0-398-06235-8) C C Thomas.

— Understanding & Preventing Suicide: New Perspectives. (Illus.). 134p. (C). 1990. text ed. 33.95x (0-398-05709-5) C C Thomas.

— Understanding Suicide: A Case Study Approach. 221p. (C). 1994. lib. bdg. 59.00 (1-56072-149-9) Nova Sci Pubs.

— Why People Kill Themselves: A 1990s Summary of Research Findings on Suicidal Behavior. 3rd ed. 464p. 1992. pap. 37.95 (0-398-06236-6) C C Thomas.

— Why People Kill Themselves: A 1990s Summary of Research Findings on Suicidal Behavior. 3rd ed. 464p. (C). 1992. text ed. 68.95x (0-398-05767-2) C C Thomas.

Lester, David, ed. Current Concepts of Suicide. LC 90-1600. 236p. (Orig.). 1990. pap. 16.95 (0-914783-45-9) Charles.

— Emile Durkheim: Le Suicide, One Hundred Years Later. LC 94-1056. 348p. 1994. lib. bdg. 42.50 (0-914783-73-4) Charles.

— Mechanical Rights. 183p. 1992. pap. 102.00 (90-6215-313-5, Pub. by Maklu Uitgevers BE) W W Gaunt.

— Why Women Kill Themselves. 160p. (C). 1988. text ed. 37.95x (0-398-05508-4) C C Thomas.

— Why Women Kill Themselves. 160p. 1988. pap. 22.95 (0-398-06237-4) C C Thomas.

Lester, David & Bijou Yang. The Economy & Suicide: Economic Perspectives on Suicide. (Studies in Modern Society: No. 23). 1993. 42.50 (0-404-61630-5) AMS Pr.

Lester, David & Brockopp, Gene W. Crisis Intervention & Counseling by Telephone. (Illus.). 336p. 1976. 47.95x (0-398-02641-6) C C Thomas.

— Crisis Intervention & Counseling by Telephone. (Illus.). 336p. 1976. pap. 29.95 (0-398-06230-7) C C Thomas.

Lester, David & Danto, Bruce L. Suicide Behind Bars: Prediction & Prevention. LC 92-27480. 176p. 1993. pap. 17.50 (0-914783-62-9) Charles.

Lester, David & Lester, Gene. Crime of Passion: Murder & the Murderer. LC 74-20788. 308p. 1975. 27.95 (0-88229-139-4) Nelson-Hall.

Lester, David & Tallmer, Margot, eds. Now I Lay Me Down: Suicide & the Elderly. LC 93-25814. 252p. (Orig.). 1994. pap. 19.95 (0-914783-65-3) Charles.

Lester, David, jt. ed. see Canetto, Silvia S.

Lester, David, jt. auth. see Peyton-Jones, Simon L.

Lester, David, et al. Correctional Counseling. 2nd ed. LC 91-72940. 271p. (C). 1992. pap. 21.95 (0-87084-372-9) Anderson Pub Co.

Lester, David, et al, eds. Suicide: A Guide to Information Sources. LC 80-71. (Social Issues & Social Problems Information Guide Ser.: Vol. 3). 1980. 68.00 (0-8103-1415-0) Gale.

Lester, David S. & Epand, Richard M., eds. Protein Kinase C: Current Concepts & Future Perspectives. LC 92-33971. (Ellis Horwood Series in Biochemistry & Biotechnology). 300p. 1993. 100.50 (0-13-720186-9, Tavistock-E Horwood) Routledge Chapman & Hall.

Lester, DeeGee. Roosevelt Research: Collections for the Study of Theodore, Franklin & Eleanor. LC 92-10072. (Bibliographies & Indexes in American History Ser.: No. 23). 224p. 1992. text ed. 59.95 (0-313-27204-2, LRC/, Greenwood Pr) Greenwood.

Lester, DeeGee, comp. Irish Research: A Guide to Collections in North America, Ireland, & Great Britain. LC 87-25150. 376p. 1987. text ed. 75.00 (0-313-24664-5, LIR/, Greenwood Pr) Greenwood.

Lester, DeeGee, jt. comp. see Weaver, Jack W.

***Lester, Donna.** Macon County, Missouri Pictorial History. (Illus.). 110p. 1993. 34.95 (0-88107-214-1) Curtis Media.

Lester, E. W., jt. auth. see Hickman, James.

Lester, Ed. Writing Research Papers: A Complete Guide. 7th ed. (C). 1992. 13.50 (0-673-46643-4); pap. text ed. 18.50 (0-673-46644-2) HarpCollege.

Lester, Elizabeth. Legendary King of San Miguel. 1979. pap. 6.50 (0-87461-027-3) McNally & Loftin.

Lester, Ellen, ed. see Hendricks, Douglas L., et al.

Lester, Ellen, ed. see Quillinan, James V., et al.

Lester, Ellen, ed. see Rehon, Peter M.

Lester, Ellen, ed. see Reinbolt, Jacob C.

Lester, Ellen C., ed. see Hendricks, Douglas L., et al.

Lester, Ellen C., ed. see Holderness, Richard A.

Lester, Ellen C., ed. see Rehon, Peter M.

Lester, Ellen C., ed. see Tussman, Davida S. & Hansen, Charles A.

Lester, Eugenia C. & Branson, Allegra. Frontiers Aflame. LC 87-8783. (Illus.). 302p. (Orig.). 1987. pap. 12.95 (0-932334-87-3, NY39027) Hrt of the Lakes.

Lester, G. A. Sir John Paston's Grete Boke: A Descriptive Catalogue with an Introduction, of British Library Ms. Lansdowne 285. 197p. 1984. 71.00 (0-85991-161-6) Boydell & Brewer.

Lester, G. A., ed. The Index of Middle English Prose Handlist II: Manuscripts Containing Middle English Prose in the John Rylands University Library & Chetham's Library, Manchester. LC 85-2105. 112p. 1985. 53.00 (0-85991-189-6) Boydell & Brewer.

Lester, Gene & Laufer, Peter. When Hollywood Was Fun: Snapshots of an Era. (Illus.). 224p. 1993. 24.95 (1-55972-197-9, Birch Ln Pr) Carol Pub Group.

Lester, Gene, jt. auth. see Lester, David.

Lester, Gregory W. Power with People: How to Handle Just about Anyone To Accomplish Just about Anything. 480p. 29.95 (0-9641458-0-4) Ashcroft Pr.

***Lester, Helen.** The Four Getters & Arf. 2nd ed. (Let Me Read, Level 2, Ser.). (Illus.). (J). 1995. bds. 2.95 (0-673-36272-8) GdYrBks.

— It Wasn't My Fault. LC 84-19212. (Illus.). 32p. (J). (gr. k-3). 1985. 14.95 (0-395-35629-6) HM.

— It Wasn't My Fault. (Illus.). (J). (ps-3). 1989. pap. 5.95 (0-395-51007-4, Sandpiper) HM.

— Lin's Backpack. 2nd ed. (Let Me Read Ser.). 8p. (J). (ps-1). 1994. text ed. 2.95 (0-673-36194-2) GdYrBks.

— Listen, Buddy. LC 94-33634. (Illus.). (J). 1995. 14.95 (0-395-72361-2) HM.

— Me First. LC 91-45808. (Illus.). 32p. (J). (ps up). 1992. 13.95 (0-395-58706-9) HM.

— Me First. LC 91-45808. (J). (ps-3). 1995. pap. 4.95 (0-395-72022-2) HM.

— La Mochila de Lin. 3rd ed. Ada, Alma F., tr. (Let Me Read, Level 2 Ser.). (Illus.). (SPA.). (J). 1995. bds. 2.95 (0-673-36291-4) GdYrBks.

— Pookins Gets Her Way. (Illus.). (J). (ps-3). 1990. pap. 4.95 (0-395-53965-X) HM.

— A Porcupine Named Fluffy. LC 85-24820. 32p. (J). (ps-3). 1986. 14.95 (0-395-36895-2) HM.

— A Porcupine Named Fluffy. LC 85-24820. 32p. (J). (ps-3). 1989. pap. 5.95 (0-395-52018-5) HM.

— The Revenge of the Magic Chicken. (Illus.). 32p. (J). (gr. k-3). 1990. 13.95 (0-395-50929-7) HM.

— Tacky the Penguin. LC 87-30684. 32p. (J). (ps-3). 1988. 14.95 (0-395-45536-7) HM.

— Tacky the Penguin. (Illus.). 32p. (J). (gr. k-3). 1990. pap. 4.95 (0-395-56233-3) HM.

— Three Cheers for Tacky. LC 93-14342. (Illus.). (J). 1994. 13.95 (0-395-66841-7) HM.

— The Wizard, the Fairy, & the Magic Chicken. (J). (ps-3). 1983. 10.95 (0-395-33885-9) HM.

— The Wizard, the Fairy, & the Magic Chicken. LC 82-21302. (Illus.). 32p. (J). (gr. k-3). 1988. pap. 5.95 (0-395-47945-2) HM.

***Lester, Helen & Lester, Robin.** Muttsy's Mystery. LC 94-24224. (Gund Children's Library). (J). 1995. write for info. (1-56402-499-7) Candlewick Pr.

Lester, Helen, jt. auth. see Lester, Robin.

Lester, J. C. & Wilson, D. L. Ku Klux Klan. LC 71-114758. (Civil Liberties in American History Ser.). (Illus.). 208p. 1973. reprint ed. lib. bdg. 29.50 (0-306-71927-4) Da Capo.

— Ku Klux Klan, Its Origin, Growth & Disbandment. LC 70-144650. reprint ed. 29.50 (0-404-00195-5) AMS Pr.

— Ku Klux Klan, Its Origin, Its Growth & Disbandment. LC 72-131766. 1973. reprint ed. 25.00 (0-403-00653-8) Scholarly.

Lester, J. N., ed. Heavy Metals in Wastewater & Sludge Treatment Processes, 2 vols. 176p. 1987. 279.90 (0-8493-4667-3, TD758) CRC Pr.

Lester, J. N. & Sterritt, R. M. Microbiology for Public Health & Environmental Engineers. 284p. 1988. text ed. 65.00 (0-419-12760-7, E & FN Spon); pap. text ed. 29.50 (0-419-12770-4, E & FN Spon) Routledge Chapman & Hall.

Lester, James. Too Marvelous for Words: The Life & Genius of Art Tatum. (Illus.). 304p. 1994. 25.00 (0-19-508365-2) OUP.

— Too Marvelous for Words: The Life & Genius of Art Tatum. (Illus.). 264p. 1995. pap. 10.95 (0-19-509640-1) OUP.

Lester, James D. Interactions: The Aims & Patterns of Writing. 403p. (C). 1988. pap. 22.95 (0-534-08076-6) Intl Thomson.

— A Writer's Handbook: Style & Grammar. 512p. (C). 1990. pap. text ed. 20.00 (0-15-597648-6) HB Coll Pubs.

— Writing Research Papers: A Complete Guide. 6th ed. (C). 1989. pap. text ed. 9.25 (0-673-38798-4) HarpCollege.

— Writing Research Papers: A Complete Guide. 7th ed. 1993. write for info. (0-318-69537-5, HarpT) HarpC.

***Lester, James D., comp.** Plato's Heirs: Classic Essays. LC 95-8290. 1995. pap. write for info. (0-8442-5878-4) NTC Pub Grp.

***Lester, James D., ed.** Daughters of the Revolution: Classic Essays by Women. LC 95-11910. 1995. pap. write for info. (0-8442-5880-6) NTC Pub Grp.

Lester, James D., Sr. & Lester, James D., Jr. The Research Paper Handbook. (Illus.). 232p. (Orig.). 1991. pap. 7.95 (0-673-36016-4) GdYrBks.

— Writing: Style & Grammar. 400p. (J). (gr. 6-10). 1994. pap. 9.95 (0-673-36093-8); spiral bd. 14.95 (0-673-36128-4) GdYrBks.

Lester, James D., Jr., jt. auth. see Lester, James D., Sr.

Lester, James P., ed. Environmental Politics & Policy: Theories & Evidence. LC 89-35743. 464p. (C). 1989. pap. text ed. 24.95 (0-8223-0942-4) Duke.

— Environmental Politics & Policy: Theories & Evidence. 2nd ed. LC 94-38244. (Illus.). 384p. 1995. lib. bdg. 59.95 (0-8223-1558-0); pap. text ed. 22.95 (0-8223-1569-6) Duke.

Lester, James P. & Bowman, Ann, eds. The Politics of Hazardous Waste Management. LC 83-16595. (Duke Press Policy Studies). x, 317p. (Orig.). 1983. text ed. 41.95 (0-8223-0507-0); pap. text ed. 18.95 (0-8223-0523-2) Duke.

Lester, James P., jt. ed. see Davis, Charles E.

Lester, James P., jt. ed. see Davis, Charles.

Lester, Jane. The House at Cheltonwood. large type ed. (Linford Romance Library). 1991. pap. 13.95 (0-7089-7100-8) Ulverscroft.

— Legacy for Lorna. large type ed. (Linford Romance Library). 320p. 1985. pap. 11.95 (0-7089-6124-X, Linford) Ulverscroft.

— Love's Golden Touch. large type ed. (Linford Romance Library). 272p. 1985. pap. 11.95 (0-7089-6055-3, Linford) Ulverscroft.

— Nurse at High Hedges. large type ed. 288p. 1988. 15.95 (0-7089-1882-4) Ulverscroft.

— Nurse in the East. large type ed. (Linford Romance Library). 336p. 1985. pap. 11.95 (0-7089-6098-7, Linford) Ulverscroft.

— Nurse Rita's Request. large type ed. 281p. 1989. 17.95 (0-7089-1933-2) Ulverscroft.

— The Reluctant Heart. large type ed. 416p. 1988. 15.95 (0-7089-1802-6) Ulverscroft.

— Sister March's Secret. large type ed. (Linford Romance Library). 296p. 1984. pap. 11.95 (0-7089-6047-2, Trailtree Bookshop) Ulverscroft.

Lester, Jean, ed. Faces of Alaska: A Glimpse of History Through Paintings, Photographs & Oral Histories. (Illus.). 150p. (Orig.). (C). 1988. 49.95 (0-940457-50-4); pap. 29.95 (0-940457-51-2) Tanana Yukon Hist Soc.

Lester, Jean & Bartlett, Doris A., intros. Faces of Alaska from Barrow to Wrangell: History Through Oral History, Photographs & Portraits. LC 92-80227. (Illus.). 182p. (Orig.). 1992. 49.95 (0-940457-59-8); pap. 29.95 (0-940457-60-1) Tanana Yukon Hist Soc.

Lester, Jim. Man For Arkansas: Sid McMath & the Southern Reform Tradition. (Illus.). 303p. 1976. 19.95 (0-914546-11-2) J W Bell.

Lester, Jim & Lester, Judy. Little Rock. 225p. 1987. 21.95 (0-89865-479-3) Donning Co.

Lester, Joan S. The Future of White Men & Other Diversity Dilemmas. 200p. (Orig.). (C). 1994. 17.95 (0-943233-65-8); pap. 9.95 (0-943233-61-5) Conari Press.

Lester, Joel. Analytical Approaches to Twentieth-Century Music. (C). 1989. text ed. 35.95 (0-393-95762-4); pap. text ed. write for info. (0-393-95816-7) Norton.

— Between Modes & Keys: German Theory 1592-1802. LC 87-14864. (Harmonologia Ser.: No. 7). (Illus.). 250p. 1990. lib. bdg. 47.00 (0-918728-77-0) Pendragon NY.

— Compositional Theory in the Eighteenth Century. (Illus.). 355p. 1993. text ed. 49.95 (0-674-15522-X) HUP.

— Compositional Theory in the Eignteenth Century. 355p. 1994. pap. 26.50 (0-674-15523-8) HUP.

— Harmony in Tonal Music, 2 vols. LC 81-12350. (C). 1982. student ed 8.00 (0-685-07494-3, KnopfC) Knopf.

— Harmony in Tonal Music, 2 vols., Vol. 1: Diatonic Practices. LC 81-12350. (C). 1982. Vol. 1, Diatonic Practices. text ed. 19.95 (0-394-32196-0, KnopfC) Knopf.

— Harmony in Tonal Music, 2 vols., Vol. 2: Chromatic Practices. LC 81-12350. (C). 1982. Vol. 2, Chromatic Practices. student ed 7.95 (0-685-07493-5, KnopfC) Knopf.

Lester, John & Spoerri, Pierre. Rediscovering Freedom. (Illus.). 149p. (Orig.). 1992. pap. 12.95 (0-685-65122-3) Grosvenor USA.

Lester, John A. Conrad & Religion. LC 87-14377. 240p. 1988. text ed. 39.95 (0-312-00979-8) St Martin.

— Journey Through Despair, 1880-1914: Transformations in British Literary Culture. LC 68-15767. 235p. reprint ed. pap. 67.00 (0-685-07754-3, 2016021) Bks Demand.

Lester, John C. Ku Klux Klan: Its Origin, Growth, & Disbandment. (History - United States Ser.). 198p. 1992. reprint ed. lib. bdg. 69.00 (0-7812-6204-6) Rprt Serv.

Lester, John R. Frontline Airline: Troop Carrier Pilot in World War II. (Illus.). 192p. 1994. pap. text ed. 17.95 (0-89745-179-1) Sunflower U Pr.

Lester, Judith L., jt. auth. see Lester, Andrew D.

Lester, Judy, jt. auth. see Lester, Jim.

Lester, Juliette N., jt. auth. see Hoyt, Kenneth B.

Lester, Julius. And All Our Wounds Forgiven. 256p. 1994. 19.95 (1-55970-258-3) Arcade Pub Inc.

— Black Folktales. 1991. pap. 9.95 (0-8021-3242-1) Grove-Atltic.

— Do Lord Remember Me. (Illus.). 224p. 1995. pap. text ed. 11.95 (1-55970-322-9) Arcade Pub Inc.

— How Many Spots Does a Leopard Have? (J). (gr. 4-7). 1994. pap. 5.95 (0-590-41972-2) Scholastic Inc.

— How Many Spots Does a Leopard Have? & Other Tales. (Illus.). (J). (gr. 2-6). 1989. pap. 15.95 (0-590-41973-0) Scholastic Inc.

— John Henry. LC 93-34583. (Illus.). 40p. (J). (ps-3). 1994. 16.99 (0-8037-1606-0); lib. bdg. 16.89 (0-8037-1607-9) Dial Bks Young.

— The Knee-High Man & Other Tales. LC 72-181785. (Pied Piper Bks.). (Illus.). 32p. (J). (ps-3). 1985. pap. 3.95 (0-8037-0234-5, 0383-120, Puff Pied Piper) Puffin Bks.

— Long Journey Home. 160p. (gr. 7 up). 1988. reprint ed. pap. 3.50 (0-590-41433-X, Point) Scholastic Inc.

— Long Journey Home: Stories from Black History. LC 75-181791. 160p. (J). (gr. 6 up). 1985. 14.99 (0-8037-4953-8) Dial Bks Young.

— Lovesong: Becoming a Jew. (Illus.). 256p. 1995. reprint ed. 11.95 (1-55970-316-4) Arcade Pub Inc.

— The Man Who Knew Too Much: A Moral Tale from the Baila of Zambia. LC 94-40810. (Illus.). (J). (gr. 4 up). 1994. 14.95 (0-395-60521-0, Clarion Bks) HM.

— Othello: A Retelling. LC 94-12833. (J). 1995. 12.95 (0-590-41967-6) Scholastic Inc.

— This Strange New Feeling. 164p. (YA). (gr. 7 up). 1985. pap. 2.75 (0-590-44047-0) Scholastic Inc.

— To Be a Slave. LC 68-28738. (Illus.). (J). (gr. 7-12). 1968. 15.99 (0-8037-8955-6) Dial Bks Young.

— To Be a Slave. (J). 1986. pap. 3.25 (0-590-42460-2) Scholastic Inc.

Lester, Julius & Seeger, Pete. Folksinger's Guide to the Twelve-String Guitar As Played by Leadbelly. (Illus.). 80p. 1965. pap. 12.95 (0-8256-0023-5, OK61440, Oak) Music Sales.

Lester, June, ed. Libraries & Information Services Today: The Yearly Chronicle 1991. (Illus.). 310p. (C). 1991. pap. text ed. 25.00 (0-8389-0566-8) ALA.

Lester, K. AS400 Security, Audit & Control. 140p. 1993. 261.00 (1-85617-182-5) Elsevier.

Lester, Kent. The Complete Guide to Being Your Own Remodeling Contractor. LC 94-15295. (Illus.). 288p. (Orig.). 1994. pap. 18.99 (1-55870-337-3) Betterway Bks.

Lester, Kent, jt. auth. see McGuerty, David L.

Lester, L. & Benning, B. Procurement in the Process Industry. 258p. 1989. 400.00 (0-685-39931-1, Inst Pur & Supply) St Mut.

Lester, Lane P. & Bohlin, Raymond G. The Natural Limits to Biological Change. 2nd ed. LC 89-70041. (Illus.). 207p. 1989. reprint ed. pap. 12.99 (0-945241-06-2) Probe Bks.

Lester, Leon. Clarinet Duets, Vol. 3. Date not set. pap. 7.95 (0-685-69011-3, Chester Music) Music Sales.

Lester, Marion, jt. auth. see Hughes, Elizabeth.

Lester, Mark, ed. Technology Transfer in Export Processing Zones the Semiconductor Industry in Malaysia. (Contemporary Studies in Economic & Financial Analysis: Vol. 47). 1989. 73.25 (0-89232-429-5) Jai Pr.

Lester, Mark, tr. see Deleuze, Gilles.

Lester, Mark, jt. auth. see Elder, Dana C.

Lester, Mark, jt. ed. see Germidis, Dimitri.

Lester, Mary. Hand Me That Corkscrew, Bacchus. LC 73-82326. 160p. 1973. 15.00 (0-87832-007-5) Piper.

— A Woman's Guide to Starting a Small Business. LC 80-24298. 32p. 1989. pap. 3.95 (0-87576-093-7) Pilot Bks.

Lester, Meera. Writing for the Ethnic Markets. 272p. (Orig.). 1991. pap. 14.95 (0-9622592-4-1) Writers Connection.

Lester, Michael, intro. Innovation & Economics in Building Conference. (Illus.). 236p. (Orig.). 1991. pap. 72.00 (0-85825-536-7) Accents Pubns.

Lester, Nancy B. & Onore, Cynthia S. Learning Change: One School District Meets Language Across the Curriculum. 220p. 1990. pap. text ed. 17.50 (0-86709-254-8, 0254) Boynton Cook Pubs.

Lester, Neal A. Ntozake Shange: A Critical Study of the Plays. LC 94-36113. (Critical Studies in Black Life & Culture: Vol. 21). 336p. 1994. 49.00 (0-8153-0314-9, H1441) Garland.

Lester, Patricia, ed. see Oklahoma Department of Libraries Staff.

***Lester, Patrick D., ed.** The Biographical Directory of Native American Painters. LC 95-69012. 704p. 1995. 49.95 (0-8061-9936-9) U of Okla Pr.

— The Biographical Directory of Native American Painters. limited ed. LC 95-69012. 704p. 1995. 245.00 (0-9640706-3-4) U of Okla Pr.

Lester, Paul. Photojournalism: An Ethical Approach. 224p. (C). 1991. text ed. 49.95 (0-8058-0671-7); pap. 24.95 (0-8058-0672-5); student ed, disk 17.95 (1-56321-081-9); student ed, disk 17.95 (1-56321-082-7); student ed, disk 17.95 (1-56321-084-3) L Erlbaum Assocs.

Lester, Paul M. Visual Communication: Images with Messages. LC 94-19173. 450p. 1995. pap. 31.95 (0-534-19530-X) Intl Thomson.

Lester, Paula E., jt. auth. see Bishop, Lloyd.

L

***Lester, Peter F.** Aviation Weather. LC 95-7862. 1995. write for info. (0-88487-178-9) Jeppesen Sanderson.
— Turbulence: A New Perspective for Pilots. LC 93-13133. 1993. write for info. (0-88487-141-X) Jeppesen Sanderson.
Lester, R. G., ed. Information Sources in Finance & Banking. 550p. 1995. 95.00 (1-85739-037-7) Bowker-Saur.
Lester, Ralph P. Look to the East. 13.00 (0-685-19484-1) Powner.
Lester, Richard A. As Unions Mature: An Analysis of the Evolution of American Unionism. 1958. pap. 11.95x (0-691-02800-1) Princeton U Pr.
— As Unions Mature: An Analysis of the Evolution of American Unionism. LC 58-10048. reprint ed. pap. 52.20 (0-7837-9373-1, 2060117) Bks Demand.
— Labor Arbitration in State & Local Government: An Examination of Experience in Eight States & New York City. 1984p. pap. 10.00 (0-318-20241-7) PU Indust Rel.
— Manpower Planning in a Free Society. LC 66-14890. 241p. reprint ed. pap. 68.70 (0-8357-8945-4, 2033398) Bks Demand.
— Monetary Experiments: Early American & Recent Scandinavian. LC 70-75796. (Reprints of Economic Classics Ser.). (Illus.). xvii, 316p. 1970. reprint ed. 39.50 (0-678-05547-5) Kelley.
Lester, Richard K., jt. auth. see Willrich, Mason.
Lester, Robert C. Buddhism. LC 86-43010. (Illus.). 144p. 1987. pap. 11.00 (0-06-065243-8) Harper SF.
— Theravada Buddhism in Southeast Asia. LC 71-185154. 1973. 15.95 (0-472-06184-4) U of Mich Pr.
***Lester, Robert M. & Dente-Cassidy, Marie.** Intravenous Medications for Critical Care. 2nd ed. LC 95-3557. 304p. 1995. pap. text ed. write for info. (0-7216-4887-8) Saunders.
***Lester, Robin.** Stagg's University: The Rise, Decline & Fall of Big-Time Football at The University of Chicago. LC 94-34018. (Sports & Society Ser.). 1995. write for info. (0-252-02128-2) U of Ill Pr.
***Lester, Robin & Lester, Helen.** Wuzzy Takes Off. LC 95-10694. (Gund Children's Library). (Illus.). (J). 1995. write for info. (1-56402-498-9) Candlewick Pr.
Lester, Robin, jt. auth. see Lester, Helen.
Lester-Smith, L. H., ed. The Universal Flame. 263p. 1975. 9.95 (0-8356-7506-8) Theos Pub Hse.
Lester, Thomas, jt. auth. see Gehrmann, James.
***Lester, V. Markham.** Victorian Insolvency: Bankruptcy, Imprisonment for Debt, & Company Winding-up in Nineteenth-Century England. (Oxford Historical Monographs). (Illus.). 368p. 1995. 65.00 (0-19-820518-X) OUP.
***Lester, Valerie.** Fasten Your Seat Belts! History & Heroism in the Pan Am Cabin. (Illus.). 304p. 1995. 30.00 (0-9626483-8-8) Paladwr Pr.
Lester, W. A., Jr., et al. Lecture Notes on Theoretical Chemistry. 436p. (C). 1994. text ed. 74.00 (981-02-0321-7); pap. text ed. 36.00 (981-02-0322-5) World Scientific Pub.
Lester, Will. Are You up There, Mister Jesus? Jones, M. L., ed. 134p. (Orig.). (J). 1992. pap. 5.95 (1-882270-00-2) Old Rugged Cross.
Lester, William, tr. see Scupoli, Dom L.
Lesterson, David. The Regal Beagle. Hoffman, Beverly et al, eds. LC 93-70504. (Illus.). 29p. (J). (gr. 3). Date not set. write for info. (0-9634122-3-X) Feather Fables.
***Lesthaeghe, Ron J.** The Decline of Belgian Fertility, 1800-1970. LC 77-71991. reprint ed. pap. 79.80 (0-7837-9374-X, 2060118) Bks Demand.
— The Decline of Belgian Fertility, 1870-1970. LC 77-71991. (Office of Population Research Ser.). 1978. 47.50x (0-691-05253-0) Princeton U Pr.
Lesthaeghe, Ron J., ed. Reproduction & Social Organization in Sub-Saharan Africa. 1989. 72.00 (0-520-06363-5) U CA Pr.
Lesthaeghe, Ron J., jt. ed. see Page, Hilary.
Lesti, Paul, et al. Structured Settlements. 2nd ed. LC 86-80969. 1993. 135.00 (0-685-59909-4) Clark Boardman Callaghan.
Lestienne, Remy. The Children of Time: Causality, Entropy, Becoming. Neher, E. C., tr. LC 94-20269. Date not set. write for info. (0-252-01959-8); pap. write for info. (0-252-06427-5) U of Ill Pr.
Lestourgeon, Diana E. Rosamond Lehmann. LC 64-8331. (Twayne's English Authors Ser.). 157p. (C). 1965. lib. bdg. 17.95 (0-8290-1723-2) Irvington.
L'Estrange, Francis L. Random Talks with the Living Christ. 107p. 1988. 30.00 (0-7223-2038-8, Pub. by A H S Ltd UK) St Mut.
LeStrange, Guy. Baghdad During the Abbasid Caliphate: From Contemporary Arabic & Persian Sources. LC 82-25143. xxxi, 381p. 1983. reprint ed. text ed. 99.75 (0-313-23198-2, LEBC, Greenwood Pr) Greenwood.
LeStrange, H. LeStrange Records: A Chronicle of the Early LeStranges of Norfolk, England, & the March of Wales, 1100-1310. (Illus.). 407p. 1993. reprint ed. lib. bdg. 71.00 (0-8328-3701-6); reprint ed. pap. 61.00 (0-8328-3702-4) Higginson Bk Co.
L'Estrange, Hamon. Alliance of Divine Offices. LC 71-172316. (Library of Anglo-Catholic Theology: No. 12). reprint ed. 27.50 (0-404-52104-5) AMS Pr.
L'Estrange, Michael G. The Internationalization of Japan's Security Policy: Challenges & Dilemmas for a Reluctant Power. LC 89-86034. (Policy Papers in International Affairs Ser.: No. 36). 52p. 1990. pap. 5.95 (0-87725-536-9) U of Cal IAS.
L'Estrange, Roger. Citt & Bumpkin: In a Dialogue over a Pot of Ale, Governing Matters of Religion & Government. LC 92-24280. (Augustan Reprints Ser.: No. 117 (1965)). reprint ed. 12.00 (0-404-70117-5, PR3541) AMS Pr.
— Selections from the Observator. LC 92-24819. (Augustan Reprints Ser.: No. 141 (1970)). reprint ed. 12.00 (0-404-70141-8, DA452) AMS Pr.
L'Estrange, Roger, tr. see Aesop.
L'Estrange, Roger, tr. see Quevedo y Villegas, Francisco G. de.
***Lestringant, Frank.** Mapping the Renaissance World: The Geographical Imagination in the Age of Discovery. (New Historicism: Studies in Cultural Poetics). 1994. 38.00 (0-520-08871-9) U CA Pr.
Lesueur, jt. auth. see Jean-Philippe.
LeSueur, Annette. Timeless Treasure: The Art of Stephen Gjertson. LC 93-70682. (Illus.). 64p. (Orig.). 1993. pap. 29.95 (0-9636180-0-8) AS Class Realism.
Lesueur, Jean F. Ossian, Ou les Bardes. Salome, Theodore, ed. (Chefs-d'oeuvre classiques de l'opera francaise Ser.: Vol. 15). (Illus.). 508p. (FRE.). 1970. reprint ed. pap. 45.00 (0-8450-1115-4) Broude.
LeSueur, Joe, ed. Homage to Frank O'Hara. 3rd rev. ed. (Illus.). 224p. 1988. pap. 12.00 (0-929844-12-2) Big Sky Bolinas.
LeSueur, Meridel. North Star Country. LC 84-7485. (Bison Book Ser.: No. BB-886). 351p. reprint ed. pap. 100.10 (0-7837-6184-8, 2045906) Bks Demand.
LeSueur, Meridel, jt. intro. see Darrow, Clarence.
LeSueur, Stephen C. The Eighteen Thirty-Eight Mormon War in Missouri. LC 86-16090. (Illus.). 296p. 1990. pap. 14.95 (0-8262-0729-4) U of Mo Pr.
Lesure, Francois, ed. see Debussy, Claude.
Lesure, Thomas B. All about Arizona. 13th rev. ed. (Illus.). 193p. 1983. pap. text ed. 5.95 (0-686-46671-3) Allsport Pub.
— All the Southwest. 2nd ed. (Illus.). 364p. 4.95 (0-686-63832-8) Allsport Pub.
Lesurf, J. C. Millimetre-Wave Optics, Devices & Systems. (Illus.). 268p. 1990. 101.00 (0-85274-129-4) IOP Pub.
***Lesurf, James C.** Information & Measurement. LC 94-46915. 1995. write for info. (0-7503-0308-5) IOP Pub.
Lesurf, James C., ed. Selected Papers on Gaussian Beam Mode Optics for Millimeter Wave & Terahertz Systems. LC 92-31312. (Milestone Ser.: Vol. 68). 1992. write for info. (0-8194-1061-6); pap. write for info. (0-8194-1060-8) SPIE.
Lesy, Michael. The Forbidden Zone. 253p. 1989. mass mkt. 7.95 (0-385-26034-2, Anchor NY) Doubleday.
— Rescues: The Lives of Heroes. 1991. 18.95 (0-374-24947-4) FS&G.
— Wisconsin Death Trip. 1991. pap. 16.95 (0-385-41215-0, Anchor NY) Doubleday.
Lesyk, Susan J. The Blue Book: Achieving Success on Essay Exams. 160p. (C). 1991. pap. text ed. 13.95 (0-8403-7087-3) Kendall-Hunt.
Leszcynski, W., jt. ed. see Lisinska, G.
Leszcz, Molyn. Treating the Elderly with Psychotherapy. Sadavoy, Joel, ed. LC 86-10487. 390p. 1987. 50.00 (0-8236-6647-6, BN-06647) Intl Univs Pr.
Leszczyc, Trishna, jt. auth. see Price, Ardin C.
Leszkiewicz, Ted. To the Top Without a Glass. LC 86-50264. 180p. (Orig.). 1986. pap. 7.95 (0-938287-00-1) Warren Bk Pub.
Leszner, Eva M. Assisi Embroidery. (Illus.). 1988. 13.50 (0-7134-5595-0) Branford.
***Letac, G.** Exercises & Solutions Manual for Integration & Probability. 152p. 1995. pap. 29.00 (0-387-94421-4) Spr-Verlag.
Letardi, T., ed. Excimer Lasers & Applications. 1990. 42.00 (0-8194-0325-3, VOL. 1278) SPIE.
Letardi, T., jt. auth. see Laude, L. D.
Letarouilly, Paul. Letarouilly on Renaissance Rome: An American Student Edition. abr. ed. Bayley, John B., ed. (Classical America Series in Art & Architecture). (Illus.). xiv, 160p. 1984. pap. text ed. 14.95 (0-8038-9250-0) Archit CT.
Letarouilly, Paul M. Edifices de Rome Moderne. (Illus.). 368p. (C). 1983. 65.00 (0-910413-00-2) Princeton Arch.
Letavet, A. A. & Kurlyandskaya, E. B. Toxicology of Radioactive Substances, Vol. 3: Iron-59. LC 61-9783. 1967. 88.00 (0-08-011705-8, Pub. by Pergamon Repr UK) Franklin.
Letch, Rachael. Special People. LC 90-48944. (Who Cares Ser.). (J). (gr. 4 up). 1990. 7.95 (0-85953-360-3); pap. 3.95 (0-85953-350-6) Childs Play.
Letch, Ralph A. Myths of the Atonement. 1985. 25.00 (0-7223-1657-7, Pub. by A H S Ltd UK) St Mut.
Letcher, Gary. Canoeing the Delaware: A Guide to the River & Shore. (Illus.). 170p. 1985. pap. 10.95 (0-8135-1077-5) Rutgers U Pr.
Letcher, Owen. The Gold Mines of Southern Africa: The History Technology & Statistics of the Gold Industry, Vol. 18. LC 74-353. (Illus.). 580p. 1974. reprint ed. 47.95 (0-405-05915-9) Ayer.
***Letchford, Frank & Naylor, A. R.** From the Inferno to Zos III: Michaelangelo in a Teacup: The Intimate Life of Austin Osman Spare. Naylor, A. R., ed. (Illus.). 1995. 125.00 (1-55818-327-2) Holmes Pub.
Letchikov, A. V. Localization of One-Dimensional Random Walks in Random Environment, Vol. 8. (SSR SEC Mathematical Physics Review Ser.: Vol. 8, No. 3). 50p. 1989. pap. text ed. 65.00 (3-7186-4866-0) Gordon & Breach.
Letchworth, L. Tom. Superlove Says. LC 77-71488. 168p. 1977. pap. 4.00 (0-9602334-0-7) Superlove.
Letchworth, William P. Homes of Homeless Children: Report on Orphan Asylums & Institutions for Care of Children, Vol. 4. LC 74-1693. (Children & Youth Ser.). 632p. 1974. reprint ed. 50.95 (0-405-05969-8) Ayer.
Letelier, P. S., Jr., jt. auth. see Rodrigues, W. A.
Letellier, ed. Real Time Signal Processing, No. X. 259p. 1987. 51.00 (0-89252-862-1, 827) SPIE.
Letellier, J. P., ed. Real-Time Signal Processing XI. 333p. 1988. 51.00 (0-8194-0012-2, VOL. 0977) SPIE.
— Real-Time Signal Processing XII. 314p. 1989. 53.00 (0-8194-0190-0, VOL. 1154) SPIE.
***Letellier, Joel, et al.** Word & Spirit No. 16: The Monastery & the City. (Word & Spirit Ser.). 160p. (Orig.). 1994. pap. write for info. (1-879007-10-X) St Bedes Pubns.
Letellier, Patrick, jt. auth. see Island, David.
Letellier, Phyllis M. Cooking with Cream--the Versatile Ingredient. LC 83-90266. (Illus.). 76p. (Orig.). 1983. pap. 4.00 (0-9611138-4-7) P M Letellier.
***Letellier, Robert.** Sir Walter Scott & the Gothic Novel. LC 94-38897. (Salzburg University Studies Ser.). 236p. 1994. text ed. 89.95 (0-7734-1276-X) E Mellen.
***Letellier, Robert I.** Day in Mamre, Night in Sodom: Abraham & Lot in Genesis 18 & 19. LC 94-47520. (Biblical Interpretation Ser.: Vol. 10). 1995. write for info. (90-04-10250-7) E J Brill.
LeTendre, Gerald K., jt. ed. see Rohlen, Thomas P.
LeTendre, Joseph & Haller, Evan, eds. Heat: Gay Erotic Fiction from the American Southwest. 176p. (Orig.). 1990. pap. 11.00 (0-938743-04-X) Lavender CT.
Letendre, Joseph L. Preparing for Confession. 1987. pap. 1.95 (0-937032-52-2) Light&Life Pub Co MN.
Letessier, Fernand, ed. see De Chateaubriand, Francois-Rene.
Letessier, Fernand, jt. auth. see De Chateaubriand, Rene.
Letessier, Fernand, ed. see De Lamartine, Alphonse.
***Letessier, Jean, et al, eds.** Hot Hadronic Matter: Theory & Experiment. (NATO ASI Series B, Physics: Vol. 346). 570p. 1995. 145.00 (0-306-45008-9) Plenum.
Leteurtre, J. & Quere, Y. Irradiation Effects in Fissile Materials. (Defects in Crystalline Solids Ser.: Vol. 6). 1972. 25.75 (0-444-10382-1, North Holland) Elsevier.
Leth, Kathryn B., ed. see Pervan, Anthony S.
Leth, Kathy, ed. see Quitko, Betsy, et al.
Leth, Kathy, ed. see Spies, Joseph R.
Lethaby, William. Architecture, Mysticism & Myth. 1995. pap. 12.95 (1-873616-05-8, Pub. by Solos UK) Atrium Pubs.
Lethaby, William R. Londinium: Architecture & the Crafts. LC 72-83273. (Illus.). 1972. reprint ed. 18.95 (0-405-08743-8) Ayer.
— Mediaeval Art: From the Peace of the Church to the Eve of the Renaissance, 312-1350. LC 70-157345. (Select Bibliographies Reprint Ser.). 1977. reprint ed. 30.95 (0-8369-5806-3) Ayer.
— Silverwork & Jewelry Handbook of Nineteen Hundred Three. (Illus.). 343p. 1988. reprint ed. pap. 25.00 (0-87556-362-7) Saifer.
— Westminster Abbey & the King's Craftsmen. LC 69-13243. (Illus.). 1972. reprint ed. 27.95 (0-405-08745-4, Pub. by Blom Pubns UK) Ayer.
— Westminster Abbey Re-Examined. LC 69-13244. (Illus.). 1972. reprint ed. 27.95 (0-405-08744-6, Pub. by Blom Pubns UK) Ayer.
Letham, D. S., jt. ed. see Stewart, P. R.
Letham, Robert. The Work of Christ. LC 93-19207. (Contours of Christian Theology Ser.). 288p. (Orig.). 1993. pap. 14.99 (0-8308-1532-5, 1532) InterVarsity.
Lethbride, T. Prominent Indians of Victorian Age: A Biographical Dictionary. 600p. 1986. 120.00 (0-317-61975-6, Pub. by Archives Pubs II) St Mut.
Lethbridge. First Presbyterian Church of Flint, Michigan, 1987. (Illus.). 100p. 1987. 19.95 (0-917231-08-2) Ferguson Comns Pubs.
Lethbridge, Alice. Genesee: Through the Years: An Illustrated History. 144p. 1985. 22.95 (0-89781-161-5) Preferred Mktg.
— Well Do I Remember. (Illus.). 1976. 3.00 (0-916536-01-7) Berwyn-London.
Lethbridge, David. Mind in the World: The Marxist Psychology of Self-Actualization. LC 91-37124. (Studies in Marxism: Vol. 26). 186p. 1992. 39.95 (0-930656-61-X); pap. 19.95 (0-930656-62-8) MEP Pubns.
Lethbridge, David G., ed. Government & Industry Relationships: The Lubbock Memorial Lectures, 1975. LC 75-38968. 200p. 1976. 90.00 (0-08-019733-7, Pub. by Pergamon Repr UK); pap. 90.00 (0-08-019732-9, Pub. by Pergamon Repr UK) Franklin.
***Lethbridge, David G & Ng Sek Hong.** The Business Environment in Hong Kong. (Illus.). 288p. 1995. 55.00 (0-19-585163-3); pap. 24.00 (0-19-586533-2) OUP.
Lethbridge, Henry J. All about Shanghai: A Basic Guidebook. (Oxford in Asia Paperbacks Ser.). (Illus.). 264p. 1986. pap. 8.95 (0-19-581594-7) OUP.
Lethbridge, Robert & Keefe, Terry, eds. Zola & the Craft of Fiction. 240p. 1990. text ed. 49.00 (0-7185-1312-6, Pub. by Pinter Pubs UK) St Martin.
— Zola & the Craft of FIction. 188p. 1993. pap. 14.95 (1-85567-166-2, Pub. by Pinter Pubs UK) St Martin.
Lethbridge, Robert, jt. ed. see Collier, Peter.
Lethbridge, Robert, ed. see Zola, Emile.
Lethbridge, Thomas C. Coastwise Craft: The Development of the Sailing Vessel. 1977. lib. bdg. 75.00 (0-8490-1639-8) Gordon Pr.
— Herdsmen & Hermits: Celtic Seafarers in the Northern Seas. 1950. 49.50 (0-317-07648-5) Elliots Bks.
— Herdsmen & Hermits: Celtic Seafarers in the Northern Seas. 1977. lib. bdg. 59.95 (0-8490-1941-9) Gordon Pr.
— Witches. LC 68-28449. (Illus.). 1969. reprint ed. 5.95 (0-8065-0221-5, Citadel Pr); reprint ed. pap. 2.45 (0-685-08138-9, Citadel Pr) Carol Pub Group.
Lethcoe, Athena. Valiant Lancer of Prince William Sound. 12p. 1987. 5.95 (0-9613146-7-2) Prince W Sound.
Lethcoe, Jim. Cruising Guide to Prince William Sound, Alaska, 2 vols., Set, Vols. 1 & 2. (Orig.). 1986. Set. 41.90 (0-9613146-4-8) Prince W Sound.
— An Observer's Guide to the Geology of Prince William Sound. (Illus.). 190p. (Orig.). 1989. pap. 19.95 (1-877900-00-1) Prince W Sound.
Lethcoe, Jim & Lethcoe, Nancy. Cruising Guide to Prince William Sound: Western Part, Vol. 1. LC 84-60075. (Illus.). 194p. (Orig.). 1984. pap. 19.95 (0-9613146-0-5); ring bd. 19.95 (0-9613146-1-3) Prince W Sound.
— Cruising Guide to Prince William Sound, Alaska: Eastern Part, Vol. 2. (Illus.). 194p. (Orig.). 1985. pap. 21.95 (0-9613146-2-1); ring bd. 21.95 (0-9613146-3-X) Prince W Sound.
Lethcoe, Jim & Lethcoe, Nancy, eds. A Brief History of Prince William Sound, Alaska. (Illus.). 80p. (Orig.). 1992. pap. 8.95 (0-9613146-5-6) Prince W Sound.
Lethcoe, Nancy & Nurnberger, Lisa, eds. Prince William Sound Environmental Reader, 1989: Exxon Valdez Oil Spill. (Illus.). 118p. (Orig.). 1989. pap. write for info. (0-9613146-9-9) Prince W Sound.
Lethcoe, Nancy, jt. auth. see Lethcoe, Jim.
Lethcoe, Nancy, jt. ed. see Lethcoe, Jim.
***Letheby.** A Bird Finding Guide to Alaska. (Illus.). 152p. (Orig.). 1994. pap. 14.95 (0-9637765-9-2) Cinclus Pubns.
Lethem, Christopher J. Police Detention: A Practical Guide to Advising the Suspect. (Waterlow Procedure Notes Ser.). (Illus.). 208p. 1991. pap. 33.90 (0-685-48858-6, Waterlow) Macmillan.
— A Practical Guide to Arrest & Detention. (Waterlow Procedure Notes Ser.). 128p. 1991. pap. 33.90 (0-08-036919-7, Waterlow) Macmillan.
***Lethem, Jonathan.** Amnesia Moon. LC 95-4127. 256p. 1995. 20.00 (0-15-100091-3) HarBrace.
— Gun, with Occasional Music. LC 93-4864. 1994. 19.95 (0-15-136458-3) HarBrace.
— Gun, with Occasional Music. 272p. 1995. pap. 10.95 (0-312-85878-7) Tor Bks.
Letheren, Carole A. & Mathieu, Richard. Marketing Healthcare. (Illus.). 250p. (C). 1991. text ed. 29.95 (1-878487-32-9) Practice Mgmt Info.
Letherman, K. M. Automatic Controls for Heating & Air Conditioning: Principles & Applications. LC 80-42155. (International Series on Heating, Ventilation & Refrigeration: Vol. 15). (Illus.). 235p. 1981. 106.00 (0-08-023222-1, Pub. by Pergamon Repr UK) Franklin.
Letiche, H. K., et al, eds. The Practitioner's Power of Choice in Staff-Development & Inservice Training. 176p. 1991. 26.00 (90-265-1124-8, Pub. by Swets Pub Serv NE) Taylor & Francis.
Letiche, Hugo K. Learning & Hatred for Meaning. 263p. (Orig.). 1984. pap. 33.00x (90-272-2016-6) Benjamins North Am.
Letiche, John M. Balance of Payments & Economic Growth. LC 66-21681. (Reprints of Economic Classics Ser.). (Illus.). 1967. reprint ed. 39.50 (0-678-00267-3) Kelley.
Letis, Theodore P. Martin Luther & Charismatic Ecumenism. (Orig.). 1979. pap. 1.95 (0-936592-00-1) Inst Ref Bibl Studies.
Letis, Theodore P., intro. Majority Text: Essays & Reviews in the Continuing Debate. 210p. (Orig.). (C). 1987. pap. 8.95 (0-944355-00-5) IBTS.
Letko, Ken, ed. see College of the Redwoods, Del Norte Staff.
Letley, Emma, ed. Travels with a Donkey in the Cevennes & Selected Travel Writings. (World's Classics Ser.). 304p. 1993. pap. 9.95 (0-19-282629-8) OUP.
Letley, Emma, ed. see Stevenson, Robert Louis.
Letman, Sloan T. Issues in Criminal Justice. 171p. (C). 1993. pap. text ed. 25.00 (1-884028-03-9) SL Pubs.
— Legal Issues in Criminal Justice: The Courts. 249p. 1984. pap. 12.95 (0-317-11217-1); boxed 22.95 (0-317-13010-2) Pilgrimage Inc.
— Urban Alcoholism. 104p. (C). 1993. pap. text ed. 25.00 (1-884028-00-4) SL Pubs.
***Letman, Sloan T., ed.** Criminal Justice at the Crossroads. 195p. (Orig.). (C). 1994. pap. text ed. 20.00 (1-884028-09-8) SL Pubs.
— International Issues in Criminal Justice. 100p. (Orig.). (C). 1994. pap. text ed. 20.00 (1-884028-07-1) SL Pubs.
***Letman, Sloan T. & May, Melvyn.** Critical Issues in Juvenile Delinquency Vol. II. 75p. (Orig.). (C). 1994. pap. text ed. 20.00 (1-884028-06-3) SL Pubs.
***Letman, Sloan T. & Tromanhauser, Edward.** Critical Issues in Juvenile Delinquency Vol. 1. 75p. (Orig.). (C). 1994. pap. text ed. 20.00 (1-884028-05-5) SL Pubs.
Letman, Sloan T., jt. auth. see Edwards, Dan W.
Letnanova, Elena. Piano Interpretations of the Seventeenth, Eighteenth & Nineteenth Centuries: A Study of Theory & Practice Using Original Documents. LC 91-52596. 196p. 1991. lib. bdg. 35.00x (0-89950-616-X) McFarland & Co.
Letner, Kenneth L., jt. auth. see Percy, Walker.
Letner, Ruth, ed. see Flora, Bittina R.
Leto, M. J. & Bode, W. K. Larder Chef: Food Preparation & Presentation. 3rd ed. 272p. 1989. pap. 26.95 (0-434-91133-X) Buttrwrth-Heinemann.
Letokhov, V. S. IR Multiple Photon. Joussot-Dubien, J. et al, eds. (Laser Chemistry Ser.: Vol. 8 Nos. 2-4). 179p. 1988. text ed. 229.00 (3-7186-4847-4) Gordon & Breach.
— Laser Photoionization Spectroscopy. 1987. text ed. 92.00 (0-12-444320-6) Acad Pr.
— Laser Picosecond Spectroscopy & Photochemistry of Biomolecules. (Optics & Optoelectronics Ser.). (Illus.). 328p. 1987. 141.00 (0-85274-469-2) IOP Pub.
— Lasers in Atomic, Molecular & Nuclear Physics: Proceedings of the Third International School on Laser Applications in Atomic, Molecular & Nuclear Physics, August 27-September 4, 1984, Vilnius, U. S. S. R. 622p. 1986. text ed. 250.00 (3-7186-0348-9) Gordon & Breach.
— Nonlinear Laser Chemistry: Multiple-Photon Excitation. (Chemical Physics Ser.: Vol. 22). (Illus.). 417p. 1983. 63.00 (0-387-11705-9) Spr-Verlag.

Letokhov, V. S., ed. Laser Analytical Spectrochemistry. (Optics & Optoelectronics Ser.). (Illus.). 424p. 1986. 168.00 (*0-85274-568-0*) IOP Pub.
— Laser Spectroscopy of Highly Vibrationally Excited Molecules. (Illus.). 396p. 1989. 166.00 (*0-85274-217-7*) IOP Pub.
Letokhov, V. S. & Chebotayev, V. P. Nonlinear Laser Spectroscopy. (Optical Science Ser.: Vol. 4). (Illus.). 1977. 46.00 (*0-387-08044-9*) Spr-Verlag.
Letokhov, V. S. & Ustinov, N. D., eds. Power Lasers & Their Applications. 136p. 1983. text ed. 106.00 (*3-7186-0166-4*) Gordon & Breach.
Letokhov, V. S. & Zharov, V. P. Laser Optoacoustic Spectroscopy. (Optical Sciences Ser.: Vol. 37). (Illus.). 345p. 1986. text ed. 105.00 (*0-387-11795-4*) Spr-Verlag.
Letokhov, V. S., ed. see Borshch, A. A., et al.
Letokhov, V. S., jt. ed. see Feld, M. S.
Letokhov, V. S., ed. see Khmanov, S. A., et al.
Letokhov, V. S., jt. auth. see Minogin, V. G.
Letokhov, V. S., ed. see Otten, E. W.
Letokhov, V. S., ed. see Rudolph, W. & Wilhelmi, B.
Letonturier, P. Mini Medical Encyclopedia: Mini-Encyclopedie Medicale. 8th ed. 416p. (FRE.). 1984. 25.00 (*0-8288-1816-9*, M8935) Fr & Eur.
Letoublon, F., ed. La Langue et les Textes en Grec Ancien: Actes Du Colloque Pierre Chantraine (Grenoble, 5-8 Septembre 1989) 369p. 1993. pap. 83.00 (*90-5063-066-9*, Pub. by Gieben NE) Benjamins North Am.
Letoublon, Francoise. Les Lieux Communs du Roman: Stereotypes Grecs d'Aventure & d'Amour. (Mnemosyne Ser.: Supplement 123). (Illus.). 248p. (FRE.). 1993. 65.75 (*90-04-09724-4*) E J Brill.
Letourneau. Manteniendo el Equilibrio en un Mundo: Keeping Your Cool in a World of. (SPA.). 4.95 (*0-317-04296-3*, 220569, Pub. by Edit Clie SP) TSELF.
Letourneau, Deborah K., jt. ed. see Barbosa, Pedro.
Letourneau, Gene. America's New Wolf. (Illus.). 116p. 1984. pap. 8.95 (*0-930096-34-7*) G Gannett.
— Midger, My Favorite Hunting Dog. 1987. pap. 7.95 (*0-930096-86-X*) G Gannett.
Letourneau, Janis G. Radiology in Organ Transplantation. 184p. 1990. 119.00 (*0-8151-5372-4*, Yr Bk Med Pubs) Mosby Yr Bk.
Letourneau, P. Hart-Parr: Photo Archive. 1994. pap. 24.95 (*1-882256-08-5*) Iconografix.
Letourneau, P. A. John Deere Model "B" Photo Archive: The "Unstyled" & "Styled" Model "B" (Photo Archive Ser.). (Illus.). 144p. 1992. pap. 24.95 (*1-882256-01-8*) Iconografix.
— John Deere Model "D" Photo Archive: The "Unstyled" Model "D", 1923-1938. (Photo Archive Ser.). (Illus.). 144p. 1992. pap. 24.95 (*1-882256-00-X*) Iconografix.
— Oliver Tractor: Photo Archive. (Illus.). 1994. pap. 24.95 (*1-882256-09-3*) Iconografix.
***Letourneau, P. A., ed.** Case Tractors: 1912-1959 Photo Archive. (Photo Archive Ser.). (Illus.). 144p. 1995. pap. 24.95 (*1-882256-28-X*) Iconografix.
— Caterpillar Military Tractors: The Vital Edge of Victory. LC 94-76266. (Photo Archive Ser.: Vol. 1). (Illus.). 144p. 1994. pap. 24.95 (*1-882256-16-6*) Iconografix.
— Caterpillar Military Tractors: Workpower on the Side of Victory. LC 94-76266. (Photo Archive Ser.). (Illus.). 144p. 1994. pap. 24.95 (*1-882256-17-4*) Iconografix.
— Caterpillar Sixty Photo Archive. (Photo Archive Ser.). (Illus.). 144p. 1993. pap. 24.95 (*1-882256-05-0*) Iconografix.
— Caterpillar Thirty Photo Archive. (Photo Archive Ser.). (Illus.). 144p. 1993. pap. 24.95 (*1-882256-04-2*) Iconografix.
— Dodge Trucks 1948-1961 Photo Archive. (Photo Archive Ser.). (Illus.). 128p. 1995. pap. 24.95 (*1-882256-37-9*) Iconografix.
— Farmall F Series Photo Archive: The Models F-12, F-14, F-20 & F-30. (Photo Archive Ser.). (Illus.). 144p. 1993. pap. 24.95 (*1-882256-02-6*) Iconografix.
— Farmall Model H Photo Archive. (Photo Archive Ser.). (Illus.). 1993. pap. 24.95 (*1-882256-03-4*) Iconografix.
— Farmall Model M Photo Archive. (Photo Archive Ser.). (Illus.). 144p. 1994. pap. 24.95 (*1-882256-15-8*) Iconografix.
— Farmall Regular Photo Archive. (Photo Archive Ser.). (Illus.). 144p. 1994. pap. 24.95 (*1-882256-14-X*) Iconografix.
— Fordson: 1917-1928 Photo Archive. (Photo Archive Ser.). (Illus.). 144p. 1995. pap. 24.95 (*1-882256-29-8*) Iconografix.
— Holt Tractors Photo Archive: An Album of Steam & Early Gas Tractors. LC 93-80439. (Photo Archive Ser.). (Illus.). 144p. 1993. pap. text ed. 24.95 (*1-882256-10-7*) Iconografix.
— Imperial 1955-1963 Photo Archive. (Photo Archive Ser.). (Illus.). 144p. 1994. pap. 24.95 (*1-882256-22-0*) Iconografix.
— Imperial 1964-1968 Photo Archive. (Photo Archive Ser.). (Illus.). 144p. 1994. pap. 24.95 (*1-882256-23-9*) Iconografix.
— John Deere Model A Photo Archive. (Photo Archive Ser.). (Illus.). 144p. 1994. pap. 24.95 (*1-882256-12-3*) Iconografix.
— John Deere Thirty Series Photo Archive. (Photo Archive Ser.). (Illus.). 144p. 1994. pap. 24.95 (*1-882256-13-1*) Iconografix.
— Minneapolis-Moline U Series Photo Archive. LC 93-79371. (Photo Archive Ser.). (Illus.). 144p. 1993. pap. text ed. 24.95 (*1-882256-07-7*) Iconografix.
— Russell Graders Photo Archive. LC 93-80438. (Photo Archive Ser.). (Illus.). 144p. 1993. pap. text ed. 24.95 (*1-882256-11-5*) Iconografix.
— Twin City Tractor Photo Archive, Vol. I. LC 93-79372. (Photo Archive Ser.). (Illus.). 144p. 1993. pap. 24.95 (*1-882256-06-9*) Iconografix.
Letourneau, Paul C., et al. The Nerve Growth Cone. 558p. 1991. 104.00 (*0-88167-816-3*) Raven.
Letourneau, Peter. Illustrated Case Tractor Buyer's Guide. (Illus.). 1993. pap. 16.95 (*0-87938-784-X*) Motorbooks Intl.
— John Deere Limited Production & Experimental Tractors. (Illus.). 160p. 1994. pap. 19.95 (*0-87938-951-6*) Motorbooks Intl.
Letourneau, Peter A. John Deere General Purpose Tractors, 1928-1953: History of the Model GP, A, B, G & H. LC 92-38246. (MBI Ser.). (Illus.). 192p. 1993. pap. 19.95 (*0-87938-723-8*) Motorbooks Intl.
LeTourneau, R. G. Mover of Men & Mountains. LC 60-8319. 1967. reprint ed. pap. 5.99 (*0-8024-3818-0*) Moody.
LeTourneau, Richard H. Democracy in Trouble: There's Only One Way Back to Greatness. LC 85-91035. (LeTourneau One-Way Ser.: Vol. 5). (Illus.). 138p. (Orig.). 1985. pap. 5.95 (*0-935899-01-4*) LeTourneau Pr.
— Finding Your Niche in Life: There's Only One Way to Live Especially When Your Father Is R. G. LeTourneau. LC 85-91033. (LeTourneau One-Way Ser.: Vol. 8). 317p. (Orig.). 1985. pap. 6.95 (*0-935899-04-9*) LeTourneau Pr.
— Latch Key: Keys to Learning about the Computer Habitat. LC 86-90140. (LeTourneau One-Way Ser.: Vol. 11). 333p. (Orig.). 1986. pap. 8.95 (*0-935899-07-3*) LeTourneau Pr.
— Laws of Success for Christians: There's Only One-Way to Success Both for Today & Forever. LC 85-91034. (LeTourneau One-Way Ser.: Vol. 7). 130p. (Orig.). 1985. pap. 5.95 (*0-935899-03-0*) LeTourneau Pr.
— More Than Knowledge: There's Only One Way to Get Education Back on Track. LC 85-91036. (LeTourneau One-Way Ser.: Vol. 6). (Illus.). 79p. (Orig.). 1985. pap. 4.95 (*0-935899-02-2*) LeTourneau Pr.
— Success Without Compromise: There's Only One Way to Succeed & Be Happy. 2nd ed. LC 77-80947. (LeTourneau One-Way Ser.: Vol. 4). 176p. 1985. reprint ed. pap. 5.95 (*0-88207-757-0*) LeTourneau Pr.
LeTourneau, Richard H., jt. ed. see Dick, Louise L.
LeTourneau, Tom. Lighting Techniques for Video Production. LC 86-27224. 172p. 1987. 45.00 (*0-86729-129-X*); student ed, pap. 27.95 (*0-86729-130-3*) Knowledge Indus.
Letournel, E. & Judet, R. Fracture to the Acetabulum. (Illus.). 420p. 1981. 175.00 (*0-387-09875-5*) Spr-Verlag.
— Fractures of the Acetabulum. 2nd enl. rev. ed. Elson, Reginald A., ed. & tr. by. LC 92-48836. 1994. 198.00 (*0-387-52189-5*) Spr-Verlag.
Letourneux, A., jt. auth. see Hanoteau, A.
Letouzey & Ane. Dictionnaire D'Archeologie Chretienne et De Liturgie, 28 vols. (FRE.). 1903. write for info. (*0-7859-0497-2*, 2706301562) Fr & Eur.
***Letouzey, J., ed.** Petroleum & Tectonics in Mobile Belts: 4th IFP Exploration & Production Research Conference, Bordeux, 1988. (Illus.). 224p. (C). 1990. text ed. 74.00 (*2-7108-0579-0*) Technip.
Letov, A. M. Stability in Nonlinear Control Systems. 1961. 55.00x (*0-691-08040-2*) Princeton U Pr.
LeTraunik. MVS-XA JCL: A Practical Approach. 320p. (C). 1990. pap. write for info. (*0-675-20916-1*, Merrill Pub Co) Macmillan.
Letrouneux, J. & Vinet, L. Quantum Groups, Integrable Models & Statistical Systems. 300p. 1993. text ed. 95.00 (*981-02-1555-X*) World Scientific Pub.
***Let's Go, Inc., Staff.** The Unofficial Guide to Life at Harvard. 327p. 1995. pap. 7.95 (*0-9634820-0-9*) Harvard Student Agencies Inc.
Letschert, U. Zum Mineralstoffhaushalt Einiger Chenopodiaceae bei Hohen Boruns Salzangeboten: Freilandstudiens in den Suedwestlichen U. S. A. und Kulturversuche mit Atriplex Halimus L. und Hortensis L. (Dissertationes Botanicae Ser.: Vol. 96). (Illus.). 244p. (GER.). 1986. pap. 64.00 (*3-443-64008-7*) Lubrecht & Cramer.
Letsinger-Miller, Lyn. The Artists of Brown County. LC 93-48931. 1994. 49.95 (*0-253-33354-7*) Ind U Pr.
***Letson, Douglas & Higgins, Michael.** The Jesuit Mystique. LC 95-20288. (Illus.). 288p. (C). 1995. 22.95 (*0-8294-0865-7*) Humanities.
Letson, Vivian I. The Heart is Highland: A True Story of Scots in Early Wyoming. (Illus.). 144p. (Orig.). 1991. pap. 9.95 (*0-9630487-3-2*) V I Letson.
Lett, James. The Human Enterprise: A Critical Introduction to Anthropological Theory. 178p. (C). 1987. pap. text ed. 20.95 (*0-8133-0422-9*) Westview.
Lett, John, et al. Reflejos: An Intermediate Reader for Communication. 2nd ed. 226p. (SPA.). (C). 1983. pap. text ed. 27.00 (*0-03-061346-9*) HB Coll Pubs.
Lett, John T. & Altman, Kurt I., eds. Advances in Radiation Biology, Vol. 15: Relative Radiation Sensitivities of Human Organ Systems, Pt. III. (Illus.). 328p. 1992. text ed. 125.00 (*0-12-035415-2*) Acad Pr.
Lett, John T. & Sinclair, Warren K., eds. Advances in Radiation Biology, Vol. 17: DNA & Chromatin Damage Caused by Radiation. (Illus.). 507p. 1993. text ed. 130.00 (*0-12-035417-9*) Acad Pr.
Lett, John T., jt. ed. see Altman, Kurt I.
Lett, John T., et al, eds. Advances in Radiation Biology, Vol. 13. (Serial Publication Ser.). 414p. 1987. text ed. 158.00 (*0-12-035413-6*) Acad Pr.
— Advances in Radiation Biology: Relative Radiation Sensitivities of Human Organ Systems, Vol. 18, Pt. IV. (Illus.). 232p. 1994. text ed. 110.00 (*0-12-035418-7*) Acad Pr.
— Advances in Radiation Biology Vol. 18: Relative Radiation Sensitivities of Human Organ Systems, Pt. IV. (Illus.). 232p. 1994. boxed 110.00 (*0-12-034518-8*) Acad Pr.
— Advances in Radiation Biology, Vol. 16: Effects of Low Dose & Low Dose Rate Radiation. (Illus.). 336p. 1992. text ed. 105.00 (*0-12-035416-0*) Acad Pr.
Lett, Monica. Rent Control: Concepts, Realities, & Mechanisms. 294p. 1976. boxed 17.95 (*0-87855-152-2*) Transaction Pubs.
Lett, Z. Anaesthesia. 400p. (C). 1983. pap. text ed. 69.00 (*962-209-048-6*, Pub. by Hong Kong U Pr HK) St Mut.
***Letta, Elisabetta M.** Pontormo-Rosso Fiorentino. Brierly, Anthony, tr. (Library of Great Masters). (Illus.). 80p. (Orig.). 1995. pap. 12.99 (*1-878351-48-6*) Riverside NY.
Letta, G. & Pratelli, M., eds. Probability & Analysis. (Lecture Notes in Mathematics Ser.: Vol. 1206). viii, 283p. 1986. pap. 43.80 (*0-387-16787-0*) Spr-Verlag.
Lettau, J., tr. see Lehman, Urich, et al.
Lettenmaier, Dennis P., jt. ed. see Cassidy, John J.
Letteri, J. M., ed. Schreiner Festschrift, George E. Journal: Mineral & Electrolyte Metabolism, Vol. 13, No. 6, 1987. (Illus.). vi, 118p. 1987. pap. 64.00 (*3-8055-4651-3*) S Karger.
Letteris, Meir H. Dibre Shir(Poems) Literaria Judaica No. 41. reprint ed. 49.50 (*0-404-13862-4*) AMS Pr.
Letteris, Meir H., ed. & tr. Megillat Esther: The Story of Esther. 1979. pap. 0.95 (*0-88482-583-3*) Hebrew Pub.
Letterman, David. Late Night Top Ten Lists. 1994. mass mkt. 5.99 (*0-671-51143-2*) PB.
— New Late Night Top Ten Lists. 1994. mass mkt. 5.99 (*0-671-51144-0*) PB.
Letterman, David, jt. auth. see Late Night with David Letterman Writers Staff.
Letterman, G. Gregory. Letterman's Law of Private International Business, 3 vols., Set. annuals rev. ed. LC 89-64180. (International Business & Law Ser.). 1990. 375.00 (*0-685-59810-1*) Clark Boardman Callaghan.
***Letterman, Gregory.** Letterman's Guide to International Business, 4 vols., Set. 2nd ed. (International Sr.). 1995. ring bd. write for info. (*0-614-06269-1*) Clark Boardman Callaghan.
Letterman, Jonathan & Clements, Bennett A. Medical Recollections of the Army of Potomac with Memoir of Jonathan Letterman. rev. ed. Archer, Edgar G., ed. (Illus.). 250p. 1991. reprint ed. write for info. (*1-877791-01-6*) Bohemian Brigade.
Letterman, Raymond D. Filtration Strategies to Meet the Surface Water Treatment Rule. 184p. 1991. pap. 31.50 (*0-89867-554-5*, 20268) Am Water Wks Assn.
Lettieri, Carol, tr. see Dib, Mohammad.
Lettieri, Carol, tr. see Spaziani, Maria L.
Lettieri, Dan J., ed. Drugs & Suicide: When Other Coping Strategies Fail. LC 78-50826. (Sage Annual Reviews of Drug & Alcohol Abuse Ser.: No. 2). (Illus.). 303p. reprint ed. pap. 86.40 (*0-8357-8448-7*, 2034712) Bks Demand.
Lettieri, Dan J., pref. Research Strategies in Alcoholism Treatment Assessment. LC 88-7212. (Drugs & Society Ser.: Vol. 2, No. 2). (Illus.). 123p. 1989. text ed. 29.95 (*0-86656-782-8*) Haworth Pr.
Lettieri, Dan J., jt. auth. see Neuringer, Charles.
Lettieri, Michael, jt. auth. see Bancheri, Salvatore.
***Lettieri, Robert A. & Stern, Judith.** QuickTime Starter Kit. (Illus.). 208p. (Orig.). 1995. pap. text ed. 24.00 (*1-56830-129-4*) Hayden.
Lettieri, Ronald J. Connecticut's Young Man of the Revolution: Oliver Ellsworth. LC 78-74735. write for info. (*0-918676-16-9*) Conn Hist Com.
Lettin, A. W., jt. auth. see Donell, S. T.
Lettinck, P. Aristotle's Physics & Its Reception in the Arabic World: With An Edition of the Unpublished Parts of Ibn Bajja's Commentary on the Physics. LC 93-46583. (Aristoteles Semitico-Latinus Ser.: Vol. 7). 1994. 171.50 (*90-04-09960-3*) E J Brill.
Lettinck, Paul, tr. see Philoponus & Simplicius.
Lettinga, Gatze, jt. auth. see Van Haandel, Adrianus C.
Lettinga, Virginia. Children's Bulletin Clip-Art Book. (REPRObooks Ser.). (Illus.). 272p. (Orig.). 1994. pap. 14.99 (*0-8010-5689-6*) Baker Bk.
Lettington, A. & Steed, J. W., eds. Thin Film Diamonds. LC 93-33950. 1993. write for info. (*0-412-49630-5*, Chap & Hall NY) Chapman & Hall.
Lettington, A. H. Infrared Technology & Applications (Sira, Jun 1990, London), Vol. 1320. 1990. 70.00 (*0-8194-0381-4*) SPIE.
Lettington, A. H., ed. International Meeting on Optical Systems for Space & Defense. 640p. 1990. 92.00 (*0-8194-0227-3*, VOL. 1191) SPIE.
Lettis, Richard. The Dickens Aesthetic. LC 87-45808. (Studies in the Nineteenth Century: No. 6). 1989. 37.50 (*0-404-61486-8*) AMS Pr.
— Dickens on Literature: A Continuing Study of His Aesthetic. LC 89-45850. (Studies in the Nineteenth Century: No. 8). 1990. 42.50 (*0-404-61488-4*) AMS Pr.
Lettner, Margot, jt. auth. see Ames, Janet.
Letton, Frances, jt. auth. see Letton, Jennette.
Letton, Francis, jt. auth. see Letton, Jennette.
Letton, Jennette. The Robsart Affair. 268p. 1976. reprint ed. lib. bdg. 19.95 (*0-89244-015-5*, Queens House) Amereon Ltd.
Letton, Jennette & Letton, Frances. The Young Elizabeth. 1976. reprint ed. lib. bdg. 21.95 (*0-89244-014-7*) Queens Hse-Focus Serv.
Letton, Jennette & Letton, Francis. The Robsart Affair. reprint ed. lib. bdg. 20.95 (*0-89190-237-6*, Rivercity Pr) Amereon Ltd.
— The Young Elizabeth. 1955. pap. 4.75 (*0-8222-1290-0*) Dramatists Play.
Lettow, Lucille J., jt. auth. see Harmes, Jeanne M.
***Letts, Barry.** The Ghosts of N-Space. (Privho Ser.). (Illus.). Date not set. pap. 5.95 (*0-426-20434-4*, London Bridge) Genl Dist Srvs.
***Letts, Billie.** Where the Heart Is. LC 94-43079. 368p. 1995. 17.95 (*0-446-51972-3*) Warner Bks.
— Where the Heart Is. 1996. pap. write for info. (*0-446-67221-1*) Warner Bks.
Letts, Malcolm. Sir John Mandeville: The Man & His Book. LC 70-161957. 192p. 1949. reprint ed. 25.00 (*0-403-01318-6*) Scholarly.
Letts, Malcolm, ed. Francis Mortoft: His Book, Being His Travels Through France & Italy in 1658-1659. (Hakluyt Society Works Ser.: No. 2, Vol. 57). 1969. reprint ed. 32.00 (*0-8115-0360-7*) Periodicals Srv.
— The Pilgrimage of Arnold Von Harff, Knight, 1496 to 1499. (Hakluyt Society Works Ser.: No. 2 ,Vol. 94). 1974. reprint ed. 52.00 (*0-8115-0390-9*) Periodicals Srv.
***Letts, Malcolm, ed. & tr.** Travels & Adventures of Pero Tafur (1435-149) (Curzon Travellers Ser.). (C). 1995. text ed. 70.00 (*0-7007-0348-9*, Pub. by Curzon Pr UK) Humanities.
Letts, Marceil F. & Quinlan, Beverly A. An Heirloom Book of the Nativity. Golden, Marcia, ed. (Heirloom Book Ser.). (Illus.). 80p. 1989. 24.95 (*0-685-26593-5*) Heirloom NJ.
Letts, Penny. Managing Other People's Money. (C). 1989. 35.00 (*0-86242-090-3*, Pub. by Age Concern Eng UK) St Mut.
Letts, R. Mervyn. Principles of Seating the Disabled. (Illus.). 384p. 1991. 105.00 (*0-8493-6021-8*, RD757) CRC Pr.
Letts, Robert M., ed. Management of Pediatric Fractures. (Illus.). 1296p. 1993. text ed. 250.00 (*0-443-08860-8*) Churchill.
Letts, Rosa M. The Renaissance. (Cambridge Introduction to Art Ser.). (C). 1981. pap. 11.95 (*0-521-29957-8*) Cambridge U Pr.
Letts, Vanessa. New York: Cadogan City Guides. 2nd ed. (Cadogan City Guides Ser.). (Illus.). 352p. (Orig.). 1993. pap. 14.95 (*1-56440-006-9*) Globe Pequot.
Lettunich, Janice, jt. auth. see Klug, Gary.
Lettvin, Maggie. Maggie's Back Book: Healing the Hurt in Your Lower Back. (Illus.). 1977. pap. 11.95 (*0-395-25147-8*) HM.
Letvin, Alice. Sacrifice in Surrealist Novel: The Impact of Early Theories of Primitive Religion on the Depiction of Violence in Modern Fiction. LC 90-23039. (Studies in Comparative Literature). 350p. 1991. reprint ed. 20.00 (*0-8240-5473-3*) Garland.
Letvin, N. L. & Desrosiers, R. C., eds. Simian Immuno-Deficiency Virus. (Currents Topics in Microbiology & Immunology Ser.: Vol. 188). (Illus.). 250p. 1994. 123.00 (*0-387-57274-0*) Spr-Verlag.
***Letwenko, Ed, illus.** Joshua & the Walls of Jericho. (Pencil Fun Bks.). 18p. (J). (ps-2). 1995. 0.89 (*0-7814-0189-5*) Chariot Family.
Letwin. Evidence Law: Commentary, Problems & Cases. 1986. write for info. (*0-8205-0141-7*, 255); teacher ed write for info. (*0-8205-0142-5*) Bender.
— Evidence Law: Commentary, Problems & Cases. suppl. ed. 1988. Supplement 1988. write for info. (*0-8205-0143-3*) Bender.
Letwin, Shirley R. The Anatomy of Thatcherism. 377p. (C). 1993. text ed. 32.95 (*1-56000-106-2*) Transaction Pubs.
— The Gentlemen in Trollope: Individuality & Moral Conduct. LC 81-6252. 315p. 1982. 34.50 (*0-674-34755-2*) HUP.
Letwin, Shirley R., ed. see Oakeshott, Michael.
Letwin, William. Law & Economic Policy in America: The Evolution of the Sherman Antitrust Act. LC 81-7551. xii, 304p. 1981. pap. text ed. 9.95 (*0-226-47353-8*) U Ch Pr.
— Law & Economic Policy in America: The Evolution of the Sherman Antitrust Act. LC 80-21868. xi, 304p. 1980. reprint ed. text ed. 35.00 (*0-313-22651-2*, LELE, Greenwood Pr) Greenwood.
— The Origins of Scientific Economics. LC 75-8721. 316p. 1975. reprint ed. text ed. 59.75 (*0-8371-8038-4*, LEOS, Greenwood Pr) Greenwood.
Letyagin, V. P., et al. Modern Approaches to the Treatment of Initial Stages of Breast Cancer, Vol. 3. (Soviet Medical Reviews Ser.: Vol. 3). 76p. 1989. pap. text ed. 54.00 (*3-7186-4912-8*) Gordon & Breach.
Letz, Hans. Music for Violin & Viola. 107p. 1993. reprint ed. lib. bdg. 69.00 (*0-7812-9690-0*) Rprt Serv.
Letzter, E. S., jt. auth. see Goodearl, K. R.
Leu, jt. auth. see Kau.
Leu, Donald J. Effective Reading Instruction: K-8. 2nd ed. 640p. (C). 1991. write for info. (*0-675-21264-2*, Merrill Pub Co) Macmillan.
***Leu, Donald J., Jr. & Kinzer, Charles K.** Effective Reading Instruction, K - 8. 3rd ed. 1995. write for info. (*0-02-370065-3*, Merrill Pub Co) Macmillan.
***Leu, George E.** A Hoghead's Random Railroad Reminiscences. 1995. 16.95 (*0-533-11331-8*) Vantage.
Leu, H. J., ed. Ruettner, J. R. Festschrift. (Journal: Experimental Cell Biology: Vol. 56, No. 4, 1988). (Illus.). 60p. 1988. pap. 32.00 (*3-8055-4923-7*) S Karger.
Leuba, James H. Psychological Study of Religion: Its Origin, Function, & Future. LC 75-98628. reprint ed. 49.50 (*0-404-03969-3*) AMS Pr.
Leubben, Craig. Knots for Climbers. (How to Rock Climb Ser.). (Illus.). 40p. (Orig.). 1993. pap. 4.95 (*0-934641-58-7*) Chockstone Pr.
***Leubbermann, Mimi.** Easy Orchids: Simple Secrets for Glorious Gardens, Indoors & Out. LC 95-15159. (Illus.). 1996. pap. write for info. (*0-8118-1033-X*) Chronicle Bks.
Leube, Kurt R., ed. The Essence of Friedman. 550p. 1987. 44.95 (*0-8179-8661-8*, P-366); pap. 24.95 (*0-8179-8662-6*) Hoover Inst Pr.
Leube, Kurt R. & Moore, Thomas G., eds. The Essence of Stigler. (Publication Ser.: No. 346). 377p. (C). 1986. text ed. 34.95 (*0-8179-8461-5*); pap. text ed. 15.95 (*0-8179-8462-3*) Hoover Inst Pr.
Leube, Kurt R., ed. see Bartley, W. W., III, et al.
Leube, Kurt R., jt. ed. see Nishiyama, Chiaki.

An Asterisk (*) at the beginning of an entry indicates that the title is appearing in BIP for the first time.

Leubuscher, Fred C., jt. auth. see Post, Louis F.
Leucht, Dagmar, jt. auth. see Leucht, Wolfgang.
Leucht, Wolfgang & Leucht, Dagmar. Teaching Atlas of Breast Ultrasound. (Illus.). 232p. 1991. text ed. 89.00 (0-86577-415-3) Thieme Med Pubs.
***Leuchtenburg, William E.** The FDR Years: On Roosevelt & His Legacy. LC 95-13282. 1995. write for info. (0-231-08298-3) Col U Pr.
— Flood Control Politics: The Connecticut River Valley Problem, 1927-1950. LC 73-38834. (FDR & the Era of the New Deal Ser.). (Illus.). 1972. reprint ed. lib. bdg. 39.50 (0-306-70446-3) Da Capo.
— Franklin D. Roosevelt & the New Deal 1932-1940. LC 63-12053. (New American Nation Ser.). 1963. pap. text ed. 14.00 (0-06-133025-6, TB3025, Torch) HarpC.
— In the Shadow of FDR: From Harry Truman to Bill Clinton. rev. ed. LC 92-54825. 408p. 1993. pap. 16.95x (0-8014-8123-6) Cornell U Pr.
— The Nineteen Eighty-Four Election in Historical Perspective. LC 86-72071. (Charles Edmondson Historical Lectures). 43p. (Orig.). 1986. pap. 4.50 (0-918954-45-2) Baylor Univ Pr.
— The Perils of Prosperity, 1914-1932. LC 92-44912. (Chicago History of American Civilization Ser.). 325p. (C). 1993. pap. text ed. 10.95 (0-226-47371-6) U Ch Pr.
— The Perils of Prosperity, 1914-1932. 2nd ed. LC 92-44912. (Chicago History of American Civilization Ser.). 325p. (C). 1993. lib. bdg. 29.95 (0-226-47370-8) U Ch Pr.
— The Supreme Court Reborn: Constitutional Revolution in the Age of Roosevelt. 352p. 1995. text ed. 30.00 (0-19-508613-9) OUP.
— A Troubled Feast. (C). 1987. pap. text ed. 15.00 (0-673-39343-7) HarpCollege.
Leuchtenburg, William E., ed. Political Parties. LC 76-54572. (Great Contemporary Issues Ser.). 1977. lib. bdg. 27.95 (0-405-09866-9) Ayer.
Leuchtenburg, William E., ed. see Anderson, David L.
Leuchtenburg, William E., ed. see Billings-Yun, Melanie.
Leuchtenburg, William E., ed. see Tucker, Nancy B.
Leuchter, Fred. Leuchter Report. 67p. 1989. pap. 15.00 (1-872197-00-0) Inst Hist Rev.
Leuchtmann, Horst. Polygot Dictionary of Musical Terms. 2nd ed. 805p. (ENG, FRE, GER, ITA, POL, RUS & SPA.). 1980. 195.00 (0-8288-2186-0, M9436) Fr & Eur.
— Woeterbuch Musik: Dictionary of Terms in Music. 3rd ed. 560p. (ENG, FRE & GER.). 1981. 125.00 (0-8288-2174-7, M6911) Fr & Eur.
Leuchtmann, Horst, ed. Dictionary of Terms in Music. 4th ed. 411p. (ENG & GER.). 1992. pap. 55.00 (3-598-10913-X) K G Saur.
Leuci, Bob. Captain Butterfly. 240p. 1987. 16.95 (0-317-58348-4) Freundlich.
— Doyle's Disciples. 272p. 1984. 14.95 (0-88191-006-6) Freundlich.
— Odessa Beach. LC 85-20716. 240p. 1985. 15.95 (0-88191-029-5) Freundlich.
***Leuci, Robert.** Fence Jumpers. 352p. 1995. 22.95 (0-312-13073-2, Pub. by Thomas Dunne Bks) St Martin.
Leuci, Susana, tr. see Lewis, Zoe.
Leuck, Laura. Night Is Calling. LC 93-22837. (Illus.). (J). 1994. pap. 15.00 (0-671-86940-X, S&S Bks Young Read) S&S Childrens.
Leucocyte Culture Conference Staff. Leucocyte Culture Conference: Proceedings, 4th, 1969, Hanover. McIntyre, O. Ross, ed. LC 69-19545. 607p. reprint ed. pap. 173.00 (0-685-15788-1, 2026302) Bks Demand.
***Leuder, Andreas.** Historie und Dogmatik: Ein Beitrag zur Genese und Entfaltung von Johann Salomo Semlers Verstaendnis des Alten Testaments. (Beihefte zur Zeitschrift fuer die Alttestamentliche Wissenschaft Ser.: No. 233). x, 259p. (GER.). (C). 1995. lib. bdg. 121.55 (3-11-014627-4) De Gruyter.
Leue, A. E., jt. auth. see Brandt, P. A.
Leue, Mary M. The Flying Bird Brings the Message: Lessons from My Life As Metaphor. (Orig.). 1993. pap. 12.95 (1-878115-06-5) Dwn-To-Erth Bks.
— India Journal - Pilgrimage Toward the Self. (Illus.). 190p. (Orig.). 1993. pap. 12.95 (1-878115-08-1) Dwn-To-Erth Bks.
— Jessica Dragonette's Fiery Breath: A Fable for Little Girls Who Love Their Daddies. 2nd ed. (Illus.). 46p. (J). (gr. k-6). 1993. reprint ed. pap. 9.95 (1-878115-00-6) Dwn-To-Erth Bks.
— Looking for One's Shadow at Noon: Finding the Self in School & Community, Vol 2. 116p. (Orig.). 1993. pap. 7.95 (1-878115-02-2) Dwn-To-Erth Bks.
— Looking for One's Shadow at Noon: Looking for the Self in Family & Society, Vol. 1. 1993. pap. 7.95 (1-878115-03-0) Dwn-To-Erth Bks.
— Rushing to Eva: A Pilgrimage in Search of the Great Brother. 3rd ed. (Illus.). 337p. reprint ed. pap. 12.95 (1-878115-04-9) Dwn-To-Erth Bks.
Leue, Mary M., ed. Challenging the Giant: The Best of EKORE, the Journal of Alternative Education. (Illus.). 488p. 1992. pap. 12.95 (1-878115-05-7) Dwn-To-Erth Bks.
— Challenging the Giant, Vol. II: The Best of Ekone, the Journal of Alternative Education. (Illus.). 500p. (Orig.). 1994. pap. text ed. 12.95 (1-878115-09-X) Dwn-To-Erth Bks.
Leue, Mary M., ed. see Free School Community Members.
Leuenberger, Beat E. Pereskia (Cactaceae) LC 86-28483. (Memoirs Ser.: Vol. 41). (Illus.). 142p. 1986. pap. text ed. 25.00 (0-89327-307-4) NY Botanical.
Leuenberger, Samuel. Archbishop Cranmer's Immortal Bequest: The Book of Common Prayer of the Church of England: An Evangelistic Liturgy. 400p. (Orig.). (C). 1990. pap. 24.99 (0-8028-0474-8) Eerdmans.
Leuenberger, Theodor & Weinstein, Martin E., eds. Europe, Japan, & America in the 1990s: Cooperation & Competition. LC 92-36244. (Europe-Asia-Pacific Studies in Economy & Technology). vi, 289p. 1992. 109.00 (0-387-55856-X) Spr-Verlag.
Leuenberger, Theodor, et al, eds. From Technology Transfer to Technology Management in China. (Europe-Asia-Pacific Studies in Economy & Technology). (Illus.). viii, 283p. 1990. 71.00 (0-387-52478-9) Spr-Verlag.
Leuenthal, Stan, ed. see Gilgun, John.
***Leuhrmann, Arthur & Peckham, Herbert.** Hands-On ClarisWorks: Mac Version 2.0. 1993. teacher ed 36.95 (0-941681-64-5) Computer Lit Pr.
Leuilliot, B., ed. Anthologie de la Poesie Francaise du XIX Siecle, de Chateaubriand a Baudelaire. (Poesie Ser.). (FRE.). pap. 18.95 (2-07-032258-0) Schoenhof.
***Leukart, Hank.** The Doom Hacker's Guide. 256p. 1995. cd-rom, pap. 21.95 (1-55828-428-1) MIS Press.
Leukefeld, C. G., et al. AIDS & Intravenous Drug Use: Community Intervention & Prevention. 300p. 1990. 37.00 (1-56032-141-5) Hemisp Pub.
Leukefeld, Carl & Tims, Frank M., eds. Compulsory Treatment of Drug Abuse: Research & Clinical Practice. (DHHS Publication ADM Series National Institute on Drug Abuse Research Monograph, Ser. 86: No. 88-1578). (Illus.). 264p. 1988. pap. 7.50 (0-16-002486-2, S/N 017-024-01352-8) USGPO.
***Leukefeld, Carl G. & Clayton, Richard R., eds.** Prevention Practice in Substance Abuse. (Drugs & Society Ser.: Vol. 8, No. 3 & 4). 141p. 1995. text ed. 19.95 (0-614-05609-8) Haworth Pr.
Leukefeld, Carl G. & Fimbres, Manuel, eds. Responding to AIDS: Psychosocial Initiatives. LC 87-15211. 95p. 1987. 12.95 (0-87101-148-4) Natl Assn Soc Wkrs.
Leukefeld, Carl G., jt. ed. see Vourlekis, Betsy S.
***Leukefeld, Carl G., et al, eds.** Prevention Practice in Substance Abuse. LC 95-13748. (Drugs & Society Ser.: Vol. 8, No. 3 & 4). 141p. 1995. 34.95 (1-56024-734-7) Haworth Pr.
Leukefeld, Karl G., jt. auth. see Ries, Joanne B.
Leukroth, K. Glossary for International Conferences. 3rd ed. 174p. (DAN, DUT, ENG, FRE, GER, ITA & SPA.). 1984. pap. 24.95 (0-8288-1508-9, F137200) Fr & Eur.
Leuner, Hanscarl, et al. Guided Affective Imagery with Children & Adolescents. LC 83-8050. (Emotions, Personality, & Psychotherapy Ser.). 208p. 1983. 55.00 (0-306-41232-2, Plenum Pr) Plenum.
Leuner, Jean D., et al. Mastering the Nursing Process: A Case Method Approach. LC 89-71523. (Illus.). 494p. (Orig.). (C). 1990. pap. text ed. 26.95 (0-8036-5588-6) Davis Co.
LeUnes, Arnold & Nation, Jack. Sport Psychology. 477p. 1989. 39.95 (0-8304-1139-9); write for info. (0-8304-1231-X) Nelson-Hall.
Leung. Development Land & Development Charge in Singapore. 1987. 74.00 (0-409-99537-1) Butterworth Legal Pubs.
Leung, jt. ed. see Szefler.
Leung, A. Y. Dynamic Stiffness & Substructures. LC 93-15461. 1993. 169.00 (0-387-19807-5) Spr-Verlag.
Leung, A. Y., jt. auth. see Cheung, Y. K.
***Leung, Albert Y.** Better Health with (Mostly) Chinese Herbs & Foods. (Illus.). 128p. 1994. pap. 9.95 (0-9634979-1-X) AYSL.
— Chinese Healing Foods & Herbs. Orig. Title: Chinese Herbal Remedies. (Illus.). 192p. reprint ed. pap. 10.95 (0-9634979-0-1) AYSL.
***Leung, Albert Y. & Foster, Steven.** Encyclopedia of Common Natural Ingredients used in Food, Drugs & Cosmetics. 2nd ed. LC 94-49668. 1995. text ed. 120.00 (0-471-50826-8) Wiley.
Leung, Beatrice. Sino-Vatican Relations: Problems in Conflicting Authority, 1976-1986. (London School of Economics Monographs in International Studies). (Illus.). 384p. (C). 1992. 79.95 (0-521-38173-8) Cambridge U Pr.
Leung, Benjamin K., jt. ed. see Pearson, Veronica.
***Leung, C. F., et al, eds.** Centrifuge 94: Proceedings of the International Conference Singapore, 31 August - 2 September 1994. (Illus.). 854p. (C). 1994. text ed. 115.00 (90-5410-352-3, Pub. by A A Balkema NE) Ashgate Pub Co.
Leung, C. K. & Ginsburg, Norton, eds. China: Urbanization & National Development. LC 80-29142. (Research Papers Ser.: No. 196). 283p. 1980. pap. 12.00 (0-89065-103-5) U Chicago Comm Geo.
Leung, Chi-Keung. China: Railway Patterns & National Goals. LC 80-17030. (Research Papers Ser.: No. 195). (Illus.). 233p. 1980. pap. 10.00 (0-89065-102-7) U Chicago Comm Geo.
— China: Railway Patterns & National Goals. LC 80-17030. (University of Chicago, Department of Geography, Research Paper Ser.: No. 195). (Illus.). 263p. reprint ed. pap. 75.00 (0-8357-3723-3, 2036445) Bks Demand.
Leung Chuen Chau. Hong Kong: A Unique Case of Development. LC 93-31250. (Lessons of East Asia Ser.). 48p. 1993. 6.95 (0-8213-2613-9, 12613) World Bank.
Leung, Debbie. Self Defense: The Womanly Art of Self-Care, Intuition & Choice. LC 91-61404. (Illus.). 176p. 1991. pap. 12.95 (0-929838-08-4) R & M Pr WA.
Leung, Donald. New Directions in the Clinical Use of Intravenous Immunoglobulin, Vol. I. (Illus.). 60p. 1989. write for info. (0-318-65779-1) Health Dimensions.
Leung, Donald, et al. Infectious Diseases: Beyond Antibiotics. Meyers, Burt, ed. (C). Date not set. pap. text ed. write for info. (1-878294-07-5) Health Dimensions.
Leung, Edwin P., ed. Historical Dictionary of Revolutionary China, 1839-1976. LC 91-15990. 576p. 1992. text ed. 85.00 (0-313-26457-0, LHD, Greenwood Pr) Greenwood.
Leung, H. F. Distributed Constraint Logic Programming. 350p. 1993. text ed. 74.00 (981-02-1456-1) World Scientific Pub.
Leung, H. M., jt. auth. see Thoburn, John T.
Leung, John, tr. see Dawson, David.
Leung, John, jt. ed. see Kau, Michael Y.
Leung, John K., jt. ed. see Kau, Michael Y.
Leung, K. C. Critical Observations Versus Physical Models for Close Binary Systems: Proceedings of the Colloquium in Beijing, China, Nov, 1985. 500p. 1988. text ed. 164.00 (0-677-22070-7) Gordon & Breach.
Leung, K. C. & Nha, I. S., eds. New Frontiers in Binary Research. (ASP Conference Series Publications: Vol. 38). 471p. 1993. 40.00 (0-937707-57-0) Astron Soc Pacific.
Leung, K. S., jt. auth. see Yam, Y.
Leung, K. S., et al. Biodegradable Implants in Fracture Fixation: Proceedings of the ISFR Symposium. 308p. 1994. text ed. 86.00 (981-02-1796-X) World Scientific Pub.
Leung, K. T. Linear Algebra & Geometry. 318p. (C). 1974. pap. text ed. 24.00 (0-85656-111-8, Pub. by Hong Kong U Pr HK) St Mut.
Leung, K. T. & Chen, Doris L. Elementary Set Theory, Pt. 1. 80p. (C). 1991. pap. text ed. 22.00 (962-209-013-3, Pub. by Hong Kong U Pr HK) St Mut.
— Elementary Set Theory, Pt. 1/11. 148p. (C). 1991. pap. text ed. 22.00 (962-209-026-5, Pub. by Hong Kong U Pr HK) St Mut.
Leung, K. T. & Cheung, P. H. Fundamental Concepts of Mathematics. 260p. (C). 1991. text ed. 23.00 (962-209-181-4, Pub. by Hong Kong U Pr HK) St Mut.
***Leung, K. T. & Suen, S. N.** Vectors, Matrices & Geometry: Introducing Finite-Dimensional Vector Spaces. 356p. 1994. pap. 29.50 (962-209-360-4, Pub. by Hong Kong Univ Pr HK) Coronet Bks.
Leung, K. T., et al. Polynomials & Equations. 240p. (C). 1992. pap. text ed. 29.00 (962-209-271-3, Pub. by Hong Kong U Pr HK) St Mut.
Leung, Laifong. Morning Sun: Interviews with Post-Mao Chinese Writers. LC 92-33902. 440p. 1994. 59.95 (1-56324-093-9); pap. 24.95 (1-56324-130-7) M E Sharpe.
Leung, Mai. The Classic Chinese Cook Book. LC 75-9354. (Illus.). 1976. 16.95 (0-685-02047-9, PL) HarpC.
Leung, Margaret Y. Simply Chinese: More Than Sixty Quick & Easy Recipes from China. Piade, Lynne, ed. 64p. 1993. 9.98 (0-681-41735-8) Longmeadow Pr.
Leung, Martha C., jt. auth. see Lin, Sharon C.
***Leung, P. C.** Jotting Writing by Surgery. 260p. 1994. pap. text ed. 10.00 (1-879771-13-6) Global Pub NJ.
***Leung, P. C. & Gu, Y. D.** Microsurgery in Orthopaedic Practice. LC 94-43237. 360p. 1995. text ed. 61.00 (9971-5-0860-5) World Scientific Pub.
Leung, Peter C. Current Trends in Bone Grafting. (Illus.). 130p. 1988. pap. 71.00 (0-387-50139-8) Spr-Verlag.
Leung, Peter C., jt. ed. see Adashi, Eli Y.
Leung, Peter C., jt. ed. see Chang, T. S.
Leung, Peter C., et al, eds. Burns: Treatment & Research. 324p. (C). 1991. text ed. 104.00 (9971-5-0674-2) World Scientific Pub.
— Endocrinology & Physiology of Reproduction. LC 87-11280. (Illus.). 372p. 1987. 95.00 (0-306-42583-1, Plenum Pr) Plenum.
— Molecular Basis of Reproductive Endocrinology. LC 92-2304. (Serono Symposia Ser.). (Illus.). 312p. 1992. 130.00 (0-387-97861-5); write for info. (3-540-97861-5) Spr-Verlag.
Leung, Ping-Chung, ed. Current Practice of Fracture Treatment: New Concepts & Common Problems. 1994. 165.00 (0-387-57367-4) Spr-Verlag.
Leung, PingSun, jt. ed. see Roecklein, John C.
Leung, Y. C. Physics of Dense Matter. 280p. 1985. text ed. 61.00 (9971-978-10-5) World Scientific Pub.
— Spatial Analysis & Planning Under Imprecision. (Studies in Regional Science & Urban Economics: Vol. 17). 376p. 1988. 84.75 (0-444-70390-X, North Holland) Elsevier.
Leung, Yuen-Sang. The Shanghai Taotai: Linkage Man in a Changing Society, 1843-1890. LC 90-11162. (Asian Studies at Hawaii: No. 39). 260p. 1991. pap. text ed. 24.00 (0-8248-1355-3) UH Pr.
Leunig. Common Prayer. 1991. pap. 7.00 (0-85924-933-6) Harper SF.
— The Prayer Tree. (Illus.). 1992. pap. 7.00 (1-86371-034-5, Pub. by Collins Dove AT) Harper SF.
Leuning, Kevin. Archie Givens Sr. Collection Curriculum Guide. x, 30p. (J). (ps-12). 1988. pap. text ed. write for info. (0-9632976-0-0) A Givens Sr Collect.
Leunissen, Jan L., jt. ed. see Verkleij, A. J.
Leunissen, K. L., jt. ed. see Widere, T. E.
***Leunissen, K. M., ed.** International Society of Blood Purification 12th Annual Meeting, Maastricht, September 1994 Abstracts: Journal: Blood Purification, Vol. 12, No. 3. (Journal: Blood Purification Ser.). (Illus.). 62p. 1995. pap. 43.25 (3-8055-6052-4) S Karger.
Leunissen, Paul M. Konsulin und Konsulare in der von Commodus bis Severus Alexander (180-235 n. Chr.) Prosopographische Untersuchungen zur Senatorischen Elite in Romischen Kaiserreich. ix, 490p. (GER.). 1989. 94.00 (90-5063-028-6, Pub. by Gieben NE) Benjamins North Am.
Leupen, P., ed. Philip of Leyden - A Fourteenth Century Jurist: A Study of His Life & Treatise De Cura Republicae et Sorte Principantis. (Rechtshistorische Studies: No. 7). xviii, 300p. 1992. pap. 68.00 (90-271-1678-4, Pub. by Egbert Forsten NE) Benjamins North Am.
Leupin, Alexandre. Barbarolexis: Medieval Writing & Sexuality. Cooper, Kate M., tr. LC 89-1999. 272p. 1989. 42.50 (0-674-06170-5) HUP.
Leupin, Alexandre, ed. Lacan & the Human Sciences. LC 90-39325. viii, 191p. 1991. 30.00 (0-8032-2894-5) U of Nebr Pr.
Leupold, Herbert C. Daniel. 1969. 22.99 (0-8010-5531-8) Baker Bk.
— Exposition of Genesis, 2 Vols, 1-19. 1993. 21.99 (0-8010-5549-0) Baker Bk.
— Exposition of Genesis, 2 Vols, 20-50. 1993. 24.99 (0-8010-5522-9) Baker Bk.
— Isaiah, 1 vol. ed. 1977. 29.99 (0-8010-5577-6) Baker Bk.
— Psalms. LC 59-9289. 1970. 29.99 (0-8010-5521-0) Baker Bk.
Leupold, Ulrich S. & Lehmann, Helmut T., eds. Luther's Works: Liturgy & Hymns, Vol. 53. LC 55-9893. 1965. 25.00 (0-8006-0353-2, 1-353, Fortress Pr) Augsburg Fortress.
Leupp, Francis E. Indian & His Problem. LC 72-137175. (Poverty U. S. A. Historical Record Ser.). 1975. reprint ed. 26.95 (0-405-03114-9) Ayer.
***Leupp, Gary P.** Male Colors: The Construction of Homosexuality in Tokugawa, Japan. 317p. 1995. 35.00 (0-520-08627-9) U CA Pr.
— Servants, Shophands, & Laborers. 1994. pap. 16.95 (0-691-02961-X) Princeton U Pr.
— Servants, Shophands, & Laborers in the Cities of Tokugawa Japan. (Illus.). 252p. 1992. text ed. 35.00 (0-691-03139-8) Princeton U Pr.
Leurquin, Regine. Theodore Meliteniote: Tribiblos Astronomique, Livre I. (Corpus des Astronomes Byzantins Ser.: Vol. 4). 436p. (FRE.). 1990. pap. 80.00 (90-5063-045-6, Pub. by Gieben NE) Benjamins North Am.
Leuschner, J. Germany in the Late Middle Ages. (Europe in the Middle Ages: Selected Studies: Vol. 17). 250p. 1980. 79.50 (0-444-85135-6, North Holland) Elsevier.
Leuschner, R. & Boehm, G., eds. Advances in Aerobiology. (BioSeries-EXS: No. 51). 300p. 1987. 85.00 (0-8176-1803-1) Birkhauser.
Leuschner, William A. Forest Regulation: Harvest Scheduling & Activities Planning. 1990. text ed. 75.00 (0-471-61405-X) Wiley.
— Introduction to Forest Resource Management. LC 91-21718. 304p. (C). 1992. reprint ed. lib. bdg. 52.50 (0-89464-641-9) Krieger.
Leusen, Isadore, ed. see International Congress of Physiological Sciences, Official Satellite Symposium Staff.
Leuser, David V. How to Send Healing Energy: Diccionari Enciclopedic D'abast Universal, 8 vols., Set. 3500p. (CAT.). 1974. 375.00 (0-8288-6053-X, S50517) Fr & Eur.
Leushina, A. M. The Development of Elementary Mathematical Concepts in Preschool Children. Steffe, Leslie P., ed. Teller, Joan, tr. LC 91-3865. (Soviet Studies in Mathematics Education). (Illus.). 481p. (Orig.). 1991. pap. 25.00 (0-87353-299-6) NCTM.
Leute, George, jt. auth. see Keefe, John.
Leute, Ulrich. Archaeometry: An Introduction to Physical Methods in Archaeology & the History of Art. LC 87-22689. (Illus.). 176p. 1987. lib. bdg. 40.00 (0-89573-612-8) VCH Pubs.
Leuthner, Stuart, jt. auth. see Jensen, Oliver.
Leuthold, David. Campaign Missouri Nineteen Ninety-Two. (Illus.). 288p. 1994. pap. 22.95 (0-8262-0977-7) U of Mo Pr.
Leuthold, Raymond M., et al. The Theory & Practice of Futures Markets. LC 87-45248. 432p. 1989. text ed. 44.95 (0-669-16260-4) Free Pr.
***Leutloff, D. & Srivastava, R. C., eds.** Computational Fluid Dynamics: Selected Topics. LC 94-48557. 1995. 98.00 (3-540-58757-8) Spr-Verlag.
Leutner, Robert W. Shikitei Sanba & the Comic Tradition in Edo Fiction. (Harvard-Yenching Institute Monograph: No. 25). 300p. 1986. 28.00 (0-674-80646-8) HUP.
Leutsch, E. & Schneidewin, F. G., eds. Corpus Paroemiographorum Graecorum. Bd. 21-22. pap. write for info. (0-318-70795-0, Pub. by Georg Olms GW) Lubrecht & Cramer.
Leutsch, E. L. & Schneidewin, F. Corpus Paroemiographorum Graecorum, 2 vols., Set. 1468p. (GER.). 1958. reprint ed. pap. write for info. (0-318-70499-4, Pub. by Georg Olms GW) Lubrecht & Cramer.
Leutwiler, Heinz, jt. auth. see Arsove, Maynard.
Leutz, H., jt. auth. see Barletta, W. A.
Leutz, Walter N., et al. Care for Frail Elders: Developing Community Solutions. LC 92-11506. 315p. 1992. text ed. 45.00 (0-86569-029-4, T029, Auburn Hse) Greenwood.
— Changing Health Care for an Aging Society: Planning for the Social Health Maintenance Organization. LC 84-40811. (University Health Policy Consortium Ser.). (Illus.). 272p. 1985. text ed. 37.95 (0-669-10139-7) Free Pr.
Leutzbach, W. Introduction to the Theory of Traffic Flow. (Illus.). 180p. 1987. 61.00 (0-387-17113-4) Spr-Verlag.
Leutze, James R. A Different Kind of Victory. LC 81-4005. (Illus.). 362p. 1981. 34.95 (0-87021-056-4) Naval Inst Pr.
Leutzeler, H. Bildwoerterbuch der Kunst. 2nd ed. 404p. (GER.). 1962. 45.00 (3-427-85012-9, M-7310) Fr & Eur.
Leutzinger, John F. The Handstamps of Wells, Fargo & Co. 1852 to 1895. 2nd ed. Spelman, Henry M., III, ed. LC 93-77466. (Illus.). 384p. 1993. 45.00 (0-917528-11-5) L H Hartmann.
Leuven, Lemli J., et al, eds. International Symposium of Senna First Rottach-Egern: Proceedings, May 1987. (Journal: Pharmacology: Vol. 36, Suppl. 1, 1988). iv, 240p. 1988. pap. 72.00 (3-8055-4718-8) S Karger.

An Asterisk (*) at the beginning of an entry indicates that the title is appearing in BIP for the first time.

*Leuverink, Margaret, ed. The Sages Speak About Life & Death. (Illus.). 107p. 1995. pap. 7.00 (1-880687-07-0) Chinmaya Pubns.

Leuw, Ed & Marshall, I. Haen, eds. Between Prohibition & Legalization: The Dutch Experiment in Drug Policy. LC 94-1664. (Studies on Crime & Justice Ser.). 1994. 47.50 (90-6299-103-3) Kugler Pubns.

Leuzinger-Bohleber, M., et al, eds. Two Butterflies on My Head: Psychoanalysis in the Interdisciplinary Scientific Dialogue. (Illus.). 280p. 1992. pap. 40.00 (0-387-53899-2) Spr-Verlag.

*Leuzinger, Elsy. Arte del Africa Negra. (Illus.). 388p. (ENG, FRE, GER & SPA.). 1993. 100.00x (84-343-0176-8) Elliots Bks.

Leuzzi, J. P., jt. ed. see Knauth, Christopher R.

*Leuzzi, Linda. Transportation. LC 94-17183. (Life 100 Years Ago Ser.). (YA). (gr. 10 up). 1995. write for info. (0-7910-2840-2) Chelsea Hse.

— Urban Life. LC 94-24617. (Life in America 100 Years Ago Ser.). (J). 1995. write for info. (0-7910-2841-0) Chelsea Hse.

Lev, Baruch. Accounting & Information Theory, Vol. 2. (Studies in Accounting Research). 84p. 1969. 12.00 (0-86539-014-2) Am Accounting.

Lev, Baruch, ed. Production Management: Methods & Studies. (Studies in Management Science & Systems: Vol. 13). 250p. 1986. 87.25 (0-444-87986-2) Elsevier.

Lev, Baruch & Weiss, H. J. Introduction to Mathematical Programming: Quantitative Tools for Decision Making. 290p. 1981. 46.00 (0-444-00591-9, North Holland) Elsevier.

Lev, Baruch, et al, eds. Analytic Techniques for Energy Planning: Proceedings of the First Symposium Organized by the Operations Research Society of America Special Interest Group on Energy, Natural Resources & the Environment. 372p. 1991. 100.00 (0-444-86884-4, I-291-84) Elsevier.

— Strategic Planning in Energy & Natural Resources: Proceedings of the 2nd Symposium in Analytic Techniques for Energy, Natural Resources, & Environmental Planning, Philadelphia PA, 3-4 April, 1986. (Studies in Management Science & Systems: No. 15). 340p. 1987. 107.75 (0-444-70230-X, North Holland) Elsevier.

Lev, Benjamin, ed. Energy Models & Studies. (Studies in Management Science & Systems: Vol. 9). 600p. 1983. 123.00 (0-444-86601-9, North Holland) Elsevier.

Lev, Donald. Footnotes. Barkan, Stanley H., ed. (Cross-Cultural Review Chapbook Ser.: No. 11: American Poetry 5). 16p. 1981. 15.00 (0-89304-850-X, CCC138); pap. 5.00 (0-89304-810-0); audio 10.00 (0-89304-835-6) Cross-Cultrl NY.

— Intercourse with the Dead. 63p. 1980. pap. 7.50 (0-685-49041-6, Downtown Poets) Cross-Cultrl NY.

— Intercourse with the Dead. 60p. 1980. per. 2.50 (0-917402-11-1) Downtown Poets.

Lev, Loseff. Tainyi Sovetnik. LC 87-35388. 128p. (Orig.). (RUS.). 1988. pap. 8.00 (0-938920-97-9) Hermitage.

Lev, M. C., jt. ed. see Martinez, M. R.

Lev, Martin. The Traveler's Key to Jerusalem. (Traveler's Key Ser.: No. 6). 1989. pap. 18.95 (0-394-55635-6) Knopf.

Lev, Maurice, jt. auth. see Bharati, Saroja.

Lev, Ovadia E., ed. Structural Optimization: Recent Developments & Applications. LC 81-69232. 220p. 1981. pap. 20.00 (0-87262-281-9) Am Soc Civil Eng.

Lev, Peter. Claude Lelouch, Film Director. LC 81-72036. (Illus.). 184p. 1983. 29.50 (0-8386-3114-2) Fairleigh Dickinson.

— The Euro-American Cinema. LC 92-42794. (Film Studies). (Illus.). 188p. (C). 1993. text ed. 27.50 (0-292-74677-6); pap. 12.95 (0-292-74678-4) U of Tex Pr.

Lev, R. Adenomatous Polyps of the Colon. (Illus.). 160p. 1989. 87.00 (0-387-96985-3, 2730) Spr-Verlag.

Lev, Yaacov. State & Society in Fatimid Egypt. LC 90-24522. (AHC Ser.: No. 1). xi, 217p. 1991. 63.00 (90-04-09344-3) E J Brill.

Lev, Yvonne, jt. ed. see Koehler, Barbara.

Leva-Skrovanova, Vera. Contemporary Bohemian Lace. 1987. 12.00 (0-85219-735-7) Robin & Russ.

Levach, John D. The Equine Ophthalmology Handbook. (Giddings Handbooks for Veterinarians Ser.). (Illus.). 480p. (Orig.). 1987. Incl. poster. pap. 35.00 (0-317-38016-8) Giddings Studio Pub.

Levacic, Rosalind. Financial Management in Education. (Management in Education Ser.). 192p. 1989. pap. 25.00 (0-335-09246-2, Open Univ Pr) Taylor & Francis.

— Local Management of Schools: Analysis & Practice. LC 95-5855. 1995. pap. write for info. (0-335-19375-7, Open Univ Pr) Taylor & Francis.

Levack, Brian, ed. Witch-Hunting in Continental Europe: Regional & Local Studies. LC 92-22856. (Witchcraft Magic, Demonology Ser.: Vol. 5). 304p. 1992. 54.00 (0-8153-1027-7) Garland.

Levack, Brian P. The Formation of the British State: England, Scotland, & the Union 1603-1707. 272p. 1987. 65.00 (0-19-820113-3) OUP.

— The Witch-Hunt in Early Modern Europe. 267p. (C). 1987. text ed. 23.75 (0-582-49122-3, 73488); pap. text ed. 22.95 (0-582-49123-1, 73488) Longman.

— The Witch-Hunt in Early Modern Europe. 2nd ed. 320p. (C). 1995. pap. text ed. 22.95 (0-582-08069-X, 76887) Longman.

Levack, Brian P., ed. Anthropological Studies of Witchcraft, Magic, & Religion. LC 92-21028. (Articles on Witchcraft, Magic, & Demonology Ser.: Vol. 1). 416p. 1992. 65.00 (0-8153-1023-4) Garland.

— The Literature of Witchcraft. LC 92-21029. (Articles on Witchcraft, Magic, & Demonology Ser.: Vol. 4). 352p. 1992. 57.00 (0-8153-1026-9) Garland.

— Possession & Exorcism. LC 92-22857. (Witchcraft, Magic, & Demonology Ser.: Vol. 9). 352p. 1992. 57.00 (0-8153-1031-5) Garland.

— Renaissance Magic. LC 92-22912. (Articles on Witchcraft, Magic, & Demonology Ser.: Vol. 11). 336p. 1992. 56.00 (0-8153-1034-X) Garland.

— Witch-Hunting in Early Modern Europe: General Studies. LC 92-21027. (Articles on Witchcraft, Magic, & Demonology Ser.: Vol. 3). 392p. 1992. 63.00 (0-8153-1025-0) Garland.

— Witchcraft & Demonology in Art & Literature. LC 92-22872. (Articles on Witchcraft, Magic, & Demonology Ser.: Vol. 12). (Illus.). 360p. 1992. 63.00 (0-8153-1035-8) Garland.

— Witchcraft in Colonial America. LC 92-22874. (Articles on Witchcraft, Magic, & Demonology Ser.: Vol. 8). 416p. 1992. 65.00 (0-8153-1030-7) Garland.

— Witchcraft in England. LC 92-21032. (Articles on Witchcraft, Magic, & Demonology Ser.: Vol. 6). 344p. 1992. 57.00 (0-8153-1028-5) Garland.

— Witchcraft in Scotland. LC 92-21033. (Articles on Witchcraft, Magic, & Demonology Ser.: Vol. 7). 408p. 1992. 63.00 (0-8153-1029-3) Garland.

— Witchcraft in the Ancient World & the Middle Ages. LC 92-20731. (Articles on Witchcraft, Magic, & Demonology Ser.: Vol. 2). 344p. 1992. 57.00 (0-8153-1024-2) Garland.

— Witchcraft, Women, & Society. LC 92-22873. (Articles on Witchcraft, Magic, & Demonology Ser.: Vol. 10). 310p. 1992. 53.00 (0-8153-1032-3) Garland.

Levack, Brian P., intro. Witchcraft, Magic & Demonology: An Anthology of Scholarly Articles, 12 vols., Set. 1992. 710.00 (0-8153-1022-6) Garland.

Levack, Daniel J. Amber Dreams: A Roger Zelazny Bibliography. 151p. 1983. text ed. 49.95 (0-313-27678-1) Greenwood.

— Dune Master: A Frank Herbert Bibliography. 300p. 1988. text ed. 59.95 (0-313-27679-X) Greenwood.

— PKD: A Philip K. Dick Bibliography. (Bibliographies on Science Fiction, Fantasy & Horror Ser.: No. 1). 160p. 1988. text ed. 65.00 (0-313-27680-3) Greenwood.

Levack, Daniel J., jt. auth. see Laughlin, Charlotte.

Levack, Nancy. Low Vision: A Resource Guide with Adaptations for Students with Visual Impairments. 120p. 1991. pap. 10.00 (1-880366-04-5) Texas Schl BVI.

— Low Vision: A Resource Guide with Adaptations for Students with Visual Impairments. LC 94-6108. 1994. pap. 20.00 (1-880366-12-6) Texas Schl BVI.

Levack, Nancy, jt. auth. see Loumiet, Robin.

Levadie, Benjamin, ed. see American Society for Testing & Materials Staff.

Levaggi, Rosella. Fiscal Federalism & Grants-in-Aid: The Problem of Asymmetrical Information. 208p. 1991. text ed. 68.95 (1-85628-242-2, Pub. by Avebury Pub UK) Ashgate Pub Co.

Levaillant, Maurice. Les Aventures du Scepticisme: Essai sur l'Evolution Intellectuelle d'Anatole France. (FRE.). 38.95 (0-8288-9969-X, F59035) Fr & Eur.

— Passionate Exiles: Madame de Stael & Madame Recamier. Barnes, Malcolm, tr. LC 73-160923. (Biography Index Reprint Ser.). 1977. reprint ed. 23.95 (0-8369-8086-7) Ayer.

Levaillant, Maurice, ed. see De Chateaubriand, Francois-Rene.

Levaillant, Maurice, jt. auth. see Merimee, Prosper.

Levaillant, Maurice, jt. auth. see Sainte-Beuve, Charles-Augustin.

Leval, Gaston. Collectives in the Spanish Revolution. Richards, Vernon, tr. 368p. 1975. 15.00 (0-900384-11-5) Left Bank.

Leval, Susana T. Artists Talk Back - Los Artistas Responden: Visual Conversations with el Museo, Pt. 1: Reclaiming History - Conversando en Imagenes Con el Museo, El Rescate de la Historia. 52p. (Orig.). (ENG & SPA.). (C). 1994. pap. 20.00 (1-882454-01-4) El Museo Barrio.

Leval, Susana T., et al. Antonio Martorell: A House for Us All. (Illus.). 56p. (Orig.). (ENG & SPA.). 1992. pap. 20.00 (1-882454-00-6) El Museo Barrio.

LeValley, Norma. A Tree for Me. LC 87-70974. (Illus.). 50p. (J). (ps-2). 1987. pap. 5.95 (0-9618740-0-7) Caring Tree.

LeValliant, Ted & Theroux, Marcel. What's the Verdict? Real Life Court Cases to Test Your Legal IQ. LC 90-28616. (Illus.). 128p. 1991. pap. 5.95 (0-8069-7466-4) Sterling.

LeVan, Gerald. Lawyers' Lives Out of Control: A Quality of Life Handbook. 96p. 1992. pap. 12.95 (1-56664-010-5, WrldComm Pr) WorldComm.

LeVan, Gerald, jt. auth. see Rubin, Alvin B.

Levan, N. Systems & Signals. (University Series in Modern Engineering). 173p. 1983. pap. 33.00 (0-387-90900-1) Spr-Verlag.

— Systems & Signals. 2nd rev. ed. LC 86-31158. (University Series in Modern Engineering). 176p. (C). 1987. text ed. 29.50 (0-911575-40-5) Optimization Soft.

— Systems & Signals. 3rd enl. rev. ed. LC 92-28882. (University Series in Modern Engineering). 240p. 1992. pap. text ed. 39.00 (0-911575-63-4) Optimization Soft.

LeVan, Timothy. Masters of the French Art Song: Translations of the Complete Songs of Chausson, Debussy, Duparc, Favre & Ravel. LC 91-41123. 457p. 1991. 42.50 (0-8108-2522-8) Scarecrow.

— Masters of the Italian Art Song: Word-by-Word & Poetic Translations of the Complete Songs for Voice & Piano. LC 90-8955. 333p. 1990. 35.00 (0-8108-2363-2) Scarecrow.

Levand, Rhonda. Sexual Evolution. LC 90-2338. 304p. (Orig.). 1991. pap. 12.95 (0-89087-626-6) Celestial Arts.

LeVander, Dyan. Where Do I Fit In? Prayers for Young Teen Girls. LC 89-205. 112p. (Orig.). 1989. pap. 5.99 (0-8066-2398-5, 10-7094, Augsburg) Augsburg Fortress.

Levander, Orville A., ed. AIN Symposium Proceedings, Nutrition '87. (Illus.). 157p. (Orig.). 1987. pap. 15.00 (0-943029-01-5) Am Inst Nutrition.

Levander, Orville A., ed. see New York Academy of Sciences Staff.

Levang, Elizabeth & Ilse, Sherokee. Remembering with Love: Messages of Hope for the First Year of Grieving & Beyond. LC 92-72158. 320p. 1991. 9.95 (0-925190-60-8) Fairview Press.

Levang, J. H. Living Lutheran Christianity. 129p. (Orig.). 1991. pap. 8.95 (0-943167-14-0) Faith & Fellowship Pr.

Levangie, Pamela K., jt. auth. see Norkin, Cynthia C.

Levanon, Nadav. Radar Principles. LC 87-29832. 320p. 1988. text ed. 79.95 (0-471-85881-1) Wiley.

*Levanoni, Amalia. A Turning Point in Mamluk History: The Third Reign of Al-Nasir Muhammad ibn Qalawun (1310-1341) (Islamic History & Civilization Ser.). 1995. 77.25 (90-04-10182-9) E J Brill.

Levant, Howard. The Novels of John Steinbeck: A Critical Study. LC 74-76251. 328p. 1983. pap. 12.00 (0-8262-0424-4) U of Mo Pr.

Levant, Jonathan. Oedipus the Anti-Sociopath: or Autumn Angst. 24p. (Orig.). 1992. pap. 5.00 (0-926935-62-3) Runaway Spoon.

Levant, Oscar. The Memoirs of an Amnesiac. LC 89-36545. 320p. 1989. pap. 12.95 (0-573-60698-6) S French Trade.

*Levant, Ronald & Pollack, William, eds. The New Psychology of Men. 352p. 1995. text ed. 40.00x (0-465-08656-X) Basic.

Levant, Ronald F. Between Father & Child: How to Become the Kind of Father You Want to Be. 256p. 1991. pap. 10.00 (0-14-015261-X, Penguin Bks) Viking Penguin.

— Family Therapy: A Comprehensive Overview. (Illus.). 384p. (C). 1984. text ed. write for info. (0-13-302885-2) P-H.

Levant, Ronald F., ed. Psychoeducational Approaches to Family Therapy & Counseling. 336p. 1986. 33.95 (0-8261-4850-6) Springer Pub.

Levant, Ronald F. & Kopecky, Gini. Masculinity Reconstructed: Changing the Rules of Manhood - at Work, in Relationships, & in Family Life. 352p. 1995. 22.95 (0-525-93846-X) NAL-Dutton.

Levant, Ronald F. & Shlien, John M., eds. Client-Centered Therapy & the Person-Centered Approach: New Directions in Theory, Research & Practice. LC 84-6832. 480p. 1984. text ed. 69.50 (0-275-91215-9, C1215, Praeger Pubs) Greenwood.

— Client-Centered Therapy & the Person-Centered Approach: New Directions in Theory, Research, & Practice. LC 84-6832. 480p. 1987. pap. text ed. 19.95 (0-275-92821-7, B2821, Praeger Pubs) Greenwood.

Levanthal, Sallye, ed. see Anthony, Robert.

Levanthal, Sallye, ed. see Hernacki, Mike.

Levantrosser, William F., ed. Harry S. Truman, the Man from Independence. LC 85-21962. (Contributions in Political Science Ser.: No. 145). 437p. 1986. text ed. 65.00 (0-313-25178-9, LTR/, Greenwood Pr) Greenwood.

Levantrosser, William F., jt. ed. see Friedman, Leon.

Levanyuk, A. P. & Sigov, A. S. Defects & Structural Phase Transitions. 244p. 1988. text ed. 194.00 (2-88124-067-4) Gordon & Breach.

Levanyuk, A. P., jt. ed. see Blinc, R.

Levanyuk, A. P., jt. ed. see Cummins, H. Z.

Levarie, Norma. The Art & History of Books. LC 82-8984. (Illus.). 328p. 1995. 45.00 (1-884718-02-7) Oak Knoll.

— The Art & History of Books. LC 82-8984. (Quality Paperbacks Ser.). (Illus.). 315p. 1982. reprint ed. pap. 24.50 (0-306-80181-7) Da Capo.

Levarie, Siegmund. Fundamentals of Harmony. (Wissenschaftliche Abhandlungen-Musicological Studies: Vol. 5). 150p. 1965. pap. 5.20 (0-912024-75-5) Inst Mediaeval Mus.

— Guillaume de Machaut. LC 70-98309. (Music Ser.). 1969. reprint ed. lib. bdg. 22.50 (0-306-71831-6) Da Capo.

— Mozart's Le Nozze Di Figaro. LC 77-5150. (Music Reprint Ser.). 1977. reprint ed. lib. bdg. 32.50 (0-306-70897-3) Da Capo.

Levarie, Siegmund & Levy, Ernest. Musical Morphology: A Discourse & a Dictionary. LC 82-21274. 355p. reprint ed. pap. 101.20 (0-7837-5124-9, 2044852) Bks Demand.

Levarie, Siegmund & Levy, Ernst. A Dictionary of Musical Morphology. (Wissenschaftliche Abhandlungen-Musicological Studies: Vol. 29). viii, 400p. 1980. lib. bdg. 34.00 (0-912024-32-1) Inst Mediaeval Mus.

— Tone: A Study in Musical Acoustics. rev. ed. LC 80-16794. 273p. 1980. pap. 8.50 (0-87338-250-1) Kent St U Pr.

— Tone: A Study in Musical Acoustics. 2nd ed. LC 80-29383. (Illus.). xvii, 256p. 1981. reprint ed. text ed. 59.75 (0-313-22499-4, LETO, Greenwood Pr) Greenwood.

Levarie, Siegmund, tr. see Mertin, Josef.

LeVarre, Deborah. Captive Mistress. 1983. pap. 3.75 (0-8217-1282-9) Zebra.

Levary, R. R., ed. Engineering Design: Better Results Through Operations Research Methods. 800p. 1988. 99.50 (0-444-01202-8, North Holland) Elsevier.

*Levasics, E. & Suranyi, M. Serbo-Croatian-Hungarian Concise Dictionary. 848p. 1988. 36.00x (963-205-216-1, Pub. by Akad Kiado HU) St Mut.

— Serbocroatian-Hungarian Concise Dictionary. 3rd ed. 848p. (HUN & SER.). 1982. 39.95 (0-8288-1668-9, M 8578) Fr & Eur.

Levason, W., jt. auth. see McAuliffe, C. A.

Levasseur, Alain A. Louisiana Law of Obligations in General: A Precis. 350p. (C). 1988. pap. 39.50 (0-409-25390-1) Michie Butterworth.

— Louisiana Law of Quasi-Contracts or Unjust Enrichment: A Precis. LC 92-28451. 1992. pap. 35.00 (0-409-25521-1) Michie Butterworth.

— Louisiana Law of Unjust Enrichment in Quasi-Contracts. 490p. 1991. ring bd. 110.00 (0-409-25600-5) Michie Butterworth.

Levasseur, Alain A. & Baker, John S., eds. An Introduction to the Law of the United States. 492p. (C). 1991. lib. bdg. 64.00 (0-8191-8462-4) U Pr of Amer.

Levasseur, Alain A. & Dahl, Enrique, eds. Multinational Corporations: Investments, Technology, Tax, Labor & Securities: European, North & Latin American Perspectives with Summaries in French & Spanish. LC 86-13192. 404p. (C). 1986. lib. bdg. 58.00 (0-8191-5496-2) U Pr of Amer.

Levasseur, Alain A., tr. see Alter, Michel.

Levasseur, Alain A., tr. see Atias, Christian.

Levasseur, Emile. The American Workman. Stein, Leon & Marburg, Theodore, eds. Adams, Thomas S., tr. LC 77-70510. (Work Ser.). 1977. lib. bdg. 47.95 (0-405-10180-5) Ayer.

— Histoire des Classes Ouvrieres et de L'industrie en France de 1789-1870, 2 Vols, Set. 2nd ed. LC 78-92175. (FRE.). reprint ed. 225.00 (0-404-03977-4) AMS Pr.

LeVasseur, Michal. Finding a Way: Encouraging Underrepresented Groups in Geography: An Annotated Bibliography. (Pathways in Geography Ser.: No. 5). 63p. (Orig.). 1993. pap. text ed. 5.00 (0-9627379-6-8) NCFGE.

Levasseur, Raymond L., jt. auth. see Blunk, Tim.

Levasseur-Regourd, A. C. & Hasegawa, H., eds. Origin & Evolution of Interplanetary Dust. 450p. (C). 1992. lib. bdg. 150.00 (0-7923-1365-8) Kluwer Ac.

*Levasseur-Regourd, A. C. & Raulin, F., eds. Prebiotic Chemistry in Space. (Advances in Space Research (RJ) Ser.: Vol. 16). 120p. 1995. pap. 94.00 (0-08-042622-0, Pergamon Pr) Elsevier.

Levasseur-Regourd, Amy C. Our Sun & the Inner Planets. (Planetary Exploration Ser.). 48p. 1989. 13.95 (0-8160-2045-0) Facts on File.

Levasseur, Robert E. Breakthrough Business Meetings: Shared Leadership in Action. 1994. pap. 8.95 (1-55850-395-1) Adams Pubng.

Levasseur, T. & Stafford, J. Rings of Differential Operators on Classical Rings of Invariants. LC 89-15147. (MEMO Ser.: Vol. 81/412). 117p. 1989. pap. 21.00 (0-8218-2475-9, MEMO 81/412) Am Math.

Levathes, Louise. When China Ruled the Seas: The Treasure Fleet of the Dragon Throne 1400-1433. LC 93-42773. 1994. 23.00 (0-671-70158-4) S&S Trade.

Levatino, Madeline. Past Masters: The History & Hauntings of Destrehan Plantation. (Illus.). 100p. (Orig.). 1991. pap. 8.99 (0-9630144-6-3) M Levatino.

Levay, Bela, jt. ed. see Vertes, Attila.

LeVay, David. Scenes from Surgical Life. 200p. 1976. 22.95 (0-8464-0813-9) Beekman Pubs.

LeVay, David, tr. see Roth, Joseph.

*LeVay, Simon. The Sexual Brain. (Illus.). 192p. 1994. pap. 10.95 (0-262-62093-6, Bradford Bks) MIT Pr.

*LeVay, Simon & Nonas, Elisabeth. City of Friends: A Portrait of the Gay & Lesbian Community in America. (Illus.). 464p. (C). 1995. 25.00 (0-262-12194-8) MIT Pr.

Levchenko, Stanislav, jt. auth. see Romerstein, Herbert.

Levchev, Lyubomir. Stolen Fire. LC 85-82112. 1986. pap. 13.95 (0-948259-04-3) Dufour.

Levchuk. Ukrainian-English Phrasebook. 2nd ed. 190p. (ENG & UKR.). 1980. 7.95 (0-8288-1730-8, F65560) Fr & Eur.

Levchuk, Helen. The Dingles. (Illus.). 24p. (J). (ps-2). 1991. pap. 4.95 (0-88899-044-8, Pub. by Groundwood-Douglas & McIntyre CN) Firefly Bks Ltd.

— Doris Dingle's Crafty Cat Activity Book: Games, Toys & Hobbies to Keep Your Cat's Mind Active. LC 91-2701. (Illus.). 96p. (Orig.). 1991. pap. 12.95 (0-88240-415-6) Alaska Northwest.

Leve, Robert. Childhood: The Study of Development. 536p. 1980. student ed 5.00 (0-685-04222-7); text ed. write for info. (0-07-555613-8) McGraw.

Leve, Robert M. Child & Adolescent Psychotherapy: Process & Integration. 1994. 49.95 (0-205-14907-3, Longwood Div) Allyn.

Levedev, Valentin N. The Museums of the Kostroma Land. 244p. 1986. 175.00 (0-317-61325-1, Pub. by Collets UK) Pro-Am Music.

Levee, Robert C., ed. see Genoa Area Centennial Homecoming, Inc. Staff.

LeVeen, E. Phillip. British Slave Trade Suppression Policies 1821-1865: Impact & Implications. Bruchey, Stuart, ed. LC 77-77179. (Dissertations in European Economic History Ser.). (Illus.). 1978. lib. bdg. 26.95 (0-405-10792-7) Ayer.

Leveen, J. The Hebrew Bible in Art. (British Academy, London, Schweich Lectures on Biblical Archaeology Series, 1930). 1969. reprint ed. pap. 30.00 (0-8115-1281-9) Periodicals Srv.

Leveen, Julie. Saurus Gang Kids Coloring Book. (J). (ps-3). 1990. pap. 1.95 (0-590-42313-4) Scholastic Inc.

*Leveen, Louis & Priver, David. Intimacy: Our Quest for Completeness. 144p. (Orig.). 1994. pap. 9.95 (1-885637-17-9) Bluefish Pr.

LeVeen, Phillip, jt. auth. see Runsten, David.

Leveille, Gilbert A. The Setpoint Diet. 272p. 1985. pap. 3.95 (0-345-90193-2) Ballantine.

Leveille, Gilbert A., et al. Nutrients in Foods. 1983. 29.95 (0-938550-00-4) Acad Guild.

*Leveille, Thomas M., ed. Tennessee Legal & Business Forms. LC 94-40878. 1994. write for info. (0-615-00380-X) Lawyers Cooperative.

An Asterisk (*) at the beginning of an entry indicates that the title is appearing in BIP for the first time.

*Level, Jeff, et al. Precision Type Font Reference Guide 5.0: The Complete Font Software Resource for Electronic Publishing. 700p. (Orig.). 1995. pap. 39.95 (0-9646252-0-2) Precision Type.

Level, June S. Two Hundred Level-Headed Ideas for School Library Media Centers: A Plan Book. 110p. 1988. pap. 13.50 (0-87287-668-3) Libs Unl.

Levelt, A. M., jt. auth. see Van den Essen, A. P.

Levelt, Willem J. Crossing the Boundaries in Linguistics. Klein, Wolfgang, ed. 1981. lib. bdg. 84.00 (90-277-1259-X) Kluwer Ac.

— Formal Grammars in Linguistics & Psycholinguistics: An Introduction to the Theory of Formal Languages & Automata, Vol. 1. Barnas, Andrew, tr. (Janua Linguarum, Ser. Minor: No. 192). (Illus.). 143p. 1974. pap. text ed. 20.80 (90-279-2666-2) Mouton.

— Formal Grammars in Linguistics & Psycholinguistics: Applications in Linguistic Theory, Vol. 2. (Janua Linguarum, Ser. Minor: No. 192-2). (Illus.). viii, 194p. (Orig.). 1974. pap. text ed. 26.15 (90-279-2708-1) Mouton.

— Formal Grammars in Linguistics & Psycholinguistics: Psycholinguistics Applications, Vol. 3. (Janua Linguarum, Ser. Minor: No. 192-3). 206p. 1974. pap. text ed. 32.35 (90-279-3352-9) Mouton.

Levelt, Willem J., ed. Lexical Access in Speech Production. LC 92-42764. (Illus.). 314p. 1993. pap. 23.95 (1-55786-355-5) Blackwell Pubs.

Levelt, Willem J. & Flores d'Arcais, G. B., eds. Studies in the Perception of Language. LC 78-2548. 353p. reprint ed. pap. 100.70 (0-685-20462-6, 2029858) Bks Demand.

Levelt, William J. M. Speaking: From Intention to Articulation. (ACL-MIT Series in Natural Language Processing). (Illus.). 584p. 1993. pap. 24.00 (0-262-62089-8, Bradford Bks) MIT Pr.

Leven, M. Photoelasticity: Frocht M. LC 68-57890. 1969. 203.00 (0-08-012998-6, Pub. by Pergamon Repr UK) Franklin.

Leven, Maurice. Income in the Various States: Its Sources & Distribution, 1919, 1920, & 1921. (General Ser.: No. 7). 306p. 1925. reprint ed. 79.60 (0-87014-006-X); reprint ed. mic. film 39.80 (0-685-61138-8) Natl Bur Econ Res.

Leven, Samuel J., jt. ed. see Levine, Daniel S.

Levenard, Jim, et al. An Anthology of the Paradoxist Literary Movement: Essays. Dinca, C., ed. (Illus.). 174p. (Orig.). 1993. pap. text ed. 9.99 (1-879585-34-0) Xiquan Pubng.

Levenberg, Haim. Military Preparations of the Arab Community in Palestine, 1945-1948. LC 92-18785. 281p. 1993. text ed. 45.00 (0-7146-3439-5, Pub. by F Cass Pubs UK) Intl Spec Bk.

*Levenberg, Juri. Russian Wristwatches: Pocket Watches, Stop Watches, Onboard Clock & Chronometers. (Illus.). 96p. 1995. pap. 19.95 (0-88740-873-7) Schiffer.

Levenberg, N., et al. The Metric Induced by the Robin Function. LC 91-13768. (MEMO Ser.). 156p. 1991. 25.00 (0-8218-2520-8, MEMO 92/448) Am Math.

Levenberg, S. The Enigma of Soviet Jewry, Historical Background By. 687p. (C). Date not set. 60.00 (1-870360-15-X) St Mut.

Levenberg, Schneier. The Jews & Palestine: A Study in Labour Zionism. LC 75-6444. (Rise of Jewish Nationalism & the Middle East Ser.). 402p. 1976. reprint ed. 33.00 (0-88355-331-7) Hyperion Conn.

*Levendasky, Charles. A Circle of Light. 74p. (Orig.). Date not set. pap. 9.95 (0-931271-32-0) Hi Plains Pr.

Levendorskii, Serge. Asymptotic Distribution of Eigenvalues of Differential Operators. (C). 1990. lib. bdg. 150.00 (0-7923-0539-6) Kluwer Ac.

— Degenerate Elliptic Equations. LC 93-13188. (Mathematics & Its Applications Ser.: Vol. 258). 460p. (C). 1993. lib. bdg. 186.50 (0-7923-2305-X) Kluwer Ac.

Levendusk, Christine, ed. see Rowson, Susanna.

Levene. Color Atlas of Hair & Nail Diagnosis. (Illus.). 1991. write for info. (0-8151-5437-2, Yr Bk Med Pubs) Mosby Yr Bk.

— Diagnostic Picture Tests in Dermatology. (SPA.). 1991. 26.15 (0-7234-1670-2, Wolfe Pub) Mosby Yr Bk.

— The Fastest Car in the County. LC 91-33539. (YA). (gr. 3-6). 1992. pap. 4.99 (1-55513-395-9, Chariot Bks) Chariot Family.

— The Pet That Never Was. LC 91-33518. (J). 1992. pap. 4.99 (1-55513-394-0, Chariot Bks) Chariot Family.

Levene, Bruce, ed. James Dean in Mendocino: The Making of the Movie East of Eden. (Illus.). 64p. (Orig.). 1994. pap. 8.95 (0-933391-13-7) Pac Transcript.

Levene, Clara M., jt. auth. see Schuchardt, Charles.

Levene, D. S. Religion in Livy. LC 93-11077. (Mnemosyne Ser.: Supplement 127). xi, 257p. 1993. 71.50 (90-04-09617-5) E J Brill.

Levene, Donald L., ed. Chest Pain: An Integrated Diagnostic Approach. LC 77-8297. 222p. reprint ed. pap. 63.30 (0-685-20936-9, 2056517) Bks Demand.

Levene, Donna D. Music Through Children's Literature: Theme & Variations. (Illus.). 120p. (Orig.). 1993. pap. text ed. 22.50 (1-56308-021-4) Teacher Ideas Pr.

Levene, G., jt. auth. see Goolamalai, S.

Levene, G. M., ed. Diagnostic Picture Tests in Dermatology. (Illus.). 128p. 1986. 14.95 (0-8151-5407-0, DTD-1, Yr Bk Med Pubs) Mosby Yr Bk.

Levene, G. M. & Calnan, D. C. Color Atlas of Dermatology. (Year Book Color Atlas Ser.). (Illus.). 368p. 1985. reprint ed. 51.95 (0-8151-1441-9, CLP-1, Yr Bk Med Pubs) Mosby Yr Bk.

Levene, John R., ed. see International Symposium on Visual Science Staff.

Levene, M. Jolly's Diseases of Children. 6th ed. 1990. 115.00 (0-632-02723-1) Blackwell Sci.

— The Nested Universal Relation Database Model. Goos, G. & Hartmanis, J., eds. LC 92-10727. (Lecture Notes in Computer Science Ser.: Vol. 595). x, 177p. 1992. pap. 31.00 (0-685-59405-X) Spr-Verlag.

Levene, Malcolm & Tudehope, David. Essentials of Neonatal Medicine. 2nd ed. LC 92-49090. 1993. 46.95 (0-632-03558-7) Blackwell Sci.

Levene, Malcolm I., et al. Ultrasound of the Infant Brain. (Clinics in Developmental Medicine Ser.: No. 92). (Illus.). 148p. (C). 1991. 37.95 (0-521-41212-9, Pub. by Mc Keith Pr UK) Cambridge U Pr.

Levene, Malcolm I., et al, eds. Fetal & Neonatal Neurology & Neurosurgery. (Illus.). 640p. 1988. text ed. 180.00 (0-443-03713-2) Churchill.

— Fetal & Neonatal Neurology & Neurosurgery. 2nd ed. LC 94-24322. 1994. write for info. (0-443-04910-6) Churchill.

Levene, Mark. War, Jews, & the New Europe: The Diplomacy of Lucien Wolf, 1914-1919. (Littman Library of Jewish Civilization). (Illus.). 352p. 1992. lib. bdg. 50.00 (0-19-710072-4, Pub. by Littman Lib Jew UK) Bnai Brith Bk.

Levene, Nancy. Cherry Cola Champions. LC 88-12294. (Alex Ser.). (Illus.). 120p. (J). (gr. 3-7). 1988. pap. 4.99 (1-55513-519-6, Chariot Bks) Chariot Family.

— French Fry Forgiveness. LC 87-5268. (J). (gr. 3-6). 1987. pap. 4.99 (1-55513-302-9, Chariot Bks) Chariot Family.

— Hot Chocolate Friendship. LC 87-5281. (J). (gr. 3-6). 1987. pap. 4.99 (1-55513-304-5, Chariot Bks) Chariot Family.

— Peach Pit Popularity. LC 89-33900. (J). (gr. 3-6). 1989. pap. 4.99 (1-55513-529-3, Chariot Bks) Chariot Family.

— Peanut Butter & Jelly Secrets. LC 87-5247. (J). (gr. 3-6). 1987. pap. 4.99 (1-55513-303-7, Chariot Bks) Chariot Family.

— Salty Scarecrow Solution. LC 89-31274. (J). (gr. 3-6). 1989. pap. 4.99 (1-55513-523-4, Chariot Bks) Chariot Family.

— Shoelaces & Brussel Sprouts. LC 87-5267. (J). (gr. 3-6). 1987. pap. 4.99 (1-55513-301-0, Chariot Bks) Chariot Family.

— T-Bone Trouble. LC 90-32906. (J). (gr. 3-6). 1990. pap. 4.99 (1-55513-765-2, Chariot Bks) Chariot Family.

Levene, Nancy S. Apple Turnover Treasure. Reck, Sue, ed. LC 91-45922. (Alex Ser.). 128p. (J). (gr. 3-6). Date not set. pap. 4.99 (1-55513-894-2, Chariot Bks) Chariot Family.

— Chocolate Chips & Trumpet Tricks. Reck, Sue, ed. LC 93-36195. 192p. (J). (gr. 3-6). 1994. pap. 5.99 (0-7814-0103-8, Chariot Bks) Cook.

— Crocodile Meatloaf. LC 92-32615. (J). (ps-6). 1993. pap. 4.99 (0-7814-0000-7, Chariot Bks) Chariot Family.

— Grapefruit Basket Upset. Reck, Sue, ed. LC 91-9359. 128p. (J). (gr. 3-6). Date not set. pap. 4.99 (1-55513-768-7, Chariot Bks) Chariot Family.

— Hero for a Season. Reck, Sue, ed. LC 93-21126. (T. J. Ser.). 96p. (J). (gr. 3-6). 1994. pap. 4.99 (0-7814-0702-8, Chariot Bks) Cook.

— Master of Disaster. LC 94-17356. (J). Date not set. write for info. (0-7814-0089-9, Chariot Bks) Chariot Family.

— Mint Cookie Miracles. LC 88-11902. (Alex Ser.). 120p. (J). (gr. 3-7). 1988. pap. 4.99 (1-55513-514-5, Chariot Bks) Chariot Family.

— Trouble in the Deep End. LC 93-16602. (T. J. Ser.). 1993. pap. 4.99 (0-7814-0701-X, Chariot Bks) Chariot Family.

Levene, Peter. How to Start & Run Your Own Shop. 192p. 1985. lib. bdg. 23.00 (0-86010-717-5); pap. text ed. 14.00 (0-86010-718-3) G & T Inc.

— How to Start & Run Your Own Shop. 2nd ed. (C). 1988. lib. bdg. 29.50 (1-85333-107-4, Pub. by Graham & Trotman UK); pap. text ed. 14.00 (1-85333-033-7, Pub. by Graham & Trotman UK) Kluwer Ac.

— The Shopkeeper's Handbook. (C). 1989. lib. bdg. 32.00 (1-85333-170-8, Pub. by Graham & Trotman UK); pap. text ed. 15.00 (1-85333-171-6, Pub. by Graham & Trotman UK) Kluwer Ac.

Levenfish, Gregory. Moscow International Chess Tournament, 1936. Adams, Jimmy, tr. (Tournament Book Ser.). (Illus.). 245p. 1988. 32.00 (0-939433-08-7) Caissa Edit.

Levenhagen, John I. HVAC Controls & Systems. 1992. text ed. 49.00 (0-07-037509-7) McGraw.

Levenkron, Steven. The Best Little Girl in the World. 1989. mass mkt. 5.99 (0-446-35865-7) Warner Bks.

— Obsessive-Compulsive Disorders: Treating & Understanding Crippling Habits. 208p. 1991. 17.95 (0-446-51435-7) Warner Bks.

— Obsessive-Compulsive Disorders: Treating & Understanding Crippling Habits. 1992. pap. 12.99 (0-446-39348-7) Warner Bks.

Levens, A. S. Graphical Methods in Research. LC 75-15676. 256p. 1975. reprint ed. 21.50 (0-88275-316-9) Krieger.

Levens, A. S. & Cooper, S. J. Problems in Mechanical Drawing. 6th ed. (Illus.). 224p. (C). 1985. write for info. (0-07-022334-3) McGraw.

Levens, A. S. & Edstrom, A. E. Problems in Mechanical Drawing. 4th ed. 1974. text ed. 23.16 (0-07-037349-3) McGraw.

Levens, Ann, jt. auth. see Renshaw, Polly.

*Levens, Mary. Magical Control of the Body: The Treatment of Eating Disorders Through Art Therapy. LC 94-23957. (Illus.). 160p. 1995. 55.00x (0-415-12217-1, C0232); pap. 17.95 (0-415-12216-3, C0393) Routledge.

Levens, Peter. Manipulus Vocabulorum. (Camden Society, London. Publications, First Ser.: No. 95). reprint ed. 90.00 (0-404-50195-8) AMS Pr.

— Manipulus Vocabulorum: Rhyming Dictionary of the English Language. (EETS, OS Ser.: No. 27). 1969. reprint ed. 50.00 (0-527-00027-2) Periodicals Srv.

Levens, R. G. Cicero: Verrine V. 250p. 1980. reprint ed. 14.95 (0-906515-74-2, Pub. by Brstl Class Pr UK) Focus Info Gr.

Levens, R. G., ed. A Book of Latin Letters. (Classical Texts Ser.). 196p. pap. 15.95 (0-631-13867-6, Pub. by Duckworth UK) Focus Info Gr.

*Levenson. Measure for Measure: A Musical History of Science. 1995. pap. 14.00 (0-684-80434-4, Fireside) S&S Trade.

Levenson, Alec R., jt. auth. see Solmon, Lewis C.

Levenson, Alvin J. Basic Psychopharmacology. 131p. 1981. text ed. write for info. (0-8261-2680-4); pap. text ed. 21.95 (0-8261-2681-2) Springer Pub.

Levenson, Alvin J. & Hall, Richard C., eds. Neuropsychiatric Manifestations of Physical Disease in the Elderly. (Aging Ser.: Vol. 14). 168p. 1981. text ed. 50.00 (0-89004-493-7) Raven.

Levenson, Ana & Eggly, Susan. Gramatica Espanola para Estudiantes de Ingles. Morton, Jacqueline, ed. 200p. (SPA.). 1993. pap. text ed. 9.95 (0-934034-17-6) Olivia & Hill.

*Levenson, Barry. Across the Blue Line. 1995. 17.95 (1-882146-46-8) A D G Prods.

— Exciting Concepts for Blues Guitar Soloing. Gordon, Andrew D., ed. (Illus.). 1994. audio 17.95 (1-882146-32-8) A D G Prods.

Levenson, Bob. Bill Bernbach's Book: A History of the Advertising that Changed the History of Advertising. LC 86-4013. (Illus.). 240p. 1987. 50.00 (0-394-54920-1, Villard Bks) Random.

Levenson, Bob, jt. auth. see McCarver, Tim.

Levenson, Carl, jt. ed. see Westphal, Jonathan.

*Levenson, Christopher. Arriving at Night. 80p. 1995. lib. bdg. 25.00 (0-8095-4524-1) Borgo Pr.

— Duplicities: New & Selected Poems. 128p. 1995. lib. bdg. 37.00 (0-8095-4802-X) Borgo Pr.

*Levenson, Christopher, ed. Reconcilable Differences: The Changing Face of Poetry by Canadian Men since 1970. (Illus.). 171p. 1995. 16.00 (1-896209-04-1, Pub. by Bayeaux Arts CN) Trafalgar.

Levenson, Christopher, tr. see Bauer, Wolfgang.

Levenson, Claire B. Temple Israel of Tallahassee, Florida: 1937-1987. 96p. 1987. text ed. 6.95 (0-9616000-1-2) Peninsular Pub Co.

Levenson, Dorothy. Mind & Body: A History of the American Psychosomatic Society. LC 94-5786. 1994. write for info. (0-683-05840-1) Williams & Wilkins.

*Levenson, Edgar. The Ambiguity of Change: An Inquiry into the Nature of Psychoanalytic Reality. LC 95-5184. 1995. pap. text ed. 25.00 (1-56821-467-7) Aronson.

*Levenson, Edgar A. The Fallacy of Understanding: An Inquiry into the Changing Structure of Psychoanalysis. LC 94-49190. 252p. 1995. pap. 25.00 (1-56821-478-2) Aronson.

— The Purloined Self: Interpersonal Perspective in Psychoanalysis. 288p. (Orig.). 1991. 39.95 (0-9629993-0-X); pap. 24.95 (0-9629993-1-8) Contemp Psycho.

Levenson, Elaine. Teaching Children about Life & Earth Science: Ideas & Activities Every Teacher & Parent Can Use. LC 93-40784. 1994. pap. text ed. 16.95 (0-07-037655-7) McGraw.

— Teaching Children about Science: Ideas & Activities Every Teacher & Parent Can Use. LC 93-34326. 1994. pap. text ed. 16.95 (0-07-037619-0) TAB Bks.

— Teaching Children about Science Ideas & Activities Teachers & Parents Can Use. 1993. pap. text ed. write for info. (0-8306-4598-5) TAB Bks.

Levenson, Eleanore, jt. auth. see Goldberg, Louis P.

Levenson-Estrada, Deborah. Trade Unionists Against Terror: Guatemala City, 1954-1985. LC 93-32054. (Illus.). 310p. (C). 1994. text ed. 45.00 (0-8078-2131-4); pap. text ed. 15.95 (0-8078-4440-3) U of NC Pr.

*Levenson, Hanna. Time-Limited Dynamic Psychotherapy: A Guide to Clinical Practice. LC 95-13934. 1995. 35.00 (0-465-08651-9) Basic.

Levenson, Harvey R. Complete Dictionary of Graphic Arts & Desktop Publishing Terminology: With Overview of Industry Growth & Technology. (Illus.). 276p. (Orig.). 1994. pap. 19.95 (0-932423-09-4) Summa Bks. THE COMPLETE DICTIONARY OF GRAPHIC ARTS & DESKTOP PUBLISHING TERMINOLOGY (WITH OVERVIEW OF INDUSTRY GROWTH, TECHNOLOGY, & SEGMENTS) is a beginner to advanced level dictionary of all aspects of Graphic Arts & Desktop Publishing: Art & Copy Preparation; Color Reproduction; Computer Hardware & Software; Desktop & Electronic Publishing; Digital Photography; Environmental Issues; Finishing; Photography; Image Assembly (Stripping); Ink; Laser Applications; Multimedia; Printing Processes; Proofing; Quality Control; Scanning; Substrates; Telecommunications; Typesetting; Imagesetting; & Typography. Every definition is cross-referenced to its primary area of focus to facilitate usage. Illustrations are provided for the traditional printing processes & for all the non- impact & digital printing processes. Plus complete bibliography & detailed information on all industry associations. Harvey R. Levenson, Ph.D. is currently Department Head, Graphic Communication Department, California Polytechnic State University at San Luis Obispo, California, with a prestigious career in the graphic arts profession & has created an authoritative dictionary for anyone working in these fields. Books can be ordered through a bookstore or directly from the publisher: Summa Books, 560 N. Moorpark Rd., Suite 134, Thousand Oaks, CA 91360. *Publisher Provided Annotation.*

Levenson, Howard. The Price of Justice, No. AJ3. 87p. (C). 1981. pap. 15.00 (0-900137-17-7, Pub. by NCCL UK) St Mut.

Levenson, J. C. The Mind & Art of Henry Adams. LC 68-13745. (Illus.). x, 430p. 1957. 52.50 (0-8047-0623-9) Stanford U Pr.

Levenson, J. C., ed. see Adams, Henry.

Levenson, J. C., ed. see Crane, Stephen.

Levenson, Jay, ed. The Age of the Baroque in Portugal. (Illus.). 256p. 1993. 60.00 (0-300-05841-1) Yale U Pr.

Levenson, Jay A. Circa 1492: Art in the Age of Exploration. LC 91-50590. (Illus.). 512p. (C). 1991. 30.00 (0-300-05167-0) Yale U Pr.

Levenson, Jay A., ed. The Age of Baroque in Portugal. LC 93-5424. 303p. 1994. pap. 25.00 (0-89468-198-2) Natl Gallery Art.

Levenson, Jon. Sinai & Zion, an Entry into the Jewish Bible. 1987. pap. text ed. 12.00 (0-06-254828-X) HarpC.

*Levenson, Jon D. Creation & the Persistence of Evil: The Jewish Prama of Divine Omnipotence. LC 94-31950. 1994. pap. 12.95 (0-691-02950-4) Princeton U Pr.

— The Death & Resurrection of the Beloved Son: The Transformation of Child Sacrifice in Judaism & Christianity. LC 93-7545. 272p. 1993. 27.50 (0-300-05532-3) Yale U Pr.

— The Hebrew Bible, the Old Testament, & Historical Criticism: Jews & Christians in Biblical Studies. LC 92-33118. 208p. (Orig.). 1993. pap. 14.99 (0-664-25407-1) Westminster John Knox.

— Sinai & Zion: An Entry Into the Jewish Bible. pap. 8.95 (0-00-003403-7) Harper SF.

— Theology of the Program of Restoration of Ezekiel 40-48. LC 76-3769. (Harvard Semitic Monographs: No. 10). 186p. reprint ed. pap. 53.10 (0-7837-5416-7, 2045180) Bks Demand.

Levenson, Jon D., jt. ed. see Halpern, Baruch.

Levenson, Jordan. How to Buy & Understand Refracting Telescopes. 3rd ed. LC 90-26742. (Illus.). 192p. (Orig.). 1991. 43.50 (0-914442-13-9) Levenson Pr.

— Your First Trip to Europe: Where, What & How, Vol. 1. LC 84-82461. 110p. 1985. pap. 18.50 (0-914442-11-2) Levenson Pr.

Levenson, Jordan, ed. Mourning Poetry from Obituaries in Ireland's Newspapers: The Book of Tears. LC 82-90968. (Orig.). 1983. pap. 15.95 (0-914442-10-4) Levenson Pr.

Levenson, Joseph R. Confucian China & Its Modern Fate: A Trilogy. 1968. reprint ed. 52.00 (0-520-00736-0); reprint ed. pap. 20.00 (0-520-00737-9) U CA Pr.

— Revolution & Cosmopolitanism: The Western Stage & the Chinese Stages. LC 73-121188. 196p. reprint ed. pap. 55.90 (0-7837-4833-7, 2044480) Bks Demand.

Levenson, L. L., ed. Surface Properties of Materials: Proceedings from the Conference on Surface Properties of Materials, Held at the University of Missouri, Rolla, June 24-27, 1974. (Journal of Surface Science Ser.: Vol. 48). 294p. 1975. reprint ed. 46.25 (0-444-10846-7, North Holland) Elsevier.

*Levenson, Laurie L. West's California Criminal Procedure. (West's Criminal Law Ser.). 1400p. (C). 1995. text ed. write for info. (0-314-07049-4) West Pub.

Levenson, Leah. With Wooden Sword: A Portrait of Francis Sheehy-Skeffington, Militant Pacifist. LC 82-22560. (Illus.). 282p. 1983. text ed. 35.00 (0-930350-42-1) NE U Pr.

Levenson, Leah & Natterstad, Jerry. Granville Hicks: The Intellectual in Mass Society. LC 93-16145. (Critical Perspectives on the Past Ser.). (Illus.). 336p. 1993. 39.95 (1-56639-104-0) Temple U Pr.

Levenson, Leah & Natterstad, Jerry H. Hanna Sheehy-Skeffington: Irish Feminist. LC 85-26223. (Irish Studies). (Illus.). 224p. 1986. 39.95x (0-8156-0199-9) Syracuse U Pr.

— Hanna Sheehy-Skeffington: Irish Feminist. LC 85-26223. (Irish Studies). (Illus.). 240p. 1989. pap. text ed. 12.95 (0-8156-2480-8) Syracuse U Pr.

Levenson, Lester. Keys to the Ultimate Freedom: Thoughts & Talks on Personal Transformation. 395p. (Orig.). 1993. pap. 17.97 (0-915721-03-1) Sedona Inst.

Levenson, M. D., et al, eds. Resonances: A Volume in Honor of Professor N. Bloembergen on His 70th Birthday. 512p. (C). 1990. text ed. 99.00 (981-02-0377-2); pap. text ed. 48.00 (981-02-0378-0) World Scientific Pub.

Levenson, Marc D. & Kano, Satoru, eds. Introduction to Nonlinear Laser Spectroscopy. 2nd ed. (Quantum Electronics - Principles & Applications Ser.). 288p. 1988. text ed. 66.00 (0-12-444722-8) Acad Pr.

Levenson, Marc D., jt. ed. see Yen, W. M.

Levenson, Marcia, tr. see Krupnik, Igor.

An Asterisk (*) at the beginning of an entry indicates that the title is appearing in BIP for the first time.

Levenson, Michael. A Genealogy of Modernism: A Study of English Literary Doctrine 1908-1922. 263p. 1986. pap. 18.95 (*0-521-33800-X*) Cambridge U Pr.

Levenson, Michael H. Modernism & the Fate of Individuality: Character & Novelistic Form from Conrad to Woolf. 224p. (C). 1991. 64.95 (*0-521-39491-0*) Cambridge U Pr.

Levenson, Roger. Women in Printing: Northern California, 1857-1890. (Illus.). 256p. 1995. 25.00 (*0-88496-365-9*); pap. 12.95 (*0-88496-366-7*) Capra Pr.

Levenson, Rosaline. Contractural Services in Government: Selected Bibliography on Practice in Federal, State & Local Agencies, Education in Foreign Countries, No. 980. 1976. 6.00 (*0-686-20386-0*) CPL Biblios.

— The Short-Lived Exploration of Isadore Meyerowitz. LC 94-77679. (Illus.). 80p. (Orig.). 1994. pap. 9.95 (*0-936029-35-8*) Western Bk Journ.

Levenson, S. Shell Collection: Os-2 2.0 Utilities. 1993. pap. 29.95 (*0-442-01585-2*) Van Nos Reinhold.

***Levenson, Steven.** Now That I Have Windows 4.0 on My Computer: What Do I Do Next? 300p. 1994. pap. 29.95 (*0-442-01835-5*) Van Nos Reinhold.

Levenson, Steven & Hertz, Eli. Now That I Have OS-2 2.1 on my Computer-What Do I Do Next? 2nd ed. LC 93-33005. 1993. pap. 24.95 (*0-442-01832-0*) Van Nos Reinhold.

Levenson, Steven A., ed. Medical Direction in Long-Term Care: A Guidebook for the Future. 2nd ed. LC 93-72380. 694p. 1993. 65.00 (*0-89089-547-3*) Carolina Acad Pr.

Levenson, Tom. Measure for Measure: A Musical History of Science. 1994. 25.00 (*0-671-78730-6*) S&S Trade.

Levenson, William B. & Stasheff, Edward. Teaching Through Radio & Television. rev. ed. LC 72-92303. 560p. 1969. reprint ed. text ed. 38.50 (*0-8371-2414-X*, LERT, Greenwood Pr) Greenwood.

Levenspiel, Octave. Chemical Reaction Engineering: An Introduction to the Design of Chemical Reactors. 2nd ed. LC 72-178146. 578p. 1972. Net. text ed. write for info. (*0-471-53016-6*) Wiley.

— Chemical Reactor Omnibook. 1989. 24.00 (*0-88246-164-8*) Oreg St U Bkstrs.

— Engineering Flow & Heat Exchange. LC 84-13448. (Chemical Engineering Ser.). 380p. 1984. 59.50 (*0-306-41599-2*, Plenum Pr) Plenum.

Levenspiel, Octave & Kunii, Daino. Fluidization Engineering. 2nd ed. (Chemical Engineering Ser.). 520p. 1991. text ed. 150.00 (*0-409-90233-0*) Buttrwrth-Heinemann.

Levenspiel, Octave, jt. auth. see Kunii, Daizo.

Levenstein, Aaron. Escape to Freedom: The Story of the International Rescue Committee. LC 82-21078. (Studies in Freedom: No. 2). (Illus.). xvi, 350p. 1983. text ed. 55.00 (*0-313-23815-4*, LSC/, Greenwood Pr) Greenwood.

Levenstein, Adolf. Die Arbeiterfrage: The Labor Question: with Particular Consideration of the Social Psychological Side of Modern Large-Scale Industry & Its Psycho-Physical Effect on Workers. LC 74-25767. (European Sociology Ser.). 410p. 1975. reprint ed. 34.95 (*0-405-06521-3*) Ayer.

Levenstein, Harvey. Paradox of Plenty: A Social History of Eating in Modern America. (Illus.). 368p. 1993. 30.00 (*0-19-505543-8*) OUP.

— Paradox of Plenty: A Social History of Eating in Modern America. (Illus.). 368p. 1994. reprint ed. pap. 12.95 (*0-19-508918-9*) OUP.

Levenstein, Harvey A. Communism, Anticommunism, & the CIO. LC 80-787. (Contributions in American History Ser.: No. 91). xii, 364p. 1981. text ed. 59.95 (*0-313-22072-7*, LEC/, Greenwood Pr) Greenwood.

— Labor Organization in the United States & Mexico: A History of Their Relations. LC 79-133498. 240p. 1971. text ed. 55.00 (*0-8371-5151-1*, LLO/, Greenwood Pr) Greenwood.

— Revolution at the Table: Transformation of the American Diet. (Illus.). 320p. 1988. 30.00 (*0-19-504365-0*) OUP.

Levenstein, Mary K. Caring for Your Cherished Possessions. 1994. pap. 12.00 (*0-517-88226-4*, Crown) Crown Pub Group.

— Everyday Cancer Risks & How to Avoid Them: Effective Ways to Lower Your Odds of Getting Cancer. LC 92-18103. 336p. (Orig.). 1992. pap. 11.95 (*0-89529-505-9*) Avery Pub.

Levenstein, Mary K. & Biddle, Cordelia F. Caring for your Cherished Possessions. (Illus.). 160p. 1989. 14.95 (*0-517-57087-4*, Crown) Crown Pub Group.

Levenstein, Phyllis. Messages from Home: The Mother-Child Home Program & the Prevention of School Disadvantage. LC 87-17315. 200p. 1988. 35.00 (*0-8142-0447-3*) Ohio St U Pr.

Levenston, E. A. The Stuff of Literature: Physical Aspects of Texts & Their Relation to Literary Meaning. LC 90-28937. 187p. (C). 1992. 59.50 (*0-7914-0889-2*); pap. 19.95 (*0-7914-0890-6*) State U NY Pr.

Levenston, Edward A. & Sivan, Reuven. The New Bantam-Megiddo Hebrew Dictionary. 736p. (HEB.). 1984. mass mkt. 5.95 (*0-553-26387-0*) Bantam.

Leventhal, Ann Z. Life-Lines. 220p. 1987. 15.00 (*0-913660-20-5*); pap. 12.00 (*0-913660-21-3*) Magic Cir Pr CT.

Leventhal, Bennett L., jt. ed. see Berlin, Irving N.

Leventhal, Brigid G. & Wittes, Robert E. Research Methods in Clinical Oncology. (Illus.). 256p. 1988. text ed. 94.00 (*0-88167-382-X*) Raven.

Leventhal, Debra. What Is Your Language? LC 93-10156. (Illus.). 32p. (J). (ps-1). 1994. 12.99 (*0-525-45133-1*, DCB) Dutton Child Bks.

***Leventhal, Jean H.** Echoes in the Text: Musical Citation in German Narratives from Theodor Fontane to Martin Walser. (Studies in Modern German Literature: Vol. 64). 272p. (C). 1995. text ed. 51.95 (*0-8204-2372-6*) P Lang Pubs.

Leventhal, Lance A. Microcomputer Experimentation with the IBM PC. 368p. (C). 1988. pap. text ed. 35.00 (*0-03-009542-5*); Solutions manual. write for info. (*0-03-009543-3*) SCP.

— Microcomputer Experimentation with the Intel SDK-86. 464p. (C). 1987. pap. text ed. 33.25 (*0-03-006703-0*); Solutions manual. write for info. (*0-03-007197-6*) SCP.

— Microcomputer Experimentation with the MOS Technology KIM-1. (Illus.). 480p. (C). 1982. pap. text ed. 41.00 (*0-13-580779-4*) P-H.

— Microcomputer Experimentation with the Motorola MC6800ECB. 368p. (C). 1988. text ed. 35.00 (*0-03-011782-8*); Solutions manual. write for info. (*0-03-011783-6*) SCP.

— Microcomputer Experimentation with the Synertek SYM-1. (Illus.). 512p. (C). 1983. text ed. 37.00 (*0-13-580910-X*) P-H.

— Turbo C. Quickstart. LC 91-53069. (Lance A. Leventhal Microtrend Ser.). 375p. (Orig.). 1992. pap. 29.95 (*0-915391-67-8*, Microtrend) Slawson Comm.

Leventhal, Lance A., ed. Modeling & Simulation on Microcomputers, 1982. 120p. 1982. pap. 20.00 (*0-686-36686-7*, MSM82) Soc Computer Sim.

Leventhal, Lance A., ed. see Antonovich, Michael.

Leventhal, Lance A., ed. see Antonvich, Michael.

Leventhal, Lance A., ed. see Chambers, Bill.

Leventhal, Lance A., ed. see Del Rossi, Robert.

Leventhal, Lance A., ed. see Heiser, Paul W.

Leventhal, Lance A., ed. see Moss, Julian V.

Leventhal, Lance A., ed. see Occhiogrosso, James.

Leventhal, Lance A., ed. see Occhiogrosso, Jim.

Leventhal, Lance A., ed. see Parker, Tim.

Leventhal, Lance A., ed. see Powe, James E.

Leventhal, Lance A., ed. see Powell, James E.

Leventhal, Lance A., ed. see Powell, Jim.

Leventhal, Lance A., ed. see Schmieder, Valerie.

Leventhal, Lance A., ed. see Spence, Rick.

Leventhal, Lance A., ed. see Taylor, Allan G.

Leventhal, Lance A., ed. see Taylor, Billy P.

Leventhal, Lance A., ed. see Teja, Ed & Johnson, Laura.

Leventhal, Lance A., ed. see Thro, Ellen.

Leventhal, Lance A., ed. see Vang, Soren.

Leventhal, Naomi, jt. auth. see Andrews, Dorine C.

Leventhal, Paul A. & Alexander, Yonah, eds. Preventing Nuclear Terrorism: The Report & Papers of the International Task Force on Prevention of Nuclear Terrorism. 480p. 1987. text ed. 56.00 (*0-669-14884-9*); pap. 24.95 (*0-669-14883-0*) Free Pr.

Leventhal, Paul L. & Tanzer, Sharon, eds. Averting a Latin American Nuclear Arms Race: New Prospects & Challenges for Argentine-Brazil Nuclear Cooperation. LC 91-31595. 273p. 1992. text ed. 69.95 (*0-312-07277-5*) St Martin.

***Leventhal, Robert S.** The Disciplines of Interpretation: Lessing, Herder, Schlegel, & Hermeneutics in Germany 1750-1800. LC 94-19772. (European Cultures Ser.: No. 5). 362p. (C). 1994. lib. bdg. 98.00 (*3-11-014424-7*) De Gruyter.

Leventhal, Robert S., ed. Reading after Foucault: Institutions, Disciplines, & Technologies of the Self in Germany, 1750-1830. LC 94-16730. (Kritik: German Literary Theory & Cultural Studies). (Illus.). 278p. 1994. text ed. 38.95 (*0-8143-2510-6*) Wayne St U Pr.

Leventhal, Ruth & Cheadle, Russell F. Medical Parasitology: A Self-Instructional Text. 3rd ed. LC 88-31019. (Illus.). 188p. (C). 1989. 33.95 (*0-8036-5599-1*) Davis Co.

— Medical Parasitology: A Self-Instructional Text. 4th ed. LC 84-14971. (Illus.). 240p. (C). 1995. pap. 33.95 (*0-8036-0041-0*) Davis Co.

Leventhal, Stan. The Black Marble Pool. 144p. (Orig.). 1990. 8.95 (*0-927200-05-8*) Amethyst NY.

— Candy Holidays. 160p. (Orig.). 1991. pap. 9.95 (*0-934411-51-4*, Banned Bks) Edward-William Austin.

— Faultlines. 148p. (Orig.). 1989. pap. 8.95 (*0-934411-26-3*, Banned Bks) Edward-William Austin.

— A Herd of Tiny Elephants. 150p. (Orig.). 1988. pap. 8.95 (*0-934411-13-1*, Banned Bks) Edward-William Austin.

— Mountain Climbing in Sheridan Square. 176p. (Orig.). 1988. pap. 8.95 (*0-934411-08-5*, Banned Bks) Edward-William Austin.

— Skydiving on Christopher Street. (Orig.). 1995. pap. text ed. 6.95 (*1-56333-287-6*) Masquerade.

Leventhal, Stan, ed. see Ameen, Mark.

Leventhal, Stan, ed. see Cooper, Dennis.

Leventhal, Stan, ed. see Houston, Bo.

Leventhal, Stan, ed. see Huston, Bo.

Leventhal, Stan, ed. see Killian, Kevin.

Leventhal, Stan, jt. auth. see Moore, Patrick.

Leventman, Seymour, jt. ed. see Figley, Charles R.

Leventon, Leonard. Brethren. 208p. 1994. pap. 7.95 (*1-56901-400-0*) NW Pub.

Leveque. Cutaneous Investigation in Health & Disease: Noninvasive Methods & Instrumentation. (Basic & Clinical Dermatology Ser.: Vol. 1). 464p. 1989. 175.00 (*0-8247-7967-3*) Dekker.

LeVeque, Ann. The Gallery As Studio. (Illus.). 18p. 1975. 1.00 (*0-915478-33-1*) Galleries Coll.

Leveque, Francois, et al, eds. Context of a Late Neanderthal: Implications of Multidisciplinary Research for the Transition to Upper Paleolithic Adaptations at Saint-Cesaire, Charente-Maritime, France. LC 93-14145. (Monographs in World Archaeology: No. 16). (Illus.). 143p. 1993. pap. 25.00 (*1-881094-05-7*) Prehistory Pr.

Leveque, H. Dictionnaire Thematique Francais-Argot. (FRE.). 1991. 49.95 (*0-685-48813-6*, F83770) Fr & Eur.

— Thematic French-Argot Dictionary: Dictionnaire Thematique Francais-Argot. (FRE.). 1991. 49.95 (*0-8288-3914-X*, F83770) Fr & Eur.

Leveque, Jean J. Degas Artists & Their Work. 1990. 12.99 (*0-517-69481-6*) Random Hse Value.

— Monet. (Artists & Their Work Ser.). 1990. 6.99 (*0-517-69480-8*) Random Hse Value.

Leveque, Jean-Luc & Agache. Aging Skin: Properties & Functional Changes. (Basic & Clinical Dermatology Ser.: Vol. 4). 320p. 1993. 150.00 (*0-8247-8791-9*) Dekker.

Leveque, Joseph D. Manual of Personnel Policies, Procedures & Operations. 2nd ed. LC 93-9305. 1993. write for info. (*0-13-020231-2*) P-H.

Leveque, Pierre. Birth of Greece. (Discoveries Ser.). 1994. pap. 12.95 (*0-8109-2843-4*) Abrams.

LeVeque, Randall J. Numerical Methods for Conservation Laws. (Lectures in Mathematics ETH Zurich: Vol. 1). 232p. 1990. 24.50 (*0-8176-2464-3*) Birkhauser.

LeVeque, W. J., ed. see Pure Mathematics Symposium Staff.

Leveque, William J. Elementary Theory of Numbers. Date not set. pap. 5.95 (*0-486-66348-5*) Dover.

LeVeque, William J., ed. Reviews in Number Theory: 1940-72, 6 vols., Set. LC 74-11335. 2931p. 1974. pap. 534.00 (*0-8218-0226-7*, REVNUM) Am Math.

— Reviews in Number Theory: 1940-72, 6 vols., Vol. 1. LC 74-11335. 420p. 1974. pap. 123.00 (*0-8218-0203-8*, REVNUM-1) Am Math.

— Reviews in Number Theory: 1940-72, 6 vols., Vol. 2. LC 74-11335. 672p. 1974. pap. 123.00 (*0-8218-0204-6*, REVNUM-2) Am Math.

— Reviews in Number Theory: 1940-72, 6 vols., Vol. 3. LC 74-11335. 377p. 1974. pap. 123.00 (*0-8218-0205-4*, REVNUM-3) Am Math.

— Reviews in Number Theory: 1940-72, 6 vols., Vol. 4. LC 74-11335. 582p. 1974. pap. 123.00 (*0-8218-0206-2*, REVNUM-4) Am Math.

— Reviews in Number Theory: 1940-72, 6 vols., Vol. 5. LC 74-11335. 470p. 1974. pap. 123.00 (*0-8218-0207-0*, REVNUM-5) Am Math.

— Reviews in Number Theory: 1940-72, 6 vols., Vol. 6. LC 74-11335. 410p. 1974. pap. 123.00 (*0-8218-0208-9*, REVNUM-6) Am Math.

Lever, A., jt. auth. see IUPAC Staff.

Lever, A. B., ed. Excited States & Reactive Intermediates Photochemistry, Photophysics, & Eletrochemistry. LC 86-7908. (ACS Symposium Ser.: No. 307). (Illus.). xii, 276p. 1986. 62.95 (*0-8412-0971-5*) Am Chemical.

— Inorganic Electronic Spectroscopy. 2nd ed. (Studies in Physical & Theoretical Chemistry: No. 33). 862p. 1984. 164.00 (*0-444-42389-3*, I-314-84) Elsevier.

Lever, A. B. & Gray, Harry B., eds. Iron Porphyrins, Pt. 1. (Physical Bioinorganic Chemistry Ser.). 256p. (C). 1982. write for info. (*0-201-05816-2*) Addison-Wesley.

— Iron Porphyrins, Pt. 2. (Physical Bioinorganic Chemistry Ser.). 256p. (C). 1982. write for info. (*0-201-05817-0*) Addison-Wesley.

Lever, A. P., jt. ed. see Leznoff, C. C.

Lever, B., ed. see Parker, John L.

Lever, B. G. Crop Protection Chemicals. (Applied Science & Industrial Technology Ser.). 1991. 81.00 (*0-13-194242-5*, 520504) P-H.

***Lever, Bernice.** Sometimes the Distance. 74p. 1995. 23.00 (*0-8095-4585-3*) Borgo Pr.

Lever, Charles J. Lord Kilgobbin: A Tale of Ireland in Our Own Time, 3 vols. in 1. LC 79-8149. reprint ed. 44.50 (*0-404-61961-4*) AMS Pr.

— The Martins of Cro-Martin. LC 79-8150. reprint ed. 44.50 (*0-404-61965-7*) AMS Pr.

— Our Mess, 3 vols. in 2, 1. LC 79-8152. (Illus.). reprint ed. write for info. (*0-404-61967-3*) AMS Pr.

— Our Mess, 3 vols. in 2, 2. LC 79-8152. (Illus.). reprint ed. write for info. (*0-404-61968-1*) AMS Pr.

— Our Mess, 3 vols. in 2, Set. LC 79-8152. (Illus.). reprint ed. 84.50 (*0-404-61966-5*) AMS Pr.

— St. Patrick's Eve; or, Three Eras in the Life of an Irish Peasant. LC 79-8151. (Illus.). reprint ed. 44.50 (*0-404-61970-3*) AMS Pr.

— Sir Brooke Fossbrooke, 3 vols. in 2, 1. LC 79-8422. reprint ed. write for info. (*0-404-61972-X*) AMS Pr.

— Sir Brooke Fossbrooke, 3 vols. in 2, 2. LC 79-8422. reprint ed. write for info. (*0-404-61973-8*) AMS Pr.

— Sir Brooke Fossbrooke, 3 vols. in 2, Set. LC 79-8422. reprint ed. 84.50 (*0-404-61971-1*) AMS Pr.

Lever, Christopher. The Mandarin Duck. 1989. pap. 25.00 (*0-7478-0055-3*, Pub. by Shire UK) St Mut.

***Lever, Darcy.** The Young Sea Officer's Sheet Anchor, or, a Key to the Leading of Rigging, or to Practical Seamanship - With Appendix. 2nd ed. (Illus.). 124p. 1995. reprint ed. lib. bdg. 35.00 (*0-8328-4490-X*) Higginson Bk Co.

Lever, J. L. & Boer, H. H., eds. Molluscan Neuro-Endocrinology. (Illus.). 268p. 1983. 32.00 (*0-444-85572-6*, North Holland) Elsevier.

Lever, J. L., jt. auth. see Cosh, J. A.

Lever, J. W., ed. Sonnets of the English Renaissance. LC 75-305102. (Renaissance Library). 186p. (C). 1974. pap. 22.00 (*0-485-12604-4*, Pub. by Athlone Pr UK) Humanities.

Lever, J. W., ed. see Shakespeare, William.

***Lever, Janet.** Soccer Madness: Brazil's Passion for the World's Most Popular Sport. rev. ed. (Illus.). 200p. (C). 1995. pap. text ed. 9.95x (*0-88133-843-5*) Waveland Pr.

Lever, Jill & Harris, John. Illustrated Dictionary of Architecture, 800-1914. 2nd ed. (Illus.). 224p. 1992. 60.00 (*0-571-13765-2*); pap. 29.95 (*0-571-13766-0*) Faber & Faber.

Lever, Maurice. Sade. 1994. pap. 15.95 (*0-15-600111-X*) HarBrace.

— Sade: A Biography. 1993. 35.00 (*0-374-20298-2*) FS&G.

Lever, O. W., ed. New Horizons in Carbonyl Chemistry: Reagents for Nucleophilic Acylation. 29p. 1976. pap. 12.75 (*0-08-021334-0*, Pergamon Pr) Elsevier.

Lever, Phillip & Gray, H. B., eds. Iron Porphyrins, Vol. 4, Pt. 3. LC 82-6786. (Physical Bioinorganic Chemistry Ser.). 309p. 1989. lib. bdg. 70.00 (*0-89573-718-3*) VCH Pubs.

Lever, Phillip, jt. ed. see Leznoff, Clifford C.

Lever, Ruth. The Consumer's Guide to Common Illnesses. LC 92-18688. (Illus.). 560p. (Orig.). 1992. pap. 13.00 (*0-671-74716-9*, Fireside) S&S Trade.

Lever, Thomas. Sermons: Fifteen Fifty. Arber, Edward, ed. 143p. 1990. pap. 15.00 (*0-87556-200-0*) Saifer.

Lever, Walter F. & Schaumburg-Lever, Gundula. Histopathology of the Skin. 7th ed. (Illus.). 976p. 1989. text ed. 180.00 (*0-397-50868-9*) Lippincott.

Lever, Walter F., jt. auth. see Schaumburg-Lever, Gundula.

Levere, Trevor H. Affinity & Matter: Elements of Chemical Philosophy, 1800-1865. LC 92-45001. (Classics in the History & Philosophy of Science Ser.: Vol. 12). 1993. pap. text ed. 36.00 (*2-88124-583-8*) Gordon & Breach.

— Chemists & Chemistry in Nature & Society, 1770-1878. (Collected Studies: No. CS 439). 304p. 1994. 89.95 (*0-86078-412-6*, Pub. by Variorum UK) Ashgate Pub Co.

— Poetry Realized in Nature: Samuel Taylor Coleridge & Early Nineteenth-Century Science. LC 81-1930. 272p. 1981. 59.95 (*0-521-23920-6*) Cambridge U Pr.

— Science & the Canadian Arctic: A Century of Exploration, 1918-1920. (Illus.). 400p. (C). 1993. 64.95 (*0-521-41933-6*) Cambridge U Pr.

Levere, Trevor H., ed. Editing Texts in the History of Science & Medicine: Papers Given at the Seventeenth Annual Conference on Editorial Problems. LC 82-15800. (Conference on Editorial Problems Ser.: No. 17). 1987. 37.50 (*0-404-63667-5*) AMS Pr.

Levere, Trevor H. & Shea, William R., eds. Nature, Experiment, & the Sciences. (C). 1990. lib. bdg. 123.00 (*0-7923-0420-9*) Kluwer Ac.

Leverenz, David. The Language of Puritan Feeling: An Exploration in Literature, Psychology, & Social History. LC 79-18579. 357p. reprint ed. pap. 101.80 (*0-8357-7948-3*, 2057023) Bks Demand.

— Manhood & the American Renaissance. LC 88-47914. 384p. 1989. 42.95 (*0-8014-2281-7*) Cornell U Pr.

— Manhood & the American Renaissance. LC 88-47914. 384p. 1990. reprint ed. pap. 16.95 (*0-8014-9743-4*) Cornell U Pr.

Leverenz, Jon, ed. see Nebenzahl, Kenneth.

Leverett, Brian. The Complete Book of Gardening. (Illus.). (Orig.). 1994. pap. 17.95 (*0-572-01986-6*, Pub. by W Foulsham UK) Trans-Atl Phila.

— Garden Design: Planning Smaller Gardens. 1992. pap. 16.95 (*1-85223-149-1*, Pub. by Crowood Pr UK) Trafalgar.

— Practical Bulb Growing. (Illus.). 64p. 1995. pap. 8.95 (*1-85223-857-7*, Pub. by Crowood Pr UK) Trafalgar.

— Water Gardens: Step by Step to Success. (Crowood Gardening Guides Ser.). (Illus.). 128p. 1991. pap. 16.95 (*1-85223-295-1*, Pub. by Crowood Pr UK) Trafalgar.

— Winemaking Month by Month. 3rd rev. ed. (Illus.). 160p. 1995. pap. 7.95 (*1-85327-096-2*, Pub. by Prism Pr UK) Atrium Pubs.

Leverett, Bruce. Sicilian Defense, Velimirovic Attack. (Illus.). 70p. (Orig.). 1983. pap. 6.00 (*0-931462-23-1*) Chess Ent Inc.

Leverett, Bruce W. Register Allocation in Optimizing Compilers. LC 83-18297. (Computer Science: Systems Programming Ser.: No. 19). 234p. reprint ed. pap. 66.70 (*0-685-20449-9*, 2070313) Bks Demand.

Leverett, James, et al, eds. New Plays U. S. A. Four. 254p. (C). 1988. 24.95 (*0-930452-80-1*); pap. 12.95 (*0-930452-81-X*) Theatre Comm.

Leverett, James & Osborn, M. Elizabeth, eds. New Plays U. S. A. Three. 300p. (Orig.). (C). 1986. text ed. 22.50 (*0-930452-53-4*); pap. 11.95 (*0-930452-54-2*) Theatre Comm.

Leverett, Rudy H. Legend of the Free State of Jones. LC 84-7513. (Illus.). 151p. (Orig.). reprint ed. pap. 43.10 (*0-7837-1070-4*, 2041593) Bks Demand.

Leverett, Trish. Birdies in the Oven: Aces in the Kitchen. (Illus.). 228p. (Orig.). 1986. pap. 10.00 (*0-317-58354-9*) Miss Annie's Pubns.

Leverett, Willard M. How to Buy a Good Used Piano. rev. ed. Roehl, Harvey, ed. LC 88-91309. (Illus.). 76p. 1988. pap. 8.95 (*0-9621063-0-5*) W Leverett.

Leverich, Bingham B., jt. auth. see Shniderman, Harry L.

Leverich, Kathleen. Best Enemies. LC 88-19150. (Illus.). (J). (gr. 1 up). 1989. 10.95 (*0-688-08316-1*) Greenwillow.

— Best Enemies. LC 88-19150. (Illus.). 80p. (J). (gr. 1-4). 1990. reprint ed. pap. 3.50 (*0-679-80156-1*) Knopf Bks Yng Read.

— Best Enemies Again. LC 90-30303. (Illus.). 96p. (J). (gr. 2 up). 1991. 12.95 (*0-688-09440-6*) Greenwillow.

— Best Enemies Forever. LC 94-26790. (Illus.). (J). 1995. 14.00 (*0-688-13963-9*) Greenwillow.

— Brigid Beware. LC 94-28614. (Illus.). Date not set. lib. bdg. write for info. (*0-679-95429-5*) Random.

— Brigid Beware. LC 94-28614. (Illus.). 1995. pap. 3.99 (*0-679-85429-0*) Random.

— Brigid, Bewitched. LC 93-43221. (First Stepping Stone Bks.). (Illus.). 80p. (Orig.). (J). (gr. 1-4). 1994. pap. 2.99 (*0-679-85433-9*) Random Bks Yng Read.

— Brigid, Bewitched. LC 93-43221. (First Stepping Stone Bks.). (Illus.). 80p. (Orig.). (J). (gr. 1-4). 1994. lib. bdg. 9.99 (*0-679-95433-3*) Random Bks Yng Read.

— Brigid the Bad. LC 95-5305. (Illus.). 1995. lib. bdg. write for info. (*0-679-97340-0*) Random.

— Brigid the Bad. LC 95-5305. (Illus.). (J). 1995. pap. 3.99 (*0-679-87340-6*) Random.

— Hilary & the Troublemakers. LC 91-15234. (J). 1992. 13.00 (*0-688-10857-1*) Greenwillow.

— Hilary & the Troublemakers. LC 91-13762. (Illus.). 144p. (J). (gr. 3-7). 1993. pap. 3.99 (0-679-84716-2, Bullseye Bks) Random Bks Yng Read.

— The Hungry Fox & the Foxy Duck. LC 78-11215. (Illus.). 48p. (J). (ps-3). 1979. 5.95 (0-8193-0987-7); lib. bdg. 5.95 (0-8193-0988-5) Parents.

Leverich, Kathleen, tr. see Hernandez, Xavier & Ballonga, Jordi.

Leverich, Kathleen, tr. see Ventura, Piero, et al.

***Leverich, Lyle.** Tom: The Unknown Tennessee Williams. LC 95-6038. 1995. 30.00 (0-517-70225-8, Crown) Crown Pub Group.

***Leveridge.** Therapy for the Burn Patient. 182p. 1991. pap. 43.25 (1-56593-013-4, 0255) Singular Publishing.

Levering, Donald. Outcroppings from Navajoland: Poems. LC 83-73475. 72p. 1985. 5.00 (0-912586-52-4) Navajo Coll Pr.

Levering, Frank & Urbanska, Wanda. Simple Living: One Couple's Search for a Better Life. 288p. 1993. pap. 10.00 (0-14-012339-3, Penguin Bks) Viking Penguin.

Levering, Joseph M. History of Bethlehem, Pennsylvania 1741-1892. LC 74-134432. reprint ed. 95.00 (0-404-07218-6) AMS Pr.

Levering, Miriam, ed. Rethinking Scripture: Essays from a Comparative Perspective. LC 87-9919. 276p. 1988. 59. 50 (0-88706-613-5); pap. 19.95 (0-88706-614-3) State U NY Pr.

Levering, Ralph B. The Cold War: 1945-1987. 2nd ed. Franklin, John H. & Eisenstadt, A. S., eds. LC 87-25459. (American History Ser.). (Illus.). 240p. (C). 1988. pap. text ed. write for info. (0-88295-858-5) Harlan Davidson.

— The Cold War, 1945-1991: A Post-Cold War History. Franklin, John H. & Eisenstadt, A. S., eds. (American History Ser.). (Illus.). 200p. (C). 1994. pap. text ed. write for info. (0-88295-912-3) Harlan Davidson.

***Levering, Robert.** Friends & Alcohol: Recovering a Forgotten Testimony. LC 94-65301. 1994. pap. 3.00 (0-87574-313-7) Pendle Hill.

— A Great Place to Work. 336p. 1990. reprint ed. pap. 9.95 (0-380-71103-6) Avon.

Levering, Robert & Moskowitz, Milton. The One Hundred Best Companies to Work for in America. LC 92-20442. 1993. 27.50 (0-385-26548-4) Doubleday.

— The One Hundred Best Companies to Work for in America. LC 93-6406. 528p. 1994. pap. 12.95 (0-452-27123-1, Plume) NAL-Dutton.

Levering, Ted. The Other Side of the Bridge. LC 91-91144. (Illus.). 400p. (Orig.). 1990. pap. 14.95 (0-9640957-7-7) Willowmead.

***Leverington, David.** A History of Astronomy from 1890 to the Present. LC 95-12034. 1995. pap. write for info. (3-540-19915-2) Spr-Verlag.

Leveriza, Jose P. Rage in the Hearts: A Historical Novel. 167p. (Orig.). (C). 1989. pap. 9.50 (971-10-0382-1, Pub. by New Day Pub PH) Cellar.

Levermore, Charles H. Forerunners & Competitors of the Pilgrims & Puritans, 2 vols., 1. 872p. 1989. reprint ed. write for info. (1-55613-210-7) Heritage Bk.

— Forerunners & Competitors of the Pilgrims & Puritans, 2 vols., 2. 872p. 1989. reprint ed. write for info. (1-55613-211-5) Heritage Bk.

— Forerunners & Competitors of the Pilgrims & Puritans, 2 vols., Set. 872p. 1989. reprint ed. pap. 42.50 (0-685-29819-1) Heritage Bk.

Levermore, G. J. Building Energy Management Systems: The Basics. (C). 1988. 140.00 (0-86022-205-5, Pub. by Build Servs Info Assn UK) St Mut.

— Building Energy Management Systems for the Operator. 1989. 80.00 (0-86022-216-0, Pub. by Build Servs Info Assn UK) St Mut.

— Control with a Building Energy Management System. (C). 1988. 140.00 (0-86022-204-7, Pub. by Build Servs Info Assn UK) St Mut.

— Monitoring & Targeting with a Building & Energy Management System. 1989. 80.00 (0-86022-239-X, Pub. by Build Servs Info Assn UK) St Mut.

— Presenting a Case for a Building & Energy Management System. 1989. 80.00 (0-86022-241-1, Pub. by Build Servs Info Assn UK) St Mut.

Levermore, J. G. Staff Reaction to Building Energy Management Systems. 1989. 80.00 (0-86022-233-0, Pub. by Build Servs Info Assn UK) St Mut.

***Levernier.** Phillis Wheatley. 1996. text ed. 22.95 (0-8057-4019-8) Macmillan.

Levernier, James A. & Cohen, Hennig, comps. The Indians & Their Captives. LC 76-57831. (Contributions in American Studies: No. 31). 291p. 1977. text ed. 59.95 (0-8371-9535-7, CIC/, Greenwood Pr) Greenwood.

Levernier, James A. & Wilmes, Douglas R., eds. American Writers Before Eighteen Hundred: A Biographical & Critical Reference Guide, 3 vols., 1. LC 82-933. 1984. text ed. 125.00 (0-313-23476-0, LWB/01) Greenwood.

— American Writers Before Eighteen Hundred: A Biographical & Critical Reference Guide, 3 vols., Set. LC 82-933. 1764p. 1984. text ed. 295.00 (0-313-22229-0, LWB/) Greenwood.

— American Writers Before Eighteen Hundred: A Biographical & Critical Reference Guide, 3 vols., Vol. 2. LC 82-933. 1984. text ed. 125.00 (0-313-23477-9, LWB/02) Greenwood.

— American Writers Before Eighteen Hundred: A Biographical & Critical Reference Guide, 3 vols., Vol. 3. LC 82-933. 1984. text ed. 125.00 (0-313-24096-5, LWB/03) Greenwood.

Levernier, James A., jt. auth. see Derounian-Stodola, Kathryn Zabelle.

Levers, Joan, ed. see McQueen, Iris.

Levers, Phyllis, ed. see Druhot, George S.

LeVert, Marianne. Crime. Leinwand, Gerald, ed. (American Issues Ser.). 160p. (YA). (gr. 9-12). 1991. 16.95 (0-8160-2102-3) Facts on File.

— The Welfare System: Help or Hindrance to the Poor? LC 94-21815. (Issue & Debate Ser.). (Illus.). 128p. (YA). (gr. 7 up). 1995. lib. bdg. 15.90 (1-56294-455-X) Millbrook Pr.

LeVert, Suzanne. AIDS: In Search of a Killer. LC 86-33218. (Illus.). 128p. (YA). (gr. 6 up). 1987. lib. bdg. 12.98 (0-671-62840-2, Julian Messner); lib. bdg. 5.95 (0-671-65662-7, Julian Messner) Silver Burdett Pr.

— Alberta. (Let's Discover Canada Ser.). (Illus.). 64p. (J). (gr. 3 up). 1991. lib. bdg. 16.95 (0-7910-1026-0) Chelsea Hse.

— British Columbia. (Let's Discover Canada Ser.). (Illus.). 64p. (YA). (gr. 3 up). 1991. lib. bdg. 16.95 (0-7910-1033-3) Chelsea Hse.

— Canada: Facts & Figures. (Let's Discover Canada Ser.). (Illus.). (J). (gr. 3 up). 1992. lib. bdg. 16.95 (0-7910-1035-X) Chelsea Hse.

— Dominion of Canada. (Let's Discover Canada Ser.). (Illus.). (J). (gr. 3 up). 1992. lib. bdg. 16.95 (0-7910-1034-1) Chelsea Hse.

— Edgar Allan Poe. (Library of Biography). (Illus.). 112p. (YA). (gr. 5 up). 1992. lib. bdg. 17.95 (0-7910-1640-4) Chelsea Hse.

— Hillary Rodham Clinton: First Lady. (Gateway Biographies Ser.). (Illus.). 48p. (J). (gr. 2-4). 1994. 13.40 (1-56294-432-0) Millbrook Pr.

Levert, Suzanne. Hillary Rodham Clinton; First Lady. (Gateway Biographies Ser.). (J). (gr. 4-7). 1994. pap. 6.95 (1-56294-726-5) Millbrook Pr.

LeVert, Suzanne. Let's Discover Canada, 14 bks. (Illus.). (YA). (gr. 3 up). 1991. lib. bdg. 237.30 (0-7910-1021-X) Chelsea Hse.

— Manitoba. (Let's Discover Canada Ser.). (Illus.). 64p. (YA). (gr. 3 up). 1991. lib. bdg. 16.95 (0-7910-1025-2) Chelsea Hse.

— New Brunswick. (Let's Discover Canada Ser.). (Illus.). (J). (gr. 3 up). 1992. lib. bdg. 16.95 (0-7910-1029-5) Chelsea Hse.

— Newfoundland. (Let's Discover Canada Ser.). (Illus.). (J). (gr. 3 up). 1992. lib. bdg. 16.95 (0-7910-1027-9) Chelsea Hse.

— Northwest Territories. (Let's Discover Canada Ser.). (Illus.). (J). (gr. 3 up). 1992. lib. bdg. 16.95 (0-7910-1031-7) Chelsea Hse.

— Nova Scotia. (Let's Discover Canada Ser.). (Illus.). (J). (gr. 3 up). 1992. lib. bdg. 16.95 (0-7910-1028-7) Chelsea Hse.

— Ontario. (Let's Discover Canada Ser.). (Illus.). 64p. (J). (gr. 3 up). 1991. lib. bdg. 16.95 (0-7910-1022-8) Chelsea Hse.

— Prince Edward Island. (Let's Discover Canada Ser.). (Illus.). 69p. (YA). (gr. 3 up). 1991. lib. bdg. 16.95 (0-7910-1023-6) Chelsea Hse.

— Quebec. (Let's Discover Canada Ser.). (Illus.). 64p. (YA). (gr. 3 up). 1991. lib. bdg. 16.95 (0-7910-1030-9) Chelsea Hse.

— Saskatchewan. (Let's Discover Canada Ser.). (Illus.). 64p. (J). (gr. 3 up). 1991. lib. bdg. 17.95 (0-7910-1024-4) Chelsea Hse.

— Teens Face to Face with Chronic Illness. LC 92-45819. (YA). 1993. lib. bdg. 13.98 (0-671-74540-9, Julian Messner); pap. 7.95 (0-671-74541-7, Julian Messner) Silver Burdett Pr.

— Yukon. (Let's Discover Canada Ser.). (Illus.). (J). (gr. 3 up). 1992. lib. bdg. 16.95 (0-7910-1032-5) Chelsea Hse.

LeVert, Suzanne, ed. see Keene, Carolyn.

LeVert, Suzanne, jt. auth. see Murphy, Kevin.

Levertoff, Paul, jt. tr. see Simon, Maurice.

Leverton, Charles W., Jr. On the Arizona Road with Bill Leverton. LC 86-15015. (Illus.). 128p. 1986. pap. 5.00 (0-914846-26-4) Golden West Pub.

Leverton, Ruth. Food Becomes You. LC 65-19382. (Illus.). 208p. 1965. pap. 11.95 (0-8138-2405-2) Iowa St U Pr.

Leverton, William H. Through the Box-Office Window. LC 79-8069. (Illus.). reprint ed. 26.50 (0-404-18379-4) AMS Pr.

Levertov, Denise. Breathing the Water. LC 86-23658. 96p. 1987. pap. 8.95 (0-8112-1027-8, NDP640) New Directions.

— Candles in Babylon. LC 81-22289. 144p. (C). 1982. pap. 7.95 (0-8112-0831-1, NDP533) New Directions.

— Collected Earlier Poems Nineteen Forty to Nineteen Sixty. LC 78-26199. 1979. pap. 7.95 (0-8112-0718-8, NDP475) New Directions.

— A Door in the Hive. LC 89-8304. 96p. 1989. 16.95 (0-8112-1118-5); pap. 8.95 (0-8112-1119-3, NDP685) New Directions.

— Evening Train. LC 92-20385. 128p. 1993. reprint ed. 17. 95 (0-8112-1219-X); reprint ed. pap. 8.95 (0-8112-1220-3, NDP750) New Directions.

— The Freeing of the Dust. LC 75-8568. 128p. 1975. pap. 6.95 (0-8112-0582-7, NDP401) New Directions.

— Life in the Forest. LC 78-9356. 1978. pap. 7.95 (0-8112-0693-9, NDP461) New Directions.

— Light up the Cave. LC 81-11295. 224p. 1981. 8.95 (0-8112-0813-3) New Directions.

— New & Selected Essays. LC 92-17887. 256p. 1992. 21.95 (0-8112-1217-3); pap. 11.95 (0-8112-1218-1, NDP749) New Directions.

— Oblique Prayers: New Poems with Fourteen Translations from Jean Joubert. LC 84-1103. 96p. 1984. pap. 6.95 (0-8112-0909-1, NDP578) New Directions.

— Poems, 1960 - 1967: Including The Jacob's Ladder, O Taste & See, & The Sorrow Dance. LC 82-2263. 256p. 1983. pap. 8.95 (0-8112-0859-1, NDP549) New Directions.

— Poems 1968-1972: Including Relearning the Alphabet, To Stay Alive & Footprints. LC 86-5389. 288p. 1987. pap. 12.95 (0-8112-1005-7, NDP629) New Directions.

— Tesserae. 160p. 1995. 18.95 (0-8112-1292-0) New Directions.

Levertov, Denise, jt. tr. see Dimock, Edward C., Jr.

Levertov, Denise, tr. see Guillevic, Eugene.

Levertov, Denise, tr. see Joubert, Jean.

Levertov, Denise, tr. see Meredith, William, ed.

Leverty, Maureen J., comp. Guide to Records of Northern Pacific Branch Lines, Subsidiaries, & Related Companies in the Minnesota Historical Society. LC 77-22701. 15p. 1977. pap. 2.00 (0-87351-117-4) Minn Hist.

Leveson, David J. Geology & the Urban Environment. (Illus.). 1980. text ed. 23.95 (0-19-502578-4) OUP.

— A Sense of the Earth. LC 82-11437. (Illus.). 176p. reprint ed. 18.00 (0-404-19149-5) AMS Pr.

Leveson, Irving, ed. Quantitative Explorations in Drug Abuse Policy. LC 79-21399. 183p. 1980. 45.00 (0-88331-192-5) Luce.

Leveson, Irving, jt. auth. see Fuchs, Victor R.

Leveson, Irving F. American Challenges: Business & Government in the World of the 1990s. LC 90-39104. 216p. 1991. text ed. 49.95 (0-275-93644-9, C3644, Praeger Pubs) Greenwood.

Leveson, L. F. Skytalk: English for Air Communication, Set 3. (C). 1984. audio 330.00 (0-85950-163-9, Pub. by S Thornes Pubs UK) St Mut.

Leveson, Nancy & Schuler, Douglas, eds. Directions & Implications of Advanced Computing, Vol. 2. (Directions & Implications of Advanced Computing Ser.). 288p. (C). 1993. text ed. 59.95 (0-89391-619-6) Ablex Pub.

Leveson, Nancy G. Safeware: System Safety & Computers. (Computer Science & Electrical Engineering Ser.). 680p. (C). 1995. text ed. 45.94x (0-201-11972-2) Addison-Wesley.

Levesque, Allen H., jt. auth. see Michelson, Arnold M.

Levesque, Allen H., jt. auth. see Pahlavan, Kaveh.

Levesque, Benoit, jt. auth. see Lacroix, Jean-Guy.

Levesque, Catherine. Journey Through Landscape in Seventeenth-Century Holland: The Harlem Print Series & Dutch Identity. LC 94-8293. 1995. 65.00 (0-271-01049-5) Pa St U Pr.

Levesque, Catherine, ed. Illustrated Bartsch, Vol. 6, Commentary: Netherlandish Artists. 1986. 140.00 (0-89835-105-7) Abaris Bks.

Levesque, Catou, ed. see Lempfrit, Honore-Timothee.

Levesque, Claude, jt. ed. see De Koninck, Jean-Marie.

Levesque, D., jt. auth. see Nadeau, M.

Levesque, George A. Black Boston: African American Life & Culture in Urban America, 1750-1860. LC 94-899. (Studies in African American History & Culture). (Illus.). 560p. 1994. 95.00 (0-8153-1593-7) Garland.

— Black Boston: African American Life in Urban America, 1750-1860. LC 94-899. (Studies in African American History & Culture). 1994. write for info. (0-8153-1003-X) Garland.

Levesque, George H. Social Credit & Catholicism. 1979. lib. bdg. 39.95 (0-8490-3006-4) Gordon Pr.

Levesque, Hector J., jt. ed. see Brachman, Ronald J.

Levesque, Jacques. Italian Communists Versus the Soviet Union: The PCI Charts a New Foreign Policy. Lavoy, Peter, tr. LC 87-82315. (Policy Papers in International Affairs Ser.: No. 34). vi, 57p. (C). 1987. pap. 5.95 (0-87725-534-2) U of Cal IAS.

Levesque, Jacques, jt. auth. see Lewis, Zack.

***Levesque, John.** Rossiter's Memory. 200p. 1995. 37.00 (0-8095-4579-9) Borgo Pr.

— Waiting for Aquarius. 200p. 1995. 37.00 (0-8095-4813-5) Borgo Pr.

Levesque, John M. & Williamson, Joel W., eds. A Guidebook to FORTRAN on Supercomputers. 370p. 1988. text ed. 59.00 (0-12-444760-0) Acad Pr.

Levesque, Joseph D. The Complete Hiring Manual: Policies, Practices & Procedures. 700p. 1991. 80.00 (0-685-52664-X) P-H.

— The Human Resource Problem-Solver's Handbook. 528p. 1992. text ed. 59.50 (0-07-037531-3) McGraw.

— Managing Discrimination Problems & Employee Needs, Vol. 1. (People in Organizations Ser.). 250p. (Orig.). 1989. pap. 24.95 (0-923606-06-8) Amer CC Pubs.

— Managing Employee Privacy Rights & Wrongful Discharge Problems, Vol. 2. (People in Organizations Ser.). 180p. (Orig.). 1989. pap. 21.95 (0-923606-09-2) Amer CC Pubs.

— Managing Policy, Behavior, & Performance Problems, Vol. 3. (People in Organizations Ser.). (Illus.). 225p. (Orig.). 1989. pap. 23.95 (0-923606-12-2) Amer CC Pubs.

— People in Organizations: A Guide to Solving Critical Human Resource Problems. (Illus.). 675p. (Orig.). 1989. 62.95 (0-923606-00-9); pap. 54.95 (0-923606-03-3) Amer CC Pubs.

Levesque-Lopman, Louise. Claiming Reality: Phenomenology & Women's Experience. (New Feminist Perspectives Ser.). 208p. 1988. 50.00 (0-8476-7580-7, DR 7580); pap. 22.50 (0-8476-7581-5, DR 7581) Rowman.

***Levesque, Paul.** The WOW Factory: Creating a Customer Focus Revolution in Your Business. LC 94-31410. 192p. 1994. 20.00 (0-7863-0386-7) Irwin Prof Pubng.

Levesque, Paul, tr. see Hermand, Jost.

Levesque, Rodrigue. History of Micronesia, Vol. 2: A Collection of Source Documents, Prelude to Conquest, 1561-1595. (Illus.). 704p. 1994. text ed. 100.00 (0-920201-02-4, Pub. by Levesque Pubns CN) UH Pr.

Levesque, Rodrigue, ed. History of Micronesia, Vol. 1: A Collection of Source Documents, European Discovery 1521-1560. (Illus.). 702p. 1994. text ed. 100.00 (0-920201-01-6, Pub. by Levesque Pubns CN) UH Pr.

Levete, Gina. Letting Go of Loneliness: A Positive Approach. 1993. pap. 12.95 (1-85230-398-0) Element MA.

— No Handicap to Dance: Creative Improvisation for People with or Without Disabilities. (Human Horizon Ser.). (Illus.). 146p. 1995. pap. 11.95 (0-285-64961-2, Pub. by Souvenir UK) Atrium Pubs.

***Levetin, Estelle & McMahon, Karen.** Plants & Society. 416p. (C). 1995. pap. write for info. (0-697-14064-4) Wm C Brown Pubs.

Leveton, Deborah. Iowa Artists, 1990. LC 90-82944. (Illus.). 50p. 1990. pap. 10.00 (1-879003-01-5) Edmundson.

— Iowa Artists, 1993. (Illus.). 48p. 1993. spiral bd., pap. 10. 00 (1-879003-09-0) Edmundson.

Leveton, Deborah & Heartney, Eleanor. Parts: Work by Rita McBride. LC 92-73382. (Illus.). 42p. 1992. pap. 16. 00 (1-879003-06-6) Edmundson.

Leveton, Deborah, ed. see Moore, Henry & Scott, Deborah E.

Leveton, Eva. Adolescent Crisis: Family Counseling Approaches. LC 84-10502. 304p. 1984. 28.95 (0-8261-4500-0) Springer Pub.

— A Clinician's Guide to Psychodrama. 2nd ed. LC 91-4823. Orig. Title: Psychodrama for the Timid Clinician. (Illus.). 192p. 1991. pap. 24.95 (0-8261-2262-0) Springer Pub.

Levett, John. The Ordering of Bees. LC 70-171773. (English Experience Ser.: No. 398). 96p. 1971. reprint ed. 35.00 (90-221-0398-6) Walter J Johnson.

Levett, M. J., tr. see Plato.

Levett, Paul N. Anaerobic Bacteria. 128p. 1991. text ed. 99. 95 (0-471-93237-X, Wiley-Liss); pap. text ed. 45.95 (0-471-93236-1, Wiley-Liss) Wiley.

— Anaerobic Bacteria: A Functional Biology. 224p. 1990. 69.00 (0-335-09206-3); pap. 33.00 (0-335-09205-5) Wiley.

Levett, Paul N., ed. Anaerobic Microbiology: A Practical Approach. (Practical Approach Ser.). (Illus.). 336p. 1992. 79.00 (0-19-963204-9, IRL Pr); pap. 44.00 (0-19-963262-6, IRL Pr) OUP.

Levey, A. B., jt. auth. see Martin, I.

***Levey, Barry.** Fishing the Oceans, Lakes - Rivers. (Illus.). 1992. 14.95 (1-885422-06-7) Fishermans Tales.

— Florida: Fishing & Diving the Wrecks & Artificial Reefs. (Illus.). 1994. 9.95 (1-885422-09-1) Fishermans Tales.

— Wonders of the Oceans: Sharks - Marine Mammals. (Illus.). 1995. spiral bd. 9.95 (1-885422-13-X) Fishermans Tales.

Levey, Gerald S., ed. Hormone-Receptor Interaction: Molecular Aspects. LC 76-583. (Modern Pharmacology-Toxicology Ser.: No. 9). (Illus.). 488p. reprint ed. pap. 139.10 (0-7837-0834-3, 2041148) Bks Demand.

Levey, Joel & Levey, Michelle. The Fine Arts of Relaxation, Concentration & Meditation: Ancient Skills for Modern Minds. rev. ed. LC 94-1269. (Illus.). 232p. 1994. pap. 14.95 (0-86171-040-1) Wisdom MA.

Levey, Joseph. The Jazz Experience: A Guide to Appreciation. 168p. (C). 1987. reprint ed. pap. text ed. 18.00 (0-8191-6068-7) U Pr of Amer.

Levey, Judith, ed. The Macmillan Dictionary for Children. rev. ed. LC 89-60916. (Illus.). 896p. (J). (gr. 3-7). 1989. text ed. 14.95 (0-02-761561-8, Mac Bks Young Read) S&S Childrens.

— The Macmillan First Dictionary. rev. ed. LC 90-6062. (Dictionaries Ser.). (Illus.). 416p. (J). (gr. k-4). 1990. text ed. 12.95 (0-02-761731-9, Mac Bks Young Read) S&S Childrens.

— The Macmillan Picture Wordbook. rev. ed. LC 90-8274. (Dictionaries Ser.). (Illus.). 64p. (J). (ps-1). 1990. text ed. 8.95 (0-02-754641-1, Mac Bks Young Read) S&S Childrens.

Levey, Judith S. The Concise Columbia Encyclopedia. large type ed. 1985. text ed. 368.00 (0-231-06026-2) Col U Pr.

Levey, Marc. The Thirty-Five Millimeter Film Source Book. 248p. 1992. 32.50 (0-240-80125-3, Focal) Buttrwrth-Heinemann.

Levey, Marc M., ed. Foreign Investment in the United States: Law, Taxation, Finance. 766p. 1989. text ed. 138. 00 (0-471-50045-3) Wiley.

— Foreign Investment in the United States: Law, Taxation, Finance. suppl. ed. 312p. 1992. 60.00 (0-471-54696-8) Wiley.

Levey, Martin & Petruck, Marvin, eds. Kushyar ibn Labban: "Principles of Hindu Reckoning" (Medieval Science Publications: No. 8). 128p. 1965. 30.00 (0-299-03610-3) U of Wis Pr.

Levey, Martin, tr. see Al-Kindi.

Levey, Martin, tr. see Shuja Ibn Aslam, Abukamil.

Levey, Michael. From Giotto to Cezanne: A Concise History of Painting. LC 84-50479. (World of Art Ser.). (Illus.). 324p. 1985. pap. 14.95 (0-500-20024-6) Thames Hudson.

— Giambattista Tiepolo: His Life & Art. (Illus.). 302p. 1994. pap. 30.00 (0-300-06046-7) Yale U Pr.

— High Renaissance. 320p. 1978. pap. 9.95 (0-14-021823-8, Penguin Bks) Viking Penguin.

— The Later Italian Pictures in the Collection of Her Majesty the Queen. 2nd ed. (Pictures in the Royal Collections). (Illus.). 492p. (C). 1991. 155.00 (0-521-26328-X) Cambridge U Pr.

— The Painter Depicted: Painters As a Subject in Painting. (Illus.). 1982. 10.95 (0-500-55013-1) Thames Hudson.

— Painting & Sculpture in France: 1700-1789. (Pelican History of Art Ser.). (Illus.). 304p. (C). 1993. text ed. 55. 00 (0-300-05344-4) Yale U Pr.

— Painting in Eighteenth-Century Venice. 3rd ed. LC 94-17558. 1994. write for info. (0-300-06194-3) Yale U Pr.

— Painting in Eighteenth-Century Venice. 3rd ed. LC 94-17558. 1994. pap. 18.00x (0-300-06057-2) Yale U Pr.

— Rococo to Revolution. (World of Art Ser.). (Illus.). 252p. 1985. pap. 14.95 (0-500-20050-5) Thames Hudson.

An Asterisk (*) at the beginning of an entry indicates that the title is appearing in BIP for the first time.

— Seventeenth & Eighteenth Century Italian Schools. (National Gallery Publications). (Illus.). 1989. pap. text ed. 25.00 (*0-300-06142-0*) Yale U Pr.

Levey, Michael, ed. see Pater, Walter.

Levey, Michelle, jt. auth. see Levey, Joel.

Levey, R. A., ed. Core & Log Analyses of Depositional Systems & Reservoir Properties of Gulf Coast Natural Gas Reservoirs: An Integrated Approach to Infield Reserve Growth in Frio, Vicksburg, & Wilcox Sandstones. (Illus.). 56p. 1992. pap. 3.50 (*0-317-05170-9*, GC92-1) Bur Econ Geology.

***Levey, R. A., et al.** Quantifying Secondary Gas Resources in Fluvial-Deltaic Reservoirs: A Case History from Stratton Field, South Texas. (Illus.). 38p. 1994. 4.00 (*0-614-01870-6*) Bur Econ Geology.

***Levey, R. A., et al, comps.** CD-ROM: Target Technology Applications for Infield Reserve Growth. 1994. 20.00 (*0-614-01873-0*) Bur Econ Geology.

— 3-D Seismic & Well Log Data Set: Fluvial Reservoir Systems-Stratton Field, South Texas. 30p. 1994. audio, 3.5 hd 40.00 (*0-614-01872-2*) Bur Econ Geology.

Levey, Samson H. The Messiah: An Aramoic Interpretation. 1974. 25.00 (*0-87820-402-4*) Ktav.

— The Targum of Ezekiel. (Aramaic Bible (The Targums) Ser.: Vol, 13). 145p. (Orig.). 1987. 37.95 (*0-8146-5482-7*) Liturgical Pr.

Levey, Samuel, ed. Hospital Leadership & Accountability. LC 92-1523. 441p. (Orig.). 1992. pap. text ed. 37.00 (*0-910701-84-9*, 0918) Health Admin Pr.

Levey, Samuel & Hill, James, eds. Alternative Delivery Systems: Approaches for the Health Care Executive. LC 88-16298. (Case Studies in Health Administration: Vol. 7). 95p. 1988. pap. 25.00 (*0-910701-40-7*, 0115) Health Admin Pr.

Levey, Santina M. & Payne, Patricia C. Le Pompe, Fifteen Hundred Fifty-Nine: Patterns for Venetian Bobbin Lace. 1983. pap. 19.95 (*0-903585-16-2*) Robin & Russ.

Levi. The Aquarian Gospel of Jesus Christ. 1972. 18.95 (*0-87516-041-7*); pap. 14.95 (*0-87516-168-5*) DeVorss.

— The Dream of Confucius. 1992. 22.95 (*0-15-126570-4*) HarBrace.

Levi, A. H., ed. Guide to French Literature: 1789 to the Present, Vol. 2. 884p. 1992. lib. bdg. 120.00 (*1-55862-159-8*) St James Pr.

Levi, A. H., ed. see Erasmus, Desiderius.

Levi, Albert W. Varieties of Experience: An Introduction to Philosophy. LC 57-6807. 537p. reprint ed. pap. 153.10 (*0-317-08882-3*, 2012555) Bks Demand.

Levi, Albert W. & Smith, Ralph A. Art Education: A Critical Necessity. (Disciplines in Art Education, Contexts of Understanding Ser.). (Illus.). 280p. 1991. 39.95 (*0-252-01813-3*); pap. 16.95 (*0-252-06185-3*) U of Ill Pr.

Levi, Anthony, ed. Guide to French Literature: Seventeen-Hundred Eighty-Nine to the Present, 2 vols., Set. 1992. 210.00 (*1-55862-320-5*, 200234-M99109) St James Pr.

— Guide to French Literature, Vol. I: 1789 to the Present. (Reference Guide to French Literature Ser.: Vol. 1). 884p. 1992. lib. bdg. 115.00 (*1-55862-086-9*, 200116) St James Pr.

Levi, Anthony, ed. see Pascal, Blaise.

Levi, Barbara G., et al, eds. The Future of Land-Based Strategic Missiles. (Illus.). 290p. 1989. 49.00 (*0-88318-619-5*) Am Inst Physics.

Levi, Carlo. Le Christ S'Est Arrete a Eboli. (FRE.). 1977. pap. 11.95 (*0-7859-4085-5*) Fr & Eur.

— Christ Stopped at Eboli. Frenaye, Frances, tr. 268p. 1947. pap. 10.00 (*0-374-50316-8*) FS&G.

Levi-Civita, Tullio. The Absolute Differential Calculus: Calculus of Tensors. Persico, Enrico, ed. Long, Marjorie, tr. LC 76-27497. (Illus.). 480p. 1977. reprint ed. pap. text ed. 9.95 (*0-486-63401-9*) Dover.

Levi, Constance A., jt. auth. see Levi, James H.

Levi, D. & Winternitz, P., eds. Painleve Transcendents: Their Asymptotics & Physical Applications. (NATO ASI Series B, Physics: Vol. 278). (Illus.). 462p. (C). 1992. 125.00 (*0-306-44050-4*, Plenum Pr) Plenum.

— Symmetries & Nonlinear Phenomena: Paipa, Columbia, Feb. 22-26, 1988. 472p. 1988. pap. 52.00 (*9971-5-0701-3*) World Scientific Pub.

Levi, Darrell E. Michael Manley: The Making of a Leader. LC 86-30826. (Illus.). 364p. 1990. 32.00 (*0-8203-1221-5*) U of Ga Pr.

— The Prados of Sao Paulo, Brazil: An Elite Family & Social Change, 1840-1930. LC 86-30826. 298p. 1987. 35.00 (*0-8203-0944-3*) U of Ga Pr.

Levi, Don S. Critical Thinking & Logic. 449p. (C). 1991. pap. text ed. 27.95 (*1-879215-01-2*) Sheffield WI.

Levi, Donald R. Evidencing Kansas Land Titles. LC 85-52469. 177p. 1986. pap. text ed. 20.00 (*0-914111-05-1*) Woodlawn Pubs.

— Evidencing Missouri Land Titles. LC 87-50052. 155p. 1987. pap. text ed. 20.00 (*0-914111-09-4*) Woodlawn Pubs.

— How to Teach Real Estate to Adults: A Handbook for Instructors. 134p. (Orig.). 1989. pap. text ed. 9.95 (*0-9621154-0-1*) Real Est Educ.

— Kansas Real Estate Principles. 4th ed. LC 86-51503. 444p. 1987. pap. text ed. 25.00 (*0-914111-08-6*) Woodlawn Pubs.

Levi, Donald R., jt. auth. see Spotts, W. P.

Levi, Donald R., et al. Evidencing Nebraska Land Titles. LC 89-51305. 163p. 1989. pap. text ed. 35.00 (*0-914111-11-6*) Woodlawn Pubs.

Levi, Dorothy. A Very Special Friend. LC 88-33410. (Illus.). 40p. (J). (gr. k-3). 1989. 9.95 (*0-930323-55-6*) Gallaudet Univ Pr.

Levi, Dorothy H. A Very Special Friend. (Illus.). 32p. (J). (gr. k-3). 9.95 (*1-878363-24-7*) Forest Hse.

— A Very Special Sister. (Awareness & Caring - Sign Language Storybook Ser.). (Illus.). 36p. (J). (gr. k-3). 1992. lib. bdg. 11.95 (*1-56674-033-9*) Forest Hse.

Levi, Edward H. Introduction to Legal Reasoning. rev. ed. LC 49-11213. 1962. pap. text ed. 6.95 (*0-226-47408-9*, P84) U Ch Pr.

Levi, Eliphas. The Book of Splendours. 191p. (ENG.). 1973. 10.95 (*0-87728-614-0*) Weiser.

— The Conjuration of the Four. Doubleday, Abner, tr. 1991. pap. 3.95 (*1-55818-140-7*, Sure Fire) Holmes Pub.

— History of Magic. 1973. 250.00 (*0-8490-0332-6*) Gordon Pr.

— History of Magic. 384p. 1970. pap. 17.95 (*0-87728-077-0*) Weiser.

— The History of Magic: Including a Clear & Precise Exposition of Its Procedures, Its Rites & Its Mysteries. Waite, Arthur E., tr. (Illus.). 560p. 1993. pap. 29.95 (*1-56459-404-1*) Kessinger Pub.

— The Kabbalistic Prayer. Westcott, W. W., tr. reprint ed. pap. 3.95 (*1-55818-119-9*, Sure Fire) Holmes Pub.

— The Magical Ritual of the Sanctum Regnum. Westcott, W. W., ed. reprint ed. pap. 9.95 (*1-55818-184-9*, Sure Fire) Holmes Pub.

— The Magical Ritual of the Sanctum Regnum. Westcott, W. Wynn, ed. 108p. 1992. reprint ed. pap. 8.95 (*0-922802-95-5*) Kessinger Pub.

— The Paradoxes of the Highest Science. 2nd ed. 172p. 1969. reprint ed. spiral bd. 6.60 (*0-7873-0555-3*) Mokelumne.

— The Paradoxes of the Highest Science. 172p. 1992. reprint ed. pap. 16.95 (*1-56459-020-8*) Kessinger Pub.

— Science of Hermes. Waite, Arthur E., tr. 1993. pap. 4.95 (*1-55818-207-1*) Holmes Pub.

— Transcendental Magic. Waite, A. E., tr. LC 72-16629. (Illus.). 438p. 1968. pap. 17.95 (*0-87728-079-7*) Weiser.

— Transcendental Magic, Its Doctrine & Ritual. 420p. 1976. reprint ed. spiral bd. 19.25 (*0-7873-0556-1*) Mokelumne.

Levi, Enrico. Polyphase Motors: A Direct Approach to Their Design. LC 83-16850. 438p. 1984. text ed. 125.00 (*0-471-89866-X*, Wiley-Interscience) Wiley.

Levi, Enrique J. Duplications: And Other Stories. Miller, Yvette E., ed. Chambers, Leland H., tr. LC 94-19375. (Discoveries Ser.). 192p. 1994. pap. 15.95 (*0-935480-65-X*) Lat Am Lit Rev Pr.

Levi, Enrique J., ed. When New Flowers Bloomed: Short Stories by Women Writers from Costa Rica & Panama. LC 91-26038. 208p. 1991. pap. 14.95 (*0-935480-47-1*) Lat Am Lit Rev Pr.

Levi, Enrique J. & Chambers, Leland H., eds. Contemporary Short Stories from Central America. (Institute of Latin American Studies). 320p. (Orig.). (C). 1994. text ed. 37.50 (*0-292-74030-1*); pap. 15.95 (*0-292-74034-4*) U of Tex Pr.

***Levi, Enzo.** The Science of Water: The Foundation of Modern Hydraulics. Edina, Daniel E., tr. LC 94-44189. 1995. write for info. (*0-7844-0005-9*) Am Soc Civil Eng.

***Levi, G. & Rodriguez-Artalejo, M., eds.** Algebraic & Logic Programming: 4th International Conference, ALP '94, Madrid, Spain, September 14 16, 1994. Proceedings. (Lecture Notes in Computer Science: Vol. 850). 304p. 1994. pap. 47.00 (*3-540-58431-5*) Spr-Verlag.

Levi, G., tr. see Segal, B., ed.

Levi, Gershon, ed. see Alon, Gedaliah.

Levi, Gerson B., ed. see Hirsch, Emil G.

***Levi, Giorgio, ed.** Advances in Logic Programming Theory. (International Schools for Computer Scientists Ser.). 268p. 1995. text ed. 72.00 (*0-19-853853-7*) OUP.

***Levi, Giorgio & Artalejo, Mario R.** Algebraic & Logic Programming: Proceedings of the 4th International Conference, ALP '94, Madrid, Spain, September 1994. LC 94-33286. (Series Lecture Notes in Computer Science Ser.: 850). 1994. write for info. (*0-387-58431-5*) Spr-Verlag.

Levi, Giorgio & Martelli, Maurizio, eds. Logic Programming: Proceedings of the Sixth International Conference. (Logic Programming - Research Reports & Notes). 700p. 1989. pap. 60.00 (*0-262-62065-0*) MIT Pr.

Levi, Giorgio, jt. ed. see Kirchner, H.

Levi, Giovanni. Inheriting Power: The Story of an Exorcist. Cochrane, Lydia G., tr. (Illus.). xviii, 210p. 1988. lib. bdg. 29.95 (*0-226-47417-8*) U Ch Pr.

Levi, Herbert W. & Levi, Lorna R. Spiders & Their Kin. rev. ed. Zim, Herbert S. & Fichter, George S., eds. (Golden Guide Ser.). (Illus.). (J). (gr. 9 up). 1969. pap. write for info. (*0-307-24021-5*, Golden Pr) Western Pub.

Levi, Hilde. George de Hevesy: Life & Work. (Illus.). 147p. 1985. 70.00 (*0-85274-555-9*) IOP Pub.

Levi, Honor, tr. see Pascal, Blaise.

Levi, Howard. Elements of Algebra. 4th ed. 189p. (C). 1990. text ed. 12.95 (*0-8284-0103-9*, 103) Chelsea Pub.

— Foundations of Geometry & Trignometry. 2nd ed. LC 74-23743. 360p. 1975. reprint ed. 36.00 (*0-88275-239-1*) Krieger.

— Topics in Geometry. LC 75-19477. 112p. 1975. reprint ed. 13.50 (*0-88275-280-4*) Krieger.

Levi, Isaac. Decisions & Revisions: Philosophical Essays on Knowledge & Value. 310p. 1984. 64.95 (*0-521-25457-4*) Cambridge U Pr.

— The Enterprise of Knowledge: An Essay on Knowledge, Credal Probability & Chance. 480p. 1980. pap. 14.50 (*0-262-62043-X*) MIT Pr.

— The Fixation of Belief & Its Undoing: Changing Beliefs Through Inquiry. 220p. (C). 1991. 44.95 (*0-521-41266-8*) Cambridge U Pr.

— Gambling with Truth: An Essay on Induction & the Aims of Science. 264p. 1974. pap. 10.95x (*0-262-62026-X*) MIT Pr.

— Hard Choices: Decision Making under Unresolved Conflict. 250p. (C). 1990. pap. 21.95 (*0-521-38630-6*) Cambridge U Pr.

Levi, J. N. & Walker, A. G., eds. Language in the Judicial Process. (Law, Society, & Policy Ser.: Vol. 5). (Illus.). 357p. 1990. 59.50 (*0-306-43551-9*, Plenum Pr) Plenum.

Levi, James H. & Levi, Constance A. Larchmont, New York, the Way It Was: Picture Postcards of Old Larchmont. (Illus.). 52p. 1990. pap. 14.95 (*0-9628437-0-9*) J H Levi.

***Levi, Jan H.** A Muriel Rukeyser Reader. Rukeyser, Muriel, ed. 320p. 1995. pap. 15.00 (*0-393-31323-9*) Norton.

Levi, Jan H., ed. see Morin, France, et al.

Levi, Jan Heller, ed. A Muriel Rukeyeser Reader. 320p. 1994. 25.00 (*0-393-03566-2*) Norton.

Levi, Jean. The Chinese Emperor. 1989. pap. 8.95 (*0-394-75996-6*, Vin) Random.

Levi, John & Havinden, Michael. Economics of African Agriculture. LC 82-165400. (Illus.). 183p. reprint ed. pap. 52.20 (*0-8357-6102-9*, 2034436) Bks Demand.

Levi, Jonathan. Guide for the Perplexed. 1992. 19.50 (*0-679-40893-2*) Random.

— A Guide for the Perplexed. LC 92-50606. 1993. pap. 12.00 (*0-679-73969-6*, Vin) Random.

***Levi, Joseph A., ed.** Alfonso X, el Sabio, Estoria De Alexandre el Grand, General Estoria (Quarta Parte) - The Life of Alexander the Great As Narrated by King Alfonso X the Wise, of Castile, in the General Estoria: Manuscript U. Vatican Urb. Lat. 539. LC 95-14847. (Hispanic Literature Ser.: Vol. 26). (Illus.). 224p. 1996. text ed. 89.95 (*0-7734-8900-2*) E Mellen.

Levi, Judith N. The Syntax & Semantics of Complex Nominals. 1978. text ed. 60.00 (*0-12-445150-0*) Acad Pr.

Levi, Ken, ed. Violence & Religious Commitment: Implications of Jim Jones's People's Temple Movement. LC 81-83147. (Illus.). 224p. (C). 1982. 28.50 (*0-271-00296-4*) Pa St U Pr.

Levi, L. Stress in Industry: Cause, Effects, & Prevention. (Occupational Safety & Health Ser.: No. 51). vi, 70p. (Orig.). 1984. pap. 10.00 (*92-2-103539-5*) Intl Labour Office.

Levi, Lennart. Stress & Distress in Response to Psychosocial Stimuli: Lab & Real-Life St on Sympatho Adrenomedullary & Rel Re-Act. LC 72-88767. 1972. 72.00 (*0-08-017125-7*, Pub. by Pergamon Repr UK) Franklin.

Levi, Lennart, ed. Society, Stress, & Disease: Vol. 5: Old Age. (Illus.). 410p. 1988. 180.00 (*0-19-264422-X*) OUP.

— Society, Stress, & Disease, Vol. 4: Working Life. 1982. text ed. 79.50 (*0-19-264421-1*) OUP.

Levi, Leo, ed. Handbook of Tables of Functions for Applied Optics, CRC. (Handbook Ser.). 640p. 1974. 152.95 (*0-87819-371-5*, QC, CRC Reprint) Franklin.

Levi, Lorna R., jt. auth. see Levi, Herbert W.

Levi, Louise L., tr. see Daumal, Rene.

Levi, M. Basic Notes in Psychopharmacology. 64p. (C). 1993. pap. text ed. 10.00 (*0-7923-8806-2*) Kluwer Ac.

— Franz Kafka & Anarchism. 1972. 250.00 (*0-87700-189-8*) Revisionist Pr.

***Levi-Malvano, E.** Montesquieu & Machiavelli. Pansini, Anthony J., tr. & intro. by. xx, 87p. (Orig.). (C). 1991. pap. 15.00x (*0-911876-05-7*) Greenvale.

Levi, Margaret. Marxism, Set, Vols. 1-2. (Schools of Thought in Politics Ser.: No. 1). 1188p. 1991. Set. text ed. 279.95 (*1-85278-355-9*, Pub. by E Elgar Pub UK) Ashgate Pub Co.

— Of Rule & Revenue. (California Series on Social Choice & Political Economy: Vol. 13). 1988. pap. 15.00 (*0-520-06750-9*) U CA Pr.

Levi, Margaret, jt. ed. see Cook, Karen S.

Levi, Mark. Qualitative Analysis of the Periodically Forced Relaxation Oscillations. LC 81-3642. (Memoirs of the American Mathematical Society Ser.: No. 32/224). 147p. 1981. pap. 17.00 (*0-8218-2244-6*, MEMO 32/244) Am Math.

Levi, Mark & Salam, Fathi, eds. Dynamical Systems Approaches to Nonlinear Problems in Systems & Circuits. LC 87-63139. (Proceedings in Applied Mathematics Ser.: No. 31). (Illus.). xvi, 413p. 1988. text ed. 49.75 (*0-89871-218-1*) Soc Indus-Appl Math.

***Levi, Maurice.** Economics & the Modern World. 637p. (C). 1994. pap. write for info. (*0-669-21668-2*) Heath.

— International Finance: The Markets & Financial Management of Multinational Business. 2nd ed. 1990. text ed. write for info. (*0-07-037483-X*) McGraw.

— Thinking Economically: How Economic Principles Can Contribute to Clear Thinking. LC 83-46090. 304p. 1987. pap. text ed. 15.00 (*0-465-08537-7*) Basic.

Levi, Maurice D., jt. auth. see Kupferman, Martin.

Levi, Michael. The Phantom Capitalists: Control of Long-Firm Fraud. Radzinowicz, Leon, ed. (Cambridge Studies in Criminology: Vol. XLIV). xv, 346p. 1981. text ed. 69.95 (*0-435-82520-8*) Ashgate Pub Co.

— Regulating Fraud: White-Collar Crime & the Criminal Process. 416p. 1990. 55.00 (*0-422-61160-3*, A0718); pap. 22.50 (*0-415-01812-9*, A3455) Routledge Chapman & Hall.

Levi, Michael I. Basic Notes in Psychiatry. rev. ed. (C). 1992. pap. text ed. 12.50 (*0-7923-8990-5*) Kluwer Ac.

— PMPs for the MRCPsych, Pt. II. (C). 1992. pap. text ed. 12.50 (*0-7923-8993-X*) Kluwer Ac.

Levi, Miriam. Effective Jewish Parenting. 1986. 15.95 (*0-87306-405-4*); pap. 12.95 (*0-685-12341-3*) Feldheim.

Levi-Montalcini, Rita. Nerve Cells, Transmitters & Behavior. 680p. 1980. 151.50 (*0-444-80243-6*) Elsevier.

Levi, Patricia E., jt. ed. see Chambers, Janice E.

Levi, Patricia E., jt. auth. see Hodgson, Ernest.

Levi, Patricia E., jt. ed. see Hodgson, Ernest.

Levi, Peter. Art of Poetry. 336p. (C). 1991. 37.00 (*0-300-04847-5*) Yale U Pr.

— Atlas of the Greek World. (Cultural Atlas Ser.). (Illus.). 240p. 1981. 45.00 (*0-87196-448-1*) Facts on File.

— Edward Lear: A Biography. 362p. 1995. 30.00 (*0-684-19688-3*, Scribners) S&S Trade.

— Knit One, Drop One. 1987. 15.95 (*0-8027-5688-3*) Walker & Co.

— The Life & Times of William Shakespeare. 400p. 1989. 29.95 (*0-8050-1199-4*) H Holt & Co.

— The Life & Times of William Shakespeare. (Illus.). 416p. 1991. pap. 14.95 (*0-8050-1552-3*, Owl) H Holt & Co.

— The Life & Times of William Shakespeare. LC 95-14375. 1995. reprint ed. 10.99 (*0-517-14698-3*, Pub. by Wings Bks) Random.

— Tennyson. (Illus.). 352p. 1994. text ed. 30.00 (*0-684-19662-X*, Scribners) S&S Trade.

Levi, Peter, ed. The Penguin Book of English Christian Verse. 384p. 1988. pap. 9.95 (*0-14-058602-4*, Penguin Bks) Viking Penguin.

Levi, Peter, tr. see Papadiamantis, Alexandros.

Levi, Peter, tr. see Pausanias.

Levi, Peter, jt. tr. see Pennington, Anne.

Levi, Peter S. Water, Rock & Sand: Poems. LC 63-2158. 1962. 13.95 (*0-8023-1071-0*) Dufour.

Levi, Primo. Collected Poems: New Edition. 2nd ed. Feldman, Ruth & Swann, Brian, trs. 128p. (Orig.). 1992. pap. 10.95 (*0-571-16539-7*) Faber & Faber.

— Drowned & Saved. Rosenthal, Raymond, tr. (International Ser.). 1989. pap. 10.00 (*0-679-72186-X*, Vin) Random.

— If Not Now, When. Weaver, William, tr. (Fiction Ser.). 352p. 1986. pap. 11.00 (*0-14-008492-4*, Penguin Bks) Viking Penguin.

— If Not Now, When? (Twentieth Century Classics Ser.). 1995. pap. 11.95 (*0-14-018893-2*, Penguin Bks) Viking Penguin.

— Moments of Reprieve. 176p. 1987. pap. 10.00 (*0-14-009370-2*, Penguin Bks) Viking Penguin.

— Moments of Reprieve. (Twentieth Century Classics Ser.). 1995. pap. 10.95 (*0-14-018895-9*, Penguin Bks) Viking Penguin.

— The Monkey's Wrench. 192p. 1987. pap. 10.00 (*0-14-010357-0*, Penguin Bks) Viking Penguin.

— The Monkey's Wrench. (Twentieth Century Classics Ser.). 1995. pap. 10.95 (*0-14-018892-4*, Penguin Bks) Viking Penguin.

— Other People's Trades. 1990. pap. 8.95 (*0-671-70519-9*) S&S Trade.

— The Periodic Table. 240p. 1995. pap. 10.00 (*0-8052-1041-5*) Schocken.

— The Reawakening. Woolf, Stuart J., tr. 240p. 1993. pap. 10.00 (*0-02-022369-2*, Collier S&S) S&S Trade.

— Survival in Auschwitz. Woolf, Stuart, tr. 176p. (ITA.). 1993. pap. 8.00 (*0-02-029192-2*, Pub. by Gebrueder Borntraeger GW) Macmillan.

— Survival in Auschwitz. 160p. 1987. pap. 5.95 (*0-02-034310-8*, Collier S&S) S&S Trade.

— Survival in Auschwitz. Bd. with Reawakening. 384p. 1986. 19.45 (*0-671-60541-0*) Summit Bks.

Levi, Primo & Regge, Tullio. Dialogo. Rosenthal, Raymond, tr. 112p. (C). 1989. pap. text ed. 15.95 (*0-691-08545-5*) Princeton U Pr.

Levi-Provencal, E., ed. see Menendez Pidal, Ramon.

Levi, S. M., jt. auth. see Zelikman, Vitalii L.

Levi, Samuel. Iginia d'Asti. Gossett, Philip, ed. (Italian Opera 1810-1840 Ser.). 250p. 1985. lib. bdg. 97.00 (*0-8240-6558-1*) Garland.

Levi-Setti, Riccardo. Elementary Particles. LC 63-22713. (Chicago Lectures in Physics Ser.). (Orig.). 1963. pap. text ed. 6.00 (*0-226-47446-1*) U Ch Pr.

— Trilobites. 2nd ed. LC 92-38716. (Illus.). 320p. (C). 1993. 45.00 (*0-226-47451-8*) U Ch Pr.

— Trilobites. 2nd ed. (Illus.). x, 342p. 1995. pap. 24.95 (*0-226-47452-6*) U Ch Pr.

— Trilobites: A Photographic Atlas. LC 74-7555. (Illus.). 222p. reprint ed. pap. 63.30 (*0-685-23835-0*, 2056616) Bks Demand.

Levi-Setti, Riccardo & Lasinski, Thomas. Strongly Interacting Particles. LC 73-83750. (Chicago Lectures in Physics). 328p. reprint ed. pap. 93.50 (*0-685-23872-5*, 2056656) Bks Demand.

Levi, Shem-tov. Fault Tolerant System Design. 1993. text ed. 50.00 (*0-07-037515-1*) McGraw.

Levi, Stephen. Daphne in Cottage D. 1968. pap. 4.75 (*0-8222-0270-0*) Dramatists Play.

***Levi, Steven.** A Destiny Going Sour. 1991. 5.00 (*0-932593-19-4*) Black Bear.

Levi, Steven & O'Meara, Jim. Bush Flying. 1992. pap. text ed. 16.95 (*0-07-157163-9*) McGraw.

— Bush Flying. (Practical Flying Ser.). 168p. 1992. pap. 16.95 (*0-8306-3462-2*, 1037) TAB Bks.

Levi, Steven C. Alascattalo Tales: A Treasury of Alaskan Humor. LC 92-56660. 264p. 1993. pap. 25.95 (*0-89950-864-2*) McFarland & Co.

— Deadwood Dick. (Orig.). 1988. pap. 2.95 (*0-87067-732-2*) Holloway.

— Our National Tapestry. 1986. 2.00 (*0-932593-06-2*) Black Bear.

Levi, Steven C., jt. auth. see Phillips, Douglas A.

Levi-Strauss, Claude. De Pres et de Loin; Entretiens; Deux Ans Apres. (FRE.). 1991. pap. 16.95 (*0-7859-3935-0*) Fr & Eur.

— Elementary Structures of Kinship. Needham, Rodney, ed. LC 68-12840. (Illus.). 1969. reprint ed. pap. 20.00x (*0-8070-4669-8*) Beacon Pr.

— Entretiens Avec Claude Live-Strauss. 188p. (FRE.). 1989. pap. 13.95 (*0-7859-4446-X*, 2266032631) Fr & Eur.

— From Honey to Ashes, Vol. 2: Mythologiques. Weightman, John & Weightman, Doreen, trs. 1990. pap. 13.00 (*0-685-48382-7*) U Ch Pr.

— L' Identite. (FRE.). 1987. pap. 20.95 (*0-7859-3008-6*) Fr & Eur.

An Asterisk (*) at the beginning of an entry indicates that the title is appearing in BIP for the first time.

— Introduction to the Work of Marcel Mauss. (ASA Monographs). 88p. 1987. pap. 13.95 (0-7100-9066-8, RKP) Routledge.

— The Jealous Potter. Chorier, Benedicte, tr. (Illus.). 208p. 1988. 19.95 (0-226-47480-1) U Ch Pr.

— Myth & Meaning. LC 78-25833. 80p. 1995. pap. 10.00 (0-8052-1038-5) Schocken.

— Myth & Meaning. LC 78-25833. 1987. reprint ed. pap. 9.00 (0-8052-0622-1) Schocken.

— Myth & Meaning: Five Talks for Radio. LC 78-5212. (Massey Lectures: 1977). 64p. reprint ed. pap. 25.00 (0-8357-8240-9, 2034030) Bks Demand.

— The Naked Man, Vol. 4: Mythologiques. Weightman, John & Weightman, Doreen, trs. LC 79-3399. (Illus.). 752p. 1990. pap. text ed. 21.95 (0-226-47496-8) U Ch Pr.

— The Origin of Table Manners, Vol. 3: Mythologiques. Weightman, John & Weightman, Doreen, trs. (Illus.). 560p. 1990. pap. text ed. 19.95 (0-226-47493-3) U Ch Pr.

— Pensee Sauvage. rev. ed. (FRE.). 1985. 13.95 (2-266-03816-8) Adlers Foreign Bks.

— Race et Histoire. (FRE.). 1987. pap. 12.95 (0-7859-3970-9) Fr & Eur.

— Race et Histoire. (Folio Essais Ser.: No. 58). 127p. (FRE.). 1987. pap. 9.95 (2-07-032413-3) Schoenhof.

— The Raw & the Cooked: Introduction to a Science of Mythology, Vol. 1. Weightman, John & Weightman, Doreen, trs. LC 82-15895. (Illus.). xiv, 388p. 1983. pap. text ed. 21.00 (0-226-47487-9) U Ch Pr.

— The Raw & the Cooked, Vol. 1: Mythologiques. Weightman, John & Weightman, Doreen, trs. 1990. pap. 21.00 (0-685-48381-9) U Ch Pr.

— Saudades do Brasil: A Photographic Memoir. Modelski, Sylvia, tr. (Illus.). 224p. (C). 1995. 39.95 (0-295-97472-9) U of Wash Pr.

— Savage Mind. LC 66-28197. (Nature of Human Society Ser.). 1968. pap. 13.95 (0-226-47484-4, P325) U Ch Pr.

— The Story of Lynx. Tihanyi, Catherine, tr. LC 94-34811. 1995. 24.95 (0-226-47471-2) U Ch Pr.

— Structural Anthropology, Vol. 1. LC 63-17344. 432p. 1974. pap. text ed. 20.00 (0-465-09516-X) Basic.

— Structural Anthropology, Vol. 2. Layton, Monique, tr. LC 82-16115. xvi, 384p. 1983. pap. text ed. 17.95 (0-226-47491-7) U Ch Pr.

— Totemism. (Orig.). 1963. pap. 12.00 (0-8070-4671-X) Beacon Pr.

— Tristes Tropiques. (Illus.). 432p. 1992. pap. 15.00 (0-14-016562-2, Penguin Bks) Viking Penguin.

— Tristes Tropiques. rev. ed. (Illus.). (FRE.). 1984. 12.95 (2-266-02612-7) Adlers Foreign Bks.

— The View from Afar. 328p. 1992. pap. 14.95 (0-226-47474-7) U Ch Pr.

— The Way of the Masks. Modelski, Sylvia, tr. LC 82-2723. (Illus.). 276p. 1988. pap. 18.95 (0-295-96636-X) U of Wash Pr.

Levi-Strauss, Claude & Eribon, Didier. Conversations with Claude Levi-Strauss. Wissing, Paula, tr. LC 90-11052. 192p. 1991. 19.95 (0-226-47475-5) U Ch Pr.

Levi-Strauss, David, jt. ed. see Trend, David.

Levi, Trude. A Cat Called Adolf. LC 94-18872. (Library of Holocaust Testimonies). 192p. 1995. pap. 19.50 (0-85303-289-0, Pub. by Vallentine Mitchell UK) Intl Spec Bk.

Levi-Valensi. Les Critiques de Notre Temps et Camus. (FRE.). 13.95 (0-7859-0036-5, F91100) Fr & Eur.

Levi, Vicki G. & Eisenberg, Lee. Atlantic City: One Hundred Twenty-Five Years of Ocean Madness. LC 93-46513. 1994. 18.95 (0-89815-613-0) Ten Speed Pr.

Levi, Wendell M. Encyclopedia of Pigeon Breeds. 1965. 56. 50 (0-910876-02-9) Levi Pub.

— Making Pigeons Pay. rev. ed. 1984. reprint ed. 20.00 (0-910876-03-7) Levi Pub.

— The Pigeon. 1986. reprint ed. 52.00 (0-910876-01-0) Levi Pub.

Levi, Werner. Australia's Outlook on Asia. LC 78-26904. 1979. text ed. 49.50 (0-313-20897-2, LEAO, Greenwood Pr) Greenwood.

— The Coming End of War. LC 80-39568. (Sage Library of Social Research: No. 117). 183p. reprint ed. pap. 52.20 (0-8357-4819-7, 2037756) Bks Demand.

— Contemporary International Law: A Concise Introduction. 2nd ed. 365p. (C). 1990. pap. text ed. 28. 50 (0-8133-1095-4) Westview.

— From Alms to Liberation: The Catholic Church, the Theologians, Poverty, & Politics. LC 88-29009. 183p. 1989. text ed. 49.95 (0-275-93171-4, C3171, Praeger Pubs) Greenwood.

— International Politics: Foundations of the System. LC 73-84786. 285p. reprint ed. pap. 81.30 (0-7837-2938-3, 2057516) Bks Demand.

Levi, Yaakov, jt. auth. see Radday, Yehuda.

Levi, Yehuda. Torah Study: A Survey of Classic Sources on Timely Issues. 15.95 (0-87306-555-7) Feldheim.

Levialdi, S. & Bernardelli, C. Representation: Relationship Betwen Language & Image. 236p. 1994. text ed. 71.00 (981-02-1690-4) World Scientific Pub.

Levialdi, Stefano, ed. Multicomputer Vision. 204p. 1988. text ed. 76.00 (0-12-444818-6) Acad Pr.

— Parallel Integrated Technology for Image Processing. 1985. text ed. 101.00 (0-12-444820-8) Acad Pr.

Leviant, Curt. The Man Who Thought He Was Messiah. 226p. 1990. 19.95 (0-8276-0371-1) JPS Phila.

— Masterpieces of Hebrew Literature: A Treasury of Two Thousand Years of Jewish Creativity. 1969. pap. 19.95 (0-87068-079-X) Ktav.

Leviant, Curt, tr. see Grade, Chaim.

Leviant, Curt, ed. see Reisen, Avraham.

Levias, Caspar. A Grammar of Galilean Aramaic (Hebrew) 35.00 (0-88125-136-4) Ktav.

Leviatan, D., jt. ed. see Baron, S.

Leviatin, David. The Followers of the Trail: A Jewish Working Class Community in America. LC 88-27766. 320p. (C). 1989. 40.00 (0-300-04354-6) Yale U Pr.

— Prague Sprung: Notes & Voices from the New World. LC 93-2869. 160p. 1993. text ed. 49.95 (0-275-94536-7, C4536, Praeger Pubs) Greenwood.

Levich, , p. On the Way to Understanding the Time Phenomenon: The Constructions of Time in Natural Science. (Series on Advances in Mathematics for Applied Sciences: Pt. 1). 500p. 1995. text ed. 48.00 (981-02-1360-3) World Scientific Pub.

Levich, A. P. On the Way to Understanding the Time Phenomenon: The Constructions of Time in Natural Science, Pt. 2. (Series on Advances in Mathematics for Applied Sciences). 500p. 1995. text ed. 109.00 (981-02-1606-8) World Scientific Pub.

Levich, Eugene W. The Kwangsi Way in Kuomintang China, 1931-1939. LC 92-37094. (Studies on Modern China). 336p. (C). 1993. 57.95 (1-56324-200-1) M E Sharpe.

Levich, Richard M. The International Money Market: An Assessment of Forecasting Techniques & Market Efficiency. Altman, Edward I. & Walter, Ingo, eds. LC 78-13841. (Contemporary Studies in Economic & Financial Analysis: Vol. 22). 178p. 1979. 73.25 (0-89232-109-1) Jai Pr.

Levich, Richard M., ed. The ECU Market: Current Developments & Future Prospects. (Salomon Brothers Center Bk.). 272p. 1987. text ed. 45.00 (0-669-13833-9) Free Pr.

Levich, Richard M., jt. auth. see Amihud, Yakov.

Levich, Richard M., jt. ed. see Choi, Frederick D. S.

Levick, Barbara. Claudius: The Corruption of Power. LC 89-51800. 272p. (C). 1993. pap. 16.00 (0-300-05831-4) Yale U Pr.

— Tiberius the Politician. (Classical Lives Ser.). (Illus.). 256p. 1986. reprint ed. pap. 16.95 (0-7099-4132-3, Pub. by Croom Helm UK) Routledge Chapman & Hall.

Levick, Barbara, jt. ed. see Hawley, Richard.

***Levick, Dwight & Grzinicic, Barbara.** Workers Compensation: Exposures, Coverages, Claims. Standard Publishing Corporation Staff, ed. 608p. 1994. 155.00 (0-923240-12-8) Stndrd Publishing.

Levick, Dwight E. Risk Management & Insurance Audit Techniques. 488p. 1988. ring bd. 137.00 (0-317-92516-4) Stndrd Publishing.

Levick, J. R. Introduction to Cardiovascular Physiology. 2nd ed. 278p. 1991. pap. text ed. 49.95 (0-7506-1028-X) Buttrwrth-Heinemann.

— An Introduction to Cardiovascular Physiology. 2nd ed. LC 94-45631. 1995. write for info. (0-7506-2167-2, Focal) Buttrwrth-Heinemann.

***Levick, Melba, photos.** The Balearic Islands. LC 95-15443. (Illus.). 1996. write for info. (0-8118-0659-6) Chronicle Bks.

— Barcelona. LC 92-30383. (Illus.). 332p. 1993. 85.00 (0-8109-3125-7) Abrams.

— Paradise Found: The Beautiful Retreats & Sanctuaries of California & the Southwest. (Illus.). 1995. pap. 18.95 (0-8118-0687-1) Chronicle Bks.

— Visiting Eden: The Public Gardens of Northern California. LC 92-17134. (Illus.). 1993. pap. 18.95 (0-8118-0107-1) Chronicle Bks.

Levick, Melba, jt. auth. see Young, Stanley.

Levick, Myra F. They Could Not Talk & So They Drew: Children's Styles of Coping & Thinking. (Illus.). 240p. 1983. 53.95x (0-398-04800-2) C C Thomas.

— They Could Not Talk & So They Drew: Children's Styles of Coping & Thinking. (Illus.). 240p. 1983. pap. 33.95x (0-398-06518-7) C C Thomas.

Levicki, Nancy. The College Cookbook, No. Two: By Students, for Students. 2nd rev. ed. (Illus.). 170p. 1993. pap. 11.95 (0-9631318-1-8) NJL Interests.

Levicki, Nancy, jt. auth. see Silkwood, Chris.

***Levicki, Nancy S.** Your Housekeeper's Cookbook: Bilingual Recipes, Menus & More. fac. ed. LC 85-5179. 151p. (ENG.). Date not set. pap. 43.10 (0-7837-7415-X, 2047210) Bks Demand.

***Levicoff, Judith, et al.** The Butterfly Garden. (Illus.). 48p. (Orig.). (J). (gr. 1-4). 1994. pap. 10.95 (1-880812-17-7) S Ink WA.

Levicoff, Steve. Christian Counseling & the Law. 13.99 (0-8024-1239-4) Moody.

— Street Smarts: A Survival Guide to Personal Evangelism & the Law. LC 93-22721. 240p. 1994. pap. 13.99 (0-8010-5688-8) Baker Bk.

Levidow, Les, jt. ed. see Gill, Dawn.

Levie, Alison, jt. auth. see Sing, Dick.

Levie, Alvin. Nicaragua: The People Speak. (Illus.). 224p. 1985. text ed. 34.94 (0-89789-083-3, Bergin & Garvey); pap. text ed. 12.95 (0-89789-084-1, Bergin & Garvey) Greenwood.

Levie, Eleanor. Great Little Quilts: Forty-Five Antique Crib & Doll-Size Quilts with Patterns & Directions. (Illus.). 144p. 1990. 29.95 (0-8109-3353-5) Abrams.

— Halloween Fun: One-Hundred-One Ways to Have a Safe & Scary Halloween. 192p. 1993. pap. text ed. 4.99 (0-425-13955-7) Berkley Pub.

Levie, Eleanor, jt. auth. see Thornton, Katharine.

Levie, Howard S. The Law of Non-International Armed Conflicts: Protocol II to the 1949 Geneva Conventions. LC 87-1706. 1987. lib. bdg. 202.50 (90-247-3491-6) Kluwer Ac.

— Law of War & Neutrality: A Selective English Language Bibliography. LC 88-12625. (Collection of Bibliographic & Research Resources). 224p. 1988. pap. text ed. 75.00 (0-379-20914-4) Oceana.

— Mine Warfare at Sea. 236p. (C). 1992. lib. bdg. 103.00 (0-7923-1526-X) Kluwer Ac.

— Protection of War Victims: Protocol One to the Nineteen Forty-Nine Geneva Conventions, 4 vols. suppl. ed. LC 79-16960. 1985. Supplement 1985. 10.00 (0-379-00799-1) Oceana.

— Protection of War Victims: Protocol One to the Nineteen Forty-Nine Geneva Conventions, 4 vols., Set Incl. Supplement "Superior Orders" LC 79-16960. 1979. Set, plus supplement - "Superior Orders". 190.00 (0-379-00786-X) Oceana.

— Terrorism in War: The Law of War Crimes. LC 93-25148. (Terrorism, Second Ser.). 721p. 1993. lib. bdg. 65.00 (0-379-20148-8) Oceana.

Levie, Hugo, jt. ed. see Hastings, Sue.

Levie, Hugo, et al, eds. Fighting Closures: De-industrialization & the Trade Unions 1979-1983. 233p. 1984. 42.50 (0-85124-361-4, Pub. by Spokesman Bks UK) Coronet Bks.

Levie, W. Howard, jt. ed. see Fleming, Malcolm.

Levien, David H. Introduction to Surgery. 2nd ed. LC 92-48894. (Illus.). 304p. 1993. pap. text ed. 27.95 (0-7216-6647-7) Saunders.

Levien, Frederic, jt. auth. see Cheung, Stephen W.

Levien, J. R., comp. Anatomy of a Crash: Nineteen Twenty-Nine. (Illus.). 1989. reprint ed. 11.00 (0-87034-037-9) Fraser Pub Co.

Levien, Julia. Duncan Dance: A Guide for Young People Ages Six to Sixteen. (Illus.). 112p. (Orig.). (J). (gr. 1-11). 1994. pap. 12.95 (0-87127-198-2) Princeton Bk Co.

Levien, Michael, ed. see Maurois, Andre.

Levien, Michael, ed. see Sadleir, Michael.

Levier, Francis A., jt. auth. see Edmunds, David R.

Levieux, Eleanor, tr. see Duby, Georges.

Levieux, Eleanor, tr. see Memmi, Albert.

Leviev, G. I. Nonlinear Effects in Metals in the Microwave Band, Vol. 11. (Soviet Scientific Reviews Ser.: Vol. 11, Pt. 2). 88p. 1989. pap. text ed. 65.00 (3-7186-4903-9) Gordon & Breach.

Levignac, J. & Wolfe, S. Anthony, eds. The Chin. (Illus.). 174p. 1990. text ed. write for info. (0-443-04221-7) Churchill.

Levignac, Jacque, jt. auth. see Aiach, Gilbert.

***Levillain, Philippe.** Dictionnaire Historique de la Papaute. 1776p. Date not set. 375.00 (0-7859-8720-7) Fr & Eur.

Levillot, B., ed. see Hugo, Victor.

***Levin.** Hopper. (Art Library). 1995. pap. 12.00 (0-517-88372-4, Crown) Crown Pub Group.

— Sleuth at Work: An Investigative Approach to Industrial Hygiene. 1995. text ed. 39.95 (0-442-01925-4) Van Nos Reinhold.

— Student's Guide to Will Drafting. 1987. write for info. (0-8205-0441-6, 691); teacher ed write for info. (0-8205-0442-4) Bender.

Levin & Riddell. Frontiers in Gastrointestinal Cancer. (Current Oncology Ser.: Vol. 1). 1984. 63.25 (0-444-00852-7) Elsevier.

Levin, jt. auth. see Fox.

Levin, jt. auth. see Ginsburg.

Levin, jt. auth. see Ueberroth.

Levin, et al. Art of the American Indian. Vandervelde, ed. 1973. 1.25 (0-89992-077-2) Coun India Ed.

Levin, A., tr. see Gedalge, Andre.

Levin, A. E., jt. auth. see Brush, Stephen G.

Levin, A. L. & Lubinsky, D. S. Christoffel Functions & Orthogonal Polynomials for Exponential Weights. LC 94-17089. (Memoirs of the American Mathematical Society Ser.: Vol. 535). 1994. write for info. (0-8218-2599-2) Am Math.

Levin, A. Leo, ed. see Wheeler, Russell R.

Levin, A. Leo, et al. Cases & Materials on Civil Procedure: Successor Edition. (University Casebook Ser.). 815p. (C). 1991. text ed. 41.95 (0-88277-942-7) Foundation Pr.

— Civil Procedure: Cases & Materials, Successor Edition, 1994 Supplement. (University Casebook Ser.). 80p. 1994. pap. text ed. 6.50 (1-56662-206-9) Foundation Pr.

— Civil Procedure, Teacher's Manual for Cases & Materials on Civil Procedure Successor Edition. (University Casebook Ser.). 106p. (C). 1992. pap. text ed. write for info. (1-56662-032-5) Foundation Pr.

Levin, Alan M. & Page, Wayne E. Everything You Need to Do to Get Hired (& How to Do It) Projects & Guides. LC 93-90356. 358p. 1993. student ed, ring bd. write for info. (1-883552-02-8) Career Adv MD.

— Getting Yourself Hired: The Self-Directed Job Search. LC 93-90357. 380p. 1993. student ed, ring bd. write for info. (1-883552-01-X) Career Adv MD.

— Gopp, Inc. The Company That Always Gets You Hired. LC 93-90358. 166p. (Orig.). 1993. write for info. (1-883552-00-1) Career Adv MD.

— My Job-Search Record: Records Project. LC 93-71441. 142p. 1993. student ed, ring bd. write for info. (1-883552-03-6) Career Adv MD.

Levin, Alex, see Alex Green, pseud..

***Levin, Alex V. & Sheridan, Mary S., eds.** Munchausen Syndrome by Proxy: Issues in Diagnosis & Treatment. LC 95-3324. 1995. 49.95 (0-02-918606-4) Free Pr.

Levin, Alexandra L., ed. Henrietta Srold & the Youth Aliyah: Family Letters, 1934-1944. 100p. (Orig.). 1986. write for info. (0-318-61349-2) Herzl Pr.

Levin, Amy, jt. auth. see Wise, Beth A.

Levin, Amy K. The Suppressed Sister: A Relationship in Novels by Nineteenth- & Twentieth-Century British Women. LC 91-55127. 160p. 1992. 29.50 (0-8387-5211-X) Bucknell U Pr.

Levin, Angela, jt. auth. see Marchioness of Tavistock.

Levin, Arnold M. The Private Practice of Psychotherapy. LC 83-47789. 208p. (C). 1983. text ed. 24.95 (0-02-918830-X) Free Pr.

Levin, Arthur & Rapoport, Mitchell, eds. Focus on Health: Issues & Events of 1978 from the New York Times Information Bank. LC 78-31464. (News in Print Ser.). 1980. lib. bdg. 30.95 (0-405-12874-6) Ayer.

Levin, Arthur H. Hillside Building Design & Construction. LC 90-81793. (Illus.). 192p. (Orig.). 1990. pap. 19.95 (0-931228-19-0) Arts & Arch.

Levin Associates Staff. Irish Book of Days. 1994. 10.95 (0-88363-294-2) H L Levin.

Levin, B. Impressions for Complete Denture. (Illus.). 200p. 1984. pap. text ed. 48.00 (0-86715-114-5) Quint Pub Co.

Levin, B., jt. auth. see Finkelstein, Michael O.

Levin, B. Y., ed. Entire & Subharmonic Functions. LC 91-640741. (Advances in Soviet Mathematics Ser.: Vol. 11). 275p. 1992. 147.00 (0-8218-4110-6, ADVSOV/11C) Am Math.

Levin, Barry & Ferrier, David O. Defending the Vietnam Combat Veteran. Caney-Peterson, Susan, ed. LC 89-193635. 345p. 1989. pap. text ed. 29.95 (0-9626742-0-6) VVLAP.

Levin, Barry B. Benji Lopez: A Picaresque Tale of Puerto Rican Emigration & Return. 202p. 1987. boxed 28.95 (0-465-00653-1) Transaction Pubs.

Levin, Beatrice. Women & Medicine: Pioneers Meeting the Challenge. 2nd ed. LC 87-60820. (Illus.). 272p. 1989. reprint ed. pap. 9.95 (0-939644-28-2) Media Pub.

Levin, Beatrice & Vanderveld, Marjorie. Me Run Fast Good: Biographies of Tewanima (Hopi), Carlos Montezuma (Apache) & John Horse (Seminole) 32p. (J). (gr. 5-9). 1983. pap. 3.95 (0-89992-087-X) Coun India Ed.

Levin, Berard. The Way We Live Now. large type ed. (Illus.). 200p. 1991. 11.47 (1-85290-019-9, Pub. by ISIS UK) Transaction Pubs.

Levin, Bernard, jt. ed. see DeMeester, Tom R.

Levin, Bernard M. Human Behavior in Fire: What We Know Now. 1984. 4.65 (0-318-03820-X, TR84-3) Society Fire Protect.

Levin, Beth. English Verb Classes & Alternations: A Preliminary Investigation. 280p. (C). 1993. lib. bdg. 45. 00 (0-226-47532-8); pap. text ed. 18.95 (0-226-47533-6) U Ch Pr.

Levin, Beth & Hovav, Malka R. Unaccusativity: At the Syntax-Lexical Semantics Interface. LC 94-17439. (Linguistic Inquiry Monographs: Vol. 26). 1994. 39.95x (0-262-12185-9); pap. 19.95x (0-262-62094-4) MIT Pr.

Levin, Betsy, ed. see Hawley, Willis D.

Levin, Betty. Away to Me, Moss. LC 93-48136. 176p. (J). 1994. 14.00 (0-688-13439-4) Greenwillow.

— Brother Moose. LC 89-34437. (J). (gr. 5 up). 1990. 12.95 (0-688-09266-7) Greenwillow.

— Fire in the Wind. LC 94-48801. (J). (gr. 3 up). 1995. 15. 00 (0-688-14299-0) Greenwillow.

— The Ice Bear. LC 86-254. 192p. (J). (gr. 5 up). 1986. 10. 25 (0-688-06431-0) Greenwillow.

— The Keeping Room. LC 80-23931. (Illus.). 248p. (J). 1989. reprint ed. 11.95 (0-688-80300-8) Greenwillow.

— Mercy's Mill. LC 91-31483. (J). (gr. 7 up). 1992. 14.00 (0-688-11122-X) Greenwillow.

— Starshine & Sunglow. LC 93-26672. (J). (gr. 4-7). 1994. 14.00 (0-688-22806-2) Greenwillow.

— Starshine & Sunglow. LC 93-26672. (Illus.). 96p. (J). (gr. 4-7). 1994. 14.00 (0-688-12806-8) Greenwillow.

— The Trouble With Gramary. LC 87-22702. 192p. (J). (gr. 5-p). 1988. 13.95 (0-688-07372-7) Greenwillow.

Levin, Betty B., jt. auth. see Christensen, Janet.

***Levin, Bob.** Fully Armed: The Autobiography of Jimmy Don Polk. 280p. 1995. 21.00 (1-880909-38-3) Baskerville.

Levin, Boris J. Distribution of Zeros of Entire Functions. rev. ed. Boas, R. et al, trs. LC 80-36891. (Translations of Mathematical Monographs: Vol. 5). 524p. 1980. pap. 70. 00 (0-8218-4505-5, MMONO-5) Am Math.

***Levin, Boris M.** Crryetbl: N35Pahhoe. (Illus.). 317p. (Orig.). 1994. 12.00 (0-9643641-0-7) B Levin.

***Levin, Bruce L. & Petrila, John, eds.** Mental Health Services: A Public Health Perspective. (Illus.). 448p. 1995. 50.00 (0-19-508800-X) OUP.

Levin, Carol. A Rosh Hashanah Walk. LC 87-3106. (Illus.). (J). (ps-3). 1987. 4.95 (0-930494-70-9) Kar Ben.

Levin, Carole. The Heart & Stomach of a King: Elizabeth I & the Politics of Sex & Power. LC 94-7315. (New Cultural Studies). (Illus.). 256p. (Orig.). (C). 1994. pap. text ed. 12.95 (0-8122-1533-8) U of Pa Pr.

— Propaganda in the English Reformation: Heroic & Villainous Images of King John. LC 87-31949. (Studies in British History: Vol. 11). 306p. 1988. lib. bdg. 99.95 (0-88946-463-4) E Mellen.

Levin, Carole & Robertson, Karen, eds. Sexuality & Politics in Renaissance Drama. LC 91-25367. (Studies in Renaissance Literature: Vol. 10). 289p. 1991. lib. bdg. 89.95 (0-88946-078-7) E Mellen.

***Levin, Carole & Sullivan, Patricia A., eds.** Political Rhetoric, Power, & Renaissance Women. (Speech Communication Ser.). 256p. 1995. text ed. 57.50x (0-7914-2545-2) State U NY Pr.

— Political Rhetoric, Power, & Renaissance Women. (Speech Communication Ser.). 256p. (C). 1995. pap. 18. 95x (0-7914-2546-0) State U NY Pr.

Levin, Carole & Watson, Jeanie, eds. Ambiguous Realities: Women in the Middle Ages & Renaissance. LC 87-21671. 264p. 1987. 39.95 (0-8143-1872-X); pap. 16.95 (0-8143-1873-8) Wayne St U Pr.

Levin, Charles, tr. see Baudrillard, Jean.

Levin, Dan. From the Battlefield: Dispatches of a World War II Marine. LC 94-19370. (Illus.). 160p. 1995. 21.95 (1-55750-515-2) Naval Inst Pr.

Levin, David. Cotton Mather: The Young Life of the Lord's Remembrancer, 1663-1703. LC 78-2355. (Illus.). 382p. 1978. 37.50 (0-674-17507-7) HUP.

— Exemplary Elders. LC 89-5075. 184p. 1990. 19.95 (0-8203-1186-3) U of Ga Pr.

— Forms of Uncertainty: Essays in Historical Criticism. 1992. text ed. 37.50 (0-8139-1379-9) U Pr of Va.

An Asterisk (*) at the beginning of an entry indicates that the title is appearing in BIP for the first time.

— Riddler's Riddle Book. 1991. pap. 3.50 (0-8125-1353-3) Tor Bks.
Levin, David, jt. ed. see Levin, Richard.
Levin, David, jt. ed. see Lynn, Kenneth S.
Levin, David, ed. see Mather, Cotton.
Levin, David, ed. see Orwell, George.
Levin, David, ed. see Parkman, Francis, Jr.
Levin, David, ed. see Parkman, Francis.
***Levin, David H.** Chess Puzzles for Children. (Illus.). 124p. (Orig.). (J). (gr. 2-6). 1994. pap. 11.95 (0-9638001-1-6) Syllogism Pr.
— Position & Pawn Tension in Chess. (Illus.). 118p. (Orig.). 1993. pap. 13.95 (0-9638001-0-8) Syllogism Pr.
Levin, David J. Opera Through Other Eyes. (Illus.). 288p. (C). 1994. 37.50 (0-8047-2239-0); pap. 14.95 (0-8047-2240-4) Stanford U Pr.
Levin, David M. The Body's Recollection of Being: Phenomenological Psychology & the Deconstruction of Nihilism. 384p. 1985. pap. 15.95 (0-7102-0478-7, 04787, RKP) Routledge.
— The Listening Self: Personal Growth, Social Change & the Closure of Metaphysics. 320p. 1989. 47.00 (0-415-02582-6, A1581); pap. 16.95 (0-415-02583-4, A3269) Routledge.
— The Opening of Vision: Nihilism & the Postmodern Situation. 480p. 1988. text ed. 59.95 (0-415-00412-8); pap. text ed. 19.95 (0-415-00173-0) Routledge.
Levin, David M., ed. Modernity & the Hegemony of Vision. LC 93-1523. 1993. 48.00 (0-520-07972-8); pap. 19.00 (0-520-07973-6) U CA Pr.
— Pathologies of the Modern Self: Postmodern Studies on Narcissism, Schizophrenia, & Depression. 548p. 1988. text ed. 60.00x (0-8147-5026-5); pap. 25.00 (0-8147-5039-7) NYU Pr.
Levin, David S. Developmental Experiences: Treatment of Developmental Disorders in Children. LC 84-24318. 352p. 1985. 40.00 (0-87668-760-5) Aronson.
— How to Use Unix & Xenix. Jonas, Jacqueline & Menges, Patricia A., eds. (Illus.). 95p. (Orig.). (C). 1991. pap. text ed. 195.00 (0-685-46011-8) OneOnOne Comp Trng.
Levin, Diane, jt. auth. see Carlsson-Paige, Nancy.
Levin, Diane E. Teaching Young Children in Violent Times: Building a Peaceable Classroom Environment. (Illus.). 176p. 1994. lib. bdg. 44.95 (0-86571-315-4); pap. 16.95 (0-86571-316-2) New Soc Pubs.
Levin, Diane E., jt. auth. see Carlsson-Paige, Nancy.
Levin, Dick. How to Create Wealth on a Salary. (Illus.). 208p. 1988. pap. 25.95 (0-13-404534-3) P-H.
— Strategy in a Nutshell. LC 92-8674. 160p. 1992. boxed 33.33 (0-13-853326-1) P-H.
Levin, Donald. The House of Grins. 330p. (Orig.). 1992. pap. 13.95 (0-9628647-0-6) Sewickley Pr.
Levin, Donna. California Street. 336p. 1992. pap. 4.50 (0-451-40303-7, Onyx) NAL-Dutton.
— Get That Novel Started! (And Keep Going 'Til You Finish) 176p. 1992. 17.95 (0-89879-517-6) Writers Digest.
***Levin, Doron P.** Behind the Wheel at Chrysler: The Iacocca Legacy. 1995. 25.00 (0-15-111703-9) HarBrace.
— Irreconcilable Differences. 1992. pap. 5.99 (0-451-17641-3, Sig) NAL-Dutton.
— Irreconcilable Differences: Ross Perot Versus General Motors. (Illus.). 320p. 1989. 18.95 (0-316-52211-2) Little.
Levin, Dov. Fighting Back: Lithuanian Jewry's Armed Resistance to the Nazis. LC 83-12605. 325p. 1985. 49.50 (0-8419-0831-1) Holmes & Meier.
— The Lesser of Two Evils: Eastern European Jewry under Soviet Rule. 1995. 45.00 (0-8276-0518-8) JPS Phila.
Levin, Edward. Alliances & Coalitions: Your Key to Personal & Business Success. 170p. 1984. text ed. 15.95 (0-07-037283-7) McGraw.
— Negotiating Tactics: Bargain Your Way to Winning. 1982. mass mkt. 6.95 (0-449-90074-6, Columbine) Fawcett.
Levin, Edward & De Santis, Daniel V. Mediation: An Annotated Bibliography. LC 78-18359. (Industrial & Labor Relations Bibliography Ser.: No. 15). 32p. 1978. pap. 3.25 (0-87546-069-0) ILR Pr.
Levin, Edward, tr. see Kotler, Yair.
Levin, Edward, tr. see Nigal, Gedalyah.
Levin, Edward, tr. see Raz, Simcha.
Levin, Edward D., et al, eds. Neurotransmitter Interactions & Cognitive Function. LC 92-17848. xiv, 362p. 1992. 99.00 (0-8176-3617-X) Birkhauser.
Levin, Edward J., jt. auth. see Albert, Charles T.
Levin, Elaine. The History of American Ceramics: 1607 to the Present from Pikkpkins & Bean Pots to Contemporary Forms. 1988. 65.00 (0-8109-1172-8) Abrams.
Levin, Elaine, et al. Paul Soldner: A Retrospective. LC 91-53090. (Illus.). 128p. 1992. pap. 24.95 (0-295-97159-2) U of Wash Pr.
Levin, Enid, et al. Families, Services & Confusion in Old Age. 338p. 1989. text ed. 58.95 (0-566-05714-X, Pub. by Avebury Pub UK) Ashgate Pub Co.
Levin, Ernest M. & McMurdie, Howard F., eds. Phase Diagrams for Ceramists, Vol. III. 514p. 1975. 150.00 (0-916094-06-5, PHASE3) Am Ceramic.
Levin, Ernest M., et al, eds. Phase Diagrams for Ceramists, Vol. II. 626p. 1969. 150.00 (0-916094-05-7, PHASE2) Am Ceramic.
— Phase Diagrams for Ceramists Vol. 1: Oxides & Salts, Vol. 1. (Illus.). 602p. 1964. 150.00 (0-916094-04-9, PHASE1) Am Ceramic.
Levin, Eve. Sex & Society in the World of the Orthodox Slavs, 900-1700. LC 89-30075. (Illus.). 344p. 1989. 36.50 (0-8014-2260-4) Cornell U Pr.
— Sex & Society in the World of the Orthodox Slavs, 900-1700. (Illus.). 344p. 1995. pap. 16.95 (0-8014-8304-2) Cornell U Pr.
Levin, Evgenii M., jt. auth. see Beletsky, Vladimir V.
Levin, F. I. Improvement of Sod-Podzolic Soils by Cultivation. 120p. 1968. text ed. 36.50 (0-7065-0672-3, Pub. by Keter Pub IS) Coronet Bks.
***Levin, F. S. & Micha, D. A., eds.** Coulomb Interactions in Nuclear & Atomic Few-Body Collisions. (Finite Systems & Multiparticle Dynamics Ser.). (Illus.). 335p. (C). 1995. write for info. (0-306-45149-2, Plenum Pr) Plenum.
— Long-Range Casimir Forces: Theory & Recent Experiments in Atomic Systems. (Finite Systems & Multiparticle Dynamics Ser.: Vol. 1). (Illus.). 348p. (C). 1993. 75.00 (0-306-44385-6, Plenum Pr) Plenum.
Levin, F. S., jt. auth. see Feshbach, H.
Levin, Flora, tr. see Nichomachus the Pythagorean.
Levin, Frank. Chord Classics. 1993. 9.95 (0-685-64656-4, 94810) Mel Bay.
Levin, Fred. Mapping the Mind: The Intersection of Psychoanalysis & Neuroscience. 290p. 1991. text ed. 39.95 (0-88163-124-8) Analytic Pr.
Levin, Fredric G. Effective Opening Statements: The Attorney's Master Key to Courtroom Victory. LC 83-14034. 1983. text ed. 59.95 (0-13-244418-6) Exec Reports.
***Levin, Gail.** Edward Hopper: A Catalogue Raisonne, 3 vols., Set. (Illus.). 1056p. 1995. boxed, cd-rom 600.00 (0-393-03786-X) Norton.
— Edward Hopper: An Intimate Biography. LC 95-2114. 1995. 30.00 (0-394-54664-4) Knopf.
— Edward Hopper: The Art & the Artist. (Illus.). 1981. reprint ed. 50.00 (0-393-01374-X) Norton.
— Edward Hopper: The Art & the Artist. (Illus.). 1986. reprint ed. pap. 35.00 (0-393-00082-6) Norton.
— Edward Hopper: The Complete Prints. (Illus.). 1979. 15.95 (0-393-01275-1) Norton.
— Hopper's Places. LC 85-40039. (Illus.). 94p. 1985. 18.45 (0-394-54414-5) Knopf.
— Hopper's Places. LC 85-40039. (Illus.). 96p. 1989. 24.95 (0-394-58320-5) Knopf.
— Marsden Hartley in Bavaria. LC 89-85500. (Illus.). 80p. 1989. pap. 19.95 (0-87451-516-5) U Pr of New Eng.
— Twentieth-Century American Painting: The Thyssen-Bornemisza Collection. LC 87-61728. (Illus.). 408p. 1988. 95.00 (0-85667-332-3, Pub. by P Wilson Pubs) Sothebys Pubns.
Levin, Gail, intro. Edward Hopper. 50p. 1993. pap. 20.00 (1-880154-06-4) Gagosian Gallery.
Levin, George. Laser Isotope Separation Research & Development in the U. S. S. R. Johnson, Anne H., ed. xi, 120p. (Orig.). 1989. pap. text ed. 75.00 (1-55831-093-2) Delphic Associates.
Levin, Gerald. The Educated Reader. 641p. (C). 1988. pap. text ed. 3.00 (0-15-520718-0) HB Coll Pubs.
— The Macmillan College Handbook. 2nd ed. 928p. (C). 1991. write for info. (0-02-370231-1) Macmillan.
— Prose Models. 8th ed. 571p. (C). 1989. pap. text ed. 20.00 (0-15-572286-7) HB Coll Pubs.
— Prose Models. 9th ed. 576p. (C). 1992. Instructor's manual. teacher ed, pap. text ed. 4.00 (0-15-500297-X) HB Coll Pubs.
— Prose Models. 9th ed. 576p. (C). 1993. pap. text ed. 21.50 (0-15-500174-4) HB Coll Pubs.
— Short Essays. 5th ed. 512p. (C). 1989. pap. text ed. 18.75 (0-15-580920-2) HB Coll Pubs.
— Short Essays. 6th ed. 544p. (C). 1992. pap. text ed. 20.00 (0-15-580922-9); pap. text ed. 28.50 (0-15-580923-7) HB Coll Pubs.
— Writing & Logic. 276p. (C). 1982. pap. text ed. 20.00 (0-15-597788-1); pap. text ed. 2.75 (0-15-597789-X) HB Coll Pubs.
Levin, Gerald R. Child Psychology. LC 82-9691. (Psychology Ser.). 576p. (C). 1983. text ed. 40.95 (0-534-01229-9) Brooks-Cole.
***Levin-Gervasi, Stephanie.** The Back Pain Sourcebook. 192p. 1995. 22.95 (1-56565-205-3) Lowell Hse.
Levin, Gloria, et al, eds. Ethical Implications of Primary Prevention. (Prevention in Human Services Ser.). 132p. 1991. text ed. 29.95 (1-56024-019-9) Haworth Pr.
Levin, H. Toward Stendhal. LC 75-22213. (Studies in French Literature: No. 45). 1975. lib. bdg. 75.00 (0-8383-2083-X) M S G Haskell Hse.
Levin, H., ed. Lawyers & Lawmakers of Kentucky. (Illus.). 777p. 1982. reprint ed. 40.00 (0-89308-319-4) Southern Hist Pr.
Levin, Harold D., jt. auth. see Perry, Jo Ellen.
***Levin, Harold L.** Ancient Invertebrates & Their Living Relatives. (Illus.). 350p. (C). 1995. write for info. (0-521-33450-0); pap. write for info. (0-521-33671-6) Cambridge U Pr.
— Contemporary Physical Geology. 3rd ed. 640p. (C). 1990. pap. text ed. 35.25 (0-03-031139-X) SCP.
— The Earth Through Time. 4th ed. 720p. (C). 1991. text ed. 55.25 (0-03-053689-8) SCP.
— The Earth Through Time. 4th ed. LC 93-17501. 25p. 1994. pap. text ed. 45.25 (0-03-098594-3) SCP.
— Essentials of Earth Science. 444p. (C). 1985. text ed. 42.75 (0-03-062411-8) SCP.
Levin, Harry. Grounds for Comparison. LC 72-75402. (Harvard Studies in Comparative Literature: No. 32). 423p. reprint ed. pap. 124.60 (0-7837-6094-9, 2059140) Bks Demand.
— James Joyce: A Critical Introduction. LC 60-9222. (C). 1960. pap. 9.95 (0-8112-0089-2, NDP87) New Directions.
— Memories of the Moderns. LC 80-36827. 256p. 1982. 15.95 (0-8112-0733-1); pap. 7.95 (0-8112-0842-7, NDP539) New Directions.
— The Power of Blackness: Hawthorne, Poe, Melville. LC 80-83221. xxii, 263p. 1980. reprint ed. pap. 14.95 (0-8214-0581-0) Ohio U Pr.
Levin, Harry L. & Gillespie, Robert W. The Use of Radio in Family Planning. 2.50 (0-686-44170-2) World Neigh.
Levin, Harry T. Playboys & Killjoys: An Essay on the Theory & Practice of Comedy. 224p. 1988. pap. 8.95 (0-19-504877-6) OUP.
— Why Literary Criticism Is Not an Exact Science. abr. ed. LC 68-7221. 27p. 1967. pap. 3.00 (0-674-95235-9) HUP.
Levin, Harry T., jt. auth. see Gibson, Eleanor J.
Levin, Harry T., ed. see Hawthorne, Nathaniel.
Levin, Harry T., ed. see Shakespeare, William.
Levin, Harvey J. Fact & Fancy in Television Regulation: An Economic Study of Policy Alternatives. LC 79-90148. 544p. 1980. 49.95 (0-87154-531-4) Russell Sage.
— The Invisible Resource: Use & Regulation of the Radio Spectrum. LC 71-148951. (Resources for the Future Ser.). (Illus.). 432p. 1971. 30.00 (0-8018-1316-6) Johns Hopkins.
— The Invisible Resource: Use & Regulation of the Radio Spectrum. LC 71-148951. (Illus.). 466p. reprint ed. pap. 132.90 (0-685-23703-6, 2032159) Bks Demand.
Levin, Harvey S., et al. Neurobehavioral Consequences of Closed Head Injury. (Illus.). (C). 1982. text ed. 45.00 (0-19-503008-7) OUP.
***Levin, Harvey S., et al, eds.** Catastrophic Brain Injury. (Illus.). 288p. 1995. 39.95 (0-19-508533-7) OUP.
— Frontal Lobe Function & Dysfunction. (Illus.). 448p. 1991. 49.95 (0-19-506284-1) OUP.
— Mild Head Injury. (Illus.). 304p. 1989. 45.00 (0-19-505301-X) OUP.
— Neurobehavioral Recovery from Head Injury. (Illus.). 446p. 1987. 49.95 (0-19-504287-5) OUP.
Levin, Henry M. Cost-Effectiveness: A Primer. (New Perspectives in Evaluation Ser.: Vol. 4). 168p. 1983. 39.95 (0-8039-2152-7); pap. 17.95 (0-8039-2153-5) Sage.
— Education & Jobs in a Technological World. 28p. 1984. 3.25 (0-318-22083-0, IN265) Ctr Educ Trng Employ.
Levin, Henry M. & Lockheed, Marlaine E., eds. Effective Schools in Developing Countries. LC 92-42862. 188p. 1993. 65.00 (0-7507-0173-0, Falmer Pr) Taylor & Francis.
Levin, Henry M. & Schutze, Hans G., eds. Financing Recurrent Education: Strategies for Increasing Employment, Job Opportunities, & Productivity. LC 83-11214. 320p. reprint ed. pap. 91.20 (0-8357-8488-6, 2034761) Bks Demand.
Levin, Henry M., jt. auth. see Carnoy, Martin.
Levin, Henry M., jt. ed. see Jackall, Robert.
Levin, Henry M., jt. ed. see James, Thomas.
Levin, Henry M., jt. auth. see Rumberger, Russell W.
***Levin, Herbert J.** Reflections of a Family Doctor: Writings of Herbert J. Levin, M.D. 185p. (Orig.). (C). 1994. pap. text ed. 19.95 (0-9642777-0-0) Levin Family.
Levin, Herman, jt. auth. see Axinn, June.
Levin, I. & Zakay, D., eds. Time & Human Cognition: A Life-Span Perspective. (Advances in Psychology Ser.: No. 59). 412p. 1989. 129.00 (0-318-43152-1, North Holland) Elsevier.
Levin, Igor, jt. auth. see Levin, Irina.
Levin, Ilya, tr. see Schmidt, Paul, ed.
Levin, Ina M. & Sterling, Mary E. Readiness Manipulatives: Alphabet. (Illus.). 28p. (Orig.). 1991. student ed, pap. 7.95 (1-55734-176-1) Tchr Create Mat.
— Readiness Manipulatives: Counting. (Illus.). 28p. (Orig.). (J). (ps-1). 1992. student ed 7.95 (1-55734-179-6) Tchr Create Mat.
— Readiness Manipulatives: Sequencing. (Illus.). 28p. (Orig.). 1992. student ed 7.95 (1-55734-181-8) Tchr Create Mat.
— Readiness Manipulatives: Shapes. (Illus.). 28p. (Orig.). (J). (ps-1). 1992. student ed 7.95 (1-55734-180-X) Tchr Create Mat.
— Readiness Manipulatives - Colors. (Illus.). 28p. (Orig.). 1991. student ed 7.95 (1-55734-177-X) Tchr Create Mat.
— Readiness Manipulatives - Numbers. (Illus.). 28p. (Orig.). 1991. student ed 7.95 (1-55734-178-8) Tchr Create Mat.
Levin, Ina M., ed. see Denny, Philip.
Levin, Ina M., jt. auth. see Herweck, Dona.
Levin, Ina M., ed. see Kane, Susan, et al.
Levin, Ina M., ed. see Larsen, Linda J.
Levin, Ina M., ed. see Schaff, Barbara & Roth, Sue.
Levin, Ina M., ed. see Thomas, Jennifer.
Levin, Ina M., ed. see Wallace, Annette H.
Levin, Ina M., et al. Using Math Manipulatives for Cooperative Problem Solving: Bear Counters. (Illus.). 48p. (Orig.). 1992. student ed, bds. 7.95 (1-55734-188-5) Tchr Create Mat.
Levin, Ina M., et al, eds. Goldilocks & the Three Bears. (Big Book of Favorite Tales Ser.). (Illus.). 28p. (Orig.). 1992. student ed 14.95 (1-55734-550-3) Tchr Create Mat.
— The Three Little Pigs. (Big Book of Favorite Tales Ser.). (Illus.). 28p. (Orig.). 1992. student ed 14.95 (1-55734-551-1) Tchr Create Mat.
— Whole Language Charts for Nursery Rhymes, Bk. 1. (Illus.). 26p. (Orig.). 1992. student ed 14.95 (1-55734-560-0) Tchr Create Mat.
— Whole Language Charts for Nursery Rhymes, Bk. 2. (Illus.). 26p. (Orig.). 1992. student ed 14.95 (1-55734-561-9) Tchr Create Mat.
— Whole Language Charts for Nursery Rhymes, Bk. 3. (Illus.). 26p. (Orig.). 1992. student ed 14.95 (1-55734-562-7) Tchr Create Mat.
— Whole Language Charts for Nursery Rhymes, Bk. 4. (Illus.). 26p. (Orig.). 1992. student ed 14.95 (1-55734-563-5) Tchr Create Mat.
Levin, Ira. The Boys from Brazil. 1991. mass mkt. 5.95 (0-553-29004-5) Bantam.
— The Boys from Brazil. 1976. 8.95 (0-394-40267-7) Random.
— Critic's Choice. 1962. pap. 4.75 (0-8222-0252-2) Dramatists Play.
— Deathtrap. 1979. pap. 4.75 (0-8222-0294-8) Dramatists Play.
— Deathtrap. 1979. 9.95 (0-394-50727-4) Random.
— Dr. Cook's Garden. 1968. pap. 4.75 (0-8222-0328-6) Dramatists Play.
— General Seeger. 1962. pap. 4.75 (0-8222-0437-1) Dramatists Play.
— A Kiss Before Dying. Peters, Sally, ed. 304p. 1991. reprint ed. mass mkt. 5.50 (0-671-68388-8) PB.
— Rosemary's Baby. 1991. lib. bdg. 21.95 (1-56849-065-8) Buccaneer Bks.
— Rosemary's Baby. limited ed. LC 90-23997. 256p. 1991. 75.00 (0-922890-86-2) Armchair Detective.
— Rosemary's Baby. LC 90-23997. 256p. 1991. reprint ed. 18.95 (0-922890-84-6); reprint ed. 25.00 (0-922890-85-4) Armchair Detective.
— Silver. 1992. 5.99 (0-685-53447-2) Bantam.
— Sliver: A Novel. large type ed. LC 93-40533. 1994. pap. 17.95 (0-8161-5939-4, Large Print Bks) Hall.
Levin, Ira, jt. auth. see Hyman, Mac.
Levin, Irina & Levin, Igor. Working on the Play & the Role: The Stanislavsky Method for Analyzing the Characters in a Drama. 192p. 1992. pap. 12.95 (0-929587-93-6) I R Dee.
— Working on the Play & the Role: The Stanislavsky Method for Analyzing the Characters in a Drama. 192p. 1992. 22.50 (0-929587-94-4) I R Dee.
Levin, Iris. Stage & Structure. Strauss, Sidney, ed. LC 85-15624. (Human Development Ser.: Vol. 1). 336p. 1986. text ed. 49.50 (0-89391-224-7) Ablex Pub.
Levin, Irwin P., et al. Experimental Psychology: Contemporary Methods & Applications. 432p. (C). 1994. boxed write for info. (0-697-12794-X) Brown & Benchmark.
Levin, Iurii D. Shakespeare & Literature in Nineteenth Century Russia. 368p. 1994. 70.00 (0-85496-891-1); pap. 25.00 (0-85496-863-6) Berg Pubs.
Levin, J. & McDevitt, J. Hate Crimes: The Rising Tide of Bigotry & Bloodshed. (Illus.). 270p. (C). 1993. 23.95 (0-306-44471-2, Plenum Pr) Plenum.
Levin, J., jt. auth. see Fox, James A.
Levin, J. R. & Allen, Vernon L., eds. Cognitive Learning in Children: Theories & Strategies. (Educational Psychology Ser.). 1976. text ed. 51.00 (0-12-444850-X) Acad Pr.
Levin, J. R., jt. ed. see Presley, M.
Levin, Jack. Bacterial Endotoxins: Cytokine Mediators & New Therapies for Sepsis. (Progress in Clinical & Biological Research Ser.). 240p. 1991. text ed. 99.95 (0-471-56096-0) Wiley.
— Mass Murder: America's Growing Menace. 1991. mass mkt. 4.99 (0-425-12443-6) Berkley Pub.
— Sociological Snapshots: Seeing Social Structure & Change in Everyday Life. LC 92-17454. 184p. (C). 1992. pap. text ed. 7.95 (0-8039-9001-4) Pine Forge.
— Sociological Snapshots 2: Seeing Social Structure & Change in Everyday Life. 2nd ed. LC 95-8239. 1995. write for info. (0-8039-9075-8) Pine Forge.
Levin, Jack & Arluke, Arnold. Gossip: The Inside Scoop. LC 87-2442. (Illus.). 262p. 1987. 17.95 (0-306-42533-5, Plenum Pr) Plenum.
Levin, Jack & Fox, James A. Elementary Statistics in Social Research. 6th ed. LC 93-21091. (C). 1993. student ed 13.00 (0-673-46959-X); text ed. 40.50 (0-673-46958-1) HarpCollege.
— Mass Murder: America's Growing Menace. LC 84-26585. 270p. 1985. 19.95 (0-306-41943-2, Plenum Pr) Plenum.
Levin, Jack & Levin, William C. The Functions of Discrimination & Prejudice. 2nd ed. LC 81-6794. 270p. reprint ed. pap. 77.00 (0-7837-4509-5, 2044286) Bks Demand.
— The Functions of Discrimination & Prejudice. 2nd ed. 258p. (C). 1990. pap. text ed. 16.00 (0-06-043964-5) HarpCollege.
Levin, Jack & Spates, James. Starting Sociology. 4th ed. 528p. (C). 1989. pap. text ed. 33.50 (0-06-044078-3) HarpCollege.
Levin, Jack, jt. auth. see Bourne, Richard.
Levin, Jack, jt. auth. see Ferman, Gerald S.
Levin, Jack, ed. see Fourth International Conference on Endotoxins Staff.
Levin, Jack, jt. auth. see Fox, James A.
Levin, Jack, et al, eds. Bacterial Endotoxin: Recognition & Effector Mechanisms: Proceedings of the Second Congress of the International Endotoxin Society, Vienna, 17-20 August 1992, Vol. 2. LC 92-48465. (International Congress Ser., Endotoxin Research Ser.: Vol. 1020). 1993. write for info. (0-444-89814-X) Elsevier.
Levin, James. Ayudar. Carter, Jackie, ed. LC 94-729. (J). 1994. write for info. (0-590-29365-6) Scholastic Inc.
Levin, James & Cederquist, Natalie. A Celebration of Wellness. (Illus.). 308p. 1990. pap. 16.95 (0-9628698-1-3) GLO Inc.
— A Vegetarian's Ecstasy. (Illus.). 321p. 1992. pap. 16.95 (0-9628698-7-2) GLO Inc.
— Vibrant Living. (Illus.). 260p. 1993. pap. 14.95 (0-9628698-2-1) GLO Inc.
Levin, James & Nolan, James. Principles of Classroom Management: A Hierarchical Approach. 272p. (C). 1990. pap. text ed. write for info. (0-13-691171-4) P-H.
Levin, Jeffrey S., ed. Religion in Aging & Health: Theoretical Foundations in Methodological Frontiers. (Focus Editions Ser.: Vol. 166). (Illus.). 320p. (C). 1993. text ed. 49.95 (0-8039-5438-7); pap. text ed. 24.95 (0-8039-5439-5) Sage.
Levin, Jenifer. The Sea of Light. LC 93-45971. 400p. 1994. pap. 10.95 (0-452-27059-6, Plume) NAL-Dutton.
— Shimoni's Lover. 1987. 18.95 (0-15-181990-4) HarBrace.
— Water Dancer. LC 93-44118. 1994. 10.95 (0-452-27257-2, Plume) NAL-Dutton.

An Asterisk (*) at the beginning of an entry indicates that the title is appearing in BIP for the first time.

L

Levin, Jerome D. Alcoholism: A Bio-Psycho-Social Approach. 250p. 1989. 47.00 (0-89116-895-8); pap. 26.00 (1-56032-023-0) Hemisp Pub.
— Introduction to Alcoholism Counselling: A Bio-Psycho-Social Approach. 2nd ed. 225p. 1995. 59.50x (1-56032-355-8); pap. 24.50x (1-56032-358-2) Taylor & Francis.
— Recovery from Alcoholism. LC 93-74242. 296p. 1994. reprint ed. pap. 25.00 (1-56821-186-4) Aronson.
— Recovery from Alcoholism: Beyond Your Wildest Dreams. LC 90-1232. 296p. 1991. 30.00x (0-87668-625-0) Aronson.
— Slings & Arrows: Narcissistic Injury & Its Treatment. LC 93-13285. 336p. 1993. 40.00 (0-87668-550-5) Aronson.
— Theories of the Self. LC 92-12864. 1992. 45.00 (1-56032-260-8); pap. 24.50 (1-56032-261-6) Hemisp Pub.
— Treatment of Alcoholism & Other Addictions: A Self-Psychology Approach. LC 87-19563. 448p. 1994. pap. 35.00x (0-87668-521-1) Aronson.
Levin, Jerome D., ed. see Weiss, Ronna H.
Levin, Joan H. Rustico di Filippo & the Florentine Lyric Tradition. (American University Studies: Romance Languages & Literature: Ser. II, Vol. 16). 197p. 1986. text ed. 29.50 (0-8204-0150-1) P Lang Pubs.
Levin, Joel. Getting Published: The Educators' Resource Book. LC 83-10042. 288p. 1983. lib. bdg. 16.95 (0-685-06781-5, Arco Test) P-H Gen Ref & Trav.
— How Judges Reason. LC 91-37405. 267p. (C). 1992. text ed. 39.95 (0-8204-1549-9) P Lang Pubs.
— How to Get a Job in Education. 2nd ed. 320p. 1995. pap. 12.95 (1-55850-510-5) Adams Pubng.
Levin, Joel, jt. ed. see Kratochwill, Thomas.
Levin, Joel M. Ascent of the Primal Eye. (Illus.). 30p. (Orig.). 1982. pap. text ed. 3.00 (1-879594-04-8) Androgyne Bks.
— Tigerskin. 14p. (Orig.). 1981. pap. text ed. 0.75 (1-879594-05-6) Androgyne Bks.
Levin, Johathan. The Banking Law Reference Guide for National Banks. 2nd ed. 250p. 1991. pap. 29.95 (0-13-093972-2, 130401) P-H.
***Levin, Jonathan V.** The Smiles Still Echo. LC 95-94370. (Illus.). 100p. (Orig.). 1995. pap. write for info. (0-9646551-0-1) Bethesda.
Levin, Jules F. The Slavic Element in the Old Prussian Elbing Vocabulary. LC 72-619636. (U. C. Publ. in Linguistics Ser.: Vol. 77). 124p. reprint ed. 35.40 (0-8357-9639-6, 2015116) Bks Demand.
Levin, Jules F., et al. Reading Modern Russian. (Illus.). vi, 321p. 1979. pap. text ed. 18.95 (0-89357-059-1) Slavica.
Levin, Karen A. Meatless Dishes in Twenty Minutes: Delicious, Easy-To-Prepare Meals Everyone Will Love! 128p. 1993. pap. 9.95 (0-8092-3810-1) Contemp Bks.
— The Twenty-Minute Low-Fat Gourmet: Mouth-Watering Recipes for Delicious Low-Fat Meals in a Flash. 144p. 1994. pap. 9.95 (0-8092-3809-8) Contemp Bks.
Levin, Kenneth. Unconscious Fantasy in Psychotherapy: Its Meaning & Mastery in Psychotherapy. LC 92-49153. 320p. 1994. 40.00 (0-87668-260-3) Aronson.
Levin, Keren & Morrissey, Kevin. Twenty-Minute Chicken Dishes: Delicious, Easy-to-Prepare Meals Everyone Will Love! 128p. 1991. pap. 8.95 (0-8092-4033-5) Contemp Bks.
Levin, Kim. Beyond Modernism: Essays on Art from the '70s & '80s. LC 87-45637. (Illus.). 258p. 1989. pap. 15.00 (0-06-430176-1, IN-176, Icon Edns) HarpC.
Levin, Kim, ed. Beyond Walls & Wars: Art, Politics, & Multiculturalism. LC 91-68502. 1993. pap. text ed. 15.50 (1-877675-11-3) Midmarch Arts-WAN.
Levin, Kim, jt. auth. see Crary, Jonathan.
Levin, L., jt. auth. see Gantmakher, F.
Levin, L. I. Electrochemistry of Non-Ferrous Metals. Murty, Ram, tr. (Illus.). 282p. (C). 1989. 40.00x (81-204-0458-0) S Asia.
Levin, L. I., ed. see Saxey, Roderick.
Levin, L. I., et al. Energy Reviews: Scientific & Technical Progress in District Heating & Cogeneration, Vol. 4. Rudenko, Y. N., ed. (Soviet Technology Reviews Ser.: Vol. 4, Pt. 3). iv, 146p. 1990. pap. text ed. 87.00 (3-7186-4899-7) Gordon & Breach.
Levin, Laurie & Bellotti, Laura G. Creative Weddings: An Up-to-Date Guide to Making Your Wedding As Unique As You Are. LC 93-31490. 192p. (Orig.). 1994. pap. 9.95 (0-452-27203-3, Plume) NAL-Dutton.
— You Can't Hurry Love: An Intimate Look at First Marriages after 40. 336p. 1993. pap. 4.99 (0-451-17499-2, Sig) NAL-Dutton.
Levin, Lawrence M., ed. see Galdos, Benito.
Levin, Leonard, jt. auth. see Holzman, Red.
Levin, Lewis M. Medical Staff Privileges. Karaffa, Melanie C., ed. 250p. (C). 1992. text ed. 49.95 (1-878487-36-1) Practice Mgmt Info.
Levin, Linda L. Mass Communication Law in Rhode Island. (State Law Ser.). 114p. (Orig.). 1993. pap. text ed. 12.95 (0-913507-45-8) New Forums.
Levin, Lois, ed. see Levin, Sidney.
Levin, Louis & Levin, Samuel. Practical Benchwork for Horologists. 8th rev. ed. (Illus.). 382p. 1988. reprint ed. pap. 19.95 (0-930163-12-5) Arlington Bk.
Levin, Lowell S., et al. Self-Care: Lay Initiatives in Health. LC 76-29361. 1976. 15.00 (0-686-57948-8); pap. 7.95 (0-88202-111-7) Watson Pub Intl.
Levin, Maksim G. Ethnic Origins of the Peoples of Northeastern Asia. Michael, Henry N., ed. LC 63-4343. (Arctic Institute of North America-Anthropology of the North; Translation from Russian Sources Ser.: No. 3). 367p. reprint ed. pap. 104.60 (0-317-09968-X, 2020499) Bks Demand.
Levin, Marc A., jt. auth. see Clatanoff, Robert M.
Levin, Marcia O. The Baby's Book. (Illus.). 64p. 1984. 19.95 (0-88363-084-2) H L Levin.
— The Bride's Book. (Illus.). 64p. 1985. 19.95 (0-88363-085-0) H L Levin.
— Grandmother's Book. 1992. 8.99 (0-517-07009-X) Random Hse Value.
Levin, Marian S. Grandparents' Little Dividends: How to Stay in Touch with Your Grandkids. (Illus.). 64p. (Orig.). 1989. pap. text ed. 7.95 (0-9623521-0-1) Grandparents Little Div.
Levin, Marshall N. & Hake, Theodore L. Buttons in Sets. (Illus.). 88p. 1984. pap. 12.00 (0-918708-04-4) Hake.
Levin, Martha, ed. see Dinesen, Isak.
Levin, Martha, ed. see Spring Hill Center Staff.
***Levin, Martin.** Be Your Own Literary Agent. 256p. 1995. 16.95 (0-89815-766-8) Ten Speed Pr.
— Hollywood & the Great Fan Magazines. 1991. 12.99 (0-517-05785-9) Random Hse Value.
— How to Be Your Own Literary Agent. 256p. 1995. 16.95 (0-89815-772-2) Ten Speed Pr.
Levin, Martin A. & Ferman, Barbara. The Political Hand: Policy Implementation & Youth Employment Programs. (Government & Politics Ser.). 160p. 1985. text ed. 37.50 (0-08-031604-2, Pergamon Pr); pap. text ed. 18.95 (0-08-031603-4, Pergamon Pr) Elsevier.
Levin, Martin A. & Sanger, M. Bryna. Making Government Work: How Entrepreneurial Executives Turn Bright Ideas into Real Results. LC 94-381. (Public Administration Ser.). 250p. 1994. 25.95 (1-55542-658-1) Jossey-Bass.
Levin, Martin A., jt. ed. see Landy, Marc K.
Levin, Marvin E., et al. The Diabetic Foot. 5th ed. LC 92-49437. 635p. 1992. 89.00 (0-8016-6878-6) Mosby Yr Bk.
Levin, Maurice I. Russian Declension & Conjugation: A Structural Description with Exercises. x, 159p. 1978. pap. 15.95 (0-89357-048-6) Slavica.
***Levin, Meir.** Walking with Fire: The Path of Novarodok Musar. 1996. write for info. (1-56821-603-3) Aronson.
Levin, Melvin R. American Experience & China's Urban Choices. (Working Paper Ser.: No. 8). 54p. 1987. 5.00 (0-913749-18-4) U MD Urban Stud.
— Ending Unemployment: Alternatives for Public Policy. LC 82-84540. (Urban Studies Monograph Ser.: No. 1). 398p. 1982. 12.00 (0-913749-06-0) U MD Urban Stud.
— Planning in Government: Shaping Programs that Succeed. (Illus.). 257p. (Orig.). (C). 1987. lib. bdg. 38.95 (0-685-16736-4); pap. 22.95 (0-918286-44-1) Planners Pr.
Levin, Melvin R., intro. The Best of Planning. LC 88-83721. (Illus.). 614p. (Orig.). 1989. lib. bdg. 45.00 (0-918286-59-X); pap. text ed. 29.95 (0-918286-60-3) Planners Pr.
Levin, Meyer. Beginnings in Jewish Philosophy. LC 76-116677. (Jewish Heritage Ser.). (Illus.). 192p. (gr. 9-11). 1971. text ed. 6.95 (0-87441-063-0) Behrman.
— Citizens: A Novel. LC 74-22793. reprint ed. 39.00 (0-404-58447-0) AMS Pr.
— Israel Haggadah. rev. ed. LC 70-99933. (Illus.). 1969. reprint ed. pap. 7.95 (0-8109-2040-9) Abrams.
— The Old Bunch. 976p. 1985. reprint ed. 19.95 (0-8065-0974-0, Citadel Pr); reprint ed. pap. 14.95 (0-8065-0967-8, Citadel Pr) Carol Pub Group.
Levin, Meyer & Kurzband, Toby. Story of the Jewish Way of Life. LC 59-13487. (Jewish Heritage Ser.: Vol. 3). (J). (gr. 4-6). 1959. pap. 6.95 (0-87441-003-7) Behrman.
Levin, Meyer, tr. see Asch, Sholem.
Levin, Michael. Alive & Kicking: A Novel. 368p. 1993. 21.00 (0-671-73190-4) S&S Trade.
— Alive & Kicking Vol. 1. 1994. pap. 4.99 (0-312-95305-4) St Martin.
— Feminism & Freedom. 490p. 1994. 39.95 (0-88738-125-1); pap. 21.95 (0-88738-670-9) Transaction Pubs.
— Marx, Engels & Liberal Democracy. LC 88-825. 172p. 1989. text ed. 39.95 (0-312-01577-1) St Martin.
— Old Yeller: A Literature Unit. (Literature Units Ser.). (Illus.). 48p. (Orig.). 1993. student ed, pap. 6.95 (1-55734-427-2) Tchr Create Mat.
— The Spectre of Democracy: The Rise of Modern Democracy As Seen by Its Opponents. 272p. 1992. text ed. 50.00x (0-8147-5060-5) NYU Pr.
Levin, Michael, ed. Ethnicity & Aboriginality: Case Studies in Ethnonationalism. 50.00 (0-8020-2918-3); pap. 19.95 (0-8020-7423-5) U of Toronto Pr.
Levin, Michael, jt. auth. see McMullan, Jim.
***Levin, Michael, et al.** Contracting with Architects: A School District's Perspective. 40p. (Orig.). 1991. pap. 25.00 (0-614-03399-3) Natl Sch Boards.
Levin, Michael E. Metaphysics & the Mind-Body Problem. (Clarendon Library of Logic & Philosophy). 1979. 55.00 (0-19-824415-0) OUP.
Levin, Michael G. Journey to Tradition: The Odyssey of a Born-Again Jew. 129p. 1986. 14.95 (0-88125-093-7) Ktav.
Levin, Michael H. Roll of Thunder, Hear My Cry: A Literature Unit. (Literature Units Ser.). (Illus.). 48p. 1994. student ed 6.95 (1-55734-439-6) Tchr Create Mat.
***Levin, Michael I.** Pennsylvania School Personnel Actions. 3rd ed. 428p. 1991. pap. 59.00 (0-8322-0511-7) Banks-Baldwin.
***Levin, Michael I., ed.** Pennsylvania School Laws & Rules, 1994-95. 905p. 1992. pap. 81.00 (0-8322-0512-5) Banks-Baldwin.
Levin, Michael J. & Retherford, Robert D. Recent Fertility Trends in the Pacific Islands. LC 86-16739. (Papers of the East-West Population Institute: No. 101). (Illus.). viii, 72p. 1986. pap. 3.00 (0-86638-083-3) EW Ctr HI.
Levin, Milton. Noel Coward. (English Authors Ser.: No. 73). 130p. 1989. text ed. 21.95 (0-8057-6978-1, TEAS 73, Twayne) Macmillan.
Levin, Miriam R. Republican Art & Ideology in Late Nineteenth- Century France. LC 85-21021. (Studies in the Fine Arts - Art Theory: No. 11). (Illus.). 355p. reprint ed. pap. 101.20 (0-8357-1670-8, 2070608) Bks Demand.
— When the Eiffel Tower Was New: French Visions of Progress at the Centennial of the Revolution. LC 88-63428. (Illus.). 128p. 1989. pap. 18.95 (0-87023-673-3) U of Mass Pr.
Levin, Monroe. Clues to American Music. (Clues to American Arts Ser.). (Illus.). 72p. (Orig.). 1992. pap. 7.95 (0-913515-62-0, Starrhill) Elliott & Clark.
Levin, Morris, jt. ed. see Vinik, Ave.
Levin, Morris A. Biotreatment of Industrial & Hazardous Waste. 1993. text ed. 60.00 (0-07-037554-2) McGraw.
Levin, Morris A., et al. Microbial Ecology: Principles, Methods & Applications. 800p. 1992. text ed. 82.00 (0-07-037506-2) McGraw.
Levin, Moshe Chaim, ed. see Schneersohn, Y. Y.
Levin, Murray B. Talk Radio & the American Dream. 192p. 1986. text ed. 29.95 (0-669-13216-0); text ed. 12.95 (0-669-13217-9) Free Pr.
Levin, Murray B. & Blackwood, George. The Compleat Politician: Political Strategy in Massachusetts. LC 62-18204. 1962. 29.50 (0-672-51133-9) Irvington.
Levin, N. Gordon, Jr. Woodrow Wilson & World Politics: America's Response to War & Revolution. LC 68-15893. 1970. pap. 15.95 (0-19-500803-0) OUP.
***Levin, Nancy E.** Free Willy: Talking to Animals. (Illus.). (J). (gr. k-2). 1995. pap. 2.50 (0-590-25352-2) Scholastic Inc.
Levin, Nicky. Kanal Griboedova. Levin, Roman, ed. 208p. (Orig.). (RUS.). 1986. write for info. (0-914265-05-9); pap. 12.00 (0-914265-04-0) New Eng Pub MA.
Levin, Nora. The Holocaust: The Nazi Destruction of European Jewry, 1933-1945. LC 89-2315. (Anvil Ser.). 384p. (C). 1990. pap. text ed. 17.50 (0-89464-223-5) Krieger.
— The Jews in the Soviet Union: Since 1917, 2 vols., Vol. 2. (Illus.). 432p. 1988. text ed. 55.00 (0-8147-5035-4) NYU Pr.
— Jews in the Soviet Union since 1917, 2 vols., 2. 1017p. 1990. pap. 20.00 (0-8147-5052-4) NYU Pr.
— Jews in the Soviet Union since 1917, 2 vols., Set. 1017p. 1990. pap. 37.50 (0-8147-5050-8) NYU Pr.
Levin, Nora J. How to Care for your Parents. 103p. 1987. pap. 5.95 (0-394-75690-8) Storm King Pr.
— How to Care for Your Parents: A Handbook for Adult Children. 1991. pap. 5.95 (0-935166-03-3) Storm King Pr.
— How to Care for Your Parents: A Handbook for Adult Children. 1,994th ed. 1994. pap. 6.95 (0-935166-09-2) Storm King Pr.
— How to Care for Your Parents: A Handbook for Adult Children-1993 Edition. 110p. 1993. pap. 6.95 (0-935166-06-8) Storm King Pr.
Levin, P., ed. see European Congress on Sleep Research Staff.
Levin, Pamela. Becoming the Way We Are. rev. ed. Stern, Nora G., ed. LC 84-70759. (Illus.). 120p. 1985. pap. text ed. 6.95 (0-939688-12-3) Directed Media.
— Susan B. Anthony: Fighter for Women's Rights. (Junior World Biographies Ser.). (Illus.). 80p. (J). (gr. 3-6). 1993. lib. bdg. 14.95 (0-7910-1762-1, Am Art Analog); pap. 4.95 (0-7910-1965-9, Am Art Analog) Chelsea Hse.
Levin, Paul. Claims & Changes: Handbook for Construction Contract Management. Jones, Bruce & Jones, Angier, eds. (Illus.). 222p. 23.50 (0-686-36279-9) Constr Ind Pr.
Levin, Paul, jt. auth. see Jervis, Bruce M.
***Levin, Phillis.** The Afterimage. 63p. (Orig.). 1995. pap. 9.95 (0-914278-67-3) Copper Beech.
— Temples & Fields. LC 88-4822. (Contemporary Poetry Ser.). 96p. 1988. 15.00 (0-8203-1052-2); pap. 7.95 (0-8203-1053-0) U of Ga Pr.
Levin, Phyllis L. Abigail Adams: A Biography. 1988. pap. 10.95 (0-345-35473-7, Ballantine Trade) Ballantine.
***Levin, Rhoda F.** From Generation to Generation: A Meditation Journal for Contemporary Jews. 256p. (Orig.). 1996. pap. 16.95 (0-9637795-7-5) MinervaPress.
— Heartmates: A Guide for the Spouse & Family of the Heart Patient. rev. ed. 368p. 1995. pap. 12.00 (0-9637795-1-6) MinervaPress.
— Heartmates: A Guide for the Spouse & Family of the Heart Patient. rev. unabridged ed. 1995. audio 24.95 (0-9637795-4-0) MinervaPress.
— The Heartmates Meditation Journal: A Companion for Partners of People with Heart Disease. 256p. (Orig.). 1995. pap. 15.00 (0-9637795-2-4) MinervaPress.
— Open Doors: A Meditation Journal for Partners of People Coping with Change & Loss. 256p. (Orig.). 1996. pap. 16.95 (0-9637795-8-3) MinervaPress.
— Roots & Wings: A Meditation Journal for Women in Transition. 256p. (Orig.). 1996. pap. 16.95 (0-9637795-9-1) MinervaPress.
***Levin, Rhonda F.** Heartmates: A Guide for the Spouse & Family of the Heart Patient. rev. ed. 1994. mass mkt. 5.99 (0-671-51095-9) PB.
Levin, Rich. Magic Johnson: Court Magician. rev. ed. LC 80-25814. (Sports Stars Ser.). (Illus.). 48p. (J). (gr. 2-8). 1981. lib. bdg. 11.85 (0-516-04313-7) Childrens.
Levin, Richard. Computer Virus Handbook. 1990. text ed. 24.95 (0-07-881647-5) Osborne-McGraw.
— Love & Society in Shakespearean Comedy: A Study of Dramatic Form & Content. LC 84-40060. 208p. 1985. 32.50 (0-87413-266-5) U Delaware Pr.
Levin, Richard & Levin, David, eds. Tragedy: Plays, Theory & Criticism. (Harbrace Sourcebooks Ser.). 217p. (Orig.). (C). 1960. pap. text ed. 17.50 (0-15-592346-3) HB Coll Pubs.
Levin, Richard, ed. see Middleton, Thomas.
Levin, Richard I. The Executive's Illustrated Primer of Long-Range Planning. (Illus.). 224p. 1983. pap. 25.95 (0-13-295493-1) P-H.
Levin, Richard I. & Rubin, David S. Statistics for Management. 5th ed. 928p. (C). 1991. text ed. write for info. (0-13-851965-X) P-H.
— Statistics for Management. 6th ed. LC 93-26067. 1994. text ed. write for info. (0-13-847781-7) P-H.
Levin, Rita. Punctuation Partners. (Language Arts Ser.). 48p. (J). (gr. 2-4). 1983. 6.95 (0-88160-098-9, LW 121) Learning Wks.
Levin, Rob & Eanes, Jennifer, eds. Seven Days in Winston-Salem. 240p. 1994. 32.95 (1-883987-02-4) Riverbend Bks.
Levin, Robert, ed. Y Basketball Dribblers Manual: For 5th-6th Grade Players. (Illus.). 40p. (J). (gr. 5-6). 1984. pap. text ed. 5.00 (0-931250-84-6, LYMC4666, YMCA USA) Human Kinetics.
— Y Basketball Passers Manual: For 3rd-4th Grade Players. (Illus.). 36p. (J). (gr. 3-4). 1984. pap. 5.00 (0-931250-83-8, LYMC4665, YMCA USA) Human Kinetics.
Levin, Robert, jt. ed. see Jefferies, Stephen C.
Levin, Robert, jt. ed. see Rivelli, Pauline.
Levin, Robert, ed. see YMCA of the U. S. A. Staff.
Levin, Robert A. Educating Elementary School Teachers: The Struggle for Coherent Vision, 1909-1978. LC 93-29001. 200p. (Orig.). (C). 1993. lib. bdg. 46.50 (0-8191-9276-7); pap. text ed. 27.50 (0-8191-9277-5) U Pr of Amer.
Levin, Robert D. Who Wrote the Mozart Four-Wind Concertante? Authenticity, Origin & Reconstruction. LC 84-26365. 1989. 62.00 (0-918728-31-2) Pendragon NY.
Levin, Robert E. Bill Clinton: The Inside Story. (Illus.). 320p. 1992. 5.50 (1-56171-177-2, S P I Bks) Sure Sellers.
Levin, Roman, ed. see Levin, Nicky.
Levin, Ronald M., jt. auth. see Gellhorn, Ernest.
***Levin, S. A., ed.** Frontiers in Mathematical Biology. LC 94-33688. (Lecture Notes in Biomathematics Ser.: Vol. 100). 1994. write for info. (0-387-58466-8) Spr-Verlag.
— Frontiers in Mathematical Biology. LC 94-33688. (Lecture Notes in Biomathematics Ser.: Vol. 100). 1995. 69.00 (3-540-58466-8) Spr-Verlag.
Levin, S. A. & Hallam, T. G., eds. Mathematical Ecology: Proceedings of the Autumn Research Seminar, Held at the International Centre for Theoretical Physics, Miramare-Trieste, Italy, November 29-December 10, 1982. (Lecture Notes in Biomathematics Ser.: Vol. 54). xii, 513p. 1984. 54.90 (0-387-12919-7) Spr-Verlag.
Levin, S. A., ed. see Busenberg, Stavros N., et al.
Levin, S. A., ed. see Cohen, J. E., et al.
Levin, S. A., ed. see Cressman, R.
Levin, S. A., ed. see Lyubich, Y. I.
Levin, S. A., ed. see Murray, J. D.
Levin, S. A., ed. see Nagylaki, T.
Levin, S. A., ed. see Taib, Ziad.
Levin, S. A., ed. see Tuljapurkar, S.
Levin, S. A., ed. see Tyson, J. J.
Levin, S. A., ed. see Wiegel, F. W.
Levin, S. A., et al, eds. Applied Mathematical Ecology. (Biomathematics Ser.: Vol. 18). (Illus.). 505p. 1989. 64.00 (0-387-19465-7, 2440) Spr-Verlag.
— Ecotoxicology: Problems & Approaches. (Advanced Texts in Life Sciences Ser.). (Illus.). 530p. 1988. 69.00 (0-387-96762-1) Spr-Verlag.
Levin, S. I. & Boyden, Edward A. Kosher Code of the Orthodox Jew. LC 76-76170. (Judaic Studies Library: No. SHP9). (Illus.). 264p. 1983. pap. 12.95 (0-87203-011-3) Hermon.
Levin, Samuel, jt. auth. see Levin, Louis.
Levin, Samuel R. Linguistic Structures in Poetry. (Janua Linguarum, Ser. Minor: No. 23). 1973. pap. text ed. 20.00 (90-279-0678-5) Mouton.
— Metaphoric Worlds: Conceptions of a Romantic Nature. LC 87-28955. (C). 1988. text ed. 30.00 (0-300-04172-1) Yale U Pr.
— The Semantics of Metaphor. LC 77-4550. 176p. reprint ed. pap. 50.20 (0-317-41827-0, 2025626) Bks Demand.
***Levin, Saul.** Semitic & Indo-European: The Principal Etymologies: With Observations on Afro-Asiatic. LC 95-19984. (Current Issues in Linguistic Theory Ser.: No. 129). 500p. 1995. student ed, lib. bdg. 97.00x (1-55619-583-4) Benjamins North Am.
Levin, Saul, jt. ed. see Bernardo, Aldo S.
Levin, Sharon G., jt. auth. see Stephan, Paula E.
Levin, Shmarya. The Arena. Samuel, Maurice, tr. LC 74-27999. (Modern Jewish Experience Ser.). (ENG.). 1975. reprint ed. 28.95 (0-405-06726-7) Ayer.
— Childhood in Exile. Samuel, Maurice, tr. LC 74-27997. (Modern Jewish Experience Ser.). 1975. reprint ed. 25.95 (0-405-06724-0) Ayer.
— Youth in Revolt. Samuel, Maurice, tr. LC 74-27998. (Modern Jewish Experience Ser.). 1975. reprint ed. 26.95 (0-405-06725-9) Ayer.
Levin, Sidney. Facilitating Psychotherapy. Levin, Lois, ed. 221p. 1987. text ed. 29.95 (0-8290-2137-X) Irvington.
Levin, Sidney & Kahana, Ralph J., eds. Psychodynamic Studies on Aging: Creativity, Reminiscing & Dying. LC 67-27427. 345p. 1967. text ed. 42.50 (0-8236-5640-3) Intl Univs Pr.
Levin, Sidney L., jt. auth. see Stillman, Deborah L.
Levin, Simon, contrib. Studies in Mathematical Biology. Incl. Vol. 15. Part 1, Cellular Behavior & Development of Pattern. 329p. 1978. 12.00 (0-88385-115-6); Vol. 16. Part 2, Populations & Communities. 328p. 1978. 12.00 (0-88385-116-4); (Studies in Mathematics). write for info. (0-318-59513-3) Math Assn.

An Asterisk (*) at the beginning of an entry indicates that the title is appearing in BIP for the first time.

Levin, Simon, ed. Population Biology. LC 83-21389. (Proceedings of Symposia in Applied Mathematics Ser.: Vol. 30). 101p. 1984. pap. 31.00 (*0-8218-0083-3*, PSAPM 30) Am Math.

Levin, Sis. Beirut Diary: A Husband Held Hostage & a Wife Determined to Set Him Free. LC 89-19750. 239p. 1989. 14.99 (*0-8308-1716-6*, 1716, Saltshaker Bk) InterVarsity.

Levin-Stankevich, Brian, jt. auth. see Popovych, Erika.

Levin, Stefan L. & Knight, Connie H., eds. Genetic & Environmental Hearing Loss: Syndromic & Nonsyndromic. (Alan R. Liss Ser.: Vol. 16, No. 7). 1980. 16.00 (*0-685-03288-4*) March of Dimes.

Levin, Steve. Seven Days in Tucson. 192p. 1994. 32.95 (*1-883987-01-6*) Riverbend Bks.

Levin, Stuart A., et al. The Clinician's Guide to Sexually Transmitted Infections. (Illus.). 150p. 1987. 31.95 (*0-8151-5401-1*, TID-1, Yr Bk Med Pubs) Mosby Yr Bk.

Levin, Sunie. Mingled Roots: A Guide for Jewish Grandparents of Interfaith Grandchildren. (Illus.). 84p. (Orig.). 1992. pap. 13.95 (*0-9632259-0-1*) Bnai Brith Wom.

Levin, Susan. Dorothy Wordsworth & Romanticism. (Douglass Series on Women's Lives & the Meaning of Gender). 259p. 1987. text ed. 40.00 (*0-8135-1146-1*) Rutgers U Pr.

*__Levin, Susan M.__ Harry the Hairy Monster. (Illus.). 16p. (Orig.). (J). (ps-2). 1994. pap. write for info. (*0-9642777-1-9*) Levin Family.

Levin, Susanna, jt. auth. see Smith, Kathy.

Levin, Sydney S., jt. ed. see Touchstone, Joseph C.

Levin, Ted. Backtracking: The Way of a Naturalist. LC 86-32717. (Illus.). 220p. 1987. pap. 9.95 (*0-930031-15-6*) Chelsea Green Pub.

— Blood Brook. 208p. 1992. 24.95 (*0-930031-56-3*) Chelsea Green Pub.

— Blood Brook: A Naturalist's Home Ground. 1992. pap. 14.95 (*0-930031-60-1*) Chelsea Green Pub.

Levin, Thomas Y., ed. see Kracauer, Siegfried.

Levin, Toby. Rainbow of Hope: A Guide for the Special Needs Child. LC 91-67611. 200p. (Orig.). 1992. pap. 12.95 (*0-9624680-1-0*) Starlight FL.

Levin, V., jt. auth. see Fuchs, B.

Levin, Victor. Death in Scarsdale. 32p. (Orig.). 1983. pap. 2.50 (*0-87129-158-4*, D40) Dramatic Pub.

Levin, Victor A., et al. Brain & Nervous System; Head & Neck; Genitourinary System. (Illus.). 105p. (Orig.). 1994. pap. text ed. 49.95 (*1-85922-620-5*) Current Science.

*__Levin-Waldman, Oren M.__ The Consolidated Assistance Program: Reforming Welfare by Synchronizing Public Assistance Benefits. (Orig.). 1995. pap. 3.00 (*0-941276-10-4*, J Levy Econ Inst) Bard Coll Pubns.

— Plant Closure, Regulation, & Liberalism: The Limits to Liberal Public Philosophy. LC 92-16876. 200p. (C). 1992. lib. bdg. 44.50 (*0-8191-8760-7*) U Pr of Amer.

— Plant Closure, Regulation, & Liberalism: The Limits to Liberal Public Philosophy. LC 92-16876. 200p. (C). 1992. pap. text ed. 21.50 (*0-8191-8761-5*) U Pr of Amer.

Levin-Waldman, Oren M., intro. Homosexuality & the Military: A Sourcebook of Official, Uncensored U. S. Government Documents. (Illus.). 256p. (Orig.). (C). 1993. pap. text ed. 34.95 (*1-56806-282-6*) Diane Pub.

Levin, Wayne, photos. Kalaupapa: A Portrait. 1989. 28.00 (*0-930897-45-5*, SP91) Bishop Mus.

Levin, William C. Sociological Ideas: Concepts & Applications. 3rd ed. 416p. (C). 1991. pap. 24.95 (*0-534-14646-5*) Intl Thomson.

— Sociological Ideas: Concepts & Applications. 4th ed. LC 93-3256. 473p. 1994. pap. 25.95 (*0-534-20856-8*) Intl Thomson.

Levin, William C., jt. auth. see Levin, Jack.

*__Levin, William E.__ Trade Dress Protection. (Intellectual Proprety Ser.). 1995. ring bd. write for info. (*0-614-06276-4*) Clark Boardman Callaghan.

Levina, Valentina M., tr. see Gorelik, Gennady E. & Frenkel, Victor Y.

Levinas, Emmanuel. Beyond the Verse: Talmudic Readings & Lectures. Mole, Gary D., tr. LC 94-8618. 1994. 27.95 (*0-253-33288-5*) Ind U Pr.

— Collected Philosophical Papers. Lingis, Alphonso, ed. 1987. lib. bdg. 95.00 (*90-247-3272-7*) Kluwer Ac.

— Difficult Freedom: Essays on Judaism. Hand, Sean, tr. LC 90-31771. (Jewish Studies). 368p. 1991. text ed. 38.50x (*0-8018-4074-0*) Johns Hopkins.

— Ethics & Infinity. Cohen, Richard, tr. LC 85-1542. 140p. 1985. pap. text ed. 12.00x (*0-8207-0178-5*) Duquesne.

— In the Time of the Nations. Smith, Michael B., tr. LC 94-8617. 1994. 29.95 (*0-253-33295-8*) Ind U Pr.

— Nine Talmudic Readings by Emmanuel Levinas. Aronwicz, Annette, tr. LC 89-46329. 236p. 1990. 29.95 (*0-253-33379-2*); pap. 10.95 (*0-253-20876-9*) Ind U Pr.

— Otherwise Than Being or Beyond Essence. Lingis, Alphonso, tr. (Martinus Nijhoff Philosophy Texts Ser.: No. 3). 273p. 1981. lib. bdg. 61.50 (*90-247-2374-4*) Kluwer Ac.

— Outside the Subject. LC 92-83918. 128p. (C). 1993. 32.50 (*0-8047-2197-1*); pap. 12.95 (*0-8047-2199-8*) Stanford U Pr.

— Theory of Intuition in Husserl's Phenomenology. 2nd ed. Orianne, Andre, tr. LC 95-14655. (Studies in Phenomenology & Existential Philosophy). 1995. pap. text ed. write for info. (*0-8101-1281-7*) Northwestern U Pr.

— The Theory of Intuition in Husserl's Phenomenology. Orianne, Andre, tr. (Studies in Phenomenology & Existential Philosophy). 163p. 1985. reprint ed. pap. 14.95 (*0-8101-0708-2*) Northwestern U Pr.

— Time & the Other. Cohen, Richard A., tr. & intro. by. LC 87-6900. 149p. (C). 1990. reprint ed. pap. text ed. 17.95 (*0-8207-0233-1*) Duquesne.

— Totalite et Infini. (Phaenomenologica Ser.: No. 8). 1981. lib. bdg. 89.00 (*90-247-5105-5*) Kluwer Ac.

— Totality & Infinity. Lingis, Alphonso, tr. LC 69-14431. (Duquesne Studies: Philosophical). 307p. 1969. pap. text ed. 21.50 (*0-8207-0245-5*) Duquesne.

— Totality & Infinity. Lingis, Alphonso, tr. (Martinus Nijhoff Philosophy Texts Ser.: Vol. 1). 307p. 1980. lib. bdg. 62.00 (*90-247-2288-8*) Kluwer Ac.

Levine. Care of the Renal Patient. 2nd ed. (Illus.). 336p. 1991. text ed. 49.50 (*0-7216-3056-1*) Saunders.

— Decision Making in Gastroenterology, No. 2. 512p. 1992. 69.00 (*1-55664-323-3*) Mosby Yr Bk.

— Economics & Jewish Law. 250p. 1987. 25.00 (*0-88125-106-2*); pap. 16.95 (*0-88125-116-X*) Ktav.

— Frommer's California, 1994. (Illus.). 1994. pap. 15.00 (*0-671-86656-7*, P-H Travel) P-H Gen Ref & Trav.

— Frommer's Walking Tour of England. 1994. pap. 12.00 (*0-671-88617-7*, P-H Travel) P-H Gen Ref & Trav.

— Radiology of the Esophagus. 1989. text ed. 132.50 (*0-7216-2906-7*) Saunders.

— Sweet Will. 1985. pap. 5.95 (*0-689-11586-5*, Atheneum S&S) S&S Trade.

Levine & Fromm. Adult Care Monitoring. 500p. 1994. 69.00 (*0-8016-6962-6*) Mosby Yr Bk.

Levine & Treacy, William. Rabbi Levine Challenges Father Treacy: Examine Your Jewish Roots. Ireland, Martha M., ed. 168p. (Orig.). (C). 1987. pap. 11.95 (*0-910303-09-6*) Writers Pub Serv.

Levine, jt. auth. see Chatelaine.

Levine, jt. auth. see Montross.

Levine, jt. auth. see Woodrow.

Levine, et al. Canada-U. S. Employment Transfers: A Guide to Personal Planning. 4th ed. 304p. 1992. pap. 30.50 (*0-685-67171-2*, 4045) Commerce.

Levine, A. Popular Dances Made Easy. (Ballroom Dance Ser.). 1984. lib. bdg. 79.95 (*0-87700-503-6*) Revisionist Pr.

Levine, A. J., jt. ed. see Knippers, R.

Levine, Aaron. Economic Public Policy & Jewish Law. LC 93-16847. (Library of Jewish Law & Ethics: Vol. 19). 1993. 25.00 (*0-88125-437-1*, Yeshiva Univ Pr) Ktav.

— Free Enterprise & Jewish Law: Aspects of Jewish Business Ethics. 1979. 16.95 (*0-87068-702-6*) Ktav.

— To Comfort the Bereaved: A Guide for Mourners & Those Who Visit Them. LC 93-39381. 288p. 1994. 30.00 (*1-56821-109-0*) Aronson.

Levine, Aaron, jt. auth. see Jung, Leo.

Levine, Abby. Ollie Knows Everything. LC 93-29600. (Illus.). (J). 1994. write for info. (*0-8075-6020-0*) A Whitman.

— Too Much Mush! Tucker, Kathy, ed. LC 88-33906. (Illus.). 32p. (J). (ps-2). 1989. lib. bdg. 13.95 (*0-8075-8025-2*) A Whitman.

— What Did Mommy Do Before You? Fay, Ann, ed. LC 87-27908. (Illus.). 32p. (J). (ps-3). 1988. lib. bdg. 13.95 (*0-8075-8819-9*) A Whitman.

— What Did Mommy Do Before You? (J). (ps-3). 1990. pap. 3.95 (*0-14-054215-9*, Puffin) Puffin Bks.

— You Push, I Ride. Tucker, Kathleen, ed. LC 87-36852. (Illus.). 32p. (J). (ps-00). 1989. lib. bdg. 13.95 (*0-8075-9444-X*) A Whitman.

Levine, Abby, ed. see Adorjan, Carol.

Levine, Abby, ed. see Albert, Burton, Jr.

Levine, Abby, ed. see Balterman, Lee.

Levine, Abby, ed. see Bernstein, Joanne E. & Cohen, Paul.

Levine, Abby, ed. see Bernstein, Sharon C.

Levine, Abby, ed. see Brillhart, Julie.

Levine, Abby, ed. see Brown, Drollene.

Levine, Abby, ed. see Chevalier, Christa.

Levine, Abby, ed. see Corey, Dorothy.

Levine, Abby, ed. see Emmert, Michelle.

Levine, Abby, ed. see Fireside, Bryna J.

Levine, Abby, ed. see Freedman, Sally.

Levine, Abby, ed. see Gay, Marie-Louise.

Levine, Abby, ed. see Girard, Linda W.

Levine, Abby, ed. see Goldman, Kelly & Davidson, Ronnie.

Levine, Abby, ed. see Hamilton, Carol.

Levine, Abby, ed. see Hickman, Martha W.

Levine, Abby, ed. see Jordan, MaryKate.

Levine, Abby, ed. see Kite, Patricia.

Levine, Abby, ed. see Krisher, Trudy.

Levine, Abby, ed. see Lawlor, Laurie.

Levine, Abby, ed. see Levine, Caroline.

Levine, Abby, ed. see Limmer, Milly J.

Levine, Abby, ed. see London, Jonathan.

Levine, Abby, ed. see Lydon, Kerry R.

Levine, Abby, ed. see Mathews, Judith & Robinson, Fay.

Levine, Abby, ed. see Monsell, Mary E.

Levine, Abby, ed. see Mueller, Virginia.

Levine, Abby, ed. see Nerlove, Miriam.

Levine, Abby, ed. see Nikola-Lisa, W.

Levine, Abby, ed. see Ostrow, William & Ostrow, Vivian.

Levine, Abby, ed. see Phillips, Tamara.

Levine, Abby, ed. see Rose, Deborah L.

Levine, Abby, ed. see Schwartz, Mary A.

Levine, Abby, ed. see Seltzer, Meyer.

Levine, Abby, ed. see Sills, Leslie.

Levine, Abby, ed. see Simon, Norma.

Levine, Abby, ed. see St. James, Synthia.

Levine, Abby, ed. see Stanek, Muriel.

Levine, Abby, ed. see Stover, Marjorie.

Levine, Abby, ed. see Sussman, Susan.

Levine, Abby, ed. see Tucker, Kathy.

Levine, Abby, ed. see Vigna, Judith.

Levine, Abby, ed. see West, Dan.

Levine, Abby, ed. see Whitelaw, Nancy.

Levine, Abby, ed. see Williams, Barbara.

Levine, Abby, ed. see Willner-Pardo, Gina.

Levine, Abby, ed. see Wolf, Sallie.

Levine, Abby, ed. see Wolf, Sylvia.

Levine, Abby, ed. see Youdovin, Susan S.

Levine, Adeline G. & Levine, Murray. Helping Children: A Social History. 304p. 1992. 39.95 (*0-19-506699-5*) OUP.

Levine, Alan, jt. auth. see Jones, Charles P.

Levine, Alan J. The Missile & Space Race. LC 93-23673. 256p. 1994. text ed. 55.00 (*0-275-94451-4*, Praeger Pubs) Greenwood.

— The Pacific War: Japan vs. the Allies. LC 94-39948. 216p. 1995. text ed. 49.95 (*0-275-95102-2*, Praeger Pubs) Greenwood.

— The Soviet Union, the Communist Movement, & the World Prelude to the Cold War. LC 89-16335. 189p. 1990. text ed. 45.00 (*0-275-93443-8*, C3443, Greenwood Pr) Greenwood.

— The Strategic Bombing of Germany, 1940-1945. LC 91-45610. 248p. 1992. text ed. 49.95 (*0-275-94319-4*, C4319, Praeger Pubs) Greenwood.

— The United States & the Struggle for Southeast Asia: 1945-1975. LC 95-6928. 200p. 1995. text ed. 49.95 (*0-275-95124-3*, Praeger Pubs) Greenwood.

Levine, Albert K., ed. Lasers, Vol. 1. LC 66-11288. (Illus.). 377p. reprint ed. pap. 107.50 (*0-317-07988-3*, 2055071) Bks Demand.

Levine, Albert K. & DeMaria, Anthony J., eds. Lasers, Vol. 3. LC 66-11288. 383p. reprint ed. pap. 109.20 (*0-685-15847-0*, 2027814) Bks Demand.

— Lasers, Vol. 4. LC 66-11288. 343p. reprint ed. pap. 97.80 (*0-7837-0022-9*, 2027814) Bks Demand.

Levine, Alexander J., tr. see Hoyningen-Huene, Paul.

Levine, Alexandra M., ed. see Bonadonna, Gianni.

Levine, Alice & Keane, Robert N., eds. Re-Reading Byron: Essays Selected from Hofstra University's Byron Bicentennial Conference. LC 92-16591. 280p. 1993. 50.00 (*0-8153-1135-4*) Garland.

Levine, Alice, ed. see Byron, George Gordon.

Levine, Alice, ed. see Byron.

Levine, Amy J. The Social & Ethnic Dimensions of Matthean Salvation History: "Go Nowhere among the Gentiles..." (Matt. 10.5b) LC 88-12701. (Studies in the Bible & Early Christianity: Vol. 14). 319p. 1989. lib. bdg. 99.95 (*0-88946-614-9*) E Mellen.

Levine, Amy-Jill, ed. Women Like This: New Perspectives on Jewish Women in the Greco-Roman World. 260p. 1991. pap. 15.95 (*1-55540-463-4*) Scholars Pr GA.

Levine, Andrew. Arguing for Socialism. 240p. 1988. pap. text ed. 16.95 (*0-86091-918-8*, Pub. by Verso UK) Routledge Chapman & Hall.

— The End of the State: A Marxist Reflection on an Idea of Rousseau's. 208p. 1987. 50.00 (*0-86091-170-5*, Pub. by Verso UK); pap. 16.95 (*0-86091-881-5*, Pub. by Verso UK) Routledge Chapman & Hall.

— The General Will: Rousseau, Marx, Communism. LC 93-2768. 240p. (C). 1993. 54.95 (*0-521-44322-9*) Cambridge U Pr.

— Liberal Democracy: A Critique of Its Theory. LC 81-1204. 224p. reprint ed. pap. 63.90 (*0-318-34856-X*, 2031015) Bks Demand.

Levine, Andrew, ed. The State & Its Critics, 2 vols., Set. (Schools of Thought in Politics Ser.: Vol. 3). 800p. 1992. text ed. 234.95 (*1-85278-413-X*, Pub. by E Elgar Pub UK) Ashgate Pub Co.

Levine, Ann, jt. auth. see Steinberg, Laurence.

Levine, Ann, et al. How to Design & Remodel Children's Rooms. Dunham, Christine, ed. LC 87-72100. (Illus.). 96p. (Orig.). 1988. pap. 9.95 (*0-89721-143-X*) Ortho Info.

*__Levine, Anne-Marie.__ Euphorbia, Vol. III. Busa, Christopher, ed. LC 94-65401. (Provincetown Poets Ser.: III). (Illus.). 76p. 1994. 28.00 (*0-944854-12-5*); pap. 10.00 (*0-944854-11-7*) Provincetown Arts.

Levine, Arnold, jt. auth. see Brockett, Patrick.

Levine, Arnold J. Viruses. (Scientific American Library). 1995. text ed. 32.95 (*0-7167-5031-7*) W H Freeman.

Levine, Arnold J., ed. Tumour Suppressor Genes, the Cell Cycle & Cancer. (Cancer Surveys Ser.: Vol. 12). (Illus.). 300p. (C). 1992. text ed. 60.00 (*0-87969-369-X*) Cold Spring Harbor.

Levine, Arnold J. & Schmidek, Henry M., eds. Molecular Genetics of Nervous System Tumors. LC 92-48694. 442p. 1993. text ed. 95.00 (*0-471-56179-7*, Wiley-Liss) Wiley.

Levine, Arnold J., et al, eds. The Transformed Phenotype. LC 83-26318. (Cancer Cells Ser.: No. 1). 320p. reprint ed. pap. 91.20 (*0-7837-2003-3*, 2042277) Bks Demand.

*__Levine, Arnold S. & Luck, Jeff.__ The New Management Paradigm: A Review of Principles & Practices. LC 94-28874. 1994. write for info. (*0-8330-1571-0*, MR458AF) Rand Corp.

Levine, Arthur. Global Copyright Issues in the Secondary Information Industry. Schipper, Wendy & Unruh, Betty, eds. (Report Series, 1990: No. 4). 100p. (Orig.). 1990. pap. 100.00 (*0-942308-28-X*) NFAIS.

— Handbook on Undergraduate Curriculum: Prepared for the Carnegie Council on Policy Studies in Higher Education. LC 78-50893. (Higher Education Ser.). (Illus.). 697p. 1978. 55.00x (*0-87589-376-7*) Jossey-Bass.

— When Dreams & Heroes Died: A Portrait of Today's College Student. LC 80-8005. (Higher & Adult Education Ser.). 177p. 1980. 29.95x (*0-87589-481-X*) Jossey-Bass.

Levine, Arthur, ed. Higher Learning in America, 1980-2000. LC 92-19746. 392p. 1993. text ed. 35.95 (*0-8018-4457-6*) Johns Hopkins.

— Higher Learning in America. 1980-2000. 392p. (C). 1994. reprint ed. pap. text ed. 15.95 (*0-8018-4861-X*) Johns Hopkins.

*__Levine, Arthur & Nidiffer, Jana.__ Beating the Odds: How the Poor Get to College. LC 95-9137. (Higher & Adult Education Ser.). 1995. 27.95 (*0-7879-0132-6*) Jossey-Bass.

Levine, Arthur & Weingart, John R. Reform of Undergraduate Education. LC 73-7154. (Jossey-Bass Higher Education Ser.). 176p. reprint ed. 50.20 (*0-8357-9343-5*, 2013960) Bks Demand.

Levine, Arthur, jt. auth. see Boyer, Ernest L.

Levine, Arthur, & Associates. Shaping Higher Education's Future: Demographic Realities & Opportunities, 1990-2000. LC 89-45576. (Higher Education Ser.). 213p. 1989. 28.95x (*1-55542-191-1*) Jossey-Bass.

Levine, Arthur A. All the Lights in the Night. LC 90-47496. (Illus.). 32p. (J). (ps-3). 1991. 14.95 (*0-688-10107-0*, Tambourine Bks); lib. bdg. 14.88 (*0-688-10108-9*, Tambourine Bks) Morrow.

— The Boardwalk Princess. LC 92-8081. (Illus.). 32p. (J). (ps up). 1993. 14.00 (*0-688-10306-5*, Tambourine Bks); lib. bdg. 13.93 (*0-688-10307-3*, Tambourine Bks) Morrow.

— Bono & Nonno. LC 93-35931. (Illus.). (J). 1995. write for info. (*0-688-13233-2*, Tambourine Bks); lib. bdg. write for info. (*0-688-13234-0*, Tambourine Bks) Morrow.

— The Boy Who Drew Cats: A Japanese Folktale. LC 91-46232. (J). (ps-3). 1994. 16.00 (*0-8037-1172-7*); 15.89 (*0-8037-1173-5*) Dial Bks Young.

— Pearl Moscowitz's Last Stand. LC 91-10652. (Illus.). 32p. (J). (ps up). 1993. 14.00 (*0-688-10753-2*, Tambourine Bks); lib. bdg. 13.93 (*0-688-10754-0*, Tambourine Bks) Morrow.

— Sheep Dreams. LC 91-44929. (Illus.). 32p. (J). (ps-3). 1993. 13.99 (*0-8037-1194-8*) Dial Bks Young.

Levine, Arthur S., ed. Etiology of Cancer in Man. (Cancer Growth & Progression Ser.). (C). 1989. lib. bdg. 137.00 (*0-89838-995-X*) Kluwer Ac.

Levine, Barbara, comp. Sidney Hook: A Checklist of Writings. LC 88-15043. 120p. 1989. 19.95 (*0-8093-1510-6*) S Ill U Pr.

Levine, Barbara G., jt. auth. see Mogil, H. Michael.

Levine, Barbara H. Your Body Believes Every Word You Say: The Language of the Body - Mind Connection. LC 90-1169. 224p. (Orig.). 1991. pap. 11.95 (*0-944031-07-2*) Aslan Pub.

Levine, Barry. Current Practice of Cardiothoracic Surgery. LC 93-49075. 1994. pap. 34.95 (*0-443-08976-0*) Churchill.

Levine, Barry, ed. The Caribbean Exodus. LC 86-21217. 300p. 1986. pap. text ed. 18.95 (*0-275-92183-2*, B2183, Praeger Pubs) Greenwood.

— The Caribbean Exodus. LC 86-21217. 300p. 1987. text ed. 55.00 (*0-275-92182-4*, C2182, Praeger Pubs) Greenwood.

Levine, Barry A. Current Practice of Gastrointestinal & Abdominal Surgery. LC 93-50705. 1994. pap. 49.95 (*0-443-08975-2*) Churchill.

— Current Practice of Pediatric Surgery. LC 93-49044. 1994. pap. 29.95 (*0-443-08978-7*) Churchill.

Levine, Barry A., ed. Current Practice of Breast, Skin & Soft Tissue Surgery. LC 93-50590. 1994. pap. 29.95 (*0-443-08974-4*) Churchill.

— Current Practice of Vascular Surgery. LC 93-50706. 1994. pap. 34.95 (*0-443-08977-9*) Churchill.

Levine, Barry A., et al. Current Practice of Trauma Surgery. LC 93-48362. 1994. pap. 29.95 (*0-443-08973-6*) Churchill.

Levine, Barry A., et al, eds. Current Practice of Surgery, 3 vols., Set. (Illus.). 2848p. 1993. ring bd. 315.00 (*0-443-08767-9*) Churchill.

— Current Practice of Surgery Essentials. LC 93-48804. 1994. pap. 39.95 (*0-443-08972-8*) Churchill.

Levine, Baruch. Group Psychotherapy: Practice & Development. (Illus.). 352p. (C). 1991. reprint ed. text ed. 29.95 (*0-88133-598-3*) Waveland Pr.

— Group Work with the Emotionally Disabled. LC 90-4281. (Social Work with Groups Ser.: Vol. 13, No. 1). 133p. 1990. text ed. 29.95 (*0-86656-994-4*) Haworth Pr.

— Numbers One - Twenty: A New Translation with Introduction & Commentary. LC 92-12262. (Anchor Bible Ser.: Vol. 4). 1993. 40.00 (*0-385-15651-0*) Doubleday.

Levine, Baruch & Gallogly, Virginia. Group Therapy with Alcoholics: Outpatient & Inpatient Approaches. (Human Services Guides Ser.: Vol. 40). 136p. (Orig.). (C). 1985. pap. text ed. 17.95 (*0-8039-2504-2*) Sage.

Levine, Baruch, jt. ed. see Ahituv, Shmuel.

Levine, Baruch A. The JPS Torah Commentary: Leviticus. 330p. 50.00 (*0-8276-0328-2*) JPS Phila.

Levine, Bernard. Levine's Guide to Knives & Their Values. 3rd ed. LC 85-71895. (Illus.). 512p. (Orig.). 1993. pap. 25.95 (*0-87349-136-X*) DBI.

— Pocket Knives: A Collector's Guide to Selecting, Restoring, & Enjoying New & Vintage Pocket Knives. (Collector's Library). (Illus.). 80p. 1994. 12.98 (*1-56138-216-7*) Courage Bks.

*__Levine, Beth.__ Divorce: Young People Caught in the Middle. LC 94-33430. (Issues in Focus Ser.). 128p. (YA). (gr. 6 up). 1995. lib. bdg. 17.95 (*0-89490-633-X*) Enslow Pubs.

*__Levine, Beverly.__ Pico, the Orphan Otter: A True Story. (Illus.). (J). 1995. write for info. (*1-56294-537-8*) Millbrook Pr.

Levine, Bobbie & Lichter, Carolyn. A Child's Walk Through Africa. (Illus.). 38p. (J). (gr. 3-6). 1987. spiral bd. 1.50 (*0-912303-38-7*) Michigan Mus.

— A Child's Walk Through Asia. (Illus.). 25p. (J). (gr. 2-6). 1984. spiral bd. 1.50 (*0-912303-31-X*) Michigan Mus.

Levine, Bobbie, et al. A Child's Walk Through Twentieth Century American Painting & Sculpture. (Illus.). 29p. (J). (gr. 2-6). 1986. spiral bd. 1.50 (*0-912303-37-9*) Michigan Mus.

Levine, Bruce. Half Slave & Half Free. Foner, Eric, ed. (American Century Ser.). 256p. 1992. pap. 11.95 (*0-374-52309-6*, Noonday) FS&G.

L

— Manhattan Living. Weisberg, Michael, ed. (Illus.). 304p. (Orig.). 1985. pap. 14.95 (*0-9614421-0-7*) M K L Ltd.

Levine, Bruce S. The Spirit of 1848: German Immigrants, Labor Conflict, & the Coming of the Civil War. (Working Class in American History Ser.). 400p. 1992. 34.95 (*0-252-01873-7*) U of Ill Pr.

Levine, C. & Berg, N. It's about Time. (Tamar Bks.). 1992. 15.95 (*0-89906-111-7*); pap. 12.95 (*0-89906-112-5*) Mesorah Pubns.

Levine, Carol, ed. A Death in the Family: Orphans of the HIV Epidemic. LC 93-21517. 1993. 10.00 (*1-881277-13-5*) United Hosp Fund.

***Levine, Carol, ed. & intro.** Taking Sides: Clashing Views on Controversial Bioethical Issues. 6th ed. LC 94-45959. 400p. 1995. 13.95 (*1-56134-328-5*) Dushkin Pub.

Levine, Carol, jt. ed. see Dane, Barbara O.

Levine, Caroline. Riddles to Tell Your Cat. Grant, Christy, ed. (Illus.). 32p. (J). (gr. 1-4). 1992. lib. bdg. 8.95 (*0-8075-7006-0*) A Whitman.

— Silly School Riddles & Other Classroom Crack-Ups. Levine, Abby, ed. LC 84-17300. (Illus.). 32p. (J). (gr. 1-5). 1984. 8.95 (*0-8075-7359-0*) A Whitman.

Levine, Caroline, jt. auth. see Levine, Summer N.

Levine, Caroline, jt. ed. see Levine, Summer N.

Levine, Caroline, tr. see Loraux, Nicole.

Levine, Caroline A. The Detective Stars & the Case of the Super Soccer Team. LC 92-28600. (Illus.). 48p. (J). (gr. 1-4). 1994. 11.99 (*0-525-65134-9*, Cobblehill Bks) Dutton Child Bks.

Levine, Celotta & Levine, Judah. Methods of Experimental Physics, Vol. 22. 1985. text ed. 151.00 (*0-12-475964-5*) Acad Pr.

Levine, Charles H., ed. Managing Fiscal Stress: The Crisis in the Public Sector. LC 79-27266. (Chatham House Series on Change in American Politics). (Illus.). 352p. reprint ed. pap. 100.40 (*0-8357-4830-8*, 2037767) Bks Demand.

— Managing Human Resources: A Challenge to Urban Governments. LC 77-79869. (Urban Affairs Annual Reviews Ser.: No. 13). 319p. reprint ed. pap. 91.00 (*0-8357-8491-6*, 2034765) Bks Demand.

— The Unfinished Agenda for Civil Servivce Reform: Implications of the Grace Commission Report. LC 85-71183. (Dialogues on Public Policy Ser.). 142p. 1985. pap. 10.95 (*0-8157-5251-2*) Brookings.

Levine, Charles H. & Rubin, Irene, eds. Fiscal Stress & Public Policy. LC 80-24515. (Sage Yearbooks in Politics & Public Policy Ser.: No. 9). 314p. reprint ed. pap. 89.50 (*0-8357-8419-3*, 2034684) Bks Demand.

Levine, Charles H., et al. The Politics of Retrenchment: How Local Governments Manage Fiscal Stress. LC 81-9241. (Sage Library of Social Research: No. 130). 224p. reprint ed. pap. 63.90 (*0-8357-8490-8*, 2034764) Bks Demand.

— Public Administration: Challenges, Choices & Consequences. (C). 1990. text ed. 48.00 (*0-673-39997-4*) HarpCollege.

Levine, D. S. Introduction to Cognitive & Neural Modeling. 456p. (C). 1990. text ed. 79.95 (*0-8058-0267-3*); pap. 22.50 (*0-8058-0268-1*) L Erlbaum Assocs.

Levine, Dan. London. (Frommer's Walking Tours Ser.). (Illus.). 176p. 1993. pap. 12.00 (*0-671-79836-7*, P-H Travel) P-H Gen Ref & Trav.

Levine, Daniel. Jane Addams & the Liberal Tradition. LC 80-18807. (Illus.). xviii, 277p. 1980. reprint ed. text ed. 38.50 (*0-313-22691-1*, LEJA, Greenwood Pr) Greenwood.

— Poverty & Society: The Growth of the American Welfare State in International Comparison. 368p. (C). 1988. text ed. 45.00 (*0-8135-1337-5*); pap. text ed. 16.00 (*0-8135-1353-7*) Rutgers U Pr.

— Varieties of Reform Thought. LC 79-28658. xiii, 149p. 1980. reprint ed. text ed. 49.75 (*0-313-22345-9*, LEVR, Greenwood Pr) Greenwood.

Levine, Daniel, ed. Americas Lost: The First Encounter, 1492-1713. 192p. 1992. pap. 39.95 (*2-04-014499-4*, GC4994, Pub. by Grp De La Cite FR) UNIPUB.

Levine, Daniel A., tr. see Vorobyov, N. N.

Levine, Daniel H. Conflict & Political Change in Venezuela. LC 75-39790. 328p. 1973. 47.50x (*0-691-07547-6*) Princeton U Pr.

— Conflict & Political Change in Venezuela. LC 75-39790. 299p. reprint ed. pap. 85.30 (*0-8357-3401-3*, 2039658) Bks Demand.

— Popular Voices in Latin American Catholicism. (Studies in Church & State). (Illus.). 424p. 1992. text ed. 55.00 (*0-691-08754-7*); pap. text ed. 19.95 (*0-691-02459-6*) Princeton U Pr.

— Religion & Politics in Latin America: The Catholic Church in Venezuela & Colombia. LC 80-7542. 356p. 1981. pap. 17.95 (*0-691-02200-3*) Princeton U Pr.

Levine, Daniel H., ed. Churches & Politics in Latin America. LC 79-23827. (Sage Focus Editions Ser.: No. 14). 288p. reprint ed. pap. 82.10 (*0-8357-8489-4*, 2034762) Bks Demand.

— Constructing Culture & Power in Latin America. (Comparative Studies in Society & History). 350p. 1993. text ed. 55.00 (*0-472-09456-4*); pap. text ed. 22.50 (*0-472-06456-8*) U of Mich Pr.

— Religion & Political Conflict in Latin America. LC 85-24525. xiii, 266p. (C). 1986. 32.50 (*0-8078-1689-2*); pap. 12.95 (*0-8078-4150-1*) U of NC Pr.

Levine, Daniel S. & Aparicio, Manuel, IV, eds. Neural Networks for Knowledge Representation & Inference. 512p. 1993. text ed. 99.95 (*0-8058-1158-3*); pap. 39.95 (*0-8058-1159-1*) L Erlbaum Assocs.

Levine, Daniel S. & Leven, Samuel J., eds. Motivation, Emotion, & Goal Direction in Neural Networks. 472p. (C). 1991. text ed. 99.95 (*0-8058-0447-1*) L Erlbaum Assocs.

Levine, Daniel U. & Havighurst, Robert J. Society & Education. 8th ed. 624p. (C). 1991. text ed. write for info. (*0-205-13371-1*) Allyn.

Levine, Daniel U., & Associates. Improving Student Achievement Through Mastery Learning Programs. LC 84-43029. (Higher Education Ser.). 324p. 1985. 38.95x (*0-87589-645-6*) Jossey-Bass.

Levine, Danny. The Birth of the Irgun Zvai Leumi: The Jewish Resistance Movement. 202p. 1992. pap. 15.95 (*965-229-071-8*, Pub. by Gefen Pub Hse IS) Gefen Bks.

***Levine, David.** In the Land of Giants: My Life in Basketball. LC 94-26479. 1994. 19.95 (*0-316-10173-7*) Little.

Levine, David & Negreiros, Almada, illus. The Man Who Never Was. LC 81-83226. 195p. (Orig.). 1982. text ed. 17.50 (*0-943722-07-1*); pap. 7.50 (*0-943722-08-X*) Gavea-Brown.

Levine, David, tr. see Ibn Al-Fayyumi, Nathanael.

Levine, David, ed. see Nebraska Symposium on Motivation Staff.

Levine, David, jt. auth. see Rightson, Keith.

Levine, David, jt. auth. see Rundgren, Todd.

***Levine, David, et al, eds.** Rethinking Schools: A Collection from the Leading Journal of School Reform. LC 94-34347. 304p. 1995. 25.00 (*1-56584-214-6*) New Press NY.

Levine, David A. Internal Combustion: The Races in Detroit 1915-1926. LC 75-35347. 224p. 1976. text ed. 65.00 (*0-8371-8588-2*, LIC/, Greenwood Pr) Greenwood.

— Reproducing Families: The Political Economy of English Population History. (Themes in Social Sciences Ser.). 272p. 1987. pap. 18.95 (*0-521-33785-2*) Cambridge U Pr.

Levine, David A., ed. Proletarianization & Family History. (Studies in Social Discontinuity). 1984. text ed. 59.00 (*0-12-444980-8*) Acad Pr.

Levine, David A. & Wrightson, Keith. The Making of an Industrial Society: Whickham 1560-1765. (Oxford Studies in Social History). (Illus.). 480p. 1991. 105.00 (*0-19-820066-8*) OUP.

***Levine, David I., ed.** Reinventing the Workplace: How Business & Employees Can Both Win. LC 94-24066. 222p. (C). 1995. 36.95x (*0-8157-5232-6*); pap. 15.95x (*0-8157-5231-8*) Brookings.

Levine, David I., jt. auth. see Kane, Mary K.

Levine, David I., et al. California Civil Procedure, Cases & Materials On. (American Casebook Ser.). 546p. 1991. text ed. 39.00 (*0-314-84826-6*) West Pub.

— California Civil Procedures: Teacher's Manual, Cases & Materials On. (American Casebook Ser.). 95p. 1991. pap. text ed. write for info. (*0-314-00482-3*) West Pub.

***Levine, David K. & Lippman, Steven A.** The Economics of Information, 2 Vols. (International Library of Critical Writings in Economics: Vol. 53). 960p. 1995. 279.95 (*1-85278-511-X*) Ashgate Pub Co.

Levine, David M., jt. auth. see Berenson, Mark L.

Levine, David M., et al. Business Statistics for Quality & Productivity. LC 94-16360. 1994. write for info. (*0-13-841719-9*) P-H.

Levine, David O. The American College & the Culture of Aspiration, 1915-1940. LC 86-4169. 288p. 1986. 42.50 (*0-8014-1884-4*); pap. 15.95 (*0-8014-9498-2*) Cornell U Pr.

Levine, David P. Needs, Rights & the Market. LC 88-4543. 158p. 1988. lib. bdg. 33.50 (*1-55587-115-1*) Lynne Rienner.

— Wealth & Freedom: An Introduction to Political Economy. (Illus.). (C). 1995. 49.95 (*0-521-44314-8*); pap. 15.95 (*0-521-44791-7*) Cambridge U Pr.

Levine, David P., jt. auth. see Caporaso, James A.

***Levine, David P., et al, eds.** Rethinking Schools: A Collection from the Leading Journal of School Reform. LC 94-34347. 304p. 1995. pap. 16.00 (*1-56584-215-4*) New Press NY.

***Levine, Deborah J.** Teaching Christian Children about Judaism. LC 94-48369. 64p. (Orig.). (J). 1995. pap. 18.00 (*1-56854-076-0*, TCCAJ) Liturgy Tr Pubns.

Levine, Deena R. & Adelman, Mara B. Beyond Language: Cross Cultural Communication. 2nd ed. LC 92-28675. 288p. 1993. pap. text ed. 19.25 (*0-13-094855-1*) P-H.

— Beyond Language: Intercultural Communication for ESL. (Illus.). 200p. (C). 1982. pap. text ed. 14.25 (*0-13-076000-5*) P-H.

Levine, Deena R., et al. The Culture Puzzle: Cross-Cultural Communication for English As a Second Language. (Illus.). 224p. (C). 1987. pap. text ed. 19.25 (*0-13-195520-9*) P-H.

Levine, Dennis & Hoffer, William. Inside Out. 432p. 1992. mass mkt. 5.99 (*0-425-13533-0*) Berkley Pub.

Levine, Donald N. The Flight from Ambiguity: Essays in Social & Cultural Theory. LC 85-8762. x, 256p. 1985. lib. bdg. 27.50 (*0-226-47555-7*) U Ch Pr.

— The Flight from Ambiguity: Essays in Social & Cultural Theory. LC 85-8762. x, 256p. 1988. pap. text ed. 12.95 (*0-226-47556-5*) U Ch Pr.

— Greater Ethiopia: The Evolution of a Multiethnic Society. LC 73-91233. (Illus.). 1977. pap. text ed. 15.95 (*0-226-47560-3*, P721) U Ch Pr.

— Simmel & Parsons: Two Approaches to the Study of Society. Zuckerman, Harriet & Merton, Robert K., eds. LC 79-9011. (Dissertations on Sociology Ser.). 1980. lib. bdg. 30.95 (*0-405-12979-3*) Ayer.

— Visions of the Sociological Tradition. LC 95-3389. 1992. pap. text ed. 16.95 (*0-226-47547-6*) U Ch Pr.

— Visions of the Sociological Tradition. LC 95-3389. 1994. 47.95 (*0-226-47546-8*) U Ch Pr.

— Wax & Gold: Tradition & Innovation in Ethiopian Culture. LC 65-18340. xvi, 316p. 1986. reprint ed. pap. 18.00 (*0-685-04997-3*, P458) U Ch Pr.

Levine, Donald N., ed. Performance Contracting in Education-an Appraisal: Toward a Balanced Perspective. LC 72-12681. 192p. 1973. pap. 19.95 (*0-87778-046-3*) Educ Tech Pubns.

Levine, Donald N., ed. see Simmel, Georg.

Levine, Donald P. & Sobel, Jack D., eds. Infections in Intravenous Drug Abusers. (Illus.). 416p. 1990. 75.00 (*0-19-506223-X*) OUP.

LeVine, Duane G. The City As a Human Environment. LC 94-1146. (Only One Earth Ser.). 216p. 1994. text ed. 55.00 (*0-275-94659-2*, Praeger Pubs) Greenwood.

LeVine, Duane G. & Upton, Arthur C., eds. Management of Hazardous Agents, Vol. 1: Industrial & Regulatory Approaches. LC 92-167. (Only One Earth Ser.). 208p. 1992. text ed. 55.00 (*0-275-94322-4*, C4322, Praeger Pubs) Greenwood.

— Management of Hazardous Agents, Vol. 2: Social, Political, & Policy Aspects, Vol. 2. LC 92-167. (Only One Earth Ser.). 200p. 1992. text ed. 55.00 (*0-275-94323-2*, C4323, Praeger Pubs) Greenwood.

Levine, E. Double Jeopardy. 1990. pap. 3.95 (*1-55817-315-3*, Pinnacle NY) Windsor NY.

— Escapes. 1991. mass mkt. 4.50 (*1-55817-568-7*, Pinnacle NY) Windsor NY.

— Interludes. 1990. mass mkt. 4.95 (*1-55817-339-0*, Pinnacle NY) Windsor NY.

— Wanderlust. 288p. 1988. pap. 3.95 (*1-55817-090-1*, Pinnacle NY) Windsor NY.

Levine, Ed. New York Eats: The Food Shopper's Guide to the Freshest Ingredients, the Best Take-out & Baked Goods, & the Most Unusual Marketplaces in All of New York. (Illus.). 384p. (Orig.). 1992. pap. 16.95 (*0-312-06981-2*) St Martin.

Levine, Edna S. Lisa & Her Soundless World. (Illus.). (J). (gr. 1-5). 1984. 18.95 (*0-87705-104-6*); pap. 10.95 (*0-89885-204-8*) Human Sci Pr.

Levine, Edna S., jt. auth. see Garrett, James.

Levine, Edward M. The Irish & Irish Politicians: A Study of Cultural & Social Alienation. LC 66-24921. 253p. reprint ed. pap. 72.20 (*0-318-34711-3*, 2031911) Bks Demand.

Levine, Elaine S. & Sallee, Alvin L. Listen to Our Children: Clinical Theory & Practice. 336p. 1992. per. 39.95 (*0-8403-7445-3*) Kendall-Hunt.

Levine, Eli. Golden Key. (Illus.). 1981. lib. bdg. 25.00 (*0-915262-52-5*) S J Durst.

Levine, Elieba. Friends. 288p. (Orig.). 1980. pap. 2.25 (*0-89083-645-0*) Zebra.

Levine, Elizabeth R. A Ceremonies Sampler. LC 90-70834. 127p. (Orig.). 1991. pap. 9.95 (*0-9608054-9-4*) Womans Inst-Cont Jewish Ed.

***Levine, Ellen.** Anna Pavlova: Genius of the Dance. LC 94-7310. (Illus.). 128p. (J). (gr. 3-7). 1995. 14.95 (*0-590-44304-6*) Scholastic Inc.

— A Fence Away from Freedom: Japanese-Americans & World War II. LC 95-13357. (J). 1995. write for info. (*0-399-22638-9*, Putnam) Putnam Pub Group.

— Freedom's Children: Young Civil Rights Activists Tell Their Own Stories. 224p. (YA). 1993. 16.95 (*0-399-21893-9*) Putnam Pub Group.

— Freedom's Children: Young Civil Rights Activists Tell Their Own Stories. large type ed. LC 93-10388. (Illus.). (J). 1993. pap. 16.95 (*1-56054-744-8*) Thorndike Pr.

— I Hate English! (Illus.). (J). (gr. k-2). 1989. pap. 14.95 (*0-590-42305-3*) Scholastic Inc.

— If You Lived At the Time of Martin Luther King. (J). 1990. pap. 4.95 (*0-590-42582-X*) Scholastic Inc.

— If You Lived at the Time of the Great San Francisco Earthquake. (Illus.). 64p. (J). 1992. pap. 4.95 (*0-590-45157-X*) Scholastic Inc.

— If You Traveled on the Underground Railroad. (Orig.). (J). (gr. 4-7). 1993. pap. 4.95 (*0-590-45156-1*) Scholastic Inc.

— If You Traveled West in a Covered Wagon. (Illus.). 80p. (Orig.). (J). (gr. 3-5). 1992. pap. 4.95 (*0-590-45158-8*) Scholastic Inc.

— If Your Name Was Changed at Ellis Island. LC 92-27940. (Illus.). 80p. (J). (gr. 2-5). 1993. 15.95 (*0-590-46134-6*) Scholastic Inc.

— If Your Name Was Changed at Ellis Island. 64p. (J). 1994. pap. 4.95 (*0-590-43829-8*) Scholastic Inc.

— Notes on the Pumpkin. 16p. (Orig.). 1979. pap. 3.00 (*0-89924-020-8*) Lynx Hse.

— Ready, Aim, Fire! The Real Adventures of Annie Oakley. (J). (gr. 5-7). 1989. pap. 2.95 (*0-590-41877-7*) Scholastic Inc.

— The Tree That Would Not Die. LC 94-8394. (J). (ps-3). 1995. 14.95 (*0-590-43724-0*) Scholastic Inc.

Levine, Ellen, ed. Freedom's Children: Young Civil Rights Activists Tell Their Own Stories. 224p. 1994. mass mkt. 3.99 (*0-380-72114-7*, Flare) Avon.

Levine, Ellen, intro. Periodical Guide for Computerists, 1982: Annual Since 1975-76. 70p. (Orig.). 1982. pap. 15.95 (*0-686-40864-0*) Applegate Comp Ent.

Levine, Erwin L. Theodore Francis Green: The Rhode Island Years, 1906-1936. LC 63-18096. (Brown University Bicentennial Publications). 234p. reprint ed. 66.70 (*0-685-15697-4*, 2027511) Bks Demand.

— Theodore Francis Green: The Washington Years, 1937-1960. LC 73-127366. 191p. reprint ed. 54.50 (*0-685-15710-5*, 2027512) Bks Demand.

Levine, Esther, ed. see Levine, Sy, et al.

Levine, Esther, ed. see Levine, Sy.

Levine, Etan. The Aramaic Version of Jonah. 2nd ed. LC 76-27614. 1979. pap. 14.75 (*0-87203-068-7*) Hermon.

— The Aramaic Version of Lamentations. LC 76-276212. 203p. 1981. pap. 16.25 (*0-87203-065-2*) Hermon.

— The Aramaic Version of Qohelet. 1979. pap. 16.25 (*0-87203-087-3*) Hermon.

— The Aramaic Version of the Bible: Contents & Context. xiv, 258p. (C). 1988. lib. bdg. 95.40 (*0-89925-459-4*) De Gruyter.

— The Aramaic Version of the Bible: Contents & Context. xiv, 258p. (C). 1988. lib. bdg. 55.40 (*3-11-011474-7*) De Gruyter.

— The Burning Bush: Jewish Symbolism & Mysticism. LC 81-52463. (Illus.). 123p. (Orig.). 1982. pap. 10.00 (*0-87203-105-5*) Hermon.

Levine, Etan, ed. Voices from Israel: Understanding the Israeli Mind. LC 85-47911. 288p. 1986. 19.95 (*0-8453-4825-6*, Cornwall Bks) Assoc Univ Prs.

Levine, Eugene, jt. auth. see Abdellah, Faye G.

Levine, Eugene, et al. Nursing Practice in the U. K. & North America. LC 92-12312. 1992. write for info. (*1-56593-024-X*) Singular Publishing.

Levine, Evan. Kids Pick the Best Videos for Kids. LC 93-43784. (J). 1994. pap. 9.95 (*0-8065-1498-1*, Citadel Pr) Carol Pub Group.

— Not the Piano, Mrs. Medley! LC 90-29085. (Illus.). 32p. (J). (ps-2). 1991. 14.95 (*0-531-05956-1*); 14.99 (*0-531-08556-2*) Orchard Bks Watts.

— Not the Piano, Mrs. Medley! LC 90-29085. (Illus.). 32p. (J). (ps-2). 1995. pap. text ed. 5.95 (*0-531-07062-X*) Orchard Bks Watts.

— What's Black & White & Came to Visit? LC 93-46418. (Illus.). 32p. (J). (ps-2). 1994. 14.95 (*0-531-06852-8*); lib. bdg. 14.99 (*0-531-08702-6*) Orchard Bks Watts.

Levine, Evelyn, jt. auth. see Grubbs, Arlene.

Levine, Frances. Individualized Education System: Soups from A - Z 1994. 59p. 1994. spiral bd. 14.95 (*0-938911-08-2*) Indiv Educ Syst.

Levine, Francis, et al. Santa Fe: History of an Ancient City. Noble, David G., ed. LC 89-4214. (Illus.). 1989. 29.95 (*0-933452-26-8*); pap. 16.95 (*0-933452-27-6*) Schol Am Res.

***Levine, Fred.** Road Construction Ahead. LC 94-35519. (J). 1995. 12.95 (*0-06-025427-0*) HarpC Child Bks.

Levine, Frederic M. & Sandeen, Evelyn. Conceptualization in Psychotherapy: The Models Approach. 232p. (C). 1985. text ed. 49.95 (*0-89859-549-5*) L Erlbaum Assocs.

Levine, Frederick G. Mysticism & the Occult: A Concise Encyclopedia. 480p. 1994. 24.95 (*0-87131-666-8*) M Evans.

— The Psychic Sourcebook: How to Choose & Use a Psychic. 368p. (Orig.). 1988. pap. 9.95 (*0-446-38729-0*) Warner Bks.

Levine, G., ed. A Guide to SPSS-X for Analysis of Variance. 176p. (C). 1990. text ed. 39.95 (*0-8058-0939-2*); pap. 22.50 (*0-8058-0941-4*) L Erlbaum Assocs.

Levine, Gary. Brushstrokes: A Novel. 179p. 1982. pap. 5.95 (*0-940118-65-3*) Moznaim.

— Legs Diamond: Anatomy of a Gangster. LC 95-13601. 159p. 1995. pap. 15.00 (*0-935796-55-X*) Purple Mnt Pr.

Levine, Gene N., ed. see Drury, Ruth.

***Levine, George.** Lifebirds. LC 94-41058. (Illus.). 180p. (C). 1995. 24.95 (*0-8135-2202-1*) Rutgers U Pr.

Levine, George, ed. Aesthetics & Ideology. LC 93-31173. 325p. (C). 1994. text ed. 48.00 (*0-8135-2058-4*); pap. text ed. 20.00 (*0-8135-2059-2*) Rutgers U Pr.

— Constructions of the Self. LC 91-27274. (Illus.). 325p. 1992. text ed. 45.00 (*0-8135-1772-9*); pap. text ed. 18.00 (*0-8135-1773-7*) Rutgers U Pr.

— One Culture: Essays in Science & Literature. LC 87-40143. (Science & Literature Ser.). 352p. 1987. pap. text ed. 12.95 (*0-299-11304-3*) U of Wis Pr.

— Realism & Representation: Essays on the Problem of Realism in Relation to Science, Literature & Culture. LC 92-26774. (Science & Literature Ser.). 346p. (Orig.). (C). 1993. 50.00 (*0-299-13630-2*); pap. 23.50 (*0-299-13634-5*) U of Wis Pr.

Levine, George L. Darwin & the Novelists: Patterns of Science in Victorian Fiction. LC 87-36201. 336p. 1988. 37.00 (*0-674-19285-0*) HUP.

— Darwin & the Novelists: Patterns of Science in Victorian Fiction. LC 87-36201. 334p. 1991. pap. text ed. 16.95 (*0-226-47574-3*) U Ch Pr.

Levine, George L., ed. An Annotated Critical Bibliography of George Eliot. LC 88-3044. 256p. 1988. text ed. 39.95 (*0-312-01959-9*) St Martin.

— One Culture: Essays in Science & Literature. LC 87-40143. (Science & Literature Ser.). 352p. (C). 1988. text ed. 45.00 (*0-299-11300-0*) U of Wis Pr.

Levine, George L. & Knoepflmacher, U. C., eds. The Endurance of Frankenstein: Essays on Mary Shelley's Novel. LC 77-20325. 1979. pap. 12.00 (*0-520-04640-4*) U CA Pr.

— The Endurance of Frankenstein: Essays on Mary Shelley's Novel. LC 77-20325. (Illus.). 361p. reprint ed. pap. 102.90 (*0-685-23525-4*, 2029050) Bks Demand.

Levine, George R., ed. see Bonner, William.

Levine, Gerald D., jt. auth. see Rosai, Juan.

Levine, Gilbert & Vookles, Laura. The Jeweler's Eye: Nineteenth-Century Jewelry in the Collection of Nancy & Gilbert Levine. LC 86-21490. (Illus.). 112p. (Orig.). 1986. pap. 9.50 (*0-943651-02-6*) Hudson Riv.

Levine, Gilbert, jt. ed. see Kahnert, Friedrich.

Levine, Glenn N. Pocket Guide to Commonly Prescribed Drugs. (Illus.). 304p. (C). 1993. pap. text ed. 16.95 (*0-8385-8023-8*, A8023-2) Appleton & Lange.

Levine, Gloria. Anne of Green Gables: A Study Guide. (Novel-Ties Ser.). (J). (gr. 6-8). 1989. student ed, teacher ed 15.95 (*0-88122-056-6*) Lrn Links.

— Children of the Sea. (Illus.). 48p. (Orig.). 1991. pap. 5.95 (*0-913839-98-1*) Bk Lures.

— Cricket in Times Square: A Study Guide. (Novel-Ties Ser.). (J). (gr. 4-7). 1987. student ed, teacher ed 15.95 (*0-88122-073-6*) Lrn Links.

— Fantastic Mr. Fox: A Study Guide. (Novel-Ties Ser.). (J). (gr. 3-5). 1985. teacher ed 14.95 (*0-88122-076-0*) Lrn Links.

— Mr. Popper's Penguins: A Study Guide. (Novel-Ties Ser.). 1989. student ed, teacher ed 15.95 (*0-88122-049-3*) Lrn Links.

An Asterisk (*) at the beginning of an entry indicates that the title is appearing in BIP for the first time.

— Pippi Longstocking: A Study Guide. (Novel-Ties Ser.). 1989. student ed, teacher ed 15.95 (*0-88122-050-7*) Lrn Links.

— Roll of Thunder, Hear My Cry - Study Guide. Friedland, Joyce & Kessler, Rikki, eds. (Novel-Ties Ser.). (YA). (gr. 6-10). 1993. pap. text ed. 15.95 (*0-88122-126-0*) Lrn Links.

— Trouble River: A Study Guide. (Novel-Ties Ser.). 1988. student ed, teacher ed 15.95 (*0-88122-065-5*) Lrn Links.

— The White Mountains: A Study Guide. (Novel-Ties Ser.). 1987. teacher ed 15.95 (*0-88122-097-3*) Lrn Links.

— The Wind in the Willows: A Study Guide. (Novel-Ties Ser.). 1989. teacher ed 15.95 (*0-88122-058-2*) Lrn Links.

Levine, Gloria & Fischer, Kathleen M. The Wave - Study Guide. Friedland, Joyce & Kessler, Rikki, eds. (Novel-Ties Ser.). (YA). (gr. 6-10). 1993. pap. text ed. 15.95 (*0-88122-132-5*) Lrn Links.

Levine, Gloria & Polette, Nancy. The ABCs of Reading Thinking & Literacy. (Illus.). 144p. (YA). (gr. 7-12). 1987. pap. 14.95 (*0-913839-64-7*) Bk Lures.

Levine, Gloria, et al. The High King: A Study Guide. (Novel-Ties Ser.). 1988. teacher ed 15.95 (*0-88122-093-0*) Lrn Links.

Levine, Gustav & Parkinson, Stanley. Experimental Methods in Psychology. 496p. 1993. text ed. 39.95 (*0-8058-1438-8*) L Erlbaum Assocs.

Levine, H. Classifying Immersions into IR4 over Stable Maps of 3-Manifolds into IR2. (Lecture Notes in Mathematics Ser.: Vol. 1157). 163p. 1985. pap. 31.10 (*0-387-15995-9*) Spr-Verlag.

Levine, H. & Slade, L., eds. Water Relationships in Foods: Advances in the 1980s & Trends for the 1990s. (Advances in Experimental Medicine & Biology Ser.: Vol. 302). (Illus.). 850p. 1991. 159.50 (*0-306-43936-0*, Plenum Pr) Plenum.

Levine, Hal B. & Levine, Marlene W. Urbanization in Papua New Guinea: A Study of Ambivalent Townsmen. LC 78-58795. 169p. reprint ed. pap. 48.20 (*0-318-34817-9*, 2031682) Bks Demand.

Levine, Harold, jt. ed. see Langness, Lewis L.

Levine, Henry D. & Witten, Roger M. Negotiating Telecommunications Contracts: Second Annual. v, 301p. write for info. (*0-318-61625-4*) HarBrace.

***Levine, Herbert.** Point-Counterpoint. 5th ed. 400p. 1994. pap. text ed. 17.00 (*0-312-09968-1*) St Martin.

Levine, Herbert A., jt. auth. see Kerrison, Irvine L.

***Levine, Herbert J.** Sing Unto God a New Song: A Contemporary Reading of the Psalms. LC 94-21826. 1995. 39.95 (*0-253-33341-5*) Ind U Pr.

— Yeats's Daimonic Renewal. LC 83-6989. (Studies in Modern Literature: No. 16). 179p. reprint ed. pap. 51.10 (*0-8357-1427-6*, 2070503) Bks Demand.

Levine, Herbert J. & Gaasch, William H., eds. The Ventricle: Basic & Clinical Aspects. LC 85-4976. 1985. lib. bdg. 165.50 (*0-89838-721-3*) Kluwer Ac.

Levine, Herbert J., jt. ed. see Gaasch, William H.

Levine, Herbert M. Political Issues Debated: An Introduction to Politics. (Illus.). 352p. (C). 1982. pap. write for info. (*0-13-685032-4*) P-H.

— Political Issues Debated: An Introduction to Politics. 4th ed. 336p. 1992. pap. text ed. write for info. (*0-13-681644-4*) P-H.

— The Politics of State & Local Government Debated. LC 84-11691. 384p. 1985. pap. text ed. write for info. (*0-13-684333-6*) P-H.

— World Politics Debated. 4th ed. 1992. text ed. write for info. (*0-07-037512-7*) McGraw.

Levine, Herbert M., ed. What If the American Political System Were Different? LC 91-26730. 308p. 1992. 51.95 (*1-56324-009-2*); pap. text ed. 20.95 (*1-56324-010-6*) M E Sharpe.

Levine, Herbert M., jt. auth. see Carlton, David.

Levine, Herbert S. Conduct of American Foreign Policy. 1990. pap. text ed. write for info. (*0-07-037489-9*) McGraw.

Levine, Herbert S., jt. ed. see Bergson, Abram.

Levine, Hillel. Economic Origins of Antisemitism. (Illus.). 288p. (C). 1991. text ed. 35.00 (*0-300-04987-0*) Yale U Pr.

— Economic Origins of Antisemitism: Poland & Its Jews in the Early Modern Period. 284p. (C). 1993. reprint ed. pap. text ed. 18.00 (*0-300-05248-0*) Yale U Pr.

Levine, Hillel & Harmon, Lawrence. The Death of an American Jewish Community: A Tragedy of Good Intentions. 400p. 1991. 27.95 (*0-02-913865-5*) Free Pr.

— The Death of an American Jewish Community: A Tragedy of Good Intentions. 370p. 1993. pap. 12.95 (*0-02-913866-3*) Free Pr.

Levine, Howard. Prisoners of the Past: Overcoming Post-Traumatic Stress Disorder. 144p. (Orig.). 1992. pap. 8.95 (*0-929162-51-X*) PIA Pr.

Levine, Howard, ed. see Mathog, Robert H., et al.

Levine, Howard B., ed. Adult Analysis & Childhood Sexual Abuse. 232p. 1990. text ed. 29.95 (*0-88163-083-7*) Analytic Pr.

Levine, Howard B., et al, eds. Psychoanalysis & the Nuclear Threat: Clinical & Theoretical Studies. 304p. 1988. text ed. 34.50 (*0-88163-062-4*) Analytic Pr.

Levine, Howard L. & May, Mark. Endoscopic Sinus Surgery. LC 92-49512. (Rhinology & Sinusology Ser.). (Illus.). 256p. 1993. 125.00 (*0-86577-474-9*) Thieme Med Pubs.

Levine, I. E. John Kennedy: Young Man in the White House. LC 90-49180. (American Cavalcade Ser.). (Illus.). 176p. (J). (gr. 6-10). 1991. lib. bdg. 9.95 (*1-55905-085-3*) Marshall Cavendish.

Levine, I. S., jt. auth. see Stoller, Robert J.

Levine, Ira A. Left-Wing Dramatic Theory in the American Theatre. LC 84-28018. (Theater & Dramatic Studies: No. 24). (Illus.). 249p. reprint ed. pap. 71.00 (*0-8357-1599-X*, 2070557) Bks Demand.

Levine, Ira N. Molecular Spectroscopy. LC 74-30477. 491p. 1975. text ed. 85.95 (*0-471-53128-6*) Wiley.

— Physical Chemistry. 3rd rev. ed. 920p. (C). 1988. text ed. write for info. (*0-07-037474-0*) McGraw.

— Physical Chemistry. 4th ed. LC 93-48561. 1994. text ed. write for info. (*0-07-037528-3*) McGraw.

— Quantum Chemistry. 4th ed. 629p. 1991. text ed. 42.00 (*0-205-12770-3*, H27709) P-H.

Levine, Isaac D. Mitchell, Pioneer of Air Power. LC 71-169426. (Literature & History of Aviation Ser.). 1972. reprint ed. 33.95 (*0-405-03777-5*) Ayer.

***Levine, J.** How to Speak New Yorkese. Date not set. pap. 2.99 (*0-517-13390-3*) Random.

Levine, J. R. & Eggleston, J. R. The Anthracite Basins of Eastern Pennsylvania: Field Trip Guide Book. (Illus.). 54p. (Orig.). (C). 1994. pap. text ed. 40.00 (*1-56806-478-0*) Diane Pub.

Levine, Jack. The Complete Graphic Work of Jack Levine. (Fine Art Ser.). (Illus.). 112p. (Orig.). 1983. pap. 11.95 (*0-486-24481-4*) Dover.

Levine, Jacob, ed. Motivation in Humor. (Controversy Ser.). 182p. (Orig.). (C). 1969. 12.95 (*0-202-25059-8*) Lieber-Atherton.

Levine, Jacques. Hitler's Secret Diaries. 160p. (Orig.). 1988. pap. 14.95 (*0-934579-00-8*) Aiglon Pr.

Levine, James. Getting Men Involved: Strategies for Early Childhood Programs. 1994. pap. 12.95 (*0-590-49605-0*) Scholastic Inc.

Levine, James A. Day Care & the Public Schools. 140p. 1978. pap. 5.00 (*0-89292-078-5*) Educ Dev Ctr.

Levine, James P. Juries & Politics. LC 91-11960. 202p. (C). 1992. pap. 17.95 (*0-534-14754-2*) Intl Thomson.

Levine, James P., jt. auth. see Abbott, David W.

Levine, Jan M. Analytical Assignments for Integrating Legal Research & Writing, 2 bks. (Orig.). 1991. Academic Yr., 1991-92. teacher ed write for info. (*0-916951-25-1*); pap. write for info. (*0-318-68471-3*); Fall 1991 Semester. write for info. (*0-916951-23-5*); Spring 1992 Semester. write for info. (*0-916951-24-3*) Adams & Ambrose.

— Analytical Assignments for Integrating Legal Research & Writing (1993-94 Edition) 2nd ed. 1993. student ed write for info. (*0-916951-26-X*) Adams & Ambrose.

— Analytical Assignments for Integrating Legal Research & Writing (1994-95) (C). 1994. write for info. (*0-916951-02-2*) Adams & Ambrose.

Levine, Jennifer. Forever in My Heart: A Story to Help Children Participate in Life As a Parent Dies. LC 92-50678. (Illus.). 32p. (Orig.). (J). (gr. 1-6). 1992. pap. 6.95 (*1-878321-08-0*) Rainbow NC.

— My Foster Home: A Story for Children Entering Foster Care. (Illus.). (J). (gr. k-6). 1993. 5.95 (*0-87868-537-5*) Child Welfare.

Levine, Jessica, tr. see Le Dantec, Denise & Le Dantec, Jean-Pierre.

Levine, Jessica, tr. see LeDentec, Denise & LeDantec, Jean-Pierre.

Levine, Jessica, tr. see Tafuri, Manfredo.

Levine, Jessica, tr. see Tarfuri, Manfredo.

Levine, Jessie, ed. see Winters, Manque.

Levine, Joel H. Exceptions Are the Rule: An Inquiry into Methods in the Social Sciences. LC 93-1256. (New Perspectives in Sociology Ser.). 312p. (C). 1993. text ed. 55.50 (*0-8133-1646-4*); pap. text ed. 19.95 (*0-8133-1647-2*) Westview.

Levine, Joel M. & Tyler, Ralph W. Secondary Instruction: A Manual for Classroom Teaching. 400p. 1989. text ed. 54.00 (*0-205-11790-2*, H17908) Allyn.

Levine, Joel S., ed. Global Biomass Burning: Atmospheric, Climatic, & Biospheric Implications. (Illus.). 395p. 1992. 80.00 (*0-262-12159-X*) MIT Pr.

— The Photochemistry of Atmospheres: Earth, the Other Planets, & Comets. 1985. text ed. 151.00 (*0-12-444920-4*) Acad Pr.

Levine, Joel S., jt. auth. see Jacobson, Eugene D.

Levine, John. Business Graphics: A C Plus Plus Toolkit for Windows Applications. 1993. disk, pap. 39.95 (*1-55851-330-2*) M&T Bks.

— Designing GUI Applications for Windows. 1993. disk, pap. 39.95 (*1-55851-328-0*) M&T Bks.

— Internet for Dummies. (Illus.). 384p. 1993. pap. 19.95 (*1-56884-024-1*) IDG Bks.

— Internet Secrets. 1995. pap. 39.99 (*1-56884-452-2*) IDG Bks.

— Internet Windows Dum Start. 1995. pap. 39.99 (*1-56884-246-5*) IDG Bks.

— The Internet Windows for Dummies Start Kit. 1995. pap. 34.99 (*1-56884-237-6*) IDG Bks.

— Mixed Language Programming for Windows. 1993. disk, pap. 39.95 (*1-55851-332-9*) M&T Bks.

— More UNIX for Dummies. 1995. pap. 19.99 (*1-56884-361-5*) IDG Bks.

— QR - Internet for Dummies. 1994. pap. 8.95 (*1-56884-168-X*) IDG Bks.

— UNIX for Dummies. (Illus.). 400p. 1993. pap. 19.95 (*1-878058-58-4*) IDG Bks.

— Unix for Dummies. 1995. pap. 19.99 (*1-56884-905-2*) IDG Bks.

***Levine, John & Baroudi, Carol.** Internet for Dummies. 2nd ed. 1994. pap. 19.99 (*1-56884-222-8*) IDG Bks.

Levine, John & Young, Margaret L. UNIX Dictionary of Commands, Terms & Acronyms. 1995. text ed. 35.50 (*0-07-037643-3*); pap. text ed. 24.95 (*0-07-037644-1*) McGraw.

Levine, John, jt. auth. see Young, Margaret L.

Levine, John, et al. Lex & Yacc. 2nd ed. (Nutshell Ser.). 366p. 1992. pap. 29.95 (*1-56592-000-7*) OReilly & Assocs.

Levine, John R. Comp-Compilers 1990 Annual. 700p. (Orig.). (C). 1991. pap. text ed. 50.00 (*0-944954-02-2*) Ctr Bk Pubs.

— Programming for Graphics Files: In C & C Plus Plus. LC 93-31897. 480p. 1994. disk 49.95 (*0-471-59856-9*); disk 20.00 (*0-471-59857-7*) Wiley.

— Programming for Graphics Files: In C & C Plus Plus. LC 93-31897. 480p. 1994. pap. text ed. 29.95 (*0-471-59854-2*) Wiley.

Levine, John R., ed. Computer Compilers Annual, 1991. 900p. (Orig.). 1992. pap. text ed. 70.00 (*0-944954-03-0*) Ctr Bk Pubs.

Levine, John R., jt. auth. see Kay, David C.

Levine, John R., jt. auth. see Kay, David.

Levine, Jon E. & Conn, P. Michael, eds. Methods in Neurosciences, Vol. 20: Pulsatility in Neuroendocrine Systems. (Illus.). 510p. 1994. text ed. 95.00 (*0-12-185289-X*) Acad Pr.

Levine, Jonathan D., ed. A Minyan of Comfort: Evening Services for the House of Mourning. 1990. 10.95 (*0-87677-078-2*) Prayer Bk.

Levine, Jonathan D., jt. auth. see Greenberg, Sidney.

Levine, Jonathan D., jt. ed. see Greenberg, Sidney.

Levine, Jonathan D., jt. auth. see Preeg, Ernest H.

Levine, Joseph. The Battle of the Books: History & Literature in the Augustan Age. (Illus.). 448p. 1994. pap. 16.95 (*0-8014-8199-6*) Cornell U Pr.

— The Coral Reef at Night. LC 93-12277. (Illus.). 1993. 39.95 (*0-8109-3190-7*) Abrams.

***Levine, Joseph & Miller, Kenneth R.** Biology: Discovering Life. 2nd ed. 988p. 1994. text ed. write for info. (*0-669-33494-4*) Heath.

Levine, Joseph & Suzuki, David. The Secret of Life: Redesigning the Living World. LC 93-4817. (Illus.). 320p. 1993. 24.95 (*0-9636881-0-3*) WGBH.

Levine, Joseph A. Synagogue Song in America. Schofield, Michael & Smith, Larry W., eds. LC 88-17178. (Performance in World Music Ser.: No. 4). xvi, 232p. 1989. 29.95 (*0-941677-12-5*); audio 30.00 (*0-941677-17-6*) White Cliffs Media.

Levine, Joseph M. The Battle of the Books: History & Literature in the Augustan Age. LC 90-55735. (Illus.). 448p. 1991. 42.50 (*0-8014-2537-9*) Cornell U Pr.

— Dr. Woodward's Shield: History, Science, & Satire in Augustan England. LC 75-27927. (Illus.). 376p. 1991. reprint ed. pap. 15.95 (*0-8014-9935-6*) Cornell U Pr.

— Humanism & History: Origins of Modern English Historiography. LC 86-16776. (Illus.). 304p. (C). 1987. 37.95 (*0-8014-1885-2*) Cornell U Pr.

Levine, Joseph S. The Complete Fishkeeper: Everything Aquarium Fishes Need to Stay Happy, Healthy, & Alive. (Illus.). 288p. 1991. 30.00 (*0-688-10146-1*) Morrow.

— Complete Fishkeeper: Everything Aquarium Fishes Need to Stay Happy, Healthy, & Alive. 1995. pap. 15.00 (*0-688-14068-8*, Quill) Morrow.

Levine, Joseph S. & Miller, Kenneth R. Biology: Discovering Life, 4 vols. LC 90-82264. 898p. (C). 1990. text ed. 37.50 (*0-669-12008-1*); Study guide. student ed 13.50 (*0-669-12009-X*); Study guide for Core Concepts vol. student ed write for info. (*0-669-28947-7*); Instr.'s guide. teacher ed 2.00 (*0-669-12014-6*); Transparencies/slides. trans. write for info. (*0-669-27697-9*) Heath.

— Biology: Discovering Life, 4 vols., Vol. I: Core Concepts. LC 90-82264. 419p. (C). 1990. Vol. I, Core Concepts, 419 p. pap. text ed. write for info. (*0-669-28840-3*) Heath.

— Biology: Discovering Life, 4 vols., Vol. II: Diversity. LC 90-82264. 97p. (C). 1990. Vol. II, Diversity, 97 p. pap. text ed. write for info. (*0-669-28841-1*) Heath.

— Biology: Discovering Life, 4 vols., Vol. III: Plant Systems. LC 90-82264. 71p. (C). 1990. Vol. III, Plant Systems, 71 p. pap. text ed. write for info. (*0-669-28842-X*) Heath.

— Biology: Discovering Life, 4 vols., Vol. IV: Animal Systems. LC 90-82264. 308p. (C). 1990. Vol. IV, Animal Systems, 308 p. pap. text ed. write for info. (*0-669-28843-8*) Heath.

Levine, Josh. Jerry Seinfeld: Much Ado about Nothing. 1993. pap. 9.95 (*1-55022-201-5*, Pub. by ECW Pr CN) InBook.

Levine, Josie. Bilingual Learners & Mainstream Curriculum: Integrated Approaches to Learning & the Teaching & Learning of English As a Second Language. 225p. 1990. 75.00 (*1-85000-494-3*, Falmer Pr); pap. 35.00 (*1-85000-495-1*, Falmer Pr) Taylor & Francis.

Levine, Judah, jt. auth. see Levine, Celotta.

Levine, Judith. My Enemy, My Love: Women, Men & the Dilemmas of Gender. LC 92-32703. 1993. 12.95 (*0-385-41080-8*, Anchor NY) Doubleday.

***Levine, Judith L.** Michael: A Memory Everlasting: A Mother's Diary. 128p. Date not set. 18.95 (*1-56167-198-3*) Noble Hse MD.

Levine, Judy & Jackson, Nancy. How to Speak New Yorkese: A Hand Guide to the World's Most Improbable Language. (Illus.). 96p. (Orig.). 1989. pap. 6.95 (*0-930753-07-0*) Spect Ln Pr.

Levine, Julius B. Winning Trial Advocacy: How to Avoid Mistakes Made by Master Trial Lawyers. 330p. 1989. text ed. 49.95 (*0-13-961319-6*) P-H.

Levine, June & Madden, Lyn. Lyn: A Story of Prostitution. 256p. (Orig.). (C). 1987. pap. 13.95 (*0-946211-45-0*, Pub. by Attic IE) InBook.

Levine, June P. Creation & Criticism: A Passage to India. LC 78-134772. 218p. reprint ed. pap. 62.20 (*0-317-27831-2*, 2055945) Bks Demand.

Levine, Kara & Temko, Erika. Breaking into the Catering Business: A Learning Annex Book. LC 94-20349. 1994. 8.95 (*0-8065-1586-4*, Citadel Pr) Carol Pub Group.

Levine, Katherine G. When Good Kids Do Bad Things. Rubenstein, Julie, ed. 272p. 1993. reprint ed. pap. 10.00 (*0-671-79296-2*) PB.

Levine, Kenneth. Social Context of Literacy. (Language, Education & Society Ser.). 247p. (C). 1986. text ed. 42.50 (*0-7100-9745-X*, RKP); pap. text ed. 19.95 (*0-685-12291-3*, RKP) Routledge.

— The Social Context of Literacy. 272p. (C). 1986. pap. 19.95 (*0-7102-1391-3*, RKP) Routledge.

***Levine, Kristin J.** Development of Pre-Writing & Scissor Skills: A Visual Analysis. 48p. 1995. pap. text ed., vdisk 79.00 (*0-88450-188-4*, 4363) Commun Skill.

Levine, L., ed. Arachidonate Metabolism in Immunologic Systems. (Progress in Allergy Ser.: Vol. 44). (Illus.). viii, 216p. 1988. 118.50 (*3-8055-4773-0*) S Karger.

Levine, Laura. Men in Women's Clothing: Anti-Theatricality & Effeminization, 1579-1642. LC 93-27476. (Studies in Renaissance Literature & Culture: No. 5). 240p. (C). 1994. pap. 16.95 (*0-521-46627-X*) Cambridge U Pr.

— Men in Women's Clothing: Anti-Theatricality & Effeminization, 1579-1642. LC 93-27476. (Studies in Renaissance Literature & Culture: No. 5). 240p. (C). 1995. 59.95 (*0-521-45507-3*) Cambridge U Pr.

Levine, Laurence W. U. S. - China Relations. 7.95 (*0-8315-0136-7*) Speller.

Levine, Lawrence C., et al, eds. A Torts Anthology. LC 92-47129. 1993. write for info. (*0-87084-849-6*) Anderson Pub Co.

Levine, Lawrence W. Black Culture & Black Consciousness: Afro-American Folk Thought from Slavery to Freedom. LC 76-9223. 1978. reprint ed. pap. 13.95 (*0-19-502374-9*) OUP.

— Defender of the Faith: William Jennings Bryan: The Last Decade 1915-1925. LC 86-25679. 400p. 1987. pap. 15.95 (*0-674-19542-6*) HUP.

— Highbrow-Lowbrow: The Emergence of Cultural Hierarchy in America. (William E. Massey Sr. Lectures in the History of American Civilization). (Illus.). 320p. 1990. pap. text ed. 15.00 (*0-674-39077-6*) HUP.

— New York One. (Orig.). 1979. pap. 2.50 (*0-89083-556-X*) Zebra.

— The Unpredictable Past: Explorations in American Cultural History. 1993. pap. 16.95 (*0-19-508297-4*) OUP.

Levine, Lee D. Bird: The Making of an American Sports Legend. 1989. mass mkt. 5.50 (*0-425-11781-2*) Berkley Pub.

Levine, Lee I. The Synagogue in Late Antiquity. (JTS & the American Schools of Oriental Research Ser.). 1987. pap. 19.95 (*0-685-19157-5*); bds. 26.95 (*0-317-64344-4*) Jewish Sem.

Levine, Lee I., ed. The Galilee in Late Antiquity. LC 92-12475. 1992. 35.00 (*0-674-34113-9*) Jewish Sem.

— The Galilee in Late Antiquity. (Jewish Theological Seminary Ser.). (Illus.). 410p. 1994. pap. 17.95 (*0-674-34114-7*, LEVGAX) HUP.

— The Synagogue in Late Antiquity: A Centennial Publication of the Jewish Theological Seminary of America. LC 86-14069. xiv, 223p. 1986. 26.95 (*0-89757-510-5*, Eisenbrauns); pap. 15.95 (*0-89757-509-1*, Eisenbrauns) Am Sch Orient Res.

Levine, Len. The Maverick Guide to Prague. (Illus.). 320p. 1993. pap. 14.95 (*0-88289-934-1*) Pelican.

Levine, Leonard P., jt. auth. see Besag, Frank P.

Levine, Leonore S., jt. ed. see New, Maria I.

Levine, Leslie B. Clinical Management of the Disabled Dental Patient: A Working Manual for Dental Professionals, Vol. 1. Mason, Leslie C., ed. (Illus.). 65p. (Orig.). (C). 1989. pap. text ed. 10.95 (*0-9622139-0-X*) Denta Pr.

Levine, Lewis & Hughey, Lucinda S. Changing Times: Toward an Integrated Approach to Reading. (Illus.). 300p. (C). 1985. pap. text ed. 20.50 (*0-13-128182-8*) P-H.

Levine, Linda, ed. Diffusion, Transfer, & Implementation of Information Technology: Proceedings of the IFIP TC8 Working Conference on Diffusion, Transfer, & Implementation of Information Technology, Pittsburgh, PA, U.S.A., 11-13 October 1993. LC 94-4643. (IFIP Transactions A: Computer Science & Technology Ser.: Vol. A-45). 1994. write for info. (*0-444-81856-1*, North Holland) Elsevier.

Levine, Linda & Barbach, Lonnie G. The Intimate Male: Candid Discussions about Women, Sex & Relationships. 400p. 1985. pap. 5.99 (*0-451-15938-1*, Sig) NAL-Dutton.

Levine, Linda G., et al, eds. Spanish Women Writers: A Bio-Bibliographical Source Book. LC 92-42432. 632p. 1993. text ed. 95.00 (*0-313-26823-1*, LSB, Greenwood Pr) Greenwood.

Levine, Lois, jt. auth. see Burros, Marian.

Levine, Louis, pseud. The Women's Garment Workers. LC 72-89752. (American Labor, from Conspiracy to Collective Bargaining Ser., No. 1). 608p. 1976. reprint ed. 23.95 (*0-405-02139-9*) Ayer.

***Levine, Louis, ed.** Genetics of Natural Populations: The Continuing Importance of Theodosius Dobzhansky. LC 94-29691. 1995. write for info. (*0-231-08116-2*) Col U Pr.

Levine, M. Man & Machine Vision. 848p. 1985. text ed. write for info. (*0-07-037446-5*) McGraw.

Levine, M. D., jt. auth. see Noble, P. B.

Levine, Madeline, tr. see Bialoszewski, Miron.

Levine, Madeline, tr. see Fink, Ida.

Levine, Madeline, ed. see Weintraub, Wiktor.

Levine, Madeline G., tr. see Milosz, Czeslaw.

Levine, Marc V. The Reconquest of Montreal: Language Policy & Social Change in a Bilingual City. (Illus.). 320p. 1990. 44.95 (*0-87722-703-9*); pap. 18.95 (*0-87722-899-X*) Temple U Pr.

Levine, Marc V., et al. The State & Democracy: Revitalizing America's Government. (Alternative Policies for America Ser.). 256p. 1988. text ed. 49.95 (0-415-90045-X, Routledge NY); pap. text ed. 17.95 (0-415-90076-X, Routledge NY) Routledge.

Levine, Marian, ed. Cookies! 64p. 1989. pap. 3.49 (0-942320-33-6) Am Cooking.

— Cooking with Old Bay. (Collector's Ser.: Vol. 27). 64p. (Orig.). 1989. pap. 3.49 (0-942320-34-4) Am Cooking.

Levine, Marian, ed. see Bloom, Leslie.

Levine, Marian, ed. see Bradley, Jane.

Levine, Marian, ed. see Clingerman, Polly.

Levine, Marian, ed. see Passin, Roy.

Levine, Marian, ed. see Rosenberg, Lawrence.

Levine, Marian, ed. see Seidita, Karla.

Levine, Marian, ed. see Slack, Susan.

Levine, Marian, ed. see Torine, Len.

Levine, Marilyn A. The Found Generation: Chinese Communists in Europe During the Twenties. LC 92-46157. (Jackson School Publications in International Studies). 296p. 1993. 35.00 (0-295-97240-8) U of Wash Pr.

Levine, Marilyn M., jt. auth. see Baldwin, Shauna S.

Levine, Mark. Debt: Poems. LC 92-37862. 1993. 20.00 (0-688-12397-X); pap. 8.00 (0-688-12398-8) Morrow.

— The Jazz Piano Book. (Illus.). 307p. (Orig.). (C). 1990. pap. text ed. 20.00 (0-9614701-5-1) Sher Music.

***Levine, Mark & Rachlis, Eugene, eds.** The Complete Book of Bible Quotations. 592p. 1994. 10.95 (1-56865-103-1, GuildAmerica) Dblday Bk Music.

Levine, Mark, jt. auth. see Pollan, Stephen M.

Levine, Mark L. Builders' Liability. 1980. write for info. (0-318-02240-0) Prof Pubns & Educ.

— Complete Book of Bible Quotations. 1989. pap. 18.00 (0-671-70551-2) PB.

— Exchanging Real Estate, 2 vols. 1995. 115.00 (0-317-01847-7) Prof Pubns & Educ.

— Landlords'-Owners' Liability (1981) 1989. write for info. (0-317-00909-5) Prof Pubns & Educ.

— Levine's Real Estate Transactions. 1991. pap. write for info. (0-314-86700-7) West Pub.

— Negotiating a Book Contract: A Guide for Authors, Agents & Lawyers. 96p. (Orig.). 1988. pap. 12.95 (0-918825-69-5) Moyer Bell.

— Real Estate Appraiser's Liabiity. 1995. write for info. (0-317-01846-9) Prof Pubns & Educ.

— Real Estate Appraisers' Liability. LC 91-60906. (Real Property-Zoning Ser.). 1991. Revised annually with supplement. 135.00 (0-685-59814-4) Clark Boardman Callaghan.

— Real Estate Fundamentals. LC 76-3508. 440p. reprint ed. pap. 125.40 (0-317-20531-5, 2022843) Bks Demand.

— Real Estate Tax Update Outline (1987) 1995. write for info. (0-318-58317-8) Prof Pubns & Educ.

— Real Estate Transactions, Tax Planning. 1995. write for info. (0-317-01848-5) Prof Pubns & Educ.

— Real Estate Transactions, Tax Planning & Consequences. 1390p. (C). 1993. pap. text ed. write for info. (0-314-02383-6) West Pub.

— Real Estate Transactions, Tax Planning & Consequences: 1995 Edition. 1450p. (C). 1995. pap. text ed. write for info. (0-314-06362-5) West Pub.

— Realtors' Liability. 1979. write for info. (0-317-00910-9) Prof Pubns & Educ.

— Realtors Liability. LC 79-4133. (Real Estate For Professional Practitioners Ser.). 285p. reprint ed. pap. 81.30 (0-317-09301-0, 2022419) Bks Demand.

Levine, Mark R., ed. Manual of Oculoplastic Surgery. LC 88-18903. (Illus.). 284p. reprint ed. pap. 81.00 (0-7837-6254-2, 2045966) Bks Demand.

Levine, Mark S. Canonical Analysis & Factor Comparison. LC 77-75941. (Quantitative Applications in the Social Sciences Ser.: Vol. 6). 62p. 1977. 9.95 (0-8039-0655-2) Sage.

Levine, Marlene W., jt. auth. see Levine, Hal B.

Levine, Marsha, ed. Professional Practice Schools: Integrating School Reform & Teacher Education. 192p. (C). 1992. text ed. 38.00 (0-8077-3176-5); pap. text ed. 17.95 (0-8077-3175-7) Tchrs Coll.

Levine, Marsha & Trachtman, Roberta, eds. American Business & the Public School: Case Studies of Corporate Involvement in Public Education. 296p. 1988. text ed. 27.95 (0-8077-2880-2) Tchrs Coll.

Levine, Marshall R. A Physician's Guide to Utilization Review. LC 86-16486. 56p. 1987. pap. 4.95 (0-8036-5602-5) Davis Co.

Levine, Martin. Curious about HDTV? 1994. pap. 15.95 (0-672-30506-2) Sams.

— Legal Education. LC 93-27764. (International Library of Essays in Law & Legal Theory: Vol. 5). 1993. 150.00 (0-8147-5065-6) NYU Pr.

Levine, Martin L. Age Discrimination & the Mandatory Retirement Controversy. LC 88-9280. 272p. 1989. text ed. 34.00 (0-8018-3357-4) Johns Hopkins.

***Levine, Martin L., ed.** Law & Psychology. LC 95-7995. (International Library of Essays in Law & Legal Theory: No. 16). 500p. 1995. 150.00x (0-8147-5064-8) NYU Pr.

Levine, Martin N. Mental Retardation Handbook. 147p. 1989. pap. text ed. 39.50 (0-87424-230-4, W-230) Western Psych.

Levine, Martin P., jt. auth. see Markisz, John A.

Levine, Marvin. Effective Problem Solving. 2nd ed. LC 93-31281. 1993. pap. text ed. write for info. (0-13-245481-5) P-H.

Levine, Marvin J. Privatization of Government: The Delivery of Public Goods & Services by Private Means. (Public Employee Relations Library: No. 72). 88p. 1990. 14.00 (0-685-41305-5) Intl Personnel Mgmt.

— Public Personnel Management: Structure, Process & Practice. 1983. 22.95 (0-913878-27-8) T Horton & Dghts.

Levine, Mel. Keeping a Head in School: A Student's Book about Learning Abilities & Learning Disorders. rev. ed. (Illus.). 312p. (J). (gr. 4-10). 1991. reprint ed. pap. text ed. 22.00 (0-8388-2069-7, 2069); reprint ed. audio 27.85 (0-8388-2070-0, 2070) Ed Pub Serv.

— Life in the Trash Lane: Cash, Cars & Corruption, a Sports Agent's True Story. LC 93-44457. 192p. 1993. pap. 9.95 (0-942963-48-2) Distinctive Pub.

Levine, Melvin D. & McAnarney, Elizabeth R., eds. Early Adolescent Transitions: An Interdisciplinary Perspective. LC 86-45939. (Johnson & Johnson Pediatric Roundtable Ser.). 304p. 1987. text ed. 40.00 (0-669-14633-1) Free Pr.

Levine, Melvin M. Fission Reactors. (Illus.). 77p. 1984. pap. 10.00 (0-318-41413-9, IO-19) Am Assn Physics.

Levine, Michael. The Address Book: Direct Access to over 3,500 Celebrities, Corporate Execs, & Other VIPs. LC 92-31749. 288p. 1993. pap. 9.95 (0-399-51793-6, Perigree Bks) Berkley Pub.

— The Address Book No. 7: How to Reach Anyone Who Is Anyone. LC 94-33188. 288p. (Orig.). 1995. pap. 11.00 (0-399-52149-6, Perigree Bks) Berkley Pub.

— Big White Lie: The CIA & the Cocaine-Crack Epidemic. 1993. 22.95 (1-56025-064-X) Thunders Mouth.

— Guerrilla PR: How You Can Wage an Effective Publicity Campaign . . . Without Going Broke. 256p. 1994. 10.00 (0-88730-664-0) Harper Busn.

— The Kid's Address Book. rev. ed. 240p. (J). 1994. pap. 9.00 (0-399-51875-4, Perigree Bks) Berkley Pub.

— Kid's Address Book: Over Fifteen Hundred Addresses of Celebrities, Athletes, Entertainers, & More. 176p. (Orig.). 1992. pap. 9.00 (0-399-51783-9, Perigree Bks) Berkley Pub.

— Lessons at the Halfway Point. 150p. 1995. pap. 12.95 (0-89087-744-0) Celestial Arts.

— The Music Address Book: How to Reach Anyone Who's Anyone in Music. 2nd ed. 256p. (Orig.). 1994. pap. 12.00 (0-06-273257-9, Harper Ref) HarpC.

— The Music Address Book: How to Reach Anyone Who's Anyone in Music. 256p. (Orig.). 1991. reprint ed. lib. bdg. 27.00x (0-8095-9074-3) Borgo Pr.

Levine, Michael & Kavanau-Levine, Laura. The Big White Lie: The Deep Cover Operation That Exposed the CIA Sabotage of the Drug War. 448p. 1994. pap. 13.95 (1-56025-084-4) Thunders Mouth.

Levine, Michael, tr. see Semyonova Tian-Shanskaia.

Levine, Michael G. Writing Through Repression: Literature, Censorship, Psychoanalysis. 232p. (C). 1994. text ed. 35.00 (0-8018-4835-0) Johns Hopkins.

Levine, Michael K. Inside International Trade Policy Formulation: A History of the 1982 US-EC Steel Arrangements. LC 85-3724. 176p. 1985. text ed. 45.00 (0-275-90136-X, C0136, Praeger Pubs) Greenwood.

Levine, Michael L. Civil Rights. Bakalar, Nick, ed. (Social Issues in American History Ser.). (Illus.). 192p. 1996. 29.95 (0-89774-859-X, 2147) Oryx Pr.

Levine, Michael P. How Schools Can Help Combat Student Eating Disorders. (Combat Ser.). 280p. 1987. pap. 12.95 (0-8106-3289-6) NEA.

— Hume & the Problem of Miracles: A Solution. (C). 1988. lib. bdg. 86.50 (0-7923-0043-2) Kluwer Ac.

— Pantheism: A Non-Theistic Concept of Deity. LC 93-34726. 400p. 1994. 65.00 (0-415-07064-3, B3909, Routledge NY) Routledge.

Levine, Michael S., jt. ed. see Franks, Jacqueline.

Levine, Michael W. & Shefner, Jeremy M. Fundamentals of Sensation & Perception. 2nd ed. 512p. (C). 1991. text ed. 53.95 (0-534-14172-2) Brooks-Cole.

Levine, Mindy N., ed. see Dance Theater Workshop Staff.

Levine, Mira, jt. ed. see Kaufman, Menahem.

Levine, Miriam. Devotion: A Memoir. LC 92-44781. 264p. 1993. 29.95 (0-8203-1555-9) U of Ga Pr.

— A Guide to Writers' Homes in New England. (Illus.). 192p. 1984. pap. 11.95 (0-918222-51-6) Applewood.

Levine, Morris E. Digital Theory & Experimentation Using Integrated Circuits. enl. rev. ed. (Illus.). 272p. (C). 1982. pap. text ed. 52.00 (0-13-212688-5) P-H.

Levine, Mortimer. The Early Elizabethan Succession Question, 1558-1568. viii, 245p. 1966. 32.50 (0-8047-0299-3) Stanford U Pr.

— The Early Elizabethan Succession Question, 1558-1568. fac. ed. LC 66-17563. 111p. 1966. reprint ed. pap. 30.00 (0-7837-7911-9, 2047667) Bks Demand.

— Tudor England, 1485-1603. LC 68-12060. (Conference on British Studies, Bibliographical Handbooks). 127p. reprint ed. pap. 36.20 (0-685-16011-4, 2027230) Bks Demand.

Levine, Murray. The History & Politics of Mental Health. 1981. pap. 12.95 (0-19-502956-9) OUP.

***Levine, Murray & Doueck, Howard J.** Psychotherapy & Mandated Reporting of Child Maltreatment. (Practice Ser.: Vol. 12). 168p. (C). 1995. 42.95 (0-8039-5472-7); pap. 18.95 (0-8039-5473-5) Sage.

Levine, Murray & Perkins, David V. Community Psychology: Perspective & Applications. (Illus.). 384p. 1987. 35.00 (0-19-503946-7) OUP.

Levine, Murray, jt. auth. see Levine, Adeline G.

***Levine, Myron A.** Presidential Campaigns & Elections: Issues & Images in the Media Age. 2nd ed. 300p. 1995. pap. text ed. 24.00 (0-87581-394-1) Peacock Pubs.

— Presidential Campaigns & Elections: Issues, Images, & Partisanship. LC 91-76459. 288p. 1992. pap. 18.00 (0-87581-357-7) Peacock Pubs.

Levine, N. The Tabernacle. (Illus.). 144p. 1990. boxed 125.00 (1-871055-15-6) Soncino Pr.

Levine, Nancy D., ed. The Older Volunteer: An Annotated Bibliography. LC 92-41898. (Bibliographies & Indexes in Gerontology Ser.: No. 21). 136p. 1993. text ed. 49.95 (0-313-28125-4, BOV, Greenwood Pr) Greenwood.

Levine, Nancy E. The Dynamics of Polyandry: Kinship, Domesticity, & Population on the Tibetan Border. (Illus.). 344p. 1988. lib. bdg. 47.50 (0-226-47568-9); pap. text ed. 17.95 (0-226-47569-7) U Ch Pr.

Levine, Naomi & Hochbaum, Martin, eds. Poor Jews: An American Awakening. LC 73-85097. 206p. 1974. 32.95 (0-87855-073-9); pap. 18.95 (0-87855-570-6) Transaction Pubs.

Levine, Nathan. Typing for Everyone. 9th ed. Lindsell-Roberts, Sheryl, ed. LC 93-31880. (Illus.). 1994. pap. 13.00 (0-671-87285-0) P-H Gen Ref & Trav.

Levine, Ned, jt. auth. see Glickfeld, Madelyn.

Levine, Neil. Colville for the Defense: A Critique of the Reports of the U. N. Special Rapporteur for Guatemala. 31p. write for info. (0-318-62436-2, Am Watch) Hum Rts Watch.

Levine, Neil, jt. auth. see Lipman, Jonathan.

Levine, Norma. The Blessing Power of the Buddhas. 1993. pap. 15.95 (1-85230-305-0) Element MA.

Levine, Norman. Pigmentation & Pigmentary Disorders. 1993. 159.95 (0-8493-7353-0, RL790) CRC Pr.

— Skin Healthy: Everyone's Guide to Great Skin. 184p. 1995. pap. 12.95 (0-87833-900-0) Taylor Pub.

Levine, Norman, ed. see Bauer, Walter K.

Levine, Norman, tr. see Lukacs, Georg.

Levine, Norman D. Veterinary Protozoology. LC 84-27867. (Illus.). 414p. 1985. text ed. 48.95 (0-8138-1861-3) Iowa St U Pr.

Levine, Norman D., ed. Natural Nidality of Diseases & Questions of Parasitology. Plous, Frederick K., Jr., tr. LC 68-11027. (Illus.). 495p. reprint ed. 141.10 (0-8357-9691-4, 2019031) Bks Demand.

— The Protozoan Phylum Apicomplexa, 2 vols., Vol. I. 240p. 1988. 124.00 (0-8493-4653-3, SF780, CRC Reprint) Franklin.

— The Protozoan Phylum Apicomplexa, 2 vols., Vol. II. 176p. 1988. 98.00 (0-8493-4654-1, CRC Reprint) Franklin.

Levine, Norman D. & Ivens, Virginia R., eds. Coccidian Parasites of Rodents. 150p. 1989. 132.00 (0-8493-4898-6, QL368) CRC Pr.

Levine, Norman D., ed. see Drake, Daniel.

Levine, Norman D., ed. see Naumov, N. P.

Levine, Norman D., ed. see Pavlovsky, Evgeny N.

Levine, Norman S. Current Treatment in Dental Practice. (Illus.). 533p. 1986. text ed. 75.50 (0-7216-1198-2) Saunders.

Levine, P. J. The Amateur & the Professional: Historians, Antiquarians & Archaeologists in Nineteenth-Century England, 1838-1886. (Illus.). 220p. 1986. 64.95 (0-521-30635-3) Cambridge U Pr.

Levine, Paul. Cabinets & Built-Ins: A Practical Guide to Building Professional Quality Cabinetry. (Illus.). 384p. 1994. 27.95 (0-87596-590-3) Rodale Pr Inc.

— False Dawn. 1994. mass mkt. 5.99 (0-553-56504-4) Bantam.

— Fool Me Twice: A Jake Lassiter Novel. LC 95-7720. 1996. write for info. (0-688-14304-0) Morrow.

— Making Kitchen Cabinets: A Foolproof System for the Home Workshop. LC 87-51674. (Illus.). 192p. 1988. pap. 19.95 (0-918804-94-9); vhs 29.95 (0-918804-95-7); bmax 29.95 (0-918804-96-5) Taunton.

— Mortal Sin. 352p. 1995. mass mkt. 5.50 (0-380-72161-9) Avon.

— Mortal Sin. LC 93-30662. 1994. 20.00 (0-688-12717-7) Morrow.

— Night Vision. 1992. mass mkt. 5.99 (0-553-29762-7) Bantam.

— Slashback. LC 94-13051. 1995. 22.00 (0-688-12718-5) Morrow.

— To Speak for the Dead. 1991. 5.99 (0-553-29172-6) Bantam.

Levine, Paul, jt. auth. see Currie, David.

Levine, Paul A., et al. Electrocardiography of Rate-Modulated Pacemaker Rhythms. (Illus.). 90p. (Orig.). (C). 1990. pap. 40.00 (0-9626364-0-1); pap. 40.00 (0-9626364-1-X) Siemens Pacesetter.

Levine, Peter. A. G. Spalding & the Rise of Baseball: The Promise of American Sport. 1986. pap. 10.95 (0-19-504220-4) OUP.

— American Sport. 224p. (C). 1989. pap. text ed. write for info. (0-13-031378-5) P-H.

— The Behavior of State Legislative Parties in the Jacksonian Era New Jersey: 1829-1844. LC 75-18248. 285p. 1977. 25.00 (0-8386-1800-6) Fairleigh Dickinson.

— Ellis Island to Ebbets Field: Sport & the American Jewish Experience. 1992. 24.95 (0-685-61042-X) OUP.

— Ellis Island to Ebbets Field: Sport & the American Jewish Experience. 400p. 1992. 25.00 (0-19-505128-9) OUP.

— Ellis Island to Ebbets Field: Sport & the American Jewish Experience. (Illus.). 340p. 1993. reprint ed. pap. 11.95 (0-19-508555-8) OUP.

— Nietzsche & the Modern Crisis of the Humanities. LC 94-11021. 302p. (C). 1995. text ed. 57.50 (0-7914-2327-1); pap. 18.95 (0-7914-2328-X) State U NY Pr.

Levine, Peter, ed. Baseball History. (Illus.). 160p. 1990. reprint ed. pap. 14.95 (0-9625132-1-0) Cyberbooks.

Levine, Peter, jt. auth. see Lipsyte, Robert.

Levine, Philip. The Bread to Time: Toward an Autobiography. LC 93-22599. 1994. 23.00 (0-679-42406-7) Knopf.

— Don't Ask. LC 80-24992. (Poets on Poetry Ser.). 192p. (C). 1981. pap. 13.95 (0-472-06327-8) U of Mich Pr.

— New Selected Poems. 1992. pap. 15.00 (0-679-74056-2) McKay.

— Not This Pig: Poems. LC 68-16006. (Wesleyan Poetry Program Ser.: Vol. 38). 80p. 1968. pap. 10.95 (0-8195-1038-6, Wesleyan Univ Pr) U Pr of New Eng.

— The Simple Truth: Poems. LC 94-14508. 1994. 20.00 (0-679-43580-8) Knopf.

— A Walk with Tom Jefferson. LC 87-46080. 80p. 1988. 16.95 (0-394-57038-3); pap. 13.00 (0-394-75859-5) Knopf.

— What Work Is. 1991. pap. 18.50 (0-679-40166-0) McKay.

— What Work Is. 1992. pap. 12.00 (0-679-74058-9) McKay.

Levine, Philip, ed. The Essential Keats. (Essential Poets Ser.: Vol. 1). 128p. 1987. pap. 8.00 (0-88001-135-1) Ecco Pr.

Levine, Philip, tr. see Fuertes, Gloria.

Levine, Philip, et al. Earth, Stars, & Writers. LC 92-36089. (National Book Week Lectures). 1992. write for info. (0-8444-0771-2) Lib Congress.

Levine, Philippa. Private Lives & Public Commitment: Feminist Resistance in England, 1860-1900. 250p. 1990. text ed. 49.95 (0-631-14802-7) Blackwell Pubs.

— Victorian Feminism, 1850-1900. LC 94-11565. 176p. 1989. 17.95 (0-8130-1321-6) U Press Fla.

***Levine, Phillip J.** Chemical Use among Older Adults: Risks, Reactions, & Concerns. 40p. 1993. pap. 3.95 (1-56246-071-4, P267) Johnsn Inst.

Levine-Provost, Gail, jt. auth. see Provost, Gary.

Levine, R. & Luft, Rolf, eds. Advances in Metabolic Disorders, Vols. 1-6. Incl. Vol. 8. Somatomedins & Some Other Growth Factors. 1975. lib. bdg. 90.00 (0-12-027384-5); (Serial Publication Ser.). write for info. (0-318-50199-6) Acad Pr.

— Advances in Metabolic Disorders, Vols. 7-10. Incl. Vol. 8. Somatomedins & Some Other Growth Factors. 1975. lib. bdg. 90.00 (0-12-027384-5); (Serial Publication Ser.). write for info. (0-318-50198-8) Acad Pr.

Levine, R. A., jt. ed. see Lovenberg, Walter.

Levine, R. D., jt. auth. see Iachello, F.

Levine, R. L. & Fitgerald, H. E., eds. Analysis of Dynamic Psychological Systems, Vol. 1: Basic Approaches to General Systems, Dynamic Systems, & Cybernetics. (Illus.). 265p. 1992. 50.00 (0-306-43745-7, Plenum Pr) Plenum.

Levine, R. L. & Fitzgerald, Hiram E., eds. Analysis of Dynamic Psychological Systems, Vol. 2: Methods & Applications. (Illus.). 370p. 1992. 60.00 (0-306-43746-5, Plenum Pr) Plenum.

Levine, Raphael D. & Bernstein, Richard B. Molecular Reaction Dynamics & Chemical Reactivity. (Illus.). 552p. 1987. 49.95 (0-19-504139-9) OUP.

Levine, Rhonda F. Class Struggle & the New Deal: Industrial Labor, Industrial Capital, & the State. LC 88-17183. (Studies in Historical Social Change). 232p. 1988. 29.95 (0-7006-0373-5); pap. 14.95 (0-7006-0496-0) U Pr of KS.

Levine, Rhonda F. & Lembeke, Jerry, eds. Recapturing Marxism: An Appraisal of Recent Trends in Sociological Theory. LC 87-11589. 264p. 1987. text ed. 59.95 (0-275-92576-5, C2576, Praeger Pubs); pap. text ed. 14.95 (0-275-92638-9, B2638, Praeger Pubs) Greenwood.

Levine, Richard, jt. auth. see Halperin, Jonathan L.

Levine, Richard A., intro. The Victorian Experience: The Novelists. LC 75-15338. 273p. 1983. text ed. 18.95 (0-8214-0190-4) Ohio U Pr.

— The Victorian Experience: The Prose Writers. LC 81-22493. x, 239p. 1983. pap. 15.00x (0-8214-0707-4) Ohio U Pr.

Levine, Richard M. Bad Blood: A Family Murder in Marin County. 352p. 1983. pap. 4.50 (0-451-15503-3, Sig); pap. 4.99 (0-451-16321-4) NAL-Dutton.

Levine, Robert. AI & Expert Systems: A Comprehensive Guide, C Version. 1990. pap. text ed. 29.95 (0-07-037500-3) McGraw.

— Conspiracy & Romance: Studies in Brockden Brown, Cooper, Hawthorne & Melville. (Cambridge Studies in American Literature & Culture: No. 33). 317p. (C). 1989. 59.95 (0-521-36654-2) Cambridge U Pr.

LeVine, Robert. The Uniform Commercial Code: An Operational Translation. LC 80-68569. 1980. pap. 16.50 (0-933718-00-4) Browning Pubns.

Levine, Robert, ed. Formal Grammar: Theory & Implementation. (Vancouver Series in Cognitive Science). 456p. 1992. 75.00 (0-19-507314-2); pap. 39.95 (0-19-507310-X) OUP.

Levine, Robert, ed. & tr. A Thirteenth-Century Life of Charlemagne. LC 91-13581. (Library of Medieval Literature: Vol. 80A). 170p. 1991. 30.00 (0-8153-0397-1) Garland.

Levine, Robert, tr. France Before Charlemagne: A Translation from the Grandes Chroniques. LC 89-13819. (Studies in French Civilization: Vol. 3). 296p. 1990. lib. bdg. 89.95 (0-88946-640-8) E Mellen.

Levine, Robert & Lutyens, Elizabeth. Opera Small Talk: Pocket Plots, Crucial Characters, & Amusing Asides. LC 93-80148. (Illus.). 100p. 1993. pap. 9.95 (0-9638743-0-6) Cherubino Pr.

Levine, Robert, tr. see Minstrel of Reims.

Levine, Robert A. The Arms Debate. LC 63-17204. 364p. reprint ed. pap. 103.80 (0-7837-4478-1, 2044186) Bks Demand.

— The SDI Debate As a Continuation of History. (CISA Working Paper Ser.: No. 55). 57p. (Orig.). Date not set. pap. 10.00 (0-86682-070-1) Ctr Intl Relations.

— Still the Arms Debate. 420p. 1990. text ed. 52.95 (1-85521-071-1, Pub. by Dartmth Pub UK) Ashgate Pub Co.

— Uniform Deterrence of Nuclear First Use. LC 93-25248. 1993. 15.00 (0-8330-1401-3, MR-231) Rand Corp.

LeVine, Robert A., ed. Culture & Personality: Contemporary Readings. LC 79-16915. 466p. 1974. pap. text ed. 29.95 (0-202-01122-4) Aldine de Gruyter.

Levine, Robert A., ed. Transition & Turmoil in the Atlantic Alliance. 250p. 1991. 47.00 (0-8448-1701-5, Crane Russak); pap. 29.00 (0-8448-1702-3, Crane Russak) Taylor & Francis.

Levine, Robert A. & Stan, Peter J. Macroeconomic Strategy for the 1990's: Getting the Long Run Right. LC 93-6415. 1993. write for info. (0-8330-1449-8, MR-325-RC) Rand Corp.

An Asterisk (*) at the beginning of an entry indicates that the title is appearing in BIP for the first time.

LeVine, Robert A., et al. Child Care & Culture: Lessons from Africa. LC 93-33584. (Illus.). 304p. (C). 1994. 49.95 (*0-521-33171-4*) Cambridge U Pr.

Levine, Robert J. Ethics & Regulation of Clinical Research. LC 87-28955. 1988. 21.00 (*0-300-04288-4*) Yale U Pr.

Levine, Robert J., jt. auth. see Young, Brugruet L.

Levine, Robert M. Cuba in the 1850's: Through the Lens of Charles DeForest Fredricks. 86p. 1990. 24.95 (*0-8130-1010-1*) U Press Fla.

— Historical Dictionary of Brazil. LC 78-10178. (Latin American Historical Dictionaries Ser.: No. 19). 309p. 1979. lib. bdg. 27.50 (*0-8108-1178-2*) Scarecrow.

— Images of History: Nineteenth- & Early Twentieth-Century Latin American Photographs As Documents. LC 88-26741. (Illus.). 228p. 1989. lib. bdg. 75.50 (*0-8223-0883-5*) Duke.

— Images of History: Nineteenth- & Early Twentieth-Century Latin American Photographs As Documents. LC 88-26741. (Illus.). 228p. (C). 1990. reprint ed. pap. text ed. 36.95 (*0-8223-0999-8*) Duke.

— Pernambuco in the Brazilian Federation, 1889-1937. LC 76-47968. (Illus.). xxiv, 236p. 1978. 35.00 (*0-8047-0944-0*) Stanford U Pr.

— Race & Ethnic Relations in Latin America & the Caribbean: An Historical Dictionary & Bibliography. LC 80-15179. 260p. 1980. 22.50 (*0-8108-1324-6*) Scarecrow.

— Tropical Diaspora: The Jewish Experience in Cuba. LC 93-12542. (Illus.). 400p. (C). 1993. lib. bdg. 34.95 (*0-8130-1218-X*) U Press Fla.

— Vale of Tears: Revisiting the Canudos Massacre in Northeastern Brazil, 1893-1897. LC 91-36011. (C). 1992. 45.00 (*0-520-07524-2*) U CA Pr.

— Vale of Tears: Revisiting the Canudos Massacre in Northeastern Brazil, 1893-1897. 1995. pap. 15.95 (*0-520-20343-7*) U CA Pr.

— The Vargas Regime. LC 78-115222. (Institute of Latin American Studies). 270p. (C). 1970. text ed. 44.00 (*0-231-03370-2*) Col U Pr.

Levine, Robert M., ed. Windows on Latin America: Understanding Society Through Photographs. (Illus.). 194p. 1987. pap. 21.95 (*0-935501-06-1*, WL001) U Miami N-S Ctr.

***Levine, Robert M. & Sebe Bom Meihy, Jose C.** The Life & Death of Carolina Maria de Jesus. LC 95-4352. (Dialogos Ser.). (Illus.). 160p. 1995. 29.95x (*0-8263-1647-6*); pap. 15.95x (*0-8263-1648-4*) Free Spirit Pub.

Levine, Robert S. & Pagni, Patrick J. Fire Science for Fire Safety. (Combustion Science & Technology Ser.). 510p. 1984. pap. text ed. 169.00 (*2-88124-115-8*) Gordon & Breach.

Levine, Roz. Palmistry: How to Chart the Lines of Your Life. (Illus.). 128p. (Orig.). 1993. pap. 14.00 (*0-671-78501-X*, Fireside) S&S Trade.

— Seasonings. 366p. (Orig.). 1993. pap. 8.95 (*1-56245-075-1*) Great Quotations.

Levine, Ruth. Pharmacology: Drug Actions & Reactions. 3rd ed. (Illus.). 1983. 24.50 (*0-316-52222-8*) Little.

Levine, S., ed. Flight Vehicle Materials, Structures, & Dynamics, Vol. 3: Ceramics & Ceramic Matrix Composites. 1992. 105.00 (*0-685-70654-0*, 100322) ASME.

Levine, S. B. Sexual Life: A Clinician's Guide. (Critical Issues in Psychiatry Ser.). (Illus.). 265p. (C). 1992. 34.50 (*0-306-44287-6*, Plenum Pr) Plenum.

Levine, S. J., tr. see Infante, G. Cabrera.

Levine, S. N. Selected Papers on Desalination & Ocean Technology. (Illus.). 11.25 (*0-8446-2459-4*) Peter Smith.

Levine, Sally S. Oh Yes, I Still Will Write My Poem. Edelman, Ann B., ed. 57p. (Orig.). 1993. pap. 10.00 (*0-9637922-2-9*) Cherry Stne Bks.

Levine, Samuel. You Take Jesus, I'll Take God. LC 80-82731. 134p. (Orig.). 1980. pap. 5.95 (*0-9604754-1-9*) Hamoroh Pr.

Levine, Samuel P. Ham, Kosher Style! LC 79-89747. 1979. 9.95 (*0-9602906-1-3*); pap. 5.95 (*0-9602906-0-5*) S P Levine.

Levine, Sanford. The Two Hundred Forty-Seven Best Movie Scenes in Film History: A Filmgoer's Guide to Cigar Scenes, Car Chase Scenes, Haircut Scenes, Whistling Scenes, Dentist Scenes, Fluttering Drapes, Funny Walks, Mirrors, Name Mispronunciations, Parking Meters, Sagging Shoulders, Steambaths, & Numerous Other Scenes Long Noted by Aficionados. LC 91-50953. 192p. 1992. lib. bdg. 27.50x (*0-89950-671-2*) McFarland & Co.

LeVine, Sarah & Correa, Clara S. Dolor y Alegria: Women & Social Change in Urban Mexico. LC 92-39037. (Life Course Studies). (Illus.). 254p. (Orig.). 1993. 37.50 (*0-299-13790-2*); pap. 12.95 (*0-299-13794-5*) U of Wis Pr.

Levine, Saul V. Radical Departures: Desperate Detours to Growing Up. LC 83-26491. 216p. 1986. pap. 4.95 (*0-15-675799-0*, Harvest Bks) HarBrace.

Levine, Saul V. & Wilcox, Kathleen. Dear Doctor. LC 86-21335. 256p. (YA). (gr. 7 up). 1987. lib. bdg. 12.93 (*0-688-07094-9*) Lothrop.

Levine, Seymour. Cyclist's Guide to Overnight Stops: Central States. 1982. pap. 3.95 (*0-345-30116-1*) Ballantine.

— Cyclist's Guide to Overnight Stops: Eastern States. 448p. 1982. pap. 3.95 (*0-345-30115-3*) Ballantine.

Levine, Seymour & Ursin, Holger, eds. Coping & Health. LC 79-28833. (NATO Conference Series III, Human Factors: Vol. 12). 372p. 1980. 85.00 (*0-306-40422-2*, Plenum Pr) Plenum.

Levine, Seymour, jt. ed. see Brush, F. Robert.

Levine, Shar. The Paper Book & Paper Maker. LC 92-72021. (Illus.). 32p. (J). (gr. k-5). 1993. 12.95 (*1-56282-235-7*) Hyprn Child.

Levine, Shar & Grafton, Allison. Projects for a Healthy Planet: Simple Environmental Experiments for Kids. (J). 1992. pap. text ed. 10.95 (*0-471-55484-7*) Wiley.

— The Science Party Book: Simple Instructions for Spy Parties, Bubble Parties, & Much, Much More. 1994. pap. text ed. 10.95 (*0-471-59646-9*) Wiley.

***Levine, Shar & Johnstone, Leslie.** Everyday Science: Fun & Easy Projects for Making Practical Things. LC 94-24700. (J). 1995. pap. text ed. 9.95 (*0-471-11014-0*) Wiley.

— Silly Science: Strange & Startling Projects to Amaze Your Family & Friends. (J). 1995. pap. text ed. 9.95 (*0-471-11013-2*) Wiley.

Levine, Sherrie, et al. Art at the Edge! LC 88-81388. (Illus.). 24p. (Orig.). 1987. pap. 7.50 (*0-939802-49-X*) High Mus Art.

Levine, Shlomo D. The Singular Problems of the Single Jewish Parent. 39p. (Orig.). 1981. pap. text ed. 1.25 (*0-8381-2115-2*) United Synagogue.

Levine, Sol & Lilienfeld, Abraham M. Epidemiology & Health Policy. (Contemporary Issues in Health, Medicine & Social Policy Ser.). 290p. 1987. text ed. 37.50 (*0-422-78000-6*, Pub. by Tavistock UK); pap. text ed. 16.95 (*0-422-78010-3*, Pub. by Tavistock UK) Routledge Chapman & Hall.

Levine, Sol, jt. auth. see Croog, Sydney.

Levine, Stacey. My Horse & Other Stories. (New American Fiction Ser.: No. 28). 150p. (Orig.). 1990. pap. 11.95 (*1-55713-124-4*) Sun & Moon CA.

Levine, Stanley & Knight, Bud. Facades. 400p. 1988. pap. 3.95 (*0-8217-2511-4*) Zebra.

***Levine, Stephen.** Embracing the Beloved: Relationship as a Path of Awakening. LC 94-19871. 1995. 21.95 (*0-385-42526-0*) Doubleday.

— Gradual Awakening. 1989. mass mkt. 8.95 (*0-385-26218-3*, Anchor NY) Doubleday.

— Guided Meditations. 1991. 11.00 (*0-385-41737-3*, Anchor NY) Doubleday.

— Healing into Life & Death. 1989. mass mkt. 9.95 (*0-385-26219-1*, Anchor NY) Doubleday.

— Meetings at the Edge. 1989. mass mkt. 9.95 (*0-385-26220-5*, Anchor NY) Doubleday.

— Paper Trails: A Guide to Public Records in California. 1994. pap. 16.95 (*0-9621793-2-9*) CA News Pubs Assn.

— Who Dies? 1989. mass mkt. 9.95 (*0-385-26221-3*, Anchor NY) Doubleday.

Levine, Stephen, jt. auth. see Dass, Ram.

Levine, Stephen B., jt. ed. see Pariser, Stephen F.

Levine, Stephen R. Planning for Strikes: Obtaining Maximum Performance with Minimum Personnel. 54p. 1975. pap. 25.00 (*0-941496-00-7*) Model Cities.

Levine, Steve. A Blue Tongue. LC 76-14297. (Illus.). 24p. 1976. pap. 3.00 (*0-915124-19-X*, Toothpaste) Coffee Hse.

— The Cycles of Heaven. (Morning Coffee Chapbook Ser.). (Illus.). 11p. (Orig.). 1988. pap. 7.50 (*0-918273-38-2*) Coffee Hse.

— Pure Notations. LC 81-16404. (Illus.). 32p. (Orig.). 1981. pap. 6.00 (*0-915124-52-1*, Toothpaste) Coffee Hse.

— To & For. LC 92-3245. (Orig.). 1992. pap. 10.95 (*0-918273-71-4*) Coffee Hse.

Levine, Steve & Star, Brenda. Living with Live Foods: A Primer. (Illus.). (Orig.). 1994. pap. 12.00 (*1-884886-02-7*) Starr Pubng.

Levine, Steven I. Anvil of Victory: The Communist Revolution in Manchuria. LC 86-19821. (Illus.). 384p. 1987. text ed. 44.00 (*0-231-06436-5*) Col U Pr.

Levine, Steven I., jt. ed. see Hsiung, James C.

Levine, Steven I., tr. see Vishnyakova-Akimova, Vera V.

Levine, Steven P., jt. ed. see Martin, William F.

Levine, Steven Z. Claude Monet. LC 94-14642. (Rizzoli Art Ser.). (Illus.). 24p. 1994. 7.95 (*0-8478-1785-7*) Rizzoli Intl.

— Monet, Narcissus, & Self-Reflection: The Modernist Myth of the Self. LC 94-1105. 1994. lib. bdg. 70.00 (*0-226-47543-3*); pap. text ed. 29.95 (*0-226-47544-1*) U Ch Pr.

Levine, Steven Z., contrib. Warren Rohrer. (Illus.). 6p. 1991. pap. 2.00 (*1-879173-06-9*) Locks Gallery.

Levine, Stuart & Levine, Susan, eds. The Short Fiction of Edgar Allan Poe: An Annotated Edition. 672p. 1990. pap. 19.95 (*0-252-06125-X*) U of Ill Pr.

***Levine, Summer N. & Levine, Caroline.** Irwin Business & Investment Almanac 1995. 1994. 75.00 (*0-7863-0240-2*) Irwin Prof Pubng.

Levine, Summer N. & Levine, Caroline, eds. The Business One Irwin Business & Investment Almanac 1994. 18th ed. 750p. 1994. 75.00 (*1-55623-926-2*) Irwin Prof Pubng.

Levine, Sumner N. The Acquisitions Manual. 1989. 64.95 (*0-13-405929-8*) P-H.

Levine, Sumner N., ed. The Acquisitions Manual: A Guide to Negotiating & Executing Business Acquisitions. 1989. 64.95 (*0-317-03936-9*) NY Inst Finance.

— The Financial Analyst's Handbook. 2nd ed. 1870p. 1988. text ed. 120.00 (*0-87094-919-5*) Irwin Prof Pubng.

Levine, Sura & Landes, Joan. Representing Revolution: French & British Images, 1789-1804. (Illus.). 56p. 1989. pap. 12.00 (*0-914337-13-0*) Mead Art Mus.

***Levine, Susan.** Degrees of Equality: The American Association of University Women & The Challenge of Twentieth Century Feminism. LC 94-44693. (Critical Perspectives on the Past Ser.). 1995. 29.95 (*1-56639-326-4*) Temple U Pr.

— A Life in the Struggle: Ivory Perry & the Culture of Opposition. (Critical Perspectives on the Past Ser.). (Illus.). 328p. 1995. pap. 18.95 (*1-56639-321-3*) Temple U Pr.

Levine, Susan, jt. ed. see Levine, Stuart.

Levine, Susan P., et al. Recreation Experiences for the Severely Impaired or Nonambulatory Child. (Illus.). 96p. 1983. spiral bd. 19.95x (*0-398-04783-9*) C C Thomas.

Levine, Suzanne J. Subversive Scribe: Translating Latin American Fiction. 224p. 1991. pap. 12.00 (*1-55597-146-6*) Graywolf.

Levine, Suzanne J., tr. see Bioy-Casares, Adolfo.

Levine, Suzanne J., tr. see Bioy Casares, Adolfo.

Levine, Suzanne J., jt. auth. see Monegal, Emir R.

Levine, Suzanne J., tr. see Puig, Manuel.

Levine, Suzanne J., tr. see Rios, Julian.

Levine, Suzanne J., tr. see Sarduy, Severo.

Levine, Suzanne Jill, tr. see Sarduy, Severo.

Levine, Suzanne M. Medical Book of Remedies. 128p. (Orig.). 1995. pap. 3.99 (*0-451-18211-1*, Sig) NAL-Dutton.

— My Feet are Killing Me! 240p. 1988. reprint ed. pap. 5.99 (*0-449-21593-8*, Crest) Fawcett.

Levine, Suzanne M. & Sandroff, Ronni. Walk It Off: Twenty Minutes a Day to Health & Fitness. (Illus.). 224p. (Orig.). 1990. pap. 10.95 (*0-452-26535-5*, Plume) NAL-Dutton.

Levine, Sy. Discrete Semiconductors & Opto-Electronics. Levine, Esther & Worthing, Jerry, eds. (Library on Basic Electronics: Vol. 2). (Illus.). 356p. 1988. text ed. 35.00 (*0-939527-01-4*) Electro Horiz.

— Integrated Circuits & Computer Concepts. Levine, Esther & Worthing, Jerry, eds. (Library on Basic Electronics: Vol. 3). (Illus.). 320p. 1989. text ed. 35.00 (*0-939527-02-2*) Electro Horiz.

Levine, Sy, et al. Basic Concepts & Passive Components, Vol. 1. Levine, Esther & Worthing, Jerry, eds. LC 85-71203. (Library on Basic Electronics). (Illus.). 305p. 1986. text ed. 35.00 (*0-939527-00-6*) Electro Horiz.

LeVine, Terry Y., ed. Inka Storage Systems. LC 92-54157. (Illus.). 400p. 1992. 34.95 (*0-8061-2440-7*) U of Okla Pr.

Levine, Toby K., et al. The Africans: Study Guide. LC 85-28166. 1986. pap. text ed. 12.95 (*0-275-92074-7*, B2074, Praeger Pubs) Greenwood.

Levine, V. Colombia. 1976. lib. bdg. 59.95 (*0-8490-1641-X*) Gordon Pr.

Levine, Victor, jt. auth. see Allen, David N.

Levine, Victoria L., jt. auth. see Howard, James H.

Levine, W. G., ed. The Chelation of Heavy Metals. LC 77-30495. 1979. 108.00 (*0-08-017719-0*, Pub. by Pergamon Repr UK) Franklin.

Levine, W. S., et al, eds. Issues in Control of Urban Traffic Systems. LC 81-71830. 268p. 1982. pap. 50.00 (*0-939204-07-X*) Eng Found.

Leviner, Betty C., jt. auth. see Gilliam, Jan K.

Levinger, Beryl. Achieving Education for All: Nutrition, Health & School Performance. 72p. 1993. pap. text ed. write for info. (*0-9637044-3-5*) PACT Pubns.

— La Nutricion, la Salud y la Educacion para Todos. Vanderschoot, Fauvette, tr. (C). 1993. pap. write for info. (*0-9637044-4-3*) PACT Pubns.

Levinger, Elma E. Beautiful Garden & Other Bible Tales. (Illus.). (J). (gr. 3-5). 6.95 (*0-8197-0253-6*) Bloch.

Levinger, George & Raush, Harold L., eds. Close Relationships: Perspectives on the Meaning of Intimacy. LC 77-900. (Illus.). 208p. 1977. 27.50x (*0-87023-238-X*) U of Mass Pr.

Levinger, Larry. Thomas Merton: His Life & Times. 1989. 19.95 (*0-317-67534-6*) Harper SF.

***Levings, Charles S., III & Vasil, Indra K., eds.** The Molecular Biology of Plant Mitochondria. (Advances in Cellular & Molecular Biology of Plants: Vol. 3). 676p. (C). 1995. lib. bdg. 325.00 (*0-7923-3224-5*) Kluwer Ac.

Levingston, Bari R., jt. auth. see Kaspers, Candace B.

Levinkind, Susan, jt. auth. see Elias, Stephen.

***Levinon, Sanford, ed.** Responding to Imperfection: The Theory & Practice of Constitutional Amendment. LC 94-27766. 1994. pap. 18.95 (*0-691-02570-3*) Princeton U Pr.

— Responding to Imperfection: The Theory & Practice of Constitutional Amendment. LC 94-27766. 1995. 59.50 (*0-691-08657-5*) Princeton U Pr.

Levins, Bruce S., jt. auth. see Modesitt, Lee E., Jr.

Levins, Richard. Evolution in Changing Environments: Some Theoretical Explorations. LC 68-20871. (Monographs in Population Biology: No. 2). (Illus.). 130p. reprint ed. pap. 37.10 (*0-7837-0558-1*, 2040902) Bks Demand.

Levins, Richard & Lewontin, Richard C. The Dialectical Biologist. LC 84-22451. (Illus.). 336p. 1987. pap. 22.00 (*0-674-20283-X*) HUP.

Levins, Richard, jt. auth. see Haila, Yrjo.

Levins, Richard, jt. auth. see Puccia, Charles J.

Levinshtein, M. A Best of Soviet Semiconductor Physics & Technology (1989-1990) 900p. 1995. text ed. 109.00 (*981-02-1579-7*) World Scientific Pub.

Levinshtein, M., et al. Getting to Know Semiconductors. 200p. (C). 1992. text ed. 36.00 (*981-02-0760-3*) World Scientific Pub.

— Handbook Series on Semiconductor Parameters, Vol. 1. 300p. 1995. text ed. 99.00 (*981-02-1420-0*) World Scientific Pub.

Levinshtein, Mikhail, ed. Best of Soviet Semiconductor Physics & Technology, 1987-1988. 360p. 1991. 95.00 (*0-88318-782-5*); pap. 45.00 (*0-88318-783-3*) Am Inst Physics.

Levinskaja. Russian-Polish Dictionary. 320p. (POL & RUS.). 1981. 14.95 (*0-8288-0488-5*, F 47670) Fr & Eur.

Levinskii, N. N. & Mkrtchian, G. A. Russian-English Technical Dictionary of Defects & Breakdowns. 334p. 1985. 59.00 (*0-317-42707-5*, Pub. by Collets UK) Pro-Am Music.

Levinsky, Jeff, jt. auth. see Targ, Joan.

Levinsky, Norman, jt. auth. see Wilkins, Richard.

Levinsky, Norman G., ed. see Institute of Medicine, Committee for the Study of the Medicare ESRD Program Staff.

Levinsky, Ruth. Nathalie Sarraute & Fedor Dostoevsky: Their Philosophy, Psychology, & Literary Techniques. (Graduate Studies: No. 3). 44p. (Orig.). 1973. pap. 2.00 (*0-89672-010-1*) Tex Tech Univ Pr.

Levinsky, Sara A. & Steindl-Rast, David. A Bridge of Dreams: The Story of Paramananda, a Modern Mystic. LC 83-82698. (Illus.). 632p. (Orig.). 1984. pap. 12.95 (*0-940262-12-6*) Lindisfarne Pr.

Levinsohn, Allan G., jt. auth. see Huxhold, William E.

***Levinsohn, Florence H.** Belgrade: Among the Serbs. 337p. 1994. 27.50 (*1-56663-061-4*) I R Dee.

Levinsohn, Florence H. & Wright, Benjamin D., eds. School Desegregation: Shadow & Substance. LC 76-17291. 224p. reprint ed. pap. 63.90 (*0-685-15771-7*, 2026781) Bks Demand.

Levinsohn, Mark E., jt. auth. see Martire, Joseph R.

Levinsohn, Stephen, ed. Discourse Features of Ten Languages of West- Central Africa. LC 94-67160. (Publications in Linguistics). (Orig.). Date not set. pap. write for info. (*0-88312-619-2*); fiche write for info. (*1-55671-983-3*) Summer Instit Ling.

Levinsohn, Stephen H. The Inga Language. (Janua Linguarum, Series Practica: No. 188). (Illus.). (Orig.). 1976. pap. text ed. 44.65 (*90-279-3381-2*) Mouton.

— Textual Connections in Acts. LC 86-20238. (Society of Biblical Literature Monographs). 197p. 1987. 30.95 (*1-55540-060-4*, 06-00-31); pap. 19.95 (*1-55540-061-2*) Scholars Pr GA.

Levinson. Devil's Creek. (Pecos Kid Ser.: No. 5). 1994. mass mkt. 3.50 (*0-06-100656-4*, Harp PBks) HarpC.

— Electronic Ceramics: Properties, Devices & Applications. (Electrical Engineering & Electronics Ser.: Vol. 44). 552p. 1987. 160.00 (*0-8247-7761-1*) Dekker.

— Encyclopedia of Marriage & the Family, 2 vols. Incl. Encyclopedia of Marriage & the Family Vol. 1. 1995. 75.00 (*0-02-897236-8*); Encyclopedia of Marriage & the Family Vol. 2. 1995. 75.00 (*0-02-897237-6*); 150.00 (*0-02-897235-X*) Macmillan.

***Levinson & Bodensteiner.** Civil Rights Legislation & Litigation, 1994. 682p. Date not set. ring bd. 48.50 (*1-879581-16-7*) Lupus Pubns.

Levinson, jt. auth. see Ember.

Levinson, A. A., ed. Apollo Eleven Lunar Science Conference, Jan., 1970: Proceedings, 3 vols, Set. Incl. Vol. 1. Mineralogy & Petrology. LC 72-119485. 1970. (*0-318-55135-7*); Vol. 2. Chemical & Isotope Analysis. LC 72-119485. 1970. (*0-318-55136-5*); Vol. 3. Physical Properties. LC 72-119485. 1970. (*0-318-55137-3*); LC 72-119485. c, 2000p. 1970. 1,032.00 (*0-08-016392-0*, Pub. by Pergamon Repr UK) Franklin.

Levinson, A. A. & Taylor, Ross. Moon Rocks & Minerals. 240p. 1971. 98.00 (*0-08-016669-5*, Pub. by Pergamon Repr UK) Franklin.

Levinson, A. A., ed. see Beus, A. A. & Grigorian, S. V.

Levinson, A. A., jt. auth. see Lunar Science Institute Staff.

Levinson, A. A., et al. Practical Problems in Exploration Geochemistry. LC 86-72694. (Illus.). 269p. 1987. 80.00 (*0-915834-05-7*) Applied Pub.

Levinson, Abraham. The Mentally Retarded Child. enl. rev. ed. LC 77-25884. (Illus.). 187p. 1978. reprint ed. text ed. 48.50 (*0-313-20123-4*, LEMR, Greenwood Pr) Greenwood.

Levinson, Andre. Andre Levinson on Dance: Writings from Paris in the Twenties. Garafola, Lynn, ed. LC 90-50911. (Illus.). 174p. 1991. 25.00 (*0-8195-5227-5*, Wesleyan Univ Pr) U Pr of New Eng.

— Bakst: The Story of the Artist's Life. LC 68-57182. (Illus.). 1978. reprint ed. 36.95 (*0-405-08233-9*) Ayer.

— Ballet Old & New. Summer, Susan C., tr. LC 81-70095. 144p. 1982. pap. 15.95 (*0-87127-130-3*, Dance Horizons) Princeton Bk Co.

Levinson, Arnold I. New Directions in the Clinical Use of Intravenous Immunoglobulin, Vol. II. (Illus.). 60p. 1990. write for info. (*0-318-65780-5*) Health Dimensions.

Levinson, Arnold I. & Paterson, Yvonne, eds. Molecular & Cellular Biology of the Allergic Response. LC 94-4449. (Clinical Allergy & Immunology Ser.: Vol. 3). 464p. 1994. 150.00 (*0-8247-8876-1*) Dekker.

Levinson, Arthur T. The Web of Their Lives: Macbeth & Human Greatness. 120p. 1984. pap. 7.95 (*0-9613268-0-8*) Byrnam Pr.

Levinson, Barry. Avalon, Tin Men, & Diner: Three Screenplays. 1990. pap. 12.95 (*0-87113-435-7*) Grove-Atltic.

— Levinson on Levinson. Thompson, David, ed. (Illus.). 170p. (Orig.). 1993. pap. 11.95 (*0-571-16731-4*) Faber & Faber.

***Levinson, Bradley A., et al, eds.** The Cultural Production of the Educated Person: Critical Ethnographiew of Schooling & Local Practice. (SUNY Series, Power, Social Identity, & Education). 384p. (C). 1996. text ed. 74.50x (*0-7914-2859-1*); pap. text ed. 24.95x (*0-7914-2860-5*) State U NY Pr.

Levinson, Charles. Food & Beverage Operations: Cost Control Systems Management. 2nd ed. 336p. 1988. text ed. 70.00 (*0-13-322819-3*) P-H.

— Industry's Democratic Revolution. 350p. 1974. 25.00 (*0-8464-1322-1*) Beekman Pubs.

Levinson, Charles, jt. auth. see Kotschevar, Lendal H.

Levinson, D., jt. auth. see Kane, T. R.

Levinson, Daniel J., et al. The Seasons of a Man's Life. LC 77-20978. 1978. 24.95 (*0-394-40694-X*) Knopf.

— The Seasons of a Man's Life. 1986. pap. 12.00 (*0-345-33901-0*, Ballantine Trade) Ballantine.

Levinson, Daniel R., et al. Using Alternative Dispute Resolution in the Federal Government. 40p. 1993. pap. text ed. 9.95 (*0-936295-41-4*) FPMI Comns.

Levinson, David. Aggression & Conflict. (Human Experience Ser.). 240p. 1994. lib. bdg. 49.50 (*0-87436-728-X*) ABC-CLIO.

An Asterisk (*) at the beginning of an entry indicates that the title is appearing in BIP for the first time.

— Ethnic Relations. (Human Experience Ser.). 304p. 1995. lib. bdg. 49.50 (*0-87436-735-2*) ABC-CLIO.
— Family Violence in Cross-Cultural Perspectives. (Frontiers of Anthropology Ser.: Vol. 1). 200p. (C). 1989. text ed. 49.95 (*0-8039-3075-5*); pap. text ed. 24.00 (*0-8039-3076-3*) Sage.
— Human Environments. (Human Experience Ser.). 350p. 1995. lib. bdg. 49.50 (*0-87436-784-0*) ABC-CLIO.
Levinson, David, ed. The Encyclopedia of World Cultures: Sponsored by the Human Relations Area Files at Yale University, 10 vols. (Illus.). 6500p. 1994. 800.00 (*0-685-40448-X*, Hall Reference) Macmillan.
— The Encyclopedia of World Cultures: Sponsored by the Human Relations Area Files at Yale University, 10 vols., Set. (Illus.). 6500p. 1995. text ed. 800.00 (*0-8161-1840-X*, Hall Reference) Macmillan.
— A Guide to Alcoholism Treatment Research. Incl. Vol. I Behavioral Medicine - Behavior Modification. 525p. (Orig.). 1981. pap. 45.00 (*0-87536-736-4*); Vol. III, Alcoholics Anonymous & Counseling. 553p. (Orig.). 1984. 45.00 (*0-87536-740-2*); (Theoretical Information Control Guides Ser.). write for info. (*0-318-57544-2*) HRAFP.
— A Guide to Alcoholism Treatment Research, Vol. 2. LC 82-105273. (HRAF Theoretical Information Control System Ser.: No. 4). 494p. reprint ed. pap. 140.80 (*0-685-15373-8*, 2027172) Bks Demand.
— A Guide to Social Theory: Worldwide Cross-Cultural Tests, 5 vols. 1700p. 1978. 495.00 (*0-317-34231-2*) HRAFP.
Levinson, David & Human Relations Area Files at Yale University & Staff, eds. The Encyclopedia of World Cultures Vol. 2: Oceania, Vol. 2. large type ed. 650p. 1991. text ed. 100.00 (*0-8161-1809-4*, Hall Reference) Macmillan.
Levinson, David & Malone, Martin J. Toward Explaining Human Culture: A Critical Review of the Findings of Worldwide Cross-Cultural Research. LC 80-83324. (Comparative Studies). 412p. 1980. 25.00 (*0-87536-339-3*) HRAFP.
Levinson, David & O'Leary, Timothy J., eds. The Encyclopedia of World Cultures, Vol. 1: North America. large type ed. 600p. 1991. text ed. 100.00 (*0-8161-1808-6*, Hall Reference) Macmillan.
Levinson, David & Sherwood, David. The Tribal Living Book: One Hundred Fifty Things to Do & Make from Traditional Cultures. rev. ed. LC 93-10533. (Illus.). 240p. 1993. pap. 16.95 (*1-55566-104-1*) Johnson Bks.
Levinson, David, ed. see Yale University Staff.
Levinson, Debra. The Truth about Chiropractic. (Illus.). 1993. 39.95 (*0-9633577-0-0*) Max Pubns.
Levinson, Deidre. Modus Vivendi. (Contemporary American Fiction Ser.). 112p. 1985. mass mkt. 6.95 (*0-14-008097-X*, Penguin Bks) Viking Penguin.
Levinson, E. D. Architectural Rendering. LC 82-17151. 256p. 1983. text ed. 29.95 (*0-07-037413-9*) McGraw.
Levinson, Edward. I Break Strikes: The Technique of Pearl L. Bergoff. LC 75-89750. (American Labor, from Conspiracy to Collective Bargaining Ser., No. 1). 314p. 1974. reprint ed. 21.95 (*0-405-02137-2*) Ayer.
— Labor on the March. (Literature of American Labor Ser.). 344p. 1995. pap. 14.95 (*0-87546-340-1*) ILR Pr.
— Labor on the March. 329p. 1993. reprint ed. lib. bdg. 89.00 (*0-7812-5249-0*) Rprt Serv.
Levinson, Edward M. Transdisciplinary Vocational Assessment: Issues in School-based Programs. LC 92-53226. 1993. pap. 42.50 (*0-88422-118-0*) Clinical Psych.
Levinson, Ellis. Hiring Contractors Without Going Through Hell: How to Find, Hire, Supervise, & Pay Professional Help. 174p. (Orig.). 1992. 23.95 (*0-8027-1194-4*); pap. 14.95 (*0-8027-7381-8*) Walker & Co.
Levinson, F. James. Addressing Malnutrition in Africa: Low-Cost Possibilities for Government Agencies & Donors. (Social Dimensions of Adjustment in Sub-Saharan Africa Working Paper Ser.: No. 13). 44p. 1991. 6.95 (*0-8213-1897-7*, 11897) World Bank.
Levinson, Frederick. The Gospel at Infant Baptism. pap. 4.95 (*0-7152-0443-2*) Outlook.
Levinson, Gerald B., jt. auth. see Laurenzi, Elise.
Levinson, Gershon, jt. auth. see Shnider, Sol M.
Levinson, Hanna, jt. auth. see Reif, Joseph A.
Levinson, Harold M. Collective Bargaining by British Local Authority Employees. LC 74-634398. (Comparative Studies in Public Employment Labor Relations Ser.). 1971. 10.00 (*0-87736-013-8*); pap. 5.00 (*0-87736-014-6*) U of Mich Inst Labor.
— Collective Bargaining by Public Employees in Sweden. LC 72-619516. (Comparative Studies in Public Employment Labor Relations Ser.). 120p. 1972. 10.00 (*0-87736-023-5*); pap. 5.00 (*0-87736-024-3*) U of Mich Inst Labor.
Levinson, Harold N. A Scientific Watergate - Dyslexia: How & Why Countless Millions Are Deprived of Breakthrough Medical Treatment. LC 93-87064. (Illus.). 456p. 1994. 24.95 (*0-9639303-0-3*) Stonebrdge Pubng.
— Smart but Feeling Dumb. LC 84-40090. 256p. 1988. pap. 10.95 (*0-446-38841-6*) Warner Bks.
— Smart But Feeling Dumb. rev. ed. 320p. 1994. pap. 11.99 (*0-446-39545-5*) Warner Bks.
— Total Concentration: How to Understand Attention Deficit Disorder, Maximize Your Mental Energy, & Reach Your Full Potential. LC 90-48943. 1990. 18.95 (*0-87131-595-5*) M Evans.
— Total Concentration: How to Understand Attention Deficit Disorder, Maximize Your Mental Energy, & Reach Your Full Potential. 1992. pap. 11.95 (*0-87131-708-7*) M Evans.
— Turning Around: The Upside-Down Kids, Helping Dyslexic Kids Overcome Their Disorder. LC 92-13440. 1992. 17.95 (*0-87131-700-1*) M Evans.
— Upside-down Kids. LC 91-4420. 164p. 1991. 17.95 (*0-87131-625-0*) M Evans.
Levinson, Harold N. & Carter, Steven. Phobia Free: A Medical Breakthrough Linking Ninety Percent of all Phobias & Panic Attacks to a Hidden Physical Problem. LC 86-6303. 300p. 1986. pap. 8.95 (*0-87131-539-4*) M Evans.
Levinson, Harry. Career Mastery: Keys to Taking Charge of Your Career Throughout Your Work Life. LC 92-20192. 240p. (Orig.). 1992. pap. 15.95 (*1-881052-05-2*) Berrett-Koehler.
— Casebook for Psychological Man. LC 82-8955. 208p. (C). 1982. teacher ed 6.95 (*0-916516-05-9*); pap. 6.95 (*0-916516-04-0*) Levinson Inst.
— Emotional Health in the World of Work. rev. ed. LC 63-20323. 298p. 1964. pap. 8.95 (*0-916516-03-2*) Levinson Inst.
— The Exceptional Executive: A Psychological Conception. LC 68-25615. 307p. reprint ed. pap. 87.50 (*0-7837-1713-X*, 2057242) Bks Demand.
— Executive. rev. ed. LC 80-26107. 382p. 1982. pap. 18.50 (*0-674-27396-6*) HUP.
— Psychological Man. LC 76-2583. 147p. (Orig.). (C). 1976. pap. text ed. 6.95 (*0-916516-02-4*) Levinson Inst.
— Ready, Fire, Aim: Avoiding Management by Impulse. LC 86-10593. 304p. 1986. 25.00 (*0-916516-06-7*); pap. 9.95 (*0-916516-07-5*) Levinson Inst.
Levinson, Harry, ed. Designing & Managing Your Career. 1989. text ed. 29.95 (*0-07-103249-5*) McGraw.
Levinson, Harry, et al. Organizational Diagnosis. LC 71-168429. (Illus.). 575p. 1976. pap. 21.00 (*0-674-64346-1*) HUP.
Levinson, Henry S. The Religious Investigations of William James. LC 80-26109. 323p. reprint ed. pap. 92.10 (*0-7837-3767-X*, 2043584) Bks Demand.
— Santayana, Pragmatism, & the Spiritual Life. LC 91-50785. (Illus.). xvi, 348p. (C). 1992. 45.00 (*0-8078-2031-8*) U of NC Pr.
— Science, Metaphysics, & the Chance of Salvation: An Interpretation of the Thought of William James. LC 78-7383. (American Academy of Religion. Dissertation Ser.: No. 24). 266p. reprint ed. pap. 75.90 (*0-7837-5467-1*, 2045232) Bks Demand.
Levinson, Henry S. & Kern, Montague. The Religious Investigations of William James. LC 80-26109. (Studies in Religion). xii, 316p. 1981. 32.50 (*0-8078-1468-7*) U of NC Pr.
Levinson, I. B. & Nikitin, A. A. Handbook for Theoretical Computation of Line Intensities. 248p. 1965. text ed. 67.50 (*0-7065-0545-X*, Pub. by Keter Pub IS) Coronet Bks.
Levinson, Irving J. Introduction to Mechanics. 2nd ed. (C). 1968. text ed. 62.00 (*0-13-487660-1*) P-H.
— Preparing for the Engineer-in-Training Examination. 3rd ed. LC 82-18251. 242p. 1992. 18.50 (*0-910554-85-4*) Engineering.
— Statics & Strength of Materials. (C). 1970. text ed. 79.00 (*0-13-844506-0*) P-H.
Levinson, James H. Another Line. 145p. 1990. pap. 7.50 (*0-922820-03-1*) Watermark Pr.
Levinson, Jay A., et al. Early Italian Engravings from the National Gallery of Art. (Illus.). 616p. 1973. pap. 150.00 (*1-55660-188-3*) A Wofsy Fine Arts.
Levinson, Jay C. Earning Money Without a Job. rev. ed. 1991. pap. 9.95 (*0-8050-1458-6*, Owl) H Holt & Co.
— Five Hundred Fifty-Five Ways to Earn Extra Money. rev. ed. LC 81-47471. 432p. (Orig.). 1992. pap. 14.95 (*0-8050-1459-4*, Owl) H Holt & Co.
— Guerilla Marketing Attack. 1989. 17.95 (*0-318-41374-4*); pap. 7.95 (*0-318-41375-2*) HM.
— Guerilla Marketing for the Nineties: The Newest Secrets for Making Big Profits from Your Small Business. LC 93-22334. 1993. pap. 12.95 (*0-395-64496-8*) HM.
— Guerrilla Advertising: Cost-Effective Tactics for Small Business Success. 1994. pap. 11.95 (*0-395-68718-7*) HM.
— Guerrilla Marketing. 1985. pap. 7.95 (*0-685-10137-1*) HM.
— Guerrilla Marketing Attack: New Strategies, Tactics, & Weapons for Winning Big Profits. 224p. 1989. pap. 10.95 (*0-395-50220-9*) HM.
— Guerrilla Marketing Excellence: The 50 Golden Rules for Small Business Success. LC 92-20533. 288p. 1993. pap. 11.95 (*0-395-60844-9*) HM.
— Guerrilla Marketing Weapons: 100 Affordable Marketing Methods for Maximizing Profits from Your Small Business. 240p. 1990. pap. 11.95 (*0-452-26519-3*, Plume) NAL-Dutton.
— The Ninety Minute Hour: Combining Time-Saving Technology with New Age Psychology to Take You Beyond Time Management. 1990. 17.95 (*0-317-02816-2*, Dutton) NAL-Dutton.
Levinson, Jay C. & Godin, Seth. The Guerilla Marketing Handbook. (Illus.). 304p. 1994. pap. 16.95 (*0-395-70013-2*) HM.
***Levinson, Jay C. & Rubin, Charles.** Guerrilla Marketing On-Line: The Entrepreneur's Guide to Earning Profits on the Internet. LC 95-6335. 320p. 1995. pap. 12.95 (*0-395-72859-2*) HM.
Levinson, Jay C., jt. auth. see Blechman, Bruce J.
Levinson, Jerome I. Unrequited Toil: Denial of Labor Rights in Mexico & Implications for NAFTA. Reding, Andrew A., ed. (North America Project Special Report Ser.). 28p. 1993. 5.00 (*0-911646-53-1*) World Policy.
— World's Bankers: The Multilateral Financial Institutions in the 1900's. 1993. pap. 9.95 (*0-87078-181-2*) TCFP-PPP.
Levinson, Jerrold. Music, Art, & Metaphysics: Essays in Philosophical Aesthetics. LC 90-55138. (Illus.). 432p. 1991. 52.50 (*0-8014-2342-2*); pap. 17.95 (*0-8014-9591-1*) Cornell U Pr.
Levinson, Jock. Embroidery: A Beginner's Workshop. (Illus.). 64p. 1993. pap. 12.95 (*1-86351-086-9*, Pub. by S Milner AT) Sterling.
Levinson, Joel B. Pittsburgh Pictorial Tour Guide. 24p. 1990. 3.75 (*0-914355-07-4*) J B Jeffers.
Levinson, Joel B., et al. Pittsburgh: Views Between the Rivers. (Illus.). 68p. 1991. pap. 12.50 (*0-914355-10-4*) J B Jeffers.
Levinson, John M. & Headley, Somers G. Shorebirds: The Birds, the Hunters, the Decoys. LC 91-50581. (Illus.). 160p. 1991. 49.95 (*0-87033-424-7*, Tidewtr Pubs) Cornell Maritime.
Levinson, L. Fundamentals of Engineering Mechanics. (Russian Monographs & Texts on the Physical Sciences). 336p. 1965. text ed. 255.00 (*0-677-20250-4*) Gordon & Breach.
Levinson, L. Harold. State Administrative Law. write for info. (*0-318-59313-0*) Little.
Levinson, L. Harold, jt. auth. see England, Arthur J., Jr.
Levinson, Lionel M. & Hirano, Shin-ichi, eds. Grain Boundaries & Interfacial Phenomena in Electronic Ceramics. LC 94-4933. (Ceramic Transactions Ser.: Vol. 41). 390p. 1994. 83.00 (*0-944904-73-4*, 1EBK00D) Am Ceramic.
***Levinson, Luisa M.** The Two Siblings & Other Stories. Miller, Yvette E., ed. Lipp, Sylvia E., tr. (Discoveries Ser.). 130p. Date not set. pap. 15.95 (*0-935480-74-9*) Lat Am Lit Rev Pr.
***Levinson, Luna, ed.** Mathematics, Science & Technology Education Programs That Work: A Collection of Exemplary Educational Programs & Practices in the National Diffusion Network. 145p. (Orig.). (C). 1994. pap. text ed. 30.00x (*0-7881-1525-1*) Diane Pub.
Levinson, Marc. Beyond Free Markets: The Revival of Activist Economics. LC 87-45775. 224p. 1990. pap. 12.95 (*0-669-16973-0*) Free Pr.
Levinson, Marc, jt. auth. see Aho, C. Michael.
Levinson, Marilyn. The Fourth-Grade Four. LC 89-31109. (Illus.). 64p. (J). (gr. 2-4). 1991. pap. 4.95 (*0-8050-1640-6*, Owlet BYR) H Holt & Co.
— No Boys Allowed. LC 93-22335. (Illus.). 128p. (J). (gr. 5-8). 1993. lib. bdg. 13.95 (*0-8167-3135-7*); pap. 2.95 (*0-8167-3136-5*) BrdgeWater.
Levinson, Marjorie. The Romantic Fragment Poem: A Critique of a Form. LC 85-28927. x, 268p. 1986. 34.95 (*0-8078-1684-1*) U of NC Pr.
Levinson, Micheal S. The Book of Lev It a Kiss, Kislev. 96p. 1972. pap. 3.00 (*0-685-26765-2*) Hse ov Day Vid.
Levinson, Nadine, jt. auth. see Schuker, Eleanor.
Levinson, Nancy & Rucklin, Joanne. Feeling Great: Reaching Out to the World, Reaching in to Yourself - Without Drugs. 2nd ed. 112p. 1991. reprint ed. lib. bdg. 23.00x (*0-8095-6322-3*) Borgo Pr.
Levinson, Nancy S. Chuck Yeager the Man Who Broke the Sound Barrier. LC 87-25431. 133p. (J). (gr. 5 up). 1988. 13.95 (*0-8027-6781-8*); lib. bdg. 14.85 (*0-8027-6799-0*) Walker & Co.
— Clara & the Bookwagon. LC 86-45773. (Harper I Can Read Bk.). (Illus.). 64p. (J). (gr. k-3). 1988. lib. bdg. 14.89 (*0-06-023838-0*) HarpC Child Bks.
— Clara & the Bookwagon. LC 86-45773. (Trophy I Can Read Bk.). (Illus.). 64p. (J). (gr. k-3). 1991. pap. 3.50 (*0-06-444134-2*, Trophy) HarpC Child Bks.
— Snowshoe Thompson. LC 90-37401. (I Can Read Bk.). (Illus.). 64p. (J). (gr. k-3). 1992. 14.95 (*0-06-023801-1*); lib. bdg. 14.89 (*0-06-023802-X*) HarpC Child Bks.
— Sweet Notes, Sour Notes. LC 92-19549. (Illus.). 64p. (J). (gr. 2-5). 1993. 12.99 (*0-525-67379-2*, Lodestar Bks) NAL-Dutton.
— Turn of the Century: Our Nation One Hundred Years Ago. LC 93-4604. (Illus.). 144p. (J). (gr. 5-9). 1994. 16.99 (*0-525-67433-0*, Lodestar Bks) Dutton Child Bks.
Levinson, Nancy S. & Rocklin, Joanne. Feeling Great: Reaching Out to the World, Reaching in to Yourself--Without Drugs. 2nd rev. ed. LC 92-16217. (Illus.). 112p. (YA). (gr. 8-12). 1992. pap. 7.95 (*0-89793-087-8*) Hunter Hse.
Levinson, Norma. Paper Children. large type ed. 560p. 1988. 15.95 (*0-7089-1852-2*) Ulverscroft.
Levinson, Norman. Gap & Density Theorems. LC 41-6147. (Colloquium Publications: Vol. 26). 246p. 1991. 34.00 (*0-8218-1026-X*, COLL-26) Am Math.
Levinson, Norman & Redheffer, Raymond. Complex Variables. 1988. text ed. write for info. (*0-07-037492-9*); Solutions manual. pap. text ed. write for info. (*0-07-037493-7*) McGraw.
Levinson, Norman, jt. auth. see Coddington, Earl A.
Levinson, Orde. The African Dream: Themes & Images of John Muafangejo. LC 92-70865. (Illus.). 120p. 1993. pap. 14.95 (*0-500-27682-X*) Thames Hudson.
Levinson, Orde, ed. & comp. John Piper: The Complete Graphic Works. (Illus.). 144p. 1988. 70.00 (*0-571-14990-1*) Faber & Faber.
Levinson, Paul. Electronic Chronicles: Columns of the Changes in Our Time. LC 92-18689. 224p. (Orig.). 1992. pap. 14.95 (*0-9631203-3-6*) Anamnesis Pr.
— Mind at Large: Knowing in the Technological Age. 271p. 1988. 73.25 (*0-89232-816-9*) Jai Pr.
Levinson, Ralph, ed. Teaching Science. LC 93-17467. 1994. write for info. (*0-415-10253-7*) Routledge.
Levinson, Richard & Link, William. Rehearsal for Murder. 1983. 4.95 (*0-87129-279-3*, R36) Dramatic Pub.
Levinson, Riki. Boys Here - Girls There. LC 92-5321. (Illus.). (J). 1993. 13.00 (*0-525-67374-1*, Lodestar Bks) Dutton Child Bks.
— Grandpa's Hotel. LC 94-45915. (Illus.). 32p. (J). (gr. k-3). 1995. 14.95 (*0-531-09475-8*); lib. bdg. 14.99 (*0-531-08775-1*) Orchard Bks Watts.
— I Go with My Family to Grandma's. LC 86-4490. (Unicorn Paperbacks Ser.). (Illus.). 32p. (J). (ps-1). 1986. pap. 3.95 (*0-525-44557-9*, DCB) Dutton Child Bks.
— I Go with My Family to Grandma's. (J). (ps-3). 1992. pap. 4.99 (*0-14-054762-2*) Puffin Bks.
— Mira Como Salen las Estrellas. (Illus.). 32p. (SPA.). (J). (ps-3). 1992. 15.99 (*0-525-44958-2*, DCB) Dutton Child Bks.
— Mira Como Salen las Estrellas. (Illus.). 32p. (SPA.). (J). 1995. pap. 4.99 (*0-14-055505-6*) Puffin Bks.
— Our Home Is the Sea. LC 87-36419. (Illus.). 32p. (J). (gr. k-3). 1988. pap. 13.95 (*0-525-44406-8*, DCB) Dutton Child Bks.
— Our Home Is the Sea. (Illus.). 32p. (J). (gr. k-3). 1992. pap. 4.99 (*0-14-054552-2*, Puff Unicorn) Puffin Bks.
— Soon, Annala. LC 92-44588. (Illus.). 32p. (J). (ps-2). 1993. 14.95 (*0-531-05494-2*) Orchard Bks Watts.
— Soon, Annala. LC 92-44588. (Illus.). 32p. (J). (ps-2). 1993. lib. bdg. 14.99 (*0-531-08644-5*) Orchard Bks Watts.
— Watch the Stars Come Out. LC 84-28672. (Illus.). 32p. (J). (ps-3). 1985. 15.00 (*0-525-44205-7*, DCB) Dutton Child Bks.
— Watch the Stars Come Out. (Illus.). 32p. (J). 1995. pap. 4.99 (*0-14-055506-4*) Puffin Bks.
Levinson, Risha. Information & Referral Networks: Doorways to Human Services. (Social Work Ser.). 256p. (C). 1987. 27.95 (*0-8261-4820-4*) Springer Pub.
Levinson, Risha W. & Haynes, Karen S., eds. Accessing Human Services: International Perspectives. LC 84-16012. (Social Science Delivery Systems Ser.: No. 7). 320p. reprint ed. pap. 91.20 (*0-8357-4820-0*, 2037757) Bks Demand.
Levinson, Robert. The Jews in the California Gold Rush. 2nd ed. (Illus.). 1994. pap. write for info. (*0-943376-62-9*) Magnes Mus.
Levinson, Robert, jt. ed. see Epstein, Susan.
Levinson, Robert E. Super Savvy: How to Get It, How to Use It, How to Make A Fortune with It! Lauer, Mark T., ed. LC 94-14016. 256p. 1994. pap. 14.95 (*1-880539-29-2*) Garrett FL.
Levinson, Robin, jt. auth. see Treiser, Susan.
Levinson, Robin K., jt. auth. see Sherrer, Yvonne.
Levinson, Ronald B., ed. see Plato.
Levinson, Rosalie B., jt. auth. see Bodensteiner, Ivan E.
Levinson, Samuel A. & MacFate, Robert P. Clinical Laboratory Diagnosis. 7th ed. LC 68-18867. 1343p. reprint ed. pap. 180.00 (*0-317-28597-1*, 2055436) Bks Demand.
Levinson, Sandra & Bruscia, Kenneth. A Curriculum for Teaching Optacon Music Reading. (Illus.). 140p. (Orig.). 1984. teacher ed 30.00 (*0-9614080-7-3*) Tembrook Pr.
Levinson, Sanford. Constitutional Faith. 216p. (Orig.). 1990. text ed. 42.50 (*0-691-07769-X*); pap. text ed. 13.95 (*0-691-02321-2*) Princeton U Pr.
Levinson, Sanford, jt. auth. see Brest, Paul.
Levinson, Sanford, jt. ed. see Mailloux, Steven.
Levinson, Sanford, ed. see McCloskey, Robert G.
Levinson, Stephen C. Pragmatics. LC 82-14701. (Cambridge Textbooks in Linguistics Ser.). 325p. 1983. pap. 29.95 (*0-521-29414-2*) Cambridge U Pr.
Levinson, Stephen C., jt. auth. see Brown, Penelope.
Levinson, Warren E. & Jawetz, Ernest. Medical Microbiology & Immunology: Examination & Board Review. 3rd ed. (Illus.). 529p. 1994. pap. text ed. 28.95 (*0-8385-6242-6*, A6242-0) Appleton & Lange.
Levinson, William A. Study Guide for Engineering & the Physical Sciences. (Illus.). 101p. (Orig.). 1988. pap. text ed. 7.00 (*0-913811-04-1*) Northeast A S.
— The Way of Strategy. LC 94-6143. 1994. 29.95 (*0-87389-227-5*) ASQC Qual Pr.
— The Way of Strategy. 1995. 24.95 (*0-87389-228-3*) Irwin.
Levinson, Y. B., jt. auth. see Gantmakher, V. F.
Levinstein, Edward. Morbid Craving for Morphia: Die Morphiumsucht. Grob, Gerald N., ed. Harrer, Charles, tr. LC 80-1259. (Addiction in America Ser.). 1981. reprint ed. lib. bdg. 15.95 (*0-405-13602-1*) Ayer.
Levinstein, Jerry. The Complete Carpet Manual. (Illus.). 376p. 1992. 59.95 (*0-912526-60-2*) Lib Res.
***Levinthal, David.** Small Wonder: Worlds in a Box. (Illus.). 1994. pap. 27.50 (*1-881616-39-8*) Dist Art Pubs.
Levinton, Jeffrey. Genetics, Paleontology, & Macroevolution. (Illus.). 550p. 1988. 54.95 (*0-521-24933-3*) Cambridge U Pr.
***Levinton, Jeffrey S.** Marine Biology: Function, Biodiversity, Ecology. (Illus.). 448p. (C). 1995. text ed. 47.95 (*0-19-508573-6*) OUP.
Levis, Albert J. Conflict Analysis-The Formal Theory of Behavior: A Theory & Its Experimental Validation. LC 88-90914. (Illus.). 500p. (C). 1989. 50.00 (*0-929642-00-7*) Normative Pubns.
— Conflict Analysis Training: A Program of Emotional Education. LC 88-90913. (Illus.). 160p. (Orig.). (C). 1989. pap. 25.00 (*0-929642-01-5*) Normative Pubns.
***Levis, Alexander & Levis, Ilze S., eds.** Science of Command & Control Pt. 3: Coping with Change. (AIP Information Systems: Vol. III). 200p. (Orig.). (C). 1994. pap. 18.95 (*0-916159-25-6*) AFCEA Intl Pr.
Levis, Alexander H., jt. ed. see Johnson, Stuart E.
Levis, Allen. General Merchandise - HBA Mgt & OPS. 1989. pap. 32.95 (*0-86730-313-1*) Lebhar Friedman.
Levis, Bob, ed. see Malmuth, Mason.
Levis, G. Liz & Beth, Vol. 1: EROS Grahic Novel, No. 6. Verre, Tom, ed. Jordan, Gil, tr. (Illus.). 88p. (Orig.). 1993. pap. 11.95 (*1-56097-205-X*) Fantagraph Bks.
Levis, Ilze S., jt. ed. see Levis, Alexander.
Levis, Larry. The Afterlife: Poems. LC 77-8598. 61p. reprint ed. pap. 25.00 (*0-8357-3840-X*, 2036572) Bks Demand.
— The Dollmaker's Ghost. 2nd ed. 72p. 1992. reprint ed. pap. 10.95 (*0-88748-125-6*) Carnegie-Mellon.
— The Widening Spell of the Leaves. LC 90-21308. (Poetry Ser.). 77p. (C). 1991. 19.95 (*0-8229-3675-5*); pap. 10.95 (*0-8229-5454-0*) U of Pittsburgh Pr.

An Asterisk (*) at the beginning of an entry indicates that the title is appearing in BIP for the first time.

— Winter Stars. LC 84-21957. (Poetry Ser.). 104p. 1985. 19.95 (0-8229-3511-2); pap. 10.95 (0-8229-5368-4) U of Pittsburgh Pr.

— Wrecking Crew. LC 78-181398. (Poetry Ser.). 1972. 19.95 (0-8229-3238-5) U of Pittsburgh Pr.

Levison, Ann, ed. see Van Dinh, Tran.

Levison, Arnold B. Knowledge & Society: An Introduction to the Philosophy of the Social Sciences. LC 72-88122. 1974. 29.50 (0-672-53661-7) Irvington.

— Knowledge & Society: An Introduction to the Philosophy of the Social Sciences. LC 72-88122. 1974. pap. 10.83 (0-672-63661-1) Pegasus.

***Levison, Fred.** The Prospect of Heaven. (C). 1993. pap. 24.95x (0-85305-334-0, Pub. by J Arthur Ltd UK) St Mut.

Levison, H. Textbook for Dental Nurses. 7th ed. (Illus.). 320p. 1991. pap. 26.50 (0-632-02956-0) Blackwell Sci.

***Levison, Harry.** Paint & Paper. (Pleasures of Home Ser.). (Illus.). 128p. 1995. 21.95 (0-304-34628-4, Pub. by Cassell UK) Sterling.

Levison, John R., jt. auth. see Pope-Levison, Priscilla.

Levison, Lee M. Community Service Programs in Independent Schools: The Processes of Implementation & Institutionalization of Peripheral Educational Innovations. rev. ed. LC 93-49428. (Non-profit Institutions in America Ser.). 208p. 1994. 51.00 (0-8153-0907-4) Garland.

Levison, Louise. Filmmakers & Financing: Business Plans for Independents. 160p. 1994. pap. 19.95 (0-240-80207-1, Focal) Buttrwrth-Heinemann.

Levison, M. & Sentance, W. A. Introduction to Computer Science. 160p. 1970. text ed. 156.00 (0-677-61440-3) Gordon & Breach.

Levison, Mary, ed. Wrestling with the Church. (C). 1992. pap. 24.00 (0-85305-307-3, Pub. by J Arthur Ltd UK) St Mut.

Levison, Matthew E., ed. The Pneumonias: Clinical Approaches to Infectious Diseases of the Lower Respiratory Tract. LC 83-10473. 592p. reprint ed. pap. 168.80 (0-8357-7864-9, 2036281) Bks Demand.

Levison, Michael, et al. The Settlement of Polynesia: A Computer Simulation. LC 72-92337. 145p. reprint ed. pap. 41.40 (0-317-39704-4, 2055888) Bks Demand.

Levison, N. The Jewish Background of Christianity: 586 B.C. to A.D. 1. 1977. lib. bdg. 59.95 (0-8490-2100-6) Gordon Pr.

Levison, Teddi, jt. auth. see Faber, Stuart J.

Levison, William H. Black Diamonds; or Humor, Satire & Sentiment... LC 75-91083. (American Humorists Ser.). reprint ed. lib. bdg. 29.50 (0-8398-1156-X) Irvington.

Levit, Fred. A Dickens Glossary. LC 89-36390. 460p. 1990. 53.00 (0-8240-5542-X, 1210) Garland.

Levit, Herschel, jt. auth. see Piranesi, Giovanni B.

Levit, Nancy, jt. auth. see Hayman, Robert L., Jr.

Levit, Robert A. & Gikakis, Christina, eds. Shared Wisdom: Development & Succession Planning. (Best Practices Ser.: No. 2). 300p. 1994. pap. text ed. 25.00 (1-881115-05-4) Human Res Plan.

Levit, Rose. With Secrets to Keep. LC 90-20947. 160p. (YA). (gr. 12 up). 1991. 12.95 (1-55870-197-4) Shoe Tree Pr.

Levit, Sarah. Fashion in Photographs, 1880-1900. (Illus.). 144p. (C). 1992. text ed. 82.50 (0-7134-6120-9) B&N Imports.

Levit, Saul D. Pennsylvania Domestic Relations Forms. 540p. 1989. disk, ring bd. 169.00 (0-8342-0075-9) Michie Butterworth.

— Pennsylvania Domestic Relations Forms. suppl. ed. 1994. ring bd. 80.00 (0-685-74634-8) Butterworth Legal Pubs.

— Pennsylvania Domestic Relations Forms, Set. 1994. disk 50.00 (0-614-03766-2) Butterworth Legal Pubs.

Levit, Steve. Quality Is Just the Beginning: Managing for Total Responsiveness. 1994. text ed. 29.95 (0-07-037592-5) McGraw.

Levitan, Alexander, jt. auth. see Jevne, Ronna F.

Levitan, B. M. Generalized Translation Operators & Some of Their Applications. 208p. 1964. text ed. 56.50 (0-7065-0554-9, Pub. by Keter Pub IS) Coronet Bks.

Levitan, B. M. & Sargsjan, I. S. Introduction to Spectral Theory: Selfadjoint Ordinary Differential Operators. Feinstein, A., tr. LC 75-15565. (Translations of Mathematical Monographs: Vol. 39). 525p. 1991. 129.00 (0-8218-1589-X, MMONO-39) Am Math.

— Strum-Liouville & Dirac Operators. (C). 1990. lib. bdg. 164.00 (0-7923-0992-8) Kluwer Ac.

Levitan, B. M. & Zhikov, V. V. Almost Periodic Functions & Differential Equations. Longdon, L. V., tr. LC 82-4352. 150p. 1983. 59.95 (0-521-24407-2) Cambridge U Pr.

Levitan, B. M., et al. Six Papers in Analysis. LC 73-15614. (Translations Ser.: No. 2, Vol. 101). 250p. 1973. 59.00 (0-8218-3051-1, TRANS 2-101) Am Math.

***Levitan, Ben.** Too Easy Gourmet: The World's First Non-Fiction Cookbook. LC 94-90329. (Orig.). 1995. pap. 6.95 (0-9640023-0-2) Too Easy Gourmet.

Levitan, Cayli H. Minister to Minister, Vol. I: Alternative Services for All Occasions. 100p. (Orig.). 1992. pap. 13.95 (0-9632747-0-8) C H Levitan.

Levitan, Donald. Consultants & Consulting: Sources & Resources. (Organizations & Interest Groups Ser.: Vol. 2). 120p. 20.00 (0-8240-5173-4, SS656) Garland.

— Guide to Grants: Governmental & Nongovernmental. 2nd ed. 230p. (C). 1985. pap. 25.00 (0-931684-09-9) Gov Res Pubns.

Levitan, Donald & Mariner, Elwyn. Your Massachusetts Government. 10th ed. LC 84-13554. (Illus.). 272p. (Orig.). 1984. pap. text ed. 25.00 (0-931684-07-2) Gov Res Pubns.

Levitan, Donald, jt. auth. see Seagrave, Jane.

Levitan, Irwin B. & Kaczmarek, Leonard K. The Neuron: Cell & Molecular Biology. (Illus.). 464p. 1991. pap. 39.95 (0-19-507071-2) OUP.

Levitan, Irwin B., jt. auth. see Kaczmarek, Leonard K.

Levitan, Jeanie, ed. see Labbance, Bob & Cornwell, David.

Levitan, Kalman L. In Search of Miniature Books. 68p. 1985. text ed. 19.95 (0-9614884-4-1) Kaycee Pr.

Levitan, Karen B., ed. Government Infostructures: A Guide to the Networks of Information Resources & Technologies at Federal, State, & Local Levels. LC 86-27119. 336p. 1987. text ed. 69.50 (0-313-24864-8, LGI/, Greenwood Pr) Greenwood.

Levitan, Linda, jt. auth. see Moore, Matthew S.

Levitan, Max. Textbook of Human Genetics. 3rd ed. (Illus.). 456p. 1988. 42.50 (0-19-504935-7) OUP.

Levitan, Nancy. Retirement Rights. LC 93-49888. 512p. (Orig.). 1994. pap. 15.00 (0-380-76894-1) Avon.

Levitan, Richard, jt. auth. see Shubik, Martin.

Levitan, Sar A. Antipoverty Work & Training Efforts: Goals & Reality. 2nd ed. (Policy Papers in Human Resources & Industrial Relations Ser.: No. 3). (Orig.). 1970. pap. 5.00 (0-87736-103-7) U of Mich Inst Labor.

— Design of Federal Antipoverty Strategy. (Policy Papers in Human Resources & Industrial Relations Ser.: No. 1). (Orig.). (C). 1967. pap. 5.00 (0-87736-101-0) U of Mich Inst Labor.

— Employment & Earnings Inadequacy: A New Social Indicator. LC 74-6831. (Policy Studies in Employment & Welfare: No. 19). 128p. reprint ed. pap. 36.50 (0-317-42113-1, 2023121) Bks Demand.

— Federal Aid to Depressed Areas: An Evaluation of the Area Redevelopment Administration. LC 64-16310. 288p. reprint ed. pap. 82.10 (0-317-28691-9, 2020470) Bks Demand.

— The Great Society's Poor Law: A New Approach to Poverty. LC 74-82450. 362p. reprint ed. pap. 103.20 (0-317-28775-3, 2020474) Bks Demand.

— Programs in Aid of the Poor. rev. ed. LC 84-28890. 176p. 1990. pap. text ed. 10.95 (0-8018-4040-6) Johns Hopkins.

— Programs in Aid of the Poor. 5th ed. LC 84-28890. 165p. reprint ed. pap. 47.10 (0-8357-6904-6, 2037962) Bks Demand.

— Programs in Aid of the Poor. 6th rev. ed. LC 84-28890. 176p. 1990. text ed. 29.50x (0-8018-4039-2) Johns Hopkins.

— Programs in Aid of the Poor for the 1980's, No. 1. 4th ed. LC 80-8093. (Policy Studies in Employment & Welfare: No. 1). 169p. reprint ed. pap. 48.20 (0-317-42065-8, 2025885) Bks Demand.

Levitan, Sar A. & Alderman, Karen Cleary. Child Care & ABC's Too. LC 75-11355. (Illus.). 136p. 1976. 20.00 (0-8018-1733-1) Johns Hopkins.

Levitan, Sar A. & Belous, Richard. Shorter Hours, Shorter Weeks: Spreading the Work to Reduce Unemployment. LC 77-4787. (Johns Hopkins University Policy Studies in Employment & Welfare: No. 30). (Illus.). 107p. reprint ed. 30.50 (0-8357-9286-2, 2016573) Bks Demand.

Levitan, Sar A. & Conway, Elizabeth A. Families in Flux: New Approaches to Meeting Challenges for Child, Elder, & Health Care in the 1990s. LC 90-1525. (Special Report Ser.). 1990. 95.00 (1-55871-162-7, BSP 171) BNA.

Levitan, Sar A. & Cooper, Martha. Business Lobbies: The Public Good & the Bottom Line. LC 83-48071. 168p. 1983. text ed. 20.00 (0-8018-3108-3) Johns Hopkins.

Levitan, Sar A. & Gallo, Frank. A Second Chance: Training for Jobs. LC 87-37266. 220p. 1988. text ed. 26.00 (0-88099-057-0); pap. text ed. 16.00 (0-88099-056-2) W E Upjohn.

Levitan, Sar A. & Johnson, Clifford M. Second Thoughts on Work. LC 82-13532. 241p. 1982. text ed. 24.00 (0-88099-000-7); pap. text ed. 14.00 (0-88099-001-5) W E Upjohn.

Levitan, Sar A. & Johnston, William B. Indian Giving: Federal Programs for Native Americans. LC 75-11354. (Policy Studies in Employment & Welfare: No. 20). 94p. reprint ed. pap. 26.80 (0-8357-8179-8, 2034150) Bks Demand.

Levitan, Sar A. & Mangum, Garth L. Federal Training & Work Programs in the Sixties. LC 78-626163. (Orig.). 1969. 13.00 (0-87736-305-6); pap. 6.50 (0-87736-306-4) U of Mich Inst Labor.

— Making Sense of Federal Manpower Policy. 2nd ed. (Policy Papers in Human Resources & Industrial Relations Ser.: No. 2). (Orig.). (C). 1973. pap. 5.00 (0-87736-102-9) U of Mich Inst Labor.

Levitan, Sar A. & Mangum, Garth L., eds. The T in CETA: Local & National Perspectives. LC 81-19791. 433p. 1981. text ed. 14.00 (0-911558-94-2); pap. text ed. 10.00 (0-911558-93-4) W E Upjohn.

Levitan, Sar A. & Noden, Alexandra B. Working for the Sovereign: Employee Relations in the Federal Government. LC 82-49064. (Policy Studies in Employment & Welfare Ser.). 160p. 1983. text ed. 22.50 (0-8018-3028-1) Johns Hopkins.

Levitan, Sar A. & Taggart, Robert. Jobs for the Disabled. LC 76-49910. (Policy Studies in Employment & Welfare: No. 28). 143p. reprint ed. pap. 40.80 (0-317-08463-1, 2017568) Bks Demand.

Levitan, Sar A. & Werneke, Diane. Productivity: Problems, Prospects, & Policies. LC 83-22184. (Policy Studies in Employment & Welfare: No. 40). 144p. 1984. pap. 10.95x (0-8018-3038-9) Johns Hopkins.

Levitan, Sar A. & Wurzburg, Gregory K. Evaluating Federal Social Programs: An Uncertain Art. LC 79-17946. 148p. 1979. text ed. 18.00 (0-911558-65-9); pap. 8.00 (0-911558-64-0) W E Upjohn.

Levitan, Sar A. & Zickler, Joyce K. The Quest for a Federal Manpower Partnership. LC 74-16541. 141p. reprint ed. pap. 40.20 (0-7837-4140-5, 2057963) Bks Demand.

Levitan, Sar A., jt. auth. see Davidson, Roger H.

Levitan, Sar A., et al. Economic Opportunity in the Ghetto: The Partnership of Government & Business. LC 70-108580. (Policy Studies in Employment & Welfare: No. 3). 94p. reprint ed. pap. 26.80 (0-317-42151-4, 2023120) Bks Demand.

— Protecting American Workers: An Assessment of Government Programs. 1986. pap. 34.00 (0-87179-521-3, 0521) BNA.

— Still a Dream: The Changing Status of Blacks Since 1960. LC 74-16539. 398p. 1976. pap. 14.95 (0-674-83856-4) HUP.

— What's Happening to the American Family: Tensions, Hopes, Realities. rev. ed. LC 87-46304. 240p. reprint ed. pap. 68.40 (0-7837-6429-4, 2046427) Bks Demand.

— What's Happening to the American Family? Tensions, Hopes, Realities. rev. ed. LC 87-46304. (Illus.). 240p. reprint ed. pap. 68.40 (0-8357-8374-X, 2034132) Bks Demand.

— Work & Welfare Go Together. LC 72-3227. (Policy Studies in Employment & Welfare Ser.: No. 13). 153p. 1972. pap. 10.95x (0-8018-1421-9) Johns Hopkins.

— Working but Poor: America's Contradiction. rev. ed. LC 92-34719. (Illus.). 160p. 1993. text ed. 32.50 (0-8018-4574-2); pap. text ed. 10.95 (0-8018-4575-0) Johns Hopkins.

Levitan, Sara & Belous, Richard S. More Than Subsistence: Minimum Wages for the Working Poor. LC 79-11688. 1979. pap. 10.95 (0-8018-2274-2) Johns Hopkins.

Levitan, Sara & Taggart, Robert. The Promise of Greatness. 325p. 1977. pap. 14.95 (0-674-71456-3) HUP.

Levitan, Stephan J. & Berkowitz, Howard L., eds. New Developments in Pain Research & Treatment. LC 84-28254. (Clinical Insights Ser.). 87p. reprint ed. pap. 25.00 (0-8357-7817-7, 2036189) Bks Demand.

Levitas, Daniel, ed. When Hate Groups Come to Town: A Handbook of Effective Community Responses. rev. ed. (Illus.). 200p. 1992. pap. 20.00 (1-881320-05-7) Black Belt Pr.

Levitas, Ruth. The Concept of Utopia. 224p. (C). 1991. text ed. 39.95x (0-8156-2513-8); pap. text ed. 16.95x (0-8156-2514-6) Syracuse U Pr.

***Levitas, Susan, ed.** Railroad Ties: Industry & Culture in Hagerstown, Maryland. LC 94-33071. (Illus.). 64p. 1994. pap. 14.00 (1-878399-64-0, MD Hist Trust) Div Hist Cult Progs.

Levitas, V. I. Large Deformation of Materials with Complex Rheological Properties at Normal & High Pressure. 323p. 1992. 97.00 (1-56072-085-9) Nova Sci Pubs.

Levite, Ariel, jt. ed. see Feldman, Shai.

Levite, Ariel, jt. ed. see Klieman, Aharon.

Levite, Ariel E. Intelligence & Strategic Surprises. LC 86-17401. 300p. 1987. text ed. 35.50 (0-231-06374-1) Col U Pr.

Levite, Ariel E., et al, eds. Foreign Military Intervention: The Dynamics of Protracted Conflict. (Illus.). 312p. 1992. text ed. 32.50 (0-231-07294-5) Col U Pr.

***Levite, Bernard L.** Structured COBOL Programming: Interactive & Batch Processing. 1994. write for info. (0-615-00038-X) Boyd & Fraser.

Levite, George. By George for Lilly - Love Letters to a Potbellied Stove. Griffis, Molly L., ed. LC 87-90704. (Illus.). 160p. 1992. pap. write for info. (0-927562-13-8) Levite Apache.

Levith, Murray J. Shakespeare's Italian Settings & Plays. LC 87-21277. 144p. 1989. text ed. 39.95 (0-312-00911-9) St Martin.

Leviticus. Sefer Ha'hinnuch: The Book of Education, Vols. 2 & 3. 1985. 33.95 (0-87306-145-4) Feldheim.

***Levitin.** Evil Encounter. (J). 1996. 15.00 (0-689-80216-1, S&S Bks Young Read) S&S Childrens.

Levitin, tr. see De Andrade, Eugenio.

Levitin, Alexis, ed. see De Andrade, Eugenio.

Levitin, Alexis, tr. see De Andrade, Eugenio.

Levitin, Alexis, tr. see Lispector, Clarice.

Levitin, Anany. Data Quality Foundations. 2nd rev. ed. Snow, Kimberly, ed. (AT&T Quality Library). 50p. 1992. pap. 22.45 (0-932764-26-6, 500-490) AT&T Customer Info.

Levitin, Dan. From Demo Tape to Record Deal. (Alfred Handy Guide Ser.). 48p. (Orig.). 1992. pap. 4.50 (0-88284-494-6, 4422) Alfred Pub.

Levitin, E. S. Perturbation Theory in Mathematical Programming and It's Application. LC 93-8778. (Interscience Series in Discrete Mathematics). 1994. text ed. 64.95 (0-471-93935-8) Wiley.

Levitin, Isabella, tr. see Yanovsky, Vassily.

Levitin, Moshe, ed. see American Institute of Certified Public Accountants Staff.

Levitin, Moshe S., ed. see American Institute of Certified Public Accountants Staff.

Levitin, Nancy. America's Health Care Crisis - Who's Responsible? Who's Responsible? LC 94-15523. (Impact Book Ser.). (Illus.). 128p. (YA). (gr. 7-12). 1994. lib. bdg. 14.56 (0-531-11187-3) Watts.

Levitin, Sonia. Adam's War. LC 93-13833. (J). 1994. 13.99 (0-8037-1506-4); lib. bdg. 13.89 (0-8037-1507-2) Dial Bks Young.

— Annie's Promise. LC 92-16819. 192p. (J). (gr. 5 up). 1993. text ed. 14.95 (0-689-31752-2, Atheneum Bks Young) S&S Childrens.

— Beyond Another Door. (YA). 1994. mass mkt. 3.99 (0-449-70425-4, Juniper) Fawcett.

— Escape from Egypt: A Novel. LC 93-29376. (YA). (gr. 7 up). 1994. 16.95 (0-316-52273-2) Little.

— The Golem & the Dragon Girl. LC 92-27665. 176p. (J). (gr. 3-7). 1993. lib. bdg. 14.89 (0-8037-1281-2) Dial Bks Young.

— The Golem & the Dragon Girl. (YA). 1994. mass mkt. 3.99 (0-449-70441-6, Expressions Three Ltd) Fawcett.

— Incident at Loring Groves. 160p. 1990. mass mkt. 3.99 (0-449-70347-9, Juniper) Fawcett.

— Journey to America. 2nd ed. LC 70-98616. (Illus.). 160p. (J). (gr. 3-7). 1993. text ed. 13.95 (0-689-31829-4, Atheneum Bks Young) S&S Childrens.

— Journey to America. LC 86-22234. (Illus.). 160p. (J). (gr. 3-6). 1987. reprint ed. pap. 3.95 (0-689-71130-1, Aladdin Paperbacks) S&S Childrens.

— Man Who Kept His Heart in a Bucket. (J). (ps-3). 1991. 14.95 (0-8037-1029-1); lib. bdg. 14.89 (0-8037-1030-5) Dial Bks Young.

— The Man Who Kept His Heart in a Bucket. (Illus.). 40p. (J). (ps-3). 1995. pap. 5.99 (0-14-055461-0, Puff Pied Piper) Puffin Bks.

— The Mark of Conte. 240p. (YA). (gr. 7 up). 1987. pap. 3.95 (0-02-044191-6, Collier Bks Young) S&S Childrens.

— A Piece of Home. (J). 1994. write for info. (0-8037-1625-7) Dial Bks Young.

— The Return. 1988. mass mkt. 3.99 (0-449-70280-4, Juniper) Fawcett.

— The Return. LC 86-25891. 224p. (J). (gr. 5 up). 1987. text ed. 14.95 (0-689-31309-8, Atheneum Bks Young) S&S Childrens.

— Rita, the Weekend Rat. (Illus.). 144p. (Orig.). (J). (gr. 3-7). 1980. pap. 1.95 (0-590-30378-3) Scholastic Inc.

— Season for Unicorns. 1987. pap. 2.50 (0-449-70227-8) Fawcett.

— Silver Days. LC 88-27491. 192p. (YA). (gr. 5 up). 1989. text ed. 14.95 (0-689-31563-5, Atheneum Bks Young) S&S Childrens.

— Silver Days. LC 91-22581. 192p. (J). (gr. 3-7). 1992. reprint ed. pap. 3.95 (0-689-71570-6, Aladdin Paperbacks) S&S Childrens.

Levitin, Teresa E., jt. auth. see Miller, Warren E.

Levitin, Victor. TraX: Simulation & Analysis of Dynamical Systems. Millstein, Jeffrey, ed. 73p. 1990. 295.00 (1-884977-10-3); teacher ed 590.00 (1-884977-11-1) Applied Biomath.

Levitine, George. Culture & Revolution: Cultural Ramifications of the French Revolution. Libby, Susan & Hall, Pam, eds. (Illus.). 336p. (C). 1989. write for info. (0-9625932-0-6) Univ MD Dept Art Hist.

Leviton. Handbook to Middle East Amphibians & Reptiles. LC 90-63909. 1992. write for info. (0-916984-23-0) SSAR.

Leviton, Alan E., jt. ed. see Kockelman, W. J.

Leviton, Alan E., jt. ed. see Taylor, Ronald J.

Leviton, Alan E., et al, eds. Frontiers of Geological Exploration of Western North America. LC 82-71290. 248p. (Orig.). 1982. 16.95 (0-934394-03-2) AAASPD.

***Leviton, Charles.** There Is No Bad Truth. 288p. 1995. per., pap. text ed. 26.25 (0-7872-1093-5) Kendall-Hunt.

Leviton, Charles D. There Is No Bad Truth: The Search for Self. 288p. (C). 1990. per. 21.95 (0-8403-5856-3) Kendall-Hunt.

Leviton, Daniel. Horrendous Deaths, Health & Well-Being. 1990. 75.00 (1-56032-033-8) Hemisp Pub.

Leviton, Daniel, ed. Horrendous Death & Health: Towards Action. (Death Education, Aging & Health Care Ser.). 408p. 1991. 75.00 (1-56032-186-5) Hemisp Pub.

Leviton, Laura C., et al, eds. Evaluating AIDS Prevention: Contributions of Multiple Disciplines. LC 85-644749. (New Directions for Program Evaluation Ser.: No. PE 46). 1990. 17.95 (1-55542-835-5) Jossey-Bass.

Leviton, Richard. Anthroposophic Medicine Today. 40p. 1988. pap. 3.95 (0-88010-265-9) Anthroposophic.

— Brain Builders: A Lifelong Guide to Sharper Thinking, Better Memory, & an Age-Proof Mind. 1995. pap. text ed. 12.95 (0-13-303603-0) P-H.

— Brain Builders: A Lifelong Guide to Sharper Thinking, Better Memory, & an Age-Proof Mind. 1995. text ed. 27.95 (0-13-303611-1) P-H.

— The Imagination of Pentecost: Rudolf Steiner & Contemporary Spirituality. 304p. (Orig.). 1994. pap. 24.95 (0-88010-379-5) Anthroposophic.

— Seven Steps to Better Vision: Easy, Practical & Natural Techniques That Will Improve Your Eyesight. (Illus.). 144p. 1992. pap. 8.95 (0-936184-13-2) E W-Nat Hlth Bks.

— Tofu, Tempeh, Miso & Other Soyfoods. Passwater, Richard A. & Mindell, Earl R., eds. (Good Health Guide Ser.). 32p. 1982. pap. 2.50 (0-87983-284-3) Keats.

— Weddings by Design: A Guide to Non-Traditional Ceremonies. LC 92-53058. 208p. 1994. pap. 14.00 (0-06-251007-X) Harper SF.

Leviton, Sharon C., jt. auth. see Greenstone, James L.

Leviton, Shirley I., jt. auth. see National Council of Jewish Women Staff.

Levitov, Leo. Solution of the Voynich Manuscript. 176p. (Orig.). 1987. lib. bdg. 44.30 (0-89412-149-9); pap. 34.80 (0-89412-148-0) Aegean Park Pr.

***Levitskiy, Semyon P. & Shulman, Zinoviy P.** Bubbles in Polymeric Liquids. LC 94-61880. 307p. 1995. pap. text ed. 85.00 (1-56676-247-2) Technomic.

Levitsky, David, jt. auth. see Garrison, Terry N.

Levitsky, David A., ed. Malnutrition, Environment, & Behavior: New Perspectives. LC 78-58016. 256p. 1978. 28.50 (0-8014-1045-2) Cornell U Pr.

Levitsky, Jacob & Prasad, Ranga N. Credit Guarantee Schemes for Small & Medium Enterprises. (Technical Paper Ser.: No. 58). 98p. 1987. 7.95 (0-8213-0866-1, 10866) World Bank.

Levitsky, Ronald. The Innocence That Kills. LC 93-42385. 254p. 1994. text ed. 20.00 (0-684-19707-3, Scribners) S&S Trade.

— The Love That Kills. 304p. 1993. pap. 4.99 (0-451-40374-6, Onyx) NAL-Dutton.

— The Love That Kills. 256p. 1991. text ed. 18.95 (0-684-19295-0, Scribners) S&S Trade.

— The Spirit That Kills. 384p. 1995. pap. 4.99 (0-451-40540-4, Onyx) NAL-Dutton.

— Stone Boy: A Nate Rosen Mystery. 224p. 1993. text ed. 20.00 (0-684-19554-2, Scribners) S&S Trade.

An Asterisk (*) at the beginning of an entry indicates that the title is appearing in BIP for the first time.

— The Truth That Kills. 352p. 1994. pap. 4.99 (0-451-40401-7, Onyx) NAL-Dutton.
— The Wisdom of Serpents: A Nate Rosen Mystery. 256p. 1992. text ed. 19.00 (0-684-19411-2, Scribners) S&S Trade.
Levitsky, Serge L. Copyright, Defamation & Privacy in Soviet Civil Law, No. 22. (Law in Eastern Europe Ser.). 517p. 1979. lib. bdg. 91.50 (90-286-0139-2) Kluwer Ac.
Levitsky, Serge L., ed. see Boguslavsky, M. M. & Smirnov, P. S.
Levitsky, Sidney & Fitzgerald, Jeanne T., eds. Using CPT for Cardiothoracic Reimbursement: A Manual for Surgeons & Insurance Billing Specialists. 105p. (Orig.). 1990. 25.00 (0-9626174-0-7) Soc Thor Surgeons.
Levitsky, Sidney, jt. ed. see Engelman, Richard M.
***Levitt.** Reorganized NHS. 1991. 52.50 (1-56593-016-9, 0259) Singular Publishing.
— Treatment of Cerebral Palsy in Motor Delay. 3rd ed. (Illus.). 312p. 1994. pap. 34.95 (0-632-03873-X, Pub. by Blckwell Sci Pubns UK) Blackwell Sci.
Levitt & Forrest, eds. The Laser Marketplace. 1988. 38.00 (0-89252-985-7, 950) SPIE.
***Levitt & Mertelsmann.** Hematopoietic Stem Cells: Biology & Therapeutic Applications. 659p. 1995. 195.00 (0-8247-9305-6) Dekker.
Levitt, jt. auth. see Unger.
Levitt, A. R., jt. auth. see MacLeod, J. S.
Levitt, Annette S. The Intertextuality of Joyce Cary's "The Horse's Mouth" LC 93-32507. 186p. 1993. text ed. 79.95 (0-7734-9353-0) E Mellen.
Levitt, Annette S., jt. ed. see Bertholf, Robert J.
Levitt, Anthony J., jt. ed. see Joffe, Russell T.
***Levitt, Atma J.** The Kripalu Cookbook: Gourmet Vegetarian Recipes. LC 94-38742. 1995. pap. 16.95 (0-936399-65-1) Berkshire Hse.
Levitt, B. Blake, jt. auth. see Sussman, John R.
***Levitt, Blake.** 50 Essential Things to Do When the Doctor Says It's Infertility. 144p. (Orig.). 1995. pap. 9.95 (0-452-27119-3, Plume) NAL-Dutton.
***Levitt, Blake B.** Electromagnetic Fields. 1995. pap. 13.00 (0-15-628100-7) HarBrace.
Levitt, Cyril. Children of Privilege: Student Revolt in the Sixties. 288p. 1984. 40.00 (0-8020-5636-9) U of Toronto Pr.
— Children of Privilege: Student Revolt in the Sixties: a Study of Student Movements in Canada, the United States & West Germany. LC 84-211030. (Illus.). 280p. reprint ed. pap. 79.80 (0-7837-0526-3, 2040852) Bks Demand.
Levitt, Cyril, ed. see DeGre, Gerard.
Levitt, Cyril, jt. ed. see Greenspan, Louis.
Levitt, David, jt. auth. see Schwanauer, Stephan.
Levitt, Diane. Private Sins. 1993. mass mkt. 4.99 (1-55817-738-8, Pinnacle NY) Windsor NY.
— Teen Families & Welfare Dependency in California: Background Briefing Report with Seminar Presentations. 137p. 1994. pap. 15.00 (0-929722-83-3) CA State Library Fndtn.
Levitt, Eleanor. Natural Food Cookery. Orig. Title: The Wonderful World of Natural-Food Cookery. (Illus.). 320p. 1979. reprint ed. pap. 5.95 (0-486-23851-2) Dover.
Levitt, Eugene E. The Clinical Application of MMPI Special Scales. 136p. 1989. 29.95 (0-8058-0047-6) L Erlbaum Assocs.
Levitt, Eugene E., et al. Depression: Concepts, Controversies & Some New Facts. 2nd ed. 264p. 1983. text ed. 39.95 (0-89859-278-X) L Erlbaum Assocs.
Levitt, Eugene E. The Psychology of Anxiety. 2nd ed. LC 80-107. 188p. 1980. text ed. 29.95 (0-89859-040-X) L Erlbaum Assocs.
Levitt, Eugene E. & Gotts, Edward E. The Clinical Application of MMPI Special Scales. 2nd ed. 200p. 1995. text ed. 29.95 (0-8058-1770-0) L Erlbaum Assocs.
Levitt, Geoffrey M. Democracies Against Terror: The Western Response to State-Supported Terrorism. 1988. write for info. (0-318-63177-6, Praeger Pubs) Greenwood.
— The Western Response to State-Supported Terrorism. LC 86-418. (Washington Papers: No. 134). (Illus.). 160p. 1988. text ed. 39.95 (0-275-93021-1, C3021, Praeger Pubs); pap. text ed. 9.95 (0-275-93022-X, B3022, Praeger Pubs) Greenwood.
Levitt, H., et al, eds. Sensory Aids for the Hearing Impaired. LC 76-28875. 576p. 1980. 49.95 (0-87942-087-1, PC01289); pap. 39.95 (0-685-55581-X, PP01297) Inst Electrical.
Levitt, Harry & Boysen, Allen E., eds. Recent Advances in Sensory Aids for Hearing Impairment. (Illus.). 136p. (Orig.). (C). 1994. pap. text ed. 55.00 (0-7881-0355-5) Diane Pub.
Levitt, Harry, ed. see Neuman, Arlene C.
Levitt, Helen. In the Street: Chalk Drawings & Messages, New York City, 1938-1948. LC 86-29367. (Illus.). 112p. 1987. pap. 24.50 (0-8223-0771-5) Duke.
— A Way of Seeing. rev. ed. LC 81-82838. (Illus.). 100p. 1989. reprint ed. pap. text ed. 19.95 (0-8223-1005-8) Duke.
Levitt, Ian. Poverty & Welfare in Scotland, 1890-1948. 200p. 1988. 45.00 (0-85224-558-0, Pub. by Edinburgh U Pr UK) Col U Pr.
— Poverty & Welfare in Scotland, 1890-1948. 256p. 1990. pap. text ed. 17.00 (0-85224-583-1, Pub. by Edinburgh U Pr UK) Col U Pr.
Levitt, J. M. & Marshall, Roy K. Star Maps for Beginners. 50th anniversary ed. (Illus.). 64p. 1992. pap. 10.00 (0-671-79187-7, Fireside) S&S Trade.
Levitt, J. Stanley. A Beginner's Guide to Investing in No-Load Mutual Funds. Craig, Barbara & Liszkowski, Ron, eds. (Illus.). 144p. (Orig.). 1993. pap. 15.95 (0-942641-46-9) Intl Pub IL.
— Do It Yourself Investing with No-Load-Mutual Funds. 112p. 1991. pap. text ed. 19.95 (0-9631039-0-3) J S Levitt.
— Mental Shorthand: Memory Training Self Taught. 55p. 1992. pap. 12.95 (0-9631039-1-1) J S Levitt.
Levitt, Jacob. Responses of Plants to Environmental Stresses: Vol. I: Chilling, Freezing, & High Temperature Stresses. 2nd ed. (Physiological Ecology Ser.). 1980. text ed. 91.00 (0-12-445501-8) Acad Pr.
— Responses of Plants to Environmental Stresses, Vol. 2: Water, Radiaton, Salt & Other Stresses. LC 79-51680. (Physiological Ecology Ser.). 1980. text ed. 104.00 (0-12-445502-6) Acad Pr.
Levitt, Jesse, jt. ed. see Thomas, T. M.
Levitt, Jesse, et al, eds. Geolinguistic Perpectives: Proceedings of the International Conference Celebrating the Twentieth Anniversary of the American Society of Geolinguistics, 1985. 398p. (Orig.). 1987. pap. text ed. 33.00 (0-8191-6046-6, American Society of Geolinguistics) U Pr of Amer.
Levitt, JoAnn & Norian, Todd, eds. Sounds of the Sacred: Chants of Love & Prayer. LC 90-62313. (Illus.). 158p. (Orig.). Date not set. pap. 14.95 (0-940258-23-4) Kripalu Pubns.
Levitt, JoAnn, ed. see Desai, Yogi A.
Levitt, JoAnn, et al. Kripalu Kitchen: A Natural Foods Cookbook & Nutritional Guide. LC 80-68122. (Illus.). 270p. (Orig.). 1980. pap. 9.95 (0-940258-01-3) Kripalu Pubns.
Levitt, Joanna J. Sex & Psychology of Sexual Offenses: Index of New Information with Authors, Subjects & Bibliography. 180p. 1993. 49.50 (1-55914-768-7); pap. 39.50 (1-55914-769-5) ABBE Pubs Assn.
Levitt, Joel. Complete Guide to Fleet Management. 220p. 1989. boxed 39.00 (0-13-159328-5) P-H.
— Managing Factory Maintenance. (Illus.). 320p. 1995. 38.95 (0-8311-3063-6) Indus Pr.
Levitt, Joel H. Small Signal Analysis: By Computer, By Inspection. LC 82-83970. (Illus.). 184p. (C). 1983. pap. text ed. 11.25 (0-9609892-0-X) Haywood Pr.
Levitt, Joseph. Pearson & Canada's Role in Nuclear Disarmament & Arms Control Negotiations, 1945-1957. (Illus.). 328p. 1993. 39.95 (0-7735-0905-4, Pub. by McGill CN) U of Toronto Pr.
Levitt, Judy, jt. ed. see Wallace, Margaret E.
Levitt, Julie G. Your Career: How to Make It Happen. 2nd ed. (C). 1990. pap. 22.95 (0-538-70167-6, CA42BB) S-W Pub.
Levitt, Lawrence P., jt. auth. see Weiner, Howard L.
Levitt, M., ed. Precast Concrete: Materials, Manufacture, Properties & Usage. (Illus.). ix, 233p. 1982. 74.00 (0-85334-994-0, Pub. by Elsevier Applied Sci UK) Elsevier.
Levitt, M. & Belforte, D., eds. Industrial Laser Handbook. (Illus.). 400p. 1992. 163.00 (0-387-97751-1) Spr-Verlag.
Levitt, M., jt. ed. see Belforte, D.
Levitt, M., jt. ed. see Forrest, G.
Levitt, M. R., jt. ed. see Belforte, D. A.
Levitt, M. R., jt. ed. see Forrest, G. T.
Levitt, Marcus C. Russian Literary Politics & the Pushkin Celebration of 1880. LC 88-43237. (Studies of the Harriman Institute). (Illus.). 240p. 1989. 32.95 (0-8014-2250-7) Cornell U Pr.
***Levitt, Marcus C., ed.** Early Modern Russian Writers: Late-Seventeenth & Eighteenth Centuries, Vol. 150. LC 95-1711. (Dictionary of Literary Biography: Vol. 150). 465p. 1995. 128.00 (0-8103-5711-9) Gale.
Levitt, Martin J. Confessions of a Union Buster. LC 93-14736. 1993. 25.00 (0-517-58330-5, Crown) Crown Pub Group.
Levitt, Michael. America's Cup 1851-1992. (Illus.). 208p. 1992. 50.00 (1-55868-105-1) Gr Arts Ctr Pub.
Levitt, Michael, jt. auth. see Conner, Dennis.
Levitt, Mimi, tr. see Durrenmatt, Friedrich & Selz, Peter.
Levitt, Morris & Belforte, Dave. Industrial Laser Annual Handbook 1988. 352p. 1988. 125.00 (0-87814-333-5, L4300) PennWell Bks.
— Industrial Laser Annual Handbook, 1989. 352p. 1989. 125.00 (0-87814-341-6, L4302) PennWell Bks.
Levitt, Morris & Belforte, David, eds. Industrial Laser Annual Handbook, 1990. (Illus.). 272p. 1990. 125.00 (0-87814-359-9, L4304) PennWell Bks.
Levitt, Morris J. State & Local Government & Politics: A Simulation. 3rd ed. 136p. 1993. spiral bd. 19.95 (0-8403-8741-5) Kendall-Hunt.
Levitt, Morris R. & Forrest, Gary T., eds. The Laser Marketplace in Nineteen Eighty-Nine. 124p. 1989. 42.00 (0-8194-0160-9, VOL. 1124) SPIE.
Levitt, Morris R., jt. ed. see Belforte, David A.
Levitt, Mortimer. The Executive Look & How to Get It: Professional Guidelines for Putting Together Executive Wardrobes for Men & Women. LC 79-18848. (AMA Management Briefing Ser.). 76p. reprint ed. pap. 25.00 (0-317-28128-3, 2055741) Bks Demand.
— How to Start Your Own Business Without Losing Your Shirt: Secrets of the Artful Entrepreneur. (Illus.). 236p. 1988. text ed. 18.00 (0-689-11958-5, Pub. by Ctrl Bur voor Schimmel NE) Macmillan.
Levitt, Morton. Freud & Dewey on the Nature of Man. LC 76-138157. 180p. 1971. reprint ed. text ed. 38.50 (0-8371-5614-9, LEFD, Greenwood Pr) Greenwood.
Levitt, Morton & Rubenstein, Ben, eds. The Mental Health Field: A Critical Appraisal. LC 70-135397. 387p. reprint ed. pap. 110.30 (0-685-15806-3, 2027681) Bks Demand.
— Youth & Social Change. LC 73-157414. 420p. reprint ed. pap. 119.70 (0-317-52059-8, 2027499) Bks Demand.
Levitt, N. J. Grassmannians & Gauss Maps in Piecewise-Linear & Piecewise-Differential Topology. (Lecture Notes in Mathematics Ser.: Vol. 1366). 203p. 1989. pap. 34.10 (0-387-50756-6) Spr-Verlag.
Levitt, Norman, jt. auth. see Gross, Paul R.
Levitt, Paul M. A Structural Approach to the Analysis of Drama. LC 79-159466. (De Proprietatibus Litterarum, Ser. Major: No. 15). 119p. 1971. text ed. 25.40 (90-279-1841-4) Mouton.
Levitt, Paul M. & Guralnick, Elissa S. You Can Make It Back: Coping with Serious Illness. LC 84-26049. 226p. reprint ed. pap. 64.50 (0-7837-1362-2, 2041510) Bks Demand.
Levitt, Paul M., et al. The Cancer Reference Book: Direct & Clear Answers to Everyone's Questions. LC 78-26046. 299p. reprint ed. pap. 85.30 (0-7837-1571-4, 2041863) Bks Demand.
— The Weighty Word Book. (Illus.). 99p. (Orig.). (J). (gr. 4-9). 1990. reprint ed. 17.95 (0-9627979-0-1) Manuscripts.
Levitt, Peter. Bright Root, Dark Root. LC 90-86382. 113p. 1991. pap. 12.95 (0-913089-20-6) Broken Moon.
— Homage: Leda As Virgin. 18p. 1986. boxed 125.00 (0-911783-03-2) Lockhart Pr.
— One Hundred Butterflies. LC 92-70016. 110p. (Orig.). 1992. pap. 10.95 (0-913089-27-3) Broken Moon.
Levitt, Peter, ed. see Dunitz, Jay.
Levitt, Peter, ed. see Nhat Hanh, Thich.
Levitt, Rachelle, ed. Cities Reborn. LC 87-50398. 203p. 1987. pap. 52.00 (0-87420-667-7, C32) Urban Land.
— Research Parks & Other Ventures: The University-Real Estate Connection. LC 85-52744. 113p. (C). 1985. pap. 42.95 (0-87420-633-2, R18) Urban Land.
Levitt, Rachelle & Kirlin, John, eds. Managing Development Through Public-Private Negotiations. 2nd ed. LC 85-51328. 184p. 1986. pap. 43.95 (0-87420-642-1, M21) Urban Land.
Levitt, Rachelle L., jt. ed. see Waite, Margaret M.
Levitt, Ray E., jt. auth. see Dym, Clive L.
Levitt, Raymond E. & Samelson, Nancy. Construction Safety Management. 2nd ed. 224p. 1993. text ed. 49.95 (0-471-59933-6) Wiley.
Levitt, Richard, ed. see Jarrell, David G.
Levitt, Ruth, tr. see Minco, Marga.
Levitt, S. H., et al. Levitt & Tapley's Technological Basis of Radiation Therapy. 2nd ed. (Illus.). 429p. 1992. text ed. 79.50 (0-8121-1466-3) Williams & Wilkins.
Levitt, Sandra G., et al, eds. Hiring Foreign Personnel, 1990: Immigration Problems & Solutions. 302p. (Orig.). 1989. pap. text ed. 49.95 (1-878677-06-3) Amer Immi Law Assn.
Levitt, Sarah. Victorians Unbuttoned: Registered Designs for Clothing, Their Makers & Wearers, 1839-1900. (Illus.). 246p. 1986. 34.95 (0-04-391013-0) Routledge Chapman & Hall.
Levitt, Saul. The Andersonville Trial. 1961. pap. 4.75 (0-8222-0042-2) Dramatists Play.
— Jim Thorpe, All American. (Orig.). (J). (gr. 4 up). 1980. 5.50 (0-87602-237-9) Anchorage.
Levitt, Sidney. The Mighty Movers. LC 92-54869. (Illus.). 48p. (J). (gr. k-3). 1994. 10.95 (1-56282-421-X); lib. bdg. 10.89 (1-56282-422-8) Hyprn Child.
Levitt, Theodore. The Marketing Imagination. LC 83-47989. 256p. (C). 1983. 9.95 (0-02-918840-7) Free Pr.
— The Marketing Imagination. enl. ed. 218p. 1986. text ed. 29.95 (0-02-919180-7); pap. 14.95 (0-02-919090-8) Free Pr.
— Thinking about Management. 160p. 1990. text ed. 19.95 (0-02-918605-6) Free Pr.
Levitt, Zola. El Espiritu De Sun Myung Moon: The Spirit of Sun Myung Moon. (SPA.). 3.95 (84-7228-388-7, 220380, Pub. by Edit Clie SP) TSELF.
Levitt, Zola, jt. auth. see McCall, Thomas S.
Levitus, Bob. Customizing Your Macintosh for Productivity & for Fun, Incl. disk. 1993. disk, pap. 39.95 (1-56686-087-3) Brady Compu Bks.
— Dr. Macintosh. 2nd ed. 1992. pap. 26.95 (0-201-57050-5) Addison-Wesley.
— Dr. Macintosh's Desktop Video: The Complete Quidktime & Animation Handbook. 1993. pap. 39.95 (1-56686-025-3) Brady Compu Bks.
— Dr. Macintosh's Guide to the On-Line Universe. 1992. pap. 24.95 (0-201-58125-6) Addison-Wesley.
— MAC System 7.5 for Dummies. 1994. pap. 19.95 (1-56884-197-3) IDG Bks.
— Son of Stupid Mac Tricks: Eighteen New Insanely Great Tricks for Your Macintosh. 1991. pap. 19.95 (0-201-56787-3) Addison-Wesley.
— Stupid-Beyond-Belief PC Tricks. 1992. pap. 19.95 (0-201-63235-7) Addison-Wesley.
— Stupid PC Tricks. 1991. pap. 19.95 (0-201-57759-3) Addison-Wesley.
— Stupid Windows Tricks: Making It All Make Nonsense. 1992. pap. 19.95 (0-201-60840-5) Addison-Wesley.
***Levitus, Bob & Evans, Jeff.** Webmaster Macintosh: How to Build Your Own World-Wide Server Without Really Trying. (Illus.). 400p. 1995. pap. write for info. (0-12-445574-3) Acad Pr.
— Webmaster Windows: How to Build Your Own World-Wide Web Server Without Really Trying. (Illus.). 400p. 1995. disk, pap. write for info. (0-12-445573-5) Acad Pr.
Levitus, Bob & Frasse, Michael. The Guide to the Macintosh Underground. 1993. pap. 19.95 (0-672-48549-4) Hayden.
Levitz, Mitchell. Count Us In: Growing up with Down Syndrome. 1994. 19.95 (0-15-150447-4); pap. 9.95 (0-15-622660-X) HarBrace.
Levitz, Nancy, ed. see Weidemann, Sela.
Levitz, Paul. Legion of Superheroes, Vol. 1. 1989. pap. 10.00 (0-912771-52-6) Mayfair Games.
Levitz, Paul, ed. see O'Neil, Dennis.
Levitzki, Alexander, jt. auth. see Schulster, Dennis.
Levitzki, Alexander, jt. ed. see Schulster, Dennis.
Levitzky, et al. Introduction to Respiratory Care. (Illus.). 608p. 1990. text ed. 57.50 (0-7216-1090-0) Saunders.
Levitzky, Michael G. Cardiopulmonary Physiology in Anesthesiology. LC 94-2822. 384p. 1995. text ed. 49.00 (0-07-037534-8) Hlth Prof Div.
— Pulmonary Physiology. 4th ed. LC 94-23506. (Illus.). 288p. 1995. pap. text ed. 25.00 (0-07-037535-6) Hlth Prof Div.
Levkoff, Alice F., jt. auth. see Whitelaw, Robert N.
Levkoff, Mary L. Rodin in His Time. LC 93-61544. (Illus.). 224p. 1994. 50.00 (0-500-23678-X) Thames Hudson.
Levkov, Ilya. Bitburg & Beyond. 1987. 29.95 (0-933503-94-6) Sure Sellers.
Levkowitz, H., jt. ed. see Grinstein, G.
Levmore, Saul. Foundations of Tort Law. LC 92-45580. (Interdisciplinary Readers in Law Ser.). 368p. 1993. 49.95 (0-19-508391-1); pap. 19.95 (0-19-508392-X) OUP.
Levoir, John, jt. auth. see Hogan, Richard.
LeVoir, John M., jt. auth. see Hogan, Richard M.
Levokove, Michael. The Selling Edge: Winning over Today's Business Customers. LC 92-75676. 200p. 1993. text ed. 18.95 (0-944435-21-1) Glenbridge Pub.
Levorsen, Arville I. Geology of Petroleum. 2nd ed. LC 65-25242. (Geology Ser.). (Illus.). 724p. (C). 1995. text ed. write for info. (0-7167-0230-4) W H Freeman.
— Stratigraphic Type Oil Fields, 2 vols. 1976. lib. bdg. 250.00 (0-8490-2694-6) Gordon Pr.
Levorsen, Arville I., ed. see American Association of Petroleum Geologists Staff.
Levorsen, Bella, ed. see Sierra Nevada Dog Drivers, Inc. Staff.
Levoy, Gregg. This Business of Writing. 224p. 1992. 19.95 (0-89879-505-2) Writers Digest.
Levoy, Myron. Alan & Naomi. LC 76-41522. (Trophy Bk.). 176p. (J). (gr. 6 up). 1987. pap. 3.95 (0-06-440209-6, Trophy) HarpC Child Bks.
— The Hanukkah of Great-Uncle Otto. LC 84-12635. (Illus.). 48p. (J). (gr. 3-7). 1984. 12.95 (0-8276-0242-1) JPS Phila.
— Kelly 'n' Me. LC 91-35807. (Charlotte Zolotow Bk.). 208p. (YA). (gr. 7 up). 1992. lib. bdg. 14.89 (0-06-020839-2) HarpC Child Bks.
— Pictures of Adam. 1995. 18.25 (0-8446-6807-9) Peter Smith.
— Pictures of Adam. LC 92-24598. 224p. (YA). (gr. 7 up). 1993. reprint ed. pap. 4.95 (0-688-11941-7, Pub. by Beech Tree Bks) Morrow.
— A Shadow Like a Leopard. LC 79-2812. (Trophy Bk.). 192p. (J). (gr. 4-7). 1994. pap. 3.95 (0-06-440458-7, Trophy) HarpC Child Bks.
— Shadow Like a Leopard. 1995. 17.50 (0-8446-6814-1) Peter Smith.
— The Witch of Fourth Street & Other Stories. (J). (gr. 3-6). 1991. 17.25 (0-8446-6450-2) Peter Smith.
— Witch of Fourth Street & Other Stories. LC 74-183174. (Illus.). 128p. (J). (gr. 3-7). 1974. pap. 3.95 (0-06-440059-X, Trophy) HarpC Child Bks.
Levoy, Robert P. Successful Professional Practice. LC 74-97581. (Illus.). 192p. 1970. 39.95 (0-13-868307-7, Busn) P-H.
Levrat, Bernard & Tagg, E. D., eds. The Computer in the Home: Its Challenge to Education. 152p. 1987. 38.50 (0-444-70213-X, North Holland) Elsevier.
Levring, Tore, ed. Tenth International Seaweed Symposium. (Illus.). 780p. 1981. 150.00 (3-11-008389-2) De Gruyter.
Levtzion, Nehemia. Ancient Ghana & Mali. LC 79-27281. 290p. (C). 1980. reprint ed. 29.50 (0-8419-0431-6, Africana) Holmes & Meier.
— Islam in West Africa: Religion, Society & Politics to 1800. (Collected Studies: CS 462). 336p. 1994. 89.95 (0-86078-444-4, Pub. by Variorum UK) Ashgate Pub Co.
Levtzion, Nehemia, ed. Conversion to Islam. LC 77-26771. 265p. 1979. 42.95 (0-8419-0343-3) Holmes & Meier.
Levtzion, Nehemia & Voll, John O., eds. Eighteenth-Century Renewal & Reform in Islam. LC 87-16188. 168p. 1987. text ed. 34.95x (0-8156-2402-6) Syracuse U Pr.
Levush, Ruth, ed. Campaign Financing of National Elections in Foreign Countries. 199p. (Orig.). (C). 1992. pap. text ed. 40.00 (1-56806-108-0) Diane Pub.
Levy. AIDS: Pathogenesis & Treatment. (Immunology Ser.: Vol. 44). 720p. 1989. 125.00 (0-8247-7684-4) Dekker.
— Arco NTE. 11th ed. 1995. audio, pap. text ed. 17.95 (0-02-860018-5, Arco Test) P-H Gen Ref & Trav.
— Cleo & Coyote. (J). 1996. 15.00 (0-06-024271-X); lib. bdg. 14.89 (0-06-024272-8) HarpC Child Bks.
— Dr. Seuss. 1994. write for info. (0-676-73211-9) Random Hse Value.
— The 403 (b) Answer Book. 300p. 1995. 79.00 (0-8342-0616-1) Aspen Pub.
— Frankenstein Moved In. (J). 1990. mass mkt. 3.50 (0-06-107013-0, Harp PBks) HarpC.
— How to Use French Verbs. 1977. pap. 8.95 (0-8120-0599-6) Barron.
— If You Were There When They Signed the Constitution. (Orig.). (J). 1992. 4.95 (0-590-45159-6) Scholastic Inc.
— Inventing & Patenting Sourcebook. 2nd ed. 1992. 90.00 (0-8103-7616-4) Gale.
— Massachusetts Zoning & Land Use Law. 1994. write for info. (1-56257-217-2) Butterworth Legal Pubs.
— National Teacher Exams. 11th ed. 1994. pap. 15.00 (0-671-84823-2, Arco Test) P-H Gen Ref & Trav.
— Return of the Jedi. 1995. 3.99 (0-679-87205-1) Random.
— Role of Procoagulant Activity in Health & Disease. 1993. 159.95 (0-8493-5566-4, QP93) CRC Pr.
— Role of Procoagulant Activity in Health & Disease. 1993. 165.00 (0-317-05735-9, QR186, CRC Reprint) Franklin.
— Welcome to. . . Networks: A Guide to LAN'S. 1993. pap. 19.95 (1-55828-259-9) MIS Press.
Levy & Hallowell. Green Perspectives: Thinking & Writing about Nature. (C). 1993. text ed. 18.75 (0-06-501500-2) HarpCollege.

An Asterisk (*) at the beginning of an entry indicates that the title is appearing in BIP for the first time.

Levy & Sarnat. Capital Investment & Financial Decisions. 5th ed. 1994. pap. text ed. 47.00 (*0-13-300112-1*) P-H.

Levy, jt. auth. see Berne, Robert M.

Levy, jt. auth. see Berne.

Levy, A. A Century of Model Trains. 2nd ed. (Illus.). 208p. (ENG & GER.). 1974. 45.00 (*0-911868-02-X*, C02) Carstens Pubns.

— Deep Inelastic Scattering & Related Subjects: Proceedings of the International Workshop. 552p. 1995. text ed. 124.00 (*981-02-2053-7*) World Scientific Pub.

Levy, A., et al, eds. Endogenous Peptides & Centrally Acting Drugs. (Progress in Biochemical Pharmacology Ser.: Vol. 16). (Illus.). xvi, 160p. 1980. 65.75 (*3-8055-0831-X*) S Karger.

Levy, A. E., jt. auth. see Butler-Sloss, Elizabeth.

Levy, A. V., ed. Proceedings: Corrosion-Erosion-Wear of Materials at Elevated Temperatures. (Illus.). 700p. 1991. 10.00 (*1-877914-18-5*) NACE Intl.

Levy, Abraham, jt. auth. see Gubby, Lucien.

Levy, Abraham J. Rashi's Commentary on Ezekiel 40-48. v, 122p. 1931. text ed. 12.95 (*0-685-65026-X*, Ctr Judaic Studies) Eisenbrauns.

Levy, Adolph J. Solving Statute of Limitations Problems. suppl. ed. 800p. 1987. 85.00 (*0-930273-65-6*) Michie Butterworth.

Levy, Alan. Ezra Pound: The Voice of Silence. LC 82-83126. 160p. (C). 1982. 16.00 (*0-932966-25-X*) Permanent Pr.

— So Many Heroes. rev. ed. LC 80-65002. Orig. Title: Rowboat to Prague. 384p. 1980. reprint ed. pap. 16.00 (*0-933256-16-7*) Second Chance.

— So Many Heroes. 2nd rev. ed. LC 80-65002. Orig. Title: Rowboat to Prague. 384p. 1980. reprint ed. 22.00 (*0-933256-12-4*) Second Chance.

— Vladimir Nabokov: The Velvet Butterfly. LC 83-63247. (Illus.). 164p. (C). 1984. pap. 16.00 (*0-932966-41-1*) Permanent Pr.

— W. H. Auden: In the Autumn of the Age of Anxiety. LC 82-84008. (Illus.). 160p. (C). 1983. pap. 16.00 (*0-932966-31-4*) Permanent Pr.

— The Wiesenthal File. LC 94-16552. (Illus.). 463p. 1994. 29.99 (*0-8028-3772-7*) Eerdmans.

Levy, Alan H. Elite Education & the Private School: Excellence & Arrogance at Phillips Exeter Academy. LC 90-38906. (Studies in Education: Vol. 11). 104p. 1990. lib. bdg. 59.95 (*0-88946-947-4*) E Mellen.

— Musical Nationalism: American Composers' Search for Identity. LC 82-12168. (Contributions in American Studies: No. 66). xi, 168p. 1983. text ed. 45.00 (*0-313-23709-3*, LMN/, Greenwood Pr) Greenwood.

— Radical Aesthetics & Music Criticism in America, 1930-1950. LC 91-35626. 80p. 1991. lib. bdg. 49.95 (*0-7734-9621-1*) E Mellen.

Levy, Alan S., et al. A Study of Nutrition Label Formats: Performance & Preference. 55p. (Orig.). (C). 1992. pap. text ed. 40.00 (*1-56806-050-5*) Diane Pub.

***Levy, Alan V.** Solid Particle Erosion & Erosion-Corrosion of Materials. 225p. 1995. 98.00 (*0-87170-519-2*) ASM.

Levy, Allan M. & Fuerst, Mark L. The Sports Injury Handbook: Professional Advice for Amateur Athletes. 304p. 1993. pap. text ed. 17.95 (*0-471-54737-9*) Wiley.

Levy, Allen, jt. auth. see Fuller, Roland.

Levy, Allen, ed. see Ottenheimer, Peter.

Levy, Amir & Merry, Uri. Organizational Transformation: Approaches, Strategies, & Theories. LC 86-9389. 347p. 1986. text ed. 59.95 (*0-275-92147-6*, C2147, Praeger Pubs) Greenwood.

Levy, Amnon. Economic Dynamics: Applications of Difference Equations, Differential Equations & Optimal Control. 213p. 1992. 68.95 (*1-85628-404-2*, Pub. by Avebury Pub UK) Ashgate Pub Co.

Levy, Amy. Reuben Sachs: A Sketch. LC 78-37699. reprint ed. 26.00 (*0-404-56758-4*) AMS Pr.

***Levy, Andre & Duffour, Jacqueline.** Dictionnaire Pratique de L'Alimentation. 1987. write for info. (*0-7859-7914-X*, 2-7021-1649-3) Fr & Eur.

Levy, Andre, ed. see Wu Cheng-en.

Levy, Andrew. The Culture & Commerce of the Short Story. LC 92-38879. (Cambridge Studies in American Literature & Culture: No. 68). 192p. (C). 1993. 47.95 (*0-521-44057-2*) Cambridge U Pr.

— Curve. 80p. 1994. 10.00 (*1-882022-20-3*) O Bks.

— Democracy Assemblages. 32p. 1990. 7.50 (*0-911623-08-6*) I Klang.

— Values Chauffeur You. LC 90-60632. 88p. 1991. 9.00 (*1-882022-06-8*) O Bks.

Levy, Anita. Other Women: The Writing of Class, Race & Gender, 1832-1898. (Illus.). 250p. 1991. text ed. 35.00 (*0-691-06865-8*); pap. text ed. 9.95 (*0-691-01493-0*) Princeton U Pr.

Levy, April. Writing College English. 340p. (C). 1988. pap. text ed. 17.50 (*0-15-597825-X*) HB Coll Pubs.

Levy, Avigdor. The Sephardim in the Ottoman Empire. LC 92-2992. (Illus.). 192p. (C). 1994. pap. 12.95 (*0-87850-089-8*) Darwin Pr.

Levy, Avigdor, ed. The Jews of the Ottoman Empire. LC 92-2991. (Illus.). 760p. (C). 1994. text ed. 49.95 (*0-87850-090-1*) Darwin Pr.

Levy, Azriel. A Hierarchy of Formulas in Set Theory. LC 52-42839. (Memoirs Ser.: No. 1/57). 76p. 1983. reprint ed. pap. 21.00 (*0-8218-1257-2*, MEMO 1/57) Am Math.

Levy, B. Barry. Planets, Potions & Parchments: Scientific Hebraica from the Dead Sea Scrolls to the Eighteenth Century. (Illus.). 124p. 1990. 60.00 (*0-7735-0793-0*, Pub. by McGill CN); pap. 29.95 (*0-7735-0791-4*, Pub. by McGill CN) U of Toronto Pr.

— Targum Neophyti One: A Textual Study: Leviticus, Numbers, Deuteronomy, Vol. 2. LC 86-11117. (Brown Classics in Judaica Ser.). 396p. (Orig.). (C). 1987. lib. bdg. 56.50 (*0-8191-6313-9*, Studies in Judaism); pap. text ed. 32.00 (*0-8191-6314-7*, Studies in Judaism) U Pr of Amer.

— Targun Neophyti One: A Textual Study: Introduction, Genesis, Exodus. LC 86-11117. (Studies in Judaism). 470p. (Orig.). (C). 1986. lib. bdg. 59.50 (*0-8191-5464-4*, Studies in Judaism); pap. text ed. 35.50 (*0-8191-5465-2*, Studies in Judaism) U Pr of Amer.

Levy, B. H. La Barbarie a Visage Humaine. (FRE.). 1985. pap. 12.95 (*0-7859-3127-9*) Fr & Eur.

— Eloge des Intellectuels. (FRE.). 1988. pap. 9.95 (*0-7859-3146-5*, 2253047759) Fr & Eur.

— Questions de Principe, Vol. 2. 1986. pap. 18.95 (*0-7859-3133-3*) Fr & Eur.

— Questions de Principe, Vol. 3: La Suite dans les Idees. (FRE.). 1990. pap. 18.95 (*0-7859-3156-2*, 2253054321) Fr & Eur.

— Questions de Principe, Vol. 4: Idees Fixes. (FRE.). 1992. pap. 22.95 (*0-7859-3172-4*, 2253061743) Fr & Eur.

— Savannah's Old Jewish Community Cemeteries. LC 83-1045. vii, 118p. 1983. 10.95 (*0-86554-076-4*, H68) Mercer Univ Pr.

Levy, B. S. The Last Open Road. 512p. 1994. 25.00 (*0-9642107-0-3*) Think Fast Ink.

Levy, Barbara. How to Draw Clowns. LC 91-17171. (Illus.). 32p. (J). (gr. 2-6). 1991. lib. bdg. 10.65 (*0-8167-2477-6*); pap. text ed. 1.95 (*0-8167-2478-4*) Troll Assocs.

Levy, Barbara W. Barbara's View: Los Angeles, California. rev. ed. (Illus.). (Orig.). 1992. pap. 7.50 (*1-882340-08-6*) Barbaras View.

— Barbara's View: Miami & South Florida. (Illus.). 1993. pap. 7.50 (*1-882340-09-4*) Barbaras View.

— Barbara's View: Miami & South Florida. rev. ed. 1994. 7.50 (*1-882340-16-7*) Barbaras View.

— Barbara's View: Miami & South Florida XXI 263-195. (Illus.). 1994. pap. 7.50 (*1-882340-17-5*) Barbaras View.

— Barbara's View: Milan, Italy. (Illus.). 1993. reprint ed. pap. 7.50 (*1-882340-14-0*) Barbaras View.

— Barbara's View: New York, New York. (Illus.). 1993. pap. 7.50 (*1-882340-11-6*) Barbaras View.

Levy, Barnet M. Handbook of Experimental Stomatology. 224p. 1982. 98.95 (*0-8493-3161-7*, RC815, CRC Reprint) Franklin.

Levy, Barnet M., et al. The Marmoset Periodontium in Health & Disease. Myers, H. M., ed. (Monographs in Oral Science: Vol. 1). 1972. 31.25 (*3-8055-1366-6*) S Karger.

Levy, Barrie. In Love & in Danger: A Teen's Guide to Breaking Free of Abusive Relationships. LC 92-41914. 107p. (Orig.). 1992. pap. 8.95 (*1-878067-26-5*) Seal Pr Feminist.

Levy, Barrie, ed. Dating Violence: Young Women in Danger. LC 90-24538. (New Leaf Ser.). 308p. (Orig.). 1991. pap. 16.95 (*1-878067-03-6*) Seal Pr Feminist.

***Levy, Barrie & Griggans, Patricia.** What Parents Need to Know about Dating Violence. 196p. (Orig.). 1995. pap. 10.95 (*1-878067-47-8*) Seal Pr Feminist.

Levy, Barry. Quakers & the American Family: British Quakers in the Delaware Valley, 1650-1765. 368p. 1992. reprint ed. pap. 18.95 (*0-19-504976-4*) OUP.

***Levy, Barry & Wegman, David, eds.** Occupational Health: Recognizing & Preventing Work-Related Disease. 3rd ed. LC 94-13146. 1994. 45.00 (*0-316-52271-6*) Little.

Levy, Bernard-Henry, jt. auth. see Giroud, Francoise.

Levy, Bernard S., ed. The Bible in the Middle Ages: Its Influence on Literature & Art. (Medieval & Renaissance Texts & Studies: Vol. 89). 224p. 1992. 25.00 (*0-86698-101-2*, MR89) MRTS.

Levy, Bernard S. & Szarmach, Paul E., eds. The Alliterative Tradition in the Fourteenth Century. LC 80-28821. 227p. reprint ed. pap. 64.70 (*0-7837-0293-0*, 2040614) Bks Demand.

Levy, Bertram L. & White, Benjamin T. Georgia Estate Planning, Will Drafting & Estate Administration Forms, 2 vols. suppl. ed. 1994. ring bd. 89.00 (*0-685-70883-7*) Butterworth Legal Pubs.

— Georgia Estate Planning, Will Drafting & Estate Administration Forms, 2 vols., Set. 980p. 1994. 5.25 hd, ring bd. 239.00 (*0-87189-062-3*) Michie Butterworth.

Levy, Beryl H. Anglo-American Philosophy of Law: An Introduction to Its Development & Outcome. 456p. (C). 1990. text ed. 49.95 (*0-88738-344-0*) Transaction Pubs.

Levy, Betty A., jt. ed. see Carr, Thomas H.

***Levy, Bill.** Knock-Off. LC 94-69936. 368p. 1995. 22.00 (*0-936385-22-7*) J Friedlander.

Levy, Brian & Wackers, Paul, eds. The Fox & Other Animals: Special Issue of "Reinardus, Yearbook of the International Reynard Society" (Illus.). vii, 212p. 1993. pap. 65.00x (*1-55619-336-X*) Benjamins North Am.

— Reinardus. (Yearbook of the International Reynard Society Ser.: Vol. 5). (Illus.). 246p. 1992. pap. 60.00 (*1-55619-335-1*) Benjamins North Am.

— Reinardus: Yearbook of the International Reynard Society, Vol. 4. (Illus.). ii, 250p. 1991. pap. 65.00 (*1-55619-334-3*) Benjamins North Am.

— Reinardus, Vol. 3: Yearbook of the International Reynard Society. 229p. 1990. pap. 65.00 (*1-55619-333-5*) Benjamins North Am.

— Reinardus, Vol. 6: Yearbook of the International Reynard Society. (Illus.). 248p. (ENG & FRE.). 1993. pap. 65.00x (*1-55619-337-8*) Benjamins North Am.

Levy, Brooks E. & Bastien, Pierre C. Roman Coins in the Princeton Library, I. Republic to Commodus. (Editions NR, 1985 Ser.). 191p. 1994. 100.00 (*0-685-72019-5*) Am Numismatic.

Levy-Bruhl, Lucien. How Natives Think. Coser, Lewis A. & Powell, Walter W., eds. Clare, Lilian A., tr. LC 79-7006. (Perennial Works in Sociology Ser.). 1980. reprint ed. lib. bdg. 31.95 (*0-405-12104-0*) Ayer.

— La Mythologie Primitive. 2nd ed. LC 75-35138. 1976. reprint ed. 57.50 (*0-404-14154-4*) AMS Pr.

— The Philosophy of Auguste Comte. 1976. lib. bdg. 59.95 (*0-8490-2430-7*) Gordon Pr.

— Primitive Mentality. Clare, Lillian A., tr. LC 75-41174. 1976. reprint ed. 69.50 (*0-404-14568-X*) AMS Pr.

— Primitives & the Supernatural. LC 73-4358. (Studies in Comparative Literature: No. 35). 1972. reprint ed. lib. bdg. 58.95 (*0-8383-1589-5*) M S G Haskell Hse.

Levy, Builder. Images of Appalachian Coalfields. LC 88-24816. (Visual Studies). (Illus.). 144p. (C). 1989. 27.95 (*0-87722-588-5*) Temple U Pr.

Levy, Carl, ed. Socialism & the Intelligentsia: 1880-1914. (History Workshop Ser.). 224p. (C). 1988. lib. bdg. 59.95 (*0-7102-0722-0*, RKP); pap. text ed. 22.00 (*0-7102-1257-7*, RKP) Routledge.

Levy, Celia, ed. Stuttering Therapies: Practical Approaches. 224p. 1987. pap. text ed. 25.95 (*0-7099-4145-5*, Pub. by Croom Helm UK) Routledge Chapman & Hall.

Levy, Charles. Crocodiles & Alligators. 1991. 9.98 (*1-55521-714-1*) Bk Sales Inc.

— Human Biology: Text & Laboratory Manual. 352p. (C). 1994. 39.95 (*0-8403-9618-X*) Kendall-Hunt.

Levy, Charles K. Biology: Human Perspectives Preliminary Edition. 256p. 1993. spiral bd. 34.95 (*0-8403-8945-0*) Kendall-Hunt.

— Elements of Biology. 3rd ed. LC 81-17556. (Biology Ser.). (Illus.). 620p. 1983. teacher ed write for info. (*0-201-04565-6*); text ed. write for info. (*0-201-04564-8*); student ed write for info. (*0-201-04566-4*) Addison-Wesley.

Levy, Charles S. Guide to Ethical Decisions & Actions for Social Service Administrators: A Handbook for Managerial Personnel. LC 81-13511. (Supplement to Administration in Social Work Ser.: No. 1). 160p. 1982. text ed. 32.95 (*0-86656-106-4*) Haworth Pr.

— Social Work Ethics. LC 75-11007. 266p. 1976. 42.95 (*0-87705-254-9*); pap. 20.95 (*0-87705-493-2*) Human Sci Pr.

— Social Work Ethics on the Line. LC 92-3349. 130p. 1993. lib. bdg. 29.95 (*1-56024-282-5*) Haworth Pr.

Levy, Charlotte L. Computer-Assisted Litigation Support: An Annotated Bibliography. LC 84-1756. (CompuBibs Ser.: No. 4). 31p. 1984. pap. 10.00 (*0-914791-02-8*) Vantage Info.

Levy, Charlotte L. & Robbins, Sara. Library Automation: A Systems & Software Sampler. (CompuBibs Ser.: No. 11). 87p. 1985. pap. 15.50 (*0-914791-10-9*) Vantage Info.

Levy, Christopher & Barrett, David S. Questions & Answers on Apley's Concise System of Orthopedics. 192p. 1991. pap. 15.95 (*0-7506-1170-7*) Buttrwrth-Heinemann.

Levy, Claude. Emancipation, Sugar, & Federalism: Barbados & the West Indies, 1833-1876. LC 79-18084. (University of Florida Latin American Monographs: No. 25). (Illus.). viii, 206p. 1980. 18.95 (*0-8130-0655-4*) U Press Fla.

Levy, Constance. I'm Going to Pet a Worm Today: And Other Poems. LC 91-7485. (Illus.). 48p. (J). (gr. k-5). 1991. text ed. 12.95 (*0-689-50535-3*, McElderry) S&S Childrens.

— A Tree Place: And Other Poems. LC 93-20586. (Illus.). 48p. (J). (gr. k-5). 1994. lib. bdg. 12.95 (*0-689-50599-X*, McElderry) S&S Childrens.

Levy, D. Heuristic Programming in Artificial Intelligence: The Second Computer Olympiad. (Artificial Intelligence Ser.). 200p. 1991. text ed. 86.00 (*0-13-382615-5*, 270305) P-H.

Levy, D. A. The Madison Poems & Collages. 1980. 12.00 (*0-685-04199-9*) Quixote.

Levy, D. A., et al. Zen Concrete & Etc. (Illus.). 245p. 1991. pap. 27.50 (*0-941160-04-1*) Ghost Pony Pr.

Levy, D. H. The Quest for Comets: An Explosive Trail of Beauty & Danger. (Illus.). 260p. (C). 1994. 23.95 (*0-306-44651-0*, Plenum Pr) Plenum.

Levy, Dana, jt. auth. see Grilli, Peter.

Levy, Daniel C. Higher Education & the State in Latin America: Private Challenges to Public Dominance. LC 85-21023. xviii, 434p. (C). 1986. 27.50 (*0-226-47608-1*) U Ch Pr.

— University & Government in Mexico: Autonomy in a Authoritarian System. LC 79-21134. 190p. 1980. text ed. 49.95 (*0-275-90512-8*, C0512, Praeger Pubs) Greenwood.

Levy, Daniel C., ed. Private Education & Public Policy: Studies in Choice & Public Policy. LC 85-15568. 1986. text ed. 48.00 (*0-19-503710-3*) OUP.

Levy, Daniel C. & Szekely, Gabriel. Mexico: Paradoxes of Stability & Change. 2nd rev. ed. (Profiles - Nations of Contemporary Africa Ser.). 297p. (C). 1987. pap. text ed. 19.95 (*0-8133-0350-8*) Westview.

Levy, Daniel J. Automobile Aerobics: Exercise Your Right to Trim Thousands Off the Price of Your Next Automobile & Make the Dealership Sweat! 160p. 1994. pap. 9.95 (*0-9637628-8-5*) Tennyson Pub.

Levy, Daniel S., et al. Conceptual & Statistical Issues in Contingent Valuation: Estimating the Value of Altered Visibility in the Grand Canyon. LC 93-48695. 54p. 1995. pap. text ed. 13.00 (*0-8330-1500-1*) Rand Corp.

Levy, Danielle. Race Relations - New Wine & Old Bottles: Creating a Newer Vision. Parker, Diane, ed. LC 92-50878. 200p. 1993. pap. 11.95 (*0-88247-980-6*, 980) R & E Pubs.

Levy, Darline G. The Ideas & Careers of Simon-Nicolas-Henri Linguet: A Study in Eighteenth-Century French Politics. LC 79-24109. (Illus.). 394p. 1980. 39.95 (*0-252-00311-X*) U of Ill Pr.

Levy, Darline G., jt. ed. see Applewhite, Harriet B.

Levy, Darline G., et al, eds. Women in Revolutionary Paris, 1789-1795. 326p. 1980. pap. 15.95 (*0-252-00855-3*) U of Ill Pr.

Levy, David. Joel: The Day of the Lord. LC 86-82328. 1986. pap. text ed. 6.95 (*0-915540-37-1*) Frnds Israel.

Levy, David, ed. see Dollars & Sense Staff, et al.

Levy, David, jt. auth. see Keene, Raymond.

Levy, David, jt. auth. see Levy, S. Jay.

Levy, David, jt. ed. see National Industrial Council Staff.

Levy, David B. Beethoven: The Ninth Symphony. (Monuments of Western Music Ser.). (Illus.). 1995. text ed. 35.00 (*0-02-871363-X*) Schirmer Bks.

Levy, David H. Clyde Tombaugh: Discoverer of Planet Pluto. LC 90-48545. (Illus.). 212p. 1992. reprint ed. pap. 15.95 (*0-8165-1317-1*) U of Ariz Pr.

— Impact Jupiter: The Crash of Comet Shoemaker-Levy 9. (Illus.). 300p. 1995. 25.95 (*0-306-45088-7*, Plenum Pr) Plenum.

— The Man Who Sold the Milky Way: A Biography of Bart Bok. LC 93-4039. (Illus.). 246p. 1993. 35.00 (*0-8165-1149-7*) U of Ariz Pr.

— The Quest for Comets: An Explosive Trail of Beauty & Danger. 304p. 1995. reprint ed. pap. 12.50 (*0-380-72526-6*) Avon.

— The Sky: A User's Guide. (Illus.). 313p. (C). 1993. pap. 14.95 (*0-521-45958-3*) Cambridge U Pr.

— Skywatching. O'Byrne, John, ed. LC 95-8609. (A Nature Company Guide Ser.). (Illus.). 288p. 1995. write for info. (*0-7835-4751-X*) Time-Life.

— Variable Star Observing. 180p. 1989. 27.95 (*0-521-32113-1*) Cambridge U Pr.

Levy, David H., ed. The Sky: A User's Guide. (Illus.). 300p. (C). 1991. 29.95 (*0-521-39112-1*) Cambridge U Pr.

Levy, David H., jt. auth. see Edberg, Stephen J.

Levy, David J. The Measure of Man: Incursions in Philosophical & Political Anthropology. 248p. (C). 1993. text ed. 34.95 (*0-8262-0899-1*) U of Mo Pr.

— Political Order: Philosophical Anthropology, Modernity, & the Challenge of Ideology. LC 87-13456. 208p. 1988. text ed. 32.50 (*0-8071-1389-1*) La State U Pr.

Levy, David L. Best Parent - Both Parents. 1993. 9.95 (*1-878901-56-7*) Hampton Roads Pub Co.

— Revolt of the Animals: or What Really Happened at Chernobyl. (Illus.). 117p. (Orig.). 1992. pap. 13.95 (*0-929492-03-X*) Nextstep Pubns.

Levy, David M. The Economic Ideas of Ordinary People: From Preferences to Trade. 304p. 1991. 69.95 (*0-415-06770-7*, A6163) Routledge.

Levy, David N., ed. Computer Chess Compendium. 450p. 1989. 53.00 (*0-387-91331-9*) Spr-Verlag.

— Computer Games I. (Illus.). 350p. 1988. 61.00 (*0-387-96496-7*) Spr-Verlag.

— Computer Games II. (Illus.). 365p. 1988. 72.00 (*0-387-96609-9*) Spr-Verlag.

— Learn Chess from the World Champions. 214p. 1979. pap. text ed. 17.95 (*0-08-021388-X*, Pergamon Pr) Elsevier.

Levy, David N. & Newborn, Monty. How Computers Play Chess. 280p. 1995. text ed. write for info. (*0-7167-8239-1*) W H Freeman.

— How Computers Play Chess. 280p. 1995. pap. text ed. write for info. (*0-7167-8121-2*) W H Freeman.

Levy, David N. & O'Connell, Kevin J. How to Play the Sicilian Defense: Primary Level. (Chess Library). (Illus.). 160p. 1988. pap. 14.95 (*0-02-029191-4*, Collier S&S) S&S Trade.

— Instant Chess. (Chess Ser.). (Illus.). 83p. 1984. 17.90 (*0-08-024122-0*, Pergamon Pr); pap. 11.90 (*0-08-024121-2*, Pergamon Pr) Elsevier.

Levy, David W. The Debate over Vietnam. LC 90-49525. (American Moment Ser.). 216p. 1991. text ed. 38.95 (*0-8018-4148-8*); pap. text ed. 12.95 (*0-8018-4149-6*) Johns Hopkins.

— The Debate over Vietnam. 2nd ed. LC 95-3385. (American Moment Ser.). 230p. 1995. pap. text ed. 13.95x (*0-8018-5114-9*) Johns Hopkins.

— The Debate over Vietnam. 2nd ed. LC 95-3385. (American Moment Ser.). 230p. 1995. text ed. 38.95x (*0-8018-5113-0*) Johns Hopkins.

Levy, David W., ed. see Brandeis, Louis D.

Levy, David W., jt. ed. see Buhite, Russell D.

Levy, David W., jt. ed. see Urofsky, Melvin I.

Levy, Deborah. Heresies & Evan & Moses. (Methuen New Theatrescripts Ser.). 34p. 1988. pap. 8.95 (*0-413-17170-1*, A0123, Pub. by Methuen UK) Heinemann.

Levy, Deborah, ed. Walks on Water. 160p. 1992. pap. 19.95 (*0-413-67120-8*, A0655, Pub. by Methuen UK) Heinemann.

***Levy, Delores G.** Branching Out: Emmy's Story. (Orig.). (YA). (gr. 8-12). 1995. audio 13.95 (*0-9642639-1-2*) Portraits West.

— Branching Out: Emmy's Story. (Illus.). 142p. (Orig.). (YA). (gr. 8-12). 1995. pap. 7.95 (*0-9642639-0-4*) Portraits West.

Levy, Dominique, jt. auth. see Dumenil, Gerard.

Levy, Donald, jt. auth. see Goldsmith, Donald.

Levy, Donald L., tr. see Haggai, J. E.

Levy, Doran J., jt. auth. see Morgan, Carol M.

Levy, Dore J. Chinese Narrative Poetry: The Tradition in Shih from the Late Han Through Tang Dynasties. LC 88-14712. 224p. (C). 1988. lib. bdg. 36.95 (*0-8223-0863-0*) Duke.

Levy, E. Provencal-Francais. 5th ed. 387p. 1973. pap. 58.00 (*3-533-01393-6*) IBD Ltd.

Levy, E., ed. Le Systeme Palatial en Orient, en Grece et a Rome: Acts du Collogie de Strasbourg, 19-22 Juin 1985. (Travaux du Centre de Recherche sur le Proche Orient et la Grece Antiques Ser.: Vol. 9). (Illus.). 502p. 1987. pap. 91.50 (*90-04-08520-3*) E J Brill.

An Asterisk (*) at the beginning of an entry indicates that the title is appearing in BIP for the first time.

L

L

*Levy, E. & Herrington, C. S., eds.** Non-Isotopic Methods in Molecular Biology: A Practical Approach. (Practical Approach Ser.: Vol. 153). (Illus.). 240p. 1995. pap. 49.00 (0-19-963455-6, IRL Pr); bds. 89.00 (0-19-963456-4, IRL Pr) OUP.

Levy, E., jt. auth. see World Association of Societies of Pathology Staff.

*Levy, Earl J.** Examination of Witnesses in Criminal Cases. 3rd ed. 490p. 1994. 90.00 (0-459-55279-1, 9552791-671) Carswell Co.

Levy, Edmond. Making A Winning Short. 1994. pap. 14.95 (0-8050-2680-0) H Holt & Co.

*Levy, Elie.** Dictionnaire de Physique. 890p. (FRE.). 1988. 250.00 (0-7859-8622-7, 213039311x) Fr & Eur.

Levy, Elizabeth. The Case of the Gobbling Squash. (Illus.). (J). (gr. 2-4). 1988. pap. 13.00 (0-671-63655-3, S&S Bks Young Read) S&S Childrens.

— The Case of the Gobbling Squash. (Illus.). (J). (gr. 2-4). 1989. pap. 2.95 (0-671-68873-1, S&S Bks Young Read) S&S Childrens.

— The Case of the Mind-Reading Mommies. (Illus.). (J). 1990. pap. 2.95 (0-671-69435-9) S&S Trade.

— The Case of the Tattletale Heart. (Illus.). 64p. (J). (gr. 2-4). 1992. pap. 3.00 (0-671-74064-4, S&S Bks Young Read) S&S Childrens.

— Cheater, Cheater. LC 92-33455. (J). 1993. 13.95 (0-590-45865-5) Scholastic Inc.

— Cheater, Cheater. (J). (gr. 4-7). 1994. pap. 3.50 (0-590-45866-3) Scholastic Inc.

— Cold As Ice. 176p. 1989. pap. 2.95 (0-380-70315-7, Flare) Avon.

— Double Standard. 160p. (J). (gr. 7 up). 1984. pap. 2.25 (0-380-87379-6, 87379-6, Flare) Avon.

— Dracula Is a Pain in the Neck. LC 82-47707. (Illus.). 80p. (J). (gr. 2-6). 1983. lib. bdg. 13.89 (0-06-023823-2) HarpC Child Bks.

— Dracula Is a Pain in the Neck. LC 82-47707. (Trophy Bk.). (Illus.). 80p. (J). (gr. 2-5). 1984. pap. 3.95 (0-06-440146-4, Trophy) HarpC Child Bks.

— Dracula Is a Pain in the Neck. (J). 1990. mass mkt. 3.50 (0-06-107014-9) HarpC.

— The Drowned. 208p. (J). (gr. 5-9). 1995. 16.95 (0-7868-0135-2) Hyprn Child.

— First Date. (Gymnasts Ser.: No. 13). (J). 1990. pap. 2.75 (0-590-42825-X) Scholastic Inc.

— Frankenstein Moved in on the Fourth Floor. LC 78-19830. (Illus.). (J). (gr. 1-5). 1979. lib. bdg. 13.89 (0-06-023811-9) HarpC Child Bks.

— Frankenstein Moved in on the Fourth Floor. LC 78-19830. (Trophy Bk.). (Illus.). 64p. (J). (gr. 2-5). 1981. pap. 3.95 (0-06-440122-7, Trophy) HarpC Child Bks.

— The Gorgonzola Zombies in the Park. LC 92-11353. (Trophy Bk.). (Illus.). 96p. (J). (gr. 2-5). 1994. pap. 3.95 (0-06-440555-9, Trophy) HarpC Child Bks.

— Keep Ms. Sugarman in the Fourth Grade. LC 91-22576. (Illus.). 96p. (J). (gr. 3-6). 1992. 13.95 (0-06-020426-5); lib. bdg. 13.89 (0-06-020427-3) HarpC Child Bks.

— Keep Ms. Sugarman in the Fourth Grade. LC 91-22576. (Trophy Bk.). 96p. (J). (gr. 3-6). 1993. pap. 3.95 (0-06-440487-0, Trophy) HarpC Child Bks.

— A Mammoth Mix-Up: A Brian & Pea Brain Mystery. LC 94-47960. (Brian & Pea Brain Mystery Ser.). (Illus.). 96p. (J). (gr. 2-5). 1995. 12.95 (0-06-024814-9, HarpT); lib. bdg. 12.89 (0-06-024815-7, HarpT) HarpC Child Bks.

— The Mystery of the Missing Dog. LC 94-38765. (Hello Reader! Ser.: Vol. 2). (Illus.). (J). 1995. pap. 3.50 (0-590-47484-7) Scholastic Inc.

— The New Coach? (Gymnasts Ser.: No. 18). 128p. (J). (gr. 3-7). 1991. pap. 2.75 (0-590-44695-9) Scholastic Inc.

— Out of Control. (Gymnasts Ser.: No. 12). (J). (gr. 4-7). 1990. pap. 2.75 (0-590-42824-1) Scholastic Inc.

— Rude, Rowdy Rumors: A Brian & Pea Brain Mystery, No. 2. LC 93-46792. (Illus.). 96p. (J). (gr. 2-5). 1994. 13.00 (0-06-023462-8); lib. bdg. 12.89 (0-06-023463-6) HarpC Child Bks.

— School Spirit Sabotage: A Brian & Pea Brain Mystery. LC 93-23029. (Illus.). 96p. (J). 1994. 14.00 (0-06-023407-5); lib. bdg. 13.89 (0-06-023408-3) HarpC Child Bks.

— The Schoolyard Mystery. (Hello Reader!, Invisible Inc. Ser.: Level 4, Bk. 1). (Illus.). 48p. (J). (gr. 2-3). 1994. pap. 3.50 (0-590-47483-9, Cartwheel) Scholastic Inc.

— Something Queer at the Ball Park. (Something Queer Ser.). (Illus.). 48p. (J). (gr. 1-4). 1984. pap. 3.50 (0-440-48116-3, YB) Dell.

— Something Queer at the Ball Park. (J). (gr. 1-3). 17.00 (0-8446-6256-9) Peter Smith.

— Something Queer at the Haunted School. (Something Queer Ser.). (Illus.). 48p. (J). (gr. 1-4). 1983. pap. 3.25 (0-440-48461-8, YB) Dell.

— Something Queer at the Library. (Something Queer Ser.). (Illus.). 48p. (J). (gr. 1-4). 1989. pap. 3.25 (0-440-48120-1, YB) Dell.

— Something Queer at the Scary Movie. LC 94-45618. (Illus.). 48p. (J). (gr. 2-5). 1995. 13.95 (0-7868-0150-6); pap. 4.95 (0-7868-1056-4) Hyprn Child.

— Something Queer in Outer Space. LC 92-54870. (Something Queer Ser.). (Illus.). 48p. (J). (gr. 2-5). 1993. 12.95 (1-56282-566-6) Hyprn Child.

— Something Queer in Outer Space. LC 92-54870. (Something Queer Ser.). (Illus.). 48p. (J). (gr. 2-5). 1995. pap. 4.95 (1-56282-279-9) Hyprn Ppbks.

— Something Queer in the Cafeteria. LC 93-31343. (Illus.). 48p. (J). (gr. 2-5). 1994. 13.95 (0-7868-0001-1); pap. 4.95 (0-7868-1000-9) Hyprn Child.

— Something Queer in the Cafeteria. (Something Queer Ser.: Bk. 2). (Illus.). 48p. (J). (gr. 2-5). 1994. pap. 4.95 (0-685-74694-1) Hyprn Ppbks.

— Something Queer Is Going On. (Something Queer Ser.). (Illus.). 48p. (J). (gr. 1-4). 1982. pap. 3.25 (0-440-47974-6, YB) Dell.

— Something Queer Is Going On. (J). (gr. 1-3). 16.50 (0-8446-6257-7) Peter Smith.

*Levy, Ellen, ed.** Tasting Life Twice: Lesbian Literary Fiction by New American Writers. LC 94-47010. (Orig.). 1995. pap. 10.00 (0-380-78123-9) Avon.

Levy, Emanuel. George Cukor, Master of Elegance: Hollywood's Legendary Director & His Stars. LC 93-31894. 1994. 25.00 (0-688-11246-3) Morrow.

— The Habima--Israel's National Theater, 1917-1977. LC 79-12486. 384p. 1979. text ed. 52.00 (0-231-04582-4) Col U Pr.

— John Wayne: Prophet of the American Way of Life. LC 87-28410. (Illus.). 399p. 1988. 39.50 (0-8108-2054-4) Scarecrow.

— Small-Town America in Film: The Decline & Fall of Community. (Illus.). 288p. 1990. 27.95 (0-8264-0484-7, F Ungar Bks) Continuum.

*Levy, Emil.** Petit Dictionnaire Provencal-Francais. 387p. (FRE & PRO.). 1990. pap. 59.95 (0-7859-8169-1, 2869712790) Fr & Eur.

Levy, Eric P. Beckett & the Voice of Species: A Study of the Prose Fiction. 145p. 1980. 44.00 (0-389-20004-2, 06781) B&N Imports.

Levy, Ernest, jt. auth. see Levarie, Siegmund.

Levy, Ernst. Pauli Sententiae: A Palingenesia of the Opening Titles As a Specimen of Research in West Roman Vulgar Law. LC 76-96338. xii, 130p. 1969. reprint ed. 25.00 (0-678-04533-X) Kelley.

— Pauli Sententiae, a Palingenesia of the Opening Titles As a Specimen of Research in West Roman Vulgar Law. xii, 130p. 1970. reprint ed. text ed. 7.50 (0-8377-2400-7) Rothman.

— A Theory of Harmony. LC 85-12604. (SUNY Series in Cultural Perspectives). (Illus.). 99p. 1985. 59.50 (0-87395-993-0); pap. 19.95 (0-87395-992-2) State U NY Pr.

Levy, Ernst, jt. auth. see Levarie, Siegmund.

Levy, Esther. Jewish Cookery Book. 200p. 1988. reprint ed. 11.95 (1-55709-109-9) Applewood.

— Jewish Cookery Book on Principles of Economy Adapted for Jewish Housekeepers. LC 74-28000. (Modern Jewish Experience Ser.). 1975. reprint ed. 23.95 (0-405-06727-5) Ayer.

Levy, Eugene. James Weldon Johnson, Black Leader, Black Voice. LC 72-95134. (Negro American Biographies & Autobiographies Ser.). 393p. pap. 112.10 (0-8357-8927-6, 2056786) Bks Demand.

Levy, Eugene, et al, eds. Protostars & Planets Three. LC 92-44841. (Space Science Ser.). (Illus.). 1596p. 1993. 90.00 (0-8165-1334-1) U of Ariz Pr.

*Levy, Faye.** Classic Techniques for Fine Cooking. LC 94-28039. (California Culinary Academy Ser.). (Illus.). 128p. 1995. pap. 11.95 (1-56426-071-2) Cole Group.

— Faye Levy's International Chicken Cookbook. 1992. 29.95 (0-446-51569-8) Warner Bks.

— Faye Levy's International Jewish Cookbook. LC 91-50083. (Illus.). 336p. 1991. 29.95 (0-446-51568-X) Warner Bks.

— Faye Levy's International Jewish Cookbook. 384p. 1995. pap. 12.99 (0-446-67126-6) Warner Bks.

— Faye Levy's International Vegetable Cookbook: Over 300 Sensational Recipes from Argentina to Zaire & Artichokes to Zucchini. LC 92-51034. (Illus.). 464p. 1993. 29.95 (0-446-51719-4) Warner Bks.

— The La Varenne Tour Book. (Illus.). 171p. 1979. pap. 7.95 (0-89716-057-6) P B Pubng.

— Sensational Chocolate. (Illus.). 192p. 1992. pap. 14.95 (1-55788-049-2, HP Books) Berkley Pub.

— Sensational Pasta. (Illus.). 192p. (Orig.). 1989. pap. 14.95 (0-89586-631-5, HP Books) Berkley Pub.

— 30 Low-Fat Meals in 30 Minutes. 208p. (Orig.). 1995. pap. 9.99 (0-446-67059-6) Warner Bks.

Levy, Fran S. Dance Movement Therapy: A Healing Art. rev. ed. (Illus.). 377p. (C). 1992. pap. text ed. 29.95 (0-88314-531-6) AAHPERD.

Levy, Francis A., ed. Crystallography & Crystal Chemistry of Materials with a Layered Structure. (Physics & Chemistry of Materials with Layered Structures Ser.: No. 2). 380p. 1976. lib. bdg. 131.50 (90-277-0586-0) Kluwer Ac.

— Fritz Hulliger: Structural Chemistry of Layer-Type Phases. LC 76-26635. (Physics & Chemistry of Materials with Layered Structures Ser.: No. 5). 1977. lib. bdg. 131.50 (90-277-0714-6) Kluwer Ac.

— Intercalated Layered Materials. (Physics & Chemistry of Materials with Layered Structures Ser.: No. 6). 1979. lib. bdg. 158.00 (90-277-0967-X) Kluwer Ac.

Levy, Frank. Dollars & Dreams: The Changing American Income Distribution. LC 86-42952. (Population of the United States in the 1980s: A Census Monograph Ser.). 256p. (Orig.). 1987. 34.95 (0-87154-523-3) Russell Sage.

— Dollars & Dreams: The Changing American Income Distribution. (Orig.). 1988. pap. 9.95 (0-393-30557-0) Norton.

Levy, Frank S. & Michel, Richard C. The Economic Future of American Families: Income & Wealth Trends. LC 90-20278. (Illus.). 148p. (Orig.). (C). 1991. lib. bdg. 42.00 (0-87766-486-2); pap. text ed. 15.25 (0-87766-487-0) Urban Inst.

Levy, Frank S., et al. Urban Outcomes: Schools, Streets, & Libraries. (Oakland Project Ser.). 1974. pap. 14.00 (0-520-03045-1) U CA Pr.

Levy, Fritz J., ed. see Bacon, Francis.

Levy, G. & De Vachon, M. La Douleur. 1993. pap. text ed. 29.00 (2-88124-893-4) Gordon & Breach.

Levy, Gail, ed. see Stodden, Norma J. & McCormick, Linda.

Levy, Gail, ed. see Stodden, Norma J.

Levy, Gail, ed. see Stodden, Norma J. & McCormick, Linda.

Levy, Gary & White, Graham, eds. Provincial & Territorial Legislatures in Canada. 369p. 1989. pap. 18.95 (0-8020-6734-4) U of Toronto Pr.

Levy, Geoffrey M. Packaging in the Envirnment. 1993. 87.50 (0-7514-0091-2, Pub. by Blackie Acad & Prof UK) Routledge Chapman & Hall.

Levy, George. To Die in Chicago: Confederate Prisons at Camp Douglas, 1862-1865. (Illus.). 328p. 1994. boxed 25.00 (1-879260-20-4) Evanston Pub.

Levy, George C., ed. Topics in Carbon-13 NMR Spectroscopy, Vol. 4. (Topics in Carbon-13 NMR Spectroscopy Ser.: 1-683). 282p. 1984. text ed. 144.00 (0-471-09857-4, Wiley-Interscience) Wiley.

Levy, George C., et al. Carbon-13 Nuclear Magnetic Resonance Spectroscopy. 2nd ed. 352p. (C). 1993. reprint ed. lib. bdg. 59.95 (0-89464-796-2) Krieger.

Levy, Gerald M., ed. Arbitration of Real Estate Valuation Disputes. LC 87-71510. 1987. pap. 19.95 (0-943001-21-8) Am Arbitration.

Levy, Gerhard, ed. see Benet, Leslie Z., et al.

Levy, Gerold H., jt. auth. see Kofke, W. Andrew.

Levy, Gertrude R. The Sword from the Rock: Investigation into the Origins of Epic Literature & Development of the Hero. 1976. lib. bdg. 59.95 (0-8490-2723-3) Gordon Pr.

Levy, H. The Universe of Science. LC 74-26272. (History, Philosophy & Sociology of Science Ser.). 1975. reprint ed. 23.95 (0-405-06600-7) Ayer.

Levy, H. & Lessman, F. Finite Difference Equations. unabridged ed. LC 92-20438. (Illus.). 278p. 1992. reprint ed. pap. text ed. 7.95 (0-486-67260-3) Dover.

Levy, H. M., Jr., ed. see Partee, Phillip E.

*Levy, Haim.** Introduction to Investments. 960p. (C). 1996. text ed. write for info. (0-201-51372-2) Addison-Wesley.

Levy, Haim, ed. Research in Finance, Vol. 1. 1979. lib. bdg. 73.25 (0-89232-043-5) Jai Pr.

— Research in Finance, Vol. 2. 250p. 1980. lib. bdg. 73.25 (0-89232-130-X) Jai Pr.

— Research in Finance, Vol. 3. 225p. 1981. 73.25 (0-89232-218-7) Jai Pr.

— Research in Finance, Vol. 4. 1983. 73.25 (0-89232-279-9) Jai Pr.

— Research in Finance, Vol. 5. 1985. 73.25 (0-89232-587-9) Jai Pr.

Levy, Haim & Sarnat, Marshall. Capital Investment & Financial Decisions. 5th ed. LC 93-25792. 1994. pap. text ed. 20.00 (0-13-115882-1) P-H Gen Ref & Trav.

Levy, Haim, jt. auth. see Ben-Horim, Moshe.

Levy, Harold B. Square Pegs, Round Holes: The Learning-Disabled Child in the Classroom & at Home. LC 73-3422. (Illus.). 288p. 1974. 8.95 (0-316-52232-5) Little.

Levy, Harold P. There Were Days Like That. DeWitt, Beverley J., ed. (Illus.). 164p. (Orig.). 1985. pap. 9.95 (0-9615303-0-8) Blue Whale Pr.

Levy, Harriet L. Nine-Twenty O'Farrell Street. LC 74-29501. (Modern Jewish Experience Ser.). (Illus.). 1975. reprint ed. 25.95 (0-405-06728-3) Ayer.

Levy, Harry L. A Latin Reader for Colleges. LC 62-18119. (Midway Reprint Ser.). xii, 264p. 1989. reprint ed. pap. text ed. 13.95 (0-226-47601-4) U Ch Pr.

Levy, Harry L., intro. Lucian: Seventy Dialogues. LC 75-5652. (American Philological Association Ser.: Vol. 4). 1977. 22.95 (0-8061-1216-6) U of Okla Pr.

Levy, Helen F. Fiction of the Home Place: Jewett, Cather, Glasgow, Porter, Welty, & Naylor. LC 91-35996. 272p. 1993. reprint ed. pap. 17.95 (0-87805-663-7) U Pr of Miss.

*Levy, Henry L.** Finding Your Self & Helping Others: The Holistic Way. Widosh, Kathleen & Widosh, Bud, eds. (Illus.). 210p. (Orig.). 1995. pap. 14.00 (0-9645413-9-4) Ctr Psychol.

Levy, Henry M. & Eckhouse, Richard H. Computer Programming & Architecture: The VAX. 2nd ed. (Illus.). 444p. (C). 1989. text ed. 39.95 (1-55558-015-7, EY-6740E-DP, Digital DEC) Buttrwrth-Heinemann.

Levy, Hermann. Economic Liberalism. LC 79-51864. 1981. reprint ed. 15.95 (0-88355-956-0) Hyperion Conn.

— Monopoly & Competition: A Study in English Industrial Organisation. Wilkins, Mira, ed. LC 76-29993. (European Business Ser.). 1977. reprint ed. lib. bdg. 31.95 (0-405-09751-4) Ayer.

Levy, Hilton B., ed. The Biochemistry of Viruses. LC 75-90149. (Illus.). 671p. reprint ed. pap. 180.00 (0-7837-0951-X, 2041256) Bks Demand.

Levy, Howard B., et al. Diagnosis & Management of the Hospitalized Child. 696p. 1984. pap. 38.00 (0-89004-913-0) Raven.

Levy, Howard S. Izumi Shikibu as a Love Poetress (Flourished 990-1020), 300 Poems. (East Asian Poetry in Translation Ser.: No. 16-18). 1981. pap. 16.00 (0-686-37538-6) Oriental Bk Store.

— Lesser Known Japanese Poetry Classics. (East Asian Poetry in Translation Ser.: No. 7). 1976. pap. 8.00 (0-89986-302-7) Oriental Bk Store.

— The Lotus Lovers: The Complete History of the Curious Erotic Custom of Footbinding in China. (Chinese Erotic & Sexual Classics Ser.). 352p. 1992. 31.95 (0-87975-687-X) Prometheus Bks.

— One Hundred Haiku. (East Asian Poetry in Translation Ser.: No. 5). 1976. pap. 8.00 (0-89986-300-0) Oriental Bk Store.

— One Hundred Shinkokinshu. (East Asian Poetry in Translation Ser.: No. 4). 1976. pap. 8.00 (0-89986-299-3) Oriental Bk Store.

Levy, Howard S., tr. Japanese Love Poems, 1-100, No. 7. (East Asian Poetry in Translation Ser.). 1976. pap. 8.00 (0-89986-304-3) Oriental Bk Store.

— Japanese Love Poems, 101-200, Vol. 8. (East Asian Poetry in Translation Ser.). 1977. pap. 8.00 (0-89986-322-1) Oriental Bk Store.

— Japanese Love Poems, 201-300, Vol. 9. (East Asian Poetry in Translation Ser.). 1977. pap. 8.00 (0-89986-323-X) Oriental Bk Store.

— Korean Love Poems, Vol. 2. 1976. pap. 8.00 (0-89986-258-6) Oriental Bk Store.

— Minamoto No Sanetomo (1192-1219) As a Love Poet (Japanese Love Poems 501-600) (East Asian Poetry in Translation Ser.: No. 14). 1980. pap. 8.00 (0-686-37536-X) Oriental Bk Store.

— One Hundred Selections from Kokinshu. (East Asian Poetry in Translation Ser.: No. 3). 1976. pap. 8.00 (0-89986-259-4) Oriental Bk Store.

— One Hundred Senryu Selections. (East Asian Poetry in Translation Ser.: No. 10). 1979. pap. 8.00 (0-89986-301-9) Oriental Bk Store.

— Saigyo: More Love Poems (101-200) (East Asian Poetry in Translation Ser.: No. 15). 1981. pap. 8.00 (0-686-37537-8) Oriental Bk Store.

— Saigyo (1112-1190) As a Love Poet: One Hundred More Selections (201-300), Japanese Love Poems (1001-1100) (East Asian Poetry in Translation Ser.: No. 20). 1981. pap. 8.00 (0-686-37540-8) Oriental Bk Store.

— Saigyo (1118-1190) As a Love Poet (Japanese Love Poems, 401-500) (East Asian Poetry in Translation Ser.: No. 12). 1980. pap. 8.00 (0-686-37534-3) Oriental Bk Store.

— Saigyo (1118-1190) the Poet of Reflective Being & Natural Scene. (East Asian Poetry in Translation Ser.: No. 13). 1980. pap. 8.00 (0-686-37535-1) Oriental Bk Store.

Levy, Howard S. & Ishihara, Akira. The Tao of Sex. 2nd ed. (Illus.). 241p. 1989. 24.95 (0-941255-43-3); pap. 12.95 (0-941255-44-1) Integral Pub.

Levy, Howard S. & Ohsawa, Junko, trs. Japanese Love Poems (301-400) (East Asian Poetry in Translation Ser.: No. 11). 1980. pap. 8.00 (0-686-37533-5) Oriental Bk Store.

Levy, Ian H. Hitomaro & the Birth of Japanese Lyricism. LC 83-42564. 200p. 1984. 29.95x (0-691-06581-0) Princeton U Pr.

Levy, Ian H., tr. The Ten Thousand Leaves: A Translation of the Man'yoshu, Japan's Premier Anthology of Classical Poetry, Vol. 1. LC 80-8561. (Library of Asian Translations). (Illus.). 280p. (C). 1981. pap. 16.95 (0-691-00029-8) Princeton U Pr.

Levy, Isaac, tr. The Pentateuch, 7 vols. 4257p. (ENG & HEB.). 1962. 100.00 (0-910818-12-6) Judaica Pr.

Levy, Isaac J. Jewish Rhodes: A Lost Culture. (Illus.). 96p. 1989. 9.95 (0-685-49192-7) Magnes Mus.

Levy, Isaac J., tr. And the World Stood Silent: Sephardic Poetry of the Holocaust. LC 88-19932. 248p. 1989. 22.50 (0-252-01580-0) U of Ill Pr.

Levy, Ivor S. MCQs for FRCOPHTH for the Royal College of Ophthalmologists Examinations. 140p. (C). 1994. pap. text ed. 16.50 (0-7923-8847-X) Kluwer Ac.

— MCQs for MRCOPHTH for the Royal College of Ophthalmologists Examinations. 80p. (C). 1994. pap. text ed. 14.75 (0-7923-8848-8) Kluwer Ac.

— MCQs in Optics & Refraction for the Royal College of Ophthalmologists Examinations. 48p. (C). 1994. pap. text ed. 14.75 (0-7923-8835-6) Kluwer Ac.

Levy, J. One Minute Reference: WordPerfect 6 for Windows. 1993. pap. 6.99 (1-56761-283-0) Alpha Bks IN.

Levy, J., jt. auth. see Hoffmann, G.

Levy, J. A., ed. The Retroviridae, Vol. 1. (Viruses Ser.). (Illus.). 316p. 1992. 95.00 (0-306-44074-1, Plenum Pr) Plenum.

— The Retroviridae, Vol. 2. (Viruses Ser.). (Illus.). 480p. (C). 1993. 89.50 (0-306-44369-4, Plenum Pr) Plenum.

— The Retroviridae, Vol. 3. (Viruses Ser.). (Illus.). 535p. (C). 1994. 110.00 (0-306-44693-6, Plenum Pr) Plenum.

Levy, J. C., jt. auth. see Delacour, J.

Levy, J. M. Urban & Metropolitan Economics. 448p. 1985. text ed. write for info. (0-07-037455-4) McGraw.

Levy, Jack, jt. ed. see Wubbels, Theo.

Levy, Jack S. War in the Modern Great Power System, 1495-1975. LC 83-10249. 232p. 1983. 25.00 (0-8131-1497-7); pap. 8.00 (0-8131-0164-6) U Pr of Ky.

Levy, Jade, jt. ed. see Levy, Lynnie.

Levy, Jane & Helzel, Florence B. The Jewish Illustrated Book. LC 86-80427. (Illus.). 150p. (Orig.). 1986. pap. 16.00 (0-943376-33-5) Magnes Mus.

Levy, Janet, jt. auth. see Levy, Nathan.

*Levy, Janice.** The Spirit of Tio Fernando: A Day of the Dead Story. Mlawer, Teresa, tr. LC 95-1318. (Illus.). (ENG & SPA.). 1995. write for info. (0-8075-7585-2) A Whitman.

Levy, Jay A. HIV & the Pathogenesis of AIDS. LC 94-20424. (Illus.). 370p. 1994. pap. 49.00 (1-55581-076-4) Am Soc Microbio.

Levy, Jay A., et al. Virology. 3rd ed. LC 93-2450. 1994. text ed. 71.00 (0-13-953753-8) P-H.

Levy, Jerrold E. & Kunitz, Stephen J. Indian Drinking: Navajo Practices & Anglo-American Theories. LC 73-17173. 271p. reprint ed. 77.30 (0-8357-9910-7, 2055122) Bks Demand.

Levy, Jerrold E. & Pepper, Barbara. Orayvi Revisited: Social Stratification in an "Egalitarian" Society. (Resident Scholar Ser.). (Illus.). 198p. 1992. 35.00 (0-933452-33-0, U of Wash Pr) Schol Am Res.

Levy, Jerrold E., jt. auth. see Kunitz, Stephen J.

Levy, Jerrold E., et al. Hand Trembling, Frenzy Witchcraft & Moth Madness. LC 87-19445. 176p. 1987. 27.95 (0-8165-1036-9) U of Ariz Pr.

Levy, Jerrold H. Anaphylactic Reactions in Anesthesia & Intensive Care. 2nd ed. 1992. 50.00 (0-7506-9064-X) Buttrwrth-Heinemann.

An Asterisk (*) at the beginning of an entry indicates that the title is appearing in BIP for the first time.

Levy, Jill & Lowe, Robert. Management Review of the Allegheny County (Pa.) Court of Common Pleas Court Reporter Division. 180p. 1991. 11.00 (0-685-50608-8, NERO251) Natl Ctr St Courts.

Levy, Jill B., jt. auth. see Hewitt, William E.

Levy, Jo, tr. see Adamov, Arthur.

Levy, Jo, tr. see Aragon, Louis.

Levy, Joan U. Advance Placement Exam in U.S. Government & Politics. 1994. pap. 15.00 (0-671-84780-5, Arco Test) P-H Gen Ref & Trav.

Levy, Joan U. & Levy, Norman. ACT: American College Testing Program. 15th ed. LC 93-48848. 1994. pap. 12.00 (0-671-88822-6, Arco Test) P-H Gen Ref & Trav.

Levy, Joan U., jt. auth. see Levy, Norman.

Levy, Joan U., et al. Advanced Placement Examination in European History. 2nd ed. LC 92-34477. 1993. 14.00 (0-671-84777-5, Arco Test) P-H Gen Ref & Trav.

Levy, JoAnn. They Saw the Elephant: Women in the California Gold Rush. LC 92-54146. (Illus.). 288p. 1992. reprint ed. pap. 12.95 (0-8061-2473-3) U of Okla Pr.

Levy, John. FormTool Made Easy. 1992. pap. text ed. 19.95 (0-07-881740-4) Osborne-McGraw.

— Suppose a Man. 1977. 4.00 (0-685-88979-3) Elizabeth Pr.

— We Don't Kill Snakes Where We Come From: Two Years in a Greek Village. 128p. 1993. pap. 8.00 (1-882168-02-X) Querencia Bks.

Levy, John M. Contemporary Urban Planning. 3rd ed. LC 93-24560. 352p. 1993. pap. text ed. write for info. (0-13-146614-3) P-H.

— Economic Development Programs for Cities, Counties & Towns. 2nd ed. LC 90-32301. 192p. 1990. text ed. 49.95 (0-275-93366-0, C3366, Praeger Pubs); pap. text ed. 14.95 (0-275-93760-7, B3760, Praeger Pubs) Greenwood.

— Essential Microeconomics for Public Policy Analysis. LC 95-7990. 1995. text ed. write for info. (0-275-94362-3, Praeger Pubs); pap. text ed. write for info. (0-275-94363-1, Praeger Pubs) Greenwood.

Levy, John M., ed. see Moliterno, James E.

Levy, Jon D. Maine Family Law, 1988-1991: Divorce, Separation & Annulment. 380p. 1994. ring bd. 85.00 (0-89442-076-3) Michie Butterworth.

— Maine Family Law, 1988-1991: Divorce, Separation & Annulment. suppl. ed. 380p. 1993. 40.00 (0-88063-790-0) Butterworth Legal Pubs.

Levy, Jonathan. Charlie the Chicken & Other Plays. 86p. (Orig.). 1990. 10.00 (0-685-32638-1) Playsmith.

— The Gymnasium of the Imagination: A Collection of Children's Plays in English, 1780-1860. LC 91-16448. (Contributions in Drama & Theatre Studies: No. 40). 296p. 1992. text ed. 55.00 (0-313-26697-2, LGN, Greenwood Pr) Greenwood.

— Marco Polo. 1977. pap. 4.75 (0-8222-0732-X) Dramatists Play.

— A Theatre of the Imagination. 56p. pap. 7.95 (0-932720-75-7) New Plays Inc.

Levy, Joseph, ed. A Practical Approach to Pediatric Gastroenterology. (Illus.). 250p. 1987. 39.95 (0-8151-5419-4, GKL-1, Yr Bk Med Pubs) Mosby Yr Bk.

Levy, Joseph, pref. Play Behavior. LC 83-6102. 250p. (C). 1983. reprint ed. text ed. 27.50 (0-89874-627-2) Krieger.

***Levy, Joseph, et al, eds.** Connectionist Models of Memory & Language. 288p. 1995. 59.95x (1-85728-368-6, Pub. by UCL Pr UK) Taylor & Francis.

Levy, Joseph R. Building LANtastic Networks. 1994. pap. 29.95 (1-55851-394-9) M&T Bks.

— Create Your Own Virtual Reality System. 1994. text ed. 44.95 (0-07-037651-4); disk, pap. 32.95 (0-07-037652-2) McGraw.

— Flight Simulator 5 Strategies & Secrets. LC 93-86066. 231p. 1993. 12.99 (0-7821-1249-8) Sybex.

— Networking Fundamentals. 2nd ed. 1995. pap. 21.95 (1-55828-404-4) MIS Press.

Levy, Joseph V. & Bach-Y-Rita, Paul. Vitamins: Their Use & Abuse. 155p. 1976. 8.95 (0-87140-616-0) Liveright.

Levy, Judith. Dad Remembers: A Treasury of Memories for My Child. (Illus.). 64p. 1993. 16.95 (0-06-017007-7, HarpT) HarpC.

— Grandfather Remembers: Memories for my Grandchild. LC 85-45645. 64p. 1986. 16.95i (0-06-015561-2, HarpT) HarpC.

— V. S. Naipaul: Displacement & Autobiography. LC 94-37551. (Reference Library of the Humanities: Vol. 1781). 176p. 1994. 26.00 (0-8153-1468-X, H1781) Garland.

Levy, Judith & Pelikan, Judy. Grandmother Remembers: A Written Heirloom for My Grandchild. (Illus.). 64p. 1983. 15.95 (0-941434-32-X) Stewart Tabori & Chang.

— Grandmother Remembers Family Recipes. (Illus.). 96p. 1984. 15.95 (0-941434-46-X) Stewart Tabori & Chang.

— Grandmother Remembers Songbook. LC 92-50287. 1992. 15.95 (1-56305-316-0, 3316) Workman Pub.

Levy, Judith, jt. auth. see Rascon, Bonnie.

Levy, Judy. Patchwork Pillows. LC 76-47804. (Illus.). 1977. pap. 4.50 (0-486-23473-8) Dover.

Levy, Julien. Surrealism. LC 68-9469. 1968. reprint ed. 18.95 (0-405-00299-8, Ind Pubns) Ayer.

— Surrealism. (Illus.). 202p. 1995. reprint ed. pap. 17.95 (0-306-80663-0) Da Capo.

Levy, Julien, ed. see Berman, Eugene.

Levy, Juliette D. Complete Herbal Handbook for the Dog & Cat. 1991. pap. 12.95 (0-571-16115-4) Faber & Faber.

— Illustrated Herbal Handbook for Everyone. (Illus.). 224p. 1992. pap. 12.95 (0-571-11894-1) Faber & Faber.

Levy, Juliette de Bairacli. The Complete Herbal Handbook for Farm & Stable. 384p. (Orig.). 1991. pap. 12.95 (0-571-16116-2) Faber & Faber.

Levy, Karen B. The Politics of Women's Health Care: Medicalization As a Form of Social Control. LC 92-39492. (Woman in History Ser.: Vol. 60). (Illus.). 133p. 1992. pap. 10.00 (0-86663-201-8) Ide Hse.

Levy, Kenneth. Music: A Listener's Introduction. 526p. (C). 1989. text ed. 53.00 (0-06-043978-5) HarpCollege.

— Music: A Listener's Introduction. 526p. (C). 1990. student ed 16.50 (0-06-044072-4); lp 56.50 (0-06-043933-5) HarpCollege.

Levy-Konesky, Nancy & Brovender, Jacqueline G. Revue. 256p. (FRE.). (C). 1990. pap. text ed. 27.00 (0-03-026422-7) HB Coll Pubs.

Levy-Konesky, Nancy & Daggett, Karen. Asi Es. (ENG & SPA.). (C). 1991. text ed., vhs write for info. (0-318-69165-5) HB Coll Pubs.

— Asi Es. (Illus.). 560p. (SPA.). (C). 1992. teacher ed write for info. (0-03-049482-6); text ed. 45.25 (0-03-033379-2) HB Coll Pubs.

— Revista. Perez-Abreu, Marilyn et al, eds. 250p. (C). 1988. pap. text ed. 22.75 (0-03-014214-8) HB Coll Pubs.

Levy-Konesky, Nancy, jt. auth. see Carrara, Antonio.

Levy-Konesky, Nancy, et al. Fronteras: Gramatica y Conversacion. 320p. (C). 1987. pap. text ed. 26.75 (0-03-004029-9) HB Coll Pubs.

— Fronteras: Gramatica y Conversacion. 2nd ed. 352p. (ENG & SPA.). (C). 1990. 23.50 (0-03-034587-1) HB Coll Pubs.

— Fronteras: Gramatica y Conversacion. 2nd ed. 352p. (ENG & SPA.). (C). 1990. pap. text ed. 17.00 (0-03-049033-2) HB Coll Pubs.

— Fronteras: Gramatica y Conversacion. 2nd ed. 352p. (ENG & SPA.). (C). 1992. student ed write for info. (0-318-69166-3); pap. text ed. 29.50 (0-03-049017-0); 31.00 (0-03-049014-6) HB Coll Pubs.

— Fronteras: Literatura y Cultura. 2nd ed. 208p. (ENG & SPA.). (C). 1992. pap. text ed. 26.00 (0-03-049018-9) HB Coll Pubs.

— Fronteras: Literatura y Cultura. 2nd ed. 208p. (ENG & SPA.). (C). 1992. pap. text ed. 22.00 (0-03-049012-X); audio 6.75 (0-03-055889-1) HB Coll Pubs.

Levy, L. Rotary International. 1990. 135.00 (0-7121-1851-9, Pub. by Northcote UK) St Mut.

Levy, L., jt. auth. see Bilgram, Hugo.

Levy, Laurie, ed. see Morton Press Staff.

Levy, Lawrence & Morgan, Brian. Golf: Tours & Detours. (Illus.). 160p. 1988. 24.95 (0-88162-362-8, Pergamon Pr) Elsevier.

Levy, Lawrence & White, Gordon S., Jr. A Victory for Jamie: The Story of Greg Norman & Jamie Hutton. (Illus.). 64p. 1989. 20.00 (0-9615344-4-3) Intl Merc OH.

Levy-Leblond, J. M. & Balibar, F. Quantics. 1990. 115.50 (0-444-87424-0); pap. 44.95 (0-444-88120-4) Elsevier.

Levy-Leblond, J. M. & Cini, M., eds. Quantum Theory Without Reduction. (Illus.). 180p. 1990. 54.00 (0-7503-0031-0) IOP Pub.

Levy-Leblond, Jean-Marc, jt. ed. see Beltrametti, Enrico E.

Levy-Leboyer, Claude. Le Psychologue et l'Entreprise. (Collection De Psychologie Appliquee). 175p. (FRE.). reprint ed. pap. 49.90 (0-7837-6951-2, 2046780) Bks Demand.

— Psychology & Environment. Canter, David & Griffiths, Ian, trs. LC 81-21382. 197p. reprint ed. pap. 56.20 (0-8357-4821-9, 2037758) Bks Demand.

Levy-Leboyer, Claude, ed. Vandalism: Behavior & Motivations. 364p. 1984. 95.00 (0-444-86775-9, I-245-84) Elsevier.

Levy-Leboyer, Maurice & Bourguignon, Francois. The French Economy in the Nineteenth Century: An Essay in Econometric Analysis. (Illus.). (C). 1990. 79.95 (0-521-33147-1) Cambridge U Pr.

Levy, Leo B., jt. ed. see McNeir, Waldo F.

Levy, Leon S. Fundamental Concepts of Computer Science: Mathematical Foundations of Programming. LC 88-392. (Illus.). 318p. (C). 1988. reprint ed. pap. 23.00 (0-932633-06-4) Dorset Hse Pub Co.

Levy, Leonard, et al, eds. Encyclopedia of The American Constitution, 2 vols. 2196p. 1990. 175.00 (0-685-47371-6) Macmillan.

Levy, Leonard A. & Hetherington, Vincent J., eds. Principles & Practice of Podiatric Medicine. (Illus.). 1171p. 1990. text ed. 174.00 (0-443-08534-X) Churchill.

Levy, Leonard A. & Thompson, Anne K., eds. Podiatric Medical Assisting. 2nd ed. (Illus.). 295p. 1992. pap. text ed. 45.00 (0-443-08760-1) Churchill.

Levy, Leonard W. Blasphemy: An Anglo-American History of Free Expression. LC 92-36345. 1993. 35.00 (0-679-40236-5) Knopf.

— Blasphemy: Verbal Offense Against the Sacred, from Moses to Salman Rushdie. LC 94-31365. 688p. 1995. pap. 18.95 (0-8078-4515-9) U of NC Pr.

— Blasphemy in Massachusetts: Freedom of Conscience & the Abner Kneeland Case. LC 70-16634. 592p. 1973. lib. bdg. 65.00 (0-306-70221-5) Da Capo.

— Constitutional Opinions: Aspects of the Bill of Rights. 288p. 1989. reprint ed. pap. 18.95 (0-19-505945-X) OUP.

— Emergence of a Free Press. rev. ed. 416p. 1987. pap. 12.95 (0-19-504240-9) OUP.

— Encyclopedia of American Presidency, Vol. 4. 1993. 80.00 (0-13-275975-6) P-H.

— Encyclopedia of the American Presidency, Vol. 1. 1993. 80.00 (0-13-276197-1) P-H.

— Encyclopedia of the American Presidency, Vol. 3. 1993. 80.00 (0-13-275967-5) P-H.

— Essays on the Making of the Constitution. 2nd ed. LC 86-16255. (Orig.). 1987. 14.95 (0-19-504902-0) OUP.

— The Establishment Clause: Religion & the First Amendment. 2nd ed. LC 94-1046. 300p. 1994. 34.95 (0-8078-2156-X); pap. 14.95 (0-8078-4466-7) U of NC Pr.

— Jefferson & Civil Liberties: The Darker Side. 264p. 1989. reprint ed. pap. 8.95 (0-929587-11-1, Elephant Paperbacks) I R Dee.

— A License to Steal: The Forfeiture of Property. LC 95-14497. 1995. write for info. (0-8078-2242-6) U of NC Pr.

— Original Intent & the Framer's Constitution. 288p. 1988. text ed. 19.95 (0-02-918791-5) Macmillan.

— Origins of the Fifth Amendment: The Right Against Self-Incrimination. 576p. 1986. reprint ed. text ed. 23.99 (0-02-919570-5); reprint ed. pap. 14.95 (0-02-919580-2) Macmillan.

— Seasoned Judgments: Constitutional Rights & American History. 410p. (C). 1994. 39.95 (1-56000-170-4) Transaction Pubs.

— Supplement to the Encyclopedia of the American Constitution. 704p. 1992. Blue binding. text ed. 100.00 (0-02-918675-7); Red binding. text ed. 100.00 (0-02-918678-1) Macmillan.

***Levy, Leonard W., ed.** Freedom of the Press from Zenger to Jefferson. (C). 1995. reprint ed. text ed. write for info. (0-89089-837-5) Carolina Acad Pr.

Levy, Leonard W. & Fisher, Louis, eds. Encyclopedia of the American Presidency, Set. LC 93-13574. 1993. 355.00 (0-13-275983-7) S&S Trade.

Levy, Leonard W. & Jones, Douglas L., eds. Jim Crow in Boston: The Origin of the "Separate but Equal Doctrine" LC 73-39622. (Civil Liberties in American History Ser.). 1974. lib. bdg. 35.00 (0-306-70157-X) Da Capo.

Levy, Leonard W. & Mahoney, Dennis J. The Framing & Ratification of the Constitution. 1987. write for info. (0-317-62103-3) Macmillan.

Levy, Leonard W. & Mahoney, Dennis J., eds. The Constitution: A History of Its Framing & Ratification. 352p. 1987. 23.99 (0-02-918790-7) Macmillan.

Levy, Leonard W., et al, eds. American Constitutional History. (Readings from the Encyclopedia of the American Constitution Ser.). 352p. (C). 1989. pap. 12.95 (0-02-897231-7) Macmillan.

— Civil Rights. (Readings from the Encyclopedia of the American Constitution Ser.). 350p. (C). 1989. pap. 12.95 (0-02-897241-4) Macmillan.

— Encyclopedia of the American Constitution, 4 vols. LC 86-3038. 1500p. 1986. 400.00 (0-02-918610-2) Macmillan.

— The Encyclopedia of the American Constitution, 2 vols., Set. 1990. lib. bdg. 175.00 (0-02-918695-1) Macmillan.

Levy, Lillian, ed. Space: Its Impact on Man & Society. LC 72-13181. (Essay Index Reprint Ser.). 1977. reprint ed. 19.95 (0-8369-8164-2) Ayer.

***Levy, Linda & Grabowski, Francine.** Low-Fat Living for Real People: The Fat-Free Chocolate-Covered Creme-Filled Mini-Cakes Diet & Other Confusions of Low-Fat Eating Explained. LC 94-76345. 208p. 1994. pap. 12.95 (0-9627403-5-7) Lake Isle Pr.

Levy, Lou, ed. Day Walks in the Santa Monica Mountains. rev. ed. 125p. (Orig.). 1986. pap. 3.95 (0-9619564-0-2) SMMTF.

Levy, Louis E. The Jewish Year. 1979. lib. bdg. 59.95 (0-685-96463-9) Revisionist Pr.

Levy, Lynnie & Levy, Jade, eds. Of a Like Mind Source Book: For Spiritually-Minded Women. 124p. 1990. pap. 10.00 (0-9626751-0-5) Triple Crescent.

Levy, M., et al, eds. Quantitative Particle Physics: Caregese 1992. (NATO ASI Series B, Physics: Vol. 311). (Illus.). 430p. (C). 1993. 120.00 (0-306-44560-3, Plenum Pr) Plenum.

Levy, M, et al, eds. Z Degree Physics: Cargese 1990. (NATO ASI Series B, Physics: Vol. 261). (Illus.). 522p. 1991. 125.00 (0-306-43934-4, Plenum Pr) Plenum.

***Levy, M. J., ed.** Perdita: The Memoirs of Mary Robinson, 1758-1800. 1995. 35.00 (0-614-07439-8) Dufour.

Levy, Marc. Rhodesia Becomes Zimbabwe: The United States & the Internal Settlement & The Lancaster House Conference. (Pew Case Studies in International Affairs). 50p. (C). 1989. pap. text ed. 2.50 (1-56927-442-8) Geo U Inst Dplmcy.

Levy, Margot, ed. Annual Obituary 1984. 1986. 95.00 (0-912289-53-8) St James Pr.

Levy, Marguerite F., ed. Research & Theory in Developmental Psychology: Awards Papers of the New York State Psychological Association. 1983. 27.50 (0-8290-1067-X) Irvington.

Levy, Marilyn. City Girl, Country Girl. (Orig.). 1993. mass mkt. 3.99 (0-449-70424-6, Juniper) Fawcett.

— Fitting In. (Orig.). (YA). 1991. mass mkt. 3.99 (0-449-70373-8, Juniper) Fawcett.

— Is That Really Me in the Mirror? 144p. (Orig.). 1991. pap. 3.95 (0-449-70343-6, Juniper) Fawcett.

— No Way Home. 1992. 17.50 (0-8446-6520-7) Peter Smith.

— Remember to Remember Me. (J). (gr. 5 up). 1988. pap. 2.95 (0-449-70278-2, Juniper) Fawcett.

Levy, Marion F. Each in Her Own Way: Five Women Leaders of the Developing World. LC 87-26844. 182p. 1988. pap. text ed. 17.95 (1-55587-094-5) Lynne Rienner.

Levy, Marion J., Jr. Maternal Influence: The Search for Social Universals. 263p. (C). 1992. pap. 19.95 (1-56000-614-5) Transaction Pubs.

— Our Mother-Tempers. 1989. 40.00 (0-520-06422-4) U CA Pr.

Levy, Mark. Joan Brown: The Golden Age. LC 86-50213. (Illus.). 40p. (Orig.). 1986. pap. 12.00 (0-937097-00-4) SDSU Univ Art.

— Technicians of Ecstasy: Shamanism & the Modern Artist. (Illus.). 360p. (Orig.). 1993. pap. 14.95 (0-9626184-4-6) Bramble Co.

Levy, Mark R., ed. The VCR Age. (Focus Editions Ser.: Vol. 105). 280p. (C). 1989. text ed. 49.95 (0-8039-3299-5); pap. text ed. 24.95 (0-8039-3300-2) Sage.

Levy, Mark R. & Gurevitch, Michael. Defining Media Studies: Reflections on the Future of the Field. (Illus.). 448p. (C). 1994. text ed. 48.00 (0-19-508787-9); pap. text ed. 19.95 (0-19-508788-7) OUP.

Levy, Mark R., jt. ed. see Biocca, Frank.

Levy, Mark R., jt. auth. see Robinson, John P.

Levy, Markus, jt. auth. see Dipert, Brian.

Levy-Marschal, Claire & Czernichow, P., eds. Epidemiology & Etiology of Insulin-Dependent Diabetes in the Young. (Pediatric & Adolescent Endocrinology Ser.: Vol. 21). (Illus.). xii, 242p. 1992. 192.00 (3-8055-5521-0) S Karger.

Levy, Martin, et al. Life & Health: Targeting Wellness. 1992. text ed. write for info. (0-07-037494-5); pap. text ed. write for info. (0-07-037523-2) McGraw.

Levy, Marvin, et al. Essentials of Life & Health. 5th ed. 486p. (C). 1987. text ed. 24.95 (0-685-18212-6) McGraw.

Levy, Matthew N. & Vassalle, Mario, eds. Excitation & Neural Control of the Heart. (American Physiological Society Book). (Illus.). 312p. 1988. 45.00 (0-19-520701-7) OUP.

Levy, Matthew N., jt. ed. see Berne, Robert M.

Levy, Matthew N., jt. ed. see Schwartz, Peter J.

Levy, Matthys. Why Buildings Fall Down. 1994. pap. 11.95 (0-393-31152-X) Norton.

Levy, Matthys, jt. auth. see Salvadori, Mario.

Levy, Maurice. Lovecraft: A Study in the Fantastic. Joshi, S. T., tr. LC 87-36470. 144p. 1988. 31.95 (0-8143-1955-6); pap. 14.95 (0-8143-1956-4) Wayne St U Pr.

Levy, Maurice, ed. Cargese Lectures in Physics, 1972, Vol. 7. x, 502p. 1977. text ed. 241.00 (0-677-15750-9) Gordon & Breach.

Levy, Maurice & Bessis, D., eds. Cargese Lectures in Physics: 1970 Lectures, Vol. 5. 556p. (C). 1972. text ed. 331.00 (0-677-15180-2) Gordon & Breach.

Levy, Maurice & Jancovici, B., eds. Cargese Lecture Notes 1964: Vol. 1, Statistical Mechanics, Vol. 64. 244p. (Orig.). (C). 1966. text ed. 218.00 (0-677-10980-6) Gordon & Breach.

Levy, Maurice & Jean, M., eds. Cargese Lectures in Physics, 1966-1968, Vol. 1. 438p. (Orig.). 1967. text ed. 342.00 (0-677-11650-0) Gordon & Breach.

— Cargese Lectures in Physics, 1966-1968, Vol. 2. 432p. (Orig.). 1968. 175.00 (0-677-12720-0) Gordon & Breach.

— Cargese Lectures in Physics, 1966-1968, Vol. 3. 686p. (Orig.). 1969. text ed. 407.00 (0-677-13580-7) Gordon & Breach.

Levy, Maurice & Kastler, D., eds. Cargese Lectures in Physics, 1969, Vol. 4. 398p. 1970. text ed. 292.00 (0-677-13910-1) Gordon & Breach.

Levy, Maurice & Lurcat, F., eds. Cargese Lecture Notes, 1965: Application of Mathematics to Problems in Theoretical Physics, Vol. 65. 516p. 1967. text ed. 304.00 (0-677-11660-8) Gordon & Breach.

Levy, Maurice & Meyer, P., eds. Cargese Lectures Notes, 1963: Elementary Particles & High Energy Physics, Vol. 63. 370p. 1965. text ed. 267.00 (0-677-10590-8) Gordon & Breach.

Levy, Maurice & Robinson, John L., eds. Energy & Agriculture: Their Interacting Futures Policy & Implications & Global Models. (Golbal Modelling & Applications Ser.: Vol. I). 384p. 1984. text ed. 196.00 (3-7186-0187-7) Gordon & Breach.

Levy, Maurice, jt. auth. see Cournand, Andre.

Levy, Maurice, et al, eds. Particle Physics: Cargese 1985. Weyers, Jacques & Castamans, Raymond, trs. (NATO ASI Series B, Physical Sciences: Vol. 150). 447p. 1987. 95.00 (0-306-42562-9, Plenum Pr) Plenum.

— Particle Physics: Cargese 1987. LC 88-4180. (NATO ASI Series B, Physics: Vol. 173). (Illus.). 684p. 1988. 145.00 (0-306-42835-0, Plenum Pr) Plenum.

— Particle Physics: Cargese 1989. (NATO ASI Series B, Physics: Vol. 223). (Illus.). 368p. 1990. 95.00 (0-306-43601-9, Plenum Pr) Plenum.

Levy, Michael. Natalie Babbit. (Twayne's United States Authors Ser.: No. 573). 136p. (C). 1991. text ed. 20.95 (0-8057-7612-5, Twayne) Macmillan.

— Political Thought in America: An Anthology. 2nd ed. 596p. (C). 1992. reprint ed. pap. text ed. 25.95 (0-88133-688-2) Waveland Pr.

Levy, Michael & Weitz, Barton A. Retailing Management. 864p. (C). 1991. text ed. 64.95 (0-256-05989-6) Irwin.

— Retailing Management. 2nd ed. LC 94-26274. (Marketing Ser.). 736p. (C). 1994. text ed. 64.95 (0-256-13661-0) Irwin.

Levy, Michael, ed. see Academy of Marketing Science Staff.

Levy, Michael, ed. see Hewson, brendan.

Levy, Michael, et al. Statmaster for Business & Economics. (C). 1987. pap. text ed. 12.75 (0-673-39523-5) HarpCollege.

Levy, Michael B., jt. ed. see Abbot, Philip.

Levy, Michael B., jt. ed. see Portis, Edward B.

Levy, Michael H., jt. auth. see Green, Helen I.

Levy, Michele F., et al, eds. Borders of Culture, Margins of Identity: Seventh Annual Colloquium of the Interdisciplinary Nineteenth Century Studies Association, New Orleans, 1992. (Occasional Publications Ser.: No. 3). (Illus.). 95p. (Orig.). 1994. pap. 8.95 (1-883275-01-6) Xavier Rev.

***Levy, Mike.** Decorated Earthenware. (Complete Potter Ser.). (Illus.). 96p. 1995. pap. 19.95 (0-7134-7714-8) Trafalgar.

Levy, Miriam J. Governance & Grievance: Habsburg Policy & Italian Tyrol in the Eighteenth Century. LC 87-15189. 272p. (Orig.). 1988. pap. 17.50 (0-911198-86-5) Purdue U Pr.

Levy, Mitchell A. Home Ownership: The American Myth: Rent vs. Buy Analysis. rev. ed. (Illus.). 160p. (Orig.). 1993. pap. 11.95 (0-9633302-1-7) Myth Breakers.

Levy, Morten. The World of the Gorrlaus Slatts: A Morphological Investigation of a Branch of Norwegian Fiddle Music Tradition, 3 vols., Set. (Illus.). 960p. (Orig.). 1989. pap. 142.50x (*87-89160-02-9*, Pub. by Almqv & Wiksell SW) Coronet Bks.

Levy, Myrna N. The Summer Kid. (J). (gr. 1-5). Date not set. pap. 5.95 (*0-929005-20-1*, Pub. by Second Story Pr CN) InBook.

Levy, Nathan. Each Life Is Once. (J). (gr. k up). 1993. pap. 7.95 (*1-878347-15-2*) NL Assocs.

— Nathan Levy's One Hundred Intriguing Questions, Bk. 1. (J). (gr. 3 up). 1993. 7.95 (*1-878347-35-7*) NL Assocs.

— Nathan Levy's One Hundred Intriguing Questions, Bk. 2. (J). (gr. 3 up). 1994. 7.95 (*1-878347-36-5*) NL Assocs.

— Nathan Levy's One Hundred Intriguing Questions, Bk. 3. (J). (gr. 3 up). 1994. 7.95 (*1-878347-37-3*) NL Assocs.

— Nathan Levy's 100 Intriguing Questions, Bk. 4. 52p. (Orig.). (YA). (gr. 3 up). 1994. pap. 7.95 (*1-878347-38-1*) NL Assocs.

— Nathan Levy's 100 Intriguing Questions, Bk. 5. 52p. (Orig.). (YA). (gr. 3 up). 1994. pap. 7.95 (*1-878347-40-3*) NL Assocs.

— Nathan Levy's 100 Intriguing Questions, Bk. 6. 52p. (Orig.). (YA). (gr. 3 up). 1994. pap. 7.95 (*1-878347-42-X*) NL Assocs.

— Personality Probe. (J). (gr. k up). 1990. pap. 19.95 (*1-878347-07-1*) NL Assocs.

— Stories with Holes. 40p. (Orig.). (YA). (gr. 3 up). 1994. pap. 6.00 (*1-878347-44-6*) NL Assocs.

— Stories with Holes, Vol. I. (Orig.). (J). (gr. 3 up). 1987. 6.00 (*0-685-63374-8*) NL Assocs.

— Stories with Holes, Vol. II. (Orig.). (J). (gr. 3 up). 1990. pap. 6.00 (*1-878347-00-4*) NL Assocs.

— Stories with Holes, Vol. III. (Orig.). (J). (gr. 3 up). 1990. pap. 6.00 (*1-878347-01-2*) NL Assocs.

— Stories with Holes, Vol. IV. (Orig.). (J). (gr. 3 up). 1990. pap. 6.00 (*1-878347-02-0*) NL Assocs.

— Stories with Holes, Vol. V. (Orig.). (J). (gr. 3 up). 1990. pap. 6.00 (*1-878347-03-9*) NL Assocs.

— Stories with Holes, Vol. VI. (Orig.). (J). (gr. 3 up). 1991. pap. 6.00 (*1-878347-09-8*) NL Assocs.

— Stories with Holes, Vol. VII. (Orig.). (J). (gr. 3 up). 1992. pap. 6.00 (*1-878347-10-1*) NL Assocs.

— Stories with Holes, Vol. VIII. 20p. (Orig.). (J). (gr. 3 up). 1992. pap. 6.00 (*1-878347-11-X*) NL Assocs.

— Stories with Holes, Vol. IX. (Orig.). (J). (gr. 3 up). 1992. pap. 6.00 (*1-878347-17-9*) NL Assocs.

— Stories with Holes, Vol. X. (Orig.). (J). (gr. 3 up). 1992. pap. 6.00 (*1-878347-21-7*) NL Assocs.

— Stories with Holes, Vol. XI. (Orig.). (J). (gr. 3 up). 1992. pap. 6.00 (*1-878347-22-5*) NL Assocs.

— Stories with Holes, Vol. XII. (Orig.). (J). (gr. 3 up). 1993. pap. 6.00 (*1-878347-26-8*) NL Assocs.

— Stories with Holes, Vol. XIII. (Orig.). (J). (gr. 3 up). 1993. pap. 6.00 (*1-878347-27-6*) NL Assocs.

— Stories with Holes, Vol. XIV. (Orig.). (J). (gr. 3 up). 1993. write for info. (*1-878347-28-4*) NL Assocs.

— Stories with Holes, Vol. XV. (Orig.). (J). (gr. 3 up). 1993. write for info. (*1-878347-29-2*) NL Assocs.

— Stories with Holes, Vol. XVI. (Orig.). (J). (gr. 3 up). 1993. write for info. (*1-878347-30-6*) NL Assocs.

— Stories with Holes, Vol. XVII. (Orig.). (J). (gr. 3 up). 1993. write for info. (*1-878347-31-4*) NL Assocs.

— Stories with Holes, Vol. XVIII. (Orig.). (J). (gr. 3 up). 1993. write for info. (*1-878347-32-2*) NL Assocs.

Levy, Nathan & Burke, Amy M. Tools of the Trade. (J). (gr. 4-12). 1992. pap. 7.95 (*1-878347-18-7*) NL Assocs.

***Levy, Nathan & Levy, Janet.** There Are Those. rev. ed. (Illus.). 40p. (J). (gr. 1-12). 1994. pap. 9.95 (*1-878347-41-1*) NL Assocs.

Levy, Nathan & Pastis, Steven. Who Am I? Inventors, Vol. 5. (J). (gr. 4-8). 1992. pap. 6.00 (*1-878347-19-5*) NL Assocs.

Levy, Nathan, et al. Who Am I? History, Vol. 1. (J). (gr. 4-8). 1990. pap. 6.00 (*1-878347-04-7*) NL Assocs.

— Who Am I? Literature Authors, Vol. 2. (J). (gr. 4-8). 1991. pap. 6.00 (*1-878347-12-8*) NL Assocs.

— Who Am I? Literature Characters, Vol. 4. (J). (gr. 2-8). 1991. pap. 6.00 (*1-878347-14-4*) NL Assocs.

— Who Am I? Music, Vol. 3. (J). (gr. 4-8). 1991. pap. 6.00 (*1-878347-13-6*) NL Assocs.

Levy, Neil M. & Golden, Michael M. California Torts, 6 vols. LC 85-61608. 1985. Updates available. ring bd. write for info. (*0-8205-1116-1*, 116) Bender.

Levy, Norman & Levy, Joan U. Mechanical Aptitude & Spatial Relations Tests. 2nd ed. 256p. 1991. pap. 12.00 (*0-13-568692-X*, Arco Test) P-H Gen Ref & Trav.

— S. A. T. Math Preparatory Set. 600p. 1989. pap. text ed. 8.95 (*1-55637-085-7*) Visual Educ Assn.

Levy, Norman, jt. auth. see Bramson, Morris.

Levy, Norman, jt. auth. see Levy, Joan U.

Levy, Norman B., ed. Psychonephrology, Vol. 1: Psychological Factors in Hemodialysis & Transplantation. LC 80-20681. 306p. 1981. 75.00 (*0-306-40586-5*, Plenum Pr) Plenum.

— Psychonephrology, Vol. 2: Psychological Problems in Kidney Failure & Their Treatment. LC 83-8015. 312p. 1983. 85.00 (*0-306-41154-7*, Plenum Pr) Plenum.

Levy, Norman B., jt. ed. see Solomon, Kenneth.

Levy, Oscar. The Revival of Aristocracy. 1972. 59.95 (*0-8490-0952-9*) Gordon Pr.

Levy, Oscar, tr. see Nietzsche, Frederich.

Levy, Owen, ed. Party Planner. (Party Planner Ser.). (Illus.). 96p. 1991. 18.95 (*0-9629770-0-4*) Langston Pr.

Levy, Patricia. Nigeria. LC 92-38754. (Cultures of the World Ser.). (J). 1993. 21.95 (*1-85435-574-0*) Marshall Cavendish.

— Puerto Rico. LC 94-22573. (Cultures of the World Ser.). (J). 1994. write for info. (*1-85435-690-9*); 21.95 (*1-85435-692-5*) Marshall Cavendish.

— Switzerland. LC 93-44260. (Cultures of the World Ser.). (J). 1994. 21.95 (*1-85435-591-0*) Marshall Cavendish.

— Women in Society: Ireland. LC 93-40414. (J). 1994. 22.95 (*1-85435-563-5*) Marshall Cavendish.

Levy, Patricia M. Ireland. LC 93-11026. (Cultures of the World Ser.). (J). (gr. 5 up). 1993. 21.95 (*1-85435-580-5*) Marshall Cavendish.

— Women in Society: Britain. LC 92-33353. (J). 1993. 22.95 (*1-85435-555-4*) Marshall Cavendish.

Levy, Paul. Random Functions: A Laplacian Random Function Depending on a Point of Hilbert Space. LC 56-8639. (University of California Publications in Social Welfare: Vol. 2, No. 10). 14p. reprint ed. pap. 25.00 (*0-317-11008-X*, 2021182) Bks Demand.

— The Turtle That Lost His Shell. (Bedtime with Barney Ser.). 24p. (J). 1995. write for info. (*1-57064-048-3*) Barney Pub.

Levy, Paul S. & Lemeshow, Stanley. Sampling of Populations: Methods & Applications. (Series in Probability & Mathematics). 1991. text ed. 69.95 (*0-471-50822-5*) Wiley.

Levy, Peter. The Complete Car Cost Guide, 1991. 368p. 1991. per., pap. 39.00 (*0-941443-11-6*) IntelliChoice.

— The Complete Car Cost Guide, 1992. 353p. 1992. per., pap. 39.00 (*0-941443-13-2*) IntelliChoice.

— The Complete Car Cost Guide, 1993. 379p. 1993. per., pap. 45.00 (*0-941443-15-9*) IntelliChoice.

— The Complete Small Truck Cost Guide, 1991. 281p. 1991. per., pap. 39.00 (*0-941443-12-4*) IntelliChoice.

— The Complete Small Truck Cost Guide, 1992. 250p. 1992. per., pap. 39.00 (*0-941443-14-0*) IntelliChoice.

— The Complete Small Truck Cost Guide, 1993. 312p. 1993. per., pap. 45.00 (*0-941443-16-7*) IntelliChoice.

Levy, Peter B. The New Left & Labor in the 1960s. LC 93-30844. (Illus.). 320p. 1994. 49.95 (*0-252-02074-X*); pap. 16.95 (*0-252-06367-8*) U of Ill Pr.

Levy, Peter B., ed. Documentary History of the Modern Civil Rights Movements. LC 91-27240. 296p. 1992. text ed. 55.00 (*0-313-27233-6*, LMR/, Greenwood Pr) Greenwood.

— Let Freedom Ring: A Documentary History of the Modern Civil Rights Movement. LC 91-27717. 272p. 1992. pap. text ed. 15.95 (*0-275-93434-9*, B3434, Praeger Pubs) Greenwood.

— One Hundred Key Documents in American Democracy. LC 93-1137. 536p. 1993. text ed. 59.95 (*0-313-28424-5*, LVK/, Greenwood Pr) Greenwood.

Levy, Philippa. Interpersonal Skills. 64p. 1993. pap. 35.00 (*1-85604-081-X*, LAP081X, Pub. by Lib Assn Pub UK) UNIPUB.

Levy-Provencal, E. Historia de Espana: 4. Espana Musulmana (711-1031) La Conquista, el Emirato, el Califato. 568p. 1992. 189.50x (*84-239-4806-4*) Elliots Bks.

— Historia de Espana: 5. Espana Musulmana (711-1031) Instituciones y Vida Social e Intelectual. 862p. 1992. 189.50x (*84-239-4807-2*) Elliots Bks.

Levy, R. A., ed. Microelectronic Materials & Processes. (C). 1989. lib. bdg. 277.50 (*0-7923-0147-1*); pap. text ed. 130.00 (*0-7923-0154-4*) Kluwer Ac.

— Novel Silicon Based Technologies. (C). 1991. lib. bdg. 98.00 (*0-7923-1112-4*) Kluwer Ac.

— Reduced Thermal Processing for ULSI. LC 89-23011. (NATO ASI Series B, Physics: Vol. 207). (Illus.). 450p. 1989. 110.00 (*0-306-43382-6*, Plenum Pr) Plenum.

Levy, R. I. Mesocosm: Hinduism & the Organization of a Traditional Newar City in Nepal. (C). 1992. 108.00 (*0-7855-0192-4*, Pub. by Ratna Pustak Bhandar) St Mut.

Levy, R. I., ed. A New Era of Lipid-Lowering Drug Alternative: Journal: Cardiology, Vol. 76, Suppl. 1, 1989. (Illus.). iv, 102p. 1989. pap. 25.50 (*3-8055-5023-5*) S Karger.

***Levy, Ran.** Wild Flowers of Japan: A Field Guide. Lancet, Barry, ed. 224p. 1995. pap. 25.00 (*4-7700-1809-6*) Kodansha.

Levy, Randolph N. Becoming an American. 1993. pap. 17.95 (*0-533-10372-X*) Vantage.

— Me: The New American Teenager, a Poem, Accompanied by Other Poetic Creations. 1993. 8.95 (*0-533-10371-1*) Vantage.

Levy, Raphael. Contribution a la Lexicographie Francaise Selon D'anciens Textes D'origies Juive. (FRE.). 1960. 75.00 (*0-89366-103-1*) Ultramarine Pub.

Levy, Raymond. Making Mechanical Marvels in Wood. LC 91-9634. (Illus.). 200p. 1991. pap. 14.95 (*0-8069-7358-7*) Sterling.

***Levy, Raymond & Howard, Robert, eds.** Developments in Dementia & Functional Disorders in the Elderly. LC 94-47442. 232p. 1995. 75.00 (*1-871816-27-0*, Pub. by Wrightson Biomed UK) Taylor & Francis.

Levy, Raymond, et al, eds. Treatment & Care in Old Age Psychiatry. LC 93-3405. 256p. 1993. pap. 85.00 (*1-871816-17-3*, Pub. by Wrightson Biomed UK) Taylor & Francis.

Levy, Rebecca A. I Remember Rhodes... Orig. Title: Mi Akodro de Rhodes... (Illus.). 256p. (ENG & LAD.). 1987. 16.95 (*0-87203-130-6*) Hermon.

Levy, Rene H. & Penry, J. Kiffin. Idiosyncratic Reactions to Valproate: Clinical Risk Patterns & Mechanisms of Toxicity. 184p. 1992. 47.50 (*0-88167-859-7*, 2344) Raven.

***Levy, Rene H., et al, eds.** Antiepileptic Drugs. 4th ed. 1056p. 1995. 163.50 (*0-7817-0246-1*) Raven.

— Metabolism of Antiepileptic Drugs. 264p. 1984. text ed. 105.00 (*0-88167-000-6*) Raven.

Levy, Richard C. Inventor's Desktop Companion: A Guide to Successfully Marketing & Protecting Your Ideas. 1990. pap. 24.95 (*0-8103-7943-0*) Visible Ink Pr.

— Inventor's Desktop Companion: The Guide to Successfully Marketing & Protecting Your Ideas. 2nd ed. 470p. 1995. pap. 24.95 (*0-7876-0490-9*) Visible Ink Pr.

— Secret of Selling Inventions. 2nd ed. Levy, Sheryl, ed. 200p. (Orig.). 1986. 49.50 (*0-931347-00-9*) Ricsher Pub Ltd.

Levy, Richard N., ed. On the Wings of Awe: A Machzor for Rosh Hashanah & Yom Kippur. 1985. 13.95 (*0-685-31415-4*) B'nai B'rith-Hillel.

— On Wings of Freedom: The Hillel Haggadah for the Nights of Passover. 1989. 5.95 (*0-685-31416-2*) B'nai B'rith-Hillel.

Levy, Richard S. The Downfall of the Anti-Semitic Political Parties in Imperial Germany. LC 74-20083. (Yale Historical Publications: Miscellany: No. 106). 345p. reprint ed. pap. 98.40 (*0-8357-8101-1*, 2033800) Bks Demand.

Levy, Richard S., ed. Antisemitism in the Modern World: An Anthology of Texts. LC 90-81852. (Sources in Modern History Ser.). 270p. (C). 1990. pap. text ed. 15.00 (*0-669-24340-X*) Heath.

— A Lie & Libel: The History of "the Protocols of the Elders of Zion" 198p. 1995. text ed. 22.50 (*0-8032-4243-3*) U of Nebr Pr.

Levy, Robert. Clan of the Shape-Changers. LC 92-36010. (YA). 1994. 13.95 (*0-395-66602-3*) HM.

— Clan of the Shape-Changers. (J). (gr. 4-7). 1994. 13.95 (*0-395-66612-0*) HM.

— Escape from Exile. LC 92-20443. 176p. (J). (gr. 5-9). 1993. 13.95 (*0-395-64379-1*) HM.

— Misfit Apprentice. LC 93-1575. (YA). (gr. 10). 1995. 14.95 (*0-395-68077-8*) HM.

— Prisons & the Law. 1995. boxed write for info. (*0-406-02514-2*, UK) Butterworth Legal Pubs.

Levy, Robert & Joseph, Joan. Robert Levy's Magic Book. LC 76-16016. (Illus.). 216p. (J). (gr. 5 up). 1976. 10.95 (*0-87131-219-0*) M Evans.

***Levy, Robert & Spillers, William R.** Analysis of Geometrically Non-Linear Structures. LC 94-38086. 1995. 49.95 (*0-412-99601-4*) Chapman & Hall.

Levy, Robert I. Mesocosm: Hinduism & the Organization of a Traditional Newar City in Nepal. 1992. 180.00 (*0-7855-0260-2*, Pub. by Ratna Pustak Bhandar) St Mut.

— Mesocosm: Hinduism & the Organization of a Traditional Newar City in Nepal. (Illus.). 800p. 1990. 72.00 (*0-520-06911-0*) U CA Pr.

— Tahitians: Mind & Experience in the Society Islands. LC 73-77136. (Illus.). xxviii, 548p. 1975. reprint ed. pap. text ed. 17.95 (*0-226-47607-3*, P649) U Ch Pr.

Levy, Robert I., et al, eds. Lipoproteins & Atherosclerosis. (Atherosclerosis Reviews Ser.: Vol. 17). (Illus.). 336p. 1988. text ed. 127.50 (*0-88167-402-8*) Raven.

— Nutrition, Lipids, & Coronary Heart Disease: A Global View. fac. ed. LC 78-67020. (Nutrition in Health & Disease Ser.: No. 1). (Illus.). 578p. Date not set. pap. 164.80 (*0-7837-7529-6*, 2046975) Bks Demand.

Levy, Robert J. Introductory Logic. 110p. (Orig.). 1984. pap. text ed. 15.00 (*0-8191-4179-8*) U Pr of Amer.

— Whistle Maker. (Anhinga Prize for Poetry Ser.). 68p. (Orig.). 1987. 8.00 (*0-938078-23-2*); pap. 8.00 (*0-938078-22-4*) Anhinga Pr.

Levy, Robert J., jt. auth. see Foote, Caleb.

Levy, Robert S., jt. auth. see Gross, Harry.

Levy, Robert S., jt. auth. see Small, Anne.

Levy, Roger. French Interests & Policies in the Far East. LC 75-30110. (Institute of Pacific Relations Ser.). 1976. reprint ed. 45.00 (*0-404-59540-5*) AMS Pr.

Levy, Rona, jt. auth. see Jayaratne, Srinika.

Levy, Rosalie M. Heavenly Friends: A Saint for Each Day. LC 59-25199. 1984. reprint ed. pap. 6.00 (*0-8198-0639-0*) Pauline Bks.

Levy, Ruth, jt. auth. see Mahrer, Debi.

Levy, S., tr. see Janich, K.

Levy, S., jt. auth. see Seroul, R.

Levy, S. B. The Antibiotic Paradox: How Miracle Drugs Are Destroying the Miracle. (Illus.). 280p. (C). 1992. 24.95 (*0-306-44331-7*, Plenum Pr) Plenum.

Levy, S. C. & Bro, P. Battery Hazards & Accident Prevention. (Illus.). 300p. (C). 1994. 49.50 (*0-306-44758-4*, Plenum Pr) Plenum.

Levy, S. C., jt. auth. see Bro, P.

***Levy, S. Jay.** The Economics of Aging: Can We Afford Grandma & Grandpa. (Public Policy Briefs Ser.). 32p. (Orig.). 1995. pap. 3.00 (*0-941276-06-6*, J Levy Econ Inst) Bard Coll Pubns.

Levy, S. Jay & Levy, David. Surviving the Contained Depression of the 1990's. LC 92-56827. 96p. 16.00 (*0-679-42401-6*) Random.

Levy, S. Leon. Nassau W. Senior, 1790-1864: Critical Essayist, Classical Economist & Adviser of Governments. rev. ed. LC 67-30861. 336p. 1970. 39.50 (*0-678-05676-5*) Kelley.

Levy, S. Leon, ed. see Senior, Nassau W.

Levy-Salomone, Rosemary. An Analysis of the Effects of Language Acquisitions Context upon the Dual Language Development of Non-English Dominant Students. Cordasco, Francesco, ed. LC 77-90557. (Bilingual-Bicultural Education in the U. S. Ser.). 1978. lib. bdg. 36.95 (*0-405-11095-2*) Ayer.

Levy, Samuel & Scheinman, Melvin, eds. Cardiac Arrhythmias: From Diagnosis to Therapy. (Illus.). 415p. 1984. 59.50 (*0-87993-213-9*) Futura Pub.

Levy, Samuel J. Applied Geometric Tolerancing II: (AGT II) 720p. 1993. pap. 59.00 (*1-883467-00-4*) Intl Geometric.

— Computer Aided Tolerancing Analysis (CATA) Manual. 175p. 1986. ring bd. 34.00 (*1-883467-02-0*) Intl Geometric.

— Summary Fact Data Sheets (SFDS) 20p. 1990. ring bd. 24.00 (*1-883467-01-2*) Intl Geometric.

Levy, Samuel L. Nassau W. Senior: The Prophet of Modern Capitalism. 1943. 20.00 (*0-686-17409-7*) R S Barnes.

Levy, Sandra & Siegel, Barbara. Electronic Keyboard for Kids. (Illus.). 80p. 1988. pap. 8.95 (*0-8256-1185-7*, AM70483) Music Sales.

Levy, Sandra M. Behavior & Cancer: Life-Style & Psychosocial Factors in the Initiation & Progression of Cancer. LC 85-45061. (Joint Publication in the Jossey-Bass Social & Behavioral Science Series & the Jossey-Bass Health Ser.). 279p. reprint ed. pap. 79.60 (*0-7837-2521-3*, 2042680) Bks Demand.

Levy, Sara G. Mother Goose Rhymes for Jewish Children. (Illus.). (J). (ps-2). 1979. reprint ed. pap. 8.95 (*0-8197-0254-4*) Bloch.

Levy, Saul. Account's Legal Reponsibility. Brief, Richard P., ed. LC 80-1509. (Dimensions of Accounting Theory & Practice Ser.). 1980. reprint ed. lib. bdg. 31.95 (*0-405-13534-3*) Ayer.

Levy-Schoen, A., jt. ed. see O'Regan, J. K.

Levy, Seymour. A Guide to Counseling: Developing Employees through Performance Reviews. LC 76-16912. 1976. 6.75 (*0-935198-01-6*) M M Bruce.

— Improving Performance Through Performance Review: A Guide to the Employee. 1970. 6.25 (*0-935198-02-4*) M M Bruce.

Levy, Sheryl, ed. see Levy, Richard C.

Levy, Shimon. Samuel Beckett's Self-Referential Drama: The Three Is. LC 89-32607. 210p. 1990. text ed. 45.00 (*0-312-03245-5*) St Martin.

Levy, Shlomit, ed. Louis Guttman on Theory & Methodology: Selected Writings. (Benchmark Ser.). 448p. 1993. 69.95 (*1-85521-389-3*, Pub. by Dartmth Pub UK) Ashgate Pub Co.

Levy, Sidney, et al. Marketing Manager's Handbook. 3rd ed. 1994. 69.95 (*0-85013-203-7*) Dartnell Corp.

— Plastics Extrusion Technology Handbook. 2nd ed. (Illus.). 352p. 1989. 39.95 (*0-8311-1185-2*) Indus Pr.

Levy, Sidney J. & Robles, Albert G. The Image of Archivists: Resource Allocators' Perceptions. 61p. (Orig.). 1984. pap. text ed. 7.00 (*0-931828-35-X*) Soc Am Archivists.

Levy, Sidney M. Construction Superintendent's Handbook: The Competitive Contractor. 1992. text ed. 55.95 (*0-442-00688-8*) Chapman & Hall.

— Japanese Construction: An American Perspective. (Illus.). 250p. 1990. text ed. 52.95 (*0-442-31865-0*) Chapman & Hall.

— Japan's Big Six: Inside Japan's Construction Industry. 320p. 1993. text ed. 40.00i (*0-07-037522-4*) McGraw.

— Project Management in Construction. 2nd ed. LC 93-21585. 1994. text ed. 49.00 (*0-07-037590-9*) McGraw.

Levy, Silvano. Understanding French Accounts: Language & Terminology. 128p. (Orig.). 1995. pap. 37.50 (*0-317-05902-5*, Pub. by Pitman Pub Ltd UK) Trans-Atl Phila.

Levy, Silvano, ed. see Donaghy, Peter & Laidler, John.

Levy, Silvano, ed. see Hofften, Adelheid & Edelsbacher, Johanna.

Levy, Silvio, jt. auth. see Knuth, Donald E.

Levy, Silvio, tr. see Schwarz, Albert S.

Levy, Solly, tr. see Kelly, Tim.

Levy, Stephen. California City & County Rankings, 1990. rev. ed. 160p. 1990. pap. text ed. 125.00 (*1-878316-07-9*) CCSCE.

— California Economic Growth, 1991: Regional Market Update & Projections. rev. ed. LC 90-660113. 250p. (C). 1991. pap. 195.00 (*1-878316-08-7*) CCSCE.

— California Population Characteristics, 1991. rev. ed. LC 90-660112. 1991. pap. 195.00 (*1-878316-09-5*) CCSCE.

— California Population Characteristics, 1992. rev. ed. LC 90-660112. 1992. pap. 195.00 (*1-878316-13-3*) CCSCE.

— Insanely Great: The Life & Times of the Macintosh, the Computer That Changed Everything. LC 93-30495. 224p. 1994. 20.95 (*0-670-85244-9*, Viking) Viking Penguin.

— The Outlook for the California Economy, May 1992. (C). 1992. pap. text ed. 45.00 (*1-878316-15-X*) CCSCE.

Levy, Stephen, ed. California City & County Rankings, 1991. rev. ed. LC 91-660231. 160p. 1991. pap. text ed. 125.00 (*1-878316-10-9*) CCSCE.

Levy, Stephen J. Children of Drug Abusers. 1991. 35.00 (*0-669-27332-5*) Heath.

Levy, Stephen T. & Ninan, Philip T., eds. Schizophrenia: Treatment of Acute Psychotic Episodes. LC 89-17556. 250p. 1990. text ed. 36.00 (*0-88048-164-1*) Am Psychiatric.

Levy, Steven. Artificial Life: A Report from the Frontier Where Computers Meet Biology. LC 92-50600. 1993. pap. 13.00 (*0-679-74389-8*, Vin) Random.

— Artificial Life: How Computers Are Transforming Our Understanding of Evolution & the Future of Life. LC 91-50749. (Illus.). 320p. 1992. 24.50 (*0-679-40774-X*) Pantheon.

— Hackers: Heroes of the Computer Revolution. 1985. pap. 12.95 (*0-385-31210-5*, Delta) Dell.

— Insanely Great: The Life & Times of Macintosh, the Computer That Changed Everything. 320p. 1995. pap. 9.95 (*0-14-023237-0*, Penguin Bks) Viking Penguin.

Levy, Steven T. Principles of Interpretation. LC 84-2808. 240p. 1990. reprint ed. 30.00x (*0-87668-705-2*) Aronson.

Levy, Stuart B. Gene Transfer in the Environment. 1989. text ed. 59.50 (*0-07-037290-X*) McGraw.

Levy, Stuart B. & Novick, Richard, eds. Antibiotic Resistance Genes: Ecology, Transfer, & Expression. LC 86-24361. (Banbury Report Ser.: No. 24). 436p. 1986. text ed. 68.00 (*0-87969-224-3*) Cold Spring Harbor.

Levy, Susan P., ed. see Cisek, Eugene & Persky, Robert S.

Levy, Susan P., ed. see Davis, Harold.

Levy, Susan P., ed. see Jackson, Zella.

Levy, Susan P., jt. auth. see Persky, Robert S.

Levy, Sydney. The Play of the Text: Max Jacob's "Le Cornet a Des" LC 80-52298. 174p. 1981. 24.50 (*0-299-08510-4*) U of Wis Pr.

An Asterisk (*) at the beginning of an entry indicates that the title is appearing in BIP for the first time.

Levy, Thomas, ed. The Archaeology of Society in the Holy Land. (Illus.). 460p. 1994. 80.00 (*0-8160-2855-9*) Facts on File.

Levy, Thomas E., jt. auth. see Holl, Augustin.

Levy, Tina. Vital Signs: Mathematics in Everyday Life. 326p. (C). 1991. pap. text ed. 23.95 (*0-89863-144-0*) Star Pub CA.

Levy, Tony. Out for a Duck. large type ed. 320p. 1988. 15.95 (*0-7089-1915-4*) Ulverscroft.

Levy, V. M. Financial Management of Hospitals. 3rd ed. xxii, 510p. 1985. pap. 74.50 (*0-455-20296-6*, Pub. by Law Bk Co) W W Gaunt.

— Financial Management of Hospitals. 4th ed. 486p. 1992. pap. 75.00 (*0-455-21060-8*, Pub. by Law Bk Co) W W Gaunt.

— Public Financial Administration. 2nd ed. ix, 317p. 1981. pap. 49.00 (*0-455-20090-4*, Pub. by Law Bk Co) W W Gaunt.

Levy, Virginia K. Let's Go to the Art Museum. (Illus.). 34p. 1988. pap. 8.95 (*0-8109-2380-7*) Abrams.

Levy, Viv. Beginner's Guide to Figure Drawing. 1993. 12.98 (*1-55521-854-7*) Bk Sales Inc.

Levy, Walter A., jt. ed. see Summer, Claire.

Levy, Walter J., jt. ed. see Keating, Helene L.

Levy, William. Basic Offset & Presswork. LC 80-730005. 1979. student ed 6.00 (*0-8064-0065-X*, 314); audio 139.99 (*0-8064-0066-8*) Bergwall.

— Black & White Copy Preparation. LC 80-730006. 1979. student ed 6.00 (*0-8064-0059-5*, 311); audio 199.00 (*0-8064-0060-9*) Bergwall.

— Color Copy Preparation. LC 80-730007. 1979. student ed 6.00 (*0-8064-0061-7*, 312); audio 139.00 (*0-8064-0062-5*) Bergwall.

Levy, William, et al, eds. Synaptic Modification, Neuron Selectivity & Nervous System Organization. 280p. (C). 1985. text ed. 59.95 (*0-89859-344-1*) L Erlbaum Assocs.

Levy, William S. Skin Problems of the Amputee. LC 78-50196. (Illus.). 324p. 1983. 49.95 (*0-87527-181-2*) Green.

Levy, William T., jt. auth. see Scherle, Victor.

Levy, Y., et al, eds. Categories & Processes in Language Acquisition. 296p. 1988. text ed. 59.95 (*0-8058-0151-0*) L Erlbaum Assocs.

Levy, Yonata, ed. Other Children, Other Languages: Issues in the Theory of Language Acquisition. 424p. 1993. text ed. 79.95 (*0-8058-1330-6*) L Erlbaum Assocs.

Levy, Ze'ev. Baruch or Benedict: On Some Jewish Aspects of Spinoza's Philosophy. LC 89-8257. (American University Studies: Philosophy: Ser. V, Vol. 81). 224p. (C). 1989. text ed. 39.50 (*0-8204-0986-3*) P Lang Pubs.

— Between Yafeth & Shem: On the Relationship Between Jewish & General Philosophy. (American University Studies: Philosophy: Ser. V, Vol. 21). 253p. 1987. text ed. 40.90 (*0-8204-0373-3*) P Lang Pubs.

— David Baumgardt & Ethical Hedonism. 1989. 39.50 (*0-88125-304-9*) Ktav.

Levy, Zvi, intro. Negotiating Positive Identity in a Group Care Community: Reclaiming Uprooted Youth. LC 93-34917. (Child & Youth Services Ser.: Vol. 16, No. 2). (Illus.). 141p. 1993. lib. bdg. 29.95 (*1-56024-514-X*) Haworth Pr.

Lew, Alan. Eight Monologs. 64p. (Orig.). 1980. pap. 3.50 (*0-931416-01-9*) Open Books.

***Lew, Alan A. & Yu, Lawrence.** Tourism in China: Geographic, Political, & Economic Perspectives. LC 94-29615. (C). 1994. text ed. 54.95 (*0-8133-8874-0*) Westview.

Lew, Alan E. Means Interior Estimating. (Illus.). 370p. 1987. 59.95 (*0-87629-067-5*, 67237) R S Means.

Lew, Amy, jt. auth. see Bettner, Betty L.

Lew, Ann & Denniston, Debra. Lew-Denniston Dental Office Injury & Illness Prevention Program. 43p. 1992. student ed 195.00 (*0-9634080-1-1*) Prof Mgmt Pubns.

— Lew-Denniston Medical Office Injury & Illness Prevention Program. 40p. 1991. student ed 195.00 (*0-9634080-0-3*) Prof Mgmt Pubns.

Lew, Christina, jt. auth. see Womack, Randy L.

Lew, Dayan. Humanity of Jewish Law. 220p. 1986. 12.95 (*0-900689-87-0*) Soncino Pr.

Lew, Edward A. & Gajewski, Jerzy, eds. Medical Risks: Trends in Mortality by Age & Time Elapsed, 2 vols., 1. LC 90-7707. 368p. 1990. text ed. 195.00 (*0-275-93787-9*, C37861, Praeger Pubs) Greenwood.

— Medical Risks: Trends in Mortality by Age & Time Elapsed, 2 vols., Set. LC 90-7707. 1512p. 1990. text ed. 195.00 (*0-275-93786-0*, C37860, Praeger Pubs) Greenwood.

— Medical Risks: Trends in Mortality by Age & Time Elapsed, 2 vols., Vol. 2. LC 90-7707. 368p. 1990. text ed. 195.00 (*0-275-93788-7*, C37862, Praeger Pubs) Greenwood.

Lew, Ellen F. Ellen Lew's Far East Favorites Cookbook. 200p. 1992. pap. 7.98 (*0-9623626-0-3*) E F Lew.

— Ellen Lew's Pacific Rim Light & Low Recipes. 200p. 1992. 10.00 (*0-9623626-1-1*) E F Lew.

Lew, Ellen F. & Akins, Harold D. Rice: A Food for All Seasons Cookbook. (Illus.). 1989. 10.00 (*0-317-93880-0*) H D Akins.

Lew, Ellen F., jt. auth. see Akins, H. D.

Lew, Gordon, tr. see Lim, Genny.

Lew, James. The Art of Stretching & Kicking. LC 80-106144. (Illus.). 104p. 1977. pap. 7.95 (*0-86568-007-8*, 206) Unique Pubns.

Lew, Jennifer F., jt. auth. see Proctor, Richard M.

Lew, Jonathan, jt. auth. see Wong, Mary.

Lew, Judy, jt. auth. see Poladitmontri, Panurat.

Lew, Julian, ed. see School of International Arbitration Staff.

Lew, Meyer S., ed. see Marmorstein, Arthur.

Lew, Mike. Victims No Longer: Men Recovering from Incest & Other Childhood Sexual Abuse. LC 89-45839. 352p. 1990. reprint ed. pap. 17.00 (*0-06-097300-5*, PL) HarpC.

Lew, Roberta A., jt. ed. see Butters, John P.

***Lew, Thomas.** Picture Book (an Autobiography) Date not set. 50.00 (*0-614-04616-5*) NFS Pr.

Lew, Walter K., contrib. Premonitions: The Kaya Anthology of New Asian American Poetry. LC 94-75916. (Illus.). 596p. 1995. 20.00 (*1-885030-13-4*); pap. 19.95x (*1-885030-14-2*) Kaya Prod.

Lew, Walter K., ed. Muae: Journal of Asian Diasporic Culture, Vol. 1. (Illus.). 250p. (Orig.). 1995. pap. 12.00 (*1-885030-15-0*) Kaya Prod.

Lewak, R., et al. Therapist Guide to the MMPI & MMPI-2: Providing Feedback & Treatment. LC 89-81012. xii, 364p. 1990. 30.95 (*1-55959-006-8*) Accel Devel.

Lewald, Ernest H., ed. The Web: Stories by Argentine Women. LC 81-51646. 135p. 1983. 26.00 (*0-89410-085-8*) Three Continents.

Lewald, Fanny. The Education of Fanny Lewald: An Autobiography. Lewis, Hanna B., ed. & anno. by. LC 91-35930. (SUNY Series, Women Writers in Translation). 341p. 1992. 59.50 (*0-7914-1147-8*); pap. 19.95 (*0-7914-1148-6*) State U NY Pr.

— Prinz Louis Ferdinand. Rogols-Siegel, Linda, tr. LC 88-13957. (Studies in German Thought & History: Vol. 6). 507p. 1989. lib. bdg. 119.95 (*0-88946-357-3*) E Mellen.

Lewald, Herald E., ed. The Cry of Home: Cultural Nationalism & the Modern Writer. LC 76-173656. 1972. 20.00 (*0-87049-135-0*) Lib Soc Sci.

— The Cry of Home: Cultural Nationalism & the Modern Writer. LC 76-173656. 412p. reprint ed. pap. 117.50 (*0-685-16029-7*, 2027559) Bks Demand.

Lewallen, Dale. PC - Computing Guide to Excel 3.0. (Guide to...Ser.). (Illus.). 434p. (Orig.). 1991. pap. 24.95 (*1-56276-019-X*) Ziff-Davis.

— PC - Computing Guide to Excel 4.0 for Windows. (Guide to...Ser.). (Illus.). 643p. (Orig.). 1992. pap. 27.95 (*1-56276-048-3*) Ziff-Davis.

— This Old PC. 1993. pap. 29.95 (*1-56276-108-0*) Ziff-Davis.

Lewallen, David, jt. ed. see Crosby, Lynn.

Lewallen, Susan, jt. auth. see Courtright, Paul.

Lewalski, Barbara K. Donne's Anniversaries & the Poetry of Praise: The Creation of a Symbolic Mode. LC 72-14027. 399p. reprint ed. pap. 113.80 (*0-8357-3689-X*, 2036413) Bks Demand.

— Milton's Brief Epic: The Genre, Meaning, & Art of Paradise Regained. LC 66-10282. (Brown University Bicentennial Publications). 448p. reprint ed. pap. 127.70 (*0-7837-2620-1*, 2042956) Bks Demand.

— Paradise Lost & the Rhetoric of Literary Forms. 370p. 1985. text ed. 57.50 (*0-691-06642-6*) Princeton U Pr.

— Protestant Poetics & the Seventeenth-Century Religious Lyric. LC 78-70305. (Illus.). 563p. reprint ed. pap. 160.50 (*0-8357-4284-9*, 2037083) Bks Demand.

— Writing Women in Jacobean England. (Illus.). 431p. (C). 1993. text ed. 47.50 (*0-674-96242-7*) HUP.

— Writing Women in Jacobean England. (Illus.). 431p. 1994. pap. text ed. 19.95 (*0-674-96243-5*, LEWWRX) HUP.

Lewalski, Barbara K., ed. Renaissance Genres. (English Studies: No. 14). 512p. 1986. 27.95 (*0-674-76040-9*); pap. 11.95 (*0-674-76041-7*) HUP.

Lewalski, Zdzislaw M. Product Esthetics: An Interpretation for Designers. (Illus.). 240p. (Orig.). 1988. pap. 17.95 (*0-944327-04-4*) Design & Dev Engineering Pr.

Lewan, Lloyd S. & Billingsley, Ronald G. Women in the Workplace: A Man's Perspective. LC 88-90731. (Illus.). 125p. (Orig.). 1988. pap. 6.95 (*0-9620360-0-5*) Remington Pr.

Lewan, M. D., jt. ed. see Pittman, E. D.

Lewand, Robert, jt. auth. see Bielawski, Larry.

Lewandoski, Theodor. Linguistics Dictionary: Linguistisches Woerterbuch, 3 vols., Set. 5th ed. 1287p. (GER.). 1985. 150.00 (*0-8288-1977-7*, M15160) Fr & Eur.

Lewandowsi, Joseph J. Alaskan Environmental Impact Statements: A Bibliography. LC 81-623250. (Occasional Papers Ser.: No. 7). 235p. 1980. pap. text ed. 7.50 (*0-937592-05-6*) U Alaska Rasmuson Lib.

Lewandowska-Tomaszczyk, Barbara, jt. ed. see Tomaszczyk, Jerzy.

Lewandowski, A. & Stanchev, I., eds. Methodology & Software for Interactive Decision Support. (Lecture Notes in Economics & Mathematical Systems Ser.: Vol. 337). viii, 308p. 1989. pap. 42.00 (*0-387-51572-0*) Spr-Verlag.

Lewandowski, A. & Volkovich, V., eds. Multiobjective Problems of Mathematical Programming: Proceedings of the International Conference on Multiobjective Problems of Mathematical Programming Held in Yalta, U. S. S. R., October 26-November 2, 1988. (Lecture Notes in Economics & Mathematical Systems Ser.: Vol. 351). (Illus.). vii, 314p. 1990. pap. 46.00 (*0-387-53432-6*) Spr-Verlag.

Lewandowski, A. & Wierzbicki, A. P., eds. Aspiration Based Decision Support Systems. (Lecture Notes in Economics & Mathematical Systems Ser.: Vol. 331). x, 399p. 1989. pap. 50.60 (*0-387-51213-6*) Spr-Verlag.

Lewandowski, A., et al, eds. Methodology, Implementation & Applications of Decision Support Systems. (CISM International Centre for Mechanical Sciences Ser.: Vol. 320). (Illus.). vi, 322p. 1991. pap. 42.00 (*0-387-82297-6*) Spr-Verlag.

LeWandowski, G., ed. Biotechnology Applications in Hazardous Waste Treatment. 423p. 1990. 82.00 (*0-8169-0484-7*, P63) Am Inst Chem Eng.

Lewandowski, R., ed. Helmet-Mounted Displays II. 1990. 53.00 (*0-8194-0341-5*, VOL. 1290) SPIE.

Lewandowski, Roger G. The Revolutionary Management Handbook. 1994. 10.95 (*0-8062-4813-0*) Carlton.

Lewandowski, Susan. Migration & Ethnicity in Urban India. 1982. 18.00 (*0-8364-0833-0*, Pub. by Manohar II) S Asia.

Lewandowski, Theodor. Dictionary of Linguistics: Diccionario de Linguistica. 2nd ed. 464p. (SPA.). 1986. pap. 59.95 (*0-7859-4953-4*) Fr & Eur.

Lewandowsky, S., et al, eds. Implicit Memory: Theoretical Issues. 352p. (C). 1990. text ed. 69.95 (*0-8058-0358-0*) L Erlbaum Assocs.

Lewandowsky, Stephen, jt. ed. see Hockley, William.

Lewanski, Richard C., ed. Guide to Polish Libraries & Archives. (East European Monographs: No. 6). 209p. 1974. text ed. 47.50 (*0-231-03896-8*) East Eur Quarterly.

Lewarch, Dennis E., jt. ed. see O'Brien, Michael J.

***LeWarne, Charles P.** Utopias on Puget Sound, 1885-1915. (Illus.). 346p. 1995. pap. 18.95 (*0-295-97444-3*) U of Wash Pr.

— Washington State. rev. ed. LC 85-20977. (Illus.). 438p. 1993. 50.00 (*0-295-97301-3*) U of Wash Pr.

LeWarne, Charles P., jt. auth. see Ficken, Robert E.

Lewart, Cass R. Modem Handbook for the Communications Professional. 320p. 1987. 40.25 (*0-444-01279-6*) P-H.

— Science & Engineering Programs for the PCjr. 200p. 1985. 14.95 (*0-13-794942-1*); disk 29.95 (*0-13-794975-8*) P-H.

— Science & Engineering Sourcebook. LC 82-80269. (Illus.). 96p. (Orig.). 1982. pap. 9.95 (*0-942412-02-8*); audio 8.95 (*0-686-98227-4*) Micro Text Pubns.

— Scientific & Engineering Sourcebook: Professional Programs for the Timex Sinclair 1000. LC 82-62818. (Illus.). 120p. (Orig.). 1983. pap. text ed. 15.95 (*0-07-037444-9*, BYTE Bks) McGraw.

Lewbel, George. Curacao Diving & Snorkeling Guide. 1990. pap. 11.95 (*1-55992-029-7*, Pisces Bks) Gulf Pub.

— Decompression Workbook. 1990. pap. 9.95 (*1-55992-011-4*, Pisces Bks) Gulf Pub.

Lewbel, George S. & Martin, Larry R. Diving & Snorkeling Guide to Cozumel. 2nd ed. 96p. 1991. 11.95 (*1-55992-034-3*, Pisces Bks) Gulf Pub.

— Diving Bonaire. (Illus.). 132p. (Orig.). 1991. pap. 18.95 (*0-9623389-4-X*) Aqua Quest.

Lewbin, Hyman J. Rebirth of Jewish Art: The Unfolding of Jewish Art in the Nineteenth Century. LC 74-76483. (Illus.). 1974. 16.95 (*0-88400-007-9*) Shengold.

Lewchuk, Wayne. American Technology & the British Vehicle Industry. 250p. 1987. 64.95 (*0-521-30269-2*) Cambridge U Pr.

Lewell, John. A-Z Guide to Computer Graphics. 1985. pap. text ed. 14.95 (*0-07-037457-0*) McGraw.

— A-Z Guide to Computer Graphics. 1985. text ed. 29.95 (*0-07-037464-3*, BYTE Bks) McGraw.

— Modern Japanese Novelists: A Biographical Dictionary. De Angelis, Paul, ed. LC 92-11324. (Illus.). 448p. (C). 1993. 50.00 (*4-7700-1649-2*) Kodansha.

***Lewellen, Gale R.** Human CNS Structure. 192p. (C). 1994. pap. text ed., spiral bd. 18.95 (*0-7872-0312-2*) Kendall-Hunt.

Lewellen, James B. A Parent's Guide to Quality Schools: Taking Charge of Your Child's Education. 1994. 12.95 (*0-533-10794-6*) Vantage.

Lewellen, John. La Luna, el Sol, y las Estrellas (Moon, Sun, & Stars) Kratky, Lada, tr. LC 81-7749. (Spanish New True Bks.). (Illus.). 48p. (SPA.). (J). (gr. k-4). 1984. lib. bdg. 12.90 (*0-516-31637-0*); pap. 4.95 (*0-516-51637-X*) Childrens.

— Moon, Sun & Stars. LC 81-7749. (New True Bks.). (Illus.). 48p. (J). (gr. k-4). 1981. lib. bdg. 12.90 (*0-516-01637-7*); pap. 4.95 (*0-516-41637-5*) Childrens.

Lewellen, Ted. The Ruthless Gun. 160p. 1981. pap. 1.75 (*0-449-12796-6*, GM) Fawcett.

***Lewellen, Ted C.** Dependency & Development: An Introduction to the Third World. LC 94-39193. 288p. 1995. text ed. 65.00 (*0-89789-399-9*, Bergin & Garvey); pap. text ed. 22.95 (*0-89789-400-6*, Bergin & Garvey) Greenwood.

— Political Anthropology: An Introduction. 2nd ed. LC 91-44660. 248p. 1992. text ed. 55.00 (*0-89789-289-5*, H289, Bergin & Garvey); pap. text ed. 17.95 (*0-89789-290-9*, G290, Bergin & Garvey) Greenwood.

Lewellen, Wilbur G. Executive Compensation in Large Industrial Corporations. (Fiscal Studies Ser.: No. 11). 396p. 1968. 103.30 (*0-87014-481-2*) Natl Bur Econ Res.

— Executive Compensation in Large Industrial Corporations. LC 67-29643. (National Bureau of Economic Research, Fiscal Studies: No. 11). (Illus.). 397p. reprint ed. pap. 113.20 (*0-8357-7573-9*, 2056894) Bks Demand.

— The Ownership Income of Management. (Fiscal Studies Ser.: No. 14). 220p. 1971. reprint ed. 57.20 (*0-87014-222-4*) Natl Bur Econ Res.

Lewellyn, Harry. Glovebox Guide to Unpaved Southern California. (Illus.). 268p. (Orig.). 1987. pap. 9.95 (*0-944781-00-4*) Glovebox Pubns.

— Glovebox Guide to Unpaved Southern California. 2nd ed. 348p. (Orig.). 1992. spiral bd. 12.95 (*0-944781-01-2*) Glovebox Pubns.

Lewen, Si. A Journey. LC 80-67120. 86p. 1980. 30.00 (*0-87982-032-2*) Art Alliance.

Lewenhak, Sheila. The Revaluation of Women's Work. 288p. 1988. lib. bdg. 57.50 (*0-415-01863-3*) Routledge.

— Women & Work. LC 80-16906. 1980. text ed. 18.95 (*0-312-88778-7*) St Martin.

Lewens, George, pseud. My Lives Between Hitler & Stalin. (Illus.). 160p. (Orig.). 1992. pap. 12.95 (*0-9631336-0-8*) Lewens Pub.

Lewenson, George, see George Lewens, pseud..

Lewenson, S., jt. ed. see Birnbach, N.

Lewenson, Sandra, jt. ed. see Birnbach, Nettie.

Lewenson, Sandra B. Taking Charge: Nursing, Suffrage, & Feminism in America, 1873-1920. LC 93-11137. (Development of American Feminism Ser.: Vol. 1). 368p. 1993. 55.00 (*0-8240-6897-1*) Garland.

Lewenstam. Applications of Ion-Selective Electrodes in Clinical Chem. 1995. write for info. (*0-8493-4209-0*) CRC Pr.

Lewenstein, M., jt. ed. see Kujawski, A.

Lewenstein, Marion, ed. see Enkelis, Liane & Olsen, Karen.

Lewenstein, Suzanne M. Stone Tool Use at Cerros: The Ethnoarchaeological & Use-Wear Evidence. LC 86-24910. (Illus.). 238p. 1987. text ed. 42.50 (*0-292-77590-3*) U of Tex Pr.

Lewenz, Marie A., tr. see Bulow, Bernhard H.

Lewenz, Susan M. Introductory Guide to Joint Ventures in the Soviet Union. 25p. 1990. pap. 1.50 (*0-16-020041-5*, S/N 003-009-00570-1) USGPO.

Lewer, Nick. Physicians & the Peace Movement. 140p. 1992. text ed. 29.50 (*0-7146-3438-7*, Pub. by F Cass Pubs UK) Intl Spec Bk.

***Lewerentz, Claus & Lindner, Thomas, eds.** Formal Development of Reactive Systems: Case Study Production Cell. LC 94-44675. (Lecture Notes in Computer Science: No. 891). 394p. 1995. pap. 62.00 (*0-387-58867-1*) Spr-Verlag.

Lewerenz, Alfred S. Antique Auto Body Brass Work for the Restorer. (Vintage Craft Ser.: No. 5). (Illus.). 1970. pap. 6.95 (*0-911160-05-1*) Post Group.

Lewerenz, Alfred S., ed. Antique Auto Body Accessories for the Restorer. (Vintage Craft Ser.: No. 7). (Illus.). 1970. pap. 6.95 (*0-911160-07-8*) Post Group.

Lewers, Irene & Lewis, Rosellen. Talk, Talk, Talk, Jesus. LC 90-61751. 109p. 1990. pap. 5.95 (*0-89221-184-9*) New Leaf.

Lewerth, Margaret. Stuyvesant Square. 464p. 1989. mass mkt. 4.50 (*0-380-70596-6*) Avon.

***Lewes, Darby.** Dream Revisionaries: Gender & Genre in Women's Utopian Fiction, 1870-1920. LC 94-40947. 1995. write for info. (*0-8173-0795-8*) U of Ala Pr.

Lewes, F. & Parker, S. Leisure & Tourism. (Reviews of United Kingdom Statistical Sources Ser.: Vol. 4). 1975. 56.00 (*0-08-022455-5*, Pub. by Pergamon Repr UK) Franklin.

Lewes, George H. Literary Criticism of George Henry Lewes. Kaminsky, Alice R., ed. LC 64-17230. (Regents Critics Ser.). 183p. reprint ed. pap. 52.20 (*0-7837-6014-0*, 2045825) Bks Demand.

— On Actors & the Art of Acting. LC 68-56038. (Illus.). 237p. 1970. reprint ed. text ed. 55.00 (*0-8371-0533-1*, LEAA, Greenwood Pr) Greenwood.

— Ranthorpe. Smalley, Barbara, ed. LC 74-82496. lvii, 369p. 1974. pap. 9.95 (*0-8214-0168-8*) Ohio U Pr.

— Rose, Blanche & Violet, 3 vols. in 2, Set. LC 79-8153. reprint ed. 84.50 (*0-404-61975-4*) AMS Pr.

— The Spanish Drama: Lope De Vaga & Calderon. 1980. lib. bdg. 59.95 (*0-8490-3201-6*) Gordon Pr.

***Lewes, Kenneth.** Psychoanalysis & Male Homosexuality. LC 94-49189. 328p. 1995. pap. 30.00 (*1-56821-484-7*) Aronson.

Lewfishman. Golf Magazine Shortcuts to Better Golf. 1993. 6.98 (*0-88365-820-8*) Galahad Bks.

Lewi, Grant. Astrology for the Millions. 6th ed. LC 90-31242. (Classics of Astrology Library). 464p. 1990. pap. 12.95 (*0-87542-438-4*) Llewellyn Pubns.

— Heaven Knows What. 9th rev. ed. LC 84-48086. (Popular Astrology Ser.). 370p. 1984. pap. 12.95 (*0-87542-444-9*) Llewellyn Pubns.

Lewi, Grant & Greene, Liz, creators. The Astrology Kit. 1987. 26.95 (*0-312-01350-7*, Pub. by Thomas Dunne Bks) St Martin.

Lewi, J., et al. Software Development by LL1 Syntax Description. 1992. text ed. 59.95 (*0-471-93148-9*) Wiley.

Lewi, Paul J. Multivariate Data Analysis in Industrial Practice. LC 82-6906. (Chemometrics Research Studies: No. 3). (Illus.). 258p. reprint ed. pap. 73.60 (*0-8357-6228-9*, 2034229) Bks Demand.

Lewi, Paul J. & Marsboom, R. P., eds. Toxicology Reference Data-Wistar Rat. (Janssen Research Foundation Ser.: Vol. 4). 358p. 1981. 97.50 (*0-444-80342-4*) Elsevier.

Lewi, Paul J., jt. auth. see Van Horebeek, I.

Lewick-Wallace, Mary. Vocabulary Building & Word Study. Raygor, Alton L., ed. (Communication Skills Ser.). 240p. (Orig.). (C). 1981. text ed. write for info. (*0-07-067902-9*) McGraw.

Lewicki, G., jt. auth. see Odyniec, W.

Lewicki, Paul. Nonconscious Social Information Processing. LC 85-15618. 1986. pap. text ed. 40.00 (*0-12-446121-2*) Acad Pr.

***Lewicki, Roy & Hiam, Alexander.** Negotiating Strategically: Tools for Resolving Disputes & Conflicts Successfully. (The Portable MBA Ser.). Date not set. text ed. 27.95 (*0-471-01321-8*) Wiley.

Lewicki, Roy J. & Litterer, Joseph A. Negotiation. 368p. (C). 1985. text ed. 49.95 (*0-256-02633-5*) Irwin.

— Negotiation: Readings, Exercises, & Cases. (C). 1985. pap. text ed. 29.95 (*0-256-02634-3*) Irwin.

Lewicki, Roy J., jt. auth. see Bowditch, James L.

Lewicki, Roy J., et al. Experiences in Management & Organizational Behavior. 3rd ed. LC 87-25353. (Management Ser.). 368p. 1988. Net. pap. text ed. write for info. (*0-471-83796-2*) Wiley.

— Negotiation. 2nd ed. LC 93-40307. 496p. (C). 1994. pap. text ed. 49.95 (*0-256-10163-9*) Irwin.

— Negotiation: Readings, Exercises, & Cases. 2nd ed. LC 92-11882. 784p. (C). 1992. text ed. 33.95 (*0-256-10164-7*) Irwin.

Lewicki, Roy J., et al, eds. Research on Negotiation in Organizations, Vol. 1. 1986. 73.25 (*0-89232-638-7*) Jai Pr.

— Research on Negotiation in Organizations, Vol. 2. 1988. 73.25 (*0-89232-639-5*) Jai Pr.

Lewicki, Zbigniew. The Bang & the Whimper: Apocalypse & Entropy in American Literature. LC 83-12678. (Contributions in American Studies: No. 71). xvii, 135p. 1984. text ed. 45.00 (*0-313-23674-7*, LBW/, Greenwood Pr) Greenwood.

Lewiecki-Wilson, Cynthia. Writing Against the Family: Gender in Lawrence & Joyce. LC 93-7829. (Illus.). 288p. 1994. 34.95 (*0-8093-1881-4*) S Ill U Pr.

Lewin & Preston. Handbook of Fiber Science & Technology. (International Fiber Science & Technology Ser.: Vol. 12). 408p. 1993. 215.00 (*0-8247-8866-4*) Dekker.

Lewin & Sello. Handbook of Fiber Science & Technology, Vol. 1, Pt. B Vol. 1, Pt. B: Chemical Processing of Fibers & Fabrics: Fundamentals & Preparation. (International Fiber Science & Technology Ser.). 368p. 1984. 199.00 (*0-8247-7117-6*) Dekker.

Lewin, A. The Law, Procedure & Conduct of Meetings in South Africa. 5th ed. 302p. 1985. pap. 32.00 (*0-7021-1528-2*, Pub. by Juta SA) W W Gaunt.

Lewin, Abraham. A Cup of Tears: A Diary of the Warsaw Ghetto. Polonsky, Antony, ed. Hutton, Chris, tr. (Illus.). 224p. 1988. 29.95 (*0-631-16215-1*) Blackwell Pubs.

Lewin, Arie Y. & Shakum, Melvin F., eds. Policy Science: Methodologies & Cases. LC 75-23356. 450p. 1976. 208.00 (*0-08-019601-2*, Pub. by Pergamon Repr UK) Franklin.

Lewin, Arthur. Electrognathographics: Atlas of Diagnostic Procedures & Interpretation. (Illus.). 168p. 1985. text ed. 80.00 (*0-86715-156-0*) Quint Pub Co.

Lewin, B. & Bruno. Small Dictionary of Japanology: Kleines Woerterbuch der Japanologie. 2nd ed. 596p. (GER & JPN.). 1981. 85.00 (*0-8288-1019-2*, M7512) Fr & Eur.

Lewin, Benjamin. Gene Expression, Vol. 1. LC 73-14382. (Illus.). 660p. reprint ed. pap. 180.00 (*0-685-23550-5*, 2027890) Bks Demand.

— Gene Expression, Vol. 2: Eucaryotic Chromosomes. 2nd ed. LC 80-10849. 1178p. reprint ed. pap. 180.00 (*0-685-16155-2*, 2056300) Bks Demand.

— Genes V. (Illus.). 1296p. (C). 1993. text ed. 65.00 (*0-19-854287-9*) OUP.

Lewin, Bertram D. The Image & the Past. LC 68-59121. 128p. 1969. text ed. 25.00 (*0-8236-2505-2*) Intl Univs Pr.

***Lewin, Betsy.** Booby Hatch. LC 94-19309. (J). 1995. 14.95 (*0-395-68703-9*, Clarion Bks) HM.

— Walk a Green Path. (J). 1995. pap. write for info. (*0-615-00072-X*) Lothrop.

***Lewin, Bruno.** Kleines Woerterbuch der Japanologie. 593p. (GER.). 1968. 125.00 (*0-7859-8365-1*, 3447005300) Fr & Eur.

Lewin, Cheryl, jt. auth. see Holland, D. K.

Lewin, David. Musical Form & Transformation: Four Analytical Essays. LC 92-42592. (Illus.). 192p. (C). 1993. text ed. 25.00 (*0-300-05686-9*) Yale U Pr.

***Lewin, David & Mitchell, Daniel J.** Human Resource Management: An Economic Approach. 2nd ed. LC 94-34201. 1995. text ed. 54.95 (*0-538-84487-6*) S-W Pub.

Lewin, David & Peterson, Richard B. The Modern Grievance Procedure in the United States. LC 87-32612. (Illus.). 301p. 1988. text ed. 69.50 (*0-89930-149-5*, LMG/, Quorum Bks) Greenwood.

Lewin, David, et al. Public Sector Labor Relations. LC 82-64038. 672p. (C). 1988. text ed. 52.95 (*0-669-17125-5*); text ed. 26.95 (*0-669-12893-7*) Free Pr.

Lewin, David, et al, eds. Research Frontiers in IR & HR. 1992. 22.50 (*0-913447-53-6*) Indus Relations Res.

Lewin, Douglas & Noaks, David. Theory & Design of Digital Computer Systems. 3rd ed. LC 92-30621. 1992. write for info. (*0-412-42880-6*) Chapman & Hall.

Lewin, Douglas, jt. ed. see Boulaye, G.

***Lewin, Elizabeth.** Financial Fitness for Newlyweds. fac. ed. LC 83-14139. 188p. 1984. reprint ed. pap. 53.60 (*0-7837-8141-5*, 2047949) Bks Demand.

— Financial Fitness Through Divorce: A Guide to the Financial Realities of Divorce. LC 86-24383. 156p. reprint ed. pap. 44.50 (*0-8357-3497-8*, 2039757) Bks Demand.

— Kiss the Rat Race Good-Bye: Achieve Financial Independence Within 15 Years: A Step-by-Step Program. LC 94-31504. 272p. 1994. pap. 13.95 (*0-8027-7438-5*) Walker & Co.

Lewin, Elizabeth & Ryan, Bernard, Jr. Simple Ways to Help Your Kids Become Dollar-Smart. LC 93-36832. 128p. (Orig.). 1994. pap. 8.95 (*0-8027-7429-6*) Walker & Co.

Lewin, Elizabeth S. Financial Fitness for New Families. 1989. pap. 12.95 (*0-8160-1980-0*) Facts on File.

— Your Personal Financial Fitness Program, 1995-1996. 1995. pap. 13.95 (*0-8160-3146-0*) Facts on File.

Lewin, Ellen. Lesbian Mothers: Accounts of Gender in American Culture. LC 92-54977. (Anthropology of Contemporary Issues Ser.). 256p. 1993. 34.95 (*0-8014-2857-2*); pap. 13.95 (*0-8014-8099-X*) Cornell U Pr.

— Mothers & Children. Cortes, Carlos E., ed. LC 79-6215. (Hispanics in the United States Ser.). (Illus.). 1981. lib. bdg. 23.95 (*0-405-13163-1*) Ayer.

Lewin-Epstein, Noah & Semyonov, Moshe. The Arab Minority in Israel's Economy: Patterns of Ethnic Inequality. 169p. (C). 1993. text ed. 50.00 (*0-8133-1525-5*) Westview.

Lewin-Epstein, Noah, jt. auth. see Semyonov, Moshe.

Lewin, Esther. Random House Thesaurus of Slang. 1989. pap. 12.00 (*0-679-72700-0*) Random.

Lewin, Esther & Lewis, Albert E. The Thesaurus of Slang: Over 165,000 Uncensored Contemporary Slang Terms, Common Idioms, & Colloquialisms, Updated for the 1990's & Arranged for Quick & Easy Reference. LC 93-42890. 1994. 50.00 (*0-8160-2898-2*) Facts on File.

Lewin, Evans. The Germans & Africa. 1977. lib. bdg. 59.95 (*0-8490-1886-2*) Gordon Pr.

Lewin, Frank & Auld, Louis E. Burning Bright: The Genesis of an Opera. (Monograph: No. 1). (Illus.). 100p. (Orig.). 1985. pap. 15.00 (*0-937129-00-3*) Lyrica.

Lewin, Hugh. Jafta. (Jafta Collection). (Illus.). 24p. (J). (ps-3). 1989. reprint ed. pap. 4.95 (*0-87614-494-6*, Lerner Publctns) Lerner Group.

— Jafta: The Homecoming. LC 93-12945. (Illus.). 32p. (J). (ps-2). 1994. 8.99 (*0-679-84722-7*); lib. bdg. 9.99 (*0-679-94722-1*) Knopf Bks Yng Read.

— Jafta - the Journey. LC 84-4326. (The Jafta Bks.). (Illus.). 24p. (J). (ps-3). 1994. lib. bdg. 15.95 (*0-87614-265-X*, First Ave Edns) Lerner Group.

— Jafta - The Journey. LC 84-4326. (The Jafta Bks.). (Illus.). 24p. (J). (ps-3). 1994. pap. 4.95 (*0-87614-644-2*, First Ave Edns) Lerner Group.

— Jafta - the Town. LC 84-4950. (The Jafta Bks.). (Illus.). 24p. (J). (ps-3). 1994. lib. bdg. 15.95 (*0-87614-266-8*, First Ave Edns) Lerner Group.

— Jafta - The Town. LC 84-4950. (The Jafta Bks.). (Illus.). 24p. (J). (ps-3). 1994. pap. 4.95 (*0-87614-645-0*, First Ave Edns) Lerner Group.

— Jafta & the Wedding. LC 82-12836. (Jafta Collection Ser.). (Illus.). 24p. (J). (ps-3). 1983. pap. 4.95 (*0-87614-497-0*, Carolrhoda) Lerner Group.

— Jafta's Father. (Jafta Collection Ser.). (Illus.). 24p. (J). (ps-3). 1983. 15.95 (*0-87614-209-9*, Carolrhoda) Lerner Group.

— Jafta's Father. (Jafta Collection). (Illus.). 24p. (J). (ps-3). 1989. reprint ed. pap. 4.95 (*0-87614-496-2*, Lerner Publctns) Lerner Group.

— Jafta's Mother. LC 82-12863. (J). (ps-3). 1988. 15.95 (*0-87614-208-0*, Carolrhoda) Lerner Group.

— Jafta's Mother. (Jafta Collection). (Illus.). 24p. (J). (ps-3). 1989. reprint ed. pap. 4.95 (*0-87614-495-4*, Lerner Publctns) Lerner Group.

— The Picture That Came Alive. (Junior African Writers Ser.). (Illus.). (J). (gr. 4-5). 1992. pap. 2.95 (*0-7910-2912-3*) Chelsea Hse.

Lewin, Isaac. Towards International Guarantees for Religious Liberty. LC 81-52086. 128p. 10.00 (*0-88400-078-8*) Shengold.

Lewin, Isaac & Gelber, Nahum M. A History of Polish Jewry During the Revival of Poland. LC 90-53261. 334p. 1990. 20.00 (*0-88400-143-1*) Shengold.

Lewin, Isaac, jt. auth. see Kranzler, David.

Lewin, Jacqueline A. & Taylor, Marilyn S. The St. Joe Road: Emigration Mid Eighteen Hundreds. 64p. 1992. pap. 12.00 (*1-884483-00-3*) St Joseph Mus.

Lewin, James. Die Lehre Von Den Ideen Bei Malebranche. (Abhandlungen Zur Philosophie und Ihrer Geschichte Ser.: No. 35). viii, 165p. 1981. reprint ed. write for info. (*3-487-06787-0*, Pub. by Georg Olms GW) Lubrecht & Cramer.

Lewin, Jane E., tr. see Genette, Gerard.

Lewin, Jonathan L. & Lewin, Myrtle H. An Introduction to Mathematical Analysis. 350p. (C). 1988. text ed. 41.95 (*0-394-37262-X*) Random.

— An Introduction to Mathematical Analysis. 2nd ed. LC 92-26695. 1992. text ed. write for info. (*0-07-037585-2*) McGraw.

Lewin, Joseph. Differential Games: Theory & Methods for Solving Game Problems with Singular Surfaces. LC 93-33448. 1993. 49.00 (*0-387-19841-5*) Spr-Verlag.

Lewin, Julius. Politics & Law in South Africa: Essays on Race Relations. 116p. reprint ed. pap. 33.10 (*0-317-11029-2*, 2001695) Bks Demand.

— Studies in African Native Law. 173p. Date not set. reprint ed. 35.95 (*0-933121-90-3*) Black Classic.

Lewin, Karl K. Brief Encounters (Brief Psychotherapy) LC 78-96987. 288p. 1970. 10.00 (*0-87527-048-4*) Green.

— Heritage of Illusions. LC 76-528. 192p. 1977. 10.60 (*0-87527-157-X*) Green.

— Sexual Self-Destruct: Conscience of the West. LC 79-54918. 166p. 1980. 15.00 (*0-87527-197-9*) Green.

Lewin, Keith, jt. auth. see Colclough, Christopher.

Lewin, Klaus J., et al. Gastrointestinal Pathology & Its Clinical Implications, 2 vols., Set. LC 88-28473. (Illus.). 1488p. 1991. 335.00 (*0-89640-153-7*) Igaku-Shoin.

Lewin, Kurt I. A Journey Through Illusions. (Illus.). 480p. (Orig.). 1993. 24.95 (*1-56474-057-9*) Fithian Pr.

Lewin, L. Structural Properties of Polylogarithms. LC 91-18172. (SURV Ser.: No. 37). 412p. 1991. 133.00 (*0-8218-1634-9*, SURV-37) Am Math.

Lewin, Larry, jt. auth. see Knight, Tanis.

Lewin, Leif. Governing Trade Unions in Sweden. LC 79-26724. (Illus.). 180p. 1980. 32.00 (*0-674-35875-9*) HUP.

— Ideology & Strategy: A Century of Swedish Politics. (Political Economy of Institutions & Decisions Ser.: No. 3). (Illus.). 425p. 1989. 69.95 (*0-521-34330-5*) Cambridge U Pr.

— Self Interest & Public Interest in Western Politics. Lavery, Donald S., tr. (Comparative European Politics Ser.). (Illus.). 160p. 1991. 48.00 (*0-19-827726-1*, 11906); pap. 17.95 (*0-19-827725-3*) OUP.

Lewin, Leif & Vedung, Evert, eds. Politics As Rational Action: Essays in Public Choice & Policy Analysis. (Theory & Decision Library: No. 23). 276p. 1980. lib. bdg. 64.00 (*90-277-1040-6*) Kluwer Ac.

Lewin, Leonard. On the Possibility & Desirability of Peace. abr. ed. LC 67-27553. 43p. (C). 1987. reprint ed. pap. 5.00 (*0-942153-18-9*) Entropy Conserv.

— Sciences & the Paranormal. 16p. 1979. pap. 4.00 (*0-904674-07-X*, Pub. by Octagon Pr UK) ISHK Bk Service.

Lewin, Leonard, ed. Telecommunications: An Interdisciplinary Survey. LC 78-26665. (Illus.). 722p. reprint ed. pap. 180.00 (*0-8357-7923-8*, 2036349) Bks Demand.

— Telecommunications: An Interdisciplinary Text. LC 84-70225. (Illus.). 709p. reprint ed. pap. 180.00 (*0-7837-1188-3*, 2041718) Bks Demand.

— Telecommunications in the U. S. Trends & Policies. LC 81-67809. (Illus.). 487p. reprint ed. pap. 138.80 (*0-8357-4190-7*, 2036968) Bks Demand.

Lewin, Leonard C. Report from Iron Mountain. 110p. 1993. reprint ed. lib. bdg. 25.95x (*0-89968-322-3*, Lghtyr Pr) Buccaneer Bks.

Lewin, Lewis M., jt. auth. see Lundervold, Duane A.

Lewin, Linda. Politics & Parentela in Paraiba: A Case Study of Family-Based Oligarchy in Brazil. LC 86-42850. (Illus.). 392p. 1987. text ed. 65.00 (*0-691-07719-3*) Princeton U Pr.

— Politics & Parentela in Paraiba: A Case Study of Family-Based Oligarchy in Brazil. LC 86-42850. reprint ed. pap. 149.40 (*0-7837-9375-8*, 2060119) Bks Demand.

Lewin, M. & Preston, J. HB of Fiber Science & Technology Pt. A: High Technology Fibers. (International Fiber Science & Technology Ser.: Vol. 5). 424p. 1985. 199.00 (*0-8247-7279-2*) Dekker.

Lewin, M. & Sello, S. Handbook of Fiber Science & Technology: Chemical Processing of Fibers & Fabrics, Pt. B: Functional Finishes. (International Fiber Science & Technology Ser.: Vol. 2). 544p. 1984. pap. 199.00 (*0-8247-7118-4*) Dekker.

Lewin, M. J. The Molecular Basis of Somatostatin Activity in the GI Tract. (Molecular Biology Intelligence Unit Ser.). write for info. (*1-57059-164-4*) R G Landes.

Lewin, Marion E., ed. Health Policy Agenda: Some Critical Questions. 126p. 1985. 32.25 (*0-8447-3584-1*) Am Enterprise.

***Lewin, Marsha.** The Overnight Consultant. LC 95-17526. 1995. text ed. 37.95 (*0-471-11944-X*); text ed. 19.95 (*0-471-11945-8*) Wiley.

Lewin, Marsha D. & Rosenau, Milton D., Jr. Software Project Management - Step by Step. 313p. 1988. text ed. 43.00 (*0-9627022-0-X*) M D Lewin Assocs.

Lewin, Menachem. Polymers for Advanced Technologies: IUPAC International Symposium. LC 88-177. 953p. 1988. lib. bdg. 150.00 (*0-89573-293-9*) VCH Pubs.

Lewin, Menachem & Goldstein, I. S., eds. Wood Structure & Composition. (International Fiber Science & Technology Ser.: Vol. 11). 512p. 1991. 199.00 (*0-8247-8233-X*) Dekker.

Lewin, Menachem, et al. Flame-Retardant Polymeric Materials, Vol. 3. LC 75-26781. 248p. 1982. 69.50 (*0-306-40868-6*, Plenum Pr) Plenum.

Lewin, Michael, ed. see Barenboim, Daniel.

Lewin, Michael Z. Called by a Panther. 1991. 17.95 (*0-89296-439-1*) Mysterious Pr.

— Family Business: A Novel of Detection. (Lunghi Family Mystery Ser.). 224p. 1995. reprint ed. 20.00 (*0-88150-348-7*, Foul Play) Countryman.

— Missing Woman. 1991. mass mkt. 4.99 (*0-446-40026-2*, Mysterious Paperbk) Warner Bks.

— Night Cover: A Leroy Powder Mystery. (Detective Leroy Powder Mystery Ser.). 254p. (Orig.). 1995. reprint ed. pap. 10.00 (*0-88150-345-2*, Foul Play) Countryman.

— Silent Salesman. 1991. mass mkt. 4.99 (*0-446-40025-4*, Mysterious Paperbk) Warner Bks.

— Underdog. 272p. 1993. 18.95 (*0-89296-440-5*) Mysterious Pr.

— Underdog. 256p. 1995. mass mkt. 5.50 (*0-446-40436-5*, Mysterious Paperbk) Warner Bks.

Lewin, Michael Z., jt. auth. see Cody, Liza.

Lewin, Michael Z., jt. ed. see Cody, Liza.

Lewin, Miriam. Understanding Psychological Research. LC 87-3507. 464p. (C). 1987. reprint ed. lib. bdg. 46.50 (*0-89464-230-8*) Krieger.

Lewin, Miriam, ed. In the Shadow of the Past: Psychology Portrays the Sexes. LC 83-10072. 338p. 1984. text ed. 50.50 (*0-231-05302-9*); pap. 17.00 (*0-231-05303-7*) Col U Pr.

Lewin, Morton H. Elements of C. LC 86-4910. (Foundations of Computer Science Ser.). 260p. 1986. 49.50 (*0-306-42182-8*, Plenum Pr) Plenum.

— Logic Design & Computer Organization. LC 81-20636. 478p. 1983. text ed. 38.36 (*0-201-04144-8*) Addison-Wesley.

Lewin, Moshe. The Gorbachev Phenomenon: A Historical Interpretation. enl. rev. ed. LC 90-46995. 208p. 1991. 25.00 (*0-520-07428-9*); pap. 13.00 (*0-520-07429-7*) U CA Pr.

— The Making of the Soviet System: Essays in the Social History of Interwar Russia. 368p. 1994. pap. 16.95 (*1-56584-125-5*) New Press NY.

— Russia - U. S. S. R. - Russia: The Drive & Drift of a Superstate. 384p. 1994. 30.00 (*1-56584-123-9*) New Press NY.

— Russian Peasants & Soviet Power: A Study of Collectivization. 544p. (C). 1975. reprint ed. pap. text ed. 18.95 (*0-393-00752-9*) Norton.

— Stalinism & the Seeds of Soviet Reform. (C). 1991. pap. text ed. 22.00 (*0-7453-0427-3*, Pub. by Pluto Pr UK) Westview.

— Stalinism & the Seeds of Soviet Reform: The Debates of the 1960s. LC 91-8701. 414p. (C). 1991. pap. text ed. 25.95 (*0-87332-858-2*) M E Sharpe.

Lewin, Myrtle H., jt. auth. see Lewin, Jonathan L.

Lewin, Peter A., jt. ed. see Ziskin, Marvin C.

Lewin, Ralph A. The Biology of Algae & Diverse Other Verses. 1987. pap. 9.95 (*0-940168-11-1*) Boxwood.

— The Genetics of Algae. LC 75-27297. (Botanical Monographs: Vol. 12). 1976. 65.00 (*0-520-03149-0*) U CA Pr.

Lewin, Ralph A., ed. Origins of Plastids: Symbiogenesis, Prochlorophytes & Evolution. (Illus.). 288p. 1992. 65.00 (*0-412-03691-6*, A7375, Chapman & Hall) Chapman & Hall.

Lewin, Ralph A., tr. see Thurber, James.

Lewin, Rhoda G., ed. Witnesses to the Holocaust: An Oral History. (Oral History Ser.: No. 2). (Illus.). 240p. 1989. text ed. 20.95 (*0-8057-9100-0*, Pub. by Royal Botanic Garden UK) Macmillan.

— Witnesses to the Holocaust: An Oral History. (Twayne's Oral History Ser.: No. 2). 240p. 1991. pap. 12.95 (*0-8057-9126-4*, Pub. by Royal Botanic Garden UK) Macmillan.

Lewin, Rod. Steel Spine, Iron Will. LC 91-78105. 320p. (Orig.). 1992. pap. 18.95 (*0-9632031-0-X*) Boomerang Bks.

Lewin, Roger. Bones of Contention: Controversies in the Search for Human Origins. (Illus.). 352p. 1988. pap. 10.95 (*0-671-66837-4*, Touchstone Bks) S&S Trade.

— Complexity: Life at the Edge of Chaos. LC 93-21652. (Illus.). 224p. 1994. pap. 10.00 (*0-02-014795-3*, Collier S&S) S&S Trade.

— Complexity: Life on the Edge of Chaos. (Illus.). 256p. 1992. text ed. 22.00 (*0-02-570485-0*) Macmillan.

— Human Evolution. 3rd ed. LC 92-48913. 1993. 21.95 (*0-86542-262-1*) Blackwell Sci.

— In the Age of Mankind: A Smithsonian Book of Human Evolution. LC 88-42686. (Illus.). 256p. 1989. 37.50 (*0-89599-022-9*); pap. 19.95 (*0-89599-025-3*) Smithsonian.

— The Origin of Modern Humans: A Scientific American Library Volume. LC 93-17647. (J). 1995. text ed. write for info. (*0-7167-5039-2*, Sci Am Yng Rdrs) W H Freeman.

— Thread of Life: The Smithsonian Looks at Evolution. LC 82-16834. (Illus.). 256p. (C). 1991. pap. 19.95 (*0-89599-029-6*) Smithsonian.

Lewin, Roger, jt. auth. see Leakey, Richard E.

Lewin, Roger, jt. auth. see Savage-Rumbaugh, Sue.

Lewin, Roger A. & Schulz, Clarence. Losing & Fusing: Borderline Transitional Object & Self Relations. LC 92-6219. 368p. 1992. 47.50 (*0-87668-490-8*) Aronson.

Lewin, Ronald. Churchill As Warlord. LC 72-96544. (Illus.). 308p. (C). 1982. pap. 10.95 (*0-8128-6099-3*, Scrbrough Hse) Madison Bks UPA.

— Hitler's Mistakes. LC 86-30649. 174p. 1987. pap. 6.95 (*0-688-07289-5*, Quill) Morrow.

Lewin, Sam. How to Win at the Races. 1979. pap. 5.00 (*0-87980-244-8*) Wilshire.

Lewin, Samuel. Between Two Abysses, Pt. 1. Leftwich, Joseph, tr. LC 85-22377. (Trilogy Ser.). 224p. 1988. 12.95 (*0-8453-4795-0*, Cornwall Bks) Assoc Univ Prs.

— Between Two Abysses: A Trilogy, 3 pts. Leftwich, Joseph, tr. Boxed Set. boxed 29.50 (*0-318-36511-1*, Cornwall Bks); Pt. 3: Shining Through the Clouds. write for info. (*0-318-63293-4*, Cornwall Bks) Assoc Univ Prs.

— Between Two Abysses: A Trilogy, 3 vols. Leftwich, Joseph, tr. 1988. Boxed set. boxed 29.50 (*0-8453-4818-3*, Cornwall Bks) Assoc Univ Prs.

— Between Two Abysses: A Trilogy, 3 pts., Pt. 1: Between Two Abysses. Leftwich, Joseph, tr. 12.95 (*0-318-36512-X*, Cornwall Bks) Assoc Univ Prs.

— Dark Mountains & Blue Valleys, Pt. 2. Leftwich, Joseph, tr. LC 85-22377. (Trilogy Ser.). 160p. 1988. 12.95 (*0-8453-4804-3*, Cornwall Bks) Assoc Univ Prs.

— Singing Through the Clouds, Pt. 3. Leftwich, Joseph, tr. LC 85-22377. (Trilogy Ser.). 160p. 1988. 12.95 (*0-8453-4805-1*, Cornwall Bks) Assoc Univ Prs.

— The Turning of the Tide. Leftwich, Joseph, tr. 8.95 (*0-8453-2087-4*, Cornwall Bks) Assoc Univ Prs.

Lewin, Susan G. Contemporary American Art Jewelry. LC 94-1413. 1994. write for info. (*0-8109-3198-2*) Abrams.

— Formica & Design: From the Countertop to High Art. LC 90-50793. (Illus.). 1991. 45.00 (*0-8478-1334-7*) Rizzoli Intl.

Lewin, Ted. Amazon Boy. LC 92-15798. (Illus.). 32p. (J). (gr. k-3). 1993. text ed. 14.95 (*0-02-757383-4*, Mac Bks Young Read) S&S Childrens.

— I Was a Teenage Professional Wrestler. LC 94-2132. 128p. (J). (gr. 5-9). 1994. pap. 6.95 (*0-7868-1009-2*) Hyprn Child.

— I Was a Teenage Professional Wrestler. LC 92-31523. (Illus.). 128p. (YA). (gr. 6 up). 1993. 17.95 (*0-531-05477-2*); 17.99 (*0-531-08627-5*) Orchard Bks Watts.

— Market! LC 95-7439. (Illus.). (J). 1996. write for info. (*0-688-12161-6*); lib. bdg. write for info. (*0-688-12162-4*) Lothrop.

— The Reindeer People. LC 93-19252. (Illus.). 40p. (J). (gr. 1-4). 1994. text ed. 14.95 (*0-02-757390-7*, Mac Bks Young Read) S&S Childrens.

— Sacred River. LC 94-18370. (J). 1999. 14.95 (*0-395-69846-4*, Clarion Bks) HM.

— Tiger Trek. LC 89-12710. (Illus.). 40p. (J). (gr. 1-5). 1990. lib. bdg. 14.95 (*0-02-757381-8*, Mac Bks Young Read) S&S Childrens.

Lewin, Thomas H. A Manual of Tibetan Being: A Guide to the Colloquial Speech of Tibet in a Series of Progressive Exercises. (C). 1985. reprint ed. 18.50 (*0-8364-2411-5*, Pub. by Asian Educ Servs II) S Asia.

Lewin, Tom. Security: Everyting You Need to Know about Household Alarm Systems. LC 82-61141. (Illus.). 99p. 1982. 16.95 (*0-9609362-0-3*); pap. 7.95 (*0-9609362-1-1*) Park Lane Ent.

Lewin, Walter H. & National Academy of Sciences Staff. High Energy Astrophysics: American & Soviet Research - Proceedings from the U. S. - U. S. S. R. Workshop. 424p. 1991. pap. 30.00 (*0-309-04334-4*) Natl Acad Pr.

Lewin, Walter H., et al, eds. X-Ray Binaries. (Cambridge Astrophysics Ser.: No. 26). (Illus.). 640p. (C). 1992. write for info. (*0-521-41684-1*) Cambridge U Pr.

Lewine, Carol F. The Sistine Chapel Walls & the Roman Liturgy. (Illus.). 192p. (C). 1993. 45.00 (*0-271-00792-3*) Pa St U Pr.

Lewine, D. A., ed. see Eighty-Eight Open Consortium Staff.

An Asterisk (*) at the beginning of an entry indicates that the title is appearing in BIP for the first time.

Lewine, Donald. POSIX Programmer's Guide. (Nutshell Handbook Ser.). 640p. 1991. pap. 34.95 (0-937175-73-0) OReilly & Assocs.

Lewine, Harris, jt. auth. see Humphrey, Mark.

Lewine, Harris, jt. ed. see Okrent, Daniel.

Lewine, Richard & Simon, Alfred. Songs of the Theater: A Definitive Index to the Songs of the Musical Stage. LC 84-13068. 916p. 1984. 82.00 (0-8242-0706-8) Wilson.

Lewine, Richard R., jt. auth. see Bernheim, Kayla F.

Lewington, Anna. Antonio's Rain Forest. (Carolrhoda Picture Bks.). (Illus.). 48p. (J). (ps-5). 1993. 21.50 (0-87614-749-X, Carolrhoda) Lerner Group.

— Plants for People. (Illus.). 240p. 1990. 40.00 (0-19-520840-4) OUP.

— Rain Forest Amerindians. LC 92-10560. (Threatened Cultures Ser.). (Illus.). 48p. (J). (gr. 5-6). 1992. lib. bdg. 22.80 (0-8114-2302-6) Raintree Steck-V.

— What Do We Know about Amazonian Indians? LC 93-1736. (What Do We Know about...? Ser.). (Illus.). 40p. (J). (gr. 3 up). 1993. lib. bdg. 16.95 (0-87226-367-3); pap. 8.95 (0-87226-262-6) P Bedrick Bks.

*Lewington, Anna & Parker, Edward. Brazil. (Illus.). 48p. (J). (gr. 6-8). Date not set. 15.95 (1-56847-339-7) Thomson Lrning.

Lewington, Peter. No Right-of-Way: How Democracy Came to the Oil Patch. LC 90-20444. (Illus.). 290p. 1991. 28.95 (0-8138-1677-7) Iowa St U Pr.

Lewington, Richard & Streeter, David. The Natural History of the Oak Tree: An Intricate Visual Exploration of the Oak & Its Environment. LC 93-18573. (Illus.). 60p. 1993. 19.95 (1-56458-307-4) Dorling Kindersley.

*Lewins, Frank. Transsexualism in Society: A Sociology of Male-to-Female Transsexuals. 184p. 1995. 49.95 (0-7329-3043-X); pap. 24.95 (0-7329-3044-8) Paul & Co Pubs.

Lewins, Frank & Ly, Judith. The First Wave: The Settlement of Australia's First Vietnam Refugees. 124p. 1985. text ed. 21.95 (0-86861-461-0) Routledge Chapman & Hall.

Lewins, Jeffery D. Advances in Nuclear Science & Technology, Vol. 22. Becker, Martin, ed. (Illus.). 242p. 1992. 85.00 (0-306-44094-6, Plenum Pr) Plenum.

— Importance of the Adjoint Function: Physical Basis of Variational & Perturbation Theory in Transport & Diffusion Problems. LC 65-142230. 1965. 84.00 (0-08-013836-5, Pub. by Pergamon Repr UK) Franklin.

— Nuclear Reactor Kinetics & Control. LC 77-8107. 1978. 120.00 (0-08-021682-X, Pub. by Pergamon Repr UK) Franklin.

Lewins, Jeffery D., ed. Teaching Thermodynamics. 538p. 1986. 125.00 (0-306-42207-7, Plenum Pr) Plenum.

Lewins, Jeffery D. & Becker, Martin, eds. Advances in Nuclear Science & Technology, Vol. 21. LC 62-13039. (Illus.). 308p. 1990. 85.00 (0-306-43614-0, Plenum Pr) Plenum.

— Advances in Nuclear Science & Technology, Vol. 13. LC 62-13039. 480p. 1981. 110.00 (0-306-40637-3, Plenum Pr) Plenum.

— Advances in Nuclear Science & Technology, Vol. 14: Sensitivity & Uncertainty Analysis of Reactor Performance Paramaters. LC 82-3654. 388p. 1982. 95.00 (0-306-40994-1, Plenum Pr) Plenum.

— Advances in Nuclear Science & Technology, Vol. 16. LC 62-13039. 596p. 1983. 135.00 (0-306-41486-4, Plenum Pr) Plenum.

— Advances in Nuclear Science & Technology, Vol. 17: Simulators for Nuclear Power. LC 85-31170. 244p. 1986. 75.00 (0-306-42234-4, Plenum Pr) Plenum.

— Advances in Nuclear Science & Technology, Vol. 18. LC 62-13059. 434p. 1987. 105.00 (0-306-42289-1, Plenum Pr) Plenum.

— Advances in Nuclear Science & Technology, Vol. 19: Festschrift in Honor of Eugene Wigner. LC 62-13039. 508p. 1987. 120.00 (0-306-42543-2, Plenum Pr) Plenum.

— Advances in Nuclear Science & Technology, Vol. 20. (Illus.). 242p. 1988. 85.00 (0-306-43082-7, Plenum Pr) Plenum.

— Advances in Nuclear Science & Technology, Vol.15. LC 62-13039. 418p. 1983. 105.00 (0-306-41392-2, Plenum Pr) Plenum.

Lewins, Jeffery D., jt. ed. see Worley, N.

Lewinska, Pelagia. Twenty Months in Auschwitz. Teichner, Albert, tr. 1968. 4.95 (0-8184-0090-0) Carol Pub Group.

Lewinski, Jan S. Money, Credit & Prices. LC 79-51865. 1980. reprint ed. 17.00 (0-88355-957-9) Hyperion Conn.

Lewinski, Jorge & Magnus, Mayotte. The Book of Portrait Photography. 160p. 1982. 60.00 (0-85223-226-8, Pub. by Ebury Pr UK) Trafalgar.

Lewinski, Ron. Guide for Sponsors. 3rd ed. Tufano, Victoria M., ed. LC 93-30922. (Font & Table Ser.). 54p. 1993. pap. 5.00 (1-56854-007-8, GSPON3) Liturgy Tr Pubns.

— El Privilegio de Ser Padrino o Madrina: Guia para los Patrocinadores del Catecumenado. Rodriquez, Pedro, tr. 68p. (SPA.). 1990. pap. 4.50 (0-929650-25-5) Liturgy Tr Pubns.

— Welcoming the New Catholic. 3rd rev. ed. LC 93-50845. (Font & Table Ser.). 98p. 1994. pap. 5.95 (1-56854-013-2, WNEW 3) Liturgy Tr Pubns.

Lewinsohn, Peter, et al. Control Your Depression. 1978. 12.95 (0-13-171702-2, Spectrum Bks) P-H.

Lewinsohn, Peter M., jt. auth. see Brown, Richard.

Lewinsohn, Peter M., jt. auth. see Teri, Linda.

Lewinsohn, Peter M., et al. The Coping with Depression Course: A Psychoeducational Intervention for Unipolar Depression. 223p. 1984. 21.95 (0-916154-11-4) Castalia Pub.

Lewinstein, Bruce, ed. When Science Meets the Public. 164p. 1992. 14.00 (0-87168-440-3, 92-06S) AAAS.

LeWinter, Martin, jt. auth. see Gaasch, William.

Lewinter-Suskind, Leslie, jt. auth. see Suskind, Robert M.

Lewis. Anatomical Workbook. 128p. 1990. pap. 19.95 (0-7506-1023-9) Buttrwrth-Heinemann.

— Art of Aesthetic Plastic Surgery, 2 vols., Set. 1989. 360.00 (0-316-52344-5) Little.

— Brewing. 1995. pap. (0-412-26420-X) Chapman & Hall.

— Carpentry. 2nd ed. 48p. 1995. teacher ed, pap. text ed. 14.95 (0-8273-7029-6) Delmar.

— The Connected Corporation: How Leading Companies Win Through Customer-Supplier Alliances. 1995. 28.00 (0-02-919055-X) Free Pr.

— Encyclopedia of Religious Fundamentalism & Modernism in America. 1996. 80.00 (0-13-061383-5) P-H.

— George MacDonald: An Anthology. Lewis, C. S., ed. 192p. 1986. pap. 7.95 (0-02-022640-3, Pub. by Gebrueder Borntraeger GW) Macmillan.

— Illustrated Dictionary of Toxicology. 1995. write for info. (0-87371-578-0) Lewis Pubs.

— Lamb Chop & Friends: Blue Ribbon Kitten. (J). 1995. pap. text ed. 1.95 (0-307-10564-4, Golden Pr) Western Pub.

— Language Therapy. 1990. 64.50 (1-56593-542-X, 0215) Singular Publishing.

— Medical-Surgical Nursing Text-Student Learning Guide Package. 240p. 1992. pap. 70.95 (0-8016-6950-2) Mosby Yr Bk.

— Practice Management for Dentists. 1989. 75.00 (0-7236-0944-6, Pub. by John Wright UK) Buttrwrth-Heinemann.

— Scientific Inventory Control. 2nd ed. 1981. text ed. 33.95 (0-408-00595-5) Buttrwrth-Heinemann.

— The Screwtape Letters. 1995. 7.99 (1-55748-622-0) Barbour & Co.

— Secret Languages of Success. 1995. 7.98 (0-88365-894-1) Galahad Bks.

— Tepoztlan: Village in Mexico, 1960. 104p. (C). 1960. pap. text ed. 13.50 (0-03-006050-8) HB Coll Pubs.

— Uncommon Knowledge. 1995. pap. 6.50 (0-671-70020-0) PB.

— When the Rivers Go Home. Date not set. pap. 4.99 (0-517-13337-7) Random.

Lewis & Collier. Medical Surgical Nursing. 1952p. 1991. 64.95 (0-8016-6039-4) Mosby Yr Bk.

Lewis & Denenberg. Data Structures & Their Algorithms. (C). 1991. pap. text ed. 67.00 (0-673-39736-X) HarpCollege.

— Data Structures & Their Algorithms: Solutions Manual. (C). 1991. teacher ed 10.00 (0-673-49381-4) HarpCollege.

Lewis & Emory. The United States Conquest of California: An Original Anthology. Cortes, Carlos E., ed. LC 76-7303. (Chicano Heritage Ser.). (Illus.). 1977. 57.95 (0-405-09542-2) Ayer.

Lewis & Hennen. West Virginia: Documents in the History of a Rural-Industrial State. 384p. (C). 1991. pap. text ed. 27.95 (0-8403-6970-0) Kendall-Hunt.

Lewis & Knortz. Orthopaedic Assessment & Treatment of the Geriatric Patient. 456p. 1993. 49.95 (0-8016-6512-4) Mosby Yr Bk.

Lewis & Luther. Primarily Speaking, Vol. 1: LDS Clip Art. pap. 5.95 (0-88494-682-7) Bookcraft Inc.

— Primarily Speaking, Vol. 2: LDS Clip Art. pap. 7.95 (0-88494-751-3) Bookcraft Inc.

— Primarily Speaking, Vol. 3: Learning Activities. pap. 6.95 (0-88494-718-1) Bookcraft Inc.

Lewis & Moore, eds. Fiber Optic Systems for Mobile Platforms. 182p. 1987. 45.00 (0-89252-875-3, 840) SPIE.

Lewis & Ryan. Medical & Surgical Retina: Advances, Controversies. 550p. 1993. 110.00 (0-8016-6797-6) Mosby Yr Bk.

Lewis & Sines, eds. Fracture Mechanics: Fourteenth Symposium: Volume 1, Theory & Analysis - STP 791. 610p. 1983. 75.00 (0-8031-0728-5, 04-791001-30) ASTM.

— Fracture Mechanics: Fourteenth Symposium - STP 791, 2 vols., Set. 1983. 135.00 (0-8031-0730-7, 04-791000-30) ASTM.

— Fracture Mechanics: Fourteenth Symposium - STP 791, 2 vols., Vol. 11. 639p. 1983. 75.00 (0-8031-0729-3, 04-791002-30) ASTM.

Lewis & Sutherland. Growing & Displaying Bonsai: A Step-by-Step Guide. (Illus.). 128p. 1995. 14.98 (0-8317-5162-2) Smithmark.

Lewis, jt. auth. see Edwardes.

Lewis, jt. auth. see Ray.

Lewis, jt. auth. see Trunkey.

Lewis, jt. auth. see WVHC Staff.

Lewis, et al. Glory Filled the Land: A Trilogy on the Welsh Revival of 1904-1905. Roberts, Richard O., ed. xvi, 204p. 1989. 17.95 (0-940033-38-0) R O Roberts.

— Management of Human Services Programs. 2nd ed. LC 90-46530. 304p. (C). 1991. text ed. 40.95 (0-534-13074-7) Brooks-Cole.

— Manual of Psychosocial Nursing Interventions: Promoting Mental Health in Medical-Surgical Settings. 288p. 1989. text ed. 37.50 (0-7216-5763-X) Saunders.

*Lewis & Clark. The Journals of the Lewis & Clark Expedition Vol. 9: The Journals of John Ordway, May 14, 1804-Sept. 23, 1806, & Charles Floyd, May 14-Aug. 18, 1804, Vol. 9. Moulton, Gary, ed. 416p. 1995. text ed. 55.00 (0-8032-2914-3) U of Nebr Pr.

*Lewis & Johnson Weiner Staff. Betrayal: The Story of Aldrich Ames, An American Spy. 1995. 25.00 (0-679-44050-X) Random.

Lewis, A. D. & Ibbetson, D. J., eds. The Roman Law Tradition. 248p. (C). 1994. 54.95 (0-521-44199-4) Cambridge U Pr.

Lewis, A. D., jt. ed. see Chen, W. F.

Lewis, A. H., jt. auth. see MacEwen, W. A.

Lewis, A. J., tr. see Romen, A. S.

Lewis, Adam. Salmon of the Pacific. LC 94-16591. (Illus.). 96p. (Orig.). 1994. pap. 14.95 (1-57061-016-9) Sasquatch Bks.

Lewis, Adele & Grappo, Gary. How to Write Better Resumes. 4th ed. 288p. 1993. pap. 9.95 (0-8120-1556-8) Barron.

Lewis, Adele, jt. auth. see Schuman, Nancy.

Lewis, Adele B. Better Resumes for Sales & Marketing Personnel. 176p. 1985. pap. 11.95 (0-8120-2981-X) Barron.

Lewis, Adele B. & Moore, David J. Best Resumes for Scientists & Engineers. 2nd ed. LC 93-2849. 1993. text ed. 37.50 (0-471-59452-0); pap. text ed. 14.95 (0-471-59451-2) Wiley.

Lewis, Adele B. & Saltman, David A. Better Resumes for Attorneys & Paralegals. 1986. pap. 9.95 (0-8120-3649-2) Barron.

Lewis, Alan & Warneryd, Karl-Erik, eds. Ethics & Economic Affairs. LC 93-45693. 368p. 1994. 69.95 (0-415-09396-1, B3923, Routledge NY) Routledge.

Lewis, Alan, et al, eds. New Perspectives in Anti-Inflammatory Therapies. (Advances in Inflammation Research Ser.: Vol. 12). (Illus.). 352p. 1988. text ed. 128.50 (0-88167-362-5) Raven.

Lewis, Alan E. Apocalypse Soon? Christian Responsibility & the Book of Revelation. 1987. 50.00 (0-317-89954-6, Pub. by Wild Goose Pubns UK) St Mut.

Lewis, Alan J. & Furst, Daniel E., eds. Nonsteroidal Anti-Inflammatory Drugs: Mechanisms & Clinical Uses. 2nd ed. LC 93-34984. 488p. 1993. 195.00 (0-8247-8856-7) Dekker.

Lewis, Albert B. Danger Insurance Fraud in Progress: How to Avoid Becoming A Victim. LC 87-71527. 381p. (Orig.). 1987. pap. text ed., spiral bd. 80.00 (0-939713-02-0) Carriage House.

— A Guide to Understanding & Using the Property & Casualty Statutory Statements for Banks, Investors & Brokers. LC 86-72094. (Orig.). 1987. pap. 15.00 (0-939713-00-4) Carriage House.

Lewis, Albert C. Albert Einstein, 1879-1955: A Centenary Exhibit. (Illus.). 40p. 1979. pap. 7.50 (0-87959-090-4) U of Tex H Ransom Ctr.

Lewis, Albert C., intro. Albert Einstein: Four Commemorative Lectures. 1979. 10.00 (0-87959-093-9) U of Tex H Ransom Ctr.

Lewis, Albert C., jt. auth. see Griffin, Nicholas.

Lewis, Albert C., ed. see Russell, Bertrand.

Lewis, Albert D., II. The Great Spiritual War. (Illus.). 300p. 1993. 19.95 (0-9633356-9-3) Harvest Time.

Lewis, Albert D., Jr. The Great Spiritual War: AIDS & Abortion, Vol. 4. (Illus.). 52p. (Orig.). Date not set. pap. 5.00 (0-9633356-4-2) Harvest Time.

— The Great Spiritual War: Idol Worship, Vol. 3. (Illus.). 20p. (Orig.). Date not set. pap. 2.50 (0-9633356-3-4) Harvest Time.

— The Great Spiritual War: My Personal Testimony, Vol. 7. (Illus.). 100p. (Orig.). Date not set. pap. 7.00 (0-9633356-7-7) Harvest Time.

— The Great Spiritual War: Our Real Foe(s) - Who Are They?, Vol. 2. (Illus.). 23p. (Orig.). Date not set. pap. 2.50 (0-9633356-2-6) Harvest Time.

— The Great Spiritual War: Suicide; Forgiveness; Repentance: The Weapons of Our Warfare & a Letter to the President, Vol. 6. (Illus.). 31p. (Orig.). Date not set. pap. 4.00 (0-9633356-6-9) Harvest Time.

— The Great Spiritual War: The Great Tribulation, Vol. 5. (Illus.). 22p. (Orig.). Date not set. pap. 2.50 (0-9633356-5-0) Harvest Time.

— The Great Spiritual War: What Is It?, Vol. 1. (Illus.). 42p. (Orig.). Date not set. pap. 4.50 (0-9633356-1-8) Harvest Time.

Lewis, Albert E., jt. auth. see Lewin, Esther.

*Lewis, Alcinda, ed. Butterfly Gardens: Luring Nature's Loveliest Pollinators to Your Yard. (21st-Century Gardening Ser.). (Illus.). 1995. per., pap. 6.95 (0-945352-88-3) Bklyn Botanic.

Lewis, Alcinda C., jt. ed. see Papaj, Daniel R.

*Lewis, Alfred. Pak: Using American Law Books. 288p. (C). 1995. boxed 29.38 (0-7872-0734-9) Kendall-Hunt.

Lewis, Alfred H. Apaches of New York. LC 73-37277. (Short Story Index Reprint Ser.). 1977. reprint ed. 23.95 (0-8369-4088-1) Ayer.

— The Boss. LC 67-29272. (Americans in Fiction Ser.). reprint ed. lib. bdg. 19.00 (0-8398-1157-8); reprint ed. pap. text ed. 6.95 (0-89197-684-1) Irvington.

— Faro Nell & Her Friends: Wolfville Stories. LC 73-163042. (Short Story Index Reprint Ser.). (Illus.). 1977. reprint ed. 24.95 (0-8369-3956-5) Ayer.

— Sandburrs. LC 72-90585. (Short Story Index Reprint Ser.). (Illus.). 1977. 21.95 (0-8369-3068-1) Ayer.

— Sandburrs. LC 72-104512. (Illus.). 318p. reprint ed. lib. bdg. 18.00 (0-8398-1158-6) Irvington.

— Sandburrs. 318p. (C). 1986. reprint ed. pap. text ed. 7.95 (0-8290-2029-2) Irvington.

— Wolfville. 1972. reprint ed. lib. bdg. 29.00 (0-8422-8090-1) Irvington.

— Wolfville. 1986. reprint ed. pap. text ed. 8.95 (0-8290-1957-X) Irvington.

Lewis, Alfred H., ed. Old Wolfville: Chapters from the Fiction of Alfred Henry Lewis. LC 68-13363. (Illus.). 274p. reprint ed. pap. 78.10 (0-317-29603-5, 2021715) Bks Demand.

Lewis, Alfred J. Using California Law Books. 100p. (C). 1994. per., pap. text ed. 16.50 (0-8403-2982-2) Kendall-Hunt.

Lewis, Alison. Subverting Patriarchy. 300p. 1994. 44.95 (0-85496-322-7) Berg Pubs.

Lewis, Alison, et al. The Lamplighters: 25 Years of Gilbert & Sullivan in San Francisco. LC 77-78710. (Illus.). 1977. 20.00 (0-9601270-2-X); pap. 10.00 (0-9601270-1-1) Opera West.

Lewis, Alison S., jt. auth. see Sykes, Beverly.

Lewis, Allen. Baseball's Greatest Streaks: The Highs & Lows of Teams, Pitchers & Hitters in the Modern Major Leagues. LC 91-51209. 272p. 1992. lib. bdg. 32.50x (0-89950-714-X) McFarland & Co.

Lewis, Allison, et al. La Ensenanza de la Sexualidad Humana en las Escuelas: Un Manual para el Educador. Jaimes, Rene, ed. (Illus.). 236p. (Orig.). 1985. write for info. (0-916683-11-7) Intl Plan Parent.

— Teaching Human Sexuality in Caribbean Schools: A Teachers Handbook. Jaimes, Rene, ed. (Illus.). 306p. (Orig.). pap. 15.00 (0-916683-07-9) Intl Plan Parent.

Lewis, Alonzo & Newhall, James. History of Lynn, Including Lynnfield, Saugus, Swampscott & Nahant. rev. ed. (Illus.). 620p. 1989. reprint ed. lib. bdg. 62.00 (0-8328-0840-7, MA0072) Higginson Bk Co.

Lewis, Alonzo & Newhall, James R. History of Lynn, Essex County, Massachusetts: Including Lynnfield, Saugus, Swampscott & Nahant. (Illus.). 628p. 1989. reprint ed. pap. 32.50 (1-55613-218-2) Heritage Bk.

Lewis, Alun. Alun Lewis: Collected Stories. 360p. 1990. 38.00 (1-85411-012-8, Pub. by Poetry Wales Pr UK) Dufour.

— Letters to My Wife. 280p. 1989. 35.00 (1-85411-004-7, Pub. by Poetry Wales Pr UK) Dufour.

Lewis, Amanda. Writing: A Fact & Fun Book. 1992. pap. 8.61 (0-201-63236-5) Addison-Wesley.

Lewis, Amy, jt. ed. see Sader, Marion.

*Lewis, Andrew, ed. Current Legal Problems Vol. 48, Pt. 1: Annual Review. 224p. 1995. pap. 39.95 (0-19-826041-5) OUP.

Lewis, Andrew W. Royal Succession in Capetian France: Studies on Familial Order & the State. LC 81-6360. (Historical Studies: No. 100). (Illus.). 374p. 1982. 37.00 (0-674-77985-1) HUP.

Lewis, Angela. Sea Change. 1971. 5.95 (0-393-08641-0) Norton.

Lewis, Ann. Chairing Child Protection Conferences: An Exploration of Role & Attitude. 135p. 1994. 51.95 (1-85628-691-6, Pub. by Avebury Pub UK) Ashgate Pub Co.

— Children's Understanding of Disability. LC 94-34162. 224p. 1995. 55.00x (0-415-10131-X, 0338); pap. 17.95 (0-415-10132-8, B4018) Routledge.

— Primary Special Needs & the National Curriculum. 224p. 1991. 74.50 (0-415-05427-3, A5849) Routledge.

— Primary Special Needs & the National Curriculum. 2nd ed. LC 95-15426. 1995. write for info. (0-415-12582-0) Routledge.

*Lewis, Ann E. Reuniting Refugee Families: An Attorney's Guide to Law & Procedure. Marks, Stephanie & Black, George, eds. 200p. (Orig.). 1994. pap. text ed. 25.00 (0-934143-70-6) Lawyers Comm Human.

*Lewis, Ann E., ed. Fifty Georgia Stories. LC 87-26193. (Illus.). 320p. 1987. pap. 14.95 (0-87797-270-2) Cherokee.

*Lewis, Annabel. The Ultimate Ribbon Book. (Illus.). 128p. 1995. 29.95 (1-57076-030-6, Trafalgar Sq Pub) Trafalgar.

Lewis, Anne. Leadership Styles. 63p. 1993. pap. 9.95 (0-87652-178-2) Am Assn Sch Admin.

— Partnerships Connecting School & Community. 124p. (Orig.). 1986. pap. 12.95 (0-87652-102-2, 021-00182) Am Assn Sch Admin.

— Restructuring America's Schools. 248p. (Orig.). 1989. pap. 15.95 (0-87652-145-6, 021-00269) Am Assn Sch Admin.

Lewis, Anne, ed. Teaching Basis Riding. 93p. (C). 1990. pap. 21.00 (0-85131-460-0, Pub. by J A Allen & Co UK) St Mut.

Lewis, Anne & Steinberger, Elizabeth. Learning Styles: Putting Research & Common Sense into Practice. 56p. 1991. pap. 5.00 (0-685-51034-4, 021-00314) Am Assn Sch Admin.

Lewis, Anne, ed. see Rambon, Sheppard.

Lewis, Anthony. Bazooka: How to Build Your Own. (Illus.). 64p. 1993. pap. 10.00 (0-87364-738-6) Paladin Pr.

— Concordance to Cordwainer Smith. 2nd ed. 1994. pap. 9.00 (0-915368-57-9) New Eng SF Assoc.

— Gideon's Trumpet. 1989. pap. 10.00 (0-679-72312-9, Vin) Random.

— Make No Law. 1993. pap. 4.99 (0-517-11212-4) Random Hse Value.

— Make No Law: The Sullivan Case & the First Amendment. LC 91-6618. 368p. 1991. 25.00 (0-394-58774-X) Random.

— Make No Law: The Sullivan Case & the First Amendment. LC 92-50104. 1992. pap. 13.00 (0-679-73939-4, Vin) Random.

Lewis, Anthony, jt. ed. see Fortune, Nigel.

Lewis, Anthony, jt. auth. see Llewellyn, Claire.

Lewis, Anthony J. The Love Story in Shakespearean Comedy. LC 91-45643. 248p. 1992. lib. bdg. 28.00 (0-8131-1786-0) U Pr of Ky.

Lewis, Anthony R. Annotated Bibliography of Recursive Science Fiction. 56p. 1990. pap. 6.00 (0-915368-47-1) New Eng SF Assoc.

Lewis, Archibald R. Medieval Society in Southern France & Catalonia. (Collected Studies: No. CS197). 280p. (C). 1984. reprint ed. lib. bdg. 87.95 (0-86078-145-3, Pub. by Variorum UK) Ashgate Pub Co.

— Nomads & Crusaders A.D. 1000-1368. LC 87-45588. (Illus.). 224p. 1988. 25.00 (0-253-34787-4); pap. 10.95 (0-253-20652-9, MB-652) Ind U Pr.

— A War in the West. (Illus.). 45p. 1989. pap. 10.00 (0-685-29004-2) A Lewis.

Lewis, Archibald R. & Runyan, Timothy J. European Naval & Maritime History, 300-1500. LC 84-48485. (Illus.). 208p. 1985. 22.95 (0-253-32082-8); pap. 9.95 (0-253-20573-5, MB-573) Ind U Pr.

Lewis, Arne. A Book of Rules. LC 83-80760. (Illus.). 48p. 1983. 22.95 (0-912810-41-6) Lustrum Pr.

Lewis, Arnold. American Country Houses of the Gilded Age: Sheldon's "Artistic Country-Seats" (Illus.). 128p. (C). 1983. pap. 9.95 (*0-486-24301-X*) Dover.

Lewis, Arnold & Morgan, Keith, eds. American Victorian Architecture. LC 73-92261. Orig. Title: L' Architecture American. (Illus.). 160p. 1975. reprint ed. pap. 10.95 (*0-486-23177-1*) Dover.

Lewis, Arnold, et al. The Opulent Interiors of the Gilded Age: All 203 Photographs from Artistic Houses, with New Text. 192p. 1987. pap. 14.95 (*0-486-25250-7*) Dover.

Lewis, Arthur. Judges & Ruth. (Everyman's Bible Commentary Ser.). (C). 1979. pap. 7.99 (*0-8024-2007-9*) Moody.

— Syndicalism & the General Strike. 1976. lib. bdg. 59.95 (*0-8490-2696-2*) Gordon Pr.

Lewis, Arthur H. The Day They Shook the Plum Tree. 250p. 1985. reprint ed. lib. bdg. 29.95 (*0-89966-600-0*) Buccaneer Bks.

— Jueces y Rut (Comentario Biblico Portavoz) Orig. Title: Judges & Ruth (Everyman's Bible Commentary). 128p. (SPA.). 1982. pap. 5.99 (*0-8254-1434-2*) Kregel.

— Lament for the Molly Maguires. 308p. 1990. reprint ed. lib. bdg. 26.95 (*0-89966-722-8*) Buccaneer Bks.

Lewis, Arthur M. Evolution-Social & Organic: Linnaeus, Darwin, Kropotkin, Marx. (Science for the Workers Ser.). 186p. 1984. 17.95 (*0-88286-088-7*) C H Kerr.

— Vital Problems in Social Evolution: An Introduction to the Materialist Conception of History. (Science for the Workers Ser.). 192p. 1984. 17.95 (*0-88286-089-5*) C H Kerr.

Lewis, Arthur M., jt. auth. see Darrow, Clarence S.

Lewis, Arthur M., jt. auth. see Darrow, Clarence.

Lewis, Arthur O., ed. American Utopias: Selected Short Fiction. LC 77-154448. (Utopian Literature Ser.). 1973. reprint ed. 23.95 (*0-405-03530-6*) Ayer.

— Utopian Literature, 41 Bks, Set. 1971. 932.50 (*0-405-03510-1*) Ayer.

Lewis, Arthur O., et al, eds. Anglo-German & American-German Crosscurrents, Vol. 4. (Illus.). 204p. (C). 1990. lib. bdg. 42.00 (*0-8191-7474-2*) U Pr of Amer.

Lewis, Arthur W. Basic Bookbinding. (Illus.). 1952. pap. 3.95 (*0-486-20169-4*) Dover.

Lewis, B., ed. Bioacoustics: A Comparative Approach. (Illus.). 1983. text ed. 128.00 (*0-12-446550-1*) Acad Pr.

Lewis, B. & Anderson, J. C. Nucleation & Growth of Thin Films. 1979. text ed. 212.00 (*0-12-446680-X*) Acad Pr.

Lewis, B. & Cribb, P. Orchids of Vanuatu. (Illus.). 171p. 1989. pap. text ed. 6.00 (*0-947643-16-8*, Pub. by Royal Botanic Garden UK) Lubrecht & Cramer.

Lewis, B. & Horabin, I. Case Studies in the Use of Algorithms. (Programmed Instruction in Industry Ser.). 18.00 (*0-08-014035-1*, Pub. by Pergamon Repr UK) Franklin.

Lewis, B., jt. ed. see Miller, Norman E.

***Lewis, B., et al, eds.** Underground Corrosion Control. (Illus.). 1993. 78.00 (*1-877914-48-7*) NACE Intl.

Lewis, B. P., jt. ed. see Brown, F.

Lewis, B. S. & Kimchi, A., eds. Heart-Failure Mechanisms & Management. (Illus.). 480p. 1991. 101.00 (*0-387-53145-9*) Spr-Verlag.

Lewis, B. Victor & Magos, Adam L., eds. Endometrial Ablation. LC 92-21014. 232p. 1993. 89.95 (*0-443-04587-9*) Churchill.

Lewis, Barbara. Young Lions. (Illus.). 243p. (Orig.). 1993. pap. 9.95 (*0-87579-771-7*) Deseret Bk.

***Lewis, Barbara A.** The Kid's Guide to Service Projects: Over 500 Service Ideas for Young People Who Want to Make a Difference. Espeland, Pamela, ed. 184p. (Orig.). (J). (gr. 4 up). 1995. pap. 10.95 (*0-915793-82-2*) Free Spirit Pub.

— A Kid's Guide to Social Action: How to Solve the Social Problems You Choose - & Turn Creative Thinking Into Positive Action. Espeland, Pamela, ed. LC 90-44297. (Self-Help for Kids Ser.). (Illus.). 208p. (Orig.). (YA). (gr. 5 up). 1991. pap. 14.95 (*0-915793-29-6*) Free Spirit Pub.

— Kids with Courage: True Stories about Young People Making a Difference. Espeland, Pamela, ed. 44p. 1992. teacher ed, pap. 5.95 (*0-915793-40-7*) Free Spirit Pub.

— Kids with Courage: True Stories about Young People Making a Difference. Espeland, Pamela, ed. LC 91-46726. 184p. (J). (gr. 5-12). 1992. pap. 10.95 (*0-915793-39-3*) Free Spirit Pub.

Lewis, Barbara C. Cote d'Ivoire. (Profiles - Nations of Contemporary Africa Ser.). 128p. 1929. text ed. 26.50 (*0-86531-023-8*) Westview.

***Lewis, Barry.** Inside Endurance. (Illus.). 192p. 1996. pap. 14.95 (*0-8117-2551-0*) Stackpole.

— Running the Trans America Footrace: Trials & Triumphs of Life on the Road. (Illus.). 160p. 1994. pap. 14.95 (*0-8117-2582-0*) Stackpole.

Lewis, Bea. Quick & Easy Low-Fat, Low-Cholesterol Recipes Kids Will Love. 128p. (Orig.). 1990. pap. 3.95 (*0-380-76079-7*) Avon.

Lewis-Beck, Michael S. Applied Regression: An Introduction. (Quantitative Applications in the Social Sciences Ser.: Vol. 22). (Illus.). 79p. 1980. pap. 9.95 (*0-8039-1494-6*) Sage.

— Data Analysis: An Introduction. (Quantitative Applications in the Social Science Ser.). 96p. 1995. pap. text ed. 9.95 (*0-8039-5772-6*) Sage.

— Economics & Elections: The Major Western Democracies. (Illus.). 200p. (C). 1990. pap. text ed. 15.95 (*0-472-08133-0*) U of Mich Pr.

— Forecasting Elections. 163p. 1992. 21.95 (*0-87187-600-0*) Congr Quarterly.

Lewis-Beck, Michael S., jt. ed. see Eulau, Heinz.

Lewis, Bernard. Arabs in History. 1960. pap. text ed. 12.00 (*0-06-131029-8*, TB 1029, Torch) HarpC.

— The Arabs in History. rev. ed. 200p. 1991. reprint ed. lib. bdg. 20.00x (*0-8095-9079-4*) Borgo Pr.

— The Arabs in History. 6th ed. LC 92-43000. 256p. (C). 1993. 12.95 (*0-19-285258-2*) OUP.

— The Assassins: A Radical Sect in Islam. 1987. pap. 9.95 (*0-19-520550-2*) OUP.

— Cultures in Conflict: Christians, Muslims, & Jews in the Age of Discovery. (Illus.). 128p. 1995. 16.95 (*0-19-509026-8*) OUP.

— Cultures in Conflict: Christians, Muslims, & Jews in the Age of Discovery. (Illus.). 120p. 1996. reprint ed. pap. 9.95 (*0-19-510283-5*) OUP.

— Emergence of Modern Turkey. 2nd ed. (Royal Institute of International Affairs Ser.). (Illus.). (C). 1969. pap. 16.95 (*0-19-500344-6*) OUP.

— Islam & the West. LC 92-26938. (Illus.). 240p. 1993. 25.00 (*0-19-507619-2*) OUP.

— Islam & the West. 238p. 1994. reprint ed. pap. 12.95 (*0-19-509061-6*) OUP.

— Islam in History: Ideas, People, & Events in the Middle East. rev. ed. LC 92-46218. 496p. 1993. pap. 27.95 (*0-8126-9217-9*) Open Court.

— Islam in History: Ideas, People, & Events in the Middle East. 2nd rev. ed. LC 92-46218. 496p. 1993. 59.95 (*0-8126-9216-0*) Open Court.

— Istanbul & the Civilization of the Ottoman Empire. (Centers of Civilization Ser.: Vol. 9). (Illus.). 1972. reprint ed. pap. 10.95 (*0-8061-1060-0*) U of Okla Pr.

— The Jews of Islam. LC 84-42575. (Illus.). 259p. 1987. pap. 12.95 (*0-691-00807-8*) Princeton U Pr.

— The Muslim Discovery of Europe. (Illus.). 352p. 1985. pap. 13.95 (*0-393-30233-4*) Norton.

— The Origins of Isma'ilism: A Study of the Historical Background of the Fatimid Caliphate. LC 74-180357. reprint ed. 22.50 (*0-404-56289-2*) AMS Pr.

— The Political Language of Islam. LC 87-19222. (Exxon Lecture Ser.). viii, 168p. 1991. pap. 9.95 (*0-226-47693-6*) U Ch Pr.

— Race & Slavery in the Middle East: A Historical Enquiry. (Illus.). 194p. 1992. pap. 10.95 (*0-19-505326-5*) OUP.

— Race & Slavery in the Middle East: An Historical Enquiry. (Illus.). 200p. 1990. 30.00 (*0-19-506283-3*) OUP.

— Semites & Anti-Semites. LC 85-26021. 1987. pap. 7.95 (*0-393-30420-5*) Norton.

— The Shaping of the Modern Middle East. rev. ed. (Illus.). 224p. (C). 1994. 29.95 (*0-19-507281-2*); pap. text ed. 12.95 (*0-19-507282-0*) OUP.

Lewis, Bernard, ed. Christians & Jews in the Ottoman Empire: The Functioning of a Plural Society. abr. ed. 320p. (C). Date not set. pap. text ed. 24.95 (*0-8419-1138-X*) Holmes & Meier.

Lewis, Bernard, ed. & tr. Islam-From the Prophet Muhammad to the Capture of Constantinople: Volume 1: Politics & War. (Illus.). 303p. 1987. pap. 14.95 (*0-19-505087-8*) OUP.

— Islam-From the Prophet Muhammad to the Capture of Constantinople: Volume 3: Religion & Society. (Illus.). 352p. 1987. pap. 15.95 (*0-19-505088-6*) OUP.

Lewis, Bernard, ed. World of Islam. LC 91-65146. (Illus.). 360p. 1992. reprint ed. pap. 29.95 (*0-500-27624-2*) Thames Hudson.

Lewis, Bernard & Schnapper, Dominique, eds. Muslims in Europe. LC 94-13756. (Social Change in Western Europe). 1994. 39.00 (*1-85567-250-2*, Pub. by Pinter Pubs UK); pap. 15.00 (*1-85567-214-6*, Pub. by Pinter Pubs UK) St Martin.

Lewis, Bernard & Von Elbe, Guenther, eds. Combustion, Flames, & Explosions of Gases. 3rd ed. 739p. 1987. text ed. 99.00 (*0-12-446751-2*) Acad Pr.

Lewis, Bernard, jt. ed. see Braude, Benjamin.

Lewis, Bernard, jt. auth. see Cohen, Amnon.

Lewis, Bernard, ed. see Goldziher, Ignaz.

Lewis, Bernard L., et al. Aspects of Radar Signal Processing. 554p. 1986. text ed. 29.00 (*0-89006-197-1*) Artech Hse.

Lewis, Bernard T. Building Maintenance Engineering Price Book 1985-86. 300p. 1986. 39.95 (*0-412-01071-2*, 9666, Chap & Hall NY) Chapman & Hall.

Lewis, Beth I. George Grosz: Art & Politics in the Weimar Republic. (Illus.). 356p. 1991. pap. text ed. 17.95 (*0-691-00291-6*) Princeton U Pr.

Lewis, Beth I., et al. Grosz-Heartfield: The Artist As Social Critic. (Germany in the Twenties Ser.). (Illus.). 94p. 1980. 24.50 (*0-8419-7504-3*) Holmes & Meier.

Lewis, Betty. Holy City: Riker's Religious Roadside Attraction. (Topics in Monterey Bay Area History Ser.). (Illus.). 100p. 1992. pap. 8.95 (*0-9617681-5-0*) Otter B Bks.

— Monterey Bay Yesterday: A Nostalgic Era in Postcards. (Illus.). 124p. (Orig.). 1987. reprint ed. pap. 4.98 (*0-9617681-1-8*) Otter B Bks.

— Watsonville: Memories That Linger, Vol. 1. LC 76-41500. 220p. 1986. 13.95 (*0-9617681-0-X*) Otter B Bks.

— Watsonville: Memories That Linger, Vol. 2. LC 76-41500. (Illus.). 154p. 1980. 13.95 (*0-934136-08-4*) Otter B Bks.

Lewis, Beverley. The Six-Hour Mystery. LC 93-35020. (Illus.). (J). (gr. 4 up). 1993. 3.99 (*0-8066-2666-6*, 9-2666) Augsburg Fortress.

Lewis, Beverly. California Christmas. (Holly's Heart Ser.: Bk. 5). 160p. (J). (gr. 6-9). 1994. pap. 5.99 (*0-310-43321-5*) Zondervan.

— The Chicken Pox Panic. (Cul-De-Sac Kids Ser.). 80p. 1995. mass mkt. 2.99 (*1-55661-626-0*) Bethany Hse.

— The Crazy Christmas Angel Mystery. (Cul-De-Sac Kids Ser.). 80p. 1995. mass mkt. 2.99 (*1-55661-627-9*) Bethany Hse.

— Curing Common Faults: Remedy Those Costly Shots. 1994. 4.98 (*0-8317-4037-X*) Smithmark.

— Curing Hooks & Slices: Straighten the Curving Shots. 1994. 4.98 (*0-8317-4039-6*) Smithmark.

— The Double Dabble Surprise. (Cul-De-Sac Kids Ser.). 80p. 1995. mass mkt. 2.99 (*1-55661-625-2*) Bethany Hse.

— Double Dabble Thanksgiving Surprise. (J). (ps-3). 1993. pap. 3.95 (*1-56233-175-2*, Squeaky Sneaker) Star Song TN.

— Godd-Bye Dressel Hills. (Holly's Heart Ser.: Bk. 7). 160p. (J). 1994. pap. 5.99 (*0-310-44410-1*) Zondervan.

— Golf for Women. 1992. 14.99 (*0-517-07296-3*) Random Hse Value.

— Holly's First Love. LC 92-47055. (J). 1993. pap. 5.99 (*0-310-38051-0*) Zondervan.

— How to Break Ninety: The Mental & Tactical Approach. 1994. 4.98 (*0-8317-4038-8*) Smithmark.

— Mountain Bikes & Garbanzo Beans. LC 93-4606. (Ready, Set, Read Ser.). (J). 1993. pap. 3.99 (*0-8066-2663-1*, 9-2663, Augsburg) Augsburg Fortress.

— Mystery at Midnight. LC 95-5845. (Ready, Set, Read! Ser.: First Chapter Bks.). (Illus.). (J). 1995. write for info. (*0-8066-2749-2*) Augsburg Fortress.

— The No-Guys Pact. (Hollys Heart Superbook Ser.: No. 1). 208p. (J). 1995. pap. 6.99 (*0-310-20193-4*) Zondervan.

— Perfecting Your Short Game: Cure Your Putting Problems. 1994. 4.98 (*0-8317-4034-5*) Smithmark.

— Power Driving: Swing on the Right Track. 1994. 4.98 (*0-8317-4035-3*) Smithmark.

— Sealed with a Kiss. (Holly's Heart Ser.: Bk. 3). 144p. (J). (gr. 6-9). 1993. pap. 5.99 (*0-310-38071-5*, Youth Spec) Zondervan.

— Second-Best Friend. (Holly's Heart Ser.: Bk. 6). 160p. (J). (gr. 6-9). 1994. pap. 5.99 (*0-310-43331-2*) Zondervan.

— Secret in the Willows. (Summerhill Secrets Ser.: Bk. 2). 144p. 1995. pap. 4.99 (*1-55661-477-2*) Bethany Hse.

— Secret Summer Heart. (Holly's Heart Ser.: Bk. 2). 160p. (J). (gr. 6-9). 1993. pap. 5.99 (*0-310-38061-8*) Zondervan.

— Shots for Lower Scoring: How to Play the Trickier Shots. 1994. 4.98 (*0-8317-4036-1*) Smithmark.

— Straight-A Teacher. (Holly's Heart Ser.: Bk. 8). 160p. (J). 1994. pap. 5.99 (*0-310-46111-1*) Zondervan.

— The Trouble with Weddings. (Holly's Heart Ser.: Bk. 4). 144p. (J). (gr. 6-9). 1993. pap. 5.99 (*0-310-38081-2*) Zondervan.

— Whispers Down the Lane. (Summerhill Secrets Ser.: Bk. 1). 144p. (J). 1995. pap. 4.99 (*1-55661-476-4*) Bethany Hse.

Lewis, Bill. West Texas Adventure. 180p. 1993. pap. 9.95 (*1-57087-007-1*) Prof Pr NC.

Lewis, Blake, jt. auth. see Williams, Basil.

Lewis, Bob. Modern Fighting Vehicles. (Concise Color Guides Ser.). (Illus.). 240p. 1988. pap. 4.50 (*0-681-40433-7*) Longmeadow Pr.

Lewis, Brad & Goldstein, Gabriella. Olympic Results, Barcelona 1992: A Complete Compilation of Results from the Games of the XXV Olympiad. LC 93-15813. (Reference Library of the Humanities: Vol. 1752). 648p. 1993. Alk. paper. 96.00 (*0-8153-0333-5*, H1752) Garland.

Lewis, Brad, ed. see Maxwell, John.

Lewis, Brad A. Assault on Lake Casitas. Moran, Ed, ed. LC 90-84461. (Illus.). 200p. (Orig.). 1990. pap. 11.95 (*1-879174-00-6*) Broad St Bks.

Lewis, Brenda J. Little Foster & Maria: A Program about Abuse. 32p. 1993. 6.95 (*1-884063-04-7*) Mar Co Prods.

— Little Foster & Sam: A Program about Drugs. 24p. 1994. 6.95 (*1-884063-18-7*) Mar Co Prods.

Lewis, Brenda R. Coins & Currency. LC 92-46359. (Hobby Handbooks Ser.). (Illus.). 80p. (J). (gr. 5 up). 1993. lib. bdg. 13.99 (*0-679-92662-3*) Random Bks Yng Read.

Lewis, Brenda R., jt. auth. see Riordan, James.

Lewis, Brian. Jean Mitry & the Aesthetics of the Cinema. Kirkpatrick, Diane, ed. LC 84-138. (Studies in Cinema: No. 25). 150p. reprint ed. 42.80 (*0-8357-1553-1*, 2070457) Bks Demand.

— The Naked Australian: Australia, Her People & the Way They Live. LC 86-72287. (Illus.). 250p. 1987. 13.95 (*0-940749-02-5*); pap. 9.95 (*0-940749-00-9*) A A Pub.

— Our War. 330p. 1980. 29.95 (*0-522-84199-6*) Intl Spec Bk.

Lewis, Brian & Watts, Burl. A Car Collection for the Common Man: A Brief History of the Towe Ford Museums. (Illus.). 120p. 1987. 12.95 (*0-940749-03-3*); pap. 7.95 (*0-940749-05-X*) A A Pub.

Lewis, Brian, jt. auth. see Horabin, Ivan.

Lewis, Brian, ed. see IPM Committee on International Affairs Staff.

Lewis, Brian, et al. Canada: North of Sixty. (Illus.). 304p. 1991. 50.00 (*0-7710-1581-X*, Pub. by McClelland & Stewart CN) Firefly Bks Ltd.

Lewis, Bruce. Four Men Went to War. 1990. mass mkt. 4.95 (*0-312-92280-9*) St Martin.

Lewis, Bruce R. & Ford, Richard K. Basic Statistics Using SAS. 2nd ed. 148p. (C). 1987. pap. text ed. 28.50 (*0-314-34736-4*) West Pub.

Lewis, Burckhardt J. Travels in Arabia. 478p. (C). 1992. 125.00 (*0-685-67239-5*, Darf Pubs Ltd) St Mut.

Lewis, Byron A. & Pucelick, R. Frank. Magic Demystified: A Pragmatic Guide to Communication & Change. 2nd ed. LC 82-223576. (Neurolinguistic Programming Book Ser.). (Illus.). 167p. 1984. 16.95 (*0-943920-09-4*) Metamorphous Pr.

Lewis, Byron A. & Pucelik, Frank. Magic of NLP Demystified: A Pragmatic Guide to Communication & Change. rev. ed. LC 90-5742. (Positive Change Guide Ser.). (Illus.). 176p. 1990. pap. 9.95 (*1-55552-017-0*) Metamorphous Pr.

Lewis, C. Employee Selection. 2nd ed. 200p. 1991. pap. 53.50 (*0-7487-1371-9*, Pub. by Stanley Thornes UK) Trans-Atl Phila.

Lewis, C., et al. Marketing Peanut Butter: A Microcomputer Simulation. 1985. Apple. 150.00 (*0-07-079587-8*); IBM-PC. 150.00 (*0-07-079588-6*); TRS-80. 150.00 (*0-07-079586-X*); Manual. pap. text ed. write for info. (*0-07-040762-2*) McGraw.

Lewis, C. Testimony. 1994. mass mkt. 5.50 (*0-06-104283-8*, Harp PBks) HarpC.

— A Wish to Be. 1994. pap. 11.95 (*1-85230-534-7*) Element MA.

Lewis, C., jt. ed. see Bennett, D.

Lewis, C., jt. auth. see Lewis, P. C.

Lewis, C., jt. auth. see Trotta, V.

Lewis, C., et al, eds. Annual Survey of South African Law 1991. 781p. 1992. write for info. (*0-7021-2939-9*, Pub. by Juta SA) W W Gaunt.

Lewis, C. D. Industrial & Business Forecasting Methods. (Illus.). 144p. 1982. text ed. 42.95 (*0-408-00559-9*) Buttrwrth-Heinemann.

Lewis, C. Day. The Complete Poems of C. Day Lewis. LC 91-68076. 752p. (C). 1992. 65.00 (*0-8047-2070-3*) Stanford U Pr.

— The Complete Poems of C. Day Lewis. 768p. 1995. 65.00x (*0-8047-2073-8*); 24.95 (*0-8047-2585-3*) Stanford U Pr.

— Revolution in Writing. LC 75-37952. (Studies in English Literature: No. 33). 1976. lib. bdg. 75.00 (*0-8383-2115-1*) M S G Haskell Hse.

Lewis, C. Day, ed. see Owen, Wilfred.

Lewis, C. E. & McGee, James O., eds. The Macrophage: The Natural Immune System. (Illus.). 448p. 1992. 50.00 (*0-19-963234-0*) OUP.

Lewis, C. F., jt. ed. see Kohel, R. J.

Lewis, C. J. & Lewis, J. Norman. Natality & Fecundity: A Contribution to National Demography. LC 75-38135. (Demography Ser.). 1976. reprint ed. 19.95 (*0-405-07988-5*) Ayer.

Lewis, C. L. & Ott, L. Analytical Chemistry of Nickel. LC 71-118320. 1970. 106.00 (*0-08-015876-5*, Pub. by Pergamon Repr UK) Franklin.

Lewis, C. P., jt. ed. see Currie, C. R. J.

Lewis, C. P., jt. auth. see Wright, A. P.

Lewis, C. Roy, jt. auth. see Carter, Harold.

Lewis, C. S. Abolition of Man. 128p. 1978. reprint ed. pap. 5.00 (*0-02-086790-5*, Collier S&S) S&S Trade.

— All My Road Before Me. 1992. pap. 14.95 (*0-15-604643-1*, Harvest Bks) HarBrace.

— All My Road Before Me: The Diary of C. S. Lewis (1922-1927) 1991. 24.95 (*0-15-104609-3*) HarBrace.

— A Book of Narnians: The Lion, the Witch & the Others. LC 94-29069. (Illus.). 96p. (J). (gr. 3 up). 1995. 16.95 (*0-06-025009-7*) HarpC Child Bks.

— A Book of Narnians: The Lion, the Witch & the Others. LC 94-29069. (Illus.). 96p. (YA). (gr. 3 up). 1995. lib. bdg. 16.89 (*0-06-025014-3*) HarpC Child Bks.

— The Business of Heaven: Daily Readings from C. S. Lewis. 1984. pap. 9.95 (*0-15-614863-3*, Harvest Bks) HarBrace.

— C. S. Lewis Letters to Children. (J). 1985. 9.95 (*0-02-570830-9*) Macmillan.

— The Case for Christianity. 64p. 1989. pap. 5.95 (*0-02-086750-6*, Collier S&S) S&S Trade.

— Christian Reflections. 1976. 18.95 (*0-8488-1077-5*) Amereon Ltd.

— Christian Reflections. 1967. pap. 9.99 (*0-8028-0869-7*) Eerdmans.

— Chronicles of Narnia, 7 bks., Set. (Illus.). (J). (gr. 3 up). 1994. boxed 105.00 (*0-06-024488-7*); boxed, pap. 27.65 (*0-06-447119-5*, Trophy); boxed, pap. 41.65 (*0-06-440537-0*, Trophy) HarpC Child Bks.

— The Dark Tower & Other Stories. Hooper, Walter, ed. LC 76-52387. 158p. 1977. pap. 8.00 (*0-15-623930-2*, Harvest Bks) HarBrace.

— The Discarded Image: An Introduction to Medieval & Renaissance Literature. (Canto Bk.). 240p. (C). 1994. pap. 9.95 (*0-521-47735-2*) Cambridge U Pr.

— The Four Loves. 19.25 (*0-8446-6214-3*) Peter Smith.

— The Four Loves. large type ed. (Large Print Inspirational Ser.). 240p. 1986. pap. 9.95 (*0-8027-2547-3*) Walker & Co.

— The Four Loves. LC 60-10920. 192p. 1971. reprint ed. pap. 6.95 (*0-15-632930-1*, Harvest Bks) HarBrace.

— The Four Loves: Modern Classic Ser. 1991. 15.95 (*0-15-132916-8*) HarBrace.

— God in the Dock. Hooper, Walter, ed. 1972. pap. 14.99 (*0-8028-0868-9*) Eerdmans.

— The Grand Miracle. (Epiphany Bks.). 176p. 1986. mass mkt. 5.99 (*0-345-33658-5*) Ballantine.

— Great Divorce. 128p. 1978. reprint ed. pap. 6.00 (*0-02-086890-1*, Pub. by Gebrueder Borntraeger GW) Macmillan.

— A Grief Observed. 1983. mass mkt. 5.50 (*0-553-27486-4*) Bantam.

— Grief Observed. 1994. pap. 10.00 (*0-06-065284-5*) Harper SF.

— A Grief Observed. large type ed. 120p. 1985. reprint ed. pap. 7.95 (*0-8027-2470-1*) Walker & Co.

— A Grief Observed: Special Gift Edition. LC 88-45674. 96p. 1989. reprint ed. 12.00 (*0-06-065273-X*) Harper SF.

— The Horse & His Boy. LC 93-14300. (Trophy Keypoint Bk.). (Illus.). 192p. (J). (gr. 3 up). 1994. pap. 3.95 (*0-06-447106-3*, Harper Keypoint) HarpC Child Bks.

— The Horse & His Boy. LC 93-14300. (Chronicles of Narnia Ser.: Bk. 3). (Illus.). 196p. (J). (gr. 3 up). 1994. 15.00 (*0-06-023488-1*) HarpC Child Bks.

— The Horse & His Boy. LC 93-14300. (Chronicles of Narnia Ser.: Bk. 3). (Illus.). 240p. (J). (gr. 3 up). 1994. lib. bdg. 14.89 (*0-06-023489-X*, Trophy) HarpC Child Bks.

— The Horse & His Boy: Chronicles of Narnia. LC 93-14300. (Trophy Bk.). (Illus.). 192p. (J). (gr. 3 up). 1994. pap. 5.95 (*0-06-440501-X*, Trophy) HarpC Child Bks.

— Inspirational Writing. 1994. 12.98 (0-88486-108-2) Arrowood Pr.

— Inspirational Writings of C. S. Lewis. 1991. 12.98 (0-88486-047-7, Inspirational Pr) Arrowood Pr.

— The Joyful Christian: 127 Readings. 256p. 1984. pap. 9.00 (0-02-086930-4, Pub. by Gebrueder Borntraeger GW) Macmillan.

— The Last Battle. (Chronicles of Narnia Ser.). (Illus.). 176p. (J). (gr. 3 up). 1994. pap. 5.95 (0-06-440503-6); pap. 3.95 (0-06-447108-X, Trophy) HarpC Child Bks.

— The Last Battle. LC 93-14302. (Chronicles of Narnia Ser.: Bk. 7). (Illus.). 176p. (J). (gr. 3 up). 1994. 15.00 (0-06-023493-8) HarpC Child Bks.

— The Last Battle. LC 93-14302. (Chronicles of Narnia Ser.: Bk. 7). (Illus.). 224p. (J). (gr. 3 up). 1994. lib. bdg. 14.89 (0-06-023494-6) HarpC Child Bks.

— Last Battle. 192p. (J). (gr. 4 up). 1970. pap. 3.95 (0-02-044210-6, Collier S&S) S&S Trade.

— Letters to an American Lady. Kilby, Clyde S., ed. 1967. pap. 4.99 (0-8028-1428-X) Eerdmans.

— Letters to Malcolm: Chiefly on Prayer. LC 64-11536. 124p. 1973. reprint ed. pap. 6.95 (0-15-650880-X, Harvest Bks) HarBrace.

— The Lion, the Witch & the Wardrobe. Robinette, Joseph, ed. 1989. 4.95 (0-87129-265-3, L62) Dramatic Pub.

— The Lion, the Witch & the Wardrobe. LC 93-8889. (Chronicles of Narnia Ser.). (Illus.). 160p. (J). (gr. 3 up). 1994. pap. 5.95 (0-06-440499-4); pap. 3.95 (0-06-447104-7, Trophy) HarpC Child Bks.

— The Lion, the Witch & the Wardrobe. Lawrie, Robin, ed. & illus. by. LC 94-13165. (Trophy Picture Bk.). 64p. (J). (gr. 3 up). 1995. pap. 7.95 (0-06-443399-4, Trophy) HarpC Child Bks.

— The Lion, the Witch & the Wardrobe. LC 83-61572. (Chronicles of Narnia Ser.). (Illus.). 160p. (J). (gr. 4 up). 1988. lib. bdg. 22.95 (0-02-758200-0, Mac Bks Young Read) S&S Childrens.

— The Lion, the Witch, & the Wardrobe. LC 93-8889. (Chronicles of Narnia Ser.: Bk. 1). (Illus.). 208p. (J). (gr. 3 up). 1994. 15.00 (0-06-023481-4) HarpC Child Bks.

— The Lion, the Witch, & the Wardrobe. LC 93-8889. (Chronicles of Narnia Ser.: Bk. 1). (Illus.). 160p. (J). (gr. 3 up). 1994. lib. bdg. 14.89 (0-06-023482-2) HarpC Child Bks.

— The Lion, the Witch, & the Wardrobe: (El Lion, la Bruja y el Armario) (SPA.). (J). 11.95 (84-204-4564-9) Santillana.

— Lion, Witch, & Wardrobe, Bk. I. (J). 1976. 18.95 (0-8488-0823-1) Amereon Ltd.

— The Magician's Nephew. LC 93-14301. (Chronicles of Narnia Ser.). (Illus.). 176p. (J). (gr. 3 up). 1994. pap. 5.95 (0-06-440505-2, Trophy) HarpC Child Bks.

— The Magician's Nephew: Chronicles of Narnia. LC 93-14301. (Trophy Keypoint Bk.). (Illus.). 176p. (J). (gr. 3 up). 1994. pap. 3.95 (0-06-447110-1, Trophy) HarpC Child Bks.

— The Magician's Nephew - Full. 1984. 5.00 (0-87129-541-5, M57) Dramatic Pub.

— The Magician's Nephew (One-Act) 1985. 4.95 (0-87129-368-4, M57) Dramatic Pub.

— Mere Christianity. 192p. 1952. text ed. 15.00 (0-02-570610-1) Macmillan.

— Mere Christianity. 192p. 1978. pap. 4.95 (0-02-086830-8) Macmillan.

— Mere Christianity. 1981. 12.95 (0-02-570590-3) Macmillan.

— Mere Christianity. 180p. 1986. pap. 7.95 (0-02-086940-1, Collier S&S) S&S Trade.

— Mere Christianity. large type ed. (Large Print Inspirational Ser.). 1987. pap. 12.95 (0-8027-2575-9) Walker & Co.

— Miracles. 192p. 1978. pap. 3.95 (0-02-086760-3, Collier S&S) S&S Trade.

— Narrative Poems. Hooper, Walter, ed. LC 78-15062. 1978. pap. 4.95 (0-15-665327-3, Harvest Bks) HarBrace.

— Of Other Worlds: Essays & Stories. Hooper, Walter, ed. LC 75-6785. 148p. 1975. pap. 6.95 (0-15-667897-7, Harvest Bks) HarBrace.

— On Stories: And Other Essays on Literature. LC 81-48014. 144p. 1982. pap. 4.95 (0-15-668788-7, Harvest Bks) HarBrace.

— Out of the Silent Planet. 1980. 14.95 (0-02-570790-6) Macmillan.

— Out of the Silent Planet. (J). Date not set. 18.95 (0-8488-0563-1) Yestermorrow.

— Out of the Silent Planet. 1991. reprint ed. lib. bdg. 21.95 (1-56849-039-9) Buccaneer Bks.

— Out of the Silent Planet. (Space Trilogy Ser.). 192p. 1990. reprint ed. text ed. 45.00 (0-02-570795-7) Macmillan.

— Perelandra. (J). 1976. 19.95 (0-8488-0564-X) Amereon Ltd.

— Perelandra. 224p. 1987. pap. 5.95 (0-02-086950-9) Macmillan.

— Perelandra. (Space Trilogy Ser.). 224p. 1990. reprint ed. text ed. 40.00 (0-02-570845-7) Macmillan.

— Pilgrims Regress. 1992. pap. 9.99 (0-8028-0641-4) Eerdmans.

— The Pilgrim's Regress: An Allegorical Apology for Christianity, Reason, & Romanticism. LC 82-101595. 221p. reprint ed. pap. 63.00 (0-317-30149-7, 2025332) Bks Demand.

— Poems. Hooper, Walter, ed. LC 77-4733. 142p. 1977. pap. 7.95 (0-15-672248-8, Harvest Bks) HarBrace.

— Present Concerns. 1987. 14.95 (0-15-173948-X, Harvest Bks); pap. 4.95 (0-15-673840-6, Harvest Bks) HarBrace.

— Prince Caspian. 224p. (J). 1970. pap. 3.95 (0-02-044240-8, Collier S&S) S&S Trade.

— Prince Caspian. LC 85-18999. (Chronicles of Narnia Ser.). (Illus.). 192p. (J). (gr. 4 up). 1986. reprint ed. pap. 7.95 (0-02-044430-3, Collier Bks Young) S&S Childrens.

— Prince Caspian: The Return to Narnia. LC 93-11514. (Chronicles of Narnia Ser.). (Illus.). 192p. (J). (gr. 3 up). 1994. pap. 5.95 (0-06-440500-1, Trophy); pap. 3.95 (0-06-447105-5, Harper Keypoint) HarpC Child Bks.

— Prince Caspian: The Return to Narnia. LC 93-11514. (Chronicles of Narnia Ser.: Bk. 2). (Illus.). 192p. (J). (gr. 3 up). 1994. 15.00 (0-06-023483-0) HarpC Child Bks.

— Prince Caspian: The Return to Narnia. LC 93-11514. (Chronicles of Narnia Ser.: Bk. 4). (Illus.). 240p. (J). (gr. 3 up). 1994. lib. bdg. 14.89 (0-06-023484-9) HarpC Child Bks.

— The Problem of Pain. 160p. 1978. pap. 4.95 (0-02-086850-2, Collier S&S) S&S Trade.

— Reflections on the Psalms. LC 58-10910. 1964. pap. 8.00 (0-15-676248-X, Harvest Bks) HarBrace.

— Reflections on the Psalms. large type ed. (Large Print Inspirational Ser.). 1985. pap. 9.95 (0-8027-2512-0) Walker & Co.

— The Screwtape Letters. 18.95 (0-89190-989-3, Am Repr) Amereon Ltd.

— The Screwtape Letters. 9.95 (1-55748-240-3); 7.99 (0-916441-33-4, Christian Lib) Barbour & Co.

— The Screwtape Letters. 160p. (J). 1992. pap. text ed. 4.95 (1-55748-315-9) Barbour & Co.

— The Screwtape Letters. (Illus.). 144p. 1978. student ed. pap. 4.99 (0-8007-8336-0, Spire) Revell.

— The Screwtape Letters. 160p. 1988. pap. 2.95 (0-451-62610-9, Ment) NAL-Dutton.

— Screwtape Letters. 1995. pap. 4.50 (0-553-21443-8, Bantam Classics) Bantam.

— The Screwtape Letters. deluxe ed. 14.95 (1-55748-080-X, Christian Lib) Barbour & Co.

— The Screwtape Letters. rev. ed. 192p. 1982. pap. 2.95 (0-02-086740-9) Macmillan.

— The Seeing Eye & Other Selected Essays from Christian Reflections. 256p. 1986. mass mkt. 4.99 (0-345-32866-3) Ballantine.

— The Silver Chair. LC 93-14299. (Chronicles of Narnia Ser.). (Illus.). 208p. (J). (gr. 3 up). 1994. pap. 3.95 (0-06-447109-8); pap. 5.95 (0-06-440504-4, Trophy) HarpC Child Bks.

— The Silver Chair. LC 93-14299. (Chronicles of Narnia Ser.: Bk. 4). (Illus.). 208p. (J). (gr. 3 up). 1994. 15.00 (0-06-023495-4) HarpC Child Bks.

— The Silver Chair. LC 93-14299. (Chronicles of Narnia Ser.: Bk. 4). (Illus.). 256p. (J). (gr. 3 up). 1994. lib. bdg. 14.89 (0-06-023496-2) HarpC Child Bks.

— Six by Lewis, 6 vols. 1978. pap. 27.95 (0-02-086770-0, Pub. by Gebrueder Borntraeger GW) Macmillan.

— Space Trilogy, 3 vols. Incl. Perelandra. 1965. 3.95 (0-02-086900-2); That Hideous Strength. 1965. 3.95 (0-02-086920-7); 768p. 1975. Boxed Set. Set pap. 11.95 (0-02-022350-1, Collier S&S) S&S Trade.

— Space Trilogy, 3 vols., Set. 2nd ed. 1986. pap. 16.95 (0-02-022360-9, Pub. by Gebrueder Borntraeger GW) Macmillan.

— Spirits in Bondage: A Cycle of Lyrics. 1984. pap. 7.00 (0-15-684748-5, Harvest Bks) HarBrace.

— Surprised by Joy. Date not set. 20.95 (0-8488-1078-3) Amereon Ltd.

— Surprised by Joy: The Shape of My Early Life. LC 56-5329. 248p. 1956. 14.95 (0-15-187011-X) HarBrace.

— Surprised by Joy: The Shape of My Early Life. LC 56-5329. 1966. pap. 7.95 (0-15-687011-8, Harvest Bks) HarBrace.

— That Hideous Strength. 384p. 1987. pap. 5.95 (0-02-086960-6, Pub. by Gebrueder Borntraeger GW) Macmillan.

— That Hideous Strength. (Space Trilogy Ser.). 584p. 1990. reprint ed. text ed. 60.00 (0-02-571255-1) Macmillan.

— Till We Have Faces: A Myth Retold. LC 79-24272. (Illus.). 320p. 1980. pap. 8.95 (0-15-690436-5, Harvest Bks) HarBrace.

— Trying to Smile. 1992. 19.95 (0-15-191312-9) HarBrace.

— The Visionary Christian: One Hundred & Thirty-One Readings from C. S. Lewis. 288p. 1984. text ed. 8.95 (0-02-086730-1, Pub. by Gebrueder Borntraeger GW) Macmillan.

— The Voyage of the Dawn Treader. (Chronicles of Narnia Ser.). (Illus.). 208p. (J). (gr. 3 up). 1994. pap. 3.95 (0-06-447107-1) HarpC Child Bks.

— The Voyage of the Dawn Treader. LC 93-11515. (Chronicles of Narnia Ser.: Bk. 3). (Illus.). 208p. (J). (gr. 3 up). 1994. 15.00 (0-06-023486-5) HarpC Child Bks.

— The Voyage of the Dawn Treader. LC 93-11515. (Chronicles of Narnia Ser.: Bk. 5). (Illus.). 256p. (J). (gr. 3 up). 1994. lib. bdg. 14.89 (0-06-023487-3) HarpC Child Bks.

— The Voyage of the Dawn Treader: Chronicles of Narnia. LC 93-11515. (Trophy Keypoint Bk.). (Illus.). 208p. (J). (gr. 3 up). 1994. pap. 5.95 (0-06-440502-8, Trophy) HarpC Child Bks.

— The Weight of Glory & Other Addresses. 2nd rev. ed. 96p. 1980. reprint ed. pap. 5.95 (0-02-095980-X, Pub. by Gebrueder Borntraeger GW) Macmillan.

— The World's Last Night & Other Essays. LC 73-4887. 113p. 1973. reprint ed. pap. 6.95 (0-15-698360-5, Harvest Bks) HarBrace.

Lewis, C. S., ed. The Collected Short Stories of Edith Wharton, Vol. 2. (Hudson River Editions Ser.). 908p. 1989. text ed. 50.00 (0-02-626161-8, Scribners) S&S Trade.

Lewis, C. S. & Baynes, Pauline. The Magician's Nephew. LC 93-14301. (Chronicles of Narnia Ser.: Bk. 6). (Illus.). 176p. (J). (gr. 3 up). 1994. 15.00 (0-06-023497-0) HarpC Child Bks.

— The Magician's Nephew. LC 93-14301. (Chronicles of Narnia Ser.: Bk. 1). (Illus.). 208p. (J). (gr. 3 up). 1994. lib. bdg. 14.89 (0-06-023498-9) HarpC Child Bks.

Lewis, C. S., ed. see Lewis.

***Lewis, C. S., et al.** Narnia - Touring-Musical. Date not set. 5.00 (0-87129-565-2, N01) Dramatic Pub.

Lewis, Candace, jt. auth. see Mann, Peter.

Lewis, Carenza, jt. ed. see Aston, Michael.

Lewis, Carl & Marx, Jeffrey. Inside Track: My Professional Life in Amateur Track & Field. 1990. 19.95 (0-685-46193-9) S&S Trade.

Lewis, Carol & Sternheimer, Stephen. Soviet Urban Management: With Comparisons to the United States. LC 78-19748. (Praeger Special Studies). 255p. 1979. text ed. 59.95 (0-275-90381-8, C0381, Praeger Pubs) Greenwood.

Lewis, Carol R. Listening to Children. LC 84-11154. 208p. 1985. 30.00 (0-87668-728-1) Aronson.

— Listening to Children. LC 84-11154. 208p. 1992. pap. 27.50x (0-87668-285-9) Aronson.

Lewis, Carol S. On Your Own: How to Escape the Corporation & Make More Money As an Independent Contractor. 1994. pap. 14.95 (1-878707-13-2) HighText.

Lewis, Carol W. The Ethics Challenge in Public Service: A Problem-Solving Guide. LC 91-3401. (Public Administration Ser.). 252p. 1991. 29.95 (1-55542-383-3) Jossey-Bass.

Lewis, Carol W. & Walker, A. Grayson, III. Casebook in Public Budgeting & Financial Management. (Illus.). 384p. (C). 1984. pap. text ed. write for info. (0-13-115402-8) P-H.

Lewis, Carol W., jt. ed. see Peterson, George E.

***Lewis, Carole B.** Aging: The Health Care Challenge. 3rd ed. (Illus.). 500p. (C). 1995. pap. text ed. 38.00 (0-8036-0042-9) Davis Co.

— Clinical Measures of Functional Outcomes: The Functional Tool Box. McNerney, Therese, ed. 240p. 1994. student ed 149.00 (0-9643582-0-4) Learn Pubns.

— Improving Mobility in Older Persons: A Manual for Geriatric Specialists. LC 88-24244. 172p. (C). 1988. 50.00 (0-8342-0020-1) Aspen Pub.

Lewis, Carole B., ed. Aging: The Health Care Challenge. 2nd ed. LC 89-25679. (Illus.). 427p. (C). 1990. text ed. 38.00 (0-8036-5615-7) Davis Co.

Lewis, Carole B. & Bottomley, Jennifer M. Geriatric Physical Therapy: A Clinical Approach. (Illus.). 656p. 1994. 49.95 (0-8385-8875-1, A8875-5) Appleton & Lange.

Lewis, Carole B. & McNerney, Therese. Exercise Handouts for Rehabilitation. (Aspen Series on Physical Therapy). 536p. 1993. ring bd. 79.00 (0-8342-0372-3, 20372) Aspen Pub.

Lewis, Carolyn D. Reporting for Television. LC 83-7568. (Illus.). 192p. 1984. text ed. 31.50 (0-231-05538-2) Col U Pr.

Lewis, Carroll. Treasures of Galveston Bay. (Illus.). 1966. 13.95 (0-87244-052-4) Texian.

Lewis, Carson M., et al. Superficial Liposculpture: Manual of Technique. LC 92-49210. 137p. 1993. 175.00 (0-387-97917-4) Spr-Verlag.

Lewis, Cass. Dead Man's Confession. LC 93-71557. (Adventures of Shelly Holmes Ser.). 232p. (YA). 1993. pap. 3.95 (1-56969-150-9) FamilyVision.

***Lewis, Catherine.** Dry Fire: A Novel. 288p. 1996. 21.00 (0-393-03835-1) Norton.

Lewis, Catherine C. Educating Hearts & Minds: Reflections on Japanese Preschool & Elementary Education. (Illus.). 308p. (C). 1995. 49.95 (0-521-45197-3); pap. 16.95 (0-521-45832-3) Cambridge U Pr.

Lewis, Catherine F., jt. auth. see Haywood, Kathleen M.

Lewis, Cathy, ed. see Bianchi, Susan & Butler, Jan.

Lewis, Catriona J., jt. auth. see Kirkwood, Evelyne.

Lewis, Cecil. All My Yesterdays: An Autobiography. LC 93-14870. 1993. 24.95 (1-85230-405-7) Element MA.

— Farewell to Wings. Gibert, James, ed. LC 79-7279. (Flight: Its First Seventy-Five Years Ser.). (Illus.). 1980. reprint ed. lib. bdg. 15.95 (0-405-12188-1) Ayer.

— Sagittarius Rising. 352p. 1993. 35.00 (1-85367-143-6, 5585) Stackpole.

— A Wish to Be: A Voyage of Discovery. LC 94-22041. 1994. pap. 11.95 (1-85230-558-4) Element MA.

Lewis, Chad T., et al. IO Enterprises, Student Manual: A Microcomputer Simulation. 40p. (C). 1993. pap. text ed. 20.00 (0-03-097741-X) Dryden Pr.

— Managerial Skills in Organizations. 350p. 1990. teacher ed, disk write for info. (0-318-66374-0, H23377) Allyn.

Lewis, Charles. Becoming a Father. LC 86-2635. 192p. 1986. 90.00 (0-335-15128-0, Open Univ Pr); pap. 32.00 (0-335-15127-2, Open Univ Pr) Taylor & Francis.

— State & Diplomatic Immunity. 3rd rev. ed. 1990. 120.00 (1-85044-254-1) Lloyds London Pr.

Lewis, Charles & O'Brien, Margaret, eds. Reassessing Fatherhood. LC 87-60199. 288p. (C). 1987. text ed. 45.00 (0-8039-8019-1); pap. text ed. 24.00 (0-8039-8020-5) Sage.

Lewis, Charles, jt. ed. see Keren, Gideon.

Lewis, Charles B. Brother Gardner's Lime-Kiln Club. LC 76-104513. (Illus.). reprint ed. lib. bdg. 19.00 (0-8398-1159-4) Irvington.

Lewis, Charles C., jt. auth. see Lord, Richard A.

Lewis, Charles F., jt. ed. see Christiansen, M. N.

Lewis, Charles J. Medical Negligence: A Practical Guide. 567p. 1992. 150.00 (0-85459-643-7, Pub. by Tolley Pubng UK) St Mut.

Lewis, Charles L. Admiral De Grasse & American Independence. LC 79-6113. (Navies & Men Ser.). (Illus.). 1980. reprint ed. lib. bdg. 44.95 (0-405-13042-2) Ayer.

— David Glasgow Farragut. LC 79-6115. (Navies & Men Ser.). (Illus.). 1980. Vol. Repr. Of 1941 Ed. lib. bdg. 38.95 (0-405-13043-0); Vol. 2, Repr, Of 1943 Ed. lib. bdg. 44.95 (0-405-13044-9) Ayer.

— Famous American Naval Officers. rev. ed. LC 76-142655. (Essay Index Reprint Ser.). 1977. 31.95 (0-8369-2170-4) Ayer.

— Famous Old-World Sea Fighters. LC 70-99708. (Essay Index Reprint Ser.). 1977. 31.95 (0-8369-1419-8) Ayer.

— Famous Sea Fighters: Outstanding Naval Engagements Over 23 Centuries of Sea History with a Bibliography of 102 Works. 1977. lib. bdg. 75.00 (0-8490-1804-8) Gordon Pr.

— How to Plan Produce & Stage Special Events. (Illus.). 250p. (Orig.). 1992. pap. 25.95 (0-685-59318-5) Evergreen IL.

— Matthew Fontaine Maury. LC 79-6116. (Navies & Men Ser.). (Illus.). 1980. reprint ed. lib. bdg. 31.95 (0-405-13045-7) Ayer.

— Matthew Fontaine Maury, the Pathfinder of the Seas. LC 72-98638. reprint ed. 34.50 (0-404-03984-7) AMS Pr.

— The Retail Business Booster: Sales Promotion with Pizzazz. (Illus.). 208p. (Orig.). 1990. pap. 25.95 (0-9625990-0-X) Evergreen IL.

— Retail Excellence: A Handbook for Retail Merchants. (Illus.). 126p. (Orig.). 1992. pap. 19.95 (0-9625990-3-4) Evergreen IL.

— The Romantic Decatur. LC 79-164614. (Select Bibliographies Reprint Ser.). 1977. reprint ed. 23.95 (0-8369-5898-5) Ayer.

— The Unique Inside Guide to Washington State. (Illus.). 420p. (Orig.). 1991. pap. 14.95 (0-9625990-2-6) Evergreen IL.

***Lewis, Charles M., ed.** Relativism & Religion. LC 94-43978. 1995. write for info. (0-312-12392-2) St Martin.

Lewis, Charles R. Heaven Is Ours. Graves, Helen, ed. 118p. 1987. 6.95 (1-55523-043-1) Winston-Derek.

Lewis, Charlton M. Prologue to the Chinese Revolution: The Transformation of Ideas & Institutions in Hunan Province, 1891-1907. (East Asian Monographs: No. 70). 216p. 1976. 21.00 (0-674-71441-5) HUP.

Lewis, Charlton T. Elementary Latin Dictionary. (ENG & LAT.). 1969. 29.95 (0-19-910205-8) OUP.

Lewis, Charlton T. & Short, Charles. Latin Dictionary: Founded on Andrews Edition of Freund's Latin Dictionary. (LAT.). 1956. 135.00 (0-19-864201-6) OUP.

Lewis, Cherry, ed. see Jekyll, Gertrude.

Lewis, Christine L., ed. Research Philosophy & Techniques: Selected Readings. 2nd ed. LC 92-71748. 172p. 1992. pap. text ed. 18.00 (0-89462-070-3) IIA.

— Strategic Management for Insurers: Selected Readings, 2 vols. LC 92-74543. 610p. (C). 1992. 26.00 (0-89462-073-8) IIA.

Lewis, Christine L., et al. Gemini: Gifted Education Manual for Individualizing Networks of Instruction. 50p. 1980. teacher ed, pap. 15.00 (0-89824-015-8) Trillium Pr.

— Pegasus: Providing Enrichment for the Gifted by Adapting Selected Units of Study. Cantor, Marjorie A., ed. 119p. 1980. teacher ed, pap. 15.00 (0-89824-017-4) Trillium Pr.

Lewis, Christopher, ed. Antiques Road Show: Tiaras, Tallboys & Teddy Bears: A Selection from Radio Times Antiques Roadshow Column. (Illus.). 93p. 1992. pap. 9.95 (0-563-36179-4, BBC-Parkwest) Parkwest Pubns.

Lewis, Christopher, jt. ed. see Cohn-Sherbok, Dan.

Lewis, Christopher O. Tonal Coherence in Mahler's Ninth Symphony. LC 84-2754. (Studies in Musicology: No. 79). 148p. reprint ed. pap. 42.20 (0-8357-1585-X, 2070558) Bks Demand.

Lewis, Chuck. All the Riches of Job, a True Story of Success, & What Came After. LC 93-83590. (Illus.). 128p. (Orig.). (C). 1993. pap. text ed. 8.95 (0-9635854-0-1) Serendpty Pr.

Lewis, Claire & Davis, Kelly. Thirty-Five Up. (Illus.). 120p. 1992. pap. 15.95 (0-563-36202-2, BBC-Parkwest) Parkwest Pubns.

Lewis, Claire, et al, eds. The Psychoimmunology of Human Cancer: Mind & Body in the Fight for Survival? LC 94-8027. (Illus.). 320p. 1995. 75.00 (0-19-262365-6) OUP.

Lewis, Claire E. & McGee, James O., eds. The Natural Killer Cell: The Natural Immune System. (Illus.). 282p. 1992. pap. 40.00 (0-19-963232-4) OUP.

Lewis, Clara M. Basic & Family Nutrition: A Self Instructional Approach. 2nd ed. 261p. (C). 1984. pap. text ed. 11.95 (0-8036-5623-8) Davis Co.

Lewis, Clara M., jt. auth. see Bailey, Carolyn S.

Lewis, Clarence E., ed. Flowering Trees. (Plants & Gardens Ser.). (Illus.). 1983. 3.95 (0-945352-42-5, Sterling) Bklyn Botanic.

Lewis, Clarence I. Mind & the World Order: Outline of a Theory of Knowledge. 1990. pap. 9.95 (0-486-26564-1) Dover.

— Values & Imperatives: Studies in Ethics. Lange, John, ed. LC 69-13181. xv, 201p. 1969. 29.50 (0-8047-0687-5) Stanford U Pr.

***Lewis, Clarissa.** The Problem with Cameron. (Illus.). 24p. (J). (gr. 4-8). 1995. 12.95 (0-9647148-0-9) Pocket Change.

Lewis, Claudia L. Indian Families of the Northwest Coast: The Impact of Change. LC 70-108776. 236p. reprint ed. pap. 67.30 (0-685-15634-6, 2026736) Bks Demand.

Lewis, Clayton, jt. ed. see Bice, Ken.

Lewis, Clement E. When It's Twilight Time: Thirty Worship Services for Health Care Centers, Retirement Homes, & Other Special Life Settings. LC 93-42515. 1994. pap. write for info. (1-55673-837-4) CSS OH.

Lewis, Cleona. International Accounts. (Brookings Institution Reprint Ser.). reprint ed. lib. bdg. 29.50 (0-697-00163-6) Irvington.

Lewis, Cleona & Schlotterbeck, Karl T. America's Stake in International Investments. Bruchey, Stuart & Bruchey, Eleanor, eds. LC 76-5015. (Essay Index Reprint Ser.). 1976. reprint ed. 62.95 (0-405-09283-0) Ayer.

Lewis, Clive S. An Experiment in Criticism. (C). 1961. 54.95 (0-521-05553-9) Cambridge U Pr.

— An Experiment in Criticism. (Canto Book Ser.). 150p. (C). 1992. pap. 8.95 (0-521-42281-7) Cambridge U Pr.

— Preface to Paradise Lost. 1961. pap. 12.95 (0-19-500345-4) OUP.
— Rehabilitations & Other Essays. LC 71-167377. (Essay Index Reprint Ser.). 1977. reprint ed. 18.95 (0-8369-2559-9) Ayer.
— Rehabilitations & Other Essays. reprint ed. 14.00 (0-403-04233-X) Somerset Pub.
— Selected Literary Essays. Hooper, Walter, ed. LC 74-85724. 1979. pap. 24.95 (0-521-29680-3) Cambridge U Pr.
— Spenser's Images of Life. Fowler, Alastair, ed. 1978. pap. 19.95 (0-521-29284-0) Cambridge U Pr.
— Studies in Medieval & Renaissance Literature. 1980. pap. 18.95 (0-521-29701-X) Cambridge U Pr.
— Studies in Words. (Canto Book Ser.). 352p. (C). 1990. pap. 11.95 (0-521-39831-2) Cambridge U Pr.
Lewis, Colin. Business Forecasting in a Lotus 1-2-3 Environment. 1989. disk, pap. text ed. 53.50 (0-471-92357-5) Wiley.
— Essence of Personal Computing. 1991. 53.33 (0-13-284720-5) P-H.
— Practical Bonsai. (Illus.). 64p. 1992. pap. 8.95 (1-85223-661-2, Pub. by Crowood Pr UK) Trafalgar.
Lewis, Colin, jt. auth. see Edwards, John.
Lewis, Colin, jt. auth. see Spooner, Ann.
Lewis, Colin A. Horse Breeding in Ireland. 232p. 1990. pap. 50.00 (0-85131-315-9, Pub. by J A Allen & Co UK) St Mut.
Lewis, Colin M. British Railways in Argentina 1857-1914: A Case Study of Foreign Investment. (Institute of Latin American Studies Monographs: No. 12). (Illus.). 259p. (C). 1983. text ed. 42.50 (0-485-17712-9, Pub. by Athlone Pr UK) Humanities.
Lewis, Colin M., jt. auth. see Abel, Christopher.
Lewis, Colleen, jt. ed. see Bryett, Keith.
Lewis, Craig. Blood Evidence. 288p. 1992. mass mkt. 5.50 (0-425-13212-9) Berkley Pub.
Lewis, Craig A. Blood Evidence. 1990. 17.95 (0-87483-116-4) August Hse.
Lewis, Cris W., jt. auth. see Peterson, Craig H.
Lewis, C.S. Inspirational Writings of C. S. Lewis. 1987. 12.98 (0-88486-016-7, Inspiratnl Pub) Arrowood Pr.
Lewis, Curtis L. & Underwood, Dennis D. The Great American Horse Race of 1976: A Photographic Documentary. (Illus.). 224p. (Orig.). 1993. pap. 16.95 (0-9638302-0-1) Buckboard Pub.
Lewis, Cynthia & Lewis, Thomas. Best Hikes with Children in Vermont, New Hampshire & Maine. LC 91-26465. (Best Hikes with Children Ser.). (Illus.). 256p. 1991. pap. 12.95 (0-89886-281-7) Mountaineers.
Lewis, Cynthia C. Hello, Alexander Graham Bell Speaking. (Taking Part Ser.). (Illus.). 64p. (J). (gr. 3 up). 1991. text ed. 13.95 (0-87518-461-8, Dillon Silver Burdett) Silver Burdett Pr.
— Mother's First Year. 1992. mass mkt. 5.50 (0-425-13271-4) Berkley Pub.
— Really Important Stuff My Kids Have Taught Me. Kovalchick, Sally, ed. 416p. (Orig.). 1994. pap. 6.95 (1-56305-700-X) Workman Pub.
Lewis, Cynthia C. & Lewis, Thomas J. Best Hikes with Children in Connecticut, Massachusetts, & Rhode Island. LC 90-28611. (Best Hikes with Children Ser.). (Illus.). 256p. 1991. pap. 12.95 (0-89886-265-5) Mountaineers.
Lewis, Cynthia C. & Lewis, Tom. Best Hikes with Children in the Catskills. LC 92-5135. (Best Hikes with Children Ser.). (Illus.). 230p. (Orig.). 1992. pap. 12.95 (0-89886-322-8) Mountaineers.
Lewis, D. Matrix Theory. 300p. (C). 1991. text ed. 44.00 (981-02-0689-5) World Scientific Pub.
Lewis, D., jt. auth. see Bartenieff, I.
Lewis, D., jt. ed. see Singh, M.
Lewis, D. A. Anti-Inflammatory Drugs from Plant & Marine Sources. (Agents & Actions Supplements Ser.: No. 27). 371p. 1989. 82.00 (0-8176-2265-9) Birkhauser.
Lewis, D. A., jt. auth. see Hawkey, P. M.
Lewis, D. Gerwyn. The University & the Colleges of Education in Wales, 1925-1978. 270p. 1980. 32.50 (0-7083-0760-4, Pub. by U of Wales UK) Bks Intl VA.
Lewis, D. Gregory. Photojournalism: Content & Technique. 352p. (C). 1991. pap. write for info. (0-697-04292-8) Brown & Benchmark.
— Photojournalism: Content & Technique. 2nd ed. 352p. (C). 1995. pap. text ed. write for info. (0-697-14629-4) Brown & Benchmark.
Lewis, D. H., ed. Induced Skeletal Muscle Ischemia in Man. (Illus.). iv, 180p. 1982. pap. 92.00 (3-8055-3427-2) S Karger.
Lewis, D. H. & Haglund, U. Shock Research. (Fernstrom Foundation Ser.: Vol. 3). 1983. 103.00 (0-444-80533-8, I-352-83) Elsevier.
Lewis, D. H., ed. see Conference of the European Society for Microcirculation, 9th, Antwerp, July 5-9, 1976.
Lewis, D. H., ed. see Conference on Microcirculation, 6th, Aalborg, 1970.
Lewis, D. H., ed. see Conference on Microcirculation, 6th European, Aalborg, 1970.
Lewis, D. H., ed. see Easter School in Agricultural Science (8th 1961, University of Nottingham) Staff.
Lewis, D. H., ed. see European Conference on Microcirculation Staff.
Lewis, D. M., et al, eds. The Fifth Century B. C. 2nd ed. (Cambridge Ancient History Ser.: Vol. 5, Pt. 2). 650p. 1992. 105.00 (0-521-23347-X) Cambridge U Pr.
— The Fourth Century B. C. 2nd ed. (Cambridge Ancient History Ser.: Vol. 6). (Illus.). 1120p. 1994. 150.00 (0-521-23348-8) Cambridge U Pr.
Lewis, D. V. P., jt. ed. see Ionnides, C.
Lewis, D. W. & McConchie, David M. Practical Sedimentology. 2nd ed. LC 92-34768. 1993. pap. 39.95 (0-442-01217-9) Chapman & Hall.

***Lewis, Dale.** Roy Houck Buffalo Man. 148p. Date not set. text ed. 20.00 (0-614-07280-8) Buffalo Pr.
Lewis, Dale & Carter, Nick. Voices from Africa: Local Perspectives on Conservation. LC 94-4758. 216p. (Orig.). 1993. pap. 19.95 (0-89164-124-6) World Wildlife Fund.
Lewis, Dallas & Lewis, Lisa. The Planet Yes. (Illus.). 32p. (Orig.). (J). (gr. 3). 1994. 13.95 (0-9634087-1-2); pap. 6.95 (0-9634087-2-0) Silly Billys Bks.
Lewis, Dallas & Lewis, Lisa M. The Last Book. (Illus.). 32p. (J). (gr. 1-2). 1992. 16.00 (0-9634087-0-4) Silly Billys Bks.
Lewis, Dan. Eight Thousand Miles of Dirt. 2nd rev. ed. (Illus.). 188p. 1992. pap. 16.95 (0-941875-16-4) Wolverine Gallery.
— Paddle & Portage: Wyoming Floater's Guide. (Illus.). 186p. 1991. pap. 12.95 (0-941875-15-6) Wolverine Gallery.
***Lewis, Dan A. & Lurigio, Arthur J.** The State Mental Patient & Urban Life: Moving in & Out of the Institution. (Illus.). 146p. 1994. pap. 22.95 (0-398-06238-2) C C Thomas.
— The State Mental Patient & Urban Life: Moving in & Out of the Institution. 146p. (C). 1994. text ed. 37.95 (0-398-05901-2) C C Thomas.
Lewis, Dan A. & Nakagawa, Kathryn. Race & Educational Reform in the American Metropolis: A Study of School Decentralization. (SUNY Series, Frontiers in Education). 176p. (C). 1994. 57.50x (0-7914-2133-3); pap. 18.95x (0-7914-2134-1) State U NY Pr.
Lewis, Dan A. & Salem, Greta W. Fear of Crime: Incivility & the Production of a Social Problem. (New Observations Ser.). 145p. (Orig.). 1986. 34.95 (0-88738-086-7) Transaction Pubs.
Lewis, Dan A., et al. The Social Construction of Reform: Crime Prevention & Community Organization. 192p. 1988. 32.95 (0-88738-138-3) Transaction Pubs.
— Worlds of the Mentally Ill: How Deinstitutionalization Works in the City. LC 89-18058. 208p. (C). 1990. text ed. 29.95 (0-8093-1477-0) S Ill U Pr.
Lewis, Dana, tr. see Koike, Kazuo.
Lewis, Dana, tr. see Manabe, Johji.
Lewis, Dana, tr. see Shirow, Masamune.
Lewis, Dana K. Working with Children: Effective Communication Through Self-Awareness. LC 81-2668. (Sage Human Services Guides Ser.: No. 22). 160p. reprint ed. pap. 45.60 (0-8357-4755-7, 2037677) Bks Demand.
Lewis, Daniel. Victorian Houses Coloring Book. (Illus.). (J). (gr. k-3). 1950. pap. 2.95 (0-486-23908-X) Dover.
Lewis, Daniel I. & Lee, Winnie. Bank President. (Chief Executive Ser.). 64p. (Orig.). 1984. disk 74.95 (0-915847-00-0); pap. 9.95 (0-915847-02-7) Lewis Lee Corp.
Lewis, Daniel M., jt. auth. see Burrell, Robert.
Lewis, Danny, tr. see Heider, Ulrike.
Lewis, Danny, jt. auth. see Lewis, JoLinda.
Lewis, Daphne. Illuminations: An Interweave of Thought, Identity, & Love. Ferguson, Wynne L., ed. LC 92-24817. 108p. 1992. 19.95 (1-880292-21-1) LangMarc.
Lewis, Darrell L., jt. auth. see Stoeppelwerth, Walter W.
Lewis, Darrell R., jt. auth. see Boyer, Carol M.
Lewis, Darrell R., jt. auth. see Clark, Shirley M.
Lewis, Darrell R., jt. ed. see Clark, Shirley M.
Lewis, Dartrey B., jt. ed. see Dove, Allan B.
***Lewis, Dave.** Complete Guide to the Music of Led Zeppelin. (Illus.). (Orig.). 1995. pap. 7.95 (0-7119-3528-9, OP 47350, Pub. by Omnibus Press UK) Omnibus NY.
— Led Zeppelin: A Celebration. (Illus.). 128p. 1991. pap. 25.95 (0-7119-2416-3, OP46135) Omnibus NY.
Lewis, David. The Basics of Business. 288p. (Orig.). 1988. pap. 22.50 (0-7121-0794-0, Pub. by Pitman Pub Ltd UK) Trans-Atl Phila.
— Chevrolet Small-Block V-8 Interchange Manual. (Illus.). 160p. 1989. pap. 17.95 (0-87938-357-7) Motorbooks Intl.
— Convention: A Philosophical Study. LC 69-12727. 227p. 1987. pap. 14.50 (0-674-17026-1) HUP.
— Counterfactuals. LC 72-78430. 1973. 10.00 (0-674-17540-9) HUP.
— Counterfactuals. LC 72-78430. 160p. 1987. pap. 12.95 (0-674-17541-7) HUP.
— The Creative Producer: A Memoir of the Studio System. Curtis, James, ed. (Filmmakers Ser.: No. 36). (Illus.). 272p. 1993. 37.50 (0-8108-2720-4) Scarecrow.
— Dying to Tell. LC 92-70085. 179p. 1992. pap. 11.95 (0-89112-152-8) Abilene Christ U.
— Essentials of Employment Law. 288p. (C). 1986. 120.00 (0-85292-357-0, Pub. by IPM Hse UK) St Mut.
— Essentials of Employment Law. 352p. 1993. pap. 125.00 (0-85292-536-0, Pub. by IPM Hse UK) St Mut.
— Finite Counterforce. (Working Papers on Nuclear Deterrence). 1988. 2.50 (0-318-33326-0, SB1) IPPP.
— On the Plurality of Worlds. 270p. 1985. pap. 23.95 (0-631-13994-X) Blackwell Pubs.
— Parts of Classes. (Illus.). 112p. 1990. pap. text ed. 15.95 (0-631-17656-X) Blackwell Pubs.
— Philosophical Papers, Vol. II. (Illus.). 1987. text ed. 49.95 (0-19-503645-X) OUP.
— The Portugal Trigger. 360p. 1995. 23.95 (1-878179-16-0) Burning Gate Pr.
— The Public Image of Henry Ford: An American Folk Hero & His Company. LC 76-807. (Great Lakes Bks.). (Illus.). 600p. 1976. pap. 18.95 (0-8143-1892-4) Wayne St U Pr.
— The Secret Language of Success: Using Body Language to Get What You Want. 1990. pap. 11.95 (0-88184-644-9) Carroll & Graf.

— Sloss Furnaces & the Rise of the Birmingham District: An Industrial Epic. LC 93-48178. (History of American Science & Technology Ser.). 632p. 1994. 39.95 (0-8173-0708-7) U of Ala Pr.
— Stress for Success: Using Your Hidden Creative Energy for Health, Achievement & Happiness. 208p. 1992. pap. 10.95 (0-88184-872-7) Carroll & Graf.
— Terry Frost. Knowles, Elizabeth, ed. (Illus.). 252p. 1994. 75.00 (1-85928-041-2, Pub. by Scolar Pr UK) Ashgate Pub Co.
— UFO: End-Time Delusion. LC 91-61713. 256p. (Orig.). 1991. pap. 8.95 (0-89221-213-6) New Leaf.
— Warren Mackenzie: American Potter. (Illus.). 232p. 1991. 65.00 (4-7700-1528-3) Kodansha.
— Warren Mackenzie: An American Potter. 192p. Date not set. 45.00 (4-7700-1991-2) FS&G.
— Warren MacKenzie, Potter: A Retrospective. Brown, Susan, ed. LC 89-51231. (Illus.). 128p. (Orig.). 1989. pap. text ed. 30.00 (0-938713-05-1) Univ MN Art Mus.
— We, the Navigators: The Ancient Art of Landfinding in the Pacific. LC 72-82139. (Illus.). 366p. 1975. pap. 10.95 (0-8248-0394-9) UH Pr.
— We, the Navigators: The Ancient Art of Landfinding in the Pacific. 2nd ed. Oulton, Derek, ed. LC 93-44019. (Illus.). 384p. (C). 1994. pap. text ed. 24.95 (0-8248-1582-3) UH Pr.
Lewis, David, ed. Oil Painting Techniques: Learn How to Master Oil Painting Working Techniques to Create Your Own Successful Paintings. (Illus.). 144p. 1983. pap. 16.95 (0-8230-3261-2, Watsn-Guptill) Watsn-Guptill.
— Pencil Drawing Techniques. (Illus.). 144p. 1984. pap. 16.95 (0-8230-3991-9, Watsn-Guptill) Watsn-Guptill.
— Watercolor Painting Techniques. (Illus.). 144p. 1983. pap. 16.95 (0-8230-5669-4, Watsn-Guptill) Watsn-Guptill.
Lewis, David & Greene, James. Thinking Better. LC 83-8389. 324p. 1983. pap. 9.95 (0-8050-0022-4, Owl) H Holt & Co.
Lewis, David & James, Philip. Discipline. 128p. (C). 1992. 70.00 (0-85292-485-2, Pub. by IPM Hse UK) St Mut.
***Lewis, David & Knowles, Elizabeth.** Terry Frost. (Illus.). 252p. 1994. 299.50 (1-85928-160-5) Ashgate Pub Co.
Lewis, David, ed. see Coleman, Kenneth.
Lewis, David, tr. see Koike, Kazuo.
Lewis, David, tr. see Manabe, Johji.
Lewis, David, tr. see Miyazaki, Hayao.
Lewis, David, tr. see Sander, Nicolas.
***Lewis, David, et al.** The Gospel According to Generation X--The Culture of Adolescent Faith. 1995. pap. 14.95 (0-89112-015-7) Abilene Christ U.
Lewis, David, et al, eds. Inscriptiones Graecae, Vol. 1, Fasc. 2: Consilio et Auctoritate Academiae Scientiarum Berolinensis et Brandenburgensis Editae. xiv, 998p. (LAT.). 1993. lib. bdg. 715.40 (3-11-010362-1) De Gruyter.
Lewis, David A. Can Israel Survive in a Hostile World? LC 93-87251. 352p. (Orig.). 1994. pap. 11.95 (0-89221-260-8) New Leaf.
— Dark Angels of Light. LC 84-61915. 138p. (Orig.). 1985. pap. 5.95 (0-89221-117-2) New Leaf.
— Magog Nineteen Eighty-Two Cancelled. LC 82-62079. 144p. 1982. pap. 4.95 (0-89221-103-2) New Leaf.
— Prophecy Two Thousand. LC 90-60310. (Illus.). 432p. 1990. pap. 11.95 (0-89221-179-2) New Leaf.
— Smashing the Gates of Hell in the Last Days. LC 86-65887. 234p. 1987. pap. 8.95 (0-89221-143-1) New Leaf.
***Lewis, David C.** Health Effects of Human Chemical Exposure. Date not set. write for info. (0-944225-28-4) Pacific Research.
— Health Effects of Quinones. 1995. write for info. (0-944225-18-7) Pacific Research.
— Medicinal Plants of Asia: A Systematic Bibliography. 1987. 60.00 (0-939781-18-2) Asia Bks CA.
Lewis, David J., jt. ed. see Farrington, John W.
Lewis, David K. Convention: A Philosophical Study. LC 69-12727. (Illus.). 1969. 15.00 (0-674-17025-3) HUP.
— Konventionen: Eine Sprachphilosophische Abhandlung. Posher, Roland & Wenzel, Detlef, trs. (Grundlagen der Kommunikation Ser.). xiv, 224p. (GER.). (C). 1975. pap. 29.25 (3-11-004608-3) De Gruyter.
***Lewis, David K., et al.** Shattering the Silence--Telling the Church the Truth about Kids & Sexuality. rev. ed. 1995. pap. 14.95 (0-89112-014-9) Abilene Christ U.
Lewis, David L. District of Columbia: A Bicentennial History. (States & the Nation Ser.). (Illus.). 1976. 14.95 (0-393-05601-5) Norton.
— Du Bois reader. 1995. 35.00 (0-8050-3263-0) H Holt & Co.
— King: A Biography. 2nd ed. (Blacks in the New World Ser.). 481p. 1978. pap. 12.95 (0-252-00680-1) U of Ill Pr.
— Neither Wolf Nor Dog: American Indians, Environment, & Agrarian Change. (Illus.). 304p. 1994. 29.95 (0-19-506297-3) OUP.
— Prisoners of Honor: The Dreyfus Affair. LC 94-31878. 1994. pap. 12.00 (0-8050-3766-7) H Holt & Co.
— The Race to Fashoda: Colonialism & African Resistance. LC 94-36013. 1995. pap. 13.95 (0-8050-3556-7, Owl) H Holt & Co.
— W. E. B. Du Bois, Vol. 2. 1997. 35.00 (0-8050-2534-0) H Holt & Co.
— W. E. B. Du Bois: A Reader. 1995. pap. 16.95 (0-8050-3264-9) H Holt & Co.
— W. E. B. Du Bois: Biography of a Race, 1868-1919. LC 93-16617. (Illus.). 700p. 1993. 35.00 (0-8050-2621-5) H Holt & Co.
— W. E. B. Du Bois: Biography of a Race, 1868-1919. 1994. pap. 17.95 (0-8050-3568-0) H Holt & Co.
— When Harlem Was in Vogue. (Illus.). 400p. 1989. pap. 13.95 (0-19-505969-7) OUP.

***Lewis, David L., ed. & intro.** The Portable Harlem Renaissance Reader. 816p. 1995. pap. 14.95 (0-14-017036-7, Penguin Bks) Viking Penguin.
Lewis, David L., intro. The Portable Harlem Renaissance Reader. LC 93-30233. 816p. 1994. 27.95 (0-670-84510-8, Viking) Viking Penguin.
Lewis, David L. & Goldstein, Laurence, eds. The Automobile & American Culture. 1983. pap. text ed. 19.95 (0-472-08044-X) U of Mich Pr.
Lewis, David M., jt. ed. see Meiggs, Russell.
Lewis, David R. Mattie Robinson's Pearly Confections. LC 91-68092. 53p. 1992. pap. 5.95 (1-55523-505-0) Winston-Derek.
Lewis, David V. Power Negotiating Tactics & Techniques. LC 81-5164. 243p. 1984. 19.95 (0-13-686808-8, Busn); pap. 5.95 (0-13-687740-0, Busn) P-H.
Lewis, David W. French for Business & International Careers: Vocabulary, Stylistics, Culture; A College Reader. (American University Studies: Foreign Language Instruction: Ser. VI, Vol. 4). 650p. 1988. text ed. 58.00 (0-8204-0513-2) P Lang Pubs.
— The Road to Europe: The Past & Future of European Integration, 1945-1993. LC 91-16050. 488p. (C). 1993. text ed. 69.95 (0-8204-1640-1) P Lang Pubs.
Lewis, David W., Jr., ed. see Fine, Norman M.
Lewis, Dawn, jt. illus. see Devine, John.
Lewis Deans, Mary. Like the Moon. 179p. (Orig.). 1989. pap. 7.95 (0-9624388-0-4) Flatrock Bks.
Lewis, Deborah. Kirkwood Fires. (Orig.). 1978. pap. 1.95 (0-89083-405-9) Zebra.
— The Wind at Winter's End. (Orig.). 1979. pap. 1.95 (0-89083-540-3) Zebra.
Lewis, Deborah S. Motherhood Stress. 176p. 1992. pap. 9.99 (0-310-57471-4) Zondervan.
Lewis, Deborah S. & Lewis, Gregg. Did I Ever Tell You About How Our Family Got Started? Building Togetherness & Values by Sharing Stories about Your Family. (Family Share Together Ser.). 112p. 1994. pap. 7.99 (0-310-42111-X) Zondervan.
— Did I Ever Tell You about the Time When You Were Little? Building Togetherness & Values by Sharing Stories about Your Family. (Family Share Together Ser.). 112p. 1994. pap. 7.99 (0-310-41071-1) Zondervan.
— Did I Ever Tell You about When Mom & Dad Were Young? Building Togetherness & Values by Sharing Stories about Your Family. (Family Share Together Ser.). 112p. 1994. pap. 7.99 (0-310-42101-2) Zondervan.
— Did I Ever Tell You about When Your Grandparents Were Children? Building Togetherness & Values by Sharing Stories about Your Family. (Family Share Together Ser.). 112p. 1994. pap. 7.99 (0-310-42121-7) Zondervan.
***Lewis, Deborah S. & Lewis, Gregg A., photos.** When You Were a Baby. LC 94-44691. (J). 1995. 13.95 (1-56145-102-9) Peachtree Pubs.
***Lewis, Deborrah.** The Sculpture of Pol Bury: Shapes in Space & Time. 1978. pap. 4.95 (0-614-02731-4) A M Huntington Art.
Lewis, Dennis & Washburn, Robert. British Point Twenty-Two RF Training Rifles. (Illus.). 64p. 1993. pap. 10.95 (1-880677-03-2) Excalibur NY.
Lewis, Denslow. Gynecologic Consideration of the Sexual Act. Hollender, Marc H., ed. 1970. 15.00 (0-87730-002-X) M&S Pr.
Lewis, Di, jt. auth. see Green, Caroline.
Lewis, Diane. Fifty Ways to Recycle Fruit Cake. 1992. pap. 5.95 (0-934860-94-7) Adventure Pubns.
***Lewis, Dianne.** Jan Compagnie in the Straits of Malacca, 1641-1795. (Monographs in International Studies Southeast Asia: No. 96). (Illus.). 175p. (Orig.). (C). 1995. pap. text ed. 18.00x (0-89680-187-X) Ohio U Pr.
Lewis, Dierde & Reeves, David, eds. Methods & Evaluation of In Vitro Models of Antimicrobial Chemotherapy. 325p. 1989. pap. text ed. 49.00 (0-12-446660-5) Acad Pr.
Lewis, Dio. Chastity: Our Secret Sins. LC 73-20634. (Sex, Marriage & Society Ser.). 324p. 1974. reprint ed. 26.95 (0-405-05809-8) Ayer.
— Our Girls. LC 74-3958. (Women in America Ser.). 388p. 1974. reprint ed. 34.95 (0-405-06106-4) Ayer.
Lewis, Dominic B. Doctor Rabelais. LC 69-10117. 274p. 1969. reprint ed. text ed. 59.75 (0-8371-0145-X, LEDR, Greenwood Pr) Greenwood.
— James Boswell, a Short Life. 2nd ed. LC 79-25846. (Illus.). 285p. 1980. reprint ed. text ed. 59.75 (0-313-22232-0, LEJB, Greenwood Pr) Greenwood.
Lewis, Dominic B. & Lee, Charles, eds. The Stuffed Owl: An Anthology of Bad Verse. LC 76-42707. (Illus.). reprint ed. 20.00 (0-404-15371-2) AMS Pr.
***Lewis, Donald.** Uptown Country Food with Style. (Illus.). 165p. 1995. reprint ed. 12.95 (0-9646944-0-9) Uptown Cntry.
Lewis, Donald J., ed. see Pure Mathematics Symposium Staff.
Lewis, Donald M. Lighten Their Darkness: The Evangelical Mission to Working-Class London, 1828-1860. LC 86-12104. (Contributions to the Study of Religion Ser.: No. 19). (Illus.). 386p. 1986. text ed. 65.00 (0-313-25577-6, LLD/, Greenwood Pr) Greenwood.
***Lewis, Donald M., intro.** The Blackwell Dictionary of Evangelical Biography 1730-1860. 1200p. 1995. lib. bdg. 150.00 (0-631-17384-6) Blackwell Pubs.
Lewis, Donovan. Pioneers of California: True Stories of Early Settlers in the Golden State. (Illus.). 567p. 1993. 26.95 (0-942087-06-2) Scottwall Assocs.
Lewis, Dorothy O., ed. Vulnerabilities to Delinquency. 343p. 1981. text ed. 37.95 (0-88331-211-5) Luce.
Lewis, Dottie L., ed. Baseball in Cincinnati: From Wooden Fences to Astroturf. (Illus.). 64p. (Orig.). 1988. pap. text ed. 7.50 (0-911497-10-2) Cinc Hist Soc.

An Asterisk (*) at the beginning of an entry indicates that the title is appearing in BIP for the first time.

— The Taft Museum: A Cincinnati Legacy. (Illus.). 63p. (Orig.). 1988. pap. text ed. 7.50 (*0-911497-09-9*) Cinc Hist Soc.

Lewis, E. Edward Carpenter. 1972. 59.95 (*0-8490-0091-2*) Gordon Pr.

***Lewis, E. E.** Introduction to Reliability Engineering. 2nd ed. LC 95-13533. 1995. text ed. write for info. (*0-471-01833-3*) Wiley.

Lewis, E. E. & Miller, W. F., Jr. Computational Methods of Neutron Transport. LC 93-36902. 1993. 50.00 (*0-89448-452-4*) Am Nuclear Soc.

Lewis, E. Glyn. Linguistics & Second Language Pedagogy: A Theoretical Study. LC 73-79891. (Janua Linguarum, Ser. Didactica: No. 10). 137p. (Orig.). 1974. pap. text ed. 32.35 (*90-279-2707-3*) Mouton.

— Multilingualism in the Soviet Union: Aspects of Language Policy & Its Implementation. (Contributions to the Sociology of Language Ser.: No. 3). (Illus.). 332p. (Orig.). 1972. pap. text ed. 70.80 (*90-279-2352-3*) Mouton.

Lewis, E. R. Network Models in Population Biology. LC 77-5873. (Biomathematics Ser.: Vol 7). 1977. 54.00 (*0-387-08214-X*) Spr-Verlag.

Lewis, E. Ridley. Acts of the Apostles & the Letters of St. Paul. (London Divinity Ser.). 160p. 1964. reprint ed. 6.50 (*0-227-67519-3*) Attic Pr.

— Johannine Writings & Other Epistles. (London Divinity Ser.). 144p. 1961. 6.50 (*0-227-67663-7*) Attic Pr.

Lewis, E. Ridley, jt. auth. see Lewis, Lionel S.

Lewis, Earl. In Their Own Interests: Race, Class & Power in Twentieth-Century Norfolk, Virginia. (Illus.). 288p. 1990. 38.00 (*0-520-06644-8*); pap. 13.00 (*0-520-08444-6*) U CA Pr.

Lewis, Earl B., illus. The New King: A Madagascan Legend. LC 93-28561. 32p. (J). 1995. 14.99 (*0-8037-1460-2*); lib. bdg. 14.89 (*0-8037-1461-0*) Dial Bks Young.

***Lewis, Eddie.** Ray Had an Idea about Love. 1995. 20.00 (*0-671-88762-9*) S&S Trade.

— The Wedding's Over: What Now? 1989. 9.95 (*0-89137-574-0*); pap. 6.75 (*0-685-35356-7*) Quality Pubns.

Lewis, Edith M. Haiku Is. . . a Feeling. LC 89-64144. (Illus.). 64p. (Orig.). (J). (gr. 1-3). 1990. pap. 5.95 (*0-9624993-0-7*) Pippin Bks.

Lewis, Edna. In Pursuit of Flavor. LC 88-45215. (Illus.). 352p. 1988. 18.95 (*0-394-54271-1*) Knopf.

— The Taste of Country Cooking. 1976. 24.95 (*0-394-48311-1*); pap. 18.00 (*0-394-73215-4*) Knopf.

Lewis, Edna & Peterson, Evangeline. The Edna Lewis Cookbook. (Cookbook Ser.). 200p. 1983. reprint ed. pap. 9.95 (*0-88001-193-9*) Ecco Pr.

Lewis, Edward. American Shortline Railway Guide. 4th ed. Emmerich, Michael, ed. (Illus.). 264p. 1990. pap. 18.95 (*0-89024-109-0*) Kalmbach.

— Bracketing: A Constructive Way to Learn Basic English Grammar. 3rd ed. 1992. 22.55 (*0-536-58238-6*) Ginn Pr.

— From a Different Angle: Observations on Being Human. (Illus.). 64p. 1993. pap. 12.95 (*1-880823-01-2*) N Star Pubns.

— I Heard My Heart Speak: Observations on Relationships. George, Tamsen E., ed. (Illus.). 64p. 1992. pap. 14.95 (*1-880823-04-7*) N Star Pubns.

Lewis, Edward, tr. see Heil, A. & Wesch.

Lewis, Edward E. The Mobility of the Negro. LC 68-58603. (Columbia University. Studies in the Social Sciences: No. 342). reprint ed. 20.00 (*0-404-51342-5*) AMS Pr.

Lewis, Edward V., ed. Principles of Naval Architecture, 3 vols., Set. LC 88-60829. 1988. 240.00 (*0-685-56498-3*) Soc Naval Arch.

— Principles of Naval Architecture, 3 vols., Set. rev. ed. 1988. 180.00 (*0-614-06723-5*) Soc Naval Arch.

— Principles of Naval Architecture, 3 vols., Vol. I. LC 88-60829. 320p. 1988. 120.00 (*0-939773-00-7*) Soc Naval Arch.

— Principles of Naval Architecture, 3 vols., Vol. II. LC 88-60829. 320p. 1988. 120.00 (*0-939773-01-5*) Soc Naval Arch.

— Principles of Naval Architecture, 3 vols., Vol. III. LC 88-60829. 507p. 1988. 120.00 (*0-939773-02-3*) Soc Naval Arch.

Lewis, Edwin. Teach Yourself Welsh Dictionary. (Teach Yourself Ser.). 1992. 15.95 (*0-8288-8412-9*) Fr & Eur.

Lewis, Edwin H. The History of the English Paragraph. 1976. lib. bdg. 59.95 (*0-8490-1996-6*) Gordon Pr.

Lewis, Edwin R., et al, eds. The Vertebrate Inner Ear. 256p. 1985. 168.00 (*0-8493-6465-5*, QP461, CRC Reprint) Franklin.

***Lewis, Elaine.** Less is More: A Practical Guide to Maximizing the Space in Your Home. 1995. 29.95 (*0-670-84239-7*, Penguin Bks) Viking Penguin.

Lewis, Elaine, jt. auth. see Lewis, Paul.

Lewis, Eleanor, ed. Darkroom. LC 76-57201. (Illus.). 184p. (Orig.). 1979. pap. 17.50 (*0-912810-19-X*) Lustrum Pr.

Lewis, Eleanor P. George Washington's Beautiful Nelly: The Letters of Eleanor Parke Custis Lewis to Elizabeth Bordley Gibson, 1794-1851. Brady, Patricia, ed. LC 91-4797. (Women's Diaries & Letters of the Nineteenth-Century South Ser.). (Illus.). 309p. 1991. 29.95 (*0-87249-754-2*) U of SC Pr.

— Nelly Custis Lewis's Housekeeping Book. Schmit, Patricia B., ed. LC 82-81038. (Illus.). x, 134p. 1982. 12.95 (*0-917860-09-8*) Historic New Orleans.

***Lewis, Elizabeth B.** A Guide to the Treasures of Early Christian Art. (Illus.). 290p. 1994. 39.95 (*0-87061-208-5*) Chr Classics.

Lewis, Elizabeth F. Young Fu of the Upper Yangtze. (J). (gr. k-6). 1990. mass mkt. 3.99 (*0-440-49043-X*, YB) Dell.

— Young Fu of the Upper Yangtze. LC 72-91654. (Illus.). 268p. (J). (gr. 4-6). 1973. 18.95 (*0-8050-0549-8*, Bks Young Read) H Holt & Co.

— Young Fu of the Upper Yangtze. braille ed. 336p. 1993. text ed. 26.88 (*1-56956-484-1*, BR9155) W A T Braille.

Lewis, Elizabeth N. Manual of Patient Classification: Systems & Techniques for Practical Application. 432p. 1988. 150.00 (*0-87189-898-5*, 510) Aspen Pub.

Lewis, Elmer E. Introduction to Reliability Engineering. 480p. 1987. Net. text ed. write for info. (*0-471-81199-8*) Wiley.

***Lewis, Elton.** Fading Back: A Personal Look Back into the History of the Virgin Islands Police Department. (Illus.). 125p. (Orig.). Date not set. pap. write for info. (*0-9627257-8-1*) Aye Aye Pr.

Lewis, Emanuel R. Seacoast Fortifications of the United States: An Introductory History. (Illus.). 145p. 1993. pap. 17.95 (*1-55750-502-0*) Naval Inst Pr.

Lewis, Eric, tr. see Alexander of Aphrodisias.

Lewis, Ernest A. The Fremont Cannon, High Up & Far Back. 2nd rev. ed. LC 92-60710. (Illus.). 96p. (C). 1992. reprint ed. pap. 14.95 (*0-9633604-1-8*) Western Trails.

— The Great Lost Fremont Cannon Expedition: The Fremont Cannon High Up & Far Back. 3rd rev. ed. LC 92-60780. (Illus.). 96p. (J). (gr. 10 up). 1992. reprint ed. pap. 12.95 (*0-9633604-2-6*) Western Trails.

Lewis, Ernest L. & Mouw, John T. The Use of Contrast Coefficients: Supplement to McNeil, Kelly, & McNeil, "Testing Research Hypotheses Using Multiple Linear Regression" LC 77-16406. 80p. 1978. pap. text ed. 2.95 (*0-8093-0868-1*) S Ill U Pr.

Lewis, Ernest L., jt. auth. see Reilly, Robert R.

***Lewis, Ethan.** Gospels of Wealth: How the Rich Portray Their Lives. LC 94-33272. 304p. 1994. text ed. 59.95 (*0-275-94643-6*, Praeger Pubs) Greenwood.

Lewis, Eugene. American Politics in a Bureaucratic Age: Citizens, Constituents, Clients & Victims. 192p. (C). 1988. reprint ed. pap. text ed. 19.50 (*0-8191-7049-6*) U Pr of Amer.

— Public Entrepreneurship: Toward a Theory of Bureaucratic Political Power. LC 79-2451. 284p. reprint ed. pap. 81.60 (*0-8357-3953-8*, 2057049) Bks Demand.

Lewis, Evelyn L. Housing Decisions. LC 93-23858. (Home Economics Ser.). (Illus.). 416p. 1994. 39.96 (*0-87006-071-6*) Goodheart.

Lewis, F. L., jt. ed. see Sadegh, N.

Lewis, F. R. & Pfeiffer, U. J., eds. Practical Applications of Fiberoptics in Critical Care Monitoring. 204p. 1990. pap. 44.00 (*0-387-51718-9*) Spr-Verlag.

Lewis, Felice F. Literature, Obscenity, & Law. LC 75-42094. 310p. 1976. 19.95 (*0-8093-0749-9*) S Ill U Pr.

— Literature, Obscenity, & Law. LC 75-42094. 310p. 1978. reprint ed. pap. 12.95 (*0-8093-0870-3*) S Ill U Pr.

Lewis-Ferguson, Julinda. Alvin Ailey, Jr. A Life in Dance. LC 93-17906. 64p. (J). (gr. 3-8). 1994. 14.95 (*0-8027-8239-6*); lib. bdg. 15.85 (*0-8027-8241-8*) Walker & Co.

Lewis, Ferris E. Our Own State, Michigan. 16th ed. LC 78-66800. (Illus.). (J). (gr. 7-10). 1978. teacher ed 13.70x (*0-910726-23-X*) Hillsdale Educ.

— The Story of the Knights Templars (1118-1315) 100p. 1994. pap. 14.95 (*1-56459-441-6*) Kessinger Pub.

Lewis, Fiona. Between Men: A Novel. 304p. 1995. 21.00 (*0-87113-586-8*) Grove-Atltic.

Lewis, Flora. Europe: Road to Unity. rev. ed. (Illus.). 592p. 1992. pap. 14.00 (*0-671-77828-5*, Touchstone Bks) S&S Trade.

Lewis, Frances M., jt. ed. see Ward, William B.

Lewis, Frank, ed. The Nation Crossword Puzzles, Vol. 7. 1994. pap. 8.00 (*0-8129-2035-X*, Times Bks) Random.

— The Nation Crossword Puzzles, Vol. 8. 1994. pap. 8.00 (*0-8129-2036-8*, Times Bks) Random.

Lewis, Frank A. Substance & Predication in Aristotle. 375p. (C). 1992. 54.95 (*0-521-39159-8*) Cambridge U Pr.

Lewis, Frank C., ed. see Haight, Ada C.

Lewis, Frank L. Optimal Control. LC 85-20312. 362p. 1986. text ed. 79.95 (*0-471-81240-4*, Wiley-Interscience) Wiley.

— Optimal Estimation with an Introduction to Stachastic Control Theory. LC 85-26554. 376p. 1986. text ed. 79.95 (*0-471-83741-5*) Wiley.

Lewis, Frank L. & Abdallah, Chaouki T., eds. Robot Control: Dynamics, Motion Planning, & Analysis. LC 92-5764. (Illus.). 552p. (C). 1993. text ed. 69.95 (*0-7803-0404-7*, PC0299-8) Inst Electrical.

***Lewis, Frank L. & Syrmos, Vassilis L.** Optimal Control. 2nd ed. LC 95-15649. 1995. text ed. 74.95 (*0-471-03378-2*) Wiley.

Lewis, Frank L., jt. auth. see Stevens, Brian L.

Lewis, Frank L., et al. Control of Robot Manipulators. LC 92-17922. (Illus.). 448p. (C). 1993. write for info. (*0-02-370501-9*) Macmillan.

Lewis, Frank R., Jr., jt. auth. see Weigelt, John A.

Lewis, Frank W. Nation Crossword Puzzles. 1993. pap. 7.50 (*0-8129-2031-7*, Times Bks); pap. 7.50 (*0-8129-2032-5*, Times Bks) Random.

— Nation Crossword Puzzles, Vol. 1. 1992. pap. 7.50 (*0-8129-2012-0*, Times Bks) Random.

— Nation Crossword Puzzles, Vol. 2. 1992. pap. 7.50 (*0-8129-2013-9*, Times Bks) Random.

— The Nation Crossword Puzzles, Vol. 5. 1993. pap. 7.50 (*0-8129-2033-3*, Times Bks) Random.

— The Nation Crossword Puzzles, Vol. 6. 1993. pap. 7.50 (*0-8129-2034-1*, Times Bks) Random.

— Solving Cipher Problems. 260p. (Orig.). 1992. pap. 30.80 (*0-89412-178-2*) Aegean Park Pr.

Lewis, Frederick. Young at Heart: The Story of Johnny Kelley - Boston's Marathon Man. Johnson, Dick, ed. LC 92-60011. (Illus.). 224p. 1992. 19.95 (*0-941539-87-3*) WRS Group.

Lewis, Frederick P. The Nationalization of Liberty. 82p. (Orig.). (C). 1990. pap. text ed. 13.50 (*0-8191-7763-6*) U Pr of Amer.

Lewis, G. Postcards from Kew. 72p. 1989. pap. 5.00 (*0-11-250037-4*, HM0374, Pub. by HMSO UK) UNIPUB.

Lewis, G., jt. auth. see Descartes, Rene.

Lewis, G., ed. see Trucks, H. E.

Lewis, G. E. Communication Services Via Satellite: A Handbook for Design, Installation & Service Engineers. 2nd ed. (Illus.). 400p. 1992. 64.95 (*0-7506-0437-9*) Buttrwrth-Heinemann.

Lewis, G. J., jt. auth. see Walmsley, D. J.

Lewis, G. L., jt. auth. see Spink, M. S.

Lewis, G. M. Neutrinos. (Wykeham Science Ser.: No. 12). 132p. 1971. pap. 18.00 (*0-85109-140-7*) Taylor & Francis.

Lewis, G. M. & Wheatley, G. A. Neutrinos. LC 73-135382. (Wykeham Science Ser.: No. 12). 132p. (C). 1970. 18.00 (*0-8448-1114-9*, Crane Russak) Taylor & Francis.

***Lewis, Gary.** A Dead Man's Treasure. 110p. (Orig.). 1995. pap. 7.95 (*0-7610-0057-7*) NW Pub.

Lewis, Gary A. The Clean-up of Codfish Cove. (Shamu & His Crew Adventure Ser.). (Illus.). 32p. (J). (gr. k-3). 1994. 5.95 (*1-884506-05-4*) Third Story.

— News from Somewhere: Connecting Health & Freedom at the Workplace. LC 85-27269. (Contributions in Political Science Ser.: No. 151). (Illus.). 226p. 1986. text ed. 55.00 (*0-313-24869-9*, LNF/, Greenwood Pr) Greenwood.

— Shamu's Best Friend. (Shamu & His Crew Adventure Ser.). (Illus.). 32p. (J). (gr. k-4). 1994. 5.95 (*1-884506-04-6*) Third Story.

Lewis, Gary L., jt. auth. see Viessman, Warren, Jr.

***Lewis, Gary M.** ORACLE Reporting: Queries with SQL Objects. LC 95-94198. (Illus.). (Orig.). 1995. pap. write for info. (*0-9644912-3-0*) Komenda Pub.

Lewis, Gaspar. Cabinetmaking, Patternmaking & Millwork. LC 79-50917. (Carpentry-Cabinetmaking Ser.). 438p. (C). 1981. teacher ed 12.00 (*0-8273-1815-4*) Delmar.

— Carpentry. LC 83-71049. 544p. 1984. teacher ed 10.00 (*0-8273-1801-4*); 10.95 (*0-8273-1808-1*); text ed. 38.95 (*0-8273-1800-6*) Delmar.

— Carpentry. 2nd ed. LC 94-8421. (Illus.). 800p. 1995. 38.95 (*0-8273-5979-9*) Delmar.

— Carpentry. LC 83-71049. (Illus.). 566p. (C). 1991. reprint ed. lib. bdg. 47.00x (*0-8095-7600-7*) Borgo Pr.

— Safety for Carpenters & Woodworkers. LC 80-66859. (Carpentry-Cabinetmaking Ser.). (C). 1981. teacher ed 10.00 (*0-8273-1870-7*); pap. text ed. 13.95 (*0-8273-1869-3*) Delmar.

Lewis, Gasper. Carpentry. LC 83-71049. (Illus.). 576p. 1988. 21.95 (*0-8069-6752-8*) Sterling.

Lewis, Gavin, jt. auth. see Greer, Thomas H.

Lewis, Gay. Bittersweet. LC 84-62706. 207p. 1985. pap. 4.95 (*0-88270-583-0*) Bridge Pub.

Lewis, Geoff. Newnes Communications Technology Handbook. (Illus.). 456p. 1994. 69.95 (*0-7506-1729-2*) Buttrwrth-Heinemann.

Lewis, Geoff E., jt. auth. see Sinclair, Ian.

Lewis, Geoffrey. Lord Atkin. 1984. U.K. boxed 48.00 (*0-406-27210-7*) Butterworth Legal Pubs.

Lewis, Geoffrey E., jt. auth. see Sinclair, Ian R.

Lewis, Geoffrey L. Teach Yourself Malay. (Teach Yourself Ser.). 1980. pap. 6.95 (*0-679-10187-X*) McKay.

— Teach Yourself Turkish. (Teach Yourself Ser.). 1979. pap. 5.95 (*0-679-10200-0*) McKay.

— Teach Yourself Turkish. (Teach Yourself Ser.). 1992. 15.95 (*0-8288-8407-2*); 45.00 (*0-8288-8408-0*) Fr & Eur.

— Turkish Grammar. 328p. 1985. pap. 39.95 (*0-19-815838-6*) OUP.

Lewis, Geoffrey L., tr. The Book of Dede Korkut. 224p. 1974. pap. 8.95 (*0-14-044298-7*, Penguin Classics) Viking Penguin.

Lewis, Geoffrey L., tr. see Taner, Haldun.

Lewis, Geoffrey L., jt. auth. see Timperley, Stuart.

Lewis, George. Encyclopedia of Massachusetts. (Encyclopedia of the United States Ser.). (Illus.). 601p. 1984. reprint ed. lib. bdg. 79.00 (*0-403-09983-8*) Somerset Pub.

Lewis, George C. An Essay on the Influence of Authority in Matters of Opinion. LC 73-14165. 440p. 1974. reprint ed. 28.95 (*0-405-05510-2*) Ayer.

— A Treatise on the Methods of Observation & Reasoning in Politics, 2 vols. in 1. LC 73-14166. (Perspectives in Social Inquiry Ser.). 984p. 1974. reprint ed. 59.95 (*0-405-05511-0*) Ayer.

Lewis, George C., tr. see Boeckh, Augustus.

Lewis, George E. The Indiana Company, 1763-1798: A Study in Eighteenth Century Frontier Land Speculation & Business Venture. LC 70-140363. (Select Bibliographies Reprint Ser.). 1977. reprint ed. 25.95 (*0-8369-5606-0*) Ayer.

Lewis, George H. All That Glitters: Country Music in America. LC 92-74544. 340p. 1993. 44.95 (*0-87972-573-7*); pap. 21.95 (*0-87972-574-5*) Bowling Green Univ.

Lewis, George S. Black Heritage Unveiled. 2nd ed. LC 86-62546. (Illus.). 200p. 1987. text ed. 15.95 (*0-937771-09-0*); lib. bdg. 14.95 (*0-937771-10-4*); pap. text ed. 10.95 (*0-937771-08-2*) Spencers Intl.

— Israel, Egypt & the Blackman. LC 86-62542. 180p. (Orig.). 1986. text ed. 15.95 (*0-937771-06-6*); lib. bdg. 15.95 (*0-937771-07-4*); pap. text ed. 10.95 (*0-937771-05-8*) Spencers Intl.

— Space Age Laws of Success. LC 87-6009. (Orig.). 1987. text ed. 15.95 (*0-937771-14-7*); pap. text ed. 10.95 (*0-937771-15-5*) Spencers Intl.

— Space Age Marriage Techniques. LC 87-60010. (Orig.). 1987. text ed. 15.95 (*0-937771-13-9*); pap. text ed. 12.95 (*0-937771-12-0*) Spencers Intl.

— Space Age Predictions. LC 86-90555. 71p. 1986. lib. bdg. 10.95 (*0-937771-00-7*); pap. text ed. 10.95 (*0-937771-02-3*) Spencers Intl.

— The Wayward Wife. LC 86-62543. 25p. (Orig.). 1986. text ed. 10.95 (*0-937771-03-1*); lib. bdg. 10.95 (*0-937771-11-2*); pap. text ed. 8.95 (*0-937771-04-X*) Spencers Intl.

Lewis, George S., intro. Message to Adam's Children: The Book of Enoch. (Orig.). 1990. text ed. 18.95 (*0-937771-16-3*); pap. 12.95 (*0-937771-17-1*) Spencers Intl.

Lewis, Geraint. Michael Tippett, O. M. A Celebration. (Illus.). 255p. 1985. 39.95 (*0-85936-140-3*, Pub. by The Baton Pr UK) Pro-Am Music.

Lewis, Gerald. Critical Incident Stress & Trauma in the Workplace. 134p. (Orig.). 1994. pap. text ed. 18.95 (*1-55959-054-8*) Accel Devel.

Lewis, Gerald & Simmons, Bill. Profitable Roadside Retailing: Making It Happen. 131p. 10.00 (*0-685-65572-5*) Petro Mktg Ed Found.

Lewis, Gerald E. How to Talk Yankee. rev. ed. LC 88-38431. (Illus.). 58p. (Orig.). 1986. pap. 3.95 (*0-945980-07-8*) Nrth Country Pr.

— So Long, Scout, & Other Stories. LC 87-7104. (Illus.). 161p. (Orig.). 1988. pap. 9.95 (*0-945432-00-3*) Nrth Country Pr.

Lewis, Geraldine A. Dying to Live. abr. ed. 320p. 1995. pap. 9.95 (*1-56901-378-0*) NW Pub.

Lewis, Gertrud J., ed. see Gertrud the Great of Helfta.

Lewis, Gertrude, ed. see Anschell, Helen & Malkin, Marsha.

Lewis, Gifford, ed. Selected Letters of Somerville & Ross. (Illus.). 352p. 1991. pap. 14.95 (*0-571-15349-6*) Faber & Faber.

Lewis, Gilbert. Knowledge of Illness in a Sepik Society: A Study of the Gnau, New Guinea. (London School of Economics Monographs on Social Anthropology: No. 52). (Illus.). 379p. (C). 1975. text ed. 55.00 (*0-485-19552-6*, Pub. by Athlone Pr UK) Humanities.

Lewis, Gilbert, jt. ed. see Frankel, Stephen.

Lewis, Gilbert N. Anatomy of Science. LC 75-156680. (Essay Index Reprint Ser.). 1977. reprint ed. 20.95 (*0-8369-2408-8*) Ayer.

Lewis, Gillian & Pettegree, Andrew, eds. Calvinism in Europe, 1555-C. 1620: A Collection of Documents. Duke, Alastair et al, trs. 288p. (C). 1992. text ed. 59.95 (*0-7190-3551-1*, Pub. by Manchester Univ Pr UK); text ed. 24.95 (*0-7190-3552-X*, Pub. by Manchester Univ Pr UK) St Martin.

Lewis, Gladys S. Message, Messenger, & Response: Puritan Forms & Cultural Reformation in Harriet Beecher Stowe's "Uncle Tom's Cabin" 438p. (C). 1994. lib. bdg. 48.00 (*0-8191-9607-X*) U Pr of Amer.

Lewis, Glen. Australian Movies & the American Dream. LC 87-14590. (Illus.). 229p. 1987. text ed. 49.95 (*0-275-92675-3*, C2675, Praeger Pubs) Greenwood.

Lewis, Glenn A. Dinner at Mario's. (Illus.). 19p. (J). (gr. k-3). 1992. pap. 5.95 (*1-895583-53-5*) MAYA Pubs.

— Funny Things. (Illus.). 15p. (J). (gr. k-3). 1992. pap. 4.95 (*1-895583-54-3*) MAYA Pubs.

Lewis, Gloria, jt. auth. see Pisano, Beverly.

Lewis, Gordon. Bible, the Christian & Jehovah's Witnesses. 1966. pap. 2.99 (*0-87552-324-2*) Presby & Reformed.

— Bible, the Christian & Latter Day Saints. 1966. pap. 2.99 (*0-87552-325-0*) Presby & Reformed.

— Bible, the Christian & Seventh Day Adventists. 1966. pap. 2.99 (*0-87552-326-9*) Presby & Reformed.

— Florida Fishing: Fresh & Salt Water. LC 56-11379. (Illus.). (Orig.). 1957. pap. 2.95 (*0-8200-0102-3*) Great Outdoors.

— Notes on the Puerto Rican Revolution: An Essay on American Dominance & Caribbean Resistance. LC 74-7791. 288p. 1976. pap. 5.95 (*0-85345-371-3*) Monthly Rev.

— Slavery, Imperialism, & Freedom: Studies in English Radical Thought. LC 78-2826. 346p. 1978. pap. 6.50 (*0-85345-501-5*) Monthly Rev.

Lewis, Gordon, ed. History of the Japanese Camera. 1990. 60.00 (*0-935398-16-3*); pap. 50.00 (*0-935398-17-1*) G Eastman Hse.

Lewis, Gordon D. & Kyrou, Emilios J. Handy Hints on Legal Practice. 2nd ed. 334p. 1993. pap. 45.00 (*0-455-21201-5*, Pub. by Law Bk Co) W W Gaunt.

Lewis, Gordon H. & Michel, Richard C., eds. Microsimulation Techniques for Tax & Transfer Analysis. LC 89-24832. (Illus.). 262p. (Orig.). 1990. lib. bdg. 57.00 (*0-87766-432-3*); pap. text ed. 24.00 (*0-87766-433-1*) Urban Inst.

Lewis, Gordon H. & Morrison, Richard J. Income Transfer Analysis. LC 89-22057. 338p. (C). 1989. reprint ed. lib. bdg. 58.00 (*0-87766-430-7*) Urban Inst.

***Lewis, Gordon K.** Grenada: The Jewel Despoiled. LC 86-46282. 251p. 1987. pap. 71.60 (*0-7837-7453-2*, 2049175) Bks Demand.

— Growth of the Modern West Indies. LC 68-13657. 512p. 1968. pap. 12.00 (*0-85345-130-3*) Monthly Rev.

— Main Currents in Caribbean Thought: The Historical Evolution of Caribbean Society in Its Ideological Aspects, 1492-1900. LC 82-17128. (Studies in Atlantic History & Culture). 400p. (C). 1983. text ed. 50.00 (*0-8018-2589-X*) Johns Hopkins.

— Main Currents in Caribbean Thought: The Historical Evolution of Caribbean Society in Its Ideological Aspects, 1492-1900. LC 82-17128. (Johns Hopkins Studies in Atlantic History & Culture Ser.). 492p. 1987. pap. text ed. 15.95 (*0-8018-3492-9*) Johns Hopkins.

— Puerto Rico: Freedom & Power in the Caribbean. LC 63-20065. reprint ed. pap. 180.00 (*0-7837-9607-2*, 2060364) Bks Demand.

Lewis, Gordon R. Confronting the Cults. LC 66-26791. 1966. pap. 8.99 (*0-87552-323-4*) Presby & Reformed.

— Decide for Yourself: A Theological Workbook. LC 71-116046. (Orig.). 1970. pap. 12.99 (*0-87784-633-2*, 633) InterVarsity.

An Asterisk (*) at the beginning of an entry indicates that the title is appearing in BIP for the first time.

— Lo Que Todos Debemos Saber sobre la Meditacion Trancendental: Transcendental Meditation. (SPA.). 3.25 (*84-7228-252-X*, 220554, Pub. by Edit Clie SP) TSELF.

— Testing Christianity's Truth Claims: Approaches to Christian Apologetics. 363p. (C). 1990. reprint ed. pap. text ed. 29.50 (*0-8191-7838-1*) U Pr of Amer.

Lewis, Gordon R. & Demarest, Bruce A. Integrative Theology: Knowing Ultimate Reality; The Living God, Vol. 1. 352p. 1987. 34.99 (*0-310-39230-6*, 12710) Zondervan.

— Integrative Theology: Our Primary Need, Christ's Atoning Provisions, Vol. 2. 544p. 1990. 34.99 (*0-310-39240-3*) Zondervan.

— Integrative Theology, Vol. 3: Spirit-Given Life; God's People Present & Future. 576p. 1994. 34.99 (*0-310-59830-3*) Zondervan.

Lewis, Grace. One Thousand One Chemicals in Everyday Products. (Illus.). 352p. 1994. text ed. 19.95 (*0-442-01458-9*) Van Nos Reinhold.

Lewis, Graham, et al, eds. Columbia Poetry Review, No. 2. 96p. (Orig.). 1989. pap. 8.00 (*0-932026-20-6*) Columbia College Chi.

Lewis, Grant, Jr. My Friends. 1995. 18.95 (*0-8062-4964-1*) Carlton.

Lewis, Gregg. Caught. 1987. pap. 6.95 (*0-89066-091-3*) World Wide Pubs.

— Hudson Taylor's Spiritual Secret. 1990. 9.99 (*0-929239-20-2*) Discovery Hse Pubs.

— A Promise Is Forever. (Christy Miller Ser.: No. 12). 1995. audio 18.99 (*1-56179-357-4*) Focus Family.

— A Promise Is Forever. 1995. 16.99 (*1-56179-350-7*) Focus Family.

Lewis, Gregg, jt. auth. see Gray, Daphne.

Lewis, Gregg, jt. auth. see Landry, Tom.

Lewis, Gregg, jt. auth. see Lewis, Deborah S.

Lewis, Gregg, jt. auth. see Lewis, Marjorie.

Lewis, Gregg, jt. auth. see Lewis, Ralph L.

Lewis, Gregg, jt. auth. see Martin, Carolyn.

Lewis, Gregg, jt. auth. see Thomas, Bob.

Lewis, Gregg A., jt. photos see Lewis, Deborah S.

Lewis, Gregory. Pricing for Profit. (Business Basics Ser.). pap. text ed. write for info. (*0-7494-0832-4*, Pub. by Kogan Page Educ UK) Taylor & Francis.

— Sudden Return. rev. ed. 1994. 9.95 (*0-8062-4888-2*) Carlton.

Lewis, Griselda. A Collector's History of English Pottery. 4th ed. (Illus.). 360p. 1987. 79.50 (*1-85149-056-6*) Antique Collect.

Lewis, Griselda, jt. auth. see Lewis, John.

Lewis, Guy & Appenzeller, Herb. Successful Sport Management. 377p. 1985. 60.00 (*0-87215-925-6*) Michie Butterworth.

***Lewis, Gwyneth.** Parables & Faxes. 77p. 1995. pap. 14.95 (*1-85224-319-8*) Dufour.

Lewis, Gwyneth, ed. see Zimmerman, R. Lee.

Lewis, Gwynne. The French Revolution: Rethinking the Debate. LC 92-44015. (Historical Connections Ser.). 128p. 1993. pap. 11.95 (*0-415-05466-4*, A7868, Routledge NY) Routledge.

— Pierre-Francois Tubeuf & the Advent of Capitalism in France, 1770-1840. 360p. 1993. 59.00 (*0-19-822895-3*) OUP.

Lewis, Gwynne, tr. see Soboul, Albert.

Lewis, H., jt. auth. see Bird, Martyn.

Lewis, H. D. The French Education System. LC 85-22247. 256p. 1986. text ed. 32.50 (*0-312-30454-4*) St Martin.

Lewis, H. Elvit. Christ among the Welsh Miners. 1987. pap. 8.99 (*0-88019-221-6*) Schmul Pub Co.

Lewis, H. G. How to Handle Your Own Public Relations. LC 76-20710. 180p. 1976. 29.95 (*0-88229-319-2*) Nelson-Hall.

Lewis, H. Gregg. Union Relative Wage Effects: A Survey. LC 85-8663. 1986. lib. bdg. 37.50 (*0-226-47721-5*) U Ch Pr.

Lewis, H. Spencer. Essays of a Modern Mystic. 6th ed. LC 63-12317. 195p. 1961. 16.95 (*0-912057-21-1*, 501820) AMORC.

— Mental Poisoning. LC 59-55270. 104p. 1987. pap. 9.95 (*0-912057-49-1*, 502010) AMORC.

— Mystical Life of Jesus. LC 54-20988. (Illus.). 320p. 1986. pap. 14.95 (*0-912057-46-7*, 501980) AMORC.

— Rosicrucian Principles for the Home & Business. LC 54-21694. 241p. 1987. pap. 12.95 (*0-912057-54-8*, 502030) AMORC.

— Rosicrucian Questions & Answers with Complete History. 17th ed. 358p. 1993. 18.95 (*0-912057-59-9*) AMORC.

— The Secret Doctrines of Jesus. 19th ed. LC 37-22922. 237p. 1965. 17.95 (*0-912057-14-9*, 501610) AMORC.

— Self Mastery & Fate with the Cycles of Life. LC 55-16785. (Illus.). 253p. 1986. pap. 14.95 (*0-912057-45-9*, 501970) AMORC.

— A Thousand Years of Yesterday. 22th ed. LC 20-9068. 156p. 1982. 15.95 (*0-912057-01-7*, 501630) AMORC.

Lewis, H. W. Technological Risk. 368p. 1992. pap. 12.95 (*0-393-30829-4*) Norton.

Lewis, Hanna B., ed. see Lewald, Fanny.

Lewis, Harold. The Intellectual Base of Social Work Practice: Tools for Thought in a Helping Profession. LC 82-5593. (Saul Horowitz Jr. Memorial Ser.). 258p. 1982. text ed. 27.95 (*0-86656-176-5*); pap. text ed. 14.95 (*0-86656-418-7*) Haworth Pr.

— Mathematics for Daily Living. rev. ed. 1979. 21.96 (*0-8009-1552-6*); teacher ed, text ed. 23.92 (*0-8009-1549-6*) Random.

Lewis, Harold G. Unionism & Relative Wages in the United States: An Empirical Inquiry. LC 63-20915. (Studies in Economics of the Economics Research Center of the University of Chicago). 325p. reprint ed. pap. 92.70 (*0-685-23873-3*, 2056657) Bks Demand.

***Lewis, Harold T.** Yet with a Steady Beat: The African American Struggle for Recognition in the Episcopal Church. (Illus.). 256p. (Orig.). (C). 1995. pap. write for info. (*1-56338-130-3*) TPI PA.

Lewis, Harriet. Jackson Whole Food Cookbook. LC 92-81137. 194p. 1992. write for info. (*0-933294-04-2*) Backroads.

— The Last Garage Sale. LC 79-57092. 56p. (Orig.). 1982. pap. 6.95 (*0-933294-02-6*) Backroads.

— Pampoody & Max. 72p. (J). 1977. pap. 4.50 (*0-933294-01-8*) Backroads.

— Within the Earth, a Mountain. LC 88-70296. 158p. 1988. pap. 9.95 (*0-933294-03-4*) Backroads.

Lewis, Harry. Home Cooking. LC 75-20729. (Haystack Ser). (Illus.). 76p. 1975. 6.00 (*0-913142-08-5*); pap. 3.50 (*0-913142-07-7*) Mulch Pr.

— Silly. 96p. (Orig.). 1992. pap. text ed. 8.00 (*1-881523-00-4*) Junction CA.

Lewis, Harry A., ed. Peter Geach: Philosophical Encounters. (Synthese Library). (C). 1991. lib. bdg. 106.50 (*0-7923-0823-9*) Kluwer Ac.

Lewis, Harry R. & Papadimitriou, Christos H. Elements of the Theory of Computation. (Software Ser.). (Illus.). 496p. 1981. text ed. write for info. (*0-13-273417-6*) P-H.

Lewis, Harvey S. Jezus Misztikus Elete. Gaal, Violetta, tr. (Illus.). (HUN.). 1993. write for info. (*0-912057-88-2*) AMORC.

— A Rozsakeresztes Rend Tortenete. Gaal, Violetta, tr. (HUN.). 1993. write for info. (*0-912057-89-0*) AMORC.

Lewis, Harvey S., et al. Commercial Banking in Mississippi, 1940-1980. 1983. pap. 5.00 (*0-938004-10-7*) U MS Bus Econ.

Lewis, Heather. House Rules. LC 93-25614. 1994. 21.95 (*0-385-47210-2*, N A Talese) Doubleday.

Lewis, Helen. A Time to Speak. 144p. 1994. 16.95 (*0-7867-0068-8*) Carroll & Graf.

— A Time to Speak. 132p. 1993. pap. 15.95 (*0-85640-491-8*, Pub. by Blackstaff Pr IE) Dufour.

Lewis, Helen B. Freud & Modern Psychology, Vol. 1: The Emotional Basis of Mental Illness. LC 80-20937. (Emotions, Personality, & Psychotherapy Ser.). 258p. 1981. 49.50 (*0-306-40525-3*, Plenum Pr) Plenum.

— Freud & Modern Psychology, Vol. 2: The Emotional Basis of Human Behavior. (Emotions, Personality, & Psychotherapy Ser.). 246p. 1983. 49.50 (*0-306-41329-9*, Plenum Pr) Plenum.

— Shame & Guilt in Neurosis. LC 75-128622. 519p. 1971. pap. text ed. 24.95 (*0-8236-8307-9*, 026075) Intl Univs Pr.

Lewis, Helen B., ed. The Role of Shame in Symptom Formation. 264p. 1987. text ed. 49.95 (*0-89859-600-9*) L Erlbaum Assocs.

Lewis, Helen F. New York's Finger Lakes, Pioneer Families Especially Tompkins County: A Genealogical Notebook. 403p. 1991. lib. bdg. 69.95 (*1-56012-111-4*) Kinship Rhinebeck.

***Lewis, Helen F., ed.** Southeastern Michigan Pioneer Families: Especially Lenawee County & New York Origins. 426p. 1994. lib. bdg. 23.95 (*1-56012-130-0*, 128) Kinship Rhinebeck.

Lewis, Helen M. & Lewis, Meharry H. The Beauty of Holiness: A Small Catechism of the Holiness Faith & Doctrine: The Church of the Living God, the Pillar & Ground of the Truth, Inc. LC 88-92506. 150p. 1988. 30.00 (*0-910003-05-X*) New & Living.

Lewis, Helen M. & Lewis, Meharry H., eds. The Church of the Living God, the Pillar & Ground of the Truth, Inc: General Assembly Programs 1978-1987. (Illus.). 200p. 1987. lib. bdg. 35.00 (*0-910003-03-3*) New & Living.

Lewis, Helen N., ed. see Pincus, Robert, et al.

Lewis, Heloise. Vamos Amigos: A Beginning Spanish Course. 1986. pap. text ed. 8.70 (*0-582-36225-3*, 74821) Longman.

Lewis, Henry. The Valley of the Mississippi Illustrated. Heilbron, Bertha L., ed. Poatgieter, A. H., tr. LC 67-65590. (Illus.). 423p. 1967. 39.75 (*0-87351-035-6*) Minn Hist.

Lewis, Henry T. Ilocano Irrigation: The Corporate Resolution. LC 90-47736. (Asian Studies at Hawaii: No. 37). (Illus.). 184p. 1991. text ed. 20.00 (*0-8248-1357-X*) UH Pr.

***Lewis, Herbert S.** After the Eagles Landed: The Yemenites of Israel. (Illus.). 277p. (C). 1994. pap. text ed. 10.95x (*0-88133-810-9*) Waveland Pr.

— Galla Monarchy: Jimma Abba Jifar, Ethiopia, 1830-1932. (Illus.). 168p. 1965. 30.00 (*0-299-03690-1*) U of Wis Pr.

Lewis, Herschell G. Big Profits from Small Budget Advertising: Increase Effectiveness at Lower Cost. (Illus.). 380p. 1992. ring bd. 91.50 (*0-85013-221-5*) Dartnell Corp.

— Blood Feast. 43p. 1991. pap. 4.95 (*0-944735-82-7*) Malibu Graphics.

— Blood Feast. 2nd ed. (Illus.). 160p. 1988. reprint ed. pap. 9.95 (*0-938782-07-X*) Fantaco.

— Copywriting Secrets & Tactics. (Illus.). 420p. 1992. ring bd. 91.50 (*0-85013-193-6*) Dartnell Corp.

— Direct Mail Copy That Sells. (Illus.). 1986. 12.95 (*0-13-214750-5*, Busn) P-H.

— Direct Marketing Strategies & Tactics. (Illus.). 360p. 1992. 49.95 (*0-85013-220-7*) Dartnell Corp.

— Herschell Gordon Lewis on the Art of Writing Copy. 416p. 1988. text ed. 49.95 (*0-13-387309-9*, Busn) P-H.

— How to Make Your Advertising Twice As Effective at Half the Cost. LC 90-80110. (Illus.). 278p. 1992. pap. 19.95 (*0-85013-219-3*) Dartnell Corp.

— How to Make Your Advertising Twice As Effective at Half the Cost. LC 85-9573. 273p. 1986. 27.95 (*0-13-417882-3*, Busn) P-H.

— How to Write Powerful Catalog Copy. LC 89-81587. (Illus.). 331p. 1992. 49.95 (*0-85013-222-3*) Dartnell Corp.

— How to Write Powerful Fund Raising Letters. LC 88-64123. 206p. 1990. 40.00 (*0-944496-05-9*) Precept Pr.

— More Than You Ever Wanted to Know about Mail Order Advertising. LC 83-4465. 330p. 1986. 10.95 (*0-13-601039-3*) P-H.

— Open Me Now! 260p. 1995. text ed. 40.00 (*1-56625-036-6*) Bonus Books.

— Power Copywriting. 335p. 1994. pap. 29.95 (*0-85013-227-4*) Dartnell Corp.

— Power Copywriting: Dynamic New Communication Techniques to Help You Sell More Products. 334p. 1992. 29.95 (*0-85013-187-1*) Dartnell Corp.

— Sales Letters That Sizzle: All the Hooks, Lines & Sinkers You'll Ever Need to Close Sales. LC 94-16176. 1994. 29.95 (*0-8442-3547-4*, NTC Busn Bks) NTC Pub Grp.

— Two Thousand Maniacs. 2nd rev. ed. (Illus.). 144p. 1988. pap. 9.95 (*0-938782-08-8*) Fantaco.

Lewis, Herschell G. & Lewis, Margo. Everybody's Guide to Plate Collecting. rev. ed. (Illus.). 240p. 1994. pap. 12.95 (*1-56625-007-2*) Bonus Books.

Lewis, Hilary & O'Connor, John. Philip Johnson: The Architect in His Own Words. LC 94-16057. (Illus.). 208p. 1994. 50.00 (*0-8478-1823-3*) Rizzoli Intl.

Lewis, Hilda. Ship That Flew. LC 58-5903. (Illus.). (J). (gr. 3-7). 1958. 26.95 (*0-87599-067-3*) S G Phillips.

Lewis, Hilda, ed. Child Art: The Beginnings of Self-Affirmation. rev. ed. LC 73-75581. (Illus.). 124p. 1973. 7.95 (*0-87297-004-3*); pap. 6.95 (*0-87297-005-1*) Diablo.

Lewis, Hilda S. Deprived Children: The Mersham Experiment; a Social & Clinical Study. LC 77-27491. 163p. 1978. reprint ed. text ed. 35.00 (*0-8371-9070-3*, LEDC, Greenwood Pr) Greenwood.

Lewis, Howard, jt. auth. see Ellis, J. Nigel.

Lewis, Hunter. A Question of Values: Six Ways We Make the Personal Choices That Shape Our Lives. LC 90-56471. 256p. 1991. reprint ed. pap. 13.00 (*0-06-250532-7*) Harper SF.

Lewis, Hylan. Blackways of Kent. 1955. pap. 13.95x (*0-8084-0064-9*) NCUP.

— Blackways of Kent. 1955. 20.00 (*0-8078-0676-5*) U of NC Pr.

Lewis, Hyman. Self Hypnosis Dynamics. 1962. pap. 3.00 (*0-87505-334-3*) Borden.

Lewis, I. & Wells, F. Millimicrosecond Pulse Techniques. 2nd rev. ed. LC 59-12608. (International Series of Monographs on Electronics & Instrumentation: Vol. 5). 1959. 183.00 (*0-08-013958-2*, Pub. by Pergamon Repr UK) Franklin.

Lewis, I., jt. auth. see Jenkins, Edgar N.

Lewis, I. M. Blood & Bone: The Call of Kinship in Somali Society. LC 93-47165. 286p. 1994. 45.95 (*0-932415-92-X*); pap. 16.95 (*0-932415-93-8*) Red Sea Pr.

— Ecstatic Religion: An Anthropological Study of Spirit Possession & Shamanism. 2nd ed. 224p. (Orig.). 1989. pap. 14.95 (*0-415-00799-2*) Routledge.

— A Pastoral Democracy. LC 81-4074. 320p. 1982. 49.50 (*0-8419-0667-X*) Holmes & Meier.

— A Pastoral Democracy: A Study of Pastoralism & Politics among the Northern Somali of the Horn of Africa. LC 81-4074. (Illus.). 349p. reprint ed. pap. 99.50 (*0-8357-3015-8*, 2057101) Bks Demand.

— Peoples of the Horn of Africa: Somali, Afar & Saho. LC 55-4468. (Ethnographic Survey of Africa: North Eastern Africa Ser.: Pt. 1). 212p. reprint ed. pap. 60.50 (*0-8357-3014-X*, 2057100) Bks Demand.

— Religion in Context: Cults & Charisma. (Essays in Social Anthropology Ser.). (Illus.). 160p. 1986. pap. 15.95 (*0-521-31596-4*) Cambridge U Pr.

— Social Anthropology in Perspective: The Relevance of Social Anthropology. 2nd ed. 400p. 1986. pap. 16.95 (*0-521-31351-1*) Cambridge U Pr.

Lewis, I. M., ed. Nationalism & Self-Determination in the Horn of Africa. (Illus.). 229p. (Orig.). 1984. pap. 12.00 (*0-685-08758-1*, Pub. by Ithaca UK) Evergreen Dist.

Lewis, I. M., et al. Women's Medicine: The Zar-Bori Cult in Africa & Beyond. 296p. 1991. text ed. 69.00 (*0-7486-0261-5*, Pub. by Edinburgh U Pr UK) Col U Pr.

Lewis, Ida B. The Education of Girls in China. LC 78-176992. (Columbia University. Teachers College. Contributions to Education Ser.: No. 104). reprint ed. 37.50 (*0-404-55104-1*) AMS Pr.

Lewis-Idema, Deborah. Increasing Provider Participation: Strategies for Improving State Perinatal Programs. 75p. (Orig.). 1988. pap. text ed. 15.00 (*1-55877-026-7*) Natl Governor.

— Monitoring Medicaid Provider Participation & Access to Care. Glass, Karen, ed. 42p. (Orig.). 1992. pap. text ed. 15.00 (*1-55877-166-2*) Natl Governor.

Lewis, Ioan M. A Modern History of Somalia: Nation & State in the Horn of Africa. rev. ed. LC 79-40569. 289p. reprint ed. pap. 82.40 (*0-317-27754-5*, 2025232) Bks Demand.

— A Modern History of Somalia: Nation & State in the Horn of Africa. 2nd exp. rev. ed. (Special Studies on Africa). (Illus.). 297p. 1988. pap. text ed. 72.50 (*0-8133-7402-2*) Westview.

Lewis, Ioan M., jt. ed. see Johoda, Gustav.

***Lewis, Ira.** Chinese Coffee. 1995. pap. 4.75 (*0-8222-1426-1*) Dramatists Play.

Lewis, Isabelle, jt. auth. see Sparling, Joseph.

Lewis, Ivor. Sahibs, Nabobs, & Boxwallahs: The Words of Anglo-India. 350p. 1992. 29.95 (*0-19-562582-X*) OUP.

Lewis, J. Mision Mundial (World Mission), Vol. I. (SPA.). Date not set. teacher ed 2.50 (*1-56063-536-3*, 498678) Editorial Unilit.

— Mision Mundial (World Mission), Vol. II. (SPA.). Date not set. teacher ed 2.50 (*1-56063-537-1*, 498679) Editorial Unilit.

— Mision Mundial (World Mission), Vol. III. (SPA.). Date not set. teacher ed 2.50 (*1-56063-538-X*, 498680) Editorial Unilit.

Lewis, J., tr. see De Gourmont, Remy.

Lewis, J., tr. see Samuda, R. J. & Kong, S. L.

Lewis, J., jt. auth. see Shaw, T.

Lewis, J. A. Economic Impact Analysis: A UK Literature Survey & Bibliography. (Progress in Planning Ser.: PRPL 30). 56p. 1990. pap. 42.00 (*0-08-036880-8*, Pergamon Pr) Elsevier.

Lewis, J. C. & Masatomi, H., eds. Crane Research Around the World. (Illus.). 259p. 1981. pap. 17.00 (*0-318-14550-2*) Intl Crane.

Lewis, J. D. Three of the Best. (C). 1989. 23.00 (*0-7223-2331-X*, Pub. by A H S Ltd UK) St Mut.

Lewis, J. David & Smith, Richard L. American Sociology & Pragmatism: Mead, Chicago Sociology, & Symbolic Interaction. LC 80-15489. (Illus.). 1981. 30.00 (*0-226-47697-9*) U Ch Pr.

Lewis, J. E. Cheese Starters: Development & Application of the Lewis System. 226p. 1987. 66.75 (*1-85166-024-0*, Pub. by Elsevier Applied Sci UK) Elsevier.

***Lewis, J. H.** Comparative Hemostasis in Vertebrates. (Illus.). 405p. 1995. write for info. (*0-306-44841-6*, Plenum Pr) Plenum.

Lewis, J. H., jt. auth. see Lewis, R. E.

Lewis, J. H., jt. ed. see Seeff, L. B.

Lewis, J. Lowell. Ring of Liberation: Deceptive Discourse in Brazilian Capoeira. (Illus.). 232p. 1992. lib. bdg. 34.95 (*0-226-47682-0*); pap. text ed. 14.95 (*0-226-47683-9*) U Ch Pr.

Lewis, J. N., jt. auth. see Headley, Joseph C.

Lewis, J. Norman, jt. auth. see Lewis, C. J.

Lewis, J. O., intro. Johnson City: The Way We Were. (Illus.). 64p. 1989. reprint ed. pap. 4.95 (*0-932807-46-1*) Overmountain Pr.

Lewis, J. O., jt. auth. see Scorer, N.

Lewis, J. P. Manual of the Vanni Districts, Ceylon. (C). 1993. text ed. 32.50 (*81-7013-113-8*, Pub. by Navrang) S Asia.

***Lewis, J. Patrick.** Black Swan, White Crow. (Illus.). 1995. 14.00 (*0-689-31899-5*, Atheneum Bks Young) S&S Childrens.

— The Bookworm's Feast: A Potluck of Poems. LC 94-31897. 1996. lib. bdg. write for info. (*0-8037-1693-1*) Dial Bks Young.

— The Bookworm's Feast: A Potluck of Poems. LC 94-31897. (J). 1996. write for info. (*0-8037-1692-3*) Dial Bks Young.

— Boshblobberbosh: Runcible Poems for Mr. Lear. LC 93-43749. (J). 1995. write for info. (*0-8037-1390-8*); lib. bdg. write for info. (*0-8037-1391-6*) Dial Bks Young.

— The Christmas of the Reddle Moon. LC 93-28049. (Illus.). (J). 1994. 15.99 (*0-8037-1566-6*); lib. bdg. 15.89 (*0-8037-1567-6*) Dial Bks Young.

— Earth Verses & Water Rhymes. LC 90-40709. (Illus.). 32p. (J). (gr. 2-5). 1991. text ed. 13.95 (*0-689-31693-3*, Atheneum Bks Young) S&S Childrens.

— The Fat-Cats at Sea. (Illus.). 40p. (J). (ps-3). 1994. 15.00 (*0-679-82639-4*, Apple Soup Bks); lib. bdg. 15.99 (*0-679-92639-9*, Apple Soup Bks) Knopf Bks Yng Read.

— A Hippopotamusn't: And Other Animal Poems. (Illus.). 40p. (J). (ps-3). 1994. pap. 4.99 (*0-14-055273-1*, Puff Pied Piper) Puffin Bks.

— July Is a Mad Mosquito. LC 93-19743. (Illus.). 32p. (J). (gr. 2-5). 1994. text ed. 14.95 (*0-689-31813-8*, Atheneum Bks Young) S&S Childrens.

— The Little Buggers: Insect & Spider Poems. LC 94-31900. (Illus.). (J). 1997. write for info. (*0-8037-1769-5*); lib. bdg. write for info. (*0-8037-1770-9*) Dial Bks Young.

— Long Was the Winter Road They Traveled: A Tale of the Nativity. (J). 1996. write for info. (*0-8037-1814-4*); lib. bdg. write for info. (*0-8037-1815-2*) Dial Bks Young.

— The Moonbow of Mr. B. Bones. LC 88-37107. (Illus.). 40p. (J). (ps-4). 1992. lib. bdg. 16.99 (*0-394-95365-7*) Knopf Bks Yng Read.

— One Dog Day. LC 92-24573. (Illus.). 64p. (J). (gr. 2-5). 1993. text ed. 12.95 (*0-689-31808-1*, Atheneum Bks Young) S&S Childrens.

— Riddle-Icious. LC 93-43759. (J). 1995. 15.00 (*0-679-84011-7*); lib. bdg. write for info. (*0-679-94011-1*) Knopf.

— Ridicholas Nicholas: More Animal Poems. LC 91-44349. (Illus.). 40p. (J). (ps-3). 1995. 14.99 (*0-8037-1327-4*); lib. bdg. 14.89 (*0-8037-1328-2*) Dial Bks Young.

Lewis, J. Slater. The Commercial Organization of Factories: A Handbook. Brief, Richard P., ed. LC 77-87274. (Development of Contemporary Accounting Thought Ser.). 1978. reprint ed. lib. bdg. 60.95 (*0-405-10902-4*) Ayer.

Lewis, J. W., jt. ed. see Akil, H.

Lewis, Jac & Lewis, Miriam S. Costume: The Performing Partner. Zapel, Arthur L., ed. LC 90-53279. (Illus.). 192p. (Orig.). 1990. pap. text ed. 11.95 (*0-916260-71-2*, B162) Meriwether Pub.

Lewis, Jack. Gun Digest Book of Sporting Clays. LC 91-71896. (Illus.). 224p. (Orig.). 1991. pap. 17.95 (*0-87349-125-4*) DBI.

Lewis, Jack, ed. Gun Digest Book of Assault Weapons. 3rd ed. LC 85-73744. (Illus.). 256p. (Orig.). 1993. pap. 18.95 (*0-87349-139-4*) DBI.

— Gun Digest Book of Modern Gun Values. 9th ed. LC 75-10067. (Illus.). 560p. (Orig.). 1993. pap. 20.95 (*0-87349-138-6*) DBI.

— Shotgun Digest. 4th ed. LC 74-80333. (Illus.). 256p. (Orig.). 1993. pap. 17.95 (*0-87349-137-8*) DBI.

Lewis, Jack & Combs, Roger. Gun Digest Book of Knifemaking. LC 88-51673. (Illus.). 224p. (Orig.). 1989. pap. 16.95 (*0-87349-035-5*) DBI.

— Gun Digest Book of Knives. 4th ed. LC 73-83465. (Illus.). 256p. (Orig.). 1992. pap. 16.95 (*0-87349-129-7*) DBI.

Lewis, Jack, ed. see Gertrud the Great of Helfta.

Lewis, Jack, tr. see Gertrud the Great of Helfta.

Lewis, Jack P. The English Bible from KJV to NIV: A History & Evaluation. 2nd ed. LC 91-258. 512p. 1991. pap. text ed. 21.99 (*0-8010-5666-7*) Baker Bk.

— The Gospel According to Matthew, Pt. 1. LC 75-21256. 1984. 12.95 (*0-915547-17-1*) Abilene Christ U.

— The Gospel According to Matthew, Pt. 2. LC 75-21256. 1984. 12.95 (*0-915547-18-X*) Abilene Christ U.

— Minor Prophets. LC 66-18308. 1966. pap. 5.99 (*0-8010-5509-1*) Baker Bk.

— Questions You've Asked about Bible Translations. 423p. (Orig.). 1991. 15.95 (*0-945441-04-5*) Res Pubns AR.

Lewis, Jack P., ed. Interpreting Second Corinthians 5: 14-21: An Exercise in Hermeneutics. LC 89-34218. (Studies in Bible & Early Christianity: Vol. 17). 204p. 1989. lib. bdg. 89.95 (*0-88946-617-3*) E Mellen.

***Lewis, Jack W.** A CrashCourse In Integral Calculus. 1995. cd-rom, pap. 39.95 (*1-878707-28-0*) HighText.

— Modeling Engineering Systems: PC-Based Techniques & Design Tools. 1993. pap. 19.95 (*1-878707-08-6*) HighText.

Lewis, Jack W., ed. Studies in General & English Phonetics: Essays in Honour of Professor J. D. O'Connor. LC 94-4050. (Illus.). 504p. 1995. 95.00x (*0-415-08068-1*, C0285) Routledge.

***Lewis, Jack W. & HighText Multimedia Development Group.** A CrashCourse In Differential Calculus. 1995. cd-rom, pap. 39.95 (*1-878707-24-8*) HighText.

Lewis, James, Jr. Achieving Excellence in Our Schools...by Taking Lessons from America's Best Run Companies. LC 85-51152. 250p. 1986. 24.95 (*0-915253-03-8*) Wilkerson Pub Co.

— Creating Excellence in Our Schools...by Taking More Lessons from America's Best Run Companies. LC 85-51533. 250p. 1986. 24.95 (*0-915253-04-6*) Wilkerson Pub Co.

Lewis, James. Everything You Always Wanted to Know about Drafting, Vol. 1, No. 1. (Illus.). 68p. 1987. pap. 10.00 (*0-9617322-1-0*) Flat Surface.

Lewis, James, Jr. Excellent Organizations: How to Develop & Organize Them Using Theory Z. LC 83-51208. (Illus.). 318p. 1985. 9.95 (*0-915253-00-3*) Wilkerson Pub Co.

Lewis, James. Hocus Pocus Stir & Cook, The Kitchen Science Magic Book. LC 91-30403. (Illus.). 79p. (YA). 1991. pap. 7.00 (*0-88166-183-X*) Meadowbrook.

— Horoscope Signs Illustrated, Vol. 1. (Illus.). 24p. 1987. pap. 2.00 (*0-9617322-5-3*) Flat Surface.

— How I Survived Prostate Cancer, & So Can You: A Guide for Diagnosing & Treating Prostate Cancer. (Illus.). 274p. (Orig.). 1994. 24.95 (*1-883257-05-0*); pap. 18.95 (*1-883257-06-9*) Hlth Edu Lit.

— How to Advertise with No Money Down: No Credit-Bad Credit, Vol. 1, No. 1. (Illus.). 126p. 1987. pap. 15.00 (*0-9617322-0-2*) Flat Surface.

— Implementing Total Quality in Education to Produce Great Schools: Transforming the American Education System. (Illus.). 306p. (C). 1993. 39.95 (*1-883257-01-8*) Hlth Edu Lit.

Lewis, James, Jr. Implementing Total Quality in Education to Produce Great Schools: Transforming the American School System. 320p. (C). 1993. 35.95 (*1-883257-00-X*) Hlth Edu Lit.

Lewis, James. Learn While You Scrub: Science in the Tub. (YA). (gr. 5 up). 1989. 7.00 (*0-671-68999-1*) S&S Trade.

— Learn While You Scrub, Science in the Tub. LC 89-33793. 96p. 1990. pap. 7.00 (*0-88166-138-4*) Meadowbrook.

— Measure, Pour & Mix: Kitchen Science Tricks. 80p. 1990. pap. 7.00 (*0-88166-134-1*) Meadowbrook.

— Over Three Hundred Anxious Gift Catalogs, Vol. 1. 96p. 1987. pap. 5.00 (*0-9617322-6-1*) Flat Surface.

Lewis, James, Jr. Recreating Our Schools for the Twenty-first Century. 280p. 1987. 24.95 (*0-915253-10-0*) Wilkerson Pub Co.

Lewis, James. Rub-a Dub-Dub, Science in the Tub. LC 88-36401. 70p. 1989. pap. 6.00 (*0-88166-161-9*) Meadowbrook.

Lewis, James, ed. see Currier, Paul J., et al.

Lewis, James A. The Final Campaign of the American Revolution: Rise & Fall of the Spanish Bahamas. Still, William N., Jr., ed. (Studies in Maritime History). (Illus.). 160p. 1991. text ed. 29.95 (*0-87249-726-7*) U of SC Pr.

— Humorous Poems with Illustrations, Vol. 1. (Illus.). 68p. 1987. pap. 10.00 (*0-9617322-2-9*) Flat Surface.

— The Miracle of Dr. George Washington Carver, Vol. 1. (Illus.). 68p. (Orig.). 1987. pap. 10.00 (*0-9617322-3-7*) Flat Surface.

— Southern Life, Vol. 1. (Illus.). 68p. 1987. pap. 10.00 (*0-9617322-4-5*) Flat Surface.

Lewis, James A., jt. auth. see Anderson, William L.

Lewis, James B., jt. auth. see Creedon, John J.

Lewis, James C. How to Think Like a Winner. 154p. (Orig.). 1989. pap. 7.95 (*0-942482-12-3*) Unity Church Denver.

— The Key to Spiritual Growth. LC 84-52070. 163p. 1985. 6.95 (*0-87159-004-2*) Unity Bks.

— Moving on to Greater Things. LC 88-50843. 294p. (Orig.). 1990. pap. 10.95 (*0-942482-11-5*) Unity Church Denver.

Lewis, James F. & Travis, William G. Religious Traditions of the World. 608p. 1991. 24.99 (*0-310-51900-4*) Zondervan.

Lewis, James H. A Pharmacologic Approach to Gastrointestinal Disorders. LC 93-13185. (Illus.). 667p. 1994. 85.00 (*0-683-04970-4*) Williams & Wilkins.

Lewis, James K. Religious Life of Fugitive Slaves & Rise of the Coloured Baptist Churches, 1820-1865, in What Is Now Ontario. Gaustad, Edwin S., ed. LC 79-52574. (Baptist Tradition Ser.). 1980. lib. bdg. 23.95 (*0-405-12442-2*) Ayer.

***Lewis, James P.** Fundamentals of Project Management. LC 94-41740. (WorkSmart Ser.). 128p. 1995. pap. 10.95 (*0-8144-7835-2*) AMACOM.

— How to Build & Manage a Winning Project Team. 224p. 1993. 26.95 (*0-8144-5137-3*) AMACOM.

— Project Management: Planning, Scheduling, & Control. 195p. 1992. student ed 95.00 (*0-9631886-0-7*) Knightsbdg.

— Project Management: Planning, Scheduling, & Control. 2nd ed. (Illus.). 252p. 1993. student ed 95.00 (*0-9631886-1-5*) Knightsbdg.

— Project Management: Tools, Principles, Practices. (Illus.). 257p. 1994. student ed 95.00 (*0-9631886-2-3*) Knightsbdg.

— Project Manager's Desk Reference: A Comprehensive Guide to Project Planning, Evaluation & Control. 525p. 1995. 29.95 (*1-55738-896-2*) Probus Pub Co.

— Project Planning, Scheduling & Control: A Hands-on Guide to Bringing Projects in on Time & on Budget. 300p. 1995. 37.50 (*1-55738-869-5*) Probus Pub Co.

— Project Workbench for Windows: Version 2.0. (Illus.). 352p. 1994. pap. 29.95 (*0-442-01764-2*) Van Nos Reinhold.

Lewis, James R. The Astrology Encyclopedia. 550p. 1994. 45.00 (*0-8103-8900-2*, 101561) Gale.

— The Astrology Encyclopedia. 550p. 1994. pap. 19.95 (*0-8103-9460-X*) Visible Ink Pr.

— Cult - Anti-Cult: How a National Mindset & Government Incompetence Aided & Abetted the Waco Disaster. (Illus.). 300p. 1994. 25.00 (*1-883322-03-0*) Agamemnon Pr.

— The Dream Encyclopedia. LC 95-10759. 1995. pap. 14.95 (*0-7876-0156-X*) Gale.

— The Dream Encyclopedia. 600p. 1995. 49.95 (*0-7876-0155-1*) Gale.

— Encyclopedia of Afterlife Beliefs & Phenomena. LC 94-29172. 420p. (YA). 1994. 37.95 (*0-8103-4879-9*) Gale.

— Encyclopedia of Afterlife Beliefs & Phenomena 1. 444p. 1995. pap. text ed. 15.95 (*0-7876-0288-4*) Visible Ink Pr.

— The Gods Have Landed: New Religions from Other Worlds. (Illus.). 320p. 1995. text ed. 59.50x (*0-7914-2329-8*); pap. text ed. 19.95 (*0-7914-2330-1*) State U NY Pr.

Lewis, James R., ed. From the Ashes: Making Sense Out of Waco. 288p. (C). 1994. lib. bdg. 54.00 (*0-8476-7914-4*); pap. text ed. 21.95 (*0-8476-7915-2*) Rowman.

— Magical Religion & Modern Witchcraft. 336p. (C). 1996. text ed. 59.50x (*0-7914-2889-3*); pap. 19.95 (*0-7914-2890-7*) State U NY Pr.

Lewis, James R. & Melton, J. Gordon, eds. Church Universal & Triumphant: In Scholarly Perspective. (Illus.). 174p. (C). 1994. pap. text ed. 20.00 (*0-8191-9634-7*) U Pr of Amer.

— Perspectives on the New Age. LC 91-39093. (SUNY Series in Religious Studies). 369p. 1992. 59.50 (*0-7914-1213-X*); pap. 19.95 (*0-7914-1214-8*) State U NY Pr.

Lewis, James W. The Protestant Experience in Gary, Indiana, 1906-1975: At Home in the City. LC 91-24752. (Illus.). 304p. (C). 1992. text ed. 41.00x (*0-87049-737-5*) U of Tenn Pr.

Lewis, James W., jt. ed. see Wind, James P.

Lewis, Jan. Math Readiness. (Rainbow Skill Builders Ser.: Level 3). 80p. (Orig.). 1985. pap. 2.95 (*0-8431-2500-4*) Price Stern.

— The Pursuit of Happiness: Family & Values in Jefferson's Virginia. LC 83-1786. (Illus.). 336p. 1985. pap. 15.95 (*0-521-31508-5*) Cambridge U Pr.

Lewis, Jan, jt. auth. see Marketing Graphics Corporation Staff.

Lewis, Jane. The Politics of Motherhood: Child & Maternal Welfare in England, 1900-1939. 240p. 1980. 37.95 (*0-7735-0521-0*, Pub. by McGill CN) U of Toronto Pr.

— Voluntary Sector, the State & Social Work in Britain: The Charity Organisation Society-Family Welfare Association since 1869. 200p. 1995. text ed. 59.95 (*1-85898-188-3*) Ashgate Pub Co.

— Women & Social Action in Victorian & Edwardian England. LC 90-71680. 336p. 1991. 42.50 (*0-8047-1905-5*) Stanford U Pr.

— Women & Social Policies in Europe: Work, Family & the State. 256p. 1993. 59.95 (*1-85278-563-2*, Pub. by E Elgar Pub UK) Ashgate Pub Co.

— Women in Britain: Women, Family, Work & the State since 1945. Seldon, A., ed. (Institute of Contemporary British History Ser.). 144p. (Orig.). (C). 1992. text ed. 39.95 (*0-631-16975-X*); pap. text ed. 14.95 (*0-631-16976-8*) Blackwell Pubs.

— Women in England, 1870-1950: Sexual Divisons & Social Change. LC 84-48437. (Illus.). 288p. 1985. 25.00 (*0-253-36608-9*); pap. 10.95 (*0-253-28926-2*) Ind U Pr.

Lewis, Jane, ed. Women & Social Policies in Europe. 264p. 1994. pap. 22.95 (*1-85278-918-2*, Pub. by E Elgar Pub UK) Ashgate Pub Co.

Lewis, Jane & Meredith, Barbara. Daughters Who Care: Daughters Caring for Mothers at Home. 200p. (C). 1988. lib. bdg. 54.00 (*0-415-00681-3*) Routledge.

Lewis, Jane, et al, eds. Women, Work & Family in the British, Canadian & Norwegian Offshore Oilfields. LC 86-31393. 200p. 1988. text ed. 45.00 (*0-312-00528-8*) St Martin.

Lewis, Janet. Against a Darkening Sky. LC 85-9770. 302p. 1985. reprint ed. text ed. 22.50 (*0-8040-0865-5*); reprint ed. pap. 9.95 (*0-8040-0866-3*) Swallow.

— Birthday of the Infanta. 22p. 1981. 25.00 (*0-936576-03-0*) Symposium Pr.

— Ghost of Monsieur Scarron. LC 65-16520. 378p. 1959. pap. 9.95 (*0-8040-0133-2*, 82-70514) Swallow.

— Goodbye, Son & Other Stories. LC 85-27731. 221p. 1986. reprint ed. text ed. 19.95 (*0-8040-0867-1*); reprint ed. pap. 10.95 (*0-8040-0868-X*) Swallow.

— The Legend: The Story of Neengay, a Libretto. LC 86-32863. 80p. (Orig.). 1987. pap. 8.95 (*0-936784-26-1*) J Daniel.

— Poems Old & New: 1918-1978. LC 80-26209. xvi, 112p. 1981. 19.95x (*0-8040-0371-8*); pap. 10.95 (*0-8040-0372-6*) Swallow.

— Trial of Soren Qvist. LC 72-94405. 256p. 1959. pap. 12.95 (*0-8040-0297-5*) Swallow.

— The Wife: A Libretto (For an Opera in Three Acts) 2nd ed. LC 88-11720. 64p. 1988. pap. 8.95 (*0-936784-63-6*) J Daniel.

— Wife of Martin Guerre. LC 82-70548. 109p. 1967. reprint ed. pap. 7.95 (*0-8040-0321-1*) Ohio U Pr.

Lewis, Janet T. & Plumb, Barbara L. Cooking with Zucchini. 3rd ed. 170p. (Orig.). 1980. pap. 8.00 (*0-9611974-0-4*) Country Garden.

Lewis, Jay. Other Men's Minds. LC 70-134108. (Essay Index Reprint Ser.). 1977. 19.95 (*0-8369-1974-2*) Ayer.

Lewis, Jean. Kate Gleeson's Kitty's Gift. (Golden Sturdy Shape Bks.). (Illus.). 14p. (J). 1994. write for info. (*0-307-12497-5*, Golden Bks) Western Pub.

— Sweet Dreams, Tweety. (J). (ps-3). 1993. pap. 1.95 (*0-307-10552-0*, Golden Pr) Western Pub.

Lewis, Jeff. Extremity of the Skies. 140p. (C). 1990. 33.00 (*1-875184-01-5*, Pub. by Pascoe Pub AT) St Mut.

— Treasures from the Beginning of the World. (Illus.). 140p. (Orig.). 1994. pap. 10.95 (*1-886028-13-3*) Savage Pr.

— The Writer's Manual: A Practical Guide to Creative & Vocational Writing. 120p. (C). 1990. 60.00 (*0-7316-2314-2*, Pub. by Pascoe Pub AT) St Mut.

***Lewis, Jel D.** The Black Virgin. 200p. (Orig.). 1995. pap. 16.95 (*0-9639917-2-8*) Writers Unltd.

— The Man Pleaser. 200p. (Orig.). 1995. pap. 12.95 (*0-9639917-3-6*) Writers Unltd.

— The Naked Girl. (Illus.). 269p. (Orig.). 1991. pap. 12.95 (*0-910303-27-4*) Writers Pub Serv.

— The Perfect Lady. 200p. 1994. pap. 12.95 (*0-9639917-0-1*) Writers Unltd.

Lewis, Jeremy, ed. see Hornung, E. W.

Lewis, Jeremy, ed. see Wells, H. G.

Lewis, Jerre G. & Renn, Leslie D. How to Start a Participative Management Program: Ten Key Steps. LC 91-90576. 104p. 1991. pap. 9.95 (*0-9628759-1-0*) Lewis Renn.

— How to Start & Manage a Bicycle Shop Business: Step-by-Step Guide to Business Success. (Illus.). 66p. (Orig.). 1994. pap. 9.95 (*0-9628759-7-X*) Lewis Renn.

— How to Start & Manage a Bookkeeping Service Business: Step-by-Step Guide to Business Success. (Illus.). 60p. (Orig.). 1994. pap. 9.95 (*1-887005-09-9*) Lewis Renn.

— How to Start & Manage a Construction Electrician Business: Step-by-Step Guide to Business Success. (Illus.). 60p. (Orig.). 1994. pap. 9.95 (*1-887005-06-4*) Lewis Renn.

— How to Start & Manage a Day Care Center: Step-by-Step Guide to Business Success. (Illus.). 64p. (Orig.). 1994. pap. 9.95 (*1-887005-04-8*) Lewis Renn.

— How to Start & Manage a Flower & Plant Store Business: Step-by-Step Guide to Business Success. (Illus.). 61p. (Orig.). 1994. pap. 9.95 (*1-887005-05-6*) Lewis Renn.

— How to Start & Manage a Garden Center Business: Step-by-Step Guide to Business Success. (Illus.). 61p. (Orig.). 1994. pap. 9.95 (*0-9628759-5-3*) Lewis Renn.

— How to Start & Manage a Hair Styling Shop Business: Step-by-Step Guide to Business Success. (Illus.). 62p. (Orig.). 1994. pap. 9.95 (*0-9628759-6-1*) Lewis Renn.

— How to Start & Manage a Health Spa Business: Step-by-Step Guide to Business Success. (Illus.). 60p. (Orig.). 1994. pap. 9.95 (*1-887005-00-5*) Lewis Renn.

— How to Start & Manage a Housecleaning Service Business: Step-by-Step Guide to Business Success. (Illus.). 61p. (Orig.). 1994. pap. 9.95 (*1-887005-07-2*) Lewis Renn.

— How to Start & Manage a Nursing Service Business: Step-by-Step Guide to Business Success. (Illus.). 65p. (Orig.). 1994. pap. 9.95 (*1-887005-08-0*) Lewis Renn.

— How to Start & Manage a Restaurant Business: Step-by-Step Guide to Business Success. (Illus.). 61p. (Orig.). 1994. pap. 9.95 (*1-887005-01-3*) Lewis Renn.

— How to Start & Manage a Secretarial Service Business: Step-by-Step Guide to Business Success. (Illus.). 62p. (Orig.). 1994. pap. 9.95 (*1-887005-10-2*) Lewis Renn.

— How to Start & Manage a Specialty Food Store Business: Step-by-Step Guide to Business Success. (Illus.). 60p. (Orig.). 1994. pap. 9.95 (*1-887005-02-1*) Lewis Renn.

— How to Start & Manage a Travel Agency Business: Step-by-Step Guide to Business Success. (Illus.). 66p. (Orig.). 1994. pap. 9.95 (*0-9628759-8-8*) Lewis Renn.

— How to Start & Manage a Welding Business: Step-by-Step Guide to Business Success. (Illus.). 63p. (Orig.). 1994. pap. 9.95 (*1-887005-03-X*) Lewis Renn.

— How to Start & Manage a Word Processing Service Business: Step by Step Guide to Business Success. (Illus.). 62p. (Orig.). 1994. pap. 9.95 (*0-9628759-4-5*) Lewis Renn.

— How to Start & Manage an Answering Service Business: Step-by-Step Guide to Business Success. (Illus.). 60p. (Orig.). 1994. pap. 9.95 (*0-9628759-9-6*) Lewis Renn.

— How to Start & Manage an Apparel Store Business: Step by Step Guide to Business Success. (Illus.). 61p. (Orig.). 1994. pap. 9.95 (*0-9628759-3-7*) Lewis Renn.

— How to Start & Manage Your Own Business: A Practical Way to Start Your Own Business. LC 91-60125. (Illus.). 104p. (Orig.). 1991. pap. 9.95 (*0-9628759-0-2*) Lewis Renn.

— Top Eighteen Business Guides for the Twentieth Century: Step-by-Step Guides to Business Success. 300p. (Orig.). 1994. pap. 178.10 (*0-9628759-2-9*) Lewis Renn.

***Lewis, Jerry, intro.** Bob Dole: The U. S. Senator Who Was Severely Wounded in WWII. (Great Achievers Ser.). (Illus.). 128p. (YA). (gr. 5 up). 1995. 18.95 (*0-7910-2084-3*) Chelsea Hse.

— Ernest Hemingway: The Writer Who Suffered from Depression. (Great Achievers Ser.). (Illus.). 128p. (YA). (gr. 5 up). 1995. 18.95 (*0-7910-2420-2*) Chelsea Hse.

— Ludwig Van Beethoven: The Composer Who Continued to Write Music after He Became Deaf. (Great Achievers). (Illus.). 128p. (YA). (gr. 5 up). 1995. 18.95 (*0-7910-2082-7*) Chelsea Hse.

— Mary Tyler Moore: The Award-Winning Actress Who Has Diabetes. (Great Achievers Ser.). (Illus.). 128p. (YA). (gr. 5 up). 1995. 18.95 (*0-7910-2416-4*) Chelsea Hse.

— Roy Campanella: The Baseball Star Who Became Paralyzed in a Car Accident. (Great Achievers Ser.). (Illus.). 128p. (YA). (gr. 5 up). 1995. 18.95 (*0-7910-2083-5*) Chelsea Hse.

— Vincent Van Gogh: The Painter Who Suffered from Depression. (Great Achievers Ser.). (Illus.). 128p. (YA). (gr. 5 up). 1995. 18.95 (*0-7910-2423-7*) Chelsea Hse.

Lewis, Jerry A. Wings for the Heart: Montana's Upland Birds & Waterfowl. 352p. 1992. pap. write for info. (*0-9632227-0-8*) W River Pr.

Lewis, Jerry M. The Birth of the Family: An Empirical Inquiry. LC 89-9911. 224p. 1989. 28.95 (*0-87630-550-8*) Brunner-Mazel.

— How's Your Family? A Guide to Identifying Your Family's Strengths & Weaknesses. LC 88-14668. 208p. 1989. pap. 17.50 (*0-87630-537-0*) Brunner-Mazel.

— Swimming Upstream: Teaching & Learning Psychotherapy in a Biological Era. LC 90-2671. 208p. 1991. 28.95 (*0-87630-612-1*) Brunner-Mazel.

Lewis, Jerry M. & Usdin, Gene, eds. Treatment Planning in Psychiatry. LC 82-3985. 453p. reprint ed. pap. 129.20 (*0-8357-7792-8*, 2036153) Bks Demand.

Lewis, Jill. Fascism & the Working Class in Austria Nineteen Eighteen to Nineteen Thirty-Four. 246p. 1991. 58.50 (*0-85496-581-5*) Berg Pubs.

Lewis, Jill, jt. auth. see Joseph, Gloria.

Lewis, Jim. Biblical Favorites. LC 85-50948. 134p. (Orig.). 1985. pap. 7.95 (*0-942482-08-5*) Unity Church Denver.

— The Great Commitment. LC 81-71542. 120p. (Orig.). 1982. pap. 7.50 (*0-942482-03-4*) Unity Church Denver.

— Mystical Teachings of Christianity. 150p. 1980. pap. 7.95 (*0-942482-01-8*) Unity Church Denver.

— Positive Thoughts for Successful Living. LC 80-50277. 138p. (Orig.). 1979. pap. 7.95 (*0-942482-00-X*) Unity Church Denver.

— Real Gone. (Illus.). 56p. 1994. 15.00 (*0-9631095-2-9*) Artspace Bks.

— Reincarnation & Translation. 31p. (Orig.). 1981. pap. 3.00 (*0-942482-02-6*) Unity Church Denver.

— Sister: A Novel. LC 92-34194. 216p. 1993. 20.00 (*1-55597-178-4*) Graywolf.

— Spiritual Gospel. LC 82-51231. 145p. (Orig.). 1982. pap. 8.95 (*0-942482-05-0*) Unity Church Denver.

— The Ten Commandments: Then & Now. LC 84-50912. 95p. (Orig.). 1984. pap. 5.95 (*0-942482-07-7*) Unity Church Denver.

— The Twelve Thrones. LC 83-91008. 85p. (Orig.). 1983. pap. 5.95 (*0-942482-06-9*) Unity Church Denver.

— The Upward Path. LC 82-60277. 150p. (Orig.). 1982. pap. 7.95 (*0-942482-04-2*) Unity Church Denver.

Lewis, Jim & Guttman, Ariel. The Astrocartography Book of Maps: The Astrology of Relocation: How 136 Famous People Found Their Place. LC 89-8070. (Modern Astrology Library). 336p. (Orig.). 1989. pap. 15.95 (*0-87542-434-1*) Llewellyn Pubns.

Lewis, Jim & Lewis, Lorrie. I Am Independent Curriculum Series, Vols. 1-8. (Illus.). 40p. 1993. Sample, 40p. pap. 5.00 (*1-878110-15-2*) Abundant Answers.

— I Am Independent Instructors Guide. (I Am Independent Curriculum Ser.: Vol. 1). (Illus.). 40p. 1991. teacher ed 28.00 (*1-878110-01-2*) Abundant Answers.

— I Am Independent Workbook Series 8 Vols., Vols. 1-8. (Illus.). 530p. 1993. student ed 280.00 (*1-878110-02-0*) Abundant Answers.

— I Can Help Myself. (I Am Independent Curriculum Ser.: Vol. 2). 82p. 1993. student ed 39.95 (*1-878110-03-9*) Abundant Answers.

— I Can Live on My Own. (I Am Independent Curriculum Ser.: Vol. 7). (Illus.). 60p. 1993. student ed 28.00 (*1-878110-08-X*) Abundant Answers.

— I Can Live Safely. (I Am Independent Curriculum Ser.: Vol. 3). 64p. 1992. 28.00 (*1-878110-05-5*) Abundant Answers.

— I Like Learning More. (I Am Independent Curriculum Ser.: Vol. 8). 64p. 1993. student ed 45.00 (*1-878110-09-8*) Abundant Answers.

— I Like to Cook Good Food. (I Am Independent Curriculum Ser.: Vol. 5). 154p. 1991. Incl. wkbk., ckbk. student ed 45.95 (*1-878110-04-7*); Wkbk., 80p. student ed 35.50 (*1-878110-11-X*); Recipe bk., 74p. pap. text ed. 28.00 (*1-878110-10-1*) Abundant Answers.

— I Like Who I Am. (I Am Independent Curriculum Ser.: Vol. 4). (Illus.). 62p. 1991. student ed 37.00 (*1-878110-06-3*) Abundant Answers.

— I Want Money. (I Am Independent Curriculum Ser.: Vol. 6). (Illus.). 128p. 1991. student ed 28.00 (*1-878110-07-1*) Abundant Answers.

Lewis, Joan, jt. auth. see Heymsfield, Carla.

Lewis, Joanna & Luther, Brenda. Gospel Fundamentals for Family Home Evening. 1994. pap. 7.95 (*0-88494-928-1*) Bookcraft Inc.

— Primarily Speaking, Vol. 4: Learning Activities on the Missions of the Church. 1991. pap. 7.95 (0-88494-815-3) Bookcraft Inc.

Lewis, Joanna, jt. auth. see Wise, Gayla.

Lewis, Joe. The World-Peacemaker. 1983. pap. 2.95 (0-87505-329-7) Borden.

Lewis, Joe O. Layman's Bible Book Commentary: First & Second Samuel & First Chronicles, Vol. 5. LC 79-54796. 1991. 8.99 (0-8054-1175-5) Broadman.

***Lewis, Johanna M.** Artisans in the North Carolina Backcountry. (Illus.). 240p. 1995. text ed. 34.95 (0-8131-1908-1) U Pr of Ky.

Lewis, John. The History of the Life & Sufferings of the Revered & Learned John Wiclif, D. D. LC 74-178543. reprint ed. 39.50 (0-404-56625-1) AMS Pr.

— Marxism & the Irrationalists. LC 72-6687. 141p. 1973. reprint ed. text ed. 49.75 (0-8371-6494-X, LEMB, Greenwood Pr) Greenwood.

— Marxism & the Open Mind. 222p. 1957. 32.95 (0-87855-032-1) Transaction Pubs.

— Printed Ephemera. (Illus.). 288p. 1990. 69.50 (1-85149-116-3) Antique Collect.

— Rowland Hilder: Painter of the English Landscape. (Illus.). 176p. 1987. 49.50 (1-85149-050-7) Antique Collect.

— So Your Doctor Recommended Surgery. LC 89-27825. 1990. 22.50 (0-942637-20-8, Dembner NY) Barricade Bks.

Lewis, John, et al. Success & Failure in Small Business. LC 83-16447. 304p. 1984. text ed. 58.95 (0-566-00645-6) Ashgate Pub Co.

Lewis, John. A Taste for Sailing. 240p. 1994. 48.00 (0-86138-077-0, Pub. by T Dalton UK) St Mut.

Lewis, John, ed. Eat No Evil Cookbook: There Is No Such Thing As a Bad, Evil or Forbidden Food! (Illus.). 1991. text ed. 18.95 (0-685-46316-8) New Outlook.

Lewis, John & Lewis, Griselda. Pratt Ware: English & Scottish Relief Decorated & Underglaze Coloured Earthenware, 1780-1840. (Illus.). 514p. 1993. 89.50 (1-85149-191-0) Antique Collect.

— Pratt Ware (Album 296) (C). 1989. pap. 25.00x (0-7478-0220-3, Pub. by Shire UK) St Mut.

Lewis, John & Shreeves, Karl. Decompression Theory, Dive Tables & Dive Computers. Talley, Tonya, ed. (Illus.). 100p. (Orig.). (C). 1990. pap. text ed. 14.95 (1-878663-06-2) PADI.

Lewis, John, jt. auth. see Green, David R.

Lewis, John, ed. see Sundermeyer, Velma & Sundermeyer, Colleen.

Lewis, John, jt. auth. see Walker, Lydia.

Lewis, John, et al, eds. Christianity & the Social Revolution. LC 79-37892. (Select Bibliographies Reprint Ser.). 1977. reprint ed. 27.95 (0-8369-6729-1) Ayer.

Lewis, John B. Analysis of Linear Dynamic Systems. (Illus.). 880p. 1977. 59.95 (0-916460-20-7, Matrix Pubs Inc) Weber Systems.

***Lewis, John F. & Hartings, Susan C.** Sexual Harassment in Education. 2nd ed. 57p. (Orig.). 1994. pap. 21.95 (1-56534-064-7) NOLPE.

Lewis, John F., et al. Drug & Alcohol Abuse in Schools: A Practical Guide for Administrators & Educators for Combatting Drug & Alcohol Abuse. 2nd ed. 40p. 1992. pap. 12.95 (1-56534-050-7) NOLPE.

— Sexual Harassment in Education. 50p. (Orig.). 1993. pap. 19.95 (1-56534-057-4) NOLPE.

Lewis, John G., jt. auth. see Miller, Virginia L.

Lewis, John G., ed. see SIAM Conference on Applied Linear Algebra Staff.

Lewis, John H. Recollections from 1860-1865. 92p. 1983. 17.50 (0-89029-074-1) Morningside Bkshop.

***Lewis, John L. & Murray, Margaret A. M.** The Method of Layer Potentials for the Heat Equation in Time-Varying Domains. LC 94-43211. (Memoirs Ser.: Vol. 545). 1995. write for info. (0-8218-0360-3) Am Math.

Lewis, John M. & Deiros, Pablo A. La Revelacion e Inspiracion de las Escrituras. (Biblioteca de Doctrina Cristiana Ser.). 162p. (SPA.). 1986. pap. 5.25 (0-311-09113-X) Casa Bautista.

Lewis, John M. & Fontrier, Tionette H. Near Misses in Anesthesia. 112p. 1988. pap. 29.95 (0-409-90111-3) Buttrwrth-Heinemann.

Lewis, John P. Asian Development: The Role of Development Assistance. (Asian Agenda Report Ser.: No. 7). (Illus.). 66p. (Orig.). 1987. pap. text ed. 8.50 (0-8191-6590-5, The Asia Society) U Pr of Amer.

— India's Political Economy: Governance & Reform. 416p. 1995. text ed. 35.00 (0-19-563515-9) OUP.

— Pro-Poor Aid Conditionality. LC 93-19137. (Policy Essay Ser.: No. 8). 72p. (C). 1993. pap. 9.95 (1-56517-009-1) Overseas Dev Council.

— Strengthening the Poor: What Have We Learned? Feinberg, Richard E. & Kallab, Valerina, eds. (U. S. Third World Policy Perspective Ser.: No. 10). 1988. 32.95 (0-88738-267-3); pap. 17.95 (0-88738-768-3) Transaction Pubs.

Lewis, John P., ed. Development Strategies: A New Synthesis. (U. S. Third World Policy Perspectives Ser.). 128p. 1985. 32.95 (0-88738-044-1); pap. 17.95 (0-87855-991-4) Transaction Pubs.

Lewis, John P. & Kallab, Valeriana, eds. U. S. Foreign Policy & the Third World: Agenda 1983. LC 83-3373. 304p. 1983. text ed. 65.00 (0-275-91034-2, C1034, Praeger Pubs) Greenwood.

Lewis, John R. Atlas of Aesthetic Plastic Surgery. (Illus.). 1973. 62.00 (0-316-52335-6) Little.

— Dragons Are Lonely. LC 93-12977. (Illus.). 32p. (J). (gr. 1-3). 1993. 14.95 (0-87797-239-7) Cherokee.

— Small Town & Other American Poems. LC 76-20235. 80p. 1976. 12.95 (0-87797-124-2) Cherokee.

***Lewis, John S., ed.** Physics & Chemistry of the Solar System. (Illus.). 556p. 1995. boxed 149.00 (0-12-446740-7) Acad Pr.

— Physics & Chemistry of the Solar System. (Illus.). 556p. 1995. pap. 69.95 (0-12-446741-5) Acad Pr.

Lewis, John S. & Lewis, Ruth A. Space Resources: Breaking the Bonds of the Earth. LC 86-32677. (Illus.). 384p. 1987. text ed. 53.00 (0-231-06498-5) Col U Pr.

Lewis, John S. & Primm, Ronald G. Planets & Their Atmospheres: Origin & Evolution (Monograph) LC 83-10001. (International Geophysics Ser.). 1983. pap. text ed. 65.00 (0-12-446582-X) Acad Pr.

Lewis, John S., et al. Resources of Near-Earth Space. LC 93-23753. (Space Science Ser.). (Illus.). 990p. 1993. 75.00 (0-8165-1404-6) U of Ariz Pr.

Lewis, John W. Leadership in Communist China. LC 77-25475. (Illus.). 305p. 1978. reprint ed. text ed. 59.75 (0-313-20119-6, LELC, Greenwood Pr) Greenwood.

— Political Networks & the Chinese Policy Process. (Occasional Paper of the Northeast Asia-United States Forum on International Policy, Stanford University). 32p. (Orig.). pap. 6.00 (0-935371-15-X) CFISAC.

Lewis, John W., ed. The City in Communist China. LC 78-130828. 120p. reprint ed. pap. 30.00 (0-8357-4633-X, 2037562) Bks Demand.

— Party Leadership & Revolutionary Power in China. LC 72-120056. (Contemporary China Institute Publications). 430p. reprint ed. pap. 122.60 (0-685-16006-8, 2027229) Bks Demand.

— Peasant Rebellion & Communist Revolution in Asia. LC 73-89860. xvi, 364p. 1974. 47.50 (0-8047-0856-8); pap. 15.95 (0-8047-0924-6) Stanford U Pr.

Lewis, John W. & Blacker, Coit D., eds. Next Steps on the Creation of an Accidental Nuclear War Prevention Center. (Special Report of the Center for International Security & Arms Control, Stanford University Ser.). 45p. (Orig.). 1983. pap. 8.00 (0-935371-07-9) CFISAC.

Lewis, John W. & Litai, Xue. China Builds the Bomb. LC 87-30404. (ISIS Studies in International Security & Arms Control: Vol. 3). (Illus.). 352p. 1988. 45.00 (0-8047-1452-5); pap. 14.95 (0-8047-1841-5) Stanford U Pr.

— China's Strategic Seapower: The Politics of Force Modernization in the Nuclear Age. LC 94-11688. (Studies in International Security & Arms Control). 1994. 45.00 (0-8047-2303-6) Stanford U Pr.

Lewis, John W., jt. auth. see Cowan, Alan.

Lewis, JoLinda & Lewis, Danny. Discover the Apocrypha. 25p. 1972. 3.95 (0-932807-02-X) Overmountain Pr.

Lewis, Jon. Industrialization & Trade Union Organisation in South Africa, 1924-1955: The Rise & Fall of the South African Trades & Labour Council. (African Studies: No. 42). (Illus.). 256p. 1985. 64.95 (0-521-26312-3) Cambridge U Pr.

— The Road to Romance & Ruin: Teen Films & Youth Culture. 1992. 45.00 (0-415-90426-9, A5772, Routledge NY); pap. 14.95 (0-415-90427-7, A5776, Routledge NY) Routledge.

— Whom God Wishes to Destroy... Francis Coppola & the New Hollywood. (Illus.). 216p. 1995. 23.95 (0-8223-1602-1) Duke.

Lewis, Jon, ed. Permanent Book of Twentieth Century Eyewitness History: An Enthralling Kaleidoscope of the Great Moments of Our Century. (Illus.). 512p. 1995. pap. 11.95 (0-7867-0161-7) Carroll & Graf.

Lewis, Jon, ed. see Sundermeyer, Colleen A.

Lewis, Jon E. D-Day: Eyewitness Accounts of the Battle of Normandy. 352p. 1994. pap. 11.95 (0-7867-0090-4) Carroll & Graf.

Lewis, Jon E., ed. The Mammoth Book of Modern War Stories. 544p. 1993. pap. 9.95 (0-88184-958-8) Carroll & Graf.

— The Mammoth Book of the Western. 576p. 1991. pap. 9.95 (0-88184-791-7) Carroll & Graf.

— The Mammoth Book of True War Stories. 544p. 1992. pap. 9.95 (0-88184-756-9) Carroll & Graf.

Lewis, Jon E. & Stempel, Penny. Cult TV: The Essential Critical Guide. (Illus.). 256p. 1994. pap. 19.95 (1-85793-053-3, Pub. by Pavilion UK) Trafalgar.

Lewis, Jonatan. Mision Mundial (World Mission), 3 vols., Set. (SPA.). Date not set. 16.99 (0-685-74961-4, 498481) Editorial Unilit.

— Mision Mundial (World Mission), Vol. I. (SPA.). 1990. 5.99 (1-56063-065-5, 498478) Editorial Unilit.

— Mision Mundial (World Mission), Vol. II. (SPA.). 1990. 5.99 (1-56063-066-3, 498479) Editorial Unilit.

— Mision Mundial (World Mission), Vol. III. (SPA.). 1990. 5.99 (1-56063-067-1, 498480) Editorial Unilit.

Lewis, Jonathan. Stalin: A Time for Judgement. 1990. 22.45 (0-394-58058-3) Pantheon.

Lewis, Jonathan D., jt. auth. see Muslin, Hyman L.

Lewis-Jones, Robert & Winkler, Michael. Sludge Parasites & Other Pathogens: Health Risks from Sewage. 240p. 1991. text ed. 32.00 (0-13-963703-6) P-H.

Lewis, Jordan D. Partnership for Profit: Structuring & Managing Strategic Alliances. 1990. 32.95 (0-02-919050-9) Free Pr.

Lewis, Joseph. Atheism & Other Addresses. LC 72-161333. (Atheist Viewpoint Ser.). (Illus.). 510p. 1972. reprint ed. 35.95 (0-405-03800-3) Ayer.

— The Bible Unmasked. 1991. lib. bdg. 69.95 (0-8490-4272-0) Gordon Pr.

— The Bible Unmasked. 236p. 1975. reprint ed. spiral bd. 6.60 (0-7873-0557-X) Mokelumne.

— The Bible Unmasked, Vol. I. 122p. 1990. pap. text ed. 13.00 (0-916157-37-7) African Islam Miss Pubns.

— The Bible Unmasked, Vol. II. 120p. 1990. pap. text ed. 13.00 (0-916157-38-5) African Islam Miss Pubns.

— Ingersoll the Magnificent. (Illus.). 342p. (C). 1985. reprint ed. pap. 10.00 (0-910309-12-4, 5216) Am Atheist.

— Spain: A Land Blighted by Religion. (Illus.). 96p. (C). reprint ed. write for info. (0-318-70299-1) Hakims Pubs.

— Spain: A Land Blighted by Religion. (Illus.). 96p. (C). 1993. reprint ed. pap. 5.95 (0-317-05574-7) Hakims Pubs.

Lewis, Judith, jt. ed. see Carlson, Jon.

Lewis, Judith A., ed. Addictions: Concepts & Strategies for Treatment. LC 94-9159. 393p. 1994. 49.00 (0-8342-0563-7) Aspen Pub.

***Lewis, Judith A. & Bernstein, Judith.** Health of Women: A Relational Perspective. (Nursing Ser.). Date not set. 45.00 (0-86720-485-0) Jones & Bartlett.

Lewis, Judith A. & Lewis, Michael D. Community Counseling. (Counseling, Human Services Ser.). 300p. (C). 1990. text ed. 38.95 (0-534-10248-4) Brooks-Cole.

Lewis, Judith A., et al. Counseling Women over the Life Span. LC 91-77048. 307p. 1992. pap. 29.95 (0-89108-222-0, 9203) Love Pub Co.

— Health Counseling. LC 92-37322. 1993. text ed. 38.95 (0-534-13446-7) Brooks-Cole.

— Substance Abuse Counseling: An Individualized Approach. LC 87-24618. 281p. (C). 1987. text ed. 35.95 (0-534-08448-6) Brooks-Cole.

— Substance Abuse Counseling: An Individualized Approach. 2nd ed. LC 93-8054. 1994. text ed. 43.95 (0-534-20053-2) Brooks-Cole.

Lewis, Judith S. In the Family Way: Childbearing in the British Aristocracy, 1760-1860. 270p. (C). 1986. text ed. 40.00 (0-8135-1116-X) Rutgers U Pr.

Lewis, Judy. Heart Beats & Soul Sounds. LC 93-93718. (Illus.). 112p. (Orig.). 1993. pap. 8.95 (0-9639332-0-5) Swamp Pond.

— Uncommon Knowledge. Grose, Bill, ed. 448p. 1994. 23.00 (0-671-70019-7) PB.

Lewis, Judy & Williams, Janice. NMS Introduction to Clinical Medicine. (National Medical Ser.). 260p. 1991. 24.00 (0-683-06212-3) Williams & Wilkins.

Lewis, Judy & Yarbrough, Jane. California People & Places. (Illus.). 32p. (J). (gr. 4). 1991. 260.00 (1-879748-01-0) Calif Perf Prods.

Lewis, Julie. Olga Masters: A Lot of Living. 1991. pap. 22.95 (0-7022-2387-5, Pub. by Univ Queensland Pr AT) Intl Spec Bk.

Lewis, June R. The Cotswolds at War. (Illus.). 288p. 1993. text ed. 30.00 (0-7509-0048-2) A Sutton Pub.

Lewis, Justin. Art, Culture & Enterprise. 196p. 1990. 52.00 (0-415-04449-9, A4234); pap. 14.95 (0-415-04450-2, A4238) Routledge.

— The Ideological Octopus. (Studies in Culture & Communication). 192p. 1991. 45.00 (0-415-90287-8, A4287, Routledge NY); pap. 13.95 (0-415-90288-6, A4291, Routledge NY) Routledge.

Lewis, Justin, jt. ed. see Cruz, Jon.

Lewis, Justin, jt. auth. see Jhally, Sut.

Lewis, K. E., jt. ed. see Limbaugh, R. H.

Lewis, K. R., jt. ed. see Riley, Ralph.

Lewis-Kane, Melody, et al. Arts Mentor Program: A Manual for Sponsors. 58p. 1986. 4.50 (0-910883-16-5, 127) Natl Coun Aging.

Lewis, Karen. From Arapesh to Zuni: A Book of Bibleless Peoples. (Illus.). 31p. 1986. pap. text ed. 4.95 (0-938978-07-1) Wycliffe Bible.

Lewis, Karen & Hathersmith, June. Harvest of Trust. (Illus.). 200p. (Orig.). 1989. pap. write for info. (0-938978-12-8) Wycliffe Bible.

Lewis, Karen G., intro. Variations on Teaching & Supervising Group Therapy. LC 89-19970. (Journal of Independent Social Work: Vol. 3, No. 4). (Illus.). 151p. 1989. text ed. 29.95 (0-86656-921-9) Haworth Pr.

Lewis, Karen G., jt. ed. see Kahn, Michael D.

Lewis, Karen Gail, ed. Family Systems Application to Social Work: Training & Clinical Practice. LC 91-26307. (Journal of Independent Social Work). 217p. 1991. pap. text ed. 14.95 (1-56024-194-2) Haworth Pr.

— Family Systems Application to Social Work: Training & Clinical Practice. LC 91-26307. (Journal of Independent Social Work). 217p. 1992. lib. bdg. 39.95 (1-56024-191-8) Haworth Pr.

Lewis, Karen W., tr. see Yasuoka, Shotaro.

Lewis, Karron G., ed. Face to Face: A Source Book of Individual Consultation Techniques for Faculty-Instructional Developers. 253p. (Orig.). 1988. pap. 10.95 (0-913507-08-3) New Forums.

Lewis, Kathryn, ed. see Evans-Tiller, Jan.

Lewis, Kathryn Roots, jt. auth. see Hefner, Christine Roots.

Lewis, Kathryn T. & Hefner, Christine R., eds. Investment Statistics Locator, Revised and Expanded. expanded rev. ed. LC 94-39014. 304p. 1995. 69.95 (0-89774-781-X) Oryx Pr.

Lewis, Kathy. Chatty Cathy Dolls. 1994. pap. 15.95 (0-89145-579-5) Collector Bks.

Lewis, Kathy A. Ancestors & Descendants of the Lewis & Sutton Families of Todd County, Minnesota. LC 92-71811. (Illus.). 247p. 1992. lib. bdg. write for info. (0-9620135-2-8) K A Lewis.

— The Norwegian Roots of the Sonsteby Family. LC 94-75407. (Illus.). 76p. 1994. lib. bdg. write for info. (0-9620135-3-6) K A Lewis.

Lewis, Kathy A. & Sonsteby, Georgine B. From Norway to the Klondike: The Adventurous & Independent Life of Georgine B. Sonsteby. LC 88-91021. (Illus.). 94p. (Orig.). 1988. 17.95 (0-9620135-0-1); pap. 12.95 (0-9620135-1-X) K A Lewis.

Lewis, Keeta & Thomson, Helen. Manual of School Health. (Illus.). 266p. (C). 1986. pap. text ed. 32.25 (0-201-15292-4, Health Sci) Addison-Wesley.

***Lewis, Keeta D.** Infants & Children with Prenatal Alcohol & Drug Exposure: A Guide to Identification & Intervention. LC 94-47669. 1995. 44.95 (0-9624814-2-4) Sunrise River Pr.

Lewis, Kenneth, jt. auth. see John, Bernard.

Lewis, Kenneth B. Steel Wire in America. 2nd ed. 1989. 30.00 (0-685-26880-2) Wire Assn Intl.

Lewis, Kenneth E. The American Frontier: An Archaeological Study of Settlement Pattern & Process. LC 83-19725. (Studies in Historical Archaeology). 1984. text ed. 68.00 (0-12-446560-9) Acad Pr.

Lewis, Kenneth H. & Bass, Joe R. Fiber Optic Fundamentals. (ABC of the Telephone Ser.: Vol. 17). (Illus.). 120p. 1991. pap. 24.95 (1-56016-044-6) ABC TeleTraining.

Lewis, Kenrich M. & Rethwisch, David G., eds. Catalyzed Direct Reactions of Silicon. LC 93-34294. (Studies in Organic Chemistry: No. 49). 1993. write for info. (0-444-81715-8) Elsevier.

Lewis, Kevin. Crown House Collection, Vol. 1: The Printed Calicos of Manchester. (Illus.). 70p. 1990. boxed write for info. (1-872669-00-X) Crown House.

— Crown House Collection, Vol. 2: Fleurs de France, Weaves, Prints & Original Designs, 1860-1905. (Illus.). 85p. 1991. boxed write for info. (1-872669-01-8) Crown House.

Lewis, Kevin, jt. auth. see Samples, Kenneth.

Lewis, Kevin M. Standards-Based Procurement. 31p. (Orig.). 1993. pap. 10.00 (0-936593-19-9) UniForum.

***Lewis, Kevin N.** Downsizing Future USAF Fighter Forces: Living Within the Constraints of History. LC 94-48047. 130p. 1995. pap. text ed. 15.00 (0-8330-1621-0) Rand Corp.

— Planning Future U. S. Fighting Forces. LC 93-23131. 1993. write for info. (0-8330-1416-1, MR-285) Rand Corp.

Lewis, Kim. Emma's Lamb. LC 90-3863. (Illus.). 32p. (J). (ps-1). 1991. text ed. 13.95 (0-02-758821-1, Four Winds Pr) S&S Childrens.

— First Snow. LC 92-54413. (Illus.). 32p. (J). (ps up). 1993. 14.95 (1-56402-194-7) Candlewick Pr.

— Floss. LC 91-71853. (Illus.). 32p. (J). (ps up). 1992. 14.95 (1-56402-010-X) Candlewick Pr.

— Floss. LC 91-71853. 32p. (J). (ps up). 1994. pap. 4.99 (1-56402-271-4) Candlewick Pr.

— The Last Train. LC 93-32370. (Illus.). 32p. (J). (ps up). 1994. 14.95 (1-56402-343-5) Candlewick Pr.

— My Friend Harry. 1995. write for info. (1-56402-617-5) Candlewick Pr.

— The Shepherd Boy. LC 89-23679. (Illus.). 32p. (J). (ps-1). 1990. text ed. 13.95 (0-02-758581-6, Four Winds Pr) S&S Childrens.

***Lewis, Klara K.** Adventures of Mr. Lewis in Russia: A Ten Act Situational Play. (In the Shoes of the Traveler Ser.). (Illus.). (Orig.). (RUS.). 1995. pap. 11.95 (1-886821-08-9); audio, pap. 24.99 (1-886821-09-7); pap. text ed. 11.95 (1-886821-21-6) Pavleen.

— In the Shoes of the Traveler. (Illus.). (Orig.). (RUS.). 1995. pap. 69.95 (0-614-03664-X); audio, pap. 129.95 (1-886821-15-1); audio, pap. text ed. 129.95 (1-886821-16-X) Pavleen.

— In the Shoes of the Traveler: Russian Language, Culture, Way of Life, 7 bks., Set. (In the Shoes of the Traveler Ser.). (Illus.). (Orig.). (RUS.). 1995. pap. 69.95 (1-886821-14-3) Pavleen.

— In the Shoes of the Traveler, Situational Russian Pt. I: Meeting People, Packing & Customs, at a Hotel, Shopping, at a Restaurant. (In the Shoes of the Traveler Ser.). (Illus.). (Orig.). (RUS.). 1995. pap. 15.95 (1-886821-04-6); audio, pap. 29.95 (1-886821-05-4); pap. text ed. 15.95 (1-886821-19-4) Pavleen.

— In the Shoes of the Traveler, Situational Russian Pt. II: In a City Using Transportation, at the Post Office, Talking on the Telephone, at a Bank, at a Doctor's Office, When Things Go Wrong, Visiting Russian Friends & Toasting. (In the Shoes of the Traveler Ser.). (Illus.). (Orig.). (RUS.). 1995. pap. 15.95 (1-886821-06-2); audio, pap. 29.95 (1-886821-07-0); pap. text ed. 15.95 (1-886821-20-8) Pavleen.

— Russian Culture Keys. 2nd ed. (In the Shoes of the Traveler Ser.). 1995. audio 16.95 (1-886821-13-5) Pavleen.

— Russian Instant Help Cards: Everyday Expressions, Frequently Asked Questions, Gratitude, Apology, Agreement, Refusal, Regret, Congratulations & Good Wishes, Requests, Wants & Needs, Compliments, Toasts. (In the Shoes of the Traveler Ser.). (Illus.). (Orig.). (RUS.). 1995. pap. 9.95 (1-886821-10-0); audio, pap. 19.99 (1-886821-11-9) Pavleen.

— Russian Picture Alphabet. (In the Shoes of the Traveler Ser.). (Illus.). (Orig.). (RUS.). 1995. pap. 9.95 (1-886821-00-3); audio, pap. 17.95 (1-886821-01-1); pap. text ed. 9.95 (1-886821-18-6) Pavleen.

— Russian Picture Dictionary: Things Around Me, Colors, Numbers, Pronouns, Professions, Days of the Week, Family, Fruits, Vegetables, Groceries, Parts of the Body, Weather, Clothing, Living Room, Kitchen, Bedroom, Office, Questions, Animals, Verbs, Time, Etc. (In the Shoes of the Traveler Ser.). (Illus.). (Orig.). (RUS.). 1995. pap. 16.95 (1-886821-02-X); audio, pap. 27.95 (1-886821-03-8); pap. text ed. 16.95 (1-886821-17-8) Pavleen.

— Russian Restaurant Menu: Food & Drink Guide for Breakfast, Lunch & Dinner. (In the Shoes of the Traveler Ser.). (Illus.). (Orig.). (RUS.). 1995. pap. 6.95 (1-886821-12-7) Pavleen.

Lewis, L. Employee Selection. (C). 1989. 110.00 (0-09-158271-7, Pub. by S Thornes Pubs UK) St Mut.

Lewis, L., ed. Electrical Installation Technology No. One: Theory & Regulations. (C). 1989. 110.00 (0-7487-0272-5, Pub. by S Thornes Pubs UK) St Mut.

Lewis, L. A. & Berry, L. African Environments & Resources. (Illus.). 352p. 1988. 49.95 (0-04-916010-9); pap. 19.95 (0-04-916011-7) Routledge Chapman & Hall.

An Asterisk (*) at the beginning of an entry indicates that the title is appearing in BIP for the first time.

Lewis, L. A. & Opplt, J. J., eds. Handbook of Electrophoresis, CRC, 3 vols., III. 1983. 173.95 (*0-8493-0573-X*, CRC Reprint) Franklin.
— Handbook of Electrophoresis, CRC, 3 vols., IV. 1983. 152.95 (*0-8493-0574-8*, CRC Reprint) Franklin.
— Handbook of Electrophoresis, CRC, 3 vols., Vol. 1: Basic Principles & Concepts. 336p. 1983. Lipoproteins: Basic Principles & Concepts, Vol. 1, 336 Pgs. 113.95 (*0-8493-0571-3*, QD117, CRC Reprint) Franklin.
— Handbook of Electrophoresis, CRC, 3 vols., Vol. 2: Lipoproteins in Disease. 400p. 1983. Lipoproteins In Disease, Vol. 2, 400 Pgs. 113.95 (*0-8493-0572-1*, CRC Reprint) Franklin.
Lewis, L. G., et al. Equivariant Stable Homotopy Theory. (Lecture Notes in Mathematics Ser.: Vol. 1213). ix, 538p. 1986. pap. 66.50 (*0-387-16820-6*) Spr-Verlag.
Lewis, L. J. Society, Schools & Progress in Nigeria. 1965. 76.00 (*0-08-011340-0*, Pub. by Pergamon Repr UK) Franklin.
Lewis, La Vaughn G., jt. ed. see Stedman, W. David.
Lewis, Larry, jt. auth. see Smyth, Vera G.
Lewis, Larry L. The Church Planter's Handbook. LC 92-25513. 1992. 8.99 (*0-8054-6068-3*) Broadman.
— Organizar para Evangelizar - Organize to Evangelize: Manual para el Crecimiento de la Iglesia - A Manual for Church Growth. Smith, Josie, tr. 112p. (Orig.). (SPA.). 1992. pap. 2.40 (*0-311-13857-8*) Casa Bautista.
— Organize to Evangelize. (Orig.). 1991. pap. 6.99 (*0-8054-6257-0*) Broadman.
Lewis, Laura. 52 Ways to Live a Long & Healthy Life. Moyer, Ann & Towle, Mike, eds. 300p. (Orig.). 1993. pap. 8.95 (*1-56530-066-1*) Summit TX.
Lewis, Laurel, jt. auth. see Nestingen, Signe L.
Lewis, Laurence A., jt. auth. see Johnson, Douglas L.
Lewis, Lee A. The Trouble with Dreams. LC 91-27503. 160p. (Orig.). (J). (gr. 4-7). 1991. pap. 5.95 (*0-8361-3571-7*) Herald Pr.
Lewis, Leland. The Baja Sea Guide. LC 85-173041. (Sea Guide Ser.). (Illus.). 368p. Date not set. reprint ed. 37.50 (*0-688-04314-3*, Hearst Marine Bks) Morrow.
Lewis, Lennox & Steeples, Joe. Lennox Lewis: The Autobiography of the WBC Heavyweight Champion of the World. (Illus.). 208p. 1994. 22.95 (*0-571-17191-5*); pap. 14.95 (*0-571-19844-9*) Faber & Faber.
Lewis, Lesle, ed. see Longacre, Celeste.
Lewis, Lesley. The Private Life of a Country House. (Illus.). 192p. 1992. 30.00 (*0-7509-0080-6*) A Sutton Pub.
— The Private Life of a Country House, 1912-1939. 2nd large type ed. (Illus.). 237p. 1993. 24.95 (*1-85695-001-8*, Pub. by ISIS UK) Transaction Pubs.
***Lewis, Leslie.** Curing Conflict. 192p. 1994. pap. 45.00 (*0-273-60559-3*, Pub. by Pitman Pubng UK) St Mut.
***Lewis, Leslie, et al.** Analytic Architecture for Joint Staff Decision Support. LC 95-1950. (MR-511-JS Ser.). (Illus.). 68p. 1995. pap. text ed. 13.00 (*0-8330-1623-7*) Rand Corp.
— The United States Special Operations Command Resource Management Process: An Application of the Strategy-to-Tasks Framework. LC 94-17803. 1994. write for info. (*0-8330-1557-5*, MR445ASOCOM) Rand Corp.
Lewis, Leslie L., ed. Poems by Favorite Poets in Large Print. large type ed. (General Ser.). 375p. 1992. text ed. 21.95 (*0-8161-5029-X*) G K Hall.
Lewis, Leslie L., jt. auth. see Altenbernd, Lynn.
Lewis, Linda. All for the Love of That Boy. 224p. (J). (gr. 7-9). 1989. pap. 2.95 (*0-671-68243-1*, Archway) PB.
— Dedicated to That Boy I Love. (Linda Story Ser.). 168p. (J). (gr. 6-9). 1990. pap. 2.75 (*0-671-68244-X*, Archway) PB.
— Honeymoon Suite. 1995. mass mkt. 2.99 (*0-373-19113-8*, 1-19113-9) Silhouette.
— Is There Life after Boys? 165p. (YA). (gr. 5-7). 1990. pap. 2.95 (*0-671-69559-2*, Archway) PB.
— Loving Two Is Hard to Do. 160p. (J). (gr. 6-9). 1990. pap. 2.95 (*0-671-70587-3*, Archway) PB.
— Pre-Teen Means Inbetween. MacDonald, Pat, ed. 160p. (Orig.). (J). (gr. 3-6). 1993. pap. 2.99 (*0-671-74535-2*, Minstrel Bks) PB.
— Two Young Two Go Four Boys. (J). (gr. 2-5). 1990. pap. 2.75 (*0-671-69560-6*, Archway) PB.
— The Ultimate Dessert Book. (Illus.). Date not set. 12.95 (*0-394-41276-1*) Random.
— Water's Edge: Women Who Push the Limits in Rowing, Kayaking & Canoeing. LC 92-4361. (Illus.). 288p. (Orig.). 1992. pap. 14.95 (*1-878067-18-4*) Seal Pr Feminist.
— We Hate Everything but Boys. (J). (gr. 5-7). 1990. pap. 2.99 (*0-671-72225-5*, Archway) PB.
— We Love only Older Boys. 176p. (Orig.). (YA). (gr. 7 up). 1990. pap. 2.95 (*0-671-69558-4*, Archway) PB.
Lewis, Linda H., ed. Addressing the Needs of Returning Women. LC 85-644750. (New Directions for Continuing Education Ser.: No. ACE 39). 1988. 16.95 (*1-55542-880-0*) Jossey-Bass.
Lewis, Linda L., jt. ed. see Dan, Alice J.
Lewis, Linda M. The Promethean Politics of Milton, Blake, & Shelley. (Illus.). 240p. (C). 1992. text ed. 34.95 (*0-8262-0805-3*) U of Mo Pr.
Lewis, Lionel S. The Cold War & Academic Governance: The Lattimore Case at Johns Hopkins. LC 92-24053. (SUNY Series, Frontiers in Education). 318p. (C). 1993. 59.50 (*0-7914-1493-0*); pap. 19.95 (*0-7914-1494-9*) State U NY Pr.
— Cold War on Campus: A Study of the Politics of Organizational Control. 314p. 1987. 37.95x (*0-88738-178-2*) Transaction Pubs.
Lewis, Lionel S. & Lewis, E. Ridley. The Life & Teaching of Jesus Christ: According to the Synoptic Gospels. (London Divinity Ser.). 160p. 1977. reprint ed. 6.50 (*0-227-67401-4*) Attic Pr.
Lewis, Lionel S., jt. ed. see Kingston, Paul W.
Lewis, Lisa. The Unbeliever. LC 94-10661. (Brittingham Prize in Poetry Ser.). 72p. (C). 1994. text ed. 17.95 (*0-299-14400-3*); pap. 10.95 (*0-299-14404-6*) U of Wis Pr.
Lewis, Lisa, ed. see Kipling, Rudyard.
Lewis, Lisa, jt. auth. see Lewis, Dallas.
Lewis, Lisa A. The Adoring Audience: Fan Culture & Popular Media. 272p. 1992. 49.95 (*0-04-445572-0*, A8162); pap. 15.95 (*0-04-445573-9*, A8187) Routledge Chapman & Hall.
— Gender Politics & MTV: Voicing the Difference. (Illus.). 248p. 1990. 39.95 (*0-87722-693-8*) Temple U Pr.
— Gender Politics & MTV: Voicing the Difference. 1992. pap. 18.95 (*0-87722-942-2*) Temple U Pr.
Lewis, Lisa A., ed. The Adoring Audience: Fan Culture & Popular Media. LC 91-37332. 256p. 1992. 55.00 (*0-415-07820-2*, A8162); pap. 16.95 (*0-415-07821-0*, A8187) Routledge.
Lewis, Lisa M., jt. auth. see Lewis, Dallas.
Lewis, Lloyd. The Assassination of Lincoln: History & Myth. xviii, 367p. 1994. pap. 12.95 (*0-8032-7949-3*, Bison Books) U of Nebr Pr.
— Captain Sam Grant, 1822-1861. 1991. pap. 13.95 (*0-316-52348-8*) Little.
— It Takes All Kinds. LC 70-117328. (Biography Index Reprint Ser.). 1977. 25.95 (*0-8369-8020-4*) Ayer.
— Myths After Lincoln. 11.25 (*0-8446-4023-9*) Peter Smith.
— Sherman: Fighting Prophet. (Civil War Ser.). 690p. 1993. 12.95 (*0-914427-78-4*) W S Konecky Assocs.
— Sherman: Fighting Prophet. LC 93-11132. (Illus.). xxi, 720p. 1993. reprint ed. pap. 20.00 (*0-8032-7945-0*, Bison Books) U of Nebr Pr.
— Sherman Fighting Prophet. 1994. 12.98 (*0-8317-3287-3*) Smithmark.
Lewis, Lloyd & Smith, Henry J. Oscar Wilde Discovers America, Eighteen Eighty-Two. LC 67-12459. (Illus.). 1972. reprint ed. 24.95 (*0-405-08746-2*) Ayer.
Lewis, Lloyd B. The Tainted War: Culture & Identity in Vietnam War Narratives. LC 84-27929. (Contributions in Military History Ser.: No. 44). xvi, 193p. 1985. text ed. 49.95 (*0-313-23723-9*, LVW/, Greenwood Pr) Greenwood.
Lewis, Loel, ed. Bluestones & Salt Hay: An Anthology of New Jersey Poets. LC 89-36067. 210p. (Orig.). 1990. text ed. 35.00 (*0-8135-1485-1*); pap. 11.95 (*0-8135-1486-X*) Rutgers U Pr.
Lewis, Loida N. How the Filipino Veteran of World War II Can Become a U. S. Citizen (According to the Immigration Act of 1990) LC 91-72022. 155p. 1991. pap. 19.95 (*0-9629516-0-9*) FR Pubns.
— One Hundred One Legal Ways to Stay in the U. S. A.: or How to Get a Green Card According to the Immigration Act of 1990, Bk. 1. Eakin, Sybil et al, eds. LC 91-77185. 308p. (Orig.). 1992. pap. 19.95 (*1-880808-00-5*) Bookmark NY.
— One Hundred One Legal Ways to Stay in the U. S. A.: or How to Get a Green Card According to the Immigration Act of 1990, Bk. 1. Wiley, Elliott et al, eds. LC 91-77185. 222p. (Orig.). 1994. 29.95 (*1-880808-01-3*) Bookmark NY.
***Lewis, Loida N. & Madlansacay, Len T.** Como Obtener la Tarjeta Verde: Maneras Legitimas de Permanecer en los EE.VV. Cambridge Translation Resources Staff, tr. (Illus.). 225p. (SPA.). 1994. pap. 24.95 (*0-87337-264-6*) Nolo Pr.
— How to Get a Green Card: Legal Ways to Stay in the U. S. A. 2nd ed. Repa, Barbara K., ed. LC 94-41017. (Illus.). 225p. 1995. pap. 24.95 (*0-87337-288-3*) Nolo Pr.
Lewis, Lois F. Carlin School, A History Book: The Story of a School in Ravenna, Ohio, U. S. A. (Illus.). 28p. (Orig.). (J). (gr. 5). 1989. pap. text ed. write for info. (*0-9620136-3-3*) L F Lewis.
— Tappan School, a History Book: The Story of a School in Ravenna, Ohio, U. S. A. (Illus.). 28p. (Orig.). (J). (gr. 5). 1989. pap. text ed. write for info. (*0-9620136-1-7*) L F Lewis.
— West Main School, a History Book: The Story of a School in Ravenna, Ohio, U. S. A. (Illus.). (Orig.). (J). (gr. 5). 1988. pap. text ed. 2.00 (*0-9620136-0-9*) L F Lewis.
Lewis, Lon D. Equine Clinical Nutrition. 1994. 105.00 (*0-683-04962-3*) Williams & Wilkins.
— Feeding & Care of the Horse. 2nd ed. LC 94-18096. 1994. write for info. (*0-683-04967-4*) Williams & Wilkins.
Lewis, Lon D., et al. Alimentation Clinique des Petits Animoux, No. III. 3rd ed. Moreau, Philippe, tr. (Illus.). 470p. (C). 1989. 18.00 (*0-945837-00-3*) M Morris Assocs.
— Feeding Dogs & Cats. rev. ed. 61p. (C). 1989. pap. text ed. 1.50 (*0-945837-01-1*) M Morris Assocs.
— Guide to Dietary Management of Small Animals. rev. ed. 37p. (C). 1989. pap. text ed. 1.50 (*0-945837-02-X*) M Morris Assocs.
Lewis, Lorene, jt. auth. see Lewis, Merrill.
Lewis, Lorrie. In Our Weakness. 96p. 1991. pap. 7.95 (*1-878110-00-4*) Abundant Answers.
Lewis, Lorrie, jt. auth. see Lewis, Jim.
Lewis, Luevester. Jackie. (Illus.). (J). (gr. k-5). 1970. pap. 1.00 (*0-685-42384-0*) Third World.
Lewis, LuVerne M., jt. auth. see Harrison.
Lewis, LuVerne W., jt. auth. see McConnell, Edwina A.
Lewis, LuVerne W., jt. auth. see Timby, Barbara K.
Lewis, Lynne, ed. see Akutagawa & Whitman Staff.
Lewis, Lynne, ed. see Farebee, Gideon, Jr.
Lewis, Lynne, ed. see Froelich, Craig.
Lewis, Lynne E., ed. see Akutagawa, Donald & Whitman, Terry.
Lewis, Lynne E., ed. see Black, Joanne C.
Lewis, Lynne E., ed. see Bolen, Steven J.
Lewis, Lynne E., ed. see Kruger, Fred J.
Lewis, M. Hay Esperanza-Padres Que Sufren (Hope for the Hurting Parent) (SPA.). Date not set. 1.79 (*0-685-74943-6*, 497414) Editorial Unilit.
Lewis, M. & Feinman, S., eds. Social Influences & Socialization in Infancy. LC 90-14308. (Genesis of Behavior Ser.: Vol. 6). (Illus.). 330p. 1990. 55.00 (*0-306-43632-9*, Plenum Pr) Plenum.
Lewis, M. & Miller, S., eds. Handbook of Developmental Psychopathology. LC 89-23243. (Illus.). 556p. 1990. 80.00 (*0-306-43190-4*, Plenum Pr) Plenum.
Lewis, M., jt. auth. see Grandison, A.
***Lewis, M. Christine.** Hey, That's Not Fair! 1995. pap. 5.95 (*0-533-11069-6*) Vantage.
Lewis, M. E. Thematic Methods & Strategies in Learning Disabilities: A Textbook for Practitioners. LC 92-42082. (Illus.). 210p. (Orig.). (C). 1993. pap. text ed. 29.95 (*1-879105-95-0*) Singular Publishing.
Lewis, M. H., ed. Glasses & Glass-Ceramics. 416p. 1989. 86.00 (*0-412-27690-9*) Chapman & Hall.
Lewis, M. J., jt. auth. see Lloyd-Jones, Roger.
Lewis, M. K. & Lewis, Rosemary R. Your Film Acting Career: How to Break into the Movies & TV & Survive in Hollywood. 3rd rev. ed. LC 92-74915. (Illus.). 320p. 1993. reprint ed. pap. 15.95 (*0-929149-01-7*) Gorham Hse.
Lewis, Mack O. How to Franchise Your Business. 3rd ed. LC 74-8015. 48p. 1990. pap. 5.95 (*0-87576-147-X*) Pilot Bks.
Lewis, Madeline D., jt. auth. see Lewis, Thomas M.
Lewis, Madeline K., jt. auth. see Lewis, Thomas M.
Lewis, Magda G. Without a Word: Teaching Beyond Women's Silence. LC 93-2318. 224p. 1993. 49.95 (*0-415-90593-1*, A7282, Routledge NY); pap. 15.95 (*0-415-90594-X*, A7286, Routledge NY) Routledge.
Lewis, Marcia A. & Tamparo, Carol D. Medical Law, Ethics, & Bioethics in the Medical Office. 3rd ed. (Illus.). 270p. (C). 1993. pap. text ed. 18.95 (*0-8036-5624-6*) Davis Co.
Lewis, Marcia A., jt. auth. see Tamparo, Carol.
Lewis, Margaret. Ngaio Marsh: A Life. 2nd large type ed. 448p. 1993. 24.95 (*1-85089-327-6*, Pub. by ISIS UK) Transaction Pubs.
Lewis, Margo, jt. auth. see Lewis, Herschell G.
Lewis, Marguerite. Hooked on Reading! LC 86-2629. 206p. 1986. spiral bd. 27.95 (*0-87628-406-3*) Ctr Appl Res.
— Hooked on Research! Ready-to-Use Projects & Crosswords for Practice in Basic Library Skills. (Illus.). 252p. 1984. spiral bd. 27.95 (*0-87628-407-1*) Ctr Appl Res.
— Randolph Caldecott: The Children's Illustrator. (Illus.). 48p. (J). (gr. 2-7). 1992. pap. 10.95 (*0-913853-22-4*, 32533, Alleyside) Highsmith Pr.
Lewis, Marguerite & Kudla, Pamela J. Hooked on Independent Study: A Programmed Approach to Library Skills for Grades 3-8. 256p. 1989. pap. 18.95 (*0-87628-405-5*) Ctr Appl Res.
— Hooked on Library Skills: A Sequential Activities Program. 288p. (J). (gr. k-6). 1988. spiral bd. 27.95 (*0-87628-408-X*) Ctr Appl Res.
— Remarkable People! Ready-to-Use Biography Activities for Grades 4-8. 256p. 1991. pap. 27.95 (*0-87628-792-5*, 710506) P-H.
Lewis, Maria C., tr. see Sargent, Dennis J.
Lewis, Maria I., ed. see Sargent, Dennis J. & Chambers, Maynard N.
Lewis, Maria I., tr. see Sargent, Dennis J. & Chambers, Maynard.
Lewis, Marjorie & Lewis, Gregg. The Hurting Parent. rev. ed. 176p. (Orig.). 1988. reprint ed. pap. 9.99 (*0-310-41631-0*, 11224P) Zondervan.
Lewis, Mark. Birding in the San Juan Islands. LC 87-23997. (Illus.). 224p. (Orig.). 1987. pap. 10.95 (*0-89886-133-0*) Mountaineers.
— Forty-Five Programs for the TRS-80 Model 4 Computer. 96p. 1984. 8.95 (*0-86668-040-3*) ARCsoft.
Lewis, Mark, jt. auth. see Shuckelman, Moe.
Lewis, Mark E. Sanctioned Violence in Early China. LC 88-37052. (Chinese Philosophy & Culture Ser.). 374p. 1989. 74.50 (*0-7914-0076-X*); pap. 24.95 (*0-7914-0077-8*) State U NY Pr.
Lewis, Martha B., des. Christmas Carols for Beginning Piano. 24p. 1991. pap. text ed. 5.95 (*0-87487-409-2*) Summy-Birchard.
Lewis, Martha W. The Official Priests of Rome under the Julio-Claudians: A Study of the Nobility from 44 B. C. to 68 A. D. LC 56-2111. (American Academy in Rome. Papers & Monographs: Vol. 16). 192p. pap. 54.80 (*0-685-15618-4*, 2026730) Bks Demand.
Lewis, Martin. A-Z of Cars of the 1980s. (Illus.). 160p. 1994. 32.95 (*1-870979-54-0*, Pub. by Bay View Bks UK) Motorbooks Intl.
Lewis, Martin G. & Rowden, Geoffrey. Histopathology: A Step-by-Step-Approach. 250p. 1984. 40.95 (*0-316-52340-2*) Little.
Lewis, Martin G., et al. Appleton & Lange's Review of General Pathology. 3rd ed. (Illus.). 195p. 1993. pap. 26.95 (*0-8385-0161-3*, A0161-8) Appleton & Lange.
Lewis, Martin W. Green Delusions: An Environmentalist Critique of Radical Environmentalism. LC 92-5671. 298p. 1992. 24.95 (*0-8223-1257-3*) Duke.
— Green Delusions: An Environmentalist Critique of Radical Environmentalism. LC 92-5671. 304p. 1994. pap. 12.95 (*0-8223-1474-6*) Duke.
— Wagering the Land: Ritual, Capital, & Environmental Degradation in the Cordillera of Northern Luzon, 1900-1986. LC 91-12307. (C). 1992. 40.00 (*0-520-07272-3*) U CA Pr.
Lewis, Martina E. Easy English: A Quick, Easy Guide to Standard English Usage. 110p. (Orig.). 1987. pap. 8.95 (*0-933109-00-8*) Probata Pr.
— Videodiscs for English Classes: Classroom Applications of Videodisc Technology: Secondary English. 120p. (Orig.). 1989. pap. text ed. 26.95 (*0-933109-02-4*) Probata Pr.
***Lewis, Marv.** Changchau: The Tiger of Burma. 270p. Date not set. pap. 8.95 (*0-7610-0421-1*) NW Pub.
***Lewis, Marvin.** From This High Hill: Conversations with a Seasonal Traveler. Howard, Morgan, ed. LC 94-34648. (Light Line Ser.). 228p. (Orig.). 1994. pap. 5.95 (*0-89084-786-X*) Bob Jones Univ Pr.
Lewis, Marvin A. Ethnicity & Identity in Contemporary Afro-Venezuelan Literature: A Culturalist Approach. 136p. (C). 1992. text ed. 24.95 (*0-8262-0840-1*) U of Mo Pr.
— From Lima to Leticia: The Peruvian Novels of Mario Vargas Llosa. LC 83-1057. 182p. (Orig.). (C). 1983. lib. bdg. 52.00 (*0-8191-3049-4*); pap. text ed. 23.00 (*0-8191-3050-8*) U Pr of Amer.
— Treading the Ebony Path: Ideology & Violence in Contemporary Afro-Colombian Prose Fiction. LC 86-30901. 152p. 1988. text ed. 20.00 (*0-8262-0638-7*) U of Mo Pr.
Lewis, Marvin E. Awakening the Marvelous Powers Within You. 345p. 1994. pap. 9.95 (*1-56901-365-9*) NW Pub.
— The Greatest Quest in the World. Van Treese, James B., ed. Ingram, tr. 376p. (Orig.). 1993. pap. 12.95 (*1-880416-16-6*) NW Pub.
— The Miracle of Success. Van Treese, James B., ed. 370p. 1992. 12.95 (*1-880416-17-4*) NW Pub.
Lewis, Marvin E. & Sadoff, Robert L. Psychic Injuries, 3 vols., Vols. 12, 12a & 12b. (Courtroom Medicine Ser.). 1975. Looseleaf updates avail. write for info. (*0-8205-1256-7*) Bender.
Lewis, Mary. Herstory: Black Female Rites of Passage. 1988. pap. 6.95 (*0-913543-08-X*) African Am Imag.
— Living & Celebrating the Advent-Christmas Seasons. rev. ed. LC 87-32905. 1988. spiral bd. 4.95 (*0-685-13939-5*); write for info. (*0-8198-4419-5*) Pauline Bks.
***Lewis, Mary, ed.** The Buglhat Motet Anthologies: Selections from Liber Cantus (Vocum Quatuor) Triginta Novem Motetos Habet. LC 95-5755. (Sixteenth-Century Motet Ser.: No. 14). 392p. 1995. 98.00 (*0-8240-7914-0*) Garland.
***Lewis, Mary E.** The Layperson's Prophecy Handbook for Everyday Use: The Revelation of Jesus Christ & Seventy Weeks of Daniel. LC 94-77966. (Illus.). 193p. (Orig.). 1994. pap. text ed. 11.95 (*0-9642873-0-7*) Lewis Pubng.
Lewis, Mary H. An Adventure with Children. Provenzo, Eugene F., Jr. & Provenzo, Therese M., eds. LC 85-15821. (Illus.). 124p. 1985. reprint ed. lib. bdg. 52.00 (*0-8191-4911-X*) U Pr of Amer.
Lewis, Mary L. Love Lives Here, Vol. 1. 100p. 1987. pap. 6.50 (*1-56770-170-1*) S Scheewe Pubns.
— Love Lives Here, Vol. 2. 100p. 1988. pap. 6.50 (*1-56770-185-X*) S Scheewe Pubns.
— Love Lives Here, Vol. 3. 100p. 1988. pap. 6.50 (*1-56770-195-7*) S Scheewe Pubns.
Lewis, Mary L. & Keane, Joyce E. Naked in the Kitchen: Everyman's Graphic-Classic Calendar-Cookbook. Spitler, Sue, ed. (Illus.). 32p. (Orig.). 1989. pap. 9.50 (*0-685-29055-7*) Order Day Ink.
Lewis, Mary S. Antonio Gardano, Venetian Music Printer, 1538-1569: A Descriptive Bibliography & Historical Study, Vol. 1, 1538-1549. LC 87-21202. (Illus.). 964p. 1988. lib. bdg. 137.00 (*0-8240-8454-3*) Garland.
Lewis, Mary T. Cezanne's Early Imagery. 300p. (C). 1989. 48.00 (*0-520-06561-1*) U CA Pr.
— Cezanne's Early Imagery. 1992. pap. 20.00 (*0-520-06563-8*) U CA Pr.
Lewis, Matthew. The Monk. Anderson, Howard, ed. (World's Classics Ser.). 1982. pap. 8.95 (*0-19-281524-5*, IRL Pr) OUP.
— The Monk. 2nd ed. McEvoy, Emma, ed. & intro. by. (World's Classics Ser.). 480p. 1996. pap. 8.95 (*0-19-282435-X*) OUP.
Lewis, Matthew G. Bravo of Venice, A Romance. LC 74-131327. (Gothic Novels Ser.). 1974. reprint ed. 51.95 (*0-405-00807-4*) Ayer.
— The Castle Spectre. LC 90-40606. 122p. 1990. reprint ed. 43.00 (*1-85477-049-7*, Pub. by Woodstock Bks UK) Cassell.
— Journal of a West India Proprietor, Kept During a Residence in the Island of Jamaica. LC 74-89041. 408p. 1970. reprint ed. text ed. 35.00 (*0-8371-1845-X*, LEJ&, Negro U Pr) Greenwood.
— The Monk. 446p. 1952. pap. 12.95 (*0-8021-5107-8*) Grove-Atltic.
Lewis, Maureen, et al. AIDS in Developing Countries: Cost Issues & Policy Tradeoffs. LC 89-35241. (Report Ser.: No. 89-5). 92p. (Orig.). (C). 1989. lib. bdg. 41.00 (*0-87766-426-9*); pap. text ed. 15.50 (*0-87766-427-7*) Urban Inst.
Lewis, Maurice. Electrical Installation Competences, Pt. One, vol. One: Theory. (Illus.). 144p. (Orig.). 1992. pap. 27.50 (*0-7487-1398-0*, Pub. by Stanley Thornes UK) Trans-Atl Phila.
— Electrical Installation Competences, Pt. One, Vol. Three: Practical. (Illus.). 112p. (Orig.). 1991. pap. 24.00 (*0-7487-1300-X*, Pub. by Stanley Thornes UK) Trans-Atl Phila.
— Electrical Installation Competences, Pt. One, Vol. Two: Science. (Illus.). 96p. (Orig.). 1991. pap. 24.00 (*0-7487-0591-0*, Pub. by Stanley Thornes UK) Trans-Atl Phila.
— Electrical Installation Competences, Pt. Two, Vol. One: Science. (Illus.). 96p. (Orig.). 1993. pap. 27.50 (*0-7487-1660-2*, Pub. by Stanley Thornes UK) Trans-Atl Phila.
— Electrical Installation Competences, Pt. Two, Vol. Three: Theory. (Illus.). 96p. (Orig.). 1994. pap. 27.50 (*0-7487-1661-0*, Pub. by Stanley Thornes UK) Trans-Atl Phila.

— Electrical Installation Competences, Pt. Two, Vol. Two: Practical. (Illus.). 112p. (Orig.). 1994. pap. 27.50 (0-7487-1659-9, Pub. by Stanley Thornes UK) Trans-Atl Phila.

— Electrical Installation Technology Pt. 1: Theory & Regulations. 3rd rev. ed. 168p. (C). 1992. pap. 30.00x (0-7487-1542-8, Pub. by S Thornes Pubs UK) St Mut.

— Electrical Installation Technology Pt. 2: Science & Calculations. 3rd ed. (Illus.). 160p. (C). 1988. pap. 30.00x (0-7487-0378-0, Pub. by S Thornes Pubs UK) St Mut.

— Electrical Installation Technology Pt. 3: Advanced Work. 2nd ed. (Illus.). 160p. (C). 1992. pap. 33.00x (0-7487-1520-7, Pub. by S Thornes Pubs UK) St Mut.

— Questions & Answers in Electrical Installation Technology. 192p. (C). 1989. pap. 30.00x (0-7487-0236-9, Pub. by S Thornes Pubs UK) St Mut.

Lewis, Maynah. The Other Side of Paradise. large type ed. 288p. 1985. 15.95 (0-7089-1379-2) Ulverscroft.

Lewis, Meharry H., ed. see Church of the Living God, the Pillar & Ground of the Truth, Inc. Supreme Executive Council Staff.

Lewis, Meharry H., jt. auth. see Lewis, Helen M.

Lewis, Meharry H., jt. ed. see Lewis, Helen M.

Lewis, Mel. Writing to Win. 160p. 1987. pap. text ed. 14.95 (0-07-084942-0) McGraw.

Lewis, Melanie, jt. auth. see Marek, Edmund A.

Lewis, Melvin. Child & Adolescent Psychiatry: A Comprehensive Textbook. (Illus.). 1318p. 1991. 135.00 (0-683-04954-2) Williams & Wilkins.

Lewis, Melvin & Volkmar, Fred R. Clinical Aspects of Child & Adolescent Development: An Introductory Synthesis of Developmental Concepts & Clinical Experience. 3rd ed. LC 89-7955. (Illus.). 475p. 1991. text ed. 49.00 (0-8121-1218-0) Williams & Wilkins.

Lewis, Meriwether. Journals of the Lewis & Clark Expedition, Vol. 8: June 10-September 26, 1806. LC 82-8510. x, 456p. (C). 1993. 55.00 (0-8032-2903-8) U of Nebr Pr.

Lewis, Meriwether & Clark, William. The History of the Lewis & Clark Expedition, 3 vols., 1. Coues, Elliot, ed. (Illus.). 1508p. 1979. pap. 8.95 (0-486-21268-8) Dover.

— The History of the Lewis & Clark Expedition, 3 vols., 2. Coues, Elliot, ed. (Illus.). 1508p. 1979. pap. 8.95 (0-486-21269-6) Dover.

— The History of the Lewis & Clark Expedition, 3 vols., 3. Coues, Elliot, ed. (Illus.). 1508p. 1979. pap. 8.95 (0-486-21270-X) Dover.

— Journals of Lewis & Clark. De Voto, Bernard A., ed. (American Heritage Library). (Illus.). 560p. 1973. pap. 12.95 (0-395-08380-X, 31, SenEd) HM.

— Journals of Lewis & Clark: A New Selection. Bakeless, John, ed. (Orig.). 1964. pap. 5.99 (0-451-62670-2, Ment) NAL-Dutton.

— The Journals of the Lewis & Clark Expedition: March 23-June 9, 1806. Moulton, Gary E., ed. LC 82-8510. (Illus.). x, 383p. 1991. 55.00 (0-8032-2898-8) U of Nebr Pr.

— Journals of the Lewis & Clark Expedition: November 2, 1805-March 22, 1806, Vol. 6. LC 82-8510. (Illus.). xii, 531p. 1990. 55.00 (0-8032-2893-7) U of Nebr Pr.

— The Journals of the Lewis & Clark Expedition, Vol. 2: August 30, 1803 - August 24, 1804. Moulton, Gary E., ed. LC 82-8510. (Illus.). x, 612p. 1986. 55.00 (0-8032-2869-4) U of Nebr Pr.

— The Journals of the Lewis & Clark Expedition, Vol. 3: August 25, 1804-April 6, 1805. Moulton, Gary E., ed. LC 82-8510. (Illus.). x, 544p. 1987. 55.00 (0-8032-2875-9) U of Nebr Pr.

— The Journals of the Lewis & Clark Expedition, Vol. 4: April 7-July 27, 1805. Moulton, Gary E., ed. LC 82-8510. (Illus.). x, 464p. 1987. 55.00 (0-8032-2877-5) U of Nebr Pr.

— The Journals of the Lewis & Clark Expedition, Vol. 5: July 28 - November 1, 1805. Moulton, Gary E., ed. LC 82-8510. (Illus.). xiii, 415p. 1988. 55.00 (0-8032-2883-X) U of Nebr Pr.

Lewis, Meriwether, et al. History of the Expedition under the Command of Captains Lewis & Clark, 3 vols., Set. LC 72-2820. (American Explorers Ser.). (Illus.). reprint ed. 165.00 (0-404-54920-9) AMS Pr.

Lewis, Merrill. Robert Cantwell. LC 85-70130. (Western Writers Ser.: No. 70). (Illus.). 54p. (Orig.). 1985. pap. 3.95 (0-88430-044-7) Boise St U W Writ Ser.

Lewis, Merrill & Lee, L. L., eds. The Westering Experience in American Literature: Bicentennial Essays. LC 77-80814. 1977. pap. 4.95 (0-930216-01-6) West Wash Univ.

Lewis, Merrill & Lewis, Lorene. Wallace Stegner. LC 72-619569. (Western Writers Ser.: No. 4). (Illus.). 48p. (Orig.). (C). 1972. pap. 3.95 (0-88430-003-X) Boise St U W Writ Ser.

Lewis, Merrill E., jt. ed. see Lee, Lawrence L.

***Lewis, Mervyn K., ed.** Financial Intermediaries. (International Library of Critical Writings in Business History: Vol. 43). 624p. 1994. 185.95 (1-85278-791-0, Pub. by E Elgar Pub UK) Ashgate Pub Co.

Lewis, Mervyn K., jt. ed. see Dowd, Kevin.

Lewis, Michael. Colorado Centennial Farms & Ranches: A Century of Seasons. (Illus.). 80p. 1994. 25.00 (1-56579-050-2) Westcliffe Pubs Inc.

— The Culture of Inequality. 2nd ed. LC 77-24214. 240p. 1993. pap. 16.95 (0-87023-857-4) U of Mass Pr.

— Liar's Poker. 1989. 18.95 (0-393-02750-3) Norton.

— Liar's Poker: Rising Through the Wreckage on Wall Street. 1990. pap. 11.00 (0-14-014345-9, Penguin Bks) Viking Penguin.

— The Money Culture. 304p. 1992. reprint ed. pap. 11.00 (0-14-017318-8, Penguin Bks) Viking Penguin.

— Pacific Rift: Adventures in the Fault Zone Between the U. S. & Japan. Rukeyser, William S. & Kiser, Anthony C., eds. LC 90-71779. (Larger Agenda Ser.). (Illus.). 88p. 1991. 11.95 (0-9624745-6-8) Whittle Comns.

— Pacific Rift: Why Americans & Japanese Don't Understand Each Other. 128p. 1993. pap. 7.95 (0-393-30986-X) Norton.

— Recycling Economic Development Through Scrap-Based Manufacturing. LC 94-5188. (Illus.). 42p. 1994. pap. text ed. 20.00 (0-917582-97-7) Inst Local Self Re.

— Research in Social Problems & Public Policy, Vol. 3. 1984. 73.25 (0-89232-339-6) Jai Pr.

— Rioters & Citizens: Mass Protest in Imperial Japan. 1990. 48.00 (0-520-06642-1) U CA Pr.

— Shame: The Exposed Self. 285p. 1992. text ed. 27.95 (0-02-918881-4) Free Pr.

— Stout. (Classic Beer Style Ser.). (Illus.). Date not set. 11.95 (0-937381-44-6) Brewers Pubns.

— Urban America: Institutions & Experience. LC 72-10944. 526p. reprint ed. pap. 150.00 (0-317-07770-8, 2013723) Bks Demand.

— World Cup Soccer. (Illus.). 288p. 1994. 22.50 (1-55921-106-7); pap. 12.95 (1-55921-107-5) Moyer Bell.

Lewis, Michael, ed. Beyond the Dyad. (Genesis of Behavior Ser.: Vol. 4). 346p. 1984. 65.00 (0-306-41446-5, Plenum Pr) Plenum.

— Origins of Intelligence: Infancy & Early Childhood. 2nd ed. 552p. 1983. 47.50 (0-306-41225-X, Plenum Pr) Plenum.

— Origins of Intelligence: Infancy & Early Childhood. LC 75-31530. 423p. reprint ed. pap. 120.60 (0-317-29329-X, 2024020) Bks Demand.

— Research in Social Problems & Public Policy, Vol. 1. 1979. lib. bdg. 73.25 (0-89232-068-0) Jai Pr.

— Research in Social Problems & Public Policy, Vol. 2. 250p. 1981. 73.25 (0-89232-195-4) Jai Pr.

— Research in Social Problems & Public Policy, Vol. 4. 1987. 73.25 (0-89232-560-7) Jai Pr.

Lewis, Michael & Haviland, Jeannette M., eds. Handbook of Emotions. LC 92-48999. 641p. 1993. text ed. 65.00 (0-89862-988-8) Guilford Pr.

Lewis, Michael & Hill, Jimmie. Source Book for Teaching English Overseas. 128p. (Orig.). (C). 1981. pap. text ed. 18.50 (0-435-28992-6, 28992) Heinemann.

Lewis, Michael & Michalson, Linda, eds. Children's Emotions & Moods: Developmental Theory & Measurement. LC 83-2456. 488p. 1983. 59.50 (0-306-41209-8, Plenum Pr) Plenum.

Lewis, Michael & Rosenblum, Leonard A., eds. The Origins of Fear. LC 74-9565. (Origins of Behavior Ser.: Vol.2). (Illus.). 298p. reprint ed. pap. 85.00 (0-317-08216-7, 2012621) Bks Demand.

— The Uncommon Child. LC 80-20601. (Genesis of Behavior Ser.: Vol. 3). 354p. 1981. 65.00 (0-306-40499-0, Plenum Pr) Plenum.

Lewis, Michael & Saarni, Carolyn, eds. Lying & Deception in Everyday Life. 368p. 1993. lib. bdg. 27.95 (0-89862-894-6) Guilford Pr.

— The Socialization of Emotions. (Genesis of Behavior Ser.: Vol. 5). 334p. 1985. 65.00 (0-306-41851-7, Plenum Pr) Plenum.

Lewis, Michael & Taft, Lawrence, eds. Developmental Disabilities: Theory, Assessment & Intervention. 288p. 1982. text ed. 35.00 (0-88331-134-8) Luce.

Lewis, Michael & Worobey, John, eds. Infant Stress & Coping. LC 85-644581. (New Directions for Child Development Ser.: No. CD 45). 1989. 17.95 (1-55542-844-4) Jossey-Bass.

Lewis, Michael, jt. auth. see Hunt, Michael.

Lewis, Michael, et al, eds. Mothers, Babies, & Cocaine: The Role of Toxins in Development. 384p. 1995. text ed. 79.95 (0-8058-1583-X); pap. 29.95 (0-8058-1584-8) L Erlbaum Assocs.

Lewis, Michael A. & Lamey, Philip-John. Clinical Oral Medicine. LC 93-20528. (Illus.). 144p. 1993. pap. 55.00 (0-7236-2255-8, Pub. by John Wright UK) Buttrwrth-Heinemann.

Lewis, Michael A., jt. auth. see Lamey, Philip-John.

Lewis, Michael A., jt. ed. see Suter, Glen W., II.

Lewis, Michael D., jt. auth. see Lewis, Judith A.

Lewis, Michael D., jt. auth. see Wallace, Sheri A.

Lewis, Michael J. The Politics of the German Gothic Revival: August Reichensperger. LC 92-38723. (Architectural History Foundation Ser.). (Illus.). 240p. 1993. 52.50 (0-262-12177-8) MIT Pr.

Lewis, Michael J., jt. ed. see Thomas, George E.

Lewis, Michael L., jt. auth. see Dodd, Carley H.

Lewis, Mike & Kelly, Graham. Twenty Training Workshops for Developing Managerial Effectiveness, Vol. 1. 288p. 1986. text ed. 154.95 (0-566-02515-9, Pub. by Gower UK) Ashgate Pub Co.

— Twenty Training Workshops for Developing Managerial Effectiveness, Vol. 1. 1992. ring bd. 139.95 (0-87425-186-9) Human Res Dev Pr.

Lewis, Mike, tr. see Pruyt, Hans.

Lewis, Milton, jt. ed. see Macleod, Roy.

Lewis, Mina B. Confessions of a Boat Lover's Wife or Is a Marriage Like This Worth Saving? Roosevelt, Constance, ed. LC 86-18438. 154p. 1987. 10.95 (0-688-06918-5, Hearst Marine Bks) Morrow.

Lewis, Miriam S., jt. auth. see Lewis, Jac.

Lewis, Morgan V. & Pratzner, Frank C., eds. Perspectives on Vocational Education: Purposes & Performance. 73p. 1984. 7.95 (0-318-17788-9, RD247) Ctr Educ Trng Employ.

Lewis, Morgan V., et al. Future Influences on Vocational Education. 17p. 1984. 2.75 (0-318-22107-1, SN46) Ctr Educ Trng Employ.

Lewis, Morris M. Infant Speech: A Study of the Beginnings of Language. LC 74-21420. (Classics in Child Development Ser.). 350p. 1978. reprint ed. 33.95 (0-405-06470-5) Ayer.

Lewis, Morton. Ted Kid Lewis: His Life & Times. (Illus.). 273p. 1992. 24.95 (0-86051-644-X, Robson-Parkwest) Parkwest Pubns.

Lewis, Mumford. The Golden Day: A Study in American Literature & Culture. LC 82-24199. xxx, 144p. 1983. reprint ed. text ed. 42.50 (0-313-23845-6, MUGO, Greenwood Pr) Greenwood.

Lewis, Myrna, II, jt. auth. see Butler, Robert N.

Lewis, Myrna I., jt. auth. see Butler, Robert N.

Lewis, N. E. & Moore, E. L. Fiber Optic Systems for Mobile Platforms IV, Vol. 1369. 1991. 53.00 (0-8194-0430-6) SPIE.

Lewis, N. E. & Moore, E. L., eds. Fiber Optic Systems for Mobile Platforms, Vol. 989, No. 2. 1988. 45.00 (0-8194-0024-6) SPIE.

Lewis, Nancy, ed. see Lewis, R. W.

Lewis, Naomi. Cry Wolf & Other Aesop Fables. (Illus.). 32p. (J). (ps up). 1988. 18.00 (0-19-520710-6) OUP.

— Hare & Badger Go to Town. (Illus.). 32p. (J). (ps-1). 1987. 9.95 (0-905478-94-0, Pub. by Century UK) Trafalgar.

Lewis, Naomi, ret. Stories from the Arabian Nights. (Illus.). 224p. 1991. 9.99 (0-517-05480-9) Random Hse Value.

Lewis, Naomi, tr. Proud Knight, Fair Lady: The Twelve Lais of Marie de France. (Illus.). 128p. (J). (gr. 5 up). 1989. pap. 19.95 (0-670-82656-1) Viking Child Bks.

Lewis, Naomi, tr. see Baumann, Kurt.

Lewis, Naomi, tr. see Grimm, Jacob & Grimm, Wilhelm K.

Lewis, Naomi, jt. auth. see Kruss, James.

Lewis, Naomi, tr. see Perrault, Charles.

Lewis, Naomi, tr. see Rupprecht, Siegfried P.

Lewis, Naphtali & Reinhold, Meyer. Roman Civilization, Vols. I & II. 3rd ed. 1990. text ed. 125.00 (0-231-07054-3); pap. text ed. 45.00 (0-231-07055-1) Col U Pr.

— The Roman Empire. (Roman Civilization Ser.: Vol. 2). 736p. 1990. text ed. 63.00 (0-231-07132-9); pap. text ed. 22.50 (0-231-07133-7) Col U Pr.

— The Roman Republic & the Principate of Augustus. (Roman Civilization Ser.: Vol. 1). (Illus.). 696p. 1990. text ed. 63.00 (0-231-07130-2); pap. text ed. 22.50 (0-231-07131-0) Col U Pr.

***Lewis, Natalie.** Novel Extenders, African-American Stories. (ECS Think & Learn Activity Book Ser.). (Illus.). 128p. (Orig.). 1995. teacher ed, pap. 15.95 (1-57022-050-6) ECS Lrn Systs.

Lewis, Neville, jt. auth. see Haag, Michael.

***Lewis, Nigel.** The Book of Babel: Words & the Way We See Things. LC 94-61461. 320p. (Orig.). 1995. pap. 19.95 (0-87745-496-5) U of Iowa Pr.

Lewis, Nigel, jt. auth. see Houston, William.

Lewis, Nolan D. Research in Dementia Precox. Grob, Gerald N., ed. LC 78-22572. (Historical Issues in Mental Health Ser.). 1980. reprint ed. lib. bdg. 25.95 (0-405-11925-9) Ayer.

Lewis, Norm. Prioridad Uno (Priority One) (SPA.). 1992. 4.25 (1-56063-079-5, 498483) Editorial Unilit.

— Priority One: What God Wants. 160p. 1988. pap. 7.95 (0-939497-10-7) Promise Pub.

— Priority One: What God Wants. LC 88-70157. 151p. 1990. reprint ed. pap. 4.95 (0-87808-215-8, WCL215-8) William Carey Lib.

Lewis, Norman. Correct Spelling Made Easy. rev. ed. 1987. mass mkt. 4.99 (0-440-31501-8, LE) Dell.

— A Dragon Apparent. (Eland Travel Classics Ser.). 317p. 1993. reprint ed. pap. 14.95 (0-907871-00-3) Hippocrene Bks.

— Empires in the East. 1994. 25.00 (0-8050-1960-X) H Holt & Co.

— A Goddess in the Stones: Travels in India. 336p. 1993. pap. 14.95 (0-8050-2666-5) H Holt & Co.

— Golden Earth: Travels in Burma. (Eland Travel Classics Ser.). 257p. 1993. reprint ed. pap. 14.95 (0-907871-65-8) Hippocrene Bks.

— Honoured Society (The Sicilian Mafia Observed) (Illus.). 266p. 1993. reprint ed. pap. 14.95 (0-907871-80-1) Hippocrene Bks.

— How to Read Better & Faster. 4th ed. (C). 1990. pap. text ed. 30.50 (0-690-01528-3) HarpCollege.

— Inner City Regeneration: The Demise of Territorial Government. (Studies in Law & Politics Ser.). 72p. 1992. pap. 20.00 (0-335-09632-8, Open Univ Pr) Taylor & Francis.

— Instant Word Power. 512p. 1982. pap. 4.95 (0-451-15646-3, Sig) NAL-Dutton.

— Naples '44: An Intelligence Officer in the Italian Labyrinth. LC 94-27642. 1994. pap. 14.95 (0-8050-3373-4) H Holt & Co.

— New American Dictionary of Good English: An A to Z Guide to Grammar & Correct Usage. 464p. 1987. pap. 4.95 (0-451-15023-6, Sig) NAL-Dutton.

— New Roget's Thesaurus in Dictionary Form. 512p. 1986. mass mkt. 4.99 (0-425-09975-X) Berkley Pub.

— Rapid Vocabulary Builder. 192p. 1988. pap. 8.95 (0-399-51400-7, Perigree Bks) Berkley Pub.

— A Suitable Case for Corruption. large type ed. 352p. 1985. 15.95 (0-7089-1390-3) Ulverscroft.

— Thirty Days to Better English. 208p. 1985. pap. 4.95 (0-451-15702-8, Sig) NAL-Dutton.

— Twenty Days to Better Spelling. (Orig.). 1989. pap. 3.95 (0-317-02802-2) NAL-Dutton.

— Twenty Days to Better Spelling. 288p. (Orig.). 1989. pap. 3.95 (0-451-15819-9, Sig) NAL-Dutton.

— Voices of the Old Sea. 208p. 1986. mass mkt. 5.95 (0-14-007780-4, Penguin Bks) Viking Penguin.

— Word Power Made Easy. 1991. mass mkt. 5.99 (0-671-74190-X) PB.

Lewis, Norman, ed. Happy & Glorious: The Constitution in Transition. (Studies in Law & Politics Ser.). 112p. 1990. pap. 20.00 (0-335-09487-2, Open Univ Pr) Taylor & Francis.

Lewis, Norman & Birkinshaw, Patrick. When Citizens Complain: Reforming Justice & Administration. LC 92-21161. (Law & Political Change Ser.). 1993. 85.00 (0-335-15745-9, Open Univ Pr); pap. 34.00 (0-335-15744-0, Open Univ Pr) Taylor & Francis.

Lewis, Norman, jt. auth. see Funk, Wilfred.

Lewis, Norman G. & Paice, Michael G., eds. Plant Cell Wall Polymers: Biogenesis & Biodegradation. LC 89-6926. (Symposium Ser.: No. 399). (Illus.). xi, 664p. 1989. 119.95 (0-8412-1658-4) Am Chemical.

Lewis, Norris E. & Moore, Emery L., eds. Fiber Optic Systems for Mobile Platforms III. 192p. 1990. 62.00 (0-8194-0209-5, VOL. 1173) SPIE.

Lewis, O. A. Plants & Nitrogen. (Studies in Biology: No. 166). 120p. (C). 1992. pap. 14.95 (0-521-42776-2) Cambridge U Pr.

Lewis, O. G. Good News. (Illus.). (J). (gr. k-6). 1978. 2.99 (3-901170-05-7) CEF Press.

Lewis, O. J. Functional Morphology of the Evolving Hand & Foot. (Illus.). 368p. 1989. 135.00 (0-19-261684-6) OUP.

Lewis, Orlando F. The Development of American Prisons & Prison Customs, 1776-1845. LC 93-39530. (Criminology, Law Enforcement, & Social Problems Ser.: No. 1). (Illus.). 1995. reprint ed. 25.00 (0-87585-706-X) Patterson Smith.

Lewis, Oscar. Bay Window Bohemia. (Illus.). 248p. 1983. reprint ed. pap. 9.95 (0-911819-01-0) Yosemite D.

— The Big Four. rev. ed. 310p. (C). 1995. reprint ed. pap. 6.95 (0-89174-042-2) Comstock Edns.

— The Big Four. 1992. reprint ed. lib. bdg. 75.00 (0-7812-5060-9) Rprt Serv.

— The Big Four: The Story of Huntington, Stanford, Hopkins, & Crocker, & of the Building of the Central Pacific. Bruchey, Stuart, ed. LC 80-1324. (Railroads Ser.). (Illus.). 1981. reprint ed. lib. bdg. 44.95 (0-405-13799-0) Ayer.

— Children of Sanchez. 1979. pap. 16.00 (0-394-70280-8, Vin) Random.

— The Effects of White Contact upon Blackfoot Culture. LC 84-45511. (American Ethnological Society Monographs: No. 6). 1988. reprint ed. 20.00 (0-404-62906-7) AMS Pr.

— Five Families: Mexican Case Studies in the Culture of Poverty. LC 59-10644. 364p. 1975. pap. text ed. 18.00 (0-465-09705-7) Basic.

— I Remember Christine. LC 88-37037. (Vintage West Ser.). 280p. 1989. reprint ed. pap. 10.95 (0-87417-151-2) U of Nev Pr.

— Sea Routes to the Gold Fields. 256p. 1987. reprint ed. 4.50 (0-89174-044-9) Comstock Edns.

Lewis, Oscar, et al. Four Men: Living the Revolution: An Oral History of Contemporary Cuba. LC 76-54878. 608p. 1976. 44.95 (0-252-00628-3) U of Ill Pr.

— Four Women: Living the Revolution: An Oral History of Contemporary Cuba. LC 79-54878. 485p. 1977. 39.95 (0-252-00639-9) U of Ill Pr.

Lewis, Owen. Energy Conscious Design: A Primer for European Architects. (Illus.). 160p. 1992. 55.00 (0-7134-6919-6, Pub. by Batsford UK) Trafalgar.

— The European Passive Solar Handbook. (Illus.). 304p. 1991. 85.00 (0-7134-6918-8, Pub. by Batsford UK) Trafalgar.

Lewis, Owen & Goulding, John, eds. European Directory of Energy Efficient Building 1993: Components-Services-Materials. (Illus.). 320p. (Orig.). (C). 1992. 75.00 (1-873936-14-1, Pub. by J & J Sci Pubs UK) Bks Intl VA.

— European Directory of Energy Efficient Building 1994: Components, Services, Materials. (Illus.). 344p. (Orig.). 1994. pap. 75.00 (1-873936-23-0, Pub. by Ponte Pr GW) Bks Intl VA.

Lewis, Owen, jt. ed. see Goulding, John.

Lewis, P. Ensene a Su Hijo Con Destreza (Terrific Tips for Parents) (SPA.). Date not set. 2.49 (1-56063-023-X, 498055) Editorial Unilit.

— Health Protection from Chemicals in the Workplace. LC 93-3158. (Applied Science & Industrial Technology Ser.). 286p. 1993. text ed. 65.00 (0-13-388240-3) P-H.

— Reason Wounded: An Experience of India's Emergency. 207p. 1978. 16.95 (0-318-36609-6) Asia Bk Corp.

Lewis, P. C. Enterprise Sandwich Shops: A Market Simulation Apple II Plus (on Apple with Applesoft) Version. 1983. 150.00 (0-07-037536-4) McGraw.

— Enterprise Sandwich Shops: A Market Simulation, Apple IIe & Apple II Plus Version. 1984. 150.00 (0-07-079636-X) McGraw.

— Enterprise Sandwich Shops: A Market Simulation TRS-80 Version. 1984. 150.00 (0-07-079181-3) McGraw.

Lewis, P. C. & Lewis, C. Student Manual for the Donut Franchise: A Microcomputer Simulation. 32p. 1985. pap. text ed. 9.15 (0-07-037604-2) McGraw.

Lewis, P. R. & Knight, D. P. Staining Methods for Sectioned Material. (Practical Methods in Electron Microscopy Ser.: Vol. 5, Pt. 1). 1977. pap. 27.00 (0-7204-0606-4, North Holland) Elsevier.

***Lewis, Pamela S., et al.** Management: Challenges in the 21st Century. LC 94-22667. 650p. 1994. pap. text ed. 64.25 (0-314-04568-6) West Pub.

Lewis, Particia J., et al. Showering, Set. (Project MORE Daily Living Skills Ser.). 48p. (Orig.). 1978. pap. text ed. 149.00 (0-685-05756-9) PRO-ED.

Lewis, Patricia, ed. see Blinks, William, et al.

Lewis, Patricia, et al. Using Deodorant, Set. (Project MORE Daily Living Skills Ser.). (Illus.). 32p. 1979. reprint ed. pap. text ed. 149.00 (0-685-05767-4) PRO-ED.

An Asterisk (*) at the beginning of an entry indicates that the title is appearing in BIP for the first time.

— Washing Your Hair, Set. (Project MORE Daily Living Skills Ser.). (Illus.). 32p. 1978. reprint ed. pap. text ed. 149.00 (*0-685-05768-2*) PRO-ED.

Lewis, Patrick. A Hippopotamusn't: And Other Animal Verses. Fogelman, Phyllis J., ed. LC 87-24579. (Illus.). 40p. (J). (ps-3). 1990. 12.95 (*0-8037-0518-2*); lib. bdg. 12.89 (*0-8037-0519-0*) Dial Bks Young.

Lewis-Patrick, Denise. Animal ABC's. (My First Golden Board Bks.). (J). (ps). 1990. bds. write for info. (*0-307-06127-2*) Western Pub.

— How Many Animals. (J). (ps). 1990. write for info. (*0-307-06129-9*) Western Pub.

— Opposites. (J). (ps). 1990. write for info. (*0-307-06133-7*) Western Pub.

— Shapes & Colors. (J). (ps). 1990. write for info. (*0-307-06134-5*) Western Pub.

— What Does Baby Hear? (J). (ps). 1990. write for info. (*0-307-06132-9*) Western Pub.

— What Does Baby See? (J). (ps). 1990. write for info. (*0-307-06130-2*) Western Pub.

Lewis, Patti & Coleman, Sara. I Laffed Till I Cried: Thirty-Six Years of Marriage to Jerry Lewis. LC 93-25671. (Illus.). 192p. 1993. 19.95 (*1-56796-035-9*) WRS Group.

Lewis, Paul. Akha-English Dictionary. LC 73-14371. (Cornell University, Southeast Asia Program, Data Paper Ser.: No. 70). 403p. reprint ed. pap. 114.90 (*0-8357-5291-7*, 2010475) Bks Demand.

— Comic Effects: Interdisciplinary Approaches to Humor in Literature. LC 88-28227. 179p. 1989. 59.50 (*0-7914-0022-0*); pap. 19.95 (*0-7914-0023-9*) State U NY Pr.

— Cuarenta Maneras-Ensenar-Nino-Valores Morales (Forty Ways to Teach Your Child Values) (SPA.). 1994. 6.99 (*1-56063-241-0*, 498405) Editorial Unilit.

— The Five Key Habits of Smart Dads: Secrest of Fast-Track Fathering. 224p. 1994. pap. 15.99 (*0-310-58580-5*); pap. 12.99 (*0-310-61688-3*) Zondervan.

— Information Systems Development: A Systematic Approach. 320p. (Orig.). 1992. pap. 53.50 (*0-273-03107-4*, Pub. by Pitman Pub Ltd UK) Trans-Atl Phila.

— Practical Employment Law: A Guide for Human Resource Managers. 384p. 1992. pap. 39.95 (*0-631-18679-4*) Blackwell Pubs.

— The Successful Management of Redundancy. (Human Resource Management in Action Ser.). 272p. 1993. pap. write for info. (*0-631-18681-6*) Blackwell Pubs.

— Twenty Years of Statutory Reduncdancy Payments in Great Britain. (C). 1988. text ed. 39.00 (*0-685-22130-X*, Pub. by Univ Nottingham UK) St Mut.

— Twenty Years of Statutory Redundancy Payments in Great Britain... (Leeds-Nottingham Occasional Papers in Industrial Relations: No. 8). (C). 1985. 35.00 (*0-900572-63-9*) St Mut.

Lewis, Paul & Lewis, Elaine. Peoples of the Golden Triangle: Six Tribes in Thailand. LC 84-50047. (Illus.). 1984. 40.00 (*0-500-97314-8*) Thames Hudson.

Lewis, Paul, jt. auth. see McDowell, Josh.

Lewis, Paul, jt. auth. see McGrew, Anthony.

Lewis, Paul G. Central Europe since Nineteen Forty-Five. LC 93-32588. (Post War World Ser.). (C). 1994. text ed. 63.95 (*0-582-03609-7*, Pub. by Longman UK) Longman.

— Central Europe since Nineteen Forty-Five. LC 93-32588. (Post War World Ser.). (C). 1995. pap. text ed. 22.95 (*0-582-03608-9*, Pub. by Longman UK) Longman.

— Political Authority & Party Secretaries in Poland, 1975-1986. (Illus.). 368p. (C). 1989. 69.95 (*0-521-36369-1*) Cambridge U Pr.

Lewis, Paul G., ed. Democracy & Civil Society in Eastern Europe. LC 92-1049. (Selected Papers from the Fourth World Congress for Soviet & East European Studies, Harrogate, 1990). 160p. 1992. text ed. 65.00 (*0-312-08042-5*) St Martin.

Lewis, Paul H. The Crisis of Argentine Capitalism. LC 89-31350. xxviii, 573p. 1992. pap. 19.95 (*0-8078-4356-3*) U of NC Pr.

— Paraguay under Stroessner. LC 79-28554. 268p. reprint ed. pap. 76.40 (*0-8357-3896-5*, 2036628) Bks Demand.

— Political Parties & Generations in Paraguay's Liberal Era, 1869-1940. LC 92-21164. xvi, 228p. 1992. 37.50 (*0-8078-2078-4*) U of NC Pr.

— Socialism, Liberalism, & Dictatorship in Paraguay. Hoover Institution Press Staff & Wesson, Robert, eds. LC 81-21092. (Politics in Latin America, A Hoover Institution Ser.). 170p. 1982. text ed. 49.95 (*0-275-90847-X*, C0847, Praeger Pubs) Greenwood.

Lewis, Paul M. Beauty of America. LC 89-38286. (Illus.). 1991. pap. 9.95 (*1-55988-002-3*) LTA Pub.

— Beauty of Arizona. rev. ed. LC 92-27400. 1992. 19.95 (*1-55988-324-3*); pap. 9.95 (*1-55988-323-5*) LTA Pub.

— Beauty of California. Shangle, Robert D., ed. (Illus.). 80p. 1989. 19.95 (*0-917630-71-8*); pap. 9.95 (*0-917630-42-4*) LTA Pub.

— Beauty of Colorado. LC 92-27402. 1992. 19.95 (*1-55988-326-X*); pap. 9.95 (*1-55988-325-1*) LTA Pub.

— Beauty of Florida. Shangle, Robert D., ed. (Illus.). 80p. (Orig.). 1990. 19.95 (*0-917630-81-5*) LTA Pub.

— Beauty of Hawaii. Shangle, Robert D., ed. (Illus.). 80p. 1989. 19.95 (*0-917630-58-0*); pap. 9.95 (*0-917630-57-2*) LTA Pub.

— Beauty of Massachusetts. Shangle, Robert D., ed. LC 89-12522. (Illus.). 80p. 1990. 19.95 (*0-917630-83-1*); pap. 9.95 (*0-917630-82-3*) LTA Pub.

— Beauty of Missouri. LC 89-38294. (Illus.). 1990. 19.95 (*1-55988-005-8*); pap. 9.95 (*1-55988-004-X*) LTA Pub.

— Beauty of New Jersey. LC 91-25684. (Illus.). 80p. 1989. 19.95 (*0-917630-85-8*); pap. 9.95 (*0-917630-84-X*) LTA Pub.

— Beauty of Oregon. rev. ed. LC 91-26980. 1991. 19.95 (*1-55988-319-7*); pap. 9.95 (*1-55988-318-9*) LTA Pub.

— Beauty of Pennsylvania. (Illus.). 80p. 1990. 19.95 (*0-917630-87-4*); pap. 9.95 (*0-917630-86-6*) LTA Pub.

— Beauty of the California Coast. Shangle, Robert D., ed. (Illus.). 80p. (Orig.). 1989. 19.95 (*0-917630-90-4*); pap. text ed. 9.95 (*0-917630-43-2*) LTA Pub.

— Beauty of Utah. LC 88-37209. 1989. 19.95 (*1-55988-328-6*); pap. 9.95 (*1-55988-327-8*) LTA Pub.

— Beauty of Washington. rev. ed. 1992. 19.95 (*1-55988-317-0*); pap. 9.95 (*1-55988-316-2*) LTA Pub.

Lewis, Paul O. Davy's Dream. (Illus.). 64p. (J). (ps-6). 1988. 14.95 (*0-941831-32-9*); pap. 9.95 (*0-941831-28-0*) Beyond Words Pub.

— Ever Wondered. (Illus.). 36p. (J). (gr. 3-6). 1991. pap. 5.95 (*0-941831-67-1*) Beyond Words Pub.

— Grasper: A Young Crab's Discovery out of His Shell. Roehm, Michelle, ed. (Illus.). 36p. (J). 1993. 14.95 (*0-941831-85-X*) Beyond Words Pub.

— P. Bear's New Years Party - A Counting Book. (Illus.). 24p. (J). (ps-1). 1989. 12.95 (*0-941831-21-3*); pap. 8.95 (*0-941831-29-9*) Beyond Words Pub.

— The Starlight Bride. (Illus.). 40p. (J). (ps-6). 1988. 14.95 (*0-941831-33-7*); pap. 9.95 (*0-941831-25-6*) Beyond Words Pub.

— Storm Boy. LC 94-44154. (Illus.). 32p. (J). (gr. k-3). 1995. 14.95 (*1-885223-12-9*) Beyond Words Pub.

Lewis, Paula G. The Aesthetics of Stephane Mallarme in Relation to His Public. LC 74-5898. 260p. (C). 1976. 25.00 (*0-8386-1615-1*) Fairleigh Dickinson.

— The Literary Vision of Gabrielle Roy. 2nd ed. LC 84-50323. 335p. 1993. 33.95 (*0-917786-05-X*) Summa Pubns.

Lewis, Paula G., ed. Traditionalism, Nationalism, & Feminism: Women Writers of Quebec. LC 84-10854. (Contributions in Women's Studies: No. 53). (Illus.). xli, 280p. 1985. text ed. 59.95 (*0-313-24510-X*, LTF/, Greenwood Pr) Greenwood.

Lewis, Penny. Creative Transformation: The Healing Power of the Arts. (Illus.). 200p. (Orig.). 1993. pap. 19.95 (*0-933029-66-7*) Chiron Pubns.

Lewis, Penny & Loman, Susan. The Kestenberg Movement Profile: Its Past, Present Applications & Future Directions. LC 90-81441. 176p. (C). 1990. pap. text ed. 12.00 (*1-881245-01-2*) Antioch New Eng.

Lewis, Peter. Alf Francis: Racing Mechanic, 1948-58. 1991. 49.95 (*0-85429-937-8*, Pub. by G T Foulis Ltd) Haynes Pubns.

— Media & Communication for Beginners. (Writers & Readers Documentary Comic Bks.). (Illus.). 176p. (Orig.). 1991. pap. 7.95 (*0-86316-115-4*) Writers & Readers.

Lewis, Peter & Booth, Jerry, eds. The Invisible Medium: Commercial, Public & Community Radio. LC 90-4357. 250p. (C). 1990. reprint ed. 24.95 (*0-88258-032-9*); reprint ed. pap. 14.95 (*0-88258-106-6*) Howard U Pr.

Lewis, Peter A. Fielding's Burlesque Drama. (University of Durham Ser.: Vol. 2). (Illus.). 200p. 1987. 25.00 (*0-85224-542-4*, Pub. by Edinburgh U Pr UK) Col U Pr.

— Maps & Statistics. 336p. 1977. pap. 22.50 (*0-416-65380-4*, NO. 6180) Routledge Chapman & Hall.

Lewis, Peter A., ed. Pigment Handbook, 3 vols., Set. 1988. text ed. 608.00 (*0-471-60021-0*) Wiley.

— Pigment Handbook, 3 vols., Vol. 1. 2nd ed. 1988. text ed. 350.00 (*0-471-82833-5*) Wiley.

— Pigment Handbook, 3 vols., Vol. 2. 2nd ed. 1973. text ed. 295.00 (*0-471-67124-X*) Wiley.

— Pigment Handbook, 3 vols., Vol. 3. 1973. text ed. 250.00 (*0-471-67126-6*) Wiley.

Lewis, Peter A. & Orav, Endel J. Simulation Methodology for Statisticians, Operations Analysts, & Engineers, Vol. I. LC 88-5536. 416p. (C). 1989. boxed 62.95 (*0-534-09450-3*) Chapman & Hall.

Lewis, Peter A. & Wood, Nigel, eds. John Gay & the Scriblerians. LC 88-18198. (Critical Studies). 224p. 1989. text ed. 39.95 (*0-312-02422-3*) St Martin.

Lewis, Peter A., et al. Enhanced Simulation & Statistics Package. LC 89-4860. 96p. (C). 1989. pap. text ed. 95.00 (*0-534-10260-3*) Chapman & Hall.

Lewis, Peter H., ed. see Hein, Peg.

Lewis, Peter J. & O'Grady, John, eds. Clinical Pharmacology of Prostacyciin. 274p. 1981. 75.50 (*0-89004-591-7*) Raven.

***Lewis, Peter J., et al, eds.** Prostacyclin in Pregnancy. LC 83-42597. (Illus.). Date not set. reprint ed. pap. 70.20 (*0-7837-9559-9*, 2060308) Bks Demand.

Lewis, Philip. Life of Death: A Novel. 253p. 1993. 18.95 (*0-932511-74-0*); pap. 8.95 (*0-932511-75-9*) Fiction Coll.

Lewis, Philip C. The American Dame. 1963. pap. 4.75 (*0-8222-0028-7*) Dramatists Play.

Lewis, Philip G. Approaching Precalculus Mathematics Discretely: Explorations in a Computer Environment. (Explorations in Logo Ser.). 350p. (Orig.). 1989. 47.50x (*0-262-12138-7*); pap. 24.95x (*0-262-62063-4*) MIT Pr.

***Lewis, Philip H.** Tomorrow by Design: A Regional Design Process for Sustainability. (Series in Sustainable Design). Date not set. text ed. 44.95 (*0-471-10935-5*) Wiley.

Lewis, Philip M., 2nd, et al. Compiler Design Theory. LC 75-9012. (Illus.). 672p. (C). 1976. text ed. write for info. (*0-201-14455-7*) Addison-Wesley.

Lewis, Philip S., ed. Law & Technology in the Pacific Community. LC 94-8107. (C). 1994. text ed. 68.50 (*0-8133-2158-1*) Westview.

Lewis, Philip S., jt. ed. see Abel, Richard L.

Lewis, Philip S.C., jt. ed. see Able, Richard L.

Lewis, Philippa, jt. auth. see Cameron, Elisabeth.

Lewis, Philippa, jt. auth. see Drury, Elizabeth.

Lewis, Phyllis H., jt. ed. see McDade, Sharon A.

***Lewis, Phyllis R.** Trapped on a Cloud. 100p. (J). Date not set. pap. 7.95 (*0-7610-0263-4*) NW Pub.

***Lewis, Preston.** The Demise of Billy the Kid. large type ed. LC 95-2476. 484p. 1995. 19.95 (*0-7838-1280-9*) Thorndike Pr.

— Demise of Billy the Kid: The Memoirs of H. H. Lomax. 1994. 5.50 (*0-553-56541-9*) Bantam.

Lewis Publishers Staff, et al. Geraghty & Miller's Groundwater Bibliography. 5th ed. 507p. 1991. 79.95 (*0-87371-642-6*, T) Lewis Pubs.

Lewis, R. Aunt Armadillo. (Illus.). 24p. (J). (ps-8). 1985. 12.95 (*0-920303-38-2*, Pub. by Annick CN); pap. 4.95 (*0-920303-39-0*, Pub. by Annick CN) Firefly Bks Ltd.

— Engineering Quantities & Systems of Units. (Illus.). 166p. 1972. 38.00 (*0-85334-530-9*, Pub. by Elsevier Applied Sci UK) Elsevier.

— Show Me the MAC. (Show Me Ser.). (Illus.). 125p. 1993. pap. 12.95 (*1-56761-265-2*) Alpha Bks IN.

Lewis, R., ed. Involving Micros in Education: Proceedings of the IFIP TC 3 & University of Lancaster Joint Working Conference, Lancaster, England, March 24-26, 1982. 240p. 1982. 48.75 (*0-444-86459-8*, North Holland) Elsevier.

Lewis, R. & Otsuki, S., eds. Advanced Research on Computers in Education: Proceedings of the IFIP TC3 International Conference, Tokyo, Japan, 18-20 July, 1990. 362p. 1991. 111.50 (*0-444-88788-1*, North Holland) Elsevier.

Lewis, R. & Tagg, E. D. Computer for Each Student. 1987. 46.50 (*0-318-32598-5*) Elsevier.

Lewis, R. & Tagg, E. D., eds. A Computer for Each Student: Proceedings of the IFIP WG 3.2 Working Conference, Delft University, The Netherlands, April 21-23, 1987. 182p. 1987. 51.50 (*0-444-70301-2*, North Holland) Elsevier.

Lewis, R., jt. ed. see Ercoli, P.

Lewis, R., jt. auth. see Rose, Carla.

Lewis, R., jt. auth. see Sax, I.

Lewis, R. B. Light & Truth. 400p. Date not set. reprint ed. 45.00 (*0-933121-73-3*) Black Classic.

Lewis, R. Barry. The Hood Site: A Late Woodland Hamlet in the Sangamon Valley of Central Illinois. (Reports of Investigations Ser.: No. 31). (Illus.). 41p. 1975. pap. 2.00 (*0-89792-057-0*) Ill St Museum.

— Mississippian Exploitative Strategies: A Southeast Missouri Example. Wood, W. Raymond, ed. LC 73-620254. (Research Ser.: No. 11). (Illus.). 63p. (Orig.). 1974. pap. 5.00 (*0-943414-12-1*) MO Arch Soc.

***Lewis, R. Barry, ed.** Kentucky Archaeology. (Illus.). 312p. 1995. text ed. 29.95 (*0-8131-1907-3*) U Pr of Ky.

Lewis, R. Barry, jt. ed. see Emerson, Thomas E.

Lewis, R. E. & Lewis, J. H. Catalogue of Invalid Genus Group & Species Group Names in Siphonaptera (Insecta) (Theses Zoologicae Ser.: Vol. 11). 263p. 1989. lib. bdg. 135.00 (*3-87429-302-5*) Koeltz Sci Bks.

Lewis, R. E., jt. ed. see Cruse, J. M.

Lewis, R. E., Jr.

Lewis, R. E.

Lewis, R. E., jt. ed. see Cruse, Julius M.

Lewis, R. E., jt. auth. see Schramm, B. A.

Lewis, R. F., Jr., jt. ed. see Cruse, J. M.

Lewis, R. I. Vortex Element Methods for Fluid Dynamic Analysis of Engineering Systems. (Engine Technology Ser.). (Illus.). 450p. (C). 1991. 145.00 (*0-521-36010-2*) Cambridge U Pr.

Lewis, R. J., III. Paraclete a Simple Tale of Magic, Love, & Happiness. LC 92-56935. 86p. 1993. 10.95 (*1-55523-579-4*) Winston-Derek.

Lewis, R. R., jt. ed. see Zorn, J. C.

Lewis, R. T., jt. ed. see Everitt, W. N.

Lewis, R. T., jt. auth. see Knowles, I. W.

Lewis, R. W. The Jameses: A Family Narrative. (Illus.). 660p. 1991. 35.00 (*0-374-17861-5*) FS&G.

— Letters of Edith Wharton. Lewis, Nancy, ed. (Illus.). 672p. 1994. pap. 16.00 (*0-02-034400-7*, Collier S&S) S&S Trade.

— Literary Reflections: A Shoring of Images, 1960-1993. 288p. 1993. text ed. 24.95 (*1-55553-160-1*) NE U Pr.

— Programming Industrial Control Systems Using IEC 1131-3. (IEE Control Engineering Ser.: No. 50). xiv, 281p. 1995. boxed 75.00 (*0-85296-827-2*) Inst Elect Eng.

Lewis, R. W., ed. The Collected Short Stories of Edith Wharton, Vol. 1. (Hudson River Editions Ser.). 752p. 1987. text ed. 60.00 (*0-02-570600-4*, Scribners) S&S Trade.

Lewis, R. W., intro. The Selected Short Stories of Edith Wharton: Introduced & Edited by R. W. B. Lewis. 416p. 1991. text ed. 24.95 (*0-684-19304-3*, Scribners) S&S Trade.

Lewis, R. W. & Pendrill, D. Advanced Financial Accounting. 4th ed. 640p. (Orig.). 1994. pap. 62.50 (*0-273-60500-3*, Pub. by Pitman Pub Ltd UK) Trans-Atl Phila.

Lewis, R. W., ed. see Schrefler, B. A.

Lewis, R. W., ed. see Technical Association of the Pulp & Paper Industry Staff.

Lewis, R. W., ed. see Wharton, Edith.

Lewis, R. W., et al. The Finite Element Method in Heat Transfer Analysis. LC 93-7789. 350p. 1993. text ed. 89.95 (*0-471-93424-0*) Wiley.

— The Finite Element Method in Heat Transfer Analysis. pap. text ed. 49.95 (*0-471-94362-2*) Wiley.

Lewis, R. W., et al, eds. Numerical Methods for Transient & Coupled Problems. (Series in Numerical Methods in Engineering). 1987. text ed. 275.00 (*0-471-91200-X*) Wiley.

— Numerical Methods in Coupled Systems. LC 82-24809. (Numerical Methods in Engineering Ser.: No. 1-405). 400p. 1984. text ed. 298.00 (*0-471-90122-9*, Wiley-Interscience) Wiley.

Lewis, R. W. B. The City of Florence: Historical Vistas & Personal Sightings. LC 94-20160. 1995. 27.50 (*0-374-12404-3*) FS&G.

— Edith Wharton: A Biography. LC 85-13035. (Illus.). 592p. (C). 1985. reprint ed. pap. 15.95 (*0-88064-020-0*) Fromm Intl Pub.

***Lewis, Ralph.** By Dead Reckoning. (Illus.). 240p. 1995. 25.00 (*0-9626483-6-1*) Paladwr Pr.

— Mental Alchemy. 3rd ed. LC 79-66799. 270p. 1978. 17.95 (*0-912057-38-6*, 501830) AMORC.

— Team-Building Skills: Trainer's Guide. LC 94-13300. (One-Day Workshop Ser.). 1994. text ed. 99.95 (*0-07-040831-9*) McGraw.

Lewis, Ralph, ed. The Immortalized Words of the Past. LC 85-63539. 308p. (Orig.). 1986. pap. 12.95 (*0-912057-42-4*, 501950) AMORC.

***Lewis, Ralph & Gardner, Keith S.** Sir William Russell Flint. 1994. 55.00 (*0-7153-9306-5*, Pub. by D & C Pub UK) Sterling.

Lewis, Ralph & Smith, Douglas. Total Quality in Higher Education. LC 93-31083. (Total Quality Ser.). (Illus.). 324p. 1994. 39.95 (*0-9634030-7-9*) St Lucie Pr.

Lewis, Ralph, jt. auth. see Lowe, Phil.

Lewis, Ralph L. & Lewis, Gregg. Inductive Preaching: Helping People Listen. LC 83-70321. 224p. 1983. pap. 10.99 (*0-89107-287-X*) Crossway Bks.

— Learning to Preach Like Jesus. LC 89-50325. 160p. 1989. pap. 9.99 (*0-89107-536-4*) Crossway Bks.

Lewis, Ralph M. The Conscious Interlude. 9th ed. LC 57-8541. 371p. 1985. 18.95 (*0-912057-20-3*, 501810) AMORC.

— Cosmic Mission Fulfilled. 3rd ed. LC 66-25243. 364p. 1978. 18.95 (*0-912057-22-X*, 501790) AMORC.

— Cosmic Mission Fulfilled: The Life of Dr. H. Spencer Lewis - a 20th Century Mystic. LC 66-25243. (Illus.). 364p. Date not set. pap. 16.95 (*0-912057-90-4*, 501790) AMORC.

— Land Buying Checklist. 4th ed. 60p. 1990. pap. 20.00 (*0-86718-358-6*) Home Builder.

— Sanctuary of Self. LC 48-17673. 351p. 1987. pap. 14.95 (*0-912057-53-X*, 502040) AMORC.

— Through the Mind's Eye. LC 81-84954. 371p. 1982. 18.95 (*0-912057-32-7*, 501890) AMORC.

Lewis, Ralph M., ed. The Universe of Numbers. LC 83-51126. 209p. (Orig.). 1984. pap. 12.95 (*0-912057-11-4*, 501920) AMORC.

Lewis, Ramon. The Discipline Dilemma. (C). 1990. 65.00 (*0-86431-083-8*, Pub. by Aust Council Educ Res AT) St Mut.

Lewis, Ramon & Lewis, Susan. The Parenting Puzzle. (C). 1990. 65.00 (*0-86431-036-6*, Pub. by Aust Council Educ Res AT) St Mut.

Lewis, Rand C. A Nazi Legacy: Right-Wing Extremism in West Germany. LC 90-24277. 208p. 1991. text ed. 42.95 (*0-275-93853-0*, C3853, Praeger Pubs) Greenwood.

Lewis, Randolph, ed. see Gilbert, Stuart.

Lewis, Reginald F. & Walker, Blair S. Why Should White Guys Have All the Fun? How Reginald Lewis Created a Billion-Dollar Business Empire. LC 94-17864. 1994. text ed. 22.95 (*0-471-04227-7*) Wiley.

***Lewis, Reina.** Gendering Orientalism: Race, Femininity, & Representation. LC 95-16143. (Gender, Racism, Ethnicity Ser.). 1996. write for info. (*0-415-12489-1*); pap. write for info. (*0-415-12490-5*) Routledge.

Lewis, Rena B. Special Education Technology: Practical Applications. LC 92-35860. 1993. pap. 32.95 (*0-534-20286-1*) Brooks-Cole.

— Teaching Special Students in the Mainstream. 3rd ed. 528p. (C). 1990. pap. write for info. (*0-675-21135-2*, Merrill Pub Co) Macmillan.

Lewis, Rena B., jt. auth. see Lynch, Eleanor W.

Lewis, Rena B., jt. auth. see McLoughlin, James A.

Lewis, Rhys. Practical Digital Image Processing. (Ellis Horwood Series in Digital & Signal Processing). 1991. 51.00 (*0-13-683525-2*, 330103) P-H.

Lewis, Richard. All of You Was Singing. LC 89-18263. (Illus.). 32p. (J). 1991. text ed. 13.95 (*0-689-31596-1*, Atheneum Bks Young) S&S Childrens.

— All of You Was Singing. LC 93-44589. (Illus.). 32p. (J). (gr. k-3). 1994. pap. 4.95 (*0-689-71853-5*, Aladdin Paperbacks) S&S Childrens.

— Compensation for Industrial Injuries. 1987. U.K. text ed. 65.00 (*0-86205-214-9*) Butterworth Legal Pubs.

— A Contemporary Approach to Fidelity & Surety Bonding. Date not set. write for info. (*1-56461-120-5*, 26020) Rough Notes.

— Contractor's Analysis. Date not set. write for info. (*1-56461-136-1*) Rough Notes.

— How to Pay for a College Education Without Going Broke. 204p. 1993. pap. 9.95 (*1-55850-255-6*) Adams Pubng.

— In the Night, Still Dark. LC 87-11538. (Illus.). 32p. (J). 1988. text ed. 13.95 (*0-689-31310-1*, Atheneum Bks Young) S&S Childrens.

— Leaders & Teachers: Adult Education & the Challenge of Labour in South Wales, 1906-40. (Studies in Welsh History Ser.: Vol. VIII). xxiv, 271p. 1993. 40.00 (*0-7083-1219-5*, Pub. by U of Wales UK) Bks Intl VA.

— Multicultural Global History. 144p. (C). 1993. per., pap. text ed. 20.95 (*0-8403-8594-3*) Kendall-Hunt.

— Sax's Dangerous Properties of Industrial Materials/ Hawley's Condensed Chemical Dictionary CD-ROM. 1995. text ed. 300.00 (*0-442-01946-7*) Van Nos Reinhold.

— When Thought Is Young: Reflections on Teaching & the Poetry of the Child. LC 91-61262. (Illus.). 80p. 1992. pap. 7.95 (*0-89823-137-X*) New Rivers Pr.

Lewis, Richard, ed. Miracles: Poems by Children of the English Speaking World. 1966. reprint ed. pap. 5.95 (*0-686-39707-X*) Touchstone Ctr Child.

L

L

Lewis, Richard & Lewis, Susan. The Power of Art. (Illus.). 528p. (Orig.). (C). 1994. pap. text ed. 44.00 (*0-15-500320-8*) HB Coll Pubs.

Lewis, Richard C. Contract Suretyship. 1991. 49.50 (*1-56461-037-3*, 46100) Rough Notes.

Lewis, Richard E., jt. ed. see Gregory, Robert G.

Lewis, Richard J. Food Additives Handbook. 1989. text ed. 99.95 (*0-442-20508-2*) Van Nos Reinhold.

Lewis, Richard J., Sr. Hawley's Condensed Chemical Dictionary. 12th ed. LC 92-18951. 1275p. 1993. text ed. 69.95 (*0-442-01131-8*) Van Nos Reinhold.

— Hazardous Chemicals Desk Reference. 3rd rev. ed. LC 92-46784. 1600p. 1993. text ed. 99.95 (*0-442-01408-2*) Van Nos Reinhold.

— Lewis: Sax's Dangerous Properties of Industrial Materials. 8th ed. 4400p. 1992. text ed. 399.95 (*0-442-01132-6*) Van Nos Reinhold.

Lewis, Richard J. Rapid Guide to Hazardous Chemicals in the Workplace. 3rd ed. 1994. pap. 19.95 (*0-442-01759-6*) Van Nos Reinhold.

Lewis, Richard J., Sr. Reproductively Active Chemicals. 1100p. 1991. text ed. 139.95 (*0-442-31878-2*) Van Nos Reinhold.

Lewis, Richard J., jt. auth. see Sax, N. Irving.

Lewis, Richard O. Conventional Functions of Black English in American Literature. 100p. 1995. 44.95 (*1-880921-64-2*); pap. 24.95 (*1-880921-53-7*) Austin & Winfield.

Lewis, Richard P., ed. see American College of Cardiology Staff.

Lewis, Richard P., jt. ed. see Warren, James V.

Lewis, Richard S. Space in the Twenty-First Century. (Illus.). 240p. 1990. 29.95 (*0-231-06304-0*) Col U Pr.

— Voyages of Columbia. 1984. text ed. 37.00 (*0-231-05924-8*) Col U Pr.

Lewis, Richard W. American Adam. LC 55-5133. 1959. pap. text ed. 10.95 (*0-226-47681-2*, P38) U Ch Pr.

Lewis, Ricki. The Beginnings of Life: An Introduction to Cell, Molecular & Developmental Biology. 368p. (C). 1991. write for info. (*0-697-12678-1*) Wm C Brown Pubs.

— The Beginnings of Life: An Introduction to Cell, Molecular & Developmental Biology. 2nd ed. 136p. 1994. student ed, spiral bd. write for info. (*0-697-24806-2*) Wm C Brown Pubs.

— Human Genetics: Concepts & Applications. 416p. (C). 1993. Case wkbk. student ed write for info. (*0-697-22287-X*) Wm C Brown Pubs.

— Human Genetics: Concepts & Applications. 416p. (C). 1993. pap. text ed. 40.00 (*0-697-13315-X*) Wm C Brown Pubs.

— Human Genetics: Concepts & Applications. 416p. (C). 1994. Study guide. student ed write for info. (*0-697-20817-6*) Wm C Brown Pubs.

— Life. 832p. (C). 1991. pap. write for info. (*0-697-14187-X*); pap. write for info. (*0-697-14193-4*); write for info. (*0-697-12059-7*) Wm C Brown Pubs.

— Life. 832p. (C). 1991. text ed. write for info. (*0-697-05392-X*); student ed write for info. (*0-697-05637-6*); student ed write for info. (*0-697-05636-8*) Wm C Brown Pubs.

Lewis, Ricki & Moore, Randall c. The Kingdoms of Life. 2nd ed. 128p. (C). 1995. pap. text ed. write for info. (*0-697-22897-5*) Wm C Brown Pubs.

— Life. 2nd ed. 920p. (C). 1994. pap. text ed. write for info. (*0-697-15924-8*) Wm C Brown Pubs.

— Life. 2nd ed. 920p. (C). 1995. text ed. write for info. (*0-697-15923-X*) Wm C Brown Pubs.

— Life, Lab Manual. 2nd ed. 192p. (C). 1994. student ed, spiral bd. write for info. (*0-697-15942-6*) Wm C Brown Pubs.

— Life, Study Art Notebook. 2nd ed. 232p. 1994. student ed, spiral bd. write for info. (*0-697-24548-9*) Wm C Brown Pubs.

— Life, Study Guide. 2nd ed. 176p. (C). 1995. student ed, spiral bd. write for info. (*0-697-15945-0*) Wm C Brown Pubs.

Lewis, Ricki, jt. auth. see Moore, Randall c.

Lewis, Rik. Dragonfly: Cycle of Fire. Black, Bill, ed. (Illus.). 52p. (Orig.). 1991. pap. 9.95 (*1-56225-000-0*) A C Comics.

Lewis, Rob. Friska, the Sheep That Was Too Small. 1989. pap. 3.95 (*0-374-42463-2*) FS&G.

— Henrietta's First Winter. (Illus.). 32p. (J). (ps-3). 1990. 11.95 (*0-374-32951-6*) FS&G.

— Jake's Birthday. (Illus.). 32p. (J). (ps-k). 1994. 17.95 (*0-370-31776-9*, Pub. by Bodley Head UK) Trafalgar.

— Tidy up, Trevor. LC 92-30327. (J). (ps-3). 1993. 13.95 (*0-15-200626-5*) HarBrace.

— The White Bicycle. LC 88-45092. (Illus.). 32p. (J). (ps up). 1988. 12.00 (*0-374-38384-7*) FS&G.

Lewis, Rob, jt. auth. see Nelson, Linda A.

Lewis, Robert. Advice to the Players. LC 79-3291. 192p. 1989. reprint ed. pap. 8.95 (*1-55936-003-8*) Theatre Comm.

— Geographic Perspectives on Soviet Central Asia. 256p. 1991. 69.95 (*0-415-07592-0*, A8175) Routledge Chapman & Hall.

Lewis, Robert, Jr. Hemingway on Love. LC 72-6772. (Studies in Fiction: No. 34). 1972. reprint ed. lib. bdg. 75.00 (*0-8383-1650-6*) M S G Haskell Hse.

Lewis, Robert. Method or Madness. 165p. 1958. 6.50 (*0-573-69033-2*) French.

Lewis, Robert & Hendricks, William. Rocking the Roles: Building a Win-Win Marriage. LC 91-61395. 252p. (Orig.). 1991. pap. 10.00 (*0-89109-641-8*) NavPress.

Lewis, Robert & Mendelsohn, Patrick, eds. Lessons from Learning: Proceedings of the IFIP TC3 - WG3.3 Wording Conference on Lessons from Learning, Archamps, France. LC 94-7739. (IFIP Transactions Ser.). 1994. write for info. (*0-444-81832-4*) Elsevier.

Lewis, Robert & Tagg, E. D., eds. Informatics & Education: An Anthology of Papers Selected from IFIP TC3 Publications since the Establishment of TC3 in 1963. 750p. 1988. 128.25 (*0-444-70417-5*, North Holland) Elsevier.

Lewis, Robert A. & Rowland, Richard H. Population Redistribution in the U. S. S. R. Its Impact on Society 1897-1977. LC 79-18076. (Praeger Special Studies). 510p. 1979. text ed. 95.00 (*0-275-90382-6*, C0382, Praeger Pubs) Greenwood.

Lewis, Robert A., jt. ed. see Culp, Robert D.

Lewis, Robert A., et al, eds. Environmental Specimen Banking & Monitoring As Related to Banking. 370p. 1983. lib. bdg. 140.00 (*0-89838-621-7*) Kluwer Ac.

Lewis, Robert C. Cases in Hospitality Marketing & Management. 1989. Net. pap. text ed. write for info. (*0-471-50898-5*) Wiley.

— Marketing Leadership in Hospitality. 2nd ed. (Hospitality, Travel & Tourism Ser.). 1994. text ed. 49.95 (*0-442-01888-6*) Van Nos Reinhold.

Lewis, Robert C., jt. auth. see Leitritz, Earl.

Lewis, Robert E. Ceratophyllidae: Currently Accepted Valid Taxa (Insecta: Siphonaptera) (Theses Zoologicae Ser.: Vol. 13). (Illus.). 267p. 1990. text ed. 143.00 (*3-87429-304-1*) Koeltz Sci Bks.

— Handbook for Contributors to the Chaucer Library. LC 73-81628. 30p. 1973. pap. 2.50 (*0-8203-0320-8*) U of Ga Pr.

— How to Conduct a Sensitivity Analysis. Burke, Sarah A., ed. LC 91-22358. (Illus.). 64p. (Orig.). 1991. pap. text ed. 55.00 (*0-936742-83-6*, 32461) Robt Morris Assocs.

Lewis, Robert E. & Williams, Mary J., eds. Middle English Dictionary: Fascicle T.1. (C). 1992. pap. text ed. 22.50 (*0-472-01211-8*) U of Mich Pr.

— Middle English Dictionary: Fascicle T.2. (C). 1992. pap. text ed. 22.50 (*0-472-01212-6*) U of Mich Pr.

Lewis, Robert E., jt. auth. see Adams, Nancy E.

Lewis, Robert E., jt. ed. see Williams, Jerry M.

Lewis, Robert E., et al. Fleas of the Pacific Northwest. LC 88-1612. (Illus.). 304p. 1988. text ed. 59.95 (*0-87071-355-8*) Oreg St U Pr.

Lewis, Robert E., et al, eds. Middle English Dictionary: Fascicle T.3. 128p. 1994. pap. text ed. 22.50 (*0-472-01213-4*) U of Mich Pr.

— Middle English Dictionary: Fascicle T.4. 128p. 1994. pap. text ed. 22.50 (*0-472-01214-2*) U of Mich Pr.

— Middle English Dictionary: Fascicle T.5. 128p. 1994. pap. text ed. 15.00 (*0-472-01215-0*) U of Mich Pr.

***Lewis, Robert F.** Last One in's a Rotten Egg. Ingram, tr. 230p. Date not set. pap. 8.95 (*0-7610-0450-5*) NW Pub.

Lewis, Robert J. Fire Station Location Studies Using a Microcomputer. 1986. pap. 5.35 (*0-318-22360-0*, TR 86-1) Society Fire Protect.

— Welsh Family Coats of Arms. (Illus.). 96p. (Orig.). 1995. pap. text ed. 22.00 (*0-7884-0156-4*) Heritage Bk.

Lewis, Robert J., jt. auth. see Koohang, Alex A.

Lewis, Robert J. C. Lewis Patriarchs of Early Virginia & Maryland with Some Arms & Origins. (Illus.). xii, 166p. (Orig.). 1991. pap. text ed. 24.00 (*1-55613-471-1*) S B Paoli.

Lewis, Robert M. & Picut, Catherine A. Veterinary Clinical Immunology: From Classroom to Clinics. LC 88-22624. 280p. reprint ed. pap. 79.80 (*0-7837-2851-4*, 2057621) Bks Demand.

Lewis, Robert O. Independent Verification & Validation: A Life Cycle Engineering Process for Quality Software. (New Dimensions in Engineering Ser.). 384p. 1992. text ed. 74.95 (*0-471-57011-7*) Wiley.

Lewis, Robert S. Elements of Mining. 3rd ed. LC 64-14990. 782p. reprint ed. pap. 180.00 (*0-317-10407-1*, 2016298) Bks Demand.

***Lewis, Robert T.** A New Look at Growing Older: Reprogramming for the Years Ahead. LC 95-67021. 200p. (Orig.). 1995. pap. 9.95 (*0-9644889-2-2*) Southland Pub.

Lewis, Robert T. & Peterson, Hugh M. Human Behavior: An Introduction to Psychology. LC 71-190207. 469p. reprint ed. pap. 133.70 (*0-317-10440-3*, 2012539) Bks Demand.

— Human Behavior: An Introduction to Psychology (Student Guide) LC 71-190207. (Illus.). 117p. reprint ed. pap. 33.40 (*0-317-10445-4*, 2012540) Bks Demand.

Lewis, Robert W. A Farewell to Arms: The War of the Words. (Masterwork Studies). 170p. (C). 1992. text ed. 21.95 (*0-8057-8052-1*, Pub. by Royal Botanic Garden UK); pap. 12.95 (*0-8057-8102-1*, Pub. by Royal Botanic Garden UK) Macmillan.

Lewis, Robert W., ed. Hemingway in Italy & Other Essays: Critical Approaches. LC 89-48747. 232p. 1990. text ed. 49.95 (*0-275-92916-7*, C2916, Greenwood Pr) Greenwood.

Lewis, Robin J. E. M. Forster's Passages to India. LC 79-843. 168p. 1979. text ed. 39.00 (*0-231-04508-5*) Col U Pr.

***Lewis, Robyn, ed.** The Legal Dictionary: English - Welsh. 500p. 1992. 114.00 (*0-86383-534-1*, Pub. by Gomer Pr UK) St Mut.

Lewis, Roger. Color & the Edgar Cayce Readings. 48p. 1973. pap. 4.00 (*0-87604-068-7*, 264) ARE Pr.

Lewis, Roger & Kelloway, Ros. Jacques & Lewis: Sex Discrimination & Occupational Pension Schemes. Vaughan, David, ed. (Current EC Legal Developments Ser.). 255p. 1994. pap. 169.00 (*0-406-00344-0*) Butterworth Legal Pubs.

Lewis, Roger, ed. see Kipling, Rudyard.

***Lewis, Roger C.** Thomas James Wise & the Trial Book Fallacy. (Illus.). 260p. 1994. 74.95 (*1-85928-036-6*, Pub. by Scolar Pr UK) Ashgate Pub Co.

Lewis, Roger K. Architect? A Candid Guide to the Profession. (Orig.). 1985. pap. 15.00x (*0-262-62048-0*) MIT Pr.

Lewis, Roland. Home Video Maker's Handbook. LC 87-15558. (Illus.). 224p. 1987. 5.99 (*0-517-05602-X*) Random Hse Value.

— Learn to Make Videos in a Weekend. LC 92-54795. 1993. 16.00 (*0-679-42230-7*) Knopf.

Lewis, Roland W. Numerical Methods in Heat Transfer, Vol. 1. LC 80-49973. (Wiley Series in Numerical Methods in Engineering). 552p. reprint ed. pap. 157.40 (*0-7837-6553-3*, 2044131) Bks Demand.

— Numerical Methods in Heat Transfer, Vol. 3. LC 80-49973. (Wiley Series in Numerical Methods in Engineering). (Illus.). 308p. reprint ed. pap. 87.80 (*0-7837-4391-2*, 2044131) Bks Demand.

***Lewis, Ron.** Flashback: The Untold Story of Lee Harvey Oswald. (Illus.). 272p. (Orig.). 1993. pap. 14.95 (*1-883305-00-4*) Lewcom Prods.

Lewis, Ronald J. Activity-Based Costing for Marketing & Manufacturing. LC 92-31710. 248p. 1993. text ed. 59.95 (*0-89930-801-5*, LYB, Quorum Bks) Greenwood.

— Activity-Based Models for Cost Management Systems. LC 94-37876. 296p. 1995. text ed. 59.95 (*0-89930-965-8*, Quorum Bks) Greenwood.

— Murder in Mackinac. LC 94-72293. 143p. 1994. pap. 12.95 (*0-9642436-0-1*) Agawa Pr.

Lewis, Ronald L. Black Coal Miners in America: Race, Class, & Community Conflict, 1780-1980. LC 87-2086. (Illus.). 256p. 1987. 28.00 (*0-8131-1610-4*) U Pr of Ky.

— Coal, Iron, & Slaves: Industrial Slavery in Maryland & Virginia, 1715-1865. LC 78-55333. (Contributions in Labor Studies: No. 6). (Illus.). 283p. 1979. text ed. 59.95 (*0-313-20522-1*, LCI/, Greenwood Pr) Greenwood.

Lewis, Ronald L., jt. ed. see Foner, Philip S.

Lewis, Ros, jt. auth. see Howe, Renate.

Lewis, Rose E. Hug 'em to Heaven. (Orig.). 1989. pap. 4.00 (*0-915541-50-5*) Star Bks Inc.

— With All My Heart. (Orig.). 1990. pap. 4.00 (*0-915541-57-2*) Star Bks Inc.

Lewis, Rosellen, jt. auth. see Lewers, Irene.

Lewis, Rosemary. Review for CLEP General English Composition. rev. ed. 245p. (C). 1988. vhs 750.00 (*1-56030-017-5*) Comex Systs.

— Review for CLEP General English Composition. rev. ed. 245p. (C). 1994. pap. text ed. 12.95 (*1-56030-001-9*) Comex Systs.

***Lewis, Rosemary, et al.** Our Children's Heritage: A History of Clarkston-Independence Township. (Illus.). (J). (gr. 2-4). 1995. text ed. 8.79 (*0-9621749-1-2*) Clarkston CHS.

— Our Children's Heritage: A History of Clarkston-Independence Township. (Illus.). 81p. (J). (gr. 2-4). 1995. 25.00 (*0-9621749-2-0*) Clarkston CHS.

— Reviewbooks for the GED Test. (Reviewbooks for the GED Test Ser.). (Illus.). (YA). 1992. pap. text ed. 90.65 (*1-56030-089-2*) Comex Systs.

Lewis, Rosemary P., ed. see Powell, Ken L.

Lewis, Rosemary R., jt. auth. see Lewis, M. K.

Lewis, Roth. Principles of Epidemiology: A Self Teaching Guide. 1982. pap. text ed. 66.00 (*0-12-593180-8*) Acad Pr.

Lewis, Roy. Bloodeagle. large type ed. LC 93-43541. 1994. 22.95 (*0-7927-1928-X*, Curley Lrg Print); pap. 20.95 (*0-7927-1927-1*, Curley Lrg Print) Chivers N Amer.

— Bloodeagle: An Arnold Landon Mystery. 224p. 1993. 19.95 (*0-312-10431-6*) St Martin.

— Choosing Your Career, Finding Your Vocation: A Step-by-Step Guide for Adults & Counselors. 1989. pap. 9.95 (*0-8091-3099-8*) Paulist Pr.

— Cross Bearer: An Arnold Landon Mystery. 1994. 18.95 (*0-312-11765-5*) St Martin.

— The Devil Is Dead. large type ed. 1990. 17.95 (*0-7451-9920-8*, C0638, Atlantic Lrg Print); pap. 15.95 (*0-7927-0370-7*, C0832, Atlantic Lrg Print) Chivers N Amer.

— Evolution Man: Or, How I Ate My Father. 1994. pap. 10.00 (*0-679-75009-6*, Vin) Random.

— Evolution Man or, How I Ate My Father. LC 93-3359. 1993. 18.00 (*0-679-42727-9*) Pantheon.

— Men of Subtle Craft. 192p. 1988. 13.95 (*0-312-81789-4*) St Martin.

— A Secret Dying. large type ed. LC 93-6729. 1993. 21.95 (*0-7927-1546-2*, Curley Lrg Print); pap. 19.95 (*0-7927-1545-4*, Curley Lrg Print) Chivers N Amer.

— A Secret Dying: An Arthur Landon Mystery. LC 92-33373. 1993. 17.95 (*0-312-08887-6*) St Martin.

Lewis, Roy H. A Cracking of Spines. large type ed. (Linford Mystery Library). 352p. 1987. pap. 11.95 (*0-7089-6459-1*, Linford) Ulverscroft.

— The Manuscript Murders. large type ed. (Linford Mystery Library). 304p. 1987. pap. 11.95 (*0-7089-6389-7*) Ulverscroft.

— A Pension for Death. large type ed. (Linford Mystery Library). 336p. 1987. pap. 11.95 (*0-7089-6395-1*) Ulverscroft.

— A Wisp of Smoke. large type ed. 326p. 1992. 21.95 (*0-7505-0355-6*) Ulverscroft.

Lewis, Roy R., III, ed. Creation & Restoration of Coastal Plant Communities. 232p. 1982. 156.00 (*0-8493-6573-2*, QK938, CRC Reprint) Franklin.

Lewis, Royce C., Jr. Primary Care Orthopaedics. (Illus.). 328p. 1988. text ed. 43.50 (*0-443-08356-8*) Churchill.

Lewis, Rudy. International Trader's IntroGuide. LC 93-72321. (Illus.). 230p. 1993. pap. 18.00 (*1-878647-10-5*) Duncan & Duncan.

Lewis, Rupert. Garvey: His Work & Impact. LC 91-70398. 1991. 49.95 (*0-86543-225-2*); pap. 14.95 (*0-86543-224-4*) Africa World.

— Marcus Garvey: Anti-Colonial Champion. LC 87-72598. 280p. 1988. 29.95 (*0-86543-061-6*); pap. 11.95 (*0-86543-062-4*) Africa World.

Lewis, Rupert & Warner-Lewis, Maureen, eds. Garvey: Africa, Europe, the Americas. 200p. 1994. 39.95 (*0-86543-415-8*); pap. 14.95 (*0-86543-416-6*) Africa World.

Lewis, Russell. The New Service Society. LC 74-169688. 187p. reprint ed. pap. 53.30 (*0-317-09733-4*, 2005887) Bks Demand.

Lewis, Russell, ed. Recent Controversies in Political Economy. LC 91-45321. 320p. 1992. 89.95 (*0-415-06163-6*, A7333) Routledge.

Lewis, Ruth A., jt. auth. see Lewis, John S.

Lewis, S. & Beumer, J. The Branemark Implant System: Clinical & Laboratory Procedures. (Illus.). 250p. 1990. 95.00 (*0-912791-62-4*) Ishiyaku Euro.

Lewis, S., jt. ed. see Appelbaum, D.

Lewis, S. J. Forgotten Legions: German Army Infantry Policy, 1918-1941. LC 85-6601. 208p. 1985. text ed. 37.50 (*0-275-90235-8*, C0235, Praeger Pubs) Greenwood.

Lewis, S. M. Myelofibrosis Pathophysiology & Clinical Management. (Hematology Ser.: Vol. 4). 224p. 1985. 125.00 (*0-8247-7411-6*) Dekker.

***Lewis, S. M. & Koepke, J. A., eds.** Hematology Laboratory Management & Practice. LC 94-35300. 1995. 95.00 (*0-7506-0964-8*) Buttrwrth-Heinemann.

Lewis, S. M., jt. auth. see Dacie, John V.

Lewis, S. M., jt. ed. see Dacie, John V.

***Lewis, Sadie & Hermes, Robert.** ATM/Sonet Explained. 159p. (Orig.). 1995. pap. 12.95 (*1-880548-53-4*) Numidia Pr.

Lewis, Sadie & Marney-Petix, V. C. Your Pocket SONET-ATM Glossary. (Quick Reference Ser.). (Illus.). 165p. (Orig.). 1993. pap. 12.95 (*1-880548-52-6*) Numidia Pr.

Lewis, Sam, ed. Talisman. (Earthdawn Ser.: No. 5). 288p. (Orig.). 1994. pap. 4.99 (*0-451-45389-1*, ROC) NAL-Dutton.

Lewis, Samella. African American Art & Artists. LC 93-40781. 1994. 50.00 (*0-520-08788-7*); pap. 25.00 (*0-520-08532-9*) U CA Pr.

— Art: African American. 2nd rev. ed. (Illus.). 312p. (Orig.). (C). 1990. reprint ed. pap. text ed. 25.00 (*0-941248-08-9*) Hancraft.

Lewis, Samella S. & Waddy, Ruth. Black Artists on Art, 2 vols, 1. rev. ed. LC 76-97788. 1971. pap. 15.00 (*0-941248-04-6*) Hancraft.

— Black Artists on Art, 2 vols, 2. rev. ed. LC 76-97788. 1971. 20.00 (*0-941248-02-X*); pap. 15.00 (*0-941248-05-4*) Hancraft.

— Black Artists on Art, 2 vols, Set. rev. ed. LC 76-97788. 1971. 40.00 (*0-941248-00-3*); pap. 30.00 (*0-941248-03-8*) Hancraft.

— Black Artists on Art, 2 vols, Vol. 1. rev. ed. LC 76-97788. 1971. 20.00 (*0-941248-01-1*) Hancraft.

Lewis, Samuel. A Topographical Dictionary of Ireland, 2 Vols., Set. LC 83-82827. 1480p. 1995. reprint ed. 85.00 (*0-8063-1063-4*) Genealog Pub.

— A Topographical Dictionary of Scotland, 2 vols. LC 89-83729. 1233p. 1989. 75.00 (*0-8063-1255-6*) Genealog Pub.

Lewis, Samuel L. The Jerusalem Trilogy. Tessler, Sitara & Jablonski, Moineddin, eds. (Illus.). 336p. (Orig.). 1975. pap. 5.95 (*0-915424-03-7*, Prophecy Pressworks) PeaceWks Intl Ctr Dances Univ Peace.

— The Rejected Avatar. (Illus.). 24p. (Orig.). 1968. pap. 1.25 (*0-915424-00-2*, Prophecy Pressworks) PeaceWks Intl Ctr Dances Univ Peace.

— Siva! Siva! Cresent & Heart: Selected Poetry of Murshid Samuel L. Lewis. (Bismillah Bks.: No. 1). (Illus.). 112p. (Orig.). 1980. pap. 3.50 (*0-915424-04-5*) PeaceWks Intl Ctr Dances Univ Peace.

— Sufi Vision & Initiation: Meetings with Remarkable Beings. Douglas-Klotz, Neil, ed. LC 86-42579. (Illus.). 398p. (Orig.). 1986. pap. 12.95 (*0-915424-10-X*) PeaceWks Intl Ctr Dances Univ Peace.

Lewis, Samuel L. & Douglas-Klotz, Neil. Spiritual Dance & Walk: An Introduction to the Dances of Universal Peace & Walking Meditations of Samuel L. Lewis. rev. ed. Demcho-Wagor, Marie, ed. (Illus.). 144p. 1990. 14.95 (*0-915424-12-6*); pap. 9.95 (*0-915424-13-4*) PeaceWks Intl Ctr Dances Univ Peace.

Lewis, Samuel L. & Khan, Hazrat I. The Bowl of Saki Commentary. Jablonski, Moineddin & Klotz, Saadi, eds. 180p. (Orig.). 1981. pap. 18.00 (*0-915424-08-8*) PeaceWks Intl Ctr Dances Univ Peace.

Lewis, Samuel M. Modes of Historical Discourse in J. G. Herder & N. M. Karamzin. LC 94-18326. (Studies on the Themes & Motifs in Literature: Vol. 12). Date not set. write for info. (*0-8204-2576-1*) P Lang Pubs.

Lewis, Samuel W., intro. The A. D. L. Handbook on Israel: Pocket Size Resource Guide. (Illus.). 170p. 1985. 9.95 (*0-88464-057-4*) ADL.

— A Directory of U. S. Resources on the Rule of Law for the Independent States of the Former Soviet Union. LC 92-33149. (Orig.). 1992. pap. 14.95 (*1-878379-16-X*) US Inst Peace.

Lewis, Sandra C. Elder Care in Occupational Therapy. LC 87-43265. 502p. 1989. pap. 36.00 (*1-55642-037-4*) SLACK Inc.

Lewis, Sangeeta P., jt. auth. see Sharma, Hari D.

Lewis, Sara. Eating Well on a Budget. (C). 1992. 30.00 (*0-86242-120-9*, Pub. by Age Concern Eng UK) St Mut.

— Heart Conditions. large type ed. LC 93-19355. 370p. 1994. 21.95 (*0-15-139805-4*) HarBrace.

— Heart Conditions. large type ed. LC 94-8001. 1994. 21.95 (*0-7862-0221-1*) Thorndike Pr.

Lewis, Sasha G. Sunday's Women: A Report on Lesbian Life Today. LC 78-53655. 229p. reprint ed. pap. 65.30 (*0-7837-1385-1*, 2041561) Bks Demand.

Lewis, Saunders. Saunders Lewis: A Presentation of His Work. Jones, Harri P., ed. 228p. 1990. pap. 14.95 (*0-87243-187-8*) Templegate.

An Asterisk (*) at the beginning of an entry indicates that the title is appearing in BIP for the first time.

Lewis, Scott. Rainforest Book. LC 90-70820. 112p. 1990. pap. 7.95 (*0-9626072-1-5*) Living Planet Pr.
— The Rainforest Book. 128p. (Orig.). 1993. pap. 3.99 (*0-425-13769-4*) Berkley Pub.
Lewis, Scott, jt. auth. see Bratman, Fred.
Lewis, Scott, ed. see Browning, Robert & Browning, Elizabeth Barrett.
Lewis, Scott, jt. auth. see Ellis, Drew.
Lewis, Scott M. Ob-Gyn Malpractice. LC 85-22450. (Medico-Legal Library). 602p. 1989. text ed. 138.00 (*0-471-81032-0*) Wiley.
— Ob-Gyn Malpractice, No. 2. suppl. ed. LC 85-22450. (Medico-Legal Library). 256p. 1993. 68.00 (*0-471-59812-7*) Wiley.
Lewis, Shannon. Personal Habits. 1984. pap. 3.50 (*0-8217-1306-X*) Zebra.
Lewis, Sharen, jt. auth. see LaMorte, Kathy.
Lewis, Shari. Air Charlie. (Lamb Chop's Play-Along Adventures Ser.). (J). (ps-3). 1994. 2.99 (*0-553-37391-9*) Bantam.
— The Boat Contest: The Lion & the Mouse. Marshall, Blaine, ed. (Lamb Chop's Fables Ser.). (Illus.). 32p. (J). (ps-3). 1993. 9.95 (*0-8094-7446-8*) Time-Life.
— Cinderella: Lamb Chop's Play-Along Fairy Tales. (J). (ps-3). 1994. pap. 2.99 (*0-553-37386-2*) Bantam.
— Goldilocks & the Three Bears: Lamb Chop's Play-along Fairy Tales. (J). (ps-3). 1994. pap. 2.99 (*0-553-37388-9*) Bantam.
— Lamb Chop's Fables: The Lamb Who Could Featuring Aesop's The Tortoise & the Hare. Doyle, Robert A., ed. (Illus.). 32p. (J). Date not set. write for info. (*0-8094-7804-8*) Time-Life.
— One-Minute Bible Stories: New Testament. (J). (ps). 1991. mass mkt. 4.99 (*0-440-40628-5*, YB) Dell.
— One-Minute Bible Stories: Old Testament. (J). (ps). 1991. mass mkt. 4.99 (*0-440-40627-7*, YB) Dell.
— One-Minute Bible Stories: Old Testament. LC 86-2011. (Illus.). 48p. (J). (ps-3). 1986. lib. bdg. 10.00 (*0-385-19565-0*) Doubleday.
— One-Minute Birthday Stories. (J). (ps-3). 1995. pap. 4.99 (*0-440-41004-5*) Dell.
— One-Minute Birthday Stories. (J). (ps-3). 1992. mass mkt. 10.00 (*0-385-41325-4*) Doubleday.
— One Minute Christmas. (J). 1993. mass mkt. 4.99 (*0-440-40856-3*) Dell.
— One-Minute Easter Stories. (J). (ps-3). 1993. mass mkt. 3.99 (*0-440-40764-8*) Dell.
— One-Minute Favorite Fairy Tales. (J). (ps). 1991. mass mkt. 3.99 (*0-440-40625-0*, YB) Dell.
— One Minute Jewish Stories. (J). 1993. mass mkt. 4.99 (*0-440-40878-4*) Dell.
— One-Minute Scary Stories. (J). (ps-3). 1993. 4.99 (*0-440-40833-4*) Dell.
— One-Minute Scary Stories. (J). (ps-3). 1991. mass mkt. 10.00 (*0-385-41778-0*) Doubleday.
— Plant Yzark. (Lamb Chop's Play-Along Adventures Ser.). (J). (ps-3). 1994. 2.99 (*0-553-37389-7*) Bantam.
— Ring. (Lamb Chop's Play-Along Adventures Ser.). (J). (ps-3). 1994. pap. 2.99 (*0-553-37390-0*) Bantam.
— Shari Lewis Presents One Hundred & One Things for Kids to Do. LC 86-43065. (Illus.). 96p. (J). (gr. 1-5). 1987. lib. bdg. 9.99 (*0-394-98966-X*) Random Bks Yng Read.
— Shari Lewis Presents One Hundred One Games & Songs for Kids to Play & Sing. LC 92-20572. (Illus.). 96p. (J). (gr. 1-5). 1993. lib. bdg. 9.99 (*0-679-92271-7*); pap. 6.99 (*0-679-82271-2*) Random Bks Yng Read.
— Three Little Pigs: Lamb Chop's Play-along Fairy Tales. (J). (ps-3). 1994. pap. 2.99 (*0-553-37387-0*) Bantam.
— You Can Do It, Lamb Chop: Featuring Aesop's the Tortoise & the Hare. Doyle, Robert A., ed. LC 93-46420. (Illus.). 32p. (J). 1994. 5.95 (*0-8094-7832-3*) Time-Life.
— You Can Do It, Lamb Chop! With Puppet. (J). 1994. pap. 16.95 (*0-8094-7833-1*) Time-Life.
Lewis, Shari & O'Kun, Lan. One-Minute Bedtime Stories. LC 79-8024. (Books for Young Readers). (Illus.). 48p. (J). (ps-3). 1982. mass mkt. 10.00 (*0-385-15292-2*) Doubleday.
Lewis, Shari & Oppenheimer, Lillian. Folding Paper Puppets. rev. ed. 1995. pap. 11.95 (*0-8128-8541-4*, Scrbrough Hse) Madison Bks UPA.
— Folding Paper Toys. rev. ed. LC 63-20060. (Illus.). 100p. (J). (gr. 4 up). 1992. reprint ed. pap. 11.95 (*0-8128-1953-5*, Scrbrough Hse) Madison Bks UPA.
Lewis, Shari & Zimmerman, Dick. Shari Lewis Presents One Hundred-One Magic Tricks for Kids to Do. LC 89-10360. (Illus.). 96p. (Orig.). (J). 1990. lib. bdg. 9.99 (*0-394-92059-7*); pap. 6.95 (*0-394-82059-2*) Random Bks Yng Read.
Lewis, Sharon. Medical Surgical Nursing: Assessment & Management of Clinical Problems. 2nd ed. 1987. 59.95 (*0-07-037568-2*) McGraw.
Lewis, Sharon & Collier, I. Medical Surgical Nursing: Assessment & Management of Clinical Problems. 1888p. (C). 1983. text ed. 59.95 (*0-07-037561-5*) McGraw.
Lewis, Sheila. Destroy Not the Dream. (Rainbow Romances Ser.). 160p. 1993. 14.95 (*0-7090-4914-5*, Hale-Parkwest) Parkwest Pubns.
— Destroy Not the Dream. large type ed. (Romance Ser.). 288p. 1994. pap. 14.95 (*0-7089-7544-5*, Trailtree Bookshop) Ulverscroft.
— For Love of Lucia. large type ed. (Linford Romance Library). 272p. 1993. pap. 14.95 (*0-7089-7319-1*, Trailtree Bookshop) Ulverscroft.
Lewis, Sherman L. Evaluating Corporate Investment & Financing Opportunities: A Handbook & Guide to Selected Methods for Managers & Finance Professionals. LC 86-623. 309p. 1986. text ed. 75.00 (*0-89930-144-4*, LCP/, Quorum Bks) Greenwood.
— The Improvement of Corporate Financial Performance: A Manager's Guide to Evaluating Selected Opportunities. LC 88-35684. 395p. 1989. text ed. 75.00 (*0-89930-432-X*, LIM/, Quorum Bks) Greenwood.
Lewis, Sherri Y., ed. see Cochran, Judith.
***Lewis, Sherry.** Call Me Mom. (Women Who Dare Ser.). 1995. 3.50 (*0-373-70628-6*, 1-70628-2) Harlequin Bks.
— No Place for Secrets. 256p. (Orig.). 1993. pap. text ed. 4.99 (*0-425-14835-1*, Prime Crime) Berkley Pub.
Lewis, Sherry L. My Trip to the Big Chicken. LC 93-80806. 32p. (J). 1993. pap. write for info. (*0-9639319-0-3*) K S Jewels.
Lewis, Shirley, jt. ed. see Dabney, Norma.
Lewis, Sian. Smoke in the Tunnel. (YA). 1991. pap. 23.00 (*0-685-60035-1*, Pub. by Gomer Pr UK) St Mut.
***Lewis, Simon.** The Art & Science of SmallTalk. LC 94-45966. (Hewlett-Packard Professional Bks.). 1995. pap. text ed. 30.00 (*0-13-371345-8*) P-H.
Lewis, Sinclair. Ann Vickers. LC 93-46687. xx, 564p. 1994. pap. 15.00 (*0-8032-7947-7*, Bison Books) U of Nebr Pr.
— Arrowsmith. 1976. 22.95 (*0-8488-0825-8*) Amereon Ltd.
— Arrowsmith. LC 25-78. (Modern Classic Ser.). 132p. 1990. 15.95 (*0-15-108216-2*) HarBrace.
— Arrowsmith. 1961. pap. 5.95 (*0-451-52225-7*, Sig Classics) NAL-Dutton.
— Arrowsmith. 1994. reprint ed. lib. bdg. 26.95x (*0-89966-402-4*) Buccaneer Bks.
— Babbitt. 1976. 22.95 (*0-8488-0826-6*) Amereon Ltd.
— Babbitt. LC 84-254209. (Book Notes Ser.). 1985. pap. 2.50 (*0-8120-3504-6*) Barron.
— Babbitt. LC 22-14419. (Modern Classic Ser.). 408p. 1989. 15.95 (*0-15-110421-2*) HarBrace.
— Babbitt. 1961. pap. 4.95 (*0-451-52242-7*, Sig Classics) NAL-Dutton.
— Babbitt. 408p. 1987. reprint ed. lib. bdg. 25.95 (*0-89966-622-1*) Buccaneer Bks.
— Cass Timberlane. 1976. 17.95 (*0-8488-1411-8*) Amereon Ltd.
— Cass Timberlane. 1982. reprint ed. lib. bdg. 18.95 (*0-89966-401-6*) Buccaneer Bks.
— Dodsworth. 1976. 24.95 (*0-8488-0565-8*) Amereon Ltd.
— Dodsworth. 336p. 1995. mass mkt., pap. 4.95 (*0-451-52598-1*, Sig Classics) NAL-Dutton.
— Elmer Gantry. 1976. 21.95 (*0-8488-0827-4*) Amereon Ltd.
— Elmer Gantry. 1967. pap. 4.95 (*0-451-52251-6*, CE1653, Sig Classics) NAL-Dutton.
— Free Air. LC 92-37702. xii, 370p. 1993. pap. 11.95 (*0-8032-7943-4*, Bison Books) U of Nebr Pr.
— Free Air. reprint ed. lib. bdg. 69.00 (*0-7812-0766-5*) Rprt Serv.
— Free Air. 1971. reprint ed. 59.00 (*0-403-01071-3*) Scholarly.
— It Can't Happen Here. 1970. pap. 4.95 (*0-451-15936-5*, Sig) NAL-Dutton.
— It Can't Happen Here. 366p. 1993. pap. 4.95 (*0-451-52582-5*, Sig Classics) NAL-Dutton.
— The Job: The American Novel. LC 93-43084. viii, 327p. 1994. pap. 13.00 (*0-8032-7948-5*, Bison Books) U of Nebr Pr.
— Main Street. 1976. 23.95 (*0-8488-0828-2*) Amereon Ltd.
— Main Street. LC 20-18934. (Modern Classic Ser.). 451p. 1989. 15.95 (*0-15-155547-8*) HarBrace.
— Main Street. 440p. 1961. pap. 4.50 (*0-451-52147-1*, Sig Classics) NAL-Dutton.
— Main Street. 448p. 1995. 9.95 (*0-14-018901-7*, Penguin Classics) Viking Penguin.
— Main Street. 297p. 1984. reprint ed. lib. bdg. 26.95 (*0-89966-495-4*) Buccaneer Bks.
— Main Street & Babbitt. Hersey, John, ed. 898p. 1992. 35.00 (*0-940450-61-5*) Library of America.
— Man Who Knew Coolidge: Being the Soul of Lowell Schmaltz, Constructive & Nordic Citizen. LC 79-157784. (Short Story Index Reprint Ser.). 1980. reprint ed. 23.95 (*0-8369-3896-8*) Ayer.
— Selected Short Stories of Sinclair Lewis. 456p. 1990. pap. 12.95 (*0-929587-22-7*, Elephant Paperbacks) I R Dee.
Lewis, Sinclair & Schary, Dore. Storm in the West. rev. ed. LC 63-13228. (Illus.). 200p. (C). 1981. pap. 5.95 (*0-8128-6079-9*, Scrbrough Hse) Madison Bks UPA.
Lewis, Sol, ed. see Hyatt, Felicia B.
Lewis, Sol, ed. see Kaplan, Helene C.
Lewis, Sol, ed. see Rosenberg, Carl.
Lewis, Sol, ed. see Stabholz, Thaddeus.
***Lewis, Sondra K. & Blakley, Lonnett D.** Allergy & Candida Cooking - Rotational Style. 384p. 1995. pap. 19.95 (*0-9643462-0-6*) Canary Connect.
***Lewis, Stanley X., Jr.** The Auditor's Guide to Sampling. 79p. 1991. pap. text ed. 60.00 (*0-933179-06-5*) Bus Account Pubns.
Lewis, Stanley X. & Glover, Robert I. Accounting for Social Responsibility: A Historical Perspective. 95p. (C). 1986. pap. text ed. 19.50 (*0-933179-00-6*) Bus Account Pubns.
***Lewis, Stanley X., Jr. & King, Jerry G.** Community (Rural) Water Associations' Accountability. 30p. 1992. pap. text ed. 19.50 (*0-614-04640-8*) Bus Account Pubns.
***Lewis, Stanley X., Jr., et al.** Developing & Implementing Business Information Systems for Small Businesses. 51p. 1990. pap. text ed. 19.50 (*0-933179-04-9*) Bus Account Pubns.
Lewis, Stephen. And Baby Makes None. 208p. 1991. 18.95 (*0-8027-5789-8*) Walker & Co.
— The Best Sellers. 320p. 1986. reprint ed. pap. 3.95 (*0-8439-2427-6*) Dorchester Pub Co.
— Cowboy Blues. 220p. (Orig.). 1985. pap. 6.95 (*0-932870-64-3*) Alyson Pubns.
— The Economics of Apartheid. (Illus.). 192p. 1989. pap. 17.95 (*0-87609-056-0*) Coun Foreign.
— Expensive Pleasures. 384p. 1986. reprint ed. pap. 3.50 (*0-8439-2323-7*) Dorchester Pub Co.
— The Monkey Rope. 192p. 1990. 18.95 (*0-8027-5761-8*) Walker & Co.
— The Regulars. 480p. (Orig.). 1985. reprint ed. pap. 3.95 (*0-8439-2197-8*) Dorchester Pub Co.
Lewis, Stephen, jt. auth. see Kleiman, Lowell.
Lewis, Stephen D., jt. auth. see Boyd, Daniel R.
***Lewis, Stephen J., et al.** Undaunted Faith: Memorial Edition: The Life Story of Jennie Dean. 149p. 1995. 18.00 (*1-886826-04-8*) Manassas Mus.
Lewis, Stephen R. Taxation for Development: Principles & Applications. LC 83-19308. 1984. pap. 18.95 (*0-19-503053-2*) OUP.
Lewis, Stephen R., Jr., ed. Henry George & Contemporary Economic Development. 96p. 1985. pap. 5.00 (*0-911312-68-4*) Schalkenbach.
Lewis, Stephen R., Jr., jt. auth. see Harvey, Charles.
Lewis, Steve, jt. ed. see Fraser, George C.
Lewis, Steven J. Aging & Health: Linking Research & Public Policy. (Illus.). 492p. 1989. 89.95 (*0-87371-160-2*, RA564) Lewis Pubs.
Lewis, Suford. Noreascon Two Memory Book. (Illus.). 56p. 1985. pap. text ed. 2.00 (*0-9603146-3-6*) MA Convent Fandom.
***Lewis, Susan.** Betrayal. 1994. pap. 5.99 (*0-06-100561-4*, Harp PBks) HarpC.
— Class Apart. 1990. mass mkt. 4.95 (*0-06-100093-0*, Harp PBks) HarpC.
— Dance While You Can. 1991. mass mkt. 4.99 (*0-06-109933-3*, Harp PBks) HarpC.
— Obession. 1993. mass mkt. 5.99 (*0-06-100560-6*, Harp PBks) HarpC.
— Stolen Beginnings. 1992. mass mkt. 5.50 (*0-06-100441-3*, Harp PBks) HarpC.
Lewis, Susan, jt. ed. see Blumenreich, Patricia E.
Lewis, Susan, jt. auth. see Lewis, Ramon.
Lewis, Susan, jt. auth. see Lewis, Richard.
Lewis, Susanna. Knitting Lace: A Workshop with Patterns & Projects. 224p. (C). 1992. pap. 24.95 (*0-942391-52-7*) Taunton.
Lewis, Suzan & Cooper, Cary L. Managing the New Work Force: The Challenge of Dual-Income Families. 254p. 1993. pap. 14.95 (*0-89384-253-2*) Pfeiffer & Co.
Lewis, Suzan, et al, eds. Dual-Earner Families: International Perspectives. 256p. 1991. 55.00 (*0-8039-8382-4*); pap. 22.50 (*0-8039-8383-2*) Sage.
Lewis, Suzanne. The Art of Matthew Paris in the Chronica Majora. LC 83-4837. (California Studies in the History of Art: No. XXI). 576p. 1986. 145.00 (*0-520-04981-0*) U CA Pr.
— Reading Images: Narrative Discourse & Reception in the Thirteenth-Century Illuminated Apocalypse. (Illus.). 448p. (C). 1995. write for info. (*0-521-47920-7*) Cambridge U Pr.
Lewis, Suzanne, ed. see Gaskell, Elizabeth C.
Lewis, Suzanne, ed. see Gaskell, Elizabeth.
Lewis, Suzanne G. & Samoff, Joel, eds. Microcomputers in African Development: Critical Perspectives. (Special Studies on Africa). 258p. (C). 1991. pap. text ed. 47.50 (*0-8133-7934-2*) Westview.
***Lewis, Sydney.** Hospital: An Oral History of Cook County Hospital. LC 94-21775. 1995. 25.00 (*1-56584-138-7*) New Press NY.
Lewis, Sylvan. Low-Cholesterol Life: The Diet & Lifestyle Way to the New, Healthier You. 1992. pap. 4.50 (*1-56171-075-X*, S P I Bks) Sure Sellers.
Lewis, Sylvan R. Cholesterol Cure Made Easy. LC 92-34868. 1993. 4.99 (*0-517-08904-1*) Random Hse Value.
— Cholesterol Cure Made Easy: A Doctor's Diet Plan to Lower Your Cholesterol Naturally. 122p. 1994. pap. 5.95 (*0-8119-0182-3*) LIFETIME.
— Diet & Exercise Made Easy. (Illus.). 128p. (Orig.). 1980. pap. 2.00 (*0-936320-00-1*) Compact Books.
— Doctor's Cholesterol & Low Salt Diet Guide. 128p. (Orig.). 1980. pap. 2.00 (*0-936320-02-8*) Compact Books.
— Heart Watchers' Complete Diet & Menu Planner. Bartimole, John, ed. 160p. 1988. pap. 6.95 (*0-8119-0719-8*) LIFETIME.
— Lose Ugly Fat Fast. 128p. 1980. pap. 2.00 (*0-936320-04-4*) Compact Books.
— Lose Weight Without Going Hungry. (Illus.). 128p. 1981. pap. 2.00 (*0-936320-10-9*) Compact Books.
Lewis, T. Revolutionary Roads. Date not set. 30.00 (*0-06-018231-8*, HarpT) HarpC.
***Lewis, T. L.** The Gospel According to the Pallbearers. 160p. (Orig.). 1995. pap. write for info. (*1-885591-95-0*) Morris Pubng.
Lewis, Tamra W. A Mother's Things to Do Organizer: Balancing It All. abr. ed. write for info. (*0-9633508-0-3*); audio 10.95 (*0-9633508-1-1*) TRB & Assocs.
Lewis, Taylor, photos. Chesapeake, the Eastern Shore: Gardens & Houses. LC 92-35045. 1993. 45.00 (*0-671-75857-8*) S&S Trade.
— Martha's Vineyard: Gardens & Houses. (Illus.). 288p. 1992. 45.00 (*0-671-75858-6*) S&S Trade.
Lewis, Taylor & Heard, Virginia. Nantucket: Gardens & Houses. (Illus.). 1990. 45.00 (*0-316-52334-8*) Little.
Lewis, Taylor, jt. auth. see Sinclair, Peg.
***Lewis, Ted, ed.** Object-Oriented Application Frameworks. LC 94-48023. 1995. write for info. (*1-884777-06-6*) Manning Pubns.
***Lewis, Ted G.** Client-Server Yellow Pages. LC 95-14772. 1995. write for info. (*1-884777-08-2*) Manning Pubns.
— Foundations of Parallel Programming: A Machine-Independent Approach. LC 84-4873. 296p. 1994. text ed. 54.00 (*0-8186-5692-1*, BP05692) IEEE Comp Soc.
Lewis, Ted G., jt. auth. see Oman, Paul W.
Lewis, Terence. Harrap's English-Brazilian Portuguese Business Dictionary. 283p. 1982. 125.00 (*0-8288-0118-5*, M14371) Fr & Eur.
Lewis, Terrance L. A Climate for Appeasement. LC 90-6166. (Studies in History & Culture: Vol. 3). 263p. (C). 1990. text ed. 44.95 (*0-8204-1314-3*) P Lang Pubs.
— Dorothy L. Sayers' Wimsey & Interwar British Society. LC 94-19556. 180p. 1994. text ed. 79.95 (*0-7734-9102-3*) E Mellen.
Lewis, Theodore G. Case: Computer-Aided Software Engineering. 1991. text ed. 54.95 (*0-442-00361-7*) Van Nos Reinhold.
— Pascal for the IBM Personal Computer. LC 82-22750. 288p. 1983. pap. 15.95 (*0-201-05464-7*) Addison-Wesley.
Lewis, Theodore J. Cults of the Dead in Ancient Israel & Ugarit. (Harvard Semitic Monographs). 1989. 21.95 (*1-55540-325-5*, 04 00 39) Scholars Pr GA.
Lewis, Theresa. Caribbean Folk Legends. LC 89-81981. (Young Reader's Ser.). 90p. (YA). (gr. 6-12). 1990. 19.95 (*0-86543-158-2*); pap. 7.95 (*0-86543-159-0*) Africa World.
Lewis, Theresa, ed. see Berry, Mary.
Lewis, Theresia J., jt. auth. see Bittrich, Louis E.
Lewis, Thomas, ed. A Source Guide to the Music of Percy Grainger. (Illus.). 352p. 1991. pap. 35.00 (*0-912483-56-3*) Pro-Am Music.
Lewis, Thomas, jt. auth. see Lewis, Cynthia.
Lewis, Thomas, jt. auth. see Lewis, Walter.
Lewis, Thomas A. The Medicine Men: Oglala Sioux Ceremony & Healing. LC 89-22508. (Studies in the Anthropology of North American Indians). (Illus.). viii, 219p. 1990. 25.00 (*0-8032-2890-2*) U of Nebr Pr.
— The Medicine Men: Oglala Sioux Ceremony & Healing. LC 89-22508. (Illus.). viii, 219p. 1990. reprint ed. pap. 9.95 (*0-8032-7939-6*, Bison Books) U of Nebr Pr.
Lewis, Thomas H. Forgotten Battles along the Yellowstone. (Illus.). 1985. pap. 4.95 (*0-916552-31-4*) Acoma Bks.
Lewis, Thomas J., jt. auth. see Lewis, Cynthia C.
Lewis, Thomas L. & Fingeret, Murray. Primary Care of the Glaucomas. (Illus.). 410p. (C). 1993. text ed. 90.00 (*0-8385-7998-1*, A7998-6) Appleton & Lange.
Lewis, Thomas M. & Kneberg, Madeline. Hiwassee Island: An Archaeological Account of Four Tennessee Indian Peoples. LC 75-130688. (Illus.). 328p. 1970. pap. 18.95 (*0-87049-420-1*) U of Tenn Pr.
— Tribes That Slumber: Indians of the Tennessee Region. LC 58-12085. (Illus.). 208p. 1958. pap. 16.95 (*0-87049-021-4*) U of Tenn Pr.
***Lewis, Thomas M. & Lewis, Madeline D.** The Prehistory of the Chickamauga Basin in Tennessee, 2 vols., Set, Vol. 1. (Illus.). 320p. (C). 1995. lib. bdg. 50.00 (*0-87049-861-4*); pap. text ed. 25.00x (*0-87049-863-0*) U of Tenn Pr.
— The Prehistory of the Chickamauga Basin in Tennessee, 2 vols., Set, Vol. 2. (Illus.). 432p. (C). 1995. lib. bdg. 50.00x (*0-87049-862-2*); pap. text ed. 25.00x (*0-87049-864-9*) U of Tenn Pr.
Lewis, Thomas M. & Lewis, Madeline K. Eva: An Archaic Site. LC 61-18403. (University of Tennessee Study in Anthropology Ser.). 188p. reprint ed. pap. 53.60 (*0-7837-3027-6*, 2042913) Bks Demand.
Lewis, Thomas P. Clipper Ship. LC 77-11858. (Harper I Can Read Bk.). (Illus.). 64p. (J). (ps-3). 1978. 11.95 (*0-06-023808-9*); lib. bdg. 11.89 (*0-06-023809-7*) HarpC Child Bks.
— Clipper Ship. LC 77-11858. (Trophy I Can Read Bk.). (Illus.). 64p. (J). (gr. k-3). 1992. pap. 3.50 (*0-06-444160-1*, Trophy) HarpC Child Bks.
— Hill of Fire. LC 70-121802. (Harper I Can Read History Bk.). (Illus.). 64p. (J). (gr. k-3). 1971. lib. bdg. 14.89 (*0-06-023804-6*) HarpC Child Bks.
— Hill of Fire. LC 70-121802. (Trophy I Can Read Book & Cassette Set). (Illus.). 64p. (J). (gr. k-3). 1983. pap. 3.50 (*0-06-444040-0*, Dealer Bank) HarpC Child Bks.
— The Pro - Am Book of Music & Mythology, Vol. 1. (Illus.). 892p. 1992. 59.95 (*0-912483-51-2*) Pro-Am Music.
— The Pro - Am Book of Music & Mythology, Vol. 2. 659p. 1992. 49.95 (*0-912483-82-2*) Pro-Am Music.
— The Pro Am Guide to U. S. Books about Music: Annotated Subject Guide to Current & Backlist Titles. (General Music Ser.: Gms-6). 211p. (Orig.). 1987. pap. 35.00 (*0-912483-03-2*) Pro-Am Music.
— Something about the Music, No. 2: Anthology of the Critical Opinions. 660p. 1991. 44.50 (*0-912483-66-0*); pap. 29.50 (*0-912483-54-7*) Pro-Am Music.
Lewis, Thomas P., ed. The Pro-Am Guide to U. S. Books about Music: Annotated Subject Guide to Current & Backlist Titles, 1987 Supplement. 173p. (Orig.). 1988. pap. 23.50 (*0-912483-14-8*) Pro-Am Music.
Lewis, Thomas P., ed. see Leppard, Raymond.
Lewis, Thomas P., ed. see Stevens, Denis.
Lewis, Thomas R. Organization, Training, Search & Recovery Procedures for the Underwater Unit. 2nd ed. LC 79-83668. (Illus.). 1979. 6.95 (*0-918616-04-2*) Northern Mich.
Lewis, Thomas S. Letters of Hart Crane & His Family. LC 73-21675. 675p. 1974. text ed. 91.50 (*0-231-03740-6*) Col U Pr.
Lewis, Thomas S., ed. see Crane, Hart.
Lewis, Thomas T., ed. see Harley, Brilliana.
Lewis, Tim, et al. Teaching Students with Behavioral Disorders: Basic Questions & Answers. 37p. 1991. 8.90 (*0-86586-205-2*, P337) Coun Exc Child.
Lewis, Timothy E. Environmental Chemistry & Toxicology of Aluminum. (Illus.). 500p. 1989. 85.95 (*0-87371-194-7*, RA1231) Lewis Pubs.
— Tree Rings As Indicators of Ecosystem Health. 224p. 1994. 99.50 (*0-8493-7651-3*, 7651) CRC Pr.
Lewis, Toby, jt. auth. see Barnett, Vic.
Lewis, Todd V. RT: A Readers Theater Ministry. 1987. 8.50 (*0-685-68712-0*, MP-641) Lillenas.
— RT 2: Two Scripts for Readers Theater. 1989. 8.50 (*0-685-68698-1*, MP-657) Lillenas.

An Asterisk (*) at the beginning of an entry indicates that the title is appearing in BIP for the first time.

Lewis, Tom. Darwin Sayonara. 104p. (C). 1990. pap. 39.00 (*0-86439-133-1*, Pub. by Boolarong Pubns AT) St Mut.

— Empire of the Air: The Men Who Made Radio. LC 90-56385. (Illus.). 432p. 1993. pap. 13.00 (*0-06-098119-9*, PL) HarpC.

— Empire of the Air: The Men Who Made Radio. braille ed. 1169p. 1993. vinyl bd. 93.52 (*1-56956-365-9*, BR9073) W A T Braille.

— Storied New Mexico: An Annotated Bibliography of Novels with New Mexico Settings. LC 90-26834. 338p. 1991. 45.00 (*0-8263-1223-3*) U of NM Pr.

Lewis, Tom, jt. auth. see Lewis, Cynthia C.

Lewis, Tom G. Karate for Kids. 120p. (Orig.). (J). (gr. 2-10). 1980. pap. 3.95 (*0-89826-005-1*) Natl Paperback.

Lewis, Tom J. & Jungman, Robert E., eds. On Being Foreign: Culture Shock in Short Fiction. LC 86-81109. 308p. (Orig.). 1986. pap. 16.95 (*0-933662-62-9*) Intercult Pr.

***Lewis, Tommi.** Pogs: The Milkcap Guide. 1994. pap. 8.95 (*0-8362-4240-8*) Andrews & McMeel.

***Lewis, Tommi, ed.** Mad about You. 128p. 1995. pap. 8.95 (*0-8362-1775-6*) Andrews & McMeel.

Lewis, Tommy & Harrell, Irene B. Isn't It Amazin'? A Book about the Love of God. 184p. (Orig.). 1983. pap. 7.00 (*0-915541-00-9*) Star Bks Inc.

Lewis, Tony. Cricket in Many Lands. 256p. 1992. 34.95 (*0-340-50889-2*, Pub. by H & S UK) Trafalgar.

— MCC Masterclass: The New MCC Coaching Book. (Illus.). 192p. 1995. 39.95 (*0-297-81431-1*, Pub. by Weidenfeld) Trafalgar.

— Wave Energy. (Illus.). 149p. 1985. pap. text ed. 60.00 (*0-86010-793-0*) G & T Inc.

***Lewis, Tracy.** Dangerous Obsessions. 740p. Date not set. pap. 12.95 (*0-7610-0307-X*) NW Pub.

Lewis, Trevor, ed. Insect Communication. 1984. text ed. 115.00 (*0-12-447175-7*) Acad Pr.

Lewis, Trudy. Private Correspondences. 180p. 1994. 19.95 (*0-8101-5033-6*) Northwestern U Pr.

Lewis, Vern, jt. auth. see Narramore, Bruce.

***Lewis, Vicki, et al.** Be Mine, Valentine; To Have It All; Cupid's Task; Only with the Heart, 4 vols. in 1. (Romance Digest Ser.: Vol. 4, No. 4). 1995. pap. 2.75 (*0-373-82722-9*, 1-82722-9) Harlequin Bks.

Lewis, Vicky A. Development & Handicap. 256p. 1987. pap. text ed. 24.95 (*0-631-13633-9*) Blackwell Pubs.

***Lewis, Victoria M.** Colorado Home Owner's Guide to Paying Less Property Taxes: Complete Step by Step Instructions to Lower Current Year Property Taxes, Receive Refunds for Past Years, Plus Interest. 216p. (C). 1995. pap. text ed. 24.95 (*0-9645932-0-3*) Xenia Pubns.

Lewis, Virginia L. Flames of Passion - Flames of Greed: Acts of Arson in German Prose Fiction 1850-1900. LC 91-3807. (Studies on Themes & Motifs in Literature: Vol. 2). 251p. 1991. 47.95 (*0-8204-1500-6*) P Lang Pubs.

Lewis, Vivian. The Traveler's Atlas. (Illus.). 230p. (Orig.). (C). 1988. pap. 9.95 (*0-945332-13-0*) Agora Inc MD.

Lewis, W. Refugees. write for info. (*0-275-90020-7*, C0020, Praeger Pubs) Greenwood.

Lewis, W. Arthur. Development Economics in the 1950s. LC 94-19438. (Occasional Papers Ser.). 1994. pap. 6.95 (*1-55815-354-3*) ICS Pr.

— Racial Conflict & Economic Development. (Illus.). 128p. 1985. 19.95 (*0-674-74579-5*) HUP.

Lewis, W. Cris, jt. auth. see Peterson, H. Craig.

Lewis, W. David. Iron & Steel in America. (Industry in America Ser.). (Illus.). 64p. 1986. reprint ed. pap. 5.95 (*0-914650-10-6*) Hagley Museum.

Lewis, W. David & Trimble, William F. The Airway to Everywhere: A History of All American Aviation 1937-1953. LC 87-25176. (Illus.). 240p. (C). 1988. 29.95 (*0-8229-3579-1*) U of Pittsburgh Pr.

Lewis, W. H. In the Arms of Our Elders. 170p. 1995. pap. 10.95 (*0-932112-35-8*) Carolina Wren.

— The Splendid Century. LC 53-9235. 1971. pap. 13.50 (*0-688-06009-9*, Quill) Morrow.

Lewis, W. H., jt. ed. see Hooper, Walter.

Lewis, W. M., ed. Developments in Water Treatment, 1. (Illus.). 1980. 66.75 (*0-85334-902-9*, Pub. by Elsevier Applied Sci UK) Elsevier.

— Developments in Water Treatment, 2. (Illus.). 1980. 66.75 (*0-85334-903-7*, Pub. by Elsevier Applied Sci UK) Elsevier.

Lewis, W. M., Jr., et al. Eutrophication & Land Use. (Ecological Studies. Analysis & Synthesis: Vol. 46). (Illus.). 275p. 1984. 91.00 (*0-387-90961-3*) Spr-Verlag.

Lewis, W. S., ed. see Walpole, Horace.

Lewis, W. T. Genealogy of the Lewis Family in America. 458p. 1989. reprint ed. lib. bdg. 76.50 (*0-8328-0767-2*); reprint ed. pap. 68.50 (*0-8328-0768-0*) Higginson Bk Co.

Lewis, Walter & Lewis, Thomas. Modern Organ Building. (Illus.). xii, 164p. 1986. reprint ed. 86.00x (*0-913746-26-6*); reprint ed. pap. 65.00x (*0-913746-27-4*) Organ Lit.

Lewis, Walter H. Ecology Field Glossary: A Naturalist's Vocabulary. LC 77-71856. 153p. 1977. text ed. 49.95 (*0-8371-9547-0*, LEF/, Greenwood Pr) Greenwood.

Lewis, Walter H. & Elvin-Lewis, Memory P. Medical Botany: Plants Affecting Man's Health. LC 76-44376. 515p. 1982. pap. text ed. 49.95 (*0-471-86134-0*) Wiley.

Lewis-Walters, Jan & Hamilton, Lyne. Integrating Environmental Education into the Curriculum... Painlessly. 119p. (Orig.). 1992. pap. 15.95 (*1-879639-18-1*) Natl Educ Serv.

Lewis, Ward B. Eugene O'Neill: The German Reception of America's First Dramatist. LC 84-47881. (Germanic Studies in America: Vol. 50). 211p. (C). 1984. text ed. 28.95 (*0-8204-0156-0*) P Lang Pubs.

Lewis, Warren. Behind Every Successful President. 1991. 18.95 (*1-56171-089-X*) Sure Sellers.

— Computer Site Integration Technique. 1993. 79.00 (*0-614-03636-4*) D White Consult.

— Franchises: Dollars & Sense. 560p. 1993. pap. text ed. 49.95 (*0-8403-8963-9*) Kendall-Hunt.

Lewis, Warren, ed. Whole Language: The Debate. 350p. (Orig.). 1994. pap. 24.95 (*0-927516-39-X*) ERIC-REC.

Lewis, Warren, ed. see Behm, Mary & Behm, Richard.

Lewis, Warren, ed. see Gottlieb, Stephen S.

Lewis, Warren, ed. see Grusko, Robin & Kramer, Judy.

Lewis, Warren, ed. see Katz, Kim & Katz, Claudia.

Lewis, Warren, ed. see McAllister, Elizabeth.

Lewis, Warren, ed. see McGowen, Carolyn S.

Lewis, Warren, ed. see Measell, James S.

Lewis, Warren, ed. see Shefelbine, John.

Lewis, Warren, ed. see Sproule, J. Michael.

Lewis, Wendy. Sarah Scrap & Her Nature Trail. (Illus.). 32p. (J). 1993. 13.95 (*0-237-51216-5*, Pub. by Evans Bros Ltd UK) Trafalgar.

— Sarah Scrap & Her Wonderful Heap! (Illus.). 32p. (J). (gr. k-2). 1992. 13.95 (*0-237-51152-5*, Pub. by Evans Bros Ltd UK) Trafalgar.

— Save the Animals. (Illus.). 32p. (J). (gr. k-2). 1992. 15.95 (*0-237-51153-3*, Pub. by Evans Bros Ltd UK) Trafalgar.

Lewis-Wild, Robin. One Hundred One Torchon Patterns. rev. ed. (Illus.). 132p. 1992. reprint ed. pap. 19.95 (*0-9633892-0-3*) Robins Bobbins.

Lewis, Wilfred, Jr. Federal Fiscal Policy in the Postwar Recessions. LC 80-16. (Brookings Institution, National Committee on Government Finance, Studies of Government Finance). (Illus.). xv, 311p. 1980. reprint ed. text ed. 38.50 (*0-313-22284-3*, LEFF) Greenwood.

Lewis, William. Will. abr. ed. 270p. 1995. pap. 8.95 (*1-56901-444-2*) NW Pub.

Lewis, William & Milano, Carol. Profitable Careers in Nonprofit. 1987. pap. text ed. 14.95 (*0-471-83699-0*) Wiley.

Lewis, William & Schuman, Nancy. Fast Track Guide to the Highest Paying Jobs. LC 87-10045. 200p. 1987. pap. text ed. 14.95 (*0-471-83801-2*) Wiley.

Lewis, William, jt. auth. see Marks, Edward.

Lewis, William, jt. ed. see Marr, Phebe.

Lewis, William, jt. auth. see Schuman, Nancy.

Lewis, William A. Overhead Costs: Some Essays in Economic Analysis. LC 70-113506. (Illus.). 200p. 1970. reprint ed. lib. bdg. 27.50 (*0-678-06014-2*) Kelley.

— Politics in West Africa. LC 81-13317. (Whidden Lectures for 1965 Ser.). 90p. 1982. reprint ed. text ed. 49.75 (*0-313-23202-4*, LEPW, Greenwood Pr) Greenwood.

Lewis, William A. & Molloy, Nancy H. How to Choose & Use Temporary Services. LC 90-53214. 260p. reprint ed. pap. 74.10 (*0-7837-7061-8*, 2046873) Bks Demand.

Lewis, William B. The Case of John Mary Jones: Are Unhappy Homosexuals Doomed to Stay That Way? Edwards, Marian, ed. 125p. (Orig.). (C). 1992. pap. text ed. 14.95 (*0-9614079-6-4*) TVR Pub Co.

Lewis, William C., jt. ed. see Greenfield, Norman S.

Lewis, William D. & Keasbey, A. Q. Miscellaneous Writings of the Late Hon. Joseph P. Bradley... & a Review of His "Judicial Record," by William Draper Lewis... & an Account of His "Dissenting Opinions," by the Late A. Q. Keasbey. Bradley, Charles, ed. xii, 435p. 1986. reprint ed. lib. bdg. 42.50 (*0-8377-0876-1*) Rothman.

Lewis, William E., jt. auth. see Albracht, E. Edward.

Lewis, William F. Soul Rebels: The Rastafari. (Illus.). 139p. (Orig.). (C). 1993. pap. text ed. 9.50 (*0-88133-739-0*) Waveland Pr.

Lewis, William J. Interpreting for Park Visitors. (Illus.). 160p. 1981. pap. 2.95 (*0-915992-11-6*) Eastern Acorn.

Lewis, William L., jt. auth. see Beker, Jerome.

Lewis, William M. From a College Platform: Addresses. LC 68-29224. (Essay Index Reprint Ser.). (Illus.). 1977. reprint ed. 20.95 (*0-8369-0617-9*) Ayer.

Lewis, William M., et al. Wharton Assembly Addresses Nineteen Thirty-Seven. LC 79-157969. (Essay Index Reprint Ser.). 1977. reprint ed. 15.95 (*0-8369-2258-1*) Ayer.

Lewis, William S. The Case of Spokane Garry. 139p. 1987. 14.95 (*0-87770-428-7*); pap. 9.95 (*0-87770-405-8*) Ye Galleon.

— Early Days in the Big Bend Country. (Shorey Historical Ser.). 40p. reprint ed. pap. 3.95 (*0-8466-0089-7*, S89) Shorey.

Lewis, William S., ed. see MacDonald, Ranald.

Lewis-Williams, ed. Rock Paintings of Natal Drakensberg. (Orig.). pap. 18.95 (*0-86980-869-9*, Pub. by Univ Natal Pr SA) Intl Spec Bk.

Lewis, Willie N. Between Sun & Sod: An Informal History of the Texas Panhandle. LC 75-40893. (Illus.). 200p. 1976. 13.95 (*0-89096-010-0*) Tex A&M Univ Pr.

— Willie, a Girl from a Town Called Dallas. LC 83-18081. (Illus.). 150p. 1984. 12.95 (*0-89096-175-1*) Tex A&M Univ Pr.

Lewis, Wilmarth S. Collector's Progress. LC 73-16738. (Illus.). 253p. 1974. reprint ed. text ed. 59.75 (*0-8371-7219-5*, LECP, Greenwood Pr) Greenwood.

— Rescuing Horace Walpole. LC 78-7590. (Illus.). 1978. 47.00 (*0-300-02278-6*) Yale U Pr.

— Three Tours Through London in the Years 1748, 1776, 1797. LC 77-104252. (Illus.). 135p. 1971. reprint ed. text ed. 49.75 (*0-8371-3977-5*, LETL, Greenwood Pr) Greenwood.

Lewis, Wilmarth S., ed. see Walpole, Horace.

Lewis, Winsome V., ed. see Wright-Lewis, Joan.

Lewis, Winston B., jt. auth. see La Monte, John L.

Lewis, Wyndham. America, I Presume. LC 72-2158. (American Literature Ser.: No. 49). 1972. reprint ed. lib. bdg. 75.00 (*0-8383-1476-7*) M S G Haskell Hse.

— The Apes of God. LC 81-7659. (Illus.). 642p. 1992. reprint ed. 25.00 (*0-87685-513-3*); reprint ed. pap. 15.00 (*0-87685-512-5*) Black Sparrow.

— The Art of Being Ruled. LC 88-32776. (Illus.). 464p. (C). 1989. reprint ed. 25.00 (*0-87685-754-3*); reprint ed. pap. 15.00 (*0-87685-753-5*) Black Sparrow.

— The Art of Being Ruled. LC 72-39603. (English Literature Ser.: No. 33). 1972. reprint ed. lib. bdg. 75.00 (*0-8383-1376-0*) M S G Haskell Hse.

— Blast One. (Illus.). 167p. (C). 1992. reprint ed. pap. 15.00 (*0-87685-521-4*) Black Sparrow.

— Blast Three. Cooney, Seamus et al, eds. (Illus.). 300p. (Orig.). 1984. pap. 20.00 (*0-87685-591-5*) Black Sparrow.

— Blast Two. (Illus.). 111p. 1993. reprint ed. pap. 15.00 (*0-87685-523-0*) Black Sparrow.

— Blasting & Bombardiering. 350p. (Orig.). 1982. pap. 11.95 (*0-7145-0130-1*) Riverrun NY.

— Blasting & Bombardiering. 2nd rev. ed. LC 67-17112. (Illus.). 359p. (Orig.). reprint ed. pap. 102.40 (*0-8357-7313-2*, 2029954) Bks Demand.

— The Childermass. LC 76-145141. (Literature Ser.). 328p. 1972. reprint ed. 49.00 (*0-403-01072-1*) Scholarly.

— The Complete Wild Body. Lafourcade, Bernard, ed. LC 82-4498. (Illus.). 418p. (Orig.). 1982. 25.00 (*0-87685-552-4*); pap. 15.00 (*0-87685-551-6*) Black Sparrow.

— Count Your Dead, They Are Alive. LC 72-82185. 1972. reprint ed. lib. bdg. 250.00 (*0-87968-007-5*) Gordon Pr.

— Creatures of Habit & Creatures of Change: Essays on Art, Literature & Society, 1914-1956. Edwards, Paul, ed. & intro. by. LC 89-14999. (Illus.). 430p. (Orig.). (C). 1989. pap. 15.00 (*0-87685-769-1*) Black Sparrow.

— Diabolical Principle & the Dithyrambic Spectator. LC 78-176495. (English Literature Ser.: No. 33). 1971. reprint ed. lib. bdg. 75.00 (*0-8383-1362-0*) M S G Haskell Hse.

— Doom of Youth. LC 72-2090. (English Literature Ser.: No. 33). 1972. reprint ed. lib. bdg. 75.00 (*0-8383-1475-9*) M S G Haskell Hse.

— The Enemy: A Review of Art & Literature, Vol. 1. (Illus.). 246p. (Orig.). (C). 1994. 25.00 (*0-87685-948-1*, 1355-820X); pap. 15.00 (*0-87685-947-3*, 1355-820X) Black Sparrow.

— The Enemy: A Review of Art & Literature, Vol. 1. deluxe ed. (Illus.). 246p. (Orig.). (C). 1994. 35.00 (*0-87685-949-X*, 1355-820X) Black Sparrow.

— The Enemy: A Review of Art & Literature, Vol. 2. (Illus.). 215p. (Orig.). (C). 1994. 25.00 (*0-87685-951-1*, 1355-280X); pap. 15.00 (*0-87685-950-3*, 1355-820X) Black Sparrow.

— The Enemy: A Review of Art & Literature, Vol. 2. deluxe ed. (Illus.). 215p. (Orig.). (C). 1994. 35.00 (*0-87685-952-X*, 1355-820X) Black Sparrow.

— The Enemy: A Review of Art & Literature, Vol. 3. (Illus.). 205p. (Orig.). (C). 1994. 25.00 (*0-87685-954-6*, 1355-820X); pap. 15.00 (*0-87685-953-8*, 1355-820X) Black Sparrow.

— The Enemy: A Review of Art & Literature, Vol. 3. deluxe ed. (Illus.). 205p. (Orig.). (C). 1994. 35.00 (*0-87685-955-4*, 1355-820X) Black Sparrow.

— Filibusters in Barbary. LC 72-2114. (English Literature Ser.: No. 33). 1972. reprint ed. lib. bdg. 49.95 (*0-8383-1477-5*) M S G Haskell Hse.

— Hitler. LC 72-82189. 1972. reprint ed. lib. bdg. 250.00 (*0-87968-005-9*) Gordon Pr.

— The Hitler Cult. LC 72-82187. 1972. reprint ed. lib. bdg. 250.00 (*0-87968-006-7*) Gordon Pr.

— Hitler, the Germans & the Jews, 5 vols, Set. 1522p. 1973. 1,500.00 (*0-8490-0366-0*) Gordon Pr.

— The Jews, Are They Human? LC 72-82188. 1972. reprint ed. lib. bdg. 250.00 (*0-87968-008-3*) Gordon Pr.

— Journey into Barbary. Fox, C. J., ed. LC 82-20784. (Illus.). 238p. (Orig.). (C). 1983. 25.00 (*0-87685-519-2*); pap. 14.00 (*0-87685-518-4*) Black Sparrow.

— Left Wings Over Europe. LC 72-82186. 1972. reprint ed. lib. bdg. 250.00 (*0-87968-004-0*) Gordon Pr.

— The Letters of Wyndham Lewis. Rose, W. K., ed. LC 61-10121. (Illus.). 1964. 10.00 (*0-8112-0305-0*) New Directions.

— Men Without Art. Cooney, Seamus, ed. LC 87-733. 330p. (Orig.). 1987. pap. 14.00 (*0-87685-686-5*) Black Sparrow.

— Monstre Gai. (Orig.). 1981. pap. 9.95 (*0-7145-0386-X*) Riverrun NY.

— The Old Gang & the New Gang. LC 72-3159. (English Literature Ser.: No. 33). 1972. reprint ed. lib. bdg. 75.00 (*0-8383-1525-9*) M S G Haskell Hse.

— Paleface. 1973. lib. bdg. 250.00 (*0-87968-018-0*) Gordon Pr.

— Paleface. LC 73-95438. (English Biography Ser.: No. 31). 1970. reprint ed. lib. bdg. 75.00 (*0-8383-0990-9*) M S G Haskell Hse.

— Paleface, the Philosophy of the Melting Pot. 1971. reprint ed. 39.00 (*0-403-01073-X*) Scholarly.

— The Revenge for Love. LC 91-4269. (Illus.). 404p. (Orig.). (C). 1991. 25.00 (*0-87685-829-9*); pap. 15.00 (*0-87685-828-0*) Black Sparrow.

— The Revenge for Love. deluxe ed. LC 91-4269. (Illus.). 404p. (Orig.). (C). 1991. 30.00 (*0-87685-830-2*) Black Sparrow.

— The Roaring Queen. 1973. 10.00 (*0-87140-576-8*) Liveright.

— Rude Assignment. Foshay, Toby, ed. LC 84-16837. (Illus.). 315p. (Orig.). 1984. 25.00 (*0-87685-604-0*); pap. 14.00 (*0-87685-603-2*) Black Sparrow.

— Self Condemned. LC 83-2836. (Illus.). 440p. (Orig.). 1983. 25.00 (*0-87685-576-1*); pap. 15.00 (*0-87685-575-3*) Black Sparrow.

— Snooty Baronet. LC 83-22472. (Illus.). 350p. (Orig.). 1984. 25.00 (*0-87685-600-8*); pap. 14.00 (*0-87685-599-0*) Black Sparrow.

— Snooty Baronet. deluxe ed. LC 83-22472. (Illus.). 350p. (Orig.). 1984. 30.00 (*0-87685-601-6*) Black Sparrow.

— Snooty Baronet. LC 77-176492. (English Literature Ser.: No. 33). (Orig.). 1971. reprint ed. lib. bdg. 59.95 (*0-8383-1359-0*) M S G Haskell Hse.

— Time & Western Man. Edwards, Paul, ed. & intro. by. LC 93-1568. 617p. (Orig.). (C). 1993. 30.00 (*0-87685-879-5*); pap. 17.50 (*0-87685-878-7*) Black Sparrow.

— Time & Western Man. deluxe ed. Edwards, Paul, ed. & intro. by. LC 93-1568. 617p. (Orig.). (C). 1993. 35.00 (*0-87685-880-9*) Black Sparrow.

— Time & Western Man. LC 78-64042. (Des Imagistes: Literature of the Imagist Movement Ser.). (Orig.). reprint ed. 36.00 (*0-404-17125-7*) AMS Pr.

— The Vulgar Streak. LC 85-6099. (Illus.). 273p. (Orig.). (C). 1985. 25.00 (*0-87685-629-6*); pap. 14.00 (*0-87685-628-8*) Black Sparrow.

— The Vulgar Streak. deluxe ed. LC 85-6099. (Illus.). 273p. (Orig.). (C). 1985. 30.00 (*0-87685-630-X*) Black Sparrow.

— Wild Body. LC 70-137666. (Studies in Poetry: No. 38). 1971. reprint ed. lib. bdg. 75.00 (*0-8383-1225-X*) M S G Haskell Hse.

— The Writer & the Absolute. LC 75-7240. 202p. 1975. reprint ed. text ed. 55.00 (*0-8371-8098-8*, LEWR, Greenwood Pr) Greenwood.

— Wyndham Lewis the Artist. LC 74-173843. (English Literature Ser.: No. 33). 1971. reprint ed. lib. bdg. 75.00 (*0-8383-1348-5*) M S G Haskell Hse.

Lewis, Wyndham, aft. Tarr: The Nineteen Eighteen Version. LC 89-29842. (Illus.). 430p. (Orig.). (C). 1990. 25.00 (*0-87685-785-3*); pap. 15.00 (*0-87685-784-5*) Black Sparrow.

Lewis, Wyndham, ed. Enemy, 1927-1929, 2 vols., Set. (Illus.). 1968. reprint ed. 85.00 (*0-7146-2107-2*, Pub. by F Cass Pubs UK) Intl Spec Bk.

— Tyro: A Review of the Arts of Painting, Sculpture & Design, Nos. 1 & 2: 1921-22. (Illus.). 120p. 1970. 65.00 (*0-7146-2116-1*, Pub. by F Cass Pubs UK) Intl Spec Bk.

Lewis, Wyndham, jt. auth. see Pound, Ezra.

***Lewis, Zack & Levesque, Jacques.** Montreal & the Casino: The Gaming Guide to Montreal. (Illus.). 192p. (Orig.). 1994. pap. 12.95 (*0-930016-21-1*) Passport Pr.

Lewis, Zack, ed. see Panet, Jean-Pierre.

***Lewis, Zoe.** Beauty & the Beast Teacup Mix-Up: A Sorting Book. LC 94-70049. (Illus.). 24p. (J). (ps-k). 1994. 10.95 (*0-7868-3013-1*) Disney Pr.

— Cenicienta. Leuci, Susana, tr. LC 94-79552. (Libros Buena Vista Ser.). (Illus.). 64p. (SPA.). (J). (gr. 2-6). 1995. pap. 3.50 (*0-7868-4045-5*) Disney Pr.

— Cinderella. LC 94-70524. (Illustrated Classics Ser.). (Illus.). 96p. 1995. 14.95 (*0-7868-3014-X*) Disney Pr.

— Cinderella. LC 94-70524. (Illustrated Classics Ser.). (Illus.). 96p. 1995. lib. bdg. 14.89 (*0-7868-5008-6*) Disney Pr.

— Cinderella. LC 94-70523. (Junior Novel Ser.). (Illus.). 64p. (J). (gr. 2-6). 1995. pap. 3.50 (*0-7868-4009-9*) Disney Pr.

Lewisehn, Leonard, tr. see Nurbakhsh, Javad.

Lewishon, Leonard, tr. see Javad, Nurbakhsh.

Lewisohn, James. Lead Us Forth from Prison. 1977. 3.00 (*0-912678-34-8*, Greenfld Rev Pr) Greenfld Rev Lit.

***Lewisohn, Leonard.** Beyond Faith & Infidelity: The Sufi Poetry & Teachings of Mahmud Shabistari. (Sufi Ser.: No. 5). 220p. (C). 1995. pap. 19.95 (*0-7007-0343-8*, Pub. by Curzon Pr UK) Humanities.

Lewisohn, Leonard, ed. Classical Persian Sufisu-from Its Origins to Rumi. (Illus.). 708p. 1994. 49.95 (*0-933546-50-5*); pap. 29.95 (*0-933546-51-3*) KNP.

— The Legacy of Medieval Persian Sufism. (Illus.). 434p. 1992. pap. 29.95 (*0-933546-46-7*) KNP.

— The Legacy of Medieval Persian Sufism. (Illus.). 450p. 1992. 44.95 (*0-685-59457-2*) KNP.

Lewisohn, Leonard, tr. see Nurbakhsh, Javad.

Lewisohn, Leonard, tr. see Nurbakhsh.

Lewisohn, Ludwig. Drama & the Stage. LC 71-84319. (Essay Index Reprint Ser.). 1977. 19.95 (*0-8369-1089-3*) Ayer.

— The Island Within. LC 74-29503. (Modern Jewish Experience Ser.). 1975. reprint ed. 33.95 (*0-405-06730-5*) Ayer.

— Israel. LC 76-138122. 279p. (C). 1971. reprint ed. text ed. 59.75 (*0-8371-5698-X*, LEIS, Greenwood Pr) Greenwood.

— Mid-Channel. LC 74-29502. (Modern Jewish Experience Ser.). 1975. reprint ed. 28.95 (*0-405-06729-1*) Ayer.

— Permanent Horizon. LC 73-117818. (Essay Index Reprint Ser.). 1977. 21.95 (*0-8369-1811-8*) Ayer.

— Up Stream: An American Chronicle. LC 24-11220. reprint ed. 29.00 (*0-403-00655-4*) Scholarly.

— Upstream. 1992. reprint ed. lib. bdg. 250.00 (*0-8490-8904-2*) Gordon Pr.

Lewisohn, Ludwig, tr. see Sudermann, Hermann.

Lewisohn, Ludwig, tr. see Werfel, Franz.

Lewisohn, Mark. Beatles Day by Day. 1990. pap. 9.95 (*0-517-57750-X*, Harmony) Crown Pub Group.

— Beatles Recording Sessions. 1990. pap. 20.00 (*0-517-58182-5*, Harmony) Crown Pub Group.

— The Beatles: Recording Sessions: The Official Abbey Road Studio Session Notes, 1962-1970. (Illus.). 204p. 1989. 27.50 (*0-517-57066-1*, Harmony) Crown Pub Group.

— The Complete Beatles Chronicle. LC 92-19561. (Illus.). 368p. 1992. 14.00 (*0-517-58100-0*, Harmony) Crown Pub Group.

Lewisohn, Mark, et al. The Beatles London. (Illus.). 144p. 1994. pap. 10.95 (*0-312-11184-3*) St Martin.

Lewisohn, Sam A. Painters & Personality: A Collector's View of Modern Art. LC 70-152188. (Essay Index Reprint Ser.). 1977. reprint ed. 42.95 (*0-8369-2238-7*) Ayer.

Lewisohn, William, jt. auth. see Arlington, Lewis C.

Lewison, Dale M. Essentials of Retailing. 592p. (C). 1989. write for info. (*0-675-20651-0*, Merrill Pub Co) Macmillan.

An Asterisk (*) at the beginning of an entry indicates that the title is appearing in BIP for the first time.

— Retailing. 5th ed. (Illus.). 912p. (C). 1994. text ed. write for info. (*0-02-370530-2*) Macmillan.

Lewison, Dale M. & Hawes. Cases in Retail Management. 272p. (C). 1989. pap. write for info. (*0-675-21083-6*, Merrill Pub Co) Macmillan.

Lewison, Jeremy. Ben Nicholson. LC 91-11556. (Illus.). 128p. 1991. 24.95 (*0-8478-1395-9*) Rizzoli Intl.

— Ben Nicholson. 277p. 1994. pap. 60.00 (*1-85437-130-4*) U of Wash Pr.

— Brice Marden: Prints 1961-1991. (Illus.). 176p. 1992. 60.00 (*1-85437-092-8*, Pub. by Tate Gallery UK); pap. 35.00 (*1-85437-091-X*, Pub. by Tate Gallery UK) U of Wash Pr.

— Genius of Industrial England: Edward Wadsworth, 1889-1949. (Illus.). 128p. (C). 1990. pap. 25.00 (*0-9505532-7-1*, Pub. by Lund Humphries UK) Antique Collect.

***Lewison, Jeremy & McMillan, Duncan.** Contemporary British Art in Print. 232p. 1995. 59.50 (*1-873968-63-9*) Dist Art Pubs.

Lewison-Singar, Rita, ed. see Lin, Jami.

Lewison, Wendy. Baby Has a Boo-Boo. (Pudgy Board Bks.). (Illus.). 18p. (J). (ps). 1994. bds. 2.95 (*0-448-40583-0*, G&D) Putnam Pub Group.

— Boo! Peekaboo! LC 90-83244. (Wee Pudgy Board Bks.). (Illus.). 24p. (J). (ps). 1991. 2.50 (*0-448-40133-9*, G&D) Putnam Pub Group.

— Christmas Cookies. (Wee Pudgy Board Bks.). (Illus.). 24p. (J). (ps). 1993. bds. 2.95 (*0-448-40554-7*, G&D) Putnam Pub Group.

— Happy Babies. (My First Golden Board Bks.). (Illus.). 24p. (J). 1994. bds. write for info. (*0-307-06145-0*, Golden Bks) Western Pub.

— Happy Thanksgiving! (Wee Pudgy Board Bks.). (Illus.). 24p. (J). (ps). 1993. bds. 2.95 (*0-448-40552-0*, G&D) Putnam Pub Group.

— Nighty-Night. (Poke & Look Bks.). (Illus.). 24p. (J). (ps). 1992. spiral bd. 9.95 (*0-448-40391-9*, G&D) Putnam Pub Group.

— Say Thank You, Theodore. (All Aboard Bks.). (Illus.). 32p. (J). (ps-3). 1992. pap. 2.25 (*0-448-40476-1*, G&D) Putnam Pub Group.

Lewison, Wendy C. Buzz Said the Bee. (Illus.). 32p. (J). 1992. pap. 2.95 (*0-590-44185-X*, Cartwheel) Scholastic Inc.

— Bye-Bye, Baby. (J). (ps). 1992. 4.95 (*0-590-45172-3*, Cartwheel) Scholastic Inc.

— Going to Sleep on the Farm. LC 91-3737. (Illus.). 32p. (J). (ps-2). 1992. 13.99 (*0-8037-1096-8*); lib. bdg. 13.89 (*0-8037-1097-6*) Dial Bks Young.

— Hello, Snow! (All Aboard Bks.). (Illus.). 32p. (J). (ps-3). 1994. pap. 2.25 (*0-448-40486-9*, G&D) Putnam Pub Group.

— I Wear Tutu Everywhere! LC 94-36629. (All Aboard Bks.). (Illus.). 1995. write for info. (*0-448-40877-5*, G&D) Putnam Pub Group.

— The Princess & the Potty. LC 93-7853. (Illus.). (J). (gr. 2 up). 1994. pap. 14.00 (*0-671-87284-2*, S&S Bks Young Read) S&S Childrens.

— The Rooster Who Lost His Crow. LC 93-28059. (Illus.). (J). 1995. 14.99 (*0-8037-1545-5*); lib. bdg. 14.89 (*0-8037-1546-3*) Dial Bks Young.

— Shy Vi. LC 91-39658. (Illus.). 40p. (J). (ps-2). 1993. pap. 14.00 (*0-671-76968-5*, S&S Bks Young Read) S&S Childrens.

— Uh-oh, Baby. (J). (ps). 1992. 4.95 (*0-590-45171-5*, Cartwheel) Scholastic Inc.

— Where's Baby? (J). 1992. 4.95 (*0-685-53516-9*) Scholastic Inc.

Lewit, Jane. Bar Bat Mitzvah Planbook. rev. ed. Date not set. pap. 14.95 (*0-8128-8546-5*) Madison Bks UPA.

— Record & Remember: Tracing Your Roots Through Oral History. 1993. pap. 10.95 (*0-8128-8550-3*, Scrbrough Hse) Madison Bks UPA.

Lewit, Jane & Epstein, Ellen. The Bar - Bat Mitzvah Planbook. 200p. 1991. pap. 14.95 (*0-8128-8529-5*, Scrbrough Hse) Madison Bks UPA.

Lewit, Karel. Manipulative Therapy in the Rehabilitation of the Motor System. 2nd ed. (Illus.). 336p. 1991. pap. 59.95 (*0-7506-1123-5*) Buttrwrth-Heinemann.

LeWita, Beatrix. French Bourgeois Culture. Underwood, J. A., tr. (Illus.). 200p. (C). 1994. pap. 17.95 (*0-521-46626-1*) Cambridge U Pr.

— French Bourgeois Culture. Underwood, J. A., tr. LC 93-29766. (C). 1994. 49.95 (*0-521-44099-8*) Cambridge U Pr.

***Lewith.** The Clinical Research Method Com. 1993. 144.50 (*1-56593-128-9*, 0449) Singular Publishing.

Lewitt, Joan. Lending a Hand in Holland, 1945-1946. (C). 1989. pap. 21.00 (*1-85072-075-4*, Pub. by W Sessions UK) St Mut.

Lewitt, S. N. Songs of Chaos. 1993. mass mkt. 4.99 (*0-441-77529-2*) Ace Bks.

Lewitt, Shariann. Memento Mori. 1995. 21.95 (*0-312-85625-3*) Tor Bks.

Lewitt, Sol. Incomplete Open Cubes. 1974. pap. 8.50 (*0-686-46773-6*) J Weber Gall.

LeWitt, Sol. Isometric Drawings. 1981. pap. 10.00 (*0-686-43403-X*) J Weber Gall.

LeWitt, Sol, tr. see Pound, Ezra.

Lewitter, L. R., ed. see Pososhkov, Ivan.

***Lewitter, Sidney R.** American Dreams: The Story of a Jewish Immigrant Family. Lehman, Sarah, ed. LC 94-70749. (YA). Date not set. write for info. (*1-56062-262-8*); pap. write for info. (*1-56062-263-6*) CIS Comm.

Lewittes, Mendell. Jewish Law: An Introduction. LC 94-17489. 312p. 1994. pap. 24.95 (*1-56821-302-6*) Aronson.

— Jewish Marriage: Rabbinic Law, Legend, & Custom. LC 94-9185. 312p. 1994. 30.00 (*1-56821-201-1*) Aronson.

— Principles & Development of Jewish Law. LC 87-11778. 298p. (Orig.). 1987. pap. 12.95 (*0-8197-0506-3*) Bloch.

— Religious Foundations of the Jewish State: The Concept & Practice of Jewish Statehood from Biblical Times to the Modern State of Israel. LC 94-17488. 284p. 1994. pap. 24.95 (*1-56821-301-8*) Aronson.

Lewittes, Mordecai, jt. auth. see Blumberg, Harry.

Lewkenor, Samuel. A Discourse for Such As Are Desirous to Know...of All Those Cities Wherein Doe Flourish Priviledged Universities. LC 70-6110. (English Experience Ser.: No. 90). 1969. reprint ed. 22.00 (*90-221-0090-1*) Walter J Johnson.

Lewko, John H., ed. How Children & Adolescents View the World of Work. LC 85-644581. (New Directions for Child Development Ser.: No. CD 35). 1987. 17.95 (*1-55542-972-6*) Jossey-Bass.

Lewkowicz, David J. & Lickliter, Robert, eds. The Development of Intersensory Perception: Comparative Perspectives. 448p. 1994. text ed. 99.95 (*0-8058-1217-2*) L Erlbaum Assocs.

Lewkowicz, John. The Complete MUMPS. 500p. 1989. pap. text ed. 63.00 (*0-13-162125-4*) P-H.

Lewkowski, J. P., jt. auth. see Mohr, V.

***Lewman, David.** Adventures with Young King Arthur - Musical. Date not set. 5.50 (*0-87129-473-7*, A07) Dramatic Pub.

Lewnes, George P. Tikla. (Illus.). 229p. (C). 1988. reprint ed. 13.95 (*0-9623211-0-9*); reprint ed. lib. bdg. 10.00 (*0-685-26168-9*) T Lewnes Pub.

Lewontin. Human Diversity. 1995. text ed. write for info. (*0-7167-1470-1*) W H Freeman.

Lewontin, Richard C. Biology as Ideology: The Doctrine of DNA. LC 92-54487. 112p. 1993. pap. 10.00 (*0-06-097519-9*, PL) HarpC.

— The Genetic Basis of Evolutionary Change. LC 73-19786. (Biological Ser.: Vol. 25). 346p. 1974. pap. text ed. 21.50 (*0-231-08318-1*) Col U Pr.

— Inside & Outside: Gene, Environment, & Organism. LC 93-39598. (C). 1994. pap. write for info. (*0-914206-35-4*) Clark U Pr.

Lewontin, Richard C., ed. see Dobzhansky, Theodosius.

Lewontin, Richard C., jt. auth. see Levins, Richard.

Lewontin, Richard C., ed. see Suzuki, David T. & Griffiths, Tony.

Lewontin, Richard C., et al. Not in Our Genes. 1985. pap. 12.76 (*0-394-72888-2*) Pantheon.

Lewontin, Timothy. Parsons' Mill. LC 88-40521. 192p. 1989. 17.95 (*0-87451-479-7*) U Pr of New Eng.

Lewrs, R. Camp Life of a Confederate Boy. 1976. 22.50 (*0-8488-1079-1*) Amereon Ltd.

Lewry, Osmund, ed. Robert Kilwardby O. P., on Time & Imagination: De Tempore, De Spiritu Fantastico. (Auctores Britannici Medii Aevi IX). 224p. 1987. 150.00 (*0-19-726054-3*) OUP.

Lewry, S., jt. auth. see Abbott, Pamela.

Lewsen, Phyllis. John X. Merriman: Paradoxical South African Statesman. LC 81-13097. 447p. reprint ed. pap. 127.40 (*0-7837-3323-2*, 2057728) Bks Demand.

Lewter, Nicholas C., jt. auth. see Mitchell, Henry H.

***Lewton, J. V.** Called to Darkness. 224p. 1995. mass mkt. 3.99 (*0-8217-4914-5*) Zebra.

— Just Pretend. 256p. 1994. mass mkt. 3.50 (*0-8217-4672-3*) Zebra.

Lewton, Kathleen L. Public Relations in Health Care: A Guide for Professionals. 367p. (Orig.). 1991. pap. 49.00 (*1-55648-066-0*, 166122) AHPI.

Lewty, Majorie. Bittersweet Honeymoon. large type ed. (Classic Romance Ser.). 1992. 18.95 (*0-263-13343-5*, Pub. by Mills & Boon Ltd UK) Chivers N Amer.

Lewty, Marjorie. Deep Water. large type ed. (Harlequin Ser.). 1992. reprint ed. lib. bdg. 18.95 (*0-263-12981-0*, Pub. by Mills & Boon UK) Thorndike Pr.

— Love Is a Dangerous Game. large type ed. (Linford Romance Library). 304p. 1985. pap. 11.95 (*0-7089-6064-2*, Linford) Ulverscroft.

— The Short Engagement. large type ed. 352p. 1984. 15.95 (*0-7089-1213-3*) Ulverscroft.

***Lewty, Peter J.** Across the Columbia Plain: Railroad Expansion on the Interior Northwest, 1885-1893. LC 94-39630. (Illus.). 286p. (Orig.). 1995. 35.00 (*0-87422-115-3*); pap. 25.00 (*0-87422-114-5*) Wash St U Pr.

— To the Columbia Gateway: The Oregon Railway & the Northern Pacific, 1879-1884. LC 87-21041. (Illus.). 202p. 1987. 30.00 (*0-87422-030-0*); pap. 20.00 (*0-87422-029-7*) Wash St U Pr.

Lewy, A. Studies in Educational Evaluation. (Reviews in Educational Evaluation Ser.: Vol. 6, No. 2). (Illus.). 116p. 1980. pap. 21.00 (*0-08-026760-2*, Pergamon Pr) Elsevier.

Lewy, Arieh & Nevo, David. Evaluation Roles in Education. 528p. 1981. text ed. 87.00 (*0-677-16290-1*) Gordon & Breach.

Lewy, Guenter. America in Vietnam. 1980. pap. 11.95 (*0-19-502732-9*) OUP.

— The Cause That Failed: Communism in American Political Life. 384p. 1990. 24.95 (*0-19-505748-1*) OUP.

— False Consciousness: An Essay on Mystification. LC 82-1985. 192p. 1982. 29.95 (*0-87855-451-3*) Transaction Pubs.

— The Federal Loyalty-Security Program: The Need for Reform. LC 83-2711. (AEI Studies: No. 378). 104p. reprint ed. pap. 29.70 (*0-8357-4480-9*, 2037330) Bks Demand.

— Peace & Revolution: The Moral Crisis of American Pacifism. LC 88-1374. 293p. reprint ed. pap. 83.60 (*0-8357-4364-0*, 2037193) Bks Demand.

Lewy, Hans, et al, eds. Three Jewish Philosophers: Philo, Saadya, Gaon, Jehuda, Halevi. LC 60-9081. 448p. (C). 1972. reprint ed. pap. 11.00 (*0-689-70126-8*, T6, Pub. by Ctrl Bur voor Schimmel NE) Macmillan.

Lewy, Julius, jt. auth. see Eisser, George.

Lewy, R. Employees at Risk. 1991. text ed. 44.95 (*0-442-00402-8*) Van Nos Reinhold.

Lewyt, C., ed. see Broad, C. D.

Lexa-Senning, Susan, jt. auth. see Alden, Laura.

Lexander, Ren, jt. auth. see Soadhi, Geraldine.

Lexau, Joan M. Don't Be My Valentine. LC 85-42621. (Harper I Can Read Bk.). (Illus.). 64p. (J). (gr. k-3). 1985. lib. bdg. 14.89 (*0-06-023873-9*) HarpC Child Bks.

— Don't Be My Valentine. LC 85-42621. (Trophy I Can Read Bk.). (Illus.). 64p. (J). (gr. k-3). 1988. pap. 3.50 (*0-06-444115-6*, Trophy) HarpC Child Bks.

— Don't Be My Valentine. (J). (gr. 1-4). 1990. audio 19.95 (*0-87499-150-1*); audio, pap. 12.95 (*0-87499-149-8*) Live Oak Media.

— Don't Be My Valentine, 4 bks., Set. (J). (gr. 1-4). 1990. audio 29.95 (*0-685-38539-6*) Live Oak Media.

— Emily & the Klunky Baby & the Next-Door Dog. LC 77-181789. (Illus.). 40p. (J). (ps-3). 1972. 5.95 (*0-8037-2309-1*) Dial Bks Young.

— Rooftop Mystery. LC 68-16821. (Harper I Can Read Mystery Bk.). (Illus.). 64p. (J). (gr. k-3). 1968. lib. bdg. 14.89 (*0-06-023865-8*) HarpC Child Bks.

— Striped Ice Cream. LC 68-10774. (Illus.). 96p. (J). (gr. k-3). 1968. lib. bdg. 14.89 (*0-397-31047-1*, Lipp Jr Bks) HarpC Child Bks.

— Striped Ice Cream. (J). 1992. 2.99 (*0-590-45729-2*, Little Apple) Scholastic Inc.

— Trouble Will Find You. LC 93-6813. (Illus.). (J). (ps-6). 1994. 13.95 (*0-395-64380-5*) HM.

Lexicon, jt. auth. see Leibniz.

Lexicon Publications Staff. The New Webster's Crossword Dictionary. 1991. mass mkt. 5.99 (*0-425-12882-2*) Berkley Pub.

Lexigraph Company Staff. Chez Game. (Illus.). 76p. (Orig.). 1985. pap. 10.00 (*0-934365-00-8*) Leco Pub.

Lexikos Publishing Staff. Short History of Portland. 1990. pap. 12.95 (*0-938530-46-1*) Lexikos.

Lexington, Daniel. The Inventor's Guide to Enterprise Founding: Stock Share Issuance in the Early Stages. 2nd ed. (How 2 of Inventing Money Ser.). (Illus.). 88p. 1994. Wkbk. student ed 9.14 (*0-9641686-1-8*) Should Know.

***Lexington Herald-Leader Staff.** Life's a Dance: The Story of John Michael Montgomery. (Illus.). 128p. 1995. pap. 14.95 (*0-8362-0567-7*) Andrews & McMeel.

Lexington School for the Deaf Staff. Auditory Skills Curriculum: Preschool Supplement. (Auditory Skills Instructional Planning System Ser.). 180p. 1988. ring bd. 35.00 (*0-943292-23-9*) Foreworks.

Lextz, Gerald S. Lancaster County Architecture, 1700-1850. (Illus.). 176p. 1992. 40.00 (*0-9635153-0-6*) Hist Preserv Trst.

Lexus, Ed. Dutch at Your Fingertips. 1987. pap. 8.95 (*0-7102-0953-3*, RKP) Routledge.

— German at Your Fingertips. 1987. pap. 6.95 (*0-7102-0954-1*, RKP) Routledge.

— Italian at Your Fingertips. 1987. pap. 6.95 (*0-7102-0955-X*, RKP) Routledge.

Lexus Ltd. Staff. Harrap's Chinese Phrase Book. 128p. 1991. pap. 3.95 (*0-13-388729-4*) P-H.

— Harrap's Concise Spanish. 992p. 1991. 17.00 (*0-13-377615-8*, Harraps) P-H Gen Ref & Trav.

— Harrap's Japanese Phrase Book. 128p. 1991. pap. 4.00 (*0-13-388737-5*) P-H.

— Harrap's Russian Phrase Book. 128p. 1991. pap. 4.00 (*0-13-388745-6*) P-H.

Lexus Ltd. Staff, et al. Harrap's Student German. 800p. 1991. pap. 12.00 (*0-13-377623-9*, Harraps) P-H Gen Ref & Trav.

***Ley.** Natural Healing Handbook. 1995. mass mkt. 14.95 (*0-9642703-5-8*) B L Pubns.

***Ley, Alice C.** At Dark of the Moon. large type ed. 352p. 1995. 23.95 (*0-7089-3263-0*) Ulverscroft.

— A Conformable Wife. large type ed. 1994. 21.95 (*0-7089-3150-2*) Ulverscroft.

— The Georgian Rake. large type ed. 1994. 20.95 (*0-7089-3168-5*) Ulverscroft.

— Intrepid Miss Haydon. 1983. pap. 2.25 (*0-449-20274-7*) Fawcett.

— The Intrepid Miss Haydon. large type ed. LC 94-29902. 1995. pap. 16.95 (*0-8161-7491-1*) Hall.

— The Jewelled Snuffbox. large type ed. 368p. 1994. 20.95 (*0-7089-3114-6*) Ulverscroft.

— The Master of Liversedge. large type ed. 1994. 20.95 (*0-7089-3203-7*) Ulverscroft.

— A Reputation Dies. large type ed. 298p. 1989. pap. 13.95 (*0-8161-4732-9*) G K Hall.

***Ley, Beth. Natural Healing Handbook: Get Back to Health...Naturally. 322p. 1994. pap. 14.95 (*0-9642703-1-5*) B L Pubns.**

Features valuable, easy-to-find, easy-to-understand information about diet & nutrition & how to avoid & treat common health problems including: Acne, Allergies, Arthritis, Cold sores, Dandruff, Fatigue, Food poisoning, Gallstones, Gout, Headaches, Heartburn, Hemorrhoids, High cholesterol, High blood pressure, Hives, Hypoglycemia, Insect bites, Insomnia, Intestinal gas, Immune deficiency, Leg cramps, Memory loss, Night blindness, Osteoporosis, Prostate trouble, Sinusitis, Stress, Varicose veins, Weight problems, Yeast infection & more! Find out: What herbs to use, what supplements to take, how to avoid illness & disease with the help of nature, not drugs! Find out what foods are high in valuable disease-fighting nutrients. This reader-friendly reference guide is designed to quickly give you the facts you are seeking, without excess meaningless information. FROM THE FOREWORD BY DR. ARNOLD SUSSER, R.Ph., Ph.D., "Whether you want to stay in good health or get back to good health naturally, this book belongs in your "Health is Wealth" library. NATURAL HEALING HANDBOOK truly offers something for everyone!" PUBLISHED BY BL PUBLICATIONS, 1638 Westcliff Drive, Newport Beach, CA 92660. 1-714-645-9718. DISTRIBUTED BY NUTRI-BOOKS, 790 West Tennessee Ave., Denver, CO 80223. 1-800-279-2048. ***Publisher Provided Annotation.***

Ley, Beth, jt. auth. see Jamieson, James.

Ley, Beth, jt. auth. see Susser, Arnold.

***Ley, Beth M.** Castor Oil: Its Healing Properties. 42p. (Orig.). 1989. pap. 3.95 (*0-614-02687-3*) B L Pubns.

— Dr. John Willard's Catalyst Altered Water. 64p. (Orig.). 1992. pap. 3.95 (*91-49-59100-2*) B L Pubns.

Ley, Charles D. Portuguese Voyages, 1498-1663. 1977. lib. bdg. 59.95 (*0-8490-2459-5*) Gordon Pr.

— Spanish Poetry Since 1939. LC 62-52819. 289p. reprint ed. pap. 82.40 (*0-685-17851-X*, 2029511) Bks Demand.

Ley, D. Forbes. The Best Seller. LC 84-50560. 1990. reprint ed. 19.95 (*0-9613319-0-9*) Sales Success.

— The Best Seller. LC 84-50560. 313p. 1995. reprint ed. pap. 19.95 (*0-9613319-2-5*) Sales Success.

— The Best Seller: Of Automobiles. LC 85-90516. 1986. 9.95 (*0-9613319-1-7*) Sales Success.

Ley, David. The Black Inner City As Frontier Outpost. LC 74-82116. (Monograph Ser.: No. 7). 1974. pap. 10.00 (*0-89291-086-0*) Assn Am Geographers.

— A Social Geography of the City. 449p. (C). 1990. pap. text ed. 57.00 (*0-06-384875-9*) HarpCollege.

Ley, David, jt. auth. see Duncan, James S.

Ley, David, jt. auth. see Hasson, Shlomo.

Ley, David F., jt. ed. see Bourne, Larry S.

Ley, Graham. A Short Introduction to the Ancient Greek Theater. (Illus.). 120p. 1991. pap. 6.95 (*0-226-47760-6*) U Ch Pr.

— A Short Introduction to the Ancient Greek Theater. (Illus.). 120p. 1991. lib. bdg. 20.00 (*0-226-47759-2*) U Ch Pr.

Ley, J. W. The Dickens Circle. LC 72-573. (Studies in Dickens: No. 52). 1972. reprint ed. lib. bdg. 75.00 (*0-8383-1415-5*) M S G Haskell Hse.

Ley, L. & Cardona, M., eds. Photoemission in Solids II: Case Studies. LC 78-2503. (Topics in Applied Physics Ser.: Vol. 27). (Illus.). 1979. 79.00 (*0-387-09202-1*) Spr-Verlag.

Ley, Philip. Communicating with Patients: Improving Communication, Satisfaction & Compliance. 240p. 1989. 49.95 (*0-7099-4161-7*); pap. 17.95 (*0-7099-4174-9*) Routledge Chapman & Hall.

Ley, Ralph, jt. auth. see Hill, Claude.

Ley, Ronald. A Whisper of Espionage: Wolfgang Kohler & the Apes of Tenerife. LC 89-36061. 292p. 1990. 19.95 (*0-89529-432-X*) Avery Pub.

Ley, Ronald, jt. ed. see Timmons, Beverly H.

Ley, Rosamond, tr. see Busoni, Ferruccio.

Ley, Rossmund, tr. see Busoni, Ferruccio B.

Ley, S. V. & Low, C. M. Ultrasound in Synthesis. (Reactivity & Structure Ser.: Vol. 27). (Illus.). 185p. 1989. 109.00 (*0-387-51023-0*) Spr-Verlag.

Ley, Thomas W., jt. ed. see Williams, Kathleen M.

Ley, Willy. Rockets, Missiles & Space Travel. 1994. reprint ed. lib. bdg. 45.95 (*1-56849-302-9*) Buccaneer Bks.

Leyburn, Ellen D. Satiric Allegory: Mirror of Man. LC 78-5886. (Yale Studies in English: Vol. 130). 142p. 1978. reprint ed. text ed. 45.00 (*0-313-20457-8*, LESM, Greenwood Pr) Greenwood.

Leyburn, James G. The Haitian People. rev. ed. LC 80-476. (Caribbean Ser.: No. 9). (Illus.). xlviii, 342p. 1980. reprint ed. text ed. 48.50 (*0-313-22155-3*, LEHA, Greenwood Pr) Greenwood.

— The Scotch-Irish: A Social History. LC 62-16063. xx, 377p. (C). 1989. reprint ed. pap. 14.95 (*0-8078-4259-1*) U of NC Pr.

— The Way We Lived: Durham, 1900-1920. Savage, Lon K., ed. 220p. 1987. 16.95 (*0-9617256-1-3*) Northcross Hse.

Leyda, Jay. An Index to the Creative Work of Alexander Dovzhenko. (Film Ser.). 1980. lib. bdg. 59.95 (*0-8490-3094-3*) Gordon Pr.

— An Index to the Creative Work of V. I. Pudovkin. (Film Ser.). 1980. lib. bdg. 59.95 (*0-8490-3092-7*) Gordon Pr.

— Kino: A History of the Russian & Soviet Film, with a New Postcript & a Filmography Brought up to the Present. rev. ed. LC 82-48563. (Illus.). 580p. 1983. reprint ed. pap. 24.95 (*0-691-00346-7*) Princeton U Pr.

Leyda, Jay, ed. Eisenstein, No. 2: A Premature Celebration of Eisenstein's Centenary. Upchurch, Alan et al, trs. (Illus.). 59p. (Orig.). (C). 1989. pap. 9.95 (*0-413-19370-5*, AO346, Pub. by Methuen UK) Heinemann.

— Film Makers Speak: Voices of Film Experience. LC 84-12041. (Quality Paperbacks Ser.). 581p. (C). 1984. reprint ed. pap. 13.95 (*0-306-80228-7*) Da Capo.

An Asterisk (*) at the beginning of an entry indicates that the title is appearing in BIP for the first time.

Leyda, Jay & Bertensson, Sergei, eds. The Musorgsky Reader: A Life of Modeste Petrovich Musorgsky in Letters & Documents. LC 70-87393. (Music Ser.). (Illus.). 1970. reprint ed. lib. bdg. 49.50 (*0-306-71534-1*) Da Capo.

Leyda, Jay, ed. see Eisenstein, Sergei M.

Leyda, Jay, et al. Before Hollywood: Turn-of-the-Century American Film. (Illus.). 172p. (Orig.). 1987. pap. 25.00 (*0-917418-81-6*) Am Fed Arts.

Leyden, D. & Collins, W. Silyated Surfaces, Vol. 7. (Midland Macromolecular Monographs). 388p. 1980. text ed. 239.00 (*0-677-13370-7*) Gordon & Breach.

Leyden, D. E. & Collins, W. T., eds. Chemically Modified Oxide Surfaces: Proceedings of the Chemically Modified Surfaces Symposium, Midland, Michigan, June 28-30, 1989. 408p. 1990. text ed. 95.00 (*2-88124-428-9*) Gordon & Breach.

Leyden, Dennis P. & Link, Albert N. Government's Role in Innovation. LC 92-20984. 224p. (C). 1992. lib. bdg. 78.00 (*0-7923-9261-2*) Kluwer Ac.

Leyden, Dennis R., et al. Measuring Patient Attitudes in a Comprehensive Health Care Setting. 62p. 1977. write for info. (*0-318-59912-0*) Assn U Busn & Econ Res.

Leyden, Dennis R., et al, eds. Bibliography of Nineteen-Seventy Five Publications of University Bureaus Business & Economic Research, Vol. 20. 209p. 1976. 7.50 (*0-318-13494-2*) Assn U Busn & Econ Res.

— Bibliography of Nineteen Seventy-Seven Publications of University Bureaus of Business & Economic Research, Vols. 22. 264p. 1978. 12.50 (*0-318-13496-9*) Assn U Busn & Econ Res.

— Bibliography of Nineteen Seventy-Six Publications of University Bureaus of Business & Economic Research, Vol. 21. 258p. 1977. 12.50 (*0-318-13497-7*) Assn U Busn & Econ Res.

Leyden, Donald E., ed. Silanes, Surfaces & Interfaces: Proceedings of the Silanes, Surfaces & Interfaces Symposium, Snowmass, Colorado, June 19-21, 1985 - Volume 1, Chemically Modified Surfaces. 584p. 1986. text ed. 169.00 (*2-88124-085-2*) Gordon & Breach.

Leyden, Donald E. & Collins, Ward T., eds. Chemically Modified Surfaces in Science & Industry. (Chemically Modified Surfaces Ser.: Vol. 2). 681p. (C). 1988. text ed. 154.00 (*2-88124-221-9*) Gordon & Breach.

Leyden, Maurice. Boys & Girls Come Out to Play: A Collection of Irish Singing Games. (Illus.). 112p. (Orig.). 1994. pap. 13.95 (*0-86281-432-4*, Pub. by Appletree Pr IE) Irish Bks Media.

Leyden, Susan. Helping the Child of Exceptional Ability. large type ed. LC 85-4137. (Special Education Ser.). 102p. (Orig.). 1985. pap. 19.95 (*0-7099-1635-3*, Pub. by Croom Helm UK) Routledge Chapman & Hall.

Leydenfrost, Robert. The Elephant Book. LC 79-87457. (Illus.). 128p. 1979. 3.95 (*0-932966-03-9*) Permanent Pr.

***Leydesdorf, Loet.** Evolutionary Economics & Chaos Theory: New Directions in Technology Studies, Vol. 1. 1994. pap. 19.95 (*0-312-12218-7*) St Martin.

Leydesdorff, Loet, et al, eds. Evolutionary Economics & Chaos Theory: New Directions in Technology Studies. LC 94-1945. 1994. write for info. (*1-85567-198-0*, Pub. by Pinter Pubs UK); pap. write for info. (*1-85567-202-2*, Pub. by Pinter Pubs UK) St Martin.

Leydesdorff, Selma. We Lived with Dignity: The Jewish Proleteriat of Amsterdam, 1900-1940. Heny, Frank, tr. (Illus.). 328p. 1994. reprint ed. text ed. 39.95 (*0-8143-2338-3*) Wayne St U Pr.

Leydet, Francois. The Coyote: Defiant Songdog of the West. LC 87-40563. (Illus.). 224p. 1981. 24.95 (*0-8061-2168-8*); pap. 12.95 (*0-8061-2123-8*) U of Okla Pr.

Leyel, C. F. Herbal Delights: Tisanes, Syrups, Confections, Electuaries, Robs, Juleps, Vinegars & Conserves. (Illus.). 320p. (Orig.). 1987. pap. 10.95 (*0-571-14850-6*) Faber & Faber.

— The Truth about Herbs. 106p. 1985. pap. 8.00 (*0-89540-145-2*, SB-145) Sun Pub.

— The Truth about Herbs. 106p. 1966. reprint ed. spiral bd. 4.40 (*0-7873-0558-8*) Mokelumne.

Leyel, C. F., ed. see Grieve, M.

Leyendecker, G., ed. see Stock, H. & Wildt, L.

Leyendecker, Liston E. Palace Car Prince: A Biography of George Mortimer Pullman. (C). 1994. pap. 14.95 (*0-87081-337-4*) Univ Pr Colo.

Leyendecker, Liston E., jt. auth. see Trenton, Patricia.

Leyendekkers, J. V. Thermodynamics of Seawater As a Multicomponent Electrolyte Solution, Pt. 1: Entropy, Volume, Expansibility, Compressibility. LC 76-18422. (Marine Science Ser.: No. 3). (Illus.). 510p. reprint ed. pap. 145.40 (*0-7837-0788-6*, 2041102) Bks Demand.

Leyens, J. P., jt. auth. see Codol, J. P.

***Leyens, Jacques-Philippe, et al.** Stereotypes & Social Cognition. 256p. 1994. 65.00 (*0-8039-8583-5*); pap. 21.95 (*0-8039-8584-3*) Sage.

Leyerle, Anne L. & Leyerle, William D. Song Anthology One. 3rd rev. ed. LC 79-90829. 159p. (J). (gr. 9 up). 1985. spiral bd. 12.95 (*0-9602296-3-9*) Leyerle Pubns.

Leyerle, Anne L. & Leyerle, William D., eds. French Diction Songs. 2nd rev. ed. 128p. 1990. pap. text ed. 12.95 (*0-9602296-9-8*) Leyerle Pubns.

— Song Anthology Two. 159p. (YA). (gr. 9 up). 1984. spiral bd. 12.95 (*0-9602296-4-7*) Leyerle Pubns.

Leyerle, Betty. Moving & Shaking American Medicine: The Structure of a Socioeconomic Transformation. LC 83-22646. (Contributions in Economics & Economic History Ser.: No. 57). vii, 218p. 1984. text ed. 49.95 (*0-313-24020-5*, LIP/, Greenwood Pr) Greenwood.

— The Private Regulation of American Health Care. 240p. 1994. text ed. 45.00 (*1-56324-288-5*); pap. text ed. 17.50 (*1-56324-289-3*) M E Sharpe.

Leyerle, John & Quick, Anne, eds. Chaucer: A Selected Bibliography. (Medieval Bibliographies Ser.). 352p. 1986. pap. 10.95 (*0-8020-6408-6*) U of Toronto Pr.

Leyerle, John, jt. ed. see Benson, Larry D.

Leyerle, John, jt. ed. see Damico, Helen.

Leyerle, William D. Vocal Development Through Organic Imagery. 2nd enl. rev. ed. LC 78-103579. (Illus.). 189p. (C). 1986. pap. 14.95 (*0-9602296-6-3*) Leyerle Pubns.

Leyerle, William D., jt. ed. see Ellingboe, Bradley.

Leyerle, William D., jt. auth. see Leyerle, Anne L.

Leyerle, William D., jt. ed. see Leyerle, Anne L.

Leyh, ed. see Anderson, Robert L. & Dunkelberg, John S.

Leyh, ed. see Austin, Larry M. & Ghandforoush, Parviz.

Leyh, ed. see Bacon, Jonathan P.

Leyh, ed. see Bacon, Jonathan . & Sindt, Robert.

Leyh, ed. see Barfield, Jesse T., et al.

Leyh, ed. see Bitter, Gary G.

Leyh, ed. see Bitter, Gary.

Leyh, ed. see Black, Ken.

Leyh, ed. see Clabaugh, Maurice G., Jr. & Forbes, Jesse L.

Leyh, ed. see Clabaugh, Maurice G., Jr., et al.

Leyh, ed. see Clabaugh, Maurice G., Jr. & Forbes, Jesse L.

Leyh, ed. see Copeland, Cody T. & Bacon, Jonathan P.

Leyh, ed. see Fandt, Patricia M.

Leyh, ed. see Fisher, Bruce D. & Phillips, Michael J.

Leyh, ed. see Fisher, Bruce & Jennings, Marianne M.

Leyh, ed. see Guay, E. Joseph.

Leyh, ed. see Harris, O. Jeff & Hartman, Sandra.

Leyh, ed. see Harrison, Jeffrey S. & St. John, Caron H.

Leyh, ed. see Heiman, Barbara & McGauley, Nancy.

Leyh, ed. see Jansen, Dennis W., et al.

Leyh, ed. see Jarboe, Glen R.

Leyh, ed. see Jennings, Daniel F.

Leyh, ed. see Jennings, Marianne M.

Leyh, ed. see Knapp, Michael C.

Leyh, ed. see Lozuk, Larry.

Leyh, ed. see Lozuk, Larry & Ketcham, Emily M.

Leyh, ed. see Lund, Patsy H.

Leyh, ed. see McDaniel, Carl, Jr. & Gates, Roger H.

Leyh, ed. see McLaren, Bruce J.

Leyh, ed. see Murphy, Kevin E.

Leyh, ed. see Nelson, Debra L. & Quick, James C.

Leyh, ed. see Nicholson, John R.

Leyh, ed. see Quain, William J. & Jarboe, Glen R.

Leyh, ed. see Raiborn, Cecily A., et al.

Leyh, ed. see Ross, Paul W., et al.

Leyh, ed. see Ross, Steven C., et al.

Leyh, ed. see Ross, Steven C.

Leyh, ed. see Ross, Steven C. & Hutson, Stephen V.

Leyh, ed. see Ross, Steven C. & Maestas, Ronald W.

Leyh, ed. see Ross, Steven C.

Leyh, ed. see Ross, Steven C. & Hutson, Stephen V.

Leyh, ed. see Ross, Steven C. & Maestas, Ronald W.

Leyh, ed. see Ross, Steven C. & Hutson, Stephen V.

Leyh, ed. see Ross, Steven C.

Leyh, ed. see Ruff, Laura B. & Weitzer, Mary K.

Leyh, ed. see Simon, Judith C.

Leyh, ed. see Smith, Larry D.

Leyh, ed. see Vonderembse, Mark A. & White, Gregory P.

Leyh, ed. see Zikmund, William G. & D'Amico, Michael.

Leyh, ed. see Zimmerman, Steven M. & Conrad, Leo.

Leyh, Gregory, intro. Legal Hermeneutics: History, Theory, & Practice. LC 90-19397. 335p. 1991. 45.00 (*0-520-07283-9*); pap. 16.00 (*0-520-07284-7*) U CA Pr.

Leylan, Thomas. Writing Applications with Clipper. 1994. pap. 39.95 (*1-55851-382-5*) M&T Bks.

Leyland, B. N., jt. ed. see Duz'minskii, A. S.

Leyland, Charles G., tr. see Heine, Heinrich & Liebermann, Max.

Leyland, Francis A. Bronte Family, 2 vols., Set. LC 70-157554. (English Literature Ser.: No. 33). 1971. reprint ed. lib. bdg. 150.00 (*0-8383-1256-X*) M S G Haskell Hse.

***Leyland, Peter, et al.** Textbook on Administrative Law. 368p. 1994. pap. 38.00 (*1-85431-318-5*, Pub. by Blackstone Pr UK) W W Gaunt.

Leyland, Valerie. Electronic Data Interchange: A Management View. LC 93-1299. (BCS Practitioner Ser.). 250p. 1993. pap. text ed. 42.00 (*0-13-249533-3*) P-H.

Leyland, Winston, ed. And Still More Meatmen: An Anthology of Gay Male Comics, Vol. 3. 2nd ed. (Illus.). 160p. 1990. reprint ed. pap. 14.95 (*0-943595-10-X*) Leyland Pubns.

— Angels of the Lyre: Anthology of Gay Poetry. LC 75-19135. (Illus.). 256p. (C). 1975. 12.95 (*0-915572-14-1*); pap. 6.95 (*0-915572-13-3*) Panjandrum.

— Boys Will Be Boys, Vol. 9: True Gay Encounters. 160p. (Orig.). 1990. pap. 10.95 (*0-943595-26-6*) Leyland Pubns.

— Eighteen & Over: True Gay Encounters, Vol. 10. 160p. (Orig.). 1991. pap. 10.95 (*0-943595-31-2*) Leyland Pubns.

— Enlisted Meat: True Homosexual Military Stories, Vol. 1. 160p. (Orig.). 1991. pap. 12.95 (*0-943595-32-0*) Leyland Pubns.

— Gay Roots, Vol. 1: Twenty Years of Gay Sunshine: An Anthology of Gay History, Sex, Politics, & Culture. (Illus.). 704p. (Orig.). 1991. lib. bdg. 40.00 (*0-940567-12-1*); pap. 22.95 (*0-940567-13-X*) Gay Sunshine.

— Gay Roots, Vol. 2: An Anthology of Gay History, Sex, Politics & Culture. (Illus.). 320p. (Orig.). 1993. lib. bdg. 50.00 (*0-940567-14-8*); pap. 19.95 (*0-940567-15-6*) Gay Sunshine.

— Gay Sunshine Interviews, Vol. 1. (Illus.). 328p. (Orig.). 1984. 25.00 (*0-917342-60-7*); pap. 14.95 (*0-917342-63-1*) Gay Sunshine.

— Gay Sunshine Interviews, Vol. 2. (Illus.). 288p. (Orig.). 1982. 25.00 (*0-917342-62-3*); pap. 14.95 (*0-685-01892-X*) Gay Sunshine.

— Hot Studs, Vol. 3: True Homosexual Encounters First Hand. (Illus.). 192p. (Orig.). 1986. pap. 10.95 (*0-917342-15-1*) Leyland Pubns.

— Lust: Licentious Underground Sexy True Gay Encounters, Vol. 1. (Illus.). 176p. (Orig.). 1994. reprint ed. pap. 14.95 (*0-943595-48-7*) Leyland Pubns.

— Manplay, Vol. 3: True Gay Encounters. 192p. (Orig.). 1986. pap. 10.00 (*0-943595-06-1*) Leyland Pubns.

— Marine Biology: True Homosexual Military Stories, Vol. 4. (Military Sex Stories Ser.: Vol. 4). 160p. (Orig.). 1994. pap. 14.95 (*0-943595-49-5*) Leyland Pubns.

— Meatmen: An Anthology of Gay Male Comics, 2 vols. (Illus.). 1989. pap. write for info. (*0-318-68338-5*) Leyland Pubns.

— Meatmen: An Anthology of Gay Male Comics, 3 vols. (Illus.). 1991. pap. write for info. (*0-318-68339-3*) Leyland Pubns.

— Meatmen: An Anthology of Gay Male Comics, 2 vols., 5. (Illus.). 1989. pap. 14.95 (*0-943595-15-0*) Leyland Pubns.

— Meatmen: An Anthology of Gay Male Comics, 2 vols., 6. (Illus.). 1989. pap. 14.95 (*0-943595-20-7*) Leyland Pubns.

— Meatmen: An Anthology of Gay Male Comics, 3 vols., 7. (Illus.). 1990. pap. 13.95 (*0-943595-22-3*) Leyland Pubns.

— Meatmen: An Anthology of Gay Male Comics, 3 vols., 8. (Illus.). 1990. pap. 13.95 (*0-943595-23-1*) Leyland Pubns.

— Meatmen: An Anthology of Gay Male Comics, 3 vols., 9. (Illus.). 1990. pap. 14.95 (*0-943595-24-X*) Leyland Pubns.

— Meatmen: An Anthology of Gay Male Comics, 3 vols., 10. (Illus.). 1991. pap. 14.95 (*0-943595-27-4*) Leyland Pubns.

— Meatmen: An Anthology of Gay Male Comics, 3 vols., 11. (Illus.). 1991. pap. 14.95 (*0-943595-28-2*) Leyland Pubns.

— Meatmen: An Anthology of Gay Male Comics, 3 vols., 12. (Illus.). 1991. pap. 15.95 (*0-943595-29-0*) Leyland Pubns.

— Meatmen: An Anthology of Gay Male Comics, Vol. 1. 2nd ed. (Illus.). 192p. 1989. reprint ed. pap. 14.95 (*0-917342-23-2*) Leyland Pubns.

— Meatmen: An Anthology of Gay Male Comics, Vol. 13. (Illus.). 160p. 1992. pap. 15.95 (*0-685-57220-X*) Leyland Pubns.

— Meatmen: An Anthology of Gay Male Comics, Vol. 14. (Illus.). 160p. 1993. pap. 15.95 (*0-943595-35-5*) Leyland Pubns.

— Meatmen: Anthology of Gay Male Comics. (Meatmen Comics Ser.: Vol. 16). (Illus.). 160p. (Orig.). 1994. pap. 15.95 (*0-943595-44-4*) Leyland Pubns.

— Meatmen: Anthology of Gay Male Comics. (Meatmen Comics Ser.: Vol. 17). (Illus.). 160p. (Orig.). 1995. pap. 15.95 (*0-943595-50-9*) Leyland Pubns.

— Meatmen: Anthology of Gay Male Comics, Vol. 15. (Illus.). 160p. (Orig.). 1993. pap. 15.95 (*0-943595-38-X*) Leyland Pubns.

— Meatmen Continues: An Anthology of Gay Male Comics, Vol. 4. (Illus.). 160p. (Orig.). 1988. pap. 14.95 (*0-943595-12-6*) Leyland Pubns.

— Military Sex: True Homosexual Stories, Vol. 3. 160p. (Orig.). 1993. pap. 14.95 (*0-943595-41-X*) Leyland Pubns.

— My Deep Dark Pain Is Love: A Collection of Latin American Gay Fiction. Lacey, E. A., tr. (Illus.). 384p. (Orig.). 1983. pap. 14.95 (*0-917342-03-8*) Gay Sunshine.

— Orgasms: Homosexual Encounters from First Hand, Vol. 2. (Illus.). 192p. (Orig.). 1985. pap. 10.95 (*0-917342-12-7*) Leyland Pubns.

— Singlehanded, Vol. 4: True Homosexual Encounters from First Hand. 192p. (Orig.). 1987. pap. 10.95 (*0-943595-05-3*) Leyland Pubns.

— Studflesh, Vol. 8: True Gay Encounters. 160p. (Orig.). 1989. pap. 10.00 (*0-943595-25-8*) Leyland Pubns.

— Ten & One-Half Inches, Vol. 6: True Gay Encounters. 160p. (Orig.). 1988. pap. 10.00 (*0-943595-18-5*) Leyland Pubns.

— Warriors & Lovers: True Homosexual Military Stories, Vol. 2. 160p. (Orig.). 1992. pap. 14.95 (*0-943595-37-1*) Leyland Pubns.

— Young Numbers, Vol. 4: True Gay Encounters. 192p. (Orig.). 1987. pap. 10.95 (*0-943595-08-8*) Leyland Pubns.

Leyland, Winston, intro. Teleny: Novel Attributed to Oscar Wilde. 184p. 1984. reprint ed. lib. bdg. 25.00 (*0-917342-32-1*); reprint ed. pap. 7.95 (*0-917342-33-X*) Gay Sunshine.

Leyland, Winston, ed. see Ginsberg, Allen & Orlovsky, Peter.

Leyland, Winston, ed. see Stoddard, Charles W.

Leyman, Jean. How Do You Feel? Koj Puas Xis Nyob (English-Hmong Medical Handbook) Ly, Xeng, tr. LC 82-91138. (Illus.). 36p. 1983. pap. 5.00 (*0-9610684-0-X*) Mulberry Tree.

Leymarie, Jean. Gauguin: Watercolors, Pastels, Drawings. LC 88-43447. (Illus.). 100p. 1989. pap. 25.00 (*0-8478-1050-X*) Rizzoli Intl.

Leymarie, Jean, ed. Georges Braque. (Illus.). 280p. 1988. 65.00 (*3-7913-0882-3*, Pub. by Prestel) TeNeues.

***Leyn, K.** Russisch-Deutsches Woerterbuch. 11th ed. 735p. (GER & RUS.). 1991. 105.00 (*0-7859-8548-4*, 3894511117) Fr & Eur.

Leyner, Mark. Et Tu, Babe. LC 93-15503. (Vintage Contemporaries Ser.). 1993. pap. 10.00 (*0-679-74506-8*, Vin) Random.

— I Smell Esther Williams: And Other Stories. LC 94-31359. 1995. pap. 10.00 (*0-679-75045-2*, Vin) Random.

— I Smell Esther Williams & Other Stories. LC 82-83107. 197p. 1983. 15.95 (*0-914590-76-6*); pap. 8.95 (*0-914590-77-4*) Fiction Coll.

— My Cousin, My Gastroenterologist. 1990. pap. 10.00 (*0-517-57579-5*, Harmony) Crown Pub Group.

— My Cousin, My Gastroenterologist. LC 93-15505. 1995. pap. 10.00 (*0-679-74579-3*, Vin) Random.

— Tooth Imprints on a Corn Dog. 1995. 19.00 (*0-517-59384-X*, Crown) Crown Pub Group.

Leyner, Mark, et al, eds. American Made. LC 86-4459. 214p. 1986. 15.95 (*0-914590-98-7*); pap. 8.95 (*0-914590-99-5*) Fiction Coll.

Leypoldt, Martha M. Forty Ways to Teach in Groups. (Orig.). 1967. pap. text ed. 9.00 (*0-8170-0376-2*) Judson.

Leys, Colin. Politics in Britain. 2nd ed. 400p. 1989. pap. 19.95 (*0-8020-6751-4*) U of Toronto Pr.

— Politics in Britain: An Introduction. LC 83-213340. (Illus.). 360p. (Orig.). reprint ed. pap. 102.60 (*0-8357-3645-8*, 2036372) Bks Demand.

Leys, Colin, ed. Politics & Change in Developing Countries: Studies in the Theory & Practice of Development. 301p. reprint ed. pap. 85.80 (*0-317-09390-8*, 2051389) Bks Demand.

Leys, Colin & Saul, John S. Namibia's Liberation Struggle: The Two-Edged Sword. LC 94-8024. (Eastern African Studies). (Illus.). 300p. (C). 1994. text ed. 44.95 (*0-8214-1103-9*); pap. text ed. 19.95 (*0-8214-1104-7*) Ohio U Pr.

Leys, Colin T. European Politics in Southern Rhodesia. LC 82-6176. xii, 323p. 1982. reprint ed. text ed. 59.75 (*0-313-23548-1*, LEEU, Greenwood Pr) Greenwood.

— Politics in Britain: From Labourism to Thatcherism. 384p. 1989. 50.00 (*0-86091-240-X*, A3888); pap. 17.95 (*0-86091-954-4*, A3892) Routledge Chapman & Hall.

— Underdevelopment in Kenya: The Political Economy of Neo-Colonialism, 1964-1971. LC 74-76387. 1975. pap. 17.00 (*0-520-02770-1*) U CA Pr.

Leys, Colin T., jt. ed. see Berman, Bruce J.

Leys, Ruth. From Sympathy to Reflex: Marshall Hall & His Opponents. LC 90-19507. (Harvard Dissertations in the History of Science Ser.). 568p. 1991. reprint ed. 117.00 (*0-8240-0042-0*) Garland.

Leys, Ruth & Evans, Rand B., eds. Defining American Psychology: The Correspondence Between Adolph Meyer & Edward Brandord Titchener. LC 89-15315. 296p. 1990. text ed. 45.00x (*0-8018-3865-7*) Johns Hopkins.

Leys, Simon. The Death of Napoleon. Clancy, Patricia, tr. 1992. 15.00 (*0-374-13565-7*) FS&G.

— Death of Napoleon. 1994. pap. 9.00 (*0-374-52395-9*, Noonday) FS&G.

***Leyser, Brady J. & Gosset, Pol, eds.** Rock Stars - Pop Stars: A Comprehensive Bibliography, 1955-1994. LC 94-28691. (Musical Reference Collection: No. 43). 302p. 1994. text ed. 59.95 (*0-313-29422-4*) Greenwood.

Leyser, K. J. Medieval Germany & Its Neighbours, 900-1250. 300p. (C). 1982. text ed. 55.00 (*0-907628-08-7*); pap. 18.00 (*0-907628-09-5*) Hambledon Press.

Leyser, Karl. Communications & Power in Medieval Europe: The Carolingian & Ottonian Centures. Reuter, Timothy, ed. LC 94-20663. 1994. 60.00 (*1-85285-013-2*) Hambledon Press.

— Communications & Power in Medieval Europe: The Gregorian Revolution & Beyond. Reuter, Timothy, ed. LC 94-25531. 1994. write for info. (*1-85285-113-9*) Hambledon Press.

Leyshon, Andrew, et al. The Rise of the British Provincial Financial Centre. (Progress in Planning Ser.: PRPL 31). 80p. 1990. pap. 42.00 (*0-08-037384-4*, Pergamon Pr) Elsevier.

Leyshon, Anna H., jt. auth. see Renner-McCaffrey, Jo.

Leyshon, Glynn, ed. see Mikalachki, Albert.

Leyshon, Glynn A. The Coach & Sport Management. Zeigler, Earle F., ed. (Stipes Monograph Series on Sport & Physical Education Management). 48p. 1992. pap. text ed. 4.80 (*0-87563-425-7*) Stipes.

Leyson, J. F., ed. Sexual Rehabilitation of the Spinal-Cord-Injured Patient. LC 90-4685. (Illus.). 548p. 1991. 125.00 (*0-89603-145-4*) Humana.

Leytham, J., jt. auth. see Schramm, W.

***Leyton-Brown, David, ed.** Canadian Annual Review of Politics & Public Affairs, 1988. 352p. 1994. 70.00 (*0-8020-5849-3*) U of Toronto Pr.

— Canadian Annual Review of Politics & Public Affairs, 1989. 320p. (C). 1995. 70.00 (*0-8020-0714-7*) U of Toronto Pr.

Leyton, Elliott. Hunting Humans. 1990. mass mkt. 4.99 (*0-671-73141-6*) PB.

Leyton, Lawrence. My First Magic Book. LC 93-22104. (Illus.). 48p. (J). (gr. k-4). 1993. 12.95 (*1-56458-319-8*) Dorling Kindersley.

Leyton, Michael. Symmetry, Causality, Mind. (Illus.). 640p. 1992. 52.50 (*0-262-12163-8*, Bradford Bks) MIT Pr.

Leyva, Josefina. Los Balseros de la Libertad. 105p. 1992. pap. write for info. (*1-882721-00-4*) Edit Ponce de Leon.

Leza, Richard L. Export Now: A Guide for Small Businesses. 3rd ed. 1993. pap. 19.95 (*1-55571-167-7*) Oasis Pr OR.

Lezak, Muriel. Neuropsychological Assessment. 3rd ed. (Illus.). 854p. 1995. 65.00 (*0-19-509031-4*) OUP.

Lezak, Roseann, ed. see Kubi, K. Appiah.

Lezama Lima, Jose. Paradiso. Rabassa, Gregory, tr. (Texas Pan American Ser.). 471p. 1988. pap. 14.95 (*0-292-76507-X*) U of Tex Pr.

Lezar, Ted. Making Government Work: A Conservative Agenda for the States. LC 93-47055. 1993. pap. 15.95 (*0-89526-730-6*) Regnery Pub.

Lezhnev, A. Pushkin's Prose. Reeder, Roberta, tr. Orig. Title: Proza Pushkina. 225p. 1986. pap. 45.00 (*0-317-40744-9*, Pub. by Collets UK) St Mut.

Lezine, I., jt. auth. see David, M.

An Asterisk (*) at the beginning of an entry indicates that the title is appearing in BIP for the first time.

L

Leznoff, C. C. & Lever, A. P., eds. Phthalocyanines: Properties & Applications, Vol. 2. (Illus.). 640p. 1993. text ed. 150.00 (*1-56081-544-2*) VCH Pubs.

Leznoff, Clifford C. & Lever, Phillip, eds. Phthalocyanines: Properties & Applications. LC 89-16518. 436p. 1989. text ed. 165.00 (*0-89573-753-1*) VCH Pubs.

Leznov, A. N. & Saveliev, M. V. Group-Theoretical Methods for Integration of Nonlinear Dynamical Systems. Leites, D. A., tr. (Progress in Physics Ser.: Vol. 15). 312p. 1992. 163.50 (*0-8176-2615-8*) Birkhauser.

Lezotte, Lawrence W. Creating the Total Quality Effective School. 110p. 1992. pap. 25.00 (*1-883247-02-0*) Effect Schls.

— Effective Schools Practices That Work. Jacoby, Barbara C., ed. 93p. 1991. pap. 17.95 (*1-883247-03-9*) Effect Schls.

— Sustainable School Reform: The District Context. Jacoby, Barbara C., ed. 283p. 1992. pap. 32.50 (*1-883247-01-2*) Effect Schls.

Lezotte, Lawrence W. & Jacoby, Barbara C. A Guide to the School Improvement Process Based on Effective Schools Research. 165p. 1990. pap. 29.95 (*1-883247-00-4*) Effect Schls.

LFA, Inc. (Lupus Foundation of America, Inc.) Staff. Successful Living with Chronic Illness. 2nd ed. 244p. 1994. per. 14.95 (*0-8403-9101-3*) Kendall-Hunt.

Lhalungpa, Lobsang P. Life of Milarepa. 256p. 1990. pap. 11.95 (*0-525-48546-5*, Dutton) NAL-Dutton.

— The Life of Milarepa: A New Translation from the Tibetan. 256p. 1992. pap. 13.95 (*0-14-019350-2*, Arkana) Viking Penguin.

Lhalungpa, Lobsang P., tr. see Takpo Tashi Namgyal.

Lhamon, W. T. Deliberate Speed: The Origins of a Cultural Style in the American 1950's. 1990. 21.95 (*0-87474-379-6*) Smithsonian.

Lhamon, W. T., Jr. Deliberate Speed: The Origins of a Cultural Style in the American 1950's. LC 89-26197. 304p. 1993. reprint ed. pap. 15.95 (*1-56098-316-7*) Smithsonian.

Lhamon, W. T., jt. auth. see Rourke, Constance.

Lhardy, Patricia, tr. see Ricard, Rene.

Lherbier, L. W., ed. see Vacuum Metallurgy Conference on Specialty Metals Melting & Processing Staff.

***L'Heritier, Philippe.** Dictionnaire de Genetique. 272p. (FRE.). 1979. pap. 69.95 (*0-7859-7824-0*, 2225526575) Fr & Eur.

L'Hermine, C. Radiology of Liver Circulation. LC 85-8905. (Radiology Ser.). 1985. lib. bdg. 142.00 (*0-89838-715-9*) Kluwer Ac.

L'Hermite, M., ed. Update on Hormonal Treatment in the Menopause. (Progress in Reproductive Biology & Medicine Ser.: Vol. 13). (Illus.). viii, 108p. 1989. 78.50 (*3-8055-4904-0*) S Karger.

L'Hermite, P. L. Processing & Use of Organic Sludge & Liquid Agricultural Wastes. 1986. lib. bdg. 169.50 (*90-277-2338-9*) Kluwer Ac.

— Treatment & Use of Sewage Sluge & Liquid Agricultural Wastes. 1991. 144.50 (*1-85166-682-6*) Elsevier.

L'Hermite, P. L. & Handtschutter, J., eds. Copper in Animal Wastes & Sewage Sludge. xiv, 378p. 1981. lib. bdg. 74.50 (*90-277-1293-X*) Kluwer Ac.

L'Hermite, P. L. & Ott, H., eds. Characterization, Treatment & Use of Sewage Sludge. xviii, 803p. 1981. lib. bdg. 154.50 (*90-277-1294-8*) Kluwer Ac.

— Processing & Use of Sewage Sludge. 600p. 1984. lib. bdg. 167.00 (*90-277-1727-3*) Kluwer Ac.

L'Hermite, P. L., jt. ed. see Barth, H.

L'Hermite, P. L., jt. ed. see Dirkzwager, A. H.

L'Heureux, Conrad, jt. auth. see Bybee, Howard C.

L'Heureux, John. Family Affairs. 192p. 1994. pap. 9.95 (*0-14-015225-3*, Penguin Bks) Viking Penguin.

— Tight White Collar. LC 93-13352. 224p. 1993. pap. 10.00 (*0-14-015526-0*, Penguin Bks) Viking Penguin.

— A Woman Run Mad. 240p. 1989. reprint ed. mass mkt. 4.99 (*0-380-70686-5*) Avon.

L'Heureux, Mother Aloysius G. Mystical Vocabulary of Venerable Mere Marie De L'Incarnation & Its Problems. LC 72-94190. (Catholic University of America. Studies in Romance Languages & Literatures: No. 53). (FRE.). reprint ed. 37.50 (*0-404-50353-5*) AMS Pr.

Lhevinne, Josef. Basic Principles in Pianoforte Playing. 2nd ed. Orig. Title: The Etude. (Illus.). 1970. reprint ed. pap. 4.50 (*0-913000-06-X*) Maestro Scope.

— Basic Principles in Pianoforte Playing. LC 74-157433. Orig. Title: The Etude. 1972. reprint ed. pap. 2.95 (*0-486-22820-7*) Dover.

L'Hevreux, Raymond. Cabinetmaking: Building Drawers. LC 81-730635. 1981. student ed 5.00 (*0-8064-0267-9*, 705); audio 109.00 (*0-8064-0268-7*) Bergwall.

— Cabinetmaking: Rod Layout. LC 80-730671. 1981. student ed 7.00 (*0-8064-0265-2*, 704); audio 189.00 (*0-8064-0266-0*) Bergwall.

Lho, Kyongsoo, jt. ed. see Henriksen, Thomas H.

Lhomeau, Franck & Coelho, Alain. Marcel Proust: Remembrance of Publishers Past. Destree, Sabine, tr. 320p. 1995. 24.95 (*1-55970-058-0*) Arcade Pub Inc.

Lhommedieu, Arthur J. Children of the Sun. (J). (ps-3). 1993. 7.95 (*0-85953-931-8*) Childs Play.

— Metamorphoses: Butterfly. (J). (ps-3). 1993. 5.95 (*0-85953-170-8*) Childs Play.

— Metamorphoses: Egg, Tadpole, Frog. (J). (ps-3). 1993. 5.95 (*0-85953-169-4*) Childs Play.

L'Hommedieu, P. H., jt. auth. see L'Hommedieu, William A.

L'Hommedieu, Toni. The Divorce Experience of Working & Middle Class Women. LC 83-17967. (Research in Clinical Psychology Ser.: No. 8). 178p. reprint ed. pap. 50.80 (*0-8357-1478-0*, 2070400) Bks Demand.

***L'Hommedieu, William A. & L'Hommedieu, P. H.** L' Hommedieu Genealogy, 2 vols., Set. (Illus.). 930p. 1994. reprint ed. lib. bdg. 135.00 (*0-8328-4341-5*); reprint ed. pap. 125.00 (*0-8328-4342-3*) Higginson Bk Co.

Lhonnrot, Elias, jt. auth. see Magoun, Francis P.

Lhote, Gilles. Cowboys of the Sky. Clyman, Jacky & Clyman, Jeff, trs. 160p. 1988. write for info. (*0-318-64033-3*) Avirex Ltd.

Lhotka, J. Medieval Feudal French Coinage. 2nd ed. (Illus.). 1990. pap. 1.00 (*0-685-36401-1*) S J Durst.

Lhotka, John F., Jr. Introduction to East Roman (Byzantine) Coinage. 2nd rev. ed. LC 88-72080. (Illus.). 128p. 1989. reprint ed. pap. 15.00 (*0-942666-53-4*) S J Durst.

— Introduction to Medieval Bracteates. 2nd rev. ed. LC 88-72318. (Illus.). 80p. 1989. reprint ed. pap. 12.00 (*0-942666-52-6*) S J Durst.

Lhotka, John F. & Anderson, P. K. Survey of Medieval Iberian Coinages. 2nd rev. ed. LC 88-72079. 128p. 1989. reprint ed. pap. 15.00 (*0-942666-54-2*) S J Durst.

Lhotsky, Oldrich, ed. see Czechoslovak Academy of Sciences Institute of Botany.

Lhotzky, Stephan, tr. see Holzach, Michael.

Lhoyd, H., tr. see Caradoc Of Llancarfan.

Lhundrub, Ngorchen K. The Beautiful Ornament of the Three Visions. Lobsand Dagpa & Goldbert, Jay, eds. 232p. 1991. pap. 12.95 (*0-937938-99-8*) Snow Lion Pubns.

***L'Hygiene Populaire Staff.** Dictionnaire Chinois-Francais des Termes Medicaux Usuels. 1990. write for info. (*0-7859-8702-9*, 7117006668) Fr & Eur.

Li. Advances in Plant Cold Hardiness. 1992. 173.00 (*0-8493-4950-8*, QK756) CRC Pr.

— Comparative Cardiovascular Dynamics of Mammals. 1994. write for info. (*0-8493-0169-6*) CRC Pr.

***Li, A. P., et al, eds.** Toxicity Testing: New Approaches & Applications in Human Risk Assessment. fac. ed. LC 84-27634. 300p. Date not set. pap. 85.50 (*0-7837-7281-5*, 2047025) Bks Demand.

Li, Albert P., ed. Genetic Toxicology. 1991. 84.95 (*0-685-48568-4*, RA1224, CRC Reprint) Franklin.

Li, Albert P. & Heflich, Robert H. Genetic Toxicology. 493p. 1991. 93.95 (*0-8493-8815-5*, RA1224) CRC Pr.

— Genetic Toxicology: A Treatise. 500p. 1990. 65.00 (*0-936923-38-5*) Telford Pr.

Li Ang. The Butcher's Wife. Goldblatt, Howard & Yeung, Ellen, trs. LC 89-46060. (Asian Voices Ser.). 142p. 1990. reprint ed. pap. 9.95 (*0-8070-8323-2*) Beacon Pr.

Li, Barbara, jt. auth. see Christensen, Kathy.

Li, C. K., et al. Children's Sexual Encounters with Adults: A Scientific Study. LC 92-43601. 343p. (C). 1993. 39.95 (*0-87975-820-1*) Prometheus Bks.

Li, C. Y., et al. Stress Induced Phenomena in Metallization. (Conference Proceeding Ser.: No. 263). 288p. 1992. 95.00 (*1-56396-082-6*) Am Inst Physics.

Li-Chan, Eunice, jt. auth. see Nakai, Shuryo.

Li, Charles & Talania, Franquintin. Professional Engineers (Civil) License Reviewer (Solved Problems) LC 89-81648. (Illus.). 300p. 1990. pap. 34.00x (*0-929176-07-3*) Burdick & Landreth Co.

Li, Charles N., ed. Mechanisms of Syntactic Change. 640p. 1977. 25.00 (*0-292-75035-8*) U of Tex Pr.

Li, Charles N. & Thompson, Sandra A. Mandarin Chinese: A Functional Reference Grammar. LC 80-6054. 1981. 65.00 (*0-520-04286-7*); pap. 20.00 (*0-520-06610-3*) U CA Pr.

Li, Charles N., jt. ed. see Hyman, Larry M.

Li Chi. Anyang. LC 75-40873. (Illus.). 324p. 1978. 30.00 (*0-295-95490-6*) U of Wash Pr.

Li Chi & Johnson, Dale. Two Studies in Chinese Literature. (Michigan Monographs in Chinese Studies: No. 3). (Illus.). 98p. 1968. pap. 1.50 (*0-89264-003-0*) Ctr Chinese Studies.

Li Ch'iao-P'ing. The Chemical Arts of Old China. LC 75-36234. reprint ed. 24.50 (*0-404-14482-9*) AMS Pr.

Li Chih. Li Chih, Fifteen Twenty-Seven to Sixteen Hundred Two, in Contemporary Chinese Historiography: New Light on His Life & Works. LC 79-57496. 231p. reprint ed. pap. 65.90 (*0-685-23734-6*, 2032775) Bks Demand.

Li Chih-Ch'ang. The Travels of an Alchemist. LC 75-36233. reprint ed. 24.50 (*0-404-14481-0*) AMS Pr.

Li, Ching C. Path Analysis: A Primer. 1975. pap. text ed. 11.95 (*0-910286-40-X*) Boxwood.

Li-Ching-Chao. Li-Ch'ing-Chao: Complete Poems. Rexroth, Kenneth & Ling Chung, eds. LC 79-15596. 1979. pap. 7.95 (*0-8112-0745-5*, NDP492) New Directions.

Li, Cho-ming. Economic Development of Communist China: An Appraisal of the First Five Years of Industrialization. LC 84-6517. xvi, 284p. 1984. reprint ed. text ed. 89.50 (*0-313-24451-0*, LEDE, Greenwood Pr) Greenwood.

Li, Christine, et al. Real Estate Closing Procedures (1992) LC 84-153773. 147p. 1992. 35.00 (*0-685-10481-8*) NJ Inst CLE.

Li, Christine, jt. auth. see Stanwick, Kathy.

Li, Chu-tsing, tr. see Nai, Xia.

Li, Chu-Tsing, et al, eds. Artists & Patrons: Some Social & Economic Aspects of Chinese Painting. LC 89-2688. (Illus.). 262p. 1991. text ed. 35.00 (*0-685-54317-X*); pap. 24.95 (*0-295-97148-7*) U of Wash Pr.

Li Chuan-Shih. Central & Local Finance in China. LC 68-57573. (Columbia University. Studies in the Social Sciences: No. 226). reprint ed. 20.00 (*0-404-51226-7*) AMS Pr.

Li, Chung-Tze. Directory of Chinese-American Librarians. 2nd ed. 45p. 1986. pap. 6.00 (*0-937256-04-8*) Chinese Cult Serv.

Li-Chung Wang. Analytic Functions with Mathematical Philosophy. LC 89-90388. 104p. (Orig.). (C). 1989. pap. text ed. 9.95 (*0-9624242-1-8*) L C Wang Pr.

Li, Chuni. Policy Deployment: Setting the Direction for Change. Hankinson, Mari-Lynn, ed. (AT&T Quality Library). 97p. (Orig.). 1992. pap. 29.95 (*0-932764-31-2*, 500-453) AT&T Customer Info.

Li Cunbao. The Wreath at the Foot of the Mountain. Hanming, Chen & Belcher, James O., trs. (Library of World Literature in Translation: Vol. 6). 133p. 1991. 46.00 (*0-8240-2992-5*) Garland.

***Li, David H.** Chess Detective: Kriegspiel Strategies, Endgames, & Problems. 191p. 1995. pap. 12.95 (*0-9637852-4-9*) Premier MD.

— The Happy Game of Mah-Jong. 136p. 1994. pap. 9.95 (*0-9637852-3-0*) Premier MD.

— Kriegspiel: Chess under Uncertainty. 144p. 1994. pap. 9.95 (*0-9637852-1-4*); Rule book. pap. 9.95 (*0-9637852-2-2*) Premier MD.

— Our Town - 1993: A Daily Record of the Twenty Remaining Days of the Bush Administration & the First 100 Days of the Clinton Administration. 144p. (Orig.). 1993. pap. 5.95 (*0-9637852-0-6*) Premier MD.

Li, David H. & Boockholdt, James L. Accounting Information Systems: Transaction Processing & Controls. 2nd ed. 824p. (C). 1990. text ed. 69.95 (*0-256-03575-X*) Irwin.

Li, Deyi. A PROLOG Database System. LC 83-26896. 207p. 1984. text ed. 119.00 (*0-471-90429-5*) Wiley.

Li, Deyi & Liu, Dongbo. A Fuzzy Prolog Database System. 1990. text ed. 81.50 (*0-471-92762-7*) Wiley.

Li Ding. Acupuncture, Meridian Theory & Acupuncture Points. You Benlin & Wang Zhaorong, trs. (Illus.). 414p. (C). 1992. reprint ed. text ed. 60.00 (*0-8351-2143-7*) China Bks.

Li, Evelyn, tr. see Yuen Liao Fan.

Li, Fei-Kan. The Family. Pa, Chin, ed. 1976. lib. bdg. 59.95 (*0-8490-1800-5*) Gordon Pr.

***Li, Feng.** The Geography of Business Information: Corporate Network & the Spatial & Functional Corporation. LC 94-35184. (Belhaven Studies in the Information Economics). Date not set. text ed. 54.95 (*0-471-94939-6*) Wiley.

Li Gotami Govinda. Tibet in Pictures: A Journey into the Past, 2 vols., Set. LC 79-21352. 1980. 85.00 (*0-913546-57-7*) Dharma Pub.

Li, H. P. Probabilities & Statistics. 300p. 1993. text ed. 95.00 (*981-02-1650-5*) World Scientific Pub.

Li, Haibo, jt. auth. see Forchheimer, Robert.

Li, Hans. Ancient Ones: Sacred Monuments of the Inca, Maya & Cliffdwellers. 1994. 35.00 (*0-9639556-0-8*) City of Light.

Li, He. Sino-Latin American Economic Relations. LC 91-19434. 192p. 1991. text ed. 55.00 (*0-275-93759-3*, C3759, Praeger Pubs) Greenwood.

Li He, tr. see Scollard, Fredrikke S., et al.

Li Heng. Dictionary of Library & Information Sciences. 400p. (CHI & ENG.). 1984. 150.00 (*0-8288-0179-7*, M15588) Fr & Eur.

Li, Hong-Chan. Social Work Education. LC 77-19339. 359p. 1978. lib. bdg. 26.00 (*0-8108-1108-1*) Scarecrow.

— Social Work Education II: A Bibliography, 1977-1987. LC 77-19339. 318p. 1989. 29.50 (*0-8108-2195-8*) Scarecrow.

***Li, Hua & Gupta, Madan.** Fuzzy Logic & Intelligent Systems. LC 95-16748. (International Series in Intelligent Technologies: Vol. 3). 1995. write for info. (*0-7923-9575-1*) Kluwer Ac.

Li, Hua, jt. ed. see Koch, Christof.

Li i, B., et al, eds. Theory & Technology of Quenching: A Handbook. (Illus.). 512p. 1992. 253.00 (*0-387-52040-6*) Spr-Verlag.

Li Itunda Yenge. Analysis of Bulk Flow of Materials under Gravity Caving Process: Pt. 1: Sublevel Caving in Relation to Flow in Bins & Bunkers. Raese, Jon W., ed. LC 81-129. (Colorado School of Mines Quarterly Ser.: Vol. 75, No. 4). (Illus.). 45p. 1981. pap. 8.00 (*0-686-74853-0*) Colo Sch Mines.

Li, Iun J. The Ageless Chinese: A History. 3rd ed. LC 73-159451. 629p. (C). 1978. pap. write for info. (*0-02-370550-7*, Scribners) S&S Trade.

Li, J. C., ed. see International Symposium on Rate Processes in Plastic Deformation Staff.

Li, J. J., et al, eds. Hormonal Carcinogenesis: Proceedings of the First International Symposia, March 19-21, 1991. (Illus.). 392p. 1992. 76.00 (*0-387-97797-X*) Spr-Verlag.

Li, J. K., jt. auth. see Wang, H. P.

Li Janchang, jt. auth. see Qu Geping.

Li, Jenny. Learning Chinese with Fun. (Illus.). (Orig.). 1967. pap. 3.75 (*0-910286-24-8*) Boxwood.

Li Jinxue & Wei Yuanping. Chinese Manipulation & Massage: Chinese Manipulative Therapy (CMT) (International Academic Publishers Ser.). 1990. text ed. 70.00 (*0-08-037488-3*, Pergamon Pr) Elsevier.

Li, John K. Arterial System Dynamics: Hemodynamics of Arteries. (Biomedical Engineering Ser.). 112p. 1986. text ed. 60.00x (*0-8147-5029-X*) NYU Pr.

Li, Jui. The Early Revolutionary Activities of Comrade Mao Tse-tung. Hsiung, James C., ed. LC 74-24422. (China Book Project Ser.). 399p. reprint ed. 113.80 (*0-685-16322-9*, 2027620) Bks Demand.

Li, K., jt. auth. see Liu, T. S.

Li, K. S. & Lo, S. C., eds. Probabilistic Methods in Geotechnical Engineering: Proceedings of the Conference on Probabilistic Methods in Geotechnical Engineering Canberra - Australia - 10-12 February, 1993. (Illus.). 342p. (C). 1993. text ed. 105.00 (*90-5410-303-5*, Pub. by A A Balkema NE) Ashgate Pub Co.

Li, K. T. Economic Transformation of Taiwan. (Illus.). 448p. 1988. text ed. 55.00 (*0-85683-108-5*, Pub. by Shepheard-Walwyn Pubs UK) Paul & Co Pubs.

— The Evolution of Policy Behind Taiwan's Development Success. 300p. 1995. text ed. 46.00 (*981-02-1838-9*) World Scientific Pub.

— The Evolution of Policy Behind Taiwan's Development Success. (C). 1988. text ed. 27.00 (*0-300-04080-6*) Yale U Pr.

***Li, Kam W.** The Availabilty Method of Energy Conversion. (Combustion: an International Ser.). 352p. 1995. 69.50x (*1-56032-349-3*) Taylor & Francis.

Li, Kam W. & Priddy, A. Paul. Power Plant System Design. LC 84-22177. 641p. 1985. Net. text ed. write for info. (*0-471-88847-8*) Wiley.

Li, Kenneth. Semiconductor Lasers. 1993. text ed. 39.95 (*0-07-037705-7*) McGraw.

Li, Kui Wai. Financial Repression & Economic Reform in China. LC 93-50074. 208p. 1994. text ed. 55.00 (*0-275-94801-3*, Praeger Pubs) Greenwood.

Li Kung Shaw. Purposive Biology. LC 81-90747. (Illus.). 359p. (C). 1982. text ed. 20.00 (*0-9607806-0-2*); pap. text ed. 15.00 (*0-9607806-1-0*) Li Kung Shaw.

***Li, Leslie.** Bittersweet. 512p. 1994. pap. 12.95 (*0-8048-3036-3*) C E Tuttle.

Li, Lillian M. China's Silk Trade: Traditional Industry in the Modern World, 1842-1937. (East Asian Monographs: No. 97). 309p. 1981. 30.00 (*0-674-11962-2*) HUP.

Li, Lillian M., jt. ed. see Rawski, Thomas G.

Li, Lincoln. Student Nationalism in China, 1924-1949. LC 93-6639. (Chinese Philosophy & Culture Ser.). 209p. (C). 1994. 59.50 (*0-7914-1749-2*); pap. 19.95 (*0-7914-1750-6*) State U NY Pr.

Li, Ling-Fong, jt. ed. see Cheng, T. P.

Li, Ling-Fong, jt. auth. see Cheng, Ta-Pei.

Li, M. & Vitanyi, Paul M. An Introduction to Kolmogorov Complexity & Its Applications. (Texts & Monographs in Computer Science). (Illus.). 530p. 1993. write for info. (*3-540-94053-7*) Spr-Verlag.

Li, Marjorie & Li, Peter, eds. Understanding Asian Americans: A Curriculum Resource Guide. 185p. (Orig.). 1990. pap. text ed. 29.95 (*1-55570-047-0*) Neal-Schuman.

Li Mei-Ge, tr. see Jackins, Harvey.

Li, Ming-Fu. Modern Semiconductor Quantum Physics. (Solid State Electronics Ser.). 500p. 1995. text ed. 84.00 (*981-02-1599-1*) World Scientific Pub.

Li, N. Recent Developments in Separation Science, 2 vols., Set. LC 72-88417. 1982. 229.00 (*0-8493-5031-X*) CRC Pr.

Li, N., ed. see Fang, Z. Y., et al.

***Li Nian Pei.** Old Tales of China. (Illus.). 206p. 1983. reprint ed. pap. 4.95 (*9971-947-34-X*) Heian Intl.

Li, Norman & Calo, Joseph M., eds. Separation & Purification Technology. LC 92-19323. 320p. 1992. 145.00 (*0-8247-8721-8*) Dekker.

Li, Norman N. Recent Developments in Separation Science, Vol. VI. 208p. 1981. 110.00 (*0-8493-5487-0*, TP156, CRC Reprint) Franklin.

— Recent Developments in Separation Science, Vol. VII. 224p. 1981. 110.00 (*0-8493-5488-9*, CRC Reprint) Franklin.

Li, Norman N. & Calo, Joseph M., eds. Recent Developments in Separation Science, Vol. IX. 352p. 1986. 169.95 (*0-8493-5490-0*, TP156, CRC Reprint) Franklin.

Li, Norman N. & Navratil, James D., eds. Recent Developments in Separation Science, Vol. VIII. 344p. 1986. 204.00 (*0-8493-5489-7*, TP156) CRC Pr.

Li, Norman N. & Strathmann, Heiner, eds. Separation Technology. LC 88-82568. 633p. 1988. 77.00 (*0-8169-0448-0*, P 58) Am Inst Chem Eng.

Li, P. K., ed. A Text of Chinese Military Terms. 390p. (CHI & ENG.). 1972. pap. 12.95 (*0-7859-0792-0*, M-9577) Fr & Eur.

Li, Paul H. Potato Physiology. 1985. text ed. 158.00 (*0-12-447660-0*) Acad Pr.

Li, Paul H., ed. Low Temperature Stress Physiology in Crops. 208p. 1988. 124.00 (*0-8493-6567-8*, SB781, CRC Reprint) Franklin.

Li, Paul M., intro. California Judges' Benchbook: Criminal Posttrial Proceedings 1991, 4 vols., Set. LC 90-82513. 368p. 1991. pap. text ed. 65.00 (*0-88124-382-5*, CR-31791) Cont Ed Bar-CA.

— California Judges' Benchbook: Criminal Pretrial Proceedings 1991, 4 vols., Set. LC 90-82514. 253p. 1991. pap. text ed. 65.00 (*0-88124-380-9*, CR-31791) Cont Ed Bar-CA.

— California Judges' Benchbook: Criminal Trials 1991, Set. LC 90-82512. 266p. 1991. pap. text ed. 65.00 (*0-88124-381-7*, CR-31791) Cont Ed Bar-CA.

— California Judges Benchbook: Nineteen Ninety-One Edition, 4 vols., Set. 1342p. 1991. pap. text ed. 65.00 (*0-88124-379-5*, CR-31791) Cont Ed Bar-CA.

Li, Peter, jt. ed. see Li, Marjorie.

Li, Peter, et al. Culture & Politics in China: An Anatomy of Tiananmen Square. 250p. (C). 1990. 34.95 (*0-88738-353-X*) Transaction Pubs.

Li, Peter S. Race & Ethnic Relations in Canada. 320p. 1990. pap. 15.95 (*0-19-540721-0*) OUP.

Li, Q. B., ed. High Energy Astrophysics: Compact Stars & Active Galaxies. 300p. (C). 1991. text ed. 98.00 (*981-02-0697-6*) World Scientific Pub.

Li, R. Wen-Hsiung. Fluid Mechanics in Water Resources Engineering. (C). 1983. text ed. write for info. (*0-205-07895-8*, H78959) P-H.

Li, S. F. Capillary Electrophoresis: Principles, Practice, & Applications. LC 92-14151. (Journal of Chromatography Library: Vol. 52). 1992. write for info. (*0-444-89433-0*) Elsevier.

— Capillary Electrophoresis: Principles, Practice, & Applications. (Journal of Chromatography Library: Vol. 52). 608p. 1993. pap. 114.25 (*0-444-81590-2*) Elsevier.

Li, S. S., ed. Semiconductor Physical Electronics. (Microdevices: Physics & Fabrication Technologies Ser.). (Illus.). 565p. 1992. 65.00 (*0-306-44157-8*, Plenum Pr) Plenum.

Li, S. X., jt. auth. see L-Z Fang.

Li, Shan L. Strategic Investment Planning & Technology Choice in Manufacturing Systems. rev. ed. LC 93-38434. (Studies on Industrial Productivity). 176p. 1994. 45.00 (*0-8153-1594-5*) Garland.

Li, Shao-ch'Ang. Popular Buddhism in China. lib. bdg. 79.95 (*0-87968-539-5*) Krishna Pr.

Li, Sheng S., jt. auth. see Cristoloveanu, Sorin.

Li, Shing T., et al. Microcomputer Tools for Communications Engineering. LC 83-71834. (Illus.). 279p. reprint ed. pap. 79.60 (*0-318-39749-8*, 2033123) Bks Demand.

***Li, Shiyou & Adair, Kent T.** Camptotheca Acuminata Decaisne, Xi Shu, a Promising Anti-Tumor & Anti-Viral Tree for the Twenty-First Century. (Illus.). 268p. Date not set. 45.00 (*0-938361-11-2*) Austin Univ Forestry.

Li Shufen, ed. Legends of Ten Chinese Traditional Festivals. (Illus.). 54p. (J). (gr. 1-3). 1992. pap. 8.95 (*0-8351-2560-2*) China Bks.

Li, Shujiang & Luckert, Karl W. Mythology & Folklore of the Hui, a Muslim Chinese People. Yu, Fenglan et al, trs. (Illus.). 459p. 1994. 59.50 (*0-7914-1823-5*); pap. 19.95 (*0-7914-1824-3*) State U NY Pr.

***Li, Sifa & Mathias, Jack, eds.** Freshwater Fish Culture in China: Principles & Practice. LC 94-39744. (Developments in Aquaculture & Fisheries Science Ser.: Vol. 28). 1994. write for info. (*0-444-88882-9*) Elsevier.

Li, T. T. & De Mottoni, P. School on Qualitative Aspects & Applications of Nonlinear Evolution Equations. 250p. 1991. text ed. 93.00 (*981-02-0504-X*) World Scientific Pub.

Li, Ta M., et al, eds. Mineral Resource Management by Personal Computer. LC 86-63422. 180p. (Orig.). reprint ed. pap. 51.30 (*0-8357-2566-9*, 2040256) Bks Demand.

— Mineral Resources of the Pacific Rim: Proceedings of the Special Programming by the Minerals Resource Management Committee During the First International SME-AIME Fall Meeting, Honolulu, Hawaii, September 5-9, 1982. LC 82-71990. (Illus.). 237p. reprint ed. pap. 67.60 (*0-7837-1217-0*, 2041748) Bks Demand.

Li Tana & Reid, Anthony, eds. Southern Vietnam under the Nguyen: Documents on the Economic History of Cochinchina (Dang Trong), 1602-1777. 177p. 1993. 36.25 (*981-3016-68-X*, Pub. by Inst SE Asian Studies SI) Ashgate Pub Co.

Li, Tien-Yi. Chinese Fiction: A Bibliography of Books & Articles in Chinese & English. 1968. 21.95 (*0-88710-017-1*) Yale Far Eastern Pubns.

— The History of Chinese Literature: A Selected Bibliography. enl. rev. ed. 1968. 15.95 (*0-88710-030-9*) Yale Far Eastern Pubns.

Li, Tien-Yi, comp. Selected Readings in Chinese Communist Literature. rev. ed. 1954. 9.95 (*0-88710-080-5*); audio write for info. (*0-88710-081-3*) Yale Far Eastern Pubns.

Li, Tien-Yi, ed. Selected Works of George A. Kennedy. 1964. 21.95 (*0-88710-082-1*) Yale Far Eastern Pubns.

Li, Tien-Yi, jt. ed. see Liu, Wu-Chi.

Li, Tingye, ed. Advances in Optical-Fiber Communications, Vol. 1. 1985. text ed. 105.00 (*0-12-447301-6*) Acad Pr.

— Topics in Lightware Transmission Systems. (Optical Fiber Communications Ser.). (Illus.). 308p. 1991. text ed. 80.00 (*0-12-447302-4*) Acad Pr.

Li, Tze-Chung. An Introduction to Online Searching. LC 84-6686. (Contributions in Librarianship & Information Science Ser.: No. 50). (Illus.). xvi, 289p. 1985. text ed. 49.95 (*0-313-24274-7*, LIO/, Greenwood Pr) Greenwood.

— A List of Doctoral Dissertations by Chinese Students in the United States: 1961-1964. LC 67-30284. 1967. pap. 5.95 (*0-686-24155-X*) Chinese Cult Serv.

— Mah Jong: The Rules for Playing the Chinese Game. 2nd ed. 79p. 1991. pap. 12.95 (*0-937256-02-1*) Chinese Cult Serv.

Li, Victor H. De-Recognizing Taiwan: The Legal Problems. LC 77-78287. 1977. pap. 1.50 (*0-87003-031-0*) Carnegie Endow.

Li, Victor H., ed. The Future of Taiwan: A Difference of Opinion, A Dialogue among Trong R. Chai et al. LC 80-50142. 200p. reprint ed. pap. 57.00 (*0-8357-2615-0*, 2040102) Bks Demand.

— Law & Politics in China's Foreign Trade. LC 76-7790. (Asian Law Ser.: No. 4). 488p. 1977. 40.00 (*0-295-95512-0*) U of Wash Pr.

Li, W., jt. ed. see Billington, R.

Li, Wai-yee. Enchantment & Disenchantment: Love & Illusion in Chinese Literature. LC 92-32032. 336p. (C). 1993. text ed. 37.50 (*0-691-05684-6*) Princeton U Pr.

Li Wan Po, A. Statistics for the Life Sciences. 1993. pap. write for info. (*0-632-03354-1*) Blackwell Sci.

Li, Wei, tr. see Lim, Wendy.

Li, Weiping, jt. auth. see Slotine, Jean-Jacques E.

Li, Wen-Hsiung & Graur, Dan. Fundamentals of Molecular Evolution. LC 90-43581. (Illus.). 284p. (C). 1991. pap. text ed. 27.50 (*0-87893-452-9*) Sinauer Assocs.

Li, Wen-Hsiung & Lam, Sau-Hai. Principles of Fluid Mechanics. 1964. write for info. (*0-201-04240-1*) Addison-Wesley.

Li, X. & Yong, J. M., eds. Control Theory of Distributed Parameter Systems & Applications: Proceedings of the IFIP WG 7.2 Working Conference, Shanghai, China, May 6-9, 1990. (Lecture Notes in Control & Information Sciences Ser.: Vol. 159). (Illus.). 227p. 1991. pap. 44.00 (*0-387-53894-1*) Spr-Verlag.

Li, X. -Y., jt. ed. see Yu, N. -T.

Li, X. B., jt. auth. see Basu, A.

***Li, Xia & Crane, Nancy B.** Electronic Style: A Guide to Citing Electronic Information. rev. ed. 100p. 1995. pap. 14.95 (*0-88736-998-7*) Mecklermedia.

Li, Xia, jt. auth. see Crane, Nancy.

Li, Xiao M., tr. The Mending of the Sky & Other Chinese Myths. (Illus.). 54p. (Orig.). (YA). (gr. 5 up). 1989. pap. 9.00 (*0-9617481-3-3*) Oyster River Pr.

Li, Xiao-Rong, jt. auth. see Bar-Shalom, Yaakov.

***Li, Xiaoming.** Disequilibria, Economic Reforms & Economic Policies: A Theoretical & Empirical Investigation for China. 255p. 1995. boxed, pap. 63.95 (*1-85972-081-1*, Pub. by Avebury Pub UK) Ashgate Pub Co.

Li Xiaoqi, jt. auth. see Liu, Irene.

Li Xuemei & Jingyi, Zhao. Acupuncture Patterns & Practice. LC 92-85309. (Illus.). 205p. 1993. text ed. 35.00 (*0-939616-16-5*) Eastland.

Li Xueqin & Chang, K. C. Eastern Zhou & Qin Civilizations. LC 85-5387. 336p. 1986. text ed. 65.00 (*0-300-03286-2*) Yale U Pr.

***Li, Xungjing & Yong, Jiongmin.** Optimal Control Theory for Infinite Dimensional Systems. (Systems & Control Ser.). 1994. 95.00 (*0-8176-3722-2*) Birkhauser.

***Li, Y. F., et al.** Progress in Robotics & Intelligent Systems, Vol. 5. 320p. 1995. write for info. (*1-56750-041-2*) Ablex Pub.

Li Yen-Hui, Audrey, jt. auth. see Aoun, Joseph.

Li Yu. Silent Operas. Hanan, Patrick, ed. & intro. by. (Illus.). xiii, 201p. (Orig.). 1990. pap. 10.95 (*962-7255-07-6*, Pub. by Renditions Papbk HK) SPD-Small Pr Dist.

***Li, Yu-cheng & Chung, Jin S., eds.** The Proceedings of the Special Offshore Symposium China: SOSC 1994 (PACOMS '94) 797p. 1994. 100.00 (*1-880653-15-X*) ISOPE.

Li, Yu-Ning, ed. Shang Yang's Reforms & State Control in China. LC 76-4301. (China Book Project Ser.). 392p. reprint ed. pap. 111.80 (*0-8357-2621-5*, 2040109) Bks Demand.

Li, Yun, jt. ed. see Rogers, Eric.

Li, Yuying, jt. ed. see Coleman, Thomas F.

Li, Z. C. Numerical Methods for Elliptic Problems with Singularities: Boundary Methods & Non-Conforming Combinations. 276p. (C). 1990. text ed. 48.00 (*981-02-0292-X*) World Scientific Pub.

Li, Z. C., et al, eds. Computer Transformation of Digital Images & Patterns. 276p. (C). 1989. text ed. 68.00 (*9971-5-0951-2*) World Scientific Pub.

Li, Z. P., et al. Retrospect & Prospect in Protein Research. 280p. 1991. text ed. 61.00 (*981-02-0518-X*) World Scientific Pub.

Li, Zexiang & Canny, J. F., eds. Nonholonomic Motion Planning. LC 92-27560. (Kluwer International Series in Engineering & Computer Science). 1992. lib. bdg. 125.00 (*0-7923-9275-2*) Kluwer Ac.

Li Zhen. Chinese Goldfish. (Illus.). 200p. 1991. 26.95 (*7-119-00408-5*, 16035) Tetra Pr.

Li Zhenjie & Wang Shixun. Newspaper Chinese ABC: An Introductory Reader. (C & T Asian Language Ser.). 189p. (Orig.). (C). 1988. reprint ed. pap. text ed. 8.95 (*0-88727-059-X*) Cheng & Tsui.

Li, Zhisui. Private Life of Chairman Mao. 1994. 30.00 (*0-679-40035-4*) Random.

Li Zi Ming. Liang Zhen Pu Eight Diagram Palm. 154p. 1993. pap. 17.95 (*1-883175-00-3*) High View Pubns.

Liachowitz, Claire H. Disability As a Social Construct: Legislative Roots. LC 88-17153. 152p. (C). 1988. text ed. 28.95x (*0-8122-8134-9*) U of Pa Pr.

Liacos, Paul J. Handbook of Massachusetts Evidence. 5th ed. 584p. 1981. 75.00 (*0-316-51813-1*) Little.

Liahona Research, Inc. Staff. Alabama Marriages, Early to Eighteen Twenty-Five. Dodd, Jordan, ed. 158p. 1991. lib. bdg. 35.00 (*1-877677-36-1*) Precision Indexing.

— Arkansas Marriages, Early to 1850. Dodd, Jordan, ed. 1990. lib. bdg. 60.00 (*1-877677-25-6*) Precision Indexing.

— Georgia Marriages, Early to 1800. Dodd, Jordan, ed. 1990. lib. bdg. 25.00 (*1-877677-27-2*) Precision Indexing.

— Illinois Marriages, Early to Eighteen Twenty-Five. Dodd, Jordan, ed. 87p. 1991. lib. bdg. 25.00 (*1-877677-31-0*) Precision Indexing.

— Indiana Marriages, Early to Eighteen Twenty-Five. Dodd, Jordan, ed. 345p. 1991. lib. bdg. 80.00 (*1-877677-34-5*) Precision Indexing.

— Kentucky Marriages, Early to 1800. Dodd, Jordan, ed. 1990. lib. bdg. 60.00 (*1-877677-30-2*) Precision Indexing.

— Mississippi Marriages, Early to Eighteen Twenty-Five. Dodd, Jordan, ed. 117p. 1991. lib. bdg. 35.00 (*1-877677-35-3*) Precision Indexing.

— Missouri Marriages, Early to Eighteen Twenty-Five. Dodd, Jordan, ed. 67p. 1991. lib. bdg. 25.00 (*1-877677-37-X*) Precision Indexing.

— North Carolina Marriages, Early to Eighteen Hundred. Dodd, Jordan, ed. 523p. 1991. lib. bdg. 95.00 (*1-877677-28-0*) Precision Indexing.

— Tennessee Marriages, Early to 1800. Dodd, Jordan, ed. 1990. lib. bdg. 25.00 (*1-877677-29-9*) Precision Indexing.

— Texas Marriages, Early to 1850. Dodd, Jordan, ed. 1990. lib. bdg. 60.00 (*1-877677-26-4*) Precision Indexing.

— Virginia Marriages, Early to Eighteen Hundred. Dodd, Jordan, ed. 1148p. 1991. lib. bdg. 145.00 (*1-877677-39-6*) Precision Indexing.

Liakas, Nicolas. New York University Institute on Securities Laws & Regulations. annuals 1977. Annual. ring bd. write for info. (*0-8205-1501-9*) Bender.

Liakopoulos, A., jt. ed. see Simpkins, P. G.

***Lial, et al.** Mathematics with Applications. 6th ed. (C). 1995. student ed, text ed. 12.00 (*0-673-46944-1*) HarpCollege.

— Intermediate Algebra. 5th ed. (C). 1994. student ed, text ed. 12.50 (*0-673-99063-X*) HarpCollege.

— Intermediate Algebra with Early Functions & Graphing. 5th ed. (C). 1994. student ed, text ed. 12.50 (*0-673-99538-0*) HarpCollege.

— Introductory Algebra. 5th ed. (C). 1994. student ed, text ed. 12.50 (*0-673-99062-1*) HarpCollege.

***Lial, Margaret L., et al.** Beginning Algebra. 7th ed. LC 95-9797. (C). 1995. write for info. (*0-673-99139-3*) HarpCollege.

— Beginning & Intermediate Algebra. LC 95-9796. (C). 1995. write for info. (*0-673-99857-6*) HarpCollege.

Lial, Margaret L. & Miller, Charles D. Algebra for College Students. (C). 1988. text ed. 37.00 (*0-673-18866-3*) HarpCollege.

— Beginning Algebra. 5th ed. (C). 1987. text ed. 32.25 (*0-673-18808-6*) HarpCollege.

— Calculus with Applications. 4th ed. (C). 1988. text ed. 43.75 (*0-673-38251-6*) HarpCollege.

— Calculus with Applications: Brief Version. 4th ed. (C). 1989. text ed. 42.75 (*0-673-38465-9*) HarpCollege.

— College Algebra. 5th ed. (C). 1988. text ed. 39.00 (*0-673-38245-1*) HarpCollege.

— Finite Mathematics. 4th ed. (C). 1989. text ed. 44.00 (*0-673-38253-2*) HarpCollege.

— Finite Mathematics & Calculus with Applications. 3rd ed. (C). 1989. text ed. 46.75 (*0-673-38255-9*) HarpCollege.

— Intermediate Algebra. 5th ed. (C). 1987. text ed. 32.25 (*0-673-18809-4*) HarpCollege.

— Precalculus. (C). 1988. text ed. 63.00 (*0-673-15872-1*) HarpCollege.

Lial, Margaret L., jt. auth. see Hornsby, E. John.

Lial, Margaret L., jt. auth. see Hornsby, E. John, Jr.

Lial, Margaret L., jt. auth. see Miller, Charles D.

Lial, Margaret L., et al. Algebra & Trigonometry. 6th ed. LC 93-26181. 654p. (C). 1994. 61.50 (*0-673-46739-2*) HarpCollege.

— Algebra for College Students. 3rd ed. LC 95-8117. (Illus.). (C). 1995. text ed. write for info. (*0-673-99061-3*) HarpCollege.

— Calculus with Applications. 5th abr. ed. LC 92-27441. (C). 1992. 47.00 (*0-673-46725-2*) HarpCollege.

— Calculus with Applications. 5th ed. LC 92-27440. (C). 1992. 48.00 (*0-673-46726-0*) HarpCollege.

— College Algebra. 6th ed. LC 92-13866. (Illus.). (C). 1992. text ed. 42.50 (*0-673-46648-5*) HarpCollege.

— Essentials of Geometry for College Students. (C). 1989. text ed. 60.50 (*0-673-38419-5*) HarpCollege.

— Finite Mathematics. 5th ed. LC 92-28348. (C). 1992. 49.25 (*0-673-46727-9*) HarpCollege.

— Finite Mathematics & Calculus: with Applications. 4th ed. (C). 1993. student ed 24.00 (*0-673-46764-3*) HarpCollege.

— Finite Mathematics & Calculus with Applications. 4th ed. LC 92-27439. (C). 1993. 52.00 (*0-673-46757-0*) HarpCollege.

— Intermediate Algebra. 7th ed. LC 95-10263. 1995. write for info. (*0-673-99059-1*) HarpCollege.

— Intermediate Algebra with Early Graphs & Functions. 2nd ed. LC 95-10057. (C). 1995. 11.00 (*0-673-99557-7*) HarpCollege.

— Mathematics with Applications: In the Management, Natural & Social Sciences. 6th ed. LC 94-13576. (Illus.). (C). 1995. text ed. 50.00 (*0-673-46943-3*) HarpCollege.

— Trigonometry. 5th ed. LC 92-13849. (Illus.). (C). 1992. text ed. 40.50 (*0-673-46647-7*) HarpCollege.

— Trigonometry. 5th ed. LC 92-22236. (C). 1992. 7.20 (*0-673-46753-8*) HarpCollege.

Liall, Margaret L. & Miller, Charles D. Math with Applications. 5th ed. (C). 1991. text ed. 51.00 (*0-673-46277-3*); 22.00 (*0-673-46278-1*) HarpCollege.

Liall, Margaret L., et al. Algebra for College Students. (C). 1991. text ed. 59.00 (*0-673-46469-5*) HarpCollege.

— Algebra for College Students. (C). 1991. 21.50 (*0-673-46471-7*); 18.50 (*0-673-46470-9*) HarpCollege.

— Beginning Algebra. (C). 1991. 21.00 (*0-673-46461-X*); 18.50 (*0-673-46460-1*) HarpCollege.

— Beginning Algebra. 6th ed. (C). 1991. text ed. 57.50 (*0-673-46459-8*) HarpCollege.

— Brief Calculus with Applications: Student Solution Manual. 5th ed. (C). 1993. text ed. 23.00 (*0-673-46755-4*) HarpCollege.

— College Algebra. 6th ed. (C). 1992. student ed 14.00 (*0-673-46816-X*); teacher ed 15.00 (*0-673-46817-8*) HarpCollege.

— Finite Mathematics. 5th ed. (C). 1993. student ed 24.00 (*0-673-46756-2*) HarpCollege.

— Intermediate Algebra. 6th ed. (C). 1991. text ed. 57.50 (*0-673-46464-4*); 21.00 (*0-673-46466-0*); 18.50 (*0-673-46465-2*) HarpCollege.

— Trigonometry. 5th ed. (C). 1992. teacher ed 14.00 (*0-673-46815-1*) HarpCollege.

Lian, Ann & Lian, Leslie. The Fourteen Carat Caper. LC 88-51031. (Illus.). 44p. (J). 1988. 5.95 (*1-55523-171-3*) Winston-Derek.

Lian, Anne, ed. Finance, 1993: A Harvard Business School Career Guide. 1993. pap. text ed. 20.00 (*0-07-103393-9*) McGraw.

Lian, J. B., jt. ed. see Glimcher, M. J.

Lian, Jane B., jt. ed. see Stein, Gary S.

Lian, Kwen F., jt. auth. see Hill, Michael.

Lian, Leslie, jt. auth. see Lian, Ann.

Lian, Ming-Gon J., jt. auth. see Holmes, Melanie R.

Lian, Tanja, ed. see Beares, Paul R.

Lian, Tongshu. Theory of Conjugation for Reflecting Prisms. (International Academic Publishers Ser.). (Illus.). 500p. 1991. 115.00 (*0-08-037935-4*, Pub. by IAP UK) Elsevier.

Liang, jt. auth. see Chandler, Alfred D., Jr.

***Liang, Amy.** The Living Art of Bonsai: Principles & Techniques of Cultivation & Propagation. (Illus.). 288p. 1995. pap. 19.95 (*0-8069-8781-2*) Sterling.

Liang, Anne. Finance, 1993. (C). 1993. pap. 20.00 (*0-87584-405-7*) Harvard Busn.

Liang Chau. How to Develop the Restaurant Business: Promotion of the Chinese Restaurant Take-out Order Business. LC 93-77774. (Illus.). 100p. (Orig.). (CHI.). 1993. pap. write for info. (*0-9636456-0-9*) Gold Town Sales.

Liang Chi-Chao. History of Chinese Political Thought. LC 70-100526. reprint ed. 17.50 (*0-404-03985-5*) AMS Pr.

Liang, Ch'I-Ch'Ao. Types of Modern & Ancient Chinese Love-Songs. (Asian Folklore & Social Life Monographs: No. 8). (CHI.). 1970. 14.00 (*0-89986-011-7*) Oriental Bk Store.

Liang, Chi-Shad. Burma's Foreign Relations: Neutralism in Theory & Practice. LC 90-31953. 288p. 1990. text ed. 55.00 (*0-275-93455-1*, C3455, Praeger Pubs) Greenwood.

Liang-Chi Tao. Guides to Clinical Aspiration Biopsy: Lung, Pleura, & Mediastinum. LC 87-29883. (Illus.). 512p. 1988. 95.00 (*0-89640-136-7*) Igaku-Shoin.

Liang, Diana F., comp. Mathematical Journals: An Annotated Guide. LC 92-18459. 246p. 1992. 29.50 (*0-8108-2585-6*) Scarecrow.

Liang, Edison P. & Petrosian, Vahe, eds. Gamma-Ray Bursts. LC 86-70761. (AIP Conference Proceedings Ser.: 141). 224p. 1986. lib. bdg. 60.00 (*0-88318-340-4*) Am Inst Physics.

Liang, Ernest P. China: Railways & Agricultural Development, 1875 to 1935. LC 82-4749. (Research Papers Ser.: No. 203). 186p. (C). 1982. pap. 10.00 (*0-89065-109-4*) U Chicago Comm Geo.

Liang Heng & Shapiro, Judith. After the Nightmare. 1986. 16.95 (*0-394-55153-2*) Knopf.

Liang, Hsi-Huey. The Rise of Modern Police & the European State System from Metternich to the Second World War. 448p. (C). 1992. 59.95 (*0-521-43022-4*) Cambridge U Pr.

Liang Huew Wang & Gar-On Yeh, eds. Keep a City Moving. 300p. 1993. pap. 15.00 (*92-833-2102-2*, APO1022, Pub. by Asian Prod Organ) UNIPUB.

Liang, James. Pronunciation Exercises for Beginning Chinese. 1978. 1.75 (*0-88710-059-7*); write for info. (*0-88710-060-0*) Yale Far Eastern Pubns.

Liang, K. S., et al, eds. Interface Dynamics & Growth. (Symposium Proceedings Ser.: Vol. 237). 1992. text ed. 60.00 (*1-55899-131-X*) Materials Res.

Liang, Matthew H., et al. Rheumatology: Problems in Primary Care. (Problems in Primary Care Ser.). 256p. 1990. pap. 39.95 (*0-87489-421-2*) Med Economics.

Liang, Robert Y., ed. see American Society of Civil Engineers Geotechnical Engineering Division Staff.

Liang, S. Y. & Wu, C. L., eds. Sensors & Signal Processing for Manufacturing. (PED Ser.: Vol. 55). 240p. 1992. 57.50 (*0-7918-0798-3*, G00692) ASME.

***Liang, Sheng.** Neo-Mohism. 200p. (Orig.). (CHI.). 1995. pap. 20.00 (*0-9642790-2-9*) Sayinga.

Liang, Shou-Yu, jt. auth. see Yang, Jwing-Ming.

Liang, Shu-Jan, jt. auth. see Losman, Donald L.

Liang, T. T. T'ai Chi Ch'uan for Health & Self-Defense: Philosophy & Practice. 1977. pap. 9.00 (*0-394-72461-5*, Vin) Random.

***Liang, Ting-Peng & Lee, Jae K.** Applied Knowledge Acquisition. Date not set. 44.95 (*1-55860-202-X*); disk 25.00 (*1-55860-204-6*) Morgan Kaufmann.

Liang, Yu-kao & Tao, L. K. Village & Town Life in China. LC 73-887. (China Studies: from Confucius to Mao Ser.). xi, 155p. 1978. reprint ed. 18.00 (*0-88355-080-6*) Hyperion Conn.

Liang, Z., et al, eds. Flow Modeling & Turbulence Measurements. 800p. 1992. 124.00 (*1-56032-209-8*) Hemisp Pub.

Liang, Zhuge & Ji, Liu. Mastering the Art of War. Cleary, Thomas, ed. & tr. by. LC 89-10264. (Dragon Editions Ser.). 152p. (Orig.). 1989. pap. 11.00 (*0-87773-513-1*, Sham Dragon Edits) Shambhala Pubns.

***Liang, Zhuge, et al.** Mastering the Art of War. Cleary, Thomas, tr. 208p. (Orig.). 1995. pap. text ed. 6.00 (*1-57062-081-4*); pap. text ed. 48.00 (*1-57062-082-2*) Shambhala Pubns.

Liao, David. The Unresponsive: Resistant or Neglected? Homogeneous Unit Principal Illustrated by the Hakka Chinese in Taiwan. LC 73-175494. 160p. 1979. reprint ed. pap. 6.95 (*0-87808-735-4*) William Carey Lib.

Liao, I-Chiu, jt. ed. see Lee, Cheng-Sheng.

Liao, S. T., et al. Dynamical Systems. (Nankai Series in Pure, Applied Mathematics & Theoretical Physics). 332p. 1993. text ed. 95.00 (*981-02-1350-6*) World Scientific Pub.

Liao, Samuel Y. Engineering Applications of Electromagnetic Theory. 455p. (C). 1988. text ed. 70.25 (*0-314-60175-9*) West Pub.

— Microwave Devices & Circuits. 3rd ed. 592p. 1990. text ed. 79.00 (*0-13-583204-7*) P-H.

Liao, Shu S., jt. auth. see Fremgen, James M.

***Liao, Sung J., et al.** Principles & Practices of Contemporary Acupuncture. LC 94-21951. 1994. 65.00 (*0-8247-9291-2*) Dekker.

Liao, Thomas T. & Miller, David C., eds. Systems Approach to Instructional Design. LC 77-86497. (Technology of Learning Systems Ser.: Vol. 1). (Illus.). 1978. pap. 10.00 (*0-89503-004-7*) Baywood Pub.

Liao, Tim F. Interpreting Probability Models: Logit, Probit, & Other Generalized Models. (Quantitative Applications in the Social Sciences Ser.: Vol. 101). 96p. 1994. pap. 9.95 (*0-8039-4999-5*) Sage.

Liao, Waysun. The Essence of T'ai Chi. LC 94-6790. (Pocket Consultant Ser.). 200p. (Orig.). 1995. pap. text ed. 6.00 (*1-57062-039-3*) Shambhala Pubns.

— The Essence of T'ai Chi. (Orig.). 1995. pap. text ed. 48.00 (*1-57062-040-7*) Shambhala Pubns.

— T'ai Chi Classics. LC 89-43316. (Illus.). 296p. (Orig.). 1990. pap. 15.00 (*0-87773-531-X*) Shambhala Pubns.

An Asterisk (*) at the beginning of an entry indicates that the title is appearing in BIP for the first time.

Liao Wen-Kuei. The Individual & the Community. LC 73-14035. (International Library of Psychology, Philosophy & Scientific Method Ser.). 314p. (C). 1974. reprint ed. text ed. 65.00 (*0-8371-7142-3*, LIIN, Greenwood Pr) Greenwood.

Liao, Woody M. & Boockholdt, James L. Cost Accounting for Managerial Planning, Decision Making & Control. 4th ed. LC 91-73135. 744p. 1992. 53.95 (*0-87393-136-X*); student ed 17.95 (*0-87393-137-8*) Dame Pubns.

Liao, Y., jt. auth. see Culshaw, B.

Liapin, Lev, tr. see Frank-Kamenetskii, Maxim D.

Liapounoff, M. A. Probleme General de la Stabilite du Mouvement. (Annals of Mathematics Studies). 1947. 23.00 (*0-527-02733-2*) Periodicals Srv.

Liapunov, Vadim, ed. see Bakhtin, M. M.

Liapunov, Vadim, tr. see Bakhtin, M. M.

Liapunov, Vadim, ed. see Bakhtin, M. M.

Liaqat, M. Muntaz, jt. ed. see Masud, Muhammad K.

Liard, P., et al. Schwindel. (Illus.). x, 102p. 1994. pap. 30.50 (*3-8055-5814-7*) S Karger.

— Le Vertige. (Illus.). xii, 96p. 1993. pap. 30.50 (*3-8055-5822-8*) S Karger.

Liardet, Frances, tr. see Al-Kharrat, Edwar.

Liardet, Frances, tr. see Ibrahim, Gamil A.

Liardet, Tim. Clay Hill. (Poetry Wales Poets Ser.: No. 12). 46p. (Orig.). 1988. pap. 8.95 (*0-907476-88-0*, Pub. by Poetry Wales Pr UK) Dufour.

— Fellini Beach. 1995. 14.95 (*0-614-07440-1*, Pub. by Seren Bks UK) Dufour.

Liardon, Roberts. Breaking Controlling Powers. rev. ed. 110p. 1991. pap. 4.95 (*1-879993-09-0*) Embassy Pub.

— A Call to Action: Killing Giants & Subduing Kingdoms. rev. ed. 108p. 1985. pap. 5.99 (*1-879993-12-0*) Embassy Pub.

— The Cry of the Spirit. rev. ed. 168p. 1989. pap. 6.95 (*1-879993-10-4*) Embassy Pub.

— Final Approach. 192p. 1993. pap. 7.99 (*0-88419-338-1*, Creation Hse) Strang Comms Co.

— Forget Not All His Benefits. 64p. (Orig.). Date not set. pap. text ed. 3.99 (*1-879993-14-7*) Embassy Pub.

— Haunted Houses, Ghosts & Demons: What You Can Do about It. 128p. (Orig.). 1993. pap. text ed. 6.99 (*1-879993-15-5*) Embassy Pub.

— I Saw Heaven. rev. ed. 64p. 1990. reprint ed. pap. 3.95 (*1-879993-11-2*) Embassy Pub.

— The Invading Force. 63p. 1987. pap. 3.95 (*0-88144-088-4*) Christian Pub.

— The Invading Force. rev. ed. 64p. 1988. pap. 3.99 (*1-879993-03-1*) Embassy Pub.

— Kathryn Kuhlman: A Spiritual Biography of God's Miracle Working Power. rev. ed. 158p. (Orig.). 1990. pap. 7.99 (*1-879993-08-2*) Embassy Pub.

— Learning to Say No. rev. ed. 64p. (Orig.). 1988. pap. 3.99 (*1-879993-05-8*) Embassy Pub.

— The Price of Spiritual Power. 47p. 1987. pap. 2.95 (*0-88144-090-6*) Christian Pub.

— The Price of Spiritual Power. rev. ed. 48p. 1987. pap. 2.99 (*1-879993-04-X*) Embassy Pub.

— The Quest for Spiritual Hunger. 43p. 1987. pap. 2.95 (*0-88144-089-2*) Christian Pub.

— The Quest for Spiritual Hunger. rev. ed. 48p. 1987. pap. 2.95 (*1-879993-13-9*) Embassy Pub.

— Religious Politics: Men Pleasers or God Pleasers. rev. ed. 34p. 1988. pap. 0.98 (*1-879993-02-3*) Embassy Pub.

— Run to the Battle. rev. ed. 137p. (Orig.). 1989. pap. 5.99 (*1-879993-06-6*) Embassy Pub.

— School of the Spirit. 1994. pap. 8.99 (*0-88419-360-8*, Creation Hse) Strang Comms Co.

— Spiritual Timing. rev. ed. 64p. (Orig.). 1990. pap. 3.99 (*1-879993-07-4*) Embassy Pub.

Lias, Godfrey, tr. see Benes, Edvard.

Lias, Kai-Lung. From Yenan to Peking. 1976. lib. bdg. 59.95 (*0-8490-1869-2*) Gordon Pr.

Lias, Sharon G., jt. ed. see Aulsoos, Pierre.

Liatov, Y. S. Colloid Chemistry of Polymers. (Polymer Science Library: No. 7). 460p. 1988. 151.50 (*0-444-43006-7*) Elsevier.

***Liaut, Jean-Noel.** Cover Girls & Supermodels: 1945-1965. Buss, Robin, tr. (Illus.). 322p. 1995. 35.00 (*0-7145-2998-2*) M Boyars Pubs.

Liautaud, Marian V. Swatting the Mosquitoes of Marriage. 240p. 1994. pap. 9.99 (*0-310-40511-4*) Zondervan.

Liaw, ed. Infrared Systems & Components, No. II. 1988. 45.00 (*0-89252-925-3*, 890) SPIE.

Liaw, P. K. & Gungor, M. N., eds. Fundamental Relationships Between Microstructure & Mechanical Properties of Metal Matrix Composites. (Illus.). 900p. 1989. 149.00 (*0-87339-092-X*) Minerals Metals.

Liaw, P. K. & Nicholas, T., eds. Effects of Load & Thermal Histories on Mechanical Behavior of Materials. LC 87-42887. (Illus.). 299p. 1987. 10.00 (*0-87339-028-8*) Minerals Metals.

Liaw, P. K., ed. see Metallurgical Society of AIME Staff.

Liaw, P. K., et al, eds. Microstructures & Mechanical Properties of Agińg Materials. (Illus.). 900p. 1993. 280.00 (*0-87339-207-8*, 466) Minerals Metals.

— Nondestructive Evaluation & Material Properties II. 253p. 1994. 98.00 (*0-87339-230-2*) Minerals Metals.

— Nondestructive Evaluation & Material Properties of Advanced Materials. (Illus.). 130p. 1992. 44.00 (*0-87339-143-8*, 424) Minerals Metals.

— Proceedings of the Morris E. Fine Symposium. (Illus.). 512p. 1990. 74.00 (*0-87339-164-0*, 383) Minerals Metals.

Liaw, Peter K., ed. see Minerals, Metals & Materials Society Staff.

Liaw, Y. F., ed. Chronic Hepatitis. 292p. 1987. 106.25 (*0-444-80822-1*) Elsevier.

Lib. Sanchez Staff. Diccionario Espanol-Ingles, Ingles-Espanol. 1704p. 1991. 55.00 (*0-7859-6246-8*, 8476300980) Fr & Eur.

Libaire, George, tr. see Caulaincourt, Armand A.

Libaire, George, ed. see Caulaincourt, Armand A.

Liban, Felicia. Cloisonne Enameling & Jewelry Making. 1989. pap. 8.95 (*0-486-25971-1*) Dover.

Libana, Susanaha, jt. auth. see Lee, Susan.

Libanio, J. B. Spiritual Discernment & Politics: Guidelines for Religious Communities. Morrow, Theodore, tr. LC 82-2257. Orig. Title: Discernment E politica. 143p. (Orig.). reprint ed. pap. 40.80 (*0-8357-7034-6*, 2033540) Bks Demand.

Libanius. Concordantiae in Libanium, Pars Tertia: Declamationes Et Progymnasmata. Date not set. write for info. (*0-318-70964-3*, Pub. by Georg Olms GW) Lubrecht & Cramer.

— Opera, 12 vols. in 13. cxi, 6513p. 1985. reprint ed. write for info. (*0-318-70965-1*, Pub. by Georg Olms GW) Lubrecht & Cramer.

— Selected Orations, 2 vols., I. Warmington, E. H., ed. (Loeb Classical Library: No. 451, 452). 590p. (ENG & GRE.). 1969. text ed. 18.95 (*0-674-99496-5*) HUP.

— Selected Orations, 2 vols., II. Warmington, E. H., ed. (Loeb Classical Library: No. 451, 452). 556p. (ENG & GRE.). 1969. 18.95 (*0-674-99497-3*) HUP.

Libaridian, Gerard J., ed. Armenia at the Crossroads: Democracy & Nationhood in the Post-Soviet Era. LC 91-70342. 172p. 1991. 29.95 (*0-9628715-1-6*); pap. 14.95 (*0-9628715-0-8*) Blue Crane Bks.

Libau, A. L. Scalpel: A Novel. 1991. pap. 10.95 (*0-533-09276-0*) Vantage.

Libb, Melva, ed. see Biros, Florence K.

Libb, Melva, ed. see Clinkscale, Lonnie.

Libb, Melva, ed. see Conningham, Jewell.

Libb, Melva, jt. auth. see Gregorino, Linda.

Libb, Melva, ed. see Ragland, Thomas E.

Libben, G., jt. auth. see Paradis, Michel.

Libberman, Cy. Mystique of the Tall Ships. 1989. 14.98 (*0-88365-747-3*) Galahad Bks.

Libberton, G. P., ed. Tenth Advances in Reliability Technology Symposium: Proceedings held at the University of Bradford, UK, 6-8 April 1988. 386p. 1988. 79.25 (*1-85166-202-2*) Elsevier.

Libbey, Elizabeth. All That Heat in a Cold Sky. (Poetry Ser.). (Orig.). 1992. lib. bdg. 16.95 (*0-88748-144-2*); pap. 9.95 (*0-88748-145-0*) Carnegie-Mellon.

— Songs of a Returning Soul. LC 81-71587. 1981. pap. 9.95 (*0-915604-67-1*) Carnegie-Mellon.

Libbey, James K. Alexander Gumberg & Soviet-American Relations, 1917-1933. LC 77-73704. 241p. reprint ed. pap. 68.70 (*0-7837-5777-8*, 2045443) Bks Demand.

— American-Russian Economic Relations, 1770s-1990s: A Survey of Issues & References, No. 4. (Guides to Historical Issues Ser.). 220p. 1989. 21.95 (*0-941690-35-0*); pap. text ed. 12.95 (*0-941690-36-9*) Regina Bks.

Libbey, Robert. Handbook of Modern Communication Technology. 1994. text ed. 69.95 (*0-442-30861-2*) Van Nos Reinhold.

Libbey, Robert L., ed. Handbook of Circuit Mathematics for Technical Engineers. 400p. 1991. 47.95 (*0-8493-7400-6*) CRC Pr.

Libbey, Ted. The NPR Guide to Building a Classical CD Collection. LC 92-50292. 1993. pap. 15.95 (*1-56305-051-X*, 3051) Workman Pub.

Libbey, Theodore, jt. auth. see Scavelli, Ramon.

Libbie, Frederick J. Tinker Family: Ancestors & Descendants of Joseph Wescot Tinker, Ellsworth, Maine, 1791-1868, a Descendant of John Tinker of Boston. 36p. 1994. reprint ed. pap. 7.50 (*0-8328-4065-3*) Higginson Bk Co.

Libbish, B. Advances in the Teaching of Modern Languages: 1964 Edition. LC 63-21902. 1964. 84.00 (*0-08-010445-2*, Pub. by Pergamon Repr UK) Franklin.

Libbrecht, Katrien. Hysterical Psychosis: A Historical Survey. LC 94-8720. 290p. (C). 1994. 39.95 (*1-56000-181-X*) Transaction Pubs.

Libby, Anthony. Mythologies of Nothing: Mystical Death in American Poetry, 1940-1970. LC 83-3460. 240p. 1984. 24.95 (*0-252-01049-3*) U of Ill Pr.

— The Secret Turning of the Earth. LC 94-33242. (Wick Poetry Chapbook Ser.: No. 5). 32p. (Orig.). 1995. pap. 3.00 (*0-87338-520-9*) Kent St U Pr.

Libby, Barbara. Old Cat. 1993. 4.99 (*0-517-09324-3*) Random Hse Value.

Libby, Bill, jt. auth. see O'Neil, Kitty.

Libby, Bob. The Forgiveness Book. LC 91-38206. 149p. (Orig.). 1992. pap. 9.95 (*1-56101-048-0*) Cowley Pubns.

— Grace Happens: Stories of Everyday Encounters with Grace. LC 93-49859. 163p. 1994. pap. 10.95 (*1-56101-091-X*) Cowley Pubns.

Libby, C. T. Libby Family in America, 1602-1881. (Illus.). 628p. 1990. reprint ed. lib. bdg. 101.50 (*0-8328-1494-6*); reprint ed. pap. 93.50 (*0-8328-1495-4*) Higginson Bk Co.

Libby, Elizabeth. The Crowd Inside. LC 79-59801. (Poetry Ser.). 1978. 16.95 (*0-915604-52-3*); pap. 9.95 (*0-915604-53-1*) Carnegie-Mellon.

Libby, Gary R. Salon & Picturesque Photography in Cuba, 1860-1920. Miller, Sandra L., ed. (Illus.). 50p. (C). 1988. pap. 20.00 (*0-933053-02-9*) Museum Art Sciences.

Libby, Gary R., ed. see Poyner, Robin.

Libby, Gary R., ed. see Rand, Harry.

Libby, Hugo L. Introduction to Electromagnetic Nondestructive Test Methods. 382p. 1979. reprint ed. 43.50 (*0-88275-964-7*) Krieger.

Libby, James A. Meat Hygiene. 4th ed. LC 73-14959. 670p. reprint ed. pap. 180.00 (*0-685-15874-8*, 2056189) Bks Demand.

Libby, Jean, ed. see Henry, Thomas W.

Libby, L. M. Carbon Dioxide & Climate: Dedicated to Williard F. Libby & Hans E. Suss. (Illus.). 270p. 1980. pap. 48.00 (*0-08-026240-6*, Pergamon Pr) Elsevier.

Libby, Larry. Someday Heaven. 48p. (J). 13.99 (*0-945564-77-5*, Gold & Honey) Questar Pubs.

— Somewhere Angels. 48p. (J). (gr. k-5). 1994. 13.99 (*0-88070-651-1*, Gold & Honey) Questar Pubs.

Libby, Larry, ed. see Anderson, Neil & Moore, Hyatt.

Libby, Larry, ed. see Dean, Chuck.

Libby, Larry, ed. see Eareckson-Tada, Joni.

Libby, Larry, ed. see Reeve, Pamela.

Libby, Larry, ed. see Stoddard, William S.

Libby, Larry, ed. see Tada, Joni E.

Libby, Larry, ed. see Weber, Stu.

Libby, Larry R., ed. see Baker, Don.

Libby, Larry R., ed. see Kimmel, Tim.

Libby, Larry R., ed. see Needham, David C.

Libby, Leona M. Past Climates: Tree Thermometers, Commodities, & People. (Illus.). 157p. 1983. text ed. 25.00 (*0-292-73019-5*) U of Tex Pr.

Libby, M. S. The Attitude of Voltaire to Magic & the Sciences. 1971. 59.95 (*0-87968-676-6*) Gordon Pr.

Libby, Margaret S. Attitude of Voltaire to Magic & the Sciences. LC 35-10134. (Columbia University. Studies in the Social Sciences: No. 408). reprint ed. 10.00 (*0-404-51408-1*) AMS Pr.

Libby, O. G., ed. Arikara Narrative of the Campaign Against the Hostile Dakotas: June 1876. (Illus.). 1920. 20.00 (*0-914074-00-8*, J M C & Co) Amereon Ltd.

Libby, P. A. & Williams, F., eds. Turbulent Reacting Flows. (Topics in Applied Physics Ser.: Vol. 44). (Illus.). 260p. 1980. 77.00 (*0-387-10192-6*) Spr-Verlag.

Libby, Paul A. & Williams, Forman A., eds. Turbulent Reacting Flows. (Combustion Treatise Ser.). (Illus.). 647p. 1994. text ed. 150.00 (*0-12-447945-6*) Acad Pr.

Libby, Peter, ed. see Peabody, Kathleen L. & Mooney, Margaret L.

Libby, Ronald T. Hawke's Law: The Politics of Mining & Aboriginal Land Rights in Australia. 208p. 1992. reprint ed. pap. text ed. 16.95 (*0-271-00835-0*) Pa St U Pr.

— The Politics of Economic Power in Southern Africa. (Illus.). 384p. 1987. text ed. 57.50 (*0-691-07723-1*); pap. text ed. 15.95 (*0-691-02256-9*) Princeton U Pr.

— Protecting Markets: U. S. Policy & the World Grain Trade. LC 91-55536. (Illus.). 176p. 1992. 28.95 (*0-8014-2617-0*) Cornell U Pr.

— Toward an Africanized U. S. Policy for Southern Africa: A Strategy for Increasing Political Leverage. LC 79-93355. (Policy Papers in International Affairs Ser.: No. 11). 120p. 1980. pap. 7.50 (*0-87725-511-3*) U of Cal IAS.

Libby, Susan, ed. see Levitine, George.

Libby, V. Data Structures & Target Classification, Vol. 1470. 1991. 62.00 (*0-8194-0579-5*) SPIE.

Libby, W. J., jt. ed. see Ahuja, M. R.

Libby, Willard F. Radiocarbon Dating. 2nd ed. LC 55-10246. 187p. reprint ed. pap. 53.30 (*0-317-08415-1*, 2005396) Bks Demand.

Libby, Yvonne, jt. auth. see Herr, Judy.

Libecap, Gary, ed. Advances in the Study of Entrepreneurship, Innovation, & Economic Growth, Vol. 4. 1991. 73.25 (*1-55938-139-6*) Jai Pr.

— Advances in the Study of Entrepreneurship, Innovation, & Economic Growth, Supplement 1: Corporate Reorganization Through Mergers, Acquisitions, & Leverage Buyouts; Proceeding of the Third Annual Business - Academic Dialogue Held December 5-6, 1986. 217p. 1989. 73.25 (*0-89232-776-6*) Jai Pr.

— Advances in the Study of Entrepreneurship, Innovation, & Economic Growth, Vol. 3: American International Competitiveness. 231p. 1989. 73.25 (*0-89232-944-0*) Jai Pr.

— Entrepreneurship & Innovation: The Impact of Venture Capital on the Development of New Enterprise. (Advances in the Study of Entrepreneurship, Innovation & Economic Growth Ser.: Vol. 1). 1987. 73.25 (*0-89232-703-0*) Jai Pr.

— Innovation in New Markets: The Impact of Deregulation on Airlines, Financial Markets, & Telecommunications. (Advances in the Study of Entrepreneurship, Innovation & Economic Growth Ser.: Vol. 2). 1988. 73.25 (*0-89232-771-5*) Jai Pr.

Libecap, Gary D. Contracting for Property Rights. (Political Economy of Institutions & Decisions Ser.). (Illus.). 100p. (C). 1990. 54.95 (*0-521-36620-8*) Cambridge U Pr.

— Contracting for Property Rights. (Political Economy of Institutions & Decisions Ser.). (Illus.). 100p. (C). 1994. pap. 15.95 (*0-521-44904-9*) Cambridge U Pr.

— The Evolution of Private Mineral Rights: Nevada's Comstock Lode. LC 77-14777. (Dissertations in American Economic History Ser.). 1978. 33.95 (*0-405-11047-2*) Ayer.

Libecap, Gary D., jt. ed. see Goldin, Claudia.

Libecap, Gary D., jt. auth. see Johnson, Ronald N.

Liben, Lynn, ed. Piaget & the Foundations of Knowledge. 272p. 1984. text ed. 59.95 (*0-89859-248-8*) L Erlbaum Assocs.

Liben, Lynn S. Development & Learning: Conflict or Congruence? (Jean Piaget Symposium Ser.). 256p. 1987. 49.95 (*0-8058-0009-3*) L Erlbaum Assocs.

Liben, Lynn S., ed. Deaf Children: Developmental Perspectives. (Developmental Psychology Ser.). 1979. text ed. 63.00 (*0-12-447950-2*) Acad Pr.

Liber de Duobus Principiis Staff. Un Traite Neo-Manicheen du XIIIe siecle. LC 78-63185. (Heresies of the Early Christian & Medieval Era Ser.: Second Ser.). 1979. reprint ed. 49.50 (*0-404-16224-X*) AMS Pr.

Liber Domicilii Regis Jacobi Quinti Staff. Excerpta E Libris Domicilii Domini Jacobi Quinti Regis Scotorum. LC 75-172317. (Bannatyne Club, Edinburgh. Publications: No. 54). reprint ed. 37.50 (*0-404-52764-7*) AMS Pr.

Liber, George O. Soviet Nationality Policy, Urban Growth, & Identity Change in the Ukrainian SSR, 1923-1934. (Cambridge Russian, Soviet & Post-Soviet Studies: No. 84). (Illus.). 280p. (C). 1992. 64.95 (*0-521-41391-5*) Cambridge U Pr.

Liber, George O. & Mostovych, Anna, comps. Nonconformity & Dissent in the Ukrainian SSR, 1955-1975: A Select Bibliography. LC 77-73709. (Sources & Documents Ser.). xv, 245p. 1978. pap. (*0-916458-01-6*) Harvard Ukrainian.

Liber Kartor AB Staff & Maps International AB Staff. Earth Mapbook: Environmental Atlas. 2nd ed. Interarts, Ltd. Staff, ed. 187p. 1993. 15.95 (*1-879856-32-8*) Interarts.

Libera, Caitlin. Creating Circles of Power & Magic: A Woman's Guide to Sacred Community. LC 94-20558. 1994. pap. 12.95 (*0-89594-712-9*) Crossing Pr.

Libera, M., et al, eds. Crystallization & Related Phenomena in Amorphous Materials - Ceramics, Metals, Polymers, & Semiconductors, Vol. 321: Materials Research Society Symposium Proceedings. 1994. text ed. 78.00 (*1-55899-220-0*) Materials Res.

Liberal Summer School Oxford Staff. Essays in Liberalism Being the Lectures & Papers Which Were Delivered at the Liberal Summer School at Oxford, 1922. 1977. 23.95 (*0-8369-0426-5*) Ayer.

Liberatore, Anthony, et al. Explorations in Macroeconomics. 3rd ed. 482p. (C). 1990. pap. text ed. 45.60 (*0-929655-96-6*) CT Pub.

Liberatore, M. J., ed. Selection & Evaluation of Advanced Manufacturing Technologies. (Illus.). vi, 324p. 1990. 83.00 (*0-387-52656-0*) Spr-Verlag.

Liberatore, Paul. The San Quentin Massacre: A True Story of Race & Violence in the Radical New Left. 1994. 22.95 (*1-879360-32-2*) Noble Pr.

Liberia Editrice Vaticana. Catecismo De la Inglesia Catolica: Catechism of the Catholic Church. 662p. (Orig.). (SPA.). 1993. pap. 9.95 (*0-89243-583-6*) Liguori Pubns.

Liberles, Robert. Religious Conflict in Social Context: The Resurgence of Orthodox Judaism in Frankfurt Am Main, 1838-1877. LC 84-27981. (Contributions to the Study of Religion Ser.: No. 13). xvi, 297p. 1985. text ed. 55.00 (*0-313-24806-0*, LRX/) Greenwood.

— Salo Wittmayer Baron: Architect of Jewish History. (Modern Jewish Masters Ser.). 1995. 45.00 (*0-8147-5088-5*) NYU Pr.

***Liberman.** Light. 1995. 16.95 (*1-879323-27-3*) Sound Horizons AV.

— Social Skills Training for Psychiatric. (C). 1989. 31.95 (*0-205-14407-1*, H4407); pap. 21.95 (*0-205-14406-3*, H4406) Allyn.

Liberman & Gordon. Biohazards Management Handbook. (Occupational Safety & Health Ser.: Vol. 17). 737p. 1989. 170.00 (*0-8247-7897-9*) Dekker.

Liberman, Aaron. Risk & Insurance Management Guide for Medical Group Organizations. 1988. 24.00 (*0-933948-14-X*) Med Group Mgmt.

Liberman, Aaron & Woodruff, Michael J. Risk Management. LC 92-44149. (Creative Pastoral Care & Counseling Ser.). 96p. 1993. 10.00 (*0-8006-2758-X*, 1-2758, Fortress Pr) Augsburg Fortress.

Liberman, Alexander. The Artist in His Studio: The Heroes of Modern Art. enl. rev. ed. LC 88-42661. (Illus.). 1988. 60.00 (*0-394-56567-3*) Random.

Liberman, Alexander & Brodsky, Joseph. Campidoglio: Michelangelo's Roman Capitol. LC 94-13750. 1994. 75.00 (*0-679-43052-0*) Random.

***Liberman, Alvin M.** Speech: A Special Code. (Learning, Development, & Conceptual Change Ser.). (Illus.). 504p. 1995. 50.00x (*0-262-12192-1*, Bradford Bks) MIT Pr.

Liberman, Anatoly. Germanic Accentology, Vol. 1: The Scandinavian Languages. LC 80-27276. (Minnesota Publications in the Humanities). 392p. reprint ed. pap. 111.80 (*0-7837-2937-5*, 2057517) Bks Demand.

Liberman, Anatoly, tr. On the Heights of Creation. LC 92-34415. (Russian & East European Studies: Vol. 2). 1992. write for info. (*1-55938-525-1*) Jai Pr.

Liberman, Anatoly, tr. see Lermontov, Mikhail.

Liberman, Anatoly, ed. see Propp, Vladimir.

Liberman, Anatoly, tr. see Trubetzkoy, N. S.

Liberman, Cy & Liberman, Pat. The Crab Book. (Illus.). 160p. 1986. pap. 4.95 (*0-912608-22-6*) Mid Atlantic.

— The Mystique of Tall Ships. (Illus.). 128p. 1986. 29.95 (*0-912608-28-5*) Mid Atlantic.

***Liberman, Daniel F.** Biohazards Management Handbook. 2nd expanded rev. ed. LC 94-1164. (Occupational Safety & Health Ser.: Vol. 26). 1995. write for info. (*0-8247-8995-4*) Dekker.

Liberman, David. The Eternal Torah: A Commentary upon the Books of Joshua-Judges-Smauel One, Samuel Two,, Pt. 2. 360p. 1983. 20.00 (*0-9609840-1-1*) Twin Pines Pr.

Liberman, Evsefi G. Economic Methods & the Effectiveness of Production. LC 70-183252. 195p. reprint ed. pap. 55.60 (*0-317-30480-1*, 2024813) Bks Demand.

Liberman, Gail & Lavine, Alan. Reducing Debt & Improving Your Credit. (ICFP Personal Wealth Building Guides Ser.). 256p. 1993. text ed. 12.95 (*0-471-58373-1*) Wiley.

— Reducing Debt & Improving Your Credit. (ICFP Personal Wealth Building Guides Ser.). 256p. 1994. pap. text ed. 14.95 (*0-471-58374-X*) Wiley.

Liberman, Hal, jt. auth. see Liberman, Rita T.

Liberman, Isabelle Y., jt. ed. see Shankweiler, Donald.

Liberman, Jacob. Light: Medicine of the Future: How We Can Use It to Heal Ourselves Now. LC 90-748. (Illus.). 288p. (Orig.). 1993. pap. 16.95 (*1-879181-01-0*) Bear & Co.

— Take off Your Glasses & See: How to Heal Your Eyesight & Expand Your Insight. LC 94-32101. 1995. 21.00 (*0-517-59859-0*) Crown Pub Group.

*Liberman, Joan. The Busy World of Richard Scarry Busytown (an OMSI Exhibit) Activity Guide for Parents & Teachers. (Illus.). 72p. (Orig.). (SPA.). 1995. pap. 5.00 (0-9617645-2-X) Oreg Mus Sci & Indus.

Liberman, Jon C. SuperCharge Your Sales Force: Applying the Power of Computers to Get the Best from Your Sales Team. 225p. 1993. 22.95 (1-55738-441-X) Probus Pub Co.

Liberman, Kenneth. Understanding Interaction in Central Australia. (Studies in Ethnomethodology). 352p. 1985. 67.50 (0-7102-0473-6, RKP) Routledge.

Liberman, Lee, ed. see Cohen, David.

Liberman, M. A. & Velikovich, A. L. Physics of Shock Waves in Gases & Plasmas. (Electrophysics Ser.: Vol. 19). (Illus.). 400p. 1986. 93.00 (0-387-15605-4) Spr-Verlag.

Liberman, Myron M. Katherine Anne Porter's Fiction. LC 73-107951. 115p. reprint ed. pap. 32.80 (0-7837-3630-4, 2043496) Bks Demand.

Liberman, Pat, jt. auth. see Liberman, Cy.

Liberman, Paul. The Fig Tree Blossoms. (Orig.). 1976. pap. 3.95 (0-89350-000-3) Fountain Pr.

Liberman, R. P. A Guide to Behavioral Analysis & Therapy. 368p. 1972. 150.00 (0-08-016645-8, Pub. by Pergamon Repr UK) Franklin.

Liberman, R. P., et al. The Handbook of Marital Therapy: A Positive Approach to Helping Troubled Relationships. LC 79-9103. (Applied Clinical Psychology Ser.). (Illus.). 278p. 1980. 39.50 (0-306-40235-1, Plenum Pr); student ed 15.00 (0-685-04074-7, Plenum Pr) Plenum.

Liberman, Rita T. & Liberman, Hal. Tot's 'n Tension. 100p. (Orig.). 1985. pap. 5.95 (0-9614923-0-9) Tranquil Pr.

Liberman, Robert P. Psychiatric Rehabilitation of Chronic Mental Patients. LC 87-1492. 312p. 1988. boxed 26.00 (0-88048-201-X, 8201) Am Psychiatric.

Liberman, Robert P., ed. Effective Psychiatric Rehabilitation. LC 85-646993. (New Directions for Mental Health Services Ser.: No. MHS 53). 120p. 1991. student ed 17.95 (1-55542-757-X) Jossey-Bass.

Liberman, Robert P. & Yager, Joel, eds. Stress in Psychiatric Disorders. LC 93-41244. 208p. 1993. 34.95 (0-8261-8310-7) Springer Pub.

Liberman, Robert P., jt. ed. see Corrigan, Patrick.

Liberman, Simon I. Building Lenin's Russia. LC 75-39057. (Russian Studies: Perspectives on the Revolution). 228p. 1977. reprint ed. lib. bdg. 23.10 (0-88355-437-2) Hyperion Conn.

Liberman, Susan, et al. Memorable Film Characters: An Index to Roles & Performers, 1915-1983. LC 84-10844. (Bibliographies & Indexes in the Performing Arts Ser.: No. 1). ix, 291p. 1984. text ed. 69.50 (0-313-23977-0, LMF/, Greenwood Pr) Greenwood.

*Liberman, Yana. My China. (C). 1994. text ed. 17.95 (1-881116-45-X) Black Forrest Pr.

Libermann, Paulette & Marle, Charles-Michel. Symplectic Geometry & Analytical Mechanics. 1987. lib. bdg. 154.50 (90-277-2438-5) Kluwer Ac.

*Libero, Chiara. Tuscany. (Illus.). 160p. 1995. 17.98 (0-8317-8018-5) Smithmark.

Libersat, Henry. Do Whatever He Tells You: Finding Joy in Pleasing God. LC 90-43483. 174p. (Orig.). 1990. pap. 7.95 (0-8198-1819-4) Pauline Bks.

— Godparents. 154p. (Orig.). 1991. pap. 7.99 (0-89283-708-X) Servant.

— Way, Truth & Life: Living with Jesus Our Personal Savior. LC 88-34206. 110p. (Orig.). 1989. pap. 7.95 (0-8198-8237-2) Pauline Bks.

Libersat, Henry, jt. auth. see McKenna, Briege.

Libersat, Henry P. Miracle in the Marketplace. LC 90-70772. 96p. (Orig.). 1990. pap. 5.95 (1-878718-03-7) Resurrection.

Liberski. Light & Electronmicroscopic Neuropathology - Slow Virus Diseases. 1992. 218.00 (0-8493-6725-5, QR201) CRC Pr.

Liberski, P. P. The Enigma of Slow Viruses: Facts & Artefacts. LC 92-48419. (Archives of Virology Ser.: No. 6). 1993. write for info. (3-211-82427-8); 179.00 (0-387-82427-8) Spr-Verlag.

*Libert, Bo. The Environmental Heritage of Soviet Agriculture. (Sustainable Rural Development Ser.). 240p. 1995. 72.50 (0-85198-961-6) CAB Intl.

Libert, Jack. Edasi. (Illus.). 96p. (Orig.). (C). 1986. pap. 10.00 (0-9614148-0-4) Edasi.

Libert, Raymond J. The Slave in the Empty Grave. 32p. 1994. pap. 6.95 (0-8059-3478-2) Dorrance.

Liberti, Lawrence, jt. auth. see Der Marderosian, Ara.

Liberti, Lorenzo & Millar, John R. Fundamentals & Applications of Ion Exchange. LC 85-18842. 1985. lib. bdg. 65.50 (0-318-18277-7) Kluwer Ac.

Libertino. Pediatric & Reconstructive Urologic Surgery. 700p. 1996. 125.00 (0-8016-7802-1) Mosby Yr Bk.

*Liberto, Nicholas, ed. Powder Coating: The Complete Finisher's Handbook. LC 94-78590. (Illus.). 1994. 75.00 (0-9643091-0-6) Powder Coat Inst.

Libertson, J. Proximity, Levinas, Blanchot, Bataille & Communication. 1982. lib. bdg. 112.50 (90-247-2506-2) Kluwer Ac.

Liberty, Arthur L. Pewter & the Revival of Its Use. (Shorey Lost Arts Ser.). 28p. reprint ed. pap. 3.95 (0-8466-6007-5, U7) Shorey.

*Liberty, Franklin P. Computer Programming Ship's Business. LC 87-5231. (Illus.). (Orig.). reprint ed. pap. 83.80 (0-7837-9064-3, 2049813) Bks Demand.

*Liberty, Jesse. Teach Yourself C Plus Plus in 21 Days. (Illus.). 848p. (Orig.). 1994. pap. 29.99 (0-672-30541-0) Sams.

— Teach Yourself More C Plus Plus Programming in 21 Days. (Illus.). 800p. (Orig.). 1995. pap. text ed. 29.99 (0-672-30657-3) Sams.

Liberty, John. Journals of Dissent & Social Change. 6th ed. 518p. 1986. pap. 20.00 (0-938847-00-7) CSU Sacto Lib.

— Journals of Dissent & Social Change. 7th ed. 554p. 1993. pap. 25.00 (0-938847-01-5) CSU Sacto Lib.

Liberty, Larry L. Leadership Wisdom: A Guide to Producing Extraordinary Results. 272p. (Orig.). 1994. pap. 19.95 (0-9641669-0-9) Liberty Cnslting.

Liberty, Leona. Counselor: National Certification & State Licensing Examinations. 320p. 1989. pap. 21.00 (0-13-183260-3) P-H.

Liberty, Margot, jt. auth. see Stands In Timber, John.

Liberty, Margot, jt. ed. see Wood, W. Raymond.

*Liberty, Margot, et al. Working Cowboy: Recollections of Ray Holmes. LC 94-29445. (Illus.). 288p. 1995. 28.95 (0-8061-2692-2) U of Okla Pr.

Liberty Pub Staff. National Park Vacation: America's Best. 1991. pap. 9.95 (0-89709-191-4) Liberty Pub.

*Libes, Don. Exploring Expect: A Tcl-Based Toolkit for Automating Interactive Programs. O'Reilly, Tim, ed. (Illus.). 550p. (Orig.). 1994. 29.95 (1-56592-090-2) OReilly & Assocs.

— Obfuscated C & Other Mysteries, Set. 432p. 1992. disk 39.95 (0-471-57805-3) Wiley.

Libes, Don & Ressler, Sandy. Life with UNIX: A Guide for Everyone. 1988. 36.95 (0-13-536657-7) P-H.

Libes, Sol, et al. Digital Electronics: Concepts & Applications. (Illus.). 292p. 1988. reprint ed. pap. text ed. 14.00 (0-86657-007-1) Buck Eng Co.

Libes, Susan. An Introduction to Marine Biogeochemistry. 752p. (C). 1992. Net. text ed. write for info. (0-471-50946-9) Wiley.

Libeskind, Daniel. Daniel Libeskind: Countersign. LC 91-62802. (Illus.). 144p. 1992. 45.00 (0-8478-1478-5) Rizzoli Intl.

*Libeskind, Daniel & LeCuyer, Annette W. 1995 Raoul Wallenberg Lecture: Daniel Libeskind: Traces of the Unborn. (Illus.). 50p. (Orig.). (C). 1995. pap. text ed. 11.50 (0-9614792-1-3) U Mich Arch.

Libeskind-Hadas, Ran. Fault Covering Problems in Reconfigurable VLSI Systems. (International Series in Engineering & Computer Science, VLSI, Computer Architecture, & Digital Screen Processing). 144p. (C). 1992. lib. bdg. 70.50 (0-7923-9231-0) Kluwer Ac.

Libet, Benjamin. Neurophysiology of Consciousness: Selected Papers of Benjamin Libet. LC 93-16896. (Contemporary Neuroscientists Ser.). (Illus.). 424p. 1993. 89.50 (0-8176-3538-6) Birkhauser.

Libey, Donald R. Libey on Change: Superforces & Socialforces in the Marketing Future. LC 94-1877. 145p. 1994. 55.00 (1-882222-07-5) Libey Pub.

— Libey on Customers. LC 92-32559. (Libey New Century Library). 288p. 1992. 65.00 (1-882222-00-8, Libey Pub) Libey Pub.

— Libey on Recency, Frequency, & Monetary Value. 126p. 1994. write for info. (1-882222-06-7) Libey Pub.

— Libey on Supercycles. 1994. 65.00 (1-882222-01-6) Libey Pub.

Libgober, A., jt. auth. see Birman, J.

*Libicki, Martin. Information Technology Standards: Quest for the Common Byte. 400p. 1995. 79.95 (1-55558-131-5, Digital DEC) Buttrwrth-Heinemann.

*Libicki, Martin C. Standards: The Rough Road to the Common Byte. (Illus.). 46p. (Orig.). 1994. pap. text ed. write for info. (1-879716-15-1, P-94-6) Ctr Info Policy.

— What Makes Industries Strategic: A Perspective on Technology, Economic Development, & Defense. (Illus.). 93p. 1990. per. 2.75 (0-16-025888-X, S/N 008-020-01115-4) USGPO.

*Libin, Laurence. Our Tuneful Heritage: American Musical Instruments from the Metropolitan Museum of Art. LC 94-42019. 90p. 1994. 19.95 (0-8425-2325-1) Brigham.

Libin, Laurence, et al. The Spanish Guitar. (Illus.). 210p. (ENG & SPA.). (C). reprint ed. pap. 60.00 (0-933224-79-6, Pub. by Opera Tres SP) Bold Strummer Ltd.

Libkind, Marcus. Ski Tours in Lassen Volcanic National Park. LC 89-92069. (Illus.). 128p. (Orig.). 1989. pap. 10.95 (0-931255-04-X) Bittersweet Pub.

— Ski Tours in the Sierra Nevada: Carson Pass, Bear Valley, Pinecrest, Vol. 2. LC 84-73452. (Illus.). 132p. (Orig.). 1985. pap. 11.95 (0-931255-01-5) Bittersweet Pub.

— Ski Tours in the Sierra Nevada: East of Sierra Crest, Vol. 4. LC 84-73452. (Illus.). 184p. (Orig.). 1986. pap. 13.95 (0-931255-03-1) Bittersweet Pub.

— Ski Tours in the Sierra Nevada: Yosemite, Kings Canyon, Sequoia, Vol. 3. LC 84-73452. (Illus.). 136p. (Orig.). 1985. pap. 11.95 (0-931255-02-3) Bittersweet Pub.

— Ski Tours in the Sierra Nevada Vol. 1: Lake Tahoe. (Illus.). 266p. 1995. pap. 16.95 (0-931255-08-2) Bittersweet Pub.

Libman, Howard & Witzburg, Robert A., eds. HIV Infection: A Clinical Manual. 2nd ed. LC 93-3548. Orig. Title: Clinical Manual for Care of the Adult Patient with HIV Infection. (Illus.). 560p. 1993. pap. 35.00 (0-316-51162-5) Little.

Libo, Kenneth & Howe, Irving. We Lived There Too: In Their Own Words & Pictures - Pioneer Jews & the Westward Movement of America 1630-1930. (Illus.). 4p. 1985. pap. 13.95 (0-312-85867-1, Pub. by Marek) St Martin.

Liboff, Richard L. Introductory Quantum Mechanics. (Illus.). 672p. 1980. text ed. 61.25 (0-201-12221-9) Addison-Wesley.

— Introductory Quantum Mechanics. 2nd ed. (Illus.). 736p. (C). 1992. text ed. 65.75 (0-201-54715-5) Addison-Wesley.

Liboff, Richard L. & Rostoker, Norman, eds. Kinetic Equations. LC 72-122848. (Illus.). 360p. 1971. text ed. 215.00 (0-677-14080-0) Gordon & Breach.

Libonati, Gerald. The Adjuster. LC 94-71378. 292p. 1995. pap. 10.95 (0-9640965-0-1) Avant G Bks.

Libonati, Michael, jt. auth. see Sands, C.

Libov, Charlotte, jt. auth. see Pashkow, Fredric J.

Libov, Charlotte, jt. auth. see Pashkow, Fredric.

Libow, Judith A., jt. auth. see Schreier, Herbert A.

Libowitz, R., ed. Faith & Freedom: A Tribute to Franklin H. Littell. LC 87-15972. 268p. 1987. 47.00 (0-08-035852-7, Pergamon Pr) Elsevier.

Libowitz, Richard. Mordecai M. Kaplan & the Development of Reconstructionism. LC 83-923. (Studies in American Religion: Vol. 9). (Illus.). 266p. 1983. lib. bdg. 89.95 (0-88946-651-3) E Mellen.

Libr. du Liban Staff. Dictionary of English Idioms. (ARA & ENG.). 1989. 29.95 (0-86685-512-2) Intl Bk Ctr.

Libra, C. A. Astrology: Its Techniques & Ethics. (Arcana Ser.). (Illus.). 272p. 1981. reprint ed. pap. 5.95 (0-87877-035-6, P-35) Newcastle Pub.

Libra, C. Aq. Astrology: Its Techniques & Ethics. LC 80-23764. xii, 259p. 1980. reprint ed. lib. bdg. 27.00x (0-89370-635-3) Borgo Pr.

Librach, Hank. Pocket Computer Primer. LC 82-80270. 96p. (Orig.). 1982. pap. 9.95 (0-942412-00-1); audio 8.95 (0-686-87024-7) Micro Text Pubns.

Librach, Hank & Behrendt, William. Using the Commodore 64 in the Home. (Illus.). 100p. 1984. pap. 10.95 (0-685-06718-1) P-H.

Librairie du Liban Dictionary Department Staff, comp. English-Arabic Dictionary of Economics & Commerce. (Libraire du Liban). (ARA & ENG.). 1983. 25.00 (0-86685-169-0); pap. 7.95 (0-86685-076-7) Intl Bk Ctr.

Librairie du Liban Staff. ABC Dictionary I: Arabic & English. (ARA & ENG.). (J). (ps-4). 1983. 6.00 (0-86685-336-7) Intl Bk Ctr.

— ABC Dictionary I: Arabic & French. (ARA & FRE.). (J). (ps-4). 1983. 6.00 (0-86685-310-3) Intl Bk Ctr.

— ABC Dictionary I: Arabic & German. (ARA & GER.). (J). (ps-4). 1983. 6.00 (0-86685-309-X) Intl Bk Ctr.

— ABC Dictionary Tamhidi: Arabic & French. (ARA & FRE.). (J). (ps-4). 1983. 6.00 (0-86685-315-4) Intl Bk Ctr.

— ABC Dictionary Tamhidi: Arabic & German. (ARA & GER.). (J). (ps-4). 1983. 6.00 (0-86685-313-8) Intl Bk Ctr.

— ABC Dictionary Tamhidi: Arabic & Italian. (ARA & ITA.). (J). (ps-4). 1983. 6.00 (0-86685-316-2) Intl Bk Ctr.

— ABC I: Arabic Italian Dictionary. (J). (ps-4). 1983. 6.00 (0-86685-308-1) Intl Bk Ctr.

— ABC Tamhidi Arabic-Spanish Dictionary. (ARA & SPA.). (J). (ps-4). 1983. 6.00 (0-86685-312-X) Intl Bk Ctr.

— English Grammar Made Easy: English - Arabic. 1990. 6.95 (0-86685-458-4) Intl Bk Ctr.

— Maroof the Cobbler. (J). 1986. 7.95 (0-86685-566-1) Intl Bk Ctr.

— The Mesopotamia. (J). 1991. 7.95 (0-86685-489-4) Intl Bk Ctr.

— My Illustrated Dictionary. (ARA & ENG.). (YA). (gr. 5-12). 1983. 9.95 (0-86685-317-0); 9.95 (0-86685-318-9); 9.95 (0-86685-319-7); 9.95 (0-86685-320-0); 9.95 (0-86685-321-9) Intl Bk Ctr.

— The Phoenicians. (J). 1991. 8.95x (0-86685-570-X) Intl Bk Ctr.

Librairie Larousse Staff. Larousse Wines & Vineyards of France. (Illus.). 640p. 1991. 29.95 (1-55970-113-7) Arcade Pub Inc.

Librairie Larousse Staff, jt. ed. see Houghton Mifflin Company Staff.

Librarie du Liban Staff. ABC Picture Dictionary: English to Arabic. 1991. 4.95 (0-86685-460-6) Intl Bk Ctr.

Library Administration & Management Association Preconference Staff. Practical Help for New Supervisors. 2nd ed. Giesecke, Joan, ed. LC 92-12302. 85p. (C). 1992. pap. text ed. 18.00 (0-8389-3408-0) ALA.

*Library Assn., Working Party on Community Info. Staff. Community Information: What Libraries Can Do: a Consultative Document. fac. ed. LC 80-508485. (Illus.). 137p. 1980. reprint ed. pap. 39.10 (0-7837-8204-7, 2047962) Bks Demand.

Library Association, Conference Staff. Preserving the Word: The Library Association Conference Proceedings, Harrogate, 1986. Palmer, R. E., ed. LC 87-16523. 159p. reprint ed. pap. 45.40 (0-7837-5316-0, 2045055) Bks Demand.

Library Association Staff. Guidelines for Training in Libraries, 9 vols. LC 81-154916. reprint ed. pap. 25.00 (0-7837-7071-5, 2046883) Bks Demand.

Library Committee Staff & Wilson, Doris L. Martin County, North Carolina Abstracts of Deed Book A 1774-1787. 136p. 1993. pap. 25.00 (0-9626609-2-2) MCH Soc NC.

Library Cooperation Committee. Multitype Library Cooperation Section Staff. The Report on Library Cooperation: 1986. 3rd ed. 450p. 1986. 25.00 (0-8389-7026-5, ASCLA) ALA.

Library Information Technology Centre Staff, ed. European Directory of Software for Libraries & Information Services. 180p. 1993. 73.95 (1-85742-092-6, Pub. by Ashgate UK) Ashgate Pub Co.

Library of American Art, jt. auth. see Ballinger, James K.

*Library of Congress, Cataloging Policy & Support Office Staff, comp. Subject Cataloging Manual. 2nd ed. LC 94-41263. 1995. write for info. (0-615-00423-7) Lib Congress.

*Library of Congress, Collections Policy Office Staff, comp. Library of Congress Collections Policy Statements. LC 94-40681. 1994. write for info. (0-615-00424-5) Lib Congress.

Library of Congress, Federal Research Div. Staff. Israel: A Country Study. 3rd ed. Metz, Helen C., ed. LC 90-6119. (Area Handbook Ser.). (Illus.). 454p. 1991. text ed. 19.00 (0-16-028017-6) USGPO.

— Uganda: A Country Study. 2nd ed. Byrnes, Rita M., ed. LC 92-513. (Area Handbook Ser.: No. 550-74). 1992. write for info. (0-8444-0749-6) Lib Congress.

Library of Congress, Federal Research Division Staff. Cyprus, a Country Study. 4th ed. Solsten, Eric, ed. LC 92-36090. (Area Handbook Ser.). 1993. write for info. (0-8444-0752-6) Lib Congress.

— Portugal Country Studies: Area Handbook. 2nd ed. Solsten, Eric, ed. LC 93-30722. (Area Handbook Ser.). 1994. 19.00 (0-8444-0776-3) Lib Congress.

— Sudan: A Country Study. 4th ed. Metz, Helen C., ed. LC 92-21336. (Area Handbook Ser.). 1992. write for info. (0-8444-0750-X) Lib Congress.

*Library of Congress, Federal Research Division Staff & Hudson, Rex A. Chile Country Studies: Area Handbook. 3rd ed. LC 94-21663. (Area Handbook DA Pam Ser.: Vol. 550-77). 1994. 25.00 (0-8444-0828-X) Lib Congress.

*Library of Congress, Federal Research Division Staff & Merrill, Tim. Nicaragua Country Studies: Area Handbook. 3rd ed. LC 94-21664. (Area Handbook DA Pam Ser.: 550-88). 1994. 18.00 (0-8444-0831-X) Lib Congress.

*Library of Congress, Federal Research Division Staff, et al, eds. Zaire Country Studies: Area Handbook. 4th ed. LC 94-25092. (Area Handbook DA Pam Ser.: 550-67). 1994. 22.00 (0-8444-0795-X) Lib Congress.

Library of Congress Federal Research Division. Saudi Arabia Country Studies: Area Handbook. Metz, Helen C., ed. LC 93-28506. (Area Handbook Ser.: No. 550-51). 1993. 20.00 (0-8444-0791-7) Lib Congress.

Library of Congress, National Library Service for the Blind & Physically Handicapped Staff. Coping Skills. LC 93-32178. 1993. write for info. (0-08-440799-9, Pergamon Pr) Elsevier.

— More Mysteries. LC 92-30160. 1992. write for info. (0-8444-0763-1) Lib Congress.

— Science Fiction & Fantasy. LC 94-35460. 1994. write for info. (0-8444-0842-5) Lib Congress.

*Library of Congress, Network Development Department. Network Advisory Committee: Proceedings of the Library of Congress Network Advisory Committee Meeting, December 12-14, 1993. LC 94-33175. (Network Planning Paper Ser.: Vol. 26). 1994. write for info. (0-8444-0824-7) Lib Congress.

Library of Congress Prints Division Staff, jt. auth. see Beall, Karen.

Library of Congress Staff. Africa South of the Sahara: Index to Periodical Literature, First Supplement. 1973. lib. bdg. 120.00 (0-8161-1048-4, Hall Library) G K Hall.

— Africa South of the Sahara: Index to Periodical Literature, 1900-1970, 4 vols, Set. 1974. lib. bdg. 400.00 (0-8161-0892-7, Hall Library) G K Hall.

— An Album of Civil War Battle Art. 128p. 1988. reprint ed. pap. 12.95 (1-55709-111-0) Applewood.

— American Prints in the Library of Congress: A Catalog of the Collection. LC 73-106134. (Illus.). 590p. reprint ed. 168.20 (0-8357-9262-5, 2051253) Bks Demand.

— Bibliographic Guide to Law: 1991, 2 vols., Vol. 2. (Bibliographic Guides Ser.). 1053p. 1992. text ed. 340.00 (0-8161-7163-7) G K Hall.

— Catalog of American Political Prints in the Library of Congress, 1766-1876. (Library Catalogs). (Illus.). 800p. 1991. lib. bdg. 135.00 (0-8161-0444-1) G K Hall.

— Catalog of Broadsides in the Rare Book Division, 4 vols., Set. 1972. lib. bdg. 490.00 (0-8161-0990-7, Hall Library) G K Hall.

— Charles Fenderich: Lithographer of American Statesmen. Miller, Lillian B., ed. LC 76-24470. (Illus.). 1978. Includes 3 black & white fiches. fiche, lib. bdg. 25.00 (0-226-69243-4) U Ch Pr.

— European Collections: An Illustrated Guide. LC 94-32368. (Illus.). 1994. write for info. (0-8444-0841-7) Lib Congress.

— Far Eastern Languages Catalog, 22 vols., Set. 1972. lib. bdg. 2,490.00 (0-8161-0980-X, Hall Library) G K Hall.

— Index to Latin American Legislation, First Supplement, 1961-1965, 2 vols., Set. 1970. lib. bdg. 240.00 (0-8161-0875-7, Hall Library) G K Hall.

— Index to Latin American Legislation, Second Supplement, 2 vols., Set. 1978. lib. bdg. 130.00 (0-8161-1020-4, Hall Library) G K Hall.

— Index to Latin American Legislation, 1950-1960, 2 Vols, Set. 1970. lib. bdg. 215.00 (0-8161-0594-4, Hall Library) G K Hall.

— Library of Congress Music, Theater, & Dance: An Illustrated Guide. LC 93-27720. (Illus.), 80p. 1993. 8.50 (0-8444-0801-8) Lib Congress.

— National Union Catalog: A Cumulative Author List, 1958-1962. Incl. Vol. 51. Music & Phonorecords - Authors List, Pt. 1. 40.00 (0-87471-731-0); Vol. 52. Music & Phonorecords - Subject Index, Pt. 2. 40.00 (0-87471-732-9); Vol. 53. Motion Pictures & Film Strips, Titles, Pt. 1. 40.00 (0-87471-733-7); Vol. 54. Motion Pictures & Film Strips, Pt. 2 - Subject Index. 40.00 (0-87471-734-5); write for info. (0-318-55560-3) Rowman.

— Southeast Asia Subject Catalog, 6 vols., Set. 1972. lib. bdg. 655.00 (0-8161-0857-9, Hall Library) G K Hall.

— Specifications for Microfilming Manuscripts. LC 80-607061. (Technical Papers). 21p. 1980. reprint ed. pap. 12.00 (0-8444-0332-6, D003) Assn Inform & Image Mgmt.

— Specifications for the Microfilming of Books & Pamphlets in the Library of Congress. rev. ed. LC 73-9756. (Technical Papers). 16p. 1982. reprint ed. pap. 12.00 (0-8444-0098-X, D005) Assn Inform & Image Mgmt.

— Specifications for the Microfilming of Library Card Catalogs. rev. ed. LC 74-16227. (Technical Papers). 10p. 1974. reprint ed. pap. 12.00 (0-8444-0138-2, D006) Assn Inform & Image Mgmt.

An Asterisk (*) at the beginning of an entry indicates that the title is appearing in BIP for the first time.

— Specifications for the Microfilming of Newspapers in the Library of Congress. LC 74-37943. (Technical Papers). 17p. 1982. reprint ed. pap. 12.00 (*0-8444-0014-9*, D004) Assn Inform & Image Mgmt.

Library of Congress Staff, ed. Music Subject Headings Used in Printed Catalog Cards of the Library of Congress. (Library Science Ser.). 1980. lib. bdg. 59.95 (*0-8490-3178-8*) Gordon Pr.

Library of Congress Staff & Arion Press Staff. The Constitution of the United States: Published for the Bicentennial of Its Adoption in 1787. LC 87-600111. 63p. 1987. 2.50 (*0-8444-0560-4*, 030-000-00190-7) Lib Congress.

Library of Congress Staff, jt. auth. see Huntington Library Staff.

Library of Congress Staff, jt. auth. see New York Public Library Art.

Library of Congress Staff, jt. auth. see New York Public Library Staff.

Library of Congress Staff, jt. comp. see New York Public Library Staff.

Library of Congress Staff, jt. auth. see New York Public Library Theatre.

Library of Congress Staff, jt. auth. see Research Libraries of the New York Public Library Staff.

Library of Congress Staff, jt. auth. see University of Texas Library, Austin, Nettie Lee Benson Latin American Collection Staff.

Library of Congress, Washington, D. C., Geography & Map Division Staff. The Bibliography of Cartography, 5 vols., Set. 1973. lib. bdg. 615.00 (*0-8161-1008-5*, Hall Library) G K Hall.

— The Bibliography of Cartography, First Supplement. 1980. lib. bdg. 285.00 (*0-8161-0259-7*, Hall Library) G K Hall.

Library of Congress, Washington, D. C., Staff. Catalog of Brazilian Acquisitions of the Library of Congress, 1964-1974. 1976. lib. bdg. 110.00 (*0-8161-0033-0*, Hall Library) G K Hall.

Library of the Kiel Institute of World Economics in the Federal Republic of Germany Staff, jt. ed. see Siefkes, Frauke.

Library of the Peabody Museum of Archaeology & Ethnology, Harvard University Staff. Tozzer Library. 2nd ed. (Library Catalogs). 1988. lib. bdg. 6,600.00 (*0-8161-1731-4*) G K Hall.

Library School Commons Conference Staff. A Search for New Insights in Librarianship: A Day of Comparative Studies - Proceedings of the Library School Commons Conference, University of Wisconsin, April 25, 1975. Williamson, William L., ed. 106p. 1976. pap. 5.00 (*0-936442-04-2*) U Wis Sch Lib.

Library Service for the Blind & Physically Handicapped, Library of Congress Staff. Classics. LC 94-9204. 1994. write for info. (*0-8444-0811-5*) Lib Congress.

Library Services Task Force Staff. Substitute Natural Gas from Hydrocarbon Liquids (Oil Gasification) A Bibliography 1960-1973. 62p. 1974. 7.00 (*0-318-12711-3*, H02074) Am Gas Assn.

Library Staff, et al. Historical American Sketches: An Illustrated Guide to the Manuscript Collections of the American Philosophical Society. American Philosophical Society Staff, ed. 300p. 1984. lib. bdg. 95.00 (*0-8161-0433-6*, Hall Library) G K Hall.

Librescu, L., ed. Non-Classical Problems of the Theory & Behavior of Structures Exposed to Complex Environmental Conditions. LC 93-71578. (AMD Ser.: Vol. 164). 183p. 1993. pap. 50.00 (*0-7918-1143-3*, G00787) ASME.

Librett, Jeffrey S., tr. Of the Sublime: Presence in Question: Essays by Jean-Francois Courtine, Michel Deguy, Eliane Escoubas, Philippe Lacoue-Labarthe, Jean-Francois Lyotard, Louis Marin, Jean-Luc Nancy, & Jacob Rogozinski. LC 91-9447. (SUNY Series, Intersections: Philosophy & Critical Theory). 255p. (C). 1993. 59.50 (*0-7914-1379-9*); pap. 19.95 (*0-7914-1380-2*) State U NY Pr.

LiBretto, Ellen V., ed. High-Low Handbook: Encouraging Literacy in the 1990s. 3rd ed. (Serving Special Needs Ser.). 304p. 1990. 43.00 (*0-8352-2804-5*) Bowker.

Libri, Guillaume. Histoire Des Sciences Mathematiques en Italie, 4 vols., Set. xxviii, 1950p. 1967. reprint ed. write for info. (*0-318-71371-3*, Pub. by Georg Olms GW) Lubrecht & Cramer.

Libros Alianza Staff. Celebremos Su Gloria (Celebrate His Glory) (SPA.). Date not set. spiral bd. pap. 7.00 (*0-685-74912-6*, 490182); pap., vinyl bd. 8.00 (*958-9269-09-5*, 490181); spiral bd., vinyl bd. 12.00 (*958-9269-10-9*, 490191); spiral bd., vinyl bd. 16.50 (*0-685-74913-4*, 490193); vinyl bd. 11.00 (*958-9269-13-3*, 490183); vinyl bd. 17.00 (*958-9269-14-1*, 490194) Editorial Unilit.

Libros Desafio Staff, ed. see Francen, Mike.

Libros, Harold. Hard-Core Liberals: A Sociological Analysis of the Philadelphia Americans for Democratic Action. 147p. 1975. boxed 29.95x (*0-87073-148-3*) Transaction Pubs.

Libucha, Mark, jt. ed. see No, Yongkyoon.

Liburdi, Joe & Sherman, Cara. The Complete Guide to Sea & Sea. (Illus.). 256p. (Orig.). 1994. pap. text ed. 10.25 (*0-9621111-2-0*) Orca Pubns.

— How to Use Sea & Sea. (Illus.). 120p. (Orig.). 1988. pap. text ed. write for info. (*0-9621111-0-4*) Orca Pubns.

Libutti, L. Robert. Systems Application Architecture: The IBM SAA Strategy. 1990. pap. 24.95 (*0-8306-3516-5*) TAB Bks.

Licari, James J. The Learning Company. 1994. text ed. 55.00 (*0-07-037715-4*) McGraw.

— Plastic Coating for Electronics. LC 79-26923. 398p. 1980. reprint ed. lib. bdg. 38.50 (*0-89874-107-6*) Krieger.

Licari, James J. & Enlow, Leonard R. Hybrid Microcircuit Technology Handbook: Materials, Processes, Design, Testing & Production. LC 87-34701. (Illus.). 429p. 1989. 72.00 (*0-8155-1152-3*) Noyes.

Licari, James J. & Hughes, Laura A. Handbook of Polymer Coatings for Electronics: Chemistry, Technology & Applications. 2nd ed. LC 89-70994. (Illus.). 392p. 1990. 75.00 (*0-8155-1235-X*) Noyes.

Licastro, Peter J. Birthplace of Legends: The Story of Corvette Production at the St. Louis Assembly Plant, 1953-1981. (Illus.). 152p. 1993. pap. 32.95 (*0-9630555-8-5*) Just The Facts.

— The Original 1973-1977 Corvette Fact Manual. 2nd ed. 152p. 1994. pap. 35.95 (*0-9630555-7-7*) Just The Facts.

Licata, David P. Advanced Placement Chemistry Student Handbook. (YA). (gr. 10-12). 1993. pap. text ed. 12.95 (*0-9636095-0-5*) Licatas Edutype.

— Basic Chemistry in Microscale. 30p. 1993. 9.95 (*0-9636095-1-3*) Licatas Edutype.

— Chemistry Labs for Distance Learning: A Microscale Laboratory Manual. (Illus.). 64p. (C). 1994. student ed 16.65 (*0-9636095-2-1*) Licatas Edutype.

Licata, Guy, jt. auth. see Garnsey, Wayne.

Licata, Renora. Everything You Need to Know about Anger. rev. ed. (Need to Know Library). (YA). (gr. 7-12). 1994. lib. bdg. 15.95 (*0-8239-2036-4*) Rosen Group.

— Princess Diana: Royal Ambassador. (Library of Famous Women). (Illus.). 64p. (J). (gr. 3-7). 1993. lib. bdg. 14.95 (*1-56711-013-4*); pap. 7.95 (*1-56711-051-7*) Blackbirch.

Licata, Salvatore & Peterson, Robert, eds. The Gay Past: A Collection of Historical Essays. LC 84-22398. 224p. 1986. pap. text ed. 14.95 (*0-918393-11-6*) Harrington Pk.

Licata, Salvatore J. & Petersen, Robert P., eds. Historical Perspectives on Homosexuality. LC 80-6262. (Journal of Homosexuality: Vol. 6, Nos. 1-2). 224p. 1982. text ed. 39.95 (*0-917724-27-5*); pap. 14.95 (*0-86656-436-5*) Haworth Pr.

Licate, Jack A. Creation of a Mexican Landscape: Territorial Organization & Settlement in the Eastern Puebla Basin, 1520-1605. LC 81-12941. (Research Papers Ser.: No. 201). (Illus.). 143p. 1981. pap. text ed. 12.00 (*0-89065-107-8*) U Chicago Comm Geo.

Liccardi, Millicent R., jt. auth. see Camp, Elizabeth L.

Lich, Glen E. Fred Gipson at Work. LC 89-39876. (Illus.). 152p. 1990. 29.95 (*0-89096-424-6*) Tex A&M Univ Pr.

Lich, Glen E., ed. Regional Studies: The Interplay of Land & People. LC 91-4133. (Essays on the American West Ser.: No. 12). (Illus.). 198p. 1992. 32.50 (*0-89096-477-7*) Tex A&M Univ Pr.

Lich, Glen E. & Reeves-Marquardt, Dona B., eds. Texas Country: The Changing Rural Scene. LC 86-40216. (Illus.). 280p. 1986. 18.95 (*0-89096-247-2*) Tex A&M Univ Pr.

Lich, Lera T. Larry McMurtry's Texas: Evolution of a Myth. Eakin, Edwin M., ed. LC 87-24314. (Illus.). 104p. 1988. 9.95 (*0-89015-613-1*) Sunbelt Media.

Lichardus, B., ed. see Natriuretic Hormone Symposium Staff.

Lichardus, R., et al, eds. Hormonal Regulation of Sodium Excretion. (Developments in Endocrinology Ser.: Vol. 10). 1981. 79.50 (*0-444-80289-4*) Elsevier.

***Lichauco, Alejandro.** The Lichauco Paper: Imperialism in the Philippines. LC 73-7953. reprint ed. pap. 36.20 (*0-7837-9603-X*, 2060360) Bks Demand.

Lichauco, Marcial P., jt. auth. see Storey, Moorfield.

Lichbach, Mark I. The Rebel's Dilemma. (Economics, Cognition, & Society Ser.). 550p. 1994. text ed. 45.00 (*0-472-10532-9*) U of Mich Pr.

Lichello, Robert. Dag Hammarskjold: A Giant in Diplomacy. Rahmas, D. Steve, ed. LC 73-185657. (Outstanding Personalities Ser.: No. 1). 32p. (Orig.). (gr. 7-12). 1972. lib. bdg. 4.95 (*0-87157-501-9*) SamHar Pr.

— Edward R. Murrow: Broadcaster of Courage. Rahmas, D. Steve, ed. LC 75-185660. (Outstanding Personalities Ser.: No. 4). 32p. (Orig.). (gr. 7-12). 1972. lib. bdg. 4.95 (*0-87157-504-3*) SamHar Pr.

— Enrico Fermi: Father of the Atomic Bomb. Rahmas, D. Steve, ed. LC 70-185667. (Outstanding Personalities Ser.: No. 11). 32p. (YA). (gr. 7-12). 1972. lib. bdg. 4.95 (*0-87157-511-6*) SamHar Pr.

— How to Make a Million Dollars in the Stock Market - Automatically. rev. ed. 1985. pap. 5.95 (*0-451-16814-3*, NAL Bks) NAL-Dutton.

— How to Make One Million Dollars in the Stock Market - Automatically! 3rd rev. ed. 256p. 1992. pap. 5.99 (*0-451-17453-4*, Sig) NAL-Dutton.

Lichenberg, Frank R. Corporate Takeovers & Productivity. (Illus.). 168p. 1992. 32.50 (*0-262-12164-6*) MIT Pr.

Lichfield, Lord, ed. see Carpenter, Sue.

Lichfield, N. & Proudlove, A. Conservation & Traffic: Planning Problems in York. (C). 1988. 80.00 (*0-900657-23-5*, Pub. by W Sessions UK) St Mut.

Lichfield, Nathaniel. Economics in Urban Conservation. (Illus.). 280p. 1989. 79.95 (*0-521-32851-9*) Cambridge U Pr.

***Lichfield, Nathaniel, et al.** Community Impact Evaluation: Principles & Practice. 352p. 1995. 95.00x (*1-85728-237-X*, Pub. by UCL Pr UK); pap. 32.00x (*1-85728-238-8*, Pub. by UCL Pr UK) Taylor & Francis.

— Evaluation in the Planning Process. 336p. 1975. 139.00 (*0-08-017843-X*, Pub. by Pergamon Repr UK) Franklin.

Lichine, Alexis. Alexis Lichine's Guide to the Wines & Vineyards of France. 3rd ed. 1986. 25.00 (*0-394-55335-7*) Knopf.

— Alexis Lichine's Guide to the Wines & Vineyards of France. 4th ed. 1989. pap. 18.95 (*0-679-72285-8*) Knopf.

— Encyclopedie des Vins et des Alcools de Tous les Pays. 945p. (FRE.). 1980. pap. 49.95 (*0-8288-1177-6*, M12622) Fr & Eur.

Lichius, J. J. Phytochemische Analyse Seltener Digitalisarten (wie Digitalis Subalpina Br.-Bl.) und Reziproker Digitaliskreuzungen. (Dissertationes Botanicae Ser.: Vol. 172). (Illus.). 298p. (GER.). 1991. pap. 82.80 (*3-443-64084-2*, Pub. by Cramer-Borntraeger GW) Lubrecht & Cramer.

Lichko, Joseph, jt. auth. see Freed, Shervin.

***Lichlitea, Vernon L.** The People from a Far Away Place. 230p. (Orig.). Date not set. pap. 8.95 (*0-7610-0285-5*) NW Pub.

Lichnerowicz, Andre. Magnetohydrodynamics: Waves & Shock Waves in Curved Space-Time. (Mathematical Physics Studies). 292p. (C). 1994. lib. bdg. 94.00 (*0-7923-2805-1*) Kluwer Ac.

Lichnewsky, A. & Sague, Z. C. Supercomputing: State of the Art. 1987. 97.50 (*0-444-70320-9*) Elsevier.

Lichnewsky, Alain, jt. auth. see Glowinski, Roland.

Lichstein, Kenneth L. Clinical Relaxation Strategies. LC 87-25296. (Personality Processes Ser.). 426p. 1988. text ed. 69.95 (*0-471-81592-6*) Wiley.

Licht. Air Pollution Control Engineering: Basic Calculations for Particulate Collection. 2nd ed. 496p. 1988. 140.00 (*0-8247-7898-7*) Dekker.

Licht, Chaim. The Legends of the Sages: The Image of the Sage in Rabbinic Literature. 25.00 (*0-88125-361-8*) Ktav.

Licht, Fred. Canova. LC 82-16309. (Illus.). 280p. 1983. 125.00 (*0-89659-327-4*) Abbeville Pr.

— Josef Albers Glass, Color, & Light. 1994. 45.00 (*0-8109-6864-9*) Abrams.

— Shelter the Pilgrim. (Classic Short Stories Ser.). 48p. (J). (gr. 6). 1990. lib. bdg. 13.95 (*0-88682-307-2*) Creative Ed.

Licht, Fred, jt. auth. see Wardropper, Ian.

Licht, Fred S., intro. Goya: The Origins of the Modern Temper in Art. (Icon Editions Ser.). (Illus.). 288p. 1983. pap. text ed. 21.00 (*0-06-430123-0*, IN-123, Icon Edns) HarpC.

Licht, Hans, pseud. Sexual Life in Ancient Greece. Dawson, Lawrence H., ed. Freese, J. H., tr. LC 72-9622. (Illus.). reprint ed. 67.50 (*0-404-57417-3*) AMS Pr.

Licht, J. Storytelling in the Bible. 2nd ed. 154p. (C). 1986. text ed. 15.00 (*965-223-542-3*, Pub. by Magnes Press IS) Eisenbrauns.

Licht, Lilla M. & Moore, William B. McKnight Genealogy, 1754-1981. LC 81-85782. (Illus.). 476p. 1981. 25.00 (*0-9607184-0-0*); pap. 22.00 (*0-9607184-1-9*) Licht Pubns.

***Licht, R. & De Villiers, B., eds.** South Africa's Crisis of Constitutional Democracy Vol. 1: Can the U.S. Constitution Help? 261p. 1994. pap. text ed. 20.00 (*0-7021-3143-1*, Pub. by Juta SA) W W Gaunt.

Licht, Robert A., ed. The Framers & Fundamental Rights. 202p. (C). 1991. 19.95 (*0-8447-3788-7*) Am Enterprise.

— Is the Supreme Court the Guardian of the Constitution? LC 92-34511. (AEI Studies). 210p. (Orig.). Date not set. pap. write for info. (*0-8447-3812-3*, AEI Pr) Am Enterprise.

— Is the Supreme Court the Guardian of the Constitution? LC 92-34511. (AEI Studies). 210p. (Orig.). 1993. 19.95 (*0-8447-3813-1*, AEI Pr) Am Enterprise.

— Old Rights & New. 213p. Date not set. pap. write for info. (*0-8447-3776-3*, AEI Pr) Am Enterprise.

— Old Rights & New. 213p. 1993. 19.95 (*0-8447-3775-5*, AEI Pr) Am Enterprise.

Licht, Robert A., jt. ed. see Goldwin, Robert A.

Licht, Robert A., et al, eds. South Africa's Crisis of Constitutional Democracy: Can the U. S. Constitution Help? LC 93-43191. 274p. 1995. pap. 20.00 (*0-8447-3834-4*, AEI Pr) Am Enterprise.

Licht, Walter. Getting Work: Philadelphia, 1840-1950. 317p. 1992. text ed. 45.00x (*0-674-35428-1*) HUP.

— Industrializing America: The Nineteenth Century. (The American Moment Ser.). 224p. 1994. text ed. 38.95x (*0-8018-5013-4*); pap. text ed. 13.95 (*0-8018-5014-2*) Johns Hopkins.

— Working for the Railroad: The Organization of Work in the Nineteenth-Century. LC 82-61372. (Illus.). 352p. 1987. pap. text ed. 17.95x (*0-691-10221-X*) Princeton U Pr.

Lichtarovicz, A., ed. Jet Cutting Technology. LC 92-35068. (Fluid Mechanics & Its Applications Ser.: Vol. 13). 1992. lib. bdg. 286.00 (*0-7923-1979-6*) Kluwer Ac.

Lichtblau, Minna. Jewish Wit & Wisdom. 1992. 5.99 (*0-517-03764-5*) Random Hse Value.

Lichtblau, Myron. Rayuela y la Creatividad Artistica. LC 88-81377. (Coleccion Polymita Ser.). 92p. (Orig.). (SPA.). 1989. pap. 12.00 (*0-89729-491-2*) Ediciones.

Lichtblau, Myron I. Manuel Galvez. LC 71-169627. (Twayne's World Authors Ser.). 152p. (C). 1972. lib. bdg. 17.95 (*0-8290-1737-2*) Irvington.

Lichtblau, Myron I., ed. Eduardo Mallea ante la Critica. LC 84-81478. (Coleccion Polymita Ser.). 92p. (Orig.). (SPA.). 1985. pap. 10.00 (*0-89729-355-X*) Ediciones.

— La Emigracion y el Exilio en la Literatura Hispanica del Siglo Veinte. LC 87-81465. (Coleccion Polymita Ser.). 156p. (Orig.). (ENG & SPA.). 1988. pap. 19.00 (*0-89729-445-9*) Ediciones.

Lichtblau, Myron I., tr. see Mallea, Eduardo.

Lichte, Rainer. More Radio Receiver: Chance or Choice. LC 87-80675. 96p. 1987. pap. 12.95 (*0-914542-18-4*) Gilfer.

— Radio Receiver--Chance or Choice. Ferrell, Jeanne C., ed. LC 85-80383. 224p. (Orig.). 1985. pap. 18.50 (*0-914542-16-8*) Gilfer.

Lichten, Eric. Class, Power & Austerity: The New York City Fiscal Crisis. LC 85-22954. (Critical Studies in Work & Community). 272p. (Orig.). 1986. text ed. 55.00 (*0-89789-090-6*, Bergin & Garvey); pap. text ed. 16.95 (*0-89789-091-4*, Bergin & Garvey) Greenwood.

Lichten, Frances. Folk Art Motifs of Pennsylvania. LC 75-28849. (Pictorial Archive Ser.). (Illus.). 96p. 1976. reprint ed. pap. 6.95 (*0-486-23303-0*) Dover.

Lichten, Jan. Wyznania Niechrzescijanskie na Drugim Soborze Watykanskim. 24p. 1965. 2.50 (*0-940962-46-2*) Polish Inst Art & Sci.

Lichten, Joanne V. Dinin' Lean in Houston: A Restaurant Guide to Lower Fat - Lower Calorie Dining in the Houston Area. 348p. 1991. pap. 14.95 (*1-880347-56-3*) Nutrifit Cnslt.

Lichten, Joseph L., jt. auth. see Graham, Robert A.

Lichtenberg, A. J. & Lieberman, M. A. Regular & Chaotic Dynamics. 2nd ed. John, F. & Marsden, Jerrold E., eds. (Applied Mathematical Sciences Ser.: Vol. 38). Orig. Title: Regular & Stochastic Motion. (Illus.). 656p. 1992. 59.95 (*0-387-97745-7*) Spr-Verlag.

— Regular & Stochastic Motion. (Applied Mathematical Sciences Ser.: Vol. 38). (Illus.). 499p. 1989. 56.00 (*0-387-90707-6*) Spr-Verlag.

Lichtenberg, Allan J., jt. auth. see Lieberman, Michael A.

Lichtenberg, Betty K., jt. auth. see Troutman, Andrai P.

Lichtenberg, Betty K., jt. auth. see Troutman, Andria P.

Lichtenberg, D. B., ed. see Conference on the Present Status of Weak Interaction Physics, Indiana Univ., Bloomington, May 16-17, 1977.

Lichtenberg, Dierdre. Poems. (Illus.). 60p. (Orig.). pap. 5.00 (*0-9617811-0-6*) Chandrabala Pr.

***Lichtenberg, Fran, ed.** Polyurethanes Ninety Four: Proceedings of the SPI - 35th Annual Technical - Marketing Conference. LC 94-61290. 690p. 1994. pap. text ed. 155.00 (*1-56676-208-1*) Technomic.

Lichtenberg, Fran W., ed. CFCs & the Polyurethane Industry: A Compilation of Technical Publications, 1986-1988. LC 88-51497. 178p. 1988. pap. 35.00 (*0-87762-653-7*) Technomic.

— CFCs & the Polyurethane Industry, Vol. 2: A Compilation of Technical Publications, 1988-1989. LC 88-51497. 360p. 1989. pap. 55.00 (*0-87762-729-0*) Technomic.

— CFCs & the Polyurethane Industry, Vol. 3: A Compilation of Technical Publications, 1990. LC 88-51497. 328p. 1990. 55.00 (*0-87762-811-4*) Technomic.

— CFCs & the Polyurethane Industry, Vol. 4: A Compilation of Technical Publications, 1991. 425p. 1992. pap. 55.00 (*0-87762-928-5*) Technomic.

— CFCs & the Polyurethane Industry, Vol. 5: A Compilation of Technical Publications, 1992. (Illus.). 312p. 1993. pap. 65.00 (*1-56676-009-7*, 760097) Technomic.

Lichtenberg, G. C. Lichtenberg's Visits to England. Mare, Margaret L. & Quarrell, W. H., eds. LC 71-91906. 1972. 24.95 (*0-405-08747-0*, Pub. by Blom Pubns UK) Ayer.

Lichtenberg, Georg C. Aphorisms. 208p. 1990. pap. 7.95 (*0-14-044519-6*, Penguin Classics) Viking Penguin.

Lichtenberg, J., et al. Recycling of Activated - Contaminated Reinforcement Metal in Concrete. 90p. 1994. pap. 16.00 (*92-826-7383-9*, Pub. by Europ Com) UNIPUB.

Lichtenberg, James, et al, eds. Chemical & Biological Characterization of Municipal Sludges, Sediments, Dredge Spoils, & Drilling Muds. LC 88-3295. (Special Technical Publication Ser.: No. 976). (Illus.). 510p. 1988. text ed. 69.00 (*0-8031-0987-3*, 04-976000-16) ASTM.

Lichtenberg, Joseph. Psychoanalysis & Infant Research. (Psychoanalytic Inquiry Book Ser.: Vol. 2). 280p. (C). 1991. pap. 24.95 (*0-88163-002-0*) Analytic Pr.

Lichtenberg, Joseph D. Psychoanalysis & Motivation. (Psychoanalytic Inquiry Book Ser.: Vol. 10). 408p. 1989. text ed. 43.95 (*0-88163-084-5*) Analytic Pr.

— The Talking Cure: A Descriptive Guide to Psychoanalysis. (Psychoanalytic Inquiry Book Ser.). 166p. (C). 1994. reprint ed. pap. 22.50 (*0-88163-192-2*) Analytic Pr.

Lichtenberg, Joseph D. & Kaplan, Samuel, eds. Reflections on Self Psychology. (Psychoanalytic Inquiry Book Ser.: Vol. 1). 448p. 1983. text ed. 49.95 (*0-88163-001-2*) Analytic Pr.

Lichtenberg, Joseph D., et al. The Self & Motivational Systems: Toward a Theory of Psychoanalytic Technique. (Psychoanalytic Inquiry Book Ser.: Vol. 13). 248p. 1992. 39.95 (*0-88163-154-X*) Analytic Pr.

Lichtenberg, Joseph D., et al, eds. Empathy, 2 vols., Vol. 1. LC 84-2862. (Psychoanalytic Inquiry Book Ser.: No. 3). (Illus.). 372p. reprint ed. pap. 96.80 (*0-8357-4386-1*, 2037218) Bks Demand.

— Empathy, 2 vols., Vol. 2. LC 84-2862. (Psychoanalytic Inquiry Book Ser.: No. 3). (Illus.). 391p. reprint ed. pap. 111.50 (*0-8357-4387-X*) Bks Demand.

Lichtenberg, Judith. Foundations & Limits of Freedom of the Press. 1987. 1.50 (*0-318-33305-8*) IPPP.

— On Alternatives to Industrial Flight: The Moral Issues. Ezorsky, Gertrude, ed. 1987. 1.50 (*0-318-33306-6*) IPPP.

Lichtenberg, Judith, ed. Democracy & the Mass Media. (Cambridge Studies in Philosophy & Public Policy). 336p. (C). 1990. pap. 21.95 (*0-521-38817-1*) Cambridge U Pr.

— Democracy & the Mass Media. 1990. 44.50 (*0-317-05240-3*); pap. 14.95 (*0-317-05241-1*) IPPP.

Lichtenberg, Kara. A Research Guide to Human Sexuality. LC 93-37236. (Reference Library of Social Science: Vol. 836). 527p. 1994. 75.00 (*0-8153-0867-1*, SS836) Garland.

Lichtenberg, Marc L., jt. auth. see Tarlow, David M.

Lichtenberg, Peter A. A Guide to Psychological Practice in Geriatric Long-Term Care. LC 92-48389. (Illus.). 210p. 1994. lib. bdg. 39.95 (*1-56024-410-0*); pap. 19.95 (*1-56024-411-9*) Haworth Pr.

Lichtenberg, Philip. Getting Even: The Equalizing Law of Relationship. 120p. (Orig.). (C). 1988. lib. bdg. 31.50 (*0-8191-6774-6*) U Pr of Amer.

— Undoing the Clinch of Oppression. LC 89-48239. (American University Studies: Psychology: Ser. VIII, Vol. 21). 235p. (C). 1990. text ed. 52.95 (0-8204-1301-1) P Lang Pubs.

Lichtenberg, Robert M. The Role of Middleman Transactions in World Trade. (Occasional Papers: No. 64). 104p. 1959. reprint ed. 27.10 (0-87014-378-6); reprint ed. mic. film 20.00 (0-685-61320-8) Natl Bur Econ Res.

Lichtenberger, Andre. Socialisme Au Dix-Huitieme Siecle: Etudes Sur les Idees Socialistes Dans les Ecrivains Francais due XVIII Siecle Avant la Revolution. LC 67-27835. viii, 471p. 1967. reprint ed. 49.50 (0-678-00329-7) Kelley.

***Lichtenberger, E. & Pecsi, M., eds.** Contemporary Essays in Austrian & Hungarian Geography: Proceedings of the First Austro-Hungarian Geographical Seminar Vienna, 17-19 November, 1986. (Studies in Geography in Hungary: No. 22). 264p. (C). 1988. 84.00x (963-05-4946-8, Pub. by Akad Kiado HU) St Mut.

Lichtenberger, E., jt. ed. see Heinritz, Gunter.

Lichtenberger, Elisabeth. Vienna: A Bridge Between Cultures. Muhlgassner, Dietlinde & Reisser, Craig, trs. LC 93-7361. (World Cities Ser.). 212p. 1993. text ed. 49.95 (0-470-22008-2, Belhaven) Halsted Pr.

— Vienna: Bridge Between Cultures. (World Cities Ser.). 1993. text ed. 59.95 (0-471-94705-9) Wiley.

Lichtenberger, F., jt. auth. see Kutzler, B.

Lichtenberger, Henri. Germany & Its Evolution in Modern Times. Ludovici, A. M., tr. 1977. lib. bdg. 59.95 (0-8490-1887-0) Gordon Pr.

— Third Reich. Pinson, Koppel S., tr. LC 73-102249. (Select Bibliographies Reprint Ser.). 1977. 35.95 (0-8369-5134-4) Ayer.

Lichtenberger, J. P. Divorce: A Social Interpretation. LC 70-169392. (Family in America Ser.). 488p. 1979. reprint ed. 28.95 (0-405-03869-0) Ayer.

Lichtenberger, James P. Divorce: A Study in Social Causation. LC 72-76685. (Columbia University. Studies in the Social Sciences: No. 94). reprint ed. 18.50 (0-404-51094-9) AMS Pr.

Lichtenberger, John. Advertising Compliance Law: Handbook for Marketing Professionals & Their Counsel. LC 85-31248. 224p. 1986. text ed. 59.95 (0-89930-122-3, LAD/, Quorum Bks) Greenwood.

Lichtenberk, Frantisek. A Grammar of Manam. LC 81-11362. (Oceanic Linguistics Special Publications: No. 18). 670p. 1984. pap. text ed. 25.00 (0-8248-0764-2) UH Pr.

Lichtenegger, E., jt. auth. see Kutschera, L.

Lichtenegger, H., jt. auth. see Hofmann-Wellenhof, B.

Lichtenstadter, Ilse. Islam & the Modern Age. 228p. 1958. text ed. 29.00 (0-8290-0179-4) Irvington.

Lichtensteiger, W., jt. ed. see Schlumpf, M.

***Lichtenstein.** Twice the Work of Free Labor: The Political Economy of Convict Labor in the New South. 240p. 1995. 64.95x (1-85984-991-1, C0513, Pub. by Verso UK); pap. 18.95 (1-85984-086-8, C0514, Pub. by Verso UK) Routledge Chapman & Hall.

Lichtenstein & Fauci. Current Therapy in Allergy, Immunology & Rheumatology. 4th ed. 391p. 1991. 75.00 (1-55664-329-2) Mosby Yr Bk.

Lichtenstein, Alexander C. & Kroll, Michael A. The Fortress Economy: The Economic Role of the U. S. Prison System. Kamel, Rachael, ed. 1990. pap. 2.00 (0-910082-16-2) Am Fr Serv Comm.

Lichtenstein, Beverly, jt. auth. see Hanlin, Jayne.

Lichtenstein, Diane. Writing Their Nations: The Tradition of Nineteenth-Century American Jewish Women Writers. LC 91-47015. 192p. 1992. 24.95 (0-253-33346-6) Ind U Pr.

Lichtenstein, E. A. Labour Law. 200p. (C). 1991. pap. 85.00 (1-85352-564-2, Pub. by HLT Pubns UK) St Mut.

Lichtenstein, E. A. & Read, P. A., eds. Contract Law. 330p. (C). 1991. 60.00 (1-85352-694-0, Pub. by HLT Pubns UK); pap. 60.00 (1-85352-832-3, Pub. by HLT Pubns UK) St Mut.

Lichtenstein, Heinz. The Dilemma of Human Identity. LC 84-45086. 416p. 1983. 40.00 (0-87668-677-3) Aronson.

Lichtenstein, Irving L. Hernia Repair Without Disability. 2nd ed. (Illus.). 268p. 1986. text ed. 90.00 (0-912791-30-6) Ishiyaku Euro.

Lichtenstein, Jack. Field to Fabric: The Story of American Cotton Growers. 350p. 1990. 19.95 (0-89672-238-4) Tex Tech Univ Pr.

Lichtenstein, Jacqueline. The Eloquence of Color: Rhetoric & Painting in the French Classical Age. McVarish, Emily, tr. (New Historicism: Studies in Cultural Poetics: No. 18). (C). 1992. 45.00 (0-520-06907-2) U CA Pr.

Lichtenstein, Judy. Dinosaur Cowboys Puppet Theatre. (J). (ps-3). 1994. 10.95 (1-55550-882-0) Universe.

Lichtenstein, L. M., ed. see Collegium Internationale Allergologicum Symposium Staff.

Lichtenstein, Michael H., jt. auth. see Patitucci, Frank M.

Lichtenstein, Michael J. Vitamin Deficiencies: Index of Modern Information with Bibliography. LC 88-47794. 150p. 1988. 44.50 (0-88164-888-4); pap. 39.50 (0-88164-889-2) ABBE Pubs Assn.

Lichtenstein, Nelson. Labor's War at Home: The CIO in World War II. LC 82-4349. 304p. 1983. 54.95 (0-521-23472-7) Cambridge U Pr.

— Labor's War at Home: The CIO in World War II. LC 82-4349. 304p. 1987. pap. 17.95 (0-521-33573-6) Cambridge U Pr.

Lichtenstein, Nelson, ed. Political Profiles, Vol. 4. LC 76-20897. 765p. reprint ed. pap. 180.00 (0-7837-6489-8, 2045089) Bks Demand.

Lichtenstein, Nelson & Harris, Howell J., eds. Industrial Democracy in America: The Ambiguous Promise. LC 92-28462. (Woodrow Wilson Center Ser.). 400p. (C). 1993. 49.95 (0-521-43121-2) Cambridge U Pr.

Lichtenstein, Nelson & Meyer, Stephen, eds. On the Line: Essays in the History of Auto Work. (Working Class in American History Ser.). (Illus.). 280p. 1989. 32.50 (0-252-01539-8); pap. 12.95 (0-252-06015-6) U of Ill Pr.

Lichtenstein, Nelson & Schoenebaum, Eleanora W., eds. Political Profiles, Vol. 3: The Kennedy Years. LC 76-20897. 647p. reprint ed. pap. 180.00 (0-7837-5346-2, 2045089) Bks Demand.

Lichtenstein, Nelson, jt. ed. see Boris, Eileen.

Lichtenstein, Peter M. China at the Brink: The Political Economy of Reform & Retrenchment in the Post-Mao Era. LC 91-9594. 176p. 1991. text ed. 45.00 (0-275-94052-7, C4052, Praeger Pubs) Greenwood.

Lichtenstein, Robert, tr. The Nibelungenlied. LC 91-44798. (Studies in German Language & Literature: Vol. 9). 260p. 1992. lib. bdg. 89.95 (0-7734-9470-7) E Mellen.

Lichtenstein, Robert, tr. see Koenig Rother.

Lichtenstein, Roy & Hendra, Tony. Brad '61: Portrait of the Artist as a Young Man. LC 93-5614. (Illus.). 96p. 1993. 21.00 (0-679-43097-0) Pantheon.

Lichtenthaler, Hartmut L., ed. Applications of Chlorophyll Fluorescence: In Photosynthesis Research, Stress Physiology, Hydrobiology & Remote Sensing. (C). 1988. lib. bdg. 122.00 (90-247-3787-7) Kluwer Ac.

Lichtenthaler, W., ed. Carbohydrates As Organic Raw Materials. (Illus.). 370p. 1991. lib. bdg. 125.00 (1-56081-131-5) VCH Pubs.

Lichtenwanger, William. The Music of Henry Cowell: A Descriptive Catalog. LC 86-81843. (I.S.A.M. Monographs: No. 23). 414p. (Orig.). 1987. pap. 18.00 (0-914678-26-4) Inst Am Music.

Lichtenwanger, William, ed. Oscar Sonneck & American Music. LC 82-13670. (Music in American Life Ser.). 304p. 1983. 29.95 (0-252-01021-3) U of Ill Pr.

Lichter, jt. auth. see Dybowski.

Lichter, Carolyn, jt. auth. see Levine, Bobbie.

Lichter, Gerhard. Fossil Collector's Handbook: Finding, Identifying, Preparing, Displaying. Reinersmann, Elisabeth E., tr. LC 93-24783. (Illus.). 160p. 1993. pap. 14.95 (0-8069-0350-3) Sterling.

Lichter, Ivan. Communication in Cancer Care. LC 86-20764. (Illus.). 209p. 1987. text ed. 60.00 (0-443-03698-5) Churchill.

***Lichter, Michael.** Sturgis: Harleys in the Hills. (Postcard Books of Photos on Biker Lifestyle Ser.). (Illus.). 48p. 1995. pap. 8.95 (1-887228-07-1) Rogue Press.

Lichter, Paul. Elvis - Behind Closed Doors. 135p. 1987. 45.00 (0-9616027-4-0) Jesse Bks.

— Elvis Magic Moments. 176p. 1994. 65.00 (0-9616027-7-5) Jesse Bks.

— Elvis-Memories: A Love Story. limited ed. 320p. 1985. 65.00 (0-9616027-2-4) Jesse Bks.

— Elvis Rebel Heart. (Illus.). 200p. 1992. 65.00 (0-9616027-6-7) Jesse Bks.

Lichter, S. Robert, jt. auth. see Sabato, Larry J.

Lichter, S. Robert, et al. The Media Elite: America's New Power Brokers. 1990. pap. 12.95 (0-8038-9350-7) Hastings.

— Prime Time: How TV Portrays American Culture. 336p. 1993. 22.95 (0-89526-491-9) Regnery Pub.

Lichter, Sigmund. Man: The Sensual Male. (Orig.). 1970. pap. 1.50 (0-87067-412-9, BH412) Holloway.

Lichtgarn, Peter. The Corporate Communicator's Quick Reference. LC 92-42083. 192p. 1993. text ed. 20.00 (1-55623-892-4) Irwin Prof Pubng.

Lichtheim, George. Marxism: A Historical & Critical Study. rev. ed. 432p. 1964. pap. 13.95 (0-7100-4645-6, RKP) Routledge.

— Marxism: An Historical & Critical Study. LC 81-17066. 424p. 1982. reprint ed. pap. text ed. 18.50 (0-231-05425-4) Col U Pr.

— Marxism in Modern France. LC 66-14788. 1968. pap. text ed. 17.50 (0-231-08584-2) Col U Pr.

— Thoughts among the Ruins: Collected Essays on Europe & Beyond. 524p. 1986. reprint ed. pap. 39.95 (0-88738-657-1) Transaction Pubs.

Lichtheim, Miriam. Ancient Egyptian Literature: A Book of Readings, Vol. 3: The Late Period. LC 75-189225. (Near Eastern Center Series, UCLA: No. 12). 248p. 1980. 45.00 (0-520-03882-7); pap. 13.00 (0-520-04020-1) U CA Pr.

— Ancient Egyptian Literature, a Book of Readings, Vol. 1: The Old & the Middle Kingdoms. LC 75-189225. (Near Eastern Center Series, UCLA: No. 12). 1973. pap. 13.00 (0-520-02899-6) U CA Pr.

— Ancient Egyptian Literature: A Book of Readings, Vol. 2: The New Kingdom. LC 75-189225. (Near Eastern Center Series, UCLA: No. 12). 1976. pap. 13.00 (0-520-03615-8) U CA Pr.

Lichti, Wayne P. Introduction to Micro Processor-Controller Design. (Illus.). 170p. (Orig.). 1991. pap. text ed. 18.95 (0-9629672-0-3) Lassen Tech Pr.

Lichtlen, P. R. & Krayenbuhl, H. P., eds. New Aspects on Nisoldipine. 1990. pap. text ed. 43.00 (0-471-56082-0) Wiley.

Lichtlen, P. R. & Reale, A., eds. Adalat: A Comprehensive Review. (Illus.). 248p. 1991. 51.00 (0-387-54033-4) Spr-Verlag.

Lichtlen, P. R., jt. ed. see Engel, H. J.

Lichtman, Allan J. Prejudice & the Old Politics: The Presidential Election of 1928. LC 78-26813. 380p. reprint ed. pap. 108.30 (0-7837-0302-3, 2040624) Bks Demand.

Lichtman, Allan J. & Challinor, Joan R. Kin & Communities: Families in America. LC 78-24246. (International Symposia Ser.). (Illus.). 336p. 1979. text ed. 32.50 (0-87474-608-6, LIKC); pap. text ed. 17.95 (0-87474-609-4, LIKCP) Smithsonian.

Lichtman, Allan J. & DeCell, Ken. The Thirteen Keys to the Presidency. 464p. 1992. pap. 14.95 (0-8191-8751-8) Madison Bks UPA.

— Thirteen Keys to Winning the Presidency: A Radically New System for Determining the Winners & Losers of American Presidential Elections. 456p. 1990. pap. 24.95 (0-8191-7008-9) Madison Bks UPA.

Lichtman, Allan J. & French, Valerie. Historians & the Living Past: The Theory & Practice of Historical Study. LC 77-86035. (C). 1978. reprint ed. pap. text ed. write for info. (0-88295-773-2) Harlan Davidson.

Lichtman, Allan J., jt. auth. see Langbein, Laura I.

Lichtman, Brenda. Innovative Games. LC 93-20454. (Illus.). 144p. 1993. pap. 16.00x (0-87322-488-4, BLIC0488) Human Kinetics.

Lichtman, David M. The Wrist & Its Disorders. (Illus.). 496p. 1988. text ed. 145.00 (0-03-011842-5) Saunders.

Lichtman, Jeff W., jt. auth. see Purves, Dale.

Lichtman, Marilyn, jt. auth. see Gerstein, Martin.

Lichtman, Richard. Essays in Critical Social Theory: Toward a Marxist Critique of Liberal Ideology. LC 92-24510. (New Directions in Philosophy Ser.: Vol. 1). 308p. (C). 1994. pap. text ed. 29.95 (0-8204-1521-9) P Lang Pubs.

— The Production of Desire: The Integration of Psychoanalysis into Marxist Theory. 317p. 1986. pap. 16.95 (0-02-919080-0) Free Pr.

Lichtman, Robert J. Biogas Systems in India. 130p. 1990. 19.25 (0-86619-167-4) Vols Tech Asst.

Lichtman, Ronnie & Papera, Susan. Gynecology: Well-Woman Care. (Illus.). 608p. 1989. boxed 80.00 (0-8385-9682-7, A9682-4) Appleton & Lange.

Lichtman, Susan A. Life Stages of Woman's Heroic Journey: A Study of the Origins of the Great Goddess Archetype. LC 91-31494. 112p. 1991. lib. bdg. 59.95 (0-7734-9699-8) E Mellen.

Lichtman, Wendy. Blew & the Death of the Mag. (Illus.). 74p. (J). (gr. 3-9). 1975. 5.00 (0-913512-53-2) Freestone Pub Co.

Lichtmann, Maria R. The Contemplative Poetry of Gerard Manly Hopkins. 256p. 1989. text ed. 37.50 (0-691-07345-7) Princeton U Pr.

Lichtner-Hoyer, Peter. Complete Cavaletti: Basic to Advanced Training of Horse & Rider. 128p. 1992. 22.50 (0-914327-40-2) Breakthrgh NY.

Lichtner, Schomer. Alphabet Drawings. (Illus.). 88p. (Orig.). (J). (gr. k up). 1973. pap. 4.50 (0-686-97176-0) Lichtner.

— Ballerina's Holiday. (Illus.). 76p. (Orig.). (J). (gr. 5 up). 1979. pap. 4.95 (0-941074-04-8) Lichtner.

— Drawings from the Nude. (Illus.). 156p. 1974. bds. 12.00 (0-941074-03-X) Lichtner.

— The Fan, Ballet & Other Drawings. LC 81-81113. (Illus.). 56p. (Orig.). 1981. pap. 4.95 (0-941074-05-6) Lichtner.

— Schomer Lichtner Drawings. (Illus.). 72p. (Orig.). 1964. pap. 5.00 (0-941074-00-5) Lichtner.

— Spotted Cow. LC 81-81117. (Illus.). 48p. (Orig.). 1969. pap. 4.50 (0-941074-01-3) Lichtner.

Lichtveld, Noni. I Lost My Arrow in a Kan Kan Tree. LC 92-56102. (J). 1993. write for info. (0-688-12748-7) Lothrop.

Lichtwardt, R. W. The Trichomycetes. (Illus.). 410p. 1986. 129.00 (0-387-96237-9) Spr-Verlag.

Lichty, Bob. Standard Catalog of Ford 1903-1990. LC 90-60574. (Standard Catalog of American Cars Ser.). (Illus.). 480p. (Orig.). 1990. pap. 19.95 (0-87341-140-4, AF01) Krause Pubns.

Lichty, Lawrence W., jt. auth. see Webster, James G.

Lichty, Robert. Collecting & Restoring Antique Fire Engines. (Illus.). 224p. 1981. pap. 9.95 (0-8306-2099-0) TAB Bks.

Lichty, Ron, jt. auth. see Eyes, David.

***Lichty, Tom.** America Online for Windows 95 Membership Kit & Tour Guide. 3rd ed. 600p. 1995. disk 27.95 (1-56604-253-4) Ventana Pr.

— America Online for Windows 95 Tour Guide. 3rd ed. 600p. 1995. 19.95 (1-56604-252-6) Ventana Pr.

— America Online's Internet: Easy, Graphical Access - the AOL Way - Macintosh Edition. 1994. Incl. diskette. disk, pap. 24.95 (1-56604-175-9) Ventana Pr.

— America Online's Internet for Windows: Easy, Graphical Access - the AOL Way. 1994. Incl. diskette. disk, pap. 24.95 (1-56604-176-7) Ventana Pr.

— Design Principles for Desktop Publishers. 2nd ed. 226p. 1994. pap. 19.95 (0-534-23082-2) Intl Thomson.

— Desktop Publishing with Word for Windows. 2nd ed. (Illus.). 352p. 1994. pap. 21.95 (1-56604-074-4) Ventana Pr.

— Mac Word & Excel Desktop Companion. 2nd ed. 1994. pap. 21.95 (1-56604-130-9) Ventana Pr.

— Mac, Word & Excel Desktop Companion: The Three-in-One Guide to the Hottest Mac Software. (Illus.). 370p. 1993. pap. 21.95 (1-56604-065-5) Ventana Pr.

— Official America Online for Macintosh Membership Kit: Tour Guide, Set. 2nd ed. (Illus.). 360p. 1994. disk, pap. 27.95 (1-56604-127-9) Ventana Pr.

— Official America Online for Windows Membership Kit: Tour Guide. 2nd ed. (Illus.). 402p. 1994. pap. 27.95 (1-56604-128-7) Ventana Pr.

— Official America Online for Windows Membership Kit & Tour Guide. (Illus.). 390p. pap. 34.95 (1-56604-013-2) Ventana Pr.

— Official America Online Membership Kit & Tour Guide: Macintosh Edition. (Illus.). 390p. (Orig.). (C). pap. 34.95 (1-56604-012-4) Ventana Pr.

— Visual Guide to Visual Basic for Applications. (Illus.). 400p. 1994. pap. 27.95 (1-56604-147-3) Ventana Pr.

Lichty, Tom & Parks, Kathy. Official America Online Membership Kit & Tour Guide: PC Edition. (Illus.). 390p. (C). pap. 34.95 (1-56604-025-6) Ventana Pr.

Lichy, Wolfgang. Besteuerung und Innenfinanzierung. (C). 1967. 67.70 (3-11-000911-0) De Gruyter.

Lick, Carol J. & Peterson, Pam. Theoretical Time, The Industrial Renaissance. 135p. (C). 1990. 23.50 (0-9622176-6-2) Air Acad Pr.

Lick, D. R. & Liu, J. Q. Graph Theory, Combinatorics, Algorithms & Applications. 500p. 1994. text ed. 109.00 (981-02-1855-9) World Scientific Pub.

Lick, Sue. The Iberian Americans. (Peoples of North America Ser.). (Illus.). 112p. (J). (gr. 5 up). 1990. 17.95 (0-87754-896-X) Chelsea Hse.

Licka, C. E., jt. auth. see Higby, Wayne.

Lickbarrow, Isabella. Poetical Effusions. LC 93-46504. 1994. 48.00 (1-85477-167-1, Pub. by Woodstock Bks UK) Cassell.

Lickei, Elizabeth, ed. see Rowe, Frank.

Licker, Paul S. The Art of Managing Software Development People. LC 84-25619. 280p. reprint ed. pap. 79.80 (0-7837-2815-8, 2057657) Bks Demand.

Lickey, Marvin E. & Gordon, Barbara. Medicine & Mental Illness. Orig. Title: Drugs for Mental Illness. (C). 1995. pap. text ed. 20.95 (0-7167-2196-1) W H Freeman.

Licklider, Patricia. At Your Command: A Basic English Workbook. 2nd ed. (C). 1987. pap. text ed. 24.00 (0-673-39276-7) HarpCollege.

Licklider, Roy, ed. Stopping the Killing: How Civil Wars End. (Illus.). 354p. (C). 1995. text ed. 50.00 (0-8147-5070-2) NYU Pr.

— Stopping the Killing: How Civil Wars End. (Illus.). 354p. 1995. pap. 18.95 (0-8147-5097-4) NYU Pr.

Lickliter, Robert, jt. ed. see Lewkowicz, David J.

Lickliter, Robert E., jt. auth. see Salmon, Terrell P.

Lickona, Thomas. Educating for Character: How Our Schools Can Teach Respect & Responsibility. 1992. pap. 12.95 (0-553-37052-9) Bantam.

— Raising Good Children. (Orig.). 1994. pap. 12.95 (0-553-37429-X) Bantam.

Lickona, Thomas, jt. ed. see Ryan, Kevin.

Lickona, Tom, et al. Sex, Love & You: Making the Right Decision. LC 94-71887. 192p. (Orig.). (YA). (gr. 9-12). 1994. pap. 6.95 (0-87793-540-8) Ave Maria.

Lickorish, John R., jt. auth. see Howells, John G.

***Lickorish, Leonard & Jenkins, Kit.** An Introduction to Tourism. 240p. 1995. pap. 24.95 (0-7506-1956-2) Buttrwrth-Heinemann.

Lickson, Charles. Ethics for Government Employees. Gerould, Philip, ed. LC 92-75718. (Fifty-Minute Ser.). 120p. (Orig.). 1993. pap. text ed. 9.95 (1-56052-208-9) Crisp Pubns.

***Lickson, Charles P.** A Legal Guide for Small Business: How to Do It Right the First Time. Manber, Beverly, ed. LC 93-72970. (Crisp Small Business & Entrepreneurship Ser.). 210p. (Orig.). 1994. pap. 15.95 (1-56052-266-6) Crisp Pubns.

Lickson, Jeffrey E. Continuously Improving Self. Crisp, Michael G., ed. LC 91-77764. (Fifty-Minute Ser.). (Illus.). 100p. (Orig.). 1992. pap. 9.95 (1-56052-151-1) Crisp Pubns.

Lico, Laurie E. Resumes for Executive Women. 128p. (Orig.). 1984. pap. 7.95 (0-671-49758-8) S&S Trade.

Licten, Danny. Quarterly Selections. Thomas, Joyce & Souter, Irene, eds. LC 83-73466. 1983. 5.00 (0-916183-00-9) Cal Poet.

Lid, J. Norwegian-Swedish-Finnish Flora: Norsk-Svensk-Finsk Flora. 837p. (FIN, NOR & SWE.). 1985. 195.00 (0-8288-1248-9, F22443) Fr & Eur.

***Lidberg, Paul, et al.** Steam Age. (Castle Falkenstein Ser.). (Illus.). 104p. (Orig.). 1995. pap. 14.00 (0-937279-56-0, CF6021) R Talsorian.

Lidbetter, Ernest J. Heredity & the Social Problem Group. 1977. lib. bdg. 59.95 (0-8490-1944-3) Gordon Pr.

Lidbetter, H. Martin. Friends Ambulance Unit. 1993. 24.00 (1-85072-128-9, Pub. by W Sessions UK) St Mut.

Lidbetter, Hubert. The Friends Meeting House: Historical Survey of Friends' Places of Worship from the Beginning of Quakerism Including Plans & Photographs. (C). 1989. pap. 21.00 (0-900657-50-2, Pub. by W Sessions UK) St Mut.

Liddament, M. Building Air Tightness & Ventilation: An Overview of International Practice. 1986. 60.00 (0-86022-143-1, Pub. by Build Servs Info Assn UK) St Mut.

Liddell & Cathcart. Being Big. (NFS Canada). (J). (ps-3). 1994. pap. 5.95 (0-929005-60-0, Pub. by Second Story Pr CN) InBook.

— Being Big. (NFS Canada). (J). (ps-3). 1995. 12.95 (0-929005-62-7, Pub. by Second Story Pr CN) InBook.

Liddell, Alex. Port & the Quintas of the Douro. (Illus.). 280p. 1992. 39.95 (0-85667-410-9) Sothebys Pubns.

Liddell, Andree, ed. The Practice of Clinical Psychology in Great Britain. LC 82-20030. 277p. reprint ed. pap. 79.00 (0-7837-3219-8, 2043237) Bks Demand.

Liddell, Eric. Manual de Discipulado Cristiano (The Disciplines of the Christian Life) 160p. (Orig.). (SPA.). 1992. pap. 4.95 (84-7645-572-0, 223667, Pub. by Edit Clie SP) TSELF.

Liddell, F. D. & Miller, Klara. Mineral Fibers & Health. (Illus.). 376p. 1991. 213.00 (0-8493-6646-1, RC1231) CRC Pr.

Liddell, Felix H., ed. I Hear a Symphony: African Americans Celebrate Love. LC 94-6742. 1994. 27.95 (0-385-47502-0, Anchor NY) Doubleday.

***Liddell, Grant.** The Privacy Act. 200p. 1995. pap. 65.00 (0-19-558313-2) OUP.

***Liddell, H. G. & Scott, R.** A Greek-English Lexicon. 9th rev. suppl. ed. Glare, P. G., ed. 2378p. 1995. text ed. 125.00 (0-19-864226-1) OUP.

Liddell-Hart, B. A Greater Than Napoleon, Scipio Africanus. LC 75-156735. 281p. 1927. 24.00 (0-8196-0269-8) Biblo.

Liddell Hart, B. H. The German Generals Talk. 1971. pap. 9.25 (0-688-06012-9, Quill) Morrow.

— The Remaking of Modern Armies. 1980. lib. bdg. 64.95 (0-8490-3189-3) Gordon Pr.

— Scipio Africanus: Greater Than Napoleon. 288p. 1992. 37.50 (1-85367-132-0) Stackpole.

An Asterisk (*) at the beginning of an entry indicates that the title is appearing in BIP for the first time.

Liddell-Hart, B. H. Tanks: The History of the Royal Tank Regiment & Its Predecessors, 1914-1915, 2 vols., Set. reprint ed. 49.95 (*0-89201-079-7*) Zenger Pub.

Liddell-Hart, B. H., intro. The Rommel Papers. (Quality Paperbacks Ser.). (Illus.). xxx, 544p. 1982. reprint ed. pap. 14.95 (*0-306-80157-4*) Da Capo.

Liddell Hart, Basil H. The Defence of Britain. LC 79-23041. 444p. 1980. reprint ed. text ed. 65.00 (*0-313-22175-8*, LHDB, Greenwood Pr) Greenwood.

— Foch, the Man of Orleans. LC 79-22870. (Illus.). 480p. 1980. reprint ed. text ed. 85.00 (*0-313-22171-5*, LHFO, Greenwood Pr) Greenwood.

— The Ghost of Napoleon. LC 79-23039. 199p. 1980. reprint ed. text ed. 35.00 (*0-313-22172-3*, LHGN, Greenwood Pr) Greenwood.

— Great Captains Unveiled. LC 67-23240. (Essay Index Reprint Ser.). 1977. 23.95 (*0-8369-0618-7*) Ayer.

— The Real War, Nineteen Fourteen to Nineteen Eighteen. 1963. pap. 15.95 (*0-316-52505-7*) Little.

— Reputations Ten Years After. LC 68-8478. (Essay Index Reprint Ser.). (Illus.). 1977. reprint ed. 23.95 (*0-8369-0619-5*) Ayer.

— The Revolution in Warfare. LC 79-22632. 125p. 1980. reprint ed. text ed. 38.50 (*0-313-22173-1*, LHRW, Greenwood Pr) Greenwood.

— Sherman: Soldier, Realist, American. (Illus.). 480p. 1993. reprint ed. pap. 15.95 (*0-306-80507-3*) Da Capo.

— Sherman: Soldier, Realist, American. LC 78-536. 456p. 1978. reprint ed. text ed. 52.50 (*0-313-20288-5*, LHSH, Greenwood Pr) Greenwood.

— Strategy. 2nd rev. ed. (Illus.). 432p. 1991. pap. 13.95 (*0-452-01071-3*, Mer) NAL-Dutton.

— T. E. Lawrence: In Arabia & After. LC 71-109768. (Illus.). 491p. 1979. reprint ed. text ed. 35.00 (*0-8371-4258-X*, LITL, Greenwood Pr) Greenwood.

Liddell, Henry G. & Scott, Robert, comps. Intermediate Greek-English Lexicon. (ENG & GRE.). 1945. text ed. 35.00 (*0-19-910206-6*) OUP.

Liddell, Henry G. & Scott, Robert, eds. Abridged Greek-English Lexicon. (ENG & GRE.). 1935. 29.95 (*0-19-910207-4*) OUP.

— Greek-English Lexicon. 9th ed. (ENG & GRE.). 1968. reprint ed. 135.00 (*0-19-864214-8*) OUP.

Liddell, J. E. & Weeks, I. Antibody Technology: A Comprehensive Overview. (Introduction to Biotechniques Ser.). 160p. (Orig.). 1995. pap. 42.50x (*1-872748-87-2*, Pub. by Bios Scientific UK) Coronet Bks.

Liddell, J. Eryl & Cryer, A. A Practical Guide to Monoclonal Antibodies. 1991. pap. text ed. 54.95 (*0-471-92905-0*) Wiley.

Liddell, Janice. Imani & the Flying Africans. (Illus.). 32p. (J). (gr. 3-8). 1993. 14.95 (*0-86543-365-8*); pap. 6.95 (*0-86543-366-6*) Africa World.

Liddell, Jill. The Patchwork Pilgrimage: How to Create Vibrant Church Decorations & Vestments with Quilting Techniques. (Illus.). 160p. 1993. 35.00 (*0-525-93689-0*, Viking Studio); pap. 25.00 (*0-525-48615-1*, Viking Studio) Studio Bks.

Liddell, Jill & Watanabe, Yuko. Japanese Quilts. (Illus.). 112p. 1988. pap. 24.95 (*0-525-48386-1*, Dutton) NAL-Dutton.

Liddell, Jill, jt. auth. see Patchwork Quilt Tsushin Staff.

***Liddell, K. C., et al, eds.** Metals & Materials: Waste Reduction, Recovery & Remediation; Proceedings of the Symposium Organized by the Reactive Metals Committee of the Light Metals Division of TMS, Rosemont, IL, 1994. LC 94-78463. 235p. 1995. 68.00 (*0-87339-244-2*) Minerals Metals.

— Refractory Metals: Extraction, Processing & Applications. (Illus.). 530p. 1991. 140.00 (*0-87339-159-4*, 399) Minerals Metals.

Liddell, Louise A. Building Life Skills. LC 93-26390. (Home Economics Ser.). (Illus.). 575p. 1994. 38.60 (*0-87006-094-5*) Goodheart.

— Clothes & Your Appearance. rev. ed. (Illus.). 496p. 1991. text ed. 39.96 (*0-87006-844-X*) Goodheart.

Liddell, Robert. The Aunts. LC 87-60977. (Illus.). 192p. 1987. 21.00 (*0-7206-0665-9*, Pub. by P Owen Ltd UK) Dufour.

— The Deep End: A Novel. 187p. 1994. 28.00 (*0-7206-0903-8*, Pub. by P Owen Ltd UK) Dufour.

— Elizabeth & Ivy. LC 86-82059. 126p. 1986. 26.00 (*0-7206-0644-6*, Pub. by P Owen Ltd UK) Dufour.

— Kind Relations: A Novel. 285p. 1994. 30.00 (*0-7206-0947-X*, Pub. by P Owen Ltd UK) Dufour.

— The Last Enchantments. 221p. 1991. 29.00 (*0-7206-0816-3*, Pub. by P Owen Ltd UK) Dufour.

— Mind at Ease: Barbara Pym & Her Novels. 144p. 1989. 29.00 (*0-7206-0731-0*, Pub. by P Owen Ltd UK) Dufour.

— Some Principles of Fiction. LC 73-433. 162p. 1974. reprint ed. lib. bdg. 9.50 (*0-8371-6764-7*, LIPF, Greenwood Pr) Greenwood.

— Stepsons. 228p. 1992. 32.00 (*0-7206-0853-8*, Pub. by P Owen Ltd UK) Dufour.

— A Treatise on the Novel. LC 83-45913. reprint ed. 21.00 (*0-404-20160-1*) AMS Pr.

— Twin Spirits: The Novels of Emily & Anne Bronte. LC 90-80795. 144p. 1990. 32.00 (*0-7206-0776-0*, Pub. by P Owen Ltd UK) Dufour.

— Unreal City. 238p. 1993. reprint ed. 30.00 (*0-7206-0884-8*, Pub. by P Owen Ltd UK) Dufour.

Liddell, Robert, tr. see Fabre, Ferdinand.

***Liddell, Scott.** Racing with the World: How States Can Build a 21st Century Workforce. 37p. 1994. 20.00 (*1-55516-807-8*, 3912) Natl Conf State Legis.

Liddell, Scott, jt. auth. see Shreve, David.

Liddell, Scott K. American Sign Language Syntax. (Approaches to Semiotics Ser.: No. 52). 194p. 1980. 50.00 (*90-279-3437-1*) Mouton.

Liddell, Viola G. A Place of Springs. 192p. 1982. pap. 14.50 (*0-8173-0121-6*) U of Ala Pr.

— With a Southern Accent. LC 82-10893. (Library of Alabama Classics). 272p. 1982. pap. 14.95 (*0-8173-0130-5*) U of Ala Pr.

***Liddell, W. E. & Howard, M.** The Pickingill Papers. Date not set. pap. 21.95 (*1-898307-10-5*, Pub. by Capall Bann Pubng UK) Holmes Pub.

Liddelow, Lorelei. Cook with Me. 126p. (Orig.). (J). (gr. k-3). 1989. pap. 11.95 (*0-920541-95-X*) Peguis Pubs Ltd.

— Fly with Me. (Illus.). 101p. (Orig.). (gr. k-3). 1989. teacher ed, pap. 11.95 (*0-920541-93-3*) Peguis Pubs Ltd.

— Talk with Me. (Illus.). 101p. (Orig.). (J). (gr. k-3). 1984. pap. 11.95 (*0-920541-97-6*) Peguis Pubs Ltd.

Liddendale, David W. The Parliament of France. LC 79-1633. 1980. reprint ed. 26.00 (*0-88355-937-4*) Hyperion Conn.

Liddiard, Jean, jt. auth. see Condell, Diana.

Liddiard, Penny, jt. ed. see Carver, Vida.

Liddiard, Roberta G. Ride the Morning Winds. LC 84-27354. 97p. (Orig.). 1985. pap. 5.95 (*0-933380-29-1*) Olive Pr Pubns.

Liddicoat, Anthony. A Grammar of the Norman French of the Channel Islands: The Dialects of Jersey & Sark. LC 93-40684. (Grammar Library: No. 13). xii, 452p. (C). 1994. lib. bdg. 221.55 (*3-11-012631-1*) Mouton.

Liddicoat, Richard T., Jr. Handbook of Gem Identification. 12th ed. (Illus.). 1987. 39.95 (*0-87311-012-9*) Gemological.

Liddil, Bob. Apothecary on the Street of Dreams: Little Shop of Poisons & Potions Two. (Illus.). (Orig.). pap. 12.00 (*0-926895-00-1*) B Liddil.

Liddington, Jill. The Road to Greenham Common: Feminism & Anti-Militarism in Britain Since 1820. (Syracuse Studies on Peace & Conflict Resolution). (Illus.). 360p. (C). 1991. reprint ed. text ed. 39.95x (*0-8156-2539-1*); reprint ed. pap. text ed. 14.95 (*0-8156-2540-5*) Syracuse U Pr.

Liddle, Ann, tr. see Cixous, Helen.

Liddle, Barry, comp. Dictionary of Sports Quotations. 1987. 24.95 (*0-7102-0785-9*, RKP) Routledge.

Liddle, Howard A., et al, eds. Handbook of Family Therapy Training & Supervision. LC 87-24848. (Guilford Family Therapy Ser.). 432p. 1988. lib. bdg. 49.95 (*0-89862-073-2*) Guilford Pr.

Liddle, Jeffrey L. & Marino, Michael F., III. Labor & Employment in New York. suppl. ed. 1994. ring bd. 39.50 (*0-685-47712-6*) Butterworth Legal Pubs.

— Labor & Employment in New York. 2nd ed. 450p. 1994. ring bd. 89.50 (*0-8240-7329-0*) Michie Butterworth.

Liddle, Joanna & Joshi, Rama. Daughters of Independence: Gender, Caste, & Class in India. 264p. (C). 1989. text ed. 40.00 (*0-8135-1435-5*); pap. text ed. 15.00 (*0-8135-1436-3*) Rutgers U Pr.

Liddle, Matt. Make Your Own Book. LC 93-83466. (Discovery Kit Ser.). (Illus.). 64p. (Orig.). (J). (gr. 3 up). 1993. 17.95 (*1-56138-337-6*) Running Pr.

Liddle, Michel, ed. see Culioli, Antoine.

Liddle, Nancy, ed. The Sculpture of Richard Stankiewicz, Nineteen Fifty-Three to Nineteen Seventy-Nine. (Illus.). 28p. (Orig.). 1979. pap. 3.00 (*0-686-47034-6*) U Albany Art Mus.

— Thom O'Connor: Prints & Drawings, A Retrospective Exhibition, 1962-1982. LC 83-60042. (Illus.). 24p. 1983. pap. 3.00 (*0-686-47031-1*) U Albany Art Mus.

Liddle, Nancy, ed. see Feroletto, Mia.

Liddle, P. H. Gallipoli: 1915: Pen, Pencils & Cameras at War. (Illus.). 165p. 1985. 31.00 (*0-08-031172-5*, Pub. by Brasseys UK) Brasseys Inc.

Liddle, Peter. Men of Gallipoli: The Dardanelles & Gallipoli Experience, August 1914 to January 1916. (Battle Standards Ser.). (Illus.). 260p. (C). 1989. reprint ed. lib. bdg. 25.00x (*0-8095-7514-0*) Borgo Pr.

Liddle, R. A. The Van Oil Field, Van Zandt County, Texas. (Bulletin Ser.: BULL 3601). 79p. 1936. 1.50 (*0-318-03307-0*) Bur Econ Geology.

Liddle, R. William. Ethnicity, Party, & National Integration: An Indonesian Case Study. LC 70-99830. (Southeast Asia Studies: No. 7). (Illus.). 256p. reprint ed. 73.00 (*0-8357-9165-3*, 2011088) Bks Demand.

Liddle, R. William, et al, eds. Political Participation in Modern Indonesia. LC 73-89521. (Monograph Ser.: No. 19). (Illus.). 206p. 1973. 9.50 (*0-938692-11-9*) Yale U SE Asia.

Liddle, William. Reading for Concepts: Bks. A-H, Bk. C. 2nd ed. (Illus.). (gr. 3-9). 1977. pap. text ed. 7.40 (*0-07-037663-8*) McGraw.

— Reading for Concepts: Bks. A-H, Bk. D. 2nd ed. (Illus.). (gr. 3-9). 1977. pap. text ed. 7.40 (*0-07-037664-6*) McGraw.

— Reading for Concepts: Bks. A-H, Bk. A. 2nd ed. (Illus.). (gr. 3-9). 1977. pap. text ed. 7.40 (*0-07-037661-1*) McGraw.

— Reading for Concepts: Bks. A-H, Bk. B. 2nd ed. (Illus.). (gr. 3-9). 1977. pap. text ed. 7.40 (*0-07-037662-X*) McGraw.

— Reading for Concepts: Bks. A-H, Bk. E. 2nd ed. (Illus.). (gr. 3-9). 1977. pap. text ed. 7.40 (*0-07-037665-4*) McGraw.

— Reading for Concepts: Bks. A-H, Bk. F. 2nd ed. (Illus.). (gr. 3-9). 1977. pap. text ed. 7.96 (*0-07-037666-2*) McGraw.

— Reading for Concepts: Bks. A-H, BK. G. 2nd ed. (Illus.). (gr. 3-9). 1977. Bk. G. pap. text ed. 7.96 (*0-07-037667-0*) McGraw.

— Reading for Concepts: Bks. A-H, Bk. H. 2nd ed. (Illus.). (gr. 3-9). 1977. pap. text ed. 7.96 (*0-07-037668-9*) McGraw.

Liddon, H. P. Divinity of Our Lord & Savior Jesus Christ. 630p. lib. bdg. 22.99 (*0-8254-5158-2*) Kregel.

Liddon, Henry P. The Russian Journal - Two: A Record Kept by Henry Parry Liddon of a Tour Taken with C. L. Dodgson in the Summer of 1867. Cohen, Morton N., ed. LC 79-83663. (Carroll Studies: No. 3). 64p. (Orig.). 1979. pap. 20.00 (*0-930326-03-2*) L Carroll Soc.

Liddon, Sim C. The Dual Brain, Religion, & the Unconscious. 265p. 1989. lib. bdg. 27.95 (*0-87975-523-7*) Prometheus Bks.

Liddy, G. Gordon. The Monkey Handlers. 352p. 1991. mass mkt. 5.99 (*0-312-92613-8*) St Martin.

— Out of Control. 352p. 1991. mass mkt. 4.99 (*0-312-92428-3*) St Martin.

— Will. 1976. 24.95 (*0-8488-0718-9*) Amereon Ltd.

— Will. 1991. mass mkt. 5.99 (*0-312-92412-7*) St Martin.

— Will: The Autobiography of G. Gordon Liddy. 1995. 23.95 (*0-312-11915-1*) St Martin.

Liddy, James. Collected Poems. 300p. (C). 1994. 24.95 (*1-881871-09-6*); pap. 14.95 (*1-881871-08-8*) Creighton U Pr.

— Esau, My Kingdom for a Drink: Homage to James Joyce on His Eightieth Birthday. 1962. pap. 2.00 (*0-910664-10-2*) Gotham.

Liddy, Richard M. Transforming Light: Intellectual Conversion in the Early Lonergan. 272p. (Orig.). 1993. pap. text ed. 14.95 (*0-8146-5839-3*, M Glazier) Liturgical Pr.

Liddy, Rosemary & Walsh, Deirdre. Surviving Sexual Abuse. (Attic Handbooks Ser.). 96p. (Orig.). (C). 1989. pap. 7.95 (*0-946211-61-2*, Pub. by Attic IE) InBook.

Lide. Handbook of Chemistry & Physics. 73th ed. 1992. 99.50 (*0-8493-0473-3*, QD) CRC Pr.

— Handbook of Organic Solvents. 1994. write for info. (*0-8493-8930-5*) CRC Pr.

— Handbook of Thermophysical & Thermochemical Data. 1994. 149.95 (*0-8493-0197-1*, QC173) CRC Pr.

Lide, David R., Jr. Basic Laboratory & Industrial Chemicals. 1993. 39.95 (*0-8493-4498-0*, QP64) CRC Pr.

Lide, David R. Handbook of Chemistry & Physics. 72th ed. 2407p. 1993. 99.50 (*0-8493-0472-5*, QD65, CRC Reprint); 39.95 (*0-8493-0565-9*, CRC Reprint) Franklin.

Lide, David R., Jr. Handbook of Chemistry & Physics. 74th ed. 1993. 99.50 (*0-8493-0474-1*, QD) CRC Pr.

Lide, David R., ed. CRC Handbook of Chemistry & Physics. 75th ed. 2624p. 1994. 99.50 (*0-8493-0475-X*, 475) CRC Pr.

— Handbook of Chemistry & Physics. 76th ed. 2624p. 1995. 99.50 (*0-8493-0476-8*, 476) CRC Pr.

— Handbook of Chemistry & Physics, 1994 Special Student Edition. 2472p. 1994. 39.95 (*0-8493-0566-7*, 566) CRC Pr.

***Lide, David R. & Milne, G. W.** Handbook of Data on Common Organic Compounds. 3000p. 1994. 995.00 (*0-8493-0404-0*, 404) CRC Pr.

— Names, Synonyms, & Structures of Organic Compounds: A CRC Reference Handbook. 3000p. 1994. 495.00 (*0-8493-0405-9*, 405) CRC Pr.

Lide, David R. & Milne, G. W., eds. Handbook of Data on Organic Compounds. 3rd ed. LC 93-40342. 1993. write for info. (*0-8493-0445-8*) CRC Pr.

— Properties of Organic Compounds: Version 4. 0. 1994. cd-rom 695.00 (*0-8493-0446-6*, 446) CRC Pr.

— Properties of Organic Compounds 5.0 on CD-ROM. 1995. cd-rom 850.00 (*0-8493-0447-4*, 447) CRC Pr.

Lide, Elizabeth. You Are What You See. 1993. 18.00 (*0-932526-47-0*) Nexus Pr.

Lide, Mary. Command of the King. large type ed. (General Ser.). 1993. 21.95 (*0-7089-2554-5*) Ulverscroft.

— Fortune's Knave: The Making of William the Conqueror: a Novel. 288p. 1993. 18.95 (*0-312-09293-8*) St Martin.

— Isobelle. LC 87-40414. 288p. 1989. pap. 12.95 (*0-446-38949-8*) Warner Bks.

— Polmena Cove. 1994. 19.95 (*0-312-11877-5*) St Martin.

— Polmena Cove. large type ed. LC 94-42979. 323p. 1995. pap. 18.95 (*0-7838-1203-5*, Large Print Bks) Hall.

— A Royal Quest. 1988. pap. 12.95 (*0-446-38791-6*) Warner Bks.

— The Sea Scape. large type ed. LC 92-26852. (Popular Ser.). 310p. 1993. reprint ed. pap. 17.95 (*1-56054-552-6*) Thorndike Pr.

— Tregaran. large type ed. (General Ser.). 300p. 1990. lib. bdg. 18.95 (*0-8161-4980-1*, Large Print Bks) Hall.

Lide, Vanessa, jt. ed. see Bleviss, Deborah L.

Lidell, Lucy. The Book of Massage. 192p. 1984. pap. 14.00 (*0-671-54139-0*, Fireside) S&S Trade.

Liden, Elisabeth. Between Water & Heaven: Carl Milles' Search for American Commissions. (Illus.). 128p. 1986. 46.50x (*91-22-00815-2*, Pub. by Almqv & Wiksell SW) Coronet Bks.

Liden, Robert. Advanced Engine Demonstration Project. 1987. pap. 4.95 (*0-685-24742-2*) Research Analysts.

Lider, Julian. British Military Thought after World War II. LC 83-20724. 200p. 1985. text ed. 74.95 (*0-566-00638-3*) Ashgate Pub Co.

— Correlation of Forces: An Analysis of Marxist-Leninist Concepts. LC 85-27841. 320p. 1986. text ed. 45.00 (*0-312-17004-1*) St Martin.

— Military Force. 360p. 1981. text ed. 85.95 (*0-566-00296-5*) Ashgate Pub Co.

— On the Nature of War. 420p. 1978. text ed. 67.95 (*0-566-00178-0*) Ashgate Pub Co.

— Origins & Development of West German Military Thought: 1949-1966, Vol. 1. 1986. text ed. 99.95 (*0-566-00946-3*, Pub. by Dartmth Pub UK) Ashgate Pub Co.

— Origins & Development of West German Military Thought: 1966-1985, Vol. 2. 500p. 1987. text ed. 113.95 (*0-566-05236-9*, Pub. by Dartmth Pub UK) Ashgate Pub Co.

Liderbach, Daniel. The Numinous Universe. 1989. pap. 9.95 (*0-8091-3060-2*) Paulist Pr.

— The Theology of Grace & the American Mind: A Representation of Catholic Doctrine. LC 83-22154. (Toronto Studies in Theology: Vol. 15). 170p. 1983. lib. bdg. 79.95 (*0-88946-761-7*) E Mellen.

— Why Do We Suffer? New Ways of Understanding. LC 92-12767. 160p. 1992. pap. 11.95 (*0-8091-3319-9*) Paulist Pr.

Lidhoo, Motilal. Child Rearing & Psycho-Social Development. (C). 1991. 12.50 (*81-7024-300-9*, Pub. by Ashish II) S Asia.

Lidiak, Edward G. & Zietz, Isidore. Interpretation of Aeromagnetic Anomalies Between Latitudes 37 Degrees N & 38 Degrees N in the Eastern & Central United States. LC 76-12278. (Geological Society of America, Special Paper Ser.: No. 167). 59p. reprint ed. pap. 25.00 (*0-317-30056-3*, 2025032) Bks Demand.

Lidiard, Alan, jt. auth. see Allnatt, Alan.

Lidicker, W. Z., jt. ed. see Stenseth, Nils C.

***Lidicker, William Z., Jr., ed.** Landscape Approaches in Mammalian Ecology & Conservation. 224p. 1995. text ed. 35.95 (*0-8166-2587-5*) U of Minn Pr.

— Rodents: A World Survey of Species of Conservation Concern. (Occasional Papers of the IUCN Species Survival Commission: No. 4). (Illus.). 64p. (Orig.). 1989. pap. 17.00 (*2-88032-971-X*, Pub. by IUCN SZ) Island Pr.

Lidin. Handbook of Inorganic Chemistry. 1993. write for info. (*0-8493-9343-4*) CRC Pr.

Lidin, G. D. Air Pollution in Mines: Theory, Hazards & Controls. 304p. 1966. text ed. 79.50 (*0-7065-0411-9*, Pub. by Keter Pub IS) Coronet Bks.

Lidinsky, William & Vlack, David, eds. Perspectives on Packetized Voice & Data Communications. LC 90-32479. (Illus.). 304p. 1991. text ed. 49.95 (*0-87942-263-7*, PC02527) Inst Electrical.

Lidis Staff. Dictionnaire Encyclopedique Lidis, 3 vols., Set. 1104p. (FRE.). 1977. 350.00 (*0-8288-5386-X*, M6138) Fr & Eur.

— Encyclopedie de l'Art, 6 vols, Set. (FRE.). 1976. 895.00 (*0-8288-5680-X*, M6189) Fr & Eur.

— Encyclopedie Medicale De la Famille, 4 vols., Set. 1200p. (FRE.). 1976. 650.00 (*0-8288-5688-5*, M6221) Fr & Eur.

— Encyclopedie Scientifique et Technique, 5 vols., Set. 2480p. (FRE.). 1975. 795.00 (*0-8288-5878-0*, M6233) Fr & Eur.

***Lidl, Andreas.** Six Sonatas for Solo Viola Da Gamba & Violoncello. Miloradovitch, Hazelle, ed. (Baroque Ser.: No. 5). 1995. 20.00 (*1-56571-095-9*) PRB Prods.

Lidl, R., ed. Papers in Algebra, Analysis & Statistics. LC 82-1826. (Contemporary Mathematics Ser.: Vol. 9). 400p. 1982. pap. 35.00 (*0-8218-5009-1*, CONM-9) Am Math.

Lidl, R. & Mullen, G. L. Dickson Polynomials. LC 92-30842. (Pitman Monographs & Surveys in Pure & Applied Mathematics). 1992. write for info. (*0-582-09119-5*) Longman.

Lidl, R. & Pilz, G. Applied Abstract Algebra. LC 84-10576. (Undergraduate Texts in Mathematics Ser.). (Illus.). 450p. 1984. 49.00 (*0-387-96035-X*) Spr-Verlag.

Lidl, R., et al. Dickson Polynomials. (Pitman Monographs & Surveys in Pure & Applied Mathematics). 207p. 1993. text ed. 125.00 (*0-470-22089-9*) Halsted Pr.

Lidl, Rudolf & Niederreiter, Harald. Introduction to Finite Fields & Their Applications. rev. ed. LC 93-49020. (Illus.). 400p. (C). 1994. 47.95 (*0-521-46094-8*) Cambridge U Pr.

Lidman, Sara. Naboth's Stone. Tate, Joan, tr. LC 89-81774. (Norvik Press Series B: No. 7). 262p. (Orig.). 1990. pap. 22.50 (*1-870041-12-7*, Pub. by Norvik Pr UK) Dufour.

Lidman, Sven. Audiovisual Combi, 8 vols., Set. 1991. 695.00 (*0-7859-6359-6*, 8485797302) Fr & Eur.

— Audiovisual Combi, Vol. 1. 312p. 1991. 95.00 (*0-685-70609-5*, 8485797310) Fr & Eur.

— Audiovisual Combi, Vol. 2. 312p. 1991. 95.00 (*0-7859-6361-8*, 8485797329) Fr & Eur.

— Audiovisual Combi, Vol. 3. 296p. 1991. 95.00 (*0-7859-6362-6*, 8485797337) Fr & Eur.

— Audiovisual Combi, Vol. 4. 304p. 1991. 95.00 (*0-7859-6363-4*, 8485797345) Fr & Eur.

— Audiovisual Combi, Vol. 5. 312p. 1991. 95.00 (*0-7859-6364-2*, 8485797353) Fr & Eur.

— Audiovisual Combi, Vol. 6. 296p. 1991. 95.00 (*0-7859-6365-0*, 8485797361) Fr & Eur.

— Audiovisual Combi, Vol. 7. 312p. 1991. 95.00 (*0-7859-6499-1*) Fr & Eur.

— Audiovisual Combi, Vol. 8. 304p. 1991. 95.00 (*0-7859-6366-9*, 8485797388) Fr & Eur.

— Enciclopedia Combi Visual, 10 vols. 7th ed. 2448p. (SPA.). 1989. write for info. (*0-7859-5075-3*) Fr & Eur.

— Enciclopedia Combi Visual, Vol. 1. 248p. 1989. 75.00 (*0-7859-6349-9*, 8485797191) Fr & Eur.

— Enciclopedia Combi Visual, Vol. 2. 248p. 1989. 75.00 (*0-7859-6351-0*, 8485797205) Fr & Eur.

— Enciclopedia Combi Visual, Vol. 3. 248p. 1989. 75.00 (*0-7859-6352-9*, 8485797213) Fr & Eur.

— Enciclopedia Combi Visual, Vol. 4. 248p. 1989. 75.00 (*0-7859-6353-7*, 8485797221) Fr & Eur.

— Enciclopedia Combi Visual, Vol. 5. 248p. 1989. 75.00 (*0-7859-6500-9*) Fr & Eur.

— Enciclopedia Combi Visual, Vol. 6. 248p. 1989. 75.00 (*0-7859-6354-5*, 8485797248) Fr & Eur.

— Enciclopedia Combi Visual, Vol. 7. 240p. 1989. 75.00 (*0-7859-6355-3*, 8485797256) Fr & Eur.

— Enciclopedia Combi Visual, Vol. 8. 240p. 1989. 75.00 (*0-7859-6356-1*, 8485797264) Fr & Eur.

— Enciclopedia Combi Visual, Vol. 10. 240p. 1989. 75.00 (*0-7859-6358-8*, 8485797280) Fr & Eur.

Lidmus, Susan B. Church Family Ministry: Changing Loneliness to Fellowship in the Church. 1985. pap. 7.95 (*0-570-03945-2*, 12-2878) Concordia.

Lido, Serge. Ballet. 1991. lib. bdg. 15.00 (*0-8288-2636-6*) Fr & Eur.

— Ballet d'Aujourd'hui of Today. (Illus.). (ENG & FRE.). 1965. lib. bdg. 9.95 (*0-8288-3984-0*) Fr & Eur.

Lidoff, Lorraine, comp. Supports for Family Caregivers of the Elderly: Highlights of a National Symposium. 60p. 1985. 9.00 (*0-910883-62-9*) Natl Coun Aging.

***Lidofsky, Lillian.** Cats & the People They Own. LC 94-5388. 144p. 1995. pap. 7.00 (*0-399-51908-4*) Berkley Pub.

***Lidofsky, Lillian, pseud.** Dogs & the People They Own. LC 94-31192. 144p. (Orig.). 1995. pap. 8.00 (*0-399-51944-0*, Perigree Bks) Berkley Pub.

Lidolt, Erwina. The Food Combining Cookbook: Recipes for the Hay System. (Illus.). 128p. 1994. pap. 10.00 (*0-7225-1269-4*) Thorsons SF.

Lidorenko, N. S., ed. see Koltun, M. M.

Lidov, Aleksei, jt. ed. see Batalov, Andrei.

***Lidova, Natalia.** Drama & Ritual of Early Hinduism. (C). 1994. text ed. 14.00 (*0-614-04134-1*, Pub. by Motilal Banarsidass II) S Asia.

***Lidskog, Rolf.** Radioactive & Hazardous Waste Management in Sweden: Movements, Politics & Science. (Studia Sociologica Upsaliensia: No. 38). 195p. (Orig.). 1994. pap. 54.50x (*91-554-3298-0*, Pub. by Almqv & Wiksell SW) Coronet Bks.

Lidsky, Theodore I., jt. auth. see Schneider, Jay S.

Lidston, L., jt. auth. see Bateman, B.

Lidstone, Herrick K., Jr., et al. Federal Income Taxation of Corporations. 6th ed. LC 89-80745. 459p. 1989. text ed. 105.00 (*0-8318-0522-6*, B522) Am Law Inst.

Lidstone, J., jt. auth. see Gerber, R.

Lidstone, John. Beyond the Pay-Packet: Proven Techniques for Leading, Motivating, & Inspiring Salespeople to Achieve Success. LC 92-21880. 1992. 24.95 (*0-07-707697-4*) McGraw.

— How to Recruit & Select Successful Salesmen. rev. ed. 320p. 1983. text ed. 73.95 (*0-566-02325-3*) Ashgate Pub Co.

— Manual of Sales Negotiation. 250p. 1991. text ed. 79.95 (*0-566-02788-7*, Pub. by Gower UK) Ashgate Pub Co.

— Marketing Planning for the Pharmaceutical Industry. 250p. 1987. text ed. 145.00 (*0-566-02630-9*, Pub. by Gower UK) Ashgate Pub Co.

— Motivating Your Sales Force. 144p. 1978. text ed. 57.95 (*0-566-02082-3*) Ashgate Pub Co.

— Motivating Your Sales Force. 144p. 1995. pap. 16.95 (*0-566-07617-9*, Pub. by Gower UK) Ashgate Pub Co.

— Profitable Selling. 240p. 1986. pap. text ed. 19.95 (*0-7045-0524-X*, Pub. by Gower UK) Ashgate Pub Co.

Lidstone, John, ed. Global Issues of Our Time. LC 93-34256. (Illus.). 192p. (J). 1995. pap. 18.95 (*0-521-42163-2*) Cambridge U Pr.

Lidstone, Ken, jt. auth. see Bevan, Vaughan.

Lidstone, R. A. Studies in Symbology: Astrology, the Tarot, Numerology, the Bible. 1991. lib. bdg. 69.95 (*0-8490-4517-7*) Gordon Pr.

— Studies in Symbology: The Tarot, Astrology, the Bible, Numerology. 1991. lib. bdg. 79.95 (*0-8490-4990-3*) Gordon Pr.

Lidstone, Ronald A. Studies in Symbology. 93p. 1961. reprint ed. spiral bd. 4.40 (*0-7873-0559-6*) Mokelumne.

Lidstrom, Anders. Discretion: An Art of the Possible. 208p. (Orig.). 1991. pap. 58.50x (*0-685-62398-X*, Pub. by Almqv & Wiksell SW) Coronet Bks.

Lidtke, Vernon L. The Alternative Culture: Socialist Labor in Imperial Germany. (Illus.). 299p. 1985. 45.00 (*0-19-503507-0*) OUP.

— Outlawed Party: Social Democracy in Germany, 1878-1890. LC 66-14311. 388p. reprint ed. 110.60 (*0-8357-9506-3*, 2011480) Bks Demand.

Lidz, B., jt. auth. see Rose, P. R.

Lidz, Carol S. Improving Assessment of Schoolchildren. LC 80-26130. (Jossey-Bass Social & Behavioral Science Ser.). 239p. reprint ed. pap. 68.20 (*0-8357-4993-2*, 2037926) Bks Demand.

— Practitioner's Guide to Dynamic Assessment. LC 91-13657. (Guilford School Practitioner Ser.). 210p. 1991. lib. bdg. 45.00 (*0-89862-363-4*); pap. 19.95 (*0-89862-242-5*) Guilford Pr.

Lidz, Carol S., ed. Dynamic Assessment: An Interactional Approach to Evaluating Learning Potential. LC 86-19375. 511p. 1987. lib. bdg. 47.50 (*0-89862-695-1*) Guilford Pr.

Lidz, Charles W., et al. The Erosion of Autonomy in Long-Term Care. 216p. 1992. 37.95 (*0-19-507394-0*) OUP.

— Informed Consent: A Study of Decision-Making in Psychiatry. LC 83-8488. (Perspectives on Law & Behavior Ser.). 365p. 1984. lib. bdg. 45.00 (*0-89862-275-1*) Guilford Pr.

Lidz, Franz. Unstrung Heroes. 176p. 1991. 17.95 (*0-394-56988-1*) Random.

Lidz, Jane, photos. Water by Design: Architecture, History, & Myth. LC 93-27389. 1994. 60.00 (*0-8109-3975-4*) Abrams.

Lidz, Ruth W., jt. auth. see Lidz, Theodore.

Lidz, Theodore. The Family & Human Adaptation. LC 63-20457. 126p. 1963. text ed. 25.00 (*0-8236-1880-3*); pap. text ed. 24.95 (*0-8236-8051-7*, 21880) Intl Univs Pr.

— Hamlet's Enemy: Madness & Myth in Hamlet. xii, 258p. 1990. reprint ed. pap. 24.95 (*0-8236-8067-3*) Intl Univs Pr.

— Origin & Treatment of Schizophrenic Disorders. 158p. 1990. reprint ed. pap. 24.95 (*0-8236-8206-4*, BN 23895) Intl Univs Pr.

— The Person: His & Her Development Throughout the Life Cycle. LC 76-22745. 625p. 1983. pap. text ed. 30.00 (*0-465-05541-9*) Basic.

— The Relevance of the Family to Psychoanalytic Theory. LC 92-1477. 266p. (C). 1992. 30.00 (*0-8236-5784-1*) Intl Univs Pr.

Lidz, Theodore & Fleck, Stephen. Schizophrenia & the Family. rev. ed. LC 65-23613. 494p. 1985. text ed. 60. 00x (*0-8236-6001-X*, 06001) Intl Univs Pr.

Lidz, Theodore & Lidz, Ruth W. Oedipus in the Stone Age: A Psychoanalytic Study of Masculinization in Papua New Guinea. LC 88-25796. 215p. 1989. text ed. 30.00 (*0-8236-3727-1*) Intl Univs Pr.

Lidz, Victor M., jt. ed. see Klausner, Samuel Z.

Lidzbarski, Mark. Handbuch der Nordsemitischen Epigraphik Nebst Ausgewahlten Inschriften, 2 vols., Set. 1969. reprint ed. write for info. (*0-318-72103-1*, Pub. by Georg Olms GW) Lubrecht & Cramer.

Lie, Arne B. & Robinson, Robby. Night & Fog. 1990. 18.95 (*0-393-02779-1*) Norton.

Lie, Hiu. Die Mandschu-Sprachkunde in Korea. LC 70-635028. (Uralic & Altaic Ser.: Vol. 114). (Illus.). 275p. (Orig.). 1972. pap. text ed. 19.00 (*0-87750-162-9*) Res Inst Inner Asian Studies.

Lie, John, ed. The Impoverished Spirit in Contemporary Japan: Selected Essays of Honda Katuichi. 320p. 1993. 34.00 (*0-85345-858-8*); pap. 16.00 (*0-85345-859-6*) Monthly Rev.

Lie, John, jt. auth. see Abelmann, Nancy.

Lie, Jonas L. The Seer & Other Norwegian Tales. Morton, Brian & Trevor, Richard, trs. 160p. (Orig.). 1990. pap. 21.00 (*0-948259-65-5*, Pub. by Forest Bks UK) Dufour.

— Weird Tales from Northern Seas, from the Danish of Jonas Lie. LC 79-81272. (Short Story Index Reprint Ser.). (Illus.). 1977. 17.95 (*0-8369-3024-X*) Ayer.

Lie, K. I., jt. ed. see Van der Wall, Ernst E.

Lie, K. I., jt. ed. see Van Zwieten, Pieter A.

Lie, Merete & Lund, Ragnhild. Renegotiating Local Values: Working Women & Foreign Industry in Malaysia. (Studies on Asian Topics (Scandinavian Institute of Asian Studies): No. 14). 288p. (C). 1994. pap. 39.95 (*0-7007-0280-6*, Pub. by Curzon Pr UK) Humanities.

Lie, Sophus. Differentialgleichungen. LC 66-12880. 39.50 (*0-8284-0206-X*) Chelsea Pub.

— Geometrie der Beruehrungstransformationen. LC 72-113134. (GER.). 1976. 39.50 (*0-8284-0291-4*) Chelsea Pub.

— Transformationsgruppen, 3 Vols, Set. 2nd ed. LC 76-113135. 1970. 125.00 (*0-8284-0232-9*) Chelsea Pub.

— Vorlesungen Uber Continuierliche Gruppen Mit Geometrischen und Anderen Anwendungen. 2nd ed. LC 66-12879. 1971. text ed. 59.95 (*0-8284-0199-3*) Chelsea Pub.

Lie, Suzanne, et al, eds. World Yearbook of Education, 1994: The Gender Gap in Higher Education. 260p. 1994. 65.00 (*0-7494-1079-5*, Pub. by Kogan Page Educ UK) Taylor & Francis.

Lie, Suzanne S. & O'Leary, Virginia. Storming the Tower: Women in the Academic World. 256p. 1990. pap. 31.95 (*0-89397-404-8*) Nichols Pub.

Lie, T. T., ed. Structural Fire Protection: Manual of Practice. 250p. 1992. text ed. 56.00 (*0-87262-888-4*) Am Soc Civil Eng.

Lieb. Baseball As I Have Known It. 1976. 28.95 (*0-8488-1549-1*) Amereon Ltd.

— Detroit Tigers. 1976. 20.95 (*0-8488-1578-5*) Amereon Ltd.

— St. Louis Cardinals: Great Baseball Club. 1976. 22.95 (*0-8488-1579-3*) Amereon Ltd.

***Lieb, Barbara, ed.** Achieving World Class Standards: The Challenge for Educating Teachers. 53p. (Orig.). (C). 1994. pap. text ed. 35.00 (*0-7881-1387-9*) Diane Pub.

Lieb, E. H., et al, eds. Studies in Mathematical Physics: Essays in Honor of Valentine Bargmann. LC 76-4057. (Physics Ser.). (Illus.). 472p. 1976. 75.00x (*0-691-08180-8*); pap. 24.95x (*0-691-08185-9*) Princeton U Pr.

Lieb, Elliott H. The Stability of Matter: From Atoms to Stars: Selecta of Elliott H. Lieb. Thirring, W., ed. viii, 565p. 1991. 89.00 (*0-387-53039-8*) Spr-Verlag.

Lieb, Elliott H. & Mattis, D. C., eds. The Many-Body Problem: An Encyclopedia of Exactly Solved Models 1D. 2nd ed. 800p. 1993. text ed. 109.00 (*981-02-0975-4*) World Scientific Pub.

Lieb, Hans H. Integrational Linguistics, 6 vols. (Current Issues in Linguistic Theory Ser.: No. 17). 1720p. Date not set. write for info. (*90-272-3535-X*) Benjamins North Am.

— Integrational Linguistics, 6 vols., Vol. 1: General Outline. (Current Issues in Linguistic Theory Ser.: No. 17). 1720p. 1984. Vol. 1, General Outline. 97.00x (*90-272-3508-2*) Benjamins North Am.

— Integrational Linguistics, 6 vols., Vol. 2: A Theory of Grammars. (Current Issues in Linguistic Theory Ser.: No. 17). 1720p. Date not set. Vol. 2, A Theory of Grammars. write for info. (*0-686-37279-4*) Benjamins North Am.

— Integrational Linguistics, 6 vols., Vol. 3, Language Universals & Language Contfasts. (Current Issues in Linguistic Theory Ser.: No. 17). 1720p. Date not set. Vol. 3, Language Universals & Language Contrasts. write for info. (*0-686-37791-5*) Benjamins North Am.

— Integrational Linguistics, 6 vols., Vol. 4: Syntax & Semantics. (Current Issues in Linguistic Theory Ser.: No. 17). 1720p. Date not set. Vol. 4, Syntax & Semantics. write for info. (*0-686-37280-8*) Benjamins North Am.

— Integrational Linguistics, 6 vols., Vol. 5: Morphology & Morphosemantics. (Current Issues in Linguistic Theory Ser.: No. 17). 1720p. Date not set. Vol. 5., Morphology & Morphosemantics. write for info. (*0-686-37281-6*) Benjamins North Am.

— Integrational Linguistics, 6 vols., Vol. 6: Lexical Semantics. (Current Issues in Linguistic Theory Ser.: No. 17). 1720p. Date not set. Vol. 6, Lexical Semantics. write for info. (*0-686-37282-4*) Benjamins North Am.

Lieb, Hans-Heinrich. Linguistic Variables: Towards a Unified Theory of Linguistic Variation. LC 93-5760. (Current Issues in Linguistic Theory Ser.: Vol. 108). xiv, 261p. 1993. 68.00x (*1-55619-562-1*) Benjamins North Am.

Lieb, Hans-Heinrich, ed. Prospects for a New Structuralism. LC 92-33520. (Current Issues in Linguistic Theory Ser.: No. 96). vi, 276p. 1992. 59.00x (*1-55619-158-8*) Benjamins North Am.

Lieb, Ingo, jt. auth. see Fischer, Wolfgang.

Lieb, Irwin C. Past, Present, & Future: A Philosophical Essay about Time. 272p. 1991. 34.95 (*0-252-01804-4*); pap. 14.95 (*0-252-06182-9*) U of Ill Pr.

Lieb, Julian. A Medical Solution to the Health Care Crisis. 129p. 1993. 19.50 (*0-87527-512-5*) Green.

Lieb, Julian, jt. auth. see Hershman, D. Jablow.

Lieb, Michael. The Dialectics of Creation: Patterns of Birth & Regeneration in "Paradise Lost" LC 71-76047. 272p. 1970. 30.00 (*0-87023-049-2*) U of Mass Pr.

— Milton & the Culture of Violence. LC 93-32279. 288p. 1994. 32.50 (*0-8014-2903-X*) Cornell U Pr.

— Poetics of the Holy: A Reading of Paradise Lost. LC 80-29159. (Illus.). 464p. reprint ed. pap. 132.30 (*0-7837-7073-1*, 2046885) Bks Demand.

— The Sinews of Ulysses: Form & Convention in Milton's Works. LC 88-25651. (Duquesne Studies: Language & Literature Ser.: Vol. 9). 190p. 1989. text ed. 28.95x (*0-8207-0205-6*) Duquesne.

— The Visionary Mode: Biblical Prophecy, Hermeneutics & Cultural Change. LC 91-9439. 352p. 1991. 36.95 (*0-8014-2273-6*) Cornell U Pr.

Lieb, Michael & Shawcross, John T., eds. Achievements of the Left Hand: Essays on the Prose of John Milton. LC 73-79506. 404p. 1974. 37.50 (*0-87023-125-1*) U of Mass Pr.

Lieb, Michael, jt. ed. see Benet, Diana T.

Lieb, Robert C. Labor in the Transportation Industry. LC 73-13343. (Special Studies in U. S. Economic, Social & Political Issues). 1974. 47.50 (*0-275-28791-2*) Irvington.

— Transportation. 3rd ed. (C). 1985. teacher ed. write for info. (*0-8359-7824-9*, Reston); text ed. write for info. (*0-8359-7823-0*, Reston) P-H.

Lieb, Sandra R. Mother of the Blues: A Study of Ma Rainey. LC 81-1168. (Illus.). 256p. 1983. pap. 16.95 (*0-87023-394-7*) U of Mass Pr.

Liebaers, H., et al, eds. New Information Technologies & Libraries. 1985. lib. bdg. 110.00 (*90-277-2105-X*) Kluwer Ac.

Liebaers, Herman. Mostly in the Line of Duty: Thirty Years with Books. 1980. lib. bdg. 56.50 (*90-247-2228-4*) Kluwer Ac.

— Small Talk about Great Books. pap. 3.00 (*0-89073-062-8*) Boston Public Lib.

Liebau, H., ed. Mechanisms & Recent Advances in Therapy of Hypertension. (Contributions to Nephrology Ser.: Vol. 8). (Illus.). 1977. 66.50 (*3-8055-2671-7*) S Karger.

Liebau, H., jt. ed. see Bahlmann, J.

Liebb, Julius, jt. auth. see Bromberg, Murray.

Liebchen, Peter A. Kontum: Battle for the Central Highlands. 104p. 1993. reprint ed. pap. 15.00 (*0-923135-66-9*) Dalley Bk Service.

— MAP Aid to Laos, 1959-1972. 200p. 1993. reprint ed. pap. 20.00 (*0-923135-51-0*) Dalley Bk Service.

Liebeault, Ambroise-Auguste. Le Sommeil Provoque et les Etats Anologues. LC 75-16716. (Classics in Psychiatry Ser.). 1976. reprint ed. 26.95 (*0-405-07444-1*) Ayer.

Liebeck, Hans, jt. auth. see Baxandall, Peter.

Liebeck, Helen, jt. ed. see Pollard, Elaine.

Liebeck, M., et al. The Maximal Factorizations of the Finite Simple Groups & Their Automorphism Groups. (MEMO Ser.: Vol. 86/432). 151p. 1990. pap. text ed. 22.00 (*0-8218-2494-5*, MEMO 86/432) Am Math.

Liebeck, Martin W. & Saxl, Jan, eds. Groups & Combinatorics. (London Mathematical Society Lecture Note Ser.: No. 165). 350p. (C). 1992. pap. 47.95 (*0-521-40685-4*) Cambridge U Pr.

Liebeck, Martin W., jt. auth. see James, Gordon D.

Liebeck, Martin W., jt. auth. see Kleidman, P. B.

Liebeck, Pamela. Vectors & Matrices. 192p. (C). 1971. 82. 00 (*0-08-015823-4*, Pub. by Pergamon Repr UK) Franklin.

Liebel-Weckowicz, H., jt. auth. see Weckowicz, T. E.

Liebelt, Robert A. & Truitt, Edward B., Jr. Let's Talk about Alcoholism. (Illus.). 248p. (Orig.). 1989. pap. 15.95 (*0-926719-00-9*) Platte River Pr.

Liebenau, Jonathan. The Challenge of New Technology: Innovation in British Business Since 1850. 200p. 1988. text ed. 58.95 (*0-566-05147-8*, Pub. by Avebury Pub UK) Ashgate Pub Co.

— Medical Science & Medical Industry: The Formation of the American Pharmaceutical Industry. LC 86-27346. 224p. 1987. text ed. 35.00 (*0-8018-3356-6*) Johns Hopkins.

Liebenau, Jonathan, jt. ed. see Davenport-Hines, R. P.

Liebenau, Jonathan, et al, eds. Pill Peddlers: Essays on the History of the Pharmaceutical Industry. 133p. (Orig.). (C). 1990. pap. 10.95 (*0-931292-22-0*) Am Inst Hist Pharm.

Liebenauer, Paul. Laboratory Manual for College Physics. 1987. pap. text ed. 16.25 (*0-89917-531-7*) Tichenor Pub.

Liebenberg. Techniques for Geographers: Book One. 160p. 1987. pap. 21.95 (*0-409-11147-3*) Buttrwrth-Heinemann.

Liebenberg, A. C. Concrete Bridges: Design & Construction. LC 92-5592. (Concrete Design & Construction Ser.). 280p. 1993. text ed. 145.00 (*0-470-21865-7*) Halsted Pr.

Liebengood, Judy. Freedom from Eating Disorders. LC 93-86776. 176p. 1994. pap. 9.99 (*0-933451-20-2*) Prescott Pr.

— Freedom from Eating Disorders - The Workbook. 96p. 1994. pap. 14.99 (*0-933451-22-9*) Prescott Pr.

***Liebengood, Judy L.** My Soul Clings to You. 240p. (Orig.). Date not set. pap. 8.95 (*0-7610-0392-4*) NW Pub.

Liebenow, J. Gus. African Politics: Crises & Challenges. LC 85-45469. (Illus.). 320p. 1986. 35.00 (*0-253-30275-7*); pap. 12.95 (*0-253-20388-0*, MB-388) Ind U Pr.

— Colonial Rule & Political Development in Tanzania: The Case of the Makonde. LC 72-126898. 374p. reprint ed. pap. 106.60 (*0-8357-9449-0*, 2014777) Bks Demand.

— Liberia: The Evolution of Privilege. LC 69-18359. (Africa in the Modern World Ser.). 269p. reprint ed. pap. 76.70 (*0-685-20412-X*, 2030230) Bks Demand.

— Liberia: The Quest for Democracy. LC 86-45956. (Illus.). 350p. 1987. pap. 12.95 (*0-253-20424-0*, MB-424) Ind U Pr.

Liebenson, Diane S. & Rubenstein, Randi S., eds. Case Management Resource Guide, 4 vols. 3000p. 1992. pap. 60.00 (*0-685-74384-5*) Ctr CHI.

— Case Management Resource Guide, 4 vols., Set. 3rd ed. 3000p. 1992. pap. 225.00 (*1-880874-00-8*) Ctr CHI.

— Case Management Resource Guide, 4 vols., Vol. 1: Eastern U. S. 3000p. 1992. Eastern U. S., Vol. 1. pap. 60.00 (*1-880874-01-6*) Ctr CHI.

— Case Management Resource Guide, 4 vols., Vol. 2: Southern U. S. 3000p. 1992. Southern U. S., Vol. 2. pap. 60.00 (*1-880874-02-4*) Ctr CHI.

— Case Management Resource Guide, 4 vols., Vol. 3: Midwestern U. S. 3000p. 1992. Midwestern U. S., Vol. 3. pap. 60.00 (*1-880874-03-2*) Ctr CHI.

— Case Management Resource Guide, 4 vols., Vol. 4: Western U. S. 3000p. 1992. Western U. S., Vol. 4. pap. 60.00 (*1-880874-04-0*) Ctr CHI.

Liebenstein, Meret, tr. see Ohlig, Adelheid.

Liebenthal, Andres, et al. Solar Energy: Lessons from the Pacific Island Experience. LC 94-13345. (Technical Paper, Energy Ser.: No. 244). 72p. 1994. write for info. (*0-8213-2802-6*) World Bank.

Liebenthal, Jean Z. Cottonwood Summer. pap. 6.95 (*0-88494-825-0*) Bookcraft Inc.

— Feathers & Rings. 1993. pap. 6.95 (*0-88494-870-6*) Bookcraft Inc.

Lieber. Frommer's Budapest. (Illus.). 1994. pap. 13.00 (*0-671-86979-5*, P-H Travel) P-H Gen Ref & Trav.

— No Common Power. 2nd ed. (C). 1990. pap. text ed. 26. 50 (*0-673-52122-2*) HarpCollege.

Lieber, jt. auth. see Greenberg.

Lieber, Charles S. Medical & Nutritional Complications of Alcoholism: Mechanisms & Management. (Illus.). 666p. 1992. 89.50 (*0-306-43558-6*, Plenum Med Bk) Plenum.

— Medical Disorders of Alcoholism: Pathogenesis & Treatment. (Major Problems in Internal Medicine Ser.: Vol. 22). (Illus.). 608p. 1982. text ed. 105.00 (*0-7216-5774-5*) Saunders.

Lieber, Charles S., ed. Recent Advances in the Biology of Alcoholism. LC 82-1033. (Advances in Alcohol & Substance Abuse Ser.: Vol. 1, No. 2). 123p. 1982. text ed. 39.95 (*0-86656-104-8*, B104) Haworth Pr.

Lieber, Constance L. & Sillito, John, eds. Letters from Exile: The Correspondence of Martha Hughes Cannon & Angus M. Cannon, 1886-1888. limited ed. LC 89-32696. 286p. 1990. 60.00 (*0-941214-77-X*) Signature Bks.

Lieber, Francis. Notes on Fallacies of American Protectionists. Bd. with Lectures on the History of Protection in the United States. (Neglected American Economists Ser.). 1974. Set lib. bdg. 61.00 (*0-8240-1018-3*) Garland.

— On Civil Liberty & Self Government. LC 76-169655. (Civil Liberties in American History Ser.). 1972. reprint ed. lib. bdg. 75.00 (*0-306-70284-3*) Da Capo.

***Lieber, James B.** Friendly Takeover: How an Employee Buyout Saved a Steel Town. LC 94-45179. 1995. 23.95 (*0-670-82075-X*, Viking) Viking Penguin.

Lieber, M., jt. auth. see Stein, M.

Lieber, Michael. Street Scenes: Afro-American Culture in Urban Trinidad. 120p. 1981. pap. 11.95 (*0-87073-874-7*) Schenkman Bks Inc.

Lieber, Michael D. More Than a Living: Fishing & Social Order on a Polynesian Atoll. (Conflict & Social Change Ser.). 235p. (C). 1993. pap. text ed. 47.50 (*0-8133-8780-9*) Westview.

Lieber, Michael D. & Dikepa, Kalio H. Kapingamarangi Lexicon. LC 73-90855. (PALI Language Texts, Polynesia Ser.). 434p. (Orig.). (PLI.). 1974. pap. text ed. 15.00 (*0-8248-0304-3*) UH Pr.

Lieber, Phyllis, et al. Grown up Children, Grown up Parents: Opening the Door to Healthy Relationships Between Parents Adult Children. 1994. 18.95 (*1-55972-243-6*) Carol Pub Group.

Lieber, Richard E. Skeletal Muscle Structure & Function. (Illus.). 314p. 1992. pap. 36.00 (*0-683-05026-5*) Williams & Wilkins.

Lieber, Robert J. American Diplomatic Response to the 1973-1974 Energy Crisis. (Pew Case Studies in International Affairs). 50p. (C). 1988. pap. text ed. 2.50 (*1-56927-148-8*) Geo U Inst Dplmcy.

— No Common Power: Understanding International Relations. LC 94-7217. (C). 1994. 25.00 (*0-673-52390-X*) HarpCollege.

— The Oil Decade: Conflict & Cooperation in the West. (Illus.). 172p. (C). 1986. reprint ed. pap. text ed. 22.50 (*0-8191-5466-0*) U Pr of Amer.

Lieber, Robert J., ed. Will Europe Fight for Oil: Energy Relations in the Atlantic Area. 240p. 1983. 38.50 (*0-275-91035-0*, C1035, Praeger Pubs) Greenwood.

Lieber, Rochelle. Deconstructing Morphology: Word Formation in Syntactic Theory. (Illus.). 232p. 1992. lib. bdg. 57.50 (*0-226-48062-3*); pap. text ed. 24.95 (*0-226-48063-1*) U Ch Pr.

— An Integrated Theory of Autosegmental Processes. LC 86-30049. (SUNY Series in Linguistics). 209p. 1987. 89. 50 (*0-88706-509-0*); pap. 29.95 (*0-88706-510-4*) State U NY Pr.

An Asterisk (*) at the beginning of an entry indicates that the title is appearing in BIP for the first time.

Lieber, Sherman. Mystics & Missionaries: The Jews in Palestine, 1799-1840. LC 92-53605. 544p. 1992. 45.00 (*0-87480-391-8*) U of Utah Pr.

Lieber, Todd M. Endless Experiments: Essays on the Heroic Experience in American Romanticism. LC 72-10658. 1973. 29.50 (*0-8142-0180-6*) Ohio St U Pr.

Lieber, William M. Lieber on Pensions, 5 vols. 4200p. 1991. ring bd. 595.00 (*0-13-085821-8*) Aspen Law.

***Lieberg, Carolyn S.** Suriname. LC 95-2692. (Enchantment of the World Ser.). (J). 1995. write for info. (*0-516-02638-0*) Childrens.

Lieberg, Godo. Poeta Creator: Studien zu einer Figur der' antiken Dichtung. ix, 179p. (Orig.). (GER.). (C). 1982. pap. 35.00 (*90-70265-53-2*, Pub. by Gieben NE) Benjamins North Am.

Lieberg, Owen S. High Temperature Water Systems. 2nd ed. LC 63-24500. 237p. reprint ed. pap. 67.60 (*0-317-10811-5*, 2001908) Bks Demand.

***Lieberman.** Coaches Guide for Women's Basketball. 1994. pap. 13.95 (*0-915611-61-9*) Sagamore Pub.

— Handbook of Psychiatric Rehabilitation. (C). 1992. 54.95 (*0-205-14557-4*, H4557, Longwood Div) Allyn.

— Preparing for the CLEP. 5th ed. 1995. pap. 11.95 (*0-02-860029-0*) Macmillan.

— Public Education: An Autopsy. 393p. 1995. pap. 14.95 (*0-674-72234-5*, LIEPUX) HUP.

Lieberman, et al. Pharmaceutical Dosage Forms: Disperse Systems, Vol. 2. 712p. 1989. 175.00 (*0-8247-8104-X*) Dekker.

— Pharmaceutical Dosage Forms: Disperse Systems, Vol. 1. 544p. 1988. 170.00 (*0-8247-7817-0*) Dekker.

— Pharmaceutical Dosage Forms: Tablets, Vol. 1. 2nd ed. 576p. 1989. 145.00 (*0-8247-8044-2*) Dekker.

— Pharmaceutical Dosage Forms: Tablets, Vol. 2. 2nd ed. 632p. 1990. 150.00 (*0-8247-8289-5*) Dekker.

— Pharmaceutical Dosage Forms, Vol. 3: Tablets. 2nd ed. 584p. 1990. 140.00 (*0-8247-8300-X*) Dekker.

Lieberman, et al, eds. Monoamine Oxidase Inhibitors in Neurological Diseases. (Neurological Disease & Therapy Ser.: Vol. 21). 400p. 1994. 150.00 (*0-8247-9082-0*) Dekker.

Lieberman, A. & Lataste, X., eds. Parkinson's Disease: The Role of Dopamine Agonists. (New Trends in Clinical Neurology Ser.). (Illus.). 120p. 1989. 55.00 (*1-85070-272-1*) Prthnon Pub.

Lieberman, A., jt. auth. see Krayevskii, N.

Lieberman, A. S., jt. auth. see Navch, Z.

Lieberman, A. S., jt. auth. see Naveh, Z.

Lieberman, Abraham, jt. ed. see Olanow, Charles W.

Lieberman, Abraham N., et al. Parkinson's Disease: The Complete Guide for Patients & Caregivers. 256p. (Orig.). 1993. pap. 11.00 (*0-671-76819-0*, Fireside) S&S Trade.

Lieberman, Adrienne, jt. auth. see Kerns, Lawrence.

Lieberman, Adrienne B. Easing Labor Pain: The Complete Guide to a More Comfortable & Rewarding Birth. rev. ed. Rosenberg, Dan, ed. LC 92-382. (Illus.). 288p. 1992. 19.95 (*1-55832-044-X*); pap. 12.95 (*1-55832-043-1*) Harvard Common Pr.

Lieberman, Alexander. Marlene: An Intimate Photographic Memoir. LC 92-50548. (Illus.). 1992. 45.00 (*0-679-42086-X*) Random.

Lieberman, Alicia. Emotional Life of the Toddler. 256p. 1993. 24.95 (*0-02-919021-5*) Free Pr.

***Lieberman, Alicia F.** The Emotional Life of the Toddler. 1995. pap. 12.00 (*0-02-874017-3*) Free Pr.

Lieberman, Alvin. Contamination Control & Cleanrooms: Problems, Engineering Solutions, & Applications. (Illus.). 384p. 1992. text ed. 59.95 (*0-442-00574-1*) Chapman & Hall.

Lieberman, Ann. Schools As Collaborative Cultures: Creating the Future Now. (School Development & the Management of Change Ser.). 256p. 1990. 75.00 (*1-85000-672-5*); pap. 31.00 (*1-85000-673-3*) Taylor & Francis.

Lieberman, Ann, ed. Building a Professional Culture in Schools. (Series on School Reform). 248p. (C). 1988. text ed. 32.95 (*0-8077-2901-9*); pap. text ed. 18.95 (*0-8077-2900-0*) Tchrs Coll.

— The Changing Contexts of Teaching. (National Society for the Study of Education Publication Ser.). 275p. 1992. 27.50 (*0-226-60157-9*) U Ch Pr.

— Rethinking School Improvement: Research, Craft & Concept. 240p. 1986. pap. text ed. 17.95 (*0-8077-2807-1*) Tchrs Coll.

— The Series on School Reform: Building from the Ground Up. (The Series on School Reform). 216p. (C). 1995. text ed. 40.00x (*0-8077-3404-7*); pap. text ed. 18.95x (*0-8077-3403-9*) Tchrs Coll.

Lieberman, Ann & McLaughlin, Milbrey W., eds. Policy Making in Education. LC 81-85130. (National Society for the Study of Education Publication Ser.: 81st; Pt. 1). 300p. (C). 1982. lib. bdg. 15.00 (*0-226-60132-3*) U Ch Pr.

Lieberman, Ann & Miller, Lynne. Teachers - Their World & Their Work: Implications for School Improvement. 160p. (C). 1991. reprint ed. pap. text ed. 13.95 (*0-8077-3165-X*) Tchrs Coll.

Lieberman, Ann & Miller, Lynne, eds. Staff Development for Education in the 90s: New Demands, New Realities, New Perspectives. 2nd ed. (Series on Schooll Reform). 288p. (C). 1991. text ed. 45.95 (*0-8077-3100-5*); pap. text ed. 20.95 (*0-8077-3099-8*) Tchrs Coll.

Lieberman, Archie. Neighbors. LC 93-3554. 1993. 40.00 (*0-00-255209-4*) Collins SF.

Lieberman, Bernhardt. Social Choice. LC 75-132954. (Monographs & Texts in the Behavioral Sciences). (Illus.). 438p. 1971. text ed. 145.00 (*0-677-14770-8*) Gordon & Breach.

Lieberman, Bernhardt, ed. see Rader, Trout.

Lieberman, Betsy & Chamberlain, Donald. Breaking New Ground: Developing Innovative AIDS Care Residences. LC 93-71111. 250p. 1993. pap. text ed. 39.95 (*0-9636595-0-2*) AIDS Hse WA.

— Breaking New Ground: Developing Innovative AIDS Care Residences. 311p. 1993. pap. 39.95 (*0-9639595-0-6*) AIDS Hse WA.

Lieberman, Carl, ed. Government & Politics in Ohio. LC 84-15205. 340p. (Orig.). 1984. pap. text ed. 27.00 (*0-8191-4207-7*) U Pr of Amer.

— Government, Politics, & Public Policy in Ohio. LC 95-94293. 300p. (C). 1995. text ed. 44.95 (*0-9646524-0-4*); pap. text ed. 24.95 (*0-9646524-1-2*) Midwest Pr.

Lieberman, Chaim. The Grave Concern. LC 68-58650. 202p. 1968. 10.00 (*0-88400-016-8*) Shengold.

***Lieberman-Cline, Nancy & Roberts, Robin.** Basketball for Women: Becoming a Complete Player. LC 95-17945. (Illus.). 264p. (Orig.). 1995. pap. 16.95 (*0-87322-610-0*, PLIE0610) Human Kinetics.

Lieberman, Dan. Renovating Your Home for Maximum Profit: Make up to 4,000 Dollars for Every 1,000 Dollars You Invest. 1991. 21.95 (*1-55958-097-6*); pap. 14.95 (*0-685-47856-4*) Prima Pub.

Lieberman, Dan & Hoffman, Paul. Getting the Most for Your Home in a Down Market or Any Market. 2nd ed. 352p. 1993. pap. 8.95 (*1-55850-249-1*) Adams Pubng.

— Renovating Your Home for Maximum Profit: Make up to 4000 Dollars for Every 1000 Dollars You Invest in Your House, Condo, Co-op, or Rental Property. 2nd rev. ed. LC 93-50094. 1994. write for info. (*1-55958-505-6*) Prima Pub.

Lieberman, David. The Eternal Torah: A Commentary Integrating All the Prophets into the Books of Kings, Bk. 3. 600p. (C). 1986. 25.00 (*0-9609840-2-X*) Twin Pines Pr.

— The Eternal Torah: A Commentary upon Torah Pentateuch Consolidating the Scholarship Throughout Hebrew Literature, Pt. 1. 570p. 1986. reprint ed. 25.00 (*0-9609840-0-3*) Twin Pines Pr.

Lieberman, David A. Learning: Behavior & Cognition. 2nd ed. (C). 1993. text ed. 48.95 (*0-534-17400-0*) Brooks-Cole.

Lieberman, Deborah, jt. auth. see Fox, Perla.

Lieberman, Devorah A. & Gurtov, Mel. Revealing the World: An Interdisciplinary Reader for International Studies. 304p. (C). 1992. per. 32.95 (*0-8403-7951-X*) Kendall-Hunt.

Lieberman, Donald. The Doctor in Your House: Dr. Lieberman's Unique Guide to Preventive Medicine & Sensible Money Saving Self Care. 80p. (Orig.). 1989. pap. 6.95 (*0-317-93298-5*) Jadon Pubns.

Lieberman, E. James. Acts of Will: The Life & Work of Otto Rank. LC 84-21121. (Illus.). 485p. 1985. text ed. 32.95 (*0-02-919020-7*) Free Pr.

— Acts of Will: The Life & Work of Otto Rank. 2nd ed. LC 93-28227. (Illus.). 536p. 1993. reprint ed. pap. 18.95 (*0-87023-871-X*) U of Mass Pr.

Lieberman, E. James, jt. auth. see Brenner, Marcella B.

Lieberman, Eli. Modern Soldering & Brazing Techniques. LC 87-30002. 212p. 1988. 16.00 (*0-912524-43-X*) Busn News.

Lieberman, Elias. American Short Story. LC 71-128995. reprint ed. 31.50 (*0-404-03986-3*) AMS Pr.

— The American Short Story: A Study of the Influence of Locality in Its Development. (BCL1-PS American Literature Ser.). 183p. 1992. reprint ed. lib. bdg. 69.00 (*0-7812-6637-8*) Rprt Serv.

Lieberman, Ellen, jt. auth. see Douglass, Catherine J.

Lieberman, Ellin, jt. auth. see Kaplan, Norman M.

Lieberman, Elliot R. Multi-Objective Programming in the U. S. S. R. (Statistical Modeling & Decision Science Ser.). (Illus.). 368p. 1991. text ed. 72.00 (*0-12-449660-1*) Acad Pr.

Lieberman, Florence. Clinical Social Workers as Psychotherapists. LC 82-3109. 1982. 29.95 (*0-89876-037-2*) Gardner Pr.

— Social Work with Children. LC 78-23287. 344p. 1979. 45. 95 (*0-87705-255-7*); pap. 26.95 (*0-87705-257-3*) Human Sci Pr.

Lieberman, Florence & Collen, Morris F. Aging in Good Health: A Quality Lifestyle for the Later Years. 300p. 1993. 26.95 (*0-306-44502-6*, Plenum Insight) Plenum.

Lieberman, Florence, et al, eds. The Foster Care Dilemma: A Special Issue of Child & Adolescent Social Work Journal. 134p. 1987. pap. 16.95 (*0-89885-367-2*) Human Sci Pr.

Lieberman, Fredric, ed. A Chinese Zither Tutor: The Mei-an ch'in-p'u. LC 82-4895. (Illus.). 156p. 1982. 40.00 (*0-295-95941-X*) U of Wash Pr.

Lieberman, Gerald F. Three Thousand Five Hundred Good Jokes for Speakers. LC 74-29354. 480p. 1975. mass mkt. 6.95 (*0-385-00545-8*, Dolp) Doubleday.

— Three Thousand Five Hundred Good Quotes for Speakers. LC 81-43552. 288p. 1987. mass mkt. 6.95 (*0-385-17769-0*) Doubleday.

Lieberman, Gerald J. & Owen, Donald B. Tables of the Hypergeometric Probability Distribution. vi, 726p. 1961. 75.00 (*0-8047-0057-5*) Stanford U Pr.

Lieberman, Gerald J., jt. auth. see Hillier, Frederick S.

Lieberman, Gerald J., jt. auth. see Resnikoff, George J.

Lieberman, Harvey. Decision Guides. (Simulation Game Ser.). 1974. pap. 35.00 (*0-89401-013-1*); 8.00 (*0-685-77376-0*); 12.00 (*0-89401-015-8*) Didactic Syst.

— Effective Supervision in Government. (Simulation Game Ser.). 1973. pap. 26.25 (*0-89401-024-7*) Didactic Syst.

— Women in Management. (Simulation Game Ser.). 1975. pap. 26.25 (*0-89401-095-6*); pap. write for info. (*0-685-78132-1*) Didactic Syst.

Lieberman, Harvey & Rausch, Erwin. Managing & Allocating Time: Industrial. 1976. pap. 26.25 (*0-89401-060-3*); pap. write for info. (*0-685-73581-8*); teacher ed, pap. 1.00 (*0-685-73582-6*) Didactic Syst.

— Managing & Allocating Time (Non-Industrial) (Simulation Game Ser.). 1976. pap. 26.25 (*0-89401-061-1*); pap. write for info. (*0-686-57894-5*) Didactic Syst.

Lieberman, Herbert H. Shadow Dancers. 1990. reprint ed. mass mkt. 5.95 (*0-312-92288-4*) St Martin.

— Shadow Dancers: A Novel. 416p. 1989. 18.95 (*0-316-52417-4*) Little.

Lieberman, Ira W. Industrial Restructuring: Policy & Practice. (Policy & Research Ser.: No. 9). 34p. 1990. 6.95 (*0-8213-1441-6*, 11441) World Bank.

***Lieberman, Ira W., et al.** Mass Privatization in Central & Eastern Europe & the Former Soviet Union: A Comparative Analysis. LC 95-3895. (Studies of Economies in Transformation: Vol. 16). 1995. write for info. (*0-8213-3199-X*) World Bank.

***Lieberman, Ira W., et al, eds.** Russia: Creating Private Enterprise & Efficient Markets. LC 94-49067. (Studies of Economies in Transformation: No. 15). 1995. write for info. (*0-8213-3187-6*) World Bank.

Lieberman, J. Ben. Type & Typefaces. 2nd ed. LC 77-24401. (Illus.). 1978. 19.95 (*0-918142-01-6*); pap. 14.95 (*0-918142-02-4*) Myriade.

Lieberman, Jack. Inherited Disease of the Lung. 1988. text ed. 58.50 (*0-7216-2763-3*) Saunders.

Lieberman, Jack, ed. Sarcoidosis. (Illus.). 224p. 1985. text ed. 79.95 (*0-8089-1728-5*, 792539, Grune) Saunders.

Lieberman, James L. A Practical Guide for Hazardous Waste Management, Administration, & Compliance. Gauiter, Gary, ed. LC 94-12877. 1994. write for info. (*1-56670-115-5*) Lewis Pubs.

— A Practical Guide for Hazardous Waste Management, Administration & Compliance: RCRA Compliance Guide. (Environmental Regulatory Compliance Ser.). 240p. (C). 1993. pap. text ed. write for info. (*0-9638274-0-5*) Envir Info Srvs.

Lieberman, Janet E., ed. Collaborating with High Schools. LC 85-644753. (New Directions for Community Colleges Ser.: No. CC 63). 1988. 16.95 (*1-55542-882-7*) Jossey-Bass.

Lieberman, Jeffrey A. & Kane, John M., eds. Predictors of Relapse in Schizophrenia. LC 86-10900. (Clinical Insights Ser.). 167p. reprint ed. pap. 47.60 (*0-8357-7847-9*, 2036223) Bks Demand.

Lieberman, Jeffrey A., jt. ed. see Kane, John M.

Lieberman, Jethro K. Business Law & the Legal Environment. 2nd ed. 1226p. (C). 1988. text ed. 56.00 (*0-15-505659-X*) HB Coll Pubs.

— The Enduring Constitution. LC 86-32458. (Illus.). 493p. 1987. text ed. 86.95 (*0-314-32026-1*) West Pub.

— The Enduring Constitution. limited ed. LC 86-32458. (Illus.). 483p. 1987. text ed. 42.95 (*0-314-32025-3*) West Pub.

— The Nineteen Ninety-Four Supplement to the Evolving Constitution. 85p. (Orig.). Date not set. pap. 16.95 (*0-9630136-1-0*) Dialogue.

Lieberman, Jethro K. & Siedel, George J., III. Business Law & the Legal Environment. 3rd ed. 1400p. (C). 1993. pap. text ed. 11.50 (*0-15-505519-4*) Dryden Pr.

— Business Law & the Legal Environment. 3rd ed. 1400p. (C). 1993. text ed. 57.25 (*0-15-505516-X*); teacher ed, pap. text ed. 11.00 (*0-15-505518-6*) Dryden Pr.

Lieberman, Jethro K., jt. auth. see Goldstein, Tom.

Lieberman, Joe. Those Amazing Tables: Teaching Multiplication Through Patterns & Color Strips. (J). (gr. 4-7). 1983. pap. 10.95 (*0-201-48019-0*) Addison-Wesley.

— Those Amazing Tables: Teaching Multiplication Through Patterns & Color Strips. 64p. (J). (gr. 3-8). 1983. pap. text ed. 9.95 (*0-914040-98-7*) Cuisenaire.

Lieberman, Joseph A., III, jt. auth. see Stuart, Marian R.

Lieberman, Joseph I. Child Support in America: Practical Advice for Negotiating & Collecting - a Fair Settlement. LC 86-5501. 128p. (C). 1988. reprint ed. 10.00 (*0-300-04210-8*) Yale U Pr.

Lieberman, Judy S. Complete Off-Premise Caterer. 1991. text ed. 49.95 (*0-442-31858-8*) Van Nos Reinhold.

Lieberman, Julie L. Blues Fiddle. (Illus.). 112p. pap. 14.95 (*0-8256-0308-0*, OK64162, Oak) Music Sales.

— Improvising Violin. (Illus.). 132p. 1995. pap. 19.95 (*0-614-04272-0*) Huiksi Music.

— Improvising Violin. rev. ed. (Illus.). 136p. 1995. pap. 19. 95 (*1-879730-10-3*) Huiksi Music.

— You Are Your Instrument: The Definitive Musician's Guide to Practice & Performance. (Illus.). 152p. 1991. pap. 20.00 (*1-879730-20-0*) Huiksi Music.

Lieberman, Julie L., ed. see Deva, Jeannie.

Lieberman, Laurence. New & Selected Poems, 1962 to 1992. LC 92-45567. 232p. 1993. 29.95 (*0-252-02010-3*); pap. 17.95 (*0-252-06314-7*) U of Ill Pr.

— Unassigned Frequencies: American Poetry in Review, 1964-77. LC 77-10072. 307p. 1977. 29.95 (*0-252-00477-9*) U of Ill Pr.

Lieberman, Leo. What Can I Be? A Guide to Five Hundred Twenty-Five Liberal Arts & Business Careers. LC 75-26001. 1976. 19.50 (*0-935198-03-2*) M M Bruce.

Lieberman, Leo & Spielberger, Jeffrey. College Board Achievement Test: English Composition. 2nd ed. 256p. 1991. pap. 11.00 (*0-13-144965-6*, Arco Test) P-H Gen Ref & Trav.

— Essential English Composition for College-Bound Students. 3rd ed. LC 93-2054. (Orig.). 1993. pap. 10.00 (*0-671-86401-7*) P-H.

— SAT II Writing. 3rd ed. LC 93-17593. 1993. pap. 12.00 (*0-671-86400-9*) P-H.

Lieberman, Leo, et al. Preparation for the CLEP: College-Level Examination Program: The Five General Exams. 4th ed. 528p. 1993. pap. 12.00 (*0-671-84711-2*, Arco Test) P-H Gen Ref & Trav.

Lieberman, Lillian. ABC: Board Games. (Illus.). 64p. (J). (ps-2). 1991. pap. 7.95 (*1-878279-31-9*) Monday Morning Bks.

— ABC: Box Games. (Illus.). 64p. 1991. pap. 7.95 (*1-878279-30-0*) Monday Morning Bks.

— ABC: Folder Games. (Illus.). 64p. 1991. pap. 7.95 (*1-878279-29-7*) Monday Morning Bks.

— Classification. 64p. (J). (gr. 2-5). 1989. 6.95 (*0-912107-89-8*, MM1906) Monday Morning Bks.

— Comprehension. (Reading Superstar Ser.). 64p. (J). (gr. 2-5). 1987. 6.95 (*0-912107-66-9*) Monday Morning Bks.

— FolderGames for Math Plus. (Illus.). 144p. (J). (gr. 1-3). 1995. teacher ed, pap. 13.95 (*1-878279-84-X*, MM 2007) Monday Morning Bks.

— FolderGames for Phonics Plus. (Illus.). 144p. (J). (gr. 1-3). 1995. teacher ed, pap. 13.95 (*1-878279-85-8*, MM 2008) Monday Morning Bks.

— Following Directions. 64p. (J). (gr. 2-5). 1989. 6.95 (*0-912107-87-1*, MM1904) Monday Morning Bks.

— KinderFolders for Math Readiness. (Illus.). 144p. (J). (ps-1). 1995. teacher ed, pap. 13.95 (*1-878279-82-3*, MM 2005) Monday Morning Bks.

— Making Inferences. (Illus.). 64p. (J). (gr. 2-5). 1989. teacher ed, pap. 6.95 (*0-912107-88-X*, MM 1905) Monday Morning Bks.

— Vocabulary. (Reading Superstar Ser.). 64p. (J). (gr. 2-5). 1987. 6.95 (*0-912107-68-5*) Monday Morning Bks.

— Word Structure. (Reading Superstar Ser.). 64p. (J). (gr. k-3). 1987. 6.95 (*0-912107-67-7*) Monday Morning Bks.

***Lieberman, Linda.** KinderFolders for Reading Readiness. (Illus.). 144p. (J). (ps-1). 1995. teacher ed, pap. 13.95 (*1-878279-83-1*, MM 2006) Monday Morning Bks.

Lieberman, Louis, jt. auth. see Westheimer, Ruth.

***Lieberman, M.** Coming Out Conservative. 1994. pap. 4.99 (*0-517-13024-6*) Random.

Lieberman, M. A., jt. auth. see Lichtenberg, A. J.

Lieberman, M. Laurence. The Dieter's Pharmacy: The Essential Guide to Drugs That Affect Your Appetite & Body Weight. 384p. 1990. pap. 9.95 (*0-685-28831-5*) St Martin.

— The Sexual Pharmacy: The Complete Guide to Drugs with Sexual Side Effects. 320p. 1988. 18.95 (*0-317-66926-5*) NAL-Dutton.

Lieberman, Marc, jt. ed. see Kennett, David.

Lieberman, Marc F. & Drake, Michael V. A Computerized Perimetry: A Simplified Guide. 2nd ed. LC 92-80659. 232p. 1992. 45.00 (*1-55642-212-1*) SLACK Inc.

Lieberman, Marc R. Your Rights As a Consumer. 2nd ed. (Layman's Law Guides Ser.). 128p. 1994. pap. 8.95 (*1-56414-083-0*) Career Pr Inc.

Lieberman, Marcia. The Outdoor Traveler's Guide to the Alps. LC 91-3146. (Illus.). 360p. 1991. pap. 25.00 (*1-55670-177-2*) Stewart Tabori & Chang.

Lieberman, Marcia & Lieberman, Philip. Walking Switzerland - the Swiss Way: From Vacation Apartments, Mountain Hotels, Inns & Huts. LC 87-12350. (Illus.). 260p. (Orig.). 1987. pap. 12.95 (*0-89886-137-3*) Mountaineers.

Lieberman, Martin. Apple Dining & Entertainment Club. rev. ed. (Illus.). 54p. 1988. pap. 6.95 (*0-943711-01-0*) Apple Dining.

Lieberman, Maurice. Ear Training & Sight Singing. (Illus.). (C). 1959. pap. text ed. 19.95 (*0-393-09519-3*) Norton.

Lieberman, Melvyn, jt. ed. see Blaustein, Mordecai P.

Lieberman, Melvyn, jt. ed. see Nelson, Phillip G.

***Lieberman, Michael A. & Lichtenberg, Allan J.** Principles of Plasma Discharges & Materials Processing. 1994. text ed. 69.95 (*0-471-00577-0*) Wiley.

Lieberman, Morris, ed. Post-Harvest Physiology & Crop Preservation. LC 82-3645. (NATO ASI Series A, Life Sciences: Vol. 46). 586p. 1983. 125.00 (*0-306-40984-4*, Plenum Pr) Plenum.

Lieberman, Morton A., jt. auth. see Tobin, Sheldon S.

Lieberman, Morton A., et al. Self-Help Groups for Coping with Crisis: Origins, Members, Processes, & Impact. LC 79-88772. (Jossey-Bass Social & Behavioral Science Ser.). 480p. reprint ed. pap. 136.80 (*0-8357-4903-7*, 2037833) Bks Demand.

Lieberman, Myron. Bargaining. LC 79-66017. 333p. (Orig.). 1979. pap. 18.95 (*0-931028-09-4*) Teach-em.

— Beyond Public Education. LC 80-25571. 272p. 1985. text ed. 49.95 (*0-275-92039-9*, C2039, Praeger Pubs) Greenwood.

— Privatization & Educational Choice. 400p. 1989. text ed. 39.95 (*0-312-02799-0*); pap. 12.95 (*0-312-02845-8*) St Martin.

— Public Education: An Autopsy. LC 92-46732. 393p. 1993. text ed. 27.95 (*0-674-72232-9*) HUP.

Lieberman, Myron, jt. auth. see Gelsert, Gene.

Lieberman, Nancy & Jennings, Debby. Lady Magic: The Autobiography of Nancy Lieberman-Cline. (Illus.). 239p. 1992. 19.95 (*0-685-75065-5*) Sagamore Pub.

Lieberman, Nathaniel, photos. Manhattan Lightscape. (Illus.). 124p. 1990. 55.00 (*1-55859-121-4*) Abbeville Pr.

Lieberman-Nissen, Karen. Nutrition & Disease: An Annotated Bibliography. LC 90-14114. 192p. 1991. 25. 00 (*0-8240-7977-9*, 548) Garland.

Lieberman, Norman P. Troubleshooting Natural Gas Processing - Wellhead to Transmission. 208p. 1987. 69. 95 (*0-87814-308-4*, P4429) PennWell Bks.

— Troubleshooting Process Operations. 3rd ed. 576p. 1991. 79.95 (*0-87814-348-3*, P4480) PennWell Bks.

Lieberman, Paul. West's Legal Forms: Business Organizations with Tax Analysis, Vol. 2A. 2nd rev. ed. Date not set. text ed. write for info. (*0-314-02897-8*) West Pub.

— West's Legal Forms, Vol. 2: Business Organizations with Tax Analysis. 2nd rev. ed. 800p. Date not set. text ed. write for info. (*0-314-02102-7*) West Pub.

Lieberman, Philip. The Biology & Evolution of Language. LC 83-22582. (Illus.). 392p. 1984. 40.28 (*0-674-07412-2*) HUP.

— The Biology & Evolution of Language. 392p. 1987. pap. 16.95 (*0-674-07413-0*) HUP.

— Speech Acoustics & Perception. LC 70-183114. (Studies in Communicative Disorders). (C). 1972. write for info. (*0-672-61293-3*, Bobbs) Macmillan.

— The Speech of Primates. (Janua Linguarum, Ser. Minor: No. 148). (Illus.). 133p. (Orig.). 1972. pap. text ed. 46.95 (*90-279-2321-3*) Mouton.

— Uniquely Human: The Evolution of Speech, Thought, & Selfless Behavior. LC 90-38130. (Illus.). 210p. 1991. 34.95 (*0-674-92182-8*, LIEUNI) HUP.

— Uniquely Human: The Evolution of Speech, Thought, & Selfless Behavior. (Illus.). 210p. (C). 1993. pap. 14.95 (*0-674-92183-6*) HUP.

Lieberman, Philip & Blumstein, Shelia E. Speech Physiology, Speech Perception, & Acoustic Phonetics. (Cambridge Studies in Speech Science & Communication). (Illus.). 260p. 1988. 69.95 (*0-521-30866-6*); pap. 19.95 (*0-521-31357-0*) Cambridge U Pr.

Lieberman, Philip, jt. auth. see Lieberman, Marcia.

***Lieberman, Philip A.** Radio's Morning Show Personalities: 27 Early Hour Broadcasters & Deejays from the 1920's to the 1990's. 144p. 1995. lib. bdg. 29.95 (*0-7864-0037-4*) McFarland & Co.

Lieberman, Philip H. & Good, Robert A., eds. Diseases of Hematopoietic System. LC 81-4946. (Anatomic Pathology Slide Seminar Ser.). (Illus.). 121p. 1981. pap. text ed. 35.00 (*0-89189-085-8*, 50-1-046-00) Am Soc Clinical.

Lieberman, R. A. & Wlodarczyk, M. T. Chemical, Biochemical, & Environmental Fiber Sensors II, Vol. 1368. 1991. 62.00 (*0-8194-0429-2*) SPIE.

Lieberman, R. A. & Wlodarczyk, M. T., eds. Chemical, Biochemical & Environmental Applications of Fibers, Vol. 990. 1988. 45.00 (*0-8194-0025-4*) SPIE.

— Chemical, Biochemical, & Environmental Fiber Sensors. 310p. 1990. 70.00 (*0-8194-0208-7*, VOL. 1172) SPIE.

Lieberman, Ralph. Cornerstones: Twenty-Six Masterpieces of Western Architecture. 1989. 25.95 (*0-525-24461-1*, Dutton); pap. 15.95 (*0-525-48259-8*, Dutton) NAL-Dutton.

— Renaissance Architecture in Venice. LC 82-22606. (Illus.). 144p. 1982. 60.00 (*0-89659-310-X*) Abbeville Pr.

Lieberman, Randy, jt. ed. see Ordway, Frederick I., III.

Lieberman, Robbie. My Song Is My Weapon: People's Songs, American Communism, & the Politics of Culture, 1930-1950. (Music in American Life Ser.). (Illus.). 232p. 1989. 24.95 (*0-252-01559-2*) U of Ill Pr.

— My Song Is My Weapon: People's Songs, American Communism, & the Politics of Culture, 1930-1950. (Music in American Life Ser.). (Illus.). 232p. (C). 1995. pap. 16.95 (*0-252-06525-5*) U of Ill Pr.

***Lieberman, Robert H.** Goobersville Breakdown. (Illus.). 221p. 1979. 11.95 (*0-933124-01-5*) Gamma Bks.

— Goobersville Breakdown. (Illus.). 221p. 1979. reprint ed. pap. 6.95 (*0-933124-00-7*) Gamma Bks.

— The Physics Ferret: A Guide to Ferreting Out the Solution to Problems in Science, Math, &...Life. (Illus.). 32p. 1994. pap. 3.95 (*0-933124-02-3*) Gamma Bks.

Lieberman, Ronald. Keystone Five - Pennsylvania Books in Print. 1978. 12.00 (*0-934630-04-6*); lib. bdg. 12.00 (*0-934630-05-4*); pap. 5.00 (*0-934630-03-8*) Family Album.

— Keystone, No. 10: "Die Alte Zeite" - German Americana. 1989. pap. 10.00 (*0-934630-18-6*) Family Album.

— Keystone Tercentenary. 1983. 15.00 (*0-934630-12-7*); lib. bdg. 15.00 (*0-934630-13-5*); pap. 10.00 (*0-934630-14-3*) Family Album.

— Tillers of the Cultural Soil: Scholar Printers. (Orig.). Date not set. pap. write for info. (*0-934630-19-4*) Family Album.

***Lieberman, Sandord R., ed.** The Soviet Empire Reconsidered: Essays in Honor of Adam B. Ulam. LC 94-23353. (C). 1994. text ed. 59.95 (*0-8133-8839-2*) Westview.

Lieberman, Saul & Hyman, Arthur, eds. Salo Wittmayer Baron Jubilee Volume: On the Occasion of His Eightieth Birthday, 3 vols, 1. LC 74-82633. 1533p. 1975. write for info. (*0-231-03911-5*) Col U Pr.

— Salo Wittmayer Baron Jubilee Volume: On the Occasion of His Eightieth Birthday, 3 vols, 2. LC 74-82633. 1533p. 1975. write for info. (*0-231-03912-3*) Col U Pr.

— Salo Wittmayer Baron Jubilee Volume: On the Occasion of His Eightieth Birthday, 3 vols, 3. LC 74-82633. 1533p. 1975. write for info. (*0-231-03913-1*) Col U Pr.

— Salo Wittmayer Baron Jubilee Volume: On the Occasion of His Eightieth Birthday, 3 vols, Set. LC 74-82633. 1533p. 1975. 119.00 (*0-685-51945-7*) Col U Pr.

Lieberman, Shari & Bruning, Nancy P. The Real Vitamin & Mineral Book: Going Beyond the RDA for Optimum Health. LC 90-40460. 326p. (Orig.). 1990. pap. 9.95 (*0-89529-449-4*) Avery Pub.

Lieberman, Sima. Curse of the Macarena. abr. ed. 326p. 1994. pap. 9.95 (*1-56901-389-6*) NW Pub.

— The Economic & Political Roots of the New Protectionism. 200p. 1988. 53.50 (*0-8476-7595-5*, JR 7595) Rowman.

— Growth & Crisis in the Spanish Economy: 1940-93. LC 95-2227. 1995. write for info. (*0-415-12428-X*) Routledge.

— Labor Movements & Labor Thought: Spain, France, Germany & the United States. LC 85-16859. 302p. 1985. text ed. 65.00 (*0-275-90214-5*, C0214, Praeger Pubs) Greenwood.

— The Long Road to a European Monetary Union. 222p. (Orig.). (C). 1992. lib. bdg. 47.50 (*0-8191-8590-6*); pap. text ed. 24.50 (*0-8191-8591-4*) U Pr of Amer.

Lieberman, Stephen J. Sumerological Studies in Honor of Thorkild Jacobsen: On His Seventieth Birthday, June 7, 1974. LC 75-42584. (Assyriological Studies: No. 20). 1977. lib. bdg. 20.00 (*0-226-62282-7*) U Ch Pr.

Lieberman, Susan, jt. auth. see Feldscher, Sharla.

Lieberman, Susan A. New Traditions: Redefining Celebrations for Today's Family. 1991. pap. 9.95 (*0-374-52262-6*, Noonday) FS&G.

***Lieberman, Syd.** Streets & Alleys: Stories with a Chicago Accent. (American Storytelling Ser.). 1995. 19.95 (*0-87483-424-4*) August Hse.

— The Wise Shoemaker of Studena. LC 93-43481. (Illus.). 32p. (J). (gr. 5-8). 1994. 15.95 (*0-8276-0509-9*) JPS Phila.

***Lieberman, Tanya.** Storybooks Teach about World Cultures. (Illus.). 48p. 1994. teacher ed, pap. text ed. 6.95 (*1-878279-77-7*, MM 1998) Evan-Moor Corp.

***Lieberman, Victor B.** Burmese Administrative Cycles: Anarchy & Conquest, c. 1580-1760. LC 83-13716. reprint ed. pap. 101.80 (*0-7837-9376-6*, 2060120) Bks Demand.

— Burmese Administrative Cycles: Anarchy & Conquest, Fifteen Eighty to Seventeen Sixty. LC 83-13716. (Illus.). 275p. 1984. 57.50x (*0-691-05407-X*) Princeton U Pr.

Lieberman, William. Images. 1982. 12.50 (*0-934630-11-9*) Family Album.

— Images. deluxe limited ed. 1982. 25.00 (*0-934630-15-1*) Family Album.

— Jackson Pollock: The Early Years. LC 88-62943. (Illus.). 35p. 1989. pap. 15.00 (*0-935037-26-8*) G Peters Gallery.

Lieberman, William S. Edvard Munch: A Selection of His Prints from American Collections. LC 79-169306. (Museum of Modern Art Publications in Reprint). (Illus.). 42p. 1972. reprint ed. 12.95 (*0-405-01565-8*) Ayer.

— Matisse: Fifty Years of His Graphic Art. 150p. 1981. reprint ed. pap. 12.95 (*0-8076-1022-4*) Braziller.

— Max Ernst. LC 72-169307. (Museum of Modern Art Publications in Reprint). (Illus.). 66p. 1972. reprint ed. 15.95 (*0-405-01566-6*) Ayer.

Lieberman, William S., ed. Picasso Linoleum Cuts: The Mr. & Mrs. Charles Kramer Collection. (Illus.). 168p. 1985. 35.00 (*0-87099-404-2*) Metro Mus Art.

— Twentieth-Century Modern Masters: The Jacques & Natasha Gelman Collection. (Illus.). 368p. 1989. 95.00 (*0-87099-568-5*, Abrams) Metro Mus Art.

Lieberman, William S. & Rewald, Sabine. Twentieth-Century Modern Masters: The Jacques & Natasha Gelman Collection. (Illus.). 336p. 1990. 60.00 (*0-8109-1037-3*) Abrams.

Liebermann. Community & Home Health Nursing. (Clinical Rotation Guide Ser.). 120p. 1989. 14.95 (*0-87434-208-2*) Springhouse Pub.

— Rapidly Solidified Alloys: Processes-Structures-Properties-Applications. (Materials Engineering Ser.: Vol. 3). 792p. 1993. 215.00 (*0-8247-8951-2*) Dekker.

Liebermann, Alvin. Contamination Control. (Illus.). 182p. (C). 1990. 100.00 (*0-918247-09-8*) Tustin Tech.

Liebermann, Jeremiah, ed. see Garvy, John W., Jr.

Liebermann, M. Coloring Books on Events of the Jewish Months: Nisan. (Learn As You Color Ser.: No. II). (J). (ps-2). 1987. 3.00 (*0-914131-86-9*, D712) Torah Umesorah.

— Coloring Books on Events of the Jewish Months: Tishrei, Cheshvan. (Learn As You Color Ser.: No. II). (J). (ps-2). 1987. 3.00 (*0-914131-84-2*, D710) Torah Umesorah.

— Coloring Books on the Parshas Hashavua: Bereishis. (Learn As You Color Ser.: No. I). (J). (ps-2). 1987. 3.00 (*0-914131-79-6*, D700) Torah Umesorah.

— Coloring Books on the Parshas Hashavua: Devorim. (Learn As You Color Ser.: No. I). (J). (ps-2). 1987. 3.00 (*0-914131-83-4*, D704) Torah Umesorah.

— Coloring Books on the Parshas Hashavua: Shemos. (Learn As You Color Ser.: No. I). (J). (ps-2). 1987. 3.00 (*0-914131-80-X*, D701) Torah Umesorah.

— Coloring Books on the Parshas Hashavua: Vayikrah. (Learn As You Color Ser.: No. I). (J). (ps-2). 1987. 3.00 (*0-914131-81-8*, D702) Torah Umesorah.

— Learn as You Color Series III: Brachos. (J). (ps-2). 1987. 3.00 (*0-914131-88-5*, D720) Torah Umesorah.

Liebermann, Max, jt. auth. see Heine, Heinrich.

Liebermann-Meffert, D., et al, eds. Greater Omentum: Anatomy, Physiology, Pathology, Surgery. (Illus.). 361p. 1983. 291.00 (*0-387-11882-9*) Spr-Verlag.

Liebermann, Mike & Daily, Bev. Paediatrics: What Shall I Do? LC 93-7817. (Illus.). 128p. 1993. pap. 20.00 (*0-7506-1402-1*) Buttrwrth-Heinemann.

Liebermann, Robert C. & Sondergeld, Carl H., eds. Experimental Techniques in Mineral & Rock Physics: The Schreiber Volume. LC 94-8954. 1994. write for info. (*3-7643-5028-8*) Birkhauser.

— Experimental Techniques in Mineral & Rock Physics: The Schreiber Volume. LC 94-8954. (Pure & Applied Geophysics Ser.). 430p. 1994. 35.00 (*0-8176-5028-8*) Birkhauser.

Lieberoff, Allen. Climb Your Own Ladder: 101 Home Businesses that Can Make You Wealthy. 224p. 1982. pap. 7.95 (*0-686-46704-3*, Fireside) S&S Trade.

Liebers, Arthur. How to Get the Job You Want Overseas. rev. ed. LC 75-1138. 39p. 1990. pap. 4.95 (*0-87576-148-8*) Pilot Bks.

— How to Start a Profitable Retirement Business. rev. ed. LC 84-25381. 48p. 1987. pap. 3.95 (*0-87576-117-8*) Pilot Bks.

Liebers, Reinhold. Wie Geschrieben Steht: Studien zu Einer Besonderen Art Fruehchristlichen Schriftbezuges. viii, 445p. (GER.). (C). 1993. lib. bdg. 136.95 (*3-11-013859-X*) De Gruyter.

Liebersath, Henry. Caught in the Middle: Meeting God in the Midst of Problems. 176p. (Orig.). 1987. 8.95 (*0-8245-0822-X*) Crossroad NY.

Liebersohn, Harry. Fate & Utopia in German Sociology. (German Social Thought Ser.). 280p. 1988. 35.00 (*0-262-12133-6*) MIT Pr.

— Fate & Utopia in German Sociology. (Studies in Contemporary German Thought). 246p. 1990. reprint ed. pap. 12.95 (*0-262-62079-0*) MIT Pr.

Lieberson, Alan. A Physician's Guide to Advance Medical Directives. Karaffa, Melanie C., ed. LC 92-48385. 350p. 1993. 69.95 (*1-878487-52-3*, ME223) Practice Mgmt Info.

Lieberson, Alan D. Advance Medical Directives. LC 92-82793. 1992. 145.00 (*0-685-59919-1*) Clark Boardman Callaghan.

Lieberson, Stanley. Language Diversity & Language Contact: Essays by Stanley Lieberson. Dil, Anwar S., ed. (Language Science & National Development Ser.). 408p. 1981. 49.50 (*0-8047-1098-8*) Stanford U Pr.

— Making It Count: The Improvement of Social Research & Theory. 1985. pap. 14.00 (*0-520-06037-7*) U CA Pr.

— Making It Count: The Improvement of Social Research & Theory. LC 84-25285. 271p. reprint ed. pap. 77.30 (*0-7837-4843-4*, 2044490) Bks Demand.

— A Piece of the Pie: Blacks & White Immigrants Since 1880. (Illus.). 420p. 1980. pap. 17.00 (*0-520-04362-6*) U CA Pr.

Lieberson, Stanley, ed. Explorations in Sociolinguistics. 4th ed. LC 67-64323. (General Publications: Vol. 44). (Orig.). 1973. pap. text ed. 18.00 (*0-317-93772-3*) Res Inst Inner Asian Studies.

Lieberson, Stanley & Waters, Mary C. From Many Strands: Ethnic & Racial Groups in Contemporary America. (Population of the United States in the 1980s: A Census Monograph Ser.). 304p. 1988. 45.00 (*0-87154-543-8*) Russell Sage.

— From Many Strands: Ethnic & Racial Groups in Contemporary America. LC 88-9651. (Population of the United States in the 1980s: A Census Monograph Ser.). (Illus.). 304p. (C). 1990. pap. 16.95 (*0-87154-527-6*) Russell Sage.

Liebert, Arthur. Mythus und Kultur: Myth & Culture. Bolle, Kees W., ed. (Mythology Ser.). (GER.). 1978. reprint ed. lib. bdg. 19.95 (*0-405-10549-5*) Ayer.

Liebert, Elizabeth. Changing Life Patterns: Adult Development in Spiritual Direction. LC 91-37118. 208p. 1992. pap. 13.95 (*0-8091-3296-6*) Paulist Pr.

Liebert, Herman. Bibliography Old & New. LC 72-619564. (Bibliographical Monograph: No. 6). (Illus.). 1974. 10.00 (*0-87959-050-5*) U of Tex H Ransom Ctr.

Liebert, J., jt. auth. see Hayes, D. S.

Liebert, Lynn Langenbach, jt. auth. see Liebert, Robert M.

***Liebert, Mary A., ed.** The Author's Guide to Biomedical Journals: Complete Manuscript Submission Instruction for 185 Leading Biomedical Periodicals. 628p. 1994. 164.00 (*0-913113-61-1*) M Liebert.

Liebert, Mike, jt. auth. see Leavengood, Betty.

Liebert, Robert M. Early Window. 6th ed. (C). 1988. pap. 19.95 (*0-205-14408-X*, H4408) Allyn.

— Osage Life & Legends: Earth People - Sky People. (Illus.). 144p. 1987. 16.95 (*0-87961-168-5*); pap. 8.95 (*0-87961-169-3*) Naturegraph.

***Liebert, Robert M. & Liebert, Lynn Langenbach.** Science & Behavior: An Introduction to Methods of Psychological Research. 4th rev. ed. LC 94-40698. 1995. text ed. 55.00 (*0-13-142721-0*) P-H.

Liebert, Robert M & Spiegler, Michael D. Personality: Strategies & Issues. 6th ed. LC 89-22097. 608p. (C). 1989. text ed. 50.95 (*0-534-12228-0*) Brooks-Cole.

— Personality: Strategies & Issues. 7th ed. LC 93-36565. 1994. text ed. 52.95 (*0-534-17580-5*) Brooks-Cole.

Liebert, Robert M., jt. auth. see Harris, Judith R.

Liebert, Robert M., jt. auth. see Houts, Arthur C.

Liebert, Robert M., jt. auth. see Johnson, Margaret H.

Liebert, Robert M., et al. The Early Window: Effects of Television on Children & Youth. 2nd ed. LC 82-5327. (General Psychology Ser.: No. 34). (Illus.). 280p. 1982. text ed. 35.00 (*0-08-027548-6*, J125, Pergamon Pr); pap. text ed. 12.95 (*0-08-027547-8*, Pergamon Pr) Elsevier.

Liebert, Robert S. Michelangelo: A Psychoanalytic Study of His Life & Images. LC 82-7042. (Illus.). xxii, 449p. 1983. text ed. 45.00 (*0-300-02793-1*) Yale U Pr.

Liebert, Robert S., jt. auth. see Oldham, John M.

Lieberthal, Edwin M. The Complete Book of Fingermath. (Illus.). 1979. text ed. 21.96 (*0-07-037680-8*) McGraw.

Lieberthal, Edwin M., jt. auth. see Gurau, Peter K.

***Lieberthal, Kenneth.** Governing China. 450p. (C). 1995. text ed. 20.95 (*0-393-96714-X*) Norton.

— Governing China: From Revolution Through Reform. (Illus.). 512p. 1995. 30.00 (*0-393-03787-8*) Norton.

Lieberthal, Kenneth & Dickson, Bruce. Research Guide to Central Party & Government Meetings in China, 1949-1986. 2nd ed. LC 88-18527. 392p. 1989. 88.95 (*0-87332-492-7*) M E Sharpe.

Lieberthal, Kenneth & Oksenberg, Michel. Policy Making in China: Leaders, Structures, & Processes. 461p. 1990. text ed. 62.50 (*0-691-05668-4*); pap. text ed. 17.95 (*0-691-01075-7*) Princeton U Pr.

Lieberthal, Kenneth, jt. ed. see Lardy, Nicholas R.

Lieberthal, Kenneth, et al. Central Documents & Politburo Politics in China. LC 78-8740. (Michigan Monographs in Chinese Studies: No. 33). 201p. 1978. pap. 6.00 (*0-89264-033-2*) Ctr Chinese Studies.

Lieberthal, Kenneth, et al, eds. Perspectives on Modern China: Four Anniversaries. LC 91-13410. (Studies on Modern China). 448p. 1991. 67.95 (*0-87332-814-0*); pap. 23.95 (*0-87332-890-6*) M E Sharpe.

Lieberthal, Kenneth G. Revolution & Tradition in Tientsin, 1949-1952. LC 79-64215. xiv, 234p. 1980. 32.50 (*0-8047-1044-9*) Stanford U Pr.

Lieberthal, Kenneth G. & Lampton, David M., eds. Bureaucracy, Politics, & Decision Making in Post-Mao China. LC 91-9476. (Studies on China: Vol. 14). (Illus.). 384p. 1992. 45.00 (*0-520-07356-8*) U CA Pr.

Liebes, Tamar & Katz, Elihu. The Export of Meaning: Cross-Cultural Readings of Dallas. 2nd ed. 200p. 1994. pap. text ed. 19.95 (*0-7456-1295-4*) Blackwell Pubs.

Liebes, Yehuda. Studies in Jewish Myth & Messianism. Stein, Batya, tr. LC 91-36470. (SUNY Series in Judaica: Hermeneutics, Mysticism, & Religion). 226p. (C). 1992. 59.50 (*0-7914-1193-1*); pap. 19.95 (*0-7914-1194-X*) State U NY Pr.

— Studies in the Zohar. Schwartz, Arnold & Nakadhe, Stephanie, trs. LC 91-36469. (SUNY Series in Judaica Hermeneutics, Mysticism, & Religion). 1993. 59.50 (*0-7914-1189-3*); pap. 19.95 (*0-7914-1190-7*) State U NY Pr.

Liebeschuetz, J. H. Barbarians & Bishops: Army, Church, & State in the Age of Arcadius & Chrysostom. 304p. 1992. pap. 35.00 (*0-19-814073-8*) OUP.

— From Diocletian to the Arab Conquest: Change in the Late Roman Empire. (Collected Studies: No. CS310). 288p. 1990. text ed. 95.00 (*0-86078-258-1*, Pub. by Variorum UK) Ashgate Pub Co.

Liebeshutz, Hans. Mediaeval Humanism in the Life & Writings of John of Salisbury, with an Epilogue: John of Salisbury & the School of Chartres. (Warburg Institute Studies: Vol. 17). 1969. reprint ed. pap. 44.00 (*0-8115-1392-0*) Periodicals Srv.

Liebeskind, J. C., jt. ed. see Fields, H. L.

Liebeskind, Joseph, ed. see Von Dittersdorf, Karl D.

Liebeskind, Lanny S., ed. Advances in Metal-Organic Chemistry, Vol. 2. 300p. 1991. 90.25 (*0-89232-948-3*) Jai Pr.

— Advances in Metal-Organic Chemistry, Vol. 3. 1991. 90.25 (*1-55938-324-0*) Jai Pr.

Liebesny, Herbert J. The Law of the Near & Middle East: Readings, Cases, & Materials. LC 75-22046. 316p. 1975. 59.50 (*0-87395-256-1*) State U NY Pr.

Liebesny, Herbert J., jt. ed. see Khadduri, Majid.

Liebetrau, Albert M. Measures of Association, Vol. 32. LC 83-60229. (Quantitative Applications in the Social Sciences Ser.: Vol. 32). 95p. 1983. 9.95 (*0-8039-1974-3*) Sage.

Liebgott. The Anatomical Basis of Dentistry. (Illus.). 511p. (C). 1986. 48.95 (*0-941158-88-8*) Mosby Yr Bk.

Liebhaber, Josephine D. The Cat Fights Back. (Illus.). 118p. (Orig.). 1993. pap. 6.95 (*0-9635609-0-5*) Action Res.

Liebhaberg, Bruno. Industrial Relations & Multinational Corporations in Europe. LC 80-83365. 122p. 1981. text ed. 49.95 (*0-275-90670-1*, C0670, Praeger Pubs) Greenwood.

Liebhardt, Paul. Odyssey: Tales of the Universe. 224p. 1991. 60.00 (*0-9628861-0-6*) Inst Shipboard.

Liebhardt, Paul W. Discovery: The Adventure of Shipboard Education. Rogers, Judy S., ed. LC 85-50383. (Illus.). 1985. 50.00 (*0-9614403-0-9*) William & Allen.

***Liebherr, James K.** Cladistic Analysis of North American Platynini & Revision of the Agonum Extensicolle Species Group (Coleoptera: Carabidae) LC 85-29034. (University of California Publications in Entomology: No. 106). 210p. 1986. pap. 59.90 (*0-7837-7490-7*, 2049212) Bks Demand.

Liebherr, James K., ed. Zoogeography of Caribbean Insects. LC 87-47868. (Illus.). 304p. 1988. 45.00 (*0-8014-2143-8*) Cornell U Pr.

Liebich, Andre, et al, eds. Citizenship, East & West. LC 94-14172. (Publications de l'Institut Universitaire de Hautes Etudes Internationales, Geneve Ser.). 1995. write for info. (*0-7103-0491-9*, Pub. by Kegan Paul Intl UK) Routledge Chapman & Hall.

Liebig, H., jt. auth. see Flik, T.

Liebig, James E. Business Ethics: Profiles in Civic Virtue. LC 89-29522. 256p. 1991. 21.95 (*1-55591-059-9*); pap. 12.95 (*1-55591-101-3*) Fulcrum Pub.

— Merchants of Vision: People Bringing New Purpose & Values to Business. LC 93-43269. 252p. 1994. 24.95 (*1-881052-42-7*) Berrett-Koehler.

Liebing, Alison & Ward, Tony. Deaths in Custody: International Perspectives. 196p. 1994. 90.00 (*1-871177-55-3*, Pub. by Whiting & Birch UK); pap. 34.95 (*1-871177-42-1*, Pub. by Whiting & Birch UK) Paul & Co Pubs.

***Liebing, Edward.** Beyond the Basics: Maintaining & Optimizing Netware Three Servers. (Illus.). 360p. (Orig.). 1995. pap. 29.95 (*0-9645751-0-8*) SevenL Pr.

— LAN Manager 2.0: A Supervisor's Guide. 1992. pap. 34.95 (*1-55851-160-1*) M&T Bks.

— The Official Novell NetWare Lite Handbook. LC 92-64215. 381p. 1992. 24.95 (*0-7821-1095-9*) Sybex.

— User's Guide to Netware X OS. 2nd ed. 1992. pap. 29.95 (*1-55851-283-7*) M&T Bks.

Liebing, Edward, et al. NetWare Workstation Troubleshooting Maintenance Handbook. 400p. 1990. pap. text ed. 32.95 (*0-07-607027-1*) McGraw.

Liebing, Ralph W. Architectural Working Drawings. 3rd ed. 1990. text ed. 69.95 (*0-471-50181-6*) Wiley.

— Construction Regulations Handbook. LC 86-19041. 368p. 1987. text ed. 53.95 (*0-471-81705-8*) Wiley.

Liebkind, Karmela. New Identities in Europe: Immigrant Ancestry & the Ethnic Identity of Youth. (Illus.). 1989. text ed. 69.95 (*0-566-05741-7*, Pub. by Gower UK) Ashgate Pub Co.

Liebknecht, Karl. Libertarian Anthology. 1972. 59.95 (*0-8490-0517-5*) Gordon Pr.

— Militarism & Anti-Militarism. 1972. 59.95 (*0-8490-0635-X*) Gordon Pr.

— Militarism & Anti-Militarism. 1969. 29.50 (*0-86527-130-5*) Fertig.

— Militarism & Anti-Militarism. 7.75 (*0-8446-4571-0*) Peter Smith.

Liebknecht, Wilhelm P. Karl Marx: Biographical Memoirs. Untermann, E., tr. LC 69-10119. 181p. 1969. reprint ed. text ed. 52.50 (*0-8371-0536-6*, LIKM, Greenwood Pr) Greenwood.

— Karl Marx, Biographical Memoirs. 1901. 13.00 (*0-403-00200-1*) Scholarly.

Lieblein, L. & McGillivray, R., trs. Jacques Grevin: Taken by Surprise. 84p. 1989. pap. 6.00 (*0-919473-51-2*, DH49, Pub. by Dovehouse CN) MRTS.

Liebler, Barbara. Hands on Weaving. LC 86-80911. (Illus.). 112p. 1986. pap. 8.95 (*0-934026-24-6*) Interweave.

Liebler, H. Baxter. Boil My Heart for Me. LC 94-17862. (Illus.). 230p. 1994. reprint ed. pap. 14.95 (*0-87480-464-7*) U of Utah Pr.

Liebler, Joan G., et al. Management Principles for Health Professionals. 2nd ed. 448p. (C). 1992. 51.00 (*0-8342-0287-5*) Aspen Pub.

Liebler, John. Frog Counts to Ten. LC 93-40116. (Illus.). 32p. (J). (gr. k-3). 1994. 13.90 (*1-56294-436-3*) Millbrook Pr.

— Frog Counts to Ten. (Illus.). 32p. (J). (gr. k-3). 1995. pap. 3.95 (*1-56294-698-6*) Millbrook Pr.

***Liebler, M. L.** Breaking the Voodoo: Poetry & Fiction. 2nd ed. LC 89-643744. 116p. (Orig.). Date not set. per., pap. text ed. 6.50 (*1-56439-038-1*) Ridgeway.

— Deliver Me: Christian Poems. (King Tree Little Book Ser.). (Illus.). 16p. (Orig.). (C). 1991. pap. text ed. 3.00 (*1-56439-006-3*) Ridgeway.

Liebler, M. L., ed. The Vision of Words: Poetry by Southeast Michigan Poets. (Illus.). 80p. (Orig.). 1992. per. 19.95 (*1-56439-022-5*) Ridgeway.

Liebler, M. L., intro. The Hollow Moon: Poetry by Five Young St. Clair Shores Poets. 40p. 1993. pap. text ed. 6.00 (*1-56439-029-2*) Ridgeway.

***Liebler, Naomi C.** Shakespeare's Festive Tragedy: The Ritual Foundations of Genre. LC 95-9687. 1995. write for info. (*0-415-08657-4*); pap. write for info. (*0-415-13183-9*) Routledge.

Lieblich, Amia. Seasons of Captivity: The Inner World of POW's. 240p. 1995. 40.00 (*0-8147-5079-6*) NYU Pr.

— Seasons of Captivity: The Inner World of POW's. 240p. 1995. pap. 16.95 (*0-8147-5095-8*) NYU Pr.

— Transition to Adulthood During Military Service: The Israeli Case. LC 89-30041. (SUNY Series in Israeli Studies). 221p. 1989. 64.50 (*0-7914-0146-4*); pap. 21.95 (*0-7914-0147-2*) State U NY Pr.

Lieblich, Amia, jt. auth. see Josselson, Ruthellen.

Lieblich, Jerome H. Dimensioning & Tolerancing Manual. 140p. 1988. pap. 19.95 (*0-912702-44-3*) Global Eng Doc.

— Drawing Requirements Manual. 8th ed. 1100p. 1992. 155.00 (*0-912702-64-8*); ring bd. 155.00 (*0-912702-65-6*) Global Eng Doc.

Lieblich, Jerome H., ed. Screw Thread Standards for Federal Services. 582p. 1978. ring bd. 195.00 (*0-912702-11-7*, FED-STD-H28) Global Eng Doc.

Lieblich, Julia. Sisters: Lives of Devotion & Defiance. 338p. 1994. reprint ed. pap. 14.95 (*0-8245-1436-X*) Crossroad NY.

Liebling, A. J. Back Where I Came From. LC 89-38678. 320p. 1990. reprint ed. pap. 11.00 (*0-86547-425-7*, North Pt Pr) FS&G.

— Between Meals: An Appetite for Paris. LC 94-26990. 1995. 12.50 (*0-679-60142-2*, Modern Lib) Random.

— The Earl of Louisiana. LC 76-130664. 252p. 1970. pap. 11.95 (*0-8071-0203-2*) La State U Pr.

— The Honest Rainmaker: The Life & Times of Colonel John R. Stingo. LC 89-8812. 176p. 1989. reprint ed. pap. 9.95 (*0-86547-396-X*, North Pt Pr) FS&G.

— A Neutral Corner: Boxing Essays. Warner, Fred & Barbour, James, eds. 256p. 1990. 19.95 (*0-86547-450-8*, North Pt Pr) FS&G.

— The Press. 1981. pap. 6.95 (*0-394-74849-2*) Pantheon.

— The Sweet Science. (Autographed Sports Classics Ser.). 1981. reprint ed. 24.95 (*0-941372-06-5*) Holtzman Pr.

Liebling, Abbott J. Mink & Red Herring, the Wayward Pressman's Casebook. LC 76-157960. 251p. 1972. reprint ed. text ed. 35.00 (*0-8371-6174-6*, LIMR, Greenwood Pr) Greenwood.

Liebling, Alison. Suicides in Prison. LC 92-4230. 256p. 1992. 69.95 (*0-415-07559-9*, A9562) Routledge.

Liebling, Emil, jt. auth. see Mathews, William S.

Liebling, Henry E. Handbook for Personal Productivity. 128p. Date not set. 9.00 (*0-915299-94-1*, PP-305) Prod Press.

Liebling, Herman I. U. S. Corporate Profitability & Capital Formation: Are Rates of Return Sufficient? (Policy Studies). 1980. 58.00 (*0-08-024622-2*, Pergamon Pr) Elsevier.

Liebling, Jerome. Jerome Liebling: A Life in Photography. LC 94-70316. (Illus.). 124p. 1995. 40.00 (*0-89381-599-3*) Aperture.

— Jerome Liebling Photographs. LC 82-6919. (Illus.). 108p. 1982. 40.00 (*0-87023-371-8*) U of Mass Pr.

Liebman. Neuroanatomy Made Easy & Understandable. 4th ed. 160p. 1991. 30.00 (*0-8342-0202-6*, 20202) Aspen Pub.

Liebman, Arthur. The Ghosts, Witches & Vampires Quiz Book. LC 91-23371. (Illus.). 128p. (J). (gr. 3-10). 1992. pap. 4.95 (*0-8069-8409-0*) Sterling.

— The Politics of Puerto Rican University Students. LC 78-630381. (Latin American Monographs: No. 20). 217p. reprint ed. pap. 61.90 (*0-8357-7719-7*, 2036076) Bks Demand.

Liebman, Arthur, et al. Latin American University Students: A Six Nation Study. LC 70-180152. (Center for International Affairs Ser.). (Illus.). 322p. 1972. 29.00 (*0-674-51275-8*) HUP.

Liebman, Charles S. Deceptive Images: Toward a Redefinition of American Judaism. 256p. 1988. 34.95 (*0-88738-218-5*) Transaction Pubs.

— Pressure Without Sanctions: The Influence of World Jewry on Israeli Policy. LC 75-18242. 304p. (C). 1976. 39.50 (*0-8386-1791-3*) Fairleigh Dickinson.

— Religious & Secular: Conflict & Accommodation Between Jews in Israel. 238p. 1990. pap. 8.95 (*0-9623723-1-5*) AVI CHAI.

Liebman, Charles S., ed. Conflict & Accommodation Between Jews in Israel: Religious & Secular. 8.95 (*0-88125-374-X*) Ktav.

Liebman, Charles S. & Cohen, Steven M. Two Worlds of Judaism: The Israeli & American Experiences. LC 89-28455. 224p. (C). 1990. 30.00 (*0-300-04726-6*) Yale U Pr.

— Two Worlds of Judaism: The Israeli & American Experiences. 213p. (C). 1992. reprint ed. pap. text ed. 14.00 (*0-300-05231-6*) Yale U Pr.

Liebman, Charles S. & Don-Yehiya, Eliezer. Civil Religion in Israel: Traditional Judaism & Political Culture in the Jewish State. LC 82-17427. 270p. 1983. 45.00 (*0-520-04817-2*) U CA Pr.

— Religion & Politics in Israel. LC 83-48172. (Jewish Political & Social Studies). 158p. reprint ed. pap. 45.10 (*0-7837-6104-X*, 2059150) Bks Demand.

Liebman, Charles S., jt. auth. see Cohen, Steven M.

Liebman, Glenn. Baseball Shorts: 1,000 of the Game's Funniest One-Liners. 240p. 1994. 9.95 (*0-8092-3644-3*) Contemp Bks.

— Golf Shorts: 1,001 of Golf's Funniest One-Liners. 256p. 1995. 12.00 (*0-8092-3489-0*) Contemp Bks.

— Sports Shorts: Two Thousand of Sports' Funniest One-Liners. LC 93-2776. 384p. 1993. 12.95 (*0-8092-3768-7*) Contemp Bks.

Liebman, J. F. & Geenberg, A., eds. Biophysical Aspects. (Molecular Structure & Energetics Ser.: Vol. 4). 407p. 1987. lib. bdg. 95.00 (*0-89573-336-6*) VCH Pubs.

Liebman, J. F. & Greenberg, A., eds. Chemical Bonding Models. (Molecular Structure & Energetics Ser.). 360p. 1986. lib. bdg. 95.00 (*0-89573-139-8*, VOL. 1) VCH Pubs.

— Physical Measurements. (Molecular Structure & Energetics Ser.: Vol. 2). 388p. 1987. lib. bdg. 95.00 (*0-89573-140-1*) VCH Pubs.

Liebman, James S. Federal Habeas Corpus Practice & Procedure, 2 vols. suppl. ed. 1992. 75.00 (*0-87473-962-4*) Michie Butterworth.

Liebman, James S. & Hertz, Randy. Federal Habeas Corpus Practice & Procedure, 2 vols., Set. 1993. 180.00 (*0-87473-409-6*) Michie Butterworth.

Liebman, Jeffrey M. & Cooper, Steven J. The Neuropharmacological Basis of Reward. (Illus.). 448p. 1989. 75.00 (*0-19-852176-6*) OUP.

Liebman, Jerome, et al, eds. Pediatric & Fundamental Eletrocardiography. (Developments in Cardiovascular Medicine Ser.). 1987. lib. bdg. 162.00 (*0-89838-815-5*) Kluwer Ac.

Liebman, Joel & Greenberg, Arthur, eds. Fluorine-Containing Molecules: Structure, Reactivity, Synthesis & Applications. LC 88-19227. (Molecular Structure & Energetics Ser.). 346p. 1988. lib. bdg. 95.00 (*0-89573-705-1*) VCH Pubs.

— Mechanistic Principles of Enzyme Activity. LC 88-19229. (Molecular Structure & Energetics Ser.). 404p. 1989. lib. bdg. 95.00 (*0-89573-706-X*) VCH Pubs.

Liebman, Joel F. & Greenberg, Arthur, eds. Environmental Influences & Recognition in Enzyme Chemistry. LC 88-19228. (Molecular Structure & Energetics Ser.). 349p. 1989. lib. bdg. 95.00 (*0-89573-707-8*) VCH Pubs.

— From Atoms to Polymers Isoelectronic Analogies to Molecular Structure & Energenitics: Isoelectronic Analogies. LC 88-36684. 473p. 1989. lib. bdg. 95.00 (*0-89573-711-6*) VCH Pubs.

— Modern Models of Bonding & Delocalization. LC 88-19226. (Molecular Structures & Energetics Ser.: Vol. 6). 461p. 1989. lib. bdg. 95.00 (*0-89573-714-0*) VCH Pubs.

Liebman, Joel F., et al, eds. Advances in Boron & the Boranes: A Volume in Honor of Anton B. Burg. LC 87-21705. (Molecular Structure & Energetics Ser.). 547p. 1988. lib. bdg. 95.00 (*0-89573-272-6*) VCH Pubs.

Liebman, John R., jt. auth. see Root, William A.

Liebman, Jon, jt. ed. see Conway, Jennifer.

Liebman, Joshua L. Peace of Mind. LC 93-45844. 1994. reprint ed. 9.95 (*0-8065-1496-5*, Citadel Pr) Carol Pub Group.

Liebman, Judith, et al. Modeling & Optimization with GINO. (Illus.). 200p. 1986. disk, pap. text ed. 37.50 (*0-89426-050-2*); 5.25 hd, pap. text ed. 47.50 (*0-89426-106-1*); 3.5 hd, pap. text ed. 47.50 (*0-89426-157-6*); mac hd, pap. text ed. 47.50 (*0-89426-158-4*) Boyd & Fraser.

Liebman, Lance, ed. Ethnic Relations in America. LC 82-552. 184p. 1982. 11.95 (*0-13-291682-7*) Am Assembly.

Liebman, Lance, ed. see American Assembly Staff.

Liebman, Lance, jt. auth. see Haar, Charles M.

Liebman, Lance, jt. auth. see Heymann, Philip B.

Liebman, Lance, jt. auth. see Rothstein, Mark A.

Liebman, Lisa, jt. auth. see Kanjo, Kathryn.

Liebman, Malvina W. Jewish Cookery from Boston to Baghdad. LC 75-2186. (Illus.). 272p. 1975. bds. 18.00 (*0-911389-02-4*) NightinGale Res.

— Tastes & Tales: Jewish Cookery for Young People with Tales from Around the World. (Illus.). 200p. (Orig.). 1986. spiral bd. 8.95 (*0-930029-02-X*) Central Agency.

Liebman, Marcel. Leninism under Lenin. (C). 1985. pap. 9.95 (*0-85036-261-X*, Pub. by Merlin Pr UK) Humanities.

Liebman, Matthew Z., jt. ed. see Altieri, Miguel.

Liebman, Michael N., ed. see American Chemical Society, Division of Agricultural & Food Chemistry Staff.

Liebman, Richard F., jt. ed. see Bernstein, Harlan.

Liebman, Robert C. & Wuthnow, Robert. The New Christian Right: Mobilization & Legitimation. (Social Institutions & Social Change Ser.). 264p. (C). 1983. lib. bdg. 42.95 (*0-202-30307-1*); pap. text ed. 22.95 (*0-202-30308-X*) Aldine de Gruyter.

Liebman, Ronald S. Grand Jury. 1983. pap. 2.95 (*0-345-29784-9*) Ballantine.

Liebman, Ronald S., jt. auth. see Stone, Scott N.

***Liebman, Roy.** Silent Film Performers: An Annotated Bibliography of Published, Unpublished & Archival Sources for over 350 Actors & Actresses. 320p. 1995. lib. bdg. 75.00 (*0-7864-0100-1*) McFarland & Co.

Liebman, Seymour. The Enlightened. 157p. 1967. pap. 10.95 (*0-87024-311-X*) U of Miami Pr.

Liebman, Seymour B. The Inquisitors & the Jews in the New World: Summaries of Procesos 1500-1810, & Bibliographical Guide. LC 72-85110. 160p. 1973. 11.95 (*0-87024-245-8*) U of Miami Pr.

— Jews in New Spain: Faith, Flame & the Inquisition. LC 70-91213. (Illus.). 381p. 1970. 13.95 (*0-87024-129-X*) U of Miami Pr.

— New World Jewry, Fourteen Ninety-Three to Eighteen Twenty-Five: Requiem for the Forgotten. 25.00 (*0-87068-277-6*) Ktav.

Liebman, Wayne. Tending the Fire: The Ritual Men's Group. 64p. 1991. pap. 7.00 (*0-915408-45-7*) Ally Pr.

***Liebmann, George W.** The Little Platoons: Local Governments in Modern History. LC 95-5308. 184p. 1995. text ed. 55.00 (*0-275-95178-2*, Praeger Pubs) Greenwood.

Liebmann, Lisa. Fauve Birds, Butterflies, & Flowers. (Giftwraps by Artists Ser.). 1990. pap. 14.95 (*0-8109-2976-7*) Abrams.

— Pat Steir: Waterfalls. (Illus.). 32p. (Orig.). 1990. pap. text ed. 10.00 (*0-614-00473-X*) Contemp Art Mus.

— Southeast Bank Collects: A Corporation Views Contemporary Art. Perez, Esther, ed. 70p. (Orig.). 1990. write for info. (*0-943411-21-1*) Norton Gal Art.

Liebmann, M. Western European Sculpture. 264p. (C). 1988. 275.00 (*0-569-53686-3*, Pub. by Collets UK) Pro-Am Music.

— Western European Sculpture from Soviet Museums: 15th & 16th Centuries. (Illus.). 264p. (C). 1988. text ed. 300.00 (*0-685-40254-1*, Pub. by Collets) St Mut.

— Western European Sculpture from Soviet Museums, 15th-16th Centuries. 264p. (C). 1988. 275.00 (*0-685-34410-X*, Pub. by Collets) St Mut.

Liebmann, Marian. Art Therapy for Groups: A Handbook of Themes, Games & Exercises. (Illus.). 226p. (Orig.). 1986. pap. text ed. 19.95 (*0-914797-24-7*) Brookline Bks.

Liebmann, Marian, ed. Art Therapy in Practice. 176p. 1990. 56.00 (*1-85302-057-5*, Pub. by J Kingsley Pubs UK); pap. 27.00 (*1-85302-058-3*, Pub. by J Kingsley Pubs UK) Taylor & Francis.

— Art Therapy with Offenders. 220p. 1994. pap. 36.00 (*1-85302-171-7*, Pub. by J Kingsley Pubs UK) Taylor & Francis.

Liebmann, R. Statistical Mechanics of Periodic Frustrated Ising Systems. (Lecture Notes in Physics Ser.: Vol. 251). vii, 142p. 1986. 27.00 (*0-387-16473-1*) Spr-Verlag.

Liebmann-Smith, Joan. In Pursuit of Pregnancy: How Couples Discover, Cope with, & Resolve Their Fertility Problems. LC 86-28656. 224p. 1987. pap. 9.95 (*1-55704-039-7*) Newmarket.

Liebmann-Smith, Richard, ed. The Question of AIDS. 89p. 1985. pap. text ed. 6.00 (*0-89766-302-0*) NY Acad Sci.

Liebnitz, Jennifer, et al. Rilke & the Visual Arts. Baron, Frank, ed. (Illus.). 150p. 1982. 12.50 (*0-87291-153-5*) Coronado Pr.

Liebo, Stephen L., ed. see Cavel, Michael P.

Liebo, Stephen L., ed. see Winer, Edward L., et al.

Liebold, Louise C. Fireworks, Brass Bands & Elephants: Promotional Events with Flair for Libraries & Other Nonprofit Organizations. LC 85-43488. (Illus.). 144p. 1986. pap. 29.95 (*0-89774-249-4*) Oryx Pr.

Liebovich, Louis W. Bylines in Despair: Herbert Hoover, the Great Depression, & the U. S. News Media. LC 93-50679. 256p. 1994. text ed. 52.95 (*0-275-94843-9*, Praeger Pubs) Greenwood.

— The Press & the Origins of the Cold War, 1944-1947. LC 87-38478. 181p. 1988. text ed. 49.95 (*0-275-92999-X*, C2999, Praeger Pubs) Greenwood.

Liebovich, Louis W., jt. ed. see Bielawski, Shraga F.

Liebovitz, Maury & Solomon, Linda, eds. Legacies: Stories of Courage, Humor, & Resilience, of Love, Loss, & Life-Changing Encounters, by New Writers Sixty & Older. LC 92-56196. 320p. 1993. 22.00 (*0-06-019045-0*, A Asher Bks) HarpC.

Liebow, Cynthia, tr. see Saumont, Annie.

Liebow, Elliot. Tally's Corners. 1968. pap. 9.95 (*0-316-52514-6*) Little.

— Tell Them Who I Am: The Lives of Homeless Women. 350p. 1993. text ed. 24.95 (*0-02-919095-9*) Free Pr.

— Tell Them Who I Am: The Lives of Homeless Women. 368p. 1995. 11.95 (*0-14-024137-X*, Penguin Bks) Viking Penguin.

Liebow, Ely. Dr. Joe Bell: Model for Sherlock Holmes. LC 81-85520. 286p. 1982. 16.95 (*0-87972-197-9*); pap. 11.95 (*0-87972-198-7*) Bowling Green Univ.

Liebow, Ely, ed. see Nieminski, John.

Liebowitz, Barry, jt. auth. see Light, Enid.

Liebowitz, Daniel. The Lion & the Flame. 320p. (Orig.). 1992. pap. 14.95 (*1-879384-15-9*) Cypress Hse.

Liebowitz, H., ed. Combined Nonlinear & Linear (Micro & Macro) Fracture Mechanics: Applications to Modern Engineering Structures - Selected Papers, U.S.-Japan Seminar. 1976. pap. 56.00 (*0-08-019982-8*, Pergamon Pr) Elsevier.

— Progress in Fatigue & Fracture, Vol. 8 No. 1. 1976. pap. 73.00 (*0-08-020866-5*, Pergamon Pr) Elsevier.

Liebowitz, H., jt. ed. see Bodner, S. R.

Liebowitz, H., jt. auth. see Eringen, A. Cemal.

Liebowitz, Harold. The Oriental Institute Excavations at Selenkahiye, Syria: Terra-Cotta Figurines & Model Vehicles. Van Loon, M., ed. LC 81-71738. (Bibliotheca Mesopotamica Ser.: Vol. 22). (Illus.). xiv, 60p. 1987. 22.00 (*0-685-05119-6*); pap. 14.50 (*0-685-05120-X*) Undena Pubns.

***Liebowitz, J. & Prereau, D.** Worldwide Intelligent Systems: Approaches to Telecommunications & Network Management. LC 94-77523. (Frontiers in Artificial Intelligence & Applications Ser.: Vol. 24). 279p. 1995. 75.00 (*90-5199-183-5*) IOS Press.

Liebowitz, Jay. Dynamics of Decision Support Systems & Expert Systems. 288p. (C). 1990. pap. text ed. 43.00 (*0-03-026383-2*) Dryden Pr.

— Expert Systems for Business & Management. 1990. text ed. 63.00 (*0-13-296468-6*) P-H.

Liebowitz, Jay, ed. Expert Systems Applications to Telecommunications. LC 87-27022. (Telecommunications Ser.). 371p. 1988. text ed. 95.00 (*0-471-62459-4*) Wiley.

— Moving Towards Expert Systems Globally in the 21st Century. LC 94-4689. (Illus.). 1573p. (C). 1994. 330.00 (*1-882345-00-2*) Cognizant Comm.

— Operational Expert System Applications in the United States. 168p. 1992. 48.00 (*0-08-041429-X*, Pergamon Pr) Elsevier.

— Worldwide Expert Systems Activities & Trends. LC 94-4690. (Illus.). 178p. (C). 1994. 48.00 (*1-882345-02-9*) Cognizant Comm.

Liebowitz, Jay & Singh, I., eds. FAX-Net Electronic Mail Source Directory. (Illus.). 228p. 1986. pap. 96.00 (*0-08-033983-2*, K125, Pergamon Pr) Elsevier.

— Fax-Net Electronic Mail Source Directory. 220p. 1987. pap. 96.00 (*0-08-034495-X*, Pergamon Pr) Elsevier.

Liebowitz, Jay & Zelde, Janet S. Kids & Computers. 2nd ed. (Illus.). 70p. (J). (gr. 3-6). 1989. reprint ed. write for info. (*0-9623252-0-1*); reprint ed. pap. write for info. (*0-9623252-2-8*) J Liebowitz.

Liebowitz, Jay, ed. see Artz, John M., et al.

Liebowitz, Jay, jt. auth. see Medsker, Larry.

Liebowitz, Jay, jt. ed. see Turban, Efraim.

Liebowitz, Martin L., jt. auth. see Homer, Sidney.

Liebowitz, Nathan. Daniel Bell & the Agony of Modern Liberalism. LC 84-15690. (Contributions in Political Science Ser.: No. 124). xii, 293p. 1985. text ed. 59.95 (*0-313-24279-8*, LID/, Greenwood Pr) Greenwood.

Liebowitz, Ronald D., jt. ed. see Kraus, Michael.

Liebowitz, Sol. Argentina. (Let's Visit Places & Peoples of the World Ser.). (Illus.). 128p. (J). (gr. 5 up). 1990. 14.95 (*0-7910-1106-2*) Chelsea Hse.

Liebrand, W. G., et al, eds. Social Psychological Approach to Social Dilemmas. (International Series in Experimental Social Psychology). 250p. 1992. 71.00 (*0-08-037775-0*, Pergamon Pr) Elsevier.

***Liebs, Chester.** Main Street to Miracle Mile: American Roadside Architecture. (Illus.). 262p. 1994. pap. 24.95 (*0-8018-5095-9*) Johns Hopkins.

Liebscher, J. J., jt. auth. see Baumgartner, A.

Liebschutz, Sarah F. Bargaining under Federalism: Contemporary New York. LC 90-39852. (SUNY Series in Public Administration). 251p. (C). 1991. 57.50 (*0-7914-0634-2*); pap. 18.95 (*0-7914-0635-0*) State U NY Pr.

— Federal Aid to Rochester. LC 83-73308. 58p. 1984. pap. 8.95 (*0-8157-5253-9*) Brookings.

Liebskind, Lanny S., ed. Advances in Metal-Organic Chemistry, Vol. 1. 1988. 73.25 (*0-89232-863-0*) Jai Pr.

***Liebson, David J. & Nowka, Richard H.** The Uniform Commercial Code of Kentucky. 2nd ed. 1151p. 1992. 95.00 (*0-87473-852-0*) Michie Butterworth.

Liebson, Donald. Electric Utility Encyclopedia, 1993. rev. ed. (Illus.). 8500p. 2,000.00 (*0-929836-28-6*); cd-rom, disk write for info. (*0-318-67989-0*) OPRI.

— Electric Utility Operations & Maintenance Costs, 1993. 500p. 500.00 (*0-929836-33-2*); disk write for info. (*0-318-67990-4*) OPRI.

— Electric Utility Sourcebook, 1993. rev. ed. 1,000.00 (*0-929836-30-8*) OPRI.

— Electric Utility Yearbook, 1993. rev. ed. 4250p. 1,500.00 (*0-929836-29-4*) OPRI.

— Natural Gas Contracts, 1993. 400p. 750.00 (*0-929836-95-2*) OPRI.

— Natural Gas LDCs, 1993. (Illus.). 1,000.00 (*0-929836-94-4*) OPRI.

— The Natural Gas Pipeline Encyclopedia, 1993. rev. ed. (Illus.). 1600p. 2,000.00 (*0-929836-91-X*); cd-rom, disk write for info. (*0-318-69931-1*) OPRI.

— The Natural Gas Pipeline Sourcebook, 1993. rev. ed. (Illus.). 1,000.00 (*0-929836-92-8*) OPRI.

— Natural Gas Pipeline Yearbook, 1993. rev. ed. (Illus.). 1000p. 1,500.00 (*0-929836-93-6*) OPRI.

— Petroleum Pipeline Encyclopedia, 1993. rev. ed. (Illus.). 4800p. 2,000.00 (*0-929836-80-4*); cd-rom, disk write for info. (*0-318-69791-2*) OPRI.

— Petroleum Pipeline Sourcebook, 1993. rev. ed. (Illus.). 600p. 1,000.00 (*0-929836-81-2*) OPRI.

— Petroleum Pipeline Yearbook, 1993. rev. ed. (Illus.). 3000p. 1,500.00 (*0-929836-82-0*) OPRI.

— United States Electric Generating Plants, 1993. 500p. 750.00 (*0-929836-32-4*) OPRI.

Liebson, Donald C. The OPRI Electric Generating Plant Database. 1000p. 1993. 2,500.00 (*0-929836-31-6*) OPRI.

Liebson, John. Exploring Wordperfect 6 for DOS. 390p. (Orig.). 1993. pap. text ed. 29.95 (0-9626660-8-4) Future Comms.

Liebson, Milt. Direct Stone Sculpture. LC 90-64436. (Illus.). 160p. 1991. text ed. 29.95 (0-88740-305-0) Schiffer.

Liebstoeckl, Hans. Secret Sciences in the Light of Our Time: Genesis, Golgotha's Mystery, Occultism, Philosopher's Stone, Rudolf Steiner. 1972. 59.95 (0-8490-1014-4) Gordon Pr.

Liechti. HE: Shiatsu. 1992. pap. 9.95 (1-85230-318-2) Element MA.

Liechty, Anna L., jt. auth. see **Wezeman, Phyllis V.**

Liechty, Daniel. Andreas Fischer & the Sabbatarian Anabaptists: An Early Reformation Episode in East Central Europe. LC 87-17727. (Studies in Anabaptist & Mennonite History: No. 29). 192p. 1988. 29.95 (0-8361-1293-8) Herald Pr.

— Early Anabaptist Spirituality: Selected Writings. LC 94-8478. (Classics of Western Spirituality Ser.). 1994. pap. 19.95 (0-8091-3475-6) Paulist Pr.

— Sabbatarianism & the Sixteenth Century: A Page in the History of the Christian Approach to Judaism. LC 93-71090. 94p. 1993. pap. 13.95 (0-943872-99-5) Andrews Univ Pr.

— Theology in Postliberal Perspective. LC 90-38708. 128p. (Orig.). (C). 1990. pap. 10.95 (0-334-02481-1) TPI PA.

— Transference & Transcendence: Ernest Becker's Contribution to Psychotherapy. LC 94-39365. 224p. 1995. 35.00 (1-56821-434-0) Aronson.

Liechty, Daniel, ed. & tr. Early Anabaptist Spiritually: Selected Writings. LC 94-8478. (Classics of Western Spirituality Ser.). 1994. 29.95 (0-8091-0466-0) Paulist Pr.

***Liechty, Elizabeth G., et al.** Fitting & Pattern Alterations: A Multi-Method Approach. 1992. per. 29.50 (0-87005-739-1) Conselle Inst.

Liechty, Elizabeth L., et al. Fitting & Pattern Alteration: A Multi-Method Approach. (Illus.). 250p. (C). 1985. text ed. 18.50 (0-87005-775-8) Fairchild.

Liechty, Jay. America's State Church: Will It Be the Dominant Religion in the Twenty First Century? 197p. (Orig.). 1994. pap. 11.95 (0-9624576-1-2) Calder Pr.

— How to Avoid a Collision (Audit) with the IRS. 120p. (Orig.). 1990. pap. 7.95 (0-685-28875-7) Calder Pr.

Lieder, F. W., ed. Popular German Stories. (Orig.). (GER.). pap. text ed. 6.95 (0-89197-351-6) Irvington.

Lieder, Paul R., ed. Eminent British Poets of the Nineteenth Century: Tennyson to Housman, Vol. 2. LC 72-448. (Granger Index Reprint Ser.). 1977. reprint ed. 38.95 (0-8369-6366-0) Ayer.

— Eminent British Poets of the Nineteenth Century: Wordsworth to Landor, Vol. 1. LC 72-448. (Granger Index Reprint Ser.). 1977. reprint ed. 40.95 (0-8369-6365-2) Ayer.

Liederbach, Clarence A. America's Thousand Bishops: From 1513 to 1974, from Abramowicz to Zuroweste. LC 73-94081. 80p. 1974. pap. 3.50 (0-913228-09-5) R J Liederbach.

— Canada's Bishops: Sixteen Fifty-Eight to Nineteen Seventy-Five. LC 73-94082. 1976. pap. 2.95 (0-913228-10-9) R J Liederbach.

Liederbach, Robert J., ed. see **Ryan, Abram.**

***Liederman, Erica.** The Book of Eleanor. 200p. (Orig.). 1995. pap. 14.00 (0-9646828-0-X) N Fork Pr.

Liederman, Judith. The Pleasure Dome. 1983. pap. 3.75 (0-8217-1134-2) Zebra.

Liedermann, David, jt. auth. see **Urvater, Michele.**

Liedl, G. L. & Hobbs, L. W., eds. Frontiers in Materials Education, Vol. 66. (Materials Research Society Symposium Proceedings Ser.). 1986. text ed. 36.00 (0-931837-31-6) Materials Res.

Liedl, Janice, tr. see **Bartlett, Kenneth, et al, eds.**

Liedl, R., et al, eds. Iteration Theory & Its Functional Equations. (Lecture Notes in Mathematics Ser.: Vol. 1163). viii, 231p. 1985. pap. 34.10 (0-387-16067-1) Spr-Verlag.

Liedlich, Raymond D., jt. auth. see **Smith, William F.**

Liedloff, Helmut. Ohne Muhe! LC 79-84596. (German Sequential Readers Ser.). (Illus.). (J). (gr. 9-10). 1980. pap. 9.44 (0-395-27931-3) HM.

Liedloff, Helmut, jt. auth. see **Moeller, Jack R.**

Liedloff, Jean. The Continuum Concept. 256p. 1985. pap. 11.54 (0-201-05071-4) Addison-Wesley.

— The Continuum Concept. 21.25 (0-8446-6267-4) Peter Smith.

Liedo, Pablo, jt. ed. see **Aluja, Martin.**

Liedtke, A. James. Current & Future Modalities of Cardiac Imaging. 250p. 1988. 50.00 (0-89335-308-6) PMA Pub Corp.

Liedtke, R. K. Dictionary of Clinical Pharmacology for Doctors & Pharmacists: Woerterbuch der Klinischen Pharmakologie Fuer Mediziner und Pharmazeuten. 245p. 1980. 49.95 (0-8288-1838-X, M15389) Fr & Eur.

Liedtke, Walter. Flemish Paintings in the Metropolitan Museum of Art, 2 vols. (Illus.). 488p. 1984. 25.00 (0-87099-356-9) Metro Mus Art.

— Royal Horse & Rider. 336p. 1989. 65.00 (0-89835-267-3) Abaris Bks.

Liedtke, Walter A. Flemish Paintings in the Metropolitan Museum of Art. 1994. 25.00 (0-8109-6461-9) Abrams.

— Masterworks from the Musee Des Beaux-Arts, Lille. 1992. 60.00 (0-8109-6417-1) Abrams.

Lief, jt. auth. see **Booth, Joe.**

Lief, Alfred. Brandeis: The Personal History of an American Ideal. LC 72-169768. (Select Bibliographies Reprint Ser.). 1977. reprint ed. 35.95 (0-8369-5988-4) Ayer.

Lief, Alfred, ed. The Dissenting Opinions of Mr. Justice Holmes. xviii, 314p. 1981. reprint ed. lib. bdg. 27.50 (0-8377-0811-7) Rothman.

Lief, Alfred, ed. see **Meyer, Adolf.**

***Lief, Bert W.** EURoad: The Complete Guide to Motoring in Europe. 24th ed. (Illus.). 64p. 1995. pap. 7.95 (0-912693-11-8) VLE Ltd.

— Walks Through London. 1992. 3.00 (0-912693-63-0, 1043) VLE Ltd.

— Walks Through Munich. 1992. 3.00 (0-912693-65-7, 1046) VLE Ltd.

Lief, Bert W. & Keely, L. M. Walks Through Amsterdam. 1991. 3.00 (0-912693-60-6, 1054) VLE Ltd.

— Walks Through Barcelona. 1992. 3.00 (0-912693-62-2, 1050) VLE Ltd.

— Walks Through Brussels. 1991. 3.00 (0-912693-61-4, 1053) VLE Ltd.

— Walks Through Dublin. 1994. 3.00 (0-912693-71-1, 1055) VLE Ltd.

— Walks Through Madrid. 1992. 3.00 (0-912693-64-9, 1044) VLE Ltd.

— Walks Through Paris. 1992. 3.00 (0-912693-66-5, 1045) VLE Ltd.

— Walks Through Rome. 1992. 3.00 (0-912693-67-3, 1047) VLE Ltd.

— Walks Through Seville. 1992. 3.00 (0-912693-68-1, 1051) VLE Ltd.

— Walks Through Stuttgart. 1988. 3.00 (0-912693-57-6, 1048) VLE Ltd.

— Walks Through Vienna. 1992. 3.00 (0-912693-69-X, 1052) VLE Ltd.

— Walks Through Zurich. 1992. 3.00 (0-912693-70-3, 1049) VLE Ltd.

Lief, Greg, jt. auth. see **Booth, Joe.**

Lief, Harold I. & Hoch, Zwi. International Research in Sexology: Selected Papers from the Fifth World Congress. LC 83-21146. 238p. 1984. text ed. 59.95 (0-275-91442-9, C1442, Praeger Pubs) Greenwood.

Lief, Harold I., jt. ed. see **Hoch, Zwi.**

Lief, Judith L., ed. see **Trungpa, Chogyam.**

Lief, Light. The Modern Age: Literature. 4th ed. 800p. (C). 1981. pap. text ed. 27.50 (0-03-055616-3) HB Coll Pubs.

Lief, Nina R. The First Year of Life: A Curriculum for Parenting Information. 362p. 24.18 (0-686-86720-5) Sadlier.

Lief, Nina R. & Fahs, Mary E. The Early Childhood Development Center's Parenting Series: The First Year of Life. 288p. 1991. 24.95 (0-8027-1153-7); pap. 12.95 (0-8027-7349-4) Walker & Co.

— The Early Childhood Development Center's Parenting Series: The Second Year of Life. 288p. 1991. 24.95 (0-8027-1154-5); pap. 12.95 (0-8027-7350-8) Walker & Co.

— The Early Childhood Development Center's Parenting Series: The Third Year of Life. 288p. 1991. 24.95 (0-8027-1155-3); pap. 12.95 (0-8027-7351-6) Walker & Co.

Lief, Patricia. Fun with Fruits & Vegetables. 1991. 13.99 (0-86653-994-8) Fearon Teach Aids.

Liefeld, Olive F. Unfolding Destinies: New Perspectives on Peter Fleming & the Auca Mission. 224p. 1990. pap. 9.99 (0-310-54001-1) Zondervan.

***Liefeld, Walter L.** Interpreting the Book of Acts. (Guides to New Testament Exegesis Ser.). 128p. (Orig.). 1995. pap. 8.99 (0-8010-2015-8) Baker Bk.

— New Testament Exposition. 1989. pap. 16.99 (0-310-45911-7) Zondervan.

Liefeld, Walter L., jt. auth. see **Tucker, Ruth A.**

Lieff & Trechsel, eds. Moisture Migration in Buildings - STP 779. 291p. 1982. 39.00 (0-8031-0605-X, 04-779000-10) ASTM.

Lieff Benderly, Beryl. Dancing Without Music. LC 90-41334. 302p. 1990. pap. 13.95 (0-930323-59-9) Gallaudet Univ Pr.

Lieff, Jonathan D. Computer Applications in Psychiatry. LC 86-17240. 384p. 1987. boxed 40.00 (0-88048-031-9, 48-031-9) Am Psychiatric.

— Computers & Other Technological Aids for Psychiatric Private Practice. LC 84-6286. (Private Practice Monograph Ser.). 123p. reprint ed. pap. 35.10 (0-8357-7846-0, 2036221) Bks Demand.

Lieff, Morris & Stumpf, S. M., eds. Fire Resistive Coatings: The Need for Standards - STP 826. LC 83-71335. 162p. 1984. pap. text ed. 22.00 (0-8031-0214-3, 04-826000-31) ASTM.

***Liefferink, J. D., et al, eds.** European Intergration & Environmental Policy. 1994. text ed. 74.95 (0-471-94811-X) Wiley.

— European Integration & Environmental Policy. 288p. 1993. text ed. 64.95 (0-470-22105-4) Halsted Pr.

Liefmann, Robert. Cartels, Concerns & Trusts. Wilkins, Mira, ed. LC 76-29997. (European Business Ser.). 1977. reprint ed. lib. bdg. 35.95 (0-405-09755-7) Ayer.

Liegeois, Jean-Pierre. Gypsies: An Illustrated History. 192p. 1993. pap. 15.00 (0-86356-025-3, Pub. by Saqi Bks UK) Interlink Pub.

Liegerot, G. F. There's No Traffic on the Extra Mile: The Courageous Battle by Bob Foerster to Overcome a Rare Paralysis & the Amazing Life of Athlete Tim Hughes. 1992. 17.95 (0-533-10211-1) Vantage.

Lieh-Tzu. The Book of Lieh-Tzu: A Classic of the Tao. Graham, A. C., tr. (Translations from the Oriental Classics Ser.). 208p. 1990. pap. text ed. 14.50 (0-231-07237-6) Col U Pr.

***Lieh-Tzu & Wong, Eva.** Lieh-Tzu: A Taoist Guide to Practical Living. LC 95-16063. 256p. (Orig.). 1995. pap. 15.00 (1-57062-153-5, Sham Dragon Edits) Shambhala Pubns.

Liehaus, Jacob L. Contraception & Family Planning: A Medical Subject Analysis with Reference Bibliography. LC 85-48080. 150p. 1987. 44.50 (0-88164-432-3); pap. 39.50 (0-88164-433-1) ABBE Pubs Assn.

— Premenstrual Syndrome: Index of Modern Information. LC 88-47618. 150p. 1990. 44.50 (1-55914-138-7); pap. 39.50 (1-55914-139-5) ABBE Pubs Assn.

— Psychiatric Status Rating Scales in Medicine & Psychology: Guidebook for Reference & Research. LC 83-46108. 150p. 1985. 37.50 (0-88164-150-2); pap. 34.50 (0-88164-151-0) ABBE Pubs Assn.

Liehm, Antonin, jt. auth. see **Liehm, Mira.**

Liehm, Antonin J. Closely Watched Films: The Czechoslovak Experience. LC 72-94987. 495p. reprint ed. 141.10 (0-685-16318-0, 2027619) Bks Demand.

— The Milos Forman Stories. LC 73-92806. (Illus.). 201p. reprint ed. pap. 57.30 (0-685-23741-9, 2032782) Bks Demand.

Liehm, Freddy. French & Dutch Lexicon of Economic & Commercial Terms: Lexique de Termes Economiques et Commerciaux. 104p. (DUT & FRE.). 1986. pap. 35.00 (0-8288-0804-X, M2365) Fr & Eur.

Liehm, Mira. Passion & Defiance: Italian Film from 1942 to the Present. LC 83-6667. (Illus.). 450p. (C). 1984. 40.00 (0-520-05020-7); pap. 15.00 (0-520-05744-9) U CA Pr.

Liehm, Mira & Liehm, Antonin. The Most Important Art: Soviet & East European Film After 1945. 467p. 1977. 45.00 (0-520-03157-1); pap. 15.00 (0-520-04128-3) U CA Pr.

Liehr, H. & Grun, M., eds. Reticuloendothelial System & Pathogenesis of Liver Disease: Proceedings of the International Biomedical Symposium, Warzberg, W. Germany, 1979. 422p. 1980. pap. 102.00 (0-444-80240-1) Elsevier.

***Liehr, M., et al, eds.** Ultraclean Semiconductor Processing: Technology & Surface Chemical Cleaning & Passivation. (Symposium Proceedings Ser.: Vol. 386). 1995. text ed. 63.00 (1-55899-289-8) Materials Res.

***Liell, Peter & Coleman, John.** Law of Education, 2 vols., Set. Date not set. ring bd. 495.00 (0-406-02647-5, UK) Butterworth Legal Pubs.

Liell, Peter & Saunders, John B. The Law of Education, 2 vols. 9th ed. 1991. U.K. ring bd. 420.00 (0-406-39643-4) Butterworth Legal Pubs.

Lielpeteris, J. & Moreau, R., eds. Liquid Metal Magnetohydrodynamics. (C). 1989. lib. bdg. 155.00 (0-7923-0344-X) Kluwer Ac.

Liem, Ann. Jacob Boehme: Insights into the Challenge of Evil. LC 77-79823. 32p. (Orig.). 1977. pap. 3.00 (0-87574-214-9) Pendle Hill.

Liem, Channing. The Korean War: An Unanswered Question. 93p. 1992. 7.00 (0-317-04972-0) Comm New Korea.

Liem Thanh Nguyen, jt. auth. see **Henkin, Alan B.**

Liem, Tik L. Invitations to Science Inquiry. 2nd ed. (Illus.). 467p. 1991. reprint ed. 40.00 (1-878106-00-7) Sci Inquiry.

— Invitations to Science Inquiry: Supplement to First & Second Edition. (Illus.). 180p. 1992. pap. text ed. 19.50 (1-878106-01-5) Sci Inquiry.

— Turning Kids on to Science in the Home: Forces & Motion, Vol. 3. (Illus.). 122p. 1992. pap. text ed. 17.50 (1-878106-06-6) Sci Inquiry.

— Turning Kids on to Science in the Home: Living Things, Vol. 4. (Illus.). 67p. 1992. pap. text ed. 12.50 (1-878106-07-4) Sci Inquiry.

— Turning Kids on to Science in the Home, Vol. 2: Energy, Vol. 2. (Illus.). 168p. 1992. pap. text ed. 20.00 (1-878106-05-8) Sci Inquiry.

— Turning Our Kids on to Science in the Home: Our Environment, 4 vols., 1. (Illus.). 185p. 1992. write for info. (1-878106-04-X) Sci Inquiry.

— Turning Our Kids on to Science in the Home: Our Environment, 4 vols., Set. (Illus.). 185p. 1992. pap. text ed. 25.00 (1-878106-08-2) Sci Inquiry.

Liemant, A., et al. Equilibrium Distributions of Branching Processes. (C). 1988. lib. bdg. 93.00 (90-277-2774-0) Kluwer Ac.

Lien. Learning Apple II Basic. 1984. pap. 14.95 (0-932760-24-4) CompuSoft.

— SAR: Side Effects & Drug Design. (Medicinal Research Ser.: Vol. 11). 384p. 1987. 180.00 (0-8247-7686-0) Dekker.

Lien, Carsten. Olympic Battleground: The Power Politics of Timber Preservation. LC 90-45255. (Illus.). 448p. 1991. 35.00 (0-87156-646-X) Sierra.

Lien, David A. The BASIC Handbook: Encyclopedia of the BASIC Computer Language. 3rd ed. LC 85-71338. 862p. (Orig.). 1986. pap. 24.95 (0-932760-33-3) CompuSoft.

— The IBM BASIC Handbook: The Encyclopedia of the BASIC Computer Language for All IBM Personal Computers & Compatibles. 2nd ed. LC 85-63823. 250p. (Orig.). 1986. pap. 16.95 (0-932760-38-4) CompuSoft.

— Learning Apple II BASIC: Includes the Enhanced IIe, IIc & II Plus. rev. ed. LC 85-71965. (CompuSoft Learning Ser.). (Illus.). 365p. (Orig.). 1985. pap. 14.95 (0-932760-35-X) CompuSoft.

— Learning IBM BASIC for the Personal Computer. rev. ed. LC 82-73471. (CompuSoft Learning Ser.). (Illus.). 494p. (Orig.). (gr. 7 up). 1984. pap. 19.95 (0-932760-13-9) CompuSoft.

— Learning Microsoft BASIC for the Macintosh: New Microsoft 2.X Version. LC 85-71339. (Illus.). 457p. (Orig.). 1985. pap. 19.95 (0-932760-34-1) CompuSoft.

— MS-DOS, Advanced Applications, Vol. 2. 3rd ed. 384p. (Orig.). (C). 1986. pap. 14.95 (0-932760-46-5) CompuSoft.

— MS-DOS-the Advanced Course. 1989. pap. 27.95 (0-932760-49-X) CompuSoft.

— MS-DOS-the Basic Course. 1989. pap. 14.95 (0-932760-48-1) CompuSoft.

— MS-DOS, The Basics, Vol. 1. 3rd ed. 145p. (Orig.). (C). 1986. pap. 7.95 (0-932760-45-7) CompuSoft.

Lien, George E., ed. see **American Society of Mechanical Engineers, Research Committee on High Temperature Steam Generation.**

Lien-Teh, Wu, jt. auth. see **Wong, Chi-Min.**

Lien-Teh, Wu, jt. auth. see **Wong, K. C.**

Lienau, C. C., ed. see **Richardson, Lewis F.**

Lienau, Paul J. & Lunis, Ben C. Geothermal Direct Use Engineering & Design Guidebook. 2nd ed. (Illus.). 443p. 1991. lib. bdg. 20.00 (1-880228-00-9) OR Inst Tech.

Lience, E., ed. Clinical Atlas of Rheumatology. (Illus.). 128p. 1986. 34.95 (0-8151-2958-0, RHD-1, Yr Bk Med Pubs) Mosby Yr Bk.

Lienert, Ursula. Typology of the Ting in the Shang Dynasty: A Tentative Chronology of the Yin-Hsu Period. 410p. (Orig.). 1979. pap. 52.50 (3-515-02808-0) Coronet Bks.

Lienesch, Michael. New Order of the Ages: Time, the Constitution, & the Making of Modern American Political Thought. 245p. (C). 1990. text ed. 39.50 (0-691-07779-7); pap. text ed. 12.95 (0-691-00611-3) Princeton U Pr.

— Redeeming America: Piety & Politics in the New Christian Right. LC 92-45782. xii, 332p. 1993. text ed. 45.00 (0-8078-2089-X); pap. 17.95 (0-8078-4428-4) U of NC Pr.

Lienesch, Michael, jt. ed. see **Gillespie, Michael A.**

Lienesch, William C. National Parks in Urban Areas. Corbett, Marjorie, ed. 29p. (Orig.). 1986. pap. 4.50 (0-940091-17-8) Natl Parks & Cons.

Lienhard, Janet. FrameMaker for Windows: Step-by-Step Calendar. Arias, Claire C., ed. & illus. by. (Trainers' Signature Ser.). 120p. (Orig.). 1993. pap. 11.95 (1-880663-47-3) Ellipsys Intl.

— FrameMaker for Windows: Step-by-Step Chart. Arias, Claire C., ed. & illus. by. (Trainers' Signature Ser.). 120p. (Orig.). 1993. pap. 11.95 (1-880663-48-1) Ellipsys Intl.

— FrameMaker for Windows: Step-by-Step Letter. 2nd ed. Arias, Claire C., ed. & illus. by. (Trainers' Signature Ser.). 120p. (Orig.). 1993. pap. 11.95 (1-880663-42-2) Ellipsys Intl.

Lienhard, John H., jt. auth. see **Tien, Chang L.**

***Lienhard, Joseph T.** The Bible, the Church, & Authority: The Canon of the Christian Bible in History & Theology. (Orig.). 1995. pap. text ed. write for info. (0-8146-5536-X, M Glazier) Liturgical Pr.

— Ministry. LC 83-83154. (Message of the Fathers of the Church Ser.: Vol. 8). 183p. 1984. 15.95 (0-8146-5348-0); pap. 11.95 (0-8146-5320-0) Liturgical Pr.

Lienhard, Joseph T., et al. Augustine: Presbyter Factus Sum. LC 93-16709. 590p. (C). 1994. text ed. 69.95 (0-8204-2199-5) P Lang Pubs.

Lienhard, M. The Origins & Characteristics of Anabaptism. (International Archives of the History of Ideas Ser.: No. 87). 1977. lib. bdg. 126.50 (90-247-1896-1) Kluwer Ac.

Lienhard, Marc. Un Temps, une Ville, une Reforme: La Reformation a Strasbourg. 310p. 1990. text ed. 95.00 (0-86078-268-9, Pub. by Variorum UK) Ashgate Pub Co.

Lienhard, S. Songs of Nepal: An Anthropology of Newar Folksongs & Hymns. 1992. 50.00 (0-7855-0287-4, Pub. by Ratna Pustak Bhandar) St Mut.

— Songs of Nepal - An Anthropology of Newar Folk Songs & Hymns. (C). 1991. text ed. 30.00 (0-7855-0155-X, Pub. by Ratna Pustak Bhandar) St Mut.

Lienhard, Siegfried. Nepalese Manuscripts, Pt. 1: Nevari & Sanskrit. (VOHD Ser.: No. 33.1). (Illus.). 254p. 1988. 124.50 (3-515-03041-7) Coronet Bks.

Lienhard, Siegfried, ed. Songs of Nepal: An Anthology of Nevar Folk-Songs & Hymns. (Asian Studies at Hawaii: No. 30). 232p. 1984. pap. text ed. 17.00 (0-8248-0680-8) UH Pr.

Lienhart, David A., jt. ed. see **McElroy, Charles H.**

***Lientz, Benent P. & Rea, Kathryn.** Project Management for the 21st Century. (Illus.). 308p. 1995. pap. 34.95 (0-12-449965-1) Acad Pr.

Lientz, Bennett P. An Introduction to Distributed Systems: Contract Title: Network Services--Managerial Evaluation. (Computer-Business Interface Ser.). 1981. pap. text ed. write for info. (0-201-04297-5) Addison-Wesley.

Lientz, Bennett P. & Swanson, E. Burton. Software Maintenance Management. LC 80-12154. 160p. 1980. pap. text ed. write for info. (0-201-04205-3) Addison-Wesley.

Lientz, Bennett P., jt. auth. see **Allen, R. J.**

Liepa, Alex, ed. see **MacDougall, Mary-Katherine.**

Liepa, George U., et al, eds. Dietary Proteins: How They Alleviate Disease & Promote Better Health. 296p. 1992. 75.00 (0-935315-41-1) AOCS Pr.

Liepins & Uppuluri. Data Quality Control: Theory & Pragmatics. (Statistics: Vol. 112). 304p. 1991. 110.00 (0-8247-8354-9) Dekker.

Liepins, Raimond, jt. auth. see **Ku, Chen C.**

Liepmann, Hans W. & Narashima, R., eds. Turbulence Management & Relaminarisation. (Illus.). xxiii, 550p. 1987. 99.00 (0-387-18574-7) Spr-Verlag.

Liepmann, Hans W. & Roshko, A. Elements of Gas Dynamics. LC 56-9823. 439p. 1957. Net. text ed. write for info. (0-471-53460-9) Wiley.

Liepmann, Heinrich. Tariff Levels & the Economic Unity of Europe: An Examination of Tariff Policy Export Movements & the Economic Integration of Europe 1913-1931. Stenning, H., tr. LC 79-12741. (Studies in International Economics: No. 3). (Illus.). 424p. 1980. reprint ed. lib. bdg. 45.00 (0-87991-852-7) Porcupine Pr.

Liepmann, Kate K. The Journey to Work: Its Significance for Industrial & Community Life. LC 73-13403. 1973. text ed. 59.75 (0-8371-7051-6, LIJW, Greenwood Pr) Greenwood.

Liepmann, Klaus. The Language of Music. LC 52-12521. reprint ed. pap. 96.00 (0-317-09947-7, 2012561) Bks Demand.

Liepmann, Lise. Winning Connections: A Program for On-Target Business Communications. LC 83-7052. (Illus.). 252p. 1984. write for info. (0-672-52743-X) Macmillan.

An Asterisk (*) at the beginning of an entry indicates that the title is appearing in BIP for the first time.

L

Liepmann, Moritz. Krieg und Kriminalitat in Deutschland. (Wirtschafts-Und Sozialgeschichte des Weltkrieges (Osterreichische Und Ungarische Serie)). (GER.). 1930. 100.00 (*0-317-27496-1*) Elliots Bks.

Lieppman, Michael E. & Sardi, Bill. Preserve Your Sight: The Definitive Nutrition & Lifestyle Guide to Preventive Eye Care. (Illus.). 467p. 1994. 39.50 (*0-9637874-8-9*) Eye Commns.

Liepsch, D. W., ed. Biofluid Mechanics: Blood Flow in Large Vessels: Proceeding of the Second International Symposium, June 25-18, 1989. (Illus.). 500p. 1991. pap. 96.00 (*0-387-52730-3*) Spr-Verlag.

Liepsch, Dieter W., ed. Blood Flow in Large Arteries: Applications to Atherogenesis & Clinical Medicine. (Monographs on Atherosclerosis: Vol. 15). (Illus.). viii, 288p. 1989. 216.00 (*3-8055-4983-0*) S Karger.

Lier, Aida Walqui Van & Barraza, Ruth A. Sendas Literarias. LC 94-11182. 1995. text ed. 39.95 (*0-8384-5126-8*) Heinle & Heinle.

Lier, Bruno, et al.

Liere, Alan. Bear Heads & Fish Tales. (Illus.). 144p. (Orig.). 1989. pap. 9.95 (*0-916771-05-9*) Alaska Angler.

— Bear Heads & Fish Tales. Batin, Christopher M., ed. LC 88-70823. (Illus.). 140p. (Orig.). 1990. pap. 9.95 (*0-916771-25-3*, SK33.L5) Alaska Angler.

***Lierena, Mario.** La Honda de David. LC 94-72078. (Coleccion Cuba y Sus Jueces). 208p. 1994. pap. 19.00 (*0-89729-747-4*) Ediciones.

Lierman, Deonna & Brewer, Karen, eds. Fun-Tastic Crafts & Fantastic Ideas. (Illus.). 96p. (Orig.). 1994. pap. text ed. 12.99 (*0-7847-0055-9*, 14-02165) Standard Pub.

— Super Crafts & Other Fun Stuff. (Illus.). 96p. (Orig.). 1995. pap. text ed. 12.99 (*0-7847-0296-9*, 14-02166) Standard Pub.

Lierman, Deonna & Rector, Andy, eds. An Ark Full of Crafts: For a Boatload of Fun. LC 92-36579. (Illus.). 96p. 1993. 12.99 (*0-87403-889-8*, 14-02150) Standard Pub.

Lierman, Terry, ed. Building a Healthy America: Conquering Disease & Disability. 2nd rev. ed. 248p. 1987. 49.00 (*0-913113-12-3*) M Liebert.

Lierse, W. Applied Anatomy of the Pelvis. (Illus.). 350p. 1987. 454.00 (*0-387-16750-1*) Spr-Verlag.

Lierse, W., ed. European Anatomical Congress: Sixth Congress Abstracts. (Journal: Acta Anatomica: Vol. 3, No. 1-2). 176p. 1981. pap. 126.50 (*3-8055-3463-9*) S Karger.

Lierse, W. & Beck, F., eds. Studies of the Normal & Abnormal Development of the Nervous System. (Bibliotheca Anatomica Ser.: No. 19). (Illus.). 1981. pap. 149.75 (*3-8055-1039-X*) S Karger.

Lies, Betty B. The Poet's Pen: Writing Poetry with Middle & High School Students. (Illus.). 100p. (Orig.). 1993. pap. 18.00 (*1-56308-111-3*) Teacher Ideas Pr.

Lies, Brian. Hamlet & the Enormous Chinese Dragon Kite. LC 93-30726. (J). 1994. 14.95 (*0-395-68391-2*) HM.

Liesbrock, Heinz. Edward Hopper: Forty Masterworks. 1991. pap. 10.95 (*0-393-30764-6*) Norton.

***Liesch, Barry.** The New Worship: Straight Talk on Music & the Church. Hazlitt, William, tr. LC 95-2576. 256p. (Orig.). 1995. pap. 15.99 (*0-8010-9001-6*) Baker Bk.

— People in the Presence of God: Models & Directions for Worship. 320p. (Orig.). 1988. pap. 19.99 (*0-310-31601-4*, 18430P) Zondervan.

Liesch, Peter. Government Mandated Countertrade: Deals of Arm Twisting. 186p. 1991. 68.95 (*1-85628-266-X*, Pub. by Avebury Pub UK) Ashgate Pub Co.

Liese, B., ed. Classical Swine Fever & Related Viral Infections. (Developments in Veterinary Virology Ser.). (C). 1987. lib. bdg. 106.00 (*0-89838-969-0*) Kluwer Ac.

Liese, Bernhard H., et al. Organizing & Managing Tropical Disease Control Programs: Case Studies. (Technical Paper Ser.: No. 167). 131p. 1992. 8.95 (*0-8213-2086-6*, 12086) World Bank.

— Organizing & Managing Tropical Disease Control Programs: Lessons of Success Technical Paper No. 159. 62p. 1991. 6.95 (*0-8213-1959-0*, 11959) World Bank.

Liesegang, jt. auth. see Bartley.

Liesener, James W. Instruments for Planning & Evaluating Library Media Programs. rev. ed. 1991. 5.00 (*0-911808-15-9*) U of Md Lib Serv.

Liesenfeld, Vincent J. The Licensing Act of Seventeen Thirty-Seven. LC 84-40153. (Illus.). 272p. 1984. text ed. 27.50 (*0-299-09810-9*) U of Wis Pr.

Liesenfelt, Joannie. Cold Paper: A Mother's Search for Her Daughter. 285p. 1992. pap. 14.95 (*0-9637547-1-8*) Arbor Hill Pr.

Lieske, Jay H. & Abalakin, Victor K., eds. Inertial Coordinate System on the Sky. (C). 1990. lib. bdg. 154.00 (*0-7923-0786-0*); pap. text ed. 68.00 (*0-7923-0787-9*) Kluwer Ac.

Lieskovsky, Gary, jt. ed. see Skinner, Donald G.

Liesner, Thelma. One Hundred Years of Economic Statistics. (Illus.). 352p. 1990. 75.00 (*0-8160-2344-1*) Facts on File.

Liess, B., et al, eds. Ruminant Pestivirus Infections: Virology, Pathogenesis, & Perspectives of Prophylaxis. (Archives of Virology Ser.: Supplementum 3). (Illus.). viii, 271p. 1993. pap. 152.00 (*0-387-82279-8*) Spr-Verlag.

Liess, Otto. Conical Refraction & Higher Microlocalization. (Lecture Notes in Mathematics Ser.: Vol. 1555). x, 389p. 1993. pap. write for info. (*3-540-57105-1*) Spr-Verlag.

— Conical Refraction & Higher Microlocalization. LC 93-26024. (Lecture Notes in Mathematics Ser.: Vol. 1555). 1993. pap. 56.00 (*0-387-57105-1*) Spr-Verlag.

Liestman, Vicki. Columbus Day. (Holiday on My Own Ser.). (Illus.). 56p. (J). (gr. k-3). 1991. lib. bdg. 15.95 (*0-87614-444-X*, Carolrhoda) Lerner Group.

— Columbus Day. (J). (gr. k-3). 1992. pap. 5.95 (*0-87614-559-4*, Carolrhoda) Lerner Group.

Lieten, G. K. Continuity & Change in Rural West Bengal. 1993. 38.00 (*0-8039-9449-4*) Sage.

— Dutch Multinational Corporations in India. (C). 1987. 32.50 (*81-85054-33-9*, Pub. by Manohar II) S Asia.

Lieten, G. K., et al, eds. Women, Migrants & Tribals: Survival Strategies in Asia. (C). 1989. 22.50 (*81-85054-77-0*, Pub. by Manohar II) S Asia.

Lieten, Georges K. The First Communist Ministry in Kerala, 1957-1959. 1983. 15.00 (*0-8364-0976-0*, Pub. by KP Bagchi IA) S Asia.

Lieter, Bernard A. European Multinationals in Latin America: A Positive Sum Game for the Exchange of Raw Materials & Technology in the 1980's. LC 79-91943. (Praeger Special Studies). 298p. 1980. text ed. 59.95 (*0-275-90513-6*, C0513, Praeger Pubs) Greenwood.

Lieth, H., et al, eds. Interactions Between Climate & Biosphere: Transactions of the C. E. C. Symposium in Osnabruck. (Progress in Biometeorology Ser.: Vol. 3). xviii, 394p. 1984. text ed. 121.95 (*90-265-0527-2*, Pub. by Swets Pub Serv NE) Swets North Am.

Lieth, Helmut & Lohmann, Martina, eds. Restoration of Tropical Forest Ecosystems. LC 92-33607. (Tasks for Vegetation Science Ser.). 272p. 1993. lib. bdg. 154.00 (*0-7923-1945-1*) Kluwer Ac.

Lieth, Helmut & Markert, Bernd, eds. Element Concentration Cadasters in Ecosystems (ECCE) Methods of Assessment & Evaluation. LC 90-11976. 448p. 1990. lib. bdg. 135.00 (*0-89573-962-3*) VCH Pubs.

Lieth, Helmut & Massoum, Ahmed A., eds. Towards Rational Use of High Salinity Tolerant Plants: Agriculture & Forestry under Marginal Soil Water Conditions. LC 92-22601. (Tasks for Vegetation Science Ser.: No. 28). 1993. lib. bdg. 255.00 (*0-7923-1866-8*) Kluwer Ac.

— Towards Rational Use of High Salinity Tolerant Plants Vol. 1: Deliberations about High Salinity Tolerant Plants & Ecosystems. 1992. lib. bdg. 290.00 (*0-7923-1865-X*) Kluwer Ac.

Lieth, Helmut & Werger, M. J., eds. Tropical Rain Forest Ecosystems: Biogeographical & Ecological Studies. (Ecosystems of the World Ser.: Vol. 14B). 732p. 1989. 243.75 (*0-444-42755-4*) Elsevier.

Lieth, Helmut & Whittaker, R. H., eds. Primary Productivity of the Biosphere. LC 74-26627. (Ecological Studies: Vol. 14). (Illus.). 350p. 1975. 119.00 (*0-387-07083-4*) Spr-Verlag.

Lieth, Helmut, jt. ed. see Pandeya, S. C.

***Lietty Raventos de Pubillones Staff.** Modales y Vida Social: Preguntas y Respuestas. 157p. (Orig.). (SPA.). 1994. pap. 9.95 (*0-931839-19-X*) Miami Herald.

Lietz, Paul S., ed. Calendar of Philippine Documents in the Ayer Collection of the Newberry Library. 259p. 1956. 8.00 (*0-911028-01-3*) Newberry.

Lietz, Robert. At Park & East Division. LC 81-8430. 76p. 1981. 7.95 (*0-934332-33-9*); pap. 4.25 (*0-934332-32-0*) LEpervier Pr.

— The Lindbergh Half-Century. (Poetry Ser.). 75p. (Orig.). (C). 1987. pap. 8.00 (*0-934332-47-9*) LEpervier Pr.

Lietze, Ernst. Modern Heliographic Processes. 1974. pap. 7.95 (*0-87992-000-9*) Visual Studies.

Lietzman, Hans. Apollinaris von Laodicea und seine Schule: Texte und Untersuchungen. LC 82-45817. (Orthodoxies & Heresies in the Early Church Ser.). reprint ed. 37.50 (*0-404-62390-5*) AMS Pr.

Lietzmann, Hans. Apollinaris Von Laodicea und Seine Schule. xvi, 323p. 1970. reprint ed. write for info. (*0-318-70966-X*, Pub. by Georg Olms GW) Lubrecht & Cramer.

— Geschichte der Alten Kirche, 4 vols. in 1. 1220p. (C). 1975. reprint ed. 167.70 (*3-11-004625-3*) De Gruyter.

Lieu, Judith. Jews among Pagans & Christians: In the Roman Empire. 1992. 39.95 (*0-415-04972-5*, Pub. by Tavistock UK) Routledge Chapman & Hall.

— The Second & Third Epistles of John. 280p. 1987. 39.95 (*0-567-09443-X*, Pub. by T & T Clark UK) Bks Intl VA.

— The Theology of the Johannine Epistles. (New Testament Theology Ser.). 148p. (C). 1991. 44.95 (*0-521-35246-0*); pap. 15.95 (*0-521-35806-X*) Cambridge U Pr.

***Lieu, Judith, et al, eds.** The Jews among Pagans & Christians: In the Roman Empire. 208p. 1994. pap. 16.95 (*0-415-11448-9*, B4737) Routledge.

***Lieu Quoc Nhi.** Duong Tinh Doinga. 314p. (Orig.). (YA). 1994. pap. 14.00 (*1-886535-02-7*) Dong Van.

— Hoang Hon Cuoi Cung. 326p. (Orig.). 1994. pap. 14.00 (*1-886535-01-9*) Dong Van.

Lieu Quoc Nhi, tr. see Quynh Dao.

Lieu, Samuel N. Manichaeism in the Later Roman Empire & Medieval China. (WissUNT Neuen Testament Ser.: No. 63). 400p. 1992. 92.50 (*3-16-145820-6*, Pub. by J C B Mohr GW) Coronet Bks.

Lieu, Samuel N., ed. The Emperor Julian: Panegyric & Polemic. 2nd ed. (Translated Texts for Historians Ser.). 160p. (C). 1989. reprint ed. pap. text ed. 15.95 (*0-85323-376-4*, Pub. by Liverpool Univ Pr UK) U of Pa Pr.

Lieu, Samuel N., ed. see Dodgeon, Michael L.

Lieu, Samuel N. C. Manichaeism in Mesopotamia & the Roman East. LC 93-48493. (Religions in the Graeco-Roman World Ser.: Vol. 118). 1994. 85.75 (*90-04-09742-2*) E J Brill.

Lieure, Jules. Callot's Graphic Work: A Catalogue Raisonne, 2 vols. (Illus.). (FRE.). 1989. reprint ed. Set, Vol. 1, 368p, Vol. 2, 364p. 295.00 (*1-55660-028-3*) A Wofsy Fine Arts.

Lieuwen, Edwin. Mexican Militarism: The Political Rise & Fall of the Revolutionary Army, 1910-1940. LC 80-28937. (Illus.). xiii, 194p. 1981. reprint ed. text ed. 52.50 (*0-313-22911-2*, LIMM, Greenwood Pr) Greenwood.

— Venezuela. LC 85-24781. xi, 223p. 1986. reprint ed. text ed. 55.00 (*0-313-24979-2*, LIVE, Greenwood Pr) Greenwood.

Lievano, M. Francisco, tr. see Cho, Paul Y. & Manzano, R. Whitney.

Lievano, M. Francisco, tr. see Foster, Richard.

Lievegoed, B. C. Mystery Streams in Europe & the New Mysteries. Van Houten, J. M. et al, trs. 87p. (Orig.). 1982. pap. 8.95 (*0-88010-002-8*) Anthroposophic.

— Phases of Childhood. 206p. 1990. pap. 14.95 (*0-88010-189-X*, 1228) Anthroposophic.

Lievegoed, Bernard. Man on the Threshold: The Challenge of Inner Development. 210p. 1990. pap. 18.95 (*0-9507062-6-4*, 1291, Pub. by Hawthorn Press UK) Anthroposophic.

— Phases: Crisis & Development in the Individual. 3rd ed. Lake, H. S., tr. 250p. (Orig.). 1988. pap. 14.95 (*0-85440-353-1*, Steinerbks) Anthroposophic.

Lieven, Anatol. The Baltic Revolution: Estonia, Latvia, Lithuania & the Path to Independence. (Illus.). 496p. (C). 1994. pap. 15.00 (*0-300-06078-5*) Yale U Pr.

Lieven, Dominic. The Aristocracy in Europe, 1815-1914. 1994. pap. 15.00 (*0-231-08113-8*) Col U Pr.

— Nicholas II: The Twilight of the Empire. (Illus.). 304p. 1993. 24.00 (*0-312-10510-X*) St Martin.

— Russia's Rulers Before the Revolution. LC 88-38155. 384p. 1989. text ed. 42.00 (*0-300-04371-6*) Yale U Pr.

— Russia's Rulers under the Old Regime. (Illus.). 384p. (C). 1991. reprint ed. pap. text ed. 22.00 (*0-300-04937-4*) Yale U Pr.

Lieven, Dominic C. The Aristocracy in Europe, 1815-1914. LC 92-23071. 308p. (C). 1993. 29.50 (*0-231-08112-X*); pap. 15.00 (*0-685-63514-7*) Col U Pr.

Lieven, Peter. The Birth of Ballets-Russes. Zarine, L., tr. (Illus.). 367p. 1973. reprint ed. pap. 6.95 (*0-486-22962-9*) Dover.

Lievrouw, Leah A., jt. ed. see Ruben, Brent D.

Lievsay, John L. Elizabethan Image of Italy. LC 64-9036. (Folger Guides to the Age of Shakespeare Ser.). 1964. pap. 4.95 (*0-918016-26-6*) Folger Bks.

— The Sixteenth Century: Skelton Through Hooker. LC 68-15229. (Goldentree Bibliographies Series in Language & Literature). (C). 1968. pap. text ed. write for info. (*0-88295-520-9*) Harlan Davidson.

— Venetian Phoenix: Paolo Sarpi & Some of His English Friends, 1606-1700. LC 73-6818. x, 262p. 1973. 29.95 (*0-7006-0108-2*) U Pr of KS.

***Lievsay, John L., ed.** The Seventeenth-Century Resolve: A Historical Anthology of a Literary Form. fac. ed. LC 79-4004. 221p. 1994. pap. 63.00 (*0-7837-7595-4*, 2047348) Bks Demand.

Lievsay, John L., ed. see Tuvill, Daniel.

Liew, F. Y., ed. Vaccination Strategies of Tropical Diseases. 304p. 1989. 179.00 (*0-8493-6189-3*, RC119) CRC Pr.

Liew, Richard, jt. ed. see Severino, Sally K.

Liewellyn, John, et al. Economic Forecasting & Policy. (International Library of Economics). 256p. 1985. 22.00 (*0-7102-0600-3*, RKP) Routledge.

Lifang, Chen, jt. auth. see Sianglin, Yu.

Lifanov, Ivan K., jt. auth. see Belotserkovsky, Sergei M.

Lifar, Serge. Serge Diaghilev: His Life, His Work, His Legend. LC 76-25041. (Series in Dance). 1976. reprint ed. lib. bdg. 32.50 (*0-306-70839-6*) Da Capo.

Lifchez, Raymond, ed. The Dervish Lodge: Architecture, Art, & Sufism in Ottoman Turkey. (Comparative Studies on Muslim Societies: No. 10). (C). 1992. 50.00 (*0-520-07060-7*) U CA Pr.

— Rethinking Architecture: Design Students & Physically Disabled People. 1986. pap. 14.00 (*0-520-05899-2*) U CA Pr.

Lifchez, Raymond & Winslow, Barbara. Design for Independent Living: The Environment & Physically Disabled People. (Illus.). 208p. 1981. pap. 16.00 (*0-520-04434-7*) U CA Pr.

Life & Work of Christiaan Huygens Symposium Staff. Studies on Christiaan Huygens: Invited Papers of the Symposium, Amsterdam, August 22-25, 1979. Bos, H. J. et al, eds. 1980. text ed. 42.00 (*90-265-0333-4*, Pub. by Swets Pub Serv NE) Swets North Am.

Life, Daniel H., jt. auth. see Friestad, Jennifer G.

Life Editors & Friend, David. More Reflections on the Meaning of Life. (Illus.). 224p. 1992. 35.00 (*0-316-29409-8*) Little.

Life Magazine Editors. Best of Life. 1988. 19.99 (*0-517-61940-7*) Random Hse Value.

— Life & Love: A Book of Embraces, Vol. 1. LC 94-32392. (Illus.). 1995. 14.95 (*0-316-52645-2*) Little.

— Life Carries On. (Illus.). 1993. pap. 14.00 (*0-671-86852-7*, Fireside) S&S Trade.

***Life Magazine Editors & Hirshberg, Charles.** Elvis: A Celebration in Pictures. (Illus.). 128p. 1995. 22.95 (*0-446-52020-9*) Warner Bks.

Life Magazine Staff. Enciclopedia Life De la Fotografia, 16 vols., Set. 3650p. 1975. 495.00 (*0-8288-5871-3*, S50551) Fr & Eur.

— Faces. (Illus.). 192p. 1993. text ed. 12.99 (*0-02-574043-1*) Macmillan.

— Life Goes to the Movies. 1987. 19.99 (*0-517-62585-7*) Random Hse Value.

— The Wall: A Day in the Life of the Vietnam Veterans Memorial. LC 93-14677. (Illus.). 96p. (Orig.). 1993. pap. 15.95 (*0-312-09478-7*, Pub. by Thomas Dunne Bks) St Martin.

— The Wall: A Day in the Life of the Vietnam Veterans Memorial. LC 93-14677. (Illus.). 96p. (Orig.). 1993. Special ed. 24.95 (*0-312-09479-5*, Pub. by Thomas Dunne Bks) St Martin.

Life, Page W. Sir Thomas Malory & the Morte D'Arthur: A Survey of Scholarship & Annotated Bibliography. LC 80-16180. 297p. 1980. 28.50 (*0-8139-0868-X*) U Pr of Va.

Life-Study Fellowship Staff. With God All Things Are Possible. 1984. mass mkt. 5.50 (*0-553-26249-1*) Bantam.

Lifesmith Fractals Staff. Fractal Cosmos: The Art of Mathematical Design. (Illus.). (Orig.). 1994. pap. 24.95 (*1-56937-064-8*) Amber Lotus.

Liff, Alvin A. Color & Black & White Television Theory & Servicing. (Illus.). 1979. text ed. 29.95 (*0-685-03795-9*) P-H.

Liff, Alvin A. & Wilson, Sam. Color & Black & White Television Theory & Servicing. 3rd ed. 608p. 1993. text ed. 65.00 (*0-13-150012-0*) P-H.

Liff, David M., et al. Corporate Advertising: The Business Response to Changing Public Attitudes. 67p. 1980. pap. 15.00 (*0-931035-56-2*) IRRC Inc DC.

Liffick, Blaise W., ed. Simulation: Programming Techniques. LC 78-8649. 1979. pap. text ed. 15.95 (*0-07-037826-6*, BYTE Bks) McGraw.

Liffring-Zug, Joan. The American Gothic Cookbook. rev. ed. Feske, Esther et al, eds. (Illus.). 62p. 1986. pap. 7.95 (*0-941016-33-1*) Penfield.

— Men: Nineteen Fifty to Nineteen Eighty-Five. Zug, John & Crum, Dorothy, eds. LC 86-63007. (Illus.). 64p. (Orig.). 1986. pap. 12.95 (*0-941016-38-2*) Penfield.

Liffring-Zug, Joan, comp. The Amanas Yesterday: A Religious Communal Society. LC 74-26353. (Illus.). 48p. 1975. pap. 7.95 (*0-9603858-8-6*) Penfield.

Liffring-Zug, Joan, photos. Women Nineteen Fifty-Seven to Nineteen Seventy-Five. LC 81-80099. (Illus.). 72p. 1981. pap. 12.95 (*0-9603858-4-3*) Penfield.

Liffring-Zug, Joan & Zug, John. The Amana Colonies. 2nd rev. ed. Shoup, Don, ed. (Illus.). 48p. 1993. pap. text ed. 6.95 (*0-941016-23-4*) Penfield.

Liffring-Zug, Joan & Zug, John, eds. The Kalona Heritage: Amish & Mennonite Culture. (Illus.). 64p. 1983. pap. 6.95 (*0-941016-09-9*) Penfield.

Liffring-Zug, Joan, ed. see Martin, Pat.

Liffring-Zug, Joan, ed. see McDonald, Julie.

Lifland, William T. State Antitrust Law. 350p. 1984. ring bd. 95.00 (*0-318-12030-5*, 00583) NY Law Pub.

Lifschitz, Alexander E. Magnetohydrodynamics & Spectral Theory. (C). 1989. lib. bdg. 217.50 (*90-247-3713-3*) Kluwer Ac.

Lifschitz, Carlos H. & Nichols, Buford, eds. Malnutrition in Chronic Diet-Associated Infantile Diarrhea: Diagnosis & Management. (Bristol-Myers Nutrition Symposia Ser.: Vol. 8). 464p. 1990. text ed. 85.00 (*0-12-450020-X*) Acad Pr.

Lifschitz, Elena, jt. auth. see Rosengrant, Sandra.

Lifschitz, Leatrice, ed. Only Morning in Her Shoes: Poems about Old Women. 176p. (Orig.). 1990. pap. 4.00 (*0-87421-145-X*) Utah St U Pr.

Lifschitz, Marvin. Freedom from Memory, Desire, & Understanding: Psychoanalysis & Gestalt Psychology. LC 93-20971. (Frontiers of Consciousness Ser.). (Illus.). 260p. (C). 1995. text ed. 34.95x (*0-8290-2452-2*) Irvington.

Lifschitz, Vladimir. Mechanical Theorem Proving in the U. S. S. R. The Leningrad School. Krafft, Rebecca, ed. (Illus.). 103p. (Orig.). 1986. pap. text ed. 75.00 (*1-55831-026-6*) Delphic Associates.

Lifschitz, Vladimir, ed. Artificial Intelligence & Mathematical Theory of Computation: Papers in Honor of John McCarthy. (Illus.). 475p. 1991. text ed. 72.00 (*0-12-450010-2*) Acad Pr.

Lifschitz, Vladimir, tr. see Maslov, S. Yu.

Lifschitz, Vladimir, jt. ed. see McCarthy, John.

Lifschultz, Lawrence, jt. ed. see Ali, Rabia.

Lifschultz, Lawrence, et al. Bordering on Treason? The Trial & Conviction of Arif Durrani. 56p. 1991. 5.50 (*0-9630587-0-3*) Pamphleteers.

Lifshay, Karen, jt. auth. see Batchelor, Doug.

Lifshin, ed. Tangled Vines: New Edition. 1992. pap. 9.95 (*0-15-688166-7*, Harvest Bks) HarBrace.

***Lifshin, E., ed.** Materials Science & Technology: A Comprehensive Treatment, Vol. 2B, Characterization of Materials, Pt. 2. 775p. 1994. 295.00 (*1-56081-128-5*) VCH Pubs.

— Materials Science & Technology, Vol. 2A: Characterization of Materials. 724p. 1992. lib. bdg. 325.00 (*0-89573-690-X*); 270.00 (*0-685-60606-6*) VCH Pubs.

Lifshin, Eric, jt. ed. see Cahn, Robert W.

Lifshin, Lyn. Apple Blossoms. 1993. 2.00 (*0-939520-03-6*) Ghost Dance.

— Blue Tattoo. 80p. 1995. pap. 9.95 (*1-880391-12-0*) Event Horizon.

— Dance Poems. (Dialogues on Dance Ser.: No. 7). 1986. pap. 6.00 (*0-941240-05-3*) Ommation Pr.

— The Doctor Poems. 136p. 1990. 25.00 (*0-930090-43-8*); pap. 9.95 (*0-930090-44-6*) Applezaba.

— The Doctor Poems. deluxe limited ed. 136p. 1990. 30.00 (*0-930090-42-X*) Applezaba.

— Leaning South. LC 76-58048. (Contemporary Poets Ser.). 1977. 10.95 (*0-87376-030-1*); pap. 4.95 (*0-87376-031-X*) Red Dust.

— The Mad Girl Drives in a Daze. (Illus.). 20p. (Orig.). 1995. 4.95 (*1-878116-37-1*) JVC Bks.

— Madonna Who Shifts for Herself. LC 82-73945. 73p. 1983. pap. 5.95 (*0-930090-18-7*) Applezaba.

— Madonna Who Shifts for Herself. deluxe limited ed. LC 82-73945. 73p. 1983. 15.00 (*0-930090-19-5*) Applezaba.

— Marilyn Monroe: Poems by Lyn Lifshin. Hamilton, Brian C. & DelMargo, Lynn D., eds. 143p. (Orig.). 1994. pap. 8.95 (*1-882550-02-1*) Quiet Lion Pr.

— Naked Charm. LC 79-12065. 1983. pap. 8.95 (*0-89807-006-6*) Illuminati.

— Not Made of Glass: Lyn Lifshin Berns, 1968-1989. 120p. (Orig.). 1989. pap. 14.95 (*0-918670-01-2*) Combinations.

— Parade. 40p. (Orig.). 1994. pap. text ed. 4.00 (*0-935390-19-7*) Wormwood Bks & Mag.

— Red Hair & the Jesuit. (Backpocket Poets Ser.). 36p. (Orig.). 1988. pap. 2.50 (*0-916155-05-6*) Trout Creek.

— Remember the Ladies. 1985. pap. 1.50 (0-317-19794-0) Ghost Dance.
— Rubbed Silk. 60p. (Orig.). 1988. pap. 8.95 (0-89807-252-2) Illuminati.
— Thirty-Five Sundays. (Offset Offshoot Ser.: No. 3). 56p. 1979. pap. 4.00 (0-317-06439-8) Ommation Pr.
Lifshin, Lyn, ed. Lips Unsealed: Confidences from Contemporary Women Writers. (Illus.). 237p. (Orig.). (C). 1990. reprint ed. lib. bdg. 33.00x (0-8095-4075-4) Borgo Pr.
Lifshin, Lyn, et al. Eye of the Beast. Lovingood, Sut, ed. (Gypsy Ser.: No. 5). 64p. (Orig.). 1986. pap. 4.95 (0-935839-02-X) Vergin Pr.
— Vergin' Mary & Madonna. (Elite Chaps: No. 4). 62p. (Orig.). 1986. pap. 3.20 (0-935839-01-1) Vergin Pr.
Lifshits, Evgenii M. & Andronikashvili, E. L. A Supplement of "Helium" LC 59-8465. 176p. reprint ed. pap. 50.20 (0-317-08930-7, 2003365) Bks Demand.
Lifshits, Il'ya M., et al. Introduction to the Theory of Disordered Systems. LC 87-15951. 512p. 1988. text ed. 140.00 (0-471-87533-3) Wiley.
***Lifshits, M. A.** Gaussian Random Functions. LC 95-3066. (Mathematics & Its Applications Ser.: Vol. 322). 352p. (C). 1995. lib. bdg. 157.00 (0-7923-3385-3) Kluwer Ac.
Lifshits, Tanya, jt. auth. see Lifshits, Yonatan.
Lifshits, V. G., et al. Surface Phases on Silicon: Preparation, Structures, & Properties. LC 94-4938. 1994. text ed. 115.00 (0-471-94846-2) Wiley.
Lifshits, Yonatan & Lifshits, Tanya. Uman, Uman, Rosh HaShanah: A Guide to Rebbe Nachmans Rosh HaShanah in Uman. Greenbaum, Avraham, ed. (Illus.). 96p. 1992. pap. 2.00 (0-930213-43-2) Breslov Res Inst.
Lifshitz. Children's Nutrition. (Health Science Ser.). 1991. boxed 50.00 (0-86720-186-X) Jones & Bartlett.
— Clinical Disorders in Pediatric Gastroenterology & Nutrition. (Pediatrics Ser.: Vol. 1). 464p. 1980. 140.00 (0-8247-6954-6) Dekker.
— Pediatric Endocrinology: A Clinical Guide. 2nd expanded rev. ed. (Clinical Pediatrics Ser.: Vol. 7). 1104p. 1990. 250.00 (0-8247-8159-7) Dekker.
Lifshitz, Assa, ed. Shock Waves in Chemistry. LC 81-5375. (Illus.). 400p. reprint ed. pap. 114.00 (0-7837-0744-4, 2041064) Bks Demand.
Lifshitz, E. M. & Pitaevskii, L. P. Physical Kinetics. Sykes, J. B. & Franklin, R. N., trs. (Course of Theoretical Physics Ser.: Vol. 10). (Illus.). 625p. 1981. text ed. 125.00 (0-08-020641-7, Pergamon Pr); pap. text ed. 52.00 (0-08-026480-8, Pergamon Pr) Elsevier.
Lifshitz, E. M., jt. auth. see Landau, L. D.
Lifshitz, Fima, ed. Carbohydrate Intolerance in Infancy. LC 82-5107. (Clinical Disorders in Pediatric Nutrition SEr.: No. 1). 271p. reprint ed. pap. 77.30 (0-318-35011-4, 2030871) Bks Demand.
— Childhood Nutrition. LC 94-14377. (Modern Nutrition Ser.). 304p. 1994. 75.00 (0-8493-2764-4, 2764) CRC Pr.
— Common Pediatric Disorders: Metabolism, Heart Disease, Allergies, Substance Abuse & Trauma. LC 84-14294. (Clinical Pediatrics Ser.: No. 1). (Illus.). 463p. reprint ed. pap. 132.00 (0-7837-0610-3, 2040958) Bks Demand.
— Pediatric Nutrition: Infant Feedings-Deficiencies-Diseases. (Clinical Disorders in Pediatric Nutrition SEr.: Vol. 2). (Illus.). 648p. 1982. 150.00 (0-8247-1430-X) Dekker.
Lifshitz, Leatrice H., ed. Her Soul Beneath the Bone: Women's Poetry on Breast Cancer. LC 88-1348. 104p. 1988. pap. 10.95 (0-252-06008-3) U of Ill Pr.
Lifshitz, Ze'ev H. The Paradox of Human Existence: A Commentary on the Book of Jonah. LC 94-6287. 296p. 1995. pap. 25.00 (1-56821-219-4) Aronson.
Lifson, Ben, ed. see Samaras, Lucas.
Lifson, David S. Sholem Aleichem's Wandering Star & Other Plays of Jewish Life. LC 86-73240. 216p. 1988. 19.95 (0-8453-4810-8, Cornwall Bks) Assoc Univ Prs.
Lifson, David S., tr. Epic & Folk Plays from the Yiddish Theatre. 224p. 1975. 36.50 (0-8386-1082-X) Fairleigh Dickinson.
***Lifson, Lawrence, ed.** The Therapeutic Actions of Psychodynamic Psychotherapy: Current Concepts of Cure. (PI Ser.: No. 1). Date not set. write for info. (0-88163-205-8) Analytic Pr.
Lifson, Thomas B., jt. auth. see Yoshino, M. Y.
Liftin, Elaine, jt. auth. see Hansen, John H.
Lifton, Bernice. Bug Busters: Poison Free Pest Controls for House & Garden. LC 90-19678. (Illus.). 272p. 1991. pap. 9.95 (0-89529-451-6) Avery Pub.
Lifton, Betsy & Lifton, Karen. Five's a Crowd. (Not for Blondes Only Ser.). 144p. (J). (gr. 3-7). 1992. pap. 2.95 (0-590-45526-5, Apple Paperbacks) Scholastic Inc.
— Show Time! (Not for Blondes Only Ser.). 144p. (J). (gr. 3-7). 1992. pap. 2.95 (0-590-45683-0, Apple Paperbacks) Scholastic Inc.
***Lifton, Betty J.** Journey of the Adopted Self: A Quest for Wholeness. 336p. 1995. pap. 12.00 (0-465-03675-9) Basic.
— Lost & Found: The Adoption Experience. LC 87-45636. 320p. 1988. reprint ed. pap. 9.95 (0-685-43848-1, PL-7132, PL) HarpC.
— A Place Called Hiroshima. Pockell & Ichiba, eds. (Illus.). 152p. 1990. reprint ed. pap. 14.95 (0-87011-961-3) Kodansha.
— Tell Me a Real Adoption Story. LC 90-26506. (J). (ps-3). 1994. 13.00 (0-679-80629-6); lib. bdg. 13.99 (0-679-90629-0) Knopf Bks Yng Read.
Lifton, Betty J., jt. auth. see Lifton, Robert J.
Lifton, David S. Best Evidence. 1981. 19.95 (0-02-571870-3) Macmillan.
— Best Evidence: Disguise & Deception in the Assassination of John F. Kennedy. 1992. pap. 6.99 (0-451-17573-5, Sig) NAL-Dutton.
Lifton, Karen, jt. auth. see Lifton, Betsy.
***Lifton, Paul.** Vast Encyclopedia: The Theatre of Thornton Wilder. LC 95-5675. (Contributions in Drama & Theatre Studies: Vol. 61). 1995. text ed. write for info. (0-313-29356-2, Greenwood Pr) Greenwood.
Lifton, Robert J. America & the Asian Revolutions. 2nd ed. 178p. (C). 1973. reprint ed. 27.95x (0-87855-065-8); reprint ed. pap. text ed. 16.95x (0-87855-562-5) Transaction Pubs.
— The Broken Connection: On Death & the Continuity of Life. 500p. Date not set. pap. write for info. (0-88048-874-3, 8874) Am Psychiatric.
— Death in Life: Survivors of Hiroshima. LC 91-50248. xii, 594p. (C). 1991. reprint ed. pap. 19.95 (0-8078-4344-X) U of NC Pr.
— Home from the War: Learning from Vietnam Veterans. LC 91-39232. 504p. 1992. pap. 18.00 (0-8070-5505-0) Beacon Pr.
— The Nazi Doctors: Medical Killing & the Psychology of Genocide. LC 85-73874. 576p. 1988. pap. 18.00 (0-465-04905-2) Basic.
— The Protean Self: Human Resilience in an Age of Fragmentation. LC 92-56174. 240p. 1993. 25.00 (0-465-06420-5) Basic.
— The Protean Self: Human Resilience in the Age of Fragmentation. 240p. 1994. pap. 13.00 (0-465-06421-3) Basic.
— Six Lives-Six Deaths. LC 78-11926. 1979. 42.00 (0-300-02266-2) Yale U Pr.
— Thought Reform & the Psychology of Totalism: A Study of "Brainwashing" in China. LC 88-40534. xiv, 510p. (C). 1989. reprint ed. pap. 17.95 (0-8078-4253-2) U of NC Pr.
Lifton, Robert J., ed. The Woman in America. LC 77-11064. 293p. 1977. reprint ed. text ed. 49.50 (0-8371-9810-0, LIWO, Greenwood Pr) Greenwood.
Lifton, Robert J. & Humphrey, Nicholas, eds. In a Dark Time. LC 84-10816. 160p. (Orig.). 1984. text ed. 22.00 (0-674-44538-4); pap. text ed. 7.95 (0-674-44539-2) HUP.
Lifton, Robert J. & Lifton, Betty J. The Journey of the Adopted Self: A Quest for Wholeness. 224p. 1994. 22.00 (0-465-00811-9) Basic.
***Lifton, Robert J. & Mitchell, Greg.** Hiroshima in America: Fifty Years of Denial. LC 95-13734. 1995. write for info. (0-615-00709-0, Putnam) Putnam Pub Group.
Ligas, J. R., jt. ed. see Epstein, M. A.
Liger, Louis. Le Jardinier Fleuriste et Historiographe. 679p. reprint ed. write for info. (0-318-71372-1, Pub. by Georg Olms GW) Lubrecht & Cramer.
***Ligertwood, A. L.** Australian Evidence. 2nd ed. 1993. 107.00 (0-409-30487-5); pap. 83.00 (0-409-30488-3, Australia) Butterworth Legal Pubs.
Ligeti, Gyorgy. Ligeti in Conversation. (Eulenburg Music Ser.). 140p. 1985. pap. 19.50 (0-903873-68-0) Da Capo.
Ligeti, L. Researches in Altaic Languages. 338p. 1975. 58.00 (0-569-08204-8, Pub. by Collets UK) Pro-Am Music.
***Ligeti, L., ed.** Proceedings of the Csoma de Koros Memorial Symposium. 586p. (C). 1978. 153.00x (963-05-1568-7, Pub. by Akad Kiado HU) St Mut.
Ligeti, Louis. Proceedings of the Cosma de Koros Memorial Symposium. 586p. 1978. 142.50 (0-569-08468-7, Pub. by Collets UK) Pro-Am Music.
Ligget, Cathy, jt. auth. see Ligget, Mark.
Ligget, Mark & Ligget, Cathy. The Complete Handbook of Songwriting: An Insider's Guide to Making It in the Music Industry. LC 85-7197. 352p. 1985. pap. 9.95 (0-452-25687-9, Plume) NAL-Dutton.
Liggett, Barbara. Archaeology at New Market. 1978. pap. 5.00 (0-916530-09-4) Athenaeum Phila.
Liggett, Cathy, jt. auth. see Liggett, Mark.
***Liggett, Helen & Perry, David C.** Spatial Practices: Critical Explorations in Social - Spatial Theory. 264p. 1995. text ed. 46.00 (0-8039-5114-0); pap. text ed. 22.95 (0-8039-5115-9) Sage.
Liggett, James A. Fluid Mechanics. LC 93-28418. 1993. text ed. write for info. (0-07-037805-3) McGraw.
Liggett, John V. Dimensional Variation Management Handbook: A Guide for Quality, Design, & Manufacturing Engineers. LC 92-28359. 320p. 1992. text ed. 84.00 (0-13-927641-6) P-H.
Liggett, Lucy A., jt. auth. see Aldridge, Henry B.
Liggett, Mark & Liggett, Cathy. The Complete Handbook of Songwriting: An Insider's Guide to Making It in the Music Industry. 2nd ed. 272p. 1993. pap. 12.00 (0-452-27011-1, Plume) NAL-Dutton.
Liggett, Sarah, jt. auth. see Halpern, Jeanne W.
Liggett, T. M. Interacting Particle Systems. (Grundlehren der Mathematischen Wissenschaften Ser.: Vol. 276). (Illus.). 500p. 1985. 87.00 (0-387-96069-4) Spr-Verlag.
Liggett, Twila C. & Mayer, Cynthia. The Reading Rainbow Guide to Children's Books: The 101 Best Titles. LC 93-46695. 1994. 19.95 (1-55972-222-3, Birch Ln Pr); pap. 12.95 (0-8065-1493-0, Birch Ln Pr) Carol Pub Group.
Liggio, Leonard P. & Martin, James J., eds. Watershed of Empire: Essays on New Deal Foreign Policy. LC 76-4291. 1976. pap. 3.95 (0-87926-020-3) R Myles.
Light. Pediatric Hand & Upper Extremity. 1991. 45.00 (0-8151-5424-0, Yr Bk Med Pubs) Mosby Yr Bk.
Light & Lan-Ying. Contemporary World Issues. 1989. pap. 20.95 (0-8384-3328-6) Heinle & Heinle.
Light, jt. auth. see Preece.
Light & Life Symposium Staff. Light & Life: Proceedings of the Symposium, Johns Hopkins University, 1960. McElroy, William D. & Glass, Bentley, eds. LC 60-16544. (Johns Hopkins University, McCollum-Pratt Institute, Contribution: No. 302). 938p. reprint ed. pap. 180.00 (0-317-20654-0, 2024139) Bks Demand.
Light, A. R. The Initial Processing of Pain & Its Descending Control: Spinal & Trigeminal Systems. (Pain & Headache Ser.: Vol. 12). (Illus.). xiv, 306p. 1992. 280.00 (3-8055-5569-5) S Karger.
Light, Alison. Forever England: Femininity, Literature & Conservatism Between the Wars. 320p. 1991. 49.95 (0-415-01661-4, A6638); pap. 15.95 (0-415-01662-2) Routledge.
Light, Arthur, et al. Opiate Addiction. Grob, Gerald N., ed. LC 80-1257. (Addiction in America Ser.). 1981. reprint ed. lib. bdg. 15.95 (0-405-13604-8) Ayer.
Light, C., ed. Village Coquettes. LC 92-85578. 1992. pap. 12.95 (1-877978-43-4, FLF Pr) Woldt.
***Light, Cassandra.** Way of the Doll. LC 94-48177. 1995. 18.95 (0-8118-0698-7) Chronicle Bks.
***Light, Dale B.** Rome & the New Republic: Conflict & Community in Philadelphia Catholicism Between the Revolution & the Civil War. LC 95-16520. (Notre Dame Studies in American Catholicism: Vol. 14). (C). 1996. text ed. 48.95 (0-268-01652-6) U of Notre Dame Pr.
Light, Danielle. Remembering Me: A Journal for You & Your Loved Ones. 136p. 1986. pap. 7.95 (0-9616478-0-9) Mt Shasta Pubns.
Light, Donald & May, Annabelle. Britain's Health System: From Welfare State to Managed Market. (International Health Policy Ser.: No. 4). 176p. Date not set. pap. 95.00 (1-881393-19-4) Faulkner & Gray.
Light, Donald, Jr., jt. auth. see Henslin, James M.
Light, Donald W. & Schuller, Alexander, eds. Political Values on Health Care: The German Experience. (Human & Social Dimensions of Medicine Ser.). (Illus.). 550p. 1985. 60.00 (0-262-12109-3) MIT Pr.
Light, Donald W., jt. auth. see Widman, Mindy.
Light, Duane. Felt Pen & Watercolor. (Artist's Library). (Illus.). 64p. (Orig.). 1992. pap. 6.95 (1-56010-123-7, AL20) W Foster Pub.
Light, Duane R. Boats in Watercolor. (How to Draw & Paint Ser.). (Illus.). 32p. (Orig.). 1989. pap. 5.95 (0-929261-70-4, HT210) W Foster Pub.
— Watercolor. (Artist's Library). (Illus.). 64p. (Orig.). 1989. pap. 6.95 (0-929261-02-X, AL02) W Foster Pub.
— Watercolor with Mixed Media. (Artist's Library). (Illus.). 64p. (Orig.). 1989. pap. 6.95 (1-56010-032-X, AL16) W Foster Pub.
Light, Enid & Lebowitz, Barry, eds. The Elderly with Chronic Mental Illness. 384p. 1991. 49.95 (0-8261-7280-6) Springer Pub.
Light, Enid & Liebowitz, Barry. Alzheimer's Disease Treatment & Family Stress: Directions for Research. 500p. 1990. 52.00 (1-56032-137-7) Hemisp Pub.
Light, Enid, et al, eds. Stress Effects on Family Caregivers of Alzheimer's & Related Dementias: Research & Interventions. 440p. 1994. 58.95 (0-8261-7890-1) Springer Pub.
Light, Fred R. CERCLA Law & Procedure. LC 91-26413. 416p. 1991. text ed. 150.00 (0-87179-707-0, 0707) BNA.
— CERCLA Law & Procedure. suppl. ed. 122p. 1993. pap. text ed. 38.00 (0-614-04035-3) BNA.
— CERCLA Law & Procedure Compendium. 1284p. 1992. text ed. 88.00 (0-87179-742-9, 0742) BNA.
Light, H. Wayne. Light's Retention Scale - 1991. 80p. 1991. student ed 65.00 (0-685-71873-5, 914-1AN); 18.00 (0-87879-916-8); pap. 17.00 (0-87879-914-1, 914-1AN); lp 22.00 (0-87879-915-X) Acad Therapy.
Light, H. Wayne & Morrison, Pam. Beyond Retention: A Survival Guide for the Regular Classroom Teacher. Kratoville, Betty L., ed. (Illus.). 112p. (Orig.). 1990. pap. text ed. 15.00 (0-87879-900-1) Acad Therapy.
Light, Ivan & Bahchu, Parminder, eds. Immigration & Entrepreneurship: Culture, Capital, & Ethnic Networks. LC 92-14137. 352p. (C). 1993. 39.95 (1-56000-070-8) Transaction Pubs.
***Light, Ivan & Rosenstein, Carolyn.** Race, Ethnicity, & Entrepreneurship in Urban America. LC 95-3418. (Sociology & Economics Ser.). 256p. 1995. lib. bdg. 47.95 (0-202-30505-8); pap. 23.95 (0-202-30506-6) Aldine de Gruyter.
Light, Ivan H., ed. Italians in America: Annotated Guide to New York Times Articles, 1890-1940, No. 824. 1975. 6.00 (0-686-20359-3) CPL Biblios.
Light, Ivan H. & Bonacich, Edna. Immigrant Entrepreneurs: Koreans in Los Angeles, 1965-1982. 1988. 50.00 (0-520-06146-2) U CA Pr.
— Immigrant Entrepreneurs: Koreans in Los Angeles, 1965-1982. (Illus.). 506p. 1991. reprint ed. pap. 16.00 (0-520-07656-7) U CA Pr.
Light, James F. John William DeForest. 192p. 1965. 49.50 (0-685-63207-5) Elliots Bks.
Light, Janice B. The Joy of Listening. LC 78-52752. 1978. pap. text ed. 10.50 (0-88200-119-1, M7992) Alexander Graham.
Light, Jeremy, jt. auth. see Harper, Peter.
Light, Joanne. Coastal Nova Scotia: An Outdoor Adventure Guide. (Illus.). 148p. (Orig.). 1993. pap. 9.95 (1-55109-043-0, Pub. by Nimbus Publishing Ltd CN) Chelsea Green Pub.
— Hiking Guide to Nova Scotia. (Illus.). 148p. 1995. pap. 11.95 (1-55109-108-9, Pub. by Nimbus Publishing Ltd CN) Chelsea Green Pub.
Light, Joey. High-Riding Heroes. 224p. (Orig.). 1993. pap. 2.95 (1-56597-051-9, Kismet) Meteor Pub.
— Sterling's Reasons. 224p. (Orig.). 1991. pap. 2.95 (1-878702-46-7) Meteor Pub.
— Veteran's Day. 224p. (Orig.). 1993. pap. 2.95 (1-56597-104-3, Kismet) Meteor Pub.
Light, John. Beachcombers. LC 91-38130. (Light Reading Ser.). (J). (gr. 4 up). 1991. 2.95 (0-85953-502-9) Childs Play.
— Dig That Hole! LC 91-39036. (Light Reading Ser.). (J). (gr. 5 up). 1991. 3.95 (0-85953-503-7) Childs Play.
— It's Great Outdoors. LC 90-34353. (Light Reading Ser.). (J). (gr. 5 up). 1991. 3.95 (0-85953-338-7) Childs Play.
— Odd Jobs. LC 90-34354. (Light Reading Ser.). (J). (gr. 4 up). 1991. 3.95 (0-85953-339-5) Childs Play.
— Playing at Home. LC 90-34356. (Light Reading Ser.). (J). (gr. 4 up). 1991. 3.95 (0-85953-336-0) Childs Play.
— Race Ace Roger. LC 91-33417. (Light Reading Ser.). (J). (gr. 4 up). 1991. 3.95 (0-85953-501-0) Childs Play.
— Snap Happy. LC 91-36610. (Light Reading Ser.). (J). (gr. 4 up). 1991. 3.95 (0-85953-504-5) Childs Play.
— What's Cooking. LC 90-34355. (Light Reading Ser.). (J). (gr. 4 up). 1991. 3.95 (0-85953-337-9) Childs Play.
Light, Ken, et al. To the Promised Land. (Illus.). 90p. 1988. 25.00 (0-89381-324-9) Aperture.
Light, Lady. Stead. 208p. 1993. write for info. (1-56167-116-9) Am Literary Pr.
Light, Laura, ed. see Bingham, Mindy, et al.
Light, Leah L. & Burke, Deborah M., eds. Language, Memory, & Aging. (Illus.). 281p. (C). 1988. 64.95 (0-521-32942-6) Cambridge U Pr.
— Language, Memory, & Aging. (Illus.). 296p. (C). 1993. pap. 21.95 (0-521-44876-X) Cambridge U Pr.
***Light, Linda.** Passions & Prejudice: The Secrets of Spindletop. (Illus.). 392p. 1995. 21.95 (0-9645617-0-0) Spindletop Prod.
Light, Margot. The Soviet Theory of International Relations. 384p. 1988. pap. 15.95 (0-312-01891-6) St Martin.
— Soviet Theory of International Relations. LC 87-34021. 1988. text ed. 45.00 (0-312-01889-4) St Martin.
Light, Margot, ed. Troubled Friendships: Moscow's Third World Venture. 288p. 1994. text ed. 59.50 (1-85043-649-5, Pub. by I B Tauris UK) St Martin.
Light, Margot, jt. ed. see Groom, A. J.
Light, Marilyn. Hypoglycemia. Passwater, Richard A. & Mindell, Earl, eds. (Good Health Guide Ser.). (Orig.). 1983. pap. 2.50 (0-87983-302-5) Keats.
Light, Marilyn H. Hypoglycemia: One of Man's Most Widespread & Misdiagnosed Diseases. 1.95 (0-317-00895-1) Hypoglycemia Foun.
— Psychology & Physiologic Findings in Psychosomatic Disorders. 3.00 (0-317-05970-X) Hypoglycemia Foun.
Light, Mary, ed. see Beck, Brandon & Grunder, Charles.
Light, Michael. Ranch. (Illus.). 96p. 1993. 35.00 (0-944092-25-X) Twin Palms Pub.
Light, Nathan. Qazaqs in the People's Republic of China: The Local Processes of History. Cuffel, Victoria J., ed. LC 93-655022. (MacArthur Scholar Ser., Occasional Paper: No. 22). (Illus.). 107p. (Orig.). 1994. pap. 4.50 (1-881157-24-5) In Ctr Global.
Light, Nicholas. Longman Food Science Handbook. 1989. pap. 6.95 (0-582-08815-1, TG7601) Longman.
Light, Nicholas & Walker, A. Cook-Chill Catering: Technology & Management. 366p. 1990. 93.75 (1-85166-437-8) Elsevier.
Light, Paul. Still Artful Work: The Continuing Politics of Social Security Reform. 2nd ed. LC 94-17594. 1994. write for info. (0-07-037949-1) McGraw.
Light, Paul & Butterworth, George, eds. Context & Cognition. 192p. 1993. text ed. 39.95 (0-8058-1392-6); pap. 19.95 (0-8058-1393-4) L Erlbaum Assocs.
Light, Paul C. America's Cube: Solving the Social Security Puzzle. 224p. (C). 1985. pap. text ed. write for info. (0-07-554485-7) McGraw.
— The Baby Boomers. 1988. 19.95 (0-393-02524-1) Norton.
— The Baby Boomers. 1990. pap. 8.95 (0-393-30639-9) Norton.
— Forging Legislation. 192p. 1991. 22.95 (0-393-03038-5) Norton.
— Forging Legislation. (C). 1991. pap. text ed. 9.95 (0-393-96071-4) Norton.
— Monitoring Government: Inspectors General & the Search for Accountability. 268p. (C). 1993. 34.95 (0-8157-5255-5); pap. 14.95 (0-8157-5256-3) Brookings.
— The President's Agenda: Domestic Policy Choice from Kennedy to Carter with Notes on Ronald Reagan. LC 81-47607. 256p. 1983. 32.50 (0-8018-2657-8) Johns Hopkins.
— The President's Agenda: Domestic Policy Choice from Kennedy to Reagan. rev. ed. LC 91-3779. 304p. 1991. pap. text ed. 14.95x (0-8018-4279-4) Johns Hopkins.
— The President's Agenda: Domestic Policy Choice from Kennedy to Reagan. 2nd rev. ed. LC 91-3779. 304p. 1991. text ed. 45.00x (0-8018-4278-6) Johns Hopkins.
— Thickening Government. 200p. (C). 1995. 29.95x (0-8157-5250-4); pap. 11.95x (0-8157-5249-0) Brookings.
— Vice-Presidential Power: Advice & Influence in the White House. LC 83-48050. 288p. 1983. text ed. 42.00x (0-8018-3058-3) Johns Hopkins.
Light, Paul C., jt. auth. see Butterworth, George E.
Light, Paul C., jt. ed. see Richards, Martin.
Light, Paul C., et al, eds. Learning to Think. (Child Development in Social Context Ser.). 320p. 1991. 72.00 (0-415-05824-4, A5453); pap. 18.95 (0-415-05825-2, A5457) Routledge.
Light, Phyllis B. Prince Charming Lives! Finding the Love of Your Life. LC 93-6409. 240p. 1993. pap. 12.95 (0-931892-78-3) B Dolphin Pub.
Light, Richard J. & Pillemer, David B. Summing up: The Science of Reviewing Research. LC 84-4506. (Illus.). 224p. 1984. 25.00 (0-674-85430-6); pap. 12.95 (0-674-85431-4) HUP.
Light, Richard J., et al. By Design: Planning Research on Higher Education. (Illus.). 288p. 1990. 36.50 (0-674-08930-8); pap. 14.95 (0-674-08931-6) HUP.
Light, Richard U. Focus on Africa. LC 73-150192. (Select Bibliographies Reprint Ser.). (Illus.). 1977. reprint ed. 60.95 (0-8369-5705-9) Ayer.
Light, Richard W. Pleural Diseases. 2nd ed. LC 89-13487. (Illus.). 331p. 1990. text ed. 69.50 (0-8121-1318-7) Williams & Wilkins.
— Pleural Diseases. 3rd ed. LC 94-44122. 1995. write for info. (0-683-05017-6) Williams & Wilkins.

Light, Roy. Criminalising the Drink-Driver. 224p. 1994. 57.95 (*1-85521-456-3*, Pub. by Dartmth Pub UK) Ashgate Pub Co.

Light, Roy, jt. auth. see Bottoms, Anthony E.

Light, Roy, et al. Car Theft: The Offender's Perspective. (Home Organist Library: No. 130). 100p. 1993. pap. 15.00 (*0-11-341069-7*, HM10697, Pub. by HMSO UK) UNIPUB.

***Light, Russel D.** On Perspective. (Illus.). 160p. 1995. pap. 24.95 (*0-7506-1694-6*, Butterwrth Archit) Buttrwrth-Heinemann.

Light, Sally. House Histories: A Guide to Tracing the Genealogy of Your Home: Including Chapters on How to Operate a Homebased "House Histories" Business. LC 88-83479. (Illus.). 302p. (Orig.). 1989. pap. text ed. 14.95 (*0-9614876-1-5*) Golden Hl Pr NY.

Light, Stephen. Shuzo Kuki & Jean Paul Sartre: Influence & Counter-Influence in the Early History of Existential Phenomenology. LC 86-11861. (Journal of the History of Philosophy Monograph Ser.). 168p. (Orig.). 1987. pap. text ed. 13.95 (*0-8093-1271-9*) S Ill U Pr.

***Light Technology Research.** Shining the Light Vol. 1. 193p. (Orig.). 1994. pap. 12.95 (*0-929385-66-7*) Light Tech Comns Servs.

— Shining the Light Vol. II. 418p. (Orig.). 1995. pap. 14.95 (*0-929385-70-5*) Light Tech Comns Servs.

Light, Timothy & Yao, Tao-Chung. The Character Book: A Workbook to Accompany "Read Chinese", Bk. 1. (Mirror Ser.). 316p. (Orig.). (CHI.). 1985. pap. text ed. 12.95 (*0-88710-137-2*) Yale Far Eastern Pubns.

Light, Timothy, jt. auth. see McCoy, John.

Light, W. A. & Cheney, E. W. Approximation Theory in Tensor Product Spaces. (Lecture Notes in Mathematics Ser.: Vol. 1169). vii, 157p. 1985. pap. 31.10 (*0-387-16057-4*) Spr-Verlag.

Light, Will, ed. Advances in Numerical Analysis: Nonlinear Partial Differential Equations & Dynamical Systems, Vol. 1. (Illus.). 224p. 1991. 52.00 (*0-19-853438-8*) OUP.

— Advances in Numerical Analysis: Wavelets, Subdivision Algorithms, & Radial Basis Functions, Vol. 2. 224p. 1992. 49.95 (*0-19-853439-6*) OUP.

***Light, William J.** Neurobiology of Alcohol Abuse. (Illus.). 190p. 1986. pap. 26.95 (*0-614-02251-7*) C C Thomas.

— Neurobiology of Alcohol Abuse. (Illus.). 190p. (C). 1986. 41.95x (*0-398-05197-6*) C C Thomas.

— Spionidae: Invertebrates of the San Francisco Bay Estuary System, Vol. 1. Lee, Welton L., ed. (Illus.). 1978. text ed. 12.50 (*0-910286-58-2*) Boxwood.

Light Work Staff & Gonchar, Nancy, eds. John Wood. (Illus.). 24p. 7.50 (*0-935445-01-3*) Light Work.

Lightband, D. A. Direct Current Traction Motor. 436p. 1970. 35.00 (*0-8464-1461-9*) Beekman Pubs.

Lightbody, A. Great Book of Fighter Planes. 1991. 24.99 (*0-517-03598-7*) Random Hse Value.

Lightbody, Andy & Poyer, Joe. Milspeak: A Dictionary of International Military Acronyms & Abbreviations. 91p. (Orig.). 1986. pap. 5.95 (*1-882391-00-4*) N Cape Pubns.

Lightbody, Audrey. Faith Is the Journey. 144p. (Orig.). (YA). (gr. 7 up). 1987. pap. 5.95 (*0-939925-10-9*) R C Law & Co.

Lightbody, Mark & Smallman, Tom. Canada: A Travel Survival Kit. 5th ed. (Illus.). 936p. 1994. pap. 19.95 (*0-86442-216-4*) Lonely Planet.

Lightbody, Nancy K. & Malley, Sarah H. Observa-Story: Portland to Cut & Color. LC 76-54460. (Illus.). (J). (gr. 1-4). 1976. pap. 1.25 (*0-9600612-5-8*) Greater Portland.

Lightbourne & Rankin. Physical Mathematics & Nonlinear Partial Differential Equations. (Lecture Notes in Pure & Applied Mathematics Ser.: Vol. 102). 280p. 1985. 110.00 (*0-8247-7343-8*) Dekker.

Lightbourne, K. A. Grandfather Played the Trumpet: Sailors Fantasies. 375p. (Orig.). (J). 1988. pap. 12.50 (*0-9621212-0-7*) Sailors Fantasies Pub.

Lightbown, Ronald. Piero Della Francesca. (Illus.). 312p. 1992. 125.00 (*1-55859-168-0*) Abbeville Pr.

— Sandro Botticelli: Life & Work. (Illus.). 340p. 1989. 125.00 (*0-89659-931-0*) Abbeville Pr.

Lightbrown, Ronald J. Mediaeval European Jewellery. (Illus.). 560p. 1992. 200.00 (*0-948107-87-1*, Pub. by Victoria & Albert Mus UK) Trafalgar.

***Lighten Up Enterprises Staff.** Best of Hearts. 10th aniversary ed. 1994. pap. 6.50 (*1-879127-30-X*) Lighten Up Enter.

— Celebrate Treasures of Friendship. 1994. pap. 7.50 (*1-879127-28-8*) Lighten Up Enter.

— Gift of Christmas. 1994. pap. 7.50 (*1-879127-40-7*) Lighten Up Enter.

— Going Home. 1994. pap. 8.50 (*1-879127-34-2*) Lighten Up Enter.

— Lessons from the Heart. 1994. pap. 8.50 (*1-879127-35-0*) Lighten Up Enter.

— Main Street Memories. 1994. pap. 8.50 (*1-879127-33-4*) Lighten Up Enter.

— Simple Treasures. 1994. pap. 8.50 (*1-879127-36-9*) Lighten Up Enter.

***Lighten-Up Staff.** Mother's Love. 1995. pap. text ed. 4.99 (*1-879127-47-4*) Adventure Pubns.

— Special Angel. 1995. pap. text ed. 4.99 (*1-879127-50-4*) Adventure Pubns.

— Sunshine & Smiles. 1995. pap. text ed. 4.99 (*1-879127-48-2*) Adventure Pubns.

— Words of Love. 1995. pap. text ed. 4.99 (*1-879127-49-0*) Adventure Pubns.

***Lighter, Dawn.** Gentle Discipline: 50 Effective Techniques for Teaching Your Children Good Behavior. 1995. pap. 6.00 (*0-671-52701-0*) Meadowbrook.

— Gentle Discipline: 50 Effective Techniques for Teaching Your Children Good Behavior. LC 95-15373. 1995. write for info. (*0-88166-233-X*) Meadowbrook.

— Gentle Discipline: 50 Simple Ways to Teach Your Child Good Behavior. 1995. pap. 6.00 (*0-88116-233-7*) Meadowbrook.

Lighter, Jonathan E. Historical Dictionary of American Slang. 1994. 55.00 (*0-394-54427-7*, Pubs Info Bureau) Random.

Lightfall, Frederick F. & Allan, Susan. Local Realities, Local Adaptations: Problem, Process, & Person in a School's Governance. 230p. 1989. 85.00 (*1-85000-587-7*, Falmer Pr); pap. 40.00 (*1-85000-588-5*, Falmer Pr) Taylor & Francis.

Lightfood, D. Teach Yourself Computer Programming in Pascal. 1984. pap. 8.95 (*0-679-10539-5*) McKay.

Lightfoot, C. S., ed. Recent Turkish Coin Hoards & Numismatic Studies. (Oxbow Monographs in Archaeology). (Illus.). 347p. 1992. pap. 68.00 (*0-946897-27-1*) David Brown.

Lightfoot, Charles R. Handbook of Business Quotations. 258p. 1990. 20.95 (*0-87201-065-1*) Gulf Pub.

Lightfoot, Claude & Patterson, William L. Four Score Years in Freedom's Fight. 16p. 1972. pap. 0.35 (*0-87898-081-4*) New Outlook.

Lightfoot, Claude M. Human Rights U. S. Style: From Colonial Times Through the New Deal. LC 77-21113. 239p. reprint ed. pap. 68.20 (*0-685-20528-2*, 2029990) Bks Demand.

— Racism & Human Survival: Lessons of Nazi Germany for Today's World. LC 72-82082. (Illus.). 304p. reprint ed. pap. 86.70 (*0-8357-3510-9*, 2034255) Bks Demand.

Lightfoot, D. J. Trail Fever: The Life of a Texas Cowboy. LC 92-5458. (Illus.). (YA). 1992. write for info. (*0-688-11537-3*) Lothrop.

Lightfoot, David. How to Set Parameters: Arguments from Language Change. (Illus.). 232p. 1991. 32.50 (*0-262-12153-0*) MIT Pr.

— How to Set Parameters: Arguments from Language Change. (Illus.). 232p. 1993. pap. 16.00 (*0-262-62090-1*, Bradford Bks) MIT Pr.

— Natural Logic & the Greek Moods. (Janua Linguarum, Series Practica: No. 230). 149p. 1975. pap. text ed. 46.95 (*90-279-3061-9*) Mouton.

Lightfoot, David & Hornstein, Norbert, eds. Verb Movement. LC 93-5481. 384p. (C). 1994. pap. 22.95 (*0-521-45661-4*) Cambridge U Pr.

— Verb Movement. LC 93-5481. 384p. (C). 1994. 64.95 (*0-521-45041-1*) Cambridge U Pr.

Lightfoot, David, jt. ed. see Webelhuth, Gert.

Lightfoot, Frederick. Nineteenth-Century New York in Rare Photographic Views. (New York Ser.). (Illus.). 96p. (Orig.). 1981. pap. 11.95 (*0-486-24137-8*) Dover.

Lightfoot, Frederick, jt. auth. see Johnson, Harry.

Lightfoot, Frederick S., et al, eds. Suffolk County, Long Island in Early Photographs. (Americana Ser.). 144p. 1984. pap. 9.95 (*0-486-24672-8*) Dover.

Lightfoot, J. B. The Apostolic Fathers, 5 vols., Set. 3024p. 1989. 99.95 (*0-943575-27-3*) Hendrickson MA.

— Biblical Essays. 459p. 1994. 19.95 (*1-56563-077-7*) Hendrickson MA.

— The Christian Ministry. LC 83-62042. 120p. 1983. pap. 8.95 (*0-8192-1331-4*) Morehouse Pub.

— J. B. Lightfoot's Commentary on the Epistles of St. Paul, 4 vols., Set. 1504p. Date not set. 74.95 (*1-56563-016-5*) Hendrickson MA.

— Padres Apostolicos: Apostolics Fathers. (SPA.). 23.95 (*84-7645-442-2*, 223461, Pub. by Edit Clie SP) TSELF.

— Philippians. LC 94-18837. (Crossway Classic Commentaries Ser.). 224p. (Orig.). 1994. pap. 10.99 (*0-89107-800-2*) Crossway Bks.

Lightfoot, J. B., ed. see Mansel, Henry L.

Lightfoot, J. D., tr. see Ignatius.

Lightfoot, John. A Commentary on the New Testament from the Talmud & Hebraica, 4 vols., Set. 1664p. 1989. 59.95 (*0-943575-26-5*) Hendrickson MA.

— Whole Works of John Lightfoot, 13 Vols, Set. Pitman, John, ed. LC 79-127318. reprint ed. write for info. (*0-404-04010-1*) AMS Pr.

Lightfoot, Joseph B., tr. & intro. The Apostolic Fathers - Patres Apostolici, 5 vols. lv, 2940p. (GER.). 1973. reprint ed. Vol. I, 1 & 2: S. Clement of Rome. write for info. (*0-318-70114-6*, Pub. by Georg Olms GW); reprint ed. Vol. II, 2 & 3: S. Ignatius, S. Polycarp. write for info. (*0-318-70116-2*, Pub. by Georg Olms GW) Lubrecht & Cramer.

— The Apostolic Fathers - Patres Apostolici, 5 vols., Set. lv, 2940p. (GER.). 1973. reprint ed. 518.70 (*3-487-04687-3*, Pub. by Georg Olms GW) Lubrecht & Cramer.

— The Apostolic Fathers - Patres Apostolici, 5 vols., Vol. II. lv, 2940p. (GER.). 1973. reprint ed. write for info. (*0-318-70115-4*, Pub. by Georg Olms GW) Lubrecht & Cramer.

Lightfoot, Kent G. Prehistoric Political Dynamics: A Case Study From the American Southwest. LC 83-25079. 193p. 1984. 25.00 (*0-87580-097-1*) N Ill U Pr.

Lightfoot-Klein, Hanny. A Woman's Odyssey into Africa: Tracks Across a Life. LC 91-18809. (Women's Studies). 150p. 1992. 39.95 (*1-56024-155-1*); pap. 17.95 (*1-56023-007-X*) Haworth Jrnl Co-Edits.

Lightfoot-Klein, Hanny, ed. Prisoners of Ritual: An Odyssey into Female Genital Circumcision in Africa. LC 89-15637. (Illus.). 306p. 1989. pap. text ed. 14.95 (*0-918393-68-X*) Harrington Pk.

Lightfoot-Klein, Hanny, pref. Prisoners of Ritual: An Odyssey into Female Genital Circumcision in Africa. LC 89-15639. (Haworth Series on Women: No. 2). (Illus.). 306p. 1989. text ed. 29.95 (*0-86656-877-8*) Haworth Pr.

Lightfoot, Lynn O., jt. auth. see Ross, Robert R.

Lightfoot, Marge. Cartooning for Kids. (Illus.). 64p. (J). 1993. 16.95 (*1-895688-03-5*, Pub. by Greey dePencier CN); pap. 8.95 (*0-920775-84-5*, Pub. by Greey dePencier CN) Firefly Bks Ltd.

Lightfoot, Marise P., jt. auth. see Garrett, Jill K.

Lightfoot, Martin & Martin, Nancy, eds. The Word for Teaching Is Learning: Essays for James Britton. LC 88-5069. xvii, 300p. 1988. pap. text ed. 20.00 (*0-86709-237-8*) Boynton Cook Pubs.

Lightfoot, Neil R. How We Got the Bible. rev. ed. LC 86-71090. (Way of Life Ser.). 95p. 1986. reprint ed. pap. 6.95 (*0-685-67509-2*) Abilene Christ U.

— How We Got the Bible. 2nd ed. LC 62-22230. 160p. 1988. 11.99 (*0-8010-5644-6*) Baker Bk.

— Jesus Christ Today: A Commentary on the Book of Hebrews. 274p. (C). reprint ed. pap. 13.95 (*0-9623823-0-2*) Bible Guides.

— Parables of Jesus, Vol. 1. 1986. reprint ed. 6.95 (*0-89112-178-1*) Abilene Christ U.

— Parables of Jesus, Vol. 2. LC 86-71089. (Way of Life Ser.). 95p. 1986. reprint ed. Vol. 1, 95p. pap. 6.95 (*0-89112-179-X*); reprint ed. pap. 6.95 (*0-685-73795-0*) Abilene Christ U.

— Role of Women: New Testament Perspectives. 1988. pap. 4.95 (*0-318-35184-6*) Student Assn.

***Lightfoot, Ricky R.** The Duckfoot Site Vol. 2: Archaeology of the House & Household. LC 94-68616. (Occasional Paper Ser.: No. 4). (Illus.). 192p. (Orig.). 1994. pap. 19.95x (*0-9624640-5-8*) Crow Canyon Archaeol.

Lightfoot, Ricky R. & Etzkorn, Mary C., eds. The Duckfoot Site Vol. 1: Descriptive Archaeology. LC 92-75597. (Occasional Paper Ser.: No. 3). (Illus.). 398p. (Orig.). 1993. pap. text ed. 29.95 (*0-9624640-2-3*) Crow Canyon Archaeol.

Lightfoot, Robert. Employment Game. 50p. 1994. pap. 7.95 (*0-939427-81-8*) Alpha Pubns OH.

— Obtaining Credit Fast & Easy. 79p. 1992. pap. 9.95 (*0-939427-73-7*) Alpha Pubns OH.

Lightfoot, Ruth. A Place for You in My Father's House. 140p. (Orig.). 1993. pap. 6.99 (*1-56043-514-3*) Destiny Image.

Lightfoot, Sara L. Balm in Gilead. 1989. pap. 14.42 (*0-201-51807-4*) Addison-Wesley.

— Good High School Portraits of Character & Culture. LC 83-70772. 416p. 1985. pap. text ed. 17.00 (*0-465-02696-6*) Basic.

Lightfoot, Sara L., jt. auth. see Carew, Jean V.

Lighthall, J. I. The Indian Household Medicine Guide. 1991. lib. bdg. 79.95 (*0-8490-4100-7*) Gordon Pr.

— The Indian Household Medicine Guide. 2nd ed. 142p. 1966. reprint ed. spiral bd. 7.15 (*0-7873-0560-X*) Mokelumne.

Lighthall, Lynne, rev. Sears List of Subject Headings: Canadian Companion. 4th ed. LC 92-27740. 1992. 18.00 (*0-8242-0832-3*) Wilson.

Lighthart, Bruce & Mohr, J. A., eds. Atmospheric Microbial Aerosols: Theoretical & Applied Aspects. LC 93-2375. 397p. 1994. 95.00 (*0-412-03181-7*) Chapman & Hall.

Lighthill, Celia. Cinema Century, Vol. I: The First Fifty Years. 240p. (C). 1993. per., pap. text ed. 33.95 (*0-8403-8788-1*) Kendall-Hunt.

Lighthill, J. Mathematical Biofluiddynamics. (CBMS-NSF Regional Conference Ser.: No. 17). vi, 281p. 1975. reprint ed. pap. text ed. 42.50 (*0-89871-014-6*) Soc Indus-Appl Math.

Lighthill, James. An Informal Introduction to Theoretical Fluid Mechanics. (Institute of Mathematics & Its Applications Conference Series, New Ser.: No. 2). (Illus.). 272p. 1988. pap. 29.95 (*0-19-853630-5*) OUP.

— Waves in Fluids. LC 77-8174. (Illus.). 1979. pap. 44.95 (*0-521-29233-6*) Cambridge U Pr.

Lighthill, M. J. Introduction to Fourier Analysis & Generalized Functions. (Cambridge Monographs on Mechanics & Applied Mathematics). (C). 1958. pap. 17.95 (*0-521-09128-4*) Cambridge U Pr.

Lightle, Juliana & Doucet, Elizabeth H. Sexual Harassment. Crisp, Michael G., ed. LC 91-78106. (Fifty-Minute Ser.). (Illus.). 100p. (Orig.). 1992. pap. 9.95 (*1-56052-153-8*) Crisp Pubns.

Lightle, Steve. Exodus II. 1983. pap. 6.95 (*0-917726-56-1*) Hunter Bks.

Lightle, Steve, jt. auth. see Nocenti, Ann.

Lightley, John W. Jewish Sects & Parties in the Time of Jesus. 1980. lib. bdg. 75.00 (*0-8490-3150-8*) Gordon Pr.

Lightman, Alan. Einstein's Dreams. 192p. 1994. mass mkt. 7.99 (*0-446-67011-1*) Warner Bks.

— Good Benito. 224p. 1996. pap. 7.99 (*0-446-67160-6*) Warner Bks.

— Time for the Stars: Astronomy in the 1990's. 144p. 1994. mass mkt. 6.99 (*0-446-67024-3*) Warner Bks.

Lightman, Alan P. Ancient Light: Our Changing View of the Universe. (Illus.). 170p. (C). 1991. text ed. 18.95 (*0-674-03362-0*) HUP.

— Ancient Light: Our Changing View of the Universe. (Illus.). 170p. (C). 1993. pap. text ed. 10.95 (*0-674-03363-9*) HUP.

— Einstein's Dreams: A Novel. LC 92-50465. (Illus.). 192p. 1992. 17.00 (*0-679-41646-3*) Pantheon.

— Good Benito. LC 94-25957. 1995. 21.00 (*0-679-43614-6*) Pantheon.

— Great Ideas in Physics. 1992. text ed. write for info. (*0-07-037935-1*); pap. text ed. write for info. (*0-07-037937-8*) McGraw.

Lightman, Alan P. & Brawer, Roberta. Origins: The Lives & Worlds of Modern Cosmologists. (Illus.). 563p. 1990. text ed. 38.00 (*0-674-64470-0*) HUP.

— Origins: The Lives & Worlds of Modern Cosmologists. (Illus.). 576p. 1992. pap. text ed. 16.95 (*0-674-64471-9*) HUP.

Lightman, Alan P., jt. auth. see Rybicki, George B.

Lightman, Alan P., et al. Problem Book in Relativity & Gravitation. 500p. 1975. 85.00 (*0-691-08160-3*); pap. 35.00 (*0-691-08162-X*) Princeton U Pr.

Lightman, Bernard, jt. ed. see Helmstadter, Richard J.

Lightman, Josie. The Faerie Way: A Novel. 106p. (Orig.). 1991. pap. text ed. 9.26 (*0-9624641-0-4*) Dayspring Pr.

Lightman, Josie, ed. The Faerie Way. 103p. (Orig.). 1991. pap. 11.81 (*0-685-48271-5*) Dayspring Pr.

Lightman, Marjorie & Negrin, Howard, eds. Outside Academe: New Ways of Working in the Humanities. LC 81-13463. 74p. 1982. pap. text ed. 12.00 (*0-86656-132-3*) Haworth Pr.

Lightman, Marjorie, jt. ed. see Hoff-Wilson, Joan.

Lightman, Robert D., ed. see Shapiro, Susan.

Lightman, Susan, ed. Immunology of Eye Diseases. (Immunology & Medicine Ser.). (C). 1989. lib. bdg. 75.00 (*0-7923-8908-5*) Kluwer Ac.

Lightner, Candy. Giving Sorrow Words: How to Cope with Grief & Get on with Your Life. 1991. pap. 12.99 (*0-446-39290-1*) Warner Bks.

Lightner, Candy & Hathaway, Nancy. Giving Sorrow Words: How to Cope With Grief & Get On With Your Life. 1990. 19.95 (*0-446-51509-4*) Warner Bks.

Lightner, D. V., jt. ed. see Sindermann, J. C.

Lightner, David L. Labor on the Illinois Central Railroad, 1852-1900: The Evolution of an Industrial Environment. Bruchey, Stuart, ed. LC 76-39834. (Nineteen Seventy-Seven Dissertations Ser.). (Illus.). 1977. lib. bdg. 36.95 (*0-405-09914-2*) Ayer.

Lightner, Helen. Class Voice & the American Art Song: A Source Book & Anthology. LC 91-7428. (Illus.). 191p. 1991. 32.50 (*0-8108-2381-0*) Scarecrow.

Lightner, Robert P. Evangelical Theology: A Survey & Review. LC 85-73722. 314p. 1990. pap. 15.99 (*0-8010-5663-2*) Baker Bk.

— Handbook of Evangelical Theology. 313p. 1995. pap. 10.99 (*0-8254-3145-X*) Kregel.

— Heaven for Those Who Can't Believe. LC 76-50303. 64p. 1977. pap. 2.25 (*0-87227-035-1*) Reg Baptist.

— James: Apostle of Practical Christianity. LC 81-70775. (Chosen Messenger Ser.). 128p. (Orig.). 1982. teacher ed 5.95 (*0-89636-105-5*); pap. text ed. 3.95 (*0-89636-079-2*) Accent CO.

Lightner, Ted. Introduction to English Derivational Morphology. (Linguisticae Investigationes Supplementa Ser.: No. 6). xxxviii, 533p. 1983. 107.00x (*90-272-3116-8*) Benjamins North Am.

***Lightning, Speaks.** Neioituonah: (Indian Issues) 2nd ed. 1995. 14.00 (*0-614-06312-4*) Spirit Talk Pr.

Lighton, Merle. Addict to Yearning: Inspirational Philosophy & Religion. 1952. 5.00 (*0-910892-00-8*, 910892) Lighton Pubns.

Lightsey, Harry M., Jr. Gems in a Crown: The People & Places of the College of Charleston - University of Charleston, South Carolina. 116p. 1993. 39.95 (*0-9638620-0-6*) Coll Charleston.

Lightsey, Harry M. & Flanagan, James F. South Carolina Civil Procedure. 1988. ring bd. 80.00 (*0-943856-12-4*, 425) SC Bar CLE.

Lightship Software Staff. Macscheme Student Edition. (C). 1990. disk, pap. text ed. 42.50 (*0-89426-141-X*) Boyd & Fraser.

— MacSheme: Users Guide & Language Reference Manual. 450p. 1990. pap. 39.95 (*0-262-62077-4*) MIT Pr.

Lightstone, A. H. Mathematical Logic: An Introduction to Model Theory. LC 77-17838. (Mathematical Concepts & Methods in Science & Engineering Ser.: Vol. 9). (Illus.). 352p. 1978. 47.50 (*0-306-30894-0*, Plenum Pr) Plenum.

Lightstone, Jack. Society, the Sacred & Scripture in Ancient Judaism. (Studies in Christianity & Judaism). 148p. (C). 1988. pap. 18.50 (*0-88920-975-8*, Pub. by Wilfrid Laurier CN) Humanities.

Lightstone, Jack N. The Commerce of the Sacred: Mediation of the Divine among Jews in the Graeco-Roman Diaspora. LC 83-20180. (Brown Judaic Studies). 234p. (C). 1984. pap. 19.75 (*0-89130-664-1*, 14 00 59) Scholars Pr GA.

— The Rhetoric of the Babylonian Talmud, Its Social Meaning & Context. (Studies in Christianity & Judaism: Vol. 6). 330p. (C). 1994. pap. 28.50 (*0-88920-238-9*, Pub. by Wilfrid Laurier CN) Humanities.

Lightstone, Jack N., jt. ed. see Fishbane, Simcha.

***Lightstone, Jack N., et al.** Ritual & Ethnic Identity: A Comparative Study of the Social Meaning of Liturgical Ritual in Synagogues. 255p. (C). 1995. pap. 35.00 (*0-88920-247-8*, Pub. by Wilfrid Laurier CN) Humanities.

Lightstone, James F., jt. ed. see Latman, Alan.

Lightwood, James T. Charles Dickens & Music. LC 76-119084. (Studies in Music: No. 42). 1970. reprint ed. lib. bdg. 48.95 (*0-8383-1080-X*) M S G Haskell Hse.

— Samuel Wesley, Musician: The Story of His Life. LC 72-83745. 1972. reprint ed. 20.95 (*0-405-08748-9*) Ayer.

Lightwood, John M. The Nature of Positive Law. xiv, 419p. 1982. reprint ed. lib. bdg. 35.00 (*0-8377-0814-1*) Rothman.

Ligi, Elio, jt. auth. see Fericano, Paul.

Ligi, Elio E. Disturbances. Trusky, Tom, ed. LC 89-80858. (Ahsahta Press Modern & Contemporary Poets of the West Ser.). 60p. (Orig.). 1990. pap. 6.95 (*0-916272-40-0*) Ahsahta Pr.

Ligibel, Ted & Wright, Richard. Island Heritage: A Guided Tour to Lake Erie's Bass Islands. LC 87-5742. (Illus.). 96p. (Orig.). 1987. pap. 12.50 (*0-8142-0442-2*) Ohio St U Pr.

Ligibel, Ted J. Clark Lake: Images of a Michigan Tradition. (Illus.). 156p. 1991. 40.00 (*0-9630645-0-9*) Clark Lke HPC.

Lignell, Kathleen. Red Horses. LC 91-61223. 56p. 1991. pap. 7.95 (*0-9621570-1-5*) North Lights.

Lignell, Kathleen, ed. The Eloquent Edge: Fifteen Maine Women Writers. LC 89-38065. 176p. 1989. 10.95 (*0-934745-12-9*) Acadia Pub Co.

Lignian, Mildred. Folks & Oaks of Olivet. (Illus.). 116p. 1975. pap. 3.50 (*0-685-55903-3*) Olivet.

An Asterisk (*) at the beginning of an entry indicates that the title is appearing in BIP for the first time.

Ligo, Larry L. The Concept of Function in Twentieth-Century Architectural Criticism. LC 84-44. (Studies in the Fine Arts - Architecture: No. 2). 233p. reprint ed. pap. 66.50 (*0-8357-1542-6*, 2070339) Bks Demand.

Ligon, Fred & Tannenbaum, Elizabeth. Picture Stories. (Illus.). 1990. pap. text ed. 12.95 (*0-8013-0366-4*, 78145) Longman.

Ligon, Fred, et al. More Picture Stories: Language & Problem Posing Activities. 128p. 1992. pap. text ed. 12.95 (*0-8013-0839-9*, 78905) Longman.

Ligon, Helen H. Successful Management Information Systems. rev. ed. LC 86-6979. (Research for Business Decisions Ser.: No. 78). 223p. reprint ed. pap. 63.60 (*0-8357-1703-8*, 2070401) Bks Demand.

Ligon, Linda, ed. The Herb Companion Cooks: Recipes from the First Five Years of the Herb Companion Magazine. (Illus.). 128p. 1994. pap. 16.95 (*0-934026-95-5*) Interweave.

Ligon, Linda, ed. see Becker, Jim & Becker, Dotti.

Ligon, Linda, ed. see Cooper, Frank M.

Ligon, Linda, ed. see Dille, Carolyn & Belsinger, Susan.

Ligon, Linda C., ed. Homespun, Handknit: Caps, Socks, Mittens & Gloves. LC 87-80522. (Illus.). 160p. (Orig.). 1987. pap. 15.00 (*0-934026-26-2*) Interweave.

— A Rug Weaver's Source Book. LC 84-82358. (Illus.). 176p. 1986. pap. 20.00 (*0-934026-16-5*) Interweave.

Ligon, Linda C., ed. see Atwater, Mary M.

Ligon, Linda C., ed. see DuBoff, Leonard D.

Ligon, Linda C., ed. see Van Stralen, Trudy.

Ligon, Lindon, ed. see Lovejoy, Sharon.

Ligon, P. C., jt. ed. see Swegle, W. E.

Ligon, Polly C., jt. ed. see Clubb, Deborah.

Ligon, Terry, jt. auth. see Enns, Peter.

Ligon, W. V. The McGehee Papers: Southside Virginia in the 1850's. (Illus.). 120p. (Orig.). 1984. pap. 9.95 (*0-930051-00-9*) Green Creek Pub Co.

***Ligon, William T., Sr.** Imparting the Blessing to Your Children: What the Jewish Patriarchs Knew. 56p. 1989. student ed 10.00 (*1-886327-00-9*) Fathers Blessing.

***Ligotti, Thomas.** Grimscribe: His Lives & Works. 240p. 1994. pap. text ed. 4.99 (*0-515-11471-5*) Jove Pubns.

— Noctuary. 224p. 1994. 18.95 (*0-7867-0003-3*) Carroll & Graf.

— Noctuary. 208p. 1995. pap. 8.95 (*0-7867-0235-4*) Carroll & Graf.

— Songs of a Dead Dreamer. 288p. 1991. pap. 4.50 (*0-88184-721-6*) Carroll & Graf.

Ligou, Daniel. Dictionnaire de la Franc-Maconnerie, 2 vols., Set. 3rd ed. 1344p. (FRE.). 1991. 175.00 (*0-7859-4767-1*, M267) Fr & Eur.

Ligou, Jacques P. Elements of Nuclear Engineering. 508p. (YA). (gr. 6 up). 1986. text ed. 342.00 (*3-7186-0363-2*) Gordon & Breach.

Ligouri, Alphonsus. The Way of the Cross: According to the Method of St. Alphonsus Liguori. 1987. reprint ed. pap. 0.75 (*0-89555-313-9*) TAN Bks Pubs.

Ligozat, Gerard, jt. auth. see Bestougeff, Helene.

Liguori, Alphonse. The Blessed Virgin Mary: Excerpt from the Glories of Mary. LC 82-50587. 96p. 1974. reprint ed. pap. 4.50 (*0-89555-177-2*) TAN Bks Pubs.

Liguori, Alphonsus. Glories of Mary. LC 90-33219. 215p. (Orig.). 1990. pap. 10.95 (*0-8189-0561-1*) Alba.

— The Holy Eucharist. LC 93-5955. 1994. pap. 8.95 (*0-8189-0676-6*) Alba.

— Love Is Prayer - Prayer Is Love. Stringraeber, John, ed. LC 72-97592. 192p. 1973. pap. 4.95 (*0-89243-047-8*) Liguori Pubns.

— Preparation for Death. abr. ed. LC 82-50596. 1982. reprint ed. pap. 7.00 (*0-89555-174-8*) TAN Bks Pubs.

— To Love Christ Jesus. LC 86-83164. 96p. 1987. pap. 2.95 (*0-89243-262-4*) Liguori Pubns.

— What Will Hell Be Like? Schaefer, J., ed. 24p. 1988. reprint ed. pap. 0.75 (*0-89555-341-4*) TAN Bks Pubs.

Liguori, Alphonsus de. Sermons of St. Alphonsus Liguori for All the Sundays of the Year. LC 82-50894. 408p. 1982. reprint ed. pap. 16.50 (*0-89555-193-4*) TAN Bks Pubs.

Liguori, Salvatore, jt. auth. see Gray, Wiliam S.

***Lih, Laras T. & Naumov, Oleg V., eds.** Stalin's Letters to Molotov, 1925-1936. Fitzpatrick, Catherine A., tr. LC 94-44050. (Annals of Communism Ser.). 1995. 25.00 (*0-300-06211-7*) Yale U Pr.

Lih, Lars T. Bread & Authority in Russia: 1914-1921. 1990. 40.00 (*0-520-06584-0*) U CA Pr.

Lihani, John. Manuscript Documents from Spain Dating from the 12th through the 18th Centuries Housed in the Special Collection of the Margaret I King Library, Univer. of Ky. LC 84-50663. (University of Kentucky Libraries Occasional Papers). 117p. (Orig.). 1984. lib. bdg. 7.00 (*0-917519-01-9*) U of KY Libs.

Lihani, John, ed. Global Demands on Language & the Mission of the Language Academies. LC 88-623526. xxxii, 219p. (Orig.). (C). 1988. pap. 14.95 (*0-929390-00-8*) KY Foreign Language Conference.

— Poema de Fernan Gonzalez. (Medieval Texts & Studies: No. 4). 188p. 1991. text ed. 22.00 (*0-937191-21-3*) Colleagues Pr Inc.

Lihn, Enrique. The Dark Room & Other Poems. Lerzundi, Patricio C., ed. Cohen, Jonathan et al, trs. LC 77-12927. 1978. 8.95 (*0-8112-0676-9*); pap. 2.45 (*0-8112-0677-7*, NDP452) New Directions.

***Liholm, Molly.** Tempting Jake. (Temptation Ser.). 1995. mass mkt. 3.25 (*0-373-25652-3*, 1-25652-8) Harlequin Bks.

***Lihong Xie.** Evolving Self in the Novels of Gail Godwin. LC 94-30115. (Southern Literary Studies). 248p. 1995. text ed. 30.00 (*0-8071-1924-5*) La State U Pr.

Lihou, David A. & Jones, Michael C. Hazard Evaluation Using Personal Computers. 500p. 1987. text ed. write for info. (*0-408-01058-4*) Buttrwrth-Heinemann.

***Lihs, Harriet R.** Jazz Dance. 2nd ed. 170p. (Orig.). 1993. pap. text ed. 8.95x (*0-614-03278-4*) American Pr.

— Teaching Gymnastics. 2nd ed. 150p. (Orig.). 1994. pap. text ed. 8.95x (*0-89641-226-1*) American Pr.

Liinder, Greg, ed. see Oberman, Lola.

Liittschwager, David, jt. auth. see Middleton, Susan.

***Liivaku, U. & Mereste, U.** Stock Exchange Dictionary: Estonian - Finnish - English - German - Russian. 217p. (EST, FIN & GER.). 1994. 118.00x (*951-640-664-5*) IBD Ltd.

Lijinsky, William. Chemistry & Biology of N-Nitroso Compounds. (Monographs on Cancer Research). 400p. (C). 1992. 175.00 (*0-521-34629-0*) Cambridge U Pr.

Lijklema, L., jt. ed. see IAWPRC Programme Committee Staff.

Lijklema, L., et al, eds. INTERURBA '92. (Water Science & Technology Ser.: Vol. 27). 1993. pap. 110.00 (*0-08-042350-7*, Pergamon Pr) Elsevier.

— Water Pollution Research & Control, Amsterdam 1984: Proceedings of the 12th Biennial Conference of the International Association on Water Pollution Research & Control Held in Amsterdam, The Netherlands, 17-20 September 1984. 1985. 330.00 (*0-08-033657-4*, Pub. by PPL UK) Elsevier.

Lijn, Liliane. Crossing Map. (Illus.). (Orig.). 1983. pap. 14.95 (*0-500-97310-5*) Thames Hudson.

Lijnen, H. R., et al, eds. Synthetic Substrates in Clinical Blood Coagulation Assays. (Developments in Hematology & Immunology Ser.: No. 1). 142p. 1980. lib. bdg. 47.00 (*90-247-2409-0*) Kluwer Ac.

***Lijnzaad, Elizabeth.** Reservations to UN-Human Rights Treaties: Ratify & Ruin? LC 94-40864. (International Studies in Human Rights: Vol. 38). 1995. lib. bdg. 142.00 (*0-7923-3256-3*, Pub. by M Nijhoff) Kluwer Ac.

Lijphart, Arend. Democracies: Patterns of Majoritarian & Consensus Government in Twenty-One Countries. LC 83-14639. 248p. 1984. pap. 12.00 (*0-300-03182-3*, Y 493) Yale U Pr.

— Democracy in Plural Societies: A Comparative Exploration. LC 77-76311. 1980. pap. 14.00 (*0-300-02494-0*) Yale U Pr.

— Electoral Systems & Party Systems: A Study of Twenty-Seven Democracies, 1945-1990. (Comparative European Politics Ser.). (Illus.). 232p. 1994. 29.95 (*0-19-827347-9*) OUP.

— Electoral Systems & Party Systems: A Study of Twenty-Seven Democracies, 1945-1990. (Comparative European Politics Ser.). (Illus.). 232p. 1995. reprint ed. pap. 17.95 (*0-19-828054-8*) OUP.

— Parliamentary vs. Presidential Government. (Oxford Readings in Politics & Government Ser.). 272p. 1992. 56.00 (*0-19-878043-5*); pap. 19.95 (*0-19-878044-3*) OUP.

— The Politics of Accommodation: Pluralism & Democracy in the Netherlands. 2nd rev. ed. LC 68-11667. 255p. reprint ed. pap. 72.70 (*0-685-23624-2*, 2029051) Bks Demand.

— Power-Sharing in South Africa. LC 85-82195. (Policy Papers in International Affairs Ser.: No. 24). x, 179p. (C). 1985. pap. 11.50 (*0-87725-524-5*) U of Cal IAS.

— The Trauma of Decolonization: The Dutch & West New Guinea. LC 66-12506. (Yale Studies in Political Science). 316p. reprint ed. pap. 90.10 (*0-317-11338-0*, 2022014) Bks Demand.

Lijphart, Arend, ed. Conflict & Coexistence in Belgium: The Dynamics of a Culturally Divided Society. LC 81-7200. (Research Ser.: No. 46). (Illus.). ix, 171p. 1981. pap. 10.50 (*0-87725-146-0*) U of Cal IAS.

Lijphart, Arend, jt. ed. see Grofman, Bernard.

Lijphart, Arent & Grofman, Bernard, eds. Choosing an Electoral System: Issues & Alternatives. LC 84-18283. (American Political Parties & Elections Ser.). 286p. 1984. text ed. 75.00 (*0-275-91216-7*, C1216, Praeger Pubs) Greenwood.

Likar, I. V. & Robinson, R. W. Atherosclerosis. (Monographs on Atherosclerosis: Vol. 12). (Illus.). viii, 176p. 1986. 109.00 (*3-8055-4069-8*) S Karger.

Liken, Shari, ed. Houston Medical Directory, 1990. 700p. 1990. 34.95 (*0-933745-06-0*) Med Prod.

— Houston Medical Directory, 1991. 710p. 1990. 39.95 (*0-933745-07-9*) Med Prod.

***Likeness, James B.** Crayons on the Wall. 128p. 1995. ring bd. 15.00 (*0-9629765-5-5*) Frederick Pubs.

Likens, Agnes. The Good Ol' Days. LC 93-91807. 162p. 1993. write for info. (*0-9639220-0-9*) A Likens.

***Likens, G. E. & Bormann, F. H.** Biogeochemistry of a Forested Ecosystem. 2nd ed. LC 94-41866. (Illus.). 168p. 1995. 49.95 (*0-387-94502-4*) Spr-Verlag.

Likens, G. E., jt. auth. see Bormann, F. H.

Likens, Gene E., ed. An Ecosystem Approach to Aquatic Ecology. (Illus.). xiv, 516p. 1985. 84.00 (*0-387-96106-2*) Spr-Verlag.

— Long-Term Studies in Ecology. (Illus.). 210p. 1990. 75.00 (*0-387-96743-5*) Spr-Verlag.

— Some Perpectives of the Major Biochemical Cycles. LC 80-42017. (Scientific Committee on Problems of the Environment Ser.: Report 17). 175p. 1981. text ed. 61.95 (*0-471-27989-7*) Wiley.

***Likens, Gene E. & Bormann, F. Herbert.** Biogeochemistry of a Forested Ecosystem. 2nd ed. LC 94-41866. (Illus.). 168p. 1995. 29.95 (*0-387-94351-X*) Spr-Verlag.

Likens, Gene E., jt. auth. see Bormann, F. H.

Likens, Gene E., jt. ed. see Groffman, Peter M.

Likens, Gene E., jt. auth. see Wetzel, Robert G.

Likens, Gene E., et al. Biogeochemistry of a Forested Ecosystem. LC 76-50113. 1991. pap. 28.00 (*0-387-90225-2*) Spr-Verlag.

***Liker, Jeffrey K., et al, eds.** Engineered to Japan: Japanese Technology - Management Practices. (Illus.). 464p. 1995. 35.00 (*0-19-509555-3*) OUP.

Likert, Jane G., jt. auth. see Likert, Rensis.

Likert, Rensis & Likert, Jane G. New Ways of Managing Conflict. LC 75-23216. (Illus.). 383p. reprint ed. pap. 109.20 (*0-8357-3611-3*, AU00396) Bks Demand.

Likes, Pat D. Twelve Plus Me. (Illus.). 160p. 1991. reprint ed. pap. 7.95 (*0-929292-09-X*) Hannibal Bks.

Likes, Robert C. & Day, Glenn R. From This Mountain-Cerro Gordo. LC 75-44236. (Illus.). 86p. 1975. pap. 8.95 (*0-912494-15-8*) Chalfant Pr.

Likhachev, A., ed. see International Agency for Research on Cancer Staff.

Likhachev, Dmitirii S. Reflections on Russia, Vol. 4. (CCRS Series on Change in Contemporary Soviet Society: No. 4). 191p. (C). 1991. text ed. 41.00 (*0-8133-7743-9*) Westview.

Likhachev, N. I., et al. Wastewater Collection & Transportation, Vol. 1. (Design Handbook of Wastewater Systems). 150p. 1986. 100.00 (*0-89864-021-0*) Allerton Pr.

Likhacheva, V. The Art of Byzantium. 310p. (RUS.). 1981. 24.00 (*0-317-57213-X*, Pub. by Collets UK) St Mut.

Likhachova, L., jt. auth. see Pleshanova, I.

Likhachova, Liudmila, ed. see Pleshanova, Ialila.

Likharev, Konstantin K. Dynamics of Josephson Junctions & Circuits. 634p. 1986. text ed. 208.00 (*2-88124-042-9*) Gordon & Breach.

Likholobov, V., jt. ed. see Yermakov, Yu.

Likhtenshtefin, Gerktis. Spin Labeling Methods in Molecular Biology. LC 76-16500. 271p. reprint ed. pap. 77.30 (*0-317-28454-1*, 2055151) Bks Demand.

Likhtenshtein, Gertz I. Biophysical Labeling Methods in Molecular Biology. LC 92-19487. (Illus.). 256p. (C). 1993. 54.95 (*0-521-43132-8*) Cambridge U Pr.

Likhtman, V. I. Physicochemical Mechanics of Metals: Adsorption Phemomena in the Process of Deformation & Failure of Metals. 247p. 1964. text ed. 66.00 (*0-317-46421-3*, Pub. by Keter Pub IS) Coronet Bks.

Likierman, Andrew. Professional Liability. 188p. 1989. pap. 35.00 (*0-11-515205-9*, HM5029) UNIPUB.

Likosky, Stephan, ed. Coming Out: An Anthology of International Gay & Lesbian Writings. LC 91-50834. 576p. (Orig.). 1992. pap. 15.00 (*0-679-74054-6*) Pantheon.

Likoudis, James. Ending the Byzantine Greek Schism: Containing: The 14th c. Apologia of Demetrios Kydones for Unity with Rome & the "Contraerrones Gracconum" of St. Thomas Aquinas. rev. ed. (Illus.). 235p. (C). 1992. pap. text ed. 14.95 (*1-879860-01-5*) Cath United Faith.

Likoudis, James & Whitehead, K. D. The Pope, the Council, & the Mass. 1981. 13.95 (*0-8158-0400-8*) Chris Mass.

Liksen, H. J. Classical Circus Equitation Liberty, High School, Quadrilles & Vaulting. Coxe, Anthony H., tr. 240p. 1990. 120.00 (*0-85131-542-9*, Pub. by J A Allen & Co UK) St Mut.

Liksom, Rosa. One Night Stands. 1994. pap. 11.99 (*1-85242-292-0*) Serpents Tail.

Likta, Michael. International Dimensions of the Legal Environment of Business. 2nd ed. 256p. (C). 1991. pap. 20.95 (*0-534-92505-7*) Intl Thomson.

Lilburn, Pat & Rawson, Pam. Let's Talk Math: Encouraging Children to Explore Ideas. LC 93-44870. 120p. 1994. pap. text ed. 15.00 (*0-435-08348-1*) Heinemann.

Lile, Laird A. Florida Probate: Discussion & Commentary on Code, Rules, & Forms. LC 94-73045. 1994. ring bd. 89.50 (*0-318-72212-7*) Bisel Co.

***Lileks.** Fresh Lies. 1995. pap. (*0-671-73704-X*) PB.

— Mr. Obvious. 1995. pap. 5.50 (*0-671-73705-8*) S&S Trade.

Lileks, James. Fresh Lies. LC 93-30993. 1994. 18.00 (*0-671-73703-1*) PB.

— Notes of a Nervous Man. Chelius, Jane, ed. 240p. 1992. reprint ed. pap. 10.00 (*0-671-73702-3*) PB.

Liles, Glennis S. The W-Hollow Cookbook. 2nd ed. Charles, Chuck D., ed. (Illus.). 320p. 1990. 24.00 (*0-945084-18-8*) J Stuart Found.

— W-Hollow Holidays & Holiday Recipes. 240p. 1995. write for info. (*1-886029-07-5*) Spider Hill Pr.

Liles, J. N. The Art & Craft of Natural Dyeing: Traditional Recipes for Modern Use. LC 90-12045. 254p. 1990. Alk. paper. text ed. 42.00x (*0-87049-669-7*); pap. 19.50 (*0-87049-670-0*) U of Tenn Pr.

Liles, Larry E. & Neimeyer, Robert A. Winning Racquetball. 192p. (C). 1993. pap. text ed. write for info. (*0-697-13151-3*) Brown & Benchmark.

Liles, Marcia T., ed. see Taggard, Genevieve.

Liles, Maurine. Kitty of Blossom Prairie. (Illus.). 128p. (J). (gr. 4-7). 1992. 14.95 (*0-89015-863-0*) Sunbelt Media.

Liles, Maurine W. The Boy of Blossom Prairie, Who Became Vice-President. (J). 1993. 14.95 (*0-89015-913-0*) Sunbelt Media.

— Rebecca of Blossom Prairie: Grandmother of a Vice President. Roberts, M., ed. (Illus.). 112p. (J). 1990. 10.95 (*0-89015-754-5*) Sunbelt Media.

— Sam & the Speaker's Chair. LC 93-42374. (J). 1994. 14.95 (*0-89015-946-7*) Sunbelt Media.

Liles, Necia D., ed. see Lord, Israel S.

Liles, Parker, et al. Typing Mailable Letters. 3rd ed. Rubin, Audrey S., ed. (Illus.). (J). (gr. 9-12). 1978. text ed. 11.24 (*0-07-037855-X*) McGraw.

Liley, D. T., jt. auth. see Kingsford, D. P.

Liley, P. E., ed. see Thermophysical Properties Symposium Staff.

Liley, Peter E. Schaum's Two Thousand Solved Problems in Mechanical Engineering Thermodynamics. 416p. 1989. pap. text ed. 19.95 (*0-07-037863-0*) McGraw.

Liley, Peter E., et al. Properties of Inorganic & Organic Fluids. (CINDAS Data Series on Material Properties: Vol. V-1). 309p. 1988. 121.00 (*0-89116-802-8*) Hemisp Pub.

Lilford, R. J. Pre-Natal Diagnosis. 245p. 1990. 135.00 (*0-407-01044-0*) Buttrwrth-Heinemann.

Lilford, Richard, jt. auth. see Chard, Tim.

Lilie, Ralph-J. Byzantium & the Crusader States 1096-1204. rev. ed. Morris, J. C. & Ridings, Jean E., trs. (Illus.). 360p. 1994. 59.00 (*0-19-820407-8*) OUP.

Lilie, Tish. The Knitting Problem Solver. Foster, Kim & Parkinson, Connie, eds. (Country Wisdom Bulletin Ser.). (Illus.). 32p. 1991. 2.95 (*0-88266-696-7*, Storey Pub) Storey Comm Inc.

Lilien, Gary L. Marketing Management: Analytic Exercises with Lotus 1-2-3. 183p. (C). 1988. 3.5 hd 32.50 (*0-89426-169-X*); 5.25 hd, pap. text ed. 32.50 (*0-89426-146-0*) Boyd & Fraser.

— Marketing Mix Analysis with Lotus 1-2-3. 250p. 1986. 3.5 hd 42.50 (*0-89426-168-1*) Boyd & Fraser.

Lilien, Gary L., jt. ed. see Eliashberg, J.

Lilienfeld, Abraham M. Epidemiology of Mongolism. LC 78-82451. (Illus.). 160p. reprint ed. 45.60 (*0-8357-9270-6*, 2011559) Bks Demand.

Lilienfeld, Abraham M., jt. auth. see Levine, Sol.

Lilienfeld, Abraham M., et al. Cancer in the United States. LC 72-80658. (Vital & Health Statistics Monographs, American Public Health Association). (Illus.). 572p. 1972. 47.50 (*0-674-09425-5*) HUP.

Lilienfeld, Robert. The Rise of Systems Theory. LC 85-5531. 310p. (C). 1988. reprint ed. text ed. 42.50 (*0-89874-857-7*) Krieger.

Lilienfeld, Robert, jt. auth. see Bensman, Joseph.

Lilienfeld, Scott O. Seeing Both Sides: Classic Controversies in Abnormal Psychology. LC 94-18083. 532p. 1995. pap. 24.95 (*0-534-25134-X*) Brooks-Cole.

Lilienfeld, David E. & Stolley, Paul D. Foundations of Epidemiology. (Illus.). 368p. 1994. 49.95 (*0-19-505035-5*); pap. 27.50 (*0-19-505036-3*) OUP.

Lilienstein, Fred M. Magnetics Engineering Fundamentals & Computer-Aided Design Solutions. LC 92-26751. 1993. text ed. 103.95 (*0-442-00738-8*) Van Nos Reinhold.

Lilienthal, Alfred. The Zionist Connection II. 904p. 1986. pap. 29.00 (*0-949667-33-1*, Pub. by Veritas Pubng AT) Noontide.

Lilienthal, B. Phosphates & Dental Caries. (Monographs in Oral Science: Vol. 6). (Illus.). 1977. 55.25 (*3-8055-2677-6*) S Karger.

Lilienthal, David E. Big Business: A New Era. LC 73-2517. (Big Business; Economic Power in a Free Society Ser.). 1973. reprint ed. 19.95 (*0-405-05097-6*) Ayer.

— Change, Hope & the Bomb. LC 63-16236. 178p. reprint ed. pap. 50.80 (*0-8357-8827-X*, 2033384) Bks Demand.

***Lilienthal, Meta.** Dear Remembered World. (American Autobiography Ser.). 248p. 1995. reprint ed. lib. bdg. 79.00 (*0-7812-8577-1*) Rprt Serv.

Lilienthal, Nancy, jt. auth. see Rohmann, Steven O.

Lilienthal, Nancy, et al. Tackling Toxics in Everyday Products: A Directory of Organizations. LC 91-29961. 192p. 1992. pap. 19.95 (*0-918780-56-X*) INFORM NY.

Lilienthal, Philip E., tr. see Bousquet, Georges H.

Lilies, W. Conrad, Jr., jt. auth. see Larson, Eric B.

Liliuokalani. Hawaii's Story by Hawaii's Queen. (American Biography Ser.). 1991. reprint ed. lib. bdg. write for info. (*0-7812-8245-4*) Rprt Serv.

Lilja, David. Architectural Alternatives for Exploring Parallelism. LC 91-33298. (Illus.). 464p. (C). 1992. text ed. 65.00 (*0-8186-2642-9*, 2642) IEEE Comp Soc.

Lilja, David J. & Bird, Peter L., eds. The Interaction of Compilation Technology & Computer Architecture. LC 94-1648. 296p. (C). 1994. lib. bdg. 95.00 (*0-7923-9451-8*) Kluwer Ac.

Lilja, Dick, jt. auth. see Lilja, Irene.

Lilja, Irene & Lilja, Dick. Suislaw Forest Hikes: A Guide to Oregon's Coast Range. (Illus.). 64p. (Orig.). 1990. pap. 8.95 (*0-910467-08-0*) Heritage Assocs.

Lilja, R., et al. Unemployment & Labour Market Flexibility in Finland. vi, 222p. 1990. pap. 24.00 (*92-2-107273-8*) Intl Labour Office.

Liljegren, S. B. American Studies in Sweden. (Essays & Studies on American Language & Literature: Vol. 14). (Orig.). 1962. pap. 18.00 (*0-8115-0194-9*) Periodicals Srv.

— Bulwer-Lytton's Novels & Isis Unveiled. (Essays & Studies on English Language & Literature: Vol. 18). (Orig.). 1957. pap. 15.00 (*0-8115-0216-3*) Periodicals Srv.

— Joseph Conrad As a "Prober of Feminine Hearts" Notes on the Novel "The Rescue" (Essays & Studies on English Language & Literature: Vol. 27). (Orig.). 1968. pap. 15.00 (*0-8115-0225-2*) Periodicals Srv.

— Revolt Against Romanticism in American Literature As Evidenced in the Work of S. L. Clemens. 59p. 1983. pap. 12.50 (*0-87556-650-2*) Saifer.

— The Revolt Against Romanticism in American Literature As Evidenced in the Works of S. L. Clemens. (Essays & Studies on American Language & Literature: Vol. 1). 1974. reprint ed. pap. 18.00 (*0-8115-0183-3*) Periodicals Srv.

— Studies on the Origin & Early Tradition of English Utopian Fiction. (Essays & Studies on English Language & Literature: Vol. 23). (Orig.). 1961. pap. 20.00 (*0-8115-0221-X*) Periodicals Srv.

Liljegren, S. B., ed. see Harrington, James.

Liljegren, Sten. American & European in the Works of Henry James. LC 71-119080. (Studies in Henry James: No. 17). (C). 1970. reprint ed. lib. bdg. 49.95 (*0-8383-1076-1*) M S G Haskell Hse.

— Revolt Against Romanticism in American Literature. (BCL1-PS American Literature Ser.). 60p. 1993. reprint ed. lib. bdg. 59.00 (*0-7812-6951-2*) Rprt Serv.

— Revolt Against Romanticism in American Literature: As Evidenced in the Works of S. L. Clemens. LC 65-15896. (Studies in Fiction: No. 34). (C). 1969. reprint ed. lib. bdg. 75.00 (*0-8383-0583-0*) M S G Haskell Hse.

An Asterisk (*) at the beginning of an entry indicates that the title is appearing in BIP for the first time.

— Studies in Milton. LC 67-30816. (Studies in Milton: No. 22). 1969. reprint ed. lib. bdg. 75.00 (*0-8383-0718-3*) M S G Haskell Hse.

Liljegren, Steven K., jt. auth. see Chiauzzi, Emil.

Liljehorn, Linda. Preschool Bible Bulletin Boards. (Christian Preschool Ser.). 96p. 1991. 10.95 (*0-86653-572-1*, SS896, Shining Star Pubns) Good Apple.

Liljencrants, Johan. Spiritism & Religion. 1926. 19.50 (*0-8159-6820-5*) Devin.

Liljencrants, Jonathan.

Liljendahl, Eva. Explosion & Other Poems. 104p. (Orig.). 1994. pap. write for info. (*0-9637979-1-3*) T Y Okosun.

Liljenstolpe, Carl & Burke, Mary A. Recruiting Volunteers. Crisp, Michael G., ed. LC 91-76308. (Fifty-Minute Ser.). (Illus.). 100p. (Orig.). 1992. pap. 9.95 (*1-56052-141-4*) Crisp Pubns.

Liljenstolpe, Carl, jt. auth. see Burke, Mary A.

Liljequist, Gosta H., ed. Weather & Weather Maps. (Contributions to Current Research in Geophysics Ser.: 10). 265p. (C). 1982. text ed. 71.95 (*0-8176-1192-4*) Birkhauser.

Liljestrand, G., jt. auth. see Holmstedt, B.

Liljestrand, G., jt. ed. see Holmstedt, B.

Liljestrand, Walter. Centrifugal Pumps & Piping Systems. LC 83-161604. (Mud Equipment Manual Ser.: No. 4). 168p. (Orig.). 1983. pap. 41.00 (*0-87201-616-1*) Gulf Pub.

Liljestrand, Walter & Lawson, Gordon. Degassers: Degassers. LC 83-161604. (Mud Equipment Manual Ser.: No. 5). (Illus.). 94p. (Orig.). 1985. pap. 25.00 (*0-87201-617-X*) Gulf Pub.

Liljestrom, Rita, jt. ed. see Tumbo-Masabo, Z.

Liljestrom, Rita, et al. Young Children in China. 262p. 1984. 79.00 (*0-905028-30-9*, Pub. by Multilingual Matters UK); pap. 29.95 (*0-905028-29-5*, Pub. by Multilingual Matters UK) Taylor & Francis.

Lilker, Shalom. Kibbutz Judaism: A New Tradition in the Making. LC 80-70886. (Norwood Editions, Kibbutz, Cooperative Societies, & Alternative Social Policy Bks.: Vol. 7). 240p. 1983. 14.95 (*0-8453-4740-3*, Cornwall Bks) Assoc Univ Prs.

Lill, Roland, jt. ed. see Neupert, Walter.

Lill, Wayne P., Jr. Decision Tables & Flowcharts: DEVA, the Decision Table Evaluation Program for Strategic Logic Design & Development. 200p. 1992. 34.95 (*1-882619-08-0*) Binary Triangles.

Lill, Wendy. All Fall Down. 108p. 1994. pap. 10.95 (*0-88922-336-X*, Pub. by Talonbooks CN) InBook.

Lilla, Mark. Arch in Public Space. 1986. pap. write for info. (*0-02-919170-X*) Macmillan.

— G. B. Vico: The Making of an Anti-Modern. (Illus.). 271p. (C). 1993. text ed. 45.00 (*0-674-33962-2*) HUP.

— G. B. Vico: The Making of an Anti-Modern. LC 92-23388. 1993. text ed. write for info. (*0-674-54305-X*) HUP.

— G. B. Vico: The Making of an Anti-Modern. (Illus.). 271p. 1994. pap. text ed. 17.95 (*0-674-33963-0*, LILVIX) HUP.

Lilla, Mark, jt. ed. see Glazer, Nathan.

Lillard, Lee A. An Essay on Human Wealth. (Explorations in Economic Research Four Ser.: No. 5). 50p. 1978. reprint ed. 35.00 (*0-685-61421-2*) Natl Bur Econ Res.

Lillard, Louise, jt. auth. see Poletti, Jacques.

Lillard, Paula P. Children Learning: A Teacher's Classroom Diary. LC 80-16151. 256p. 1987. write for info. (*0-8052-3745-3*) Schocken.

— Montessori: A Modern Approach. LC 78-163334. (Illus.). 192p. (C). 1988. 12.00 (*0-8052-0920-4*) Schocken.

Lillard, Richard G. The Great Forest. LC 72-8129. (Illus.). 452p. 1973. reprint ed. lib. bdg. 49.50 (*0-306-70534-6*) Da Capo.

— My Urban Wilderness in the Hollywood Hills: A Year of Years on Quito Lane. (Illus.). 218p. (Orig.). (C). 1983. lib. bdg. 52.00 (*0-8191-3317-5*); pap. text ed. 24.00 (*0-8191-3318-3*) U Pr of Amer.

Lillard, Stewart. Meigs County, Tennessee: A Documented Account of Its European Settlement & Growth. rev. ed. (Illus.). 202p. 1983. reprint ed. 20.00 (*0-317-39990-X*) Southern Hist Pr.

Lillard, Thomas, jt. auth. see Hurtik, Emil.

Lillberg, John & Oothoudt, Michael, eds. Computing for High Luminosity & High Intensity Facilities. LC 90-55634. (AIP Conference Proceedings Ser.: No. 209). (Illus.). 704p. 1990. 95.00 (*0-88318-786-8*) Am Inst Physics.

Lillegard, Dee. Brass. LC 87-32990. (Introduction to Musical Instruments Ser.). (Illus.). 32p. (J). (ps-3). 1988. lib. bdg. 11.85 (*0-516-02218-0*) Childrens.

— The Hee Haw River. (J). 1995. 14.95 (*0-8050-2375-5*) H Holt & Co.

— I Can Be a Carpenter. LC 86-9676. (I Can Be Bks.). (Illus.). 32p. (J). (gr. k-3). 1986. lib. bdg. 11.85 (*0-516-01884-1*); pap. 3.95 (*0-516-41884-X*) Childrens.

— I Can Be a Secretary. LC 86-29947. (I Can Be Bks.). (Illus.). 32p. (J). (gr. k-3). 1987. lib. bdg. 11.85 (*0-516-01907-4*) Childrens.

— James A. Garfield. LC 87-18200. (Encyclopedia of Presidents Ser.). (Illus.). 100p. (J). (gr. 3 up). 1987. lib. bdg. 14.40 (*0-516-01394-7*) Childrens.

— James K. Polk. LC 87-35188. (Encyclopedia of Presidents Ser.). (Illus.). 100p. (J). (gr. 3 up). 1988. lib. bdg. 14.40 (*0-516-01351-3*) Childrens.

— John Tyler. LC 87-18202. (Encyclopedia of Presidents Ser.). (Illus.). 100p. (J). (gr. 3 up). 1987. lib. bdg. 14.40 (*0-516-01393-9*) Childrens.

— My First Columbus Day Book. LC 87-10304. (My First Holiday Bks.). (Illus.). 32p. (J). (ps-2). 1987. lib. bdg. 11.55 (*0-516-02909-6*); pap. 3.95 (*0-516-42909-4*) Childrens.

— My First Martin Luther King Book. LC 86-31670. (My First Holiday Bks.). (Illus.). 32p. (J). (ps-2). 1987. lib. bdg. 11.55 (*0-516-02908-8*); pap. 3.95 (*0-516-42908-6*) Childrens.

— My Yellow Ball. LC 92-27003. (Illus.). (J). (gr. k-3). 1993. 12.99 (*0-525-45078-5*, DCB) Dutton Child Bks.

— Nevada. braille ed. 195p. (J). 1993. vinyl bd. 15.40 (*1-56956-139-7*, BR9036) W A T Braille.

— Percussion. LC 87-18217. (Introduction to Musical Instruments Ser.). (Illus.). 32p. (J). (ps-3). 1987. lib. bdg. 11.85 (*0-516-02216-4*) Childrens.

— Potatoes on Tuesday. 2nd ed. (Let Me Read Ser.). (Illus.). 8p. (J). (ps-2). 1995. pap. 2.95 (*0-673-36235-3*) GdYrBks.

— Richard Nixon. LC 87-35185. (Encyclopedia of Presidents Ser.). (Illus.). 100p. (J). (gr. 3 up). 1988. lib. bdg. 14.40 (*0-516-01356-4*) Childrens.

— Sitting in My Box. LC 89-31609. (Illus.). 32p. (J). (ps-2). 1989. 12.95 (*0-525-44528-5*, DCB) Dutton Child Bks.

— Sitting in My Box. (Illus.). 32p. (J). (ps-2). 1992. pap. 4.99 (*0-14-054819-X*, Puff Unicorn) Puffin Bks.

— Sitting in My Box. (Giant Bk. Ser.). (Illus.). 32p. (J). (ps-2). 1993. pap. 17.99 (*0-14-054886-6*, Puff Unicorn) Puffin Bks.

— Strings. LC 87-32994. (Introduction to Musical Instruments Ser.). (Illus.). 32p. (J). (ps-3). 1988. lib. bdg. 11.85 (*0-516-02219-9*) Childrens.

— Where Is It? LC 84-7005. (Rookie Reader Ser.). (Illus.). 32p. (J). (ps-2). 1984. lib. bdg. 10.35 (*0-516-02065-X*); pap. 2.95 (*0-516-42065-8*) Childrens.

— Woodwinds. LC 87-18232. (Introduction to Musical Instruments Ser.). (Illus.). 32p. (J). (ps-3). 1987. lib. bdg. 11.85 (*0-516-02217-2*) Childrens.

Lillegard, Dee & Stoker, Wayne. I Can Be a Plumber. LC 86-30950. (I Can Be Bks.). (Illus.). 32p. (J). (gr. k-3). 1987. lib. bdg. 11.85 (*0-516-01906-6*) Childrens.

— Nevada. LC 90-34665. (America the Beautiful Ser.). (Illus.). 144p. (J). (gr. 4 up). 1990. lib. bdg. 20.55 (*0-516-00474-3*) Childrens.

Lillegard, Wade A. & Rucker, Karen S., eds. Handbook of Sports Medicine: A Symptom-Oriented Approach. (Illus.). 350p. 1993. 60.00 (*1-56372-052-3*, Andover Med Pubs) Buttrwrth-Heinemann.

Lillegraven, Jason A., et al. Evolutionary Relationships of Middle Eocene & Younger Species of Centetodon (Mammalia, Insectivora, Geolabididae) with a Description of the Dentition of Ankylodon (Adapisoricidae) LC 81-53020. (Illus.). 116p. (C). 1981. pap. 12.50 (*0-941570-00-2*) U of Wyoming.

— Vertebrates, Phylogeny, & Philosophy. Flanagan, K., ed. LC 86-50857. (Illus.). 372p. 1986. lib. bdg. 30.00 (*0-941570-02-9*) U of Wyoming.

Lillegraven, Jason A., et al, eds. Mesozoic Mammals: The First Two-Thirds of Mammalian History. 1979. pap. 18.00 (*0-520-03951-3*) U CA Pr.

Lillehagen, Frank M., jt. ed. see Bo, Ketil.

Lillehoj, Erik P., jt. ed. see Malik, Vedpal S.

Lillen, Linda. Testing Peripheries: U.S.-Yugoslav Economic Relations in the Interwar Years. LC 93-72245. (East European Monographs: No. CCCLXXXII). 234p. 1994. 48.00 (*0-88033-279-4*) East Eur Quarterly.

Liller, William. The Ancient Solar Observations of Rapanui: The Archaeoastronomy of Easter Island. LC 93-25642. (Easter Island Foundation Ser.). 1993. 12.00 (*1-880636-01-8*) Cloud Mtn.

— The Cambridge Guide to Astronomical Discovery. (Illus.). 240p. (C). 1992. 29.95 (*0-521-41839-9*) Cambridge U Pr.

Liller, William & Mayer, Ben. The Cambridge Astronomy Guide: A Practical Introduction to Astronomy. (Illus.). 170p. (C). 1990. pap. 22.95 (*0-521-39915-7*) Cambridge U Pr.

Lillesand, Thomas M. & Keifer, Ralph W. Remote Sensing & Image Interpretation. 2nd ed. 721p. 1987. Net. text ed. write for info. (*0-471-84517-5*) Wiley.

Lillesand, Thomas M. & Kiefer, Ralph W. Remote Sensing & Image Interpretation. 3rd ed. LC 93-32253. 1994. text ed. write for info. (*0-471-57783-9*) Wiley.

***Lillethorup, Galen K.** Can Your Cat Do That? A Whimsical Aid to Expanding a Child's Imagination. Lillethorup, Kragh, ed. & illus. by. LC 95-92189. 32p. (J). (ps). 1995. pap. 8.95 (*0-9646015-0-8*) Sibling Pr.

— A Guide to Understanding ADF Navigation & NDB Instrument Approaches. 2nd ed. (Illus.). 54p. Date not set. pap. text ed. 12.95 (*0-9646015-1-6*) Sibling Pr.

Lillethorup, Kragh, ed. see Lillethorup, Galen K.

Lilley. Pharmacology & the Nursing Process. 1996. 35.95 (*0-8016-7893-5*) Mosby Yr Bk.

Lilley, Alan A. A Handbook of Segmental Paving. (Illus.). 160p. 1991. 83.95 (*0-442-31381-0*) Chapman & Hall.

Lilley, D. M. J., jt. ed. see Eckstein, F.

***Lilley, David M., ed.** DNA-Protein: Structural Interactions: Frontiers in Molecular Biology. (Frontiers in Molecular Biology Ser.). (Illus.). 220p. 1995. pap. text ed. 43.00 (*0-19-963453-X*, IRL Pr) OUP.

— DNA-Protein: Structural Interactions: Frontiers in Molecular Biology. (Frontiers in Molecular Biology Ser.). (Illus.). 220p. 1995. text ed. 85.00 (*0-19-963454-8*, IRL Pr) OUP.

Lilley, David M., jt. ed. see Eckstein, F.

Lilley, David M., jt. ed. see Eckstein, G.

Lilley, David M., et al, eds. Structural Tools for the Analysis of Protein-Nucleic Acid Complexes. LC 92-30658. (Advances in Life Sciences Ser.). ix, 469p. 1992. 99.50 (*0-8176-2776-6*) Birkhauser.

Lilley, Dorothy B. & Trice, Ronald W. A History of Information Science, 1945-1985. (Library & Information Science Ser.). 192p. 1989. text ed. 48.00 (*0-12-450060-9*) Acad Pr.

***Lilley, Edward R.** Making It Click! Starting a Successful Photography Studio. 348p. Date not set. 29.95 (*0-614-07445-2*) SOS Pubng.

Lilley, George. Anthony Powell: A Bibliography. (Illus.). 320p. 1993. 78.00 (*0-938768-46-8*) Oak Knoll.

Lilley, Irene M., jt. auth. see Froebel, Friedrich.

Lilley, James R. & Willkie, Wendell L., III. Beyond MFN: Trade with China & American Interests. LC 94-8228. 192p. (Orig.). 1994. 29.95 (*0-8447-3856-5*, AEI Pr); pap. 12.95 (*0-8447-3857-3*, AEI Pr) Am Enterprise.

Lilley, John F., jt. ed. see Clark, Asa A., IV.

Lilley, Kate, ed. see Cavendish, Margaret.

Lilley, Lucy. Vivien Alone. large type ed. 1990. 21.95 (*0-7089-2237-6*) Ulverscroft.

Lilley, Mary B. My Best to You from the Lilley Pad. LC 91-90243. 152p. 1991. pap. 9.95 (*0-9629488-0-2*) Lilley Pub.

***Lilley, Steve.** Hernando Cortes. LC 95-1279. (Importance of Ser.). (J). 1995. 16.95 (*1-56006-066-2*) Lucent Bks.

Lilleyman, J. S. & Hann, M., eds. Paediatric Haematology. (Illus.). 498p. 1992. text ed. 119.95 (*0-443-04366-3*) Churchill.

Lilleyman, J. S., jt. ed. see Hinchliffe, R. F.

Lilleyman, John S. Childhood Leukaemia: The Facts. (Facts Ser.). (Illus.). 176p. 1994. pap. 14.95 (*0-19-262451-2*) OUP.

Lillford, Peter J., jt. ed. see Vincent, Julian F.

***Lillian, Georgianna.** Some of My Best Friends Are Angels. (Illus.). (Orig.). 1994. pap. text ed. 12.95 (*0-931667-06-2*) New Dream Publishing Co.

Lillibridge, E. Michael. The Love Book for Couples: Building a Healthy Relationship. LC 83-81431. 144p. (Orig.). (C). 1984. pap. 14.95 (*0-89334-048-0*) Humanics Ltd.

— The Love Book for Couples: Building a Healthy Relationship. LC 83-81431. 144p. (Orig.). 1984. lib. bdg. 24.95 (*0-89334-209-2*, 209-2) Humanics Ltd.

Lillibridge, E. Michael & Mathis, Andrew G. Impact-Parent Training: Becoming a Successful Parent. (Illus.). 132p. (Orig.). 1982. pap. 4.95 (*0-936098-38-4*) Intl Marriage.

***Lillibridge, G. D.** The Innocent Years: Growing up in a Small Town in the 1920s & 1930s. 140p. 1995. pap. 10.00 (*0-9644027-0-X*) G D Lillibridge.

Lillibridge, Laurence F. Hard Marches, Hard Crackers, & Hard Beds: The Edward Rolfe Civil War Letters & Diaries. LC 93-91604. (Illus.). 216p. 1993. 25.65 (*0-9637276-0-5*) Lillibrdge Pub.

Lillich, Barbara, et al, eds. The Bosler Cookbook of Hors D'Oeuvres & Other Savory Recipes. (Illus.). 1988. spiral bd., pap. 10.95 (*0-9620870-0-9*) Friends Bosler.

Lillich, Meredith, et al, eds. Studies in Cistercian Art & Architecture, I. (Cistercian Studies: No. 66). (Illus.). (Orig.). 1982. pap. 12.95 (*0-87907-866-9*) Cistercian Pubns.

Lillich, Meredith P. The Armor of Light: Stained Glass in Western France, 1250-1325, Vol. 23. LC 92-30564. (California Studies in the History of Art). 1993. 150.00 (*0-520-05186-6*) U CA Pr.

— Rainbow Like an Emerald: Stained Glass in Lorraine in the Thirteenth & Early Fourteenth Centuries. (Illus.). 256p. 1991. 49.50 (*0-271-00702-8*) Pa St U Pr.

Lillich, Meredith P., ed. Studies in Cistercian Art & Architecture, Vol. IV. (Cistercian Studies: No. 134). (Illus.). 300p. (Orig.). 1993. 49.95 (*0-87907-634-8*); pap. 24.95 (*0-87907-534-1*) Cistercian Pubns.

— Studies in Cistercian Art & Architecture, II. (Cistercian Studies: No. 69). (Illus.). pap. 14.95 (*0-87907-869-3*) Cistercian Pubns.

— Studies in Cistercian Art & Architecture, III. (Cistercian Studies: No. 89). (Orig.). 1987. 49.95 (*0-87907-789-1*); pap. 22.95 (*0-685-11922-X*) Cistercian Pubns.

Lillich, Richard B. Economic Coercion & the New International Economic Order. 401p. (Orig.). 1976. 40.00 (*0-318-50090-6*) Proced Aspects Intl.

— Human Rights Documents. 1991. 11.50 (*0-316-52619-3*) Little.

— International Human Rights: Problems of Law, Policy, & Practice. 2nd ed. 1991. 49.00 (*0-316-52616-9*) Little.

— International Human Rights Instruments. 2nd ed. LC 90-24440. 888p. 1990. ring bd. 95.00 (*0-89941-750-7*, 302000) W S Hein.

Lillich, Richard B., ed. Fact-Finding Before International Tribunals. 300p. (C). 1991. lib. bdg. 60.00 (*0-941320-71-5*) Transnatl Pubs.

— The United Nations Compensation Commission: Thirteenth Sokol Colloquium. LC 94-44756. 1995. write for info. (*0-941320-73-1*) Transnatl Pubs.

— The Valuation of Nationalized Property in International Law, Vol. 1. LC 70-177376. 188p. reprint ed. pap. 53.60 (*0-317-26811-2*, 2024314) Bks Demand.

Lillich, Richard B. & Brower, Charles N., eds. International Arbitration in the Twenty-First Century: Towards Judicialization & Uniformity? LC 93-37218. (Twelfth Sokol Colloquium Ser.). 350p. (C). 1994. lib. bdg. 75.00 (*0-941320-72-3*) Transnatl Pubs.

Lillich, Richard B. & Newman, Frank C. International Human Rights: Problems of Law & Policy. 1979. 38.00 (*0-316-52612-6*) Little.

Lillich, Richard B., jt. auth. see Hannum, Hurst.

Lillico, Joris. Freedom Handbook. 36p. 1978. pap. 2.50 (*0-931116-03-1*) Ralston-Pilot.

Lillico, Michael. Managerial Communication. LC 77-188641. 168p. (C). 1972. text ed. 76.00 (*0-08-016633-4*, Pub. by Pergamon Repr UK) Franklin.

***Lillicrap, Denis R.** Food & Beverage Service. 3rd ed. 1993. pap. text ed. 23.95 (*0-470-23355-9*) Wiley.

Lillie, Anne S., ed. see Mass Tech Times, Inc. Staff.

Lillie, Arthur. The Influence of Buddhism on Primitive Christianity. LC 78-70094. 1980. reprint ed. 28.75 (*0-404-17343-8*) AMS Pr.

— Modern Mystics & Modern Magic. LC 72-5680. (Essay Index Reprint Ser.). 1977. reprint ed. 20.95 (*0-8369-2996-9*) Ayer.

Lillie, David. Beyond Charisma. 127p. 1981. pap. 7.50 (*0-85364-325-3*, Pub. by Paternoster UK) Attic Pr.

Lillie, David L., ed. Teaching Parents to Teach: Education for the Handicapped. (First Chance Ser.). (Illus.). 1976. pap. 9.95 (*0-8027-7262-5*) Walker & Co.

Lillie, David W. Our Radiant World. (Illus.). 240p. 1987. pap. 13.95 (*0-8306-2851-7*) TAB Bks.

Lillie, E., et al, eds. Electronic Packaging Materials Science IV: Materials Research Society Symposium Proceedings, Vol. 154. 1989. text ed. 42.00 (*1-55899-027-5*) Materials Res.

Lillie, E. D., et al, eds. Electronic Packaging Materials Science V: Materials Research Society Symposium Proceedings, Vol. 203. 455p. 1991. text ed. 50.00 (*1-55899-095-X*) Materials Res.

***Lillie, Helen.** Home to Strathblane. 352p. (C). 1993. pap. 32.00x (*1-874640-40-8*, Pub. by Argyll Pubng UK) St Mut.

Lillie, John H. & Bauer, Brent A. Sectional Anatomy of the Head & Neck: A Detailed Atlas. (Illus.). 224p. 1994. 55.00 (*0-19-504297-2*) OUP.

Lillie, Mary P. A Decade of Dreams. LC 79-53015. (Living Poets' Library Ser.: Vol. 23). 1979. pap. 3.50 (*0-686-81663-3*) Dragons Teeth.

— Times & Seasons. (Poetry Ser.). (Illus.). 100p. (Orig.). 1986. pap. 9.95 (*0-942996-06-2*) Post Apollo Pr.

Lillie, Mary P., ed. see Stampa, Gaspara.

Lillie, Mary P., tr. see Stampa, Gaspara.

Lillie, Mary P., jt. ed. see Stortoni, Laura A.

Lillie, Mary P., tr. see Stortoni, Laura A. & Lillie, Mary P., eds.

Lillie, Patricia. Everything Has a Place. LC 90-23497. (Illus.). 24p. (J). (ps up). 1993. 14.00 (*0-688-10082-1*); lib. bdg. 13.93 (*0-688-10083-X*) Greenwillow.

— Floppy Teddy Bear. LC 93-26516. (Illus.). 32p. (J). 1995. 15.00 (*0-688-12570-0*) Greenwillow.

— Jake & Rosie. LC 87-14939. (Illus.). 24p. (J). (ps up). 1989. 11.95 (*0-688-07624-6*); lib. bdg. 11.88 (*0-688-07625-4*) Greenwillow.

— When the Rooster Crowed. LC 90-30783. (Illus.). 32p. (J). (ps up). 1991. 13.95 (*0-688-09378-7*); lib. bdg. 13.88 (*0-688-09379-5*) Greenwillow.

— When This Box Is Full. LC 92-28743. (Illus.). 24p. (J). 1993. 14.00 (*0-688-12016-4*); lib. bdg. 13.93 (*0-688-12017-2*) Greenwillow.

Lillie, R. J., jt. ed. see Malinconico, L. L., Jr.

Lillie, Virginia H. From the Sycamore Tree. 40p. 1992. pap. 5.00 (*1-878149-12-1*) Counterpoint Pub.

— Shades of Jade. (Illus.). (Orig.). 1991. pap. 5.95 (*1-878149-04-0*) Counterpoint Pub.

Lilliedahl, Ann. Henry James in Scandinavia: His Literary Reputation. LC 91-58146. (Henry James Studies: No. 2). 1992. 39.95 (*0-404-62462-6*) AMS Pr.

Lilliefors, Jim. Highway 50: Ain't That America! LC 92-54766. (Illus.). 240p. 1993. 19.95 (*1-55591-073-4*) Fulcrum Pub.

— The Running Mind. LC 78-58053. (Illus.). 182p. 1979. pap. 4.95 (*0-89037-144-X*) Anderson World.

Lilliford, P., jt. ed. see Blanshard, J. M.

***Lillington, J. N.** Light Water Reactor Safety: The Development of Advanced Models & Codes for Light Water Reactor Safety Analysis. LC 95-2322. 1995. write for info. (*0-444-89741-0*) Elsevier.

Lillington, Kenneth. Jonah's Mirror. 160p. (YA). (gr. 7 up). 1992. pap. 6.95 (*0-571-16736-5*) Faber & Faber.

— Josephine. (Children's Paperbacks Ser.). 148p. (J). (gr. 3-6). 1991. pap. 4.95 (*0-571-16118-9*) Faber & Faber.

— The Mad Detective. 160p. (YA). (gr. 7 up). 1992. 15.95 (*0-571-16593-1*) Faber & Faber.

— The Real Live Dinosaur & Other Stories. (Children's Paperbacks Ser.). (Illus.). 144p. (J). (gr. 3-7). 1992. pap. 4.95 (*0-571-16318-1*) Faber & Faber.

Lillington, Kenneth, text. A Christmas Carol. (Easy Piano Picture Book Ser.). (Illus.). 32p. (Orig.). (J). (gr. k up). 1988. pap. 9.95 (*0-571-10093-7*) Faber & Faber.

— The Mikado: Easy Piano Picture Book. (Easy Piano Picture Book Ser.). (Illus.). 32p. (J). (gr. k up). 1988. pap. 9.95 (*0-571-10085-6*) Faber & Faber.

***Lillios, Katina T., ed.** The Origins of Complex Societies in Late Prehistoric Iberia. LC 95-1561. (Archaeological Ser.: Vol. 8). 1995. text ed. write for info. (*1-879621-19-3*); pap. text ed. write for info. (*1-879621-18-5*) Intl Mono Prehstry.

Lillis, B. Lauren. Instant Speaking Course. (Illus.). 29p. 1981. Discounts 10-49 copies $2.63 ea., 50-99 copies $2.10 ea., 100 or more copies $1.75 ea. pap. text ed. 3.50 (*0-8134-2176-4*) Interstate.

Lillis, Carol A. Brady's Introduction to Medical Terminology. 3rd ed. (Illus.). 254p. 1990. pap. text ed. 21.95 (*0-8385-0813-8*, A0813-4) Appleton & Lange.

Lillis, K., jt. ed. see Lauglo, J.

Lillis, Tony, ed. see Clark, Stephen P.

Lillis, Tony, ed. see Klein, Jean H.

Lillis, Tony, ed. see Snyder, W. C.

Liliuokalani. Hawaii's Story by Hawaii's Queen. 464p. 1990. pap. 6.95 (*0-935180-85-0*) Mutual Pub HI.

Lillo, George. The Works: With Some Account of His Life, 2 vols. in 1. (Anglistica & Americana Ser.: No. 140). xlviii, 610p. 1973. reprint ed. 102.70 (*3-487-04677-6*, Pub. by Georg Olms GW) Lubrecht & Cramer.

Lillo, George & McBurney, William H. The London Merchant. LC 65-11521. (Regents Restoration Drama Ser.). xxvi, 106p. 1965. pap. 5.95 (*0-8032-5365-6*) U of Nebr Pr.

Lillo, George & Noble, Richard. The Dramatic Works of George Lillo. Steffensen, James L., Jr., ed. (Oxford English Texts Ser.). (Illus.). 784p. 1993. 145.00 (*0-19-812714-6*) OUP.

An Asterisk (*) at the beginning of an entry indicates that the title is appearing in BIP for the first time.

Lillo-Martin, Diane C. Universal Grammar & American Sign Language: Setting the Null Argument Parameters. (Studies in Theoretical Psycholinguistics). 264p. (C). 1991. lib. bdg. 90.00 (*0-7923-1419-0*) Kluwer Ac.

Lillrank, Paul & Kano, Noriaki. Continuous Improvement: Quality Control Circles in Japanese Industry. LC 89-7202. (Michigan Papers in Japanese Studies: No. 19). (Illus.). xvi, 294p. (Orig.). 1989. pap. 13.95 (*0-939512-37-8*) U MI Japan.

Lilly, Anne L. & Frew, Mary A. Workbook for Comprehensive Medical Assisting: Competencies for Administrative & Clinical Practice. 3rd ed. (Illus.). (C). 1994. student ed, pap. text ed. 14.95 (*0-8036-3872-8*) Davis Co.

***Lilly-Burmeister, Angela.** How to Make Money: Personal Training. 55p. 1995. 10.00 (*0-9645658-9-7*) Catered Fitness Pub.

Lilly, Catherine M., ed. see Ramm, Charles A.

Lilly, Don. How to Earn Fifteen Dollars to Fifty Dollars an Hour & More with a Pick-up Truck or Van. rev. ed. LC 86-71695. (Illus.). 128p. 1987. pap. 12.95 (*0-910899-09-6*) Darian Bks.

Lilly, Douglas E. Lehigh & New England Railroad: A Color Retrospect. LC 88-82320. (Illus.). viii, 136p. 1988. 45.00 (*0-962844-0-9*) Garrigues Hse.

Lilly Endowment, Inc. Staff, jt. auth. see APPA Staff.

Lilly, Fred, jt. auth. see Bertolucci, John.

Lilly, Graham C. Evidence: Introduction to the Law. 2nd ed. 585p. (C). 1990. reprint ed. text ed. 26.50 (*0-314-59288-1*) West Pub.

Lilly, J. Robert, jt. ed. see Russell, Ken.

Lilly, J. Robert, et al. Criminological Theory: Context & Consequences. (Studies in Crime, Law, & Justice: Vol. 5). 240p. (C). 1989. text ed. 46.00 (*0-8039-2638-3*); pap. text ed. 19.95 (*0-8039-2639-1*) Sage.

— Criminological Theory: Context & Consequences. 1994. pap. 18.95 (*0-8039-5901-X*) Sage.

— Criminological Theory: Context & Consequences. 2nd ed. 240p. 1994. 39.95 (*0-8039-5900-1*) Sage.

Lilly, John C., jt. auth. see Gold, E. J.

Lilly, Julie, ed. see Hagen, Ross.

Lilly, Kathryn W. Efficient Dynamic Simulation of Robotic Mechanisms. LC 92-33226. (International Series in Engineering & Computer Science, VLSI, Computer Architecture, & Digital Screen Processing: Vol. 203). 1992. lib. bdg. 78.00 (*0-7923-9286-8*) Kluwer Ac.

Lilly, Kenneth, jt. auth. see Pope, Joyce.

Lilly, Kenneth E., Jr. Marine Weather of Western Washington. LC 83-50478. (Illus.). 150p. (Orig.). 1983. pap. 12.95 (*0-916682-38-2*) Starpath.

Lilly, L. R. Diesel Engine Reference Book. LC 83-26240. (Illus.). 720p. 1984. text ed. 170.00 (*0-408-00443-6*) Buttrwrth-Heinemann.

Lilly, Leonard. Pathophysiology of Heart Disease. (Illus.). 300p. 1992. pap. 24.50 (*0-8121-1566-X*) Williams & Wilkins.

Lilly, Mark. Gay Men's Literature in the Twentieth Century. LC 93-15241. 256p. (C). 1993. text ed. 45.00 (*0-8147-5071-0*); pap. text ed. 14.95 (*0-8147-5081-8*) NYU Pr.

— The NCCL - The First Fifty Years. (C). 1988. 30.00 (*0-685-33955-6*, Pub. by NCCL UK) St Mut.

Lilly, Mark, ed. Lesbian & Gay Writing: An Anthology of Critical Essays. 220p. 1990. 24.95 (*0-87722-706-3*) Temple U Pr.

Lilly, Mark, ed. see Bronte, Charlotte.

Lilly, Michael A. If You Die Tomorrow. 128p. 1990. pap. text ed. 12.95 (*0-9640614-0-6*) KC Collins.

Lilly, Paul R., Jr. Words in Search of Victims: The Achievement of Jerzy Kosinksi. LC 88-3021. 212p. 1988. 18.50 (*0-87338-366-4*) Kent St U Pr.

Lilly, Reginald, tr. see Haar, Michel.

Lilly, Reginald, tr. see Heidegger, Martin.

Lilly, Reginald, tr. see Marx, Werner.

Lilly, Roy S., jt. auth. see Graham, John R.

***Lilly, Sharon.** Tree Climber's Guide. (Illus.). (C). 1994. pap. 30.00 (*1-881956-08-3*) Int Soc Arboricult.

Lilly, Susan C., jt. auth. see Dale, Nell B.

Lilly, Susan C., jt. auth. see Dale, Nell.

Lilly, W. S., ed. see Newman, John H.

Lilly, Willene J. The Petroleum Secretary's Handbook. 2nd ed. LC 84-27384. 352p. 1985. 25.00 (*0-87814-278-9*, P4369) PennWell Bks.

Lilly, William. Astrologer's Guide. 112p. 1970. 7.00 (*0-86690-123-X*, L1294-014) Am Fed Astrologers.

— Christian Astrology, 3 vols. (Illus.). 893p. (C). 1986. reprint ed. Vol. I, Introduction to Astrology. write for info. (*0-318-68005-X*); reprint ed. Vol. II, Horary Astrology. write for info. (*0-318-68006-8*); reprint ed. Vol. III, Natal Astrology & Predictive Astrology. write for info. (*0-318-68007-6*) JustUs & Assocs.

— Christian Astrology, 3 vols., Set. (Illus.). 893p. (C). 1986. reprint ed. pap. text ed. 80.00 (*1-878935-03-8*) JustUs & Assocs.

— Christian Astrology, Vol. I: Introduction to Astrology - The Basics. (Illus.). 147p. (C). 1985. reprint ed. pap. text ed. 20.00 (*1-878935-00-3*) JustUs & Assocs.

— Christian Astrology, Vol. II: Horary Astrology (Traditional Method) (Illus.). 367p. (C). 1985. reprint ed. pap. 30.00 (*1-878935-01-1*) JustUs & Assocs.

— Christian Astrology, Vol. III: Natal Astrology & Predictive Astrology. (Illus.). 379p. (C). 1986. reprint ed. pap. 30.00 (*1-878935-02-X*) JustUs & Assocs.

— An Introduction to Astrology. 556p. 1966. reprint ed. spiral bd. 19.25 (*0-7873-0561-8*) Mokelumne.

— An Introduction to the Study of Astrology: With Numerous Emendations, Adapted to the Improved State of Science. 575p. 1993. pap. 33.00 (*1-56459-406-8*) Kessinger Pub.

Lilly, William, ed. The Astrological Aphorisms of Cardan. 1990. reprint ed. pap. 3.95 (*1-55818-101-6*, Sure Fire) Holmes Pub.

Lilly, William, ed. see Bonatus, Guido.

Lillyman, William J. Reality's Dark Dream: The Narrative Fiction of Ludwig Tieck. (C). 1979. 100.00 (*3-11-007710-8*) De Gruyter.

Lillyman, William J., ed. Goethe's Narrative Fiction: The Irvine Goethe Symposium. LC 83-18848. viii, 299p. 1983. 83.85 (*3-11-008734-0*) De Gruyter.

Lillyman, William J., et al, eds. Critical Architecture & Contemporary Culture. LC 92-22185. (University of California Humanities Research Institute Ser.). 224p. (C). 1994. 39.95 (*0-19-507819-5*) OUP.

Lillystone, Simon, ed. see Pecar, Branko.

***Lilo.** A Shadow over My Life. (Illus.). 81p. (YA). 1994. text ed. 9.95 (*965-229-110-2*, Pub. by Gefen Pub Hse IS) Gefen Bks.

Lily, Don, ed. see Juray, G. John.

Lily Toy Hong. Two of Everything. Mathews, Judith, ed. LC 92-29880. (Illus.). 32p. (J). (gr. k-3). 1993. lib. bdg. 14.95 (*0-8075-8157-7*) A Whitman.

Lily, William. A Shorte Introduction of Grammar. LC 45-4059. 1977. reprint ed. 50.00 (*0-8201-1208-9*) Schol Facsimiles.

Lilya, Mary, ed. see Mayer, Steven E. & Scheie, David.

Lilya, Wagner. Peer Teaching: Historical Perspective. LC 82-939. (Contributions to the Study of Education Ser.: No. 5). 256p. 1982. text ed. 55.00 (*0-313-23230-X*, WPT/, Greenwood Pr) Greenwood.

Lilyquist, C., et al. Studies in Early Egyptian Glass. LC 93-24451. (Illus.). 77p. 1993. pap. 20.00 (*0-87099-683-5*) Metro Mus Art.

Lim & Smalzer. Noteworthy. 1989. pap. 20.95 (*0-8384-2946-7*) Heinle & Heinle.

— Noteworthy. 1990. audio 50.00 (*0-8384-2948-3*); audio 10.00 (*0-8384-2949-1*) Heinle & Heinle.

Lim & Soter. Clinical Photomedicine. (Basic & Clinical Dermatology Ser.: Vol. 6). 428p. 1993. 140.00 (*0-8247-8862-1*) Dekker.

Lim, jt. auth. see Grady.

Lim, Arthur M., ed. Fison's Retinal Detachment Surgery. (Illus.). 1978. 62.50 (*3-8055-2862-0*) S Karger.

Lim, Arthur S. A Colour Atlas of Posterior Chamber Implants. (Illus.). 692p. 1985. text ed. 121.00 (*0-7216-1573-2*) Saunders.

Lim, Arthur S., ed. Ocular Microsurgery. (Developments in Ophthalmology Ser.: Vol. 1). (Illus.). viii, 96p. 1981. 40.00 (*3-8055-1106-X*) S Karger.

Lim, Arthur S., jt. auth. see Constable, Ian J.

Lim, B. S., ed. Computer Integrated Manufacturing (ICCIM '91) 800p. (C). 1991. text ed. 118.00 (*981-02-0684-4*) World Scientific Pub.

Lim, Bill B. Solar Energy Application in the Tropics. 1982. lib. bdg. 117.00 (*90-277-1506-8*) Kluwer Ac.

Lim, Bill P., pref. Selected Papers on the Indoor Environment. (Illus.). 160p. (Orig.). (C). 1989. pap. text ed. 15.00 (*0-939493-03-9*) Coun Tall Bldg.

***Lim, C. E. & Sessa, D. J., eds.** Nutrition & Utilization Technology in Aquaculture. 1995. 70.00 (*0-935315-54-3*) AOCS Pr.

Lim, Catherine. Little Ironies: Stories of Singapore. (Writing in Asia Ser.). 106p. (C). 1978. pap. 5.00 (*0-435-00224-4*, 00224) Heinemann.

— Or Else, the Lightning God & Other Stories. (Writing in Asia Ser.). 194p. (Orig.). 1980. pap. 5.00 (*0-435-00251-1*, 00251) Heinemann.

— Or Else the Lightning God & Other Stories. (Writing in Asia Ser.). 194p. (C). 1980. pap. 5.00 (*9971-64-014-7*, 00251) Heinemann.

Lim Ching San & Lee, Gim. MAC-Graphics. 2nd ed. 288p. 1992. pap. 49.95 (*0-8306-4234-X*, 4285, Design Pr) TAB Bks.

— MAC-Graphics: A Designer's Visual Guide to Graphics for the Apple Macintosh. (Illus.). 288p. 1991. pap. 49.95 (*0-8306-1072-3*, 3864, Windcrest) TAB Bks.

Lim, Christina, et al. In the Shadow of the Tiger: The 407th Air Service Squadron, 14th Air Service Group, 14th Air Force, World War II. (Illus.). 225p. 1993. 32.00 (*0-9637207-0-8*) Lim & Lim.

Lim, Daniel & Stewart, Greg. Introduction to Microbiology: A Laboratory Textbook. (Illus.). 220p. (Orig.). (C). 1993. pap. text ed. 29.95 (*0-89892-112-0*) Contemp Pub Co of Raleigh.

Lim, David. Export Instability & Compensatory Financing. 224p. (C). 1991. text ed. 74.00 (*0-415-03645-3*, A5245) Routledge.

— Spiritual Gifts: A Fresh Look. LC 90-23950. 336p. 1991. pap. 8.95 (*0-88243-636-8*, 02-0636) Gospel Pub.

Lim, Edward C. & Innes, K. Keith, eds. Excited States: Rotational Effects on the Behavior of Excited Molecules, Vol. 7. 247p. 1988. text ed. 158.00 (*0-12-227207-2*) Acad Pr.

Lim, Franklin, ed. Biomedical Applications of Microencapsulation. 192p. 1984. 119.00 (*0-8493-5440-4*, RS201, CRC Reprint) Franklin.

Lim, Genny. Paper Angels - Bitter Cane: Two Plays by Genny Lim. (Orig.). (C). 1991. pap. text ed. 8.95 (*0-9623102-1-2*) Kalamaku Pr.

— Wings for Lai Ho. Lew, Gordon, tr. (Illus.). 48p. (Orig.). (J). (gr. 5-8). 1982. pap. 5.95 (*0-934788-01-4*) E-W Pub Co.

Lim, H. A., jt. auth. see Kolchanov, N. A.

Lim, H. A., et al. Bioinformatics, Supercomputing & Complex Genome Analysis: International Conference. 400p. 1993. text ed. 118.00 (*981-02-1157-0*) World Scientific Pub.

Lim, Henry C. & Venkatqsubramanian, K., eds. Biochemical Engineering IV. (Annals Ser.: Vol. 469). 112.00 (*0-89766-333-0*); pap. 112.00 (*0-89766-334-9*) NY Acad Sci.

***Lim-Hing, ed.** The Very Inside: An Anthology of Writings by Asian & Pacific Islander Lesbians. 1994. per. 16.95 (*0-920813-97-6*, Pub. by Sister Vision CN) InBook.

Lim, J. L. The Science of Beauty: The Skin, Vol. 1. (Illus.). 256p. 1992. pap. write for info. (*0-632-02798-3*) Blackwell Sci.

Lim, Jaime A. Literature & Politics: The Colonial Experience in Nine Philippine Novels. 182p. (Orig.). 1993. pap. 11.75 (*971-10-0478-X*, Pub. by New Day Pub PH) Cellar.

Lim, Jessie. China. (Focus On Ser.). (Illus.). 32p. (J). (gr. 4-8). 1992. 17.95 (*0-237-60301-2*, Pub. by Evans Bros Ltd UK) Trafalgar.

Lim, Joe S. Two-Dimensional Signal & Image Processing. 880p. 1989. text ed. 82.00 (*0-13-935322-4*) P-H.

Lim, Joe S. & Oppenheim, Alan V. Advanced Topics in Signal Processing. (Illus.). 512p. 1987. text ed. 77.00 (*0-13-013129-6*) P-H.

***Lim, Kee Y. & Long, John.** The MUSE Method for Usability Engineering. (Series in Human-Computer Interaction: No. 8). (Illus.). 350p. (C). 1995. 49.95 (*0-521-47494-9*) Cambridge U Pr.

Lim, Linda & Fong, Pang Eng. Trade Employment & Industrialisation in Singapore. (Employment, Adjustment & Industrialisation Ser.: No. 2). vi, 110p. 1986. pap. 20.00 (*92-2-105231-1*) Intl Labour Office.

Lim, Lucy. Six Contemporary Chinese Women Artists. LC 91-74138. (Illus.). 102p. 1993. pap. 24.95 (*0-9609784-1-0*) CCF San Francisco.

Lim, Lucy, ed. Wu Guanzhong: A Contemporary Chinese Artist. LC 89-60262. (Illus.). 184p. 1989. 60.00 (*0-295-96992-X*) U of Wash Pr.

Lim, Lucy, et al. Stories from China's Past: Han Dynasty Pictorial Tomb Reliefs & Archaeological Objects from Sichuan Province, People's Republic of China. LC 87-70422. (Illus.). 210p. 1988. reprint ed. pap. 35.00 (*0-295-96797-8*) U of Wash Pr.

Lim, Pacifico A. COBOL for the IBM PC. 292p. 1986. text ed. 49.95 (*0-442-25970-0*) Van Nos Reinhold.

— Db2 for Application Programmers. 1989. text ed. 57.00 (*0-13-199795-5*) P-H.

Lim, Paulino, Jr. Passion Summer & Other Stories. 81p. (Orig.). (C). 1989. pap. 5.75 (*971-10-0326-0*, Pub. by New Day Pub PH) Cellar.

— Sparrows Don't Sing in the Philippines. 133p. (Orig.). 1994. pap. 9.50x (*971-10-0527-1*, Pub. by New Day Pub PH) Cellar.

— Tiger Orchids on Mount Mayon: A Novella. 94p. (Orig.). (C). 1990. pap. 7.50 (*971-10-0410-0*, Pub. by New Day Pub PH) Cellar.

Lim, Phyllis, jt. auth. see Dunkel, Patricia.

Lim, Phyllis L. & Kurtin, Mary. TOEFL Grammar Workbook. 2nd ed. Wellman, Laurie, ed. 256p. 1992. pap. 11.00 (*0-13-921917-X*, Arco Test) P-H Gen Ref & Trav.

Lim, Phyllis L., jt. auth. see Dunkel, Patricia.

Lim, Phyllis L., jt. auth. see Smalzer, William.

Lim Pui Huen, P. The Malay World of Southeast Asia. 472p. 1987. text ed. 54.75 (*9971-988-36-4*, Pub. by Inst SE Asian Studies SI) Ashgate Pub Co.

Lim, R. K., ed. Pharmacology of Pain: Proceedings - Vol. 9. 1968. 112.00 (*0-08-012374-0*, Pub. by Pergamon Repr UK) Franklin.

Lim, R. P., et al. Sustainable Clean Water. (Advances in Limnology Ser.: Heft 28). (Illus.). 571p. 1987. pap. text ed. 180.00 (*3-510-47026-5*) Lubrecht & Cramer.

Lim, Richard. Public Disputation, Power, & Social Order in Late Antiquity. LC 93-43761. (Transformation of the Classical Heritage: No. 23). 1995. 48.00 (*0-520-08577-9*) U CA Pr.

Lim, Robin. After the Baby's Birth: A Woman's Way to Wellness. LC 90-1802. 272p. (Orig.). 1990. pap. 14.95 (*0-89087-590-1*) Celestial Arts.

Lim, Shirley & Spencer, Norman K. One World of Literature. (C). 1992. pap. 28.76 (*0-395-58880-4*) HM.

***Lim, Shirley G.** Monsoon History. (Skoob Pacifica Ser.). 1995. pap. 11.95 (*1-871438-44-6*) Atrium Pubs.

— Moving Her Self: Feminism in the Shadow of Empire. (Cross-Cultural Memoir Ser.). (Orig.). 1996. 21.95 (*1-55861-105-3*) Feminist Pr.

— Nationalism & Literature: English-Language Writing from the Philippines & Singapore. 186p. (Orig.). 1994. pap. 13.50 (*971-10-0525-5*, Pub. by New Day Pub PH) Cellar.

— Writing South East Asia in English. (Skoob Pacifica Ser.). 1995. pap. 24.95 (*1-871438-49-7*) Atrium Pubs.

Lim, Shirley G., ed. Approaches to Teaching Kingston's The Woman Warrior. LC 91-27413. (Approaches to Teaching World Literature Ser.: No. 39). xi, 178p. 1991. text ed. 37.50 (*0-87352-703-8*, AP39C); pap. text ed. 18.00x (*0-87352-704-6*, AP39P) Modern Lang.

Lim Siew Ming, A. Practical Ophthalmic Microsurgery. (Illus.). 1980. 31.25 (*3-8055-3036-6*) S Karger.

Lim, Sing. West Coast Chinese Boy. LC 79-67110. (Illus.). 64p. (J). (gr. 5 up). 1991. pap. 7.95 (*0-88776-270-0*) Tundra Bks.

Lim, Wayne C. Managing Software Reuse. 224p. 1993. boxed 38.00 (*0-13-552373-7*) P-H.

Lim, Wendy. Chinatown, DC: A Photographic Journal. Chow, Esther N. & Ho, Chi-Kwan, eds. Li, Wei & Sun, Yumei, trs. (Illus.). 111p. (Orig.). (CHI.). (C). 1991. write for info. (*0-9629267-0-1*) Asian Amer Arts.

Lim, Wendy, jt. ed. see Hiro.

Lim, Y. K. Introduction to Classical Electrodynamics. 433p. 1986. text ed. 47.00 (*9971-978-51-2*); pap. text ed. 30.00 (*9971-978-85-7*) World Scientific Pub.

— Problems & Solutions on Mechanics: Major American Universities Ph.d. Qualifying Questions & Solutions. 768p. 1994. text ed. 99.00 (*981-02-1295-X*); pap. text ed. 48.00 (*981-02-1298-4*) World Scientific Pub.

— Problems & Solutions on Optics: Major American Univ. PhD Qualifying Questions & Solutions. 204p. 1991. text ed. 59.00 (*981-02-0438-8*); pap. text ed. 30.00 (*981-02-0439-6*) World Scientific Pub.

— Problems & Solutions on Solid State Physics, Relativity & Miscellaneous Topics. 364p. 1994. text ed. 99.00 (*981-02-1892-3*); pap. text ed. 53.00 (*981-02-1893-1*) World Scientific Pub.

Lim, Y. K., ed. Problems & Solutions on Electromagnetism. 550p. (C). 1993. text ed. 78.00 (*981-02-0625-9*); pap. text ed. 39.00 (*981-02-0626-7*) World Scientific Pub.

— Problems & Solutions on Thermodynamics & Statistical Mechanics. 420p. (C). 1990. text ed. 74.00 (*981-02-0055-2*); pap. text ed. 36.00 (*981-02-0056-0*) World Scientific Pub.

Lim, Y. S., tr. see Johnson, Jerry A.

Lim, Yong, ed. The Directory of Buyout Financing Sources. 520p. Date not set. 225.00 (*0-914470-68-X*) SDC Pubng.

— The Directory of M&A Intermediaries. 564p. Date not set. 225.00 (*0-914470-69-8*) SDC Pubng.

— The Merger Yearbook. 15th ed. (Illus.). 1200p. Date not set. 395.00 (*0-914470-66-3*) SDC Pubng.

— The Merger Yearbook. 16th ed. text ed. 395.00 (*0-914470-71-X*) SDC Pubng.

***Lim, Yong & Weissberg, Ted, eds.** Directory of Buyout Financing Sources. 579p. 1994. 225.00 (*0-914470-72-8*) Venture Econ Inc.

— Directory of M&A Intermediaries. 597p. 1994. 225.00 (*0-914470-73-6*) Venture Econ Inc.

— Pratt's Guide to Venture Capital Sources. 18th ed. 724p. 1995. 225.00 (*0-914470-70-1*) Venture Econ Inc.

Lima, jt. auth. see Fontes.

Lima, Anthony K. The DBASE II for Beginners. LC 84-22897. (Personal Computing Ser.). (Illus.). 160p. 1986. 16.50 (*0-13-196080-6*); pap. text ed. 24.33 (*0-13-196098-9*) P-H.

— Mastering dBASE III in Less Than a Day. (Illus.). 160p. 1986. 20.50 (*0-13-559816-8*) P-H.

Lima, Carolyn W. & Lima, John A. A to Zoo: Subject Access to Children's Picture Books. 4th ed. 1158p. 1993. 55.00 (*0-8352-3201-8*) Bowker.

Lima-de-Faria, A. Evolution Without Selection. 1990. pap. 101.25 (*0-444-81255-5*) Elsevier.

— Evolution Without Selection: Form & Function by Autoevolution. 373p. 1988. 164.00 (*0-444-80963-5*) Elsevier.

— Molecular Evolution & Organization of the Chromosome. 1162p. 1986. 252.50 (*0-444-80407-2*, I-451-83); pap. 119.50 (*0-444-80765-9*) Elsevier.

Lima-de-Faria, J. Structural Minerology: An Introduction. LC 94-10374. (Solid Earth Sciences Library: Vol. 7). 1994. lib. bdg. 150.00 (*0-7923-2821-3*) Kluwer Ac.

Lima-de-Faria, J., ed. Historical Atlas of Crystallography. (C). 1990. lib. bdg. 36.00 (*0-7923-0649-X*) Kluwer Ac.

Lima, John A., jt. auth. see Lima, Carolyn W.

Lima, Jose L. Paradiso. Vitier, Cintio, ed. (Latin American Series - Coleccion Archivos). 797p. (SPA.). (C). 1988. pap. 41.95x (*84-00-06880-7*) U of Pittsburgh Pr.

Lima, Joseph A. & Otterman, George R., eds. Manual on Selection & Use of Engine Coolants & Cooling System Chemicals. 4th ed. LC 89-342. (Manual Ser.: No. MNL 6). (Illus.). 16p. 1989. pap. text ed. 12.00 (*0-8031-1265-3*, 28-006089-15) ASTM.

Lima, Luiz C. The Dark Side of Reason: Fictionality & Power. Britto, Paulo H., tr. LC 91-24853. 360p. (C). 1992. 37.50 (*0-8047-1976-4*) Stanford U Pr.

Lima, Patrick. The Harrowsmith Perennial Garden: Flowers for Three Seasons. (Illus.). 160p. (Orig.). 1987. pap. 19.95 (*0-920656-74-9*, Pub. by Camden Hse CN) Firefly Bks Ltd.

Lima, Patrick & Forsyth, Turid. Harrowsmith Illustrated Book of Herbs. 176p. 1986. pap. 19.95 (*0-920656-45-5*, Pub. by Camden Hse CN) Firefly Bks Ltd.

Lima, Patrick & Scanlan, John. The Natural Food Garden: Growing Vegetables & Fruits Chemical-Free. (Illus.). 160p. 1992. pap. 19.95 (*1-55958-202-2*) Prima Pub.

Lima, R. F. Arco Motor Vehicle Dictionary. 362p. (ENG & SPA.). 1980. pap. 39.95 (*0-8288-0049-9*, S36349) Fr & Eur.

***Lima, Robert.** Dark Prisms: Occultism in Hispanic Drama. 208p. 1995. text ed. 29.95 (*0-8131-1909-X*) U Pr of Ky.

— Fathoms. LC 81-68921. 38p. 1981. pap. 5.00 (*0-87601-006-0*) Carnation.

— Ramon Del Valle-Inclan. LC 72-186643. (Columbia Essays on Modern Writers Ser.: No. 59). 1972. pap. text ed. 7.50 (*0-231-03499-7*) Col U Pr.

— Valle-Inclan: The Theatre of His Life. LC 87-19119. (Illus.). 392p. 1988. text ed. 35.00 (*0-8262-0661-1*) U of Mo Pr.

Lima, Robert, tr. see Del Valle-Inclan, Ramon.

Lima, Robert, tr. see Halsey, Martha T., ed.

Lima, Robert, tr. see Tatum, Charles M., ed.

***Lima, Susan D., et al, eds.** The Reality of Linguistic Rules. LC 94-27030. (Studies in Language Companion Ser.: No. 26). xxiii, 472p. 1994. lib. bdg. 115.00x (*1-55619-378-5*) Benjamins North Am.

Lima, Tony. Developing dBASE IV Applications: Programming with the dBASE Template Language. 400p. 1989. pap. 24.95 (*0-201-19798-7*) Addison-Wesley.

— Developing Foxpro for Windows Applications. 1993. pap. 26.95 (*0-201-62456-7*) Addison-Wesley.

— Developing Paradox Applications. LC 92-31141. 1993. pap. 29.95 (*0-201-63210-1*) Addison-Wesley.

— Inside dBASE IV. 1989. pap. 21.95 (*0-201-16638-0*) Addison-Wesley.

Liman, A. V. A Critical Study of the Literary Style of Ibuse Musuji: As Sensitive as Waters. LC 91-41402. 632p. 1992. lib. bdg. 129.95 (*0-7734-9614-9*) E Mellen.

Liman, Anthony, tr. see Ibuse, Masuji.

An Asterisk (*) at the beginning of an entry indicates that the title is appearing in BIP for the first time.

Limardo, Miguel. Luces Encendidas Para Cada Dia. 376p. 1985. reprint ed. 7.50 (*0-311-40038-8*) Casa Bautista.

Limato, Susan. Baby Basics for New Parents: Quick Answers When You Need Them. 160p. (Orig.). 1994. mass mkt. 4.99 (*0-380-77378-3*) Avon.

Limaye, jt. ed. see Kulkarni.

Limaye, Dilip, jt. auth. see Gellings, Clark W.

Limaye, Dilip R., ed. Industrial Cogeneration Applications. LC 85-45873. 300p. 1986. text ed. 57.00 (*0-88173-022-X*) Fairmont Pr.

Limaye, Dilip R., jt. auth. see Gellings, Clark W.

Limaye, Madhu. Cabinet Government in India. 135p. 1989. text ed. 35.00 (*81-7027-138-X*, Pub. by Radiant Pubs II) S Asia.

— Contemporary Indian Politics. 400p. 1987. text ed. 40.00 (*81-7027-104-5*, Pub. by Radiant Pubs II) S Asia.

— Janata Party Experiment, 2 vols., Set. (C). 1994. 88.50x (*81-7018-711-7*, Pub. by BR Pub II) S Asia.

— Mahatma Gandhi & Jawaharlal Nehru: A Historic Partnership Since 1916-1948, Vol. II. 1989. 62.00 (*0-685-34763-X*, Pub. by BR Pub II) S Asia.

— Mahatma Gandhi & Jawaharlal Nehru: A Historic Partnership 1916-1948, Vol. 3. 1990. 50.00 (*81-7018-583-1*, Pub. by BR Pub II) S Asia.

— Mahatma Gandhi & Jawaharlal Nehru, Vol. I: A Historic Partnership, 1916-1948. (C). 1989. 27.50 (*81-7018-548-3*) S Asia.

— Mahatma Gandhi & Jawaharlal Nehru, Vol. 3: A Historic Partnership, Set. (C). 1990. text ed. 50.00 (*81-7018-547-5*, Pub. by BR Pub II) S Asia.

— Prime Movers: Role of the Individual in History. xii, 448p. 1986. text ed. 45.00 (*81-7027-087-1*, Pub. by Radiant Pubs II) S Asia.

— Religious Bigotry: A Threat to Ordered State. (C). 1995. 18.00x (*81-202-0409-3*, Pub. by Ajanta II) S Asia.

— Socialist Communist Interactions in India. (C). 1991. 36.00 (*81-202-0319-4*, Pub. by Ajanta II) S Asia.

Limaye, Madhu, ed. Mahatma Gandhi & Jawaharlal Nehru, Vol. IV. (C). 1991. 40.00 (*0-685-49094-7*, Pub. by BR Pub II) S Asia.

Limaye, Madhu, et al, eds. Documentary History of the Janata Party, 3 vols., Set. 1993. text ed. 150.00 (*0-685-44991-2*, Pub. by Radiant Pubs II) S Asia.

Limaye, Santosh Y., jt. ed. see Stinton, David P.

Limaye, Surekha V., tr. Mahayanasutralamkara by 'Asanga' (Bibliotheca Indo-Buddhica Ser.: No. 94). (C). 1992. 54.00 (*81-7030-347-8*) S Asia.

Limb, Peter. The ANC & Black Workers in South Africa, 1912-1992: An Annotated Bibliography. LC 93-26607. 394p. 1993. 95.00 (*1-873836-95-3*, Pub. by H Zell Pubs UK) Bowker-Saur.

Limb, Sue. Come Back, Grandma. LC 92-43534. (Illus.). 32p. (J). (ps-2). 1994. 13.00 (*0-679-84720-0*) Knopf Bks Yng Read.

— Dulcie Domum's Bad Housekeeping. 224p. 1995. pap. 13.95 (*1-85702-066-9*, Pub. by Fourth Estate UK) Trafalgar.

— More Bad Housekeeping. 192p. 1993. 22.95 (*1-85702-013-8*, Pub. by Fourth Estate UK) Trafalgar.

— More Bad Housekeeping. 176p. 1995. pap. 13.95 (*1-85702-151-7*, Pub. by Fourth Estate UK) Trafalgar.

Limbacher, James L. Four Aspects of the Film. Jowett, Garth S., ed. LC 77-11379. (Aspects of Film Ser.). (Illus.). 1978. reprint ed. lib. bdg. 30.95 (*0-405-11138-X*) Ayer.

— Keeping Score: Film Music Nineteen Seventy-Two to Nineteen Seventy-Nine. LC 80-26474. 519p. 1981. 45.00 (*0-8108-1390-4*) Scarecrow.

— A Reference Guide to Audiovisual Information. LC 72-1737. 107p. reprint ed. pap. 30.50 (*0-317-10299-0*, 2050190) Bks Demand.

— Sexuality in World Cinema, 2 vols. LC 83-3019. 1535p. 1983. 85.00 (*0-8108-1609-1*) Scarecrow.

— Sexuality in World Cinema, Vol. 1: A-K. 1535p. 1983. write for info. (*0-318-57572-8*) Scarecrow.

— Sexuality in World Cinema, Vol. 2: L-Z. 1535p. 1983. write for info. (*0-318-57573-6*) Scarecrow.

Limbacher, James L., ed. Haven't I Seen You Somewhere Before? Remakes, Sequels & Series in Motion Pictures, Video, & Television, 1896-1990. LC 79-84272. 1991. 65.00 (*0-87650-244-3*) Pierian.

— The Song List: A Guide to Contemporary Music from Classical Sources. LC 73-78293. 1973. 16.50 (*0-87650-041-6*) Pierian.

Limbacher, James L. & Wright, H. Stephen. Keeping Score: Film & Television Music, 1980-1988 (with Additional Coverage of 1921-1979) LC 91-21180. 928p. 1991. 92.50 (*0-8108-2453-1*) Scarecrow.

Limbaugh, R. H. & Lewis, K. E., eds. The John Muir Papers, 1858-1957: Guide & Index to the Microfilm Edition. 190p. 1986. pap. 55.00 (*0-89887-050-X*) Chadwyck-Healey.

Limbaugh, Rush. See, I Told You So. Regan, Judith, ed. 320p. 1993. 24.00 (*0-671-87120-X*) PB.

— See, I Told You So. 1994. reprint ed. pap. 6.99 (*0-671-87121-8*, Pocket Star Bks) PB.

— See, I Told You So: Gift Edition. 1993. 45.00 (*0-671-88807-2*) PB.

— The Way Things Ought to Be. Regan, Judith, ed. 320p. 1992. 22.00 (*0-671-75145-X*) PB.

— The Way Things Ought to Be. Regan, Judith, ed. 352p. 1993. reprint ed. pap. 6.99 (*0-671-75150-6*, Pocket Star Bks) PB.

Limbaugh, Rush H., III. See, I Told You So. large type ed. LC 94-1662. 1994. 24.95 (*0-8161-7427-X*, Large Print Bks) Hall.

— See, I Told You So. large type ed. LC 94-1662. 1995. pap. 17.95 (*0-8161-7428-8*, Large Print Bks) Hall.

— The Way Things Ought to Be. braille ed. 591p. 1993. text ed. 47.28 (*1-56956-523-6*, BR9107) W A T Braille.

— The Way Things Ought to Be. large type ed. LC 92-38202. (General Ser.). 1993. 22.95 (*0-8161-5731-6*, Large Print Bks) Hall.

Limbell Art Museum Curatorial Staff, et al. In Pursuit of Quality: An Illustrated History of the Art & Architecture. LC 87-27559. (Kimbell Art Museum Ser.). (Illus.). 344p. 1988. 75.00 (*0-8109-1124-8*) Abrams.

Limberis, Vasiliki. Divine Heiress: The Virgin Mary & the Creation of Christian Constantinople. LC 93-47960. 208p. 1994. 45.00 (*0-415-09677-4*, B3246, Routledge NY) Routledge.

Limbert, Charles P., & Co. Staff. Limbert Arts & Crafts Furniture: The Complete 1903 Catalog. (Illus.). 96p. 1992. reprint ed. pap. 7.95 (*0-486-27120-X*) Dover.

Limbert, Paul M. Denominational Policies in the Support & Supervision of Higher Education. LC 75-176994. (Columbia University. Teachers College. Contributions to Education Ser.: No. 378). reprint ed. 37.50 (*0-404-55378-8*) AMS Pr.

Limbird, Lee E., ed. The Alpha-2 Adrenergic Receptors. LC 88-6833. (Receptors Ser.). (Illus.). 384p. 1988. 99.50 (*0-89603-135-7*) Humana.

Limbo, Rana K. & Wheeler, Sara R. When a Baby Dies: A Handbook for Healing & Helping. 168p. 1986. pap. 8.95 (*0-9612310-3-3*) Harsand Pr.

Limbrick, Elaine & Thomson, Douglas F., eds. Franciscus Sanchez: That Nothing Is Known. 300p. 1989. 74.95 (*0-521-35077-8*) Cambridge U Pr.

Limbrunner, Alfred, jt. auth. see Richardz, Klaus.

Limbrunner, George F., jt. auth. see Spiegel, Leonard.

Limburg, James. Easter: Proclamation 5, Series B. 1994. pap. 4.50 (*0-8006-4189-2*, Fortress Pr) Augsburg Fortress.

— Hosea Micah. LC 87-46293. (Interpretation: a Bible Commentary for Preaching & Teaching Ser.). 204p. 1988. 20.00 (*0-8042-3128-1*, John Knox) Westminster John Knox.

— Jonah: A Commentary. Mays, James L. et al, eds. LC 93-17160. (Old Testament Library). 144p. 1993. text ed. 20.00 (*0-664-21296-4*) Westminster John Knox.

— Psalms for Sojourners. LC 86-2621. (Illus.). 112p. (Orig.). 1986. pap. 8.99 (*0-8066-2206-7*, 10-5306, Augsburg) Augsburg Fortress.

Limburg, James, ed. Judaism: An Introduction for Christians. LC 87-9189. (Illus.). 288p. (Orig.). 1987. pap. 8.99 (*0-8066-2263-6*, 10-3610, Augsburg) Augsburg Fortress.

Limburg, K. E., et al. The Hudson River Ecosystem. (Environmental Management Ser.). (Illus.). xiv, 331p. 1986. 119.00 (*0-387-96220-4*) Spr-Verlag.

***Limburg, Michael.** The Essentials of Computer-to-Plate Technology. Gruff, Pamela & Destree, Thomas, eds. LC 95-75590. 110p. (Orig.). Date not set. pap. text ed. 40.00 (*0-88362-178-9*) Graphic Arts Tech Found.

Limburg, Peter. Stories Behind Words. LC 85-26398. 288p. 1986. 35.00 (*0-8242-0718-1*) Wilson.

Limburg, Peter R. Weird! The Complete Book of Halloween Words. 176p. (J). 1991. pap. 3.50 (*0-380-71172-9*, Camelot) Avon.

— Weird! The Complete Book of Halloween Words. LC 88-38678. (Illus.). 128p. (J). (gr. 4-10). 1989. text ed. 13.95 (*0-02-759050-X*, Bradbury S&S) S&S Childrens.

Limburg, Val. Electronic Media Ethics. 160p. 1994. pap. 19.95 (*0-240-80145-8*, Focal) Buttrwrth-Heinemann.

***Limburgher, Rush N. & Namey, Rick.** Buy This Book & Make Me Rich. 169p. (Orig.). 1994. pap. 4.99 (*0-312-95402-6*) St Martin.

Limebeer, David J. N., jt. auth. see Green, Michael.

Limentani, Adam, ed. see Gaddini, Eugenio.

***Limeres, Rene & Pedersen, Gunnar.** Alaska Fishing: The Complete Guide. (Illus.). 608p. (Orig.). 1995. pap. 19.95 (*0-935701-27-3*) Foghorn Pr.

Limerick, David & Cunnington, Bert. Managing the New Organization: A Blueprint for Networks & Strategic Alliances. (Management Ser.). 290p. 1993. 29.95 (*1-55542-581-X*) Jossey-Bass.

Limerick, Patricia N. Desert Passages: Encounters with the American Deserts. LC 84-28032. 224p. reprint ed. pap. 63.90 (*0-7837-5168-0*, 2044897) Bks Demand.

— The Legacy of Conquest: The Unbroken Past of the American West. LC 86-23883. 1988. pap. 11.95 (*0-393-30497-3*) Norton.

Limerick, Patricia N., jt. auth. see Jensen, Joan M.

Limerick, Patricia N., jt. auth. see White, Richard.

Limerick, Patricia N., et al, eds. Trails: Toward a New Western History. LC 91-25640. (Illus.). 250p. 1991. pap. 12.95 (*0-7006-0501-0*) U Pr of KS.

— Trails: Toward a New Western History. LC 91-25640. (Illus.). 250p. 1991. 29.95 (*0-7006-0500-2*) U Pr of KS.

Limic. Mathematical Modelling of Trace Elements in Biological Systems. 1995. write for info. (*0-8493-4576-6*, CRC Reprint) Franklin.

Liming, Gary. Working with Clarion. 1990. pap. text ed. 19.95 (*0-07-156499-3*) McGraw.

— Working with Clarion. (Illus.). 304p. 1990. 29.95 (*0-8306-9403-X*, 3403); pap. 19.60 (*0-685-45395-2*) TAB Bks.

— Working with Clarion. (Illus.). 304p. 1990. 19.95 (*0-8306-3403-7*, 3403, Windcrest) TAB Bks.

Limjoco, Lenny. Larawan: Portraits of Filipinos. (Illus.). 72p. (Orig.). (C). 1989. pap. text ed. 15.00 (*0-9616181-2-4*) Rutgers U Pr.

Limkemann, William O. Application Programming in CTOS. 300p. 1993. pap. text ed. 38.00 (*0-13-041872-2*) P-H.

Limmer, Milly J. Where Do Little Girls Grow? Levine, Abby, ed. LC 92-22936. (Illus.). 32p. (J). (ps-2). 1993. lib. bdg. 14.95 (*0-8075-8924-1*) A Whitman.

— Where Will You Swim Tonight? Fay, Ann, ed. LC 90-38938. (Illus.). 32p. (J). (ps-1). 1991. 14.95 (*0-8075-8949-7*) A Whitman.

***Limoge, Y. & Bocquet, J. L.** Reactive Phase Formation at Interfaces & Diffusion Processes. (Materials Science Forum Ser.: Vols. 155-156). (Illus.). 598p. (C). 1994. text ed. 164.00 (*0-87849-680-7*, Pub. by Trans Tech SZ) LPS Dist Ctr.

Limoges, Camille, jt. ed. see Coleman, William R.

Limoli, Tom M. The Dental Consultant Looks at Insurance. 3rd rev. ed. 304p. 1992. 95.00 (*0-685-71299-0*, D7203) PennWell Bks.

Limolli, Howard, tr. see Duras, Marguerite.

Limon, Graciela. In Search of Bernabe. LC 93-12813. 200p. (Orig.). (C). 1993. pap. 9.50 (*1-55885-073-2*) Arte Publico.

— Maria de Belen: The Autobiography of an Indian Woman. 315p. 1990. 16.95 (*0-533-08381-8*) Vantage.

— The Memories of Ana Calderon. LC 94-8663. 1994. 19.95 (*1-55885-116-X*) Arte Publico.

Limon, Janet, jt. auth. see Minear, Tish.

Limon, Jerzy. Dangerous Matter: English Drama & Politics in 1623-24. (Illus.). 174p. 1986. 69.95 (*0-521-30664-7*) Cambridge U Pr.

— Gentlemen of a Company: English Players in Central & Eastern Europe, 1590 to 1660. (Illus.). 208p. 1985. 54.95 (*0-521-26304-2*) Cambridge U Pr.

— The Masque of Stuart Culture. LC 89-40475. (Illus.). 240p. 1990. 40.00 (*0-87413-396-3*) U Delaware Pr.

Limon, Jerzy & Halio, Jay L., eds. Shakespeare & His Contemporaries: Eastern & Central European Studies. LC 92-53788. (International Studies in Shakespeare & His Contemporaries). 272p. (C). 1993. 39.50 (*0-87413-475-7*) U Delaware Pr.

Limon, John. The Place of Fiction in the Time of Science: A Disciplinary History of American Writing. (Cambridge Studies in American Literature & Culture: No. 39). 224p. (C). 1990. 49.95 (*0-521-35251-7*) Cambridge U Pr.

— Writing after War: American War Fiction from Realism to Postmodernism. 288p. 1994. 45.00 (*0-19-508758-5*); pap. 17.95 (*0-19-508759-3*) OUP.

Limon, Jose E. Dancing with the Devil: Society & Cultural Poetics in Mexican-American South Texas. LC 93-39968. (New Directions in Anthropological Writing Ser.). 256p. 1994. 42.00 (*0-299-14220-5*); pap. 15.95 (*0-299-14224-8*) U of Wis Pr.

— Mexican Ballads, Chicano Poems: History & Influence in Mexican-American Social Poetry. (New Historicism: Studies in Cultural Poetics: No. 17). (C). 1992. 38.00 (*0-520-06865-3*); pap. 15.00 (*0-520-07633-8*) U CA Pr.

Limon, Martin. Jade Lady Burning. LC 92-27572. 224p. 1992. 19.95 (*0-939149-71-0*) Soho Press.

— Jade Lady Burning. LC 92-27572. 224p. 1994. pap. 10.00 (*1-56947-020-0*) Soho Press.

Limon, Sharlene, jt. auth. see Waters, Verle.

Limon, Will. Beginning Again: Beyond the End of Love. 86p. (Orig.). 1991. pap. 8.00 (*0-89486-706-7*, 5070A) Hazelden.

Limonov, Eduard. Eto Ia - Edichka. 3rd ed. 290p. (RUS.). 1989. pap. 16.00 (*0-89830-132-7*) Russica Pubs.

— U Nas Byla Velikaia Epokha. 150p. (Orig.). (RUS.). 1989. pap. 15.50 (*0-89830-124-6*) Russica Pubs.

Limouris, Gennadios & Vaporis, N. M., eds. Orthodox Perspectives on Baptism, Eucharist & Ministry. xii, 168p. (Orig.). 1985. pap. 7.95 (*0-917651-22-7*) Holy Cross Orthodox.

Limousin, Odile. The Story of Paper. Matthews, Sarah, tr. LC 87-31752. (Illus.). 38p. (J). (gr. k-5). 1988. 5.95 (*0-944589-16-2*, 162) Young Discovery Lib.

Limousin, Odile & Neumann, Daniele. TV & Films: Behind the Scenes. (Young Discovery Library). (Illus.). 40p. (J). (gr. k-5). 1993. lib. bdg. 9.95 (*1-56674-073-8*, HTS Bks) Forest Hse.

— TV & Films: Behind the Scenes. Bogard, Vicki, tr. LC 92-966. (Illus.). (J). (gr. k-5). 1992. 5.95 (*0-944589-36-7*) Young Discovery Lib.

Limouze, Henry S., jt. ed. see Cary, Cecile W.

Limouzy, Pierre & Bourgeacq, Jacques A. Manuel de Composition Francaise. 2nd ed. 1990. teacher ed 7.95 (*0-07-037904-1*); text ed. write for info. (*0-07-037903-3*) McGraw.

— Vouz Avez la Parole: Manuel de Conversation. (Illus.). 300p. 1988. pap. text ed. write for info. (*0-13-943804-1*) P-H.

Limper, Mary G., ed. see Mills, Kenneth G.

Limpert, Dana. Swan Flyway: The Tundra Swan. LC 92-42381. (Smithsonian Wild Heritage Collection). (Illus.). (J). (gr. k-3). 1993. 11.95 (*0-924483-95-4*); audio 16.95 (*0-924483-96-2*); audio 25.95 (*0-924483-97-0*); audio 39.95 (*0-924483-98-9*); audio write for info. (*0-924483-99-7*) Soundprints.

Limpert, E., jt. ed. see Wolfe, M. S.

Limpert, Rudolf. Motor Vehicle Accident Reconstruction & Cause Analysis. 3rd ed. (Illus.). 876p. 1994. 85.00 (*0-87473-462-2*) Michie Butterworth.

Limpert, Rudolph. Brake Design & Safety. LC 92-25978. 460p. 1992. 99.00 (*1-56091-261-8*, R-120) Soc Auto Engineers.

Limprecht, Jane E. ConAgra Who? The Story of ConAgra's First 70 Years. Amsden, Don B., ed. (Illus.). 301p. 1990. 19.95 (*0-9627100-0-8*) Conagra.

***Limpumba, N.** Africa Beyond Adjustment. LC 94-36132. (Policy Essay Ser.: Vol. 15). 1994. pap. 9.95 (*1-56517-016-4*) Overseas Dev Council.

Limpus, Bruce. Lights! Camera! Action! 88p. 1994. pap. text ed. 19.95 (*1-882664-08-6*) Prufrock Pr.

Limson, Stella G. Primary Health Care in Omaha Nebraska: A Case Study of Nine Primary Health Care Centers. (Illus.). 50p. (Orig.). 1986. pap. 3.50 (*1-55719-025-9*) U NE CPAR.

Limulus Inc. Staff. Fast Food & Quick Service Restaurant Franchises: The North American Directory. LC 94-76699. (Franchise Information Ser.). 136p. (Orig.). 1994. pap. 19.95 (*1-885177-00-3*) Limulus.

Limur, Charles de, jt. auth. see Highman, Arthur.

Lin, ed. Handbook of Digital System Design. 2nd ed. 1990. 65.00 (*0-8493-4272-4*, TK868) CRC Pr.

— Optical-Laser Microlithography. 1988. 65.00 (*0-89252-957-1*, 922) SPIE.

Lin & Simons. Nonlinear & Convex Analysis: Proceedings in Honor of Ky Fan. (Lecture Notes in Pure & Applied Mathematics Ser.: Vol. 107). 320p. 1987. 140.00 (*0-8247-7777-8*) Dekker.

Lin, et al. Dawn over Chungking. LC 74-31239. (China in the 20th Century Ser.). 240p. 1975. reprint ed. lib. bdg. 29.50 (*0-306-70692-X*) Da Capo.

Lin, A. N. & Carter, D. M., eds. Epidermolysis Bullosa: Basic & Clinical Aspects. (Illus.). xiv, 302p. 1992. 98.00 (*0-387-97796-1*) Spr-Verlag.

Lin, A. T. M., jt. ed. see Krisch, A. D.

Lin, Adet, tr. see Hsieh Pingying.

Lin, Alice. Grandmother Had No Name. 1988. pap. 9.95 (*0-8351-2034-1*) China Bks.

Lin, Anna. Handbook of TCM Urology & Male Sexual Dysfunction. Flaws, Bob, ed. LC 92-73392. 220p. (Orig.). 1992. pap. 16.95 (*0-936185-36-8*) Blue Poppy.

Lin, Anna, jt. tr. see Flaws, Bob.

Lin, Anor, tr. see Hsieh Pingying.

Lin, B., ed. Banach Space Theory. LC 88-38106. (CONM Ser.: Vol. 85). 521p. 1989. pap. 59.00 (*0-8218-5092-X*, CONM-85) Am Math.

Lin, Ben C., jt. auth. see Dunphy, Robert T.

Lin, Bih-Jaw & Myers, James T. Forces for Change in Contemporary China. LC 93-15124. 400p. (C). 1993. 34.95 (*0-87249-969-3*) U of SC Pr.

Lin, Bih-Jaw, jt. ed. see Myers, James T.

Lin, Burn J., ed. Optical - Laser Microlithography II. 581p. 1989. 77.00 (*0-8194-0123-4*, VOL. 1088) SPIE.

Lin, C. & Au-Yang, M. K., eds. Seismic Analysis of Power Plant Systems & Components. (PVP Ser.: Vol. 73). 200p. 1983. pap. text ed. 12.00 (*0-317-02647-X*, H00259) ASME.

Lin, C. C. & Segel, L. A. Mathematics Applied to Deterministic Problems in the Natural Sciences. (Classics in Applied Mathematics Ser.: No. 1). xxi, 609p. 1988. pap. 30.25 (*0-89871-229-7*) Soc Indus-Appl Math.

Lin, C. C., jt. auth. see Bertin, G.

Lin, C. D. Fundamental Processes & Applications of Atoms & Ions, Review. 628p. 1993. text ed. 164.00 (*981-02-1537-1*) World Scientific Pub.

***Lin, C. W., ed.** Natural Hazard Phenomena & Mitigation: Proceedings of the Pressure Vessels & Piping Conference, Minneapolis, MN, 1994. LC 94-71661. (PVP Ser.: Vol. 271). 163p. 1994. pap. 50.00 (*0-7918-1194-8*) ASME.

— Seismic Modal Analysis & System Interaction. (PVP Ser.: Vol. 249). 156p. 1993. 45.00 (*0-7918-0976-5*, H00808) ASME.

Lin, Cantian, jt. auth. see Gregory, John.

Lin, Charles. The Atmosphere & Climate Change: An Introduction. 144p. (C). 1994. per., pap. text ed. 20.95 (*0-8403-9202-8*) Kendall-Hunt.

Lin, Cheng-hung & Fu, Daiwie, eds. Philosophy & Conceptual History of Science in Taiwan. LC 92-12852. (Boston Studies in the Philosophy of Science: Vol. 141). (C). 1993. lib. bdg. 122.00 (*0-7923-1766-1*) Kluwer Ac.

Lin-chi. Zen Teachings of Master Lin-chi. Watson, Burton, tr. LC 92-56455. 112p. (Orig.). 1993. pap. 10.00 (*0-87773-891-2*, Sham Dragon Edits) Shambhala Pubns.

Lin, Chia-Ch'iao. Statistical Theories of Turbulence. (Princeton Aeronautical Paperbacks Ser: No. 10). 67p. reprint ed. pap. 25.00 (*0-317-09284-7*, 2001133) Bks Demand.

Lin, Chia-Ch'iao, ed. Turbulent Flows & Heat Transfer. LC 58-50928. (High Speed Aerodynamics & Jet Propulsion Ser.: Vol. 5). 569p. reprint ed. pap. 162.20 (*0-317-09274-X*, 2001132) Bks Demand.

Lin, Chin-Chu, et al, eds. The High-Risk Fetus: Pathophysiology, Diagnosis, & Management. LC 92-2378. (Illus.). 696p. 1992. 99.00 (*0-387-97836-4*) Spr-Verlag.

Lin, Chin-Teng. Neural Fuzzy Control Systems with Structure & Parameter Learning. 150p. 1994. text ed. 39.00 (*981-02-1613-0*) World Scientific Pub.

Lin, Ching-Fang. Modeling, Design, Analysis, Simulation & Evaluation. 450p. 1993. text ed. 45.00 (*0-13-596388-5*) P-H.

— Modern Navigation, Guidance, & Control Processing. 560p. 1991. text ed. 82.00 (*0-13-596230-7*) P-H.

Lin, Ching-Yuan. Latin America vs. East Asia: A Comparative Development Perspective. LC 89-4128. 256p. 1989. 51.95 (*0-87332-526-5*) M E Sharpe.

Lin, Chinlon, ed. Optoelectronic Technology & Lightwave Communications Systems. (Illus.). 640p. 1989. text ed. 84.95 (*0-442-26050-4*) Van Nos Reinhold.

Lin, D., et al, eds. Computer Applications in the Automation of Shipyard Operation & Ship Design: Proceedings of the IFIP WG5.6 Sixth International Conference, Shanghai, People's Republic of China, 15-16 Sept., 1988, Vol. VI. 370p. 1989. 95.00 (*0-444-87343-0*, North Holland) Elsevier.

Lin, David. China Letters. 470p. (Orig.). 1993. pap. 9.95 (*0-923309-05-5*) Hartland Pubns.

Lin, David J. Free Radicals & Disease Prevention: What You Must Know. LC 93-2753. (Illus.). 80p. (Orig.). 1993. pap. 9.95 (*0-87983-587-7*) Keats.

Lin, Doris, jt. auth. see Dugre, Donald.

Lin, E. C., et al. Bacteria, Plasmids, & Phages: An Introduction to Molecular Biology. LC 83-22784. (Illus.). 325p. reprint ed. pap. 92.70 (*0-7837-6077-9*, 2059123) Bks Demand.

Lin, Elizabeth L., ed. see Wei-Chuan Cultural Educational Foundation.

An Asterisk (*) at the beginning of an entry indicates that the title is appearing in BIP for the first time.

Lin, Emil T. & Sadee, Wolfgang, eds. Drug Level Monitoring, Vol. 2. LC 85-17833. 375p. reprint ed. pap. 106.90 (*0-7837-2814-X*, 2057658) Bks Demand.

Lin, Florence. Florence Lin's Complete Book of Chinese Noodles, Dumplings & Breads. 1993. pap. 12.00 (*0-688-12845-9*, Quill) Morrow.

Lin, Forest. The DOS Coursebook. 620p. (Orig.). 1991. pap. 25.00 (*0-9624230-3-3*) Scott Jones Inc.

— The DOS 5 Coursebook. (Illus.). 664p. (Orig.). (C). 1992. pap. text ed. 33.95 (*0-9624230-9-2*) Scott Jones Inc.

— The DOS 6 Coursebook. 700p. (Orig.). 1993. pap. 33.95 (*1-881991-28-8*) Scott Jones Inc.

— The One-Two-Three Coursebook. (Illus.). 742p. (Orig.). (C). 1992. pap. text ed. 30.00 (*0-9624230-7-6*) Scott Jones Inc.

— The One Two Three Primer. 380p. (Orig.). (C). 1993. pap. text ed. 17.00 (*1-881991-26-1*) Scott Jones Inc.

— Quickstart in DOS. 120p. pap. 8.00 (*1-881991-25-3*) Scott Jones Inc.

— The Visual BASIC Coursebook. 800p. 1995. 31.00 (*1-881991-37-7*) Scott Jones Inc.

***Lin, Fu & Jianren, Wu.** The Sea of Regret: Two Turn-of-the Century Chinese Romantic Novels. Hanan, Patrick, tr. LC 94-49173. 220p. 1995. text ed. 32.00x (*0-8248-1666-8*); pap. text ed. 15.95x (*0-8248-1709-5*) UH Pr.

Lin Gen Hwa. The Paintings of Lin Gen Hwa. (Illus.). 64p. 1983. pap. 5.95 (*0-934788-05-7*) E-W Pub Co.

***Lin, Geoge & Stewart, Gayla.** AS/400: Systems, Utilities, Database & Programming. LC 95-15988. 1995. text ed. 49.00 (*0-13-382060-2*) P-H.

Lin, Grier C. Learning AutoCAD by Example. 148p. 1989. pap. text ed. 32.80 (*0-13-528266-7*) P-H.

Lin, H. K. & Rao, P. D. Ferric Chloride Leaching of the Delta Sulfide Ores & Gold Extraction from the Leaching Residue. (MIRL Report Ser.: No. 84). (Illus.). 18p. (Orig.). (C). 1987. pap. 4.00 (*0-911043-08-X*) UAKF Min Ind Res Lab.

Lin, Helen T. Beginning Standard Chinese. 188p. (Orig.). (C). 1992. pap. 15.95 (*0-8351-1940-8*) China Bks.

— Essential Grammar for Modern Chinese. 2nd ed. LC 81-67784. (Cheng & Tsui Language Ser.). x, 312p. (CHI.). (C). 1984. pap. 14.95 (*0-917056-10-8*) Cheng & Tsui.

Lin, Herbert S., ed. see National Research Council, Steering Committee on Rights & Responsibilities in Networked Communities.

Lin Hsin Hsin. Love at First Byte. 300p. 1992. pap. text ed. 21.00 (*981-02-1026-4*) World Scientific Pub.

***Lin, Huaxin.** C*-Algebra Extensions of C(X) LC 95-3280. (Memoirs Ser.: Vol. 550). 1995. write for info. (*0-8218-2611-5*) Am Math.

Lin, Hui-Sheng, jt. auth. see Thornton, Arland.

Lin, Ian B., intro. MECH 'Ninety-One Australia: Engineering for a Competitive World, Conference 1: Improving the Manufacturing Environment. (Illus.). 58p. (Orig.). 1991. pap. 38.50 (*0-85825-525-1*, Pub. by Inst Engrs Aust-EA Bks AT) Accents Pubns.

Lin, J. Steenrod Connections & Connectivity in H Spaces. LC 87-12589. (MEMO Ser.: No. 68-369). 87p. 1987. pap. text ed. 18.00 (*0-8218-2431-7*, MEMO 68/369) Am Math.

Lin, J. C., ed. Advances in Electromagnetic Fields in Living Systems, Vol. 1. 215p. (C). 1994. 69.50 (*0-306-44738-X*, Plenum Pr) Plenum.

Lin, J. T., ed. Growth, Characterization, & Applications of Laser Host & Nonlinear Crystals. 286p. 1989. 53.00 (*0-8194-0140-4*, VOL. 1104) SPIE.

Lin, Jain I. The Death of a Kaiser. (Illus.). 128p. (Orig.). 1985. pap. 5.95 (*0-913428-56-6*) Landfall Pr.

Lin, James C., ed. Electromagnetic Interaction with Biological Systems. (Illus.). 292p. 1989. 79.50 (*0-306-43109-2*, Plenum Pr) Plenum.

Lin, James C., jt. auth. see Michaelson, Sol M.

***Lin, Jami.** Earth Design: The Added Dimension. Lewison-Singar, Rita, ed. (Illus.). 256p. (Orig.). 1995. pap. 24.21 (*0-9643060-9-3*) Earth Design.

Lin, Jian H., jt. auth. see Grub, Phillip D.

Lin, Jing. Education in Post-Mao China. LC 92-19593. 152p. 1992. text ed. 39.95 (*0-275-94270-8*, C4270, Praeger Pubs) Greenwood.

— The Opening of the Chinese Mind: Democratic Changes in China Since 1978. LC 93-50073. 208p. 1994. text ed. 49.95 (*0-275-94594-4*, Praeger Pubs) Greenwood.

— The Red Guards' Path to Violence: Political, Educational, & Psychological Factors. LC 91-2272. 200p. 1991. text ed. 49.95 (*0-275-93872-7*, C3872, Praeger Pubs) Greenwood.

***Lin, Jonathon & Shiue, Tony.** CNC Programming Using Mastercam Version Four & Five. Sterzik, Karen L., ed. (Illus.). 880p. (C). 1995. pap. text ed. 55.00 (*1-886552-00-2*) Scholars Intl.

Lin, Julia. Essays on Contemporary Chinese Poetry. LC 85-2972. 195p. (C). 1985. text ed. 28.50 (*0-8214-0804-6*) Ohio U Pr.

Lin, Julia C. Modern Chinese Poetry: An Introduction. LC 70-152330. (Asia of the School of International Studies: No. 21). 278p. 1972. pap. 10.00 (*0-295-95281-4*) U of Wash Pr.

Lin, Julia C., tr. Women of the Red Plain: An Anthology of Contemporary Chinese Women's Poetry. 208p. 1993. pap. 10.00 (*0-14-058647-4*, Penguin Bks) Viking Penguin.

Lin, Key-Ming, et al, eds. Psychopharmacology & Psychobiology of Ethnicity. LC 92-49996. (Progress in Psychiatry Ser.: No. 39). 272p. 1993. text ed. 33.50 (*0-88048-471-3*) Am Psychiatric.

Lin, Lee H., ed. see Weichuan.

Lin, M. J., jt. auth. see Hwang, L.

Lin, Mike W. Architectural Rendering Techniques: A Color Reference. LC 84-25812. (Illus.). 256p. 1985. text ed. 54.95 (*0-442-25953-0*) Van Nos Reinhold.

— Drawing & Designing with Confidence. (Illus.). 224p. 1993. text ed. 54.95 (*0-442-00176-2*) Van Nos Reinhold.

Lin, Nan. The Struggle for Tiananmen: Anatomy of the 1989 Mass Movement. LC 92-15780. 232p. 1992. text ed. 45.00 (*0-275-93656-2*, C3656, Praeger Pubs) Greenwood.

Lin, Nan, jt. ed. see Marsden, Pater V.

Lin, Nan, et al, eds. Social Support, Life Events, & Depression. 1985. text ed. 99.00 (*0-12-450660-7*); pap. text ed. 58.00 (*0-12-450661-5*) Acad Pr.

Lin, Nancy T., tr. see En-Lai, Chou.

Lin, O. C. & Chao, E. Y., eds. Perspectives on Biomaterials. (Materials Science Monographs). 366p. 1986. 123.00 (*0-444-42672-8*) Elsevier.

Lin, O. C. C., et al, eds. Development & Transfer of Industrial Technology. LC 94-5799. (Advances in Industrial Engineering Ser.: Vol. 20). 292p. 1994. 200.00 (*0-444-81686-0*) Elsevier.

Lin, P. Mangrove Vegetation. 150p. 1988. 29.50 (*0-387-15718-2*) Spr-Verlag.

Lin, P. M. Symbolic Network Analysis. (Studies in Electrical & Electronic Engineering: No. 41). 310p. 1991. 137.25 (*0-444-87389-9*) Elsevier.

Lin, Paul J. A Translation of Lao Tzu's "Tao Te Ching" & Wang Pi's "Commentary." (Michigan Monographs in Chinese Studies: No. 30). 232p. (Orig.). 1977. pap. 8.50 (*0-89264-030-8*) Ctr Chinese Studies.

Lin, Pei-Jan P., et al, eds. Acceptance Testing of Radiological Imaging Equipment: Proceedings of the Symposium Held on October 1-2, 1981. (American Association of Physicists in Medicine Symposium Ser.: No. 1). 310p. 1982. 40.00 (*0-88318-400-1*) Am Inst Physics.

Lin, Qingson, jt. ed. see Byrd, William A.

Lin, R. Y., ed. see Symposium on Interfaces in Metal-Ceramics Composites Staff.

Lin, Ray Y. & Fishman, Steven G., eds. Control of Interfaces in Metal & Ceramics Composites. LC 93-80902. 1994. 84.00 (*0-87339-259-0*) Minerals Metals.

***Lin, Robert I., ed.** Garlic in Biology & Medicine: Proceedings Of The First World Congress On The Health Significance of Garlic & Garlic Constituents. (Illus.). 275p. (Orig.). 1995. pap. text ed. 150.00 (*0-9640678-0-3*) Nutrit Intl.

***Lin, S. C., et al.** CNC Process Modeling Using SmartCAM. Sterzik, Karen L., ed. (Illus.). 700p. (C). 1995. pap. 65.00 (*1-886552-02-9*) Scholars Intl.

Lin, S. C. Computer Numerical Control from Programming to Networking. 106p. 1994. teacher ed 12.00 (*0-8273-4716-2*) Delmar.

***Lin, S. C. & Shiue, F. C.** Mastercam Book for Windows. Sterzik, Karen L., ed. (Illus.). 900p. 1995. pap. 69.00 (*1-886552-01-0*) Scholars Intl.

Lin, S. H., ed. Advances in Multiphoton Processes & Spectroscopy, Vol. 7. 320p. (C). 1991. text ed. 98.00 (*981-02-0718-2*) World Scientific Pub.

Lin, S. H., et al. Advances in Multiphoton Processes & Spectroscopy, Vol. 8. 408p. 1993. text ed. 91.00 (*981-02-1543-6*) World Scientific Pub.

— Density Matrix Method & Femtosecond Processes. 228p. (C). 1991. text ed. 36.00 (*981-02-0709-3*) World Scientific Pub.

Lin, S. H., et al, eds. Multiphoton Spectroscopy of Molecules: Quantum Electronics: Principles & Applications. LC 83-2584. 1984. text ed. 126.00 (*0-12-450520-1*) Acad Pr.

Lin, S. P. & Lai, W. Michael. Selected Papers of Chia-Shun Yih, 2 vols. (Advanced Series on Fluid Mechanics). 1064p. (C). 1991. text ed. 193.00 (*981-02-0543-0*) World Scientific Pub.

— Selected Papers of Chia-Shun Yih: Advanced Series on Fluid Mechanics, 2 vols. 1064p. (C). 1991. text ed. 153.00 (*0-318-67155-7*) World Scientific Pub.

Lin, S. P., et al, eds. Nonlinear Instability of Nonparallel Flows. LC 94-19338. 1994. 154.00 (*0-387-57679-7*) Spr-Verlag.

Lin, Sein, ed. see Lincoln Institute of Land Policy Staff.

Lin Shan. Name Your Baby in Chinese. (Illus.). 210p. 1988. pap. 8.95 (*0-89346-304-3*) Heian Intl.

Lin, Sharon C. & Leung, Martha C. Chinese Libraries & Librarianship: An Annotated Bibliography. 1986. pap. 14.95 (*0-937256-03-X*) Chinese Cult Serv.

Lin, Shiow-Ching & Pearce, Eli M. High Performance Thermosets: Chemistry, Properties, Applications. LC 93-37466. 368p. (C). 1993. text ed. write for info. (*1-56990-155-4*) Hanser-Gardner.

Lin, Shu. Introduction to Error-Correcting Codes. LC 76-124417. 1970. 32.95 (*0-685-03876-9*) P-H.

Lin, Shuen-Fu. The Transformation of a Chinese Lyrical Tradition: Chaing K'uei & Southern Sung Tz'u Poetry. LC 77-85549. (Illus.). 1978. 39.50x (*0-691-06351-6*) Princeton U Pr.

Lin, Shuen-Fu & Owen, Stephen. The Vitality of the Lyric Voice: Shih Poetry from the Late Han to the T'ang. 400p. 1986. text ed. 62.50x (*0-691-03134-7*) Princeton U Pr.

Lin, Shwu Yeng T., jt. auth. see Lin, You-Feng.

Lin, Sophia, ed. see Wei Chuan Publishing Staff.

Lin, Su-Chen J. Computer Numerical Control: Essentials in Programming & Networking. 1994. text ed. 49.95 (*0-8273-4715-4*) Delmar.

Lin, T. Y. & Burns, Ned H. Design of Prestressed Concrete Structures. 3rd ed. LC 80-20619. 646p. (C). 1981. Net. text ed. write for info. (*0-471-01898-8*) Wiley.

Lin, T. Y. & Kelly, J. W., eds. Prestressed Concrete Buildings. (Illus.). 334p. 1962. text ed. 171.00 (*0-677-10310-7*) Gordon & Breach.

Lin, Timothy. The Secret of Church Growth. Taniguchi, Ruth W., tr. 118p. (Orig.). 1992. pap. write for info. (*0-945304-01-3*) FCBC.

Lin, Timothy T. The Life & Thought of Soren Kierkegaard. (Masterworks of Literature Ser.). 1974. pap. 13.95x (*0-8084-0377-X*) NCUP.

Lin, Tung-Hai. Development of the Agrarian Movement & Agrarian Legislation in China, 1912-1930. 1976. lib. bdg. 34.95 (*0-8490-1714-9*) Gordon Pr.

Lin, Vivian. Health, Women's Work, & Industrialization: Semiconductor Workers in Singapore & Malaysia. LC 91-18133. (Developing Economies of the Third World Ser.). 192p. 1991. 49.00 (*0-8153-0632-6*) Garland.

***Lin, Vladimir & Pinchover, Yehuda.** Manifolds with Group Actions & Elliptic Operators. LC 94-26456. 1994. write for info. (*0-8218-2604-2*) Am Math.

Lin, W. Thomas, jt. auth. see Vasarhelyi, Miklos.

Lin, Wei-Ying. The Future of Foreign Business & Foreign Investments in China. LC 75-30068. (Institute of Pacific Relations Ser.). reprint ed. 22.00 (*0-404-59541-3*) AMS Pr.

Lin, Wen C. Handbook of Digital Systems for Scientists & Engineers. 272p. 1981. 69.95 (*0-8493-0671-X*, TK868, CRC Reprint) Franklin.

Lin, Y. C., jt. auth. see Volakis, John L.

Lin, Y. K. Probabilistic Theory of Structural Dynamics. LC 75-42154. 380p. 1976. reprint ed. 38.00 (*0-88275-377-0*) Krieger.

Lin, Y. K., ed. Probabilistic Mechanics & Structural & Geotechnical Reliability: Proceedings of the Sixth Specialty Conference Sponsored by the Engineering Mechanics, Structural, & Geotechnical Engineering Divisions, American Society of Civil Engineers, Denver, Colorado, July 8-10, 1992. LC 92-15903. 616p. 1992. pap. text ed. 56.00 (*0-87262-873-6*) Am Soc Civil Eng.

Lin, Y. K. & Cai, G. Q. Probabilistic Structure Dynamics: Advanced Theory Applications. rev. ed. LC 94-13102. 1994. text ed. write for info. (*0-07-038038-4*) McGraw.

Lin, Y. K. & Elishakoff, I., eds. Stochastic Structural Dynamics 1: New Theoretical Developments. xiii, 356p. 1991. 95.00 (*0-387-54167-5*) Spr-Verlag.

Lin, Y. K. & Schueller, G. I., eds. Stochastic Structural Mechanics. (Lecture Notes in Engineering Ser.: Vol. 31). xi, 507p. 1987. pap. 79.00 (*0-387-18463-5*) Spr-Verlag.

Lin, Y. K., jt. ed. see Elishakoff, I.

Lin, Y. W. & Srinivasan, R., eds. Digital Image Processing Applications. 449p. 1989. 77.00 (*0-8194-0110-2*, VOL. 1075) SPIE.

Lin, You-Feng & Lin, Shwu Yeng T. Set Theory with Applications. (Illus.). ix, 221p. 1985. reprint ed. pap. text ed. 25.50 (*0-931541-04-2*) Mancorp Pub.

Lin, You-Feng, jt. auth. see McWaters, Marcus M.

Lin, Yu-Chong & Shida, Kathleen K., eds. Man in the Sea, Vol. I. (Illus.). 330p. 1990. text ed. 35.50 (*0-941332-12-8*) Best Pub Co.

— Man in the Sea, Vol. II. (Illus.). 232p. 1990. text ed. 33.00 (*0-941332-13-6*) Best Pub Co.

Lin Yu-T'ang. The Gay Genius: The Life & Times of Su Tungpo. LC 71-112327. (Illus.). 370p. 1971. reprint ed. text ed. 35.00 (*0-8371-4715-8*, LIGG, Greenwood Pr) Greenwood.

Lin, Yu-T'Ang. The Little Critic: Essays, Satires & Sketches on China. (First Series: 1930-1932) LC 79-2831. 299p. 1988. reprint ed. 28.00 (*0-8305-0009-X*) Hyperion Conn.

— The Little Critic: Essays, Satires & Sketches on China (Second Series: 1933-1935. LC 79-2832. 258p. 1988. reprint ed. 26.00 (*0-8305-0010-3*) Hyperion Conn.

Lin Yu-T'ang. Widow, Nun & Courtesan: Three Novelettes from the Chinese. LC 75-112328. vi, 266p. 1971. reprint ed. text ed. 38.50 (*0-8371-4716-6*, LIWN, Greenwood Pr) Greenwood.

Lin Yu-T'ang, ed. The Importance of Understanding: Translations from the Chinese. (Essay Index Reprint Ser.). 1977. reprint ed. 29.95 (*0-518-10115-0*) Ayer.

Lin, Yu-T'Ang, jt. auth. see Hu, Shih.

Lin Yun, jt. auth. see Rossbach, Sarah.

Lin, Zhiguang, jt. auth. see Zhang, Jiacheng.

Lin, Zhiling & Robinson, Thomas W., eds. The Chinese & Their Future: Beijing, Taipei, & Hong Kong. LC 93-21227. 536p. 1994. 39.75 (*0-8447-3805-0*, AEI Pr); pap. 19.95 (*0-8447-3804-2*, AEI Pr) Am Enterprise.

Linacre, Anthea, jt. auth. see Bowskill, Derek.

Linacre, Edward. Climate Data & Resources: A Reference & Guide. (Illus.). 384p. (C). 1992. 75.00 (*0-415-05702-7*, A6535); pap. 31.50 (*0-415-05703-5*, A6539) Routledge.

Linacre, John M. Many-Facet Rasch Measurement. 2nd ed. LC 94-76939. (Illus.). 157p. 1994. pap. text ed. 30.00 (*0-941938-02-6*) Mesa Pr.

***Linahon, Gail.** Hancock County, IA. (Illus.). 417p. 1993. 60.00 (*0-88107-222-2*) Curtis Media.

Linam, Gail. The Bible Speaks to Children. LC 88-7529. (Orig.). 1989. pap. 4.99 (*0-8054-4931-0*) Broadman.

Linam, Shawn L. & Jarvis, M. Todd. Biotechnology Sourcebook. LC 88-45788. 372p. 1989. pap. text ed. 95.00 (*0-88173-073-4*) Fairmont Pr.

Linamen, Karen S. The Parent Warrior. 204p. 1993. pap. 9.99 (*1-56476-127-4*, Victor Books) SP Pubns.

Linamen, Karen S. & Holland, Linda. Working Women, Workable Lives: Creative Solutions for Managing Home & Career. 256p. 1993. reprint ed. pap. 9.99 (*0-87788-851-5*) Shaw Pubs.

Linan, Amable & Williams, Forman A. Fundamental Aspects of Combustion. LC 92-23050. (Oxford Engineering Science Ser.: No. 34). (Illus.). 192p. 1993. 35.00 (*0-19-507626-5*) OUP.

Linant de Bellefonds, Y. Traite De Droit Musulman Compare: Filiation - Incapacites - Liberalites Entre Vifs, Tome 3. (Recherches Mediterraneennes Ser.: No. 9). 1973. pap. 52.25 (*90-279-7199-4*) Mouton.

***Linard, Brian.** A Way to the Heart of Christmas. 1994. pap. 6.95 (*1-56548-025-2*) New City.

Linardakis, Constantina & Linardakis, Nikos M. Recipes Sworn to Secrecy. (Illus.). 64p. (Orig.). 1995. pap. 12.95 (*1-884084-08-7*) Michaelis Med.

Linardakis, Nikos M. Digging up the Bones... Pharmacology, Microbiology, Pathology & Biochemistry, 4 vols., Set B. 400p. (Orig.). (C). 1994. Vol. 1, Pharmacology. pap. text ed. 16.00 (*1-884084-00-1*); Vol. 2, Microbiology. pap. text ed. 16.00 (*1-884084-01-X*); Vol. 3, Pathology. pap. text ed. 16.00 (*1-884084-02-8*); Vol.4, Biochemistry. pap. text ed. write for info. (*1-884084-04-4*) Michaelis Med.

— Digging up the Bones... Pharmacology, Microbiology, Pathology & Biochemistry, 4 vols., Set B, Set. 400p. (Orig.). (C). 1994. pap. text ed. 64.00 (*1-884084-10-9*) Michaelis Med.

— Digging up the Bones... Vol. 5: Behavioral Science. (Illus.). 80p. (C). 1995. pap. text ed. 16.00 (*1-884084-11-7*) Michaelis Med.

Linardakis, Nikos M., jt. auth. see Golbin, Alexander Z.

Linardakis, Nikos M., jt. auth. see Linardakis, Constantina.

Linares, Enrique. A Scientific Approach to the Metaphysics of Astrology. Robertson, Arlene, ed. 170p. (Orig.). 1982. per. 7.95 (*0-930706-10-2*) Seek-It Pubns.

Linares, Filadelfo. Jean-Jacques Rousseaus Bruch Mit David Hume. (Studien und Materialien Zur Geschichte der Philosophie Ser.: No. 30). xi, 127p. 1991. write for info. (*3-487-09478-9*, Pub. by Georg Olms GW) Lubrecht & Cramer.

Linares, Olga F. Prayer, Power & Production: The Jola of Casamance, Senegal. (Cambridge Studies in Social & Cultural Anthropology: No. 82). (Illus.). 240p. (C). 1992. 64.95 (*0-521-40132-1*) Cambridge U Pr.

Linari, F., et al, eds. Pathogenesis & Treatment of Nephrolithiasis. (Contributions to Nephrology Ser.: Vol. 58). x, 298p. 1987. 141.75 (*3-8055-4554-1*) S Karger.

Linaweaver, Brad. Moon of Ice. 288p. 1993. mass mkt. 4.99 (*0-8125-2020-3*) Tor Bks.

Linaweaver, F. Pierce, ed. Environmental Engineering. LC 92-23894. 688p. 1992. pap. text ed. 56.00 (*0-87262-878-7*) Am Soc Civil Eng.

Linberg, G. & Heard, A. Dictionary of Names of Marine Food-Fishes of World Fauna. 562p. (C). 1980. 135.00 (*0-685-54129-0*, Pub. by Collets) St Mut.

— Dictionary of Names of Marine Food Fishes of World Fauna. 562p. (C). 1980. 135.00 (*0-89771-913-1*, Pub. by Collets) St Mut.

Linberg, John V. Oculoplastic & Orbital Emergencies. (Illus.). 237p. (C). 1990. boxed 50.00 (*0-8385-3626-3*, A3626-7) Appleton & Lange.

Linberg, John V., ed. Lacrimal Surgery. (Contemporary Issues in Ophthalmology Ser.: Vol. 5). (Illus.). 348p. 1988. text ed. 87.00 (*0-443-08582-X*) Churchill.

Linblad, B. S., ed. Perinatal Nutrition. (Bristol-Myers Nutrition Symposia Ser.: No. 6). 394p. 1988. text ed. 99.00 (*0-12-450285-7*) Acad Pr.

***Linblom, Steven.** Fly the Hot Ones. LC 89-29491. (J). (gr. 4-7). 1995. pap. 6.95 (*0-395-72023-0*) HM.

Linc, Deb, intro. Women's Wheels. 38p. (Orig.). 1982. pap. 7.95 (*0-9610084-0-7*) Amelia Pub.

Lincecum, Jerry B. Adventures of the Good Humor Man. LC 90-81801. (Illus.). 145p. (Orig.). 1990. pap. 10.00 (*0-9626851-0-0*) Big Barn Pr.

Lincecum, Jerry B., ed. Adventures of a Frontier Naturalist: The Life & Times of Dr. Gideon Lincecum. LC 94-11122. (Illus.). 344p. 1994. 35.00 (*0-89096-592-7*); pap. 14.95 (*0-89096-603-6*) Tex A&M Univ Pr.

Linch, Adrian L. Evaluation of Ambient Air Quality by Personnel Monitoring, Vol. 1. 2nd ed. 384p. 1981. 129.95 (*0-8493-5293-2*, TD890, CRC Reprint) Franklin.

— Evaluation of Ambient Air Quality by Personnel Monitoring, Vol. 2. 2nd ed. 336p. 1981. 119.00 (*0-8493-5294-0*, CRC Reprint) Franklin.

Linch, David & Yates, A. P. Haematology. LC 85-16585. (Colour Aids Ser.). (Illus.). 124p. (Orig.). (C). 1986. pap. 19.95 (*0-443-02842-7*) Churchill.

Linch-Zadel, Lauri, ed. see Burbank, Doreen C.

Linche, Richard, tr. see Cartari, Vincenzo.

Linchitz, Joel. The Complete Guide to Telemarketing Management. LC 89-46218. 360p. 1990. 59.95 (*0-8144-5885-8*) AMACOM.

— The Complete Guide to Telemarketing Management. 333p. 1993. pap. 24.95 (*0-8144-7863-8*) AMACOM.

***Lincicome, Mark E.** Priciple, Praxis, & the Politics of Educational Reform in Meiji Japan. LC 94-35279. (Illus.). 328p. (C). 1995. text ed. 45.00x (*0-8248-1620-X*) UH Pr.

Linck, Ernestine S. Eats: A Folk History of Texas Foods. 1989. pap. 12.95 (*0-87565-035-X*) Tex Christian.

Linck, Ernestine S. & Roach, Joyce. Eats: A Folk History of Texas Food. LC 88-20158. (Illus.). 258p. 1989. 23.50 (*0-87565-032-5*) Tex Christian.

Linck, Orville F. A Passage Through Pakistan. LC 59-15364. 283p. reprint ed. 80.70 (*0-685-16278-8*, 2027610) Bks Demand.

Lincoff, Gary H. S&S Guide to Mushrooms. 1982. pap. 15.00 (*0-671-42849-7*) S&S Trade.

Lincoff, Gary H., jt. auth. see Audubon Society Staff.

Lincold, Roger N., ed. see Howe, Donald W.

***Lincoln.** Psychosexual Medicine: A Study of Underlying Themes. 206p. 1992. pap. 47.75 (*1-56593-049-5*, 0297) Singular Publishing.

Lincoln, et al. Mechanical Fastening of Plastics: An Engineering Handbook. (Mechanical Engineering Ser.: Vol. 26). 240p. 1984. 89.75 (*0-8247-7078-1*) Dekker.

***Lincoln, Abraham.** Abraham Lincoln: Autobiographical Narrative. (American Autobiography Ser.). 77p. 1995. reprint ed. lib. bdg. 69.00 (*0-7812-8578-X*) Rprt Serv.

— Abraham Lincoln: His Speeches & Writings. Basler, Roy P., ed. LC 46-11909. 1968. reprint ed. 73.00 (*0-527-57100-8*) Periodicals Srv.

— Abraham Lincoln: His Speeches & Writings. (History - United States Ser.). 843p. 1993. reprint ed. lib. bdg. 199.00 (*0-7812-4898-1*) Rprt Serv.

An Asterisk (*) at the beginning of an entry indicates that the title is appearing in BIP for the first time.

— Abraham Lincoln's Autobiography. (American Autobiography Ser.). 45p. 1995. reprint ed. lib. bdg. 69.00 (0-7812-8579-8) Rprt Serv.
— Calligraphy Is Fun. 80p. (Orig.). 1990. pap. 12.95 (0-943295-13-0) Graphics Plus FL.
— The Essential Lincoln. LC 93-3373. 1993. 8.99 (0-517-09345-6, Pub. by Gramercy) Random Hse Value.
— Famous Speeches of Abraham Lincoln. LC 78-90652. (Essay Index Reprint Ser.). 1977. 18.95 (0-8369-1207-1) Ayer.
— Four Speeches by Abraham Lincoln, Hitherto Unpublished or Unknown. 1969. reprint ed. 20.00 (0-527-57106-7) Periodicals Srv.
— The Gettysburg Address. (Illus.). (J). 1995. 14.95 (0-395-69824-3) HM.
— Great Speeches. (Thrift Editions Ser.). 128p. reprint ed. pap. 1.00 (0-486-26872-1) Dover.
— The Hunt Speedball Calligraphy Workbook...: An Italic Notebook. LC 78-56645. (Illus.). 120p. (YA). (gr. 7-12). 1978. pap. 12.95 (0-942032-00-4) Calligrafree.
— Italic. 60p. (Orig.). 1989. pap. 9.95 (0-943295-11-4) Graphics Plus FL.
— The Life & Writings of Abraham Lincoln. (History - United States Ser.). 863p. 1993. reprint ed. lib. bdg. 119.00 (0-7812-4899-X) Rprt Serv.
— Lincoln Dictionary. Winn, Ralph, ed. pap. 1.45 (0-685-19407-8, 43, Citadel Pr) Carol Pub Group.
— The Lincoln Encyclopedia: The Spoken & Written Words of A. Lincoln Arranged for Ready Reference. Shaw, Archer H., ed. LC 80-12651. xii, 395p. 1980. reprint ed. text ed. 45.50 (0-313-22471-4, SHLE, Greenwood Pr) Greenwood.
— Lincoln's Letters. 1995. audio 16.95 (1-883049-50-4); audio, lib. bdg. 18.95 (1-883049-51-2) Commuters Lib.
— Lincoln's Prose. 1995. audio 16.95 (1-883049-52-0); audio, lib. bdg. 18.95 (1-883049-53-9) Commuters Lib.
— Poems of Abraham Lincoln. 1991. 8.95 (1-55709-133-1) Applewood.
— Selected Speeches & Writings. LC 91-50227. (Vintage Books - the Library of America). 608p. 1992. pap. 12.50 (0-679-73731-6, Vin) Random.
— Selected Writings & Speeches. Williams, T. Harry, ed. (University Classics Ser.). 334p. 1980. pap. 12.95 (0-87532-136-4) Hendricks House.
— Speeches & Letters. 316p. 1993. pap. 6.95 (0-460-87146-3, Everyman's Classic Lib) C E Tuttle.
— Speeches & Writings, 2 vols., Set. Fehrenbacher, Don E., ed. 1989. 70.00 (0-940450-68-2) Library of America.
— Speeches & Writings, 2 vols., Vol. I, 1832-1858. Fehrenbacher, Don E., ed. LC 89-2362. 889p. 1989. 35.00 (0-940450-43-7) Library of America.
— Speeches & Writings, 2 vols., Vol. II, 1859-1865. Fehrenbacher, Don E., ed. LC 89-45349. 788p. 1989. 35.00 (0-940450-63-1) Library of America.
— Speeches & Writings: Presidential Messages & Proclamations, 1859-1865, Vol. 2. 1990. write for info. (0-318-66783-5, Penguin Bks) Viking Penguin.
— Speeches & Writings: The Lincoln-Douglas Debates, 1832-1858, Vol. 1. 1990. write for info. (0-318-66782-7, Penguin Bks) Viking Penguin.
— Wisdom & Wit. (J). (gr. 8 up). 1965. 7.99 (0-88088-359-6) Peter Pauper.
Lincoln, Abraham & Douglas, Stephen. Lincoln-Douglas Debates of 1858. Johannsen, Robert W., ed. (Orig.). 1965. pap. 15.95 (0-19-500921-5) OUP.
Lincoln, Adams W., ed. Sunlight & Shadow. LC 76-24669. (Sources of Modern Photography Ser.). (Illus.). 1979. reprint ed. lib. bdg. 19.95 (0-405-09646-1) Ayer.
Lincoln, Alan J. & Lincoln, Carol Z. Library Crime & Security: An International Perspective. LC 87-12059. (Library & Archival Security Ser.: Vol. 8, Nos. 1 & 2). 163p. 1987. text ed. 39.95 (0-86656-480-2) Haworth Pr.
Lincoln, Alan J. & Straus, Murray A., eds. Crime & the Family. (Illus.). 276p. (C). 1985. 44.95x (0-398-05144-5) C C Thomas.
— Crime & the Family. (Illus.). 276p. 1985. pap. 29.95 (0-398-06240-4) C C Thomas.
*__Lincoln, Andrew.__ Spiritual History: A Reading of William Blake's the Four Zoas. 288p. 1995. 49.95 (0-19-818314-3) OUP.
— WBC, Vol. 42: Ephesians. 432p. 1990. write for info. (0-8499-0241-X) Word Inc.
Lincoln, Andrew, ed. see Blake, William, et al.
Lincoln, Andrew T. & Wedderburn, A. J. The Theology of the Later Pauline Letters. LC 92-31674. (New Testament Theology Ser.). 175p. (C). 1993. 49.95 (0-521-36460-4); pap. 15.95 (0-521-36721-2) Cambridge U Pr.
Lincoln, Anna & Fothergill, Dorothy. Escape to China. (Illus.). 271p. 1983. 13.95 (0-87141-076-1) Manyland.
Lincoln Beta Club Staff, jt. auth. see Marshall, Ed.
Lincoln, Bill, et al. Encyclopedia of Wood: A Tree-by-Tree Guide to the World's Most Valuable Resource. 224p. 1989. 29.95 (0-8160-2159-7) Facts on File.
Lincoln, Bruce. Authority: Construction & Corrosion. 224p. 1994. 22.50 (0-226-48197-2) U Ch Pr.
— Death, War, & Sacrifice: Studies in Ideology & Practice. LC 90-26902. (Illus.). 344p. 1991. pap. text ed. 17.95 (0-226-48200-6) U Ch Pr.
— Death, War, & Sacrifice: Studies in Ideology & Practice. LC 90-26902. (Illus.). 344p. 1991. lib. bdg. 45.00 (0-226-48199-9) U Ch Pr.
— Discourse & the Construction of Society: Comparitive Studies of Myth, Ritual, & Classification. (Illus.). 256p. 1992. pap. 19.95 (0-19-507909-4) OUP.
— Emerging from the Chrysalis: Rituals of Women's Initiation. (Illus.). 184p. (C). 1991. pap. text ed. 14.95 (0-19-506910-2) OUP.
— Emerging from the Chrysalis: Studies in Rituals of Women's Initiation. LC 80-24189. 167p. reprint ed. pap. 47.60 (0-7837-2062-9, 2042337) Bks Demand.
Lincoln, Bruce, ed. Religion, Rebellion, Revolution: An Interdisciplinary & Cross-Cultural Collection of Essays. LC 85-1992. 312p. 1985. text ed. 39.95 (0-312-67061-3) St Martin.
Lincoln, C. Eric. The Avenue, Clayton City. (Black History Titles Ser.). 1989. mass mkt. 4.99 (0-345-36034-6) Ballantine.
— The Black Muslims in America. 3rd rev. ed. 328p. (C). 1994. pap. text ed. 16.99 (0-8028-0703-8) Eerdmans.
— Race, Religion, & the Continuing American Dilemma. 304p. 1986. pap. 9.95 (0-8090-0163-2) Hill & Wang.
— This Road since Freedom. 92p. (Orig.). 1990. 17.50 (0-932112-30-7); pap. 10.00 (0-932112-31-5) Carolina Wren.
Lincoln, C. Eric & Mamiya, Lawrence. The Black Church in the African American Experience. LC 90-34050. 472p. (C). 1990. pap. text ed. 21.95 (0-8223-1073-2) Duke.
Lincoln, C. Eric, jt. auth. see Frazier, E. Franklin.
Lincoln, C. I., jt. auth. see Chalofsky, N.
Lincoln, C. Z. Constitutional History of New York, 5 vols., Set. 1993. reprint ed. lib. bdg. 375.00 (0-7812-5189-3) Rprt Serv.
Lincoln, Carol Z., jt. auth. see Lincoln, Alan J.
Lincoln, Charles H. Manuscript Records of the French & Indian War in the Library of the American Antiquarian Society. 267p. 1993. reprint ed. pap. text ed. 20.00 (1-55613-739-7) Heritage Bk.
Lincoln, Charles H., ed. see Shirley, William.
Lincoln, Colm. Dublin As a Work of Art. (Illus.). 224p. 1993. 45.00 (0-86278-313-5, Pub. by OBrien Pr IE) Dufour.
Lincoln, Dennis W., jt. ed. see Edwards, Christopher R.
Lincoln, E. Eric. Black Muslims in America. 1993. pap. 16.95 (0-86543-400-X) Africa World.
Lincoln, Edmond E., tr. Du Pont De Nemours on the Dangers of Inflation: An Address by Pierre Sanvel DuPont, 1790. (Kress Library of Business & Economics Publication: No. 7). 58p. 1949. pap. 9.95 (0-678-09902-2, Kress Lib Business) Kelley.
Lincoln, Edward J. Japan: Facing Economic Maturity. LC 87-18235. 298p. (C). 1988. 34.95 (0-8157-5260-1); pap. 14.95 (0-8157-5259-8) Brookings.
— Japan's Economic Role in Northeast Asia. LC 86-22439. (Asian Agenda Report Ser.: No. 10). (Illus.). 86p. (Orig.). (C). 1987. lib. bdg. 25.50 (0-8191-5677-9, The Asia Society); pap. text ed. 8.00 (0-8191-5678-7, The Asia Society) U Pr of Amer.
— Japan's New Global Role. (Integrating National Economies: Promise & Pitfalls Ser.). 320p. (Orig.). (C). 1995. 36.95x (0-8157-5258-X) Brookings.
— Japan's New Global Role. (Integrating National Economies: Promise & Pitfalls Ser.). 320p. (Orig.). (C). 1995. pap. 16.95x (0-8157-5257-1) Brookings.
— Japan's Unequal Trade. 180p. 1990. 31.95 (0-8157-5262-8); pap. 12.95 (0-8157-5261-X) Brookings.
Lincoln, Edward J., ed. Japan & the Middle East. LC 90-53699. 82p. (C). 1990. pap. text ed. 5.00 (0-916808-38-6) Mid East Inst.
Lincoln, Eugene, ed. see Williams-Wilson, Miriam J.
Lincoln, Evelyn. Art in Transition: Post-Impressionist Prints & Drawings from the Achenbach Foundation for Graphic Arts. LC 88-80186. (Illus.). 15p. (C). 1988. pap. 4.00 (0-88401-058-9) Fine Arts Mus.
Lincoln, F. Catalog of Papal Medals. 1990. reprint ed. pap. 10.00 (0-915262-83-5) S J Durst.
Lincoln, Francis G. Mining Districts & Mineral Resources of Nevada. (Illus.). 1982. 14.95 (0-913814-48-2) Nevada Pubns.
Lincoln, George. History of the Town of Hingham, Vol. I. (Illus.). 805p. 1992. reprint ed. lib. bdg. 77.50 (0-8328-2494-1) Higginson Bk Co.
— History of the Town of Hingham, Vol. II. (Illus.). 915p. 1992. reprint ed. lib. bdg. 62.50 (0-8328-2495-X) Higginson Bk Co.
— The History of the Town of Hingham, MA Vol. II: The Genealogy. LC 82-80017. 927p. 1994. reprint ed. 60.00 (0-89725-029-X) Picton Pr.
Lincoln, Harry B. The Italian Madrigal & Related Repertories: Indexes to Printed Collections. LC 87-51189. (C). 1988. text ed. 100.00 (0-300-03683-3) Yale U Pr.
— Latin Motet: Indices to Printed Collections, 1500-1600. (Wissenschaftliche Abhandlungen-Musicological Studies: Vol. 59). xii, 835p. 1993. lib. bdg. 220.00 (0-931902-80-0) Inst Mediaeval Mus.
Lincoln, Harry B., ed. & tr. L' Amorosa Ero. LC 66-64729. 134p. 1968. 49.50 (0-87395-030-5) State U NY Pr.
Lincoln, Harry B. & Bonta, Stephen. Study Scores of Historical Styles, Vol. 1. 400p. 1986. text ed. write for info. (0-13-698267-0) P-H.
— Study Scores of Historical Styles, Vol. II. (Illus.). 400p. 1987. pap. text ed. write for info. (0-13-858853-8) P-H.
Lincoln Highway Association Staff. A Complete Official Road Guide of the Lincoln Highway. 5th ed. (Illus.). 542p. 1993. reprint ed. pap. text ed. 17.95 (1-880397-05-6) Patrice Pr.
Lincoln, I. T. Revelations of an International Spy. 1972. 59.95 (0-8490-0949-9) Gordon Pr.
Lincoln Institute of Land Policy Staff. Agribusiness Education in Transition: Strategies for Change, Report of the National Agribusiness Education Commission, June 1989. Downey, W. David, ed. 80p. reprint ed. pap. 25.00 (0-7837-2162-5, 2042467) Bks Demand.
— American Federalism in the 1980s: Changes & Consequences: Conference Summary & Papers May 19-20, 1981. (Lincoln Institute Monograph Ser.: No. 81-7). 86p. reprint ed. pap. 25.00 (0-7837-2171-4, 2042494) Bks Demand.
— Land Management Issues & Development Strategies in Developing Countries, Vol. 2. Lin, Sein & Zaman, Wasin, eds. 134p. reprint ed. pap. 38.20 (0-7837-3873-0, 2043712) Bks Demand.
— Land Policy in Developing Countries. (Lincoln Institute Monograph Ser.: No. 84-4). 78p. reprint ed. pap. 25.00 (0-7837-2156-0, 2042456) Bks Demand.
Lincoln, J. D. & Lincoln, Rosemary. People of Portsmouth & Some Who Came to Town. LC 82-16543. (Illus.). 112p. 1982. pap. 13.95 (0-914339-00-1) P E Randall Pub.
Lincoln, Jack, ed. see Birch, Stephen & Ida, Junko.
Lincoln, Jack, ed. see Hacker, Edward.
Lincoln, James. Clock. (J). 1992. pap. 15.00 (0-385-30037-9, Delta) Dell.
Lincoln, James H. & Donahue, James L. Fiery Trial. LC 84-62633. (Illus.). 68p. 1984. 12.00 (0-9614344-0-6) Historical Soc MI.
Lincoln, James R. Prescription Filled. LC 81-51752. (Illus.). 202p. 1981. 12.50 (0-88492-039-9) W S Sullwold.
Lincoln, James R. & Kalleberg, Arne L. Culture, Control & Commitment: A Study of Work Organization & Work Attitudes in the United States & Japan. (Illus.). 264p. (C). 1992. pap. 21.95 (0-521-42866-1) Cambridge U Pr.
Lincoln, John. Rich Grass Sweet Water. 1989. 19.95 (0-89096-387-8) Tex A&M Univ Pr.
Lincoln, John C. Ground Rent, Not Taxes: The Natural Source of Revenue for the Government. 72p. reprint ed. pap. 25.00 (0-7837-2170-6, 2042492) Bks Demand.
Lincoln, John E., jt. auth. see Heffernan, James W.
Lincoln, John E., jt. auth. see Heffernan, James.
Lincoln, Jonathan T. The City of the Dinner-Pail. Stein, Leon, ed. LC 77-70511. (Work Ser.). 1977. reprint ed. lib. bdg. 23.95 (0-405-10181-3) Ayer.
Lincoln, Joseph C. Cape Cod Stories. 1976. reprint ed. lib. bdg. 21.95 (0-88411-791-X, Aeonian Pr) Amereon Ltd.
— Cap'n Eri. 1976. reprint ed. lib. bdg. 25.95 (0-88411-792-8, Aeonian Pr) Amereon Ltd.
— Partners of the Tide. LC 72-98402. reprint ed. 24.95 (0-404-03987-1) AMS Pr.
— Storm Girl. 1976. reprint ed. lib. bdg. 21.95 (0-88411-793-6, Aeonian Pr) Amereon Ltd.
Lincoln, Kenneth. Indi'n Humor: Bicultural Play in Native America. (Illus.). 288p. 1993. 42.00 (0-19-506887-4) OUP.
— Native American Renaissance. LC 82-17450. 320p. 1983. pap. 15.00 (0-520-05457-1) U CA Pr.
— Native American Renaissance. LC 82-17450. (Illus.). 323p. reprint ed. pap. 92.10 (0-7837-4752-7, 2044499) Bks Demand.
Lincoln, Kenneth, ed. see Alexie, Sherman.
Lincoln, Kenneth, ed. see TallMountain, Mary.
Lincoln, Kenneth R., jt. auth. see Arpad, Joseph J.
Lincoln, Key. Submission Holds. (Orig.). 1994. pap. text ed. 4.95 (1-56333-266-3) Masquerade.
Lincoln, Lillian. Bellwood Treasure. 1987. pap. 2.50 (0-449-21187-8) Fawcett.
Lincoln, Louise, ed. Southwest Indian Silver from the Doneghy Collection. (Illus.). 189p. 1982. text ed. 29.95 (0-292-72440-3) U of Tex Pr.
Lincoln, Louise, et al. An Assemblage of Spirits: Idea & Image in New Ireland. LC 87-15779. (Illus.). 168p. 1987. pap. 17.95 (0-8076-1188-3) Braziller.
Lincoln, Margaret. Amazing Boats. LC 92-3045. (Eyewitness Juniors Ser.). (Illus.). 32p. (Orig.). (J). (gr. 1-5). 1992. lib. bdg. 9.99 (0-679-92770-0); pap. 7.99 (0-679-82770-6) Knopf Bks Yng Read.
*__Lincoln, Margarette.__ The Pirate's Handbook. LC 94-46512. (J). 1995. 12.99 (0-525-65209-4, Cobblehill Bks) Dutton Child Bks.
*__Lincoln, Patrick D.__ Computational Aspects of Linear Logic. (Foundations of Computing Ser.). (Illus.). 250p. (C). 1995. 35.00x (0-262-12195-6) MIT Pr.
Lincoln, R., jt. ed. see Tietze, S. L.
Lincoln, R. J. & Boxshall, G. A. The Cambridge Illustrated Dictionary of Natural History. (Illus.). 408p. 1987. 39.95 (0-521-30551-9) Cambridge U Pr.
— The Cambridge Illustrated Dictionary of Natural History. (Illus.). 420p. (C). 1990. pap. 19.95 (0-521-39941-6) Cambridge U Pr.
Lincoln, R. J., et al, eds. A Dictionary of Ecology, Evolution & Systematics. LC 81-18013. 298p. 1984. pap. 27.95 (0-521-26902-4) Cambridge U Pr.
Lincoln Residents, photos. Five Roads: Photographic Essay by the Lincoln 1975 Bicentennial Commission. (Illus.). 34p. (Orig.). 1990. reprint ed. pap. 4.00 (0-944856-02-0) Lincoln Hist Soc.
Lincoln, Richard, ed. see Alan Guttmacher Institute Staff.
Lincoln, Rosemary, jt. auth. see Lincoln, J. D.
Lincoln, Rufus, ed. Papers of Captain Rufus Lincoln of Wareham, Mass. LC 74-140872. (Eyewitness Accounts of the American Revolution Ser., No. 1). 1971. reprint ed. 23.95 (0-405-01220-9) Ayer.
Lincoln, T. M. Cyclic GMP. (Molecular Biology Intelligence Unit Ser.). 119p. 1994. 89.95 (1-57059-146-6, LN9146) R G Landes.
Lincoln, Tim. Managing Information System for Profit. 1990. text ed. 65.50 (0-471-92554-3) Wiley.
Lincoln, Victoria. Teresa: A Woman: A Biography of Teresa of Avila. Rivers, Elias & De Nicolas, Antonio T., eds. LC 84-8561. (SUNY Series in Cultural Perspectives). 440p. 1985. 59.50 (0-87395-936-1); pap. 19.95 (0-87395-937-X) State U NY Pr.
Lincoln, W. Genealogy of the Waldo Family: A Record of the Descendants of Cornelius Waldo of Ipswich, Massachusetts, from 1647 to 1900, 2 vols. in 1. (Illus.). 1129p. 1989. reprint ed. lib. bdg. 177.00 (0-8328-1214-5); reprint ed. pap. 169.00 (0-8328-1215-3) Higginson Bk Co.
Lincoln, W. Bruce. The Great Reforms: Autocracy, Bureaucracy, & the Politics of Change in Imperial Russia. 293p. (C). 1990. text ed. 30.00 (0-87580-155-2); pap. text ed. 12.00 (0-87580-549-3) N Ill U Pr.
— In the Vanguard of Reform: Russia's Enlightened Bureaucrats, 1825-1861. LC 82-6509. (Illus.). 297p. (C). 1986. pap. 12.00 (0-87580-536-1) N Ill U Pr.
— In War's Dark Shadow: The Russians Before the Great War. (Illus.). 592p. 1994. pap. 16.95 (0-19-508953-7) OUP.
— Nicholas I: Emperor & Autocrat of All the Russias. 424p. 1989. reprint ed. pap. text ed. 12.50 (0-87580-548-5) N Ill U Pr.
— Passage Through Armageddon: The Russians in War & Revolution, 1914-1918. (Illus.). 656p. 1994. pap. 18.95 (0-19-508954-5) OUP.
— The Romanovs: Autocrats of All the Russias. LC 80-39902. (Illus.). 864p. 1983. pap. 18.95 (0-385-27908-6, Dial) Doubleday.
Lincoln, W. Bruce, et al. Moscow: Treasures & Traditions. LC 90-30271. (Illus.). 320p. 1990. 50.00 (0-295-96994-6, Smithsonian Traveling); pap. 24.95 (0-295-96995-4, Smithsonian Traveling) U of Wash Pr.
Lincoln, W. E. Lincoln: Some Descendants of Stephen Lincoln of Wymondham, England; Edmund Larkin of England; Thomas Oliver of Bristol, England. 322p. 1993. reprint ed. lib. bdg. 59.50 (0-8328-3703-2); reprint ed. pap. 49.50 (0-8328-3704-0) Higginson Bk Co.
Lincoln, Wanda. Write Through the Year. (Illus.). 112p. (J). (gr. 2-6). 1989. teacher ed. pap. 9.95 (0-912107-90-1, MM 1907) Monday Morning Bks.
Lincoln, Wanda, jt. auth. see Suid, Murray.
Lincoln, William. Alton Trials - of Winthrop S. Gilman, Enoch Long & Others. LC 70-125703. (American Journalists Ser.). 1978. reprint ed. 18.95 (0-405-01684-0) Ayer.
*__Lincoln, William A.__ Complete Manual of Wood Veneering. rev. ed. (Illus.). 400p. 1995. pap. 19.95 (0-941936-32-5) Linden Pub Fresno.
— The Marquetry Manual. LC 90-40525. (Illus.). 272p. (Orig.). 1990. reprint ed. pap. 19.95 (0-941936-19-8) Linden Pub Fresno.
— World Woods in Color. LC 90-23574. (Illus.). 320p. 1991. reprint ed. 49.95 (0-941936-20-1) Linden Pub Fresno.
Lincoln, William F., jt. ed. see Huelsberg, Nancy A.
Lincoln, Yvonna S. Organizational Theory & Inquiry. (Focus Editions Ser.: Vol. 75). 320p. 1985. 49.95 (0-8039-2494-1); pap. 24.95 (0-8039-2495-X) Sage.
Lincoln, Yvonna S. & Guba, Egon G. Naturalistic Inquiry. LC 84-26295. 416p. 1985. 39.95 (0-8039-2431-3) Sage.
Lincoln, Yvonna S., jt. ed. see Denzin, Norman K.
Lincoln, Yvonna S., jt. auth. see Guba, Econ G.

*__Lincourt, John.__ Ethics Without a Net. 128p. (C). 1994. pap. text ed., spiral bd. 10.48 (0-7872-0276-2) Kendall-Hunt.
*__Lind.__ Up from Conservatism. Date not set. 23.00 (0-02-874109-9) Free Pr.
Lind, jt. auth. see Dreke.
Lind, A. Forsikerungs Ordbok. 57p. (ENG & NOR.). 1989. 59.95 (0-8288-7876-5) Fr & Eur.
Lind, A. R. Lyric Poetry of the Italian Renaissance: An Anthology with Verse Translations. 1954. 59.50 (0-685-26673-7) Elliots Bks.
Lind, Alan. Black Bear Cub. LC 93-31130. (Smithsonian Wild Heritage Collection). (Illus.). 32p. (J). (gr. k-3). 1994. audio 16.95 (1-56899-050-2); audio 39.95 (1-56899-053-7); audio 25.95 (1-56899-052-9); audio write for info. (1-56899-051-0) Soundprints.
— Black Bear Cub. LC 93-31130. (Smithsonian Wild Heritage Collection). (Illus.). 32p. (J). (gr. k-3). 1994. 11.95 (1-56899-030-8) Soundprints.
— Black Bear Cub. (Smithsonian Wild Heritage Collection). (Illus.). 32p. (J). (gr. k-3). 1995. pap. 4.95 (1-56899-200-9); pap. 14.95 (1-56899-206-8) Soundprints.
Lind, Andrew W. Nanyang Perspective: Chinese Students in Multiracial Singapore. LC 74-75816. (Asian Studies at Hawaii: No. 13). 1974. pap. text ed. 10.00 (0-8248-0330-2) UH Pr.
Lind, Andrew W., jt. auth. see Coman, Katherine.
Lind, Andrew W., ed. see Conference on Race Relations in World Perspective, Honolulu, 1954.
Lind, Aulis O. Coastal Landforms of Cat Island, Bahamas: A Study of Holocene Accretionary Topography & Sea Level Change. LC 76-77892. (Research Papers Ser.: No. 122). 156p. 1969. pap. 12.00 (0-89065-029-2) U Chicago Comm Geo.
— Coastal Landforms of Cat Island, Bahamas: A Study of Holocene Accretionary Topography & Sea Level Change. LC 76-77892. (University of Chicago, Department of Geography, Research Paper Ser.: No. 122). (Illus.). 175p. reprint ed. pap. 49.90 (0-7837-0399-6, 2040720) Bks Demand.
*__Lind, Beth B.__ Multicultural Children's Literature: An Annotated Bibliography. 216p. 1996. lib. bdg. 37.50 (0-7864-0038-2) McFarland & Co.
Lind, Brenda. The Conservation Easement Stewardship Guide: Designing, Monitoring, & Enforcing Conservation Easements. (Illus.). 72p. (Orig.). 1991. pap. 16.00 (0-943915-07-4) Land Trust DC.
Lind, Carl S., jt. auth. see Lind, Marilyn.
Lind, Carla. Frank Lloyd Wright's Life & Homes. LC 94-7923. (Wright at a Glance Ser.). (Illus.). 60p. 1994. 9.95 (1-56640-996-9) Pomegranate Calif.
— Frank Lloyd Wright's Lost Buildings. LC 94-7935. (Wright at a Glance Ser.). (Illus.). 60p. 1994. 9.95 (1-56640-999-3) Pomegranate Calif.

An Asterisk (*) at the beginning of an entry indicates that the title is appearing in BIP for the first time.

— Frank Lloyd Wright's Prairie Houses. LC 94-7924. (Wright at a Glance Ser.). (Illus.). 60p. 1994. 9.95 (*1-56640-997-7*) Pomegranate Calif.

— Frank Lloyd Wright's Usonian Houses. LC 94-7934. (Wright at a Glance Ser.). (Illus.). 60p. 1994. 9.95 (*1-56640-998-5*) Pomegranate Calif.

— The Wright Style: Re-Creating the Spirit of Frank Lloyd Wright. (Illus.). 224p. 1992. 50.00 (*0-671-74959-5*) S&S Trade.

Lind Centennial Publication Committee Staff. From Sagebrush to Satellite: Facts & Folklore about Lind, Washington, 1888-1988. (Illus.). 176p. (Orig.). 1988. pap. 12.95 (*0-940151-08-1*) Statesman Exam.

Lind, Dave & Wright, Meg, illus. Building. (Visualized Songs Ser.). 20p. (J). (gr. 1-8). 1983. pap. 4.50 (*0-86508-135-2*) BCM Pubn.

***Lind, Douglas & Marcus, Brian.** An Introduction to Symbolic Dynamics & Coding. (Illus.). 484p. (C). 1995. write for info. (*0-521-55124-2*); pap. write for info. (*0-521-55900-6*) Cambridge U Pr.

Lind, Douglas A. & Mason, Robert D. Basic Statistics for Business & Economics. LC 93-3530. 528p. (C). 1993. text ed. 60.95 (*0-256-12222-9*) Irwin.

Lind, Douglas A., jt. auth. see Mason, Robert D.

Lind, E. A. & Tyler, T. R., eds. The Social Psychology of Procedural Justice. LC 87-38473. (Critical Issues in Social Justice Ser.). (Illus.). 280p. 1988. 37.50 (*0-306-42726-5*, Plenum Pr) Plenum.

Lind, Earl, et al. Autobiography of an Androgyne. LC 75-12333. (Homosexuality). 1975. reprint ed. 23.95 (*0-405-07400-X*) Ayer.

— The Female Impersonators: A Sequel to "the Autobiography of an Androgyne" LC 75-12334. (Homosexuality Ser.). (Illus.). 1975. reprint ed. 23.95 (*0-405-07358-5*) Ayer.

Lind, Edna M. & Brook, Alan J. Desmids of the English Lake District. 1980. 39.00 (*0-686-75592-8*) St Mut.

Lind, Edna M. & Morrison, M. E. S. East African Vegetation. LC 73-85206. 274p. reprint ed. pap. 78.10 (*0-317-28443-6*, 2051260) Bks Demand.

Lind, Ekard. Exercises for Musicians: How to Control & Prevent Postural Stress. Plucked String, Inc. Staff, ed. Harris, Keith, tr. LC 87-60423. (Illus.). 68p. (Orig.). 1987. pap. 9.95 (*0-9614120-1-1*) Plucked.

Lind, Ernie. The Complete Book of Trick & Fancy Shooting. 1977. pap. 3.95 (*0-8065-0588-5*, Citadel Pr) Carol Pub Group.

Lind, Georg, et al. Moral Development & Social Environment: Studies in the Philosophy & Psychology of Moral Judgement & Education. Wakenhut, Roland & Hartman, Hans, eds. 314p. 1985. 32.95 (*0-913750-27-1*) Transaction Pubs.

Lind, Henry C., ed. The Long Road for Home: The Civil War Experiences of Four Farmboy Soldiers of the Twenty-Seventh Massachusetts Regiment of Volunteer Infantry as Told by Their Personal Correspondence, 1861-1864. LC 91-58579. (Illus.). 216p. (C). 1992. 36.50 (*0-8386-3464-8*) Fairleigh Dickinson.

Lind, Hope K. Apart & Together: Mennonites in Oregon & Neighboring States, 1876-1976. (Studies in Anabaptist & Mennonite History). (Illus.). 416p. 1990. 26.95 (*0-8361-3106-1*) Herald Pr.

Lind, J., et al, eds. Children & Parents in Hospitals. (Journal: Pediatrician: Vol. 9, No. 3-4). (Illus.). 120p. 1980. pap. 16.00 (*3-8055-1476-X*) S Karger.

Lind, Jakov. The Stove. LC 82-10824. 77p. 1983. pap. 7.95 (*0-935296-27-1*) Sheep Meadow.

Lind, Jane. Kids' Northwoods Activity Book with Glossary. (Illus.). 26p. (Orig.). 1987. pap. 4.95 (*0-910259-06-2*) Womens Times.

Lind, Jane, ed. see Holte, Ingeborg.

Lind, Jennifer, ed. see Cornesky, Robert A.

Lind, Judi. Heartsong. 224p. (Orig.). 1992. pap. 2.95 (*1-56597-016-0*, Kismet) Meteor Pub.

— Quinn's Inheritance. 224p. (Orig.). 1991. pap. 2.75 (*1-878702-38-6*, Kismet) Meteor Pub.

— Veil of Fear. (Intrigue Ser.). 1995. pap. 3.50 (*0-373-22310-2*, 1-22310-6) Harlequin Bks.

— Without a Past. (Intrigue Ser.). 1994. mass mkt. 2.99 (*0-373-22260-2*, 1-22260-3) Harlequin Bks.

Lind, Karen, jt. auth. see Charlesworth, Rosalind.

Lind, Karen K. Exploring Science in Early Childhood: A Developmental Approach. 352p. 1991. teacher ed 8.00 (*0-8273-4723-5*); pap. text ed. 25.95 (*0-8273-4722-7*) Delmar.

Lind, Karen K., ed. Water, Stones, & Fossil Bones. (CESI Sourcebook Ser.: Vol. VI). (Illus.). 140p. 1991. pap. text ed. 18.50 (*0-87355-101-X*) Natl Sci Tchrs.

***Lind, Kate.** From Hazelbrush to Cornfields: Amish Mennonites of Iowa, 1846-1946. (Illus.). 765p. 1994. 40.00 (*0-9636151-3-0*) St Andrews IA.

Lind-Kyle, Patricia. When Sleeping Beauty Wakes Up: A Woman's Tale of the Healing of the Immune System & the Awakening of the Feminine. LC 92-93335. 256p. 1992. pap. 14.95 (*0-9632310-1-4*) Swan Raven.

Lind, L. R. Berengario da Carpi, on Fracture of the Skull or Cranium. LC 90-55267. (Transactions Ser.: Vol. 80, Pt. 4). (Illus.). 164p. (C). 1990. pap. 20.00 (*0-87169-804-8*, T804-LIL) Am Philos.

— An Epitaph Years After. LC 89-81153. 75p. 1990. 10.00 (*0-9624631-0-8*) Bennett & Kitchel.

— Gabriele Zerbi, Gerontocomia: On the Care of the Aged & Maximianus, Elegies on Old Age & Love. LC 87-72873. (Memoirs Ser.: Vol. 182). (Illus.). 346p. (C). 1988. 20.00 (*0-87169-182-5*, M182-LIL) Am Philos.

— The Letters of Giovanni Garzoni: Bolognese Humanist & Physician (1419-1505) (American Philological Association Philological Monographs). 600p. 1992. 69.95 (*1-55540-111-2*, 400033) Scholars Pr GA.

Lind, L. R., ed. Twentieth Century Italian Poetry: A Bilingual Anthology. LC 73-11343. (Library of Liberal Arts). 432p. 1974. pap. 10.50 (*0-672-61220-8*, Bobbs) Macmillan.

Lind, L. R., tr. see Vergil.

Lind, Laura J., jt. auth. see Haring, Joen I.

Lind, Levi R., ed. Latin Poetry in Verse Translation. LC 57-59176. (YA). (gr. 9 up). 1957. pap. 9.96 (*0-395-05118-5*, RivEd) HM.

Lind, Lew. Battle of the Wine Dark Sea: The Aegean Sea Campaign, 1940-45. (Illus.). 192p. 1994. 29.95 (*0-86417-562-0*, Pub. by Kangaroo Pr AT) Seven Hills Bk.

Lind, Loren J. The Learning Machine: A Hard Look at Toronto Schools. 228p. (Orig.). 1974. pap. 9.95 (*0-88784-646-7*, Pub. by Hse of Anansi Pr CN) Genl Dist Srvs.

Lind, Louise. Southeast Asians in Rhode Island: The New Americans. (Rhode Island Ethnic Heritage Pamphlet Ser.). (Illus.). (Orig.). 1989. pap. 4.75 (*0-917012-86-0*) RI Pubns Soc.

— William Blackstone: Sage of the Wilderness. (Illus.). 108p. (Orig.). 1993. pap. text ed. 11.00 (*1-55613-910-1*) Heritage Bk.

Lind, Marilyn. Continuing Your Genealogical Research in Minnesota. LC 85-80942. (Illus.). 161p. 1986. pap. text ed. 14.50 (*0-937463-09-4*) Linden Tree.

— Immigration, Migration & Settlement in the United States: A Genealogical Guidebook. LC 85-809040. (Illus.). 144p. (Orig.). (C). 1985. pap. 12.95 (*0-937463-08-6*) Linden Tree.

— Printing & Publishing Your Family History. LC 86-8100. (Illus.). 63p. (Orig.). 1986. pap. text ed. 7.50 (*0-937463-10-8*) Linden Tree.

— Researching & Finding Your German Heritage. 2nd enl. rev. ed. LC 90-62026. (Illus.). 150p. (Orig.). 1991. reprint ed. pap. 13.25 (*0-937463-12-4*) Linden Tree.

— Researching Your Family & Heritage. LC 90-62025. (Illus.). 176p. (Orig.). (C). 1991. pap. 14.50 (*0-937463-13-2*) Linden Tree.

— Supplement to Using Maps & Aerial Photography in Your Genealogical Research. LC 85-80941. (Illus.). 43p. (Orig.). 1985. pap. text ed. 5.50 (*0-937463-07-8*) Linden Tree.

— Thiem, Christoph & August-A Dream & a Promise. LC 81-90330. (Illus.). 187p. (Orig.). 1981. text ed. 35.00 (*0-937463-01-9*); pap. text ed. 30.00 (*0-937463-02-7*) Linden Tree.

— Using Maps & Aerial Photography in Your Genealogical Research. LC 84-81793. (Illus.). 137p. 1984. pap. text ed. 9.95 (*0-937463-05-1*) Linden Tree.

— Using Maps & Aerial Photography in Your Genealogical Research-With Supplement on Foreign Aerial Photography. rev. ed. LC 85-80941. (Illus.). 217p. (Orig.). 1985. pap. text ed. 15.50 (*0-937463-06-X*) Linden Tree.

— Volkszahlung: Birth Census 1856-1878, Evangelical Kirchengemeinde Kreis Wiristz, Provinz Posen German Kaiser Reich. LC 94-79225. (Illus.). 103p. (Orig.). 1995. pap. 14.95 (*0-937463-14-0*) Linden Tree.

Lind, Marilyn & Lind, Carl S. Looking Backward to Sweden: A Genealogical Research Book, & the Lind-Bure Family, 1000-1986. LC 86-81744. (Illus.). 154p. (Orig.). 1986. pap. text ed. 14.50 (*0-937463-11-6*) Linden Tree.

Lind, Mary A. Asia: A Christian Perspective. 1994. reprint ed. 8.99 (*0-9615534-4-8*) YWAM Pub.

Lind, Mary Ann. The Compassionate Memsahibs: Welfare Activities of British Women in India, 1900-1947. LC 87-24953. (Contributions in Woman Studies). 144p. 1988. text ed. 45.00 (*0-313-26059-1*, LRJ/, Greenwood Pr) Greenwood.

Lind, MaryAnn. From Nirvana to the New Age. LC 90-46026. 1991. pap. 7.99 (*0-8007-5381-X*) Revell.

Lind, Mecka. Cackle Goes A-Courting. (J). (ps-3). 1992. 18.95 (*0-87614-715-5*, Carolrhoda) Lerner Group.

Lind, Michael. The Next American Nation: The New Nationalism and the Fourth American Revolution. 350p. 1995. 25.00 (*0-02-919103-3*) Free Pr.

— Postclassic & Early Colonial Mixtec Houses in the Nochixtlan Valley, Oaxaca, Mexico. (Publications in Anthropology: No. 23). 79p. 1979. pap. 6.25 (*0-935462-12-0*) Vanderbilt Pubns.

— The Sociocultural Dimensions of Mixtec Ceramics. Spores, Ronald & McNutt, Paula M., eds. (Publications in Anthropology: No. 33). (Illus.). 120p. (Orig.). 1987. pap. text ed. 13.85 (*0-935462-24-4*) Vanderbilt Pubns.

Lind, Millard C. Monotheism, Power & Justice: Collected Old Testament Essays. (Text-Reader Ser.: No. 3). 273p. (Orig.). 1990. pap. text ed. 10.00 (*0-936273-16-X*) Inst Mennonite.

— Yahweh Is a Warrior. LC 80-16038. (Christian Peace Shelf Ser.). 248p. 1980. pap. 12.95x (*0-8361-1233-4*) Herald Pr.

Lind, N. C., jt. ed. see Eggwertz, Sigge.

Lind, Nancy S. & Elder, Ann, eds. The Small City & Regional Community, Vol. 8: Proceedings of the 1988 Conference. vii, 295p. 1988. pap. text ed. 19.00 (*0-932310-10-9*, 79-644450) U of Wis-Stevens Point.

Lind, O. T., ed. Reservoir Eutrophication. (Water Science & Technology Ser.: Vol. 28). 112p. 1993. pap. 110.00 (*0-08-042354-X*, Pergamon Pr) Elsevier.

Lind, Per. Computerization in Developing Countries: Model & Reality. 160p. (C). 1991. text ed. 75.00 (*0-415-03818-9*, A5215) Routledge.

Lind, Richard E., jt. auth. see Hall, Calvin S.

Lind, Richard W., jt. auth. see Hinkel, Arthur R.

Lind, Robert C., et al. Discounting for Time & Risk in Energy Policy. 468p. 1982. 42.50 (*0-8018-2709-4*) Resources Future.

Lind, Robert W. Brother Van: Montana Pioneer Circuit Rider. (Illus.). 208p. (Orig.). 1992. pap. 12.95 (*1-56044-145-3*) Falcon Pr MT.

Lind, Robin. Pedaling Northwards: A Father & Son's Bicycle Adventure from Virginia to Canada. 108p. 1993. pap. 8.95 (*0-9639531-0-9*) Hope Springs.

Lind, Roger M., jt. auth. see Tropman, John E.

Lind, Stephen, et al. Fundamentals of Partnership Taxation: Cases & Materials. 4th ed. (University Casebook Ser.). 504p. 1994. text ed. 39.00 (*1-56662-169-0*) Foundation Pr.

***Lind, Stephen A. & Schwarz, Stephen.** Fundamentals of Partnership Taxation: Cases & Materials. 4th ed. Lathrope, Daniel J. & Rosenberg, Joshua D., eds. (University Casebook Ser.). 232p. 1994. teacher ed, pap. text ed. write for info. (*1-56662-196-8*) Foundation Pr.

Lind, Stephen A., jt. auth. see Freeland, James J.

Lind, Stephen A., jt. auth. see Hudson, David M.

Lind, Stephen A., et al. Cases & Materials on Fundamentals of Partnership Taxation: Teacher's Manual. 3rd ed. (University Casebook Ser.). 271p. 1991. pap. text ed. write for info. (*0-88277-978-8*) Foundation Pr.

— Fundamentals of Corporate Taxation: Cases & Materials, 1994 Supplement. 3rd ed. (University Casebook Ser.). 43p. 1994. pap. text ed. 4.50 (*1-56662-202-6*) Foundation Pr.

— Fundamentals of Corporate Taxation, Cases & Materials On. 3rd ed. (University Casebook Ser.). 809p. 1991. text ed. 39.25 (*0-88277-877-3*) Foundation Pr.

— Fundamentals of Corporate Taxation, Teacher's Manual to Accompany Cases & Materials On. 3rd ed. (University Casebook Ser.). 297p. 1991. pap. text ed. write for info. (*0-88277-905-2*) Foundation Pr.

— Fundamentals of Corporate Taxation, 1993 Supplement to Cases & Materials On. 3rd ed. (University Casebook Ser.). 36p. 1993. pap. text ed. 4.50 (*1-56662-105-4*) Foundation Pr.

— Fundamentals of Partnership Taxation: Cases & Materials. 3rd ed. (University Casebook Ser.). 483p. (C). 1991. text ed. 36.25 (*0-88277-954-0*) Foundation Pr.

— Fundamentals of Partnerships Taxation, 1993 Supplement to Cases & Materials. 3rd ed. (University Casebook Ser.). 73p. 1993. pap. text ed. 5.50 (*1-56662-109-7*) Foundation Pr.

Lind, T. & Mackay, G. A. Norwegian Oil Policies. 158p. reprint ed. pap. 45.10 (*0-7837-1170-0*, 2041699) Bks Demand.

Lind, T., jt. ed. see Huisjes, H. J.

Lind, Vibeke. Knitting in the Nordic Tradition. Jensen, Annette A., tr. LC 84-81825. (Illus.). 128p. 1992. 24.95 (*0-937274-15-1*) Lark Books.

Lind, William S. Maneuver Warfare Handbook. (Replica Edition Ser.). 133p. (C). 1985. pap. text ed. 31.95 (*0-86531-862-X*) Westview.

Linda, C. Majka, jt. ed. see Voydanoff, Patricia.

Linda, Mary F., ed. see Zabel, Craig.

***Linda, Parry, ed.** Bedtime Prayers. LC 94-3642. (Little Prayers Ser.). (Illus.). (J). 1995. 3.99 (*0-8499-1148-6*) Word Pub.

Lindabury, Richard V. Study of Patriotism in the Elizabethan Drama. LC 68-54170. (Studies in Drama: No. 39). 1969. reprint ed. lib. bdg. 75.00 (*0-8383-0584-9*) M S G Haskell Hse.

Lindabury, Tryon. One Magnificent Moment. 140p. (Orig.). 1991. pap. 6.95 (*1-879366-09-6*) Hearthstone OK.

Lindahl, Anders. Information Through Sherds: A Case Study of the Early Glazed Earthenware from Dalby Scania. (Illus.). xvi, 200p. (Orig.). 1987. pap. 93.00x (*91-7810-717-2*) Coronet Bks.

Lindahl, Barry A., jt. auth. see Lee, J. D.

Lindahl, Carl. Earnest Games: Folkloric Patterns in the Canterbury Tales. LC 86-45469. (Illus.). 208p. 1987. pap. 10.95 (*0-253-20550-6*, MB-550) Ind U Pr.

Lindahl, Carl, jt. ed. see Burlakoff, Nikolai.

Lindahl, Erik R. Studies in the Theory of Money & Capital. LC 70-117915. (Reprints of Economic Classics Ser.). (Illus.). 391p. 1970. reprint ed. 39.50 (*0-678-00655-5*) Kelley.

Lindahl, Ingemar B. The Soviet Union & the Nordic Nuclear-Weapons-Free-Zone Proposal. LC 87-13133. 200p. 1988. text ed. 55.00 (*0-312-01187-3*) St Martin.

Lindahl, Ingemar B., jt. ed. see Nordenfelt, Lennart.

Lindahl, Judy. Decorating with Fabric: An Idea Book. rev. ed. 128p. 1980. pap. 6.95 (*0-9603032-1-9*) Lindahl.

— Energy Saving Decorating. rev. ed. LC 81-90134. (Illus.). 128p. (Orig.). 1981. pap. 6.95 (*0-9603032-3-5*) Lindahl.

— The Shade Book. rev. ed. (Illus.). 152p. pap. 9.95 (*0-9603032-2-7*) Lindahl.

Lindahl, Lars. Position & Change. Needham, Paul, tr. (Synthese Library: No. 112). 1977. lib. bdg. 112.50 (*90-277-0787-1*) Kluwer Ac.

Lindahl, Lars-Ake & Poulsen, F., eds. Thin Sets in Harmonic Analysis: Seminars Held at Institute Mittag-Leffler, 1969-70. LC 79-163310. (Lecture Notes in Pure & Applied Mathematics Ser.: No. 2). 197p. reprint ed. pap. 56.20 (*0-7837-3419-0*, 2052465) Bks Demand.

***Lindahl, Laurel.** Twin Cities' Best Seats. 80p. (Orig.). 1994. pap. text ed. 14.95 (*0-9643511-2-9*) MN Monthly.

Lindahl, Wesley E. Strategic Planning for Fund Raising: How to Bring in More Money Using Strategic Resource Allocation. LC 92-25900. (Nonprofit Sector-Public Administration Ser.). 152p. 1992. 37.95 (*1-55542-495-3*) Jossey-Bass.

Lindahn, Ronald P. The Human Being Handbook. 200p. 1991. write for info. (*1-877652-08-3*) Valet Pub.

Lindall, Robert J., et al. Minnesota Condemnation Law. 450p. 1992. ring bd. 115.00 (*0-86678-646-5*) Michie Butterworth.

— Minnesota Condemnation Law. suppl. ed. 450p. 1992. 35.00 (*0-685-74268-7*) Butterworth Legal Pubs.

Lindamood, Phyllis. Drawing with Language: Using Verbalizing & Visualizing to Solve Visual-Motor Problems. (Illus.). 200p. 1993. pap. 19.00 (*0-945856-04-0*) Nancibell Inc.

Lindamood, Phyllis, jt. auth. see Bell, Nanci.

Lindamood, Suzanne & Hanna, Sherman D. Housing, Society & Consumers: An Introduction. (Illus.). 498p. 1979. text ed. 55.25 (*0-8299-0230-9*) West Pub.

***Lindars, Barnabas.** Judges First-Fifth. Mayes, A. D., ed. 352p. 1994. text ed. 49.95 (*0-567-09696-3*, Pub. by T & T Clark UK) Bks Intl VA.

— NCBC John. 1981. pap. 22.99 (*0-8028-1864-1*) Eerdmans.

— Theology of the Letter to Hebrews. (New Testament Theology Ser.). 1991. pap. 15.95 (*0-521-35748-9*) Cambridge U Pr.

— Theology of the Letter to the Hebrews. (New Testament Theology Ser.). 176p. (C). 1991. 44.95 (*0-521-35487-0*) Cambridge U Pr.

Lindau, Buff, ed. see Casey, Eileen L.

Lindau, Gustav. Die Flechten. vii, 252p. 1971. reprint ed. 59.00 (*3-87429-023-9*) Koeltz Sci Bks.

Lindau, Gustav, ed. Kryptogamenflora Fuer Anfaenger, Bande 1-6. 1971. reprint ed. 539.00 (*3-87429-030-1*) Koeltz Sci Bks.

— Kryptogamenflora Fuer Anfaenger, Bande 1: Die Hoeheren Pilze. xii, 497p. 1971. reprint ed. lib. bdg. 110.00 (*3-87429-021-2*) Koeltz Sci Bks.

— Kryptogamenflora Fuer Anfaenger, Bande 5: Die Laubmoose. 1971. reprint ed. 59.00 (*3-87429-026-3*) Koeltz Sci Bks.

— Kryptogamenflora Fuer Anfaenger, Bande 6: Die Torf- und Lebermoose. 1971. reprint ed. 79.00 (*3-87429-027-1*) Koeltz Sci Bks.

Lindau, Joan. Letting in the Night. LC 89-1331. 180p. (Orig.). 1989. lib. bdg. 18.95 (*0-932379-60-5*); pap. 8.95 (*0-932379-59-1*) Firebrand Bks.

***Lindauer, David L. & Nunberg, Barbara, eds.** Rehabilitating Government: Pay & Employment Reform in Africa. LC 94-26924. (World Bank Regional & Sectoral Studies). 1994. write for info. (*0-8213-3000-4*) World Bank.

Lindauer, David L. & Roemer, Michael. Development in Asia & Africa: Legacies & Opportunities. LC 94-7211. 1994. pap. 19.95 (*1-55815-320-9*) ICS Pr.

Lindauer, Harry, tr. see Lochner, R. K.

***Lindauer, Lois L. & Sampson, Sally.** The Diet Workshop's Recipes for Healthy Living. LC 94-26401. 1995. 25.00 (*0-385-47251-X*) Doubleday.

Lindauer, M., jt. ed. see Wohlfarth-Bottermann, K. E.

Lindauer, M. S. Perceptual Psychology. 1978. text ed. 23.50 (*0-685-04011-9*, Pergamon Pr); pap. text ed. 17.00 (*0-685-04012-7*, Pergamon Pr) Elsevier.

Lindauer, Martin. Communication among Social Bees. LC 61-5579. (Harvard Bks. in Biology: No. 2). (Illus.). 152p. reprint ed. pap. 44.20 (*0-7837-1714-8*, 2057243) Bks Demand.

Lindauer, Martin S. The Psychological Study of Literature: Limitations, Possibilities & Accomplishments. LC 73-80499. 250p. 1974. 33.95 (*0-911012-74-5*) Nelson-Hall.

Lindauer, Steve. Secrets of a Satisfying Lovelife. LC 91-73491. 1991. 17.95 (*0-9630158-1-8*); pap. 14.95 (*0-9630158-2-6*) Baker-Hill.

— Secrets of a Satisfying Lovelife. 2nd rev. ed. LC 91-73491. 196p. 1992. pap. 9.95 (*0-9630158-3-4*) Baker-Hill.

Lindauer, Thea, tr. see Lochner, R. K.

Lindbeck, A. Nobel Lectures in Economic Sciences 1969-1980. 500p. 1992. text ed. 86.00 (*981-02-0833-2*); pap. text ed. 46.00 (*981-02-0834-0*) World Scientific Pub.

Lindbeck, A., ed. Inflation & Employment in Open Economics: Essays by Members of the Institute for International Economic Studies, Univ. of Stockholm, Sweden. (Studies in International Economics: Vol. 5). 1979. 97.50 (*0-444-85227-1*, North Holland) Elsevier.

Lindbeck, Assar. The Collected Essays of Assar Lindbeck, 2 vols. (Economists of the Twentieth Century Ser.). 600p. 1993. Vol. I: Macroeconomics & Economic Policy. 67.95 (*1-85278-720-1*, Pub. by E Elgar Pub UK) Ashgate Pub Co.

— The Collected Essays of Assar Lindbeck, 2 vols. (Economists of the Twentieth Century Ser.). 600p. 1993. Vol. II: The Welfare State. 64.95 (*1-85278-721-X*, Pub. by E Elgar Pub UK) Ashgate Pub Co.

— Unemployment & Macroeconomics. LC 92-29465. (Ohlin Lectures: Vol. 3). (Illus.). 120p. 1993. 25.00 (*0-262-12175-1*) MIT Pr.

Lindbeck, Assar & Snower, Dennis J. The Insider-Outsider Theory of Employment & Unemployment. 304p. 1990. reprint ed. pap. 16.95 (*0-262-62074-X*) MIT Pr.

Lindbeck, Assar, et al. Turning Sweden Around. (Illus.). 180p. 1994. 32.50 (*0-262-12181-6*) MIT Pr.

Lindbeck, George A. Infallibility. (Pere Marquette Lectures). 1972. 10.00 (*0-87462-504-1*) Marquette.

— The Nature of Doctrine: Religion & Theology in a Postliberal Age. LC 83-27332. 142p. 1984. pap. 13.99 (*0-664-24618-4*, Westminster) Westminster John Knox.

Lindbeck, John R. Metric Practices in Drafting. 1979. pap. 7.92 (*0-02-665240-4*) Bennett IL.

Lindbeck, John R. & Kruppa. Basic Manufacturing. (gr. 9-12). 1984. text ed. 12.80 (*0-02-662590-3*) Bennett IL.

Lindbeck, John R. & Wygant, Robert M. Product Design & Manufacture. LC 94-20422. 1994. text ed. 67.00 (*0-13-034257-2*) P-H.

Lindbeck, John R., jt. auth. see Feirer, John L.

Lindbeck, John R., et al. Basic Crafts. (gr. 7-12). 1979. text ed. 18.60 (*0-02-662430-3*); student ed 5.20 (*0-02-662440-0*) Bennett IL.

— Manufacturing Technology. 640p. 1989. text ed. 83.00 (*0-13-487315-7*) P-H.

Lindbeck, Susan, jt. auth. see Amoriell, Amelia.

An Asterisk (*) at the beginning of an entry indicates that the title is appearing in BIP for the first time.

Lindberg. Digital Broadband Networks & Services. 1994. text ed. 50.00 (0-07-037936-X) McGraw.

Lindberg, Alf, jt. ed. see Garegg, Per.

Lindberg, Anne. The Worry Week. (J). (gr. 3-7). 1988. pap. 2.95 (0-380-70394-7, Camelot) Avon.

Lindberg, Barbro. Understanding Rett Syndrome: A Practical Guide for Parents, Teachers & Therapists. LC 90-34409. (Illus.). 184p. 1992. text ed. 26.00 (0-88937-033-8) Hogrefe & Huber Pubs.

Lindberg, Becky T. Chelsea Martin Turns Green. Tucker, Kathy, ed. LC 92-31613. (Illus.). 144p. (J). (gr. 2-4). 1993. lib. bdg. 11.95 (0-8075-1134-X) A Whitman.

— Speak up, Chelsea Martin! Tucker, Kathleen, ed. LC 91-313. (Illus.). 128p. (J). (gr. 2-4). 1991. 11.95 (0-8075-7552-6) A Whitman.

— Thomas Tuttle Just in Time. LC 93-38606. (Illus.). (J). (gr. 4-7). 1994. 11.95 (0-8075-7898-3) A Whitman.

Lindberg, Bertil C. Troubleshooting Communications Facilities. 1990. text ed. 89.95 (0-471-61286-3) Wiley.

Lindberg, Carter. Beyond Charity: Reformation Initiatives for the Poor. LC 92-29963. 208p. 1993. pap. 15.00 (0-8006-2569-2, 1-2569) Augsburg Fortress.

— The European Reformations. (Illus.). 400p. (C). 1996. write for info. (1-55786-574-4); pap. write for info. (1-55786-575-2) Blackwell Pubs.

— The Third Reformation: Charismatic Movements & the Lutheran Tradition. LC 83-11371. x, 346p. 1983. 24.95 (0-86554-075-6, MUP/H83) Mercer Univ Pr.

Lindberg, Carter, ed. Piety, Politics, & Ethics: Reformation Studies in Honor of George Wolfgang Forell. (Sixteenth Century Essays & Studies: Vol. III). (Illus.). 200p. 1984. 35.00 (0-940474-03-4) Sixteenth Cent.

Lindberg, D. A., ed. see O'Moore, R. R., et al.

Lindberg, David C. The Beginnings of Western Science: The European Scientific Tradition in Philosophical, Religious, & Institutional Context, 600 B. C. to A. D. 1450. LC 91-37741. (Illus.). 424p. 1992. lib. bdg. 57.00 (0-226-48230-8); pap. text ed. 19.95 (0-226-48231-6) U Ch Pr.

— Theories of Vision from Al-Kindi to Kepler. LC 75-19504. 324p. 1981. pap. text ed. 10.00 (0-226-48235-9) U Ch Pr.

Lindberg, David C., ed. John Pecham: Tractatus De Perspectiva. (Text Ser.). 1972. 13.00 (0-686-11561-9) Franciscan Inst.

— Science in the Middle Ages. LC 78-5367. (Chicago History of Science & Medicine Ser.). (Illus.). 1980. pap. text ed. 20.00 (0-226-48233-2, P870) U Ch Pr.

Lindberg, David C. & Numbers, Ronald L., eds. God & Nature: Historical Essays on the Encounter Between Christianity & Science. 1986. pap. 20.00 (0-520-05692-2) U CA Pr.

— God & Nature: Historical Essays on the Encounter Between Christianity & Science. LC 85-7548. (Illus.). 528p. reprint ed. pap. 150.50 (0-7837-4751-9, 2044498) Bks Demand.

Lindberg, David C. & Westman, Robert S., eds. Reappraisals of the Scientific Revolution. (Illus.). 530p. (C). 1990. 74.95 (0-521-34262-7); pap. 24.95 (0-521-34804-8) Cambridge U Pr.

Lindberg, David C., ed. see Pecham, John.

Lindberg, David R. Acmaeidae: Invertebrates of the San Francisco Bay Estuary System, Vol. 2. Lee, Welton L., ed. (Illus.). 1981. text ed. 12.50 (0-910286-72-8) Boxwood.

Lindberg, David S., ed. see Williams, Margaret R.

Lindberg, Duane R. Men of the Cloth & the Social-Cultural Fabric of the Norwegian Ethnic Community in North Dakota. Cordasco, Francesco, ed. LC 80-877. (American Ethnic Groups Ser.). 1981. lib. bdg. 42.95 (0-405-13438-X) Ayer.

Lindberg, G. U. Multilingual Dictionary of Names of Marine Food-Dishes of World Fauna. 562p. 1980. 79.00 (0-686-44732-8, Pub. by Collets UK) Pro-Am Music.

Lindberg, G. U. & Krasykova, Z. V., eds. Fishes of the Sea of Japan & the Adjacent Areas of the Sea of Okhotsk & the Yellow Sea, Pt. 4: Gobiodei (CXLV. Fam. Anarhichadidae - CLXXV. Fam. Periophthalmidae) (Russian Translation Ser.: No. 71). (Illus.). 628p. (C). 1989. 110.00 (90-6191-415-9, Pub. by A A Balkema NE) Ashgate Pub Co.

Lindberg, H. E. & Florence, A. L. Dynamic Pulse Buckling: Theory & Experiment. (C). 1987. lib. bdg. 144.00 (90-247-3566-1) Kluwer Ac.

***Lindberg, Jana H.** Cross Stitch Animals: More Than Sixty Captivating Designs from the World of Nature. (Illus.). 128p. 1995. 24.95 (0-304-34296-3, Pub. by Cassell UK) Sterling.

— Flowers in Cross Stitch. (Illus.). 128p. 1992. 27.95 (0-304-34129-0, Pub. by Cassell UK) Sterling.

— Flowers in Cross Stitch: More Than Eighty Beautiful Floral Charted Designs. (Illus.). 128p. (Orig.). 1994. pap. 14.95 (0-304-34359-5, Pub. by Cassell UK) Sterling.

Lindberg, Janice B., et al. Introduction to Nursing: Concepts, Issues, & Opportunities. 2nd ed. LC 93-25212. (Illus.). 464p. (C). 1994. pap. text ed. 26.95 (0-397-54986-5, Lippincott Nursing) Lippincott.

Lindberg, John. Foundations of Social Survival. LC 72-9590. 260p. 1973. reprint ed. text ed. 59.75 (0-8371-6586-5, LIFS, Greenwood Pr) Greenwood.

Lindberg, John D., ed. see Weise, Christian.

Lindberg, Kathryne V. Reading Pound Reading: Modernism after Nietzsche. 288p. 1987. 48.00 (0-19-504165-8) OUP.

***Lindberg, Kathryne V. & Kronick, Joseph G., eds.** America's Modernisms: Revaluing the Canon Essays in Honor of Joseph N. Riddel. (Horizons in Theory & American Culture Ser.). 256p. (C). 1995. text ed. 35.00 (0-8071-2018-9) La State U Pr.

Lindberg, Kelley. Netware for Macintosh User's Guide. (Illus.). 400p. (Orig.). 1990. pap. 29.95 (1-55851-126-1) M&T Bks.

Lindberg, Kelley J. Novell's Guide to Managing Small NetWare Networks. LC 93-83421. 311p. 1993. 24.99 (0-7821-1238-2) Sybex.

— Novell's 3.12 Administrator's Handbook. LC 94-69701. 350p. 1994. 24.99 (0-7821-1635-3) Sybex.

Lindberg, Kreg. Policies for Maximizing Nature Tourism's Ecological & Economic Benefits. 30p. 1991. Large format. pap. 12.95 (0-915825-67-8, LIEPP) World Resources Inst.

Lindberg, Kreg & Hawkins, Donald E., eds. Ecotourism: A Guide for Planners & Managers. LC 93-70175. (Illus.). 176p. (Orig.). 1993. pap. 14.95 (0-9636331-0-4) Ecotourism Soc.

***Lindberg, Kreg, et al.** Attitudes, Concerns, & Priorities of Oregon Coast Residents Regarding Tourism & Economic Development: Results from Surveys of Residents in Eight Communities. 48p. 1994. pap. 6.00 (1-881826-04-X) OR Sea Grant.

Lindberg, Leon N. The Political Dynamics of European Economic Integration. LC 63-14129. 120p. reprint ed. pap. 30.00 (0-318-35030-0, 2030976) Bks Demand.

Lindberg, Leon N. & Maier, Charles S., eds. The Politics of Inflation & Economic Stagnation. LC 84-23263. 612p. 1985. 39.95 (0-8157-5264-4); pap. 18.95 (0-8157-5263-6) Brookings.

Lindberg, Leon N. & Scheingold, Stuart A., eds. Regional Integration: Theory & Research. LC 77-139717. (Illus.). 439p. 1971. pap. 15.95 (0-674-75327-5) HUP.

Lindberg, Lois, et al, eds. Alba's Medical Technology Board Exam Review, 1991, Vol. I. 11th rev. ed. 747p. 1991. text ed. 39.00 (0-910224-13-7) Berkeley Sci.

— Alba's Medical Technology Board Examination Review, Vol. 2: Questions & Answers. 7th rev. ed. (Illus.). 550p. 1993. spiral bd. 36.00 (0-910224-14-5) Berkeley Sci.

Lindberg Press Staff. Butterfly Charted Designs. (Illus.). 48p. (Orig.). 1988. pap. 2.95 (0-486-25639-1) Dover.

— Charted Bird Designs. 1989. pap. 2.95 (0-486-26138-7) Dover.

— Charted Christmas Designs for Counted Cross-Stitch & Other Needlecrafts: From the Archives of the Lindberg Press. (Illus.). 42p. (Orig.). 1982. pap. 2.95 (0-486-24356-7) Dover.

— Knitting for Babies. 1980. pap. 3.95 (0-486-23953-5) Dover.

— Scandinavian Charted Designs. (Illus.). 1979. pap. 2.50 (0-486-23787-7) Dover.

Lindberg Press Staff, ed. Charted Designs for the Kitchen. 48p. (Orig.). 1987. pap. 2.95 (0-486-25496-8) Dover.

— Hearts & Flowers Charted Designs. 48p. (Orig.). 1986. pap. 2.95 (0-486-25111-X) Dover.

— Roses Charted Designs. (Illus.). 32p. (Orig.). 1987. pap. 3.50 (0-486-25523-9) Dover.

— Zodiac Charted Designs for Cross-Stitch Needlepoint & Other Techniques. 48p. 1985. pap. 2.95 (0-486-24932-8) Dover.

Lindberg, R. A. & Braton, N. R. Welding & Other Joining Processes. 1985. 30.00 (0-9606344-6-0) Blitz Pub Co.

***Lindberg, Richard.** Chicago by Gaslight: A History of Chicago's Underworld: 1880-1920. (Illus.). 280p. 1995. pap. 14.00 (0-89733-421-3) Academy Chi Pubs.

— Stealing First in a Two-Team Town: The White Sox from Comiskey to Reinsdorf. (Illus.). 275p. 1994. 19.95 (0-915611-93-7) Sagamore Pub.

Lindberg, Richard C. To Serve & Collect: Chicago Politics & Police Corruption from the Lager Beer Riot to the Summerdale Scandal. LC 90-38713. 384p. 1991. text ed. 49.95 (0-275-93415-2, C3415, Praeger Pubs) Greenwood.

Lindberg, Rick. Stuck on the Sox. 192p. (Orig.). 1978. pap. 1.95 (0-930528-02-6) Sassafras Pr.

Lindberg, Robert E. Feeling Good after Forty. 272p. 1991. pap. text ed. 15.95 (0-8403-6799-6) Kendall-Hunt.

— Marital Magic: How the Five C's Create Magic or Madness in Your Marriage. 272p. 1991. pap. text ed. 15.95 (0-8403-6789-9) Kendall-Hunt.

Lindberg, Roy A. Processes & Materials of Manufacture. 4th ed. (Illus.). 848p. 1989. text ed. write for info. (0-205-11817-8, H18179) P-H.

— Processes & Materials of Manufacture. 4th ed. (Illus.). 848p. 1990. teacher ed write for info. (0-318-63888-6, H18187); teacher ed write for info. (0-318-63887-8, H18195) P-H.

Lindberg, Roy A., jt. auth. see Cohn, Theodore.

Lindberg, S. E., et al, eds. Acidic Precipitation. (Advances in Environmental Science Ser.: Vol. 3). (Illus.). xiv, 332p. 1989. 129.00 (0-685-31289-5, 2993) Spr-Verlag.

Lindberg, Sarah, ed. see Hoyland, Terri R.

Lindberg, Stanley W. The Legacy of Erskine Caldwell. (Georgia Humanities Council Publications). (Illus.). 64p. 1989. pap. 9.95 (0-8203-1315-7) U of Ga Pr.

Lindberg, Stanley W. & Corey, Stephen, eds. Keener Sounds: Selected Poems from The Georgia Review. LC 86-25086. 240p. 1987. pap. 14.95 (0-8203-0937-0) U of Ga Pr.

— Necessary Fictions: Selected Stories from the Georgia Review. LC 86-16079. 352p. 1986. pap. 14.95 (0-8203-0883-8) U of Ga Pr.

Lindberg, Stanley W., jt. auth. see Patterson, L. Ray.

Lindberg, T., et al. Ecology of Arable Land: Organisms, Carbon & Nitrogen Cycling. Andren, O., ed. (Ecological Bulletins Ser.: No. 40). 221p. 1990. 300.00 (87-16-10605-9, Yr Bk Med Pubs) Mosby Yr Bk.

Lindberg, Thomas, ed. Strategies & Tactics in Organic Synthesis, Vol. 1. (Illus.). 370p. 1993. reprint ed. pap. text ed. 39.95 (0-12-450275-X) Acad Pr.

— Strategies & Tactics in Organic Synthesis, Vol. 2. 507p. 1988. text ed. 125.00 (0-12-450281-4) Acad Pr.

— Strategies & Tactics in Organic Synthesis, Vol. 3. (Illus.). 544p. 1991. text ed. 138.00 (0-12-450282-2) Acad Pr.

Lindbergh, Anne. Nick of Time. LC 93-20777. (J). 1994. 15.95 (0-316-52629-0) Little.

— Three Lives to Live. (J). (gr. 3-6). 1995. reprint ed. pap. 3.50 (0-671-86732-6, Minstrel Bks) PB.

Lindbergh, Anne M. Bailey's Window. 144p. (YA). 1991. pap. 3.50 (0-380-70767-5, Camelot) Avon.

— Bailey's Window. LC 83-18360. (Illus.). 115p. (J). (gr. 3-7). 1984. 14.95 (0-15-205642-4, HB Juv Bks) HarBrace.

— Bring Me a Unicorn: Diaries & Letters of Anne Morrow Lindbergh, 1922-1928. 1993. pap. 8.95 (0-15-614164-7) HarBrace.

— Dearly Beloved. 202p. 1991. reprint ed. lib. bdg. 28.95x (0-89966-790-2) Buccaneer Bks.

— Flower & the Nettle: Diaries & Letters of Anne Morrow Lindbergh, 1936-1939. 1994. pap. 15.95 (0-15-631942-X) HarBrace.

— Gift from the Sea. 1992. pap. write for info. (0-394-58449-X) Pantheon.

— Gift from the Sea. LC 77-14351. 1978. pap. 5.50 (0-394-72455-0, Vin) Random.

— Gift from the Sea. LC 90-50140. 144p. 1991. pap. 7.00 (0-679-73241-1, Vin) Random.

— Gift from the Sea. (Chatto Pocket Library). 138p. 1994. 13.95 (0-7011-4963-9, Pub. by Chatto & Windus UK) Trafalgar.

— Hour of Gold, Hour of Lead: Diaries & Letters of Anne Morrow Lindbergh, 1929-1932. 1993. pap. 9.95 (0-15-642183-6) HarBrace.

— The Hunky-Dory Dairy. LC 85-16408. (Illus.). 147p. (J). (gr. 4-6). 1986. 14.95 (0-15-237449-3, HB Juv Bks) HarBrace.

— Hunky-Dory Dairy. 160p. (J). (gr. 3-7). 1987. pap. 2.75 (0-380-70320-3, Camelot) Avon.

— Locked Rooms & Open Doors: Diaries & Letters of Anne Morrow Lindbergh, 1933-1935. 32p. 1993. pap. 12.95 (0-15-652956-4) HarBrace.

— Nobody's Orphan. (J). (gr. 3-7). 1987. pap. 2.95 (0-380-70395-5, Camelot) Avon.

— North to the Orient. LC 35-27279. 1966. pap. 6.95 (0-15-667140-9, Harvest Bks) HarBrace.

— The People in Pineapple Place. 160p. (J). (gr. 4-5). 1990. pap. 2.95 (0-380-70766-7, Camelot) Avon.

— The Prisoner of Pineapple Place. 192p. (J). 1990. pap. 2.95 (0-380-70765-9, Camelot) Avon.

— The Shadow on the Dial. (J). (gr. 3-7). 1988. pap. 2.75 (0-380-70545-1, Camelot) Avon.

— Three Lives to Live. 192p. (J). (gr. 3-7). 1992. 14.95 (0-316-52628-2) Little.

— Tidy Lady. LC 88-10905. (Illus.). 30p. (J). (gr. k-3). 1989. 13.95 (0-15-287150-0) HarBrace.

— Travel Far, Pay No Fare. LC 91-35886. 192p. (J). (gr. 5-8). 1992. 14.95 (0-06-021775-8); lib. bdg. 14.89 (0-06-021776-6) HarpC Child Bks.

— The Unicorn & Other Poems. LC 56-9810. 112p. 1993. 14.00 (0-679-42540-3) Pantheon.

— The Unicorn & Other Poems. LC 72-4548. 1972. pap. 7.00 (0-394-71822-4, Vin) Random.

— War Within & Without. 1995. pap. 14.95 (0-15-694703-X) HarBrace.

— War Within & Without: Diaries & Letters, Nineteen Thirty-Nine to Nineteen Forty-Four. LC 79-21614. 536p. 1980. 14.95 (0-15-194661-2) HarBrace.

Lindbergh, Anne M. & Hoguet, Susan R. Next Time, Take Care. (Illus.). 32p. (J). (ps-3). 1988. 13.95 (0-15-257200-7, HB Juv Bks) HarBrace.

Lindbergh, Anne Morrow. Gift from the Sea. large type ed. 268p. 1985. reprint ed. pap. 9.95 (0-8027-2466-3) Walker & Co.

Lindbergh, Charles A. The Autobiography of Values. LC 77-7873. 448p. 1978. 19.95 (0-15-110202-3) HarBrace.

— Autobiography of Values. 1992. pap. 14.95 (0-15-609402-9, Harvest Bks) HarBrace.

— Banking, Currency, the Money Trust & War, 3 vols. 1972. 300.00 (0-87968-704-5) Gordon Pr.

Lindbergh, Charles A., Sr. Lindbergh on the Federal Reserve. 249p. 1989. reprint ed. pap. 9.00 (0-939482-15-0) Noontide.

Lindbergh, Charles A. Radio Speeches of Charles A. Lindbergh: 1939-1940. 1982. lib. bdg. 69.95 (0-87700-455-2) Revisionist Pr.

— Spirit of St. Louis. (Illus.). 576p. 1975. text ed. 60.00 (0-684-14421-2, Scribners) S&S Trade.

— Spirit of St. Louis. LC 93-4148. 562p. 1993. reprint ed. pap. 14.95 (0-87351-288-X, Borealis Book) Minn Hist.

— The Spirit of St. Louis. 512p. 1991. reprint ed. lib. bdg. 33.95 (0-89966-793-7) Buccaneer Bks.

— The Wartime Journals of Charles A. Lindbergh. LC 78-124830. 1038p. 1970. 19.95 (0-15-194625-6) HarBrace.

— We. 1976. 23.95 (0-8488-1412-6) Amereon Ltd.

— We. (Illus.). 318p. 1991. reprint ed. lib. bdg. 35.95 (0-89966-832-1) Buccaneer Bks.

Lindbergh, Ernest A. International Law Dictionary: English - French - German. 448p. (C). 1992. 72.00 (1-85431-119-0, Pub. by Blackstone Pr UK) W W Gaunt.

Lindbergh, Reeve. Benjamin's Barn. (Illus.). 32p. (J). (ps-3). 1990. 13.95 (0-8037-0613-8) Dial Bks Young.

— Benjamin's Barn. (Illus.). 24p. (J). (ps-3). 1994. pap. 5.99 (0-14-050863-5, Puff Pied Piper) Puffin Bks.

— Day the Goose Got Loose. LC 87-28959. (Illus.). 32p. (J). (ps-3). 1990. 12.95 (0-8037-0408-9); lib. bdg. 12.89 (0-8037-0409-7) Dial Bks Young.

— The Day the Goose Got Loose. (Illus.). 32p. (J). 1995. pap. 4.99 (0-14-055337-1) Puffin Bks.

— Grandfather's Lovesong. LC 92-22212. (Illus.). 32p. (J). 1993. 14.99 (0-670-84842-5) Viking Child Bks.

— Grandfather's Lovesong. (Illus.). 32p. (J). 1995. pap. 4.99 (0-14-055481-5) Puffin Bks.

— If I'd Known Then What I Know Now. LC 93-24058. (Illus.). (J). 1994. 13.99 (0-670-85351-8) Viking Child Bks.

— Johnny Appleseed. (J). (ps-4). 1990. 15.95 (0-316-52618-5, Joy St Bks) Little.

— Johnny Appleseed. (J). (ps-3). 1993. mass mkt. 5.95 (0-316-52634-7) Little.

— The Midnight Farm. LC 86-1722. 32p. (J). (ps-2). 1987. 15.99 (0-8037-0331-7) Dial Bks Young.

— The Midnight Farm. (Illus.). 32p. (J). (ps-2). 1995. 5.99 (0-14-055668-0, Puff Pied Piper) Puffin Bks.

— The Names of the Mountains. large type ed. LC 93-18466. 344p. 1993. reprint ed. Alk. paper. lib. bdg. 20.95 (1-56054-695-6) Thorndike Pr.

— The Names of the Mountains: A Novel. 224p. 1992. 19.00 (0-671-73148-3) S&S Trade.

— There's a Cow in the Road! LC 92-34883. (Illus.). 32p. (J). (ps-2). 1993. 13.99 (0-8037-1335-5); lib. bdg. 13.89 (0-8037-1336-3) Dial Bks Young.

— View from the Air: Charles Lindbergh's Earth & Sky. (Illus.). 32p. (J). 1992. 15.00 (0-670-84660-0) Viking Child Bks.

— What Is the Sun? LC 93-3557. (Illus.). 32p. (J). (ps up). 1994. 14.95 (1-56402-146-7) Candlewick Pr.

Lindbery, J. How to Play Drums Today. 1990. 4.95 (0-685-32225-4, H022) Hansen Ed Mus.

Lindblad, A. S., et al, eds. Continuous Ambulatory Peritoneal Dialysis in the U. S. A. (Developments in Nephrology Ser.). (C). 1989. lib. bdg. 137.00 (0-7923-0179-X) Kluwer Ac.

Lindblad, Carl & Druben, Laurel. Small Farm Grain Storage, 3 vols., Set. (Illus.). 1990. 18.00 (0-685-45921-7) Vols Tech Asst.

— Small Farm Grain Storage, Vol. I. (Illus.). 204p. 1976. 8.50 (0-86619-052-X) Vols Tech Asst.

— Small Farm Grain Storage, Vol. II. (Illus.). 170p. 1976. 8.50 (0-86619-053-8) Vols Tech Asst.

— Small Farm Grain Storage, Vol. III. (Illus.). 148p. 1976. 8.50 (0-86619-054-6) Vols Tech Asst.

— Small Farm Grain Storage: Almaceniamento del Grano. (Illus.). 331p. 1976. Spanish. 12.00 (0-685-17951-6) Vols Tech Asst.

Lindblad, Carl, jt. auth. see Harris, Kenton.

Lindblad, Goran. Non-Equilibrium Entropy & Irreversibility. 1983. lib. bdg. 72.00 (90-277-1640-4) Kluwer Ac.

Lindblad, Ishrat & Ljung, Magnus, eds. Proceedings from the Third Nordic Conference for English Studies, 2 vols., Set. (Stokholm Studies in English: LXXIII). 806p. (Orig.). 1987. pap. text ed. 108.00x (91-22-00870-5, Pub. by Almqv & Wiksell SW) Coronet Bks.

Lindblad, K. E. Noah Webster's Pronunciation & Modern New England Speech. (Essays & Studies on American Language & Literature: Vol. 11). (Orig.). 1954. pap. 18.00 (0-8115-0191-4) Periodicals Srv.

Lindblad, Lisa & Lindlbad, Sven-Olof. Serengeti Migration. LC 93-26338. (Illus.). 40p. (J). (gr. 3-7). 1994. 15.95 (1-56282-668-9); lib. bdg. 15.89 (1-56282-669-7) Hyprn Child.

Lindblad, Ulrika, tr. see Braulik, Georg.

Lindblom, Bjorn & Ohman, Sven, eds. Frontiers of Speech Communication Research. 1979. text ed. 157.00 (0-12-449850-7) Acad Pr.

Lindblom, Charles E. Inquiry & Change: The Troubled Attempt to Understand & Shape Society. 336p. (C). 1992. reprint ed. pap. text ed. 17.00 (0-300-05667-2) Yale U Pr.

— Policy Making Process. 2nd ed. 1979. pap. text ed. write for info. (0-13-686543-7) P-H.

— Politics & Markets: The World's Political-Economic Systems. LC 77-75250. 416p. 1980. pap. text ed. 20.00 (0-465-05958-9) Basic.

— The Science of "Muddling Through" (Reprint Series in Social Sciences). (C). 1993. reprint ed. pap. text ed. 1.00 (0-8290-3504-4, PS-169) Irvington.

Lindblom, Charles E. & Cohen, Davis K. Usable Knowledge. 1979. 25.00 (0-300-02335-9); pap. 10.00 (0-300-02336-7) Yale U Pr.

Lindblom, Charles E. & Woodhouse, Edward J. The Policy Making Process: Foundations of Modern Political Science Ser. 3rd ed. LC 92-28729. 160p. (C). 1992. pap. text ed. write for info. (0-13-682360-2) P-H.

Lindblom, Charles E., jt. auth. see Braybrooke, David.

Lindblom, Charles E., jt. auth. see Dahl, Robert A.

Lindblom, Johannes. Prophecy in Ancient Israel. LC 63-907. 480p. reprint ed. pap. 136.80 (0-317-55778-5, 2029298) Bks Demand.

Lindblom, Peter D., jt. auth. see Emery, Donald W.

Lindblom, Steve. Flying the Hot Ones. (J). (gr. 3-7). 1990. write for info. (0-318-66741-X) HM.

Lindblom, Steven. Golden Book of Snakes & Other Reptiles. (Golden Favorites Ser.). (J). 1990. write for info. (0-307-15852-7, Golden Bks) Western Pub.

Lindblom, U. E. & Gnirk, P. F. Nuclear Waste Disposal: Can We Rely on Bedrock? 80p. 1982. text ed. 36.00 (0-08-027608-3, Pub. by Pergamon Repr UK) Franklin.

Lindbloom, Carl G., jt. auth. see Moskowitz, Harvey S.

Lindbloom, Eric, photos. Angels at the Arno. LC 93-50142. (Illus.). 1994. 35.00 (0-87923-974-3) Godine.

— Angels at the Arno: Photographs by Eric Lindbloom. (Illus.). 84p. 1995. pap. 19.95 (0-87923-994-8) Godine.

Lindbolm, Steven. Fly the Hot Ones. LC 89-29491. (Illus.). 128p. (J). (gr. 4 up). 1991. 17.95 (0-395-51075-9) HM.

Lindbom, Annie, jt. ed. see Venge, Per.

Lindbom, Annie, jt. ed. see Venge, Per.

Lindbom, Tage. The Tares & the Good Grain or the Kingdom of Man at the Hour of Reckoning. Moore, Alvin, tr. LC 83-944. 161p. 1983. pap. 11.95 (0-86554-079-9, MUP-H69) Mercer Univ Pr.

Lindborg, Bonnie, ed. see Kubsch, Erwin.

An Asterisk (*) at the beginning of an entry indicates that the title is appearing in BIP for the first time.

Linde, A. Particle Physics & Inflationary Cosmology. Feshbach, H., ed. (Contemporary Concepts in Physics Ser.: Vol. 1). xviii, 362p. 1990. text ed. 62.00 (*3-7186-0489-2*); pap. text ed. 29.00 (*3-7186-0490-6*) Gordon & Breach.

Linde, Anders. Dentin & Dentinogenesis. 176p. 1984. Vol. I, 176 p. 132.00 (*0-8493-5200-2*, QM569, CRC Reprint); Vol. II., 168 p. 132.00 (*0-8493-5201-0*, QM569, CRC Reprint) Franklin.

Linde, Andrei D. Inflation & Quantum Cosmology. 216p. 1990. text ed. 49.00 (*0-12-450145-1*) Acad Pr.

Linde, Charlotte. Life Stories: The Creation of Coherence. LC 92-25763. (Oxford Studies in Sociolinguistics). 1993. 49.95 (*0-19-507372-X*); pap. 17.95 (*0-19-507373-8*) OUP.

Linde, H. M., tr. The Recorder Player's Handbook. rev. ed. 1974. pap. 29.95 (*0-930448-11-1*, ST12322) Eur-Am Music.

Linde, Hans A., et al. Legislative & Administrative Processes. 2nd ed. LC 81-4738. (University Casebook Ser.). 887p. 1991. reprint ed. text ed. 35.00 (*0-88277-026-8*) Foundation Pr.

Linde, Karen. Winning Womens Softball. 1990. pap. 12.95 (*0-13-356148-8*) P-H.

Linde, Karen & Hoehn, Robert G. Girls' Softball: A Complete Guide for Players & Coaches. LC 85-3653. 195p. 1985. text ed. 21.95 (*0-13-356734-6*, Parker Publishing Co) P-H.

Linde, Lavaun & Quishenberry, Mary. Daniel & the Big Cats: Level One. (Bible Stories for Early Readers Ser.: Bk. 5). (Illus.). 32p. (J). (gr. 1). 1986. pap. text ed. 4.99 (*0-945107-04-8*) Bradshaw Pubs.

— God Adds Oil: Level Two. (Bible Stories for Early Readers Ser.: Bk. 1). (Illus.). 32p. (Orig.). (J). (gr. 1). 1988. pap. text ed. 4.99 (*0-945107-05-6*) Bradshaw Pubs.

— I Will Help: Level One. (Bible Stories for Early Readers Ser.: Bk. 2). (Illus.). 32p. (Orig.). (J). (gr. 1). 1986. pap. text ed. 4.99 (*0-945107-01-3*) Bradshaw Pubs.

— Jonah's Ride: Level Two. (Bible Stories for Early Readers Ser.: Bk. 5). (Illus.). 32p. (Orig.). (J). (gr. 1). 1988. pap. text ed. 4.99 (*0-945107-09-9*) Bradshaw Pubs.

— The Lad's Bag: Level One. (Bible Stories for Early Readers Ser.: Bk. 4). (Illus.). 32p. (J). (gr. 1). 1986. pap. text ed. 4.99 (*0-945107-03-X*) Bradshaw Pubs.

— Mom & the Lad: Level One. (Bible Stories for Early Readers Ser.: Bk. 3). (Illus.). 32p. (J). (gr. 1). 1986. pap. text ed. 4.99 (*0-945107-02-1*) Bradshaw Pubs.

— Not a Bed: Level One. (Bible Stories for Early Readers Ser.: Bk. 1). (Illus.). 32p. (Orig.). (J). (gr. 1). 1986. pap. text ed. 4.99 (*0-945107-00-5*) Bradshaw Pubs.

— Seven Dips: Level Two. (Bible Stories for Early Readers Ser.: Bk. 4). (Illus.). 32p. (Orig.). (J). (gr. 1). 1988. pap. text ed. 4.99 (*0-945107-08-0*) Bradshaw Pubs.

— Three Brave Men: Level Two. (Bible Stories for Early Readers Ser.: Bk. 3). (Illus.). 32p. (Orig.). (J). (gr. 1). 1988. pap. text ed. 4.99 (*0-945107-07-2*) Bradshaw Pubs.

— Zacchaeus' Cash Bag: Level Two. (Bible Stories for Early Readers Ser.: Bk. 2). (Illus.). 32p. (Orig.). (J). (gr. 1). 1988. pap. text ed. 4.99 (*0-945107-06-4*) Bradshaw Pubs.

Linde, Peter. Numerical Modelling & Capacity Design of Earthquake-Resistant Reinforced Concrete Walls. LC 93-37013. (Report of the Institute of Structural Engineering ETH Zurich Ser.: No. 200). 236p. 1994. pap. text ed. 64.00 (*0-8176-2968-8*) Birkhauser.

Linde, Richard M., jt. auth. see Wakita, Osamu A.

Linde, Shirley & Carrow, Donald J., eds. The Directory of Holistic Medicine & Alternate Health Care Services in the U. S. LC 85-13193. 264p. 1986. pap. 6.95 (*0-932090-18-4*) Mosby Yr Bk.

Linde, Shirley & Lane, Lea. Hippocrene Insider's Guide to the World's Most Exciting Cruises, So Far. (Insiders Guide Ser.). (Illus.). 230p. (Orig.). 1994. pap. 18.95 (*0-7818-0258-X*) Hippocrene Bks.

Linde, Shirley, jt. auth. see Allen, Robert F.

Linde, Shirley M., jt. auth. see Breecher, Maury M.

Linde, Shirley M., jt. auth. see Hauri, Peter J.

Linde, Werner. Infinitely Divisible & Stables Measures on Banach Spaces. 202p. (C). 1983. 70.00 (*0-685-36895-5*, Pub. by Collets) St Mut.

— Probability in Banach Spaces Stable & Infinitely Divisible Distributions. 1986. text ed. 145.00 (*0-471-90893-2*) Wiley.

Lindeberg, J. F., ed. Safety of Computer Control Systems, 1991: Proceedings of the IFAC-IFIP-EWICS-SRE Symposium, Trondheim, Norway, 30 October - 1 November 1991. (IFAC Symposia Ser.). 197p. 1991. 78.00 (*0-08-041697-7*, Pergamon Pr) Elsevier.

Lindeberg, Tony. Scale-Space Theory in Computer Vision. LC 93-23648. 440p. (C). 1993. lib. bdg. 130.00 (*0-7923-2636-9*) Kluwer Ac.

— Scale-Space Theory in Computer Vision. 440p. (C). 1994. lib. bdg. 130.00 (*0-7923-9418-6*) Kluwer Ac.

Lindeberry, Heather S. Benito Huerta: Preserve, Negate, Transcend. (Illus.). 32p. 1994. pap. write for info. (*1-879286-08-4*) AZ Bd Regents.

Lindeboom, G. A. The Letters of Jan Swammerdam to Melchisedec Thevenot, with English Translation & a Biographical Sketch. 202p. 1975. text ed. 57.00 (*90-265-0222-2*, Pub. by Swets Pub Serv NE) Swets North Am.

Lindeboom, M. Empirical Duration Models for the Labor Market. (Tinbergen Institute Research Ser.). 172p. 1992. pap. 25.00 (*90-5170-147-0*, Pub. by Thesis Pubs NE) IBD Ltd.

***Lindeburg.** Solutions Manual for the Mechanical Engineering Reference Manual. 9th ed. 1995. pap. text ed. 17.95 (*0-912045-84-1*) Prof Pubns CA.

Lindeburg, Michael R. Civil Engineering Quick Reference Cards. (Engineering Reference Manual Ser.). 48p. (Orig.). 1986. spiral bd. 19.95 (*0-932276-59-8*) Prof Pubns CA.

— Civil Engineering Reference Manual. 6th ed. (Engineering Reference Manual Ser.). 712p. 1992. 51.95 (*0-912045-45-0*) Prof Pubns CA.

— Civil Engineering Sample Examination. 3rd ed. (Engineering Reference Manual Ser.). 72p. 1992. pap. text ed. 13.95 (*0-912045-51-5*) Prof Pubns CA.

— Consolidated Gas Dynamics Tables: Data for Isentropic, Rayleigh, & Fanno Flow, & Normal Shock Waves. (Engineering Reference Manual Ser.). 88p. (C). 1989. pap. text ed. 18.95 (*0-932276-96-2*) Prof Pubns CA.

— EIT Review Manual. (Illus.). 600p. (Orig.). 1995. pap. 39.95 (*0-912045-85-X*) Prof Pubns CA.

— Engineer-in-Training Reference Manual. 8th ed. LC 91-66398. (Engineering Reference Manual Ser.). 1056p. (C). 1992. text ed. 48.95 (*0-912045-56-6*) Prof Pubns CA.

— Engineer-in-Training Sample Examinations. LC 90-63739. (Engineering Reference Manual Ser.). 144p. 1991. pap. text ed. 16.95 (*0-912045-24-8*) Prof Pubns CA.

— Engineering Economic Analysis: An Introduction. (Engineering Reference Manual Ser.). (Illus.). 240p. (Orig.). 1993. pap. 16.95 (*0-912045-60-4*) Prof Pubns CA.

— Engineering Fundamentals Quick Reference Cards. 4th ed. (Engineering Reference Manual Ser.). 48p. 1991. spiral bd. 13.95 (*0-912045-34-5*) Prof Pubns CA.

— Engineering Unit Conversions. 3rd ed. 160p. 1993. text ed. 22.95 (*0-912045-63-9*) Prof Pubns CA.

— Fire & Explosion Protection Systems: A Design Professional's Introduction. 2nd ed. LC 94-23456. (Engineering Reference Manual Ser.). 1995. pap. 16.95 (*0-912045-82-5*) Prof Pubns CA.

— Mechanical Engineering Quick Reference Cards. (Engineering Reference Manual Ser.). 56p. (Orig.). 1992. spiral bd. 21.95 (*0-912045-49-3*) Prof Pubns CA.

— Mechanical Engineering Quick Reference Cards. 3rd ed. (Orig.). 1994. pap. 22.95 (*0-912045-75-2*) Prof Pubns CA.

— Mechanical Engineering Reference Manual. 9th ed. (Illus.). 672p. 1994. 49.95 (*0-912045-72-8*) Prof Pubns CA.

— Mechanical Engineering Sample Examination. 2nd ed. (Engineering Reference Manual Ser.). 36p. (C). 1989. pap. text ed. 13.95 (*0-912045-07-8*) Prof Pubns CA.

— Mini-Exams for the Engineer-In-Training Exam. (Engineering Reference Manual Ser.). 88p. 1990. pap. 15.95 (*0-932276-34-2*) Prof Pubns CA.

— One Hundred & One Solved Civil Engineering Problems. LC 94-9618. (Engineering Reference Manual Ser.). 194p. (Orig.). 1994. pap. 24.95 (*0-912045-64-7*) Prof Pubns CA.

— One Hundred One Solved Mechanical Engineering Problems. (Engineering Reference Manual Ser.). (Illus.). 128p. (C). 1989. pap. text ed. 25.95 (*0-932276-95-4*) Prof Pubns CA.

— Seismic Design of Building Structures: A Professional's Introduction to Earthquake Forces & Design Details. 6th ed. (Illus.). 170p. 1994. pap. 21.95 (*0-912045-76-0*) Prof Pubns CA.

— Solutions Manual for the Civil Engineering Reference Manual. 6th ed. (Engineering Reference Manual Ser.). 168p. 1992. pap. 17.95 (*0-912045-43-4*) Prof Pubns CA.

— Solutions Manual for the Engineer-in-Training Reference Manual: SI Units. 8th ed. (Engineering Reference Manual Ser.). 256p. 1992. pap. text ed. 17.95 (*0-912045-40-X*) Prof Pubns CA.

— Solutions Manual for the Mechanical Engineering Reference Manual. 8th ed. (Engineering Reference Manual Ser.). 134p. 1990. pap. text ed. 17.95 (*0-912045-23-X*) Prof Pubns CA.

— Solutions Manual for the Mechanical Engineering Reference Manual. 9th ed. 134p. 1994. pap. 16.95 (*0-912045-73-6*) Prof Pubns CA.

Lindeburg, Micheal R. 1001 Solved Engineering Fundamentals Problems. (Engineering Reference Manual Ser.). (Illus.). 760p. (C). 1988. 23.00 (*0-932276-90-3*) Prof Pubns CA.

Lindee, M. Susan. Suffering Made Real: American Science & the Survivors at Hiroshima. LC 94-1832. 1994. 29.95 (*0-226-48237-5*) U Ch Pr.

Lindee, M. Susan, jt. auth. see Nelkin, Dorothy.

Lindeen, James W. Governing America's Economy. LC 93-17155. 1993. pap. text ed. write for info. (*0-13-097031-X*) P-H.

Lindegaard, Annette, jt. ed. see Dollerup, Cay.

Lindeke, B., jt. ed. see Cho, A. K.

Lindeke, Wolfgang. Dictionary of Ventilation & Health. 186p. 1980. 65.00 (*0-569-08522-5*, Pub. by Collets UK) St Mut.

— Heating, Ventilation & Health Technology. 186p. (ENG, GER, RUS & SLO.). 1988. 50.00 (*0-317-59470-2*, Pub. by Collets UK) Pro-Am Music.

— Technical Veterinary Dictionary. 185p. (ENG, GER, RUS & SLV.). 1972. 95.00 (*0-8288-6421-7*, M-9894) Fr & Eur.

Lindekugel, D. M. Shooters: TV News Photographers & Their Work. LC 93-23672. 192p. 1994. text ed. 49.95 (*0-275-94603-7*, Praeger Pubs) Greenwood.

Lindell, Anne. Audio Tape Program: A Workbook. (C). 1983. pap. text ed. 13.95 (*0-472-08573-5*) U of Mich Pr.

— Intensive English for Communication, Bk. 2. (Illus.). 294p. 1980. pap. text ed. 13.95 (*0-472-08572-7*) U of Mich Pr.

Lindell, Anne & Hagiwara, M. Peter. Intensive English for Communication, Bk. 1. LC 78-58152. (Illus.). 1979. student ed. 13.95 (*0-472-08571-9*); pap. text ed. 13.95 (*0-472-08570-0*) U of Mich Pr.

Lindell, Bo. How Safe Is Safe Enough? LC 88-22075. (Taylor Lecture Ser.: No. 12). 1988. 20.00 (*0-913392-99-5*) NCRP Pubns.

Lindell, Ethel B., jt. auth. see Lindell, John E.

Lindell, G. L., jt. auth. see Zines, L.

***Lindell, Geoffrey, ed.** Future Directions in Australian Constitutional Law: Essays in Honour of Professor Leslie Zines. 304p. 1994. 54.00 (*1-86287-147-7*, Pub. by Federation Pr AU) W W Gaunt.

Lindell, Ismo V. Methods for Electromagnetic Field Analysis. (Oxford Engineering Science Ser.: No. 30). (Illus.). 304p. 1992. 83.00 (*0-19-856239-X*) OUP.

Lindell, John E. & Lindell, Ethel B. Oh God, Help Me! LC 88-91189. (Illus.). 209p. (Orig.). 1988. pap. 10.00 (*0-9620643-0-0*) J E Lindell.

— Oh God, Help Me! A True Story of Faith in the Life of a Polio Survivor. (Illus.). 210p. (Orig.). 1988. pap. text ed. write for info. (*0-318-63145-8*) J E Lindell.

Lindell, Kristina. Folk Tales from Kammu, Vol. 1: A Story Listeners Tales. (C). 1977. pap. 18.50 (*0-7007-0108-7*, Pub. by Curzon Pr UK) Humanities.

— Folk Tales from Kammu, Vol. 2: A Story Tellers Tales. (C). 1980. pap. 18.50 (*0-7007-0131-1*, Pub. by Curzon Pr UK) Humanities.

— Folk Tales from Kammu, Vol. 4: A Master Tellers Tales. (C). 1989. pap. 17.50 (*0-7007-0214-8*, Pub. by Curzon Pr UK) Humanities.

— The Student Lovers. DeFrancis, John, ed. LC 70-189615. (PALI Language Texts, Chinese Ser.). (Illus.). 40p. (Orig.). (C). 1975. pap. text ed. 8.00 (*0-8248-0225-X*) UH Pr.

Lindell, Kristina, ed. Kammu Year: Its Lore & Music. (C). 1989. pap. 19.95 (*0-7007-0151-6*, Pub. by Curzon Pr UK) Humanities.

Lindell, Kristina, jt. auth. see Tayanin, Damrong.

Lindell, Kristina, et al. Folk Tales from Kammu: Pearls of Kammu Literature, No. 3. (Scandinavian Institute of Asian Studies Monograph: No. 51). 325p. (C). 1984. pap. 25.00 (*0-7007-0170-2*, Pub. by Curzon Pr UK) Humanities.

— Folk Tales from Kammu-IV: A Master Teller's Tales. 220p. (C). 1988. 65.00 (*0-685-32850-3*, Pub. by Curzon Pr UK) Humanities.

— Folk Tales from Kammu, Vol. 5: A Young Story-Teller's Tales. (Scandinavian Institute of Asian Studies Monograph: No. 66). (Illus.). 220p. (C). 1995. pap. 29.95 (*0-7007-0297-0*, Pub. by Curzon Pr UK) Humanities.

Lindell, Michael K., jt. auth. see Perry, Ronald W.

Lindeman & McAthie. Readings in Nursing Trends & Issues. 1990. 24.95 (*0-87434-232-5*) Springhouse Pub.

Lindeman, Anne. State Concerns in the Future Development of Vocational Education. 22p. 1984. 3.00 (*0-318-22201-9*, OC98) Ctr Educ Trng Employ.

Lindeman, Bruce. Real Estate Brokerage. 450p. (C). 1981. text ed. 27.00 (*0-8359-6517-1*, Reston) P-H.

— Real Estate Brokerage Management. 3rd ed. 323p. 1993. text ed. 47.00 (*0-13-763459-5*, 160801) P-H.

Lindeman, Carl, illus. The Valley Outfitter: Your Complete Recreational Guide to Montana's Flathead Valley. 1994. pap. write for info. (*0-9640756-0-1*) Whitefish Mag.

Lindeman, Carol A., ed. Alternate Conceptions of Work & Society: Implications for Professional Nursing. 225p. (Orig.). 1988. pap. 20.00 (*0-922148-00-7*) AACN.

Lindeman, Carol A., jt. ed. see Tanner, Christine.

Lindeman, Carolynn A. PianoLab: An Introduction to Class Piano. 2nd ed. 343p. (C). 1991. pap. 31.95 (*0-534-13944-2*) Intl Thomson.

Lindeman, Carolynn A. & Hackett, Patricia. MusicLab: An Introduction to the Fundamentals of Music. 442p. (C). 1989. pap. 32.95 (*0-534-09558-5*) Intl Thomson.

Lindeman, Carolynn A., jt. auth. see Hackett, Patricia.

Lindeman, Eduard. The Meaning of Adult Education. LC 89-61231. 150p. (C). 1989. pap. 19.95 (*0-9622488-1-9*) U OK PMC.

Lindeman, Eduard C. Wealth & Culture. 155p. 1987. 39.95 (*0-88738-170-7*) Transaction Pubs.

***Lindeman, Eric D. & Blumenthal, Anita.** Handbook: The International Nuclear Fuel Cycle. 80p. 1995. 15.00 (*0-9646545-0-4*) NY Nuclear.

***Lindeman, J. Bruce.** How to Prepare for the Real Estate Licensing Examinations: Salesperson, Broker, Appraiser. 1995. student ed. pap. 12.95 (*0-8120-2994-1*) Barron.

— Microeconomics. (E Z 101 Study Keys Ser.). 144p. 1992. pap. 5.95 (*0-8120-4601-3*) Barron.

Lindeman, J. Bruce & Friedman, Jack P. How to Prepare for Real Estate Licensing Examinations: Salesperson & Broker. 4th ed. 352p. 1990. pap. 11.95 (*0-8120-4355-3*) Barron.

Lindeman, J. C., jt. auth. see Cowan, R. S.

Lindeman, J. F., jt. ed. see Holman, B. L.

Lindeman, Jack. Twenty-One Poems. 1963. pap. 6.00 (*0-685-62609-1*) Atlantis Edns.

Lindeman, Lee & Harste, Pat. Country Kitchen Cutouts. LC 93-43891. (Illus.). 136p. 1994. pap. 12.95 (*0-8069-0370-8*) Sterling.

Lindeman, Lee & Harte, Patricia. Wildlife Toys in Wood. LC 92-41345. (Illus.). 128p. 1993. pap. 12.95 (*0-8069-8666-2*) Sterling.

Lindeman, Peter V. Introductory Biology: Laboratory Manual. (Illus.). 85p. (C). 1991. write for info. (*0-944324-49-5*) Am Artist Pub.

***Lindeman, Stephen P.** Nutshells. 12p. (Orig.). 1994. pap. write for info. (*1-885206-05-4*, Iliad Pr) Cader Pubng.

Lindeman, William, tr. see Steiner, Rudolf.

Lindemann, A., jt. auth. see Conzelmann, H.

Lindemann, Alan & Haugen, Diane. Modern Medicine: What You're Dying to Know. (Illus.). 256p. 1992. 14.95 (*0-9632244-0-9*) Persnl Best ND.

Lindemann, Albert S. A History of European Socialism. LC 82-40167. xxi, 386p. 1983. text ed. 50.00 (*0-300-02797-4*) Yale U Pr.

— A History of European Socialism. LC 82-40167. 406p. 1984. reprint ed. pap. 19.00 (*0-300-03246-3*, Y-505) Yale U Pr.

— The Jew Accused: Three Anti-Semitic Affairs - Dreyfus, Beilis, Frank - 1894-1915. (Illus.). 304p. (C). 1992. pap. 14.95 (*0-521-44761-5*) Cambridge U Pr.

— The Jew Accused: Three Anti-Semitic Affairs - Dreyfus, Beiliss, Frank - 1894-1915. (Illus.). 350p. (C). 1991. 42.95 (*0-521-40302-2*) Cambridge U Pr.

Lindemann, Barbara & Grossman, Paul. Employment Discrimination Law. 2nd ed. LC 82-12801. 1720p. 1983. Price includes most recent supplement. text ed. 145.00 (*0-87179-386-5*, 9386) BNA.

***Lindemann, Barbara & Kadue, David.** Preventing Sexual Harassment: A Fact Sheet for Employees. 1994. text ed. 0.95 (*0-87179-866-2*) BNA.

Lindemann, Barbara & Kadue, David D. Primer on Sexual Harassment. LC 92-25748. 319p. 1992. pap. text ed. 45.00 (*0-87179-764-X*, 0764) BNA.

— Sexual Harassment in Employment Law. LC 91-41340. 882p. 1992. pap. text ed. 128.00 (*0-87179-704-6*, 0704) BNA.

Lindemann, Bonnie, jt. auth. see Harstad, Peter T.

Lindemann, Carol. The Handbook of Phobia Therapy: Rapid Symptom Relief in Phobias & Anxiety Disorders. LC 89-6535. 456p. 1989. 50.00 (*0-87668-866-0*) Aronson.

Lindemann, Constance. This Is How Seventy Looks: Stories of My Life. 147p. (Orig.). 1993. pap. 9.50 (*0-9637014-0-1*) Compage Pr.

Lindemann, Elizabeth B. Erich Lindemann: A Biographical Sketch. LC 87-80018. (Illus.). (Orig.). 1987. pap. 14.40 (*0-9618299-0-7*) E B Lindemann.

***Lindemann, Eric.** Crisis Intervention. LC 94-47404. 1995. pap. 30.00 (*1-56821-468-5*) Aronson.

Lindemann, Erika. A Rhetoric for Writing Teachers. 3rd ed. (Illus.). 320p. (C). 1995. pap. text ed. 18.95 (*0-19-508844-1*) OUP.

Lindemann, Erika & Fleming, Sandra M., eds. CCCC Bibliography of Composition & Rhetoric, 1989. annot. ed. 224p. (C). 1991. 29.95 (*0-8093-1712-5*) S Ill U Pr.

Lindemann, Erika & Harding, Mary B., eds. CCCC Bibliography of Composition & Rhetoric, 1988. 224p. (C). 1990. 29.95 (*0-8093-1669-2*); pap. 19.95 (*0-8093-1670-6*) S Ill U Pr.

Lindemann, Erika, et al, eds. CCCC Bibliography of Composition & Rhetoric 1987. 216p. (C). 1990. 29.95 (*0-8093-1647-1*); pap. 19.95 (*0-8093-1648-X*) S Ill U Pr.

Lindemann, Erika C. Longman Bibliography of Composition & Rhetoric, Vol. I, 1984-1985. 318p. 1987. text ed. 44.76 (*0-582-28376-0*, 71409) Longman.

Lindemann, Erika C., ed. Longman Bibliography of Composition & Rhetoric, Vol. II: 1986. 216p. (C). 1988. text ed. 42.36 (*0-8013-0254-4*, 75907) Longman.

Lindemann, Erika C. & Tate, Gary, eds. An Introduction to Composition Studies. (Illus.). 208p. (C). 1991. pap. text ed. 15.95 (*0-19-506363-5*, 11255) OUP.

Lindemann, G. Lexikon der Kunststile, 2 vols., Set. 360p. (GER.). 1980. pap. 24.95 (*0-8288-1421-X*, M7251) Fr & Eur.

Lindemann, James E., et al. Psychological & Behavioral Aspects of Physical Disability: A Manual for Health Practitioners. LC 81-17885. 452p. (C). 1981. 59.50 (*0-306-40776-0*, Plenum Pr) Plenum.

Lindemann, Jeff W., jt. auth. see Cole, SuzAnne C.

Lindemann, Joann. Portrait. (Illus.). 28p. (Orig.). 1987. pap. 4.95 (*0-929688-03-1*) Bear Hse Pub.

Lindemann, Kelvin. The Red Umbrellas. LC 74-30367. 214p. 1975. reprint ed. text ed. 55.00 (*0-8371-7521-6*, LIRU, Greenwood Pr) Greenwood.

Lindemann, Mark & Rose, William. Role of U. S. in a Changing World. (Illus.). 192p. (Orig.). (C). 1993. pap. text ed. 13.95 (*1-56134-110-X*) Dushkin Pub.

Lindemann, Mary. Patriots & Paupers: Hamburg, 1712-1830. 352p. 1990. 49.95 (*0-19-506140-3*) OUP.

Lindemann, Michael. UFOs & the Alien Presence: Six Viewpoints. 240p. (Orig.). 1991. pap. 12.95 (*0-9630104-0-9*) Twenty Twenty Grp.

Lindemans, Fred W., jt. ed. see Kappenberger, Lukas.

Lindemeyer, Nancy, jt. auth. see McCaffery, Janet.

Linden. Canadian Tort Law. 4th ed. 840p. 1988. 150.00 (*0-409-80191-7*) Butterworth Legal Pubs.

— Compute in Comfort: Practical Simple Exercises & Techniques for Preventing Physical & Mental. 1995. pap. text ed. 18.95 (*0-13-309915-6*) P-H.

***Linden, Allen & Firestone, S. E.** Butterworths Ontario Motor Vehicle Law Practice & Procedure Manual. Date not set. ring bd. 150.00 (*0-409-91920-9*, CN) Butterworth Legal Pubs.

***Linden, Allen & Klar, Lewis.** Canadian Tort Law: Cases, Notes & Materials. 10th ed. 864p. 1994. pap. 85.00 (*0-409-91188-7*, CN) Butterworth Legal Pubs.

Linden, Allen M. Canadian Tort Law. 5th ed. 864p. 1993. text ed. 155.00 (*0-409-90596-8*); student ed. pap. text ed. 80.00 (*0-409-91429-0*) Butterworth Legal Pubs.

***Linden, Ann M.** One Smiling Grandma. (Illus.). 32p. (J). 1995. pap. 4.99 (*0-14-055341-X*) Puffin Bks.

***Linden, Anne.** Emerald Blue. (J). 1994. 15.95 (*0-689-31946-0*, Atheneum Bks Young) S&S Childrens.

Linden, Anne & Spalding, Murray. The Enneagram & NLP: A Journey of Evolution. 240p. (Orig.). 1994. pap. 15.95 (*1-55552-042-1*) Metamorphous Pr.

Linden, Carl A. Khrushchev & the Soviet Leadership: With an Epilogue on Gorbachev. rev. ed. LC 89-43532. 291p. 1990. pap. text ed. 14.95 (*0-8018-4009-0*) Johns Hopkins.

— Khrushchev & the Soviet Leadership: With an Epilogue on Gorbachev. 2nd rev. ed. LC 89-43532. 291p. 1990. text ed. 45.00x (*0-8018-4008-2*) Johns Hopkins.

— Khrushchev & the Soviet Leadership, 1957-1964. LC 66-16035. 282p. 1966. reprint ed. pap. 80.70 (*0-8357-6909-7*, 2037967) Bks Demand.

— The Soviet Party-State: Aspects of Ideocratic Despotism. LC 83-13984. 144p. 1983. text ed. 45.00 (*0-275-91037-7*, C1037, Praeger Pubs) Greenwood.

An Asterisk (*) at the beginning of an entry indicates that the title is appearing in BIP for the first time.

Linden, Catherine. Highland Flame. 448p. (Orig.). 1991. pap. 4.50 (*0-8439-3159-0*) Dorchester Pub Co.

— Highland Rose. 480p. (Orig.). 1988. pap. 4.50 (*0-8439-2692-9*) Dorchester Pub Co.

— Lover's Moon. 448p. (Orig.). 1991. pap. 4.50 (*0-8439-3076-4*) Dorchester Pub Co.

***Linden, David, ed.** Handbook of Batteries. 2nd ed. LC 94-29189. 1995. text ed. 125.00 (*0-07-037921-1*) McGraw.

Linden, Eugene. Silent Partners: The Legacy of Ape Language Experiments. 208p. 1987. pap. 3.95 (*0-345-34234-8*) Ballantine.

Linden, Eugene, jt. auth. see Wang, An.

Linden, F. Taschenlexikon der Logistik. 130p. (ENG & GER.). 1991. pap. 95.00 (*0-8288-3882-8*, F112511) Fr & Eur.

Linden, Fabian, jt. auth. see Gates, Theodore R.

Linden, Frans P., ed. Transition of the Human Dentition. (Craniofacial Growth Monograph Ser.: Vol. 13). (Illus.). 150p. reprint ed. pap. 42.80 (*0-685-24149-1*, 2033022) Bks Demand.

***Linden, G. & Hurst, W. Jeffrey, eds.** Analytical Techniques for Foods & Agricultural Products. Dieter, Lance, tr. LC 95-14991. (Analysis & Control Methods for Foods & Agricultural Products Ser.). 1995. write for info. (*1-56081-687-2*) VCH Pubs.

***Linden, Glenn M. & Pressly, Thomas J.** Voices from the House Divided: The United States Civil War as Personal Experience. LC 94-26795. 1994. write for info. (*0-07-037934-3*) McGraw.

Linden, H. R. & Pettyjohn, E. S. Selection of Oils for High-Btu Oil Gas. (Research Bulletin Ser.: No. 12). iv, 48p. 1952. 5.00 (*0-317-56810-8*) Inst Gas Tech.

— Selection of Oils for High-Btu Oil Gas. suppl. ed. (Research Bulletin Ser.: No. 12). iv, 48p. 1952. 1.50 (*0-317-56811-6*) Inst Gas Tech.

Linden, H R., jt. auth. see Bair, W G.

Linden, H R., jt. auth. see Dirksen, H A.

Linden, H R., jt. auth. see Schultz, E B., Jr.

Linden, H. R., jt. auth. see Tarman, P. B.

Linden Hills Press Staff. Container Gardening: The Northern Gardener's Library. 1992. pap. 9.95 (*0-9628378-3-0*) Linden Hills Pr.

— Flower Gardens. 1991. pap. 9.95 (*0-9628378-1-4*) Linden Hills Pr.

— Good Gardener. 1991. pap. 9.95 (*0-9628378-0-6*) Linden Hills Pr.

— Landscaping with Trees & Shrubs: The Northern Gardener's Library. 1992. pap. 9.95 (*0-9628378-2-2*) Linden Hills Pr.

Linden, Ian. Emirs & Evangelicals. 1986. 29.50 (*0-7146-3146-9*, BHA-03146, Pub. by F Cass Pubs UK) Intl Spec Bk.

Linden, James D., jt. auth. see Shertzer, Bruce E.

Linden, Jonathan, ed. see CAD-CAM Alert Editors.

Linden, Jonathan, ed. see Johnson, Robert H.

Linden, Jonathan, ed. see Mayer, Ralph.

Linden Lane Press Staff, ed. see Arango, Guillermo.

Linden-Laufer, S., jt. auth. see Colvin, E.

Linden, Lena. Development Change & Linear Structural Equations: Application of LISREL Models. (IEA Monograph Studies: No. 13). 114p. (Orig.). 1986. pap. text ed. 38.00x (*91-22-00803-9*, Pub. by Almqv & Wiksell SW) Coronet Bks.

Linden, Mary, jt. auth. see Glass, Jane.

Linden, Mary S. Suzie's Story: The Autobiography of Socialite, Philanthropist & World Traveler, Mary Sue McCulloch Linden. LC 92-25761. 1992. 29.95 (*0-935834-87-7*) Rainbow Books.

Linden, Millicent. Living in a State of Orgasm. LC 62-22285. (Illus.). (Orig.). 1967. pap. 5.00 (*0-912628-01-4*) M Linden NY.

— The Orgasm is a Vacuum, Tension-in-Repose, the Fountain of Youth Foundation: Unifying the Body in the Universal Field of Unification Through Tension-in-Repose. (Illus.). 1985. 8.00 (*0-912628-11-1*) M Linden NY.

— Preparing Your Body to Fly, Vol. 1. 1977. pap. 7.00 (*0-912628-05-7*) M Linden NY.

— Tension-in-Repose: A Basic Home Series Course. (Illus.). 100p. 1971. 4.95 (*0-912628-08-1*) M Linden NY.

— Tension-in-Repose: An Introduction to Living in a State of Orgasm, Vol. 1. LC 62-22285. (Illus.). 1975. 5.00 (*0-912628-09-X*) M Linden NY.

— The Yawn, et Al: A Key to Reserve Buoyancy for Human Flight. LC 78-64375. (Evolutionary New Material from Tension in Repose Ser.). (Illus.). 1978. 7.00 (*0-912628-06-5*) M Linden NY.

Linden, Myra J. & Whimbey, Arthur. Analytical Writing & Thinking: Facing the Tests. 472p. 1990. 69.95 (*0-8058-0908-2*); teacher ed write for info. (*0-8058-0932-5*); pap. 22.50 (*0-8058-0648-2*) L Erlbaum Assocs.

— Why Johnny Can't Write: How to Improve Writing Skills. 136p. 1990. 19.95 (*0-8058-0852-3*); pap. 10.95 (*0-8058-0853-1*) L Erlbaum Assocs.

Linden, Paula & Gross, Susan. Taking Care of Mommy. (Family Bk. Ser.). 239p. 1983. pap. 7.95 (*0-318-19491-0*) M E Pinkham.

Linden, Philip Van. Knowing Christ Through Mark's Gospel. 1977. pap. 1.95 (*0-8199-0727-8*, Frncscn Herld) Franciscan Pr.

Linden, R. Ruth. Making Stories, Making Selves: Feminist Reflections on the Holocaust. LC 92-20410. (Helen Hooven Santmyer Prize in Women's Studies). (Illus.). 191p. (C). 1993. text ed. 39.50 (*0-8142-0583-6*) Ohio St U Pr.

Linden, Richard, jt. auth. see Newkirk, William.

Linden, Robin R., et al, eds. Against Sadomasochism: A Radical Feminist Analysis. LC 81-15284. 224p. (Orig.). (C). 1981. pap. 7.95 (*0-9603628-3-5*) Frog in Well.

Linden, Ronald H. Bear & Foxes: The International Relations of the East European States, 1965-1969. (East European Monographs: No. 50). 318p. 1979. text ed. 54.00 (*0-914710-45-1*) East Eur Quarterly.

***Linden, Ronald H. & Rockman, Bert A., eds.** Elite Studies & Communist Politics: Essays in Memory of Carl Beck. LC 83-21637. 366p. 1984. pap. 104.40 (*0-7837-8540-2*, 2049355) Bks Demand.

Linden, Russell M. Seamless Government: A Practical Guide to Re-Engineering in the Public Sector. (Public Administration Ser.). 256p. 1994. 25.95 (*0-7879-0015-X*) Jossey-Bass.

Linden, Stanton J. William Cooper's - A Catalogue of Chymicall Books, 1673-88: A Verified Version. LC 86-27165. (Reference Library of the Humanities). 224p. 1987. lib. bdg. 20.00 (*0-8240-8557-4*, H670) Garland.

Linden, Stanton J., ed. see Bachon, Roger.

Linden, Stanton J., jt. ed. see Dixon, Laurinda.

Linden, W. Psychological Perspectives of Essential Hypertension. (Biobehavioral Medicine Ser.: Vol. 3). (Illus.). x, 130p. 1984. pap. 55.25 (*3-8055-3662-3*) S Karger.

— Psychologiche Perspektiven des Bluthochdrucks. (Illus.). vii, 132p. 1983. 53.75 (*3-8055-3642-9*) S Karger.

Linden, W., ed. Biological Barriers in Behavioral Medicine. LC 87-36137. (Behavioral Psychophysiology Ser.). (Illus.). 348p. 1988. 60.00 (*0-306-42651-X*, Plenum Pr) Plenum.

Linden-Ward, Blanche. Silent City on a Hill: Landscapes of Memory & Boston's Mount Auburn Cemetery. (Urban Life & Urban Landsapes Ser.). (Illus.). 400p. 1989. 56.50 (*0-8142-0469-4*) Ohio St U Pr.

Linden-Ward, Blanche & Green, Carol H. American Women in the Nineteen Sixties: Changing the Future. LC 92-592. (American Women in the Twentieth Century Ser.). 608p. 1992. text ed. 55.00 (*0-8057-9905-2*, Twayne); pap. 19.95 (*0-8057-9913-3*, Twayne) Macmillan.

Linden, William, jt. auth. see Newkirk, William.

Linden, Wolfgang. Autogenic Training: A Clinical Guide. LC 90-13970. 180p. 1990. lib. bdg. 40.00 (*0-89862-551-3*); pap. text ed. 17.95 (*0-89862-454-1*) Guilford Pr.

Lindenauer, Isak. August Tiesselinck: A Lifetime in Metal, 1890-1972. (Illus.). 82p. 1990. pap. 20.00 (*0-9624994-0-4*) Lindenauer.

Lindenbauer, Leo. Diets, Diets, Diets Made You Fat, Fat, Fat: Diets Don't Work. (Health Ser.). 95p. 1993. reprint ed. pap. write for info. (*0-9639616-0-8*) L Lindenbauer.

Lindenbaum, Pija. Boodil, My Dog. LC 92-13172. (Illus.). 48p. (J). (ps-2). 1992. 14.95 (*0-8050-2444-1*, Bks Young Read) H Holt & Co.

— Boodil, My Dog. LC 92-13172. (Illus.). 48p. (J). (PS-2). 1995. pap. 5.95 (*0-8050-3940-6*, Owlet BYR) H Holt & Co.

Lindenbaum, S. J., ed. Experimental Meson Spectroscopy, 1983: Seventh International Conference, Brookhaven. LC 84-70910. (AIP Conference Proceedings Ser.: No. 113). 506p. 1984. lib. bdg. 46.00 (*0-88318-312-9*) Am Inst Physics.

Lindenbaum, S. J., jt. ed. see Chung, S. U.

Lindenbaum, Samuel D. Analytical Dynamics - Course N. 316p. 1994. text ed. 74.00 (*981-02-1467-7*) World Scientific Pub.

Lindenbaum, Shirley. Kuru Sorcery: Disease & Danger in the New Guinea Highlands. Edgerton, Robert B. & Langness, L. L., eds. LC 78-64596. 174p. (C). 1979. pap. 14.95 (*0-87484-362-6*) Mayfield Pub.

Lindenbaum, Shirley & Lock, Margaret M., eds. Knowledge, Power, & Practice: The Anthropology of Medicine & Everyday Life. LC 92-28208. (Comparative Studies of Health Systems & Medical Care: Vol. 36). 1993. 50.00 (*0-520-07784-9*); pap. 15.00 (*0-520-07785-7*) U CA Pr.

Lindenbaum, Shirley, jt. auth. see Herdt, Gilbert.

Lindenberg, et al. Chemical Thermodynamics. 352p. 1996. pap. 20.00 (*0-8016-6750-X*) Mosby Yr Bk.

Lindenberg, Christoph. Teaching History: Suggested Themes of the Curriculum in Waldorf Schools. Luborsky, Peter, tr. 204p. (Orig.). 1989. pap. text ed. 10.00 (*0-9623978-0-6*) Assn Waldorf Schls.

Lindenberg, J., jt. ed. see Kolkman, P. A.

Lindenberg, Katja, tr. see Honerkamp, Josef.

Lindenberg, Marc & Crosby, Benjamin. Managing Development: The Political Dimension. LC 80-83345. (Library of Management for Development). 217p. (Orig.). 1981. 34.95 (*0-931816-49-1*); pap. 16.25 (*0-685-02928-X*) Transaction Pubs.

— Managing Development: The Political Dimension. fac. ed. LC 80-83345. (Illus.). 231p. (Orig.). 1994. pap. 65.90 (*0-7837-7579-2*, 2047332) Bks Demand.

Lindenberg, Marc & Ramirez, Noel. Managing Adjustment in Developing Countries: Economic & Political Perspectives. LC 89-20119. 328p. 1990. 34.95 (*1-55815-053-6*); pap. 14.95 (*1-55815-054-4*) ICS Pr.

Lindenberg, Marc M. The Human Development Race: Improving the Quality of Life in Developing Countries. LC 93-14619. 233p. 1993. 29.95 (*1-55815-277-6*); pap. 14.95 (*1-55815-278-4*) ICS Pr.

Lindenberg, Nita. Strangers to Themselves: Encounters with Retarded & Insane People. 110p. 1990. pap. 12.95 (*0-86315-087-X*, 1421, Pub. by Floris Books UK) Anthroposophic.

Lindenberg, Richard, et al. Neuropathology of Vision: An Atlas. LC 73-12319. 510p. reprint ed. pap. 145.40 (*0-317-28596-3*, 2055437) Bks Demand.

Lindenberg, Siegwart, et al, eds. Approaches to Social Theory. LC 85-62806. 450p. (C). 1986. text ed. 45.00 (*0-87154-205-6*) Russell Sage.

Lindenberg, Siegwart M. & Schreuder, Hein, eds. Interdisciplinary Perspectives on Organization Studies. LC 92-33026. 1993. text ed. 96.00 (*0-08-040814-1*, Pergamon Pr) Elsevier.

Lindenberger, Herbert. Georg Trakl. 166p. 1971. 49.50 (*0-685-63212-1*) Elliots Bks.

— Opera: The Extravagant Art. LC 84-7092. 298p. 1984. 37.50 (*0-8014-1698-1*); pap. 15.95 (*0-8014-9425-7*) Cornell U Pr.

— Saul's Fall: A Critical Fiction. LC 78-22003. 1979. 38.50 (*0-8018-2176-2*) Johns Hopkins.

Lindenberger, Herbert S. The History in Literature: On Value, Genre, & Institutions. 269p. 1992. text ed. 39.50 (*0-231-07252-X*) Col U Pr.

— On Wordsworth's Prelude. LC 75-25493. 316p. 1976. reprint ed. text ed. 60.50 (*0-8371-8417-7*, LIOW, Greenwood Pr) Greenwood.

Lindenberger, James M. Ancient Aramaic & Hebrew Letters. LC 93-6657. (SB Writings from the Ancient World Ser.: No. 4). 172p. 1994. 44.95 (*1-55540-839-7*, 061504) Scholars Pr GA.

Lindenberger, James M., ed. Ancient Aramaic & Hebrew Letters. LC 93-6657. (Writings from the Ancient World Ser.: No. 4). 1994. pap. 29.95 (*1-55540-840-0*) Scholars Pr GA.

Lindenberger, Jan. Black Memorabilia Around the House: A Handbook & Price Guide. LC 92-63106. (Illus.). (Orig.). 1993. pap. 16.95 (*0-88740-487-1*) Schiffer.

— Black Memorabilia for the Kitchen: A Handbook & Price Guide. LC 96-60635. (Illus.). 144p. 1992. pap. 15.95 (*0-88740-432-4*) Schiffer.

— Collecting Plastics: A Handbook & Price Guide. LC 91-65648. (Illus.). 144p. 1991. pap. 15.95 (*0-88740-335-2*) Schiffer.

— Collecting the Fifties & Sixties: A Handbook & Price Guide. (Illus.). 160p. 1993. pap. 16.95 (*0-88740-543-6*) Schiffer.

— The Fifties & Sixties Kitchen: A Handbook & Price Guide. LC 93-87048. (Illus.). 160p. 1994. pap. 16.95 (*0-88740-591-6*) Schiffer.

— More Black Collectibles: A Handbook & Price Guide. LC 94-37616. (Illus.). 160p. (Orig.). 1995. pap. 16.95 (*0-88740-733-1*) Schiffer.

— Raggedy Ann & Andy Collectibles: A Handbook & Price Guide. (Illus.). 160p. (Orig.). 1995. pap. 19.95 (*0-88740-782-X*) Schiffer.

***Lindenberger, Jan & Spontak, Joyce.** Planters Peanuts Collectibles 1906-1961: Handbook & Price Guide. LC 95-10515. (Illus.). 160p. (Orig.). 1995. pap. 19.95 (*0-88740-792-7*) Schiffer.

Lindenburg, Katja & West, Bruce J. Open & Closed Systems: The Nonequilibrium Statistical Mechanics of Nonlinear Processes. 464p. 1990. lib. bdg. 55.00 (*0-89573-347-1*) VCH Pubs.

Lindenbusch, John, ed. see Harris, NiNi.

Lindenfeld, Frank. When Workers Decide: Workplace Democracy Takes Root in North America. Krimerman, Len, ed. 304p. (Orig.). 1992. pap. 16.95 (*0-86571-201-8*) New Soc Pubs.

— When Workers Decide: Workplace Democracy Takes Root in North America. Krimerman, Len, ed. 304p. (Orig.). 1992. lib. bdg. 39.95 (*0-86571-200-X*) New Soc Pubs.

Lindenfeld, Frank, ed. Radical Perspectives on Social Problems: Readings in Critical Sociology. 3rd ed. 414p. (Orig.). 1987. lib. bdg. 38.95 (*0-930390-74-1*); pap. text ed. 18.95 (*0-930390-73-3*) Gen Hall.

Lindenfeld, Frank & Rothschild-Whitt, Joyce, eds. Workplace Democracy & Social Change. LC 82-80137. 456p. (C). 1982. 20.00 (*0-87558-101-3*, Extending Hor Bks); pap. 12.00 (*0-87558-102-1*, Extending Hor Bks) Porter Sargent.

Lindenfeld, Jacqueline. Speech & Sociability at French Urban Marketplaces. LC 90-31713. (Pragmatics & Beyond New Ser.: Vol. 7). viii, 173p. 1990. 47.00x (*1-55619-109-X*) Benjamins North Am.

Lindenfeld, Jacqueline, tr. see Cohen, Daniel.

Lindenfeld, P., jt. auth. see Fillo, J. A.

Lindenfeld, Peter. Radioactive Radiations & Their Biological Effects. 2nd ed. 75p. 1985. reprint ed. 10.00 (*0-318-41548-8*, IO13) Am Assn Physics.

— Summary of Some Properties of Nuclei, Nuclear Radiation, & Reactors. 26p. 1981. 5.00 (*0-318-41554-2*, MS3) Am Assn Physics.

Lindenmann, J., jt. auth. see Edelhart, M.

Lindenmann, Walter K. Attitude & Opinion Research. 3rd ed. 83p. 1983. 24.00 (*0-89964-221-7*) Coun Adv & Supp Ed.

Lindenmayer, A., jt. auth. see Prusinkiewicz, P.

Lindenmayer, Clem. Trekking in the Patagonian Andes: A Walking Guide. (Illus.). 224p. (Orig.). 1992. pap. 13.95 (*0-86442-144-3*) Lonely Planet.

Lindenmayer, Jean-Pierre & Kay, Stanley R., eds. New Biological Vistas on Schizophrenia. LC 91-45371. (Einstein Clinical & Experimental Psychiatry Monograph Ser.: No. 6). 288p. 1992. 45.95 (*0-87630-654-7*) Brunner-Mazel.

Lindenmeyer, Leonard. DOS Operating System: With Coverage of 5.0. 540p. (C). 1993. pap. 35.95 (*0-87835-752-1*, BF7521) S-W Pub.

Lindenstrauss, J. & Milman, V. D., eds. Geometric Aspects of Functional Analysis. (Lecture Notes in Mathematics Ser.: Vol. 1267). vii, 212p. 1987. pap. 30.00 (*0-387-18103-2*) Spr-Verlag.

— Geometric Aspects of Functional Analysis. (Lecture Notes in Mathematics Ser.: Vol. 1376). vii, 288p. 1989. pap. 37.30 (*0-387-51303-5*) Spr-Verlag.

— Geometric Aspects of Functional Analysis. (Lecture Notes in Mathematics Ser.: Vol. 1469). xi, 191p. 1991. pap. 32.00 (*0-387-54024-5*) Spr-Verlag.

— Geometric Aspects of Functional Analysis: Israel Seminar (GAFA) 1992-94. LC 95-10775. (Operator Theory, Advances & Applications Ser.: Vol. 77). 1995. write for info. (*0-8176-5207-8*) Birkhauser.

Lindenstrauss, J. & Tzafriri, L. Classical Banach Spaces II: Function Spaces. (Ergebnisse der Mathematik und Ihrer Grenzgebiete Ser.: Vol. 97). 1979. 79.00 (*0-387-08888-1*) Spr-Verlag.

Lindenstrauss, Joram. Extension of Compact Operators. 4th ed. LC 52-42839. (Memoirs Ser.: No. 1/48). 112p. 1987. reprint ed. pap. 18.00 (*0-8218-1248-3*, MEMO 1/48) Am Math.

Lindenthal. The Health of the American Jew. write for info. (*0-275-90018-5*, C0018, Praeger Pubs) Greenwood.

Lindenthal, Jacob J. & Schneider, Mareleyn. Health Concerns of Hispanics in New York City. LC 91-21072. 256p. 1991. lib. bdg. 89.95 (*0-7734-9852-4*) E Mellen.

Lindenthal, Jacob J., jt. auth. see Thomas, Claudewell S.

Linder. Transdisciplinary Play-Based Assessment & Intervention: Child & Program Summary Forms. 58p. 1993. 27.00 (*1-55766-163-4*) P H Brookes.

Linder, jt. auth. see Damjanov.

Linder, A. Planen und Auswerten von Versuchen. 3rd ed. (Reihe der Experimentellen Biologie Ser.: No. 13). (Illus.). 344p. (GER.). 1980. 94.00 (*0-8176-0248-8*) Birkhauser.

Linder, Amnon, tr. & comment. The Jews in Roman Imperial Legislation. LC 87-6290. 437p. 1987. 44.95 (*0-8143-1809-6*) Wayne St U Pr.

Linder, Bert. Condemned Without Judgment: The Three Lives of a Holocaust Survivor. 1994. 19.95 (*1-56171-340-6*) Sure Sellers.

***Linder, Bonnie S.** Dear Mr. President: When Parents Are Sent to War. (Children in the Military Ser.). (J). (ps-4). 1995. pap. text ed. 4.95 (*0-9643966-2-9*) Sylvan Crest.

— Just a Toy: Dealing with Weapons. (Children in the Military Ser.). (J). (ps-4). 1995. pap. text ed. 4.95 (*0-9643966-3-7*) Sylvan Crest.

— On My Way: Dealing with a Move. LC 94-92235. (Children in the Military Ser.). 20p. (J). (ps-4). 1994. pap. 4.95 (*0-9643966-0-2*) Sylvan Crest.

— Time Apart: Dealing with Family Separation. LC 94-92271. (Children in the Military Ser.). 18p. (J). (ps-4). 1994. pap. text ed. 4.95 (*0-9643966-1-0*) Sylvan Crest.

Linder, Erik H. Hjalmar Bergman. LC 74-23060. (Twayne's World Authors Ser.). 197p. (C). 1975. lib. bdg. 17.95 (*0-8057-2147-9*) Irvington.

Linder, Greg, ed. see Allen, Hayward.

Linder, Greg, ed. see Backes, David.

Linder, Greg, ed. see Breining, Greg.

Linder, Greg, ed. see Fitzharris, Tim.

Linder, Harry, jt. auth. see Linder, Olive.

Linder, Harry P. Techniques of Code Drafting: The Lively Art of Personal Weaving Drafts. LC 83-72938. (Illus.). 140p. (Orig.). 1983. 16.95 (*0-915113-00-7*) Bizarre Butterfly.

Linder, James, ed. Check Sample Stack: Cytopathology. 1992. disk 200.00 (*0-89189-323-7*, D69-3-002-33) Am Soc Clinical.

Linder, James & Rennard, Steven. Atlas of Bronchoalveolar Lavage. LC 87-31924. (Illus.). 257p. 1988. 105.00 (*0-89189-261-3*, 16-1-042-00); sl. 125.00 (*0-89189-272-9*) Am Soc Clinical.

Linder, Leo & Dromberg, D. A. The Serpentine Rouletted Stamps of Finland: Issues of 1860 & 1866. Koplowitz, G. B., ed. Aro, Kauko, tr. (Illus.). 106p. (Orig.). 1983. pap. text ed. 17.50 (*0-936493-00-3*) Scand Philatelic.

Linder, Leslie. The Journal of Beatrix Potter. 480p. 1990. 29.95 (*0-7232-3625-9*) Warne.

Linder, M. C. Biochemistry of Copper. (Biochemistry of the Elements Ser.: Vol. 10). (Illus.). 430p. 1991. 95.00 (*0-306-43658-2*, Plenum Pr) Plenum.

Linder, M. C., ed. Nutritional Biochemistry & Metabolism: With Clinical Applications. 2nd ed. 310p. 1991. 59.50 (*0-8385-7084-4*) Appleton & Lange.

Linder, Marc. The Employment Relationship in Anglo-American Law: A Historical Perspective. LC 89-7492. (Contributions in Legal Studies: No. 54). 309p. 1989. text ed. 65.00 (*0-313-26824-X*, LER/, Greenwood Pr) Greenwood.

— Farewell to the Self-Employed: Deconstructing a Socioeconomic & Legal Solipsism. LC 91-39643. (Contributions in Labor Studies: No. 41). 200p. 1992. text ed. 47.95 (*0-313-28466-0*, LFW/, Greenwood Pr) Greenwood.

— Labor Statistics & Class Struggle. LC 94-34677. 130p. 1994. pap. 7.50 (*0-7178-0711-8*) Intl Pubs Co.

— Migrant Workers & Minimum Wages: Regulating the Exploitation of Agricultural Labor in the United States. LC 92-19439. 322p. (C). 1992. pap. text ed. 54.50 (*0-8133-8616-0*) Westview.

— Projecting Capitalism: A History of the Internationalization of the Construction Industry. LC 93-50546. (Contributions in Economics & Economic History Ser.). 288p. 1994. text ed. 59.95 (*0-313-29293-0*, Greenwood Pr) Greenwood.

— The Supreme Labor Court in Nazi Germany. 290p. 1987. 65.00 (*0-685-58348-1*) Transnatl Pubs.

Linder, Mark. Little Boy Blue. 1992. 22.50 (*0-679-40981-5*) Random.

Linder, Mark, et al, contribs. Scogin, Elam, & Bray: A Critical Monograph. LC 92-15638. (Illus.). 224p. 1992. 60.00 (*0-8478-1534-X*); pap. 35.00 (*0-8478-1535-8*) Rizzoli Intl.

***Linder, Mats.** The ECITC Guide to IT&T Testing & Certification. (Illus.). 110p. (Orig.). (C). 1994. pap. text ed. 45.00 (*0-7881-1493-X*) Diane Pub.

Linder, O. D. The Gibson & Related Families. 1991. 42.50 (*0-9627513-1-6*) Linder.

Linder, O. D., jt. auth. see Linder, Penny.

Linder, Olive & Linder, Harry. Handspinning Cotton. (Illus.). 100p. 1985. pap. 8.95 (*0-915113-02-3*) Bizarre Butterfly.

— Handspinning Flax. (Illus.). 80p. 1986. 9.95 (*0-915113-04-X*) Bizarre Butterfly.

Linder, P. W., et al. Analysis Using Glass Electrodes. 160p. 1984. 65.00 (*0-335-10420-7*, Open Univ Pr) Taylor & Francis.

Linder, Pamela, jt. auth. see Holstead, Christy.

Linder, Patrick, jt. ed. see Hall, Michael N.

Linder, Penny & Linder, O. D. The Linder Family. 1991. 32.50 (*0-9627513-0-8*) Linder.

***Linder, Ray.** Making the Most of Your Money: How to Develop a Personal Financial Strategy for Maximum Impact. 180p. Date not set. pap. 10.99 (*1-56476-389-7*, Victor Books) SP Pubns.

Linder, Ron. Animals on the Roof. 136p. (Orig.). 1993. pap. 9.95 (*0-9635886-3-X*) R Linder.

Linder, Roscoe G. An Evaluation of the Courses in Education of a State Teachers College by Teachers in Service. LC 79-176995. (Columbia University. Teachers College. Contributions to Education Ser.: No. 664). reprint ed. 22.50 (*0-404-55664-7*) AMS Pr.

***Linder, S. Wayne.** Loan Review Deskbook: How to Establish, Maintain & Regulate an Effective Program. 276p. 1989. 135.00 (*1-55520-203-9*) Probus Pub Co.

— Total Quality Loan Management: Applying the Principles of TQM for Superior Lending Performance. 1993. 50.00 (*1-55738-371-5*) Probus Pub Co.

Linder, Staffan B. The Harried Leisure Class. LC 73-92909. 182p. 1971. pap. text ed. 15.50 (*0-231-08649-0*) Col U Pr.

— The Pacific Century: Economic & Political Consequences of Asian-Pacific Dynamism. 168p. 1986. 25.00 (*0-8047-1294-8*); pap. 10.95 (*0-8047-1305-7*) Stanford U Pr.

Linder, Steven. The Measure of Justice. LC 92-11520. 194p. 1992. 19.95 (*0-8027-4134-7*) Walker & Co.

— Wager. 192p. 1986. 14.95 (*0-8027-4061-8*) Walker & Co.

***Linder, Sune & Kellomaki, Seppo, eds.** Management of Structure & Productivity of Boreal & Subalpine Forests. (Studia Forestalia Suecica Ser.: No. 191). (Illus.). 94p. (Orig.). 1994. pap. 33.50x (*91-576-4822-0*, Pub. by Almqv & Wiksell SW) Coronet Bks.

Linder, Toni W. Transdisciplinary Play-Based Intervention: Guidelines for Developing a Meaningful Curriculum for Young Children. LC 93-426. 1993. 47.00 (*1-55766-130-8*) P H Brookes.

Linderer, Gary. The Eyes of the Eagle. 224p. (Orig.). 1991. mass mkt. 5.99 (*0-8041-0733-5*) Ivy Books.

Linderer, Gary A. Eyes Behind the Lines. 1991. mass mkt. 4.99 (*0-8041-0819-6*) Ivy Books.

***Linderman, Carol.** Womb with a View. (J). Date not set. 7.95 (*1-56901-581-3*) NW Pub.

Linderman, Charles W., ed. International Technical Conference on Slurry Tranportation, 2nd: Proceedings. LC 77-81416. (Illus.). 152p. 1977. pap. 100.00 (*0-932066-02-X*) Coal Slurry Tech.

— International Technical Conference on Slurry Transportation, 4th: Proceedings. LC 79-63397. (Illus.). 248p. 1971. pap. 100.00 (*0-932066-04-6*) Coal Slurry Tech.

Linderman, Charles W. & Skedgell, David W., eds. International Technical Conference on Slurry Transportation, 5th: Proceedings. 5th ed. LC 80-92621. (Illus.). 296p. (Orig.). 1980. pap. 100.00 (*0-932066-05-4*) Coal Slurry Tech.

Linderman, David A., et al. Alzheimer's Day Care: A Basic Guide. 152p. 1990. 57.00 (*0-89116-106-6*); pap. 29.00 (*1-56032-152-0*) Hemisp Pub.

Linderman, Earl W. & Linderman, Marlene M. Arts & Crafts in the Classroom. 2nd ed. (Illus.). 528p. (C). 1984. text ed. write for info. (*0-02-370860-3*) Macmillan.

Linderman, F. B., jt. auth. see Reiss, W.

***Linderman, Frank B.** Indian Lodge-Fire Stories. (Illus.). 96p. (Orig.). 1995. pap. 10.95 (*0-943972-39-6*) Homestead WY.

— Indian Why Stories. LC 95-12885. (Illus.). 1995. pap. write for info. (*0-486-28800-5*) Dover.

— Montana Adventure: The Recollections of Frank B. Linderman. Merriam, H. G., ed. LC 85-1051. 236p. reprint ed. pap. 67.30 (*0-7837-4277-0*, 2043969) Bks Demand.

— Plenty-Coups: Chief of the Crows. LC 30-11369. (Illus.). x, 325p. 1962. pap. 10.95 (*0-8032-5121-1*, Bison Books) U of Nebr Pr.

— Pretty-Shield. (Native American Voices Ser.). (Illus.). 256p. reprint ed. write for info. (*0-7835-1758-0*) Time-Life.

— Pretty-Shield: Medicine Woman of the Crows. LC 72-3273. (Illus.). 256p. 1974. reprint ed. pap. 9.95 (*0-8032-5791-0*, Bison Books) U of Nebr Pr.

— Quartzville. Barsness, Larry, ed. LC 85-15431. (Illus.). 200p. 1985. 15.95 (*0-87842-194-7*); pap. 9.95 (*0-87842-195-5*) Mountain Pr.

— Recollections of Charley Russell. LC 63-18074. (Illus.). 196p. 1988. pap. 13.95 (*0-8061-2112-2*) U of Okla Pr.

— Wolf & the Winds. LC 86-40075. 224p. 1986. 21.95 (*0-8061-2007-X*) U of Okla Pr.

***Linderman, Frank B. & Russell, Charles M.** Indian Old-Man Stories: More Sparks from War Eagle's Lodge-Fire. (Illus.). 208p. 1995. pap. 16.95 (*1-56044-357-X*) Falcon Pr MT.

— Indian Why Stories: Sparks from War Eagle's Lodge-Fire. (Illus.). 256p. 1995. pap. 16.95 (*1-56044-356-1*) Falcon Pr MT.

Linderman, Gerald F. Embattled Courage: The Experience of Battle in the American Civil War. 288p. 1987. 24.95 (*0-02-919760-0*) Free Pr.

— Embattled Courage: The Experience of Combat in the American Civil War. 357p. 1989. pap. 12.95 (*0-02-919761-9*) Free Pr.

Linderman, Hank. Hot Tips for the Home Recording Studio. 160p. 1994. 18.99 (*0-89879-651-2*) Writers Digest.

Linderman, Jennifer J., jt. auth. see Lauffenburger, Douglas A.

***Linderman, Joan M. & Funk, Virginia.** The New Complete Akita. (Illus.). 256p. 1995. 25.95 (*0-87605-031-3*) Howell Bk.

Linderman, Joan M. & Funk, Virginia B. The Complete Akita. LC 83-6180. (Complete Breed Book Ser.). (Illus.). 216p. 1983. 25.95 (*0-87605-006-2*) Howell Bk.

***Linderman, Marlene G.** Art in the Elementary School: Drawing, Painting & Creating for the Classroom. 272p. (C). 1995. pap. write for info. (*0-697-12500-9*) Brown & Benchmark.

— Art in the Elementary School: Drawing, Painting, & Creating for the Classroom. 4th ed. 320p. (C). 1990. pap. write for info. (*0-697-03341-4*) Brown & Benchmark.

Linderman, Marlene M., jt. auth. see Linderman, Earl W.

Linderman, R. G., jt. ed. see Bethlenfalvay, G. J.

Linderman, R. G., jt. ed. see Pfleger, F. L.

Linderman, Sheila, jt. auth. see Hayot, Roger.

Lindermeyer, Vivian & Howell, Leon, eds. Ethics in the Present Tense: Christianity & Crisis 1966-1991. 200p. (Orig.). 1991. 21.95 (*0-377-00239-9*); pap. 12.95 (*0-377-00230-5*) Friendship Pr.

Linders, B. E. Strategic Planning in South East England 1968-78: A Case Study. (Illus.). 83p. 1985. pap. 22.00 (*0-08-032720-6*, Pergamon Pr) Elsevier.

Linders, Tullia & Alroth, Brita, eds. Economics of Cult in the Ancient Greek World: Proceedings of the Uppsala Symposium 1990. (Uppsala Studies in Ancient Mediterranean & Near Eastern Civilizations: No. 21). (Illus.). 99p. (Orig.). (C). 1993. pap. 41.50x (*91-554-3031-7*, Pub. by Uppsala Universitet SW) Coronet Bks.

Lindert, Peter H. International Economics. 9th ed. 672p. (C). 1990. text ed. 63.95 (*0-256-07900-5*) Irwin.

— International Economics. 9th ed. 256p. (C). 1991. student ed 20.95 (*0-256-07901-3*) Irwin.

— Key Currencies & Gold, Nineteen Hundred to Nineteen Thirteen. LC 76-93955. (Princeton Studies in International Finance Ser.: No. 24). 89p. reprint ed. pap. 25.40 (*0-317-28387-1*, 2022391) Bks Demand.

Lindert, Peter H., jt. ed. see Eichengreen, Barry.

Lindert, Peter H., jt. auth. see Williamson, Jeffrey G.

Lindesay, James, et al. Delirium & the Elderly. (Illus.). 132p. 1991. 45.00 (*0-19-261862-8*) OUP.

Lindesay, William. Alone on the Great Wall. LC 91-71367. 234p. 1991. pap. 14.95 (*1-55591-079-3*) Fulcrum Pub.

— Marching with Mao: A Biographical Journey. (Illus.). 224p. 1995. 39.95 (*0-340-55664-1*, Pub. by H & S UK) Trafalgar.

Lindesmith, Alfred R., et al. Social Psychology. 6th ed. (Illus.). 512p. (C). 1988. text ed. write for info. (*0-13-817990-5*) P-H.

Lindestrom, Peter. Geographia Americae with an Account of the Delaware Indians. Scott, Franklyn D., ed. LC 78-15195. (Scandinavians in America Ser.). (Illus.). 1979. reprint ed. lib. bdg. 40.95 (*0-405-11648-9*) Ayer.

Lindey, Alexancer. Separation Agreements & Ante-Nuptial Contracts, 3 vols. 1964. Updates. ring bd. write for info. (*0-8205-1360-1*) Bender.

Lindey, Alexander & Landau, Michael. Lindey on Entertainment, Publishing & the Arts: Agreements & the Law, 4 vols. 2nd ed. LC 80-10991. (Entertainment & Communication Law Ser.). 1980. disk, ring bd. 580.00 (*0-87632-005-1*) Clark Boardman Callaghan.

Lindey, Christine. Art in the Cold War. (Illus.). 224p. (C). 1991. 30.00 (*1-56131-010-7*) New Amsterdam Bks.

Lindfield, G. R. & Penny, J. E. Microcomputers in Numerical Analysis. LC 93-23169. (Mathematics & Its Applications Ser.: Statistics, Operational Research, & Computational Mathematics Section). 1993. 23.95 (*0-13-336744-4*, Tavistock-E Horwood) Routledge Chapman & Hall.

Lindfield, George, jt. auth. see Penny, John.

***Lindfors.** Popular Literatures in Africa. Date not set. per. 12.95 (*0-86543-221-X*) Africa World.

Lindfors, Bernth. Black African Literature in English, 1982-86. 550p. 1989. lib. bdg. 85.00 (*0-905450-75-2*, Pub. by H Zell Pubs UK) Bowker-Saur.

— Black African Literature in English, 1987-1991. (Bibliographical Research in African Literature Ser.: No. 3). 472p. 1995. 125.00 (*1-873836-16-3*, Pub. by H Zell Pubs UK) Bowker-Saur.

— Folklore in Nigerian Literature. LC 72-91804. 200p. (C). 1974. 35.00 (*0-8419-0134-1*, Africana) Holmes & Meier.

— Long Drums & Canons: Teaching & Researching African Literatures. LC 94-37182. 1994. write for info. (*0-86543-436-0*); pap. write for info. (*0-86543-437-9*) Africa World.

Lindfors, Bernth, ed. Approaches to Teaching Achebe's Things Fall Apart. LC 91-26230. (Approaches to Teaching World Literature Ser.: No. 37). x, 145p. 1991. 37.50 (*0-87352-547-7*, AP37C); pap. 18.00x (*0-87352-548-5*, AP37P) Modern Lang.

— Black African Literature in English: A Guide to Information Sources. LC 73-16983. (American Literature, English Literature, & World Literatures in English Information Guide Ser.: Vol. 23). 512p. 1978. 68.00 (*0-8103-1206-9*) Gale.

— Contemporary Black South African Literature: A Symposium. 2nd ed. LC 85-50381. (African Literature Association Annuals Ser.: No. 1). 145p. 1985. reprint ed. 22.00 (*0-89410-454-3*); reprint ed. pap. 14.00 (*0-89410-455-1*) Three Continents.

— Critical Perspectives on Amos Tutuola. LC 75-13706. (Illus.). 318p. (Orig.). 1975. 25.00 (*0-914478-05-2*); pap. 15.00 (*0-914478-06-0*) Three Continents.

— Critical Perspectives on Nigerian Literatures. LC 75-27391. 1976. boxed 25.00 (*0-914478-27-3*) Three Continents.

— Mazungumzo: Interviews with East African Writers, Publishers, Editors & Scholars. LC 80-25684. (Papers in International Studies: Africa Ser.: No. 41). 187p. reprint ed. pap. 53.30 (*0-7837-1327-4*, 2041475) Bks Demand.

— South African Voices. 36p. 1975. pap. 10.00 (*0-87959-125-0*) U of Tex H Ransom Ctr.

Lindfors, Bernth & Kothandaraman, Bata, eds. South Asian Responses to Chinua Achebe. 200p. (C). 1993. text ed. 27.50 (*81-85218-66-8*, Pub. by Prestige II) Advent Bks Div.

Lindfors, Bernth & Schild, Ulla. Neo-African Literature & Culture: Essays in Memory of Janheinz Jahn. 352p. 1982. text ed. 49.50 (*3-593-32821-6*) Irvington.

Lindfors, Bernth, ed. see Veit-Wild, Flora.

Lindfors, Berth. Early Nigerian Literature. LC 81-12719. 180p. 1982. 35.50 (*0-8419-0740-4*, Africana) Holmes & Meier.

Lindfors, Eula A., ed. Guild Musicianship. 64p. (gr. 3-12). 1974. pap. text ed. 9.95 (*0-87487-638-9*) Summy-Birchard.

Lindfors, Judith W. Children's Language & Learning. 2nd ed. (Illus.). 512p. (C). 1987. text ed. 53.00 (*0-13-131962-0*) P-H.

Lindfors, Judith W., ed. Delicate Balances: Collaborative Research in Language Education. LC 93-8097. (Illus.). 148p. (Orig.). 1993. pap. 14.95 (*0-8141-1077-0*) NCTE.

Lindfors, Viveca & Austin, Paul, eds. I Am a Woman. 96p. 1991. pap. 7.95 (*1-55783-048-7*) Applause Theatre Bk Pubs.

***Lindgaard, Gitte.** Using the Data Warehouse: A Guide for Designing Useful Computer Systems. LC 94-142590. (Computing Ser.). 393p. 1994. pap. 54.95 (*0-412-46100-5*) Chapman & Hall.

Lindgreen, P., jt. ed. see Falkenberg, E. D.

Lindgren, Alvin J. Foundations for Purposeful Church Administration. LC 65-16459. 1965. 17.95 (*0-687-13339-4*) Abingdon.

Lindgren, Alvin J. & Shawchuck, Norman. Let My People Go: Empowering Laity for Ministry. 144p. (Orig.). (C). 1989. reprint ed. pap. text ed. 10.95 (*0-938180-15-0*) Spiritual Growth.

Lindgren, Alvin J., jt. auth. see Shawchuck, Norman.

Lindgren, Amy, ed. see Kelnhofer, Guy, Jr.

Lindgren, Astrid. A Calf for Christmas. Lucas, Barbara, tr. (Illus.). 32p. (J). (ps up). 1991. bds. 13.95 (*91-29-59920-2*, Pub. by R & S Bks) FS&G.

— The Children of Noisy Village. (J). (gr. 3-7). 1988. pap. 5.99 (*0-14-032609-X*, Puffin) Puffin Bks.

— The Children on Troublemaker Street. LC 91-15647. (Illus.). 112p. (J). (gr. 1-4). 1991. reprint ed. pap. 3.50 (*0-689-71515-3*, Aladdin Paperbacks) S&S Childrens.

— Christmas in Noisy Village. LC 64-21473. (Picture Puffins Ser.). 32p. (J). (ps-3). 1981. pap. 4.99 (*0-14-050344-7*, Puffin) Puffin Bks.

— Christmas in the Stable. (Sandcastle Ser.). (Illus.). 32p. (J). 1991. 5.95 (*0-698-20677-0*, Sandcastle Bks) Putnam Pub Group.

— I Don't Want to Go to Bed. Lucas, Barbara, tr. (Illus.). 32p. (J). (ps up). 1988. 12.95 (*91-29-59066-3*, Pub. by R & S Bks) FS&G.

— I Want a Brother or Sister. Bibb, Eric, tr. (Illus.). 32p. (J). (ps up). 1988. 10.95 (*91-29-58778-6*, Pub. by R & S Bks) FS&G.

— I Want to Go to School, Too! Lucas, Barbara, tr. (Illus.). 32p. (J). (ps up). 1987. 10.95 (*91-29-58328-4*, Pub. by R & S Bks) FS&G.

— Lotta on Troublemaker Street. Bothmer, Gerry, tr. LC 90-25169. (Illus.). 64p. (J). (gr. 1-4). 1991. reprint ed. pap. 2.95 (*0-689-71443-2*, Aladdin Paperbacks) S&S Childrens.

— Lotta's Christmas Surprise. (Illus.). 32p. (J). (ps-3). 1990. 13.95 (*91-29-59782-X*, Pub. by R & S Bks) FS&G.

— Lotta's Easter Surprise. Lucas, Barbara, tr. (Illus.). 32p. (J). (ps up). 1991. bds. 13.95 (*91-29-59862-1*) FS&G.

— Mio My Son. (J). (gr. 3-7). 1988. pap. 4.99 (*0-14-032608-1*, Puffin) Puffin Bks.

— Mischievous Meg. Bothmer, Gerry, tr. LC 85-575. (Illus.). (J). (ps-00). 1985. pap. 4.99 (*0-14-031954-9*, Puffin) Puffin Bks.

— Pippi Goes on Board. 172p. (J). 1980. lib. bdg. 12.95 (*0-89967-014-8*) Harmony Raine.

— Pippi Goes on Board. (J). 1977. pap. 3.95 (*0-14-032774-6*, Puffin); pap. 3.99 (*0-14-030959-4*, Puffin) Puffin Bks.

— Pippi Goes on Board. (Illus.). (J). (gr. 4-6). 1957. pap. 13.99 (*0-670-55677-7*) Viking Child Bks.

— Pippi Goes on Board. 192p. (J). 1981. reprint ed. lib. bdg. 16.95 (*0-89966-339-7*) Buccaneer Bks.

— Pippi in the South Seas. Bothmer, Gerry, tr. (Illus.). 128p. (J). (gr. 3-7). 1977. pap. 3.99 (*0-14-030958-6*, Puffin) Puffin Bks.

— Pippi in the South Seas. (J). 1988. pap. 3.95 (*0-14-032773-8*, Puffin) Puffin Bks.

— Pippi in the South Seas. Bothmer, Gerry, tr. (Illus.). (J). (gr. 4-6). 1959. pap. 13.99 (*0-670-55711-0*) Viking Child Bks.

— Pippi Longstocking. Lamborn, Florence, tr. (Illus.). 158p. (J). (gr. 4-6). 1977. pap. 3.99 (*0-14-030957-8*, Puffin) Puffin Bks.

— Pippi Longstocking. (J). 1988. pap. 3.95 (*0-14-032772-X*, Puffin) Puffin Bks.

— Pippi Longstocking. Lamborn, Florence, tr. (Illus.). (J). (gr. 4-6). 1950. pap. 13.99 (*0-670-55745-5*) Viking Child Bks.

— Pippi Longstocking. 192p. (J). 1981. reprint ed. lib. bdg. 21.95 (*0-89966-338-9*) Buccaneer Bks.

— Pippi Longstocking. 175p. (J). 1980. reprint ed. lib. bdg. 12.95 (*0-89967-013-X*) Harmony Raine.

— Ronia, the Robber's Daughter. (J). (gr. 3-7). 1993. 17.25 (*0-8446-6649-1*) Peter Smith.

— Ronia, the Robber's Daughter. (Illus.). 176p. (J). (gr. 4-7). 1985. pap. 4.99 (*0-14-031720-1*, Puffin) Puffin Bks.

— The Tomten. (Sandcastle Ser.). (Illus.). 32p. (J). (ps-3). 1990. pap. 5.95 (*0-698-20680-0*, Sandcastle Bks) Putnam Pub Group.

— The Tomten. LC 61-10658. (Illus.). (J). (gr. 1-3). 1979. reprint ed. 14.95 (*0-698-20147-7*, Coward) Putnam Pub Group.

— The Tomten & the Fox. (Illus.). 32p. (J). (ps-3). 1989. pap. 5.95 (*0-698-20644-4*, Sandcastle Bks) Putnam Pub Group.

***Lindgren, Babro.** Louie. Murray, Steve, tr. (Illus.). 32p. (J). 1994. 10.95 (*91-29-62916-0*) FS&G.

Lindgren, Barbro. Sam's Ball. LC 83-722. (Illus.). 32p. (J). (ps-00). 1983. 6.95 (*0-688-02359-2*) Morrow Jr Bks.

— Sam's Bath. LC 83-724. (Illus.). 32p. (J). (ps-00). 1983. 6.95 (*0-688-02362-2*) Morrow Jr Bks.

— Sam's Car. LC 82-3437. Orig. Title: Max Bil. (Illus.). 32p. (J). (gr. k-3). 1982. 6.95 (*0-688-01263-9*) Morrow Jr Bks.

— Sam's Cookie. LC 82-3419. Orig. Title: Max Kaka. (Illus.). 32p. (J). (gr. k-3). 1982. 6.95 (*0-688-01267-1*) Morrow Jr Bks.

— Sam's Potty. LC 86-864. (Illus.). 32p. (J). (ps-00). 1986. 6.95 (*0-688-06603-8*) Morrow Jr Bks.

— Sam's Teddy Bear. LC 82-3418. (Illus.). 32p. (J). (gr. k-3). 1982. 6.95 (*0-688-01270-1*) Morrow Jr Bks.

— Sam's Wagon. LC 86-865. (Illus.). 32p. (J). (ps-00). 1986. 6.95 (*0-688-05802-7*) Morrow Jr Bks.

— The Wild Baby. Prelutsky, Jack, tr. LC 81-2151. (Illus.). (J). (gr. k-3). 1981. lib. bdg. 15.88 (*0-688-00601-9*) Greenwillow.

— The Wild Baby Gets a Puppy: Swedish Edition. Prelutsky, Jack, tr. LC 87-212. Orig. Title: Vilda bebin far en hund. (Illus.). 32p. (J). (ps-3). 1988. reprint ed. 11.95 (*0-688-06711-5*); reprint ed. lib. bdg. 11.88 (*0-688-06712-3*) Greenwillow.

Lindgren, Bernard W. Statistical Theory. 4th ed. LC 93-1042. 633p. 1993. 57.95 (*0-412-04181-2*) Chapman & Hall.

Lindgren, Bruce, jt. auth. see Judd, Peter.

Lindgren, Carl E. Panola Remembers: Education in a Southern Community. 240p. (Orig.). 1994. pap. write for info. (*0-9631249-4-3*) Morris Pubng.

Lindgren, Claire. Classical Art Forms & Celtic Mutations: Figural Art in Roman Britain. LC 80-18987. (Illus.). 244p. (Orig.). 1981. 24.00 (*0-8155-5057-X*, NP) Noyes.

Lindgren, Dorothy, jt. auth. see Crafton, Helen.

Lindgren, Gary F. Managing Industrial Hazardous Waste: A Practical Handbook. (Illus.). 390p. 1989. 79.95 (*0-87371-147-5*, TD1040) Lewis Pubs.

Lindgren, Gunilla W., ed. Growth As a Mirror of Conditions in Society. 116p. (Orig.). 1990. pap. 48.00x (*91-7656-224-7*, Pub. by Almqv & Wiksell SW) Coronet Bks.

Lindgren, H. Elaine. Land in Her Own Name: Women As Homesteaders in North Dakota. LC 89-64484. (Illus.). 300p. 1991. 25.00 (*0-911042-39-3*) N Dak Inst.

Lindgren, Henry C. Leadership, Authority & Powersharing. LC 81-18644. 186p. (Orig.). 1982. lib. bdg. 16.50 (*0-89874-251-X*) Krieger.

— Lindgren Three: Ancient Greek Bronze Coins from the Lindgren Collection. LC 93-74078. (Illus.). 228p. 1993. 90.00 (*0-9636738-1-5*) Classical Numismatic Grp.

— The Psychology of College Success: A Dynamic Approach. LC 79-25614. 158p. 1980. reprint ed. lib. bdg. 12.50 (*0-89874-035-5*) Krieger.

— The Psychology of Money. 342p. (C). 1991. lib. bdg. 37.50 (*0-89464-399-1*) Krieger.

Lindgren, Henry C., jt. auth. see Suter, W. Newton.

Lindgren, I. & Morrison, J. Atomic Many-Body Theory. 2nd ed. (Atoms & Plasmas Ser.: Vol. 3). (Illus.). xv, 469p. 1986. pap. 67.00 (*0-387-16649-1*) Spr-Verlag.

Lindgren, I., et al. Heavy Ion Spectroscopy & QED Effects in Atomic Systems: Proceedings of the Nobel Symposium. 272p. 1993. text ed. 95.00 (*981-02-1337-9*) World Scientific Pub.

Lindgren, J. Ralph & Taub, Nadine. The Law of Sex Discrimination. 2nd ed. Hannan, ed. LC 93-25946. 550p. (C). 1993. pap. text ed. 50.75 (*0-314-02708-4*) West Pub.

***Lindgren, James M.** Preserving Historic New England: Preservation, Progressivism, & the Remaking of Memory. (Illus.). 288p. 1995. 35.00 (*0-19-509363-1*) OUP.

— Preserving the Old Dominion: Historic Preservation & Virginia Traditionalism. LC 92-46301. (Illus.). 400p. 1993. 39.95 (*0-8139-1450-7*) U Pr of Va.

Lindgren, K. E. Time in the Performance of Contracts. 2nd ed. 1982. Australia. 62.00 (*0-409-30390-9*) Butterworth Legal Pubs.

Lindgren, K. E., jt. auth. see Vermeesch, R. B.

Lindgren, Kevin E., jt. auth. see Shtein, Basil J.

Lindgren, Marcia, jt. auth. see Dettmer, Helena.

Lindgren, Mereth, et al. A History of Swedish Art. (Illus.). 278p. 1987. 125.00x (*91-85330-78-7*, Pub. by Signum SW) Coronet Bks.

Lindgren, Merri V., ed. see Cooperative Children's Book Center Staff.

Lindgren, Michael. Glory & Failure: The Difference Engines of Johann Muller, Charles Babbage, & Georg & Edvard Scheutz. McKay, Craig G., tr. (Illus.). 1990. pap. 47.50x (*0-262-12146-8*) MIT Pr.

Lindgren, Nilo, jt. auth. see Wildes, Karl.

An Asterisk (*) at the beginning of an entry indicates that the title is appearing in BIP for the first time.

Lindgren, Raymond E. Norway-Sweden: Union, Disunion, & Scandinavian Integration. LC 78-13451. 298p. 1979. reprint ed. text ed. 38.50 (0-313-21043-8, LINS, Greenwood Pr) Greenwood.

Lindgren, S., ed. Modern Concepts in Neurotraumatology. (Acta Neurochirugica - Supplementum Ser.: No. 36). (Illus.). viii, 159p. 1987. pap. 114.00 (0-387-81931-2) Spr-Verlag.

Lindgren, S., jt. auth. see Jonsson, A.

***Lindgren, Torgny.** In Praise of Truth. Geddes, Tom, tr. 224p. 1995. 23.00 (0-00-271255-5, HarpT) HarpC.

— Light. 288p. 1994. pap. 13.00 (0-00-271172-9, IntlDept) HarpC.

— Light: A Novel. Geddes, Tom, tr. 288p. 1993. 24.00 (0-00-271171-0, Pub. by HarpC UK) HarpC.

Lindgrenson, Sonja, tr. see Hallberg, Peter.

Lindh, E. & Thorell, Jan, eds. Clinical Impact of Bone & Connective Tissue Markers. 350p. 1989. text ed. 92.00 (0-12-450740-9) Acad Pr.

Lindh, Thomas. Essays on Expectations in Economic Theory. (Studia Oeconomica Upsaliensia: No. 21). 112p. 1992. pap. text ed. 40.00x (91-554-2850-9, Pub. by Almqv & Wiksell SW) Coronet Bks.

Lindh, Wilborta, jt. auth. see Indovina, Theresa.

Lindh, Wilburta O., jt. auth. see Tamparo, Carol D.

Lindh, Wilburta Q., jt. auth. see Indovina, Theresa.

Lindh, Wilburta Q., jt. auth. see Tamparo, Carol D.

Lindhal, Erik, ed. see Wicksell, Knut.

Lindhardt, Jan. Martin Luther: Knowledge and Mediation in the Renaissance. LC 86-17940. (Texts & Studies in Religion: Vol. 29). 270p. 1986. lib. bdg. 89.95 (0-88946-817-6) E Mellen.

Lindhe, E. Textbook of Clinical Periodontology. 1989. 94.95 (87-16-06453-4, Yr Bk Med Pubs) Mosby Yr Bk.

Lindhe, Richard & Grossman, Steven D. Accounting Information Systems. LC 80-67524. 380p. (C). 1980. text ed. 69.95 (0-931920-23-X) Dame Pubns.

Lindhe, Richard, et al. The Business Policy Game. rev. ed. LC 84-73026. 112p. 1985. pap. 16.95 (0-931920-98-1) Dame Pubns.

Lindheim, Richard D., jt. auth. see Blum, Richard A.

Lindheim, Roslyn, et al. Changing Hospital Environments for Children. LC 75-188969. (Illus.). 218p. reprint ed. pap. 62.20 (0-7837-1715-6, 2057244) Bks Demand.

Lindheimer, jt. auth. see Barron.

Lindholdt, Paul, jt. ed. see Friedman, Mitch.

Lindholdt, Paul J., ed. see Josselyn, John.

Lindholm, Byron W., jt. ed. see Touliatos, John.

Lindholm, Charles. Charisma. 1990. 39.95 (1-55786-021-1) Blackwell Pubs.

— Charisma. 224p. 1993. pap. 17.95 (1-55786-453-5) Blackwell Pubs.

— The Islamic Middle East: An Historical Anthropology. (Illus.). Date not set. pap. write for info. (1-55786-421-7) Blackwell Pubs.

— The Islamic Middle East: An Historical Anthropology. (Illus.). 320p. (C). Date not set. write for info. (1-55786-420-9) Blackwell Pubs.

Lindholm, E. & Asbrink, L. Molecular Orbitals & Their Energies, Studied by the Semiempirical HAM Method. (Lecture Notes in Chemistry Ser.: Vol. 38). x, 288p. 1985. pap. 33.00 (0-387-15659-3) Spr-Verlag.

Lindholm, Lars B. Pilgrims of the Night: Pathfinders of the Magical Way. LC 93-36883. (Western Magic Historical Ser.). (Illus.). 256p. 1993. pap. 12.00 (0-87542-474-0) Llewellyn Pubns.

Lindholm, Megan, jt. auth. see Brust, Steven.

Lindholm, Paul R. First Fruits: Stewardship Thoughts & Stories from Around the World. LC 93-15679. 128p. (Orig.). 1993. lib. bdg. 18.95 (0-932727-67-0); pap. 11.95 (0-932727-66-2) Hope Pub Hse.

Lindholm, Richard W. Land Value Taxation, Progress & Poverty Centenary. LC 80-52299. 238p. 1981. 20.00 (0-299-08520-1) U of Wis Pr.

— Money & Banking. (Quality Paperback Ser.: No. 19). 271p. (Orig.). 1969. pap. 8.00 (0-8226-0019-6) Littlefield.

— Money Management & Institutions. 334p. 1978. pap. 8.00 (0-8226-0334-9) Littlefield.

— Value-Added Tax & Other Tax Reforms. LC 76-24827. (Illus.). 338p. 1976. 42.95 (0-911012-87-7) Nelson-Hall.

Lindholm, Richard W., ed. Examination of Basic Weaknesses of Income As the Major Federal Tax Base. LC 86-518. 336p. 1986. text ed. 59.95 (0-275-92148-4, C2148, Praeger Pubs) Greenwood.

— Flexible Manufacturing Systems 4: Proceedings of the 4th International Conference, Stockholm, Sweden, 15-17 October 1985. 500p. 1986. 128.25 (0-444-87814-9, North Holland) Elsevier.

— Property Taxation & the Finance of Education. LC 73-2046. (TRED Ser.). (Illus.). 346p. 1974. 32.50 (0-299-06440-9) U of Wis Pr.

— Property Taxation, U. S. A. Proceedings. (Committee on Taxation, Resources & Economic Development Ser.: No. 2). (Illus.). 332p. 1969. pap. 8.00 (0-299-04544-7) U of Wis Pr.

Lindholm, Roy. A Practical Approach to Sedimentology. (Illus.). 192p. 1987. text ed. 45.00 (0-04-551131-4); pap. text ed. 21.95 (0-04-551132-2) Routledge Chapman & Hall.

Lindholm, Ulric S., jt. auth. see Francis, Philip H.

Lindig, Carmen. The Path from the Parlor: Louisiana Women, 1879-1920. 195p. 1986. 17.50 (0-940984-30-X) U of SW LA Ctr LA Studies.

Lindinger, Herbert. Ulm Design: The Morality of Objects. Britt, David, tr. (Illus.). 288p. 1990. 50.00 (0-262-12147-6) MIT Pr.

Lindinger, W., et al, eds. Swarms of Ions & Electrons in Gases. (Illus.). 320p. 1984. 55.00 (0-387-81823-5) Spr-Verlag.

Lindisfarne, Nancy, jt. ed. see Cornwall, Andrea.

Lindkvist, K. G. Studies on the Local Sense of the Prepositions "in", "at", "on", "to" in Modern English. (Lund Studies in English: Vol. 20). 1974. reprint ed. pap. 40.00 (0-8115-0563-4) Periodicals Srv.

Lindlahr, H. Acute Diseases, Pts. I-II: Their Uniform Treatment by Natural Methods: Mental, Emotional & Psychic Disorders. 54p. 1973. spiral bd. 5.50 (0-7873-0562-6) Mokelumne.

Lindlahr, Henry. Natural Therapeutics, Vol. VI: Iridiagnosis & Other Diagnostic Methods. 5th ed. 327p. 1974. reprint ed. spiral bd. 19.25 (0-7873-0563-4) Mokelumne.

— Natural Therapeutics, Vol. 1: Philosophy. 354p. (Orig.). Date not set. pap. 35.95 (0-8464-4258-2) Beekman Pubs.

— Natural Therapeutics, Vol. 2: Practice. 328p. Date not set. 26.95 (0-8464-4259-0) Beekman Pubs.

— Natural Therapeutics, Vol. 3: Natural Dietics. 184p. Date not set. 19.95 (0-8464-4260-4) Beekman Pubs.

— Natural Therapeutics, Vol. 4: Iridiagnosis. 284p. Date not set. 31.50 (0-8464-4261-2); pap. 26.95 (0-685-71020-3) Beekman Pubs.

Lindlahr, Victor H. Eat & Reduce. (Illus.). 194p. 1972. pap. 4.95 (0-87877-015-1, H-15) Newcastle Pub.

— For Women After Forty. 1976. pap. 1.00 (0-87904-035-1) Lust.

— The Natural Way to Health. 255p. 1973. pap. 5.95 (0-87877-017-8, H-17) Newcastle Pub.

— The Natural Way to Health. LC 80-19863. 255p. 1980. reprint ed. lib. bdg. 27.00x (0-89370-617-5) Borgo Pr.

— You Are What You Eat. LC 80-19722. 128p. 1990. reprint ed. 25.00x (0-89370-604-3); reprint ed. pap. 15.00x (0-89370-990-5) Borgo Pr.

Lindland, Frances K. Memories of the Morning Calm. Brown, Darlene, ed. (Illus.). 228p. 1992. pap. 13.95 (0-9617572-3-X) Times Journal Pub.

Lindlar, H. Rororo Musikhandbuch, 2 vols. (GER.). 1976. pap. 35.00 (0-8288-5753-9, M7605) Fr & Eur.

***Lindlar, Heinrich.** Woerterbuch der Musik. 331p. (GER.). 1989. 59.95 (0-7859-8378-3, 3458160329) Fr & Eur.

Lindlbad, Sven-Olof, jt. auth. see Lindblad, Lisa.

***Lindle, Jane C.** Surviving School Micropolitics: Strategies for Administrators. LC 94-60924. 168p. 1994. text ed. 35.00 (1-56676-175-1) Technomic.

Lindle, Jane C., jt. auth. see Steffy, Betty E.

Lindley, B., jt. auth. see Nesbitt Hawes, R.

Lindley, Betty & Lindley, Ernest K. A New Deal for Youth: The Story of the National Youth Administration. LC 72-172687. (FDR & the Era of the New Deal Ser.). (Illus.). 316p. 1972. reprint ed. lib. bdg. 39.50 (0-306-70382-3) Da Capo.

Lindley, Celeste M. & Deloatch, Kimberly H. Infusion Technology: A Self-Instructional Approach. 120p. 1993. pap. 219.00 (1-879907-40-2) Am Soc Hlth-Syst.

— Infusion Technology Manual: A Self-Instructional Approach. (Illus.). 120p. 1993. pap. 63.00 (1-879907-38-0) Am Soc Hlth-Syst.

Lindley, Charles. The Ghost Book: Of Charles Lindley, Viscount Halifax. 512p. 1994. pap. 10.95 (0-7867-0151-X) Carroll & Graf.

***Lindley, Craig.** Photographic Imaging Techniques in C - C++ for Windows & Windows NT. LC 94-49718. 1995. pap. 44.95 (0-471-11568-1) Wiley.

Lindley, Craig A. Practical Image Processing in C: Acquisition Manipulation Storage. 1991. pap. text ed. 49.95 (0-471-53062-X); disk 49.95 (0-471-53240-1); disk 94.90 (0-471-54377-2) Wiley.

— Practical Ray Tracing in C. 528p. 1992. disk 49.95 (0-471-57301-9) Wiley.

Lindley, Curtis H. A Treatise on the American Law Relating to Mines & Mineral Lands Within the Public Land States & Territories & Governing the Acquisition & Enjoyment of Mining Rights in Lands of the Public Domain, 2 vols. 2nd ed. LC 72-2853. (Use & Abuse of America's Natural Resources Ser.). 1972. reprint ed. 145.95 (0-405-04517-4) Ayer.

— A Treatise on the American Law Relating to Mines & Mineral Lands Within the Public Land States & Territories & Governing the Acquisition & Enjoyment of Mining Rights in Lands of the Public Domain, 3 vols. 3rd ed. cclii, 2810p. 1988. reprint ed. Set, Vol. 1, cclii, 730p., Vol.2, 954p., Vol.3, 1126p. lib. bdg. 195.00 (0-8377-2411-2) Rothman.

— A Treatise on the American Law Relating to Mines & Mineral Lands Within the Public Land States & Territories & Governing the Acquisition & Enjoyment of Mining Rights in Lands of the Public Domain, 2 vols, 1. 2nd ed. LC 72-2853. (Use & Abuse of America's Natural Resources Ser.). 1972. reprint ed. 72.95 (0-405-04546-8) Ayer.

— A Treatise on the American Law Relating to Mines & Mineral Lands Within the Public Land States & Territories & Governing the Acquisition & Enjoyment of Mining Rights in Lands of the Public Domain, 2 vols, 2. 2nd ed. LC 72-2853. (Use & Abuse of America's Natural Resources Ser.). 1972. reprint ed. 72.95 (0-405-04547-6) Ayer.

Lindley, D. V. Bayesian Statistics, A Review. (CBMS-NSF Regional Conference Ser.: No. 2). v, 83p. (Orig.). 1972. reprint ed. pap. text ed. 16.00 (0-89871-002-2) Soc Indus-Appl Math.

***Lindley, D. V. & Scott, W. F.** New Cambridge Elementary Statistical Tables. 2nd ed. (Illus.). 100p. (C). 1995. pap. write for info. (0-521-48485-5) Cambridge U Pr.

Lindley, Daniel A. This Rough Magic: The Life of Teaching. LC 93-25009. 160p. 1993. text ed. 49.95 (0-89789-363-8, G366, Bergin & Garvey); pap. text ed. 15.95 (0-89789-366-2, H363, Bergin & Garvey) Greenwood.

Lindley, David. The End of Physics: The Myth of a Unified Theory. 320p. 1994. pap. 13.00 (0-465-01976-5) Basic.

— Thomas Campion. (Medieval & Renaissance Authors Ser.: Vol. 7). xii, 242p. 1986. 48.75 (90-04-07601-8) E J Brill.

— The Trials of Frances Howard: Fact & Fiction in the Court of King James. LC 93-654. 224p. 1993. 59.95 (0-415-05206-8, B2563) Routledge.

***Lindley, David, ed.** Court Masques. (World's Classics Ser.). (Illus.). 400p. 1995. 56.00 (0-19-812164-4); pap. 13.95 (0-19-282569-0) OUP.

Lindley, David, et al, eds. Cosmology & Particle Physics. 1991. 18.00 (0-917853-42-3, RB-57) Am Assn Physics.

Lindley, Dennis V. Making Decisions. 2nd ed. LC 08-512010. 1991. pap. text ed. 32.95 (0-471-90808-8) Wiley.

Lindley, Dennis V., jt. ed. see Clarotti, Carlo A.

Lindley, Denver, tr. see Hesse, Hermann.

Lindley, Denver, tr. see Remarque, Erich M.

Lindley, Dwight N., ed. see Mill, John Stuart.

Lindley, Ernest K. Franklin Delano Roosevelt: A Career in Progressive Democracy. rev. ed. LC 73-21771. (FDR & the Era of the New Deal Ser.). 366p. 1974. reprint ed. lib. bdg. 39.50 (0-306-70634-2) Da Capo.

— Half Way with Roosevelt. LC 75-8789. (FDR & the Era of the New Deal Ser.). x, 449p. 1975. reprint ed. lib. bdg. 49.50 (0-306-70706-3) Da Capo.

— The Roosevelt Revolution, First Phase. LC 74-637. (FDR & the Era of the New Deal Ser.). 328p. 1974. reprint ed. lib. bdg. 39.50 (0-306-70651-2) Da Capo.

Lindley, Ernest K., jt. auth. see Lindley, Betty.

Lindley, H., ed. New Harmony As Seen by Participants & Travelers: Pt. 1. Letters of William Pelham. Pt. 2. Diary & Recollections of Victor Colin Duclos. Pt. 3. Report of a Visit to New Harmony by Karl Bernhard. LC 74-32002. (American Utopian Adventure Ser.). (Illus.). 128p. 1976. reprint ed. lib. bdg. 25.00 (0-87991-028-3) Porcupine Pr.

***Lindley, Harlow.** Indiana As Seen by Early Travelers. 596p. 1992. pap. 17.75 (1-885323-05-0) IN Hist Bureau.

Lindley, I. J. D., et al, eds. The Chemokines: Biology of the Inflammatory Peptide Supergene Family II. (Advances in Experimental Medicine & Biology Ser.: Vol. 351). (Illus.). 234p. (C). 1994. 75.00 (0-306-44710-X) Plenum.

Lindley, John. Contribution to the Orchidology of India. 100p. (C). 1982. 30.00 (0-685-22346-9, Scientific) St Mut.

— Folia Orchidacea. 400p. (C). 1983. 80.00 (0-685-22345-0, Scientific) St Mut.

— Folia Orchidacea: A Enumeratiion of the Known Species of Orchids, 2 vols. in 1. 1983. reprint ed. 50.00 (90-6123-088-8) S Asia.

— The Genera & Species of Orchidaceous Plants, 7 vols. in 1. 1984. reprint ed. 50.00 (90-6123-091-8) Lubrecht & Cramer.

— Medical & Economical Botany. (C). 1988. 50.00 (0-317-92359-5, Scientific) St Mut.

— Medicinal & Economical Botany. 274p. (C). 1984. 65.00 (0-685-22359-0, Scientific) St Mut.

— Orchidaceous Plants. 553p. (C). 1983. 80.00 (0-685-22347-7, Scientific) St Mut.

— Rosarum Monographia: Or a Botanical History of Roses. (Old Roses Ser.). (Illus.). 1979. reprint ed. text ed. 27.50 (0-930576-17-9) E M Coleman Ent.

Lindley, John M. A Soldier Is Also a Citizen: The Controversy over Military Justice, 1917-1920. LC 90-45122. (Distinguished Studies in American Legal & Constitutional History: Vol. 15). 264p. 1990. reprint ed. 59.00 (0-8240-0026-9) Garland.

Lindley, L. Flora Medica: Botanical Account of More Important Plants Used in Medicine. (C). 1988. 120.00 (0-317-92360-9, Scientific) St Mut.

— The Genera & Species of Orchideous Plants. (C). 1988. 60.00 (0-685-22334-5, Scientific) St Mut.

Lindley, Lester G. The Constitution Faces Technology: The Relationship of the National Government to the Telegraph, 1866-1884. LC 75-2586. (Dissertations in American Economic History Ser.). 1975. 28.95 (0-405-07206-6) Ayer.

— Contract, Economic Change, & the Search for Order in Industrialized America. LC 93-5722. (Distinguished Studies in American Legal & Constitutional History). 344p. 1993. 57.00 (0-8153-0895-7, 93-5722) Garland.

Lindley, M. G., jt. ed. see Birch, Gordon G.

***Lindley, Mary E.** A Manual on Investigating Child Custody Reports. 194p. 1988. pap. 24.95 (0-398-06241-2) C C Thomas.

— A Manual on Investigating Child Custody Reports. 194p. (C). 1988. text ed. 42.95x (0-398-05487-8) C C Thomas.

Lindley, Mary E., jt. auth. see Plumb, Gordon B.

Lindley, Nathaniel, tr. see Thibaut, Anton F.

Lindley, P. G., ed. see Gunn, S. J.

Lindley, Richard, tr. see Calderwood, Michael.

Lindley, Richard, jt. auth. see Holmes, Jeremy.

Lindley, Richard B. Haciendas & Economic Development: Guadalajara, Mexico, at Independence. (Latin American Monographs: No. 58). 172p. (C). 1983. text ed. 19.95 (0-292-72042-4) U of Tex Pr.

Lindley, Ricky, illus. Refreshings: A Book of Renewal. 210p. (Orig.). 1990. pap. 9.95 (0-942727-18-5) NC Yrly Pubns Bd.

Lindley, Robert, ed. Higher Education & the Labor Market. 184p. 1981. 21.00 (0-900868-83-X, Open Univ Pr) Taylor & Francis.

***Lindley, William R.** Hard Times, Good Times in Oregon: Recollections of the 1930s. (Illus.). 112p. 1994. pap. 14.95 (0-89745-186-4) Sunflower U Pr.

— Twentieth-Century American Newspapers. (Illus.). 116p. 1993. pap. 14.95 (0-89745-160-0) Sunflower U Pr.

Lindlof, Thomas R. Natural Audiences: Qualitative Research of Media Uses & Effects. Voigt, Melvin J., ed. LC 86-17425. (Communication & Information Science Ser.). 288p. 1987. text ed. 45.00 (0-89391-341-3) Ablex Pub.

— Qualitative Communications Research Methods. (Current Communication: An Advanced Text Ser.: Vol. 3). 364p. 1994. 52.00 (0-8039-3517-X); pap. 24.95 (0-8039-3518-8) Sage.

Lindman, jt. ed. see Friberg.

Lindman, B., et al, eds. Surfactants & Macromolecules: Self-Assembly at Interfaces & in Bulk. (Progress in Colloid & Polymer Science Ser.: Vol. 82). 200p. 1991. 148.00 (0-387-91367-X) Spr-Verlag.

Lindman, H. R. Analysis of Variance in Experimental Designs. (Texts in Statistics Ser.). (Illus.). ix, 531p. 1991. 49.95 (0-387-97571-3) Spr-Verlag.

***Lindman, Maj.** Flicka, Ricka, Dicka & a Little Dog. LC 94-37260. (J). 1995. write for info. (0-8075-2486-7) A Whitman.

— Flicka, Ricka, Dicka & the Big Red Hen. LC 95-916. (J). 1995. write for info. (0-8075-2493-X) A Whitman.

— Flicka, Ricka, Dicka & the Little Dog. (J). (ps-3). 1995. pap. 6.95 (0-8075-2497-2) A Whitman.

— Flicka, Ricka, Dicka & the New Dotted Dresses. (Albert Whitman Prairie Bks.). (Illus.). 32p. (J). (ps-2). 1994. pap. 6.95 (0-8075-2494-8) A Whitman.

— Flicka, Ricka, Dicka & the Three Kittens. (Albert Whitman Prairie Bks.). (Illus.). 32p. (J). (ps-2). 1994. pap. 6.95 (0-8075-2500-6) A Whitman.

— Flicka, Ricka, Dicka & Their New Friend. LC 95-1050. (Illus.). (J). 1995. pap. write for info. (0-8075-2498-0) A Whitman.

— Flicka, Ricka, Dicka Bake a Cake. (J). (ps-3). 1995. pap. 6.95 (0-8075-2492-1) A Whitman.

— Flicka, Ricka, Dicka Bake a Cake. LC 94-37261. (J). 1995. write for info. (0-8075-2480-8) A Whitman.

— Snipp, Snapp, Snurr & Gingerbread. 1976. 9.95 (0-8488-1413-4) Amereon Ltd.

— Snipp, Snapp, Snurr & the Big Farm. (Illus.). 32p. (J). 1993. reprint ed. lib. bdg. 14.95 (1-56849-004-6) Buccaneer Bks.

— Snipp, Snapp, Snurr & the Big Surprise. (Illus.). 32p. (J). 1993. reprint ed. lib. bdg. 14.95 (1-56849-003-8) Buccaneer Bks.

— Snipp, Snapp, Snurr & the Buttered Bread. (J). (ps-3). 1995. pap. 6.95 (0-8075-7491-0) A Whitman.

— Snipp, Snapp, Snurr & the Buttered Bread. LC 94-37262. (J). 1995. write for info. (0-8075-7504-6) A Whitman.

— Snipp, Snapp, Snurr & the Buttered Bread. (Illus.). 32p. (J). 1993. reprint ed. lib. bdg. 14.95 (1-56849-002-X) Buccaneer Bks.

— Snipp, Snapp, Snurr & the Gingerbread. (Albert Whitman Prairie Bks.). (Illus.). 32p. (J). (ps-2). 1994. pap. 6.95 (0-8075-7493-7) A Whitman.

— Snipp, Snapp, Snurr & the Gingerbread. (Illus.). 30p. (J). 1991. reprint ed. pap. 10.95 (0-89966-829-1) Buccaneer Bks.

— Snipp, Snapp, Snurr & the Magic Horse. (Illus.). 32p. (J). 1993. reprint ed. lib. bdg. 14.95 (1-56849-001-1) Buccaneer Bks.

— Snipp, Snapp, Snurr & the Red Shoes. (Albert Whitman Prairie Bks.). (Illus.). 32p. (J). (ps-2). 1994. pap. 6.95 (0-8075-7496-1) A Whitman.

— Snipp, Snapp, Snurr & the Red Shoes. (Illus.). 32p. (J). 1993. reprint ed. lib. bdg. 14.95 (1-56849-000-3) Buccaneer Bks.

— Snipp, Snapp, Snurr & the Reindeer. LC 95-1048. (Illus.). (J). 1996. pap. write for info. (0-8075-7497-X) A Whitman.

— Snipp, Snapp, Snurr & the Reindeer. (Illus.). 32p. (J). 1993. reprint ed. lib. bdg. 14.95 (1-56849-005-4) Buccaneer Bks.

— Snipp, Snapp, Snurr & the Seven Dogs. (Illus.). 32p. (J). 1993. reprint ed. lib. bdg. 14.95 (1-56849-007-0) Buccaneer Bks.

— Snipp, Snapp, Snurr & the Yellow Sled. LC 95-1049. (J). 1995. write for info. (0-8075-7499-6) A Whitman.

— Snipp, Snapp, Snurr & the Yellow Sled. (Illus.). 30p. (J). 1991. reprint ed. pap. 10.95 (0-89966-828-3) Buccaneer Bks.

— Snipp, Snapp, Snurr Learn to Swim. (J). (ps-3). 1995. pap. 6.95 (0-8075-7494-5) A Whitman.

— Snipp, Snapp, Snurr Learn to Swim. (Illus.). 32p. (J). 1993. reprint ed. lib. bdg. 14.95 (1-56849-006-2) Buccaneer Bks.

Lindman, N., jt. ed. see Chadwick, M. J.

***Lindmier, Thomas A. & Mount, Steven R.** I Can Tell By Your Outfit That You Are a Cowboy: Wyoming Cowboy Gear, 1870-1928. (Illus.). 160p. (Orig.). 1995. 24.95 (0-931271-34-7); pap. 14.95 (0-931271-33-9) Hi Plains Pr.

Lindner, Al. Pike. 1994. pap. 11.95 (0-929384-52-0) In-Fisherman.

Lindner, Al, et al. Pike: An In-Fisherman Handbook of Strategies. (Illus.). 234p. (Orig.). 1983. pap. 11.95 (0-9605254-2-4) In-Fisherman.

— Smallmouth Bass: An In-Fisherman Handbook of Strategies. (Illus.). 246p. (Orig.). 1984. pap. 11.95 (0-9605254-3-2) In-Fisherman.

— Walleye Wisdom: An In-Fisherman Handbook of Strategies. (Illus.). 388p. (Orig.). 1983. pap. 11.95 (0-9605254-1-6) In-Fisherman.

Lindner, Carl. Angling into Light. LC 94-83572. 72p. (Orig.). 1994. pap. 7.95 (0-943512-15-8) Linwood Pub.

Lindner, Eileen W., et al. When Churches Mind the Children: A Study of Day Care in Local Parishes. LC 83-22545. 192p. (Orig.). 1983. pap. 10.95 (0-931114-23-3) High-Scope.

Lindner, Elsbeth, jt. ed. see Collins, Judith.

Lindner, Harold H. Clinical Anatomy. (Illus.). 690p. 1988. pap. text ed. 29.00 (0-8385-1259-3, A1259-9) Appleton & Lange.

Lindner, John B., ed. By Faith: Christian Students among the Cloud of Witnesses. (Orig.). 1991. pap. 9.95 (0-377-00236-4) Friendship Pr.

An Asterisk (*) at the beginning of an entry indicates that the title is appearing in BIP for the first time.

Lindner, Kurt. Bibliographie der Deutschen und der Niederlaendischen Jagdliteratur von 1480 bis 1850. (Illus.). (C). 1977. 384.60 (*3-11-006640-8*) De Gruyter.
Lindner, L. Cockatiels: Look & Learn. (Illus.). 64p. 1993. 7.95 (*0-7938-0069-2*, KD009) TFH Pubns.
Lindner, Lindy, jt. auth. see Means, Beth.
Lindner, M., jt. ed. see Buras, A. J.
Lindner, P. & Zemb, T. Neutron X-Ray & Light Scattering: Introduction to an Investigative Tool for Colloidal & Polymeric Systems. 1991. 89.75 (*0-444-88946-9*, NHD 8) Elsevier.
Lindner, Peter G. Doctor Lindner's Special Weight Control Method. 1979. pap. 2.00 (*0-87980-030-5*) Wilshire.
— Mind over Platter. 1972. pap. 5.00 (*0-87980-099-2*) Wilshire.
Lindner, R., jt. ed. see Muller, W.
Lindner, Rudi. Nomads & Ottomans in Medieval Anatolia. LC 82-61287. (Uralic & Altaic Ser.: Vol. 144). 190p. 1983. 20.00 (*0-933070-12-8*) Res Inst Inner Asian Studies.
Lindner, Thomas, jt. ed. see Lewerentz, Claus.
Lindner, Vicki, jt. auth. see Ohashi, Watari.
Lindner, Vicki, ed. see Ohashi, Watari.
Lindnerer, Wolf-Volker, jt. auth. see Konig, Karl.
Lindners, Al, et al. Crappie Wisdom: An In-Fisherman Handbook of Strategies. (Illus.). 258p. (Orig.). 1985. pap. 11.95 (*0-9605254-4-0*) In-Fisherman.
Lindo, David K. Supervision Can Be Easy! LC 79-17682. 282p. reprint ed. pap. 80.40 (*0-317-26952-6*, 2023582) Bks Demand.
Lindo, Elias H., tr. see Ben-Israel, Manasseh.
Lindo-Fuentes, Hector. Weak Foundations: The Economy of El Salvador in the Nineteenth Century, 1821-1898. (Illus.). 275p. 1990. 40.00 (*0-520-06927-7*) U CA Pr.
Lindo-Fuentes, Hector, jt. auth. see Gudmundson, Lowell.
Lindo, Howard. Making Dreams Come True. (YA). 1993. 7.95 (*0-533-10406-8*) Vantage.
Lindo, Hugo. Only the Voice. Miller, Elizabeth G., tr. Orig. Title: Solo La Voz. 110p. (Orig.). 1984. pap. 8.00 (*0-939378-04-3*) Mundus Artium.
— Ways of Rain. Miller, Yvette E., ed. Miller, Elizabeth G., tr. LC 86-18577. 160p. (ENG & SPA.). 1986. pap. 10.95 (*0-935480-24-2*) Lat Am Lit Rev Pr.
Lindo Systems Staff. Lindo Student Version. text ed. 3.00 (*0-13-121062-9*) P-H.
Lindofrs & Gibbs, eds. Research on Wole Soyinka. 45.00 (*0-86543-218-X*); pap. 14.95 (*0-86543-219-8*) Africa World.
Lindon, J. C., jt. auth. see Emsley, James W.
Lindon, James A. & Raber, Laura L. The Pen Is in My Hand...Now What? Exciting & Practical Ideas for Teaching Writing. Elletro Productions Staff, ed. LC 93-18914. (Illus.). 145p. 1993. pap. 11.95 (*1-56875-048-X*) R & E Pubs.
Lindop, Audrey E. I Start Counting. 320p. 1992. reprint ed. 16.50 (*0-86220-833-5*, Black Dagger) Chivers N Amer.
***Lindop, Barbara.** Sekoto: The Art of Gerard Sekoto. (Illus.). 64p. 1995. 24.95 (*1-85793-461-X*, Pub. by Pavilion UK) Trafalgar.
Lindop, Edmund. Assassinations That Shook America. LC 92-15082. (Illus.). 144p. (YA). (gr. 9-12). 1992. lib. bdg. 14.98 (*0-531-11049-4*) Watts.
— The Bill of Rights & Landmark Cases. LC 89-8960. (Illus.). 144p. (J). (gr. 7-9). 1989. lib. bdg. 14.98 (*0-531-10790-6*) Watts.
— Birth of the Constitution. LC 86-13380. (Illus.). 160p. (J). (gr. 6 up). 1987. lib. bdg. 18.95 (*0-89490-135-4*) Enslow Pubs.
— The Changing Supreme Court. LC 95-13842. (Democracy in Action Ser.). (Illus.). (YA). (gr. 7-12). 1995. lib. bdg. 15.33 (*0-531-11224-1*) Watts.
— Presidents by Accident. LC 91-17056. (Non-Fiction Ser.). (Illus.). 208p. (YA). (gr. 9-12). 1991. lib. bdg. 16.52 (*0-531-11059-1*) Watts.
— Presidents vs. Congress: Conflict & Compromise. LC 93-30784. (Democracy in Action Ser.). (Illus.). 168p. (YA). (gr. 9-12). 1994. lib. bdg. 14.21 (*0-531-11165-2*) Watts.
Lindop, G. B., jt. auth. see Semple, P. F.
Lindop, Grevel, ed. see De Quincey, Thomas.
***Lindorf, W.** Mountain Bike: Repair & Maintenance. (Illus.). 72p. 1995. pap. 12.95 (*0-7063-7420-7*, Pub. by Ward Lock UK) Sterling.
Lindow, C. W. & Blanchard, Homer D. A Little Organ Lexicon. (Little Organ Book Ser.: No. 2). 40p. 1981. pap. 7.50 (*0-930112-04-0*) Organ Lit.
Lindow, John. Comitatus, Individual & Honor: Studies in North Germanic Institutional Vocabulary. LC 75-620093. (University of California Publications in Social Welfare: Vol. 83). 193p. reprint ed. pap. 55.10 (*0-317-08268-X*, 2015111) Bks Demand.
— Myths & Legends of the Vikings. (Illus.). 1980. pap. 3.95 (*0-88388-071-7*) Bellerophon Bks.
— Swedish Legends & Folktales. LC 77-7830. 1978. 35.00 (*0-520-03520-8*) U CA Pr.
— Viking Ships. (J). (gr. 1-9). 1992. pap. 5.95 (*0-88388-078-4*) Bellerophon Bks.
Lindow, John, jt. ed. see Clover, Carol J.
Lindow, John, et al, eds. Structure & Meaning in Old Norse Literature: New Approaches to Textual Analysis & Literary Criticism. (Studies in Northern Civilization: No.3). 454p. 1986. pap. text ed. 67.50 (*87-7492-607-1*, Pub. by Odense Universitets Forlag DK) Coronet Bks.
Lindow, S. E., jt. ed. see Windels, C. E.
Lindow, Sandra. Rooted in the Earth. Moore, Eugenia & Leiper, Esther M., eds. (Illus.). 32p. (Orig.). (YA). (gr. 9 up). 1989. pap. 3.95 (*0-9617284-8-5*) Sand & Silk.
Lindoy, Leonard F. The Chemistry of Macrocyclic Ligand Complexes. 250p. (C). 1989. 89.95 (*0-521-25261-X*) Cambridge U Pr.
— The Chemistry of Macrocyclic Ligand Complexes. 288p. (C). 1990. pap. 27.95 (*0-521-40985-3*) Cambridge U Pr.
Lindpaintner, Klaus & Ganten, Detlev, eds. The Cardiac Renin-Angiotensin System. (Illus.). 392p. 1994. 75.00 (*0-87993-571-5*) Futura Pub.
Lindquist. Answers to Milady's Standard Theory Workbook. 160p. 1991. pap. 25.50 (*1-56253-006-2*) Milady Pub.
— Milady's Standard Theory Workbook 91. 160p. 1991. pap. 15.50 (*1-56253-005-4*) Milady Pub.
— Ophthalmic Surgery Update, No. 1. 50p. 1992. 75.00 (*0-8151-5459-3*) Mosby Yr Bk.
— Ophthalmic Surgery Update, No. 2. 1993. 75.00 (*0-8151-5460-7*, Yr Bk Med Pubs) Mosby Yr Bk.
— Ophthalmic Surgery Update, No. 3. Date not set. write for info. (*0-8151-5463-1*, Yr Bk Med Pubs) Mosby Yr Bk.
— Ophthalmic Surgery Update, No. 4. Date not set. write for info. (*0-8151-5461-5*, Yr Bk Med Pubs) Mosby Yr Bk.
— Ophthalmic Surgery Update, No. 5. Date not set. write for info. (*0-8151-5462-3*, Yr Bk Med Pubs) Mosby Yr Bk.
Lindquist, A. Ophthalmic Surgery: Core Workbook. 1989. 195.00 (*0-8151-5458-5*, Yr Bk Med Pubs) Mosby Yr Bk.
Lindquist, A., jt. ed. see Byrnes, Christopher I.
Lindquist, A., jt. auth. see Hanon.
Lindquist, Barbara, jt. auth. see Molnar, Alex.
***Lindquist, C.** Advances in Radiosurgery I. 124p. 1995. 94.00 (*3-211-82612-2*) Spr-Verlag.
Lindquist, Carol. The Banana Lover's Cookbook. LC 92-41399. 1993. pap. 10.95 (*0-312-08702-0*) St Martin.
Lindquist, Charles. Lenawee County: A Harvest of Pride & Promise. 208p. 1990. 25.95 (*0-89781-337-5*) Preferred Mktg.
Lindquist, Claude S. Active Network Design with Signal Filtering Applications. LC 76-14238. 1977. 49.95 (*0-917144-01-5*) Steward & Sons.
— Active Network Design with Signal Filtering Applications: Solutions Manual. 1978. 19.95 (*0-917144-02-3*) Steward & Sons.
— Adaptive & Digital Signal Processing with Digital Filtering Applications. 1988. 49.95 (*0-917144-03-1*) Steward & Sons.
Lindquist, David P. English & Continental Furniture with Prices. 240p. 1994. pap. 18.95 (*0-87069-662-9*, Wallace-Hmestead) Chilton.
— The Official Price Guide to Antiques & Collectibles. 1994. 13th ed. (Illus.). 704p. 1993. pap. 14.00 (*0-87637-872-6*, House of Collect) Ballantine.
***Lindquist, David P. & Waren, Caroline C.** Victorian Furniture with Prices. LC 95-10554. 248p. 1995. pap. 22.95 (*0-87069-664-5*, Wallace-Hmestead) Chilton.
Lindquist, David P. & Warren, Caroline C. Colonial Revival Furniture with Prices. LC 92-50671. 184p. 1993. pap. 14.95 (*0-87069-660-2*) Chilton.
Lindquist, Emory K. Bethany in Kansas: The History of a College. LC 75-18910. (Illus.). 320p. 1975. 5.00 (*0-916030-03-2*) Bethany Coll KS.
— Birger Sandzen: An Illustrated Biography. LC 92-23467. (Illus.). 200p. 1993. 29.95 (*0-7006-0575-4*) U Pr of KS.
— Hagbard Brase: Beloved Music Master. Pearson, A. John, ed. LC 84-16773. (Illus.). 166p. 1984. 10.00 (*0-916030-06-7*) Bethany Coll KS.
— An Immigrant's American Odyssey: A Biography of Ernst Skarstedt. LC 74-21137. (Augustana Historical Society Publication Ser.: No. 24). (Illus.). 240p. 1974. 5.95 (*0-910184-24-0*) Augustana.
— An Immigrant's Two Worlds: A Biography of Hjalmar Edgren. LC 72-80673. (Augustana Historical Society Publication Ser.: No. 23). (Illus.). 97p. 1972. 4.95 (*0-910184-23-2*) Augustana.
— Shepherd of an Immigrant People: The Story of Erland Carlsson. LC 78-108120. (Augustana Historical Society Publication Ser.: No. 26). 236p. 1978. 7.50 (*0-910184-26-7*) Augustana.
Lindquist, Emory K., et al. G. N. Malm: A Swedish Immigrant's Varied Career. Pearson, A. John, ed. LC 89-32481. (Illus.). 244p. 1989. 15.00 (*0-918331-01-3*) Smoky Valley Hist.
Lindquist, Eric N. The Origins of the Center for Hellenic Studies. (Illus.). 96p. 1991. text ed. 15.95 (*0-691-03174-6*) Princeton U Pr.
Lindquist, Grace C. Claudia of Pompeii. 1990. 16.95 (*0-533-09301-5*) Vantage.
Lindquist, Gustavus E. The Indian in American Life. LC 74-7977. reprint ed. 17.50 (*0-404-11867-4*) AMS Pr.
— Red Man in the United States: An Intimate Study of the Social, Economic & Religious Life of the American Indian. LC 68-56243. (Illus.). xxvii, 461p. 1973. reprint ed. lib. bdg. 49.50 (*0-678-00798-5*) Kelley.
Lindquist, Hal, ed. see Groneman, Chris H.
Lindquist, Hal, ed. see Helsel, Jay D. & Urbanick, Byron.
Lindquist, Jack. Strategies for Change. 1978. text ed. 14.95 (*0-937012-05-X*) Coun Indep Colleges.
Lindquist, Jack, ed. Designing Teaching Improvement Programs. LC 79-51475. 1978. reprint ed. pap. 12.95 (*0-937012-07-6*) Coun Indep Colleges.
Lindquist, Jennie D. The Crystal Tree. (J). (gr. 2-6). 19.50 (*0-8446-6287-9*) Peter Smith.
— The Little Silver House. (Illus.). (J). (gr. 2-6). 15.50 (*0-8446-6190-2*) Peter Smith.
Lindquist, John H. Misdemeanor Crime: Trivial Criminal Pursuit. LC 87-34664. (Studies in Crime, Law & Justice: No. 4). 197p. reprint ed. pap. 56.20 (*0-7837-6584-3*, 2046149) Bks Demand.
Lindquist, Kenneth H., intro. Catalogue of the Permanent Collection. (Illus.). 175p. 1973. 7.95 (*1-877885-00-2*) Arnot Art.
— Transients: Paintings by Thomas S. Buechner. (Orig.). 1985. pap. 14.95 (*1-877885-04-5*) Arnot Art.
***Lindquist, Lareau.** Too Soon To Quit: The Daily Encouragement Factor. 192p. 1994. 17.95 (*1-885481-00-4*) Quadrus Media.
— Too Soon To Quit: The Daily Encouragement Factor. 192p. 1994. pap. 9.95 (*1-885481-01-2*) Quadrus Media.
Lindquist, Linnea. Teaching Tips for Cosmetology. 24p. (C). 1981. pap. text ed. 16.00 (*0-314-63395-2*) West Pub.
Lindquist, Marie. Holding Back: Why We Hide the Truth about Ourselves. 148p. 1989. pap. 9.00 (*0-89486-419-X*, 5012A) Hazelden.
— In a Perfect World. 160p. (J). (gr. 6-12). 1991. per. 3.95 (*0-89486-775-X*, T5127) Hazelden.
Lindquist, Mark. Sculpting Wood: Contemporary Tools & Techniques. LC 86-70901. (Illus.). 304p. (Orig.). 1986. pap. 29.00 (*0-87192-228-2*) Davis Mass.
Lindquist, Mark A. & Zanger, Martin N., eds. Buried Roots & Indestructible Seeds: The Survival of American Indian Life in Story, History, & Spirit. LC 93-39068. (Illus.). 160p. 1995. pap. text ed. 12.95 (*0-299-14444-5*) U of Wis Pr.
— Buried Roots & Indestructible Seeds: The Survival of American Indian Life in Story, History, & Spirit. LC 94-39068. (Illus.). 160p. (C). 1995. lib. bdg. 42.00 (*0-299-14440-2*) U of Wis Pr.
Lindquist, Mary M., ed. Learning & Teaching Geometry, K-12: 1987 Yearbook. (Illus.). 250p. 1987. 20.00 (*0-87353-235-X*, 359E1) NCTM.
— Results from the Fourth Mathematics Assessment of the National Assessment of Educational Progress. LC 89-3335. (Illus.). 173p. 1989. pap. 15.00 (*0-87353-274-0*) NCTM.
— Selected Issues in Mathematics Education. LC 80-82903. (National Society for the Education Series on Contemporary Education Issues). 276p. (C). 1981. 27.50 (*0-8211-1114-0*); text ed. write for info. (*0-685-03242-6*) McCutchan.
Lindquist, Mary M., et al. Making Sense of Data. LC 92-41881. (Curriculum & Evaluation Standards for School Mathematics Addenda Ser.: Grades K-6). (Illus.). 48p. (Orig.). 1993. pap. 9.50 (*0-87353-318-6*) NCTM.
Lindquist, Nancy. Best of Friends. 1991. pap. 4.99 (*0-8024-1081-2*) Moody.
Lindquist, Patricia, jt. ed. see Azarnoff, Pat.
***Lindquist, Patricia E.** The Pictorial History of Fayetteville & Lincoln County, Tennessee. LC 94-22425. (Illus.). 1994. write for info. (*0-89865-926-4*) Donning Co.
Lindquist, Richard K., jt. auth. see Powell, Charles C.
Lindquist, Robert, jt. auth. see Bologna, G. Jack.
Lindquist, Robert A. Spinnin' How to Score a Hit As a Mobile DJ for Fun & Profit. Warner, David & Dygert, Clare, eds. (Illus.). 110p. 1987. pap. 15.00 (*0-943047-00-5*) TNT Prodns.
Lindquist, Robert J., jt. auth. see Bologna, G. Jack.
Lindquist, S., jt. ed. see Maresca, B.
Lindquist, Scott. Before He Takes You Out: The Safe Dating Guide for the 90's. LC 89-51783. 172p. 1989. pap. 9.95 (*0-9623779-0-2*) Vigal Pubs.
Lindquist, Susan H. Walking the Rim. LC 91-76966. 144p. (YA). (gr. 7 up). 1992. 14.95 (*1-56397-098-8*) Boyds Mills Pr.
***Lindquist, Tarry.** Seeing the Whole Through Social Studies. LC 94-48190. 206p. 1995. pap. text ed. 19.50 (*0-435-08902-1*) Heinemann.
***Lindquist, Timothy & Koehnemann, Harry, eds.** Proceedings of the PCTE '94 Conference. (PCTE Technical Journal Ser.: No. 2). 1994. pap. 50.00 (*0-9644599-0-6*) Mark V Systs.
Lindquist, W. Current Progress in Hyperbolic Systems: Riemann Problems & Computations. LC 89-17780. 367p. 1989. pap. 49.00 (*0-8218-5106-3*, CONM-100) Am Math.
Lindqvist, Cecilia. China. 1991. 38.95 (*0-201-57009-2*) Addison-Wesley.
Lindqvist, Maria. Infant Multinationals: The Internationalization of Young, Technology-Based Swedish Firms. 274p. (Orig.). 1991. pap. 115.00x (*91-971005-8-7*, Pub. by Almqv & Wiksell SW) Coronet Bks.
Lindqvist, S., et al, eds. Order & Chaos in Nonlinear Physical Systems. LC 88-15113. (Physics of Solids & Liquids Ser.). (Illus.). 488p. 1988. 115.00 (*0-306-42847-4*, Plenum Pr) Plenum.
Lindqvist, Svante, ed. Center on the Periphery: Historical Aspects of 20th-Century Swedish Physics. LC 93-32830. (Uppsala Studies in the History of Science: No. 17). (Illus.). 576p. (C). 1993. 50.00 (*0-88135-157-1*, Sci Hist) Watson Pub Intl.
Lindroos & Cermakova, H. Finnish-Czech, Czech-Finnish Pocket Dictionary: Suomi-Tsekki-Suomi Taskusankirja. 447p. (CZE & FIN.). 1984. 95.00 (*0-8288-1688-3*, F12200) Fr & Eur.
Lindros, Eric. Fire on Ice. 1991. pap. 14.95 (*0-00-637747-5*, Pub. by Angus & Robertson AT) HarpC.
— Fire on Ice. 1992. mass mkt. 5.50 (*0-06-109121-9*, Harp PBks) HarpC.
Lindros, K. O. & Eriksson, C. J., eds. The Role of Acetaldehyde in the Actions of Ethanol: Satellite Symposium to the Sixth International Congress of Pharmacology. (Finnish Foundation for Alcohol Studies: Vol. 23). (Illus.). 1975. pap. 8.00 (*951-9191-23-2*) Rutgers Ctr Alcohol.
Lindroth, Carl H. The Carabidae (Coleoptera) of Fennoscandia & Denmark, Pt. 1. (Fauna Entomologica Scandinavica Ser.: No. 15-1). (Illus.). 226p. 1985. text ed. 64.00 (*90-04-07727-8*) Lubrecht & Cramer.
— The Carabidae (Coleoptera) of Fennoscandia & Denmark, Pt. 2. (Fauna Entomologica Scandinavica Ser.: Vol. 15/2). (Illus.). 274p. 1986. 45.75 (*90-04-08182-8*) Lubrecht & Cramer.
— Ground Beetles (Carbidae) of Fennoscandia, Pt. II. (Illus.). (C). 1988. 30.00 (*81-205-0085-7*, Pub. by Oxford IBH II) S Asia.
***Lindroth, Colette & Lindroth, James.** Rachel Crothers: A Research & Production Sourcebook. LC 94-41267. (Modern Dramatists Research & Production Sourcebooks Ser.: Vol. 8). 160p. 1995. text ed. 59.95 (*0-313-27815-6*, Greenwood Pr) Greenwood.
Lindroth, James, jt. auth. see Lindroth, Colette.
Lindroth, James, jt. auth. see Sweeney, John D.
Lindroth, Mildred. Rhymes of the Times: Taken from the Nursery, Ironic Take-Offs on Mother Goose. 2nd ed. (Illus.). 24p. 1992. reprint ed. pap. 4.95 (*1-879009-09-9*) S P-Persephone Pr.
Lindroth, S. E. & Rynaenen, S. S., eds. Food Technology in the Year Two Thousand. (Bibliotheca Nutritio et Dieta Ser.: No. 47). (Illus.). xiv, 22p. 1990. 105.75 (*3-8055-5243-2*) S Karger.
Lindrup, Garth. Butterworths Competition Law Handbook. 3rd ed. 826p. 1993. pap. 100.00 (*0-406-02280-1*, UK) Butterworth Legal Pubs.
Lindsa, Sandra K., ed. see Acin-Kosta, Milos.
Lindsay. Follow Your Heart. large type ed. 1991. 17.95 (*0-7451-9781-7*, C0294, Atlantic Lrg Print); pap. 15.95 (*0-7927-0222-0*, C0428, Atlantic Lrg Print) Chivers N Amer.
— Food Microbiology. 1995. write for info. (*0-8493-4282-1*) CRC Pr.
— Functional Human Anatomy. 1994. 25.00 (*0-8016-6472-1*); 54.95 (*0-8016-6471-3*) Mosby Yr Bk.
Lindsay, A. A., jt. auth. see Sawyer, J. O.
Lindsay, A. B., tr. see Kuropatkin, Aleksei N.
Lindsay, A. Brook, III. The Cygnus Conspiracy. Amthor, Terry, ed. (Space Master Ser.). 32p. (Orig.). (YA). (gr. 10-12). 1987. pap. 12.00 (*0-915795-92-2*, 9102) Iron Crown Ent Inc.
Lindsay, A. Brooke, III. Raiders from the Frontier. Amthor, Terry K., ed. (Space Master Ser.). (Illus.). 64p. (Orig.). (C). 1989. pap. 9.00 (*1-55806-026-X*, 9800) Iron Crown Ent Inc.
Lindsay, A. D., tr. see Plato.
***Lindsay, Alan.** A. 150p. 1996. pap. 7.95 (*0-7610-0466-1*) NW Pub.
Lindsay, Alan & Neumann, Ruth. The Challenge for Research in Higher Education: Harmonizing Excellence & Utility. Fife, Jonathan D., ed. & frwd. by. LC 89-83630. (ASHE-ERIC Higher Education Report Ser.: No. 8, 1988). 150p. (Orig.). (C). 1989. pap. 15.00 (*0-913317-52-7*) GWU Schl E&HD.
Lindsay, Alan E. & Budkin, Alberto. The Cardiac Arrhythmias: An Approach to Their Electrocardiographic Recognition. 2nd ed. (Illus.). 178p. 1975. pap. 26.50 (*0-8151-5428-3*, Yr Bk Med Pubs) Mosby Yr Bk.
Lindsay, Alexander D. Karl Marx's 'Capital' LC 73-7456. (Illus.). 128p. 1973. reprint ed. text ed. 48.50 (*0-8371-6935-6*, LIMC, Greenwood Pr) Greenwood.
— Religion, Science, & Society in the Modern World. LC 70-37847. (Essay Index Reprint Ser.). 1977. reprint ed. 15.95 (*0-8369-2604-8*) Ayer.
Lindsay, Alexander D. & Erskine-Hall, Howard, eds. Congreve: The Critical Heritage. 496p. 1989. 112.00 (*0-415-02535-4*) Routledge.
Lindsay, Alexander D., tr. see Plato.
Lindsay, Alexander J., Jr., et al. Survey & Excavations North & East of Navajo Mountain, Utah, 1959-1962. (Glen Canyon Ser.: No. 8). 400p. 1968. pap. 12.50 (*0-685-14708-8*, BS-45) Mus Northern Ariz.
Lindsay, Anne. American Cancer Society Cookbook. 1990. 9.98 (*0-671-07484-9*) S&S Trade.
— Low-Cholesterol Cuisine. 1992. pap. 10.00 (*0-688-11616-7*, Quill) Morrow.
Lindsay, Anne & Fine, Diane J. American Cancer Society Cookbook: A Menu for Good Health. LC 87-28230. (Illus.). 256p. 1988. 25.00 (*0-688-07484-7*) Hearst Bks.
Lindsay, Beverly, ed. Comparative Perspectives of Third World Women: The Impact of Race, Sex, & Class. LC 78-19793. (Praeger Special Studies). 334p. 1980. text ed. 38.50 (*0-275-90514-4*, C0514, Praeger Pubs) Greenwood.
Lindsay, Beverly, jt. ed. see Ginsburg, Mark B.
***Lindsay, Cecile.** Reflexivity & Revolution in the New Novel: Claude Ollier's Ficional Cycle. 215p. 1990. 44.50 (*0-8142-0527-5*) Ohio St U Pr.
Lindsay, Cecile, tr. see Derrida, Jacques.
Lindsay, Cecile, tr. see Lyotard, Jean-Francois.
Lindsay, Charles, Jr. Have Fun Playing Jazz. (Music for Millions Ser.: Vol. 46). 1976. pap. 9.95 (*0-8256-4046-6*) Music Sales.
Lindsay, Charles. Mentawai Shaman: Shaman: Keeper of the Rain Forest. (Illus.). 120p. 1992. 39.95 (*0-89381-520-9*) Aperture.
— Turtle Islands: Balinese Ritual & the Green Turtle. LC 94-60220. (Illus.). 124p. 1995. 39.50 (*1-883489-10-5*) Takarajima.
Lindsay, Charles L. Trident: A Trading Strategy. 1991. 50.00 (*0-930233-48-4*) Windsor.
Lindsay, Cotton M. Equal Pay for Comparable Work: An Economic Analysis of a New Antidiscrimination Dotrine. 1980. pap. 2.50 (*0-916770-11-7*) Law & Econ U Miami.
— New Directions in Public Health Care: A Prescription for the 1980's. 308p. 1980. pap. 18.95 (*0-917616-37-5*) Transaction Pubs.
— New Directions in Public Health Care: A Prescription for the 1980's. 3rd ed. 308p. 1980. 29.95 (*0-87855-394-0*) Transaction Pubs.
Lindsay, Crawford. For Fun & Profit: Self-Employment Opportunities in Recreation, Sports & Travel. LC 84-47761. 179p. (Orig.). 1984. pap. 9.95 (*0-911781-01-3*) Live Oak Pubns.
***Lindsay, Cynthia.** Dear Boris: The Life of William Henry Pratt a.k.a. Boris Karloff. (Illus.). (Orig.). 1995. pap. 20.00 (*0-614-06773-1*) Limelight Edns.

An Asterisk (*) at the beginning of an entry indicates that the title is appearing in BIP for the first time.

— Dear Boris: The Life of William Henry Pratt a.k.a. Boris Karloff. (Illus.). 288p. (Orig.). 1995. reprint ed. pap. 20.00 (*0-87910-076-1*) Limelight Edns.

Lindsay, D. R. Breeding the Flock: Modern Research & Reproduction in Sheep. 1988. pap. 33.00 (*0-909605-45-9*, Pub. by Inkata Pr AT) Intl Spec Bk.

Lindsay, D. R. & Pearce, D. T., eds. Reproduction in Sheep. 427p. 1985. 115.00 (*0-521-30659-0*) Cambridge U Pr.

Lindsay, D. T. & Price, W. L. Information Security. 1991. 110.25 (*0-444-89219-2*) Elsevier.

Lindsay, David. Ane Satyre of the Thrie Estaits. LC 75-26333. (English Experience Ser.: No. 137). 156p. 1969. reprint ed. 45.00 (*90-221-0137-1*) Walter J Johnson.

— Devil's Tor. Reginald, R. & Melville, Douglas, eds. LC 77-84249. (Lost Race & Adult Fantasy Ser.). 1978. reprint ed. lib. bdg. 44.95 (*0-405-10995-4*) Ayer.

— A Voyage To Arcturus. 248p. 1985. pap. 5.95 (*0-8065-0944-9*, Citadel Pr) Carol Pub Group.

— A Voyage to Arcturus. 1993. reprint ed. lib. bdg. 18.95 (*0-89968-406-8*, Lghtyr Pr) Buccaneer Bks.

— The Warkis of the Famous & Worthie Knicht, Schir David Lyndesay. Newly Correctit & Augmentit. LC 75-171797. (English Experience Ser.: No. 352). 362p. 1971. reprint ed. 44.00 (*90-221-0352-8*) Walter J Johnson.

— Works, Pt. V. Small, J. & Hall, F., eds. (EETS, OS Ser.: Nos. 11, 19, 35, 37). 1974. reprint ed. 17.00 (*0-686-66918-5*) Periodicals Srv.

— Works, Pts. I-IV. Small, J. & Hall, F., eds. (EETS, OS Ser.: Nos. 11, 19, 35, 37). 1974. reprint ed. Pts. I-iV. 45.00 (*0-527-00013-2*) Periodicals Srv.

Lindsay, David L. Black Gold, Red Death. 256p. 1986. mass mkt. 5.99 (*0-449-13121-1*, GM) Fawcett.

— Body of Truth. 1993. mass mkt. 6.50 (*0-553-28964-0*) Bantam.

— In the Lake of the Moon. 1990. 5.99 (*0-553-28344-8*) Bantam.

Lindsay, David W., ed. see Gay, John, et al.

Lindsay, Debra. Science in the Subarctic: Trappers, Traders, & the Smithsonian Institution. LC 92-29811. (Illus.). 192p. (C). 1993. text ed. 34.00 (*1-56098-233-0*) Smithsonian.

***Lindsay, Dennis G.** The Birth of Planet Earth & the Age of the Universe. (Creation Science Ser.: Vol. 8). 1993. per. 8.95 (*0-89985-285-8*) Christ for the Nations.

— The Canopied Earth: World That Was. (Creation Science Ser.: Vol. 9). 1991. per. 7.95 (*0-89985-281-5*) Christ for the Nations.

— The Dinosaur Dilemma: Fact or Fantasy. (Creation Science Ser.: Vol. 7). 1990. per. 6.95 (*0-89985-279-3*) Christ for the Nations.

— The Dismantling of Evolutionism's Sacred Cow: Radiometric Dating. (Creation Science Ser.: Vol. 9). 1992. per. 8.95 (*0-89985-286-6*) Christ for the Nations.

— Foundations for Creationism. (Creation Science Ser.: Vol. 1). 1990. per. 5.95 (*0-89985-277-7*) Christ for the Nations.

— The Genesis Flood: Continents in Collision. (Creation Science Ser.: Vol. 5). 1992. per. 7.95 (*0-89985-282-3*) Christ for the Nations.

— Harmony of Science & Scripture. (Creation Science Ser.: Vol. 2). 1991. per. 6.95 (*0-89985-278-5*) Christ for the Nations.

— The Original Star Wars & the Age of Ice. (Creation Science Ser.: Vol. 6). 1992. per. 8.95 (*0-89985-284-X*) Christ for the Nations.

— The Origins Controversy: Creation or Chance. (Creation Science Ser.: Vol. 3). 1991. 6.95 (*0-89985-280-7*) Christ for the Nations.

Lindsay, Dennis R. Josephus & Faith: Pistis & Pisteuein As Faith Terminology in the Writings of Flavius Josephus & in the New Testament. LC 93-29156. (Arbeiten zur Geschichte des Antiken Judentums & des Urchristentums Ser.: Bd. 19). xiv, 212p. 1993. 63.00 (*90-04-09858-5*) E J Brill.

Lindsay, Diana, jt. ed. see Lindsay, Lowell.

Lindsay, Dorothy & Lindsay, Steele. Destiny at Cracker Creek. LC 84-61590. 192p. 1984. pap. 8.50 (*0-88100-047-7*) Natl Writ Pr.

Lindsay, E. H., et al, eds. European Neogene Mammal Chronology. LC 89-26648. (NATO ASI Series A, Life Sciences: Vol. 180). (Illus.). 668p. 1990. 139.50 (*0-306-43391-5*, Plenum Pr) Plenum.

Lindsay, Eldress B. Seasoned with Grace: My Generation of Shaker Cooking. Boswell, Mary R., ed. LC 87-19933. (Illus.). 164p. (Orig.). 1988. pap. 13.00 (*0-88150-099-2*) Countryman.

Lindsay, F. Panama, 2 vols. 1976. lib. bdg. 200.00 (*0-8490-2403-X*) Gordon Pr.

Lindsay, Fay D. A Special Kind of Freedom. (Illus.). 99p. (Orig.). 1982. pap. 7.00 (*0-943980-01-1*) AIGA Pubns.

Lindsay, Forbes. Cuba & Her People of Today. 1976. lib. bdg. 59.95 (*0-8490-1689-4*) Gordon Pr.

***Lindsay, Franklin.** Beacons in the Night: With the OSS & Tito's Partisans in Wartime Yugoslavia. (Illus.). 428p. 1995. pap. 14.95 (*0-8047-2588-8*) Stanford U Pr.

— Beacons in the Night: With the OSS & Tito's Partisans in Wartime Yugoslavia. LC 92-36774. (Illus.). 428p. (C). 1995. 45.00x (*0-8047-2123-8*) Stanford U Pr.

Lindsay, Franklin A., intro. Improving Management of the Public Work Force: The Challenge to State & Local Government. LC 78-11075. 138p. 1978. pap. 5.00 (*0-87186-067-8*) Comm Econ Dev.

— Jobs for the Hard-to-Employ: New Directions for a Private Partnership. LC 77-28272. (CED Statement on National Policy Ser.). 1978. lib. bdg. 4.50 (*0-87186-766-4*); pap. 3.00 (*0-87186-066-X*) Comm Econ Dev.

Lindsay, Frannie. The Aerial Tide Coming In. (Illus.). 16p. 1981. pap. 3.00 (*0-934714-24-X*); bds. 25.00 (*0-934714-23-1*) Swamp Pr.

— The Harp of the First Day. (Illus.). 34p. 1980. pap. 24.00 (*0-934714-13-4*) Swamp Pr.

— The Horse We Lie Down In: Eight Poems. (Poetry Chapbooks Ser.: No. 1). 10p. 1980. pap. 1.00 (*0-936044-02-0*) Pikestaff Pr.

Lindsay, G. C. Contract. 2nd ed. (LBC Nutshell Ser.). xiii, 157p. 1987. pap. 11.95 (*0-455-20767-4*, Pub. by Law Bk Co) W W Gaunt.

— Guide to the Practice of the Supreme Court of New South Wales. xxv, 246p. 1989. pap. 39.50 (*0-455-20929-4*, Pub. by Law Bk Co) W W Gaunt.

Lindsay, G. H. Conversion of an Oil Fired Boiler to an Atmospheric Fluidized Bed Burning Coal, EUR 14322. 90p. 1993. pap. 16.00 (*92-826-5487-7*, CS-NA-14322-EN-C, Pub. by Europ Com) UNIPUB.

Lindsay, George E., ed. see Cordy-Collins, Alana & Nicholson, H. B.

***Lindsay, Godon.** Is Jesus the Son of God? (Es Jesus el Hijo De Dios?) (Literature Crusade Ser.). (SPA.). 1965. pap. 0.95 (*0-89985-373-0*) Christ for the Nations.

***Lindsay, Gordon, pseud.** The ABC's for Godly Living. 1992. 8.95 (*0-89985-283-1*) Christ for the Nations.

Lindsay, Gordon. Abraham, Friend of God. (Old Testament Ser.: Vol. 4). 1964. 1.95 (*0-89985-126-6*) Christ for the Nations.

— Acts in Action, Vol. 1. (Book of Acts Ser.). 1979. pap. 1.95 (*0-89985-962-3*) Christ for the Nations.

— Adam & Eve. (Old Testament Ser.: Vol. 2). 1964. 1.95 (*0-89985-124-X*) Christ for the Nations.

— Alcohol - the Nationalized Sin. 1962. per. 2.95 (*0-89985-274-2*) Christ for the Nations.

— Amazing Discoveries in the Words of Jesus. 1960. per. 6.95 (*0-89985-112-6*) Christ for the Nations.

— Amazing Prophecies Prove the Bible. 1971. 2.95 (*0-89985-053-7*) Christ for the Nations.

— The Antichrist & His Forerunner. (End of the Age Ser.: Vol. 2). 1973. 1.95 (*0-89985-068-5*) Christ for the Nations.

— The Antichrist's Rise to Power. (End of the Age Ser.: Vol. 3). 1973. 1.95 (*0-89985-069-3*) Christ for the Nations.

— Apostles, Prophets & Administrators. 1960. per. 2.95 (*0-89985-121-5*) Christ for the Nations.

— Armageddon. (Revelation Ser.: Vol. 14). 1962. 1.95 (*0-89985-047-2*) Christ for the Nations.

— The Art of Successful Praying. 1967. 1.95 (*0-89985-079-0*) Christ for the Nations.

— The Astounding Diary of Dr. John G. Lake. 1987. per. 2.95 (*0-89985-273-4*) Christ for the Nations.

— Astrology, Reincarnation & Psychics. (Sorcery in America Ser.: Vol. 2). 1968. 1.95 (*0-89985-951-8*) Christ for the Nations.

— The Beast from the Bottomless Pit. (Revelation Ser.: Vol. 10). 1962. 1.95 (*0-89985-043-X*) Christ for the Nations.

— Bible Days Are Here Again. 1960. per. 5.95 (*0-89985-194-0*) Christ for the Nations.

— The Bible Is a Scientific Book. 1971. per. 3.95 (*0-89985-117-7*) Christ for the Nations.

— The Bible Secret of Divine Health. 1960. 1.95 (*0-89985-023-5*) Christ for the Nations.

— The Chaos of the Psychics, Vol. 4 of 4. (Sorcery in America Ser.: Vol. 4). 2.95 (*0-89985-094-4*) Christ for the Nations.

— Charismatic Ministry. 1968. per. 4.95 (*0-89985-122-3*) Christ for the Nations.

— Charles G. Finney, Vol. 5 of 7. (Men Who Changed the World Ser.: Vol. 5). 1972. 1.50 (*0-89985-258-0*) Christ for the Nations.

— Christ the Great Physician. 1960. 1.95 (*0-89985-024-3*) Christ for the Nations.

— A Citizen of Two Worlds. 1974. 2.95 (*0-89985-000-6*) Christ for the Nations.

— The Creation. (Old Testament Ser.: Vol. 1). 1964. 1.95 (*0-89985-123-1*) Christ for the Nations.

— D. L. Moody, Vol. 7 of 7. (Men Who Changed the World Ser.: Vol. 7). 1972. 1.50 (*0-89985-260-2*) Christ for the Nations.

— David Comes into the Kingdom. (Old Testament Ser.: Vol. 22). 1965. 1.95 (*0-89985-142-8*) Christ for the Nations.

— David Reaping the Whirlwind. (Old Testament Ser.: Vol. 23). 1966. 1.95 (*0-89985-143-6*) Christ for the Nations.

— Death & the Hereafter. 1972. 1.95 (*0-89985-096-0*) Christ for the Nations.

— The Death Cheaters. 1971. 2.95 (*0-89985-081-2*) Christ for the Nations.

— The Decline & Fall of Israel & Judah. (Old Testament Ser.: Vol. 33). 1967. 1.95 (*0-89985-153-3*) Christ for the Nations.

— Demons & the Occult. (Powers of Darkness Ser.: Vol. 6). 1969. 2.95 (*0-89985-089-8*) Christ for the Nations.

— Did Politics Influence Jesus? 1979. per. 3.95 (*0-89985-113-4*) Christ for the Nations.

— Difficult Questions About the Bible Answered. 1971. 1.95 (*0-89985-114-2*) Christ for the Nations.

— The Early Kings of Israel. (Old Testament Ser.: Vol. 27). 1966. 1.95 (*0-89985-147-9*) Christ for the Nations.

— The Early Kings of Judah & the Revolution. (Old Testament Ser.: Vol. 26). 1966. 1.95 (*0-89985-146-0*) Christ for the Nations.

— The Early Life of David. (Old Testament Ser.: Vol. 21). 1965. 1.95 (*0-89985-141-X*) Christ for the Nations.

— Elijah, the Man Who Did Not Die. (Old Testament Ser.: Vol. 29). 1967. 1.95 (*0-89985-149-5*) Christ for the Nations.

— Elijah, the Whirlwind Prophet. (Old Testament Ser.: Vol. 28). 1967. 1.95 (*0-89985-148-7*) Christ for the Nations.

— Elisha-Prophet of the Supernatural. (Old Testament Ser.: Vol. 31). 1967. 1.95 (*0-89985-151-7*) Christ for the Nations.

— Elisha-The Man Who Received the Double Portion. (Old Testament Ser.: Vol. 30). 1967. 1.95 (*0-89985-150-9*) Christ for the Nations.

— Enoch & Noah, Patriarchs of the Deluge. (Old Testament Ser.: Vol. 3). 1964. 1.95 (*0-89985-125-8*) Christ for the Nations.

— ESP, Ouija Boards & Hypnotism. (Sorcery in America Ser.: Vol. 1). 1968. pap. 2.95 (*0-89985-950-X*) Christ for the Nations.

— Evolution-The Incredible Hoax. 1961. 1.50 (*0-89985-115-0*) Christ for the Nations.

— Ezra & Nehemiah & the Return from Babylon. (Old Testament Ser.: Vol. 34). 1967. 1.95 (*0-89985-154-1*) Christ for the Nations.

— Facts about the Seventh Day. (Books for Ministers & Workers Ser.). 1964. 1.95 (*0-89985-116-9*) Christ for the Nations.

— False Christs, False Prophets. per. 3.95 (*0-89985-054-5*) Christ for the Nations.

— The Forgotten Miracles of the Bible, Vol. 6 of 7. (Miracles in the Bible Ser.: Vol. 6). 1977. 2.95 (*0-89985-183-5*) Christ for the Nations.

— Forty Signs of the Soon Coming of Christ. 1960. 3.95 (*0-89985-055-3*) Christ for the Nations.

— 450-Year Judgment Cycles. (Miracles in the Bible Ser.: Vol. 5). 1977. 2.95 (*0-89985-182-7*) Christ for the Nations.

— The 400 Silent Years. (Old Testament Ser.: Vol. 38). 1968. 1.95 (*0-89985-158-4*) Christ for the Nations.

— Francis, the Poor Man of Assisi, Vol. 1 of 7. (Men Who Changed the World Ser.: Vol. 1). 1972. 1.50 (*0-89985-254-8*) Christ for the Nations.

— Freda. 1984. per. 4.95 (*0-89985-268-8*) Christ for the Nations.

— George Muller & General Booth, Vol. 6 of 7. (Men Who Changed the World Ser.: Vol. 6). 1972. 1.50 (*0-89985-259-9*) Christ for the Nations.

— Gideon & the Early Judges. (Old Testament Ser.: Vol. 15). 1965. 1.95 (*0-89985-135-5*) Christ for the Nations.

— The Gifts of the Spirit. (Literature Crusade Ser.). 1965. pap. 0.95 (*0-89985-357-9*) Christ for the Nations.

— Gifts of the Spirit, 4 vols., 2. (Gifts of the Spirit Ser.). 1963. per. 4.95 (*0-89985-196-7*) Christ for the Nations.

— Gifts of the Spirit, 4 vols., 3. (Gifts of the Spirit Ser.). 1963. per. 4.95 (*0-89985-197-5*) Christ for the Nations.

— Gifts of the Spirit, 4 vols., 4. (Gifts of the Spirit Ser.). 1963. per. 4.95 (*0-89985-199-1*) Christ for the Nations.

— Gifts of the Spirit, Vol. 1. (Gifts of the Spirit Ser.). 1963. per. 4.95 (*0-89985-195-9*) Christ for the Nations.

— The Gifts of the Spirit (Dones Del Espirtu) (Literature Crusade Ser.). (SPA.). 1965. pap. write for info. (*0-89985-370-6*) Christ for the Nations.

— God's Master Key to Prosperity. 1960. per. 2.50 (*0-89985-001-4*) Christ for the Nations.

— God's Plan of the Ages. 1971. per. 6.95 (*0-89985-056-1*) Christ for the Nations.

— The Gordon Lindsay Story. Christ for the Nations Staff, ed. (Orig.). 1964. per. 6.95 (*0-89985-002-2*) Christ for the Nations.

— The Great Day of the Lord. (Revelation Ser.: Vol. 4). 1962. 1.95 (*0-89985-037-5*) Christ for the Nations.

— The Great Tribulation. (End of the Age Ser.: Vol. 4). 1973. 2.95 (*0-89985-070-7*) Christ for the Nations.

— The Great Trumpets & the Vial Judgments. (End of the Age Ser.: Vol. 6). 1973. 2.95 (*0-89985-072-3*) Christ for the Nations.

— The Great White Throne. (End of the Age Ser.: Vol. 9). 1974. 1.95 (*0-89985-075-8*) Christ for the Nations.

— Hades-Abode of the Unrighteous Dead. 1968. 1.95 (*0-89985-082-0*) Christ for the Nations.

— The House the Lord Built. 1973. 2.95 (*0-89985-015-4*) Christ for the Nations.

— How to Be a Successful Christian. (Literature Crusade Ser.). 1965. pap. 0.95 (*0-89985-359-5*) Christ for the Nations.

— How to Be a Successful Christian (Como Vivar Una Vida) rev. ed. (Literature Crusade Ser.). (SPA.). 1965. pap. 0.95 (*0-89985-372-2*) Christ for the Nations.

— How to Be Enriched by Giving. 1974. per. 2.50 (*0-89985-012-X*) Christ for the Nations.

— How to Deal With Violence, Vol. 4. (Powers of Darkness Ser.). per. 4.95 (*0-89985-087-1*) Christ for the Nations.

— How to Find the Perfect Will of God. 1967. 2.95 (*0-89985-003-0*) Christ for the Nations.

— How to Receive the Baptism of the Holy Spirit. (Literature Crusade Ser.). Date not set. pap. 0.95 (*0-89985-354-4*) Christ for the Nations.

— How to Receive the Baptism of the Holy Spirit (Como Reciber El Bautismo Del Espiritu Santo) (Literature Crusade Ser.). (SPA.). 1965. pap. 0.95 (*0-89985-367-6*) Christ for the Nations.

— How You Can Be Healed. 1965. 1.95 (*0-89985-026-X*) Christ for the Nations.

— How You Can Be Healed. (Literature Crusade Ser.). 1965. pap. 0.95 (*0-89985-353-6*) Christ for the Nations.

— How You Can Be Healed (Como Puede Usted Ser Sanado) (Literature Crusade Ser.). (SPA.). 1965. pap. 0.95 (*0-89985-366-8*) Christ for the Nations.

— How You Can Have Divine Health. 1961. 1.95 (*0-89985-027-8*) Christ for the Nations.

— Increase Your Prayer Power Tenfold. 1972. 1.95 (*0-89985-080-4*) Christ for the Nations.

— Is Jesus the Son of God? (Literature Crusade Ser.). 1965. pap. 0.95 (*0-89985-360-9*) Christ for the Nations.

— Isaac & Rebekah. (Old Testament Ser.: Vol. 6). 1964. 1.95 (*0-89985-127-4*) Christ for the Nations.

— Isaiah & Jeremiah. (Old Testament Ser.: Vol. 35). 1967. 1.95 (*0-89985-155-X*) Christ for the Nations.

— Israel: Prophetic Signs. 1964. per. 3.95 (*0-89985-189-4*) Christ for the Nations.

— Israel, the False Prophet & the Two Witnesses, Vol. 5. (End of the Age Ser.). 1964. 1.95 (*0-89985-071-5*) Christ for the Nations.

— Israel's 48 Signs of Christ's Return. 1965. per. 3.00 (*0-89985-186-X*) Christ for the Nations.

— It's Sooner Than You Think. 1967. 1.95 (*0-89985-057-X*) Christ for the Nations.

— Jacob & His Son, Joseph. (Old Testament Ser.: Vol. 8). 1964. 1.95 (*0-89985-129-0*) Christ for the Nations.

— Jacob, the Supplanter Who Became a Prince with God. (Old Testament Ser.: Vol. 7). 1964. 1.95 (*0-89985-128-2*) Christ for the Nations.

— Jephthah & Sampson. (Old Testament Ser.: Vol. 16). 1965. 1.95 (*0-89985-136-3*) Christ for the Nations.

— John Alexander Dowie: A Life of Tragedies & Triumphs. 1980. 6.95 (*0-89985-985-2*) Christ for the Nations.

— John G. Lake - Apostle to Africa. 1972. 3.95 (*0-89985-011-1*) Christ for the Nations.

— John G. Lake Sermons on Dominion over Demons, Disease, & Death. 1960. per. 4.95 (*0-89985-028-6*) Christ for the Nations.

— John Wesley & William Carey, Vol. 4 of 7. (Men Who Changed the World Ser.: Vol. 4). 1972. 1.50 (*0-89985-257-2*) Christ for the Nations.

— Joseph & His Brethren. (Old Testament Ser.: Vol. 9). 1964. 1.95 (*0-89985-130-4*) Christ for the Nations.

— Joshua, Conqueror of Canaan. (Old Testament Ser.: Vol. 14). 1965. 1.95 (*0-89985-134-7*) Christ for the Nations.

— The Judgment Seat of Christ, Vol. 7. (End of the Age Ser.). 1973. 2.95 (*0-89985-073-1*) Christ for the Nations.

— The Judgment Throne & the Seven Seals. (Revelation Ser.: Vol. 3). 1962. pap. 1.95 (*0-89985-036-7*) Christ for the Nations.

— The Key to Israel's Future-The Forgotten Covenant. 1972. 3.95 (*0-89985-191-6*) Christ for the Nations.

— The Last Days of David & His Contemporaries. (Old Testament Ser.: Vol. 24). 1966. 1.95 (*0-89985-144-4*) Christ for the Nations.

— Life after Death. 1960. per. 3.95 (*0-89985-083-9*) Christ for the Nations.

— Life after Death. (Literature Crusade Ser.). 1965. pap. 0.95 (*0-89985-351-X*) Christ for the Nations.

— Life after Death (Vida Despues De la Muerta) (Literature Crusade Ser.). (SPA.). 1965. pap. 0.95 (*0-89985-364-1*) Christ for the Nations.

— Life & Teachings of Christ, Vol. 1. (Orig.). 1963. per. 6.95 (*0-89985-967-4*) Christ for the Nations.

— Life & Teachings of Christ, Vol. 2. (Orig.). 1963. per. 6.95 (*0-89985-968-2*) Christ for the Nations.

— Life & Teachings of Christ, Vol. 3. (Orig.). 1963. reprint ed. per. 6.95 (*0-89985-969-0*) Christ for the Nations.

— The Lord, the Lion & Multi (Cristo, el Leon y Pablo) (Literature Crusade Ser.). (SPA.). Date not set. pap. 0.95 (*0-89985-377-3*) Christ for the Nations.

— Lot & Lot's Wife. (Old Testament Ser.: Vol. 5). 1964. pap. 1.95 (*0-89985-958-5*) Christ for the Nations.

— Marriage, Divorce & Remarriage. 1962. 3.95 (*0-89985-004-9*) Christ for the Nations.

— Martin Luther & George Fox, Vol. 3 of 7. (Men Who Changed the World Ser.: Vol. 3). 1965. 1.50 (*0-89985-256-4*) Christ for the Nations.

— Messiah Witness-Israel's Destiny & Coming Deliverer. 1.95 (*0-89985-187-8*) Christ for the Nations.

— The Millennium. (Revelation Ser.: Vol. 15). 1962. 1.95 (*0-89985-048-0*) Christ for the Nations.

— Ministry of Angels. 1964. 1.95 (*0-89985-018-9*) Christ for the Nations.

— Ministry of Casting Out Demons, Vol. 7. (Powers of Darkness Ser.). 1967. 1.95 (*0-89985-090-1*) Christ for the Nations.

— The Minor Prophets: Hosea, Joel, Amos, Obadiah, Jonah, Micah. (Old Testament Ser.: Vol. 36). 1968. 1.95 (*0-89985-156-8*) Christ for the Nations.

— The Minor Prophets: Nahum, Habakkuk, Zephaniah, Haggai. Zechariah, Malachi. (Old Testament Ser.: Vol. 37). 1968. 1.95 (*0-89985-157-6*) Christ for the Nations.

— The Miracle of Israel. 3.95 (*0-89985-188-6*) Christ for the Nations.

— Miracles of Christ, Pt. I, Vol. 2. (Miracles in the Bible Ser.: Vol. 7). 1979. Vol. 2. 2.95 (*0-89985-960-7*) Christ for the Nations.

— Miracles of Christ, Pt. II, Vol. 3. (Miracles in the Bible Ser.: Vol. 7). 1979. 2.95 (*0-89985-961-5*) Christ for the Nations.

— The Miracles of Divine Discipline, Vol. 7 of 7. (Miracles in the Bible Ser.: Vol. 7). 1977. 1.95 (*0-89985-184-3*) Christ for the Nations.

— Miracles of the Apostles, Vol. 4 of 7. (Miracles in the Bible Ser.: Vol. 4). 1977. 1.95 (*0-89985-181-9*) Christ for the Nations.

— Moses: The Lawgiver. (Old Testament Ser.: Vol. 11). 1964. pap. 1.95 (*0-89985-959-3*) Christ for the Nations.

— Moses & His Contemporaries. (Old Testament Ser.: Vol. 13). 1965. 1.95 (*0-89985-133-9*) Christ for the Nations.

— Moses & the Church in the Wilderness. (Old Testament Ser.: Vol. 12). 1964. 1.95 (*0-89985-132-0*) Christ for the Nations.

— Moses, The Deliverer. (Old Testament Ser.: Vol. 10). 1964. 1.95 (*0-89985-131-2*) Christ for the Nations.

— Mutu Finds the Way to Heaven (Pablo Encuentra el Camino Al Cielo) (Literature Crusade Ser.). (SPA.). Date not set. pap. 0.95 (*0-89985-376-5*) Christ for the Nations.

— My Diary Secrets. 1976. per. 4.95 (*0-89985-021-9*) Christ for the Nations.

— The Mystery of Jeane Dixon. 1966. 1.95 (*0-89985-084-7*) Christ for the Nations.

— The New Heavens & the New Earth. (Revelation Ser.: Vol. 16). 1962. 1.95 (*0-89985-049-9*) Christ for the Nations.

An Asterisk (*) at the beginning of an entry indicates that the title is appearing in BIP for the first time.

— The New John G. Lake Sermons. 1971. 3.95 (*0-89985-987-9*) Christ for the Nations.

— Old Testament Healings, Vol. 1 of 7. (Miracles in the Bible Ser.: Vol. 1). 1976. 2.95 (*0-89985-179-7*) Christ for the Nations.

— One Body, One Spirit, One Lord. 1982. per. 3.95 (*0-89985-991-7*) Christ for the Nations.

— The 144,000 on Mt. Zion. (Revelation Ser.: Vol. 11). 1962. 1.95 (*0-89985-044-8*) Christ for the Nations.

— One in Every Other Family. 1973. 3.95 (*0-89985-016-2*) Christ for the Nations.

— The Origin of Demons & Their Orders, Vol. 5. (Powers of Darkness Ser.). 2.95 (*0-89985-088-X*) Christ for the Nations.

— Out of the Dark Valley. 1975. per. 2.95 (*0-89985-019-7*) Christ for the Nations.

— Parables of Jesus Christ. (Life & Teachings of Christ Ser.: Vol. 1). (SPA.). 1973. 3.95 (*0-89985-261-0*) Christ for the Nations.

— Parables of Jesus Christ, Vols. 1 & 2 of 9. (Life & Teachings of Christ Ser.). (SPA.). 3.95 (*0-89985-980-1*) Christ for the Nations.

— Paradise-Abode of the Righteous Dead. 1967. 1.95 (*0-89985-085-5*) Christ for the Nations.

— Prayer & Fasting. 1960. 3.95 (*0-89985-076-6*) Christ for the Nations.

— Prayer That Moves Mountains. 1960. per. 4.95 (*0-89985-078-2*) Christ for the Nations.

— Prayer That Moves Mountains. (Literature Crusade Ser.). 1965. pap. 0.95 (*0-89985-352-8*) Christ for the Nations.

— Prayer That Moves Mountains (La Oracion Que Nueve las Montanas) (Literature Crusade Ser.). (SPA.). 1965. pap. 0.95 (*0-89985-365-X*) Christ for the Nations.

— The Prophecies of Daniel. 1969. per. 4.95 (*0-89985-052-9*) Christ for the Nations.

— The Rapture. 1969. 2.95 (*0-89985-063-4*) Christ for the Nations.

— The Rapture & the Second Coming of Christ. (Revelation Ser.: Vol. 8). 1965. 1.95 (*0-89985-041-3*) Christ for the Nations.

— Red China in Prophecy. (Prophecy Ser.). 1972. per. 2.25 (*0-89985-059-6*) Christ for the Nations.

— The Revolution & After. (Old Testament Ser.: Vol.. 32). 1967. 1.95 (*0-89985-152-5*) Christ for the Nations.

— The Rhyming Bible. 1967. 1.00 (*0-89985-250-5*) Christ for the Nations.

— The Rise of the Antichrist. (Revelation Ser.: Vol. 9). 1962. 1.95 (*0-89985-042-1*) Christ for the Nations.

— Ruth, The Gleaner, & the Boy Samuel. (Old Testament Ser.: Vol. 17). 1965. 1.95 (*0-89985-137-1*) Christ for the Nations.

— Samuel, the Prophet. (Old Testament Ser.: Vol. 18). 1965. 1.95 (*0-89985-138-X*) Christ for the Nations.

— Satan, Demon Manifestations & Delusions, Vol. 3. rev. ed. (Powers of Darkness Ser.). 1967. pap. 2.95 (*0-89985-955-0*) Christ for the Nations.

— Satan, Fallen Angels & Demons. (Literature Crusade Ser.: Vol. 2). 1965. pap. 0.95 (*0-89985-350-1*) Christ for the Nations.

— Satan, Fallen Angels & Demons, Vol. 2. (Powers of Darkness Ser.). 1960. pap. 1.95 (*0-89985-954-2*) Christ for the Nations.

— Satan, Fallen Angels & Demons (Los Angeles Caidos) (Literature Crusade Ser.). (SPA.). 1965. pap. 0.95 (*0-89985-363-3*) Christ for the Nations.

— Satan's Rebellion & Fall, 7 vols., Vol. 1. (Powers of Darkness Ser.). 1967. 1.95 (*0-89985-953-4*) Christ for the Nations.

— Saul & Jonathan. (Old Testament Ser.: Vol. 20). 1965. 1.95 (*0-89985-140-1*) Christ for the Nations.

— Saul, Israel's First King. (Old Testament Ser.: Vol. 19). 1965. 1.95 (*0-89985-139-8*) Christ for the Nations.

— The Second Coming of Christ. (Literature Crusade Ser.). 1965. pap. 0.95 (*0-89985-358-7*) Christ for the Nations.

— The Second Coming of Christ. 1967. 1.95 (*0-89985-061-8*) Christ for the Nations.

— The Second Coming of Christ (La Segunda Venida De Cristo) (Literature Crusade Ser.). (SPA.). 1965. pap. 0.95 (*0-89985-371-4*) Christ for the Nations.

— The Seven Churches of Prophecy, Vol. 1. (Revelation Ser.: Vol. 2). 1962. 1.95 (*0-89985-977-1*) Christ for the Nations.

— The Seven Churches of Prophecy, 2, Vol. 2. (Revelation Ser.: 2). 1962. 1.95 (*0-89985-978-X*) Christ for the Nations.

— Seven Master Keys to Triumphant Christian Living. 1967. 2.95 (*0-89985-006-5*) Christ for the Nations.

— Should Christians Attend Movies? 1964. 1.95 (*0-89985-007-3*) Christ for the Nations.

— Signs of the Coming of the Antichrist. (End of the Age Ser.: Vol. 1). 1.95 (*0-89985-067-7*) Christ for the Nations.

— Signs of the Soon Coming Christ (Senates De la Pronla Venida De Cristo) (Literature Crusade Ser.). (SPA.). 1960. pap. 0.95 (*0-89985-368-4*) Christ for the Nations.

— Signs of the Soon Coming of Christ. (Literature Crusade Ser.). 1965. pap. 0.95 (*0-89985-355-2*) Christ for the Nations.

— Signs of the Times in the Heavens. 1967. 1.95 (*0-89985-062-6*) Christ for the Nations.

— Solomon & Rehoboam. (Old Testament Ser.: Vol. 25). 1966. 1.95 (*0-89985-145-2*) Christ for the Nations.

— Spiritual Hunger (John G. Lake Sermons) 1960. per. 3.95 (*0-89985-020-0*) Christ for the Nations.

— Spiritualism, Vol. 3 of 4. (Sorcery in America Ser.: Vol. 3). 1969. 2.95 (*0-89985-093-6*) Christ for the Nations.

— The Sun-Clothed Woman & the Manchild. (Revelation Ser.: Vol. 7). 1962. 1.95 (*0-89985-040-5*) Christ for the Nations.

— They Saw It Happen. 1972. 2.95 (*0-89985-010-3*) Christ for the Nations.

— Thirty Bible Reasons Why Christ Heals Today. 1968. 2.95 (*0-89985-031-6*) Christ for the Nations.

— A Thousand Years of Peace, Vol. 8 of 9. (End of the Age Ser.: Vol. 8). 1974. 1.95 (*0-89985-074-X*) Christ for the Nations.

— The Tribulation Temple. (Revelation Ser.: Vol. 5). 1962. 1.95 (*0-89985-038-3*) Christ for the Nations.

— Triunity of the Godhead. 1986. per. 3.95 (*0-89985-272-6*) Christ for the Nations.

— Twenty-Five Objections to Divine Healing & the Bible Answers. 1971. 1.95 (*0-89985-030-8*) Christ for the Nations.

— 21 Reasons Why Christians Should Speak in Other Tongues. 1971. 1.95 (*0-89985-269-6*) Christ for the Nations.

— Twenty-One Things Shortly to Come to Pass in Israel. 1964. 1.95 (*0-89985-192-4*) Christ for the Nations.

— 22 Questions Most Frequently Asked by the Unsaved. 1970. 2.95 (*0-89985-118-5*) Christ for the Nations.

— The Two Babylons. (Revelation Ser.: Vol. 13). 1962. 1.95 (*0-89985-046-4*) Christ for the Nations.

— The Two Witnesses. (Revelation Ser.: Vol. 6). 1962. 1.95 (*0-89985-039-1*) Christ for the Nations.

— The Vial Judgments. (Revelation Ser.: Vol. 12). 1962. 1.95 (*0-89985-045-6*) Christ for the Nations.

— Visitation: Key to Church Growth. 1966. 2.95 (*0-89985-119-3*) Christ for the Nations.

— Visitation (La Llave Al Crecimiento De Su Iglesia) (Literature Crusade Ser.). (SPA.). 1965. pap. 0.95 (*0-89985-375-7*) Christ for the Nations.

— The Way to Eternal Life. (Literature Crusade Ser.). 1965. pap. 0.95 (*0-614-06170-9*) Christ for the Nations.

— The Way to Eternal Life (El Camino A la Vida Eterna) (SPA.). 1965. pap. 0.95 (*0-89985-374-9*) Christ for the Nations.

— Why Christians Are Sick. 1960. per. 3.95 (*0-89985-029-4*) Christ for the Nations.

— Why Do the Righteous Suffer? 1963. 2.95 (*0-89985-032-4*) Christ for the Nations.

— Why Do They Do It? 1971. 1.00 (*0-89985-120-7*) Christ for the Nations.

— Why Some Are Not Healed. 1967. 1.95 (*0-89985-033-2*) Christ for the Nations.

— Why the Bible Is the Word of God. (Literature Crusade Ser.). 1965. pap. 0.95 (*0-89985-356-0*) Christ for the Nations.

— Why the Bible Is the Word of God (La Biblia el la Palabrade Dios Por Que? (Literature Crusade Ser.). (SPA.). 1965. pap. 0.95 (*0-89985-369-2*) Christ for the Nations.

— Will Christians Go Through the Great Tribulation? 1971. 2.95 (*0-89985-065-0*) Christ for the Nations.

— Will Our President Die in Office? 1962. per. 2.25 (*0-89985-984-4*) Christ for the Nations.

— Will the Antichrist Come Out of Russia? 1966. 1.95 (*0-89985-066-9*) Christ for the Nations.

— The World: 2000 A. D. 1968. 3.95 (*0-89985-064-2*) Christ for the Nations.

Lindsay, Gordon, sel. The World's Best Loved Christian Poems. 1972. 1.95 (*0-89985-251-3*) Christ for the Nations.

Lindsay, Gordon, ed. see Davis, Marietta.

Lindsay, Gordon, ed. see Wright, Marilyn.

Lindsay, Griff. Maya the Illusion. 168p. 1994. pap. 7.95 (*1-56901-250-4*) NW Pub.

Lindsay, Howard & Crouse, Russel. The Great Sebastians. LC 56-7735. (Illus.). 177p. 1956. 14.95 (*0-910278-35-0*) Boulevard.

— Life with Mother. 1950. pap. 4.75 (*0-8222-0662-5*) Dramatists Play.

Lindsay, Howard & Crouse, Russell. The Great Sebastians. 1956. pap. 4.75 (*0-8222-0484-3*) Dramatists Play.

Lindsay, Ian G. & Cosh, Mary. Inveraray & the Dukes of Argyll. (Illus.). 508p. 1988. pap. 30.00 (*0-85224-577-7*, Pub. by Edinburgh U Pr UK) Col U Pr.

Lindsay, J. F. & Ramachandran, V. Modeling & Analysis of Linear Physical Systems. (Illus.). 780p. (C). 1990. text ed. 69.95 (*0-929704-19-3*) Weber Systems.

Lindsay, J. V., et al. Urban Crisis: A Symposium. LC 71-146555. (Symposia on Law & Society Ser.). 1971. reprint ed. lib. bdg. 19.50 (*0-306-70115-4*) Da Capo.

Lindsay, Jack. Gainsborough: His Life & Art. (Illus.). 244p. 1983. pap. 7.95 (*0-586-05613-0*, Pub. by Granada UK) Academy Chi Pubs.

— The Monster City: Defoe's London, 1688-1730. LC 78-58316. 1978. text ed. 29.95 (*0-312-54612-2*) St Martin.

— Song of a Falling World: Culture During the Break-up of the Roman Empire, A.D. 350-600. 303p. 1979. reprint ed. 27.50 (*0-88355-701-0*) Hyperion Conn.

— Turner. (Illus.). 383p. 1981. reprint ed. pap. 8.95 (*0-586-03852-3*) Academy Chi Pubs.

— William Blake: Creative Will & the Poetic Image. LC 70-118005. (Studies in Blake: No. 3). 1970. reprint ed. lib. bdg. 59.95 (*0-8383-1061-3*) M S G Haskell Hse.

Lindsay, Jack, tr. see Apuleius, Lucius.

Lindsay, Jack, tr. see Bruno, Giordano.

Lindsay, James A. Annual & Semiannual Promotion, with Special Reference to the Elementary School. LC 72-176996. (Columbia University. Teachers College. Contributions to Education Ser.: No. 570). reprint ed. 22.50 (*0-404-55570-5*) AMS Pr.

Lindsay, James F. & Katz, Silas. Dynamics of Physical Circuits & Systems. (Illus.). 480p. 1978. 59.95 (*0-916460-21-5*, Matrix Pubs Inc) Weber Systems.

Lindsay, James F. & Rashid, Muhammad H. Electromechanics & Electrical Machinery. (Illus.). 240p. (C). 1985. text ed. 77.00 (*0-13-250093-0*) P-H.

Lindsay, James J., jt. auth. see Wildman, John B.

Lindsay, James M. Congress & Nuclear Weapons. LC 90-49522. 304p. 1991. text ed. 32.00 (*0-8018-4141-0*) Johns Hopkins.

— Congress & the Politics of U. S. Foreign Policy. LC 94-1246. 228p. 1994. text ed. 42.50x (*0-8018-4881-4*); pap. text ed. 13.95x (*0-8018-4882-2*) Johns Hopkins.

— Gottfried Keller: Life & Works. LC 69-14390. 1968. 30.00 (*0-8023-1205-5*) Dufour.

Lindsay, James M., jt. ed. see Ripley, Randall B.

Lindsay, Jean. Miss Elizabeth B. Mitchell. (C). 1989. pap. text ed. 40.00 (*1-85821-023-2*, Pub. by Pentland Pr UK) St Mut.

Lindsay, Jeanne W. Caring, Commitment & Change: How to Build a Relationship That Lasts. (Teenage Couples Ser.). (Illus.). (Orig.). (YA). (gr. 7 up). 1995. student ed, pap. 2.50 (*0-930934-96-2*) Morning Glory.

— Caring, Commitment & Change: How to Build a Relationship That Lasts. (Teenage Couples Ser.). (Illus.). 208p. (Orig.). (YA). (gr. 7 up). 1995. pap. 9.95 (*0-930934-93-8*) Morning Glory.

Lindsay, Jeanne W. Caring, Commitment & Change: How to Build a Relationship That Lasts. (Teenage Couples Ser.). (Illus.). 208p. (Orig.). (YA). (gr. 7 up). 1995. 15.95 (*0-930934-92-X*) Morning Glory.

Lindsay, Jeanne W. Coping with Reality: Handling Money, In-Laws, Babies & Other Details of Daily Life. (Teenage Couples Ser.). (Illus.). (Orig.). (YA). (gr. 7 up). 1995. student ed 2.50 (*0-930934-88-1*) Morning Glory.

— Coping with Reality: Handling Money, In-Laws, Babies & Other Details of Daily Life. (Teenage Couples Ser.). (Illus.). 192p. (Orig.). (YA). (gr. 7 up). 1995. 15.95 (*0-930934-87-3*); pap. 9.95 (*0-930934-86-5*) Morning Glory.

— Do I Have a Daddy? A Story about a Single-Parent Child. 2nd ed. LC 90-49676. (Illus.). 48p. (J). 1991. 12.95 (*0-930934-45-8*); pap. 5.95 (*0-930934-44-X*) Morning Glory.

— Open Adoption: A Caring Option. LC 86-21807. (Illus.). 256p. (Orig.). 1987. 15.95 (*0-930934-22-9*); teacher ed 2.50 (*0-930934-24-5*); pap. 9.95 (*0-930934-23-7*) Morning Glory.

— Parents, Pregnant Teens, & the Adoption Option: Help for Families. LC 88-8359. 208p. (Orig.). 1988. pap. 8.95 (*0-930934-28-8*) Morning Glory.

— Pregnant Too Soon: Adoption Is an Option. rev. ed. LC 87-22042. (Illus.). 224p. (YA). (gr. 7-12). 1987. teacher ed 2.50 (*0-930934-27-X*); pap. 9.95 (*0-930934-25-3*) Morning Glory.

— School-Age Parents: The Challenge of Three-Generation Living. LC 90-6039. (Illus.). 224p. (Orig.). 1990. 15.95 (*0-930934-37-7*); teacher ed 2.50 (*0-930934-56-3*); pap. 10.95 (*0-930934-36-9*) Morning Glory.

— Teen Dads: Rights, Responsibilities & Joys. (Illus.). 192p. (Orig.). (YA). (gr. 7 up). 1993. 15.95 (*0-930934-77-6*); pap. 9.95 (*0-930934-78-4*); teacher ed, pap. 2.50 (*0-930934-80-6*); student ed, pap. 2.50 (*0-930934-79-2*) Morning Glory.

— Teenage Couples Series Curriculum Guide. (Teenage Couples Ser.). 136p. 1995. pap. 19.95 (*0-930934-89-X*) Morning Glory.

— Teenage Marriage: Coping with Reality. rev. ed. LC 83-19638. (Illus.). 208p. (YA). 1988. pap. 9.95 (*0-930934-30-X*) Morning Glory.

— Teens Parenting - The Challenge of Toddlers: Parenting Your Child from One to Three. LC 91-30316. (Teens Parenting Ser.). (Illus.). 192p. (Orig.). 1991. text ed. 15.95 (*0-930934-59-8*); pap. 9.95 (*0-930934-58-X*); teacher ed, pap. 7.95 (*0-930934-67-9*); student ed, pap. 2.50 (*0-930934-65-2*) Morning Glory.

— Teens Parenting - Your Baby's First Year: A How-to-Parent Book Especially for Teenage Parents. rev. ed. LC 91-21513. (Teens Parenting Ser.). (Illus.). 192p. (J). (gr. 6 up). 1991. text ed. 15.95 (*0-930934-53-9*); pap. text ed. 9.95 (*0-930934-52-0*) Morning Glory.

— Teens Parenting - Your Baby's First Year: A How-to-Parent Book Especially for Teenage Parents. rev. ed. LC 91-21513. (Teens Parenting Ser.). (Illus.). 48p. (YA). (gr. 6 up). 1991. student ed, pap. 2.50 (*0-930934-64-4*) Morning Glory.

— Yo Tengo Papa? Do I Have a Daddy? Un Cuento Sobre Un Nino de Madre Soltera, A Story about a Single-Parent Child. Palacios, Argentina, tr. (Illus.). 48p. (Orig.). (SPA.). (J). (ps-3). 1994. 12.95 (*0-930934-83-0*); pap. 5.95 (*0-930934-82-2*) Morning Glory.

— You Can Help Pregnant & Parenting Teens, Bk. 2: Curriculum Guide. (Teens Parenting Ser.). (Illus.). 192p. (Orig.). 1993. teacher ed, pap. 24.95 (*0-930934-73-3*) Morning Glory.

Lindsay, Jeanne W. & Brunelli, Jean. Adolescentes Como Padres - La Jornada de tu Embarazo y el Nacimiento de tu Bebe: Como Cuidar de ti Misma y de tu Recien Nacido si Eres una Adolescente Embarazada. Palacios, Argentina, tr. LC 92-43626. (Illus.). 24p. (SPA.). 1993. teacher ed 2.50 (*0-930934-72-5*); student ed 2.50 (*0-930934-71-7*); pap. text ed. 9.95 (*0-930934-69-5*) Morning Glory.

— Teens Parenting - Your Pregnancy & Newborn Journey: How to Take Care of Yourself & Your Newborn When You're a Pregnant Teen. LC 91-3712. (Teens Parenting Ser.). (Illus.). 192p. (Orig.). (YA). (gr. 6 up). 1991. text ed. 15.95 (*0-930934-51-2*); student ed, pap. 2.50 (*0-930934-60-1*); pap. text ed. 9.95 (*0-930934-50-4*) Morning Glory.

— Teens Parenting - Your Pregnancy & Newborn Journey (Easier Reading) How to Take Care of Yourself & Your Newborn When You're a Pregnant Teen - Easy Reading Edition. LC 91-3712. (Illus.). 192p. (Orig.). (YA). (gr. 6 up). 1992. text ed. 15.95 (*0-930934-62-8*); teacher ed, pap. 2.50 (*0-930934-68-7*); student ed, pap. 2.50 (*0-930934-63-6*); pap. text ed. 9.95 (*0-930934-61-X*) Morning Glory.

Lindsay, Jeanne W. & McCullough, Sally. Teens Parenting - Discipline from Birth to Three: How to Prevent & Deal with Discipline Problems with Babies & Toddlers. LC 91-3711. (Teens Parenting Ser.). (Illus.). 192p. (Orig.). (YA). (gr. 6 up). 1991. text ed. 15.95 (*0-930934-55-5*); student ed, pap. 2.50 (*0-930934-66-0*); pap. text ed. 9.95 (*0-930934-54-7*) Morning Glory.

Lindsay, Jeanne W. & Monserrat, Catherine P. Adoption Awareness: A Guide for Teachers, Counselors, Nurses, & Caring Others. LC 88-34540. (Illus.). 288p. (Orig.). 1989. 15.95 (*0-930934-33-4*); pap. 9.95 (*0-930934-32-6*) Morning Glory.

Lindsay, Jeanne W. & Rodine, Sharon. Teen Pregnancy Challenge, Bk. 1, Strategies for Change. LC 89-14491. (Illus.). 256p. (Orig.). 1989. 14.95 (*0-930934-35-0*) Morning Glory.

— Teen Pregnancy Challenge, Bk. 2, Programs for Kids. LC 89-14491. (Illus.). 256p. (Orig.). 1989. 14.95 (*0-930934-39-3*); pap. 9.95 (*0-930934-38-5*) Morning Glory.

— Teen Pregnancy Challenge, 2 bks., Set. LC 89-14491. (Illus.). (Orig.). 1989. 24.95 (*0-930934-41-5*) Morning Glory.

Lindsay, Jeff, jt. auth. see Hemingway, Hilary.

Lindsay, Jennifer. Javanese Gamelan. 2nd ed. (Images of Asia Ser.). (Illus.). 102p. 1992. 14.95 (*0-19-588582-1*) OUP.

Lindsay, Jennifer & Greaves, Dana. Paradox for Windows Power Programming. (Illus.). (Orig.). 1992. pap. 39.95 (*1-56529-091-7*) Que.

Lindsay, Jennifer, jt. auth. see Greaves, Dana.

Lindsay, Jessie & Tress, Helen. What Every Cook Should Know. 1974. lib. bdg. 69.95 (*0-685-51386-6*) Revisionist Pr.

Lindsay, Joan. Picnic at Hanging Rock. 1976. 16.95 (*0-8488-1415-0*) Amereon Ltd.

— Picnic at Hanging Rock. 1988. 4.95 (*0-87129-248-3*, P62) Dramatic Pub.

— Picnic at Hanging Rock. 192p. 1986. reprint ed. lib. bdg. 25.95 (*0-89966-560-8*) Buccaneer Bks.

***Lindsay, Joan V.** Chicago from the River. (Illus.). 48p. (Orig.). 1995. pap. 14.95 (*0-9647350-0-8*) J V & D Lindsay.

Lindsay, Joe. Picture Discs of the World Price Guide: International Reference Book for Picture Records, 1923-1989. Bukoski, Pete & Grobman, Marc, eds. (Illus.). 80p. (Orig.). 1990. pap. 20.00 (*0-9617347-2-8*, 190ABI) BIODISC.

— The Record Label Guide for Domestic LPs. (Illus.). 200p. (Orig.). 1986. pap. 14.95 (*0-9617347-0-1*) BIODISC.

Lindsay, Joe, jt. auth. see Cox, Perry.

***Lindsay, John & Ellis, Norman, eds.** Making Sense of Pensions & Retirement. LC 95-14243. 1995. write for info. (*1-85775-090-X*, Radcliffe Med Pr) Scovill Paterson.

Lindsay, John F. Fundamentals of Air Transportation. 112p. 1992. spiral bd. 19.95 (*0-8403-8077-1*) Kendall-Hunt.

Lindsay, John W. & Steele, D. Whedon's Commentary on the Old Testament, Vol. 2: Leviticus-Deuteronomy. 21.99 (*0-88019-129-5*) Schmul Pub Co.

Lindsay, Joseph. Diseases of the Aorta. (Illus.). 370p. 1993. 75.00 (*0-8121-1694-1*) Williams & Wilkins.

Lindsay, Joyce & Lindsay, Maurice. A Pleasure of Gardens: A Literary Companion. (Aberdeen University Press Bks.). (Illus.). 224p. 1991. pap. text ed. 16.95 (*0-08-041209-2*, Pub. by Aberdeen U Pr) Macmillan.

Lindsay, Joycey H. Marriages of Henrico County, Virginia, 1680-1808. 96p. 1983. reprint ed. pap. 15.00 (*0-89308-364-X*) Southern Hist Pr.

Lindsay, Karen, ed. see Ryan, Gary & Ryan, Bob.

Lindsay, Kathleen. Forever You'll Be Mine. large type ed. 393p. 1982. 15.95 (*0-7089-0792-X*) Ulverscroft.

Lindsay, Kenneth. European Assemblies: The Experimental Period, 1949 to 1959. LC 81-6877. xxi, 267p. 1981. reprint ed. text ed. 59.75 (*0-313-20846-8*, LIEA, Greenwood Pr) Greenwood.

Lindsay, Kenneth, tr. see Kandinsky, Wassily.

Lindsay, Kenneth L. Three-D & the MAFIA Club. viii, 228p. (Orig.). 1981. pap. 10.00 (*0-943980-00-3*) AIGA Pubns.

Lindsay, Kenneth W., jt. auth. see Jennett, Bryan.

Lindsay, Kenneth W., et al. Neurology & Neurosurgery Illustrated. 2nd ed. (Illus.). 576p. 1991. pap. text ed. 59.00 (*0-443-04345-0*) Churchill.

Lindsay, Laura L., jt. auth. see Rasberry, Robert W.

Lindsay, Lausier Betty A. A Historical Genealogy for Roy-DesJardins Dit Lauzier, Dionne, Gendrea, Boucher. LC 93-2222. 1993. 40.00 (*0-87152-474-0*) Reprint.

Lindsay, Len. Captain COMAL Gets Organized. (Amazing Adventures of Captain COMAL Ser.). (Illus.). 102p. 1984. pap. 14.95 (*0-928411-01-X*) COMAL Users.

— COMAL Handbook: Commodore 64 Version (2.00) 1986. 38.95 (*0-8359-0785-6*, Reston); 24.95 (*0-8359-0784-8*, Reston) P-H.

Lindsay, Lord & Gillin, Donald. Chinese Communism & the U. S. Proceedings of a Mini-Symposium, 1935-1936. 69p. 1975. pap. 6.00 (*0-939252-03-1*) ASU Ctr Asian.

***Lindsay, Lowell & Lindsay, Diana, eds.** Anza-Borrego Desert Region. 4th ed. LC 84-52660. (Illus.). 175p. 1996. pap. 13.95 (*0-89997-187-3*) Wilderness Pr.

Lindsay, Lowell, ed. see Clifford, H. J., et al.

Lindsay, Lowell, jt. auth. see Remeika, Paul.

Lindsay, Margie. Developing Capital Markets in Eastern Europe: A Business Reference. 336p. (C). 1992. text ed. 65.00 (*0-8147-5067-2*) NYU Pr.

— International Business in Gorbachev's Soviet Union. 218p. 1989. text ed. 55.00 (*0-312-03552-7*) St Martin.

Lindsay, Margot. Communicating with Neurological Patients. 182p. 1990. pap. 25.00 (*1-871364-37-X*) Ishiyaku Euro.

An Asterisk (*) at the beginning of an entry indicates that the title is appearing in BIP for the first time.

Lindsay, Maurice. Collected Poems, Nineteen Forty to Nineteen Ninety. 270p. 1990. pap. text ed. 25.00 (*0-08-040910-5*, Pub. by Aberdeen U Pr) Macmillan.
— History of Scottish Literature. 1977. 42.00 (*0-7091-5642-1*) Dufour.
Lindsay, Maurice, jt. auth. see Lindsay, Joyce.
Lindsay, Mela M. Shukar Balan: The White Lamb. 1976. 16.50 (*0-914222-02-3*) Am Hist Soc Ger.
— The Story of Johann: The Boy Who Longed to Come to Amerika. LC 90-85324. (Illus.). 190p. (YA). 1991. 14.50 (*0-914222-18-X*) Am Hist Soc Ger.
Lindsay, Mercedes E. A Normal Family & Grandma's Potpourri Writings. 1992. 12.95 (*0-533-10217-0*) Vantage.
Lindsay, Michael. China & the Cold War: A Study in International Politics. LC 79-2834. 286p. 1984. reprint ed. 25.75 (*0-8305-0011-1*) Hyperion Conn.
Lindsay, Michael, et al. Notes on Educational Problems in Communist China, 1941-47. LC 77-10962. 194p. 1977. reprint ed. text ed. 49.75 (*0-8371-9815-1*, LINE, Greenwood Pr) Greenwood.
Lindsay, Mrs. Gordon, see Gordon Lindsay, pseud..
Lindsay, Nancy S. Friends in the Kitchen. 2nd ed. 280p. 1995. pap. 16.95 (*0-9639320-3-9*) LaLo-Lin.
Lindsay, Norene. Pathfinder - Exploring Career & Educational Paths: Career & Educational Planning for Junior High & High School Students. Adams, Sara, ed. (Illus.). 112p. (YA). (gr. 8-12). 1994. student ed, pap. 4.95 (*1-56370-120-0*, PFP) JIST Works.
Lindsay, Norman. Saturdee. LC 75-41175. (Illus.). reprint ed. 18.45 (*0-404-14716-X*) AMS Pr.
***Lindsay, Paul.** Gentkill: A Novel of the FBI. LC 95-1858. 304p. 1995. 23.00 (*0-679-42616-7*, Villard Bks) Random.
— Harbour My Heart. large type ed. LC 93-28616. 1993. 18.95 (*0-7927-1805-4*, Curley Lrg Print); pap. 17.95 (*0-7927-1804-6*, Curley Lrg Print) Chivers N Amer.
— The Synagogues of London. LC 92-21435. (Illus.). 144p. 1992. text ed. 35.00 (*0-85303-241-6*, Pub. by Vallentine Mitchell UK); pap. 19.50 (*0-85303-258-0*, Pub. by Vallentine Mitchell UK) Intl Spec Bk.
— Witness to the Truth. large type ed. (Cloak & Dagger Ser.). 630p. 1993. reprint ed. lib. bdg. 20.95 (*1-56054-637-9*) Thorndike Pr.
— Witnesses of the Truth. 1994. mass mkt. 5.99 (*0-449-14794-0*, GM) Fawcett.
Lindsay, Paula. Awake, My Heart. large type ed. (Linford Romance Library). 320p. 1989. pap. 11.95 (*0-7089-6704-3*, Linford) Ulverscroft.
— Charity Child. large type ed. 1990. 21.95 (*0-7089-2238-4*) Ulverscroft.
— Country Doctor. large type ed. (Linford adj Romance Library). 1988. pap. text ed. 10.95 (*0-7089-6540-7*, Linford) Ulverscroft.
— Dream of Destiny. large type ed. (Linford Romance Library). 288p. 1993. pap. 14.95 (*0-7089-7409-0*, Trailtree Bookshop) Ulverscroft.
— Magic in the Rain. large type ed. (Linford Romance Library). 304p. 1993. pap. 14.95 (*0-7089-7337-X*, Linford) Ulverscroft.
— Promise of Happiness. large type ed. 288p. 1988. 16.95 (*0-7089-1868-9*) Ulverscroft.
— Ride a Rainbow. large type ed. LC 92-23385. 1993. 19.95 (*0-7927-1407-5*, Curley Lrg Print) Chivers N Amer.
— Spring Fever. large type ed. LC 93-46290. 1994. 18.95 (*0-7927-1948-4*, Curley Lrg Print); pap. 17.65 (*0-7927-1947-6*, Curley Lrg Print) Chivers N Amer.
— This Bright Mantle. large type ed. 1990. 21.95 (*0-7089-2141-8*) Ulverscroft.
— Wild Rose. large type ed. LC 92-43473. 1993. 19.95 (*0-7927-1560-8*, Curley Lrg Print) Chivers N Amer.
Lindsay, Peter H. & Norman, Donald A. Human Information Processing: An Introduction to Psychology. 2nd ed. 777p. (C). 1977. text ed. 44.00 (*0-15-540377-X*, LIND2); write for info. (*0-15-540379-6*) HB Coll Pubs.
Lindsay, Philip. The Haunted Man: A Portrait of Edgar Allan Poe. 1976. 20.95 (*0-89190-968-0*, Am Repr) Amereon Ltd.
— Mirror for Ruffians. LC 72-303. (Essay Index Reprint Ser.). 1977. reprint ed. 23.95 (*0-8369-2799-0*) Ayer.
Lindsay, R. B. Introduction of Physical Statistics. 13.25 (*0-8446-2471-3*) Peter Smith.
— Julius Robert Mayer, Prophet of Energy. LC 72-8045. (Men of Physics Ser.). (C). 1973. 107.00 (*0-08-016985-6*, Pub. by Pergamon Repr UK) Franklin.
— Lord Rayleigh, the Man & His Work. LC 79-94934. (Men of Physics Ser.). 1970. 112.00 (*0-08-006821-9*, Pub. by Pergamon Repr UK) Franklin.
Lindsay, R. B., ed. The Journal of Acoustical Society of America, Cumulative Index: Volumes 31-35. 1140p. 1963. 90.00 (*0-318-12201-4*) Acoustical Soc Am.
— Journal of the Acoustical Society of America: Cumulative Index, Vols. 65-74. 1983. pap. 75.00 (*0-318-01688-5*) Acoustical Soc Am.
— Journal of the Acoustical Society of America: Cumulative Index, Vols. 11-20. 395p. 1948. pap. 10.00 (*0-317-05546-1*) Acoustical Soc Am.
— Journal of the Acoustical Society of America: Cumulative Index, Vols. 21-30. 952p. 1956. pap. 75.00 (*0-318-19080-X*) Acoustical Soc Am.
— Journal of the Acoustical Society of America: Cumulative Index, Vols. 45-54. 540p. 1974. pap. 60.00 (*0-318-19081-8*) Acoustical Soc Am.
— Journal of the Acoustical Society of America: Cumulative Index, Vols. 55-64. 816p. 1979. pap. 60.00 (*0-318-19082-6*) Acoustical Soc Am.
— The Journal of the Acoustical Society of America, Cumulative Index: Volumes 1-10. 131p. 1938. pap. 10.00 (*0-318-12202-2*) Acoustical Soc Am.
— Journal of the Acoustical Society of America, Vols. 36-44: Cumulative Index. (Contemporary Literature Ser.: Vol. 1). 1060p. 1968. 125.00 (*0-317-02844-8*) Acoustical Soc Am.
Lindsay, R. Bruce & Margenau, Henry. Foundations of Physics. LC 80-84973. 1981. 40.00 (*0-918024-18-8*); pap. 19.50 (*0-918024-17-X*) Ox Bow.
Lindsay, R. C. & Willis, B. J. Biotechnology Challenges for the Flavour & Food Industry: Proc Intern Symp Organ by Quest Intern, Va., May 2-5, 1988. 1990. 63.00 (*1-85166-405-X*) Elsevier.
Lindsay, R. C., jt. auth. see Kaylegian, K. E.
Lindsay, R. W., ed. Quality Requirements of Super-Duty Steels. LC 59-14904. (Metallurgical Society Conference Ser.: Vol. 3). 319p. reprint ed. pap. 91.00 (*0-317-10903-0*, 2000666) Bks Demand.
Lindsay, Rachel. Mask of Gold. large type ed. 405p. 1981. 12.00 (*0-7089-0706-7*) Ulverscroft.
***Lindsay, Randy L.** Immortal: Third Reich. 1995. 14.95 (*1-885681-04-6*) Precedence.
Lindsay, Richard P. In These Difficult Times. 10.95 (*0-88494-758-0*) Bookcraft Inc.
Lindsay, Robert. A Guide to Diagnosis, Prevention & Treatment: A General Guide to Diagnosis & Treatment. LC 92-14302. 52p. 1992. pap. 19.00 (*0-88167-941-0*) Raven.
Lindsay, Robert B. The Nature of Physics: A Physicist's Views on the History & Philosophy of Science. LC 68-10642. 220p. reprint ed. pap. 62.70 (*0-685-15727-X*, 2027513) Bks Demand.
— The Role of Science in Civilization. LC 73-3234. (Illus.). 318p. 1973. reprint ed. text ed. 35.00 (*0-8371-6837-6*, LIRS, Greenwood Pr) Greenwood.
Lindsay, Robert G. This High Name: Public Relations & the U. S. Marine Corps. LC 57-5238. (Illus.). 126p. reprint ed. pap. 36.00 (*0-317-08238-8*, 2021140) Bks Demand.
Lindsay, Robert O. & Neu, John. Mazarinades: A Checklist of Copies in Major Collections in the United States. LC 74-150720. 507p. 1972. 23.50 (*0-8108-0369-0*) Scarecrow.
Lindsay, Robert O. & Neu, John, eds. French Political Pamphlets, Fifteen Forty-Seven to Sixteen Forty-Eight: A Catalog of Major Collections in American Libraries. LC 78-84953. 522p. 1969. 35.00 (*0-299-04990-6*) U of Wis Pr.
***Lindsay, Ruth, illus.** Animals That Change: Metamorphsis. LC 95-4062. (J). 1995. 15.99 (*0-525-67496-9*, Lodestar Bks) Dutton Child Bks.
Lindsay, S. J. & Powell, G. E. Handbook of Clinical Adult Psychology. 550p. 1987. text ed. 129.95 (*0-566-05102-8*, Pub. by Avebury Pub UK) Ashgate Pub Co.
Lindsay, S. K., jt. auth. see Acin-Kosta, Milos.
Lindsay, S. K., ed. see Acin-Kosta, Milos.
Lindsay, Sandie. High Performance Liquid Chromatography. 2nd ed. (Analytical Chemistry by Open Learning Ser.). 300p. 1992. pap. text ed. 57.95 (*0-471-93115-2*) Wiley.
Lindsay, Sandy. High Performance Liquid Chromatography. LC 87-8158. (Analytical Chemistry by Open Learning Ser.). 244p. 1987. pap. text ed. 49.95 (*0-471-91373-1*) Wiley.
Lindsay, Sarah. Bodies of Water. 48p. 1986. pap. 8.00 (*0-87775-186-2*) Unicorn Pr.
— Insomniac's Lullaby. (Illus.). 48p. (Orig.). 1989. pap. 8.00 (*0-87775-221-4*) Unicorn Pr.
Lindsay, Sheila. Time Travels of an Irish Psychic. LC 89-81669. 87p. 1990. pap. 11.95 (*0-85342-896-4*, Pub. by Mercier Pr IE) Dufour.
Lindsay, Stan & Powell, Graham. An Introduction to Clinical Child Psychology. 1988. text ed. 68.95 (*0-566-05103-6*, Pub. by Avebury Pub UK) Ashgate Pub Co.
Lindsay, Stan & Powell, Graham, eds. The Handbook of Clinical Adult Psychology. LC 93-33181. 1994. pap. 45.00 (*0-415-07216-6*, B3734, Routledge NY) Routledge.
— The Handbook of Clinical Adult Psychology. 2nd ed. LC 93-33181. 840p. 1994. 89.95x (*0-415-07215-8*, B3730, Routledge NY) Routledge.
Lindsay, Steele, jt. auth. see Lindsay, Dorothy.
Lindsay, Suzanne G. Mary Cassatt & Philadelphia. LC 84-29623. (Illus.). 100p. 1985. pap. 14.95 (*0-87633-061-8*) Phila Mus Art.
Lindsay, Sylvia, jt. ed. see Altschul, Jeffrey H.
Lindsay, T. F., tr. see Dalbiez, Roland.
Lindsay, Thomas M. A History of the Reformation, 2 vols., Set. LC 83-45664. reprint ed. 105.00 (*0-404-19814-7*) AMS Pr.
— A History of the Reformation, 2 vols., Set. LC 72-37893. (Select Bibliographies Reprint Ser.). 1977. reprint ed. 78.95 (*0-8369-6730-5*) Ayer.
— Luther & the Germany Reformation. LC 71-133524. (Select Bibliographies Reprint Ser.). 1977. reprint ed. 20.95 (*0-8369-5556-0*) Ayer.
Lindsay, Tomas. Reforma & Su Desarrollo Social: Reformation & Its Social Influence. (SPA.). 17.95 (*84-7645-119-9*, 223177, Pub. by Edit Clie SP) TSELF.
— La Reforma en Su Contexto Historico: Historic Foundations of the Reformation. (SPA.). 17.95 (*84-7645-020-6*, 223082, Pub. by Edit Clie SP) TSELF.
Lindsay, Vachel. Art of the Moving Picture. LC 75-114381. 1970. reprint ed. pap. 3.45 (*0-87140-204-1*) Liveright.
— The Congo & Other Poems. alternate unabridged ed. 96p. 1992. reprint ed. pap. text ed. 1.00 (*0-486-27272-9*) Dover.
— Johnny Appleseed & Other Poems. 138p. (J). 1981. lib. bdg. 21.95 (*0-89967-039-3*) Harmony Raine.
— Johnny Appleseed & Other Poems. 129p. (J). 1981. reprint ed. lib. bdg. 23.95 (*0-89966-365-6*) Buccaneer Bks.
— The Poetry of Vachel Lindsay, Vol. 1. Camp, Dennis, ed. 1984. 24.95 (*0-933180-45-4*) Spoon Riv Poetry.
— Poetry of Vachel Lindsay, Vol. 2. Camp, Dennis, ed. 1984. 24.95 (*0-933180-67-5*) Spoon Riv Poetry.
— The Progress & Poetry of the Movies: A Second Book of Film Criticism. LC 94-16749. 1994. write for info. (*0-8108-2917-7*) Scarecrow.
— The Prose of Vachel Lindsay, Vol. 1. Camp, Dennis, ed. 340p. 1989. 24.95 (*0-944024-08-4*) Spoon Riv Poetry.
— Selected Poems of Vachel Lindsay. 1986. 12.95 (*0-02-548270-X*) Macmillan.
— Una Tortuga Encantadora - Turtle Magic. LC 90-62625. (Illus.). 12p. (J). 1991. bds. 5.95 (*1-877779-22-9*) Schneider Educational.
Lindsay, W. M., ed. Nonius Marcellus: Dictionary of Republican Latin. (St. Andrews University Publications: No. 1). 120p. 1985. reprint ed. 25.87 (*3-487-01092-5*, Pub. by Georg Olms GW) Lubrecht & Cramer.
Lindsay, W. M., ed. see Festus, Sextus P.
Lindsay, W. M., ed. see Marcellus, Nonius.
Lindsay, W. M., ed. see Marcellus Nonius.
Lindsay, W. M., ed. see Martial.
Lindsay, W. M., ed. see Nonius Marcellus.
Lindsay, W. M., ed. see Plautus.
Lindsay, W. M., ed. see Terence.
Lindsay, W. M., et al, eds. Glossaria Latina, Bd. I: Glossarium Ansileubi Sive Librum Glossarum. xxi, 1990p. 1965. reprint ed. write for info. (*0-318-71131-1*, Pub. by Georg Olms GW) Lubrecht & Cramer.
— Glossaria Latina, Bd. II: Arma, Abavus Philoxenus. xxi, 1990p. 1965. reprint ed. write for info. (*0-318-71132-X*, Pub. by Georg Olms GW) Lubrecht & Cramer.
— Glossaria Latina, Bd. III: Abstrusa, Abolita. xxi, 1990p. 1965. reprint ed. write for info. (*0-318-71133-8*, Pub. by Georg Olms GW) Lubrecht & Cramer.
— Glossaria Latina, Bd. IV: Placidi Glossae. xxi, 1990p. 1965. reprint ed. write for info. (*0-318-71134-6*, Pub. by Georg Olms GW) Lubrecht & Cramer.
— Glossaria Latina, Bd. V: (Abba, AA) xxi, 1990p. 1965. reprint ed. write for info. (*0-318-71135-4*, Pub. by Georg Olms GW) Lubrecht & Cramer.
— Glossaria Latina, 5 vols., Set. xxi, 1990p. 1965. reprint ed. write for info. (*0-318-71130-3*, Pub. by Georg Olms GW) Lubrecht & Cramer.
Lindsay, Wallace M. The Codex Turnebi of Plautus & Plauti Codicis Senonsensis. (Illus.). 59p. (GER.). 1972. reprint ed. 76.70 (*3-487-04312-2*, Pub. by Georg Olms GW) Lubrecht & Cramer.
— Early Irish Minuscule Script. (St. Andrews University Publications: No. 6). 74p. 1971. reprint ed. 32.37 (*3-487-04026-3*, Pub. by Georg Olms GW) Lubrecht & Cramer.
— Die Lateinische Sprache. xiii, 747p. 1984. reprint ed. write for info. (*3-487-07484-2*, Pub. by Georg Olms GW) Lubrecht & Cramer.
— Notae Latinae. xxiv, 500p. 1972. reprint ed. Incl. Doris Bains' "A Supplement to Notae Latinae," xii, 72p. write for info. (*0-318-71161-3*, Pub. by Georg Olms GW) Lubrecht & Cramer.
— Notae Latinae: An Account of Abbreviation in Latin MSS. of the Early Minuscule Period. suppl. ed. xxiv, 500p. 1972. Abbreviations in Latin MSS. of 850 to 1050 AD. write for info. (*0-318-72043-4*, Pub. by Georg Olms GW) Lubrecht & Cramer.
— Notae Latinae: An Account of Abbreviation in Latin MSS. of the Early Minuscule Period. xxiv, 500p. 1972. reprint ed. write for info. (*0-318-72042-6*, Pub. by Georg Olms GW) Lubrecht & Cramer.
— Palaeographia Latina, 6 pts. in 1. (St. Andrews University Publications: Nos. 14, 16, 19, 20, 23, 28). 456p. 1989. reprint ed. 128.70 (*3-487-05308-X*, Pub. by Georg Olms GW) Lubrecht & Cramer.
Lindsay, Wallace M., ed. see Festus, Sextus P.
Lindsay, William. Barosaurus. LC 92-52819. (American Museum of Natural History Ser.). (Illus.). 32p. (J). (gr. 3 up). 1993. 12.95 (*1-56458-123-3*) Dorling Kindersley.
— Corythosaurus. LC 92-54309. (American Museum of Natural History Ser.). (Illus.). 32p. (J). (gr. 3 up). 1993. 12.95 (*1-56458-225-6*) Dorling Kindersley.
— Great Dinosaur Atlas. (Illus.). (J). (gr. 3 up). 1991. 16.00 (*0-671-74480-1*, Julian Messner); lib. bdg. 16.98 (*0-671-74479-8*, Julian Messner) Silver Burdett Pr.
— Prehistoric Life. LC 93-32076. (Eyewitness Bks.). (J). (gr. 5 up). 1994. 16.00 (*0-679-86001-0*); lib. bdg. 16.99 (*0-679-96001-5*) Knopf Bks Yng Read.
— Triceratops. LC 92-54308. (American Museum of Natural History Ser.). (Illus.). 32p. (J). (gr. 3 up). 1993. 12.95 (*1-56458-226-4*) Dorling Kindersley.
— Tyrannosaurus. LC 92-52820. (American Museum of Natural History Ser.). (Illus.). 32p. (J). (gr. 3 up). 1993. 12.95 (*1-56458-124-1*) Dorling Kindersley.
Lindsay, William, jt. auth. see Clark, Neil.
Lindsay, William M., jt. auth. see Evans, James R.
Lindsay, William S. History of Merchant Shipping & Ancient Commerce, 4 Vols, 1. LC 05-41460. reprint ed. 30.00 (*0-404-04031-4*) AMS Pr.
— History of Merchant Shipping & Ancient Commerce, 4 Vols, 2. LC 05-41460. reprint ed. 30.00 (*0-404-04032-2*) AMS Pr.
— History of Merchant Shipping & Ancient Commerce, 4 Vols, 3. LC 05-41460. reprint ed. 30.00 (*0-404-04033-0*) AMS Pr.
— History of Merchant Shipping & Ancient Commerce, 4 Vols, 4. LC 05-41460. reprint ed. 30.00 (*0-404-04034-9*) AMS Pr.
— History of Merchant Shipping & Ancient Commerce, 4 Vols, Set. LC 05-41460. reprint ed. 120.00 (*0-404-04030-6*) AMS Pr.
***Lindsell, Harold.** When You Pray. Liu, Jonathan, tr. 288p. (CHI.). 1991. pap. 5.00 (*1-56582-092-4*) Christ Renew Min.
***Lindsell-Roberts.** Business Letter Writing. 1995. pap. 11.95 (*0-02-860014-2*) Macmillan.
Lindsell-Roberts, Sheryl. Business Letter Writing. LC 94-18524. 1994. write for info. (*0-671-88637-1*) Macmillan.
— Loony Laws & Silly Statutes. LC 93-42066. (Illus.). 128p. 1994. pap. 5.95 (*0-8069-0472-0*) Sterling.
— Mastering Computer Typing: Learning the ABCs of the Computer Keyboard. LC 94-41777. (Illus.). 208p. 1995. 10.95 (*0-395-71406-0*) HM.
— Office Professional's Quick Reference Hanbook. 1995. pap. 7.95 (*0-02-860027-4*) Macmillan.
— The Office Professional's Quick Reference Handbook. 4th rev. ed. LC 94-32827. 1995. write for info. (*0-671-89919-8*, Arco Test) P-H Gen Ref & Trav.
Lindsell-Roberts, Sheryl, ed. see Levine, Nathan.
Lindsell-Roberts, Sheryl L. The Secretary's Quick Reference Handbook. 3rd ed. (Illus.). 304p. 1992. pap. 8.00 (*0-13-799396-X*, Arco Test) P-H Gen Ref & Trav.
Lindseth, Roy O. Digital Processing of Geophysical Data: A Review. (Course Notes Ser.: No. 1). 282p. 1982. reprint ed. pap. 46.00 (*0-931830-50-8*, 456) Soc Expl Geophys.
***Lindsey.** Absence of Light. 1995. mass mkt. (*0-553-56941-4*) Bantam.
***Lindsey, Aa.** Natural Areas of Indiana & Their Preservation. 1969. 18.00 (*1-883362-07-5*) IN Acad Sci.
— Natural Features of Indiana. 1976. 18.00 (*1-883362-06-7*) IN Acad Sci.
Lindsey, Alton A. Naturalist on Watch. (Illus.). 228p. (Orig.). 1983. 10.00 (*0-913859-00-1*); pap. 4.75 (*0-913859-01-X*) Goshen Coll.
Lindsey, Alton A., et al. The Bicentennial of John James Audubon. LC 84-47791. (Illus.). 192p. 1985. 25.00 (*0-253-10650-8*) Ind U Pr.
***Lindsey, Andrea, pseud.** Becoming Intimately One: Wisdom for Excellence in Marriage. 160p. (Orig.). 1995. pap. write for info. (*1-57502-001-7*) Morris Pubng.
Lindsey, Anne H., jt. auth. see Bell, C. Ritchie.
Lindsey, Ben B. & Borough, Rube. The Dangerous Life. LC 73-11938. (Metropolitan America Ser.). 468p. 1974. reprint ed. 33.95 (*0-405-05400-9*) Ayer.
Lindsey, Ben B. & Evans, Wainwright. The Companionate Marriage. LC 73-169393. (Family in America Ser.). 400p. 1977. reprint ed. 21.95 (*0-405-03870-4*) Ayer.
— The Revolt of Modern Youth. LC 73-8818. (Americana Library Ser.: No. 28). 388p. 1973. reprint ed. 25.00 (*0-295-95298-9*) U of Wash Pr.
Lindsey, Betina. The Serpent Beguiled. Tolley, Carolyn, ed. 256p. (Orig.). 1992. mass mkt. 4.99 (*0-671-74467-4*) PB.
— Swan Bride. Tolley, Caroline, ed. 288p. (Orig.). 1990. mass mkt. 5.50 (*0-671-68914-2*) PB.
— Swan Star. 1994. mass mkt. 5.50 (*0-671-79939-8*) PB.
— Swan Witch. Tolley, Carolyn, ed. 256p. (Orig.). 1993. mass mkt. 4.99 (*0-671-75171-9*) PB.
Lindsey, Bonnie J. & Rayburn, Francis M. The Professional Medical Assistant: Clinical Practice. LC 92-18589. 316p. 1993. pap. text ed. 32.95 (*0-8273-4150-4*) Delmar.
— The Professional Medical Assistant Clinical Practice: Instructor's Resource Guide. 216p. 1993. 19.95 (*0-8273-4151-2*) Delmar.
— The Professional Medical Assistant Clinical Practice Workbook. 134p. 1993. 14.95 (*0-8273-4155-5*) Delmar.
Lindsey, Byron, jt. ed. see Goscilo, Helena.
Lindsey, C. H. & Vander Meulen, S. V. Informal Introduction to Algol 68. 2nd ed. 362p. 1977. 69.25 (*0-7204-0504-1*, North Holland) Elsevier.
Lindsey, Carol C., ed. Ideas on Wings. (Illus.). 72p. 1978. 17.95 (*0-87510-120-8*) Christian Sci.
Lindsey, Crawford W., Jr. Teaching Students to Teach Themselves. 148p. 1988. pap. 27.95 (*0-89397-315-7*) Nichols Pub.
***Lindsey, Dana.** Julie's Garden. (Sil Romance Ser.). 1995. pap. 2.99 (*0-373-19071-9*, 1-19071-9) Silhouette.
Lindsey, Darryl. Electromechanical Package Design. 1992. text ed. write for info. (*0-07-037877-0*) McGraw.
***Lindsey, Dave & Lindsey, Matt.** The Great American Stock Car Racing Trivia Book. 128p. 1994. reprint ed. pap. 5.95 (*0-9637733-4-8*) Premium Pr TN.
***Lindsey, David A. & Clark, Reino F.** Copper & Uranium in Pennsylvanian & Permian Sedimentary Rocks, Northern Sangre de Cristo Range, Colorado. LC 94-41507. (Bulletin Ser.: No. 2116). 1995. write for info. (*0-615-00389-3*) US Geol Survey.
Lindsey, David C. Bye Bye Backache. LC 81-67080. (Illus.). 256p. 1981. 17.95 (*0-939342-00-6*); pap. 10.95 (*0-939342-01-4*) DCarlin Pub.
Lindsey, David E., jt. auth. see Dolan, Edwin C.
Lindsey, David E., jt. auth. see Dolan, Edwin G.
Lindsey, David L. An Absence of Light. 1994. 23.00 (*0-385-42311-X*) Doubleday.
— A Cold Mind. 352p. 1990. mass mkt. 5.99 (*0-671-73338-9*) PB.
— Cold Mind. 1994. mass mkt. 6.50 (*0-553-56081-6*) Bantam.
— Heat from Another Sun. 1985. mass mkt. 5.95 (*0-671-54632-5*) PB.
— Mercy. 1991. mass mkt. 6.50 (*0-553-28972-1*) Bantam.
— Spiral. (Orig.). 1990. pap. 5.99 (*0-671-73337-0*) S&S Trade.
Lindsey, David M. Creating a Happier Life. 1990. pap. 9.95 (*1-878040-00-6*) Personal Growth.
— Discovering Life's Purpose. 1990. pap. 8.95 (*1-878040-01-4*) Personal Growth.
— Understanding Death & Grief. 1991. pap. 9.95 (*1-878040-03-0*) Personal Growth.
***Lindsey, Dawn.** The American Cousin. (Regency Romance Ser.). 224p. 1995. 3.99 (*0-451-17946-3*, Sig) NAL-Dutton.
— An English Alliance. (Regency Romance Ser.). 224p. (Orig.). 1995. mass mkt. 3.99 (*0-451-17947-1*, Sig) NAL-Dutton.
— The Great Lady Tony. (Regency Romance Ser.). 224p. 1986. pap. 3.99 (*0-451-14382-5*, Sig) NAL-Dutton.

An Asterisk (*) at the beginning of an entry indicates that the title is appearing in BIP for the first time.

— An Independent Woman. (Regency Romance Ser.). 224p. (Orig.). 1994. pap. 3.99 (*0-451-17874-2*, Sig) NAL-Dutton.
— The Nonpareil. 1986. pap. 3.99 (*0-451-14117-2*, Sig) NAL-Dutton.
— The Reluctant Heroine. (Signet Regency Romance Ser.). 224p. (Orig.). 1993. pap. 3.99 (*0-451-17525-5*, Sig) NAL-Dutton.
— The Reluctant Heroine. large type ed. LC 93-37451. (Orig.). 1994. bds. 18.95 (*0-7862-0097-9*) Thorndike Pr.
Lindsey, Donal F. Indians at Hampton Institute, 1877-1923. LC 93-45510. 356p. 1994. 43.95 (*0-252-02106-1*) U of Ill Pr.
Lindsey, Duncan. The Art of Playing Real Life Monopoly: The Wage Earner's Guide to Building an Estate. (Illus.). 224p. (Orig.). 1986. pap. 9.95 (*0-936667-00-1*) Oregon Pr.
— Personal Finances with Excel. 304p. (Orig.). pap. 59.95 (*0-936667-14-1*) Oregon Pr.
— Personal Monopoly: Lotos Compatible Tools for Building Your Personal Estate. 300p. (Orig.). 1987. pap. 19.95 (*0-317-56265-7*); disk 39.95 (*0-317-56266-5*) Oregon Pr.
— The Scientific Publication System in Social Science. LC 78-62570. (Jossey-Bass Social & Behavioral Science Ser.). 189p. reprint ed. pap. 53.90 (*0-8357-4994-0*, 2037927) Bks Demand.
— The Welfare of Children. (Illus.). 288p. 1994. 29.95 (*0-19-508518-3*) OUP.
Lindsey, Edmon. Mastering Word Problems the Easy Way. 170p. 1991. pap. text ed. 15.25 (*0-9634346-0-8*) S Paul Pub.
Lindsey, Esther H. & Homes, Virginia. Key Events in Executives' Lives. McCall, Morgan W., Jr., ed. (Technical Report Ser.: No. 132G). 1987. pap. 65.00 (*0-912879-30-0*) Ctr Creat Leader.
Lindsey, Forrest. Pipefitters Handbook. 464p. 1967. 21.95 (*0-8311-3019-9*) Indus Pr.
Lindsey, G., et al. CGnet Story: A Case Study in International Computer Networking. 140p. 1994. pap. 16.95 (*0-88936-678-0*, IDRC6780, Pub. by IDRC CN) UNIPUB.
Lindsey, George, jt. ed. see Nelson, Walter.
***Lindsey, George, et al.** Goober in a Nutshell. LC 94-34456. 192p. (Orig.). 1995. pap. 10.00 (*0-380-77739-8*) Avon.
Lindsey, George G. & Boysen, Marcia, eds. Nelson's Directory of Investment Research, 1989. Orig. Title: Nelson's Directory of Wall Street Research. 1300p. 1988. reprint ed. Incl. suppl. subscription. per. 315.00 (*0-922460-01-9*) Nelson Pubns.
Lindsey, George R., jt. auth. see Legault, Albert.
Lindsey, Hal. Combat Faith. 256p. (Orig.). 1986. pap. 9.95 (*0-553-34342-4*) Bantam.
— Greatest Works of Hal Lindsey. 1994. 10.98 (*0-88486-104-X*) Arrowood Pr.
— Israel & the Last Days. (Harvest Pocket Bks.). 48p. 1991. pap. 2.50 (*0-89081-911-4*) Harvest Hse.
— La Liberacion del Planeta Tierra. 192p. (SPA.). 1986. reprint ed. pap. 7.75 (*0-311-13823-3*) Casa Bautista.
— Liberation of Planet Earth. 1992. mass mkt. 5.50 (*0-06-104192-0*, Harp PBks) HarpC.
— Planet Earth Two Thousand A. D. 1994. pap. 12.99 (*0-9641058-0-2*) Western Front.
— A Prophetical Walk Through the Holy Land. LC 83-80121. 200p. (Orig.). 1983. 29.99 (*0-89081-381-7*) Harvest Hse.
— Satan Is Alive & Well on Planet Earth. 1992. mass mkt. 5.50 (*0-06-104191-2*, Harp PBks) HarpC.
— There's a New World Coming. 320p. 1984. mass mkt. 4.99 (*0-553-24555-4*) Bantam.
— There's a New World Coming: An In-Depth Analysis of the Book of Revelation. 288p. 1984. pap. 9.99 (*0-89081-440-6*) Harvest Hse.
Lindsey, Hal & Carlson, C. C. The Late Great Planet Earth. 1992. mass mkt. 4.99 (*0-06-104190-4*, Harp PBks) HarpC.
— Late Great Planet Earth. 1973. pap. 5.99 (*0-310-27772-8*, 18093P) Zondervan.
— Satan Is Alive & Well on Planet Earth. 224p. 1972. pap. 9.99 (*0-310-27791-4*, 18189P) Zondervan.
Lindsey, Howard. History of Black America. 1994. 17.98 (*1-55521-960-8*) Bk Sales Inc.
Lindsey, Howard & Crouse, Russel. The Prescott Proposals. 1954. pap. 4.75 (*0-8222-0909-8*) Dramatists Play.
— State of the Union. 1947. pap. 4.75 (*0-8222-1074-6*) Dramatists Play.
Lindsey, Howard, ed. see Nemerov, Howard.
Lindsey, J. K. The Analysis of Stochastic Processes Using GLIM. (Lecture Notes in Statistics Ser.: Vol. 72). vi, 294p. 1992. pap. 49.00 (*0-387-97761-9*) Spr-Verlag.
— Introductory Statistics: The Modelling Approach. (Illus.). 240p. 1995. 63.00 (*0-19-852346-7*); pap. 29.95 (*0-19-852345-9*) OUP.
— Modelling Frequency & Count Data. (Oxford Statistical Science Ser.: No. 15). (Illus.). 304p. 1995. 43.00 (*0-19-852331-9*) OUP.
— Models for Repeated Measurements. (Oxford Statistical Science Ser.: No. 10). (Illus.). 432p. 1993. 56.95 (*0-19-852299-1*) OUP.
Lindsey, J. P. & Gilbertson, R. L. Basidiomycetes That Decay Aspen in North America. (Bibliotheca Mycologica Ser.: No. 63). 1978. lib. bdg. 78.00 (*3-7682-1193-2*) Lubrecht & Cramer.
Lindsey, Jack. Applied Illumination Engineering. LC 88-45787. 500p. 1990. text ed. 69.00 (*0-88173-060-2*) Fairmont Pr.
Lindsey, Jack L., jt. auth. see Fairmont Press Staff.
Lindsey, Jennifer. Start-up Money: Raise What You Need for Your Small Business. 1989. pap. text ed. 17.95 (*0-471-50031-3*) Wiley.
Lindsey, Jennifer, ed. Applied Clinical Trials Conference & Exhibition Proceedings. 93p. 1993. pap. text ed. 90.00 (*0-929870-16-6*) Advanstar Commns.
Lindsey, Jennifer, jt. ed. see Thornton, Alice.
Lindsey, Jim, tr. see Sosa, Robert.
Lindsey, Jimmy D., ed. Computers & Exceptional Individuals. 2nd ed. LC 91-48182. 416p. 1993. pap. text ed. 29.00 (*0-89079-547-9*, 6548) PRO-ED.
Lindsey, Johanna. Angel. 416p. (Orig.). 1992. mass mkt. 5.99 (*0-380-75628-5*) Avon.
— Angel. large type ed. (Romance Ser.). (Orig.). 1993. 22.95 (*0-8161-5760-X*) Hall.
— Angel. large type ed. 362p. (Orig.). 1994. pap. 16.95 (*0-8161-5761-8*) Thorndike Pr.
— Brave the Wild Wind. 352p. 1984. mass mkt. 5.99 (*0-380-89284-7*) Avon.
— Captive Bride. 1977. mass mkt. 5.99 (*0-380-01697-4*, 88799-1) Avon.
— Captive Bride. large type ed. (General Ser.). 342p. 1992. text ed. 19.95 (*0-8161-5291-8*, Large Print Bks); pap. 15. 95 (*0-8161-5292-6*, Large Print Bks) Hall.
— Defy Not the Heart. 416p. (Orig.). 1989. mass mkt. 5.99 (*0-380-75299-9*) Avon.
— Fires of Winter. large type ed. LC 93-13157. 437p. 1994. reprint ed. pap. 17.95 (*0-8161-5290-X*) Hall.
— Fires of Winter. 368p. 1980. reprint ed. mass mkt. 5.99 (*0-380-75747-8*) Avon.
— A Gentle Feuding. 336p. 1984. mass mkt. 5.99 (*0-380-87155-6*) Avon.
— Gentle Rogue. 432p. 1990. mass mkt. 5.99 (*0-380-75302-2*) Avon.
— Gentle Rogue. braille ed. 581p. 1992. vinyl bd. 46.48 (*1-56956-239-3*, BR8438) W A T Braille.
— Gentle Rogue. large type ed. (General Ser.). 442p. 1991. text ed. 19.95 (*0-8161-5228-4*, Large Print Bks) Hall.
— Glorious Angel. 320p. (Orig.). 1982. mass mkt. 5.99 (*0-380-79202-8*) Avon.
— Glorious Angel. LC 93-46126. (Orig.). (J). 1994. write for info. (*0-8161-5285-3*); pap. write for info. (*0-8161-5286-1*) G K Hall.
— Heart of Thunder. 368p. 1983. mass mkt. 5.99 (*0-380-85118-0*) Avon.
— Heart of Thunder. large type ed. LC 93-35910. 1994. 22. 95 (*0-8161-5293-4*) Hall.
— Heart of Thunder. large type ed. LC 93-35910. 1994. pap. 16.95 (*0-8161-5294-2*) Hall.
— A Heart So Wild. 352p. 1986. mass mkt. 5.99 (*0-380-75084-8*) Avon.
— Hearts Aflame. 368p. 1987. reprint ed. mass mkt. 5.99 (*0-380-89982-5*) Avon.
— Keeper of the Heart. 416p. (Orig.). 1993. mass mkt. 5.99 (*0-380-77493-3*) Avon.
— Love Me Forever. LC 95-13549. 1995. 22.00 (*0-688-14286-9*) Morrow.
— Love Only Once. 352p. 1985. mass mkt. 5.99 (*0-380-89953-1*) Avon.
— The Magic of You. 416p. (Orig.). 1993. mass mkt. 5.99 (*0-380-75629-3*) Avon.
— Man of My Dreams. 432p. (Orig.). 1992. mass mkt. 5.99 (*0-380-75626-9*) Avon.
— Man of My Dreams. braille ed. 471p. (Orig.). 1993. text ed. 37.68 (*1-56956-508-2*, BR9074) W A T Braille.
— Man of My Dreams. large type ed. LC 92-27195. (General Ser.). (Orig.). 1993. pap. 16.95 (*0-8161-5636-0*) G K Hall.
— Once a Princess. 432p. 1991. mass mkt. 5.99 (*0-380-75625-0*) Avon.
— Once a Princess. large type ed. (General Ser.). 403p. 1992. text ed. 21.95 (*0-8161-5312-4*); pap. 16.95 (*0-8161-5313-2*) G K Hall.
— Paradise Wild. 320p. 1981. mass mkt. 5.99 (*0-380-77651-0*) Avon.
— Paradise Wild. large type ed. LC 93-19644. 1993. 21.95 (*0-8161-5287-X*) Hall.
— Paradise Wild. large type ed. LC 93-19644. 1994. pap. 16. 95 (*0-8161-5288-8*) Hall.
— A Pirate's Love. 1988. mass mkt. 5.99 (*0-380-40048-0*) Avon.
— Prisoner of My Desire. 400p. (Orig.). 1991. mass mkt. 5.99 (*0-380-75627-7*) Avon.
— Prisoner of My Desire. braille ed. 508p. (Orig.). 1992. vinyl bd. 40.64 (*1-56956-082-X*, BR8762) W A T Braille.
— Prisoner of My Desire. large type ed. LC 92-23459. (General Ser.). 400p. (Orig.). 1993. lib. bdg. 20.95 (*0-8161-5459-7*); pap. 16.95 (*0-8161-5460-0*) G K Hall.
— Savage Thunder. 416p. (Orig.). 1989. mass mkt. 5.99 (*0-380-75300-6*) Avon.
— Savage Thunder. large type ed. LC 90-38576. 490p. (Orig.). 1990. reprint ed. lib. bdg. 19.95 (*1-56054-029-X*) Thorndike Pr.
— Secret Fire. 416p. 1987. mass mkt. 5.99 (*0-380-75087-2*) Avon.
— Silver Angel. 432p. (Orig.). 1988. mass mkt. 5.99 (*0-380-75294-8*) Avon.
— So Speaks the Heart. 368p. 1983. mass mkt. 5.99 (*0-380-81471-4*) Avon.
— Surrender My Love. 432p. (Orig.). 1994. mass mkt. 6.50 (*0-380-76256-0*) Avon.
— Surrender My Love. large type ed. LC 94-34502. 403p. 1994. 21.95 (*0-7838-1124-1*) Hall.
— Tender Is the Storm. 336p. 1985. mass mkt. 5.99 (*0-380-89693-1*) Avon.
— Tender Rebel. 384p. (Orig.). 1988. mass mkt. 5.99 (*0-380-75086-4*) Avon.
— Until Forever. 416p. (Orig.). 1995. mass mkt. 6.50 (*0-380-76259-5*) Avon.
— Warrior's Woman. 432p. (Orig.). 1990. mass mkt. 5.99 (*0-380-75301-4*) Avon.
— When Love Awaits. 352p. 1986. mass mkt. 5.99 (*0-380-89739-3*) Avon.
— You Belong to Me. 432p. (Orig.). 1994. mass mkt. 6.50 (*0-380-76258-7*) Avon.
— You Belong to Me. large type ed. LC 95-15707. (Large Print Bks.). 1995. 25.95 (*1-56895-213-9*) Wheeler Pub.
Lindsey, Jonathan A., ed. Performance Evaluation: A Management Basic for Librarians. LC 86-42746. 232p. 1986. 39.50 (*0-89774-313-X*) Oryx Pr.
Lindsey, Jonathan A. & Prentice, Ann E. Professional Ethics & Librarians. LC 83-43244. 112p. 1985. 41.95 (*0-89774-133-1*) Oryx Pr.
Lindsey, K., ed. Plant Tissue Culture Manual, Supplement 2. (Looseleaf Product Code: LS Ser.). 75p. (C). 1992. ring bd. 32.00 (*0-7923-1516-2*) Kluwer Ac.
— Plant Tissue Culture Manual B - W. 585p. (C). 1991. lib. bdg. 143.00 (*0-7923-1115-9*) Kluwer Ac.
***Lindsey, Karen.** Divorced, Beheaded, Survived: A Feminist Reinterpretation of the Wives of Henry VIII. LC 94-34505. 320p. 1995. 24.00 (*0-201-60895-2*) Addison-Wesley.
— Falling Off the Roof. LC 75-21788. 64p. 1975. pap. 9.95 (*0-914086-08-1*) Alicejamesbooks.
Lindsey, Karen, jt. auth. see Love, Susan M.
Lindsey, Linda, jt. auth. see Schimelpfenig, Tod.
Lindsey, Linda L. & Christy, Sandra. Gender Roles: A Sociological Perspective. 2nd ed. LC 93-34999. 448p. 1994. pap. text ed. write for info. (*0-13-350307-0*) P-H.
Lindsey, Margaret. Training Teachers of the Gifted & Talented. Tannenbaum, Abraham J., ed. LC 80-11867. (Perspectives on Gifted & Talented Education Ser.). (Orig.). 1980. pap. text ed. 7.95 (*0-8077-2590-0*) Tchrs Coll.
Lindsey, Margaret, jt. auth. see Stratemeyer, Florence B.
Lindsey, Marilyn L. The Little Lost Sheep. LC 87-91993. (Happy Day Bks.). (Illus.). (J). (gr. k-2). 1988. 2.50 (*0-87403-398-5*, 24-03808) Standard Pub.
Lindsey, Matt, jt. auth. see Lindsey, Dave.
Lindsey, May P. Dictionary of Mental Handicap. 304p. 1989. 55.00 (*0-415-02810-8*) Routledge.
Lindsey, Michael, et al. AMEND - Philosophy & Curriculum for Treating Batterers. LC 91-73217. (Illus.). 124p. (Orig.). 1993. pap. 16.95 (*1-880197-04-9*) Gylantic Pub.
— AMEND - Philosophy & Curriculum for Treating Batterers, Set. LC 91-73217. (Illus.). 124p. (Orig.). 1993. 28.90 (*1-880197-06-5*) Gylantic Pub.
Lindsey, Neil M. Tales of a Wilderness Trapper. 66p. 1973. pap. 3.00 (*0-936622-21-0*) A R Harding Pub.
Lindsey, Olive. Never Go Back. large type ed. 1992. 18.95 (*0-7451-8400-6*, Atlantic Lrg Print); pap. 16.96 (*0-7927-1160-2*, Atlantic Lrg Print) Chivers N Amer.
Lindsey, Patrice. Golden Gamble. 224p. (Orig.). 1991. pap. 2.95 (*1-878702-52-1*, Kismet) Meteor Pub.
Lindsey, Robert. Irresistible Impulse. 1993. mass mkt. 4.99 (*0-440-21668-0*, Dell Trade Pbks) Dell.
Lindsey, Robert, jt. auth. see Brando, Marlon.
Lindsey, Robert L. Jesus, Rabbi & Lord: The Hebrew Story of Jesus Behind Our Gospels. LC 89-62723. 228p. (Orig.). 1990. pap. 11.95 (*0-9623950-0-5*) Cornerstn Pub.
Lindsey, Ruth & Gorrie, Douglas D. Survival Kit for Those Who Sit: Simple Office Exercises to Boost Your Energy & Productivity. LC 89-10211. (Illus.). 128p. (Orig.). 1989. pap. 8.95 (*0-913581-10-0*); 7.50 (*0-913581-11-9*) Publitec.
Lindsey, Ruth, jt. auth. see Corbin, Charles B.
Lindsey, Ruth, jt. auth. see Corbin, Charles.
Lindsey, Ruth, et al. Fitness for the Health of It. 6th ed. 192p. (C). 1989. pap. write for info. (*0-697-07282-7*) Brown & Benchmark.
***Lindsey, Scott.** Wisdom for Everyday Living. LC 94-69839. 128p. (Orig.). 1995. pap. 6.95 (*0-89221-284-5*) New Leaf.
Lindsey, Sharon, jt. ed. see Orsund-Gassiot, Cindy A.
Lindsey, Stephen, et al. Guide to Write-up Services. 1993. ring bd. 88.00 (*1-56433-410-4*) Prctnrs Pub Co.
***Lindsey, Stephen W., et al.** Guide to Write-up Services. 1994. ring bd. 92.00 (*1-56433-535-6*) Prctnrs Pub Co.
Lindsey, Terence, ed. see Forshaw, John.
Lindsey, Terri. Going My Way? large type ed. 261p. 1992. reprint ed. lib. bdg. 13.95 (*1-56054-490-2*) Thorndike Pr.
Lindsey, W. C. & Chie, C. M., eds. Phase-Locked Loops. 352p. 1985. 59.95 (*0-87942-200-9*, PC01917) Inst Electrical.
Lindsey, Wallace M., jt. auth. see Isidori.
Lindsey, Wallace M., ed. see Plautus.
Lindsey, William C. & Simon, Mark K., eds. Phase-Locked Loops & Their Application. LC 85-19725. 440p. 1978. 49.95 (*0-87942-101-0*, PC00984) Inst Electrical.
Lindsey, William D. Singing in a Strange Land: Praying & Acting with the Poor. LC 90-63488. 120p. (Orig.). (C). 1991. pap. 8.95 (*1-55612-415-5*, LL1415) Sheed & Ward MO.
Lindsey, William H. & Quint, Bruce. The Oasis Technique. 91p. 1986. 15.00 (*0-317-01541-9*) Fla Atlantic.
Lindsey, Wm C. & Simon, Marvin K. Telecommunication Systems Engineering. (Illus.). 592p. reprint ed. pap. 14. 95 (*0-486-66838-X*) Dover.
Lindskog, B. I. & Zetterberg, B. L. Lexicon of Medical Terminology: Medicinsk Terminologi Lexikon. 620p. 1981. 250.00 (*0-8288-1884-3*, F22400) Fr & Eur.
Lindskog, Robert E., jt. auth. see Newnan, Donald G.
***Lindskold, Jane.** Brother to Dragons, Companion to Owls. 224p. (Orig.). 1994. mass mkt. 4.99 (*0-380-77527-1*, AvoNova) Avon.
— Marks of Our Brothers. 256p. (Orig.). 1995. mass mkt. 4.99 (*0-380-77847-5*, AvoNova) Avon.
Lindskold, Jane M. Roger Zelazny. LC 93-29505. (Twayne's United States Authors Ser.). 192p. 1993. text ed. 22.95 (*0-8057-3953-X*, Twayne) Macmillan.
Lindskold, Svenn. You & Me: The Why & How of Interpersonal Behavior. LC 81-16978. 246p. 1982. 25.95 (*0-88229-621-3*) Nelson-Hall.
Lindskoog. Light in the Shadowlands: Protecting the Real C. S. Lewis. 10.99 (*0-88070-695-3*) Questar Pubs.
Lindskoog, John & Lindskoog, Kathryn. How to Grow a Young Reader: A Parent's Guide to Books for Kids. LC 88-23205. 200p. (Orig.). 1989. pap. 9.99 (*0-87788-353-X*) Shaw Pubs.
Lindskoog, Kathryn. Creative Writing: For People Who Can't Not Write. 288p. 1989. pap. 18.99 (*0-310-25321-7*) Zondervan.
— Fakes, Frauds, & Other Malarkey: 301 Amazing Stories & How Not to Be Fooled. 256p. 1993. pap. 12.99 (*0-310-57731-4*) Zondervan.
— Finding the Landlord: A Guidebook to C. S. Lewis's Pilgrim's Regress. (Illus.). 160p. (Orig.). 1995. pap. 9.95 (*0-940895-35-8*, 58) Cornerstone IL.
Lindskoog, Kathryn, ed. see Alcott, Louisa May.
Lindskoog, Kathryn, jt. auth. see Lindskoog, John.
Lindsley, A. L. Sketches of an Excursion to Southern Alaska. fac. ed. (Shorey Historical Ser.). 76p. pap. 4.95 (*0-8466-0091-9*, S91) Shorey.
Lindsley, Charles E. Fundamentals of Singing for Voice Classes. 264p. (C). 1985. Spiralbound. pap. 27.95 (*0-534-04608-8*) Intl Thomson.
Lindsley, D. H., ed. Oxide Minerals: Petrologic & Magnetic Significance. (Reviews in Mineralogy Ser.: Vol. 25). 509p. 1991. per. 25.00 (*0-939950-30-8*) Mineralogical Soc.
Lindsley, Dan L. & Grell, E. H. Genetic Variations of Drosophila Melanogaster. LC 68-15915. (Illus.). 472p. 1968. 17.00 (*0-87279-638-8*, 627) Carnegie Inst.
Lindsley, Dan L. & Zimm, Georgianna G. The Genome of Drosophilia Melanogaster. (Illus.). 1133p. 1992. text ed. 85.00 (*0-12-450990-8*) Acad Pr.
Lindsley, David. Boiler Control Systems. 1991. text ed. 43. 00 (*0-07-707374-6*) McGraw.
Lindsley, Donald B., ed. see Blinkov, Samuil Mikha'ilovich & Smirnov, N. A.
***Lindsley, James E.** The Church Club of New York: The First Hundred Years. 256p. 1994. 20.00 (*0-9638146-0-5*) Church Club.
Lindsley, Karen B., ed. Cave Research Foundation Annual Report, 1981. (Illus.). 55p. (Orig.). 1984. pap. 5.00 (*0-939748-04-5*) Cave Bks MO.
— Cave Research Foundation Annual Report, 1984. (Illus.). 60p. (Orig.). 1985. pap. 5.00 (*0-939748-17-7*) Cave Bks MO.
— Cave Research Foundation Annual Report, 1986. (Illus.). 51p. (Orig.). 1987. pap. 5.00 (*0-939748-22-3*) Cave Bks MO.
— Cave Research Foundation Annual Report, 1987. (Illus.). 74p. (Orig.). 1987. pap. 5.00 (*0-939748-23-1*) Cave Bks MO.
— Cave Research Foundation Annual Report, 1988. (Illus.). 91p. (Orig.). 1989. pap. 5.00 (*0-939748-24-X*) Cave Bks MO.
— Cave Research Foundation Annual Report, 1989. (Illus.). 85p. (Orig.). 1990. pap. 5.00 (*0-939748-26-6*) Cave Bks MO.
— Cave Research Foundation Annual Report, 1990. (Illus.). 80p. (Orig.). 1991. pap. 5.00 (*0-939748-33-9*) Cave Bks MO.
— Cave Research Foundation Annual Report, 1991. (Illus.). 76p. (Orig.). 1992. pap. 5.00 (*0-939748-35-5*) Cave Bks MO.
— Cave Research Foundation Annual Report, 1992. (Illus.). 68p. (Orig.). 1993. pap. 5.00 (*0-939748-38-X*) Cave Bks MO.
Lindsley, Karen B., jt. ed. see Bridgemon, Rondal R.
Lindsley, Margaret. Andrew Henry: Mine & Mountain Major. (Illus.). 370p. (J). 1990. pap. 15.95 (*0-936204-78-8*) Jelm Mtn.
Lindsley, Michelle L. Tutorial: Bridging the Gap Between MIL-STD-810 & MIL-STD-781. LC 62-38584. 221p. 1990. pap. text ed. 100.00 (*0-915414-32-5*) Inst Environ Sci.
— Tutorial: The Environmental Engineering Specialist's Role in Procurement: A Systems Acquisition Primer. LC 62-38584. 93p. (Orig.). 1988. pap. text ed. 75.00 (*0-915414-39-2*) Inst Environ Sci.
Lindsley, Steven. New Orleans: An Artist's Sketchbook. (Illus.). 50p. 1994. pap. 9.50 (*1-884824-03-X*) Tryon Pubng.
Lindsley, Thomas. Building a Workforce Investment System for America. 42p. 1992. pap. text ed. 9.95 (*0-88713-654-0*) Nat Alliance.
***Lindsted, Rob.** The Cost of Revival. 40p. (Orig.). 1994. pap. 2.50 (*1-879366-46-0*) Hearthstone OK.
— The Sound of the Trumpet. 50p. (Orig.). 1994. pap. 2.50 (*1-879366-57-6*) Hearthstone OK.
— Travel Guide to Israel. (Illus.). 126p. (Orig.). (C). 1990. pap. 5.95 (*0-9624517-5-4*) Hearthstone OK.
***Lindsted, Rob & Gaverluk, Emil.** Why the Church Will Not Go Through the Great Tribulation. 40p. (Orig.). 1994. pap. 2.50 (*1-879366-58-4*) Hearthstone OK.
***Lindsted, Rob & Werner, Earl.** End-Time Prophetic Chronology. 242p. (Orig.). 1994. pap. 2.50 (*1-879366-59-2*) Hearthstone OK.
Lindsted, Rob, jt. auth. see Gaverluk, Emil.
***Lindsted, Rob, et al.** Years That Changed the World. 92p. (Orig.). 1995. pap. 7.95 (*1-879366-92-4*) Hearthstone OK.
***Lindsted, Robert.** Can You Really Know Your Future? 100p. (Orig.). 1992. pap. 7.95 (*1-879366-32-0*) Hearthstone OK.
— Certainty of Bible Prophecy. 72p. (Orig.). 1991. pap. 5.95 (*1-879366-07-X*) Hearthstone OK.

An Asterisk (*) at the beginning of an entry indicates that the title is appearing in BIP for the first time.

Lindsten, J. Nobel Lectures in Physiology or Medicine 1971-1980. 690p. 1992. text ed. 122.00 (*981-02-0790-5*); pap. text ed. 61.00 (*981-02-0791-3*) World Scientific Pub.
— Nobel Lectures in Physiology or Medicine 1981-1990. 640p. 1993. text ed. 118.00 (*981-02-0792-1*); pap. text ed. 55.00 (*981-02-0793-X*) World Scientific Pub.
Lindsten, Jan & Pettersson, Ulf. Etiology of Human Disease at the DNA Level: Nobel Symposium 80. 336p. 1991. 94.00 (*0-88167-761-2*) Raven.
***Lindstrand, Doug.** Doug Lindstrand's Alaska Sketchbook. LC 94-96881. (Illus.). 200p. (Orig.). 1995. pap. text ed. 25.00 (*0-9608290-8-3*) Sourdough Studio.
— Doug Lindstrand's Alaska Sketchbook Vol. 2. LC 94-96881. (Illus.). 200p. (Orig.). 1995. pap. text ed. 25.00 (*0-9608290-9-1*) Sourdough Studio.
***Lindstrand, Eric.** Fair Games. 600p. Date not set. pap. 12. 95 (*1-56901-616-X*) NW Pub.
Lindstrm, Tom, et al, eds. Stochastic Analysis & Application: Proceedings Oslo-Silivri, July 1992. LC 93-28190. (Stochastics Monographs: Vol. 8). 1993. text ed. 84.00 (*2-88124-948-5*) Gordon & Breach.
***Lindstrom.** Business Week Guide to the Information Highway: Strategies & Solutions. 1995. pap. text ed. 21. 95 (*0-07-882124-X*) Osborne-McGraw.
Lindstrom, Bengt & Spencer, Nick, eds. Social Pediatrics. (Illus.). 550p. 1995. 125.00 (*0-19-262179-3*) OUP.
Lindstrom, Carl, jt. auth. see Lindstrom, Virginia.
Lindstrom, Christina, jt. auth. see Schaffer, Judith.
Lindstrom, Dan, jt. ed. see Moses, Leon N.
Lindstrom, Diane. Economic Development in the Philadelphia Region, 1810-1850. LC 77-23582. 255p. 1978. text ed. 53.00 (*0-231-04272-8*) Col U Pr.
Lindstrom, Eva. The Cat Hat. Croall, Stephen, tr. (Illus.). 40p. (J). (gr. 1-4). 1989. 12.95 (*0-916291-23-5*); pap. 6.95 (*0-916291-24-3*) Kane-Miller Bk.
***Lindstrom, Fred B., et al, eds.** Kimball Young on Sociology in Transition, 1912-1968: An Oral Account by the 35th President of the ASA. (Illus.). 184p. (C). 1995. lib. bdg. 39.00 (*0-8191-9788-2*) U Pr of Amer.
— Kimball Young on Sociology in Transition, 1912-1968: An Oral Account by the 35th President of the ASA. (Illus.). 184p. (Orig.). (C). 1995. pap. text ed. 29.50 (*0-8191-9789-0*) U Pr of Amer.
Lindstrom, Fredrik. God & the Origin of Evil: A Contextual Analysis of Alleged Monistic Evidence in the Old Testament. (Coniectanea Biblica. Old Testament Ser.: No. 21). (Orig.). 1983. pap. 49.00x (*0-317-65797-6*) Coronet Bks.
— Suffering & Sin: Interpretations of Illness in the Individual Complaint Psalms. (Coniectanea Biblica Old Testament Ser.: No. 37). 500p. (Orig.). 1994. pap. 72. 50x (*91-22-01580-9*, Pub. by Almqv & Wiksell SW) Coronet Bks.
Lindstrom, Gaell. Thomas Moran in Utah. 21p. 1983. pap. 1. 00x (*0-87421-146-8*) Utah St U Pr.
Lindstrom, Joyce. Idaho's Vigilantes. LC 84-50763. (Illus.). 104p. (Orig.). 1984. pap. 7.95 (*0-89301-101-0*) U of Idaho Pr.
Lindstrom, Lamont. Cargo Cult: Strange Stories of Desire from Melanesia & Beyond. LC 93-5399. (Illus.). 288p. (C). 1993. lib. bdg. 36.00 (*0-8248-1526-2*); pap. text ed. 14.95 (*0-8248-1563-7*) UH Pr.
— Knowledge & Power in a South Pacific Society. LC 90-53172. (Ethnographic Inquiry Ser.). (Illus.). 240p. 1990. 39.95 (*0-87474-365-6*); pap. 16.95 (*0-87474-357-5*) Smithsonian.
Lindstrom, Lamont & White, Geoffrey M. Island Encounters: Black & White Memories of the Pacific War. LC 90-9613. (Illus.). 208p. 1990. 24.95 (*0-87474-457-1*) Smithsonian.
Lindstrom, Lamont, jt. ed. see White, Geoffrey M.
Lindstrom, Lars. Managing Alcoholism: Matching Clients to Treatment. (Illus.). 390p. 1992. 65.00 (*0-19-261902-0*) OUP.
Lindstrom, Lars G. Christian Spiritual Healing: A Psychological Study. Ideology & Experience in the British Healing Movement. (Psychologia et Sociologica Religionum Ser.: No. 7). 207p. (Orig.). 1992. pap. text ed. 46.50x (*91-554-2962-9*, Pub. by Almqv & Wiksell SW) Coronet Bks.
Lindstrom, M., jt. auth. see Reid, Joy M.
Lindstrom, Marilyn. The Voice from Inner Space: Answers Who Am I? Why Am I Here? Beckman, Jean, ed. LC 90-35087. 112p. (Orig.). (J). 1990. pap. 7.95 (*0-941992-20-9*) Los Arboles Pub.
Lindstrom, Mary E., et al, eds. Methods in Enzymology, Vol. 188: Hydrocarbons & Methylotrophy. 504p. 1990. text ed. 94.00 (*0-12-182089-0*) Acad Pr.
Lindstrom, Miriam. Children's Art: A Study of Normal Development in Children's Modes of Visualization. LC 57-10499. (Illus.). 1957. reprint ed. pap. 11.00 (*0-520-00752-2*) U CA Pr.
Lindstrom, Naomi. Jewish Issues in Argentine Literature: From Gerchunoff to Szichman. LC 88-27635. 216p. 1989. text ed. 24.00 (*0-8262-0708-1*) U of Mo Pr.
— Jorge Luis Borges. (Twayne's Studies in Short Fiction). 208p. (C). 1990. text ed. 22.95 (*0-8057-8327-X*, Twayne) Macmillan.
— Literary Expressionism in Argentina. LC 77-24558. 100p. 1978. pap. 2.00 (*0-87918-038-2*) ASU Lat Am St.
— Macedonio Fernandez. LC 80-53826. 138p. (Orig.). 1981. pap. 18.00 (*0-89295-018-8*) Society Sp & Sp-Am.
— Twentieth-Century Spanish American Fiction. LC 93-42557. (Texas Pan American Ser.). 256p. (C). 1994. text ed. 37.50 (*0-292-78119-9*); pap. 15.95 (*0-292-74682-2*) U of Tex Pr.
— Woman's Voice in Latin American Literature. LC 86-51313. 200p. (Orig.). 1990. 26.00 (*0-89410-295-8*); pap. 16.00 (*0-89410-296-6*) Three Continents.
Lindstrom, Naomi, tr. see Agosin, Marjorie.
Lindstrom, Naomi, tr. see Parente Cunha, Helena.
Lindstrom, Naomi, jt. auth. see Virgillo, Carmelo.
Lindstrom, Peter. Not for the Short Winded: Congressional Reform, 1961-1986. (Congressional Operations Ser.). 116p. (Orig.). (C). 1986. pap. text ed. 13.50 (*0-939715-05-8*) Ctr Politics.
Lindstrom, Peter & Miller, Ellen. Soft Money: A Loophole for the 80's. 28p. (Orig.). (C). 1985. pap. text ed. 5.95 (*0-939715-03-1*) Ctr Politics.
Lindstrom, R. L. Cataract Surgery & Lens Implantation. (Current Opinion in Ophthalmology 1993 Ser.). (Illus.). 112p. (Orig.). 1993. pap. 59.95 (*1-870485-67-X*) Current Science.
Lindstrom, Richard L. Cataract Surgery & Lens Implantation. (Current Opinion in Ophthalmology 1994 Ser.). (Illus.). 110p. (Orig.). 1994. pap. text ed. 59.95 (*1-85922-624-8*) Current Science.
— Cataract Surgery & Lens Implantation. (Current Opinion in Ophthalmology Ser.). (Illus.). 65p. (Orig.). 1995. pap. text ed. 59.95 (*1-85922-730-9*) Current Science.
Lindstrom, Richard L., jt. auth. see Smith, S. Gregory.
Lindstrom, S. C. & Gabrielson, P. W., eds. Thirteenth International Seaweed Symposium. (Developments in Hydrobiology Ser.). (C). 1990. lib. bdg. 307.00 (*0-7923-0763-1*) Kluwer Ac.
Lindstrom, Talbot & Tighe, Kevin P. Trade Regulation by Negotiation: Federal Trade Commission Consent Decrees. LC 73-93919. 1181p. reprint ed. pap. 180.00 (*0-317-26772-8*, 2024341) Bks Demand.
Lindstrom, Tom. Brownian Motion on Nested Fractals. LC 89-18138. (Memoirs of the American Mathematical Society Ser.: Vol. 420). 128p. 1990. 22.00 (*0-8218-2484-8*, MEMO/83/420C) Am Math.
***Lindstrom, Virginia & Lindstrom, Carl.** Golden Cocoon. 154p. (C). 1995. 19.95 (*0-942597-88-5*) White Mane Pub.
Lindstrom, Wendell D., jt. auth. see Finkbeiner, Daniel T.
Lindstromberg, Seth, ed. The Recipe Book: Practical Ideas for the Language Classroom. (Pilgrims Resource Bks.). 91p. 1990. pap. text ed. 17.95 (*0-582-03764-6*, 78673) Longman.
Lindt, Gillian, ed. Religion in America. LC 75-54571. (Great Contemporary Issues Ser.). 1977. lib. bdg. 27.95 (*0-405-09865-0*) Ayer.
Lindt, J. T., ed. see Society of Plastics Engineers Staff.
***Lindt, Peggy.** Buddies. (Illus.). 32p. (J). 1995. 9.95 (*0-87905-663-0*) Gibbs Smith Pub.
Lindtner, Christian, tr. Master of Wisdom: Writings of the Buddhist Master Nagarjuna. LC 86-29111. (Tibetan Translation Ser.: Vol. 14). 413p. 1986. 36.00 (*0-89800-139-0*) Dharma Pub.
Linduff, Katheryn M., jt. auth. see Hsu, Cho-Yun.
Lindup, Mike, jt. auth. see Evans, Dewi.
***L'Industrie Aeronautique Staff.** Dictionnaire Francias-Chinois de l'Aeronautique & de l'Espa. 1991. write for info. (*0-7859-8707-X*, 7800463672) Fr & Eur.
***Lindvall.** Read-Aloud Bible Stories Vol. 4. 1995. 17.99 (*0-8024-7166-8*) Moody.
Lindvall, Ella K. Bible Illustrated for Little Children. (Illus.). (J). (ps-2). 1991. text ed. 9.99 (*0-8024-0569-X*) Moody.
— My Friend Jesus. (Illus.). 32p. (Orig.). (J). (gr. 1-3). 1989. pap. 2.99 (*0-8024-5949-8*) Moody.
— My Teacher Jesus. (Illus.). (J). (ps-2). pap. 2.99 (*0-8024-5946-3*) Moody.
— Read-Aloud Bible Stories, Vol. 1. LC 82-2114. 160p. (J). (ps-2). 1982. 17.99 (*0-8024-7163-3*) Moody.
— Read-Aloud Bible Stories, Vol. 2. (Illus.). 1985. text ed. 17.99 (*0-8024-7164-1*) Moody.
— Read Aloud Bible Stories, Vol. 3. (J). (ps-2). 1990. 17.99 (*0-8024-7165-X*) Moody.
Lindvall, O., ed. Restoration of Brain Function by Tissue Transplantation. LC 92-49462. (Basic & Clinical Aspects of Neuroscience Ser.: Vol. 5). 1993. 35.00 (*0-387-55823-3*) Spr-Verlag.
Lindvall, O., et al, eds. Intracerebral Transplantation in Movement Disorders, Vol. 5: Restorative Neurology. 360p. 1991. 248.25 (*0-444-81364-0*) Elsevier.
Lindvall, Terry. Surprised by Laughter: C. S. Lewis & the Comic Spirit. 512p. 1994. 22.99 (*1-56233-105-1*) Star Song TN.
Lindvall, Torgny. Lectures on the Coupling Method. LC 92-12811. (Probability & Mathematical Statistics Ser.). 272p. 1992. text ed. 68.95 (*0-471-54025-0*) Wiley.
Lindwall, Bo, et al. The World of Carl Larsson. LC 84-152789. (Illus.). 196p. (Orig.). (YA). 1991. 39.95 (*0-914676-93-8*, Green Tiger S&S) S&S Childrens.
Lindway, Russ. The Superior Person's Guide to Everyday Irritations. Carle, Cliff, ed. (Illus.). 224p. (Orig.). 1990. pap. 4.95 (*0-918259-23-1*) CCC Pubns.
Lindwer, Willy. Last Seven Months of Anne Frank. 1992. pap. 12.00 (*0-385-42360-8*, Anchor NY) Doubleday.
Lindy, Jacob D., jt. ed. see Wilson, John P.
Lindy, Jacob D., et al, eds. Vietnam: A Casebook. LC 87-15062. (Psychosocial Stress Ser.: No. 10). 384p. 1987. 45.95 (*0-87630-471-4*) Brunner-Mazel.
Lindzen, Richard S. Dynamics in Atmospheric Physics. (Illus.). 352p. (C). 1990. 47.95 (*0-521-36101-X*) Cambridge U Pr.
Lindzen, Richard S., jt. auth. see Chapman, S.
Lindzen, Richard S., et al, eds. The Atmosphere - A Challenge: The Science of Jule Gregory Charney. (Illus.). 320p. 1990. 65.00 (*1-878220-03-9*) Am Meteorological.
Lindzey, Gardner. Projective Techniques & Cross-Cultural Research. LC 61-15951. (Century Psychology Ser.). 1976. reprint ed. 29.75 (*0-89197-361-3*); reprint ed. pap. text ed. 12.95 (*0-89197-908-5*) Irvington.
Lindzey, Gardner, ed. History of Psychology in Autobiography, Vol. VIII. LC 30-20129. (Illus.). 504p. 1989. 52.50 (*0-8047-1492-4*) Stanford U Pr.
Lindzey, Gardner & Aronson, E. Handbook of Social Psychology, 5 vols. 2nd ed. Incl. Vol. 1. Systematic Positions. 1968. (*0-201-04262-2*); Vol. 2. Research Methods. 1968. (*0-201-04263-0*); Vol. 3. Individual in a Social Context. 1968. (*0-201-04264-9*); Vol. 4. Group Psychology & Phenomena of Interaction. 1968. (*0-201-04265-7*); Vol. 5. Applied Social Psychology. 1968. (*0-201-04266-5*); 1968. write for info. (*0-318-50120-1*) Addison-Wesley.
Lindzey, Gardner & Aronson, Elliot, eds. Handbook of Social Psychology, 2 vols., Set. 3rd ed. (C). 1985. text ed. 150.00 (*0-89859-720-X*) L Erlbaum Assocs.
— Handbook of Social Psychology, Vol. 1. 3rd ed. 1985. text ed. write for info. (*0-07-554876-3*) McGraw.
— Handbook of Social Psychology, Vol. 2. 3rd ed. 1985. text ed. write for info. (*0-07-554877-1*) McGraw.
— Handbook of Social Psychology: Vol. I, Theory & Method. 3rd ed. 832p. (C). 1985. text ed. 70.00 (*0-89859-718-8*) L Erlbaum Assocs.
Lindzey, Gardner & Aronson, Elliott, eds. Handbook of Social Psychology: Vol. II, Special Fields & Applications. 3rd ed. 1136p. (C). 1985. text ed. 80.00 (*0-89859-719-6*) L Erlbaum Assocs.
Lindzey, Gardner & Thiessen, Delbert D., eds. Contributions to Behavior - Genetic Analysis. LC 73-92661. (Century Psychology Ser.). 1970. 34.50 (*0-89197-109-2*) Irvington.
Lindzey, Gardner, jt. ed. see Boring, Edwin G.
Lindzey, Gardner, jt. auth. see Hall, Calvin S.
Lindzey, Gardner, et al. Psychology. 3rd ed. (C). 1988. text ed. 53.95 (*0-87901-361-3*); student ed. pap. 11.95 (*0-87901-354-0*) Worth.
Lindzey, Gardner, et al, eds. Theories of Personality: Primary Sources & Research. 2nd ed. LC 87-21943. 502p. 1988. reprint ed. lib. bdg. 43.50 (*0-89464-254-5*) Krieger.
***Line, Dave.** The Big Book of Brewing. (Illus.). 254p. (Orig.). pap. 12.95 (*0-9619072-9-0*) G W Kent.
— Brewing Beer Like Those You Buy. (Illus.). 158p. (Orig.). 1993. reprint ed. pap. 10.95 (*0-9619072-3-1*) G W Kent.
Line, Francis R. Adventure Unlimited: Searching the Globe with Francis Raymond Line. (Illus.). 206p. (Orig.). 1988. pap. 8.95 (*0-938109-05-7*) Wide Horiz Pr.
— Scrapbook on America. (Orig.). 1990. pap. 8.95 (*0-938109-07-3*) Wide Horiz Pr.
— Sheep, Stars, & Solitude: Adventure Saga of a Wilderness Trail. LC 86-11154. (Illus.). 166p. (Orig.). 1986. pap. 8.95 (*0-938109-02-2*) Wide Horiz Pr.
— Super Seniors, Their Stories & Secrets. (Illus.). 175p. (Orig.). 1989. pap. 8.95 (*0-938109-06-5*) Wide Horiz Pr.
Line, Francis R. & Line, Helen E. Grand Canyon Love Story: A True Living Adventure. 2nd ed. (Illus.). 300p. 1988. reprint ed. pap. 8.95 (*0-938109-04-9*) Wide Horiz Pr.
Line, Francis R. & Line, Winfield H. Foot by Foot Through the U. S. A. A High Adventure Odyssey to Every State in the Union. LC 86-28939. (Illus.). 312p. (Orig.). 1987. pap. 8.95 (*0-938109-03-0*) Wide Horiz Pr.
Line, Helen E., jt. auth. see Line, Francis R.
Line, Julia. Discover Numerology: Understanding & Using the Power of Numbers. LC 93-24780. (Illus.). 224p. 1993. pap. 9.95 (*0-8069-0464-X*) Sterling.
Line, Lee E., et al. Austin, Vol. 1: The Pictorial. Hudspeth, Patrick D. & Cooke, Barbara V., eds. 68p. (Orig.). 1989. 16.00 (*0-317-93913-0*); pap. 8.00 (*0-317-93914-9*) Strictly TX Inc.
Line, Lorie. Selections from Sharing the Season, Vol. 2. Maybery, Paul, ed. (Illus.). 36p. (YA). 1993. pap. text ed. 9.95 (*0-9638000-0-0*) Time Line Prods.
Line, Maurice, ed. Librarianship & Information Work Worldwide, 1993. 274p. 1994. 110.00 (*1-85739-082-2*) Bowker-Saur.
***Line, Maurice B.** Lines of Thought: Selected Papers of Maurice B. Line. Anthony, L. J., ed. LC 88-24376. reprint ed. pap. 100.90 (*0-7837-9269-7*, 2060006) Bks Demand.
— A Little Off Line. 70p. (C). 1988. 69.00 (*0-946139-06-7*, Pub. by Elm Pubns UK) St Mut.
***Line, Maurice B., et al, eds.** Librarianship & Information Work Worldwide 1994: An Annual Survey. 274p. 1995. 100.00 (*1-85739-059-8*) Bowker-Saur.
Line, Walter C. News Writing for Non-Professionals. LC 78-20771. 176p. 1979. 25.95 (*0-88229-348-6*) Nelson-Hall.
Line, Winfield H., jt. auth. see Line, Francis R.
Lineal, Irv, ed. & intro. Lineal Industrial Distributors Register: Asia-Africa-Middle East-Pacific Basin Edition. 420p. 1988. ring bd. 190.00 (*0-9612412-4-1*) Lineal Pub Co.
Lineal, Irv, ed. Lineal's Plant Engineering & Maintenance Idea Book. (Illus.). 222p. 1988. ring bd. 70.00 (*0-9612412-5-X*) Lineal Pub Co.
— Manual de Ideas Lineal Sobre Ingenieria de Fabricas y Mantenimiento. Loinaz, Jorge, tr. 315p. (SPA.). 1989. ring bd. 70.00 (*0-9612412-6-8*) Lineal Pub Co.
Lineau, Richard M. Night Run. Hill, Renais J., ed. LC 92-52642. 274p. 1992. pap. 10.95 (*1-55666-078-2*) Pubs Grp Toluca.
Lineaweaver, Marion. The Season Within. 1967. 5.95 (*0-87233-836-3*) Bauhan.
Lineaweaver, Thomas H., III & Backus, Richard H. The Natural History of Sharks. (Illus.). 256p. 1986. pap. 14. 95 (*0-8052-0766-X*) Lyons & Burford.
Lineback, Kent L. Being the Boss: The Craft of Managing People. LC 86-27751. 192p. 1987. 29.95 (*0-87942-212-2*, PCO2055) Inst Electrical.
Lineback, Mark. Corporate Madness. (Illus.). 104p. (Orig.). 1994. pap. 9.95 (*0-9641121-0-8*) Madness.
***Lineback, Richard H., ed.** International Directory of Philosophy & Philosophers, 1995-96. 9th ed. 450p. 1995. 99.00 (*0-912632-98-4*) Philos Document.
— The Philosopher's Index: A Retrospective Index to Non-U. S. English Language Publications from 1940, 3 vols., Set. 1265p. 1980. 375.00 (*0-912632-12-7*) Philos Document.
— The Philosopher's Index: Cumulative Edition, 1967-1968, Vols. I & II. 708p. 1969. 80.00 (*0-912632-00-3*) Philos Document.
— The Philosopher's Index: Cumulative Edition, 1969, Vol. III. 611p. 1970. 80.00 (*0-912632-01-1*) Philos Document.
— The Philosopher's Index: Cumulative Edition, 1970, Vol. IV. 872p. 1971. 80.00 (*0-912632-02-X*) Philos Document.
— The Philosopher's Index: Cumulative Edition, 1971, Vol. V. 911p. 1972. 80.00 (*0-912632-03-8*) Philos Document.
— The Philosopher's Index: Cumulative Edition, 1972, Vol. VI. 1027p. 1973. 95.00 (*0-912632-04-6*) Philos Document.
— The Philosopher's Index: Cumulative Edition, 1973, Vol. VII. 1216p. 1974. 95.00 (*0-912632-05-4*) Philos Document.
— The Philosopher's Index: Cumulative Edition, 1974, Vol. VIII. 1397p. 1975. 95.00 (*0-912632-06-2*) Philos Document.
— The Philosopher's Index: Cumulative Edition, 1975, Vol. IX. 403p. 1976. 95.00 (*0-912632-07-0*) Philos Document.
— The Philosopher's Index: Cumulative Edition, 1976, Vol. X. 403p. 1977. 110.00 (*0-912632-08-9*) Philos Document.
— The Philosopher's Index: Cumulative Edition, 1977, Vol. XI. 410p. 1978. 110.00 (*0-912632-10-0*) Philos Document.
— The Philosopher's Index: Cumulative Edition, 1978, Vol. XII. 447p. 1979. 110.00 (*0-912632-11-9*) Philos Document.
— The Philosopher's Index: Cumulative Edition, 1979, Vol. XIII. 555p. 1980. 110.00 (*0-912632-13-5*) Philos Document.
— The Philosopher's Index: Cumulative Edition, 1980, Vol. XIV. 576p. 1981. 120.00 (*0-912632-14-3*) Philos Document.
— Philosopher's Index: Cumulative Edition, 1981, Vol. XV. 570p. 1982. 120.00 (*0-912632-15-1*) Philos Document.
— The Philosopher's Index: Cumulative Edition, 1982, Vol. XVI. 540p. 1983. 120.00 (*0-912632-16-X*) Philos Document.
— The Philosopher's Index: Cumulative Edition, 1983, Vol. XVII. 482p. 1984. 120.00 (*0-912632-17-8*) Philos Document.
— The Philosopher's Index: Cumulative Edition, 1984, Vol. XVIII. 532p. 1985. 130.00 (*0-912632-18-6*) Philos Document.
— The Philosopher's Index: 1991 Cumulative Edition, Vol. 25. 750p. 1992. 155.00 (*0-912632-53-4*) Philos Document.
— Philosopher's Index, Vol. 26: 1992 Cumulative Edition. 534p. 1993. 162.00 (*0-912632-54-2*) Philos Document.
— Philosopher's Index, Vol. 27: 1993 Cumulative Edition. 779p. 1994. 172.00 (*0-912632-55-0*) Philos Document.
— The Philosopher's Index, 1986: Cumulative Edition, Vol. XX. 624p. 1987. 130.00 (*0-912632-21-6*) Philos Document.
— Philosopher's Index, 1987: Cumulative Edition, Vol. XXI. 672p. 1988. 130.00 (*0-912632-22-4*) Philos Document.
— Philosopher's Index, 1988: Cumulative Edition, Vol. XXII. 649p. 1989. 140.00 (*0-912632-24-0*) Philos Document.
— Philosopher's Index, 1989: Cumulative Edition, Vol. XXIII. 695p. 1990. 140.00 (*0-912632-51-8*) Philos Document.
— The Philosopher's Index 1990 Cumulative Edition, Vol. 24. 774p. 1991. 150.00 (*0-912632-52-6*) Philos Document.
— The Philosopher's Index, 1994: Cumulative Edition, Vol. 28. 800p. 1995. 181.00 (*0-912632-56-9*) Philos Document.
— The Philosophers's Index, 1985: Cumulative Edition, Vol. XIX. 488p. 1986. 130.00 (*0-912632-19-4*) Philos Document.
— Searching "The Philosopher's Index" Database on Dialog. 63p. 1988. 15.00 (*0-912632-50-X*) Philos Document.
Linebarger, Paul M. The Political Doctrines of Sun Yat-Sen. LC 73-3926. 278p. 1973. text ed. 38.50 (*0-8371-6855-4*, LISY, Greenwood Pr) Greenwood.
— Political Doctrines of Sun Yat-Sen: An Exposition of the San Min Chu I. LC 78-64293. (Johns Hopkins University. Studies in the Social Sciences. Thirtieth Ser. 1912: 24). reprint ed. 13.00 (*0-404-61393-4*) AMS Pr.
— The Political Doctrines of Sun Yat-Sen: An Exposition of the San Min Chu-I. LC 73-889. (China Studies: from Confucius to Mao Ser.). xiv, 278p. 1973. reprint ed. 21. 50 (*0-88355-082-2*) Hyperion Conn.
— Psychological Warfare. LC 72-4671. (International Propaganda & Communications Ser.). (Illus.). 318p. 1977. reprint ed. 27.95 (*0-405-04755-X*) Ayer.
— Sun Yat Sen & the Chinese Republic. LC 70-96469. 1969. reprint ed. 22.50 (*0-404-03989-8*) AMS Pr.
Linebaugh, Donald W. & Robinson, Gary C., eds. Spatial Patterning in Historical Archaeology: Selected Studies of Settlement. (Occasional Papers in Archaeology: No. 2). (Illus.). 144p. (Orig.). (C). 1994. pap. 17.00 (*0-9615670-6-6*, King & Queen Pr) Soc Alu Wm.
Linebaugh, Peter. The London Hanged: Crime & Civil Society in the Eighteenth Century. (Illus.). 512p. (C). 1992. 49.95 (*0-521-41842-9*) Cambridge U Pr.
— The London Hanged: Crime & Civil Society in the Eighteenth Century. (Illus.). 512p. (C). 1993. pap. 16.95 (*0-521-45758-0*) Cambridge U Pr.

Lineberry, John. That We May Have Fellowship: Studies in First John. LC 86-24841. 112p. 1986. pap. 4.95 (*0-87227-115-3*, RBP5143) Reg Baptist.

Lineberry, Robert L. American Government: Brief Edition. (C). 1993. 34.00 (*0-06-500721-2*) HarpCollege.

— American Government: Brief Edition. (C). 1993. student ed 14.75 (*0-06-501761-7*) HarpCollege.

— Equality & Urban Policy: The Distribution of Municipal Public Services. LC 76-53962. (Sage Library of Social Research: No. 39). 207p. 1977. reprint ed. pap. 59.00 (*0-7837-1127-1*, 2041657) Bks Demand.

Lineberry, Robert L. & Masotti, Louis, eds. Urban Policy Problems. (C). 1975. pap. 12.00 (*0-918592-11-9*) Pol Studies.

Lineberry, Robert L. & Masotti, Louis H. Urban Problems & Public Policy. 240p. 1985. reprint ed. lib. bdg. 37.50 (*0-8191-5142-4*, Pol Studies) U Pr of Amer.

Lineberry, Robert L. & Masotti, Louis H., eds. Urban Problems & Public Policy. 240p. 1976. boxed 34.95x (*0-669-00017-5*) Transaction Pubs.

Lineberry, Robert L., et al. Government in America: People, Politics, & Policy. 6th ed. LC 93-11155. (C). 1993. text ed. 40.00 (*0-673-52323-3*) HarpCollege.

— Government in America, Brief: People, Politics, & Policy. 2nd ed. LC 94-36374. (C). 1995. text ed. 23.50 (*0-673-99658-1*) HarpCollege.

Lineberry, Tommy. Twice a Champion: The Toney Lineberry Story. 2nd ed. Talbolt, Frederick, ed. 200p. 1988. 14.95 (*0-685-23257-3*); pap. 8.95 (*0-685-23258-1*) T Lineberry.

Linecar, Howard W., ed. The Milled Coinage of England. 1971. 15.00 (*0-685-51502-8*) S J Durst.

Linecar, Howard W. & Stone, A. G. English Proof & Pattern Crown Size Pieces. 1968. 18.00 (*0-685-51507-9*) S J Durst.

Linecraft, Inc. Staff, ed. see Virchik, Henrietta.

***Linedecker.** Deadly Obsessions. 1995. mass mkt. 4.99 (*0-7860-0112-7*, Pinnacle NY) Windsor NY.

Linedecker, Clifford. Blood Money. (Illus.). 384p. 1993. mass mkt. 4.99 (*1-55817-773-6*, Pinnacle NY) Windsor NY.

Linedecker, Clifford L. Deadly White Female. 1994. mass mkt. 4.99 (*0-312-95165-5*) St Martin.

— Gun for Hire: The Soldier of Fortune Killings. 392p. (Orig.). 1992. mass mkt. 4.99 (*0-380-76204-8*) Avon.

— Killer Kids: Shocking True Stories of Children Who Murdered Their Parents. 1993. mass mkt. 4.99 (*0-312-95006-3*) St Martin.

— The Man Who Killed Boys. 1993. mass mkt. 4.99 (*0-312-95228-7*) St Martin.

— Massacre at Waco: The Shocking True Story of Cult Leader David Koresh & the Branch Davidians. 1993. mass mkt. 4.99 (*0-312-95226-0*) St Martin.

— Night Stalker. 1991. mass mkt. 4.95 (*0-312-92505-0*) St Martin.

— Nurses Who Kill: The Frightening True Crime Accounts of Healthcare Workers Who Murder Their Patients. 1990. pap. 3.95 (*1-55817-449-4*, Pinnacle NY) Windsor NY.

— Prison Groupies. (Illus.). 320p. 1993. mass mkt. 4.99 (*1-55817-702-7*, Pinnacle NY) Windsor NY.

***Linedecker, Clifford L. & Osanka, Frank M.** Deadly Obsessions. 352p. 1995. pap. 4.99 (*0-8217-0112-6*) Zebra.

Linehan, Marsha M. Cognitive Behavioral Treatment of Borderline Personality Disorder. LC 93-20483. (Diagnosis & Treatment of Mental Disorders Ser.). 558p. 1993. lib. bdg. 39.50 (*0-89862-183-6*) Guilford Pr.

— Skills Training Manual for Treating Borderline Personality Disorder. LC 93-15216. (Diagnosis & Treatment of Mental Disorders Ser.). 180p. (Orig.). 1993. student ed 24.95 (*0-89862-034-1*) Guilford Pr.

***Linehan, Patricia & Landreth, Patrick.** Mayas. deluxe ed. 160p. 1995. 25.00 (*0-614-04527-4*) Donald R Hoflin.

Linehan, Peter. History & the Historians of Medieval Spain. LC 92-21842. 700p. (C). 1993. 105.00 (*0-19-821945-8*, Clarendon Pr) OUP.

— Past & Present in Medieval Spain. (Collected Studies: No. CS384). 360p. 1992. 89.95 (*0-86078-341-3*, Pub. by Variorum UK) Ashgate Pub Co.

Linehard, Marc, jt. ed. see Krieger, Christian.

***Lineker, Bruce, et al.** Tim Rollins & K. O. S. The Red Badge of Courage. Margolis, Nancy H., ed. (Illus.). 1994. 8.00 (*0-9611560-4-X*) SEC Contemp Art-Ava.

Lineker, Gary. The Young Soccer Player. LC 93-41145. (Illus.). 32p. (J). (gr. 2-6). 1994. 7.95 (*1-56458-592-1*) Dorling Kindersley.

***Lineman, Rose.** Eclipse Interpretation Manual. 147p. 1986. 13.00 (*0-86690-301-1*, L2356-014) Am Fed Astrologers.

— Eclipses: Astrological Guideposts. LC 83-72326. 128p. 1984. 13.00 (*0-86690-258-9*, L2403-014) Am Fed Astrologers.

Lineman, Rose & Popelka, Jan. The Compendium of Astrology. LC 83-63067. 1984. pap. 14.95 (*0-914918-43-5*, Whitford Pr) Schiffer.

Linenthal, Amy, jt. ed. see Sharp, Robert V.

Linenthal, Arthur J. First A Dream: The History of Boston's Jewish Hospitals, 1896-1928. LC 90-82277. (Illus.). xxii, 727p. 1990. 33.00 (*0-9626606-0-4*) A J Linenthal.

Linenthal, Edward T. Changing Images of the Warrior Hero in America: A History of Popular Symbolism. LC 82-22885. (Studies in American Religion: Vol. 6). 296p. 1983. lib. bdg. 89.95 (*0-88946-921-0*) E Mellen.

— Preserving Memory: The Struggle to Create America's Holocaust Museum. (Illus.). 320p. 1995. 27.95 (*0-670-86067-0*, Viking) Viking Penguin.

— Sacred Ground: Americans & Their Battlefields. (Illus.). 320p. 1991. 29.95 (*0-252-01783-8*) U of Ill Pr.

— Sacred Ground: Americans & Their Battlefields. 2nd ed. LC 93-23925. (Illus.). 320p. 1993. pap. 19.95 (*0-252-06171-3*) U of Ill Pr.

— Symbolic Defense: The Cultural Significance of the Strategic Defense Initiative. fac. ed. LC 88-32111. (Illus.). 160p. 1989. reprint ed. pap. 45.60 (*0-7837-8076-1*, 2047829) Bks Demand.

Linenthal, Edward T., jt. ed. see Chernus, Ira.

Linenthal, Edward T., jt. ed. see Chidester, David.

***Liner.** Scientific & Common Names for the Amphibians & Reptiles of Mexico. 1994. write for info. (*0-916984-32-X*) SSAR.

Liner, Charles D., ed. Shared Responsibility. 48p. (Orig.). (C). 1985. pap. text ed. 4.50 (*1-56011-144-5*, 85.07) Institute Government.

— State & Local Government Relations in North Carolina: Their Evolution & Current Status. 2nd ed. (C). 1995. pap. text ed. write for info. (*1-56011-244-1*) Institute Government.

***Liner, E. Blaine, ed.** Compacts & Coalitions in Metropolitan Governance. fac. ed. (Lincoln Institute of Land Policy Ser.: No. 86-6). 54p. 1986. reprint ed. pap. 25.00 (*0-7837-7825-2*, 2047581) Bks Demand.

— A Decade of Devolution: Perspectives of State & Local Relations. LC 89-31871. (Illus.). 260p. (Orig.). 1989. lib. bdg. 57.00 (*0-87766-464-1*); pap. text ed. 31.50 (*0-87766-463-3*) Urban Inst.

— Intergovernmental Land Management Innovations. 57p. 1985. 12.00 (*0-317-01540-0*) Fla Atlantic.

— Intergovernmental Land Management Innovations. (Lincoln Institute of Land Policy Monograph Ser.: No. 85-7). 67p. reprint ed. pap. 25.00 (*0-7837-5760-3*, 2045422) Bks Demand.

— Local Agenda Setting Processes. fac. ed. (Lincoln Institute of Land Policy Monograph Ser.: No. 85-10). 61p. 1985. reprint ed. pap. 25.00 (*0-7837-7827-9*, 2047583) Bks Demand.

— Local Agenda Setting Processes: Part I: The Conceptual & Historical Framework. (Lincoln Institute Monograph: No. 85-10). 53p. 1985. pap. 5.25 (*1-55844-090-9*) Lincoln Inst Land.

***Liner, Tom & Butler, Deborah.** Rooms to Grow: Natural Language Arts in the Middle School. LC 93-74700. (Illus.). 428p. (C). 1995. pap. text ed. 27.95 (*0-89089-577-5*) Carolina Acad Pr.

Linerode, Darla. Introduction to Art. (Illus.). (Orig.). (J). (gr. 3-6). 1992. pap. 63.00 (*0-935493-29-8*) Modern Learn Pr.

— An Introduction to Art. (Illus.). 18p. 1991. pap. text ed. 49.50 (*1-56762-329-8*) Modern Learn Pr.

— Let's Look at Art. (Illus.). (Orig.). (J). (gr. 1-6). 1992. pap. write for info. (*0-935493-30-1*) Modern Learn Pr.

— Let's Look at Art, 9 vols., Set. (Illus.). 168p. (Orig.). Date not set. pap. text ed. 410.00 (*1-56762-044-2*) Modern Learn Pr.

— Let's Look at Faces. (Illus.). 18p. 1991. pap. text ed. 49.50 (*1-56762-042-6*) Modern Learn Pr.

— Let's Look at Landscapes. (Illus.). 18p. 1991. pap. text ed. 49.50 (*1-56762-043-4*) Modern Learn Pr.

— Let's Look at Line. (Illus.). 18p. 1991. pap. text ed. 49.50 (*1-56762-039-6*) Modern Learn Pr.

— Let's Look at Portraits. (Illus.). 18p. 1991. pap. text ed. 49.50 (*1-56762-041-8*) Modern Learn Pr.

— Let's Look at Transportation. (Illus.). 18p. 1991. pap. text ed. 49.50 (*1-56762-040-X*) Modern Learn Pr.

Lines. Power Supplies. 1992. pap. 10.95 (*0-7906-1024-8*, Prompt Pubns) H W Sams.

Lines, Amelia A. To Raise Myself a Little: The Diaries & Letters of Jennie, a Georgia Teacher, 1851-1886. Dyer, Thomas, ed. LC 81-301. 288p. 1982. 25.00 (*0-8203-0562-6*) U of Ga Pr.

Lines, Anni M. Vitamins & Minerals: The Health Connection. LC 85-7638. 188p. 1985. pap. 6.95 (*0-932090-14-1*) Health Plus.

Lines, Anni M., jt. auth. see Airola, Paavo O.

Lines, Anni M., jt. auth. see Airola, Paavo.

Lines, C. Fragile Planet. (Down to Earth Ser.). (C). 1987. 40.00 (*0-09-172361-2*, Pub. by S Thornes Pubs UK) St Mut.

— Leisure & Tourism. (Down to Earth Ser.). (C). 1988. 60.00 (*0-09-173193-3*, Pub. by S Thornes Pubs UK) St Mut.

— Living in the City. (Down to Earth Ser.). (C). 1988. 30.00 (*0-09-173065-1*, Pub. by S Thornes Pubs UK) St Mut.

Lines, Clifford J. Companion to the Industrial Revolution. 256p. 1990. 27.50 (*0-8160-2157-0*) Facts on File.

Lines, Kathleen. Lavender's Blue. (Illus.). 180p. (J). (ps-7). 1990. pap. 12.00 (*0-19-272208-5*) OUP.

Lines, Kathleen, ed. The Faber Book of Greek Legends. (Illus.). 268p. (J). (gr. 4 up). 1986. pap. 11.95 (*0-571-13920-5*) Faber & Faber.

— The Faber Book of Magical Tales. LC 85-4437. (Illus.). 176p. (Orig.). (J). (gr. 5-9). 1985. pap. 7.95 (*0-571-13648-6*) Faber & Faber.

Lines, Kathleen, ed. see Uttley, Alison.

Lines, Laurence R., ed. Inversion of Geophysical Data. LC 88-60485. (Geophysics Reprint Ser.: No. 9). 560p. 1988. pap. text ed. 55.00 (*0-931830-58-3*, 469) Soc Expl Geophys.

Lines, Malcolm E. A Number for Your Thoughts: Facts & Speculations about Numbers from Euclid to the Latest Computers. (Illus.). 220p. 1986. pap. 18.00 (*0-85274-495-1*) IOP Pub.

— Think of a Number. (Illus.). 172p. 1990. pap. 18.00 (*0-85274-183-9*) IOP Pub.

***Lines, Malcom E.** On the Shoulders of Giants. LC 94-30118. 1994. 90.00 (*0-7503-0104-X*); pap. 30.00 (*0-7503-0103-1*) IOP Pub.

Lines, Malcom E. & Glass, Alastair M. Principles & Applications of Ferroelectrics & Related Materials. (International Series of Monographs on Physics). (Illus.). 1977. 135.00 (*0-19-851286-4*) OUP.

Lines, Marianna. Sacred Stones, Sacred Places. 128p. (C). 1991. text ed. 95.00 (*0-685-49634-1*, Pub. by St Andrew UK) St Mut.

— Sacred Stones, Sacred Places. (Illus.). 160p. (C). 1992. 65.00 (*0-685-60678-3*, Pub. by St Andrew UK) St Mut.

— Sacred Stones, Sacred Places. 176p. 1993. 80.00 (*0-7152-0652-4*, Pub. by St Andrew UK) St Mut.

Lines, Timothy A. Functional Images of the Religious Educator. 540p. (Orig.). 1992. pap. 18.95 (*0-89135-087-X*) Religious Educ.

— Systemic Religious Education. LC 86-20383. 264p. (Orig.). 1987. pap. 17.95 (*0-89135-057-8*) Religious Educ.

Lines, William J. Taming the Great South Land: A History of the Conquest of Nature in Australia. 1992. 30.00 (*0-520-07830-6*) U CA Pr.

Linesch, Debra, ed. Art Therapy with Families in Crisis: Overcoming Resistance Through Nonverbal Expression. LC 92-27839. (Illus.). 192p. 1993. 25.00 (*0-87630-638-5*) Brunner-Mazel.

Linesch, Debra G. Adolescent Art Therapy. LC 87-21866. 256p. 1988. 29.95 (*0-87630-486-2*) Brunner-Mazel.

Linet, Martha S. The Leukemias: Epidemiologic Aspects, No. 6. (Illus.). 1985. 49.95 (*0-19-503448-1*) OUP.

Linett, Deena. The Translator's Wife. 1986. pap. 6.50 (*0-317-53674-5*) Humanities Arts Pr.

Linfert, Carl. Bosch. (Masters of Art Ser.). (Illus.). 128p. 1989. 22.95 (*0-8109-0719-4*) Abrams.

Linffors, Bernth, jt. ed. see Sander, Reinhard W.

Linfield, Jordan, jt. auth. see Krevisky, Joseph.

Linfield, Jordan L. & Kay, Joe. Your Mother Wears Army Boots! A Treasure Trove of Insults, Slurs & Putdowns. 288p. (Orig.). 1992. pap. 9.00 (*0-380-76591-8*) Avon.

Linfield, Jordan L. & Krevisky, Joseph. Word Traps: A Dictionary of the Seven Thousand Most Confusing Sound-Alike & Look-Alike Words. LC 92-25760. 374p. 1993. pap. 12.00 (*0-02-052751-9*, Pub. by Gebrueder Borntraeger GW) Macmillan.

Linfield, Michael. Freedom under Fire: U. S. Civil Liberties in Times of War. 256p. (Orig.). (C). 1990. 40.00 (*0-89608-375-6*); pap. 14.00 (*0-89608-374-8*) South End Pr.

***Linfield, Robert F.** Telecommunications: Present Status & Future Trends. LC 94-31267. (Advanced Computing & Telecommunications Ser.). (Illus.). 169p. 1995. 42.00 (*0-8155-1368-2*) Noyes.

Linfield, Trudy. English Spoken Here: Series Guide. (English Spoken Here (ESL) Ser.). 1988. pap. text ed. write for info. (*0-8428-0862-0*) Cambridge Bk.

Linfield, Warner A., ed. Anionic Surfactants, Pt. 1. LC 75-22777. (Surfactant Science Ser.: No. 7). (Illus.). 328p. reprint ed. pap. 93.50 (*0-8357-5490-1*, 2032990) Bks Demand.

Linfoot, Ken, ed. Communication Strategies for People with Developmental Disabilities: Issues from Theory & Practice. LC 93-50222. 208p. 1994. 33.00 (*1-55766-170-7*, Pub. by MacLennan & Petty AT) P H Brookes.

Linford, M. Mary Wollstonecraft. 1972. lib. bdg. 250.00 (*0-8490-0588-4*) Gordon Pr.

Linford, Marilynne T. ABCs for Young LDS. rev. ed. 1991. pap. 5.95 (*0-88494-794-7*) Bookcraft Inc.

— Is Anyone Out There Building Mother's Self-Esteem? 2nd ed. LC 86-16657. 114p. 1992. reprint ed. pap. 6.95 (*0-87579-618-4*) Deseret Bk.

Linford, R. G., ed. Electrochemical Science & Technology of Polymers, Vol. 1. 344p. 1987. 101.00 (*1-85166-031-3*, Pub. by Elsevier Applied Sci UK) Elsevier.

— Electrochemical Science & Technology of Polymers, Vol. 2. 424p. 1990. 122.50 (*1-85166-469-6*) Elsevier.

Linfors, Bernth, ed. Black African Literature in English: 1977-1981. LC 86-1021. 412p. 1986. 45.00 (*0-8419-0962-8*, Africana) Holmes & Meier.

— Black African Literature in English: 1982-1986. Date not set. write for info. (*0-8419-1241-6*, Africana) Holmes & Meier.

Linforth, Ivan M. The Arts of Orpheus. LC 72-9296. (Philosophy of Plato & Aristotle Ser.). 1977. reprint ed. 35.95 (*0-405-04847-5*) Ayer.

Linforth, Veda. Toy Shop Tales. (J). 1993. 7.95 (*0-533-10266-9*) Vantage.

Ling, Agnes H., jt. auth. see Ling, Daniel.

Ling, Amy. Between Worlds: Women Writers of Chinese Ancestry. (Athene Ser.). 292p. 1990. text ed. 37.50 (*0-08-037464-6*, Pub. by PPI UK); pap. text ed. 16.95 (*0-08-037463-8*, Pub. by PPI UK) Elsevier.

— Between Worlds: Women Writers of Chinese Ancestry. (Athene Ser.). 232p. (C). text ed. 37.50 (*0-8077-6237-7*); pap. text ed. 16.95 (*0-8077-6238-5*) Tchrs Coll.

Ling, Amy & White-Parks, Annette, eds. The Spring of Chinese North American Literature: Collected Writings of Sui Sin Far. LC 94-14202. (Asian American Experience Ser.). 1995. write for info. (*0-252-02133-9*); pap. write for info. (*0-252-06419-4*) U of Ill Pr.

Ling, Amy, jt. ed. see Brown, Wesley.

Ling, Amy, jt. ed. see Geok-Lin Lim, Shirley.

Ling, Bing-Chung. Form Discrimination As a Learning Cue in Infants. LC 41-14185. (Comparative Psychology Monographs: Vol. 17). 1941. pap. 40.00 (*0-527-02665-4*) Periodicals Srv.

Ling, C. Clifton, et al, eds. Computed Tomography in Radiation Therapy. (Illus.). 284p. 1983. text ed. 104.00 (*0-89004-831-2*) Raven.

Ling Chung, ed. see Li-Ching-Chao.

Ling, Curtis C. An Integrated 94GHz Monopulse Tracking Receiver. (University of Michigan Report Ser.: No. RL900). 188p. reprint ed. pap. 53.60 (*0-7837-6782-X*, 2046612) Bks Demand.

Ling, Daniel. Cumulative Record of Speech Skill Acquisition. LC 77-93949. 1977. pap. text ed. 10.50 (*0-88200-115-9*, A1983) Alexander Graham.

— Speech & the Hearing Impaired Child: Theory & Practice. LC 76-21920. (Illus.). 1976. text ed. 25.95 (*0-88200-074-8*, A0669) Alexander Graham.

— Teacher-Clinician Planbook & Guide to the Development of Speech Skills. LC 77-93949. 1978. pap. text ed. 10.50 (*0-88200-116-7*, A2092) Alexander Graham.

Ling, Daniel, ed. Early Intervention for Hearing Impaired Children: Total Communication Options. LC 84-11396. (Illus.). 256p. 1984. pap. text ed. 25.50 (*0-316-52685-1*) Singular Publishing.

Ling, Daniel & Ling, Agnes H. Aural Habilitation: The Foundations of Verbal Learning in Hearing-Impaired Children. LC 78-56077. 1978. pap. text ed. 24.95 (*0-88200-121-3*, C2441) Alexander Graham.

— Basic Vocabulary & Language Thesaurus for Hearing-Impaired Children. LC 76-52826. 1977. 9.95 (*0-88200-078-0*, C1437) Alexander Graham.

Ling, David A., jt. auth. see Thomas, Richard W.

Ling, Ding. I Myself Am a Woman: Selected Writings of Ding Ling. Bjorge, Gary, ed. Barlow, Tani & Bjorge, Gary, trs. LC 88-43313. (Asian Voices Ser.). 364p. 1990. reprint ed. pap. 17.00 (*0-8070-6747-4*) Beacon Pr.

— Miss Sophie's Diary. 274p. (Orig.). 1995. lib. bdg. 27.00 (*0-8095-4515-2*) Borgo Pr.

— Miss Sophie's Diary. Jenner, W. J., tr. 271p. (Orig.). 1985. pap. 7.95 (*0-8351-1078-8*) China Bks.

Ling, Dorothy. The Original Art of Music. LC 88-19117. 190p. 1990. 35.00 (*0-8191-7117-4*); pap. 20.00 (*0-8191-7118-2*) U Pr of Amer.

Ling, Dwight L. Tunisia: From Protectorate to Republic. LC 67-63013. (Indiana University International Studies). (Illus.). 284p. reprint ed. pap. 81.00 (*0-317-11307-0*, 2055232) Bks Demand.

Ling, Edwin R. One Family, Many Animals. LC 88-18580. 166p. 1988. 13.75 (*0-930950-21-6*); pap. 8.75 (*0-930950-22-4*) Nopoly Pr.

Ling, Edwin R., Sr. Space Crescent. 1984. 24.95 (*0-87397-264-3*) Strode.

Ling, Evan, ed. see Metallurgical Society of AIME Staff.

Ling, Evelyn R. Archives in the Church or Synagogue Library. LC 81-7650. (Guide Ser.: No. 10). 24p. 1981. pap. 6.00 (*0-915324-18-0*); pap. 4.75 (*0-685-01322-7*) CSLA.

Ling, Frank W., jt. ed. see Stovall, Thomas G.

Ling, Frederick F. Surface Mechanics. LC 72-10012. 336p. reprint ed. pap. 95.80 (*0-317-11062-4*, 2006492) Bks Demand.

Ling, Frederick F., ed. Springer Texts in Mechanical Engineering. 1991. text ed. write for info. (*0-318-68929-4*) Spr-Verlag.

Ling, Frederick F. & Pan, C. H., eds. Approaches to Modeling of Friction & Wear. (Illus.). xiii, 173p. 1987. 73.00 (*0-387-96656-0*) Spr-Verlag.

Ling, Frederick F., ed. see American Society of Mechanical Engineers.

Ling, Frederick F., ed. see Chryssolouris, G. & Sheng, P.

Ling, Frederick F., ed. see Costello, G. A.

Ling, Frederick F., ed. see DeVries, W. R.

Ling, Frederick F., ed. see Kuznetsov, E. N.

Ling, Frederick F., ed. see Miu, Denny K.

Ling, Frederick F., et al. Boundary Lubrication: An Appraisal of World Literature. LC 70-79165. 586p. reprint ed. pap. 167.10 (*0-8357-7367-1*, 2016847) Bks Demand.

***Ling, Gerald V.** Lower Urinary Tract Diseases of Dogs & Cats. LC 94-41538. 1995. write for info. (*0-8151-5446-1*) Mosby Yr Bk.

Ling, Gilbert N. In Search of the Physical Basis of Life. LC 83-26919. 822p. 1984. 145.00 (*0-306-41409-0*, Plenum Pr) Plenum.

— A Revolution in the Physiology of the Living Cell & Beyond. LC 89-11068. 404p. 1992. lib. bdg. 64.50 (*0-89464-398-3*) Krieger.

Ling, H., ed. see Symposium on Materials & Processes for Wireless Communications Staff, et al.

***Ling-hsia Yeh.** Practical Chinese Reader II: Patterns & Exercises, Simplified Character Edition. expanded ed. (C & T Asian Language Ser.). 128p. (Orig.). (C). 1994. student ed 10.95 (*0-88727-208-8*) Cheng & Tsui.

— Practical Chinese Reader II: Patterns & Exercises, Traditional Character Edition. expanded ed. (C & T Asian Language Ser.). 198p. (Orig.). (C). 1994. student ed 14.95 (*0-88727-200-2*) Cheng & Tsui.

Ling Hsu, Vivian. A Reader in Post-Cultural Revolution Chinese Literature. (Illus.). (Orig.). (CHI.). (C). 1988. pap. text ed. 29.95 (*0-88710-162-3*) Yale Far Eastern Pubns.

Ling, Hung C., et al, eds. Materials in Microelectronic & Optoelectronic Packaging. LC 93-11050. (Ceramic Transactions Ser.: Vol. 33). 471p. 1993. 69.00 (*0-944904-63-7*, TRANS033) Am Ceramic.

Ling, Linzho. Goldfish for Those Who Care. (Illus.). 32p. 1994. pap. 3.95 (*0-7938-1378-6*, B103) TFH Pubns.

Ling, M. How to Increase Sales & Put Yourself Across by Telephone. 1980. pap. 10.00 (*0-13-413112-6*) P-H.

Ling, M., ed. see Shabana, A. A.

Ling, Mary. Amazing Crocodiles & Other Reptiles. LC 90-19239. (Eyewitness Juniors Ser.: No. 10). (Illus.). 32p. (Orig.). (J). (gr. 1-5). 1991. lib. bdg. 9.99 (*0-679-90689-4*); pap. 7.99 (*0-679-80689-X*) Knopf Bks Yng Read.

— Amazing Fish. LC 90-49651. (Eyewitness Juniors Ser.: No. 11). (Illus.). 32p. (Orig.). (J). (gr. 1-5). 1991. pap. 7.99 (*0-679-81516-3*) Knopf Bks Yng Read.

— Amazing Fish. LC 90-49651. (Eyewitness Juniors Ser.: No. 11). (Illus.). 32p. (Orig.). (J). (gr. 1-5). 1991. lib. bdg. 9.99 (*0-679-91516-8*) Knopf Bks Yng Read.

— Amazing Wolves, Dogs, & Foxes. LC 91-6514. (Eyewitness Juniors Ser.). (Illus.). 32p. (Orig.). (J). (gr. 1-5). 1991. pap. 7.99 (*0-679-81521-X*) Knopf Bks Yng Read.

An Asterisk (*) at the beginning of an entry indicates that the title is appearing in BIP for the first time.

— Amazing Wolves, Dogs, & Foxes. LC 91-6514. (Eyewitness Juniors Ser.). (Illus.). 32p. (Orig.). (J). (gr. 1-5). 1991. lib. bdg. 9.99 (*0-679-91521-4*) Knopf Bks Yng Read.

— Butterfly. LC 92-52808. (See How They Grow Ser.). (Illus.). 24p. (J). (ps-1). 1992. 7.95 (*1-56458-112-8*) Dorling Kindersley.

— Calf. LC 92-53486. (See How They Grow Ser.). (Illus.). 24p. (J). (ps-1). 1993. 7.95 (*1-56458-205-1*) Dorling Kindersley.

— Foal. LC 92-52809. (See How They Grow Ser.). (Illus.). 24p. (J). (ps-1). 1992. 7.95 (*1-56458-113-6*) Dorling Kindersley.

— Fox. LC 92-52810. (See How They Grow Ser.). (Illus.). 24p. (J). (ps-1). 1992. 7.95 (*1-56458-114-4*) Dorling Kindersley.

— Giraffe. LC 93-3041. (See How They Grow Ser.). (Illus.). 24p. (J). (ps-1). 1993. 7.95 (*1-56458-311-2*) Dorling Kindersley.

— Owl. LC 92-52811. (See How They Grow Ser.). (Illus.). 24p. (J). (ps-1). 1992. 7.95 (*1-56458-115-2*) Dorling Kindersley.

— Penguin. LC 93-22105. (See How They Grow Ser.). (Illus.). 24p. (J). (ps-1). 1993. 7.95 (*1-56458-312-0*) Dorling Kindersley.

— Pig. LC 92-53487. (See How They Grow Ser.). (Illus.). 24p. (J). (ps-1). 1993. 7.95 (*1-56458-204-3*) Dorling Kindersley.

Ling, N. R. & Kay, J. E., eds. Lymphocyte Stimulation. 2nd rev. ed. LC 74-83274. 397p. 1975. 151.00 (*0-444-10701-0*, North Holland) Elsevier.

Ling, Peter. Halfway to Heaven. 592p. 1994. 25.95 (*1-85797-076-4*) Trafalgar.

— Happy Tomorrow. 416p. 1995. 27.00 (*1-85797-629-0*, Pub. by Orion) Trafalgar.

— High Water. 406p. 1992. 24.95 (*0-7126-2144-X*, Pub. by Century UK) Trafalgar.

Ling, Peter J. America & the Automobile: Technology, Reform & Social Change, 1893-1923. 208p. 1992. pap. 24.95 (*0-7190-3808-1*, Pub. by Manchester Univ Pr UK) St Martin.

Ling, Richard C. & Goddard, Walter E. Orchestrating Success: Improve Control of the Business with Sales & Operations Planning. LC 88-50483. 157p. 1988. 116.00 (*0-939246-11-2*) Oliver Wight.

Ling, Robert V., jt. auth. see Farmer, Randolph W.

Ling, Roger. The Greek World. LC 88-819. (Making of the Past Ser.). (Illus.). 160p. (gr. 8 up). 1990. 19.95 (*0-87226-301-0*) P Bedrick Bks.

— Roman Painting. (Illus.). 236p. (C). 1991. 94.95 (*0-521-30614-0*); pap. 34.95 (*0-521-31595-6*) Cambridge U Pr.

— Romano-British Wall Painting. 1989. pap. 25.00 (*0-85263-715-2*, Pub. by Shire UK) St Mut.

Ling, Roger, jt. auth. see Strong, Donald.

Ling, Roger, et al, eds. Roman Art. (Pelican History of Art Ser.). (Illus.). 406p. (C). 1988. reprint ed. pap. text ed. 25.00 (*0-300-05293-6*) Yale U Pr.

Ling, Shao-Wen. Aquaculture in Southeast Asia: A Historical Overview. Mumaw, Laura, ed. LC 77-3828. (Washington Sea Grant Ser.). (Illus.). 108p. 1977. pap. 10.00 (*0-295-95563-5*) U of Wash Pr.

Ling, Sheilah W. Saints Alive! 240p. (C). 1990. 39.00 (*0-85439-367-6*, Pub. by St Paul Pubns UK) St Mut.

— Your Glory Reflected: Twenty Outstanding Christians of the Twentieth Century. 192p. 1993. 35.00 (*0-85439-457-5*, Pub. by St Paul Pubns UK) St Mut.

Ling, Tok-Wang, ed. see International Conference on Database Systems for Advanced Applications Staff.

Ling, Trevor. The Significance of Satan: New Testament Demonology & Its Contemporary Relevance. LC 79-8110. (Satanism Ser.). 120p. 1985. reprint ed. 21.50 (*0-404-18424-3*) AMS Pr.

Ling, Trevor, ed. Buddhist Trends in Southeast Asia. 189p. 1993. 38.45 (*981-3035-80-3*, Pub. by Inst SE Asian Studies SI); pap. 25.00 (*981-3035-81-1*, Pub. by Inst SE Asian Studies SI) Ashgate Pub Co.

Ling, Trevor, tr. & intro. Buddha's Philosophy of Man. 256p. 1993. pap. 6.95 (*0-460-87207-9*, Everyman's Classic Lib) C E Tuttle.

Ling, Vivian. The Girl in Red: A Study Guide for the Film. 1994. pap. 18.00 (*0-89264-116-9*) Ctr Chinese Studies.

— Under the Bridge: A Study Guide for the Film. 325p. 1994. pap. 18.00 (*0-89264-113-4*) Ctr Chinese Studies.

Ling, Vivian & Dew, James E. Studying in China: A Practical Text for Spoken Chinese. 160p. 1994. pap. text ed. 14.95 (*0-88727-196-0*) Cheng & Tsui.

Ling, Zhu. Rural Reform & Peasant Income in China: The Impact of China's Post-Mao Rural Reforms in Selected Regions. LC 90-44603. 130p. 1991. text ed. 65.00 (*0-312-05325-8*) St Martin.

Lingaiah, K. Machine Design Data Handbook. 1994. text ed. 136.50 (*0-07-037933-5*) McGraw.

Lingaiah, Karnati, et al. Indian Economy. 1990. text ed. 27.95 (*81-207-1236-6*, Pub. by Sterling Pubs II) Apt Bks.

Lingam, S., jt. auth. see Hall, C. M.

LIngappa, B. T., jt. auth. see Lingappa, Yamuna.

Lingappa, Yamuna & LIngappa, B. T. Wholesome Nutrition for Mind, Body, & Microflora: The Goal of Lacto-Vegetarianism (Recipes of Udipi Cuisine Included) 416p. 1992. pap. 16.00 (*0-9634999-0-4*) Ecobiol Fnd.

Lingard, Anne, jt. auth. see Spencer, Peggy.

Lingard, Bob, et al, eds. Schooling Reform in Hard Times. LC 92-38081. 324p. 1993. 90.00 (*0-7507-0119-6*, Falmer Pr); pap. 33.00 (*0-7507-0120-X*, Falmer Pr) Taylor & Francis.

***Lingard, James R.** Bank Security Documents. 2nd ed. 1993. 175.00 (*0-406-00581-8*, U.K.) Butterworth Legal Pubs.

— Corporate Rescues & Insolvencies. 2nd ed. 1989. 84.00 (*0-406-10601-0*, U.K.) Butterworth Legal Pubs.

— Tolley's Commercial Loan Agreements. 136p. 1990. 105.00 (*0-85459-453-1*, Pub. by Tolley Pubng UK) St Mut.

***Lingard, Joan.** After Colette. 315p. 1995. 24.95 (*1-85619-328-4*, Sinclair-Stevenson) Trafalgar.

— Between Two Worlds. 192p. (J). (gr. 7 up). 1993. pap. 4.50 (*0-14-036505-2*, Puffin) Puffin Bks.

— Tug of War. 192p. (J). (gr. 5 up). 1992. pap. 4.50 (*0-14-036072-7*, Puffin) Puffin Bks.

Lingard, Tim, ed. see Marion, Dawn D.

Lingas, A., et al, eds. Automata, Languages & Programming: Proceedings of the 20th International Colloquium, ICALP 93, Lund, Sweden, July 5-9, 1993. (Lecture Notes in Computer Science Ser.: Vol. 700). vii, 697p. 1993. pap. 101.00 (*0-387-56939-1*) Spr-Verlag.

Lingat, Robert. The Classic Law of India. Derrett, J. D., tr. 323p. 1993. 43.50 (*81-215-0610-7*, Pub. by M Manoharial II) Coronet Bks.

Linge, Godfrey J., ed. Peripheralisation & Industrial Change Impacts on Nations, Regions, Firms, & People. 272p. 1988. lib. bdg. 57.50 (*0-7099-4865-4*, Pub. by Croom Helm UK) Routledge Chapman & Hall.

Linge, Godfrey J. & Forbes, D. K., eds. China's Spatial Economy: Recent Developments & Reforms. (Illus.). 240p. 1991. 45.00 (*0-19-585296-6*) OUP.

Linge, Godfrey J. & Van Der Knaap, G. A., eds. Labour, Environment & Industrial Change. 256p. 1989. 57.50 (*0-415-00928-6*) Routledge.

Linge, Godfrey J., jt. ed. see Rich, D. C.

Lingelbach, Jenepher R., ed. Hands-on Nature: Information & Activities for Exploring the Environment with Children. LC 86-28268. (Illus.). 240p. 1987. pap. 16.95 (*0-9617627-0-5*) VT Inst Nat Sci.

Lingelbach, William E. Austria-Hungary: Based on the Work of Paul Louis Leger, College De France. LC 70-135846. (Eastern Europe Collection Ser.). 1971. reprint ed. 33.95 (*0-405-02788-5*) Ayer.

Lingeman & Underberg. Detection-Oriented Derivatization Techniques in Liquid Chromatography. (Chromatographic Science Ser.: Vol. 48). 432p. 1990. 140.00 (*0-8247-8287-9*) Dekker.

Lingeman, James E. & Newman, D. M., eds. Shock Wave Lithotripsy, Vol. 1: State of the Art. (Illus.). 432p. 1988. 110.00 (*0-306-43112-2*, Plenum Pr) Plenum.

— Shock Wave Lithotripsy, Vol. 2: Urinary & Biliary Lithotripsy. LC 89-70948. (Illus.). 476p. 1989. 110.00 (*0-306-43416-4*, Plenum Pr) Plenum.

Lingeman, James E., et al. Urinary Calculi: ESWL, Endourology, & Medical Therapy. Moster, Mary B., ed. LC 88-38144. 476p. reprint ed. pap. 135.70 (*0-7837-2725-9*, 2043105) Bks Demand.

Lingeman, Richard. Theodore Dreiser: An American Journey. abr. ed. LC 92-40559. 672p. 1993. pap. text ed. 19.95 (*0-471-57426-0*) Wiley.

Lingen, L. Russian-German Legal Dictionary: Juristisches Woerterbuch: Russisch-Deutsch. 608p. (GER & RUS.). 1985. 85.00 (*0-8288-0982-8*, M8601) Fr & Eur.

Lingenberg, R., jt. auth. see Scherk, Peter.

Lingenfelter, Mary R. Vocations in Fiction: An Annotated Bibliography. LC 74-3102. (Studies in Fiction: No. 34). 1974. lib. bdg. 75.00 (*0-8383-2052-X*) M S G Haskell Hse.

Lingenfelter, R. E., et al, eds. Gamma-Ray Transients & Related Astrophysical Phenomena: La Jolla Institute. LC 81-715443. (AIP Conference Proceedings Ser.: No. 77). 500p. 1982. lib. bdg. 37.00 (*0-88318-176-2*) Am Inst Physics.

Lingenfelter, Richard E. Death Valley & the Amargosa: A Land of Illusion. (Illus.). 622p. 1986. pap. 18.00 (*0-520-06356-2*) U CA Pr.

— Steamboats on the Colorado River, 1852-1916. LC 78-16241. (Illus.). 211p. reprint ed. pap. 60.20 (*0-7837-1908-6*, 2042112) Bks Demand.

Lingenfelter, Richard E., ed. Dan De Quille, The Washoe Giant: A Biography & Anthology. LC 89-16584. (Western Literature Ser.). 464p. (Orig.). 1990. pap. 19.95 (*0-87417-152-0*) U of Nev Pr.

Lingenfelter, Richard E. & Dwyer, Richard A., eds. Death Valley Lore: Classic Tales of Fantasy, Adventure, & Mystery. LC 88-17277. (Illus.). 360p. 1988. 24.95 (*0-87417-136-9*) U of Nev Pr.

Lingenfelter, Richard E. & Gash, Karen R. The Newspapers of Nevada: A History & Bibliography, 1854-1979. LC 83-16790. (Illus.). 368p. 1984. 50.00 (*0-87417-075-3*) U of Nev Pr.

Lingenfelter, Scott, ed. Ethics in the Russian Marketplace: An Anthology. Molodyi, Boris & Molodyi, Vadim, trs. 213p. (Orig.). 1992. pap. text ed. 20.00 (*1-879089-10-6*) B Graham Ctr.

Lingenfelter, Sherwood. Transforming Culture: A Challenge for Christian Mission. LC 92-4276. 218p. 1992. pap. 14.99 (*0-8010-5674-8*) Baker Bk.

Lingenfelter, Sherwood G. & Mayers, Marvin K. Ministering Cross-Culturally: An Incarnation Model for Personal Relationships. LC 86-71157. 1986. pap. 5.99 (*0-8010-5632-2*) Baker Bk.

— Questionnaire for Ministering Cross-Culturally: A Personal Profile of Basic Values. 1991. 0.99 (*0-8010-5652-7*) Baker Bk.

Lingenfelter, Sherwood G., jt. auth. see Koop, Gordon.

Lingengelter, Richard & Pisarowicz, James, eds. Proceedings Death Valley Conference on History & Prehistory, 1st. LC 91-74080. (Death Valley History Conference Ser.). (Illus.). 120p. (Orig.). (C). 1992. pap. 10.95 (*1-878900-22-6*) DVNH Assn.

Linger, Daniel T. Dangerous Encounters: Meanings of Violence in a Brazilian City. LC 91-28599. (Illus.). 300p. (C). 1993. 45.00x (*0-8047-1926-8*) Stanford U Pr.

— Dangerous Encounters: Meanings of Violence in a Brazilian City. (Illus.). 300p. 1995. pap. 14.95 (*0-8047-2589-6*) Stanford U Pr.

Linger, Juyne, ed. see Bosek, Rita.

Linger, Juyne, ed. see Malone, Lawrence.

Linger, Juyne, ed. see Rosenblum, Joseph.

Linger, Richard C., et al. Structured Programming: Theory & Practice. LC 78-18641. (C). 1979. text ed. 51.75 (*0-201-14461-1*) Addison-Wesley.

***Lingerm.** Journeys into Meditation & Music. 1994. 14.95 (*0-8356-2094-8*, Quest) Theos Pub Hse.

Lingerman, Hal A. The Book of Numerology: Taking a Count of Your Life. (Illus.). 160p. (Orig.). 1994. pap. 9.95 (*0-87728-804-6*) Weiser.

— Healing Energies of Music. 2nd ed. LC 94-36151. 300p. (J). 1995. pap. 12.00 (*0-8356-0722-4*, Quest) Theos Pub Hse.

— Life Streams. LC 87-40522. (Illus.). 309p. (Orig.). 1988. pap. 7.95 (*0-8356-0629-5*, Quest) Theos Pub Hse.

— Living Your Destiny. LC 92-7903. 224p. (Orig.). 1992. pap. 10.95 (*0-87728-746-5*) Weiser.

Linggard, Robert. Electronic Synthesis of Speech. (Illus.). 175p. 1985. 44.95 (*0-521-24469-2*) Cambridge U Pr.

Linggard, Robert, et al, eds. Neural Networks for Vision, Speech, & Natural Language. 456p. 1992. 69.95 (*0-442-31579-1*) Chapman & Hall.

Lingham, Brian, ed. Harry Truman: The Man-His Music. LC 85-80165. (Illus.). 100p. 1985. 19.95 (*0-913504-98-X*); pap. 12.95 (*0-913504-97-1*) Lowell Pr.

Lingham, Gretchen, ed. see Murray, Cindy C.

Lingham, Sundara & Harvey, David R. Manual of Child Development. LC 87-15861. (Manual Ser.). (Illus.). 120p. 1988. pap. text ed. 24.95 (*0-443-03784-1*) Churchill.

Lingis, Alphonso. Abuses. LC 93-40254. 1994. 25.00 (*0-520-08631-7*) U CA Pr.

— Abuses. 1995. pap. 13.95 (*0-520-20344-5*) U CA Pr.

— The Community of Those Who Have Nothing in Common. LC 93-23955. (Studies in Continental Thought). 1994. 29.95 (*0-253-33438-1*); pap. 12.95 (*0-253-20852-1*) Ind U Pr.

— Deathbound Subjectivity. LC 88-45450. (Studies in Phenomenology & Existential Philosophy). 222p. 1989. 34.95 (*0-253-31660-X*) Ind U Pr.

— Excesses: Eros & Culture. LC 83-9122. (Illus.). 166p. 1984. 59.50 (*0-87395-797-0*); pap. 24.95 (*0-87395-796-2*) State U NY Pr.

— Foreign Bodies. LC 93-49537. 1994. 52.50 (*0-415-90989-9*, Routledge NY); pap. 16.95 (*0-415-90990-2*, Routledge NY) Routledge.

— Libido: The French Existential Theories. LC 84-48483. (Studies in Phenomenology & Existential Philosophy). 144p. reprint ed. pap. 41.10 (*0-7837-3715-7*, 2057893) Bks Demand.

Lingis, Alphonso, tr. see Klossowski, Pierre.

Lingis, Alphonso, ed. see Levinas, Emmanuel.

Lingis, Alphonso, tr. see Levinas, Emmanuel.

Lingis, Alphonso, tr. see Merleau-Ponty, Maurice.

Lingl, James P. The California Community Association Reference Guide, 1993. 356p. 1993. text ed. 40.00 (*0-9629533-2-6*) CAPCO.

— The California Community Association Reference Guide, 1993. 2nd ed. 360p. 1993. text ed. 40.00 (*0-9629533-3-4*) CAPCO.

— The California Community Association Reference Guide, 1994. 366p. 1994. text ed. 40.00 (*0-9629533-4-2*) CAPCO.

Lingle, Gary R. Birding Crane River: Nebraska's Platte. 124p. 1994. spiral bd. 11.95 (*0-9641219-0-5*) Harrier Pubng.

***Lingle, Walter.** Memories of Davidson College. (American Autobiography Ser.). 157p. 1995. reprint ed. lib. bdg. 69.00 (*0-7812-8580-1*) Rprt Serv.

Lingle, Walter L. & Kuykendall, John W. Presbyterians, Their History & Beliefs. LC 77-15750. 1958. reprint ed. pap. 5.99 (*0-8042-0985-5*, John Knox) Westminster John Knox.

***Lingle, Wilbur.** Approaching Jehovah's Witnesses in Love: How to Witness Effectively Without Arguing. 250p. (Orig.). 1994. pap. 8.95 (*0-87508-702-7*) Chr Lit.

Lingley, Anne, tr. see Silvan, Matthew.

Lingley, Charles R. Transition in Virginia from Colony to Commonwealth. LC 10-14656. (Columbia University. Studies in the Social Sciences: No. 96). reprint ed. 20.00 (*0-404-51096-5*) AMS Pr.

Lingley, William S., Jr., jt. auth. see Palmer, Stephen P.

Lingner, Michael, ed. see von Bismark, Beatrice.

Lingo, Susan. Easy to Prepare Activities for Busy Teachers. (New Testament Ser.). (Illus.). 32p. 1992. teacher ed 8.99 (*0-87403-980-0*, 14-03508) Standard Pub.

— Easy to Prepare Learning Activities for Busy Teachers. (Old Testament Ser.). (Illus.). 32p. (Orig.). 1992. teacher ed 8.99 (*0-87403-979-7*, 14-03507) Standard Pub.

— I Can Read the Bible: Rebus Verses for Young Readers. (Illus.). (Orig.). (J). (gr. 1-4). 1994. pap. 3.99 (*0-570-04764-1*) Concordia.

Lingo, Susan, ed. Teachers Guide: Toddlers & Two's, Fall 1995. (Hands-on Bible Curriculum Ser.). (Illus.). 160p. 1995. teacher ed. pap. 19.99 (*1-55945-401-6*) Group Pub.

— Teachers Guide: Toddlers & 2s, Winter 1995-1996. (Hands-on Bible Curriculum Ser.). (Illus.). 160p. 1995. pap. 19.99 (*1-55945-403-2*) Group Pub.

Lingo, Susan L. Teaching Our Children to Pray. Gambill, Henrietta, ed. (Illus.). 80p. 1994. pap. 9.99 (*0-7847-0190-3*, 18-03217) Standard Pub.

Lingo, Susan L. & Downey, Melissa C. Abraham. (Graded Activity - Resource Bks.). (Illus.). 32p. (J). (ps-7). 1992. student ed 3.99 (*0-87403-915-0*, 23-02525) Standard Pub.

— Daniel. (Graded Activity - Resource Bks.). (Illus.). 32p. (J). (ps-7). 1992. student ed 3.99 (*0-87403-919-3*, 23-02529) Standard Pub.

— David. (Graded Activity - Resource Bks.). (Illus.). 32p. (J). (ps-7). 1992. student ed 3.99 (*0-87403-918-5*, 23-02528) Standard Pub.

— Joshua. (Graded Activity - Resource Bks.). (Illus.). 32p. (J). (ps-7). 1992. student ed 3.99 (*0-87403-917-7*, 23-02527) Standard Pub.

— Moses. (Graded Activity - Resource Bks.). (Illus.). 112p. (J). (ps-7). 1992. student ed 3.99 (*0-87403-916-9*, 23-02526) Standard Pub.

— Noah. (Graded Activity - Resource Bks.). (Illus.). 32p. (J). (ps-7). 1992. student ed 3.99 (*0-87403-914-2*, 23-02524) Standard Pub.

Lingo, Susan L., jt. auth. see Downey, Melissa C.

Lingoes, J., jt. auth. see Borg, I.

Lingpa, Dudjom. Buddhahood Without Meditation: A Visionary Account Known As Refining Apparent Phenomena, Nangjang. Barron, Richard, tr. LC 93-34038. (Illus.). 245p. 1994. reprint ed. 100.00 (*1-881847-01-2*) Chagdud Gonpa-Padma.

Lingquist, David G. & Page, Lawrence M., eds. Environmental Biology of Darters. (Developments in Environmental Biology of Fishes Ser.). 1984. lib. bdg. 98.00 (*90-6193-506-7*) Kluwer Ac.

***Lingren, Art.** Thompson River, BC. (River Journal Ser.: Vol. 2, No. 3). (Illus.). 48p. 1994. pap. 14.95 (*1-878175-47-5*) F Amato Pubns.

Lingren, Arthur J. Fly Patterns of Roderick Haig-Brown. (Illus.). 72p. 1993. 21.95 (*1-878175-39-4*) F Amato Pubns.

Lingren, Herbert, et al, eds. Family Strengths Eight-Nine: Pathways to Well-Being. 1987. pap. 10.00 (*0-934949-03-4*) U Nebr Dept Human.

Lingren, Minnie. Hops Cultivation in Lewis County. 54p. 1989. reprint ed. pap. 7.50 (*0-685-30404-3*) Fernwood Pr.

Lingren, Torgny. Bathsheba. Geddes, Tom, tr. 250p. 1993. pap. 11.00 (*0-00-271271-7*, Pub. by HarpC UK) HarpC.

***Lings.** Eleventh Hour. 1995. 22.95 (*0-946621-07-1*) Atrium Pubs.

— Symbol & Archetype, Vol. 1. 1995. pap. 14.95 (*1-870196-05-8*) Atrium Pubs.

Lings, Brian. Information Structures: A Uniform Approach Using Pascal. 250p. 1986. 52.50 (*0-412-26490-0*, 9565); pap. 19.95 (*0-412-26500-1*, 9566) Chapman & Hall.

Lings, Martin. Collected Poems. (Illus.). 51p. (Orig.). 1987. pap. 14.95 (*0-900588-28-4*) S Perennis.

— Muhammad. 368p. 1987. pap. 16.95 (*0-89281-170-6*) Inner Tradit.

— The Quranic Art of Calligraphy & Illumination. LC 86-27505. (Illus.). 242p. 1987. reprint ed. text ed. 59.95 (*0-940793-00-8*) Interlink Pub.

— The Secret of Shakespeare. 144p. (Orig.). 1984. pap. 8.95 (*0-89281-059-9*) Inner Tradit.

— A Sufi Saint of the Twentieth Century: Shaikh Ahmad Al-Alawi. 242p. 1995. pap. 15.95 (*0-946621-50-0*) Atrium Pubs.

— What Is Sufism? 133p. 1995. pap. 8.95 (*0-946621-41-1*, Pub. by Islamic Texts UK) Atrium Pubs.

— What Is Sufism? 136p. 1988. pap. 9.95 (*0-04-297039-3*) Routledge Chapman & Hall.

Lings, Martin, see Abu B. Ad-Din, pseud..

Lings, Martin, ed. see Guenon, Rene, Jr.

Lings, Martin, jt. ed. see Guenon, Rene.

Lingua Press Staff. Lingua Press Collection One Catalogue, Vol. 1. Gaburo, Kenneth, ed. (Illus.). 44p. 1976. 1.50 (*0-939044-00-5*) Lingua Pr.

— Lingua Press Collection Three Catalogue, Vol. 3. Gaburo, Kenneth, ed. (Illus.). 150p. Date not set. pap. 8.50 (*0-939044-23-4*) Lingua Pr.

— Lingua Press Collection Two Catalogue, Vol. 2. Gaburo, Kenneth, ed. (Illus.). 132p. 1978. pap. 3.95 (*0-939044-17-X*) Lingua Pr.

LinguaFranca Language Services Staff, tr. see Degauque, Pierre & Hamelin, Joel, eds.

Linguaphone Staff. Linguaphone Afrikaans Course for English Speakers: Beginner's Course. (AFR & ENG.). 1991. Afrikaans Language - Self-Instruction & Conversation. student ed, digital audio 250.00 (*0-8288-4050-4*, F60960) Fr & Eur.

— Linguaphone American Course for Finnish Speakers: Beginner's Course. (ENG & FIN.). 1991. American Language - Self-Instruction & Conversation. student ed, audio 295.00 (*0-8288-4273-6*) Fr & Eur.

— Linguaphone American Course for French Speakers: Beginner's Course. (ENG & FRE.). 1991. American Language - Self-Instruction & Conversation. student ed, audio 295.00 (*0-8288-4274-4*) Fr & Eur.

— Linguaphone American Course for German Speakers: Beginner's Course. (ENG & GER.). 1991. American Language - Self-Instruction & Conversation. student ed, audio 295.00 (*0-8288-4277-9*) Fr & Eur.

— Linguaphone American Course for Italian Speakers: Beginner's Course. (ENG & ITA.). 1991. American Language - Self-Instruction & Conversation. student ed, audio 295.00 (*0-8288-4282-5*) Fr & Eur.

— Linguaphone American Course for Japanese Speakers: Beginner's Course. (ENG & JPN.). 1991. American Language - Self-Instruction & Conversation. student ed, audio 295.00 (*0-8288-4284-1*); American Language - Self-Instruction & Conversation. student ed, cd-rom 395.00 (*0-8288-4287-6*) Fr & Eur.

— Linguaphone American Course for Japanese Speakers: Intermediate Course. (ENG & JPN.). 1991. American Language - Self-Instruction & Conversation. student ed, audio 225.00 (*0-8288-4285-X*) Fr & Eur.

— Linguaphone American Course for Portuguese Speakers: Beginner's Course. (ENG & POR.). 1991. American Language - Self-Instruction & Conversation. student ed, audio 295.00 (*0-8288-4294-9*) Fr & Eur.

— Linguaphone American Course for Portuguese Speakers: Intermediate Course. (ENG & POR.). 1991. American Language - Self-Instruction & Conversation. student ed, audio 225.00 (*0-8288-4295-7*) Fr & Eur.

— Linguaphone American Course for Spanish Speakers: Beginner's Course. (ENG & SPA.). 1991. American Language - Self-Instruction & Conversation. student ed, audio 295.00 (*0-685-52094-3*) Fr & Eur.

— Linguaphone American Course for Spanish Speakers: Intermediate Course. (ENG & SPA.). 1991. American Language - Self-Instruction & Conversation. student ed, audio 225.00 (*0-8288-4297-3*) Fr & Eur.

— Linguaphone Arabic Course for English Speakers: Beginner's Course. (ARA & ENG.). 1991. Arabic Language - Self-Instruction & Conversation. student ed, digital audio 295.00 (*0-8288-4051-2*, F127355) Fr & Eur.

— Linguaphone Arabic Course for French Speakers: Beginner's Course. (ARA & FRE.). 1991. Arabic Language - Self-Instruction & Conversation. student ed, digital audio 295.00 (*0-8288-4052-0*, F43160) Fr & Eur.

— Linguaphone Arabic Course for Indonesian Speakers: Beginner's Course. (ARA & IND.). 1991. Arabic Language - Self-Instruction & Conversation. student ed, audio 295.00 (*0-8288-3288-9*) Fr & Eur.

— Linguaphone Arabic Course for Malaysian Speakers: Beginner's Course. (ARA & MAY.). 1991. Arabic Language - Self-Instruction & Conversation. student ed, audio 295.00 (*0-8288-4288-4*) Fr & Eur.

— Linguaphone Arabic Course for Turkish Speakers: Beginner's Course. (ARA & TUR.). 1991. Arabic Language - Self-Instruction & Conversation. student ed, audio 295.00 (*0-8288-4301-5*) Fr & Eur.

— Linguaphone Business English Course for Cantonese-Chinese Speakers: Beginner's Course. (CHI & ENG.). 1991. English Language - Self-Instruction & Conversation; Business English - Self-Instruction & Conversati. student ed, audio 250.00 (*0-8288-3277-3*) Fr & Eur.

— Linguaphone Business English Course for Dutch Speakers: Beginner's Course. (DUT & ENG.). 1991. English Language - Self-Instruction & Conversation; Business English - Self-Instruction & Conversati. student ed, digital audio 295.00 (*0-8288-4053-9*) Fr & Eur.

— Linguaphone Business English Course for English Speakers: Beginner's Course. 1991. English Language - Self-Instruction & Conversation; Business English - Self-Instruction & Conversati. student ed, audio 250.00 (*0-8288-4270-1*) Fr & Eur.

— Linguaphone Business English Course for Finnish Speakers: Beginner's Course. (ENG & FIN.). 1991. English Language - Self-Instruction & Conversation; Business English - Self-Instruction & Conversati. student ed, digital audio 250.00 (*0-8288-4057-1*); English Language - Self-Instruction & Conversation; Business English - Self-Instruction & Conversati. student ed, audio 250.00 (*0-8288-4272-8*) Fr & Eur.

— Linguaphone Business English Course for French Speakers: Beginner's Course. (ENG & FRE.). 1991. English Language - Self-Instruction & Conversation; Business English - Self-Instruction & Conversati. student ed, digital audio 250.00 (*0-8288-4054-7*) Fr & Eur.

— Linguaphone Business English Course for German Speakers: Beginner's Course. (ENG & GER.). 1991. English Language - Self-Instruction & Conversation; Business English - Self-Instruction & Conversati. student ed, digital audio 250.00 (*0-8288-4055-5*) Fr & Eur.

— Linguaphone Business English Course for Greek Speakers: Beginner's Course. (ENG & GRE.). 1991. English Language - Self-Instruction & Conversation; Business English - Self-Instruction & Conversati. student ed, audio 250.00 (*0-8288-3287-0*) Fr & Eur.

— Linguaphone Business English Course for Indonesian Speakers: Beginner's Course. (ENG & IND.). 1991. English Language - Self-Instruction & Conversation; Business English - Self-Instruction & Conversati. student ed, audio 250.00 (*0-8288-3291-9*) Fr & Eur.

— Linguaphone Business English Course for Italian Speakers: Beginner's Course. (ENG & ITA.). 1991. English Language - Self-Instruction & Conversation; Business English - Self-Instruction & Conversati. student ed, audio 250.00 (*0-8288-3292-7*) Fr & Eur.

— Linguaphone Business English Course for Japanese Speakers: Beginner's Course. (ENG & JPN.). 1991. English Language - Self-Instruction & Conversation; Business English - Self-Instruction & Conversati. student ed, audio 250.00 (*0-8288-3296-X*) Fr & Eur.

— Linguaphone Business English Course for Malaysian Speakers: Beginner's Course. (ENG & MAY.). 1991. English Language - Self-Instruction & Conversation; Business English - Self-Instruction & Conversati. student ed, audio 250.00 (*0-8288-3297-8*) Fr & Eur.

— Linguaphone Business English Course for Mandarin-Chinese Speakers: Beginner's Course. (CHI & ENG.). 1991. English Language - Self-Instruction & Conversation; Business English - Self-Instruction & Conversati. student ed, digital audio 250.00 (*0-8288-4056-3*) Fr & Eur.

— Linguaphone Business English Course for Norwegian Speakers: Beginner's Course. (ENG & NOR.). 1991. English Language - Self-Instruction & Conversation; Business English - Self-Instruction & Conversati. student ed, audio 250.00 (*0-8288-3302-8*) Fr & Eur.

— Linguaphone Business English Course for Spanish Speakers: Beginner's Course. (ENG & SPA.). 1991. English Language - Self-Instruction & Conversation; Business English - Self-Instruction & Conversati. student ed, audio 250.00 (*0-8288-4298-1*) Fr & Eur.

— Linguaphone Business English Course for Swedish Speakers: Beginner's Course. (ENG & SWE.). 1991. English Language - Self-Instruction & Conversation; Business English - Self-Instruction & Conversati. student ed, audio 250.00 (*0-8288-4299-X*) Fr & Eur.

— Linguaphone Continental Spanish Course for Danish Speakers: Beginner's Course. (DAN & SPA.). 1991. Spanish Language - Self-Instruction & Conversation. student ed, digital audio 295.00 (*0-8288-4077-6*) Fr & Eur.

— Linguaphone Continental Spanish Course for Dutch Speakers: Beginner's Course. (DUT & SPA.). 1991. Spanish Language - Self-Instruction & Conversation. student ed, digital audio 295.00 (*0-8288-4078-4*) Fr & Eur.

— Linguaphone Continental Spanish Course for Finnish Speakers: Beginner's Course. (FIN & SPA.). 1991. Spanish Language - Self-Instruction & Conversation. student ed, digital audio 295.00 (*0-8288-4063-6*) Fr & Eur.

— Linguaphone Continental Spanish Course for French Speakers: Beginner's Course. (FRE & SPA.). 1991. Spanish Language - Self-Instruction & Conversation. student ed, digital audio 295.00 (*0-8288-4062-8*) Fr & Eur.

— Linguaphone Continental Spanish Course for German Speakers: Beginner's Course. (GER & SPA.). 1991. Spanish Language - Self-Instruction & Conversation. student ed, audio 295.00 (*0-8288-4064-4*) Fr & Eur.

— Linguaphone Continental Spanish Course for Italian Speakers: Beginner's Course. (ITA & SPA.). 1991. Spanish Language - Self-Instruction & Conversation. student ed, digital audio 295.00 (*0-8288-4065-2*) Fr & Eur.

— Linguaphone Continental Spanish Course for Japanese Speakers: Beginner's Course. (JPN & SPA.). 1991. Spanish Language - Self-Instruction & Conversation. student ed, digital audio 295.00 (*0-8288-4066-0*) Fr & Eur.

— Linguaphone Continental Spanish Course for Norwegian Speakers: Beginner's Course. (NOR & SPA.). 1991. Spanish Language - Self-Instruction & Conversation. student ed, digital audio 295.00 (*0-8288-4067-9*) Fr & Eur.

— Linguaphone Czech Course for English Speakers: Beginner's Course. (CZE & ENG.). 1991. Czech Language - Self-Instruction & Conversation. student ed, digital audio 95.00 (*0-8288-3272-2*) Fr & Eur.

— Linguaphone Danish Course for English Speakers: Beginner's Course. (DAN & ENG.). 1991. Danish Language - Self-Instruction & Conversation. student ed, digital audio 250.00 (*0-8288-4068-7*) Fr & Eur.

— Linguaphone Danish Course for Icelandic Speaking People: Beginner's Course. (DAN & ICE.). 1991. Danish Language - Self-Instruction & Conversation. student ed, digital audio 250.00 (*0-8288-4069-5*) Fr & Eur.

— Linguaphone Dutch Course for English Speakers: Beginner's Course. (DUT & ENG.). 1991. Dutch Language - Self-Instruction & Conversation. student ed, digital audio 250.00 (*0-8288-4070-9*) Fr & Eur.

— Linguaphone Dutch Course for French Speakers: Beginner's Course. (DUT & FRE.). 1991. Dutch Language - Self-Instruction & Conversation. student ed, digital audio 295.00 (*0-8288-3284-6*) Fr & Eur.

— Linguaphone English Course for Arabic Speakers: Beginner's Course. (ARA & ENG.). 1991. English Language - Self-Instruction & Conversation. student ed, digital audio 295.00 (*0-8288-4074-1*) Fr & Eur.

— Linguaphone English Course for Arabic Speakers: Intermediate Course. (ARA & ENG.). 1991. English Language - Self-Instruction & Conversation. student ed, digital audio 225.00 (*0-8288-4079-2*) Fr & Eur.

— Linguaphone English Course for Cantonese Speakers: Beginner's Course. (CHI & ENG.). 1991. English Language - Self-Instruction & Conversation. student ed, digital audio 225.00 (*0-8288-4080-6*); English Language - Self-Instruction & Conversation. student ed, cd-rom 395.00 (*0-685-52090-0*) Fr & Eur.

— Linguaphone English Course for Catalan Speakers: Beginner's Course. (CAT & ENG.). 1991. English Language - Self-Instruction & Conversation. student ed, audio 225.00 (*0-8288-4256-6*); English Language - Self-Instruction & Conversation. student ed, audio 225.00 (*0-8288-3275-7*) Fr & Eur.

— Linguaphone English Course for Croatian Speakers: Beginner's Course. (CRO & ENG.). 1991. English Language - Self-Instruction & Conversation. student ed, audio 225.00 (*0-685-54563-6*) Fr & Eur.

— Linguaphone English Course for Czech Speakers: Beginner's Course. (CZE & ENG.). 1991. English Language - Self-Instruction & Conversation. student ed, digital audio 225.00 (*0-8288-4087-3*) Fr & Eur.

— Linguaphone English Course for Danish Speakers: Beginner's Course. (DAN & ENG.). 1991. English Language - Self-Instruction & Conversation. student ed, digital audio 295.00 (*0-8288-4088-1*); English Language - Self-Instruction & Conversation. student ed, cd-rom 395.00 (*0-8288-4089-X*) Fr & Eur.

— Linguaphone English Course for Dutch Speakers: Beginner's Course. (DUT & ENG.). 1991. English Language - Self-Instruction & Conversation. student ed, digital audio 295.00 (*0-8288-3280-3*) Fr & Eur.

— Linguaphone English Course for Dutch Speakers: Intermediate Course. (DUT & ENG.). 1991. English Language - Self-Instruction & Conversation. student ed, digital audio 225.00 (*0-8288-4091-1*) Fr & Eur.

— Linguaphone English Course for English Speakers: Advanced Course. 1991. English Language - Self-Instruction & Conversation. student ed, audio 225.00 (*0-8288-4269-8*) Fr & Eur.

— Linguaphone English Course for English Speakers: Beginner's Course. 1991. English Language - Self-Instruction & Conversation. student ed, audio 295.00 (*0-8288-4266-3*); English Language - Self-Instruction & Conversation. student ed, cd-rom 395.00 (*0-685-52093-5*) Fr & Eur.

— Linguaphone English Course for English Speakers: Intermediate Course. 1991. English Language - Self-Instruction & Conversation. student ed, audio 250.00 (*0-8288-4268-X*) Fr & Eur.

— Linguaphone English Course for Finnish Speakers: Beginner's Course. (ENG & FIN.). 1991. English Language - Self-Instruction & Conversation. student ed, cd-rom 395.00 (*0-8288-4094-6*); English Language - Self-Instruction & Conversation. student ed, audio 295.00 (*0-8288-4092-X*) Fr & Eur.

— Linguaphone English Course for Finnish Speakers: Intermediate Course. (ENG & FIN.). 1991. English Language - Self-Instruction & Conversation. student ed, digital audio 225.00 (*0-8288-4093-8*) Fr & Eur.

— Linguaphone English Course for French Speakers: Advanced Course. (ENG & FRE.). 1991. English Language - Self-Instruction & Conversation. student ed, digital audio 225.00 (*0-8288-3285-4*) Fr & Eur.

— Linguaphone English Course for French Speakers: Beginner's Course. (ENG & FRE.). 1991. English Language - Self-Instruction & Conversation. student ed, digital audio 295.00 (*0-8288-4072-5*); English Language - Self-Instruction & Conversation. student ed, cd-rom 395.00 (*0-8288-4097-0*) Fr & Eur.

— Linguaphone English Course for French Speakers: Intermediate Course. (ENG & FRE.). 1991. English Language - Self-Instruction & Conversation. student ed, digital audio 225.00 (*0-8288-4073-3*) Fr & Eur.

— Linguaphone English Course for German Speakers: Beginner's Course. (ENG & GER.). 1991. English Language - Self-Instruction & Conversation. student ed, cd-rom 395.00 (*0-8288-4100-4*); English Language - Self-Instruction & Conversation. digital audio 295.00 (*0-8288-4098-9*) Fr & Eur.

— Linguaphone English Course for German Speakers: Intermediate Course. (ENG & GER.). 1991. English Language - Self-Instruction & Conversation. student ed, digital audio 225.00 (*0-8288-4099-7*) Fr & Eur.

— Linguaphone English Course for Greek Speakers: Beginner's Course. (ENG & GRE.). 1991. English Language - Self-Instruction & Conversation. student ed, digital audio 295.00 (*0-8288-4101-2*) Fr & Eur.

— Linguaphone English Course for Greek Speakers: Intermediate Course. (ENG & GRE.). 1991. English Language - Self-Instruction & Conversation. student ed, digital audio 225.00 (*0-8288-4102-0*) Fr & Eur.

— Linguaphone English Course for Hebrew Speakers: Beginner's Course. (ENG & HEB.). 1991. English Language - Self-Instruction & Conversation. student ed, digital audio 295.00 (*0-8288-4103-9*) Fr & Eur.

— Linguaphone English Course for Hungarian Speakers: Beginner's Course. (ENG & HUN.). 1991. English Language - Self-Instruction & Conversation. student ed, digital audio 225.00 (*0-8288-4105-5*) Fr & Eur.

— Linguaphone English Course for Icelandic Speakers: Beginner's Course. (ENG & ICE.). 1991. English Language - Self-Instruction & Conversation. student ed, digital audio 295.00 (*0-8288-4104-7*) Fr & Eur.

— Linguaphone English Course for Indonesian Speakers: Beginner's Course. (ENG & IND.). 1991. English Language - Self-Instruction & Conversation. student ed, audio 295.00 (*0-8288-3289-7*) Fr & Eur.

— Linguaphone English Course for Italian Speakers: Beginner's Course. (ENG & ITA.). 1991. English Language - Self-Instruction & Conversation. student ed, digital audio 295.00 (*0-8288-4106-3*) Fr & Eur.

— Linguaphone English Course for Italian Speakers: Intermediate Course. (ENG & ITA.). 1991. English Language - Self-Instruction & Conversation. student ed, digital audio 225.00 (*0-8288-4107-1*) Fr & Eur.

— Linguaphone English Course for Japanese Speakers: Intermediate Course. (ENG & JPN.). 1991. English Language - Self-Instruction & Conversation. student ed, digital audio 295.00 (*0-8288-4108-X*) Fr & Eur.

— Linguaphone English Course for Malay Speakers: Beginner's Course. (ENG & MAY.). 1991. English Language - Self-Instruction & Conversation. student ed, digital audio 295.00 (*0-8288-4109-8*) Fr & Eur.

— Linguaphone English Course for Mandarin Speakers: Beginner's Course. (CHI & ENG.). 1991. English Language - Self-Instruction & Conversation. student ed, digital audio 295.00 (*0-8288-4110-1*); English Language - Self-Instruction & Conversation. student ed, cd-rom 395.00 (*0-8288-4112-8*) Fr & Eur.

— Linguaphone English Course for Mandarin Speakers: Intermediate Course. (CHI & ENG.). 1991. English Language - Self-Instruction & Conversation. student ed, digital audio 225.00 (*0-8288-4111-X*) Fr & Eur.

— Linguaphone English Course for Norwegian Speakers: Beginner's Course. (ENG & NOR.). 1991. English Language - Self-Instruction & Conversation. student ed, digital audio 295.00 (*0-8288-4113-6*); English Language - Self-Instruction & Conversation. student ed, cd-rom 395.00 (*0-8288-4115-2*) Fr & Eur.

— Linguaphone English Course for Norwegian Speakers: Intermediate Course. (ENG & NOR.). 1991. English Language - Self-Instruction & Conversation. student ed, digital audio 225.00 (*0-8288-4114-4*) Fr & Eur.

— Linguaphone English Course for Persian Speakers: Beginner's Course. (ENG & PER.). 1991. English Language - Self-Instruction & Conversation. student ed, digital audio 225.00 (*0-8288-4116-0*) Fr & Eur.

— Linguaphone English Course for Polish Speakers: Beginner's Course. (ENG & POL.). 1991. English Language - Self-Instruction & Conversation. student ed, digital audio 225.00 (*0-8288-4117-9*) Fr & Eur.

— Linguaphone English Course for Portuguese Speakers: Beginner's Course. (ENG & POR.). 1991. English Language - Self-Instruction & Conversation. student ed, digital audio 295.00 (*0-8288-3307-9*) Fr & Eur.

— Linguaphone English Course for Portuguese Speakers: Intermediate Course. (ENG & POR.). 1991. English Language - Self-Instruction & Conversation. student ed, digital audio 225.00 (*0-8288-3308-7*) Fr & Eur.

— Linguaphone English Course for Russian Speakers: Beginner's Course. (ENG & RUS.). 1991. English Language - Self-Instruction & Conversation. student ed, digital audio 295.00 (*0-8288-4118-7*, F60960) Fr & Eur.

— Linguaphone English Course for Serbian Speakers: Beginner's Course. (ENG & SER.). 1991. English Language - Self-Instruction & Conversation. student ed, digital audio 295.00 (*0-8288-4119-5*, F43160) Fr & Eur.

— Linguaphone English Course for Serbo-Croatian Speakers: Beginner's Course. (ENG & SER.). 1991. English Language - Self-Instruction & Conversation. student ed, digital audio 295.00 (*0-8288-4121-7*) Fr & Eur.

— Linguaphone English Course for Slovenian Speakers: Beginner's Course. (ENG & SLV.). 1991. English Language - Self-Instruction & Conversation. student ed, digital audio 295.00 (*0-8288-4120-9*) Fr & Eur.

— Linguaphone English Course for Spanish Speakers: Beginner's Course. (ENG & SPA.). 1991. English Language - Self-Instruction & Conversation. student ed, digital audio 295.00 (*0-8288-4085-7*) Fr & Eur.

— Linguaphone English Course for Spanish Speakers: Intermediate Course. (ENG & SPA.). 1991. English Language - Self-Instruction & Conversation. student ed, digital audio 225.00 (*0-8288-4086-5*) Fr & Eur.

— Linguaphone English Course for Swedish Speakers: Beginner's Course. (ENG & SWE.). 1991. English Language - Self-Instruction & Conversation. student ed, digital audio 295.00 (*0-8288-4122-5*); English Language - Self-Instruction & Conversation. student ed, cd-rom 395.00 (*0-8288-4124-1*) Fr & Eur.

— Linguaphone English Course for Swedish Speakers: Intermediate Course. (ENG & SWE.). 1991. English Language - Self-Instruction & Conversation. student ed, digital audio 225.00 (*0-8288-4123-3*) Fr & Eur.

— Linguaphone English Course for Thai Speakers: Beginner's Course. (ENG & THA.). 1991. English Language - Self-Instruction & Conversation. student ed, digital audio 295.00 (*0-8288-4125-X*) Fr & Eur.

— Linguaphone English Course for Thai Speakers: Intermediate Course. (ENG & THA.). 1991. English Language - Self-Instruction & Conversation. student ed, digital audio 225.00 (*0-8288-4126-8*) Fr & Eur.

— Linguaphone English Course for Turkish Speakers: Beginner's Course. (ENG & TUR.). 1991. English Language - Self-Instruction & Conversation. student ed, digital audio 295.00 (*0-8288-4127-6*) Fr & Eur.

— Linguaphone English Course for Turkish Speakers: Intermediate Course. (ENG & TUR.). 1991. English Language - Self-Instruction & Conversation. student ed, digital audio 225.00 (*0-8288-4128-4*) Fr & Eur.

— Linguaphone English Course for Vietnamese Speakers: Beginner's Course. (ENG & VIE.). 1991. English Language - Self-Instruction & Conversation. student ed, digital audio 225.00 (*0-8288-4129-2*) Fr & Eur.

— Linguaphone Finnish Course for English Speakers: Beginner's Course. (ENG & FIN.). 1991. Finnish Language - Self-Instruction & Conversation. student ed, digital audio 225.00 (*0-8288-4130-6*) Fr & Eur.

— Linguaphone Finnish Course for Swedish Speakers: Beginner's Course. (FIN & SWE.). 1991. Finnish Language - Self-Instruction & Conversation. student ed, digital audio 225.00 (*0-8288-4131-4*) Fr & Eur.

— Linguaphone French Course for Arabic Speakers: Beginner's Course. (ARA & FRE.). 1991. French Language - Self-Instruction & Conversation. student ed, digital audio 225.00 (*0-8288-4132-2*) Fr & Eur.

— Linguaphone French Course for Cantonese-Chinese Speakers: Beginner's Course. (CHI & ENG.). 1991. French Language - Self-Instruction & Conversation. student ed, cd-rom 395.00 (*0-8288-4260-4*) Fr & Eur.

— Linguaphone French Course for Croatian Speakers: Beginner's Course. (CRO & FRE.). 1991. French Language - Self-Instruction & Conversation. student ed, audio 225.00 (*0-8288-4263-9*) Fr & Eur.

— Linguaphone French Course for Czech Speakers: Beginner's Course. (CZE & FRE.). 1991. French Language - Self-Instruction & Conversation. student ed, digital audio 225.00 (*0-8288-4137-3*) Fr & Eur.

— Linguaphone French Course for Danish Speakers: Beginner's Course. (DAN & FRE.). 1991. French Language - Self-Instruction & Conversation. student ed, digital audio 295.00 (*0-8288-4138-1*); French Language - Self-Instruction & Conversation. student ed, cd-rom 395.00 (*0-8288-4139-X*) Fr & Eur.

— Linguaphone French Course for Dutch Speakers: Beginner's Course. (DUT & FRE.). 1991. French Language - Self-Instruction & Conversation. student ed, digital audio 295.00 (*0-8288-3281-1*) Fr & Eur.

— Linguaphone French Course for Dutch Speakers: Intermediate Course. (DUT & FRE.). 1991. French Language - Self-Instruction & Conversation. student ed, digital audio 225.00 (*0-8288-3282-X*) Fr & Eur.

— Linguaphone French Course for English Speakers: Beginner's Course. (ENG & FRE.). 1991. French Language - Self-Instruction & Conversation. student ed, digital audio 295.00 (*0-8288-4142-X*); French Language - Self-Instruction & Conversation. student ed, cd-rom 395.00 (*0-8288-4144-6*) Fr & Eur.

An Asterisk (*) at the beginning of an entry indicates that the title is appearing in BIP for the first time.

— Linguaphone French Course for English Speakers: Intermediate Course. (ENG & FRE.). 1991. French Language - Self-Instruction & Conversation. student ed, digital audio 225.00 (*0-8288-4143-8*) Fr & Eur.

— Linguaphone French Course for Finnish Speakers: Beginner's Course. (FIN & FRE.). 1991. French Language - Self-Instruction & Conversation. student ed, digital audio 295.00 (*0-8288-4145-4*); French Language - Self-Instruction & Conversation. student ed, cd-rom 395. 00 (*0-8288-4147-0*) Fr & Eur.

— Linguaphone French Course for Finnish Speakers: Intermediate Course. (FIN & FRE.). 1991. French Language - Self-Instruction & Conversation. student ed, digital audio 225.00 (*0-8288-4146-2*) Fr & Eur.

— Linguaphone French Course for German Speakers: Beginner's Course. (FRE & GER.). 1991. French Language - Self-Instruction & Conversation. student ed, digital audio 295.00 (*0-8288-4148-9*); French Language - Self-Instruction & Conversation. student ed, cd-rom 395. 00 (*0-8288-4149-7*) Fr & Eur.

— Linguaphone French Course for German Speakers: Intermediate Course. (FRE & GER.). 1991. French Language - Self-Instruction & Conversation. student ed, digital audio 225.00 (*0-8288-4150-0*) Fr & Eur.

— Linguaphone French Course for Greek Speakers: Beginner's Course. (FRE & GRE.). 1991. French Language - Self-Instruction & Conversation. student ed, digital audio 295.00 (*0-8288-4151-9*) Fr & Eur.

— Linguaphone French Course for Greek Speakers: Intermediate Course. (FRE & GRE.). 1991. French Language - Self-Instruction & Conversation. student ed, digital audio 225.00 (*0-8288-4152-7*) Fr & Eur.

— Linguaphone French Course for Italian Speakers: Beginner's Course. (FRE & ITA.). 1991. French Language - Self-Instruction & Conversation. student ed, digital audio 295.00 (*0-8288-4153-5*) Fr & Eur.

— Linguaphone French Course for Italian Speakers: Intermediate Course. (FRE & ITA.). 1991. French Language - Self-Instruction & Conversation. student ed, digital audio 225.00 (*0-8288-4154-3*) Fr & Eur.

— Linguaphone French Course for Japanese Speakers: Beginner's Course. (FRE & JPN.). 1991. French Language - Self-Instruction & Conversation. student ed, digital audio 295.00 (*0-8288-4155-1*) Fr & Eur.

— Linguaphone French Course for Mandarin-Chinese Speakers: Beginner's Course. (CHI & ENG.). 1991. French Language - Self-Instruction & Conversation. student ed, audio 295.00 (*0-8288-3278-1*); French Language - Self-Instruction & Conversation. student ed, cd-rom 395.00 (*0-8288-4259-0*) Fr & Eur.

— Linguaphone French Course for Norwegian Speakers: Beginner's Course. (FRE & NOR.). 1991. French Language - Self-Instruction & Conversation. student ed, digital audio 295.00 (*0-8288-3298-6*); French Language - Self-Instruction & Conversation. student ed, cd-rom 395. 00 (*0-8288-4158-6*) Fr & Eur.

— Linguaphone French Course for Norwegian Speakers: Intermediate Course. (FRE & NOR.). 1991. French Language - Self-Instruction & Conversation. student ed, digital audio 225.00 (*0-8288-3299-4*) Fr & Eur.

— Linguaphone French Course for Persian Speakers: Beginner's Course. (FRE & PER.). 1991. French Language - Self-Instruction & Conversation. student ed, digital audio 225.00 (*0-8288-4159-4*) Fr & Eur.

— Linguaphone French Course for Portuguese Speakers: Beginner's Course. (FRE & POR.). 1991. French Language - Self-Instruction & Conversation. student ed, digital audio 295.00 (*0-8288-3303-6*) Fr & Eur.

— Linguaphone French Course for Portuguese Speakers: Intermediate Course. (FRE & POR.). 1991. French Language - Self-Instruction & Conversation. student ed, digital audio 225.00 (*0-8288-3304-4*) Fr & Eur.

— Linguaphone French Course for Serbian Speakers: Beginner's Course. (FRE & SER.). 1991. French Language - Self-Instruction & Conversation. student ed, digital audio 295.00 (*0-8288-4160-8*) Fr & Eur.

— Linguaphone French Course for Slovenian Speakers: Beginner's Course. (FRE & SLV.). 1991. French Language - Self-Instruction & Conversation. student ed, digital audio 295.00 (*0-8288-4161-6*) Fr & Eur.

— Linguaphone French Course for Spanish Speakers: Beginner's Course. (FRE & SPA.). 1991. French Language - Self-Instruction & Conversation. student ed, digital audio 295.00 (*0-8288-4134-9*) Fr & Eur.

— Linguaphone French Course for Spanish Speakers: Intermediate Course. (FRE & SPA.). 1991. French Language - Self-Instruction & Conversation. student ed, digital audio 225.00 (*0-8288-3311-7*) Fr & Eur.

— Linguaphone French Course for Swedish Speakers: Beginner's Course. (FRE & SWE.). 1991. French Language - Self-Instruction & Conversation. student ed, digital audio 295.00 (*0-8288-4163-2*); French Language - Self-Instruction & Conversation. student ed, cd-rom 395. 00 (*0-8288-4164-0*) Fr & Eur.

— Linguaphone French Course for Swedish Speakers: Intermediate Course. (FRE & SWE.). 1991. French Language - Self-Instruction & Conversation. student ed, digital audio 225.00 (*0-8288-4162-4*) Fr & Eur.

— Linguaphone French Course for Turkish Speakers: Beginner's Course. (FRE & TUR.). 1991. French Language - Self-Instruction & Conversation. student ed, digital audio 295.00 (*0-8288-4165-9*) Fr & Eur.

— Linguaphone German Course for Cantonese Chinese Speakers: Beginner's Course. (CHI & GER.). 1991. German Language - Self-Instruction & Conversation. student ed, cd-rom 395.00 (*0-8288-4187-X*) Fr & Eur.

— Linguaphone German Course for Chinese-Mandarin Speakers: Beginner's Course. (CHI & GER.). 1991. Italian Language - Self-Instruction & Conversation. student ed, cd-rom 395.00 (*0-8288-4261-2*) Fr & Eur.

— Linguaphone German Course for Croatian Speakers: Beginner's Course. (CRO & GER.). 1991. German Language - Self-Instruction & Conversation. student ed, audio 225.00 (*0-8288-4264-7*) Fr & Eur.

— Linguaphone German Course for Danish Speakers: Beginner's Course. (DAN & GER.). 1991. German Language - Self-Instruction & Conversation. student ed, digital audio 295.00 (*0-8288-3279-X*); German Language - Self-Instruction & Conversation. student ed, cd-rom 395.00 (*0-8288-4170-5*) Fr & Eur.

— Linguaphone German Course for Dutch Speakers: Beginner's Course. (DUT & GER.). 1991. German Language - Self-Instruction & Conversation. student ed, digital audio 295.00 (*0-8288-4171-3*) Fr & Eur.

— Linguaphone German Course for Dutch Speakers: Intermediate Course. (DUT & GER.). 1991. German Language - Self-Instruction & Conversation. student ed, digital audio 225.00 (*0-8288-4172-1*) Fr & Eur.

— Linguaphone German Course for English Speakers: Beginner's Course. (ENG & GER.). 1991. German Language - Self-Instruction & Conversation. student ed, digital audio 295.00 (*0-8288-4173-X*); German Language - Self-Instruction & Conversation. student ed, cd-rom 395.00 (*0-8288-4175-6*) Fr & Eur.

— Linguaphone German Course for English Speakers: Intermediate Course. (ENG & GER.). 1991. German Language - Self-Instruction & Conversation. student ed, digital audio 225.00 (*0-8288-4174-8*) Fr & Eur.

— Linguaphone German Course for Finnish Speakers: Beginner's Course. (FIN & GER.). 1991. German Language - Self-Instruction & Conversation. student ed, digital audio 295.00 (*0-8288-4176-4*); German Language - Self-Instruction & Conversation. student ed, cd-rom 395.00 (*0-8288-4178-0*) Fr & Eur.

— Linguaphone German Course for Finnish Speakers: Intermediate Course. (FIN & GER.). 1991. German Language - Self-Instruction & Conversation. student ed, digital audio 225.00 (*0-8288-4177-2*) Fr & Eur.

— Linguaphone German Course for French Speakers: Beginner's Course. (FRE & GER.). 1991. German Language - Self-Instruction & Conversation. student ed, digital audio 295.00 (*0-8288-4179-9*); German Language - Self-Instruction & Conversation. student ed, cd-rom 395.00 (*0-8288-4181-0*) Fr & Eur.

— Linguaphone German Course for French Speakers: Intermediate Course. (FRE & GER.). 1991. German Language - Self-Instruction & Conversation. student ed, digital audio 225.00 (*0-8288-4180-2*) Fr & Eur.

— Linguaphone German Course for Greek Speakers: Beginner's Course. (GER & GRE.). 1991. German Language - Self-Instruction & Conversation. student ed, digital audio 295.00 (*0-8288-4182-9*) Fr & Eur.

— Linguaphone German Course for Greek Speakers: Intermediate Course. (GER & GRE.). 1991. German Language - Self-Instruction & Conversation. student ed, digital audio 225.00 (*0-8288-4183-7*) Fr & Eur.

— Linguaphone German Course for Italian Speakers: Beginner's Course. (GER & ITA.). 1991. German Language - Self-Instruction & Conversation. student ed, digital audio 295.00 (*0-8288-4184-5*) Fr & Eur.

— Linguaphone German Course for Italian Speakers: Intermediate Course. (GER & ITA.). 1991. German Language - Self-Instruction & Conversation. student ed, digital audio 225.00 (*0-8288-4185-3*) Fr & Eur.

— Linguaphone German Course for Japanese Speakers: Beginner's Course. (GER & JPN.). 1991. German Language - Self-Instruction & Conversation. student ed, digital audio 295.00 (*0-8288-4186-1*) Fr & Eur.

— Linguaphone German Course for Mandarin Chinese Speakers: Beginner's Course. (CHI & GER.). 1991. German Language - Self-Instruction & Conversation. student ed, digital audio 295.00 (*0-8288-4188-8*) Fr & Eur.

— Linguaphone German Course for Norwegian Speakers: Beginner's Course. (GER & NOR.). 1991. German Language - Self-Instruction & Conversation. student ed, audio 295.00 (*0-8288-3300-1*); German Language - Self-Instruction & Conversation. student ed, cd-rom 395.00 (*0-8288-4293-0*) Fr & Eur.

— Linguaphone German Course for Norwegian Speakers: Intermediate Course. (GER & NOR.). 1991. English Language - Self-Instruction & Conversation. student ed, audio 225.00 (*0-8288-3301-X*) Fr & Eur.

— Linguaphone German Course for Portuguese Speakers: Beginner's Course. (GER & POR.). 1991. German Language - Self-Instruction & Conversation. student ed, digital audio 295.00 (*0-8288-3305-2*) Fr & Eur.

— Linguaphone German Course for Serbian Speakers: Beginner's Course. (GER & SER.). 1991. German Language - Self-Instruction & Conversation. student ed, digital audio 295.00 (*0-8288-4189-6*) Fr & Eur.

— Linguaphone German Course for Slovenian Speakers: Beginner's Course. (GER & SLV.). 1991. German Language - Self-Instruction & Conversation. student ed, digital audio 295.00 (*0-8288-4190-X*) Fr & Eur.

— Linguaphone German Course for Spanish Speakers: Beginner's Course. (GER & SPA.). 1991. German Language - Self-Instruction & Conversation. student ed, digital audio 295.00 (*0-8288-4167-5*) Fr & Eur.

— Linguaphone German Course for Spanish Speakers: Intermediate Course. (GER & SPA.). 1991. German Language - Self-Instruction & Conversation. student ed, digital audio 225.00 (*0-8288-4168-3*) Fr & Eur.

— Linguaphone German Course for Swedish Speakers: Beginner's Course. (GER & SWE.). 1991. German Language - Self-Instruction & Conversation. student ed, digital audio 295.00 (*0-8288-4192-6*); German Language - Self-Instruction & Conversation. student ed, cd-rom 395.00 (*0-8288-4193-4*) Fr & Eur.

— Linguaphone German Course for Swedish Speakers: Intermediate Course. (GER & SWE.). 1991. German Language - Self-Instruction & Conversation. student ed, digital audio 225.00 (*0-8288-4191-8*) Fr & Eur.

— Linguaphone German Course for Turkish Speakers: Beginner's Course. (GER & TUR.). 1991. German Language - Self-Instruction & Conversation. student ed, digital audio 295.00 (*0-8288-4194-2*) Fr & Eur.

— Linguaphone Greek Course for English Speakers: Beginner's Course. (ENG & GRE.). 1991. Greek Language - Self-Instruction & Conversation. student ed, digital audio 250.00 (*0-8288-4195-0*) Fr & Eur.

— Linguaphone Greek Course for French Speakers: Beginner's Course. (FRE & GRE.). 1991. Greek Language - Self-Instruction & Conversation. student ed, digital audio 225.00 (*0-8288-4196-9*) Fr & Eur.

— Linguaphone Greek Course for German Speakers: Beginner's Course. (GER & GRE.). 1991. Greek Language - Self-Instruction & Conversation. student ed, digital audio 250.00 (*0-8288-4197-7*) Fr & Eur.

— Linguaphone Hebrew Course for English Speakers: Beginner's Course. (ENG & HEB.). 1991. Hebrew Language - Self-Instruction & Conversation. student ed, digital audio 250.00 (*0-8288-4198-5*) Fr & Eur.

— Linguaphone Hebrew Course for French Speakers: Beginner's Course. (FRE & HEB.). 1991. Hebrew Language - Self-Instruction & Conversation. student ed, digital audio 250.00 (*0-8288-4199-3*) Fr & Eur.

— Linguaphone Hindi Course for English Speakers: Beginner's Course. (ENG & HIN.). 1991. Hindi Language - Self-Instruction & Conversation. student ed, digital audio 225.00 (*0-8288-3273-0*) Fr & Eur.

— Linguaphone Icelandic Course for English Speakers: Beginner's Course. (ENG & ICE.). 1991. Icelandic Language - Self-Instruction & Conversation. student ed, digital audio 225.00 (*0-8288-4200-0*) Fr & Eur.

— Linguaphone Indonesian Course for Dutch Speakers: Beginner's Course. (DUT & IND.). 1991. Indonesian Language - Self-Instruction & Conversation. student ed, audio 250.00 (*0-8288-4203-5*) Fr & Eur.

— Linguaphone Indonesian Course for English Speakers: Beginner's Course. (ENG & IND.). 1991. Indonesian Language - Self-Instruction & Conversation. student ed, audio 250.00 (*0-8288-4202-7*) Fr & Eur.

— Linguaphone Irish Course for English Speakers: Beginner's Course. (DUT & IRI.). 1991. Irish Language - Self-Instruction & Conversation. student ed, audio 225. 00 (*0-8288-4204-3*) Fr & Eur.

— Linguaphone Italian Course for Danish Speakers: Beginner's Course. (DAN & ITA.). 1991. Italian Language - Self-Instruction & Conversation. student ed, digital audio 295.00 (*0-8288-4207-8*) Fr & Eur.

— Linguaphone Italian Course for Dutch Speakers: Beginner's Course. (DUT & ITA.). 1991. Italian Language - Self-Instruction & Conversation. student ed, audio 295.00 (*0-8288-3283-8*) Fr & Eur.

— Linguaphone Italian Course for English Speakers: Beginner's Course. (ENG & ITA.). 1991. Italian Language - Self-Instruction & Conversation. student ed, audio 295.00 (*0-8288-4208-6*) Fr & Eur.

— Linguaphone Italian Course for Finnish Speakers: Beginner's Course. (FIN & ITA.). 1991. Italian Language - Self-Instruction & Conversation. student ed, audio 225. 00 (*0-8288-4209-4*) Fr & Eur.

— Linguaphone Italian Course for French Speakers: Beginner's Course. (FRE & ITA.). 1991. Italian Language - Self-Instruction & Conversation. student ed, audio 295.00 (*0-8288-4210-8*) Fr & Eur.

— Linguaphone Italian Course for German Speakers: Beginner's Course. (GER & ITA.). 1991. Italian Language - Self-Instruction & Conversation. student ed, audio 295.00 (*0-685-52091-9*) Fr & Eur.

— Linguaphone Italian Course for Greek Speakers: Beginner's Course. (GRE & ITA.). 1991. Italian Language - Self-Instruction & Conversation. student ed, audio 295.00 (*0-8288-4211-6*) Fr & Eur.

— Linguaphone Italian Course for Norwegian Speakers: Beginner's Course. (ITA & NOR.). 1991. Italian Language - Self-Instruction & Conversation. student ed, audio 295.00 (*0-8288-4212-4*) Fr & Eur.

— Linguaphone Italian Course for Portuguese Speakers: Beginner's Course. (ITA & POR.). 1991. Italian Language - Self-Instruction & Conversation. student ed, audio 295.00 (*0-8288-3306-0*) Fr & Eur.

— Linguaphone Italian Course for Spanish Speakers: Beginner's Course. (ITA & SPA.). 1991. Italian Language - Self-Instruction & Conversation. student ed, digital audio 295.00 (*0-8288-4206-X*) Fr & Eur.

— Linguaphone Italian Course for Swedish Speakers: Beginner's Course. (ITA & SWE.). 1991. Italian Language - Self-Instruction & Conversation. student ed, audio 295.00 (*0-8288-4213-2*) Fr & Eur.

— Linguaphone Japanese Course for Cantonese Chinese Speakers: Beginner's Course. (CHI & JPN.). 1991. Japanese Language - Self-Instruction & Conversation. student ed, audio 225.00 (*0-8288-3276-5*) Fr & Eur.

— Linguaphone Japanese Course for English Speakers: Beginner's Course. (ENG & JPN.). 1991. Japanese Language - Self-Instruction & Conversation. student ed, audio 225.00 (*0-8288-4214-0*) Fr & Eur.

— Linguaphone Japanese Course for French Speakers: Beginner's Course. (FRE & JPN.). 1991. Japanese Language - Self-Instruction & Conversation. student ed, audio 225.00 (*0-8288-4215-9*) Fr & Eur.

— Linguaphone Japanese Course for German Speakers: Beginner's Course. (GER & JPN.). 1991. Japanese Language - Self-Instruction & Conversation. student ed, audio 225.00 (*0-8288-4216-7*) Fr & Eur.

— Linguaphone Japanese Course for Indonesian Speakers: Beginner's Course. (IND & JPN.). 1991. Japanese Language - Self-Instruction & Conversation. student ed, audio 225.00 (*0-8288-3290-0*) Fr & Eur.

— Linguaphone Korean Course for English Speakers: Beginner's Course. (ENG & KOR.). 1991. Korean Language - Self-Instruction & Conversation. student ed, audio 250.00 (*0-8288-4217-5*) Fr & Eur.

— Linguaphone Korean Course for Japanese Speakers: Beginner's Course. (JPN & KOR.). 1991. Korean Language - Self-Instruction & Conversation. student ed, audio 250.00 (*0-8288-4218-3*) Fr & Eur.

— Linguaphone (Latin-American) Spanish Course for English Speakers: Beginner's Course. (ENG & SPA.). 1991. Latin-American Spanish Language - Self-Instruction & Conversation. student ed, audio 250.00 (*0-8288-3274-9*) Fr & Eur.

— Linguaphone Malay Course for English Speakers: Beginner's Course. (ENG & MAY.). 1991. Malay Language - Self-Instruction & Conversation. student ed, audio 225.00 (*0-8288-4221-3*) Fr & Eur.

— Linguaphone Mandarin Chinese Course for English Speakers: Beginner's Course. (CHI & ENG.). 1991. Mandarin Chinese Language - Self-Instruction & Conversation. student ed, audio 295.00 (*0-8288-4222-1*) Fr & Eur.

— Linguaphone Mandarin Chinese Course for Japanese Speakers: Beginner's Course. (CHI & JPN.). 1991. Mandarin Chinese Language - Self-Instruction & Conversation. student ed, audio 295.00 (*0-8288-4223-X*) Fr & Eur.

— Linguaphone Norwegian Course for Dutch Speakers: Beginner's Course. (DUT & NOR.). 1991. Norwegian Language - Self-Instruction & Conversation. student ed, audio 225.00 (*0-8288-4224-8*) Fr & Eur.

— Linguaphone Norwegian Course for English Speakers: Beginner's Course. (ENG & NOR.). 1991. Norwegian Language - Self-Instruction & Conversation. student ed, audio 225.00 (*0-8288-4225-6*) Fr & Eur.

— Linguaphone Norwegian Course for French Speakers: Beginner's Course. (FRE & NOR.). 1991. Norwegian Language - Self-Instruction & Conversation. student ed, audio 225.00 (*0-8288-4226-4*) Fr & Eur.

— Linguaphone Norwegian Course for German Speakers: Beginner's Course. (GER & NOR.). 1991. Norwegian Language - Self-Instruction & Conversation. student ed, audio 225.00 (*0-8288-4227-2*) Fr & Eur.

— Linguaphone Persian Course for English Speakers: Beginner's Course. (ENG & PER.). 1991. Persian Language - Self-Instruction & Conversation. student ed, digital audio 95.00 (*0-8288-4254-X*) Fr & Eur.

— Linguaphone Polish Course for English Speakers: Beginner's Course. (ENG & POL.). 1991. Polish Language - Self-Instruction & Conversation. student ed, audio 250.00 (*0-8288-4228-0*) Fr & Eur.

— Linguaphone Polish Course for French Speakers: Beginner's Course. (FRE & POL.). 1991. Polish Language - Self-Instruction & Conversation. student ed, audio 250.00 (*0-8288-3286-2*) Fr & Eur.

— Linguaphone Portuguese Course for Danish Speakers: Beginner's Course. (DAN & POR.). 1991. Portuguese Language - Self-Instruction & Conversation. student ed, digital audio 225.00 (*0-8288-4059-8*) Fr & Eur.

— Linguaphone Portuguese Course for Dutch Speakers: Beginner's Course. (DUT & POR.). 1991. Portuguese Language - Self-Instruction & Conversation. student ed, digital audio 225.00 (*0-8288-4058-X*) Fr & Eur.

— Linguaphone Portuguese Course for English Speakers: Beginner's Course. (ENG & POR.). 1991. Polish Language - Self-Instruction & Conversation. student ed, audio 250.00 (*0-8288-4230-2*) Fr & Eur.

— Linguaphone Portuguese Course for French Speakers: Beginner's Course. (FRE & POR.). 1991. Portuguese Language - Self-Instruction & Conversation. student ed, digital audio 250.00 (*0-8288-4060-1*) Fr & Eur.

— Linguaphone Portuguese Course for Norwegian Speakers: Beginner's Course. (NOR & POR.). 1991. Portuguese Language - Self-Instruction & Conversation. student ed, digital audio 225.00 (*0-8288-4076-8*) Fr & Eur.

— Linguaphone Portuguese Course for Swedish Speakers: Beginner's Course. (POR & SWE.). 1991. Portuguese Language - Self-Instruction & Conversation. student ed, audio 225.00 (*0-8288-4300-7*) Fr & Eur.

— Linguaphone Portuguese (European) Course for German Speakers: Beginner's Course. (GER & POR.). 1991. Portuguese Language - Self-Instruction & Conversation. student ed, audio 225.00 (*0-8288-4275-2*) Fr & Eur.

— Linguaphone Russian Course for Danish Speakers: Beginner's Course. (DAN & RUS.). 1991. Russian Language - Self-Instruction & Conversation. student ed, audio 295.00 (*0-8288-4231-0*) Fr & Eur.

— Linguaphone Russian Course for English Speakers: Beginner's Course. (ENG & RUS.). 1991. Russian Language - Self-Instruction & Conversation. student ed, audio 295.00 (*0-8288-4232-9*) Fr & Eur.

— Linguaphone Russian Course for Finnish Speakers: Beginner's Course. (FIN & RUS.). 1991. Russian Language - Self-Instruction & Conversation. student ed, audio 295.00 (*0-8288-4234-5*) Fr & Eur.

— Linguaphone Russian Course for French Speakers: Beginner's Course. (FRE & RUS.). 1991. Russian Language - Self-Instruction & Conversation. student ed, audio 295.00 (*0-8288-4233-7*) Fr & Eur.

— Linguaphone Russian Course for German Speakers: Beginner's Course. (GER & RUS.). 1991. Russian Language - Self-Instruction & Conversation. student ed, audio 295.00 (*0-8288-4235-3*) Fr & Eur.

— Linguaphone Russian Course for Italian Speakers: Beginner's Course. (ITA & RUS.). 1991. Russian Language - Self-Instruction & Conversation. student ed, audio 295.00 (*0-8288-3293-5*) Fr & Eur.

— Linguaphone Russian Course for Japanese Speakers: Beginner's Course. (JPN & RUS.). 1991. Russian Language - Self-Instruction & Conversation. student ed, audio 295.00 (*0-8288-4236-1*) Fr & Eur.

— Linguaphone Russian Course for Norwegian Speakers: Beginner's Course. (NOR & RUS.). 1991. Russian Language - Self-Instruction & Conversation. student ed, audio 295.00 (*0-8288-4238-8*) Fr & Eur.

— Linguaphone Russian Course for Spanish Speakers: Beginner's Course. (RUS & SPA.). 1991. Russian Language - Self-Instruction & Conversation. student ed, audio 295.00 (*0-8288-4239-6*) Fr & Eur.

— Linguaphone Russian Course for Swedish Speakers: Beginner's Course. (RUS & SWE.). 1991. Russian Language - Self-Instruction & Conversation. student ed, audio 295.00 (*0-8288-4240-X*) Fr & Eur.

— Linguaphone Serbo-Croatian Course for English Speakers: Beginner's Course. (ENG & SER.). 1991. Serbo-Croatian Language - Self-Instruction & Conversation. student ed, audio 250.00 (*0-8288-4241-8*) Fr & Eur.

— Linguaphone Serbo-Croatian Course for German Speakers: Beginner's Course. (GER & SER.). 1991. Serbo-Croatian Language - Self-Instruction & Conversation. student ed, audio 250.00 (*0-8288-4242-6*) Fr & Eur.

— Linguaphone Spanish (Castillian) Course for English Speakers: Beginner's Course. (ENG & SPA.). 1991. Spanish Language - Self-Instruction & Conversation. student ed, audio 295.00 (*0-8288-4271-X*) Fr & Eur.

— Linguaphone Spanish (Continental) Course for German Speakers: Beginner's Course. (GER & SPA.). 1991. Spanish Language - Self-Instruction & Conversation. student ed, audio 295.00 (*0-8288-4276-0*) Fr & Eur.

— Linguaphone Spanish Course for Swedish Speakers: Beginner's Course. (SPA & SWE.). 1991. Spanish Language - Self-Instruction & Conversation. student ed, audio 295.00 (*0-8288-4245-0*) Fr & Eur.

— Linguaphone Swedish Course for English Speakers: Beginner's Course. (ENG & SWE.). 1991. Swedish Language - Self-Instruction & Conversation. student ed, audio 295.00 (*0-8288-4247-7*) Fr & Eur.

— Linguaphone Swedish Course for Finnish Speakers: Beginner's Course. (FIN & SWE.). 1991. Swedish Language - Self-Instruction & Conversation. student ed, audio 295.00 (*0-8288-4248-5*) Fr & Eur.

— Linguaphone Swedish Course for Finnish Speakers: Intermediate Course. (FIN & SWE.). 1991. Swedish Language - Self-Instruction & Conversation. student ed, audio 225.00 (*0-8288-4249-3*) Fr & Eur.

— Linguaphone Swedish Course for German Speakers: Beginner's Course. (GER & SWE.). 1991. Swedish Language - Self-Instruction & Conversation. student ed, audio 295.00 (*0-8288-4250-7*) Fr & Eur.

— Linguaphone Thai Course for English Speakers: Beginner's Course. (ENG & THA.). 1991. Thai Language - Self-Instruction & Conversation. student ed, audio 250.00 (*0-8288-4251-5*) Fr & Eur.

— Linguaphone Welsh Course for English Speakers: Beginner's Course. (ENG & WEL.). 1991. Welsh Language - Self-Instruction & Conversation. student ed, audio 250.00 (*0-8288-4252-3*) Fr & Eur.

***Linguistic Symposium on Romance Languages Staff.** Contemporary Research in Romance Linguistics: Papers from the 22nd Linguistics Symposium on Romance Languages, El Paso-Cd. Juarez, February 1992. Amastae, Jon et al, eds. LC 95-15320. (Current Issues in Linguistic Theory Ser.: No. 123). 400p. 1995. lib. bdg. 95.00x (*1-55619-577-X*) Benjamins North Am.

— Contemporary Studies in Romance Linguistics. fac. ed. Suner, Margarita, ed. LC 78-13028. (Illus.). 414p. 1978. reprint ed. pap. 118.00 (*0-7837-7786-8*, 2047541) Bks Demand.

— Linguistic Studies in Romance Languages: Proceedings of the Third Linguistic Symposium on Romance Languages. Campbell, R. Joe et al, eds. LC 74-76135. 271p. reprint ed. pap. 77.30 (*0-7837-6310-7*, 2046025) Bks Demand.

LinguiSystems Staff. Access - The Parent Guide. 1993. 11.95 (*1-55999-395-2*) LinguiSystems.

— Access to Literature: A Chair for My Mother. 1993. student ed 16.95 (*1-55999-363-4*) LinguiSystems.

— Access to Literature: A Wrinkle in Time. 1993. student ed 16.95 (*1-55999-384-7*) LinguiSystems.

— Access to Literature: Julie of the Wolves. 1993. student ed 16.95 (*1-55999-381-2*) LinguiSystems.

— Access to Literature: Maniac Magee. 1993. student ed 16.95 (*1-55999-387-1*) LinguiSystems.

— Access to Literature: Mr. Popper's Penguins. 1993. student ed 16.95 (*1-55999-369-3*) LinguiSystems.

— Access to Literature: Shiloh. 1993. student ed 16.95 (*1-55999-378-2*) LinguiSystems.

— Access to Literature: Summer of the Swans. 1993. student ed 16.95 (*1-55999-375-8*) LinguiSystems.

— Access to Literature: The Boxcar Children. 1993. student ed 16.95 (*1-55999-360-X*) LinguiSystems.

— Access to Literature: The Mixed-Up Files of Mrs. Basil E. Frankweiler. 1993. student ed 16.95 (*1-55999-372-3*) LinguiSystems.

— Access to Literature: The Mouse & the Motorcycle. 1993. student ed 16.95 (*1-55999-366-9*) LinguiSystems.

— Access to Reading & Language Arts - 2 Grade Set. 1993. student ed 77.70 (*1-55999-269-7*) LinguiSystems.

— Access to Reading & Language Arts - 2 Literary Concepts: Student Book. 1993. student ed 14.95 (*1-55999-273-5*) LinguiSystems.

— Access to Reading & Language Arts - 2 Study Skills: Study Book. 1993. student ed 14.95 (*1-55999-307-3*) LinguiSystems.

— Access to Reading & Language Arts - 2 Vocabulary: Student Book. 1993. student ed 14.95 (*1-55999-267-0*) LinguiSystems.

— Access to Reading & Language Arts - 2 Word Analysis: Student Book. 1993. student ed 14.95 (*1-55999-270-0*) LinguiSystems.

— Access to Reading & Language Arts - 2 Writing: Teachers Guide & Student Book. 1993. student ed 14.95 (*1-55999-310-3*) LinguiSystems.

— Access to Reading & Language Arts - 3 Grade Set. 1993. student ed 77.70 (*1-55999-277-8*) LinguiSystems.

— Access to Reading & Language Arts - 3 Literary Concepts: Teachers Guide & Student Book. 1993. student ed 14.95 (*1-55999-322-7*) LinguiSystems.

— Access to Reading & Language Arts - 3 Reading & Listening Comprehension: Teachers Guide & Student Book. 1993. student ed 14.95 (*1-55999-303-0*) LinguiSystems.

— Access to Reading & Language Arts - 3 Study Skills: Teachers Guide & Student Book. 1993. student ed 14.95 (*1-55999-275-1*) LinguiSystems.

— Access to Reading & Language Arts - 3 Vocabulary: Teachers Guide & Student Book. 1993. student ed 14.95 (*1-55999-316-2*) LinguiSystems.

— Access to Reading & Language Arts - 3 Word Analysis: Teachers Guide & Student Book. 1993. student ed 14.95 (*1-55999-319-7*) LinguiSystems.

— Access to Reading & Language Arts - 3 Writing: Teachers Guide & Student Book. 1993. student ed 14.95 (*1-55999-278-6*) LinguiSystems.

— Access to Reading & Language Arts - 4 Grade Set. 1993. student ed 77.70 (*1-55999-283-2*) LinguiSystems.

— Access to Reading & Language Arts - 4 Literary Concepts: Teachers Guide & Student Book. 1993. student ed 14.95 (*1-55999-287-5*) LinguiSystems.

— Access to Reading & Language Arts - 4 Reading & Listening Comprehension: Teachers Guide & Student Book. 1993. student ed 14.95 (*1-55999-296-4*) LinguiSystems.

— Access to Reading & Language Arts - 4 Study Skills: Teachers Guide & Student Book. 1993. student ed 14.95 (*1-55999-290-5*) LinguiSystems.

— Access to Reading & Language Arts - 4 Vocabulary: Teachers Guide & Student Book. 1993. student ed 14.95 (*1-55999-281-6*) LinguiSystems.

— Access to Reading & Language Arts - 4 Word Analysis: Teachers Guide & Student Book. 1993. student ed 14.95 (*1-55999-284-0*) LinguiSystems.

— Access to Reading & Language Arts - 4 Writing: Teachers Guide & Student Book. 1993. student ed 14.95 (*1-55999-293-X*) LinguiSystems.

— Access to Reading & Language Arts - 5 Grade Set. 1993. student ed 77.70 (*1-55999-326-X*) LinguiSystems.

— Access to Reading & Language Arts - 5 Literary Concepts: Teachers Guide & Student Book. 1993. student ed 14.95 (*1-55999-330-8*) LinguiSystems.

— Access to Reading & Language Arts - 5 Reading & Listening Comprehension: Teachers Guide & Student Book. 1993. student ed 14.95 (*1-55999-339-1*) LinguiSystems.

— Access to Reading & Language Arts - 5 Study Skills: Teachers Guide & Student Book. 1993. student ed 14.95 (*1-55999-333-2*) LinguiSystems.

— Access to Reading & Language Arts - 5 Vocabulary: Teachers Guide & Student Book. 1993. student ed 14.95 (*1-55999-299-9*) LinguiSystems.

— Access to Reading & Language Arts - 5 Word Analysis: Teachers Guide & Student Book. 1993. student ed 14.95 (*1-55999-327-8*) LinguiSystems.

— Access to Reading & Language Arts - 5 Writing: Teachers Guide & Student Book. 1993. student ed 14.95 (*1-55999-336-7*) LinguiSystems.

— Access to Reading & Language Arts - 6 Grade Set. 1993. student ed 77.70 (*1-55999-344-8*) LinguiSystems.

— Access to Reading & Language Arts - 6 Literary Concepts: Teachers Guide & Student Book. 1993. student ed 14.95 (*1-55999-348-0*) LinguiSystems.

— Access to Reading & Language Arts - 6 Reading & Listening Comprehension: Teachers Guide & Student Book. 1993. student ed 14.95 (*1-55999-357-X*) LinguiSystems.

— Access to Reading & Language Arts - 6 Study Skills: Teachers Guide & Student Book. 1993. student ed 14.95 (*1-55999-351-0*) LinguiSystems.

— Access to Reading & Language Arts - 6 Vocabulary: Teachers Guide & Student Book. 1993. student ed 14.95 (*1-55999-342-1*) LinguiSystems.

— Access to Reading & Language Arts - 6 Word Analysis: Teachers Guide & Student Book. 1993. student ed 14.95 (*1-55999-345-6*) LinguiSystems.

— Access to Reading & Language Arts - 6 Writing: Teachers Guide & Student Book. 1993. student ed 14.95 (*1-55999-354-5*) LinguiSystems.

— ACHIEV-Blue Lesson Plans: Activities for Children Involving Everyday Vocabulary. 1990. student ed, spiral bd. 27.95 (*1-55999-098-8*) LinguiSystems.

— ACHIEV-Red Lesson Plans: Activities for Children Involving Everyday Vocabulary. 1990. student ed, spiral bd. 27.95 (*1-55999-099-6*) LinguiSystems.

— ACHIEV-Red Sing-a-Longs Manual (Activities for Children Involving Everyday Vocabulary - Home & Family Vocabulary) (J). (ps-3). 1989. 27.95 (*1-55999-006-6*) LinguiSystems.

— Sydney's World. 1993. 11.95 (*1-55999-266-2*) LinguiSystems.

Lingwall, James B., et al. Caseload Issues in Schools: How to Make Better Decisions. Snope, Trudy, ed. (Professional Practices Ser.). 56p. 1985. pap. text ed. 16.50 (*0-910329-25-7*) Am Speech Lang Hearing.

Lingwood, James, ed. Erik Bulatov: Moscow. 96p. (Orig.). 1989. pap. 25.00 (*3-907509-03-X*, Pub. by Parkett Pubs SZ) Dist Art Pubs.

— Ilya Kabakov: Ten Characters. 72p. (Orig.). 1989. pap. 22.50 (*0-905263-47-2*, Pub. by Parkett Pubs SZ) Dist Art Pubs.

Lingwood, James, ed. see Bird, Jon, et al.

Linh, Mark. You: Prayer for Beginners & Those Who Have Forgotten How. LC 76-41584. 156p. (Orig.). 1976. pap. 6.95 (*0-913592-78-1*) Tabor Pub.

Linhart, H. & Zucchini, W. Model Selection. LC 86-7763. (Probability & Mathematical Statistics Ser.). 304p. 1986. text ed. 104.00 (*0-471-83722-9*) Wiley.

Linhart, J. F., ed. Plasma Physics: Proceedings of the EUR-CNEN Association Meeting, 1969. 1975. pap. 16.25 (*0-08-020450-3*, Pergamon Pr) Elsevier.

Linhart, Peter B., et al, eds. Bargaining with Incomplete Information. (Economic Theory, Econometrics & Mathematical Economics Ser.). (Illus.). 553p. 1992. text ed. 79.00 (*0-12-451050-7*) Acad Pr.

Linhart, Robert. The Assembly Line. Crosland, Margaret, tr. LC 81-1703. Orig. Title: L'Etabli. 160p. (Orig.). 1981. pap. text ed. 12.95x (*0-87023-322-X*) U of Mass Pr.

Linial, Andrew V., jt. auth. see Gerhardt, John J.

Linick, Andrew S. Nunchaku, Karate's Deadliest Fighting Sticks. 3rd ed. LC 75-6144. (Illus.). 240p. 1982. reprint ed. 29.95 (*0-917098-01-3*); reprint ed. pap. 17.95 (*0-917098-00-5*) LKA Inc.

— Picture Profits: Let Your Camera Make Money for You. 4th ed. 1981. pap. 7.95 (*0-917098-02-1*) LKA Inc.

Liniger, C., jt. ed. see Assal, J. P.

Liniger-Goumaz, Max. Historical Dictionary of Equatorial Guinea. 2nd ed. LC 88-11409. (African Historical Dictionaries Ser.: No. 21). (Illus.). 270p. 1988. 32.50 (*0-8108-2120-6*) Scarecrow.

— Small Is Not Always Beautiful: The Story of Equatorial Guinea. 200p. (C). 1989. lib. bdg. 50.00 (*0-389-20861-2*, N8419) B&N Imports.

Lininger, Clarence. Best War at the Time. 10.95 (*0-8315-0068-9*) Speller.

Lininger, Skye. Using Ventura Publisher 4 for Windows. (Illus.). (Orig.). 1992. pap. 29.95 (*0-88022-929-2*) Que.

Linington. Date with Death. large type ed. 1991. 17.95 (*0-7451-8096-5*, AH0154, Atlantic Lrg Print); pap. 15.95 (*0-7927-0574-2*, AS0190, Atlantic Lrg Print) Chivers N Amer.

Linington, George E. & Gardlund, Sharon L. Experiments & Exercises for General Chemistry. rev. ed. 208p. (C). 1994. pap. text ed., spiral bd. 17.95 (*0-8403-9443-8*) Kendall-Hunt.

— Experiments & Exercises for General Chemistry. 4th ed. 208p. 1992. spiral bd. 16.95 (*0-8403-7777-0*) Kendall-Hunt.

Link, Albert N. Evaluating Economic Damages: A Handbook for Attorneys. LC 91-47571. 256p. 1992. text ed. 59.95 (*0-89930-763-9*, LV#, Quorum Bks) Greenwood.

— Link's International Dictionary of Business Economics. 350p. 1993. 45.00 (*1-55738-495-9*); pap. 24.95 (*1-55738-505-X*) Probus Pub Co.

— Mastering the Business Cycle: How to Keep Your Company on Track in Times of Economic Change. (Entrepreneur's Guide Ser.). 1990. pap. 22.95 (*1-55738-144-5*) Probus Pub Co.

— Research & Development in U. S. Manufacturing. LC 80-21542. 144p. 1981. text ed. 45.00 (*0-275-90672-8*, C0672, Praeger Pubs) Greenwood.

— Technological Change & Productivity Growth. (Fundamentals of Pure & Applied Economics Ser.: Vol. 13). 90p. 1987. pap. text ed. 28.00 (*3-7186-0347-0*) Gordon & Breach.

Link, Albert N., ed. Cooperative Research & Development: The Industry, University, Government Relationship. (C). 1989. lib. bdg. 64.00 (*0-89838-303-X*) Kluwer Ac.

Link, Albert N. & Bauer, Laura L. Cooperative Research in U.S. Manufacturing: Assessing Policy Initiatives & Corporate Strategies. LC 87-45771. 128p. 1988. text ed. 35.00 (*0-669-16969-2*) Free Pr.

Link, Albert N. & Tassey, Gregory. Strategies for Technology-Based Competition: Meeting the New Global Challenge. LC 86-45885. 160p. 1987. text ed. 35.00 (*0-669-14574-2*) Free Pr.

Link, Albert N., jt. auth. see Bozeman, Barry.

Link, Albert N., jt. auth. see Hebert, Robert F.

Link, Albert N., jt. auth. see Leyden, Dennis P.

Link, Arthur, ed. The Deliberations of the Council of Four, March 24-June 28, 1919: Notes of the Official Interpreter, Paul Mantoux, 2 vols., Set. (Papers of Woodrow Wilson). (Illus.). 1283p. 1992. text ed. 99.50 (*0-691-04793-6*) Princeton U Pr.

— The Papers of Woodrow Wilson: April 8, 1922-February 6, 1924, Vol. 68. 375p. 1993. text ed. 69.50 (*0-691-04812-6*) Princeton U Pr.

— The Papers of Woodrow Wilson: December 24, 1920-April 7, 1922, Vol. 67. (Illus.). 655p. 1992. text ed. 69.50 (*0-691-04799-5*) Princeton U Pr.

— The Papers of Woodrow Wilson, Vol. 65: February 28-July 31, 1920. (Illus.). 673p. 1992. text ed. 69.50 (*0-691-04792-8*) Princeton U Pr.

— The Papers of Woodrow Wilson, Vol. 66: August 2-December 23, 1920. (Illus.). 583p. 1992. text ed. 69.50 (*0-691-04798-7*) Princeton U Pr.

— The Papers of Woodrow Wilson, 1918-1924: Contents & Index, Vols. 53-68, Vol. 69. 375p. 1993. text ed. 69.50 (*0-685-62626-1*) Princeton U Pr.

Link, Arthur S. Higher Realism of Woodrow Wilson & Other Essays. LC 73-138987. 1971. 24.95 (*0-8265-1163-5*) Vanderbilt U Pr.

— Woodrow Wilson: Revolution, War, & Peace. LC 79-50909. 152p. (C). 1979. pap. text ed. write for info. (*0-88295-798-8*) Harlan Davidson.

Link, Arthur S., ed. The Papers of Woodrow Wilson: September 14 to November 8, 1918, Vol. 51. LC 66-10880. (Illus.). 648p. 1985. text ed. 69.50 (*0-691-04730-8*) Princeton U Pr.

— The Papers of Woodrow Wilson, Vol. 47: March 13-May 12, 1918. LC 66-10880. (Papers of Woodrow Wilson). (Illus.). 632p. 1984. text ed. 69.50 (*0-691-04707-3*) Princeton U Pr.

— The Papers of Woodrow Wilson, Vol. 48: May 13-July 17, 1918. LC 66-10880. (Illus.). 585p. 1985. text ed. 69.50 (*0-691-04708-1*) Princeton U Pr.

— The Papers of Woodrow Wilson, Vol. 49: July 18-September 18, 1918. LC 66-10880. (Illus.). 665p. 1985. text ed. 69.50 (*0-691-04709-X*) Princeton U Pr.

— The Papers of Woodrow Wilson, Vol. 60: June 1 - June 17, 1919. 752p. 1989. text ed. 69.50 (*0-691-04762-6*) Princeton U Pr.

— The Papers of Woodrow Wilson, Vol. 61: June 18 - July 25, 1919. 620p. (C). 1989. pap. text ed. 69.50 (*0-691-04766-9*) Princeton U Pr.

— The Papers of Woodrow Wilson, Vol. 62: July 26-September 3, 1919. (Illus.). 688p. 1990. text ed. 69.50 (*0-691-04767-7*) Princeton U Pr.

— The Papers of Woodrow Wilson, Vol. 63: September 4-November 5, 1919. (Illus.). 546p. 1990. text ed. 69.50 (*0-691-04775-8*) Princeton U Pr.

— Woodrow Wilson & a Revolutionary World, 1913-1921. fac. ed. LC 82-2565. (Supplementary Volumes to The Papers of Woodrow Wilson). 249p. 1982. reprint ed. pap. 71.00 (*0-7837-8053-2*, 2047806) Bks Demand.

Link, Arthur S. & Catton, William B. American Epoch: A History of the United States since the 1890's, 3 Vols., 2. 5th ed. (Illus.). 1980. 12.00 (*0-394-32358-0*) Knopf.

Link, Arthur S. & Coben, Stanley. The Democratic Heritage: A History of the United States. LC 69-11030. 688p. (Orig.). 1971. 32.50 (*0-686-81279-4*) Krieger.

Link, Arthur S. & Hilderbrand, Robert C., eds. The Papers of Woodrow Wilson: The Complete Press Conferences, 1913-1919, Vol. 50. LC 66-10880. (Illus.). 688p. 1985. text ed. 69.50 (*0-691-04710-3*) Princeton U Pr.

Link, Arthur S. & Hirst, David W., eds. The Papers of Woodrow Wilson: November 9, 1918-January 11, 1919, Vol. 53. LC 66-10880. (Illus.). 736p. 1985. 69.50 (*0-691-04731-6*) Princeton U Pr.

Link, Arthur S. & Link, William A. The Twentieth Century: A Brief American History in Two Volumes, Vol. 1. 2nd ed. (Illus.). 210p. 1992. pap. text ed. write for info. (*0-88295-890-9*) Harlan Davidson.

— The Twentieth Century: A Brief American History in Two Volumes, Vol. 2. 2nd ed. (Illus.). 376p. 1992. pap. text ed. write for info. (*0-88295-892-5*) Harlan Davidson.

Link, Arthur S. & McCormick, Richard L. Progressivism. Franklin, John H. & Eisenstadt, A. S., eds. LC 82-15857. (American History Ser.). 164p. (C). 1983. pap. text ed. write for info. (*0-88295-814-3*) Harlan Davidson.

Link, Arthur S., ed. see Axson, Stockton.

Link, Arthur S., jt. auth. see Link, William A.

Link, Arthur S., ed. see Wilson, Woodrow.

Link, Arthur S., et al. The American People: A History. LC 80-69272. (Illus.). 1008p. (C). 1981. text ed. write for info. (*0-88295-804-6*) Harlan Davidson.

— The American People: A History, Vol. 1 to 1877. 2nd rev. ed. LC 86-24261. (Illus.). 504p. (C). 1987. pap. text ed. write for info. (*0-88295-848-8*) Harlan Davidson.

— The American People: A History, Vol. 2 since 1865. 2nd rev. ed. LC 86-24261. (Illus.). 582p. (C). 1987. pap. text ed. write for info. (*0-88295-849-6*) Harlan Davidson.

— A Concise History of the American People. LC 83-23184. (Illus.). 622p. (C). 1984. pap. text ed. write for info. (*0-88295-817-8*); teacher ed, pap. text ed. write for info. (*0-88295-821-6*) Harlan Davidson.

— A Concise History of the American People, Vol. 1. LC 83-23184. (Illus.). 622p. (C). 1984. student ed, pap. text ed. write for info. (*0-88295-822-4*) Harlan Davidson.

— A Concise History of the American People, Vol. 1: To 1877. LC 83-23184. (Illus.). 622p. (C). 1984. pap. text ed. write for info. (*0-88295-818-6*) Harlan Davidson.

— A Concise History of the American People, Vol. 2. LC 83-23184. (Illus.). 622p. (C). 1984. student ed, pap. text ed. write for info. (*0-88295-823-2*) Harlan Davidson.

— A Concise History of the American People, Vol. 2: Since 1865. LC 83-23184. (Illus.). 622p. (C). 1984. pap. text ed. write for info. (*0-88295-819-4*) Harlan Davidson.

— The Papers of Woodrow Wilson: February 8-March 16, 1919, Vol. 55. Hirst, David W. et al, eds. (Illus.). 604p. 1986. text ed. 69.50 (*0-691-04737-5*) Princeton U Pr.

— The Papers of Woodrow Wilson, Vol. 57: April 5 - April 22, 1919. Aandahl, Frederick, ed. (Illus.). 704p. 1987. text ed. 69.50x (*0-691-04743-X*) Princeton U Pr.

Link, Arthur S., et al, eds. The Papers of Woodrow Wilson: January 11-February 7, 1919, Vol. 54. (Illus.). 616p. 1986. text ed. 69.50 (*0-691-04736-7*) Princeton U Pr.

— The Papers of Woodrow Wilson: November 6, 1919 - February 27, 1920, Vol. 64. 565p. 1990. text ed. 69.50 (*0-691-04791-X*) Princeton U Pr.

— The Papers of Woodrow Wilson, Vol. 39: Content & Index to Volumes 27-38, 1913-1916. LC 66-10880. 300p. 1985. text ed. 69.50 (*0-691-04696-4*) Princeton U Pr.

— The Papers of Woodrow Wilson, Vol. 52: Contents & Index, Vol. 40-49, 51. 240p. 1987. text ed. 69.50x (*0-691-04744-8*) Princeton U Pr.

— The Papers of Woodrow Wilson, Vol. 56: March 17 - April 4, 1919. (Illus.). 696p. 1987. text ed. 69.50x (*0-691-04742-1*) Princeton U Pr.

— The Papers of Woodrow Wilson, Vol. 58: April 23 to May 9, 1919. (Illus.). 696p. 1988. text ed. 69.50 (*0-691-04748-0*) Princeton U Pr.

An Asterisk (*) at the beginning of an entry indicates that the title is appearing in BIP for the first time.

— The Papers of Woodrow Wilson, Vol. 59: May 10 - May 31, 1919. (Illus.). 744p. 1988. 69.50x (*0-691-04754-5*) Princeton U Pr.

*Link, Charles E.** Jesus' Epilogue to the Sermon on the Mount: A Study of the Lord's Prayer. LC 94-24369. 88p. (Orig.). 1995. pap. 8.25 (*0-7880-0374-7*) CSS OH.

— A Meal for the Road: Fourteen Sermons on the Lord's Prayer. LC 93-30840. 92p. 1994. pap. 7.95 (*1-55673-702-5*) CSS OH.

Link, D. A., jt. auth. see Busch, D. A.

Link, David & Soderquist, Larry. Law of Federal Estate & Gift Taxation: 1978-1990, 1 vol. rev. ed. 100.00 (*0-317-11947-8*) Clark Boardman Callaghan.

Link, Eugene P. Democratic-Republican Societies, 1790-1800. (History - United States Ser.). 256p. 1993. reprint ed. lib. bdg. 79.00 (*0-7812-4881-7*) Rprt Serv.

— The Social Ideas of American Physicians, 1776-1976: Studies of the Humanitarian Tradition in Medicine. LC 91-50603. (Illus.). 320p. 1993. 46.50 (*0-945636-34-2*) Susquehanna U Pr.

Link, Floyd. Looking over the Shoulder. 127p. 1993. pap. 9.95 (*1-878208-26-8*) Guild Pr IN.

Link, Frances R., ed. Essays on the Intellect. LC 84-81488. 160p. (Orig.). 1985. pap. 5.00 (*0-87120-132-1*, 611-85408) Assn Supervision.

Link, Frances R. & Almquist, S. Thinking to Write: A Work Journal Program. 62p. (Orig.). 1987. pap. 2.50 (*0-86631-120-3*); teacher ed 5.00 (*0-317-62982-4*) Curriculum Dev Assocs.

Link, Frederick, ed. see Behn, Aphra.

Link, Frederick M., ed. see Dryden, John.

Link, Frederick M., ed. see Scott, Sir Walter.

Link, Gail. All I Ask of You. 448p. (Orig.). 1994. pap. 4.99 (*0-8439-3606-1*) Dorchester Pub Co.

— Encantadora. 448p. (Orig.). 1991. pap. 4.50 (*0-8439-3178-7*) Dorchester Pub Co.

— Never Call It Loving. 448p. (Orig.). 1993. pap. 4.99 (*0-8439-3519-7*) Dorchester Pub Co.

— There Never Was a Time. 448p. (Orig.). 1995. mass mkt., pap. text ed. 4.99 (*0-505-52025-7*) Dorchester Pub Co.

— Wolf's Embrace. 448p. 1992. reprint ed. pap. 4.50 (*0-8439-3358-5*) Dorchester Pub Co.

Link, George K., ed. see Theophrastus.

Link, George K., tr. see Theophrastus.

Link, Gloria. The Lady's Lion. (Illus.). 1995. pap. 10.95 (*0-9627860-8-X*) Lone Oak MN.

***Link, Grants.** Corporate Funders Operating in Missouri. 1994. pap. 50.00 (*0-9631907-1-7*) Grants Link.

Link, Hans-Georg, ed. The Roots of Our Common Faith: Faith in the Scriptures & in the Early Church. (Faith & Order Paper Ser.: No. 119). (Illus.). 143p. reprint ed. pap. 40.80 (*0-7837-6002-7*, 2045812) Bks Demand.

Link-Heer, Ursula. Prousts "A la Recherche du Temps Perdu" und die Form der Autobiographie. (Beihefte zu Poetica Ser.: Vol. 18). 348p. (GER.). 1987. 56.00x (*90-6032-214-2*, Pub. by B R Gruener NE) Benjamins North Am.

Link, Howard A. The Art of Shibata Zeshin: The Mr. & Mrs. James E. O'Brien Collection at the Honolulu Academy of Arts. (Illus.). 196p. (C). 1979. 25.00 (*0-937426-23-7*) Honolu Arts.

— The Feminine Image: Women of Japan. (Illus.). 146p. (Orig.). (C). 1985. pap. 12.50 (*0-937426-06-7*) Honolu Arts.

— Prints by Utagawa Hiroshige: The James A. Michener Collection, 2 vols., Vol. 1. (Illus.). 167p. (Orig.). (ENG & JPN.). (C). 1995. pap. 32.50 (*0-937426-13-X*, 6222) Honolu Arts.

— Prints by Utagawa Hiroshige: The James A. Michener Collection, 2 vols., Vol. 2. (Illus.). 62p. (Orig.). (ENG & JPN.). (C). 1992. pap. 17.50 (*0-685-64840-0*) Honolu Arts.

— Prints by Utagawa Hiroshige: The James A. Michener Collection, 2 vols., Vol. 2. (Illus.). 64p. (Orig.). (ENG & JPN.). (C). 1995. Set. pap. 49.95 (*0-937426-18-0*, 618-0) Honolu Arts.

— Waves & Plagues: The Art of Masami Teraoka. (Illus.). 96p. 1989. 29.95 (*0-87701-602-X*); pap. 16.95 (*0-87701-590-2*) Chronicle Bks.

Link, Howard A., text. The Art of Shibata Zeshin: The Mr. & Mrs. James E. O'Brien Collection. LC 79-24341. (Illus.). 195p. 1995. 25.00 (*0-903697-05-X*, 237) Honolu Arts.

Link, Howard A., et al. Primitve Ukiyo-E: From the James A. Michener Collection in the Honolulu Academy of Arts. LC 79-6397. (Illus.). 344p. 1980. 55.00 (*0-8248-0483-X*) UH Pr.

Link, Irene, jt. auth. see Farnham, Rebecca.

Link, J., et al. In-Vivo Magnetic Resonance Spectroscopy I: Probesheads & Radiofrequency Pulses, Spectrum Analysis. LC 91-30593. 284p. 1992. 119.00 (*0-387-54547-6*, QP519) Spr-Verlag.

Link, John E., jt. auth. see Bailey, John J.

Link, Kurt H. Doctor's Prescription: For Getting the Best Medical Care. LC 89-30969. 1990. 19.95 (*0-942637-15-1*, Dembner NY) Barricade Bks.

Link, Linda P. Numbers Rule the World: Ancient Secrets in the Alphabet: Others Being Finished. (Illus.). (Orig.). 1989. write for info. (*0-318-65407-5*) Pearls Pub.

Link, Mae M. & Coleman, Hubert A. Medical Support: Army Air Forces in World War II. 1027p. 1992. pap. text ed. write for info. (*0-912799-69-2*) Off Air Force.

Link, Margaret S., ret. The Pollen Path: A Collection of Navajo Myths. LC 56-7272. (Illus.). xiv, 210p. 1956. 27.50 (*0-8047-0473-2*) Stanford U Pr.

Link, Marion, jt. auth. see Van Hock, Susan.

Link, Mark. Action 2000: Praying Scripture in a Contemporary Way, Cycle C. (Mark Link, S. J., Library). 416p. 1994. pap. 8.95 (*0-7829-0362-2*, 22047) Tabor Pub.

— Bible 2000: Genesis to Revelation - for Busy People. 343p. (Orig.). (YA). Date not set. lib. bdg. 8.95 (*0-7829-0459-9*) Tabor Pub.

— The Catholic Vision. (Illus.). 128p. (Orig.). 1989. teacher ed 5.95 (*1-55924-073-3*, 59110); pap. text ed. 15.00 (*1-55924-071-7*, S9100) Tabor Pub.

— Challenge 2000: Daily Meditations Based on the Spiritual Exercises of St. Ignatius. (Mark Link, S. J., Library). 392p. 1993. pap. 8.95 (*0-7829-0363-0*, 22049) Tabor Pub.

— Illustrated Daily Homilies: Year I & II, Gospel. 148p. 1986. 36.70 (*0-89505-391-8*, 25340) Tabor Pub.

— Illustrated Daily Homilies: Year I, Reading I. 128p. 1988. ring bd. 37.95 (*0-89505-586-4*, 25400) Tabor Pub.

— Illustrated Daily Homilies: Year II, Reading I. 128p. 1987. ring bd. 37.95 (*0-89505-574-0*, 25370) Tabor Pub.

— Illustrated Sunday Homilies: Year B, Series II. 125p. (Orig.). 1990. pap. 32.95 (*0-89505-931-2*, 25510) Tabor Pub.

— Illustrated Sunday Homilies: Year C, Series II. 125p. (Orig.). 1991. pap. 32.95 (*0-89505-932-0*, 25520) Tabor Pub.

— Illustrated Sunday Homilies: Year C, Series I. 128p. 1988. ring bd. 32.95 (*0-89505-587-2*, 25410) Tabor Pub.

— Illustrated Sunday Homilies, Year A, Series II. (Illus.). 125p. 1989. ring bd. 32.95 (*0-89505-794-8*, 25500) Tabor Pub.

— Illustrated Sunday Homilies, Year A, Series I. 124p. 1986. ring bd. 32.95 (*0-89505-392-6*, 25350) Tabor Pub.

— Illustrated Sunday Homilies, Year B, Series I. 124p. 1987. ring bd. 32.95 (*0-89505-573-2*, 25380) Tabor Pub.

— Lent Two Thousand. 62p. 1994. 1.95 (*0-7829-0446-7*, 22050) Tabor Pub.

— Lord, Who Are You? LC 82-70106. 214p. (Orig.). 1982. pap. 14.50 (*0-89505-066-8*, 21048) Tabor Pub.

— Lord, Who Are You? Teacher's Manual. 169p. (Orig.). 1982. teacher ed 21.95 (*0-89505-095-1*, 21049) Tabor Pub.

— The Mark Link, S. J., Library, 5 vols., Set. Date not set. pap. 39.95 (*0-7829-0524-2*, 22054) Thomas More.

— Mission 2000: Daily Meditations Based on the Lectionary, Cycle B. (Mark Link, S. J., Library). 416p. 1993. pap. 8.95 (*0-7829-0048-8*, 22046) Tabor Pub.

— One Hundred Stories for Special Occasion Homilies. 1992. 32.95 (*0-7829-0049-6*, 25650) Tabor Pub.

— Path Through Catholicism. (Illus.). 224p. (Orig.). (YA). (gr. 9-12). 1991. pap. 14.50 (*1-55924-543-3*, 22039) Tabor Pub.

— Path Through Catholicism Resource Manual. 247p. (Orig.). 1991. teacher ed, pap. 27.50 (*1-55924-544-1*, 22M39) Tabor Pub.

— Path Through Scripture. (Illus.). 288p. (YA). (gr. 9-12). 1987. pap. 14.50 (*0-89505-402-7*, 21095) Tabor Pub.

— Path Through Scripture: Teacher's Resource Manual. 328p. (YA). (gr. 9-12). 1987. 27.50 (*0-89505-403-5*, 253X1) Tabor Pub.

— Prayer Paths: Search for Serenity & God in an Age of Stress. (Illus.). 161p. (Orig.). 1990. pap. 7.50 (*1-55924-480-1*, 22037) Tabor Pub.

— The Seventh Trumpet. LC 78-53943. 1978. 14.50 (*0-89505-014-5*, 21004) Tabor Pub.

— The Seventh Trumpet: Teacher's Manual. 207p. (YA). (gr. 9-12). 1978. 21.95 (*0-89505-030-7*, 21005) Tabor Pub.

— Spirit Two Thousand. 62p. 1994. 1.95 (*0-7829-0447-5*, 22051) Tabor Pub.

— These Stones Will Shout: A New Voice for the Old Testament. (Illus.). 236p. 1975. pap. text ed. 14.50 (*0-89505-117-6*, 21033) Tabor Pub.

— These Stones Will Shout: Teacher's Manual. 297p. 1975. 21.95 (*0-89505-046-3*, 21034) Tabor Pub.

— Vision 2000: Daily Meditations Based on the Lectionary, Cycle A. (Mark Link, S. J., Library). 407p. 1992. pap. 8.95 (*0-7829-0103-4*, 22043) Tabor Pub.

Link, Martin, jt. auth. see Blood, Charles L.

Link, Martin A., ed. Navajo: A Century of Progress, 1868-1968. LC 68-15787. (Illus.). 110p. 1968. 6.00 (*0-318-19652-2*) Navajo.

Link, Mike. Black Hills - Badlands: The Web of the West. (Voyageur Wilderness Ser.). (Illus.). 120p. 1980. reprint ed. pap. 14.95 (*0-89658-017-2*) Voyageur Pr.

— Minnesota State Parks: Celebrating 100 Years. LC 89-77801. (Illus.). 112p. (Orig.). 1990. pap. 14.95 (*0-89658-103-9*) Voyageur Pr.

Link, Mike & Crowley, Kate. Following the Pack: Leading Wolf Researchers. LC 93-21358. 1994. 19.95 (*0-89658-199-3*) Voyageur Pr.

— Romancing Minnesota: Intimate Places to Stay & Dine. (Orig.). 1995. pap. 12.95 (*1-57025-043-X*) Pfeifer-Hamilton.

Link, Mike, jt. auth. see Crowley, Kate.

Link, Mike, et al. Journeys to Door County. (Illus.). 136p. 1985. pap. 14.95 (*0-89658-049-0*) Voyageur Pr.

Link, Nelle W. Smocking & Gathering for Fabric Manipulation. Kliot, Jules & Kliot, Kaethe, eds. (Illus.). 112p. 1987. pap. 10.00 (*0-916896-25-0*) Lacis Pubns.

***Link, O. Winston.** Steam, Steel & Stars: America's Last Steam Railroad. 1994. pap. 19.95 (*0-8109-2587-7*) Abrams.

***Link, O. Winston, photos.** The Last Steam Railroad in America: From Tidewater to Whitetop. LC 95-7406. 1995. write for info. (*0-8109-3575-9*) Abrams.

Link, P. K., et al, eds. Regional Geology of Eastern Idaho & Western Wyoming. (Memoir Ser.: No. 179). (Illus.). 1992. 88.75 (*0-8137-1179-7*) Geol Soc.

Link, Paul. A Time to Sow & a Time to Reap. (Illus.). 178p. 1990. pap. text ed. write for info. (*0-318-66612-X*) P Link.

— A Time to Sow & a Time to Reap. rev. ed. 182p. 1991. pap. text ed. write for info. (*0-9625216-1-2*) P Link.

Link, Paul K. & Hackett, William R., eds. Guidebook to the Geology of Central & Southern Idaho. 335p. (Orig.). 1988. pap. 35.00 (*1-55765-026-8*) ID Geog Survey.

Link, Peggy W., illus. Nebraska Pioneer Cookbook. LC 74-77089. x, 164p. 1974. pap. 5.95 (*0-8032-5801-1*) U of Nebr Pr.

Link, Perry. Evening Chats in Beijing. 448p. 1992. 24.95 (*0-393-03052-0*) Norton.

— Evening Chats in Beijing. 336p. 1993. pap. 11.95 (*0-393-31065-5*) Norton.

— Roses & Thorns: The Second Blooming of the Hundred Flowers in Chinese Fiction, 1979-80. LC 83-9147. (Illus.). 300p. (C). 1984. pap. 14.00 (*0-520-04980-2*) U CA Pr.

Link, Perry, ed. Stubborn Weeds: Popular & Controversial Chinese Literature after the Cultural Revolution. LC 82-48268. (Chinese Literature in Translation Ser.). (Illus.). 304p. 1984. reprint ed. 30.00 (*0-253-35512-5*) Ind U Pr.

Link, Perry, ed. see Liu Binyan.

Link, Perry, et al, eds. Unofficial China: Popular Culture & Thought in the People's Republic. 238p. (C). 1989. pap. text ed. 19.95 (*0-8133-0924-7*) Westview.

Link, Peter K. Basic Petroleum Geology. 2nd rev. ed. LC 81-83909. 426p. 1990. 50.00 (*0-930972-10-4*, P7140) Oil & Gas.

Link, Phil. Another Time: A Fictional Story of the Truth about Fraternities at Chapel Hill in the Thirties. 200p. 1990. pap. 9.95 (*0-9628079-0-7*) Carolina Cerulean.

Link, Richard F., jt. auth. see Koch, George S., Jr.

Link, Robert C. Cash, Cash Who's Got the Cash? Practical Management Techniques for Mom & Pop Business Owners. 120p. (Orig.). 1988. student ed 13.95 (*0-9621819-0-0*); pap. 9.95 (*0-9621819-1-9*) Bobolink Busn Bks.

Link, Robert G. English Theories of Economic Fluctuations, 1815-1848. LC 68-54282. (Columbia University. Studies in the Social Sciences: No. 598). reprint ed. 18.50 (*0-404-51598-3*) AMS Pr.

Link, S. Gordden. Personal Journal for Yesterday, Now, & Tomorrow: And Other Selected Poems. 128p. 1992. 12.50 (*0-9634744-0-5*) B Souders.

Link, S. W., ed. The Wave Theory of Difference & Similarity. (Scientific Psychology Ser.). 384p. (C). 1991. text ed. 79.95 (*0-8058-0926-0*) L Erlbaum Assocs.

Link-Salinger, Ruth. Jewish Law in Our Time. 183p. 17.95x (*0-8197-0486-5*); pap. 12.95 (*0-8197-0487-3*) Bloch.

Link-Salinger, Ruth & Herrera, Robert, eds. Scholars, Savants & Their Tests: Studies in Philosophy & Religious Thought: Essays in Honor of Arthur Hyman. 271p. (C). 1989. text ed. 48.95 (*0-8204-0834-4*) P Lang Pubs.

Link-Salinger, Ruth, ed. see Halakah & Kabbala.

Link-Salinger, Ruth, et al, eds. A Straight Path: Studies in Medieval Philosophy & Culture. LC 87-18403. (Essays in Honor of Arthur Hyman Ser.). 309p. 1988. 35.00 (*0-8132-0648-0*) Cath U Pr.

Link, Terry. Thematic Book Reports for Social Studies: Literature Lists & Ready-to-Use Book Reports. (Illus.). 64p. 1995. student ed 6.95 (*1-56472-024-1*) Edupress.

Link, Tom. Universal City & North Hollywood. 1991. 27.95 (*0-89781-393-6*) Preferred Mktg.

Link, Werner. The East-West Conflict: The Organization of International Relations in the Twentieth Century. Bennett-Ruete, Jackie, tr. LC 85-22322. 208p. 1986. text ed. 32.50 (*0-312-22495-8*) St Martin.

Link, William. A Fatherless Country. LC 78-26468. 1979. pap. 6.95 (*0-87233-049-4*) Bauhan.

Link, William, jt. auth. see Levinson, Richard.

Link, William A. A Hard Country & a Lonely Place: Schooling, Society, & Reform in Rural Virginia, 1870-1920. LC 86-1412. (Fred W. Morrison Series in Southern Studies). xvi, 275p. (C). 1986. 32.50 (*0-8078-1706-6*) U of NC Pr.

— The Paradox of Southern Progressivism, 1880-1930. LC 92-1328. (Fred W. Morrison Series in Southern Studies). (Illus.). xviii, 440p. (C). 1993. text ed. 45.00 (*0-8078-2040-7*) U of NC Pr.

— The Rebuilding of the Old Commonwealth: Documents of Social Reform in the Progressive Era South. 160p. 1995. pap. text ed. 8.65 (*0-312-10590-8*) St Martin.

— William Friday: Power, Purpose, & American Higher Education. LC 94-5723. (Illus.). 530p. 1995. 29.95 (*0-8078-2167-5*) U of NC Pr.

Link, William A. & Link, Arthur S. American Epoch: A History of the United States since 1900. 7th ed. LC 92-16975. 1992. pap. text ed. write for info. (*0-07-037951-3*) McGraw.

— American Epoch - A History of the United States since 1900: Affluence & Anxiety, 1940-1992, Vol. 2. 7th ed. 1992. pap. text ed. write for info. (*0-07-037952-1*) McGraw.

Link, William A., jt. auth. see Link, Arthur S.

Linke, Anita. French for Business. 137p. 1989. audio 185.00 (*0-88432-267-X*, SFR225); 11.95 (*0-88432-546-6*, BFR225) Audio-Forum.

Linke, David, jt. auth. see Barbeito, Carol.

Linke, Esther, ed. see West, John R.

Linke, Frances. Space Patrol Comics. (Space Patrol Ser.: No. 2). 70p. (Orig.). 1977. pap. 15.00 (*0-933276-05-2*) Nin-Ra Ent.

— Space Patrol III. Linke, Ray, ed. (Space Patrol Ser.: No. 3). (Illus.). 205p. 1980. 30.00 (*0-933276-06-0*); lib. bdg. 40.00 (*0-933276-07-9*) Nin-Ra Ent.

Linke, Frances, pseud. Space Patrol Memories, by Tonga. Wahle, Ted, ed. (Space Patrol Ser.: No. 1). (Illus.). 173p. (Orig.). 1976. 35.00 (*0-933276-00-1*); lib. bdg. 40.00 (*0-933276-01-X*); pap. 30.00 (*0-933276-03-6*) Nin-Ra Ent.

Linke, Horst. Labyrinth Fish: The Bubble Nest Builders. (Illus.). 170p. Date not set. 21.95 (*3-89356-137-4*, 16071) Tetra Pr.

Linke, Lilo. Ecuador: Country of Contrasts. 1976. lib. bdg. 59.95 (*0-8490-1750-5*) Gordon Pr.

***Linke, P.** Time Flies When You're Alive. 1994. pap. 3.99 (*0-517-13193-5*) Random.

Linke, Paul. Time Flies When You're Alive: A Love Story. LC 92-37589. 1993. 16.95 (*1-55972-183-9*, Birch Ln Pr) Carol Pub Group.

Linke, Ray, ed. see Linke, Frances.

Linke, Robert T., ed. see Squires, Frank H.

Linke, Steven R. Managing Crises in Defense Industry: The PEPCON & AVTEX Cases. 52p. 1990. pap. 1.75 (*0-16-023485-9*, S/N 008-020-01212-2) USGPO.

Linke, William F. Solubilities: Inorganic & Metal-Organic Compounds: A Compilation of Solubility Data from the Periodical Literature, Vol. 1. 4th ed. LC 65-6490. 1491p. reprint ed. pap. 180.00 (*0-8357-4124-9*, 2052335) Bks Demand.

Linke, William F., ed. Seidell's Solubilities: Inorganic & Metal-Organic Compounds, 2 vols. 4th ed. Incl. A-J1486p. 1958. 39.95 (*0-8412-0097-1*); K-Z1914p. 1966. 49.95 (*0-8412-0098-X*); write for info. (*0-318-50483-9*) Am Chemical.

Linkemer, B., jt. auth. see Weiss, Donald H.

Linkemer, Bobbi. How to Run a Meeting. LC 86-47815. (Successful Office Skills Ser.). 64p. 1987. pap. 4.00 (*0-8144-7671-6*) AMACOM.

— How to Write an Effective Resume. LC 86-47813. (Successful Office Skills Ser.). 64p. 1987. pap. 4.00 (*0-8144-7669-4*) AMACOM.

— Polishing Your Professional Image. LC 86-47814. (Successful Office Skills Ser.). 64p. 1987. pap. 4.00 (*0-8144-7670-8*) AMACOM.

Linkens. CAD for Control Systems. 600p. 1993. 165.00 (*0-8247-9060-X*) Dekker.

Linkens, Derek A., jt. auth. see Nie, Junhong.

Linker, Corinne. Circle of Seasons. (Science & Nature Ser.). (Illus.). 32p. (J). (ps-2). Date not set. 11.95 (*1-56065-157-1*) Capstone Pr.

Linker, Jerry M. Designing Instructional Visuals. (Bridges for Ideas Handbook Ser.). 1968. pap. text ed. 6.00 (*0-913648-01-9*) U Tex Austin Film Lib.

— Instructional Display Boards. (Bridges for Ideas Handbook Ser.). 1973. pap. text ed. 6.00 (*0-913648-02-7*) U Tex Austin Film Lib.

Linker, Kate. Love for Sale: The Words & Pictures of Barbara Kruger. (Illus.). 96p. 1990. 29.95 (*0-8109-1219-8*) Abrams.

— Vito Acconci. LC 92-37681. (Illus.). 224p. 1994. 50.00 (*0-8478-1645-1*) Rizzoli Intl.

Linker, Kate, et al. Individuals: A Selected History of Contemporary Art, 1945-1986. (Illus.). 372p. 1986. 65.00 (*0-89659-676-1*) Abbeville Pr.

Linker, Robert W. A Bibliography of Old French Lyrics. LC 79-11948. (Romance Monographs: No. 31). 1979. 52.00 (*84-499-2809-5*) Romance.

— Music of the Minnesinger & Early Meistersinger. LC 73-181946. (North Carolina. University. Studies in the Germanic Languages & Literatures: No. 32). reprint ed. 27.00 (*0-404-50932-0*) AMS Pr.

Linker, Sue. Sunbonnet Sue Through the Year. LC 94-6365. 1994. 19.95 (*1-56477-058-3*) That Patchwork.

Linkert, Lo. Golf Epidemic. 96p. 1992. pap. 9.95 (*0-929097-02-5*) Spect Ln Pr.

Linkh, Richard M. American Catholicism & European Immigrants (1900-1924) LC 74-79914. 200p. 1975. 5.00 (*0-913256-17-X*) Ctr Migration.

Linkhart, Douglas K. Microwave Circulator Design. (Artech House Microwave Library). (Illus.). 208p. (C). 1989. text ed. 68.00 (*0-89006-329-X*) Artech Hse.

Linkhart, Luther. Sawtooth National Recreation Area. 2nd ed. LC 87-40156. (Illus.). 224p. 1988. pap. 14.95 (*0-89997-085-0*) Wilderness Pr.

— The Trinity Alps: A Hiking & Backpacking Guide. 3rd ed. LC 94-27756. 240p. 1994. pap. 15.95 (*0-89997-176-8*) Wilderness Pr.

Linkhorn, Renee, ed. see Chedid, Andree.

***Linklater.** Before Sunrise. 1995. pap. 13.95 (*0-312-13345-6*) St Martin.

— Color Atlas of Diseases & Disorders of Sheep. 304p. 1993. 89.00 (*0-8151-5438-0*, Yr Bk Med Pubs) Mosby Yr Bk.

Linklater, Andrew. Beyond Realism & Marxism: Critical Theory & International Relations. LC 89-32801. 212p. 1990. text ed. 49.95 (*0-312-03249-8*) St Martin.

Linklater, Andrew, jt. ed. see MacMillan, John.

Linklater, Andro. Wild People: Travels with Borneo's Head Hunters. 216p. 1992. pap. 10.95 (*0-87113-477-2*) Grove-Atltic.

Linklater, Elizabeth. A Child under Sail. (C). 1987. 60.00 (*0-85174-302-1*, Pub. by Brwn Son Ferg) St Mut.

Linklater, Eric. The Men of Ness. (C). 1986. 40.00 (*0-907618-03-0*, Pub. by Orkney Pr UK) St Mut.

— Seaskin Trousers. large type ed. (Illus.). 200p. 1991. 11.47 (*1-85290-021-0*, Pub. by ISIS UK) Transaction Pubs.

— A Spell for Old Bones. Reginald, R. & Melville, Douglas, eds. LC 77-84250. (Lost Race & Adult Fantasy Ser.). 1978. reprint ed. lib. bdg. 23.95 (*0-405-10996-2*) Ayer.

Linklater, Kristin. Freeing the Natural Voice. LC 75-28172. (Illus.). 224p. (C). 1985. pap. 19.95 (*0-89676-071-5*) Drama Bk.

Linklater, Peter, ed. Education & the World of Work: Positive Partnerships. 220p. 1987. 95.00 (*0-335-15602-9*, Open Univ Pr) Taylor & Francis.

Linklater, Richard. Dazed & Confused. LC 93-868. (Illus.). 160p. (Orig.). 1993. pap. 13.95 (*0-312-09466-3*) St Martin.

— Slacker. 1992. pap. 14.95 (*0-312-07797-1*) St Martin.

An Asterisk (*) at the beginning of an entry indicates that the title is appearing in BIP for the first time.

Linkletter, Art. Kids Say the Darndest Things. LC 54-11661. (Illus.). 262p. (YA). (gr. 7 up). 1977. reprint ed. pap. 3.50 (*0-89559-010-7*) Green Hill.

Linkletter, Eve. Collin-O. LC 84-52307. (Illus.). 183p. (Orig.). 1985. 8.95 (*0-931683-02-5*, Pub. by Oracle Bks); pap. 4.95 (*0-931683-00-9*, Pub. by Oracle Bks) Sci Fict & Fant Prodns.

Linkman, Audrey. The Victorians: A Photographic Portrait. (Illus.). 192p. 1993. 39.95 (*1-85043-738-6*, Pub. by I B Tauris UK) St Martin.

Linko, P., et al, eds. Extrusion Cooking. LC 89-83945. (Illus.). 471p. 1989. 99.00 (*0-913250-67-8*) Am Assn Cereal Chem.

— Food Process Engineering: Vol. 1: Food Processing Systems. (Illus.). xii, 981p. 1980. 255.75 (*0-85334-896-0*, Pub. by Elsevier Applied Sci UK) Elsevier.

— Food Process Engineering: Volume 2: Enzyme Engineering in Food Processing. (Illus.). vii, 328p. 1980. 93.75 (*0-85334-897-9*, Pub. by Elsevier Applied Sci UK) Elsevier.

Linkon, Neal. The Blade. Van Treese, James B., ed. 299p. 1993. pap. 9.95 (*1-56901-097-8*) NW Pub.

Linkov, V. & Saakyants, A. Lev Tolstoi: His Life & Work. 272p. (C). 1979. 30.00 (*0-317-92433-8*, Pub. by Collets UK) Pro-Am Music.

Linkow, Leonard I. Implant Dentistry Today: A Multidisciplinary Approach, 3 vols. 1624p. 1990. text ed. 665.00 (*1-57235-001-6*) Piccin NY.

***Links, Bo.** Follow the Wind. 1995. 21.00 (*0-671-51058-4*) S&S Trade.

***Links, J. G.** Canaletto. rev. ed. (Illus.). 240p. (C). 1994. reprint ed. 49.95 (*0-7148-3170-0*, Pub. by Phaidon Press UK) Chronicle Bks.

— Venice for Pleasure. 4th rev. ed. (Illus.). 272p. 1991. pap. 12.95 (*1-55921-048-6*) Moyer Bell.

— Venice for Pleasure. 5th ed. (Illus.). 272p. 1995. pap. 14.95 (*1-55921-143-1*) Moyer Bell.

Links, J. G. & Baetjer, Katherine. Canaletto. (Illus.). 384p. 1990. 45.00 (*0-8109-3155-9*, Abrams); pap. 35.00 (*0-87099-561-8*, Abrams) Metro Mus Art.

Links, J. G., ed. see Constable, W. G.

Links, J. G., ed. see Ruskin, John.

Links, Marty. There's No Such Thing As Too Much Love. LC 83-71146. (Illus.). 1984. 5.95 (*0-915696-84-3*) Determined Prods.

— Yes I Can: Yes I Did. Lins, Barbara, ed. (Illus.). 32p. (Orig.). (J). (ps). 1990. pap. write for info. (*1-878079-00-X*) Arts Pubns.

Links, Marty & Knight, Marilyn. Yes I Can. (Illus.). (J). 1990. 4.95 (*0-685-57229-3*) Arts Pubns.

Links, Marty & Linse, Barbara. Love the Earth: An Ecology Resource Book. (Illus.). (J). 1991. 5.95 (*1-878079-01-8*); 4.95 (*0-685-59046-1*) Arts Pubns.

***Links, Paul S., ed.** Clinical Assessment & Management of Severe Personality Disorders. (Clinical Practice Ser.: No. 35). 1995. boxed 33.00 (*0-88048-488-8*, 8488) Am Psychiatric.

— Family Environment & Borderline Personality Disorder. LC 89-18574. (Progress in Psychiatry Ser.). 160p. 1990. text ed. 25.00 (*0-88048-188-9*) Am Psychiatric.

Links Staff, jt. auth. see Borton, Brett.

***Linksman, Ricki.** How to Solve Your Child's Reading Problems. 292p. 1995. pap. 12.95 (*0-8065-1618-6*, Citadel Pr) Carol Pub Group.

— Solving Your Child's Reading Problems. Date not set. pap. write for info. (*0-614-01893-5*, Citadel Pr) Carol Pub Group.

Linksman, Ricki, jt. auth. see Scotti, Juliet.

Linkugel, Wil A. & Solomon, Martha. Anna Howard Shaw: Suffrage Orator & Social Reformer. LC 90-38414. (Great American Orators: Critical Studies, Speeches & Sources: No. 10). 256p. 1990. text ed. 49.95 (*0-313-26345-0*, LKA, Greenwood Pr) Greenwood.

Linkwitz, K. & Hangleiter, U., eds. High Precision Navigation. (Illus.). 650p. 1989. 104.00 (*0-387-50921-6*) Spr-Verlag.

Linkwitz, K., et al, eds. Applications of Geodesy to Engineering. LC 93-34455. (International Association of Geodesy Symposia Ser.: No. 108). 448p. 1993. pap. 136.00 (*0-387-56233-8*) Spr-Verlag.

Linky, Donald, ed. The New Jersey Directory: The Insider Guide to New Jersey Leaders, 1992-1993 Edition. 456p. 1992. pap. 86.00 (*1-879171-00-7*) Joshua Comns.

— The New Jersey Directory, 1993-94: The Insider Guide to New Jersey Leaders. 3rd ed. 486p. pap. 86.00 (*1-879171-02-3*) Joshua Comns.

Linl, Arthur S., ed. see Wilson, Woodrow.

Linley, David. Classical Furniture. LC 93-603. (Illus.). 1993. 60.00 (*0-8109-3188-5*) Abrams.

Linley, Eliza, jt. ed. see Welch, Marni.

Linley, John. The Georgia Catalog, Historic American Buildings Survey: A Guide to the Architecture of the State. LC 81-19856. (Wormsloe Foundation Publications Ser.: No. 15). (Illus.). 432p. 1982. 34.95 (*0-8203-0613-4*); pap. 19.95 (*0-8203-0614-2*) U of Ga Pr.

Linley, Mike. The Frog & the Toad: Masters of Land & Water. Stefoff, Rebecca, ed. LC 92-10246. (Wildlife Survival Library). (Illus.). 31p. (J). (gr. 3-6). 1992. lib. bdg. 17.26 (*1-56074-050-7*) Garrett Ed Corp.

— The Lizard in the Jungle. LC 87-42612. (Animal Habitats Ser.). (Illus.). 32p. (J). (gr. 4-6). 1988. lib. bdg. 17.27 (*1-55532-303-0*) Gareth Stevens Inc.

— The Penguin: The Fastest Flightless Birds. Stefoff, Rebecca, ed. LC 92-10245. (Wildlife Survival Library). (Illus.). 31p. (J). (gr. 3-6). 1992. lib. bdg. 17.26 (*1-56074-052-3*) Garrett Ed Corp.

— The Snake: Smooth Scaly & Successful. Stefoff, Rebecca, ed. LC 92-10248. (Wildlife Survival Library). (Illus.). 32p. (J). (gr. 3-6). 1992. lib. bdg. 17.26 (*1-56074-053-1*) Garrett Ed Corp.

— The Snake in the Grass. LC 89-4621. (Animal Habitats Ser.). (Illus.). 32p. (J). (gr. 4-6). 1989. lib. bdg. 17.27 (*0-8368-0118-0*) Gareth Stevens Inc.

— Snakes. LC 91-8558. (Weird & Wonderful Ser.). 32p. (J). (gr. 2-5). 1993. 14.95 (*1-56847-006-1*) Thomson Lrning.

— Snakes. (Weird & Wonderful Ser.). (Illus.). 32p. (J). (gr. 2-5). 1995. reprint ed. pap. 5.95 (*1-56847-304-4*) Thomson Lrning.

Linley, Neil, ed. see At-Tayyib, Ibn.

***Linmark, R. Zamora.** Rolling the R's. LC 94-75595. 130p. 1995. 19.95 (*1-885030-04-5*) Kaya Prod.

Linn, Beth. The Niche Series. (Illus.). 48p. 1991. pap. 16.95 (*0-89822-066-1*) Visual Studies.

Linn, Brian M. The U. S. Army & Counterinsurgency in the Philippine War, 1899-1902. LC 88-20741. (Illus.). xviii, 258p. (C). 1989. 39.95 (*0-8078-1834-8*) U of NC Pr.

— The United States Army & Counterinsurgency in the Philippine War, 1899-1902. LC 88-20741. (Illus.). reprint ed. pap. 77.60 (*0-7837-9038-4*, 2049789) Bks Demand.

Linn, Christopher. The Everglades: Exploring the Unknown. LC 75-23414. (Illus.). 32p. (J). (gr. 5-10). 1976. lib. bdg. 10.79 (*0-89375-006-9*) Troll Assocs.

Linn, D. M., ed. see Soil Science Society of America, Division S-3 Staff.

Linn, Dennis & Linn, Matthew. Healing Life's Hurts: Healing Memories Through the Five Stages of Forgiveness. LC 77-14794. 324p. 1978. pap. 8.95 (*0-8091-2059-3*) Paulist Pr.

Linn, Dennis, jt. auth. see Linn, Matthew.

Linn, Dennis, et al. Belonging: Bonds of Healing & Recovery. LC 92-29855. 288p. 1993. pap. 9.95 (*0-8091-3365-2*) Paulist Pr.

— Good Goats: Healing Our Image of God. LC 93-41067. 1994. pap. 11.95 (*0-8091-3463-2*) Paulist Pr.

— Healing the Greatest Hurt: Healing Grief & the Family Tree. LC 85-60407. 258p. (Orig.). 1985. pap. 8.95 (*0-8091-2714-8*) Paulist Pr.

— Praying with One Another for Healing. 1984. pap. 5.95 (*0-8091-2619-2*) Paulist Pr.

— Sleeping with Bread: Holding What Gives You Life. LC 95-2305. (Illus.). 80p. (Orig.). 1995. pap. 9.95 (*0-8091-3579-5*) Paulist Pr.

Linn-Desmond, Nancy. Men Who Hate Women & the Women Who Hate Them: The Masochistic Art of Dating. (Illus.). 160p. 1992. pap. 4.50 (*0-8216-2518-7*, Carol Paperbacks) Carol Pub Group.

Linn, Don. Detail & Scale, Vol. 28, Av-8 Harrier, Part 1. (Illus.). 72p. 1987. pap. 10.95 (*0-8306-8038-1*, 25038) TAB Bks.

— F-18 Hornet Developmental & Early Production. (Detail & Scale Ser.: Vol. 6). (Illus.). 72p. 1982. pap. 8.95 (*0-8168-5016-X*, 25016, TAB-Aero) TAB Bks.

— F4F Wildcat in Action. (Aircraft in Action Ser.). (Illus.). 50p. 1988. pap. 8.95 (*0-89747-200-4*) Squad Sig Pubns.

— MiG-21 Fishbed in Action. (Aircraft in Action Ser.). (Illus.). 50p. 1993. pap. 8.95 (*0-89747-290-X*, 1131) Squad Sig Pubns.

Linn, Ed. Hitter: Life & Turmoils of Ted Williams. 1994. pap. 12.95 (*0-15-600091-1*) HarBrace.

— Hitter: The Life & Turmoils of Ted Williams. LC 93-42460. 1993. 23.95 (*0-15-193100-3*, Harvest Bks) HarBrace.

Linn, Ed & Durslag, Mel. The One Hundred Million Dollar Game. 320p. 1985. 16.95 (*0-671-47054-X*) S&S Trade.

Linn, Ed, jt. auth. see Veeck, Bill.

Linn, Elbridge B. That They May All Be One. 1969. 4.50 (*0-88027-020-9*) Firm Foun Pub.

Linn, Emily, tr. see Sheffer, Susannah, ed.

Linn, Erin. Children Are Not Paper Dolls: A Visit with Bereaved Siblings. (Illus.). 121p. (Orig.). (J). (gr. k-8). 1982. pap. 8.95 (*0-9614636-0-0*) Pub Mark.

— I Know Just How You Feel... Avoiding the Cliches of Grief. Erickson, Claire L., ed. LC 85-90509. (Illus.). 128p. (Orig.). 1986. pap. 7.00 (*0-9614636-1-9*) Pub Mark.

— One Hundred Fifty Facts about Grieving Children. 96p. (Orig.). 1990. pap. 6.00 (*0-9614636-3-5*) Pub Mark.

— Premonitions, Visitations & Dreams of the Bereaved. Saulisbury, Jo, ed. (Orig.). 1991. pap. 6.95 (*0-9614636-4-3*) Pub Mark.

Linn, Henry H. Safeguarding School Funds. LC 76-176997. (Columbia University. Teachers College. Contributions to Education Ser.: No. 387). reprint ed. 22.50 (*0-404-55387-7*) AMS Pr.

Linn, Ian. Application Refused: Employment Vetting by the State. 96p. (C). 1991. pap. text ed. 25.00 (*0-900137-33-9*, Pub. by NCCL UK) St Mut.

Linn, James R. The Little Green Hummingbird. Huston, Dwayne L., ed. LC 92-75969. (Illus.). 44p. (J). (gr. 3). 1993. pap. 7.98 (*1-882798-01-5*) Erth & Sky Pub.

Linn, Jan. What Ministers Wish Church Members Knew. LC 92-32944. 144p. (Orig.). 1993. pap. 12.99 (*0-8272-4230-1*) Chalice Pr.

Linn, Jan G. Living Inside Out: Learning How to Pray the Serenity Prayer. 176p. (Orig.). Date not set. pap. 9.99 (*0-8272-2123-1*) Chalice Pr.

— What Church Members Wish Ministers Knew. 160p. (Orig.). 1995. pap. 12.99 (*0-8272-4234-4*) Chalice Pr.

Linn, Jo W. Abstracts of the Minutes of the Court of Pleas & Quarter Sessions, Rowan Co., N.C., 1753-1762. 177p. 1978. 30.00 (*0-918470-02-1*) J W Linn.

— Abstracts of the Minutes of the Court of Pleas & Quarter Sessions, Rowan Co., N.C., 1763-1774. 208p. 1979. 30.00 (*0-918470-03-X*) J W Linn.

— Abstracts of the Minutes of the Court of Pleas & Quarter Sessions, Rowan County, N.C., 1775-1789. LC 81-84591. 250p. 1982. 35.00 (*0-918470-13-7*) J W Linn.

— Abstracts of the Wills & Estates Records of Rowan County, N.C., 1753-1805 & Tax Lists of 1759-1778. 216p. 1980. 30.00 (*0-918470-04-8*) J W Linn.

— Ancestry of Moore-Rowan Families with Related Lines of Fleming, Renick, Bosley, Green, Girault, Beatty, Reading, Armitage, Royston, Rapelje. LC 94-73608. (Illus.). 185p. 1995. pap. 25.00 (*0-918470-23-4*) J W Linn.

— Ancestry of Sims-Hallman Families with Related Lines of Jernigan, Boon, Bryan. LC 94-73561. (Illus.). 148p. 1995. pap. 25.00 (*0-918470-22-6*) J W Linn.

— Census of Rowan County, North Carolina, 1850: A Genealogical Compilation of the Schedules. LC 91-77702. (Illus.). 158p. 1992. lib. bdg. 28.00 (*0-918470-20-X*); pap. 26.00 (*0-918470-21-8*) J W Linn.

— The Diary of Elizabeth Dick Lindsay 1831-1861: Guilford County, N. C. (Illus.). 110p. 1975. 18.50 (*0-918470-10-2*) J W Linn.

— Drake, Arrington, White, Turner, Linn, Brown: And Two Dozen Related Southern Lines. LC 84-81760. (Illus.). 1984. 35.00 (*0-918470-17-X*) J W Linn.

— Gray Family & Allied Lines: Bowman, Lindsay, Millis, Disk, Peebles, Wiley, Shannon, Lamar, McGee. 607p. 1994. reprint ed. lib. bdg. 85.00 (*0-8328-4322-9*); reprint ed. pap. 75.00 (*0-8328-4323-7*) Higginson Bk Co.

— A Holmes Family of Rowan & Davidson Counties, NC. LC 88-91003. (Illus.). 316p. 1988. 25.00 (*0-918470-19-6*) J W Linn.

— People Named Hanes. LC 80-52426. (Illus.). 281p. 1980. 25.00 (*0-918470-12-9*) J W Linn.

— Rowan County, N. C., Tax List 1815. LC 87-92111. (Illus.). 1987. pap. 12.00 (*0-918470-18-8*) J W Linn.

— Surry County, North Carolina, Wills, 1771-1827: Annotated Genealogical Abstracts. 215p. 1992. 25.00 (*0-8063-1346-3*, 3380) Genealog Pub.

Linn, Jo W. & Gray, Gordon. The Ancestry of Nathalie Fontaine Lyons: Lyons, Nunes Miranda, Luria, Cohen, Hart, Clayland, Maffitt, Beach. LC 81-84236. (Illus.). 265p. 1981. 25.00 (*0-918470-14-5*) J W Linn.

Linn, Johannes F., jt. auth. see Bahl, Roy W.

Linn, Johannes F., jt. auth. see Bhattacharya, Amar.

Linn, John B. Annals of Buffalo Valley, Pennsylvania, 1755-1855. (Illus.). 630p. 1989. reprint ed. pap. 30.00 (*1-55613-206-9*) Heritage Bk.

— History of Centre & Clinton Counties, Pennsylvania. (Illus.). 672p. 1994. reprint ed. lib. bdg. 69.50 (*0-8328-3621-4*) Higginson Bk Co.

Linn, John B. & Egle, William H. Lists of Officers of the Colonies on the Delaware & the Province of Pennsylvania, 1614-1776. 221p. 1992. reprint ed. pap. 25.00 (*0-685-66230-6*, 9284) Clearfield Co.

— Muster Rolls of the Pennsylvania Volunteers in the War of 1812-1814. (Pennsylvania Archives, Second Ser.: Vol. XII, 1890). 560p. 1994. pap. 39.95 (*0-614-00889-1*, 3385) Clearfield Co.

— Pennsylvania Marriages Prior to 1790: Names of Persons for Whom Marriage Licenses Were Issued in the Province of Pennsylvania Previous to 1790. rev. ed. LC 75-37471. 376p. 1994. reprint ed. 25.00 (*0-8063-0709-9*, 3390) Genealog Pub.

— Persons Naturalized in the Province of Pennsylvania, 1740-1773. 139p. 1991. reprint ed. 18.50 (*0-685-60428-4*, 3395) Clearfield Co.

— Record of Pennsylvania Marriages Prior to 1810, 2 vols. 1987. reprint ed. 75.00 (*0-8063-0214-3*, 3400) Genealog Pub.

Linn, John J. Reminiscences of Fifty Years in Texas. LC 86-60968. (Illus.). 397p. 1986. reprint ed. 21.95 (*0-938349-00-7*) State House Pr.

Linn, Joseph. Behold the Man: Exalting the Christ of Easter. 1989. 5.25 (*0-8341-9204-7*, ME-40); audio 10.98 (*0-685-68617-5*, BCTA-9112C) Lillenas.

— Bound for the Kingdom. 1992. 6.50 (*0-8341-9279-9*, MB-636); audio 15.98 (*0-685-71337-7*, TA-9139C); audio 85.00 (*0-685-71339-3*, MU-9139C); cd-rom 85.00 (*0-685-71340-7*, MU-9139T); 7.00 (*0-685-71338-5*, L-9139C) Lillenas.

— Can You Imagine? (J). 1983. 5.95 (*0-8341-9273-X*, BCMB-519); ring bd. 0.75 (*0-685-68207-2*, MU-728); audio 12.98 (*0-685-68208-0*, TA-9045C) Lillenas.

— Find Us Faithful. 1988. spiral bd. 6.50 (*0-8341-9162-8*, MB-598) Lillenas.

— Glorybound. 1985. 6.50 (*0-8341-9286-1*, MB-552) Lillenas.

— Heart Songs. 1991. 5.95 (*0-8341-9008-7*, MB-632); audio 12.98 (*0-685-68446-5*, TA-9137C); audio 60.00 (*0-685-68448-2*, MU-9137C); cd-rom 60.00 (*0-685-68449-0*, MU-9137T); 6.00 (*0-685-68447-4*, L-9137C) Lillenas.

— Heaven's Child: Unto Us a Son Is Given. 1989. 5.95 (*0-685-68457-1*, MC-70); audio 10.98 (*0-685-68458-X*, TA-9117C) Lillenas.

— Highest Praise. 1982. 5.95 (*0-685-74878-2*, MB-513) Lillenas.

— Ladies Praise. 1979. 5.25 (*0-8341-9126-1*, MB-469) Lillenas.

— Lift up a Song. 1984. 5.25 (*0-685-74881-2*, MB-533) Lillenas.

— Little Child...Mighty King. 1983. 5.25 (*0-685-68506-3*, MC-51); audio 10.98 (*0-685-68507-1*, TA-9054C) Lillenas.

Linn, Joseph, contrib. Call Him Jesus. 1987. 5.25 (*0-685-68478-4*, MC-62); audio 10.98 (*0-685-68479-2*, TA-9084C) Lillenas.

— Instrumental Solotrax, Vol. 1: Violin, Flute. 1986. 11.95 (*0-8341-9223-3*, MB-534); digital audio 10.98 (*0-685-68355-9*, TA-9081C) Lillenas.

— Instrumental Solotrax, Vol. 2: B Flat Trumpet. 1987. 10.95 (*0-8341-9263-2*, MB-572); audio 10.98 (*0-685-68357-5*, TA-9082C) Lillenas.

— Instrumental Solotrax, Vol. 3: Trombone. 1989. 10.95 (*0-685-68358-3*, BCMB-603); audio 10.98 (*0-685-69273-6*, TA-9109C) Lillenas.

— Instrumental Solotrax, Vol. 4: E Flat Alto Saxophone. 1989. 10.95 (*0-685-69274-4*, MB-604); audio 10.98 (*0-685-69275-2*, TA-9110C) Lillenas.

— A Living Hope. 1976. 4.95 (*0-685-68637-X*, ME-22) Lillenas.

— Promise of Peace. 1985. 5.25 (*0-685-68488-1*, MC-54); digital audio 10.98 (*0-685-68489-X*, TA-9061C) Lillenas.

Linn, Joseph, des. Lift High the Lord: Songs & Sketches for Contemporary Praise. 1993. 5.95 (*0-8341-9028-1*, MB-678); digital audio 12.98 (*0-685-72855-2*, TA-9164C); digital audio 60.00 (*0-685-72857-9*, MU-9164C); digital audio 60.00 (*0-685-72860-9*, MU-9164S); cd-rom 60.00 (*0-685-72858-7*, MU-9164T); 6.00 (*0-685-72856-0*, L-9164C); 172.00 (*0-685-72859-5*, OR-9164) Lillenas.

— Soldiers of the Cross: Flexible Voicings for Men's Choir or Ensemble. 1994. 5.95 (*0-8341-9107-5*, MB-685) Lillenas.

— Soldiers of the Cross: Flexible Voicings for Men's Choir or Ensemble. 1994. digital audio 12.98 (*0-614-01734-3*, TA-9170C) Lillenas.

— Soldiers of the Cross: Flexible Voicings for Men's Choir or Ensemble. 1994. digital audio 60.00 (*0-614-01735-1*, MU-9170C) Lillenas.

— Soldiers of the Cross: Flexible Voicings for Men's Choir or Ensemble. 1994. cd-rom 60.00 (*0-614-01736-X*, MU-9170T) Lillenas.

— Soldiers of the Cross: Flexible Voicings for Men's Choir or Ensemble. suppl. ed. 1994. 6.00 (*0-614-01737-8*, L-9170C) Lillenas.

Linn, Joseph, jt. auth. see Fettke, Tom.

Linn, Julius, intro. Guide to UAB Medical Center: And Other Health Related Resources Available to the General Public. 511p. 1988. 5.00 (*0-685-22958-0*) UAB Med Ctr.

Linn, Karen. That Half-Barbaric Twang: The Banjo in American Popular Culture. (Music in American Life Ser.). (Illus.). 208p. 1991. 29.95 (*0-252-01780-3*) U of Ill Pr.

— That Half-Barbaric Twang: The Banjo in American Popular Culture. 1994. pap. 12.95 (*0-252-06433-X*) U of Ill Pr.

Linn, Louis. Handbook of Hospital Psychiatry: A Practical Guide to Therapy. LC 55-8237. 1955. pap. text ed. 24.95 (*0-8236-8069-X*, 22300) Intl Univs Pr.

Linn, Louis, ed. Frontiers in General Hospital Psychiatry. LC 61-10147. 483p. 1961. text ed. 52.50 (*0-8236-2080-8*); pap. text ed. 24.95 (*0-8236-8055-X*, 22080) Intl Univs Pr.

Linn, Marcia C., jt. auth. see Clancy, Michael J.

Linn, Marcia C., jt. ed. see Hyde, Janet S.

Linn, Mary J., et al. Healing the Dying. LC 79-53111. 128p. 1979. pap. 6.95 (*0-8091-2212-X*) Paulist Pr.

Linn, Matthew & Linn, Dennis. Healing of Memories: Prayers & Confession-Steps to Inner Healing. LC 74-17697. 112p. (Orig.). 1974. pap. 4.95 (*0-8091-1854-8*) Paulist Pr.

Linn, Matthew, jt. auth. see Linn, Dennis.

Linn, Matthew, et al. Healing Spiritual Abuse & Religious Addiction. LC 94-13408. 160p. 1994. pap. 8.95 (*0-8091-3488-8*) Paulist Pr.

— Healing the Eight Stages of Life. 272p. 1988. pap. 8.95 (*0-8091-2980-9*) Paulist Pr.

— Prayer Course for Healing Life's Hurts: Book. 128p. 1983. pap. 8.95 (*0-8091-2522-6*) Paulist Pr.

Linn, Michael D. & Cleary, Linda M. Linguistics for Teachers. LC 92-26665. 1993. pap. text ed. write for info. (*0-07-037946-7*) McGraw.

Linn, Michael D., jt. auth. see Allen, Harold B.

Linn, Michael D., jt. auth. see Allen, Harold E.

***Linn, Nancy.** Early Photography. (Illus.). 64p. (Orig.). 1994. pap. 6.00 (*0-9613812-0-5*) A White Pub.

— Madonna & Child. (Illus.). 160p. 1984. pap. 5.00 (*0-9613812-1-3*) A White Pub.

Linn, R. H. Journeys in the Night. 1994. 16.95 (*0-533-10680-X*) Vantage.

Linn, Richard J. & Uyar, M. Umit, eds. Conformance Testing Methodologies & Architecture for OSI Protocols. LC 93-45664. 512p. 1994. text ed. 60.00 (*0-8186-5352-3*, 5352) IEEE Comp Soc.

Linn, Robert L. Staying Thin. 1982. pap. 2.95 (*0-89083-916-6*) Zebra.

Linn, Robert L., ed. Educational Measurement. LC 93-16503. (American Council on Education-Oryx Press Series on Higher Education). (Illus.). 624p. 1988. boxed 65.00 (*0-89774-802-6*) Oryx Pr.

— Educational Measurement. 3rd ed. (Ace-Macmillan Series on Higher Education). 784p. 1988. write for info. (*0-318-41133-4*) Macmillan.

— Intelligence: Measurement, Theory, & Public Policy--Proceedings of a Symposium in Honor of Lloyd G. Humphreys. 240p. 1989. 24.95 (*0-252-01535-5*) U of Ill Pr.

Linn, Robert L. & Gronlund, Norman E. Measurement & Assessment in Teaching. 7th ed. LC 94-9006. 576p. (C). 1994. write for info. (*0-02-348261-3*) Macmillan.

Linn, Robert L. & Stuart, Sandra L. The Last Chance Diet. 1976. 10.00 (*0-8184-0239-3*) Carol Pub Group.

Linn, Robert L., jt. auth. see Gronlund, Norman E.

Linn, Rolf N. Schillers Junge Idealisten. LC 71-182546. (University of California Publications in Social Welfare: Vol. 106). 96p. reprint ed. pap. 27.40 (*0-317-29557-8*, 2021258) Bks Demand.

***Linn, Ruth.** Conscience at War: The Israeli Soldier As a Moral Critic. (SUNY Series in Israeli Studies). 224p. (C). 1996. text ed. 54.50x (*0-7914-2777-3*); pap. text ed. 17.95x (*0-7914-2778-1*) State U NY Pr.

— Not Shooting & Not Crying: Psychological Inquiry into Moral Disobedience. LC 88-24720. (Contributions in Military Studies: No. 85). 174p. 1989. text ed. 49.95 (*0-313-26497-X*, LNS, Greenwood Pr) Greenwood.

An Asterisk (*) at the beginning of an entry indicates that the title is appearing in BIP for the first time.

Linn, S. L., et al. Monte Carlo Simulation in High Energy & Nuclear Physics: Proceedings of the 93 International Conference. 400p. 1994. text ed. 112.00 (*981-02-1621-1*) World Scientific Pub.

Linn, S. P., comp. Golden Gleams of Thought. LC 74-121925. (Granger Index Reprint Ser.). 1977. 21.95 (*0-8369-6166-8*) Ayer.

Linn, Stuart M. & Roberts, Richard J., eds. Nucleases. LC 85-9653. (Cold Spring Harbor Monograph Ser.: No. 14). 402p. reprint ed. pap. 114.60 (*0-7837-2004-1*, 2042278) Bks Demand.

Linn, W., jt. auth. see Drury, Kitty.

Linn, W. A. Story of Mormonism. 637p. 1993. reprint ed. lib. bdg. 109.00 (*0-7812-5311-X*) Rprt Serv.

Linn, W. A., et al. The Mormons & Mormonism, 15 vols. 1973. lib. bdg. 50.00 (*0-8490-0675-9*) Gordon Pr.

***Linn-Watson, TerriAnn.** Radiographic Pathology. LC 95-13455. (Illus.). 256p. 1995. text ed. write for info. (*0-7216-4129-6*) Saunders.

Linn, William A. Horace Greeley, Founder & Editor of the New York Tribune. 1977. 18.95 (*0-8369-7115-9*, 7949) Ayer.

Linnaeus, Carl. Bibliotheca Botanica. 1968. 12.00 (*0-934454-13-2*) Lubrecht & Cramer.
— Hortus Cliffortianus. (Illus.). 1968. reprint ed. 162.50 (*3-7682-0543-6*) Lubrecht & Cramer.
— Mantissa Plantarum: 1767-71, 2 Vols. in 1. 1960. 97.50 (*3-7682-0037-X*) Lubrecht & Cramer.
— Miscellaneous Tracts Relating to Natural History, Husbandry, & Physick: Calender of Flora Is Added. Egerton, Frank N., 3rd, ed. LC 77-74237. (History of Ecology Ser.). 1978. reprint ed. lib. bdg. 31.95 (*0-405-10406-5*) Ayer.
— Philosophia Botanica. (Illus.). 1966. reprint ed. 97.50 (*3-7682-0350-6*) Lubrecht & Cramer.
— Select Dissertations from the Amoenitates Academicae: Supplement to Mr. Stillingfleet's Tracts, Relating Natural History. Egerton, Frank N., 3rd, ed. Brand, F. J., tr. LC 77-74238. (History of Ecology Ser.). 1978. reprint ed. lib. bdg. 42.95 (*0-405-10407-3*) Ayer.
— Systema Naturae: Tomus II, Vegetabilia. 10th ed. 1964. reprint ed. 112.50 (*3-7682-0219-4*) Lubrecht & Cramer.
— Systema Naturae 1735. 30p. 1964. reprint ed. text ed. 44.00 (*90-6004-104-6*, Pub. by B De Graaf NE) Coronet Bks.

Linnaeus, Carl, ed. see Artedi, P.

Linnainmaa, S., jt. ed. see Jaakkola, H.

Linnard, W. Forestry & Wood Dictionary: Russian-English. 109p. 1966. 49.95 (*0-8288-6717-8*, M-9709) Fr & Eur.

Linnard, W., ed. Russian-English Forestry & Wood Dictionary. 109p. (C). 1966. 30.00 (*0-00-000025-6*) CAB Intl.

Linnard, W., jt. auth. see Ussovsky, B. N.

Linnartz, Jean-Paul. Narrowband Land-Mobile Radio Networks. LC 92-32244. (Telecommunications Ser.). 445p. (C). 1993. text ed. 88.00 (*0-89006-645-0*) Artech Hse.

Linne, jt. auth. see Clerc.

Linne, Eric B., jt. ed. see Lerman, Dan.

Linne, H. Key Factors for Industrial Partnership in European Community Programmes, EUR 13991. 90p. 1992. pap. 10.00 (*92-826-3270-9*, CD-NA-13991-EN-C, Pub. by Europ Com) UNIPUB.

Linne, Jean J. Basic Techniques for the Medical Laboratory. 2nd ed. (Illus.). 1979. text ed. 39.95 (*0-07-037948-3*) McGraw.

Linne, Jean J. & Ringsrud. Basic Techniques in Clinical Laboratory Science. 3rd ed. 580p. 1991. 32.95 (*0-8016-2864-4*) Mosby Yr Bk.

Linne, Olga, jt. ed. see Hamelink, Cees J.

Linnea. A Doll's House & Hedda Gabler (Ibsen) (Book Notes Ser.). (J). (gr. 9-12). 1985. pap. 2.95 (*0-8120-3511-9*) Barron.
— Romeo & Juliet (Shakespeare) (Book Notes Ser.). (C). 1984. pap. 2.95 (*0-8120-3440-6*) Barron.

***Linnea, Ann.** Deep Water Passage. LC 94-48635. 1995. 22.95 (*0-316-52683-5*) Little.

Linnea, Sharon. Raoul Wallenberg: The Man Who Stopped Death. (Illus.). 168p. (YA). (gr. 10 up). 1993. 17.95 (*0-8276-0440-8*); pap. 9.95 (*0-8276-0448-3*) JPS Phila.

Linnegar, Sidney & Hewitt, Jennifer. Irises. (Wisley Ser.). (Illus.). 64p. 1991. pap. 5.95 (*0-304-31853-1*, Pub. by Cassell UK) Sterling.

Linnekin, Jocelyn. Sacred Queens & Women of Consequence: Rank, Gender, & Colonialism in the Hawaiian Islands. (Women & Culture Ser.). (Illus.). 296p. 1990. text ed. 39.50 (*0-472-09423-8*); pap. text ed. 16.95 (*0-472-06423-1*) U of Mich Pr.

Linnekin, Jocelyn & Poyer, Lin, eds. Cultural Identity & Ethnicity in the Pacific. LC 89-5228. 336p. 1990. text ed. 35.00 (*0-8248-1208-5*) UH Pr.

Linnekin, Richard. Eighty Knots to Mach 2: Forty-Five Years in the Cockpit. LC 90-28950. (Illus.). 404p. 1991. 28.95 (*1-55750-500-4*) Naval Inst Pr.

Linnell, Andrew & Auer, Varvara. The Dance of the Elves. (Illus.). 32p. (Orig.). (J). (ps). 1984. pap. 13.50 (*0-936132-68-X*) Merc Pr NY.

Linnell, Dennis. SAA Handbook. 1990. pap. 24.95 (*0-201-51786-8*) Addison-Wesley.

Linnell, Naomi, jt. auth. see Postgate, Oliver.

Linneman, R. Shirt Sleeve Approach to Long Range Planning for the Smaller Growing Corporation. 1980. text ed. 53.33 (*0-13-808972-8*) P-H.

Linneman, Robert E. Making Niche Marketing Work: How to Grow Bigger by Acting Smaller. 1991. text ed. 22.95 (*0-07-037954-8*) McGraw.
— Making Niche Marketing Work: How to Grow Bigger by Acting Smaller. 1992. pap. text ed. 14.95 (*0-07-037971-8*) McGraw.

***Linneman, Robert E. & Stanton, John L.** Marketing Planning in a Total Quality Environment. LC 94-48363. (Illus.). 461p. 1995. lib. bdg. 49.95 (*1-56024-938-2*) Haworth Pr.

Linnemann, Eta. Historical Criticism of the Bible: Methodology or Ideology? LC 90-34958. 176p. (Orig.). 1990. pap. text ed. 9.99 (*0-8010-5662-4*) Baker Bk.
— Is There a Synoptic Problem? Rethinking the Literary Dependence of the First Three Gospels. Yarbrough, Robert W., tr. LC 92-8555. 208p. 1992. pap. 10.99 (*0-8010-5679-9*) Baker Bk.

Linnemann, Hans. South-South Trade Preferences: The GSTP & Trade in Manufactures. (Illus.). 236p. (C). 1992. text ed. 29.95 (*0-8039-9421-4*) Sage.

Linnemann, Hans, et al, eds. Model of International Relations in Agriculture (MOIRA) Report of Project Group Food for a Growing World Population. (Contributions to Economic Analysis Ser.: Vol. 124). 380p. 1979. 77.00 (*0-444-85169-0*, North Holland) Elsevier.

Linnemann, Russell J., ed. Alain Locke: Reflections on a Modern Renaissance Man. LC 82-7211. xv, 146p. (C). 1982. text ed. 27.50 (*0-8071-1036-1*) La State U Pr.

Linnenkohl, Susan. Basic Nutrition Workbook. 160p. (C). 1993. pap. text ed. 14.95 (*0-8403-8388-6*) Kendall-Hunt.

Linner, John H. Surgery for Morbid Obesity. (Illus.). 275p. 1984. 138.00 (*0-387-90888-9*) Spr-Verlag.

Linner, John H., jt. auth. see Philo, Ron.

***Linner, Rachelle.** City of Silence: Listening to Hiroshima. LC 94-45689. 150p. 1995. 16.95 (*1-57075-014-9*) Orbis Bks.

***Linnert, G. E.** Welding Metallurgy: Fundamentals, Vol. 1. 4th ed. (Illus.). 950p. 1995. 80.00 (*0-87171-457-4*, wM1) Am Welding.
— Welding Metallurgy, Carbon & Alloy Steels: Technology, Vol. 2. 3rd ed. (Illus.). 674p. 1967. 36.00 (*0-686-95605-2*, WM2) Am Welding.

Linnert, Peter. Lexikon Angloamerikanischer und Deutscher Managementbegriffe: Lexicon of Anglo-American & german Management Terminology. (GER.). 1972. 45.00 (*0-8288-6406-3*, M-7286) Fr & Eur.

Linnett, J., jt. auth. see Peacock, T.

Linney, Barbara J., jt. auth. see Linney, George E., Jr.

Linney, George E., Jr. & Linney, Barbara J. Medical Directors: What, Why, How. 44p. (Orig.). (C). 1993. pap. text ed. 20.00 (*0-924674-19-9*) Am Coll Phys Execs.

Linney, Jean A. & Wandersman, Abraham. Prevention Plus III: Assessing Alcohol & Other Drug Prevention Programs at the School & Community Level: A Four-Step Guide to Useful Program Assessment. (Illus.). 461p. (Orig.). (C). 1993. pap. text ed. 50.00 (*0-7881-0085-8*) Diane Pub.

Linney, Romulus. Ambrosio. 1993. 4.75 (*0-8222-1320-6*) Dramatists Play.
— The Captivity of Pixie Shedman. 1981. pap. 4.75 (*0-8222-0180-1*) Dramatists Play.
— Childe Byron. 1981. pap. 4.75 (*0-8222-0201-8*) Dramatists Play.
— The Death of King Philip. 1984. pap. 2.75 (*0-8222-0291-3*) Dramatists Play.
— Democracy. 1976. pap. 4.75 (*0-8222-0299-9*) Dramatists Play.
— Heathen Valley. 1988. pap. 4.75 (*0-8222-0508-4*) Dramatists Play.
— El Hermano. 1981. pap. 2.75 (*0-8222-0355-3*) Dramatists Play.
— Holy Ghosts. 1989. pap. 4.75 (*0-8222-0526-2*) Dramatists Play.
— Juliet - Yancey - April Snow. 1989. pap. 4.75 (*0-8222-0063-5*) Dramatists Play.
— Laughing Stock: Three Short Plays. 1984. pap. 4.75 (*0-8222-0643-9*) Dramatists Play.
— The Love Suicide at Schofield Barracks: Full Length. 1972. pap. 4.75 (*0-8222-0702-8*) Dramatists Play.
— The Love Suicide at Schofield Barracks: One-Act. 1985. pap. 2.75 (*0-8222-0701-X*) Dramatists Play.
— Old Man Joseph & His Family. 1978. pap. 4.75 (*0-8222-0841-5*) Dramatists Play.
— Pops. 65p. 1987. pap. 4.75 (*0-8222-0906-3*) Dramatists Play.
— Romulus Linney, Seventeen Short Plays. LC 92-27781. (Plays for Actors Ser.). 276p. 1992. 14.95 (*1-880399-21-0*) Smith & Kraus.
— Sand Mountain. 1985. pap. 4.75 (*0-8222-0985-3*) Dramatists Play.
— The Sorrows of Frederick. 1976. pap. 4.75 (*0-8222-1058-4*) Dramatists Play.
— The Sorrows of Frederick & Holy Ghosts. LC 76-47904. 1977. pap. 3.95 (*0-15-683848-6*, Harvest Bks) HarBrace.
— Spain. 1994. pap. 4.75 (*0-8222-1376-1*) Dramatists Play.
— Tennessee. 1980. pap. 2.75 (*0-8222-1119-X*) Dramatists Play.
— Three Poets. 1990. pap. 4.75 (*0-8222-1141-6*) Dramatists Play.
— 2. 1993. pap. 4.75 (*0-8222-1486-5*) Dramatists Play.
— Unchanging Love. 1991. pap. 4.75 (*0-8222-1188-2*) Dramatists Play.
— A Woman without a Name. 57p. 1986. pap. 4.75 (*0-8222-1269-2*) Dramatists Play.

Linnik, I. Old Master Paintings in Soviet Museums. (Illus.). 211p. (C). 1989. text ed. 235.00 (*0-569-09217-5*, Pub. by Collets) St Mut.

Linnik, I. V. Dutch Paintings in the Museums of the Soviet Union: Gollandskaia Zhivopis'v Muzeiakh Sovetskogo Soiuza. (Illus.). 520p. (RUS.). 1984. 289.00 (*0-317-57325-X*, Pub. by Collets UK) St Mut.

Linnik, J. V., ed. see Steklov Institute of Mathematics, Academy of Sciences, U. S. S. R. Staff.

Linnik, Jurii V. Dispersion Method in Binary Additive Problems. Schuur, S., tr. LC 63-15660. (Translations of Mathematical Monographs: Vol. 4). 186p. 1990. reprint ed. pap. 55.00 (*0-8218-1554-7*, MMONO-4) Am Math.
— Ergodic Properties of Algebraic Fields. (Ergenbnisse der Mathematik und Ihrer Grenzebiete Ser.: Vol. 45). 1968. 65.00 (*0-387-04101-X*) Spr-Verlag.
— Statistical Problems with Nuisance Parameters. Technica, S., tr. LC 67-30101. (Translations of Mathematical Monographs: Vol. 20). 258p. 1968. 44.00 (*0-8218-1570-9*, MMONO-20) Am Math.

Linnik, Jurii V., ed. Articles on Mathematical Statistics & the Theory of Probability. LC 66-26640. (Proceedings of the Steklov Institute of Mathematics Ser.: No. 79). 259p. 1966. 75.00 (*0-8218-1879-1*, STEKLO-79) Am Math.

Linnik, Jurii V. & Ostrovskii, Iosif V. Decomposition of Random Variables & Vectors. LC 76-51345. (Translations of Mathematical Monographs: Vol. 48). 380p. 1977. 89.00 (*0-8218-1598-9*, MMONO-48) Am Math.

Linnik, Jurii V., ed. see Steklov Institute of Mathematics, Academy of Sciences, U. S. S. R. Staff.

Linnik, P., jt. auth. see Aizerman, M.

Linnik, Y. & Johnson, N. I. Method of Least Squares & Principal Theory of Observations. LC 60-13826. 1961. 157.00 (*0-08-009433-3*, Pub. by Pergamon Repr UK) Franklin.

Linnoila, Markku, jt. ed. see Davidson, Lucy.

Linosay, T. J. Capt. Gougar & His Steamboats. 1987. pap. 5.95 (*0-917914-67-8*) Lindsay Pubns.

Linowes, David F. Managing Growth Through Acquisition. LC 68-31542. 192p. reprint ed. pap. 54.80 (*0-317-09717-2*, 2050394) Bks Demand.
— Privacy in America: Is Your Private Life in the Public Eye? LC 88-20645. 206p. 1989. 19.95 (*0-252-01604-1*) U of Ill Pr.

Linowes, David F., ed. Privatization: Toward More Effective Government--Report of the President's Commission on Privatization. 304p. 1988. pap. 10.95 (*0-252-06058-X*) U of Ill Pr.

Linowitz, Sol M. World Hunger: A Challenge to American Policy. LC 80-85486. (Headline Ser.: No. 252). (Illus.). 64p. 1980. pap. 5.95 (*0-87124-065-3*) Foreign Policy.

Linowtiz, Sol M. & Mayer, Martin. Betrayers of the Profession: Lawyering at the End of the Twentieth Century. LC 93-31995. 320p. 1994. text ed. 25.00 (*0-684-19416-3*, Scribners) S&S Trade.

Linquist, Luann. Secret Lovers. 1991. pap. 12.95 (*0-669-27666-9*) Free Pr.
— Secret Lovers: Affairs Happen - How to Cope. 240p. 1989. text ed. 19.95 (*0-669-19931-1*) Free Pr.

Lins, Barbara, ed. see Links, Marty.

Lins, Charles. The Modula-2 Software Component Library. (Compass International Ser.). (Illus.). xix, 450p. 1989. 43.00 (*0-387-97074-6*) Spr-Verlag.
— The Modula-2 Software Component Library, Vol. 1. (Compass International Ser.). (Illus.). xvi, 312p. 1988. 49.00 (*0-387-96867-9*) Spr-Verlag.
— The Modula-2 Software Component Library, Vol. 2. (Compass International Ser.). (Illus.). xviii, 368p. 1989. 49.00 (*0-387-96939-X*) Spr-Verlag.
— The Modula-2 Software Component Library, Vol. 4. Muchnik, S. S. & Schnupp, P., eds. (Compass International Ser.). (Illus.). xvii, 371p. 1990. 43.00 (*0-387-97255-2*) Spr-Verlag.

Lins, David A., et al. Farmland. LC 81-71618. 340p. (Orig.). 1982. 19.95 (*0-930264-60-6*); 14.95 (*0-930264-57-6*) Century Comm.

Lins, Gerald T., jt. auth. see Lemke, Thomas.

Lins, Osman. Avalovara. Rabassa, Gregory, tr. (Texas Pan American Ser.). 344p. 1990. reprint ed. pap. 14.95 (*0-292-70416-X*) U of Tex Pr.
— The Queen of the Prisons of Greece. Frizzi, Adria, tr. 192p. 1995. pap. 12.95 (*1-56478-056-2*) Dalkey Arch.

Linsalata, Carmine R. Smollett's Hoax: Don Quixote in English. LC 77-181947. (Stanford University. Stanford Studies in Language & Literature: No. 14). reprint ed. 24.00 (*0-404-51824-9*) AMS Pr.

***Linsay, Art.** I Can: Coach Ron Brown's Search for Success. 162p. (Orig.). (YA). 1992. pap. 8.95 (*1-887002-01-4*) Cross Trng.

Linscheid, Adolph. In-Service Improvement of the State Teachers College Faculty: A Study of the Efforts at in-Service Improvement of the Faculties of State Teachers Colleges in the United States. LC 70-176998. (Columbia University. Teachers College. Contributions to Education Ser.: No. 309). reprint ed. 22.50 (*0-404-55309-5*) AMS Pr.

Linscott, Eloise H. Folk Songs of Old New England. 368p. 1993. reprint ed. pap. text ed. 9.95 (*0-486-27827-1*) Dover.

Linscott, Eloise H., ed. Folk Songs of Old New England. 2nd ed. 370p. reprint ed. pap. 105.50 (*0-317-09660-5*, 2010217) Bks Demand.

***Linscott, Gillian.** Easy Day for a Lady. 1995. 19.95 (*0-312-11811-2*) St Martin.
— An Easy Day for a Lady. large type ed. LC 94-39578. 326p. 1995. pap. 18.95 (*0-7862-0362-5*) Thorndike Pr.
— Hanging on the Wire. LC 92-33295. 1992. 17.95 (*0-312-08806-X*) St Martin.
— Hanging on the Wire. large type ed. LC 94-19730. 1995. pap. 17.95 (*0-7862-0309-9*) Thorndike Pr.
— Murder, I Presume. large type ed. (Keating's Choice Ser.). 312p. 1992. 10.97 (*1-85089-428-0*, Pub. by ISIS UK) Transaction Pubs.
— Stage Fright. 192p. 1993. 17.95 (*0-312-09812-X*, Pub. by Thomas Dunne Bks) St Martin.
— Stage Fright. large type ed. LC 94-11736. 1994. 20.95 (*0-7927-2044-X*, Curley Lrg Print); pap. 19.95 (*0-7927-2043-1*, Curley Lrg Print) Chivers N Amer.

Linscott, Robert N., ed. State of Mind. LC 72-8483. (Essay Index Reprint Ser.). 1977. reprint ed. 28.95 (*0-8369-7321-6*) Ayer.

Linscott, Steve & Frame, Randy. Maximum Security. LC 93-41997. 224p. 1994. 12.99 (*0-89107-787-1*) Crossway Bks.

Linscott, Walt A., jt. auth. see Blattner, J. Wray.

Linse, jt. auth. see Yeldin.

Linse, A. R., jt. ed. see Stein, J. K.

Linse, Barbara. The Art of the Mexican Folk. (Illus.). 78p. 1991. text ed. 7.95 (*1-878079-03-4*) Arts Pubns.
— Arts & Crafts for All Seasons. LC 68-57698. (J). (gr. k-6). 1969. pap. 8.99 (*0-8224-0490-7*) Fearon Teach Aids.

Linse, Barbara & Knight, Marilyn. Love the Earth. Dresser, Ginny, ed. (Illus.). 32p. (J). 1991. pap. write for info. (*0-318-68833-6*) Arts Pubns.

Linse, Barbara, jt. auth. see Judd, Dick.

Linse, Barbara, jt. auth. see Links, Marty.

Linse, Barbara B. & Kuska, George, eds. Live Again Our Mission Past: California Missions Through Children's Eyes. (Story of Spanish California through the Missions Ser.). (Illus.). 200p. (YA). (gr. 7-12). 1984. pap. 13.95 (*0-9607458-1-5*) Arts Pubns.

Linse, Barbara B., ed. see Andrews, Janice H.

Linse, Barbara B., ed. see Christensen, Kathy.

Linse, C., tr. see Maffesoli, Michel.

***Linse, Doris.** Woerterbuch der Datentechnik: German-French, French-German. 2nd ed. 394p. (FRE & GER.). 1993. 125.00 (*0-7859-7068-1*) Fr & Eur.

Linsell, Stewart. Hickling Broad. 200p. 1994. 57.00 (*0-86138-072-X*, Pub. by T Dalton UK) St Mut.

***Linsell, Tony.** Anglo-Saxon: Mythology, Migration & Magic. (Illus.). 167p. 1994. 29.95 (*1-898281-09-2*, Pub. by Anglo-Saxon Bks UK) Paul & Co Pubs.

***Linsell, Tony & Partridge, Brian.** Rune Cards. 1994. 19.95 (*0-9516209-7-5*, Pub. by Anglo-Saxon Bks UK) Paul & Co Pubs.

***Linsenman, Bob & Nevala, Steve.** Great Lakes Steelhead: A Guided Tour for Fly-Anglers. (Illus.). (Orig.). 1995. pap. 22.00 (*0-88150-312-6*, Backcountry) Countryman.
— Michigan Trout Streams: A Fly-Angler's Guide. (Illus.). 272p. (Orig.). 1993. pap. 16.00 (*0-88150-271-5*, Backcountry) Countryman.

Linsenman-Schuh, Norma. Presenting Ali Marie in Cabin Fever. (Happy to Be Me Ser.). (Illus.). 32p. (Orig.). (J). (gr. k-5). 1993. pap. 5.95 (*1-884073-03-4*); pap. 24.95 (*1-884073-00-X*) Esteem Intl.
— Presenting Jessica Lyn in King Purple. (Happy to Be Me Ser.). (Illus.). 32p. (Orig.). (J). 1993. pap. 5.95 (*1-884073-04-2*); pap. 24.95 (*1-884073-01-8*) Esteem Intl.

Linsenmeyer, Helen. From Fingers to Finger Bowls: California Cooking from Indian Times Until the Turn of the Century, with Lore & Recipes. Pourade, Richard, ed. (Illus.). 141p. (C). 1991. reprint ed. pap. 14.95 (*0-945092-08-3*) EZ Nature.

Linsey, Adrian & Fieldhouse, Ken. Landscape Design Guide, Vol. I: Soft Landscape. Dodd, Jeremy, ed. 224p. 1990. text ed. 73.95 (*0-566-09017-1*, Pub. by Gower UK) Ashgate Pub Co.

Linsk, et al. Clinical Aspiration Cytology. 2nd ed. LC 65-9913. (Illus.). 432p. 1989. text ed. 125.00 (*0-397-50826-3*, Lippincott Medical) Lippincott.

Linsk, Nathan, et al, eds. Wages for Caring: Compensating Family Care of the Elderly. LC 91-37512. 296p. 1992. text ed. 59.95 (*0-275-93635-X*, C3635, Praeger Pubs) Greenwood.

Linskens, H. F. & Heslop-Harrison, J., eds. Cellular Interactions. (Encyclopedia of Plant Physiology Ser.). (Illus.). 850p. 1984. 278.00 (*0-387-12738-0*) Spr-Verlag.

Linskens, H. F. & Jackson, J. F. Essential Oils & Waxes: With the Assistance of Numerous Experts. (Modern Methods of Plant Analysis Ser.: Vol. 12). (Illus.). xviii, 337p. 1991. 198.00 (*0-387-51915-7*) Spr-Verlag.

Linskens, H. F. & Jackson, J. F., eds. Analysis of Non-Alcoholic Beverages. (Modern Methods of Plant Analysis Ser.: Vol. 8). (Illus.). 450p. 1988. 224.00 (*0-387-18820-7*) Spr-Verlag.
— Cell Components. (Modern Methods of Plant Analysis Ser.: Vol. 1). (Illus.). 430p. 1986. 239.00 (*0-387-15822-7*) Spr-Verlag.
— Gases in Plant & Microbial Cells. (Modern Methods of Plant Analysis, New Ser.: Vol. 9). (Illus.). 385p. 1989. 201.00 (*0-387-18821-5*) Spr-Verlag.
— High Performance Liquid Chromatography in Plant Sciences. (Modern Methods of Plant Analysis Ser.: Vol. 5). (Illus.). 255p. 1987. 126.00 (*0-387-17243-2*) Spr-Verlag.
— Immunology in Plant Sciences. (Modern Methods of Plant Analysis Ser.: Vol. 4). (Illus.). 305p. 1986. 179.00 (*0-387-16842-7*) Spr-Verlag.
— Physical Methods in Plant Sciences. (Modern Methods of Plant Analysis Ser.: Vol. 11). (Illus.). 320p. 1990. 167.00 (*0-387-50332-3*) Spr-Verlag.
— Plant Fibers. (Modern Methods of Plant Analysis Ser.: Vol. 10). (Illus.). 420p. 1989. 230.00 (*0-387-18822-3*) Spr-Verlag.
— Plant Toxin Analysis. (Modern Methods of Plant Analysis Ser.: Vol. 13). (Illus.). 368p. 1992. 229.00 (*0-387-52328-6*) Spr-Verlag.
— Seed Analysis. (Modern Methods of Plant Analysis Ser.: Vol. 14). (Illus.). 384p. 1992. 245.00 (*0-387-52737-0*) Spr-Verlag.
— Vegetables & Vegetable Products. (Modern Methods of Plant Analysis Ser.: Vol. 16). 208p. 1994. 136.00 (*0-387-55843-8*) Spr-Verlag.

Linskens, H. F., jt. ed. see Jackson, J. F.

Linskens, H. F., et al, eds. Gas Chromatography-Mass Spectrometry. (Modern Methods of Plant Analysis Ser.: Vol. 3). (Illus.). 330p. 1986. 193.00 (*0-387-15911-8*) Spr-Verlag.

L

— Nuclear Magnetic Resonance. (Modern Methods of Plant Analysis Ser.: Vol. 2). (Illus.). 215p. 1986. 139.00 (*0-387-15910-X*) Spr-Verlag.

*__Linskey, Tom.__ Race Winning Strategies: Smart Lessons with Deep Dacron. (Illus.). 250p. 1995. pap. 17.95 (*0-924486-88-0*) Sheridan.

Linskie, Rosella. The Learning Process: Theory & Practice. LC 83-16882. 320p. 1983. reprint ed. pap. text ed. 25.00 (*0-8191-3591-7*) U Pr of Amer.

Linskill, Joseph, ed. see Raimbaut de Vaqueiras.

Linsky, Arnold S. & Straus, Murray A. Social Stress in the United States: Links to Regional Patterns in Crime & Illness. LC 86-14192. 174p. 1986. text ed. 49.95 (*0-86569-149-5*, Auburn Hse) Greenwood.

*__Linsky, Arnold S., et al.__ Stress, Culture, & Aggression. LC 94-48643. 1995. write for info. (*0-300-05706-7*) Yale U Pr.

Linsky, B., jt. ed. see Matthen, M.

Linsky, Benjamin, ed. Chicago Association of Commerce & Industry, Committee of Investigationon Smoke Abatement. Chicago Report on Smoke Abatement: A Landmark Survey of the Technology & History of Air Pollution Control. write for info. (*0-318-61059-0*, Pergamon Pr) Elsevier.

Linsky, Jeffrey L. & Stencel, R. E., eds. Cool Stars, Stellar Systems & the Sun. (Lecture Notes in Physics Ser.: Vol. 291). 537p. 1988. 66.00 (*0-387-18653-0*) Spr-Verlag.

Linsky, Leonard, ed. Semantics & the Philosophy of Language. 2nd ed. LC 52-10465. 304p. 1952. reprint ed. pap. 12.95 (*0-252-00093-5*) U of Ill Pr.

Linsky, Martin, et al. Impact: How the Press Affects Federal Policy Making. (C). 1988. pap. text ed. 8.95 (*0-393-95793-4*) Norton.

*__Linsley, E. Gorton & Chemsak, John A.__ The Cerambycidae of North America Pt. VII, No.2: Taxonomy & Classification of the Subfamily Lamiinae, Tribes Acanthocinini Through Hemilophini. (Publications in Entomology). (Illus.). 304p. 1995. pap. 38.00 (*0-520-09795-5*) U CA Pr.

Linsley, Earle G. Nesting Biology & Associates of Melitoma (Hymenoptera, Anthophoridae) LC 80-12433. (University of California Publications in Social Welfare: No. 90). 53p. reprint ed. pap. 25.00 (*0-685-24001-0*, 2031586) Bks Demand.

Linsley, Earle G. & Chemsak, John A. Taxonomy & Classification of the Subfamily Lamiinae: Tribes Parmenini Through Acanthoderini. (Publications in Entomology: Vol. 102). 1985. pap. 28.00 (*0-520-09690-8*) U CA Pr.

Linsley, Earle G. & Sterling, Keir B., eds. Beetles from the Early Russian Explorations of the West Coast of North America: 1815-1857. (Biologists & Their World Ser.). (Illus.). (FRE, GER & LAT.). 1978. lib. bdg. 58.95 (*0-405-10691-2*) Ayer.

— The Principal Contributions of Henry Walter Bates to a Knowledge of the Butterflies & Longicorn Beetles of the Amazon Valley: Original Anthology. LC 77-81106. (Biologists & Their World Ser.). (Illus.). 1978. lib. bdg. 72.95 (*0-405-10690-4*) Ayer.

Linsley, Horace E. Broaching: Tooling & Practice. LC 61-9128. 224p. reprint ed. pap. 63.90 (*0-8357-7437-6*, 2001909) Bks Demand.

— Machine Tools, What They Are & How They Work: An Introduction to the Fundamentals of Mass Production. Hall, Herbert D., ed. LC 57-7456. 448p. reprint ed. pap. 127.70 (*0-317-10939-1*, 2001907) Bks Demand.

Linsley, Judith, jt. auth. see Foy, Jessica.

Linsley, Leslie. Key West Houses. LC 91-28698. (Illus.). 96p. (Orig.). 1992. pap. 17.95 (*0-8478-1494-7*) Rizzoli Intl.

— Leslie Linsley's Weekend Decorating: 1,001 Quick Home Decorating Ideas, Tips & How-To's. 366p. (Orig.). 1993. pap. 10.99 (*0-446-39411-4*) Warner Bks.

— More Weekend Quilts. LC 92-41318. 1993. 24.95 (*0-312-08849-3*) St Martin.

— More Weekend Quilts: Nineteen Classic Quilts to Make with Shortcuts & Quick Techniques. 1994. pap. 14.95 (*0-312-11858-9*) St Martin.

— Nantucket Style. LC 89-43255. 1990. 40.00 (*0-8478-1165-4*) Rizzoli Intl.

— Nantucket Style. 228p. 1994. 29.95 (*0-8478-1830-6*) Rizzoli Intl.

— Pretty Patchwork. 1993. 24.95 (*0-696-02389-X*) Meredith Bks.

— Quilter's Country Christmas. 1990. 21.95 (*0-312-03691-4*) St Martin.

— Scrimshaw: A Traditional Folk Art, a Contemporary Craft. (Illus.). 1979. pap. 14.95 (*0-8015-6609-6*, Dutton) NAL-Dutton.

— The Weekend Quilt. (Illus.). 160p. 1992. pap. 14.95 (*0-685-50332-1*) St Martin.

Linsley, Ray K. Water Resources Engineering. 4th ed. 1992. text ed. write for info. (*0-07-038010-4*) McGraw.

— Water Resources Engineering. 4th ed. 1993. Solutions manual. student ed, pap. text ed. write for info. (*0-07-038012-0*) McGraw.

Linsley, Ray K., et al. Hydrology for Engineers. 3rd ed. (Water Resources & Environmental Engineering Ser.). (Illus.). 496p. 1982. text ed. write for info. (*0-07-037956-4*) McGraw.

Linson, Art. A Pound of Flesh: Perilous Tales of How to Produce Movies in Hollywood. LC 93-22889. 208p. 1993. 18.00 (*0-8021-1543-8*) Grove-Atltic.

— A Pound of Flesh: Producing in Hollywood--Perilous Tales from the Trenches. 208p. 1995. pap. 9.00 (*0-380-72401-4*) Avon.

Linson, Connell. Images-Glimpses & Other Sightings: Poetry. LC 91-76392. 66p. (Orig.). 1992. pap. 8.95 (*1-55618-111-6*) Brunswick Pub.

Linss, Wilhelm C., tr. see Luz, Ulrich.

Linssen, Robert. Living Zen. Abrahams-Curiel, Diana, tr. 348p. 1988. pap. 12.95 (*0-8021-3136-0*) Grove-Atltic.

Linster, Tom. Blue Food: A Case of National Indigestion. (Illus.). 90p. (Orig.). 1992. pap. 8.95 (*1-881631-00-1*) Byfor Fnd.

Linstone, Harold A. Multiple Perspectives for Decision Making: Bridging the Gap Between Analysis & Action. 400p. 1984. 41.00 (*0-444-00803-9*) P-H.

Linstone, Harold A. & Mitroff, Ian I. The Challenge of the Twenty-First Century: Managing Technology & Ourselves in a Shrinking World. LC 93-296698. (Illus.). 406p. 1994. 64.50x (*0-7914-1949-5*); pap. 21.95x (*0-7914-1950-9*) State U NY Pr.

Linstone, Harold A., jt. auth. see Mitroff, Ian I.

Linstrom, Dag, jt. auth. see Osterberg, Eva.

Linstromberg, Lillian. Taking Time. LC 89-61707. (Illus.). 96p. (Orig.). 1989. pap. 7.95 (*0-9623452-0-2*) Oregon Coast Cmnty Col.

Linstromberg, Walter W. & Baumgarten, Henry E. Organic Chemistry: A Brief Course. 6th ed. LC 86-81385. 517p. (C). 1987. text ed. 35.50 (*0-669-12660-8*); Study guide. student ed 14.00 (*0-669-12661-6*); Test item file. write for info. (*0-669-17411-4*) Heath.

— Organic Experiments. 6th ed. 404p. (C). 1987. pap. text ed. 19.00 (*0-669-12662-4*); Instr.'s manual. teacher ed 2.00 (*0-669-12663-2*) Heath.

Linstrum, Helen. Taking Your Show on the Road: A Guide for New Student Recruiters. 1990. 23.00 (*0-89964-274-8*) Coun Adv & Supp Ed.

Lint, Gregg L. & Taylor, Robert J., eds. The Papers of John Adams, Vols. 7 & 8: September 1778-February 1780, Set. LC 77-4707. (Adams Papers: General Correspondence & Other Papers of the Adams Statesmen Ser.). (Illus.). 480p. 1989. 100.00 (*0-674-65444-7*) Belknap Pr.

Lintas, Claudia, jt. ed. see Fabriani, Giuseppe.

Linten, Harold. Sketching the Concept. 1993. 45.95 (*0-07-157805-6*) McGraw.

Lintermans, Gloria. Cheap Chic: A Guide to LA's Resale Boutiques. (Illus.). 218p. (Orig.). 1990. pap. 12.95 (*0-9625807-0-8*) A Lintermans Pubs.

— The Newly Divorced Book of Protocol. LC 94-44570. 1995. 17.95 (*1-56980-037-5*) Barricade Bks.

Lintermans, J. P. Two-Dimensional Echocardiography in Infants & Children. 1986. lib. bdg. 185.00 (*0-89838-778-7*) Kluwer Ac.

Lintern, Paul. As the Ancient World Turns: Around the Guiding Light of the Days of All Our Ancestors Lives. (Orig.). 1992. pap. 6.95 (*1-55673-495-6*) CSS OH.

Linthicum, et al. ADA Handbook: A Guide to the Americans with Disability Act. 176p. (C). 1992. pap. text ed. 17.95 (*0-8403-7882-3*) Kendall-Hunt.

Linthicum, Bob, ed. see Boyland, Anita W.

Linthicum, Bob, ed. see Jacobs, Carl.

Linthicum, Bob, ed. see MBA Ethics Task Force Staff.

Linthicum, D. S. & Farid, Nadir R., eds. Anti-Idiotypes, Receptors, & Molecular Mimicry. 345p. 1987. 106.00 (*0-387-96548-3*) Spr-Verlag.

Linthicum, David. UNIX Desktop Guide to UUCP. (Illus.). 400p. (Orig.). 1992. pap. 27.95 (*0-672-48517-6*) Sams.

Linthicum, Dorothy S. The Dry Pipeline: Increasing the Flow of Minority Faculty. 62p. reprint ed. pap. 25.00 (*0-7837-5163-X*, 2044892) Bks Demand.

Linthicum, Fred H., Jr. & Schwartzman, Jorge A. An Atlas of Micropathology of the Temporal Bone. (Illus.). 104p. (C). 1994. text ed. 125.00 (*1-56593-377-X*, 0755) Singular Publishing.

Linthicum, Robert C. City of God, City of Satan: A Biblical Theology for the Urban Church. 384p. (Orig.). 1991. pap. 18.99 (*0-310-53141-1*) Zondervan.

— Empowering the Poor. 128p. 1991. pap. 8.95 (*0-912552-75-1*) MARC.

Linthorst, Ann T. A Gift of Love: Marriage As a Spiritual Journey. 166p. 1985. reprint ed. pap. 9.95 (*0-913105-17-1*) PAGL Pr.

— Mothering As a Spiritual Journey: Learning to Let God Nurture Your Children & You along with Them. 140p. (Orig.). 1993. pap. 11.95 (*0-8245-1250-2*) Crossroad NY.

— Thus Saith the Lord: Giddyap: Metapsychiatric Commentaries on Human Experience & Spiritual Growth. 106p. (Orig.). 1986. pap. 11.00 (*0-913105-18-X*) PAGL Pr.

Linthorst, Jan. A Primer on Metapsychiatry. 79p. 1987. pap. 7.00 (*0-913105-21-X*) PAGL Pr.

Linthwaite, Illona, comp. Ain't I a Woman! LC 87-35577. 214p. 1991. pap. 7.95 (*0-87226-209-X*) P Bedrick Bks.

Linthwaite, Illona, ed. Ain't I a Woman! A Book of Women's Poetry from Around the World. LC 93-13201. 1993. 7.99 (*0-517-09365-0*, Pub. by Wings Bks) Random Hse Value.

Lintner, Bertil. Burma in Revolt: Opium & Insurgency since 1948. LC 94-25846. 1994. text ed. 59.95 (*0-8133-2344-4*) Westview.

— Land of Jade: A Journey Through Insurgent Burma. (Illus.). 334p. (C). 1995. pap. 25.00 (*1-870838-45-9*, Pub. by Kiscadale UK) Weatherhill.

— Outrage: Burma's Struggle for Democracy. (Illus.). 256p. (C). 1995. reprint ed. pap. 25.00 (*0-9515814-1-4*, Pub. by Kiscadale UK) Weatherhill.

— The Rise & Fall of the Communist Party of Burma (CPB) (Southeast Asia Program Ser.: No. 6). (Illus.). 124p. (Orig.). 1990. 10.00 (*0-87727-123-2*) Cornell SE Asia.

Lintner, Grace. Bond & Free. LC 79-38656. (Black Heritage Library Collection). 1977. reprint ed. 22.95 (*0-8369-9014-5*) Ayer.

Lintner, John. Economic Research: Retrospect & Prospect, Vol. 2: Finance & Capital Markets. (General Ser.: No. 96). 87p. 1972. reprint ed. 22.70 (*0-87014-252-6*) Natl Bur Econ Res.

— Interest Rate Expectations & Optimal Forward Commitments for Institutional Investors. (Explorations in Economic Research Three Ser.: No. 4). 76p. 1976. reprint ed. 35.00 (*0-685-66196-2*) Natl Bur Econ Res.

Lintner, John, et al. Forward Commitment Decisions on Life Insurance Companies for Investments in Bonds & Mortgages. (Explorations in Economic Research Four Ser.: No. 5). 50p. 1978. reprint ed. 35.00 (*0-685-61418-2*) Natl Bur Econ Res.

Lintner, Mildred D. Introduction to WordPerfect 4.2. 76p. 1990. pap. 14.95 (*0-9624073-1-3*) Pippin Publishing.

Lintner, Mildred D., jt. auth. see Lauckner, Kurt F.

Lintner, Valerio. A Traveller's History of Italy. LC 89-15345. (Traveller's History Ser.). (Illus.). 288p. 1993. pap. 13.95 (*0-940793-46-6*) Interlink Pub.

Linton, Adelin, jt. auth. see Linton, Ralph.

*__Linton, Adrainne, et al.__ Introductory Nursing Care of Adults. (Illus.). 1216p. 1995. text ed. 44.95 (*0-7216-3319-6*) Saunders.

Linton, Alan H. Microbes, Man & Animals: The Natural History of Microbia - Interactions. LC 81-14719. 270p. 1982. text ed. 129.00 (*0-471-10083-8*) Wiley.

— Microbes, Man & Animals: The Natural History of Microbial Interactions. LC 81-14719. (Illus.). 358p. reprint ed. pap. 102.10 (*0-685-20721-8*, 2030509) Bks Demand.

Linton, Anthony. Newes of the Complement of the Art of Navigation & of the Mightie Empire of Cataia. LC 72-215. (English Experience Ser.: No. 204). 1969. reprint ed. 30.00 (*90-221-0204-1*) Walter J Johnson.

Linton, Calvin D. Effective Revenue Writing Two. rev. ed. 206p. 1984. reprint ed. boxed 5.50 (*0-16-004615-7*, S/N 048-004-00037-7) USGPO.

Linton, Clarence. A Study of Some Problems Arising in the Admission of Students As Candidates for Professional Degrees in Education. LC 73-176999. (Columbia University. Teachers College. Contributions to Education Ser.: No. 285). reprint ed. 22.50 (*0-404-55285-4*) AMS Pr.

Linton, D. & Boston, R. The Newspaper Press in Britain: An Annotated Bibliography. 384p. 1987. text ed. 130.00 (*0-7201-1792-5*, Mansell Pub) Cassell.

Linton, David & Boston, Ray. The Twentieth-Century Newspaper Press in Britain: An Annotated Bibliography. 416p. 1995. 120.00 (*0-7201-2159-0*, Mansell Pub) Cassell.

Linton, Derek S. Who Has the Youth, Has the Future: The Campaign to Save Young Workers in Imperial Germany. 256p. (C). 1991. 59.95 (*0-521-38537-7*) Cambridge U Pr.

Linton, Fred E., tr. see Caratheodory, Constantin.

Linton, George & Hanson, V. Reader's Guide to the Mahatma Letters. 1988. 19.95 (*81-7059-113-9*) Theos Pub Hse.

Linton, Harold. Architectural Sketching in Markers. 1991. pap. 39.95 (*0-442-31883-9*) Van Nos Reinhold.

— Color Consulting: A Survey of International Color Design. LC 90-42282. (Illus.). 208p. 1991. text ed. 64.95 (*0-442-23352-3*) Van Nos Reinhold.

— Color Forecasting: A Survey of International Color Marketing. 1994. text ed. 59.95 (*0-442-01160-1*) Van Nos Reinhold.

Linton, Harold & Matthews, Henry. Harold Linton: Paintings 1976-1986. LC 86-23605. (Illus.). 12p. (Orig.). 1986. pap. 5.00 (*0-940623-00-5*) Muskegon Art.

Linton, Harold & Sutton, Scott. Sketching the Concept. (Illus.). 160p. 1992. 45.95 (*0-8306-4070-3*, 3858, Design Pr) TAB Bks.

Linton, Harold, jt. auth. see Rochon, Richard.

Linton, Ian. Building Customer Loyalty. 192p. (Orig.). 1993. pap. 39.50x (*0-273-60080-X*, Pub. by Pitman Pub Ltd UK) Trans-Atl Phila.

— Creating a Customer Focused Company: 25 Proven Customer Service Strategies. (Financial Times Management Ser.). 224p. 1995. 72.50x (*0-273-60711-1*, Pub. by Pitman Pub Ltd UK) Trans-Atl Phila.

— Database Marketing: How to Manage Customer Information for Profit. (Financial Times Management Ser.). 300p. 1995. 67.50 (*0-273-61179-8*, Pub. by Pitman Pub Ltd UK) Trans-Atl Phila.

— The Spider Principle: Improving Local Marketing Performance. (Financial Times Management Ser.). 224p. 1993. 77.50x (*0-273-60328-0*, Pub. by Pitman Pub Ltd UK) Trans-Atl Phila.

— Twenty-Five Tips for Customer Service: An Action Plan for Service Success. (Institute of Management Ser.). 192p. 1995. 67.50x (*0-273-60973-4*, Pub. by Pitman Pub Ltd UK); pap. 39.50x (*0-273-60974-2*, Pub. by Pitman Pub Ltd UK) Trans-Atl Phila.

*__Linton, Ian & Morley, Kevin.__ Integrated Marketing Communications. 162p. 1995. pap. 29.95 (*0-7506-1938-4*) Buttrwrth-Heinemann.

*__Linton, Isobel.__ A Gentleman's Daughter. 304p. 1995. mass mkt. 3.99 (*0-8217-4946-3*) Windsor NY.

Linton, James M., jt. auth. see Jowett, Garth.

Linton, Karin. The Temporal Horizon: A Study of the Theme of Time in Anne Tyler's Major Novels. (Studia Anglistica Upsaliensia Ser.: No. 68). 143p. (Orig.). 1989. pap. 40.00x (*91-554-2339-6*, Pub. by Almqv & Wiksell SW) Coronet Bks.

Linton, Margaret. Children's Camp in Canada. 1982. pap. 7.95 (*0-452-25346-2*, Plume) NAL-Dutton.

Linton, Marigold & Gallo, Phillip S., Jr. The Practical Statistician: Simplified Handbook of Statistics. LC 73-91423. (Illus.). 384p. (C). 1975. pap. 24.95 (*0-8185-0127-8*) Brooks-Cole.

Linton, Patricia, jt. auth. see Bussell, Darcy.

Linton, Ralph. Age & Sex Categories. (Reprint Series in Social Sciences). (C). 1993. reprint ed. pap. text ed. 1.00 (*0-8290-2710-6*, S-173) Irvington.

— Archaeology of the Marquesas Islands. (BMB Ser.: No. 23). 1972. reprint ed. 30.00 (*0-527-02126-1*) Periodicals Srv.

— The Cultural Background of Personality. LC 80-29240. xix, 157p. 1981. reprint ed. text ed. 35.00 (*0-313-22783-7*, LICU, Greenwood Pr) Greenwood.

— Tanala, a Hill Tribe of Madagascar. (Chicago Field Museum of Natural History Fieldiana Anthropology Ser.). 1974. 36.00 (*0-527-01882-1*) Periodicals Srv.

Linton, Ralph & Linton, Adelin. We Gather Together: The Story of Thanksgiving. (Illus.). 100p. 1990. reprint ed. lib. bdg. 34.00 (*1-55888-883-7*) Omnigraphics Inc.

Linton, Ralph & Wingert, Paul. Arts of the South Seas. LC 76-169308. (Museum of Modern Art Publications in Reprint). (Illus.). 200p. 1980. reprint ed. 29.95 (*0-405-01567-4*) Ayer.

Linton, Stanley. Music Fundamentals & Functional Skills. (Illus.). 320p. 1984. pap. text ed. 43.00 (*0-13-606939-8*) P-H.

Linton, Steve & Rust, Damon. Ice Rescue. 1982. pap. text ed. 2.00 (*0-943717-13-2*) Concept Sys.

Linton, Steve J., et al. Dive Rescue Specialist Training Manual. 81p. 1986. pap. text ed. 14.95 (*0-943717-42-6*) Concept Sys.

Linton, Thomas, ed. The Linton Register, 1990-1991: The Trainer's Resource Directory. 2000p. (C). 1992. 350.00 (*0-9626607-0-1*) Linton Pub Co.

Linton, Virginia. Heading Out. LC 80-23182. 1981. 10.95 (*0-87233-054-0*) Bauhan.

Linton, William A., Jr. A Primer on Computer System Interoperability. (Orig.). Date not set. pap. 19.95 (*0-939547-00-7*) SMC.

Linton, William J. Memories. LC 69-13753. vi, 236p. 1970. reprint ed. 37.50 (*0-678-00596-6*) Kelley.

— Victorian American Wood Engraving. LC 75-22525. (Athenaeum Library of 19th Century America). (Illus.). 1976. reprint ed. text ed. 25.00 (*0-89257-010-5*) Am Life Foun.

Lintott, Andrew. Imperium Romanum: Politics & Administration. LC 92-26011. 1993. write for info. (*0-415-01594-4*) Routledge.

— Judicial Reform & Land Reform in the Roman Republic: A New Edition, with Translation & Commentary, of the Laws from Urbino. (Illus.). 318p. (C). 1993. 95.00 (*0-521-40373-1*) Cambridge U Pr.

— Violence, Civil Strife, & Revolution in the Classical City. 288p. (C). 1987. pap. text ed. 14.95 (*0-7099-4170-6*, Pub. by Croom Helm UK) Routledge Chapman & Hall.

*__Lintott, Pam & Miller, Rosemary.__ The Quilt Room. LC 95-13637. (Illus.). 1995. write for info. (*1-56477-097-4*) That Patchwork.

— The Quilt Room: Patchwork & Quilting Workshops. (Illus.). 160p. 1993. 29.95 (*0-943955-63-7*, Trafalgar Sq Pub) Trafalgar.

— The Quilter's Workbook: A Practical Source & Record Book for Quilters. (Illus.). 112p. 1993. 17.95 (*1-85238-422-0*, Pub. by New Holland Pubs UK) Sterling.

Lints, F. A. Genetics & Aging. (Interdisciplinary Topics in Gerontology Ser.: Vol. 14). (Illus.). 1978. pap. 47.25 (*3-8055-2891-4*) S Karger.

Lints, F. A., ed. Non-Mammalian Models for Research on Ageing. (Interdisciplinary Topics in Gerontology Ser.: Vol. 21). (Illus.). viii, 288p. 1985. 158.50 (*3-8055-4019-1*) S Karger.

Lints, F. A., et al. Aging in Drosophila. (Aging Ser.). 179p. 1977. text ed. 24.50 (*0-8422-7244-5*) Irvington.

Lints, Richard. The Fabric of Theology: A Prolegomenon to Evangelical Theology. LC 93-35443. 376p. 1993. pap. text ed. 19.99 (*0-8028-0674-0*) Eerdmans.

Lintz, Christopher R. Architecture & Community Variability Within the Antelope Creek Phase of the Texas Panhandle. (Studies in Oklahoma's Past). (Illus.). 380p. (C). 1986. pap. text ed. 13.00 (*1-881346-07-2*) Univ OK Archeol.

*__Linver.__ The Leader's Edge. 1995. pap. 10.00 (*0-684-80433-6*, Fireside) S&S Trade.

Linver, Sandy. Leader's Edge. 1994. 20.00 (*0-671-88179-5*) S&S Trade.

— Speak & Get Results. 1994. pap. 11.00 (*0-671-89316-5*, Fireside) S&S Trade.

— Speak & Get Results: Complete Guide to Presentations & Speeches That Work in Any Business Situation. 256p. 1983. 14.70 (*0-671-44204-X*) Summit Bks.

Linver, Sandy & Mengert, Jim. Speak & Get Results: The Complete Guide to Speeches & Presentations That Work in Any Business Situation. rev. ed. LC 93-46040. 1994. 22.00 (*0-671-88996-6*) S&S Trade.

Linville, Barbara. Christy's Pouting Again. (Ark Angel Bks.). (Illus.). 32p. (J). (gr. k-2). 1989. 2.99 (*0-87403-627-5*, 3891) Standard Pub.

— Joey's Too Much TV. (Ark Angel Bks.). (Illus.). 32p. (J). (gr. k-2). 1989. 2.99 (*0-87403-628-3*, 3892) Standard Pub.

— Susie's Afraid of the Dark. (Ark Angel Bks.). (Illus.). 32p. (J). (gr. k-2). 1989. 2.99 (*0-87403-629-1*, 3893) Standard Pub.

— Tommy's Afraid to Try. (Ark Angel Bks.). (Illus.). 32p. (J). (gr. k-2). 1989. 2.99 (*0-87403-630-5*) Standard Pub.

Linville, Bill, ed. Reservoir Characterization III. LC 92-43076. 1056p. 1993. 99.95 (*0-87814-392-0*, P4522) PennWell Bks.

Linville, Chi L. & Anderson, Jim. Scapegoat...a Money, Sex, Love Story. 250p. 1991. 9.95 (*0-932574-13-0*) Brun Pr.

Linville, James, ed. see Smith, J. P.

Linville, Linda K. Academic Skills Achievement Program. LC 93-14480. 352p. (C). 1993. pap. text ed. 23.50 (*0-256-14219-X*) Irwin.

Linworth Publishing, Inc. Staff. Computers & the School Library. (Illus.). 125p. 1990. pap. text ed. 24.95 (*0-87436-607-0*) ABC-CLIO.

— Tips & Other Bright Ideas for School Librarians. (Professional Growth Ser.). (Illus.). 202p. 1993. reprint ed. pap. text ed. 24.95 (*0-87436-605-4*) Linworth Pub.

Linworth Publishing, Inc. Staff, ed. The Book Report & Library Talk Author Profile Collection. (Professional Growth Ser.). (Illus.). 109p. 1992. 26.95 (*0-938865-12-9*) Linworth Pub.

— The Book Report & Library Talk Directory of Sources. 2nd rev. ed. (Professional Growth Ser.). 100p. 1994. pap. text ed. 19.95 (*0-938865-34-X*) Linworth Pub.

— Instant Art Notebook. (Professional Growth Ser.). (Illus.). 140p. 1992. ring bd. 34.95 (*0-938865-17-X*) Linworth Pub.

— Library Research Skills: Grades 7-12. (Professional Growth Ser.). (Illus.). 138p. 1990. pap. text ed. 19.95 (*0-938865-00-5*) Linworth Pub.

— Reading Motivation. 2nd ed. (Professional Growth Ser.). (Illus.). 120p. 1993. pap. text ed. 19.95 (*0-938865-26-9*) Linworth Pub.

— Shoptalk Ideas for Elementary School Librarians. (Professional Growth Ser.). (Illus.). 75p. 1994. pap. text ed. 16.95 (*0-938865-30-7*) Linworth Pub.

— Skills for Life: Library Information Literacy for Grades K-6. LC 93-21178. (Professional Growth Ser.). 299p. 1993. 34.95 (*0-938865-19-6*) Linworth Pub.

— Skills for Life: Library Information Literacy for Grades 6-8. LC 93-33733. (Professional Growth Ser.). 292p. 1993. 34.95 (*0-938865-20-X*) Linworth Pub.

— Skills for Life: Library Information Literacy for Grades 9-12. LC 93-39622. (Professional Growth Ser.). 328p. 1993. 34.95 (*0-938865-21-8*) Linworth Pub.

— Teaching Information Literacy Using Electronic Resources for Grades K-6. (Professional Growth Ser.). 250p. 1995. 36.95 (*0-938865-44-7*) Linworth Pub.

— Teaching Information Literacy Using Electronic Resources for Grades 6-12. (Professional Growth Ser.). 250p. 1995. 36.95 (*0-938865-45-5*) Linworth Pub.

***Linz, Cathie.** Baby Wanted. (Montana Mavericks Ser.). 1995. mass mkt. 3.99 (*0-373-50174-9*, 1-50174-1) Harlequin Bks.

— Bridal Blues. 1994. mass mkt. 2.99 (*0-373-05894-2*, 1-05894-0) Harlequin Bks.

— Escapades. (Silhouette Desire Ser.). 1993. mass mkt. 2.99 (*0-373-05804-7*, 5-05804-5) Silhouette.

— Midnight Ice. (Silhouette Desire Ser.). 1994. mass mkt. 2.99 (*0-373-05846-2*, 5-05846-6) Silhouette.

— One of a Kind Marriage. large type ed. LC 94-45657. 235p. 1995. pap. 18.95 (*0-7838-1234-5*) Hall.

— A Wife in Time. 1995. mass mkt. 3.25 (*0-373-05958-2*, 1-05958-3) Silhouette.

Linz, Daniel & Malamuth, Neil. Pornography. (Communication Concepts Ser.: Vol. 5). 88p. (C). 1993. text ed. 24.00 (*0-8039-4480-2*); pap. text ed. 10.95 (*0-8039-4481-0*) Sage.

Linz, Juan J., ed. Breakdown of Democratic Regimes: Crisis, Breakdown, & Requalibrium. LC 78-571. (BDR Ser.: Vol. 1). 144p. (Orig.). 1978. pap. text ed. 10.95x (*0-8018-2009-X*) Johns Hopkins.

Linz, Juan J. & Stepan, Alfred, eds. The Breakdown of Democratic Regimes: Latin America. LC 78-594. (BDR Ser.: Vol. 3). (Orig.). 1978. pap. text ed. 12.95x (*0-8018-2023-5*) Johns Hopkins.

Linz, Juan J. & Valenzuela, Arturo, eds. The Failure of Presidential Democracy. LC 93-27221. 454p. 1994. text ed. 65.00 (*0-8018-4639-0*) Johns Hopkins.

— Failure of Presidential Democracy, Vol. 1: Comparative Perspectives. LC 93-27222. 1994. pap. 13.95 (*0-8018-4640-4*) Johns Hopkins.

— Failure of Presidential Democracy, Vol. 2: The Case of Latin America. LC 93-27222. 1994. pap. 16.95 (*0-8018-4784-2*) Johns Hopkins.

Linz, Juan J., jt. auth. see Shain, Yossi.

Linz, Mary H., et al, eds. Case Management: Historical, Current & Future Perspectives. (Illus.). 140p. (Orig.). 1990. pap. text ed. 24.95 (*0-914797-65-4*) Brookline Bks.

Linz, Peter. Analytical & Numerical Methods for Volterra Equations. LC 84-51968. (Studies in Applied Mathematics: No. 7). xiii, 227p. 1985. text ed. 40.75 (*0-89871-198-3*) Soc Indus-Appl Math.

— An Introduction to Formal Languages & Automata. LC 89-85747. 373p. (C). 1990. text ed. 37.00 (*0-669-17342-8*); Instr.'s guide. teacher ed 2.00 (*0-669-17344-4*) Heath.

Linz, Susan, ed. The Impact of World War II on the Soviet Union. (Illus.). 312p. 1985. pap. 22.50 (*0-8476-7379-0*) Rowman.

Linz, Susan & Moskoff, William, eds. Reorganization & Reform in the Soviet Economy. LC 87-35630. 150p. 1988. 51.95 (*0-87332-472-2*) M E Sharpe.

Linz, Werner M., ed. see Gentry, Francis G.

Linzee, J. W. Parker: The History of Peter Parker & Sarah Ruggles. (Illus.). 609p. 1991. reprint ed. lib. bdg. 99.50 (*0-8328-2894-7*); reprint ed. pap. 89.50 (*0-8328-2893-9*) Higginson Bk Co.

Linzell, J. L., jt. auth. see Peaker, M.

Linzer, Estelle, ed. Guide to Albert Schweitzer Collections. 2nd ed. 64p. (Orig.). 1992. pap. text ed. 7.50 (*1-881815-25-0*) Albert Schweitzer.

Linzer, M., ed. see International Conference on Hot Isostatic Pressing Staff.

Linzer, Norman. The Jewish Family: Authority & Tradition in Modern Perspectives. 317p. 1984. 43.95 (*0-89885-149-1*); pap. 20.95 (*0-89885-191-2*) Human Sci Pr.

— Suicide: The Will to Live vs the Will to Die. 240p. 1984. 35.95 (*0-89885-156-4*); pap. 20.95 (*0-89885-190-4*) Human Sci Pr.

***Linzer, Norman, et al, eds.** Crisis & Continuity: The Jewish Family in the 21st Century. LC 94-42914. 1995. 39.50 (*0-88125-507-6*); pap. text ed. 19.95 (*0-88125-508-4*) Ktav.

Linzer, Peter. A Contracts Anthology. 459p. 1989. pap. 24.00 (*0-87084-417-2*) Anderson Pub Co.

Linzey, Alicia V. & Linzey, Donald W. Mammals of Great Smoky Mountains National Park. LC 74-111048. 148p. (Orig.). reprint ed. pap. 42.20 (*0-317-55797-1*, 2029377) Bks Demand.

***Linzey, Andrew.** Animal Theology. LC 94-35580. 1995. write for info. (*0-252-02170-3*); pap. write for info. (*0-252-06467-4*) U of Ill Pr.

— Christianity & the Rights of Animals. 224p. 1987. pap. 12.95 (*0-8245-0875-0*) Crossroad NY.

***Linzey, Andrew & Clarke, Paul A.** Dictionary of Ethics, Society & Theology. 600p. 1995. 99.95 (*0-415-06212-8*, B0385) Routledge.

Linzey, Andrew & Regan, Tom. Animals & Christianity. 360p. (Orig.). 1988. pap. 14.95 (*0-8245-0902-1*) Crossroad NY.

Linzey, Andrew & Regan, Tom, eds. Animals & Christianity. (Orig.). 1992. 23.00 (*0-8446-6531-2*) Peter Smith.

Linzey, Andrew, jt. ed. see Clarke, Paul A.

***Linzey, Donald W.** Mammals of Great Smoky Mountains National Park. (Illus.). 152p. (Orig.). 1995. pap. text ed. 14.95 (*0-939923-48-3*) M & W Pub Co.

— Mammals of Virginia. (Illus.). 500p. 1995. 49.95 (*0-939923-36-X*) M & W Pub Co.

Linzey, Donald W. & Clifford, Michael J. Snakes of Virginia. LC 81-12951. (Illus.). 224p. (C). 1995. pap. 24.95 (*0-8139-0826-4*) U Pr of Va.

— Snakes of Virginia. LC 81-12951. 207p. reprint ed. pap. 59.00 (*0-7837-1244-8*, 2041381) Bks Demand.

Linzey, Donald W., jt. auth. see Linzey, Alicia V.

Linzey, Sharon, et al, eds. East-West Christian Organizations: A Directory of Western Christian Organizations Working in East Central Europe & the Former Soviet Union. 240p. 1993. pap. text ed. 15.00 (*0-9635856-0-6*) Berry Pub Srv.

Linzmayer, Owen. Bitchin Mac Programs. LC 93-87703. 135p. 1994. pap. 19.99 (*0-7821-1507-1*) Sybex.

— Mac Bathroom Reader. LC 94-67199. 306p. 1994. pap. 12.99 (*0-7821-1531-4*) Sybex.

— The Macintosh Joker. 156p. 1994. disk, pap. 19.95 (*1-56830-079-4*); pap. 19.95 (*0-685-71534-5*) Hayden.

Linzmayer, Owen W. Totally Rad Mac. 2nd ed. LC 93-86587. 138p. 1994. 19.99 (*0-7821-1456-3*) Sybex.

Linzmeyer, Peter, see Peter D. Wit, pseud..

Linzner, Gordon. The Spy Who Drank Blood. LC 84-14127. 144p. (Orig.). 1984. pap. 5.95 (*0-917053-01-X*) Space And.

Linzy, Jan. A Century of Pointers - Field & Show. (Illus.). 450p. 1996. text ed. 59.95 (*1-55893-024-8*) Camino E E & Bk.

Linzy, Jan, jt. auth. see Camino Book Co. Staff.

Lio, Frederick F. A Military History of Modern China, 1924 to 1949. LC 81-6577. xii, 312p. 1981. reprint ed. text ed. 59.75 (*0-313-23012-9*, LIMH, Greenwood Pr) Greenwood.

Lio, I-ming, jt. auth. see Chang Po-tuan.

Liogier, Henri A. Descriptive Flora of Puerto Rico & Adjacent Islands: Spermatophyta, Vol. I. LC 84-22668. 352p. 1985. pap. 20.00 (*0-8477-2334-8*) U of PR Pr.

— Descriptive Flora of Puerto Rico & Adjacent Islands, Vol. II: Leguminosae to Anacardiaceae. LC 84-25668. 481p. 1988. pap. 23.00 (*0-8477-2333-X*) U of PR Pr.

Liogier, Henri A. & Martorell, Luis F. Flora of Puerto Rico & Adjacent Islands: A Systematic Synopsis. LC 82-16431. 342p. (Orig.). 1982. pap. 15.00 (*0-8477-2329-1*) U of PR Pr.

Lion Books Staff. First Easter. (J). (ps-3). 1994. pap. 1.99 (*0-7459-1793-3*) Lion USA.

Lion, Edgar. Shopping Centers: Planning, Development, & Administration. LC 75-33374. 208p. reprint ed. pap. 59.30 (*0-685-16180-3*, 2056295) Bks Demand.

Lion, Gerard & Vergne, Michele, eds. The Weil Representation, Maslov Index & Theta Series. (Progress in Mathematics Ser.: No. 6). 346p. 1980. pap. text ed. 46.50 (*0-8176-3007-4*) Birkhauser.

Lion Publishing Staff. Felicidades: Es un Varon (Congratulations It's a Boy) (SPA.). Date not set. 4.99 (*1-56063-312-3*, 490343) Editorial Unilit.

— Felicidades: Es una Nina (Congratulations It's a Girl) (SPA.). Date not set. 4.99 (*1-56063-313-1*, 490344) Editorial Unilit.

— Jesus Is Born. (Puzzle Bks.). (J). (ps). 1992. bds. 6.99 (*0-7459-2203-1*) Lion USA.

Lion Staff. It's a Boy! 1992. 5.99 (*0-7459-2207-4*) Lion USA.

— It's a Girl! 1992. 5.99 (*0-7459-2226-0*) Lion USA.

— Libro Despegable (Concertina Puzzle Book) Animales En Pareja (Aminals Two by Two) (SPA.). Date not set. 4.99 (*1-56063-204-6*, 494004) Editorial Unilit.

— Libro Despegable (Concertina Puzzle Book) Animales Grandes y Chicos (All the Animals) (SPA.). Date not set. 4.99 (*1-56063-205-4*, 494005) Editorial Unilit.

— Libro Despegable (Concertina Puzzle Book) Dios Cuida De Mi (God Cares for Me) (SPA.). Date not set. 4.99 (*1-56063-206-2*, 494006) Editorial Unilit.

— Libro Despegable (Concertina Puzzle Book) Dios Cuida De Su Creacion (God Cares for the Earth) (SPA.). Date not set. 4.99 (*1-56063-201-1*, 494001) Editorial Unilit.

— Libro Despegable (Concertina Puzzle Book) El Bebe De Navidad (The Christmas Baby) (SPA.). Date not set. 4.99 (*1-56063-203-8*, 494003) Editorial Unilit.

— Libro Despegable (Concertina Puzzle Book) Regalos En la Primera Navidad (The First Christmas Present) (SPA.). Date not set. 4.99 (*1-56063-202-X*, 494002) Editorial Unilit.

Lion The Printer. Seven Days a Week. (Illus.). (J). (gr. k-5). 1977. spiral bd. 2.00 (*0-914080-62-8*) Shulsinger Sales.

Lionel, et al. Nevada Environmental Law Handbook. 2nd ed. (State Environmental Law Ser.). 339p. 1993. pap. text ed. 79.00 (*0-86587-335-6*) Gov Insts.

Lionel Corporation Staff. How to Operate & Maintain Lionel Trains & Accessories. LC 92-70952. (Illus.). 60p. 1992. reprint ed. pap. 10.00 (*0-930429-02-8*) Bibliographic Pr.

Lionel, Frederic. Challenge. 164p. Date not set. 13.95 (*0-8464-4200-0*) Beekman Pubs.

— Mirrors of Truth: Reflections of Living Mastery. Wise Thinking Staff, tr. 128p. (Orig.). 1991. pap. 10.95 (*0-944135-10-2*) Archedigm Pubns.

***Lionells, Marylou, et al, eds.** Handbook of Interpersonal Psychoanalysis. 992p. 1995. text ed. 180.00 (*0-88163-120-5*) Analytic Pr.

Lionetti, Harold E., jt. auth. see De Castells, Matilda O.

Lionnet, Francoise. Autobiographical Voices: Race, Gender, Self-Portraiture. LC 88-43236. (Reading Women Writing Ser.). 280p. 1989. 34.95 (*0-8014-2091-1*) Cornell U Pr.

— Autobiographical Voices: Race, Gender, Self-Portraiture. LC 88-43236. (Reading Women Writing Ser.). 280p. 1991. reprint ed. pap. 13.95 (*0-8014-9927-5*) Cornell U Pr.

— Postcolonial Representations: Women, Literature, Identity. (Reading Women Writing Ser.). 208p. 1995. 32.50 (*0-8014-2984-6*); pap. 12.95x (*0-8014-8180-5*) Cornell U Pr.

Lionnet, G., jt. auth. see D'Offay, Danielle.

***Lionni.** Matthew's Dream. 1995. 4.99 (*0-679-87318-X*) Random.

Lionni, Leo. Alexander & the Wind-up Mouse. LC 76-77423. (Illus.). 32p. (J). (ps-2). 1969. 15.00 (*0-394-80914-5*); lib. bdg. 15.99 (*0-394-90914-3*) Knopf Bks Yng Read.

— Alexander & the Wind-up Mouse. LC 74-2088. (Pinwheel Bks.). (Illus.). 32p. (J). (ps-3). 1974. reprint ed. pap. 5.99 (*0-394-82911-5*) Pantheon.

— Biggest House in the World. LC 68-12646. (Illus.). (J). (gr. k-3). 1968. lib. bdg. 14.99 (*0-394-90944-5*) Pantheon.

— The Biggest House in the World. LC 68-12646. (Children's Paperbacks Ser.). (Illus.). 32p. (J). (ps-6). 1973. pap. 4.99 (*0-394-82740-6*) Knopf Bks Yng Read.

— A Busy Year. LC 91-29149. (Illus.). 36p. (J). (ps-2). 1992. 7.99 (*0-679-82464-2*); lib. bdg. 10.99 (*0-679-92464-7*) Knopf Bks Yng Read.

— A Busy Year. 1992. pap. 10.99 (*0-685-52501-5*) McKay.

— A Color of His Own. LC 75-28456. (Illus.). 40p. (J). (ps-00). 1993. 8.99 (*0-679-84197-0*); lib. bdg. 9.99 (*0-679-94197-5*) Knopf Bks Yng Read.

— Cornelius. LC 82-6442. (Dragonfly Bks.). (Illus.). (J). (ps-2). 1994. pap. 4.99 (*0-679-86040-1*) Knopf Bks Yng Read.

— An Extraordinary Egg. LC 93-28565. (Illus.). 40p. (J). (ps-2). 1994. 15.00 (*0-679-85840-7*); lib. bdg. 15.99 (*0-679-95840-1*) Knopf Bks Yng Read.

— Fish Is Fish. LC 78-117452. (Knopf Children's Paperbacks Ser.). 32p. (J). (ps-6). 1974. pap. 4.99 (*0-394-82799-6*) Knopf.

— Fish Is Fish. LC 78-117452. (Illus.). (J). (gr. k-3). 1970. lib. bdg. 13.99 (*0-394-90440-0*) Pantheon.

— A Flea Story. (J). Date not set. write for info. (*0-679-86203-X*) Random Bks Yng Read.

— A Flea Story: I Want to Stay Here! I Want to Go There! LC 77-4322. (Illus.). (J). (ps-2). 1977. 15.00 (*0-394-83498-4*); lib. bdg. 15.99 (*0-394-93498-9*) Pantheon.

— Frederick. LC 66-10355. (Illus.). 40p. (J). (ps-2). 1967. 17.00 (*0-394-81040-6*) Knopf Bks Yng Read.

— Frederick. LC 66-10355. (Illus.). 40p. (J). (ps-2). 1967. lib. bdg. 16.99 (*0-394-91040-0*) Knopf Bks Yng Read.

— Frederick. LC 66-10355. (Pinwheel Bks.). (Illus.). 32p. (J). (gr. k-3). 1973. pap. 4.99 (*0-394-82614-0*) Knopf Bks Yng Read.

— Frederick's Fables: A Leo Lionni Treasury of Favorite Stories. LC 85-5186. (Illus.). 144p. (J). (ps-3). 1993. 20.00 (*0-394-87710-1*) Knopf Bks Yng Read.

— Inch by Inch. (Illus.). (J). (gr. k-1). 1962. 10.95 (*0-8392-3010-9*) Astor-Honor.

— Inch by Inch. Cohn, Amy, ed. LC 94-6483. (Illus.). 32p. (J). (ps up). 1994. reprint ed. pap. 4.95 (*0-688-13283-9*, Mulberry) Morrow.

— It's Mine. LC 85-190. (Illus.). 32p. (J). (ps-1). 1986. 15.00 (*0-394-87000-X*); lib. bdg. 15.99 (*0-394-97000-4*) Knopf Bks Yng Read.

— Let's Play. (Chunky Bks.). (Illus.). 28p. (J). (ps). 1993. 3.25 (*0-679-84030-3*) Random Bks Yng Read.

— Little Blue & Little Yellow. (Illus.). (J). (gr. k-1). 1959. 10.95 (*0-8392-3018-4*) Astor-Honor.

— Little Blue & Little Yellow. Cohn, Amy, ed. LC 94-7324. (Illus.). 48p. (J). (ps up). 1994. reprint ed. pap. 4.95 (*0-688-13285-5*, Mulberry) Morrow.

— Mr. McMouse. LC 92-8963. (Illus.). 40p. (J). (ps-1). 1992. 15.00 (*0-679-83890-2*); lib. bdg. 15.99 (*0-679-93890-7*) Knopf Bks Yng Read.

— On My Beach There Are Many Pebbles. (Illus.). (J). (gr. k-1). 1961. 10.95 (*0-8392-3024-9*) Astor-Honor.

— On the Beach There Are Many Pebbles. Cohn, Amy, ed. LC 94-6484. (Illus.). 32p. (J). (ps up). 1994. reprint ed. pap. 4.95 (*0-688-13284-7*, Mulberry) Morrow.

— Pouce par Pouce. (Illus.). (FRE.). (J). (gr. k-1). 1961. 10.95 (*0-8392-3028-1*) Astor-Honor.

— Pulgada a Pulgada. (Illus.). (SPA.). (J). (gr. k-1). 1961. 10.95 (*0-8392-3030-3*) Astor-Honor.

— Six Crows. LC 87-3141. (Illus.). 32p. (J). (ps-2). 1988. lib. bdg. 13.99 (*0-394-99572-4*) Knopf Bks Yng Read.

— Swimmy. LC 63-8504. (Illus.). 40p. (J). (ps-2). 1963. 16.00 (*0-394-81713-3*); lib. bdg. 15.99 (*0-394-91713-8*) Knopf Bks Yng Read.

— Swimmy. LC 63-8504. (Children's Paperbacks Ser.). (Illus.). 32p. (J). (ps-6). 1973. pap. 4.99 (*0-394-82620-5*) Knopf Bks Yng Read.

— Tico & the Golden Wings. (J). (gr. 1-4). 1993. 17.75 (*0-8446-6663-7*) Peter Smith.

— Tillie & the Wall. LC 88-9316. (Illus.). 32p. (J). (ps-2). 1989. 12.95 (*0-394-82155-6*); lib. bdg. 13.99 (*0-394-92155-0*) Knopf Bks Yng Read.

Lionni, Paolo. The Leipzig Connection. (Basics of Education Ser.: No. 1). (Illus.). xii, 119p. (Orig.). (C). 1980. pap. 4.95 (*0-89739-001-6*) Heron Bks OR.

Lions, J. L. Control of Distributed Singular System. 576p. 1987. text ed. 69.95 (*0-471-91858-X*) Wiley.

— Optimal Control of Systems Governed by Partial Differential Equations. Mitter, S. K., tr. LC 78-113638. (Grundlehren der Mathematischen Wissenschaften Ser.: Vol. 170). (Illus.). 1971. 79.00 (*0-387-05115-5*) Spr-Verlag.

— Some Aspects of the Optimal Control of Distributed Parameter Systems. (CBMS-NSF Regional Conference Ser.: No. 6). vi, 92p. (Orig.). 1972. pap. text ed. 17.00 (*0-89871-004-9*) Soc Indus-Appl Math.

— Some Methods in Mathematical Analysis of Systems & Their Control. 572p. 1981. text ed. 289.00 (*0-677-60200-6*) Gordon & Breach.

— Vistas in Applied Mathematics. Balakrishnan, A. V. et al, eds. xii, 384p. 1986. 120.00 (*0-387-96376-6*) Spr-Verlag.

Lions, J. L. & Magenes, E. Non-Homogeneous Boundary Value Problems & Applications, Vol. 1. Kenneth, P., tr. LC 71-151407. (Grundlehren der Mathematischen Wissenschaften Ser.: Vol. 181). 355p. 1972. 45.00 (*0-387-05363-8*) Spr-Verlag.

— Non-Homogeneous Boundary Value Problems & Applications, Vol. 3. Kenneth, P., tr. LC 71-151407. (Grundlehren der Mathematischen Wissenschaften Ser.: Vol. 183). 330p. 1973. 79.00 (*0-387-05832-X*) Spr-Verlag.

Lions, J. L., jt. auth. see Benoussan, Alain.

Lions, J. L., jt. ed. see Benoussan, Alain.

Lions, J. L., jt. ed. see Bensoussan, A.

Lions, J. L., ed. see Ciarlet, P. G.

Lions, J. L., jt. ed. see Ciarlet, P. G.

Lions, J. L., ed. see Crouzeix, M. & Rappaz, J.

Lions, J. L., jt. auth. see Dautray, R.

Lions, J. L., jt. auth. see Duvant, G.

Lions, J. L., jt. auth. see Glowinski, R.

Lions, J. L., jt. ed. see Glowinski, R.

Lions, J. L., ed. see Grisvard, P.

Lions, J. L., jt. auth. see Kang, F.

Lions, J. L., jt. auth. see Lagnese, J. E.

Lions, J. L., ed. see Le Tallec, P. V.

Lions, J. L., ed. see Rabier, P. J. & Oden, J. Tinsley.

Lions of Illinois Foundation Staff. Illinois Directory of Services for the Visually Impaired. large type ed. 1985. 10.00 (*0-317-01849-3*) Lions IL Foun.

Lions, P. L., jt. ed. see Fleming, W.

Liontas, jt. auth. see Baginski.

Liontos, Lynn B. At-Risk Families & Schools: Becoming Partners. LC 91-77519. xii, 156p. 1992. pap. 12.95 (*0-86552-113-1*) U of Oreg ERIC.

Lior, N., ed. Measurements & Control in Water Desalination. 464p. 1986. 154.00 (*0-444-42671-X*) Elsevier.

Lior, N. & Tanasawa, I., eds. Heat & Mass Transfer Materials Processing. 700p. 1991. 105.00 (*1-56032-192-X*) Hemisp Pub.

Liorzou, G. Knee Ligaments: Clinical Examination. Finlayson, D., tr. (Illus.). xii, 108p. 1991. 96.00 (*0-387-53761-9*) Spr-Verlag.

Liotta, Charles, et al. Phase-Transfer Catalysis: Fundamentals, Applications & Industrial Perspectives. LC 93-19659. 1993. 89.95 (*0-412-04071-9*) Chapman & Hall.

Liotta, Dennis, ed. Advances in Molecular Modeling, Vol. 3. 1992. 90.25 (*1-55938-326-7*) Jai Pr.

— Applications of Molecular Orbital Theory in Organic Chemistry, Vol. 1. 1988. 73.25 (*0-89232-871-1*) Jai Pr.

Liotta, Dennis C. Organoselenium Chemistry. LC 86-5582. 422p. 1987. text ed. 105.00 (*0-471-88867-2*) Wiley.

Liotta, Dennis C. & Volmer, Mark. Organic Syntheses Reaction Guide. (Organic Syntheses Collective Volumes Ser.). 1991. text ed. 74.95 (*0-471-54261-X*) Wiley.

Liotta, Lance A., ed. Influence of Tumor Development on the Host. (Cancer Growth & Progression Ser.). (C). 1988. lib. bdg. 140.00 (*0-89838-992-5*) Kluwer Ac.

Liotta, Lance A. & Hurt, I. R. Tumor Invasion & Metastasis. 1982. lib. bdg. 242.00 (*90-247-2611-5*) Kluwer Ac.

Liotta, Mary A., ed. see Brady, Joan.

Liotta, Mary A., ed. see Clark, Carolyn C.

Liotta, Mary A., ed. see Farese, Susan J.

Liotta, Mary A., ed. see Zagury, Carolyn S.

Liotta, Mary Ann, ed. see Clark, Carolyn C.

Liotta, P. H. Diamond's Compass: A Novel. LC 92-33371. 1993. 18.95 (*0-945575-74-2*) Algonquin Bks.

— Learning to Fly: A Season with the Peregrine Falcon. LC 88-35016. (Illus.). 271p. 1989. 16.95 (*0-945575-15-7*) Algonquin Bks.

— Rules of Engagement. (CSU Poetry Ser.: No. XXXIV). 137p. (Orig.). 1991. 15.00 (*0-914946-88-9*); pap. 10.00 (*0-914946-89-7*) Cleveland St Univ Poetry Ctr.

Liotti, G., jt. auth. see Guidano, Vittorio F.

Liou, Juin J. Advanced Semiconductor Device Physics. LC 93-42250. 1993. 89.00 (*0-89006-696-5*) Artech Hse.

Liou, Kuo-Nan. Radiation & Cloud Processes in the Atmosphere: Theory, Observation & Modeling. (Oxford Monographs on Geology & Geophysics: No. 21). (Illus.). 512p. 1992. 85.00 (*0-19-504910-1*) OUP.

Lioy, Paul & Lippmann, Morton, eds. Toxic Air Pollutant Guidelines: Review of Recent Progress & Problems. (Illus.). (C). 1988. pap. text ed. 8.00 (*0-936712-77-5*) Am Conf Govt Indus Hygienist.

Lioy, Paul J., jt. ed. see Kneip, Theo J.

Liozbanski, jt. auth. see Persobke.

***Lip, Evelyn.** Chinese Beliefs & Superstitions. (Illus.). 80p. (Orig.). 1985. pap. 6.95 (*9971-947-88-9*) Heian Intl.

— Chinese Numbers: Significance, Symbolism & Traditions. (Illus.). 121p. (Orig.). 1992. pap. 9.95 (*0-89346-376-0*) Heian Intl.

— Chinese Proverbs & Sayings. 111p. 1984. pap. 5.95 (*9971-947-61-7*) Heian Intl.

— Feng Shui: A Layman's Guide to Chinese Geomancy. (Illus.). 132p. 1987. pap. 9.95 (*0-89346-286-1*) Heian Intl.

— Feng Shui for Business. (Illus.). 112p. 1990. pap. 9.95 (*0-89346-326-4*) Heian Intl.

— Feng Shui for the Home. (Illus.). 91p. 1990. pap. 9.95 (*0-89346-327-2*) Heian Intl.

— Fun with Astrology. (Illus.). 84p. (Orig.). 1983. pap. 6.50 (*9971-947-54-4*) Heian Intl.

— Fun with Chinese Horoscopes. rev. ed. (Illus.). 104p. 1987. reprint ed. pap. 6.50 (*9971-947-11-0*) Heian Intl.

— Notes on Things Chinese. (Illus.). 128p. Date not set. pap. 6.95 (*9971-4-9061-7*) Heian Intl.

— Out of China: Culture & Traditions. LC 93-23966. (Illus.). 1993. 29.90 (*0-685-65618-7*) Addison-Wesley.

Lipanovich, Marianne, ed. see Hodges, Larry & Powell, Charles C.

Lipanovich, Marianne, ed. see Hodgson, Larry, et al.

Lipanovich, Marianne, ed. see Lauwers, Susan, et al.

Lipanovich, Marianne, ed. see ORTHO Books Staff.

Lipari, Joanna, jt. auth. see Brandstein, Eve.

***Lipari, Joseph & Jobin, Leonard.** Isn't That Romantic: Imaginative Ways to Express Your Love. LC 94-21294. 1995. pap. 8.95 (*0-89529-634-9*) Avery Pub.

Lipartito, Kenneth. The Bell System & Regional Business: The Telephone in the South, 1877-1920. LC 89-32037. (AT&T Series in Telephone History). (Illus.). 304p. 1989. text ed. 42.50x (*0-8018-3797-9*) Johns Hopkins.

Lipartito, Kenneth J. & Pratt, Joseph A. Baker & Botts in the Development of Modern Houston. (Illus.). 276p. 1991. 24.95 (*0-292-70782-7*) U of Tex Pr.

Lipatov, Y. S. Adsorption of Polymers. 188p. 1974. text ed. 47.75 (*0-7065-1434-3*, Pub. by Keter Pub IS) Coronet Bks.

Lipay, Raymond J. Accounting Services for Your Small Business: A Guide for Evaluating Company Performance, Obtaining Financing, Selling Your Business. LC 82-13647. 270p. reprint ed. pap. 77.00 (*0-7837-3512-X*, 2057845) Bks Demand.

— Keys to Choosing a Financial Specialist. (Business Keys Ser.). 160p. (Orig.). 1992. pap. text ed. 4.95 (*0-8120-4545-9*) Barron.

Lipchitz, Leslie & McDonald, Donogh, eds. German Unification: Economic Issues. LC 90-26503. (Occasional Paper Ser.: No. 75). xiii, 171p. (Orig.). 1991. pap. 10.00 (*1-55775-200-1*) Intl Monetary.

Lipcon, Charles R. Seaman's Rights in the United States When Involved in an Accident. Professional Translating Services, Inc. Staff, tr. 50p. (Orig.). (FRE, GER, GRE, ITA, KOR, POR & SPA.). 1989. pap. 9.95 (*0-932557-01-5*) Adels Inc.

Lipe, Betty & Lipe, Robert. Clean Your Shells & Other Sealife. 40p. (Orig.). 1993. pap. 4.95 (*0-9637681-1-5*) Shell Store.

Lipe, David, jt. auth. see Andre, Lee.

Lipe, Karen. The Big Book of Boat Canvas: A Complete Guide to Fabric Work on Boats. (Illus.). 256p. 1991. pap. 18.95 (*0-915160-34-X*, 60210P) Intl Marine.

— The Big Book of Boat Canvas: A Complete Guide to Fabric Work on Boats. 1991. pap. 19.95 (*0-07-038000-7*) McGraw.

— Big Book of Boat Canvas: A Complete Guide to Fabric Work on Boats. 1991. pap. 19.95 (*0-915160-35-8*) Seven Seas.

Lipe, Robert. Marginellas. 40p. (Orig.). 1991. pap. 15.95 (*0-9637681-0-7*) Shell Store.

Lipe, Robert, jt. auth. see Lipe, Betty.

Lipe, Robert E. & Abbott, R. Tucker. Living Shells of the Caribbean & Florida Keys. (Illus.). 80p. (Orig.). 1991. pap. 5.95 (*0-915826-25-9*) Am Malacologists.

Lipe, Roger. The Road to Ground Zero. 126p. (Orig.). 1993. pap. 6.99 (*1-56043-755-3*) Destiny Image.

Lipe, William D. Excavations, Glen Canyon Area, 1958. (Glen Canyon Ser.: No. 11). reprint ed. 47.50 (*0-404-60644-X*) AMS Pr.

Lipe, William D., ed. The Sand Canyon Archaeological Project: A Progress Report. LC 91-76321. (Occasional Paper Ser.: No. 2). (Illus.). 160p. (Orig.). 1992. pap. text ed. 21.95x (*0-9624640-1-5*) Crow Canyon Archaeol.

Lipe, William D. & Hegmon, Michelle, eds. The Architecture of Social Integration in Prehistoric Pueblos. LC 89-81117. (Occasional Paper Ser.: No. 1). (Illus.). 175p. (Orig.). 1990. pap. text ed. 21.95x (*0-9624640-0-7*) Crow Canyon Archaeol.

Lipe, William D., et al. Excavations, Glen Canyon Area, 1959. (Glen Canyon Ser.: No. 13). reprint ed. 47.50 (*0-404-60649-0*) AMS Pr.

Lipeck, Udo W. & Thalheim, Bernhard. Modelling Database Dynamics: Selected Papers from the Fourth International Workshop on Foundations of Models & Languages for Data & Objects, Volkse, Germ 19-22 October 1992. 4th ed. LC 93-3307. (Workshops in Computing Ser.). 1993. 59.00 (*0-387-19803-2*) Spr-Verlag.

Lipenius, Martin. Bibliotheca Realis Iuridica, 6 vols., Set. 1967. reprint ed. write for info. (*0-318-71838-3*, Pub. by Georg Olms GW) Lubrecht & Cramer.

— Bibliotheca Realis Philosophica, 2 vols., Set. 1967. reprint ed. write for info. (*0-318-71839-1*, Pub. by Georg Olms GW) Lubrecht & Cramer.

— Bibliotheca Realis Theologica, 2 vols., Set. 1973. reprint ed. write for info. (*3-487-04594-X*, Pub. by Georg Olms GW) Lubrecht & Cramer.

Lipetz, Ben-Ami. Guide to Case Studies of Scientific Activity. LC 65-23580. 1965. 20.00 (*0-910788-02-2*) Intermedia.

— Measurement of Efficiency of Scientific Research. LC 65-23581. 1965. 20.00 (*0-910788-01-4*) Intermedia.

Lipetz, Marcia J. Routine Justice: Processing Cases in Women's Court. (New Observations Ser.). 128p. 1983. 28.95 (*0-87855-483-1*) Transaction Pubs.

Lipetz, Marcia J., jt. auth. see Ellis, R. L.

Lipetz, P. Good Calorie Diet. 288p. 1994. 23.00 (*0-06-017112-X*, HarpT) HarpC.

Lipez, Richard, ed. see Coben, Harlan.

Lipfert, Frederick W. Air Pollution & Community Health: A Critical Review & Data Sourcebook. LC 93-1364. 1994. text ed. 69.95 (*0-442-01444-9*) Van Nos Reinhold.

— The Association of Human Mortality with Air Pollution 1984. Dixon, Eustace A., ed. (Illus.). 240p. (C). 1984. pap. 15.95 (*0-942848-03-9*) Eureka Pubns.

Lipfert, Helmut & Girbig, Werner. The War Diary of Hauptmann Helmut Lipfert: JG 52 on the Russian Front 1943-1945. Johnston, David, tr. LC 92-61775. (Illus.). 224p. 1993. 29.95 (*0-88740-446-4*) Schiffer.

Lipfert, Nathan R., jt. auth. see Martin, Kenneth R.

Lipgens, Walter, ed. Documents on the History of European Integration: Vol. 2, Plans for European Union in Great Britain & in Exile, 1939-1945. (European University Institute, Series B (History): Vols. 1/2). xxiv, 852p. 1986. 216.00 (*0-89925-212-5*) De Gruyter.

— Documents on the History of European Integration Vol. 1: Continental Plans for European Union 1939-1945. LC 84-19842. (European University Institute, Series B (History)). (Illus.). xxiv, 823p. 1984. 290.80 (*3-11-009724-9*; fiche 290.80 (*0-318-59211-8*) De Gruyter.

— Documents on the History of European Integration Vol. 2: Plans for European Union in Great Britain & in Exile, 1939-1945. (European University Institute, Series B (History): Vols. 1/2). xxiv, 852p. 1986. 261.55 (*3-11-010338-9*) De Gruyter.

***Lipgens, Walter & Loth, Wilfried, eds.** Documents on the History of European Integration Vol. 3: The Struggle for the European Union by Political Parties & Pressure Groups in Western European Countries, 1945-1950. xliv, 824p. (C). 1988. lib. bdg. 284.65x (*3-11-011429-1*) De Gruyter.

— Documents on the History of European Integration, Vol. 3: The Struggle for the European Union by Political Parties & Pressure Groups in Western European Countries, 1945-1950. xliv, 824p. (C). 1988. lib. bdg. 284.65x (*0-89925-416-0*) De Gruyter.

Lipham, James M. Effective Principal, Effective School. LC 81-154085. 36p. (Orig.). reprint ed. pap. 25.00 (*0-685-23753-2*, 2032795) Bks Demand.

Lipham, James M., et al. The Principalship: Concepts, Competencies, & Cases. 335p. (C). 1985. text ed. 32.95 (*0-582-28581-X*, 71607) Longman.

Lipiec, Jerzy, jt. ed. see Glinski, Jan.

Lipietz, Alain. The Enchanted World: Inflation, Credit & the World Crisis. 188p. (C). 1988. text ed. 50.00 (*0-86091-098-9*, A0876, Pub. by Verso UK); pap. text ed. 14.95 (*0-86091-806-8*, A0880, Pub. by Verso UK) Routledge Chapman & Hall.

— Green Hopes: The Future of Political Ecology. Slater, Malcolm, tr. 169p. 1995. write for info. (*0-7456-1325-X*, Pub. by Polity Pr UK); pap. write for info. (*0-7456-1327-6*, Pub. by Polity Pr UK) Blackwell Pubs.

— Mirages & Miracles: The Crises of Global Fordism. 240p. 1988. 50.00 (*0-86091-152-7*, Pub. by Verso UK); pap. 15.95 (*0-86091-865-3*, Pub. by Verso UK) Routledge Chapman & Hall.

— Towards a New Economic Order: Postfordism, Ecology & Democracy. LC 92-11305. (Europe & the International Order Ser.). 196p. (C). 1992. text ed. 42.50 (*0-19-520961-3*); pap. text ed. 15.95 (*0-19-520962-1*) OUP.

Lipin, B. R., ed. see Boynton, William V., et al.

Lipin, Lawrence M. Producers, Proletarians, & Politicians: Workers & Party Politics in Evansville & New Albany, Indiana, 1850-87. LC 92-41298. 328p. 1993. 42.50 (*0-252-02019-7*) U of Ill Pr.

Lipincot, Don & Treverton, Gregory F. Negotiations Concerning the Falklands - Maldives Dispute: Breakdown of Negotiations & the Haig Mediation Effort. (Pew Case Studies in International Affairs). 56p. (C). 1988. pap. text ed. 2.50 (*1-56927-406-1*) Geo U Inst Dplmcy.

***Lipinski, Klaus.** Lexikon der Datenkommunikation. 380p. (GER.). 1994. 185.00 (*0-7859-8541-7*, 3892380732) Fr & Eur.

Lipinski, jt. auth. see Kelly.

Lipinski, Alex. The Directory of Jobs & Careers Abroad. 8th ed. 352p. 1993. pap. 16.95 (*1-85458-025-6*, Pub. by Vacation-Work UK) Petersons Guides.

Lipinski, Arlene L. Work, Jobs & Occupations--Distress, Dangers & Diseases: Index of New Information. (Illus.). 150p. 1994. 44.50 (*0-7883-0014-8*); pap. 39.50 (*0-7883-0015-6*) ABBE Pubs Assn.

Lipinski, Boguslaw, ed. Electronic Conduction & Mechanoelectrical Transduction in Biological Materials. LC 82-12998. (Illus.). 319p. reprint ed. pap. 91.00 (*0-7837-0888-2*, 2041194) Bks Demand.

***Lipinski, Edouard.** Dictionnaire de la Civilisation Phenicienne et Punique. 501p. (FRE.). 1993. 285.00 (*0-7859-7902-6*, 2503500331) Fr & Eur.

Lipinski, Hubert & Adler, Richard. The HUB Project: Computer-Based Support for Group Problem Solving. 218p. 1982. 15.00 (*0-318-19196-2*, R-51) Inst Future.

Lipinski, Kathleen A. & Lipinski, Robert A. Professional Guide to Alcoholic Beverages. (Illus.). 480p. (C). 1989. 20.95 (*0-442-31913-4*) Van Nos Reinhold.

— Professional Guide to Alcoholic Beverages. (Illus.). 480p. (C). 1989. text ed. 44.95 (*0-442-25837-2*) Van Nos Reinhold.

Lipinski, Kathleen A., jt. auth. see Lipinski, Robert A.

Lipinski, Martha E., ed. Role of the Civil Engineer in Highway Safety. 215p. 1983. pap. 25.00 (*0-87262-374-2*) Am Soc Civil Eng.

Lipinski, Miroslaw, ed. Treasury of Polish Love Poems, Quotations & Proverbs. 128p. 1994. 9.00 (*0-7818-0297-0*) Hippocrene Bks.

Lipinski, Miroslaw, ed. see Sienkiewicz, Henryk.

Lipinski, Miroslaw, tr. see Sienkiewicz, Henryk.

Lipinski, Rick, tr. see Cernuda, Luis.

Lipinski, Robert A. & Lipinski, Kathleen A. The Complete Beverage Dictionary. 416p. 1992. text ed. 39.95 (*0-442-23987-4*) Van Nos Reinhold.

Lipinski, Robert A., jt. auth. see Lipinski, Kathleen A.

Lipinski, Thomas. The Fall-Down Artist. 304p. 1994. 20.95 (*0-312-10461-8*, Pub. by Thomas Dunne Bks) St Martin.

Lipinsky, Edward S. Handbook Bisolar Resources. McClure, Thomas A., ed. (Handbook of Biosolar Resources Ser.: Vol. 2). 608p. 1981. 119.00 (*0-8493-3473-X*, TP360, CRC Reprint) Franklin.

Lipinsky, Miroslaw, tr. see Sienkiewicz, Henryk.

Lipis, Allen H., et al. Electronic Banking. LC 84-20831. (Professional Banking & Finance Ser.). 220p. 1985. text ed. 65.00 (*0-471-88224-0*) Wiley.

Lipis, Joan R. Celebrate Passover Haggadah: A Christian Presentation of the Traditional Jewish Festival. LC 93-18254. 1993. 2.95 (*1-881022-03-X*) Purple Pomegranate.

Lipitakis, A. Computer Mathematics, Lecture Notes: Advances on Computer Mathematics & Its Applications. 384p. 1993. text ed. 74.00 (*981-02-1292-5*) World Scientific Pub.

Lipka, Charles, ed. see Jud, Brian.

Lipka, Leonard. Semantic Structure & Word Formation: Verb-Particle Constructions in Contemporary English. 1973. bds. 47.75 (*3-7705-0947-1*) Adlers Foreign Bks.

Lipka, Richard P. & Brinthaupt, Thomas M., eds. Self-Perspectives Across the Life Span. LC 91-16383. (SUNY Series, Studying the Self). 282p. (C). 1992. 59.50 (*0-7914-1003-X*); pap. 19.95 (*0-7914-1004-8*) State U NY Pr.

Lipka, Richard P., jt. auth. see Beane, James A.

Lipka, Richard P., jt. ed. see Brinthaupt, Thomas M.

Lipka, Richard P., et al. Community Service Projects: Citizenship in Action. LC 85-61790. (Fastback Ser.: No. 231). 50p. 1985. pap. 1.25 (*0-87367-231-3*) Phi Delta Kappa.

Lipke, Ken & Swiatek, Frank. The American Leader. (Illus.). 250p. (C). 1989. write for info. (*0-318-65231-5*) Gibraltar LIF.

Lipke, Paul, ed. see Ansel, Willits, et al.

Lipke, William C. Thomas Waterman Wood, PNA, 1823-1903. (Illus.). 1970. pap. 4.00 (*0-89073-032-6*) Boston Public Lib.

Lipke, William C. & Grime, Philip N., eds. Vermont Landscape Images, 1776-1976. LC 76-19178. (Illus.). 119p. 1976. pap. 15.95 (*0-87451-991-8*) U Pr of New Eng.

Lipkin, Barbara, ed. see Charischak, Ihor.

Lipkin, Bernice. String Processing & Text Manipulation in C: Selected Data Structures & Tech. 464p. 1994. pap. text ed. 36.80 (*0-13-121443-8*) P-H.

Lipkin, Catherine & Solotaroff, Virginia. Words on the Page, Bk. 1. 1990. pap. 9.00 (*0-06-096367-0*, PL) HarpC.

Lipkin, Catherine, jt. auth. see Solotaroff, Virginia.

Lipkin, David P., jt. auth. see Nolan, James.

Lipkin, Gladys B. & Cohen, Roberta G. Effective Approaches to Patients' Behavior. 4th ed. LC 91-4806. 312p. (C). 1992. pap. text ed. 27.95 (*0-8261-1496-2*) Springer Pub.

Lipkin, H. J. Quantum Mechanics: New Approaches to Selected Topics. LC 72-79733. 478p. 1986. reprint ed. pap. 32.50 (*0-444-87010-5*, North Holland) Elsevier.

Lipkin, Lawrence. Accountant's Handbook of Formulas & Tables. 3rd ed. 608p. 1988. text ed. 59.95 (*0-13-002957-2*, Busn) P-H.

Lipkin, M., Jr., ed. see White, K. L.

Lipkin, Mack. The Care of Patients: Perspectives & Practices. rev. ed. LC 86-24599. 235p. 1987. text ed. 14.00 (*0-300-03771-6*) Yale U Pr.

— Psychosocial Factors Affecting Health. LC 82-11249. 396p. 1982. text ed. 75.00 (*0-275-91371-6*, C1371, Praeger Pubs) Greenwood.

Lipkin, Mack & Lybrand, William A., eds. Population-Based Medicine. LC 81-21116. 220p. 1982. text ed. 55.00 (*0-275-91370-8*, C1370, Praeger Pubs) Greenwood.

Lipkin, Mack, ed. see Tahir-Kheli, Shirin.

Lipkin, Mack, Jr., et al. The Medical Interview. LC 94-6511. 1994. write for info. (*0-387-94257-2*); 138.00 (*3-540-94257-2*) Spr-Verlag.

Lipkin, Marjorie B. The School Search Guide to Private Schools in the Northeast. 351p. 1988. pap. text ed. 12.95 (*0-9620326-0-3*) Schoolsearch Pr.

Lipkin, Martin, jt. ed. see Zedeck, Morris S.

Lipkin, Martin, et al. Calcium, Vitamin D, & Prevention of Colon Cancer. (Illus.). 416p. 1991. 115.00 (*0-8493-4264-3*, RC280) CRC Pr.

Lipkin, Midge. The Schoolsearch Guide to Colleges with Programs or Services for Students with Learning Disabilities. 928p. (Orig.). 1993. pap. text ed. 34.95 (*0-9620326-5-4*) Schoolsearch Pr.

— The Schoolsearch Guide to Private Schools with Programs or Services for Students with Learning Disabilities. 650p. (Orig.). 1992. pap. 34.95 (*0-9620326-4-6*) Schoolsearch Pr.

Lipkin, W. I., jt. ed. see Koprowski, H.

Lipkind, William. Days to Remember. (Illus.). (J). (gr. 3 up). 1961. 10.95 (*0-8392-3006-0*) Astor-Honor.

Lipking, Lawrence. The Life of the Poet: Beginning & Ending Poetic Careers. LC 81-1067. (Illus.). (C). 1985. pap. 7.95 (*0-226-48451-3*) U Ch Pr.

Lipking, Lawrence, ed. High Romantic Argument: Essays for M. H. Abrams. 192p. 1981. 29.95 (*0-8014-1307-9*) Cornell U Pr.

Lipking, Lawrence I. The Ordering of the Arts in Eighteenth-Century England. LC 76-90953. 523p. reprint ed. pap. 149.10 (*0-8357-2780-7*, 2039906) Bks Demand.

Lipkov, Alexander, jt. auth. see Konchalovsky, Andrei.

Lipkowitz, Brenda, ed. see Dickens, Nathaniel A.

Lipkowitz, Kenneth B. & Boyd, Donald B., eds. Reviews in Computational Chemistry. LC 89-21466. 419p. 1990. lib. bdg. 115.00 (*0-89573-754-X*) VCH Pubs.

— Reviews in Computational Chemistry, Vol. 2. 520p. 1991. text ed. 125.00 (*1-56081-515-9*) VCH Pubs.

Lipkowitz, Kenny B. & Boyd, Donald B. Reviews in Computational Chemistry, Vol. 4. 280p. 1993. 79.00 (*1-56081-620-1*) VCH Pubs.

— Reviews in Computational Chemistry, Vol. 5. 458p. 1994. 110.00 (*1-56081-658-9*) VCH Pubs.

Lipkowitz, Kenny B. & Boyd, Donald B., eds. Reviews in Computational Chemistry, Vol. 3. LC 92-30192. 272p. 1993. 75.00 (*1-56081-619-8*) VCH Pubs.

Lipkowitz, Marcel. French Royal & Administrative Acts, Twelve Fifty-Six to Seventeen Ninety-Four: A Subject Guide to the New York Public Library Collection of Sixteen Thousand Pamphlets Now on Microfilm. LC 78-8497. 206p. 1978. 90.00 (*0-89235-011-3*) Res Pubns CT.

Lipkowitz, Myron, jt. auth. see Navarra, Tova.

Lipkowski, Jacek & Ross, Philip N., eds. Adsorption of Molecules at Metal Electrodes. LC 92-19438. (Frontiers of Electrochemistry Ser.: Vol. 1). 1992. 145.00 (*0-89573-786-8*) VCH Pubs.

— The Eletrochemistry of Novel Materials. LC 93-40037. 1994. write for info. (*0-89573-788-4*) VCH Pubs.

Lipman, Aaron. Colombian Entrepreneur in Bogota. LC 69-15926. (Hispanic-American Studies Ser.: No. 22). (Illus.). 1969. 9.95 (*0-87024-111-7*) U of Miami Pr.

Lipman, Andrew D. Telecom Deregulation. LC 87-82644. 260p. 1987. 60.00 (*0-917845-06-4*) Intertec IL.

Lipman-Blumen, Jean. Gender Roles & Power. 224p. (C). 1984. text ed. write for info. (*0-13-347518-2*); pap. text ed. write for info. (*0-13-347500-X*) P-H.

Lipman, Bradford C., ed. ECG Pocket Guide. (Illus.). 224p. 1986. 24.95 (*0-8151-5450-X*, COL-1, Yr Bk Med Pubs) Mosby Yr Bk.

Lipman, Bradford C. & Cascio, Toni. ECG Assessment & Interpretation. (Illus.). 295p. 1994. pap. 22.95 (*0-8036-5646-7*) Davis Co.

Lipman, Burton E. The Executive Job Search Program. LC 82-90123. (Illus.). 175p. (Orig.). 1982. pap. 24.95 (*0-943064-01-5*) Bell Pub.

— How to Become a Vice-President in Two Weeks (More or Less) (Illus.). 130p. 1982. pap. 24.95 (*0-943064-04-X*) Bell Pub.

— How to Control & Reduce Inventory. rev. ed. LC 72-4485. (Illus.). 210p. 1988. pap. 49.50 (*0-943064-02-3*) Bell Pub.

Lipman, Doug. Story Games: Fun Activities for Telling, Creating, Collecting, & Writing. LC 94-38939. (Illus.). 160p. 1994. pap. 24.95 (*0-89774-848-4*) Oryx Pr.

— The Storytelling Coach. (American Storytelling Ser.). 1995. 24.95 (*0-87483-435-X*); pap. 14.95 (*0-87483-434-1*) August Hse.

— We All Go Together: Creative Activities for Children to Use with Multicultural Folksongs. (Illus.). 232p. 1994. pap. 34.50 (*0-89774-764-X*) Oryx Pr.

Lipman, Ed. No Capital Crime. 1975. pap. 5.00 (*0-915016-04-4*) Second Coming.

Lipman, Elinor. Into Love & Out Again. 1988. pap. 6.95 (*0-671-65676-7*) PB.

— Isabel's Bed. Rosenman, Jane, ed. 400p. 1995. 20.00 (*0-671-88160-4*) PB.

— Then She Found Me. Rosenman, Jane, ed. 320p. 1991. reprint ed. pap. 12.00 (*0-671-68615-1*, WSP) PB.

Lipman, Eva, jt. auth. see Graves, Ken.

Lipman, Frederick D. Being Public. 3rd ed. 26p. 1987. pap. text ed. 15.00 (*0-936093-06-4*) Packard Pr Fin.

— Going Public: Everything You Need to Know to Successfully Turn a Private Enterprise into a Publicly Traded Company. LC 93-23557. 1994. boxed 24.95 (*1-55958-425-4*) Prima Pub.

Lipman, Frederick D. & Wiseman, Lawrence R. Being Public: Banks & Bank Holding Companies. 28p. (Orig.). 1988. pap. 15.00 (*0-936093-10-2*) Packard Pr Fin.

Lipman, Henry & Blazey, Mark. Students of the Third Age: University - College Programs for Retired Adults. Fischer, Richard B. et al, eds. (ACE-Oryx Series on Higher Education). (Illus.). 192p. 1992. 29.95 (*0-02-897143-4*, ACE-Oryx) Oryx Pr.

Lipman, Ira A., ed. The Private Security Industry: Issues & Trends. (Annals Ser.: Vol. 498). 1988. 26.00 (*0-8039-3102-6*); pap. 17.00 (*0-8039-3103-4*) Sage.

Lipman, J. & Gau, Y. Topological Invariants of Quasi-Ordinary Singularities & Embedded Topological Classification of Quasi-Ordinary Singularities. LC 88-10559. (MEMO Ser.: No. 74/388). 129p. 1989. reprint ed. 22.00 (*0-8218-2451-1*, MEMO 74/388) Am Math.

***Lipman, J. & Teissier, B., eds.** Oscar Zariski: Collected Papers Vol. 4: Equisingularity on Algebraic Varieties. (Mathematicians of Our Time Ser.). 1979. 75.00x (*0-262-24022-X*) MIT Pr.

Lipman, Jean. American Folk Art in Wood, Metal & Stone. pap. 8.95 (*0-486-22816-9*) Dover.
— American Primitive Painting. LC 79-184124. (Illus.). 158p. 1972. reprint ed. pap. 9.95 (*0-486-22815-0*) Dover.
Lipman, Jean & Aspinwall, Margaret. Alexander Calder & His Magical Mobiles. LC 81-1811. (Illus.). 96p. (J). (ps up). 1981. 19.95 (*0-933920-17-2*) Hudson Hills.
Lipman, Jean & Mevlendyke, Eve. American Folk Decoration. (Illus.). xii, 163p. 1972. reprint ed. pap. 8.95 (*0-486-22217-9*) Dover.
Lipman, Jean & Winchester, Alice. Primitive Painters in America, Seventeen Fifty - Nineteen Fifty: An Anthology. LC 70-179732. (Biography Index Reprint Ser.). 1980. reprint ed. 16.95 (*0-8369-8100-6*) Ayer.
Lipman, Jean, et al. Five-Star Folk Art: One Hundred American Masterpieces. (Illus.). 176p. 1990. 39.95 (*0-8109-3302-0*) Abrams.
***Lipman, John C., ed.** Quick Reference to Radiology. LC 94-33452. 1994. pap. text ed. 39.95 (*0-8385-8196-X*) Appleton & Lange.
Lipman, Jonathan. Frank Lloyd Wright & the Johnson Wax Buildings. LC 85-43489. (Illus.). 1986. pap. 29.95 (*0-8478-0706-1*) Rizzoli Intl.
Lipman, Jonathan & Levine, Neil. The Wright State: Frank Lloyd Wright in Wisconsin. LC 92-30063. 1992. pap. 19.95 (*0-944110-27-4*) Milwauk Art Mus.
Lipman, Jonathan N. & Harrell, Stevan, eds. Violence in China: Essays in Culture & Counterculture. LC 88-32411. (SUNY Series in Chinese Local Studies). 249p. 1990. 64.50 (*0-7914-0113-8*); pap. 21.95 (*0-7914-0115-4*) State U NY Pr.
Lipman, Joseph. Residues & Traces of Differential Forms Via Hochschild Homology. LC 86-28698. (Contemporary Mathematics Ser.: Vol. 61). 95p. 1987. 22.00 (*0-8218-5070-9*, CONM/61C) Am Math.
Lipman, Kennard, ed. see Norbu, Namkhai.
***Lipman, Linda.** Real Estate Advertising That Works! (Illus.). 298p. 1992. reprint ed. pap. 19.95 (*1-887145-01-X*) Argyle Pr NV.
***Lipman, M., et al.** An Atlas for the Differential Diagnosis of AIDS. LC 94-21470. (Encyclopedia of Visual Medicine Ser.). 1994. 78.00 (*1-85070-474-0*) Prthnon Pub.
Lipman, Marc E., jt. ed. see Dickson, Robert B.
Lipman, Matthew. Elfie, 3 bks., Set. (Philosophy for Children Ser.). 184p. 1987. pap. 10.50x (*0-916834-24-7*) Inst Advncmnt Philos Child.
— Harry Prime. 213p. 1991. pap. 8.00 (*0-916834-23-9*) Inst Advncmnt Philos Child.
— Harry Stottlemeier's Discovery. rev. ed. LC 76-9315. (Philosophy for Children Ser.). 96p. (J). (gr. 5-6). 1982. pap. 10.50 (*0-916834-06-9*, TX516-633) Inst Advncmnt Philos Child.
— Kio & Gus. LC 79-9315. (Philosophy for Children Ser.). 77p. (J). (gr. 3-4). 1982. pap. 10.50 (*0-916834-19-0*, TX942-173) Inst Advncmnt Philos Child.
— Lisa. (Philosophy for Children Ser.). 96p. (YA). (gr. 7-10). 1983. pap. 10.50 (*0-916834-21-2*) Inst Advncmnt Philos Child.
— Mark. LC 80-80849. (Philosophy for Children Ser.). 86p. (gr. 11-12). 1980. pap. 10.50 (*0-916834-13-1*, TX 752-903) Inst Advncmnt Philos Child.
— Philosophy Goes to School. LC 87-18071. 250p. (C). 1988. 34.95 (*0-87722-537-0*); pap. 16.95 (*0-87722-555-9*) Temple U Pr.
Lipman, Matthew, et al. Philosophy in the Classroom. 2nd ed. 248p. 1980. pap. 22.95 (*0-87722-183-9*) Temple U Pr.
Lipman, Matthew. Pixie. LC 81-67706. (Philosophy for Children Ser.). 98p. (Orig.). (J). (gr. 3-4). 1981. pap. 10.50 (*0-916834-17-4*, TX782-682) Inst Advncmnt Philos Child.
— Suki. (Philosophy for Children Ser.). 153p. (Orig.). (gr. 9-10). 1978. pap. 10.50 (*0-916834-08-5*, TX86-788) Inst Advncmnt Philos Child.
— Thinking Children & Education. 768p. 1993. per. 39.95 (*0-8403-8584-6*) Kendall-Hunt.
— Thinking in Education. (C). 1991. 59.95 (*0-521-40032-5*); pap. 19.95 (*0-521-40911-X*) Cambridge U Pr.
— What Happens in Art. LC 66-27473. (Century Philosophy Ser.). (Orig.). 1967. pap. text ed. 9.95 (*0-89197-470-9*) Irvington.
Lipman, Matthew, ed. Contemporary Aesthetics. LC 73-76197. 1973. 39.50 (*0-89197-711-2*); pap. text ed. 15.95 (*0-89197-712-0*) Irvington.
Lipman, Matthew & Gazzard, Ann. Getting Our Thoughts Together: Instructional Manual to Accompany Elfie. 600p. 1988. 45.00 (*0-685-25529-8*) Inst Advncmnt Philos Child.
Lipman, Matthew & Sharp, A. M. Ethical Inquiry: Instructional Manual to Accompany Lisa. rev. ed. LC 76-9316. 1985. 45.00x (*0-916834-05-0*, TX 508-097) Inst Advncmnt Philos Child.
— Looking for Meaning: Instructional Manual to Accompany Pixie. LC 81-71564. 390p. 1982. teacher ed 45.00x (*0-916834-18-2*, TX932-050) Inst Advncmnt Philos Child.
Lipman, Matthew & Sharp, Ann M. Social Inquiry: Instructional Manual to Accompany Mark. 396p. 1980. teacher ed 45.00 (*0-916834-15-8*, TX 758-975) Inst Advncmnt Philos Child.
— Wondering at the World: Instructional Manual to Accompany KIO & GUS. (Philosophy for Children Ser.). 500p. 1986. 45.00x (*0-916834-20-4*) Inst Advncmnt Philos Child.
Lipman, Matthew & Sharp, Ann M., eds. Writing How & Why: Instructional Manual to Accompany Suki. 384p. 1980. teacher ed 45.00x (*0-916834-14-X*, TX 726-631) Inst Advncmnt Philos Child.
Lipman, Matthew, et al, eds. Philosophical Inquiry: Instructional Manual to Accompany Harry Stottlemeier's Discovery. 2nd ed. LC 76-9315. 1979. 45.00x (*0-916834-12-3*, TX467-188) Inst Advncmnt Philos Child.
Lipman, Michel. Medical Law & Ethics. LC 93-1344. 1993. pap. 14.85 (*0-13-064585-0*) P-H.
— You Are the Justice. 80p. pap. 10.00 (*0-87879-982-6*) High Noon Bks.
Lipman, Michel & Furniss, Cathy. Legal Eagle Series, 5 novels, Set. Kratoville, Betty L., ed. (Illus.). 240p. (Orig.). (J). (gr. 4-12). 1988. pap. 17.00 (*0-87879-594-4*) High Noon Bks.
Lipman, P. W., et al, eds. Cenozoic Volcanism in the Western United States. 1989. 42.00 (*0-87590-242-1*) Am Geophysical.
Lipman, Samuel. Music & More: Essays, 1968-1991. 318p. (Orig.). 1994. 35.00 (*0-8101-1051-2*); pap. 14.95 (*0-8101-1076-8*) Northwestern U Pr.
Lipman, Samuel, ed. see Arnold, Matthew.
Lipman, Sonia, jt. ed. see Lipman, V. D.
Lipman, Steve. Laughter in Hell: The Use of Humor During the Holocaust. LC 90-28101. 296p. 1992. 29.95 (*0-87668-585-8*) Aronson.
— Laughter in Hell: The Use of Humor During the Holocaust. LC 90-28101. 296p. 1993. pap. 24.95 (*1-56821-112-0*) Aronson.
Lipman, V. D. History of the Jews in Britain since 1858. LC 90-4865. 255p. 1990. 45.00 (*0-8419-1288-2*) Holmes & Meier.
Lipman, V. D. & Lipman, Sonia, eds. The Century of Moses Montefiore. LC 84-27225. (Littman Library of Jewish Civilization). (Illus.). 396p. 1985. 17.50 (*0-19-710041-4*, Pub. by Littman Lib Jew UK) Bnai Brith Bk.
Lipman-Wulf, Peter. Period of Internment: Letters & Drawings from Les Milles 1939-1940. LC 91-73296. (Illus.). 98p. (Orig.). 1993. pap. 15.00 (*0-9630164-5-8*) Canios Edit.
Lipman, Zada, ed. Local Government & Environmental Control in New South Wales. 160p. 1991. pap. 35.00 (*1-86287-074-8*, Pub. by Federation Pr AU) W W Gaunt.
Lipmann, Joel. Sweet Home Chicago. 1980. pap. 2.00 (*0-686-70612-9*) Quixote.
Lipmanson, Don, tr. see Crepin, Joseph.
Lipnack, Jessica & Stamps, Jeffrey. The Age of the Network: Organising Principles for the 21st Century. 224p. (C). 1994. 66.00x (*0-939246-71-6*) Oliver Wight.
— The TeamNet Factor: Bringing the Power of Boundary-Crossing Teams into the Heart of Your Business. LC 92-85207. 256p. 1993. 27.50 (*0-939246-34-1*) Oliver Wight.
Lipner & Kalman, David M. Computer Law. 624p. (C). 1989. write for info. (*0-675-21104-2*, Merrill Pub Co) Macmillan.
Lipner, jt. auth. see Fredericks.
Lipner, Barbara. Cloze for Comprehension: American Pioneers, 10 bks., Set. (Illus.). 1983. pap. text ed. 19.95 (*0-87594-212-1*) Book-Lab.
— Cloze for Comprehension: Celebrities of the Civil War, 10 bks., Set. (Illus.). 1983. pap. text ed. 19.95 (*0-87594-211-3*) Book-Lab.
— Cloze for Comprehension: Changing America, New Ideas, 10 bks., Set. (Illus.). 1983. pap. text ed. 19.95 (*0-87594-213-X*) Book-Lab.
— Cloze for Comprehension: Revolutionary War & Its Heroes, 10 bks., Set. (Illus.). 1983. pap. text ed. 19.95 (*0-87594-210-5*) Book-Lab.
Lipner, Barbara & Fredericks, Robert. Cloze for Comprehension: Outstanding Woman, 10 bks., Set. (Illus.). 1983. pap. text ed. 19.95 (*0-87594-203-2*) Book-Lab.
— Cloze for Comprehension: Show Business Greats, 10 bks., Set. (Illus.). 1983. pap. text ed. 19.95 (*0-87594-205-9*) Book-Lab.
— Cloze for Comprehension: Sports Personalities, 10 bks., Set. (Illus.). 1983. pap. text ed. 19.95 (*0-87594-204-0*) Book-Lab.
Lipner, Julius. Hindus: Their Religious Beliefs & Practices. LC 93-3813. 1993. write for info. (*0-415-05181-9*) Routledge.
Lipner, Julius J. The Face of Truth: A Study of Meaning & Metaphysics in the Vedantic Theology of Ramanuja. LC 84-24075. 183p. 1986. 59.50 (*0-88706-038-2*); pap. 19.95 (*0-88706-039-0*) State U NY Pr.
Lipner, Seth E. The Legal & Economic Aspects of Gray Market Goods. LC 90-30008. 240p. 1990. text ed. 59.95 (*0-89930-466-4*, LLC/, Quorum Bks) Greenwood.
Lipniacka, Ewa. Asleep at Last. LC 92-33326. (Jamie & Luke Ser.). (Illus.). (J). 1993. 6.95 (*1-56656-118-3*, Crocodile Bks) Interlink Pub.
— It's Mine! LC 92-33324. (Jamie & Luke Ser.). (Illus.). (J). 1993. 6.95 (*1-56656-119-1*, Crocodile Bks) Interlink Pub.
— School Trip. LC 92-33325. (Jamie & Luke Ser.). (Illus.). (J). 1993. 6.95 (*1-56656-121-3*, Crocodile Bks) Interlink Pub.
— To Bed...or Else! LC 91-22118. (Illus.). 32p. (J). (ps-3). 1992. 13.95 (*0-940793-85-7*, Crocodile Bks) Interlink Pub.
— Tooth Fairy. LC 92-33328. (Jamie & Luke Ser.). (Illus.). (J). 1993. 6.95 (*1-56656-120-5*, Crocodile Bks) Interlink Pub.
Lipnick, Robert L., ed. see Overton, Charles E.
Lipo, Carl P., jt. auth. see Dales, George F.
Lipoprotein Research Group Staff & Vance, Dennis E., eds. Phosphatidylcholine Metabolism. 248p. 1989. 180.00 (*0-8493-6338-1*, QP752) CRC Pr.
Liposits, Zsolt. Ultrastructural Immunocytochemistry of the Hypothalamic Corticotropin Releasing Hormone Synthesizing System: Anatomical Basis of Neuronal & Humoral Regulatory Mechanisms. (Progress in Histochemistry & Cytochemistry Ser.: Vol. 21-2). 98p. (Orig.). 1990. 65.00 (*0-685-48102-6*); pap. 80.00 (*0-89574-317-5*) G F Verlag.
Lipovcan, Srecko, ed. The Musical Heritage of the Nations & Nationalities of Yugoslavia from the 16th to the 19th Century, Vol. I. 252p. 1980. pap. 12.00 (*0-918660-42-4*) Ragusan Pr.
Lipovetsky, Gilles. The Empire of Fashion: Dressing Modern Democracy. Porter, Catherine, tr. LC 94-4830. (New French Thought Ser.). 1994. 24.95 (*0-691-03373-0*) Princeton U Pr.
Lipovski, G. J. Object-Oriented Interfacing to 16-Bit Microcontrollers. LC 92-15063. 612p. 1992. text ed. 57.00 (*0-13-629221-6*) P-H.
— Single & Multiple Chip Microcomputer Interfacing. (Illus.). 528p. (C). 1987. text ed. 74.00 (*0-13-810557-X*) P-H.
Lipovski, G. J., jt. auth. see Wagner, T. J.
Lipovski, Jack & Malek, Miroslav. Parallel Computing: Theory & Comparisons. 384p. 1987. text ed. 89.95 (*0-471-82262-0*) Wiley.
Lipovsky, Igor P. The Socialist Movement in Turkey, 1960-1980. LC 92-18122. (Social, Economic & Political Studies of the Middle East: Vol. 45). 190p. 1992. 51.50 (*90-04-09582-9*) E J Brill.
Lipovsky, James. A Historiographical Study of Livy. rev. ed. Connor, W. R., ed. LC 80-2657. (Monographs in Classical Studies). 1981. lib. bdg. 24.95 (*0-405-14043-6*) Ayer.
Lipovszky, G., et al. Vibration Testing of Machines & Their Maintenance. (Studies in Mechanical Engineering: No. 10). 312p. 1990. 123.25 (*0-444-98808-4*) Elsevier.
Lipow, Anne G., ed. Rethinking Reference in Academic Libraries. (Illus.). 242p. (Orig.). 1993. pap. 32.00 (*1-882208-02-1*) Library Solns.
Lipow, Anne G., ed. see LAMA Development Committee Staff.
Lipow, Arthur. Authoritarian Socialism in America: Edward Bellamy & the Nationalist Movement. 332p. 1991. reprint ed. pap. 15.00 (*0-520-07543-9*) U CA Pr.
Lipow, Arthur, jt. ed. see Haberkern, Ernest E.
Lipow, Myron, jt. auth. see Lloyd, David K.
Lipowitz, jt. auth. see Caywood.
Lipowitz, Alan J., et al. Small Animal Orthopedics Illustrated. LC 92-30767. (Illus.). 336p. 1993. 70.00 (*0-8016-7477-8*) Mosby Yr Bk.
Lipowski, Adam, jt. auth. see Kulig, Jan.
Lipowski, Jacek & Ross, Philip N., eds. Structure of Electrified Interfaces. LC 92-44292. (Frontiers of Electrochemistry Ser.). 406p. 1993. 125.00 (*0-89573-787-6*) VCH Pubs.
Lipowski, Zbigniew J. Delirium: Acute Confusional States. 512p. 1990. 75.00 (*0-19-506150-0*) OUP.
— Psychosomatic Medicine & Liaison Psychiatry: Selected Papers. LC 85-12474. 470p. 1985. 75.00 (*0-306-42038-4*, Plenum Med Bk) Plenum.
Lipowski, Zbigniew J., et al, eds. Psychosomatic Medicine: Current Trends & Clinical Applications. (Illus.). 1977. text ed. 45.00 (*0-19-502169-X*) OUP.
Lipowsky, R., et al, eds. The Structure & Conformation of Amphiphilic Membranes: Proceedings of the International Workshop on Amphiphilic Membranes, Julich, Germany, September 16-18, 1991. LC 92-14296. (Proceedings in Physics Ser.: Vol. 66). (Illus.). xi, 298p. 1992. 80.00 (*0-387-55452-1*) Spr-Verlag.
***Lipowsky, Reinhard & Sackmann, Erich, eds.** Structure & Dynamics of Membranes - Generic & Specific Interactions: From Cells to Visicles. LC 95-8846. (Handbook of Biological Physics Ser.: Vol. 1A). 1995. write for info. (*0-444-81975-4*) Elsevier.
Lipp, Frank J. The Mixe of Oaxaca: Religion, Ritual & Healing. (Illus.). 275p. (C). 1991. text ed. 35.00 (*0-292-76517-7*) U of Tex Pr.
Lipp, Frank J., Jr., jt. auth. see Von Reis, Siri V.
Lipp, Markus D., et al. Local Anesthesia. Coldwell, Mark et al, trs. LC 93-12264. 1993. text ed. 68.00 (*0-86715-263-X*) Quint Pub Co.
Lipp, Martin. Medical Landmarks, U.S.A. A Travel Guide to Historical Sites, Architectural Gems, Remarkable. 384p. 1991. pap. text ed. 35.00 (*0-07-037974-2*) Hlth Prof Div.
Lipp, Martin R. & Whitten, David N. To Your Health: Two Physicians Explore the Health Benefits of Wine. LC 93-5437. 176p. 1994. 18.00 (*0-06-258514-2*) Harper SF.
***Lipp, Muriel S.** What's in the Green, Dark Woods? (Illus.). 32p. (J). (gr. 3-8). 1995. 11.95 (*1-55971-456-5*) NorthWord.
Lipp, Reiner, jt. ed. see Brogyanyi, Bela.
Lipp, Solomon, ed. U. S. A. - Spanish America: Challenge & Response. (Series A: Monagrafias: No. 154). 192p. (C). 1993. text ed. 53.00 (*1-85566-033-4*, Pub. by Tamesis Bks Ltd UK) Boydell & Brewer.
Lipp, Sylvia E., tr. see Levinson, Luisa M.
Lippa, Erik A. Mathematics for Freshman in the Life Sciences. (Illus.). 319p. (Orig.). (C). 1977. pap. text ed. 25.00 (*0-9607980-0-5*) E A Lippa.
Lippa, Richard A. Introduction to Social Psychology. 643p. (C). 1989. text ed. 50.95 (*0-534-11772-4*) Brooks-Cole.
— Introduction to Social Psychology. 2nd ed. LC 93-35816. 1994. text ed. 53.95 (*0-534-17388-8*) Brooks-Cole.
Lippard, George. Blanche of Brandywine. LC 77-76926. (American Fiction Reprint Ser.). 1977. 18.95 (*0-8369-7005-5*) Ayer.
— Empire City. LC 70-76927. (American Fiction Reprint Ser.). 1977. 18.95 (*0-8369-7006-3*) Ayer.
— New York: Its Upper Ten & Lower Million. LC 70-104514. reprint ed. lib. bdg. 29.50 (*0-8398-1161-6*); reprint ed. pap. text ed. 9.95 (*0-8290-1855-7*) Irvington.
— The Quaker City: or The Monks of Monk Hall: A Romance of Philadelphia Life, Mystery, & Crime. Reynolds, David S., ed. & intro. by. LC 94-44599. 632p. 1995. pap. 19.95 (*0-87023-971-6*) U of Mass Pr.
— Washington & His Generals: Or, Legends of the American Revolution. LC 70-164570. (American Fiction Reprint Ser.). Orig. Title: The Legends of the American Revolution, 1776. 1977. reprint ed. 35.95 (*0-8369-7047-0*) Ayer.
Lippard, George, jt. auth. see Clymer, R. Swinburne.
Lippard, Karl C. Perazzi Shotguns. (Illus.). 121p. 1993. pap. 13.95 (*0-9611880-2-2*) Viet Nam Mar.
— The Warriors, the United States Marines. LC 83-90360. (Illus.). 239p. 1983. 34.95 (*0-9611880-0-6*); 250.00 (*0-9611880-1-4*) Viet Nam Mar.
Lippard, Lucy, et al. Ethics of Change. Fetscher, Elmar, ed. (Proceedings of the February Forum Ser.). 150p. (Orig.). 1992. pap. text ed. write for info. (*1-882070-07-0*) Atlantic Ctr Arts.
Lippard, Lucy. Eva Hesse. (Illus.). 251p. 1992. reprint ed. pap. 18.95 (*0-306-80484-0*) Da Capo.
— Overlay: Contemporary Art & the Art of Prehistory. 296p. 1995. pap. 20.00 (*1-56584-238-3*) New Press NY.
Lippard, Lucy & Middlebrook, Diane. Backtalk. (Illus.). 48p. (Orig.). 1993. pap. write for info. (*1-880658-06-2*) San Barb CAF.
Lippard, Lucy, jt. auth. see Brookman, Philip.
***Lippard, Lucy, et al.** Dialogo - Dialogue - Comhra. (Illus.). 272p. Date not set. pap. 29.95 (*0-9646426-1-1*) Dist Art Pubs.
— Jimmie Durham: The Bishop's Moose & the Pinkerton Men. Colo, Papo, ed. (Illus.). 36p. (Orig.). 1990. pap. 15.00 (*0-913263-31-1*) Exit Art.
— Papo Colo: Will, Power, & Desire. (Illus.). 48p. (Orig.). 1986. pap. 15.00 (*0-913263-14-1*) Exit Art.
Lippard, Lucy R. A Different War: Vietnam in Art. LC 89-70103. (Illus.). 120p. (Orig.). 1990. pap. 18.95 (*0-941104-43-5*) Real Comet.
— Mixed Blessings: New Art in a Multicultural America. LC 89-43203. (Illus.). 320p. 1990. 49.50 (*0-394-57759-0*); pap. 24.95 (*0-679-72966-6*) Pantheon.
— Overlay: Contemporary Art & the Art of Prehistory. LC 82-22331. (Illus.). 266p. 1983. pap. 25.00 (*0-394-71145-9*) Pantheon.
— Partial Recall: Photographs of Native North Americans. LC 92-53737. (Illus.). 200p. 1992. 35.00 (*1-56584-016-X*); pap. 19.95 (*1-56584-041-0*) New Press NY.
— The Pink Glass Swan: Selected Feminist Essays on Art. LC 94-23406. 352p. 1995. pap. 20.00 (*1-56584-213-8*) New Press NY.
— Pop Art. (World of Art Ser.). (Illus.). 216p. 1985. pap. 14.95 (*0-500-20052-1*) Thames Hudson.
Lippard, Lucy R., intro. Voices of Women: Three Critics on Three Poets on Three Artist-Heroines. 2nd rev. ed. LC 80-80281. (Illus.). 1990. pap. text ed. 8.00 (*0-9602476-1-0*) Midmarch Arts-WAN.
Lippard, Lucy R. & Goldman, Shifra M. Juan Sanchez: Rican-Structed Convictions. (Illus.). 32p. (Orig.). 1989. pap. 15.00 (*0-913263-28-1*) Exit Art.
Lippard, Lucy R., jt. auth. see Martin-Crosa, Ricardo.
Lippard, Stephen, jt. auth. see Berg, Jeremy.
Lippard, Stephen J. Progress in Inorganic Chemistry, 8 vols., Vol. 30. LC 82-20111. (Progress in Inorganic Chemistry Ser.). 528p. (Orig.). 1983. text ed. 190.00 (*0-471-87022-6*, Wiley-Interscience) Wiley.
— Progress in Inorganic Chemistry, 8 vols., Vol. 33. LC 82-20111. (Progress in Inorganic Chemistry Ser.). 528p. (Orig.). 1985. text ed. 185.00 (*0-471-80334-0*, Wiley-Interscience) Wiley.
— Progress in Inorganic Chemistry, 8 vols., Vol. 34. LC 82-20111. (Progress in Inorganic Chemistry Ser.). 528p. (Orig.). 1986. text ed. 199.00 (*0-471-81948-4*, Wiley-Interscience) Wiley.
— Progress in Inorganic Chemistry, 8 vols., Vol. 35. LC 82-20111. (Progress in Inorganic Chemistry Ser.). 528p. (Orig.). 1987. text ed. 185.00 (*0-471-84291-5*, Wiley-Interscience) Wiley.
— Progress in Inorganic Chemistry, 8 vols., Vol. 36. LC 82-20111. (Progress in Inorganic Chemistry Ser.). 528p. (Orig.). 1988. text ed. 160.00 (*0-471-61144-1*, Wiley-Interscience) Wiley.
— Progress in Inorganic Chemistry, 8 vols., Vol. 37. LC 82-20111. (Progress in Inorganic Chemistry Ser.). 528p. (Orig.). 1989. text ed. 180.00 (*0-471-62297-4*, Wiley-Interscience) Wiley.
— Progress in Inorganic Chemistry, 8 vols., Vol. 38. LC 82-20111. (Progress in Inorganic Chemistry Ser.). 528p. (Orig.). 1990. text ed. 175.00 (*0-471-50397-5*, Wiley-Interscience) Wiley.
— Progress in Inorganic Chemistry, 8 vols., Vol. 38. LC 82-20111. (Progress in Inorganic Chemistry Ser.). 528p. (Orig.). 1991. pap. text ed. 62.95 (*0-471-52945-1*, Wiley-Interscience) Wiley.
— Progress in Inorganic Chemistry, 8 vols., Vol. 39. LC 82-20111. (Progress in Inorganic Chemistry Ser.). 528p. (Orig.). 1991. text ed. 166.00 (*0-471-54489-2*, Wiley-Interscience) Wiley.
Lippard, Stephen J., ed. Platinum, Gold, & Other Metal Chemotherapeutic Agents. LC 82-24333. (Symposium Ser.: No. 209). 453p. 1983. lib. bdg. 65.95 (*0-8412-0758-5*) Am Chemical.
— Progress in Inorganic Chemistry, Vol. 40. 608p. (Orig.). 1992. text ed. 180.00 (*0-471-57191-1*) Wiley.
Lippart, Lucy. Michelle Stuart: The Elements 1973-1979. 1992. pap. 15.00 (*0-9634941-0-4*) Fanbush.
Lippe, Aschwin. The Freer Indian Sculptures. (Occasional Studies: No. 8). 1970. 15.00 (*0-934686-12-2*) Freer.

Lippe, Toinette, ed. see Dass, Ram & Gorman, Paul.

Lippe, Toinette, ed. see West, John A.

Lippenyi, T. & Vari, S. G., eds. Lasers & Optics in Medicine: The First Joint Congress of the Hungarian & Israel Medical Laser Societies, Budapest, Hungary, June, 1991. 1992. write for info. (*0-8194-0753-4*, 1616) SPIE.

Lipper Analytical Services International Corporation Staff. Lipper International Closed-End Funds Service, 2 vols., Set. McBride, William et al, eds. Orig. Title: Lipper Directory of Emerging Funds. 1200p. 1994. 4,000.00 (*0-9640376-4-5*) Lipper Analytical.

***Lipper, Susan, photos.** Grapevine. (Illus.). 112p. 1995. 50.00 (*0-948797-13-4*) Dist Art Pubs.

Lippert, ed. see Ferdico, John N.

Lippert, ed. see Peck, Robert S.

Lippert, ed. see Weaver, Jefferson H. & Ellison, Maria E.

Lippert, Barbara, et al. German Unification & EC Integration: German & British Perspectives. LC 93-15273. 1993. 14.95 (*0-87609-147-8*) Coun Foreign.

Lippert, Catherine B. Eighteenth Century English Porcelain in the Collection of the Indianapolis Museum of Art. LC 82-84076. (Indianapolis Museum of Art: Centennial Catalogue Ser.). (Illus.). 320p. (Orig.). 1988. 45.00 (*0-936260-11-4*); pap. 30.00 (*0-936260-12-2*) Ind Mus Art.

Lippert, Donald F. Mister B. (Illus.). 32p. (J). (ps). 1989. write for info. (*0-318-64642-0*) Pastel Pubns.

— Polly Popcan. (Illus.). 32p. (J). (ps). 1989. write for info. (*0-318-64640-4*) Pastel Pubns.

— Shag & the Bouncing Ball. (Illus.). 32p. (J). (ps). 1989. write for info. (*0-318-64643-9*) Pastel Pubns.

— The Tale of the Two Golden Doves. 64p. (Orig.). 1989. pap. 7.95 (*0-925737-00-3*) Pastel Pubns.

Lippert, E. Dictionary of Political Psychology: Handwoerterbuch der Politischen Psychologie. 380p. (GER.). 1983. 65.00 (*0-8288-2256-5*, M15264) Fr & Eur.

***Lippert, E. & Macomber, J. D., eds.** Dynamics During Spectroscopic Transitions: Relaxation Processes in Condensed Matter. LC 94-41054. 1995. write for info. (*3-540-58703-9*); write for info. (*0-387-58703-9*) Spr-Verlag.

Lippert, Frederick G. & Teitz, Carol C. Diagnosing Musculoskeletal Problems: A Practical Guide. 156p. 1987. pap. text ed. 22.00 (*0-683-05052-4*) Williams & Wilkins.

Lippert, JoAnn L., ed. see McMenamin, R. W. & Kralovec, William P.

Lippert, JoAnn L., ed. see McMenamin, Robert W.

Lippert, Julius. The Evolution of Culture, 2 vols. 1975. 500.00 (*0-87968-158-6*) Gordon Pr.

Lippert, Laurel H., ed. see Huggins, Ellie.

Lippert, Laurel H., jt. auth. see Lippert, Tom.

Lippert, Laurel H., ed. see Prosor, Larry & Popoff, Leo.

Lippert, Laurel H., ed. see Prosor, Larry & Moreno, Richard.

Lippert, Margaret H. La Hija de la Serpiente Marina - the Sea Serpent's Daughter: Una Leyenda Brasilena. LC 92-21438. (J). (gr. 4-7). 1993. lib. bdg. 11.89 (*0-8167-3124-1*); pap. 3.95 (*0-8167-3074-1*) Troll Assocs.

— The Sea Serpent's Daughter: A Brazilian Legend. LC 92-21438. (Legends of the World Ser.). (Illus.). 32p. (J). (gr. 2-5). 1993. lib. bdg. 11.89 (*0-8167-3053-9*); pap. text ed. 3.95 (*0-8167-3054-7*) Troll Assocs.

Lippert, Raymond & Segal, Richard A., Jr. Traditions: A Tribute to Wedding Cake Decorating. (Orig.). 1990. write for info. (*0-9627704-0-X*) Bakery Crafts.

Lippert, T., et al. Science on the Connection Machine: Proceedings of the 1st European Users Meeting. 236p. 1992. text ed. 81.00 (*981-02-1206-2*) World Scientific Pub.

Lippert, Tom & Lippert, Laurel H. The Woodstove Cookerybook. LC 82-102151. (Illus.). 60p. (Orig.). 1981. pap. 3.95 (*0-941800-00-8*) Tulip Pr.

***Lippert, Wayne R.** Stay Alive: How to Street Fight with a Pistol. LC 95-90017. (Illus.). 270p. (Orig.). Date not set. pap. text ed. write for info. (*0-9645362-0-X*) Fair Winds.

Lippett, Ingrid, ed. & concept. Trust Your Feelings: A Protective Behaviours Resource Manual for Primary School Teachers. (C). 1989. pap. text ed. 80.00 (*0-89771-037-1*, Pub. by Essence Pubns AT) St Mut.

***Lippi-Green, Rosina.** Language Ideology & Language Change in Early Modern German: A Sociolinguistic Study of the Consonantal System of Nuremburg. LC 94-31088. (Current Issues in Linguistic Theory Ser.: No. 119). 150p. 1994. lib. bdg. 48.00x (*1-55619-573-7*) Benjamins North Am.

Lippi-Green, Rosina, ed. Recent Developments in Germanic Linguistics. LC 92-34480. (Current Issues in Linguistic Theory Ser.: No. 93). xii, 163p. 1992. 47.00x (*1-55619-154-5*) Benjamins North Am.

Lippi, Robert. How to Buy Good Printing & Save Money: A Printing Buyers Guide. (Illus.). 144p. 1987. 17.95 (*0-88108-041-1*); pap. 14.50 (*0-88108-042-X*) Art Dir.

Lippiatt, Arthur & Wright, Graham. Architecture of Small Computer Systems. 2nd ed. (Illus.). 240p. (C). 1986. pap. text ed. 19.95 (*0-13-044744-7*) P-H.

Lippiello, Patrick M., et al, eds. The Biology of Nicotine: Current Research Issues. 240p. 1992. 89.50 (*0-88167-860-0*) Raven.

Lippin, Paula, ed. see Cannon, James S.

Lippin, Tobi, ed. Working Women. (Southern Exposure Ser.). (Illus.). 128p. (Orig.). (C). 1982. pap. 4.00 (*0-943810-12-4*) Inst Southern Studies.

***Lippincott.** American Drug Index, 1995. 1994. 45.00 (*0-932686-32-X*) Facts & Comparisons.

Lippincott, Benjamin E. Democracy's Dilemma: The Totalitarian Party in a Free Society. LC 65-12755. 303p. reprint ed. pap. 86.40 (*0-317-07886-0*, 2012420) Bks Demand.

Lippincott, Benjamin E., ed. see Lange, Oscar & Taylor, Fred M.

Lippincott, David, jt. auth. see Philyaw, Chuck.

Lippincott, E. P., jt. ed. see Farrar, Harry, IV.

Lippincott, Isaac. A History of Manufactures in the Ohio Valley to the Year 1860. LC 73-2518. (Big Business; Economic Power in a Free Society Ser.). 1977. reprint ed. 19.95 (*0-405-05098-4*) Ayer.

— A History of Manufactures in the Ohio Valley to the Year 1860. LC 73-19608. (Perspectives in American History Ser.: No. 14). viii, 214p. 1974. reprint ed. lib. bdg. 29.50 (*0-87991-340-1*) Porcupine Pr.

***Lippincott, J. B.** Bates: Pocket Guide to Physical Examination & History Taking. 1994. pap. 19.95 (*0-397-55057-X*) Lippincott.

Lippincott, Kristen. Astronomy. LC 93-33102. (Eyewitness Science Ser.). (J). 1994. 15.95 (*1-56458-680-4*) Dorling Kindersley.

Lippincott, Lillian. A Bibliography of the Writings & Criticisms of Edwin Arlington Robinson. LC 74-1423. (American Literature Ser.: No. 49). 1974. lib. bdg. 49.95 (*0-8383-2049-X*) M S G Haskell Hse.

Lippincott, Louise. Edvard Munch: Starry Night. LC 88-13061. (Getty Museum Studies on Art). (Illus.). 102p. 1988. pap. 15.95 (*0-89236-139-5*) J P Getty Trust.

— Lawrence Alma Tadema, Spring. LC 90-49669. (Getty Museum Studies on Art). (Illus.). 100p. 1991. pap. 15.95 (*0-89236-186-7*) J P Getty Trust.

Lippincott, Mary. NOLAW: North Lansing Against the World. (Illus.). viii, 208p. 1981. 12.00 (*0-941366-00-6*) Matthew Pubs.

— Twin Lions. 781p. reprint ed. pap. 14.95 (*0-941366-01-4*) Matthew Pubs.

Lippincott, Ronald C., jt. auth. see Begun, James W.

Lippincott, Sara J. Haps & Mishaps of a Tour in Europe. (American Biography Ser.). 437p. 1991. reprint ed. lib. bdg. 89.00 (*0-7812-8246-2*) Rprt Serv.

Lippincott, Sharon M. Meetings: Do's, Don'ts, & Donuts: The Complete Handbook for Successful Meetings. LC 94-75075. 204p. 1994. pap. 12.95 (*0-9637966-3-1*) Lghthse Pt Pr.

Lippincott, W. T., ed. Cumulative Index to Journal of Chemical Education, 4 vols., 4. 1994. 18.00 (*0-910362-28-9*, 1969-1978) Chem Educ.

— Essays in Physical Chemistry: A Sourcebook for Physical Chemistry Teachers. (Illus.). v, 174p. 1988. pap. 39.95 (*0-8412-1478-6*) Am Chemical.

Lippincott, W. T., jt ed. see Kieffer, W. F.

Lippisch, Alexander. The Delta Wing: History & Development. Lippisch, Gertrude L., tr. LC 81-8166. 136p. reprint ed. pap. 38.80 (*0-317-27916-5*, 2025130) Bks Demand.

Lippisch, Gertrude L., tr. see Lippisch, Alexander.

Lippit, Norika M. & Selden, Kyoko I., eds. Japanese Women Writers: Twentieth Century Short Fiction. Selden, Kyoko I., tr. LC 91-2924. 312p. 1991. 49.95 (*0-87332-859-0*); pap. text ed. 18.95 (*0-87332-860-4*) M E Sharpe.

Lippit, Victor D. The Economic Development of China. LC 86-20410. 278p. 1987. pap. text ed. 20.95 (*0-87332-404-8*) M E Sharpe.

— Land Reform & Economic Development in China: A Study of Institutional Change & Development Finance. LC 74-15391. 194p. reprint ed. pap. 55.30 (*0-8357-2614-2*, 2040105) Bks Demand.

Lippit, Victor D., ed. Studies in Radical Political Economy. 384p. 1995. 50.00 (*0-87332-606-7*); pap. 21.95 (*0-87332-607-5*) M E Sharpe.

Lippitt, Gordon L. & Lippitt, Ronald. The Consulting Process in Action. 2nd rev. ed. LC 86-19693. (Illus.). 213p. 1986. pap. 24.95 (*0-88390-201-X*) Pfeiffer & Co.

Lippitt, Gordon L., et al. Implementing Organizational Change: A Practical Guide to Managing Change Efforts. LC 84-47990. (Management Ser.). 205p. 1985. 27.95 (*0-87589-622-7*) Jossey-Bass.

Lippitt, Henry F. Jeannie Lippitt & the Mastery of Silence. 1974. pap. 1.00 (*0-685-67664-1*) RI Hist Soc.

Lippitt, Jill, ed. The National Women's Information Exchange Directory. LC 93-41914. 192p. (Orig.). 1994. pap. 10.00 (*0-380-77570-0*) Avon.

Lippitt, Peggy, et al. Cross-Age Helping Package. LC 78-164709. 242p. 1972. pap. 8.00 (*0-87944-108-9*) Inst Soc Res.

— Cross-Age Helping Program: Orientation, Training & Related Materials. LC 78-164709. 242p. reprint ed. pap. 69.00 (*0-7837-5274-1*, 2045012) Bks Demand.

Lippitt, Ronald, jt. auth. see Lippitt, Gordon L.

Lippitt, Ronald, et al. Futuring. 176p. 1986. pap. text ed. write for info. (*0-201-15792-6*) Addison-Wesley.

***Lippke, Richard L.** Radical Business Ethics. 240p. (C). 1995. text ed. 58.50 (*0-8476-8069-X*); pap. text ed. 22.95 (*0-8476-8070-3*) Rowman.

Lippman Abu-Lughod, Janet, et al. From Urban Village to "East Village" The Battle for New York's Lower East Side. (Illus.). 320p. (Orig.). (C). 1994. text ed. 54.95 (*1-55786-523-X*); pap. text ed. 21.95 (*1-55786-525-6*) Blackwell Pubs.

Lippman, Anna. The Babies. 36p. 1969. 2.50 (*0-87129-154-1*, B10) Dramatic Pub.

Lippman, Carlee. Representations of Innocence in Literatures of the World: Strategies of Multicultural Narrative. LC 93-34509. 196p. 1993. text ed. 79.95 (*0-7734-9394-8*) E Mellen.

Lippman, Deborah & Colin, Paul. How to Make Amulets & Charms: What They Mean & How to Use Them. LC 94-17781. 1994. 12.95 (*0-8065-1572-4*) Carol Pub Group.

Lippman, Edward. A History of Western Musical Aesthetics. viii, 551p. 1992. pap. text ed. 25.00 (*0-8032-7951-5*, Bison Books) U of Nebr Pr.

— A History of Western Musical Aesthetics. LC 91-47076. vii, 551p. 1992. 70.00 (*0-8032-2863-5*) U of Nebr Pr.

Lippman, Edward A. Musical Thought in Ancient Greece. LC 74-23415. (Music Reprint Ser.). 1975. reprint ed. lib. bdg. 32.50 (*0-306-70669-5*) Da Capo.

Lippman, Edward A., ed. Musical Aesthetics: A Historical Reader - The Nineteenth Century. LC 85-28415. (Aesthetics in Music Ser.: No. 4, Vol.II). 450p. 1988. lib. bdg. 73.00 (*0-918728-90-8*) Pendragon NY.

— Musical Aesthetics: A Historical Reader, the Twentieth Century. LC 85-28415. (Aesthetics in Music Ser.: No. 4, Vol. 3). 350p. 1990. lib. bdg. 73.00 (*0-945193-10-6*) Pendragon NY.

Lippman, Helen & Reardon, Patricia. Enjoying New Jersey Outdoors: A Year-Round Guide to Outdoor Recreation in the Garden State & Nearby. LC 90-44574. (Illus.). 216p. (C). 1991. text ed. 34.00 (*0-8135-1654-4*); pap. 11.95 (*0-8135-1655-2*) Rutgers U Pr.

Lippman, Leopold D. & Goldberg, I. Ignacy. Right to Education: Anatomy of the Pennsylvania Case & Its Implications for Exceptional Children. LC 73-78038. (Teachers College Series in Special Education). 153p. reprint ed. pap. 43.70 (*0-685-20394-8*, 2030172) Bks Demand.

Lippman, Marc E. Diagnoses & Management of Breast Cancer. 1987. text ed. 68.50 (*0-7020-0993-8*) Saunders.

Lippman, Marc E. & Dickson, Robert B., eds. Regulatory Mechanisms in Breast Cancer: Advances in Cellular & Molecular Biology of Breast Cancer. (Cancer Treatment & Research Ser.). (C). 1991. lib. bdg. 158.50 (*0-7923-0868-9*) Kluwer Ac.

Lippman, Marc E., jt. ed. see Dickson, Robert B.

Lippman, Marc E., jt. auth. see Thompson, E. Brad.

Lippman, Marc E., et al. Diagnosis & Management of Breast Cancer. (Illus.). 480p. 1988. text ed. 84.00 (*0-7216-1958-4*) Saunders.

Lippman, Matthew, et al. Islamic Criminal Law & Procedure: An Introduction. LC 88-4037. 183p. 1988. text ed. 49.95 (*0-275-93009-2*, C3009, Praeger Pubs) Greenwood.

Lippman, Morton, ed. Critical Reviews of Environmental Toxicants: Human Exposures & Their Health Effects. 1000p. 1992. text ed. 99.95 (*0-442-00549-0*) Van Nos Reinhold.

Lippman, Paul. American Typewriters: A Collector's Encyclopedia. 288p. 1992. 55.00 (*0-9633201-0-6*) Orig & Copy.

— American Typewriters: A Collector's Encyclopedia. 288p. 1995. pap. 39.95 (*0-614-05026-X*) Orig & Copy.

Lippman, Peter. Busy Trains. LC 77-86145. (Pictureback Ser.). (Illus.). 32p. (J). (ps-3). 1981. lib. bdg. 5.99 (*0-394-93748-1*); pap. 2.50 (*0-394-83748-7*) Random Bks Yng Read.

— Firehouse Co., No. 1: Mini House Book. (J). (ps). 1994. 9.95 (*1-56305-663-1*) Workman Pub.

— From Here to There. LC 75-19947. (Illus.). 48p. (J). (gr. 1 up). 1975. pap. 5.00 (*0-912846-11-9*) Bookstore Pr.

— Mini House Books: Haunted House. Kovalchick, Sally, ed. (Illus.). 20p. (J). 1994. 9.95 (*1-56305-731-X*) Workman Pub.

— Mini House Books: Old Macdonald's Barn. (Illus.). 20p. (J). (ps-1). 1993. bds. 9.95 (*1-56305-500-7*, 3500) Workman Pub.

— Mini House Books: Santa's Workshop. (Illus.). 20p. (J). (ps-1). 1993. bds. 9.95 (*1-56305-499-X*, 3499) Workman Pub.

— Noah's Ark: Mini House Book. (J). (ps). 1994. 9.95 (*1-56305-662-3*) Workman Pub.

Lippman, Richard & Maldonado, Jose. Eating In: The Official Single Man's Cookbook. LC 88-70598. (Illus.). 144p. (Orig.). 1988. pap. 8.95 (*0-944042-00-7*) CorkScrew Pr.

Lippman, Sid. With This Song, I Thee Wed. (Illus.). 40p. 1992. pap. 14.95 (*0-685-65827-9*, AM87508) Music Sales.

Lippman, Sidney, et al. A You're Adorable. LC 93-931. (Illus.). 32p. (J). (ps up). 1994. 9.95 (*1-56402-237-4*) Candlewick Pr.

***Lippman, Stanley.** Inside the C++ Program & Object Models. (C). 1995. pap. text ed. write for info. (*0-201-83454-5*) Addison-Wesley.

Lippman, Stanley B. A-C Plus Plus Primer. (Illus.). 448p. (C). 1989. pap. text ed. 23.96 (*0-201-16487-6*) Addison-Wesley.

— C Plus Plus Primer. 2nd ed. (Illus.). 544p. (C). 1991. pap. text ed. 39.75 (*0-201-54848-8*) Addison-Wesley.

Lippman, Steven A., jt. auth. see Levine, David K.

Lippman, Susannah, ed. see Weiss, Bonnie.

Lippman, Thomas W. Understanding Islam. 1982. pap. 4.99 (*0-451-62760-1*, Ment) NAL-Dutton.

— Understanding Islam: An Introduction to the Moslem World. LC 81-85142. 208p. 1982. pap. 3.95 (*0-451-62666-4*, ME2079, Ment) NAL-Dutton.

Lippman, Thomas W., comp. The Washington Post Deskbook on Style. 2nd ed. 1989. pap. text ed. 9.95 (*0-07-068414-6*) McGraw.

Lippman, Walter. A Preface to Morals. LC 82-2035. (Social Science Classics Ser.). 375p. 1982. reprint ed. pap. 19.95 (*0-87855-907-8*) Transaction Pubs.

— U. S. War Aims. LC 76-16079. 235p. 1976. reprint ed. lib. bdg. 29.50 (*0-306-70773-X*) Da Capo.

Lippmann, H., ed. see CISM (International Center for Mechanical Sciences), Department for General Mechanics Staff.

Lippmann, John. Deeper into Diving. (Illus.). 610p. (Orig.). 1991. pap. 39.95 (*0-9590306-3-8*) Aqua Quest.

— The Essentials of Deeper Sport Diving. (Illus.). 320p. (Orig.). 1992. pap. 21.95 (*0-9623389-3-1*) Aqua Quest.

— Oxygen First Aid for Divers. (Illus.). 150p. (Orig.). 1992. pap. 14.95 (*0-9590306-5-4*) Aqua Quest.

Lippmann, John & Bugg, Stan. The Dan Emergency Handbook: A Guide to the Identification of & First Aid for Scuba (Air) Diving Injuries. 2nd ed. 1991. spiral bd. 12.95 (*0-9590306-1-1*) Aqua Quest.

Lippmann, Morton & Schlesinger, Richard B. Chemical Contamination in the Human Environment. (Illus.). 1979. text ed. 35.00 (*0-19-502441-9*) OUP.

Lippmann, Morton, jt. ed. see Kneip, T. J.

Lippmann, Morton, jt. ed. see Lioy, Paul.

Lippmann, Richard P., et al, eds. Advances in Neural Information Processing Systems, Vol. 3. 1130p. 1991. 49.95 (*1-55860-184-8*) Morgan Kaufmann.

Lippmann, Walter. American Inquisitors. LC 92-16068. 142p. (C). 1992. pap. 19.95 (*1-56000-635-8*) Transaction Pubs.

— Drift & Mastery. LC 85-40764. 192p. 1986. reprint ed. pap. 10.95 (*0-299-10604-7*) U of Wis Pr.

— An Inquiry into the Principles of the Good Society. LC 72-7871. 402p. 1973. reprint ed. text ed. 70.00 (*0-8371-6522-9*, LIGS, Greenwood Pr) Greenwood.

— Liberty & the News. LC 94-44023. (History of Ideas Ser.). 1995. pap. write for info. (*1-56000-809-1*) Transaction Pubs.

— The Method of Freedom. 146p. (C). 1991. pap. text ed. 19.95 (*1-56000-559-9*) Transaction Pubs.

— The Phantom Public: Library of Conservative Thought. rev. ed. LC 92-41593. 225p. (C). 1993. pap. text ed. 19.95 (*1-56000-677-3*) Transaction Pubs.

— Public Opinion. 1965. pap. 14.95 (*0-02-919130-0*) Free Pr.

— Public Persons. Harrison, Gilbert A., ed. 1976. 7.95 (*0-87140-620-9*) Liveright.

— The Public Philosophy. 209p. 1989. pap. 19.95 (*0-88738-791-8*) Transaction Pubs.

Lipponer, George. The End of Forever. 200p. 1993. write for info. (*0-89962-624-6*) Dove Pub NY.

— Mending Fences. 350p. (Orig.). 1989. pap. write for info. (*0-9624158-0-4*) Dove Pub NY.

Lipps, Gottlob F. Mythenbildung und Erkenntnis: Eine Abhandlung Uber Die Grundlagen der Philosophie. Bolle, Kees W., ed. LC 77-79141. (Mythology Ser.). 1978. lib. bdg. 30.95 (*0-405-10550-9*) Ayer.

Lipps, J. H. Fossil Prokaryotes & Protists. (Illus.). 1993. pap. 49.95 (*0-86542-073-4*) Blackwell Sci.

Lipps, J. H. & Signor, P. W., eds. Origin & Early Evolution of the Metazoa. (Topics in Geobiology Ser.: Vol. 10). (Illus.). 560p. 1992. 95.00 (*0-306-44067-9*, Plenum Pr) Plenum.

Lipps, Jere H., ed. Foraminiferal Ecology & Paleoecology. (Short Course Notes Ser.: No. 6). 198p. 1979. 14.00 (*0-918985-38-2*) SEPM.

Lipps, Theodor. Psychological Studies. 2nd ed. LC 73-2972. (Classics in Psychology Ser.). 1974. reprint ed. 23.95 (*0-405-05145-X*) Ayer.

***Lipps, Theodore.** Consonance & Dissonance in Music. 142p. 1995. 21.95 (*0-940459-18-3*) Everett Bks.

Lippson, Alice J., ed. & illus. The Chesapeake Bay in Maryland: An Atlas of Natural Resources. LC 72-12352. 64p. 1973. 30.00 (*0-8018-1467-7*); pap. 13.95 (*0-8018-1468-5*) Johns Hopkins.

Lippson, Alice J. & Lippson, Robert L. Life in the Chesapeake Bay. LC 83-11278. 240p. 1984. text ed. 39.95 (*0-8018-3012-5*); pap. text ed. 16.95 (*0-8018-3013-3*) Johns Hopkins.

Lippson, Alice J., et al, eds. Environmental Atlas of the Potomac Estuary. (Illus.). 285p. 1981. 32.50 (*0-8018-2618-7*) Johns Hopkins.

Lippson, Robert L., jt. auth. see Lippson, Alice J.

Lippy, Charles H. Being Religious, American Style: A History of Popular Religiosity in the United States. LC 93-50545. 296p. 1994. pap. text ed. 19.95 (*0-275-94901-X*, Praeger Pubs) Greenwood.

— Being Religious, American Style: A History of Popular Religiosity in the United States. LC 93-50545. (Series Contributions to the Study of Religion: Vol. 37). 296p. 1994. text ed. 65.00 (*0-313-27895-4*, Greenwood Pr) Greenwood.

— Bibliography of Religion in the South. LC 85-13575. xvi, 498p. 1985. text ed. 49.95 (*0-86554-161-2*, MUP-H151) Mercer Univ Pr.

Lippy, Charles H., ed. Religion in South Carolina. LC 92-46310. 247p. 1993. 24.95 (*0-87249-891-3*) U of SC Pr.

— Religious Periodicals of the United States: Academic & Scholarly Journals. LC 85-9861. (Historical Guides to the World's Periodicals & Newspapers Ser.). 626p. 1986. text ed. 79.50 (*0-313-23420-5*, LRP/, Greenwood Pr) Greenwood.

— Twentieth-Century Shapers of American Popular Religion. LC 88-15487. 519p. 1989. text ed. 89.50 (*0-313-25356-0*, LTW/, Greenwood Pr) Greenwood.

Lippy, Charles H. & Williams, Peter W., eds. Encyclopedia of the American Religious Experience. 3 vols., Set. 1872p. 1987. text ed. 295.00 (*0-684-18062-6*, Scribners) S&S Trade.

Lippy, Charles H., jt. ed. see Fackler, P. Mark.

Lippy, Charles H., et al. Christianity Comes to the Americas, 1492-1776. (Illus.). 384p. 1992. 29.95 (*1-55778-234-2*) Paragon Hse.

— Christianity Comes to the Americas, 1492-1776: 1492-1776. LC 92-8490. 400p. 1992. pap. 18.95 (*1-55778-501-5*) Paragon Hse.

Lippy, Elsie. God's Story. (Illus.). 10p. (J). (gr. k-6). 1989. pap. text ed. 2.50 (*1-55976-128-8*) CEF Press.

Lippy, Jane. Alpha to Omega. LC 88-50832. 17p. 1988. pap. 5.95 (*1-55523-162-4*) Winston-Derek.

Lippy, John. Chemical Magic. 164p. pap. 4.00 (*0-913022-32-2*) Angriff Pr.

Lips. Plant Nitrogen Metabolism. 1995. write for info. (*0-8493-6256-3*) CRC Pr.

Lips, Hilary M. Sex & Gender: An Introduction. 2nd rev. ed. LC 92-20228. 482p. (C). 1993. pap. text ed. 32.95 (*1-55934-090-8*) Mayfield Pub.

— Women, Men, & Power. LC 90-41065. 245p. (C). 1991. pap. text ed. 22.95 (*0-87484-916-0*) Mayfield Pub.

Lips, Julius E. Savage Hits Back. 1966. 10.00 (*0-8216-0147-4*, Univ Bks) Carol Pub Group.

Lipschitz, Alexander S., tr. see Grzesinski, Albert C.

Lipschitz, Chaim U. Franco, Spain, the Jews & the Holocaust. 1983. 25.00 (*0-88125-025-2*) Ktav.

Lipschitz, David A., jt. ed. see Chernoff, Ronni.

Lipschitz, Leslie, et al. Federal Republic of Germany: Adjustment in a Surplus Country. (Occasional Paper Ser.: No. 64). ix, 103p. 1989. pap. 7.50 (*1-55775-088-2*) Intl Monetary.

Lipschitz, Rudolf. Briefwechsel Mit Cantor, Dedekind, Helmholtz, Kronecker, Weierstrass, und Anderen. (Dokumente zur Geschichte der Mathematik Ser.: Vol. 2). xviii, 253p. (GER.). (C). 1986. 34.00 (*3-528-08969-5*, Pub. by Vieweg & Sohn GW) Ballen Bkslr.

Lipschultz. Infertility in the Male. 2nd ed. 480p. 1990. 89.00 (*0-8151-5447-X*, Yr Bk Med Pubs) Mosby Yr Bk.

Lipschultz, Mark R. & Rasmussen, R. Kent. Dictionary of African Historical Biography. enl. ed. 1986. pap. 16.00 (*0-520-06611-1*) U CA Pr.

— Dictionary of African Historical Biography. 2nd enl. ed. 1986. 55.00 (*0-520-05179-3*) U CA Pr.

Lipschutz, Barbara. Contractions. 1974. pap. 2.50 (*0-912786-28-0*) Know Inc.

Lipschutz, Kurt. The Good Neighbor Policy. (End of the Century Bks.). 88p. 1989. pap. 5.95 (*0-926664-03-4*) Bay Area Ctr Art & Tech.

Lipschutz, Mark. Selected Still Projection Apparatus for Scenic Effects Projection. 2nd ed. 1976. pap. 5.95 (*0-685-83023-3*) Scenographic.

Lipschutz, Martin. Differential Geometry. (Schaum's Outline Ser.). 1969. pap. text ed. 12.95 (*0-07-037985-8*) McGraw.

Lipschutz, Ronnie D. & Conca, Ken, eds. The State & Social Power in Global Environmental Politics. LC 93-15878. (New Directions in World Politics Ser.). 363p. 1993. 55.00 (*0-231-08106-5*); pap. 17.05 (*0-231-08107-3*) Col U Pr.

Lipschutz, Seymour. Finite Mathematics. (Schaum's Outline Ser.). (C). 1966. pap. text ed. 12.95 (*0-07-037987-4*) McGraw.

— General Topology. (Orig.). (C). 1965. pap. text ed. 13.95 (*0-07-037988-2*) McGraw.

— Outline of Discrete Mathematics. (Schaum's Outline Ser.). (Illus.). 1976. pap. text ed. 12.95 (*0-07-037981-5*) McGraw.

— Schaum's Outline of Data Structure. (Schaum Outline Ser.). 320p. 1986. pap. text ed. 12.95 (*0-07-038001-5*) McGraw.

— Schaum's Outline of Data Structures with Pascal. (Schaum's Outline Ser.). 1993. text ed. write for info. (*0-07-038009-0*) McGraw.

— Schaum's Outline of Essential Computer Mathematics. 256p. (C). 1982. pap. text ed. 12.95 (*0-07-037990-4*) McGraw.

— Schaum's Outline of Finite Mathematics: Including Hundreds of Solved Problems. 2nd ed. (Schaum's Outline Ser.). 1994. pap. text ed. 14.95 (*0-07-038002-3*) McGraw.

— Schaum's Outline of Linear Algebra. 2nd ed. (Schaum's Outline Ser.). 1991. pap. text ed. 13.95 (*0-07-038007-4*) McGraw.

— Schaum's Outline of Set Theory. 2nd ed. (Schaum's Outline Ser.). 1988. pap. text ed. write for info. (*0-07-038003-1*) McGraw.

— Schaum's Three Thousand Solved Problems in Linear Algebra. 4960p. 1989. pap. text ed. 19.95 (*0-07-038023-6*) McGraw.

— Set Theory & Related Topics. (Orig.). (C). 1964. pap. text ed. 12.95 (*0-07-037986-6*) McGraw.

— Two Thousand Solved Problems in Discrete Mathematics. (Schaum's Solved Problems Ser.). 544p. 1992. pap. text ed. 16.95 (*0-07-038031-7*) McGraw.

Lipschutz, Seymour & Poe, Arthur. Schaum's Outline of Programming with FORTRAN IV. (Schaum's Outline Ser.). 1978. pap. text ed. 12.95 (*0-07-037984-X*) McGraw.

— Schaum's Outline of Structured FORTRAN. (Schaum's Outline Ser.). 1993. write for info. (*0-07-037997-1*) McGraw.

Lipschutz, Yacov. Kashruth: A Comprehensive Reference to the Principles of Kosher. (ArtScroll Ser.). (Illus.). 168p. 1988. 17.95 (*0-89906-558-9*); pap. 14.95 (*0-89906-559-7*) Mesorah Pubns.

Lipscomb, jt. auth. see Hufford.

Lipscomb, Anne S. & Hutchison, Kathleen. Tracing Your Mississippi Ancestors. (Illus.). 160p. 1994. 32.50 (*0-87805-697-1*); pap. 14.95 (*0-87805-698-X*) U Pr of Miss.

***Lipscomb, David M., ed.** Hearing Conservation in Industry, Schools, & the Military. LC 94-26675. (Illus.). 344p. 1994. pap. text ed. 45.00 (*1-56593-380-X*, 0559) Singular Publishing.

Lipscomb, Diana. Organic Evolution. 200p. (C). 1994. spiral bd. 24.95 (*0-8403-9478-0*) Kendall-Hunt.

Lipscomb, Elizabeth J., et al, eds. The Several Worlds of Pearl S. Buck: Essays Presented at a Centennial Symposium, Randolph-Macon Woman's College, March 26-28, 1992. LC 93-43752. (Contributions in Women's Studies: No. 144). 184p. 1994. text ed. 49.95 (*0-313-29152-7*, Greenwood Pr) Greenwood.

Lipscomb, Ernest B., III. Walker on Patents, 11 vols., Set. 3rd ed. LC 84-81078. (IP Ser.). 1984. 950.00 (*0-685-65399-4*) Clark Boardman Callaghan.

— Walker on Patents, 11 vols., Set. annuals 3rd rev. ed. LC 84-81078. (IP Ser.). 1984. 950.00 (*0-685-59817-9*) Clark Boardman Callaghan.

Lipscomb, Ernest B., 3rd, jt. auth. see Deller, Anthony W.

Lipscomb, Guy. Watercolor: Go with the Flow. LC 92-34438. (Illus.). 144p. 1993. 29.95 (*0-8230-3189-6*, Watsn-Guptill) Watsn-Guptill.

Lipscomb, James L. Structuring Complex Real Estate Transactions: Law, Procedure, Forms. LC 88-198. 471p. 1988. text ed. 123.00 (*0-471-84713-5*) Wiley.

Lipscomb, Joseph, ed. Physician Staffing for the VA, Vol. I. 432p. 1991. 39.95 (*0-309-04549-5*) Natl Acad Pr.

Lipscomb, Mance & Alyn, Glen. I Say Me for a Parable: The Oral Autobiography of Mance Lipscomb, Texas Bluesman. LC 92-46560. 340p. 1993. 28.00 (*0-393-03500-X*) Norton.

— I Say Me for a Parable: The Oral Autobiography of Mance Lipscomb, Texas Bluesman. LC 94-37446. (Illus.). 508p. 1995. pap. 16.95 (*0-306-80610-X*) Da Capo.

Lipscomb, Patricia, tr. see Gehlen, Arnold.

Lipscomb, Susan D. & Zuanich, Margaret A. BASIC Fun: Computer Games, Puzzles & Problems Children Can Write. 176p. (J). (gr. k-7). 1982. pap. 2.95 (*0-380-80606-1*, Camelot) Avon.

Lipscomb, Terry W. The Carolina Lowcountry April 1775-June 1776 & the Battle of Fort Moultrie. rev. ed. Andrews, Judith M., ed. (South Carolina Revolutionary War Studies: No. 1). 56p. 1994. pap. write for info. (*1-880067-25-0*) SC Dept of Arch & Hist.

— South Carolina Becomes a State. (Illus.). 56p. 1976. write for info. (*1-880067-00-5*) SC Dept of Arch & Hist.

— South Carolina in Seventeen Ninety-One: George Washington Tours the State. Andrews, Judith M., ed. 112p. 1993. pap. write for info. (*1-880067-21-8*) SC Dept of Arch & Hist.

— South Carolina Revolutionary War Battles, Vol. 1: The Carolina Low Country, April 1775-June 1776. Brimelow, Judith M., ed. (South Carolina Revolutionary War Battles Ser.). (Illus.). 56p. 1991. pap. text ed. write for info. (*1-880067-04-8*) SC Dept of Arch & Hist.

Lipscomb, William L. The Armenian Apocryphal Adam Literature. (Armenian Texts & Studies). 298p. 1990. 28.95 (*1-55540-455-3*, 21 02 08) Scholars Pr GA.

Lipscombe, B. P. Boat Owner's Guide to Coastwise Navigation. (C). 1987. 40.00 (*0-685-45082-1*, Pub. by Brwn Son Ferg) St Mut.

Lipsedge, Maurice, jt. auth. see Littlewood, Ronald.

Lipset, Seymour M. Consensus & Conflict in Political Sociology. (Illus.). 275p. 1985. 39.95 (*0-88738-051-4*); pap. 21.95 (*0-88738-608-3*) Transaction Pubs.

— Continental Divide: The Values & Institutions of the United States & Canada. 1990. 29.95 (*0-415-90309-2*, A4356, Routledge NY) Routledge.

— Continental Divide: The Values & Institutions of the United States & Canada. 337p. 1990. pap. 15.95 (*0-415-90385-8*, A5389, Routledge NY) Routledge.

— The Emergence of the One-Party South: The Election of 1860. (Irvington Reprint Series in American History). (C). 1991. reprint ed. pap. text ed. 1.00 (*0-8290-2608-8*, H-130) Irvington.

— Emerging Coalitions in American Politics. 530p. 1978. pap. text ed. 21.95 (*0-917616-22-7*) Transaction Pubs.

— Exceptionalism: The Persistence of An American Ideology. 320p. 1995. 25.00 (*0-393-03725-8*) Norton.

— The First New Nation: The United States in Historical & Comparative Perspective. 1979. reprint ed. pap. 9.95 (*0-393-00911-4*) Norton.

— Political Man: The Social Bases of Politics. LC 80-8867. 608p. (C). 1981. reprint ed. pap. text ed. 16.95 (*0-8018-2522-9*) Johns Hopkins.

— The Radical Right: A Problem for American Democracy. (Reprint Series in Social Sciences). (C). 1993. reprint ed. pap. text ed. 2.90 (*0-8290-2661-4*, S-445) Irvington.

— Rebellion in the University. LC 92-14855. (Foundations of Higher Education Ser.). 372p. (C). 1992. pap. 21.95 (*1-56000-596-3*) Transaction Pubs.

— Revolution & Counterrevolution: Change & Persistence in Social Structure. rev. ed. 436p. 1987. pap. 21.95 (*0-88738-694-6*) Transaction Pubs.

— Some Social Requisites of Democracy: Economic Development & Political Legitimacy. (Reprint Series in Social Sciences). (C). 1993. reprint ed. pap. text ed. 2.90 (*0-8290-3810-8*, S-175) Irvington.

— The Third Century: America As a Post-Industrial Society. 1980. pap. text ed. 7.95 (*0-226-48458-0*, P884) U Ch Pr.

Lipset, Seymour M., ed. American Pluralism & the Jewish Community. 220p. 1989. 24.95 (*0-88738-286-X*) Transaction Pubs.

— Party Coalitions in the Nineteen Eighties. LC 81-83095. 464p. 1981. text ed. 32.95 (*0-917616-45-6*); pap. text ed. 16.95 (*0-917616-43-X*) Transaction Pubs.

Lipset, Seymour M. & Bendix, Reinhard. Social Mobility in Industrial Society. 316p. (C). 1991. pap. text ed. 21.95 (*1-56000-606-4*) Transaction Pubs.

***Lipset, Seymour M. & Raab, Earl.** Jews & the New American Scene. LC 94-32358. 251p. 1995. pap. text ed. 22.95 (*0-674-47493-7*, LIPJEW) HUP.

— The Politics of Unreason: Right-Wing Extremism in America, 1790-1970. (Patterns of American Prejudice Ser.). 420p. reprint ed. 12.50 (*0-686-95046-1*); reprint ed. pap. 7.95 (*0-686-99454-X*) ADL.

Lipset, Seymour M. & Schneider, William. The Confidence Gap: Business, Labor & Government in the Public Mind. rev. ed. LC 86-27416. 480p. 1987. pap. text ed. 14.95 (*0-8018-3044-3*) Johns Hopkins.

Lipset, Seymour M., jt. ed. see Laslett, John H.

Lipset, Seymour M., ed. see Martineau, Harriet.

Lipset, Seymour M., et al. Union Democracy: The Internal Politics of the International Typographical Union. LC 56-6202. (Illus.). 1977. pap. 18.95 (*0-02-919210-2*) Free Pr.

***Lipset, Seymour M., et al, eds.** The Encyclopedia of Democracy, 4 vols. (Illus.). 1800p. 1995. 395.00 (*0-87187-675-2*) Congr Quarterly.

Lipsett, Laurence. Back to Work: How to Rejoin the Workforce after an Absence. 135p. (Orig.). 1993. pap. 15.95 (*0-9637107-0-2*) Curtice Pub.

— How to Hire Winners Legally. LC 94-23334. 150p. 1994. pap. 14.95 (*0-87425-982-7*) Human Res Dev Pr.

— How to Test Sales Applicants Legally. 101p. 1994. pap. 29.95 (*0-9637107-1-0*) Curtice Pub.

Lipsett, Linda O. Pieced from Ellen's Quilt: Ellen Spaulding Reed's Letters & Story. LC 91-16329. (Illus.). 224p. (Orig.). 1991. pap. text ed. 13.95 (*0-9629399-0-0*) Halstead Meadows.

Lipsett, Linda O., jt. auth. see Price, Esther.

Lipsett, Mortimer B., jt. ed. see Merriam, George R.

Lipsett, Roger, et al. VHDL: Hardware Description & Design. 320p. (C). 1989. lib. bdg. 78.00 (*0-7923-9030-X*) Kluwer Ac.

Lipsett, Suzanne. Remember Me. LC 90-49382. 145p. 1991. 17.95 (*0-916515-98-2*) Mercury Hse Inc.

— Surviving a Writer's Life. LC 93-22857. 240p. 1994. 18.00 (*0-06-250657-9*) Harper SF.

— Surviving a Writer's Life. LC 93-22857. 240p. 1995. pap. 10.00 (*0-06-250658-7*) Harper SF.

Lipsett, Suzanne, ed. see Manahan, William.

Lipsett, Suzanne, jt. auth. see Marshall, John R.

Lipsett, Suzanne, ed. see Patten, Leslie & Patten, Terry.

Lipsett, Suzanne, ed. see Rascon, Armando.

Lipsett, Suzanne, ed. see Roads, Michael J.

Lipsett, Suzanne, jt. auth. see Siano, Nick.

Lipsett, Suzanne, ed. see Silva, Jose & Stone, Robert B.

Lipsey, B. An Art of Our Own: The Spiritual in 20th Century Art. (C). 1990. 320.00 (*0-685-34378-2*, Pub. by Collets) St Mut.

— Art of the Avant-Garde in Russia - Selections from the G. Costakis-Solomon Guggenheim Museum Exhibition. (C). 1990. pap. 170.00 (*0-685-34377-4*, Pub. by Collets) St Mut.

Lipsey, Mark W. Design Sensitivity: Statistical Power for Experimental Research. (Illus.). 224p. (C). 1989. text ed. 49.95 (*0-8039-3062-3*); pap. text ed. 24.00 (*0-8039-3063-1*) Sage.

***Lipsey, Richard A. Sports Market Place. 1074p. 1995. pap. 199.00 (*0-935644-02-4*) Sportsguide. All inclusive resource reference book. Over 9,000 sports organizations, with detailed descriptions of services & products, calendars, marketing services, supplier advertising agencies, five different indexes, & other essential information. Over 26,000 business executives. To order call 1-800-776-7877 & 1-602-954-8106 or FAX: 1-602-955-3441. Mail orders to: Sports Market Place, P.O. Box 10129, Phoenix, AZ 85064.** *Publisher Provided Annotation.*

— Sports Market Place Register 1995. 600p. 1995. pap. 59.00 (*0-935644-03-2*) Sportsguide.

Lipsey, Richard A., ed. Baseball Market Place. 320p. 1990. pap. 19.95 (*0-685-34606-4*) Sportsguide.

Lipsey, Richard G. Economics. 10th ed. (C). 1992. 64.50 (*0-06-501022-1*) HarpCollege.

— Economics. 10th ed. (C). 1993. student ed 24.00 (*0-06-501093-0*) HarpCollege.

— Macro. (C). 1993. student ed 22.50 (*0-06-501094-9*) HarpCollege.

— Macroeconomics. (C). 1992. 47.00 (*0-06-501023-X*) HarpCollege.

— Micro. (C). 1993. student ed 22.50 (*0-06-501095-7*) HarpCollege.

— Microeconomics. (C). 1992. 47.00 (*0-06-501024-8*) HarpCollege.

Lipsey, Richard G., jt. auth. see Harbury, Colin.

Lipsey, Richard G., et al. Economics. 8th ed. (C). 1994. Canadian. text ed. 41.00 (*0-673-46979-4*); Canadian. text ed. 24.00 (*0-673-46983-2*) HarpCollege.

— Economics. 8th ed. (C). 1994. Study guide. student ed 14.50 (*0-673-46980-8*); Study guide. student ed 12.00 (*0-673-46984-0*) HarpCollege.

— Economics. 9th ed. 1040p. (C). 1990. text ed. 39.50 (*0-06-043908-4*) HarpCollege.

— Macroeconomics. 9th ed. 540p. (C). 1989. pap. text ed. 28.00 (*0-06-044112-7*) HarpCollege.

— Micro Economics. 8th ed. (C). 1994. text ed. 27.00 (*0-673-46981-6*) HarpCollege.

— Micro Economics. 8th ed. (C). 1994. 12.00 (*0-673-46982-4*) HarpCollege.

— Microeconomics. 9th ed. 540p. (C). 1990. pap. text ed. 26.25 (*0-06-044113-5*) HarpCollege.

Lipsey, Robert E. Price & Quantity Trends in the Foreign Trade of the United States. (Studies in International Economic Relations: No. 2). 505p. 1963. reprint ed. 131.30 (*0-87014-154-6*) Natl Bur Econ Res.

Lipsey, Robert E. & Preston, Doris. Source Book of Statistics Relating to Construction. (General Ser.: No. 82). 319p. 1966. reprint ed. 83.00 (*0-87014-082-5*) Natl Bur Econ Res.

Lipsey, Robert E. & Tice, Helen S., eds. The Measurement of Saving, Investment, & Wealth. LC 88-4669. (National Bureau of Economic Research Studies in Income & Wealth: Vol. 52). (Illus.). 744p. 1989. lib. bdg. 85.00 (*0-226-48468-8*) U Ch Pr.

Lipsey, Robert E. & Weiss, Merle Y. The Structure of Ocean Transport Costs. (Explorations in Economic Research One Ser.: No. 1). 42p. 1974. reprint ed. 35.00 (*0-685-61371-2*) Natl Bur Econ Res.

Lipsey, Robert E., jt. auth. see Cagan, Phillip.

Lipsey, Robert E., jt. auth. see Fabricant, Solomon.

Lipsey, Robert E., jt. auth. see Kravis, Irving B.

Lipsey, Roger, ed. see Coomaraswamy, Ananda K.

Lipsey, Roger, ed. see Coomaraswamy.

Lipsey, Sally I. & Ignatavicius, Donna D. Math for Nurses: A Problem Solving Approach. (Illus.). 256p. 1993. pap. text ed. 24.50 (*0-7216-6481-4*) Saunders.

Lipshitz, Abe. Studies on Abraham Ibn Ezra. 118p. (C). 1969. 7.95 (*0-935982-43-4*, AL-01) Spertus Coll.

Lipshitz, Abe, intro. The Commentary of Abraham Ibn Ezra on Hosea. 190p. 1988. 19.95 (*0-87203-127-6*) Hermon.

Lipshitz, Arye. We Built Jerusalem: Tales of Pioneering Days. Louvish, Misha, tr. LC 84-45016. 176p. 1985. 14.95 (*0-8453-4787-X*, Cornwall Bks) Assoc Univ Prs.

Lipshitz, E. M., ed. see Landau, L. D.

***Lipshitz, Howard D.** Localized RNAs. (Molecular Biology Intelligence Unit Ser.). 411p. 1995. write for info. (*1-57059-276-4*) R G Landes.

Lipshitz, Hymie. X-Rated Drinks. 1991. pap. 6.90 (*0-9617655-0-X*) Foley Pub.

Lipshitz, J., et al, eds. Perinatal Development of the Heart & Lung. LC 86-30529. (Research in Perinatal Medicine Ser.: No. V). 1987. 65.00 (*0-916859-38-X*) Perinatology.

Lipshultz, Larry I., et al, eds. Surgery of the Male Reproductive Tract. (Clinics in Andrology Ser.: No. 2). (Illus.). 275p. 1980. lib. bdg. 140.00 (*90-247-2315-9*) Kluwer Ac.

Lipshutz, Nelson R. The Regulatory Economics of Title Insurance. LC 93-5440. 168p. 1994. text ed. 49.95 (*0-275-94742-4*, Praeger Pubs) Greenwood.

Lipsite, Edmond. Hebrew Olam Shalem, 3 cass., Set. 66p. (HEB.). 1985. audio 59.50 (*0-88432-579-2*, AFHE10) Audio-Forum.

Lipsitt, Lewis P., ed. Advances in Infancy Research, Vol. 1. (Advances in Infancy Research Ser.). 300p. 1981. text ed. 65.00 (*0-89391-045-7*) Ablex Pub.

Lipsitt, Lewis P. & Field, Tiffany M., eds. Perinatal Risk & Newborn Behavior. LC 82-8909. 208p. (C). 1982. text ed. 39.50 (*0-89391-123-2*) Ablex Pub.

Lipsitt, Lewis P. & Mitnick, Leonard L. Self-Regulatory Behavior & Risk Taking: Causes & Consequences. 432p. (C). 1991. text ed. 65.00 (*0-89391-818-0*) Ablex Pub.

Lipsitt, Lewis P. & Rovee-Collier, Carolyn. Advances in Infancy Research, Vol. 3. (Advances in Infancy Research Ser.). 320p. 1984. text ed. 65.00 (*0-89391-208-5*) Ablex Pub.

Lipsitt, Lewis P. & Rovee-Collier, Carolyn, eds. Advances in Infancy Research, Vol. 2. (Advances in Infancy Research Ser.). 344p. 1983. text ed. 65.00 (*0-89391-113-5*) Ablex Pub.

— Advances in Infancy Research, Vol. 4. 300p. 1986. text ed. 65.00 (*0-89391-309-X*) Ablex Pub.

Lipsitt, Lewis P. & Spiker, C. C., eds. Advances in Child Development, Vol. 17. (Serial Publication Ser.). 318p. 1982. text ed. 116.00 (*0-12-009717-6*) Acad Pr.

— Advances in Child Development, Vol. 18. (Serial Publication Ser.). 1984. text ed. 116.00 (*0-12-009718-4*) Acad Pr.

Lipsitt, Lewis P., ed. see Moerk, Ernst L.

Lipsitt, Lewis P., ed. see Plooij, Frans X.

Lipsitt, Lewis P., jt. ed. see Reese, H. W.

Lipsitt, Lewis P., jt. ed. see Reese, Hayne W.

Lipsitt, Lewis P., jt. ed. see Rovee-Collier, Carolyn.

Lipsitt, Lewis P

Lipsitz-Bem, Sandra. The Lenses of Gender: Transforming the Debate on Sexual Inequality. 256p. 1994. pap. 14.00 (*0-300-06163-3*) Yale U Pr.

Lipsitz, George. Class & Culture in Cold War America: A Rainbow at Midnight. 264p. 1981. 29.95 (*0-03-059207-0*, Bergin & Garvey) Greenwood.

— Dangerous Crossroads: Popular Music, Postmodernism & the Poetics of Place. LC 94-20455. 320p. 1994. 27.95 (*1-85984-935-0*, B4542, Pub. by Verso UK) Routledge Chapman & Hall.

— A Life in the Struggle: Ivory Perry & the Culture of Opposition. (Critical Perspectives on the Past Ser.). (Illus.). 328p. (C). 1988. 37.95 (*0-87722-550-8*) Temple U Pr.

— Rainbow at Midnight: Labor & Culture in the 1940s. LC 93-36425. 376p. (C). 1994. 49.95 (*0-252-02094-4*); pap. 15.95 (*0-252-06394-5*) U of Ill Pr.

— The Sidewalks of St. Louis: Places, People & Politics in an American City. (Illus.). 152p. (C). 1991. 16.95 (*0-8262-0814-2*) U of Mo Pr.

— Time Passages: Collective Memory & American Popular Culture. 323p. 1989. text ed. 34.95 (*0-8166-1805-4*); pap. text ed. 14.95 (*0-8166-1806-2*) U of Minn Pr.

Lipsitz, Helyn K. Rose-Colored Glasses. 120p. 1992. pap. text ed. 6.95 (*0-9633233-0-X*) Chicago Rose.

Lipsitz, Joan. Growing up Forgotten. LC 79-67002. 267p. (Orig.). 1980. pap. text ed. 19.95 (*0-87855-792-X*) Transaction Pubs.

— Successful Schools for Young Adolescents. 240p. 1983. 32.95 (*0-87855-487-4*); pap. text ed. 18.95 (*0-87855-947-7*) Transaction Pubs.

Lipsitz, Lawrence, ed. Technology & Education: Articles from Educational Technology Magazine. LC 79-125873. 192p. 1971. 27.95 (*0-87778-011-0*) Educ Tech Pubns.

— The Test Score Decline: Meaning & Issues. LC 76-13169. (Illus.). 240p. 1977. 32.95 (*0-87778-095-1*) Educ Tech Pubns.

Lipsitz, Lawrence, jt. ed. see Ackerman, Jerrold.

Lipsitz, Lewis & Speak, David M. American Democracy. 3rd ed. LC 92-50017. (Illus.). 736p. (C). 1993. pap. text ed. 30.50 (*0-312-06663-5*) St Martin.

— American Democracy. 3rd ed. LC 92-50017. (Illus.). 736p. (C). 1993. pap. text ed. 13.00 (*0-312-08080-8*) St Martin.

Lipsius, Justus. A Direction for Travailers for the Behoofe of the Young Earle of Bedford, Being Now Ready to Travell. LC 77-7414. (English Experience Ser.: No. 878). 1977. reprint ed. lib. bdg. 15.00 (*90-221-0878-3*) Walter J Johnson.

— Opera Omnia, 4 vols., Set. xii, 5010p. (GER.). reprint ed. write for info. (*0-318-70500-1*, Pub. by Georg Olms GW) Lubrecht & Cramer.

— Principles of Letter-Writing: A Bilingual Text of Justi Lipsii Epistolica Institutio. Young, R. V. & Hester, M. Thomas, eds. Hester, M. Thomas, tr. LC 93-41720. (Library of Renaissance Humanism: Vol. 3). 136p. (ENG & LAT.). (C). 1995. 34.95x (*0-8093-1958-6*) S Ill U Pr.

— The Roman Colosseum, 2 vols. (Printed Sources of Western Art Ser.). (Illus.). (LAT.). 1981. reprint ed. pap. 55.00 (*0-915346-58-3*) A Wofsy Fine Arts.

— Sixe Bookes of Politickes or Civil Doctrine. Jones, W., tr. LC 79-25633. (English Experience Ser.: No. 287). 1970. reprint ed. 22.00 (*90-221-0287-4*) Walter J Johnson.

Lipsius, Justus H. Das Attische Recht und Rechtsverfahren, 3 vols. in 1. iv, 1041p. 1984. reprint ed. write for info. (*3-487-01434-3*, Pub. by Georg Olms GW) Lubrecht & Cramer.

Lipsius, Richard A. Acta Apostolorum Apocrypha, 2 vols. in 3, Set. Bonnet, Max, ed. cxc, 1174p. (GER.). 1990. reprint ed. write for info. (*3-487-00044-X*, Pub. by Georg Olms GW) Lubrecht & Cramer.

Lipska, Ewa. Poet? Criminal? Madman? Plebanke, Barbara & Howard, Tony, trs. 95p. (Orig.). 1991. pap. 16.95 (*1-85610-011-1*, Pub. by Forest Bks UK) Dufour.

Lipske, Michael, jt. auth. see Center for Science in the Public Interest Staff.

Lipskerov, M. F. Samy Malenky Gnom (a Very Small Gnome) (Illus.). 18p. (Orig.). (RUS.). (J). 1991. pap. 14. 95 (*0-934393-23-0*) Rector Pr.

— Volk u Telonok: Wolf & Calf. (Childrens Ser.). (Illus.). 18p. (Orig.). (RUS.). (J). 1989. pap. 14.95 (*0-934393-15-X*) Rector Pr.

Lipski, Alexander. Life & Teaching of Sri Anandamayi Ma. (C). 1988. 9.00 (*81-208-0530-5*, Pub. by Motilal Banarsidass II) S Asia.

— Thomas Merton & Asia: His Quest for Utopia. (Cistercian Studies: No. 74). 1983. 17.95 (*0-87907-874-X*); pap. 7.95 (*0-87907-974-6*) Cistercian Pubns.

Lipski, John M. Language of the Islenos: Vestigial Spanish in Louisiana. LC 89-13508. 144p. 1990. text ed. 24.95 (*0-8071-1534-7*) La State U Pr.

— Latin American Spanish. LC 93-31346. (Linguistics Library). 1994. write for info. (*0-582-08761-9*, Pub. by Longman UK); pap. write for info. (*0-582-08760-0*, Pub. by Longman UK) Longman.

— The Speech of the Negros Congos of Panama. LC 88-7617. (Creole Language Library: Vol. 4). vii, 159p. (C). 1989. 59.00x (*1-55619-049-2*) Benjamins North Am.

Lipski, John M., jt. auth. see Neale-Silva, Eduardo.

Lipski, John M., jt. ed. see Roca, Ana.

Lipski, Jozef. Diplomat in Berlin, 1933-1939: Papers & Memoirs of Jozef Lipski, Ambassador of Poland. Jedrzejewicz, Waclaw, ed. LC 67-25871. 727p. reprint ed. pap. 180.00 (*0-317-09473-4*, 2006109) Bks Demand.

***Lipskin, Beth A., et al, eds.** The Tenth National Space Symposium Proceedings Report. 244p. 1994. pap. 50.00 (*0-9616962-8-1*) Univelt Inc.

Lipsky & Lipton. Student's Guide to Accounting for Lawyers. 1985. write for info. (*0-8205-0356-8*, 642) Bender.

Lipsky, Abram. John Wesley: A Portrait. LC 76-155619. reprint ed. 20.50 (*0-404-03994-4*) AMS Pr.

Lipsky, D. & Lipton, D. S. G. to Accounting, Set. 2nd ed. 1992. write for info. (*0-8205-0357-6*) Bender.

Lipsky, David B., ed. Advances in Industrial & Labor Relations, Vol. 2. 1985. 73.25 (*0-89232-444-9*) Jai Pr.

— Advances in Industrial & Labor Relations, Vol. 3. 1986. 73.25 (*0-89232-642-5*) Jai Pr.

— Advances in Industrial & Labor Relations, Vol. 4. 1988. 73.25 (*0-89232-715-4*) Jai Pr.

Lipsky, David B. & Donn, Clifford B., eds. Collective Bargaining in American Industry: Contemporary Perspectives & Future Directions. LC 85-45936. 368p. (C). 1987. text ed. 22.95 (*0-669-12594-6*); text ed. 21.95 (*0-669-12595-4*) Free Pr.

Lipsky, David B. & Douglas, Joel M., eds. Advances in Industrial & Labor Relations, Vol. 1. 1983. 73.25 (*0-89232-250-0*) Jai Pr.

Lipsky, George A., et al. Ethiopia. LC 62-13515. (Area & Country Surveys Ser.). 392p. 1962. 20.00x (*0-87536-917-0*) HRAFP.

— Saudi Arabia. LC 59-8227. (Area & Country Surveys Ser.). 381p. 1959. 20.00x (*0-87536-907-3*) HRAFP.

Lipsky, Lester. Queuing Theory: A Linear Algebraic Approach. 400p. (C). 1992. write for info. (*0-02-370952-9*) Macmillan.

Lipsky, Louis. Thirty Years of American Zionism, Vol.1. Davis, Moshe, ed. LC 77-70718. (America & the Holy Land Ser.). 1977. reprint ed. lib. bdg. 29.95 (*0-405-10263-1*) Ayer.

Lipsky, Michael. Street-Level Bureaucracy: Dilemmas of the Individual in Public Services. LC 79-7350. 275p. 1983. pap. 12.95 (*0-87154-526-8*) Russell Sage.

Lipsky, Michael, ed. Law & Order: Police Encounters. LC 72-91468. 144p. 1970. reprint ed. pap. text ed. 14.95 (*0-87855-563-3*) Transaction Pubs.

Lipsky, Michael & Olson, David J. Commission Politics: The Processing of Racial Crisis in America. LC 74-20192. 492p. 1977. 39.95x (*0-87855-078-X*) Transaction Pubs.

— Commission Politics: The Processing of Racial Crisis in America. LC 74-20192. 490p. reprint ed. pap. 139.70 (*0-318-34655-9*, 2056584) Bks Demand.

Lipsky, Michael, jt. auth. see Rathgeb, Steven.

Lipsky, Michael, jt. auth. see Smith, Steven R.

Lipsky, Peter E., et al, eds. Structure, Function, & Regulation of Molecules Involved in Leukocyte Adhesion: Proceedings of the Second International Conferences on "Structure & Function of Molecules Involved in Leukocyte Adhesion II" Held in Titisee, Germany, October 2-6, 1991. LC 92-2337. (Illus.). 567p. 1992. 98.00 (*0-387-97870-4*) Spr-Verlag.

Lipsky, Stephen. Microwave Passive Direction Finding. 1987. text ed. 110.00 (*0-471-83454-8*) Wiley.

Lipsky, Suzanne. Internalized Racism. 1978. pap. 2.00 (*0-913937-24-X*) Rational Isl.

Lipsman, Samuel L. & Weiss, Stephen. A False Peace. Manning, Robert, ed. (Vietnam Experience Ser.: Vol. XVI). (Illus.). 192p. 1985. 16.95 (*0-939526-15-8*) Boston Pub Co.

Lipsman, Samuel L., jt. auth. see Dougan, Clark.

Lipsman, Samuel L., jt. auth. see Doyle, Edward G.

Lipsomb, Jane. A Young Colonel from Virginia. LC 92-64468. 64p. 1993. pap. 8.00 (*1-56002-199-3*, Univ Edtns) Aegina Pr.

Lipson & Wixson. Assessment & Instruction of Reading Disabilities. (C). 1991. text ed. 58.50 (*0-673-18335-1*) HarpCollege.

Lipson, Abigail & Perkins, David N. Block: Getting out of Your Own Way. 1990. 18.95 (*0-8184-0516-3*) Carol Pub Group.

Lipson, Alexander. A Russian Course: Pt. 1. (Illus.). ix, 338p. (Orig.). (C). 1981. pap. text ed. 16.95 (*0-89357-080-X*) Slavica.

— A Russian Course: Pt. 2. (Illus.). 343p. (Orig.). (C). 1981. pap. text ed. 16.95 (*0-89357-081-8*) Slavica.

— A Russian Course: Pt. 3. (Illus.). iv, 105p. (Orig.). 1981. pap. text ed. 12.95 (*0-89357-082-6*) Slavica.

Lipson, Ashley. Documentary Evidence. (Art of Advocacy Ser.). 1986. Looseleaf updates available. write for info. (*0-8205-1028-9*) Bender.

Lipson, Ashley S. Art of Advocacy: Demonstrative Evidence. 1988. ring bd. write for info. (*0-8205-1082-3*) Bender.

— Law Office Automation for Paralegals, Administrators & Legal Secretaries. 384p. 1989. text ed. 59.95 (*0-13-526583-5*) P-H.

Lipson, Carol, jt. auth. see Fischer, Ernst P.

Lipson, Charles. Standing Guard: Protecting Foreign Capital in the 19th & 20th Centuries. LC 83-24260. (Studies in International Political Economy: Vol. 11). 330p. 1985. pap. 15.00 (*0-520-05327-3*) U CA Pr.

Lipson, Charles & Sheth, N. J. Statistical Design & Analysis of Engineering Experiments. (Illus.). 544p. (C). 1973. text ed. write for info. (*0-07-037991-2*) McGraw.

Lipson, E. History of the Woolen & Worsted Industries. 273p. 1965. reprint ed. 30.00 (*0-7146-2339-3*, Pub. by F Cass Pubs UK) Intl Spec Bk.

Lipson, Eden R. The New York Times Parent's Guide to the Best Books for Children. (Illus.). 448p. 1988. 22.00 (*0-8129-1649-2*, Times Bks); pap. 12.95 (*0-8129-1688-3*, Times Bks) Random.

— The New York Times Parent's Guide to the Best Books for Children. LC 91-2675. (Illus.). 464p. 1991. pap. 15. 00 (*0-8129-1889-4*, Times Bks) Random.

Lipson, Edward D., jt. ed. see Cerda-Olmedo, Enrique.

Lipson, Ephraim. Europe in the Nineteenth Century, 1815-1914. 11th ed. LC 78-16548. (Illus.). 298p. 1979. reprint ed. text ed. 59.75 (*0-313-20593-0*, LIEN, Greenwood Pr) Greenwood.

Lipson, Eric. Passover Haggadah: A Messianic Celebration. LC 85-82168. (Illus.). 128p. 1986. 10.95 (*0-9616148-0-3*); pap. 7.95 (*0-9616148-5-4*) Purple Pomegranate.

Lipson, Eric, jt. auth. see Lipson, Greta.

Lipson, Fran, jt. auth. see Molyneux, Lynn.

Lipson, Greta. A Book for All Seasons. 160p. (J). (gr. 5-9). 1990. 12.95 (*0-86653-540-3*, GA1153) Good Apple.

— Fact, Fantasy, Folklore. 160p. (J). (gr. 3-12). 1977. 12.95 (*0-916456-11-0*, GA71) Good Apple.

— Famous Fables for Little Troupers. 168p. (J). (gr. k-6). 1984. 13.95 (*0-86653-202-1*, GA 554) Good Apple.

— Fast Ideas for Busy Teachers. 160p. 1989. 12.95 (*0-86653-504-7*, GA1082) Good Apple.

Lipson, Greta & Bolkosky, Sidney. Mighty Myth. 152p. (J). (gr. 5-12). 1982. 12.95 (*0-86653-064-9*, GA 419) Good Apple.

Lipson, Greta & Greenberg, Bernice. Extra! Extra! Read All about It! 160p. (J). (gr. 4-8). 1981. 12.95 (*0-86653-006-1*, GA234) Good Apple.

Lipson, Greta & Lipson, Eric. Everyday Law for Young Citizens. 160p. (J). (gr. 5 up). 1988. student ed 12.95 (*0-86653-447-4*, GA1056) Good Apple.

Lipson, Greta & Romantowski, Jane. Calliope. 160p. (gr. 4-8). 1981. 12.95 (*0-86653-025-8*, GA230) Good Apple.

Lipson, Greta & Romatowski, Jane. Ethnic Pride. (Illus.). 152p. (J). (gr. 4-9). 1983. student ed 12.95 (*0-86653-121-1*, GA 464) Good Apple.

Lipson, Greta & Solomon, Susan. Romeo & Juliet: Plainspoken. (Illus.). 256p. (J). (gr. 7-12). 1985. 15.95 (*0-86653-283-8*, GA 659) Good Apple.

Lipson, Greta B. Audacious Poetry. (Illus.). 128p. (J). (gr. 6-12). 1992. student ed 11.95 (*0-86653-683-3*, 1417) Good Apple.

— A Leash on Love: A Book for All Ages. LC 93-176359. (Illus.). 32p. (J). 1992. 9.95 (*0-9630637-0-7*) Barclay Bks.

— More Fast Ideas for Busy Teachers: One Hundred Productive Activities for Teachers, Substitutes, & Parents. (Illus.). 144p. (J). (gr. 4-8). 1994. 12.95 (*0-86653-821-6*, GA1513) Good Apple.

— Tales with a Twist. 160p. (J). (gr. 5-9). 1991. 12.95 (*0-86653-609-4*, GA1328) Good Apple.

Lipson, H., ed. see Bragg, Lawrence.

Lipson, H., jt. auth. see Lipson, S. G.

Lipson, John D. Elements of Algebra & Algebraic Computing. 342p. (C). 1981. text ed. 39.95 (*0-201-04115-4*, Adv Bk Prog); pap. 39.95 (*0-201-04480-3*, Adv Bk Prog) Addison-Wesley.

Lipson, Joseph I. Educational Technology in Voc Ed. 28p. 1984. 3.25 (*0-318-22085-7*, IN268) Ctr Educ Trng Employ.

Lipson, Juliene G. Jews for Jesus: An Anthropological Study. LC 89-45372. (Studies in Anthropology: No. 5). 1990. 42.50 (*0-404-62605-X*) AMS Pr.

Lipson, Lawrence, tr. see Gleijeses, Piero.

Lipson, Leslie. The Ethical Crises of Civilization: Moral Meltdown or Advance. (Illus.). 416p. 1993. 55.00 (*0-8039-5242-2*); pap. 25.00 (*0-8039-5243-0*) Sage.

— The Great Issues of Politics. 7th ed. (Illus.). 416p. (C). 1985. text ed. write for info. (*0-13-363912-6*) P-H.

— Great Issues of Politics. 8th ed. 416p. (C). 1989. text ed. write for info. (*0-13-363920-7*) P-H.

— The Great Issues of Politics: An Introduction to Political Science. 9th ed. LC 92-17866. 432p. 1992. text ed. write for info. (*0-13-364407-3*) P-H.

Lipson, Michael. How the Wind Plays. (Illus.). 32p. (J). (ps-1). 1994. 14.95 (*1-56282-325-6*); lib. bdg. 14.89 (*1-56282-326-4*) Hyprn Child.

Lipson, Michael, tr. see Kuhlewind, Georg.

Lipson, Michael, tr. see Rudnicki, Konrad.

Lipson, Michael, tr. see Steiner, Rudolf.

Lipson, Michelle. The Fantastic Costume Book: Forty Complete Patterns to Amaze & Amuse. (Illus.). 128p. (J). (gr. 4 up). 1993. pap. 14.95 (*0-8069-8377-9*) Sterling.

— Sew a Dinosaur. LC 90-45158. (Illus.). 128p. 1992. pap. 14.95 (*0-8069-8213-6*) Sterling.

Lipson, Michelle, et al. The Fantastic Costume Book: Forty Complete Patterns to Amaze & Amuse. LC 92-11365. (Illus.). 128p. (J). (gr. 4 up). 1992. 21.95 (*0-8069-8376-0*) Sterling.

Lipson, Ruth. Modeh Ani Means Thank You. (Illus.). (J). (ps-2). 1986. 9.95 (*0-87306-392-9*) Feldheim.

— Shabbos Is Coming. (Sifrei Rimon Ser.). 1985. pap. 2.95 (*0-87306-383-X*) Feldheim.

Lipson, S. G. & Lipson, H. Optical Physics. 2nd ed. LC 79-8963. (Illus.). 496p. 1981. pap. 37.95 (*0-521-29584-X*) Cambridge U Pr.

Lipson, S. G., jt. auth. see Kuper, C. G.

***Lipson, S. G., et al.** Optical Physics. (Illus.). 464p. (C). 1995. pap. write for info. (*0-521-43631-1*) Cambridge U Pr.

— Optical Physics. 3rd ed. (Illus.). 464p. (C). 1995. write for info. (*0-521-43047-X*) Cambridge U Pr.

Lipson, Steve. Windows As a Second Language. LC 93-87705. 288p. 1994. pap. 17.99 (*0-7821-1369-9*) Sybex.

Lipson, Steven, jt. ed. see Braun, Judith V.

***Lipson, Tony.** From Conception to Birth: Our Most Important Journey. (Illus.). 168p. (Orig.). 1994. pap. 12. 95 (*1-86429-006-4*) Morehouse Pub.

Lipstadt, Deborah. Beyond Belief: The American Press & the Coming of the Holocaust. 336p. (C). 1985. text ed. 32.95 (*0-02-919160-2*) Free Pr.

— Beyond Belief: The American Press & the Coming of the Holocaust. 370p. 1993. pap. 12.95 (*0-02-919161-0*) Free Pr.

— Denying the Holocaust: The Growing Assault on Truth & Memory. LC 93-9952. 300p. 1993. text ed. 22.95 (*0-02-919235-8*) Free Pr.

— The Zionist Career of Louis Lipsky, 1900-1921. 1981. 38. 95 (*0-405-14086-X*) Ayer.

Lipstadt, Deborah E. Denying the Holocaust: The Growing Assault on Truth & Memory. LC 93-45586. 288p. 1994. pap. 10.95 (*0-452-27274-2*, Plume) NAL-Dutton.

Lipstein, Kurt. Principles of the Conflict of Laws: National & International. 160p. 1981. 21.50 (*90-286-0750-1*) Kluwer Ac.

Lipstein, Norman J., ed. see ASME Staff.

Lipstein, Sherman, ed. see Palmer, Paul M.

Lipstiz, George, jt. auth. see Berns, Marla C.

Lipsyte, Marjorie. Hot Type. 224p. 1981. pap. 2.25 (*0-449-24415-6*, Crest) Fawcett.

Lipsyte, Robert. Arnold Schwarzenegger: Hercules in America. LC 92-46901. (Superstar Lineup Ser.). (Illus.). 96p. (J). (gr. 5-9). 1993. 14.00 (*0-06-023002-9*); lib. bdg. 14.89 (*0-06-023003-7*) HarpC Child Bks.

— Arnold Schwarzenegger: Hercules in America. LC 92-46901. (Superstar Lineup: A Trophy Nonfiction Bk.). (Illus.). 96p. (J). (gr. 3-7). 1995. pap. 3.95 (*0-06-446142-4*, Trophy) HarpC Child Bks.

— The Brave. LC 90-25396. (Charlotte Zolotow Bk.). 208p. (YA). (gr. 7 up). 1991. 15.00 (*0-06-023915-8*) HarpC Child Bks.

— The Brave. LC 90-25396. (Charlotte Zolotow Bk.). 208p. (YA). (gr. 7 up). 1993. pap. 3.95 (*0-06-447079-2*, Trophy) HarpC Child Bks.

— The Chemo Kid. LC 91-55500. (Trophy Keypoint Bk.). 176p. (YA). (gr. 7 up). 1992. lib. bdg. 14.89 (*0-06-020285-8*); pap. 3.95 (*0-685-59055-0*) HarpC Child Bks.

— The Chemo Kid. LC 91-55500. (Trophy Keypoint Bk.). 176p. (YA). (gr. 7 up). 1993. pap. 3.95 (*0-06-447101-2*, Trophy) HarpC Child Bks.

— The Chief. LC 92-54502. 240p. (YA). (gr. 7 up). 1993. 15.00 (*0-06-021064-8*); lib. bdg. 14.89 (*0-06-021068-0*) HarpC Child Bks.

— Chief. LC 92-54502. (Trophy Book). 240p. (YA). (gr. 7 up). 1995. pap. 3.95 (*0-06-447097-0*) HarpC Child Bks.

— The Contender. LC 67-19623. 190p. (YA). (gr. 7-9). 1967. lib. bdg. 14.89 (*0-06-023920-4*) HarpC Child Bks.

— The Contender. LC 67-19623. (Trophy Keypoint Bk.). 176p. (YA). (gr. 7 up). 1987. pap. 3.95 (*0-06-447039-3*, Trophy) HarpC Child Bks.

— Free to Be Muhammad Ali. LC 77-25640. (Ursula Nordstrom Bk.). (J). (gr. 5 up). 1978. lib. bdg. 14.89 (*0-06-023902-6*) HarpC Child Bks.

— Jim Thorpe: Twentieth-Century Jock. LC 92-44069. (Superstar Lineup Ser.). (Illus.). 112p. (J). (gr. 5-9). 1993. 14.00 (*0-06-022988-8*); lib. bdg. 13.89 (*0-06-022989-6*) HarpC Child Bks.

— Jim Thorpe: Twentieth-Century Jock. LC 92-44069. (J). (gr. 4-7). 1995. pap. 3.95 (*0-06-446141-6*) HarpC Child Bks.

— Joe Louis: A Champ for all America. LC 93-48767. (Superstar Lineup Ser.). (Illus.). 96p. (J). (gr. 5-9). 1994. lib. bdg. 14.89 (*0-06-023410-5*) HarpC Child Bks.

— Joe Louis: A Champ for All America. LC 93-48767. (Superstar Lineup Ser.). (Illus.). 96p. (J). (gr. 5-9). 1994. pap. 3.95 (*0-06-446155-6*, Trophy) HarpC Child Bks.

— Michael Jordan: A Life Above the Rim. LC 93-50561. (Superstar Lineup Ser.). (Illus.). 96p. (J). (gr. 5-9). 1994. lib. bdg. 14.89 (*0-06-024235-3*) HarpC Child Bks.

— Michael Jordan: A Life above the Rim. (Superstar Lineup Ser.). (Illus.). 96p. (J). (gr. 5-9). 1994. pap. 3.95 (*0-06-446156-4*, Trophy) HarpC Child Bks.

— One Fat Summer. LC 76-49746. (YA). (gr. 7 up). 1977. lib. bdg. 14.89 (*0-06-023896-8*) HarpC Child Bks.

— One Fat Summer. LC 76-49746. (Charlotte Zolotow Bk.). 240p. (YA). (gr. 7 up). 1991. pap. 3.95 (*0-06-447073-3*, Trophy) HarpC Child Bks.

— Summer Rules. LC 79-2816. (Ursula Nordstrom Bk.). 160p. (YA). (gr. 7 up). 1981. lib. bdg. 14.89 (*0-06-023898-4*) HarpC Child Bks.

— Summer Rules. LC 79-2816. (Trophy Keypoint Bk.). 208p. (YA). (gr. 7 up). 1992. pap. 3.95 (*0-06-447071-7*, Trophy) HarpC Child Bks.

Lipsyte, Robert & Brown, Gene. Sports & Society. (Great Contemporary Issues Ser.). 35.00 (*0-405-13143-7*) Ayer.

***Lipsyte, Robert & Levine, Peter.** Idols of the Game: A Sporting History of the American Century. (Illus.). 368p. 1995. 23.95 (*1-57036-154-1*) Turner Pub GA.

Lipsyte, Robert, jt. auth. see Gregory, Dick.

Liptak, Andras, et al. Handbook of Oligosaccharides: Trisaccharides, 2 vols., 1. 256p. 1990. 173.95 (*0-8493-2901-9*, QP702) CRC Pr.

— Handbook of Oligosaccharides: Trisaccharides, 2 vols., 2. 256p. 1990. 173.95 (*0-8493-2902-7*) CRC Pr.

Liptak, Bela G. Analytical Instrumentation. LC 93-48731. 496p. 1994. pap. 44.95 (*0-8019-8397-5*) Chilton.

— Flow Measurement. LC 92-56585. 224p. 1993. pap. 34.95 (*0-8019-8386-X*) Chilton.

— Municipal Waste Disposal. LC 90-55321. 512p. 1991. 69. 95 (*0-8019-7867-X*) Chilton.

— Temperature Measurement. LC 92-56586. 128p. 1993. pap. 29.95 (*0-8019-8385-1*) Chilton.

Liptak, Bela G., ed. Instrument Engineers' Handbook: Process Control. 3rd ed. LC 94-20792. 1584p. 1995. 125.00 (*0-8019-8242-1*) Chilton.

Liptak, D., ed. see Dennehy, R. & Grisez, G.

Liptak, D., ed. see Lawler, R. & May, W.

Liptak, David Q. The New Code & the Sacraments. 140p. 1983. pap. 7.95 (*0-941850-12-9*) Liturgical Pubns.

— Preaching Mary's Praises - Homilies. 1992. 5.95 (*1-56036-013-5*) AMI Pr.

— Sacramental & Occasional Homilies. LC 80-29287. 96p. (Orig.). 1981. pap. 5.95 (*0-8189-0408-9*) Alba.

— The Saints As Models: Preaching & Prayer. rev. ed. 159p. 1990. pap. 8.95 (*0-940169-07-X*) Liturgical Pubns.

Liptak, David Q. & Sheridan, Philip A. The New Code: Laity & Deacons. 128p. (Orig.). 1986. pap. 7.95 (*0-941850-19-6*) Liturgical Pubns.

Liptak, Diana. And Thy House. 123p. (Orig.). 1985. pap. 3.00 (*0-9615057-0-2*) D Liptak.

Liptak, Dolores. European Immigrants & the Catholic Church in Connecticut, 1870-1920. LC 86-6859. (CMS Migration & Ethnicity Ser.). 1987. 19.50 (*0-913256-79-X*); pap. text ed. 14.50 (*0-913256-80-3*) Ctr Migration.

Liptak, Dolores, ed. A Church of Many Cultures: Selected Historical Essays on Ethnic American Catholicism. (Heritage of American Catholicism Ser.). 416p. 1988. lib. bdg. 20.00 (*0-8240-4081-3*) Garland.

Liptak, Dolores, jt. auth. see Stepsis, M. U.

Liptak, Karen. Adoption Controversies. LC 93-19810. (Changing Family Ser.). (Illus.). 160p. 1993. lib. bdg. 14. 49 (*0-531-13032-0*) Watts.

— Astronomy Basics. (Illus.). 48p. (J). (gr. 3-7). 1986. 10.95 (*0-13-049966-8*) P-H.

— Coming-of-Age: Traditions & Rituals Around the World. LC 93-1414. (Illus.). 128p. (YA). (gr. 7 up). 1994. lib. bdg. 15.90 (*1-56294-243-3*) Millbrook Pr.

— Dating Dinosaurs & Other Old Things. LC 91-23072. (Illus.). 72p. (YA). (gr. 7 up). 1992. lib. bdg. 14.90 (*1-56294-134-8*) Millbrook Pr.

— Endangered Peoples. LC 92-41391. (Impact Book Ser.). (J). 1993. lib. bdg. 14.42 (*0-531-10987-9*) Watts.

— Indians of the Pacific Northwest. (First Americans Ser.). (Illus.). 96p. (J). (gr. 5-8). 1990. 18.95 (*0-8160-2384-0*) Facts on File.

— Indians of the Southwest. (First Americans Ser.). (Illus.). 96p. (J). (gr. 5-8). 1990. 18.95 (*0-8160-2385-9*) Facts on File.

— Inside Biosphere 2: The Rainforest. (From Inside Biosphere 2 Ser.). 64p. (J). (gr. 3 up). 1993. pap. text ed. 8.95 (*1-882428-06-4*) Biosphere Pr.

— North American Indian Ceremonies. Mathews, V., ed. LC 90-12337. (First Bks.). (Illus.). 64p. (J). (gr. 3-6). 1992. lib. bdg. 13.93 (*0-531-20100-7*) Watts.

An Asterisk (*) at the beginning of an entry indicates that the title is appearing in BIP for the first time.

L

— North American Indian Ceremonies. (First Bks.). (Illus.). 64p. (J). (gr. 5-8). 1992. pap. 5.95 (*0-531-15639-7*) Watts.

— North American Indian Medicine People. LC 90-12337. (Full-Color First Bks.). (Illus.). 64p. (J). (gr. 5-8). 1990. lib. bdg. 13.93 (*0-531-10868-6*) Watts.

— North American Indian Medicine People. (First Bks.). (Illus.). 64p. (J). (gr. 5-8). 1992. pap. 5.95 (*0-531-15640-0*) Watts.

— North American Indian Sign Language. LC 90-12336. (First Bks.). (Illus.). 64p. (J). (gr. 5-8). 1990. lib. bdg. 13. 93 (*0-531-10869-4*) Watts.

— North American Indian Sign Language. (First Bks.). (Illus.). 64p. (J). (gr. 5-8). 1992. pap. 5.95 (*0-531-15641-9*) Watts.

— North American Indian Survival Skills. LC 90-12354. (First Bks.). (Illus.). 64p. (J). (gr. 5-8). 1990. lib. bdg. 13. 93 (*0-531-10870-8*) Watts.

— North American Indian Survival Skills. (First Bks.). (Illus.). 64p. (J). (gr. 5-8). 1992. pap. 5.95 (*0-531-15642-7*) Watts.

— North American Indian Tribal Chiefs. Mathews, V., ed. LC 91-30261. (First Bks.). (Illus.). 64p. (J). (gr. 3-6). 1992. lib. bdg. 13.93 (*0-531-20101-5*) Watts.

— North American Indian Tribal Chiefs. (First Bks.). (Illus.). 64p. (J). (gr. 5-8). 1992. pap. 5.95 (*0-531-15643-5*) Watts.

— Saving Our Wetlands & Their Wildlife. LC 91-4682. (First Bks.). (Illus.). 64p. (J). (gr. 5-8). 1991. lib. bdg. 13. 93 (*0-531-20092-2*) Watts.

— Saving Our Wetlands & Their Wildlife. (First Bks.). (Illus.). 64p. (J). (gr. 5-8). 1992. pap. 5.95 (*0-531-15648-6*) Watts.

***Liptak, P.** Avars & Ancient Hungarians. 208p. (C). 1983. 57.00x (*963-05-2956-4*, Pub. by Akad Kiado HU) St Mut.

Liptak, Pal. Avars & Ancient Hungarians. 208p. 1983. 82.50 (*0-685-16982-0*, Pub. by Collets UK) Pro-Am Music.

Liptay, Lynne, jt. auth. see Mueser, Anne M.

Lipton, jt. auth. see Lipsky.

Lipton, Alfred. Cinderella, Vol. 512. rev. ed. Caban, Janice, ed. & illus. by. (Once upon a Tale Ser.). 10p. (J). (gr. k). 1989. pap. 2.00 (*1-878501-01-1*) Ntrl Science Indus.

— Goldilox & the Three Bears, Vol. 514. rev. ed. Caban, Janice, ed. & illus. by. (Once upon a Tale Ser.). 10p. (J). (gr. k). 1989. pap. 2.00 (*1-878501-02-X*) Ntrl Science Indus.

— Jack & the Beanstalk, Vol. 510. rev. ed. Caban, Janice, ed. & illus. by. (Once upon a Tale Ser.). 10p. (J). (gr. k). 1989. pap. 2.00 (*1-878501-00-3*) Ntrl Science Indus.

— Little Red Riding Hood, Vol. 520. rev. ed. Caban, Janice, ed. & illus. by. (Once upon a Tale Ser.). 10p. (J). (gr. k). 1989. pap. 2.00 (*1-878501-05-4*) Ntrl Science Indus.

— Pinocchio, Vol. 516. rev. ed. Caban, Janice, ed. & illus. by. (Once upon a Tale Ser.). 10p. (J). (gr. k). 1989. pap. 2.00 (*1-878501-03-8*) Ntrl Science Indus.

— Sleeping Beauty, Vol. 518. rev. ed. Caban, Janice, ed. & illus. by. (Once upon a Tale Ser.). 10p. (J). (gr. k). 1989. pap. 2.00 (*1-878501-04-6*) Ntrl Science Indus.

Lipton, Allan, jt. ed. see Bijvoet, Olav L.

Lipton, Barbara. Survival: Life & Art of the Alaskan Eskimo. LC 76-53613. 1977. 7.95 (*0-932828-04-3*) Newark Mus.

— Treasures of Tibetan Art: The Collections of the Jacques Marchais Museum of Tibetan Art. (Illus.). 352p. 1996. 59.95 (*0-19-509713-0*); pap. 29.95 (*0-19-509714-9*) OUP.

Lipton, Carolee, jt. auth. see Lipton, Chet.

Lipton, Charles, jt. auth. see Haynes, J. H.

Lipton, Chet & Lipton, Carolee. Walking Easy in the Austrian Alps: A Hiking Guide for Active Adults. (Walking Easy Ser.). 192p. (Orig.). 1994. pap. 10.95 (*0-933469-16-0*) Gateway Bks.

— Walking Easy in the French Alps: A Hiking Guide for Active Adults. (Walking Easy Ser.). (Illus.). 224p. (Orig.). 1995. pap. 11.95 (*0-933469-21-7*) Gateway Bks.

— Walking Easy in the Italian Alps: A Hiking Guide for Active Adults. (Walking Easy Ser.). (Illus.). 224p. (Orig.). 1995. pap. 11.95 (*0-933469-22-5*) Gateway Bks.

— Walking Easy in the Swiss Alps: A Hiking Guide for Active Adults. (Illus.). 192p. 1993. pap. 10.95 (*0-933469-15-2*) Gateway Bks.

Lipton, D., jt. auth. see Lipsky, D.

***Lipton, David.** A Visit to Portland. 39p. (J). 1990. 3.50 (*0-9643034-0-X*) White Truffle Bks.

Lipton, David A. Broker-Dealer Regulation. (Securities Law Ser.). 1988. ring bd. 145.00 (*0-87632-599-1*) Clark Boardman Callaghan.

Lipton, David R. Ernst Cassirer: The Dilemma of a Liberal Intellectual in Germany, 1914-1933. LC 78-6945. 226p. reprint ed. pap. 64.50 (*0-8357-8119-4*, 2033992) Bks Demand.

Lipton, Douglas W. & Strand, Ivar E. Maryland's Ocean Fisheries: A Bioeconomic Assessment. pap. 1.50 (*0-943676-22-3*) MD Sea Grant Col.

Lipton, Eunice. Alias Olympia: A Woman's Search for Manet's Notorious Model & Her Own Desire. 192p. 1994. pap. 9.95 (*0-452-01135-3*, Mer) NAL-Dutton.

— Alias Olympia: A Woman's Search for Manet's Notorious Model & Her Own Desire. 192p. 1993. text ed. 20.00 (*0-684-19417-1*, Scribners) S&S Trade.

— Looking into Degas: Uneasy Images of Women & Modern Life. (Illus.). 1986. 47.50 (*0-520-05604-3*); pap. 16.00 (*0-520-06340-6*) U CA Pr.

***Lipton, G.** French Bilingual Dictionary Beginner. (YA). 1975. pap. 7.95 (*0-8120-0470-1*) Barron.

Lipton, Gladys. Practical Handbook to Elementary Foreign Language Programs. 2nd ed. 224p. 1991. pap. 19.95 (*0-8442-9332-6*, Natl Textbk) NTC Pub Grp.

Lipton, Gladys C. Beginning French Bilingual Dictionary. 2nd rev. ed. 368p. 1989. pap. 5.95 (*0-8120-4273-5*) Barron.

Lipton, Gladys C. & Colaneri, John. Beginning Italian Bilingual Dictionary. 2nd rev. ed. 464p. 1989. pap. 5.95 (*0-8120-4272-7*) Barron.

Lipton, Gladys C. & Munoz, Olivia. Beginning Spanish Bilingual Dictionary. 2nd rev. ed. 400p. 1989. pap. 5.95 (*0-8120-4274-3*) Barron.

Lipton, Gladys C., ed. see American Association of Teachers of French.

Lipton, Helene L. & Lee, Philip R. Drugs & the Elderly: Clinical, Social, & Policy Perspectives. LC 87-33574. 280p. 1988. 37.50 (*0-8047-1295-6*) Stanford U Pr.

Lipton, Howard L., jt. ed. see Gilden, Donald H.

Lipton, James. An Exaltation of Home & Family. 1993. 10. 00 (*0-679-41871-7*, Villard Bks) Random.

— An Exaltation of Larks: The Ultimate Edition. (Illus.). 336p. 1993. reprint ed. pap. 12.50 (*0-14-017096-0*, Penguin Bks) Viking Penguin.

— Exaltation of Romance & Raunch. 1994. 10.00 (*0-679-41872-5*, Villard Bks) Random.

Lipton, June, jt. auth. see O'Donnell, Asta.

***Lipton, Kathryn L.** Dictionary of Agriculture: From Abaca to Zoonosis. LC 94-25260. 375p. 1995. lib. bdg. 70.00 (*1-55587-523-8*) Lynne Rienner.

Lipton, Lenny. Independent Filmmaking. (Illus.). 448p. 1983. 12.95 (*0-686-46243-2*, Fireside) S&S Trade.

— Puff the Magic Dragon. 19p. (Orig.). (YA). Date not set. pap. 14.95 (*0-89524-863-8*, 02502143) Cherry Lane.

Lipton, Martin & Steinberger, Erica H. Takeovers & Freezeouts, 5 vols., Set. 2000p. 1978. 290.00 (*0-317-01347-5*, 00551) NY Law Pub.

Lipton, Martin, jt. auth. see Oakes, Jeannie.

Lipton, Merle & Simkins, Charles, eds. State & Market: In Post Apartheid South Africa. LC 94-19869. (C). 1994. pap. text ed. 45.00 (*0-8133-2234-0*) Westview.

***Lipton, Merrill I.** Posttraumatic Stress Disorder: Additional Perspectives. LC 93-37142. 258p. 1994. pap. 29.95 (*0-398-06242-0*) C C Thomas.

— Posttraumatic Stress Disorder: Additional Perspectives. LC 93-37142. 258p. (C). 1994. text ed. 49.95x (*0-398-05899-7*) C C Thomas.

Lipton, Michael & Longhurst, Richard. New Seeds & Poor People. LC 88-23079. (Studies in Development). 432p. 1989. text ed. 50.00 (*0-8018-3795-2*) Johns Hopkins.

Lipton, Michael & Paarlberg, Robert. Role of the World Bank in Agricultural Development in the 1990s. large type ed. 56p. 1990. 10.00 (*0-89629-315-7*) Intl Food Policy.

Lipton, Michael & Toye, John. Does Aid Work in India? A Country Study of the Impact of Offical Development Assistance. 304p. 1990. 75.00 (*0-415-01096-9*, A1555) Routledge.

— Does Aid Work in India? A Country Study of the Impact of Official Development Assistance. (Illus.). 304p. (Orig.). 1991. pap. 25.00 (*0-415-07160-7*, A6624) Routledge.

Lipton, Michael & Van der Gaag, Jacques. Including the Poor. LC 93-34793. (Regional & Sectoral Studies). 624p. 1993. 35.95 (*0-8213-2674-0*, 12674) World Bank.

Lipton, Michael, jt. auth. see Payne, Philip.

Lipton, Mimi, ed. The Tiger Rugs of Tibet. LC 88-51136. (Illus.). 1989. 60.00 (*0-500-97369-5*) Thames Hudson.

Lipton, Mimi & Dueser, Thorsten, photos. Stacking Wood. LC 92-62137. (Illus.). 124p. 1993. pap. 19.95 (*0-500-97407-1*) Thames Hudson.

Lipton, Peter. Inference to the Best Explanation. 240p. (C). 1991. text ed. 49.95 (*0-415-05886-4*, A5544) Routledge.

— Inference to the Best Explanation. (Philosophical Issues in Science Ser.). 192p. 1993. pap. 15.95 (*0-415-10029-1*, B2454) Routledge.

***Lipton, Phillip & Herzberg, Abe.** Essential Corporations Legislation. (Essential Legislation Ser.). 600p. 1995. pap. 30.00 (*0-455-21307-0*, Pub. by Law Bk Co) W W Gaunt.

— Understanding Company Law. 4th ed. 590p. 1991. pap. 49.00 (*0-455-21022-5*, Pub. by Law Bk Co) W W Gaunt.

— Understanding Company Law: Supplement, July, 1992. 4th ed. 1992. 15.00 (*0-455-21155-8*, Pub. by Law Bk Co) W W Gaunt.

— Understanding Company Law: With Computer Tutorials. 5th ed. 730p. 1993. disk, pap. 69.00 (*0-455-21215-5*, Pub. by Law Bk Co) W W Gaunt.

Lipton, R. P. User Guide to Focus. 272p. 1987. pap. text ed. 29.95 (*0-07-038006-6*) McGraw.

Lipton, Richard B., et al. Migraine Beating the Odds: The Doctors'Guide to Reducing Your Risk. (Illus.). 160p. 1992. pap. 8.61 (*0-201-57785-2*) Addison-Wesley.

Lipton, Rose C., jt. auth. see Provence, Sally.

Lipton, Russell C. Multimedia Toolkit: Build Your Own Solutions with DocuSource. 1992. disk, pap. 45.00 (*0-679-74084-8*) Random.

— Users Guide to FOCUS. 2nd ed. (Illus.). 320p. 1988. pap. text ed. 24.95 (*0-07-038013-9*) McGraw.

Lipton, Sampson. The Control of Chronic Pain. (Current Topics in Anesthesia Ser.: Vol. 2). (Illus.). 1979. 40.50 (*0-8151-5504-2*, Yr Bk Med Pubs) Mosby Yr Bk.

Lipton, Sampson, et al. The Pain Clinic. (Advances in Pain Research & Therapy Ser.: Vol. 13). 400p. 1990. 112.50 (*0-88167-582-2*) Raven.

Lipton, Sydney & Lynch, Jeremiah. Handbook of Health Hazard Control in the Chemical Process Industry. rev. ed. LC 94-2360. 1994. text ed. 99.95 (*0-471-55464-2*) Wiley.

— Health Hazard Control in the Chemical Process Industry. LC 87-16042. 358p. 1987. text ed. 94.95 (*0-471-84478-0*) Wiley.

Lipton, Zelda, jt. auth. see Vadakin, Charles E.

Liptser, R. S. & Shiryayev, A. N. Theory of Martingales. (C). 1989. lib. bdg. 296.00 (*0-7923-0395-4*) Kluwer Ac.

***Liptzin, Sol.** Arthur Schnitzler. LC 94-48728. (Studies in Austrian Literature, Culture, & Thought). 1995. pap. 19. 95 (*1-57241-013-2*) Ariadne CA.

Liptzin, Solomon. Biblical Themes in World Literature. LC 84-19457. 316p. 1985. 25.00 (*0-88125-063-5*) Ktav.

— Germany's Stepchildren. LC 75-167378. (Essay Index Reprint Ser.). 1977. reprint ed. 24.95 (*0-8369-2462-2*) Ayer.

— Historical Survey of German Literature. LC 72-89407. (Illus.). xiii, 300p. 1972. reprint ed. lib. bdg. 35.00 (*0-8154-0441-7*) Cooper Sq.

— Lyric Pioneers of Modern Germany. LC 28-5277. reprint ed. 16.45 (*0-404-03995-2*) AMS Pr.

— Shelley in Germany. LC 24-14279. (Columbia University. Germanic Studies, Old Ser.: No. 27). reprint ed. 17.00 (*0-404-50427-2*) AMS Pr.

Liptzin, Solomon, ed. see Peretz, Isaac L.

Lipuma, Anthony, jt. auth. see Rooney, Robert.

Lipuma, Edward S., jt. auth. see Meltzoff, Sarah K.

Lipunov, M. Astrophysics of Neutron Stars. Borner, Gerhard et al, eds. Wadhwa, R. S., tr. (Astronomy & Astrophysics Library). 344p. (C). 1992. text ed. 98.00 (*0-387-53568-3*) Spr-Verlag.

Lipworth, E., jt. ed. see Chretien, M.

Liquian, E. & Sobrevinas, Irene. Filipino Cooking: Here & Abroad. 194p. 1970. 12.95 (*0-318-36288-0*) Asia Bk Corp.

Liquid Chromatography Symposium Staff. Biological - Biomedical Applications of Liquid Chromatography. Hawk, Gerald L. et al, eds. LC 78-26628. (Chromatographic Science Ser.: No. 10). (Illus.). 756p. reprint ed. pap. 180.00 (*0-7837-0794-0*, 2041108) Bks Demand.

— Biological - Biomedical Applications of Liquid Chromatography, No. II. Hawk, Gerald L. et al, eds. LC 79-18918. (Chromatographic Science Ser.: No. 12). (Illus.). 520p. reprint ed. pap. 148.20 (*0-7837-0798-3*, 2041112) Bks Demand.

Liquid Scintillation Counting Symposium Staff. Liquid Scintillation Counting: Proceedings of a Symposium on Liquid Scintillation Counting, 5th, Bath, England, September 13-16, 1977, Vol. 3. Crook, M. A. & Johnson, P., eds. LC 70-156826. 321p. reprint ed. pap. 91.50 (*0-317-29707-4*, 2024009) Bks Demand.

— Liquid Scintillation Counting: Proceedings of a Symposium on Liquid Scintillation Counting, 5th, Bath, England, September 13-16, 1977, Vol. 4. Crook, M. A. & Johnson, P., eds. LC 70-156826. 279p. reprint ed. pap. 79.60 (*0-317-29709-0*, 2024010) Bks Demand.

— Liquid Scintillation Counting: Proceedings of a Symposium on Liquid Scintillation Counting, 5th, Bath, England, September 13-16, 1977, Vol. 5. Crook, M. A. & Johnson, P., eds. 232p. reprint ed. pap. 66.20 (*0-317-29406-7*, 2024011) Bks Demand.

Liquori, Alfonso M., jt. auth. see Redemptorists Staff.

Liquorman, Wayne, ed. see Balsekar, Ramesh S.

Lira, David M. Bankruptcy. 184p. 1988. text ed. 29.95 (*0-13-056532-6*, Busn) P-H.

Lira, Gloria G. Maria Luisa Bombal: Realidad y Fantasia. 28.50 (*0-916379-25-6*) Scripta.

Lira-Powell, Julianne H. Fifty Things You Can Do to Promote World Peace. Moran, Ran, ed. (Illus.). 144p. (Orig.). 1991. pap. 9.95 (*0-9629881-8-9*) Adelitas Pubs.

Liria, Pilar, tr. see Garcia-Godoy, Cristian.

Liritzis, Y., ed. Radioactivity Alert: A Guide to Radiation Effects. (Illus.). 129p. 1992. pap. 9.95 (*960-220-069-3*) Paul & Co Pubs.

Liroff, Richard A. A National Policy for the Environment: NEPA & Its Aftermath. LC 75-28910. 284p. reprint ed. pap. 81.00 (*0-685-20430-8*, 2056429) Bks Demand.

Lirtzman, Sidney I., jt. ed. see O'Connor, Charles J.

Lis, Catharina. Social Change & the Labouring Poor: Antwerp, 1770-1860. LC 85-52070. 224p. 1986. 32.00 (*0-300-03610-8*) Yale U Pr.

Lis, Halina, jt. auth. see Sharon, Nathan.

Lis-Turlejska, Maya, tr. see Jackins, Harvey.

Lisa, M. P., ed. see Rajneesh, Osho.

***Lisa, P. Joseph.** The Assault on Medical Freedom. 336p. (Orig.). 1994. pap. 14.95 (*1-57174-003-1*) Hampton Roads Pub Co.

Lisa, Philip, jt. auth. see Pfeiffer, Lee.

Lisagore, W. Barry, ed. see Leis, Brian N.

Lisak. Handbook of Myasthenia Gravis & Myastenic Syndromes. (Neurological Disease & Therapy Ser.: Vol. 23). 440p. 1994. 150.00 (*0-8247-8825-7*) Dekker.

Lisak, Janet M., jt. auth. see Tenney, Colleen C.

Lisandrelli, Elaine, jt. auth. see Bartoletti, Susan.

Lisanevich, Xenia, ed. see Adisa, Opal P., et al.

Lisann, Maury. Broadcasting to the Soviet Union: International Politics & Radio. LC 74-14046. (Illus.). 224p. 1975. 34.95 (*0-275-05590-6*, Praeger Pubs) Greenwood.

Lisano, Michael. Lab Manual for Physiology. 1993. spiral bd. 10.50 (*0-88252-124-1*) Paladin Hse.

Lisansky, Edith S., jt. auth. see Schilit, Rebecca.

Lisante, James. Let's Talk: The Gospel Challenge for American Catholics. 144p. (Orig.). (C). 1994. pap. 7.95 (*1-878718-20-7*) Resurrection.

Lisante, Joan. We Deliver. LC 87-46262. 1988. pap. 7.95 (*1-55611-079-0*) D I Fine.

Lisanti, Suzana, jt. auth. see Melin, Nancy J.

Lisausky, Michael A. Study Smarter-Save Time-Learn More: A Home Study Course. (Home Study Ser.). 40p. student ed 30.00 (*0-939926-36-9*); audio (*0-939926-35-0*) Fruition Pubns.

***Lisboa, Eugenio, ed.** Dedalus Book of Portuguese Fantasy. (Dedalus Anthology Ser.). 384p. (Orig.). (POR.). 1995. pap. 16.95 (*0-7818-0386-1*) Hippocrene Bks.

Lisboa, J. C. List of Bombay Grasses & Their Uses. 142p. 1979. reprint ed. 95.00 (*0-685-21855-4*, Pub. by Intl Bk Distr II) St Mut.

Lisboa, J. C., ed. List of Bombay Grasses & Their Uses. 142p. (C). 1979. text ed. 125.00 (*0-89771-579-9*, Pub. by Intl Bk Distr II) St Mut.

Lisboa, P. G., ed. Neural Networks: Current Applications. 288p. 1992. pap. 59.95 (*0-442-31564-3*) Chapman & Hall.

Lisboa, P. G. & Taylor, M. J. Techniques & Applications of Neural Networks. LC 93-11635. (Ellis Horwood Workshop Ser.). 1993. write for info. (*0-13-062183-8*, Tavistock-E Horwood) Routledge Chapman & Hall.

Lisboa, Rosendo C. Diccionari Castella-Valencia, Valencia-Castella. 1100p. 1989. 19.95 (*0-7859-6400-2*, 8486488036) Fr & Eur.

Lisbon, Alan, jt. auth. see Fink, Mitchell P.

Lisburn, David, jt. auth. see Baxter, Stephen.

Lisby, Gregory C. Mass Communication Law in Georgia. (State Law Ser.). 120p. (C). 1992. pap. text ed. 8.95 (*0-913507-32-6*) New Forums.

Lisca, Peter. The Wide World of John Steinbeck. 338p. (C). 1981. 50.00 (*0-87752-217-0*) Gordian.

Lisca, Peter, ed. see Steinbeck, John.

Lisch, W. Hereditary Vitreoretinal Degeneration. (Developments in Ophthalmology Ser.: Vol. 8). (Illus.). viii, 92p. 1983. 52.00 (*3-8055-3615-1*) S Karger.

Lischer, Henry J., Jr. Gifts to Minors. 3rd ed. (Tax Management Portfolio Ser.: No. 403). 1988. ring bd. 50. 00 (*1-55871-074-4*) BNA.

***Lischer, Richard.** The Preacher King: Martin Luther King, Jr. & the Word That Moved America. 304p. 1995. text ed. 25.00 (*0-19-508779-8*) OUP.

— A Theology of Preaching: The Dynamics of the Gospel. 115p. (Orig.). 1993. reprint ed. pap. 9.95 (*0-939464-53-5*) Labyrinth Pr.

Lischer, Richard, ed. Theories of Preaching: Selected Readings in the Homiletical Tradition. LC 87-3504. 384p. 1987. 30.00 (*0-939464-46-2*); pap. 15.95 (*0-939464-45-4*) Labyrinth Pr.

Lischer, Richard, jt. ed. see Willimon, William H.

***Lisciandro.** Jim Morrison: An Hour for Magic. Date not set. per. 19.95 (*0-85965-162-2*, Pub. by Plexus Pub UK) InBook.

Lisciandro, Frank. Morrison: A Feast of Friends. 1991. pap. 16.99 (*0-446-39276-6*) Warner Bks.

Liscomb, Kathlyn M. Learning from Mt. Hua: A Chinese Physician's Illustrated Travel Record & Painting Theory. (RES Monographs on Anthropology & Aesthetics). (Illus.). 240p. (C). 1993. 80.00 (*0-521-41112-2*) Cambridge U Pr.

Liscomb, Robie. Grand River Suite. (Orig.). 1986. pap. 11.00 (*0-937596-10-8*) Pentagram.

Liscombe, Rhodri W. Altogether American: Robert Mills, Architect & Engineer, 1781-1855. LC 92-40045. 384p. 1994. 45.00 (*0-19-508019-X*) OUP.

— The Church Architecture of Robert Mills. (Illus.). 160p. 1985. 30.00 (*0-89308-542-1*) Southern Hist Pr.

— William Wilkins, Seventeen Seventy-Eight to Eighteen Thirty-Nine. LC 78-73247. 320p. 1980. 95.00 (*0-521-22528-0*) Cambridge U Pr.

Liscombe, Rhodri W., jt. auth. see Wadell, Gene.

Liscouski, Joe. Laboratory & Scientific Computing: A Strategic Approach. LC 94-9276. (Wiley-Interscience Series on Laboratory Automation: Vol. 1). 1994. text ed. 44.95 (*0-471-59422-9*) Wiley.

Liscouski, Joseph G., ed. Computers in the Laboratory: Current Practice & Future Trends. LC 84-18518. (Symposium Ser.: No. 265). 136p. 1984. lib. bdg. 43.95 (*0-8412-0867-0*) Am Chemical.

Liscovitch, Mordechai. Signal-Activated Phospholipases. (Molecular Biology Intelligence Unit Ser.). 124p. 1994. 89.95 (*1-57059-109-1*, LN9109) R G Landes.

Lisella, Frank S., ed. Van Nostrand Reinhold Dictionary of Environmental Health & Safety. LC 93-25838. 356p. 1994. text ed. 49.95 (*0-442-00508-3*) Van Nos Reinhold.

Lisensky, Robert P., jt. auth. see Ewell, Peter T.

Lisensky, Robert P., et al. The New Liberal Learning: Technology & the Liberal Arts. 1985. pap. 10.00 (*0-317-39617-X*) Coun Indep Colleges.

Lisetor. Crash. 1985. pap. 2.50 (*0-87879-297-X*) Acad Therapy.

Lish, Gordon. Extravaganza. 1990. 10.00 (*1-877727-05-9*) White Pine.

— My Romance. 144p. 1993. pap. 8.95 (*0-393-31104-X*) Norton.

— Quarterly, No. 6. (Vintage Original Ser.). 256p. 1988. pap. 6.95 (*0-394-75719-X*, Vin) Random.

— Quarterly, No. 25. 1993. pap. 12.00 (*0-679-74501-7*, Vin) Random.

— The Quarterly #30. 246p. Date not set. pap. 10.00 (*1-896356-01-X*) Dist Art Pubs.

— Quarterly #31. 246p. Date not set. pap. 10.00 (*1-896356-03-6*) Dist Art Pubs.

— Zimzum. LC 93-3360. 1993. 18.00 (*0-679-42685-X*) Pantheon.

Lish, Gordon, ed. Quarterly, No. 1. (Vintage Original Ser.). 256p. 1987. pap. 6.95 (*0-394-74697-X*, Vin) Random.

— Quarterly, No. 3. (Vintage Original Ser.). 256p. 1987. pap. 5.95 (*0-394-75536-7*, Vin) Random.

— Quarterly, No. 4. (Vintage Original Ser.). 256p. 1987. pap. 5.95 (*0-394-75537-5*, Vin) Random.

— Quarterly, No. 5. (Vintage Original Ser.). 256p. 1988. pap. 6.95 (*0-394-75718-1*, Vin) Random.

— The Quarterly, No. 9, Spring 1989. 256p. (Orig.). 1989. pap. 7.95 (*0-679-72139-8*, Vin) Random.

— The Quarterly, No. 11. (Orig.). 1989. pap. 7.95 (*0-679-72173-8*, Vin) Random.

— The Quarterly, No. 12. (Orig.). 1989. pap. 7.95 (*0-679-72153-3*, Vin) Random.

— Quarterly, No. 15. 1990. pap. 9.95 (*0-679-73231-4*, Vin) Random.

— The Quarterly, No. 16. (Orig.). 1990. pap. 9.95 (*0-679-73244-6*, Vin) Random.

— The Quarterly, No. 17. 256p. (Orig.). 1991. 10.00 (0-679-73494-5, Vin) Random.

— Quarterly, No. 18. 256p. 1991. pap. 10.00 (0-679-73495-3, Vin) Random.

— Quarterly, No. 19. (Vintage Original Ser.). 256p. 1991. pap. 10.00 (0-679-73690-5, Vin) Random.

— Quarterly, No. 20. (Vintage Original Ser.). 256p. 1991. pap. 10.00 (0-679-73691-3, Vin) Random.

— The Quarterly, No. 21. (Orig.). 1992. 10.00 (0-679-73862-2, Vin) Random.

— The Quarterly, No. 22. (Orig.). 1992. 12.00 (0-679-74050-3) McKay.

— The Quarterly, No. 23. (Orig.). 1992. 12.00 (0-679-74224-7, Vin) Random.

— The Quarterly, No. 24. (Orig.). 1992. 12.00 (0-679-74225-5, Vin) Random.

— The Quarterly: Winter 1988, No. 8. 256p. (Orig.). 1988. pap. 6.95 (0-394-75937-0, Vin) Random.

— The Quarterly, No. 10. 1989. pap. 7.95 (0-679-72172-X, Vin) Random.

— Quarterly, No. 13. 1990. pap. 8.95 (0-679-72893-7, Vin) Random.

— Quarterly, No. 14. 1990. pap. 8.95 (0-679-72894-5, Vin) Random.

— The Quarterly, No. 7: Fall 1988. 256p. (Orig.). 1988. pap. 6.95 (0-394-75936-2, Vin) Random.

Lish, Gordon, ed. see Hannah, Barry.

Lishka, Gerald R. A Handbook for the Ballet Accompanist. LC 78-2051. 146p. reprint ed. pap. 42.20 (0-7837-6105-8, 2059151) Bks Demand.

***Lishman, Bill.** Father Goose. Date not set. 23.00 (0-517-70133-2) Random.

— Father Goose & His Goslings. (Illus.). 72p. (Orig.). (J). (gr. k-8). 1992. pap. 10.95 (0-9623072-8-9) S Ink WA.

Lishman, Joyce, ed. Developing Services for the Elderly. 2nd ed. LC 85-40083. (Research Highlights in Social Work Ser.). 185p. 1985. text ed. 29.95 (0-312-19715-2) St Martin.

— Handbook of Theory for Accredited Practice Teachers in Social Work. 200p. 1991. pap. 29.95 (1-85302-098-2, Pub. by J Kingsley Pubs UK) Taylor & Francis.

Lishman, W. Organic Psychiatry. 2nd ed. 1988. pap. 95.00 (0-632-01496-2) Blackwell Sci.

Lishner, Kris M. & Bruya, Margaret A. Creating a Health Camp Community: A Nurse's Role. LC 94-4060. 1994. 19.95 (0-87603-135-1) Am Camping.

Lisi, Albert. Jungle Trips. 325p. 1990. per. 11.95 (0-89697-349-2) Intl Univ Pr.

Lisi, Patrick. Guide to Wisconsin Waterfalls. 1992. pap. 9.95 (1-879483-09-2) Prairie Oak Pr.

***Lisi, Victoria.** Llewellyn's 1996 Astrological Calendar. (Illus.). 24p. 1995. pap. 12.00 (1-56718-917-2) Llewellyn Pubns.

Lisi, Victoria, illus. March of the Wooden Soldiers. (Read-to-Me Ser.). 48p. (J). (ps-2). 1992. 5.95 (0-88101-261-0) Unicorn Pub.

Lisicky, Paul. Dominican Republic. (Let's Visit Places & Peoples of the World Ser.). (Illus.). 96p. 1987. lib. bdg. 14.95 (1-55546-163-8) Chelsea Hse.

— Uganda. (Places & Peoples of the World Ser.). (Illus.). 96p. (J). (gr. 5 up). 1988. lib. bdg. 14.95 (1-55546-189-1) Chelsea Hse.

Lisiewicz, M., et al. Destiny Can Wait: The Polish Air Force in World War II. (Aviation Ser.). (Illus.). 401p. 1988. reprint ed. 29.95 (0-89839-113-X) Battery Pr.

Lisine, Richard & Epping, Jay, eds. Minkus Germany Catalog. rev. ed. (Illus.). 1994. write for info. (0-912236-32-9, Minkus Pubns) Novus Debut.

Lisinska, G. & Leszcynski, W., eds. Potato Science & Technology. 380p. 1989. 104.50 (1-85166-307-X) Elsevier.

Lisio, Donald J. Hoover, Blacks, & Lily-Whites: A Study of Southern Strategies. LC 84-22002. (Fred W. Morrison Series in Southern Studies). xxii, 373p. 1985. 39.95 (0-8078-1645-0) U of NC Pr.

— The President & Protest: Hoover, MacArthur, & the Bonus March. viii, 378p. 1994. reprint ed. 32.00 (0-8232-1571-7); reprint ed. pap. 17.95 (0-8232-1572-5) Fordham.

Lisita, M. P., et al. Fiber Optics. 280p. 1971. text ed. 73.00 (0-7065-1102-6, Pub. by Keter Pub IS) Coronet Bks.

Lisitsa, V. S. Atoms & Plasmas. LC 93-46645. (Atoms & Plasmas Ser.: Vol. 14). 1994. 98.00 (0-387-57580-4) Spr-Verlag.

Lisitzin, Alexander P. Sedimentation in the World Ocean with Emphasis on the Nature, Distribution & Behavior of Marine Suspensions. Rodolfo, Kelvin S., ed. LC 72-172081. (Society of Economic Paleontologists & Mineralogists, Special Publication Ser.: No. 17). 232p. reprint ed. pap. 66.20 (0-317-27149-0, 2024744) Bks Demand.

Lisitzin, E. Sea Level Changes. (Oceanography Ser.: Vol. 8). 286p. 1974. 97.50 (0-444-41157-7) Elsevier.

Lisius, James D., ed. see Technical Association of the Pulp & Paper Industry Ser.

Lisk, Anna L., jt. auth. see Traister, Robert J.

Lisk, Anna L., jt. auth. see Traister, Robert J., Sr.

Lisk, Edward S. The Creative Director: Alternative Rehearsal Techniques. 3rd ed. LC 87-90906. (Illus.). 221p. 1987. pap. text ed. 24.95 (0-9624308-0-3) Meredith Music.

Lisk, Eunice A., jt. auth. see Rosen, Marcia.

Lisk, Franklyn. Popular Participation in Planning for Basic Needs: Concept, Methods & Practices. LC 85-18436. 286p. 1986. text ed. 35.00 (0-312-63060-3) St Martin.

Liska, Allen E. Perspectives on Deviance. 2nd ed. (Illus.). 240p. (C). 1986. text ed. write for info. (0-13-660408-0) P-H.

Liska, Allen E., ed. Social Threat & Social Control. LC 91-7550. (SUNY Series in Deviance & Social Control). (Illus.). 288p. (C). 1992. 59.50 (0-7914-0903-1); pap. 19.95 (0-7914-0904-X) State U NY Pr.

Liska, F., jt. auth. see Volke, J.

Liska, George. Alliances & the Third World. LC 68-17254. (Washington Center of Foreign Policy Research. Studies in International Affairs: No. 5). 71p. reprint ed. pap. 25.00 (0-8357-5320-4, 2023128) Bks Demand.

— Beyond Kissinger: Ways of Conservative Statecraft. LC 75-10838. (Washington Center of Foreign Policy Research. Studies in International Affairs: No. 26). 170p. reprint ed. pap. 48.50 (0-8357-7158-X, 2023127) Bks Demand.

— Fallen Dominions, Reviving Powers: Germany, the Slavs, & Europe's Unfinished Agenda. 63p. 1991. pap. 7.50 (0-941700-68-2) JH FPI SAIS.

— Imperial America: The International Politics of Primacy. LC 67-21584. (Studies in International Affairs: No. 2). 115p. (Orig.). 1967. pap. 9.95x (0-8018-0379-9) Johns Hopkins.

— Nations in Alliance: The Limits of Interdependence. LC 62-14359. 313p. reprint ed. pap. 89.30 (0-8357-8242-5, 2034146) Bks Demand.

— Nations in Alliance: The Limits of Interdependence. LC 62-14359. 320p. 1962. reprint ed. pap. 14.95 (0-8018-0381-0) Johns Hopkins.

— Quest for Equilibrium: America & the Balance of Power on Land & Sea. LC 77-4780. (Studies in International Affairs). 280p. 1977. text ed. 39.50 (0-8018-1968-7) Johns Hopkins.

— Return to the Heartland & Rebirth of the Old Order: Reconceptualizing the Environment of Strategies for East-Central Europe & Beyond. LC 94-16108. 1994. write for info. (0-941700-87-9) JH FPI SAIS.

— Russia & the Road to Appeasement: Cycles of East-West Conflict in War & Peace. LC 81-48188. 288p. 1982. text ed. 39.50 (0-8018-2763-9) Johns Hopkins.

— Russia & World Order: Strategic Choices & the Laws of Power in History. LC 79-22872. 1980. 14.50 (0-8018-2314-5) Johns Hopkins.

— Russia & World Order: Strategic Choices & the Laws of Power in History. LC 79-22872. 208p. reprint ed. pap. 59.30 (0-317-20468-8, 2023001) Bks Demand.

— War & Order: Reflections on Vietnam & History. LC 68-9697. (Washington Center of Foreign Policy Research. Studies in International Affairs: No. 11). 127p. reprint ed. pap. 36.20 (0-317-19922-6, 2023126) Bks Demand.

— The Ways of Power: World Politics As Drama & Destiny. 416p. (C). 1990. text ed. 44.95 (0-631-17188-6) Blackwell Pubs.

Liska, Jo & Cronkhite, Gary. An Ecological Perspective on Human Communication Theory. LC 94-18914. 1994. pap. text ed. 41.25 (0-15-500271-6) HB Coll Pubs.

Liska, Judith M., jt. auth. see Liska, Roger W.

Liska, Ken. Drugs & the Human Body: With Implications for Society. 4th ed. (Illus.). 464p. (C). 1993. pap. write for info. (0-02-371091-8) Macmillan.

— The Pharmacist's Guide to the Most Misused & Abused Drugs in America: Prescription Drugs - Over-the-Counter Drugs - Designer Drugs. 1988. 23.99 (0-02-572970-5) Macmillan.

Liska, Roger W. Means Facilities Maintenance Standards. (Illus.). 600p. (C). 1988. 149.95 (0-87629-096-9, 67246) R S Means.

Liska, Roger W. & Liska, Judith M. Handbook of Building & Plant Maintenance Forms & Checklists. 416p. 1988. text ed. 59.95 (0-13-375999-7, Busn) P-H.

Liska, Roger W., jt. auth. see Schuette, Stephen D.

Liske, Craig, et al, eds. Comparative Public Policy: Issues, Theories, & Methods. LC 73-91354. (Comparative Political Economy & Public Policy Ser.: Vol. 1). 302p. reprint ed. pap. 86.10 (0-317-29609-4, 2021868) Bks Demand.

Lisken-Gasparro. Testing & Teaching for Oral Proficiency. 171p. 1987. pap. 22.95 (0-8384-1505-9) Heinle & Heinle.

Lisker, Carol, ed. see Trotsky, Leon, et al.

Lisker, Leigh. Spoken Telugu. LC 63-12992. (Spoken Language Ser.). xxvii, 345p. (gr. 9-12). 1976. audio 95.00 (0-87950-377-7); audio 110.00 (0-87950-378-5); audio 50.00 (0-87950-379-3) Spoken Lang Serv.

— Spoken Telugu, Bk. 1, Units 1-30. LC 63-12992. (Spoken Language Ser.). xxvii, 345p. (gr. 9-12). 1976. pap. 15.00 (0-87950-376-9) Spoken Lang Serv.

***Liskevych, Terry.** Youth Volleyball. (Illus.). (Orig.). 1995. pap. 12.95 (1-57028-028-2) Masters Pr IN.

Liskey, Nathan & Hill, Justine. Body-Self Appreciation. rev. ed. Loam, Jason, ed. LC 88-6487. 116p. 1987. pap. 8.95 (1-55599-019-3) Elysium.

Liskin-Gasparro. Testing & Teaching for Oral Proficiency: ETS Familiarization Kits. 1987. German Kit. pap. 50.00 (0-8384-1897-X) Heinle & Heinle.

Liskin-Gasparro, Judith E., ed. Building Bridges & Making Connections. (Reports of the Northeast Conference on the Teaching of Foreign Languages). 190p. 1991. pap. 10.95 (0-915432-91-9) NE Conf Teach Foreign.

Liskin, Miriam. DBASE III Plus: The Pocket Reference. 1992. pap. text ed. 9.95 (0-07-881831-1) Osborne-McGraw.

— The dBASE III Plus Made Easy. 350p. 1988. pap. text ed. 19.95 (0-07-881294-1) Osborne-McGraw.

— Fox Pro for Windows Expert Solutions. 1995. cd-rom, pap. 49.99 (0-7897-0075-1) Que.

— HELP! Microsoft Access. 1993. pap. 29.95 (1-56276-099-8) Ziff-Davis.

— Liskin's dBase IV: 1.1 Handbook. 2nd ed. 1991. pap. text ed. 34.95 (0-07-881016-7) Osborne-McGraw.

— Liskin's dBASE IV Programming Book. 1990. Incl. disk. disk 39.95 (0-07-881617-3); pap. text ed. 28.95 (0-07-881530-4) McGraw.

— Liskin's dBASE IV 1.1 Programming Book. 1991. pap. text ed. 34.95 (0-07-881681-5) Osborne-McGraw.

— PC Magazine Programming FoxPro for Windows. Date not set. pap. 39.95 (1-56276-173-0) Ziff-Davis.

— PC Magazine Programming FoxPro 2.0. (Programming Ser.). (Illus.). 1516p. (Orig.). 1992. disk 39.95 (1-56276-038-6) Ziff-Davis.

— PC Magazine Programming FoxPro 2.5. (Programming Ser.). 1993. disk 39.95 (1-56276-164-1) Ziff-Davis.

— Your First Access Database. LC 94-65687. 424p. 1994. pap. 19.99 (0-7821-1540-3) Sybex.

Liskofsky, Sidney. U. N. Declaration on the Elimination of Religious Intolerance & Discrimination. 20p. 1982. pap. 2.00 (0-87495-041-4) Am Jewish Comm.

Liskow, George. Wildflowers of the Mount Wilson Trails & San Gabriel Mountains. (Illus.). 87p. (Orig.). 1990. pap. 10.95 (0-9628024-0-9) G Liskow.

***Lisle.** Forest. 1995. pap. (0-590-48680-2) Scholastic Inc.

Lisle, Clifton. Diamond Rock: A Tale of the Paoli Massacre. 1993. reprint ed. lib. bdg. 89.00 (0-7812-5483-3) Rprt Serv.

— Lenape Trails. 1993. reprint ed. lib. bdg. 89.00 (0-7812-5482-5) Rprt Serv.

Lisle, George. Accounting in Theory & Practice. LC 75-18475. (History of Accounting Ser.). (Illus.). 1979. reprint ed. 34.95 (0-405-07557-X) Ayer.

Lisle, George & Brief, Richard P., eds. Selections from Enclycopaedia of Accounting, 1903: Original Anthology. LC 77-87310. (Contemporary Accounting Thought Ser.). 1978. lib. bdg. 41.95 (0-405-10923-7) Ayer.

***Lisle, Harvey.** The Enlivened Rock Powders. LC 94-71840. 208p. 1994. 15.00 (0-911311-48-3) Halcyon Hse.

Lisle, Holly. Bones of the Past. 336p. 1993. mass mkt. 4.99 (0-671-72160-7) Baen Bks.

— Fire in the Mist. 304p. 1992. mass mkt. 5.99 (0-671-72132-1) Baen Bks.

— Mind of the Magic. 320p. 1995. mass mkt. 5.99 (0-671-87654-6) Baen Bks.

— Minerva Wakes. 288p. 1994. mass mkt. 4.99 (0-671-72202-6) Baen Bks.

***Lisle, Holly & Guin, Chris.** Mall, Mayhem & Magic. 1995. mass mkt. 5.99 (0-671-87678-3) Baen Bks.

Lisle, Holly, jt. auth. see Lackey, Mercedes.

Lisle, Holly, jt. auth. see Stirling, S. M.

Lisle, Janet T. Afternoon of the Elves. LC 88-35099. 128p. (J). (gr. 4-6). 1989. 14.95 (0-531-05837-9); lib. bdg. 14.99 (0-531-08437-X) Orchard Bks Watts.

— Afternoon of the Elves. (J). (gr. 4-7). 1991. pap. 2.75 (0-590-43944-8, Apple Paperbacks) Scholastic Inc.

— The Dancing Cats of Applesap. LC 92-1654. (Illus.). 176p. (J). (gr. 3-7). 1993. reprint ed. pap. 3.95 (0-689-71687-7, Aladdin Paperbacks) S&S Childrens.

— Forest. LC 93-9630. 160p. (YA). (gr. 5 up). 1993. 15.95 (0-531-06803-X); lib. bdg. 15.99 (0-531-08653-4) Orchard Bks Watts.

— The Gold Dust Letters. LC 93-11806. 128p. (J). (gr. 3-5). 1994. 14.95 (0-531-06830-7); lib. bdg. 14.99 (0-531-08680-1) Orchard Bks Watts.

— The Great Dimpole Oak. LC 87-11092. (Illus.). 144p. (J). (gr. 4-6). 1987. 14.95 (0-531-05716-X); lib. bdg. 14.99 (0-531-08316-0) Orchard Bks Watts.

— The Lampfish of Twill. LC 91-8279. (Illus.). 176p. (YA). (gr. 5 up). 1991. 15.95 (0-531-05963-4); 15.99 (0-531-08563-5) Orchard Bks Watts.

— The Lampfish of Twill. (Illus.). 176p. (J). (gr. 3-7). 1993. pap. 2.95 (0-590-46040-4, Apple Paperbacks) Scholastic Inc.

— Looking for Juliette. LC 94-6922. 128p. (J). (gr. 3-5). 1994. 14.95 (0-531-06870-6); lib. bdg. 14.99 (0-531-08720-4) Orchard Bks Watts.

— A Message from the Match Girl. LC 95-6036. (Investigators of the Unknown Ser.: Bk. 3). 128p. (J). (gr. 4-6). 1995. 14.95 (0-531-09487-1); lib. bdg. 14.99 (0-531-08787-5) Orchard Bks Watts.

— Sirens & Spies. LC 84-21518. 192p. (YA). (gr. 7 up). 1985. text ed. 14.95 (0-02-759150-6, Bradbury S&S) S&S Childrens.

— Sirens & Spies. LC 90-185. 176p. (YA). (gr. 7 up). 1990. reprint ed. pap. 3.95 (0-02-044341-2, Collier Bks Young) S&S Childrens.

Lisle, Jeff, tr. see Abuli, Sanchez.

Lisle, Jeff, tr. see Giardino, Vittorio.

Lisle, Jeff, tr. see Riera, Marti.

Lisle, Jeff, tr. see Sampayo, Carlos.

Lisle, Jennifer. Chic Simple Storage. Gross, Kim J. & Stone, Jeff, eds. (Chic Simple Components Ser.). 1994. 12.50 (0-679-43222-1) Knopf.

Lisle, John, tr. see Del Vecchio, Giorgio.

Lisle, Laurie. Portrait of an Artist: A Biography of Georgia O'Keeffe. 486p. 1985. mass mkt. 5.99 (0-671-60040-0, WSP) PB.

Lisle, R. J. Geological Strain Analysis. (Illus.). 99p. 1985. text ed. 47.00 (0-08-032590-4, Pub. by PPL UK); pap. text ed. 29.00 (0-08-032589-0, Pub. by PPL UK) Elsevier.

— Geological Structures & Maps: A Practical Guide. LC 88-5807. (Illus.). 160p. 1988. text ed. 47.00 (0-08-034854-8, Pergamon Pr); pap. text ed. 23.00 (0-08-034853-X, Pergamon Pr) Elsevier.

Lisle, Robert. Photography Remembered. LC 90-84178. 80p. 1990. pap. 19.95 (0-940744-61-9) Chrysler Museum.

***Lismore.** Here We Go: Kindergarten Level. 3rd ed. (Illus.). 48p. (J). (gr. k). 1994. student ed, pap. text ed. 8.50 (0-13-186024-0) P-H.

— Here We Go: Level One. 3rd ed. (Illus.). 64p. (J). (gr. k). 1994. student ed, pap. text ed. 8.50 (0-13-186032-1) P-H.

— Here We Go: Level Three. 3rd ed. (Illus.). 112p. 1995. student ed, pap. text ed. 8.50 (0-13-186057-7) P-H.

— Welcome to English: Let's Begin, Bk. 4. 1980. pap. 11.20 (0-13-949694-7) Prentice ESL.

***Lisnek, Paul & Kaufman, Michael.** Depositions: Procedure, Strategy & Technique. 2nd ed. 275p. 1994. text ed. write for info. (0-314-04475-2) West Pub.

Lisnek, Paul M. A Lawyer's Guide to Effective Negotiation & Mediation: CLE Edition. 225p. 1992. pap. text ed. write for info. (0-314-01679-1) West Pub.

Lisnek, Paul M. & Kaufman, Michael J. Depositions: Procedure, Strategy & Technique. 255p. 1990. pap. write for info. (0-314-65444-5) West Pub.

— Depositions: Procedures, Strategy & Technique: Professional Education Edition. 230p. (C). 1995. pap. text ed. write for info. (0-314-06262-9) West Pub.

***Lisnek, Paul M. & Oliver, Eric G.** The Complete Litigator: Reality, Perception & Persuasion in & Out of Court. LC 94-33504. 1994. 90.00 (0-9636246-5-2) Andrews Pubns.

Lisney, Adrian & Fieldhouse, Ken. Landscape Design Guide, Vol. II: Hard Landscape: The Design of Paved Spaces, Landscape Enclosure & Landscape Furniture. 224p. 1990. text ed. 73.95 (0-566-09019-8, Pub. by Gower UK) Ashgate Pub Co.

Lisney, M. I., tr. see Makrakis, Apostolos.

***Lisnik, Paul.** Quality Mind, Quality Life. LC 95-76817. 220p. 1995. 19.95 (0-916990-35-4) META Pubns.

Lison, Karen C., jt. auth. see Poston, Carol.

Lison Tolosana, Carmelo. La Imagen del Rey. Monarquia, Realeza y Poder Ritual en la Casa de los Austrias. (Nueva Austral Ser.: Vol. 249). (SPA.). 1991. pap. text ed. 24.95x (84-239-7249-6) Elliots Bks.

***Lisoskie, Pete.** Profits Hidden, Profits Found: 12 Steps to Making a Big Fortune in Any Business. (Orig.). 1995. pap. 14.95 (1-879141-13-2) Busn Toolbox.

Lisoskie, Pete & Lisoskie, Shelly. Customers for Keeps: The Network System to Smash Your Profit Barrier. LC 93-90414. (Illus.). 352p. (Orig.). 1994. pap. 19.95 (1-879141-10-8) Busn Toolbox.

Lisoskie, Pete, jt. auth. see Lisoskie, Shelly.

Lisoskie, Shelly & Lisoskie, Pete. Your IIGS Guide. (Illus.). 308p. (Orig.). 1990. pap. 21.95 (1-879141-01-9) Busn Toolbox.

Lisoskie, Shelly, jt. auth. see Lisoskie, Pete.

Lisovskii, F. & Kalugin, I. English-Russian Dictionary of Radio-Electronics. 752p. (C). 1987. 125.00 (0-685-46844-5, Pub. by Collets) St Mut.

Lisowski. The Turgai Project. 1994. 12.95 (1-881116-27-1) Black Forrest Pr.

Lisowski, Joseph. Near the Narcotic Sea. 64p. (Orig.). 1992. pap. 10.00 (0-9624155-4-5) Cottage Wordsmiths.

Lisowski, Joseph, ed. Caribbean Perspectives: The Social Structure of a Region. 224p. (C). 1990. pap. 21.95 (0-88738-838-8) Transaction Pubs.

— Environment & Labor in the Caribbean, Vol. 2: Caribbean Perspectives. 128p. (C). 1992. pap. 19.95 (1-56000-584-X) Transaction Pubs.

Lisowski, P., jt. auth. see Ho, P. Y.

Lispector, Clarice. The Apple in the Dark. Rabassa, Gregory, tr. (Texas Pan American Ser.). 378p. 1986. reprint ed. pap. 14.95 (0-292-70392-9) U of Tex Pr.

— An Apprenticeship or The Book of Delights. Mazzara, Richard A. & Parris, Lorri A., trs. (Texas Pan American Ser.). 140p. 1986. text ed. 18.95 (0-292-79030-9); pap. 8.95 (0-292-79031-7) U of Tex Pr.

— Family Ties. Pontiero, Giovanni, tr. (Texas Pan American Ser.). 156p. 1984. pap. 10.95 (0-292-72448-9) U of Tex Pr.

— The Foreign Legion. Pontiero, Giovanni, tr. & aft. by. LC 91-29992. 224p. 1992. reprint ed. pap. 10.95 (0-8112-1189-4, NDP732) New Directions.

— The Hour of the Star. Pontiero, Giovanni, tr. & aft. by. LC 91-29995. 96p. 1992. reprint ed. pap. 8.95 (0-8112-1190-8, NDP733) New Directions.

— Near to the Wild Heart. Pontiero, Giovanni, tr. & aft. by. LC 90-33455. 192p. 1990. reprint ed. 9.95 (0-8112-1139-8) New Directions.

— A Paixao Segundo G. H. Nunes, Benedito, ed. (Latin American Series - Coleccion Archivos). 366p. (POR.). (C). 1989. pap. 27.95 (85-7028-008-4) U of Pittsburgh Pr.

— The Passion According to G. H. Sousa, Ronald W., tr. LC 88-4763. (Emergent Literatures Ser.). ix, 173p. (Orig.). 1988. text ed. 24.95 (0-8166-1711-2); pap. 10.95 (0-8166-1712-0) U of Minn Pr.

— Soulstorm: Stories. Levitin, Alexis, tr. LC 89-2938. 160p. 1989. 19.95 (0-8112-1090-1); pap. 10.95 (0-8112-1091-X, NDP671) New Directions.

— The Stream of Life. Lowe, Elizabeth & Fitz, Earl, trs. (Emergent Literatures Ser.). Orig. Title: Agua Viva. 128p. (Orig.). 1989. text ed. 24.95 (0-8166-1781-3); pap. 9.95 (0-8166-1782-1) U of Minn Pr.

Lisper, B. Synthesizing Synchronous Systems by Static Scheduling in Space-Time. (Lecture Notes in Computer Science Ser.: Vol. 362). vi, 263p. 1989. pap. 37.00 (0-387-51156-3) Spr-Verlag.

Liss, A. N., et al. Russian Speakers Guide to English Through Proverbs, Vol. 1. (Illus.). 173p. (Orig.). 1992. pap. 14.95 (0-934393-51-6) Rector Pr.

— Russian Speakers Guide to English Through Proverbs, Vol. 2. (Illus.). 96p. (Orig.). (ENG & RUS.). 1992. pap. 14.95 (0-934393-50-8) Rector Pr.

Liss, Andrea & Bedoya, Roberto. James Luna: Actions & Reactions: An Eleven Year Survey of Installation-Performance Work 1981-1992. Castellon, Rolando & Hesse, Andrea, eds. LC 92-62251. (UCSC Biennial Ser.). (Illus.). 32p. (Orig.). (C). 1992. pap. text ed. 12.00 (0-939982-17-X) Sesnon Art Gall.

***Liss, Andrea & Snyder, Jill.** Impossible Evidence: Contemporary Artists View the Holocaust. (Illus.). 40p. (Orig.). Date not set. pap. 20.00 (0-614-01852-8) Freedman.

Liss, Douglas, jt. auth. see Aderton, Mimi.

An Asterisk (*) at the beginning of an entry indicates that the title is appearing in BIP for the first time.

Liss, Howard. The Giant Book of More Strange but True Sports Stories. LC 82-13236. (Illus.). 160p. (J). (gr. 5-10). 1983. pap. 8.95 (*0-394-85633-3*) Random Bks Yng Read.
— The Giant Book of Strange but True Sports Stories. LC 76-8132. (Illus.). (J). (gr. 5-9). 1976. 9.00 (*0-394-83287-6*) Random Bks Yng Read.
— Great Black Americans in Science. (Illus.). 160p. (J). (gr. 3-9). 1995. lib. bdg. 14.95 (*0-87460-392-7*) Lion Bks.
— Making of a Rookie. (NFL Punt, Pass & Kick Library: No. 9). (Illus.). (J). (gr. 5-9). 1968. lib. bdg. 3.69 (*0-394-90199-1*) Random Bks Yng Read.
Liss, Howard, jt. auth. see Devaney, John.
Liss, Howard, jt. auth. see Graziano, Rocky.
Liss, Jason, reader. Twelve. (Illus.). 84p. (J). 1989. audio 9.95 (*0-9611266-2-0*) Optext.
Liss, Jeffrey G. & Chapman, Glenn H., eds. Annual International Space Development Conference Proceedings, 8th. (Illus.). 636p. 1992. pap. text ed. 60.00 (*0-912183-09-8*) Univelt Inc.
***Liss-Levinson, Nechama.** When a Grandparent Dies: A Kid's Own Workbook for Dealing with Shiva & the Year Beyond. LC 95-5379. (J). (gr. 2-6). 1995. 14.95 (*1-879045-44-3*) Jewish Lights.
Liss, Marsha B., ed. Social & Cognitive Skills: Sex Roles & Children's Play. LC 82-24349. (Developmental Psychology Ser.). 1983. text ed. 51.00 (*0-12-451880-X*) Acad Pr.
Liss, Peggy K. Atlantic Empires: The Network of Trade & Revolution, 1713-1826. LC 82-13099. (Johns Hopkins Studies in Atlantic History & Culture Ser.). 364p. reprint ed. pap. 103.80 (*0-8357-6908-9*, 2037966) Bks Demand.
— Isabel the Queen: Her Life & Times. (Illus.). 424p. 1992. 30.00 (*0-19-507356-8*) OUP.
Liss, Peggy K., jt. ed. see Knight, Franklin W.
Liss, Per-Erik. Health Care Needs: Meaning & Measurement. 147p. 1993. 54.95 (*1-85628-453-0*, Pub. by Avebury Pub UK) Ashgate Pub Co.
Liss, Sheldon B. Fidel: Castro's Political & Social Thought. (Latin American Perspectives Ser.). 256p. (C). 1994. text ed. 63.00 (*0-8133-8678-0*); pap. text ed. 19.95 (*0-8133-8679-9*) Westview.
— Marxist Thought in Latin America. LC 83-4838. (C). 1984. pap. 12.00 (*0-520-05022-3*) U CA Pr.
— Radical Thought in Central America, Vol. 7. 290p. (C). 1991. pap. text ed. 19.95 (*0-8133-8209-2*) Westview.
— Radical Thought in Central America, Vol. 7. 290p. 1991. text ed. 61.00 (*0-8133-8208-4*) Westview.
— Roots of Revolution: Radical Thought in Cuba. LC 86-7109. xxvi, 269p. 1987. 30.00 (*0-8032-2873-2*); pap. 10.95 (*0-8032-7920-5*) U of Nebr Pr.
Liss, Susan M. & Taylor, William L., eds. New Opportunities: Civil Rights at a Crossroads. LC 92-56191. 300p. 1993. pap. 20.00 (*0-9622865-2-4*) CCCR.
Liss, Susan M., ed. see Citizens' Commission on Civil Rights.
Lissa. Core & the Elephants. LC 94-9153. (J). (gr. 3 up). 1995. 14.99 (*0-670-84335-0*, Viking) Viking Penguin.
Lissa, Zofia, ed. see Feicht, Hieronim.
***Lissak, K.** Neural & Neurohumoral Organization of Motivated Behaviour: Fourth Conference in Interbrain Held in Pecs, Hungary, May 19-23, 1975. 267p. (C). 1978. 48.00x (*963-05-1316-1*, Pub. by Akad Kiado HU) St Mut.
— Results in Neuroanatomy, Motor Organization, Cerebral Circulation & Modelling. (Recent Developments of Neurbiology in Hungary Ser.: No. 8). 242p. (C). 1979. 63.00x (*963-05-1594-6*, Pub. by Akad Kiado HU) St Mut.
— Results in Neuroanatomy, Neurochemistry, Neurophysiology & Neuropathology. (Recent Developments of Neurobiology in Hungary Ser.: No. 9). 232p. (C). 1982. 72.00x (*963-05-2947-5*, Pub. by Akad Kiado HU) St Mut.
— Results in Neuroanatomy, Neurochemistry, Neurophysiology & Neuropathy: Recent Developments of Neurobiology in Hungary 1X. 234p. 1982. 143.00 (*0-569-08739-2*, Pub. by Collets UK) Pro-Am Music.
— Results in Neuroendocrinology, Neurochemistry & Sleep Research. (Recent Developments of Neurobiology in Hungary Ser.: No. 7). 189p. (C). 1978. 50.00x (*963-05-1587-3*, Pub. by Akad Kiado HU) St Mut.
Lissak, K., ed. Results in Neuroanatomy, Motor Organization, Cerebral Circulation & Modelling: Recent Developments in Neurobiology in Hungary, Vol. VIII. 1981. 60.00 (*0-569-08549-7*, Pub. by Collets UK) Pro-Am Music.
Lissak, K. & Endroczi, E. Neuroendocrine Control of Adaptation. LC 64-22225. (International Series of Monographs on Pure & Applied Mathematics: Vol. 25). 1965. 84.00 (*0-08-010795-8*, Pub. by Pergamon Repr UK) Franklin.
***Lissak, K. & Molnar, P.** Motivation & the Neural & Neurohumoral Factors in Regulation of Behaviour. (Recent Developments of Neurobiology in Hungary Ser.: No. 10). 331p. (C). 1982. 86.00x (*963-05-2993-9*, Pub. by Akad Kiado HU) St Mut.
Lissak, Moshe. Social Mobility in Israeli Society. 136p. 1969. 32.95 (*0-87855-176-X*) Transaction Pubs.
Lissak, Moshe, ed. Israeli Society & Its Defense Establishment: The Social & Political Impact of a Protracted Violent Conflict. (Illus.). 162p. 1984. 35.00 (*0-7146-3235-X*, BHA-03235, Pub. by F Cass Pubs UK) Intl Spec Bk.
Lissak, Moshe, jt. auth. see Horowitz, Dan.
Lissak, Rivka S. Pluralism & Progressives: Hull House & the New Immigrants, 1890-1919. (Illus.). 266p. 1989. 35.00 (*0-226-48502-1*) U Ch Pr.
Lissaman, P. B., jt. auth. see Wilson, R. F.
Lissant, Kenneth J. Emulsions & Emulsion Technology, Pt. III. (Surfactant Science Ser.: Vol. 6). 272p. 1984. 125.00 (*0-8247-7083-8*) Dekker.
Lissant, Kenneth J., ed. Emulsions & Emulsion Technology, Pt. II. (Surfactant Science Ser.: Vol. 6). 544p. 1974. pap. 190.00 (*0-8247-1892-5*) Dekker.
Lissarrague, Francois. The Aesthetics of the Greek Banquet: Images of Wine & Ritual. Szegedy-Maszak, Andrew, tr. (Illus.). 165p. (C). 1990. text ed. 26.95 (*0-691-03595-4*) Princeton U Pr.
Lissarrague, Pierre, jt. auth. see Christienne, Charles.
Lissau, Rudi. Rudolf Steiner: Life, Work, Inner Path & Social Initiatives. 192p. 1990. pap. 14.95 (*1-869890-06-X*, 1230, Pub. by Hawthorn Press UK) Anthroposophic.
***Lissauer, Bob.** Lissauer's Encyclopedia of Popular Music in America. LC 95-14169. 1996. reprint ed. write for info. (*0-614-05435-4*) Facts on File.
Lisse, G. Barany, jt. ed. see Kiraly, B. K.
Lissfelt, J. Fred. The Dutchman Died, & Other Tales of Pittsburgh's Southside. LC 92-11734. (Illus.). 152p. (C). 1992. text ed. 29.95 (*0-8229-3726-3*); pap. text ed. 10.95 (*0-8229-5483-4*) U of Pittsburgh Pr.
Lissi-Caronna, Elisa. Il Mitreo dei Castra Peregrinorum: S. Stefano Rotondo. (Etudes Preliminaires aux Religions Orientales dans l'Empire Romain Ser.: Vol. 104). (Illus.). viii, 52p. 1986. pap. 54.50 (*90-04-07493-7*) E J Brill.
Lissi, Thru L. Buddhist Handbook. (Salamander Ser.: No. 3). 32p. 1993. reprint ed. pap. 2.95 (*1-56640-593-9*) Pomegranate Calif.
Lissitzky, El & Arp, Hans. Kunstismen: The Isms of Art. LC 69-9230. (Contemporary Art Ser.). (Illus.). (ENG, FRE & GER.). 1979. reprint ed. 15.95 (*0-405-00710-8*) Ayer.
Lissitzky, El & Railings, Patricia. About Two Squares - More about Two Squares, 2 vol., Set. (Illus.). 140p. 1991. boxed 40.00 (*0-262-12158-1*) MIT Pr.
Lissitzky-Kuppers, Sophie. El Lissitzky. LC 79-83561. (Illus.). 410p. 1992. 70.00 (*0-500-23090-0*) Thames Hudson.
Lissitzyn, Oliver J. International Air Transport & National Policy. (Airlines History Project Ser.). reprint ed. 52.00 (*0-404-19327-7*) AMS Pr.
— The International Court of Justice: Its Role in the Maintenance of International Peace & Security, Vol. 6. LC 78-2885. (Carnegie Endowment for International Peace, United Nations Studies: No. 6). 118p. 1978. reprint ed. text ed. 45.00 (*0-313-20333-4*, LICJ) Greenwood.
Lissner, tr. see Jackins, Harvey & Meyer.
Lissner, David. Laboratory Manual for the Casio Fx 7700G Graphing Calculator. Pullins, ed. 145p. (C). Date not set. pap. text ed. write for info. (*0-314-02385-2*) West Pub.
— Laboratory Manual for the TI-81 Graphing Calculator. Pullins, ed. 145p. (C). Date not set. pap. text ed. 17.75 (*0-314-02386-0*) West Pub.
Lissner, Dorothy, jt. ed. see Lissner, Will.
Lissner, Dorothy B., ed. see Lawrence, Elwood P., et al.
Lissner, Dorothy B., jt. ed. see Lissner, Will.
Lissner, Will & Lissner, Dorothy, eds. George & the Scholars: A Century of Scientific Research Reveals the Reformer Was an Original Economist & a World-Class Social Philosopher. LC 91-1901. (George Studies Program: Vol. 1). 528p. (Orig.). (C). 1991. pap. 10.00 (*0-911312-86-2*) Schalkenbach.
Lissner, Will & Lissner, Dorothy B., eds. George & Ohio's Civic Revival: The American Democratic Philosopher Inspired a Successful Fight Against Political Bossism, Ending Many Exactions of the System of Privilege. (George Studies Program: Vol. 3). (Orig.). (C). 1995. pap. 12.00 (*0-911312-89-7*) Schalkenbach.
Lissner, Will, ed. see Lawrence, Elwood P., et al.
Lissok, Charlotte. Teste Dein Wirtschaftsdeutsch. 112p. (GER.). 1973. pap. 9.95 (*3-468-38527-7*) Langenscheidt.
Lissovsky, F. V. & Kalugin, J. K. English-Russian Dictionary of Electronics. 718p. (ENG & RUS.). 1984. 95.00 (*0-8288-0302-1*, F17530) Fr & Eur.
Lissowski, W. & Syskind, J. Capital Output Employment Rations in Industrial Programming. LC 64-195890. 1965. 102.00 (*0-08-010732-X*, Pub. by Pergamon Repr UK) Franklin.
List, Charles J. & Plum, Stephen H., eds. Library Research Guide to Philosophy. (Library Research Guide Ser.: No. 9). 1990. pap. 18.00 (*0-87650-264-8*) Pierian.
List, E. John & Jirka, Gerhard H., eds. Stratified Flows. LC 90-41159. 1120p. 1990. pap. text ed. 97.00 (*0-87262-775-6*) Am Soc Civil Eng.
List, Eugene, ed. see Gottschalk, Louis M.
List, Friedrich. The National System of Political Economy. Lloyd, Sampson S., tr. LC 90-35160. (Reprints of Economic Classics Ser.). xxxi, 454p. 1991. reprint ed. lib. bdg. 45.00 (*0-678-01454-X*) Kelley.
— Natural System of Political Economy, 1837. Henderson, W. O., ed. 206p. 1983. text ed. 35.00 (*0-7146-3206-6*, Pub. by F Cass Pubs UK) Intl Spec Bk.
List, Gary R., jt. ed. see Szuhaj, B. F.
List, George. Singing about It: Folk Song in Southern Indiana. 450p. 1991. pap. 32.00 (*0-87195-086-3*) Ind Hist Soc.
— Stability & Variation in Hopi Song. LC 92-73156. (Memoirs Ser.: Vol. 204). 205p. 1992. 28.00 (*0-87169-204-X*, M204-LIG) Am Philos.
List, Hans. Engines: My Life & My Work. 1990. pap. 15.00 (*1-56091-086-0*, SP-841) Soc Auto Engineers.
List, Harvey L. Petrochemical Technology: An Overview for Decision Makers in the International Petrochemical Industry. (Illus.). 256p. (C). 1986. text ed. 105.00 (*0-13-661992-4*) P-H.
List, Harvey L., jt. auth. see Schmidt, Alois X.
List, Herbert, photos. Herbert List: Junge Maenner. (Illus.). 112p. 1988. 55.00 (*0-944092-03-9*) Twin Palms Pub.
List, Jeffrey H. Atlas of Sea-Floor Changes from 1878-1989: Louisiana Coast. Vol. I-2150-B; Vol. I-2150-B. 1994. write for info. (*0-318-72670-X*) US Geol Survey.
List, Julie. The Day the Loving Stopped. 1986. pap. 2.50 (*0-449-70211-1*) Fawcett.
List, Lynne K., jt. auth. see Lerner, Janet W.
List, M., jt. auth. see Hofmann, M.
List, Peter C. Radical Environmentalism: Philosophy & Tactics. 276p. (C). 1993. pap. 17.95 (*0-534-17790-5*) Intl Thomson.
List, W., ed. see Clark, R.
List, W. F., jt. ed. see Steinbereithner, K.
Lista, Giovanni. Balla (Giacomo) Catalogue of the Work. limited ed. (Illus.). 540p. 1982. Numbered ed. 225.00 (*1-55660-165-4*) A Wofsy Fine Arts.
Listak, Jeffrey M., jt. auth. see Chekan, Gregory J.
Liste-Ghoode Peace Foundation Women's Delegation Staff. Indian Women Spirituality, & Social Change. (Common Ground Ser.: Vol. V). (Illus.). 54p. (Orig.). 1990. pap. 5.00 (*1-884478-04-2*) Common Grnd.
Listen & Enjoy Staff. Listen & Enjoy French Poetry. (Listen & Enjoy Cassettes Ser.). 1991. audio 7.95 (*0-486-99927-0*) Dover.
— Listen & Enjoy German Poetry. (Listen & Enjoy Cassettes Ser.). 1991. audio 7.95 (*0-486-99929-7*) Dover.
— Listen & Enjoy Italian Poetry. (Listen & Enjoy Cassettes Ser.). 1991. audio 7.95 (*0-486-99930-0*) Dover.
— Listen & Enjoy Spanish Poetry. (Listen & Enjoy Cassettes Ser.). 1991. audio 7.95 (*0-486-99928-9*) Dover.
Listenberger, Dick, illus. Winners: Winning Recipes from the Junior League of Indianapolis. 336p. 1985. 14.95 (*0-9614447-0-3*) Jr League Indianapolis.
Lister, jt. auth. see Wilber.
Lister, A. M. & Eager, R. D. Fundamentals of Operating Systems. 5th ed. 240p. 1993. pap. 29.00 (*0-387-91462-5*) Spr-Verlag.
Lister, Adrian. Mammoths. 1994. 30.00 (*0-02-572985-3*) P-H.
***Lister, Annabel.** Creative Pressed Flowers. (Illus.). 64p. (Orig.). 1994. pap. 10.95 (*0-86417-592-2*) Seven Hills Bk.
Lister, Barbara T. & Driver, Sherri B. Quilting Bees: Swarms of Ideas & Projects for Friends. (Illus.). 96p. 1993. pap. 19.95 (*1-880972-08-5*, DreamSpinners) Pssblts Denver.
***Lister, C. Michael, II.** The Song of Suffering: Meditations from Job. 120p. (Orig.). 1995. pap. write for info. (*1-57502-021-1*) Morris Pub.
***Lister, Charles.** The Regulation of Food Law by the EC. 300p. 1992. pap. text ed. 175.00 (*0-406-01305-5*, UK) Butterworth Legal Pubs.
Lister, David G., ed. In Vivo Measurement of Body Composition in Meat Animals: Proceedings of a Workshop Held at the Agricultural & Food Research Council's Meat Research Institute, Langford, Bristol, U. K., 30 November-1 December 1983. 252p. 1984. 74.00 (*0-85334-319-5*, Pub. by Elsevier Applied Sci UK) Elsevier.
Lister, Ed & Silva, A., eds. A Primer for Psychiatric Nurses. 159p. (Orig.). (C). 1990. pap. text ed. 24.95 (*0-9627287-9-9*) Cnslts Psych Nursing.
Lister, Eugene C. Electric Circuits & Machines. 6th ed. 1983. text ed. 40.95 (*0-07-038028-7*); text ed. write for info. (*0-07-038032-5*) McGraw.
Lister, Eugene C. & Rusch, Robert J. Electric Circuits & Machines. 7th ed. LC 92-33286. 1993. 53.50 (*0-02-801809-5*) Glencoe.
Lister, Florence & Wilson, Lynn. Windows of the Past: The Ruins of the Colorado Plateau. Leach, Nicky, ed. (Wish You Were Here Ser.). (Illus.). 96p. (Orig.). 1993. 24.95 (*0-939365-22-7*); pap. 14.95 (*0-939365-21-9*) Sierra Pr CA.
Lister, Florence C. Ceramic Studies of the Historic Periods in Ancient Nubia. (Nubian Ser.: No. 2). reprint ed. 30.00 (*0-404-60686-5*) AMS Pr.
— In the Shadow of the Rocks: Archaeology of the Chimney Rock District in Southern Colorado. LC 93-13293. (Illus.). 160p. 1993. 22.50 (*0-87081-292-0*) Univ Pr Colo.
— Kaiparowits Plateau & Glen Canyon Prehistory: An Interpretation Based on Ceramics. (Glen Canyon Ser.: No. 23). reprint ed. 23.00 (*0-404-60671-7*) AMS Pr.
Lister, Florence C. & Lister, Robert H. Andalusian Ceramics in Spain & New Spain: A Cultural Register from the Third Century B.C. to 1700. LC 87-23781. 411p. 1988. 70.00 (*0-8165-0974-3*) U of Ariz Pr.
— The Chinese of Early Tucson: Historic Archaeology from the Tucson Urban Renewal Project. LC 89-5105. (Anthropological Papers: No. 52). 131p. (Orig.). 1990. pap. 29.95 (*0-8165-1151-9*) U of Ariz Pr.
— Earl Morris & Southwestern Archaeology. rev. ed. LC 93-83414. (Illus.). 204p. 1993. pap. 14.95 (*1-877856-30-4*) SW Pks Mnmts.
— Sixteenth-Century Maiolica Pottery in the Valley of Mexico. LC 81-16203. (Anthropological Papers: No. 39). 110p. 1982. 12.95 (*0-8165-0748-1*) U of Ariz Pr.
Lister, Florence C., jt. auth. see Lister, Robert H.
Lister, Graham. The Hand, Diagnosis & Indications. 3rd ed. LC 92-49326. 593p. 1993. text ed. 105.00 (*0-443-04545-3*) Churchill.
Lister, Irene. Cambridge Characters. (Cambridge Town, Gown & County Ser.: Vol. 20). (Illus.). 1978. pap. 4.95 (*0-900891-25-4*) Oleander Pr.
Lister, James & Irving, Irene M., eds. Neonatal Surgery. 3rd ed. 1990. text ed. 350.00 (*0-407-01490-X*) Buttrwrth-Heinemann.
Lister, John. By the London Post. Relman, Arnold S., ed. 248p. (Orig.). 1985. pap. text ed. 13.95 (*0-910133-13-1*) MA Med Soc.
***Lister, Kate & Harnish, Tom.** Finding Money: The Small Business Guide to Financing. LC 95-878. (Small Business Editions Ser.). 1995. text ed. 39.95 (*0-471-10983-5*) Wiley.
***Lister, Kate & Harnish, Tome.** Finding Money: The Small Business Guide to Financing. LC 95-878. (Small Business Editions Ser.). 1995. pap. text ed. 17.95 (*0-471-10984-3*) Wiley.
Lister, L. & Renshaw, R. Understanding Chemistry for A-Level. (C). 1990. text ed. 150.00 (*0-7487-0216-4*, Pub. by S Thornes Pubs UK) St Mut.
Lister, Larry, ed. Human Sexuality, Ethnoculture & Social Work. LC 86-14899. (Journal of Social Work & Human Sexuality: Vol. 4, No. 3). 163p. 1987. text ed. 39.95 (*0-86656-609-0*) Haworth Pr.
Lister, Larry & Shore, David A., eds. Human Sexuality in Medical Social Work. LC 83-26449. (Journal of Social Work & Human Sexuality: Vol. 2, No. 1). 130p. 1984. text ed. 39.95 (*0-86656-254-0*) Haworth Pr.
***Lister, Laurie-Jeanne.** Humor as a Concept in Music: A Theoretical Study of Expression in Music, the Concept of Humor, & Humor in Music, with an Analytical Example, W.A. Mozart, Ein Musikalischer Spass, KV 522. LC 94-37796. (Publikationen des Instituts fur Musikanalytik Wien: Bd. 2). 1994. pap. 37.80 (*3-631-47091-6*) P Lang Pubs.
Lister, Marcie & Lovell, Sandra. Healing Together. Johnson, Joy, ed. (Illus.). 24p. 1991. pap. 2.95 (*1-56123-023-5*) Centering Corp.
Lister, Margot. Costume: An Illustrated Survey from Ancient Times to the Twentieth Century. LC 67-29412. (Illus.). 1968. 30.00 (*0-8238-0096-2*) Plays.
Lister, Marjorie. The European Community & the Developing World: The Role of the Lome Convention. 240p. 1988. text ed. 68.95 (*0-566-05609-7*, Pub. by Avebury Pub UK) Ashgate Pub Co.
Lister, Mark, et al. Trektoons. (Illus.). 100p. (Orig.). 1991. pap. 7.95 (*0-9629570-0-3*) Starland.
***Lister, Martin.** The Photographic Image in Digital Culture. LC 94-38082. (Comedia Ser.). 256p. 1995. pap. 19.95 (*0-415-12157-4*, C0590) Routledge.
***Lister, Martin, ed.** The Photographic Image in Digital Culture. LC 94-38082. (Comedia Ser.). (Illus.). 256p. 1995. 69.95 (*0-415-12156-6*, C0589) Routledge.
Lister, Mosie. Ever New. 1982. 5.95 (*0-318-72868-0*, MB-507) Lillenas.
— Everlasting Lord. 1986. 5.25 (*0-685-68476-8*, MC-59); audio 10.98 (*0-685-68477-6*, TA-9073C) Lillenas.
— Good Ol' Gospel. 1994. audio 10.88 (*0-614-01714-9*, TA-4014C); audio 19.88 (*0-614-01716-5*, TA-4014S) Lillenas.
— Good Ol' Gospel, CD. 1994. 14.88 (*0-614-01715-7*, DC-4014); 24.88 (*0-614-01717-3*, DC-4014T) Lillenas.
— Grace & Glory. 1984. spiral bd. 6.50 (*0-8341-9189-X*, MB-523) Lillenas.
— Hallelujah Celebration. 1980. 5.95 (*0-8341-9047-8*, MB-485) Lillenas.
— Hallelujah Fountain. 1987. spiral bd. 6.50 (*0-8341-9032-X*, MB-562) Lillenas.
— Joy Overflowing. 1985. 5.25 (*0-685-74880-4*, MB-532) Lillenas.
— Living Waters. 1989. spiral bd. 6.50 (*0-8341-9282-9*, MB-600) Lillenas.
— Love, Light, & Life. 1988. 5.25 (*0-8341-9156-3*, MC-64); audio 10.98 (*0-685-68481-4*, TA-9094C) Lillenas.
— Now Men Sing! 1970. 5.25 (*0-685-74886-3*, MB-141) Lillenas.
— Reason to Rejoice. 1983. 5.25 (*0-685-68502-0*, MC-49); audio 10.98 (*0-685-68503-9*, TA-9043C) Lillenas.
— Rise & Rejoice. 1986. 5.25 (*0-8341-9225-X*, MB-557) Lillenas.
— Sweet Assurance. 1987. 5.95 (*0-8341-9187-3*, MB-576) Lillenas.
— Tree of Life. 1985. 4.95 (*0-685-68635-3*, ME-38); audio 10.98 (*0-685-68636-1*, TA-9066C) Lillenas.
Lister, Mosie, comp. Lord of All. 1979. 12.95 (*0-8341-9159-8*, MB-465) Lillenas.
Lister, Mosie, contrib. Name above All Names. 1990. 5.25 (*0-685-68463-6*, MC-69); audio 10.98 (*0-685-68464-4*, TA-9116C) Lillenas.
— Rock of Faith. 1988. 5.25 (*0-685-68622-1*, ME-39); audio 10.98 (*0-685-68623-X*, TA-9098C) Lillenas.
— Til the Storm Passes by. 1985. 5.95 (*0-8341-9120-2*, MB-538); audio 12.98 (*0-685-68256-0*, TA-9060C) Lillenas.
Lister, Mosie, des. Great Day! A Choral Celebration for Christmas. 1994. 5.25 (*0-8341-9067-2*, MC-84) Lillenas.
— Great Day! A Choral Celebration for Christmas. 1994. digital audio 10.98 (*0-614-01728-9*, TA-9166C) Lillenas.
— Great Day! A Choral Celebration for Christmas. 1994. digital audio 60.00 (*0-614-01729-7*, MU-9166C) Lillenas.
— Great Day! A Choral Celebration for Christmas. 1994. cd-rom 60.00 (*0-614-01730-0*, MU-9166T) Lillenas.
— Great Day! A Choral Celebration for Christmas. suppl. ed. 1994. 6.00 (*0-614-01731-9*, L-9166C) Lillenas.
— Great Day! A Choral Celebration for Christmas. suppl. ed. 1994. digital audio 45.00 (*0-614-01732-7*, MU-9166R) Lillenas.
— Great Day! A Choral Celebration for Christmas. suppl. ed. 1994. 8.00 (*0-614-01733-5*, MC-84SF) Lillenas.
— It's Campmeeting Time (in the Choir Loft) Easy to Prepare, Fun to Sing. 1994. digital audio 12.98 (*0-614-01681-9*, TA-9176C) Lillenas.
— It's Campmeeting Time (in the Choir Loft) Easy to Prepare, Fun to Sing. 1994. digital audio 60.00 (*0-614-01682-7*, MU-9176C) Lillenas.
— It's Campmeeting Time (in the Choir Loft) Easy to Prepare, Fun to Sing. 1994. digital audio 60.00 (*0-614-01683-5*, MU-9176S) Lillenas.
— It's Campmeeting Time (in the Choir Loft) Easy to Prepare, Fun to Sing. 1994. cd-rom 60.00 (*0-614-01684-3*, MU-9176T) Lillenas.

— It's Campmeeting Time (in the Choir Loft) Easy to Prepare, Fun to Sing. 1994. 5.95 (0-8341-9214-4, MB-699) Lillenas.

— It's Campmeeting Time (in the Choir Loft) Easy to Prepare, Fun to Sing. suppl. ed. 1994. 6.00 (0-614-01685-1, L-9176C) Lillenas.

Lister, Mosie & Bolton, Martha. Good Ol' Gospel. 1994. 9.95 (0-8341-9068-0, MB-695) Lillenas.

Lister, P. F., jt. auth. see Halsall, F.

Lister, R. P. Allotments. (Illus.). (C). 1989. 75.00 (1-85183-025-1, Silent Bks) St Mut.

— Genghis Khan. (Reprints Ser.). 232p. 1990. reprint ed. 16.95 (0-88029-406-X) Dorset Pr.

Lister, Raymond. British Romantic Painting. (Illus.). 176p. (C). 1989. 59.95 (0-521-35604-0) Cambridge U Pr.

— British Romantic Painting. (Illus.). 176p. (C). 1990. pap. 27.95 (0-521-35687-3) Cambridge U Pr.

— A Catalogue Raisonne of the Works of Samuel Palmer. (Illus.). 300p. 1988. 170.00 (0-521-34455-7) Cambridge U Pr.

— The Paintings of Samuel Palmer. (Illus.). 176p. 1987. pap. 29.95 (0-521-31855-6) Cambridge U Pr.

— The Paintings of William Blake. (Illus.). 175p. 1986. 64.95 (0-521-30538-1) Cambridge U Pr.

— The Paintings of William Blake. (Illus.). 175p. 1988. pap. 27.95 (0-521-31557-3) Cambridge U Pr.

— Samuel Palmer: His Life & Art. (Illus.). 296p. 1987. 74.95 (0-521-32850-0) Cambridge U Pr.

Lister, Raymond G. With My Own Wings: The Memoirs of Raymond Lister. (Illus.). 224p. (Orig.). 1994. pap. 23.95 (0-906672-66-X) Oleander Pr.

Lister, Richard G., jt. ed. see Weingartner, Herbert J.

Lister, Robert H. & Lister, Florence C. Anasazi Pottery. LC 78-6825. (Illus.). 103p. 1978. pap. 16.95 (0-8263-0473-7) U of NM Pr.

— Chaco Canyon: Archaeology & Archaeologists. LC 80-54566. (Illus.). 296p. 1984. reprint ed. pap. 18.95 (0-8263-0756-6) U of NM Pr.

— Mesa Verde National Park: Preserving the Past. (Illus.). 80p. 1989. 15.95 (0-917859-13-8) Sunrise SBCA.

— Those Who Came Before: Southwestern Archaeology in the National Park System: Featuring Photographs from the George A. Grant Collection & a Portfolio by David Muench. LC 83-60100. (Illus.). 184p. reprint ed. pap. 52.50 (0-8357-3617-2, 2036148) Bks Demand.

— Those Who Came Before: Southwestern Archeology in the National Park System. rev. ed. (Illus.). 232p. 1994. 45.00 (0-8263-1543-7) U of NM Pr.

— Those Who Came Before: Southwestern Archeology in the National Park System. 2nd ed. Priehs, T. J. & Scott, Sandra, eds. LC 93-86265. (Illus.). 238p. 1994. pap. 16.95 (1-877856-38-X) SW Pks Mnmts.

Lister, Robert H., jt. auth. see Lister, Florence C.

Lister, Robert H., et al. The Coombs Site, 3 pts. in 2 vols. (Glen Canyon Ser.). reprint ed. Pts. I-II. 65.00 (0-404-60720-9); reprint ed. Pt. III. 32.50 (0-404-60721-7) AMS Pr.

— The Coombs Site, 3 pts. in 2 vols., Set. (Glen Canyon Ser.). reprint ed. 97.50 (0-404-60641-5) AMS Pr.

Lister, Robin. Legend of King Arthur. 1990. 18.95 (0-385-26369-4) Doubleday.

Lister, Roger C. Bank Behavior, Regulation, & Economic Development: California, 1860-1910. LC 92-40629. (Financial Sector of the American Economy Ser.). 288p. 1993. 62.00 (0-8153-0967-8) Garland.

Lister, Ruth & Wilson, Leo. The Unequal Breadwinner. 1976. 20.00 (0-901108-57-X, Pub. by NCCL UK) St Mut.

Lister, Susan, jt. auth. see Wilber, Cynthia J.

Lister, Susan M., tr. see Camesasca, Ettore.

***Lister, Ted & Renshaw, Janet.** Understanding Chemistry for Advanced Level. 608p. (C). 1994. 57.00x (0-7478-0216-5) St Mut.

Lister, Thomas H. Arlington: A Novel, 3 vols. in 2, 1. LC 79-8154. reprint ed. write for info. (0-404-61980-0) AMS Pr.

— Arlington: A Novel, 3 vols. in 2, 2. LC 79-8154. reprint ed. write for info. (0-404-61981-9) AMS Pr.

— Arlington: A Novel, 3 vols. in 2, Set. LC 79-8154. reprint ed. 84.50 (0-404-61979-7) AMS Pr.

— Granby: A Novel, 3 vols. in 2, 1. LC 79-8156. reprint ed. write for info. (0-404-61984-3) AMS Pr.

— Granby: A Novel, 3 vols. in 2, 2. LC 79-8156. reprint ed. write for info. (0-404-61985-1) AMS Pr.

— Granby: A Novel, 3 vols. in 2, Set. LC 79-8156. reprint ed. 84.50 (0-404-61983-5) AMS Pr.

Lister, Timothy R. & Yourdon, Edward. Learning to Program in Structured COBOL, Part 2. LC 77-99232. 224p. (C). 1977. pap. 29.00 (0-685-05484-5, Yourdon) P-H.

Lister, Timothy R., jt. auth. see DeMarco, Tom.

Lister, Timothy R., jt. ed. see DeMarco, Tom.

Lister, Timothy R., jt. auth. see Goldschlager.

Listerman, Randall, tr. Hans Sachs: Nine Carnival Plays. 100p. 1985. 8.00 (0-919473-68-7, DH56, Pub. by Dovehouse CN) MRTS.

Listerman, Randall W., tr. Lope de Rueda: The Interludes. 118p. 1985. pap. 8.00 (0-919473-65-2, DH52, Pub. by Dovehouse CN) MRTS.

Listfield, Emily. Acts of Love. 320p. 1994. 21.95 (0-670-85278-3, Viking) Viking Penguin.

— Acts of Love. 384p. 1995. pap. 10.95 (0-14-023281-8, Penguin Bks) Viking Penguin.

Listgarten, M. A., jt. auth. see Schroeder, H. E.

Listick, Barton E. Lotus Guide to Add in Toolkit 123. 1990. pap. 22.95 (0-201-52324-8) Addison-Wesley.

Listokin, David. Land Use Controls: Present Problems & Future Reform. 406p. 1974. boxed 10.00 (0-87855-103-4) Transaction Pubs.

— Landmark Preservation. (Center for Urban Policy Research Bk.). 166p. 1982. pap. 20.00 (0-88285-077-6) Transaction Pubs.

Listokin, David & Casey, Stephen. Mortgage Lending & Race: Conceptual & Analytical Perspectives of the Urban Financing Dilemma. LC 79-12209. 225p. 1980. text ed. 1.00 (0-88285-060-1) Ctr Urban Pol Res.

Listokin, David & Walker, Carole. The Subdivision & Site Plan Handbook. 461p. 1989. 54.95 (0-88285-123-3) Ctr Urban Pol Res.

Listokin, David, jt. auth. see Burchell, Robert W.

***Liston, B. & Choate, C.** Exploring Literature Theme Kit. (J). 1995. pap. text ed. write for info. (0-201-59542-7) Addison-Wesley.

— Farm Animals. (Exploring Literature Theme Ser.: Bk. 3). 1995. pap. text ed. write for info. (0-201-59547-8) Addison-Wesley.

— The Five Senses. (Exploring Literature Theme Ser.: Bk. 5). (J). 1995. pap. write for info. (0-201-59548-6) Addison-Wesley.

— Growing & Changing. (Exploring Literature Theme Ser.: Bk. 6). (J). 1995. pap. write for info. (0-201-59546-X) Addison-Wesley.

— Home & Family. (Exploring Literature Theme Ser.: Bk. 1). (J). 1995. pap. text ed. write for info. (0-201-59544-3) Addison-Wesley.

— Marvelous Me. (Exploring Literature Theme Ser.: Bk. 4). (J). 1995. pap. text ed. write for info. (0-201-59543-5) Addison-Wesley.

— School & Friends. (Exploring Literature Theme Ser.: Bk. 2). (J). 1995. pap. text ed. write for info. (0-201-59545-1) Addison-Wesley.

Liston, Beverly. Family Camping Made Simple: Tent & RV Camping with Children. LC 89-7430. (Illus.). 288p. 1989. pap. 12.95 (0-87106-612-2) Globe Pequot.

Liston, Daniel P. Capitalist Schools: Explanation & Ethics in Radical Studies of Schooling. (Critical Social Thought Ser.). 208p. 1988. text ed. 35.00 (0-415-90044-1, A1561, Routledge NY); pap. 12.95 (0-415-90341-6, A4779, Routledge NY) Routledge.

Liston, Daniel P. & Zeichner, Kenneth M. Teacher Education & the Social Conditions of Schooling. (Critical Social Thought Ser.). 288p. 1991. 39.95 (0-415-90071-9, A2423, Routledge NY); pap. 14.95 (0-415-90233-9, A5174, Routledge NY) Routledge.

Liston, David & Reeves, Nigel. The Invisible Economy: A Profile of Britain's Invisible Exports. 320p. 1988. 42.50 (0-273-02704-2, Pub. by Pitman Pub Ltd UK) Trans-Atl Phila.

Liston, David, ed. see International Committee on Museum Security Staff.

Liston, John, jt. auth. see Kramer, D. E.

Liston, Linda L., jt. auth. see Conway, H. McKinley.

Liston, Linda L., jt. ed. see Conway, H. McKinley.

Liston, Maureen R. Gertrude Stein: An Annotated Critical Bibliography. LC 78-21971. (Serif Series: Bibliographies & Checklists: No. 35). 244p. reprint ed. pap. 69.60 (0-8357-5573-8, 2035200) Bks Demand.

Liston, Paul. Gold in the Fire. (Illus.). 162p. (Orig.). 1987. pap. 5.95 (0-317-93969-6) Abbeyfeale Pubs.

Liston, Robert A. The Pueblo Surrender: A Covert Action by the National Security Agency. LC 88-39716. 1988. 18.95 (0-87131-554-8) M Evans.

Liston, William T., ed. see Quarles, Francis.

***Listorti, James A.** Environmental Health Components for Water Supply, Sanitation, & Urban Projects. (Technical Paper Ser.: No. 121). 156p. 1990. 9.95 (0-614-02778-0, 11537) World Bank.

Listowel, Judith. A Habsburg Tragedy: Crown Prince Rudolf. (Illus.). 316p. 1987. 16.95 (0-88029-105-2) Dorset Pr.

Listowel, W. A. A Critical History of Modern Aesthetics. 1972. 59.95 (0-87968-966-8) Gordon Pr.

Listri, Massimo, jt. auth. see Cresti, Carlo.

Listro, John P. Accounting & Reporting for Nonprofit Organizations. 280p. 1992. per. 24.95 (0-8403-8067-4) Kendall-Hunt.

— Accounting for Nonprofit Organizations. 136p. 1983. per. 19.95 (0-8403-2912-1) Kendall-Hunt.

Liswood, Laura A. Serving Them Right: Innovative & Powerful Customer Retention Strategies. 1992. pap. 12.00 (0-88730-525-3) Harper Busn.

Lisyansky, A. A., jt. auth. see Ivanchenko, Y. M.

***Lisyuk, Michael B. & Tush, Paul J.** The Traveller's Yellow Pages & Handbook: For St. Petersburg: July Supplement. 64p. 1994. write for info. (1-881832-05-8) InfoSrvs Int.

Lisyuk, Michael B., jt. auth. see Dohan, Michael R.

Liszka, James J. The Semiotic of Myth: A Critical Study of the Symbol. LC 88-45500. (Advances in Semiotics Ser.). (Illus.). 256p. 1990. 35.00 (0-253-33513-2) Ind U Pr.

Liszka, Thomas R., ed. Index to Reviews of Bibliographic Publications: An International Annual, 1982, Vol. VII. LC 78-645642. 265p. 1985. 25.00 (0-87875-317-6) Whitston Pub.

— Index to Reviews of Bibliographic Publications, Vol. VIII: 1983. LC 78-645642. xxii, 310p. 1987. 28.50 (0-87875-340-0) Whitston Pub.

— Index to Reviews of Bibliographic Publications Vol. X, 1985. 265p. 1991. 35.00 (0-87875-405-9) Whitston Pub.

— Index to Reviews of Bibliographic Publications, 1984, Vol. IX. LC 78-645642. 346p. 1989. 40.00 (0-87875-376-1) Whitston Pub.

Liszkowski, Ron, ed. see Cochran, John S.

Liszkowski, Ron, ed. see Danenberg, Alvin H.

Liszkowski, Ron, ed. see Edleson, Michael E.

Liszkowski, Ron, ed. see Evans, Richard L.

Liszkowski, Ron, ed. see Levitt, J. Stanley.

Liszkowski, Ron, ed. see Shim, Jae K., et al.

Liszt, Catherine A., jt. auth. see Easton, Dossie.

Liszt, Franz. An Artist's Journey: Lettres d'un Bachelier es Musique, 1835-1841. Suttoni, Charles, tr. (Illus.). 304p. 1989. 24.95 (0-226-48510-2) U Ch Pr.

— The Gipsy in Music, 2 vols. 1990. reprint ed. lib. bdg. 140.00 (0-7812-9069-4) Rprt Serv.

— Letters of Franz Liszt, 2 vols. 1990. reprint ed. lib. bdg. 140.00 (0-7812-0410-0) Rprt Serv.

— Letters of Franz Liszt, 2 Vols, Set. LC 68-25294. (Studies in Music: No. 42). 1969. reprint ed. lib. bdg. 150.00 (0-8383-0307-2) M S G Haskell Hse.

— Letters of Franz Liszt, 2 vols., Set. 1980. reprint ed. lib. bdg. 95.00 (0-403-00360-1) Scholarly.

— Letters of Franz Liszt to Marie Zu Sayn-Wittgenstein. Hugo, Howard E., ed. & tr. by. LC 71-142931. 376p. 1971. reprint ed. text ed. 65.00 (0-8371-1428-4, LILM, Greenwood Pr) Greenwood.

— The Letters of Franz Liszt to Olga Von Meyendorff, 1871-1886: In the Mildred Bliss Collection at Dumbarton Oaks. 553p. (C). 1979. 32.50 (0-88402-078-9) HUP.

— The Letters of Franz Liszt to Olga von Meyendorff, 1871-1886, in the Mildred Bliss Collection at Dumbarton Oaks. Tyler, William R., tr. (Illus.). 553p. (C). 1979. text ed. 32.50 (0-685-02129-7) HUP.

— Liszt's Complete Piano Transcriptions from Wagner's Operas. Suttoni, Charles, ed. 1981. pap. 7.95 (0-486-24126-2) Dover.

— Piano Transcriptions from French & Italian Operas. (Illus.). 256p. 1982. pap. 9.95 (0-486-24273-0) Dover.

— Thirty Songs, for High Voice. Armbruster, Carl, ed. 1979. 11.25 (0-8446-5502-3) Peter Smith.

— Thirty Songs for High Voice. Armbruster, Carl, ed. LC 75-17172. 160p. 1975. reprint ed. pap. 7.95 (0-486-23197-6) Dover.

Liszt, Franz & La Mara. Letters, 2 vols., 1. Bache, Constance, tr. LC 69-13973. 1970. reprint ed. text ed. 45.00 (0-313-21285-6, LILA) Greenwood.

— Letters, 2 vols., Set. Bache, Constance, tr. LC 69-13973. 1970. reprint ed. text ed. 65.00 (0-8371-1104-8, LILE) Greenwood.

— Letters, 2 vols., Vol. 2. Bache, Constance, tr. LC 69-13973. 1970. reprint ed. text ed. 45.00 (0-8371-1105-6, LILB) Greenwood.

Liszt, Rudolph. The Last Word in Make-up: A Practical Illustrated Handbook. rev. ed. (Illus.). 1964. pap. 13.00 (0-8222-0640-4) Dramatists Play.

Litai, Xue, jt. auth. see Lewis, John W.

Litaize, Alain, jt. auth. see Lanher, Jean.

L'Italien, J. J. Proteins: Structure & Function. 810p. 1987. 135.00 (0-306-42299-9, Plenum Pr) Plenum.

Litan, Robert, ed. Verdict: Assessing the Civil Jury System. 542p. (C). 1993. 48.95 (0-8157-5282-2); pap. 24.95 (0-8157-5281-4) Brookings.

Litan, Robert, et al. Physical Damage & Human Loss: The Economic Impact of Earthquake Mitigation Measures. LC 92-28616. (Insurance & Society Ser.). 98p. (Orig.). 1992. pap. 15.00 (0-932387-35-7) Insur Info.

Litan, Robert E. The Revolution in U. S. Finance. 55p. (C). 1991. pap. 6.95 (0-8157-5279-2) Brookings.

— What Should Banks Do? LC 87-18235. 207p. 1987. 29.95 (0-8157-5270-9); pap. 11.95 (0-8157-5269-5) Brookings.

Litan, Robert E. & Lawrence, Robert Z., eds. American Living Standards: Threats & Challenges. LC 88-26238. 250p. 1988. 31.95 (0-8157-5274-1); pap. 12.95 (0-8157-5273-3) Brookings.

Litan, Robert E. & Nordhaus, William D. Reforming Federal Regulation. LC 83-3622. (Yale Fastback Ser.: No. 27). 224p. 1983. text ed. 40.00 (0-300-03045-2); pap. 12.00 (0-300-03107-6) Yale U Pr.

Litan, Robert E. & Winston, Clifford, eds. Liability: Perspectives & Policy. LC 88-7254. 248p. 1988. 34.95 (0-8157-5272-5); pap. 14.95 (0-8157-5271-7) Brookings.

Litan, Robert E., jt. ed. see Boltuck, Richard.

Litan, Robert E., jt. auth. see Herring, Richard J.

Litan, Robert E., jt. auth. see Huber, Peter W.

Litan, Robert E., jt. ed. see Kaufman, George G.

Litan, Robert E., jt. auth. see Lawrence, Robert Z.

Litchfield, Ada B. A Button in Her Ear. Rubin, Caroline, ed. LC 75-28390. (Albert Whitman Concept Bks.). (Illus.). 32p. (J). (gr. 2-4). 1976. lib. bdg. 13.95 (0-8075-0987-6) A Whitman.

— A Cane in Her Hand. Rubin, Caroline, ed. LC 77-14255. (Albert Whitman Concept Bks.). (Illus.). (J). (gr. 1-3). 1977. lib. bdg. 13.95 (0-8075-1056-4) A Whitman.

— Making Room for Uncle Joe. Tucker, Kathleen, ed. LC 83-17036. (Albert Whitman Concept Bks.). (Illus.). 32p. (J). (gr. 3-5). 1984. lib. bdg. 11.95 (0-8075-4952-5) A Whitman.

— Words in Our Hands. Tucker, Kathleen, ed. LC 79-28402. (Albert Whitman Concept Bks.: Level 2). (Illus.). (J). (gr. 2-4). 1980. lib. bdg. 13.95 (0-8075-9212-9) A Whitman.

Litchfield, C. D. & Seyfried, P. L., eds. Methodology for Biomass Determinations & Microbial Activities in Sediments-STP 673. 199p. 1979. 22.50 (0-8031-0511-8, 04-673000-16) ASTM.

Litchfield, Carolyn, jt. auth. see Vorndran, Barbara S.

Litchfield, Carter. History of Oleomargarine Tax Stamps & Licenses in the United States. LC 86-21799. (Illus.). 128p. 1988. 27.50 (0-917526-03-1) Olearius Edns.

Litchfield, Carter, et al. The Bethlehem Oil Mill Seventeen Forty-Five to Nineteen Thirty-Four: German Technology in Early Pennsylvania. LC 82-61069. (Illus.). 128p. 1984. 25.00 (0-917526-02-3) Olearius Edns.

Litchfield, Grace D. As a Man Sows, & Other Stories. LC 77-160940. (Short Story Index Reprint Ser.). 1977. reprint ed. 23.95 (0-8369-3919-0) Ayer.

— Little Venice & Other Stories. LC 72-98583. (Short Story Index Reprint Ser.). 1977. 20.95 (0-8369-3157-2) Ayer.

Litchfield, Harry R. Live & Be Well. LC 72-76583. 300p. 1972. 12.95 (0-87212-022-8) Libra.

Litchfield, Jack. The Canadian Jazz Discography. 945p. 1982. 40.00 (0-8020-2448-3) U of Toronto Pr.

Litchfield, Michael, jt. auth. see National Insecurity Council Staff.

Litchfield, Michael W. Renovation: A Complete Guide. 2nd rev. ed. 640p. 1990. boxed 36.00 (0-13-159336-6) P-H.

Litchfield, R. B. Tom Wedgwood, the First Photographer. LC 72-9217. (Literature of Photography Ser.). 1979. reprint ed. 21.95 (0-405-04924-2) Ayer.

Litchfield, R. Burr. Emergence of a Bureaucracy: The Florentine Patricians, 1530-1790. (Illus.). 392p. 1987. text ed. 65.00 (0-691-05487-8) Princeton U Pr.

Litchfield, R. Burr, tr. see Venturi, Franco.

Litchfield, W. J. The Litchfield Family in America, Pt. 1, Nos. 1-5. 384p. 1989. reprint ed. lib. bdg. 65.00 (0-8328-0771-0); reprint ed. pap. 57.00 (0-8328-0772-9) Higginson Bk Co.

Litchford, Mary & Yordy, Laura. Hypertension: Instructors Guide. (C). 1990. 5.00 (1-880989-23-9); 3.5 hd 99.00 (1-880989-07-7); 3.5 hd 99.00 (1-880989-05-0); 5.25 hd 99.00 (1-880989-06-9); 5.25 hd 99.00 (1-880989-04-2); 5.00 (1-880989-22-0) Case Sftware.

Litchford, Mary, et al. Food Menu Systems & Applications: Instructor's Guide. (C). 1992. 5.00 (1-880989-29-8); student ed 5.00 (1-880989-28-X); 3.5 hd 99.00 (1-880989-19-0); 3.5 hd 99.00 (1-880989-17-4); 5.25 hd 99.00 (1-880989-18-2); 5.25 hd 99.00 (1-880989-16-6) Case Sftware.

Litchford, Mary D. & Yordy, Laura. Diabetes: Instructor's Guide. (C). 1991. 5.00 (1-880989-25-5); 3.5 hd 99.00 (1-880989-11-5); 3.5 hd 99.00 (1-880989-09-3); 5.25 hd 99.00 (1-880989-10-7); 5.25 hd 99.00 (1-880989-08-5); 5.00 (1-880989-24-7) Case Sftware.

— Malnutrition & Stress: Instructor's Guide. (C). 1990. 5.00 (1-880989-21-2); 5.00 (1-880989-20-4); 99.00 (1-880989-03-4); 99.00 (1-880989-02-6); 99.00 (1-880989-01-8); 99.00 (1-880989-00-X) Case Sftware.

— Reading the Medical Record: Instructor's Guide. (C). 1991. 5.00 (1-880989-27-1); student ed 5.00 (1-880989-26-3); disk 99.00 (1-880989-12-3); disk 99.00 (1-880989-13-1); disk 99.00 (1-880989-14-X); disk 99.00 (1-880989-15-8) Case Sftware.

Litchford, Mary D., jt. auth. see Hogue, Mary A.

Litehiser, Joe J., ed. Observation Seismology: A Centennial Symposium for the Berkeley Seismographic Stations. 1990. 55.00 (0-520-06582-4) U CA Pr.

Litell, Julia. Building Strong Foundations: Evaluation Strategies for Family Resource Programs. 148p. 1986. pap. 30.00 (1-885429-00-2) Family Resource.

Literacy Volunteers Computer Task Force Staff. Computer Assisted Instruction (CAI) Review. Carlin, Chip & Lawson, V. K., eds. 1986. pap. text ed. 3.00 (0-318-41221-7) Lit Vol Am.

Literacy Volunteers of America-Chippewa Valley Staff. Put It in Print: How to Produce a Book of Student Writings. (Celebrate Writing Ser.). 90p. 1995. pap. text ed. 8.00 (1-885474-19-9) Chipp Valley.

Literacy Volunteers of America Staff. ESL Tutor Training Workshop. 1980. Slide & tape cassette with guidebooks. student ed, audio 550.00 (0-930713-43-5) Lit Vol Am.

Literacy Volunteers of New York City Staff, ed. Bars Coming Near: An Anthology by New Writers in Prison. (New Writers' Voices Ser.). 64p. (Orig.). 1992. pap. text ed. 3.50 (0-929631-64-1, Signal Hill) New Readers.

— From My Imagination: An Anthology of Poetry & Short Stories by New Writers. (New Writers' Voices Ser.). 64p. (Orig.). 1990. pap. text ed. 3.50 (0-929631-17-X, Signal Hill) New Readers.

— My Native Land: An Anthology by New Writers. 64p. (Orig.). 1992. pap. text ed. 3.50 (0-929631-65-X, Signal Hill) New Readers.

— Speaking from the Heart: An Anthology of Writing by New Writers. (New Writers' Voices Ser.). 64p. (Orig.). 1990. pap. text ed. 3.50 (0-929631-16-1, Signal Hill) New Readers.

— Speaking Out on Health: An Anthology. (New Writers' Voices Ser.). 64p. (Orig.). 1989. pap. text ed. 3.50 (0-929631-05-6, Signal Hill) New Readers.

— Speaking Out on Home & Family: An Anthology of Writing by New Writers. (New Writers' Voices Ser.). (Illus.). 64p. (Orig.). 1990. pap. text ed. 3.50 (0-929631-08-0, Signal Hill) New Readers.

— Speaking out on Work: An Anthology of Writing by New Writers. (New Writers' Voices Ser.). (Illus.). 64p. (Orig.). 1991. pap. text ed. 3.50 (0-929631-35-8, Signal Hill) New Readers.

— Taking Charge of My Life: An Anthology of Writing by New Writers. (New Writers' Voices Ser.). 64p. (Orig.). 1991. pap. text ed. 3.50 (0-929631-37-4, Signal Hill) New Readers.

Literacy Volunteers of New York City Staff, ed. see Abdul-Jabbar, Kareem & Knobler, Peter.

Literacy Volunteers of New York City Staff, ed. see Alvarez, Lynne, et al.

Literacy Volunteers of New York City Staff, ed. see Benchley, Peter.

Literacy Volunteers of New York City Staff, ed. see Bly, Robert, et al.

Literacy Volunteers of New York City Staff, ed. see Carbone, Sonny.

Literacy Volunteers of New York City Staff, ed. see Clark, Mary Higgins.

Literacy Volunteers of New York City Staff, ed. see Fargo, Jean.

Literacy Volunteers of New York City Staff, ed. see Feiffer, Jules, et al.

Literacy Volunteers of New York City Staff, ed. see Fulghum, Robert.

Literacy Volunteers of New York City Staff, ed. see Goodall, Jane.

An Asterisk (*) at the beginning of an entry indicates that the title is appearing in BIP for the first time.

Literacy Volunteers of New York City Staff, ed. see Gum, Lori.

Literacy Volunteers of New York City Staff, ed. see Hijuelos, Oscar.

Literacy Volunteers of New York City Staff, ed. see Jackson, Katherine & Wiseman, Richard.

Literacy Volunteers of New York City Staff, ed. see King, Stephen.

Literacy Volunteers of New York City Staff, ed. see Kingston, Maxine H.

Literacy Volunteers of New York City Staff, ed. see Krantz, Judith.

Literacy Volunteers of New York City Staff, ed. see Lynn, Loretta & Vecsey, George.

Literacy Volunteers of New York City Staff, ed. see McMurtry, Larry.

Literacy Volunteers of New York City Staff, ed. see Miles, Calvin.

Literacy Volunteers of New York City Staff, ed. see Monette, Paul.

Literacy Volunteers of New York City Staff, ed. see Moore, Mamie.

Literacy Volunteers of New York City Staff, ed. see Sanservino, Theresa.

Literacy Volunteers of New York City Staff, ed. see Tan, Amy.

Literacy Volunteers of New York City Staff, ed. see Walker, Alice.

Literacy Volunteers of New York City Staff, ed. see Williams, Ted & Underwood, John.

Literary & Philosophical Society of New York Staff, Jr. & Clinton, Dewitt. An Introductory Discourse: Proceedings of the Literary & Philosophical Society of New York, May 1814. Albritton, Claude C., ed. LC 77-6515. (History of Geology Ser.). 1978. reprint ed. lib. bdg. 19.95 (*0-405-10437-5*) Ayer.

Literary Volunteers of America Staff. Intercultural Communications - Trainer's Guide. 1980. Guidebook, slides, cassettes. student ed, audio 90.00 (*0-930713-50-8*) Lit Vol Am.

Lites, Emily & Lehman. Visions: A Low Intermediate Grammar. 256p. (C). 1990. pap. text ed. 19.25 (*0-13-328816-1*) P-H.

— Visions: Writing One. 164p. (C). 1989. pap. text ed. 15.50 (*0-13-946070-5*) P-H.

Litewka, Albert. Warsaw: A Novel of Resistance. 512p. 1989. 21.95 (*0-685-31318-2*) IMA NYC.

Litext, Inc. Staff & Solorzano, Porfirio R., intros. The Nirex Collection: Nicaraguan Revolution Extracts. (Collection of Documents Ser.: Vols. 1-10). (Illus.). 9440p. (C). 1989. pap. 425.00 (*0-685-27216-8*) LITEXT Inc.

***Litfin, Dave.** Dave Litfin's Expert Handicapping: Winning Insights into Betting Thoroughbreds. LC 95-8508. 1995. 24.95 (*0-316-52781-5*) Little.

Litfin, Duane. Public Speaking: A Handbook for Christians. 2nd ed. LC 91-42786. 368p. (Orig.). 1992. pap. 19.99 (*0-8010-5675-6*) Baker Bk.

— St. Paul's Theology of Proclamation: 1 Corinthians 1-4 & Greco-Roman Rhetoric. (Society for New Testament Studies Monographs: No. 79). 310p. (C). 1994. 64.95 (*0-521-45178-7*) Cambridge U Pr.

Litfin, Karen. Ozone Discourse: Science & Politics in Global Environmental Cooperation. LC 94-8867. (New Directions in World Politics Ser.). (Illus.). 296p. 1994. 45.00 (*0-231-08136-7*) Col U Pr.

Litherland, Caren, tr. see Paganini, Maria.

Litherland, Donna. Learning & Remembering from Text: Buttonhole Your Buddy. (Illus.). 14p. 1983. pap. text ed. 1.50 (*0-9607888-1-6*) Barney Pr.

— Reading for Executives. (Illus.). 100p. (Orig.). (C). 1982. pap. text ed. 12.50 (*0-9607888-0-8*) Barney Pr.

— Speed Reading for Progressive Adults. (Illus.). 128p. (Orig.). 1993. pap. 14.95 (*1-56474-075-7*) Fithian Pr.

— Speed Reading for Progressive Adults. rev. ed. (Illus.). 128p. (Orig.). (C). 1993. lib. bdg. write for info. (*1-56474-657-7*) Fithian Pr.

Litherland, Janet. Absolutely Unforgettable Parties: Great Ideas for Party People. Zapel, Arthur, ed. LC 89-13519. (Illus.). 192p. (Orig.). 1990. pap. 9.95 (*0-916260-63-1*, B135) Meriwether Pub.

— Clown Ministry Handbook. 4th ed. Meyer, Sheila & Zapel, Arthur L., eds. LC 82-61091. (Illus.). 160p. (Orig.). 1982. pap. text ed. 9.95 (*0-916260-20-8*, B-163) Meriwether Pub.

— The Complete Banner Handbook: A Creative Guide for Banner Design & Construction. Gallardo, Michelle Z., ed. & illus. by. LC 87-71778. 122p. (Orig.). 1987. pap. 12.95 (*0-916260-48-8*, B-172) Meriwether Pub.

— Everything New & Who's Who in Clown Ministry: With 75 Skits for Special Days. Zapel, Arthur L. & Wray, Rhonda, eds. LC 93-14652. (Illus.). 288p. (Orig.). 1993. pap. 10.95 (*0-916260-99-2*, B126) Meriwether Pub.

— Getting Started in Drama Ministry: A Complete Guide to Christian Drama. Zapel, Arthur L., ed. LC 88-42538. (Illus.). 144p. (Orig.). 1988. pap. text ed. 9.95 (*0-916260-50-X*, B-154) Meriwether Pub.

— Storytelling from the Bible: Make Scripture Live for All Ages Through the Art of Storytelling. Zapel, Arthur L. & Wray, Rhonda, eds. LC 91-29871. 176p. (Orig.). 1991. pap. 9.95 (*0-916260-80-1*, B145) Meriwether Pub.

Lithgow, Scott. Training & Working Dogs: For Quiet Confident Control of Stock. 2nd ed. (Orig.). 1991. pap. 16.95 (*0-7022-2394-8*, Pub. by Univ Queensland Pr AT) Intl Spec Bk.

Lithman, Yngve G., jt. ed. see Gerholm, Tomas.

Lithmond, Greta T. Child Welfare & Foster Home Care: Index of Modern Information. LC 88-47999. 150p. 1990. 39.50 (*1-55914-078-X*); pap. 34.50 (*1-55914-079-8*) ABBE Pubs Assn.

— Psychiatric Nursing: International Subject Analysis with Reference Bibliography. LC 85-48185. 150p. 1987. 37.50 (*0-88164-482-X*); pap. 34.50 (*0-88164-483-8*) ABBE Pubs Assn.

Lithogow, William. A Most Delectable & True Discourse of a Peregrination in Europe, Asia, Etc. LC 70-171774. (English Experience Ser.: No. 399). 152p. 1971. reprint ed. 21.00 (*90-221-0399-4*) Walter J Johnson.

***Lithographic Technical Foundation Staff.** How To Run an Offset Press. (Illus.). 300p. 1994. reprint ed. 29.95 (*1-57002-033-7*); reprint ed. pap. 19.95 (*1-57002-008-6*) Univ Publng Hse.

Lithuanian Educational Council of the USA Staff. Lithuanian: Easy Way. 292p. 1992. 22.95 (*0-88432-531-8*); audio 135.00 (*0-88432-448-6*, AFLT10) Audio-Forum.

Lithuanian Philatelic Societies of New York & Toronto Staff. Postage Stamps of Lithuania. 237p. 1979. 18.00 (*0-912574-33-X*) Collectors.

Lithwick, Dahlia, ed. I Will Sing Life: Voices from the Hole in the Wall Gang Camp. (Illus.). 288p. (J). 1992. 22.95 (*0-316-09273-8*) Little.

Lithwick, Harvey, jt. ed. see Gradus, Yehuda.

Litiche, John M., ed. International Economic Policies & Their Theoretical Foundations: A Sourcebook. 2nd ed. (Economic Theory, Econometrics & Mathematical Economics Ser.). (Illus.). 988p. 1992. pap. text ed. 69.95 (*0-12-444281-1*) Acad Pr.

Litigation Section Staff. Proposed Amendments to the Federal Rules of Evidence. 155p. 1985. 25.00 (*0-685-14430-5*, 531-0047) Amer Bar Assn.

***Litka, Michael P. & Blodgett, Mark S.** International Dimensions of the Legal Environment of Business. 3rd ed. LC 94-11693. 1995. pap. 20.95 (*0-538-84492-2*) S-W Pub.

Litkei, Andrea F. Crossings. (Illus.). 60p. 1990. reprint ed. 9.95 (*1-880165-01-5*) Hanlit Pubns.

— ESP (Extrasensory Perception) 144p. 1967. pap. 6.95 (*1-880165-04-X*) Hanlit Pubns.

— Horn of the Unicorn. (Illus.). 121p. 1985. 9.95 (*1-880165-02-3*) Hanlit Pubns.

— Plums from a Tree. (Illus.). 102p. 1978. 9.95 (*1-880165-03-1*) Hanlit Pubns.

— Psychological Territories. 176p. 1992. 14.95 (*1-880165-00-7*) Hanlit Pubns.

— Thalassa. (Illus.). 61p. 1967. pap. 6.95 (*1-880165-05-8*) Hanlit Pubns.

***Litkowski, Mary P.** Father Damien, Loving Neighbor. LC 94-77541. 64p. (Orig.). 1994. pap. 5.95 (*0-916927-20-2*) Growth Unltd.

— A Friend to All - St. John Nepomucene Neumann C. SS. R. LC 87-80716. 64p. 1987. pap. 5.95 (*0-916927-07-5*) Growth Unltd.

— Kateri Tekakwitha: Joyful Lover. LC 89-84104. (Illus.). 64p. 1989. pap. 5.95 (*0-916927-10-5*) Growth Unltd.

Litman, Robert. Wynnefield & Limer. 237p. 1983. pap. 4.95 (*0-918921-00-7*) Ivy League Pr.

Litman, Robert B. Allergy Shots. LC 92-70081. 254p. (Orig.). 1993. pap. text ed. 9.95 (*0-918921-04-X*) Ivy League Pr.

— The Treblinka Virus. LC 90-82034. 289p. 1991. pap. 8.95 (*0-918921-02-3*) Ivy League Pr.

Litman, Robert E., ed. Psychoanalysis in the Americas. LC 66-24394. 328p. 1966. text ed. 40.00 (*0-8236-5200-9*) Intl Univs Pr.

Litman, Theodor J. Health Politics & Policy. 2nd ed. 1991. text ed. 45.95 (*0-8273-4555-0*) Delmar.

Litman, Theodor J. & Robins, Leonard S. Health Politics & Policy. LC 83-26042. (Health Services Ser.: No. 1-456). 403p. (C). 1984. text ed. 45.95 (*0-8273-4289-6*) Delmar.

***Litman, Todd.** Efficient Electric Motor Systems Handbook. LC 94-43747. 1995. write for info. (*0-88173-197-8*) Fairmont Pr.

Litman, Todd & Kort, Suzanne. The Best Bike Rides in the Pacific Northwest: British Columbia, Idaho, Oregon, & Washington. LC 91-39354. (Best Bike Rides Ser.). (Illus.). 288p. (Orig.). 1995. pap. 12.95 (*1-56440-014-X*) Globe Pequot.

— Washington: Off the Beaten Path. LC 92-42524. (Voyager Book Ser.). (Illus.). 160p. (Orig.). 1993. pap. 9.95 (*1-56440-140-5*) Globe Pequot.

Lito, Mario, jt. auth. see Bode, Willi.

Litoff, Judy B. The American Midwife Debate: A Sourcebook on Its Modern Origins. LC 85-17694. (Contributions in Medical Studies: No. 18). (Illus.). 251p. 1986. text ed. 55.00 (*0-313-24191-0*, LMD/, Greenwood Pr) Greenwood.

— American Midwives: Eighteen Sixty to Present. LC 77-83893. (Contributions in Medical History Ser.: No. 1). 197p. 1978. text ed. 38.50 (*0-8371-9824-0*, LAM/) Greenwood.

***Litoff, Judy B. & McDonnell, Judith, eds.** European Immigrant Women in the United States: A Biographical Dictionary. LC 94-29001. (Biographical Dictionaries of Minority Women Ser.: Vol. 3). (Illus.). 384p. 1994. 55.00 (*0-8240-5306-0*, SS651) Garland.

***Litoff, Judy B. & Smith, David C., eds.** Since You Want Away: World War II Letters from American Women on the Home Front. (Illus.). 310p. 1995. pap. 15.95 (*0-7006-0714-5*) U Pr of KS.

— Since You Went Away: World War II Letters from American Women on the Home Front. (Illus.). 312p. 1991. 27.50 (*0-19-506795-9*) OUP.

— We're in This War Too: World War II Letters from American Women in Uniform. LC 93-36523. (Illus.). 288p. 1994. 25.00 (*0-19-507504-8*) OUP.

Litoff, Judy B., ed. see Somerville, Mrs. Keith.

Litoff, Judy B., et al. Miss You: The World War II Letters of Barbara Woodall Taylor & Charles E. Taylor. LC 89-4874. (Illus.). 376p. 1990. 29.95 (*0-8203-1145-6*) U of Ga Pr.

Litovchenko, V. G., jt. auth. see Dobrovolsky, V. N.

Litovsky, Haydee. Sephardic Playwrights of the Seventeenth & Eighteenth Centuries in Amsterdam. 184p. (Orig.). (C). 1990. lib. bdg. 41.00 (*0-8191-7843-8*) U Pr of Amer.

Litowinsky, Olga. Writing & Publishing Books for Children in the 1990s: The Inside Story, from the Editor's Desk. 144p. (Orig.). 1992. 17.95 (*0-8027-8130-6*); pap. 11.95 (*0-8027-7375-3*) Walker & Co.

Litowitz, Bonnie E. & Epstein, Phillip S., eds. Semiotic Perspectives on Clinical Theory & Practice: Medicine, Neuropsychiatry & Psychoanalysis. (Approaches to Semiotics Ser.: No. 98). (Illus.). xii, 206p. (C). 1991. lib. bdg. 84.30 (*3-11-012632-X*, 140-91) Mouton.

Litrides, Carol, jt. auth. see Axler, Bruce H.

***Litrides, Carol A. & Axler, Bruce H.** Restaurant Service: Beyond the Basics. 1994. text ed. 34.95 (*0-471-51476-4*) Wiley.

Litschauer, R. Vocabularium Polyglottum Vitae Silvarum. 126p. (ENG, FRE, GER, LAT, RUM & SPA.). 1955. 55.00 (*0-8288-6869-7*, M-7679) Fr & Eur.

Litschel, David R., jt. auth. see Rand, Glenn M.

Litschgi, M., ed. Genitalendometriose. (Illus.). viii, 112p. 1985. 47.25 (*3-8055-3984-3*) S Karger.

Litsey, Sarah. Reading the Sky. LC 89-84745. 80p. 1989. 9.00 (*0-8233-0458-2*) Golden Quill.

— The Silver Darlings. LC 93-80690. 64p. 1994. 10.00 (*0-8233-0490-6*) Golden Quill.

Litt, jt. auth. see Vaughan.

Litt, D., jt. auth. see Arya, Usharbudh.

Litt, D., jt. auth. see Harris, Errol E.

Litt, D., jt. tr. see Thomas, Edward J.

Litt, Iris F., intro. Evaluation of the Adolescent Patient. LC 90-81222. (Illus.). 211p. (Orig.). 1990. pap. text ed. 26.00 (*0-932883-98-2*) Hanley & Belfus.

Litt, Jerome Z. & Pawlak, Walter A., Jr. Drug Eruption Reference Manual. 400p. 1992. ring bd. 100.00 (*0-9634973-0-8*); 100.00 (*0-9634973-1-6*) Wal-Zac Ent.

— Drug Eruption Reference Manual. 470p. 1993. Australian Version. write for info. (*0-9634973-2-4*); U.S.A. Version. write for info. (*0-9634973-3-2*) Wal-Zac Ent.

Litt, M. A., jt. auth. see Dobbie, A. M.

Litt, Paul. The Muses, the Masses, & the Massey Commission. (Illus.). 336p. (Orig.). 1992. 50.00 (*0-8020-5003-4*); pap. 19.95 (*0-8020-6932-0*) U of Toronto Pr.

***Litta, Pompeo.** Celebrated Families of Italy: The Vitelli Family. Vitelli, Tom, ed. & tr. by. LC 95-60157. (Illus.). 120p. 1995. 50.00 (*1-883696-03-8*) EveryWare Bks.

Littauer. Chariots & Related Equipment from the Tomb of Tutankhamun. (Tutankhamuns Tomb Ser.: Vol. 8). 1986. 110.00 (*0-900416-39-4*, Pub. by Aris & Phillips UK) David Brown.

— Silver Boxes: The Gift of Encouragement. 1994. (*0-8499-5073-2*) Word Inc.

Littauer, F. Atrevete a Sonar (Dare to Dream) (SPA.). Date not set. 7.99 (*1-56063-143-0*, 498516) Editorial Unilit.

Littauer, Florence. After Every Wedding Comes a Marriage. LC 81-80023. 208p. (Orig.). 1981. pap. 7.99 (*0-89081-289-6*) Harvest Hse.

— Blow Away the Black Clouds. LC 79-50380. 1986. pap. 7.99 (*0-89081-285-3*) Harvest Hse.

— Blow Away the Black Clouds: A Woman's Answer to Depression. large type ed. 1988. pap. 14.95 (*0-8027-2606-2*) Walker & Co.

— Dare to Dream. 1991. 15.99 (*0-8499-0736-5*) Word Inc.

— Dare to Dream. 1993. pap. 5.99 (*0-8499-3501-6*) Word Inc.

— Enriquezca Su Personalidad (Personality Plus) (SPA.). 1993. 5.99 (*1-56063-317-4*, 498498) Editorial Unilit.

— Hope for Hurting Women. 255p. 1985. pap. write for info. (*0-8499-3128-2*) Word Inc.

— How to Get Along with Difficult People. LC 83-83371. 1984. pap. 7.99 (*0-89081-429-5*) Harvest Hse.

— It Takes so Little to Be above Average. 192p. 1983. pap. 7.99 (*0-89081-376-0*) Harvest Hse.

— Personality Plus. exp. ed. LC 92-13275. 1992. 8.99 (*0-8007-5445-X*); disk 24.99 (*0-8007-7097-8*) Revell.

— Put Power in Your Personality: Match Your Potential with America's Leaders. 288p. 1995. reprint ed. pap. 9.99 (*0-8007-5563-4*) Revell.

— Raising the Curtain on Raising Children. 305p. 1988. pap. 9.95 (*0-8499-3139-8*) Word Inc.

— Silver Boxes. 154p. 1989. write for info. (*0-8499-0720-9*) Word Inc.

— Wake up, Women! Submission Doesn't Mean Stupidity. LC 93-42471. 1994. pap. 10.99 (*0-8499-3830-9*) Word Pub.

— Your Personality Tree. 237p. 1986. pap. write for info. (*0-8499-3169-X*) Word Inc.

Littauer, Florence & Littauer, Marita. Personality Puzzle: Understanding the People You Work With. LC 92-5608. 224p. 1992. 9.99 (*0-8007-1676-0*) Revell.

Littauer, Fred. Wake up, Men! Headship Doesn't Mean Lordship. LC 93-42446. 1994. pap. 10.99 (*0-8499-3831-7*) Word Pub.

Littauer, Joel. Manual of Motivational Strategies: Text & Transparencies in Composition & Grammar. Ashkenas, Joan, ed. & intro. by. 60p. 1989. ring bd. 45.00 (*0-943327-05-9*) JAG Pubns.

Littauer, Marita, jt. auth. see Larson, Gaylen.

Littauer, Marita, jt. auth. see Littauer, Florence.

Littauer, Mary, tr. see Spruytte, J.

Littauer, Stephan. How-to Buy Stocks the Smart Way. 304p. 1995. pap. 19.95 (*0-7931-1090-4*, 568008-01) Dearborn Finan.

***Littauer, Stephen.** How to Buy Bonds the Smart Way. 240p. (Orig.). 1995. pap. 19.95 (*0-7931-1528-0*, 5680-2201) Dearborn Finan.

— How to Buy Mutual Funds the Smart Way. 216p. (Orig.). 1992. pap. 16.95 (*0-7931-0478-5*, 560873) Dearborn Finan.

Littauer, Stephen L. How to Buy Mutual Funds the Smart Way. LC 89-90240. 224p. (Orig.). 1989. pap. 9.95 (*0-9622593-1-4*, Montebello Pr) You Can Do It.

Littauer, Susan H. How to Start Your Business the Smart Way: 20 Common Mistakes to Avoid. 64p. (Orig.). 1989. pap. 6.95 (*0-9622593-0-6*) You Can Do It.

Littauer, U. Z., et al, eds. Neurotransmitters & Their Receptors: Based on a Workshop Sponsored by the European Molecular Biology Organisation & the Weizmann Institute of Science, Rehovot, February, 1980. LC 80-41130. (Illus.). 576p. reprint ed. pap. 164.20 (*0-685-20722-6*, 2030510) Bks Demand.

Littauer, Vladimer. Russian Hussar: A Story of the Imperial Cavalry, 1911-1920. LC 93-2299. (Illus.). 300p. (C). 1993. 24.95 (*0-942597-53-2*) White Mane Pub.

Littel, Franklin, et al, eds. In Answer . . . The Holocaust: Is the Story True. Foster, Claude R. & Van Sice, Mildred M., trs. 410p. 1989. 24.95 (*0-926193-00-7*); text ed. 24.95 (*0-926193-02-3*); lib. bdg. 24.95 (*0-926193-01-5*) Sylvan PA.

Littel, Franklin H., et al, eds. In Answer... Is the Story True? 409p. 1988. write for info. (*0-318-68671-6*) Sylvan PA.

Littell, David, jt. auth. see Kogler, Alador.

Littell, David A. & Cardamone, Donald C. Retirement Savings Plans: Design, Regulation & Administration of Cash or Deffered Arrangements. Gruszecki, Wilhelm, ed. (Employee Benefits - Human Resources Library). 600p. 1992. text ed. 118.00 (*0-471-57112-1*) Wiley.

Littell, David A., jt. auth. see Castagnera, James O.

Littell, David A., jt. auth. see Tacchino, Kenn B.

Littell, David A., et al. Financial Decision Making at Retirement. LC 94-70832. 300p. (Orig.). (C). 1994. pap. text ed. 26.00 (*0-943590-59-0*) Amer College.

— Financial Decision Making at Retirement. 2nd ed. 350p. (Orig.). (C). 1995. text ed. 28.50 (*0-943590-68-X*) Amer College.

Littell, Elizabeth H. Basic Neuroscience for the Health Professions. LC 88-43482. 300p. 1990. 38.00 (*1-55642-053-6*) SLACK Inc.

Littell, Franklin H. The Crucifixion of the Jews. (Reprints of Scholarly Excellence (ROSE) Ser.: No. 12). 160p. (C). 1986. reprint ed. pap. 10.95 (*0-86554-227-9*, P31) Mercer Univ Pr.

— The German Phoenix: Men & Movements in the Church in Germany. Garber, Zev, ed. (Studies in the Shoah: Vol. 2). 242p. (Orig.). (C). 1992. lib. bdg. 47.50 (*0-8191-8583-3*); pap. text ed. 19.50 (*0-8191-8584-1*) U Pr of Amer.

— Religious Liberties in the Crossfire of Creeds. 169p. (Orig.). 1978. 5.00 (*0-931214-01-7*) Ecumenical Phila.

Littell, Franklin H., ed. A Half Century of Religious Dialogue, 1939-1989: Making the Circles Larger. LC 89-49749. (Toronto Studies in Theology: Vol. 46). 356p. 1990. lib. bdg. 99.95 (*0-88946-926-1*) E Mellen.

Littell, Franklin H. & Locke, Hubert G., eds. The German Church Struggle & the Holocaust. LC 90-34203. 336p. 1990. lib. bdg. 99.95 (*0-7734-9995-4*) E Mellen.

Littell, Franklin H., ed. see International Scholars' Conference Staff.

Littell, Franklin H., ed. see Shur, Irene G. & Foster, Claude R., Jr.

Littell, Franklin H., jt. auth. see Shur, Irene G.

Littell, Franklin H., et al, eds. What Have We Learned? Telling the Story & Teaching the Lessons of the Holocaust. LC 93-24623. (Symposium Ser.: Vol. 30). 400p. 1993. text ed. 99.95 (*0-7734-9336-0*) E Mellen.

Littell, J., et al. Building English Skills: The McDougal, Littell English Program. large type ed. Incl. Green Level, 3 vols. 725p. (J). (gr. 8). 1984. 209.00 (*0-317-02124-9*, J-03150-00); (J). 1984. 103.40 (*0-317-04890-2*) Am Printing Hse.

Littell, John, jt. auth. see Caleel, Richard T.

Littell, John S., ed. see Graydon, Alexander.

Littell, Joseph F. The Man Who Found the Loch Ness Monster: And Other Fables for Grown-ups. LC 91-90212. (Illus.). 128p. 1991. 12.95 (*1-880243-00-8*) New World.

Littell, Marcia S., ed. Holocaust Education: A Resource Book for Teachers & Professional Leaders. LC 85-2919. (Symposium Ser.: Vol. 13). 128p. 1985. lib. bdg. 59.95 (*0-88946-704-8*) E Mellen.

— The Holocaust Forty Years After. LC 89-12980. (Symposium Ser.: Vol. 22). 1989. lib. bdg. 79.95 (*0-88946-714-5*) E Mellen.

— Liturgies on the Holocaust. LC 86-23507. 208p. 1986. lib. bdg. 89.95 (*0-88946-030-2*) E Mellen.

Littell, Marcia S., jt. ed. see Colijn, G. Jan.

Littell, Norman M. My Roosevelt Years. Dembo, Jonathan, ed. LC 87-10523. (Illus.). 436p. 1987. 35.00 (*0-295-96525-8*) U of Wash Pr.

Littell, Philip. Books & Things. LC 71-90653. (Essay Index Reprint Ser.). 1977. 21.95 (*0-8369-1221-7*) Ayer.

Littell, Richard. Endangered & Other Protected Species: Federal Law & Regulation. LC 92-16020. 613p. 1992. 72.00 (*0-87179-747-X*) BNA.

Littell, Richard, ed. Controlled Wildlife, Vol. I: Federal Permit Procedures. 2nd ed. (Orig.). 1993. pap. 40.00 (*0-942924-16-9*) Assn Syst Coll.

Littell, Robert. Read America First. LC 68-16947. (Essay Index Reprint Ser.). 1977. reprint ed. 23.95 (*0-8369-0620-9*) Ayer.

— The Visiting Professor. LC 93-26109. 1994. 21.00 (*0-679-43048-2*) Random.

Litten, Harold. The Joy of Solo Sex. Orig. Title: Solo Sex: Advanced Techniques. (Orig.). 1994. reprint ed. pap. 12.95 (*0-9626531-4-4*) Factor Pr.

— More Joy... Solosexuals Tell Their Stories. 200p. (Orig.). 1995. pap. 14.95 (*0-9626531-8-7*) Factor Pr.

L

Litten, Raye Z. & Allen, John P., eds. Measuring Alcohol Consumption: Psychosocial & Biochemical Methods. LC 92-1536. 256p. 1992. 59.50 (*0-89603-231-0*) Humana.

Litter, Jonathan. There Were These Two Guys. (Orig.). 1988. pap. 3.50 (*0-945926-01-4*) Paradigm RI.

Litteral, Linda L. Boobies, Iguanas, & Other Critters: Nature's Story in the Galapagos. (Biosphere Reserve Ser.). (Illus.). 71p. (J). (gr. 5-9). 1994. 23.00 (*1-883966-01-9*) Am Kestrel Pr.

Litteral, Robert L. Community Partnership in Communications for Ministry. (BGC Monograph Ser.). 139p. (Orig.). 1988. pap. 3.25 (*1-879089-01-7*) B Graham Ctr.

Litteral, Thomas R. Mountain Biking in the High Country of Steamboat Springs, Colorado. 104p. 1993. pap. 10.95 (*1-883966-00-0*) Am Kestrel Pr.

Litterer, Joseph A. Organizations: Structure & Behavior. 3rd ed. LC 80-15645. (Series in Management). 638p. 1986. pap. 37.50 (*0-471-07786-0*) Krieger.

— Organizations: Structure & Behavior, Vol. 1. 2nd ed. LC 77-88314. 510p. 1969. reprint ed. pap. 145.40 (*0-317-28452-5*, 2055160) Bks Demand.

— Organizations: Structure & Behavior, Vol. 2. 2nd ed. LC 77-88314. (Wiley Series in Management & Administration). (Illus.). 4431p. 1969. reprint ed. pap. 122.90 (*0-7837-3421-2*, 2055160) Bks Demand.

Litterer, Joseph A., jt. auth. see Lewicki, Roy J.

Littig, M. D., et al. Littig: Descendants of Peter Littig, Godfrey Rogge & Others. 40p. 1994. reprint ed. pap. 8.00 (*0-8328-4125-0*) Higginson Bk Co.

***Littke, Lael.** The Bridesmaids' Dress Disaster. LC 94-30487. (Bee There Ser.: Bk. 5). viii, 155p. (Orig.). (J). (gr. 3-7). 1994. pap. 4.95 (*0-87579-940-X*, Cinnamon Tree) Deseret Bk.

— Getting Rid of Rhoda. LC 92-25016. (Bee There Ser.: No. 1). 156p. (Orig.). (J). (gr. 3-7). 1992. pap. 4.95 (*0-87579-636-2*) Deseret Bk.

— The Mystery of Ruby's Ghost. LC 92-25015. (Bee There Ser.: No. 2). 166p. (Orig.). (J). (gr. 3-7). 1992. pap. 4.95 (*0-87579-656-7*) Deseret Bk.

— Prom Dress. 176p. (YA). (gr. 6-10). 1989. pap. 3.50 (*0-590-44237-6*) Scholastic Inc.

— Star of the Show. LC 93-27258. (Bee There Ser.). 162p. (Orig.). (J). (gr. 5-9). 1993. pap. 4.95 (*0-87579-785-7*) Deseret Bk.

— There's a Snake at Girls' Camp. LC 94-751. (Bee There Ser.: No. 4). (Orig.). (J). (gr. 3-7). 1994. pap. 4.95 (*0-87579-845-4*) Deseret Bk.

— Watcher. (YA). 1994. pap. 3.50 (*0-590-47088-4*) Scholastic Inc.

Littke, Ralf. Deposition, Diagenesis, & Weathering of Organic Matter-Rich Sediments. LC 93-17490. (Lecture Notes in Earth Sciences Ser.: Vol. 47). (Illus.). ix, 216p. 1993. pap. 61.00 (*0-387-56661-9*) Spr-Verlag.

Little. Color Atlas & Text of Ear Diseases in the Dog. 1994. 99.50 (*0-8151-5445-3*, Yr Bk Med Pubs) Mosby Yr Bk.

— David Braves the Giant. 2.99 (*0-679-87518-2*) Random.

— Diesel Mechanics an Introduction. 1982. 35.95 (*0-534-01054-7*) Delmar.

— Noah Saves the Animals. 2.99 (*0-679-87517-4*) Random.

— Torts: The Civil Law of Reparation for Harm Done by Wrongful Act. 1985. write for info. (*0-8205-0506-4*, 742); Incl. '88 Update. teacher ed write for info. (*0-8205-0507-2*) Bender.

***Little, ed.** La Danse Noble: An Inventory of Dances & Sources. (Illus.). 1993. pap. 85.00 (*0-8450-0092-6*) Broude.

Little & Falace. Dental Management of the Medically Compromised Patient. 3rd ed. (Illus.). 464p. 1988. pap. text ed. 36.95 (*0-8016-2459-2*) Mosby Yr Bk.

— Dental Management of the Medically Compromised Patient. 4th ed. 528p. 1993. pap. 37.95 (*0-8016-6837-9*) Mosby Yr Bk.

***Little & Prengaman.** Making the Transition to Client/Server Systems. Date not set. pap. text ed. 34.95 (*0-471-06095-X*) Wiley.

Little & Weinberg, eds. Electroorganic Synthesis: Festschrift for Manuel M. Baizer. 472p. 1991. 190.00 (*0-8247-8584-3*) Dekker.

Little, jt. ed. see Campbell, Jim.

Little, jt. auth. see Siskin.

Little, A. D., ed. Study on State-of-the-Art of Dioxin from Combustion Sources. 1981. 6.00 (*0-686-34520-7*, H00180) ASME.

Little, A. H. Water Supplies & the Treatment & Disposal of Effluents. 71p. 1975. 60.00 (*0-686-63808-5*) St Mut.

— Water Supplies & the Treatment & Disposal of Effluents. 71p. (C). 1975. pap. text ed. 70.00 (*0-900739-21-5*, Pub. by Textile Institue UK) St Mut.

Little, A. J. Planning Controls & Their Enforcement. 1982. pap. 160.00 (*0-7219-0492-0*, Scientific) St Mut.

Little, A. J., ed. Schofield's Election Law. (C). 1982. ring bd. 650.00 (*0-7219-0344-4*, Scientific) St Mut.

Little, Alan. Decor, Drama, & Design. 1977. 6.50 (*0-89679-007-X*) Moretus Pr.

— Roman Bridal Drama. 1978. 6.50 (*0-89679-009-6*) Moretus Pr.

— Roman Perspective Painting. 1976. 6.50 (*0-686-75219-8*) Moretus Pr.

Little, Alastair & Whittington, Richard. Keep It Simple: A Fresh Look at Classic Cooking. (Illus.). 192p. 1994. 29.95 (*0-87951-547-3*) Overlook Pr.

***Little, Alex G., et al, eds.** Diseases of the Esophagus Vol. 2: Benign Diseases. (Illus.). 448p. 1990. 75.00 (*0-87993-368-2*) Futura Pub.

Little, Amy, jt. ed. see Burger, Dan.

Little, Anastazia & Little, Stuart. Grandparent's Book. 1989. pap. 7.95 (*0-930753-04-6*) Spect Ln Pr.

Little, Andrew G., et al. Essays in Medieval History Presented to Thomas Frederick Tout. 1977. 26.95 (*0-8369-0427-3*) Ayer.

Little, Arthur D., Inc. Staff. DSD Development Program Report. 1990. 15.00 (*0-318-50035-3*) Uniform Code.

— DSD Store Level Study Report. 1990. 15.00 (*0-318-50034-5*) Uniform Code.

— Evaluation of LNG Vapor Control Methods. 150p. 1974. pap. 7.00 (*0-318-12609-5*, M19875) Am Gas Assn.

Little, Arthur W. From Harlem to the Rhine. LC 74-31101. (Studies in Black History & Culture: No. 54). 1974. lib. bdg. 75.00 (*0-8383-2033-3*) M S G Haskell Hse.

Little, Barbara J. Text-Aided Archaeology. 1991. 64.95 (*0-8493-8853-8*, E159) CRC Pr.

Little, Barbara J., jt. ed. see Shackel, Paul A.

Little, Barbara V. Frederick County, Virginia, Militia Records 1755-61. 68p. (Orig.). 1991. pap. text ed. 10.00 (*0-9624041-3-6*) Dominion Market.

— Orange County, Virginia Order Book One, 1734-1739, Pt. 1: 1734-1736. iv, 114p. 1990. pap. 15.00x (*0-8095-8657-6*) Borgo Pr.

— Orange County, Virginia Order Book One, 1734-1739 Pt. O: 1734-1736. iv, 114p. 1990. 37.00x (*0-8095-8187-6*) Borgo Pr.

— Orange County, Virginia, Order Book One 1734-1739, Pt. One: 1734-1736. 114p. (Orig.). 1990. pap. 15.00 (*0-9624041-2-8*) Dominion Market.

— Orange County, Virginia, Tithables, 1734-1782. 281p. (Orig.). 1988. pap. text ed. 18.50 (*0-685-29189-8*) Dominion Market.

Little Bear, Leroy, et al, eds. Pathways to Self Determination: Canadian Indians & the Canadian State. 192p. (Orig.). 1984. pap. 15.95 (*0-8020-6539-2*) U of Toronto Pr.

— Pathways to Self-Determination: Canadian Indians & the Canadian State. LC 84-162255. (Illus.). 223p. reprint ed. pap. 63.60 (*0-8357-4729-8*, 2037645) Bks Demand.

Little, Bentley. The Summoning. 544p. 1993. mass mkt. 4.50 (*0-8217-4221-3*) Zebra.

— University. 416p. (Orig.). 1995. mass mkt., pap. 4.99 (*0-451-18390-8*) NAL-Dutton.

Little, Bertis B., jt. ed. see Gilstrap, Larry C., III.

***Little, Bill L.** Eight Ways to Take an Active Role in Your Health. LC 95-2546. 1995. write for info. (*0-87788-382-3*) Shaw Pubs.

Little, Billie. Recipes for Diabetics. 1991. mass mkt. 5.99 (*0-553-29378-8*) Bantam.

— Recipes For Diabetics. rev. ed. 288p. 1990. pap. 11.00 (*0-399-51643-3*, Perigree Bks) Berkley Pub.

***Little, Brenda.** Herbal Teas. (Home Herbalist Ser.). (Illus.). 64p. 1995. 14.95 (*0-85091-650-X*, Pub. by Lothian Pub AT) Seven Hills Bk.

Little, Brenda J., jt. ed. see Kearns, Jeffrey R.

Little, Brian A., jt. ed. see Tulchinsky, Dan.

Little, Brown & Company Staff, ed. Little, Brown & Company Rights Guide: Including Atlantic Monthly Press Books & New York Graphic Society Books. 1984. write for info. (*0-318-57553-1*) Little.

Little Brown Staff. George Balanchine's the Nutcracker, Vol. 1: A Keepsake Edition. (J). (gr. 4-7). 1993. 8.95 (*0-316-23154-1*) Little.

— Washington Manual of Medical Therapeutics. 28th ed. 1995. pap. 32.95 (*0-316-92433-4*) Little.

Little, Bruce, tr. see Fridenson, Patrick, ed.

Little, Bruce, tr. see Geyer, Dietrich.

Little, Bruce, tr. see Kaelble, Hartmut.

Little, Bruce, tr. see Muller, Rolf-Dieter & Ueberschar, Gerd R.

Little, Bruce, tr. see Ziebura, Gilbert.

Little, Bruce E., ed. Secondary Art Education: An Anthology of Issues. 200p. (C). 1990. pap. text ed. 20.00 (*0-937652-53-9*) Natl Art Ed.

Little, C. Challenge of the Land. 1969. 71.00 (*0-08-006913-4*, Pub. by Pergamon Repr UK) Franklin.

Little, Carl. Edward Hopper's New England. LC 93-17447. (Essential Paintings Ser.). (Illus.). 82p. 1993. 21.95 (*1-56640-315-4*) Pomegranate Calif.

— Three Thousand Dreams Explained. Page, Carolyn, ed. (Illus.). 48p. (Orig.). 1992. pap. 7.95 (*1-879205-27-0*) Nightshade Pr.

Little, Carl, ed. see Farrar, Susan C.

Little, Carl, ed. see Gjelfriend, George E.

Little, Carl, ed. see May, Daryl & Bansemer, Roger.

Little, Carl, ed. see McMahon, James.

Little, Carolyn. The Game Cook. (Illus.). 224p. 1994. 24.95 (*1-85223-776-7*, Pub. by Crowood Pr UK) Trafalgar.

Little, Chad M. Becoming a Computer Artist. 1994. disk, pap. 39.95 (*0-672-30397-3*) Sams.

Little, Charles. Ten Thousand Illustrations from the Bible. 640p. 1991. pap. 24.99 (*0-8010-5606-3*) Baker Bk.

Little, Charles E. Cyclopedia of Classified Dates, with Exhaustive Index. 1992. reprint ed. 87.00 (*1-55888-952-3*) Omnigraphics Inc.

— The Dying of the Trees: The Pandemic in America's Forests. LC 94-46136. 1995. 22.95 (*0-670-84135-8*, Viking) Viking Penguin.

— Green Fields Forever: The Conservation Tillage Revolution in America. LC 87-4157. 192p. (Orig.). 1987. 29.95 (*0-933280-35-1*); pap. 19.95 (*0-933280-34-3*) Island Pr.

— Greenways for America. LC 90-34149. (Creating the North American Landscape Ser.). (Illus.). 288p. 1990. 24.95 (*0-8018-4066-X*) Johns Hopkins.

— Greenways for America. (Creating the Northern Landscape Ser.). (Illus.). 288p. 1994. pap. 18.95 (*0-8018-5140-8*) Johns Hopkins.

— Hope for the Land. LC 91-33963. 288p. 1992. 24.95 (*0-8135-1802-4*) Rutgers U Pr.

Little, Charles E., ed. Louis Bromfield at Malabar: Writings on Farming & Country Life. LC 88-37841. 256p. 1988. 25.95 (*0-8018-3674-3*) Johns Hopkins.

Little, Charles T., jt. auth. see Parker, Elizabeth C.

Little, Christopher. Rockbound Coast: Travels in Maine. 1994. 39.95 (*0-393-03635-9*) Norton.

Little, Colin. The Colonisation of Land: Origins & Adaptations of Terrestrial Animals. LC 83-1787. (Illus.). 480p. 1984. 145.00 (*0-521-25218-0*) Cambridge U Pr.

— The Terrestrial Invasion: An Ecophysiological Approach to the Origins of Land Animals. (Cambridge Studies in Ecology). (Illus.). 320p. (C). 1990. 84.95 (*0-521-33447-0*); pap. 37.95 (*0-521-33669-4*) Cambridge U Pr.

Little, Craig & O'Brian, Mark, eds. Reimaging America: The Arts of Social Change. (Illus.). 384p. 1990. lib. bdg. 49.95 (*0-86571-168-2*); pap. 18.95 (*0-86571-169-0*) New Soc Pubs.

Little, Craig B. Deviance & Control: Theory, Research & Social Policy. LC 88-64161. 419p. 1989. pap. 30.00 (*0-87581-341-0*) Peacock Pubs.

— Deviance & Control: Theory, Research, & Social Policy. 3rd ed. 420p. 1995. pap. text ed. write for info. (*0-87581-395-X*) Peacock Pubs.

Little, Craig B., jt. ed. see Traub, Stuart.

Little Crow. From the Gathering: The Wisdom of Little Crow. Clark, C. F., ed. LC 92-63392. 168p. 1993. 29.95 (*0-9635440-0-4*); pap. 12.95 (*0-9635440-1-2*) One Wrld Pub.

Little, D. Richard. Governing the Soviet Union. 416p. (C). 1989. pap. text ed. 17.56 (*0-582-28484-8*, 71515) Longman.

Little, Daniel. The Scientific Marx. LC 86-1384. 256p. 1986. text ed. 44.95 (*0-8166-1504-7*); pap. text ed. 16.95 (*0-8166-1505-5*) U of Minn Pr.

— Understanding Peasant China: Case Studies in the Philosophy of Social Science. LC 88-37233. 336p. (C). 1989. text ed. 35.00 (*0-300-04399-6*) Yale U Pr.

— Understanding Peasant China: Case Studies in the Philosophy of Social Science. (Illus.). 333p. (C). 1992. reprint ed. pap. text ed. 20.00 (*0-300-05477-7*) Yale U Pr.

— Varieties of Social Explanation: An Introduction to the Philosophy of Social Science. 258p. (C). 1990. pap. text ed. 21.50 (*0-8133-0566-7*) Westview.

Little, Danity. How Women Executives Learn Success: Experiences & Lessons from the Public Sector. LC 93-37027. 208p. 1994. text ed. 49.95 (*0-89930-867-8*, Quorum Bks) Greenwood.

Little, David. American Foreign Policy & Moral Rhetoric: The Example of Vietnam. LC 74-77373. (Special Studies Ser.). 1969. pap. 2.00 (*0-87641-206-1*) Carnegie Ethics & Intl Affairs.

— Religion, Order, & Law: A Study in Pre-Revolutionary England. LC 84-2611. 270p. (C). 1984. pap. text ed. 11.00 (*0-226-48546-3*) U Ch Pr.

— Sri Lanka: The Legacy of Intolerance. LC 94-1061. (Series on Religion, Nationalism, & Intolerance). (Orig.). 1994. pap. text ed. 14.95 (*1-878379-15-1*) US Inst Peace.

— Tabernacle in the Wilderness. LC 89-36832. 1989. pap. 2.50 (*0-87213-520-9*) Loizeaux.

— Tabernacle in the Wilderness, Set. LC 89-36832. 1989. Pkg. of 5. pap. 12.50 (*0-87213-561-6*) Loizeaux.

— Ukraine: The Legacy of Intolerance. LC 91-20695. (Orig.). 1991. pap. 14.95 (*1-878379-12-7*) US Inst Peace.

— Vintage Denim. LC 95-11531. (Illus.). 160p. 1995. 29.95 (*0-87905-664-9*) Gibbs Smith Pub.

Little, David, ed. see French, Allen.

Little, David, jt. ed. see Khare, R. S.

Little, David, et al. Adult Learning in Vocational Education. 137p. (C). 1991. 65.00 (*0-7300-1279-4*, Pub. by Deakin Univ AT) St Mut.

Little, David M., Jr. Classical Anesthesia Files. LC 85-12088. 335p. 1985. 35.00 (*0-9614932-0-8*) Wood Lib-Mus.

***Little, Denise, ed.** Irish Magic. 1995. pap. 12.00 (*0-8217-4882-3*) Kensington MI.

Little, Donald M. Catalytic Reforming. 256p. 1985. 79.95 (*0-87814-281-9*, P4348) PennWell Bks.

Little, Donald P. History & Historiography of the Mamluks. (Collected Studies: No. CS240). (Illus.). 328p. (C). 1986. reprint ed. lib. bdg. 95.00 (*0-86078-188-7*, Pub. by Variorum UK) Ashgate Pub Co.

Little, Donald P., jt. ed. see Hallaq, Wael B.

Little, Dorothy, ed. Cross-Border Practice Compendium. 1991. ring bd. 100.00 (*90-6544-948-5*) Kluwer Law Tax Pubs.

Little, Douglas. Electric Boats: The Handbook of Clean, Quiet Boating. 1994. pap. text ed. 17.95 (*0-07-038104-6*) Intl Marine.

— The Little Known Facts About Hippopotamuses. LC 95-1926. (Illus.). (J). 1995. write for info. (*0-395-73975-6*) Ticknor & Flds Bks Yng Read.

— Malevolent Neutrality: The United States, Great Britain, & the Origins of the Spanish Civil War. LC 84-19930. 288p. (C). 1985. 35.00 (*0-8014-1769-4*) Cornell U Pr.

Little, E., jt. auth. see Cotterill, C. C.

Little, E., ed. see Pushkin, Aleksandr.

Little, E. G., ed. Experimental Mechanics: Technology Transfer Between High Tech Engineering & Biomechanics: Proceedings of the International Conference on Experimental Mechanics, Limerick Ireland, 4-5 September 1992. LC 92-24957. (Clinical Aspects of Biomedicine Ser.: Vol. 3). 1992. write for info. (*0-444-89580-9*) Elsevier.

Little, Edward H., jt. auth. see Foster, Mary N.

Little, Elbert L., Jr. Forest Trees of the United States & Canada, & How to Identify Them. LC 79-52527. (Illus.). 1980. pap. text ed. 3.95 (*0-486-23902-0*) Dover.

Little, Elbert L., Jr., jt. auth. see Audubon Society Staff.

Little, Elbert L., Jr., jt. auth. see Viereck, Leslie A.

Little, Emily. David & the Giant. LC 86-22079. (Step into Reading Bks.). (Illus.). 48p. (J). (ps-1). 1987. lib. bdg. 7.99 (*0-394-98867-1*); pap. 3.50 (*0-394-88867-7*) Random Bks Yng Read.

— The Trojan Horse: How the Greeks Won the War. LC 87-43118. (Step into Reading Bks.). (Illus.). 48p. (Orig.). (J). (gr. 2-4). 1988. pap. 3.99 (*0-394-89674-2*) Random Bks Yng Read.

Little, Fiona. The String Quartet at the Oettingen-Wallerstein Court: Iganaz von Beecks & His Contemporaries. Caldwell, John, ed. (British Music Theses Ser.: Vol. 32). 640p. 1989. reprint ed. 50.00 (*0-8240-2343-9*) Garland.

Little, Frances. Love & Gold in a High Desert Valley. pap. 9.95 (*0-922006-06-7*) Geste Pub.

***Little, Frank A.** Little Notes from the Office: Do's, Don'ts & Basic Observations That's Made a Difference. (Illus.). (Orig.). 1994. pap. 5.99 (*0-9641206-3-1*) E W Franklin.

Little, G. E. Cyclopedia of Classified Dates. 1972. 75.00 (*0-87968-983-8*) Gordon Pr.

— Historical Lights. 1972. 59.95 (*0-8490-0309-1*) Gordon Pr.

Little, G. T. The Descendants of George Little Who Came to Newbury, Mass., in 1640. (Illus.). 638p. 1989. reprint ed. lib. bdg. 90.00 (*0-8328-0773-7*); reprint ed. pap. 80.00 (*0-8328-0774-5*) Higginson Bk Co.

— Little: Genealogy of the Little Family: Descendants of George Little, Who Came to Newbury, Massachusetts, in 1640. (Illus.). 82p. 1993. reprint ed. lib. bdg. 26.50 (*0-8328-3365-7*); reprint ed. pap. 16.50 (*0-8328-3366-5*) Higginson Bk Co.

Little, Gary B. Exploring Apple ProDos: Programming with ProDos 8 & ProDos 16. 384p. 1989. pap. 21.95 (*0-201-15008-5*) Addison-Wesley.

— Inside the Apple IIe. (Illus.). 18.95 (*0-685-09669-6*) P-H.

Little, Gary B. & Swihart, Tina. Programming for System 7. (Illus.). 400p. 1991. pap. 26.95 (*0-201-56770-9*) Addison-Wesley.

Little, Gary B., jt. auth. see Holt, Russell.

Little Gems Publishing Staff. Golf Course Memory Aid. 1991. pap. 4.95 (*0-9613410-1-7*) Little Gems FL.

Little, Geraldine. Hush, You Nightingales! Four Bulgarian Poets. Wilson, Don D., tr. (Illus.). 40p. 1994. pap. 5.00 (*1-880286-19-X*) Singular Speech Pr.

Little, Geraldine C. Contrasts in Keening: Ireland. LC 82-60038. 50p. (Orig.). 1982. pap. 4.00 (*0-943710-00-6*) Silver App Pr.

— More Light, Larger Vision. (Orig.). 1992. pap. 9.00 (*0-944676-38-3*) AHA Bks.

— Out of Darkness. LC 92-32571. 110p. (C). 1993. lib. bdg. 28.50 (*0-8191-8907-3*) U Pr of Amer.

— Star-Mapped. 72p. 1989. 6.00 (*0-943710-02-2*) Silver App Pr.

— A Well-Tuned Harp. LC 87-28838. (Illus.). 72p. (Orig.). 1988. pap. 7.00 (*0-938158-09-0*) Saturday Pr.

— Women: In the Mask & Beyond. (QRL Poetry Book Ser.: Vol. XXX). 20.00 (*0-614-06436-8*); pap. 10.00 (*0-614-06437-6*) Quarterly Rev.

Little, Geraldine C., ed. see Mandel, Charlotte.

Little, Gilbert. Como Vencer la Tension Nerviosa. Orig. Title: Nervous Christians. 128p. 1987. pap. 3.99 (*0-8254-1443-1*) Kregel.

***Little Golden Book Staff.** Cat That Climbed the Christmas Tree Little Golden Book. (J). 1994. pap. 1.59 (*0-307-00150-4*) Western Pub.

***Little Golden Books Staff.** Addition & Subtraction No. 2. (J). Date not set. pap. 3.59 (*0-307-03654-5*) Western Pub.

— Aladdin. (J). Date not set. 1.59 (*0-307-00124-5*, Golden Pr) Western Pub.

— Aladdin - Magic Carpet Ride. (J). Date not set. 1.59 (*0-307-30144-3*, Golden Pr) Western Pub.

— Baby Lambchop. (J). Date not set. 1.39 (*0-307-04016-X*, Golden Pr) Western Pub.

— Bambi. (J). Date not set. pap. 1.59 (*0-307-01061-9*, Golden Pr) Western Pub.

— Barbie Big Splash. (J). Date not set. 1.59 (*0-307-00122-9*, Golden Pr) Western Pub.

— Beauty & the Beast. (J). Date not set. 1.59 (*0-307-00644-1*, Golden Pr) Western Pub.

— Big Bird Brings Spring to Sesame Street. (J). Date not set. pap. 1.59 (*0-307-02019-3*, Golden Pr) Western Pub.

— Cinderella. (J). Date not set. 1.59 (*0-307-01035-X*) Western Pub.

— Dinosaurs. (J). Date not set. 1.39 (*0-307-08571-6*, Golden Pr) Western Pub.

— Disney's Ghostship Little Gold. (J). Date not set. 1.59 (*0-307-00112-1*, Golden Pr) Western Pub.

— Dumbo. (J). Date not set. 1.59 (*0-307-01040-6*, Golden Pr) Western Pub.

— E Wilkins Mother Goose. (J). Date not set. 1.59 (*0-307-00307-8*, Golden Pr) Western Pub.

— Elmo. (J). Date not set. 2.59 (*0-307-08326-8*, Golden Pr) Western Pub.

— First Counting Book. (J). Date not set. 1.59 (*0-307-02067-3*, Golden Pr) Western Pub.

— Flintstones. (J). Date not set. 1.39 (*0-307-08577-5*, Golden Pr) Western Pub.

— Jasmine. (J). Date not set. 1.39 (*0-307-08576-7*, Golden Pr) Western Pub.

— Lady & the Tramp. (J). Date not set. 1.59 (*0-307-00113-X*, Golden Pr) Western Pub.

— Little Golden Picture Dictionary. (J). 1981. 1.59 (*0-307-02055-X*, Golden Pr) Western Pub.

— Little Mermaid. (J). Date not set. pap. 1.95 (*0-307-01747-8*, Golden Pr) Western Pub.

— Little Red Riding Hood. (J). Date not set. 1.59 (*0-307-00134-2*, Golden Pr) Western Pub.

— Mickey Head for the Sky. (J). Date not set. 1.59 (*0-307-01000-7*) Western Pub.

— New Baby. (J). Date not set. 1.59 (*0-307-02051-7*, Golden Pr) Western Pub.

— One Hundred One Dalmatians. (J). Date not set. 1.59 (*0-307-00116-4*, Golden Pr) Western Pub.

An Asterisk (*) at the beginning of an entry indicates that the title is appearing in BIP for the first time.

— Peter Pan. (J). Date not set. 1.59 (*0-307-00104-0*, Golden Pr) Western Pub.
— Pinocchio. (J). Date not set. 1.59 (*0-307-02185-8*, Golden Pr) Western Pub.
— Pinocchio with Sixteen Crayons. (J). Date not set. pap. 1.79 (*0-307-04964-7*, Golden Pr) Western Pub.
— Scarry Busiest Firefighters Ever. (J). Date not set. 1.59 (*0-307-30140-0*, Golden Pr) Western Pub.
— Sesame Street up in the Attic. (J). Date not set. 1.59 (*0-307-01008-2*, Golden Pr) Western Pub.
— Seseme Street Mother Goose Rhymes. (J). Date not set. pap. 1.59 (*0-307-30122-2*, Golden Pr) Western Pub.
— Sleeping Beauty. Date not set. 1.59 (*0-307-02025-8*, Golden Pr) Western Pub.
— Sleepy Book. (J). Date not set. 1.59 (*0-307-03010-5*, Golden Pr) Western Pub.
— Snow White. (J). Date not set. 1.59 (*0-307-01036-8*, Golden Pr) Western Pub.
— Three Bears. (J). 1987. pap. 1.59 (*0-307-02140-8*, Golden Pr) Western Pub.
— Underwater Ad Little Mermaid. (J). Date not set. 1.59 (*0-307-00105-9*, Golden Pr) Western Pub.
— United States Map. (J). 1906. pap. 2.59 (*0-307-04560-9*, Golden Pr) Western Pub.
— Velveteen Rabbit. (J). (ps). Date not set. 1.59 (*0-307-00135-0*, Golden Pr) Western Pub.
— Very Busy Barbie. (J). Date not set. 1.59 (*0-307-30121-4*, Golden Pr) Western Pub.
— Walt Disney's Winnie-the-Pooh & the Pebble Hunt. (J). Date not set. 1.19 (*0-307-68121-1*, Golden Pr) Western Pub.
— Whole Story Lil Mermaid. (J). Date not set. 1.59 (*0-307-00106-7*) Western Pub.
— Winnie the Pooh & Eeyore Be Happy. (J). Date not set. 1.59 (*0-307-00645-X*, Golden Pr) Western Pub.

*Little Golden Books Staff, told to.** Beauty & Beast - Mrs. Potts Story. (J). Date not set. 1.59 (*0-307-30120-6*, Golden Pr) Western Pub.

Little, Gordon, ed. Selected Papers on Fundamentals of Optoelectronics. LC 93-38813. 1993. write for info. (*0-8194-1498-0*); pap. write for info. (*0-8194-1497-2*) SPIE.

Little, Graham. Faces on the Campus: A Psychosocial Study. 1975. pap. 19.95 (*0-522-84084-1*) Intl Spec Bk.

Little, Gregory L. Grand Illusions: The Spectral Reality Underlying Sexual UFO Abductions, Crashed Saucers, Afterlife Experiences, Sacred Ancient Ritual Sites, & Other Enigmas. (Illus.). 271p. (Orig.). 1994. pap. 19.95 (*0-940829-10-X*) Eagle Wing Bks. In GRAND ILLUSIONS, Dr. Greg Little continues to solve & piece together the world's most profound enigmas into a comprehensive & understandable theory. Illustrated with 90 pictures & drawings, GRAND ILLUSIONS takes readers on an adventure through reports of crashed saucers, cattle mutilations, government conspiracy, & mysterious appearances & disappearances providing the solution to these often-sensationalized topics. GRAND ILLUSIONS further shows how glowing objects & apparitions, angelic appearances, UFO abductions, ancient rituals at sacred sites, & the near death experience are a genuine mystery. The book enters the realm of physics & neurochemistry to show how intrusions from the electromagnetic (EM) energy spectrum interact with humanity producing angelic, mystical, & alien experiences. The roots of the EM theory spring from a complex interplay of Jung's concept of archetypes, Biblical reports, Native American Spirituality, & mythic-mystical lore. GRAND ILLUSIONS shows how the energy forms associated with mystical experiences are electromagnetic, adaptable & fluid in assuming their physical appearance, & have an underlying intelligence & purpose. To order: Eagle Wing Books, Inc., P.O. Box 9972, Memphis, TN 38190. ***Publisher Provided Annotation.***

— People of the WEB. Robinson, Kenneth D., ed. (Illus.). 300p. 1989. pap. 19.95 (*0-940829-03-7*) Eagle Wing Bks.

—People of the WEB: What Indian Mounds, Ancient Rituals, & Stone Circles Tell Us about Modern UFO Abductions, Apparitions, & the Near Death. Robinson, Kenneth D., ed. LC 89-85686. (Illus.). 229p. 1990. pap. 19.95 (*0-940829-02-9*) Eagle Wing Bks. PEOPLE OF THE WEB is a provocative & penetrating analysis of the paranormal that has been called a "real-life adventure book" by reviewers. The author, a scientist, private pilot, & part American Indian reports on his investigations of paranormal reports at sacred sites in the Americas, UFO & abduction cases, mystical & altered states, & bizarre manifestations of other-worldly creatures. Illustrated with 94 pictures & figures, PEOPLE OF THE WEB shows how specific rituals, performed at specific ancient sites (where electromagnetic anomalies are present), done at specific times in accordance with stellar & lunar alignments produce a myriad of apparitional & bizarre mental manifestations. The book shows how modern UFO & apparitional phenomena are recent cultural adaptations of a long-occurring phenomenon. To order: Eagle Wing Books, Inc. P.O. Box 9972 Memphis, TN 38190. ***Publisher Provided Annotation.***

Little, Gregory L. & Robinson, Kenneth D. How to Escape Your Prison. (Illus.). 82p. (Orig.). 1989. reprint ed. student ed, pap. 15.00 (*0-940829-01-0*) Eagle Wing Bks.
— Your Inner Enemy. (Illus.). 105p. (Orig.). 1989. pap. 8.95 (*0-940829-00-2*) Eagle Wing Bks.

Little, Greta D., ed. see Montgomery, Michael B.

Little, H. Clay. Agricultural Credit & Finance. 112p. 1988. per., pap. 22.95 (*0-8403-4726-X*) Kendall-Hunt.

Little, H. Ganse. Decision & Responsibility: A Wrinkle in Time. LC 74-24729. (American Academy of Religion. Studies in Religion: No. 8). (Illus.). 82p. reprint ed. pap. 25.00 (*0-7837-5488-4*, 2045253) Bks Demand.

Little, Harry A. Potential Economies in the Reorganization of Local School Attendance Units. LC 72-177900. (Columbia University. Teachers College. Contributions to Education Ser.: No. 628). reprint ed. 22.50 (*0-404-55628-0*) AMS Pr.

***Little, Henry G.** Early Days in Newington, CT, 1833-1836. 122p. 1994. reprint ed. pap. 17.50 (*0-8328-4402-0*) Higginson Bk Co.

Little, I. M., jt. auth. see Joshi, Vijay.

Little, Ian M. Macroeconomic Analysis & the Developing Countries, 1970-1990. LC 93-19069. 1993. pap. 6.95 (*1-55815-257-1*) ICS Pr.

Little, Ian M., jt. auth. see Rayner, Anthony C.

Little, Ian M., et al. Boom, Crisis, & Adjustment: The Macroeconomic Experience of Developing Countries. (World Bank Publication Ser.). 472p. 1994. 42.95 (*0-19-520891-9*, 60891) OUP.
— Boom, Crisis, & Adjustment: The Macroeconomic Experience of Developing Countries. 472p. 1993. 42.95 (*0-685-71263-X*, 60891) World Bank.
— Small Manufacturing Enterprises: A Comparative Study of India & Other Economies. (World Bank Research Publications Ser.). 376p. 1989. reprint ed. pap. 18.95 (*0-19-520779-3*) OUP.

Little, Ida & Walsh, Michael. Beachcruising & Coastal Camping. Wiiensky, Julius M., ed. LC 92-60226. (Illus.). 352p. 1992. pap. 17.95 (*0-918752-15-9*) Wescott Cove.

Little, J. Diaries of George Bird, Victorian Wheelwright, 1862-83. (C). 1980. text ed. 35.00 (*0-685-22180-6*, Pub. by Univ Nottingham UK) St Mut.

Little, J. I. Crofters & Habitants: Settler Society, Economy, & Culture in a Quebec Township, 1848-1881. 1991. 49.95 (*0-7735-0807-4*, Pub. by McGill CN) U of Toronto Pr.
— Nationalism, Capitalism, & Colonization in Nineteenth-Century Quebec: The Upper St. Francis District. 336p. (C). 1989. text ed. 49.95 (*0-7735-0699-3*, Pub. by McGill CN) U of Toronto Pr.

***Little, J. I., ed.** The Child Letters: Public & Private Life in a Canadian Merchant-Politician's Family, 1841-1845. (Illus.). 200p. 1995. 39.95 (*0-7735-1260-8*) U of Toronto Pr.

Little, J. Wesley & Brigham, Arthur J. Emerging Strategies in Early Childhood Education. (Illus.). (C). 1973. 29.50 (*0-8422-5089-1*) Irvington.

Little, Jack. Business Writing for Adults. 137p. 1983. pap. 5.00 (*0-934768-02-1*) Altair Pr.
— Love Songs & Graffiti. 82p. (Orig.). pap. 7.00 (*0-913057-08-8*) L I U Press.
— Love Songs & Graffiti. deluxe limited ed. 82p. (Orig.). 20.00 (*0-913057-07-X*) L I U Press.
— Moon of Isis. LC 76-8728. (J). (gr. 5 up). 1976. pap. 4.00 (*0-934768-00-5*) Altair Pr.
— Thunder Egg. LC 77-94288. (J). (gr. 5 up). 1978. pap. 4.00 (*0-934768-01-3*) Altair Pr.

Little, Jack, ed. see Knepp, Jay.

Little, James A. Jacob Hamblin. LC 72-164615. (Select Bibliographies Reprint Ser.). 1977. reprint ed. 19.95 (*0-8369-5899-3*) Ayer.

Little, James J., jt. auth. see Manis, Vincent C.

Little, James M., jt. auth. see Rothstein, Nancy H.

***Little, Jan.** If It Weren't for the Honor, I Would've Rather Walked. Garee, Betty, ed. 300p. (Orig.). 1995. pap. 14.50 (*0-915708-41-8*) Cheever Pub.

Little, Jane. Plumas Sketches. LC 83-50356. (Illus.). 112p. (Orig.). 1983. 12.95 (*0-9611886-1-8*) Wolf Creek Pr.
— Sneaker Hill. LC 90-23766. (Illus.). 192p. (J). (gr. 3-7). 1991. reprint ed. pap. 3.95 (*0-689-71477-7*, Aladdin Paperbacks) S&S Childrens.
— Spook. LC 90-31296. (Illus.). 128p. (J). (gr. 2-5). 1990. reprint ed. pap. 3.95 (*0-689-71417-3*, Aladdin Paperbacks) S&S Childrens.

Little, Jean. Different Dragons. (Illus.). 144p. (J). (gr. 3-7). 1989. pap. 3.95 (*0-14-031998-0*, Puffin) Puffin Bks.
— From Anna. LC 72-76505. (Illus.). 208p. (J). (gr. 4-6). 1972. lib. bdg. 14.89 (*0-06-023912-3*) HarpC Child Bks.
— From Anna. LC 72-76505. (Trophy Bk.). (Illus.). 208p. (J). (gr. 4-6). 1973. reprint ed. pap. 3.95 (*0-06-440044-1*, Trophy) HarpC Child Bks.
— Hey, World, Here I Am! LC 88-10987. (Illus.). 96p. (J). (gr. 3-7). 1989. lib. bdg. 13.89 (*0-06-024006-7*) HarpC Child Bks.
— Hey World, Here I Am! LC 88-10987. (Trophy Bk.). (Illus.). 96p. (J). (gr. 4 up). 1990. pap. 3.95 (*0-06-440384-X*, Trophy) HarpC Child Bks.
— His Banner Over Me. (Illus.). 224p. (J). (gr. 3-7). 1995. 13.99 (*0-670-85664-9*) Viking Child Bks.
— Jess Was the Brave One. (Illus.). 32p. (J). 1995. pap. 4.99 (*0-14-054309-0*) Puffin Bks.
— Jess Was the Brave One. (Illus.). 32p. (J). (ps-3). 1992. 13.95 (*0-670-83495-5*) Viking Child Bks.
— Kate. LC 20-148419. (Trophy Bk.). 174p. (J). (gr. 5-8). 1973. pap. 3.95 (*0-06-440037-9*, Trophy) HarpC Child Bks.
— Listen for the Singing. LC 90-40250. (Trophy Bk.). 272p. (J). (gr. 4-7). 1991. pap. 3.95 (*0-06-440394-7*, Trophy) HarpC Child Bks.
— Little by Little: A Writer's Childhood. (Illus.). 224p. (J). (gr. 5-9). 1988. pap. 13.95 (*0-670-81649-3*) Viking Child Bks.
— Little by Little: A Writer's Education. (Illus.). 240p. (J). (gr. 5-9). 1991. pap. 3.95 (*0-14-032325-2*, Puffin) Puffin Bks.
— Look Through My Window. LC 71-105470. (Illus.). 270p. (J). (gr. 4-7). 1970. lib. bdg. 14.89 (*0-06-023924-7*) HarpC Child Bks.
— Mama's Going to Buy You a Mockingbird. (Novels Ser.). 208p. (J). (gr. 5-9). 1986. pap. 3.99 (*0-14-031737-6*, Puffin) Puffin Bks.
— Mama's Going to Buy You a Mockingbird. LC 84-20877. 208p. (J). (gr. 4-6). 1985. pap. 13.95 (*0-670-80346-4*) Viking Child Bks.
— Mine for Keeps. 208p. (J). (gr. 3-7). 1995. 13.99 (*0-670-85967-2*) Viking Child Bks.
— One to Grow On. (J). (gr. 4-7). 1991. pap. 3.95 (*0-14-034667-8*, Puffin) Puffin Bks.
— Revenge of the Small Small. (Illus.). 32p. (J). (ps-3). 1993. 14.00 (*0-670-84471-3*) Viking Child Bks.
— Stars Come Out Within. (J). (gr. 4-7). 1991. 15.00 (*0-670-82965-X*) Viking Child Bks.

Little, Jean & De Vries, Maggie. Once upon a Golden Apple. (Illus.). 32p. (J). (ps-3). 1994. pap. 4.99 (*0-14-054164-0*) Puffin Bks.
— Once upon a Golden Apple. (Illus.). 32p. (J). (ps-3). 1991. 12.95 (*0-670-82963-3*) Viking Child Bks.

***Little, Jean & Mckay, Claire.** Bats about Baseball. (Illus.). 32p. (J). (ps-3). 1995. 11.99 (*0-670-85270-8*) Viking Child Bks.

Little, Jeffrey B. Dean Witter: Understanding Wall Street. 1991. 3.25 (*0-8306-5326-0*) TAB Bks.
— Investing & Trading. (Basic Investors Library). (Illus.). 48p. 1988. lib. bdg. 12.95 (*1-55546-627-3*) Chelsea Hse.
— The Principles of Technical Analysis. (Basic Investors Library). (Illus.). 48p. 1988. lib. bdg. 12.95 (*1-55546-626-5*) Chelsea Hse.
— Reading the Financial Pages. (Basic Investors Library). (Illus.). 48p. 1988. lib. bdg. 12.95 (*1-55546-623-0*) Chelsea Hse.
— Understanding a Company. (Basic Investors Library). (Illus.). 48p. 1988. lib. bdg. 12.95 (*1-55546-622-2*) Chelsea Hse.
— Wall Street---How It Works. (Basic Investors Library). (Illus.). 48p. 1988. lib. bdg. 12.95 (*1-55546-621-4*) Chelsea Hse.
— What Is a Share of Stock? (Basic Investors Library). (Illus.). 48p. 1988. lib. bdg. 12.95 (*1-55546-620-6*) Chelsea Hse.

Little, Jeffrey B. & Rhodes, Lucien. Como Entender a Wall Street. 1991. pap. text ed. 10.95 (*0-07-104045-5*) McGraw.
— Growth Stocks. 1977. pap. 2.95 (*0-8306-3005-8*, 30005, Liberty Hse) TAB Bks.
— Investing & Trading. 1977. pap. 2.95 (*0-8306-3008-2*, 30008, Liberty Hse) TAB Bks.
— The Principles of Technical Analysis. 1977. pap. 2.95 (*0-8306-3007-4*, 30007, Liberty Hse) TAB Bks.
— Reading the Financial Pages. 1977. pap. 2.95 (*0-8306-3004-X*, 30004, Liberty Hse) TAB Bks.
— Stock Options. 32p. 1977. pap. 2.95 (*0-89709-009-8*, 30009P) TAB Bks.
— Understanding Wall Street. 1991. pap. text ed. 10.95 (*0-07-038102-X*) McGraw.
— Understanding Wall Street. rev. ed. 240p. 1991. pap. 9.95 (*0-8306-0479-0*, Liberty Hall Pr) TAB Bks.
— Understanding Wall Street. 2nd ed. 240p. 1987. 19.95 (*0-8306-3120-8*, Liberty Hse); pap. 9.95 (*0-8306-3020-1*, 30020, Liberty Hse) TAB Bks.
— Understanding Wall Street. 3rd ed. 1991. text ed. 21.95 (*0-07-038103-8*) McGraw.
— Understanding Wall Street. 3rd rev. ed. 240p. 1991. 21.95 (*0-8306-0482-0*, 3686, Liberty Hall Pr) TAB Bks.
— Understanding Your Company. 1977. pap. 2.95 (*0-8306-3003-1*, 30003, Liberty Hse) TAB Bks.
— Wall Street - How It Works. 1977. pap. 2.95 (*0-8306-3002-3*, 30002, Liberty Hse) TAB Bks.
— What Is a Share of Stock. 1977. pap. 2.95 (*0-8306-3001-5*, 30001, Liberty Hse) TAB Bks.

Little, Jeffrey B. & Samuelson, Paul A. Bonds, Preferred Stocks & the Money Market. (Basic Investors Library). (Illus.). 48p. 1988. lib. bdg. 12.95 (*1-55546-625-7*) Chelsea Hse.
— Growth Stocks. (Basic Investors Library). (Illus.). 48p. 1988. lib. bdg. 12.95 (*1-55546-624-9*) Chelsea Hse.
— Stock Options. (Basic Investors Library). (Illus.). 48p. 1988. lib. bdg. 12.95 (*1-55546-628-1*) Chelsea Hse.

Little, Jess. America, She Ain't What She Used to Be. 1993. 18.95 (*0-533-10409-2*) Vantage.

Little, Jo. Gender, Planning, & the Policy Process. LC 93-49389. (Policy Planning & Critical Theory Ser.). 1994. text ed. 93.00 (*0-08-040481-2*, Pergamon Pr); pap. text ed. 40.00 (*0-08-040480-4*, Pergamon Pr) Elsevier.

Little, Jo, jt. auth. see Cloke, Paul J.

Little, Jo, jt. auth. see Marsden, Terry.

Little, Jocelyn. World's Strangest Animal Facts. LC 93-47248. (Illus.). 96p. (J). 1994. 13.95 (*0-8069-8520-8*) Sterling.
— World's Strangest Animal Facts. (Illus.). 96p. (J). 1995. pap. 4.95 (*0-8069-8521-6*) Sterling.

Little, John. Clinical Neurosurgery, Vol. 34. (Illus.). 718p. 1987. 64.95 (*0-683-02029-3*) Williams & Wilkins.

Little, John B., jt. auth. see Damiano, David B.

Little, John R. Clinical Neurosurgery: Proceedings of the Congress of Neurological Surgeons, Vol. 33. (Illus.). 702p. 1986. write for info. (*0-683-02028-5*) Williams & Wilkins.

Little, John R., ed. Clinical Neurosurgery: Proceedings of the Congress of Neurological Surgeons, Vol. 32. (Illus.). 680p. 1985. 54.00 (*0-683-02027-7*) Williams & Wilkins.

Little, John R. & Awad, Issam A. Reoperative Neurosurgery. (Illus.). 379p. 1992. 135.00 (*0-683-05080-X*) Williams & Wilkins.

Little, Joseph R., jt. auth. see Nguyen, Tim.

Little, Joseph R., et al, eds. Micros for Managers: A Software Guide for School Administrators. rev. ed. LC 84-62050. xxi, 298p. (Orig.). 1984. pap. 25.00 (*0-912337-05-2*) NJ Schl Bds.

Little, Joseph W. Administration of Justice in Drunk Driving Cases. LC 75-11643. (University of Florida Monographs: Social Sciences: No. 53). (Illus.). 238p. reprint ed. pap. 67.90 (*0-7837-4956-2*, 2044622) Bks Demand.

Little, Joseph W., et al. Workers' Compensation, Cases & Materials. (American Casebook Ser.). 520p. (C). 1992. text ed. 40.50 (*0-314-00965-5*) West Pub.

Little, Joyce A. The Significance of Mary for Women. 1989. 0.50 (*0-911988-86-6*) AMI Pr.
— Toward a Thomist Theology. LC 87-34963. (Toronto Studies in Theology: Vol. 34). 576p. 1988. lib. bdg. 119.95 (*0-88946-779-X*) E Mellen.

Little, Judith W. & McLaughlin, Milbrey W., eds. Teacher's Work: Individuals, Colleagues, & Contexts. LC 92-34794. (Series on School Reform). 208p. (C). 1993. text ed. 39.00 (*0-8077-3229-X*); pap. text ed. 17.95 (*0-8077-3228-1*) Tchrs Coll.

Little, Judith W. & Nelson, Linda, eds. A Leader's Guide to Mentor Training. LC 89-80829. viii, 323p. (Orig.). 1990. 20.00 (*0-86552-099-2*); ring bd. 25.00 (*0-317-99603-7*) U of Oreg ERIC.

Little, Judith W., jt. auth. see Siskin, Leslie S.

Little, Judy. Comedy & the Woman Writer: Woolf, Spark, & Feminism. LC 82-19999. xii, 224p. 1983. 25.00x (*0-8032-2859-7*) U of Nebr Pr.
— Keats As a Narrative Poet: A Test of Invention. LC 74-81365. 175p. reprint ed. pap. 49.90 (*0-7837-6015-9*, 2045826) Bks Demand.

Little, Karen. Frank Bridge: A Bio-Bibliography. LC 90-23779. (Bio-Bibliographies in Music Ser.: No. 36). 288p. 1991. text ed. 55.00 (*0-313-26232-2*, LFB/, Greenwood Pr) Greenwood.

Little, Karen E. Monkey Match. (J). (ps-1). 1981. 4.50 (*0-913545-03-1*) Moonlight FL.
— Penguin Partners. (Illus.). (J). (ps-1). 1981. 4.50 (*0-913545-05-8*) Moonlight FL.

Little, Karen E. & Thomas, A. Things That Fly. (Explainers Ser.). (Illus.). 24p. (J). (gr. 2-4). 1987. pap. 4.50 (*0-7460-0104-5*) EDC.
— Wings, Wheels & Water. (Explainers Ser.). (Illus.). 72p. (J). (gr. 2-4). 1988. 12.95 (*0-7460-0106-1*) EDC.

***Little, Karen R.** Notes: An Index to Volumes 1-50. LC 95-6324. 1995. write for info. (*0-914954-50-4*) Music Library Assn.

Little, Keith, jt. ed. see Robertson, Colin.

Little, Kenneth L. The Sociology of Urban Women's Image in African Literature. 174p. 1980. 38.50 (*0-8476-6290-X*) Rowman.
— West African Urbanization: A Study of Voluntary Associations in Social Change. LC 65-14349. 187p. reprint ed. pap. 53.30 (*0-317-20625-7*, 2024579) Bks Demand.

Little, L. P. Imprisoned Preachers & Religious Liberty in Virginia. 1987. reprint ed. 28.00 (*0-317-60755-3*) Church History.

***Little, Larry F.** Studying for Chemistry. LC 94-37734. (C). 1995. text ed. 12.50 (*0-06-500651-8*) HarpCollege.

Little, Lawrence C. Wider Horizons in Christian Adult Education. LC 62-14381. 348p. reprint ed. pap. 99.20 (*0-8357-9763-5*, 2017871) Bks Demand.

Little, Lawson, jt. auth. see Wells, Sharon.

Little League Baseball Inc. Staff. Official Little League Baseball Rules in Pictures. rev. ed. (Illus.). 80p. 1989. pap. 8.95 (*0-399-51531-3*, Perigee Bks) Berkley Pub.

Little, Lessie J. & Greenfield, Eloise. I Can Do It by Myself. LC 77-11554. (Illus.). (J). (gr. k-2). 1978. lib. bdg. 15.89 (*0-690-03851-8*, Crowell Jr Bks) HarpC Child Bks.

Little, Lessie J., jt. auth. see Greenfield, Eloise.

Little, Lester K. Benedictine Maledictions: Liturgical Cursing in Romanesque France. (Illus.). 312p. 1993. 32.50 (*0-8014-2876-9*) Cornell U Pr.
— Liberty, Charity, Fraternity: Lay Religious Confraternities at Bergamo in the Age of the Commune. LC 89-154929. (Studies in History: Vol. 51). (Illus.). 228p. 1989. pap. 25.00 (*0-87391-040-0*) Smith Coll.

— Religious Poverty & the Profit Economy in Medieval Europe. LC 78-58630. 268p. 1983. pap. 14.95 (0-8014-9247-5) Cornell U Pr.

Little, Linda & Greenberg, Ingrid. Problem Solving: Critical Thinking & Communication Skills. 128p. 1991. pap. text ed. 13.95 (0-8013-0603-5, 78533) Longman.

Little, M., et al, eds. Becoming a Family Physician. (Illus.). 288p. 1989. 54.00 (0-387-96949-7, 2588) Spr-Verlag.

Little, Manon. Essays on Robert Browning. LC 73-21773. (Studies in Browning: No. 4). 1974. lib. bdg. 75.00 (0-8383-1819-3) M S G Haskell Hse.

Little, Margaret I. Psychotic Anxieties & Containment: A Personal Record of an Analysis with Winnicott. LC 90-712. 132p. 1990. 20.00x (0-87668-785-0) Aronson.

— Transference Neurosis & Transference Psychosis. LC 80-66925. 352p. 1993. pap. 30.00 (1-56821-074-4) Aronson.

Little, Marie, jt. auth. see Little, Paul.

Little, Marilyn. Family Breakup. LC 82-48068. (Jossey-Bass Social & Behavioral Science Ser.). 251p. reprint ed. pap. 71.60 (0-8357-4904-5, 2037834) Bks Demand.

Little, Marjorie. Diabetes. (Medical Disorders & Their Treatment Ser.). (Illus.). 112p. (YA). (gr. 6-12). 1991. 18.95 (0-7910-0061-3) Chelsea Hse.

— The Endocrine System. (Healthy Body Ser.). (Illus.). 112p. (YA). (gr. 6-12). 1990. 18.95 (0-7910-0016-8) Chelsea Hse.

— Sexually Transmitted Diseases. (Medical Disorders & Their Treatment Ser.). (Illus.). 112p. (YA). (gr. 6-12). 1991. 18.95 (0-7910-0080-X) Chelsea Hse.

Little, Mark, ed. New French Thought: Political Philosophy. LC 94-8848. (New French Thought Ser.). 1994. 45.00 (0-691-03434-6); pap. 14.95 (0-691-00105-7) Princeton U Pr.

Little, Mary A. & Karlson, Kevin W. Loving Your Children Better: Matching Parenting Strategies to the Age & Stage of Your Child. LC 90-72034. 196p. 1991. pap. 9.95 (0-933701-53-5) Westport Pubs.

Little, Mary E. Julian's Cat: An Imaginary History of a Cat of Destiny. LC 88-31750. 96p. 1993. reprint ed. pap. 8.95 (0-8192-1609-7) Morehouse Pub.

— Old Cat & the Kitten. LC 93-30376. 128p. (J). (gr. 3-7). 1994. reprint ed. pap. 3.95 (0-689-71800-4, Aladdin Paperbacks) S&S Childrens.

Little, Meredith & Jenne, Natalie. Dance & the Music of J. S. Bach. LC 90-42362. (Music: Scholarship & Performance Ser.). (Illus.). 270p. 1991. 39.95 (0-253-33514-0) Ind U Pr.

Little, Meredith, jt. auth. see Foster, Steven.

***Little, Michael.** A Life Without Problems? The Achievements of a Therapeutic Community. 235p. 1995. boxed, pap. 59.95 (1-85742-317-8, Pub. by Arena UK); pap. write for info. (1-85742-316-X, Pub. by Arena UK) Ashgate Pub Co.

— Young Men in Prison: The Criminal Identity Explored Through the Rules of Behaviour. 174p. 1990. pap. text ed. 19.95 (1-85521-093-2, Pub. by Dartmth Pub UK) Ashgate Pub Co.

Little, Michael A. & Haas, Jere D., eds. Human Population Biology: A Transdisciplinary Science. (Research Monographs on Human Population Biology). (Illus.). 352p. 1989. 59.95 (0-19-505016-9) OUP.

Little, Michael R. A War of Information: The Conflict Between Public & Private U. S. Foreign Policy on El Salvador, 1979-1992. (Illus.). 210p. (C). 1993. lib. bdg. 36.50 (0-8191-9311-9) U Pr of Amer.

Little, Mickey. Camper's Guide to Colorado Parks, Lakes, and Forests. 160p. 1990. pap. 14.95 (0-87201-124-0) Gulf Pub.

— Camper's Guide to Florida Parks, Trails, Rivers, & Beaches: Where to Go & How to Get There. 2nd ed. LC 94-11410. 160p. 1994. pap. 15.95 (0-88415-180-8) Gulf Pub.

— Camper's Guide to Indiana & Ohio Parks, Lakes, & Forests: Where to Go & to Get There. LC 92-31304. 160p. 1993. 15.95 (0-87201-223-9) Gulf Pub.

— Camper's Guide to Michigan Parks, Lakes, & Forests. 162p. 1992. pap. 15.95 (0-87201-207-7) Gulf Pub.

— Camper's Guide to Minnesota: Parks, Lakes, Forests, & Trails. (Illus.). 160p. 1989. pap. 12.95 (0-87201-472-X) Gulf Pub.

— Hiking & Backpacking Trails of Texas. 4th ed. (Illus.). 1995. pap. 15.95 (0-88415-253-7, 5253) Gulf Pub.

Little, Mickey & Morava, Lillian. Camper's Guide to U. S. National Parks: East of the Rockies; Where to Go & How to Get There, Vol. 2. 192p. Date not set. pap. 18. 95 (0-88415-064-X) Gulf Pub.

Little, Mickey, jt. auth. see Morava, Lillian B.

Little, Mildred J. Camper's Guide to Texas Parks, Lakes, & Forests. 3rd ed. 160p. 1990. pap. 14.95 (0-88415-097-6, Lone Star Bks) Gulf Pub.

***Little, Miles.** Humane Medicine. (Illus.). 208p. (C). 1995. 49.95 (0-521-49513-X); pap. 16.95 (0-521-49863-5) Cambridge U Pr.

Little, N., jt. auth. see Henry, G.

***Little, Nanci.** The Grass Widow. 1995. pap. write for info. (1-886231-01-X) Madwoman Pr.

— Thin Fire. LC 93-6312. 1993. pap. 9.95 (0-9630822-4-8) Madwoman Pr.

Little, Nina F. Early Years of the McLean Hospital, Recorded in the Journal of George William Folsom, Apothecary at the Asylum in Charlestown. LC 72-181085. (Countway Library Associates Historical Publication Ser.: No. 1). (Illus.). 176p. 1972. 9.95 (0-686-05704-X) F A Countway.

Little, Nina F., jt. ed. see Smith, Philip C.

Little, Otis. State of Trade in the Northern Colonies Considered. LC 79-141124. (Research Library of Colonial Americana). 1972. reprint ed. 20.95 (0-405-03336-2) Ayer.

***Little, Paul.** Affirming the Will of God. Chen, Y. P., tr. 42p. (CHI.). 1988. pap. 0.75 (1-56582-074-6) Christ Renew Min.

— The Autobiography of a Flea, No. III. (Orig.). 1991. mass mkt. 4.95 (1-878320-94-7) Masquerade.

— Chinese Justice & Other Stories. (Orig.). 1994. pap. text ed. 4.95 (1-56333-153-5) Masquerade.

— Dangerous Lessons. 2nd ed. 176p. 1994. reprint ed. pap. 4.95 (1-878320-32-7) Masquerade.

— The Discipline of Odette. 2nd ed. 1995. pap. text ed. 5.95 (1-56333-334-1) Masquerade.

— How to Give Away Your Faith. rev. ed. LC 88-12809. 192p. 1988. pap. 9.99 (0-8308-1217-2, 1217) InterVarsity.

— Know What You Believe. 192p. 1985. pap. 8.99 (0-89693-045-9, Victor Books) SP Pubns.

— The Lustful Turk. 2nd ed. 1994. pap. text ed. 4.95 (1-56333-163-2) Masquerade.

— The Prisoner. 2nd ed. 1995. pap. text ed. 5.95 (1-56333-330-9) Masquerade.

— Slaves of Cameroon. rev. ed. (Orig.). 1992. mass mkt. 4.95 (1-56333-026-1) Masquerade.

— Tears of the Inquisition. (Orig.). 1993. pap. text ed. 4.95 (1-56333-146-2) Masquerade.

Little, Paul & Little, Marie. Know Why You Believe. 3rd ed. LC 88-12810. 168p. 1988. pap. 8.99 (0-8308-1218-0, 1218) InterVarsity.

Little, Paul E. The Answer to Life. LC 86-72378. Orig. Title: Faith is for People. 96p. 1987. reprint ed. pap. 4.99 (0-89107-429-5) Crossway Bks.

— Como Compartir Su Fe. 144p. 1988. reprint ed. pap. 4.95 (0-311-13025-9) Casa Bautista.

— Know Why You Believe. 160p. 1984. pap. 8.99 (0-89693-080-7, Victor Books) SP Pubns.

Little, Peter D. The Elusive Granary: Herder, Farmer & State in Northern Kenya. (African Studies: No. 73). (Illus.). 212p. (C). 1992. 64.95 (0-521-40552-1) Cambridge U Pr.

Little, Peter D. & Watts, Michael, eds. Living under Contract: Contract Farming & Agrarian Transformation in Sub-Saharan Africa. LC 93-6315. 288p. 1994. 68.50 (0-299-14060-1); pap. 27.50 (0-299-14064-4) U of Wis Pr.

Little, R. E. & Ekvall, J. C., eds. Statistical Analysis of Fatigue Data - STP 744. 151p. 1981. 16.50 (0-8031-0716-1, 04-744000-30) ASTM.

Little, R. E. & Jebe, E. H. Statistical Design of Fatigue Experiments. (Illus.). 280p. 1975. 84.75 (0-85334-587-2, Pub. by Elsevier Applied Sci UK) Elsevier.

Little, R. H., et al. Post-Disposal Safety Assessment of Toxic & Radioactive Waste: Waste Types. (EUR Ser.: No. 14627). 225p. 1993. pap. 35.00 (92-826-5610-1, CD-NA-14627-EN-C, Pub. by Europ Com) UNIPUB.

Little, Reg & Reed, Warren, eds. The Confucian Renaissance. 110p. (C). 1990. text ed. 20.00 (1-86287-007-1, Pub. by Federation Pr AU) W W Gaunt.

Little, Rhodes. Fidelity: Understanding Wall Street. 1991. 2.20 (0-8306-5327-9) TAB Bks.

Little, Richard & Smith, Michael, eds. Perspectives on World Politics. 2nd ed. 448p. 1991. pap. 21.00 (0-415-05624-1, A5502) Routledge.

Little, Richard, jt. auth. see McKinlay, Robert D.

Little, Richard D. Dinosaurs, Dunes, & Drifting Continents: The Geohistory of the Connecticut Valley. 2nd ed. (Illus.). 107p. 1986. pap. 8.50 (0-9616520-0-4) Val Geol Pubns.

— Exploring Franklin County: A Geology Guide. (Illus.). 101p. (Orig.). 1989. pap. 10.95 (0-9616520-1-2) Val Geol Pubns.

Little, Richard L. Metalworking Technology. (Illus.). (C). 1976. text ed. 43.95 (0-07-038097-X) McGraw.

Little, Robert C. Physiology of the Heart & Circulation. 4th ed. 392p. 1988. 26.95 (0-8151-5478-X, Yr Bk Med Pubs) Mosby Yr Bk.

Little, Robert D., jt. auth. see Kim, Choong H.

Little, Robert E. Tables for Estimating Median Fatigue Limits. LC 80-69062. (ASTM Special Technical Publication Ser.: No. 731). 184p. reprint ed. pap. 52.50 (0-8357-5555-X, 2035185) Bks Demand.

Little, Roderick. Statistical Analysis with Missing Data. 1987. text ed. 69.95 (0-471-80254-9) Wiley.

Little, Roger G. The Parlement of Poitiers: War, Government & Politics in France, 1418-1436, No. 42. (Royal Historical Society Ser.). 251p. 1984. 59.00 (0-901050-98-9) Boydell & Brewer.

Little, Ruth. Food for Thought: A Potpourri of Delicious Recipes. LC 89-85755. (Illus.). 224p. 1990. lib. bdg. 15. 95 (0-9624294-4-9) Brack Pubns.

— Language of Flowers. (Illus.). 32p. 6.00 (0-685-26791-1) R Little.

— Old Lamps & New: Restoring & Decorating. LC 64-17394. (Illus.). 15.00 (0-685-22811-8) R Little.

— Painting China for Pleasure & Profit. (Illus.). 290p. 20.00 (0-685-22812-6) R Little.

— La Pintura de la Porcelana por Placery Provecho. Mariotte, F., tr. 1976. 20.00 (0-685-69412-7) R Little.

Little, Sara. To Set One's Heart: Belief & Teaching in the Church. LC 82-49020. 160p. 1986. pap. 10.99 (0-8042-1442-5, John Knox) Westminster John Knox.

Little, Stephen. Realm of the Immortals: Daoism in the Arts of China. LC 87-35473. 76p. 1988. 14.95 (0-910386-92-7) Cleveland Mus Art.

— Visions of the Dharma: Japanese Buddhist Paintings & Prints in the Collection of the Honolulu Academy of Arts. (Illus.). 200p. (Orig.). (C). 1991. pap. 35.00 (0-937426-14-8) Honolu Arts.

Little, Stephen, jt. auth. see Curtis, Julia B.

Little, Stuart. After the Fact. 1975. 15.95 (0-405-06661-9) Ayer.

Little, Stuart, jt. auth. see Little, Anastazia.

Little, T. E., ed. see Pushkin.

Little, T. M. Agricultural Experimentation Design & Analysis: Design & Analysis. Hills, F. J., ed. LC 77-26745. 350p. (C). 1978. Net. pap. text ed. write for info. (0-471-02352-3) Wiley.

Little, T. W., jt. ed. see Ellis, W. A.

Little, Tony. Technique! Target Training for a Fat-Free Body. 240p. 1994. pap. 13.99 (0-446-67072-3) Warner Bks.

Little, W. A., jt. ed. see Kresin, Vladimir Z.

Little, Wallace, ed. see Chennault, Max, et al.

Little, Wallace H. & Goodman, Charles. Tiger Sharks! (Illus.). 246p. 1987. pap. 17.95 (0-916693-08-2) Castle Bks.

***Little, Wayne A.** Shared Expectations: Sustaining Customer Relations. LC 95-12450. (Management Master Ser.: Vol. 17). (Illus.). 50p. 1995. 15.95 (1-56327-096-X) Prod Press.

Little, William. The History of Wannen, a Mountain Hamlet Located among the White Hills of New Hampshire. (Illus.). iii, 592p. 1993. reprint ed. pap. text ed. 35.00 (1-55613-774-5) Heritage Bk.

— History of Warren, a Mountain Hamlet Located among the White Hills of New Hampshire. (Illus.). 594p. 1995. reprint ed. lib. bdg. 59.50 (0-8328-4611-2) Higginson Bk Co.

— The History of Weare, New Hampshire, 1735-1888. (Illus.). 1064p. 1988. reprint ed. lib. bdg. 106.00 (0-8328-0079-1, NH0048) Higginson Bk Co.

Little, William T., tr. Garci Rodriguez de Montalvo: The Labors of the Very Brave Knight Esplandian. (Medieval & Renaissance Texts & Studies: Vol. 92). 650p. 1992. 40.00 (0-86698-106-3) MRTS.

Littlebird, Harold. On Mountains' Breath. (Illus.). 72p. 1982. pap. 6.00 (0-940510-03-0) Tooth of Time.

Littleboy, Bruce. On Interpreting Keynes: A Study in Reconciliation. 304p. 1991. 49.95 (0-415-04475-8, A5025) Routledge.

Littlebury, F. E. & Praeger, D. K. Invisible Combat - C3CM: A Guide for the Tactical Commander. LC 86-28853. (AIP Monograph Ser.: Vol. II). (Illus.). 90p. (Orig.). 1986. pap. text ed. 8.95 (0-916159-11-6) AFCEA Intl Pr.

Littlebury, Isaac, tr. see Herodotus.

Littlechild, George. This Land Is My Land. (Illus.). 32p. (J). (gr. 3-8). 1993. 15.95 (0-89239-119-7) Childrens Book Pr.

Littlechild, Stephen C., ed. Austrian Economics, 3 vols., Set. (Schools of Thought in Economics Ser.: No. 10). (Illus.). 1348p. 1990. text ed. 399.95 (1-85278-120-3, Pub. by E Elgar Pub UK) Ashgate Pub Co.

Littledale, A., tr. see Von Balthasar, Hans U.

Littledale, Freya. Brave Little Tailor. (J). 1990. pap. 2.50 (0-590-42797-0) Scholastic Inc.

— The Elves & the Shoemaker. 32p. (J). 1991. pap. 3.95 (0-590-44855-2, Blue Ribbon Bks) Scholastic Inc.

— The Magic Fish. (Easy to Read Folktales Ser.). (Illus.). 32p. (Orig.). (J). (gr. k-3). 1986. pap. 2.50 (0-590-41100-4) Scholastic Inc.

— Peter & the North Wind. (Illus.). 32p. (J). (gr. k-3). 1989. pap. 2.50 (0-590-40629-9) Scholastic Inc.

— Rip Van Winkle. (Illus.). 40p. (J). 1991. pap. 3.95 (0-590-43113-7) Scholastic Inc.

— Stories of Ghosts, Witches, & Demons. (J). (gr. 4-7). 1992. pap. 2.95 (0-590-45556-7) Scholastic Inc.

Littledale, Freya, adapt. The Legend of Sleepy Hollow. (J). 1992. 3.95 (0-590-45050-6) Scholastic Inc.

Littledale, Harold. Essays on Lord Tennyson's Idylls of the King. 1977. lib. bdg. 59.95 (0-8490-1786-6) Gordon Pr.

Littledale, Richard F. Offices from the Service Books of the Holy Eastern Church. LC 77-133819. 1970. reprint ed. 24.50 (0-404-03996-0) AMS Pr.

LittleDog, Pat. In Search of the Holy Mother of Jobs. LC 91-61487. 128p. 1991. pap. 9.95 (0-938317-15-6) Cinco Puntos.

Littlefair, Alison B. Reading All Types of Writing. (Rethinking Reading Ser.). 128p. 1990. 80.00 (0-335-09278-0, Open Univ Pr); pap. 27.00 (0-335-09277-2, Open Univ Pr) Taylor & Francis.

Littlefield, Alice & Gates, Hill, eds. Marxist Approaches in Economic Anthropology. (Monographs in Economic Anthropology: No. 9). 280p. 1991. 50.00 (0-8191-7926-4); pap. 31.50 (0-8191-7927-2) U Pr of Amer.

Littlefield, Bancroft, Jr. & Kindler, James M. Problems & Cases in Criminal Trial Advocacy: Lawyer's Edition. 231p. 1985. 19.95 (1-55681-070-9, FBPCCTAL) Natl Inst Trial Ad.

Littlefield, Bill. Baseball Days: From the Sandlots to the Show. LC 93-6468. (Illus.). 160p. 1993. 24.95 (0-8212-1955-3) Bulfinch Pr.

— Champions: Their Glory & Beyond. LC 92-31390. (J). 1993. 22.95 (0-316-52805-6) Little.

Littlefield, Carroll D. Birds of Malheur National Wildlife Refuge, Oregon. LC 89-77930. (Illus.). 304p. 1990. text ed. 29.95 (0-87071-360-4); pap. 18.95 (0-87071-361-2) Oreg St U Pr.

Littlefield, Charles W. Man, Minerals, & Masters. (Illus.). 172p. 1980. pap. 9.50 (0-89540-059-6, SB-059) Sun Pub.

Littlefield, Daniel C. Rice & Slaves: Ethnicity & the Slave Trade in Colonial South Carolina. (Blacks in the New World Ser.). 216p. 1991. pap. 11.95 (0-252-06214-0) U of Ill Pr.

Littlefield, Daniel F., Jr. Africans & Creeks: From the Colonial Period to the Civil War. LC 78-75238. (Contributions in Afro-American & African Studies: No. 47). (Illus.). 286p. 1979. text ed. 55.00 (0-313-20703-8, LAF/, Greenwood Pr) Greenwood.

— Africans & Seminoles: From Removal to Emancipation. LC 77-86. (Contributions in Afro-American & African Studies: No. 32). 278p. 1977. text ed. 49.95 (0-8371-9529-2, LAS/, Greenwood Pr) Greenwood.

— Alex Posey: Creek Poet, Journalist, & Humorist. LC 91-14538. (American Indian Lives Ser.). viii, 331p. 1992. 39.95 (0-8032-2899-6) U of Nebr Pr.

— The Cherokee Freedmen: From Emancipation to American Citizenship. LC 78-53659. (Contributions in Afro-American & African Studies: No. 40). 281p. 1978. text ed. 59.95 (0-313-20413-6, LCH/, Greenwood Pr) Greenwood.

— The Chickasaw Freedmen: A People Without a Country. LC 79-6192. (Contributions in Afro-American & African Studies: No. 54). xii, 248p. 1980. text ed. 55.00 (0-313-22313-0, LCF/, Greenwood Pr) Greenwood.

Littlefield, Daniel F., Jr. & Parins, James W. American Indian & Alaska Native Newspapers & Periodicals, 1826-1924. LC 83-1483. (Historical Guides to the World's Periodicals & Newspapers Ser.). xxxv, 482p. 1984. text ed. 105.00 (0-313-23426-4, LNA/01) Greenwood.

— A Biobibliography of Native American Writers 1772-1924: A Supplement. LC 85-2045. (Native American Bibliography Ser.: No. 5). 350p. 1985. 29.50 (0-8108-1802-7) Scarecrow.

Littlefield, Daniel F., Jr. & Parins, James W., eds. American Indian and Alaska Native Newspapers & Periodicals, 1925-1970. LC 83-1483. (Historical Guides to the World's Periodicals & Newspapers Ser.). 577p. 1986. text ed. 105.00 (0-313-23427-2, LNA/02) Greenwood.

— American Indian & Alaska Native Newspapers & Periodicals, 1971-1985. LC 83-1483. (Historical Guides to the World's Periodicals & Newspapers Ser.). 629p. 1986. text ed. 105.00 (0-313-24834-6, LNA/03/) Greenwood.

— Native American Writing in the Southeast: An Anthology, 1875-1935. 232p. 1995. text ed. 40.00 (0-87805-827-3); pap. 16.95 (0-87805-828-1) U Pr of Miss.

Littlefield, Daniel F., Jr., jt. ed. see Parins, James W.

Littlefield, Daniel F., Jr., ed. see Posey, Alexander.

Littlefield, Daniel R., Jr., ed. see Tubbee, Okah.

Littlefield, Frank C. Germany & Yugoslavia, Nineteen Thirty-Three to Nineteen Forty-One: The German Conquest of Yugoslavia. (East European Monographs: No. 244). 176p. 1988. text ed. 30.00 (0-88033-141-0) East Eur Quarterly.

Littlefield, George E. Early Boston Booksellers. 1972. 59.95 (0-8490-0068-8) Gordon Pr.

— Early Schools & Schoolbooks of New England. 1972. 59. 95 (0-8490-0075-0) Gordon Pr.

Littlefield, John W., jt. auth. see Commonwealth Fund Staff.

Littlefield, Kathy M. & Littlefield, Robert S. Let's Debate! (Illus.). 36p. (Orig.). (J). (gr. 3-6). 1989. pap. text ed. 8.95 (1-879340-03-8, K0104) Kidspeak.

— Let's Work Together! (Illus.). 32p. (Orig.). (J). (gr. 3-6). 1991. pap. text ed. 8.95 (1-879340-08-9, K0109) Kidspeak.

— Read to Me! (Illus.). 28p. (Orig.). (J). (gr. 3-6). 1990. pap. text ed. 8.95 (1-879340-04-6, K0105) Kidspeak.

— Speak Up! (Illus.). 32p. (Orig.). (J). (gr. 3-6). 1989. pap. text ed. 8.95 (1-879340-00-3, K0101) Kidspeak.

— Tell Me a Story! (Illus.). 32p. (Orig.). (J). (gr. 3-6). 1989. pap. text ed. 8.95 (1-879340-02-X, K0103) Kidspeak.

— What Did You Say? (Illus.). 32p. (Orig.). (J). (gr. 3-6). 1989. pap. text ed. 8.95 (1-879340-01-1, K0102) Kidspeak.

— What's Your Point? (Illus.). 32p. (Orig.). (J). (gr. 3-6). 1990. pap. text ed. 8.95 (1-879340-05-4, K0106) Kidspeak.

Littlefield, Keith E., jt. ed. see Jones, Richard H.

Littlefield, Kinney & Morgan, Kitty. Dine Orange County: The Orange County Register Guide to Great Eating. (Register Bookshelf Ser.). (Illus.). 128p. (Orig.). 1994. pap. text ed. 1.37 (0-9635868-9-0) OC Register.

Littlefield, Mark G. A Bibliographic Index to Romance Philology, Vols. 1-25. LC 73-76118. 274p. reprint ed. pap. 78.10 (0-8357-7167-9, 2031537) Bks Demand.

Littlefield, Mark G., ed. Biblia Romanceada I.I.8: The Thirteenth-Century Spanish Bible Contained in Escorial MS. I. I. 8. (Dialect Ser.: No. 4). (Illus.). xiv, 334p. 1983. fiche 35.00 (0-942260-34-1) Hispanic Seminary.

— Escorial Bible I.ii.19. (Spanish Ser.: No. 66). (Illus.). xlvi, 484p. 1992. 40.00 (0-685-55405-8) Hispanic Seminary.

Littlefield, Mark G., jt. ed. see Hauptmann, Oliver H.

Littlefield, Neil. Metropolitan Area Problems & Municipal Home Rule. LC 63-62226. (Michigan Legal Publications). vi, 83p. 1985. reprint ed. lib. bdg. 34.00 (0-89941-383-8, 303530) W S Hein.

Littlefield, Robert S. & Ball, Jane A. The Teacher's Guide to Kidspeak. (Illus.). 24p. (C). 1991. pap. text ed. 8.95 (1-879340-09-7, K0110) Kidspeak.

— Tell Me the Way It Was ... (Illus.). 32p. (Orig.). (J). (gr. 3-6). 1990. pap. text ed. 8.95 (1-879340-07-0, K0108) Kidspeak.

— Who Am I? Who Are They? (Illus.). 28p. (Orig.). (J). (gr. 3-6). 1990. pap. text ed. 8.95 (1-879340-06-2, K0107) Kidspeak.

Littlefield, Robert S., jt. auth. see Littlefield, Kathy M.

Littlefield, Susan, jt. auth. see Schinz, Marina.

Littlefield, Thomson, ed. see Robbins, Daniel.

Littlefield, Warren M. DBASE - From the Dot Prompt: An Introduction to Structured Programming Using dBASE IV. LC 93-18937. 591p. (C). 1993. pap. 24.95 (0-7914-1780-8) State U NY Pr.

Littleford, John C. & Lee, Valerie. Faculty Salary Systems in Independent Schools. 1983. pap. 45.00 (0-934338-50-7) NAIS.

An Asterisk (*) at the beginning of an entry indicates that the title is appearing in BIP for the first time.

Littleford, Michael S. & Whitt, James R., eds. Giambattista Vico, Post-Mechanical Thought, & Contemporary Psychology. (American University Studies: Psychology: Ser. VIII, Vol. 11). 321p. (C). 1988. text ed. 40.00 (*0-8204-0589-2*) P Lang Pubs.

Littlegreen, Inc.'s Think Tank Staff. Transfiguration Diet. LC 85-91090. (Illus.). 176p. (Orig.). 1986. pap. 7.95 (*0-936863-04-8*, Littlegreen) Chris Pub UT.

Littlehales, Bates. Birdwatch. (Illus.). 136p. 1990. 34.95 (*0-912347-58-9*) Fulcrum Pub.

***Littlehales, Bates, photos.** The Smithsonian Guides to Natural America: The Atlantic Coast & Blue Ridge-Maryland, Washington, D. C., Virginia, & North Carolina. LC 95-1486. 1995. write for info. (*0-679-76314-7*) Smithsonian Bks.

Littlehales, Henry, ed. English Fragments from Latin Medieval Service-Books. (EETS, ES Ser.: No. 90). 1972. reprint ed. pap. 15.00 (*0-527-00294-1*) Periodicals Srv.

— St. Mary at Hill Church: The Medieval Records of a London City Church A.D. 1420-1559, Set, Pts. 1 & 2. (EETS, OS Ser.: Nos. 125, 128). 1974. reprint ed. Set. 70.00 (*0-527-00121-X*) Periodicals Srv.

Littlehales, Henry, intro. Road from London to Canterbury in the Middle Ages. (Chaucer Society Second Ser.: No. 30). 56p. reprint ed. pap. 5.95 (*0-935005-79-X*) Lincoln-Rembrandt.

Littlehales, Lillian. Pablo Casals. rev. ed. LC 72-97385. 232p. 1970. reprint ed. text ed. 49.50 (*0-8371-3010-7*, LIPC, Greenwood Pr) Greenwood.

Littlejohn, et al. Exploring the Living World. 176p. (C). 1990. spiral bd. 17.25 (*0-8403-5952-7*) Kendall-Hunt.

Littlejohn, Alice C., jt. auth. see Womack, Carol Z.

Littlejohn, Andrew. Company to Company: A New Approach to Business Correspondence in English. (Cambridge Professional English Ser.). (Illus.). 96p. 1988. Tchr's. bk., 96p. teacher ed, pap. 13.95 (*0-521-33809-3*) Cambridge U Pr.

— Company to Company: A New Approach to Business Correspondence in English. (Cambridge Professional English Ser.). (Illus.). 128p. 1988. Student's bk., 128p. student ed, pap. 12.95 (*0-521-33808-5*) Cambridge U Pr.

Littlejohn, Beth, ed. see Russell, Ching Y.

Littlejohn, Bruce. Littlejohn's Half Century at the Bench & Bar (1936-1986) (Illus.). 232p. 1987. 25.00 (*0-318-23731-8*) SC Bar Found.

— Littlejohn's Political Memoirs 1934-1988. 256p. (C). 1990. 19.95 (*0-685-30008-0*) B Littlejohn.

Littlejohn, Bruce & Labatt, Lori, eds. Islands of Hope: Ontario's Parks & Wilderness. (Illus.). 288p. 1992. 35.00 (*1-895565-10-3*) Firefly Bks Ltd.

***Littlejohn, D. & Thorburn, D., eds.** Reviews on Analytical Chemistry: Euroanalysis VIII. 376p. 1994. 159.95 (*0-85186-982-3*, R6982, Pub. by Royal Soc Chem UK) CRC Pr.

Littlejohn, David. Foreign Legions of the Third Reich, Vol. 1. (Illus.). 208p. 1987. 24.95 (*0-912138-17-3*) Bender Pub CA.

— Foreign Legions of the Third Reich, Vol. 2. (Illus.). 288p. 1987. 24.95 (*0-912138-22-X*) Bender Pub CA.

— Foreign Legions of the Third Reich, Vol. 3. (Illus.). 320p. 1994. reprint ed. 35.95 (*0-912138-29-7*) Bender Pub CA.

— Foreign Legions of the Third Reich, Vol. 4. (Illus.). 384p. 1994. reprint ed. 35.95 (*0-912138-36-X*) Bender Pub CA.

— The Hitler Youth. LC 87-73304. (Illus.). 377p. 1987. 35. 00 (*0-934870-21-7*) Johnson Ref Bks.

— The SA 1921-45: Hitler's Stormtroopers. (Men-at-Arms Ser.: No. 220). (Illus.). 48p. 1990. pap. 11.95 (*0-85045-944-3*, 9177, Pub. by Osprey Pubng Ltd UK) Stackpole.

— The Ultimate Art: Essays Around & about Opera. 1992. 25.00 (*0-520-07608-7*) U CA Pr.

— The Ultimate Art: Essays Around & about Opera. (Illus.). 320p. (C). 1994. pap. 15.00 (*0-520-07609-5*) U CA Pr.

Littlejohn, David, jt. auth. see Angolia, John R.

Littlejohn, Duffy. Hopping Freight Trains in America. (Illus.). 372p. (Orig.). 1993. pap. 13.95 (*0-944627-34-X*) Sand River Pr.

Littlejohn, E. G. Texas History Stories. LC 86-62880. (Illus.). 188p. (J). (gr. 3-7). 1986. student ed 6.95 (*0-938349-10-4*) State House Pr.

— Texas History Stories. LC 86-62880. (Illus.). 188p. (J). (gr. 3-7). 1986. reprint ed. pap. 9.95 (*0-938349-07-4*) State House Pr.

Littlejohn, Frances J. The Duodenary System of Astrology. 1967. 11.00 (*0-86690-371-2*, L2241-074) Am Fed Astrologers.

Littlejohn, Gary, jt. ed. see Cox, Terry.

Littlejohn, Gary, jt. auth. see Warwick, Dennis.

Littlejohn, Geoffrey. Rheumatism: A Consumer's Guide. large type ed. (Illus.). 218p. 1992. 21.95 (*1-85695-005-0*, Pub. by ISIS UK) Transaction Pubs.

Littlejohn, M. J. & Ladiges, Pauline Y., eds. Ecological Gradients & Boundaries. 178p. (C). 1981. text ed. 75.00 (*0-909436-04-5*, Pub. by Surrey Beatty & Sons AT) St Mut.

Littlejohn, Pat. South West Climbs: A Selection of Rock Climbs from Cornwall, Devon, Somerset, Dorset & Jersey. (Illus.). 300p. 1992. 34.95 (*0-906371-82-1*, Pub. by H & S UK) Trafalgar.

Littlejohn, Ronnie. Exploring Christian Theology. 542p. (Orig.). 1985. lib. bdg. 70.00 (*0-8191-4459-2*); pap. text ed. 34.00 (*0-8191-4460-6*) U Pr of Amer.

Littlejohn, Ronnie L. Ethics: Studying the Art of Moral Appraisal. LC 92-2481. 190p. (Orig.). (C). 1992. pap. text ed. 17.50 (*0-8191-8918-9*) U Pr of Amer.

Littlejohn, Shannon, ed. see Portenier, Bob.

Littlejohn, Stephen W. Theories of Human Communication. 4th ed. 417p. (C). 1992. text ed. 45.95 (*0-534-16134-0*) Intl Thomson.

— Theories of Human Communication. 5th ed. LC 95-4224. 1996. text ed. 46.95 (*0-534-26052-7*) Intl Thomson.

Littlejohn, Stephen W. & Jabusch, David M. Persuasive Transactions. (C). 1987. text ed. 21.50 (*0-673-15987-6*) HarpCollege.

Littlejohn, Stephen W., jt. auth. see Jabusch, David M.

Littlejohn, Stuart, jt. auth. see Stewart, R. J.

Littlemeyer, Mary H., ed. see Conference on the Optimal Preparation for the Study of Medicine, (1967: University of Chicago).

Littlepage, John D. & Bess, Demaree. In Search of Soviet Gold. LC 75-115558. (Russia Observed, Series I). 1970. reprint ed. 20.95 (*0-405-03044-4*) Ayer.

Littlepage, Loyd. How to Make Your Dreams Come True. (Illus.). 32p. 1981. pap. 5.95 (*0-911336-85-0*) Sci of Mind.

Littler. Family Practice Handbook. 736p. 1990. pap. 23.95 (*0-8151-8944-3*, Yr Bk Med Pubs) Mosby Yr Bk.

Littler, A., jt. auth. see Amery, H.

Littler, Angela. What Can You See. (Illus.). 20p. (J). (ps-1). 1988. write for info. (*0-318-63362-0*) S&S Trade.

Littler, C. R. Technology & the Organisation of Work. 1992. pap. 45.00 (*0-7300-1309-X*, Pub. by Deakin Univ AT) St Mut.

Littler, Craig R., ed. The Experience of Work. LC 84-18318. 304p. 1985. text ed. 29.95 (*0-312-27678-8*) St Martin.

Littler, Craig R., jt. auth. see Fosh, Patricia.

Littler, D. J., ed. Thermal Stresses & Thermal Fatigue. LC 72-182668. (Proceedings of the International Conferences on Basement Tectonics Ser.). 586p. reprint ed. pap. 167.10 (*0-317-41713-4*, 2055831) Bks Demand.

Littler, Dale & Wilson, Dominic, eds. Marketing Reader. (Management Reader Ser.). 300p. 1995. pap. 34.50 (*0-7506-0662-2*) Buttrwrth-Heinemann.

Littler, Diane S., jt. ed. see Littler, Mark M.

Littler, Diane S., et al. Marine Plants of the Caribbean: A Field Guide from Florida to Brazil. LC 88-43157. (Illus.). 272p. (C). 1989. pap. 22.50 (*0-87474-607-8*) Smithsonian.

***Littler, E., et al.** Antiviral Therapy. (Medical Perspectives Ser.). 160p. 1995. pap. 52.50 (*1-85996-070-7*, Pub. by Bios Scientific UK) Coronet Bks.

Littler, J. G., jt. auth. see Hancock, C. J.

Littler, J. G., jt. auth. see Hancock, C.

Littler, John & Thomas, Randall. Design with Energy: The Conservation & Use of Energy in Buildings. (Cambridge Urban & Architectural Studies: 8). (Illus.). 320p. 1984. 89.95 (*0-521-24562-1*); pap. 47.95 (*0-521-28787-1*) Cambridge U Pr.

Littler, June D. The Church of Scientology & L. Ron Hubbard. LC 92-15175. 400p. 60.00 (*0-8240-4345-6*, SS468) Garland.

Littler, Margaret. Alfred Andersch (1914-1980) & the Reception of French Thought in the Federal Republic of Germany. LC 91-26228. (Studies in German Language & Literature: Vol. 8). 404p. 1991. lib. bdg. 109.95 (*0-7734-9679-3*) E Mellen.

Littler, Mark M. & Littler, Diane S., eds. Handbook of Phycological Methods: Ecological Field Methods: Macroalgae. (Illus.). 624p. 1986. 94.95 (*0-521-24915-5*) Cambridge U Pr.

Littler, T. & Cole, G. Physics of the Ear. LC 63-18925. (International Series of Monographs on Physics: Vol. 3). 1965. 156.00 (*0-08-010124-0*, Pub. by Pergamon Repr UK) Franklin.

Littler, W. A. Clinical Ambulatory Monitoring. (Illus.). 174p. 1981. 60.00 (*0-8151-5482-8*, ACT-1, Yr Bk Med Pubs) Mosby Yr Bk.

Littler, William A., et al. Illustrated Case Histories in Cardiovascular Medicine. LC 93-15158. 128p. 1993. pap. 24.95 (*0-8151-5484-4*, Yr Bk Med Pubs) Mosby Yr Bk.

Littles, Lorenzo. The Happiness Handbook. (Illus.). 90p. 1993. pap. text ed. 9.95 (*0-9639222-1-1*) LSL Enterprises.

Littlesugar, Amy. The Spinner's Daughter. (Illus.). 40p. (J). (gr. 1-4). 1994. lib. bdg. 14.95 (*0-945912-22-6*) Pippin Pr.

Littleton, A. C. Structure of Accounting Theory. (Monograph No. 5). 234p. 1953. 12.00 (*0-86539-026-6*) Am Accounting.

Littleton, A. C., jt. auth. see Paton, W. A.

Littleton, Ananias C., et al, eds. Studies in the History of Accounting. LC 77-87275. (Development of Contemporary Accounting Thought Ser.). 1978. reprint ed. lib. bdg. 34.95 (*0-405-10903-2*) Ayer.

Littleton, C. Scott. The New Comparative Mythology: An Anthropological Assessment of the Theories of Georges Dumezil. 3rd ed. (C). 1980. pap. 14.00 (*0-520-04103-8*) U CA Pr.

Littleton, C. Scott & Malcor, Linda A. From Scythia to Camelot: A Radical Reassessment of the Legends of King Arthur, the Knights of the Round Table, & the Holy Grail. LC 94-8776. (Reference Library of the Humanities: Vol. 1795). (Illus.). 440p. 1994. 66.00 (*0-8153-1496-5*, H1795) Garland.

Littleton, Christine & Hembacher, Brian. EEO Update: Sexual Harassment. (Current Issues Ser.: No. 5). 48p. 1987. pap. 7.50 (*0-89215-142-0*) U Cal LA Indus Rel.

Littleton, George & Williams, Randall. Montgomery Quizine: The Definitive Guide to Dining & Drinking in the Capital City. (Illus.). 64p. (Orig.). 1989. pap. 5.95 (*0-9622815-0-6*) Black Belt Pr.

Littleton, J. T. & Durizch, M. L. Chest Atlas: Correlated Thin-Section Anatomy in Five Planes. LC 92-49474. 336p. 1993. 250.00 (*0-387-97928-X*); write for info. (*3-540-97928-X*) Spr-Verlag.

***Littleton, Lucy.** Al Fresco in Athens: The Owl Bay Guide to Georgia Bulldog Tailgating. 1994. pap. 8.95 (*0-9638568-6-3*) Owl Bay Pubs.

— In the Grove at Oxford: The Owl Bay Guide to Ole Miss Tailgating. 1994. pap. 8.95 (*1-885623-05-4*) Owl Bay Pubs.

— Picnics on the Plains: The Owl Bay Guide to Auburn Tiger Tailgating. 1994. pap. 8.95 (*0-9638568-3-9*) Owl Bay Pubs.

— Rocky Top Saturdays: The Owl Bay Guide to Tennessee Volunteer Tailgating. 1994. pap. 8.95 (*0-9638568-7-1*) Owl Bay Pubs.

— South Bend Saturdays: A Recipe Guide to Notre Dame Tailgating. 1995. pap. 8.95 (*1-885623-06-2*) Owl Bay Pubs.

— Sunshine Sensations: The Owl Bay Guide to Florida Gator Tailgating. 1994. pap. 8.95 (*0-9638568-5-5*) Owl Bay Pubs.

— Tailgating at Texas: A Recipe Guide to Texas Longhorn Tailgating. 1995. pap. 8.95 (*1-885623-07-0*) Owl Bay Pubs.

— Tailgating in T-Town: The Owl Bay Guide to Crimson Tide Tailgating. 1994. pap. 8.95 (*0-9638568-4-7*) Owl Bay Pubs.

— Tarheel Tailgating: A Recipe Guide to North Carolina Tailgating. 1995. pap. 8.95 (*1-885623-08-9*) Owl Bay Pubs.

***Littleton, Mark.** Baseball. (Sports Heroes Ser.). 112p. 1995. pap. 5.99 (*0-310-49551-2*) Zondervan.

— The Basics: Nailing down What Builds You Up. (Illus.). 200p. 1994. pap. 7.99 (*0-87509-549-6*) Chr Pubns.

— Basketball. (Sports Heroes Ser.). 112p. 1995. pap. 5.99 (*0-310-49561-X*) Zondervan.

— Danger on Midnight Trail. LC 94-11458. 1994. mass mkt. 3.99 (*1-56507-246-4*) Harvest Hse.

— Death Trip. 1992. pap. 11.99 (*0-8024-1730-2*) Moody.

— Escape of the Grizzly. LC 93-29408. (Crista Chronicles Ser.). (J). 1994. mass mkt. 3.99 (*1-56507-099-2*) Harvest Hse.

— Fillin' Up. 168p. (YA). 1992. 8.99 (*0-945564-72-4*, Gold & Honey) Questar Pubs.

— Football. (Sports Heroes Ser.). 112p. 1995. pap. 5.99 (*0-310-49571-7*) Zondervan.

— Friends No Matter What. LC 94-5306. (Crista Chronicles Ser.: No. 6). (Orig.). (J). (gr. 8-11). 1995. mass mkt. 3.99 (*1-56507-256-1*) Harvest Hse.

— Pairin' Up. 180p. 1994. pap. 8.99 (*0-88070-671-6*, Multnomah Bks) Questar Pubs.

— Robbers on Rock Road. (Crista Chronicles Ser.: Bk. 3). 1993. mass mkt. 3.99 (*1-56507-090-9*) Harvest Hse.

— Secrets of Moonlight Mountain. (J). 1993. mass mkt. 3.99 (*0-89081-960-2*) Harvest Hse.

— Track & Field. (Sports Heroes Ser.). 112p. 1995. pap. 5.99 (*0-310-49581-4*) Zondervan.

— Tree Fort Wars. (J). (gr. 4 up). 1993. pap. 5.99 (*1-55513-764-4*, Chariot Bks) Chariot Family.

— Tunin' Up: Daily Jammin' for Tight Relationships. Heaney, Liz, ed. 208p. (YA). 1992. pap. 8.99 (*0-88070-454-3*, Gold & Honey) Questar Pubs.

— When They Invited Me to Fellowship I Thought They Meant a Cruise. LC 92-81349. 166p. (Orig.). (YA). 1992. pap. 7.99 (*0-87509-496-1*) Chr Pubns.

— Winter Thunder. LC 92-5433. (Crista Chronicles Ser.: Bk. 2). (J). 1993. mass mkt. 3.99 (*1-56507-008-9*) Harvest Hse.

Littleton, Mark, jt. auth. see Minirth, Frank B.

Littleton, Mark L. Battle Ready: Winning the War with Temptation. 2nd ed. 1992. pap. 1.80 (*0-89693-577-9*, Victor Books) SP Pubns.

Littleton, Mark R. Adventure at Rocky Creek. Norton, LoraBeth, ed. LC 92-8047. (Rocky Creek Adventures Ser.). 208p. (J). (gr. 4-6). Date not set. pap. 5.99 (*1-55513-761-X*, Chariot Bks) Chariot Family.

— Beefin' Up: Daily Feed for Amazing Grazing. Heaney, Liz, ed. LC 89-29297. 181p. (Orig.). (YA). (gr. 7-12). 1990. pap. 8.99 (*0-88070-317-2*, Gold & Honey) Questar Pubs.

— Life from the Inside Up: Why Live a Godly Life? LC 90-84820. 1991. pap. 8.99 (*0-89636-266-3*, LifeJourney) Chariot Family.

— The Storm Within. LC 93-30564. 1994. pap. 7.99 (*0-8423-7207-5*) Tyndale.

— Trouble Down the Creek. Norton, LoraBeth, ed. 208p. (J). (gr. 4-6). Date not set. pap. 5.99 (*0-7814-0082-1*, Chariot Bks) Chariot Family.

— When God Seems Far Away. LC 87-4701. 192p. (Orig.). 1987. pap. 7.99 (*0-87788-938-4*) Shaw Pubs.

***Littleton, Michael, intro.** Prize-Winning Irish Radio Stories. 160p. 1995. pap. 13.95 (*1-85635-081-9*) Dufour.

Littleton, Suellen M. The Wapping Dispute: An Examination of the Conflict & Its Impact on the National Newspaper Industry. 237p. 1992. 68.95 (*1-85628-201-5*, Pub. by Avebury Pub UK) Ashgate Pub Co.

***Littleton, Taylor.** Happy Valley Saturdays: The Owl Bay Guide to Penn State Nittany Lions Tailgating. 1994. pap. 8.95 (*1-885623-01-1*) Owl Bay Pubs.

— Picnics in Paradise: The Owl Bay Guide to Miami Hurricanes Tailgating. 1994. pap. 8.95 (*1-885623-03-8*) Owl Bay Pubs.

Littleton, Taylor, ed. The Rights of Memory: Essays on History, Science & American Culture, Vol. V. LC 85-13972. (Franklin Lectures in the Sciences & the Humanities). (Illus.). 240p. 1986. 24.95 (*0-8173-0278-6*) U of Ala Pr.

Littleton, Taylor & Sykes, Maltby. Advancing American Art: Painting, Politics, & Cultural Confrontation at Mid-Century. LC 88-27655. (Illus.). 176p. (C). 1989. pap. 19. 95 (*0-8173-0426-6*) U of Ala Pr.

Littleton, Taylor D., jt. auth. see Bailey, Wilford S.

Littleton, Thomas. Littleton's Tenures in English. Wambaugh, Eugene, ed. (Legal Classics Ser.). lixxxiv, 425p. 1991. reprint ed. 37.50 (*0-8377-0818-4*) Rothman.

Littlewood. Landscape Detailing. 2nd ed. 1986. pap. 37.95 (*0-85139-860-X*, Butterwrth Archit) Buttrwrth-Heinemann.

Littlewood, A. B., ed. see International Symposium on Gas Chromatography Staff.

Littlewood, Audrey, tr. see Catteau, Jacques.

Littlewood, B. & Miller, D., eds. Software Reliability & Safety. 232p. 1991. 90.00 (*1-85166-533-1*) Elsevier.

Littlewood, B., jt. ed. see Fenton, N. E.

Littlewood, B., jt. ed. see Ktichenham, B. A.

Littlewood, Barbara S., jt. auth. see Davies, Julian.

***Littlewood, Ian.** A Literary Companion to Venice. LC 95-5220. 1995. pap. 14.95 (*0-312-13113-5*) St Martin.

— The Writings of Evelyn Waugh. LC 82-18513. 256p. (C). 1983. text ed. 58.50 (*0-389-80350-2*, 07208) B&N Imports.

Littlewood, J. E. Collected Papers of J. E. Littlewood, 2 vols., 1. Cassels, J. W., ed. 1983. 175.00 (*0-19-853353-5*) OUP.

Littlewood, Jane. Aspects of Grief: Bereavement in Adult Life. LC 91-21388. 192p. 1992. 69.50 (*0-415-02816-7*, A6589); pap. 16.95 (*0-415-07176-3*, A6593) Routledge.

Littlewood, Jenny. Anthropology & Nursing. Holden, Pat, ed. 256p. 1991. 74.50 (*0-415-00612-0*, A4905) Routledge.

Littlewood, John. Chess Coaching. (Illus.). 153p. 1991. pap. 19.95 (*1-85223-239-0*, Pub. by Crowood Pr UK) Trafalgar.

Littlewood, Karin, illus. Science Fiction Stories. LC 92-26453. (Story Library). 256p. (J). (gr. 4-9). 1993. 6.95 (*1-85697-889-3*, Kingfisher LKC) LKC.

Littlewood, Michael. Landscape Detailing, 2 vols., 1. 3rd ed. LC 92-34847. 1993. 49.50 (*0-7506-1304-1*, Butterwrth Archit) Buttrwrth-Heinemann.

— Landscape Detailing, 2 vols., 2. 3rd ed. LC 92-34847. 1993. 49.50 (*0-7506-1303-3*, Butterwrth Archit) Buttrwrth-Heinemann.

— Tree Detailing. (Illus.). 193p. 1988. pap. 37.95 (*0-408-50002-6*) Buttrwrth-Heinemann.

Littlewood, Paul. Chess Tactics. (Crowood Chess Library). 136p. 1989. pap. 16.95 (*0-946284-95-4*, Pub. by Crowood Pr UK) Trafalgar.

Littlewood, R., jt. auth. see Kareem, J.

Littlewood, Robert A. Physical Anthropology of the Eastern Highlands of New Guinea. LC 70-117730. (Anthropological Studies in the Eastern Highlands of New Guinea: No. 2). (Illus.). 264p. 1972. 40.00 (*0-295-95133-8*) U of Wash Pr.

Littlewood, Roland. Pathology & Identity: The Work of Mother Earth in Trinidad. LC 92-18251. (Cambridge Studies in Social & Cultural Anthropology: No. 90). (Illus.). 424p. (C). 1993. 74.95 (*0-521-38427-3*) Cambridge U Pr.

Littlewood, Ronald & Lipsedge, Maurice. Aliens & Alienists: Ethnic Minorities & Psychiatry. 2nd ed. 256p. 1989. 40.00 (*0-04-445317-5*); pap. 15.95 (*0-04-445316-7*) Routledge Chapman & Hall.

Littlewood, Thomas B. Coals of Fire: The "Alton Telegraph" Libel Case. LC 87-9844. 247p. 1988. text ed. 24.50 (*0-8093-1401-0*) S Ill U Pr.

Littlewood, Valerie. Scarecrow. (Illus.). 32p. (J). (gr. 2-6). 1992. 15.00 (*0-525-44948-5*, DCB) Dutton Child Bks.

— Scarecrow! 32p. (J). (gr. 2-6). 1995. 4.99 (*0-14-055614-1*, Puff Unicorn) Puffin Bks.

Littlewood, William. Communicative Language Teaching: An Introduction. LC 80-41563. (Cambridge English Language Learning Ser.). (Illus.). 108p. 1981. pap. 14.95 (*0-521-28154-7*) Cambridge U Pr.

***Littleworth, Arthur L. & Garner, Eric L.** California Water. (Orig.). 1995. pap. 47.50 (*0-923956-25-5*) Solano Pr.

Littman, Barbara & Ray, Michael. The Women's Business Resource Guide: A National Directory. 144p. 1994. pap. 21.95 (*1-884565-01-8*, Resource Group) Informat Design.

Littman, Ian D., jt. auth. see Carr, David K.

Littman, M., tr. Approaching Infinity: Selected Mathematical Writings of Rabeynu Shlomo of Chelme (Author of Mirkeves Hamishna) 1989. pap. 12.95 (*0-685-29637-7*) Feldheim.

Littman, Mark. Planets Beyond: Discovering the Outer Solar System. (Science Editions Ser.). 1988. text ed. 22. 95 (*0-471-61128-X*) Wiley.

— Planets Beyond: Discovering the Outer Solar System. (Illus.). 304p. 1990. pap. text ed. 16.95 (*0-471-51053-X*) Wiley.

Littman, Robert J. Kinship & Politics in Athens, 600-400 B. C. LC 90-6046. (Studia Classica: Vol. 2). 286p. (C). 1990. text ed. 60.95 (*0-8204-1159-0*) P Lang Pubs.

Littman, Robert J., jt. auth. see Pasachoff, Naomi.

***Littman, Sol.** Quebec's Jews: Vital Citizens or Eternal Strangers. (Special Reports). (Illus.). 35p. (Orig.). Date not set. pap. write for info. (*0-943058-11-2*) S Wiesenthal Ctr.

***Littman, Sol, ed.** Holocaust Denial: Bigotry in the Guise of Scholarship. (Special Reports). (Illus.). 66p. (Orig.). 1994. pap. 6.95 (*0-943048-19-2*) S Wiesenthal Ctr.

Littman, W., ed. Polymer Flooding. (Developments in Petroleum Science Ser.: No. 24). 222p. 1988. 89.75 (*0-444-43001-6*) Elsevier.

Littman, W., jt. auth. see Friedman, A.

Littman, Walter, ed. Studies in Partial Differential Equations. LC 82-62782. (MAA Studies in Mathematics: No. 23). 280p. 1983. 12.00 (*0-88385-125-3*) Math Assn.

Littmann, Mark & Willcox, Ken. Totality: Eclipses of the Sun. LC 90-23823. (Illus.). 264p. (Orig.). (YA). 1991. pap. 14.95 (*0-8248-1371-5*) UH Pr.

Littmann, Mark & Yeomans, Donald. Comet Halley: Once in a Lifetime. 190p. 1985. 21.95 (*0-8412-0905-7*); pap. 14.95 (*0-8412-0911-1*) Am Chemical.

An Asterisk (*) at the beginning of an entry indicates that the title is appearing in BIP for the first time.

Litto, Fredric M. American Dissertations on the Drama & the Theatre: A Bibliography. LC 71-76761. 529p. reprint ed. pap. 150.80 (*0-8357-5362-X*, 2027306) Bks Demand.

Litton. Win Lose & Drew. 1987. pap. 7.95 (*0-914807-06-4*) Denver Pub Co.

Litton, Brougham. The Fallen Star: History of a False Religion. 129p. 1971. reprint ed. 5.50 (*0-7873-0564-2*) Mokelumne.

Litton, Evie. The Hiker's Guide to Hot Springs in the Pacific Northwest. rev. ed. LC 92-54612. (Falcon Guide Ser.). (Illus.). 312p. (Orig.). 1993. pap. 14.95 (*1-56044-167-4*) Falcon Pr MT.

Litton, Freddie W., jt. auth. see Love, Harold D.

Litton, Gaston, jt. auth. see Dale, Edward E.

Litton, Gerry. Guide to Ami Pro 4.0. (Illus.). (Orig.). 1995. pap. 24.95 (*1-56276-243-5*) Ziff-Davis.

— PC Magazine Guide to Ami Pro. (Guide to...Ser.). 1991. pap. 24.95 (*1-56276-017-3*) Ziff-Davis.

— PC Magazine Guide to Ami Pro 2.0 & 3.0. (Guide to... Ser.). (Illus.). 753p. (Orig.). 1992. pap. 24.95 (*1-56276-090-4*) Ziff-Davis.

— PC Magazine Guide to Professional Write Plus. (Guide to...Ser.). (Illus.). 422p. (Orig.). 1991. pap. 24.95 (*1-56276-027-0*) Ziff-Davis.

— Take Ami Pro 3.0 to the Edge. (Customizing Ser.). (Illus.). 560p. (Orig.). 1993. pap. 29.95 (*1-56276-089-0*) Ziff-Davis.

— Understanding Professional Write. LC 89-63173. 385p. (Orig.). 1989. pap. 24.95 (*0-89588-656-1*) Sybex.

Litton, Glenn, jt. auth. see Smith, Cecil.

Litton, Helen. The Irish Famine: An Illustrated History. (Illus.). 128p. (Orig.). 1994. pap. 11.95 (*0-937702-14-5*) Irish Bks Media.

Litton, Helen, intro. Revolutionary Woman: Kathleen Clarke an Autobiography, 1878-1972. (Illus.). 240p. (Orig.). 1992. pap. 8.95 (*0-86278-294-5*, Pub. by OBrien Pr IE) Dufour.

Litton, Melvin. Geminga: Sword of the Shining Path. 256p. (Orig.). 1993. pap. 9.95 (*0-9622937-4-1*) III Pub.

Litton, Pamela. Brides of the West, No. 3: Scoundrel. 304p. (Orig.). 1994. mass mkt. 4.99 (*0-515-11251-8*) Jove Pubns.

Litton, R. Burton, Jr., et al. Water & Landscape: An Aesthetic Overview of the Role of Water in the Landscape. LC 74-79147. (Illus.). 314p. 1974. pap. text ed. 20.00 (*0-912394-10-2*) Water Info.

Litton, Roger A. Crime & Crime Prevention for Insurance Practice. (Illus.). 198p. 1990. text ed. 63.95 (*0-566-07076-6*, Pub. by Avebury Pub UK) Ashgate Pub Co.

Littre, Paul-Emile. Dictionnaire de la Langue Francaise. 6809p. (FRE.). 1983. lib. bdg. 1,150.00 (*0-7859-4626-8*) Fr & Eur.

Littrell. Cardiovascular & Pulmonary Word Book. (Word Book Ser.). 1991. 17.95 (*0-87434-415-8*) Springhouse Pub.

— Cardiovascular & Pulmonary Word Book. 2nd ed. 1993. 18.95 (*0-87434-519-7*) Springhouse Pub.

— Dental & Otolaryngology Word Book. 1992. 16.95 (*0-87434-476-X*) Springhouse Pub.

— Immunologic & AIDS Word Book. 1992. 14.95 (*0-87434-475-1*) Springhouse Pub.

— Neurologic & Psychiatric Wordbook. 1992. 18.95 (*0-87434-474-3*) Springhouse Pub.

— Obstetric & Gynecologic Word Book. (Word Book Ser.). 1991. 17.95 (*0-87434-416-6*) Springhouse Pub.

Littrell, Harold, tr. The English Study Bible New Testament Translation & Notes. 1994. pap. 14.95 (*1-56794-069-2*) Star Bible.

Littrell, Helen E. The Oncology Word Book. 354p. (C). 1993. pap. text ed. 30.00 (*0-8036-5649-1*) Davis Co.

Littrell, J. Understanding & Treating Alcoholism, 1. 408p. (C). 1991. text ed. 75.00 (*0-8058-0870-1*) L Erlbaum Assocs.

— Understanding & Treating Alcoholism, 2. 296p. (C). 1991. text ed. 49.95 (*0-8058-0871-X*) L Erlbaum Assocs.

— Understanding & Treating Alcoholism, Set, Vols. 1 & 2. (C). 1991. Set. text ed. 99.95 (*0-8058-0872-8*) L Erlbaum Assocs.

Littrell, Joseph J. From School to Work. (Illus.). 416p. 1991. text ed. 36.40 (*0-87006-827-X*) Goodheart.

Littrup. Analecta Hafniensia: Southeast Asian Studies in Copenhagen. (C). 1988. text ed. 60.00 (*0-7007-0199-0*, Pub. by Curzon Pr UK) Humanities.

***Littrup, Lisbeth, ed.** Identity in Asian Literature. (Studies in Asian Topics: No. 21). 280p. 1995. 70.00 (*0-7007-0367-5*, Pub. by Curzon Pr UK); pap. 19.95 (*0-7007-0368-3*, Pub. by Curzon Pr UK) Humanities.

Litts, Elyce. The Collector's Encyclopedia of Geisha Girl Porcelain. (Illus.). 176p. 1988. 19.95 (*0-89145-353-9*, 1813) Collector Bks.

Liturgical Commission Publishings Diocese of Lansing Staff. Server at the Lord's Table. Gilliland, Mary J., ed. (Illus.). 28p. (Orig.). 1984. pap. text ed. 2.00 (*0-685-28959-1*) Lit Comm Pubs.

— Special Minister of the Eucharist, Vol. 1: First Steps in Ministry. Gilliland, Mary J., ed. 31p. (Orig.). (C). 1987. pap. text ed. 2.00 (*0-685-28960-5*) Lit Comm Pubs.

— To Love & to Honor: A Pre-Marriage Ministry Resource Manual. Hawkins, Myron, ed. 235p. (Orig.). (C). 1983. ring bd. 25.00 (*0-685-28963-X*) Lit Comm Pubs.

Litvack, Frank. Coronary Laser Angioplasty. (Interventional Cardiology Ser.). (Illus.). 276p. 1992. 70.00 (*0-86542-189-7*) Blackwell Sci.

Litvack, Leon. J. M. Neale & the Quest for Sobornost. 312p. 1994. 52.00 (*0-19-826351-1*) OUP.

Litvak, A. G., ed. High-Frequency Plasma Heating. 450p. 1991. 160.00 (*0-88318-765-5*) Am Inst Physics.

Litvak, Barry. Slow Memories. 1972. pap. 2.75 (*0-8222-1044-4*) Dramatists Play.

Litvak, Eugene. Soviet Telecommunications Systems Reliability Theory. Possehl, Suzanne, ed. (Illus.). 102p. (Orig.). 1989. pap. 75.00 (*1-55831-111-4*) Delphic Associates.

Litvak, Joseph. Caught in the Act: Theatricality in the Nineteenth-Century English Novel. LC 91-10222. (C). 1992. 42.00 (*0-520-07452-1*); pap. 15.00 (*0-520-07454-8*) U CA Pr.

Litvak, Lawrence. Pension Funds & Economic Renewal. Barker, Michael, ed. (Studies in State Development Policy: Vol. 11). 136p. (C). 1981. pap. 16.95 (*0-934842-10-8*) CSPA.

Litvak, Lawrence & Daniels, Belden. Innovations in Development Finance. Barker, Michael, ed. LC 79-67381. (Studies in State Development Policy: Vol. 3). 167p. 1979. pap. 11.95 (*0-934842-02-7*) CSPA.

Litvak, Lawrence, et al. South Africa: Foreign Investment & Apartheid. 100p. 1978. write for info. (*0-318-59935-X*); pap. 3.95 (*0-685-43367-6*) Inst Policy Stud.

— South Africa: Foreign Investment & Apartheid. Hopps, Helen, ed. 100p. 1979. pap. 4.95 (*0-89758-009-5*) Inst Policy Stud.

Litvak, Lily. A Dream of Arcadia: Anti-Industrialism in Spanish Literature. LC 74-22463. 300p. reprint ed. pap. 85.50 (*0-8357-7751-0*, 2036108) Bks Demand.

***Litvak, Marilyn M.** Edward James Lennox: "Builder of Toronto" (Illus.). 150p. 1995. 29.99 (*0-614-06793-6*) Dun.

Litvak, Stuart. Seeking Wisdom: The Sufi Path. LC 82-60163. 128p. (Orig.). 1985. pap. 6.95 (*0-87728-543-8*) Weiser.

— Unstress Yourself. LC 79-89639. 172p. (Orig.). 1980. pap. 5.95 (*0-9602890-0-3*) R-E CA.

Litvak, Stuart & Senzee, A. Wayne. Toward a New Brain: Evolution & the Human Mind. 250p. 1985. 17.95 (*0-13-926056-0*) P-H.

— Toward a New Brain: Evolution & the Human Mind. write for info. (*0-318-59680-6*) S&S Trade.

Litvakovskii, A. A. Fused Cast Refractories. 280p. 1959. text ed. 68.00 (*0-317-46418-3*, Pub. by Keter Pub IS) Coronet Bks.

Litvan, G. G., jt. ed. see Sereda, P. J.

Litvan, Irene & Agid, Yves, eds. Progressive Supranuclear Palsy: Clinical & Research Approaches. (Illus.). 304p. 1992. 65.00 (*0-19-507229-4*) OUP.

Litvin, D. B. & Wike, T. R. Character Tables & Compatibility Relations of the Eighty Layer Groups & Seventeen Plane Groups. (Illus.). 250p. 1991. 85.00 (*0-306-43917-4*, Plenum Pr) Plenum.

Litvin, Danny. Pentecost Is Jewish. 112p. (Orig.). 1987. pap. 2.95 (*0-939497-03-4*) Promise Pub.

Litvin, Faydor. Theory of Gearing. LC 89-600204. (Illus.). 482p. 1989. 40.00 (*0-16-004274-7*) USGPO.

Litvin, Faydor L. Gear Geometry & Applied Theory. 752p. 1994. pap. text ed. 90.00 (*0-13-211095-4*) P-H.

Litvin, Faydor L., et al. Generation of Conjugate Spiral Bevel Gears & Their Tooth Contact Analysis. (Fall Technical Meeting Papers). (Illus.). 11p. 1986. pap. 30.00 (*1-55589-466-6*, 86FTM2) AGMA.

— Helical Gears with Pinion Circular Arc Teeth & Gear Screw Involute Teeth. (Fall Technical Meeting Papers). (Illus.). 5p. 1986. pap. 30.00 (*1-55589-467-4*, 86FTM3) AGMA.

Litvin, Jay, jt. auth. see Salk, Lee.

Litvin, Martin. I'm Going to Be Somebody! A Biography of George Fitch. LC 91-65514. (Illus.). viii, 153p. (Orig.). 1991. pap. 9.50 (*0-938463-05-5*) Western Bks.

Litvin, Valentin. The Soviet Agro-Industrial Complex: Structure & Performance: From Research to Production. McSharry, Patra, ed. (Illus.). 158p. (Orig.). 1985. pap. text ed. 75.00 (*1-55831-027-4*) Delphic Associates.

Litvinchuk, G. & Spitkovskii, I. Factorization of Measurable Matrix Functions. (Operator Theory Ser.: No. 25). 384p. 1988. 100.00 (*0-8176-1883-X*) Birkhauser.

Litvinchuk, Georgii S., jt. auth. see Kravchenko, Victor G.

Litvinne, Felia. Ma Vie et Mon Art Souvenirs. Farkas, Andrew, ed. LC 76-29950. (Opera Biographies Ser.). (Illus.). (FRE.). 1977. reprint ed. lib. bdg. 28.95 (*0-405-09691-7*) Ayer.

Litvinoff, Barnet. Fourteen Ninety-Two: The Decline of Medievalism & the Rise of the Modern Age. 256p. 1991. text ed. 24.95 (*0-684-19210-1*, Scribners) S&S Trade.

— Fourteen Ninety-Two: The Decline of Medievalism & the Rise of the Modern Age. 296p. 1992. reprint ed. pap. 11.00 (*0-380-71917-7*) Avon.

— The Letters & Papers of Chaim Weizmann: 1898-1931, Vol. I. (Series B Papers). 700p. 1984. 59.95x (*0-87855-279-0*) Transaction Pubs.

— The Letters & Papers of Chaim Weizmann: 1931-1952, Vol. II. (Series B Papers). 750p. 1984. 59.95x (*0-87855-297-9*) Transaction Pubs.

Litvinoff, Barnet, ed. The Essential Chaim Weizmann: the Man, the Statesman, the Scientist. 292p. 1983. 29.75 (*0-8419-0823-0*) Holmes & Meier.

Litvinoff, Barnet, jt. ed. see Weisgal, Meyer W.

Litvinoff, Emanuel, ed. Penguin Book of Jewish Short Stories. 1979. pap. 11.00 (*0-14-004728-X*, Penguin Bks) Viking Penguin.

Litvinoff, Sarah, ed. The Illustrated Guide to the Supernatural. (Illus.). 160p. 1986. text ed. 25.00 (*0-8161-8904-8*, Hall Reference) Macmillan.

Litvinoff, Saul. The Law of Obligations in the Louisiana Jurisprudence: A Coursebook. 3rd ed. 928p. 1991. text ed. write for info. (*0-940448-21-1*) LSU Law Pubns.

— Sale & Lease in the Louisiana Jurisprudence: A Coursebook. 2nd ed. LC 86-62791. 730p. 1986. lib. bdg. 38.00 (*0-940448-14-9*) LSU Law Pubns.

Litvinov, I., jt. tr. see Miller, A.

Litvinov, Ivy, jt. tr. see Alpatov, Mikhail V.

Litvinov, Ivy, tr. see Pisemskii, Aleksei F.

Litvinov, Ju. V., tr. see Vakhrameev, V. A.

Litvinova, I., tr. see Pisemskii, Aleksei F.

***Litvinsky, A., et al, eds.** The Crossroads of Civilizations: AD 250 to 750. (History of the Civilizations of Central Asia Ser.: Vol. III). (Illus.). 550p. 1995. text ed. 42.50 (*1-85043-871-4*) St Martin.

Litwack. Post Anesthesia Care Nursing. (Illus.). 323p. 1990. 39.95 (*0-8016-6081-5*) Mosby Yr Bk.

— Post Anesthesia Care Nursing, No. 2. 600p. 1995. spiral bd. 41.95 (*0-8016-7818-8*) Mosby Yr Bk.

Litwack, jt. auth. see Shekleton.

Litwack, D. M., jt. auth. see Davidson, I.

Litwack, David M., jt. auth. see Blum, Daniel J.

Litwack, Gerald. Receptor Purification. LC 90-4689. (Illus.). 1990. 99.50 (*0-89603-167-5*) Humana.

Litwack, Gerald, ed. Receptor Purification, Vol. 2: Receptors for Steroid Hormones, Thyroid Hormones, Water-Balancing Hormones, & Others. LC 90-4689. (Illus.). 432p. 1990. 99.50 (*0-89603-183-7*) Humana.

— Vitamins & Hormones, Vol. 48. (Illus.). 306p. 1994. text ed. 80.00 (*0-12-709848-8*) Acad Pr.

— Vitamins & Hormones, Vol. 51. (Illus.). 500p. 1995. boxed write for info. (*0-614-04655-6*) Acad Pr.

— Vitamins & Hormones Vol. 49: Steroids. (Illus.). 512p. 1994. text ed. 89.00 (*0-12-709849-6*) Acad Pr.

— Vitamins & Hormones Vol. 50, Vol. 50. (Illus.). 496p. 1995. boxed 85.00 (*0-12-709850-X*) Acad Pr.

Litwack, Gerald, jt. auth. see Norman, Anthony W.

Litwack, Kim, ed. Core Curriculum for Post Anesthesia Nursing Practice. 3rd ed. LC 94-13579. (Illus.). 544p. 1994. pap. text ed. 42.50 (*0-7216-5051-1*) Saunders.

***Litwack, Larry, ed.** Journal of Reality Therapy: A Compendium of Articles, 1981-1993. (Illus.). 392p. (Orig.). 1994. pap. 24.00 (*0-944337-19-8*) New View Pubns.

Litwack, Lawrence L., et al. Evaluation in Nursing: Principles & Practice. (Illus.). 270p. 1985. 21.95 (*0-88737-156-6*, 15-1976) Natl League Nurse.

Litwack, Leon & Meier, August. Black Leaders of the Nineteenth Century. (Blacks in the New World Ser.). (Illus.). 360p. 1991. pap. 11.95 (*0-252-06213-2*) U of Ill Pr.

Litwack, Leon F. Been in the Storm So Long: The Aftermath of Slavery. LC 80-11073. 672p. 1980. pap. 15.96 (*0-394-74398-9*, Vin) Random.

— North of Slavery: The Negro in the Free States, 1790-1860. LC 61-10869. 1965. pap. text ed. 13.95 (*0-226-48586-2*, P179) U Ch Pr.

Litwack, Leon F. & Meier, August, eds. Black Leaders of the Nineteenth Century. LC 87-19439. (Blacks in the New World Ser.). 360p. 1988. 29.95 (*0-252-01506-1*) U of Ill Pr.

Litwack, Leon F., jt. auth. see Jordan, Winthrop D.

Litwack, Leon F., jt. ed. see Stampp, Kenneth M.

Litwak, Eugene. Helping the Elderly: The Complementary Roles of Informal Networks & Formal Systems. LC 85-7985. (Perspectives on Marriage & the Family Ser.). 306p. 1985. text ed. 40.00 (*0-89862-077-5*) Guilford Pr.

Litwak, Eugene & Meyer, Henry J. School, Family & Neighborhood: The Theory & Practice of School-Community Relations. LC 73-17274. 316p. reprint ed. pap. 90.10 (*0-8357-4275-X*, 2037073) Bks Demand.

Litwak, Leo. Waiting for the News. LC 89-5577. (Great Lakes Bks.). 333p. 1990. reprint ed. text ed. 39.95 (*0-8143-2274-3*); reprint ed. pap. text ed. 19.95 (*0-8143-2275-1*) Wayne St U Pr.

Litwak, Mark. Contracts for the Film & Television Industry. 320p. (Orig.). 1994. pap. 29.95 (*1-879505-17-7*) Silman James Pr.

— Dealmaking in the Film & Television Industry: From Negotiations Through Final Contracts. LC 94-1939. 405p. (Orig.). 1993. pap. 26.95 (*1-879505-15-0*) Silman James Pr.

— Reel Power: The Struggle for Influence & Success in The New Hollywood. LC 94-2909. 336p. pap. 14.95 (*1-879505-19-3*) Silman James Pr.

Litwak, Robert. Sources of Inter-State Conflict. LC 80-28448. (Security in the Persian Gulf Ser.: Vol. 2): 100p. 1981. pap. text ed. 19.50 (*0-86598-045-4*) Rowman.

Litwak, Robert S. Detente & the Nixon Doctrine. (International Studies). 240p. 1986. pap. 19.95 (*0-521-33834-4*) Cambridge U Pr.

Litwak, Robert S., jt. ed. see Bullock, Mary B.

Litwak, Robert S., jt. ed. see Reiss, Mitchell.

Litweiler, John. The Freedom Principle: Jazz after 1958. (Quality Paperbacks Ser.). (Illus.). 324p. 1990. reprint ed. pap. 12.95 (*0-306-80377-1*) Da Capo.

— Ornette Coleman: A Harmolodic Life. (Illus.). 266p. 1994. reprint ed. pap. 13.95 (*0-306-80580-4*) Da Capo.

— Ornette Coleman: A Life in Harmolodics. LC 92-22969. 1993. 23.00 (*0-688-07212-7*) Morrow.

Litwiller, Bonnie H., jt. auth. see Duncan, David R.

Litwin. Color Atlas of Congenital Heart Surgery. 1994. 195.00 (*0-8151-5511-5*, Yr Bk Med Pubs) Mosby Yr Bk.

— Genetic Determinants of Pulmonary Disease. (Lung Biology in Health & Disease Ser.: Vol. 11). 304p. 1978. 130.00 (*0-8247-6608-3*) Dekker.

— Human Immunogenetics: Basic Principles & Clinical Relevance. (Immunology Ser.: Vol. 43). 856p. 1989. 199.00 (*0-8247-7899-5*) Dekker.

Litwin, Bennett. Where Exactly Is Heaven: Science, God & Common Sense. LC 89-69867. (Illus.). 184p. (Orig.). 1990. pap. 8.95 (*0-9615743-7-2*) SunShine CO.

***Litwin, Howard.** Uprooted in Old Age: Russian Jews & Their Social Networks in Israel. LC 94-29825. (Contributions to the Study of Aging Ser.: Vol. 25). 208p. 1995. text ed. 52.95 (*0-313-29280-9*, Greenwood Pr) Greenwood.

Litwin, Jan A. Light Microscopic Histochemistry on Plastic Sections. LC 85-26328. (Progress in Histochemistry & Cytochemistry Ser.: Vol. 16, No. 2). 84p. 1986. pap. 45.00 (*0-89574-212-8*, Pub. by Gustav Fischer Verlag) VCH Pubs.

***Litwin, Paul.** Microsoft Access Developers Handbook. LC 94-67532. 1994. disk, pap. 44.99 (*0-7821-1327-3*) Sybex.

Litwin, Paul, jt. auth. see Getz, Ken.

Litwin, Sharon, ed. see Zagat, Eugene H., Jr. & Zagat, Nina S.

Litwin, Witold. Introduction to Interoperable Multidatabase Systems. 1993. 34.00 (*0-13-497918-4*) P-H.

Litwin, Witold & Risch, Tore, eds. Applications of Databases: First International Conference, ADB-94, Vadstena, Sweden, June 1994, Proceedings. LC 94-21761. (Lecture Notes in Computer Science: Vol. 819). 1994. 62.00 (*0-387-58183-9*) Spr-Verlag.

Litwin, Witold & Schek, H. J., eds. Foundations of Data Organization & Algorithms. (Lecture Notes in Computer Science Ser.: Vol. 367). 367). viii, 531p. 1989. pap. 55.00 (*0-387-51295-0*) Spr-Verlag.

Litwin, Witold, jt. ed. see Schreiber, F. A.

Litz, A. Walton. Major American Short Stories. 3rd ed. (Illus.). 896p. (C). 1994. pap. text ed. 22.00 (*0-19-507899-3*) OUP.

Litz, A. Walton, ed. American Writers: Supplement I, 2 Vols. LC 73-1759. 1979. lib. bdg. 160.00 (*0-684-15797-7*, Scribners) S&S Trade.

— American Writers Supplement II, 2 vols. LC 73-1759. 1981. lib. bdg. 160.00 (*0-684-16482-5*, Scribners) S&S Trade.

Litz, A. Walton, ed. see Agha, Shahid A.

Litz, A. Walton, jt. ed. see Baechler, Lea.

Litz, A. Walton, ed. see Baker, Paul G.

Litz, A. Walton, ed. see Bishop, George.

Litz, A. Walton, ed. see Boren, Lynda S.

Litz, A. Walton, ed. see Butterworth, Keen.

Litz, A. Walton, ed. see Callander, Marilyn B.

Litz, A. Walton, ed. see Davidson, Arnold E.

Litz, A. Walton, ed. see Dobrinsky, Joseph.

Litz, A. Walton, ed. see Emerson, O. B.

Litz, A. Walton, ed. see Fogelman, Bruce.

Litz, A. Walton, ed. see Fraser, Gail.

Litz, A. Walton, ed. see Fryer, Sarah B.

Litz, A. Walton, ed. see Gladstein, Mimi R.

Litz, A. Walton, ed. see Hardy, Thomas.

Litz, A. Walton, ed. see Hooker, Joan F.

Litz, A. Walton, ed. see MacDonald, Bonney.

Litz, A. Walton, ed. see Maika, Patricia.

Litz, A. Walton, ed. see Maini, Darshan S.

Litz, A. Walton, ed. see Malamud, Randy.

Litz, A. Walton, ed. see McArthur, Murray.

Litz, A. Walton, ed. see Meyers, Jeffrey.

Litz, A. Walton, ed. see Parkinson, Thomas.

Litz, A. Walton, ed. see Pound, Ezra & Shakespear, Dorothy.

Litz, A. Walton, ed. see Powers, Lyall H.

Litz, A. Walton, ed. see Ragan, David P.

Litz, A. Walton, ed. see Schnitzer, Deborah.

Litz, A. Walton, ed. see Sensibar, Judith L.

Litz, A. Walton, ed. see Soldo, John J.

Litz, A. Walton, ed. see Tintner, Adeline R.

Litz, A. Walton, ed. see Tobin, David N.

Litz, A. Walton, ed. see Whelan, P. T.

Litz, A. Walton, ed. see Williams, William Carlos.

Litz, Brian. Colorado Hut to Hut: Skiing & Biking Colorado's Back Country. (Illus.). 240p. (Orig.). 1992. pap. 19.95 (*0-929969-85-5*) Westcliffe Pubs Inc.

Litz, Brian & Lankford, Kurt. Skiing Colorado's Backcountry: Northern Mountains - Trails & Tours. LC 89-33451. (Illus.). 302p. 1989. pap. 14.95 (*1-55591-044-0*) Fulcrum Pub.

Litz, R., jt. ed. see Hammerschlag, F.

Litzenberger, Robert H., jt. auth. see Huang, Chi-Fu.

Litzenburg, Thomas V., Jr., jt. auth. see Diamond, Malcolm L.

Litzinger, Boyd. The Heath Reader. 2nd ed. LC 85-82555. 530p. (C). 1987. teacher ed 2.00 (*0-669-12299-8*); pap. text ed. 15.50 (*0-669-12298-X*) Heath.

Litzinger, Boyd & Buscemi, Santi V. The Heath Reader. 3rd ed. LC 89-81685. 602p. (C). 1990. pap. text ed. 15.50 (*0-669-20597-4*); Instr.'s ed. teacher ed 2.00 (*0-669-20598-2*); Instr.'s guide. teacher ed write for info. (*0-669-24382-5*) Heath.

Litzinger, Boyd & Knickerbocker, K. L. The Browning Critics. LC 65-27008. (Kentucky Paperbacks Ser.). 448p. reprint ed. pap. 127.70 (*0-8357-7448-1*, 2031523) Bks Demand.

Litzinger, Boyd & Oates, Joyce Carol. Story: Fictions Past & Present. LC 84-81089. 1077p. (C). 1985. pap. text ed. 19.00 (*0-669-06687-7*); Instr.'s guide. teacher ed 2.00 (*0-669-06688-5*) Heath.

Litzinger, Mary E., jt. ed. see Baker, Betsy.

Litzinger, Rosanne. The Old Woman & Her Pig: An Old English Tale. LC 91-38227. (J). (ps). 1993. 13.95 (*0-15-257802-1*) HarBrace.

Litzman, Warren. Jesus Lost in the Church. 252p. (Orig.). 1993. pap. 8.99 (*1-56043-097-4*) Destiny Image.

Litzman, Warren, et al. Church Unity. LC 91-76171. 87p. 1991. pap. 7.95 (*0-940232-47-2*) Seedsowers.

Litzmann, Berthold. Clara Schumann, 3 vols., Set. 1971. reprint ed. write for info. (*0-318-71925-8*, Pub. by Georg Olms GW) Lubrecht & Cramer.

— Clara Schumann: An Artist's Life, 2 vols., Set. LC 79-20823. (Music Reprint Ser.). 1979. reprint ed. lib. bdg. 95.00 (*0-306-79582-5*) Da Capo.

Litzmann, Berthold, ed. see Schumann, Clara J. & Brahms, Johannes.

Litzmann, Berthold, ed. see Schumann, Clara & Brahms, Johannes.

An Asterisk (*) at the beginning of an entry indicates that the title is appearing in BIP for the first time.

Liu. Physical Cleaning of Coal: Present & Developing Methods. (Energy, Power & Environment Ser.: Vol. 15). 576p. 1982. 175.00 (*0-8247-1862-3*) Dekker.
— Principles & Procedures in Anesthesiology. (Illus.). 448p. 1992. text ed. 65.00 (*0-397-50948-2*) Lippincott.
— Taoist Health Exercise Book. 1994. pap. 10.95 (*1-56924-901-6*) Marlowe & Co.
***Liu & Blosseville.** Transportation Systems Theory & Application of Advanced Technology, 2 vols. (IPPV Ser.). 1995. pap. text ed. write for info. (*0-08-042226-8*, Pergamon Pr) Elsevier.
Liu & Dutka. Toxicity Screening Procedures Using Bacterial Systems. (Drug & Chemical Toxicology Ser.: Vol. 1). 496p. 1984. 165.00 (*0-8247-7171-0*) Dekker.
Liu & Roxin. Differential Games & Control Theory III: Proceedings of the Third Kingston Conference, Pt. A. (Lecture Notes in Pure & Applied Mathematics Ser.: Vol. 44). 256p. 1979. 115.00 (*0-8247-6845-0*) Dekker.
Liu & Sutinen. Control Theory & Mathematical Economics Pt. B: Proceedings of the Third Kingston Conference. (Lecture Notes in Pure & Applied Mathematics Ser.: Vol. 47). 256p. 1979. 115.00 (*0-8247-6852-3*) Dekker.
Liu, jt. auth. see Chow.
Liu, jt. ed. see Chow.
Liu, jt. ed. see Schenker.
Liu, Aimee E. Face. LC 93-47143. 368p. 1994. 21.95 (*0-446-51829-8*) Warner Bks.
— Face. 368p. 1995. pap. 10.99 (*0-446-67135-5*) Warner Bks.
Liu, Aimee E., jt. auth. see Katz, Stan J.
Liu, Alan. Wordsworth: The Sense of History. (Illus.). 742p. 1989. 59.50 (*0-8047-1373-1*); pap. 19.95 (*0-8047-1893-8*) Stanford U Pr.
Liu, Alan P. Phoenix & the Lame Lion: Modernization in Taiwan & Mainland China, 1950-1980. (Publication Ser.: No. 358). 182p. 1987. pap. 14.95 (*0-8179-8582-4*) Hoover Inst Pr.
Liu, Albert Z., tr. see Tang, Sun L.
Liu, B., et al, eds. Large Scale Systems: Theory & Applications: Selected Papers from the 6th IFAC-FORS-IMACS Symposium, Beijing, PRC, 23-25 August 1992. LC 93-33127. (IFAC Symposia Ser.: Vol. 1993, No. 10). 1993. 140.00 (*0-08-041895-3*, Pergamon Pr) Elsevier.
Liu, Bao-Lin & Fiala, Alan D. Canon of Lunar Eclipses, 1500 B.C. to 3000 A.D. LC 92-429. 1992. 24.95 (*0-943396-37-9*) Willmann-Bell.
Liu, Bede, jt. auth. see Peled, Abraham.
Liu, Benjamin M. & Monroe, James T. Ten Hispano-Arabic Strophic Songs in the Modern Oral Tradition: Music & Texts. (Publications in Modern Philology: Vol. 125). (Illus.). 101p. 1990. pap. 15.00 (*0-520-09751-3*) U CA Pr.
Liu Binyan. People or Monsters? And Other Stories & Reportage from China after Mao. Link, Perry, ed. LC 82-48594. (Chinese Literature in Translation Ser.). 160p. 1983. 20.00 (*0-253-34329-1*); pap. 8.95 (*0-253-20313-9*, MB-313) Ind U Pr.
Liu Binyan, et al. Tell the World: What Happened in China & Why. LC 89-43171. 1989. 18.95 (*0-394-58370-1*) Pantheon.
Liu, C., jt. auth. see Evett, Jack B.
Liu, C. C., jt. ed. see Seymour, Richard K.
Liu, C. S. & Tripathi, V. K. Interaction of Electromagnetic Wave with Electron Beams & Plasma. 180p. 1994. text ed. 68.00 (*981-02-1577-0*) World Scientific Pub.
Liu, C. T., et al, eds. High Temperature Ordered Intermetallic Alloys III: Materials Research Society Symposium Proceedings, Vol. 133. 1989. text ed. 59.00 (*1-55899-006-2*) Materials Res.
— Ordered Intermetallics - Physical Metallurgy & Mechanical Behaviour: Proceedings of the NATO Advanced Research Workshop, Irsee, Germany, June 23-28, 1991. LC 92-10360. (NATO Advanced Study Institutes Series E, Applied Sciences: Vol. 213). 712p. (C). 1992. lib. bdg. 219.00 (*0-7923-1726-2*) Kluwer Ac.
— Shape-Memory Materials & Phenomena: Fundamental Aspects & Applications. (Symposium Proceedings Ser.: Vol. 246). 1992. text ed. 57.00 (*1-55899-140-9*) Materials Res.
Liu, C. Y. & Chien, S., eds. Fibrinogen, Thrombosis, Coagulation, & Fibrinolysis. LC 90-14299. (Advances in Experimental Medicine & Biology Ser.: Vol. 281). (Illus.). 440p. 1990. 115.00 (*0-306-43726-0*, Plenum Pr) Plenum.
Liu, Cengdian & Nichols, R. W., eds. Pressure Vessel Technology: Proceedings of the International Conference, 6th, Beijing, People's Republic of China, 11-15 September 1988, 2 vols. (Illus.). 1750p. 1989. 734.00 (*0-08-035896-9*, Pub. by Pergamon Repr UK); 260.00 (*0-08-035897-7*, Pub. by Pergamon Repr UK) Franklin.
***Liu, Charles, ed.** Artists of Taiwan. (Illus.). 312p. 1994. 75.00 (*1-885594-01-1*) Pt Fine Arts.
— Ting Shao Kuang Serigraphs. (Illus.). 110p. 1991. 30.00 (*0-9623747-4-1*) Segal Fine Art.
Liu, Charles, jt. ed. see Zhen, Sheng T.
Liu, Cheng & Evett, Jack B. Soils & Foundations. 3rd ed. 464p. 1991. text ed. 69.00 (*0-13-816182-8*, 510802) P-H.
Liu, Cheng, jt. auth. see Evett, Jack B.
Liu, Christine. More Nutritional Chinese Cooking with Christine Liu. 2nd ed. LC 81-90263. (Illus.). 414p. 1983. 17.95 (*0-9610566-4-9*) Graphique Pubs.
— Nutrition & Diet with Chinese Cooking. 6th rev. ed. (Illus.). 338p. 1985. pap. 12.95 (*0-685-61119-1*, A837797) Graphique Pubs.
— Nutritional Cooking with Tofu. 2nd rev. ed. LC 83-32385. (Illus.). 174p. 1992. pap. 12.95 (*0-9610566-8-1*) Graphique Pubs.
Liu Chun-Jo. Controversies in Modern Chinese Intellectual History: An Analytical Bibliography of Periodical Articles, Mainly of the May Fourth & Post-May Fourth Era. LC 64-56634. (East Asian Monographs: No. 15). 214p. 1964. pap. 11.00 (*0-674-17000-8*) HUP.
Liu, Chung L. Elements of Discrete Mathematics. 2nd ed. (Computer Science Ser.). 448p. 1985. text ed. write for info. (*0-07-038133-X*) McGraw.
Liu, Chung L., jt. auth. see Belford, G.
Liu, Cricket & Albitz, Paul. DNS & BIND. (Nutshell Handbook Ser.). (Illus.). 418p. (Orig.). 1992. pap. 29.95 (*1-56592-010-4*) OReilly & Assocs.
***Liu, Cricket, et al.** Managing Internet Information Services: World Wide Web, Gopher, FTP, & More. (Illus.). 400p. (Orig.). 1994. 29.95 (*1-56592-062-7*) OReilly & Assocs.
Liu Da. T'ai Chi Ch'uan & I Ching: A Choreography of Body & Mind. LC 79-183640. 1987. pap. 10.00 (*0-06-091309-6*, PL-1309, PL) HarpC.
Liu, Da. T'ai Chi Ch'uan & Meditation. LC 85-25071. (Illus.). 192p. 1991. pap. 14.00 (*0-8052-0993-X*) Schocken.
Liu, Darrell T. Tao Te Ching. 1988. pap. 10.00 (*0-14-019060-0*, Penguin Bks) Viking Penguin.
Liu, Darrell T. & Fairweather, D. V. Labour Ward Manual. (Illus.). 144p. (C). 1985. pap. text ed. 32.95 (*0-407-00245-6*) Buttrwrth-Heinemann.
— Labour Ward Manual. 2nd ed. (Illus.). 136p. 1991. pap. 45.00 (*0-7506-1096-4*) Buttrwrth-Heinemann.
Liu, Darrell T., jt. ed. see Marshak, Daniel R.
Liu, David & Lachelin, Gillian. Practical Gynaecology. (Illus.). 216p. 1989. pap. text ed. 60.00 (*0-407-00580-3*) Buttrwrth-Heinemann.
Liu, David T., ed. A Practical Guide to Chorion Villus Sampling. (Illus.). 168p. 1991. 62.00 (*0-19-262006-1*); pap. 32.00 (*0-19-262005-3*) OUP.
Liu, Derong & Michel, Anthony N. Dynamical Systems with Saturation Nonlinearities: Analysis & Design. LC 94-12280. (Lecture Notes in Control & Information Sciences Ser.). 1994. 40.00 (*0-387-19888-1*) Spr-Verlag.
Liu, Dongbo, jt. auth. see Li, Deyi.
***Liu, E.** Travels of Lao Can. 180p. 1995. 27.00 (*0-8095-4520-9*) Borgo Pr.
— The Travels of Lao Ts'an. Shadick, Harold, tr. & intro. by. LC 86-1867. 301p. 1986. reprint ed. text ed. 59.75 (*0-313-25164-9*, LITR, Greenwood Pr) Greenwood.
Liu, Edison T., jt. ed. see Benz, Christopher C.
Liu, Eric. Next: Young American Writers on the New Generation. 1994. pap. 12.95 (*0-393-31191-0*) Norton.
Liu, Eric, ed. Next: Young American Writers on the New Generation. LC 93-38794. 1994. 21.00 (*0-393-03585-9*) Norton.
Liu, Eric S. Frequency Dictionary of Chinese Words. (Linguistic Structures, First Ser.). (CHI.). 1973. pap. text ed. 61.35 (*90-279-2627-1*) Mouton.
Liu, F. & L. Yan Mau. Chinese Medical Terminology: English to Chinese. 262p. (CHI & ENG.). 1980. 39.95 (*0-8288-0559-8*, M9399) Fr & Eur.
Liu, F. C. & Liu, T. P., eds. Nonlinear Analysis - 1989 Conference. 384p. (C). 1991. text ed. 113.00 (*981-02-0136-2*) World Scientific Pub.
Liu, F. T. United Nations Peacekeeping & the Non-Use of Force. LC 92-6760. (International Peace Academy Occasional Paper Ser.). 47p. 1992. pap. text ed. 6.95 (*1-55587-337-5*) Lynne Rienner.
Liu, Feng. Tackling Environmental Problems Across the Media of Air, Water, & Land. LC 93-379. (CPL Bibliographies Ser.: No. 289). 1993. 18.00 (*0-86602-289-9*) Coun Plan Librarians.
***Liu, Gretchen.** Pastel Portraits. (Illus.). 156p. 1995. 40.00 (*9971-88-020-2*, Pub. by Select Bks SI) Weatherhill.
Liu, Guoli. States & Markets. (C). 1994. text ed. 49.95 (*0-8133-8799-X*) Westview.
Liu, H. C., et al, eds. Quantum Well Intersubband Transition Physics & Devices: Proceedings of the NATO Advanced Research Workshop, Whistler, Canada, September 7-10, 1993. LC 94-12285. (NATO ASI Series E: Applied Sciences: Vol. 270). 588p. (C). 1994. lib. bdg. 230.00 (*0-7923-2877-9*) Kluwer Ac.
Liu, Haiping & Swortzell, Lowell, eds. Eugene O'Neill in China: An International Centenary Celebration. LC 91-28744. (Contributions in Drama & Theatre Studies: No. 44). 360p. 1992. text ed. 57.95 (*0-313-27379-0*, LEO/, Greenwood Pr) Greenwood.
Liu, Henry. Wind Engineering: A Handbook for Structural Engineering. 224p. 1990. text ed. 76.00 (*0-13-960279-8*) P-H.
Liu, Herman C. Non-Verbal Intelligence Tests for Use in China. LC 76-177001. (Columbia University. Teachers College. Contributions to Education Ser.: No. 126). reprint ed. 22.50 (*0-404-55126-2*) AMS Pr.
Liu, Hua-Yih. Concordance of Proverbs. 250p. 1993. pap. write for info. (*0-9631789-5-4*) Evan Formosan.
Liu I-Ming. Awakening to the Tao. Cleary, Thomas, tr. LC 88-17478. 96p. (Orig.). 1988. pap. 12.00 (*0-87773-447-X*) Shambhala Pubns.
Liu, Irene & Li Xiaoqi. A Chinese Text for a Changing China, Revised Edition. rev. ed. (C & T Asian Language Ser.). 250p. 1994. pap. text ed. 18.95 (*0-88727-199-5*) Cheng & Tsui.
Liu, J. P., jt. ed. see Hu, Z. X.
Liu, J. Q., jt. auth. see Lick, D. R.
Liu, J. Y., tr. see Carlson, Dwight L.
***Liu, James C.** The Road. 509p. 1994. pap. write for info. (*0-9631789-8-9*) Evan Formosan.
Liu, James J. The Art of Chinese Poetry. LC 62-7475. xii, 164p. 1966. pap. text ed. 10.95 (*0-226-48687-7*) U Ch Pr.
— The Chinese Knight Errant. LC 66-14112. 256p. reprint ed. pap. 73.00 (*0-317-28155-0*, 2024097) Bks Demand.
— Essentials of Chinese Literary Art. 150p. 1979. 4.95 (*0-318-36953-2*) Asia Bk Corp.
— The Interlingual Critic: Interpreting Chinese Poetry. LC 81-47010. 151p. reprint ed. pap. 43.90 (*0-685-23888-1*, 2056707) Bks Demand.
— Language - Paradox - Poetics: A Chinese Perspective. Lynn, Richard J., ed. 204p. 1988. 37.50 (*0-691-06741-4*) Princeton U Pr.
Liu, James J. & Wang, Stephen. Christians True in China. Shelly, Maynard, ed. LC 88-80007. 114p. 1988. pap. 10.95 (*0-87303-127-X*) Faith & Life.
Liu, James T. China Turning Inward: Intellectual-Political Changes in the Early Twelfth Century, Vol. 132. LC 80-3579. (East Asian Monographs). 225p. 1989. 28.00 (*0-674-11755-7*) HUP.
— Ou-yang Hsiu: An Eleventh-Century Neo-Confucianist. viii, 227p. 1967. 32.50 (*0-8047-0262-4*) Stanford U Pr.
— Reform in Sung China: Wang An-Shih, 1021-1086, & His New Policies. LC 59-9281. (East Asian Monographs: No. 3). 1959. 5.00 (*0-674-75300-3*) HUP.
Liu, John & Bassett, William A. Elements, Oxides & Silicates: High Pressure Phases with Implications for the Earth's Interior. 1986. 75.00 (*0-19-503681-6*) OUP.
Liu, John, tr. see Boice, James M.
Liu, Jonathan, jt. auth. see Hibbert, Edgar.
Liu, Jonathan, tr. see Lindsell, Harold.
Liu, Julius L., jt. auth. see Wang, Simon.
***Liu, K. & Wagner, A.** The Chemical Dynamics & Kinetics of Small Radicals. (Advanced Series in Physical Chemistry). 600p. 1995. text ed. 112.00 (*981-02-2985-2*) World Scientific Pub.
— The Chemical Dynamics & Kinetics of Small Radicals. (Advanced Series in Physical Chemistry). 1995. text ed. 128.00 (*981-02-1754-4*) World Scientific Pub.
Liu, K. F., ed. Chiral Solitons. 578p. 1987. pap. 47.00 (*9971-5-0323-9*) World Scientific Pub.
Liu Kang. Chop Suey. 96p. 1991. pap. text ed. 5.00 (*981-00-2730-3*) World Scientific Pub.
Liu, Kang & Tang, Xiaobing, eds. Politics, Ideology, & Literary Discourse in Modern China: Theoretical Interventions & Cultural Critique. LC 93-4448. (Illus.). 328p. 1994. lib. bdg. 39.95 (*0-8223-1403-7*); pap. text ed. 17.95 (*0-8223-1416-9*) Duke.
Liu, Kwang-Ching. Anglo-American Steamship Rivalry in China, 1862-1874. LC 62-9426. (Harvard East Asian Studies: No. 8). (Illus.). 234p. reprint ed. pap. 66.70 (*0-7837-1716-4*, 2057245) Bks Demand.
Liu Kwang-Ching, ed. American Missionaries in China: Papers from Harvard Seminars. LC 66-31226. (East Asian Monographs: No. 21). 316p. 1966. pap. 11.00 (*0-674-02600-4*) HUP.
Liu, Lawrence S., jt. ed. see Cheng, Chia-Jui.
Liu-Lengyel, Hongying, jt. auth. see Lengyel, Alfonz.
Liu, Lesley, jt. auth. see Chang, Monica.
Liu Lianshou. Proceedings of the International Symposium on Multiparticle Dynamics, XXI: Wu-han, China, 23-27 September, 1991. Wu Yuanfang, ed. LC 92-11996. 700p. 1992. text ed. 137.00 (*981-02-0949-5*) World Scientific Pub.
Liu, Lily. The American Dream. Peng, H. L., ed. 240p. (Orig.). Date not set. pap. 14.98 (*0-9639426-0-3*) Think Big Pubng.
***Liu, Lydia H.** Translingual Practice: Literature, National Culture, & Modernity - China, 1900-1937. LC 94-45961. (Illus.). 368p. 1995. 49.50x (*0-8047-2534-9*); pap. 19.95 (*0-8047-2535-7*) Stanford U Pr.
Liu Mau-Tsai. Chinesisch-Deutsches Stilwoerterbuch fuer Konversation. 816p. (CHI & GER.). 1980. 185.00 (*0-8288-1007-9*, F34990) Fr & Eur.
Liu, Michael T., ed. Chemistry of Diazirines, 2 vols., Set. 352p. 1987. 189.00 (*0-8493-5047-6*, QD341, CRC Reprint) Franklin.
Liu, Ming-Wood. Madhyamaka Thought in China. LC 94-953. (Sinica Leidensia Ser.: Vol. 30). 1994. 100.00 (*90-04-09984-0*) E J Brill.
Liu, Monica, illus. Kao & the Golden Fish: A Folktale from Thailand. LC 93-298. (Adventures in Storytelling Ser.). 32p. (J). (ps-3). 1993. lib. bdg. 13.95 (*0-516-05145-8*); pap. 12.95 (*0-516-07093-2*) Childrens.
Liu, Nancy, tr. see Qing, Dai.
Liu, Nancy, ed. see Rung, Ming.
Liu, Paul I. Introduction to Energy & the Environment. LC 93-7906. 1993. text ed. 44.95 (*0-442-01557-7*) Van Nos Reinhold.
Liu, Paul L. Blue Book of Diagnostic Tests. (Blue Book Ser.). (Illus.). 521p. 1986. pap. text ed. 30.95 (*0-7216-1417-5*) Saunders.
Liu Qian. Panda Bear Goes Visiting. (Illus.). 22p. (J). (gr. 3-4). 1982. 3.95 (*0-8351-1108-3*); pap. 2.95 (*0-8351-1139-3*) China Bks.
***Liu, Robert K.** Collectible Beads. LC 94-68696. 256p. 1995. text ed. 44.95 (*0-9641023-0-7*) Ornament.
Liu, Ruey-Wen. Selected Papers on Analog Fault Diagnosis. LC 87-3957. 148p. 1987. pap. 24.95 (*0-87942-222-X*, PP02139) Inst Electrical.
Liu, Ruey-Wen, ed. Testing & Diagnosis of Analog Circuits & Systems. LC 90-45217. (Illus.). 240p. 1991. text ed. 64.95 (*0-442-25932-8*) Van Nos Reinhold.
Liu, Samuel M., ed. Hymns of Praise: The Hymnal of the True Jesus Church. 608p. 1993. 10.00 (*0-9638077-0-6*) Genl Assem True.
***Liu Sanders, Tao T.** Dragons, Gods & Spirits from Chinese Mythology. LC 94-8354. (World Mythology Ser.). (Illus.). 132p. 1994. lib. bdg. 22.50 (*0-87226-922-1*) P Bedrick Bks.
Liu, Sarah & Vittitow, Mary L. Learning Games Without Losers. (Illus.). 96p. (J). (gr. 2-6). 1985. student ed 8.95 (*0-86530-039-9*, IP 39-9) Incentive Pubns.
Liu, Sarah, jt. auth. see Vittitow, Mary L.
Liu, Shao. Study of Human Abilities. (American Oriental Ser.: Vol. 11). 1937. 20.00 (*0-527-02685-9*) Periodicals Srv.
Liu, Shih S. Extraterritoriality: Its Rise & Decline. LC 72-82238. (Columbia University. Studies in the Social Sciences: No. 263). reprint ed. 20.00 (*0-404-51263-1*) AMS Pr.
Liu, Shih S., tr. see Chen, Liu F.
Liu-Shing-I. Dictionary of Legal & Commercial Terms: Woerterbuch der Rechtssprache & Wirtschaftssprache. 410p. (CHI & GER.). 1984. 250.00 (*0-8288-0974-7*, M15021) Fr & Eur.
Liu Sola Cliu. Blue Sky Green Sea: And Other Stories. Cheung, Martha, tr. & intro. by. xxv, 145p. (Orig.). 1993. pap. 11.95 (*962-7255-12-2*, Pub. by Renditions Papbk HK) SPD-Small Pr Dist.
Liu, Stella, ed. Holdings of the Haverhill Public Library: John Greenleaf Whittier Collection. (Illus.). 68p. (Orig.). 1976. pap. 10.00 (*1-878651-02-1*) HPL Pr.
Liu, Stephen S., jt. auth. see Chen, Thomas M.
Liu, T. Nonlinear Stability of Shock Waves for Viscous Conservation Laws. LC 85-9153. (Memoirs of the AMS Ser.: Vol. 56/328). 109p. 1988. reprint ed. pap. text ed. 21.00 (*0-8218-2329-9*, MEMO 56/328) Am Math.
Liu, T. P., jt. ed. see Liu, F. C.
Liu, T. S. & Li, K. Accelerator Mass Spectrometry. Chen, C. E. et al, eds. (Beijing Inst of Modern Phys Ser.: Vol. 4). 350p. 1992. text ed. 94.00 (*981-02-0493-0*) World Scientific Pub.
Liu, Tai. Puritan London: A Study of Religion & Society in the City Parishes. LC 85-40534. 256p. 1986. 45.00 (*0-87413-283-5*) U Delaware Pr.
Liu, Tai-Ping. Admissible Solutions of Hyperbolic Conservation Laws. LC 80-28506. (Memoirs Ser.: No. 30/240). 78p. 1981. pap. 16.00 (*0-8218-2240-3*, MEMO 30/240) Am Math.
Liu, Tessie P. The Weaver's Knot: The Contradictions of Class Struggle & Family Solidarity in Western France, 1750-1914. (Illus.). 296p. 1994. 42.50 (*0-8014-2738-X*); pap. 17.95 (*0-8014-8019-1*) Cornell U Pr.
Liu, Thelma. Just Thelma. 450p. (Orig.). 1993. pap. write for info. (*0-915214-29-6*, Wrds Worth Pr) Current.
***Liu, Timothy.** Burnt Offerings. 84p. (Orig.). 1995. pap. 12.00 (*1-55659-104-7*) Copper Canyon.
— Vox Angelica. LC 92-10732. 72p. (Orig.). 1992. pap. 9.95 (*0-914086-97-9*) Alicejamesbooks.
***Liu, Victoria & Durra, Joseph.** Let's Talk Cantonese. (Illus.). 270p. 1994. audio, pap. 49.95 (*1-881906-03-5*) JBD Pub.
Liu, Victoria & Durra, Joseph B. Let's Talk Advanced American English. (Let's Talk Ser.). 100p. 1992. audio, vdisk 158.00 (*1-881906-02-7*) JBD Pub.
— Let's Talk American English: Beginning & Intermediate. rev. ed. (Let's Talk Ser.). 100p. 1992. reprint ed. vhs 238.00 (*1-881906-01-9*) JBD Pub.
Liu Wei-ping, et al, eds. Readings in Modern Chinese. 162p. 1986. pap. text ed. 25.00 (*0-9590735-4-X*, Pub. by Wild Peony Pty AT) UH Pr.
Liu, William T., ed. China Social Statistics, 1986. (China Statistics Ser.). 294p. 1989. text ed. 95.00 (*0-275-93273-7*, C3273, Praeger Pubs) Greenwood.
— China Statistical Abstract, 1988. LC 88-28571. 144p. 1988. text ed. 55.00 (*0-275-93214-1*, C3214, Praeger Pubs) Greenwood.
Liu, William T., ed. see Notre Dame Conference on Population Staff.
Liu, William T., et al, eds. Modernization in East Asia: Political, Economic, & Social Perspectives. LC 92-9117. 200p. 1992. text ed. 55.00 (*0-275-93222-2*, C3222, Praeger Pubs) Greenwood.
Liu Wu-Chi. Confucius, His Life & Time. LC 73-138159. 189p. (C). 1972. reprint ed. text ed. 35.00 (*0-8371-5616-5*, LICO, Greenwood Pr) Greenwood.
Liu, Wu-Chi. An Introduction to Chinese Literature. LC 66-12729. 349p. reprint ed. pap. 99.50 (*0-685-16283-4*, 2056246) Bks Demand.
— K'uei Yeh Chi: Li Tai Tz'u Ch'hu Hshuan Chi - Sunflower Splendor: Three Thousand Years of Chinese Poetry. LC 76-12366. 310p. reprint ed. pap. 88.40 (*0-7837-3716-5*, 2057894) Bks Demand.
— A Short History of Confucian Philosophy. LC 78-20480. 1987. reprint ed. 22.50 (*0-88355-857-2*) Hyperion Conn.
Liu, Wu-Chi & Li, Tien-Yi, eds. Readings in Modern Literature, Vol. 2: Stories, Vol. 2. 368p. (C). 1953. pap. text ed. write for info. (*0-318-59856-6*) Yale Far Eastern Pubns.
Liu, Wu-Chi & Lo, Irving Y., eds. Sunflower Splendor: Three Thousand Years of Chinese Poetry. 696p. 1990. reprint ed. 39.95 (*0-253-35580-X*); reprint ed. pap. 19.95 (*0-253-20607-3*, MB-607) Ind U Pr.
Liu, X. L., jt. auth. see Chen, W. F.
Liu, Xiaogan. Classifying the Zhuangzi Chapters. LC 93-50079. (Michigan Monographs in Chinese Studies: No. 65). 1994. write for info. (*0-89264-106-1*); pap. write for info. (*0-89264-107-X*) Ctr Chinese Studies.
***Liu, Xiaolian.** The Odyssey of the Buddhist Mind: The Allegory of the Later Journey to the West. 336p. (C). 1994. lib. bdg. 54.00 (*0-8191-9670-3*) U Pr of Amer.
***Liu, Xinru.** Ancient India & Ancient China: Trade & Religious Exchanges AD 1-600. (Oxford India Paperbacks Ser.). 256p. 1995. pap. 7.95 (*0-19-563587-6*) OUP.
Liu Xinwu. Blackwalls & Other Stories. Cohn, Don J., ed. xiii, 200p. 1992. reprint ed. pap. 9.50 (*962-7255-06-8*, Pub. by Renditions Papbk HK) SPD-Small Pr Dist.
Liu, Xinzhi & Siegel, David, eds. Comparison Methods & Stability Theory. LC 94-20391. (Lecture Notes in Pure & Applied Mathematics Ser.: Vol. 162). 384p. 1994. 145.00 (*0-8247-9270-X*) Dekker.
***Liu, Xuecheng.** The Sino-Indian Border Dispute & Sino-Indian Relations. 236p. (C). 1994. lib. bdg. 46.50 (*0-8191-9699-1*) U Pr of Amer.

Liu, Y. A., et al, eds. Recent Developments in Chemical Process & Plant Design. 1987. text ed. 165.00 (0-471-84780-1) Wiley.

Liu, Y. A., jt. auth. see Quantrille, Thomas E.

Liu, Yameng, jt. ed. see Young, Richard E.

Liu Yanchi. The Essential Book of Traditional Chinese Medicine, Vol. 2. 1988. text ed. 107.00 (0-231-06518-3) Col U Pr.

Liu, Yang. The Costimulatory Pathway for T Cell Responses. LC 93-45549. (Molecular Biology Intelligence Unit Ser.). 128p. 1993. 89.95 (1-57059-052-4) R G Landes.

Liu, Yong-chuan. Patterns & Results of the Third Democratization Wave. 142p. (C). 1993. lib. bdg. 39.50 (0-8191-9124-8) U Pr of Amer.

Liu, Yongquan, jt. ed. see Mair, Victor H.

Liu, Yu-Cheng. The M68000 Microprocessor Family: Fundamentals of Assembly Language Programming & Interface Design. 464p. 1990. pap. text ed. 70.00 (0-13-566399-7) P-H.

Liu, Yu-Cheng & Gibson, Glenn A. Microcomputer Systems: The 8086-8088 Family, Architecture, Programming, & Design. LC 83-4552. (Illus.). 544p. (C). 1984. write for info. (0-13-580944-4) P-H.

Liu Yuehua, jt. auth. see Shou-hsin Teng.

Liu, Ziaxing. The Economic Geography of China. Jingshi, Sun, ed. (Illus.). 500p. 1988. 49.95 (0-19-584079-8) OUP.

Liu Zongren. Two Years in the Melting Pot. rev. ed. 1988. reprint ed. 16.95 (0-8351-2048-1); reprint ed. pap. 9.95 (0-8351-2035-X) China Bks.

Liubimov, G. A., et al, eds. Fluid Mechanics. (Series in Mechanical Engineering & Applied Mechanics: Vol. 2). 400p. 1991. 158.00 (0-89116-725-0) Hemisp Pub.

Liubimov, Nikolai. Nesgoraemye Slova. 304p. 1983. 39.00 (0-685-43463-X, Pub. by Collets UK) St Mut.

Liudmila, Pozhar, ed. Mori-Xwanzig Theory in Statistical Mechanics: Fundamentals & Applications. LC 94-37468. (Series in Contemporary Chemical Physics). 200p. 1995. text ed. 53.00 (981-02-1750-1) World Scientific Pub.

Liudprand of Cremona. The Embassy to Constantinople: And Other Works. 224p. 1993. pap. 10.95 (0-460-87235-4, Everyman's Classic Lib) C E Tuttle.

Liukkonen, J., jt. ed. see Hofmann, K. H.

Liulevicius, Arunas. The Factorization of Cyclic Reduced Powers by Secondary Cohomology Operations. LC 52-42839. (Memoirs Ser.: No. 1/42). 112p. 1989. reprint ed. pap. 17.00 (0-8218-1242-4, MEMO 1/42) Am Math.

Liulevicius, Arunas, ed. see Pure Mathematics Symposium Staff.

*Liungman, C. Thought Signs: The Semiotics of Symbols - Western Ideograms. LC 94-79555. 660p. 1995. 82.00 (90-5199-197-5) IOS Press.

Liungman, Carl G. Dictionary of Symbols. 608p. 1995. pap. 18.00 (0-393-31236-4) Norton.

— The Dictionary of Symbols: Western Ideograms. 596p. 1991. lib. bdg. 65.00 (0-87436-610-0) ABC-CLIO.

Liutkus, A., jt. auth. see Knystautasand, A.

*Liuzza, Roy M., ed. The Old English Versions of the Gospels Vol. I: Text & Introduction. (Early English Text Society-Original Ser.: No. 304). (Illus.). 280p. 1994. text ed. 49.95 (0-19-722306-0) OUP.

Liuzzi, Fernando. La Lauda e i Primordi Della Melodia Italiana, 2 vols. LC 80-2238. 1981. reprint ed. 185.00 (0-404-19037-5) AMS Pr.

Livadas, Panos E. & Ward, Christopher. Computer Organization & the MC68000. LC 92-24684. 720p. 1993. text ed. 74.00 (0-13-158940-7) P-H.

Livadeas, Themistocles & Charitos, Minas. The Real Truth Concerning Apostolos Makrakis. Orthodox Christian Educational Society Staff, ed. Cummings, Denver, tr. 230p. (Orig.). 1952. pap. 5.95 (0-938366-30-0) Orthodox Chr.

Livadic, P. Dizionario Italiano-Serbocroato-Italiano. 554p. (ITA & SER.). 1980. 9.95 (0-8288-1640-9, M9180) Fr & Eur.

Livanov, M. N. Spatial Organization of Cerebral Processes. 178p. 1975. text ed. 48.00 (0-7065-1514-5, Pub. by Keter Pub IS) Coronet Bks.

Livanov, M. N. & Rusinov, V. S., eds. Mathematical Analysis of the Electrical Activity of the Brain. Barlow, John S., tr. LC 68-17621. (Illus.). 113p. 1968. 19.95 (0-674-55400-0) HUP.

Livanov, V. A. Hydrogen in Titanium. 208p. 1965. text ed. 52.50 (0-7065-0576-X, Pub. by Keter Pub IS) Coronet Bks.

Livanova, Anna. L. D. Landau. Sykes, J. B., tr. 1980. text ed. 77.00 (0-08-023076-8, Pergamon Pr) Elsevier.

— Landau. Sykes, J. B., tr. 214p. 1985. 60.00 (0-317-40731-7, Pub. by Collets) St Mut.

Livanova, Elena, illus. The Tempest. LC 92-14526. (Shakespeare: The Animated Tales Ser.). 48p. (J). (gr. 5 up). 1993. pap. 6.99 (0-679-83873-2) Knopf Bks Yng Read.

Livas, Haris. Contemporary Greek Artists. 1993. 40.00 (0-533-10045-3) Vantage.

*Livdahl, et al. Stories from Response-Centered Classrooms. 160p. (C). 1995. text ed. 35.00x (0-8077-3458-6) Tchrs Coll.

*Livdahl, Barbara S., et al. Stories from Response-Centered Classrooms. 160p. (C). 1995. pap. text ed. 16.95x (0-8077-3457-8) Tchrs Coll.

Live, Anna H. Yesterday & Today in the U. S. A. Intermediate ESL Reader. 2nd ed. (Illus.). 288p. (C). 1988. pap. text ed. write for info. (0-318-62497-4) P-H.

Live, Anna H. & Sankowsky, Suzanne H. From Sea to Shining Sea: An Elementary ESL Reader. (Illus.). (C). 1985. pap. text ed. 13.00 (0-13-330796-4) P-H.

Lively, et al. Liens: En Paroles. (Bridging the Gap Ser.). 1994. pap. 31.95 (0-8384-4607-8) Heinle & Heinle.

Lively, Adam & Lively, Jack, eds. Democracy in Britain: A Reader. 360p. 1993. 54.94 (0-631-18829-0); pap. 24.95 (0-631-18831-2) Blackwell Pubs.

Lively, C. E. & Taeuber, Conrad. Rural Migration in the United States. LC 71-165601. (Research Monograph Ser.: Vol. 19). 1971. reprint ed. 25.00 (0-306-70351-3) Da Capo.

Lively, Chauncy. Chauncy Lively's Flybox. 1991. pap. 18.95 (0-8117-2078-0) Stackpole.

Lively, Donald E. The Constitution & Race. LC 91-30280. 208p. 1992. text ed. 55.00 (0-275-93914-6, C3914, Praeger Pubs); pap. text ed. 17.95 (0-275-94228-7, B4228, Praeger Pubs) Greenwood.

— Dissenting Judicial Opinions: Foreshadows of Constitutional Law. LC 92-19827. 200p. 1992. text ed. 59.95 (0-275-94382-8, C4382, Praeger Pubs); pap. text ed. 17.95 (0-275-94383-6, B4386, Praeger Pubs) Greenwood.

— Essential Principles of Communication Law. LC 91-6303. 336p. 1991. text ed. 39.95 (0-275-93912-X, C3912, Praeger Pubs) Greenwood.

— Judicial Review & the Consent of the Governed: Activist Ways & Popular Ends. LC 89-43699. 164p. 1990. lib. bdg. 28.50x (0-89950-524-4) McFarland & Co.

— Modern Communications Law. LC 90-7504. 576p. 1991. text ed. 49.95 (0-275-93735-6, C3735, Praeger Pubs) Greenwood.

Lively, Donald E., et al, eds. First Amendment Anthology. LC 94-9984. 1994. write for info. (0-87084-265-X) Anderson Pub Co.

Lively, Edwin, jt. auth. see Lively, Virginia.

Lively, Jack & Reeve, Andrew. Modern Political Theory from Hobbes to Marx: Key Debates. 320p. 1989. pap. 14.95 (0-415-01351-8) Routledge.

Lively, Jack, jt. ed. see Lively, Adam.

Lively, John, ed. see Tolpin, James.

Lively, Ken, ed. see Magid, Lynn H. & Kahn, Beth F.

Lively, Penelope. According to Mark. 1989. pap. 10.00 (0-06-097199-1, PL) HarpC.

— The Cat, the Crow, & the Banyan Tree. LC 93-22355. (Illus.). 32p. (J). (ps up). 1994. 14.95 (1-56402-325-7) Candlewick Pr.

— City of the Mind. large type ed. 319p. 1992. 22.95 (1-85089-342-X, Pub. by ISIS UK) Transaction Pubs.

— City of the Mind: A Novel. LC 90-56365. 1992. pap. 11.00 (0-06-092216-8, PL) HarpC.

— Cleopatra's Sister. large type ed. 1993. 23.95 (1-56895-039-X) Wheeler Pub.

— Cleopatra's Sister: A Novel. 240p. 1994. pap. 11.00 (0-06-092217-6, PL) HarpC.

— Dragon Trouble. (Banana Bks.). (Illus.). 42p. (J). (gr. 2-4). 1989. 3.95 (0-8120-6136-5) Barron.

— The Ghost of Thomas Kempe. LC 73-77456. (Illus.). 192p. (J). (gr. 3-6). 1973. 14.95 (0-525-30495-9, DCB) Dutton Child Bks.

— The Ghost of Thomas Kempe. (Illus.). 192p. (J). (gr. 3-7). 1995. pap. 3.99 (0-14-037794-8) Puffin Bks.

— Jacaranda, Oleander: A Memoir. LC 93-39760. 160p. 1994. 20.00 (0-06-017106-5, HarpT) HarpC.

— Judgment Day. LC 88-45596. 224p. 1989. reprint ed. pap. 7.95 (0-06-097198-3, PL 7198, PL) HarpC.

— Moon Tiger. LC 88-45594. 224p. 1989. reprint ed. pap. 12.00 (0-06-097200-9, PL 7200, PL) HarpC.

— Oleander, Jacaranda. 1995. pap. 10.00 (0-06-092622-8, PL) HarpC.

— Pack of Cards: Stories. LC 89-46104. 336p. 1990. reprint ed. pap. 12.00 (0-06-097315-3, PL) HarpC.

— Passing On. large type ed. 342p. 1990. 19.95 (1-85089-329-2, Pub. by ISIS UK) Transaction Pubs.

— Passing On: A Novel. LC 90-55666. 224p. 1991. reprint ed. pap. 11.00 (0-06-097370-6, PL) HarpC.

— The Road to Lichfield: A Novel. LC 91-57910. 224p. 1992. reprint ed. pap. 11.00 (0-06-097461-3, PL) HarpC.

— A Stitch in Time. large type ed. 264p. (J). (gr. 5 up). 1988. 16.95 (0-7451-0726-5, Galaxy Child Lrg Print) Chivers N Amer.

— The Voyage of QV66. large type ed. (Illus.). 280p. (J). 1992. 16.95 (0-7451-1548-9, Galaxy Child Lrg Print) Chivers N Amer.

Lively, Virginia & Lively, Edwin. Sexual Development of Young Children. 1991. teacher ed 8.00 (0-8273-4199-7); pap. text ed. 19.95 (0-8273-4198-9) Delmar.

Livens, Leslie. Share Valuation Handbook: Techniques for the Valuation of Shares in Private Companies. 207p. (C). 1986. 104.00 (0-906840-98-8, Pub. by Fourmat Pub UK) St Mut.

— Share Valuation Handbook: Techniques for the Valuation of Shares in Private Companies. 2nd ed. 250p. 1993. 96.00 (0-85459-811-1, Pub. by Tolley Pubng UK) St Mut.

Liverani, P., ed. see Andreade, B., et al.

Liverett, David, jt. auth. see Stephens, Christie S.

Liveright, A. A. National Trends in Higher Adult Education. 1960. 2.50 (0-87060-020-6, OCP 2) Syracuse U Cont Ed.

— University Adult Education: The Career for Experiment in Education. 1961. 2.50 (0-87060-080-X, PUC 21) Syracuse U Cont Ed.

Liveright, James. Simple Methods for Detecting Buying & Selling Points in Securities. LC 68-21699. 1968. reprint ed. 11.00 (0-87034-028-X) Fraser Pub Co.

*Liverman, H. J. High Days & Holidays: Scenes from a Tyrrell County Childhood. 1994. per., pap. 9.95 (0-9643396-0-9) Sweet Bay Tree.

Livermore. Numbers & Losses in the Civil War. rev. ed. 20.00 (0-685-51649-0) Morningside Bkshop.

Livermore, Abiel A. The War with Mexico Reviewed. Cortes, Carlos E., ed. LC 76-1287. (Chicano Heritage Ser.). 1977. reprint ed. 26.95 (0-405-09511-2) Ayer.

Livermore, Alton D. Zidovudine in Therapeutic Uses: Index of New Information. 150p. 1994. 44.50 (0-7883-0104-7); pap. 39.50 (0-7883-0105-5) ABBE Pubs Assn.

Livermore, Ann. Artists & Aesthetics in Spain. (Tamesis Bks.). (Illus.). 168p. 1990. 45.00 (0-7293-0294-6) Boydell & Brewer.

— A Short History of Spanish Music. LC 72-196469. 272p. reprint ed. pap. 77.60 (0-317-42003-8, 2026116) Bks Demand.

Livermore, George. Historical Research Respecting the Opinion of the Founders of the Republic on Negroes As Slaves, As Citizens & As Soldiers. LC 68-18599. 1970. reprint ed. 29.50 (0-678-00547-8) Kelley.

— Historical Research Respecting the Opinions of the Founders of the Republic on Negroes As Slaves, As Citizens, & As Soldiers. LC 69-18541. (American Negro: His History & Literature, Ser. No. 2). 1968. reprint ed. 13.95 (0-405-01878-9) Ayer.

Livermore, Gordon. Soviet Foreign Policy Today, 1986-1989. 3rd ed. Current Digest of the Soviet Press Staff, tr. 192p. (Orig.). (C). 1989. pap. 10.00 (0-913601-62-4) Current Digest.

— Soviet Foreign Policy Today, 1989-1990. 4th ed. Current Digest of the Soviet Press Staff, tr. 220p. (Orig.). 1990. pap. 10.00 (0-913601-63-2) Current Digest.

Livermore, Gordon, ed. Russian Foreign Policy Today: The Soviet Legacy & Post-Soviet Beginnings. 5th ed. (Current Digest Foreign Policy Readers Ser.). 228p. (Orig.). (C). 1992. pap. 15.00 (0-913601-64-0) Current Digest.

— Russia's Evolving Foreign Policy, 1992-1994: A Supplement to the 5th Edition of Russian Foreign Policy Today. (Foreign Policy Readers Ser.). 118p. 1994. pap. 21.00 (0-913601-65-9) Current Digest.

— Soviet Foreign Policy Today, 1983-1986. 2nd ed. 200p. (Orig.). (C). 1986. 10.00 (0-913601-61-6) Current Digest.

Livermore, Gordon, jt. ed. see Schulze, Fred.

Livermore, Gordon, et al, eds. U. S. S. R. Today: Perspectives from the Soviet Press, 1989-1991. 8th ed. 180p. 1991. pap. 18.00 (0-913601-78-0) Current Digest.

Livermore, Harold, ed. University of British Columbia Hispanic Studies. (Serie A: Monografias, XL). 86p. (Orig.). (ENG & SPA.). (C). 1974. pap. 27.00 (0-900411-82-1, Pub. by Tamesis Bks Ltd UK) Boydell & Brewer.

Livermore, Harold V., tr. see De la Vega, Garcilaso.

Livermore, Harold V., tr. see Vega, Garcilaso de la.

Livermore, Jesse L. How to Trade in Stocks: The Livermore Formula for Combining Time Element & Price. 116p. 1991. reprint ed. pap. 19.95 (0-934380-20-1) Traders Pr.

Livermore, John. Exemption Clauses & Implied Obligations in Contracts. xxxviii, 190p. 1986. pap. 68.00 (0-455-20681-3, Pub. by Law Bk Co) W W Gaunt.

Livermore, John, jt. auth. see Clark, E. Eugene.

Livermore, Marlin, jt. auth. see Smirnov, Mark.

Livermore, Mary A. My Story of the War: A Woman's Narrative of Four Year's Personal Experience As Nurse in the Union Army. LC 72-2612. (American Women Ser.: Images & Realities). (Illus.). 704p. 1975. reprint ed. 44.95 (0-405-04466-6) Ayer.

— My Story of the War: A Women's Narrative of Four Years Personal Experience As Nurse in the Union Army. 700p. 1978. reprint ed. 27.50 (0-87928-100-6) Corner Hse.

— My Story of the War: The Civil War Memoirs of the Famous Nurse, Relief Organizer, & Suffragette. (Illus.). 710p. 1995. reprint ed. pap. 19.95 (0-306-80658-4) Da Capo.

— The Story of My Life. (American Biography Ser.). 730p. 1991. reprint ed. lib. bdg. 119.00 (0-7812-8247-0) Rprt Serv.

— The Story of My Life; or, the Sunshine & Shadow of Seventy Years...to Which Is Added Six of Her Most Popular Lectures. LC 74-3960. (Women in America Ser.). (Illus.). 760p. 1974. reprint ed. 57.95 (0-405-06108-0) Ayer.

Livermore, Putnam, jt. auth. see Barrett, Thomas S.

Livermore, Robert. Bostonians & Bullion: The Journal of Robert Livermore. Gressley, Gene M., ed. LC 68-12703. (Illus.). 222p. reprint ed. pap. 63.30 (0-8357-5608-4, 2056848) Bks Demand.

Livermore, Samuel & Reams, Bernard D., Jr. Treatise on the Law of Principal & Agent: And of Sales by Auction, Set, Vols. I & II. Helmholz, R. H., ed. LC 86-62943. (Historical Writings in Law & Jurisprudence Ser.: No. 11). 1986. reprint ed. Set. lib. bdg. 95.00 (0-89941-526-1, 304620) W S Hein.

Livermore, Shaw. Twilight of Federalism: The Disintegration of the Federalist Party - 1815-1830. LC 73-150413. 302p. 1972. reprint ed. 75.00 (0-87752-137-9) Gordian.

— The Twilight of Federalism: The Disintegration of the Federalist Party, 1815-1830. LC 62-7410. 305p. reprint ed. pap. 87.00 (0-317-09983-3, 2000593) Bks Demand.

Livermore, Thomas L. Numbers & Losses in the Civil War in America, 1861-65. LC 57-10726. (Indiana University Civil War Centennial Ser.). 1957. 25.00 (0-527-57600-X) Periodicals Srv.

Livernash, E. Robert, ed. Comparable Worth: Issues & Alternatives. 2nd ed. LC 84-81267. 299p. 1984. pap. 11.00 (0-937856-08-8) Equal Employ.

Livernash, E. Robert, jt. auth. see Foulkes, Fred K.

Livernash, E. Robert, jt. auth. see Peach, David A.

*Livernois, Jay. Archetypal Sex: Spring 57. Hillman, James & Boer, Charles, eds. (Journal Ser.). 176p. (Orig.). 1995. pap. 15.00 (1-882670-05-1) Spring Jrnl.

Livernois, Jay, ed. see Hillman, James.

Liverpool, Charles J. Collection of All the Treaties of Peace, Alliance & Commerce Between Great Britain & Other Powers, 3 vols., Set, Vols. 1-3. LC 69-16554. 1969. reprint ed. 150.00 (0-678-00486-2) Kelley.

— Treatise on the Coins of the Realm: In a Letter to the King. LC 67-29513. (Reprints of Economic Classics Ser.). 1968. reprint ed. 39.50 (0-678-00412-9) Kelley.

Liverpool, Hollis. Calypsonians to Remember. 2nd ed. King, Darwin A., ed. 1987. pap. text ed. 10.95 (0-937421-02-2) VICY.

— Kaiso & Society. King, Darwin, ed. (Illus.). 62p. 1986. pap. text ed. 6.95 (0-317-52921-8) VICY.

Liverpool, N. J., jt. ed. see Hewlett, Cecil E.

Liversidge, Michael, et al. Canaletto & England. (Illus.). 192p. 1994. 50.00 (1-85894-002-8) U of Wash Pr.

Liverwright, A. A. & Goldmann, Freda H. Significant Developments in Continuing Higher Education. 1965. 2.50 (0-87060-016-8, OCP 12) Syracuse U Cont Ed.

Liverziani, Filippo. Reincarnation & Its Phenomena. 192p. (C). 1989. pap. 39.00 (0-7212-0789-8, Pub. by Regency Press) St Mut.

Livesay. Economics. 1990. pap. 35.95 (0-434-91174-7) Buttrwrth-Heinemann.

Livesay, Billy R., jt. auth. see Mandel, C. E., Jr.

*Livesay, Corine R. Getting & Staying Organized. (AMI How-to Ser.). 100p. 1995. 9.95 (1-884926-43-6) Amer Media.

Livesay, Corinne. Getting & Staying Organized. 112p. 1994. pap. 10.00 (0-7863-0254-2) Irwin Prof Pubng.

Livesay, Dorothy. The Woman I Am. 96p. 1991. pap. 10.00 (0-920717-37-3) SPD-Small Pr Dist.

Livesay, Harold C. American Made: Men Who Shaped the American Economy. LC 79-15971. (C). 1987. reprint ed. pap. text ed. 24.00 (0-673-39346-1) HarpCollege.

— Andrew Carnegie & the Rise of Big Business. (Library of American Biography). (C). 1987. pap. text ed. 16.00 (0-673-39344-5) HarpCollege.

— Andrew Carnegie & the Rise of Big Business. (Library of American Biography). 200p. 1995. reprint ed. pap. 15.95 (1-886746-26-5) Talman Pub.

— Samuel Gompers & Organized Labor in America. (Library of American Biography). (C). 1987. pap. text ed. 10.00 (0-673-39345-3) HarpCollege.

— Samuel Gompers & Organized Labor in America. 195p. (C). 1993. reprint ed. pap. text ed. 9.95 (0-88133-751-X) Waveland Pr.

*Livesay, Harold C., ed. Entrepreneurship & the Growth of Firms. LC 95-11872. (International Library of Critical Writings in Business History: Vol. 12). 1995. write for info. (1-85278-768-6, Pub. by E Elgar Pub UK) Ashgate Pub Co.

Livesay, Harold C., jt. auth. see Porter, Glenn.

Livesay, June. Candle in Darkness: A Novel. 280p. 1990. pap. 8.95 (0-914984-22-5) Starburst.

Livesay, Pete. Rock Climbing. 1990. 21.95 (1-55591-061-0) Fulcrum Pub.

Livesay, S. Survey of Legal Literature on Woman Offenders. i, 16p. 1975. pap. 2.00 (0-938876-01-5) Entropy Ltd.

Livesay, Thomas. Ruth Abrams: Paintings, 1940-1985. LC 86-80994. (Illus.). 94p. (Orig.). 1986. pap. 12.00 (0-934349-03-7) Grey Art Gallery Study Ctr.

Livesey, Anthony. Great Battles of World War I. 200p. 1989. text ed. 39.95 (0-02-583131-3) Macmillan.

— Great Commanders & Their Battles. LC 93-70593. (Illus.). 200p. 1993. reprint ed. 19.98 (1-56138-330-9) Courage Bks.

Livesey, Brian, jt. auth. see Allan, Barbara.

Livesey, Frank. Dictionary of Economics. 320p. (Orig.). 1993. pap. 33.50 (0-273-60034-6, Pub. by Pitman Pub Ltd UK) Trans-Atl Phila.

— Textbook of Economics. 4th ed. LC 94-30854. 1995. write for info. (0-582-23867-6) Longman.

Livesey, J. C., et al. Radiation-Protective Drugs & Their Reaction Mechanisms. LC 85-15451. (Illus.). 146p. 1986. 32.00 (0-8155-1051-9) Noyes.

Livesey, Margot, jt. auth. see Klamkin, Lynn.

Livesey, P. J. Learning & Emotion: A Biological Synthesis. 328p. (C). 1986. text ed. 59.95 (0-89859-552-5) L Erlbaum Assocs.

Livesey, Peter. Rock Climbing. (Illus.). 160p. 1990. 21.95 (0-938567-22-5) Cloudcap.

Livesey, Rupert & Proctor, Astrid. Barron's Diccionario Juvenile Illustrado: Ingles para Hispanos. (Illus.). 180p. (J). (gr. 2 up). 1994. 14.95 (0-8120-6457-7) Barron.

Livesey, Steven J. Antonius de Carlenis O. P. Four Questions on the Subalternation of the Sciences. LC 94-72415. (Transactions Ser.: Vol. 84, Pt. 4). 125p. (C). 1994. pap. 20.00 (0-87169-844-7, T844-LIS) Am Philos.

— Theology & Science in the Fourteenth Century: Three Questions on the Unity & Subalternation of the Sciences from John of Reading's Commentary on the Sentences. LC 89-909. (Studien und Texte zur Geistesgeschichte des Mittelalters Ser.: Vol. XXV). viii, 229p. (Orig.). 1989. pap. text ed. 68.75 (90-04-09023-1) E J Brill.

Livesey, V. B., jt. ed. see Sumner, G.

Livesey, W. A. Motor Trade Handbook. Date not set. text ed. write for info. (0-408-01135-1) Buttrwrth-Heinemann.

Livesley, John, ed. The DSM-IV Personality Disorders. 1995. lib. bdg. 50.00 (0-89862-257-3, 2257) Guilford Pr.

Livesley, R. K. Matrix Methods of Structural Analysis. 2nd ed. 208p. 1975. 164.00 (0-08-018888-5, Pub. by Pergamon Repr UK) Franklin.

Livesley, W. J. & Bromley, D. B. Person Perception in Childhood & Adolescence. LC 72-8606. 332p. reprint ed. pap. 94.70 (0-317-26323-4, 2025204) Bks Demand.

Livesly. History Atlas of World War I. 1994. 45.00 (0-8050-2651-7) H Holt & Co.

Liveson, Jay A. Peripheral Neurology: Case Studies in Electrodiagnosis. 2nd ed. LC 90-14135. (Illus.). 476p. (C). 1991. text ed. 60.00 (0-8036-5652-1) Davis Co.

Liveson, Jay A. & Ma, Dong M. Laboratory Reference for Clinical Neurophysiology. LC 92-9993. 513p. (C). 1992. text ed. 65.00 (0-8036-5651-3) Davis Co.

*Livesy. Merged Interests: Harvard's Greatest Legacy: The Class of '49. 1995. 22.00 (1-56977-877-9) Cadell & Davies.

An Asterisk (*) at the beginning of an entry indicates that the title is appearing in BIP for the first time.

Livet, Charles L. Lexique De la Langue De Moliere, 3 vols., Set. xiii, 2022p. 1970. reprint ed. write for info. (*0-318-71373-X*, Pub. by Georg Olms GW) Lubrecht & Cramer.

Livezeanu, Irina. Cultural Politics in Greater Romania: Regionalism, Nation Building, & Ethnic Struggle, 1918-1930. (Illus.). 356p. 1995. 45.00 (*0-8014-2445-3*) Cornell U Pr.

Livezey, Ariel W. Numberland. (Illus.). 160p. 1995. pap. 9.95 (*0-9642628-1-9*) Mtntop Pubng. NUMBERLAND is a book in which numbers are the characters, & characters they are! Have you ever met a perfect 10? She believes that "everyone wants to be a perfect 10. There's something so, well, perfect about it, in every which way." These numbers live in Chalkland, which is a poor simulation of Numberland, & are required, within the context of a special school, to solve life's problems. Their attempts are often comical, their attitudes ludicrous, but they also succeed in changing, for they have to conform to the perfect Principle that governs Numberland. About this Principle, a teacher asks, "Would this perfect Principle think of one number as more valuable than another?" NUMBERLAND is dedicated to all those who have to deal with numbers, figures, characters or calculations. Numbers (enough in your bank account?). Figures (happy with the way you look or feel?). Characters (most everyone you know?). Calculations (what is life adding up to?) This book is further dedicated to those weary of fluctuating standards of perfection, those who earnestly desire to solve the problem of being by understanding the permanent, perfect Principle that lovingly governs all. To order contact: Mountaintop Publishing, P.O. Box 15316, Long Beach, CA 90815. Tel. (310) 431-0707.** ***Publisher Provided Annotation.

Livezey, Bradley C. & Humphrey, Philip S. Taxonomy & Identification of Steamer-Ducks (Anatidae: Tachyeres) (Monograph Ser.: No. 8). 210p. 1992. pap. 14.95 (*0-89338-042-3*) U of KS Mus Nat Hist.

Livezey, Bradley C., jt. auth. see Humphrey, Philip S.

Livezey, Lowell W. Nongovernmental Organizations & the Ideas of Human Rights. (World Order Studies Program Occasional Paper: No. 15). 199p. (Orig.). 1988. pap. text ed. 11.00 (*0-945101-00-7*) Princeton CIS.

— Nongovernmental Organizations & the Ideas of Human Rights. LC 87-34939. (World Order Studies Program Occasional Paper: No. 15). 201p. (Orig.). reprint ed. pap. 57.30 (*0-8357-8527-0*, 2034825) Bks Demand.

Livezey, Robert, jt. auth. see Brown, Vinson.

Livezey, William E. Mahan on Sea Power. rev. ed. LC 79-6720. (Illus.). 444p. (Orig.). 1986. pap. 19.95 (*0-8061-1918-7*) U of Okla Pr.

Livgren, Kerry, jt. auth. see Boa, Kenneth.

Livi Bacci, Massimo. A Century of Portuguese Fertility. LC 70-120758. (Office of Population Research Ser.). 1970. 37.50 (*0-691-09307-5*) Princeton U Pr.

Livi-Bacci, Massimo. Population & Nutrition: An Essay on European Demographic History. Croft-Murray, Tania, tr. (Studies in Population, Economy & Society in Past Time). 152p. (C). 1991. 49.95 (*0-521-36325-X*); pap. 14.95 (*0-521-36871-5*) Cambridge U Pr.

Livi, R. & Politi, A., eds. Advances in Nonlinear Dynamics & Stochastic Processes: Proceedings of the meeting on Nonlinear Dynamics Arcetri, Florence, January 7-8 1985. 232p. 1985. 41.00 (*9971-5-0018-3*) World Scientific Pub.

Livi, R., et al, eds. Chaos & Complexity: Proceedings of the Workshop on Chaos & Complexity. 452p. (C). 1988. pap. 46.00 (*9971-5-0568-1*) World Scientific Pub.

— Complex Dynamics. 320p. (C). 1993. text ed. 97.00 (*1-56072-086-7*) Nova Sci Pubs.

Livia, Anna. Incidents Involving Mirth. LC 90-42348. 216p. (Orig.). 1990. 22.95 (*0-933377-14-2*); pap. 9.95 (*0-933377-13-4*) Eighth Mount Pr.

— Minimax. LC 90-42350. 250p. 1991. lib. bdg. 22.95 (*0-933377-12-6*); pap. 9.95 (*0-933377-11-8*) Eighth Mount Pr.

Livia, Anna, tr. see Barney, Natalie C.

Livia, Anna, tr. see Delarue-Mardrus, Lucie.

Liviano, David. The Official Guide to Adoptions in Eastern Europe 1994-1995, 3 vols., Set. 2820p. 1994. pap., vhs 200.00 (*0-9640536-0-8*) Melador Pubng.

Liviatan, Nissan, ed. Proceedings of a Conference on Currency Substitution & Currency Boards. LC 93-26386. (Discussion Paper Ser.: No. 207). 128p. 1993. 7.95 (*0-8213-2521-3*, 12521) World Bank.

LiviBacci, Massimo. A History of Italian Fertility During the Last Two Centuries. LC 76-3271. (Office of Population Research Ser.). 1976. 50.00 (*0-691-09369-5*) Princeton U Pr.

Living Bible Staff. Family Devotional Bible. LC 92-31145. 1993. 29.99 (*0-8423-1223-4*); pap. 19.99 (*0-8423-1224-2*) Tyndale.

Living Bible Staff, tr. Life Application Bible Study Guide: Acts. 144p. 1990. 4.99 (*0-8423-2730-4*, 012730-4) Tyndale.

— Life Application Bible Study Guide: Hosea & Jonah. 1990. 4.99 (*0-8423-2724-X*, 012724-X) Tyndale.

— Life Application Bible Study Guide: Joshua. 112p. 1990. 4.99 (*0-8423-2723-1*, 012723-1) Tyndale.

Living Earth Foundation Staff, comp. The Rainforests: A Celebration. (Illus.). 224p. 1992. 35.00 (*0-87701-790-5*); pap. 22.95 (*0-8118-0155-1*) Chronicle Bks.

***Living, Martha S., ed.** Handmade Christmas. 1995. pap. 20.00 (*0-517-88476-3*, C P Pubs) Crown Pub Group.

Living Waters Pubns. Staff, ed. see Comfort, Ray.

Living Waters Staff, ed. see Comfort, Ray.

Livingood, J., et al, eds. Christmas I Remember Best. (Illus.). (Orig.). write for info. (*0-910901-00-7*); pap. 5.95 (*0-910901-01-5*) Deseret News.

***Livingood, James W.** Chattanooga: An Illustrated Histo. 1981. 19.95 (*0-89781-027-9*) Preferred Mktg.

— Philadelphia-Baltimore Trade Rivalry 1780-1860. LC 70-112557. (Rise of Urban America Ser.). (Illus.). 1976. reprint ed. 21.95 (*0-405-02463-0*) Ayer.

Livingood, James W., jt. auth. see Govan, Gilbert E.

Livingood, James W., jt. auth. see Raulston, J. Leonard.

***Livingood, Jay K.** Development & Operation Manual for a Golf Practice Range Facility. (Illus.). 300p. 1992. 195.00 (*0-9645721-0-9*) Livingood Consult.

Livings, Henry. Eh? 1968. pap. 4.75 (*0-8222-0351-0*) Dramatists Play.

Livings, Henry, tr. see Lorca, Federico G.

Livingston. Only Spring. Date not set. pap. 10.00 (*0-06-251061-4*, HarpT) HarpC.

— Only Spring. 1995. 20.00 (*0-06-251060-6*, HarpT) HarpC.

Livingston, jt. auth. see Butler.

Livingston, A., tr. see Croce, Benedetto.

***Livingston, A. D.** Bass Cookbook. 160p. 1996. pap. 12.95 (*0-8117-2509-X*) Stackpole.

— Bass on the Fly. 2nd rev. ed. LC 93-47194. 1994. pap. text ed. 16.95 (*0-07-038151-8*, Ragged Mntn) McGraw.

— Cast Iron Cooking. 1991. pap. 12.95 (*1-55821-115-2*) Lyons & Burford.

— Good Vittles: One Man's Meat, a Few Vegetables & a Drink or Two. 1990. pap. 13.95 (*1-55821-079-2*) Lyons & Burford.

— Grilling, Smoking, & Barbecuing. 224p. 1992. 19.95 (*1-55821-151-9*) Lyons & Burford.

— Luremaking: The Art & Science of Spinnerbaits, Buzzbaits, Jigs, & Other Leadheads. 1993. pap. 16.95 (*0-87742-372-5*) Intl Marine.

— Luremaking: The Art & Science of Spinnerbaits, Buzzbaits, Jigs, & Other Leadheads. 1994. pap. text ed. 16.95 (*0-07-038152-6*) McGraw.

— Poker Strategy & Winning Play. 1991. pap. 12.95 (*1-55821-111-X*) Lyons & Burford.

— Trout Cookbook. 160p. 1996. pap. 12.95 (*0-8117-2581-2*) Stackpole.

— Venison Cookbook. LC 93-4400. (Illus.). 128p. 1993. pap. 12.95 (*0-8117-2594-4*) Stackpole.

— Wild Turkey Cookbook. LC 94-20652. 192p. 1995. pap. 12.95 (*0-8117-3097-2*) Stackpole.

Livingston, A. D. & Livingston, Helen. Edible Plants & Animals: A Compendium of Unusual Foods from Aardvark to Zamia. 1993. 25.95 (*0-8160-2744-7*) Facts on File.

Livingston, Alan & Livingston, Isabella. The Thames & Hudson Encyclopaedia of Graphic Design & Designers. LC 92-70862. (World of Art Ser.). (Illus.). 216p. 1992. pap. 12.95 (*0-500-20259-1*) Thames Hudson.

Livingston, Anne H. Nancy Shippen, Her Journal Book: The International Romance of a Young Lady of Fashion of Colonial Philadelphia. (American Biography Ser.). 348p. 1991. reprint ed. lib. bdg. 79.00 (*0-7812-8248-9*) Rprt Serv.

Livingston, Arthur, tr. see Montessori, Maria.

Livingston, Arthur, ed. see Mosca, Gaetano.

Livingston, Arthur, ed. see Pareto, Vilfredo.

Livingston, Arthur, tr. see Scheffer, Paul.

Livingston, Beverly, tr. see Tristan, Flora.

Livingston, Bob. Trailer Life's RV Repair & Maintenance Manual. LC 89-4637. 1989. pap. 29.95 (*0-934798-12-5*) TL Enterprises.

Livingston, Brian. More Windows 3.1 Secrets. 720p. 1993. disk 39.95 (*1-56884-019-5*) IDG Bks.

— Windows NT SECRETS. Date not set. pap. 39.95 (*1-878058-71-1*) IDG Bks.

— Windows 3.1 Secrets. 2nd ed. LC 92-70931. (InfoWorld Technical Bks.). 980p. 1992. pap. 39.95 (*1-878058-43-6*) IDG Bks.

— Windows 95 Secrets. 1995. pap. 39.99 (*1-56884-453-0*) IDG Bks.

Livingston, Brian & Gruman, Galen. Windows Gizmos. (Illus.). 624p. 1992. pap. 39.95 (*1-878058-66-5*) IDG Bks.

Livingston, C. H. Jongleur Gauthier le Leu: Etude Sur les Fabliaux. (Harvard Studies in Romance Languages: Vol. 24). 1951. 64.00 (*0-527-01122-3*) Periodicals Srv.

Livingston, Carl. A Laywoman's Primer of Breast Cancer. (Illus.). 24p. (Orig.). 1980. pap. 1.50 (*0-937816-03-5*) Tech Data.

Livingston, Carol. Teachers as Leaders: Evolving Roles. 176p. 1992. 15.95 (*0-8106-1848-6*) NEA.

Livingston, Carol & Castle, Shari, eds. Teachers & Research in Action. 104p. 1989. 10.95 (*0-8106-3004-4*) NEA.

Livingston, Carole. I'll Never Be Fat Again. LC 91-40267. 1992. pap. 12.95 (*0-942637-49-6*) Barricade Bks.

— Why Was I Adopted? (Illus.). (J). (gr. 1 up). 1978. text ed. 12.00 (*0-8184-0257-1*) Carol Pub Group.

— Why Was I Adopted? (Illus.). 48p. 1986. pap. 8.95 (*0-8184-0400-0*) Carol Pub Group.

Livingston, Carole & Ciliotta, Claire. Why Am I Going to the Hospital? (Illus.). (J). (gr. 1 up). 1981. 12.00 (*0-8184-0316-0*) Carol Pub Group.

Livingston, Carole, jt. auth. see Ciliotta, Claire.

Livingston, Carole R. British Broadside Ballads of the Sixteenth Century Vol. I: A Catalogue of the Extant Sheets & an Essay. LC 90-48731. 928p. 1991. 96.00 (*0-8240-7226-X*, 1390) Garland.

Livingston, Charles. Knot Theory. (Carus Monograph Ser.). (Illus.). 264p. 1993. 34.00 (*0-88385-027-3*) Math Assn.

Livingston, Cohn. Space Songs. (Illus.). (J). (ps-3). 1993. reprint ed. pap. 5.95 (*0-8234-1029-3*) Holiday.

Livingston College, Faculty of Comparative Literature. A Syllabus of Comparative Literature. 2nd ed. McCormick, John O., ed. LC 72-8502. 233p. 1972. 16.50 (*0-8108-0555-3*) Scarecrow.

Livingston County, Historical & Genealogical Society Staff & Turner Publishing Co., Staff. History & Families Livingston County, Kentucky. LC 89-50666. 502p. 1990. 49.95 (*0-938021-46-X*) Turner Pub KY.

Livingston, D. I., jt. ed. see Fleming, R. A.

Livingston, Donald & Martin, Marie, eds. Hume As Philosopher of Society, Politics & History. (Library of the History of Ideas: No. IV). 188p. 1991. text ed. 55.00 (*1-878822-03-9*) Univ Rochester Pr.

Livingston, Donald W. Hume's Philosophy of Common Life. LC 83-18227. xiv, 378p. 1986. pap. text ed. 13.95 (*0-226-48715-6*) U Ch Pr.

Livingston, Donald W. & King, James T., eds. Hume: A Re-Evaluation. LC 76-13968. 431p. reprint ed. pap. 122.90 (*0-8357-6874-0*, 2035572) Bks Demand.

Livingston, Donald W., jt. ed. see Capaldi, Nicholas.

Livingston, Donald W., ed. see Hume, David.

Livingston, E. A. President Lincoln's Third Largest City: Brooklyn & the Civil War. 187p. (Orig.). 1993. pap. 19.95 (*0-9638981-0-8*) E A Livingston.

— Studia Patristica Nineteen-Two, Vol. 2: Critica-Classica-Ascetica-Liturgica Papers of the 1983 Oxford Patristics Conference. (Cistercian Studies). 416p. (Orig.). pap. 55.00 (*0-87907-351-9*) Cistercian Pubns.

Livingston, E. A., ed. Studia Patristica Nineteen-Three, Vol. 3: Second Century-Tertullian to Nicaea in the West-Clement & Origen-The Cappadocian Fathers. Papers of the 1983 Oxford Patristics Conference. (Cistercian Studies). 584p. pap. 55.00 (*0-685-37892-6*) Cistercian Pubns.

Livingston, E. B. The Livingstones of Livingston Manor, Being the History of the Branch Which Settled in the Province of New York with an Account of Robert Livingston & Albany & His Principal Descendants. (Illus.). 623p. 1989. reprint ed. lib. bdg. 101.50 (*0-8328-0777-X*); reprint ed. pap. 93.50 (*0-8328-0778-8*) Higginson Bk Co.

Livingston, Edward. Complete Works on Criminal Jurisprudence: Consisting of Systems of Penal Law for the State of Louisiana & for the United States of America, with Introductory Reports to the Same, 2 vols., Set. LC 68-55775. (Criminology, Law Enforcement, & Social Problems Ser.: No. 7). 1968. reprint ed. 45.00 (*0-87585-007-3*) Patterson Smith.

Livingston, Elizabeth & Starbuck, Carol. Miami for Kids: A Family Guide to Greater Miami Including Everglades National Park & the Florida Keys. LC 81-65980. (Illus.). 80p. 1981. pap. 4.95 (*0-916224-63-5*) Banyan Bks.

***Livingston, Eric.** An Anthropology of Reading. LC 94-39577. 1995. write for info. (*0-253-33509-4*) Ind U Pr.

— The Ethnomethodological Foundations of Mathematics. (Studies in Ethnomethodology). 256p. 1986. 49.95 (*0-7102-0335-7*, RKP) Routledge.

— Making Sense of Ethnomethodology. 160p. (C). 1988. text ed. 55.00 (*0-7102-1261-5*, RKP); pap. write for info. (*0-7102-1262-3*, RKP) Routledge.

Livingston, G. E., ed. Nutritional Status Assessment of the Individual. 479p. 1989. 125.00 (*0-917678-25-7*) Food & Nut Pr.

Livingston, G. E., et al. The Role of Food Product Development in Implementing Dietary Guidelines. 212p. 1982. 50.00 (*0-685-67749-4*) Food & Nut Pr.

Livingston, G. Herbert. The Pentateuch in Its Cultural Environment. 2nd ed. LC 73-92978. 1974. pap. 19.99 (*0-8010-5646-2*) Baker Bk.

***Livingston, Georgette.** A Choice of Love. 256p. 1995. pap. 4.99 (*0-7860-0159-3*) Windsor NY.

— A Choice of Love. 256p. 1995. pap. 4.99 (*0-8217-0159-2*) Zebra.

— Ekahi. 1994. 17.95 (*0-8034-9087-9*, 094531) Bouregy.

— Ekolu, No. 3. 1995. 17.95 (*0-8034-9106-9*, 095132) Bouregy.

— Elua. 1995. 17.95 (*0-8034-9097-6*, 094631) Bouregy.

— The House in the Trees. 1993. 13.95 (*0-8034-9030-5*) Bouregy.

— Masquerade for Love. 1995. 17.95 (*0-8034-9094-1*, 094611) Bouregy.

— Mountain Love Song. 1993. 13.95 (*0-8034-9010-0*) Bouregy.

— Reach for Tomorrow. 1995. 17.95 (*0-8034-9105-0*, 095124) Bouregy.

Livingston, Harold. No Trophy, No Sword: An American Volunteer in the Israeli Air Force During the 1948 War of Independence. LC 93-49571. (Illus.). 262p. 1994. 21.95 (*1-883695-03-1*) Edition Q.

— Ride a Tiger. 1988. mass mkt. 4.95 (*0-312-90487-8*) St Martin.

— To Die in Babylon. 400p. 1993. 21.95 (*0-312-09923-1*, Pub. by Thomas Dunne Bks) St Martin.

Livingston, Helen, jt. auth. see Livingston, A. D.

Livingston, Ira, jt. ed. see Halberstam, Judith.

Livingston, Isabella, jt. auth. see Livingston, Alan.

Livingston, Ivor L. The ABCs of Stress Management: Taking Control of Your Life. Van Treese, James B., ed. (Illus.). 212p. 1990. pap. 7.95 (*1-880416-58-1*) NW Pub.

Livingston, Ivor L., ed. Handbook of Black American Health: The Mosaic of Conditions, Issues, Policies, & Prospects. LC 93-4852. 453p. 1994. text ed. 85.00 (*0-313-28640-X*, LHB/, Greenwood Pr) Greenwood.

Livingston, J. B. If I Were a Teenager: Pupil Book, 4 vols. (J). 1966. pap. 2.75 (*0-685-74307-1*) Quality Pubns.

— If I Were a Teenager: Teacher's Manual, 4 vols. 1966. teacher ed. pap. 3.50 (*0-685-47447-X*) Quality Pubns.

— Love Yourself. 1972. 4.50 (*0-89137-421-3*) Quality Pubns.

— Today's Victorious Woman, Vol. I. 1983. pap. 5.25 (*0-89137-426-4*) Quality Pubns.

— Today's Victorious Woman, Vol. 2. 1983. pap. 5.25 (*0-89137-427-2*) Quality Pubns.

Livingston, James. Origins of the Federal Reserve System: Money, Class, & Corporate Capitalism, 1890-1913. LC 85-48199. 272p. 1986. 39.95 (*0-8014-1844-5*); pap. 14.95 (*0-8014-9681-0*) Cornell U Pr.

— Pragmatism & the Political Economy of Cultural Revolution, 1850-1940. LC 94-5736. (Cultural Studies of the United States). 480p. 1994. text ed. 39.95 (*0-8078-2157-8*) U of NC Pr.

Livingston, James, jt. auth. see Kestner, Franklin D., Sr.

Livingston, James A., et al. Accountability & Objectives for Music Education. LC 49-626. (Contemporary Music Education Ser.). 29p. (Orig.). 1972. reprint ed. pap. 4.95 (*0-930424-00-X*) Music Educ Pubns.

Livingston, James C. Anatomy of the Sacred: An Introduction to Religion. 2nd ed. LC 92-32308. (Illus.). 480p. (C). 1993. pap. write for info. (*0-02-371401-8*) Macmillan.

— Modern Christian Thought: From the Enlightenment to Vatican Two. 523p. (C). 1971. text ed. write for info. (*0-02-371420-4*) Macmillan.

Livingston, Jane. Lee Miller: A Photographer Rediscovered. LC 88-50222. (Illus.). 1989. 50.00 (*0-500-54139-6*) Thames Hudson.

— Lee Miller Photographer. (Illus.). 176p. 1989. 60.00 (*0-917571-07-X*); pap. 28.95 (*0-917571-06-1*) CA Intl Arts.

— Lee Miller Photographs. 1989. 50.00 (*0-500-55413-7*) Thames Hudson.

— The New York School: Photographs, 1936-1963. LC 92-9852. (Illus.). 404p. 1992. 75.00 (*1-55670-239-6*) Stewart Tabori & Chang.

Livingston, Jane, contrib. Thomas Chimes: The Hermes Cycle. (Illus.). 52p. 1992. pap. 15.00 (*1-879173-11-5*) Locks Gallery.

Livingston, Jane, intro. Odyssey: The Art of Photography at National Geographic. LC 88-50159. (Illus.). 364p. 1988. 34.98 (*0-934738-45-9*) Thomasson-Grant.

Livingston, Jane & Beardsley, John. Black Folk Art in America, 1930-1980. LC 81-24072. (Illus.). 176p. 1989. reprint ed. lib. bdg. 45.00 (*0-87805-398-0*); reprint ed. pap. 29.95 (*0-87805-158-9*) U Pr of Miss.

Livingston, Jay. Crime & Criminology. 624p. (C). 1991. text ed. write for info. (*0-13-192782-5*) P-H.

Livingston, Jay C. The Fount of Dreams. LC 77-84640. 1977. 3.50 (*0-931412-00-5*, PB-001) Metatron Pr.

— The Romantic Muse. LC 78-71646. (Illus.). 1978. pap. 3.50 (*0-931412-10-2*) Metatron Pr.

Livingston, Jay C., see Livingston Edwards, pseud..

Livingston, Jay C., ed. see Edwards, Livingston, pseud.

Livingston, John & Rischin, Moses, eds. Jews of the American West. LC 90-44864. (American Jewish Civilization Ser.). 232p. 1991. pap. 14.95 (*0-8143-2171-2*) Wayne St U Pr.

Livingston, John, jt. auth. see Largay, James A.

Livingston, John A., et al. Skinned: Activists Condemn the Horrors of the Fur Trade. 256p. (Orig.). (C). 1989. pap. text ed. 6.95 (*0-685-26109-3*) Intl Wildlife.

Livingston, Julie, ed. see Gray, John.

Livingston, Julie, ed. see Kawasaki, Guy.

Livingston, Julie, ed. see Menuez, Doug & Kounalakis, Markos.

Livingston, Julie, ed. see Sollie, Eddie C.

Livingston, Julie, ed. see Strauss, Susan.

Livingston, Julie, ed. see Wang, Rosalind.

Livingston, Julie, ed. see Wood, Wendy A.

Livingston, K. C. & Graham, T. C., eds. Manufacturing Processes in Canada. LC 60-4680. (Illus.). 308p. reprint ed. pap. 87.80 (*0-317-11048-9*, 2014301) Bks Demand.

Livingston, Kathryn. Chic Simple Bed Linens. 1994. 12.50 (*0-679-43216-7*) Knopf.

Livingston, Kathryn E., ed. Fashion Photography: Patrick Demarchelier. (American Photographer Master Ser.: Vol. 2). (Illus.). 144p. 1989. 40.00 (*0-8212-1682-1*); 24.95 (*0-8212-1736-4*) Bulfinch Pr.

Livingston, Kenneth E., jt. ed. see Doane, Benjamin K.

Livingston, Leon R. From Coast to Coast with Jack London by A-No. 1. LC 74-101741. (Illus.). 1969. reprint ed. 10.00 (*0-912382-01-5*) Black Letter.

Livingston, Lida & Schrader, Constance. Wrinkles. 1980. pap. 2.50 (*0-345-29418-1*) Ballantine.

Livingston, Marco. R. B. Kitaj. enl. rev. ed. LC 92-80824. (Illus.). 160p. 1992. reprint ed. pap. 24.95 (*0-500-01549-X*) Thames Hudson.

Livingston, Margit, jt. auth. see Butler, Lynda L.

Livingston, Marius H., ed. International Terrorism in the Contemporary World. LC 77-84773. (Contributions in Political Science Ser.: No.3). (Illus.). 522p. 1978. text ed. 45.00 (*0-8371-9884-4*, LIT/, Greenwood Pr) Greenwood.

Livingston, Martin S. Near & Far: Closeness & Distance in Psychotherapy. LC 91-40451. 225p. 1992. 18.95 (*0-944957-34-X*) Rivercross Pub.

An Asterisk (*) at the beginning of an entry indicates that the title is appearing in BIP for the first time.

L

***Livingston, Michael K.** Mental Discipline: The Pursuit of Peak Performance. LC 88-34807. (Illus.). 280p. 1989. pap. text ed. 22.00x (*0-87322-440-X*, BLIV0440) Human Kinetics.

Livingston, Michael M. Beyond Backache: A Personal Guide to Back & Neck Pain Relief. LC 87-92101. 1988. 12.95 (*0-87212-212-3*) Libra.

Livingston, Mike, ed. User Conference Proceedings 1994, Vol. 1. (Illus.). 872p. (Orig.). (C). 1994. pap. text ed. 25.00 (*1-879102-22-6*) ERS Inst.

— User Conference Proceedings 1994, Vol. 2. (Illus.). 808p. (Orig.). (C). 1994. pap. text ed. 25.00 (*1-879102-23-4*) ERS Inst.

— User Conference Proceedings 1994 & 1994 User Conference Technical Handouts, 3 vols. (Illus.). 590p. (Orig.). (C). 1994. pap. text ed. 25.00 (*1-879102-19-6*); cd-rom 30.00 (*1-879102-20-X*) ERS Inst.

— User Conference Proceedings 1994 & 1994 User Conference Technical Handouts, 3 vols., Set. (Illus.). (Orig.). (C). 1994. pap. text ed. 75.00 (*1-879102-21-8*) ERS Inst.

Livingston, Miles. Money & Capital Markets. LC 92-72604. 683p. 1993. pap. 36.00 (*1-878975-15-3*) Kolb Pub.

— Money & Capital Markets. 2nd ed. LC 93-22907. 1993. 39.95 (*0-13-054405-1*) NY Inst Finance.

— Money & Capital Markets: Financial Instruments & Their Uses. 352p. 1989. pap. text ed. 42.00 (*0-13-600131-9*) P-H.

Livingston, Milton S. Particle Accelerators: A Brief History. LC 69-18038. (Illus.). 128p. reprint ed. pap. 36.50 (*0-7837-4167-7*, 2059016) Bks Demand.

Livingston, Myra C. Abraham Lincoln: A Man for All the People: A Ballad. LC 93-2731. (Illus.). 32p. (J). (ps-3). 1993. lib. bdg. 15.95 (*0-8234-1049-8*) Holiday.

— Animal, Vegetable, Mineral: Poems about Small Things. LC 93-43712. (Illus.). 80p. (J). (gr. 3-7). 1994. 14.00 (*0-06-023008-8*); lib. bdg. 13.89 (*0-06-023009-6*) HarpC Child Bks.

— Birthday Poems. LC 89-2114. (Illus.). 32p. (J). (ps-3). 1989. lib. bdg. 13.95 (*0-8234-0783-7*) Holiday.

— Celebrations. LC 84-19216. (Illus.). 32p. (J). (ps-3). 1985. lib. bdg. 15.95 (*0-8234-0550-8*); pap. 5.95 (*0-8234-0654-7*) Holiday.

— The Child As Poet: Myth or Reality? 356p. 1984. 24.95 (*0-87675-287-3*) Horn Bk.

— A Circle of Seasons. LC 81-20305. (Illus.). 32p. (J). (ps-3). 1982. lib. bdg. 15.95 (*0-8234-0452-8*); pap. 5.95 (*0-8234-0656-3*) Holiday.

— Dilly Dilly Piccalilli: Poems for the Very Young. (Illus.). 80p. (J). (gr. 1 up). 1989. text ed. 13.95 (*0-689-50466-7*, McElderry) S&S Childrens.

— Flights of Fancy & Other Poems. LC 94-14476. (J). (gr. 3-7). 1994. text ed. 13.95 (*0-689-50613-9*, Mac Bks Young Read) S&S Childrens.

— Higgledy-Piggledy: Verses & Pictures. LC 86-8789. (Illus.). 32p. (J). (gr. 3-7). 1986. text ed. 12.95 (*0-689-50407-1*, McElderry) S&S Childrens.

— I Like You, If You Like Me: Poems of Friendship. LC 86-21108. 160p. (YA). (gr. 5 up). 1987. text ed. 14.95 (*0-689-50408-X*, McElderry) S&S Childrens.

— I Never Told: And Other Poems. LC 91-20475. 48p. (J). (gr. 3-7). 1992. text ed. 12.95 (*0-689-50544-2*, McElderry) S&S Childrens.

— If the Owl Calls Again: A Collection of Owl Poems. LC 89-27659. (Illus.). 128p. (YA). (gr. 5 up). 1990. text ed. 13.95 (*0-689-50501-9*, McElderry) S&S Childrens.

— Keep on Singing: A Ballad of Marian Anderson. LC 93-46909. (Illus.). 32p. (J). (ps-3). 1994. lib. bdg. 15.95 (*0-8234-1098-6*) Holiday.

— Let Freedom Ring: A Ballad of Martin Luther King, Jr. LC 91-28245. (Illus.). 32p. (J). (ps-3). 1992. lib. bdg. 15.95 (*0-8234-0957-0*) Holiday.

— Light & Shadow. LC 91-22355. (Illus.). 32p. (J). (ps-3). 1992. lib. bdg. 14.95 (*0-8234-0931-7*) Holiday.

— Monkey Puzzle & Other Poems. LC 84-3050. (Illus.). 64p. (J). (gr. 6 up). 1984. text ed. 13.95 (*0-689-50310-5*, McElderry) S&S Childrens.

— Poem-Making: Ways to Begin Writing Poetry. LC 90-5012. (Charlotte Zolotow Bk.). 176p. (J). (gr. 4-8). 1991. 16.00 (*0-06-024019-9*); lib. bdg. 15.89 (*0-06-024020-2*) HarpC Child Bks.

— Poems of Christmas. LC 80-13627. 192p. (YA). (gr. 5 up). 1980. text ed. 14.95 (*0-689-50180-3*, McElderry) S&S Childrens.

— Remembering & Other Poems. LC 89-2654. 64p. (J). (gr. 3-7). 1989. text ed. 13.95 (*0-689-50489-6*, McElderry) S&S Childrens.

— Sky Songs. LC 83-12955. (Illus.). 32p. (J). (ps-4). 1984. lib. bdg. 14.95 (*0-8234-0502-8*) Holiday.

— Space Songs. LC 87-19628. (Illus.). 32p. (J). (ps-3). 1988. lib. bdg. 15.95 (*0-8234-0675-X*) Holiday.

— There Was a Place: And Other Poems. LC 88-12832. 40p. (J). (gr. 3-7). 1988. lib. bdg. 12.95 (*0-689-50464-0*, McElderry) S&S Childrens.

— A Time to Talk: Poems of Friendship. LC 91-42234. 128p. (YA). (gr. 7 up). 1992. lib. bdg. 13.95 (*0-689-50558-2*, McElderry) S&S Childrens.

— Up in the Air. LC 88-23293. (Illus.). 32p. (J). (ps-3). 1989. lib. bdg. 14.95 (*0-8234-0736-5*) Holiday.

— Valentine Poems. LC 85-31723. (Illus.). 32p. (J). (ps-3). 1987. lib. bdg. 14.95 (*0-8234-0587-7*) Holiday.

— Why Am I Grown So Cold? Poems of the Unknowable. LC 82-6646. 264p. (J). (gr. 5-p). 1982. text ed. 14.95 (*0-689-50242-7*, McElderry) S&S Childrens.

— Worlds I Know & Other Poems. LC 85-7344. (Illus.). 64p. (J). (gr. 4-7). 1985. text ed. 13.95 (*0-689-50332-6*, McElderry) S&S Childrens.

Livingston, Myra C., ed. Dog Poems. LC 89-2061. (Illus.). 32p. (J). (ps-3). 1990. lib. bdg. 12.95 (*0-8234-0776-4*) Holiday.

— Easter Poems. LC 84-15866. (Illus.). 32p. (J). (ps-3). 1985. lib. bdg. 13.95 (*0-8234-0546-X*) Holiday.

— Poems for Fathers. LC 88-17010. (Illus.). 32p. (J). (ps-3). 1989. lib. bdg. 13.95 (*0-8234-0729-2*) Holiday.

— Roll Along: Poems on Wheels. LC 92-32714. 80p. (J). (gr. 4 up). 1993. text ed. 11.95 (*0-689-50585-X*, McElderry) S&S Childrens.

— Thanksgiving Poems. LC 85-762. (Illus.). 32p. (J). (ps-4). 1985. lib. bdg. 14.95 (*0-8234-0570-2*) Holiday.

***Livingston, Myra C., sel.** Call down the Moon: Poems of Music. LC 95-8283. (J). 1995. write for info. (*0-689-80416-4*, McElderry) S&S Childrens.

Livingston, Myra C. & Dominguez, Joseph F., trs. Platero. LC 92-11634. (Illus.). (ENG & SPA.). (YA). 1994. 14.95 (*0-395-62365-0*, Clarion Bks) HM.

Livingston, Myra C., jt. ed. see Farber, Norma.

Livingston, Myra C., tr. see Jimenez, Juan R.

Livingston, Myra C., jt. auth. see Sutherland, Zena.

Livingston, Nancy. Incident at Parga. 1993. mass mkt. 3.99 (*0-373-28001-7*, 1-28001-5) Harlequin Bks.

— Never Were Such Times. large type ed. LC 91-28384. 763p. 1992. reprint ed. lib. bdg. 19.95 (*1-56054-256-X*) Thorndike Pr.

— Quiet Murder. 1995. pap. 3.99 (*0-373-26186-1*, 1-26186-6, Wrldwide Lib) Harlequin Bks.

— Quiet Murder. LC 92-44214. 1993. 17.95 (*0-312-08878-7*) St Martin.

— Quiet Murder. large type ed. LC 93-26074. 1993. 23.95 (*0-7927-1797-X*, Curley Lrg Print); pap. 21.95 (*0-7927-1796-1*, Curley Lrg Print) Chivers N Amer.

— Two Sisters. 592p. 1994. 25.95 (*0-312-11346-3*) St Martin.

— Unwillingly to Vegas. large type ed. LC 92-39380. 1993. 21.95 (*0-7927-1488-1*, Curley Lrg Print); pap. 19.95 (*0-7927-1487-3*, Curley Lrg Print) Chivers N Amer.

Livingston, Neil C. & Arnold, Terrell E., eds. Beyond the Iran-Contra Crisis: The Shape of U. S. Anti-Terrorism Policy in the Post-Reagan Era. LC 87-45376. (Issues in Low-Intensity Conflict Ser.). 352p. 1988. text ed. 45.00 (*0-669-16466-6*); pap. 19.95 (*0-669-16467-4*) Free Pr.

Livingston, Noel B. Sketch Pedigrees of Some of the Early Settlers in Jamaica: Compiled from the Records of the Court of Chancery of the Island with a List of the Inhabitants in 1670 & Other Matter. 139p. 1992. reprint ed. pap. 14.50 (*0-685-62562-1*, 9212) Clearfield Co.

Livingston, P. Gullible the Seagull. (Illus.). (Orig.). (J). (gr. k-6). 1992. pap. 9.95 (*0-9629860-2-X*) Sound Pub WA.

Livingston, P., et al. Disorder Order: Proceedings of the Stanford International Symposium. (Stanford Literature Studies: Vol. 1). 302p. 1984. pap. 46.50 (*0-915838-01-X*) Anma Libri.

Livingston, Paisley. Ingmar Bergman & the Rituals of Art. LC 81-17440. (Illus.). 288p. 1982. 36.95 (*0-8014-1452-0*) Cornell U Pr.

— Literary Knowledge: Humanistic Inquiry & the Philosophy of Science. LC 87-47821. 296p. 1988. 37.50 (*0-8014-2110-1*); pap. 14.95 (*0-8014-9422-2*) Cornell U Pr.

— Literature & Rationality: Ideas of Agency in Theory & Fiction. 290p. (C). 1992. 64.95 (*0-521-40540-8*) Cambridge U Pr.

— Models of Desire: Rene Girard & the Psychology of Mimesis. 248p. 1992. text ed. 33.50x (*0-8018-4385-5*) Johns Hopkins.

Livingston, Patricia H. Lessons of the Heart: Celebrating the Rhythms of Life. LC 92-72924. 128p. (Orig.). 1992. pap. 6.95 (*0-87793-486-X*) Ave Maria.

Livingston, Phil. Team Penning. (Illus.). 144p. 1991. 12.95 (*0-911647-24-4*) Western Horseman.

Livingston, Philip A., ed. see West, Franklin H., et al.

Livingston, R. J., et al, eds. The Rivers of Florida. (Ecological Studies: Vol. 83). (Illus.). 240p. 1990. 72.00 (*0-387-97363-X*) Spr-Verlag.

Livingston, Ray F. The Traditional Theory of Literature. LC 62-10830. 198p. reprint ed. pap. 56.50 (*0-317-41714-2*, 2055889) Bks Demand.

Livingston, Rik. Mr. Verlin's Zono Comix. LC 87-50993. (Showcase Comic Ser.: No. 2). (Illus.). 128p. (Orig.). 1988. pap. 7.95 (*0-917976-76-2*) Thunder Baas Pr.

Livingston, Robert. Resource Atlas of the Apalachicola Estuary: SGR-55. 64p. 1983. write for info. (*0-318-60283-0*) U Fla Law.

Livingston, Robert A. Livingston's Complete Music Business Directory - East. 200p. 1995. 39.95 (*0-932303-18-8*) GLGLC Music.

— Livingston's Complete Music Business Directory - West. 200p. 1995. 39.95 (*0-932303-19-6*) GLGLC Music.

— Livingston's Complete Music Business Reference, Vol. I. 380p. 1993. 39.95 (*0-932303-14-5*) GLGLC Music.

— Livingston's Complete Music Business Reference, Vol. II. 418p. 1993. 39.95 (*0-932303-16-1*) GLGLC Music.

— The Recording Contract. 1988. 15.00 (*0-932303-07-2*) GLGLC Music.

— The Songwriter-Publisher Contract. 1985. 15.00 (*0-932303-04-8*) GLGLC Music.

— The Tax Deduction Checklist: Songwriters, Musicians, Performers. 1988. 11.95 (*0-9607558-4-5*) GLGLC Music.

Livingston, Robert B., ed. Lung Cancer. (Cancer Treatment & Research Ser.: No. 1). (Illus.). 320p. 1981. lib. bdg. 94.00 (*90-247-2394-9*) Kluwer Ac.

Livingston, Robert G., ed. see Radunski, Peter, et al.

Livingston, Robert R. Essay on Sheep: Their Varieties - Account of the Merinoes of Spain, France, Etc. 186p. (Orig.). 1994. reprint ed. pap. 12.00 (*0-9633659-1-6*) US Hist Res Srv.

Livingston, Rodney, tr. see Marx, Karl.

Livingston, Samuel A. & Stoll, Clarice S. Simulation Games: An Introduction for the Social Studies Teacher. LC 77-171567. (Orig.). 1973. pap. text ed. 14.95 (*0-02-919240-4*) Free Pr.

Livingston, Stephanie D. & Nials, Fred L. Archaeological & Paleoenvironmental Investigations in the Ash Meadows National Wildlife Refuge, Nye County, Nevada. (Illus.). 212p. 1990. 25.00 (*0-945920-70-9*) Desert Rsch Inst.

Livingston, Stephanie D. & Pierce, Christopher. Prehistoric Archaeology of the West Sinter Quarry, Cortez Mountains, Nevada. (Quaternary Sciences Center Technical Report Ser.: No. 61). (Illus.). 130p. (C). 1988. spiral bd. 13.00 (*0-945920-61-X*) Desert Rsch Inst.

Livingston, Stephanie D., et al. Evaluation of Site 26CK3905, Range 62, Nellis Air Force Base, Nevada. (Illus.). 25p. 1989. 5.00 (*0-945920-71-7*) Desert Rsch Inst.

Livingston, Steven. Terrorism Spectacle. 221p. (C). 1993. text ed. 52.50 (*0-8133-8776-0*) Westview.

Livingston, Valerie A. W. Elmer Schofield: Proud Painter of Modest Lands. (Illus.). 64p. (Orig.). (C). 1988. pap. 15.00 (*0-9621345-0-3*) Moravian Coll.

Livingston-Wheeler, Virginia & Addeo, Edmond G. The Conquest of Cancer: Vaccines & Diet. 1993. pap. 9.95 (*0-9627145-1-8*, Cyrus Pr) Waterside Prodns.

Livingston, William, ed. Selected Papers on Instrumentation in Astronomy. LC 93-23374. (Milestone Ser.: Vol. MS 87). 1993. write for info. (*0-8194-1396-8*); pap. write for info. (*0-8194-1395-X*) SPIE.

Livingston, William, jt. auth. see Lynch, David K.

Livingston, William, et al. Independent Reflector or, Weekly Essays on Sundry Important Subjects More Particularly Adapted to the Province of New York. Klein, Milton M., ed. LC 62-13268. (John Harvard Library). 469p. 1963. 37.00 (*0-674-44850-2*) HUP.

Livingston, William S. Federalism & Constitutional Change. LC 74-9226. 380p. 1974. reprint ed. text ed. 69.50 (*0-8371-7623-9*, LIFC, Greenwood Pr) Greenwood.

Livingston, William S., ed. The Legacy of the Constitution: An Assessment for the Third Century. (Symposia Ser.). 164p. 1987. 12.00 (*0-89940-421-9*) LBJ Sch Pub Aff.

— A Prospect of Liberal Democracy. LC 79-63171. 239p. 1979. text ed. 17.50 (*0-292-76454-5*) U of Tex Pr.

— A Prospect of Liberal Democracy. LC 79-63171. 239p. reprint ed. pap. 68.20 (*0-7837-1015-1*, 2041326) Bks Demand.

Livingston, William S. & Louis, W. Roger, eds. Australia, New Zealand, & the Pacific Islands since the First World War. 261p. 1979. text ed. 20.00 (*0-292-70344-9*) U of Tex Pr.

Livingston, William S., et al, eds. The Presidency & the Congress: A Shifting Balance of Power? 450p. 1979. pap. 7.00 (*0-89940-407-3*) LBJ Sch Pub Aff.

Livingstone, Alasdair, ed. Court Poetry & Literary Miscellanea. (State Archives of Assyria Ser.: Vol. 3). (Illus.). xxxvii, 183p. 1989. text ed. 49.50 (*951-570-044-2*, Pub. by Helsinki Univ Pr FI); pap. 36.00 (*951-570-043-4*, Pub. by Helsinki Univ Pr FI) Eisenbrauns.

Livingstone, Alasdair, et al, eds. Muster Roll of Prince Charles Edward Stuart's Army, 1745-1746. 228p. 1984. 29.50 (*0-08-030385-4*, Pergamon Pr) Elsevier.

Livingstone, Angela. Pasternak: "Doctor Zhivago" (Landmarks of World Literature Ser.). (Illus.). (C). 1989. 29.95 (*0-521-32811-X*); pap. 10.95 (*0-521-31698-7*) Cambridge U Pr.

— Pasternak on Art & Creativity. 304p. 1985. 69.95 (*0-521-23842-0*) Cambridge U Pr.

Livingstone, Angela, ed. Salome: Her Life & Work. (Illus.). 256p. 1987. pap. 9.95 (*0-918825-61-X*) Moyer Bell.

Livingstone, Angela, ed. see Schweitzer, Viktoria.

Livingstone, Bruce & Morewitz, Stephen. The Medical Malpractice Handbook: The Plaintiff. 185p. 1995. 54.95 (*1-880921-66-9*); pap. 34.95 (*1-880921-65-0*) Austin & Winfield.

Livingstone, Carol. Role Play in Language Learning. Byrne, Donn, ed. (Handbooks for Language Teachers Ser.). (Illus.). 94p. (Orig.). 1983. pap. 13.50 (*0-582-74611-6*) Longman.

Livingstone, Churchill. Churchill Livingstone Nurse's Dictionary. 16th ed. 480p. 1989. pap. text ed. 7.00 (*0-443-02242-9*) Churchill.

— Medical Directory, 1994. (Illus.). 4672p. 1994. text ed. 295.00 (*0-582-23418-2*) Churchill.

Livingstone Corporation Staff, ed. Bible for Little Hearts. LC 94-9694. (J). (gr. k up). 1995. 8.99 (*0-8423-1306-0*) Tyndale.

***Livingstone, David.** Data Analysis for Chemists: Applications to QSAR & Chemical Product Design. (Illus.). 250p. 1995. 56.00 (*0-19-855728-0*) OUP.

— Family Letters: 1841-1856, 2 vols., 1. LC 75-17198. (Illus.). 1975. reprint ed. text ed. 45.00 (*0-8371-8355-3*, LIFM) Greenwood.

— Family Letters: 1841-1856, 2 vols., Set. LC 75-17198. (Illus.). 1975. reprint ed. text ed. 65.00 (*0-8371-8290-5*, LIFL) Greenwood.

— Family Letters: 1841-1856, 2 vols., Vol. 2. LC 75-17198. (Illus.). 1975. reprint ed. text ed. 45.00 (*0-8371-8356-1*, LIFN) Greenwood.

— Livingstone's Africa. LC 70-138340. (Black Heritage Library Collection). 1977. 52.95 (*0-8369-8732-2*) Ayer.

— Missionary Travels & Researches in South Africa. LC 72-5439. (Select Bibliographies Reprint Ser.). 1977. reprint ed. 68.95 (*0-8369-6918-9*) Ayer.

Livingstone, David N. Darwin's Forgotten Defenders: The Encounter Between Evangelical Theology & Evolutionary Thought. LC 87-13469. 220p. (Orig.). reprint ed. pap. 62.70 (*0-7837-3186-8*, 2042790) Bks Demand.

— The Geographical Tradition: Episodes in the History of a Contested Enterprise. LC 92-15681. 1992. 49.95 (*0-631-18535-6*); pap. 21.95 (*0-631-18586-0*) Blackwell Pubs.

— Nathaniel Southgate Shaler & the Culture of American Science. LC 85-28982. (History of American Science & Technology Ser.). 416p. 1987. 37.50 (*0-8173-0305-7*) U of Ala Pr.

— The Preadamite Theory & the Marriage of Science & Religion. LC 92-76986. (Transactions Ser.: Vol. 82, Pt. 3). 89p. (C). 1992. pap. 16.00 (*0-87169-823-4*, T821-LID) Am Philos.

Livingstone, David N., jt. ed. see Boal, F. W.

Livingstone, David N., ed. see Hodge, Charles.

Livingstone, David W. Class Ideologies & Educational Futures. LC 83-8514. 250p. 1983. 36.00 (*0-905273-40-0*, Falmer Pr); pap. 20.00 (*0-905273-39-7*, Falmer Pr) Taylor & Francis.

— Critical Pedagogy & Cultural Power. LC 86-17176. (Critical Studies in Education). 368p. 1986. text ed. 59.95 (*0-89789-112-0*, Bergin & Garvey); pap. text ed. 18.95 (*0-89789-116-3*, Bergin & Garvey) Greenwood.

Livingstone, Dinah. Saving Grace - New & Selected Poems: 1967-1987 - Dinah Livingstone. (Illus.). (C). 1988. pap. 32.00 (*0-947612-26-2*, Pub. by Rivelin Grapheme Pr) St Mut.

Livingstone, Dinah, tr. see Beyerlin, Walter.

Livingstone, Dinah, tr. see Bloom, Anthony & LeFebvre, George.

Livingstone, Dinah, tr. see Camara, Helder.

Livingstone, Dinah, tr. see Cardenal, Ernesto.

Livingstone, Dinah, tr. see Vigil, Maria L., ed.

Livingstone, Dinah, tr. see Voillaume, Rene.

Livingstone, Elizabeth A., ed. The Concise Oxford Dictionary of the Christian Church. 576p. 1980. pap. 12.95 (*0-19-283014-7*) OUP.

— Studia Patristica XVII, 3 vols., Set. 1520p. 1982. 597.00 (*0-08-025779-8*, Pub. by Pergamon Repr UK) Franklin.

Livingstone, Elizabeth A., jt. auth. see Cross, F. L.

Livingstone, Frank B. Data on the Abnormal Hemoglobins & Glucose-Six-Phosphate Dehydrogenase Deficiency in Human Populations. (Technical Reports: No. 3). 1973. pap. 2.00 (*0-932206-12-3*) U Mich Mus Anthro.

— Frequencies of Hemoglobin Variants. 1985. spiral bd. 39.95 (*0-19-503634-4*) OUP.

Livingstone, Greg. Planting Churches in Muslim Cities: A Team Approach. LC 93-6623. 240p. 1993. pap. 14.99 (*0-8010-5682-9*) Baker Bk.

Livingstone, Harrison E. Harvard, John. 1987. 10.00 (*0-941401-00-6*) Conservatory.

— High Treason Two: The Great Cover-Up: the Assassination of John F. Kennedy. (Illus.). 480p. 1992. 25.95 (*0-88184-809-3*) Carroll & Graf.

— High Treason Two: The Great Cover-Up: the Assassination of President John F. Kennedy. (Illus.). 656p. 1993. pap. 16.95 (*0-7867-0017-3*) Carroll & Graf.

— Killing the Truth: Deceit & Deception in the JFK Case. (Illus.). 640p. 1993. 23.00 (*0-88184-428-4*) Carroll & Graf.

— Killing the Truth: Deceit & Deception in the JFK Case. (Illus.). 752p. 1994. pap. 15.95 (*0-7867-0154-4*) Carroll & Graf.

Livingstone, Harrison E., jt. auth. see Groden, Robert J.

Livingstone, Harrison E., jt. auth. see Groden, Robert.

Livingstone, Harrison E., ed. see Moore, Gilbert.

***Livingstone, Harry E.** Killing Kennedy: And the Hoax of the Century. 512p. 1995. 26.00 (*0-7867-0195-1*) Carroll & Graf.

***Livingstone, Ian.** Darkmoon's Curse. (Adventures of Goldhawk Ser.). (Illus.). 64p. (J). (gr. 2-6). 1995. 5.99 (*0-14-037727-1*) Puffin Bks.

— The Demon Spider. (Adventures of Goldhawk Ser.). (Illus.). 64p. 1995. 4.99 (*0-14-037728-X*) Puffin Bks.

Livingstone, Ian, jt. auth. see Hazlewood, A.

Livingstone, J. M. The Internationalization of Business. 280p. 1989. text ed. 45.00 (*0-312-02418-5*) St Martin.

Livingstone, J. M., jt. auth. see Branton, N.

***Livingstone, John L.** The Portable MBA in Finance & Accounting. Date not set. pap. text ed. 19.95 (*0-471-11983-0*) Wiley.

— The Portable MBA in Finance & Accounting. 1992. text ed. 27.95 (*0-471-53226-6*) Wiley.

Livingstone, John L., et al. Portable MBA in Marketing & Portable MBA in Finance & Accounting Set. 1992. text ed. write for info. (*0-471-57551-8*) Wiley.

Livingstone, Ken. Livingstone's Labour: A Programme for the Nineties. 299p. 1990. text ed. 24.95 (*0-04-440346-1*) Routledge Chapman & Hall.

Livingstone-Learmonth, John. Wines of the Rhone. 3rd ed. (Faber Books on Wine Ser.). (Illus.). 384p. 1992. 39.95 (*0-571-15111-6*) Faber & Faber.

Livingstone-Learmonth, John & Master, Melvyn C. The Wines of the Rhone. 3rd ed. LC 82-24207. (Books on Wine Ser.). 255p. 1983. pap. 10.95 (*0-571-13055-0*) Faber & Faber.

***Livingstone, Marco.** Buckley, Stephen Many Angles. 84p. 1985. pap. 28.00 (*0-905836-49-9*, Pub. by Museum Modern Art UK) St Mut.

— David Hockney. rev. ed. LC 87-50185. (World of Art Ser.). (Illus.). 1988. reprint ed. pap. 11.95 (*0-500-20224-9*) Thames Hudson.

— David Hockney Faces. LC 86-83167. (Illus.). 96p. 1987. pap. 19.95 (*0-500-27464-9*) Thames Hudson.

— Hockney Etchings & Lithographs. (Illus.). 1989. pap. 24.95 (*0-500-27546-7*) Thames Hudson.

— Jim Dine: Botanical Drawings. LC 93-25858. (Illus.). 1994. write for info. (*0-8109-3214-8*) Abrams.

— Pop Art: A Continuing History. (Illus.). 272p. 1990. 49.50 (*0-8109-3707-7*) Abrams.

— Tress, Arthur: Talisman. (Illus.). 156p. (C). 1986. pap. 48.00x (*0-905836-55-3*, Pub. by Museum Modern Art UK) St Mut.

An Asterisk (*) at the beginning of an entry indicates that the title is appearing in BIP for the first time.

Livingstone, Marco, ed. Pop Art: An International Perspective. LC 91-62786. (Illus.). 1992. 60.00 (*0-8478-1475-0*); pap. 35.00 (*0-8478-1476-9*) Rizzoli Intl.

***Livingstone, Marco, text.** Allen Jones: Prints. (Illus.). 144p. Date not set. text ed. 45.00 (*3-7913-1481-5*) Pegasus.

— Farthing, Stephen: Mute Accomplices. (Illus.). 70p. 1987. pap. 32.00 (*0-905836-58-8*, Pub. by Museum Modern Art UK) St Mut.

Livingstone, Marco, jt. auth. see Compton, Michael.

Livingstone, Mark J. The Peacemaker. 352p. (Orig.). 1990. pap. 10.99 (*1-55661-156-0*) Bethany Hse.

Livingstone, Neil C. The Complete Security Guide for Executives: How to Protect Your Life, Corporate Assets, & Employees Against Crime, Sabotage, Terrorism, & Other Threats. (Issues in Low-Intensity Conflict Ser.). 240p. 1989. text ed. 34.95 (*0-669-16777-0*) Free Pr.

— Complexity Security Guide for Executives: How to Protect Yourself, Employees, & Corporate... 1991. pap. 18.95 (*0-669-27667-7*) Free Pr.

Livingstone, Neil C. & Arnold, Terrell E., eds. Fighting Back: Winning the War Against Terrorism. 288p. 1985. text ed. 42.95 (*0-669-10808-1*); text ed. 13.95 (*0-669-11139-2*) Free Pr.

Livingstone, Neil C. & Douglass, Joseph D. CBW: the Poor Man's Atomic Bomb. Tower, John, tr. LC 84-47502. (National Security Papers). 36p. 1984. 7.50 (*0-89549-057-9*) Inst Foreign Policy Anal.

Livingstone, Neil C., jt. auth. see Douglass, Joseph D., Jr.

Livingstone, Richard W. Education & the Spirit of the Age. LC 78-14130. 1979. reprint ed. 25.00 (*0-88355-804-1*) Hyperion Conn.

— Greek Ideals & Modern Life. LC 72-82814. 1969. reprint ed. 18.00 (*0-8196-0245-0*) Biblo.

Livingstone, Richard W., jt. auth. see Thucydides.

Livingstone, Rodney, tr. see Adorno, Theodor W.

Livingstone, Rodney, tr. see Lukacs, Georg.

Livingstone, Rodney, ed. see Marx, Karl & Engels, Frederick.

Livingstone, Rodney, tr. see Marx, Karl.

Livingstone, Sonia M. Making Sense of Television: The Psychology of Audience Interpretation. (International Series in Experimental Social Psychology). (Illus.). 390p. 1990. 54.00 (*0-08-036760-7*, 2605; 2704, Pergamon Pr) Elsevier.

Livingstone, Sonia M. & Lunt, Peter. Talk on Television: Audience Participation & Public Debate. LC 93-15440. (Communication & Society Ser.). 1993. write for info. (*0-415-07737-0*); pap. write for info. (*0-415-07738-9*) Routledge.

Livingstone, Sonia M., jt. auth. see Lunt, Peter K.

Livingstone, Stephen & Morison, John. Law, Society, & Change. 206p. 1990. text ed. 49.95 (*1-85521-105-X*, Pub. by Dartmth Pub UK) Ashgate Pub Co.

Livingstone, Stephen, jt. auth. see Owen, Tim.

Livingstone, W. P. La Reina Blanca de Okoyong: White Queen of Okoyong-Mary. (SPA.). 5.25 (*84-7228-319-4*, 220756, Pub. by Edit Clie SP) TSELF.

Livingwell, Catherine E., intro. Miss Livingwells's Criss-Cross Directory to Persons of Polite Society & Old Wealth, Illinois Edition 1987. (Illus.). (Orig.). 1987. pap. 50.00 (*0-933883-04-8*) Aquarius Rising Pr.

Livinstone, Dinah, tr. see Aquino, Maria P.

Livio, Mario & Shaviv, Giora, eds. Twelfth Texas Symposium on Relativistic Astrophysics, Vol. 470. 100.00 (*0-89766-335-7*); 100.00 (*0-89766-336-5*) NY Acad Sci.

Livio, Mario & Shaviv, Giori, eds. Cataclysmic Variables & Related Objects. 1983. lib. bdg. 103.00 (*90-277-1570-X*) Kluwer Ac.

Livio, Mario, jt. ed. see Williams, Robert E.

Livnat, Joshua, jt. auth. see Hackel, Kenneth S.

Livneh, Hanoch, jt. auth. see Antonak, Richard F.

Livngstone, W. P. Black Jamaica: A Study in Evolution. 1976. lib. bdg. 59.95 (*0-8490-1512-X*) Gordon Pr.

Livo, Lauren J., et al. Of Bugs & Beasts: Fact, Folklore, & Activities. (Illus.). 190p. 1995. pap. text ed. 23.50 (*1-56308-179-2*) Teacher Ideas Pr.

Livo, Norma J. Who's Afraid ...? Facing Children's Fear with Folktales. (Illus.). 150p. 1994. pap. text ed. 18.50 (*0-87287-950-X*) Teacher Ideas Pr.

Livo, Norma J. & Cha, Dia. Folk Stories of the Hmong: Peoples of Laos, Thailand, & Vietnam. 135p. 1991. lib. bdg. 22.00 (*0-87287-854-6*) Libs Unl.

Livo, Norma J. & Reitz, Sandra A. Storytelling: Process & Practice. LC 85-23681. xvi, 462p. 1986. lib. bdg. 35.00 (*0-87287-443-5*) Libs Unl.

Livo, Norma J. & Rietz, Sandra A. Storytelling Activities. LC 86-33727. xiv, 140p. 1987. pap. text ed. 17.50 (*0-87287-566-0*) Libs Unl.

— Storytelling Folklore Sourcebook. 400p. 1991. lib. bdg. 34.00 (*0-87287-601-2*) Libs Unl.

Livo, Norma J., jt. auth. see McGlathery, Glenn.

Livo, Norma J., ed. see Miller, Teresa & Pellowski, Anne.

Livolsi, Virginia A. Pathology of the Thyroid MPP. (Illus.). 448p. 1990. text ed. 78.50 (*0-7216-5782-6*) Saunders.

LiVolsi, Virginia A. & DeLellis, Ronald A., eds. Pathology of the Parathyroid & Thyroid Glands. LC 92-48313. (Monographs in Pathology: No. 35). (Illus.). 203p. 1993. 90.00 (*0-683-04817-1*) Williams & Wilkins.

Livolsi, Virginia A. & Logerfo, Paul. Thyroiditis. 224p. 1981. 113.95 (*0-8493-5705-5*, RC657, CRC Reprint) Franklin.

LiVolsi, Virginia A., et al, eds. Pathology. 3rd ed. LC 93-16371. (National Medical Series for Independent Study). (Illus.). 530p. 1994. pap. 25.00 (*0-683-06243-3*) Williams & Wilkins.

Livonen, Jyrki. The Changing Soviet Union in the New Europe: Towards a New Europe. 256p. 1991. text ed. 63.95 (*1-85278-532-2*, Pub. by E Elgar Pub UK) Ashgate Pub Co.

Livov, M. R. Dictionary of Antonyms of the Russian Language. 381p. (RUS.). 1984. 19.95 (*0-8288-2005-8*, M15178) Fr & Eur.

***Livre De Poche Staff.** L' Opera, Dictionnaire Chronologique de 1597 a nos Jours. (FRE.). 1986. pap. 16.95 (*0-7859-7852-6*, 2253038687) Fr & Eur.

Livrea & Packer. Retinoids: Progress in Research & Clinical Applications. (Basic & Clinical Dermatology Ser.: Vol. 5). 672p. 1993. 199.00 (*0-8247-8758-7*) Dekker.

Livrea, M. A. & Vidali, G., eds. Retinoids: From Basic Science to Clinical Applications. LC 94-16145. (Molecular & Cell Biology Updates Ser.). 1994. 98.00 (*0-8176-2812-6*) Birkhauser.

Livsey, Karen E. Western New York Land Transactions, 1804-1824: Extracted from the Archives of the Holland Land Company. 472p. 1991. 35.00 (*0-8063-1294-7*, 3422) Genealog Pub.

Livshits, Benedikt. The One & a Half-Eyed Archer. Bowlt, John E., ed. (Illus.). 1977. 35.00 (*0-89250-102-2*) Orient Res Partners.

Livshitz, A. V. Surgery of the Spinal Cord. Tatarchenko, V. E., tr. LC 90-4997. 440p. 1991. 65.00 (*0-8236-6257-8*) Intl Univs Pr.

Livshitz, August. Test Your Chess I. Q., Bk. 2. 2nd ed. Neat, Kenneth P., tr. (Russian Chess Ser.). (Illus.). 125p. 1988. 33.90 (*0-08-032072-4*, Pergamon Pr); pap. 19.90 (*0-08-032071-6*, Pergamon Pr) Elsevier.

— Test Your Chess IQ, Bk. 3. 1992. 20.00 (*1-85744-002-1*, Maxwell Macmillan) Macmillan.

***Livsic, M. S.** Theory of Commuting Nonselfadjoint Operators. (Mathematics & Its Applications Ser.). 332p. (C). 1995. lib. bdg. 174.00 (*0-7923-3588-0*) Kluwer Ac.

Livsic, M. S. & Waksman, L. L. Commuting Nonselfadjoint Operations in Hilbert Space. (Lecture Notes in Mathematics Ser.: Vol. 1272). iii, 115p. 1987. pap. 28.10 (*0-387-18316-7*) Spr-Verlag.

Livy. Ab Urbe Condita, Bk. 6. Kraus, Christina S., ed. (Cambridge Greek & Latin Classics Ser.). 368p. (C). 1995. 64.95 (*0-521-41002-9*); pap. 22.95 (*0-521-42238-8*) Cambridge U Pr.

— Book XXXVI. Walsh, P. G., ed. (Classical Texts Ser.). 144p. (C). 1991. text ed. 49.95 (*0-85668-523-2*, Pub. by Aris & Phillips UK); pap. text ed. 19.95 (*0-85668-524-0*, Pub. by Aris & Phillips UK) David Brown.

— Early History of Rome. De Selincourt, Aubrey, tr. (Classics Ser.). (Orig.). 1960. pap. 9.95 (*0-14-044104-2*, Penguin Classics) Viking Penguin.

— Livy, Ab Urbe Condita, Books I & II. Greenough, J. B., ed. (College Classical Ser.). 1988. 32.50 (*0-89241-026-4*); text ed. 16.00 (*0-89241-448-0*) Caratzas.

— Rome & Italy. 1982. pap. 9.95 (*0-14-044388-6*, Penguin Classics) Viking Penguin.

— Rome & the Mediterranean. Bettenson, Henry, tr. (Classics Ser.). 1976. pap. 12.95 (*0-14-044318-5*, Penguin Classics) Viking Penguin.

— Stories of Rome. Nichols, Roger, tr. LC 81-10227. (Translations from Greek & Roman Authors Ser.). (Illus.). 112p. 1982. pap. 10.95 (*0-521-22816-6*) Cambridge U Pr.

— War with Hannibal. De Selincourt, Aubrey, tr. (Classics Ser.). (Orig.). 1965. pap. 9.95 (*0-14-044145-X*, Penguin Classics) Viking Penguin.

Livy, Bryan. Management & People in Banking. 2nd ed. 1985. 75.00 (*0-85297-143-5*, Pub. by Inst Bankers UK) St Mut.

***Livy, Didier.** Albert. LC 94-48721. (Illus.). 1995. 14.95 (*1-85697-621-1*, Kingfisher LKC) LKC.

Liwschitz-Garik, Michael & Gentilini, Celso. Winding Alternating Current Machines: A Book for Winders, Repairmen, & Designers of Electric Machines. 772p. 1950. 83.00 (*0-911740-03-1*) Datarule.

Liwschitz, Y., jt. ed. see Reinhold, L.

Lixfeld, Hannjost. Folklore & Fascism: The Reich Institute for German Volkskunde. Dow, James R., ed. & tr. by. LC 93-10014. (Folklore Studies in Translation). (C). 1994. 35.00 (*0-253-33512-4*) Ind U Pr.

Lixfeld, Hannjost, jt. ed. see Dow, James R.

Lixfeld, Hannjost, tr. see Dow, James R. & Lixfeld, Hannjost, eds.

Lixfeld, Hannjost, jt. ed. see Dow, James R.

Lixfeld, Hannjost, tr. see Dow, James R. & Lixfeld, Hannjost, eds.

***Lixi, Christian.** Dictionnairede Mathematiques. 239p. (FRE.). 1988. 42.95 (*0-7859-7726-0*, 2091889512) Fr & Eur.

Lixinga, Zhou. Theory & Numerical Modeling of Turbulent Gas-Particle Flows & Combustion. LC 92-38051. 200p. 1993. 69.95 (*0-8493-7721-8*, Q) CRC Pr.

Lixl-Purcell, Andreas. Stimmen Eines Jahrhunderts, 1888-1990: Deutsche Autobiographien, Tagebucher, Bilder und Briefe. LC 89-77885. (Illus.). 304p. (C). 1991. pap. text ed. 22.00 (*0-03-049182-7*) HB Coll Pubs.

Lixl-Purcell, Andreas, ed. Women of Exile: German-Jewish Autobiographies Since Nineteen Thirty-Three. LC 87-24952. (Contributions in Women's Studies: No. 91). 241p. 1988. text ed. 49.95 (*0-313-25921-6*, LXP/, Greenwood Pr) Greenwood.

***Liyuan, Zhu & Blocker, Gene, eds.** Contemporary Chinese Aesthetics. (Asian Thought & Culture Ser.: Vol. 17). 360p. (C). 1995. text ed. 55.95 (*0-8204-2527-3*) P Lang Pubs.

Lizakowski, Adam, tr. see Wisnicki, Adrian.

Lizano, Eduardo. Economic Policy Making: Lessons from Costa Rica. 32p. 1991. pap. 5.00 (*1-55815-117-6*) ICS Pr.

Lizardos, jt. tr. see Papadopoulos.

Lizardos, Georgia, jt. tr. see Papadopulos, Leonidas J.

Lizardy, Andoni. Closing Tactics: How to Use Fast & Effective Closing Techniques. 192p. 1993. pap. 12.95 (*0-89384-235-4*) Pfeiffer & Co.

Lizarraga, Angelica, tr. see Behm, Mary & Behm, Richard.

Lizaso, Felix. Marti, Martyr of Cuban Independence. LC 73-20502. (Illus.). 260p. 1974. reprint ed. 60.00 (*0-8371-7329-9*, LIMA, Greenwood Pr) Greenwood.

Lizeng, Gong, tr. see Zehou, Li.

Lizhi, Fang. Bringing Down the Great Wall. 1991. 20.00 (*0-685-41162-1*) McKay.

— Bringing Down the Great Wall: Writings on Science, Culture, & Democracy in China. 384p. 1992. pap. 10.95 (*0-393-30885-5*) Norton.

— Galaxies, Quasars & Cosmology. Ruffini, Remo, ed. (Advanced Series in Astrophysics & Cosmology: Vol. 2). 232p. 1985. pap. 28.00 (*9971-5-0083-3*) World Scientific Pub.

— Selected Speeches & Writings by Fang Lizhi, Vol. 1. 176p. 1989. text ed. 17.00 (*962-362-003-9*); pap. text ed. 9.00 (*962-362-004-7*) World Scientific Pub.

— Selected Speeches & Writings by Fang Lizhi, Vol. 2. 267p. 1989. pap. text ed. 10.00 (*962-362-006-3*) World Scientific Pub.

Lizhi, Fang, ed. Origin, Structure & Evolution of Galaxies: Proceedings of the Yellow Mountain Summer School of Astrophysics. 344p. (Orig.). (C). 1988. pap. 47.00 (*9971-5-0522-3*) World Scientific Pub.

Lizhi, Fang & Chu, Y. Q. From Newton's Laws to Einstein's Theory of Relativity. 120p. (C). 1987. text ed. 58.00 (*9971-978-36-9*) World Scientific Pub.

Lizhi, Fang & Ruffini, Remo. Cosmology of the Early Universe. (Advanced Series in Astrophysics & Cosmology: Vol. 1). 316p. (C). 1984. 54.00 (*9971-950-92-8*); pap. 30.00 (*9971-950-93-6*) World Scientific Pub.

Lizhi, Fang & Ruffini, Remo, eds. Basic Concepts in Relativistic Astrophysics. 230p. 1983. text ed. 47.00 (*9971-950-66-9*) World Scientific Pub.

— Quantum Cosmology. (Advanced Series in Astrophysics & Cosmology: Vol. 3). 340p. (C). 1987. text ed. 98.00 (*9971-5-0293-3*); pap. text ed. 47.00 (*9971-5-0312-3*) World Scientific Pub.

Lizhong, Liu. Buddhist Art of the Tibetan Plateau. (Illus.). 358p. 1988. 100.00 (*0-8351-2128-3*) China Bks.

Lizon, Karen H. Colonial American Holidays & Entertainment. LC 92-40262. (Colonial America Ser.). (YA). 1993. lib. bdg. 13.72 (*0-531-12546-7*) Watts.

Lizon, Lulu. Travel & Tourism Careers Guide Book. Parkerson, Janet, ed. (Illus.). 133p. (Orig.). (C). 1987. pap. 19.95 (*0-935423-05-2*) Educ Pubns.

Lizon, Peter. Palace of the Soviets: Change & Direction in Soviet Architecture (1940-1950) (Illus.). 246p. 1994. pap. 40.00 (*0-89410-049-1*) Three Continents.

— Palace of the Soviets: Change & Direction in Soviet Architecture (1940-1950) (Illus.). 246p. 1995. 55.00 (*0-89410-004-1*) Three Continents.

Lizos, Peter, jt. auth. see Pratt, Brian.

Lizot, Jacques. Tales of the Yanomami: Daily Life in the Venezuelan Forest. (Canto Book Ser.). (Illus.). 216p. (C). 1991. pap. 10.95 (*0-521-40672-2*) Cambridge U Pr.

***Lizza, Chris I.** South America Ski Guide. (Bradt Guides Ser.). (Illus.). 312p. 1994. 16.95 (*1-56440-559-1*) Globe Pequot.

Lizza, Richard W. & Joyaux, Alain G. Byron Browne: Studies in Gouache from the 1940's. 16p. (Orig.). 1987. pap. 3.50 (*0-915511-06-1*) Ball State Art.

Ljapin, E. S. Semigroups. 4th ed. Brown, A. et al, trs. LC 63-15659. (Translations of Mathematical Monographs: Vol. 3). 519p. 1978. reprint ed. pap. 62.00 (*0-8218-1553-9*, MMONO-3) Am Math.

Ljiri, Yuji, jt. auth. see Cooper, W. W.

Ljung, Inger. Tradition & Interpretation: A Study of the Use & Application of Formulaic Language in the So-Called Ebed YHWH-Psalms. (Coniectanea Biblica. Old Testament Ser.: No. 12). (Orig.). 1987. pap. 39.00x (*0-317-65796-8*) Coronet Bks.

Ljung, Lennart. System Identification: Theory for the User. (Illus.). 384p. 1987. text ed. 75.00 (*0-13-881640-9*) P-H.

Ljung, Lennart & Glad, Torkel. Modeling Simulation of Dynamic Systems. 368p. 1994. text ed. 63.00 (*0-13-597097-0*) P-H.

Ljung, Lennart, jt. ed. see Anderson, B. D.

Ljung, Lennart, et al. Stochastic Approximation & Optimization of Random Systems. LC 92-10322. (DMV Seminar Ser.: No. Bd. 17). 120p. 1992. 24.50 (*3-7643-2733-2*, Pub. by Birkhauser Vlg SZ); 24.50 (*0-8176-2733-2*, Pub. by Birkhauser Vlg SZ) Birkhauser.

Ljung, Magnus, jt. ed. see Lindblad, Ishrat.

Ljungberg, Otto. Biopsy Pathology of the Thyroid & Parathyroid. LC 92-49004. (Biopsy Pathology Ser.). 1992. write for info. (*0-412-34890-X*) Chapman & Hall.

Ljunggren, Bengt. Great Men with Sick Brains & Other Essays. LC 89-81019. (Illus.). 112p. (Orig.). 1989. pap. text ed. 35.00 (*0-9624246-0-9*) Am Assn Neuro.

Ljunggren, Borje, ed. The Challenge of Reform in Indochina, Vol. 2. LC 92-26516. (Studies in International Development). 416p. 1993. text ed. 30.00 (*0-674-10712-8*) HUP.

Ljunggren, G. & Dornic, S., eds. Psychophysics in Action. (Illus.). 170p. 1989. 69.00 (*0-387-50686-1*) Spr-Verlag.

Ljunggren, Magnus. The Dream of Rebirth: A Study of Andrej Belyj's Novel Petersburg. (Stockholm Studies in Russian Literature). (Illus.). 180p. (Orig.). 1982. pap. 34.50x (*91-22-00586-2*, Pub. by Almqv & Wiksell SW) Coronet Bks.

— The Russian Mephisto: A Study of the Life & Work of Emilii Medtner. (Stockholm Studies in Russian Literature: No. 27). (Illus.). 240p. 1994. pap. 49.50 (*91-22-01656-2*, Pub. by Almqv & Wiksell SW) Coronet Bks.

Ljungmark, Lars. Swedish Exodus. 165p. 1979. 19.95 (*0-318-16623-2*) Swedish-Am.

Ljungquist, Kent P. The Grand & the Fair: Poe in the American Landscape. 1982. pap. 2.90 (*0-910556-20-2*) Enoch Pratt.

— The Grand & the Fair: Poe's Landscape Aesthetic & Pictorial Techniques. 1985. 27.50 (*0-916379-20-5*) Scripta.

Ljungstedt, N., jt. ed. see Bostrom, H.

***Ljunguist, Bengt.** Practical Dressage Manual. (Illus.). 164p. 1983. 22.95 (*0-939481-36-7*); pap. 12.95 (*0-939481-37-5*) Half Halt Pr.

Ljusternik, L. A. The Topology of Function Spaces & the Calculus of Variations in the Large. LC 66-25298. (Translations of Mathematical Monographs: Vol. 16). 96p. 1989. reprint ed. pap. 31.00 (*0-8218-1566-0*, MMONO-16) Am Math.

Lkett, C., jt. auth. see Lorr, M.

Llabres De Charneco, Amalia, jt. auth. see Charneco Babilonia, Efrain.

Llach, Francisco. Papper's Clinical Nephrology. 3rd ed. LC 93-20505. (Illus.). 640p. 1993. 100.00 (*0-316-52920-6*) Little.

***Llamas, Andreu.** Birds Conquer the Sky. LC 95-3967. (Development of the Earth Ser.). (Illus.). (ENG & SPA.). (J). 1996. write for info. (*0-7910-3455-0*) Chelsea Hse.

— The Era of Dinosaurs. LC 95-3963. (Development of the Earth Ser.). (Illus.). (ENG & SPA.). (J). 1996. write for info. (*0-7910-3452-6*) Chelsea Hse.

— The First Amphibians. LC 95-3964. (Development of the Earth Ser.). (Illus.). (ENG & SPA.). (J). 1996. write for info. (*0-7910-3453-4*) Chelsea Hse.

— The Great Marine Reptiles. LC 95-3965. (Development of the Earth Ser.). (Illus.). (ENG & SPA.). (J). 1996. write for info. (*0-7910-3454-2*) Chelsea Hse.

— Life Starts in the Sea. LC 95-3962. (Development of the Earth Ser.). (Illus.). (ENG & SPA.). (J). 1996. write for info. (*0-7910-3451-8*) Chelsea Hse.

— Mammals Dominate the Earth. LC 95-3966. (Development of the Earth Ser.). (Illus.). (ENG & SPA.). (J). 1996. write for info. (*0-7910-3456-9*) Chelsea Hse.

— Sight. (Five Senses of the Animal World Ser.). (Illus.). (J). 1996. write for info. (*0-7910-3491-7*) Chelsea Hse.

— Touch. LC 95-14781. (Five Senses of the Animal World Ser.). (Illus.). (J). 1996. write for info. (*0-7910-3494-1*) Chelsea Hse.

***Llamas, Andreu, ed.** Sight. LC 95-10514. (Five Senses of the Animal World Ser.). (Illus.). 1996. pap. write for info. (*0-7910-3496-8*) Chelsea Hse.

***Llamas, Andreu & Arredondo, Francisco.** Touch. LC 95-14781. (Five Senses of the Animal World Ser.). (Illus.). 1996. pap. write for info. (*0-7910-3499-2*) Chelsea Hse.

Llamazares, J. L., jt. ed. see Leccabue, F.

Llamzon, Teodoro A. Modern Tagalog: A Functional-Structural Description. LC 78-88212. (Janua Linguarum, Series Practica: No. 122). (Orig.). 1976. pap. text ed. 37.35 (*90-279-3493-2*) Mouton.

Llana, Christopher B. & Wisneskey, George P. Handbook of the Nautical Rules of the Road. 2nd ed. LC 90-46486. 1991. 24.95 (*1-55750-504-7*) Naval Inst Pr.

Llanes, Eduardo, tr. see Johns, Helen.

Llanes, Flor A., ed. see Uceda, Mario A.

Llang, Henry R. Das Liederbuch des Konigs Denis von Portugal. cxviii, 174p. (GER.). 1972. reprint ed. write for info. (*3-487-04245-2*, Pub. by Georg Olms GW) Lubrecht & Cramer.

Llano, Carlos. El Empresario Ante la Responsibilidad y la Motovacion. 1991. pap. text ed. 9.95 (*0-07-104041-2*) McGraw.

— El Empresario y Su Accion. 1991. pap. text ed. 9.95 (*0-07-104040-4*) McGraw.

— El Empresario y Su Mundo. 1991. pap. text ed. 9.95 (*0-07-104039-0*) McGraw.

Llano, George A., ed. Antarctic Terrestrial Biology. LC 72-92709. (Antarctic Research Ser.: Vol. 20). (Illus.). 322p. 1972. 39.00 (*0-87590-120-4*) Am Geophysical.

— Biology of the Antarctic Seas 2. LC 64-60030. (Antarctic Research Ser.: Vol. 5). (Illus.). 280p. 1965. 15.00 (*0-87590-105-0*) Am Geophysical.

Llano, George A. & Schmitt, Waldo L., eds. Biology of the Antarctic Seas Three. LC 64-60030. (Antarctic Research Ser.: Vol. 11). (Illus.). 261p. 1967. 17.00 (*0-87590-111-5*) Am Geophysical.

Llano, George A. & Wallen, I. Eugene, eds. Biology of the Antarctic Seas 4. LC 64-60030. (Antarctic Research Ser.: Vol. 17). (Illus.). 362p. 1971. 39.00 (*0-87590-117-4*) Am Geophysical.

***Llanos, Bernardita.** Re-Descubrimiento y Re-Conquista de America en la Illustracion Espanola. LC 93-2313. (Sociocritism Ser.: Vol. 6). 217p. (C). 1994. text ed. 47.95 (*0-8204-2269-X*) P Lang Pubs.

***Llanos, Hector.** Proceso Historico Prehispanico de San Agustin en el Valle de Laboyos (Pitalito-Huila) (Illus.). 122p. (SPA.). 1990. pap. 8.50 (*1-877812-31-5*) UPLAAP.

Llanso, Steven L., jt. auth. see Laur, Timothy M.

Llarch, Juan. Dali's Universal Tarot. 44p. 90.00 (*0-88079-090-3*) US Games Syst.

Llarena, Ray. Setting Your House in Order. 182p. 1993. pap. 6.95 (*1-884369-02-2*) McDougal Pubng.

Llast, Robin. Discover a New World of Healing: Answers for Successful Living in These Times. (Illus.). 234p. (Orig.). 1992. pap. text ed. 12.95 (*0-929240-52-9*) Essential Med Info Syst Inc.

Llaurens, Jose M., tr. see Sede, Santa.

Llavona, J. G. Approximation of Continuously Differentiable Functions. (North-Holland Mathematics Studies: No. 130). 242p. 1986. 64.00 (*0-444-70128-1*, North Holland) Elsevier.

Lleonart, Augusti B. Dictionary of Mythology (Diccionario de Mitologia) 2nd ed. 216p. (SPA.). 1985. 29.95 (*0-7859-4963-1*, S39844) Fr & Eur.

Llera, Humberto P. Idea, Sentimiento y Sensibilidad de Jose Marti. LC 79-56227. (Coleccion Cuba y Sus Jueces Ser.). 490p. (Orig.). (SPA.). 1982. pap. 25.00 (*0-89729-242-1*) Ediciones.

Lleras, Eduardo. Trigoniaceae. LC 77-91706. (Flora Neotropica Monograph Ser.: No. 19). (Illus.). 73p. 1978. pap. 7.25 (*0-89327-198-5*) NY Botanical.

*__Lleras, Roberto.__ Arqueologia del Alto Valle de Tenza. (Illus.). 148p. (SPA.). 1989. pap. 8.50 (*1-877812-12-9*) UPLAAP.

Llerena, Mario. The Unsuspected Revolution: The Birth & Rise of Castroism. LC 77-3119. (Illus.). 324p. 1978. 33.50 (*0-8014-1094-0*) Cornell U Pr.

Llerena, Mario, ed. see Wilson, William P. & Slattery, Kathryn.

Lleu, J. English-French Glossary of Marketing Terms. 2nd ed. 533p. 1983. pap. 95.00 (*0-8288-0084-7*, M8908) Fr & Eur.

Llewellyn, Ann, jt. auth. see Swyer, P. R.

Llewellyn, Caroline. The Lady of the Labyrinth. 352p. 1990. text ed. 19.95 (*0-684-18920-8*, Scribners) S&S Trade.

— The Lady of the Labyrinth. large type ed. (General Ser.). 400p. 1991. text ed. 20.95 (*0-8161-5071-0*) G K Hall.

— Life Blood. large type ed. LC 93-46458. 1994. 20.95 (*0-8161-5940-8*, Large Print Bks) Hall.

— Life Blood: A Novel of Suspense. 352p. 1993. text ed. 20.00 (*0-684-19402-3*, Scribners) S&S Trade.

— The Masks of Rome. 320p. 1989. pap. 3.95 (*0-8041-0375-5*) Ivy Books.

— The Masks of Rome. large type ed. (General Ser.). 432p. 1989. 20.95 (*0-8161-4752-3*, Large Print Bks) Hall.

*__Llewellyn, Carolyn.__ Life Blood. 1994. mass mkt. 5.99 (*0-8041-1263-0*) Ivy Books.

Llewellyn, Chris. Steam Dummy & Fragments from the Fire: Poems. rev. ed. (Midwest Writers Ser.). (Illus.). 124p. (Orig.). 1993. pap. 8.95 (*0-933087-29-2*) Bottom Dog Pr.

Llewellyn, Claire. First Look at Clothes. LC 91-9425. (First Look Ser.). (Illus.). 32p. (J). (gr. 1-2). 1991. lib. bdg. 17.27 (*0-8368-0677-8*) Gareth Stevens Inc.

— First Look at Growing Food. LC 91-9424. (First Look Ser.). (Illus.). 32p. (J). (gr. 1-2). 1991. lib. bdg. 17.27 (*0-8368-0678-6*) Gareth Stevens Inc.

— First Look at Keeping Warm. LC 91-9423. (First Look Ser.). (Illus.). 32p. (J). (gr. 1-2). 1991. lib. bdg. 17.27 (*0-8368-0704-9*) Gareth Stevens Inc.

— First Look in the Air. (First Look Ser.). (Illus.). 32p. (J). (gr. 1-2). 1991. lib. bdg. 17.27 (*0-8368-0701-4*) Gareth Stevens Inc.

— My First Book of Time. LC 91-58194. (Illus.). 32p. (J). (ps-3). 1992. 14.95 (*1-879431-78-5*) Dorling Kindersley.

— Tractors & Other Farm Machines. LC 94-24403. (Mighty Machines Ser.). (Illus.). 24p. (J). (ps-3). 1995. 9.95 (*1-56458-515-8*) Dorling Kindersley.

— Trucks. LC 95-10739. (Worldwise Ser.). (Illus.). 48p. (J). (gr. 4-6). 1995. lib. bdg. 14.98 (*0-531-14378-3*) Watts.

— Trucks & Other Building Machines. (Mighty Machines Ser.). (Illus.). 24p. (J). (ps-3). 1995. 9.95 (*1-56458-516-6*) Dorling Kindersley.

— Wind & Rain. LC 94-39686. (Why Do We Have? Ser.). (Illus.). (J). 1995. write for info. (*0-8120-6508-5*); pap. write for info. (*0-8120-9279-1*) Barron.

*__Llewellyn, Claire & Lewis, Anthony.__ Day & Night. LC 94-45156. (Why Do We Have? Ser.). (J). 1995. write for info. (*0-8120-6509-3*); pap. write for info. (*0-8120-9280-5*) Barron.

Llewellyn, D. J., jt. ed. see Dennis, E. S.

Llewellyn, D. T. Steels: Metallurgy & Applications. (Illus.). 256p. 1992. 110.00 (*0-7506-1090-5*) Buttrwrth-Heinemann.

— Steels Metallurgy & Applications. 2nd ed. 320p. 1994. pap. 39.95 (*0-7506-2086-2*) Buttrwrth-Heinemann.

Llewellyn, Dara, jt. auth. see Frazier, Claude A.

Llewellyn, David & Holmes, Mark. Competition or Credit Controls? 103p. (C). 1991. text ed. 70.00 (*0-255-36300-1*, Pub. by Inst Economic Affairs UK) St Mut.

Llewellyn, David T. The Evolution of the British Financial System. 1985. 65.00 (*0-85297-136-2*, Pub. by Inst Bankers UK) St Mut.

— The Regulation & Supervision of Financial Institutions. 1986. 50.00 (*0-85297-174-5*, Pub. by Inst Bankers UK) St Mut.

Llewellyn, David T., ed. Reflections on Money. LC 89-39231. 215p. 1990. text ed. 59.95 (*0-312-03997-2*) St Martin.

Llewellyn, David T., jt. ed. see Green, Christopher J.

Llewellyn, G. C. & O'Rear, C. E., eds. Biodeterioration Research, Vol. 1. LC 87-25494. (Illus.). 406p. 1988. 95.00 (*0-306-42764-8*, Plenum Pr) Plenum.

— Biodeterioration Research: Mycotoxins, Biotoxins, Wood Decay, Air Quality, Cultural Properties, General Deterioration & Degradation, Vol. 3. (Illus.). 690p. 1990. 135.00 (*0-306-43697-3*, Plenum Pr) Plenum.

Llewellyn, G. C., jt. ed. see O'Rear, C. E.

Llewellyn, G. C., et al, eds. Biodeterioration Research Four: Mycotoxins, Wood Decay, Plant Stress, Biocorrosion & General Biodeterioration. (Illus.). 702p. (C). 1994. 149.50 (*0-306-44638-3*, Plenum Pr) Plenum.

Llewellyn, Grace. The Teenage Liberation Handbook: How to Quit School & Get a Real Life & Education. 401p. (YA). (gr. 7-12). 1991. pap. 14.95 (*0-9629591-0-3*) Lowry Hse.

Llewellyn, Grace, intro. Real Lives: Eleven Teenagers Who Don't Go to School. (Illus.). 320p. (Orig.). (YA). (gr. 7-12). 1993. pap. 14.95 (*0-9629591-3-8*, LC32.R) Lowry Hse.

Llewellyn, J. Bells & Bell-Founding. (Illus.). 57p. 1987. reprint ed. pap. 25.00 (*0-87556-696-0*) Saifer.

Llewellyn, J., see Wyvern, pseud..

Llewellyn, J. A., jt. auth. see Gilbert, Richard A.

Llewellyn, J. E. Arya Samaj as a Fundamentalist Movement: A Study in Comparative Fundamentalism. (C). 1994. 30.00 (*81-7304-015-X*) S Asia.

Llewellyn, John & Potter, Stephen J. Economic Policies for the 1990s. (Illus.). 448p. 1991. text ed. 64.95 (*0-631-17662-4*) Blackwell Pubs.

Llewellyn-Jones, Derek. The A-Z of Women's Health. 2nd ed. (Oxford Paperback Reference Ser.). (Illus.). 272p. 1990. pap. 14.95 (*0-19-286112-3*) OUP.

— Everybody: The Healthy Eating Handbook. LC 92-19159. 1993. 5.99 (*0-19-286155-7*) OUP.

Llewellyn-Jones, Derek, jt. auth. see Abraham, Suzanen.

Llewellyn-Jones, Derek, jt. auth. see Abraham, Suzanne A.

Llewellyn-Jones, Margaret, jt. auth. see Griffiths, Trevor R.

Llewellyn-Jones, Rosie. A Very Ingenious Man: Claude Martin in Early Colonial India. (Illus.). 250p. 1993. 22.00 (*0-19-563131-5*) OUP.

Llewellyn, K. N. The Constitution As an Institution. (Reprint Series in Social Sciences). (C). 1993. reprint ed. pap. text ed. 1.00 (*0-8290-2737-8*, PS-171) Irvington.

Llewellyn, Karl N. Bramble Bush: On Our Law & Its Study. LC 51-1727. 192p. 1981. reprint ed. lib. bdg. 25.00 (*0-379-20738-9*); reprint ed. pap. text ed. 18.50 (*0-379-00073-3*) Oceana.

— The Case Law System in America. Ansaldi, Michael, tr. LC 89-32341. 160p. 1989. 24.95 (*0-226-48790-3*) U Ch Pr.

— The Common Law Tradition: Deciding Appeals. 565p. 1960. 45.00 (*0-316-52935-4*) Little.

Llewellyn, Karl N. & Hoebel, E. Adamson. The Cheyenne Way: Conflict & Case Law in Primitive Jurisprudence. LC 41-23735. (Civilization of the American Indian Ser.: Vol. 21). (Illus.). 374p. 1983. reprint ed. 34.95 (*0-8061-0099-0*); reprint ed. pap. 16.95 (*0-8061-1855-5*) U of Okla Pr.

Llewellyn, Keith, jt. ed. see Chekaluk, Eugene.

Llewellyn, Nigel. The Art of Death: Visual Culture in the English Death Ritual, c. 1500-1800. (Illus.). 160p. 1991. pap. 22.95 (*0-948462-16-7*) U of Wash Pr.

Llewellyn, Nigel, jt. auth. see Gent, Lucy.

Llewellyn Publications Staff. Llewellyn 1993 Daily Planetary Guide: The Astrologer's Datebook. 208p. 1992. spiral bd. 6.95 (*0-87542-903-3*) Llewellyn Pubns.

— Llewellyn's Daily Planetary Guide & Astrologer's Datebook, 1991. (Llewellyn Annual Ser.). (Illus.). 174p. (Orig.). 1990. pap. 6.95 (*0-87542-461-9*) Llewellyn Pubns.

— Llewellyn's Moon Sign Book, 1991. (Llewellyn Annual Ser.). (Illus.). 432p. 1990. pap. 4.95 (*0-87542-458-9*) Llewellyn Pubns.

— Llewellyn's Moon Sign Book, 1992. (Llewellyn Annual Ser.). (Illus.). 448p. 1991. pap. 4.95 (*0-87542-467-8*) Llewellyn Pubns.

— Llewellyn's Sun Sign Book, 1991. (Llewellyn Annual Ser.). (Illus.). 384p. (Orig.). 1990. pap. 4.95 (*0-87542-459-7*) Llewellyn Pubns.

— Llewellyn's Sun Sign Book, 1992. (Llewellyn Annual Ser.). (Illus.). 406p. (Orig.). 1991. pap. 4.95 (*0-87542-468-6*) Llewellyn Pubns.

— Llewellyn's 1990 Moon Sign Book. Buske, Terry, ed. (Llewellyn Annual Ser.). (Illus.). 448p. 1989. pap. 3.95 (*0-87542-451-1*) Llewellyn Pubns.

— Llewellyn's 1990 Sun Sign Book. Buske, Terry, ed. (Llewellyn Annual Ser.). (Illus.). 352p. 1989. pap. 3.95 (*0-87542-454-6*) Llewellyn Pubns.

— Llewellyn's 1993 Astrological Calendar. (Illus.). 48p. 1992. 9.95 (*0-87542-902-5*) Llewellyn Pubns.

— Llewellyn's 1993 Lunar Organic Gardener. Buske, Terry, ed. (Illus.). 256p. 1992. 3.95 (*0-87542-905-X*) Llewellyn Pubns.

— Llewellyn's 1993 Magical Almanac. Cunningham, Scott & Buckland, Ray, eds. (Illus.). 272p. 1992. 7.95 (*0-87542-906-8*) Llewellyn Pubns.

— Llewellyn's 1993 Moon Sign Book & Lunar Planning Guide. (Illus.). 400p. 1992. 4.95 (*0-87542-900-9*) Llewellyn Pubns.

— Llewellyn's 1993 Sun Sign Book: 1993 Horoscopes for Every Sign. (Illus.). 422p. 1992. pap. 4.95 (*0-87542-901-7*) Llewellyn Pubns.

— The Truth about Astral Projection. (Llewellyn's Truth about Ser.). 32p. (Orig.). 1983. pap. 2.00 (*0-87542-350-7*) Llewellyn Pubns.

— The Truth about Creative Visualization. (Llewellyn's Truth about Ser.). 32p. (Orig.). 1984. pap. 2.99 (*0-87542-353-1*) Llewellyn Pubns.

— The Truth about Psychic Powers. (Llewellyn's Truth about Ser.). 32p. (Orig.). 1987. pap. 2.00 (*0-87542-355-8*) Llewellyn Pubns.

— The Truth about Subliminals. (Llewellyn's Truth about Ser.). 32p. (Orig.). 1985. pap. 2.00 (*0-87542-356-6*) Llewellyn Pubns.

— The Truth about What Astrology Can Do for You. rev. ed. (Llewellyn's Truth about Ser.). 32p. (Orig.). 1990. pap. 2.00 (*0-87542-375-2*) Llewellyn Pubns.

Llewellyn, Richard. How Green Was My Valley. 1980. 17.95 (*0-02-573430-X*) Macmillan.

— How Green Was My Valley. LC 92-9684. 512p. 1992. pap. 10.00 (*0-02-022372-2*, Pub. by Gebrueder Borntraeger GW) Macmillan.

— How Green Was My Valley. 512p. 1987. text ed. 40.00 (*0-02-573420-2*, Scribners) S&S Trade.

— How Green Was My Valley. 1983. reprint ed. lib. bdg. 28.95 (*0-88411-936-X*, Aeonian Pr) Amereon Ltd.

Llewellyn, Richard, jt. auth. see Edwards, Keith.

Llewellyn, Robert. Boston. Patrick, James B., ed. (Scenic Discovery Ser.). (Illus.). 128p. 1984. 30.00 (*0-89909-046-X*) Foremost Pubs.

— Washington D. C. 176p. 1994. 14.98 (*0-8317-9472-0*) Smithmark.

Llewellyn, Robert, photos. The Cathedral of St. Peter & St. Paul. LC 88-80088. (Illus.). 120p. 1988. 19.95 (*0-943231-07-8*) Howell Pr VA.

— Mr. Jefferson's Upland Virginia. LC 83-50396. (Illus.). 80p. 1979. 25.00 (*0-934738-06-8*) Thomasson-Grant.

— Virginia: An Aerial Portrait. LC 84-52617. (Illus.). 120p. 1985. 32.00 (*0-934738-12-2*) Thomasson-Grant.

— Washington: The Capital. LC 81-69086. 120p. 1981. 19.95 (*0-934738-02-5*) Thomasson-Grant.

Llewellyn, Robert, jt. auth. see Griggs, Irwin.

Llewellyn, Robert L., photos. The Academical Village: Thomas Jefferson's University. LC 82-50830. (Illus.). 80p. 1982. 25.00 (*0-934738-03-3*) Thomasson-Grant.

Llewellyn, S. Mathematics: The Basic Skills. 3rd ed. Greer, A., ed. 288p. (C). 1988. 65.00 (*0-85950-718-1*, Pub. by S Thornes Pubs UK) St Mut.

— Mathematics - the Basic Skills for the Bahamas. (C). 1986. text ed. 55.00 (*0-85950-515-4*, Pub. by S Thornes Pubs UK) St Mut.

— Mathematics - the Basic Skills for the Bahamas - Teacher's Notes. (C). 1986. text ed. 40.00 (*0-85950-575-8*, Pub. by S Thornes Pubs UK) St Mut.

*__Llewellyn, S. & Greer, D. A.__ Mathematics-The Basic Skills. 304p. (C). 1991. 39.00x (*0-7478-0598-9*, Pub. by S Thornes Pubs UK); pap. 27.00x (*0-7487-0598-8*, Pub. by S Thornes Pubs UK) St Mut.

Llewellyn, S., jt. auth. see Farrow, L.

Llewellyn, S. P., jt. ed. see Broome, A. K.

Llewellyn, Sam. Blood Knot. large type ed. 497p. (Orig.). 1993. 21.95 (*0-7505-0403-X*, Pub. by Magna Print Bks) Ulverscroft.

— Blood Knot. Chelius, Jane, ed. 336p. (Orig.). 1993. reprint ed. mass mkt. 4.99 (*0-671-86951-5*) PB.

— Blood Orange. large type ed. 1990. 21.95 (*0-7089-2174-4*) Ulverscroft.

— Clawhammer. Chelius, Jane, ed. 384p. 1995. mass mkt. 5.50 (*0-671-78994-5*) PB.

— Clawhammer. large type ed. LC 94-10666. 516p. 1994. pap. 18.95 (*0-8161-7401-6*) Hall.

— Clawhammer. large type ed. 548p. 1994. 26.95 (*0-7505-0684-9*) Ulverscroft.

— Dead Reckoning. 1989. pap. 3.50 (*0-685-25346-5*) PB.

— Dead Reckoning. large type ed. 400p. 1988. 16.95 (*0-7089-1916-2*) Ulverscroft.

— Deadeye. Chelius, Jane, ed. 288p. 1992. reprint ed. mass mkt. 4.99 (*0-671-67044-1*) PB.

— Death Roll. Chelius, Jane, ed. 256p. 1991. reprint ed. pap. 3.95 (*0-671-67043-3*) PB.

— Gurney's Release. large type ed. 555p. 1981. 12.00 (*0-7089-0727-X*) Ulverscroft.

— Gurney's Revenge. large type ed. 403p. 1981. 12.00 (*0-7089-0655-9*) Ulverscroft.

— Gurney's Reward. large type ed. 467p. 1981. 12.00 (*0-7089-0699-0*) Ulverscroft.

— Maelstrom. Chelius, Jane, ed. 416p. (Orig.). 1994. 20.00 (*0-671-78995-3*) PB.

— Riptide. Chelius, Jane, ed. 288p. (Orig.). 1994. mass mkt. 5.50 (*0-671-89307-6*) PB.

Llewellyn-Williams, Hilary. Book of Shadows. 104p. (Orig.). 1990. pap. 17.95 (*1-85411-041-1*, Pub. by Seren Bks UK) Dufour.

Llewelyn-Bowen, Laurence, jt. auth. see Hall, Katrina.

Llewelyn, David T. & Milner, Chris, eds. Current Issues in International Monetary Economics. LC 90-8101. (Current Issues in Economics Ser.). 288p. 1990. text ed. 45.00 (*0-312-04755-X*) St Martin.

Llewelyn-Davies, R. & Macaulay, H. M. Hospital Planning & Administration. (Monograph Ser.: No. 54). (Illus.). 215p. (ENG, FRE, RUS & SPA.). 1966. 12.80 (*92-4-140054-4*) World Health.

Llewelyn, John. Beyond Metaphysics? The Hermeneutic Circle in Contemporary Philosophy. LC 84-4638. 256p. (C). 1989. pap. 18.50 (*0-391-03619-X*) Humanities.

— Emmanuel Levinas: The Genealogy of Ethics. LC 94-33895. (Warwick Studies in European Philosophy). 248p. 1995. 55.00x (*0-415-10729-6*, C0128); pap. 16.95 (*0-415-10730-X*, C0129) Routledge.

— The Middle Voice of Ecological Conscience: A Chiasmic Reading of Responsibility in the Neighbourhood of Levinas, Heidegger & Others. LC 90-28464. 320p. 1991. text ed. 49.95 (*0-312-06173-0*) St Martin.

Llewelyn, Morgan. Bard: The Odyssey of the Irish. 480p. 1987. mass mkt. 5.99 (*0-8125-8515-1*) Tor Bks.

Llewelyn, Robert. Joy of the Saints: Spiritual Readings Throughout the Year. 1992. pap. 16.95 (*0-87243-191-6*) Templegate.

Llewelyn, Robert, ed. Daily Readings from the Cloud of Unknowing. (Daily Readings Ser.). 1986. pap. 4.95 (*0-87243-149-5*) Templegate.

— Fire of Divine Love: Readings from Jean-Pierre de Caussade. 128p. 1995. pap. 10.95 (*0-89243-827-4*) Liguori Pubns.

Llewelyn, Robert, ed. see Brother Lawrence.

LLewelyn, Robert, ed. see De Caussade, Jean-Pierre.

Llewelyn, Robert, ed. see Julian of Norwich.

Llewelyn, Robert, ed. see Law, William.

Llewelyn, Robert, ed. see St. Augustine.

LLewelyn, Robert, ed. see St. Francis de Sales.

Llewelyn, Robert, ed. see St. Francis of Assisi.

Llewelyn, Robert, ed. see St. John of the Cross.

LLewelyn, Robert, ed. see St. Teresa of Avila.

Llewelyn, Robert, ed. see St. Therese of Lisieux.

Llewelyn, Robert, et al. Praying Home: The Contemplative Journey. LC 87-20194. 117p. (Orig.). 1987. pap. 7.95 (*0-936384-52-2*) Cowley Pubns.

Llewelyn, Sue. Women's Lives. 336p. 1990. pap. 12.95 (*0-415-01702-5*, A4304) Routledge.

Llewelyn, Sue, jt. ed. see Broome, Annabel.

Lliboutry, Louis A. Very Slow Flows of Solids: Basics of Modeling in Geodynamics & Glaciology. (C). 1987. lib. bdg. 216.50 (*90-247-3482-7*) Kluwer Ac.

Llibre, J., jt. auth. see Lacomba, E. A.

Llibre, Jaume & Nunes, Ana. Separatrix Surfaces & Invariant Manifolds of a Class of Integrable Hamiltonian Systems & Their Perturbations. LC 93-39026. (Memoirs of the American Mathematical Society Ser.: No. 513). 208p. 1994. pap. 36.00 (*0-8218-2581-X*) Am Math.

Llibre, Jaume, jt. auth. see Casasayas, Josefina.

Llinas, James, jt. auth. see Waltz, Edward L.

Llinas, R. & Sotelo, C., eds. The Cerebellum Revisited. (Illus.). 320p. 1992. 89.00 (*0-387-97693-0*) Spr-Verlag.

Llinas, Rodolfo R. The Workings of the Brain: Development, Memory & Perception. 224p. (C). 1995. text ed. 13.95 (*0-7167-2071-X*) W H Freeman.

Llinas, Rodolfo R., ed. The Biology of the Brain: From Neurons to Networks. (Illus.). 192p. (C). 1995. text ed. 13.95 (*0-7167-2037-X*) W H Freeman.

Llinas, Salvador O. Diccionari Catala-Angles. 3rd ed. 1088p. 1991. 59.95 (*0-7859-6498-3*) Fr & Eur.

Llines, Salvador O. & Buxton, A. English-Catalan Dictionary: Diccionari Angles-Catala. 3rd ed. 1088p. (CAT & ENG.). 1991. write for info. (*0-7859-4903-8*) Fr & Eur.

Llistosella-Matzky, I., jt. auth. see Von Kunhardt, A.

*__Lliteras, D. S.__ Half Hidden by Twilight: A Novel. 176p. (Orig.). 1994. pap. 9.95 (*1-57174-000-7*) Hampton Roads Pub Co.

— In a Warrior's Romance. 1991. pap. 11.95 (*1-878901-05-2*) Hampton Roads Pub Co.

— In the Heart of Things. 1991. pap. 8.95 (*1-878901-22-2*) Hampton Roads Pub Co.

— Into the Ashes. 256p. (Orig.). 1993. pap. 9.95 (*1-878901-77-X*) Hampton Roads Pub Co.

LLlewellyn, Sam. Riptide. large type ed. (Charnwood Ser.). 416p. 1994. 25.95 (*0-7089-8754-0*, Charnwood) Ulverscroft.

Llobera, Jose, jt. auth. see Brambilla, Massimo.

*__Llobera, Josep R.__ The God of Modernity: The Development of Nationalism in Western Europe. Nelson, Brian, ed. (European Studies Ser.). 288p. 1994. 54.95 (*0-85496-921-7*); pap. 19.95 (*0-85496-940-3*) Berg Pubs.

Llombart, Felipe V. Treasures of the Prado. (Tiny Folios Ser.). 1993. pap. 11.95 (*1-55859-558-9*) Abbeville Pr.

*__Llompart, Gabriel.__ Pintura Gotica en Mallorca. (Illus.). 128p. (SPA.). 1993. 100.00 (*84-343-0477-5*) Elliots Bks.

Llompart, Miguel F. Diccionario de l'Art I Els Oficis de la Construccion. 5th ed. 440p. (CAT.). 1988. pap. 69.95 (*0-7859-5107-5*) Fr & Eur.

*__Llonch, Carme & Blanco, Laura.__ Habitats. LC 95-12371. (Discover My World Ser.). (Illus.). (J). 1995. write for info. (*0-8120-6526-3*) Barron.

— Out & About. LC 95-15148. (Discover My World Ser.). (Illus.). (J). 1995. write for info. (*0-8120-6529-8*) Barron.

Llorens, Lela A. & Rubin, Eli Z. Developing Ego Functions in Disturbed Children: Occupational Therapy in Milieu. LC 66-24385. (Lafayette Clinic Monographs in Psychiatry: No. 1). (Illus.). 147p. (Orig.). reprint ed. pap. 41.90 (*0-7837-3638-X*, 2043505) Bks Demand.

Llorens, Washington. Humor, Epigram & Satire in Puerto Rican Literature. (Puerto Rico Ser.). 1979. lib. bdg. 59.95 (*0-8490-2941-4*) Gordon Pr.

— La Magia de la Palabra. LC 80-19972. (Coleccion Mente y Palabra). x, 171p. (SPA.). 1981. 6.00 (*0-8477-0576-5*); pap. 5.00 (*0-8477-0577-3*) U of PR Pr.

Llorente, Pilar M. Apprentice. (J). (gr. 4-7). 1993. 13.00 (*0-374-30389-4*) FS&G.

— The Apprentice. (Illus.). 112p. (J). (gr. 5 up). 1994. pap. 4.50 (*0-374-40432-1*, Sunburst Bks) FS&G.

Llorente, Segundo. Memoirs of a Yukon Priest. LC 89-27434. (Illus.). 1990. pap. 17.95 (*0-87840-494-5*) Georgetown U Pr.

Llosa, Alvaro V. The Madness of Things Peruvian: Democracy under Siege. LC 93-12632. 230p. (C). 1994. text ed. 32.95 (*1-56000-114-3*) Transaction Pubs.

Llosa, J., ed. Relativistic Action at a Distance: Classical & Quantum Aspects, Barcelona, Spain 1981, Proceedings. (Lecture Notes in Physics Ser.: Vol. 162). 263p. 1982. pap. 29.00 (*0-387-11573-0*) Spr-Verlag.

Llosa, M. Vargas. Who Killed Palomino Molero. 1988. 16.95 (*0-685-46246-3*, Collier S&S) S&S Trade.

*__Llosa, Mario V.__ Aunt Julia & the Scriptwriter. 384p. 1995. 11.95 (*0-14-024892-7*, Penguin Bks) Viking Penguin.

— A Fish in the Water. 544p. 1995. 13.95 (*0-14-024890-0*, Penguin Bks) Viking Penguin.

— A Fish in the Water: A Memoir. Lane, Helen, tr. LC 93-42603. 1994. 25.00 (*0-374-15509-7*) FS&G.

— In Praise of the Stepmother. (Illus.). 160p. 1991. reprint ed. pap. 11.95 (*0-14-015708-5*, Penguin Bks) Viking Penguin.

— A Writer's Reality. 192p. 1992. pap. 11.95 (*0-395-62234-4*) HM.

*__LLosa, Mario Vargas.__ In the Andes. Grossman, Edith, tr. 336p. Date not set. 24.00 (*0-374-14001-4*) FS&G.

Llove, T. R. How to Be Macho. 328p. (Orig.). 1984. pap. 14.95 (*0-918483-09-3*) Galahad Pub.

— How to Satisfy a Woman. 123p. (Orig.). 1985. pap. 7.95 (*0-918483-17-4*) Galahad Pub.

Lloy, Owen, et al. An Atlas of Mortality in Scotland: Including the Geography of Selected Socio-Economic Characteristics. (Illus.). 192p. 1987. 140.00 (*0-7099-4122-6*, Pub. by Croom Helm UK) Routledge Chapman & Hall.

*__Lloyd.__ In My Garden. 1995. 22.00 (*0-02-860033-9*) Macmillan.

— Secured Transactions. 1988. write for info. (*0-8205-0486-6*, 721); teacher ed write for info. (*0-318-67319-3*) Bender.

— Sexual Harassment: How to Keep Your Company Out of Court. 88p. 1992. 45.00 (*1-878375-47-4*, 75474) Panel Pubs.

An Asterisk (*) at the beginning of an entry indicates that the title is appearing in BIP for the first time.

*Lloyd & Freeman, M. C. Lloyd's Introduction to Jurisprudence. 6th ed. 1994. pap. text ed. 55.00 (0-421-45680-9, Pub. by Sweet & Maxwll) W W Gaunt.
Lloyd, ed. see De Vega.
Lloyd, jt. auth. see Guiberson.
Lloyd, A., jt. auth. see Dawson, A.
Lloyd, A. L., ed. see Brailoiu, Constantin.
Lloyd, A. L., tr. see Fallada, Hans.
Lloyd, A. L., tr. see Garcia Lorca, Federico.
*Lloyd, A. R. Wingfoot. large type ed. 1994. 23.95 (0-7089-3188-X) Ulverscroft.
Lloyd, A. T. C-119 Flying Boxcar. 228p. 1992. 41.95 (0-918805-37-6); pap. 29.95 (0-918805-38-4) Pac Aero Pr.
Lloyd, Al, et al. Folk Songs of the Americas. 276p. Date not set. pap. 12.95 (0-8256-0056-1) Music Sales.
Lloyd, Alan. The Gliders: The Story of the Wooden Chariots of World War II. (Airborne Ser.: No. 17). (Illus.). 196p. 1982. 24.95 (0-89839-066-4) Battery Pr.
— Making of the King Ten Sixty-Six. 243p. 1990. 19.95 (0-88029-473-6) Marboro Bks.
Lloyd, Alan, jt. auth. see Dickson, Gary.
Lloyd, Alan B., comp. Gods, Priests & Men: Studies in the Religion of Pharaonic Egypt by Aylward Blackman. (Studies in Egyptology). 280p. 1993. 95.00 (0-7103-0412-9, A6984, Pub. by Kegan Paul Intl UK) Routledge Chapman & Hall.
Lloyd, Alan C. The Anatomy of Neoplatonism. 208p. 1990. 55.00 (0-19-824229-8) OUP.
Lloyd, Alan C., et al. Gregg College Typing: Complete Course. 5th ed. (College Typing Ser.: No. 5). 368p. 1985. Lessons 151-225. 12.95 (0-07-038327-8) McGraw.
— Gregg Typing, Complete Course. 8th ed. (Series Eight). 1986. General Course, Typing 1. text ed. 20.32 (0-07-038342-1); pap. text ed. 25.24 (0-07-038344-8); Advanced Course, Typing 2. pap. text ed. 20.32 (0-07-038343-X) McGraw.
— Personal Typing. 4th ed. (Illus.). 1978. text ed. 19.96 (0-07-038208-5) McGraw.
Lloyd, Alan C. & Krevolin, R. You Learn to Type. 1966. text ed. 26.52 (0-07-038160-7) McGraw.
Lloyd, Alan C., et al. Gregg College Typing. (Gregg Typing Ser.: No. 5, Kit 3). 1985. text ed. 26.90 (0-07-038324-3) McGraw.
— Gregg College Typing: Complete Course. 5th ed. (College Typing Ser.: No. 5). 368p. 1985. text ed. 32.95 (0-07-038320-0); Lessons 151-225. pap. text ed. 6.15 (0-07-038330-8) McGraw.
— Gregg College Typing, Series Five, Typing 75, Basic Kit. 320p. 1984. text ed. 26.90 (0-07-038322-7) McGraw.
— Gregg Typing for Colleges: Intensive Course. (Gregg College Typing Ser.: No. 5). 240p. 1984. text ed. 25.75 (0-07-038321-9) McGraw.
— Gregg Typing for Colleges: Proofguide for Lessons 1-75. Rubin, Audrey S., ed. (Gregg College Typing Ser.: No. 5). 48p. (C). 1984. pap. text ed. 6.15 (0-07-038328-6) McGraw.
— Gregg Typing, Personal Keyboarding & Applications Series Eight. 160p. 1987. pap. text ed. 15.96 (0-07-038341-3) McGraw.
— Proofguides for Gregg Typing for Colleges: Lessons 1-75. (Gregg College Typing Ser.: Ser. 4). 48p. 1978. pap. text ed. 6.95 (0-07-038260-3) McGraw.
— Selective Practice Typing Drills. 1974. text ed. 10.88 (0-07-038147-X) McGraw.
— Series Seven Typing Complete Course, Gregg Typing. 496p. (gr. 11-12). 1982. text ed. 27.96 (0-07-038280-8) McGraw.
— Typing One: General Course Gregg Typing. LC 81-15629. (Gregg Typing Ser.: No. 7). (Illus.). 288p. 1982. text ed. 21.96 (0-07-038281-6) McGraw.
— Typing Power Drills. 3rd ed. LC 83-8592. (Illus.). 96p. 1984. text ed. 12.96 (0-07-038176-3) McGraw.
— Typing Seventy-Five: Intermediate. (Gregg College Typing Ser.: No. 5). 1984. text ed. 26.90 (0-07-038323-5) McGraw.
— Typing Skill Drives. 2nd ed. 1974. text ed. 13.96 (0-07-038161-5) McGraw.
— Typing Two: Advanced Course Gregg Typing. LC 81-15629. (Gregg Typing Ser.: No. 7). (Illus.). 288p. 1982. text ed. 21.96 (0-07-038282-4) McGraw.
Lloyd, Alan C., et al, eds. Typing Seventy Five: Advanced. (Gregg College Typing Ser.: No. 4). 1979. text ed. 24.50 (0-07-038257-3) McGraw.
— Typing Seventy Five: Expert. 4th ed. (Gregg College Typing Ser.: No. 4). 1978. text ed. 24.50 (0-07-038258-1) McGraw.
*Lloyd, Albert. Etymologisches Woerterbuch des Althochdeutschen, 8 vols., Set. (GER.). Date not set. 350.00 (0-7859-8411-9, 3525207670) Fr & Eur.
Lloyd, Albert L. Anatomy of the Verb: The Gothic Verb As a Model for a Unified Theory of Aspect, Actional Types, & Verbal Velocity. (Studies in Language Companion: No. 4). x, 351p. 1979. 71.00x (90-272-3003-X, 4) Benjamins North Am.
Lloyd, Alfred H. Dynamic Idealism. LC 75-3243. reprint ed. 17.00 (0-404-59233-3) AMS Pr.
*Lloyd, Alison, ed. The Painter in Glass. 74p. 1993. pap. 38.00 (0-86383-976-2, Pub. by Gomer Pr UK) St Mut.
Lloyd, Alwyn T. B-17 Flying Fortress: Part 2. LC 81-67592. (Detail & Scale Ser.: Vol. 11). (Illus.). 72p. 1983. pap. 8.95 (0-8168-5021-6, 25021, TAB-Aero) TAB Bks.
— B-29 Superfortress: Part 1. LC 83-2789. (Detail & Scale Ser.: Vol. 10). (Illus.). 72p. (Orig.). 1982. pap. 8.95 (0-8168-5019-4, 25019, TAB-Aero) TAB Bks.
— B-47 Stratojet. Spohn, Terry, ed. LC 93-12806. (Detail & Scale Ser.: Vol. 18). (Illus.). 72p. 1993. reprint ed. pap. 11.95 (0-89024-170-8) Kalmbach.
— Detail & Scale: Boeing 707 & AWACS, Vol. 23. (Illus.). 64p. 1987. pap. 10.95 (0-8306-8533-2, NO. 25033, TAB-Aero) TAB Bks.
— Detail & Scale, Vol. 27: B-52 Stratofortress. (Illus.). 72p. 1988. pap. 10.95 (0-8306-8037-3, 25037) TAB Bks.
— Details & Scale, Vol. 25, the B-29 Superfortress, Pt. 2 Derivatives. (Illus.). 78p. (Orig.). 1987. pap. 10.95 (0-8306-8035-7, 25035) TAB Bks.
— KC-135 Stratotanker in Detail & Scale. (Detail & Scale Ser.: Vol. 44). (Illus.). 72p. 1994. per. 11.95 (0-89024-203-8, 05059) Kalmbach.
— Liberator: America's Global Bomber. LC 93-86687. (Illus.). 560p. 1994. 39.95 (0-929521-82-X) Pictorial Hist.
Lloyd, Alwyn T. & Moore, Terry D. B-17 Flying Fortress in Detail & Scale: Part 1 (Production Versions) LC 81-67592. (Detail & Scale Ser.: Vol. 2). (Illus.). 72p. (Orig.). 1981. pap. 8.95 (0-8168-5012-7, 25012, TAB-Aero) TAB Bks.
Lloyd, Alwyn T., et al. B-17 Flying Fortress, Vol. 2: In Detail & Scale. Spohn, Terry, ed. LC 93-1657. (Illus.). 72p. 1993. pap. 11.95 (0-89024-185-6) Kalmbach.
Lloyd, Ann. The Films of Stephen King. LC 93-18424. (Illus.). 1994. 22.95 (0-312-11329-3) St Martin.
— The Films of Stephen King. LC 93-18424. (Illus.). 1994. pap. 14.95 (0-312-11274-2) St Martin.
— Movie Book: The Nineteen Forties. 1988. 2.00 (0-517-62975-5) Random Hse Value.
Lloyd, Ann, jt. auth. see Gillon, Raanan.
Lloyd, Ann W., jt. auth. see Keough, Jeffrey.
*Lloyd, Annie. Beginning Welsh Research. 155p. 1993. 15.00 (0-9644567-0-2) A Lloyd.
— How to Plan a Research Trip to Wales. 100p. (Orig.). 1995. pap. 15.00 (0-9644567-1-0) A Lloyd.
Lloyd, Arnold. Quaker Social History: Sixteen Sixty-Nine to Seventeen Thirty-Eight. LC 79-4398. 207p. 1979. reprint ed. text ed. 55.00 (0-313-20943-X, LLQU, Greenwood Pr) Greenwood.
Lloyd, Arthur. The Creed of Half Japan: Historical Sketches of Japanese Buddhism. LC 78-70095. reprint ed. 40.50 (0-404-17344-6) AMS Pr.
*Lloyd, B. M. Not a Total Waste: The True Story of a Mother, a Son, & AIDS. 325p. 1995. lib. bdg. 41.00 (0-8095-4820-8) Borgo Pr.
Lloyd, Barbara. The Colours of India. LC 88-50595. (Illus.). 160p. 1989. pap. 19.95 (0-500-27531-9) Thames Hudson.
Lloyd, Barbara & Archer, John, eds. Exploring Sex Differences. 1976. text ed. 124.00 (0-12-453550-X) Acad Pr.
Lloyd, Barbara, jt. auth. see Archer, John.
Lloyd, Barbara, jt. ed. see Duveen, Gerard.
Lloyd, Barbara B., jt. ed. see Rosch, Eleanor.
Lloyd, Beth. Explore Jersey. 128p. 1987. pap. 30.00 (0-86368-007-0) St Mut.
Lloyd, Beverly, jt. ed. see Weller, Patrick.
Lloyd-Bostock, Sally M. Law in Practice: Applications of Psychology to Legal Decision Making & Legal Skills. LC 89-14573. 177p. (C). 1989. reprint ed. pap. text ed. 27.95 (0-925065-06-4) Lyceum IL.
Lloyd-Bostock, Sally M. & Clifford, Brian R. Evaluating Witness Evidence. LC 82-7107. 305p. 1983. text ed. 156.00 (0-471-10463-9, Wiley-Interscience) Wiley.
Lloyd-Bostock, Sally M. & Clifford, Brian R., eds. Evaluating Witness Evidence: Recent Psychological Research & New Perspectives. LC 82-7107. 315p. reprint ed. pap. 89.80 (0-7837-4410-2, 2044153) Bks Demand.
Lloyd, Bruce, ed. Entrepreneurship: Creating & Managing New Ventures. (Best of Long Range Planning Ser.: Vol. 1, No. 2). 200p. 1989. pap. text ed. 47.00 (0-08-037407-7) Elsevier.
— Entrepreneurship: Creating & Managing New Ventures. (Best of Long Range Planning Ser.: Vol. 1, No. 2). 200p. 1989. text ed. 99.00 (0-08-037108-6, Pergamon Pr) Elsevier.
*Lloyd, C. Forensic Psychiatry for Health Professionals. 240p. 1994. pap. text ed. 47.75 (1-56593-183-1, 0498) Singular Publishing.
Lloyd, C., jt. auth. see Geffner, R.
Lloyd, C. J. Parliament & the Press. 1988. 24.95 (0-522-84372-7) Intl Spec Bk.
Lloyd, Camille, jt. ed. see Hendrie, Hugh C.
Lloyd, Charles. Edmund Oliver. LC 90-31305. 568p. 1990. reprint ed. 65.00 (1-85477-051-9, Pub. by Woodstock Bks UK) Cassell.
Lloyd, Charles, ed. The Roman Family: A Bridge to Roman Culture, Values & Literature. 191p. (Orig.). 1991. spiral bd. 11.30 (0-939507-35-8, B308) Amer Classical.
Lloyd, Charlotte, tr. see Fallada, Hans.
*Lloyd, Chris & Beard, Jeff. Managing Classroom Collaboration. (Cassell Practical Handbooks Ser.). (Illus.). 128p. 1995. pap. 23.95 (0-304-32988-6) Cassell.
Lloyd, Christoper. Fra Angelico. (Color Library). (Illus.). 128p. (C). 1994. reprint ed. pap. 14.95 (0-7148-2785-1, Pub. by Phaidon Press UK) Chronicle Bks.
Lloyd, Christopher. British Seaman. LC 76-118123. (Illus.). 319p. 1975. 32.50 (0-8386-7708-8) Fairleigh Dickinson.
— Christopher Lloyd's Flower Garden. LC 92-53449. (Illus.). 192p. 1993. 29.95 (1-56458-167-5) Dorling Kindersley.
— Fra Angelico. (Color Library). (Illus.). 128p. (C). 1994. reprint ed. 19.95 (0-7148-3214-6, Pub. by Phaidon Press UK) Chronicle Bks.
— Italian Paintings Before Sixteen Hundred in the Art Institute of Chicago: A Catalogue of the Collection. LC 93-12237. (Illus.). 336p. 1993. text ed. 90.00 (0-691-03351-X) Princeton U Pr.
— J-K Huysmans & the Fin-de-Siecle Novel. 1991. text ed. 40.00 (0-7486-0171-6, Pub. by Edinburgh U Pr UK) Col U Pr.
— J-K Huysmans & the Fin-de-Siecle Novel. 192p. 1992. pap. 25.00 (0-7486-0234-8, Pub. by Edinburgh U Pr UK) Col U Pr.
— The Mixed Border. (Wisley Handbooks: The Royal Horticultural Society Ser.). (Illus.). 64p. 1991. pap. 5.95 (0-304-32015-3, Pub. by Cassell UK) Sterling.
— Pacific Horizons, the Exploration of the Pacific Before Captain Cook. LC 75-41177. reprint ed. 18.00 (0-404-14710-0) AMS Pr.
— Pisarro. (Color Library). (Illus.). 128p. (C). 1994. reprint ed. 19.95 (0-7148-3228-6, Pub. by Phaidon Press UK) Chronicle Bks.
— Pissarro. (Color Library). (Illus.). 128p. (C). 1994. reprint ed. pap. 14.99 (0-7148-2729-0, Pub. by Phaidon Press UK) Chronicle Bks.
— The Structures of History. LC 92-32022. (Studies in Social Discontinuity). 272p. 1993. 49.95 (0-631-18464-3); pap. 22.95 (0-631-18465-1) Blackwell Pubs.
Lloyd, Christopher, ed. Social Theory & Political Practice. (Wolfson College Lectures). 1983. pap. 15.95 (0-19-827448-3) OUP.
— Studies on Camille Pissaro. (Illus.). 192p. 1986. pap. 37.50 (0-7102-0928-2, 09882, RKP) Routledge.
Lloyd, Christopher & Bennett, Tom. Clematis. rev. ed. LC 88-63334. (Illus.). 264p. 1989. 32.50 (0-913643-04-1) Capabilitys.
Lloyd, Christopher & Bird, Richard. The Cottage Garden. 192p. 1990. pap. 29.95 (0-13-181231-9, P-H Gardening) P-H Gen Ref & Trav.
Lloyd, Christopher & Rice, Graham. Garden Flowers from Seed. (Illus.). 276p. 1994. pap. 19.95 (0-88192-296-X) Timber.
Lloyd, Christopher, ed. see Popham, A. E.
Lloyd, Christopher, et al. Italian Paintings Before Sixteen Hundred in the Art Institute of Chicago: A Catalogue of the Collection. LC 93-12237. (Illus.). 272p. 1993. 90.00 (0-86559-110-5) Art Inst Chi.
— Planting Your Garden. (Wisley Gardening Companions Ser.). (Illus.). 256p. 1993. 19.95 (0-304-32043-9, Pub. by Cassell UK) Sterling.
Lloyd, Clare S., et al. The Status of Seabirds in Britain & Ireland. (Illus.). 355p. 1991. text ed. 39.95 (0-85661-061-5, 784661) Acad Pr.
Lloyd, Clem & Rees, Jacqui. The Last Shilling: A History of Repatriation in Australia. (Illus.). 476p. 1993. text ed. 49.95 (0-522-84508-8) Intl Spec Bk.
Lloyd, Clive W., ed. The Cytoskeletal Basis of Plant Growth & Form. (Illus.). 330p. 1991. text ed. 109.00 (0-12-453770-7) Acad Pr.
— The Plant Cytoskeleton in Growth & Development. 1983. text ed. 145.00 (0-12-453780-4) Acad Pr.
Lloyd, Clive W., jt. ed. see Hyams, Jeremy S.
Lloyd, Colin, jt. auth. see Sujita, Etsuko.
Lloyd, Cynthia B., ed. Fertility, Family Size & Structure: Consequences for Families & Children. 522p. 1993. pap. 18.00 (0-87834-077-7) Population Coun.
Lloyd, Cynthia B. & Marquette, Catherine M. Directory of Surveys in Developing Countries: Data on Families & Households, 1975-1992. LC 92-62578. 1992. pap. 25.00 (0-87834-074-2) Population Coun.
Lloyd, Cynthia B. & Niemi, Beth T. The Economics of Sex Differentials. LC 79-9569. 1981. text ed. 50.00 (0-231-04038-5) Col U Pr.
Lloyd, Cynthia B., et al, eds. Women in the Labor Market. LC 79-15547. 393p. 1979. text ed. 56.00 (0-231-04638-3) Col U Pr.
Lloyd, D., jt. ed. see Boffey, S. A.
Lloyd, D., jt. auth. see Degn, H.
Lloyd, D., jt. auth. see Evans, H. J.
Lloyd, D., et al, eds. Biochemistry & Molecular Biology of "Anaerobic" Protozoa. xii, 290p. 1989. pap. text ed. 95.00 (3-7186-4943-8) Gordon & Breach.
Lloyd, D. A. Electrostatic Precipitator Handbook. (Illus.). 232p. 1988. 105.00 (0-85274-492-7) IOP Pub.
Lloyd, D. G. Modern Syllabus Algebra. 1971. 107.00 (0-08-015965-6, Pub. by Pergamon Repr UK) Franklin.
Lloyd, D. H. Bible Bob Responds to a Jesus Honker. 68p. 1986. 15.95 (0-930090-54-3); pap. 6.95 (0-930090-53-5) Applezaba.
— Bible Bob Responds to a Jesus Honker. deluxe limited ed. 68p. 1986. 25.00 (0-930090-52-7) Applezaba.
— Dreams, Myths & Other Realities. 32p. (Orig.). 1984. pap. 3.00 (0-917554-24-8) Maelstrom.
— If Gravity Wasn't Discovered. 1979. pap. 3.95 (0-930090-06-3) Applezaba.
— Mog & Glog. LC 78-51718. (Illus.). 1978. pap. 4.95 (0-930090-01-2) Applezaba.
Lloyd, D. H., ed. see Locklin, Gerald.
Lloyd, D. Myrddin, tr. see Gruffydd, W. J.
Lloyd, Dan. Simple Minds. 330p. 1989. 32.50 (0-262-12140-9) MIT Pr.
Lloyd, Dana O. Ho Chi Minh. (World Leaders - Past & Present Ser.). (Illus.). 112p. (YA). (gr. 5 up). 1987. lib. bdg. 17.95 (0-87754-571-5) Chelsea Hse.
Lloyd, David. Anomalous States: Irish Writing & the Post-Colonial Moment. LC 93-3105. (Post-Contemporary Interventions Ser.). 184p. 1993. lib. bdg. 42.95 (0-8223-1326-X); pap. text ed. 14.95 (0-8223-1344-8) Duke.
— Dinosaur Days. Incl. Silly Games. 1985. 3.95 (0-394-87380-7); Breakfast. 1985. 3.95 (0-394-87378-5); Terrible Thing. 1985. 3.95 (0-394-87381-5); (Illus.). 32p. (J). (ps-1). 1985. write for info. (0-318-59173-1) Random Bks Yng Read.
— Hello, Goodbye. 2nd ed. (Illus.). (J). 1995. write for info. (1-56402-510-1) Candlewick Pr.
— Historic Towns of South-East England: Kent, Surrey, Sussex & Hampshire. (Illus.). 160p. 1988. 34.95 (0-575-03689-3, Pub. by V Gollancz UK) Trafalgar.
— The I AM Discourses, Vol. 10. (Illus.). 438p. 1980. 19.00 (1-878891-44-8); pap. 16.00 (1-878891-45-6) St Germain Pr.
— Nationalism & Minor Literature: James Clarence Mangan & the Emergence of Irish Cultural Nationalism. (New Historicism: Studies in Cultural Poetics: No. 3). 336p. 1987. 40.00 (0-520-05824-0) U CA Pr.
Lloyd, David, ed. Flow Cytometry in Microbiology. LC 92-38958. 1993. 119.00 (0-387-19796-6) Spr-Verlag.
— The Urgency of Identity: Contemporary English-Language Poetry from Wales. (TriQuarterly Bks.). 200p. (Orig.). 1994. 39.95 (0-8101-5032-8); pap. 14.95 (0-8101-5007-7) Northwestern U Pr.
Lloyd, David & Geldard, William. My First Library. (Illus.). 300p. (J). (ps). 1993. pap. 16.00 (0-89577-527-1) RD Assn.
Lloyd, David & Rossi, Ernest L., eds. Ultradian Rhythms in Life Processes: An Inquiry into Fundamental Principles of Chronobiology & Psychobiology. LC 92-2298. xiii, 419p. 1992. 185.00 (0-387-19746-X) Spr-Verlag.
Lloyd, David, jt. auth. see Delano, Jamie.
Lloyd, David, jt. ed. see JanMohamed, Abdul R.
Lloyd, David, jt. auth. see Moore, Alan.
LLoyd, David, jt. auth. see Ormerod, Jan.
Lloyd, David, et al. The Cell Division: Temporal Organization & Control of Cellular Growth & Reproduction. 1982. text ed. 161.00 (0-12-453760-X) Acad Pr.
*Lloyd, David G. & Barrett, Spencer C., eds. Floral Biology: Studies on Floral Evolution in Animal-Pollinated Plants. LC 94-42927. 1995. 75.00 (0-412-04341-6) Chapman & Hall.
Lloyd, David K. & Lipow, Myron. Reliability: Management, Methods & Mathematics. 2nd ed. 616p. 1977. 38.95 (0-318-13241-9, P 140) ASQC Qual Pr.
— Reliability: Management, Methods & Mathematics. 2nd ed. 589p. (C). 1984. pap. 24.95 (0-87389-000-0) ASQC Qual Pr.
Lloyd, David W. The Making of English Towns: Two Thousand Years of Evolution. (Illus.). 290p. 1993. pap. 22.95 (0-575-05311-9, Pub. by V Gollancz UK) Trafalgar.
*Lloyd, David W., ed. Traditional Native American Healing & Child Sexual Abuse. 62p. (Orig.). (C). 1994. pap. text ed. 27.95x (0-7881-1306-2) Diane Pub.
Lloyd-Davies. Color Atlas of Urology. 2nd ed. 288p. 1994. 85.00 (0-7234-1912-4, Wolfe Pub) Mosby Yr Bk.
*Lloyd-Davies, Victoria. The Tomato Cookbook. LC 94-30358. 96p. 1994. 9.98 (0-8317-8661-2) Smithmark.
Lloyd-Davies, Victoria, jt. auth. see Dettmer, Anne.
*Lloyd, Debbie. Time Management Skills: Leadership Skills for Women. Edwards, Judith, ed. 72p. (Orig.). 1994. pap. text ed. 5.95 (1-56309-102-X, New Hope) Womans Mission Union.
Lloyd, Diane V. & Stavrou, Marta B. The Physician's Assistant, No. 1210-1211. 1977. 10.00 (0-686-19685-6) CPL Biblios.
Lloyd, Donna H. The Physics of Metaphysics: Everything You Wanted to Know about the Universe & Your Place in It, but Did Not Know What to Ask. (Illus.). 300p. (C). 1993. pap. 13.95 (0-9627291-3-2) Deltaran Pub.
— The View from Olympus: Evolution of Consciousness Through Astrological - Historical Ages. (Illus.). 300p. (C). 1992. 19.95 (0-9627291-0-8); pap. 13.95 (0-9627291-1-6) Deltaran Pub.
Lloyd, Douglas. The Chemistry of Conjugated Cyclic Compounds: To Be or Not to Be Like Benzene? 1990. text ed. 115.00 (0-471-91721-4) Wiley.
— A First Course in Organic Chemistry. 1989. text ed. 173.00 (0-471-92408-3) Wiley.
Lloyd, Douglas, ed. Topics in Carbocyclic Chemistry, Vol. 1. LC 74-80937. 383p. reprint ed. pap. 109.20 (0-685-15923-X, 2026310) Bks Demand.
Lloyd, Douglas, tr. see Beyer, Hans & Walter, Wolfgang.
Lloyd, Douglas R., ed. Materials Science of Synthetic Membranes. LC 84-21652. (ACS Symposium Ser.: No. 269). 494p. 1984. lib. bdg. 87.95 (0-8412-0887-5) Am Chemical.
Lloyd, Douglas R., jt. ed. see Sirkar, Kamalesh K.
Lloyd, Douglas R., et al, eds. Inverse Gas Chromatography: Characterization of Polymers & Other Materials. LC 89-15. (ACS Symposium Ser.: No. 391). (Illus.). xi, 358p. 1989. 69.95 (0-8412-1610-X) Am Chemical.
Lloyd, E. M. Food & Inflation in the Middle East, 1940-45. xiv, 375p. 1956. 47.50 (0-8047-0468-6) Stanford U Pr.
Lloyd, Edward. Metal-Forming: An Introduction to Some Theory, Principles & Practice. (C). 1989. 300.00 (0-685-36808-4, Pub. by Fuel Metallurgical Jrnl UK) St Mut.
Lloyd, Edwards A., et al. Doses in Radiation Accidents Investigated by Chromosome Aberration Analysis: XVII: A Review of Cases Investigated, 1986. (National Radiological Protection Board R Ser.: No. 207). (Orig.). 1987. pap. text ed. 8.00 (0-85951-284-3, HM1123, Pub. by HMSO UK) UNIPUB.
Lloyd-Eley, Lesley. Tolley's VAT Penalty & Compliance Provisions. 3rd ed. 200p. 1994. 150.00 (0-85459-805-7) St Mut.
Lloyd, Elisabeth. The Structure & Confirmation of Evolutionary Theory. 247p. 1993. pap. text ed. 14.95 (0-691-00046-8) Princeton U Pr.
Lloyd, Elisabeth A. The Structure & Confirmation of Evolutionary Theory. LC 88-3123. (Contributions in Philosophy Ser.: No. 37). 243p. 1988. text ed. 49.95 (0-313-25563-6, LVY/, Greenwood Pr) Greenwood.
Lloyd, Elisabeth A., jt. ed. see Keller, Evelyn F.
Lloyd, Elizabeth. Witch Child. 352p. 1987. pap. 3.95 (0-8217-2230-1) Zebra.
— Witch Daughter. 384p. 1988. pap. 3.95 (0-8217-2353-7) Zebra.
Lloyd, Elizabeth A., jt. ed. see Keller, Evelyn F.
Lloyd, Elizabeth J. Watercolor Still Life. LC 93-47008. (DK Art School Ser.). (Illus.). 72p. 1994. 16.95 (1-56458-490-9) Dorling Kindersley.

An Asterisk (*) at the beginning of an entry indicates that the title is appearing in BIP for the first time.

Lloyd-Elliott, Martin. City Ablaze: Life with the World's Busiest Firefighters. 2nd large type ed. 273p. 1993. 23.95 (1-85695-085-9, Pub. by ISIS UK) Transaction Pubs.

Lloyd, Ernest, ed. Scrapbook Stories: Character Building Stories from Yesteryear. (Pioneer Ser.). (Illus.). 96p. (YA). (gr. 5 up). 1990. reprint ed. pap. 5.95 (0-945460-08-2) Upward Way.

Lloyd, Ernest M. A Review of the History of Infantry. LC 70-84277. 1982. reprint ed. text ed. 100.50 (0-8371-5015-9, LLHI, Greenwood Pr) Greenwood.

Lloyd, Errol. Sasha & the Bicycle Thieves. (Banana Bks.). (Illus.). 42p. (J). (gr. 2-4). 1989. 3.95 (0-8120-6141-1) Barron.

Lloyd, Evan. The Methodist: A Poem. LC 92-1718. (Augustan Reprints Ser.: No. 151-152 (1972)). reprint ed. 18.50 (0-404-70151-5, PR3541) AMS Pr.

Lloyd-Evans, Barbara, tr. see Bronte, Emily.

Lloyd, Eyre. The Succession Laws of Christian Countries with Special Reference to the Law of Primogeniture As It Exists in England. xi, 108p. 1985. reprint ed. lib. bdg. 20.00 (0-8377-0816-8) Rothman.

Lloyd-Fern, Susan, jt. auth. see Davis, Paul R.

Lloyd, Francis E. Guayule (Parthenium Argentatum Gray): A Rubber-Plant of the Chihuahuan Desert. (Illus.). 213p. 1911. pap. 10.00 (0-87279-140-8, 139) Carnegie Inst.

Lloyd, Frank W., jt. auth. see Ferris, Charles D.

Lloyd, Frederick E., ed. Lloyd's Church Musicians Directory. LC 72-1733. reprint ed. 14.75 (0-404-08319-6) AMS Pr.

Lloyd, G. Disco Dancing. (Ballroom Dance Ser.). 1986. lib. bdg. 69.95 (0-8490-3294-6) Gordon Pr.

— Disco Dancing. (Ballroom Dance Ser.). 1985. lib. bdg. 79.00 (0-87700-821-3) Revisionist Pr.

Lloyd, G. A. Egypt Since Cromer, 2 Vols, Set. LC 68-9625. 1970. reprint ed. 95.00 (0-86527-056-2) Fertig.

Lloyd, G. A., jt. auth. see Phelps, P. D.

Lloyd, G. E. Aristotle: Growth & Structure of His Thought. LC 68-21195. (Orig.). (C). 1968. pap. 19.95 (0-521-09456-9) Cambridge U Pr.

— Demystifying Mentalities. (Themes in the Social Sciences Ser.). 264p. (C). 1990. pap. 17.95 (0-521-36680-1) Cambridge U Pr.

— Demystifying Mentalities. (Themes in the Social Sciences Ser.). 264p. (C). 1990. 59.95 (0-521-36661-5) Cambridge U Pr.

— Early Greek Science: Thales to Aristotle. Finley, M. I., ed. (Ancient Culture & Society Ser.). (Illus.). (C). 1974. pap. text ed. 7.95 (0-393-00583-6) Norton.

— Greek Science after Aristotle. LC 72-11959. (Ancient Culture & Society Ser.). (Illus.). 208p. (C). 1975. pap. text ed. 10.95 (0-393-00780-4) Norton.

— Magic, Reason & Experience: Studies in the Origin & Development of Greek Science. LC 78-25710. (Illus.). 1979. 79.95 (0-521-22373-3); pap. 29.95 (0-521-29641-2) Cambridge U Pr.

— Methods & Problems in Greek Science: Selected Papers. (Illus.). 512p. (C). 1993. pap. 27.95 (0-521-39762-6) Cambridge U Pr.

— Polarity & Analogy: Two Types of Argumentation in Early Greek Thought. LC 92-17832. 512p. (C). 1992. reprint ed. pap. text ed. 16.95 (0-87220-140-6) Hackett Pub.

— The Revolution of Wisdom: Studies in the Claims & Practice of Ancient Greek Science. 1988. pap. 15.00 (0-520-06742-8) U CA Pr.

— Science: Studies in the Life Sciences in Ancient Greece. LC 82-19808. 300p. 1983. 74.95 (0-521-25314-4); pap. 27.95 (0-521-27307-2) Cambridge U Pr.

Lloyd, G. E., ed. Hippocratic Writings. Chadwick, John & Nann, W. N., trs. (Classics Ser.). 400p. 1984. pap. 9.95 (0-14-044451-3, Penguin Classics) Viking Penguin.

Lloyd, Gary G. The Lewis Families of Putnam County, Missouri, Vol. 2: Lewis Ancestors, Research Data, Maps & Obituaries. LC 89-91322. (Illus.). 166p. 1989. pap. 13.00 (0-9622972-2-4) G G Lloyd.

— The Young Families of Adair & Putnam Counties, Missouri. LC 87-119004. (Illus.). 208p. 1986. pap. 20.00 (0-9622972-0-8) G G Lloyd.

Lloyd, Genevieve. Being in Time: Self-Consciousness, Time & Narrative in Philosophy & Literature. LC 92-44132. (Ideas Ser.). 208p. 1993. 49.95 (0-415-07195-X, B2361, Routledge NY); pap. 15.95 (0-415-07196-8, B2365, Routledge NY) Routledge.

— The Man of Reason: "Male" & "Female" in Western Philosophy. 2nd ed. LC 93-17468. 166p. 1993. pap. text ed. 11.95x (0-8166-2414-3) U of Minn Pr.

— The Man of Reason: Male & Female in Western Philosophy. LC 84-10396. 148p. 1985. pap. text ed. 11.95 (0-8166-1382-6) U of Minn Pr.

— Part of Nature: Self-Knowledge in Spinoza's Ethics. LC 94-3195. 192p. 1994. 26.50x (0-8014-2999-4) Cornell U Pr.

Lloyd, Geoffrey. Textbook of General Hospital Psychiatry. 256p. 1991. pap. text ed. 36.00 (0-443-02469-3) Churchill.

Lloyd, Geoffrey E. The Revolutions of Wisdom: Studies in the Claims & Practice of Ancient Greek Science. LC 86-16055. (Sather Classical Lectures: No. 52). 480p. reprint ed. pap. 136.80 (0-7837-4847-7, 2044494) Bks Demand.

Lloyd, George, ed. see Gerard, Alexander.

Lloyd, George A. Egypt Since Cromer, 2 Vols. LC 75-107074. reprint ed. 22.00 (0-404-04024-1) AMS Pr.

Lloyd George, David. War Memoirs of David Lloyd George, 6 vols., Set. LC 75-41179. reprint ed. 295.00 (0-404-15040-3) AMS Pr.

Lloyd, George I. Cutlery Trades. (Illus.). 493p. 1968. reprint ed. 37.50 (0-7146-1403-3, Pub. by F Cass Pubs UK) Intl Spec Bk.

***Lloyd, Gill & Jefferis, David.** The History of Optics. (Science Discovery Ser.). (Illus.). 48p. (J). (gr. 6-9). 1995. 15.95 (1-56847-255-2) Thomson Lrning.

Lloyd, Gordon B. Don't Call It "Dirt"! Improving Your Garden Soil. (Illus.). 128p. 1976. 6.95 (0-916302-12-1); pap. 3.95 (0-916302-02-4) Bookworm Pub.

Lloyd, Grant & Lloyd, Mary L. Faith Blossoms at Cherry Hill. 128p. 1993. 7.98 (0-88290-473-6, 2016) Horizon Utah.

Lloyd, H. David. A Book of Work Sheets for the I-Ching (Yi-Jing). (Illus.). 65p. 1991. student ed 15.95 (1-880107-14-7) D Lloyd Eng.

Lloyd, H. Evans, tr. see Von Feuchtersleben, Ernst F.

Lloyd, H. S. The Cocker Spaniel. 1991. lib. bdg. 75.00 (0-8490-5208-4) Gordon Pr.

Lloyd, Harold C. & Stout, Wesley W. American Comedy. LC 75-91907. (Illus.). 1972. 20.95 (0-405-08749-7, Pub. by Blom Pubns UK) Ayer.

Lloyd, Harvey. Isles of Eden: Life in the Southern Family Islands of the Bahamas - Columbus Quincentennial Edition. (Illus.). 96p. 1992. 65.00 (0-9629806-0-9) Benjamin OH.

— Sacred Lands of the Southwest. (Illus.). 224p. 1995. 60.00 (1-885254-11-3) Monacelli Pr.

— Sacred Lands of the Southwest, 4 vols., Set. (Illus.). 224p. 1995. 240.00 (1-885254-18-0) Monacelli Pr.

Lloyd, Henry D. Lords of Industry. LC 73-2519. (Big Business; Economic Power in a Free Society Ser.). 1973. reprint ed. 24.95 (0-405-05099-2) Ayer.

— Man, the Social Creator. LC 75-335. (Radical Tradition in America Ser.). 279p. 1975. reprint ed. 23.65 (0-88355-238-8) Hyperion Conn.

— Men, the Workers. Withington, Anne & Stallbohen, Caroline, eds. LC 79-89751. (American Labor, from Conspiracy to Collective Bargaining Ser., No. 1). 280p. 1974. reprint ed. 21.95 (0-405-02138-0) Ayer.

Lloyd, Henry D., ed. Wealth Against Commonwealth. LC 76-7. 184p. 1976. reprint ed. text ed. 45.00 (0-8371-8726-5, LLWA, Greenwood Pr) Greenwood.

***Lloyd, Hollis.** How to Draw Cartoons & Animation. (J). 1994. 12.98 (0-7858-0040-9) Bk Sales Inc.

Lloyd, Holly & Ingalls, Lee, eds. University Science Facilities: 100 Project Profiles. (Illus.). 250p. (Orig.). 1992. pap. 95.00 (0-9627204-1-0) Tradeline.

Lloyd, Howell A., ed. see Loyseau, Charles.

Lloyd, Humphrey. High Profit-Low Risk Options Strategies. 1984. 34.95 (0-318-04209-6) Windsor.

— The Moving Balance System: A New Technique for Stock & Option Trading. 1976. 50.00 (0-685-68982-4) Windsor.

Lloyd, Humphrey E. RSL Market Timing Method. 1990. 50.00 (0-930233-45-X) Windsor.

***Lloyd, Ian.** Information Technology & the Law. 1986. boxed 50.00 (0-406-02446-4, UK) Butterworth Legal Pubs.

Lloyd, Idwal. Celtic Word Craft. (C). 1989. 30.00 (1-85022-008-5, Pub. by Dyllansow Truran UK) St Mut.

***Lloyd, J.** Full Circle Summer. 50p. 1995. pap. 6.95 (1-887589-01-5) Sea Lore Pub.

— I Found My Porpoise. 50p. 1995. pap. 6.95 (1-887589-00-7) Sea Lore Pub.

Lloyd, J. A. Dostoevsky. LC 75-30857. (Studies in Russian Literature & Life: No. 100). 1975. lib. bdg. 42.95 (0-8383-2099-6) M S G Haskell Hse.

Lloyd, J. Gordon, tr. see Arrian.

Lloyd, J. M., ed. Thermal Imaging Systems. LC 75-9635. (Optical Physics & Engineering Ser.). 456p. 1975. 89.50 (0-306-30848-7, Plenum Pr) Plenum.

Lloyd, J. R., et al, eds. Materials Reliability Issues in Microelectronics: Materials Research Society Symposium Proceedings, Vol. 225. 1991. text ed. 70.00 (1-55899-119-0) Materials Res.

Lloyd, J. Timothy, jt. ed. see Elshtain, Jean B.

Lloyd, J. W. Foundations of Logic Programming. (Symbolic Computation Ser.). xii, 212p. 1993. 69.00 (0-387-18199-7) Spr-Verlag.

Lloyd, J. W., ed. Computational Logic: Symposium Proceedings, Brussels, November 13-14, 1990. (ESPRIT Basic Research Ser.). (Illus.). xi, 211p. 1990. 34.95 (0-387-53437-7) Spr-Verlag.

Lloyd, J. W., et al, eds. The Regular Education Initiative: Alternative Perspectives on Concepts, Issues, & Methods. (Illus.). 330p. (C). 1991. text ed. 36.95 (0-9625233-3-X) Sycamore Pub.

Lloyd, J. William. Iris Heart. 1972. 59.95 (0-8490-0423-3) Gordon Pr.

— The Karezza Method: Magnetation, the Art of Connubial Love. 64p. 1964. reprint ed. spiral bd. 5.50 (0-7873-0565-0) Mokelumne.

— The Karezza Method, or Magnetation, the Art of Connubial Love. 1991. lib. bdg. 79.95 (0-87700-930-9) Revisionist Pr.

Lloyd, James G., ed. Lives of Mississippi Authors, 1817-1967. LC 81-2515. 513p. reprint ed. pap. 146.30 (0-8357-4346-2, 2037149) Bks Demand.

Lloyd, Janet, tr. see Aries, Philippe.

Lloyd, Janet, tr. see De Planhol, Xavier.

Lloyd, Janet, tr. see de Polignac, Francois.

Lloyd, Janet, tr. see De Romilly, Jacqueline.

Lloyd, Janet, tr. see Detienne, Marcel & Vernant, Jean-Pierre.

Lloyd, Janet, tr. see Detienne, Marcel.

Lloyd, Janet, tr. see Garlan, Yvon.

Lloyd, Janet, tr. see Gernet, Jacques.

Lloyd, Janet, tr. see Hartog, Francois.

Lloyd, Janet, tr. see Jullien, Francois.

Lloyd, Janet, tr. see Laroque, Francois.

Lloyd, Janet, tr. see Meny, Yves.

Lloyd, Janet, tr. see Vernant, Jean-Pierre.

Lloyd, Janet, tr. see Vernant, Jean-Pierre & Vidal-Naquet, Pierre.

***Lloyd, Janet E.** Joy & Wonder in All God's Works: Year C. 142p. (J). 1994. pap. 14.95 (0-9646362-4-7) Via Media.

Lloyd, Janet E., tr. see Svenbro, Jesper.

***Lloyd, Jeremy.** Listen Very Carefully, I Shall Say This Only Once: An Autobiography. (Illus.). 170p. 1995. 21.95 (0-563-36203-0, BBC-Parkwest) Parkwest Pubns.

— Woodland Gospels: According to Captain Beaky & His Band. LC 83-20790. (Illus.). 63p. (J). (gr. k up). 1984. pap. 4.95 (0-571-14285-0) Faber & Faber.

Lloyd, Jill. German Expressionism: Primitivism & Modernity. (Illus.). 272p. (C). 1991. text ed. 65.00 (0-300-04373-2) Yale U Pr.

Lloyd, Joan. The Career Decisions Planner: When to Move, When to Stay, & When to Go Out on Your Own. 272p. 1992. text ed. 49.95 (0-471-54733-6); pap. text ed. 14.95 (0-471-54732-8) Wiley.

— Guatemala, Land of the Mayas. LC 74-2557. (Illus.). 175p. 1974. reprint ed. text ed. 49.75 (0-8371-7415-5, LLGU, Greenwood Pr) Greenwood.

***Lloyd, Joan E.** Bedtime Stories for Lovers. 96p. (Orig.). 1996. pap. 10.99 (0-446-67139-8) Warner Bks.

— Black Satin. 256p. 1995. pap. 8.95 (0-7867-0236-2) Carroll & Graf.

— Come Play with Me: Games & Toys for Creative Lovers. 272p. (Orig.). 1994. pap. 11.99 (0-446-39538-2) Warner Bks.

— If It Feels Good: Using the Five Senses to Enhance Your Lovemaking. 240p. (Orig.). 1993. pap. 10.99 (0-446-39450-5) Warner Bks.

— Nice Couples Do: How to Turn Your Secret Dreams into Sensational Sex. 1991. pap. 11.99 (0-446-39258-8) Warner Bks.

Lloyd, Joan E. & Herman, Edwin B. Rescue Alert. 240p. (Orig.). 1994. mass mkt. 4.99 (0-425-14052-0) Berkley Pub.

Lloyd, John. Flammability of Materials. 1989. 49.50 (0-89116-289-5) CRC Pr.

— The Pimm's Book of Polo. (Illus.). 240p. 1989. 24.98 (0-943955-17-3, Trafalgar Sq Pub) Trafalgar.

***Lloyd, John, ed.** Logic Programming: Proceedings of the 1995 International Symposium. (Logic Programming Ser.). (Illus.). 800p. (C). 1995. pap. 75.00x (0-262-62099-5) MIT Pr.

Lloyd, John, jt. auth. see Hill, Patricia.

Lloyd, John, jt. ed. see Morton, Ron.

Lloyd, John B. Eighteen Miles of History on Long Beach Island. 2nd rev. ed. (Illus.). 208p. (Orig.). 1994. 38.00 (0-945582-17-X) Down the Shore Pub.

— Six Miles at Sea. Buchholz, Margaret T., ed. (Illus.). 176p. (Orig.). 1990. 32.00 (0-945582-03-X); pap. 18.95 (0-9615208-9-2) Down the Shore Pub.

Lloyd, John K., ed. see Navratil, Sidney J., et al.

Lloyd, John S., ed. How to Evaluate Residents. LC 86-72620. 400p. 1986. lib. bdg. 39.95 (0-934277-09-5) Am Bd Med Spec.

— Residency Director's Role in Specialty Certification. LC 85-70465. (Illus.). 255p. 1985. lib. bdg. 34.95 (0-934277-05-2) Am Bd Med Spec.

Lloyd, John S., jt. ed. see Langsley, Donald G.

Lloyd, John U. Etidorhpa or the End of Earth. 386p. 1974. pap. 30.00 (0-89540-004-9, SB-004) Sun Pub.

— Etidorhpa: or The End of Earth: The Strange History of a Mysterious Being & the Account of a Remarkable Journey. enl. ed. (Illus.). 375p. 1992. pap. 24.95 (1-56459-243-X) Kessinger Pub.

— Etidorpha & the Account of a Remarkable Journey: The End of the Earth, the Strange History of a Mysterious Being. 5th ed. 397p. 1966. spiral bd. 19.25 (0-7873-0566-9) Mokelumne.

Lloyd-Jones, Antonia, tr. see Huelle, Pawel.

Lloyd-Jones, Bethan. Memories of Sandfields. (Illus.). 96p. 1983. pap. 5.95 (0-85151-366-2) Banner of Truth.

Lloyd-Jones, D. Martyn. Authority. 94p. 1992. reprint ed. pap. 4.95 (0-85151-386-7) Banner of Truth.

— The Best of Martyn Lloyd-Jones. Catherwood, Christopher, ed. 144p. (Orig.). 1993. pap. 9.99 (0-8010-5686-1) Baker Bk.

— Christian Soldier. 1977. 24.99 (0-8010-5583-0) Baker Bk.

— Christian Unity: An Exposition of Ephesians 4: 1-16. 280p. 1981. 24.99 (0-8010-5607-1) Baker Bk.

— The Christian Warfare: An Exposition of Ephesians 6: 10-13. 1977. reprint ed. 24.99 (0-8010-5574-1) Baker Bk.

— The Cross. LC 85-72911. 192p. 1986. pap. 11.99 (0-89107-382-5) Crossway Bks.

— Cross: The Vindication of God. 1976. pap. 1.95 (0-85151-266-6) Banner of Truth.

— Darkness & Light: An Exposition of Ephesians 4 17-5 17. 408p. 1983. reprint ed. 24.99 (0-8010-5617-9) Baker Bk.

— De la Angoisse a la Foi. 96p. (FRE.). 1986. 3.95 (0-8297-0694-1) Life Pubs Intl.

— Evangelistic Sermons. 294p. (Orig.). 1983. pap. 15.95 (0-85151-362-X) Banner of Truth.

— Faith Tried & Triumphant. 232p. (Orig.). 1988. pap. 9.99 (0-8010-5649-7) Baker Bk.

— La Fe a Prueba. Orig. Title: Faith on Trial. 188p. (SPA.). 1976. pap. 3.75 (0-8254-1446-6) Kregel.

— First Book of Daily Readings. 1970. pap. 9.99 (0-8028-1354-2) Eerdmans.

— God's Ultimate Purpose. (Illus.). 1978. 24.99 (0-8010-5591-1) Baker Bk.

— God's Way of Reconciliation: Studies in Ephesians II. 1972. 24.99 (0-8010-5519-9) Baker Bk.

— Growing in the Spirit. LC 89-50326. (John Seventeen Ser.). 160p. 1989. 14.99 (0-89107-535-6) Crossway Bks.

— The Heart of the Gospel. LC 91-14593. 192p. 1991. reprint ed. pap. 13.99 (0-89107-638-7) Crossway Bks.

— I Am Not Ashamed: Advice to Timothy. Catherwood, Christopher, ed. 1986. pap. 7.99 (0-8010-5634-9) Baker Bk.

— Knowing the Times. 400p. 1989. 31.95 (0-85151-556-8) Banner of Truth.

— Letters of D. Martyn Lloyd-Jones. 248p. 1994. 25.95 (0-85151-674-2) Banner of Truth.

— Life in the Spirit: In Marriage, Home & Work, an Exposition of Ephesians 5: 18-6: 9. 372p. 1975. reprint ed. 24.99 (0-8010-5550-4) Baker Bk.

— The Life of Joy: An Exposition of Philippians 1 & 2. 240p. (Orig.). 1989. pap. 16.99 (0-8010-5658-6) Baker Bk.

— The Life of Peace: An Exposition of Philippians 3 & 4. 272p. 1992. 16.99 (0-8010-5678-0) Baker Bk.

— Lloyd-Jones Expositions of Ephesians, 8 Vols. 1983. 149.95 (0-8010-5623-3) Baker Bk.

— Love So Amazing: An Exposition of Colossians. (Lloyd-Jones New Testament Commentaries Ser.). 288p. 1995. reprint ed. 16.99 (0-8010-1011-X) Baker Bk.

— The Plight of Man & the Power of God. (Summit Bks.). 96p. 1982. reprint ed. pap. 4.99 (0-8010-5621-7) Baker Bk.

— Por Que lo Permite Dios? Orig. Title: Why Does God Allow War?. 96p. (SPA.). 1992. pap. 3.50 (0-8254-1448-2) Kregel.

— Preaching & Preachers. 325p. 1972. 21.99 (0-310-27870-8, 10573) Zondervan.

— The Puritans: Their Origins & Successors. 436p. (C). 1987. 32.95 (0-85151-496-0) Banner of Truth.

— Reflections: A Treasury of Daily Readings. 384p. 1995. 14.99 (0-529-10251-X) World Bible.

— Revival. LC 86-72057. 320p. (Orig.). 1987. pap. 12.99 (0-89107-415-5) Crossway Bks.

— Romans: An Exposition of Chapter 1. (Gospel of God Ser.). 416p. 1986. 22.99 (0-310-27950-X, 10571) Zondervan.

— Romans: Assurance, Chapter 5. 272p. 1972. 22.99 (0-310-27890-2, 10542) Zondervan.

— Romans: Atonement & Justification; an Exposition of Chapters 3 : 20 - 4 : 35, Vol. 1. 1971. 22.99 (0-310-27880-5, 10561) Zondervan.

— Romans: Exposition of Chapters 2, Verse 1-3, Verse 20. (Lloyd-Jones Series on Romans). 246p. 1989. 22.99 (0-310-27960-7, 10572) Zondervan.

— Romans: God's Sovereign Purpose (Exposition of Chapter 9: 1-33) 336p. 1992. 22.99 (0-310-27500-8) Zondervan.

— Romans: Sons of God -(Chapter 8 : 17 - 39) 448p. 1975. 22.99 (0-310-27920-8, 10576) Zondervan.

— Romans: The Final Perseverance of the Saints (8: 17-39) 457p. 1976. 22.99 (0-310-27930-5, 10592) Zondervan.

— Romans: The Law (Chapter 7: 1 to 8: 4) 368p. 1974. 22.99 (0-310-27910-0, 10574) Zondervan.

— Romans: The New Man (Chapter 6), Vol. 3. (C). 1973. 22.99 (0-310-27900-3, 10534) Zondervan.

— Romans: The Righteous Judgment of God, an Exposition of 2.1-3.20. 256p. 1989. 17.95 (0-310-27970-4) Zondervan.

— Safe in the World. LC 87-70457. (John Seventeen Ser.). 160p. 1988. 14.99 (0-89107-493-7) Crossway Bks.

— Sanctified Through the Truth. LC 88-71810. (John Seventeen Ser.). 160p. 1989. 14.99 (0-89107-515-1) Crossway Bks.

— Saved in Eternity: The Assurance of Our Salvation. LC 87-70457. (John Seventeen Ser.). 192p. 1988. 14.99 (0-89107-448-1) Crossway Bks.

— Second Peter. 1983. 23.95 (0-85151-379-4) Banner of Truth.

— El Sermon del Monte, 1. 1978. 10.95 (0-85151-631-9) Banner of Truth.

— El Sermon del Monte, 2. 1978. 7.95 (0-85151-509-6) Banner of Truth.

— The Sovereign Spirit: Discerning His Gifts. LC 86-6513. 160p. 1986. pap. 8.99 (0-87788-697-0) Shaw Pubs.

— Spiritual Depression: Its Causes & Cure. 1965. pap. 12.99 (0-8028-1387-9) Eerdmans.

— Studies in the Sermon on the Mount. 1971. 19.99 (0-8028-0036-X) Eerdmans.

— Unidad Cristiana. 68p. (SPA.). 1973. pap. 2.25 (0-8254-1449-0) Kregel.

— Unsearchable Riches of Christ: An Exposition of Ephesians 3. 1980. 24.99 (0-8010-5597-0) Baker Bk.

— La Vida en el Espiritu. 331p. 1987. reprint ed. pap. 10.00 (0-939125-37-4) Evangelical Lit.

Lloyd-Jones, D. Martyn, ed. Joy Unspeakable: Power & Renewal in the Holy Spirit. LC 85-1929. 284p. 1985. pap. 9.99 (0-87788-441-2) Shaw Pubs.

Lloyd-Jones, David, ed. see Mussorgsky, Modeste.

Lloyd-Jones, David, tr. see Mussorgsky, Modeste.

Lloyd-Jones, David M. What Is an Evangelical? 91p. 1993. pap. 3.95 (0-85151-626-2) Banner of Truth.

Lloyd-Jones, Hugh. Blood for the Ghosts: Classical Influences in the Nineteenth & Twentieth Centuries. LC 82-49061. 312p. 1983. text ed. 45.00x (0-8018-3017-6) Johns Hopkins.

— Greek Comedy, Hellenistic Literature, Greek Religion, & Miscellanea: Academic Papers of Sir Hugh Lloyd-Jones. (Illus.). 440p. 1991. 115.00 (0-19-814745-7) OUP.

— Greek Epic, Lyric, & Tragedy: Academic Papers of Sir Hugh Lloyd-Jones. 488p. 1991. 135.00 (0-19-814680-9) OUP.

— Greek in a Cold Climate. 248p. (C). 1991. text ed. 70.00 (0-389-20967-8) B&N Imports.

— The Justice of Zeus. 2nd ed. (Sather Classical Lectures: No. 41). 290p. 1971. pap. 14.00 (0-520-04688-9) U CA Pr.

Lloyd-Jones, Hugh, ed. The Greeks. (New Reprints in Essay & General Literature Index Ser.). 1977. reprint ed. 29.95 (0-518-10204-1, 10204) Ayer.

— Sophocles II, 2 vols., 2. LC 92-19295. (Loeb Classical Library: Nos. 20-21). 528p. 1994. 18.95 (0-674-99557-0) HUP.

Lloyd-Jones, Hugh & Wilson, N. G., eds. Sophoclea: Studies in the Text of Sophocles. 288p. 1990. 65.00 (0-19-814041-X) OUP.

Lloyd-Jones, Hugh, tr. see Aeschylus.

Lloyd-Jones, Hugh, ed. see Sophocles.

An Asterisk (*) at the beginning of an entry indicates that the title is appearing in BIP for the first time.

Lloyd-Jones, Martin. Unity in Truth. 1991. pap. 11.99 (*0-85234-288-8*, Pub. by Evangel Pr UK) Presby & Reformed.

Lloyd-Jones, Martyn. Children of God. LC 92-21507. (Studies in First John: Vol. 3). 144p. (Orig.). 1994. pap. 9.99 (*0-89107-777-4*) Crossway Bks.

— Depresion Espiritual. 319p. (SPA.). 1994. pap. 6.95 (*0-939125-61-7*) Evangelical Lit.

— Enjoying the Presence of God. 168p. (Orig.). (C). 1992. pap. 8.99 (*0-89283-757-8*, Vine Bks) Servant.

— Fellowship with God. LC 92-21507. (Studies in First John). 160p. 1993. pap. 9.99 (*0-89107-705-7*) Crossway Bks.

— The Kingdom of God. LC 92-5768. 224p. 1992. 13.99 (*0-89107-648-4*) Crossway Bks.

— Life in God. LC 92-2507. (Studies in I John: Bk. 5). 208p. (Orig.). 1995. pap. 9.99 (*0-89107-829-0*) Crossway Bks.

— The Love of God. LC 94-153867. (Studies in First John: Bk. 4). 208p. (Orig.). 1994. pap. 9.99 (*0-89107-814-2*) Crossway Bks.

— Truth Unchanged, Unchanging. 2nd ed. LC 93-376. 128p. 1993. reprint ed. pap. 6.99 (*0-89107-706-5*) Crossway Bks.

— Walking with God. LC 92-21507. (Studies in First John: Vol. 2). 144p. (C). 1993. pap. 9.99 (*0-89107-735-9*) Crossway Bks.

— Why Does God Allow Suffering? 128p. (Orig.). 1994. pap. 7.99 (*0-89107-776-6*) Crossway Bks.

***Lloyd-Jones, Martyn D.** Out of the Depths: Restoring Fellowship with God. LC 94-33867. 112p. 1994. pap. 7.99 (*0-89107-838-X*) Crossway Bks.

Lloyd Jones, Peter. Taste Today: The Role of Appreciation in Consumerism & Design. (Illus.). 260p. 1991. 94.00 (*0-08-040251-8*, Pergamon Pr) Elsevier.

Lloyd-Jones, Roger & Lewis, M. J. Manchester in the Age of the Factory: The Business Structure of Cottonoplis in the Industrial Revolution. 272p. 1988. lib. bdg. 75.00 (*0-7099-4158-7*, Pub. by Croom Helm UK) Routledge Chapman & Hall.

Lloyd, Justin. The Possession of Tony Saurian. LC 86-70176. (Illus.). 242p. (Orig.). 1987. pap. 4.95 (*0-937059-00-5*) AM to PM.

Lloyd, K. M., ed. Kew Index for 1987: Names of Seed-Bearing Plants, Ferns, & Fern Allies at the Rank of Family & Below Published During 1987 with Some Omissions from Earlier Years. 176p. 1988. pap. 49.95 (*0-19-854245-3*) OUP.

— Kew Index for 1988. 208p. 1989. pap. 39.95 (*0-19-854264-X*) OUP.

Lloyd, K. M., jt. ed. see Davies, R. A.

***Lloyd, Kathleen.** Times One-Thousand Mots Pour Parler. (Illus.). 95p. (Orig.). (FRE.). (J). (gr. 2-6). 1992. pap. 9.95 (*88-85148-54-9*, Pub. by Europ Lang Inst IT) Midwest European Pubns.

— Times One-Thousand Words to Talk About. (Illus.). 95p. (Orig.). (J). (gr. 2-6). 1992. pap. 9.95 (*981-01-0384-0*, Pub. by Europ Lang Inst IT) Midwest European Pubns.

— Times One-Thousand Worter Zum Sprechen. (Illus.). 95p. (Orig.). (GER.). (J). (gr. 2-6). 1992. reprint ed. pap. 9.95 (*88-85148-55-7*, Pub. by Europ Lang Inst IT) Midwest European Pubns.

Lloyd, Kenneth, jt. auth. see Moine, Donald J.

Lloyd, Kent, et al. Knowledge Revolution - Creating Responsible Learning Cultures: Competing in Our Global Economy: Empowering Federal Education Programs for All American Students. 1000p. (Orig.). Date not set. pap. 75.00 (*0-9634636-2-4*) Know Netwk Amer.

— Knowledge Revolution for All Americans: Winning the War Against Ignorance: Empowering Public Schools. 77p. 1992. 7.00 (*0-9634636-0-8*) Know Netwk Amer.

Lloyd-Kolkin, Donna & Tyner, Kathleen R. Media & You: An Elementary Media Literacy Curriculum. LC 90-42205. (Illus.). 170p. 1991. pap. 29.95 (*0-87778-226-1*) Educ Tech Pubns.

Lloyd, L. S. The Musical Ear. LC 88-31967. 104p. 1990. reprint ed. text ed. 45.00 (*0-313-26666-2*, LLME, Greenwood Pr) Greenwood.

Lloyd, Les, ed. Administrative Computing in Higher Education: Issues in Enterprise-Wide Networks & Systems. (Supplement to Computers in Libraries Ser.: Vol. 78). 225p. 1994. pap. text ed. 40.00 (*0-88736-898-0*) Learned Info.

— Technology & Higher Education: Class Studies on the Use of Computers, Networks, & Multimedia in the Classroom. (Supplement to Computers in Libraries Ser.: No. 62). Orig. Title: Integrating Technology into the Curriculum. 200p. 1994. pap. 49.50 (*0-88736-867-0*) Learned Info.

Lloyd, Lewis E. Tariffs: The Case for Protectionism. 9.50 (*0-8159-6902-3*) Devin.

Lloyd, Linda. Classroom Magic: Amazing Technology for Teachers & Homeschoolers. 4th ed. (Illus.). 160p. (Orig.). 1982. reprint ed. pap. 15.95 (*1-55552-014-6*) Metamorphous Pr.

— Journey to Joy: A Day by Day Guide to Getting in Touch with Your Inner Child. (Illus.). (Orig.). 1994. pap. 10.00 (*0-914003-04-6*) Twiggs Comm.

Lloyd, Linda, et al. The Ma Cuisine Cooking School Cookbook. LC 87-43221. (Illus.). 288p. 1988. 19.95 (*0-394-55289-X*) Random.

— Ma Cuisine Cooking School Cookbook. 248p. 1991. 7.99 (*0-517-69936-2*) Random Hse Value.

Lloyd, Llewelyn. Peasant Life in Sweden. LC 77-87710. 496p. reprint ed. 47.50 (*0-404-16501-X*) AMS Pr.

Lloyd, Llewelyn S. Music & Sound. LC 70-107815. (Select Bibliographies Reprint Ser.). 1977. 20.95 (*0-8369-5188-3*) Ayer.

— Music & Sound. (Music Book Index Ser.). 181p. 1992. reprint ed. lib. bdg. 69.00 (*0-7812-9477-0*) Rprt Serv.

Lloyd, Louise, ed. see Chesman, Andrea.

Lloyd, Louise, ed. see Garden Way Publishing Editors.

Lloyd, Lucy C., jt. auth. see Bleek, Whilhelm H.

Lloyd, Lyle L., jt. ed. see Schiefelbusch, Richard L.

Lloyd, Maggie H., jt. auth. see Wolfensohn, Sarah E.

Lloyd, Margaret. This Particular Earthly Scene. LC 92-38198. 80p. (Orig.). 1993. 9.95 (*0-914086-99-5*) Alicejamesbooks.

Lloyd, Margaret A., jt. auth. see Weiten, Wayne.

Lloyd, Margaret G. William Carlos William's Paterson: A Critical Appraisal. LC 77-89775. (Illus.). 305p. 1979. 35.00 (*0-8386-2152-X*) Fairleigh Dickinson.

Lloyd, Marjorie L. It Must Have Been an Angel. (Redwood Ser.). 1980. pap. 6.95 (*0-8163-0363-0*) Pacific Pr Pub Assn.

Lloyd, Marjorie S. Tombstone Names in Suffolk County, New York. (Illus.). 86p. (Orig.). 1986. pap. 15.00 (*0-9617988-0-7*) M Sones Lloyd.

Lloyd, Mark. The Guinness Book of Espionage. LC 94-8562. (Illus.). 256p. 1994. reprint ed. pap. 16.95 (*0-306-80584-7*) Da Capo.

— Modern Combat Uniforms. (Illus.). 215p. 1988. pap. 19.95 (*0-89747-226-8*) Squad Sig Pubns.

— Special Forces: The Changing Face of Warfare. (Illus.). 272p. 1995. 24.95 (*1-85409-170-0*, Pub. by Arms & Armour UK) Sterling.

Lloyd, Mark F. & Moak, Jefferson M., eds. Pennsylvania Society of Sons of the Revolution: Centennial Register, 1888-1988. LC 90-61497. (Illus.). x, 994p. 1990. 35.00 (*0-9626507-0-6*) PA Soc Sons Rev.

Lloyd, Mary. Pepsi-Cola Collectibles: The Everett Lloyd Book. (Illus.). 160p. 1993. pap. 29.95 (*0-88740-533-9*) Schiffer.

***Lloyd, Mary J.** Call It Paradise. 512p. 1995. pap. 4.99 (*0-8217-5045-3*) Zebra.

Lloyd, Mary L., jt. auth. see Lloyd, Grant.

Lloyd, Matthew & Blackmore, Janet. Glass for a Beautiful Home. (Beautiful Home Ser.). 160p. 1990. 19.95 (*0-8120-6172-1*) Barron.

Lloyd, Megan, illus. Baba Yaga: A Russian Folktale. LC 90-39215. 32p. (J). (ps-3). 1991. lib. bdg. 15.95 (*0-8234-0854-X*) Holiday.

— The Gingerbread Man. 32p. (J). (ps-3). 1993. lib. bdg. 15.95 (*0-8234-0824-8*); pap. 5.95 (*0-8234-1137-0*) Holiday.

— The Gingerbread Man. (J). (gr. k-3). 1994. audio, pap. 14.95 (*0-87499-318-0*) Live Oak Media.

— The Gingerbread Man. (J). (gr. k-3). 1994. audio 22.95 (*0-87499-319-9*) Live Oak Media.

— The Gingerbread Man, 4 bks., Set. (J). (gr. k-3). 1994. audio, pap. 33.95 (*0-87499-320-2*) Live Oak Media.

Lloyd, Michael. The Agon in Euripides. 224p. 1992. 45.00 (*0-19-814778-3*) OUP.

Lloyd, Michael E., jt. auth. see McNeil, Bruce J.

Lloyd, Michael G. Legal Databases in Europe: User Attitudes & Supplier Strategies. 218p. 1986. 95.00 (*0-444-70048-X*) Elsevier.

Lloyd-Morris, Caroline, tr. see Kogon, Eugen, et al, eds.

Lloyd, N. G., et al, eds. Nonlinear Diffusion Equations & Their Equilibrium States Three: Proceedings from a Conference Held August 20-29, 1980 in Gregynog, Wales. (Progress in Nonlinear Differential Equations & Their Applications Ser.: Vol. 7). x, 572p. 1992. 120.00 (*0-8176-3531-9*) Spr-Verlag.

***Lloyd, Nathaniel.** Garden Craftsmanship in Yew & Box. (Illus.). 170p. 1995. 39.50 (*1-870673-14-X*) Antique Collect.

— A History of English Brickwork. (Illus.). 464p. 1983. 89.50 (*0-907462-36-7*) Antique Collect.

— A History of English Brickwork. LC 72-87653. (Illus.). 1972. reprint ed. lib. bdg. 36.95 (*0-405-08750-0*, Pub. by Blom Pubns UK) Ayer.

Lloyd, Nelson M. Six Stars. LC 75-125229. (Short Story Index Reprint Ser.). 1977. 20.95 (*0-8369-3596-9*) Ayer.

Lloyd, Noppe, jt. auth. see Fergus, Hughes.

Lloyd, Norman. Stages: Norman Lloyd. LC 89-77810. (Directors Guild of America Oral History Ser.: No. 9). (Illus.). 296p. 1990. 32.50 (*0-8108-2290-3*) Scarecrow.

— Stages: Of Life in Theatre, Film & Television. LC 92-30285. (Illus.). 278p. 1993. reprint ed. pap. 14.95 (*0-87910-166-0*) Limelight Edns.

Lloyd, Norman, jt. auth. see Fish, Arnold.

Lloyd, P. & Beveridge, Michael. Information & Meaning in Child Communication. (Applied Language Studies). 1981. text ed. 105.00 (*0-12-453520-8*) Acad Pr.

Lloyd, P. J., ed. see Particle Size Analysis Conference Staff.

Lloyd, Pamela. How Writers Write. 149p. 1990. pap. 13.95 (*0-435-08512-3*) Heinemann.

Lloyd, Patti. Acuenergy. 208p. 1982. 12.95 (*0-89557-060-2*) Woodland UT.

Lloyd, Paul. From Latin to Spanish. LC 86-72883. (Memoirs Ser.: Vol. 173). (C). 1987. 40.00 (*0-87169-173-6*, M173-LLP) Am Philos.

Lloyd, Percy, tr. see Lama Yongden.

Lloyd, Peter. The French Are Coming! The Invasion Scare, 1803-5. 240p. (C). 1991. 125.00 (*0-946771-77-4*, Pub. by Spellmount UK) St Mut.

— Groupware in the 21st Century: Computer Supported Cooperative Working Toward the Millennium. LC 94-28284. (Praeger Studies on the Twenty-First Century). 336p. 1994. text ed. 65.00 (*0-275-95091-3*, Praeger Pubs); pap. text ed. 21.95 (*0-275-95092-1*, Praeger Pubs) Greenwood.

— Perspectives & Identities: The Elizabethan Writer's Search to Know His World. 1989. 35.00 (*0-948695-11-0*, Pub. by Rubicon Pr UK) Intl Spec Bk.

Lloyd, Peter, jt. ed. see King, Stephen.

Lloyd, Peter C. A Third World Proletariat? (Controversies in Sociology Ser.: No. 11). 144p. 1982. pap. text ed. 11.95 (*0-04-301141-1*) Routledge Chapman & Hall.

Lloyd, Peter E., jt. auth. see Dicken, Peter.

Lloyd, Peter J. International Trade Problems of Small Nations. LC 67-28850. 146p. reprint ed. pap. 41.70 (*0-317-20457-2*, 2023420) Bks Demand.

Lloyd-Prichard, M. F., ed. see Keymer, John.

Lloyd, R., jt. auth. see Muller, R.

Lloyd, Ricardo V. Endocrine Pathology. (Illus.). 256p. 1990. 94.00 (*0-387-97166-1*) Spr-Verlag.

— Surgical Pathology of the Pituitary Gland. (Illus.). 271p. 1992. text ed. 60.95 (*0-7216-6459-8*) Saunders.

Lloyd, Richard. Pollution & Freshwater Fish. (Illus.). 1992. 54.95 (*0-85238-187-5*) Blackwell Sci.

Lloyd, Richard, jt. ed. see Davidson, Joan.

***Lloyd, Richmond M., et al.** Strategy & Force Planning. LC 95-2794. 1995. write for info. (*0-615-00487-3*) Naval War Coll.

Lloyd, Robert C., jt. auth. see Carey, Raymond G.

Lloyd, Robert M. Systematics of the Onocleoid Ferns. LC 72-170330. (University of California Publications in Social Welfare: Vol. 61). (Illus.). 99p. reprint ed. pap. 28.30 (*0-685-23659-5*, 2014704) Bks Demand.

Lloyd, Robert M. & Mitchell, Richard S. A Flora of the White Mountains, California & Nevada. LC 79-172393. (Illus.). 1973. 40.00 (*0-520-02119-3*) U CA Pr.

Lloyd, Roger B. Golden Middle Age. LC 75-90654. (Essay Index Reprint Ser.). 1977. 20.95 (*0-8369-1208-X*) Ayer.

— Revolutionary Religion: Christianity, Fascism, & Communism. LC 78-63686. (Studies in Fascism: Ideology & Practice). reprint ed. 24.50 (*0-404-16903-1*) AMS Pr.

Lloyd, Roseann. Tap Dancing for Big Mom. 1990. pap. 4.50 (*0-89823-073-X*) New Rivers Pr.

Lloyd, Roseann & Fossum, Merle. True Selves: Twelve Step Recovery from Codependency. 128p. (Orig.). 1991. pap. 9.95 (*0-89486-765-2*, 5140A) Hazelden.

***Lloyd, Roseann & Solly, Richard.** Journeynotes: Writing for Recovery & Spiritual Growth. 236p. (Orig.). 1989. pap. 1.95 (*0-89486-606-0*) Hazelden.

Lloyd, Roseann, jt. ed. see Keenan, Deborah.

Lloyd, Roseann, jt. auth. see Solly, Richard.

Lloyd, Roseann, tr. see Wassmo, Herbjorg.

Lloyd, Rosemary. Baudelaire et Hoffmann: Affinites et Influences. LC 78-58796. 403p. reprint ed. pap. 114.90 (*0-8357-5999-7*, 2031683) Bks Demand.

— Closer & Closer Apart: Jealousy in Literature. 224p. 1995. 32.50 (*0-8014-3151-4*) Cornell U Pr.

— The Land of Lost Content: Children & Childhood in Nineteenth-Century French Literature. (Illus.). 296p. 1992. 65.00 (*0-19-815173-X*) OUP.

— Madame Bovary. (Unwin Critical Library). 336p. 1989. 44.95 (*0-04-800084-1*) Routledge Chapman & Hall.

Lloyd, Rosemary, tr. see Baudelaire, Charles P.

Lloyd, Rosemary, ed. see Baudelaire, Charles P.

Lloyd, Rosemary, ed. see Mallarme, Stephane.

Lloyd, Rosemary, tr. see Sand, George.

Lloyd, Russell F. & Rehg, Virgil R. Quality Circles: Applications in Vocational Education. 47p. 1983. 4.95 (*0-318-22183-7*, IN249) Ctr Educ Trng Employ.

Lloyd, S. The Ruined Cities of Iraq. (Illus.). 72p. 1980. 15.00 (*0-89005-375-8*) Ares.

Lloyd, S. A. Ideals As Interests in Hobbes's Leviathan: The Power of Mind over Matter. 350p. (C). 1992. 69.95 (*0-521-39243-8*) Cambridge U Pr.

Lloyd, S. D., jt. ed. see Coss, P. R.

Lloyd, S. D., jt. ed. see Ross, P. R.

Lloyd, Sam & Berthelot, Christine. Self-Empowerment. Crisp, Michael G., ed. LC 91-76251. (Fifty-Minute Ser.). 90p. (Orig.). 1992. pap. 9.95 (*1-56052-128-7*) Crisp Pubns.

***Lloyd, Sam R.** Developing Positive Assertiveness: Practical Techniques for Personal Success. rev. ed. Gerould, Philip, ed. LC 94-72612. (Fifty-Minute Ser.). (Illus.). 70p. 1995. pap. 9.95 (*1-56052-313-1*) Crisp Pubns.

Lloyd, Sampson S., tr. see List, Friedrich.

Lloyd, Sandra J., jt. auth. see Lamit, Louis G.

Lloyd, Sarah. An Indian Attachment. (Eland Travel Classics Ser.). 272p. 1992. pap. 14.95 (*0-7818-0018-8*) Hippocrene Bks.

— Indian Attachment. 1992. pap. 14.95 (*0-907871-12-7*) Hippocrene Bks.

Lloyd, Seton. Ancient Turkey: A Traveller's History of Anatolia. 1989. 35.00 (*0-520-06787-8*) U CA Pr.

— Foundations in the Dust: A Story of Mesopotamian Exploration. LC 76-46179. reprint ed. 21.50 (*0-404-15364-X*) AMS Pr.

Lloyd, Seton & Muller, Hans W. Ancient Architecture: Mesopotamia, Egypt, Crete. LC 85-30006. (History of World Architecture Ser.). (Illus.). 220p. 1986. pap. 29.95 (*0-8478-0692-8*) Rizzoli Intl.

Lloyd, Seton, jt. auth. see Jacobsen, Thorkild.

Lloyd, Simon. English Society & the Crusade, Twelve Sixteen to Thirteen Seven. (Oxford Historical Monographs). 344p. 1988. 69.00 (*0-19-822949-6*) OUP.

***Lloyd, Simon & Coss, Peter, eds.** Thirteenth Century England V: Proceedings of the Newcastle upon Tyne Conference 1993. (Thirteenth Century England Ser.). (Illus.). 256p. (C). 1995. text ed. 71.00 (*0-85115-565-0*) Boydell & Brewer.

Lloyd, Simon, jt. ed. see Coss, Peter.

Lloyd, Simon, ed. see Richard, Jean.

Lloyd, Siobhan, jt. auth. see Hall, Liz.

Lloyd, Stephen. The Barclays Guide to Law for the Small Business. 180p. (Orig.). 1991. pap. 24.95 (*0-631-17349-8*) Blackwell Pubs.

— H. Balfour Gardiner. LC 83-14227. (Illus.). 300p. 1984. 69.95 (*0-521-25609-7*) Cambridge U Pr.

Lloyd, Steven. Ivory Diptych Sundials, 1570-1750. (Illus.). 150p. 1992. text ed. 50.00 (*0-685-53271-2*) Contigo Pubns.

— Ivory Diptych Sundials, 1570-1750. (Illus.). 169p. 1992. text ed. 50.00 (*0-674-46977-1*) HUP.

Lloyd, Sue. The Phonics Handbook. (Illus.). 218p. (J). (ps-3). 1993. pap. 19.95 (*1-870946-08-1*, Pub. by Jolly Lrning UK) Am Intl Dist.

Lloyd, Sue, ed. The Penguin Roget's Thesaurus. rev. ed. (Reference Ser.). 800p. 1985. pap. 7.95 (*0-14-051155-5*, Penguin Bks) Viking Penguin.

Lloyd, Sue & Keys, Jacquie. Passion for Pasta: Delicious New Recipes for Fresh Pasta. (Illus.). 137p. 1994. 24.95 (*0-85572-222-3*, Pub. by Hill Content Pubng AT) Seven Hills Bk.

Lloyd, Sue & Wernham, Sara. Finger Phonics, 7 bks., Set. (Illus.). (J). (ps-2). 1994. 39.50 (*1-870946-31-6*, Pub. by Jolly Lrning UK) Am Intl Dist.

— Finger Phonics, Bk. 1: S, A, T, I, P, N. (Illus.). 14p. (J). (ps-2). 1994. 5.95 (*1-870946-24-3*, Pub. by Jolly Lrning UK) Am Intl Dist.

— Finger Phonics, Bk. 2: CK, E, H, R, M, D. (Illus.). 14p. (J). (ps-2). 1994. 5.95 (*1-870946-25-1*, Pub. by Jolly Lrning UK) Am Intl Dist.

— Finger Phonics, Bk. 3: G, O, U, L, F, B. (Illus.). 14p. (J). (ps-2). 1994. 5.95 (*1-870946-26-X*, Pub. by Jolly Lrning UK) Am Intl Dist.

— Finger Phonics, Bk. 4: AI, J, OA, IE, EE, OR. (Illus.). 14p. (J). (ps-2). 1994. 5.95 (*1-870946-27-8*, Pub. by Jolly Lrning UK) Am Intl Dist.

— Finger Phonics, Bk. 5: Z, W, NG, V, OO, OO. (Illus.). 14p. (J). (ps-2). 1994. 5.95 (*1-870946-28-6*, Pub. by Jolly Lrning UK) Am Intl Dist.

— Finger Phonics, Bk. 6: Y, X, CH, SH, TH, TH. (Illus.). 14p. (J). (ps-2). 1994. 5.95 (*1-870946-29-4*, Pub. by Jolly Lrning UK) Am Intl Dist.

— Finger Phonics, Bk. 7: QU, OU, OI, UE, ER, AR. (Illus.). 14p. (J). (ps-2). 1994. 5.95 (*1-870946-30-8*, Pub. by Jolly Lrning UK) Am Intl Dist.

— Phonic Wall Frieze. (Illus.). (J). (ps-2). 1994. 8.95 (*1-870946-32-4*, Pub. by Jolly Lrning UK) Am Intl Dist.

Lloyd, Susan C. No Pictures in My Grave: A Spiritual Journey in Sicily. LC 91-35598. 1992. pap. 12.95 (*1-56279-023-4*) Mercury Hse Inc.

Lloyd, Susan M. Roget's Thesaurus of English Words & Phrases. 1250p. 1989. 9.95 (*0-582-55635-X*, TV2782) Longman.

Lloyd, Susette H. Sketches of Bermuda. (Illus.). 1977. text ed. 18.95 (*0-8369-9228-8*, 9082) Ayer.

Lloyd, T. H. England & the German Hanse, 1157-1611: A Study of Their Trade & Commercial Diplomacy. 428p. (C). 1992. 89.95 (*0-521-40442-8*) Cambridge U Pr.

Lloyd, T. O. The British Empire, Fifteen Fifty-Eight to Nineteen Eighty-Three. (Short Oxford History of the Modern World Ser.). (Illus.). 1984. pap. 19.95 (*0-19-873025-X*) OUP.

— Empire, Welfare State, Europe: English History 1906-1992. 4th ed. (Short Oxford History of the Modern World). (Illus.). 600p. 1993. pap. 22.00 (*0-19-873111-6*) OUP.

Lloyd, Tim & Morrissey, Oliver, eds. Poverty, Inequality, & Rural Development. LC 93-47023. 1994. text ed. 69.95 (*0-312-12099-0*) St Martin.

Lloyd, Timothy & Glatt, Hillary. Folklife Resources in the Library of Congress. (Publications of the American Folklore Center Ser.: Vol. 8). 1993. write for info. (*0-8444-0371-7*) Lib Congress.

Lloyd, Timothy C. & Mullen, Patrick B. Lake Erie Fisherman: Work, Identity & Tradition. (Illus.). 216p. 1990. 19.95 (*0-252-01662-9*) U of Ill Pr.

Lloyd, Tom. The Charity Business: The New Philanthropists. 288p. 1994. 45.00 (*0-7195-5046-7*, Pub. by John Murray UK) Trafalgar.

— The Nice Company: Why "Nice" Companies Make More Profits. (Illus.). 224p. 1991. 29.95 (*0-7475-0346-X*, Pub. by Bloomsbury Pub Ltd UK) Trafalgar.

Lloyd, Tracey. The Old Man & the Rabbit. (Junior African Writers Ser.). (Illus.). (J). (gr. 5-6). 1992. pap. 3.95 (*0-7910-2917-4*) Chelsea Hse.

Lloyd, Trevor, jt. auth. see Perham, Michael.

Lloyd, W. Eugene, ed. Safety Evaluation of Drugs & Chemicals. LC 84-12912. (Illus.). 487p. (C). 1986. text ed. 99.50 (*0-89116-352-2*) Hemisp Pub.

Lloyd, W. Francis, jt. auth. see Austin, Bertram, Jr.

Lloyd, Ward, jt. auth. see Klein, Dan.

Lloyd-Watts, Valery, jt. auth. see Bigler, Carole.

Lloyd, William, jt. auth. see Salter, Christopher.

Lloyd's Aviation Dept. Staff, comp. Aircraft Types & Price Guidelines 1994-1995. 1994. 80.00 (*1-85044-463-3*) Lloyds London Pr.

Lloyds Bank Staff, ed. Monetarism & Keynesians. (Lloyds Bank Annual Review Ser.: Vol. 4). 1991. text ed. 49.00 (*0-86187-121-9*, Pub. by Pinter Pubs UK) St Martin.

Lloyd's of London Press, Inc. Staff. Lloyd's Ports of the World, 1994. 1993. 270.00 (*1-85044-325-4*) Lloyds London Pr.

— Lloyd's Survey Handbook. 5th ed. 1991. 85.00 (*1-85044-395-5*) Lloyds London Pr.

— Mediterranean Shipping Directory, 1993. 1993. pap. 130.00 (*1-85044-332-7*) Lloyds London Pr.

Lloyd's of London Press Staff. Capital for Shipping. (Orig.). 1994. pap. 60.00 (*1-85044-504-4*) Lloyds London Pr.

— Guide to International Ship Registers, Ship Managers & Manning Agents, 1993-1994. 1994. 80.00 (*1-85044-360-2*) Lloyds London Pr.

— Leading Developments in International Marine Insurance: An Industry Report. (Leading Developments in International Insurance Ser.). 96p. 1991. pap. 155.00 (*1-85044-407-2*) Lloyds London Pr.

— Lloyd's Cruise Industry Direct, 1994. (Illus.). 104p. 1994. pap. 80.00 (*1-85044-478-1*) Lloyds London Pr.

— Lloyd's Law Reports Citator 1919-1986. 1988. 300.00 (*1-85044-170-7*) Lloyds London Pr.

— Lloyd's Law Reports Subject Index 1919-1986. 1988. 445.00 (*1-85044-171-5*) Lloyds London Pr.

— Lloyd's Nautical Yearbook, 1994. 1993. 75.00 (*1-85044-421-8*) Lloyds London Pr.

— Lloyd's Shipping Connections, 1993 Edition. 1993. 55.00 (*1-85044-330-0*) Lloyds London Pr.

— Lloyd's War Losses - The First World War 1919-1918. 1990. 150.00 (*1-85044-314-9*) Lloyds London Pr.

— Lloyd's War Losses - The Second World War 1939-1945. 1989. 150.00 (*1-85044-217-7*) Lloyds London Pr.

— Marine Equipment Buyers' Guide, 1994. 1994. pap. 185. 00 (*1-85044-553-2*) Lloyds London Pr.

Lloyd's Ship Manager Staff. Guide to Worldwide Marine Training, 1994. 1994. pap. 85.00 (*1-85044-378-5*) Lloyds London Pr.

Lloyd's Shipping Economist Staff. Shipping & the Environment. (Orig.). 1991. pap. 30.00 (*0-685-66240-3*) Lloyds London Pr.

Lloyd's Training Centre Staff, ed. An Introduction to Lloyd's Market Procedures & Practices. 121p. (C). 1987. 105.00 (*0-948691-22-0*, Pub. by Witherby & Co UK) St Mut.

***Lluch, Alex & Lluch, Elizabeth.** Easy Wedding Planning. 208p. 1994. pap. 6.95 (*0-9639654-6-8*) Wedding Solns.

— Easy Wedding Planning. 224p. 1995. pap. 6.95 (*0-9639654-8-4*) Wedding Solns.

— Easy Wedding Planning Kit. 1995. pap. 8.31 (*0-9639654-1-7*) Wedding Solns.

— The Indispensable Groom's Guide. 124p. 1995. pap. 5.95 (*0-9639654-0-9*) Wedding Solns.

— Wedding Party Responsibility Cards: Christian Edition. 48p. 1995. pap. 6.95 (*0-9639654-9-2*) Wedding Solns.

Lluch, Elizabeth. Wedding Party Responsibility Cards: Christian Edition. 40p. 1994. pap. 6.95 (*0-9639654-4-1*) Wedding Solns.

— Wedding Party Responsibility Cards: Jewish Edition. 40p. 1994. pap. 6.95 (*0-9639654-5-X*) Wedding Solns.

Lluch, Elizabeth, jt. auth. see Lluch, Alex.

***Lluch-Mora, Francisco.** La Huella del Latido. 195p. (SPA.). 1994. 15.00 (*1-881708-06-3*) Edcnes Mairena.

Lluch-Velez, Amalia. La Decima Culta en la Literatura Puertorriquena. LC 85-22643. 1988. pap. 10.00 (*0-8477-3804-3*) U of PR Pr.

Lluelles Cardona, Victor. Diccionari Politic de Catalunya. 344p. (CAT.). 1977. pap. 24.95 (*0-8288-5306-1*, S50183) Fr & Eur.

Lluelles, Manuel F. Diccionari De Sinonims. 5th ed. 1234p. (CAT.). 1986. 59.95 (*0-7859-5117-2*) Fr & Eur.

***Lluesma, Elisa.** Communication for Business. 240p. (C). 1994. per., pap. text ed. 26.95 (*0-7872-0278-9*) Kendall-Hunt.

Llull, Ramon. Tree of Love: Ramon Llull's "Tree of the Philosophy of Love" (Historical & Scholarly Resources Ser.). 100p. 1994. pap. 19.95 (*1-883938-11-2*) Dry Bones Pr.

Llyinsky, M. Afghanistan: Onward March of the Revolution. 88p. 1982. 11.95 (*0-318-37223-1*) Asia Bk Corp.

Llyne, Jennifer, ed. see Batik, Albert.

Llyod, Frank W. Cable Television Law Nineteen Ninety-Two: Cable Faces Congress, the Courts & Competition, 2 vols., Set. (Patents, Copyrights, Trademarks, & Literary Property Ser.). 1743p. 1992. pap. text ed. 80.00 (*0-685-56909-8*, G4-3877) PLI.

Llywelyn, Morgan. Brian Boru: Emperor of the Irish. 160p. (Orig.). (J). (gr. 4 up). 1990. pap. 8.95 (*0-86278-230-9*, Pub. by OBrien Pr IE) Dufour.

— Brian Boru: Emperor of the Irish. (Illus.). 160p. (Orig.). (YA). (gr. 6 up). 1995. 14.95 (*0-312-85623-7*) Tor Bks.

— Druids. 1993. mass mkt. 5.99 (*0-8041-0844-7*) Ivy Books.

— The Elementals. 320p. 1993. 21.95 (*0-312-85568-0*) Tor Bks.

— The Elementals. 384p. 1994. mass mkt. 5.99 (*0-8125-1815-2*) Tor Bks.

— Elementals. 1994. pap. 5.99 (*0-312-51815-3*) Tor Bks.

— Finn Mac Cool. 432p. 1994. 23.95 (*0-312-85476-5*) Tor Bks.

— Finn Mac Cool. 528p. 1995. mass mkt. 6.99 (*0-8125-2401-2*) Tor Bks.

— Pride of Lions. 1995. 24.95 (*0-312-85700-4*) Tor Bks.

— Red Branch. 528p. 1990. mass mkt. 5.95 (*0-8041-0591-X*) Ivy Books.

— Strong Bow. (YA). 1995. 14.95 (*0-614-03853-7*) Tor Bks.

— Strongbow: The Story of Richard & Aoife. (Illus.). 155p. 1993. pap. 10.95 (*0-86278-274-0*, Pub. by OBrien Pr IE) Dufour.

— Xerxes. (World Leaders - Past & Present Ser.). (Illus.). 112p. (YA). (gr. 5 up). 1988. lib. bdg. 17.95 (*0-87754-447-6*) Chelsea Hse.

***Llywelyn, Morgan & Scott.** Ireland: A Graphic History. 1995. pap. text ed. 16.95 (*1-85230-627-0*) Element MA.

***Llywelyn, Morgan & Scott, Michael.** Silverhand: The Arcana, Bk. I. (Arcana Ser.: Bk. I). 432p. (Orig.). 1995. pap. 22.00 (*0-671-87652-X*) Baen Bks.

LMS Associate Staff. Library Media & Information Skills. (School Library Media Ser.). 1991. pap. text ed. 24.95 (*0-87436-665-8*) ABC-CLIO.

LMS Staff. Children's Literature: Promotion, Use, & Teaching in the School Media Center. (School Library Media Ser.). 1991. lib. bdg. 24.95 (*0-87436-666-6*) ABC-CLIO.

Lnag, James. Anglo-Saxon Sculpture. 1989. pap. 25.00 (*0-85263-927-9*, Pub. by Shire UK) St Mut.

Lo. Antenna Handbook, 4 vols. 1993. pap. 150.95 (*0-442-01674-3*) Van Nos Reinhold.

***Lo, Andrew W., ed.** The Industrial Organization & Regulation of the Securities Industry. LC 95-18033. (National Bureau of Economic Research Conference Report Ser.). 1995. write for info. (*0-226-48847-0*) U Ch Pr.

Lo, Arlene, jt. ed. see Ford, Donis W.

Lo Bello, Nino. English Well Speeched Here. (Illus.). 1986. 2.95 (*0-8431-1245-X*) Putnam Pub Group.

— Travel Trivia Handbook of Oddball European Sights. (Illus.). 224p. 1992. pap. 12.95 (*0-8065-1333-0*, Citadel Pr) Carol Pub Group.

Lo, Bernard. Resolving Ethical Dilemmas: A Guide for Clinicians. LC 93-44523. (Illus.). 366p. 1994. 29.00 (*0-683-05138-5*) Williams & Wilkins.

Lo Bosco, Rocco. Across a Distance of Knives. Taylor, Chuck, ed. (Orig.). 1982. pap. 4.95 (*0-941720-08-X*) Slough Pr TX.

Lo Bue, Erberto, jt. auth. see Ricca, Franco.

Lo Bue, F., ed. The Turin Fragments of Tyconius' Commentary on Revelation. (Texts & Studies, New Ser.: Vol. 7). 1974. reprint ed. 28.00 (*0-8115-1720-9*) Periodicals Srv.

Lo, C. H. Ten Thousand - A Dictionary of New Chinese-English-Chinese. 474p. (CHI & ENG.). 1980. 25.00 (*0-8288-1606-9*, M9266) Fr & Eur.

Lo, C. P. Hong Kong. LC 92-21730. 200p. 1992. text ed. 53. 95 (*0-470-21957-2*) Halsted Pr.

— Hong Kong. (World Cities Ser.). 1993. text ed. 59.95 (*0-471-94706-7*) Wiley.

***Lo, Carlos.** China's Legal Awakening: Legal Theory & Criminal Justice in Deng's Era. 400p. 1995. pap. 67.50 (*962-209-342-6*, Pub. by Hong Kong Univ Pr HK) Coronet Bks.

Lo Cascio, Thomas S. Alcohol Sellers & Servers: Professionals, Not Professional Servants. 153p. (C). 1993. teacher ed write for info. (*0-9636613-0-2*); student ed write for info. (*0-9636613-1-0*) Adv Desgn & Concept.

Lo Chai Chen. Aquaculture in Taiwan. (Illus.). 273p. 1990. 65.00 (*0-85238-165-4*) Blackwell Sci.

Lo Chi-kin, jt. ed. see Brosseau, Maurice.

Lo, Chor Pang. Applied Remote Sensing. 1986. text ed. 49. 95 (*0-470-20689-6*) Wiley.

Lo, Clarence Y. Small Property Versus Big Government: Social Origins of the Property Tax Revolt. 1990. 35.00 (*0-520-05971-9*) U CA Pr.

***Lo, Clarence Y.H.** Small Property vs. Big Government: Expanded & Updated Edition. 306p. 1995. pap. 14.00 (*0-520-20028-4*) U CA Pr.

Lo-dro of Drepung. Prince Who Became a Cuckoo: A Tale of Liberation. Geshe Wangyal, tr. (Bhaisajaguru Ser.). 1982. pap. 12.95 (*0-87830-574-2*, Theatre Arts Bks) Routledge Chapman & Hall.

Lo Duca, Joseph Marie. Bayard. Bunnell, Peter C. & Sobieszek, Robert A., eds. LC 76-23069. (Sources of Modern Photography Ser.). (Illus.). (FRE.). 1979. reprint ed. lib. bdg. 15.95 (*0-405-09634-8*) Ayer.

Lo Hui-Min, ed. see Morrison, G. E.

Lo, Irving Y. & Schultz, William, eds. Waiting for the Unicorn: Poems & Lyrics of China's Last Dynasty, 1644-1911. LC 85-42816. (Chinese Literature in Translation Ser.). (Illus.). 456p. (C). 1986. 37.95 (*0-253-36321-7*); pap. 17.95 (*0-253-20575-1*, MB-575) Ind U Pr.

Lo, Irving Y., jt. ed. see Liu, Wu-Chi.

Lo, Jeannie. Office Ladies-Factory Women: Life & Work at a Japanese Company. LC 89-70365. 140p. 1990. 30.95 (*0-87332-598-2*); pap. 18.95 (*0-87332-599-0*) M E Sharpe.

Lo-Johansson, Ivar. Breaking Free. Wright, Rochelle, tr. LC 89-24971. (Modern Scandinavian Literature in Translation Ser.). viii, 478p. 1990. 45.00 (*0-8032-2891-0*) U of Nebr Pr.

— Only a Mother. Bjork, Robert E., tr. & pref. by. LC 90-13059. (Modern Scandinavian Literature in Translation Ser.). viii, 505p. 1991. 45.00 (*0-8032-2882-1*) U of Nebr Pr.

— Peddling My Wares. Wright, Rochelle, tr. & intro. by. LC 94-42896. (SCAND). 1995. 44.95 (*1-57113-015-2*) Camden Hse.

Lo, K. S. The Stonewares of Yixing: From the Ming Period to the Present Day. LC 85-50363. (Illus.). 288p. 1986. 125.00 (*0-85667-181-9*, Pub. by P Wilson Pubs) Sothebys Pubns.

***Lo, Kenneth.** Chinese Vegetable & Vegetarian Cooking. 176p. (Orig.). 1995. pap. 10.95 (*0-571-10652-8*) Faber & Faber.

— Encyclopedia of Chinese Cooking. 1990. pap. 9.95 (*0-88486-035-3*) Arrowood Pr.

— Encyclopedia of Chinese Cooking. 1992. 10.98 (*0-88365-532-2*) Galahad Bks.

— The Top One Hundred Chinese Dishes. LC 92-12158. 128p. 1992. pap. 15.95 (*0-89815-497-9*) Ten Speed Pr.

Lo, Kuan-Chung. Romance of the Three Kingdoms. Brewitt-Taylor, C. H., tr. 1280p. 1990. pap. 32.95 (*0-8048-1649-2*) C E Tuttle.

Lo, Laotou, tr. see Mattison, Wendy & Scareth, Thomas, eds.

Lo, Lee. Traumatology As Treated by Traditional Chinese Medicine: A Comprehensive Text. 80p. (Orig.). (C). 1989. pap. text ed. 24.95 (*0-685-29019-0*) Zee Lo.

Lo Pinto, Maria. Honey Cookbook. 172p. 1993. reprint ed. pap. 8.95 (*0-7818-0149-4*) Hippocrene Bks.

Lo Pinto, Richard W. Pollution. Head, J. J., ed. LC 86-72203. (Carolina Biology Readers Ser.: No. 192). (Illus.). 16p. (Orig.). (YA). (gr. 10 up). 1987. pap. text ed. 2.75 (*0-89278-392-3*, 45-9792) Carolina Biological.

***Lo Proto, Frank.** High Tide. 330p. 1995. pap. text ed. 9.95 (*0-7610-0049-6*) NW Pub.

Lo, R. E., ed. Earth Observation & Remote Sensing by Satellites: Proceedings of the Symposium on Earth Observation & Remote Sensing by Satellites, Hannover, West Germany, 21 May 1982. 56p. 1984. pap. 45.00 (*0-08-031152-0*, Pergamon Pr) Elsevier.

Lo Romer, David. Merchants & Reform in Livorno, 1814-1868. 1987. 55.00 (*0-520-05649-3*) U CA Pr.

Lo Russo, Andrew P. Sing & Cook Italian. Cook, Jim, ed. 160p. (Orig.). 1993. pap. 19.95 (*0-9622020-1-0*) Happy Heart.

Lo, Ruth E. & Kinderman, Katharine S. In the Eye of the Typhoon: An American Woman in China During the Cultural Revolution. 1987. pap. 10.95 (*0-306-80283-X*) Da Capo.

Lo, S. C., jt. ed. see Li, K. S.

Lo, S. S. Glossary of Hydrology. 1770p. 1992. 110.00 (*0-918334-74-8*) WRP.

Lo, S. Y., ed. Geometrical Pictures in Hadronic Collisions. 412p. 1987. reprint ed. text ed. 108.00 (*9971-978-48-2*); reprint ed. pap. text ed. 60.00 (*9971-978-59-8*) World Scientific Pub.

***Lo, Sai-Lai.** A Modular & Extensible Network Storage Architecture. (Distinguished Dissertations in Computer Science Ser.: No. 11). (Illus.). 150p. (C). 1995. write for info. (*0-521-55115-3*) Cambridge U Pr.

Lo, Steven C. The Incorporation of Eric Chung. 220p. 1989. 14.95 (*0-945575-18-1*) Algonquin Bks.

Lo, T. Wing. Corruption & Politics in Hong Kong & China. LC 92-20666. (New Directions in Criminology Ser.). 1993. 95.00 (*0-335-15799-8*, Open Univ Pr) Taylor & Francis.

— Corruption & Politics in Hong Kong & China. LC 92-20666. (New Directions in Criminology Ser.). 176p. 1994. pap. 32.00x (*0-335-19385-4*, Open Univ Pr) Taylor & Francis.

Lo, Tec C., et al, eds. Handbook of Solvent Extraction. 1006p. (C). 1991. reprint ed. lib. bdg. 169.00 (*0-89464-546-3*) Krieger.

Lo-Tien, F. Beginner's Translation Handbook: English-Chinese. 364p. 1974. pap. 14.95 (*0-8288-5974-4*, M9581) Fr & Eur.

***Lo, Tien-When & Inderwiesen, Philip L.** Fundamentals of Seismic Tomography. LC 94-23818. (Geophysical Monograph Ser.: No. 6). 1994. pap. 22.00 (*1-56080-028-3*) Soc Expl Geophys.

Lo, Winston W. An Introduction to the Civil Service of Sung China: With Emphasis on Its Personnel Administration. LC 87-19038. 320p. 1987. text ed. 36.00 (*0-8248-1108-9*) UH Pr.

— The Life & Thought of Yeh Shih. LC 73-92410. 216p. reprint ed. pap. 61.60 (*0-7837-5014-5*, 2044681) Bks Demand.

— The Life & Thought of Yeh Shih (1150-1223) x, 206p. 1974. text ed. 26.50 (*962-201-016-4*, Pub. by Chinese Univ HK) Coronet Bks.

Lo, Y. T. & Lee, S. W., eds. The Antenna Handbook, Vol. 1: Fundamentals & Mathematical Techniques. LC 93-6502. 1993. Vol. 1, Fundamentals & Mathematical Techniques. text ed. 39.95 (*0-442-01592-5*) Van Nos Reinhold.

— The Antenna Handbook, Vol. 2: Antenna Theory. LC 93-6502. 1993. Vol. 2, Antenna Theory. text ed. 49.95 (*0-442-01593-3*) Van Nos Reinhold.

— The Antenna Handbook, Vol. 3: Applications. LC 93-6502. 1993. Vol. 3, Applications. text ed. 49.95 (*0-442-01594-1*) Van Nos Reinhold.

— The Antenna Handbook, Vol. 4: Related Topics. LC 93-6502. 1993. Vol. 4, Related Topics. text ed. 39.95 (*0-442-01596-8*) Van Nos Reinhold.

— Antenna Handbook: Theory, Applications, & Design. (Illus.). 2162p. 1988. text ed. 189.95 (*0-442-25843-7*) Van Nos Reinhold.

Lo Yang, G., jt. auth. see Le Cam, Lucien M.

Loach, Jennifer. Parliament Under the Tudors. 184p. 1991. 49.95 (*0-19-873092-6*, 9474); pap. 18.95 (*0-19-873091-8*) OUP.

Load-Curve Coverage in Future Electrical Power Generating Systems Symposium Staff. Electrical Load-Curve Coverage: Proceedings of the Symposium, Rome, Oct. 1977. United Nations Economic Commission for Europe, ed. LC 78-40342. (Illus.). 1979. 227.00 (*0-08-022422-9*, Pub. by Pergamon Repr UK) Franklin.

Loader, Anne, et al, eds. Pregnancy & Parenthood: For the National Childbirth Trust. 2nd ed. 1985. pap. 7.95 (*0-19-286060-7*) OUP.

Loader, Brian, jt. ed. see Burrows, Roger.

Loader, J. A. Ecclesiastes: A Practical Commentary. Vriend, John, tr. LC 86-4266. (Text & Interpretation Ser.). 142p. reprint ed. pap. 40.50 (*0-7837-3190-6*, 2042794) Bks Demand.

Loader, Jamer A. Polar Structures in the Book of Qohelet. (Beiheft zur Zeitschrift fuer die Alttestamentliche Wissenschaft Ser.). 150p. (C). 1979. text ed. 65.40 (*3-11-007636-5*) De Gruyter.

Loader, Jeff & Loader, Jennie. Making Board, Peg & Dice Games. (Illus.). 160p. 1993. pap. 17.95 (*0-946819-40-8*, Pub. by Guild Mstr Craftsman UK) Sterling.

— Making Wooden Toys & Games. (Illus.). 176p. 1995. pap. 14.95 (*0-946819-55-6*, Pub. by Guild Mstr Craftsman UK) Sterling.

Loader, Jennie, jt. auth. see Loader, Jeff.

Loader, Mandy. Guide to Spain. LC 93-38366. (Little Library). (Illus.). 32p. (J). (gr. 1-4). 1994. 3.95 (*1-85697-961-X*, Kingfisher LKC) LKC.

Loader, William. The Johannine Epistles. (Epworth Commentary Ser.). 144p. (Orig.). 1992. pap. 13.95 (*0-7162-0480-0*, Epworth Pr) TPI PA.

Loades, Ann. For God & Clarity: New Essays in Honor of Austin Farrer. Eaton, Jeffrey C., ed. LC 83-2451. (Pittsburgh Theological Monographs, New Ser.: No. 4). 206p. 1983. pap. 12.00 (*0-915138-52-2*) Pickwick.

— Searching for Lost Coins: Explorations in Christianity & Feminism. LC 88-1056. (Princeton Theological Monograph Ser.: No. 14). 128p. (Orig.). 1988. reprint ed. pap. 12.00 (*1-55635-000-7*) Pickwick.

Loades, Ann, ed. Dorothy L. Sayers: Spiritual Writings. LC 93-15410. 184p. 1993. pap. 13.95 (*1-56101-066-9*) Cowley Pubns.

— Feminist Theology: A Reader. 324p. (Orig.). 1990. pap. 19.99 (*0-664-25129-3*) Westminster John Knox.

Loades, Ann & McLain, Michael, eds. Hermeneutics, the Bible & Literary Criticism. LC 91-24686. 199p. 1992. text ed. 49.95 (*0-312-06881-6*) St Martin.

Loades, Ann & Rue, Loyal D., eds. Contemporary Classics in Philosophy of Religion. 616p. (C). 1991. 50.00 (*0-8126-9168-7*); pap. 21.00 (*0-8126-9169-5*) Open Court.

Loades, David. Mary Tudor: A Life. 1992. pap. 17.95 (*0-631-18449-X*) Blackwell Pubs.

— Revolution in Religion: The English Reformation, 1530-1570. (Past in Perspective Ser.). 134p. 1992. pap. 12.00 (*0-7083-1141-5*, Pub. by U of Wales UK) Bks Intl VA.

— The Tudor Navy: An Administrative Political & Military History. (Studies in Naval History). 304p. 1992. 69.95 (*0-85967-922-5*, Pub. by Scolar Pr UK) Ashgate Pub Co.

Loades, David & Walsh, Katherine. Faith & Identity: Christian Political Experience. (Studies in Church History). 256p. 1989. text ed. 59.95 (*0-631-17163-0*) Blackwell Pubs.

Loades, David M. The Reign of Mary Tudor. (Illus.). 448p. (C). 1991. pap. text ed. 31.50 (*0-582-05759-0*, 78831) Longman.

Loades, David M., ed. Politics, Censorship & the English Reformation. 227p. 1992. text ed. 65.00 (*0-86187-861-2*, Pub. by Pinter Pubs UK) St Martin.

Loam, Jason, jt. auth. see Gersh-Young, Marjorie.

Loam, Jason, ed. see Hartman, Williams & Fithian, Marilyn.

Loam, Jason, ed. see Liskey, Nathan & Hill, Justine.

Loam, Jayson, et al. Day Trips in Nature: California. (Illus.). 192p. (Orig.). 1991. pap. 14.95 (*0-9624830-3-6*) Aqua Thermal.

Loan, Edwyn, jt. auth. see Gruffudd, Heini.

Loan, Linda B. The Edge of Survival: Vietnam, the Other Side. 270p. (Orig.). 1993. pap. 8.95 (*0-9637167-0-0*) Ashley Pub.

Loan, Raymond W., ed. Bovine Respiratory Disease: A Symposium. LC 83-40491. (Illus.). 544p. 1984. 27.50 (*0-89096-187-5*) Tex A&M Univ Pr.

Loane, Helen. Industry & Commerce of the City of Rome. LC 78-64171. (Johns Hopkins University. Studies in the Social Sciences. Thirtieth Ser. 1912: 2). reprint ed. 20.50 (*0-404-61280-6*) AMS Pr.

Loane, Helen J. Industry & Commerce of the City of Rome: (50 B. C.-200 A. D.) Finley, Moses, ed. LC 79-4990. (Ancient Economic History Ser.). 1979. reprint ed. lib. bdg. 22.95 (*0-405-12378-7*) Ayer.

Loane, I. T. & Gould, J. S. Aerial Suppression of Bushfires. 1986. pap. 40.00 (*0-643-04023-4*, Pub. by CSIRO AT) Intl Spec Bk.

Loane, Marcus. Grace & the Gentiles. 149p. (Orig.). 1981. pap. text ed. 9.95 (*0-85151-327-1*) Banner of Truth.

Loasby, Brian J. Choice, Complexity, & Ignorance: An Inquiry into Economic Theory & the Practice of Decision-Making. LC 75-22558. 252p. reprint ed. pap. 71.90 (*0-685-20559-2*, 2030606) Bks Demand.

— The Mind & Method of the Economist: A Critical Appraisal of Major Economists in the 20th Century. 300p. 1989. text ed. 69.95 (*1-85278-124-6*, Pub. by E Elgar Pub UK) Ashgate Pub Co.

Loasby, Wren. Creative Interiors: A Complete Practical Course in Interior Design. (Illus.). 288p. 1992. 34.95 (*0-7153-9935-7*, Pub. by D & C Pub UK) Sterling.

Loase, John F. Sigfluence: Enduring Positive Influence. (American University Studies: Psychology: Ser. VIII, Vol. 10). 269p. 1988. 46.50 (*0-8204-0534-5*) P Lang Pubs.

— Sigfluence: Long-Term Positive Influence. LC 93-48962. 168p. (Orig.). Date not set. lib. bdg. 44.50 (*0-8191-9449-2*); pap. text ed. 27.50 (*0-8191-9450-6*) U Pr of Amer.

Loayza, Eduardo A., ed. Managing Fishery Resources: Proceedings of a Symposium, Held in Lima, Peru, June 1992. LC 93-42031. (Discussion Paper Ser.: No. 217). 130p. 1994. write for info. (*0-8213-2684-8*) World Bank.

Loayza, Eduardo A. & Sprague, Lucian M. A Strategy for Fisheries Development. (Discussion Paper Ser.: No. 135). 103p. 1992. pap. 7.95 (*0-8213-1950-7*, 11950) World Bank.

Lob, jt. auth. see Pichard.

Lob, Susan, jt. auth. see Cunningham, Patricia.

Loba, Mark. Developments in Soviet Coking Technology. Gross, Janna, ed. (Institute of Minerals Fuels IGA Ser.). 159p. (Orig.). 1986. pap. text ed. 75.00 (*1-55831-028-2*) Delphic Associates.

Loback, Tom. Halls of the Elven-King. Ruemmler, John D., ed. (Fortresses of Middle Earth Ser.). (Illus.). 32p. (Orig.). (YA). (gr. 12). 1988. pap. 6.00 (*1-55806-015-4*, 8204) Iron Crown Ent Inc.

Lobanoff, Val S. & Ross, Robert R. Centrifugal Pumps. 2nd ed. 592p. 1992. 70.00 (*0-87201-200-X*) Gulf Pub.

— Centrifugal Pumps: Design & Application. LC 84-15769. 384p. reprint ed. pap. 109.50 (*0-8357-2578-2*, 2040269) Bks Demand.

Lobanov, Grace, tr. see Leon-Portilla, Miguel.

Lobanov, Igor & Shepard-Lobanov, Silvia. Keys to Choosing a Doctor. (Retirement Keys Ser.). 160p. 1991. pap. 5.95 (*0-8120-4621-8*) Barron.

Lobanov, Mikhail. Ostrovskii. 382p. (RUS.). 1979. 39.00 (*0-317-40822-4*, Pub. by Collets UK) Pro-Am Music.

Lobanov-Rostovsky, Andrei A. Russia & Asia. 1951. 20.00x (*0-911586-18-0*) Wahr.

— Russia & Europe 1825-1878. 1954. 20.00x (*0-911586-19-9*) Wahr.

Lobanov, Y. Yu & Zhidkov, E. P. Programming & Mathematical Techniques in Physics. 324p. 1994. text ed. 109.00 (*981-02-1706-4*) World Scientific Pub.

An Asterisk (*) at the beginning of an entry indicates that the title is appearing in BIP for the first time.

Lobao, Linda M. Locality & Inequality: Farm & Industry Structure & Socioeconomic Conditions. LC 90-30748. (SUNY Series, the New Inequalities). 291p. 1990. 64.50 (0-7914-0475-7); pap. 21.95 (0-7914-0476-5) State U NY Pr.

Lobas, Vladimir. Taxi from Hell: Confessions of a Russian Hack. LC 91-5680. 304p. 1991. 20.95 (0-939149-58-3) Soho Press.

— Taxi from Hell: Confessions of a Russian Hack. LC 91-5680. 304p. 1992. pap. 12.00 (0-939149-86-9) Soho Press.

Lobato. Brothers, Sisters & Special Needs: Information & Activities for Helping Young Siblings of Children with Chronic Illnesses & Developmental Disabilities. LC 90-1518. 224p. 1990. pap. text ed. 30.00 (1-55766-043-3) P H Brookes.

Lobato, Arcadio. The Greatest Treasure. LC 89-3612. (Illus.). 28p. (J). (ps up). 1991. pap. 14.95 (0-88708-093-6, Picture Book Studio) S&S Childrens.

— Just One Wish. Clements, Andrew, tr. LC 89-49263. (Illus.). 32p. (J). (ps up). 1991. pap. 14.95 (0-88708-134-7, Picture Book Studio) S&S Childrens.

— Paper Bird. LC 93-24469. (Illus.). (J). (ps-3). 1994. 18.95 (0-87614-817-8, Carolrhoda) Lerner Group.

Lobato, Monteiro. Brazilian Short Stories. 1977. lib. bdg. 59.95 (0-8490-1550-2) Gordon Pr.

Lobaw, G. A Genealogy of the Warne Family in America, Principally the Descendants of Thomas Warne 1652-1722, One of the Proprietors of East N. J. (Illus.). 701p. 1989. reprint ed. lib. bdg. 107.00 (0-8328-1226-9); reprint ed. pap. 99.00 (0-8328-1227-7) Higginson Bk Co.

Lobb, Edward, ed. Eliot's Four Quartets: Critical Essays. 250p. (C). 1993. text ed. 39.50x (0-472-10488-8) U of Mich Pr.

Lobb, Frances, tr. see Mussolini, Benito.

Lobb, Michael L. & Watts, Thomas D. Native American Youth & Alcohol: An Annotated Bibliography. LC 88-32345. (Bibliographies & Indexes in Sociology Ser.: No. 16). 210p. 1989. text ed. 55.00 (0-313-25618-7, WNY/, Greenwood Pr) Greenwood.

Lobban, Christopher S., et al, eds. Experimental Phycology: A Laboratory Manual. (Illus.). 225p. 1988. pap. 21.95 (0-521-34834-X) Cambridge U Pr.

Lobban, Christopher S. & Harrison, Paul J. Seaweed Ecology & Physiology. LC 93-21306. (Illus.). 416p. (C). 1994. 69.95 (0-521-40334-0) Cambridge U Pr.

Lobban, Christopher S. & Schefter, Marla. Successful Lab Reports: A Manual for Science Students. (Illus.). 95p. (C). 1992. 34.95 (0-521-40404-5); pap. 12.95 (0-521-40741-9) Cambridge U Pr.

Lobban, Christopher S. & Wynne, Michael J., eds. The Biology of Seaweeds. LC 81-69858. (Botanical Monographs: Vol. 17). (Illus.). 784p. 1982. 100.00 (0-520-04585-8) U CA Pr.

Lobban, J. H., ed. English Essays. LC 72-320. (Essay Index Reprint Ser.). 1977. reprint ed. 23.95 (0-8369-2800-8) Ayer.

Lobban, Marjorie, jt. auth. see Clyde, Laurel A.

Lobban, Michael. Common Law & English Jurisprudence, 1760-1850. (Illus.). 336p. 1991. 65.00 (0-19-825293-5) OUP.

— White Man's Justice: Political Trials in South Africa 1970-1980. 350p. 1995. 55.00 (0-19-825809-7) OUP.

Lobban, Richard & Forrest, Joshua. Historical Dictionary of the Republic of Guinea-Bissau. 2nd ed. LC 87-32298. (African Historical Dictionaries Ser.: No. 22). (Illus.). 233p. 1988. 27.50 (0-8108-2086-2) Scarecrow.

Lobban, Richard & Halter, Marilyn. Historical Dictionary of the Republic of Cape Verde. 2nd ed. LC 87-34559. (African Historical Dictionaries Ser.: No. 42). (Illus.). 193p. 1988. 22.50 (0-8108-2087-0) Scarecrow.

Lobban, Richard & Lopes, Marlene. Historical Dictionary of the Republic of Cape Verde. 3rd ed. LC 94-17116. (African Historical Dictionaries Ser.: No. 62). (Illus.). 404p. 1995. 49.50 (0-8108-2918-5) Scarecrow.

***Lobban, Richard A., Jr.** Cape Verde: Criulo Colony to Independent Nation. LC 94-45454. (Nations of the Modern World Ser.). 1995. text ed. 55.00 (0-8133-8451-6) Westview.

Lobban, Richard A., jt. auth. see Coli, Waltraud B.

Lobby, Ted. Jessica & the Wolf: A Story for Children Who Have Bad Dreams. LC 92-56872. (Books to Help Children Ser.). (Illus.). (J). 1993. lib. bdg. 17.27 (0-8368-0933-5) Gareth Stevens Inc.

— Jessica & the Wolf: A Story for Children Who Have Bad Dreams. LC 89-29688. (Illus.). 32p. (J). (gr. k-3). 1990. 16.95 (0-945354-22-3); pap. 8.95 (0-945354-21-5) Magination Pr.

Lobdell, jt. tr. see Blais.

Lobdell, Ann E. Handbook for Hospital Secretaries. LC 87-12426. 195p. (Orig.). 1987. pap. 19.95 (1-55648-006-7, 049151) AHPI.

Lobdell, David, tr. see Brault, Jacques.

Lobdell, J. H. Simon Lobdell, 1646 of Milford, Connecticut, & His Descendants, Also of Nicholas Lobden (Lobdell), 1635 of Hingham, Mass., & Some Descendants. (Illus.). 425p. 1989. reprint ed. lib. bdg. 71.50 (0-8328-0779-6); reprint ed. pap. 63.50 (0-8328-0780-X) Higginson Bk Co.

Lobdell, Jared. England & Always: Tolkien's World of the Rings. LC 81-12651. 108p. reprint ed. pap. 30.80 (0-317-20012-7, 2023219) Bks Demand.

Lobdell, Jared C. Recollections of Lewis Bonnett, Jr. (1778-1850), & the Bonnett & Wetzel Families. 139p. (Orig.). 1991. pap. 18.00 (1-55613-517-3) Heritage Bk.

***Lobdell, Jared C., ed.** Further Materials on Lewis Wetzel & the Upper Ohio Frontier: The Historical Narrative of George Edgington Peter Henry's Account, the Narrative of Spencer Records, the Reminiscences of Stephen Burkam. 111p. (Orig.). 1994. pap. text ed. 17.00 (0-7884-0073-8) Heritage Bk.

— Indian Warfare in Western PA & North WV at the Time of the American Revolution: Including the Narrative of Indian & Tory Depredations by John Crawford, the Military Reminiscences of Capt. Henry Jolly, & the Narrative of Lydia Boggs Shepherd Cruger. 155p. (Orig.). 1992. pap. 16.50 (1-55613-653-6) Heritage Bk.

— A Tolkien Compass. 224p. 1980. pap. 2.50 (0-345-28855-6, Del Rey) Ballantine.

Lobdell, Jared C., ed. see Draper, Lyman C.

Lobdell, Jared C., tr. see Larison, C. W.

Lobdell, Terri, jt. auth. see Watahara, Alan.

Lobe, Mira. Ben & the Child of the Forest. (Illus.). 96p. (J). (gr. 3-4). 1988. pap. 2.95 (0-8120-3936-X) Barron.

— Christoph Wants a Party. LC 95-8395. (Illus.). (J). 1995. write for info. (0-916291-59-6) Kane-Miller Bk.

— The Snowman Who Went for a Walk. LC 83-27298. (Illus.). 32p. (J). (ps-2). 1984. 11.95 (0-688-03865-4); lib. bdg. 11.88 (0-688-03866-2) Morrow Jr Bks.

***Lobe, Thom E.** Medical Malpractice: A Physician's Guide. 440p. (Orig.). 1995. pap. 34.95 (0-07-600758-8) Hlthcare Mgmt Grp.

— Tracheal Reconstruction in Infancy. 1991. text ed. 97.95 (0-7216-5779-6) Saunders.

Lobe, Thom E. & Schropp, Kurt P. Pediatric Laparoscopy & Thoracoscopy. (Illus.). 272p. 1993. text ed. 89.50 (0-7216-4610-7) Saunders.

Lobe, Thomas. United States National Security Policy & Aid to the Thailand Police. (Monograph Series in World Affairs: Vol. 14, 1976-77 Ser., Bk. 2). 161p. (Orig.). 1977. pap. 5.95 (0-87940-051-X) Monograph Series.

Lobeck, Anne. Ellipsis: Functional Heads, Licensing, & Identification. (Illus.). 224p. 1995. 45.00 (0-19-509181-7) OUP.

Lobeck, Armin K. Things Maps Don't Tell Us: An Adventure into Map Interpretation. (Illus.). xiv, 160p. (C). 1993. pap. text ed. 17.95 (0-226-48877-2) U Ch Pr.

Lobeck, C. August. Pathologiae Graeci Sermonis Elementa, 2 vols., Set. xxv, 1099p. 1966. reprint ed. write for info. (0-318-70968-6, Pub. by Georg Olms GW) Lubrecht & Cramer.

— Phrynichi Eclogae Nominum Et Verborum Atticorum. lxxx, 841p. 1965. reprint ed. write for info. (0-318-70969-4, Pub. by Georg Olms GW) Lubrecht & Cramer.

Lobeck, Christian A. Paralipomena Grammaticae Graecae, 2 vols in 1. xii, 622p. 1967. reprint ed. Bd. I: Qua Continentur Dissertationes de Praeceptis Euphonicis de Nominibus Monosyllabis, de Adjecti. write for info. (0-318-70967-8, Pub. by Georg Olms GW); reprint ed. write for info. (0-318-72044-2, Pub. by Georg Olms GW) Lubrecht & Cramer.

— Phrynichi Eclogae Nominum et Verborum Atticorum. lxxx, 841p. 1965. reprint ed. write for info. (0-318-72045-0, Pub. by Georg Olms GW) Lubrecht & Cramer.

Lobel, Anita. Alison's Zinnia. LC 89-23700. (Illus.). 32p. (J). (ps up). 1990. 15.00 (0-688-08865-1); lib. bdg. 15.93 (0-688-08866-X) Greenwillow.

— Away from Home. LC 93-36521. (Illus.). 32p. (J). 1994. 16.00 (0-688-10354-5); lib. bdg. 15.93 (0-688-10355-3) Greenwillow.

— The Dwarf Giant. LC 95-6790. (Illus.). 32p. (J). 1996. 15.00 (0-688-14407-1) Greenwillow.

— On Market Street. (J). 1993. pap. 19.95 (0-590-71697-2) Scholastic Inc.

— Pierrot's ABC Garden. (Little Golden Bks.). (Illus.). 24p. (J). (ps-00). 1992. write for info. (0-307-00139-3, 312-04, Golden Pr) Western Pub.

— Pierrot's ABC Garden. (J). (ps-3). 1993. 12.95 (0-307-17551-0, Artsts Writrs) Western Pub.

— Sven's Bridge. LC 91-29544. (Illus.). 32p. (J). (ps-4). 1992. 14.00 (0-688-11251-X); lib. bdg. 13.93 (0-688-11252-8) Greenwillow.

Lobel, Anita, illus. The Cat & the Cook & Other Fables of Krylov. 32p. (J). (gr. k up). 1995. 15.00 (0-688-12310-4); lib. bdg. 14.93 (0-688-12311-2) Greenwillow.

Lobel, Arnold. The Book of Pigericks. LC 82-47730. (Illus.). 48p. (J). (gr. k-3). 1983. lib. bdg. 14.89 (0-06-023983-2) HarpC Child Bks.

— The Book of Pigericks (Pig Limericks) LC 82-47730. (Trophy Picture Bk.). (Illus.). 48p. (J). (ps up). 1988. pap. 5.95 (0-06-443163-0, Trophy) HarpC Child Bks.

— Days with Frog & Toad. LC 78-21786. (Harper I Can Read Bk.). (Illus.). 64p. (J). (gr. k-3). 1979. 14.00i (0-06-023963-8); lib. bdg. 14.89 (0-06-023964-6) HarpC Child Bks.

— Days with Frog & Toad. LC 78-21786. (Trophy I Can Read Book & Cassette Set). (Illus.). 64p. (J). (ps-3). 1984. pap. 3.50 (0-06-444058-3, Dealer Bank) HarpC Child Bks.

— Days with Frog & Toad. unabridged ed. (I Can Read Book Ser.). (Illus.). (J). (ps-3). 1990. audio, pap. 6.95 (1-55994-227-4, Caedmon) HarperAudio.

— Days with Frog & Toad: (Dios con Sapo y Sepo) (SPA.). (J). (gr. 1-6). 8.95 (84-204-3743-3) Santillana.

— Fables. LC 79-2004. (Illus.). 48p. (J). (gr. 1-4). 1980. 15.00 (0-06-023973-5); lib. bdg. 14.89 (0-06-023974-3) HarpC Child Bks.

— Fables. LC 79-2004. (Trophy Picture Bk.). (Illus.). 48p. (J). (gr. 1-4). 1983. pap. 5.95 (0-06-443046-4, Trophy) HarpC Child Bks.

— Fables: (Fabulas) (SPA.). (J). (gr. 1-6). 21.95 (84-204-4552-5) Santillana.

— Frog & Toad. (Coloring Book Classics Ser.). (Illus.). 32p. (J). (ps-3). 1995. 3.50 (0-694-00710-2, Festival) HarpC Child Bks.

— Frog & Toad All Year. LC 76-2343. (Harper I Can Read Bk.). (Illus.). 64p. (J). (gr. k-3). 1976. 14.95 (0-06-023950-6); lib. bdg. 14.89 (0-06-023951-4) HarpC Child Bks.

— Frog & Toad All Year. LC 76-2343. (Trophy I Can Read Book & Cassette Set). (Illus.). 64p. (J). (ps-3). 1984. pap. 3.50 (0-06-444059-1, Dealer Bank) HarpC Child Bks.

— Frog & Toad All Year. unabridged ed. (I Can Read Book Ser.). (Illus.). (J). (ps-3). 1990. pap. 6.95 (1-55994-228-2, Caedmon) HarperAudio.

— Frog & Toad Are Friends. LC 73-105492. (Harper I Can Read Bk.). (Illus.). 64p. (J). (gr. k-3). 1970. 14.95 (0-06-023957-3); lib. bdg. 14.89 (0-06-023958-1) HarpC Child Bks.

— Frog & Toad Are Friends. LC 73-105492. (Trophy I Can Read Book & Cassette Set). (Illus.). 64p. (J). (ps-3). 1979. pap. 3.50 (0-06-444020-6, Dealer Bank) HarpC Child Bks.

— Frog & Toad Are Friends. unabridged ed. (I Can Read Book Ser.). (Illus.). (J). (ps-3). 1990. pap. 6.95 (1-55994-229-0, Caedmon) HarperAudio.

— Frog & Toad Are Friends: (Sapo y Sepo Son Amigos) (SPA.). (J). (gr. 1-6). 9.95 (84-204-3043-9) Santillana.

— Frog & Toad Book Buddy: I Can Read (Trophy ICR of one Book Frog & Toad Dolls in Box) (I Can Read Ser.). (Illus.). 64p. (J). (ps-3). 1995. 10.95 (0-694-00720-X, Festival) HarpC Child Bks.

— Frog & Toad Boxed Set, 4 bks. (Trophy I Can Read Bk.). (Illus.). 64p. (J). (gr. k-3). Date not set. pap. 14.00 (0-06-444167-9, Trophy) HarpC Child Bks.

— The Frog & Toad Pop-Up Book. LC 85-45373. (Illus.). 12p. (J). (ps-3). 1986. 9.95i (0-06-023986-7) HarpC Child Bks.

— Frog & Toad Together. LC 73-183163. (Harper I Can Read Bk.). (Illus.). 64p. (J). (gr. k-3). 1972. 14.95 (0-06-023959-X); lib. bdg. 14.89 (0-06-023960-3) HarpC Child Bks.

— Frog & Toad Together. LC 73-183163. (Trophy I Can Read Book & Cassette Set). (Illus.). 64p. (J). (ps-3). 1979. pap. 3.50 (0-06-444021-4, Dealer Bank) HarpC Child Bks.

— Frog & Toad Together. unabridged ed. (I Can Read Book Ser.). (Illus.). (J). (ps-3). 1990. pap. 6.95 (1-55994-230-4, Caedmon) HarperAudio.

— Frog & Toad Together: (Sapo y Sepo Inseparables) (SPA.). (J). 8.95 (84-204-3047-1) Santillana.

— Giant John. LC 64-16639. (Illus.). 32p. (J). (gr. k-3). 1964. lib. bdg. 14.89 (0-06-022946-2) HarpC Child Bks.

— Grasshopper on the Road. LC 77-25653. (Harper I Can Read Bk.). (Illus.). 64p. (J). (gr. k-3). 1978. lib. bdg. 14.89 (0-06-023962-X) HarpC Child Bks.

— Grasshopper on the Road. LC 77-25653. (Trophy I Can Read Bk.). (Illus.). 64p. (J). (gr. k-3). 1986. pap. 3.50 (0-06-444094-X, Trophy) HarpC Child Bks.

— Gregory Griggs: And Other Nursery Rhyme People. LC 77-22209. (Illus.). 48p. (J). (ps up). 1987. pap. 3.95 (0-688-07042-6, Mulberry) Morrow.

— Holiday for Mister Muster. LC 63-15323. (Illus.). 32p. (J). (gr. k-3). 1963. lib. bdg. 12.89 (0-06-023956-5) HarpC Child Bks.

— Lucille. LC 64-11616. (Harper I Can Read Bk.). (Illus.). 64p. (J). (gr. k-3). 1964. lib. bdg. 12.89 (0-06-023966-2) HarpC Child Bks.

— Martha the Movie Mouse. LC 66-18654. (Trophy Picture Bk.). (Illus.). 32p. (J). (ps-3). 1993. pap. 4.95 (0-06-443318-8, Trophy) HarpC Child Bks.

— Ming Lo Moves the Mountain. LC 81-13327. (Illus.). 32p. (J). (gr. k-3). 1982. lib. bdg. 14.93 (0-688-00611-6) Greenwillow.

— Ming Lo Moves the Mountain. (One World Friends & Neighbors Ser.). (Illus.). (J). (gr. k-4). 1993. 14.95 (0-685-64815-X); audio 11.00 (1-882869-76-1) Varsity Read Servs.

— Ming Lo Moves the Mountain. LC 92-47364. (Illus.). 32p. (J). (ps up). 1993. pap. text ed. 4.95 (0-688-10995-0, Mulberry) Morrow.

— Mouse Soup. LC 76-41517. (Harper I Can Read Bk.). (Illus.). 64p. (J). (gr. k-3). 1977. 14.95 (0-06-023967-0); lib. bdg. 14.89 (0-06-023968-9) HarpC Child Bks.

— Mouse Soup. LC 76-41517. (Trophy I Can Read Book & Cassette Set). (Illus.). 64p. (J). (gr. k-3). 1983. pap. 3.50 (0-06-444041-9, Trophy) HarpC Child Bks.

— Mouse Tales. LC 66-18654. (Harper I Can Read Bk.). (Illus.). 64p. (J). (gr. k-3). 1972. 14.95 (0-06-023941-7); lib. bdg. 14.89 (0-06-023942-5) HarpC Child Bks.

— Mouse Tales. LC 72-76511. (Trophy I Can Read Bk.). (Illus.). 64p. (J). (ps-3). 1978. pap. 3.50 (0-06-444013-3, Trophy) HarpC Child Bks.

— On Market Street. LC 80-21418. (Illus.). 40p. (J). (gr. k-3). 1981. 14.00 (0-688-80309-1); lib. bdg. 13.93 (0-688-84309-3) Greenwillow.

— On Market Street. LC 80-21418. (Illus.). 40p. (J). (ps up). 1989. pap. 4.95 (0-688-08745-0, Mulberry) Morrow.

— On the Day Peter Stuyvesant Sailed into Town. LC 75-148420. (Trophy Picture Bk.). (Illus.). 48p. (J). (ps-3). 1987. pap. 5.95 (0-06-443144-4, Trophy) HarpC Child Bks.

— Owl at Home. LC 74-2630. (Harper I Can Read Bk.). (Illus.). 64p. (J). (gr. k-3). 1975. lib. bdg. 14.89 (0-06-023949-2) HarpC Child Bks.

— Owl at Home. LC 74-2630. (Trophy I Can Read Book & Cassette Set). (Illus.). 64p. (J). (gr. k-3). 1982. pap. 3.50 (0-06-444034-6, Trophy) HarpC Child Bks.

— The Rose in My Garden. LC 83-14097. (Illus.). 40p. (J). (gr. k-3). 1984. 16.00 (0-688-02586-2); lib. bdg. 15.93 (0-688-02587-0) Greenwillow.

— The Rose in My Garden. LC 92-24588. (Illus.). 40p. (J). (ps up). 1993. reprint ed. pap. 4.95 (0-688-12265-5, Mulberry) Morrow.

— Small Pig. LC 69-10213. (Harper I Can Read Bk.). (Illus.). 64p. (J). (gr. k-3). 1969. lib. bdg. 14.89 (0-06-023932-8) HarpC Child Bks.

— Small Pig. LC 69-10213. (Trophy I Can Read Bk.). (Illus.). 64p. (J). (gr. k-3). 1988. pap. 3.50 (0-06-444120-2, Trophy) HarpC Child Bks.

— Summer Days with Frog & Toad. (Illus.). (J). (ps-3). 1994. 9.95 (0-694-00475-8, Festival) HarpC Child Bks.

— Treeful of Pigs. LC 78-1810. (Illus.). 32p. (J). (gr. k-3). 1979. 16.00 (0-688-80177-3); lib. bdg. 15.93 (0-688-84177-5) Greenwillow.

— The Turnaround Wind. LC 87-45293. (Illus.). 32p. (J). (ps-3). 1988. lib. bdg. 14.89 (0-06-023988-3) HarpC Child Bks.

— Uncle Elephant. LC 80-8944. (Harper I Can Read Bk.). (Illus.). 64p. (J). (gr. k-3). 1981. 14.95 (0-06-023979-4); lib. bdg. 14.89 (0-06-023980-8) HarpC Child Bks.

— Uncle Elephant. LC 80-8944. (Trophy I Can Read Bk.). (Illus.). 64p. (J). (gr. k-3). 1986. pap. 3.75 (0-06-444104-0, Trophy) HarpC Child Bks.

— Uncle Elephant - Tio Elefante. (SPA.). (J). 9.95 (84-204-3716-6) Santillana.

— Whiskers & Rhymes. LC 83-25424. (Illus.). 48p. (J). (gr. k-3). 1985. 13.00 (0-688-03835-2); lib. bdg. 12.88 (0-688-03836-0) Greenwillow.

— Whiskers & Rhymes. LC 83-25424. (Illus.). 48p. (J). 1988. pap. 4.95 (0-688-08291-2, Mulberry) Morrow.

— Zoo for Mister Muster. LC 62-7313. (Illus.). 32p. (J). (ps-3). 1962. lib. bdg. 13.89 (0-06-023991-3) HarpC Child Bks.

Lobel, Arnold, illus. The Just Right Mother Goose: Just Right for 3's & 4's. LC 88-43156. (Just Right Bks.). 32p. (J). (ps). 1989. lib. bdg. 5.99 (0-394-92860-1) Random Bks Yng Read.

Lobel, Arnold, illus. & sel. The Random House Book of Mother Goose: A Treasury of 306 Timeless Nursery Rhymes. LC 86-47532. 176p. (J). (gr. 2-6). 1986. 16.00 (0-394-86799-8); lib. bdg. 16.99 (0-394-96799-2) Random Bks Yng Read.

Lobel, Arnold, jt. auth. see Parish, Peggy.

Lobel, Edgar. Medieval Latin Poetics. (Studies in Comparative Literature: No. 35). 1972. reprint ed. pap. 39.95 (0-8383-0051-0) M S G Haskell Hse.

Lobel, Eli, jt. auth. see Kodsy, Ahmad El.

Lobel, Ira B. & Manchise, Louis J. Training Russian Mediators: Advent of a New Era? (Current Issues Ser.: No. 19). 1993. 5.00 (0-89215-182-X) U Cal LA Indus Rel.

Lobel, Kerry, ed. & intro. Naming the Violence: Speaking Out about Lesbian Battering. LC 86-15561. (New Leaf Ser.). 233p. (Orig.). 1986. pap. 12.95 (0-931188-42-3) Seal Pr Feminist.

Lobel, Mary D., ed. British Atlas of Historic Towns Vol. III: The City of London from Prehistoric Times to c. 1520. (Illus.). 144p. 1990. 160.00 (0-19-822979-8) OUP.

Lobene, Ralph & Kerr, Alix. The Forsyth Experiment: An Alternative System for Dental Care. (Illus.). 162p. (C). 1979. 22.00 (0-674-31035-7) HUP.

Lobenthal, Joel. Radical Rags: Fashions of the Sixties. (Illus.). 256p. 1990. 14.98 (0-89659-930-2) Abbeville Pr.

***Lober.** Treeful of Pigs. 1988. pap. (0-590-48979-8) Scholastic Inc.

Lober, Irene. Promoting Your School: A Public Relations Handbook. LC 92-62396. 325p. 1992. text ed. 39.00 (0-87762-687-1) Technomic.

— School Facilities Maintenance & Operations Manual. 125p. (Orig.). 1988. pap. text ed. 16.00 (0-910170-51-7) Assn Sch Busn.

Lober, Lawrence & Kirk, J. Robert. Fear Itself: A Legal & Personnel Analysis of Drug Testing, AIDS, Secondary Smoke, & VDTs. 68p. 1987. pap. 20.00 (0-685-53366-2, PF04) Soc Human Resc Mgmt.

Loberg, T. Addictive Behaviors: Prevention & Early Intervention. 240p. 1989. 48.50 (90-265-0934-0, Pub. by Swets Pub Serv NE) Taylor & Francis.

Loberger, Gordon J. A Concise Guide to Standard English Usage. 384p. (C). 1993. per., pap. text ed. 34.95 (0-8403-8573-0) Kendall-Hunt.

LoBianco, Lorraine, ed. see Renoir, Jean.

Lobingier, Charles S. The Ancient & Accepted Scottish Rite of Freemasonry. 170p. 1992. pap. 19.95 (1-56459-289-8) Kessinger Pub.

— The Evolution of the Roman Law from Before the Twelve Tables to the Corpus Juris. 2nd ed. 319p. 1987. reprint ed. lib. bdg. 40.00 (0-8377-2409-0) Rothman.

Lobiondo-Wood & Haber. Nursing Research: Methods, Critical Appraisal, & Utilization. 2nd ed. (Illus.). 496p. 1990. pap. 29.95 (0-8016-3269-2) Mosby Yr Bk.

LoBiondo-Wood, Geri & Haber, Judith, eds. Nursing Research: Methods, Critical Appraisal, & Utilization. 3rd ed. LC 93-32240. 504p. 1993. pap. 29.95 (0-8016-7727-0) Mosby Yr Bk.

Lobitz, Sabine H., jt. auth. see Couper, David C.

Lobjoit, Mary, jt. ed. see Brazier, Margaret.

Lobkowicz, N. Marxismus-Leninismus in der CSR: Die tschechoslowakische Philosophie seit 1945. (Sovietica Ser.: No. 8). 267p. (GER.). 1962. lib. bdg. 56.50 (90-277-0058-3) Kluwer Ac.

— Das Widerspruchsprinzip in der neueren sowjetischen Philosophie. (Sovietica Ser.: No. 4). 89p. (GER.). 1960. lib. bdg. 16.00 (0-685-02830-5) Kluwer Ac.

Lobl, T. J. & Hafez, E. S. Male Fertility & It's Regulation. (Advances in Reproductive Health Care Ser.). 1985. lib. bdg. 213.00 (0-85200-805-8) Kluwer Ac.

Lobley, Steven J., ed. see Millard, Peter J.

Lobo-Cobb, Angela. The Water & the Leaf: Oriental Poems for Meditation. (Illus.). pap. write for info. (0-318-57646-5) Bloomsberry Pr.

Lobo-Cobb, Angela, ed. A Confluence of Colors: The First Anthology of Wisconsin Minority Poets, Vol. I. 79p. (C). 1984. pap. text ed. 5.00 (0-916783-04-9) Blue Reed.

— Winter Nest: A Poetry Anthology of Midwestern Women Poets of Color. (Poetics of Colors Ser.). 110p. (Orig.). 1987. pap. text ed. 5.00 (0-916783-05-7) Blue Reed.

Lobo, George V. A Guide to Christian Living: A New Compendium of Moral Theology. 420p. 1984. pap. 16.95 (0-87061-092-9) Chr Classics.

L

Lobo, Jeronymo. A Voyage to Abyssinia. Johnson, Samuel, tr. LC 74-15064. reprint ed. 40.00 (0-404-12105-5) AMS Pr.

Lobo, Jorge, et al. Foundations of Disjunctive Logic Programming. (Illus.). 300p. 1992. 47.50 (0-262-12165-4) MIT Pr.

Lobo, Lance C., ed. see Nadi, Aldo.

Lobo, R. A. & Naftolin, F., eds. Progesterone in Hormonal Replacement Therapy. (Illus.). 64p. (C). 1992. text ed. 34.00 (1-85070-440-6) Prthnon Pub.

Lobo, Rogerio A., ed. Treatment of the Postmenopausal Woman: Basic & Clinical Aspects. 464p. 1994. 138.00 (0-7817-0113-9) Raven.

Lobo, Susan. A House of My Own: Social Organization in the Squatter Settlements of Lima, Peru. LC 81-16275. 190p. (C). 1982. pap. 11.95 (0-8165-0761-9) U of Ariz Pr.

Lobo, V. M. Handbook of Electrolyte Solutions, Set, Pts. A & B. (Physical Sciences Data Ser.: Nos. 41A & 41B). 234p. 1990. Set. 718.00 (0-444-98847-5) Elsevier.

Lobo, V. M., jt. auth. see Mills, R.

Lobo, Virginia, tr. see Engstrom, Ted W.

***Lobodzinska, Barbara, ed.** Family, Women, & Employment in Central-Eastern Europe. LC 94-25155. (Contributions in Sociology Ser.: Vol. 112). 344p. 1995. text ed. 65.00 (0-313-29402-X, Greenwood Pr) Greenwood.

Lobrano, Gustav, jt. auth. see Flick, Alexander C.

***Lobrovich, Mitch.** The Shoemaker & the Elves. (Illus.). 24p. (J). (ps-3). 1995. 4.95 (1-57064-046-7) Barney Pub.

— The Turnip: A Folktale about Cooperation. (Bedtime with Barney Ser.). 24p. (J). 1995. write for info. (1-57064-047-5) Barney Pub.

***Lobrutto.** Elia Kazan. 1997. text ed. 26.95 (0-8057-4507-6); pap. 14.95 (0-8057-4508-4) Macmillan.

LoBrutto, Vincent. By Design: Interviews with Film Production Designers. LC 92-5849. 296p. 1992. text ed. 59.95 (0-275-94030-6, C4030, Praeger Pubs); pap. text ed. 18.95 (0-275-94031-4, B4031, Praeger Pubs) Greenwood.

— Selected Takes: Film Editors on Editing. LC 90-24262. 264p. 1991. text ed. 59.95 (0-275-93378-4, C3378, Praeger Pubs); pap. text ed. 17.95 (0-275-93395-4, B3395, Praeger Pubs) Greenwood.

Lobrutto, Vincent. Sound-On-Film: Interviews with Creators of Film Sound. LC 93-50686. 320p. 1994. text ed. 65.00 (0-275-94442-5, Praeger Pubs); pap. text ed. 19.95 (0-275-94443-3, Praeger Pubs) Greenwood.

Lobsand Dagpa, ed. see Lhundrub, Ngorchen K.

Lobsenz, Johanna. The Older Woman in Industry. LC 74-3961. (Women in America Ser.). (Illus.). 298p. 1974. reprint ed. 24.95 (0-405-06110-2) Ayer.

***Lobsenz, Norman M. & Piercy, Fred P.** Stop Marital Fights Before They Start. 224p. 1994. pap. text ed. 4.99 (0-425-14402-X) Berkley Pub.

Lobstein, Dennis D., jt. auth. see Sandler, Ronald D.

Lobue, Marie. Dinosaurs & Love. LC 92-91075. 64p. 1994. pap. 7.00 (1-56002-247-7, Univ Edtns) Aegina Pr.

LoBue, Tony. Take My Hand: Physical Guided Action. Burke, Barbara, ed. (Illus.). (Orig.). 1989. pap. text ed. 5.95 (0-9625492-0-7) T LoBue.

LoBuglio, Albert F., ed. Clinical Immunotherapy. LC 80-15386. (Immunology Ser.: No. 11). (Illus.). 351p. reprint ed. pap. 100.10 (0-8357-6057-X, 2034546) Bks Demand.

Lobus, Catherine O. Careers As a Flight Attendant. rev. ed. Rosen, Ruth, ed. (Careers in Depth Ser.). (YA). (gr. 7-12). 1994. lib. bdg. 14.95 (0-8239-1179-9) Rosen Group.

Local Government Commission Staff, ed. The County Code, 1985. rev. ed. 125p. 1985. pap. 2.80 (0-8182-0063-4) Commonweal PA.

Local History Coordination Project Staff. Locating Australia's Past: A Practical Guide to Writing Local History. 1989. pap. 19.95 (0-86840-211-7, Pub. by New South Wales Univ Pr AT) Intl Spec Bk.

Localio, S. Arthur, et al. Anorectal, Presacral & Sacral Tumors: Anatomy, Physiology, Pathogenesis & Management. (Illus.). 378p. 1987. text ed. 115.00 (0-7216-1982-7) Saunders.

LoCascio, Catherine H., jt. auth. see Stafford, Alan D.

***LoCascio, Eric M.** The Weight Training Cardiovascular Logbook. 132p. (Orig.). 1994. pap. text ed. 19.95 (0-9645470-0-7) Trng Logbk.

Locatelli, Carla. Unwording the World: Samuel Beckett's Prose Works after the Nobel Prize. LC 89-28854. 288p. (C). 1990. text ed. 32.95x (0-8122-8232-9) U of Pa Pr.

Locatis, Craig & Atkinson, Francis. Media & Technology for Education & Training. (C). 1984. write for info. (0-675-20112-8, Merrill Pub Co) Macmillan.

Locche, Daniel, jt. auth. see Alesii, Brenda.

Locche, Daniel, ed. see Stedler, Richard.

Locche, Daniel A. & Alesii, Brenda C. Buffalo Jock Rap: The "Settle Your Bet" Pro Sports Trivia Book. 264p. (Orig.). 1989. 8.95 (1-877697-00-1) Brendan Ventures.

Loch, C. S. Poor Relief in Scotland: Its Statistics & Development, 1791-1891. LC 75-38137. (Demography Ser.). 1976. reprint ed. 17.95 (0-405-07990-7) Ayer.

Loch, E. G. Ultrasonic Tomography in Obstetrics & Gynaecology. (Advances in Obstetrics & Gynaecology Ser.: Vol. 51). (Illus.). 1973. 39.25 (3-8055-1585-5) S Karger.

Loch, Karen, jt. ed. see Khosrowpour, Mehdi.

Loch, Sydney. Three Predatory Women. LC 70-125230. (Short Story Index Reprint Ser.). 1977. 19.95 (0-8369-3597-7) Ayer.

Loch, Sylvia. The Royal Horse of Europe. 256p. 1990. 110.00 (0-85131-422-8, Pub. by J A Allen & Co UK) St Mut.

***Locha, Larry N.** Dear Mom Letters: Russia - Insights & Highlights. 1995. pap. 9.95 (0-533-11275-3) Vantage.

Lochak, P. & Meunier, C. Averaging in Classical Dynamical Systems. (Applied Mathematical Sciences Ser.: Vol. 72). (Illus.). 370p. 1988. pap. 44.00 (0-387-96778-8) Spr-Verlag.

Locher, Barry J., ed. One Hundred Fifty Capital years. 96p. 1990. 20.00 (0-9627462-0-7) City Springfield IL.

***Locher, Dick.** The Daze of Whine & Neurosis. (Editorial Cartoonists Ser.). (Illus.). 160p. (Orig.). 1995. pap. 8.95 (1-56554-156-1) Pelican.

Locher, Dick, ed. Dick Tracy's Fiendish Foes: A Sixtieth Anniversary Celebration. limited ed. (Illus.). 288p. (Orig.). 1991. 50.00 (0-312-06337-7) St Martin.

Locher, Dick, jt. comp. see Collins, Max A.

Locher, Ernst. Arithmetik und Algebra. 4th ed. 72p. (GER.). 1980. pap. 10.00 (0-8176-0774-9) Birkhauser.

Locher, J. C., jt. auth. see Escher, M. C.

Locher, J. L., ed. M. C. Escher: His Life & Complete Graphic Work. (Illus.). 352p. 1982. 65.00 (0-8109-0858-1) Abrams.

— M. C. Escher: His Life & Complete Graphic Work. (Illus.). 352p. 1992. pap. 29.98 (0-8109-8113-0, Abradale Pr) Abrams.

Locher, J. L., ed. see Coxeter, H. S.

Locher, Nancy C. College -- A Complete Guide for Parents & Students. 172p. (Orig.). 1989. pap. 8.95 (0-89709-166-3) Liberty Pub.

Locher, R. C., Jr. The Complete DX'er. 2nd ed. (Illus.). (Orig.). 1989. pap. 12.00 (0-9617577-0-1) Idiom Pr.

Lochhaas, Philip H. How to Respond to Islam. 1981. pap. 2.79 (0-570-07687-0, 12-2788) Concordia.

— How to Respond to Secular Humanism. 1991. pap. 2.79 (0-570-04549-5, 12-3149) Concordia.

— How to Respond to the New Age Movement. (How to Respond Ser.). 32p. 1989. pap. 2.79 (0-570-04523-1, 12-003123) Concordia.

— The New Age Movement. LC 95-8596. (How to Respond Ser.). 1995. write for info. (0-570-04679-3) Concordia.

Lochhaas, Thomas. Study Guide to Accompany Bloomfield-Fairley: Business Communication: A Process Approach. 257p. (C). 1991. pap. text ed. 15.00 (0-15-505670-0) HB Coll Pubs.

Lochhead. Care of the Patient in Radiotherapy. (Illus.). 186p. 1984. pap. 36.95 (0-632-01138-6, B30312) Blackwell Sci.

Lochhead, David. The Dialogical Imperative: A Christian Reflection on Interfaith Encounter. LC 88-1570. (Faith Meets Faith Ser.). 120p. 1988. 39.95 (0-88344-612-X); pap. 16.95 (0-88344-611-1) Orbis Bks.

Lochhead, Douglas. Dykelands. (Illus.). 72p. (C). 1989. 80.00 (0-7735-0722-1, Pub. by McGill CN) U of Toronto Pr.

Lochhead, Ian. The Spectator & the Landscape in the Art Criticism of Diderot & His Contemporaries. LC 82-4770. (Studies in the Fine Arts: Criticism: No. 14). 133p. reprint ed. pap. 38.00 (0-685-20813-3, 2070027) Bks Demand.

Lochhead, Jack & Clement, John, eds. Cognitive Process Instruction: Research on Teaching Thinking Skills. LC 78-22122. (Illus.). 339p. 1979. pap. 59.95 (0-89859-729-3) L Erlbaum Assocs.

Lochhead, Jack, jt. auth. see Whimbey, Arthur.

Lochhead, Jewell. The Education of Young Children in England. LC 70-177002. (Columbia University. Teachers College. Contributions to Education Ser.: No. 521). reprint ed. 22.50 (0-404-55521-7) AMS Pr.

Lochin, David S. Geometrical Optics Workbook. 224p. 1991. pap. text ed. 26.95 (0-7506-9052-6) Buttrwrth-Heinemann.

Lochman, Jan M. Encountering Marx: Bonds & Barriers between Christians & Marxists. Robertson, Edwin H., tr. LC 76-55827. 156p. reprint ed. pap. 44.50 (0-685-15974-4, 2026917) Bks Demand.

Lochmandy, Paula J. Beauty Knows No Pain: The Anatomy of a Successful Facelift. LC 93-61905. (Illus.). 128p. (Orig.). 1994. pap. 20.00 (0-9639890-7-3) Tattersall Pr.

Lochmann, W. J. & Indig, M., eds. Materials & Corrosion Problems in Energy Systems. (Illus.). 211p. 1980. 10.00 (0-915567-57-1) NACE Intl.

Lochnan, Katharine. The Etchings of James McNeil Whistler. LC 84-40185. (Illus.). 320p. 1984. text ed. 55.00 (0-300-03275-7) Yale U Pr.

Lochnan, Katharine A. Whistler's Etchings & the Sources of His Etching Style, 1855-1880. LC 87-30034. (Outstanding Theses in the Fine Arts Ser.). 734p. 1988. 53.00 (0-8240-0091-9) Garland.

Lochner, Edna. Searching for Jesus: The Spiritual Journey of Leah Mthembu. 68p. 1990. pap. 3.50 (0-8341-1368-6) Beacon Hill.

***Lochner, John S.** Joey's Toy Box: The Voyage to Zendell. LC 93-93946. (Illus.). 64p. (Orig.). 1994. pap. 8.00 (1-56002-358-9, Univ Edtns) Aegina Pr.

Lochner, Louis P. Fritz Kreisler. 1988. reprint ed. lib. bdg. 49.00 (0-7812-0138-1) Rprt Serv.

— Fritz Kreisler. LC 76-181203. 1951. reprint ed. 24.00 (0-403-01613-4) Scholarly.

Lochner, Louis P., tr. see Goebbels, Joseph.

Lochner, R. K. The Last Gentleman-of-War: Raider Exploits of the Cruiser Emden. Lindauer, Thea & Lindauer, Harry, trs. LC 87-32432. (Illus.). 385p. 1988. 24.95 (0-87021-015-7) Naval Inst Pr.

Lochner, Robert H. & Matar, Joseph E. Designing for Quality: An Introduction to the Best of Taguchi & Western Methods of Statistical Experimental Design. (Illus.). 250p. 1990. 37.50 (0-527-91633-1, 916331) Qual Resc.

Lochovsky, F., ed. Entity-Relationship Approach to Database Design & Querying: Proceedings of the 8th International Conference, Toronto, Ontario, Canada, 18-20 Oct., 1989. 436p. 1990. write for info. (0-444-88716-4, North Holland) Elsevier.

Lochovsky, Frederick H. & Allen, Robert, eds. COIS, '90: Conference on Office Information Systems, Held in Cambridge, MA, April 25-27, 1990. (Illus.). viii, 291p. 1990. pap. text ed. 22.00 (0-89791-358-2, 611900) Assn Compu Machinery.

Lochran, John. The Grotto Was My Heaven: Meditations on the Message of Lourdes. 86p. (Orig.). 1993. pap. 7.95 (1-85607-075-1) Twenty-Third.

Lochray, Paul I. The Financial Planner's Guide to Estate Planning. rev. ed. 280p. 1989. boxed 34.95 (0-13-316076-9) P-H.

— Financial Planner's Guide to Estate Planning. 3rd ed. 4164p. 1991. text ed. write for info. (0-13-318502-8) P-H.

***Lochrie.** Margery Kempe & Translations of the Flesh. 1994. pap. text ed. (0-8122-1557-5) U of Pa Pr.

Lochrie, Karma. Margery Kempe & Translations of the Flesh. LC 91-26069. (New Cultural Studies). 268p. (C). 1992. text ed. 26.95 (0-8122-3107-4) U of Pa Pr.

Lochte, Dick. Blue Bayou. (Southern Mysteries Ser.). 1994. mass mkt. 4.99 (0-8041-1145-6) Ivy Books.

— Neon Smile. 1995. 21.00 (0-671-74712-6) S&S Trade.

***Lochte-Holtgreven, W.** Plasma Diagnostics. (AVS Classics Ser.). (Illus.). 945p. (C). 1995. text ed. 60.00x (1-56396-388-4) Am Inst Physics.

LoCicero, Don. The Twisted Star. LC 92-70490. 299p. (Orig.). 1992. pap. 14.95 (1-880664-00-3) E M Pr.

Lock, Charles. Thomas Hardy. LC 92-22237. (Criticism in Focus Ser.). 1992. text ed. 29.95 (0-312-08604-0) St Martin.

Lock, D. Project Management. 300p. (C). 1989. 115.00 (0-685-46417-2, Inst Pur & Supply) St Mut.

Lock, D., ed. Project Management Handbook. 625p. (C). 1987. 475.00 (0-685-39876-5, Inst Pur & Supply) St Mut.

Lock, D. S. Engineers' Metric Manual & Buyers' Guide. 1974. 440.00 (0-08-018220-8, Pub. by Pergamon Repr UK) Franklin.

Lock, Dennis. Gower Handbook of Management. 3rd ed. 1002p. 1992. 99.95 (0-566-02974-X, Pub. by Gower UK) Ashgate Pub Co.

— The Gower Handbook of Management. 3rd ed. 1044p. 1993. pap. 33.95 (0-566-07477-X, Pub. by Gower UK) Ashgate Pub Co.

— Gower Handbook of Quality Management. 2nd ed. 1994. 99.95 (0-566-07451-6, Pub. by Gower UK) Ashgate Pub Co.

— Project Management. 3rd ed. LC 84-40114. 290p. 1984. text ed. 35.00 (0-312-65108-2) St Martin.

— Project Planner. (Illus.). 168p. 1990. text ed. 189.95 (0-566-02845-X, Pub. by Gower UK) Ashgate Pub Co.

Lock, Dennis, ed. Gower Handbook of Project Management. 2nd ed. LC 93-11068. 671p. 1994. 89.95 (0-566-07391-9, Pub. by Gower UK) Ashgate Pub Co.

— Handbook of Engineering Management. (Illus.). 828p. 1989. 150.00 (0-434-91170-4) Buttrwrth-Heinemann.

— Handbook of Engineering Management. 2nd ed. LC 93-14758. (Illus.). 828p. 1993. 95.00 (0-7506-0786-6) Buttrwrth-Heinemann.

— Project Management. 5th ed. 555p. 1992. 69.95 (0-566-07339-0, Pub. by Gower UK) Ashgate Pub Co.

Lock, Diane E. True Love. 512p. 1994. mass mkt. 4.99 (0-8217-4462-3) Zebra.

Lock, E. A., jt. ed. see Bach, Peter H.

Lock, F. P. Swift's Tory Politics. LC 83-8155. 100p. 1984. 32.50 (0-87413-252-5) U Delaware Pr.

Lock, F. P., jt. ed. see Rawson, Claude.

Lock, G. & Maunder, W. General Sources of Statistics. (Reviews of United Kingdom Statistical Sources Ser.: Vol. 5). 1976. 37.00 (0-08-022456-3, Pub. by Pergamon Repr UK) Franklin.

Lock, G. S. The Growth & Decay of Ice. (Studies in Polar Research). (Illus.). 450p. (C). 1991. 110.00 (0-521-33133-1) Cambridge U Pr.

— Latent Heat Transfer: An Introduction to Fundamentals. LC 94-11638. (Engineering Science Ser.: Vol. 43). (Illus.). 320p. 1994. 85.00 (0-19-856285-3) OUP.

— The Tubular Thermosyphon: Variations on a Theme. (Oxford Engineering Science Ser.: No. 33). (Illus.). 320p. 1992. 98.00 (0-19-856247-0) OUP.

***Lock, Gary & Stancic, Zoran, eds.** Archaeology & Geographic Information Systems: A European Perspective. 400p. 1995. 99.50x (0-7484-0208-X, Pub. by Tay Francis Ltd UK) Taylor & Francis.

Lock, Gary & Wilcock, John. Computer Archaeology. 1989. pap. 25.00 (0-85263-877-9, Pub. by Shire UK) St Mut.

Lock, Graham. Forces in Motion: The Music & Thoughts of Anthony Braxton. (Quality Paperbacks Ser.). (Illus.). 446p. 1989. pap. 13.95 (0-306-80342-9) Da Capo.

— Functional English Grammar: An Introduction for Second Language Teachers. (Cambridge Language Education Ser.). (Illus.). 256p. (C). 1995. write for info. (0-521-45305-4); pap. write for info. (0-521-45922-2) Cambridge U Pr.

Lock, Helen. A Case of Mistaken Identity Vol. 9: Detective Undercurrents in Recent African American Fiction. (Studies on Themes & Motifs in Literature: Vol. 9). 147p. (C). 1994. text ed. 35.95 (0-8204-2382-3) P Lang Pubs.

Lock, J. & McElhinny, Michael W., eds. The Global Paleomagnetic Database: Design, Installation & Use with Oracle. (C). 1991. lib. bdg. 80.50 (0-7923-1327-5) Kluwer Ac.

Lock, J. M. Legumes of Africa. 570p. 1989. pap. text ed. 45.00 (0-947643-10-9, Pub. by Royal Botanic Garden UK) Lubrecht & Cramer.

Lock, J. M. & Simpson, K. Legumes of West Asia. 263p. 1991. pap. text ed. 45.00 (0-947643-29-X, Pub. by Royal Botanic Garden UK) Lubrecht & Cramer.

Lock, James E., et al. Diagnostic & Interventional Catherization in Cogenital Heart Disease. 208p. (C). 1987. lib. bdg. 93.00 (0-89838-831-7) Kluwer Ac.

Lock, John & Dixon, Canon. A Man of Sorrow: The Life, Letters & Times of the Reverend Patrick Bronte. 566p. 1979. reprint ed. text ed. 85.00 (0-313-27686-2) Greenwood.

***Lock, Kath.** Anansi & the Rubber Man. 32p. (J). 1995. 12.95 (1-86374-073-2, Pub. by ERA Pubns AT) Pubs Dist MI.

— Jennifer & Nicholas. 32p. (J). 1995. 12.95 (0-908507-99-2, Pub. by ERA Pubns AT); pap. 5.95 (0-947212-58-2, Pub. by ERA Pubns AT) Pubs Dist MI.

— The King's Gift. 32p. (J). 1995. 12.95 (1-86374-072-4, Pub. by ERA Pubns AT) Pubs Dist MI.

— Little Burnt-Face. 32p. (J). 1995. 12.95 (1-86374-070-8, Pub. by ERA Pubns AT) Pubs Dist MI.

— The Sea of Gold. 32p. (J). 1995. 12.95 (1-86374-071-6, Pub. by ERA Pubns AT) Pubs Dist MI.

— The Tiger, the Brahmin & the Jackal. 32p. (J). 1995. 12.95 (1-86374-069-4, Pub. by ERA Pubns AT) Pubs Dist MI.

Lock, Lee H. Central Banking in Malaysia. 520p. 1987. 150.00 (0-409-99533-9) Butterworth Legal Pubs.

Lock, Margaret. Encounters with Aging: Mythologies of Menopause in Japan & North America. LC 93-21379. 1995. 38.00 (0-520-08221-4) U CA Pr.

— Encounters with Aging: Mythologies of Menopause in Japan & North America. LC 93-21379. 439p. 1995. pap. 16.00 (0-520-20162-0) U CA Pr.

— Health, Illness, & Medical Care in Japan: Cultural & Social Dimensions. Norbeck, Edward, ed. LC 87-10753. 232p. 1987. text ed. 21.00 (0-8248-1102-X) UH Pr.

Lock, Margaret M. East Asian Medicine in Urban Japan: Varieties of Medical Experience. (Comparative Studies of Health Systems & Medical Care: Vol. 3). (Illus.). 1979. 45.00 (0-520-03820-7); pap. 18.00 (0-520-05231-5) U CA Pr.

Lock, Margaret M. & Gordon, Deborah, eds. Biomedicine Examined. (C). 1988. lib. bdg. 140.00 (1-55608-071-9) Kluwer Ac.

Lock, Margaret M., jt. ed. see Lindenbaum, Shirley.

Lock, Maurice A. & Williams, D. D., eds. Perspectives In Running Water Ecology. LC 81-17838. 440p. 1981. 95.00 (0-306-40898-8, Plenum Pr) Plenum.

Lock, Michael D., jt. auth. see Tarter, Michael E.

***Lock, Peter.** The Franks in the Aegean, 1204-1500. LC 94-39822. (C). 1995. text ed. 54.95 (0-582-05140-1) Longman.

— The Franks in the Aegean, 1204-1500. LC 94-39822. (C). 1996. pap. text ed. 24.95 (0-582-05139-8) Longman.

Lock, Peter, jt. ed. see Brzoska, Michael.

Lock, Robert C. The Traditional Potters of Seagrove, North Carolina: And Surrounding Areas from the 1800s to the Present. (Illus.). 224p. 1994. 34.95 (0-9641247-0-X) Antiques & Collect.

Lock, Robert D. Job Search: Career Planning Guide, Bk. 2. 2nd ed. LC 91-17843. 256p. (C). 1992. pap. 17.95 (0-534-13657-5) Brooks-Cole.

— Student Activities for Taking Charge of Your Career Direction & Job Search: Career Planning Guide, Bk. 3. 2nd ed. 136p. (YA). 1992. pap. 14.95 (0-534-13659-1) Brooks-Cole.

— Taking Charge of Your Career Direction: Career Planning Guide, Bk. 1. 2nd ed. LC 91-17083. 400p. (C). 1992. pap. 21.95 (0-534-13656-7) Brooks-Cole.

***Lock, Ron.** Blood on the Painted Mountain: Zulu Victory & Defeat, Hlobane & Kambula, 1879. (Illus.). 208p. 1995. 35.00 (1-85367-201-7, Pub. by Greenhill Bks UK) Stackpole.

Lock, Simon, jt. auth. see Kacew, Sam.

Lock, Stephen & Wells, Frank, eds. Fraud & Misconduct in Medical Research. 202p. 1993. text ed. 45.00 (0-7279-0757-3, BMJ Pubng Grp) Amer Coll Phys.

Lock, Walter. Pastoral Epistles: Critical & Exegetical Commentary. Driver, Samuel R. et al, eds. (International Critical Commentary Ser.). 212p. 1928. 32.95 (0-567-05033-5, Pub. by T & T Clark UK) Bks Intl VA.

Lock, Ward. Smart Alec's Revolting Jokes for Kids. 1989. pap. 3.50 (0-345-35527-X) Ballantine.

Lockaby, George W. Real Revival Sermon Outlines. (Sermon Outline Ser.). 80p. (Orig.). 1991. pap. 3.99 (0-8010-5669-1) Baker Bk.

— Thirty-Two Sermon Outlines on Romans. (Sermon Outline Ser.). 72p. 1991. pap. 3.99 (0-8010-5668-3) Baker Bk.

Lockamy, Archie. Reingeneering Performance Measurement: How to Align Systems to Improve Processes, Products, & Profits. 312p. 1993. 45.00 (1-55623-916-5) Irwin Prof Pubng.

***Lockard, Anna-Marie.** The Quest for a Child. 120p. (Orig.). 1993. pap. 6.95 (0-89228-081-6) Impact Christian.

Lockard, Craig A. From Kampong to City: A Social History of Kucing, Malaysia, 1820-1970. LC 87-11237. (Monographs in International Studies, Southeast Asia Ser.: No. 75). 287p. 1986. pap. text ed. 20.00x (0-89680-136-5, Ohio U Ctr Intl) Ohio U Pr.

Lockard, Helen. Those Motivated Methodists - You Are There: A Play in Seven Acts. 1993. pap. 4.95 (1-55673-587-1) CSS OH.

Lockard, I. Desk Reference for Neuroscience. 2nd ed. (Illus.). 344p. 1991. pap. 43.00 (0-387-97715-5) Spr-Verlag.

Lockard, James. Instructional Software: Practical Design & Development. 368p. (C). 1992. pap. text ed. write for info. (0-697-13233-1) Brown & Benchmark.

Lockard, James, et al. Microcomputers for Twenty-First Century Educators. LC 93-5898. 485p. (C). 1994. pap. text ed. 45.50 (0-673-52216-4) HarpCollege.

An Asterisk (*) at the beginning of an entry indicates that the title is appearing in BIP for the first time.

*Lockard, James L. Survival Thinking: For Police & Corrections Officers. 260p. 1991. pap. 29.95 (0-398-06243-9) C C Thomas.
— Survival Thinking: For Police & Corrections Officers. 260p. (C). 1991. text ed. 49.95x (0-398-05728-1) C C Thomas.
*Lockard, Joan S. & Ward, Arthur A., Jr., eds. Epilepsy: A Window to Brain Mechanisms. fac. ed. LC 79-5503. (Illus.). 296p. Date not set. pap. 84.40 (0-7837-7167-3, 2047130) Bks Demand.
Lockard, Joan S., jt. ed. see Kirkevold, Barbara C.
Lockard, John R. Bee Hunting. 72p. pap. 3.00 (0-936622-00-8) A R Harding Pub.
Lockard, Karen, jt. auth. see Bigler, Philip.
*Lockard, Nathan. The Good, the Bad, & the Bogus: Nathan Lockard's Complete Guide to Video Games. LC 94-78034. 270p. 1994. pap. 14.95 (1-881583-04-X) Advent Pr WA.
Lockard, W. Duane. Basic Cases in Constitutional Law. 3rd ed. 1991. 20.95 (0-87187-610-8) Congr Quarterly.
Lockard, William K. Design Drawing. LC 93-21971. 1993. reprint ed. 23.95 (1-56052-222-4) Crisp Pubns.
— Design Drawing Experiences. LC 93-21981. 1993. reprint ed. 20.95 (1-56052-204-6) Crisp Pubns.
— Drawing As a Means to Architecture. (Illus.). 112p. 1995. reprint ed. pap. 19.95 (1-56052-223-2) Crisp Pubns.
— Drawing Techniques for Designers: Advocating Line & Tone Drawing. LC 93-21976. 1993. reprint ed. 10.95 (1-56052-224-0) Crisp Pubns.
— Freehand Perspective for Designers: Including Shadow-Casting & Entourage. LC 93-22080. 1993. reprint ed. 10.95 (1-56052-225-9) Crisp Pubns.
Lockart, Douglas G., et al, eds. The Development Process in Small Island States. LC 92-26122. (Illus.). 224p. 1993. 59.95 (0-415-06984-X, B0204) Routledge.
Lockart, William B., et al. Constitutional Law, Cases-Comments-Questions. 7th ed. (American Casebook Ser.). 1643p. 1991. text ed. 56.50 (0-314-86319-2) West Pub.
Lockborn, Paul, et al. Blood & Lust. Shirley, Sam, ed. (Pendragon Roleplaying Game System Ser.). (Illus.). 128p. (Orig.). (J). (gr. 7 up). 1991. pap. 18.95 (0-933635-84-2, 2711) Chaosium.
Locke & Colligan. The Healer Within. 1987. pap. 5.99 (0-451-62554-4, Ment) NAL-Dutton.
Locke, A., ed. The New Negro: An Interpretation. 1972. 59.95 (0-8490-0723-2) Gordon Pr.
Locke, Alain. Race Contacts & Interracial Relations. Stewart, Jeffrey, ed. LC 91-43415. 114p. 1992. 22.95 (0-88258-137-6); pap. 14.95 (0-88258-158-9) Howard U Pr.
Locke, Alain L. Negro & His Music. Bd. with Negro Art: Past & Present. LC 69-18592. (0-88143-079-X) LC 69-18592. (American Negro His History & Literature, Ser. 2). 1979. reprint ed. 27.95 (0-88143-078-1) Ayer.
— The New Negro. 480p. 1992. reprint ed. pap. 14.95 (0-689-70821-1, Atheneum S&S) S&S Trade.
— Plays of Negro Life: A Sourcebook of Native American Drama. LC 77-132077. 430p. 1971. reprint ed. text ed. 35.00 (0-8371-5037-X, IPN&, Greenwood Pr) Greenwood.
— When People Meet, a Study in Race & Culture Contacts. rev. ed. Stern, Bernhard J., ed. LC 76-44750. reprint ed. 67.50 (0-404-15947-8) AMS Pr.
Locke, Alain L., ed. The New Negro. LC 68-55749. (Studies in American Negro Life). (Illus.). (C). 1968. pap. text ed. 13.95 (0-689-70128-4, NL10, Atheneum S&S) S&S Trade.
— New Negro: An Interpretation. LC 68-29008. (American Negro: His History & Literature, Ser. No. 1). 1968. reprint ed. 40.95 (0-405-01826-6) Ayer.
— Survey Graphic. (Illus.). 92p. 1980. reprint ed. pap. 10.00 (0-933121-05-9) Black Classic.
Locke, Arthur H. A History & Genealogy of Captain John Locke, 1627-1696. (Illus.). 720p. 1993. reprint ed. pap. text ed. 40.00 (1-55613-889-X) Heritage Bk.
Locke, Arthur W. Music & the Romantic Movement in France. LC 72-83508. 1977. reprint ed. 24.95 (0-405-08751-9, Pub. by Blom Pubns UK) Ayer.
— Selected List of Choruses for Women's Voices. 2nd ed. 253p. 1993. reprint ed. lib. bdg. 79.00 (0-7812-9691-9) Rprt Serv.
*Locke, Baden. Chrysanthemums: The Complete Guide. (Illus.). 192p. 1995. pap. 19.95 (1-85223-890-9, Pub. by Crowood Pr UK) Trafalgar.
Locke, Bette, ed. Great Register of Stanislaus County, California, 1890. LC 92-75212. 110p. (Orig.). 1992. pap. 15.00 (0-9635514-0-X) Geneal Soc.
— Great Register of Stanislaus County, California 1890. LC 92-75212. 110p. 1993. reprint ed. pap. 15.00 (0-9635514-2-6) Geneal Soc.
Locke, Carl E., jt. auth. see Riggs, Olen L., Jr.
Locke, David. Drum Damba: Talking Drum Lessons. Smith, Larry W., ed. LC 88-20455. (Performance in World Music Ser.: No. 2). (Illus.). 224p. 1992. 34.95 (0-941677-18-4); pap. 17.95 (0-941677-10-9); spiral bd. 29.95 (0-941677-13-3); audio 12.95 (0-941677-15-X); Accompanies the bk. Drum Damba: Talking Drum Lessons. 59.95 (0-941677-21-4); 59.95 (0-941677-20-6); 250.00 (0-685-58748-7); 275.00 (0-685-58749-5) White Cliffs Media.
— Drum Gahu: A Systematic Method for an African Percussion Piece. Smith, Larry W., ed. LC 87-50298. (Performance in World Music Ser.). (Illus.). x, 142p. (C). 1988. 26.95 (0-941677-03-6); pap. 15.95 (0-941677-02-8); spiral bd. 25.95 (0-941677-04-4) White Cliffs Media.
— Drum Gahu: A Systematic Method for an African Percussion Piece, Set. Smith, Larry W., ed. LC 87-50298. (Performance in World Music Ser.). (Illus.). x, 142p. (C). 1988. audio 30.00 (0-941677-08-7) White Cliffs Media.
— The Episcopal Church. 196p. 1991. 14.95 (0-87052-900-5) Hippocrene Bks.
— Kpegisu: A War Drum of the Ewe. LC 92-3213. (Performance in World Music Ser.: Vol. 7). 1992. 39.95 (0-941677-38-9); pap. 19.95 (0-941677-39-7); spiral bd. 29.95 (0-941677-41-9); digital audio 12.95 (0-685-59283-9) White Cliffs Media.
— Science As Writing. 256p. (C). 1992. text ed. 30.00 (0-300-05452-1) Yale U Pr.
Locke, David R. The Demagogue: A Political Novel. LC 73-104515. 465p. reprint ed. lib. bdg. 29.50 (0-8398-1163-2) Irvington.
— The Demagogue: A Political Novel. 465p. (C). 1986. reprint ed. pap. text ed. 9.95 (0-8290-1912-X) Irvington.
— The Morals of Abou Ben Adhem. LC 76-91086. (American Humorists Ser.). reprint ed. lib. bdg. 22.50 (0-8398-1164-0) Irvington.
— Nasby in Exile. LC 77-104516. (Illus.). reprint ed. lib. bdg. 19.50 (0-8398-1165-9) Irvington.
— A Paper City. LC 68-57539. (Muckrakers Ser.). 431p. reprint ed. lib. bdg. 39.00 (0-8398-1166-7) Irvington.
— A Paper City. (Muckrakers Ser.). 431p. (C). 1986. reprint ed. pap. text ed. 7.95 (0-8290-1861-1) Irvington.
— Swingin' Round the Cirkle. LC 72-91085. (American Humorists Ser.). (Illus.). 307p. reprint ed. lib. bdg. 26.50 (0-8398-1167-5) Irvington.
Locke, David R. & Maurer, Kent L. Defense Strategy for Women: Be Your Own Risk Manager. Runyon, Daniel V., ed. (Illus.). 136p. (Orig.). 1991. pap. 9.50 (1-878559-02-8) Saltbox Pr.
Locke, Don. Multicultural Understanding: A Comprehensive Model. (Multicultural Aspects of Counseling Ser.: Vol. 1). 220p. (C). 1992. text ed. 34.00 (0-8039-4593-0); pap. text ed. 15.95 (0-8039-4594-9) Sage.
Locke, Don, jt. ed. see Weinreich-Haste, Helen.
Locke, Don C. & Ciechalski, Joseph C. Psychological Techniques for Teachers. LC 84-70093. xx, 362p. 1985. pap. text ed. 20.95 (0-915202-34-4) Accel Devel.
— Psychological Techniques for Teachers. 2nd ed. LC 95-10447. 286p. 1995. 59.95x (1-56032-388-4); pap. 29.95x (1-56032-389-2) Accel Devel.
*Locke, Duane. Watching Wisteria: Poems by Duane Locke. 100p. 1995. 19.95 (0-9632547-4-X); pap. 9.95 (0-9632547-5-8) Vida Pub.
Locke, E. V., jt. ed. see Evans, J. D.
Locke, Edwin A. The Essence of Leadership: The Four Keys to Leading Effectively. 128p. 1992. 22.95 (0-669-27880-7) Free Pr.
— Generalizing from Laboratory to Field Settings: Research Findings from Industrial-Organizational Psychology, Organizational Behavior, & Human Resource Management. LC 84-48566. (Issues in Organization & Management Ser.). 304p. 1985. pap. 22.95 (0-669-16640-5) Free Pr.
— A Guide to Effective Study. LC 74-79409. 224p. (C). 1975. pap. text ed. 21.95 (0-8261-1580-2) Springer Pub.
Locke, Edwin A. & Latham, Gary P. A Theory of Goal Setting & Task Performance. 544p. 1989. text ed. 54.00 (0-13-913138-8) P-H.
Locke, Eleanor G., ed. Sail Away. (Illus.). 164p. (Orig.). (J). 1987. pap. 17.00 (0-913932-24-8) Boosey & Hawkes.
Locke, Elsie & Paul, Janet, eds. Mrs. Hobson's Album. (Illus.). 168p. 1990. 36.00 (1-86940-035-6) OUP.
Locke, Flora, jt. auth. see Busche, Don.
Locke, Frederick W. Quest for the Holy Grail. LC 70-181948. (Stanford University. Stanford Studies in Language & Literature: No. 21). reprint ed. 22.50 (0-404-51831-1) AMS Pr.
Locke, George H. Builders of the Canadian Commonwealth. LC 67-28755. (Essay Index Reprint Ser.). 1977. 21.95 (0-8369-0621-7) Ayer.
Locke, Harvey J., jt. auth. see Sutherland, Edwin H.
Locke, Hubert G. The Black Anti-Semitism Controversy: Protestant Views & Perspectives. LC 93-50999. 144p. 1994. text ed. 29.50 (0-945636-51-2) Susquehanna U Pr.
— The Detroit Riot of Nineteen Sixty-Seven. LC 76-79479. (Illus.). 168p. reprint ed. pap. 47.90 (0-7837-3816-1, 2043636) Bks Demand.
Locke, Hubert G., ed. The Barmen Confession: Papers from the Seattle Assembly. LC 86-23874. (Toronto Studies in Theology: Vol. 26). 370p. 1987. lib. bdg. 99.95 (0-88946-770-6) E Mellen.
— The Church Confronts the Nazis: Barmen Then & Now. LC 84-10556. (Toronto Studies in Theology: Vol. 16). 248p. 1984. lib. bdg. 89.95 (0-88946-762-5) E Mellen.
Locke, Hubert G., ed. see International Scholars' Conference Staff.
Locke, Hubert G., jt. ed. see Littell, Franklin H.
Locke, Hubert G., ed. see Niemoller, Martin.
Locke, Ian. The Chip & How It Changed the World. LC 94-15227. (History & Invention Ser.). 1995. write for info. (0-8160-3144-4) Facts on File.
— The Wheel & How It Changed the World. LC 94-15228. (History & Invention Ser.). 1995. write for info. (0-8160-3143-6) Facts on File.
Locke, J. Courtney, tr. see De Grillot, Givry.
Locke, Jane T., jt. auth. see Locke, Joseph H.
Locke, Jim. The Well-Built House. rev. ed. 320p. 1992. pap. 11.95 (0-395-62951-9, R Todd) HM.
Locke, John. Correspondence of John Locke & Edwin Clarke. LC 72-10623. (Select Bibliographies Reprint Ser.). 1977. reprint ed. 36.95 (0-8369-7116-7) Ayer.
— The Correspondence of John Locke, Vol. 4: Letters 1242-1701, Covering the Years 1690-1693. De Beer, E. S., ed. (Clarendon Edition of the Works of John Locke Ser.). 1979. 135.00 (0-19-824561-0) OUP.
— The Correspondence of John Locke, Vol. 6: Letters 2199 to 2664. De Beer, E. S., ed. (Clarendon Edition of the Works of John Locke Ser.). 806p. (C). 1981. text ed. 145.00 (0-19-824563-7) OUP.
— The Correspondence of John Locke, Vol. 8: Letters 3287-3648. De Beer, E. S., ed. 808p. 1989. 115.00 (0-19-824565-3) OUP.
— Dos Ensayos Sobre el Gobierno Civil. Abellan, Joaquin, ed. Jimenez Gracia, Francisco, tr. (Nueva Austral Ser.: Vol. 240). (SPA.). 1991. pap. text ed. 29.50x (84-239-7240-2) Elliots Bks.
— Drafts for the Essay Concerning Human Understanding, & Other Philosophical Writings, Vol. 1, Drafts A & B. Nidditch, Peter H. & Rogers, G. A., eds. (Clarendon Edition of the Works of John Locke Ser.). (Illus.). 330p. 1990. 98.00 (0-19-824545-9) OUP.
— An Essay Concerning Human Understanding. Goldie, Mark, ed. 420p. 1993. pap. 8.95 (0-460-87355-5, Everyman's Classic Lib) C E Tuttle.
— An Essay Concerning Human Understanding. 1989. 9.95 (0-452-00941-3) NAL-Dutton.
— An Essay Concerning Human Understanding, 2 vols. (Great Books in Philosophy). 640p. (C). 1994. pap. text ed. 9.95 (0-87975-917-8) Prometheus Bks.
— Essay Concerning Humanity. 1974. pap. 12.95 (0-452-01019-5, Mer) NAL-Dutton.
— Isometric Perspective Designs & How to Create Them. (Illus.). 64p. (Orig.). 1981. pap. 3.95 (0-486-24123-8) Dover.
— A Letter Concerning Toleration. Tully, James, ed. LC 83-281. (HPC Classics Ser.). 72p. (C). 1983. lib. bdg. 21.50 (0-87220-100-7); pap. text ed. 3.95 (0-915145-60-X) Hackett Pub.
— A Letter Concerning Toleration. (Great Books in Philosophy). 78p. (C). 1990. reprint ed. pap. 4.95 (0-87975-598-9) Prometheus Bks.
— Locke on Money, 2 vols., Vol. 1. Kelly, Patrick H., ed. (Clarendon Edition of the Works of John Locke Ser.). (Illus.). 362p. 1991. 118.00 (0-19-824546-7) OUP.
— Locke on Money, 2 vols., Vol. 2. Kelly, Patrick H., ed. (Clarendon Edition of the Works of John Locke Ser.). (Illus.). 336p. 1991. 95.00 (0-19-824837-7) OUP.
— Of the Conduct of the Understanding. Garforth, Francis W., ed. LC 20-49589. (Classics in Education Ser.: Vol. 31). 144p. 1966. reprint ed. pap. 41.10 (0-7837-8878-9, 6620498) Bks Demand.
— A Paraphrase & Notes on the Epistles of St. Paul, 2 vols., Vol. 1. Wainright, Arthur W., ed. (Clarendon Edition of the Works of John Locke Ser.). (Illus.). 490p. 1988. 98.00 (0-19-824801-6) OUP.
— A Paraphrase & Notes on the Epistles of St. Paul, 2 vols., Vol. 2. Wainright, Arthur W., ed. (Clarendon Edition of the Works of John Locke Ser.). (Illus.). 360p. 1988. 89.00 (0-19-824806-7) OUP.
— Political Writings of John Locke. 592p. (Orig.). 1993. pap. 5.99 (0-451-62861-6, Ment) NAL-Dutton.
— Questions Concerning the Law of Nature. Clay, Diskin et al, eds. Clay, Jenny S., tr. LC 89-46178. (Illus.). 256p. 1990. 35.00 (0-8014-2348-1) Cornell U Pr.
— The Reasonableness of Christianity. LC 89-38836. 224p. 1989. reprint ed. pap. 9.95 (0-89526-753-5) Regnery Pub.
— Reasonableness of Christianity, & A Discourse of Miracles. Ramsey, I. T., ed. 104p. 1958. pap. 8.95 (0-8047-0341-8) Stanford U Pr.
— Second Treatise of Government. Macpherson, C. B., ed. LC 80-15052. (HPC Classics Ser.). 148p. (C). 1980. lib. bdg. 21.50 (0-915144-93-X); pap. text ed. 3.95 (0-915144-86-7) Hackett Pub.
— Second Treatise of Government. Cox, Richard H., ed. LC 82-25160. (Crofts Classics Ser.). 200p. 1982. pap. text ed. write for info. (0-88295-125-4) Harlan Davidson.
— The Second Treatise on Civil Government. (Great Books in Philosophy). 132p. 1986. pap. 4.95 (0-87975-337-4) Prometheus Bks.
— Several Papers Relating to Money, Interest & Trade, Etc. LC 87-17243. (Reprints of Economic Classics Ser.). 1989. reprint ed. 49.50 (0-678-00334-3) Kelley.
— Some Thoughts Concerning Education. Yolton, John W. & Yolton, Jean, eds. (Clarendon Edition of the Works of John Locke Ser.). (Illus.). 352p. 1989. 92.00 (0-19-824582-3) OUP.
— Treatise of Civil Government & a Letter Concerning Toleration. Sherman, Charles L., ed. 1965. pap. text ed. 10.95 (0-89197-519-5) Irvington.
— Two Treatises of Government. Goldie, Mark, ed. 298p. 1993. pap. 6.95 (0-460-87356-3, Everyman's Classic Lib) C E Tuttle.
— Two Treatises of Government. Cook, Thomas I., ed. & intro. by. Bd. with Patriarcha. (Library of Classics: No. 2). 352p. 1970. Set pap. 11.95 (0-02-848500-9) Hafner.
— Two Treatises of Government. rev. ed. Laslett, Peter, ed. (Cambridge Texts in the History of Political Thought Ser.). 200p. 1988. pap. 9.95 (0-521-35730-6) Cambridge U Pr.
— Two Treatises of Government. 3rd rev. ed. Laslett, Peter, ed. (Cambridge Texts in the History of Political Thought Ser.). 200p. 1988. 59.95 (0-521-35448-X) Cambridge U Pr.
— Works, 10 Vols, Set. 1963. reprint ed. 775.00 (3-511-02600-8) Adlers Foreign Bks.
— Works of John Locke, 2 Vols, 1. LC 74-94275. (Select Bibliographies Reprint Ser.). 1977. 30.95 (0-8369-9980-0) Ayer.
— Works of John Locke, 2 Vols, 2. LC 74-94275. (Select Bibliographies Reprint Ser.). 1977. 30.95 (0-8369-9981-9) Ayer.
— Works of John Locke, 2 Vols, Set. LC 74-94275. (Select Bibliographies Reprint Ser.). 1977. 61.95 (0-8369-5049-6) Ayer.
*Locke, John C., ed. First Englishmen in India. LC 75-43767. Date not set. reprint ed. 37.50 (0-404-06615-1) AMS Pr.
Locke, John F., tr. see Maquet, Jacques P.
Locke, John L. The Child's Path to Spoken Language. LC 92-34661. (Illus.). 530p. (Orig.). 1993. text ed. 42.50 (0-674-11640-2) HUP.
— The Child's Path to Spoken Language. (Illus.). 536p. (Orig.). (C). 1995. pap. text ed. 19.95 (0-674-11639-9) HUP.
Locke, John L., jt. ed. see Smith, Michael D.
Locke, Joseph. Deadly Relations. (Blood & Lace Ser.: No. 2). (YA). 1994. pap. 3.50 (0-553-56617-2) Bantam.
— Game Over. (YA). 1993. pap. 3.50 (0-553-29652-3) Bantam.
— Kill the Teacher's Pet. (YA). 1991. pap. 2.99 (0-553-29058-4) Bantam.
— Nightmare on Elm Street. 1989. pap. 3.95 (0-312-91764-3) St Martin.
— One-Nine-Hundred-Killer. (YA). 1994. pap. 3.50 (0-553-56079-4) Bantam.
— Vampire Heart. (Blood & Lace Ser.: No. 1). (YA). 1994. pap. 3.50 (0-553-56614-8) Bantam.
— Vendetta. (YA). (gr. 9-12). 1994. pap. 3.50 (0-553-56080-8) Bantam.
Locke, Joseph H. & Locke, Jane T. Locke Art Glass: A Guide for Collectors with Photographic Illustrations of 190 Examples. 64p. (Orig.). 1987. pap. 9.95 (0-486-25400-3) Dover.
Locke, Kathy, jt. auth. see Buzby, Beth M.
Locke, Lafe. Film Animation Techniques: A Beginner's Guide & Handbook. (Illus.). 160p. 1992. pap. 12.95 (1-55870-236-9) Betterway Bks.
— Making Movies Without a Camera: Inexpensive Fun with Flip Books & Other Animation Gadgets. (Illus.). 128p. (Orig.). 1992. pap. 7.95 (1-55870-261-X, 70152) Betterway Bks.
— The Name of the Game: How Sports Talk Got That Way. (Illus.). 160p. (Orig.). 1992. pap. 8.95 (1-55870-234-2) Betterway Bks.
Locke, Lawrence F., et al. Proposals That Work: A Guide for Planning Dissertations & Grant Proposals. 3rd ed. (Illus.). 320p. (C). 1993. text ed. 48.00 (0-8039-5066-7); pap. text ed. 21.50 (0-8039-5067-5) Sage.
Locke, Lee J., ed. Essentials of Upholstery & Trim, for Vintage & Classic. (Illus.). 176p. 1970. pap. 8.95 (0-911160-48-5) Post Group.
Locke, Lisa K. Love, Lisa. LC 91-22699. (Illus.). 288p. 1991. pap. 9.95 (0-9628579-0-4) Vision WY.
Locke, Marianne, ed. see Daddy, S. Kwaku.
*Locke, Marianne, et al. Being in Motion. 75p. 1994. teacher ed 40.00 (0-9643923-0-5) Young Imag.
Locke, Mary. My China: The Way It Was. LC 91-3839. (Illus.). 96p. (Orig.). 1991. pap. 8.95 (0-931832-95-0) Fithian Pr.
— Thirteen Pieces: Life with a Multiple. 272p. (Orig.). 1993. pap. 10.00 (0-9635966-0-8) Atlan St Pub.
Locke, Mary E. Fundamentals of Word Processing in Business: Introduction to Word Processing. 1986. teacher ed write for info. (0-8359-2207-3, Reston) P-H.
Locke, Mary E., jt. ed. see Binnendijk, Hans.
Locke, Maryel & Warren, Charles, eds. Jean-Luc Godard's Hail Mary: Women & the Sacred in Film. LC 92-29569. (Illus.). 280p. (C). 1993. 29.95 (0-8093-1824-5); pap. 14.95 (0-8093-1891-1) S Ill U Pr.
Locke, Mattie. Nursing Management in the 90's - An OBRA Guideline for Directors of Nursing in Long Term Care. 224p. (Orig.). (C). 1991. pap. text ed. 19.95 (1-877735-31-0, 176) M&H Pub Co TX.
— Nursing Procedures Manual. 4th ed. (Illus.). 227p. (C). 1991. ring bd. 35.50 (1-877735-02-7, 103) M&H Pub Co TX.
— Quality Assurance with Care Planning. 300p. (C). 1992. ring bd. 42.50 (1-877735-36-1, 185) M&H Pub Co TX.
— Texas Policies & Procedures Manual. 6th ed. 383p. (C). 1993. ring bd. 75.00 (1-877735-01-9, 102) M&H Pub Co TX.
Locke, Mattie, jt. auth. see Manning, Maxine.
Locke, Mattie, et al. Care Plans That Work with the MDS. 190p. (C). 1992. pap. text ed. 54.45 (1-877735-03-5, 104) M&H Pub Co TX.
Locke, May S. Anti-Slavery in America from the Introduction of African Slaves to the Prohibition of the Slave Trade (1619-1808) 1988. 11.25 (0-8446-1284-7) Peter Smith.
*Locke, Meryl L. BBQ Raccoon. LC 94-90217. 152p. (Orig.). 1995. pap. 6.95 (1-56002-464-X) Aegina Pr.
Locke, Norton. The Land of Milk & Honey. Costa, Gwen, ed. LC 90-40784. (Illus.). 350p. 1992. 29.95 (0-87949-343-7) Ashley Bks.
*Locke, P. Harvey, et al, eds. Manual of Small Animal Dermatology. (Illus.). 280p. 1995. pap. 69.95 (0-905214-20-X) Iowa St U Pr.
Locke, Philip, jt. auth. see Downing, Angela.
Locke, Ralph, ed. The Poetic Debussy: A Collection of His Song Texts & Selected Letters. rev. ed. Miller, Richard, tr. LC 93-21462. (Eastman Studies in Music: Vol. 1). (Illus.). 320p. (C). 1994. reprint ed. pap. text ed. 19.95 (1-878822-34-9) Univ Rochester Pr.
— The Poetic Debussy: A Collection of His Song Texts & Selected Letters. 2nd rev. ed. Miller, Richard, tr. LC 93-21462. (Eastman Studies in Music: Vol. 1). (Illus.). 320p. (C). 1994. reprint ed. text ed. 45.00 (1-878822-33-0) Univ Rochester Pr.
Locke, Ralph G., jt. auth. see Kelly, Edward F.
Locke, Ralph P. Music, Musicians, & the Saint-Simonians. LC 85-20915. (Illus.). xviii, 400p. (C). 1986. lib. bdg. 55.00 (0-226-48901-9); pap. text ed. 24.95 (0-226-48902-7) U Ch Pr.
Locke, Ray. Seldom Sung Songs. LC 83-63200. 192p. 1984. 13.95 (0-915677-02-4) Roundtable Pub.
— Sweet Salt. LC 89-60774. 224p. (Orig.). 1990. pap. 12.95 (0-915677-43-1) Roundtable Pub.

An Asterisk (*) at the beginning of an entry indicates that the title is appearing in BIP for the first time.

Locke, Raymond F. The Book of the Navajo. 4th ed. 512p. (Orig.). 1989. pap. 5.95 (*0-87687-400-6*, BM 400) Mankind Pub.
— Jim Beckwourth. 208p. 1995. 4.95 (*0-87067-590-7*, Melrose Sq) Holloway.
— Joachin Murieta. (Orig.). (J). (ps-12). 1980. pap. 2.25 (*0-87067-009-3*, BH009) Holloway.
— Marie Leveau: Voodoo Queen of New Orleans. 1994. pap. 3.95 (*0-87067-750-0*, Melrose Sq) Holloway.
Locke, Raymond F., ed. The American Indian. (Great Adventures of History Ser.). 1976. 1.75 (*0-87687-003-5*, BM003) Mankind Pub.
— The Civil War. (Great Adventures of History Ser.). 1.75 (*0-87687-006-X*, BM006) Mankind Pub.
— The Human Side of History. (Great Adventures of History Ser.). 1970. 1.75 (*0-87687-004-3*, BM004) Mankind Pub.
Locke, Raymond F., ed. see Neyland, James.
Locke, Raymond F., jt. auth. see Ruth, Marianne.
Locke, Raymond F., ed. see Ruuth, Marianne.
Locke, Reginald. A Naturalists Book of Poetry. 64p. 1984. 45.00 (*0-905418-85-9*, Pub. by Gresham Bks UK) St Mut.
Locke, Richard. Locke Out: The Collected Writings of Richard Locke. (Illus.). 192p. (Orig.). 1993. pap. 12.95 (*0-943383-06-4*) FirstHand Ltd.
***Locke, Richard, et al, eds.** Employment Relations in a Changing World Economy. 1995. 40.00 (*0-262-12191-3*); pap. 19.95 (*0-262-62098-7*) MIT Pr.
Locke, Richard A. Moon Walk Eighteen Thirty-Five: Was Neil Armstrong Really the First Man on the Moon? 5th ed. Tazewell, C. W., ed. LC 90-81467. (Illus.). 80p. 1990. pap. 10.00 (*1-878515-34-9*) W S Dawson.
***Locke, Richard M.** Remaking the Italian Economy: Policy Failures & Local Successes in the Contemporary Polity. (Studies in Political Economy). 256p. 1995. 29.95x (*0-8014-2891-2*) Cornell U Pr.
Locke, Robert. Tracks. (J). (gr. 5 up). 1986. 14.95 (*0-395-40571-8*) HM.
Locke, Robert R. The End of the Practical Man, Entrepreneurship & Higher Education, in Germany, France & Great Britain: 1880 to 1940. McKay, John, ed. (Industrial Development & the Social Fabric Ser.: Vol. 7). 1984. 73.25 (*0-89232-433-3*) Jai Pr.
— Management & Higher Education since 1940: The Influence of America & Japan on West Germany, Great Britain & France. (Illus.). 428p. (C). 1989. 64.95 (*0-521-34102-7*) Cambridge U Pr.
Locke, Sam. Fair Game. 1958. pap. 4.75 (*0-8222-0379-0*) Dramatists Play.
***Locke, Shirley A.** Coping with Loss: A Guide for Caregivers. LC 94-7441. 238p. 1994. pap. 29.95 (*0-398-06244-7*) C C Thomas.
— Coping with Loss: A Guide for Caregivers. LC 94-7441. 238p. (C). 1994. text ed. 48.95 (*0-398-05912-8*) C C Thomas.
Locke, Stephen W., jt. ed. see Heintz, Bruce D.
Locke, Steven & Hornig-Rohan, Mady. Mind & Immunity: Behavioral Immunology. LC 83-81107. 248p. 1983. text ed. 75.00 (*0-275-91400-3*, C1400, Praeger Pubs) Greenwood.
Locke, Sue. Nursery Rhyme Knits: Clothes, Toys & Accessories from Birth to Six Years. (Illus.). 128p. 1990. 24.95 (*0-943955-23-8*, Trafalgar Sq Pub) Trafalgar.
Locke, Tates & Ibach, Bob. Caught in the Net. LC 81-86382. (Illus.). 176p. (Orig.). 1982. text ed. 17.95 (*0-88011-044-9*, PLOC0044) Human Kinetics.
Locke, Thomas. Delta Factor. 1994. pap. 7.99 (*1-55661-501-9*) Bethany Hse.
— Dream Voyager. (Spectrum Chronicles Ser.: Bk. 2). 176p. (J). 1995. pap. 5.99 (*1-55661-433-0*) Bethany Hse.
— Light Weaver. (Lightweaver Chronicles Ser.). (YA). 1994. pap. 4.99 (*1-55661-432-2*) Bethany Hse.
— The Omega Network. (Thomas Locke Mystery Ser.: Bk. 2). 240p. 1995. pap. 7.99 (*1-55661-502-7*) Bethany Hse.
Locke, Virginia O., jt. auth. see Stevenson, Russell.
Locke, W. N. Pronunciation of the French Spoken at Brunswick, Maine. (Publications of the American Dialect Society: No. 12). 201p. 1949. pap. 8.25 (*0-8173-0612-9*) U of Ala Pr.
Locke, William H., Jr. & Novak, Ralph M., Jr. Texas Foreclosure Manual. LC 91-65392. 484p. 1991. ring bd. 150.00 (*0-938160-63-X*, 6207) State Bar TX.
Locke, William J. Town of Tombarel. LC 71-150548. (Short Story Index Reprint Ser.). 1977. reprint ed. 20.95 (*0-8369-3845-3*) Ayer.
Locke, William N. Scientific French: A Concise Description of the Structural Elements of Scientific & Technical French. LC 78-11669. 124p. 1979. reprint ed. pap. 8.50 (*0-88275-771-7*) Krieger.
Locke, William N. & Booth, E. Donald, eds. Machine Translation of Languages: Fourteen Essays. LC 75-29339. 243p. 1976. reprint ed. text ed. 38.50 (*0-8371-8434-7*, LOMT, Greenwood Pr) Greenwood.
Lockemann, P. C., jt. ed. see Bracchi, G.
Lockemann, P. C., jt. ed. see Encarnacao, J. L.
Locker, David. Disability & Disadvantage: The Consequences of Chronic Illness. LC 83-4971. 220p. 1984. pap. 15.95 (*0-422-78740-X*, NO. 3972) Routledge Chapman & Hall.
Locker, John. Two Treatises of Government with a Supplement Containing Sir Robert Filmer's Patriarcha. 1974. pap. 10.95 (*0-317-60442-2*) Free Pr.
***Locker, John & Klopfenstein, Kenneth F.** Analytic Trigonometry. Davies Associates Staff, ed. & illus. by. 149p. 1994. pap. 12.00 (*0-9630076-3-7*) Davies & Assocs.
— Numerical Trigonometry. Davies Associates Staff, ed. & illus. by. 222p. 1994. pap. 16.00 (*0-9630076-2-9*) Davies & Assocs.
Locker, Kitty. Business & Administrative Communication. 2nd ed. 704p. (C). 1991. text ed. 58.95 (*0-256-08747-4*, 12-2304-02) Irwin.
Locker, Kitty O. Business & Administrative Communication. 3rd ed. LC 94-17702. 720p. (C). 1994. text ed. 58.95 (*0-256-14064-2*) Irwin.
***Locker, Sari.** Mindblowing Sex in the Real World: Hot Tips for Doing It in the Age of Anxiety. 208p. 1995. pap. 10.00 (*0-06-095099-4*, PL) HarpC.
Locker, Thomas. Anna & the Bagpiper. LC 92-42350. (Illus.). 32p. (J). (ps). 1994. 15.95 (*0-399-22546-3*, Philomel Bks) Putnam Pub Group.
— Boy Who Held Back the Sea. (J). (ps-3). 1991. pap. 4.95 (*0-8037-1049-6*, Puff Pied Piper) Puffin Bks.
— The Boy Who Held Back the Sea. (J). 1993. pap. 4.99 (*0-14-054613-8*, Puff Pied Piper) Puffin Bks.
— Family Farm. LC 87-19645. (Illus.). 32p. (J). (ps up). 1988. lib. bdg. 14.89 (*0-8037-0490-9*) Dial Bks Young.
— Family Farm. LC 87-19645. (Illus.). 32p. (J). (ps up). 1988. 16.99 (*0-8037-0489-5*) Dial Bks Young.
— Family Farm. (Illus.). 32p. (J). 1994. pap. 5.99 (*0-14-050351-X*, Puff Pied Piper) Puffin Bks.
— The Land of Gray Wolf. LC 90-3915. (Illus.). 32p. (J). (ps up). 1991. 16.99 (*0-8037-0936-6*); lib. bdg. 15.89 (*0-8037-0937-4*) Dial Bks Young.
— The Mare on the Hill. LC 85-1684. (Illus.). 32p. (J). (gr. k-12). 1985. lib. bdg. 15.89 (*0-8037-0208-6*) Dial Bks Young.
— The Mare on the Hill. (Illus.). 32p. 1995. pap. 5.99 (*0-14-055339-8*) Puffin Bks.
— Miranda's Smile. LC 93-28050. (J). 1994. 15.99 (*0-8037-1688-5*); lib. bdg. 15.89 (*0-8037-1689-3*) Dial Bks Young.
— Sailing with the Wind. LC 85-23381. (Illus.). 32p. (J). (ps up). 1986. lib. bdg. 14.89 (*0-8037-0312-0*) Dial Bks Young.
— Sailing with the Wind. (J). (gr. 3 up). 1992. pap. 5.99 (*0-14-054698-7*, Puff Pied Piper) Puffin Bks.
— Sky Tree: Seeing Science Through Art. LC 94-38342. (Illus.). 40p. (J). (gr. k-4). 1995. 15.95 (*0-06-024883-1*); lib. bdg. 15.89 (*0-06-024884-X*) HarpC Child Bks.
— Where the River Begins. LC 84-1709. (Illus.). 32p. (J). (gr. k-3). 1984. 16.95 (*0-8037-0089-X*); lib. bdg. 14.89 (*0-8037-0090-3*) Dial Bks Young.
— Where the River Begins. (Illus.). 32p. (J). 1993. pap. 4.99 (*0-14-054595-6*) Puffin Bks.
— The Young Artist. (Illus.). 32p. (J). (ps up). 1989. lib. bdg. 15.89 (*0-8037-0627-8*) Dial Bks Young.
— The Young Artist. (Illus.). 32p. (J). 1993. pap. 4.99 (*0-14-054923-4*, Puff Pied Piper) Puffin Bks.
Locker, Thomas, illus. The Boy Who Held Back the Sea. LC 86-32893. (J). 1987. 15.99 (*0-8037-0406-2*) Dial Bks Young.
Locker, Thomas, illus. & adapt. Rip Van Winkle. LC 87-24448. 32p. (J). (ps up). 1988. 15.95 (*0-8037-0520-4*); lib. bdg. 15.89 (*0-8037-0521-2*) Dial Bks Young.
Locker, Thomas, illus. Snow Toward Evening, a Year in a River Valley. LC 89-48307. 32p. (J). 1990. 16.99 (*0-8037-0810-6*); lib. bdg. 15.89 (*0-8037-0811-4*) Dial Bks Young.
Locker, Thomas, illus. & adapt. Washington Irving's Rip Van Winkle. 40p. (J). 1994. pap. 5.99 (*0-14-055284-7*, Puff Pied Piper) Puffin Bks.
Lockerbie & Olson. Daktar. (SPA.). Date not set. 1.95 (*0-685-74926-6*, 540099) Editorial Unilit.
Lockerbie, D. Bruce. A Passion for Learning: A History of Christian Thought on Education. 600p. (C). 1994. text ed. 29.99 (*0-8024-6581-1*) Moody.
Lockerbie, D. Bruce & Fonseca, Donald R. College: Getting in & Staying In. LC 90-32755. 208p. reprint ed. pap. 59.30 (*0-7837-5559-7*, 2045334) Bks Demand.
Lockerbie, Jeanette. A Cup of Sugar, Neighbor. (Quiet Time Books for Women). 128p. 1974. pap. 3.99 (*0-8024-1681-0*) Moody.
— More Salt in My Kitchen. LC 80-12357. (Quiet Time Books for Women). 1980. pap. 3.99 (*0-8024-5668-5*) Moody.
— Morning Glories. (Quiet Time Books for Women). (Orig.). 1987. pap. 3.99 (*0-8024-6861-6*) Moody.
— A Plate of Hot Toast. (Quiet Time Books for Women). 128p. (Orig.). 1971. pap. 3.99 (*0-8024-6625-7*) Moody.
— Salt in My Kitchen. (Quiet Time Books for Women). 1967. pap. 3.99 (*0-8024-7500-0*) Moody.
— Springtime of Faith. pap. 3.99 (*0-8024-7696-1*) Moody.
— Time Out for Coffee. (Quiet Time Books for Women). 1978. pap. 3.99 (*0-8024-8759-9*) Moody.
Lockerby, Robert, ed. Mountaineering & Mountain Club Serials: A Guide to English Language Titles. LC 90-20890. 202p. 1990. 25.00 (*0-8108-2395-0*) Scarecrow.
Lockerby, Susan C., ed. see International SAMPE Electronics Conference Staff.
Lockerd, Benjamin G., Jr. The Sacred Marriage: Psychic Integration in the Faerie Queene. LC 85-48293. (Illus.). 216p. 1987. 35.00 (*0-8387-5106-7*) Bucknell U Pr.
Lockeretz, William, ed. Environmentally Sound Agriculture. LC 83-4231. 444p. 1983. text ed. 44.95 (*0-275-91401-1*, C1401, Praeger Pubs) Greenwood.
Lockeretz, William & Anderson, Molly D. Agricultural Research Alternatives. LC 92-47113. (Our Sustainable Future Ser.: Vol. 3). x, 248p. 1993. 30.00 (*0-8032-2901-1*) U of Nebr Pr.
Lockeridge, Frances & Lockeridge, Richard. The Norths Meet Murder. 17.95 (*0-89190-916-8*, Am Repr) Amereon Ltd.
Lockeridge, Richard, jt. auth. see Lockeridge, Frances.
Lockert, Jan. An Infinite Journey. Shaw, Pat, tr. 230p. (Orig.). 1993. pap. 12.95 (*0-9631750-2-5*) Muse Pubns.
Lockert, Lacy. Studies in French-Classical Tragedy. LC 59-298. 1958. 24.95 (*0-8265-1049-3*) Vanderbilt U Pr.
Lockert, Lacy, tr. Chief Rivals of Corneille & Racine. LC 56-14366. 1956. 29.95 (*0-8265-1047-7*) Vanderbilt U Pr.
— Moot Plays of Corneille. LC 59-15968. 1959. 24.95 (*0-8265-1053-1*) Vanderbilt U Pr.
— More Plays by Rivals of Corneille & Racine. LC 68-17282. 1968. 29.95 (*0-8265-1110-4*) Vanderbilt U Pr.
Lockert, Lucia, ed. see Fox, Lucia.
Lockery, Glen, ed. Songs of Idaho. 94p. 1988. 25.00 (*0-9619700-0-6*); pap. 8.00 (*0-9619700-1-4*) Univ ID Alumni Assn.
Lockery, Shirley A. & Schoenrock, Susan A., eds. Ethnicity & Aging: Mental Health Issues. LC 90-71303. 73p. (C). 1990. pap. text ed. 8.00 (*1-879167-00-X*) SDSU Univ Ctr on Aging.
Lockett, A. G. & Islei, G., eds. Improving Decision Making in Organizations. (Lecture Notes in Economics & Mathematical Systems Ser.: Vol. 335). (Illus.). ix, 606p. 1989. pap. 68.50 (*0-387-51795-2*) Spr-Verlag.
***Lockett, Brian.** Construction Craft Jurisdiction Agreements, 1995. LC 94-43299. 1995. pap. 45.00 (*0-87179-851-4*) BNA.
Lockett, Cari L., comp. Archaeological Data Recovery at Drill Pad U19ay, Nye County, Nevada. (Illus.). 94p. 1991. 10.00 (*0-945920-62-8*) Desert Rsch Inst.
Lockett, David. Building Your Advertising Business: A Complete Guide To Get New Business Leads. 1989. pap. 14.95 (*0-8442-3168-1*, NTC Busn Bks) NTC Pub Grp.
Lockett, Hattie G. The Unwritten Literature on the Hopi. LC 76-43767. (Arizona Univ. Social Science Bulletin Ser.: No. 2). reprint ed. 18.00 (*0-404-15621-5*) AMS Pr.
Lockett, Hazel, ed. see Charles, Melvin.
Lockett, Keith. Physics in the Real World. 208p. (C). 1990. pap. 18.50 (*0-521-36690-9*) Cambridge U Pr.
Lockett, Martin & Spear, Roger, eds. Organizations As Systems. 244p. 1980. pap. 38.00 (*0-335-00263-3*, Open Univ Pr) Taylor & Francis.
Lockett, R., jt. auth. see Fish, W. F.
Lockett, Raymond. World Civilization Readings. 1992. 18.70 (*0-536-58217-3*) Ginn Pr.
Lockett, Terence A. Collecting Victorian Tiles. (Illus.). 235p. 1979. 29.50 (*0-902028-82-0*) Antique Collect.
Lockette, Kevin F. & Keyes, Ann M. Conditioning with Physical Disabilities. LC 93-47606. 288p. 1994. pap. 22.95 (*0-87322-614-3*, PLOC0614) Human Kinetics.
Lockey, Joseph B. Pan-Americanism: Its Beginnings. LC 79-111723. (American Imperialism: Viewpoints of United States Foreign Policy, 1898-1941 Ser.). 1970. reprint ed. 28.95 (*0-405-02034-1*) Ayer.
Lockey, Richard & Bukantz, Samuel, eds. Allergen Immunotherapy. (Allergic Disease & Therapy Ser.: Vol. 4). 312p. 1991. 110.00 (*0-8247-8534-7*) Dekker.
Lockey, Richard F. & Bukantz, Samuel C. Fundamentals of Immunology & Allergy. (Illus.). 352p. 1987. pap. text ed. 33.95 (*0-7216-2054-X*) Saunders.
***Lockhart, Alexander.** Positive Charges: 544 Ways to Stay Upbeat During Downbeat Times. 224p. (Orig.). 1994. pap. 6.95 (*0-9643035-5-8*) Zander Pr.
— School Teaching in Canada. 224p. 1991. 40.00 (*0-8020-2748-2*); pap. 19.95 (*0-8020-6788-3*) U of Toronto Pr.
Lockhart, Audrey. Some Aspects of Irish Emigration from Ireland to the North American Colonies Between 1660-1775. LC 76-6351. (Irish Americans Ser.). 1976. 23.95 (*0-405-09345-4*) Ayer.
Lockhart-Ball, H., jt. auth. see Norton, B.
Lockhart, Barbara. Christmas Tall Books, 3 bks. (Illus.). 36p. (J). (ps). 1993. Set, incl. snowman. bds. 14.95 (*1-56828-044-0*) Red Jacket Pr.
— The Christmas Tree. (Illus.). 12p. (J). (ps). 1993. 4.95 (*1-56828-025-4*) Red Jacket Pr.
— Santa. (Illus.). 12p. (J). 1993. 4.95 (*1-56828-026-2*) Red Jacket Pr.
— The Snowman. (Illus.). 12p. (J). (ps). 1993. 4.95 (*1-56828-024-6*) Red Jacket Pr.
Lockhart, Barbara & Lockhart, Lynne. Once a Pony Time at Chincoteague. (Illus.). 30p. (J). (gr. k-5). 1992. 8.95 (*0-87033-436-0*, Tidewtr Pubs) Cornell Maritime.
Lockhart, Barbara, jt. auth. see Lockhart, Lynne N.
***Lockhart, Betty A.** A Calf Grows Up: The Story of Dairying with a Guide to Teaching & Learning. Lockhart, Donald G., ed. (Illus.). 1992. teacher ed 7.00 (*1-880327-23-6*) Perceptions.
— The Maple Sugaring Story: A Guide for Teaching & Learning the Maple Industry. Lockhart, Donald G., ed. (Illus.). 84p. 1990. teacher ed 4.50 (*1-880327-04-X*) Perceptions.
— Visiting a Farm? "Be Safe & Sound" Says Safety Hound: A Guide to Teaching & Learning about Farm Visit Safety. Lockhart, Donald G., ed. (Illus.). 1994. teacher ed 2.50 (*1-880327-32-5*) Perceptions.
***Lockhart, Bicknell.** The Stock Market Game. Ingram, tr. 60p. 1996. pap. 12.95 (*0-7610-0488-2*) NW Pub.
Lockhart, Bruce M. The End of the Vietnamese Monarchy. LC 93-60072. (Lax-Viet Series - Yale University Southeast Asia Studies: No. 15). 242p. (Orig.). 1993. pap. 15.00 (*0-938692-50-X*) Yale U SE Asia.
Lockhart, Charles. Bargaining in International Conflicts. LC 78-23334. 224p. 1979. text ed. 42.00 (*0-231-04560-3*) Col U Pr.
— Gaining Ground: Tailoring Social Programs to American Values. 1989. 32.00 (*0-520-06437-2*) U CA Pr.
Lockhart, Charles, jt. auth. see Richards, Jack C.
Lockhart, Charles, jt. ed. see Utter, Glenn H.
Lockhart, Charlotte F. Adult Education Intensive Phonics Manual. LC 87-70692. 214p. 1987. teacher ed, audio 61.00 (*0-9605654-5-0*) Char-L.
— Discover Intensive Phonics for Yourself. rev. ed. LC 83-71502. 452p. (J). 1983. teacher ed 49.95 (*0-9605654-1-8*) Char-L.
— Discover Intensive Phonics for Yourself. 4th rev. ed. LC 88-91180. 420p. reprint ed. teacher ed, audio 70.00 (*0-9605654-6-9*) Char-L.
— Intensive Phonics Mini Manual. LC 86-70531. 95p. (Orig.). 1986. pap. text ed. 30.00 (*0-9605654-3-4*) Char-L.
— Intermediate & Adult Education Intensive Phonics Manual. LC 90-81351. 288p. 1990. teacher ed, ring bd. 109.00 (*0-9605654-7-7*) Char-L.
— Intermediate & Adult Education Intensive Phonics Workpack. LC 90-73112. 288p. 1990. student ed, ring bd. 39.00 (*0-9605654-8-5*) Char-L.
— Kindergarten & Pre-First Grade Intensive Phonics Kit. LC 86-71330. 89p. 1986. 40.00 (*0-9605654-4-2*) Char-L.
— Parents Intensive Phonics Mini Manual. LC 91-91750. 187p. (Orig.). 1991. pap. 34.00 (*0-9605654-9-3*) Char-L.
Lockhart, Darcy. Private Viewing. 1989. pap. 3.95 (*0-8217-2786-9*) Zebra.
Lockhart, Donald G., ed. see Lockhart, Betty A.
Lockhart, Earl G., comp. My Vocation, by Eminent Americans; or, What Eminent Americans Think of Their Callings. LC 72-5602. (Essay Index Reprint Ser.). 1977. reprint ed. 35.95 (*0-8369-2997-7*) Ayer.
Lockhart, Estes J. Communicating with Kids: A Practical Guide to the Forgotten Language. 224p. (Orig.). 1990. 21.95 (*0-9623538-2-5*); pap. 16.95 (*0-9623538-0-9*) Undercurrents Pr.
Lockhart, Eugene. Simple Annals. 132p. (Orig.). 1987. pap. 7.65 (*0-9618581-3-3*) E Lockhart.
Lockhart, G. B. BASIC Digital Signal Processing. (BASIC Bks.). (Illus.). 160p. 1989. pap. text ed. 24.95 (*0-408-01578-0*) Buttrwrth-Heinemann.
Lockhart, G. W. Highland Balls & Village Halls. 1989. 35.00 (*0-946487-12-X*, Pub. by Luath Pr UK) St Mut.
— The Scot & His Oats: A Survey of the Part Played by Oats & Oatmeal in Scottish History, Legend, Romance, & the Scottish Character. 72p. 1989. pap. 35.00 (*0-946487-05-7*, Pub. by Luath Pr UK) St Mut.
Lockhart, Gary. The Weather Companion: An Album of Meteorological History, Science, Legend, & Folklore. (Illus.). 1988. pap. text ed. 16.95 (*0-471-62079-3*) Wiley.
Lockhart, Greg. Nation in Arms: The Origins of the People's Army of Vietnam. 314p. 1991. 38.95 (*0-04-301294-9*, Pub. by Allen Unwin AT); pap. 24.95 (*0-04-324012-7*, Pub. by Allen Unwin AT) Paul & Co Pubs.
Lockhart, Greg, tr. see Lang, Tam, et al.
Lockhart, Harold. OSF DCE: Guide to Developing Distributed Applications. 1994. disk 59.95 (*0-07-911481-4*) McGraw.
Lockhart, J. A. & Wiseman, A. J. Introduction to Crop Husbandry. 5th ed. (Illus.). 300p. 1983. text ed. 48.00 (*0-08-029793-5*, Pergamon Pr); pap. text ed. 19.25 (*0-08-029792-7*, Pergamon Pr) Elsevier.
— Introduction to Crop Husbandry: Including Grassland. 6th ed. (Illus.). 334p. 1988. text ed. 62.00 (*0-08-034201-9*, Pergamon Pr); pap. text ed. 24.00 (*0-08-034200-0*, Pergamon Pr) Elsevier.
Lockhart, James. Nahuas After the Conquest: A Social & Cultural History of the Indians of Central Mexico. 1994. pap. 24.95 (*0-8047-2317-6*) Stanford U Pr.
— The Nahuas after the Conquest: A Social & Cultural History of the Indians of Central Mexico, Sixteenth Through Eighteenth Centuries. LC 91-29972. (Illus.). 672p. (C). 1992. 60.00 (*0-8047-1927-6*) Stanford U Pr.
— Nahuas & Spaniards: Postconquest Central Mexican History & Philology. LC 91-9895. 320p. 1991. 45.00 (*0-8047-1953-5*); pap. 18.95 (*0-8047-1954-3*) Stanford U Pr.
— Spanish Peru, Fifteen Thirty-Two to Fifteen Sixty: A Colonial Society. LC 68-14032. (Illus.). 298p. 1967. 30.00 (*0-299-04660-5*) U of Wis Pr.
— Spanish Peru, 1532-1560: A Colonial Society. LC 68-14032. (Illus.). 298p. 1974. pap. 14.95 (*0-299-04664-8*) U of Wis Pr.
— Spanish Peru, 1532-1560: A Social History. 2nd ed. LC 93-23338. 342p. 1994. 50.00 (*0-299-14160-8*); pap. 14.95 (*0-299-14164-0*) U of Wis Pr.
Lockhart, James, ed. & tr. We People Here: Nahuatl Accounts of the Conquest of Mexico. (Repertorium Columbianum Ser.: No. 1). 304p. 1994. 45.00 (*0-520-07875-6*) U CA Pr.
Lockhart, James & Otte, E. Letters & People of the Spanish Indies. LC 75-6007. (Cambridge Latin American Studies: No. 22). 322p. 1976. pap. 18.95 (*0-521-09990-0*) Cambridge U Pr.
Lockhart, James & Schwartz, Stuart. Early Latin America: A History of Colonial Spanish America & Brazil. LC 82-23506. (Cambridge Latin American Studies: No. 46). (Illus.). 427p. 1983. pap. 18.95 (*0-521-29929-2*) Cambridge U Pr.
Lockhart, James, jt. auth. see Karttunen, Frances.
Lockhart, James, et al. The Tlaxcalan Actas: A Compendium of the Records of the Cabildo of Tlaxcala (1545-1627) LC 85-31510. (Illus.). 160p. 1986. 30.00 (*0-87480-253-9*) U of Utah Pr.
Lockhart, John G. Life of Robert Burns. Douglas, William S., ed. LC 70-144515. reprint ed. 20.00 (*0-404-08517-2*) AMS Pr.
— Life of Sir Walter Scott, 10 Vols, Set. LC 73-144426. (Illus.). 7536p. 1983. reprint ed. 345.00 (*0-404-07700-5*) AMS Pr.
— Peacemakers, Eighteen Fourteen to Eighteen Fifteen. LC 68-8479. (Essay Index Reprint Ser.). 1977. reprint ed. 21.95 (*0-8369-0622-5*) Ayer.
— Reginald Dalton: A Story of English University Life, 3 vols. in 2, Set. LC 79-8157. reprint ed. 84.50 (*0-404-61987-8*) AMS Pr.
Lockhart, John G., ed. Ancient Spanish Ballads, Historical & Romantic. LC 69-13245. (Illus.). 1972. reprint ed. 24.95 (*0-405-08752-7*, Pub. by Blom Pubns UK) Ayer.
Lockhart, Julie, ed. see Alexander, Skye.
Lockhart, Julie, ed. see Bunker, Dusty.
Lockhart, Julie, jt. auth. see Devin, Mary.
Lockhart, Julie, ed. see Javane, Faith.

An Asterisk (*) at the beginning of an entry indicates that the title is appearing in BIP for the first time.

Lockhart, Julie, ed. see Kelynda.

Lockhart, Julie, ed. see Neville, E. W.

Lockhart, Julie, ed. see Steiger, Brad & Steiger, Francie.

Lockhart, Kimball, tr. see Haineault, Doris-Louise & Roy, Jean-Yves.

Lockhart, Laurence. Nadir Shah: A Critical Study Based Mainly Upon Contemporary Sources. LC 78-180358. reprint ed. 28.45 (*0-404-56290-6*) AMS Pr.

Lockhart, Lisa, jt. auth. see Smith, Jodi T.

Lockhart, Lynn. Date with an Outlaw. (American Romance Ser.). 1993. mass mkt. 3.50 (*0-373-16498-X*, 1-16498-7) Harlequin Bks.

— Nickie's Ghost. (American Romance Ser.). 1994. mass mkt. 3.50 (*0-373-16527-7*, 1-16527-3) Harlequin Bks.

Lockhart, Lynne, jt. auth. see Lockhart, Barbara.

Lockhart, Lynne N. & Lockhart, Barbara. Rambling Raft. LC 89-50761. (Illus.). 30p. (J). (gr. k-5). 1989. 7.95 (*0-87033-392-5*, Tidewtr Pubs) Cornell Maritime.

Lockhart, Monique, tr. see Lang, Tam, et al.

Lockhart, Robert H. Comes the Reckoning. LC 72-4672. (International Propaganda & Communications Ser.). 392p. 1972. reprint ed. 23.95 (*0-405-04756-8*) Ayer.

— Two Revolutions. LC 67-24887. 1967. 16.95 (*0-8023-1124-5*) Dufour.

Lockhart, Robin B. First Man. write for info. (*0-670-80735-4*) Viking Penguin.

Lockhart, Russell A., jt. auth. see Dallett, Janett.

Lockhart, S. F. To My Pocket. 1984. 39.00 (*0-946270-09-0*, Pub. by Pentland Pr UK) St Mut.

Lockhart, Sally. I Feel a Symphony. (Illus.). 16p. (Orig.). 1986. pap. 4.00 (*0-9616899-1-9*) Anapauo Farm.

— Random & Rainbow Feelings. (Illus.). 16p. (Orig.). 1986. pap. 4.00 (*0-9616899-0-0*) Anapauo Farm.

***Lockhart, Sharon L.** Educational Malpractice: A Pathfinder. LC 95-5749. (Legal Research Guides Ser.: Vol. 22). 1995. write for info. (*0-89941-926-7*) W S Hein.

Lockhart, Shawna D. AutoCAD Release. LC 93-41523. (C). 1994. pap. text ed. 39.75 (*0-201-62344-7*) Addison-Wesley.

***Lockhart, Shawna D. & Reagh, Kevin P.** The Autodesk Collection: Professional Design Software for Collegiate Users. 528p. (C). 1994. pap. text ed. write for info. (*0-201-65623-X*) Addison-Wesley.

Lockhart, Vickie, ed. Catalog of California State Funding Sources 1993. 426p. 1993. pap. text ed. 35.00 (*0-929722-53-1*) CA State Library Fndtn.

Lockhart, Vincent. Dragons Yet to Slay. 288p. 1993. pap. 5.95 (*0-9635610-0-6*) A-L Pub.

Lockhart, William B., et al. The American Constitution, Cases - Comments - Questions. 7th ed. (American Casebook Ser.). 1193p. (C). 1991. text ed. 50.00 (*0-314-88939-6*) West Pub.

— Constitutional Law - The American Constitution - Constitutional Rights & Liberties. 7th suppl. ed. (American Casebook Ser.). 226p. 1993. pap. text ed. 12.50 (*0-314-02543-X*) West Pub.

— Constitutional Law - the American Constitution - Constitutional Rights & Liberties, 1994: Cases - Comments. suppl. ed. (American Casebook Ser.). 265p. 1994. pap. text ed. 14.00 (*0-314-04417-5*) West Pub.

— Constitutional Rights & Liberties, Cases - Comments - Questions. 7th ed. (American Casebook Ser.). 1333p. (C). 1991. text ed. 50.00 (*0-314-88940-X*) West Pub.

Lockhart, William E. English & Pre-Test: Placement Tests. (Michigan Prescriptive Program Ser.). (gr. 10). 1979. student ed 1.50 (*0-87879-838-2*, Ann Arbor Div); teacher ed 2.00 (*0-87879-840-4*, Ann Arbor Div) Acad Therapy.

— English Response Sheets & Prescription Sheets. (Michigan Prescriptive Program, High School Equivalency-GED Ser.). 1975. 3.00 (*0-87879-839-0*, Ann Arbor Div) Acad Therapy.

— English Study Material: High School Equivalency-GED. (Michigan Prescriptive Program Ser.). 1975. pap. text ed. 6.00 (*0-87879-837-4*, Ann Arbor Div) Acad Therapy.

— Michigan Prescriptive Program in Math. 200p. student ed 10.00 (*0-87879-841-2*); 15.00 (*0-87879-842-0*); 3.00 (*0-87879-843-9*); 2.00 (*0-87879-844-7*) Acad Therapy.

Lockhart, William J., jt. auth. see Martin, Terri.

Lockhead, Gregory & Pomerantz, James, eds. The Perception of Structure. 353p. 1991. text ed. 40.00 (*1-55798-125-6*) Am Psychol.

— The Perception of Structure. 353p. 1994. pap. 19.95 (*1-55798-263-5*) Am Psychol.

Lockhead, Jack, jt. auth. see Whimbey, Arthur.

Lockheed Aircraft Corporation Staff. Of Men & Stars: A History of Lockheed Aircraft Corporation. Gilbert, James B., ed. LC 79-7280. (Flight: Its First Seventy-Five Years Ser.). (Illus.). 1980. reprint ed. lib. bdg. 26.95 (*0-405-12189-X*) Ayer.

Lockheed, Marlaine E. & Longford, Nicholas T. A Multilevel Model of School Effectiveness in a Developing Country. (Discussion Paper Ser.). 74p. 1989. 7.95 (*0-8213-1417-3*, 11417) World Bank.

Lockheed, Marlaine E. & Verspoor, Adriaan M. Improving Primary Education in Developing Countries. (Illus.). 432p. 1992. 39.95 (*0-19-520872-2*, 60872) OUP.

Lockheed, Marlaine E., jt. ed. see Hannaway, Jane.

Lockheed, Marlaine E., jt. ed. see Levin, Henry M.

Lockheed Research Symposium on Space Science Staff. Auroral Phenomena: Experiments & Theory, Proceedings of the Lockheed Research Symposium on Space Science, 1st, Palo Alto, Calif., 1964. Walt, Martin, ed. LC 78-17993. 180p. reprint ed. pap. 51.30 (*0-8357-5885-0*, 2015528) Bks Demand.

Lockheed Symposium on Magnetohydrodynamics Staff. The Plasma in a Magnetic Field: A Symposium on Magnetohydrodynamics, 2nd, 1957, Palo Alto. LC 58-11698. 139p. reprint ed. pap. 39.70 (*0-317-07849-6*, 2000317) Bks Demand.

— Propagation & Instabilities in Plasmas: Proceedings of the Lockheed Symposium on Magnetohydrodynamics, Palo Alto, Calif, 1962. 7th ed. LC 63-19236. 155p. reprint ed. pap. 44.20 (*0-317-12970-8*, 2000318) Bks Demand.

— Radiation & Waves in Plasmas: Proceedings of the Lockheed Symposium on Magnetohydrodynamics, 5th, Palo Alto, Calif, 1960. Mitchner, Morton, ed. LC 61-14651. 167p. reprint ed. pap. 47.60 (*0-317-07864-X*, 2000319) Bks Demand.

Lockhoven, Hans B., jt. auth. see Nelson, Thomas B.

Lockie, Andrew. The Family Guide to Homeopathy: Symptoms & Natural Solutions. (Illus.). 464p. 1993. pap. 15.00 (*0-671-76771-2*, Fireside) S&S Trade.

***Lockie, Andrew & Geddes, Nicola.** Complete Guide to Homeopathy: The Principles & Practice of Treatment with a Comprehensive Range of Self-Help Remedies for Common Ailments. LC 95-6746. 240p. 1995. 29.95 (*0-7894-0148-7*, 6-70479) Dorling Kindersley.

— The Women's Guide to Homeopathy. 352p. (Orig.). 1994. pap. 14.95 (*0-312-09944-4*) St Martin.

Lockie, D. M., tr. see Tapie, Victor L.

Lockitch. Handbook of Diagnostic Biochemistry & Hematology. 1992. 99.95 (*0-8493-3518-3*, RG558) CRC Pr.

Locklear, Edmond, Jr. How to Avoid Dangerous Sexual Situations. LC 93-61886. (Sex in Religion Ser.: Vol. 1). 256p. (Orig.). 1994. pap. 16.95 (*0-9614336-1-2*) WFCPr.

Locklear, Elliot. Arnold Schwarzenegger's "Fitness for Kids" 56p. (J). (gr. k-6). 1994. student ed 2.95 (*1-885453-00-0*) Chldrns Better Hlth.

***Locklear, Paul J.** My Journey. 1995. 16.95 (*0-533-11174-9*) Vantage.

Lockler, et al. Historias y Cuentos le Todos los Tiempos. (Illus.). (gr. 3). 1977. teacher ed, text ed. 10.48 (*0-87443-014-3*) Benson.

Lockley, Andrew. The Pursuits of Quality: A Guide for Lawyers. 150p. 1993. 60.00 (*0-85459-751-4*, Pub. by Tolley Pubng UK) St Mut.

Lockley, Arthur S. Giant Schnauzers. (KW Ser.). (Illus.). 192p. 1993. text ed. 11.95 (*0-86622-574-9*, KW-204) TFH Pubns.

Lockley, Fred. Across the Plains by Prairie Schooner. (Shorey Historical Ser.). 23p. pap. 3.75 (*0-8466-0190-7*, S190) Shorey.

— The Lockley Files, Vol. 1: Conversations with Pioneer Women. Helm, Mike, ed. LC 81-50485. (Illus.). 310p. (Orig.). 1981. pap. 13.95 (*0-931742-08-0*) Rainy Day Oreg.

— The Lockley Files, Vol. 2: Bullwhackers, Muleskinners, Pioneers, Prospectors, 49ers, Indian Fighters, Trappers, Ex-Barkeepers, Authors, Preachers, Poets & Near-Poets, & All Sorts & Conditions of Men. LC 81-50845. 358p. 1981. pap. 11.95 (*0-931742-09-9*) Rainy Day Oreg.

— The Lockley Files, Vol. 3: Visionaries, Mountain Men & Empire Builders. LC 81-50845. 396p. 1982. pap. 13.95 (*0-931742-10-2*) Rainy Day Oreg.

— The Lockley Files, Vol. 4: A Bit of Verse: Poems from the Lockley Files. Helm, Mike, ed. & intro. by. LC 81-50845. 164p. (Orig.). 1983. pap. 7.95 (*0-931742-13-7*) Rainy Day Oreg.

— Recollections of Benjamin Franklin Bonney. 1971. reprint ed. pap. 2.50 (*0-87770-060-5*) Ye Galleon.

— Reminiscences of Colonel Henry Ernst Dosch. 19p. 1972. pap. 2.50 (*0-87770-081-8*) Ye Galleon.

— To Oregon by Ox Team in '47. 18p. reprint ed. pap. 2.95 (*0-8466-0145-1*, S145) Shorey.

— Vigilante Days at Virginia City. 21p. reprint ed. pap. 2.95 (*0-8466-0146-X*, SJS146) Shorey.

Lockley, M. & Rice, A., eds. Volcanism & Fossil Biotas. (Special Paper Ser.: No. 244). (Illus.). 136p. 1990. 27.50 (*0-8137-2244-6*) Geol Soc.

Lockley, Martin. Tracking Dinosaurs: A New Look at an Ancient World. (Illus.). 249p. (C). 1991. pap. 16.95 (*0-521-42598-0*) Cambridge U Pr.

— Tracking Dinosaurs: A New Look at an Ancient World. (Illus.). 249p. (C). 1991. 44.95 (*0-521-39463-5*) Cambridge U Pr.

***Lockley, Martin & Hunt, Adrian.** Dinosaur Tracks & Other Fossil Footprints of the Western United States. 1995. 29.50 (*0-231-07926-5*) Col U Pr.

Lockley, Martin, jt. ed. see Gillette, David D.

***Lockley, Paul.** Counselling Heroin & Other Drug Users. 315p. 1995. 50.00 (*1-85343-312-8*); pap. 24.95 (*1-85343-304-7*) NYU Pr.

Lockley, R. M. Birds & Islands: The Nature Diaries of Ronald Lockley. 224p. (C). 1989. 110.00 (*0-685-36404-6*, Pub. by Witherby & Co UK) St Mut.

— Dream Island: A Record of the Simple Life. (Illus.). 166p. 1989. pap. 13.95 (*0-85493-162-7*, Pub. by V Gollancz UK) Trafalgar.

— Grey Seal, Common Seal. (Illus.). 1966. 12.50 (*0-8079-0060-5*) October.

Lockley, Ronald M. Puffins. 10.00 (*0-8159-6511-7*) Devin.

— Saga of the Grey Seal. 8.50 (*0-8159-6801-9*) Devin.

Locklin, D. W. & Hazard, H. R. Power Plant Utilization of Coal. (Battelle Energy Program Report Ser.: No. 3). 109p. reprint ed. pap. 31.10 (*0-317-09957-4*, 2005135) Bks Demand.

Locklin, David P. Economics of Transportation. 7th ed. LC 76-187057. (Irwin Series in Economics). 924p. reprint ed. pap. 180.00 (*0-317-27981-5*, 2055816) Bks Demand.

Locklin, Gerald. The Case of the Missing Blue Volkswagen. LC 84-12442. 114p. (Orig.). 1984. pap. 6.95 (*0-930090-22-5*) Applezaba.

— The Case of the Missing Blue Volkswagen. deluxe limited ed. LC 84-12442. 114p. (Orig.). 1984. 15.00 (*0-930090-21-7*) Applezaba.

— The Chase. LC 76-5706. (Illus.). 1976. pap. 3.00 (*0-916918-00-9*) Duck Down.

— The Criminal Mentality. 1976. pap. 2.50 (*0-88031-031-6*) Invisible-Red Hill.

— The Cure: A Novel for Speed Readers. LC 78-69789. 1979. pap. 3.95 (*0-930090-04-7*) Applezaba.

— The Death of Jean-Paul Sartre & Other Poems. 32p. 1988. pap. 4.50 (*0-941160-10-6*) Ghost Pony Pr.

— The Firebird Poems. LC 91-74040. 128p. 1992. pap. 12.95 (*0-9627501-8-2*) Event Horizon.

— Frisco Epic. 1978. 3.00 (*0-917554-07-8*) Maelstrom.

— Gerald Haslam. LC 87-70032. (Western Writers Ser.: No. 77). (Illus.). 51p. (Orig.). 1987. pap. 3.95 (*0-88430-076-5*) Boise St U W Writ Ser.

— The Gold Rush & Other Stories. LC 89-6768. 174p. 1989. 24.95 (*0-930090-40-3*); pap. text ed. 8.95 (*0-930090-41-1*) Applezaba.

— The Gold Rush & Other Stories. deluxe ed. LC 89-6768. 174p. 1989. 30.00 (*0-930090-39-X*) Applezaba.

— Locked in. 1973. 5.00 (*0-917554-18-3*) Maelstrom.

— The Old Mongoose & Other Poems. 35p. (Orig.). 1993. pap. 6.00 (*0-9628094-6-2*) Pearl Edit.

— On the Rack. 24p. (Orig.). 1988. pap. 4.00 (*0-916155-09-9*) Trout Creek.

— The Phantom of the Johnny Carson Show. (Talltales Ser.). 10p. (Orig.). 1984. pap. 1.95 (*0-89807-115-1*) Illuminati.

— Scenes from a Second Adolescence, & Other Poems. 1979. pap. 4.95 (*0-930090-08-X*) Applezaba.

— Son of Poop. 1973. 5.00 (*0-917554-14-0*) Maelstrom.

— Toad Turns Fifty: Selected Poems by Gerald Locklin. Lloyd, D. H., ed. 128p. 1993. 23.95 (*0-930090-60-8*); pap. 10.95 (*0-930090-62-4*) Applezaba.

— Toad Turns Fifty: Selected Poems by Gerald Locklin. deluxe ed. Lloyd, D. H., ed. 128p. 1993. 30.00 (*0-930090-61-6*) Applezaba.

— Two Summer Sequences. 1979. 4.00 (*0-917554-10-8*) Maelstrom.

Locklin, Gerald & Stetler, Charles, eds. A New Geography of Poets. LC 91-46003. 376p. 1992. 30.00 (*1-55728-240-4*); pap. 16.95 (*1-55728-241-2*) U of Ark Pr.

Locklin, Gerald & Zepeda, Rafael. By Land, Sea & Air. (Illus.). 60p. (Orig.). 1982. pap. 3.00 (*0-917554-21-3*) Maelstrom.

Locklin, Gerald, et al. Tarzan & Shane Meet the Toad. limited ed. 1975. 4.00 (*0-917554-01-9*) Maelstrom.

Lockman, Barbara. A Century's Child: The Story of Thompson Children's Home. Dixon, Stern, ed. LC 85-52345. (Illus.). 145p. 1986. 10.00 (*0-912081-02-3*) Delmar Co.

Lockman, F. J., jt. ed. see Blitz, Leo.

Lockman Foundation Staff. Biblia de las Americas. LC 86-81191. 1752p. 1986. text ed. 32.95 (*0-910618-41-0*) Foun Pubns.

— Biblia de las Americas. deluxe ed. LC 86-81191. 1752p. 1986. 44.95 (*0-910618-40-2*) Foun Pubns.

— La Biblia de las Americas. deluxe ed. 1752p. (SPA.). 1986. 59.95 (*0-910618-45-3*) Foun Pubns.

— NAS Ultra Thin Reference Bible: Dusty Rose Bonded Leather. (NAS UltraThin Reference Ser.). (Illus.). 1184p. 1988. 45.99 (*1-55819-084-8*, 4611-36) Holman Bible Pub.

— NAS Ultra Thin Reference Bible: Dusty Rose Bonded Leather. deluxe ed. (NAS UltraThin Reference Ser.). (Illus.). 1184p. 1988. 39.99 (*1-55819-083-X*, 4611-35) Holman Bible Pub.

Lockman, J. J. & Hazen, N. L., eds. Action in Social Context: Perspectives on Early Development. (Perspectives in Developmental Psychology Ser.). (Illus.). 326p. 1989. 54.50 (*0-306-43139-4*, Plenum Pr) Plenum.

Lockman, Vic. Biblical Economics in Comics. (Illus.). 112p. (Orig.). 1985. pap. 6.95 (*0-936175-00-1*) V Lockman.

— The Big Book of Cartooning, Bk. I. (Illus.). 104p. (Orig.). 1990. spiral bd., pap. 12.00 (*0-936175-08-7*) V Lockman.

— The Big Book of Cartooning, Bk. II: Animals. (Illus.). 48p. 1991. spiral bd. 8.00 (*0-936175-15-X*) V Lockman.

— Big Book of Cartooning Drawing for Girls. (Illus.). 70p. 1993. spiral bd. 10.00 (*0-936175-26-5*) V Lockman.

— The Book of Revelation: A Cartoon Illustrated Commentary. 60p. 1993. 6.00 (*0-936175-24-9*) V Lockman.

— Cartooning for Young Children, Bk. I. (Illus.). 48p. 1991. spiral bd. 6.95 (*0-936175-16-8*) V Lockman.

— Cartooning for Young Children, Bk. II. (Illus.). 48p. (J). (ps-8). 1992. 6.95 (*0-936175-23-0*) V Lockman.

— The Catechism for Young Children with Cartoons, Bk. 1. (Illus.). 45p. (Orig.). (J). (ps-6). 1984. pap. 1.50 (*0-936175-01-X*); pap. text ed. 1.00 (*0-936175-03-6*) V Lockman.

— Catechism for Young Children with Cartoons, Bk II. (Illus.). 45p. (Orig.). 1985. pap. 1.50 (*0-936175-02-8*) V Lockman.

— God's Law for Modern Man. (Illus.). 60p. (YA). 1993. 6.00 (*0-936175-25-7*) V Lockman.

— In These Last Days. (Illus.). 60p. 1994. 6.00 (*0-936175-27-3*) V Lockman.

— Machines. (Big Book of Cartooning Ser.: No. 5). (Illus.). 48p. (Orig.). (YA). (gr. 8 up). 1992. pap. 5.95 (*0-936175-20-6*) V Lockman.

— Miracle Art: Trick Cartoons. (Illus.). 48p. (Orig.). (YA). (gr. 8 up). 1992. pap. 5.95 (*0-936175-19-2*) V Lockman.

— Money, Banking, & Usury. (Illus.). 36p. 1991. 3.95 (*0-936175-09-5*) V Lockman.

— Reading & Understanding the Bible. (Illus.). 56p. (J). (gr. 6). 1992. 5.95 (*0-936175-18-4*) V Lockman.

— Super Bug Leads Tim Burr to the Gospel in the Woods. (Biblical Educational & Recreational Story Book Ser.). (Illus.). 24p. (Orig.). (J). (gr. 8 up). 1991. pap. 2.95 (*0-936175-14-1*) V Lockman.

— Water, Water...Everywhere. 36p. 1992. 3.95 (*0-936175-17-6*) V Lockman.

— Who Stopped the Clock? The Seventy Weeks of Daniel. (Illus.). 24p. 1993. 3.00 (*0-936175-21-4*) V Lockman.

Lockman, Vic, jt. auth. see Schiff, Irwin A.

Lockman, Zachary, ed. Workers & Working Classes in the Middle East: Struggles, Histories, Historiographies. LC 92-42701. (SUNY Series in the Social & Economic History of the Middle East). 341p. (C). 1993. 64.50 (*0-7914-1665-8*); pap. 21.95 (*0-7914-1666-6*) State U NY Pr.

Lockman, Zachary & Beinin, Joel, eds. Intifada: The Palestinian Uprising Against Israeli Occupation. LC 89-11595. 423p. 1989. 35.00 (*0-89608-365-9*); pap. 15.00 (*0-89608-363-2*) South End Pr.

Lockman, Zachary, jt. auth. see Beinin, Joel.

Lockmiller, David A. Scholars on Parade. 290p. 1993. pap. 15.95 (*1-57087-002-0*) Prof Pr NC.

Lockridge. Death Has a Small Voice. 1976. 18.95 (*0-89190-905-2*) Amereon Ltd.

Lockridge, Ernest, ed. Twentieth Century Interpretations of The Great Gatsby. (Orig.). (YA). (gr. 9-12). 1968. 22.50 (*0-13-363820-0*, Spectrum Bks); pap. 2.95 (*0-13-363812-X*, Spectrum Bks) P-H.

Lockridge, F. & Lockridge, R. Death Takes a Bow. (Mr. & Mrs. North Mysteries Ser.). 19.95 (*0-89190-918-4*, Am Repr) Amereon Ltd.

Lockridge, Frances & Lockridge, Richard. And Left for Dead. (Mr. & Mrs. North Mystery Ser.). 18.95 (*0-89190-912-5*, Am Repr) Amereon Ltd.

— Catch As Catch Can. 1976. 18.95 (*0-89190-913-3*) Amereon Ltd.

— Cats & People. Rao, Maya & Turner, Philip, eds. (Kodansha Globe Ser.). (Illus.). 288p. 1996. pap. 12.00 (*1-56836-115-7*, Kodansha Globe) Kodansha.

— A Client Is Cancelled. large type ed. (Popular Ser.). 280p. 1993. reprint ed. pap. 17.95 (*1-56054-299-3*) Thorndike Pr.

— Curtain for a Jester. large type ed. 316p. 1992. reprint ed. lib. bdg. 19.95 (*1-56054-238-1*) Thorndike Pr.

— Curtain for a Jester. (Mr. & Mrs. North Ser.). 222p. 1975. reprint ed. lib. bdg. 19.95 (*0-89190-904-4*, Rivercity Pr) Amereon Ltd.

— Dead As a Dinosaur. large type ed. 333p. 1991. reprint ed. lib. bdg. 19.95 (*1-56054-129-6*) Thorndike Pr.

— Dead As a Dinosaur. (Mr. & Mrs. North Ser.). 185p. 1975. reprint ed. lib. bdg. 19.95 (*0-89190-903-6*, Rivercity Pr) Amereon Ltd.

— Dead As a Dinosaur. 1993. reprint ed. lib. bdg. 17.95 (*1-56849-208-1*) Buccaneer Bks.

— Death Has a Small Voice. large type ed. LC 90-10809. 224p. 1990. lib. bdg. 19.95 (*0-89621-991-7*) Thorndike Pr.

— Death Has a Small Voice. 1993. reprint ed. lib. bdg. 17.95 (*1-56849-209-X*) Buccaneer Bks.

— Death of an Angel. large type ed. LC 90-44505. 296p. 1990. reprint ed. lib. bdg. 19.95 (*1-56054-058-3*) Thorndike Pr.

— Death of an Angel. (Mr. & Mrs. North Ser.). 1975. reprint ed. lib. bdg. 19.95 (*0-89190-907-9*, Rivercity Pr) Amereon Ltd.

— The Dishonest Murderer. 223p. 1975. reprint ed. lib. bdg. 19.95 (*0-89190-901-X*) Amereon Ltd.

— The Judge Is Reversed. large type ed. 279p. 1991. reprint ed. bds. 19.95 (*1-56054-103-2*) Thorndike Pr.

— Judge Is Reversed. 1975. reprint ed. lib. bdg. 19.95 (*0-89190-910-9*, Rivercity Pr) Amereon Ltd.

— A Key to Death. large type ed. LC 91-3570. 285p. 1991. reprint ed. bds. 19.95 (*1-56054-183-0*) Thorndike Pr.

— Key to Death. 224p. 1975. reprint ed. lib. bdg. 19.95 (*0-89190-906-0*, Rivercity Pr) Amereon Ltd.

— Long Skeleton. 1975. reprint ed. lib. bdg. 19.95 (*0-89190-909-5*, Rivercity Pr) Amereon Ltd.

— Murder by the Book. large type ed. LC 91-22667. 290p. 1991. reprint ed. bds. 19.95 (*1-56054-222-5*) Thorndike Pr.

— Murder Can't Wait. large type ed. LC 90-36323. 297p. 1990. reprint ed. bds. 19.95 (*1-56054-026-5*) Thorndike Pr.

— Murder Comes First. 192p. 1975. reprint ed. lib. bdg. 20.95 (*0-89190-902-8*, Rivercity Pr) Amereon Ltd.

— Murder Has Its Points. large type ed. LC 91-39570. 295p. 1992. reprint ed. bds. 19.95 (*1-56054-239-X*) Thorndike Pr.

— Murder out of Turn. 16.95 (*0-89190-914-1*, Am Repr) Amereon Ltd.

— A Pinch of Poison. 16.95 (*0-89190-917-6*, Am Repr) Amereon Ltd.

— Untidy Murder. large type ed. LC 92-23912. 333p. 1992. reprint ed. lib. bdg. 17.95 (*1-56054-298-5*) Thorndike Pr.

— Voyage into Violence. 1975. reprint ed. lib. bdg. 19.95 (*0-89190-908-7*, Rivercity Pr) Amereon Ltd.

— Voyage Into Violence: A Mr. & Mrs. North Mystery. large type ed. LC 93-12738. 1993. Alk. paper. pap. 17.95 (*1-56054-300-0*) Thorndike Pr.

Lockridge, Frances, jt. auth. see Lockridge, Richard.

Lockridge, Kenneth A. The Diary & Life, of William Bryd II of Virginia, 1674-1744. 1991. pap. 10.95 (*0-393-95682-2*) Norton.

— The Diary, & Life, of William Byrd II of Virginia, 1674-1744. LC 86-40425. (Institute of Early American History & Culture Ser.). xiv, 202p. 1987. 27.50 (*0-8078-1736-8*) U of NC Pr.

— Literacy in Colonial New England: An Inquiry into the Social Context of Literacy in the Early Modern West. (Illus.). (C). 1974. text ed. 6.95 (*0-393-05522-1*) Norton.

— Literacy in Colonial New England: An Inquiry into the Social Context of Literacy in the Early Modern West. (Illus.). (C). 1975. pap. text ed. 3.95 (*0-393-09263-1*) Norton.

— A New England Town: The First Hundred Years. 2nd ed. (Essays in American History Ser.). (C). 1985. pap. text ed. 9.95 (*0-393-95459-5*) Norton.

An Asterisk (*) at the beginning of an entry indicates that the title is appearing in BIP for the first time.

— On the Sources of Patriarchal Rage: The Commonplace Books of William Byrd II & Thomas Jefferson & the Gendering of Power in the Eighteenth Century. (Illus.). 133p. (C). 1993. text ed. 40.00 (*0-8147-5069-9*); pap. text ed. 15.00 (*0-8147-5089-3*) NYU Pr.

Lockridge, Larry. Shade of the Raintree: The Life & Death of Ross Lockridge, Jr. (Illus.). 528p. 1994. 27.95 (*0-670-85440-9*, Viking) Viking Penguin.

— Shade of the Raintree: The Life & Death of Ross Lockridge, Jr. (Illus.). 528p. 1995. pap. 14.95 (*0-14-015871-5*, Penguin Bks) Viking Penguin.

Lockridge, Laurence S. The Ethics of Romanticism. (C). 1989. 74.95 (*0-521-35256-8*) Cambridge U Pr.

Lockridge, Laurence S., et al, eds. Nineteenth-Century Lives: Essays Presented to Jerome Hamilton Buckley. (Illus.). 210p. (C). 1989. 69.95 (*0-521-34181-7*) Cambridge U Pr.

Lockridge, R., jt. auth. see Lockridge, F.

Lockridge, Richard. Darling of Misfortune: Edwin Booth. LC 79-91908. 1972. 30.95 (*0-405-08753-5*, Pub. by Blom Pubns UK) Ayer.

— Die Laughing. large type ed. LC 91-40154. 303p. 1992. lib. bdg. 19.95 (*1-56054-240-3*) Thorndike Pr.

Lockridge, Richard & Lockridge, Frances. Accent on Murder: A Captain Heimrich Mystery. large type ed. LC 93-13220. 1993. 17.95 (*1-56054-301-9*) Thorndike Pr.

— Death by Association. large type ed. LC 94-25980. 322p. 1995. pap. 17.95 (*1-56054-306-X*) Thorndike Pr.

— I Want to Go Home. large type ed. LC 93-13224. 1993. bds. 17.95 (*1-56054-302-7*) Thorndike Pr.

— Killing the Goose. 20.95 (*0-89190-911-7*, Am Repr) Amereon Ltd.

— Let Dead Enough Alone: A Captain Heimrich Mystery. large type ed. LC 94-33676. 235p. 1995. pap. 17.95 (*0-7838-1159-4*, Large Print Bks) Hall.

— Show Red for Danger: A Captain Heimrich Mystery. large type ed. LC 93-31000. (Popular Series: First Library Edition, 1985 (Condensed Print)). 1994. pap. 17. 95 (*1-56054-303-5*) Thorndike Pr.

— Stand Up & Die: A Captain Heimrich Mystery. large type ed. LC 94-19359. 296p. Date not set. lib. bdg. 17.95 (*1-56054-305-1*) Thorndike Pr.

Lockridge, Richard, jt. auth. see Lockridge, Frances.

Lockridge, Ross, Jr. Raintree County. 1066p. 1991. reprint ed. lib. bdg. 49.95 (*0-89966-865-8*) Buccaneer Bks.

— Raintree County: A Great American Novel about Love, Tragedy, & the American Dream. 1088p. 1994. pap. 18. 95 (*0-14-023666-X*, Penguin Bks) Viking Penguin.

Lockridge, Ross F. The Labyrinth. LC 75-336. (Radical Tradition in America Ser.). (Illus.). 94p. 1975. reprint ed. 15.00 (*0-88355-239-6*) Hyperion Conn.

Locks, Doris C. Multistate Sales & Use Tax Manual, 2 vols. 1993. ring bd. 295.00 (*0-685-69588-3*, CSTC) Warren Gorham & Lamont.

Locks, Marian, contrib. Thomas Chimes. LC 90-60705. (Orig.). 1990. pap. text ed. 15.00 (*0-9623799-2-1*) Locks Gallery.

***Locks, Mitchell O.** Reliability, Maintainability, & Availability Assessment. 2nd ed. LC 94-40648. 1995. 65. 00 (*0-87389-293-3*) ASQC Qual Pr.

Locks, Sueyun, frwd. Wonsook Kim Linton. (Illus.). 6p. 1991. pap. 2.00 (*0-685-62372-6*) Locks Gallery.

Lockshin, Martin I., tr. see Ben Meir, Samuel.

Lockshin, R., jt. auth. see Bowen, I. D.

Lockshin, Stephanie, jt. auth. see Romanczyk, Raymond G.

***Lockton, Deborah.** Employment Law. (Student Statutes Ser.). 352p. 1993. pap. text ed. 18.00 (*0-406-02302-6*, UK) Butterworth Legal Pubs.

Lockton, Deborah J. Effective Contracts of Employment. 165p. 1992. 60.00 (*1-85190-159-0*, Pub. by Tolley Pubng UK) St Mut.

Lockward, A. Algunas Cruces Altas (Some High Crosses) (SPA.). Date not set. 6.99 (*1-56063-159-7*, 490218) Editorial Unilit.

Lockward, Alonso. La Responsabilidad Social Del Creyente (The Christian's Social Responsibility) (SPA.). 1993. 4.50 (*1-56063-303-4*, 498523) Editorial Unilit.

Lockwood, A., jt. ed. see Cooper, C. P.

Lockwood, A

Lockwood, A., jt. ed. see Cooper, C.P.

Lockwood, A. P., ed. Effects of Pollutants on Aquatic Organisms. LC 75-32448. (Society for Experimental Biology Seminar Ser.: No. 2). 180p. 1976. pap. 24.95 (*0-521-29044-9*) Cambridge U Pr.

Lockwood, Alan H. Hepatic Encephalopathy. LC 92-16162. (Illus.). 160p. 1992. text ed. 75.00 (*0-7506-9234-0*) Buttrwrth-Heinemann.

Lockwood, Alan L. & Harris, David E. Reasoning with Democratic Values: Ethical Problems in United States History, 2 vols. (gr. 9-12). 1985. teacher ed 11.95 (*0-8077-6101-X*) Tchrs Coll.

— Reasoning with Democratic Values: Ethical Problems in United States History, 2 vols., Vol. I: 1607-1876. (gr. 9-12). 1985. 9.95 (*0-8077-6094-3*) Tchrs Coll.

— Reasoning with Democratic Values: Ethical Problems in United States History, 2 vols., Vol. II: 1877 to Present. (gr. 9-12). 1985. 12.95 (*0-8077-6095-1*) Tchrs Coll.

Lockwood, Albert. Notes on the Literature of the Piano. LC 67-30400. (Music Ser.). 1968. reprint ed. lib. bdg. 32.50 (*0-306-70983-X*) Da Capo.

Lockwood, Allison. Passionate Pilgrims. LC 78-66808. (Illus.). 551p. 1981. 37.50 (*0-8453-4725-X*, Cornwall Bks) Assoc Univ Prs.

— Passionate Pilgrims: The American Traveler in Great Britain, 1800-1914. LC 78-66808. 650p. 1981. 37.50 (*0-8386-2272-0*) Fairleigh Dickinson.

Lockwood, Allison M. Children of Paradise: A Northampton Memoir. (Illus.). 166p. (Orig.). 1986. pap. 9.95 (*0-9618052-0-X*) Daily Hampshire.

— No Ordinary Man: Judge Forbes & His Library. (Illus.). 136p. (Orig.). 1994. pap. 12.95 (*0-9618052-4-2*) Daily Hampshire.

— Touched with Fire: An American Community in WWII. (Illus.). 216p. (Orig.). 1993. pap. 19.95 (*0-9618052-3-4*) Daily Hampshire.

***Lockwood, Andrew & Davis, Bernard.** Food & Beverage Management: A Selection of Readings. 250p. 1995. pap. 37.95 (*0-7506-1950-3*) Buttrwrth-Heinemann.

Lockwood, Antony P. Animal Body Fluids & Their Regulation. LC 64-9913. (Illus.). 184p. 1963. 21.50 (*0-674-03700-6*) HUP.

Lockwood, Barbara & McAuley, Marilyn. Bible Surprises. LC 87-71384. (Peek & Find Ser.). (J). (ps). 1992. bds. 4.99 (*1-55513-120-4*, Chariot Bks) Chariot Family.

— God Keeps Them Safe. LC 87-62019. (Peek & Find Ser.). (J). (ps). 1988. bds. 4.99 (*1-55513-518-8*, Chariot Bks) Chariot Family.

— God Made Little & Big. LC 87-62019. (Peek & Find Ser.). (J). (ps). 1988. bds. 4.99 (*1-55513-517-X*, Chariot Bks) Chariot Family.

— Good Gifts from God. LC 87-71383. (Peek & Find Ser.). (J). (ps). 1988. bds. 4.99 (*1-55513-366-5*, Chariot Bks) Chariot Family.

Lockwood, Brocton & Mendenhall, Harlan H. Operation Greylord: The Brocton Lockwood Story. LC 89-6022. (Illus.). 224p. (C). 1989. 19.95 (*0-8093-1545-9*) S Ill U Pr.

Lockwood, C. C. Atchafalaya. 1984. 35.00 (*0-87511-695-7*) Claitors.

— C. C. Lockwood's Louisiana Nature Guide for Kids. LC 94-38613. (Illus.). 94p. (J). 1995. 19.95 (*0-8071-1989-X*) La State U Pr.

Lockwood, C. C., photos & text. Discovering Louisiana. LC 83-25614. (Illus.). vii, 150p. 1986. 39.95 (*0-8071-1335-2*) La State U Pr.

— Gulf Coast: Where Land Meets Sea. LC 83-25614. (Illus.). xvii, 150p. 1984. 34.95 (*0-8071-1170-8*) La State U Pr.

— The Yucatan Peninsula. LC 88-27260. (Illus.). xiv, 160p. 1989. 34.95 (*0-8071-1524-X*) La State U Pr.

Lockwood, Charles. Bricks & Brownstone: The New York Row House, 1783-1929. (Illus.). 288p. 1988. 39.95 (*0-89659-785-7*) Abbeville Pr.

***Lockwood, D.** The Physics of Semiconductors: Proceedings of the 22nd International Conference, 3 vols. 2400p. 1995. text ed. 446.00 (*981-02-2021-9*) World Scientific Pub.

Lockwood, D. J. & Young, J. F., eds. Light Scattering in Semiconductor Structures & Superlattices. (NATO ASI Series B, Physics: Vol. 273). (Illus.). 610p. 1991. 145.00 (*0-306-44036-9*, Plenum Pr) Plenum.

Lockwood, David. The Blackcoated Worker: A Study in Class Consciousness. 2nd ed. 272p. 1989. 64.00 (*0-19-827840-3*) OUP.

— Francis Kilvert. 160p. 1990. 27.95 (*1-85411-032-2*, Pub. by Seren Bks UK) Dufour.

— Solidarity & Schism: The Problem of Disorder in Durkheimian & Marxist Sociology. 472p. 1992. 87.00 (*0-19-827717-2*) OUP.

— Winter Wheat. 61p. (C). 1986. pap. 20.00x (*0-86383-229-6*, Pub. by Gomer Pr UK) St Mut.

Lockwood, David, ed. Kilvert, the Victorian: A New Selection from Kilvert's Diaries. (Illus.). 288p. 1992. 35. 00 (*1-85411-077-2*, Pub. by Seren Bks UK) Dufour.

Lockwood, David G., jt. auth. see Makkai, Adam.

Lockwood, David J. & Pinczuk, Aron, eds. Optical Phenomena in Semiconductor Structures of Reduced Dimensions: Proceedings of the NATO Advanced Research Workshop on Frontiers of Optical Phenomena in Semiconductor Structures of Reduced Dimensions, Yountville, California, U. S. A. July 27-31, 1992. LC 93-31755. (NATO Advanced Study Institutes Series E, Applied Sciences: No. 248). 466p. (C). 1993. lib. bdg. 186.50 (*0-7923-2512-5*) Kluwer Ac.

Lockwood, David J., jt. auth. see Cottam, Michael G.

Lockwood, Dean H., jt. auth. see Streck, William F.

Lockwood, Deborah, comp. Library Instruction: A Bibliography. LC 78-20011. 166p. 1979. text ed. 42.95 (*0-313-20720-8*, LLI/, Greenwood Pr) Greenwood.

Lockwood, DeLauna, ed. Cumulative Index to Nursing & Allied Health Literature, Vol. 31. LC 79-642922. 1986. 96.00 (*0-910478-23-6*) Cum Index Nursing.

— Cumulative Index to Nursing & Allied Health Literature, Vol. 32. LC 79-642922. 1987. 175.00 (*0-910478-24-4*) Cum Index Nursing.

— Cumulative Index to Nursing & Allied Health Literature, Vol. 33. LC 79-642922. 1988. 175.00 (*0-910478-25-2*) Cum Index Nursing.

— Cumulative Index to Nursing & Allied Health Literature, Vol. 34. LC 79-642922. 1989. 150.00 (*0-910478-26-0*) Cum Index Nursing.

— Cumulative Index to Nursing & Allied Health Literature, Vol. 35. LC 79-642922. 1990. 198.00 (*0-910478-30-9*) Cum Index Nursing.

— Cumulative Index to Nursing & Allied Health Literature, Vol. 36. LC 79-642922. 1991. write for info. (*0-910478-33-3*) Cum Index Nursing.

— Cumulative Index to Nursing & Allied Health Literature, Vol. 37. LC 79-642922. 1992. write for info. (*0-910478-39-2*) Cum Index Nursing.

— Cumulative Index to Nursing & Allied Health Literature, Vol. 38. LC 79-642922. 1993. write for info. (*0-910478-45-7*) Cum Index Nursing.

— Cumulative Index to Nursing & Allied Health Literature, Vol. 39. LC 79-642922. 1994. write for info. (*0-910478-48-1*) Cum Index Nursing.

Lockwood, E., jt. ed. see Strickland, L. H.

Lockwood, E. D., jt. auth. see Holden, F. A.

Lockwood, Edgar. South Africa's Moment of Truth. 196p. 1988. pap. 5.95 (*0-377-00180-5*) Friendship Pr.

Lockwood, Elinor. Miranda. 1977. pap. 1.95 (*0-8439-0508-5*) Dorchester Pub Co.

Lockwood, Frank. The Law & Lawyers of Pickwick. LC 72-1862. (Studies in Dickens: No. 52). 1972. reprint ed. lib. bdg. 49.95 (*0-8383-1445-7*) M S G Haskell Hse.

Lockwood, Frank C. The Apache Indians. LC 86-25103. (Illus.). xxxii, 388p. 1987. reprint ed. pap. 11.95 (*0-8032-7925-6*) U of Nebr Pr.

— Thumbnail Sketches of Famous Arizona Desert Riders, 1538-1946. LC 73-148224. (Biography Index Reprint Ser.). 1977. 16.95 (*0-8369-8071-9*) Ayer.

Lockwood, Frank C., ed. see Barnes, Will C.

Lockwood, Fred. Activities in Self Instructional Texts. (Illus.). 160p. (C). 1992. pap. text ed. 29.95 (*0-89397-379-3*) Nichols Pub.

— Data Collection in Distance Education Research: The Use of Self-Recorded Audiotape. (C). 1991. pap. 24.00x (*0-7300-1351-0*, IDE806, Pub. by Deakin Univ AT) St Mut.

— How to Design & Produce Flexible Learning Materials. (Flexible Learning Staff Development Program Ser.). 192p. 1995. pap. 39.95x (*0-7494-1455-3*, Pub. by Kogan Page Educ UK) Taylor & Francis.

— How to Present & Evaluate Flexible Learning Materials. (Flexible Learning Staff Development Program Ser.). 192p. 1995. pap. 39.95x (*0-7494-1456-1*, Pub. by Kogan Page Educ UK) Taylor & Francis.

***Lockwood, Fred, ed.** Open & Distance Learning Today. LC 95-8130. (Studies in Distance Education). 1995. write for info. (*0-415-12758-0*); pap. write for info. (*0-415-12759-9*) Routledge.

Lockwood, Fred, ed. see Calder, Judith.

Lockwood, Fred, ed. see Evans, Terry.

Lockwood, Fred, ed. see Henry, Jane.

Lockwood, Fred, ed. see Mason, Robin.

Lockwood, Fred, ed. see Robinson, Bernadette.

Lockwood, Fred, ed. see Rowntree, Derek.

Lockwood, G. New Harmony Communities. 1972. 59.95 (*0-8490-0722-4*) Gordon Pr.

Lockwood, Gayle R. Libbie Sims, Worry Wart. 144p. (J). (gr. 3-7). 1993. 13.99 (*0-670-84863-8*) Viking Child Bks.

Lockwood, George B. The New Harmony Communities. LC 72-134410. reprint ed. 34.50 (*0-404-08456-7*) AMS Pr.

— New Harmony Movement. LC 76-134411. reprint ed. 25. 00 (*0-404-08457-5*) AMS Pr.

— New Harmony Movement. LC 68-56245. (Illus.). 1970. reprint ed. 45.00 (*0-678-00667-9*) Kelley.

Lockwood, Glenda. Diary of a Human Shield. (Illus.). 230p. 1992. pap. 17.95 (*0-7475-1090-3*, Pub. by Bloomsbury Pub Ltd UK) Trafalgar.

Lockwood, Helen D. Tools & the Man. LC 21-12534. reprint ed. 14.75 (*0-404-03999-5*) AMS Pr.

Lockwood, Ingersoll. Baron Trump's Marvellous Underground Journey. 235p. 1972. reprint ed. spiral bd. 10.45 (*0-7873-0567-7*) Mokelumne.

Lockwood, James R., jt. auth. see Runion, Garth E.

Lockwood, Jill, jt. auth. see Martin, M.

Lockwood, Joanne. Scroll Saw Woodcrafting Magic! 2nd ed. 304p. 1995. pap. 16.95 (*1-56523-024-8*) Fox Chapel Pub.

Lockwood, John, jt. ed. see Smith, William.

Lockwood, Jonathan S. The Soviet View of U. S. Strategic Doctrine: Implications for Decisionmaking. LC 82-14191. (Illus.). 202p. 1983. 34.95 (*0-87855-467-X*) Transaction Pubs.

Lockwood, Jonathan S. & Lockwood, Kathleen O. The Russian View of U. S. Strategy: Its Past - Its Future. 2nd ed. 233p. (C). 1992. 32.95 (*1-56000-031-7*) Transaction Pubs.

Lockwood, Karen. Harvest Song. (Homespun Ser.). 336p. (Orig.). 1993. mass mkt. 4.99 (*1-55773-841-6*) Diamond.

— Stolen Kisses. (Orig.). 1994. pap. 4.99 (*0-515-11490-1*) Jove Pubns.

— Winter Song. 1993. mass mkt. 4.99 (*1-55773-958-7*) Diamond.

Lockwood, Katherine. Edwin & Johanna. (Illus.). 116p. (Orig.). 1989. pap. 9.99 (*0-925037-07-9*) Great Lks Poetry.

Lockwood, Kathleen O., jt. auth. see Lockwood, Jonathan S.

Lockwood, Lee. Castro's Cuba, Cuba's Fidel: Reprinted with a New Concluding Chapter. rev. ed. 380p. (C). 1990. pap. text ed. 21.50 (*0-8133-1086-5*) Westview.

— A Photographic Patron: The Carl Siembab Gallery. (Illus.). 1981. pap. 8.00 (*0-685-10376-5*) ICA Inc.

Lockwood, Lewis. Beethoven: Studies in the Creative Process. (Illus.). 283p. (C). 1992. 45.00 (*0-674-06362-7*) HUP.

Lockwood, Lewis, et al, eds. Beethoven Essays: Studies in Honor of Elliot Forbes. 288p. 1984. 28.00 (*0-674-06378-3*) HUP.

Lockwood, Lewis, ed. see Palestrini, Giovanni P.

Lockwood, Lewis C. & Forten, Charlotte L. Two Black Teachers During the Civil War: Mary S. Peake: The Colored Teacher at Fortress Monroa. 1970. 12.95 (*0-405-01931-9*, 16381) Ayer.

***Lockwood, Lisa.** The Woman's Study. 119p. 1994. spiral bd. 15.00 (*0-9643021-8-7*) Reality Living.

Lockwood, Loni, tr. see Steiner, Rudolf.

Lockwood, Luke V. Furniture Collector's Glossary. LC 67-27460. (Architecture & Decorative Art Ser.). 1967. reprint ed. lib. bdg. 16.50 (*0-306-70968-6*) Da Capo.

Lockwood, Margo. Black Dog. LC 86-80007. 64p. 1986. 15. 95 (*0-914086-60-X*); pap. 9.95 (*0-914086-61-8*) Alicejamesbooks.

— Left-Handed Happiness. (Illus.). 60p. (Orig.). 1987. pap. 12.00 (*0-9617521-0-6*) Dirty Dish Pr.

Lockwood, Margo, jt. auth. see Nyhart, Nina.

Lockwood, Michael. Mind, Brain & the Quantum: The Compound "I" (C). 1991. pap. 21.95 (*0-631-18031-1*) Blackwell Pubs.

Lockwood, Michael, jt. ed. see Flood, Raymond.

***Lockwood, Peter.** Virginia's Civil War Battlefields. (Virginia Heritage Ser.). 72p. 1995. pap. 7.95 (*1-885937-01-6*) Casco Commns.

Lockwood, Robert S. & Hillier, Carol M. Legislative Analysis: With An Emphasis on National Security Affairs. LC 81-67633. 109p. 1982. 17.50 (*0-89089-185-0*) Carolina Acad Pr.

Lockwood, Russ. Fish Cookery. 256p. 1993. 22.95 (*1-55821-246-9*) Lyons & Burford.

Lockwood, Samuel, tr. see Steiner, Rudolf.

Lockwood, Sarah. New Lyrics. LC 72-77822. (Living Poets' Library Ser.). pap. 2.50 (*0-686-02576-8*) Dragons Teeth.

Lockwood, Stephen C. Augustine Heard & Company: American Merchants in China. LC 78-120318. (East Asian Monographs: No. 37). 171p. 1971. pap. 11.00 (*0-674-05270-6*) HUP.

Lockwood, Thomas. Post-Augustan Satire: Charles Churchill & Satirical Poetry, 1750-1800. LC 78-4366. 208p. 1979. 30.00 (*0-295-95612-7*) U of Wash Pr.

Lockwood, Victoria, et al. Contemporary Pacific Societies: Studies in Development & Change. 384p. 1992. pap. text ed. 32.00 (*0-13-174723-1*) P-H.

Lockwood, Victoria S. Tahitian Transformation: Gender & Capitalist Development in a Rural Society. LC 92-24045. (Women & Change in the Developing World Ser.). 180p. (C). 1993. lib. bdg. 37.50 (*1-55587-317-0*); pap. text ed. 16.95 (*1-55587-391-X*) Lynne Rienner.

Lockwood, W. B. The Oxford Book of British Bird Names. 1984. 18.95 (*0-19-214155-4*) OUP.

— The Oxford Dictionary of British Bird Names. rev. ed. (OxfordPaperback Reference Ser.). 192p. 1993. pap. 14. 95 (*0-19-866196-7*) OUP.

Lockwood, William G. & Salo, Sheila. Gypsies & Travelers in North America: An Annotated bibliography. LC 94-18876. (Publication Ser.: No. 6). (Orig.). 1994. pap. 20. 00 (*0-9617107-5-6*) Gypsy Lore Soc.

Lockwood, William W. The Economic Development of Japan: Growth & Structural Change. enl. ed. LC 68-56833. 702p. reprint ed. pap. 180.00 (*0-317-27571-2*, 2014876) Bks Demand.

— The Economic Development of Japan: Growth & Structural Change, 1868-1938. LC 93-5709. (Michigan Classics in Japanese Studies: No. 10). xv, 603p. 1993. pap. 18.95 (*0-939512-62-9*) U MI Japan.

Lockwood, William W., ed. State & Economic Enterprise in Japan. LC 65-15386. (Studies in the Modernization of Japan). 763p. reprint ed. 180.00 (*0-8357-9514-4*, 2015225) Bks Demand.

Lockwood, Yvonne, ed. see Reuss, Richard A.

Lockwood, Yvonne R. Text & Context Folksong in a Bosnian Muslim Village. (Illus.). 220p. (Orig.). 1983. pap. 17.95 (*0-89357-120-2*) Slavica.

— Yugoslav Folklore: An Annotated Bibliography of Contributions in English. LC 75-38305. 1976. per. 8.00 (*0-88247-401-4*) Ragusan Pr.

Lockwood, Yvonne R., jt. ed. see Dewhurst, C. Kurt.

Lockyear, Frank & Gray, Robert. Trees for Tomorrow. (Illus.). 240p. 1993. pap. 12.95 (*1-56796-019-7*) WRS Group.

Lockyer, Allan. Clamdiggers & Downeast Country Stores: Eastern Maine's Vanishing Culture. LC 93-84637. (Illus.). 12p. (Orig.). 1993. pap. 14.95 (*1-880811-12-X*) North Lights.

Lockyer, Herbert. All the Divine Names & Titles. 1988. pap. 17.99 (*0-310-28041-9*, 10077P) Zondervan.

— All the Doctrines. 1988. pap. 17.99 (*0-310-28051-6*, 10082P) Zondervan.

— All the Messianic Prophecies. 1988. pap. 17.99 (*0-310-28091-5*, 10076P) Zondervan.

— All the Miracles of the Bible. 1988. pap. 17.99 (*0-310-28101-6*, 10066P) Zondervan.

— All the Parables. 1988. pap. 17.99 (*0-310-28111-3*, 10075P) Zondervan.

— All the Prayers of the Bible. 1990. pap. 17.99 (*0-310-28121-0*) Zondervan.

— All the Promises of the Bible. 1990. pap. 17.99 (*0-310-28131-8*) Zondervan.

— All the Teachings of Jesus. 1991. pap. 14.00 (*0-06-065274-8*) Harper SF.

— All the Women of the Bible. 1988. pap. 17.99 (*0-310-28151-2*, 10038P) Zondervan.

— Last Words of Saints & Sinners. LC 78-85429. 240p. 1975. pap. 9.99 (*0-8254-3111-5*) Kregel.

— The Mystery & Ministry of Angels. 111p. (YA). 1994. text ed. 9.95 (*0-942516-13-3*) Plymouth Rock Found.

Lockyer, Herbert, Sr. The Psalms: A Devotional Commentary. LC 92-15243. 640p. 1993. 27.99 (*0-8254-3146-8*); pap. 22.99 (*0-8254-3137-9*) Kregel.

Lockyer, Herbert. Retratos del Salvador. 192p. (SPA.). 1986. 4.95 (*0-8297-0741-7*) Life Pubs Intl.

Lockyer, J. Norman. The Dawn of Astronomy. 432p. (Orig.). 1992. pap. 45.00 (*1-56459-112-3*) Kessinger Pub.

Lockyer, Judith. Ordered by Words: Language & Narration in the Novels of William Faulkner. LC 90-39842. 224p. (C). 1991. 27.50 (*0-8093-1702-8*) S Ill U Pr.

Lockyer, K. G. Introduction to Critical Path Analysis. 1969. 34.95 (*0-8464-0522-9*) Beekman Pubs.

Lockyer, Keith & Gordon, James. Critical Path Analysis & Other Project Network Techniques. 5th ed. 272p. (Orig.). 1991. pap. text ed. 36.50 (*0-273-03416-2*, Pub. by Pitman Pub Ltd UK); 33.50 (*0-273-03442-1*, Pub. by Pitman Pub Ltd UK) Trans-Atl Phila.

Lockyer, L., et al. Production & Operations Management. 576p. (C). 1988. 185.00 (*0-685-39897-8*, Inst Pur & Supply) St Mut.

— Production & Operations Management. 576p. (C). 1989. 147.00 (*0-685-36159-4*, Inst Pur & Supply) St Mut.

Lockyer, Roger. The Early Stuarts: A Political History of England, 1603-1642. (Illus.). 411p. (Orig.). (C). 1989. pap. text ed. 22.95 (*0-582-49338-2*, 78201) Longman.

An Asterisk (*) at the beginning of an entry indicates that the title is appearing in BIP for the first time.

— Tudor & Stuart Britain. 2nd ed. (Illus.). 1985. pap. text ed. 22.00 (*0-312-82254-5*) St Martin.

— Tudor & Stuart Britain, 1471-1714. 2nd ed. LC 84-10085. 494p. reprint ed. pap. 140.80 (*0-7837-1587-0*, 2041879) Bks Demand.

Lockyer, Roger & O'Sullivan, Dan. Tudor England. LC 93-23514. (Sources & Opinions Ser.). 1993. 11.99 (*0-582-02202-9*, Pub. by Longman UK) Longman.

Lockyer, Roger, jt. ed. see Pincess, Gerald M.

Lockyer, Roger, jt. ed. see Pinciss, Gerald M.

Lockyer, Thomas N. Vector Particle Physics: Mathematically Consistent Models for the Structures of Subatomic Particles. LC 91-90733. 112p. (C). 1992. 12.95 (*0-9631546-0-5*); pap. 6.95 (*0-9631546-1-3*) TNL Pr.

Locock, F. A. Biographical Guide to the Divina Commedia of Dante. 1972. 59.95 (*0-87968-750-9*) Gordon Pr.

Locock, Frances. Biographical Guide to the Divinnia Commedia. LC 74-6466. (Studies in Dante: No. 9). 1974. lib. bdg. 49.95 (*0-8383-1986-6*) M S G Haskell Hse.

Locock, K. B., ed. see De Deguileville, Guillaume.

***Locock, Martin, ed.** Meaningful Architecture: Social Interpretations of Buildings. (Worldwide Architecture Ser.: Vol. 9). 320p. 1994. 59.95 (*1-85628-708-4*, Pub. by Avebury Pub UK) Ashgate Pub Co.

Locurto, Charles. Sense & Nonsense about IQ: The Case for Uniqueness. LC 90-23133. 224p. 1991. text ed. 55.00 (*0-275-93803-4*, C3803, Praeger Pubs); pap. text ed. 16.95 (*0-275-93911-1*, B3911, Praeger Pubs) Greenwood.

***Loczy, D.** Land Evaluation Studies in Hungary. (Studies in Geography in Hungary: No. 23). 95p. (C). 1988. 36.00x (*963-05-5231-0*, Pub. by Akad Kiado HU) St Mut.

Loda, Charles J., jt. auth. see Winder, Alan A.

Lodahl, Michael. The Story of God: Wesleyan Theology & Biblical Narrative. 257p. (C). 1994. pap. 19.95 (*0-8341-1479-8*) Beacon Hill.

Lodahl, Michael E. Shekhinah - Spirit: Divine Presence in Jewish & Christian Religion. LC 92-5525. (Stimulus Book Ser.). 272p. 1992. pap. 11.95 (*0-8091-3311-3*) Paulist Pr.

Lodato, Francis J., jt. auth. see Ryan, John B.

Loday, Jean-Louis. Cyclic Homology. LC 92-34146. (Grundlehren der Mathematischen Wissenschaften Ser.: Vol. 301). 1992. 149.00 (*0-387-53339-7*) Spr-Verlag.

Loddegaard, Anne, jt. ed. see Dollerup, Cay.

Lodder, Carol & Lodder, Nigel. Making Dolls' House Interiors: Decor & Furnishings in 1-12 Scale. (Illus.). 192p. 1994. 29.95 (*0-7153-0089-X*, Pub. by D & C Pub UK) Sterling.

Lodder, Christina. Russian Constructivism. LC 83-40002. (Illus.). 328p. 1983. 60.00 (*0-300-02727-3*, Y-516) Yale U Pr.

— Russian Constructivism. LC 83-40002. (Illus.). 328p. 1985. pap. 24.95 (*0-300-03406-7*, Y-516) Yale U Pr.

Lodder, Nigel, jt. auth. see Lodder, Carol.

Lodder, V. Russian Avantgarde: Art & Russian Constructivism. (C). 1990. 450.00 (*0-685-34347-2*, Pub. by Collets); pap. 170.00 (*0-685-34348-0*, Pub. by Collets) St Mut.

Lodding, William, ed. Gas Effluent Analysis. LC 67-19950. (Thermal Analysis Ser.: Vol. 13). (Illus.). 231p. reprint ed. pap. 65.90 (*0-317-07981-6*, 2055006) Bks Demand.

Lode, Juliet, ed. The Election of the European Parliament, 1989. LC 89-70326. 235p. 1990. text ed. 55.00 (*0-312-04494-1*) St Martin.

Loden, D. John. Megabrands: How to Build Them; How to Beat Them. 200p. 1991. 32.50 (*1-55623-469-4*) Irwin Prof Pubng.

***Loden, Marilyn.** Implementing Diversity: Best Practices for Making Diversity Work in Your Organization. 200p. 1995. 20.00 (*0-7863-0460-X*) Irwin Prof Pubng.

Loden, Marilyn & Rosener, Judy B. Workforce America! Managing Employee Diversity As A Vital Resource. 192p. 1990. 35.00 (*1-55623-386-8*) Irwin Prof Pubng.

Loder, Ann. The Wet Hat: And Other Stories from Beyond the Black Stump. (Illus.). 102p. (Orig.). (J). (gr. 4 up). 1993. pap. write for info. (*0-9636643-0-1*) A L Loder.

Loder, Eileen P., ed. Bibliography of the History & Organisation of Horse Racing & Thoroughbred Breeding in Great Britain & Ireland. 352p. 1990. 110.00 (*0-85131-297-7*, Pub. by J A Allen & Co UK) St Mut.

Loder, James E. The Transforming Moment. 2nd ed. 256p. 1989. reprint ed. pap. text ed. 15.95 (*0-939443-17-1*) Helmers Howard Pub.

Loder, James E. & Neidhardt, W. Jim. The Knight's Move: The Relational Logic of the Spirit in Theology & Science. LC 92-17033. 1992. pap. 27.95 (*0-939443-25-2*) Helmers Howard Pub.

Loder, Kurt. Bat Chain Puller: Rock & Roll in the Age of Celebrity. (Illus.). 320p. 1991. pap. 9.95 (*0-312-06301-6*) St Martin.

Loder, Kurt, jt. auth. see Turner, Tina.

Loder, Ted. Eavesdropping on the Echoes: Voices from the Old Testament. Broucek, Marcia, ed. LC 87-21526. 192p. (Orig.). 1988. reprint ed. 5.95 (*0-931055-42-3*); reprint ed. pap. 11.95 (*0-931055-58-X*) LuraMedia.

— Guerrillas of Grace: Prayers for the Battle. 2nd ed. Broucek, Marcia, ed. LC 84-26096. (Illus.). 136p. (Orig.). 1984. pap. 13.95 (*0-931055-04-0*) LuraMedia.

— Tracks in the Straw: Tales Spun from the Manger. Broucek, Marcia, ed. LC 85-23046. (Illus.). 176p. (Orig.). 1985. pap. 11.95 (*0-931055-06-7*) LuraMedia.

— Wrestling the Light: Ache & Awe in the Human-Divine Struggle. Broucek, Marcia, ed. LC 91-37123. (Illus.). 176p. (Orig.). 1991. pap. 14.95 (*0-931055-79-2*) LuraMedia.

Lodewick, Peter A. A Diabetic Doctor Looks at Diabetes: His & Yours. (Illus.). 204p. 1984. pap. 7.95 (*0-910117-00-4*) RMI.

Lodewick, Peter A., et al. Diabetic Man: A Guide to Health & Success in All Areas of Your Life. 336p. 1992. pap. 15.00 (*0-929923-78-2*) Lowell Hse.

Lodewyk, Christian P. Love in a Hate Situation. 156p. 1987. pap. 5.95 (*0-88144-107-4*) Christian Pub.

Lodgaard, Sverre, ed. Naval Arms Control. (International Peace Research Institute Ser.). (Illus.). 288p. (C). 1990. text ed. 49.95 (*0-8039-8387-5*) Sage.

Lodgaard, Sverre & Thee, Marek, eds. Nuclear Disengagement in Europe. 272p. 1983. 63.00 (*0-85066-244-3*) Taylor & Francis.

Lodgaard, Sverre, ed. see Stockholm International Peace Research Institute Staff.

***Lodge.** Students Cookbook. (Quick & Easy Ser.). 1995. pap. 7.95 (*0-572-01804-5*, Pub. by Foulsham UK) Atrium Pubs.

Lodge, A. E., ed. see Institute of Petroleum, London Staff.

Lodge, Arthur. Opportunities in Accounting Careers. LC 76-42889. (Illus.). (YA). (gr. 8 up). 1983. 13.95 (*0-8442-6341-9*, VGM Career Bks); pap. 10.95 (*0-8442-6342-7*, VGM Career Bks) NTC Pub Grp.

Lodge, Arthur S., et al. Viscoelasticity & Rheology. 1985. text ed. 97.00 (*0-12-454940-3*) Acad Pr.

Lodge, Barton, ed. see Palladius, Rutilius T.

Lodge, Bernard. Door to Door. LC 93-22203. (Illus.). 32p. (J). (ps-3). 1993. 14.95 (*1-879085-80-1*) Whsprng Coyote Pr.

— The Half-Mile Hat. LC 94-724. (Illus.). 32p. (J). (ps-4). 1995. 14.95 (*1-879085-89-5*) Whsprng Coyote Pr.

— There Was an Old Woman Who Lived in a Glove: A Picture Book. LC 92-12967. (Illus.). 32p. (J). (ps-4). 1992. 14.95 (*1-879085-55-0*) Whsprng Coyote Pr.

Lodge, Bernard, illus. & ret. Prince Ivan & the Firebird: A Russian Folk Tale. LC 93-12343. (J). (ps-5). 1993. 14.95 (*1-879085-86-0*) Whsprng Coyote Pr.

Lodge, Caroline, ed. see Best, Ron, et al.

Lodge, David. After Bakhtin: Essays on Fiction & Criticism. 208p. 1990. 49.95 (*0-415-05037-5*, A4556); pap. 14.95 (*0-415-05038-3*, A4560) Routledge.

— The Art of Fiction. 288p. 1994. 10.95 (*0-14-017492-3*, Penguin Bks) Viking Penguin.

— The British Museum Is Falling Down. 192p. 1989. pap. 10.95 (*0-14-012419-5*, Penguin Bks) Viking Penguin.

— Changing Places. 256p. (Orig.). 1979. pap. 10.00 (*0-14-017098-7*, Penguin Bks); mass mkt. 5.95 (*0-14-004656-9*, Penguin Bks) Viking Penguin.

— Evelyn Waugh. LC 78-136497. (Columbia Essays on Modern Writers Ser.: No. 58). 48p. 1971. pap. text ed. 7.50 (*0-231-03258-7*) Col U Pr.

— Modern Criticism & Theory. 480p. (C). 1988. pap. text ed. 28.50 (*0-582-49460-5*, 73622) Longman.

— Nice Work. 288p. 1990. pap. 10.95 (*0-14-013396-8*, Penguin Bks) Viking Penguin.

— Nice Work. large type ed. 432p. 1989. reprint ed. lib. bdg. 19.95 (*1-85089-293-8*, Pub. by ISIS UK) Transaction Pubs.

— Out of the Shelter. 272p. 1989. pap. 11.95 (*0-14-012279-6*, Penguin Bks) Viking Penguin.

— Paradise News. 304p. 1993. pap. 10.00 (*0-14-016521-5*, Penguin Bks) Viking Penguin.

— Paradise News. large type ed. LC 92-11067. 509p. 1992. reprint ed. lib. bdg. 20.95 (*1-56054-450-3*) Thorndike Pr.

— Small World. 400p. 1995. pap. 10.95 (*0-14-024486-7*, Penguin Bks) Viking Penguin.

— Small World: An Academic Romance. 1991. pap. 9.99 (*0-446-39327-4*) Warner Bks.

— Souls & Bodies. 256p. 1990. pap. 11.95 (*0-14-013018-7*, Penguin Bks) Viking Penguin.

— Therapy. 1995. 22.95 (*0-670-86358-0*, Viking) Viking Penguin.

Lodge, David, ed. Twentieth Century Literary Criticism: A Reader. 683p. (C). 1972. pap. text ed. 30.50 (*0-582-48422-7*, 73253) Longman.

Lodge, David, ed. see Eliot, George.

Lodge, Derek, jt. auth. see Cushway, Barry.

Lodge, Diana. Patchwork: More than Twenty-Five Nostalgic Step-by-Step Projects. LC 94-16516. (Traditional Needle Arts Ser.). (Illus.). 1994. write for info. (*1-57145-010-6*) Thunder Bay CA.

Lodge, Diana, jt. auth. see Mack, Lorrie.

Lodge, E. C., ed. The Account Book of a Kentish Estate, 1616-1704. (British Academy, London, Records of the Social & Economic History of England & Wales Ser.: Vol. 6). 1972. reprint ed. pap. 75.00 (*0-8115-1246-0*) Periodicals Srv.

Lodge, Elizabeth. Cassandra. (Orig.). 1980. pap. 2.25 (*0-8439-8009-5*) Dorchester Pub Co.

Lodge, G., jt. auth. see Gildersleeve, Basil L.

Lodge, G. A., ed. see Easter School in Agricultural Science (14th 1967, University of Nottingham) Staff.

Lodge, George C. American Disease. LC 86-8668. 354p. 1986. pap. 20.00 (*0-8147-5028-1*) NYU Pr.

— Perestroika for America: Restructuring Business-Government Relations for World Competitiveness. 235p. 1990. 22.95 (*0-87584-234-8*) Harvard Busn.

— Perestroika for America: Restructuring Business-Government Relations for World Competitiveness: A Harvard Business School Press Book. 1990. text ed. 22.95 (*0-07-103250-9*) McGraw.

— The Song of the Wave & Other Poems. LC 70-104517. 135p. reprint ed. lib. bdg. 19.00 (*0-8398-1168-3*) Irvington.

— Song of the Wave & Other Poems. 135p. (C). 1986. reprint ed. pap. text ed. 5.95 (*0-8290-2030-6*) Irvington.

Lodge, George C. & Vogel, Ezra F. Ideology & National Competitiveness: An Analysis of Nine Countries. 1987. text ed. 27.50 (*0-07-103520-6*) McGraw.

Lodge, George C., jt. auth. see Hubbard, Lee A.

Lodge, George C., jt. auth. see Scott, Bruce R.

Lodge, Gonzales. Lexicon Plautinum, 2 vols., Set. xxiv, 1863p. (GER.). 1971. reprint ed. write for info. (*3-487-04170-7*, Pub. by Georg Olms GW) Lubrecht & Cramer.

Lodge, Gonzalez. The Vocabulary of High School Latin. LC 73-177003. (Columbia University. Teachers College. Contributions to Education Ser.: No. 9). (LAT.). reprint ed. 22.50 (*0-404-55009-6*) AMS Pr.

Lodge, H. C. & Redmond, C. F., eds. Selections from the Correspondence of Theodore Roosevelt & Henry Cabot Lodge, 1884-1918, 2 Vols, Set. LC 72-146156. (American Public Figures Ser.). 1971. reprint ed. lib. bdg. 125.00 (*0-306-70129-4*) Da Capo.

Lodge, Henry C. Alexander Hamilton. Morse, John T., Jr., ed. LC 72-128971. (American Statesmen Ser.: No. 7). reprint ed. 35.00 (*0-404-50857-X*) AMS Pr.

— Alexander Hamilton. (BCL1 - U. S. History Ser.). 317p. 1991. reprint ed. lib. bdg. 89.00 (*0-7812-6125-2*) Rprt Serv.

— Certain Accepted Heroes. LC 79-37119. (Essay Index Reprint Ser.). 1977. reprint ed. 23.95 (*0-8369-2514-9*) Ayer.

— Daniel Webster. Morse, John T., Jr., ed. LC 71-128960. (American Statesmen Ser.: No. 21). reprint ed. 35.00 (*0-404-50871-5*) AMS Pr.

— Democracy of the Constitution, & Other Addresses & Essays. LC 67-22101. (Essay Index Reprint Ser.). 1977. 20.95 (*0-8369-0623-3*) Ayer.

— The Democracy of the Constitution & Other Addresses & Essays. (Essay Index Reprint Ser.). 297p. 1972. reprint ed. lib. bdg. 17.00 (*0-8290-0512-9*) Irvington.

— Early Memories. LC 75-1853. (Leisure Class in America Ser.). 1975. reprint ed. 26.95 (*0-405-06919-7*) Ayer.

— Fighting Frigate & Other Essays & Addresses. LC 79-90655. (Essay Index Reprint Ser.). 1977. 23.95 (*0-8369-1222-5*) Ayer.

— Frontier Town & Other Essays. LC 67-30220. (Essay Index Reprint Ser.). 1977. 21.95 (*0-8369-1975-0*) Ayer.

— George Washington, 2 Vols, 1. Morse, John T., Jr., ed. LC 74-128969. (American Statesmen Ser.: Nos. 4-5). reprint ed. write for info. (*0-404-50854-5*) AMS Pr.

— George Washington, 2 Vols, 2. Morse, John T., Jr., ed. LC 74-128969. (American Statesmen Ser.: Nos. 4-5). reprint ed. write for info. (*0-404-50855-3*) AMS Pr.

— George Washington, 2 Vols, Set. Morse, John T., Jr., ed. LC 74-128969. (American Statesmen Ser.: Nos. 4-5). reprint ed. 70.00 (*0-404-50890-1*) AMS Pr.

— Historical & Political Essays. LC 72-282. (Essay Index Reprint Ser.). 1977. reprint ed. pap. 19.95 (*0-8369-2801-6*) Ayer.

— A Short History of the English Colonies in America. 560p. (Orig.). 1995. pap. text ed. 35.00 (*0-7884-0189-0*) Heritage Bk.

— Studies in History. LC 70-39132. (Essay Index Reprint Ser.). 1977. reprint ed. 28.95 (*0-8369-2698-6*) Ayer.

— War with Spain. LC 70-111702. (American Imperialism: Viewpoints of United States Foreign Policy, 1898-1941 Ser.). 1970. reprint ed. 24.95 (*0-405-02035-X*) Ayer.

Lodge, Henry C., ed. see Cabot, George.

Lodge, Henry C., ed. see Hamilton, Alexander.

Lodge, Jack. Hollywood: Fifty Great Years. 1989. 29.88 (*0-88365-743-0*) Galahad Bks.

Lodge, James P., Jr., ed. Methods of Air Sampling & Analysis. 3rd ed. (Illus.). 780p. 1988. 105.00 (*0-87371-141-6*, TD890) Lewis Pubs.

Lodge, Jane. Computerized Litigation Support. 105p. 1990. pap. 37.50 (*1-86287-029-2*, Pub. by Federation Pr AU) W W Gaunt.

Lodge, Jim, tr. see Denaerde, Stefan & Stevens, Wendelle C.

***Lodge, John.** I Remember Detroit. (American Autobiography Ser.). 208p. 1995. reprint ed. lib. bdg. 79.00 (*0-7812-8581-X*) Rprt Serv.

— Peerage of Ireland, or a Genealogical History of the Present Nobility of That Kingdom, 7 Vols, Set. Archdall, Mervyn, ed. LC 77-172749. reprint ed. 150.00 (*0-404-07970-9*) AMS Pr.

Lodge, John, ed. Computer Data Handling in the Primary School. (Roehampton Teaching Studies Ser.). 128p. 1991. pap. 27.00 (*1-85346-178-4*, Pub. by D Fulton UK) Taylor & Francis.

Lodge, Joseph H. Drug & Alcohol Abuse in the Workplace: An Assessment of Economic & Productivity Losses. LC 87-627. 107p. reprint ed. pap. 30.50 (*0-7837-0683-9*, 2041016) Bks Demand.

Lodge, Juliet, ed. Direct Elections to the European Parliament, 1984. LC 85-10791. 309p. 1986. text ed. 32.50 (*0-312-21213-5*) St Martin.

— The European Community & the Challenge of the Future. 2nd ed. LC 93-17954. 1993. 19.95 (*0-312-09978-9*) St Martin.

— European Union: The European Community in Search of a Future. LC 85-24971. 240p. 1986. text ed. 35.00 (*0-312-27084-4*) St Martin.

Lodge, Lee D. A Study in Corneille. 1976. lib. bdg. 59.95 (*0-8490-2707-1*) Gordon Pr.

***Lodge, Marc.** Within the Bounds. 336p. 1994. pap. 5.99 (*0-425-14457-7*) Berkley Pub.

— Within the Bounds. LC 93-22982. 352p. 1993. 21.95 (*0-399-13881-1*, Putnam) Putnam Pub Group.

Lodge, Milton. Magnitude Scaling. (Quantitative Applications in the Social Sciences Ser.: Vol. 25). 88p. 1981. pap. 9.95 (*0-8039-1747-3*) Sage.

***Lodge, Milton & McGraw, Kathleen M., eds.** Political Judgement: Structure & Process. 300p. (C). 1995. text ed. 39.50x (*0-472-10541-8*) U of Mich Pr.

Lodge, Nicholas, frwd. Victorian Book of Cakes. (Illus.). 336p. 1991. 19.99 (*0-517-05694-1*) Random Hse Value.

Lodge, Nicholas & Tann, Graham. Cake Styling: Presenting & Photographing Your Cakes. (Illus.). 90p. 1992. 14.95 (*1-85238-137-X*, Pub. by New Holland Pubs UK) Sterling.

Lodge, O. R. The Recapture of Guam. reprint ed. pap. 12.00 (*0-915266-16-4*) Awani Pr.

— The Recapture of Guam. (Elite Unit Ser.: No. 28). (Illus.). 248p. 1991. reprint ed. 32.50 (*0-89839-160-1*) Battery Pr.

Lodge, Olive. Peasant Life in Yugoslavia. LC 77-87722. (Illus.). 352p. reprint ed. 44.50 (*0-404-16582-6*) AMS Pr.

Lodge, Oliver. The Ether of Space. 1991. lib. bdg. 69.95 (*0-8490-4931-8*) Gordon Pr.

— Spiritual Works, 4 vols. 1972. 400.00 (*0-8490-1114-0*) Gordon Pr.

Lodge, Oliver J. Raymond, or, Life & Death. (Collector's Library of the Unknown). (Illus.). 403p. reprint ed. write for info. (*0-8094-8145-6*) Time-Life.

— Signalling Through Space Without Wires: Being a Description of the Work of Hertz & His Successors. 3rd ed. LC 74-9688. (Telecommunications Ser.). (Illus.). 138p. 1974. 17.95 (*0-405-06051-3*) Ayer.

Lodge, Oliver J., tr. see Richet, Charles.

Lodge, R. Anthony. French: From Dialect to Standard. 272p. 1993. 59.95 (*0-415-08070-3*, A9862); pap. 17.95 (*0-415-08071-1*, A9866) Routledge.

Lodge, Richard. History of England from the Restoration to the Death of William Third. LC 70-5629. (Political History of England Ser.: No. 8). reprint ed. 45.00 (*0-404-50778-6*) AMS Pr.

— History of England from the Restoration to the Death of William Third: Sixteen-Sixty to Seventeen Hundred-Two (Polo Hist. of Eng., Vol. 8. 1969. reprint ed. 45.00 (*0-527-00853-2*) Periodicals Srv.

— Studies in Eighteenth-Century Diplomacy, 1740-1748. LC 73-109771. 421p. 1970. reprint ed. text ed. 65.00 (*0-8371-4261-X*, LODI, Greenwood Pr) Greenwood.

Lodge, Sally. Cheyenne. (Native American People Ser.). (Illus.). 32p. (J). (gr. 5-8). 1990. lib. bdg. 15.94 (*0-86625-387-4*); lib. bdg. 11.95 (*0-685-36388-0*) Rourke Corp.

Lodge, Thomas. Rosalynde, Being the Original of Shakespeare's As You Like It. Greg, W. W., ed. LC 75-128890. (Select Bibliographies Reprint Ser.). 1977. reprint ed. 18.95 (*0-8369-5510-2*) Ayer.

— A Treatise of the Plague: Containing the Nature, Signes & Accidents of the Same. LC 79-84119. (English Experience Ser.: No. 938). 92p. 1979. reprint ed. lib. bdg. 20.00 (*90-221-0938-0*) Walter J Johnson.

— Wits Miserie & the Worlds Madnesse. LC 70-25896. (English Experience Ser.: No. 198). 112p. 1969. reprint ed. 14.00 (*90-221-0198-3*) Walter J Johnson.

— The Wounds of Civil War. Houppert, J. W., ed. LC 68-63050. xxii, 115p. 1969. pap. 5.95 (*0-8032-5268-4*) U of Nebr Pr.

Lodge, Thomas & Greene, Robert. Looking-Glass for London & England. LC 71-133697. (Tudor Facsimile Texts. Old English Plays Ser.: No. 67). reprint ed. 49.50 (*0-404-53367-1*) AMS Pr.

Lodge, Thomas E. The Everglades Handbook: Understanding the Ecosystem. LC 93-48083. (Illus.). 200p. 1994. pap. 29.95 (*1-884015-06-9*) St Lucie Pr.

— The Everglades Handbook: Understanding the Ecosystem. 1995. pap. 29.95 (*1-57003-061-8*) U of SC Pr.

Lodge, Tom, ed. Resistance & Ideology in Settler Societies. (South African Studies: Vol. 4). 222p. (Orig.). 1987. pap. text ed. 15.95 (*0-86975-304-5*, Pub. by Ravan Pr ZA) Ohio U Pr.

Lodha, R. M. & Jain, P. S. Medieval Jainism: Culture & Environment. 1990. 22.50 (*81-7024-272-X*, Pub. by Ashish II) S Asia.

Lodhi, A., jt. auth. see Otterbrandt, T.

Lodhi, M. A. & International Institute of Islamic Thought Staff, eds. The Islamization of Attitudes & Practices in Science & Technology: Proceedings of a Workshop on Islamization of Attitudes & Practices in Science & Technology. LC 89-15332. (Illus.). 150p. (C). 1989. pap. text ed. 8.95 (*0-912463-42-2*) IIIT VA.

Lodi, jt. auth. see Ellis, Jr.

Lodi, Ed, jt. auth. see Ellis, Wade, Jr.

Lodi, Enzo. Saints of the Roman Calender: Including Feasts Proper to the English-Speaking World. Auman, Jordan, tr. & adapt. by. LC 92-20261. 419p. 1992. pap. 9.95 (*0-8189-0652-9*) Alba.

***Lodi, Pat.** With Love All Things Are Possible. 1995. 9.95 (*0-8062-5166-2*) Carlton.

Loding, Darlene. Economic Texts from the Third Dynasty. (Ur Excavations Texts Ser.: No. 9). 84p. 1976. 25.00 (*0-934718-37-7*) U PA Mus Pubns.

Lodish. Molecular Cell Biology. (Illus.). 1152p. (C). 1995. text ed. write for info. (*0-7167-2380-8*) W H Freeman.

Lodish, Leonard M. The Advertising Promotion Challenge: Vaguely Right or Precisely Wrong. (Illus.). 192p. 1986. 25.00 (*0-19-503702-2*) OUP.

Lodl, Ann & Longguan, Zhang, eds. Enterprise Crime: Asian & Global Perspectives. LC 92-28793. 190p. 1992. pap. 15.00 (*0-942511-60-3*) OICJ.

Lodo, Venerable L. Bardo Teachings: The Way of Death & Rebirth. 2nd ed. Clark, Nancy & Parke, Caroline, eds. LC 87-20663. 73p. (C). 1987. reprint ed. pap. 8.95 (*0-937938-60-2*) Snow Lion Pubns.

Lodo, Venerable Larma. The Quintessence of the Animate & Inanimate: A Discourse on the Holy Dharma. Clark, Nancy & Parke, Caroline, eds. LC 85-2290. (Illus.). 238p. 1985. pap. 11.95 (*0-910165-01-7*) KDK Pubns.

***Lodovico, Gerald J.** Interviewing Power. 86p. 1995. pap. 6.95 (*0-7610-0081-X*) NW Pub.

L

L

Lodro, Geshe G. Walking Through Walls: A Presentation of Tibetan Meditation. Hopkins, Jeffrey et al, eds. LC 92-16321. 1992. 35.00 (*1-55939-008-5*); pap. 19.95 (*1-55939-004-2*) Snow Lion Pubns.

Lods, Adolphe. Israel, from Its Beginning to the Middle of the Eighth Century. Hooke, S. H., tr. LC 75-41180. 1948. 34.75 (*0-404-14569-8*) AMS Pr.

— Prophets & the Rise of Judaism. Hooke, Samuel H., tr. LC 77-109772. (Illus.). 378p. (C). 1971. reprint ed. text ed. 65.00 (*0-8371-4262-8*, LOPR, Greenwood Pr) Greenwood.

Lodwick, John. Raiders from the Sea. (Illus.). 256p. 1990. 24.95 (*1-55750-525-X*) Naval Inst Pr.

Lodwick, Kathleen, ed. The Chinese Recorder Index: A Guide to Christian Missions in Asia, 1867-1941, 2 vols. LC 85-26125. 1200p. 1986. 150.00 (*0-8420-2250-3*) Scholarly Res Inc.

***Lodwick, Kathleen L.** Crusaders Against Opium: Protestant Missionaries in China, 1847-1917. (Illus.). 208p. 1996. text ed. 29.95 (*0-8131-1924-3*) U Pr of Ky.

— Educating the Women of Hainan: The Career of Margaret Moninger in China, 1915-1942. LC 94-29319. (Illus.). 248p. 1995. lib. bdg. 35.00x (*0-8131-1882-4*) U Pr of Ky.

***Lodwick, Robert C., ed.** Remembering the Future: The Challenge of the Churches in Europe. LC 94-39489. 1995. pap. 8.95 (*0-377-00290-9*) Friendship Pr.

Lody, M. E., ed. see White, Betty W.

Lodz, J., jt. ed. see Lawrynowicz, Julian.

Lodziak, Conrad. The Power of Television: A Critical Appraisal. LC 86-17706. 233p. 1986. text ed. 32.50 (*0-312-63397-1*) St Martin.

— Towards a Culture of Opposition. (C). 1995. text ed. 57.00 (*0-7453-0853-8*, Pub. by Pluto Pr UK); pap. text ed. 18.95 (*0-7453-0854-6*, Pub. by Pluto Pr UK) Westview.

Loe, H. & Kleinman, D. V., eds. Dental Plaque Control Measures & Oral Hygiene Practices. 352p. 1986. pap. 60.00 (*0-947946-48-9*, IRL Pr) OUP.

Loe, K. F. & Goto, E. DC Flux Parametron. (Series in Computer Science: Vol. 6). 216p. 1986. text ed. 47.00 (*9971-5-0113-9*) World Scientific Pub.

Loe, K. F., jt. ed. see Goto, E.

Loe, K. F., jt. auth. see Wang, P. Z.

Loe, Kelley, jt. auth. see Neuberger, Richard L.

Loe, Mary, jt. ed. see Brottman, May.

Loe, Mary L., jt. auth. see Molson-Chesaw-Knob Hill Community Development Staff.

Loeb, Arthur L. Color & Symmetry. LC 78-13084. 196p. 1978. reprint ed. 26.50 (*0-88275-745-8*) Krieger.

— Concepts & Images: Visual Mathematics. (Design Science Collections). (Illus.). xi, 228p. 1992. 49.50 (*0-8176-3620-X*) Birkhauser.

— Space Structures: Their Harmony & Counterpoint. 192p. 1976. pap. text ed. 35.50 (*0-201-04651-2*) Addison-Wesley.

— Space Structures: Their Harmony & Counterpoint. 5th rev. ed. (Design Science Collections). xviii, 169p. 1991. 34.50 (*0-8176-3588-2*) Birkhauser.

Loeb, Arthur L., tr. see Blotkamp, Carel, et al.

Loeb, Ben F., Jr. Dental Practice Law: North Carolina Cases & Materials. rev. ed. 114p. (C). 1987. pap. text ed. 9.00 (*1-56011-019-8*, 87.11) Institute Government.

— Eminent Domain Procedure for North Carolina Local Governments. rev. ed. 82p. (C). 1984. pap. text ed. 7.00 (*1-56011-056-2*, 84.24) Institute Government.

— Fire Protection Law in North Carolina. 5th ed. 216p. (C). 1993. pap. text ed. 8.50 (*1-56011-251-4*, 93.04) Institute Government.

— 1995 Supplement to Motor Vehicle Law in North Carolina. (Orig.). (C). Date not set. pap. text ed. write for info. (*1-56011-243-3*, 90.06A) Institute Government.

Loeb, Ben F., Jr. & Drennan, James C. Punishment Chart for Motor Vehicle Offenses. rev. ed. 1993. pap. text ed. 6.00 (*1-56011-252-2*) Institute Government.

Loeb, Ben F., Jr. & Lazar, John I. Animal Control Law Supplement, 1988: Civil Liability for the Misdeeds of Animals. 43p. (Orig.). (C). 1989. pap. text ed. 5.00 (*1-56011-004-X*, 86.10A) Institute Government.

Loeb, Ben F., Jr. & Loeb, Ben F., Jr. Motor Vehicle Law of North Carolina. rev. ed. 230p. (C). 1990. pap. text ed. 8.50 (*1-56011-103-8*) Institute Government.

Loeb, Ben F. & Watts, L. Poindexter. Animal Control Law for North Carolina Local Governments, 1986. 2nd ed. LC 86-225342. 69p. 1986. 12.00 (*1-56011-003-1*) Institute Government.

Loeb, Ben F., Jr., jt. auth. see Loeb, Ben F., Jr.

Loeb, Ben F., Jr., jt. comp. see Rubin, John.

Loeb, Benjamin S., jt. auth. see Seaborg, Glenn T.

Loeb, C. The Black Art of Cooking: How Cooked Food Produces Disease, an Introduction to the Unfired Diet. 1991. lib. bdg. 79.95 (*0-8490-4547-9*) Gordon Pr.

Loeb, C. W., jt. ed. see Fieschi, C.

Loeb, Carl. The Black Art of Cooking. 127p. 1993. reprint ed. spiral bd. 5.50 (*0-7873-0568-5*) Mokelumne.

Loeb, Charlotte I., tr. see Blotkamp, Carel, et al.

Loeb, D., ed. see Camarda, Renato.

Loeb, David. Nine Fantasias for the Japanese Consort (Three to Six Viols) (Contemporary Consort Ser.: No. 13). ii, 45p. 1991. 12.00 (*1-56571-015-0*) PRB Prods.

— Six Fantasias on Sephardic Themes for Solo Bass Viol. (Contemporary Instrumental Ser.: No. 6). 12p. 1992. 9.00 (*1-56571-058-4*, CI006) PRB Prods.

Loeb, David & Brown, David. How to Change Your Name in California. 6th ed. (Illus.). 144p. 1994. pap. 24.95 (*0-87337-258-1*) Nolo Pr.

Loeb, David, ed. see Villalobos, Joaquin.

Loeb, E. M. History & Traditions of Niue. (BMB Ser.). 1969. reprint ed. 35.00 (*0-527-02135-0*) Periodicals Srv.

Loeb, Edwin M. Blood Sacrifice Complex. LC 24-4020. (American Anthropological Association Memoirs Ser.: No. 30). 1924. pap. 15.00 (*0-527-00529-0*) Periodicals Srv.

— Sumatra: Its History & People. (Oxford in Asia Paperbacks Ser.). 358p. 1990. pap. 14.95 (*0-19-588944-4*) OUP.

Loeb, Evelyn, comp. Love Poems & Love Letters. (Keepsakes Ser.). (Illus.). 56p. 1994. 7.99 (*0-88088-875-X*) Peter Pauper.

— A Token of Love. (Keepsakes Ser.). (Illus.). 56p. 1994. 7.99 (*0-88088-877-6*) Peter Pauper.

Loeb, G. I., jt. ed. see Schrader, M. E.

Loeb, Gerald E. & Gans, Carl. Electromyography for Experimentalists. LC 85-28934. (Illus.). xx, 374p. 1986. lib. bdg. 60.00 (*0-226-49014-9*); pap. text ed. 22.00 (*0-226-49015-7*) U Ch Pr.

Loeb, Gerald M. The Battle for Investment Survival. LC 88-81705. 320p. 1988. reprint ed. pap. text ed. 18.00 (*0-87034-084-0*) Fraser Pub Co.

— Battle for Stock Market Profits. LC 70-130483. 1974. 7.95 (*0-671-20751-2*) S&S Trade.

Loeb, Helen M., jt. auth. see Woolever, Kristen R.

Loeb, Isidor. Legal Property Relations of Married Parties: A Study in Comparative Legislation. LC 68-56668. (Columbia University Studies in the Social Sciences Ser.: No. 34). reprint ed. 18.00 (*0-404-51034-5*) AMS Pr.

***Loeb, J.** Batman: Ghosts, Legend of the Dark Knight Halloween Special. Goodwin, ed. (Illus.). 48p. 1995. pap. write for info. (*1-56389-234-0*) DC Comics.

Loeb, J., jt. auth. see Bertin, J.

***Loeb, J. David.** Jack Rabbit Jack. (Illus.). 24p. (Orig.). (J). (ps-5). 1994. pap. 4.95 (*1-885744-01-3*) Otter Creek.

— The Pool on Otter Creek. (Illus.). 28p. (Orig.). (J). (ps-5). 1994. pap. 5.95 (*1-885744-00-5*) Otter Creek.

— The Train Ride. (Illus.). 24p. (Orig.). (J). (ps-3). 1994. pap. 3.95 (*1-885744-02-1*) Otter Creek.

Loeb, Jacques. Comparative Physiology of the Brain & Comparative Psychology. LC 73-2973. (Classics in Psychology Ser.). 1978. reprint ed. 26.95 (*0-405-05146-8*) Ayer.

— Forced Movements, Tropisms, & Animal Conduct. (Illus.). 9.00 (*0-8446-4776-4*) Peter Smith.

Loeb, James, tr. see Couat, A.

Loeb, James, tr. see Croiset, Maurice.

***Loeb, James E.** City Risk Kit. 500p. 1991. 335.00 (*0-9628164-4-2*) Indep Risk Insur Mgmt.

Loeb, Jo. Cathletics. 1990. 4.98 (*0-89009-728-3*) Bk Sales Inc.

Loeb, Jo & Loeb, Paul. You Can Train Your Cat. 1990. mass mkt. 5.50 (*0-671-73906-9*) PB.

Loeb, Judy, ed. Feminist Collage: Educating Women in the Visual Arts. LC 79-15468. 335p. reprint ed. pap. 95.50 (*0-7837-1196-4*, 2041726) Bks Demand.

Loeb, Karen. Jump Rope Queen: And Other Stories. LC 92-64073. (Minnesota Voices Project Ser.). 136p. (Orig.). 1993. pap. 9.95 (*0-89823-145-0*) New Rivers Pr.

Loeb, L., ed. Outcaste: Jewish Life in Southern Iran. (Library of Anthropology). 354p. 1977. text ed. 72.00 (*0-677-04530-1*) Gordon & Breach.

Loeb, Lawrence A., jt. auth. see Fry, Michael.

***Loeb, Leonore A., et al, eds.** Violence & the Prevention of Violence. LC 94-28007. (Illus.). 248p. 1995. text ed. 55.00 (*0-275-94873-0*, Praeger Pubs) Greenwood.

Loeb, Lori A. Consuming Angels: Advertising & Victorian Women. LC 93-46094. (Illus.). 256p. 1994. 29.95 (*0-19-508596-5*) OUP.

Loeb, Marcia. Art Deco Designs & Motifs. (Pictorial Archive Ser.). (Illus.). 96p. (Orig.). 1972. pap. 5.95 (*0-486-22826-6*) Dover.

— New Art Deco Alphabets. LC 74-29015. (Pictorial Archive Ser.). (Illus.). 80p. (Orig.). 1975. pap. 4.95 (*0-486-23149-6*) Dover.

— Pennsylvania Dutch Needlepoint Designs. (Needlework Ser.). (Illus.). 137p. (Orig.). 1976. pap. 2.95 (*0-486-23299-9*) Dover.

Loeb, Marshall. Loeb's Money Guide, 1991. 1990. pap. 14.95 (*0-316-53071-9*) Little.

— Marshall Loeb's Money Guide, 1989. rev. ed. 512p. 1988. pap. 12.95 (*0-316-53067-0*) Little.

— Marshall Loeb's Money Guide, 1990, Vol. 1. 1989. pap. 13.95 (*0-316-53064-6*) Little.

— Money Guide '92. 1991. pap. 14.95 (*0-316-53072-7*) Little.

Loeb, Michel. Noise & Human Efficiency. LC 85-16781. (Wiley Series on Studies in Human Performance). (Illus.). 283p. reprint ed. pap. 80.70 (*0-7837-4409-9*, 2044152) Bks Demand.

Loeb, P. A., jt. auth. see Hurd, A. E.

Loeb, Paul. Supertraining Your Dog. 1990. pap. 5.99 (*0-671-73209-9*) S&S Trade.

Loeb, Paul, jt. auth. see Loeb, Jo.

Loeb, Paul R. Generation at the Crossroads: Apathy & Action on the American Campus. LC 94-16186. 420p. (C). 1994. 24.95 (*0-8135-2144-0*) Rutgers U Pr.

— Generations at the Crossroads: Apathy & Action on the American Campus. 460p. (Orig.). (C). 1995. pap. 16.95 (*0-8135-2256-0*) Rutgers U Pr.

Loeb, Peter D., et al. Causes & Deterrents of Transportation Accidents: An Analysis by Mode. LC 94-8541. 240p. 1994. text ed. 59.95 (*0-89930-806-6*, Quorum Bks) Greenwood.

Loeb, Sal, ed. The Garden Book. (Illus.). 136p. (Orig.). write for info. (*0-318-61323-9*) Corpus Christi Area.

Loeb, Sorel G. & Kadden, Barbara B. Jewish History - Moments & Methods: An Activity Source Book for Teachers. LC 82-71283. (Illus.). 150p. (Orig.). 1982. pap. text ed. 10.00 (*0-86705-008-X*) A R E Pub.

— Teaching Torah: A Treasury of Activities & Insights. LC 84-70318. 300p. 1984. pap. text ed. 18.75 (*0-86705-013-6*) A R E Pub.

Loeb, Walter & Quimby, Fred W. The Clinical Chemistry of Laboratory Animals. 519p. 1989. text ed. 69.50 (*0-07-105293-3*) Hlth Prof Div.

Loebbeck, James, jt. auth. see Arens, Alvin.

Loebbecke, James K. & Luria, Edward M., eds. Accountant's Workbook Series, 22 vols. 1986. Looseleaf updates avail. write for info. (*0-8205-1019-X*) Bender.

Loebbecke, James K., jt. auth. see Arens, Alvin A.

Loebel & Mueller, Peter. Lexikon der Datenverarbeitung. 704p. (GER.). 1975. 165.00 (*0-8288-5918-3*, M7264) Fr & Eur.

Loebel, Arnold B. Chemical Problem-Solving by Dimensional Analysis, 3 Vols. 3rd ed. LC 86-8913. 448p. (C). 1986. pap. 33.56 (*0-395-35678-4*) HM.

— Chemistry: Concepts & Calculations. LC 77-26720. 576p. reprint ed. pap. 164.20 (*0-317-09888-8*, 2022508) Bks Demand.

Loebell, E., ed. International Association of Logopedics & Phoniatrics, Abstracts: 22nd World Congress, Hannover, August, 1992. (Journal: Folia Phoniatrica: Vol. 44, No. 1-2, 1992). 100p. 1992. pap. 58.50 (*3-8055-5652-7*) S Karger.

— International Association of Logopedics & Phoniatrics, Main Reports: 22nd World Congress, Hannover, August, 1992. (Journal: Folia Phoniatrica: Vol. 44, No. 3-4, 1992). (Illus.). 84p. 1992. pap. 58.50 (*3-8055-5653-5*) S Karger.

Loebell, E., ed. see International Association of Logopedics & Phoniatrics Staff.

Loebell, E., ed. see International Congress of Logopedics & Phoniatrics Staff.

Loebelson, Andrew. How to Profit in Contract Design. (Interior Design Bks.). 192p. 1983. text ed. 32.50 (*0-685-06953-2*) Inter Design.

Loeber, D. A., ed. Ruling Communist Parties & Their Status under Law. 1986. lib. bdg. 216.50 (*90-247-3209-3*) Kluwer Ac.

Loeber, Dietrich A., et al, eds. Regional Identity under Soviet Rule: The Case of the Baltic States. (Illus.). xx, 469p. 1989. 50.00 (*0-685-29788-8*) Assn Advan Baltic Studies.

Loebl, Herbert. Government Factories & the Origins of British Regional Policy, 1934-1948. 439p. 1988. text ed. 69.95 (*0-566-05343-8*, Pub. by Avebury Pub UK) Ashgate Pub Co.

Loebl, Suzanne, et al. The Nurse's Drug Handbook. 5th ed. 1989. pap. text ed. 32.95 (*0-8273-4291-8*) Delmar.

Loebl, Suzanne & Spratto, George R. The Nurse's Drug Handbook. 6th ed. 1991. text ed. 33.95 (*0-8273-4527-5*) Delmar.

Loebl, Suzanne, et al. RN Magazine's the Nurse's Drug Handbook. 7th ed. LC 93-36203. 1420p. 1994. pap. text ed. 33.95 (*0-8273-5710-9*) Delmar.

Loeblein, John M. Memoirs of Kelly Field, 1917-1918. 61p. 1974. pap. text ed. 17.95 (*0-89126-010-2*) MA-AH Pub.

Loeblich, A. B., et al. Studies in Foraminifera. 1970. 42.00 (*0-934454-75-2*) Lubrecht & Cramer.

Loeblich, Alfred R. & Tappan, Helen. Foraminiferal Genera & Their Classification. (Illus.). 1728p. 1987. text ed. 269.95 (*0-442-25937-9*) Chapman & Hall.

Loeblich, Alfred R., Jr. & Tappan, Helen. Treatise on Invertebrate Paleontology, Pt. C: Protista 2: Sarcodina, Chiefly "Thecamoebians" & Foraminiferida, 2 vols. Moore, Raymond C., ed. LC 53-12913. 936p. 1964. 43.00 (*0-8137-3003-1*) Geol Soc.

Loecher, Barbara, jt. auth. see Bascom, Lionel C.

Loeckx, Jacques & Sieber, Kurt. The Foundations of Program Verification. 2nd ed. LC 86-19008. (Computer Science Ser.). 230p. 1987. text ed. 89.95 (*0-471-91282-4*) Wiley.

Loeckx, Jacques, et al. Foundations of Programming Languages. 426p. 1988. pap. text ed. 93.95 (*0-471-92139-4*) Wiley.

Loeding, Wilfried. The ABCs of Cockatiels. (Illus.). 93p. 1986. 9.95 (*0-86622-836-5*, KW-150) TFH Pubns.

Loeffelbein, Robert L. Knight Life: Jousting in the United States. LC 78-53984. (Illus.). 1978. pap. 4.95 (*0-9601258-1-7*) Golden Owl Pub.

— The Recreation Handbook: Three-Hundred Forty-Two Games & Other Activities for Teams & Individuals. LC 92-50310. (Illus.). 255p. (J). 1992. pap. 27.50x (*0-89950-744-1*) McFarland & Co.

Loeffelbein, Robert L., ed. Script Tease: The Treasury of Surprise Endings. (Illus.). 192p. (Orig.). 1979. pap. 4.95 (*0-9601258-2-5*) Golden Owl Pub.

Loeffelholz, M. Experimental Lives: Women & Literature 1900-1945. (Women & Literature Ser.). 250p. (Orig.). 1992. text ed. 22.95 (*0-8057-8976-6*, Pub. by Royal Botanic Garden UK); pap. 13.95 (*0-8057-8977-4*, Pub. by Royal Botanic Garden UK) Macmillan.

Loeffelholz, Mary. Dickinson & the Boundaries of Feminist Theory. 192p. 1991. 32.50 (*0-252-01789-7*); pap. 13.95 (*0-252-06175-6*) U of Ill Pr.

— Experimental Lives: Women & Literature, 1900-1945. 1995. pap. 12.95 (*0-8057-8574-4*, Twayne) Macmillan.

Loeffler. Virtual Realities. 1994. pap. 29.95 (*0-442-01776-6*) Van Nos Reinhold.

Loeffler, Carl & Tong, Darlene, eds. Performance Anthology: Source Book of California Performance Art. (Illus.). 532p. 1990. pap. 24.95 (*0-86719-366-2*) Last Gasp.

Loeffler, Carl E. & Tong, Darlene, eds. Performance Anthology: Source Book for a Decade of California Performance Art. LC 79-55054. (Contemporary Documents Ser.: Vol. 1). (Illus.). 500p. 1980. pap. 15.95 (*0-931818-01-X*) Contemporary Arts.

Loeffler, Chris, jt. auth. see Hunsberger, Eydie M.

Loeffler, Donald L. An Analysis of the Treatment of the Homosexual Character in Dramas Produced in the New York Theater from 1950-1968. LC 75-14262. (Homosexuality Ser.). 1975. reprint ed. 19.95 (*0-405-07398-4*) Ayer.

Loeffler, F. J., ed. see Materials Handling Conference Staff.

Loeffler, Friedrich. Dust Collection with Bag Filters & Envelope Filters. (Illus.). x, 274p. 1988. 154.00 (*3-528-08933-4*, Pub. by Vieweg & Sohn GW) Ballen Bkslr.

Loeffler, Fritz. Otto Dix: The Complete Paintings. (Illus.). 330p. (GER.). 1981. 160.00 (*1-55660-003-8*) A Wofsy Fine Arts.

Loeffler, H., ed. Neue Therapeutische Strategien in der Haematologischen Onkologie. (Beitraege zur Onkologie Ser.: Vol. 36). (Illus.). vi, 115p. 1989. 43.25 (*3-8055-5046-4*) S Karger.

Loeffler, Jack. Poem & Revolution Before Breakfast: The Life of Edward Abbey. Date not set. 25.00 (*0-517-58632-0*, Crown) Crown Pub Group.

***Loeffler, Jack, contrib.** Tesoros del Espiritu - Treasures of the Spirit: A Portrait in Sound of Hispanic New Mexico. 1995. audio 20.00 (*0-8263-1618-2*) U of NM Pr.

Loeffler, Jay, jt. ed. see Mauch, Peter.

Loeffler, L., ed. see Nelson, Mark E.

Loeffler, M., jt. ed. see Wichmann, H. E.

Loeffler, M. P. Oskar Waelterlin: Ein Profil. 256p. (GER.). 1979. 16.95 (*0-8176-1133-9*) Birkhauser.

Loeffler, Margaret, ed. Montessori in Contemporary American Culture. LC 92-523. 298p. 1992. pap. text ed. 21.50 (*0-435-08709-6*, 08709) Heinemann.

Loeffler, Reinhold. Islam in Practice: Religious Beliefs in a Persian Village. LC 87-12175. 312p. 1988. 64.50 (*0-88706-678-X*); pap. 21.95 (*0-88706-679-8*) State U NY Pr.

Loeffler, Robert F. Step-by-Step Compo & Mold Making. LC 92-7144. (Illus.). 112p. 1992. 24.95 (*0-9632387-5-2*) LVI Pubns.

Loeffler, Robert H. A Guide to Preparing Cost-Effective Press Releases. LC 91-36042. (Illus.). 124p. 1992. lib. bdg. 29.95 (*1-56024-141-1*) Haworth Pr.

— A Guide to Preparing Cost-Effective Press Releases. 116p. 1993. pap. 12.95 (*1-56024-882-3*) Haworth Pr.

Loeffler, W., ed. see Sartor, K.

***Loehle, Craig.** On the Shoulders of Giants. 201p. (Orig.). 1994. pap. 9.95 (*0-85398-362-3*) G Ronald Pub.

Loehlein, D., jt. ed. see Doelp, R.

Loehlein, Patricia. Management Information Systems: An Information Sourcebook. (Sourcebook Series in Business & Management: No. 14). 232p. 1988. 57.50 (*0-89774-375-X*) Oryx Pr.

Loehlin, John C. Genes & Environment in Personality Development. (Individual Differences & Development Ser.: Vol. 2). (Illus.). 160p. (C). 1992. 42.95 (*0-8039-4450-0*); pap. 18.95 (*0-8039-4451-9*) Sage.

— Latent Variable Models: An Introduction to Factor, Path, Structural Analysis. 2nd ed. 304p. 1992. text ed. 59.95 (*0-8058-1083-8*); pap. 24.50 (*0-8058-1084-6*) L Erlbaum Assocs.

Loehlin, John C. & Nichols, Robert C. Heredity, Environment & Personality: A Study of 850 Sets of Twins. LC 75-33794. 214p. (C). 1976. 17.50 (*0-292-73003-9*) U of Tex Pr.

Loehman, Edna, jt. ed. see Conner, J. Richard.

Loehman, Edna T., jt. ed. see Dinar, Ariel.

Loehman, Ronald E. Characterization of Ceramics. LC 92-21549. (Materials Characterization Ser.). 312p. 1993. 59.95 (*0-7506-9253-7*) Buttrwrth-Heinemann.

***Loehner, R.** Introduction to Computational Fluid Dynamics Methods for Aerodynamics Applications. (Computational Methods in Mechanics & Aerodynamics Ser.). Date not set. text ed. 54.95 (*0-471-94276-6*) Wiley.

***Loehr.** Little Little Book. LC 93-83959. 1995. 3.25 (*0-679-85288-3*) Random.

— Little Red Barn. (J). 3.99 (*0-679-86006-1*) Random.

Loehr, Franklin. The Development of Religion As a Science. LC 83-81796. 92p. (Orig.). 1983. pap. 3.95 (*0-915151-05-7*) Religious Res Pr.

— Diary after Death. rev. ed. LC 83-82486. 148p. 1992. reprint ed. pap. 7.50 (*0-915151-04-9*) Religious Res Pr.

Loehr, Franklin, ed. see Amidon, Horton W.

Loehr, Franklin, ed. see Hussey, Helen N.

Loehr, Franklin, ed. see Hussey, Helen & Sherrod, Sandra.

Loehr, Franklin, ed. see Pinkston, Isabel.

Loehr, Franklin, ed. see Roberts, Helen.

***Loehr, Hermut.** Umkehr und Suende im Hebraeerbrief. (Beihefte zur Zeitschrift fuer die Neuetestamentliche Wissenschaft Ser.: Bd. 73). 375p. (GER.). (C). 1994. lib. bdg. 129.25 (*3-11-014202-3*) De Gruyter.

Loehr, James E. The Mental Game. 1990. pap. 11.95 (*0-452-26666-1*, Plume) NAL-Dutton.

— The Mental Game. 192p. 1990. pap. 10.95 (*0-8289-0758-7*) Viking Penguin.

— Mental Toughness Training for Sports: Achieving Athletic Excellence. 256p. 1986. pap. 9.95 (*0-8289-0574-6*) Viking Penguin.

Loehr, James E., et al. Mentally Tough: The Principles of Winning At Sports Applied to Winning In Business. LC 86-19654. 240p. 1986. pap. 8.95 (*0-87131-540-8*) M Evans.

***Loehr, James E.** The New Toughness Training for Sports. (Illus.). 224p. 1995. 11.95 (*0-452-26998-9*, Plume) NAL-Dutton.

— The New Toughness Training for Sports: Achieving Athletic Excellence. LC 94-8921. 1994. 21.95 (*0-525-93839-7*, Dutton) NAL-Dutton.

— Toughness Training for Life. (Illus.). 208p. 1993. 22.00 (*0-525-93612-2*, Dutton) NAL-Dutton.

— Toughness Training for Life: A Revolutionary Program for Maximizing Health, Happiness, & Productivity. 320p. 1994. pap. 11.95 (*0-452-27243-2*, Plume) NAL-Dutton.

Loehr, James E. & McLaughlin, Peter J. Mentally Tough. rev. ed. 1993. pap. 10.95 (*0-87131-723-0*) M Evans.

Loehr, James E., ed. see Henderson, Joe.

An Asterisk (*) at the beginning of an entry indicates that the title is appearing in BIP for the first time.

Loehr, Louise M. Willow Pattern China Price Guide. 4.00 (0-685-56581-5) H S Worth.

Loehr, Louise M., jt. auth. see Worth, Veryl M.

Loehr, Mallory. The Little Country Book. (Chunky Bks.). (Illus.). 28p. (J). (ps). 1994. 3.25 (0-679-85289-1) Random Bks Yng Read.

— Trucks. LC 91-75344. (Chunky Shape Bks.). (Illus.). 22p. (J). (ps). 1992. 3.25 (0-679-83061-8) Random Bks Yng Read.

Loehr, Raymond C. Pollution Control for Agriculture. 2nd ed. 1984. text ed. 79.00 (0-12-455270-6) Acad Pr.

Loehr, Thomas M., ed. Iron Carriers & Iron Proteins, Vol. 5. LC 89-5667. (Physical Bioinorganic Chemistry Ser.). 533p. 1989. lib. bdg. 180.00 (0-89573-298-X) VCH Pubs.

Loehr, William & Powelson, John P. The Economics of Development & Distribution. 436p. (C). 1981. text ed. 46.75 (0-15-518905-0) HB Coll Pubs.

Loehr, William & Sandler, Todd, eds. Public Goods & Public Policy. LC 77-17865. (Comparative Political Economy & Public Policy Ser.: Vol. 3). 240p. reprint ed. pap. 68.40 (0-317-09000-3, 2021923) Bks Demand.

Loehrlein, Myrna & Nylin, Dawn. Preschool Bible Lessons. (Christian Preschool Ser.). 96p. (J). (ps-1). 1990. 10.95 (0-86653-541-1, SS1875, Shining Star Pubns) Good Apple.

Loehry, H. The Oral Method of Latin Teaching. (C). 1982. pap. text ed. 55.00 (0-900269-10-3, Pub. by Old Vicarage UK) St Mut.

***Loeillet.** Werken voor Clavecimbel. 1973. pap. 20.00 (0-8450-0106-X) Broude.

Loeks, Mary, jt. auth. see DeVries, Betty.

Loeks, Mary F. Mom's Quiet Corner. (Comtempo Ser.). 1977. pap. 2.99 (0-8010-5576-8) Baker Bk.

Loeks, Mary Foxwell. Object Lessons for Children's Worship. (Object Lesson Ser.). 1979. pap. 5.99 (0-8010-5584-9) Baker Bk.

Loellgen, H., ed. Oberrheinisches Kardiologen-Symposium, Freiburg, May 1982: Journal: Cardiology, Vol. 70, Suppl. 1, 1983. (Illus.). iv, 140p. 1983. pap. 38.50 (3-8055-3688-7) S Karger.

Loellgen, H. & Mellerowicz, H., eds. Progress in Ergometry: Quality Control & Test Criteria, Fifth International Seminar on Ergometry. (Illus.). 260p. 1984. pap. 45.40 (0-387-13570-7) Spr-Verlag.

Loelling, Carol. Whose House Is This? (Surprise Bks.). (Illus.). 24p. (J). (gr. 3-6). 1979. 5.95 (0-8431-0444-9) Price Stern.

Loemker, Leroy E., ed. Gottfried Wilhelm Leibniz: Philosophical Papers & Letters. (Synthese Historical Library: No. 2). 1975. lib. bdg. 112.50 (90-277-0008-7) Kluwer Ac.

Loen, Raymond O. Superior Supervision: The Ten Percent Solution. 180p. 1994. text ed. 19.95 (0-02-919091-6) Free Pr.

Loendorf, Lawrence L., jt. ed. see Whitley, David S.

Loengard, John. Faces: Life. LC 93-41493. (gr. 5 up). 1994. 15.99 (0-517-10175-0) Random Hse Value.

— Georgia O'Keefe at Ghost Ranch. (Illus.). 80p. 1995. 35.00 (1-55670-423-2) Stewart Tabori & Chang.

— Speaking for the Negative. LC 94-14301. (Illus.). 96p. 1994. 29.95 (1-55970-282-6) Arcade Pub Inc.

Loening, K., et al. Polynuclear Aromatic Hydrocarbons Nomenclature Guide. LC 90-39042. 96p. 1990. pap. text ed. 19.95 (0-935470-59-X) Battelle.

Loening, K. L., ed. List of Standard Abbreviations, (Symbols) for Synthetic Polymers & Polymeric Materials: Basic Definitions of Terms Relating to Polymers. 1978. pap. 8.00 (0-08-022371-0, Pub. by Pergamon Repr UK) Franklin.

Loening, Kurt L., jt. ed. see Sonneveld, Helmi B.

Loening, Richard. Die Zurechungslehre Des Aristoteles. Bd. 1. xx, 359p. 1967. reprint ed. write for info. (0-318-70970-8, Pub. by Georg Olms GW) Lubrecht & Cramer.

Loening, Stefan A., jt. ed. see Culp, David A.

Loening, W. E., jt. ed. see Coovadia, H. M.

Loenneoken, S. Spansk-Norsk Ordbok: Spanish-Norwegian Dictionary. 2nd ed. 411p. (NOR & SPA.). 1980. 39.95 (0-8288-1033-8, S37620) Fr & Eur.

Loennroth, Erik, et al, eds. Conceptions of National History: Proceedings of Nobel Symposium 78. LC 93-33859. viii, 315p. (C). 1994. lib. bdg. 124.65 (3-11-013504-3, 3-94) De Gruyter.

Loeper, John J. Crusade for Kindness: Henry Bergh & the ASPCA. LC 90-27682. (Illus.). 112p. (J). (gr. 3-7). 1991. text ed. 13.95 (0-689-31560-0, Atheneum Bks Young) S&S Childrens.

— Going to School in 1776. LC 72-86940. (Illus.). 112p. (J). (gr. 4-7). 1973. text ed. 14.95 (0-689-30089-1, Aladdin Paperbacks) S&S Childrens.

— Going to School in 1876. LC 83-15669. (Illus.). 96p. (J). (gr. 4-7). 1984. text ed. 15.00 (0-689-31015-3, Aladdin Paperbacks) S&S Childrens.

Loeppky, Richard N. & Michejda, Christopher J., eds. Nitrosamines & Related N-Nitroso Compounds: Chemistry & Biochemistry. LC 94-2014. (Symposium Ser.: Vol. 553). 388p. 1994. 89.95 (0-8412-2856-6) Am Chemical.

Loer, Barbara. Das Absolute & die Wirklichkeit in Schellings Philosophie: Mit der Erstedition einer Handschrift aus dem Berliner Schelling-Nachlass. LC 73-93164. (Quellen & Studien zur Philosophie: Vol. 7). (Illus.). viii, 288p. (C). 1974. 134.65 (3-11-004329-7) De Gruyter.

Loera, Gabriel, ed. see Colle, Marie-Pierre.

Loerke, Jean Penn, jt. ed. see Langill, Ellen D.

Loertscher, David V. Biographical Index to Children's & Young Adult Authors & Illustrators: 1993 Edition. 400p. 1993. ring bd. 55.00 (0-931510-47-3) Hi Willow.

— Statistics of School Library Media Centers, 1985. 1990. 30.00 (0-931510-31-7) Hi Willow.

— Taxonomies of the School Library Media Program. xvi, 336p. 1988. pap. text ed. 26.50 (0-87287-662-4) Libs Unl.

Loertscher, David V. & Castle, Lance. A State-by-State Guide to Children's & Young Adult Authors & Illustrators. 344p. 1991. ring bd. 37.50 (0-931510-33-3); disk 30.50 (0-931510-35-X); disk 31.00 (0-931510-36-8); disk 31.50 (0-931510-37-6) Hi Willow.

Loertscher, David V. & Ho, May L. Computerized Collection for School Library Media Centers. (Excellence in School Library Media Centers: No. 2). 1986. 40.00 (0-931510-22-8) Hi Willow.

Loertscher, David V., jt. auth. see Studwell, William E.

Loertscher, David V., et al, eds. School Library Media File, No. 1. 200p. 1989. 27.50 (0-87287-685-3) Libs Unl.

Loes, Augustine, ed. see De la Salle, John B.

Loesberg, Jonathan. Aestheticism & Deconstruction: Pater, Derrida, & De Man. 276p. 1991. text ed. 32.50 (0-691-06884-4) Princeton U Pr.

— Fictions of Consciousness: Mill, Newman & the Reading of Victorian Prose. 280p. (C). 1986. pap. text ed. 20.00 (0-8135-1204-2) Rutgers U Pr.

Loesch, Danuta Z. Quantitative Dermatoglyphics: Classification, Genetics, & Pathology. (Oxford Monographs on Medical Genetics). (Illus.). 1983. 75.00 (0-19-261305-7) OUP.

Loesch, Larry C., jt. auth. see Vacc, Nicholas A.

Loeschcke, V., jt. ed. see Seitz, A.

Loeschcke, V., et al, eds. Conservation Genetics. LC 93-49017. (Experientia Supplementa Ser.: No. 68). 1994. 98.00 (0-8176-2939-4) Birkhauser.

Loesche, Walter J. Dental Caries: A Treatable Infection. rev. ed. (Illus.). 550p. (C). 1994. pap. 29.50 (0-9639689-0-4) Automat Diag.

Loeschen, John R. The Divine Community: Trinity, Church, & Ethics in Reformation Theologies. (Sixteenth Century Essays & Studies: Vol. I). 238p. 1981. 35.00 (0-940474-01-8) Sixteenth Cent.

Loeschen, R., jt. auth. see Bauer, Raymond A.

***Loescher, Elizabeth.** The Conflict Center's Conflict Management Middle School Curriculum. 64p. (J). (gr. 6-8). 1990. teacher ed 20.00 (1-887249-01-X) Conflict Ctr.

— Haciendo la Paz En Lo Practico: Un Programa De Estudios Para la Resolucion De Problemas Para la Escuela Primaria. 84p. (SPA.). (J). (gr. 1-5). 1991. teacher ed 25.00 (1-887249-02-8) Conflict Ctr.

— Peacemaking Made Practical: A Conflict Management Curriculum for the Elementary School. 86p. (J). (gr. 1-5). 1991. teacher ed 25.00 (1-887249-03-6) Conflict Ctr.

***Loescher, Elizabeth & Vobejda, Virginia.** How to Avoid World War III at Home: Conflict Management for the Family. 126p. 1994. pap. 9.00 (1-887249-00-1) Conflict Ctr.

***Loescher, Gil.** Beyond Charity: International Cooperation & the Global Refugee Crisis: A Twentieth Century Fund Book. (Illus.). 272p. 1995. reprint ed. pap. 19.95 (0-19-510294-0) OUP.

— The Global Refugee Crisis: A Reference Handbook. (Contemporary World Issues Ser.). 225p. 1994. lib. bdg. 39.50 (0-87436-753-0) ABC-CLIO.

Loescher, Gil, ed. Refugees & the Asylum Dilemma in the West. 184p. 1992. pap. 13.95 (0-271-00856-3) Pa St U Pr.

Loescher, Gil, jt. ed. see Nichols, Bruce.

Loescher, Gil D. Beyond Charity: International Cooperation & the Global Refugee Crisis. LC 92-39365. (Twentieth Century Fund Ser.). 272p. 1993. 35.00 (0-19-508183-8) OUP.

Loescher, Gil D. & Scanlan, John A. Calculated Kindness: Refugees & America's Half-Open Door, 1945 to the Present. 320p. 1986. text ed. 35.00 (0-02-927340-4) Free Pr.

Loeschke, Maravene S. Mime: Techniques & Class Formats: A Movement Program for the Visually Handicapped. (American Foundation for the Blind Practice Report Ser.). 79p. reprint ed. pap. 25.00 (0-7837-0132-2, 2040420) Bks Demand.

— The Path Between: An Historical Novel of the Dickinson Family of Amherst. LC 88-63314. (Illus.). 300p. (Orig.). (C). 1988. pap. 15.95 (0-931832-11-2) C H Fairfax.

Loeschnig, Louis. Simple Chemistry Experiments with Everyday Materials. LC 94-16757. (Illus.). 128p. 1994. 13.95 (0-8069-0688-X) Sterling.

***Loeschnig, Louis V.** Simple Chemistry Experiments with Everyday Materials. (Illus.). 128p. (Orig.). 1995. pap. 4.95 (0-8069-0689-8) Sterling.

Loeser, Angela, et al. Chemotherapie - Kompendium fuer das Pflegepersonal. (Illus.). viii, 48p. 1990. pap. 13.00 (3-8055-5295-5) S Karger.

Loeser, Harrison T. Sonar Engineering Handbook. 216p. 1993. reprint ed. 39.95 (0-932146-59-7) Peninsula CA.

Loeser, John D. & Egan, Kelly J., eds. Managing the Chronic Pain Patient: Theory & Practice at the University of Washington Multidiscipliney Pain Center. 270p. 1989. text ed. 96.50 (0-88167-464-8) Raven.

Loeser, John D., jt. auth. see Chapman, C. Richard.

Loeser, Pamela. Secret Harmony. 224p. (Orig.). 1993. pap. 2.95 (1-56597-101-9, Kismet) Meteor Pub.

Loesser, Arthur. Men Women & Pianos: A Social History. 1990. pap. 11.95 (0-486-26543-9) Dover.

Loesser, Susan. A Most Remarkable Fella: Frank Loesser & the Guys & Dolls in His Life: A Portrait by His Daughter. LC 92-54985. 1993. 23.00 (1-55611-364-1) D I Fine.

Loessin, Bruce A., jt. auth. see Duronio, Margaret A.

***Loethen, Mark L., ed.** National Symposium on Water Management in Urban Areas. (Technical Publication Ser.: No. 95-4). 350p. 1995. pap. write for info. (1-882132-35-1) Am Water Resources.

Loether, Herman & McTavish, Donald G. Descriptive & Inferential Statistics: An Introduction. rev. ed. 512p. (C). 1988. Instr's. manual avail. write for info. (0-318-62200-9, H11877) Allyn.

— Descriptive & Inferential Statistics: An Introduction. 3rd rev. ed. 512p. (C). 1988. text ed. 46.00 (0-205-11186-6, H11869) Allyn.

Loetscher, Andreas. Semantische Strukturen im Bereich der alt und mittelhochdeutschen Schallwoerter. (Quellen und Forschungen zur Sprach und Kulturgeschichte der Germanischen Voelker Ser.: NF 53). (C). 1973. 86.15 (3-11-003870-6) De Gruyter.

Loetscher, Lefferts A. A Brief History of the Presbyterians: With a New Chapter by George Laird Hunt. 4th ed. LC 83-21652. 224p. 1984. pap. 6.99 (0-664-24622-2, Westminster) Westminster John Knox.

— Facing the Enlightenment & Pietism: Archibald Alexander & the Founding of Princeton Theological Seminary. LC 82-11995. (Contributions to the Study of Religion Ser.: No. 8). x, 303p. 1983. text ed. 59.95 (0-313-23677-1, LOE/) Greenwood.

Loetterle, Bridget C. Ageless Prose: A Study of the Media-Projected Images of Aging. LC 93-34528. 328p. 1993. 72.00 (0-8153-1534-1) Garland.

Loev, Irv. Conflict Means I Love You. 3rd ed. 96p. (Orig.). 1985. pap. 9.95 (0-9615931-7-2) D & J Pr TX.

Loeve, M. Probability Theory I. 4th ed. LC 76-28332. (Graduate Texts in Mathematics Ser.: Vol. 45). 1977. 49.00 (3-540-90210-4) Spr-Verlag.

— Probability Theory II. (Graduate Texts in Mathematics Ser.: Vol. 46). 1994. 49.95 (0-387-90262-7) Spr-Verlag.

Loevgren, Sven. The Genesis of Modernism. LC 81-81720. (Illus.). xvi, 184p. 1983. reprint ed. lib. bdg. 40.00 (0-87817-280-7) Hacker.

Loevinger, J., ed. Scientific Ways in the Study of Ego Development. (Heinz Werner Lecture Ser.: No. 12). 1978. pap. 6.00 (0-914206-14-1) Clark U Pr.

Loevinger, Jane. Ego Development: Conceptions & Theories. LC 75-44880. (Social & Behavioral Science Ser.). (Illus.). 524p. 1976. 47.95x (0-87589-275-2) Jossey-Bass.

— Paradigms of Personality. (Psychology Ser.). (Illus.). 269p. (C). 1995. pap. text ed. write for info. (0-7167-1840-5) W H Freeman.

Loevinger, Jane, jt. auth. see Hy, Le-Xuan.

Loevinger, Jane, et al. Measuring Ego Development. Incl. Vol. 1. Construction & Use of a Sentence Completion Test. LC 71-92891. 265p. 1970. (0-87589-059-8); Vol. 2. Scoring Manual for Women & Girls. LC 71-92891. 475p. 1970. (0-87589-069-5); LC 71-92891. (Social & Behavioral Science Ser.). 1970. Set. 75.00 (0-87589-425-9) Jossey-Bass.

— Measuring Ego Development, Vol. 1. LC 71-92891. (Jossey-Bass Behavioral Science Ser.). 265p. pap. 71.60 (0-7837-0179-9, 2040476) Bks Demand.

— Measuring Ego Development, Vol. 2. LC 71-92891. (Jossey-Bass Behavioral Science Ser.). 477p. pap. 136.00 (0-7837-0180-2) Bks Demand.

Loevinger, Robert, et al, eds. MIRD Primer for Absorbed Dose Calculations. rev. ed. LC 91-4858. (Illus.). 128p. 1991. text ed. 50.00 (0-932004-38-5) Soc Nuclear Med.

Loevy, Hannelore. Dental Management of the Child Patient. 1981. text ed. 80.00 (0-931386-40-3) Quint Pub Co.

Loevy, Robert D. The Flawed Path to the Presidency, 1992: Unfairness & Inequality in the Presidential Selection Process. LC 93-48105. (SUNY Series on the Presidency: Contemporary Issues). 319p. (C). 1994. 59.50 (0-7914-2187-2); pap. 19.95 (0-7914-2188-0) State U NY Pr.

— To End All Segregation: The Politics of the Passage of the Civil Rights Act of 1964. 382p. (Orig.). (C). 1990. lib. bdg. 58.00 (0-8191-7688-5); pap. text ed. 28.50 (0-8191-7689-3) U Pr of Amer.

Loevy, Robert D., jt. auth. see Cronin, Thomas E.

Loevy, Steven R. William Carlos Williams's A Dream of Love. LC 83-4909. (Studies in Modern Literature: No. 22). 94p. reprint ed. pap. 26.80 (0-8357-1450-0, 2070559) Bks Demand.

Loew & Dunlop. The Illustrated History of Veterinary Medicine. (Illus.). 480p. 1991. 79.95 (0-8016-3209-9) Mosby Yr Bk.

Loew, Clemens. Dream Interpretation: A Comparative Review. rev. ed. Fosshage, James, ed. LC 85-27874. 1987. 37.50 (0-89335-241-1) PMA Pub Corp.

Loew, F., jt. ed. see Auer, L. M.

Loew, Leslie M., ed. Spectroscopic Membrane Probes. 1988. write for info. (0-318-62936-4, QH601) CRC Pr.

— Spectroscopic Membrane Probes, Vol. I. 240p. 1988. 137.00 (0-8493-4535-9, CRC Reprint) Franklin.

— Spectroscopic Membrane Probes, Vol. II. 208p. 1988. 137.00 (0-8493-4536-7, CRC Reprint) Franklin.

— Spectroscopic Membrane Probes, Vol. III. 240p. 1988. 137.00 (0-8493-4537-5, CRC Reprint) Franklin.

Loew, M. H. Medical Imaging Five, Vol. 1445: Image Processing. 1991. 100.00 (0-8194-0540-X) SPIE.

Loew, Sebastian. Local Planning. (Illus.). 165p. 1979. 28.50 (0-86206-000-1) Shoe String.

Loewald, Hans W. Papers on Psychoanalysis. LC 80-12012. 400p. 1989. pap. 20.00 (0-300-04617-0) Yale U Pr.

Loewe, Busso. Ancient Greek Theophoric Toponyms. 128p. 1980. 15.00 (0-89005-332-2) Ares.

Loewe, Edward E. Being Real: Rediscovering Truth & Reality in an Age of Deception & Illusion. Wright, Betty, ed. LC 90-30265. 350p. (Orig.). 1990. pap. 12.95 (0-935834-76-1) Rainbow Books.

Loewe, Frederick, jt. auth. see Lerner, Alan J.

Loewe, Heinz. Von Cassiodor zu Dante: Ausgewaehlte Aufsaetze Zur Geschichtsschreibung und Politischen Ideenwelt des Mittelalters. LC 73-75491. 342p. (C). 1973. 142.30 (3-11-003739-4) De Gruyter.

Loewe, Johann C. Dr. Carl Loewes Selbstbiographie. xxiii, 458p. 1976. reprint ed. write for info. (3-487-05988-6, Pub. by Georg Olms GW) Lubrecht & Cramer.

Loewe, Michael. Crisis & Conflict in Han China: Fourteen B. C. to A. D. Nine. LC 75-308728. 342p. reprint ed. pap. 97.50 (0-317-11325-9, 2012162) Bks Demand.

— Divination, Mythology & Monarchy in Han China. LC 93-28327. (University of Cambridge Oriental Publications: No. 48). (Illus.). 362p. (C). 1994. 69.95 (0-521-45466-2) Cambridge U Pr.

Loewe, Michael, ed. Early Chinese Texts: A Bibliographical Guide. LC 93-40281. (Early China Special Monographs: No. 2). 560p. 1994. 35.00 (1-55729-043-1) IEAS.

Loewe, Michael, jt. ed. see Twitchett, Denis C.

Loewe, Ralph E. A Reader for College Writers. 2nd ed. (Illus.). 368p. (C). 1985. pap. text ed. write for info. (0-13-753641-0) P-H.

— The Writing Clinic: Writing-Grammar-Readings. 4th ed. (Illus.). 384p. 1988. pap. text ed. write for info. (0-13-970112-5) P-H.

Loewe, Raphael. The Rylands Haggadah: A Medieval Sephardi Masterpiece in Facsimile. 1988. 75.00 (0-8109-1568-5) Abrams.

Loewe, Raphael, tr. see Kaplan, Yosef.

Loewe, Robert, jt. ed. see Kulp, Karel.

***Loewe, Roland.** A Grandfather's Story. 436p. 1995. pap. 33.00 (0-940121-30-1) Cross Cultural Pubns.

Loewen. Food in France. (International Food Library: Set II). (J). 1991. 11.95 (0-86625-344-0) Rourke Pubns.

— Food in Germany. (International Food Library: Set II). (J). 1991. 11.95 (0-86625-347-5) Rourke Pubns.

— Food in Greece. (International Food Library: Set II). (J). 1991. 11.95 (0-86625-348-3) Rourke Pubns.

— Food in Israel. (International Food Library: Set II). (J). 1991. 11.95 (0-86625-349-1) Rourke Pubns.

— Food in Korea. (International Food Library: Set II). (J). 1991. 11.95 (0-86625-345-9) Rourke Pubns.

— International Food Library, 6 bks., Set II. (J). 1991. 71.70 (0-86625-324-6) Rourke Pubns.

Loewen, Don, ed. Committed to World Missions: A Focus on International Strategy. 129p. (Orig.). 1990. pap. 4.95 (0-921788-00-2) Kindred Prods.

Loewen, Eleanor, jt. auth. see Toews, John.

Loewen, Eleanor M. Make My Joy Complete. Shelly, Maynard, ed. LC 87-83120. (Bible Studies). 80p. 1988. pap. 4.95 (0-87303-123-7) Faith & Life.

Loewen, Harry. No Permanent City: Stories from Mennonite History & Life. 224p. (Orig.). 1993. pap. 10.95 (0-8361-3612-8) Herald Pr.

Loewen, Harry, ed. Why I Am a Mennonite: Essays on Mennonite Identity. LC 87-62522. 352p. (Orig.). 1988. pap. 14.95 (0-8361-3463-X) Herald Pr.

Loewen, Howard J., ed. One Lord, One Church, One Hope, & One God: Mennonite Confessions of Faith. (Text-Reader Ser.: No. 2). 369p. 1985. pap. text ed. 12.00 (0-936273-08-9) Inst Mennonite.

Loewen, Jacob A. Culture & Human Values: Christian Intervention in Anthropological Perspective. Smalley, William A., ed. LC 75-12653. (Applied Cultural Anthropology Ser.). 443p. (Orig.). 1975. pap. 11.95 (0-87808-722-2) William Carey Lib.

— The Practice of Translating: Drills for Training Translators. (Helps for Translators Ser.). xiv, 260p. 1981. pap. 6.75 (0-8267-0028-4, 102703) Untd Bible Soc.

Loewen, James W. Lies My Teacher Told Me: Everything Your American History Textbook Got Wrong. 1995. 24.95 (1-56584-100-X) New Press NY.

— The Mississippi Chinese: Between Black & White. 2nd ed. 240p. (C). 1988. reprint ed. pap. text ed. 10.50x (0-88133-312-3) Waveland Pr.

— Truth about Columbus: A Subversively True Poster Book for a Dubiously Celebration Occasion. 48p. 1992. pap. 12.95 (1-56584-008-9) New Press NY.

Loewen, L. The Beatles. (Profiles in Music Ser.). (Illus.). 112p. (J). (gr. 5 up). 1989. lib. bdg. 18.60 (0-86592-610-7); lib. bdg. 13.95 (0-685-58616-2) Rourke Corp.

— Beethoven. (Profiles in Music Ser.). (Illus.). 112p. (J). (gr. 5 up). 1989. lib. bdg. 18.60 (0-86592-609-3); lib. bdg. 13.95 (0-685-58617-0) Rourke Corp.

— Elvis. (Profiles in Music Ser.). (Illus.). 112p. (J). (gr. 5 up). 1989. 13.95 (0-685-58614-6); lib. bdg. 18.60 (0-86592-606-9) Rourke Corp.

— James Brown. (Profiles in Music Ser.). (Illus.). 112p. (J). (gr. 5 up). 1989. 13.95 (0-685-58615-4); lib. bdg. 18.60 (0-86592-607-7) Rourke Corp.

— Johnny Cash. (Profiles in Music Ser.). (Illus.). 112p. (J). (gr. 5 up). 1989. 13.95 (0-685-58613-8); lib. bdg. 18.60 (0-86592-608-5) Rourke Corp.

— Mozart. (Profiles in Music Ser.). (Illus.). 112p. (J). (gr. 5 up). 1989. 13.95 (0-685-58618-9); lib. bdg. 18.60 (0-86592-605-0) Rourke Corp.

***Loewen, Melvin J.** The Descendants of Cornelius W. Loewen & Helena Bartel. 2nd ed. viii, 339p. Date not set. pap. 22.00 (0-9640876-2-6) Heritageclassics.

***Loewen, Melvin J., comp.** The Believer's Way of Life Vol. 2: Selections of Bible Readings for Daily Devotions. xviii, 365p. 1994. pap. 9.95 (0-9640876-1-8) Heritageclassics.

— God's Way of Salvation Vol. 1: Selections of Bible Readings for Daily Devotions. xviii, 365p. 1994. pap. 9.95 (0-9640876-0-X) Heritageclassics.

Loewen, N. Atlanta. (Great Cities of the U. S. A. Ser.). (Illus.). 48p. (J). (gr. 5 up). 1989. lib. bdg. 15.94 (0-86592-543-7); lib. bdg. 11.95 (0-685-58591-3) Rourke Corp.

— Philadelphia. (Great Cities of the U. S. A. Ser.). (Illus.). (J). (gr. 5 up). 1989. 11.95 (0-685-58593-X); lib. bdg. 15.94 (0-86592-542-9) Rourke Corp.

— Seattle. (Great Cities of the U. S. A. Ser.). (Illus.). (J). (gr. 5 up). 1989. 11.95 (0-685-58592-1); lib. bdg. 15.94 (0-86592-545-3) Rourke Corp.

— Washington, D. C. (Great Cities of the U. S. A. Ser.). (Illus.). (J). (gr. 5 up). 1989. lib. bdg. 15.94 (0-86592-544-5); lib. bdg. 11.95 (0-685-58590-5) Rourke Corp.

Loewen, Nancy. Food in Spain. LC 90-43595. (International Food Library: Set II). 32p. (J). (gr. 3-5). 1991. 11.95 (0-86625-346-7) Rourke Pubns.

— Jack London. LC 92-3739. (Profiles Ser.). (YA). (gr. 6 up). 1995. 18.95 (0-88682-510-5) Creative Ed.

— John Steinbeck. LC 93-1176. (Profiles Ser.). (YA). (gr. 6 up). 1995. 18.95 (0-88682-511-3) Creative Ed.

— Pearl Buck. LC 93-17133. (Profiles Ser.). (YA). (gr. 6 up). 1995. 18.95 (0-88682-514-8) Creative Ed.

— Poe. LC 93-17095. (Illus.). (J). 1993. lib. bdg. 17.95 (0-88682-509-1) Creative Ed.

— Poe. (Illus.). 64p. (YA). (gr. 6-12). 1993. 16.95 (1-56846-084-8) Creative Ed.

— Profiles in Music, 6 bks., Reading Level 6. (Illus.). 602p. (J). (gr. 5 up). 1989. 83.70 (0-685-58764-9) Rourke Corp.

— Profiles in Music, 6 bks., Set, Reading Level 6. (Illus.). 602p. (YA). (gr. 5 up). 1989. Set. lib. bdg. 111.60 (0-86592-604-2) Rourke Corp.

— Walt Whitman. LC 93-15081. 1994. lib. bdg. 16.95 (0-88682-608-X) Creative Ed.

— Walt Whitman. 48p. (YA). (gr. 7 up). 1994. 16.95 (1-56846-096-1) Creative Ed.

Loewen, Nancy & Stewart, Gail. Great Cities of the U. S., 8 bks., Reading Level 6. (Illus.). 384p. (J). (gr. 5 up). 1989. 95.60 (0-685-58767-3) Rourke Corp.

— Great Cities of the U. S., 8 bks., Set, Reading Level 6. (Illus.). 384p. (YA). (gr. 5 up). 1989. Set. lib. bdg. 127.52 (0-86592-537-2) Rourke Corp.

Loewen, Philip D. Optimal Control via Nonsmooth Analysis. LC 93-4143. (CRM Proceedings & Lecture Notes Ser.: Vol. 2). 153p. 1993. pap. 45.00 (0-8218-6996-5) Am Math.

*__Loewen, Roland.__ Small Scale Refining of Jewelers Wastes. 1995. write for info. (0-931913-19-5) Met-Chem Rsch.

Loewen, Royden. Family, Church, & Market: A Mennonite Community in the Old & New Worlds 1850-1930. LC 92-34007. 370p. 1993. 55.00 (0-8020-2937-X); pap. 24.95 (0-685-67884-9) U of Toronto Pr.

Loewen, Royden K. Family, Church, & Market: A Mennonite Community in the Old & New Worlds, 1850-1930. LC 92-34007. (Statue of Liberty-Ellis Island Centennial Ser.). (Illus.). 416p. (C). 1993. 42.50 (0-252-01980-6); pap. 19.95 (0-252-06325-2) U of Ill Pr.

Loewenberg, Alfred. Annals of Opera, Fifteen Ninety-Seven to Nineteen Forty, 2 vols., Set. 1988. reprint ed. lib. bdg. 149.00 (0-7812-0999-4) Rprt Serv.

— Early Dutch Librettos & Plays with Music in the British Museum: In the Journal of Documentation. 60p. 1993. reprint ed. lib. bdg. 69.00 (0-7812-9700-1) Rprt Serv.

Loewenberg, Bert J. & Bogin, Ruth, eds. Black Women in Nineteenth-Century American Life: Their Words, Their Thoughts, Their Feelings. LC 75-27175. 350p. (C). 1976. 30.00 (0-271-01207-2); pap. 15.95 (0-271-00507-6) Pa St U Pr.

Loewenberg, Frank M. Fundamentals of Social Intervention. 2nd ed. LC 82-22025. 448p. 1983. text ed. 35.50 (0-231-05722-9) Col U Pr.

— Religion & Social Work Practice in Contemporary American Society. 184p. 1988. text ed. 28.00 (0-231-06452-7) Col U Pr.

Loewenberg, Frank M. & Dolgoff, Ralph. Ethical Decisions for Social Work Practice. 4th ed. LC 91-66465. 280p. 1992. pap. 25.00 (0-87581-356-9) Peacock Pubs.

Loewenberg, Gerhard. Handbook of Legislative Research. Patterson, Samuel C. & Jewell, Malcolm E., eds. LC 84-29059. (Illus.). 864p. 1985. 45.00 (0-674-37075-9) HUP.

Loewenberg, Gerhard, ed. Modern Parliaments: Change or Decline. (Controversy Ser.). 1971. 12.95 (0-202-24075-4) Lieber-Atherton.

Loewenberg, Gerhard & Patterson, Samuel C. Comparing Legislatures. (Illus.). 362p. (C). 1988. reprint ed. pap. text ed. 31.00 (0-8191-7050-X) U Pr of Amer.

Loewenberg, Jacob. Dialogues from Delphi. LC 77-121485. (Essay Index Reprint Ser.). 1977. 21.95 (0-8369-1886-X) Ayer.

*__Loewenberg, Peter.__ Fantasy & Reality in History. (Illus.). 272p. 1995. 29.95 (0-19-506763-0) OUP.

Loewenberg, Robert J. An American Idol: Emerson & the "Jewish Idea" LC 84-7206. 148p. (Orig.). (C). 1984. lib. bdg. 40.00 (0-8191-3955-6); pap. text ed. 19.50 (0-8191-3956-4) U Pr of Amer.

— Equality on the Oregon Frontier: Jason Lee & the Methodist Mission, 1834-43. LC 75-40876. 300p. 1976. 25.00 (0-295-95491-4) U of Wash Pr.

— Freedom's Despots: The Critique of Abolition. LC 85-73324. 186p. 1986. lib. bdg. 19.95 (0-89089-287-3) Carolina Acad Pr.

Loewenberg, Robert J. & Alexander, Edward, eds. The Israeli Fate of Jewish Liberalism: Proceedings of a Conference in Jerusalem, at the Institute for Advanced Strategic & Political Studies, 1985. LC 88-20517. 158p. (Orig.). (C). 1988. lib. bdg. 47.00 (0-8191-7062-3); pap. text ed. 22.50 (0-8191-7063-1) U Pr of Amer.

Loewenfeld, Claire. Herb Gardening: Why & How to Grow Herbs. 256p. 1989. pap. 12.95 (0-571-09475-9) Faber & Faber.

Loewenfeld, Irene E. The Pupil: Anatomy, Physiology, & Clinical Applications, 2 Vols., Vol. I. LC 90-5180. (Illus.). 1606p. (C). 1993. text ed. 395.00 (0-8138-1908-3) Iowa St U Pr.

— The Pupil: Anatomy, Physiology, & Clinical Applications, Vol. II. (Illus.). 720p. (C). 1993. write for info. (0-318-68232-X); write for info. (0-318-68233-8) Iowa St U Pr.

Loewenfeld-Russ, Hans. Die Regelung der Volks-Ernahrung im Kriege. (Wirtschafts-Und Sozialgeschichte des Weltkrieges (Osterreichische Und Ungarische Serie)). (GER.). 1926. 150.00 (0-317-27542-9) Elliots Bks.

Loewenheim, Francis, et al. Roosevelt & Churchill: Their Secret Wartime Correspondence. (Quality Paperbacks Ser.). (Illus.). 840p. 1990. reprint ed. pap. 17.95 (0-306-80390-9) Da Capo.

Loewenson, Rene. Modern Plantation Agriculture: Corporate Wealth & Labour Squalor. 208p. (C). 1992. text ed. 55.00 (0-86232-996-5, Pub. by Zed Books UK); pap. 19.95 (0-86232-997-3, Pub. by Zed Books UK) Humanities.

Loewenstamm, Samuel E. The Evolution of the Exodus Tradition. Schwartz, Baruch J., tr. 310p. 1992. text ed. 27.00 (0-685-72548-0, Pub. by Magnes Press IS) Eisenbrauns.

— From Babylon to Canaan: Studies in the Bible & Its Oriental Background. xvii, 495p. 1992. text ed. 37.00x (965-223-784-1, Pub. by Magnes Press IS) Eisenbrauns.

*__Loewenstein, Andrea F.__ Loathsome Jews & Engulfing Women: Metaphors of Projection in the Works of Wyndham Lewis, Charles Williams & Graham Greene. LC 93-16362. 412p. 1995. pap. 18.95 (0-8147-5096-6) NYU Pr.

— Loathsome Jews & Engulfing Women: Metaphors of Projection in the Works of Wyndham Lewis, Charles Williams & Graham Greene. LC 93-16362. (Literature & Psychoanalysis Ser.: Vol. 2). 412p. 1995. 45.00 (0-8147-5063-X) NYU Pr.

— The Worry Girl: Stories from a Childhood. LC 92-8021. 160p. (Orig.). 1992. lib. bdg. 18.95 (1-56341-017-6); pap. 8.95 (1-56341-016-8) Firebrand Bks.

Loewenstein, C. Jared. A Descriptive Catalogue of the Jorge Luis Borges Collection at the University of Virginia Library. 150p. 1993. text ed. 35.00 (0-8139-1333-0) U Pr of Va.

Loewenstein, David. Milton: "Paradise Lost" LC 92-35914. (Landmarks of World Literature Ser.). (Illus.). 160p. (C). 1993. 34.95 (0-521-39303-5); pap. 11.95 (0-521-39899-1) Cambridge U Pr.

— Milton & the Drama of History: Historical Vision, Iconoclasm & the Literary Imagination. (Illus.). 228p. (C). 1990. 64.95 (0-521-37253-4) Cambridge U Pr.

Loewenstein, David & Turner, James G., eds. Politics, Poetics & Hermeneutics in Milton's Prose. (Illus.). 250p. (C). 1990. 64.95 (0-521-34458-1) Cambridge U Pr.

Loewenstein, Hubertus Z. Germans in History. LC 78-95395. reprint ed. 34.50 (0-404-04008-X) AMS Pr.

Loewenstein, K. L. The Manufacturing Technology of Continuous Glass Fibres. 2nd rev. ed. (Glass Science & Technology Ser.: Vol. 6). 354p. 1983. 138.50 (0-444-42185-8) Elsevier.

Loewenstein, Karl. Hitler's Germany. LC 72-7104. (Select Bibliographies Reprint Ser.). 1977. reprint ed. 21.95 (0-8369-6947-2) Ayer.

— Max Weber's Political Ideas in the Perspective of Our Time. LC 66-16541. 120p. 1966. pap. 9.95 (0-87023-009-3) U of Mass Pr.

Loewenstein, Louis K. Streets of San Francisco: The Origins of Street & Place Names. 2nd ed. LC 82-49331. (Illus.). 120p. (Orig.). 1984. pap. 6.95 (0-938530-27-5) Lexikos.

— The Transformation of Railroad Stations. (Railway History Monograph). (Illus.). 20p. 1992. pap. 9.00 (0-916170-43-8) J-B Pub.

Loewenstein, Prince H. & Von Zuhlsdorff, Volkmar. NATO & the Defense of the West. Fitzgerald, Edward, tr. LC 74-20276. 383p. 1975. reprint ed. text ed. 65.00 (0-8371-7855-X, LONA, Greenwood Pr) Greenwood.

Loewenstein, Rudolph M., ed. Drives, Affects, Behavior, 2 vols., Vol. 1. LC 53-11056. 399p. 1960. text ed. 55.00x (0-8236-1480-8) Intl Univs Pr.

— Drives, Affects, Behavior, 2 vols., Vol. 2. LC 53-11056. 502p. 1960. text ed. 65.00 (0-8236-1500-6) Intl Univs Pr.

*__Loewenthal.__ Mental Health & Religion. 256p. 1994. pap. 41.50 (1-56593-356-7, 0680) Singular Publishing.

Loewenthal, H. J. A Guide for the Perplexed Organic Experimentalist. 2nd ed. 1992. pap. text ed. 42.95 (0-471-93533-6) Wiley.

Loewenthal, Lillian. The Search for Isadora: The Legend & Legacy of Isadora Duncan. 1993. 26.95 (0-87127-179-6) Princeton Bk Co.

Loewenthal, Naftali. Communicating the Infinite: The Emergence of the Habad School. (Illus.). 368p. 1990. 39.95 (0-226-49045-9) U Ch Pr.

Loewenthal, Rudolf. The Sino-Judaic Bibliographies of Rudolf Loewenthal. Pollak, Michael, ed. (Bibliographica Judaica Ser.: No. 12). 208p. 1988. pap. 20.00 (0-87820-910-7) Hebrew Union Coll Pr.

Loewenthal, Rudolf, jt. auth. see Pokotilov, Dmitri.

Loewenthal, Rudolph. Turkic Languages & Literature of Central Asia. (Central Asiatic Studies: No. 1). 1957. pap. text ed. 46.00 (90-279-0014-0) Mouton.

Loewer, Barry & Reys, Georges, eds. Meaning in Mind: Fodor & His Critics. (Philosophers & Their Critics Ser.). 384p. 1993. pap. 24.95 (0-631-18701-4) Blackwell Pubs.

*__Loewer, Otto, et al.__ On-Farm Drying & Storage Systems. LC 94-72087. 576p. 1994. 55.00 (0-929355-53-9) Am Soc Ag Eng.

*__Loewer, Peter.__ American Gardens: A Tour of the Nation's Finest Private Gardens. LC 95-7409. 1995. 19.99 (0-517-14712-2, Pub. by Wings Bks) Random.

— The Evening Garden. (Illus.). 288p. 1993. text ed. 25.00 (0-02-574041-5) Macmillan.

— The New Small Garden: Plans & Plants That Make Every Inch Count. (Illus.). 192p. 1994. pap. 19.95 (0-8117-2568-5) Stackpole.

— Organic Gardener's Annuals. rev. ed. (Organic Gardener's Ser.). (Illus.). 144p. 1993. reprint ed. 19.95 (1-878823-13-2); reprint ed. pap. 9.95 (1-878823-08-6) Van Patten Pub.

— Organic Gardener's Landscape Design. (Organic Gardener's Ser.). (Illus.). 144p. 1994. pap. 9.95 (1-878823-10-8) Van Patten Pub.

— Organic Gardener's Year of Flowers. (Organic Gardener's Ser.). (Illus.). 144p. 1994. pap. 9.95 (1-878823-09-4) Van Patten Pub.

— Pond Water Zoo: An Introduction to Microscopic Life. LC 93-18468. (Illus.). 32p. (J). (gr. 1-8). 1995. text ed. 13.95 (0-689-31736-0, Atheneum Bks Young) S&S Childrens.

— Rodale's Annual Garden. LC 92-36480. 1993. 9.99 (0-517-08926-2, Pub. by Wings Bks) Random Hse Value.

— Thoreau's Garden: Native Plants for the American Landscape. (Illus.). 192p. 1995. 19.95 (0-8117-1728-3) Stackpole.

— Tough Plants for Tough Places: How to Grow 101 Easy-Care Plants for Every Part of Your Yard. LC 91-29449. (Illus.). 272p. 1991. 24.95 (0-87857-986-9, 01-030-0) Rodale Pr Inc.

— The Wild Gardener: On Flowers & Foliage for the Natural Border. LC 91-15394. 256p. 1991. 19.95 (0-8117-0885-3) Stackpole.

— A Year of Flowers. LC 93-14060. 1993. reprint ed. 9.99 (0-517-09375-8, Pub. by Wings Bks) Random Hse Value.

Loewer, Peter, jt. auth. see Tufts, Craig.

Loewer, Peter H., ed. Garden Ornaments. (Plants & Gardens Ser.). (Illus.). 1989. ring bd. 3.95 (0-945352-15-8, Sterling) Bklyn Botanic.

Loewes, Gustav & Von Hartel, Wilhelm, eds. Bibliotheca Patrum Latinorum Hispaniensis, 4 vols., Set. (Sitzungsberichte der Pilosophisch-Historischen Classe der Kaiserlichen Akademie der Wissenschaften Ser.: Vols. 111-113 & 169). 6385p. 1973. reprint ed. write for info. (3-487-04428-5, Pub. by Georg Olms GW) Lubrecht & Cramer.

Loewestein, George & Elster, Jon. Choice over Time. LC 91-42816. (Illus.). 352p. 1992. 39.95 (0-87154-558-6) Russell Sage.

Loewinsohn, Ron. Goat Dances. LC 76-43291. 145p. (Orig.). 1976. pap. 4.00 (0-87685-266-5) Black Sparrow.

Loewinson-Lessing, V. & Egorova, Zh. Rembrandt Harmensz Van Rijn: Paintings from Soviet Museums. (Illus.). 183p. (C). 1987. text ed. 330.00 (0-569-09129-2, Pub. by Collets) St Mut.

Loewisch, Dieter-Juergen, jt. ed. see Martin, Gottfried.

Loewke, Eileen, see Egan Roberta, pseud..

Loewner, Charles, et al, eds. Charles Loewner: Theory of Continuous Groups. (Mathematicians of Our Time Ser.). 1971. text ed. 30.00 (0-262-06041-8) MIT Pr.

Loewus, D. I., tr. see Cramer, F.

Loewus, F. A. & Tanner, W., eds. Plant Carbohydrates I: Intracellular Carbohydrates. (Encyclopedia of Plant Physiology Ser.: Vol. 13 a). (Illus.). 880p. 1982. 257.00 (0-387-11060-7) Spr-Verlag.

Loewus, F. A., jt. ed. see Tanner, W.

Loewy, Ariel G., et al. Cell Structure & Function. 3rd ed. 896p. (C). 1991. text ed. 57.00 (0-03-047439-6) SCP.

Loewy, Arnold, jt. auth. see LaFrance, Arthur B.

Loewy, Arnold H. Criminal Law in a Nutshell. 2nd ed. (Nutshell Ser.). 321p. 1993. reprint ed. pap. text ed. 16.00 (0-314-58529-X) West Pub.

Loewy, Arnold H., ed. A Criminal Law Anthology. LC 92-20849. 1992. write for info. (0-87084-182-3) Anderson Pub Co.

Loewy, Arthur D. & Spyer, K. Michael, eds. Central Regulation of Autonomic Functions. (Illus.). 416p. 1990. 85.00 (0-19-505106-8) OUP.

Loewy, E. H. Textbook of Medical Ethics. (Illus.). 270p. 1989. 39.50 (0-306-43280-3, Plenum Med Bk) Plenum.

Loewy, E. M. Inschriften Griechischer Bildhauer. xl, 410p. 1976. 25.00 (0-89005-112-7) Ares.

Loewy, Erich H. Ethical Dilemmas in Modern Medicine: A Physician's Viewpoint. LC 86-23460. (Studies in Health & Human Services: Vol. 8). 352p. 1986. lib. bdg. 99.95 (0-88946-133-3) E Mellen.

— Freedom & Community: The Ethics of Interdependence. LC 92-24773. 261p. (C). 1993. pap. 19.95 (0-7914-1514-7) State U NY Pr.

— Suffering & the Beneficent Community: Beyond Libertarianism. LC 90-46087. (SUNY Series in Ethical Theory). 159p. (C). 1991. 64.50 (0-7914-0745-4); pap. 21.95 (0-7914-0746-2) State U NY Pr.

Loewy, Raymond. Industrial Design. LC 79-15104. (Illus.). 250p. 1987. 85.00 (0-87951-098-6); 350.00 (0-87951-102-8); pap. 40.00 (0-87951-260-1) Overlook Pr.

Lof, George, ed. Active Solar Systems. (Illus.). 825p. 1992. 80.00x (0-262-12167-0) MIT Pr.

Lof, George O., jt. auth. see Ackerman, Edward A.

Lof, George O., jt. auth. see Cootner, Paul H.

Lof, George O. G. & Kneese, Allen V. The Economics of Water Utilization in the Beet Sugar Industry. LC 68-16166. (Resources for the Future Ser.). (Illus.). 135p. reprint ed. 38.50 (0-8357-9268-4, 2015741) Bks Demand.

Lof, P. Elsevier's Periodic Table of the Elements. 1987. pap. 122.50 (0-444-42653-1) Elsevier.

Lof, P., comp. Elsevier's Mineral & Rock Table. 1982. pap. 122.50 (0-444-42081-9) Elsevier.

— Minerals of the World Table. 1983. 122.50 (0-444-42135-1) Elsevier.

*__Lofaro.__ James Agee: Reconsiderations. LC 92-1405. (Tennessee Studies in Literature: Vol. 33). 184p. (C). 1995. pap. text ed. 16.00x (0-87049-886-X) U of Tenn Pr.

Lofaro, jt. auth. see USMA Staff.

Lofaro, Michael A. The Life & Adventures of Daniel Boone. LC 85-31513. 168p. 1986. 18.00 (0-8131-1593-0) U Pr of Ky.

— The Tall Tales of Davy Crockett: The Second Nashville Series of Crockett Almanacs, 1839-1841. LC 86-29369. (Tennesseana Editions Ser.). (Illus.). 164p. 1987. reprint ed. 30.00x (0-87049-525-9); reprint ed. pap. 15.00x (0-87049-526-7) U of Tenn Pr.

Lofaro, Michael A., ed. Davy Crockett: The Man, the Legend, the Legacy, 1786-1986. LC 84-25737. (Illus.). 228p. 1985. 35.00x (0-87049-459-7); pap. 16.00x (0-87049-507-0) U of Tenn Pr.

— James Agee: Reconsiderations. LC 92-1405. (Tennessee Studies in Literature: Vol. 33). 184p. 1992. text ed. 28.00x (0-87049-756-1) U of Tenn Pr.

Lofaro, Michael A. & Cummings, Joe, eds. Crockett at Two Hundred: New Perspectives on the Man & the Myth. LC 88-29369. 280p. 1989. 30.00x (0-87049-592-5) U of Tenn Pr.

*__Lofas, Jeanette & Sova, Dawn B.__ Stepparenting: Everything You Need to Know to Make It Work. 1995. pap. 12.00 (0-8217-4958-7) Zebra.

Lofas, Jeanette & Sova, Dawn E. Stepparenting. 256p. 1987. pap. 2.95 (0-8217-1683-2) Zebra.

*__Lofas, Jeannette & MacMillan, Joan.__ He's OK, She's OK: Honoring the Differences Between Men & Women. 144p. 1995. pap. 12.95 (0-929999-11-8) Tzedakah Pubns.

Lofas, Jeannette, jt. auth. see Roosevelt, Ruth.

Lofbarg, John O. & Barkan, Irving. Sycophancy in Athens & Capital Punishment in Ancient Athens. Vlastos, Gregory, ed. LC 78-14609. (Morals & Law in Ancient Greece Ser.). 1979. reprint ed. lib. bdg. 17.95 (0-405-11585-7) Ayer.

Lofberg, J., jt. auth. see Epperlein, H. H.

Lofberg, Jan. Spiritual or Human Value? An Evaluation-Systematical Reconstruction & Analysis of the Preaching of Jesus in the Synoptical Gospels. (Studia Philosophiae Religionis: No. 10). (Orig.). 1982. pap. 37.50x (0-317-65795-X) Coronet Bks.

Lofchie, Michael F. The Policy Factor: Agricultural Performance in Kenya & Tanzania. LC 88-18396. (Food in Africa Ser.). 236p. 1988. lib. bdg. 35.00 (1-55587-136-4) Lynne Rienner.

*__Lofer, Jennifer & Greeley, Hugh.__ Quality Improvement Techniques for Respiratory Care. (Health Care Quality Improvement Ser.). 220p. 1993. pap. text ed. 42.00 (1-885829-05-1) Opus Communs.

*__Lofer, Jennifer I. & Greeley, Hugh.__ Quality Improvement Techniques for Medical Records. (Health Care Quality Improvement Ser.). 217p. 1992. pap. text ed. 42.00 (1-885829-04-3) Opus Communs.

*__Lofer, Jennifer I., 10th & Greeley, Hugh.__ Quality Improvement Techniques for Radiology. (Health Care Quality Improvement Ser.). 230p. 1993. pap. text ed. 47.00 (1-885829-06-X) Opus Communs.

Lofer, Jennifer I., jt. auth. see Greeley, Hugh.

*__Lofer, Jennifer I., et al.__ Information Management: A Guide to the JCAHO Standards. 144p. 1994. pap. text ed. 57.00 (1-885829-09-4) Opus Communs.

Loffborough, M. & Cain, E. Pine Needle Basketry: How to Do Hand Crafts. rev. ed. LC 76-25409. (Illus.). 1978. pap. 12.95 (0-87282-110-2) Am Life Foun.

Loffer, F., jt. auth. see Bieber, E.

Lofficier, tr. see Andreas.

Lofficier, J. M., tr. see Schuiten, Peeters.

Lofficier, J. M., tr. see Tardi, Jacques.

Lofficier, Jean M., tr. see Bissette, Stephen R. & O'Connor, Nancy J., eds.

Lofficier, Jean M., tr. see Giraud, Jean.

Lofficier, Jean-Marc, tr. see Cailleteau, Thierry & Vatine, Olivier.

Lofficier, Jean-marc

Lofficier, Jean-Marc, tr. see Giraud, Jean M.

Lofficier, Jean-Marc, tr. see Giraud, Jean.

Lofficier, Jean-Marc, tr. see Jodorowsky, Alexandro & Giraud, Jean.

L'Officier, Jean-Marc, jt. ed. see L'Officier, Randy.

Lofficier, R., ed. see Giraud, Jean M.

Lofficier, R., tr. see Schuiten, Peeters.

Lofficier, R., tr. see Tardi, Jacques.

L'Officier, R. J. The Keep of Two Moons. Baisden, Greg, ed. (Arzach Ser.: No. 3). (Illus.). 12p. 1992. 12.95 (1-879450-25-9) Tundra MA.

Lofficier, R. J. Legends of Arzach, No. 5: The Keeper of the Earth's Treasures. (Illus.). 12p. 1992. 12.95 (1-879450-27-5) Tundra MA.

— Legends of Arzach, No. 6: The Fountains of Summer. (Illus.). 12p. 1992. 12.95 (1-879450-28-3) Tundra MA.

Lofficier, R. J., jt. auth. see Giraud, Jean M.

Lofficier, R. J., jt. auth. see Moebius.

L'Officier, Randy & L'Officier, Jean-Marc, eds. Visions of Arzach. (Illus.). 64p. (YA). (gr. 6 up). 1993. reprint ed. 14.95 (0-87816-233-X) Kitchen Sink.

Lofficier, Randy, tr. see Bissette, Stephen R. & O'Connor, Nancy J., eds.

Lofficier, Randy, tr. see Cailleteau, Thierry & Vatine, Olivier.

Lofficier, Randy, tr. see Giraud, Jean M.

Lofficier, Randy, tr. see Giraud, Jean.

Lofficier, Randy, tr. see Jodorowsky, Alexandro & Giraud, Jean.

Loffler, Eduard. Die Osterreichische Pferdeankaufmission Unter Dem K. K. Obersten Ritter v. Brudermann in Syrien, Palastina und der Wuste In Den Jahren 1856 und 1857. (Documenta Hippologica Ser.). xv, 240p. 1978. reprint ed. write for info. (3-487-08174-1, Pub. by Georg Olms GW) Lubrecht & Cramer.

Loffler, Fritz. Josef Hegenbarth. 352p. (GER.). 1980. 144.00 (0-317-57246-6, Pub. by Collets UK) St Mut.

An Asterisk (*) at the beginning of an entry indicates that the title is appearing in BIP for the first time.

— Otto Dix: Life & Work. Hollingdale, R. J., tr. LC 81-2947. (Illus.). 424p. 1982. 95.00 (*0-8419-0578-9*) Holmes & Meier.

Loffler, H. Paleolimnology. (Developments in Hydrobiologia Ser.). 1987. lib. bdg. 220.00 (*90-6193-624-1*) Kluwer Ac.

Loffler, H., ed. Neusiedlersee: The Limnology of a Shallow Lake in Central Europe. (Monographiae Biologicae Ser.: No. 37). (Illus.). x, 559p. 1980. lib. bdg. 206.00 (*90-6193-089-8*) Kluwer Ac.

Loffler, H. & Danielopol, D., eds. Ecology & Zoogeography of Ostracoda. (Illus.). 1978. lib. bdg. 154.50 (*90-6193-581-4*) Kluwer Ac.

Loffler, Hans & Goldman, Leonard. English Synonyms & How to Use Them, No. 1. 324p. 1974. 30.00 (*0-317-56610-5*, Pub. by Collets UK) Pro-Am Music.

Loffler, L., jt. auth. see Brauns, C. D.

Loffler, Ullrich, jt. auth. see Berthold, Werner.

***Loffler, Wolfgang & Waeterloos, Kristin.** Dictionnaire Francais-Allemand, Allemand-Francais. 1993. write for info. (*0-7859-7616-7*, 2010206576); write for info. (*0-7859-7619-1*) Fr & Eur.

Loffman, Tom. Sacramento Weather Guide: 1990 Edition. Mann, Randy, ed. & illus. by. 64p. (Orig.). 1989. pap. 2.95 (*0-941687-01-5*) Weather Pr.

Loffman, Tom & Mann, Randy. International Traveler's Weather Guide. rev. ed. LC 90-70281. (Illus.). 104p. 1990. pap. 10.95 (*0-941687-02-3*) Weather Pr.
When you're on vacation or a business trip, there's no doubt about it--if the weather is "bad" you're going to be miserable. And, you're going to be even more unhappy when you figure out how much money the whole thing cost you. The INTERNATIONAL TRAVELER'S WEATHER GUIDE can help you avoid vacation disasters by giving you concise weather information for over 150 cities in the U.S. & around the world. Not only does this book include information on temperature, rainfall, & humidity, but it also tells you the best & worst times to visit. The INTERNATIONAL TRAVELER'S WEATHER GUIDE is the most popular & easiest to use weather guide available & is designed specifically for travelers. The guide was researched & written by two meteorologists who make it easy for you to locate your destination in the tables & quickly plan your trip around the weather. The INTERNATIONAL TRAVELER'S WEATHER GUIDE is a must for travel agents, pilots, business travelers or anyone who wants to get the most out of his/her vacation. Call (800) 972-0201. ***Publisher Provided Annotation.***

Loffredo, William, jt. auth. see Milio, Frank.

Loffredo, William M., jt. auth. see Milio, Frank R.

Loffredo, William M., jt. auth. see Schreck, James O.

Lofgren, Charles A. Government from Reflection & Choice: Constitutional Essays on War, Foreign Relations & Federalism. 256p. 1986. text ed. 39.95 (*0-19-504007-4*) OUP.

— The Plessy Case: A Legal-Historical Interpretation. 288p. 1988. reprint ed. pap. 17.95 (*0-19-505684-1*) OUP.

Lofgren, Devid E. Managing Grounds Maintenance. Robinette, Gary O., ed. 181p. (Orig.). 1994. pap. text ed. 29.95 (*1-882240-02-2*) Agora Comms.

Lofgren, Don J. Dangerous Premises: An Insider's View of OSHA Enforcement. 256p. 1989. pap. 15.95 (*0-87546-150-6*) ILR Pr.

***Lofgren, Donald L.** The Bug Creek Problem & the Cretaceous-Tertiary Transition at McGuire Creek, Montana. LC 95-12046. (Geological Sciences Publications: Vol. 140). 1995. pap. write for info. (*0-520-09800-5*) U CA Pr.

Lofgren, M. J. Handbook for the Accident Reconstructionist. 318p. (C). 1983. pap. text ed. 24.00 (*1-884566-01-4*) Inst Police Tech.

Lofgren, Mikal. Wheat: Humor & Wisdom of J. Golden Kimball. LC 80-81556. 95p. 1980. 6.50 (*0-936718-04-8*) Moth Hse.

Lofgren, Orvar, jt. auth. see Frykman, Jonas.

Lofgren, Ulf. Alvin & the Unruly Elves. (J). (ps-3). 1992. 18.95 (*0-87614-590-X*, Carolrhoda) Lerner Group.

— Alvin the Knight. (J). (ps-3). 1992. 18.95 (*0-87614-698-1*, Carolrhoda) Lerner Group.

— Alvin the Pirate. (Illus.). 32p. (J). (ps-3). 1990. lib. bdg. 18.95 (*0-87614-402-4*, Carolrhoda) Lerner Group.

— Alvin the Pirate: Picture Book. (J). (ps-3). 1991. pap. 5.95 (*0-87614-551-9*, Carolrhoda) Lerner Group.

— Alvin the Zookeeper. (Picture Bks.). (Illus.). 32p. (J). (ps-3). 1991. lib. bdg. 18.95 (*0-87614-689-2*, Carolrhoda) Lerner Group.

Lofgren, William W. & Sexton, Richard R. Air War in Northern Laos: 1 April - 30 November 1971. 113p. 1993. reprint ed. pap. 14.00 (*0-923135-52-9*) Dalley Bk Service.

Lofland, Cheryl H. The National Soft Drink Association: A Tradition of Service. (Illus.). 136p. 1986. 24.95 (*0-87491-840-5*) Natl Soft Drink.

Lofland, Donald J. Powerlearning: Memory & Learning Techniques for Personal Power. (Illus.). 288p. 1992. 12.95 (*0-681-41574-6*) Longmeadow Pr.

— Powerlearning: Memory & Learning Techniques for Personal Power. 1994. pap. 8.95 (*0-681-00460-6*) Longmeadow Pr.

Lofland, John. Doomsday Cult: A Study of Conversion, Proselytization, & Maintenance of Faith. enl. ed. LC 77-23028. 1981. 29.00 (*0-8290-1111-0*); pap. text ed. 14.95 (*0-8290-0095-X*) Irvington.

— Polite Protesters: The American Peace Movement of the 1980s. (Studies on Peace & Conflict Resolution). 320p. (C). Date not set. text ed. 39.95 (*0-8156-2604-5*); pap. text ed. 16.95 (*0-8156-2605-3*) Syracuse U Pr.

— Protest: Studies of Collective Behavior & Social Movements. 361p. 1991. 36.95 (*0-88738-031-X*); pap. 39.95 (*0-88738-876-0*) Transaction Pubs.

Lofland, John & Lofland, Lyn H. Analyzing Social Settings: A Guide to Qualitative Observation & Analysis. 2nd ed. 186p. (C). 1984. pap. 18.95 (*0-534-02814-4*) Intl Thomson.

— Analyzing Social Settings: A Guide to Qualitative Observation & Analysis. 3rd ed. LC 94-25337. 267p. 1995. pap. 17.95 (*0-534-24780-6*) Intl Thomson.

Lofland, John, jt. ed. see Marullo, Sam.

Lofland, John, et al, eds. Peace Movement Organizations & Activists in the U. S. An Analytic Bibliography. LC 90-5380. (Behavioral & Social Sciences Librarian Ser.). 168p. 1990. 39.95 (*1-56024-075-X*) Haworth Pr.

Lofland, Lyn H. A World of Strangers: Order & Action in Urban Public Space. 223p. (C). 1985. reprint ed. pap. text ed. 12.50 (*0-88133-136-8*) Waveland Pr.

Lofland, Lyn H., jt. auth. see Lofland, John.

Loflin, Marvin D. & Silverberg, James, eds. Discourse & Inference in Cognitive Anthropology: An Approach to Psychic Unity & Enculturation. (World Anthropology Ser.). xiv, 314p. 1978. 50.80 (*3-10-800185-X*) Mouton.

Lofman, Ron. Celebrity Vocals. LC 93-80695. 1994. pap. 16.95 (*0-87341-292-3*) Krause Pubns.

Lofmark, Carl. What is the Bible? 118p. (C). 1992. 19.95 (*0-87975-781-7*) Prometheus Bks.

Lofmark, Carl, tr. see Soderberg, Hjalmar.

Lofmarker, R. & Pioud, G. Swedish-French Dictionary: Svensk-Fransk Fackordbok. 320p. (FRE & SWE.). 1984. 125.00 (*0-8288-0831-7*, F63000) Fr & Eur.

Lofqquist, William A. Discovering the Meaning of Prevention: A Practical Approach to Positive Change. LC 83-72268. (Illus.). 151p. 1983. pap. 12.00 (*0-913951-00-5*) Assocs Youth Dev.

Lofquist, Lloyd H. & Dawis, Rene V. Essentials of Person-Environment-Correspondence Counseling. (Illus.). 192p. 1991. text ed. 39.95 (*0-8166-1889-5*); pap. text ed. 14.95 (*0-8166-2066-0*) U of Minn Pr.

Lofquist, Lloyd H., jt. auth. see Dawis, Rene V.

Lofquist, Thelma J. Frail Elders & the Wounded Caregiver. LC 90-82851. 85p. (Orig.). 1990. pap. 8.00 (*0-8323-0483-2*) Binford Mort.

Lofshult, Diane & Bourn, Scott, eds. Case Studies in Prehospital Care. (Illus.). 128p. (Orig.). (C). 1991. teacher ed 24.95 (*0-936174-09-9*); student ed 36.00 (*0-936174-08-0*); pap. text ed. 29.95 (*0-936174-07-2*) Jems Comm.

Lofstedt. Mereness' Essentials of Psychiatric Nursing: Learning & Activity Guide. 3rd ed. (Illus.). 320p. 1990. pap. 15.95 (*0-8016-5300-2*) Mosby Yr Bk.

Lofstedt, Ragnar. Dilemma of Swedish Energy Policy: Implications for International Policymakers. LC 93-24407. (Studies in Green Research). 233p. 1993. 59.95 (*1-85628-217-1*, Pub. by Avebury Pub UK) Ashgate Pub Co.

Lofstrom, Mark D. & Wedemeyer, Dan J. Regional Interests & Global Issues: The Challenge of Telecommunications Integration for the Pacific. (PTC '92 Proceedings Ser.). 800p. 1992. 75.00 (*1-880672-01-4*) Pac Telecom.

Lofstrom, Mark D., jt. ed. see Wedemeyer, Dan J.

Loft, Abram. Ensemble! A Rehearsal Guide to Thirty Great Works of Chamber Music. LC 91-26180. (Illus.). 360p. 1992. 34.95 (*0-931340-45-4*, Amadeus Pr) Timber.

— Violin & Keyboard, Set, Vols. 1-2. LC 90-20922. 800p. 1991. reprint ed. Set. 68.00 (*0-931340-38-1*, Amadeus Pr) Timber.

— Violin & Keyboard, Vol. LC 90-20922. 364p. 1991. reprint ed. 34.00 (*0-931340-36-5*, Amadeus Pr) Timber.

— Violin & Keyboard, Vol. 2. LC 90-20922. 436p. 1991. reprint ed. 34.00 (*0-931340-37-3*, Amadeus Pr) Timber.

Loft, Randi, ed. see Aries, Ruby.

Loft, Randi, ed. see Pasquini-Masopust, Katie.

Lofthouse, Barbara, illus. The Story of Robin Hood. LC 94-651. 96p. (J). (gr. 5 up). 1994. 16.95 (*1-85697-988-1*, Kingfisher LKC) LKC.

Lofthouse, Brenda, comp. The Study of Primary Education: A Source Book: The Curriculum, Vol. 2. 285p. 1990. 90.00 (*1-85000-718-7*, Falmer Pr); pap. 31.00 (*1-85000-719-5*, Falmer Pr) Taylor & Francis.

Lofthouse, Brenda, ed. The Study of Primary Education: A Source Book: Classroom & Teaching Studies, Vol. 4. 285p. 1990. 75.00 (*1-85000-737-3*, Falmer Pr); pap. 31.00 (*1-85000-738-1*, Falmer Pr) Taylor & Francis.

— The Study of Primary Education: A Source Book: Perspectives, Vol. 1. 2nd ed. 285p. 1990. 95.00 (*1-85000-734-9*, Falmer Pr); pap. 31.00 (*1-85000-779-9*, Falmer Pr) Taylor & Francis.

Lofthouse, Brenda, jt. comp. see Southworth, Geoff.

Lofthouse, Erin, tr. see Borja, Luis E.

Lofthouse, Mary. The Gypsy Lady. 141p. 1987. 30.00 (*0-7223-2136-8*, Pub. by A H S Ltd UK) St Mut.

Lofthouse, Nigel. Pocket Guide to Wood Finishes. (Illus.). 64p. 1993. spiral bd. 16.95 (*1-55870-272-5*) Betterway Bks.

Lofthouse, Stephen. Equity Investment Management: How to Select Stocks & Markets. LC 93-29957. 1993. pap. text ed. write for info. (*0-471-94170-0*) Wiley.

— Equity Investment Management: How to Select Stocks & Markets. LC 93-29957. 1994. text ed. 59.95 (*0-471-94169-7*) Wiley.

***Lofthouse, Stephen, ed.** Readings in Investments. Date not set. text ed. 60.00 (*0-471-95209-5*) Wiley.

— Readings in Investments. 1995. pap. text ed. 39.95 (*0-471-95208-7*) Wiley.

Lofthouse, William F. Israel after the Exile: Sixth & Fifth Centuries B. C. LC 78-10629. (Illus.). 1979. reprint ed. text ed. 65.00 (*0-313-21008-X*, LOIS, Greenwood Pr) Greenwood.

Lofthus, Myrna. A Spiritual Approach to Astrology: A Complete Textbook of Astrology. LC 78-62936. (Illus.). 428p. 1983. 14.95 (*0-916360-10-5*) CRCS Pubns CA.

Loftie, W. J. The Inns of Court & Chancery. (Illus.). xii, 302p. 1994. reprint ed. lib. bdg. 42.50 (*0-8377-2416-3*) Rothman.

Loftin, Glenda. Grits for Brains. Bledsoe, Jerry, ed. LC 94-71654. (Illus.). 96p. (Orig.). 1994. pap. 7.95 (*1-878086-29-4*) Down Home NC.

Loftin, John D. Religion & Hopi Life in the Twentieth Century. LC 90-37968. (Religion in North America Ser.). 192p. 1991. 19.95 (*0-253-33517-5*); pap. 8.95 (*0-253-20857-2*) Ind U Pr.

Loftin, T. L. Contest for a Capital. (Illus.). 352p. (YA). (gr. 9-12). 1989. pap. 19.95 (*0-934812-04-7*) Tee Loftin.

Loftin, Tee, ed. see Nault, Andy.

Loftin, Tee, tr. see Zarambouka, Sofia.

***Lofting.** Story of Mrs. Tubbs. (J). Date not set. 14.00 (*0-671-79694-1*, Litl Simon S&S) S&S Childrens.

***Lofting, Hugh.** Doctor Dolittle. 1976. write for info. (*0-87129-390-0*, D18) Dramatic Pub.

— Doctor Dolittle: A Treasury. (Orig.). (J). 1990. reprint ed. lib. bdg. 25.95 (*0-89966-674-4*) Buccaneer Bks.

— Gub-Gub's Book. LC 91-4672. (J). (gr. 4-7). 1992. pap. 15.00 (*0-671-78355-6*, S&S Bks Young Read) S&S Childrens.

— The Twilight of Magic. LC 92-15766. (Illus.). (J). 1993. pap. 15.00 (*0-671-78358-0*, S&S Bks Young Read) S&S Childrens.

— The Voyage of Doctor Dolittle. (J). (gr. 4-7). 1988. mass mkt. 4.50 (*0-440-40002-3*, YB) Dell.

Loftis. Decision Making in Gerontologic Nursing. 352p. 1993. pap. 32.95 (*1-55664-186-9*) Mosby Yr Bk.

***Loftis, Chris.** The Words Hurt. LC 94-66754. (Illus.). 40p. (J). (ps-4). 1994. pap. 9.95 (*0-88282-132-6*) New Horizon NJ.

Loftis, James R., jt. auth. see American Bar Association, Section of Antitrust Law Staff.

Loftis, John. Comedy & Society from Congreve to Fielding. LC 76-51940. (Stanford University. Stanford Studies in Language & Literature: 19). reprint ed. 21.50 (*0-404-51829-X*) AMS Pr.

— Renaissance Drama in England & Spain: Topical Allusion & History Plays. (Illus.). 296p. 1987. text ed. 42.50 (*0-691-06706-6*) Princeton U Pr.

Loftis, John, ed. see Addison, Joseph.

Loftis, John, ed. see Lee, Nathaniel.

Loftis, John, ed. see Sheridan, Richard B.

Loftis, John C. Sheridan & the Drama of Georgian England. 186p. 1976. 23.50 (*0-674-80632-8*) HUP.

— The Spanish Plays of Neoclassical England. LC 87-8685. 280p. 1987. reprint ed. text ed. 67.50 (*0-313-25133-9*, LSPA, Greenwood Pr) Greenwood.

Loftis, John C. & Hardacre, Paul H., eds. Colonel Joseph Bampfield's Apology: "Written by Himself & Printed at His Desire," 1685. LC 91-58963. (Illus.). 312p. 1993. Incl. "Bampfield's Later Career: A Biographical Supplement" by John Loftis. 48.50 (*0-8387-5231-4*) Bucknell U Pr.

Loftis, N. J. Black Anima. (New Writers Ser.). 1973. 4.95 (*0-87140-562-8*) Liveright.

Loftis, Norman. Condition Zero. LC 91-17805. (American University Studies: Philosophy: Ser. V, Vol. 123). 148p. (C). 1993. text ed. 34.95 (*0-8204-1698-3*) P Lang Pubs.

Loftness, John & Mahaney, C. J. Disciplined for Life: Steps to Spiritual Strength. Somerville, Greg, ed. 112p. (Orig.). 1992. pap. 6.50 (*1-881039-00-5*) People of Destiny.

Loftness, Marvin O. Power Line Interference: A Practical Handbook. LC 92-27686. 1992. write for info. (*0-917599-07-1*) Natl Rural.

Lofton, Edgar K. Getting Started in Futures. 2nd ed. Grau, W., ed. 288p. 1993. pap. text ed. 18.95 (*0-471-57988-2*) Wiley.

Lofton, Fred C. A Crying Shepherd: A Therapy of Tears. 214p. (Orig.). 1993. pap. 9.95 (*0-9625423-7-7*) Four-G Pubs.

— Teach Us to Pray: The Disciples Request Cast Anew. 96p. 1983. pap. 4.00 (*0-89191-751-9*) Prog Bapt Pub.

Lofton, Fred C., jt. ed. see Pleasure, Mose, Jr.

***Lofton, J. Mack, Jr.** Healing Hands: An Alabama Medical Mosaic. LC 94-23119. (Illus.). 320p. (Orig.). 1995. pap. 29.95 (*0-8173-0779-6*) U of Ala Pr.

— Voices from Alabama: A Twentieth-Century Mosaic. LC 92-36110. (Illus.). 350p. (Orig.). 1993. pap. 24.95 (*0-8173-0684-6*) U of Ala Pr.

Lofton, John. Denmark Vesey's Revolt: The Slave Plot That Lit a Fuse to Fort Sumter. LC 83-11267. 316p. reprint ed. pap. 90.10 (*0-7837-4054-9*, 2043885) Bks Demand.

Lofton, Marie C., jt. auth. see Norris, Donald M.

***Lofton, Saab.** A. D. 320p. (Orig.). 1995. pap. 12.00 (*0-9622937-8-4*) III Pub.

Lofton, Todd, jt. auth. see Jones, Charles P.

Lofts. Dead March in Three Keys. (Black Dagger Crime Ser.). 16.50 (*0-86220-817-3*, BD016, Black Dagger) Chivers N Amer.

Lofts, B. & Holmes, W. N., eds. Current Trends in Comparative Endocrinology. 1318p. (C). 1985. pap. text ed. 300.00 (*962-209-039-7*, Pub. by Hong Kong U Pr HK) St Mut.

Lofts, Norah. Bless This House. 352p. 1982. pap. 2.95 (*0-449-24471-7*, Crest) Fawcett.

— Bless This House. reprint ed. lib. bdg. 21.95 (*0-89190-225-2*, Rivercity Pr) Amereon Ltd.

— Bless This House. 1977. reprint ed. lib. bdg. 24.95 (*0-89244-048-1*) Queens Hse-Focus Serv.

— The Claw. large type ed. 384p. 1983. 15.95 (*0-7089-1045-9*) Ulverscroft.

— Gads Hall. 1979. pap. 2.25 (*0-449-24040-1*) Fawcett.

— Her Own Special Island. large type ed. 1975. 21.95 (*0-85456-354-7*) Ulverscroft.

— The House at Old Vine. 1978. pap. 1.95 (*0-449-23792-3*, Crest) Fawcett.

— The House at Old Vine. reprint ed. lib. bdg. 25.95 (*0-89190-226-0*, Rivercity Pr) Amereon Ltd.

— House at Old Vine. 408p. 1990. reprint ed. lib. bdg. 24.95x (*0-89244-049-X*) Queens Hse-Focus Serv.

— The House at Sunset. reprint ed. lib. bdg. 24.95 (*0-89190-227-9*, Rivercity Pr) Amereon Ltd.

— How Far to Bethlehem? 1976. 22.95 (*0-8488-1417-7*) Amereon Ltd.

— How Far to Bethlehem? 300p. 1991. reprint ed. lib. bdg. 23.95 (*0-89966-787-2*) Buccaneer Bks.

— The Lonely Furrow. large type ed. (Large Print Contemporary Ser.). 426p. 1989. 23.95 (*0-7089-8513-0*, Charnwood) Ulverscroft.

— Scent of Cloves. reprint ed. lib. bdg. 22.95 (*0-89190-228-7*, Rivercity Pr) Amereon Ltd.

— The Silver Nutmeg. reprint ed. lib. bdg. 24.95 (*0-89190-229-5*, Rivercity Pr) Amereon Ltd.

— The Town House. reprint ed. lib. bdg. 25.95 (*0-89190-230-9*, Rivercity Pr) Amereon Ltd.

— A Wayside Tavern. large type ed. 1982. 15.95 (*0-7089-0838-1*) Ulverscroft.

Lofts, Vicki G. Purr-Oems. 1993. pap. 21.00 (*1-85183-047-2*, Silent Bks) St Mut.

***Loftus, Bill.** Idaho Handbook. 2nd ed. (Illus.). 282p. (Orig.). 1995. pap. 14.95 (*1-56691-061-7*) Moon Pubns CA.

— Idaho State Parks Guidebook. (Illus.). 130p. 1991. pap. 9.95 (*0-9607506-5-7*) News Rev Pub.

Loftus, C. ADA Yearbook, 1994. LC 94-75423. (Studies in Computer & Communications Ser.). 460p. 1994. 94.00 (*90-5199-155-X*) IOS Press.

Loftus, C., ed. ADA Yearbook 1993. LC 92-63411. (Studies in Computer & Communications Systems: Vol. 5). 450p. 1993. 94.00 (*90-5199-124-X*, Pub. by IOS Pr NE) IOS Press.

Loftus, Christopher. Carotid Endarterectomy: Principles & Technique. 1995. 130.00 (*0-942219-69-4*) Quality Med Pub.

Loftus, Christopher, ed. Neurosurgical Emergencies Vol. 1. 233p. 1994. 90.00 (*1-879284-24-3*) Am Assn Neuro.

— Neurosurgical Emergencies Vol. 2. 179p. 1994. 90.00 (*1-879284-29-4*) Am Assn Neuro.

Loftus, Christopher M. & Traynelis, Vinent C. Intraoperative Monitoring Techniques in Neurosurgery. (Illus.). 295p. 1994. text ed. 85.00 (*0-07-038431-2*) Hlth Prof Div.

Loftus, Diana S., jt. auth. see Thompson, Kimberly B.

Loftus, Elizabeth. Memory. (Illus.). 207p. 1980. pap. text ed. 20.95 (*0-912675-28-4*) Ardsley.

Loftus, Elizabeth & Ketcham, Katherine. The Myth of Repressed Memory: False Memories & the Accusations of Sexual Abuse. 336p. 1994. 22.95 (*0-312-11454-0*) St Martin.

Loftus, Elizabeth F. Eyewitness Testimony. LC 79-13195. (Illus.). 268p. 1980. 26.00 (*0-674-28775-4*) HUP.

— Eyewitness Testimony. LC 79-13195. (Illus.). 268p. 1981. pap. 15.95 (*0-674-28776-2*) HUP.

— Eyewitness Testimony: Psychological Perspectives. Wells, Gary L., ed. LC 83-7615. 384p. 1984. 69.95 (*0-521-25564-3*) Cambridge U Pr.

— Witness for the Defense: The Accused, the Eyewitness, & the Expert who puts Memory on Trial. 1991. 19.95 (*0-312-05537-4*) St Martin.

Loftus, Elizabeth F. & Doyle, James M. Eyewitness Testimony: Civil & Criminal. 2nd ed. 475p. 1992. write for info. (*0-318-69710-6*); write for info. (*0-318-69712-2*) Michie Butterworth.

— Eyewitness Testimony: Civil & Criminal. 2nd ed. 478p. 1992. 85.00 (*0-87473-983-7*) Michie Butterworth.

Loftus, Elizabeth F. & Ketcham, Katherine. Witness for the Defense: The Accused, the Eyewitness, & the Expert Who Puts Memory on Trial. (Illus.). 304p. 1992. pap. 12.95 (*0-312-08455-2*) St Martin.

Loftus, Elizabeth F., jt. auth. see Loftus, Geoffrey R.

Loftus, Elizabeth F., jt. auth. see Wortman, Camille B.

Loftus, Geoffrey R. & Loftus, Elizabeth F. Human Memory: The Processing of Information. 192p. 1976. pap. text ed. 27.50 (*0-89859-135-X*) L Erlbaum Assocs.

Loftus, John. The Belarus Secret. Miller, Nathan, ed. LC 82-48483. (Illus.). 196p. 1982. 18.95 (*0-394-52292-3*) Knopf.

— John Loftus at Seventy: Work from the Fifties to the Present. (Illus.). 52p. (Orig.). 1991. pap. 20.00 (*0-910969-01-9*) Hobart & Wm Smith.

— Valhalla's Wake. 1990. mass mkt. 4.50 (*0-06-100077-9*, Icon Edns) HarpC.

Loftus, John, jt. auth. see Aarons, Mark.

Loftus, John A. Investment Management: An Analysis of the Experience of American Management Investment Trusts. LC 78-64181. (Johns Hopkins University. Studies in the Social Sciences. Thirtieth Ser. 1912: 1). 136p. 1983. reprint ed. 24.50 (*0-404-61289-X*) AMS Pr.

Loftus, John H., tr. see Nayatani, Yoshinobu, et al.

An Asterisk (*) at the beginning of an entry indicates that the title is appearing in BIP for the first time.

Loftus, Joseph & Walfish, Beatrice, eds. Breakthroughs in Union-Management Cooperation. LC 77-24837. 49p. 1977. pap. text ed. 7.00 (*0-89361-002-X*) Work in Amer.

Loftus, Joseph P., Jr., ed. Orbital Debris from Upper-Stage Breakup. (PAAS Ser.: Vol. 121). 227p. 1989. 65.95 (*0-930403-58-4*) AIAA.

Loftus, Michele. How to Start & Operate a Home Based Word Processing or Desktop Publishing Business. 192p. 1990. pap. 9.95 (*1-55850-854-6*) Adams Pubng.

Loftus, Simon. Puligny-Montrachet. 1994. pap. 14.95 (*0-8050-3175-8*) H Holt & Co.

— Puligny-Montrachet: Journal of a Village in Burgundy. LC 92-54786. (Borzoi Reader Ser.). 1993. 24.00 (*0-679-41814-8*) Knopf.

Loftus, Tom. The Art of Legislative Politics. 150p. 1994. 28. 95 (*0-87187-981-6*); pap. 18.95 (*0-87187-980-8*) Congr Quarterly.

Lofty, J. R., jt. auth. see Edwards, C. A.

Lofty, John S. Time to Write: The Influence of Time & Culture on Learning to Write. LC 91-21447. (SUNY Series, Literacy, Culture, & Learning: Theory & Practice). (Illus.). 292p. 1992. 64.50 (*0-7914-0901-5*); pap. 21.95 (*0-7914-0902-3*) State U NY Pr.

Lofvenberg, M. T. On the Syncope of the Old English Present Endings. (Essays & Studies on English Language & Literature: Vol. 1). 1974. reprint ed. pap. 15.00 (*0-8115-0199-X*) Periodicals Srv.

— Studies on Middle English Local Surnames. (Lund Studies in English: Vol. 11). 1974. reprint ed. pap. 35.00 (*0-8115-0554-5*) Periodicals Srv.

***Lofy, Chuck.** A Grain of Wheat: Giving Voice to the Spirit of Change. 127p. 1993. 11.95 (*0-933173-56-3*) Prince Peace Pub.

Logan. The Foot & Ankle: A Clinical Application. 1994. 45. 00 (*0-8342-0605-6*) Aspen Pub.

— Reclaiming Surrendered Ground: Protecting Your Family from Spiritual Attacks. 1995. pap. 9.99 (*0-8024-3948-9*) Moody.

— Strength of Materials. (C). 1991. text ed. 82.00 (*0-06-044108-9*) HarpCollege.

***Logan & Rowe.** The Low Back & Pelvis: Clinical Applications. 200p. 1995. 46.00 (*0-8342-0689-7*) Aspen Pub.

Logan, jt. auth. see Leach.

Logan, A. H. & Wedderburn, A. J., eds. New Testament & Gnosis. 272p. 1983. 39.95 (*0-567-09344-1*, Pub. by T & T Clark UK) Bks Intl VA.

Logan, A. L. The Knee: Clinical Applications. LC 93-39114. 192p. 1994. 45.00 (*0-8342-0522-X*, 20522) Aspen Pub.

Logan, Adelphena. Memories of Sweet Grass. LC 79-65401. (Illus.). 79p. 1979. 6.95 (*0-89488-006-3*) Am Indian Arch.

Logan, Alan. Holocene Reefs of Bermuda. (Sedimenta Ser.: Vol. XI). (Illus.). 63p. 1988. 9.00 (*0-932981-10-0*) Univ Miami CSL.

Logan, Albert B. & Cheney, William R. Strategy to Revitalize the American Dream: Justice in Jeopardy. (Illus.). 260p. 1973. 8.95 (*0-317-01152-9*); pap. 5.95 (*0-317-01153-7*) NIJD Colorado.

Logan, Alistair H., ed. see Westermann, Claus.

Logan, Alistair H., tr. see Westermann, Claus.

Logan, Ann. Dial D for Destiny. (Superromance Ser.). 1994. mass mkt. 3.50 (*0-373-70585-9*, 1-70585-4) Harlequin Bks.

Logan, Anna & Koehler, Ed. The Jesus Tree Activity Book. (Illus.). 48p. (Orig.). (J). (ps-2). 1991. pap. 4.99 (*0-570-04197-X*) Concordia.

Logan, Anne. School's Out! (Illus.). 80p. 22.95 (*0-317-05897-5*, Pub. by Boston Mills Pr CN) Genl Dist Srvs.

— Twin Oaks. (Superromance Ser.). 1993. mass mkt. 3.50 (*0-373-70550-6*, 1-70550-8) Harlequin Bks.

Logan, Anne-Marie. British Artists Authority List. 1987. 20. 00 (*0-685-54075-8*) Visual Resources Assn.

— Flemish Drawings in the Age of Rubens. (Illus.). 273p. 1993. text ed. 30.00 (*1-881894-01-0*) WC Davis Mus & Cult.

— Flemish Drawings in the Age of Rubens: Selected Works from American Collections. 1994. 45.00 (*0-295-97316-1*) U of Wash Pr.

Logan, Barbara & Dawkins, Cecilia. Family-Centered Nursing in the Community. 809p. (C). 1986. text ed. 45. 25 (*0-201-12684-2*, Health Sci) Addison-Wesley.

***Logan, Beatrice & Blumenthal, Caroline.** The On-Line Library Information System (OLLI) 80p. (C). 1994. 5.16 (*0-8403-9572-8*) Kendall-Hunt.

Logan, Ben. Empty Meadow. LC 91-7977. 1991. pap. 12.95 (*1-879483-03-3*) Prairie Oak Pr.

— The Land Remembers. 290p. 1975. pap. 11.95 (*1-55971-014-4*, 0153, Heartlnd Pr); audio 19.95 (*1-55971-013-6*, Heartlnd Pr) NorthWord.

— Land Remembers: Collectors Edition. 1992. 29.95 (*1-55971-184-1*) NorthWord.

Logan, Beryl. A Religion Without Talking, No. 7: Religious Beliefs & Natural Belief in Hume's Philosophy of Religion Studies in European Thought. LC 93-16910. 184p. (C). 1993. text ed. 42.95 (*0-8204-2201-0*) P Lang Pubs.

***Logan, Cait.** Delilah. 336p. (Orig.). 1995. pap. text ed. 4.99 (*0-515-11565-7*) Jove Pubns.

— Night Fire. 352p. (Orig.). 1994. pap. text ed. 4.99 (*1-55773-986-2*) Diamond.

— Wild Dawn. 1992. mass mkt. 4.99 (*1-55773-732-0*) Diamond.

Logan, Carole, jt. auth. see Stewart, John.

Logan, Carolyn J. Winning the Land Use Game: A Guide for Developers & Citizen Protesters. LC 81-15710. 208p. 1982. text ed. 49.95 (*0-275-90849-6*, C0849, Praeger Pubs) Greenwood.

Logan, Charles H. Private Prisons: Cons & Pros. 328p. 1990. 45.00 (*0-19-506353-8*) OUP.

Logan, Charles H., jt. auth. see Sacks, Howard R.

Logan, Chris, jt. auth. see Thomas, Henk.

Logan, Cordell E. Medicine At the Crossroads: A Global View from Agriculture to Complementary Medicine. (Illus.). 444p. (Orig.). (C). 1993. pap. 19.95 (*0-9636519-0-0*) C E Logan.

Logan County Century Book Committee. History of Logan County Colorado. (Illus.). 534p. 1987. 60.00 (*0-88107-085-8*) Curtis Media.

Logan, Dan P. Tilling the Good Earth. LC 89-83521. 185p. 1989. lib. bdg. 17.95 (*0-944419-08-9*) Everett Cos Pub.

Logan, Daryl L. A First Course in the Finite Element Method. 2nd ed. 640p. 1992. text ed. 69.95 (*0-534-92964-8*) PWS Pubs.

***Logan, David A. & Logan, Wayne A.** North Carolina Tort Law. LC 94-73844. 624p. (C). 1995. lib. bdg. 95.00 (*0-89089-844-8*) Carolina Acad Pr.

Logan, Deborah, ed. see Penn, William.

Logan, Donn, jt. auth. see Attoe, Wayne.

Logan, Donna, ed. see Sterett, Betty.

***Logan, E. M. & Winterton, J. R., eds.** Information Sources in Law. 2nd ed. 500p. 1996. 95.00 (*1-85739-041-5*) Bowker-Saur.

***Logan, Earl, Jr.** Handbook of Turbomachinery. LC 94-22880. (Mechanical Engineering Ser.: Vol. 93). 1994. 160.00 (*0-8247-9263-7*) Dekker.

Logan, Earl. Turbomachinery: Basic Theory & Applications. 2nd rev. ed. (Mechanical Engineering Ser.: Vol. 85). 288p. 1993. 65.00 (*0-8247-9138-X*) Dekker.

Logan, Eunice S. & Speights, Elizabeth L. Charleston Receipts Repeats. (Illus.). 376p. 1986. pap. 12.95 (*0-9607854-5-0*) Jun League Charl SC.

Logan, F. Donald. Vikings in History. 1991. pap. 19.95 (*0-04-446040-6*); pap. 19.95 (*0-415-08396-6*, Pub. by Tavistock UK) Routledge Chapman & Hall.

Logan, Frank. A Cave House Ranch in Arizona. 1987. 5.95 (*0-685-38470-5*) Intl Univ Pr.

— Westward to a Cave-House Ranch. write for info. (*0-89697-382-4*) Intl Univ Pr.

Logan, Frank A. College Learning: Ways & Whys. 320p. (C). 1991. pap. text ed. 17.95 (*0-8403-6861-5*) Kendall-Hunt.

Logan-Frank, Lynda, et al. Wealthy Women. 1985. 14.95 (*0-910019-35-5*) United Support.

Logan, Gary W., jt. auth. see Young, Leonard M.

Logan, George M. The Meaning of More's Utopia. LC 82-16147. (Illus.). 320p. 1983. 47.50 (*0-691-06557-8*) Princeton U Pr.

Logan, George M. & Teskey, Gordon, eds. Unfolded Tales: Essays on Renaissance Romance. LC 88-47920. (Illus.). 368p. 1989. 42.50 (*0-8014-2268-X*) Cornell U Pr.

Logan, George M., ed. see More, Thomas.

Logan, Gordon D., jt. ed. see Dulany, Donelson E.

Logan, Greg. This Universe of Men. (Illus.). 150p. 1992. pap. 10.95 (*0-943383-04-8*) FirstHand Ltd.

Logan, H. M. The Dialect of the "Life of Saint Katherine" A Linguistic Study of the Phonology & Inflections. (Janua Linguarum, Series Practica: No. 130). 1973. pap. text ed. 57.50 (*90-279-3200-X*) Mouton.

***Logan, Heather.** Exploration into Cultures: An Oral History Biography of Hap Gilliland. 112p. 1995. pap. 12. 95 (*0-89992-514-6*) Coun India Ed.

Logan, Ikubolajeh, jt. ed. see Mengisteab, Kidane.

Logan, J. David. Applied Mathematics: A Contemporary Approach. LC 87-13318. 572p. 1987. text ed. 91.95 (*0-471-85083-7*) Wiley.

— An Introduction to Nonlinear Partial Differential Equations. LC 93-29705. (Pure & Applied Mathematics Ser.). 1994. text ed. 62.95 (*0-471-59916-6*) Wiley.

Logan, Jake. Ambush at Apache Rocks. (Jake Logan Ser.: No. 177). 1993. pap. 3.99 (*0-425-13981-6*) Berkley Pub.

— Ghost Town. (Slocum Ser.: No. 181). 192p. (Orig.). 1994. pap. text ed. 3.99 (*0-425-14128-4*) Berkley Pub.

— Pikes Peak Shoot-Out No. 185. (Jake Logan: No. 185). 192p. (Orig.). 1994. pap. text ed. 3.99 (*0-425-14294-9*) Berkley Pub.

— Revenge at Devils Tower. (Slocum Ser.: No. 175). 192p. (Orig.). 1993. pap. 3.99 (*0-425-13904-2*) Berkley Pub.

— Slocum: BoomTown Showdown, No. 195. 192p. (Orig.). 1995. pap. text ed. 3.99 (*0-425-14729-0*) Berkley Pub.

— Slocum No. 186: Blood Trail. (Jake Logan Ser.). 192p. (Orig.). 1994. pap. text ed. 3.99 (*0-425-14341-4*) Berkley Pub.

— Slocum No. 192: The Snake Gulch Swindlers. 192p. (Orig.). 1995. pap. text ed. 3.99 (*0-425-14570-0*) Berkley Pub.

— Slocum No. 193: Slocum & the Shoshone Whiskey. 192p. (Orig.). 1995. pap. text ed. 3.99 (*0-425-14647-2*) Berkley Pub.

— Slocum No. 194: Slocum & the Lady 'Niners. 192p. (Orig.). 1995. pap. text ed. 3.99 (*0-425-14684-7*) Berkley Pub.

— Slocum No. 197: The Silver Stallion. 192p. (Orig.). Date not set. pap. text ed. 4.99 (*0-515-11654-8*) Jove Pubns.

— Slocum No. 198: Slocum & the Spotted Horse. 192p. (Orig.). 1995. pap. text ed. 3.99 (*0-515-11679-3*) Jove Pubns.

— Slocum & Quantrill No. 188. 192p. (Orig.). 1994. pap. text ed. 3.99 (*0-425-14400-3*) Berkley Pub.

— Slocum & the Cow Town Kill. (Jake Logan Ser.: No. 184). 192p. (Orig.). 1994. pap. 3.99 (*0-425-14255-8*) Berkley Pub.

— Slocum & the Fort Worth Ambush. (Slocum Ser.: No. 190). 192p. (Orig.). 1994. pap. text ed. 3.99 (*0-425-14496-8*) Berkley Pub.

— Slocum & the Ghost Rustlers, No. 189. (Slocum Ser.: No. 189). 192p. (Orig.). 1994. pap. text ed. 3.99 (*0-425-14462-3*) Berkley Pub.

— Slocum & the Gold Slaves, No. 187. 192p. (Orig.). 1994. pap. text ed. 3.99 (*0-425-14363-5*) Berkley Pub.

— Slocum & the Invaders, No. 182. 192p. (Orig.). 1994. pap. text ed. 3.99 (*0-425-14182-9*) Berkley Pub.

— Slocum & the Mountain of Gold. (Jake Logan Ser.: No. 183). 192p. (Orig.). 1994. pap. 3.99 (*0-425-14231-0*) Berkley Pub.

— Slocum & the Phantom Gold. (Slocum Ser.: No. 180). 192p. (Orig.). 1994. pap. 3.99 (*0-425-14100-4*) Berkley Pub.

— Slocum & the Pirates, No. 196. 192p. (Orig.). 1995. pap. text ed. 3.99 (*0-515-11633-5*) Berkley Pub.

— Slocum at Dog Leg Creek, No. 199. 192p. (Orig.). 1995. pap. text ed. 3.99 (*0-515-11701-3*) Jove Pubns.

— Slocum Busts Out. 1990. pap. 3.50 (*0-425-12270-0*) Berkley Pub.

— Slocum, No. Slocum's War. 1992. pap. 3.99 (*0-425-13273-0*) Berkley Pub.

— Slocum, No. 150: Trail of Death. 1991. pap. 3.50 (*0-425-12778-8*) Berkley Pub.

— Slocum, No. 154: Slocum's Standoff. 1991. pap. 3.50 (*0-425-13037-1*) Berkley Pub.

— Slocum, No. 155: Death Control. 1991. pap. 3.50 (*0-425-13081-9*) Berkley Pub.

— Slocum, No. 156: Timber King. 1992. pap. 3.50 (*0-425-13138-6*) Berkley Pub.

— Slocum, No. 157: Railroad Baron. 1992. pap. 3.50 (*0-425-13187-4*) Berkley Pub.

— Slocum, No. 158: River Chase. 1992. pap. 3.50 (*0-425-13214-5*) Berkley Pub.

— Slocum, No. 159: Tombstone Gold. 1992. pap. 3.50 (*0-425-13241-2*) Berkley Pub.

— Slocum, No. 163: Slocum & the Bushwackers. 192p. (Orig.). 1992. pap. 3.99 (*0-425-13401-6*) Berkley Pub.

— Slocum, No. 165: San Angelo Shootout. 192p. (Orig.). 1992. pap. 3.99 (*0-425-13508-X*) Berkley Pub.

— Slocum, No. 166: Blood Fever. 192p. (Orig.). 1992. pap. 3.99 (*0-425-13532-2*) Berkley Pub.

— Slocum, No. 167: Helltown Trail. 192p. (Orig.). 1993. pap. 3.99 (*0-425-13579-9*) Berkley Pub.

— Slocum, No. 168: Sheriff Slocum. 192p. (Orig.). 1993. pap. 3.99 (*0-425-13624-8*) Berkley Pub.

— Slocum, No. 170: Slocum & the Forty Thieves. 192p. (Orig.). 1993. pap. 3.99 (*0-425-13797-X*) Berkley Pub.

— Slocum, No. 171: Powder River Massacre. 192p. (Orig.). 1993. pap. 3.99 (*0-425-13665-5*) Berkley Pub.

— Slocum, No. 173: Slocum & the Tin Star Swindle. 192p. (Orig.). 1993. pap. 3.99 (*0-425-13811-9*) Berkley Pub.

— Slocum, No. 174: Slocum & the Nightriders. 192p. (Orig.). 1993. pap. 3.99 (*0-425-13839-9*) Berkley Pub.

— Slocum, No. 176: Slocum at Outlaw's Haven. 1993. pap. 3.99 (*0-425-13951-4*) Berkley Pub.

— Slocum, No. 179: Slocum & the Buffalo Soldiers. 192p. (Orig.). 1994. pap. 3.99 (*0-425-14050-4*) Berkley Pub.

— Slocum's Silver. (Slocum Ser.: No. 200). 192p. (Orig.). 1995. pap. 3.99 (*0-515-11729-3*) Jove Pubns.

— Virginia City Showdon. (Slocum Ser.: No. 169). 192p. (Orig.). 1993. pap. 3.99 (*0-425-13761-9*) Berkley Pub.

— West Texas Plunder. (Slocum Ser.: No. 191). 192p. (Orig.). 1995. pap. text ed. 3.99 (*0-425-14535-2*) Berkley Pub.

Logan, James. Correspondence Between William Penn & James Logan, 2 vols., Set. 1993. reprint ed. lib. bdg. 150. 00 (*0-7812-5484-1*) Rprt Serv.

— The Scottish Gael: Or, Celtic Manners As Preserved among the Highlanders, 2 vols., Set. LC 77-87679. reprint ed. 59.50 (*0-404-16560-5*) AMS Pr.

Logan, James C., ed. Theology & Evangelism in the Wesleyan Heritage: Essays in the Theology of Evangelism. LC 93-6428. (Kingswood Ser.). 224p. (Orig.). 1994. pap. 14.95 (*0-687-41395-8*) Abingdon.

Logan, James K., jt. auth. see Leach, W. Barton.

Logan, James V. Wordsworthian Criticism. LC 74-7025. 304p. 1974. reprint ed. 50.00 (*0-87752-171-9*) Gordian.

Logan, Janice L. Breaking the Language Barrier with Spanish. 1977. pap. text ed. 9.55 (*0-89420-035-6*, 176040); audio 237.60 (*0-89420-127-1*, 176000) Natl Book.

Logan, Jeanne. Your Gift...Should You Decide to Accept: Communications from Aristotle. 243p. (Orig.). 1987. pap. write for info. (*0-9619742-0-6*) Harmony Haus.

Logan, Jennifer. Not Just Any Man. 192p. 1989. 13.99 (*0-8499-0662-8*) Word Inc.

Logan, Jesse A. & Hain, Fred P., eds. Chaos & Insect Ecology: Does Chaos Exist in Ecological Systems? (Illus.). 109p. (Orig.). (C). 1993. pap. text ed. 40.00 (*0-7881-0092-0*) Diane Pub.

Logan, Joan S. Two Turtles of Paradise: A Love Story for Children & Adults. (Illus.). 20p. (Orig.). (J). 1988. pap. 1.95 (*0-944208-01-0*) Seventh-Wing Pubns.

Logan, Joanna. Winter Harvest. large type ed. 1991. pap. 13. 95 (*0-7089-6980-1*) Ulverscroft.

Logan, John. The Anonymous Lover. 1973. 5.95 (*0-87140-564-4*) Liveright.

— A Ballet for the Ear: Interviews, Essays, & Reviews. Poulin, A., Jr., ed. (Poets on Poetry Ser.). 304p. 1983. pap. 13.95 (*0-472-06336-7*) U of Mich Pr.

— The Bridge of Change: Poems 1974-1980. (American Poets Continuum Ser.: No. 7). pap. 8.00 (*0-918526-35-3*) BOA Edns.

— Christianity. (World Religions Ser.). (Illus.). 48p. (J). (gr. 5-7). 1995. 15.95 (*1-56847-374-5*) Thomson Lrning.

— John Logan: The Collected Fiction. (American Poets Continuum Ser.: No. 21). 256p. 1991. 25.00 (*0-918526-78-7*); pap. 12.50 (*0-918526-79-5*) BOA Edns.

— John Logan: The Collected Poems. 1989. 30.00 (*0-918526-64-7*); pap. 15.00 (*0-918526-65-5*) BOA Edns.

— Only the Dreamer Can Change the Dream: Selected Poems. LC 80-23184. (American Poetry Ser.: No. 21). 209p. (Orig.). 1982. pap. 7.95 (*0-912946-78-4*) Ecco Pr.

— Poem in Progress. (Illus.). 1975. pap. 9.95 (*0-931848-09-1*) Dryad Pr.

— The Transformation: Poems January to March 1981. 22p. (Orig.). 1983. pap. 6.95 (*0-942908-06-6*) Pancake Pr.

Logan, John A., Jr. Dowered with Gifts: The Second Quarter of the Second Century of Christ Church Cathedral, Houston. (Illus.). 306p. (C). 1989. 20.00 (*0-317-01834-5*) Christ Church.

Logan, John A. The Great Conspiracy. LC 76-37311. (Black Heritage Library Collection). 1977. reprint ed. 71.95 (*0-8369-8948-1*) Ayer.

— No Transfer: An American Security Principle. 1961. 79. 50 (*0-685-69838-6*) Elliots Bks.

— The Volunteer Soldier of America, with Memoir of the Author & Military Reminiscences from General Logan's Private Journal. Kohn, Richard H., ed. LC 78-22385. (American Military Experience Ser.). (Illus.). 1980. reprint ed. lib. bdg. 55.95 (*0-405-11861-9*) Ayer.

Logan, John H. A History of the Upper Country of S.C., Part. 2. 118p. 1980. reprint ed. 17.50 (*0-89308-195-7*) Southern Hist Pr.

Logan, John R. & Molotch, Harvey L., eds. Urban Fortunes: The Political Economy of Place. (C). 1987. 42.50 (*0-520-05577-2*); pap. 14.00 (*0-520-06341-4*) U CA Pr.

Logan, John R. & Swanstrom, Todd, eds. Beyond the City Limits: Urban Policy & Economic Restructuring in Comparative Perspective. (Conflicts in Urban & Regional Development Ser.). 288p. 1990. pap. 22.95 (*0-87722-944-9*) Temple U Pr.

***Logan, John W.** Ten-Shun: The Making of a Soldier. Bird, Linda A., ed. 216p. (Orig.). 1995. pap. write for info. (*1-878151-04-5*) J & J Bks NY.

Logan, John W., et al. Phonics Competencies for Reading Teachers. 2nd ed. 96p. 1992. per. 12.95 (*0-8403-7406-2*) Kendall-Hunt.

Logan, Joshua & Heggen, Thomas. Mister Roberts. 1951. pap. 4.75 (*0-8222-0765-6*) Dramatists Play.

Logan, Judy. Teaching Stories. LC 93-91529. 110p. 1993. pap. text ed. 11.95 (*0-9636822-0-2*) J Logan.

Logan, Julie. World According to He & She. 1992. mass mkt. 8.00 (*0-440-50378-7*) Dell.

Logan, Kate V. My Confederate Girlhood. Baxter, Annette K., ed. LC 79-8803. (Signal Lives Ser.). (Illus.). 1980. reprint ed. lib. bdg. 26.95 (*0-405-12849-5*) Ayer.

***Logan, Kathleen.** Haciendo Pueblo: he Development of a Guadalajaran Suburb. LC 83-3650. (Illus.). 157p. 1984. pap. 44.80 (*0-7837-8391-4*, 2059202) Bks Demand.

Logan, Kevin. Close Encounters with the New Age. (Orig.). 1991. pap. 15.95 (*0-86065-879-1*) Trans-Atl Phila.

Logan, Kristina. The Man Behind the Magic. (Silhouette Romance Ser.). 1993. pap. 2.75 (*0-373-08950-3*, 5-08950-3) Silhouette.

— A Man Like Jake. (Silhouette Romance Ser.). 1994. pap. 2.75 (*0-373-08998-8*, 5-08998-2) Silhouette.

— The Right Man for Loving. large type ed. 251p. 1992. reprint ed. lib. bdg. 13.95 (*1-56054-538-0*) Thorndike Pr.

— To the Rescue. (Silhouette Romance Ser.). 1993. pap. 2.69 (*0-373-08918-X*, 5-08918-0) Silhouette.

— To the Rescue. large type ed. LC 93-20049. 226p. 1993. reprint ed. Alk. paper. lib. bdg. 13.95 (*1-56054-682-4*) Thorndike Pr.

— Two to Tango. large type ed. 240p. 1992. reprint ed. lib. bdg. 13.95 (*1-56054-461-9*) Thorndike Pr.

Logan, Laurel O. Gillian. LC 86-70911. 176p. (Orig.). 1986. pap. 3.99 (*0-87123-873-X*) Bethany Hse.

— Janette Oke: A Heart for the Prairie; the Untold Story of the Most Beloved Novelist of Our Time. 1993. 15.99 (*1-55661-326-1*) Bethany Hse.

***Logan, Leandra.** Angel Baby. 1995. mass mkt. 3.25 (*0-373-25664-7*) Harlequin Bks.

— Bargain Basement Baby. (Temptation Ser.). 1995. mass mkt. 3.25 (*0-373-25635-3*, 1-25635-3) Harlequin Bks.

— Dillon after Dark. (Temptation Ser.: No. 362). 1991. mass mkt. 2.99 (*0-373-25462-8*) Harlequin Bks.

— Happy Birthday, Baby. (Temptation Ser.). 1994. mass mkt. 2.99 (*0-373-25619-1*, 1-25619-7) Harlequin Bks.

— Her Favorite Husband. 1994. 2.99 (*0-373-25591-8*) Harlequin Bks.

— Joyride. (Temptation Ser.). 1993. mass mkt. 2.99 (*0-373-25572-1*, 1-25572-8) Harlequin Bks.

— The Last Bridesmaid. 1995. mass mkt. 3.50 (*0-373-16601-X*, 1-16601-6) Harlequin Bks.

— Secret Agent Dad. 1994. mass mkt. 3.50 (*0-373-16559-5*, 1-16559-6) Harlequin Bks.

Logan, Leanne, jt. auth. see Robinson, Daniel.

***Logan, Leanne, et al.** India: Travel Survival Kit. 6th ed. (Illus.). 1104p. 1996. pap. 24.95 (*0-86442-321-7*) Lonely Planet.

— New Caledonia: A Travel Survival Kit. 2nd ed. (Illus.). 288p. 1994. pap. 13.95 (*0-86442-201-6*) Lonely Planet.

Logan, Margaret. C.A.T. Caper. 192p. 1990. 18.95 (*0-8027-5762-6*) Walker & Co.

— Deathampton Summer. 1988. 16.95 (*0-8027-5699-9*) Walker & Co.

— The End of an Altruist. 288p. 1993. 21.95 (*0-312-10459-6*) St Martin.

— A Killing in Venture Capital. 224p. 1989. 19.95 (*0-8027-5734-0*) Walker & Co.

— Never Let a Stranger in Your House. 256p. 1995. 21.95 (*0-312-13130-5*, Pub. by Thomas Dunne Bks) St Martin.

Logan, Marie. Mississippi-Louisiana Border Country: History of Rodney Mississippi & Environs. 1974. 12.95 (*0-87511-072-X*) Claitors.

Logan, Marie-Rose & Rudnytsky, Peter L., eds. Contending Kingdoms: Historical, Psychological, & Feminist Approaches to the Literature of Sixteenth-Century England & France. LC 90-12798. 373p. (C). 1991. text ed. 44.95 (*0-8143-2149-6*); pap. text ed. 24.95 (*0-8143-2150-X*) Wayne St U Pr.

Logan, Mary S. The Part Taken by Women in American History. LC 72-2613. (American Women Ser.: Images & Realities). (Illus.). 956p. 1978. reprint ed. 59.95 (*0-405-04467-4*) Ayer.

An Asterisk (*) at the beginning of an entry indicates that the title is appearing in BIP for the first time.

*Logan, Matt. Coffin Creek. large type ed. (Western Library). 272p. 1995. pap. 14.95 (0-7089-7686-7, Linford) Ulverscroft.

*Logan, Michael F. Fighting Sprawl & City Hall: Resistance to Urban Growth in the Southwest. LC 95-5590. 1995. write for info. (0-8165-1512-3); pap. write for info. (0-8165-1553-0) U of Ariz Pr.

Logan, Mike. Bronc to Breakfast. LC 88-91264. (Illus.). 80p. (Orig.). 1988. pap. 7.95 (0-937959-53-7) Falcon Pr MT.

— Laugh Kills Lonesome & Other Poems. (Illus.). 80p. (Orig.). 1990. pap. 7.95 (1-56044-056-2) Falcon Pr MT.

— Little Friends: In Verse & Photography. (J). (ps-3). 1992. pap. 7.95 (1-56044-139-9) Falcon Pr MT.

— Men of the Open Range & Other Poems. 80p. (Orig.). 1993. pap. 7.95 (1-56044-247-6) Falcon Pr MT.

— Montana Is . . . Montana in Verse & Photography. rev. ed. LC 89-91009. (Illus.). 96p. 1989. pap. 11.95 (0-937959-82-0) Falcon Pr MT.

— Yellowstone Is... (Illus.). 96p. 1987. pap. 11.95 (0-937959-20-0) Falcon Pr MT.

Logan, Muriel B. & Crumpacker, Emily. Dining In - Portland. (Dining in Ser.). 189p. (Orig.). 1979. pap. 7.95 (0-89716-043-6) P B Pubng.

Logan, Nancy R. Children of a Lost Spirit. 396p. (Orig.). 1993. pap. 10.00 (1-883763-02-9) Kideko Hse.

Logan, Niall A. Bacterial Systematics. LC 93-26811. (Illus.). 256p. 1994. pap. 32.95 (0-632-03775-X) Blackwell Sci.

Logan, Patrick. The Holy Wells of Ireland. 1980. 21.00 (0-86140-026-7, Pub. by Colin Smythe Ltd UK); pap. 9.95 (0-86140-046-1, Pub. by Colin Smythe Ltd UK) Dufour.

— Irish Country Cures. LC 93-43393. 160p. (Orig.). 1994. pap. 6.95 (0-8069-0718-5) Sterling.

Logan, Rayford W. The Senate & the Versailles Mandate System. LC 74-14357. 112p. 1975. reprint ed. text ed. 55.00 (0-8371-7798-7, LOVM, Greenwood Pr) Greenwood.

Logan, Rayford W. & Cohen, Irving S. American Negro: Old World Background & New World Experience. rev. ed. Anderson, Howard R., ed. (Illus.). (gr. 7-12). 1970. pap. 20.12 (0-395-03157-5) HM.

Logan, Rayford W. & Winston, Michael R., eds. Dictionary of American Negro Biography. LC 81-9629. 1983. 65.00 (0-393-01513-0) Norton.

Logan, Richard. Alone: A Fascinating Study of Those Who Have Survived Long, Solitary Ordeals. LC 92-44228. 240p. 1993. pap. 16.95 (0-8117-2500-6) Stackpole.

*Logan, Richard K. Logan: A Directory of the Descendants of Andrew & Lydia Logan of Albany, NY & Abbeville, SC. 329p. (Orig.). 1994. pap. text ed. 25.00 (1-55613-993-4) Heritage Bk.

Logan, Robert A. Environmental Issues for the Nineties: A Handbook for Journalists. 2nd ed. LC 93-86547. 337p. 1993. 44.95 (0-937790-49-4, 4430) Media Institute.

— Environmental Issues for the Nineties: A Handbook for Journalists 1995. 3rd ed. 340p. 1994. 44.95 (0-937790-50-8) Media Institute.

Logan, Robert E. Beyond Church Growth. LC 89-30490. (Orig.). 1989. pap. 10.99 (0-8007-5332-1) Revell.

Logan, Robert E. & Short, Larry. Mobilizing for Compassion. LC 93-38029. 208p. (Orig.). 1994. pap. 9.99 (0-8007-5506-5) Revell.

Logan, Robert E., jt. auth. see George, Carl F.

Logan, Roderick M., jt. auth. see Carroll, John E.

Logan, Ron & McClure, Michael. HumanStory: Human History from the Dawn of Time to the Dawn of the New Age. LC 89-27959. (Illus.). 96p. (Orig.). 1989. pap. 8.95 (0-945934-01-7) New Wrld Lib.

Logan, Rosie. Rosie in Rachel. 220p. 1993. 24.95 (0-7475-1115-2, Pub. by Bloomsbury Pub Ltd UK) Trafalgar.

Logan, Sadye L., et al. Social Work Practice with Black Families: A Culturally Specific Approach. 288p. (Orig.). (C). 1990. pap. text ed. 31.95 (0-8013-0012-6, 75678) Longman.

Logan, Samuel T., Jr., ed. The Preacher & Preaching: Reviving the Art in the Twentieth Century. LC 85-32558. 480p. 1986. 19.99 (0-87552-294-7) Presby & Reformed.

Logan, Shirley W. With Pen & Voice: The Rhetoric of Nineteenth-Century African-American Women. LC 94-11166. 200p. (C). 1995. 24.95x (0-8093-1874-1); pap. 14.95x (0-8093-1875-X) S Ill U Pr.

Logan, Terence P. & Smith, Denzell S., eds. The Later Jacobean & Caroline Dramatists. LC 77-25265. (Survey & Bibliography of Recent Studies in English Renaissance Drama). 295p. reprint ed. pap. 84.10 (0-8357-2912-5, 2039150) Bks Demand.

— The New Intellectuals. LC 75-38051. (Survey & Bibliography of Recent Studies in English Renaissance Drama). xiv, 370p. 1977. 35.00 (0-8032-0859-6) U of Nebr Pr.

— The Popular School. LC 74-81364. (Survey & Bibliography of Recent Studies in English Renaissance Drama). 313p. reprint ed. pap. 89.30 (0-7837-1467-X, 2057162) Bks Demand.

Logan, Terry J., et al, eds. Effects of Conservation Tillage on Groundwater Quality: Nitrates & Pesticides. (Illus.). 300p. 1987. 59.95 (0-87371-080-0, S604, CRC Reprint) Franklin.

Logan, Tom. Acting in the Million Dollar Minute: The Art & Business of Performing in TV Commercials. LC 84-12048. (Illus.). 175p. (Orig.). 1984. pap. 7.95 (0-89461-041-4) Broadcasting Pubns.

— How to Act & Eat at the Same Time: The Business of Landing a Professional Acting Job. 2nd rev. ed. (Illus.). 144p. 1988. pap. 7.95 (0-89461-048-1, Comm Pr DC) Broadcasting Pubns.

Logan, Tom & Paige, Marvin. How To Act & Eat At the Same Time: The Business of Landing a Professional Acting Job. LC 83-110850. (Illus.). 132p. (Orig.). 1982. pap. 6.95 (0-89461-039-2); boxed 13.95 (0-89461-038-4) Broadcasting Pubns.

Logan, W. H., ed. see Cokain, Aston.

Logan, W. H., ed. see Crowne, John.

Logan, W. H., ed. see Lacy, John.

Logan, W. H., ed. see Marmion, Shakerley.

Logan, W. H., ed. see Tatham, John.

Logan, W. H., ed. see Wilson, John.

Logan, Wayne A., jt. auth. see Logan, David A.

Logan, Wende W. Breast Carcinoma: The Radiologist's Expanded Role. LC 77-13047. 396p. reprint ed. 112.90 (0-8357-9848-8, 2015195) Bks Demand.

Logan, Wende W. & Muntz, E. Phillip. Reduced Dose Mammography. LC 79-63202. (Illus.). 576p. 1979. 62.00 (0-89352-060-8, Yr Bk Med Pubs) Mosby Yr Bk.

Logan, William. Difficulty. LC 85-70928. 64p. 1986. 12.95 (0-87923-588-8) Godine.

— Moorhen: Poems. 1984. 22.50 (0-317-40770-8) Abattoir.

— Sullen Weedy Lakes. LC 87-46289. 1988. pap. 9.95 (0-87923-730-9) Godine.

Logan, William & Kaiser, Harvey. Vain Empires. (Illus.). 96p. 1995. 19.95 (1-56792-005-5) Godine.

Logan, William, ed. see Golliher, Jeffrey.

*Logan, William B. Dirt: The Excitable Skin of the Earth. 1995. 21.95 (1-57322-004-3) Riverhead Bks.

— The Gardener's Book of Sources. 272p. 1988. 24.95 (0-670-81223-4) Viking Penguin.

— Mathematics in Marketing. 2nd ed. Dorr, Eugene L., ed. (Occupational Manuals & Projects in Marketing Ser.). (Illus.). (gr. 11-12). 1978. text ed. 12.28 (0-07-038462-2) McGraw.

Logan, William B. & Freeman, M. Herbert. Merchandising Mathematics. (Illus.). 160p. (C). 1973. text ed. 19.65 (0-07-038470-3) McGraw.

Logan, William B. & Muse, Vance. The Smithsonian Guide to Historic America: The Deep South: Georgia, Florida, Alabama, Mississippi, Louisiana. Kennedy, Roger G., ed. LC 88-33091. (Smithsonian Guide to Historic America Ser.). (Illus.). 464p. 1989. 24.95 (1-55670-069-5); pap. 18.95 (1-55670-068-7) Stewart Tabori & Chang.

Logan, William B. & Ochshorn, Susan. The Smithsonian Guide to Historic America: The Pacific States: Washington, Oregon, California, Hawaii, Alaska. Kennedy, Roger G., ed. LC 89-4591. (Smithsonian Guide to Historic America Ser.). (Illus.). 496p. 1989. 24.95 (1-55670-102-0); pap. 18.95 (1-55670-106-3) Stewart Tabori & Chang.

Logan, William B., ed. see Garcia Lorca, Federico.

Logan, William S., jt. auth. see Askew, Marc.

Logan, Willis H., ed. The Kairos Covenant: Standing with South African Christians. 176p. 1988. pap. 7.95 (0-377-00189-9) Friendship Pr.

Logan-Young, Wende W. & Yanes-Hoffman, Nancy. Breast Cancer: A Practical Guide to Diagnosis, Vol. 1. (Illus.). 500p. 1994. Vol. 2. 160.00 (0-9640886-2-2); Set. write for info. (0-9640886-0-6) Mount Hope Pub.

— Breast Cancer: A Practical Guide to Diagnosis, Vol. 1. (Illus.). 500p. 1994. 160.00 (0-9640886-1-4) Mount Hope Pub.

Loganbill, Dean, jt. ed. see Gruber, Loren C.

Logar, Cyril M. Location of Responsibility for Product Policy Decisions of United States-Based Multinational Firms Manufacturing Consumer Goods. Bruchey, Stuart, ed. LC 80-581. (Multinational Corporations Ser.). (Illus.). 1980. lib. bdg. 25.95 (0-405-13373-1) Ayer.

Logasa, Hannah. Index to One-Act Plays for Stage, Radio, & Television, Suppl. 4, 1948-57. (Useful Reference Ser. of Library Bks.: Vol. 87). 1958. lib. bdg. 12.00 (0-87305-087-8) Faxon.

— Index to One-Act Plays for Stage, Radio, & Television, Suppl. 5, 1956-64. LC 24-21477. (Useful Reference Ser. of Library Bks.: Vol. 94). 1966. lib. bdg. 11.00 (0-87305-094-0) Faxon.

Logasa, Hannah & Ver Nooy, Winifred. Index to One-Act Plays, Suppl. 1, 1924-31. (Useful Reference Ser. of Library Bks.: Vol. 46). 1932. lib. bdg. 11.00 (0-87305-046-0) Faxon.

Logsdon, Gene. At Nature's Pace: Farming & the American Dream. LC 93-25589. 224p. 1994. 23.00 (0-679-42741-4) Pantheon.

Loge, Marc, tr. see Steinilber-Oberlin, Emile.

Logeman, H., ed. see Benedictus, Saint, Abbot of Monte Cassino: The Rule of S. Benet. (EETS, OS Ser.: No. 90). 1972. reprint ed. 32.00 (0-527-00089-2) Periodicals Srv.

Logeman, Robert E. Michigan No-Fault Automobile Cases: Law & Practice. LC 88-82096. 540p. 1988. ring bd. 110.00 (0-685-22735-9, 88-011) U MI Law CLE.

— Michigan No-Fault Automobile Cases: Law & Practice. LC 88-82096. 540p. 1992. Suppl. only, 1992. 45.00 (0-685-22736-7, 92-015) U MI Law CLE.

Logemann, Jeri A. Manual for the Videofluorographic Study of Swallowing. 2nd rev. ed. LC 92-41623. (C). 1993. spiral bd. 29.00 (0-89079-584-3, 6599) PRO-ED.

Logemann, Jerilyn A. Evaluation & Treatment of Swallowing Disorders. LC 90-52769. (Illus.). 249p. (C). 1983. text ed. 35.00 (0-89079-274-7, 1729) PRO-ED.

Logemann, Jerilyn A. & Sasaki, Clarence T. Speech Therapy & Rehabilitation; General Otolaryngology. (Current Opinion in Otolaryngology & Head & Neck Surgery Ser.). (Illus.). 87p. 1994. pap. text ed. 39.95 (1-85922-632-9) Current Science.

*Loger, Fred C. Ben & Jerry's: The Inside Scoop. 1995. 14.00 (0-517-88370-8) Random.

Logerfo, Paul, jt. auth. see Livolsi, Virginia A.

*Logerloff, Selma. The Girl from the Marsh Croft. Zug, John, ed. 1995. pap. 9.95 (1-57216-014-4) Penfield.

Loggans, Susan E., et al. Products Liability Litigation, 4 vols. LC 88-19303. 1988. ring bd. 500.00 (0-685-24501-2) Clark Boardman Callaghan.

*Loggerwit, Gina S. Lesbianism: Index of New Information. 140p. 1995. 37.50 (0-7883-0478-X); pap. 34.50 (0-7883-0479-8) ABBE Pubs Assn.

Logghe, Joan. What Makes a Woman Beautiful. 1993. pap. 6.00 (0-938631-15-2) Pennywhistle Pr.

Loggia, Marjorie, jt. ed. see Young, Glenn.

Loggie, Jennifer. Pediatric & Adolescent Hypertension. (Illus.). 416p. 1992. 165.00 (0-86542-097-1) Blackwell Sci.

Loggins, Richard. AppleWriter: Beginning & Beyond. 1986. 14.95 (0-89303-442-8) S&S Trade.

— Excel: Business Solutions for the Macintosh. write for info. (0-318-60207-5) Addison-Wesley.

— Using Appleworks: The Complete Guide to Applications. 1985. 17.95 (0-89303-911-X) S&S Trade.

Loggins, Vernon. Hawthornes: The Story of Seven Generations of an American Family. LC 69-10121. (Illus.). 365p. 1968. reprint ed. text ed. 35.00 (0-8371-0149-2, LOH, Greenwood Pr) Greenwood.

— I Hear America. LC 67-18431. 1937. 18.00 (0-8196-0197-7) Biblo.

— Where the Word Ends: The Life of Louis Moreau Gottschalk. fac. ed. LC 58-7553. 289p. 1958. reprint ed. pap. 82.40 (0-7837-7804-X, 2047560) Bks Demand.

Loggins, Vernon P. The Life of Our Design: Organization & Related Strategies in Troilus & Cressida. 116p. (C). 1992. lib. bdg. 29.50 (0-8191-8510-8) U Pr of Amer.

Logic Symposium Staff. Logic Colloquium: Proceedings of the Symposium, Boston, 1972-73. Parikh, R., ed. (Lecture Notes in Mathematics Ser.: Vol. 453). iv, 251p. (Orig.). 1975. pap. 23.00 (0-387-07155-5) Spr-Verlag.

Logical Operations Staff. Database Development in Lotus Notes. (Illus.). (Orig.). 1994. pap. 29.95 (1-56276-283-4) Ziff-Davis.

Logie, Gordon. Elsevier's Dictionary of Physical Planning: Defined in English. 468p. (DUT, ENG, FRE, GER, ITA & SWE.). 1989. 295.00 (0-8288-9322-5) Fr & Eur.

— Elsevier's Dictionary of Physical Planning: In English (with Definitions), French, Italian, Dutch, German & Swedish. 468p. 1989. 179.50 (0-444-70509-0) Elsevier.

— Elsevier's Dictionary of Transport in English, German, Italian, Dutch & Swedish. 296p. (DUT, ENG, FIN, FRE, GER, ITA, POR, SPA & SWE.). 1987. pap. 195.00 (0-8288-7878-1, F86700) Fr & Eur.

— Elsevier's Glossary of Employment & Industry in English, French, Italian, Dutch, German & Swedish. 290p. (DUT, ENG, FRE, GER, ITA & SWE.). 1982. 195.00 (0-8288-1537-2, M14395) Fr & Eur.

— Elsevier's Glossary of Land Resources in English, French, Italian, Dutch, German & Swedish, No. 4: International Planning Glossaries. 304p. 1984. 195.00 (0-8288-0946-1, F96331) Fr & Eur.

— Elsevier's Glossary of Planning & Development in English, French, Italian, Dutch, German & Swedish. 254p. (DUT, ENG, FRE, GER, ITA & SWE.). 1986. 195.00 (0-8288-1406-6, F117630) Fr & Eur.

— Glossary of Employment & Industry. (International Planning Glossaries Ser.: Vol. 3). 290p. (DUT, ENG, FRE, GER, ITA & SWE.). 1982. 97.50 (0-444-42064-9) Elsevier.

— Glossary of Land Resources. (International Planning Glossaries Ser.: Vol. 4). 1984. 97.50 (0-444-42281-1, I-032-84) Elsevier.

— Glossary of Planning & Development: English, French, Italian, Dutch, German & Swedish. (International Planning Glossaries Ser.: Vol. 5). 254p. 1986. 97.50 (0-444-42608-6) Elsevier.

— Glossary of Population & Housing. 266p. (DUT, ENG, FRE, GER, ITA & SWE.). 1978. 195.00 (0-8288-9321-7, F65480) Fr & Eur.

— Glossary of Populations & Housing. (International Planning Glossaries Ser.: Vol. 1). 266p. (DUT, ENG, FRE, GER, ITA & SWE.). 1978. 97.50 (0-444-41730-3) Elsevier.

— Glossary of Transport. (International Planning Glossaries Ser.: Vol. 2). 296p. 1980. 97.50 (0-444-41888-1) Elsevier.

Logie, Laura, jt. auth. see Klepsch, Marvin.

*Logie, Patricia R. Chronicles of Pride: A Journey of Discovery. (Illus.). 196p. 1990. lib. bdg. 27.95x (1-55059-012-X, Pub. by Detselig CN) Temeron Bks.

*Logie, Patricia R., et al. Chronicles of Pride: A Teacher Resource Guide. 127p. 1991. 17.95x (1-55059-027-8) Temeron Bks.

Logie, Robert, jt. ed. see Cornoldi, Cesare.

Logie, Robert H. & Denis, M. Mental Images in Human Cognition. (Advances in Psychology Ser.: Vol. 80). 1991. 100.00 (0-444-88894-2, AIP 80) Elsevier.

Logie, Robert H., jt. ed. see Davies, Graham M.

Logier, Eugene B. The Snakes of Ontario. LC 67-110673. (Canadian University Paperbooks Ser.: No. 64). (Illus.). 106p. reprint ed. pap. 30.30 (0-8357-6384-6, 2035739) Bks Demand.

Logier, Johann B. Logier's Comprehensive Course in Music, Harmony & Practical Composition. LC 76-15186. (Music Reprint Ser.). 1976. reprint ed. lib. bdg. 42.50 (0-306-70794-2) Da Capo.

— A System of the Science of Music & Practical Composition: Incidentally Comprising What Is Usually Understood by the Term Through Bass. LC 76-20715. (Music Reprint Ser.). 1976. reprint ed. lib. bdg. 42.50 (0-306-70793-4) Da Capo.

Logigian, Martha, jt. ed. see Jacobs, Karen.

Logigian, Martha K. Adult Rehabilitation: A Team Approach for Therapists. 1982. 31.50 (0-316-53083-2) Little.

Logio, George C. Bulgaria: Past & Present. LC 73-480409. reprint ed. 42.00 (0-404-56133-0) AMS Pr.

LoGiudice, James. Teaching Philosophy to Gifted Students: A Secondary Level Course of Study for Teachers & Administrators. 1985. 12.00 (0-910609-09-8) Gifted Educ Pr.

Logiudice, James & Walters, Michael E. The Philosophy of Ethics Applied to Everyday Life: A Course of Study for Gifted Students at the Secondary & Post-Secondary Levels. 1987. pap. text ed. 10.00 (0-910609-16-0) Gifted Educ Pr.

LoGiudice, James, jt. auth. see Walters, Michael E.

Logiudici, Frank. Basic Plumbing: Plastic Piping. LC 85-702621. 1985. student ed 7.00 (0-8064-0295-4, 731); audio 199.00 (0-8064-0296-2) Bergwall.

— Basic Plumbing & Pipe Fitting. LC 84-730277. 1984. student ed 8.00 (0-8064-0293-8, 730); audio 319.00 (0-8064-0294-6) Bergwall.

Logofet, Dmitrii O. Matrices & Graphs: Stability Problems in Mathematical Ecology. 1993. 69.95 (0-8493-4246-5, QH541) CRC Pr.

Logoreci, Anton, jt. ed. see Gjecov, Shtjefen.

*Logothetis, N. & Wynn, H. P. Quality Through Design: Experimental Design, Off-line Quality Control, & Taguchi's Contributions. (Oxford Series on Advanced Manufacturing: No. 7). (Illus.). 480p. 1995. pap. text ed. 47.50 (0-19-859395-3) OUP.

Logothetis, Nicholas. Managing for Total Quality. 300p. 1992. pap. text ed. 44.00 (0-13-553512-3) P-H.

Logothetis, Nicholas & Wynn, H. P. Quality Through Design: Experimental Design, Off-Line Quality Control, & Taguchi's Contributions. (Oxford Series on Advanced Manufacturing: No. 7). (Illus.). 480p. 1990. 115.00 (0-19-851993-1) OUP.

Logreyra, Jose L., jt. auth. see Cross, Manuel B.

Logrippo, L., et al, eds. Protocol Specification, Testing & Verification, X: Proceedings of the IFIP WG 6.1 Tenth International Symposium Ottawa, Ontario, Canada, 12-15 June, 1990. 416p. 1990. 102.50 (0-444-88810-1, North Holland) Elsevier.

*Logrippo, Ro. In My World: Designing Living & Learning Environments for the Young. LC 94-41907. 1995. text ed. 24.95 (0-471-11162-7) Wiley.

Logsdail, D. H. & Slater, M. J., eds. Solvent Extraction in the Process Industries, 3 Vols., 1. LC 93-5518. 1993. write for info. (1-85861-039-7) Elsevier.

— Solvent Extraction in the Process Industries, 3 Vols., 2. LC 93-5518. 1993. write for info. (1-85861-040-0) Elsevier.

— Solvent Extraction in the Process Industries, 3 Vols., 3. LC 93-5518. 1993. write for info. (1-85861-041-9) Elsevier.

— Solvent Extraction in the Process Industries, 3 Vols., Set. LC 93-5518. 1993. write for info. (1-85861-042-7) Elsevier.

Logsdom, David R., ed. Eyewitnesses at the Battle of Stones River, No. 2. (Illus.). 82p. (Orig.). 1990. pap. text ed. 5.95 (0-9626018-1-0) Kettle Mills Pr.

*Logsdon, Bette, et al. Physical Education Teaching Units for Program Development, Grades K-3. LC 94-22290. 384p. 1994. pap. text ed. 25.00x (0-87322-788-3, BLOG0788) Human Kinetics.

— Physical Education Teaching Units for Program Development, Grades 4-6. LC 94-22291. 320p. 1994. pap. text ed. 25.00x (0-87322-789-1, BLOG0789) Human Kinetics.

Logsdon, Bette J. Physical Education for Children: A Focus on the Teaching Process. 2nd ed. LC 83-11964. (Illus.). 476p. reprint ed. pap. 135.70 (0-8357-7648-4, 2056974) Bks Demand.

Logsdon, Carole. Million Dollar Promise Workbook. 120p. (Orig.). 1990. pap. 9.95 (0-939497-20-4) Promise Pub.

Logsdon, David R., ed. Eyewitnesses at the Battle of Franklin, No. 1. 3rd rev. ed. (Illus.). 96p. (Orig.). 1991. pap. text ed. 5.95 (0-9626018-0-2) Kettle Mills Pr.

— Eyewitnesses at the Battle of Shiloh, No. 3. (Illus.). 112p. (Orig.). 1994. pap. text ed. 6.95 (0-9626018-2-9) Kettle Mills Pr.

Logsdon, Duane & Wooding, Dan. Million Dollar Promise. 248p. (Orig.). 1986. pap. 8.95 (0-939497-00-X) Promise Pub.

Logsdon, Franklin S. Church Will Not Go Through the Tribulation. 24p. 1980. pap. 1.45 (0-87227-077-7, RBP5092) Reg Baptist.

Logsdon, Gary S., ed. Controlling Waterborne Giardiasis. 118p. 1988. 18.00 (0-87262-633-4) Am Soc Civil Eng.

— Slow Sand Filtration. LC 91-28171. 227p. 1991. pap. text ed. 21.00 (0-87262-847-7) Am Soc Civil Eng.

*Logsdon, Gene. At Nature's Pace: Farming & the American Dream. 224p. 1995. pap. 12.00 (0-679-75844-5) Pantheon.

— The Contrary Farmer. 256p. 1994. 21.95 (0-930031-67-9) Chelsea Green Pub.

— The Contrary Farmer. 288p. 1995. pap. 16.95 (0-930031-74-1) Chelsea Green Pub.

*Logsdon, Guy. The Whorehouse Bells Were Ringing & Other Songs Cowboys Sing. (Illus.). 416p. 1995. pap. 16.95 (0-252-06488-7) U of Ill Pr.

Logsdon, Guy, ed. The Whorehouse Bells Were Ringing & Other Songs Cowboys Sing. LC 88-19931. (Music in American Life Ser.). (Illus.). 416p. 1989. 24.95 (0-252-01583-5) U of Ill Pr.

Logsdon, Guy, et al. Saddle Serenaders, Set, incl. CD. LC 94-1776. (Illus.). 144p. 1994. pap. 29.95 (0-87905-604-5) Gibbs Smith Pub.

Logsdon, Joseph. Horace White, Nineteenth Century Liberal. LC 77-105982. (Contributions in American History Ser.: No. 10). (Illus.). 418p. 1971. text ed. 65.00 (0-8371-3309-2, LHW/, Greenwood Pr) Greenwood.

Logsdon, Joseph, jt. ed. see Hirsch, Arnold R.

Logsdon, Joseph, ed. see Northup, Solomon.

Logsdon, Linda. Establishing a Psychiatric Private Practice. LC 85-7422. (Private Practice Monograph Ser.). 99p. reprint ed. pap. 28.30 (0-8357-7842-8, 2036217) Bks Demand.

Logsdon, Loren & Mayer, Charles W., eds. Since Flannery O'Connor: Essays on the Contemporary American Short Story. LC 87-61274. (Essays in Literature Book Ser.: No. 7). (Illus.). 152p. (Orig.). (C). 1987. pap. 8.00 (0-934312-06-0) WIU Essays Lit.

Logsdon, Phyllis, jt. auth. see Lamb, Beth.

Logsdon, Thomas S. Breaking Through: Creative Problem Solving Using Six Successful Strategies. 1993. pap. 16.95 (0-201-63321-3) Addison-Wesley.

Logsdon, Tom. BASIC Programming with Structure & Style. Marshall, ed. 589p. (C). 1990. pap. text ed. 50.75 (0-314-47012-3) West Pub.

— Mobil Communications Satellites: Theory & Applications. 1995. text ed. 50.00 (0-07-038476-2) McGraw.

— The Navstar Global Positioning System. LC 92-10521. 1992. text ed. 49.95 (0-442-01040-0) Van Nos Reinhold.

— Understanding Navstara: GPS, GIS, IVHS. 1995. text ed. 49.95 (0-442-02054-6) Van Nos Reinhold.

***Logsdon, Wendy & Rapoport, Roger.** Walking Easy in the San Francisco Bay Area: A Hiking Guide for Active Adults. (Walking Easy Ser.). (Illus.). 184p. (Orig.). 1995. pap. 11.95 (0-933469-20-9) Gateway Bks.

Logsdon, Wendy, ed. see Rogoff, Marianne.

Logston, Anne. Dagger's Edge. 240p. (Orig.). 1994. pap. text ed. 4.99 (0-441-00036-3) Ace Bks.

— Greendaughter. 224p. (Orig.). 1993. pap. 4.50 (0-441-30273-4) Ace Bks.

— Shadow Hunt. 1992. pap. 4.50 (0-441-76007-4) Ace Bks.

— Wild Blood. 240p. (Orig.). 1995. pap. text ed. 4.99 (0-441-00243-9) Ace Bks.

Logston, Robert. The End-Times Blood Bath. LC 91-65923. 114p. 1992. pap. 7.95 (1-55523-450-X) Winston-Derek.

***Logstrup, Knud.** Metaphysics, 2 vols., Set. Dees, Russell, ed. (Orig.). 1995. pap. text ed. 70.00 (0-614-07297-2) Marquette.

— Metaphysics, Vol. 1. Dees, Russell, ed. (Orig.). 1995. pap. text ed. 40.00 (0-87462-603-X) Marquette.

— Metaphysics, Vol. 2. Dees, Russell, ed. (Orig.). 1995. pap. text ed. 40.00 (0-87462-607-2) Marquette.

Logue, A. W. Self-Control: Waiting Tommorrow for What You Want Today. LC 94-5478. 224p. 1994. pap. text ed. 18.00 (0-13-803750-7) P-H.

Logue, Alexandra. The Psychology of Eating & Drinking. 2nd ed. (Illus.). 352p. (C). 1995. pap. text ed. write for info. (0-7167-2197-X) W H Freeman.

Logue, Barbara. Last Rights: Death Control & the Elderly in America. LC 92-39452. (Lexington Book Series on Social Issues). 1993. text ed. 24.95 (0-669-27370-8) Free Pr.

Logue, Barbara, jt. auth. see Rosenwaike, Ira.

Logue, Cal M., ed. No Place to Hide: The South & Human Rights, 2 vols., 2. 766p. 1984. write for info. (0-318-57997-9) Mercer Univ Pr.

— No Place to Hide: The South & Human Rights, 2 vols., Set. LC 84-1044. 766p. 1984. 40.00 (0-86554-109-4, MUP-H101) Mercer Univ Pr.

— No Place to Hide: The South & Human Rights, 2 vols., Vol. 1 & 2. LC 84-1044. 766p. 1984. write for info. (0-86554-108-6, MUP-H101) Mercer Univ Pr.

Logue, Calvin M. & Dorgan, Howard, eds. New Diversity in Contemporary Southern Rhetoric. LC 86-21152. 272p. 1987. text ed. 37.50 (0-8071-1312-3) La State U Pr.

— Oratory of Southern Demagogues. LC 81-3759. (Illus.). xxii, 234p. 1981. text ed. 35.00 (0-8071-0792-1) La State U Pr.

Logue, Calvin M. & Talmadge, Eugene. Rhetoric & Response: Great American Orators: Critical Studies, Speeches, & Sources, No. 3. LC 88-24748. 325p. 1989. text ed. 59.95 (0-313-25855-4, LUE, Greenwood Pr) Greenwood.

Logue, Calvin M, ed. see McGill, Ralph.

Logue, Calvin M., et al. Briefly Speaking: A Guide to Public Speaking in College & Career. 4th ed. 350p. (C). 1991. pap. text ed. 16.00 (0-205-12913-7) Allyn.

Logue, Charles. Outplace Yourself: Secrets of an Executive Outplacement Counselor. 504p. 1993. 25.00 (1-55850-253-X) Adams Pubng.

— Outplace Yourself: Secrets of an Executive Outplacement Counselor. 504p. 1995. pap. 15.95 (1-55850-505-9) Adams Pubng.

***Logue, Christopher.** The Husbands: An Account of Books III & IV of Homer's Iliad. LC 95-13117. 96p. 1995. 17.00 (0-374-17391-5) FS&G.

— Kings: An Account of Books One to Four of Homer's Iliad. 96p. 1991. 16.95 (0-374-18151-9) FS&G.

— Kings: An Account of Books 1 & 2 of Homer's Iliad. 1992. pap. 9.00 (0-374-52368-1, Noonday) FS&G.

— Songs. 1960. 10.95 (0-8392-1106-6) Astor-Honor.

— War Music: An Account of Books 16 to 19 of Homer's Iliad. 192p. 1988. pap. 7.95 (0-374-52089-5) FS&G.

Logue, Dennis E. Handbook of Modern Finance. 1989. 145.00 (0-7913-0311-X) Warren Gorham & Lamont.

— Handbook of Modern Finance. suppl. ed. 1991. Supplemented annually; write for info. 53.75 (0-685-56109-7) Warren Gorham & Lamont.

***Logue, Dennis E., ed.** Handbook of Modern Finance. 3rd ed. LC 93-60975. 1994. 145.00 (0-7913-1762-5) Warren Gorham & Lamont.

— The WG&L Handbook of Financial Markets. LC 94-20612. 1995. text ed. 18.95 (0-538-84250-4) S-W Pub.

— The WG&L Handbook of Financial Strategy & Policy. LC 94-20887. 1995. text ed. 18.95 (0-538-84252-0) S-W Pub.

— The WG&L Handbook of International Finance. LC 94-20613. 1995. text ed. 18.95 (0-538-84253-9) S-W Pub.

— The WG&L Handbook of Securities & Investment Management. LC 94-20685. 1995. text ed. 18.95 (0-538-84249-0) S-W Pub.

— The WG&L Handbook of Short-Time & Long-Term Financial Management. LC 94-20686. 1995. text ed. 18.95 (0-538-84251-2) S-W Pub.

Logue, Dennis E. & Rogalski, Richard J. Managing Corporation Pension Plans: The Impacts of Inflation. LC 83-25786. (AEI Studies: No. 355). 78p. reprint ed. pap. 25.00 (0-7837-1083-6, 2041614) Bks Demand.

***Logue, Frank.** Stretching & Massage for Hikers & Backpackers. (Nuts-n-Bolts Ser.). (Illus.). 32p. (Orig.). 1994. pap. 4.95 (0-89732-167-7) Menasha Ridge.

Logue, Frank & Logue, Victoria. Appalachian Trail Fun Book. (J). (ps-3). 1993. pap. 6.95 (0-917953-60-6) Appalachian Trail.

— Best of the Appalachian Trail: Overnight Hikes. (Illus.). 242p. 1994. pap. 12.95 (0-89732-139-1) Menasha Ridge.

— Best of the Appalachian Trail, Day Hikes. (Illus.). 198p. 1994. pap. 12.95 (0-89732-138-3) Menasha Ridge.

— Food & Cooking for Hikers & Backpackers. (Nuts-N-Bolts Guides Ser.). 1995. pap. 4.95 (0-89732-175-8) Menasha Ridge.

— Georgia Outdoors. (Illus.). (Orig.). 1995. pap. 14.95 (0-89587-131-9) Blair.

— Knots for Hikers & Backpackers. (Illus.). 32p. pap. 4.95 (0-89732-146-4) Menasha Ridge.

***Logue, Frank, et al.** The New Blueridge Milepost Guide. 1995. pap. 9.95 (0-614-01236-8) Menasha Ridge.

***Logue, James.** Projective Probability. (Oxford Philosophical Monographs). (Illus.). 192p. 1995. text ed. 39.95 (0-19-823959-9) OUP.

Logue, John. Toward a Theory of Trade Union Internationalism. LC 80-153679. (University of Gothenberg (Sweden), Research Section Post-War History Publications Ser.: No. 7). 66p. (Orig.). 1980. pap. 2.95 (0-933522-02-9) Kent Popular.

Logue, John, ed. see Belton, Beth.

Logue, John, jt. auth. see Callesen, Gerd.

Logue, John, jt. auth. see Dye, Pat.

Logue, John, jt. auth. see Einhorn, Eric S.

Logue, John, jt. auth. see Einhorn, Eric.

Logue, John, jt. ed. see Einhorn, Eric.

Logue, John, jt. auth. see Ivancic, Catherine.

Logue, John, jt. auth. see Keremetsky, Jacob.

Logue, John, et al. Buyout! Employee Ownership as an Alternative to Plant Shutdowns: The Ohio Experience. LC 86-623028. (Illus.). 104p. (Orig.). 1986. pap. text ed. 9.95 (0-933522-15-0) Kent Popular.

***Logue, John, et al, eds.** Transforming Russian Enterprises: From State Control to Employee Ownership. LC 95-6666. (Contributions in Economics & Economic History Ser.: No. 168). 1995. text ed. write for info. (0-313-28748-1, Greenwood Pr) Greenwood.

Logue, John J. The Great Debate on Charter Reform: A Proposal for a Stronger United Nations. LC 67-47309. (Publications in the Social Sciences: No. 2). 39p. reprint ed. pap. 25.00 (0-7837-5571-6, 2045349) Bks Demand.

Logue, Larry. Sermon in the Desert: Belief and Behavior in Early St. George, Utah. LC 87-19181. (Illus.). 192p. 1988. 24.95 (0-252-01474-X) U of Ill Pr.

***Logue, Larry M.** The Lives of Civil War Soldiers: From Fort Sumter to the Twentieth Century. (American Ways Ser.). 224p. 1995. 24.95 (1-56663-093-2) I R Dee.

Logue, Mary. Discriminating Evidence. (First Poetry Ser.). 70p. 1990. pap. 8.95 (0-922811-09-1) Mid-List.

— The Haunting of Hunter House. (Author's Signature Collection). (J). (gr. 3-8). 1992. lib. bdg. 12.79 (0-89565-877-1) Childs World.

— The Missing Statue of Minnehaha. (Author's Signature Collection). (J). (gr. 3-8). 1992. lib. bdg. 12.79 (0-89565-902-6) Childs World.

— Still Explosion. LC 92-43990. 248p. 1993. text ed. 18.95 (1-878067-29-X) Seal Pr Feminist.

— Still Explosion. LC 92-43990. 248p. 1994. pap. 9.95 (1-878067-48-6) Seal Pr Feminist.

Logue, Mary, ed. see Green, Kate, et al.

Logue, Patricia H. One Child at a Time: A Parent's Guide to Rebuilding American Mindpower. (Illus.). 96p. (Orig.). 1992. pap. 10.00 (0-9630488-0-5) Mindbuilder.

Logue, Tom J. God, Could You Talk a Little Louder? The Father of a Dying Son Struggles with His Faith. 102p. (Orig.). 1990. pap. 6.95 (0-933522-21-5) Kent Popular.

Logue, Victoria. Backpacking in the Nineties: Tips, Techniques & Secrets. LC 92-43314. (Illus.). 1992. pap. 14.95 (0-89732-163-4) Menasha Ridge.

— Camping in the 90's. (Illus.). 224p. 1995. pap. 14.95 (0-89732-181-2) Menasha Ridge.

Logue, Victoria, jt. auth. see Logue, Frank.

Logue, William. Charles Renouvier, Philosopher of Liberty. LC 92-15585. 224p. (C). 1992. text ed. 35.00x (0-8071-1788-9) La State U Pr.

— From Philosophy to Sociology: The Evolution of French Liberalism, 1870-1914. LC 82-22263. 278p. 1983. 25.00 (0-87580-088-2) N Ill U Pr.

— Leon Blum: The Formative Years, 1872-1914. LC 72-7515. 345p. 1973. 24.00 (0-87580-030-0) N Ill U Pr.

Logunov, A., ed. Current Problems of Mathematics: Differential Equations, Mathematical Analysis & Their Applications. LC 86-10929. (STEKLO Ser.: Vol. 166). 271p. 1986. pap. text ed. 128.00 (0-8218-3093-7, STEKLO-166) Am Math.

— Current Problems of Mathematics: Mathematical Analysis, Algebra, Topology. LC 86-20640. (STEKLO Ser.: Vol. 167). 304p. 1986. pap. text ed. 137.00 (0-8218-3095-3, STEKLOV-167) Am Math.

Logunov, A. A. Gravitation & Elementary Particle Physics. 296p. 1983. 45.00 (0-569-20104-7, Pub. by Collets UK) Pro-Am Music.

— Lectures in Relativity & Gravitation: A Modern Look. Repyev, Alexander, tr. (Illus.). 243p. 1991. 94.00 (0-08-037939-7, Pergamon Pr) Elsevier.

***Loh.** Southeast Asia Writes Back!, Vol. 1. (Skoob Pacifica Ser.). 1995. pap. 11.95 (1-871438-19-5) Atrium Pubs.

Loh, ed. A Festival of Asian Christmas Music: Christmas Music from Hongkong, India, Indonesia, Malaysia, Philippines & Taiwan. (Asian Inst. for Liturgy & Music Anthems Ser.: No. 2). 68p. (Orig.). 1984. pap. 8.75 (971-10-0228-0, Pub. by New Day Pub PH) Cellar.

***Loh, C. Y. & Ong, I. K., eds.** Skoob Pacifica Anthology. 2nd ed. (Skoob Pacifica Ser.). 1995. pap. 11.95 (1-871438-54-3) Atrium Pubs.

Loh, Carolyn. Let's Celebrate Valentine's Day: A Book of Things to Draw. LC 87-50429. (Illus.). 32p. (J). (gr. 2-6). 1988. lib. bdg. 10.65 (0-8167-1035-X); pap. text ed. 1.95 (0-8167-1036-8) Troll Assocs.

Loh, Eudora & Medford, Roberta, comps. Statistical Sources on the California Hispanic Population: Update. pap. 25.00 (0-915745-06-2) Floricanto Pr.

Loh, Eudora, jt. auth. see Medford, Roberta.

Loh, Horace H. & Ross, David H., eds. Neurochemical Mechanisms of Opiates & Endorphins. LC 78-24623. (Advances in Biochemical Psychopharmacology Ser.: No. 20). (Illus.). 575p. reprint ed. pap. 163.90 (0-7837-7129-0, 2046958) Bks Demand.

Loh, Lily. Lily Loh's Chinese Seafood & Vegetables. Addison-Licameli, Amy, ed. (Illus.). 222p. 1991. 22.95 (0-9630299-0-8) Solana Pub.

Loh, Morag. Tucking Mommy In. LC 87-16740. (Illus.). 40p. (J). (ps-2). 1988. 14.95 (0-531-05740-2); lib. bdg. 14.99 (0-531-08340-3) Orchard Bks Watts.

— Tucking Mommy In. LC 87-16740. (Illus.). 40p. (J). (ps-2). 1991. pap. 4.95 (0-531-07025-5) Orchard Bks Watts.

Loh, Pichon P. The Early Chiang Kai-Shek: A Study of His Personality & Politics, 1887-1924. LC 70-158461. (Columbia University East Asian Institute Occasional Papers). 230p. reprint ed. pap. 65.60 (0-317-10172-2, 2006869) Bks Demand.

Loh, Y. Peng, ed. Mechanisms of Intracellular Trafficking & Processing of Proteins. 1992. 125.95 (0-8493-6870-7, QH450) CRC Pr.

***Loha-Unchit, Kasma.** It Rains Fishes: The Legends, the Traditions & the Joys of Thai Cooking. (Illus.). 224p. (Orig.). 1995. pap. 24.95 (0-87654-356-5) Pomegranate Calif.

Lohan, Frank J. The Drawing Handbook: Comprehensive, Easy-To-Master Lessons on Composition & Techniques Using Pencil & Pen & Ink. 224p. 1993. pap. 14.95 (0-8092-3786-5) Contemp Bks.

— Pen & Ink Techniques. 96p. 1978. pap. 12.95 (0-8092-7438-8) Contemp Bks.

Lohani, Bindu N. Environmental Quality Management. Varshney, C. K., ed. (C). 1984. 28.50 (0-8364-2409-3, Pub. by S Asia Pubs II) S Asia.

Lohaus, Arnold, jt. auth. see Thomas, Hoben.

Lohaus, Sara & White, Jan, eds. A Colorado Christmas Anthology. 2nd ed. (State Anthologies Ser.: No. 3). (Illus.). 1990. pap. 10.95 (0-9621085-9-6) Partridge Pr.

Lohbeck, Kurt. Holy War, Unholy Victory: Eyewitness to the CIA's Secret War in Afghanistan. LC 93-24344. (Illus.). 320p. 1993. 24.00 (0-89526-499-4) Regnery Pub.

Lohberg, Rolf. Diccionario Basico Del Ordenador. 2nd ed. 48p. 1987. pap. 8.95 (0-7859-6449-5) Fr & Eur.

Lohf, Kenneth A. & Ellenbogen, Rudolph, eds. The Rare Book & Manuscript Library of Columbia University: Collections & Treasures. 138p. 1985. pap. 25.00 (0-9607862-1-X) Columbia U Libs.

Lohf, Sabine. Building Your Own Toys. LC 89-22276. (Craft Bks.). 64p. (J). (gr. 5 up). 1989. lib. bdg. 15.45 (0-516-09251-0); pap. 8.95 (0-516-49251-9) Childrens.

— Christmas Crafts. LC 89-22255. (Craft Bks.). 64p. (J). 1989. lib. bdg. 15.45 (0-516-09252-9); pap. 8.95 (0-516-49252-7) Childrens.

— I Made It Myself. LC 89-22252. (Craft Bks.). 64p. (J). 1989. lib. bdg. 15.45 (0-516-09254-5); pap. 8.95 (0-516-49254-3) Childrens.

— Making Things for Easter. LC 89-22254. (Craft Bks.). 64p. (J). (gr. 3 up). 1989. pap. 8.95 (0-516-49253-5) Childrens.

— Things I Can Make. LC 93-40881. (J). (ps-3). 1994. 12.95 (0-8118-0667-7) Chronicle Bks.

Lohf, Sabine & Schael, Hannelore. Making Things with Yarn. LC 89-22256. (Craft Bks.). 64p. (J). (gr. 2 up). 1989. pap. 8.95 (0-516-49255-1) Childrens.

Lohfert, Walter, jt. auth. see Scherling, Theo.

Lohfink, Gerhard. The Gospels: God's Word in Human Words. Poehlmann, William R., tr. (Herald Biblical Bklts.). 80p. 1972. pap. 1.95 (0-8199-0516-X, Frncscn Herld) Franciscan Pr.

— The Gospels: God's Word in Human Words. Poehlmann, William R., tr. (Herald Biblical Bklts. Ser.). 80p. 1972. pap. 1.95 (0-8199-0212-8, Frncscn Herld) Franciscan Pr.

— Jesus & Community: The Social Dimension of Christian Faith. Galvin, John P., tr. LC 84-47928. 224p. 1984. pap. 15.00 (0-8006-1802-5, 1-1802, Fortress Pr) Augsburg Fortress.

Lohfink, Norbert. The Covenant Never Revoked: Biblical Reflections on Christian-Jewish Dialogue. 1991. pap. 7.95 (0-8091-3228-1) Paulist Pr.

— Great Themes from the Old Testament. 1981. 12.95 (0-8199-0801-0, Frncscn Herld) Franciscan Pr.

— Theology of the Pentateuch: Themes of the Priestly Narrative & Deuteronomy. 1994. pap. 18.00 (0-8006-2593-5, Fortress Pr) Augsburg Fortress.

Lohfink, Norbert F. The Inerrancy of Scripture & Other Essays. Wilson, R. A., tr. LC 91-2720. 183p. 1992. pap. 13.95 (0-941037-20-7) BIBAL Pr.

— Option for the Poor: The Basic Principle of Liberation Theology in the Light of the Bible. LC 86-72979. (Berkeley Lectures: No. 1). 85p. 1987. pap. 7.95 (0-941037-00-2) BIBAL Pr.

***Lohia, Sushama.** Lalitavajra's Manual of Buddhist Iconography. (C). 1994. text ed. 88.00 (81-85689-97-0, Pub. by Popular Prakashan II) S Asia.

***Lohkamp, Nicholas.** Jesus at the Heart of Life: The Spirituality of Being Human. 96p. 1994. 6.95 (0-86716-225-2) St Anthony Mess Pr.

Lohman, Anne A. Clay Lifting. Thompson, Bill, ed. LC 85-90939. 60p. (Orig.). 1985. pap. text ed. 7.95 (0-685-71262-1) Scott Pubns MI.

Lohman, Jack & Kirkpatrick, Arnold. Successful Thoroughbred Investment in a Changing Market. (Illus.). 253p. 1984. 25.00 (0-929346-10-6) R Meerdink Co Ltd.

Lohman, Karen, ed. see Pizzuti, Mary R. & Pizzuti, John A.

Lohman, Ruud. A House for the Third Millennium. (Illus.). 100p. (Orig.). 1986. pap. 7.95 (0-89071-335-9) Aurobindo Assn.

Lohman, Timothy G. Advances in Body Composition Assessment. LC 92-1476. (Current Issues in Exercise Science Ser.: Monograph No. 3). (Illus.). 160p. 1992. pap. 19.00x (0-87322-327-6, BLOH0327) Human Kinetics.

Lohman, Timothy G., et al. Anthropometric Standardization Reference Manual. abr. ed. LC 90-29003. (Illus.). 96p. 1991. text ed. 19.00x (0-87322-331-4, BLOH0331) Human Kinetics.

Lohman, Timothy G., et al, eds. Anthropometric Standardization Reference Manual. LC 87-8623. (Illus.). 184p. 1988. text ed. 44.00x (0-87322-121-4, BLOH0121) Human Kinetics.

Lohmann, Christoph K., ed. Discovering Difference: Contemporary Essays in American Culture. LC 92-41566. 1993. 29.95 (0-253-33607-4); pap. 12.95 (0-253-20815-7) Ind U Pr.

Lohmann, Dieter. Die Andromache-Szenen in der Ilias. (Spudasmata Ser.: Bd. 42). iv, 82p. (GER.). 1988. write for info. (3-487-09009-0, Pub. by Georg Olms GW) Lubrecht & Cramer.

Lohmann, G. P., jt. auth. see Tjalsma, R. C.

Lohmann, Hans. Drohung und Verheissung: Exegetische Untersuchungen zur Eschatologie bei den Apostolischen Vaetern. (Beiheft zur Zeitschrift fuer die Neuetestamentliche Wissenschaft Ser.: No. 55). ix, 266p. (GER.). (C). 1989. lib. bdg. 79.25x (3-11-012018-6) De Gruyter.

Lohmann, Jeanne. Between Silence & Answer: New & Selected Poems. LC 94-21462. (Illus.). 98p. 1994. pap. 10.00 (0-87574-919-4) Pendle Hill.

— Gathering a Life. LC 89-32034. 72p. (Orig.). 1989. pap. 7.50 (0-936784-77-6) J Daniel.

— Steadying the Landscape. (Illus.). 102p. 1982. pap. 5.95 (0-9607688-1-5) J A Lohmann.

Lohmann, Larry, jt. ed. see Colchester, Marcus.

Lohmann, Martina, jt. ed. see Lieth, Helmut.

Lohmann, Melane, ed. Recherche Recipes from Sound Food Restaurant & Bakery. (Illus.). 51p. (Orig.). 1984. pap. 6.95 (0-9615672-0-1) Sound Food Co.

Lohmann, Roger A. Breaking Even: Financial Management in Human Service Organizations. LC 79-23692. 336p. 1981. pap. text ed. 24.95 (0-87722-247-9) Temple U Pr.

— The Commons: New Perspectives on Nonprofit Organization & Voluntary Action. LC 92-13058. (Nonprofit Sector Ser.). 368p. 1992. 35.95 (1-55542-476-7) Jossey-Bass.

Lohmann, U., tr. see Jungel, Eberhard.

Lohmann, W. J., Jr. The Cultural Shocks of Rudyard Kipling. LC 89-13330. (American University Studies: English Language & Literature: Ser. IV, Vol. 73). 309p. (C). 1990. text ed. 46.95 (0-8204-0649-X) P Lang Pubs.

Lohmann, William T. Construction Specifications: Managing the Review Process. 320p. 1992. pap. 45.00 (0-7506-9148-4, Butterwrth Archit) Buttrwrth-Heinemann.

Lohmar, Ceil. Buying More House for Less Money. 1990. pap. 9.95 (1-55738-162-3) Probus Pub Co.

— For Sale by Owner. 1990. pap. 11.95 (1-55738-161-5) Probus Pub Co.

Lohmar, Dieter. Phanomenologie der Mathematik: Elemente Einer Phanomenologischen Aufklarung der Mathematischen Erkenntnis Nach Husserl. (Phaenomenologica Ser.: No. 114). 252p. 1989. lib. bdg. 112.50 (0-7923-0187-0) Kluwer Ac.

Lohmeyer, Henno, ed. see Shaginyan, Aleksandr.

Lohmus, J., et al. Nonassociative Algebras in Physics. (Monographs in Mathematics). 280p. Date not set. pap. text ed. 75.00 (0-911767-71-1) Hadronic Pr Inc.

Lohnes, Paul R., jt. auth. see Cooley, William W.

Lohnes, Walter F. & Nollendorfs, Valters, eds. German Studies in the United States: Assessment & Outlook. LC 76-13346. 272p. 1976. 17.50 (0-299-97009-4); pap. 7.50 (0-299-97010-8) U of Wis Pr.

Lohnes, Walter F., et al. German: A Structural Approach. (C). 1988. Language tapes avail. student ed, pap. text ed. 21.95 (0-393-95467-6) Norton.

— German: A Structural Approach. (C). 1989. Tchr's. manual. teacher ed, pap. text ed. 4.95 (0-393-95470-6) Norton.

— German: A Structural Approach. 4th ed. (C). 1988. text ed. 49.95 (0-393-95464-1) Norton.

Lohof, Bruce A. American Commonplace: Essays on the Popular Culture of the United States. LC 82-73977. 1983. 16.95 (0-87972-221-5); pap. 8.95 (0-87972-222-3) Bowling Green Univ.

Lohr, Albrecht, jt. auth. see Jakobi, Gunter.

Lohr, Albrecht, jt. ed. see Jakobi, Gunter.

An Asterisk (*) at the beginning of an entry indicates that the title is appearing in BIP for the first time.

Lohr, Andrew. Born of Water & Spirit: Teachings in Mystic Christianity. LC 90-82118. 256p. (Orig.). 1990. pap. 11.95 (*0-9626563-4-8*) Folsom Lee.
— Talks on Mystic Christianity. Challgren, Crafer, ed. LC 84-90346. (Illus.). 143p. (Orig.). 1984. pap. text ed. 6.50 (*0-9613401-0-X*) Fiery Water.
***Lohr, Eberhard & Sievers, Klaus, eds.** Urological Radiology: Radiological Diagnosis of Urological Diseases: Plain Film, Sonography, Angiography, CT, & MRI. LC 94-34633. (Illus.). 256p. 1995. text ed. 89.00 (*0-88937-131-8*) Hogrefe & Huber Pubs.
***Lohr, Eberhard, et al, eds.** Clinical Neuroradiology: A Textbook. LC 94-35189. (Illus.). 336p. 1995. text ed. 135.00 (*0-88937-132-6*) Hogrefe & Huber Pubs.
Lohr, J. E. Your First Budgerigar. (YF Ser.). (Illus.). 36p. (Orig.). (YA). 1991. pap. 1.95 (*0-86622-058-5*, YF-102) TFH Pubns.
— Your First Cockatiel. (YF Ser.). (Illus.). 36p. (Orig.). (YA). 1991. pap. 1.95 (*0-86622-060-7*, YF-104) TFH Pubns.
Lohr, Jacob A. Pediatric Outpatient Procedures. (Illus.). 400p. 1991. text ed. 49.50 (*0-397-50897-2*) Lippincott.
Lohr, James A. Computer Graphics for Aerospace & Military Applications. (Illus.). 352p. 1989. 34.95 (*0-8306-3303-0*, TAB/TPR) TAB Bks.
Lohr, James B. & Wisniewski, Alexander A. Movement Disorders: A Neuropsychiatric Approach. LC 86-27163. (Guilford Foundations of Modern Psychiatry Ser.). 387p. 1987. lib. bdg. 60.00 (*0-89862-176-3*) Guilford Pr.
Lohr, Jeffrey, jt. auth. see Hamberger, Kevin.
Lohr, Kathleen N., ed. Breast Cancer: Setting Priorities for Effectiveness Research: Report of a Study by a Committee of the Institute of Medicine, Division of Health Care Services. LC 89-64426. 72p. reprint ed. pap. 25.00 (*0-8357-2694-0*, 2040231) Bks Demand.
Lohr, Kathleen N., ed. see Committee of the Institute of Medicine Division of Health Care Services Staff.
Lohr, Kathleen N., jt. ed. see Heithoff, Kim A.
Lohr, Kathleen N., ed. see Institute of Medicine, Committee on Pediatric Emergency Medical Services Staff.
Lohr, Kathleen N., ed. see Institute of Medicine Committee on Regional Health Data Networks Staff.
Lohr, Kathleen N., ed. see Institute of Medicine, Committee to Design a Strategy for Quality Review & Assurance in Medicare Staff.
Lohr, Kathleen N., ed. see Institute of Medicine (US), Div. of Health Care.
Lohr, Paul & Meyer, Manfred, eds. Fernsehen und Jugend, Vol. 7: Eine Bibliographie Internationaler Fachliteratur 1967-1989. (Bibliographischer Dienst Ser.). 204p. (GER.). 1989. pap. 19.00 (*3-598-20687-9*) K G Saur.
Lohren, Carl & Barkow, Al. Getting Set for Golf. LC 94-16357. 1995. 18.95 (*0-670-85562-6*, Viking) Viking Penguin.
Lohrengel, J., jt. auth. see Janssen, D.
Lohrentz, Kenneth P., jt. auth. see Easterbrook, David L.
Lohrenz, Mary & Stamper, Anita. Mississippi Homespun: Nineteenth Century Textiles & the Women Who Made Them. (Illus.). 79p. 1989. pap. 15.00 (*0-938896-56-3*) Mississippi Archives.
Lohrke, E. W. Armageddon: The World War in Literature. 1971. 69.95 (*0-87968-660-X*) Gordon Pr.
Lohrman. Competency Based Orientation for Critical Care Nursing. 219p. 1992. 49.95 (*1-55664-207-5*) Mosby Yr Bk.
Lohrmann, Charles J., jt. auth. see Kapoun, Robert.
Lohrmann, Dietrich, jt. ed. see Butzer, Paul L.
Lohrmann, H. P. & Schreml, W., eds. Cytotoxic Drugs & the Granulopoietic System. (Recent Results in Cancer Research Ser.: Vol. 81). (Illus.). 235p. 1981. 65.00 (*0-387-10962-5*) Spr-Verlag.
Lohs, Karlheinz, jt. ed. see Stock, Thomas.
Lohse, Bernhard. Martin Luther: An Introduction to His Life & Work. Schultz, Robert C., tr. LC 85-45496. 304p. 1986. pap. 19.00 (*0-8006-1964-1*, 1-1964, Fortress Pr) Augsburg Fortress.
— A Short History of Christian Doctrine: From the First Century to the Present. rev. ed. Stoeffer, F. Ernest, tr. LC 66-21732. 320p. 1978. pap. 16.00 (*0-8006-1341-4*, 1-1341, Fortress Pr) Augsburg Fortress.
Lohse, Edward. Colossians & Philemon. Koester, Helmut, ed. Poehlman, William R. & Karris, Robert J., trs. LC 76-157550. (Hermeneia A Critical & Historical Commentary on the Bible Ser.). 256p. 1971. 27.00 (*0-8006-6001-3*, 1-6001, Fortress Pr) Augsburg Fortress.
Lohse, Edward. The New Testament Environment. Steely, John E., tr. LC 75-43618. 320p. 1976. pap. 14.95 (*0-687-27944-5*) Abingdon.
Lohse, Friedrich, jt. auth. see Batzer, Hans.
Lohse, Joyce B. A Yellowstone Savage: Life in Nature's Wonderland. LC 87-34212. (Illus.). 144p. (Orig.). 1988. pap. 7.95 (*0-944915-00-0*) J D Charles.
Lohwater, A. J. Russian-English Dictionary of the Mathematical Sciences. LC 90-270. 343p. (ENG & RUS.). 1990. reprint ed. pap. 38.00 (*0-8218-0133-3*, REDS) Am Math.
Lohwater, A. J., jt. auth. see Collingwood, Edward F.
Lohwater, J., tr. see Ladyzhenskaya, Olga A.
Loi, Isidoro. The Woman. 1992. 8.95 (*0-533-09661-8*) Vantage.
Loibl, Gerhard. A Collection of International Concessions & Related Instruments Index. 1982. 30.00 (*0-379-20666-8*) Oceana.
Loida, A. & Peisa, R. Long Term Behaviour of Tru Waste Bearing Ceramics Task 3 Characterization of, No. EUR 13602. 54p. 1991. pap. 8.00 (*92-826-2931-7*, CD-NA-13602-EN-C) UNIPUB.
Loike, John D., jt. auth. see Ayres, David C.
Loimer, N., et al, eds. Drug Addiction & AIDS. (Illus.). x, 431p. 1991. pap. 69.00 (*0-387-82298-4*) Spr-Verlag.
Loinaz, George, tr. see Heintzelman, John E., ed.
Loinaz, Jorge, tr. see Lineal, Irv, ed.
Loinaz, Jorge, tr. see Moffat, Donald W.
Loire, Rene. The Design Way: An Essay. 456p. 1990. 14.95 (*0-9611614-5-0*) A Ghosh.
— Place Au Dessineur! Essai sur la Conception Technique. (Illus.). 630p. (Orig.). (FRE.). 1991. pap. 25.00 (*0-9611614-7-7*) A Ghosh.
Loiry, William S. The United States-European Community Trade Directory. 288p. 1993. text ed. 55.00 (*0-471-55667-X*) Wiley.
Loiry, William S., ed. The U. S. - Eastern European Trade Sourcebook. 250p. 1991. lib. bdg. 45.00 (*1-55862-156-3*) St James Pr.
— The U. S. - Soviet Trade Sourcebook. 283p. 1990. lib. bdg. 45.00 (*1-55862-142-3*) St James Pr.
Loiry, William S., et al, eds. The U. S. - Vietnam Business Guide, 1994. 200p. (Orig.). 1994. pap. 34.95 (*1-885264-01-1*) Global Business.
Lois, George & Pitts, Bill. What's the Big Idea? How to Win with Outrageous Ideas (That Sell) LC 92-21351. (Illus.). 304p. 1993. pap. 12.95 (*0-452-26938-5*, Plume) NAL-Dutton.
Lois, Lamya, jt. auth. see Al Faruqi, Isma'il.
Loiseaux, Pierre R., jt. auth. see Fessler, Daniel W.
Loisel, Regis. Peter Pan: Neverland, Bk. 2. Baisden, Greg, ed. Irwin, Mary, tr. (Illus.). 1992. 14.95 (*1-56862-000-4*) Tundra MA.
— Peter Pan, Bk. 1: London. Baisden, Greg S., ed. Irwin, Mary, tr. (Illus.). (C). reprint ed. 14.95 (*1-879450-42-9*) Tundra MA.
***Loiselle, Andre & McIlroy, Brian, eds.** Auteur - Provocateur: The Films of Denys Arcand. LC 95-3998. 208p. 1995. pap. text ed. 19.95 (*0-275-95297-5*, Praeger Pubs) Greenwood.
— Auteur - Provocateur: The Films of Denys Arcand. LC 95-3998. (Contributions to the Study of Popular Culture: Vol. 45). 1995. text ed. 59.95 (*0-313-29672-3*, Greenwood Pr) Greenwood.
Loiselle, Beth. The Healing Power of Whole Foods. LC 93-91693. (Illus.). 384p. (Orig.). 1993. pap. 17.95 (*0-9637478-0-0*) Hlthways Nutrit.
Loiselle, Emery J. Doctor Your Own Compound Bow. (Illus.). 148p. 1976. pap. 9.95 (*0-9613281-0-X*) E J Loiselle.
— Sensabout Bow Tuning. (Illus.). 20p. (Orig.). 1971. pap. 3.00 (*0-9613281-1-8*) E J Loiselle.
***Loiselle, Mindy B. & Wright, Leslie B.** Shining Through: Pulling It Together after Sexual Abuse. 100p. (Orig.). (J). (gr. 4-10). 1994. student ed, pap. 14.00 (*1-884444-13-X*) Safer Soc.
Loiselle, P. V. & Pool, David. Hobbyist Guide to Catfish & Loaches. (Illus.). 144p. 1994. 12.95 (*3-89356-138-2*, 16580) Tetra Pr.
Loiselle, Paul. Cichlid Aquarium. (Illus.). 285p. Date not set. 23.95 (*3-923880-20-0*, 16077) Tetra Pr.
— Fishkeeper's Guide to African Cichlids. (Illus.). 116p. Date not set. 10.95 (*3-923880-39-1*, 16037) Tetra Pr.
Loiselle, Paul, jt. auth. see Baensch, Hans.
Loiselle, Paul, jt. auth. see Weiser, K. H.
***Loiselle, Paul V.** Cichlid Aquarium. 1994. 39.95 (*1-56465-146-0*) Tetra Pr.
***Loiselle, Paul V., et al.** Tetra's Popular Guide to Tropical Cichlids. LC 94-23254. 1994. 21.95 (*1-56465-147-9*) Tetra Pr.
Loiskandl, Helmut, tr. see Simmel, Georg.
Loison, R., et al. Coke: Quality & Production. 2nd ed. (Illus.). 555p. 1989. text ed. 270.00 (*0-408-02870-X*) Buttrwrth-Heinemann.
Loisy, Alfred F. My Duel with the Vatican: The Autobiography of a Catholic Modernist. Boynton, Richard W., tr. LC 68-19290. 357p. 1968. reprint ed. text ed. 59.75 (*0-8371-0148-4*, LODV, Greenwood Pr) Greenwood.
Loisy, Alfred F. & Hoffman, R. Joseph. The Gospel & the Church. LC 87-3262. (Classics of Biblical Criticism Ser.). 268p. 1988. 29.95 (*0-87975-441-9*) Prometheus Bks.
Loit, Aleksander, ed. The Baltic Countries, 1900-1914: Essays, 2 vols., Set. (Studia Baltica Stockholmiensia: No. 5, Vols. 1-2). 787p. (Orig.). (ENG & GER.). 1990. pap. 115.00x (*91-22-01389-X*, Pub. by Almqv & Wiksell SW) Coronet Bks.
— National Movements in the Baltic Countries During the 19th Century. (Studia Baltica Stockholmiensia). 572p. (Orig.). 1985. pap. 53.00x (*91-22-00776-8*, Pub. by Almqv & Wiksell SW) Coronet Bks.
Loit, Aleksander, jt. ed. see Hiden, John.
***Loit, Alexander, ed.** Emancipation & Interdependence: The Baltic States As New Entities in the International Economy, 1918-1940. (Studia Baltica Stockholmiensia Ser.: No. 13). 385p. 1994. pap. 57.50 (*91-22-01643-0*, Pub. by Almqv & Wiksell SW) Coronet Bks.
Loitsyanskii. Mechanics of Liquids & Solids. 1993. write for info. (*0-8493-9912-2*) CRC Pr.
Loitsyanskii, L. & Jones, R. Mechanics of Liquids & Gases. LC 63-9822. (International Series of Monographs in Aeronautics & Astronautics: Vol. 6). 1966. 335.00 (*0-08-010125-9*, Pub. by Pergamon Repr UK) Franklin.
Loiy, Paul J. & Daisey, Joan M. Toxic Air Pollution. (Illus.). 300p. 1987. 79.95 (*0-87371-057-6*, RA576) Lewis Pubs.
Loizeaux. Classic Houses of the Twenties. unabridged ed. LC 92-30766. Orig. Title: Loizeaux's Plan Book. (Illus.). 192p. 1993. reprint ed. pap. text ed. 12.95 (*0-486-27388-1*) Dover.
Loizeaux, Elizabeth B. Yeats & the Visual Arts. (Illus.). 264p. (C). 1986. text ed. 40.00 (*0-8135-1175-5*) Rutgers U Pr.
Loizeaux, William. Anna: A Daughter's Life. 240p. 1993. 19.95 (*1-55970-197-8*) Arcade Pub Inc.
— Anna: A Daughter's Life. 1993. pap. 9.95 (*1-55970-231-1*) Arcade Pub Inc.
Loizes, Peter. Innovation in Ethnographic Film: From Innocence to Self-Consciousness, 1955-1985. LC 93-6877. 212p. 1993. lib. bdg. 42.50 (*0-226-49226-5*); pap. text ed. 16.95 (*0-226-49227-3*) U Ch Pr.
Loizos, Peter & Papataxiarchis, Evthymios, eds. Contested Identities: Gender & Kinship in Modern Greece. (Modern Greek Studies). (Illus.). 264p. 1991. text ed. 49.50 (*0-691-09460-8*); pap. text ed. 15.95 (*0-691-02859-1*) Princeton U Pr.
Loizou, Andros & Lesser, Harry. Polis & Politics: Essays in Greek Moral & Political Philosophy. (Avebury Series in Philosophy). 166p. 1990. text ed. 59.95 (*1-85628-052-7*, Pub. by Avebury Pub UK) Ashgate Pub Co.
***Loizou, Nicos.** The Ultimate Grand Master Casino. Ingram, tr. 60p. 1996. pap. 7.95 (*0-7610-0487-4*) NW Pub.
Lojasiewicz, Stanislaw. Introduction to Complex Analytic Geometry. Klimek, Maciej, tr. 540p. 1991. 148.00 (*0-8176-1935-6*) Birkhauser.
— Introduction to the Theory of Real Functions. LC 87-30432. 250p. 1988. text ed. 175.00 (*0-471-91414-2*) Wiley.
Lojek, Bohumil, jt. ed. see Fair, Richard B.
Lojek, Michael A. & Bement, Patricia. Cardiac Rehabilitation. Grin, Oliver D. & Bouwman, Dorothy L., eds. (Patient Education Ser.). (Illus.). 26p. (Orig.). 1992. pap. text ed. 3.00 (*0-929689-48-8*) Ludann Co.
Lojk, Kelly, ed. see Boffey, Barnes.
Lojk, Kelly, ed. see Good, E. Perry.
Lojk, Kelly, ed. see Gossen, Diane C.
Lok, Ivan. Pro Audio Spectrum: The Official Book. 1993. pap. text ed. 29.95 (*0-07-881979-2*) McGraw.
Lok Raj Baral. Regional Migrations, Ethnicity & Security. (South Asian Case Ser.). 1989. text ed. 27.95 (*81-207-1103-3*, Pub. by Sterling Pubs II) Apt Bks.
Lokaj, Stanley, jt. ed. see Galloway, Rodney G.
Lokan, Jan & McKenzie, Phillip. Teacher Appraisal. (C). 1990. 65.00 (*0-86431-045-5*, Pub. by Aust Council Educ Res AT) St Mut.
Lokanathan, P. S. Industrial Organization in India. (London School of Economics & Political Science Monographs on Social Anthropology: Vol. 4). 1969. reprint ed. pap. 35.00 (*0-8115-3301-8*) Periodicals Srv.
Loke. Pathophysiology & Treatment of Inhalation Injuries. (Lung Biology in Health & Disease Ser.: Vol. 34). 576p. 1988. 199.00 (*0-8247-7795-6*) Dekker.
Loke, Wing H. A Guide to Journals in Psychology & Education. LC 90-33603. 415p. 1990. 39.50 (*0-8108-2327-6*) Scarecrow.
— Perspectives on Judgement & Decision Making. 330p. 1992. 37.50 (*0-8108-2642-9*) Scarecrow.
Loke, Y. W. Immunology & Immunopathology of the Human Foetal-Maternal Interaction. 328p. 1978. 121.00 (*0-444-80055-7*) Elsevier.
Loke, Y. W. & Whyte, A., eds. Biology of Trophoblast. 706p. 1983. 224.75 (*0-444-80477-3*, I-333-83) Elsevier.
Loken, Joan K. The HACCP Food Safety Manual. LC 94-17915. 1995. pap. text ed. 55.00 (*0-471-05685-5*) Wiley.
Loken, Michael R., jt. auth. see Owens, Marilyn A.
Loken, Robert D. Nela Test of Color Vision. LC 43-13479. (Comparative Psychology Monographs: Vol. 17). 1942. pap. 40.00 (*0-527-24925-4*) Periodicals Srv.
Loken, S., ed. High Energy Physics - Twenty-Third International Conference on High Physics: Proceedings of the International Conference, Berkeley, California, U. S. A., July 16-23, 1986, 2 vols. 1636p. 1987. pap. 102.00 (*9971-5-0184-8*) World Scientific Pub.
Lokensgard, Ole. The Nantucket Collection. LC 89-50229. (Illus.). 128p. (Orig.). 1989. pap. 8.95 (*0-9622429-0-X*) Wright Impressions.
Lokenvitz, Judith, jt. auth. see Duffy, Karen.
Loker, Donald E. Lewis Leffman: Ordnance Sergeant United States Army. 64p. (Orig.). 1974. pap. 3.50 (*0-685-29131-6*) Niagara Cnty Hist Soc.
Loker, Donald E., ed. News of the Day . . . Yesterday. (Illus.). 94p. (Orig.). 1971. pap. 3.00 (*0-685-29126-X*) Niagara Cnty Hist Soc.
Lokesh, M. B. Prout & the End of Capitalism & Communism. 126p. (Orig.). (C). 1990. pap. 6.95 (*0-685-35763-5*) Proutist Universal.
***Lokeswarananda.** The Way to God as Taught by Sri Ramakrishma. 475p. Date not set. pap. 14.95 (*0-87481-693-9*) Vedanta Ctr.
— Way to God As Taught by Sri Ramakrishna. 457p. (Orig.). 1993. pap. 14.95 (*0-87481-572-X*, Pub. by Ramakrishna Math II) Vedanta Pr.
Lokhorst, Gijsbert M. Taxonomic Studies in the Genus Heterococcus (Tribophyceae, Tribonematalas, Heteropediaceae) A Combined Cultural & Electron Microscopy Study. (Cryptogamic Studies: Vol. 3). (Illus.). 246p. 1992. pap. 120.00 (*1-56081-346-6*) VCH Pubs.
Lokich, Jacob J., ed. Cancer Chemotherapy by Infusion. 2nd ed. LC 90-61367. 712p. 1990. 129.00 (*0-944496-14-8*) Precept Pr.
Lokich, Jacob J. & Byfield, John E., eds. Combined Modality Cancer Therapy: Radiation & Infusional Chemotherapy. LC 91-61357. 264p. 1991. 99.00 (*0-944496-22-9*) Precept Pr.
Lokin, C. J., et al, eds. Subseciva Groningana II. iv, 146p. (FRE, GER & ITA.). (C). 1985. pap. 32.00 (*90-6980-006-3*, Pub. by Egbert Forsten NE) Benjamins North Am.
Lokin, J. H. & Stolte, B. H., eds. Subseciva Groningana IV: Studies in Roman & Byzantine Law. x, 274p. (Orig.). (ENG, GER & ITA.). 1990. pap. 39.50 (*90-6980-040-3*, Pub. by Egbert Forsten NE) Benjamins North Am.
Lokin, J. H., jt. ed. see Wal, N.
Lokin, J. H., et al, eds. Subseciva Groningana: Studies in Roman & Byzantine Law, No. V. ix, 94p. 1992. pap. 30.00 (*90-6980-058-6*, Pub. by Egbert Forsten NE) Benjamins North Am.
— Subseciva Groningana I. 142p. (Orig.). (ENG & GER.). 1984. pap. 30.00 (*90-6088-086-2*, Pub. by Boumas Boekhuis NE) Benjamins North Am.
— Subseciva Groningana III: Studies in Byzantine Law: Proceedings of the Symposium on the Occasion of the Completion of a New Edition of the Basilica, Groningen, June 1-4, 1988. x, 154p. (Orig.). (FRE & GER.). 1989. pap. 34.00 (*90-6980-025-X*, Pub. by Egbert Forsten NE) Benjamins North Am.
Lokke, Carl L. France & the Colonial Question. LC 75-76632. (Columbia University. Studies in the Social Sciences: No. 365). reprint ed. 12.50 (*0-404-51365-4*) AMS Pr.
Lokke, Kari. Gerard de Nerval: The Poet As Social Visionary. LC 86-82649. (French Forum Monographs: No. 66). 165p. (Orig.). 1987. pap. 13.95 (*0-917058-67-4*) French Forum.
Lokke, Virgil, jt. ed. see Koelb, Clayton.
Lokke, Virgil L., jt. ed. see Thompson, G. R.
Lokken, Lawrence, jt. auth. see Bittker, Boris I.
Lokken, Roscoe L. Iowa: Public Land Disposal. LC 72-2854. (Use & Abuse of America's Natural Resources Ser.). 320p. 1972. reprint ed. 25.95 (*0-405-04518-2*) Ayer.
Lokken, Roy N. David Lloyd, Colonial Lawmaker. LC 59-13419. (Publications in History Ser.). (Illus.). 319p. 1959. 20.00 (*0-295-73762-X*) U of Wash Pr.
Lokos, Ellen D. The Solitary Journey: Cervantes' Voyage to Parnassus. LC 90-2224. (Studies on Cervantes & His Times: Vol. 1). 230p. (C). 1991. text ed. 48.95 (*0-8204-1452-2*) P Lang Pubs.
Lokotsch, Karl. Etymologisches Woerterbuch der Europaeischen Woerter Orientalischen Ursprungs. 2nd ed. (GER.). 1975. pap. 89.95 (*0-8288-5886-1*, M7369) Fr & Eur.
Lokra. The Lady & the Fly. (I Love to Read Collection). (Illus.). 48p. (J). (gr. 3-8). 1990. lib. bdg. 12.79 (*0-89565-812-7*) Childs World.
Lokshin, A. A. & Sagomonyan, E. A. Nonlinear Waves in Inhomogeneous & Hereditary Media. (Research Reports in Physics). (Illus.). x, 121p. 1992. pap. 69.00 (*0-387-54536-0*) Spr-Verlag.
Lokshin, V. A., et al, eds. Standard Methods of Hydraulic Design for Power Boilers. Bronstein, Henri A., tr. 345p. 1988. 228.00 (*0-89116-359-X*) Hemisp Pub.
Loktev, V. M., jt. ed. see Davydov, A. S.
Lokvam, Marian, et al. Sonja. Lovas, Emily & Pollack, Rhoda-Gale, eds. LC 81-82156. (Illus.). 100p. 1981. 12.95 (*0-940316-00-5*) E J Hill & Co Inc.
Lokvig, Gaston. San Diego Coloring Book. (Illus.). 16p. (J). 1985. pap. 1.25 (*0-9607696-8-4*) Carol Mendel.
Lokvig, Tor, jt. auth. see De Brunhoff, Jean.
Loll, Leo M., jt. auth. see Buckley, Julian G., Jr.
Lollar, Amanda. The Bat in My Pocket: A Memorable Friendship. LC 91-37907. (Illus.). 100p. (Orig.). 1992. pap. 9.95 (*0-88496-347-0*) Capra Pr.
— The Bat in My Pocket: A Memorable Friendship. 160p. (Orig.). 1992. reprint ed. lib. bdg. 27.00x (*0-8095-4094-0*) Borgo Pr.
Lolley, W. Randall, et al. Servant Songs: Reflections on the History and Mission of Southeastern Baptist Theological Seminary, 1950-1988. Bland, Thomas A., Jr., ed. LC 94-4441. 264p. (Orig.). 1994. pap. 14.95 (*1-880837-94-3*) Smyth & Helwys.
Lolli, G., et al, eds. Logic Colloquium '82: Proceedings of the Colloquium Held in Florence, 23-28, Aug. 1982. (Studies in Logic & the Foundations of Mathematics: Vol. 112). 358p. 1984. 82.00 (*0-444-86876-3*) Elsevier.
Lolli, Giorgio, et al. Alcohol in Italian Culture: Food & Wine in Relation to Sobriety Among Italians & Italian Americans. LC 58-9167. (Monograph Ser.: No. 3). 1958. 7.50 (*0-911290-27-3*) Rutgers Ctr Alcohol.
Lolling, Atsuko G. Aki & the Banner of Names: And Other Stories from Japan. (Orig.). (J). (gr. 1-6). pap. 4.95 (*0-377-00218-6*) Friendship Pr.
— Teacher's Guide to Aki & the Banner of Names. (Orig.). 1991. pap. 5.95 (*0-377-00221-6*) Friendship Pr.
Lollobrigida, Gina. The Wonder of Innocence. LC 94-1412. 1994. write for info. (*0-8109-3573-2*) Abrams.
Lom, Jiri & Dykova, Iva. Protozoan Parasites of Fishes. LC 92-15825. (Developments in Aquaculture & Fisheries Science Ser.: No. 24). 1992. write for info. (*0-04-448943-9*) Elsevier.
Lom, Jiri, jt. auth. see Canning, Elizabeth U.
Lom, W. L. Liquified Natural Gas. (Illus.). 178p. 1977. 63.00 (*0-85334-583-X*, Pub. by Elsevier Applied Sci UK) Elsevier.
Loma, Dalai. Opening the Eye of New Awareness. Lopez, Donald S., Jr. & Hopkins, Jeffrey, trs. (Intermediate Book - White Ser.). 143p. 1985. pap. 12.95 (*0-86171-036-3*) Wisdom MA.
Lomahaftewa, Gloria A. Glass Tapestry: Plateau Beaded Bags from the Elaine Horwitch Collection. LC 93-41282. (Illus.). 56p. (Orig.). 1993. pap. 15.00 (*0-934351-42-2*) Heard Mus.
Lomami-Tshibamba, Paul, et al. Ngando, Victoire de l'Amour, Le Mystere de l'Enfant Disparu, Set 3 in 1. (B. E. Ser.: No. 28). (FRE.). 1962. Three works in one unit. 26.00 (*0-8115-2979-7*) Periodicals Srv.
Loman, Jim & Loman, Laurie. Family Ski Adventures: In Colorado. LC 93-90789. 170p. (Orig.). 1993. pap. 12.95 (*0-9638271-0-3*) Diversif Pubns.
Loman, Laurie, jt. auth. see Loman, Jim.
Loman, Roberta K., illus. All about Hands. (Happy Day Bks.). 28p. (J). (ps). 1992. 2.50 (*0-87403-951-7*, 24-03591) Standard Pub.

An Asterisk (*) at the beginning of an entry indicates that the title is appearing in BIP for the first time.

L

Loman, Susan & Brandt, Rose. The Body Mind Connection in Human Movement Analysis. LC 92-70393. 235p. (C). 1992. pap. text ed. 12.00 (1-881245-00-4) Antioch New Eng.

Loman, Susan, jt. auth. see Lewis, Penny.

Lomando, A. J. & Harris, P. M., eds. Giant Oil & Gas Fields. (Core Workshop Notes Ser.: No. 12). (Illus.). 876p. (Orig.). 1988. pap. text ed. 63.00 (0-918985-72-2) SEPM.

— Mixed Carbonate-Siliciclastic Sequences. (Core Workshop Notes Ser.: No. 15). 580p. 1991. pap. 64.00 (0-918985-87-0) SEPM.

***Lomando, A. J., et al, eds.** Lacustrine Reservoir & Depositional Systems. (Core Workshop Notes Ser.: No. 19). (Illus.). 388p. 1994. pap. 52.00 (1-56576-015-8) SEPM.

Lomanto, Valeria & Marinone, Nino, eds. Index Grammaticus: An Index to Latin Grammartexts, 3 vols., Set. (Alpha-Omega, Reihe A Ser.: Vol. LXXXI). x, 2568p. (GER.). 1990. 637.00 (3-487-09271-9, Pub. by Georg Olms GW) Lubrecht & Cramer.

— Index Grammaticus: An Index to the Latin Grammarians, 3 vols., Set. (Alpha-Omega, Reihe A Ser.: Vol. LXXXI). 2578p. 1990. 625.00 (3-487-09178-X, Pub. by Georg Olms GW) Lubrecht & Cramer.

Lomanto, Valeria, ed. see Symmachus, Quintus A.

Lomas, Charles. Fundamentals of Hot Wire Anemometry. (Illus.). 256p. 1986. 79.95 (0-521-30340-0) Cambridge U Pr.

Lomas, Clara, ed. see De Magnon, Leonor V.

Lomas Garza, Carmen. Family Pictures: Cuadros de familia. (Illus.). 32p. (ENG & SPA.). (J). (gr. 1-7). 1993. pap. 5.95 (0-89239-108-1) Childrens Book Pr.

— Family Pictures (Cuadros de familia) LC 89-27845. (Illus.). 32p. (ENG & SPA.). (J). (gr. 1-7). 1990. 13.95 (0-89239-050-6) Childrens Book Pr.

***Lomas, Graham.** Five Little Kittens. 1994. 7.95 (0-533-11017-3) Vantage.

Lomas, Graham M. & Wood, Peter A. Employment Location in Regional Economic Planning. 186p. 1970. 26.00 (0-7146-1587-0, Pub. by F Cass Pubs UK) Intl Spec Bk.

Lomas, Herbert, ed. & tr. Contemporary Finnish Poetry. 256p. (Orig.). 1990. pap. 19.95 (1-85224-147-0, Pub. by Bloodaxe Bks UK) Dufour.

Lomas, Herbert, ed. Letters in the Dark. 68p. 1986. pap. 7.95 (0-19-281959-3) OUP.

Lomas, Herbert, tr. see Paasilinna, Arto.

Lomas, Herbert, tr. see Stenberg, Eira.

Lomas, Jeanette, jt. auth. see Lacey, Penny.

Lomas, Jonathan. First & Foremost in Community Health Centres: The Community Health Centre at Sault Ste. Marie & the CHC Alternatives. 215p. 1985. 30.00 (0-8020-5635-0); pap. 13.95 (0-8020-6532-5) U of Toronto Pr.

Lomas, K., ed. see University College, London Staff.

Lomas, Kathryn. Rome & the Western Greeks, 350 BC-AD 200: Conquest & Acculturation in Southern Italy. LC 92-40807. 1993. write for info. (0-415-05022-7, Routledge NY) Routledge.

Lomas, Owen & McEldowney, John. Frontiers of Environmental Law. 153p. 1992. pap. text ed. 45.00 (0-471-93663-4, Pub. by Wiley Chancery Law UK) Wiley.

Lomas, Peter. Cultivating Intuition: An Introduction to Psychotherapy. LC 93-9517. 232p. 1993. 30.00x (0-87668-528-9) Aronson.

— The Limits of Interpretation. LC 90-282. 168p. 1990. 20.00x (0-87668-797-4) Aronson.

— The Limits of Interpretation. LC 90-282. 176p. 1993. pap. 10.00 (0-14-013538-3, Penguin Bks) Viking Penguin.

— The Psychotherapy of Everyday Life. LC 92-456. 168p. (C). 1992. pap. 19.95 (1-56000-629-3) Transaction Pubs.

— True & False Experience: The Human Element in Psychotherapy. 170p. (C). 1994. pap. 19.95 (1-56000-733-8) Transaction Pubs.

Lomas, R. A. North East England in the Middle Ages. 200p. (C). 1989. text ed. 66.00 (0-685-65185-1, Pub. by J Donald) St Mut.

Lomas, Richard. North-East England in the Middle Ages. 200p. (C). 1989. 66.00 (0-85976-361-7, Pub. by J Donald) St Mut.

***Lomas, Thomas.** Forty Days to Freedom. (Illus.). 176p. (Orig.). 1995. pap. 8.95 (1-883928-11-7) Longwood.

Lomask, Milton. Great Lives: Exploration. LC 88-15744. (Great Lives Ser.). (Illus.). 272p. (J). (gr. 4-6). 1988. text ed. 23.00 (0-684-18511-3, C Scribner Sons Young) S&S Childrens.

— Great Lives: Invention & Technology. LC 90-27619. (Illus.). 272p. (J). (gr. 4-6). 1991. text ed. 22.95 (0-684-19106-7, C Scribner Sons Young) S&S Childrens.

— Spirit of 1787 Making of the Constitution. 1987. pap. 2.50 (0-449-70262-6) Fawcett.

— St. Isaac & the Indians. 2nd rev. ed. LC 90-85767. (Illus.). 170p. (J). (gr. 6-8). 1991. reprint ed. pap. 9.95 (0-89870-355-7) Ignatius Pr.

Lomask, Milton, jt. auth. see Green, Constance.

Lomasky, Loren E. Persons, Rights, & the Moral Community. (Illus.). 296p. 1990. reprint ed. pap. 18.95 (0-19-506474-7) OUP.

Lomasky, Loren E., jt. ed. see Brennan, Harold G.

Lomatewama, Ramson. Ascending the Reed: Poems. 63p. (Orig.). 1987. pap. 5.00 (0-935825-01-0); vhs 24.95 (0-934351-36-8) Heard Mus.

— Drifting Through Ancestor Dreams: New & Selected Poems. LC 92-82838. (Illus.). 72p. (Orig.). 1993. pap. 9.95 (0-87358-552-6, Entrada Bks) Northland AZ.

— Silent Winds: Poetry of One Hopi. 3rd ed. LC 83-61654. 64p. 1983. reprint ed. pap. 5.00 (0-685-11806-1) Badger Claw Pr.

— Silent Winds: Poetry of One Hopi. 4th ed. 1987. pap. 5.00 (0-934351-32-5) Heard Mus.

Lomatuway'ma, Michael, jt. auth. see Geertz, Armin W.

Lomatuway'ma, Michael, jt. auth. see Malotki, Ekkehart.

Lomatuway'ma, Michael, et al. Hopi Ruin Legends. Malotki, Ekkehart, ed. & tr. by. LC 93-358. xiv, 510p. 1993. 50.00 (0-8032-2905-4) U of Nebr Pr.

Lomawaima, K. Tsianina. They Called It Prairie Light: The Story of Chilocco Indian School. LC 93-30255. (Illus.). xx, 205p. 1994. text ed. 25.00 (0-8032-2904-6) U of Nebr Pr.

***Lomawaima, Tsianina.** They Called It Prairie Light: The Story of Chilocco Indian School. 205p. (C). 1995. pap. 12.00 (0-8032-7957-4, Bison Books) U of Nebr Pr.

Lomax, ed. God & Man in Medieval Spain: Essays in Honour of J. R. L. Highfield. 1989. 49.95 (0-85668-443-0, Pub. by Aris & Phillips UK); pap. 24.95 (0-85668-486-4, Pub. by Aris & Phillips UK) David Brown.

Lomax, ed. see Lopes.

Lomax, Alan. The Land Where the Blues Began. LC 91-52627. 544p. 1993. 25.00 (0-679-40424-4) Pantheon.

— Land Where the Blues Began. 1995. pap. 14.95 (0-385-31285-7, Delta) Dell.

— Mister Jelly Roll: The Fortunes of Jelly Roll Morton, New Orleans Creole & "Inventor of Jazz" LC 92-50469. 384p. 1993. pap. 15.00 (0-679-74064-3) Pantheon.

Lomax, Alan, ed. Folk Song Style & Culture. LC 68-21545. 384p. 1994. reprint ed. pap. 21.95 (0-87855-640-0) Transaction Pubs.

Lomax, Alan & Crowell, Sidney R. American Folksong & Folklore: A Regional Bibliography. LC 70-181204. 59p. 1942. reprint ed. 49.00 (0-403-03504-X) Scholarly.

Lomax, Alan & Lomax, Crowe. American Folksong & Folklore: A Regional Bibliography. 1988. reprint ed. lib. bdg. 59.00 (0-7812-0767-3) Rprt Serv.

Lomax, Alan, jt. auth. see Asch, Moses.

Lomax, Alan, jt. auth. see Lomax, John A.

Lomax, Bill, ed. Eyewitness in Hungary: The Soviet Invasion of 1956. 183p. 1981. pap. 22.50 (0-85124-327-4, Pub. by Spokesman Bks UK) Coronet Bks.

— The Hungarians Workers' Councils in 1956. 1990. text ed. 59.00 (0-88033-191-7) Col U Pr.

Lomax, Crowe, jt. auth. see Lomax, Alan.

Lomax, Derek W. The Reconquest of Spain. LC 77-3030. reprint ed. pap. 56.00 (0-317-27796-0, 2025242) Bks Demand.

Lomax, Don. Vietnam Journal: Delta to Dak To. (Vietnam Journal Graphic Story Collection Ser.: Vol. 3). (Illus.). 144p. (Orig.). 1991. pap. 13.95 (0-927203-07-3) Apple Pr PA.

— Vietnam Journal: Indian Country. (Vietnam Journal Graphic Story Collection Ser.: Vol. 1). (Illus.). 144p. (Orig.). 1990. pap. 12.95 (0-927203-02-2) Apple Pr PA.

— Vietnam Journal: The Iron Triangle. (Vietnam Journal Graphic Story Collection Ser.: Vol. 2). (Illus.). 144p. (Orig.). 1991. pap. 12.95 (0-927203-06-5) Apple Pr PA.

***Lomax, Eric.** The Railway Man: A True Story of War, Brutality & Forgiveness. (Illus.). 224p. 1995. 22.00 (0-393-03910-2) Norton.

Lomax, Ian, jt. ed. see Bazell, Chris.

Lomax, Ian S. & Reynolds, Steven. Enforcement in the Magistrates Courts: A Guide to Enforcing Money Payments. 178p. (C). 1988. 90.00 (1-85190-045-4, Pub. by Fourmat Pub UK) St Mut.

Lomax, J. Harvey, tr. see Meier, Heinrich.

Lomax, James D. Geriatric Ambulatory & Institutional Care. 210p. 1986. text ed. 27.50 (0-912791-33-0) Ishiyaku Euro.

Lomax, John. American Ballads & Folk Songs. 1993. reprint ed. lib. bdg. 75.00 (0-7812-5942-8) Rprt Serv.

— Cowboy Songs & Other Frontier Ballads. 1993. reprint ed. lib. bdg. 75.00 (0-7812-5890-1) Rprt Serv.

— Sezz Who? LC 73-83916. 1974. 21.95 (0-87949-021-7) Ashley Bks.

***Lomax, John A. & Lomax, Alan.** American Ballads & Folk Songs. unabridged ed. (Illus.). 672p. 1994. pap. text ed. 12.95 (0-486-28276-7) Dover.

Lomax, John A., jt. auth. see Ledbetter, H.

Lomax, John F., Jr., jt. ed. see Sanders, John L.

Lomax, Joseph F., ed. see McGee, M. W.

Lomax, Joseph F., ed. see Miller, Vassar.

Lomax, Joseph J., ed. see Miller, Vassar.

Lomax, Judy. Walking in the Clouds. large type ed. 352p. 1983. 15.95 (0-7089-0960-4) Ulverscroft.

Lomax, Louis. To Kill a Black Man. (Orig.). (J). (ps-12). 1987. pap. 3.25 (0-87067-731-4) Holloway.

Lomax, Louis E. When the Word Is Given... A Report on Elijah Muhammad, Malcolm X, & the Black Muslim World. LC 78-14002. (Illus.). 192p. 1979. reprint ed. text ed. 45.00 (0-313-21002-0, LOWW, Greenwood Pr) Greenwood.

Lomax, Marion. Peep-Show Girl. 1989. pap. 11.95 (1-85224-072-5, Pub. by Bloodaxe Bks UK) Dufour.

— Stage Images & Traditions: Shakespeare to Ford. LC 86-31062. (Illus.). 220p. 1987. 54.95 (0-521-32659-1) Cambridge U Pr.

Lomax, Marion, ed. see Ford, John.

Lomax, P. & Schoenbaum, E. Environment, Drugs & Thermoregulation: International Symposium on the Pharmacology of Thermoregulation, 5th, Saint-Paul-de-Vence, November 1982. (Illus.). xvi, 224p. 1983. 63.25 (3-8055-3654-2) S Karger.

Lomax, P. & Schoenbaum, E., eds. Thermoregulation: The Pathophysiological Basis of Clinical Disorders: Eighth International Symposium on the Pharmacology of Thermoregulation, Kananaskis, Alberta, August 1991. (Illus.). xiv, 200p. 1992. 125.00 (3-8055-5513-X) S Karger.

Lomax, P. & Schonbaum, E., eds. Thermoregulation: Research & Clinical Applications: International Symposium on the Pharmacology of Thermoregulation, 7th, Odense, August, 1988. xiv, 250p. 1989. 127.25 (3-8055-4921-0) S Karger.

Lomax, P., ed. see International Congress on Pharmacology Staff.

Lomax, P., jt. auth. see Schonbaum, E.

Lomax, Pamela. Managing Staff Development in Schools: An Action Research Approach. 110p. 1990. 59.00 (1-85359-108-4, Pub. by Multilingual Matters UK); pap. 19.95 (1-85359-107-6, Pub. by Multilingual Matters UK) Taylor & Francis.

Lomax, Pamela, ed. The Management of Change: Increasing School Effectiveness & Facilitating Staff Development Through Action Research. (BERA Dialogues Ser.: No. 1). 200p. 1989. 69.00 (1-85359-061-4, Pub. by Multilingual Matters UK); pap. 24.95 (1-85359-060-6, Pub. by Multilingual Matters UK) Taylor & Francis.

— Managing Better Schools & Colleges: The Action Research Way. (BERA Dialogues Ser.: No. 5). 134p. 1991. 69.00 (1-85359-145-9, Pub. by Multilingual Matters UK); pap. 24.95 (1-85359-144-0, Pub. by Multilingual Matters UK) Taylor & Francis.

Lomax, Peter & Schonbaum, Eduard, eds. Body Temperature: Regulation, Drug Effects, & Therapeutic Implications. LC 79-879. (Modern Pharmacology-Toxicology Ser.: No. 16). (Illus.). 680p. reprint ed. pap. 180.00 (0-7837-0809-2, 2041124) Bks Demand.

Lomax, Richard G. Statistical Concepts: A Second Course for Education & the Behavioral Sciences. 362p. (C). 1992. text ed. 55.95 (0-8013-0238-2, 75894) Longman.

Lomazzi, Brad S. Railroad Timetables, Travel Brochures & Posters: A History & Guide for Collectors. (Illus.). 208p. 1995. 49.95 (0-9614876-8-2) Golden Hl Pr NY.

Lomazzo, Giovanni P. Idea Del Tempio Della Pittura. 700p. 1968. reprint ed. write for info. (0-318-71587-2, Pub. by Georg Olms GW) Lubrecht & Cramer.

***Lombana, Judy H.** Guidance for Students with Disabilities. 2nd ed. 198p. 1992. pap. 29.95 (0-398-06245-5) C C Thomas.

— Guidance for Students with Disabilities. 2nd ed. 198p. (C). 1992. text ed. 47.95x (0-398-05804-0) C C Thomas.

Lombard. An Outline History of the Japanese Drama. (C). 1928. text ed. 90.00 (0-7007-0265-2, Pub. by Curzon Pr UK) Humanities.

Lombard, Bruce. Lombard Plums. 51p. 1993. pap. 4.00 (1-884983-08-1) Homegrown Bks.

Lombard, Carl. Mortal Beings. 224p. 1994. pap. 17.95 (1-85702-103-7, Pub. by Fourth Estate UK) Trafalgar.

Lombard, Charles M. Joseph de Maistre. LC 76-13846. (Twayne's World Authors Ser.). (C). 1976. text ed. 17.95 (0-8057-6247-7) Irvington.

— Lamartine. (Twayne's World Authors Ser.). (C). 1973. lib. bdg. 17.95 (0-8057-2510-5) Irvington.

— Xavier De Maistre. LC 76-58855. (Twayne's World Authors Ser.). 155p. (C). 1977. 17.95 (0-8057-6284-1) Irvington.

Lombard, Charles M., jt. auth. see Chivers, Thomas H.

Lombard, Frank A. Outline History of Japanese Drama. LC 68-717. (Studies in Drama: No. 39). 1969. reprint ed. lib. bdg. 75.00 (0-8383-0585-7) M S G Haskell Hse.

Lombard, Frederica K. Readings in Family Law: Divorce & Its Consequences. 182p. 1989. pap. text ed. 9.50 (0-88277-787-4) Foundation Pr.

Lombard, G. L., jt. auth. see Lawrence, M. L.

Lombard, Gene. It's Good to Give Thanks. (Illus.). 24p. (J). (gr. k-6). 1991. 4.25 (1-55976-156-3) CEF Press.

Lombard, George, jt. auth. see Savage, Charles H., Jr.

Lombard, Kathy. Rock Riffs for Keyboard. (Illus.). 40p. 1988. pap. 9.95 (0-8256-1191-1, AM63926) Music Sales.

Lombard, Lawrence B. Events: A Metaphysical Study. (International Library of Philosophy). 268p. (C). 1986. text ed. 35.00 (0-7102-0354-3, RKP) Routledge.

Lombard, R. E. Comparative Morphology of the Inner Ear in Salamanders: Caudata-Amphibia. (Contributions to Vertebrate Evolution Ser.: Vol. 2). 1977. 60.00 (3-8055-2408-0) S Karger.

Lombard, Rudy, jt. auth. see Burton, Nathaniel.

Lombard, Shirley C. Iliahi: Poems of Hawaii. (Illus.). 1975. pap. 1.00 (0-914916-03-3) Ku Paa.

Lombard, Sylvia J. Yao-English Dictionary. Purnell, Herbert C., Jr., ed. LC 76-29799. (Cornell University, Southeast Asia Program, Data Paper Ser.: No. 69). 392p. reprint ed. pap. 111.80 (0-317-10129-3, 2010474) Bks Demand.

Lombardero, Oscar J. Los Nombres Cientificos de los Parasitos y Su Significado. 2nd ed. 90p. (SPA.). 1978. 12.95 (0-8288-5257-X, S33068) Fr & Eur.

Lombardi, Cathryn & Lombardi, John V. Latin American History: A Teaching Atlas. LC 83-675775. (Illus.). 136p. 1983. pap. text ed. 9.95 (0-299-09714-5) U of Wis Pr.

Lombardi, Donald N. Handbook for the New Health Care Manager: Practical Strategies for Challenging Times. LC 93-26300. 484p. 1993. 52.00 (1-55648-109-8, 001121) AHPI.

— Handbook of Personnel Selection & Performance Evaluation in Healthcare: Guidelines for Hourly, Professional, & Managerial Employees. LC 88-42792. (Health-Management Ser.). 397p. 1988. 45.95x (1-55542-106-7) Jossey-Bass.

— The Health Care Organizational Survey System. LC 94-4528. 200p. 1994. 50.00 (1-55648-118-7, 088175) AHPI.

— Progressive Health Care Management Strategies. LC 92-49632. 383p. (Orig.). 1992. 49.95 (1-55648-092-X, 088300) AHPI.

— Stress & the Health Care Environment: Practical Guidelines for Executives & Managers. LC 90-5069. 131p. (Orig.). 1990. pap. text ed. 37.00 (0-910701-61-X, 0821) Health Admin Pr.

Lombardi, Donald P., jt. auth. see Pariser, E. R.

Lombardi, Emilia L., ed. see Russell, Lao.

Lombardi, Emilia L., ed. see Russell, Walter.

Lombardi, Fabrizio & Sami, Mariagiovanna, eds. Testing & Diagnosis of VLSI & ULSI. (C). 1988. lib. bdg. 133.00 (90-247-3794-X) Kluwer Ac.

Lombardi, Frances G., jt. auth. see Lombardi, Gerald S.

Lombardi, Gerald S. & Lombardi, Frances G. The Circle Without End: A Sourcebook of American Indian Ethics. LC 82-12481. 208p. 1982. lib. bdg. 16.95 (0-87961-114-6); pap. 8.95 (0-87961-115-4) Naturegraph.

Lombardi, Joan, jt. auth. see Goffin, Stacie G.

Lombardi, John. Black Studies in the Community College. LC 72-186575. (ERIC Clearinghouse for Junior Colleges, American Association of Junior Colleges, Monograph Ser.: No. 13). 74p. reprint ed. pap. 25.00 (0-8357-7298-5, 2020551) Bks Demand.

— Labor's Voice in the Cabinet. LC 68-58604. (Columbia University. Studies in the Social Sciences: No. 496). reprint ed. 25.00 (0-404-51496-0) AMS Pr.

Lombardi, John A. & Jude, Charles V. Mechanical Excavation Systems. 1994. write for info. (0-318-72562-2) US Interior.

Lombardi, John R. Three Lost Bears. (J). 1993. 7.95 (0-533-10648-6) Vantage.

Lombardi, John R., jt. ed. see Garetz, Bruce A.

Lombardi, John V. Computer Literacy: The Basic Concepts & Language. LC 83-48122. 128p. 1983. 15.00 (0-253-31401-1); pap. 6.95 (0-253-21075-5) Ind U Pr.

— Decline & Abolition of Negro Slavery in Venezuela, 1820-1854. LC 74-105976. (Contributions in Afro-American & African Studies: No. 1). (Illus.). 217p. 1971. text ed. 55.00 (0-8371-3303-3, LOD/, Greenwood Pr) Greenwood.

— People & Places in Colonial Venezuela. LC 75-25433. 500p. reprint ed. pap. 142.50 (0-317-27832-0, 2056043) Bks Demand.

Lombardi, John V., jt. auth. see Lombardi, Cathryn.

Lombardi, Linda. Laryngeal Features & Laryngeal Neutralization. rev. ed. LC 93-33844. (Outstanding Dissertations in Linguistics Ser.). 208p. 1994. 51.00 (0-8153-1687-9) Garland.

Lombardi, Louis G. Moral Analysis: Foundations, Guides, & Applications. LC 87-12469. (SUNY Series in Philosophy). 185p. 1988. 59.50 (0-88706-665-8); pap. 19.95 (0-88706-666-6) State U NY Pr.

Lombardi, Marilyn M. The Body & the Song: Elizabeth Bishop's Poetics. LC 94-10653. 267p. (C). 1995. 29.95x (0-8093-1885-7) S Ill U Pr.

Lombardi, Marilyn M., ed. Elizabeth Bishop: The Geography of Gender. LC 93-908. 288p. (C). 1993. 37.50 (0-8139-1444-2); pap. 15.95 (0-8139-1445-0) U Pr of Va.

Lombardi, Mary. Brazilian Serial Documents: A Selective & Annotated Guide. LC 73-16533. (Indiana University Latin American Studies Program). 485p. reprint ed. pap. 138.30 (0-8357-7387-6, 2015828) Bks Demand.

Lombardi, Michael A., jt. auth. see Kamas, George.

Lombardi-Nash, Michael A., tr. see Borneman, Ernest.

Lombardi-Nash, Michael A., tr. see Hirschfeld, Magnus.

Lombardi-Nash, Michael A., tr. see Ulrichs, Karl H.

Lombardi, Richard W. Debt Trap: Rethinking the Logic of Development. LC 84-18303. 240p. 1985. text ed. 55.00 (0-275-90137-8, C0137, Praeger Pubs) Greenwood.

Lombardi, Roberto. Doors, Windows & Skylights: Selecting & Installing. rev. ed. Ahlstrand, Alan, ed. (Illus.). 112p. 1992. pap. text ed. 9.95 (0-89721-241-X) Ortho Info.

Lombardi, Tarky & Hoffman, Gerald N. Medical Malpractice Insurance: A Legislator's View. LC 78-6409. 232p. reprint ed. pap. 66.20 (0-8357-3985-6, 2036683) Bks Demand.

***Lombardi, Thomas F.** Portfolio of the Earth. LC 94-32367. 64p. 1995. pap. 12.95 (0-7734-0003-6, Mellen Poetry Pr) E Mellen.

Lombardi, Vincent P. Beginning Weight Training. 256p. (C). 1989. pap. write for info. (0-697-05496-9) Brown & Benchmark.

Lombardini, J. B., et al, eds. Taurine: New Dimensions on Nutrition & Mechanisms of Action. (Advances in Experimental Medicine & Biology Ser.: Vol. 315). (Illus.). 402p. (C). 1992. 105.00 (0-306-44224-8, Plenum Pr) Plenum.

***Lombardini, Siro & Padoan, Pier C., eds.** Europe Between East & South. LC 94-23316. 272p. (C). 1994. lib. bdg. 109.00 (0-7923-3122-2) Kluwer Ac.

Lombardino, Joseph G., ed. Nonsteroidal Antiinflammatory Drugs. LC 85-12018. (Chemistry & Pharmacology of Drugs Ser.: Vol. 5). 464p. reprint ed. pap. 132.30 (0-7837-2399-7, 2040084) Bks Demand.

Lombardino, Linda, jt. ed. see Langley, Beth.

***Lombardo, Bill & Bui, Thach.** Cheap Thrills Cuisine with Chef Peppi: A Collection of Quick, Tasty, Creative Recipes. 1995. pap. 8.95 (0-316-53092-1) Little.

Lombardo, Carole A., ed. see Youngson, Jeanne.

Lombardo, Daniel. Tales of Amherst: A Look Back. LC 85-23791. 140p. 1986. pap. 7.95 (0-9616559-0-9) Jones Lib.

Lombardo, David A. Advanced Aircraft Systems. (Practical Flying Ser.). 1993. text ed. 30.00 (0-07-038602-1); pap. text ed. 18.95 (0-07-038603-X) McGraw.

— Advanced Aircraft Systems: Understanding Your Airplane. (Illus.). 304p. 1993. text ed. 29.95 (0-8306-3997-7, 4170); pap. text ed. 18.95 (0-8306-3998-5, 4170) TAB Bks.

— Aircraft Systems: Understanding Your Airplane. 1988. pap. text ed. 19.95 (0-07-155265-0) McGraw.

— Aircraft Systems: Understanding Your Airplane. (Practical Flying Ser.). (Illus.). 304p. pap. 19.95 (0-8306-0823-0, 2423) TAB Bks.

— Aircraft Systems: Understanding Your Airplane. (Practical Flying Ser.). (Illus.). 208p. 1988. 27.95 (0-8306-9426-9, 2423H); pap. 16.95 (0-8306-2426-0, 2423P) TAB Bks.

An Asterisk (*) at the beginning of an entry indicates that the title is appearing in BIP for the first time.

Lombardo, Frank A., jt. auth. see Schroeder, Donald J.

Lombardo, Frank J. Buffalo Breath. (Illus.). 130p. (Orig.). 1988. 6.95 (*0-945702-01-9*) Vertizon Bks.

— S.O.S. 320p. (Orig.). 1991. pap. write for info. (*0-945702-02-7*) Vertizon Bks.

— A Squiggley Line & Other Oddities: Investigations into the Corners of the World. (Illus.). 130p. (Orig.). 1988. pap. 6.95 (*0-945702-00-0*) Vertizon Bks.

Lombardo, Gregory J. St. Augustine: On Faith & Works. (Ancient Christian Writers Ser.: No. 48). 128p. 1988. 14. 95 (*0-8091-0406-7*) Paulist Pr.

Lombardo, Jill A. WordPerfect 5.1 Recipes: News from Jill's Quill. (Potpourri Ser.: Vol. 1). 45p. (Orig.). 1991. student ed, spiral bd. 12.00 (*0-9629906-0-4*) Lombardo Comp Srvs.

Lombardo, John, jt. auth. see Johnson, Robert J.

Lombardo, Lucien X. Guards Imprisoned: Correctional Officers at Work. 2nd ed. LC 89-80456. 260p. (C). 1989. pap. text ed. 19.95 (*0-932930-79-4*) Anderson Pub Co.

Lombardo, Michael M. & Eichinger, Robert W. Preventing Derailment: What to Do Before It's Too Late. (Technical Report Ser.: No. 138G). 62p. 1989. pap. 20.00 (*0-912879-36-X*) Ctr Creat Leader.

Lombardo, Michael M. & McCall, Morgan W., Jr. Coping with an Intolerable Boss. (Special Report Ser.: No. 305G). 13p. 1984. pap. 10.00 (*0-912879-54-8*) Ctr Creat Leader.

Lombardo, Michael M., jt. auth. see McCall, Morgan W., Jr.

Lombardo, Patrizia. Edgar Poe et la Modernite. LC 85-61598. 187p. (FRE.). 1985. 16.95 (*0-917786-07-6*) Summa Pubns.

— The Three Paradoxes of Roland Barthes. LC 88-39328. 160p. 1990. 25.00 (*0-8203-1139-1*) U of Ga Pr.

Lombardo, Skip. How to Turn a Small Real Estate Holding into a Big Fortune: Using Your Spare Time to Propel Yourself to Wealth to Become a Real-Estate Tycoon. 142p. (Orig.). 1991. pap. 22.50 (*0-934311-95-1*) Intl Wealth.

— Real Estate on the Brink: Making Money in Distressed Properties. 225p. 1992. pap. 24.95 (*1-55738-469-X*) Probus Pub Co.

Lombardo, Stan & Duermeier, Dennis, eds. Ten Gates: The Kong-An Teaching of Zen Master Seung Sahn. (Illus.). 148p. (Orig.). 1987. pap. 10.95 (*0-942795-01-6*) Primary Point Pr.

Lombardo, Stanley, pref. Parmenides & Empedocles. LC 81-7212. 76p. (Orig.). 1982. pap. 4.95 (*0-912516-66-6*) Grey Fox.

Lombardo, Stanley & Rayor, Diane, trs. Callimachus: Hymns, Epigrams, Select Fragments. LC 87-45479. 144p. 1987. pap. text ed. 12.95x (*0-8018-3281-0*) Johns Hopkins.

Lombardo, Stanley, jt. ed. see Addiss, Stephen.

Lombardo, Stanley, tr. see Aratus.

Lombardo, Stanley, tr. see Hesiod.

Lombardo, Stanley, tr. see Lao-Tzu.

Lombardo, Stanley, tr. see Plato.

Lombardo, Thomas J. The Reciprocity of Perceiver & Environment: The Evolution of James J. Gibson's Ecological Psychology. 416p. 1987. pap. text ed. 39.95 (*0-8058-0049-2*) L Erlbaum Assocs.

Lombardy, Anthony. Severe. LC 94-18349. (Illus.). 67p. 1995. 20.00 (*0-9624631-7-5*) Bennett & Kitchel.

Lombardy, William. Modern Chess Opening Traps. 1978. pap. 10.95 (*0-679-14400-5*) McKay.

Lombardy, William & Marshall, Bette. Chess for Children Step by Step: A New, Easy Way to Learn the Game. (Illus.). (J). 1977. 18.95i (*0-316-53091-3*); pap. 18.95i (*0-316-53090-5*) Little.

Lombeida, Ernesto, tr. see Rojas, Mary H.

Lomben, David O. & Mark, James. Differential Equations. 432p. (C). 1987. text ed. write for info. (*0-13-211558-1*) P-H.

Lombness, jt. auth. see Frank.

Lomboldt, O. The Sphecidae (Hymenoptera) of Fennoscandia & Denmark. (Fauna Entomologica Scandinavica Ser.: No. 4). (Illus.). 452p. 1984. text ed. 67.50 (*87-87491-06-0*) Lubrecht & Cramer.

Lomborg, Bjorn. The Structure of Solutions in the Iterated Prisoner's Dilemma. (CISA Working Paper Ser.: No. 4). 25p. (Orig.). (C). Date not set. pap. text ed. 10.00 (*0-86682-095-7*) Ctr Intl Relations.

Lombreglia, Ralph. Make Me Work. LC 93-26485. 1994. 20.00 (*0-374-20004-1*) FS&G.

— Make Me Work: Stories. 224p. 1995. 9.95 (*0-14-024222-8*, Penguin Bks) Viking Penguin.

— Men under Water. Rosenman, Jane, ed. 224p. 1991. reprint ed. pap. 7.95 (*0-671-73260-9*, WSP) PB.

Lombriser, Roman. Top Intrapreneurs: How Successful Senior Executives Manage Strategic Change. (Financial Times Management Ser.). 256p. 1993. 77.50 (*0-317-06161-5*, Pub. by Pitman Pub Ltd UK) Trans-Atl Phila.

— Top Intrapreneurs: How Successful Senior Executives Move to Business & Strategy. 256p. 1993. 105.00 (*0-273-60624-7*, Pub. by Pitman Pubng UK) St Mut.

Lombroso, Cesar & Ferrero, William. The Female Offender. (Illus.). xxvi, 313p. 1980. reprint ed. lib. bdg. 32.50 (*0-8377-0807-9*) Rothman.

Lombroso, Cesare. Gli Anarchi. (History of Political Violence Ser.). (ITA.). 1985. reprint ed. lib. bdg. 35.00 (*0-527-41196-5*) Periodicals Srv.

— Crime, Its Causes & Remedies. Horton, Henry P., tr. LC 68-55776. (Criminology, Law Enforcement, & Social Problems Ser.: No. 14). 1968. reprint ed. 35.00 (*0-87585-014-6*) Patterson Smith.

Lombroso-Ferrero, Gina & Savitz, Leonard D. Criminal Man: According to the Classification of Cesare Lombroso. LC 70-129338. (Criminology, Law Enforcement, & Social Problems Ser.: No. 134). (Illus.). 395p. (C). 1972. reprint ed. lib. bdg. 25.00 (*0-87585-134-7*) Patterson Smith.

Lomeli, Francisco, ed. The Handbook of Hispanic Culture of the United States Literature & Art. LC 93-13348. 1993. 60.00 (*1-55885-074-0*) Arte Publico.

Lomeli, Francisco, jt. ed. see Anaya, Rudolfo A.

Lomeli, Francisco A., jt. ed. see Martinez, Julio A.

Lomeli, Francisco A., jt. ed. see Shirley, Carl R.

Lomen, G. J. Lomen: Genealogies of the Lomen (Ringstad), Brandt & Joys Families. (Illus.). 361p. 1992. reprint ed. lib. bdg. 65.50 (*0-8328-2321-X*); reprint ed. pap. 55.50 (*0-8328-2322-8*) Higginson Bk Co.

Lomen, Mary. The Original American Wheat Dolly. (Illus.). 224p. (Orig.). 1992. pap. 19.95 (*0-942323-15-7*) N Amer Heritage Pr.

Lomer, C. J., jt. ed. see Prior, C.

Lomer, Cecile, jt. ed. see Zell, Hans.

Lomer, Georg. Your Hand. 244p. Date not set. pap. 9.95 (*0-87728-651-5*) Weiser.

Lomer, Gerhard R. The Concept of Method. LC 70-177005. (Columbia University. Teachers College. Contributions to Education Ser.: No. 34). reprint ed. 22.50 (*0-404-55034-7*) AMS Pr.

Lomer, Mary. Robert of Normandy. large type ed. 490p. 1992. 21.95 (*0-7505-0308-4*) Ulverscroft.

Lomer, W. & Gardner, W. Electronic Structure of Pure Metals, Pts. A & B. LC 49-50107. (Progress in Materials Science Ser.: Vol. 1413). 1969. 38.00 (*0-08-006419-1*, Pub. by Pergamon Repr UK) Franklin.

Lomerson, Edwin O., Jr. Fundamentals of Nondestructive Testing: A Home-Study Course. Huber, Oren J., ed. (Illus.). 375p. (Orig.). 1977. pap. 221.50 (*0-931403-51-0*, 1945) Am Soc Nondestructive.

Lomet, David B., ed. Foundations of Data Organization & Algorithms: Fourth International Conference, FODO '93, Chicago, Illinois, U. S. A., October 13-15, 1993, Proceedings. LC 93-32226. (Lecture Notes in Computer Science Ser.: Vol. 730). 1993. 60.00 (*0-387-57301-1*) Spr-Verlag.

Lominadze, D. G. Cyclotron Waves in Plasma. Hamberger, S. M., ed. Dellis, A. N., tr. (International Series of Natural Philosophy: Vol. 102). (Illus.). 220p. 1981. 88.00 (*0-08-021680-3*, Pub. by Pergamon Repr UK) Franklin.

Lommasson, Robert C. Nebraska Wild Flowers. LC 70-188343. (Illus.). 243p. reprint ed. pap. 69.30 (*0-8357-6597-0*, 2035995) Bks Demand.

Lommatzsch, Ernst, jt. auth. see Segebade, Johannes.

Lommatzsch, Klaus. Anwendngen der Linearen Parametrischen Optimierung. (Mathematische Reihe Ser.: No. 69). 200p. (GER.). 1980. reprint ed. 44.50 (*0-8176-1058-8*) Birkhauser.

Lommax, P., ed. see Pharmacology of Thermoregulation Symposium Staff.

Lommel, Cookie. Madame C. J. Walker. 1993. pap. 3.95 (*0-87067-597-4*, Melrose Sq) Holloway.

— Robert Church: And the Church Family of Memphis. (Black American Ser.). (Illus.). 208p. (YA). 1995. 4.95 (*0-87067-789-6*) Holloway.

Lommel, Herman, tr. see De Saussure, Ferdinand.

Lomnicka, Eva, jt. auth. see Ellinger, E. P.

Lomnicki, A. J. Law of Town & Country Planning: Including Compulsory Purchase & Compensation. 200p. (C). 1991. pap. 68.00 (*1-85352-901-X*, Pub. by HLT Pubns UK) St Mut.

Lomnicki, Adam. Population Ecology of Individuals. May, Robert M., ed. (Monographs in Population Biology: No. 25). 220p. 1988. text ed. 55.00 (*0-691-08471-8*); pap. text ed. 17.95 (*0-691-08462-9*) Princeton U Pr.

Lomnitz-Adler, Claudio. Exits from the Labyrinth: Culture & Ideology in the Mexican National Space. LC 92-20242. 1992. 45.00 (*0-520-07788-1*) U CA Pr.

Lomnitz, Cinna. Fundamentals of Earthquake Prediction. 1994. text ed. 79.95 (*0-471-57419-8*) Wiley.

— Global Tectonics & Earthquake Risk. LC 72-87960. (Developments in Geotectonics Ser.: Vol. 5). 330p. 1974. 123.00 (*0-444-41076-7*) Elsevier.

Lomnitz, Larissa & Meinick, Ana. Chile's Middle Class: A Struggle for Survival in the Face of Neoliberalism. LC 91-19118. (LACC Studies on Latin America & the Caribbean). 180p. 1991. lib. bdg. 34.00 (*1-55587-258-1*) Lynne Rienner.

Lomnitz, Larissa A. & Perez-Lizaur, Marisol. A Mexican Elite Family, 1820-1980: Kinship, Class, & Culture. (Illus.). 300p. 1988. pap. text ed. 17.95 (*0-691-02284-4*) Princeton U Pr.

Lomnitz, Larissa A., jt. auth. see Fortes, Jacqueline.

LoMonaco, Martha S. Every Week, A Broadway Revue: The Tamiment Playhouse, 1921-1960. LC 91-34159. (Contributions in Drama & Theatre Studies: No. 45). 208p. 1992. text ed. 47.95 (*0-313-27996-9*, LBY/, Greenwood Pr) Greenwood.

***Lomonaco, Michael & Forsman, Donna.** The "21" Cookbook: Recipes & Lore from New York's Fabled Restaurant. LC 95-5983. 1995. write for info. (*0-385-47570-5*) Doubleday.

***LoMonaco, Palmyra.** Night Letters. LC 94-36988. 1996. 13.99 (*0-525-45387-3*) Dutton Child Bks.

Lomonaco, Roberta. One & One Make Three: The Diary of a Pregnancy & the Child's First Years. Griffin, Luke, tr. 85p. (Orig.). 1989. pap. 6.95 (*1-85390-023-0*, Pub. by Veritas Pubns IE) Irish Bks Media.

Lomonaco, Samuel J., Jr., ed. Low Dimensional Topology. LC 83-10022. (Contemporary Mathematics Ser.: Vol. 20). 346p. 1983. pap. 38.00 (*0-8218-5016-4*, CONM-20) Am Math.

Lomonosov, Mikhail. Kratkoi Rossiiskoi Letopisets s Rodosloviem. xii, 75p. (RUS.). (C). 1993. reprint ed. pap. 12.00 (*0-933884-89-3*) Berkeley Slavic.

Lomonosov, Mikhail V. Mikhail Vasil'evich Lomonosov on the Corpuscular Theory. Leicester, Henry M., tr. LC 73-95927. 297p. 1970. 30.00 (*0-674-57420-6*) HUP.

Lomont, J. S. Applications of Finite Groups. unabridged ed. LC 92-34875. (Illus.). 346p. 1993. reprint ed. pap. text ed. 9.95 (*0-486-67376-6*) Dover.

Lomotey, Kofi. African-American Principals: School Leadership & Success. LC 89-1881. (Contributions in Afro-American & African Studies: No. 124). 188p. 1989. text ed. 45.00 (*0-313-26375-2*, LBP, Greenwood Pr) Greenwood.

Lomotey, Kofi, ed. Going to School: The African-American Experience. LC 89-38816. (SUNY Series, Frontiers in Education). 242p. 1990. 64.50 (*0-7914-0317-3*); pap. 21. 95 (*0-7914-0318-1*) State U NY Pr.

Lomotey, Kofi & Altbach, Philip G., eds. The Racial Crisis in American Higher Education. LC 90-33700. (Frontiers in Education Ser.). 275p. (C). 1991. 64.50 (*0-7914-0520-6*); pap. 21.95 (*0-7914-0521-4*) State U NY Pr.

Lomov, S. A. Introduction to the General Theory of Singular Perturbations. Ivanov, Simeon, ed. Schulenberger, J. R., tr. LC 92-26927. (Translations of Mathematical Monographs: Vol. 112). 375p. 1992. 201.00 (*0-8218-4569-1*) Am Math.

Lomperis, Linda & Stanbury, Sarah, eds. Feminist Approaches to the Body in Medieval Literature. LC 92-33033. (New Cultural Studies). 272p. (Orig.). (C). 1993. text ed. 36.95 (*0-8122-3117-1*); pap. text ed. 16.95 (*0-8122-1364-5*) U of Pa Pr.

Lomperis, Timothy J. Reading the Wind: The Literature of the Vietnam War. LC 86-23982. xii, 174p. 1986. 36.95 (*0-8223-0705-7*); pap. 15.95 (*0-8223-0749-9*) Duke.

— The War Everyone Lost - & Won: America's Intervention in Viet Nam's Twin Struggles. rev. ed. LC 92-36594. 1992. 19.95 (*0-87187-825-9*) Congr Quarterly.

Lompscher, jt. auth. see Glaser.

Lomsky, Gerry. The Beanstalk Bandit: The Giant's Version of "Jack & the Beanstalk" (J). (gr. 2-7). 1993. Story cass. audio 6.95 (*1-883499-01-1*) Princess NJ.

— The Beanstalk Bandit: The Giant's Version of "Jack & the Beanstalk" (Illus.). 30p. (J). (gr. 2-7). 1993. pap. 4.95 (*1-883499-00-3*) Princess NJ.

Lona, Horacio E. Ueber die Auferstehung des Fleisches: Studien zur Fruenchristlichen Eschatologie. (Beiheft zur Zeitschrift fuer die Neuetestamentliche Wissenschaft Ser.: Bd. 66). xiv, 304p. (GER.). (C). 1993. lib. bdg. 98. 50 (*3-11-013828-X*) De Gruyter.

Lonard, Robert I. Guide to Grasses of the Lower Rio Grande Valley, Texas. (Illus.). 400p. (Orig.). (C). 1993. pap. text ed. write for info. (*0-938738-08-9*) U TX Pan Am Pr.

***Lonbay, Jules.** Single European Market. 1995. pap. text ed. write for info. (*0-406-60940-3*, UK) Butterworth Legal Pubs.

***Lonbay, Julian, ed.** Frontiers of Competition Law. 1994. text ed. 65.00 (*0-471-94303-7*) Wiley.

Lonbay, Julian & Spedding, Linda. International Professional Practice. 310p. 1993. ring bd. 235.00 (*0-471-93658-8*, Pub. by Wiley Chancery Law UK) Wiley.

Lonberg-Holm, K. & Philipson, L. Early Interaction Between Animal Viruses & Cells. Melnick, J. L., ed. (Monographs in Virology: Vol. 9). (Illus.). 160p. 1974. 71.25 (*3-8055-1764-5*) S Karger.

Lonberg-Holm, Karl, ed. see American Society for Microbiology Staff.

***Lonberger, William.** Tips on How to Stay Safe & Survive Almost Anything! A Watchdog Resource for Students in Grades K Through 12 & Their Parents. 1994. 14.00 (*0-910609-28-4*) Gifted Educ Pr.

***Lonborg, Rosemary.** Helpin' Bugs. (Illus.). 32p. (J). (ps-3). 1995. 14.95 (*0-9641285-2-7*) Little Frnd.

— The Quiet Hero - A Baseball Story. (Illus.). 32p. (J). (gr. 2-6). 1993. per. 7.95 (*0-8283-1958-8*) Branden Pub Co.

Lonchamp, Jean P. Science & Belief. 160p. (C). 1993. text ed. 50.00 (*0-85439-434-6*, Pub. by St Paul Pubns UK) St Mut.

Loncin, Marcel & Merson, Richard L. Food Engineering: Principles & Selected Applications. LC 78-31231. (Food Science & Technology Ser.). 1979. text ed. 158.00 (*0-12-454550-5*) Acad Pr.

Loncke, F., et al, eds. Recent Research on European Sign Languages. vi, 166p. 1984. 24.00 (*90-265-0465-9*, Pub. by Swets Pub Serv NE) Taylor & Francis.

Londay, Jim. Close for Success: The Key to Real Estate Sales. 162p. 1989. 18.95 (*0-88462-739-X*, 1913-04) Dearborn Finan.

Londeix, Bernard. Cost Estimation for Software Development. 209p. (C). 1987. text ed. 29.25 (*0-201-17451-0*) Addison-Wesley.

***Londeix, Jean-Marie.** One Hundred Fifty Years of Music for Saxophone: Bibliographical Index of Music & Educational Literature for the Saxophone: 1844-1994. Ronkin, Bruce, ed. LC 94-67611. 448p. (ENG & FRE.). 1994. 54.95 (*0-939103-04-4*) Roncorp.

Londero, Eleanor. Diccionario Collins Gem Espanol-Italiano, Italiano-Spagnolo. 5th ed. 640p. 1990. pap. 14. 95 (*0-7859-5805-3*) Fr & Eur.

— Diccionario Collins Italiano-Espanol, Espanol-Italiano "Pocket" 6th ed. 416p. 1990. 24.95 (*0-7859-5804-5*) Fr & Eur.

Londero, Elio. Beneficios y Beneficiarios: Una Introduccion a la Estimacion de los Efectos Distributivos en el Analisis Costo Beneficio. 312p. 1987. write for info. (*0-940602-24-5*) IADB.

— Benefits & Beneficiaries: An Introduction to Estimating Distributional Effects in Cost-Benefit Analysis. 304p. 1987. write for info. (*0-940602-23-7*) IADB.

Londero, Elio, ed. Precios De Cuenta. 440p. 1992. 24.00 (*0-940602-53-9*) IADB.

Londesborough, Kate, jt. auth. see O'Callaghan, Karen.

Londgraf, R. W., jt. ed. see Mindlin, H.

Londner, Henry D., jt. auth. see Seisler, Jeffrey M.

Londner, Renee. Morgan's Whistle. LC 92-14390. (Illus.). 32p. (J). (ps-2). Date not set. 11.95 (*1-56065-162-8*) Capstone Pr.

Londo, Richard J. Common Sense in Business Writing, Vols. I & II. 480p. (C). 1991. per., pap. text ed. 29.95 (*0-8403-7068-7*) Kendall-Hunt.

***London.** Affordable Space Launch. 1997. write for info. (*0-89464-057-7*) Krieger.

— A Colour Atlas of Diagnosis after Recent Injury. 146p. 1991. 92.00 (*0-8016-6295-8*) Mosby Yr Bk.

— Imaging Drug Action in the Brain. 1992. 167.95 (*0-8493-8843-0*, RM301) CRC Pr.

— Photography. 5th ed. 1994. pap. text ed. (*0-8230-4975-2*) Watsn-Guptill.

— Short Course in Photography. 2nd ed. 1994. pap. text ed. (*0-8230-4976-0*) Watsn-Guptill.

London, Abraham, tr. see Adler, Jacob.

London, Anne. Best Recipes from America's Kitchen: A Comprehensive Survey of Painting. 1988. 15.99 (*0-517-66554-9*) Random Hse Value.

London, Anne & Bishov, Bertha K. The Complete American-Jewish Cookbook. LC 88-45726. 672p. 1989. reprint ed. pap. 17.00 (*0-06-091590-0*, PL 1590, PL) HarpC.

London, Anne, et al. Multicultural Diversity Module to Accompany Boone-Kurtz, Contemporary Business. 7th ed. 34p. (C). 1993. pap. text ed. 10.50 (*0-03-097685-5*) Dryden Pr.

London, Barbara. Short Course in Photography. 2nd ed. (C). 1991. pap. text ed. 27.00 (*0-673-52121-4*) HarpCollege.

— Video Spaces: Eight Installations. 80p. 1995. pap. 22.50 (*0-87070-646-2*, 0-8109-6146-6) Mus of Modern Art.

London, Barbara & Upton, John. Photography. 5th ed. LC 93-2366. (C). 1993. text ed. 46.00 (*0-673-52223-7*, Harper Ref) HarpC.

London, Barbara, jt. auth. see Baker, Robert.

London, Barry, jt. auth. see Ritholz, Jules.

London, Bette. The Appropriated Voice: Narrative Authority in Conrad, Forster & Woolf. LC 89-48925. 208p. 1990. text ed. 37.50 (*0-472-10160-9*) U of Mich Pr.

London, Bette M., ed. Edward Christiana: Retrospective Exhibition. (Illus.). 24p. (Orig.). 1989. pap. 7.50 (*0-915895-09-9*) Munson Williams.

***London, Bill.** Country Roads of Idaho. (Country Roads Ser.). 140p. (Orig.). 1995. pap. 9.95 (*1-56626-069-8*) Country Rds.

— Umbrella Guide to Interior Northwest Antique Stores. (Illus.). 160p. 1992. pap. 12.95 (*0-945397-13-5*, Umbrella Bks) Epicenter Pr.

— Umbrella Guide to the Inland Empire. (Illus.). 192p. 1990. pap. 10.95 (*0-914143-26-3*, Umbrella Bks) Epicenter Pr.

London, Bill & Powell, Charles. Natural Wonders of Idaho. LC 93-44679. (Natural Wonders Ser.). (Illus.). 148p. (Orig.). 1994. pap. 9.95 (*1-56626-059-0*) Country Rds.

London, Bobby. Mondo Popeye. 112p. (Orig.). 1988. pap. 5.95 (*0-312-02611-0*) St Martin.

London, Bonne R. Hi-Tech Jewish Cooking: Recipes for the Microwave, Processsor, Blender, & Crock Pot. (Illus.). 378p. 1990. 14.95 (*0-944007-82-1*) Sure Sellers.

London, Bonnie. A History of Georgia. Sims, Sarah E. & Andress, Faye, eds. (Illus.). 116p. 1992. teacher ed 15.95 (*0-9623319-7-X*); teacher ed 29.95 (*0-9623319-8-8*); 4.95 (*0-9623319-5-3*); text ed. 26.95 (*0-9623319-4-5*); 3.95 (*0-9623319-6-1*) Clairmont Pr.

London Borough of Sutton Staff. Croissants at Croydon: The Memoirs of Jack Bamford. (C). 1985. 45.00 (*0-907335-15-2*, Pub. by Sutton Libs & Arts) St Mut.

London, Bruce, jt. ed. see Palen, J. John.

***London Business School Staff.** London Business School Sourceguide to Central & East European Company Information. Scott, Julie, ed. (London Business School Sourceguide Ser.). 1994. text ed. 108.00 (*1-873477-70-8*, Gale Res Intl) Gale.

London, Cait. The Bride Says No. 1994. mass mkt. 2.99 (*0-373-05891-8*, 1-05891-6) Harlequin Bks.

— Every Girl's Guide to... 1995. mass mkt. 3.50 (*0-373-52005-0*, 1-52005-5) Silhouette.

— Maybe No, Maybe Yes. (Silhouette Desire Ser.). 1993. pap. 2.89 (*0-373-05782-2*, 5-05782-3) Silhouette.

— Miracles & Mistletoe. 1995. pap. 3.25 (*0-373-05968-X*, 1-05968-2) Silhouette.

— Mr. Easy: (Man of the Month, Hawk's Way) (Desire Ser.). 1995. mass mkt. 3.25 (*0-373-05919-1*, 1-05919-5) Silhouette.

— The Seduction of Jake Tallman: Man of the Month. (Silhouette Desire Ser.). 1993. mass mkt. 2.99 (*0-373-05811-X*, 5-05811-0) Silhouette.

London, Carolyn. Adventures of a Jeeponary. (J). (ps-3). 1982. pap. 2.50 (*0-915374-19-6*) Rapids Christian.

— Stolen Ice Cream Bar. (Illus.). 12p. (J). (gr. k-6). 1981. pap. text ed. 4.25 (*1-55976-151-2*) CEF Press.

London, Cathy. Look Inside: A Woman's Thoughts on Love. LC 91-76180. 96p. 1991. pap. 8.95 (*0-936385-07-3*) J Friedlander.

London, Charmian. Book of Jack London, 2 vols. 1976. 60. 95 (*0-8488-0886-X*) Amereon Ltd.

— The Book of Jack London, 2 vols. 1992. reprint ed. lib. bdg. 150.00 (*0-7812-5061-7*) Rprt Serv.

***London, Christopher W., ed.** Architecture in Victorian & Edwardian India. (C). 1994. 94.00 (*81-85026-26-2*, Pub. by Marg) S Asia.

L

London Cigarette Co. Staff. Complete Catalog of British Cigarette Cards. 24.95 (*0-906671-48-5*) Viking Penguin.

— Complete Catalog of British Cigarette Cards. 2nd ed. 24.95 (*0-906671-85-X*) Viking Penguin.

London City Literary Institute Staff. Tradition & Experiment in Present-Day Literature. LC 68-761. (Studies in Comparative Literature: No. 35). (C). 1972. reprint ed. lib. bdg. 75.00 (*0-8383-0544-X*) M S G Haskell Hse.

London, Clement B. On Wings of Change: Self-Portrait of a Developing Country, Trinidad-Tobago. 201p. (Orig.). 1991. pap. 13.95 (*0-685-59146-8*) Calaloux Pubns.

— Through Caribbean Eyes: Reflections on an Era of Independence. LC 89-84287. 491p. pap. 12.95 (*0-938818-18-X*) ECA Assoc.

London, Clement B., jt. auth. see Carrasquillo, Angela L.

London College of Physicians Staff. Certain Necessary Directions As well for the Cure of the Plague As for Preventing the Infection: Also Certaine Select Statutes. LC 79-84120. (English Experience Ser.: No. 939). 148p. 1979. reprint ed. lib. bdg. 14.00 (*90-221-0939-9*) Walter J Johnson.

London County Council Staff. Bankside. LC 78-138274. (London County Council. Survey of London Ser.: No. 22). reprint ed. 84.50 (*0-404-51672-6*) AMS Pr.

— The Parishes of Christ Church & All Saints & the Liberties of Norton Folgate & the Old Artillery Ground. LC 74-6547. (London County Council. Survey of London Ser.: No. 27). reprint ed. 8.50 (*0-404-51677-7*) AMS Pr.

***London, David T.** Twain's Tales. 38p. (Orig.). 1994. pap. 4.00 (*1-57514-125-6*, 1165) Encore Perform Pub.

London Dialectical Society Staff. Report on Spiritualism: Together with the Evidence, Oral & Written. LC 75-36849. (Occult Ser.). 1976. reprint ed. 35.95 (*0-405-07965-6*) Ayer.

London, Dick. Graduation: The Revision of Estimates. LC 85-23001. (Illus.). 183p. (Orig.). 1985. pap. text ed. 40.00 (*0-936031-00-X*) Actex Pubns.

— Survival Models & Their Estimation. LC 88-22118. (Illus.). 326p. (Orig.). 1988. pap. text ed. 40.00 (*0-936031-02-6*) Actex Pubns.

London East Anglian Group. GASP Easy Question Bank: Bank One. (C). 1989. text ed. 300.00 (*0-7487-0213-X*, Pub. by S Thornes Pubs UK) St Mut.

— GASP Easy Question Bank: Bank Two. (C). 1989. text ed. 300.00 (*0-7487-0214-8*, Pub. by S Thornes Pubs UK) St Mut.

— GASP Explorations Resource Book. (C). 1990. text ed. 300.00 (*0-7487-0444-2*, Pub. by S Thornes Pubs UK) St Mut.

— GASP Graded Assessment Evaluation Pack. (C). 1989. text ed. 220.00 (*0-09-175897-1*, Pub. by S Thornes Pubs UK) St Mut.

— GASP Hard Question Bank: Bank One. (C). 1989. text ed. 300.00 (*0-7487-0453-1*, Pub. by S Thornes Pubs UK) St Mut.

— GASP Hard Question Bank: Bank Two. (C). 1989. text ed. 300.00 (*0-7487-0454-X*, Pub. by S Thornes Pubs UK) St Mut.

— GASP Medium Question Bank One. (C). 1990. text ed. 300.00 (*0-7487-0446-9*, Pub. by S Thornes Pubs UK) St Mut.

— GASP Medium Question Bank Two. (C). 1990. text ed. 300.00 (*0-685-39381-X*, Pub. by S Thornes Pubs UK) St Mut.

— GASP Process Skills Resource Book. (C). 1990. text ed. 320.00 (*0-7487-0443-4*, Pub. by S Thornes Pubs UK) St Mut.

— GASP Pupil Record Cards. (C). 1989. text ed. 120.00 (*0-09-175768-1*, Pub. by S Thornes Pubs UK) St Mut.

— GASP Summary Teacher's Guide. (C). 1988. text ed. 35.00 (*0-09-175646-4*, Pub. by S Thornes Pubs UK) St Mut.

— GASP Teacher's Handbook. (C). 1989. text ed. 200.00 (*0-09-175675-8*, Pub. by S Thornes Pubs UK) St Mut.

— GASP Training Manual. (C). 1990. text ed. 350.00 (*0-7487-0442-6*, Pub. by S Thornes Pubs UK) St Mut.

London, H. B., Jr. & Wiseman, Neil B. The Heart of a Great Pastor: How to Grow Strong & Thrive Wherever God Has Planted You. Rea, Dean & Woodard, Virginia, eds. LC 94-12657. (Illus.). 252p. 1994. 15.99 (*0-8307-1674-2*, 5112462) Regal.

***London, H. B. & Wiseman, Neil B.** Married to a Pastor's Wife. 240p. 1995. 15.99 (*1-56476-392-7*, 6-3392, Victor Books) SP Pubns.

London, H. B., Jr. & Wiseman, Neil B. Pastors at Risk. Hosask, Robert N., ed. LC 93-3616. (Illus.). 204p. 1993. 18.99 (*1-56476-111-8*, Victor Books) SP Pubns.

London, Herbert. The Broken Apple: New York City in the 1980's. 256p. 1989. 34.95 (*0-88738-296-7*) Transaction Pubs.

London, Herbert & Rubenstein, Edwin S. From the Empire State to the Vampire State: New York in a Downward Transition. LC 94-20687. 210p. (Orig.). (C). reprint ed. pap. text ed. 24.95 (*0-8191-9605-3*) U Pr of Amer.

London, Herbert I. Armageddon in the Classroom: An Examination of Nuclear Education. 146p. (Orig.). 1987. pap. text ed. 18.50 (*0-8191-6548-4*) U Pr of Amer.

— Closing the Circle: A Cultural History of the Rock Revolution. LC 84-2016. 208p. 1984. pap. 19.95 (*0-8304-1118-6*) Nelson-Hall.

— Military Doctrine & the American Character: Reflections on Airland Battle. LC 84-62054. (Agenda Paper Ser.: No. 14). 79p. reprint ed. pap. 25.00 (*0-7837-2122-6*, 2042404) Bks Demand.

— Social Science Theory: Structure & Application. 375p. 1989. pap. text ed. 21.95 (*0-88738-774-8*) Transaction Pubs.

London, Herbert I., ed. A Strategy for Victory Without War. LC 89-5731. 126p. (Orig.). (C). 1989. lib. bdg. 35.50 (*0-8191-7437-8*, Pub. by Hudson Inst); pap. text ed. 17.50 (*0-8191-7438-6*, Hudson Instit IN) U Pr of Amer.

London, Herbert I. & Weeks, Albert. Myths That Rule America. LC 80-5866. 176p. (C). 1981. pap. text ed. 15.00 (*0-8191-1447-2*) U Pr of Amer.

London, Hilary. Scent of Gold. large type ed. (General Ser.). 416p. 1993. 21.95 (*0-7089-2845-5*) Ulverscroft.

London, Howard B., jt. ed. see Zwerling, L. Steven.

London, Jack. The Angry Mammoth. (Illus.). 40p. 1984. pap. 1.95 (*0-932458-21-1*) Star Rover.

— The Assassination Bureau, Ltd. reprint ed. lib. bdg. 18.95 (*0-89190-655-X*, Rivercity Pr) Amereon Ltd.

— Batard. Orig. Title: The Faith of Men. (Illus.). 292p. 1987. pap. 6.95 (*0-932458-13-0*) Star Rover.

— Before Adam. (Illus.). 242p. 1992. pap. 6.95 (*0-932458-09-2*) Star Rover.

— Before Adam. reprint ed. lib. bdg. 18.95 (*0-89190-651-7*, Rivercity Pr) Amereon Ltd.

— The Best Short Stories of Jack London. reprint ed. lib. bdg. 18.95 (*0-89190-656-8*, Rivercity Pr) Amereon Ltd.

— Burning Daylight. (Illus.). 362p. 1991. pap. 9.95 (*0-932458-34-3*) Star Rover.

— The Call of the Wild. 14.95 (*0-8488-0106-7*, Amereon Hse) Amereon Ltd.

— The Call of the Wild. 64p. 1990. pap. 1.00 (*0-486-26472-6*) Dover.

— The Call of the Wild. (Illustrated Classics Collection 1). 64p. (J). (gr. 6-12). 1994. pap. 3.60 (*1-56103-417-7*) Lake Pub Co.

— The Call of the Wild. LC 94-13622. (Illus.). 1994. pap. 2.95 (*0-681-00695-1*) Longmeadow Pr.

— The Call of the Wild. LC 93-18409. (Illus.). (J). 1994. text ed. 19.95 (*0-02-759455-6*) Macmillan.

— The Call of the Wild. Platt, Kin, ed. LC 73-75461. (Now Age Illustrated Ser.). (Illus.). 64p. (J). (gr. 5-10). 1973. pap. 2.95 (*0-88301-095-X*) Pendulum Pr.

— The Call of the Wild. (Classics Ser.). 128p. (J). (gr. 3-7). 1983. pap. 2.99 (*0-14-035000-4*, Puffin) Puffin Bks.

— The Call of the Wild. (Classics Ser.). 128p. (J). (gr. 5 up). 1994. pap. 2.99 (*0-14-036669-5*) Puffin Bks.

— The Call of the Wild. LC 79-24464. (Short Classics Ser.). (Illus.). 48p. (J). (gr. 4 up). 1980. Pub. 1980. lib. bdg. 22.80 (*0-8172-1656-1*) Raintree Steck-V.

— The Call of the Wild. (Children's Classics Ser.). (J). 1991. 12.99 (*0-517-06003-5*) Random Hse Value.

— The Call of the Wild. LC 90-50182. (Vintage-Library of America Ser.). 1990. pap. 8.50 (*0-679-72535-0*, Vin) Random.

— The Call of the Wild. LC 63-14831. (Illus.). 144p. (YA). (gr. 6 up). 1970. 13.95 (*0-02-759510-2*, Mac Bks Young Read) S&S Childrens.

— The Call of the Wild. Bd. with White Fang. 1984. Set pap. 2.95 (*0-671-53147-6*, WSP) PB.

— Call of the Wild. Bd. with White Fang. LC 85-60633. LC 85-60633. (Illus.). 304p. 1985. 12.95 (*0-89577-211-6*) RD Assn.

— The Call of the Wild. Bd. with White Fang (Classics Ser.). 293p. (gr. 7-12). 1991. 3.95 (*0-553-21233-8*) Bantam.

— The Call of the Wild. 271p. 1983. reprint ed. lib. bdg. 19.95 (*0-89966-473-3*) Buccaneer Bks.

— The Call of the Wild & Selected Stories. 176p. (J). (gr. 6). 1960. pap. 3.95 (*0-451-52390-3*, Sig Classics) NAL-Dutton.

— The Call of the Wild Readalong. (Illustrated Classics Collection 1). 64p. 1994. audio, pap. 13.50 (*1-56103-419-3*) Lake Pub Co.

— The Call of the Wild, White Fang, & Other Stories. Leitz, Robert C., III, ed. (World's Classics Ser.). 400p. 1990. pap. 5.95 (*0-19-282709-X*) OUP.

— The Call of the Wild, White Fang, & Other Stories. Sinclair, Andrew, ed. 416p. 1993. 7.95 (*0-14-018651-4*, Penguin Classics) Viking Penguin.

— Captain David Grief. Orig. Title: Son of the Sun. 332p. 1987. reprint ed. pap. 5.95 (*0-935180-34-6*) Mutual Pub HI.

— Cargo. 42p. 1992. 1.95 (*0-932458-45-9*) Star Rover.

— Collected Works of Jack London. Kasdin, Steven J., ed. 1058p. 1991. 24.95 (*0-88029-596-1*) Marboro Bks.

— The Cruise of the Dazzler. (Illus.). 250p. 1981. pap. 6.95 (*0-932458-06-8*) Star Rover.

— Cruise of the Dazzler. reprint ed. lib. bdg. 15.95 (*0-89190-652-5*, Rivercity Pr) Amereon Ltd.

— The Cruise of the Snark. (Illus.). 340p. 1984. 22.50 (*0-85036-152-4*, Pub. by Seafarer Bks UK) Sheridan.

— Cruise of the Snark. 340p. 1971. reprint ed. pap. 25.00 (*0-87556-437-2*) Saifer.

— The Cruise of the Snark. 1992. reprint ed. lib. bdg. 18.95 (*0-89966-954-9*) Buccaneer Bks.

— The Cruise of the Snark. (Illus.). 340p. 1993. reprint ed. pap. 14.95 (*0-924486-46-5*) Sheridan.

— The Cruise of the Snark: A Pacific Voyage. 300p. 1986. 14.95 (*0-7103-0139-1*, Pub. by Kegan Paul Intl UK) Routledge Chapman & Hall.

— Daughter of the Snows. (Illus.). 336p. 1987. pap. 6.95 (*0-932458-36-X*) Star Rover.

— Daughters of the Rich: A Play. 1971. Octavo wrappers. 5.00 (*0-910740-18-6*) Holmes.

— Faith of Men, & Other Stories. LC 73-122729. (Short Story Index Reprint Ser.). 1980. 18.95 (*0-8369-3562-4*) Ayer.

— Five Great Short Stories. (Thrift Editions Ser.). 96p. 1992. reprint ed. pap. 1.00 (*0-486-27063-7*) Dover.

— The Fuzziness of Hoockla-Heen & To Build a Fire. (Illus.). 40p. 1983. pap. 1.95 (*0-932458-16-5*) Star Rover.

— The Game. (Illus.). 182p. 1982. pap. 5.95 (*0-932458-10-6*) Star Rover.

— God of His Fathers & Other Stories. LC 72-103523. (Short Story Index Reprint Ser.). 1977. 21.95 (*0-8369-3265-X*) Ayer.

— Gold-Hunters of the North. (Shorey Historical Ser.). 12p. reprint ed. pap. 2.95 (*0-8466-0176-1*, S176) Shorey.

— Great Short Works of Jack London. 1942. mass mkt. 6.50 (*0-06-083041-7*, HarpT) HarpC.

— Hearts of Three. Reginald, R. & Melville, Douglas, eds. LC 77-84251. (Lost Race & Adult Fantasy Ser.). 1978. reprint ed. lib. bdg. 35.95 (*0-405-10997-0*) Ayer.

— The Hobo & the Fairy. reprint ed. lib. bdg. 16.95 (*0-89190-653-3*, Rivercity Pr) Amereon Ltd.

— Iron Heel. 1976. 24.95 (*0-8488-0566-6*) Amereon Ltd.

— Iron Heel. 1992. pap. 9.95 (*0-932458-50-5*) Star Rover.

— The Iron Heel. large type ed. 425p. 1995. lib. bdg. 22.00 (*0-939495-75-9*) North Bks.

— The Iron Heel. rev. ed. LC 80-81804. 240p. 1980. pap. 7.95 (*1-55652-071-9*) L Hill Bks.

— The Iron Heel. 224p. (C). 1990. reprint ed. pap. text ed. 8.95 (*0-904526-01-1*) Westview.

— Jack London Illustrated. (Illus.). 1988. 9.99 (*0-517-30980-7*) Random Hse Value.

— Jack London in the High School Aegis. Sisson, James E., ed. (Illus.). 125p. (Orig.). (J). (gr. 7-12). 1980. pap. 5.95 (*0-932458-01-7*) Star Rover.

— Jack London Novels. 1987. 6.98 (*0-671-08621-9*) S&S Trade.

— Jack London on the Road: The Tramp Diary & Other Hobo Writings. Etulain, Richard W., ed. LC 78-17039. (Illus.). 227p. reprint ed. pap. 64.70 (*0-7837-7067-7*, 2046879) Bks Demand.

— The Jack London Reader. LC 93-85539. (Courage Literary Classics Ser.). 272p. 1994. 5.98 (*1-56138-367-8*) Courage Bks.

— Jack London's Stories of the North. 256p. (J). (gr. 4 up). 1989. pap. 3.50 (*0-590-44229-5*) Scholastic Inc.

— Jack London's Tales of Hawaii. LC 81-23492. 80p. 1984. pap. 4.95 (*0-916630-25-0*) Pr Pacifica.

— John Barleycorn. 1976. 20.95 (*0-8488-1080-5*) Amereon Ltd.

— John Barleycorn: Or, Alcoholic Memoirs. LC 78-55743. 1978. reprint ed. lib. bdg. 16.00 (*0-8376-0423-0*) Bentley.

— John Barleycorn or Alcoholic Memoirs. 1990. pap. 3.95 (*0-451-52428-4*, Sig) NAL-Dutton.

— John Barleycorn or Alcoholic Memoirs. Sutherland, John, ed. (World's Classics Ser.). 288p. 1989. pap. 8.95 (*0-19-281804-X*) OUP.

— John Barleycorn: or Alcoholic Memoirs. (American Biography Ser.). 210p. 1991. reprint ed. lib. bdg. 69.00 (*0-7812-8249-7*) Rprt Serv.

— The Letters of Jack London, 3 vols., Set. Labor, Earle G. et al, eds. LC 83-45346. (Illus.). 1768p. 1988. 149.50 (*0-8047-1227-1*); boxed 199.50 (*0-8047-1507-6*) Stanford U Pr.

— The Letters of Jack London, 3 vols., Vol. I: 1896-1905. Labor, Earle G. et al, eds. (Illus.). 1768p. 1988. Vol. 1: 1896-1905. write for info. (*0-318-62866-X*) Stanford U Pr.

— The Letters of Jack London, 3 vols., Vol. 2: 1906-1912. Labor, Earle G. et al, eds. (Illus.). 1768p. 1988. write for info. (*0-318-62867-8*) Stanford U Pr.

— The Letters of Jack London, 3 vols., Vol. 3: 1913-1916. Labor, Earle G. et al, eds. (Illus.). 1768p. 1988. write for info. (*0-318-62868-6*) Stanford U Pr.

— Lost Face. 310p. 1991. pap. 9.95 (*0-932458-42-4*) Star Rover.

— Love of Life. (Illus.). 266p. 1988. pap. 7.95 (*0-932458-38-6*) Star Rover.

— Love of Life. rev. ed. (Read-along Radio Dramas Ser.). (YA). (gr. 6-12). 1986. 35.00 (*1-878298-21-6*) Balance Pub.

— The Man with the Gash. (Illus.). 304p. 1981. pap. 6.95 (*0-932458-04-1*) Star Rover.

— Martin Eden. (Airmont Classics Ser.). (J). (gr. 9 up). 1969. pap. 3.50 (*0-8049-0209-7*, CL-209) Airmont.

— Martin Eden. 1992. pap. 9.95 (*0-932458-51-3*) Star Rover.

— Martin Eden. (American Library). 496p. (C). 1984. pap. 7.95 (*0-14-039036-7*, Penguin Classics) Viking Penguin.

— Martin Eden. 480p. 1994. 9.95 (*0-14-018772-3*, Penguin Classics) Viking Penguin.

— Moon-Face. (Illus.). 272p. 1991. pap. 6.95 (*0-932458-12-2*) Star Rover.

— Moon-Face, & Other Stories. LC 71-140334. (Short Story Index Reprint Ser.). 1977. 15.95 (*0-8369-3726-0*) Ayer.

— Mutiny on the Elsinore: A Novel of Seagoing Gangsters. (Tales of the Pacific Ser.). 375p. 1987. pap. 5.95 (*0-935180-40-0*) Mutual Pub HI.

— Nam Bok. Orig. Title: Children of the Frost. (Illus.). 272p. (Orig.). reprint ed. pap. 6.95 (*0-932458-03-3*) Star Rover.

— Novels & Social Writings. Pizer, Donald, ed. Incl. People of the Abyss. LC 82-6940. 1982. (*0-318-63061-3*); Road. LC 82-6940. 1982. (*0-318-63062-1*); Iron Heel. LC 82-6940. 1982. (*0-318-63063-X*); Martin Eden. LC 82-6940. 1982. (*0-318-63064-8*); John Barleycorn. LC 82-6940. 1982. (*0-318-63065-6*); LC 82-6940. 1192p. 1982. 27.50 (*0-940450-06-2*) Library of America.

— The People of the Abyss. LC 93-2947. (Illus.). 320p. 1995. pap. 14.95 (*1-55652-167-7*) L Hill Bks.

— The People of the Abyss. (Illus.). 320p. 1982. pap. 9.95 (*0-932458-08-4*) Star Rover.

— People of the Abyss. (C). 1993. pap. text ed. 8.95 (*0-904526-17-8*, Pub. by Journeyman Pr UK) Westview.

— The Road. (Illus.). 320p. 1991. pap. 9.95 (*0-932458-46-7*) Star Rover.

— The Road. 150p. 1993. 17.95 (*1-56723-073-3*) Yestermorrow.

— Road. Date not set. 18.95 (*0-8488-0880-0*) Yestermorrow.

— The Road. (American Biography Ser.). 224p. 1991. reprint ed. lib. bdg. 69.00 (*0-7812-8250-0*) Rprt Serv.

— The Scab. (Illus.). 42p. 1992. pap. 1.95 (*0-932458-23-8*) Star Rover.

— The Scarlet Plague. LC 74-16506. (Science Fiction Ser.). (Illus.). 181p. 1978. reprint ed. 20.95 (*0-405-06304-0*) Ayer.

— Science Fiction Stories. 1976. 21.95 (*0-8488-1081-3*) Amereon Ltd.

— The Science Fiction Stories of Jack London. 1994. reprint ed. lib. bdg. 27.95 (*1-56849-303-7*) Buccaneer Bks.

— Sea Wolf. (Airmont Classics Ser.). (J). (gr. 6 up). 1965. pap. 2.50 (*0-8049-0064-7*, CL-64) Airmont.

— Sea Wolf. 1985. 15.95 (*0-02-574630-8*) Macmillan.

— Sea Wolf. (Illus.). 370p. 1981. pap. 9.95 (*0-932458-05-X*) Star Rover.

— The Sea Wolf. (Bantam Classics Ser.). 256p. (gr. 7 up). 1984. pap. 3.95 (*0-553-21225-7*) Bantam.

— The Sea Wolf. (Illustrated Classics Collection 4). 64p. 1994. pap. 3.60 (*1-56103-609-9*) Lake Pub Co.

— The Sea Wolf. Fago, John C., ed. (Now Age Illustrated IV Ser.). (Illus.). (gr. 4-12). 1978. student ed 1.25 (*0-88301-346-0*); pap. text ed. 2.95 (*0-88301-322-3*) Pendulum Pr.

— The Sea Wolf. 320p. 1993. pap. 2.50 (*0-8125-2276-1*) Tor Bks.

— Sea-Wolf. 1993. pap. 5.95 (*0-19-282931-9*) OUP.

— The Sea Wolf. 351p. reprint ed. lib. bdg. 21.95 (*0-89190-657-6*, Rivercity Pr) Amereon Ltd.

— The Sea-Wolf & Other Selected Stories. 1990. reprint ed. lib. bdg. 19.95 (*0-89968-539-0*) Buccaneer Bks.

— The Sea-Wolf & Other Stories. 320p. 1989. mass mkt. 8.95 (*0-14-018357-4*, Penguin Classics) Viking Penguin.

— The Sea Wolf & Selected Stories. 352p. (J). (gr. 8). 1964. pap. 3.95 (*0-451-52356-3*, Sig Classics) NAL-Dutton.

— The Sea Wolf Readalong. (Illustrated Classics Collection 4). 64p. 1994. audio 13.50 (*1-56103-611-0*) Lake Pub Co.

— Short Stores of Jack London. braille ed. 1802p. 1992. vinyl bd. 144.16 (*1-56956-090-0*, BR8649) W A T Braille.

— Short Stories. (Airmont Classics Ser.). (J). (gr. 9 up). 1969. pap. 2.50 (*0-8049-0198-8*, CL-198) Airmont.

— The Short Stories of Jack London: The Authorized Edition with Definitive Texts Selected by Earle Labor, Robert C. Leitz, III, & I. Milo Shepard. Labor, Earle G. et al, eds. 832p. 1990. 35.00 (*0-02-567180-4*) Macmillan.

— Smoke Bellew. unabridged ed. LC 92-16275. (Illus.). 240p. 1992. reprint ed. pap. text ed. 7.95 (*0-486-27364-4*) Dover.

— Smoke Bellew. 1992. reprint ed. lib. bdg. 19.95 (*0-89966-952-2*) Buccaneer Bks.

— The Son of the Wolf. 1900. 39.00 (*0-403-08613-2*) Somerset Pub.

— Son of the Wolf. reprint ed. lib. bdg. 16.95 (*0-89190-654-1*, Rivercity Pr) Amereon Ltd.

— Son of the Wolf. (Illus.). 256p. 1980. reprint ed. pap. 6.95 (*0-932458-02-5*) Star Rover.

— The Son of the Wolf. 1992. reprint ed. lib. bdg. 18.95 (*0-89966-953-0*) Buccaneer Bks.

— Son of Wolf. reprint ed. lib. bdg. 75.00 (*0-7812-0202-7*) Rprt Serv.

— South Sea Tales. 324p. 1985. reprint ed. pap. 5.95 (*0-935180-14-1*) Mutual Pub HI.

— The Star Rover. 348p. 1983. pap. 8.95 (*0-911842-31-4*) Valley Sun.

— Star Rover. 1976. 21.95 (*0-8488-1082-1*) Amereon Ltd.

— The Star Rover. 320p. (C). 1990. reprint ed. pap. text ed. 12.95 (*0-904526-10-0*) Westview.

— Stories of Hawaii. Day, A. Grove, ed. LC 65-11682. 282p. 1985. reprint ed. pap. 4.95 (*0-935180-08-7*) Mutual Pub HI.

— Strength of the Strong. 1976. 19.95 (*0-8488-1083-X*) Amereon Ltd.

— Surfing, a Royal Sport. Ash, A. S., ed. 19p. (C). 1994. pap. 2.00 (*0-942208-12-9*) Bandanna Bks.

— Tales of the Fish Patrol. (Illus.). 244p. 1982. pap. 6.95 (*0-932458-07-6*) Star Rover.

— Tales of the Fish Patrol. LC 72-4454. (Short Story Index Reprint Ser.). 1977. reprint ed. 24.95 (*0-8369-4181-0*) Ayer.

— Tales of the North. 1989. 7.98 (*0-89009-439-X*) Bk Sales Inc.

— Tales of the Pacific. 240p. 1989. mass mkt. 9.95 (*0-14-018358-2*, Penguin Classics) Viking Penguin.

— Thirteen Tales of Terror. 21.95 (*0-8488-0096-6*, Amereon Hse) Amereon Ltd.

— A Thousand Deaths. (Illus.). 40p. 1984. pap. 1.95 (*0-932458-22-X*) Star Rover.

— To Build a Fire. (Creative's Classic Short Stories Ser.). (Illus.). 48p. (J). (gr. 6 up). 1980. lib. bdg. 13.95 (*0-87191-769-6*) Creative Ed.

— To Build a Fire & Other Stories. (Bantam Classics Ser.). 400p. 1986. 4.95 (*0-553-21335-0*) Bantam.

— To Build a Fire & The Mexican. (Canto Bello Ser.: No. 4). 58p. 1989. reprint ed. 45.00 (*0-939489-06-6*) Engdahl Typo.

— The Tramp. (Illus.). 51p. 1984. pap. 1.95 (*0-932458-24-6*) Star Rover.

— The Unabridged Jack London. Teacher, Lawrence & Nicholls, Richard, eds. LC 81-4383. (Illus.). 1150p. (Orig.). 1981. pap. 16.95 (*0-89471-124-5*) Running Pr.

— The Valley of the Moon. (Illus.). 192p. (Orig.). 1988. reprint ed. pap. 12.95 (*0-9614181-1-7*) Rejl.

— W. H. Chaney. 42p. 1992. 1.95 (*0-685-65598-9*) Star Rover.

— War of the Classes. (Illus.). 278p. 1982. pap. 6.95 (*0-932458-11-4*) Star Rover.

— What Life Means to Me & the Dreams of Debs. (Illus.). 42p. 1991. pap. 1.95 (*0-932458-15-7*) Star Rover.

— When God Laughs. 272p. 1992. pap. write for info. (*0-932458-40-8*) Star Rover.

— White Fang. (Airmont Classics Ser.). (J). (gr. 6 up). 1964. pap. 2.50 (*0-8049-0036-1*, CL-36) Airmont.

— White Fang. 1976. 20.95 (*0-8488-0567-4*) Amereon Ltd.

An Asterisk (*) at the beginning of an entry indicates that the title is appearing in BIP for the first time.

— White Fang. 208p. Date not set. pap. 14.95 (0-88839-260-5) Hancock House.

— White Fang. (Illustrated Classics Collection 3). 64p. 1994. pap. 3.60 (1-56103-549-1) Lake Pub Co.

— White Fang. LC 94-18650. 1994. 2.95 (0-681-00649-8) Longmeadow Pr.

— White Fang. 1986. 14.95 (0-02-574750-9) Macmillan.

— White Fang. LC 85-42971. (Classics Ser.). 272p. (J). (gr. 4-6). 1985. pap. 3.99 (0-14-035045-4, Puffin) Puffin Bks.

— White Fang. (Classics Ser.). 272p. (J). (gr. 5 up). 1994. pap. 3.99 (0-14-036667-9) Puffin Bks.

— White Fang. 256p. (J). (gr. 6 up). 1986. pap. 3.25 (0-590-42591-9) Scholastic Inc.

— White Fang. 224p. (J). 1989. pap. 2.50 (0-8125-0512-3) Tor Bks.

— White Fang. abr. ed. Farr, Naunerle, ed. (Now Age Illustrated III Ser.). (Illus.). (J). (gr. 4-12). 1977. pap. text ed. 2.95 (0-88301-271-5) Pendulum Pr.

— White Fang. large type ed. LC 93-32332. 1993. 19.95 (0-8161-5889-4) Hall.

— White Fang. large type ed. LC 93-32332. 1994. pap. 13. 95 (0-8161-5892-4) Hall.

— White Fang. (Thrift Editions Ser.). 160p. reprint ed. pap. 1.00 (0-486-26968-X) Dover.

— White Fang: Illustrated Classics. Arneson, D. J., ed. (Illus.). 128p. (Orig.). (J). 1990. pap. 2.95 (0-942025-84-9) Kidsbks.

— White Fang & The Call of the Wild. 288p. 1991. pap. 3.95 (0-451-52558-2, Sig Classics) NAL-Dutton.

— White Fang & the Call of the Wild. large type ed. 530p. 1995. lib. bdg. 22.00 (0-939495-87-2) North Bks.

— White Fang Readalong. (Illustrated Classics Collection 3). (Illus.). 64p. 1994. pap. 13.50 (1-56103-551-3) Lake Pub Co.

— The Worker & the Tramp. 1983. reprint ed. pap. 1.00 (0-915046-29-6) Wolf Hse.

— Works of Jack London. 1990. 16.99 (0-517-05359-4) Random Hse Value.

— Works of Jack London. 1993. 12.99 (0-517-09342-1) Random Hse Value.

— The Works of Jack London: Call of the Wild, White Fang, Sea-Wolf, Short Stories. LC 94-27054. 1994. 19.95 (0-681-00725-7) Longmeadow Pr.

***London, Jack & Dyer, Daniel.** The Call of the Wild. LC 95-15717. (Illus.). 1995. write for info. (0-8061-2757-0) U of Okla Pr.

London, Jack & Heron, Herbert. Gold: A Play. limited ed. 1972. 14.95 (0-910740-19-4) Holmes.

London, Jack & Strunski, Anna. The Kempton-Wace Letters. Robillard, Douglas, ed. (Masterworks of Literature Ser.). 1991. 10.95 (0-8084-0436-9) NCUP.

London, Jack & Strunsky, Anna B. Kempton-Wace Letters. LC 67-30817. (American Biography Ser.: No. 32). 1969. reprint ed. lib. bdg. 75.00 (0-8383-0719-1) M S G Haskell Hse.

London, Jack, jt. auth. see Gilman, Charlotte P.

London, Jack, et al. The Assassination Bureau, LTD. LC 94-9213. 208p. 1994. 8.95 (0-14-018677-8, Penguin Classics) Viking Penguin.

— The Call of the Wild. (Classics Illustrated Ser.). (Illus.). 52p. (YA). Date not set. pap. 4.95 (1-57209-010-3) Classics Int Ent.

— World Premiere Performance of "Gold" 32p. 1973. pap. 3.00 (0-918466-03-2) Quintessence.

— World Premiere Performance of "Scorn of Women" 1979. pap. 3.00 (0-918466-04-0) Quintessence.

London, Joan. Jack London & His Daughters. (Illus.). 224p. (Orig.). 1990. pap. 10.95 (0-930588-43-6) Heyday Bks.

London, Johnathan. Old Salt, Young Salt. LC 94-14593. (J). 1995. write for info. (0-688-12975-7); lib. bdg. write for info. (0-688-12976-5) Lothrop.

London, Jonathan. Condor's Egg. LC 93-31001. (Illus.). 32p. (J). 1994. 13.95 (0-8118-0260-4) Chronicle Bks.

— Dancer at the Waterfall. LC 94-24575. 1995. write for info. (0-688-13929-9); lib. bdg. write for info. (0-688-13930-2) Lothrop.

— The Eyes of Grey Wolf. LC 92-35987. (Illus.). (J). (gr. 4 up). 1993. 13.95 (0-8118-0285-X) Chronicle Bks.

— Fall Rap. LC 94-33713. (Illus.). 1995. write for info. (0-688-13994-9); lib. bdg. write for info. (0-688-13995-7) Lothrop.

— Froggy Gets Dressed. (Illus.). 32p. (J). (ps-3). 1994. pap. 4.99 (0-14-054457-7) Puffin Bks.

— Froggy Gets Dressed. (Illus.). 32p. (J). 1995. pap. 18.99 (0-14-055378-9) Puffin Bks.

— Froggy Gets Dressed. (Illus.). 32p. (J). (ps-1). 1992. 13.00 (0-670-84249-4) Viking Child Bks.

— Froggy Learns to Swim. LC 94-43077. (Illus.). 32p. (J). (ps-1). 1995. 12.99 (0-670-85551-0, Viking) Viking Penguin.

— Gray Fox. LC 92-20653. (Illus.). 32p. (J). (gr. 3-8). 1993. 13.99 (0-670-84490-X) Viking Child Bks.

— Hip Cat. LC 93-1179. (Illus.). (J). 1993. 13.95 (0-8118-0315-5) Chronicle Bks.

— Honey Paw & Lightfoot. (J). (ps-3). 1995. 13.95 (0-8118-0533-6) Chronicle Bks.

— In a Season of Birds. (Rockbook Ser.: No. 7). 24p. (Orig.). 1978. pap. 3.00 (0-685-20119-8) J Mudfoot.

— Into This Night We Are Rising. LC 92-27471. (Illus.). (J). (ps-3). 1993. 13.99 (0-670-84905-7) Viking Child Bks.

— Island Hurricane. LC 94-14518. (J). 1994. write for info. (0-688-08117-7); lib. bdg. write for info. (0-688-08118-5) Lothrop.

— Jackrabbit. LC 94-1082. (J). 1995. write for info. (0-517-59657-1); lib. bdg. write for info. (0-517-59658-X) Crown Bks Yng Read.

— A Koala for Katie. LC 93-16085. (Illus.). (J). 1993. write for info. (0-8075-4209-1) A Whitman.

— Let's Go, Froggy! LC 93-24059. (Illus.). 32p. (J). (ps-3). 1994. lib. bdg. 12.99 (0-670-85055-1) Viking Child Bks.

— Like Butter on Pancakes. LC 94-9154. (Illus.). (J). 1995. 13.99 (0-670-85130-2, Viking) Viking Penguin.

— The Lion Who Had Asthma. Levine, Abby, ed. LC 91-16553. (Illus.). 32p. (J). (ps-1). 1992. lib. bdg. 13.95 (0-8075-4559-7) A Whitman.

— Liplap's Wish. LC 93-31007. (Illus.). (J). 1994. 12.95 (0-8118-0505-0) Chronicle Bks.

— The Owl Who Became the Moon. LC 92-14699. (Illus.). (J). (ps-2). 1993. 13.99 (0-525-45054-8, DCB) Dutton Child Bks.

— Red Wolf Country. LC 95-10384. (Illus.). (J). 1996. write for info. (0-525-45191-9, DCB) Dutton Child Bks.

— The Sugaring-off Party. LC 93-21911. (YA). 1995. 14.99 (0-525-45187-0, DCB) Dutton Child Bks.

— The Village Basket Weaver. LC 95-10383. (Illus.). (J). 1996. write for info. (0-525-45314-8, DCB) Dutton Child Bks.

— Voices of the Wild. LC 92-27651. (Illus.). 32p. (J). (ps up). 1993. 15.00 (0-517-59217-7); lib. bdg. 15.99 (0-517-59218-5) Crown Bks Yng Read.

— Where's Home? LC 94-39237. (J). 1995. 13.99 (0-670-86028-X, Viking) Viking Penguin.

London, Jonathan, ed. Thirteen Moons on Turtle's Back: A Native American Year of Moons. (Illus.). 32p. (J). (ps-8). 1992. lib. bdg. 15.95 (0-399-22141-7, Philomel Bks) Putnam Pub Group.

London, Jonathan & Pinola, Lanny. Fire Race: A Karuk Coyote Tale about How Fire Came to the People. LC 92-32352. (Illus.). (J). 1993. 13.95 (0-8118-0241-8) Chronicle Bks.

London, Jonathon. Master Elk & the Mountain Lion. LC 94-1754. (Illus.). (J). 1995. write for info. (0-517-59917-1); write for info. (0-517-59918-X) Crown Bks Yng Read.

London, Keith, jt. auth. see Wooldridge, Susan.

London, Kurt. Film Music. LC 70-124016. (Literature of Cinema Ser.). 1974. reprint ed. 31.95 (0-405-01622-0) Ayer.

London, Kurt, ed. see International Conference on World Politics Staff.

London, Larry. The Seven-Day Scriptural Rosary. LC 88-63552. (Orig.). 1989. pap. 4.95 (0-87973-524-4, 524); audio 12.95 (0-87973-192-3) Our Sunday Visitor.

London, Lawrence F. & Lemmon, Sarah M., eds. The Episcopal Church in North Carolina, 1701-1959. (Illus.). 627p. 1987. 21.95 (0-9617935-0-3) Episcopal DNC.

London, M. D., ed. see ASTM Committee D-19 on Water.

London Magazine Editors. Coming to London. Lehmann, John, ed. LC 73-152189. (Essay Index Reprint Ser.). 1977. reprint ed. 19.95 (0-8369-2409-6) Ayer.

***London, Manual.** Interpersonal Insight: How People Gain Understanding of Themselves & Others in Organizations. (Industrial-Organizational Psychology Ser.). (Illus.). 304p. 1995. text ed. 45.00 (0-19-509077-2) OUP.

***London, Manuel.** Achieving Performance Excellence in University Administration: A Team Approach to Organizational Change & Employee Development. LC 95-14427. 272p. 1995. text ed. 59.95 (0-275-95246-0, Praeger Pubs) Greenwood.

— Change Agents: New Roles & Innovation Strategies for Human Resource Professionals. LC 88-42793. (Management Ser.). 311p. 1988. 33.95 (1-55542-107-5) Jossey-Bass.

— Developing Managers: A Guide to Motivating & Preparing People for Successful Managerial Careers. LC 84-43030. (Management Ser.). 276p. 1985. 33.95x (0-87589-646-4) Jossey-Bass.

— Managing the Training Enterprise: High-Quality, Cost-Effective Employee Training in Organizations. LC 89-45573. (Management Ser.). 365p. 1989. 34.95 (1-55542-183-0) Jossey-Bass.

***London, Manuel, ed.** Employees, Careers, & Job Creation: Developing Growth-Oriented Human Resource Strategies & Programs. (Management, Social & Behavioral Studies). 1995. 29.95 (0-7879-0125-3) Jossey-Bass.

London, Manuel & Mone, Edward M. Career Management & Survival in the Workplace: Helping Employees Make Tough Career Decisions, Stay Motivated, & Reduce Career Stress. LC 86-46334. (Management Ser.). 244p. 1987. 32.95x (1-55542-043-5) Jossey-Bass.

London, Manuel & Mone, Edward M., eds. Career Growth & Human Resource Strategies: The Role of the Human Resource Professional. LC 87-32281. 357p. 1988. text ed. 65.00 (0-89930-229-7, LHR/, Quorum Bks) Greenwood.

London, Manuel & Stempf, Stephen A. Managing Careers. (Management Ser.). (Illus.). 324p. 1982. pap. text ed. 17. 56 (0-201-04559-1) Addison-Wesley.

London, Manuel & Wueste, Richard A. Human Resource Development in Changing Organizations. LC 92-16208. 292p. 1992. text ed. 55.00 (0-89930-741-8, LCC, Quorum Bks) Greenwood.

London, Manuel, et al, eds. Human Resource Forecasting & Strategy Development: Guidelines for Analyzing & Fulfilling Organizational Needs. LC 89-24365. 280p. 1990. text ed. 55.00 (0-89930-436-2, LHS/, Greenwood Pr) Greenwood.

London, Mark. Masonry: How to Care for Old & Historic Brick & Stone. National Park Service Staff, ed. LC 86-25270. (Respectful Rehabilitation Ser.). (Illus.). 208p. (Orig.). 1988. pap. 12.95 (0-89133-125-5) Preservation Pr.

London, Martin, jt. auth. see Dill, Barbara.

London, Mel. Getting into Film. LC 77-78329. 1980. pap. 9.95 (0-345-28977-3, Ballantine Trade) Ballantine.

London, Mel & London, Sheryl. The Versatile Grain & the Elegant Bean: A Celebration of the World's Most Healthful Foods. (Illus.). 448p. 1992. pap. 27.50 (0-671-76106-4) S&S Trade.

London, Mel, jt. auth. see London, Sheryl.

London Mercury Staff. Second Mercury Story Book. LC 79-37553. (Short Story Index Reprint Ser.). 1977. reprint ed. 25.95 (0-8369-4112-8) Ayer.

London, Ministry of Defense, Naval Library Staff. Author & Subject Catalogues of the Naval Library, Ministry of Defence, 5 vols., Set. 1970. lib. bdg. 545.00 (0-8161-0755-6, Hall Library) G K Hall.

London Missionary Society Staff. London Missionary Society's Report of the Proceedings Against the Late Rev. J. Smith of Demerara, Who Was Tried Under Martial Law & Condemned to Death, on a Charge of Aiding & Assisting in a Rebellion of Negro Slaves. LC 78-79809. 204p. 1970. reprint ed. text ed. 45.00 (0-8371-1506-X, LMS&, Negro U Pr) Greenwood.

London, Nancy & Wolfe, Gary. Mansfield (OH) Municipal Court Fine Collection Improvement Project: A Technical Assistance Report. 59p. 1992. 3.50 (0-685-64935-0, NERO TA-565) Natl Ctr St Courts.

London, Nancy, jt. auth. see Adams, Lorraine.

London, Nancy, et al. Management Review of Lucas County Court of Common Pleas Automation Activities. 284p. 1990. 17.00 (0-685-38118-8, NERO-244) Natl Ctr St Courts.

London, Nancy R. Japanese Corporate Philanthropy. 160p. 1990. 35.00 (0-19-506424-0) OUP.

London, Oscar. Dr. Sunshine: A Novel. LC 92-34863. 1993. pap. 9.95 (0-89815-526-6) Ten Speed Pr.

— Kill As Few Patients As Possible: And Fifty-Six Other Essays on How to Be the World's Best Doctor. 1987. 14. 95 (0-89815-255-0); pap. 7.95 (0-89815-197-X) Ten Speed Pr.

— Take One As Needed. 224p. (Orig.). 1989. pap. 8.95 (0-89815-297-6) Ten Speed Pr.

London, P. S. Anatomy of Injury & Its Surgical Implications. 128p. 1991. text ed. 85.00 (0-7506-1251-7) Buttrwrth-Heinemann.

London, Perry. The Modes & Morals of Psychotherapy. 2nd ed. LC 84-29769. (Clinical & Community Psychology Ser.). 350p. (C). 1986. text ed. 26.00 (0-89116-290-9); pap. 24.50 (0-89116-350-6) Hemisp Pub.

London, Peter. No More Secondhand Art: Awakening the Artist Within. LC 89-42618. 208p. (Orig.). 1989. pap. 13.00 (0-87773-482-8) Shambhala Pubns.

— Step Outside: Community-Based Art Education. LC 93-11569. (Illus.). 128p. (C). 1994. pap. text ed. 32.50 (0-435-08794-0, 08794) Heinemann.

London, Rick. Dreaming Close By. LC 86-70316. 64p. 1986. 5.00 (0-917588-14-2) O Bks.

London, Robert. Nonroutine Problems: Doing Mathematics. (Illus.). 60p. (Orig.). (YA). (gr. 10-12). 1989. pap. text ed. 19.95 (0-939765-30-6, G117) Janson Pubns.

London, Roy. The Amazing Activity of Charley Contrare & the Ninety-Eighth Street Gang. 1975. pap. 4.75 (0-8222-0023-6) Dramatists Play.

— Disneyland on Parade: Three Related Short Plays. 1985. pap. 4.75 (0-8222-0315-4) Dramatists Play.

— Mrs. Murray's Farm. 1977. pap. 4.75 (0-8222-0788-5) Dramatists Play.

London, Samuel B. & Stile, Stephen W. The School's Role in the Prevention of Child Abuse. LC 81-86312. (Fastback Ser.: No. 172). 50p. (Orig.). 1982. pap. 1.25 (0-87367-172-4) Phi Delta Kappa.

London, Sandy. Smoke Screen. (Orig.). 1994. mass mkt. 4.99 (0-449-14901-3, GM) Fawcett.

London School of Economics & Political Science Department of Law Staff. Annual Survey of English Law, 1928-1940, 13 vols., Set. LC 87-83497. 5000p. 1988. reprint ed. Price per volume $82.50. lib. bdg. 1, 024.00 (0-912004-63-0) W W Gaunt.

London School of Economics, British Library of Political & Economic Science Staff. Economics 1986, Vol. 35. (International Bibliography of the Social Sciences Ser.). 768p. 1990. 170.00 (0-415-00086-6, A2740) Routledge.

— Sociology 1987, Vol. 37. (International Bibliography of the Social Sciences Ser.). 450p. 1990. 150.00 (0-685-50228-7, A5053) Routledge.

London School of Hygiene & Tropical Medicine Second Annual Public Health Forum Staff. Europe Without Frontiers: The Implications for Health. Normand, Charles E. & Vaughan, Patrick, eds. LC 92-49575. 320p. 1993. text ed. 135.00 (0-471-93759-2) Wiley.

London, Sheldon I. How to Comply with Federal Employee Laws. 1991. pap. 19.95 (0-9613262-2-0) London Pub.

— How to Comply with Federal Employee Laws: Practical Advice for Employers. 160p. 1990. pap. 19.95 (0-9613262-1-2) London Pub.

***London, Sherry.** Photoshop Special Effects: The Definitive Macintosh Photoshop Problem Solver. 550p. 1994. cd-rom, pap. 39.95 (1-878739-76-X) Waite Group Pr.

London, Sheryl & London, Mel. A Seafood Celebration: Healthful, Festive, Easy-to-Prepare Recipes for the Casual Cook or the Connoisseur. LC 93-19727. (Illus.). 1993. 30.00 (0-671-76813-1) S&S Trade.

London, Sheryl, jt. auth. see London, Mel.

***London, Sondra.** Knockin' on Joe. (Illus.). 312p. (Orig.). 1992. pap. 15.95 (1-897743-05-X, Pub. by Nemesis UK) AK Pr Dist.

London, Steve & Chihal, H. Jane. Menopause: Clinical Concepts. (Orig.). 1989. pap. 12.95 (0-929240-04-9) Essential Med Info Syst Inc.

London, Steve, jt. auth. see Chihal, H. Jane.

London, Steven H., et al, eds. The Re-Education of the American Working Class. LC 90-36778. (Contributions in Labor Studies: No. 31). 312p. 1990. text ed. 59.95 (0-313-26785-5, LRB, Greenwood Pr) Greenwood.

London Stock Exchange Staff. Stock Exchange Official Yearbook, 1993-1994. 1140p. 1994. 415.00 (1-56159-105-X, Stockton Pr) Groves Dictionaries.

London Times Staff. American Writing Today. Angoff, Allan, ed. LC 74-134144. (Essay Index Reprint Ser.). 1977. 30.95 (0-8369-2030-9) Ayer.

— Fifty Years: Memories & Contrasts. LC 71-843431. (Essay Index Reprint Ser.). 1977. reprint ed. 30.95 (0-8369-1935-1) Ayer.

— Modern Essays. LC 73-86788. (Essay Index Reprint Ser.). 1977. 23.95 (0-8369-1630-1) Ayer.

— Third Leaders, Reprinted from the Times. LC 68-16980. (Essay Index Reprint Ser.). 1977. 19.95 (0-8369-0946-1) Ayer.

— The Times Atlas of China. 1974. text ed. 29.95 (0-7230-0118-9) Van Nos Reinhold.

London, Todd. The Artistic Home. LC 87-33600. 112p. (Orig.). (C). 1988. pap. 3.95 (0-930452-76-3) Theatre Comm.

London University, Board of Studies in History Staff. Tudor Studies Presented to Albert Frederick Pollard. Seton-Watson, Robert W., ed. LC 69-17582. (Essay Index Reprint Ser.). 1977. 20.95 (0-8369-0083-9) Ayer.

London, Victoria. Destiny's Desire. 464p. 1987. pap. 3.95 (0-8217-2089-9) Zebra.

— Seductive Scoundrel. 448p. 1989. pap. 3.95 (0-8217-2677-3) Zebra.

London, W. T., ed. see International Symposium on Basic Progress in Blood Transfusion Staff.

Londong, W., et al, eds. Long-Term Intragastric pH Measurement in Man: Basic & Methodological Aspects - Journal: Digestive Diseases, Vol. 8, Suppl. 1, 1990. (Illus.). vi, 98p. 1990. pap. 27.25 (3-8055-5274-2) S Karger.

Londono & Fischer, eds. Recent Trends in Optical Systems Design: Computer Lens Design. 307p. 1987. 50.00 (0-89252-801-X, 766) SPIE.

Londre, Felicia, tr. see Chedid, Andree.

Londre, Felicia H. The History of World Theater: From the English Restoration to the Present. (Illus.). 656p. 1991. 49.50 (0-8264-0485-5, F Ungar Bks) Continuum.

— Tom Stoppard. LC 80-53698. (Literature & Life Ser.). 192p. 1981. 19.95 (0-8044-2538-8, F Ungar Bks) Continuum.

Londregan, R. P. Life Safety in Underground Rail Systems, TR 833: The Australian Effort. 1983. 4.35 (0-685-07672-5, TR83-3) Society Fire Protect.

Londres, Albert. The Road to Buenos Aires. 260p. 1974. lib. bdg. 59.95 (0-8490-0959-6) Gordon Pr.

Lone, Farooq A. Palaeoethnobotany: Plants & Ancient Man in Kashmir. (C). 1993. text ed. 42.00 (81-204-0717-2, Pub. by Oxford IBH II) S Asia.

Lone, Farooq A., et al. Palaeoethnobotany: Plants & Ancient Man in Kashmir. (Illus.). 288p. (C). 1993. text ed. 70.00 (90-6191-944-4, Pub. by A A Balkema NE) Ashgate Pub Co.

Lone, Stewart & McCormack, Gavan. Korea since 1850. LC 93-12490. 320p. 1993. text ed. 49.95 (0-312-09685-2); pap. 16.95 (0-312-09686-0) St Martin.

Lone, Stuart. Japan's First Modern War: Army & Society in the Conflict with China, 1894-95. LC 94-16292. 1994. text ed. 55.00 (0-312-12277-2) St Martin.

Lone Wolf Circles. Full Circle: A Song of Ecology & Earthen Spirituality. LC 91-24532. (Illus.). 208p. (Orig.). 1991. pap. 12.95 (0-87542-347-7) Llewellyn Pubns.

Lonegren, Sig. Pendulum Kit. 1990. pap. 19.95 (0-671-69140-6) S&S Trade.

***Lonegren, Sig, comp.** The Dowsing Rod Kit. (Illus.). 160p. 1995. boxed 27.95 (0-8048-3049-5) C E Tuttle.

Loneragan, J. F. Copper in Soils & Plants. 1981. text ed. 103.00 (0-12-455520-9) Acad Pr.

Loneregan, Mark. Blues-Rock Guitar Handbook. 1993. 4.95 (0-87166-405-4, 94172); audio 13.95 (0-87166-407-0, 94172); audio 9.98 (0-87166-406-2, 94172) Mel Bay.

Lonergan, Anne & Richards, Caroline, eds. Thomas Berry & the New Cosmology: In Dialogue with Gregory Baum, Margaret Brennan, Stephen Dunn, James Farris, Caroline Richards, Donald Senior, & Brian Swimme. LC 87-40528. 144p. (Orig.). (C). 1987. pap. 7.95 (0-89622-337-X) Twenty-Third.

Lonergan, Bernard. Doctrinal Pluralism. LC 70-155364. (Pere Marquette Lectures). 1971. 10.00 (0-87462-503-3) Marquette.

— Insight. Crowe, Frederick E. & Doran, Robert M., eds. (Collected Works of Bernard Lonergan: No. 3). 900p. 1992. 95.00 (0-8020-3454-3); pap. 35.00 (0-8020-3455-1) U of Toronto Pr.

— Method in Theology. 403p. 1990. pap. text ed. 19.95 (0-8020-6809-X) U of Toronto Pr.

— Subject. LC 68-22238. (Aquinas Lectures). (C). 1968. 10. 00 (0-87462-133-X) Marquette.

— Topics in Education: Lectures on the Philosophy of Education. Doran, Robert M. & Crowe, Frederick E., eds. (Collected Works of Bernard Lonergan: No. 10). 304p. 1993. 60.00 (0-8020-3440-3); pap. 24.95 (0-8020-3441-1) U of Toronto Pr.

— Understanding & Being. Crowe, Frederick E. & Doran, Robert M., eds. (Collected Works of Bernard Lonergan: Vol. 5). 476p. 1990. 60.00 (0-8020-3987-1); pap. 19.95 (0-8020-3989-8) U of Toronto Pr.

Lonergan, Bernard J. Collected Works of Bernard J. Lonergan. Crowe, Frederick E. & Doran, Robert M., eds. 349p. 1988. 37.50 (0-8020-3438-1) U of Toronto Pr.

— Insight: A Study of Human Understanding. LC 77-20441. 1978. pap. text ed. 26.00 (0-06-065269-1, RD 251) Harper SF.

Lonergan, Bernard J. F. Understanding & Being: An Introduction & Companion to Insight. Morelli, Elizabeth A. & Morelli, Mark D., eds. (Toronto Studies in Theology: Vol. 5). xii, 368p. 1980. lib. bdg. 99.95 (0-88946-909-1) E Mellen.

Lonergan, Carroll V. Brave Boys of Old Fort Ticonderoga. LC 87-22144. 192p. (YA). (gr. 6 up). 1987. write for info. (0-932334-57-1, Empire State Bks); pap. 7.95 (1-55787-018-7, NY16028, Empire State Bks) Hrt of the Lakes.

Lonergan, Elaine. The Sea's Many Color. (Shamu's Little Library). (Illus.). 12p. (J). (ps-00). 1994. 5.95 (1-884506-01-1) Third Story.

— Sir Winston Walrus & the Great Rescue. (Shamu & His Crew Adventure Ser.). (Illus.). 32p. (J). (gr. k-3). 1994. 5.95 (1-884506-06-2) Third Story.

Lonergan, Elaine C. Group Intervention: How to Begin & Maintain Groups in Medical & Psychiatric Settings. LC 81-66759. 328p. 1989. reprint ed. 40.00x (0-87668-887-3) Aronson.

Lonergan, Jack. Video in Language Teaching. (New Directions in Language Teaching Ser.). (Illus.). 160p. 1984. pap. 14.95 (0-521-27263-7) Cambridge U Pr.

Lonergan, Joan P. Unlocking Your Potential: A Handbook for Personal Growth. (Illus.). 72p. 1993. student ed 9.95 (1-884168-00-0) Chameleon Pub.

Lonergan, Leonard. The Iron Road. LC 81-51173. 68p. (Orig.). 1981. pap. 6.00 (0-912292-66-0) The Smith.

Lonergan, Mark. Rock Guitar Handbook. 1993. 4.95 (0-685-64041-8, 94173); audio 9.98 (0-685-64042-6, 94173); audio 13.95 (0-685-64043-4, 94173) Mel Bay.

— Rock Studies for Guitar: Rock Lines. 1993. 4.95 (0-685-64020-5, 94172); audio 9.98 (0-685-64021-3, 94172); audio 13.95 (0-685-64022-1, 94172) Mel Bay.

Lonergan, Mark, jt. auth. see Bay, William.

***Lonergan, Stephen & Brooks, David.** Watershed - Role of Fresh Water in Israeli-Palestinian Conflict. 220p. 1994. pap. 19.50 (0-88936-719-1, IDRC7191, Pub. by IDRC CN) UNIPUB.

Lonero, Peter. For Love & Duty. LC 93-93769. 176p. 1994. pap. 9.95 (1-56002-299-X, Univ Edtns) Aegina Pr.

Lones, T. East, ed. see Wright, A. R.

Lonetto, Richard. Children's Conceptions of Death. LC 79-24334. (Death & Suicide Ser.: Vol. 3). (Illus.). 238p. 1980. 27.95 (0-8261-2550-6) Springer Pub.

Loney, Glenn, ed. California Gold-Rush Plays. LC 83-61191. Orig. Title: American Pioneer Drama. 1983. 34.00 (0-933826-34-6); pap. 12.95 (0-933826-35-4) PAJ Pubns.

— Staging Shakespeare. 1990. 52.00 (0-8240-6613-8, 798) Garland.

Loney, Glenn & Boswell, William. Creating Careers in Music Theatre. 294p. (C). 1988. text ed. 39.00 (0-8204-0545-0) P Lang Pubs.

Loney, Glenn M., ed. The House of Mirth: The Play of the Novel. LC 78-75192. 184p. 1970. 29.50 (0-8386-2416-2) Fairleigh Dickinson.

— Musical Theatre in America: Papers & Proceedings of the Conference on the Musical Theatre in America. LC 83-8913. (Contributions in Drama & Theatre Studies: No. 8). (Illus.). xxi, 441p. 1984. text ed. 55.00 (0-313-23524-4, LMT/) Greenwood.

Loney, Jan, ed. The Young Hyperactive Child: Answers to Questions about Diagnosis, Prognosis & Treatment. LC 87-178. (Journal of Children in Contemporary Society Ser.: Vol. 19, Nos. 1-2). 178p. (Orig.). 1987. text ed. 49.95 (0-86656-670-8) Haworth Pr.

Loney, Kevin. Oracle DBA Handbook. 1994. pap. text ed. 34.95 (0-07-881182-1) McGraw.

Loney, Martin, et al, eds. Social Policy & Social Welfare. 352p. 1983. pap. 27.00 (0-335-10408-8, Open Univ Pr) Taylor & Francis.

— The State or the Market: Politics & Welfare in Contemporary Britain. 288p. (C). 1987. text ed. 35.00 (0-8039-8104-X); pap. text ed. 16.50 (0-8039-8105-8) Sage.

Loney, Robert A., jt. auth. see Himmelberg, Glen R.

***Long.** Atlas of Historical County Boundaries: Missouri. 1997. 60.00 (0-13-366428-7) S&S Trade.

— Atlas of Operative Neurosurgical Technique, Vol. 1. (Illus.). 390p. 1989. 240.00 (0-683-05148-2) Williams & Wilkins.

— Current Therapy in Neurological Surgery, Vol. 2. 2nd ed. 755p. (C). 1989. 61.00 (1-55664-022-6) Mosby Yr Bk.

— Current Therapy in Neurosurgery. 3rd ed. Date not set. 69.00 (1-55664-348-9) Mosby Yr Bk.

— De Paseo. (College Spanish Ser.). 1995. pap. 124.95 (0-8384-2583-6) Heinle & Heinle.

— Fetal & Neonatal Cardiology. (Illus.). 902p. 1989. text ed. 250.00 (0-7216-1887-1) Saunders.

— Medical-Surgical Nursing, No. 3. 3rd ed. 1992. 66.95 (0-8016-7416-6) Mosby Yr Bk.

— Medical-Surgical Nursing, No. 3: Student Learning Guide. 193p. 1992. pap. 12.95 (0-8016-7417-4) Mosby Yr Bk.

— Self-Assessment Picture Tests in Veterinary Medicine: Small Animal. (Illus.). 198p. 1992. pap. 26.50 (0-7234-1745-8) Mosby Yr Bk.

— Transmission: Communication Skills for Technicians. (Illus.). 1980. teacher ed write for info. (0-8359-7818-4, Reston) P-H.

Long & Doucet. French-Russian - Russian-French Dictionary of Legal & Economic Terms. 848p. 1984. pap. 72.50 (2-85608-019-7) IBD Ltd.

Long & Macian. A Concernos! 1992. pap. 29.95 (0-8384-2344-2); audio write for info. (0-318-69351-8) Heinle & Heinle.

— De Paseo. 1995. pap. 32.95 (0-8384-2585-2); pap. 27.95 (0-8384-2582-8) Heinle & Heinle.

Long & Phipps. Medical-Surgical Nursing: A Nursing Process Approach. 1600p. 1989. pap. 25.00 (0-8016-3230-7) Mosby Yr Bk.

Long & Prophit. Understanding-Responding. 2nd ed. (Nursing-Health Science Ser.). 1992. pap. text ed. 33.75 (0-86720-433-8) Jones & Bartlett.

Long, jt. auth. see Jacquot.

Long, ed. see Reich.

Long, et al. The World of CB Radio. rev. ed. LC 87-70878. (Illus.). 240p. 1987. pap. 11.95 (0-913990-53-1) Book Pub Co.

Long, A. A. Hellenistic Philosophy: Stoics, Epicureans, Sceptics. 2nd ed. 1986. pap. 16.00 (0-520-05808-9) U CA Pr.

Long, A. A. & Sedley, D. N. The Hellenistic Philosophers, Vol. 1: Translations of the Principal Sources, with Philosophical Commentary. (Illus.). 544p. 1987. 89.95 (0-521-25561-9); pap. 32.95 (0-521-27556-3) Cambridge U Pr.

— The Hellenistic Philosophers, Vol. 2: Greek & Latin Texts with Notes & Bibliography. (C). 1989. pap. 34.95 (0-521-27557-1) Cambridge U Pr.

Long, A. A., jt. ed. see Dillon, J. M.

Long, A. J., jt. auth. see Wege, D. C.

***Long, A. L.** Personal Memoirs of Robert E. Lee. 1994. 19.99 (0-517-10333-8) Random Hse Value.

Long, A. R., jt. ed. see Davies, J. H.

Long, Ada, tr. see Fuertes, Gloria.

Long, Al, ed. The Big Scam - Religion. 1994. 12.95 (0-533-10820-9) Vantage.

Long, Alice M., ed. Marriage Records of Hancock County, Maine Prior to 1892. LC 91-67682. 576p. 1992. 45.00 (0-929539-55-9) Picton Pr.

— Marriage Returns of Washington County, Maine, Prior to 1892. 128p. 1993. 22.50 (0-89725-140-7) Picton Pr.

Long, Alice M., jt. ed. see Gray, Ruth.

Long, Alton, jt. auth. see Martell, Alan R.

Long, Andrew, ed. see Dobson, Austin.

Long, Andrew F. Research into Health & Illness: Issues in Design, Analysis & Practice. LC 84-18791. 204p. 1984. text ed. 49.50 (0-566-00755-X) Ashgate Pub Co.

Long, Andrew F. & Lubben-Dunkelaar, Marrianne. Population: Theory & Policy: A Teaching Module for Those Working Towards Public Health. 120p. 1992. 89.95 (1-85742-097-7, Pub. by Ashgate UK) Ashgate Pub Co.

Long, Andrew F., et al, eds. Health Manpower: Planning, Production & Management. 300p. 1987. lib. bdg. 49.50 (0-7099-4172-2, Pub. by Croom Helm UK) Routledge Chapman & Hall.

Long, Andrew S. The Financial Responsibilities of Nonprofit Boards. No. 38. 32p. (Orig.). (C). 1993. pap. text ed. 22.00 (0-925299-25-1) Natl Ctr Nonprofit.

Long, Ann, jt. ed. see Long, Norman.

Long, Anne. The Windwalker: A Happening in the Smokies. 192p. (Orig.). 1991. pap. 7.95 (0-925591-19-X) Covenant Hse Bks.

Long, Anthony, et al, eds. Governments in Conflict? Provinces & Indian Nations in Canada. 304p. (C). 1988. text ed. 40.00 (0-8020-5779-9); pap. 19.95 (0-8020-6690-9) U of Toronto Pr.

***Long Ashton Research Station Staff.** Ecology & Integrated Farming Systems: Proceedings of the 13th Long Ashton International Symposium. Glen, D. M. et al, eds. 1995. text ed. 95.00 (0-471-95534-5) Wiley.

Long, Asphodel P. In a Chariot Drawn by Lions: The Search for the Female in Deity. 220p. 1993. pap. 10.95 (0-89594-575-4) Crossing Pr.

Long, Augustus W., jt. auth. see Parrott, Thomas M.

Long, B. J. Naval Fighters, No. 23: Convair XF24-1 & YF24-1 Seadart. (Illus.). 74p. 1993. pap. 13.95 (0-942612-23-X) Naval Fighters.

Long, Barbara B. Des Moines & Polk County: Flag on the Prairie. 136p. 1988. 29.95 (0-89781-273-5, 5175) Preferred Mktg.

Long, Barbara C. Medical-Surgical Nursing: A Nursing Process Approach. 3rd ed. 1695p. 1992. 61.95 (0-8016-6672-4) Mosby Yr Bk.

Long, Bill, jt. auth. see Carney, Glandion.

Long, Bill, jt. auth. see Jageman, Larry W.

Long, Bob. Fishing the Queen Charlotte Islands. (Illus.). 127p. (Orig.). 1989. pap. 8.95 (0-9693727-0-1) Gordon Soules Bk.

Long, Bob, ed. The Genesis of Power Chess: Effective Winning Technique for Strategy & Tactics by Leslie Ault, National Master. 352p. 1993. pap. 25.95 (0-938650-50-5) Thinkers Pr.

Long, Bob, ed. see Gordon, Stephen W.

Long, Bonita C. & Kahn, Sharon E., eds. Women, Work, & Coping: A Multidisciplinary Approach to Workplace Stress. 368p. 1993. 49.95 (0-7735-1128-8, Pub. by McGill CN); pap. 17.95 (0-7735-1129-6, Pub. by McGill CN) U of Toronto Pr.

Long, Brian. Borland Pascal Solver. 1994. disk, pap. 34.95 (0-201-59383-1) Addison-Wesley.

Long, Brian, jt. auth. see Reck, Ross R.

Long, Brian G., jt. auth. see Reck, Ross R.

Long, Bruce. William Desmond Taylor: A Dossier. LC 91-32607. (Filmmakers Ser.: No. 28). (Illus.). 471p. 1991. 47.50 (0-8108-2490-6) Scarecrow.

Long, Bruce W. & Rafert, John A. Orthopaedic Radiography. LC 94-14941. (Illus.). 560p. 1994. text ed. 65.00 (0-7216-6649-3) Saunders.

Long, Burke O. First Kings, with an Introduction to Historical Literature, 24 Vols., Vol. 9. Knierim, Rolf & Tucker, Gene, eds. (Forms of the Old Testament Literature Ser.). 288p. (Orig.). 1984. pap. 24.99 (0-8028-1920-6) Eerdmans.

— The Problem of Etiological Narrative in the Old Testament. (Beiheft 108 zur Zeitschrift fuer die Alttestamentliche Wissenschaft Ser.). (C). 1968. 33.85 (3-11-005590-2) De Gruyter.

— Second Kings. (Forms of the Old Testament Literature Ser.). xiv, 324p. 1991. pap. 24.99 (0-8028-0535-3) Eerdmans.

Long, C., et al. The Second Hand Price Guide, 1990-91. (Illus.). 200p. 1990. pap. 9.95 (0-929091-14-0, Pub. by Camden Hse CN) Firefly Bks Ltd.

Long, C. J., jt. ed. see Williams, J. Mark.

Long, C. J., et al. Behind Bars: Bar Coding Principles & Applications. LC 89-3167. (Illus.). 280p. 1989. 49.95 (0-945456-03-4) PT Pubns.

Long, C. J., et al, eds. Handbook of Head Trauma: Acute Care to Recovery. (Critical Issues in Neuropsychology Ser.). (Illus.). 426p. 1992. 75.00 (0-306-43947-6, Plenum Pr) Plenum.

Long, C. Michael. Understanding Census Data: A Quick & Simplified Reference. 71p. reprint ed. 25.00 (0-685-44383-3) West Econ Rsch.

Long, C. Thomas & Vartanian, Thomas P. Thrift Financing Devices. 246p. write for info. (0-318-60936-3) HarBrace.

***Long, Calvin T.** Elementary Introduction to Number Theory. 3rd ed. (Illus.). 292p. (C). 1995. text ed. 39.95x (0-88133-836-2) Waveland Pr.

Long, Calvin T. & DeTemple, Duane W. Mathematical Reasoning for Elementary Teachers. LC 94-20863. (C). 1994. 58.50 (0-673-46483-0) HarpCollege.

Long, Carlton. From the Gary Convention to the Present (1972-) (Milestones in Black American History Ser.). (Illus.). 1994. 18.95 (0-685-65667-5, Am Art Analog) Chelsea Hse.

Long, Cathryn J. Middle East in Search of Peace. LC 93-42274. (Headlines Ser.). (Illus.). 64p. (J). (gr. 5-8). 1994. lib. bdg. 15.90 (1-56294-510-6) Millbrook Pr.

Long, Charles. The Backyard Stonebuilder: Stonebuilding Projects for the Weekend Mason. (Illus.). 160p. (Orig.). 1991. pap. 14.95 (0-920197-19-1, Pub. by Warwick Pub CN) Firefly Bks Ltd.

— How to Survive Without a Salary: Living the Conserver Lifestyle. (Illus.). 232p. 1992. pap. 12.95 (1-895629-02-0, Pub. by Warwick Pub CN) Firefly Bks Ltd.

— Life after the City: A Harrowsmith Guide to Rural Living. 208p. 1989. pap. 12.95 (0-920656-14-5, Pub. by Camden Hse CN) Firefly Bks Ltd.

— Undefended Borders. 256p. 1995. pap. 14.95 (1-895629-46-2, Pub. by Warwick Pub CN) Firefly Bks Ltd.

Long, Charles, jt. ed. see Sbordone, Robert J.

Long, Charles E. Discovering the Universe. (C). 1990. 80.00 (0-06-364038-4) HarpCollege.

Long, Charles E., ed. see Symonds, Richard.

Long, Charles H. Alpha: The Myths of Creation. LC 82-21532. (American Academy of Religion, Classics in Religious Studies). 320p. (C). 1983. reprint ed. 20.95 (0-89130-604-8, 01-05-04) Scholars Pr GA.

— Significations: Signs, Symbols & Images in the Interpretation of Religion. LC 85-45495. 208p. 1986. pap. 15.00 (0-8006-1892-0, 1-1892, Fortress Pr) Augsburg Fortress.

Long, Charles H., ed. see Allen, Roland.

Long, Charles H., et al. Who Are the Anglicans? 88p. (Orig.). 1988. pap. 2.75 (0-88028-080-8, 940) Forward Movement.

Long, Charles J., jt. ed. see Williams, J. Michael.

Long, Charles K. Stonebuilder's Primer: A Harrowsmith Step-by-Step Guide for Owner-Builders. (Illus.). 126p. (Orig.). 1981. pap. 11.95 (0-920656-20-X, Pub. by Camden Hse CN) Firefly Bks Ltd.

***Long, Charlie.** To Vietnam with Love: The Story of Charlie & E. G. Long. (Jaffray Collection of Missionary Portraits: Bk. 12). 204p. 1995. pap. 7.99 (0-87509-582-8) Chr Pubns.

Long, Charlotte J. Until Tomorrow. 48p. (Orig.). 1983. pap. 3.95 (0-88100-036-1) Marsh Creek.

Long, Cheryl. How to Make Danish Fruit Liqueurs. Fischborn, Cynthia, ed. 80p. 1984. 5.95 (0-914667-03-3) Culinary Arts Ltd.

Long, Cheryl, ed. The Best of Scanfest: An Authentic Treasury of Scandinavian Recipes & Proverbs. 1992. pap. 14.95 (0-914667-13-0) Culinary Arts Ltd.

— Lamb Country Cooking: Lamb with All the Trimmings. LC 94-31657. (Illus.). 128p. (Orig.). 1995. pap. 10.95 (0-914667-16-5) Culinary Arts Ltd.

Long, Cheryl & Kibbey, Heather. Classic Liqueurs: The Art of Making & Cooking with Liqueurs. LC 90-37387. 128p. (Orig.). 1990. pap. 8.95 (0-914667-11-4) Culinary Arts Ltd.

Long, Cheryl, jt. auth. see Fischborn, Cynthia.

Long, Cheryl, jt. auth. see Kibbey, Heather.

Long, Cheryl, ed. see Sawyer, Helene.

Long, Chris. The Actuary in Practice, Tolley's. (C). 1989. 150.00 (0-685-33803-7, Pub. by Witherby & Co UK) St Mut.

***Long, Chris & Long, Yolanda.** You Can Have What You Say: It Works It Really Works. 78p. (Orig.). 1995. pap. write for info. (1-885591-85-3) Morris Pubng.

Long, Cindy, jt. auth. see Long, Steve.

Long, Clarence D. The Labor Force in War & Transition: Four Countries. (Occasional Papers: No. 36). 70p. 1952. reprint ed. 20.00 (0-87014-351-4) Natl Bur Econ Res.

— The Labor Force in Wartime America. (Occasional Papers: No. 14). 76p. 1944. reprint ed. 20.00 (0-87014-329-8); reprint ed. mic. film 20.00 (0-685-61250-3) Natl Bur Econ Res.

— The Labor Force under Changing Income & Employment. (General Ser.: No. 65). 464p. 1958. reprint ed. 120.70 (0-87014-064-7); reprint ed. mic. film 40.40 (0-685-61316-X) Natl Bur Econ Res.

— Wages & Earnings in the United States, 1860-1890. LC 75-19725. (National Bureau of Economic Research Ser.). (Illus.). 1975. reprint ed. 18.95 (0-405-07603-7) Ayer.

— Wages & Earnings in the United States, 1860-1890. (General Ser.: No. 67). 186p. 1960. reprint ed. 48.90 (0-87014-066-3); reprint ed. mic. film 24.50 (0-685-61323-2) Natl Bur Econ Res.

Long, Clarence D., jt. auth. see Mills, Frederick C.

Long, Claudia & Strader, Britt. Dogs. 192p. 1994. 19.95 (0-934429-73-1) Thunder Bay CA.

— Encyclopedia of Dogs. (Illus.). 112p. 1991. 12.99 (0-517-06517-7, Crescent) Random Hse Value.

Long, Cleta M. Across the Bridge. (Illus.). 101p. 1990. pap. 9.95 (0-9619468-2-2) McClain.

Long, Cloyd D. School-Leaving Youth & Employment: Some Factors Associated with the Duration of Early Employment of Youth Whose Formal Education Ended at High School Graduation or Earlier. LC 74-177006. (Columbia University. Teachers College. Contributions to Education Ser.: No. 845). reprint ed. 22.50 (0-404-55845-3) AMS Pr.

***Long, Courtney.** Dearest Brothers, Love Awaits, Much Peace, the Sisters: African American Women Talk about Sex, Love & Life. LC 94-22167. 1995. 21.95 (0-553-09702-4) Bantam.

Long, D. Law & Its Limitations in the GATT Multilateral Trade System. 1985. lib. bdg. 80.50 (90-247-3189-5) Kluwer Ac.

Long, D. A. Raman Spectroscopy. 1977. text ed. write for info. (0-07-038675-7) McGraw.

Long, D. A., jt. ed. see Clark, R. J.

Long, D. G. Sedimentology & Coal Resources of the Early Oligocene Australian Creek Formation Near Quesnel, British Columbia. (GSC Paper Ser.: No. 92-11). 73p. (Orig.). 1993. pap. 10.70 (0-660-14551-0, Pub. by Canada Commun Grp CN) Accents Pubns.

Long, D. M. Surgery of Skull Base Tumors. (Contemporary Issues in Neurological Surgery Ser.). (Illus.). 288p. 1992. 85.00 (0-86542-090-4) Blackwell Sci.

Long, D. M., jt. ed. see Gildenberg, P. L.

Long, D. Stephen. Tragedy, Tradition, Transformism: The Ethics of Paul Ramsey. LC 93-29459. 221p. (C). 1993. text ed. 52.50 (0-8133-8747-7) Westview.

Long, Dana A., jt. auth. see Prufer, Olaf H.

Long, Dani L., ed. Canadian Life & Health Insurance Law: Student Guide. (FLMI Insurance Education Program Ser.). (Orig.). (C). 1992. pap. text ed. 17.00 (0-939921-31-6) LOMA.

Long, Dani L. & Morton, Gene A. Principes des Assurances de Personnes. 2nd ed. Basarich, Joel V., ed. (FLMI Insurance Education Program Ser.). 378p. (FRE.). 1989. text ed. 66.00 (0-939921-10-3) LOMA.

— Principles of Life & Health Insurance. 2nd ed. (FLMI Insurance Education Program Ser.). (Illus.). 378p. 1988. text ed. 26.00 (0-915322-96-X) LOMA.

Long, Daryl. Jazz for Beginners. 1994. pap. 11.00 (0-86316-165-0) Writers & Readers.

— Miles Davis for Beginners. (Illus.). 100p. (Orig.). 1992. 18.00 (0-86316-154-5); pap. 8.00 (0-86316-153-7) Writers & Readers.

***Long, David.** Blue Spruce. 1995. 22.00 (0-684-80033-0) S&S Trade.

— The Flood of 'Sixty-Four: Stories. 213p. (C). 1988. pap. 8.50 (0-88001-108-4) Ecco Pr.

— The Flood of '64: Stories. 250p. 1987. 16.95 (0-88001-127-0) Ecco Pr.

— Gold Braid & Foreign Relations: Diplomatic Activities of U. S. Naval Officers, 1798-1883. LC 87-34879. (Illus.). 448p. 1988. 39.95 (0-87021-228-1) Naval Inst Pr.

— The Hajj Today: A Survey of the Contemporary Pilgrimage to Makkah. LC 78-7473. (Illus.). 180p. 1979. 49.50 (0-87395-382-7) State U NY Pr.

***Long, David & Noice, Marshall. Glacier: Images from the Crown of the Continent. (Illus.). 52p. (Orig.). 1995. pap. 24.95 (0-9645477-5-9) Whitefish Ed.**

Glacier National Park is one of the truly spectacular places in the United States. Photographer Marshall Noice has spent his life creating fine black-&-white images of the park. Until now, these images could only be appreciated in his Kalispell, Montana, gallery or through exhibits traveling around the Western U.S. Noice employs the highest quality large format photographic techniques & a grasp of the darkroom which places him among a handful of late 20th century masters of black-&-white technique. Each of the photos in this volume has been painstakingly reproduced using sheet fed printing on highest quality paper. The printing was personally supervised by the artist, who signed off on each tri-tone reproduction during printing. Anyone who follows black-&-white fine-art photography will find this book enthralling. Complementing the photography is an essay by well-known Montana writer David Long. Long's essay gives insight into Noice's art & craft & details some of the feelings Noice & Long share for Glacier National Park. This book can be ordered from: Whitefish Editions, P.O. Box 4763, Whitefish, MT 59937. Phone/FAX: 800-893-0963. The price is $24.95 available only in softbound. ISBN 0-9645477-5-9. Book is 52 pages.

Publisher Provided Annotation.

***Long, David & Wilson, Peter C.** Thinkers of the Twenty Years' Crisis: Inter-War Idealism Reassessed. 400p. 1995. 65.00 (0-19-827855-1) OUP.

An Asterisk (*) at the beginning of an entry indicates that the title is appearing in BIP for the first time.

Long, David, et al. Cross Country for Coaches & Runners. 90p. (Orig.). 1981. pap. 9.95 (*0-932741-97-5*) Championship Bks & Vid Prodns.

Long, David A., jt. ed. see Cole, Charles A.

Long, David E. Anatomy of Terrorism. 1990. text ed. 27.95 (*0-02-919345-1*) Free Pr.

— A Call to Manhood: In a Fatherless Society. LC 92-78464. 208p. 1994. pap. 9.99 (*1-56384-047-2*) Huntington Hse.

— The Jewel of Liberty: Abraham Lincoln's Re-election & the End of Slavery. (Illus.). 416p. 1994. 24.95 (*0-8117-0217-0*) Stackpole.

Long, David E., ed. see Reich, Bernard.

Long, David E., jt. auth. see Shaw, John A.

Long, David F. A Documentary History of U. S. Foreign Relations: From Seventeen Sixty to the Mid-Eighteen Nineties, Selections from Ruhl J. Bartlett's "The Record of American Diplomacy", Vol. I. LC 79-5349. 132p. 1980. pap. text ed. 19.50 (*0-8191-1038-8*) U Pr of Amer.

— Mad Jack: The Biography of Captain John Percival, USN, 1779-1862. LC 92-31763. (Contributions in Military Studies: No. 136). 288p. 1993. text ed. 57.95 (*0-313-28567-5*, LMJ, Greenwood Pr) Greenwood.

— Ready to Hazard: A Biography of Commodore William Bainbridge, 1774-1833. LC 80-29146. 359p. reprint ed. pap. 102.40 (*0-317-30023-7*, 2025021) Bks Demand.

— Sailor-Diplomat: A Biography of Commodore James Biddle, 1783-1848. LC 82-22236. (Illus.). 328p. 1983. 40.00 (*0-930350-39-1*) NE U Pr.

Long, David M. How to Tell the Future. Mortimer, Pamela, ed. 26p. (Orig.). 1993. pap. text ed. write for info. (*0-9632399-1-0*) Premier PA.

Long, Dean, jt. auth. see Frazier, Mary.

Long, Dean, jt. auth. see Long, Mary.

***Long, Deborah H.** Doing the Right Thing: A Real Estate Practitioner's Guide to Ethical Decision Making. LC 94-41398. 144p. 1995. per. 15.00 (*0-89787-939-2*) Gorsuch Scarisbrick.

— Florida Real Estate Post Licensing. (Illus.). 224p. 1995. pap. text ed. write for info. (*0-614-03566-X*) Gorsuch Scarisbrick.

Long, Dennis. Island Style. (Illus.). 128p. (Orig.). 1992. pap. 7.95 (*1-880188-22-8*) Bess Pr.

Long, Derek & Garigliano, Roberto. Reasoning by Analogy & Causality: A Model & Application. LC 93-44284. (Ellis Horwood Series in Artificial Intelligence). 1993. 69.86 (*0-13-690132-8*, Tavistock-E Horwood) Routledge Chapman & Hall.

Long, Diana E. & Golden, Janet, eds. The American General Hospital: Communities & Social Contexts. LC 89-7264. (Illus.). 216p. 1989. 36.00 (*0-8014-2349-X*); pap. 14.95 (*0-8014-9604-7*) Cornell U Pr.

***Long, DJ.** I Wish I Was the Baby. LC 94-40664. (Illus.). 32p. (J). (ps-2). 1995. 9.95 (*1-57102-035-7*, Ideals Child) Hambleton-Hill.

Long, Don L., et al. Introduction to Agribusiness Management. Lee, Jasper S., ed. (Career Preparation for Agriculture-Agribusiness Ser.). 1979. text ed. 15.96 (*0-07-038665-X*) McGraw.

Long, Donlin M. Brain Edema: Pathogenesis, Imaging, & Therapy. (Advances in Neurology Ser.: Vol. 52). 640p. 1990. 149.00 (*0-88167-625-X*) Raven.

Long, Donlin M. & McAfee, Paul C. Atlas of Spinal Surgery. (Illus.). 464p. 1992. 180.00 (*0-683-05149-0*) Williams & Wilkins.

Long, Donlin M., jt. ed. see Hopkins, Leo N.

Long, Donna A., ed. see Holmes, Janet.

***Long, Donna J., et al, eds.** Isle of Flowers: Poems by Florida Individual Artists Fellows. 200p. (Orig.). (C). 1995. pap. 15.95 (*0-938078-39-9*) Anhinga Pr.

Long, Doris E. Unfair Competition & Section 43(a) of the Lanham Act. LC 93-3995. 540p. 1993. 95.00 (*0-87179-785-2*) BNA.

Long, Dorothy R., jt. auth. see Long, Ralph B.

Long, Doucet. Dictionnaire Juridique et Economique: Russian - French, French - Russian. 1984. lib. bdg. 175.00 (*0-8288-2492-4*) Fr & Eur.

Long Doucet. Russian-French, French-Russian Legal & Economic Dictionary: Dictionnaire Juridique et Economique Russe-Francais-Russe. 844p. (FRE & RUS.). 1984. 175.00 (*0-8288-0402-8*, F80) Fr & Eur.

Long, Douglas E., jt. auth. see Young, Carol D.

Long, Douglas G. Learner Managed Learning: The Key to Lifelong Learning & Development. LC 90-63784. 176p. 1991. text ed. 39.95 (*0-312-06088-2*) St Martin.

Long, Duncan. AK47: The Complete Kalashnikov Family of Assault Rifles. (Illus.). 192p. 1988. pap. 14.00 (*0-87364-477-8*) Paladin Pr.

— Antigrav Unlimited. 176p. 1988. pap. 2.95 (*0-380-75357-X*) Avon.

— AR-15 - M16 Super Systems. (Illus.). 144p. 1989. pap. 19.95 (*0-87364-511-1*) Paladin Pr.

— The AR-15-M16: A Practical Guide. LC 85-160984. (Illus.). 168p. 1985. pap. 16.95 (*0-87364-321-6*) Paladin Pr.

— AR-7 Super Systems. (Illus.). 144p. 1990. pap. 17.00 (*0-87364-573-1*) Paladin Pr.

— Assault Pistols, Rifles & Submachine Guns. 1987. pap. 12.95 (*0-8065-1042-0*, Citadel Pr) Carol Pub Group.

— Assault Pistols, Rifles & Submachine Guns. (Illus.). 152p. 1986. pap. 21.95 (*0-87364-353-4*) Paladin Pr.

— Automatics: Fast Firepower, Tactical Superiority. (Illus.). 144p. 1986. pap. 18.00 (*0-87364-397-6*) Paladin Pr.

— Avenging Storm. (Night Stalkers Ser.: No. 9). (Orig.). 1992. mass mkt. 3.99 (*0-06-100438-3*, Harp PBks) HarpC.

— Buddha's Crown. (Night Stalkers Ser.: No. 8). 1992. mass mkt. 3.99 (*0-06-100346-8*, Harp PBks) HarpC.

— Combat Ammo of the Twenty-First Century. (Illus.). 216p. 1991. 30.00 (*0-87364-628-2*) Paladin Pr.

— Combat Ammunition: Everything You Need to Know. 1987. pap. 12.95 (*0-8065-1043-9*, Citadel Pr) Carol Pub Group.

— Combat Rifles of the Twenty-First Century: Futuristic Firearms for Tomorrow's Battlefields. (Illus.). 88p. 1990. pap. 15.00 (*0-87364-585-5*) Paladin Pr.

— The Complete AR-15 - M16 Sourcebook. (Illus.). 1992. pap. 35.00 (*0-87364-687-8*) Paladin Pr.

— Defeating Industrial Spies. LC 91-61944. (Illus.). 144p. 1991. pap. 16.95 (*1-55950-073-5*, 55086) Loompanics.

— Desert Wind. 1991. mass mkt. 3.95 (*0-06-100139-2*, Harp PBks) HarpC.

— Hand Cannons: The World's Most Powerful Handguns. (Illus.). 208p. 1994. pap. 20.00 (*0-87364-809-9*) Paladin Pr.

— Homemade Ammo: How to Make It, How to Reload It, How to Cache It. (Illus.). 96p. 1995. pap. 14.00 (*0-87364-816-1*) Paladin Pr.

— How to Survive a Nuclear Accident. LC 87-81612. (Illus.). 160p. (Orig.). 1987. pap. 10.95 (*0-915179-67-9*, 11095) Loompanics.

— Making Your AR-15 into a Legal Pistol. (Illus.). 88p. 1991. 14.00 (*0-87364-622-3*) Paladin Pr.

— The Mini-14: The Plinker, Hunter, Assault, & Everything Else Rifle. (Illus.). 120p. 1987. pap. 12.00 (*0-87364-407-7*) Paladin Pr.

— Mini-14 Super Systems. (Illus.). 200p. 1991. pap. 16.95 (*0-87364-589-8*) Paladin Pr.

— Modern Ballistic Armor: Clothing, Bomb Blankets, Shields, Vehicle Protection... Everything You Need to Know. (Illus.). 104p. 1986. pap. 12.00 (*0-87364-391-7*) Paladin Pr.

— Modern Camouflage. 2nd rev. ed. LC 91-73266. (Illus.). 80p. 1992. pap. text ed. 8.95 (*0-939427-65-6*) Alpha Pubns OH.

— Modern Combat Blades. (Illus.). 128p. 1992. text ed. 25.00 (*0-87364-670-3*) Paladin Pr.

— Modern Sniper Rifles. (Illus.). 120p. 1988. pap. 16.95 (*0-87364-470-0*) Paladin Pr.

— Neptune Thunder. (Night Stalkers Ser.: No. 7). (Orig.). 1991. mass mkt. 3.99 (*0-06-100271-2*, Harp PBks) HarpC.

— Night Stalkers. 1990. mass mkt. 3.95 (*0-06-100061-2*, Harp PBks) HarpC.

— Night Stalkers: Twilight Justice. 1990. mass mkt. 3.95 (*0-06-100096-5*, Harp PBks) HarpC.

— Night Stalkers, No. 2: Grim Reaper. 1990. mass mkt. 3.95 (*0-06-100078-7*, Harp PBks) HarpC.

— Night Stalkers, No. 5: Sea Wolf. 1991. mass mkt. 3.95 (*0-06-100158-9*, Harp PBks) HarpC.

— Night Stalkers, No. 6: Shining Path. 1991. mass mkt. 3.95 (*0-06-100183-X*, Harp PBks) HarpC.

— The Poor Man's Fort Knox: Home Security with Inexpensive Safes. (Illus.). 48p. 1991. pap. 10.00 (*0-87364-645-2*) Paladin Pr.

— Powerhouse Pistols: The Colt 1911 & Browning Hi-Power Sourcebook. (Illus.). 152p. 1990. pap. 19.95 (*0-87364-542-1*) Paladin Pr.

— The Ruger .22 Automatic Pistol: Standard-Mark I-Mark II Series. (Illus.). 168p. 1988. pap. 12.00 (*0-87364-488-3*) Paladin Pr.

— Streetsweepers: The Complete Book of Combat Shotguns. (Illus.). 160p. 1987. pap. 17.95 (*0-87364-424-7*) Paladin Pr.

— The Sturm, Ruger 10-22 Rifle & .44 Magnum Carbine. (Illus.). 108p. 1988. pap. 12.00 (*0-87364-449-2*) Paladin Pr.

— Super Shotguns. (Illus.). 96p. 1992. pap. 18.00 (*0-87364-691-6*) Paladin Pr.

— Survival Bartering. LC 86-80537. 56p. 1986. pap. text ed. 6.95 (*0-915179-37-7*) Loompanics.

— The Terrifying Three: Uzi, Ingram, & Intratec Weapons Families. (Illus.). 136p. 1989. pap. 20.00 (*0-87364-523-5*) Paladin Pr.

— To Break a Tyrant's Chains: Neo-Guerrilla Techniques for Combat. LC 91-70479. (Illus.). 152p. (Orig.). 1991. pap. 12.00 (*0-939427-91-5*, 09053) Alpha Pubns OH.

— You Can Be an Information Writer. LC 91-60974. 176p. (Orig.). 1991. pap. 16.95 (*1-55950-066-2*, 64112) Loompanics.

Long, Duncan, jt. auth. see Hoy, Michael.

Long, Dwight C. Europe in Modern Times, Guide & Outline. 1952. pap. 7.50 (*0-911586-20-2*) Wahr.

— Introduction to the Study of History & Outline of the Growth of Western Civilization from Its Beginnings to about 1648. 1951. pap. 7.50 (*0-911586-21-0*) Wahr.

Long, E., jt. auth. see Kuklick, H.

Long, E. B. The Civil War Day by Day: An Almanac 1861-1865. (Quality Paperbacks Ser.). (Illus.). xiv, 1135p. 1985. reprint ed. pap. 19.95 (*0-306-80255-4*) Da Capo.

— The Saints & the Union: Utah Territory During the Civil War. LC 80-16775. (Illus.). 326p. 1981. 27.50 (*0-252-00821-9*) U of Ill Pr.

Long, E. Croft, ed. see Arbona, Guillermo, et al.

Long, Earlene R. Gone Fishing. LC 83-22558. (Illus.). 32p. (J). (ps-3). 1987. pap. 4.95 (*0-395-44236-2*) HM.

Long, Earnest, jt. ed. see Long, Ida.

Long, Earnest A., ed. see Davidson, Al.

Long, Earnest A., jt. auth. see Long, Ernest A.

Long, Edward. History of Jamaica, 3 vols., Set. (Illus.). 1631p. 1970. reprint ed. 295.00 (*0-7146-1942-6*, Pub. by F Cass Pubs UK) Intl Spec Bk.

Long, Edward L., Jr. Higher Education As a Moral Enterprise. LC 92-13886. 224p. (Orig.). (C). 1992. pap. text ed. 25.00 (*0-87840-531-3*) Georgetown U Pr.

Long, Edward L. Peace Thinking in a Warring World. LC 83-14675. 118p. reprint ed. pap. 33.70 (*0-7837-2634-1*, 2042984) Bks Demand.

Long, Edward L., Jr. A Survey of Christian Ethics. 1982. pap. 17.95 (*0-19-503242-X*) OUP.

— A Survey of Recent Christian Ethics. 1982. pap. 15.95 (*0-19-503160-1*) OUP.

Long, Edward S. Two Nativity Dramas. 1984. 5.00 (*0-89536-697-5*, 4874) CSS OH.

Long, Elaine. Bittersweet Country. 1993. mass mkt. 4.99 (*0-312-92916-1*) St Martin.

Long, Eleanor R. Wilderness to Washington. LC 81-51895. 166p. 1981. reprint ed. pap. 7.95 (*0-89917-324-1*) Guild Pr IN.

Long, Elizabeth. The American Dream & the Popular Novel. 224p. 1985. 32.50 (*0-7100-9934-7*, RKP) Routledge.

— Ysabella de Trastamara - First Lady of the Renaissance: The Epic Reign of Queen Isabella of Spain. Douglas, Auriole, ed. 414p. 1992. 26.95 (*0-9631244-5-5*); pap. 16.95 (*0-9631244-6-3*) Alhamar Pub.

Long, Elizabeth, jt. auth. see Kuklick, Henrika.

Long, Elizabeth T., jt. comp. see Clark, Jewell T.

Long, Elliot. The Brothers Gant. large type ed. (Dales Western Ser.). 194p. 1992. pap. 16.95 (*1-85389-357-9*, Dales) Ulverscroft.

— Death on High Mesa. large type ed. (Linford Western Library). 224p. 1994. pap. 14.95 (*0-7089-7492-9*, Linford) Ulverscroft.

— Trail to Nemesis. large type ed. (Linford Western Large Pr. Ser.). 1994. pap. 14.95 (*0-7089-7642-5*) Ulverscroft.

— Wassala Valley Shootout. large type ed. (Linford Western Library). 224p. 1993. pap. 14.95 (*0-7089-7444-9*, Linford) Ulverscroft.

Long, Ernest A. & Long, Earnest A. Dictionary of Toys Sold in America, Vol. I. (Illus.). 83p. (Orig.). 1987. reprint ed. pap. 15.00 (*0-9604406-3-1*) Longs Americana.

Long, Eugene T. Existence, Being & God: An Introduction to the Philosophical Theology of John MacQuarrie. LC 84-16566. 124p. 1985. 17.95 (*0-913729-02-7*) Paragon Hse.

— Jaspers & Bultmann: A Dialogue Between Philosophy & Theology in the Existentialist Tradition. LC 68-31725. 165p. reprint ed. pap. 47.10 (*0-317-42165-4*, 2026208) Bks Demand.

Long, Eugene T., ed. Experience, Reason & God. LC 80-11334. (Studies in Philosophy & the History of Philosophy: No. 8). 186p. reprint ed. pap. 53.10 (*0-685-17831-5*, 2029499) Bks Demand.

— Prospects for a Natural Theology. LC 91-41756. (Studies in Philosophy & the History of Philosophy: Vol. 25). 242p. 1992. text ed. 51.95 (*0-8132-0755-X*) Cath U Pr.

Long, Evelyn. Grandma Tellmie about Ant, Wars Snake-Feeders, Blood-Drinking Bugs & Butterfly. Plott, Dave et al, eds. (Grandma Tellmie Bks.). 31p. (J). 1984. pap. 4.00 (*0-931881-00-5*) Collaborare Pub.

— Grandma Tellmie About...Big Deer, Little Deer ... Reindeer. Plott, Dave & Longmeyer, Carole M., eds. (Grandma Tellmie Bks.). 46p. (J). 1985. pap. 3.00 (*0-931881-01-3*) Collaborare Pub.

Long, F., ed. Ada Yearbook, 1992. 336p. 1992. 69.95 (*0-442-31581-3*) Chapman & Hall.

Long, F. A. & Schweitzer, Glenn E., eds. Risk Assessment at Hazardous Waste Sites. LC 82-16376. (Symposium Ser.: No. 204). 129p. 1982. lib. bdg. 38.95 (*0-8412-0747-X*) Am Chemical.

Long, F. W., ed. Software Engineering Environments: Proceedings of the International Workshop in Environments Chinon, France, September 18-20, 1989. (Lecture Notes in Computer Science Ser.: Vol. 467). vi, 313p. 1990. pap. 38.00 (*0-387-53452-0*) Spr-Verlag.

Long, Frank. Desirable Physical Facilities for an Activity Program. LC 78-177007. (Columbia University. Teachers College. Contributions to Education Ser.: No. 593). reprint ed. 22.50 (*0-404-55593-4*) AMS Pr.

— Restrictive Business Practices, Transnational Corporations & Development. (Dimensions of International Business Ser.). 192p. 1981. lib. bdg. 49.50 (*0-89838-057-X*) Kluwer Ac.

Long, Frank, ed. Economic Planning Studies. (International Studies in Economics & Econometrics: No. 8). 198p. 1980. pap. text ed. 36.50 (*90-277-1194-1*) Kluwer Ac.

— The Political Economy of EEC Relations with African, Caribbean & Pacific States: Contributions to the Understanding of the Lome Convention on North-South Relations. 192p. 1980. 83.00 (*0-08-024077-1*, Pub. by Pergamon Repr UK) Franklin.

— Ragnar Frisch: Economic Planning Studies. LC 75-44219. (International Studies in Economics & Econometrics: No. 8). 1975. lib. bdg. 70.00 (*90-277-0245-4*) Kluwer Ac.

Long, Frank B. Autobiographical Memoir. 35p. (Orig.). pap. 4.95 (*0-318-04708-X*) Necronomicon.

— In Mayan Splendor. LC 77-78595. (Illus.). 1977. 6.00 (*0-87054-080-7*) Arkham.

Long, Freda M. The Dressmaker. large type ed. 1990. 21.95 (*0-7089-2125-6*) Ulverscroft.

Long, G. Gilbert & Hentz, Forrest C. Problem Exercises for General Chemistry. 3rd ed. LC 86-13347. 464p. 1986. Net. pap. text ed. 18.00 (*0-471-82840-8*) Wiley.

Long, G. Gilbert, jt. auth. see Hentz, F. C., Jr.

Long, G. J., ed. Mossbauer Spectroscopy Applied to Inorganic Chemistry, Vol. 2. LC 84-13417. (Modern Inorganic Chemistry Ser.). (Illus.). 642p. 1987. 125.00 (*0-306-42507-6*, Plenum Pr) Plenum.

Long, G. J. & Grandjean, Fernande, eds. Mossbauer Spectroscopy Applied to Inorganic Chemistry, Vol. 3. (Modern Inorganic Chemistry Ser.). (Illus.). 598p. 1989. 125.00 (*0-306-43073-8*, Plenum Pr) Plenum.

Long, Gabrielle M. World's Wonder & Other Essays. (Essay Index Reprint Ser.). 1977. 23.95 (*0-8369-1223-3*) Ayer.

Long, Gary. Doctrine of Salvation, No. III. pap. 4.99 (*0-87377-066-8*) GAM Pubns.

— Doctrine of Salvation, Nos. I-II. pap. 3.99 (*0-87377-065-X*) GAM Pubns.

— This River the Muskoka. (Illus.). 184p. 35.00 (*1-55046-012-9*, Pub. by Boston Mills Pr CN) Genl Dist Srvs.

Long, Gary J., ed. Industrial Applications of the Mossbauer Effect. LC 86-22669. 806p. 1987. 135.00 (*0-306-42463-0*, Plenum Pr) Plenum.

— Mossbauer Spectroscopy Applied to Inorganic Chemistry, Vol. 1. LC 84-13417. (Modern Inorganic Chemistry Ser.). 686p. 1984. 125.00 (*0-306-41647-6*, Plenum Pr) Plenum.

Long, Gary J. & Grandjean, Fernande, eds. Mossbauer Spectroscopy Applied to Magnetism & Materials Science, Vol. 1. LC 93-14059. (Modern Inorganic Chemistry Ser.). 1993. 95.00 (*0-306-44447-X*, Plenum Pr) Plenum.

— Supermagnets, Hard Magnetic Materials. (C). 1991. lib. bdg. 220.00 (*0-7923-1092-6*) Kluwer Ac.

— The Time Domain in Surface & Structural Dynamics. (C). 1988. lib. bdg. 197.00 (*90-277-2688-4*) Kluwer Ac.

Long, George. The Folklore Calendar. LC 89-63255. (Illus.). 240p. 1990. reprint ed. lib. bdg. 38.00 (*1-55888-875-6*) Omnigraphics Inc.

— The Thoughts of Marcus Aurelius Antoninus. 195p. 1995. pap. 25.00 (*0-87556-785-1*) Saifer.

— A Treatise on the Law Relative to Sales of Personal Property. xvi, 288p. 1982. reprint ed. lib. bdg. 30.00 (*0-8377-2403-1*) Rothman.

Long, George, tr. The Meditations of Marcus Aurelius: A Practical Guide for Living in an Irrational World. 128p. (Orig.). 1993. pap. 7.50 (*0-380-72216-X*) Avon.

Long, George, tr. see Aurelius, Marcus.

Long, George F., III, jt. auth. see McKenney, Charles E.

Long, George R., comp. All the Words of Jesus. 510p. 1993. text ed. 9.95 (*1-56794-041-2*, C-2323) Star Bible.

Long, Greg. Examining the Earthlight Theory: The Yakima UFO Microcosm. (Illus.). 185p. (C). 1990. pap. text ed. 17.95 (*0-929343-57-3*) J A Hynek Ctr UFO.

Long, H. W. Sane Sex Life. 14.95 (*0-685-22094-X*) Wehman.

Long, Haniel. Cabeza de Vaca: His Relation of the Journey Florida to the Pacific 1528-1536. (Illus.). 40p. 1988. reprint ed. 60.00 (*0-942067-00-2*) Okeanos Pr.

— The Marvelous Adventure of Cabeza de Vaca. (Basket of Tolerance Ser.). (Illus.). 112p. (Orig.). 1992. pap. 11.95 (*0-918801-46-X*) Dawn Horse Pr.

— My Seasons. 2nd ed. Maguire, James H., ed. LC 77-72389. (Ahsahta Press Modern & Contemporary Poets of the West Ser.). 68p. 1977. pap. 6.95 (*0-916272-06-0*) Ahsahta Pr.

— Pinon Country. LC 86-4309. xiv, 327p. 1986. reprint ed. pap. 8.95 (*0-8032-7919-1*, Bison Books) U of Nebr Pr.

— Pittsburgh Memoranda. LC 90-33956. 88p. 1990. reprint ed. 14.95 (*0-8229-3657-7*) U of Pittsburgh Pr.

Long, Haniel, ed. see De Vaca, Cabeza.

Long, Harold & Wheeler, Allen. Counter-Attack: Isshinryu Self Defense for Men & Women. Condry, Steve, ed. (Illus.). 96p. 1983. pap. 5.95 (*0-89826-010-8*) Natl Paperback.

— Dynamics of Isshinryu Karate Black & Brown Belt, Bk. 3. Condry, Steve, ed. (Isshinryu Karate Ser.). (Illus.). 146p. (Orig.). 1980. pap. 6.95 (*0-89826-006-X*) Natl Paperback.

— Dynamics of Isshinryu Karate Blue & Green Belt, Bk. 2. Condry, Steve, ed. (Illus.). (Orig.). 1979. pap. 5.95 (*0-89826-004-3*) Natl Paperback.

— Dynamics of Isshinryu Karate Orange Belt, Bk. 1. Condry, Steve, ed. (Isshinryu Karate Ser.). (Illus.). 1978. pap. 6.95 (*0-89826-002-7*) Natl Paperback.

Long, Harold, et al. Who's Who in Isshinryu Karate. 110p. (Orig.). 1981. pap. 3.95 (*0-89826-007-8*) Natl Paperback.

Long, Harold S. Getting Started in the Illicit Drug Business. LC 88-81529. 88p. 1988. pap. 12.00 (*0-915179-81-4*, 85078) Loompanics.

— How to Collect Illegal Debts. LC 90-62065. 80p. (Orig.). 1990. pap. 8.95 (*1-55950-041-7*, 40067) Loompanics.

— Making Crime Pay. LC 88-81589. 88p. (Orig.). 1988. pap. text ed. 9.95 (*0-915179-83-0*) Loompanics.

— Successful Armed Robbery. LC 89-63706. 56p. (Orig.). 1990. pap. 8.00 (*1-55950-023-9*, 40065) Loompanics.

— Surviving in Prison. LC 90-62804. (Illus.). 136p. (Orig.). 1990. pap. 14.95 (*1-55950-044-1*, 40070) Loompanics.

Long, Harry, illus. In the Beginning. (Orig.). 1993. pap. 10.95 (*0-943383-07-2*) FirstHand Ltd.

Long, Harry, ed. see Allee, et al.

***Long, Hei.** Da Qiang Ji: Power Striking. (Illus.). 176p. 1994. pap. 15.00 (*0-87364-803-X*) Paladin Pr.

— Da Zhimingde: Striking Deadly Blows to Vital Organs. (Illus.). 200p. 1993. pap. 15.00 (*0-87364-700-9*) Paladin Pr.

— Danger Zones: Defending Yourself Against Surprise Attack. (Illus.). 128p. 1991. pap. 14.00 (*0-87364-590-1*) Paladin Pr.

— Dragons Touch: Weaknesses of the Human Anatomy. (Illus.). 184p. 1983. pap. 12.00 (*0-87364-271-6*) Paladin Pr.

— Iron Hand of the Dragon's Touch: Secrets of Breaking Power. (Illus.). 112p. 1987. pap. 12.00 (*0-87364-434-4*) Paladin Pr.

— Master's Death Touch: Unarmed Killing Techniques. (Illus.). 96p. 1990. pap. 12.00 (*0-87364-543-X*) Paladin Pr.

— Master's Guide to Basic Self-Defense: Progressive Retraining of the Reflexive Response. (Illus.). 124p. 1990. pap. 14.00 (*0-87364-574-X*) Paladin Pr.

***Long, Helen V.** Dotchka. 290p. Date not set. pap. 8.95 (*0-7610-0301-0*) NW Pub.

Long, Hollis M. Public Secondary Education for Negroes in North Carolina. LC 71-177008. (Columbia University. Teachers College. Contributions to Education Ser.: No. 529). reprint ed. 22.50 (*0-404-55529-2*) AMS Pr.

Long, Howard. Kingsport: A Romance of Industry. (Illus.). 218p. 1993. reprint ed. 21.95 (*0-932807-89-5*) Overmountain Pr.

Long, Howard R., ed. Main Street Militants: An Anthology from "Grassroots Editor" LC 78-16336. (Arcturus Books Paperbacks). 178p. 1979. reprint ed. pap. 6.95 (*0-8093-0894-0*) S Ill U Pr.

Long, Howard R., jt. auth. see Lawhorne, Clifton O.

Long, Hua. The Moon Maiden & Other Asian Folktales. (Illus.). 32p. (J). 1993. 12.95 (*0-8351-2494-0*); pap. 8.95 (*0-8351-2493-2*) China Bks.

Long, Huey. My First Days in the White House. 1992. lib. bdg. 88.95 (*0-8490-5514-8*) Gordon Pr.

Long, Huey B. Adult Education in Church & Synagogue. LC 73-13292. (Occasional Papers: No. 37). 1973. pap. 2.50 (*0-87060-061-3*, OCP 37) Syracuse U Cont Ed.

— Adult Learning. 367p. 1988. text ed. 25.00 (*0-8428-2202-X*) Cambridge Bk.

— Continuing Education of Adults in Colonial America. LC 75-38925. (Occasional Papers: No. 45). 75p. 1976. pap. text ed. 2.75 (*0-87060-070-2*, OCP 45) Syracuse U Cont Ed.

— Early Innovators in Adult Education. (Theory & Practice of Adult Education in North America Ser.). 224p. 1991. 49.95 (*0-415-00557-4*, A5451) Routledge.

Long, Huey B. & Reddy, Terrence R. Self-Directed Learning Dissertation Abstracts 1966-1991. 1991. pap. 19.95 (*0-9622488-4-3*) U OK PMC.

Long, Huey B., et al. Advances in Research & Practice in Self-Directed Learning. 295p. (Orig.). (C). 1990. pap. 19.95 (*0-9622488-2-7*) U OK PMC.

— Changing Approaches to Studying Adult Education. LC 78-62579. (Jossey-Bass Series in Higher Education). 174p. reprint ed. pap. 49.60 (*0-7837-2520-5*, 2042679) Bks Demand.

— Self-Directed Learning: Consensus & Conflict. 300p. (Orig.). (C). 1991. pap. 19.95 (*0-9622488-3-5*) U OK PMC.

Long, Huey P. My First Days in the White House. LC 70-171695. (FDR & the Era of the New Deal Ser.). (Illus.). 146p. 1972. reprint ed. lib. bdg. 19.50 (*0-306-70383-1*) Da Capo.

Long, Hugh W., ed. Confronting the Budget & Trade Deficits. LC 86-8077. (ITT Key Issues Lecture Ser.). 99p. 1986. pap. 15.00 (*0-86569-144-4*, R144, Auburn Hse) Greenwood.

Long, Ida & Long, Earnest, eds. Dictionary of Toys in America, Vol. II. (Illus.). 72p. 1987. reprint ed. pap. 15.00 (*0-9604406-4-X*) Longs Americana.

Long, Ida, ed. see Davidson, Al.

Long, Inez. Faces among the Faithful. LC 62-5029. 194p. reprint ed. pap. 55.30 (*0-317-28388-X*, 2022414) Bks Demand.

Long Island Library Resources Council Committee on Government Information Staff. A Directory of Government Documents Collections in Nassau & Suffolk Counties, New York. 3rd ed. 1992. pap. 16.50 (*0-938435-33-7*) LI Lib Resources.

Long, J., ed. Consumer Know-How. 64p. (Orig.). 1988. pap. text ed. write for info. (*0-8428-7408-9*) Cambridge Bk.

— Job Success Know-How. 64p. (Orig.). 1988. pap. text ed. 2.70 (*0-8428-7407-0*) Cambridge Bk.

— Money Know-How. 64p. (Orig.). 1988. pap. text ed. write for info. (*0-8428-7411-9*) Cambridge Bk.

Long, J. & Whitefield, A., eds. Cognitive Ergonomics & Human Computer Interaction. (Cambridge Series on Human-Computer Interaction: No. 1). 250p. (C). 1989. 64.95 (*0-521-37179-1*) Cambridge U Pr.

Long, J., tr. see Raspe, G., ed.

Long, J. Anthony, jt. ed. see Boldt, Menno.

Long, J. B., ed. Judaism & the Christian Seminary Curriculum. 166p. pap. 2.95 (*0-686-95180-8*) ADL.

Long, J. L., jt. auth. see Oberst, B. B.

Long, J. P., jt. ed. see Gerald, M. C.

Long, J. S., jt. ed. see Myers, Raymond R.

Long, J. Scott. Common Problems - Proper Solutions: Avoiding Error in Quantitative Research. (Focus Editions Ser.: Vol. 94). 360p. 1988. 49.95 (*0-8039-2806-8*); pap. 24.95 (*0-8039-2807-6*) Sage.

— Confirmatory Factor Analysis. (Quantitative Applications in the Social Sciences Ser.: Vol. 33). 88p. 1983. pap. text ed. 9.95 (*0-8039-2044-X*) Sage.

— Covariance Structure Models. LC 83-50602. (University Papers: Vol. 34). 95p. 1983. pap. text ed. 9.95 (*0-8039-2045-8*) Sage.

Long, J. Scott, jt. ed. see Bollen, Kenneth A.

Long, J. Scott, jt. ed. see Fox, John.

Long, Jacqueline, jt. auth. see Cameron, Alan.

Long, James. What Is Man? Leader's Guide. Chao, Lorna Y., tr. (Basic Doctrine Ser.). 1986. pap. write for info. (*0-941598-36-5*) Living Spring Pubns.

— Why Is God Silent When We Need Him the Most? 256p. 1994. 14.99 (*0-310-58750-6*) Zondervan.

Long, James, jt. auth. see Harding, Steven.

Long, James, jt. auth. see Williams, Robert.

Long, James A. Expanding Horizons. LC 65-24093. 254p. 1990. pap. 7.00 (*0-911500-75-8*); audio 24.00 (*0-911500-49-9*) Theos U Pr.

— Expanding Horizons. LC 65-24093. 254p. 1990. reprint ed. 12.00 (*0-911500-87-1*) Theos U Pr.

— Oregon Firsts: Oregon's Trailblazing Past & Present. (Illus.). 224p. (Orig.). (YA). 1993. pap. 24.95 (*1-882635-00-0*) Pumpkin Ridge.

Long, James D. Battletech D. R. T. 288p. (Orig.). 1994. pap. 4.99 (*0-451-45366-2*, ROC) NAL-Dutton.

Long, James D. & Frye, Virginia H. Making It till Friday: A Guide to Successful Classroom Management. 4th ed. LC 89-10450. (Illus.). 213p. (C). 1989. pap. text ed. 14.95 (*0-916622-91-6*) Princeton Bk Co.

Long, James D. & Williams, Robert L., eds. Classroom Management with Adolescents. LC 73-3077. 164p. 1973. pap. text ed. 12.95 (*0-8422-0288-9*) Irvington.

Long, James P. & Warmbrod, Catharine P. Preparing for High Technology, Bk. III: A Guide for Community Colleges. 15p. 1982. 2.75 (*0-318-22174-8*, RD231) Ctr Educ Trng Employ.

Long, James P., et al. How to Phase Out a Program. 47p. 1983. 4.95 (*0-318-22127-6*, SN42) Ctr Educ Trng Employ.

***Long, James W.** The Essential Guide to Chronic Disorders. 1995. 18.00 (*0-06-273137-8*, Harper Ref) HarpC.

— Experiments in General Chemistry. 2nd ed. 272p. (C). 1992. spiral bd. 21.95 (*0-8403-8116-6*) Kendall-Hunt.

— From Privileged to Dispossessed: The Volga Germans, 1860-1917. LC 88-1144. (Illus.). xvi, 337p. 1988. 35.00x (*0-8032-2881-3*) U of Nebr Pr.

***Long, James W. & Rybacki, James J.** The Essential Guide to Prescription Drugs, 1995. (Illus.). 1184p. (Orig.). 1994. pap. 19.00 (*0-06-273317-6*, Harper Ref) HarpC.

Long, James W., jt. auth. see Rybacki, James J.

Long, Jean. Chinese Painting Techniques: A Complete Course. (Illus.). 224p. 1994. 19.95 (*0-289-80114-1*, Pub. by Studio Vista Bks UK) Sterling.

Long, Jean, ed. see Brown, Bernita J.

***Long, Jean M.** Beneath a Lakeland Moon. (Rainbow Romances Ser.). 160p. 1994. 14.95 (*0-7090-5397-5*, 916, Hale-Parkwest) Parkwest Pubns.

— The Enchanted Isle. large type ed. 1992. pap. 16.95 (*0-7927-0902-0*, Curley Lrg Print) Chivers N Amer.

— Island Serenade. large type ed. (Linford Romance Library). 1990. pap. 12.95 (*0-7089-6822-8*, Trailtree Bookshop) Ulverscroft.

— Music of the Heart. large type ed. 1990. pap. 12.95 (*0-7089-6882-1*, Linford) Ulverscroft.

— To Dream of Gold Apples. large type ed. (Linford Romance Library). 320p. 1989. pap. 11.95 (*0-7089-6664-0*, Linford) Ulverscroft.

Long, Jeanne. Kaleidoscope. (Pathways to Poetry Ser.). 115p. 1984. pap. 15.95 (*0-86617-031-6*) Multi Media TX.

Long, Jeanne, et al. Pathways to Poetry Series: Kaleidoscope, Mosaics, Visions. Miller, Jo & Monroe, Laura, eds. (J). (gr. 1-12). 1984. Set of 3. pap. text ed. 39.95 (*0-685-62412-9*) Multi Media TX.

Long, Jeb. DBase IV Programming Language. (Illus.). (Orig.). 1992. pap. 29.95 (*0-672-22840-8*) Sams.

— FoxPro for Windows Developer's Guide. (Illus.). (Orig.). 1992. pap. 44.95 (*0-672-30020-6*) Sams.

— FoxPro for Windows Developer's Guide. 3rd ed. (Illus.). 1500p. (Orig.). 1995. pap. text ed. 49.99 (*0-672-30653-0*) Sams.

— FoxPro 2.5 for DOS Developers Guide. 1993. pap. 44.95 (*0-672-30159-8*) Sams.

— FoxPro 2.6 for Windows Developers Guide. 2nd ed. 1994. pap. 45.00 (*0-672-30565-8*) Sams.

Long, Jeb J. & Dallas, Alastair W. The dBASE IV Programming Language. 550p. 1989. 34.95 (*0-13-199647-9*) P-H.

Long, Jeff. Duel of Eagles: The Mexican & U. S. Fight for the Alamo. (Illus.). 432p. 1991. pap. 12.00 (*0-688-10967-5*, Quill) Morrow.

— Empire of Bones: A Novel of Sam Houston & the Texas Revolution. LC 92-38397. 1993. 22.00 (*0-688-12252-3*) Morrow.

Long, Jeffrey E., jt. ed. see Finn, Marie T.

Long, Jerry & Tenzer, Jeff. The Cambridge Program for the High School Equivalency Examination. Schenk, Brian, ed. (GED Preparation Ser.). (Illus.). 816p. (Orig.). 1988. pap. text ed. write for info. (*0-8428-9385-7*) Cambridge Bk.

Long, Jerry H. How to Successfully Plan Your Church's Future: An Interactive Guide to Church Planning for the Small, Medium, & Large Church. Spear, Cindy G. & Pierce, Tim, eds. 350p. 1994. ring bd. 89.95 (*1-57052-006-2*) Chrch Grwth VA.

Long, Jim. Comment Dieu A-T-Il Pu Permett. 160p. (FRE.). 1991. 4.95 (*0-8297-1496-0*) Life Pubs Intl.

— Main Event. (BattleTech Ser.). 288p. (Orig.). 1993. pap. 4.99 (*0-451-45245-3*, ROC) NAL-Dutton.

— Por Que Lo Permite Dios? 144p. (SPA.). 1991. 3.95 (*0-8297-0428-0*) Life Pubs Intl.

Long, Joann M., ed. see Warren, Betsy.

***Long, Joanna O.** Come Life Eternal. 192p. 1995. pap. 14.95 (*1-881576-59-0*) Providence Hse.

Long, John. Climbing Anchors. (How to Rock Climb Ser.). (Illus.). 120p. (Orig.). 1993. pap. 11.95 (*0-934641-37-4*) Chockstone Pr.

— Gorilla Monsoon. 176p. (Orig.). 1989. 12.95 (*0-934641-03-X*) Chockstone Pr.

— Gym Climb. (How to Rock Climb Ser.). (Illus.). 64p. 1994. pap. 4.95 (*0-934641-75-7*) Chockstone Pr.

— How to Rock Climb! 2nd ed. (Illus.). 192p. (Orig.). 1993. pap. 11.95 (*0-934641-64-1*) Chockstone Pr.

— The Law of Illinois, Vol. 1: Lincoln's Cases Before the Illinois Supreme Court, from His Entry into the Practice of Law until His Entry into Congress. (Illus.). 301p. (Orig.). (C). 1993. pap. text ed. 20.00 (*0-9635192-0-4*) Illinois Co.

— More Climbing Anchors. (How to Rock Climb Ser.). (Illus.). 120p. (Orig.). 1995. pap. 11.95 (*0-614-05453-2*) Chockstone Pr.

— The Rise of Fishes: Their Five Hundred-Million Year History. (Illus.). 208p. 49.95 (*0-86840-078-5*, Pub. by New South Wales Univ Pr AT) Intl Spec Bk.

— Rock Jocks, Wall Rats, & Hang Dogs: Rock Climbing on the Edge of Reality. LC 94-6416. 1994. pap. 11.00 (*0-671-88466-2*, Fireside) S&S Trade.

— Rock Junction. 180p. (Orig.). 1994. pap. 12.95 (*0-934641-68-4*) Chockstone Pr.

— Sport & Face Climbing. (How to Rock Climb Ser.). (Illus.). 160p. 1994. pap. 11.95 (*0-934641-56-0*) Chockstone Pr.

Long, John, ed. Campfire Howlers. 160p. 1994. pap. 11.99 (*1-57034-000-5*) ICS Bks.

— Campfire Legends. LC 93-26008. 192p. (Orig.). 1993. pap. 11.99 (*0-934802-16-5*) ICS Bks.

Long, John & Baddeley, Alan, eds. Attention & Performance IX. (Attention & Performance Ser.). 672p. 1981. 125.00 (*0-89859-156-2*) L Erlbaum Assocs.

Long, John & McCord, Grace D. McCord of Alaska. LC 74-28612. (Illus.). 150p. 1975. 7.95 (*0-913228-15-X*) Dillon-Liederbach.

***Long, John & Middendorf, John.** Big Walls. (How to Rock Climb Ser.). (Illus.). 160p. 1994. pap. 11.95 (*0-934641-63-3*) Chockstone Pr.

***Long, John & Raleight, Duane.** Clip & Go! (How to Rock Climb Ser.). (Illus.). 64p. 1994. pap. text ed. 5.95 (*0-934641-84-6*) Chockstone Pr.

Long, John, jt. auth. see Kee Yong Lim.

Long, John, jt. auth. see Lim, Kee Y.

Long, John, et al. Tales from the Steep: John Long's Favorite Climbing Literature. LC 92-45869. 184p. (Orig.). 1993. pap. 11.99 (*0-934802-92-0*) ICS Bks.

Long, John A. Motor Abilities of Deaf Children. LC 75-177009. (Columbia University. Teachers College. Contributions to Education Ser.: No. 514). reprint ed. 22.50 (*0-404-55514-4*) AMS Pr.

— The Rise of Fishes: 500 Million Years of Evolution. LC 94-24692. (Illus.). 224p. 1994. text ed. 49.95x (*0-8018-4992-6*) Johns Hopkins.

Long, John A., ed. Palaeozoic Vertebrate Biostratigraphy & Biogeography. LC 93-11551. 383p. 1994. reprint ed. pap. text ed. 40.00 (*0-8018-4779-6*) Johns Hopkins.

Long, John D. After Dinner & Other Speeches. LC 72-4550. (Essay Index Reprint Ser.). 1977. reprint ed. 20.95 (*0-8369-2958-6*) Ayer.

— Ethics, Morality, & Insurance: A Long-Range Outlook. LC 71-633786. (Sesquicentennial Insurance Ser.). 1971. 8.50 (*0-685-00047-8*) Ind U Busn Res.

— The New American Navy, 2 vols. in one. Kohn, Richard H., ed. LC 78-22386. (American Military Experience Ser.). (Illus.). 1980. reprint ed. lib. bdg. 61.95 (*0-405-11862-7*) Ayer.

Long, John H. Atlas of Historical County Boundaries: Maine, Massachusetts, Connecticut, & Rhode Island. (Illus.). 144p. 1994. 50.00 (*0-13-051947-2*) S&S Trade.

— Atlas of Historical County Boundaries: Mississippi. (Illus.). 192p. 1992. 55.00 (*0-13-051970-7*) S&S Trade.

— Atlas of Historical County Boundaries: New Hampshire & Vermont. (Illus.). 112p. 1992. 45.00 (*0-13-051954-5*) S&S Trade.

— Atlas of Historical County Boundaries: New York. (Illus.). 192p. 1992. 50.00 (*0-13-051962-6*) S&S Trade.

— Music in English Renaissance Drama. LC 68-12969. 200p. reprint ed. pap. 57.00 (*0-317-10069-6*, 2001609) Bks Demand.

— Shakespeare's Use of Music: A Study of the Music & Its Performance in the Original Production of Seven Comedies. LC 77-4643. (Music Reprint Ser.). 1977. reprint ed. lib. bdg. 32.50 (*0-306-77423-2*) Da Capo.

— Shakespeare's Use of Music: The Final Comedies. LC 77-5644. (Music Reprint Ser.). 1977. reprint ed. lib. bdg. 29.50 (*0-306-77424-0*) Da Capo.

— Shakespeare's Use of Music: Vol. 3, The Histories & Tragedies. LC 61-17588. 1971. 24.95 (*0-8130-0311-3*) U Press Fla.

Long, John H., ed. Atlas of Historical County Boundaries: Alabama. LC 94-15023. 1995. 45.00 (*0-13-309568-1*) S&S Trade.

— Atlas of Historical County Boundaries: Indiana. LC 94-15021. 1995. 45.00 (*0-13-309550-9*) S&S Trade.

— Atlas of Historical County Boundaries: Pennsylvania. LC 94-15024. 1995. 45.00 (*0-13-315532-3*) S&S Trade.

Long, John H. & DenBoer, Gordon, eds. Atlas of Historical County Boundaries: Kentucky. LC 94-15022. 1995. 45.00 (*0-13-309543-6*) S&S Trade.

Long, John H., jt. auth. see Smith Center for the History of Cartography Staff.

Long, John L. Madame Butterfly. 1972. reprint ed. lib. bdg. 27.00 (*0-8422-8092-8*) Irvington.

— Sixty Jane. LC 76-103524. (Short Story Index Reprint Ser.). 1977. 19.95 (*0-8369-3266-8*) Ayer.

Long, John V., jt. auth. see Green, Samuel.

Long, Jonathan & Paul, Korky. The Dog That Dug. LC 92-15093. (Illus.). 32p. (J). (ps-3). 1993. 13.95 (*0-916291-44-8*) Kane-Miller Bk.

Long, Josefina, tr. see Finn, Ken.

Long, Joseph. Theatre des Varietes. (Theatre in Focus Ser.). (Illus.). 120p. (Orig.). 1980. sl. 105.00 (*0-85964-063-9*) Chadwyck-Healey.

Long, Joseph C. Blue Sky Law, 2 vols. LC 85-11377. (Securities Law Ser.). 1985. ring bd. 250.00 (*0-87632-468-5*) Clark Boardman Callaghan.

Long, Joseph K., ed. Extrasensory Ecology: Parapsychology & Anthropology. LC 77-6367. 437p. 1977. 30.00 (*0-8108-1036-0*) Scarecrow.

Long, Judith. Ministers of Grace: Women in the Early Church. 151p. (C). 1990. 39.00 (*0-85439-298-X*, Pub. by St Paul Pubns UK) St Mut.

Long, Judith R. Gene Stratton-Porter: Novelist & Naturalist. 286p. 1990. 19.95 (*0-87195-052-9*) Ind Hist Soc.

Long, Judy A., jt. auth. see Hemphill, Charles F., Jr.

Long, Justin T. Engineering for Nuclear Fuel Reprocessing. LC 78-50886. 1023p. 1978. 78.00 (*0-89448-012-X*, 300012) Am Nuclear Soc.

Long, K. & Reim, T. Fatal Facts. 5.98 (*0-517-63216-0*) Random Hse Value.

Long, Kathi. Mexican Light Cooking. 192p. 1992. bds. 16.95 (*0-399-51741-3*, Perigree Bks) Berkley Pub.

Long, Kathy. Hallelujah the Clown: A Story of Blessing & Discovery. LC 92-70384. (Illus.). 32p. (J). (ps-00). 1992. pap. 4.99 (*0-8066-2560-0*, 9-2560, Augsburg) Augsburg Fortress.

— No! No! No! (Illus.). 144p. (Orig.). 1994. pap. 10.95 (*0-399-51845-2*, Perigree Bks) Berkley Pub.

— A Surprise for Mrs. Dodds: A Little Boy's Friendship Changes a Lonely Woman's Life. LC 89-84939. (Illus.). 32p. (J). (gr. 3-5). 1989. pap. 5.99 (*0-8066-2437-X*, 9-2437) Augsburg Fortress.

***Long, Kathy A.** Taylor Twinkle Finds a Home: A Christmas Story for All Seasons. 32p. (J). (gr. k-4). 1994. pap. 5.00 (*0-9642063-0-7*) Best Frnds.

Long, Kenneth R. The Music of the English Church. (Illus.). 480p. 1991. lib. bdg. 87.50 (*0-340-14962-0*, Pub. by Hodder & Stoughton Ltd UK) Lubrecht & Cramer.

Long, Kevin, jt. auth. see Siembieda, Kevin.

Long, Kevin G. Anti-Catholicism in the Nineteen Eighties. 112p. (Orig.). 1988. pap. text ed. 3.95 (*0-945775-03-2*) Cath League Rts.

Long, Kim. Almanac of Anniversaries. LC 92-28945. 1992. lib. bdg. 40.00 (*0-87436-675-5*) ABC-CLIO.

— The American Forecaster Almanac, 1994: Business Edition. (Illus.). 279p. 1994. pap. 27.50 (*0-936889-25-X*); disk 39.95 (*0-936889-28-4*); mac hd 39.95 (*0-936889-27-6*) American Demo.

— The American Forecaster Almanac 1995. 288p. (Orig.). 1994. pap. 14.95 (*0-9644540-0-9*); disk 14.95 (*0-9644540-1-7*) Am Forecaster.

— Astronaut Training Book for Kids. (Illus.). 160p. (J). (gr. 5-p). 1990. 15.95 (*0-525-67296-6*, Lodestar Bks) Dutton Child Bks.

— Directory of Educational Contests for Students K-12. 300p. 1991. lib. bdg. 40.00 (*0-87436-586-4*) ABC-CLIO.

— Encyclopedia of Field Trips & Educational Destinations. 200p. 1991. lib. bdg. 40.00 (*0-87436-585-6*) ABC-CLIO.

— The Moon Book: The Meaning of the Methodical Movements of the Magnificent, Mysterious Moon & Other Interesting Facts about Earth's Nearest Neighbor. LC 88-81081. (Illus.). 128p. (Orig.). 1988. pap. 7.95 (*1-55566-028-2*) Johnson Bks.

— Squirrels. (Wildlife Handbooks Ser.). (Illus.). 192p. (Orig.). 1995. pap. 14.95 (*1-55566-152-1*) Johnson Bks.

— Wolves. (Wildlife Handbooks Ser.). (Illus.). 192p. (Orig.). 1995. pap. 14.95 (*1-55566-158-0*) Johnson Bks.

Long, L. Dupre, jt. auth. see Gibson, Martin L.

***Long, L. Kristi.** Empowering Employees. (Business Skills Express Ser.). 1995. pap. 10.00 (*0-7863-0314-X*) Irwin Prof Pubng.

Long, Larry. Introduction to Computers & Information Systems. 4th ed. LC 93-34287. 1993. pap. text ed. write for info. (*0-13-497884-6*) P-H.

— Management Information Systems. 576p. (C). 1989. text ed. write for info. (*0-13-551599-8*) P-H.

— An MIS Case Study: Zimco Enterprises. (Illus.). 224p. (C). 1987. pap. text ed. 41.00 (*0-13-585837-2*) P-H.

— Turnaround Time: The Best of Computerworld's Q & A's. 192p. 1987. 17.50 (*0-13-933029-1*) P-H.

Long, Larry & Kreutzer, Nathan. Introduction to Computers & Information Processing: Study Guide. 256p. (C). 1984. teacher ed, pap. text ed. (*0-318-57545-0*) P-H.

Long, Larry & Long, Nancy. Computers. 3rd ed. 704p. 1992. pap. text ed. write for info. (*0-13-156241-X*) P-H.

— Computers: Instructor's Edition. 3rd annot. ed. LC 92-32920. 1993. write for info. (*0-13-156258-4*) P-H.

— Computing. LC 94-32975. 1994. pap. text ed. write for info. (*0-13-309956-3*) P-H.

— Microcomputer: Concepts. 2nd ed. 304p. 1992. pap. text ed. 33.33 (*0-13-584525-4*) P-H.

— Microcomputer: Concepts & Software. 1992. write for info. (*0-318-68776-3*) P-H.

— Microcomputers. (Illus.). 496p. (C). 1988. pap. text ed. 64.00 (*0-13-580101-X*) P-H.

Long, Larry E. Migration & Residential Mobility in the United States. LC 88-15758. (Population of the United States in the 1980s: A Census Monograph Ser.). 400p. 1988. 49.95 (*0-87154-555-1*) Russell Sage.

Long, Laurette, tr. see Meral, Jean.

Long, Leland R. With Strings Attached. 1993. 16.95 (*0-533-10570-6*) Vantage.

***Long, Leon E.** Geology. 6th ed. (Illus.). 536p. 1994. pap. text ed. 34.95x (*0-89641-265-2*) American Pr.

Long, Lilian P. Wine of the Spirit: Prayer. LC 87-91322. 208p. (Orig.). 1988. pap. 9.95 (*0-9619722-1-1*) L P Long Pub.

Long, Lois, jt. auth. see Cage, John.

***Long, Lowell.** Country Images. 37p. 1995. per., pap. 4.95 (*0-614-04034-5*) Sage Pr OK.

Long, Lynellyn D. Ban Vinai: The Refugee Camp. (Illus.). 288p. 1992. text ed. 45.00 (*0-231-07862-5*); pap. text ed. 16.50 (*0-231-07863-3*) Col U Pr.

Long, Lynellyn D. & Podnecky-Spiegel, Janet. In Print: Beginning Literacy Through Cultural Awareness. (Literacy Ser.). (Illus.). 128p. (J). 1988. teacher ed 7.95 (*0-201-12024-0*); text ed. 11.44 (*0-201-12023-2*) Addison-Wesley.

Long, Lynette & Hershberger, Eileen. One Year to a College Degree. LC 91-72905. 208p. (Orig.). 1992. pap. 9.99 (*1-56384-001-4*) Huntington Hse.

Long, Lynette & Prophit, Penny. Understanding-Responding: A Communication Manual for Nurses. LC 80-17977. (C). 1981. pap. text ed. 30.00 (*0-87872-284-X*) Jones & Bartlett.

Long, M. B. & Mitchell, B. T. ICALEO '89, Vol. 1404: Optical Methods in Flow & Particle Diagnostics (Oct 1989, Orlando) 1990. 53.00 (*0-8194-0488-8*) SPIE.

Long, Maria, jt. auth. see Metcalfe, Fray.

Long, Marjorie, tr. see Levi-Civita, Tullio.

Long, Mark. The World of Home Video Entertainment. (Illus.). 202p. (Orig.). 1990. pap. 15.95 (*0-929548-01-9*) MLE Inc.

An Asterisk (*) at the beginning of an entry indicates that the title is appearing in BIP for the first time.

— The World Satellite Almanac: The Complete Guide to Satellite Transmission & Technology. 3rd ed. Birkill, Stephen J., ed. (Illus.). 1072p. 1992. pap. 99.95 (*0-929548-04-3*) MLE Inc.

— World Satellite Almanac, 1985. Kinnaird, Bruce, ed. (Illus.). 544p. (Orig.). 1985. pap. 39.95 (*0-934543-00-3*) CommTek Pub.

— World Satellite Annual, 1993. (World Satellite Almanac Ser.: Vol. IV). (Illus.). 440p. (Orig.). 1992. pap. 59.95 (*0-929548-09-4*) MLE Inc.

Long, Mark, illus. World Satellite Annual, 1990. (World Satellite Almanac Ser.: Vol. II). 432p. 1989. pap. 39.95 (*0-685-21883-X*) MLE Inc.

Long, Mark & Keating, Jeffrey. The Inclined Orbit Satellite Tracking Guidebook, 1993. 98p. 1993. pap. 24.95 (*0-929548-12-4*) MLE Inc.

— Satellite Installation Handbook. (Illus.). 256p. 1993. 29.95 (*0-929548-11-6*) MLE Inc.

— The World of Satellite TV: International Edition for Asia, the Middle East, & the Pacific Rim. (Illus.). 220p. (Orig.). 1992. pap. 19.95 (*0-929548-08-6*) MLE Inc.

— World of Satellite TV: International Edition for Europe & Africa. (Illus.). 1993. pap. 24.95 (*0-929548-10-8*) MLE Inc.

— World of Satellite TV: North & South America. 6th ed. LC 92-81289. (Illus.). 308p. (Orig.). (C). 1992. pap. text ed. 24.95 (*0-929548-07-8*) MLE Inc.

Long, Marshall & Wilkinson, Robert, eds. It Was a Beautiful Country: A Southwest Florida Anthology. LC 73-87597. (Illus.). 64p. 1974. pap. 1.95 (*0-87208-023-4*) Island Pr Pubs.

Long, Martin. The Dark Gateway. large type ed. 1989. 17.95 (*0-7089-2076-4*) Ulverscroft.

Long, Mary. Stretchercize: Is Your Limber Lost? (Illus.). 75p. (Orig.). 1985. pap. 3.95 (*0-916005-03-8*) Silver Sea.

Long, Mary & Long, Dean. Old Georgia Privies. 3rd ed. (Illus.). 50p. 1988. write for info. (*0-318-68538-8*) Frazier-Long.

Long, Mary C. Fair Were Their Dreams: A History of the Family of John Boone of Boone Hall Plantation. (Illus.). 300p. 1990. write for info. (*0-9617517-1-1*) Bear Hllow TX.

— The Farrow Family Tales, Exaggerations, Lies: A History of the Farrow Family from South Carolina to Texas 1770-1780 - 1995. (Illus.). 150p. 1995. 75.00 (*0-9617517-3-8*) Bear Hllow TX.

***Long, Matthew & Long, Thomas.** The Spectacled Bear & Other Curious Creatures. LC 94-46642. (Illus.). (J). 1995. 12.95 (*0-8118-0809-2*) Chronicle Bks.

Long, Maurice W. Radar Reflectivity of Land & Sea. 2nd ed. LC 75-13435. (Illus.). 421p. reprint ed. pap. 120.00 (*0-8357-3937-6*, 2036672) Bks Demand.

Long, Maurice W., ed. Airborne Early Warning Systems Concepts. (Radar Library). 528p. 1992. text ed. 89.00 (*0-89006-491-1*) Artech Hse.

Long, Max F. Growing into Light. 1955. pap. 9.95 (*0-87516-043-3*) DeVorss.

— Huna Code in Religions. 1965. pap. 15.95 (*0-87516-495-1*) DeVorss.

— Mana, or Vital Force. 5th ed. 1976. pap. 4.00 (*0-910764-04-2*) Huna Res Inc.

— Psychometric Analysis. 1959. pap. 8.95 (*0-87516-045-X*) DeVorss.

— Recovering the Ancient Magic. (Illus.). 1978. reprint ed. pap. 6.95 (*0-910764-01-8*) Huna Res Inc.

— Secret Science at Work. 1953. pap. 13.95 (*0-87516-046-8*) DeVorss.

— Secret Science Behind Miracles. 1948. pap. 13.95 (*0-87516-047-6*) DeVorss.

— Self-Suggestion & the New Huna Theory of Mesmerism & Hypnosis. 1958. pap. 7.95 (*0-87516-048-4*) DeVorss.

— Short Talks on Huna. 2nd rev. ed. 1978. pap. 5.00 (*0-910764-02-6*) Huna Res Inc.

— Tarot Card Symbology. 3rd rev. ed. Wingo, E. Otha, ed. (Illus.). 1983. pap. 10.00 (*0-910764-07-7*) Huna Res Inc.

— What Jesus Taught in Secret. (Illus.). 144p. 1983. pap. 8.95 (*0-87516-510-9*) DeVorss.

Long, Michael. Introduction to the Medical Care System: An Integrated Conceptual Approach. 175p. 1994. pap. write for info. (*1-56793-016-6*, 0946) Health Admin Pr.

— Macbeth. (Twayne's New Critical Introduction to Shakespeare Ser.: No. 9). 160p. 1989. lib. bdg. 20.95 (*0-8057-8720-8*, Twayne); pap. 11.95 (*0-8057-8721-6*, Twayne) Macmillan.

Long, Michael, jt. auth. see Rosier, Malcolm.

Long, Michael H. & Richards, Jack C. Methodology in TESOL. 475p. 1987. pap. 23.95 (*0-8384-2695-6*, Newbury) Heinle & Heinle.

Long, Michael W. & Wicha, Max S., eds. The Hematopoietic Microenvironment: The Functional & Structural Basis of Blood Cell Development. LC 92-49721. (Johns Hopkins Series in Hematology - Oncology). 336p. 1993. text ed. 140.00 (*0-8018-4566-1*) Johns Hopkins.

Long, Mike. Understanding Census Data. 71p. 1990. reprint ed. 25.00 (*0-923172-02-5*) West Econ Rsch.

Long, Milbra. Fostoria Stemware: The Crystal for America. 1994. 24.95 (*0-89145-586-8*) Collector Bks.

Long, Mildred. Listen to the Silence. (Orig.). 1970. pap. 2.50 (*0-87516-049-2*) DeVorss.

Long, Nancy, jt. auth. see Long, Larry.

Long, Neville. Lights of East Anglia. 182p. (C). 1988. 36.00 (*0-86138-028-2*, Pub. by T Dalton UK) St Mut.

— Lights of East Anglia. 182p. (C). 1994. pap. 27.00 (*0-86138-029-0*) St Mut.

Long, Ngo V. Before the Revolution. 1991. text ed. 55.00 (*0-231-07678-9*) Col U Pr.

Long, Ngo V., jt. ed. see Allen, Douglas.

Long, Ngo V., jt. auth. see Leonard, Daniel.

Long, Nguyen & Kendall, Harry H. After Saigon Fell: Daily Life under the Vietnamese Communists. LC 81-85304. (Research Papers & Policy Studies: No. 4). (Illus.). (Orig.). 1981. pap. 4.00 (*0-912966-46-7*) IEAS.

Long, Nicholas, jt. auth. see Wood, Mary.

Long, Norman & Long, Ann, eds. Battlefields of Knowledge. LC 92-2785. 370p. 1992. 59.95 (*0-415-07205-0*, A7631); pap. 19.95 (*0-415-07206-9*, A7635) Routledge.

Long, Norton E. Aristotle & the Study of Local Government. (Reprint Series in Social Sciences). (C). 1993. reprint ed. pap. text ed. 1.00 (*0-8290-3492-7*, PS-173) Irvington.

— The Polity. (Reprint Series in Sociology). reprint ed. lib. bdg. 24.50 (*0-685-70258-8*); reprint ed. pap. 9.95 (*0-685-70259-6*) Irvington.

Long, Oliver. Law & Its Limitations in the GATT Multilateral Trade System. 172p. (C). 1987. pap. text ed. 60.00 (*0-86010-959-3*) Kluwer Ac.

Long, Olivia. The Dandelion Queen. (Our Precious Planet Ser.). (Illus.). 32p. (J). (ps-4). Date not set. 9.95 (*1-880042-08-8*, SL12461) Shelf-Life Bks.

— Diary of a Dog. (Pets & Their People Ser.). (Illus.). 32p. (J). (ps-4). Date not set. 9.95 (*1-880042-06-1*, SL12456) Shelf-Life Bks.

— A Horse of a Different Color. (Kaleidoscope Ser.). (Illus.). 32p. (J). (ps-4). Date not set. 9.95 (*1-880042-01-0*, SL12451) Shelf-Life Bks.

Long, Olivier. Public Scrutiny of Protection. 114p. 1989. text ed. 22.95 (*0-566-05780-8*, Pub. by Avebury Pub UK) Ashgate Pub Co.

Long, Orie. Literary Pioneers: Early American Explorers of European Culture. (BCL1-PS American Literature Ser.). 267p. 1993. reprint ed. lib. bdg. 79.00 (*0-7812-6576-2*) Rprt Serv.

Long, Orie W. Literary Pioneers. 1975. 250.00 (*0-87968-301-5*) Gordon Pr.

Long, Pamela O., intro. Science & Technology in Medieval Society. (Annals Ser.: Vol. 441). 224p. 1984. lib. bdg. 50.00 (*0-89766-276-8*); pap. 50.00 (*0-89766-277-6*) NY Acad Sci.

Long, Patricia J. & Shannon, Barbara. Focus on Nutrition. (Illus.). 336p. 1983. pap. text ed. write for info. (*0-13-322800-2*) P-H.

— Nutrition: An Inquiry into the Issues. (Illus.). 608p. (C). 1983. pap. text ed. write for info. (*0-13-627802-7*) P-H.

Long, Paul. Training Pointing Dogs. (Illus.). 112p. 1985. pap. 12.95 (*0-941130-08-8*) Lyons & Burford.

Long, Paul E. & Graening, Jay. Finite Mathematics. (C). 1993. student ed 24.00 (*0-06-500623-2*) HarpCollege.

— Finite Mathematics: An Applied Approach. LC 92-26647. (Illus.). (C). 1992. 67.50 (*0-06-500391-8*) HarpCollege.

Long, Paul V. Big Eyes: The Southwestern Photographs of Simeon Schwemberger, 1902-1908. LC 91-24923. (Illus.). 220p. 1992. 35.00 (*0-8263-1302-7*) U of NM Pr.

Long, Peter L., ed. Coccidiosis of Man & Domestic Animals. 352p. 1990. 205.00 (*0-8493-6269-5*, QR201) CRC Pr.

Long, Peter L., ed. see McDougald, Larry R.

Long, Phil. Performance Appraisal Revisited. 200p. (C). 1986. 105.00 (*0-85292-367-8*, Pub. by IPM Hse UK) St Mut.

— Retirement: Planned Liberation? 116p. (C). 1981. 102.00 (*0-85292-294-9*, Pub. by IPM Hse UK) St Mut.

Long, Phil & Hill, Margaret. Special Leave. 84p. (C). 1988. 90.00 (*0-85292-400-3*, Pub. by IPM Hse UK) St Mut.

Long, Phil, jt. auth. see Armstrong, Michael.

Long, Philip D. & Siefert, Beth L. Basic Bible for Real People: Six Key Books of the Bible in One Year of Daily Devotional Readings. 384p. 1991. pap. text ed. 9.95 (*0-9631735-0-2*) E Lib Luth Church.

Long, Priscilla, ed. New Left: A Collection of Essays. LC 69-15528. (Extending Horizons Ser.). (Illus.). 500p. (C). 1970. 6.00 (*0-87558-042-4*); pap. 3.00 (*0-87558-043-2*) Porter Sargent.

Long, Quincy. The Johnstown Vindicator. 1988. pap. 4.75 (*0-8222-0599-8*) Dramatists Play.

Long, R. A., jt. auth. see Jackman, E. R.

Long, R. Brad. Collecting Grand Army of the Republic Memorabilia. 2nd ed. (Illus.). 52p. 1991. reprint ed. pap. 8.95 (*0-9617584-1-8*) R B Long.

Long, R. E., tr. see Chekhov, Anton P.

Long, Ralph B. Structure Worksheets for Contemporary English. 253p. reprint ed. pap. 72.20 (*0-317-26521-0*, 2024056) Bks Demand.

Long, Ralph B. & Long, Dorothy R. The System of English Grammar. LC 75-159449. 531p. (C). 1980. reprint ed. text ed. 12.00 (*0-8477-3325-4*); reprint ed. pap. text ed. 9.60 (*0-8477-3326-2*) U of PR Pr.

Long, Ralph G. The Conductor's Workshop: A Workbook for Instrumental Conducting. 2nd ed. 280p. 1977. spiral bd. write for info. (*0-697-03515-8*) Brown & Benchmark.

Long, Richard. Mountains & Waters. LC 92-54548. 65p. 1993. 35.00 (*0-8076-1293-6*) Braziller.

Long, Richard A. African-Americans. 1993. 17.99 (*0-517-08792-8*) Random Hse Value.

— Black Tradition in American Dance. (Illus.). 192p. 1995. 19.98 (*0-8317-0763-1*) Smithmark.

Long, Richard A. & Collier, Eugenia W., eds. Afro-American Writing: An Anthology of Prose & Poetry. 2nd enl. ed. 784p. 1990. 15.95 (*0-271-00376-6*) Pa St U Pr.

Long, Richard J. New Office Information Technology: Human & Managerial Implications. (New Information Technology & Management Ser.). 352p. 1987. lib. bdg. 29.95 (*0-7099-4103-X*, Pub. by Croom Helm UK) Routledge Chapman & Hall.

Long, Richard J. & Skinner, Stephen C. Closed Loop Electrohydraulic Systems Manual. (Illus.). (C). 1992. text ed. write for info. (*0-9634162-1-9*) Vickers Inc Trng Ctr.

Long, Robert. Algebraic Number Theory. (Pure & Applied Mathematics Ser.: Vol. 41). 208p. 1977. 110.00 (*0-8247-6540-0*) Dekker.

— Long Island Poets. LC 86-61406. 192p. 1986. 16.00 (*0-932966-73-X*) Permanent Pr.

— The Sonnets. (Orig.). 1988. pap. 8.95 (*0-89807-255-7*) Illuminati.

— What Happens. LC 88-9423. 68p. (Orig.). 1988. pap. 9.95 (*0-913123-19-6*) Galileo.

***Long, Robert, ed.** For David Ignatow: An Anthology: Forty-Seven Poets Celebrate His 80th Birthday. 69p. (Orig.). 1994. pap. 10.00 (*0-9630164-6-6*) Canios Edit.

— The Last of the Dinosaurs. (Illus.). 1978. pap. 3.95 (*0-88388-054-7*) Bellerophon Bks.

Long, Robert, ed. see Roberts, J. S., pseud.

Long, Robert A. & Houk, Rose. Dawn of the Dinosaurs: The Triassic of Petrified Forest. (Illus.). (Orig.). (C). 1988. pap. 14.95 (*0-945695-02-0*) Petrified Forest Mus Assn.

Long, Robert A. & Welles, Samuel P. All New Dinosaurs. (J). (gr. 7 up). 1975. pap. 3.95 (*0-88388-031-8*) Bellerophon Bks.

***Long, Robert B.** Separation Processes in Waste Minimization. LC 95-2944. (Environmental Science & Pollution Control Ser.: Vol. 16). 1995. write for info. (*0-8247-9634-9*) Dekker.

Long, Robert B., ed. see Christiansen, Larry, et al.

Long, Robert B., ed. see Dunne, Alex.

Long, Robert B., ed. see Gerzadowicz, Stephan.

Long, Robert B., ed. see Parr, Larry.

Long, Robert B., ed. see Raingruber, Bob & Maser, Lou.

Long, Robert B., ed. see Unger, Tom.

Long, Robert B., ed. see Wetzell, Rolf.

Long, Robert C. The Achieving of the Great Gatsby: F. Scott Fitzgerald, 1920-1925. LC 77-92572. 224p. 1981. 32.50 (*0-8387-2192-3*); pap. 17.95 (*0-8387-5026-5*) Bucknell U Pr.

Long, Robert E. Barbara Pym. (Literature & Life Ser.). 263p. (C). 1986. 19.95 (*0-8044-2545-0*, F Ungar Bks) Continuum.

— Film & Stage Work of Ingmar Bergman. LC 93-26853. 1994. 45.00 (*0-8109-3322-5*) Abrams.

— The Films of Merchant Ivory. (Illus.). 208p. 1991. 49.50 (*0-8109-3618-6*) Abrams.

— Films of Merchant Ivory. (Illus.). 208p. 1993. pap. 19.95 (*0-8065-1470-1*, Citadel Pr) Carol Pub Group.

— The Great Succession: Henry James & the Legacy of Hawthorne. LC 79-922. (Critical Essays in Modern Literature Ser.). 215p. reprint ed. pap. 61.30 (*0-7837-2146-3*, 2042432) Bks Demand.

— Henry James: The Early Novels. (United States Authors Ser.: No. 440). 1983. text ed. 23.95 (*0-8057-7379-7*, Twayne) Macmillan.

— James Thurber. (Literature & Life Ser.). 184p. (C). 1988. 19.95 (*0-8044-2546-9*, F Ungar Bks) Continuum.

— John O'Hara. LC 83-12387. (Literature & Life Ser.). 210p. (C). 1983. 19.95 (*0-8044-2541-8*, F Ungar Bks) Continuum.

— Nathanael West. LC 84-24488. (Literature & Life Ser.). 200p. (C). 1985. 19.95 (*0-8044-2543-4*, F Ungar Bks) Continuum.

— Suicide. LC 95-11850. (References Shelf Ser.: Vol. 67, No. 2). 1995. write for info. (*0-8242-0869-2*) Wilson.

Long, Robert E., ed. Banking Scandals: The S & Ls & BCCI. LC 93-16882. (Reference Shelf Ser.: Vol. 65, No. 3). 1993. 15.00 (*0-8242-0842-0*) Wilson.

— Criminal Sentencing. LC 95-2365. (Reference Shelf Ser.: Vol. 67 No. 1). 1995. write for info. (*0-8242-0868-4*) Wilson.

— Drugs in America. LC 85-26604. (Reference Shelf Ser.: Vol. 57, No. 6). 206p. 1986. pap. 15.00 (*0-8242-0714-9*) Wilson.

— Drugs in America. LC 93-16881. (Reference Shelf Ser.: Vol. 65, No. 4). 1993. 15.00 (*0-8242-0843-9*) Wilson.

— Energy & Conservation, No. 4, Vol. 61. (Reference Shelf Ser.). 180p. (C). 1989. pap. text ed. 15.00 (*0-8242-0783-1*) Wilson.

— Immigration & the U. S. LC 92-28399. (Reference Shelf Ser.: Vol. 64, No. 4). 1992. 15.00 (*0-8242-0828-5*) Wilson.

— Religious Cults in America. LC 94-16329. (Reference Shelf Ser.: Vol. 66, No. 4). 1994. 15.00 (*0-8242-0855-2*) Wilson.

— The Reunification of Germany. LC 91-43545. (Reference Shelf Ser.: Vol. 64, No. 1). 132p. 1992. pap. 15.00 (*0-8242-0825-0*, DD262) Wilson.

Long, Robert E., ed. & pref. The State of American Education. LC 84-22110. (Reference Shelf Ser.: Vol. 56, No. 5). 231p. 1984. pap. 15.00 (*0-8242-0699-1*) Wilson.

Long, Robert E., ed. Vietnam Ten Years After. LC 86-1642. (Reference Shelf Ser.: Vol. 58, No. 2). 161p. 1986. pap. text ed. 15.00 (*0-8242-0724-6*) Wilson.

— The Welfare Debate, No. 3, Vol. 61. (Reference Shelf Ser.). 206p. (C). 1989. pap. text ed. 15.00 (*0-8242-0782-3*) Wilson.

Long, Robert Emmet, ed. The Crisis in Health Care, Vol. 63, No. 1. 1991. pap. 15.00 (*0-8242-0811-0*) Wilson.

Long, Robert F., ed. Youth Development Professionals: Connecting Competencies & Curriculum. (Youth Development Professionals Monograph Ser.: No. 1). 64p. (C). 1992. pap. text ed. 10.00 (*1-881516-00-8*) U of NI Inst Youth Lead.

— Youth Develpment Professionals: Common Ground for Professional Development. (Youth Development Professionals Monograph Ser.: No. 2). 62p. (C). 1992. pap. text ed. 10.00 (*1-881516-01-6*) U of NI Inst Youth Lead.

Long, Robert F. & Martinez, Cathy L., eds. Youth Development Professionals: Building Practice on Knowledge. (Youth Development Professionals Monograph Ser.: No. 3). 162p. (C). 1993. pap. text ed. 10.00 (*1-881516-02-4*) U of NI Inst Youth Lead.

Long, Robert H. The Power to Die. (CSU Poetry Ser.: Vol. XXIV). 108p. (Orig.). 1987. pap. 6.00 (*0-914946-63-3*) Cleveland St Univ Poetry Ctr.

Long, Robert L. & O'Brien, Paul, eds. Fast Burst Reactors: Proceedings. LC 73-603552. (AEC Symposium Ser.). 646p. 1969. pap. 24.25 (*0-87079-208-3*, CONF-690102); fiche 9.00 (*0-87079-209-1*, CONF-690102) DOE.

Long, Robert P. Wood Type & Printing Collectibles. (Illus.). 1980. pap. 7.95 (*0-9600064-0-0*) R P Long.

Long, Roger. Final Commitment: A Third Anthology of Murders in Old Berkshire. (Illus.). 128p. 1994. pap. 15.00 (*0-7509-0495-X*) A Sutton Pub.

— Japanese Shadow Theatre: Movement & Characterization in Ngayogyakarta Wayang Kulit. LC 81-16164. (Theater & Dramatic Studies: No. 11). (Illus.). 207p. reprint ed. pap. 59.00 (*0-8357-1283-4*, 2070274) Bks Demand.

***Long, Roger D.** The Man on the Spot: Essays on British Empire History. LC 95-9667. (Contributions in Comparative Colonial Studies: Vol. 31). 1995. text ed. write for info. (*0-313-29524-7*, Greenwood Pr) Greenwood.

Long, Roland H. Law of Liability Insurance, 5 vols., Set. 1976. ring bd. write for info. (*0-8205-1354-7*) Bender.

Long, Ron E. & Barrett, Joanne. Hark, the Herald Angel. (J). 1983. 4.95 (*0-685-68531-4*, MC-48); audio 10.98 (*0-685-68532-2*, TA-9039C) Lillenas.

Long, Ronald E. & Clark, J. Michael. AIDS, God & Faith: Continuing the Dialogue on Constructing Gay Theology. LC 92-18829. (Gay Men's Issues in Religious Studies: Vol. 2, Suppl.). 90p. 1992. pap. 7.00 (*0-930383-25-7*) Monument Pr.

Long, Roy C. The Long Family History. (Illus.). 304p. 1989. write for info. (*0-318-65517-9*) R C Long.

— The Long Family History. McClain Printing Co., Staff, ed. (Illus.). 267p. 1990. 30.00 (*0-9623739-0-7*) R C Long.

Long, Ruilin. Martingale Spaces & Inequalities. viii, 246p. 1993. 64.00 (*3-528-08397-2*, Pub. by Vieweg & Sohn GW) Ballen Bkslr.

Long, Ruth Y. Crackdown on Cancer with Good Nutrition. 2nd rev. ed. 172p. 1991. reprint ed. pap. 10.00 (*0-916243-15-X*) Nutrit Educ.

— Home Study Course in the New Nutrition. 280p. (Orig.). 1989. pap. 17.95 (*0-87983-381-5*) Keats.

Long, S., ed. Six Group Therapies. LC 87-7187. 358p. 1987. 65.00 (*0-306-42642-0*, Plenum Pr) Plenum.

Long, S. P. & Woodward, F. I., eds. Plants & Temperature. (Society for Experimental Biology Symposia Ser.: No. 42). 450p. 1989. text ed. 77.00 (*0-948601-20-5*) Portland NC.

Long, S. P., jt. auth. see Baker, N. R.

Long, S. P., jt. ed. see Ireland, C. R.

Long, S. P., et al, eds. Primary Productivity of Grass Ecosystems. (Illus.). 224p. 1991. 85.00 (*0-412-41020-6*, A6291) Chapman & Hall.

Long, Samuel. Research in Micropolitics: Voting Behavior, Vol. 1. 1986. 73.25 (*0-89232-365-5*) Jai Pr.

Long, Samuel, ed. Annual Review in Political Science, Vol. III. 256p. (C). 1990. text ed. 65.00 (*0-89391-501-7*) Ablex Pub.

— Annual Review of Political Science, Vol. I. 256p. (C). 1986. text ed. 65.00 (*0-89391-393-6*) Ablex Pub.

— Annual Review of Political Science, Vol. II. (Annual Review of Political Science Ser.). 288p. 1987. text ed. 65.00 (*0-89391-401-0*) Ablex Pub.

— Research in Micropolitics, Vol. 3. 1989. 73.25 (*0-89232-791-X*) Jai Pr.

— Voting Behavior II. (Research in Micropolitics Ser.: Vol. II). 304p. 1987. 73.25 (*0-89232-562-3*) Jai Pr.

Long, Samuel L., ed. The Handbook of Political Behavior, 5 vols., Vol. 1. 388p. 1981. 110.00 (*0-306-40601-2*, Plenum Pr) Plenum.

— The Handbook of Political Behavior, 5 vols., Vol. 2. 380p. 1981. 110.00 (*0-306-40602-0*, Plenum Pr) Plenum.

— The Handbook of Political Behavior, 5 vols., Vol. 3. 422p. 1981. 110.00 (*0-306-40603-9*, Plenum Pr) Plenum.

— The Handbook of Political Behavior, 5 vols., Vol. 4. 386p. 1981. 110.00 (*0-306-40604-7*, Plenum Pr) Plenum.

— The Handbook of Political Behavior, 5 vols., Vol. 5. 392p. 1981. 110.00 (*0-306-40605-5*, Plenum Pr) Plenum.

Long, Sandra, jt. auth. see Phillips, Marcus.

Long, Sara G. The Warming of Bornoir's Bed. LC 90-70447. (Illus.). 464p. (Orig.). 1992. pap. 12.00 (*1-56002-104-7*) Aegina Pr.

Long, Sharon K., et al. The Evaluation of the Washington State Family Independence Program. LC 94-818. (Urban Institute Report Ser.: No. 94-1). 174p. 1994. lib. bdg. 46.50 (*0-87766-621-0*); pap. 19.50 (*0-87766-622-9*) Urban Inst.

Long, Sheila M. A Quick Reference to Dining Etiquette. Batson, Rose, ed. (Illus.). 128p. (Orig.). 1993. lib. bdg. 7.95 (*0-9636770-0-4*) Redbird Pubng.

***Long, Shepard, ed.** So You Think You're a Sports Fan! 802 Questions to Challenge Your Knowledge. LC 94-31927. 160p. 1994. pap. 8.95 (*0-8027-7439-3*) Walker & Co.

Long, Sheppard. Carl Yastrzemski. (Baseball Legends Ser.). (Illus.). 64p. (J). (gr. 3 up). 1994. lib. bdg. 14.95 (*0-7910-1195-X*, Am Art Analog) Chelsea Hse.

Long, Sheri S., jt. auth. see Gerrard, Lisa.

Long, Sheron. The Goat in the Chile Patch. (ESL Theme Links Ser.). (Illus.). 16p. (Orig.). 1992. pap. write for info. (*1-56334-199-9*); pap. text ed. 6.00 (*1-56334-184-0*) Hampton-Brown.

— The Goat in the Chile Patch. (ESL Theme Links Ser.). (Illus.). 16p. (Orig.). (J). (gr. k-3). 1992. pap. text ed. 29.95 (*1-56334-181-6*) Hampton-Brown.

— The Goat in the Chile Patch. (ESL Theme Links Ser.). (Illus.). (Orig.). 1993. audio 10.50 (*1-56334-309-6*); 35.00 (*1-56334-310-X*) Hampton-Brown.

— The Goat in the Chile Patch, Set. (ESL Theme Links Ser.). (Illus.). (Orig.). 1993. 99.50 (*1-56334-311-8*) Hampton-Brown.

Long, Sherry, jt. auth. see Tripp, Valerie.

Long Standing Bear Chief. Ni-Kso-Ko-Wa: Blackfoot Spirituality, Traditions, Values & Beliefs. 70p. 1992. pap. 9.95 (*0-9635148-1-4*) Spirit Talk Pr.

— Ni-Kso-Ko-Wa: Blackfoot Spirituality, Traditions, Values & Beliefs. 1995. 9.95 (*0-614-06313-2*) Spirit Talk Pr.

Long, Stephen. The Song of the Spirit & the Bride: Finding Jesus in the Song of Songs. 76p. (Orig.). 1991. pap. 4.95 (*0-9629550-0-0*) Word in Action.

— The Word Personalized, Vol. 1: Names of God. 44p. 1993. pap. 10.97 (*0-9629550-2-7*) Word in Action.

Long, Stephen G. Meeting Places with Jesus. (Illus.). 60p. (Orig.). 1992. pap. 4.95 (*0-9629550-1-9*) Word in Action.

Long, Stephen I. Gallium Arsenide Digital Integrated Circuit Design. (Illus.). 416p. 1990. text ed. write for info. (*0-07-038687-0*) McGraw.

Long, Steve & Long, Cindy. Marketing Your Arts & Crafts. (Illus.). 192p. (Orig.). (C). 1987. pap. text ed. 14.95 (*0-9618894-0-3*) Idahome Pubns.

— You Can Make Money from Your Arts & Crafts: The Arts & Crafts Marketing Book. rev. ed. Strickland, Al, ed. (Be Your Own Boss Ser.). (Illus.). 224p. 1988. pap. 14.95 (*0-937769-04-5*) Mark Inc CA.

Long, Stewart L. The Development of the Television Network Oligopoly. Sterling, Christopher H., ed. LC 78-21725. (Dissertations in Broadcasting Ser.). (Illus.). 1980. lib. bdg. 17.95 (*0-405-11764-7*) Ayer.

Long Sun Tong. Principles of Design Improvement for Light Water Reactors. 393p. 1988. 121.00 (*0-89116-416-2*) Hemisp Pub.

Long, Susan. A Structural Analysis of Small Groups. 192p. 1991. 69.50 (*0-415-06501-1*, A6456) Routledge.

Long, Susan O. Family Change & the Life Course in Japan. (Cornell East Asia Ser.: No. 44). 82p. (Orig.). 1987. pap. 9.00 (*0-939657-44-9*) Cornell East Asia Pgm.

Long, Sylvester, jt. auth. see Chief Buffalo Child.

Long, Sylvia. Sylvia Long's Little Rabbits. (Art Card Ser.). 1994. boxed 5.95 (*0-8118-0556-5*) Chronicle Bks.

Long, Sylvia, jt. auth. see Ervin, Gary W.

Long, Teddy C. Fantastic Paper Holiday Decorations. LC 93-39110. 96p. 1993. 19.95 (*1-895569-18-4*, Pub. by Tamos Bks CN) Sterling.

— Make Your Own Performing Puppets. LC 94-35536. (Illus.). 96p. (J). 1995. 19.95 (*1-895569-32-X*, Pub. by Tamos Bks CN) Sterling.

Long, Teddy C., jt. auth. see Fryatt, Evelyn H.

Long, Teddy C., jt. auth. see Walter, F. Virginia.

***Long, Thomas.** Whispering the Lyrics. 1995. pap. write for info. (*0-7880-0492-1*) CSS OH.

Long, Thomas, jt. auth. see Long, Matthew.

Long, Thomas E. Basic Mathematics Skills & Vocational Education. 28p. 1980. 2.80 (*0-318-22041-5*, IN199) Ctr Educ Trng Employ.

Long, Thomas G. Preaching & the Literary Forms of the Bible. LC 88-45243. 144p. 1988. pap. text ed. 12.00 (*0-8006-2313-4*, 1-2313, Fortress Pr) Augsburg Fortress.

— The Senses of Preaching. LC 88-9148. 96p. 1988. pap. 11.99 (*0-8042-1570-7*) Westminster John Knox.

— The Witness of Preaching. 216p. (Orig.). 1989. pap. 13.99 (*0-8042-1571-5*) Westminster John Knox.

Long, Thomas G. & McCarter, Neely D., eds. Preaching in & out of Season. 132p. (Orig.). 1990. pap. 12.99 (*0-664-25149-8*) Westminster John Knox.

Long, Thomas G. & Plantinga, Conelius, Jr., eds. A Chorus of Witnesses: Model Sermons for Today's Preacher. 320p. (Orig.). 1994. pap. 17.99 (*0-8028-0132-3*) Eerdmans.

Long, Thomas G., jt. ed. see O'Day, Gail R.

Long, Thomas J. Safe at Home, Safe Alone. (Illus.). 64p. (Orig.). (J). (gr. 3-5). 1985. pap. 4.95 (*0-917917-01-4*) Miles River.

Long, Thomas J., et al. Completing Dissertations in the Behavioral Sciences & Education: A Systematic Guide for Graduate Students. LC 85-45063. (Higher & Adult Education Ser.). 238p. 1985. 28.95x (*0-87589-658-8*) Jossey-Bass.

Long, Timothy. Barbarians in Greek Comedy. LC 85-18363. 328p. (C). 1986. text ed. 29.95 (*0-8093-1248-4*) S Ill U Pr.

***Long, Toby M. & Cintas, Holly M.** Handbook of Pediatric Physical Therapy. LC 94-38122. 1995. write for info. (*0-683-05155-5*) Williams & Wilkins.

Long, V. Philips. The Art of Biblical History. (Foundations of Contemporary Interpretation Ser.: Vol. 5). 160p. 1994. pap. 17.99 (*0-310-43180-8*) Zondervan.

— The Reign & Rejection of King Saul: A Case for Literary & Theological Coherence. 294p. 1989. 23.95 (*1-55540-391-3*); pap. 11.95 (*1-55540-392-1*, 06 21 18) Scholars Pr GA.

Long, Valentine. Angels in Religion & Art. LC 77-117712. 1971. reprint ed. pap. 9.95 (*0-8199-0430-9*, Frncscn Herld) Franciscan Pr.

— Upon This Rock. 1983. 12.00 (*0-8199-0834-7*, Frncscn Herld) Franciscan Pr.

Long, Virginia L. All Roads Lead to Bushy Fork. Hathaway, Michael, ed. (Illus.). 63p. (Orig.). 1992. pap. 6.00 (*0-943795-22-2*) Chiron Rev.

***Long, Vonda O.** Communication Skills in Helping Relationships: A Framework for Facilitating Personal Growth. LC 95-8350. 1996. text ed. 30.95 (*0-534-33869-0*) Brooks-Cole.

Long, W. G. Long: History of the Long Family of Pennsylvania. 365p. 1993. reprint ed. lib. bdg. 66.00 (*0-8328-3705-9*); reprint ed. pap. 56.00 (*0-8328-3706-7*) Higginson Bk Co.

Long, Walter. Fingertip Japanese. 192p. 1994. pap. 9.95 (*0-8348-0270-8*) Weatherhill.

— Sumo: A Pocket Guide. LC 89-50474. (Illus.). 128p. 1989. pap. 9.95 (*0-8048-1594-1*) C E Tuttle.

Long, Walter S., illus. Brushwork Diary: Watercolors of Early Nevada. LC 91-12179. 136p. 1991. 24.95 (*0-87417-174-1*) U of Nev Pr.

Long, Wayne A., jt. auth. see McMullen, W. Edward.

Long, William, jt. auth. see Carney, Glandion.

Long, William B., jt. ed. see Elton, W. R.

Long, William J. Northern Trails: Some Studies of Animal Life in the Far North. (Illus.). xxv, 390p. 1989. reprint ed. pap. 14.95 (*0-936041-05-6*) Barbary Coast Bks.

— United States Export Control Policy: The National Organization of Power. 200p. 1989. text ed. 40.50 (*0-231-06798-4*) Col U Pr.

Long, William S. The Nationalists: The Australians, Vol. II. braille ed. 902p. 1993. vinyl bd. 72.16 (*1-56956-377-2*, BR9148) W A T Braille.

Long, Yolanda, jt. auth. see Long, Chris.

Long, Zeb B. & McMurry, Douglas. The Collapse of the Brass Heaven: Rebuilding Our Worldview to Embrace the Power of God. 272p. (Orig.). 1994. pap. 11.99 (*0-8007-9215-7*) Revell.

Long, Zhang, ed. Chinese Modern Folk Paintings. (Illus.). 400p. (CHI & ENG.). 1992. 178.00 (*1-880132-05-2*) Sci Pr NY.

Long, Zhang, tr. see Wang Yaoan, ed.

Long, Zhang, tr. see Wang Yao'an, ed.

Longabaugh, Karen, jt. auth. see Longabaugh, Rick.

Longabaugh, Rick & Longabaugh, Karen. Collapsible Basket Patterns. (Illus.). 128p. 1992. pap. 12.95 (*0-9633112-0-4*) Berry Basket.

— 400 Full-Size Mini-Clock Patterns. 128p. 1994. 14.95 (*0-9633112-6-3*) Berry Basket.

— Miniature Multi-Use Collapsible Basket Patterns. (Illus.). 128p. Date not set. pap. 12.95 (*0-9633112-2-0*) Berry Basket.

— Multi-Use Collapsible Basket Patterns. (Illus.). 128p. 1992. pap. 12.95 (*0-9633112-1-2*) Berry Basket.

— Multi-Use Collapsible Basket Patterns, Bk. 2. (Illus.). 128p. Date not set. pap. 12.95 (*0-9633112-3-9*) Berry Basket.

Longabaugh, Rick, jt. auth. see Spielman, Patrick.

Longaberger, Dave, jt. auth. see Williford, Steve.

Longacre, Celeste. Star Mates for Aries. Lewis, Lesle, ed. (Illus.). (Orig.). 1994. pap. 6.95 (*0-930043-01-4*) Sweet Fern.

— Star Mates for Cancer. Lewis, Lesle, ed. (Illus.). (Orig.). 1994. pap. 6.95 (*0-930043-04-9*) Sweet Fern.

— Star Mates for Capricorn. Lewis, Lesle, ed. (Illus.). (Orig.). 1995. pap. 6.95 (*0-930043-10-3*) Sweet Fern.

— Star Mates for Gemini. Lewis, Lesle, ed. (Illus.). (Orig.). 1994. pap. 6.95 (*0-930043-03-0*) Sweet Fern.

— Star Mates for Leo. Lewis, Lesle, ed. (Illus.). (Orig.). 1994. pap. 6.95 (*0-930043-05-7*) Sweet Fern.

— Star Mates for Libra. Lewis, Lesle, ed. (Illus.). (Orig.). 1994. pap. 6.95 (*0-930043-07-3*) Sweet Fern.

— Star Mates for Sagittarius. Lewis, Lesle, ed. (Illus.). (Orig.). 1995. pap. 6.95 (*0-930043-09-X*) Sweet Fern.

— Star Mates for Scorpio. Lewis, Lesle, ed. (Illus.). (Orig.). 1994. pap. 6.95 (*0-930043-08-1*) Sweet Fern.

— Star Mates for Taurus. Lewis, Lesle, ed. (Illus.). (Orig.). 1994. pap. 6.95 (*0-930043-02-2*) Sweet Fern.

— Star Mates for Virgo. Lewis, Lesle, ed. (Illus.). (Orig.). 1994. pap. 6.95 (*0-930043-06-5*) Sweet Fern.

— Visitor's Guide to Planet Earth: An Astrological Primer. (Orig.). 1984. pap. 5.00 (*0-930043-00-6*) Sweet Fern.

Longacre, Doris. Living More with Less. LC 80-15461. 304p. 1980. pap. 8.95 (*0-8361-1930-4*) Herald Pr.

— More-with-Less Cookbook. LC 75-23563. 320p. 1976. pap. 15.95 (*0-8361-1786-7*) Herald Pr.

— Weniger Ist Mehr. 352p. (Orig.). (GER.). 1983. pap. 19.95 (*0-8361-1266-0*) Herald Pr.

Longacre, Edward G. The Cavalry at Gettysburg: A Tactical Study of Mounted Operations During the Civil War's Pivotal Campaign, 9 June-14 July 1863. LC 92-37790. 338p. (C). 1993. pap. 12.95 (*0-8032-7941-8*) U of Nebr Pr.

— Jersey Cavalliers: A History of the First New Jersey Cavalry, 1861-1865. (Illus.). 423p. 1992. 35.00 (*0-944413-19-6*) Longstreet Hse.

— The Man Behind the Gun. 294p. 1977. 20.00 (*0-942211-99-5*) Olde Soldier Bks.

— Mounted Raids of the Civil War. LC 93-48611. (Illus.). 348p. (C). 1994. pap. 12.95 (*0-8032-7946-9*, Bison Books) U of Nebr Pr.

— To Gettysburg & Beyond: The Twelfth New Jersey Volunteer Infantry, II Corps, Army of the Potomac, 1862-1865. LC 87-82809. (Illus.). 467p. (C). 1988. 36.00 (*0-944413-06-4*) Longstreet Hse.

Longacre, Edward G., ed. From Antietam to Fort Fisher: The Civil War Letters of Edward King Wightman, 1862-1865. LC 83-49343. (Illus.). 296p. 1985. 39.50 (*0-8386-3210-6*) Fairleigh Dickinson.

Longacre, James B., jt. auth. see Herring, James.

Longacre, Paul, jt. auth. see Heisey, Nancy.

Longacre, R. E. An Anatomy of Speech Notions. v, 394p. (Orig.). (C). 1986. pap. text ed. 82.00 (*3-11-013322-9*) Mouton.

Longacre, Robert E. Discourse Grammar: Studies in Indigenous Languages of Colombia, Panama & Ecuador, 3 vols., 1. (Publications in Linguistics & Related Fields: No. 52). fiche 20.00 (*0-88312-463-7*) Summer Instit Ling.

— Discourse Grammar: Studies in Indigenous Languages of Colombia, Panama & Ecuador, 3 vols., 2. (Publications in Linguistics & Related Fields: No. 52). fiche 16.00 (*0-88312-464-5*) Summer Instit Ling.

— Discourse Grammar: Studies in Indigenous Languages of Colombia, Panama & Ecuador, 3 vols., 3. (Publications in Linguistics & Related Fields: No. 52). fiche 16.00 (*0-88312-465-3*) Summer Instit Ling.

— Discourse Grammar: Studies in Indigenous Languages of Colombia, Panama & Ecuador, 3 vols., Set. (Publications in Linguistics & Related Fields: No. 52). fiche 28.00 (*0-88312-460-2*) Summer Instit Ling.

— Grammar Discovery Procedures: A Field Manual. (Janua Linguarum, Series Minor: No. 33). (Orig.). 1964. pap. text ed. 18.00 (*90-279-2431-7*) Mouton.

— The Grammar of Discourse. LC 83-3993. (Topics in Language & Linguistics Ser.). 446p. 1983. 69.50 (*0-306-41273-X*, Plenum Pr) Plenum.

— Joseph: A Story of Divine Providence: A Text Theoretical & Textlinguistic Analysis of Genesis 37 & 39-48. LC 88-19754. xiv, 322p. (C). 1989. text ed. 30.00 (*0-931464-42-0*) Eisenbrauns.

Longacre, Robert E. & Jones, Linda K., eds. Discourse Studies in Meso American Languages, 2 vols., 1. (Publications in Linguistics: No. 58). 1979. fiche 16.00x (*0-88312-578-1*) Summer Instit Ling.

— Discourse Studies in Meso American Languages, 2 vols., 2. (Publications in Linguistics: No. 58). 1979. fiche 12.00x (*0-88312-480-7*) Summer Instit Ling.

— Discourse Studies in Meso American Languages, 2 vols., Set. (Publications in Linguistics: No. 58). 1979. fiche 28.00x (*0-88312-478-5*) Summer Instit Ling.

***Longacre, Sean.** Client-Centered Hypnotherapy. 96p. 1994. per., pap. text ed. 20.95 (*0-7872-0074-3*) Kendall-Hunt.

— Prin.-Clin. Applications. 96p. 1994. per., pap. text ed. 20.95 (*0-7872-0073-5*) Kendall-Hunt.

Longacre, William A. Archaeology As Anthropology: A Case Study. LC 79-113089. (Anthropological Papers: No. 17). 57p. 1970. pap. 6.95 (*0-8165-0219-6*) U of Ariz Pr.

Longacre, William A., ed. Ceramic Ethnoarchaeology. LC 90-20982. (Illus.). 307p. 1991. 50.00 (*0-8165-1198-5*) U of Ariz Pr.

Longacre, William A. & Skibo, James M. Kalinga Ethnoarchaeology: Expanding Archaeological Method & Theory. (Archaeological Inquiry Ser.). (Illus.). 256p. (C). 1994. text ed. 49.50 (*1-56098-272-1*) Smithsonian.

Longacre, William A., et al, eds. Multidisciplinary Research at Grasshopper Pueblo, Arizona. LC 82-13715. (Anthropological Papers: No. 40). 138p. 1982. pap. 14.95 (*0-8165-0425-3*) U of Ariz Pr.

Longair, M. S. High Energy Astrophysics Vol. 2: Stars, the Galaxy & Interstellar Medium. (Illus.). 416p. (C). 1994. 69.95 (*0-521-43439-4*); pap. 34.95 (*0-521-43584-6*) Cambridge U Pr.

Longair, Malcolm. Alice & the Space Telescope. LC 85-23924. (Illus.). 208p. 1989. 34.95 (*0-8018-2831-7*) Johns Hopkins.

Longair, Malcolm S. High Energy Astrophysics, Vol. 1: Particles, Photons & Their Detection. 2nd ed. (Illus.). 350p. (C). 1992. 69.95 (*0-521-38374-9*); pap. 34.95 (*0-521-38773-6*) Cambridge U Pr.

Longair, Malcolm S., jt. ed. see Einasto, Jaan.

Longaker, M. T., jt. ed. see Adzick, N. S.

Longaker, Mark, ed. see Dowson, Ernest.

Longaker, Richard P., ed. see Rossiter, Clinton.

***Longan, Kandis.** It's Great to Be Short...Not. 28p. (J). 1992. pap. 5.00 (*1-886210-07-1*) Tyketoon Yng Author.

***Longanecker, Diane.** Foal-Leading Success: A Natural Approach to Teaching Foals to Lead. (Illus.). 1996. write for info. (*0-614-04984-9*) Roustabout Pr.

— Trailer-Loading Success: A Step-by-Step Guide for Training Horses to Load. LC 92-91182. (Illus.). 103p. (Orig.). 1993. spiral bd. 28.50 (*0-9635320-0-6*) Roustabout Pr.

Longanecker, Georgia. Howdy Out There! Phonics Fun. LC 76-62681. (Illus.). (J). (ps-3). 1977. pap. 6.95 (*0-9601126-1-8*) Longanecker.

Longboat, Dianne, ed. see Green, Richard G.

Longbotham, Elisabeth P. & Longbotham, Jack H. The Adventures of Buffalo Bill & Cody: Meeting in the Mountains. (Young West Collection: Bk. 1). (Illus.). 28p. (J). (ps-3). 1995. 8.95 (*0-9645947-0-6*) West Heritage Pub. THE ADVENTURES OF BUFFALO BILL & CODY is a delightful story of two real live buffalo written as children's fiction. It is a tale which centers around the basic instincts of the largest native mammal of the American West. This book will be enjoyed by any age child who loves animal stories. It will stir their imagination from the very beginning through an encounter with the traditional enemy-the wolf-& on to their lifetime companionship, it will excite the youngster. This first book of the Young West Collection deals with the adventures of these two buffalo. It provides understanding of one of America's most beloved animals, which almost became extinct. The authors have written & designed the book for the young reader at pre-school & primary grade levels. At the same time, it provides a learning opportunity for the early reader to make the association & meaning between words & pictures. The beautiful four color illustrations preserve both color & dimension & capture the authenticity of the Buffalo. The authors are Christian educators & writers who own their own ranch where quarter horses, cattle & buffalo are raised - including Buffalo Bill & Cody. To order: Western Heritage Publishers, P.O. Box 3703, Abilene, TX 79604. Phone: 915-893-4345.** ***Publisher Provided Annotation.

Longbotham, Jack H., jt. auth. see Longbotham, Elisabeth P.

Longbotham, Lori. Quick & Easy Recipes to Boost Your Immune System. 112p. (Orig.). 1991. pap. 3.95 (*0-380-76080-0*) Avon.

Longbotham, Lori & Sonberg, Lynn. Quick & Easy Recipes to Lower Your Cholesterol. 112p. 1989. pap. 3.50 (*0-380-75871-7*) Avon.

Longbottom, Roy. Computer System Reliability. LC 79-40649. (Wiley Series in Computing). 345p. reprint ed. pap. 98.40 (*0-685-44425-2*, 2032661) Bks Demand.

Longchamp, Ferdinand. Asmodeus in New York. LC 75-1854. (Leisure Class in America Ser.). 1975. reprint ed. 26.95 (*0-405-06920-0*) Ayer.

Longdom, Danny G., ed. see Mentzer, Richard C.

Longdon, L. V., tr. see Levitan, B. M. & Zhikov, V. V.

***Longe, Bob.** Easy Card Tricks. LC 94-25142. (Illus.). 128p. 1995. pap. 4.95 (*0-8069-0950-1*) Sterling.

— Easy Magic Tricks. LC 94-11207. (Illus.). 128p. (J). 1994. 13.95 (*0-8069-1264-2*) Sterling.

— Great Card Tricks. LC 95-12702. (Illus.). 128p. 1995. pap. 4.95 (*0-8069-3894-3*) Sterling.

— Nutty Challenges & Zany Dares. LC 93-32391. (Illus.). 128p. (J). 1994. pap. 4.95 (*0-8069-0454-2*) Sterling.

— One Hundred One Amazing Card Tricks. LC 93-23861. (Illus.). 128p. 1993. pap. 4.95 (*0-8069-0342-2*) Sterling.

— World's Best Card Tricks. LC 90-46641. (Illus.). 128p. (YA). 1992. pap. 4.95 (*0-8069-8233-0*) Sterling.

— World's Best Coin Tricks. LC 92-11370. (Illus.). 128p. (J). (gr. 5-10). 1993. pap. 4.95 (*0-8069-8661-1*) Sterling.

Longe, G., ed. Multi-User Communication Systems. (CISM International Centre for Mechanical Sciences Ser.: Vol. 265). (Illus.). 259p. 1981. pap. 39.00 (*0-387-81612-7*) Spr-Verlag.

Longe, Karen M. & Brenner, Lisa B. Bar Code Technology in Health Care: A Tool for Enhancing Quality, Productivity & Cost Management. LC 93-71570. (Illus.). 131p. 1993. pap. 29.95 (*0-929870-20-4*) Advanstar Commns.

Longe, Mary E., jt. auth. see Kimble, Cathy S.

Longe, R. Leon & Calvert, John C. Physical Assessment: A Guide for Evaluating Drug Therapy. Young, Lloyd Y., ed. 250p. (Orig.). (C). 1994. pap. text ed. write for info. (*0-915486-20-2*) Applied Therapeutics.

Longe, Robert. The Files of a Counterfeit Sex Therapist. LC 76-56729. 1977. 22.95 (*0-87949-061-6*) Ashley Bks.

Longenbach, James. Modernist Poetics of History: Pound, Eliot & the Sense of the Past. 288p. 1987. text ed. 45.00 (*0-691-06707-4*) Princeton U Pr.

— Stone Cottage: Pound, Yeats, & Modernism. (Illus.). 352p. 1991. reprint ed. pap. 18.95 (*0-19-506662-6*) OUP.

— Wallace Stevens: The Plain Sense of Things. 352p. 1991. pap. 22.00 (*0-19-507022-4*) OUP.

Longenecker, Clarence E. How to Recover from a Stroke & Make a Successful Comeback. LC 77-79690. 1977. 18.95 (*0-87949-105-1*) Ashley Bks.

Longenecker, Gesina L. How Drugs Work. (Illus.). 256p. (Orig.). 1994. pap. 24.95 (*1-56276-241-9*) Ziff-Davis.

Longenecker, Gesina L., ed. The Platelets. 1985. text ed. 134.00 (*0-12-455555-1*) Acad Pr.

***Longenecker, Harold L.** Growing Leaders by Design: How to Develop Leadership Biblically. 160p. 1995. pap. 7.99 (*0-8254-3131-X*, 94-077) Kregel.

***Longenecker, John B., et al, eds.** Nutrition & Biotechnology in Heart Disease & Cancer: Proceedings of a Conference Held in Research Triangle Park, North Carolina, December 5-7, 1993. LC 95-7574. (Advances in Experimental Medicine & Biology Ser.: Vol. 369). 275p. 1995. 85.00 (*0-306-44994-3*, Plenum Pr) Plenum.

Longenecker, Justin G. & Moore, Carlos W. Small Business Management. 8th ed. 768p. (C). 1991. text ed. 55.95 (*0-538-80789-X*, GG70HA) S-W Pub.

Longenecker, Justin G. & Pringle, Charles D. Management. 6th ed. (C). 1984. write for info. (*0-675-20099-7*, Merrill Pub Co); pap. write for info. (*0-675-20164-0*, Merrill Pub Co) Macmillan.

Longenecker, Martha, comment. First Collections: Dolls & Folk Toys of the World. LC 87-62951. 160p. 1988. pap. 29.95 (*0-295-96661-0*) U of Wash Pr.

— Folk Toys of the World. (Illus.). 48p. 1978. 5.00 (*0-317-68011-0*) Mingei Intl Mus.

Longenecker, Martha, ed. Folk Art of the Soviet Union: Reflections of a Rich Cultural Diversity of the Fifteen Republics. LC 89-63305. (Illus.). 168p. (Orig.). 1991. 35.00 (*0-914155-06-7*, U of Wash Pr) Mingei Intl Mus.

— Laura Andreson: A Retrospective in Clay. LC 82-80626. (Illus.). 96p. 1982. 25.00 (*0-317-68018-8*) Mingei Intl Mus.

— Laura Andreson: A Retrospective in Clay. deluxe limited ed. LC 82-80626. (Illus.). 96p. 1982. 45.00 (*0-317-68019-6*) Mingei Intl Mus.

Longenecker, Martha W., ed. A Transcultural Mosaic: Folk Art from the Collection of Mingei International Museum. (Illus.). 130p. 1989. 35.00 (*0-914155-03-2*) Mingei Intl Mus.

— A Transcultural Mosaic: Selections from the Permanent Collection of Mingei International Museum of World Folk Art. (Illus.). 168p. 1994. 45.00 (*0-295-96913-X*) U of Wash Pr.

Longenecker, Richard. WBC, Vol. 41: Galatians. 432p. 1990. write for info. (*0-8499-0240-1*) Word Inc.

An Asterisk (*) at the beginning of an entry indicates that the title is appearing in BIP for the first time.

Longenecker, Richard N. Ministry & Message of Paul. (Contemporary Evangelical Perspective Ser.). 1971. 14.99 (*0-310-28341-8*, 12234P) Zondervan.

Longenecker, Richard N., jt. auth. see Tenney, Merrill C.

Longenecker, Sharon. Crushed but Not Destroyed. 232p. (Orig.). 1984. pap. 7.95 (*0-9614244-0-0*) Sun Ray Pub.

Longenecker, Stephen. The Christopher Sauers. 160p. (Orig.). 1981. 14.95 (*0-87178-139-5*); pap. 8.95 (*0-87178-141-7*) Brethren.

Longenecker, Stephen L. Piety & Tolerance: Pennsylvania German Religion, 1700-1850. LC 93-49988. (Pietist & Wesleyan Studies: No. 6). 216p. 1994. 27.50 (*0-8108-2771-9*) Scarecrow.

Longer, V. Defence & Foreign Policies of India. 390p. 1988. text ed. 40.00 (*81-207-0738-9*, Pub. by Sterling Pubs II) Apt Bks.

Longere, Jean. Les Sermons Latins de Maurice de Sully, Eveque de Paris (1196) Contribution a l'Histoire de la Tradition Manuscrite. (C). 1989. pap. text ed. 186.50 (*0-7923-0282-6*) Kluwer Ac.

Longes Mac Nusnig. Longesmacnuislenn: The Exile of the Sons of Uisliu. Hill, Vernan, ed. (MLA MS). 1949. 23.00 (*0-527-58150-X*) Periodicals Srv.

Longest, Beaufort B., Jr. Administrative Coordination in General Hospitals. LC 74-621513. (Research Monograph: No. 55). (Illus.). 224p. 1973. spiral bd. 30.00 (*0-88406-018-7*) GA St U Busn Pr.

— Health Policymaking in the United States. LC 94-18790. 240p. 1994. 38.00 (*1-56793-017-4*, 0947) Health Admin Pr.

— Health Professionals in Management. LC 94-43677. (C). 1995. pap. text ed. 27.95 (*0-8385-3679-4*) Appleton & Lange.

— Management Practices for the Health Professional. 4th ed. (Illus.). 221p. 1990. boxed 38.95 (*0-8385-6123-3*, A6123-2) Appleton & Lange.

Longest, David. Character Toys & Collectibles. (Illus.). 160p. 1990. 19.95 (*0-89145-266-4*) Collector Bks.

— Toys: Antique to Modern. 1994. 24.95 (*0-89145-596-5*) Collector Bks.

— Toys Antique & Collectible. 1990. pap. 14.95 (*0-89145-402-0*) Collector Bks.

Longest, George C. Genius in the Garden: Charles F. Gillette & Landscape Architecture in Virginia. LC 92-12464. 1992. 39.95 (*0-88490-172-6*) VA State Lib.

***Longeway, C. E.** Twelve. 190p. Date not set. pap. 7.95 (*0-7610-0229-4*) NW Pub.

Longfellow, Henry Wadsworth. Children's Own Longfellow. (Illus.). 109p. (J). (gr. 4-6). 1908. 19.95 (*0-395-06889-4*) HM.

— Complete Poems. 1992. reprint ed. lib. bdg. 35.95 (*0-89968-291-X*, Lghtyr Pr) Buccaneer Bks.

— Complete Writings, 11 vols., Set. (BCL1-PS American Literature Ser.). 1992. reprint ed. lib. bdg. 900.00 (*0-7812-6779-X*) Rprt Serv.

— Evangeline: A Tale of Acadia. (Illus.). 1995. 14.95 (*1-55109-116-X*, Pub. by Nimbus Publishing Ltd CN) Chelsea Green Pub.

— Evangeline: A Tale of Acadie. 109p. 1991. pap. 5.95 (*0-920852-13-0*, Pub. by Nimbus Publishing Ltd CN) Chelsea Green Pub.

— Evangeline & Other Poems. (Airmont Classics Ser.). (J). (gr. 7 up). pap. 1.50 (*0-8049-0094-9*, CL-94) Airmont.

— Evangeline & Other Poems. 64p. 1994. pap. text ed. 1.00 (*0-486-28255-4*) Dover.

— Evangeline & Selected Tales & Poems. Gregory, Horace, ed. 1964. pap. 4.95 (*0-451-52003-3*, CE1724, Sig Classics) NAL-Dutton.

— Favorite Poems. Orig. Title: The Complete Poetical Works of Henry Wadsworth Longfellow. 96p. 1992. reprint ed. pap. text ed. 1.00 (*0-486-27273-7*) Dover.

— Hiawatha. (Illus.). 32p. (J). (gr. k up). 1983. 16.99 (*0-8037-0013-X*); lib. bdg. 14.89 (*0-8037-0014-8*) Dial Bks Young.

— Hiawatha. LC 83-26972. (Legends & Folktales Ser.). (Illus.). (J). (gr. 2-5). 1984. lib. bdg. 19.97 (*0-8172-2106-9*); lib. bdg. 29.28 (*0-8172-2237-5*); pap. 23.95 (*0-8172-2265-0*) Raintree Steck-V.

— Hiawatha, with Its Original Indian Legends. (BCL1-PS American Literature Ser.). 255p. 1993. reprint ed. lib. bdg. 79.00 (*0-7812-6984-9*) Rprt Serv.

— Hiawatha's Childhood. (Illus.). 32p. (J). (gr. k up). 1984. 15.00 (*0-374-33065-4*) FS&G.

— Hiawatha's Childhood. (J). (ps-3). 1994. pap. 5.95 (*0-374-42997-9*, Sunburst Bks) FS&G.

— Hiawatha's Childhood. (Illus.). (J). (ps-3). 1987. pap. 3.99 (*0-14-050562-8*, Puffin) Puffin Bks.

— Kavanagh: A Tale. Downey, Jean, ed. (Masterworks of Literature Ser.). 1965. 15.95 (*0-8084-0198-X*); pap. 13.95x (*0-8084-0199-8*) NCUP.

— The Letters of Henry Wadsworth Longfellow, 6 vols. Hilen, Andrew R., ed. Incl. Set. 1814-36; 1837-43, 2 vols. LC 66-18248. 1164p. 1967. 95.00 (*0-674-52725-9*); Set. 1844-1856; 1857-1865, 2 vols. LC 66-18248. 1126p. 1972. 95.00 (*0-674-52728-3*); Set. 1866-1875; 1876-1882, 2 vols. LC 66-18248. 1792p. 1983. 127.50 (*0-674-52729-1*); LC 66-18248. write for info. (*0-318-53094-5*) Belknap Pr.

— Life of Henry Wadsworth Longfellow, with Extracts from His Journals & Correspondence, 3 vols., Set. Longfellow, Samuel, ed. LC 04-17165. 1968. reprint ed. 55.00 (*0-403-00078-5*) Scholarly.

— Paul Revere's Ride. LC 89-25630. (Illus.). 40p. (J). (gr. k-4). 1990. 14.99 (*0-525-44610-9*, DCB) Dutton Child Bks.

— Paul Revere's Ride. LC 84-4139. (Illus.). 48p. (J). (gr. 1 up). 1985. 14.95 (*0-688-04014-4*); lib. bdg. 14.88 (*0-688-04015-2*) Greenwillow.

— Paul Revere's Ride. LC 92-23319. (Illus.). 48p. (J). (gr. 1 up). 1993. reprint ed. pap. 4.95 (*0-688-12387-2*, Mulberry) Morrow.

— Selected Poems. Thwaite, Anthony, ed. 384p. 1993. pap. 12.95 (*0-460-87229-X*, Everyman's Classic Lib) C E Tuttle.

— Selected Poems. 240p. 1988. pap. 9.95 (*0-14-039064-2*, Penguin Classics) Viking Penguin.

— Selected Poems of Henry Wadsworth Longfellow. 1992. 6.99 (*0-517-08246-2*) Random Hse Value.

— Song of Hiawatha. 1982. 7.99 (*0-517-00197-7*) Random Hse Value.

— The Song of Hiawatha. Aaron, Daniel, ed. 176p. 1993. pap. 2.95 (*0-460-87268-0*, Everyman's Classic Lib) C E Tuttle.

— Works, 14 vols., Set. reprint ed. write for info. (*0-404-04040-3*) AMS Pr.

— Your Life Depends On It!, 2 vol. set. Molina, Tarea, ed. & intro. by. (Illus.). 1994. student ed write for info. (*0-9642779-2-1*) T Molina Ent.

Longfellow, S., ed. see Johnson, Samuel.

Longfellow, Samuel. Life of Henry Wadsworth Longfellow: With Extracts from His Journals & Correspondence, 3 vols., Set. (BCL1-PS American Literature Ser.). 1992. reprint ed. lib. bdg. 225.00 (*0-7812-6781-1*) Rprt Serv.

Longfellow, Samuel, ed. see Longfellow, Henry Wadsworth.

Longfellow, Sandra P., jt. ed. see Nelson, James B.

Longfellow, William W. The Children's Hour. 1993. 17.95 (*0-87923-971-9*) Godine.

Longfield, Bradley J. The Presbyterian Controversy: Fundamentalists, Modernists, & Moderates. (Religion in America Ser.). (Illus.). 352p. 1993. reprint ed. pap. 18.95 (*0-19-508674-0*) OUP.

Longfield, Bradley J., jt. ed. see Marsden, George M.

Longfield, Diane M. Passage to ESL Literacy. (Illus.). 422p. (Orig.). 1981. teacher ed, pap. 22.95 (*0-937354-03-1*); student ed, pap. text ed. 10.50 (*0-937354-01-5*) Delta Systems.

— Passage to ESL Literacy Visuals. (Illus.). 182p. (Orig.). 1981. teacher ed, pap. 23.95 (*0-937354-11-2*) Delta Systems.

Longfield, Jeanette & Rayner, Mike. Preventing Cardiovascular Disease in Europe. 135p. 1993. pap. 30.00 (*0-11-701755-8*, HM17558, Pub. by HMSO UK) UNIPUB.

Longfield, Mountiford. Economic Writings of Mountiford Longfield. Black, R. D., ed. LC 73-144801. (Reprints of Economic Classics Ser.). 1971. 49.50 (*0-678-00836-1*) Kelley.

Longfish, George C., jt. auth. see Penney, David W.

***Longford.** Mishka & Plishka. (J). Date not set. 16.00 (*0-689-80244-7*, Aladdin Paperbacks) S&S Childrens.

Longford, E. Wellington: Pillar of State. 547p. 1975. 10.00 (*0-586-04155-9*, Pub. by Granada UK) Academy Chi Pubs.

***Longford, Elizabeth.** The Oxford Book of Royal Anecdotes. braille ed. 1489p. 1991. text ed. 119.12 (*1-56956-315-2*, BR8085) W A T Braille.

Longford, Elizabeth, ed. The Oxford Book of Royal Anecdotes. (Illus.). 572p. 1989. 24.95 (*0-19-214153-8*) OUP.

— The Oxford Book of Royal Anecdotes. (Illus.). 576p. 1992. reprint ed. pap. 13.95 (*0-19-282851-7*) OUP.

Longford, Elizabeth, sel. Poets' Corner: An Anthology of Prose & Poetry by Those Commemorated at Westminster Abbey. 256p. 1993. 34.95 (*1-85592-058-1*, Pub. by Chapmans UK) Trafalgar.

Longford, Lindsay. Annie & the Wise Men: Under the Mistletoe. (Silhouette Romance Ser.). 1993. pap. 2.75 (*0-373-08977-5*, 5-08977-6) Silhouette.

— The Cowboy & the Princess. 1995. mass mkt. 2.99 (*0-373-19115-4*, 1-19115-4) Silhouette.

— The Cowboy, the Baby & the: (Bundles of Joy) (Sil Romance Ser.). 1995. mass mkt. 2.99 (*0-373-19073-5*, 1-19073-5) Silhouette.

— Dark Moon. (Shadows Ser.). 1995. mass mkt. 3.50 (*0-373-27053-4*, 1-27053-7) Silhouette.

— Lover in the Shadows. (Shadows Ser.). 1994. mass mkt. 3.50 (*0-373-27029-1*, 5-27029-3) Silhouette.

— Sullivan's Miracle. (Silhouette Intimate Moments Ser.). 1993. mass mkt. 3.50 (*0-373-07526-X*, 5-07526-2) Silhouette.

Longford, Nicholas T. Random Coefficient Models. LC 93-35629. (Oxford Statistical Science Ser.: No. 11). (Illus.). 288p. (C). 1994. 45.00 (*0-19-852264-9*, Clarendon Pr) OUP.

Longford, Nicholas T., jt. auth. see Lockheed, Marlaine E.

***Longford, Nick.** Models for Uncertainty in Educational Testing. LC 95-8145. (Series in Statistics). 1995. write for info. (*0-387-94513-X*) Spr-Verlag.

Longgood, William. The Queen Must Die & Other Affairs of Bees & Men. (Illus.). 1988. pap. 11.95 (*0-393-30528-7*) Norton.

Longguan, Zhang, jt. ed. see Lodl, Ann.

Longheed, L. Business Communication: Ten Steps to Success. (Business for Career Success Ser.). 1994. pap. text ed. 12.00 (*0-201-51676-4*) Longman.

— Business Correspondence: Letters, Faxes & Memos. (English for Business Success Ser.). (Illus.). 143p. 1993. pap. text ed. 12.00 (*0-201-55537-9*) Addison-Wesley.

— Business Small Talk: Five Steps to Success. (Business for Career Success Ser.). (YA). 1995. pap. text ed. 12.00 (*0-201-54261-7*); audio write for info. (*0-201-54262-5*) Longman.

— Words More Words, & Ways to Use Them. (YA). (gr. 7 up). 1993. pap. text ed. 10.95 (*0-201-53961-6*) Longman.

Longhetto, A. Atmospheric Planetary Boundary Layer Physics: Proceedings of the International Course Held in Erice, Sicily, February, 1978. (Developments in Atmospheric Science Ser.: Vol. 11). 424p. 1980. 110.25 (*0-444-41885-7*) Elsevier.

Longhi, Jon. Bricks & Anchors. 128p. (Orig.). 1991. pap. 8.95 (*0-916397-12-2*) Manic D Pr.

— The Rise & Fall of Third Leg. 160p. (Orig.). 1994. pap. 9.95 (*0-916397-27-0*) Manic D Pr.

— Zucchini & Other Stories. (Illus.). 20p. 1990. 3.00 (*0-916397-07-6*) Manic D Pr.

***Longhurst, A. H.** The Story of the Stupa. (C). 1995. 18.00x (*81-206-0160-2*, Pub. by Asian Educ Servs II) S Asia.

Longhurst, Alan R. & Pauly, Daniel, eds. Ecology of Tropical Oceans. 407p. 1987. text ed. 66.00 (*0-12-455562-4*) Acad Pr.

Longhurst, Audrey, jt. auth. see Longhurst, Jean.

Longhurst, Brian. Karl Mannheim & the Contemporary Sociology of Knowledge. LC 88-4627. 230p. 1988. text ed. 45.00 (*0-312-02017-1*) St Martin.

— Popular Music & Society. 278p. (C). 1995. text ed. write for info. (*0-7456-1437-X*); pap. text ed. write for info. (*0-7456-1464-7*) Blackwell Pubs.

Longhurst, Brian & Adler, Michael. Discourse, Power & Justice: Towards a New Sociology of Improvement. LC 93-46106. (International Library of Sociology). 304p. 1993. 79.95x (*0-415-04237-2*, B3563) Routledge.

Longhurst, C. A., ed. see De Unamuno, Miguel.

Longhurst, Derek, ed. Gender, Genre & Narrative Pleasure. 176p. 1989. text ed. 49.95 (*0-318-41096-6*); pap. text ed. 12.95 (*0-04-445009-5*) Routledge Chapman & Hall.

Longhurst, J. W., ed. Acid Deposition: Origins, Impacts & Abatement Strategies. (Illus.). 364p. 1991. 218.00 (*0-387-53741-4*) Spr-Verlag.

Longhurst, Jean & Longhurst, Audrey. COBOL. (Illus.). 656p. (C). 1989. pap. text ed. 34.00 (*0-13-139387-1*) P-H.

Longhurst, Jean, jt. auth. see Singelmann, Jay.

Longhurst, Jean, jt. auth. see Singlemann, Jay.

Longhurst, John E. The Age of Torquemada. 146p. 1964. 10.00 (*0-87291-052-0*) Coronado Pr.

— Will the Faculty Please Come to Order. 68p. 1969. pap. 2.50 (*0-87291-003-2*) Coronado Pr.

Longhurst, John E., intro. The Spartan Rhetra. 76p. 1970. pap. 5.00 (*0-87291-008-3*) Coronado Pr.

Longhurst, Nancy A. The Self-Advocacy Movement by People with Developmental Disabilities: A Demographic Study & Directory of Self-Advocacy Groups in the United States. LC 93-48121. 1994. 21.95 (*0-940898-32-2*) Am Assn Mental.

Longhurst, Rey D. How to Start & Operate Your Own Major Appliance Repair Business, Without Capital or Experience: For Major Appliances. Barber, Carolyn, ed. (Illus.). 137p. (Orig.). 1988. pap. 30.00 (*1-56302-109-9*) R Longhurst.

Longhurst, Richard, jt. auth. see Lipton, Michael.

Longhurst, Thomas M., ed. Linguistic Analysis of Children's Speech: Readings. 1974. 29.00 (*0-8422-5173-1*); pap. text ed. 9.95 (*0-8422-0404-0*) Irvington.

Longino, jt. auth. see Waas, Lane.

***Longino, Charles & Murphy, John.** The Old Age Challenge to the Biomedical Model: Paradigm Strain & Health Policy. LC 94-30642. (Society & Aging Ser.). (C). 1995. text ed. 21.95 (*0-89503-165-5*); text ed. 16.45 (*0-89503-167-1*) Baywood Pub.

***Longino, Charles F.** Retirement Migration in America: An Analysis of the Size, Trends & Economic Impact of the Country's Newest Growth Industry. Fox, R. Alan, ed. & frwd. by. (Illus.). 185p. (Orig.). 1995. pap. 39.95 (*0-9644216-1-5*) Vacation Pubns.

Longino, Helen E. Science As Social Knowledge: Value & Objectivity in Scientific Inquiry. 252p. (Orig.). 1990. pap. text ed. 15.95 (*0-691-02051-5*) Princeton U Pr.

Longino, Helen E. & Miner, Valerie, eds. Competition: A Feminist Taboo? LC 87-8515. 208p. 1987. text ed. 35.00 (*0-935312-75-7*); pap. 12.95 (*0-935312-74-9*) Feminist Pr.

Longinovic, Tomislav Z. Borderline Culture: The Politics of Identity in Four Twentieth-Century Slavic Novels. LC 92-20696. 216p. 1993. 24.00 (*1-55728-262-5*) U of Ark Pr.

Longinus. Longinus - Longini De Sublimitate Lexicon. Neuberger, Ruth, ed. (Alpha-Omega, Reihe A Ser.: Bd. LXXXVIII). viii, 118p. (GER.). 1987. write for info. (*3-487-07896-1*, Pub. by Georg Olms GW) Lubrecht & Cramer.

— On Great Writing on the Sublime. Grube, G. M., tr. LC 57-14628. 1957. pap. 2.40 (*0-672-60261-X*, LLA79, Bobbs) Macmillan.

— On Great Writing (On the Sublime) Grube, G. M., tr. & intro. by. LC 90-49700. 88p. (C). 1991. reprint ed. lib. bdg. 24.50 (*0-87220-081-7*); reprint ed. pap. text ed. 5.95 (*0-87220-080-9*) Hackett Pub.

Longinus, Cassius. Longinus on the Sublime. LC 78-41181. reprint ed. 22.50 (*0-404-14743-7*) AMS Pr.

— Longinus on the Sublime: The Peri Hupsous in Translations by Nicolas Boileau-Despreaux (1674) & William Smith (1739) LC 75-8892. 390p. 1975. lib. bdg. 60.00 (*0-8201-1153-8*) Schol Facsimiles.

Longland, W. How to Read Workshop Drawings. 6.00 (*0-85344-057-3*) Apple Blossom.

Longley. Data & Security. 1989. 46.95 (*0-8493-7110-4*) CRC Pr.

Longley, A. J. What You Don't Know Can Hurt You: A Guide to the Medical Literature. (Orig.). (C). 1981. pap. 3.00 (*0-937038-00-8*) Star Pr.

Longley, Alcander. What Is Communism. 2nd enl. rev. ed. LC 73-8710. (Communal Societies in America Ser.). reprint ed. 42.50 (*0-404-10727-3*) AMS Pr.

Longley-Cook, L. H. Fun with Brain Puzzles. 128p. 1982. pap. 1.95 (*0-449-13755-4*, GM) Fawcett.

Longley, Denise, ed. see Stephens, Frances H.

***Longley, Dennis.** Parat Lexikon Information und Kommunilation. 637p. (GER.). 1993. 195.00 (*0-7859-8683-9*, 352726843x) Fr & Eur.

Longley, Dennis & Shain, M. Expanding & Networking Microcomputers: The Complete & Up-to-Date Guide to over 600 Boards for Apple & IBM-PCs. 200p. 1985. 48.00 (*0-685-10213-0*, North Holland) Elsevier.

Longley, Dennis & Shain, Michael. Dictionary of Information Technology. 2nd ed. (Illus.). 382p. 1986. 29.95 (*0-19-520519-7*) OUP.

Longley, Dennis, et al. Dictionary of Information Security Standards Concepts & Terms. 2nd ed. 632p. 1993. 130.00 (*1-56159-069-X*, Stockton Pr) Groves Dictionaries.

Longley, Diane. Public Law & Health Service Accountability. LC 92-13011. (State of Health Ser.). 1993. 90.00 (*0-335-09686-7*, Open Univ Pr); pap. 32.50 (*0-335-09685-9*, Open Univ Pr) Taylor & Francis.

Longley, Edna. Dorothy Hewett: Selected Poems. 128p. 1990. pap. 21.00 (*1-85224-125-X*, Pub. by Bloodaxe Bks UK) Dufour.

— The Living Stream: Literature & Revisionism in Ireland. 302p. 1995. 55.00 (*1-85224-216-7*, Pub. by Bloodaxe Bks UK); pap. 25.00 (*1-85224-217-5*, Pub. by Bloodaxe Bks UK) Dufour.

— Poetry in the Wars. LC 86-25069. 264p. 1987. 38.50 (*0-87413-322-X*) U Delaware Pr.

Longley, Edna, ed. see Hewett, Dorothy.

Longley, Enda, ed. From Cathleen to Anorexia: The Breakdown of Irelands. (C). 1989. 35.00 (*0-946211-99-X*, Pub. by Attic Pr IE) St Mut.

Longley, James W. Least Squares Computations Using Orthogonalization Methods. LC 84-14939. (Lecture Notes in Pure & Applied Mathematics Ser.: No. 93). 328p. reprint ed. pap. 93.50 (*0-8357-2529-4*, 2052408) Bks Demand.

Longley, John L. The Tragic Mask: A Study of Faulkner's Heroes. LC 63-22806. 254p. reprint ed. pap. 72.40 (*0-8357-4414-0*, 2037234) Bks Demand.

Longley, John L., ed. Robert Penn Warren: A Collection of Critical Essays. LC 78-25757. 259p. 1979. reprint ed. text ed. 35.00 (*0-313-20807-7*, LORW, Greenwood Pr) Greenwood.

Longley, Judy. Rowing Past Eden. Page, Carolyn, ed. & illus. by. (Chapbook Ser.). 36p. (Orig.). 1992. pap. text ed. 6.00 (*1-879205-34-3*) Nightshade Pr.

Longley, Kateryna, jt. auth. see Gunew, Sneja.

Longley, L. Thomas: Poems - Last Poems. 1990. pap. 21.00 (*0-7121-0146-2*, Pub. by Northcote UK) St Mut.

Longley, Lawrence D. Bicameral Politics: Conference Committees in Congress. LC 88-27766. 400p. (C). 1989. 20.00 (*0-300-04544-1*) Yale U Pr.

— Changing the System. (New Directions in Comparative Politics Ser.). 192p. 1929. text ed. 38.50 (*0-8133-1506-9*) Westview.

— Changing the System. (New Directions in Comparative Politics Ser.). 192p. (C). 1929. pap. text ed. 16.95 (*0-8133-1507-7*) Westview.

Longley, Lawrence D. & Braun, Alan G. The Politics of Electoral College Reform. 2nd ed. LC 72-75202. 238p. reprint ed. pap. 67.90 (*0-8357-8277-8*, 2033805) Bks Demand.

Longley, Lawrence D., jt. auth. see Peirce, Neal R.

Longley, Mark. Analysis for Well Completion. Leecraft, Jodie, ed. (Oil & Gas Production Ser.). (Illus.). 108p. (Orig.). (C). 1984. pap. text ed. 15.00 (*0-88698-084-4*, 3.31110) PETEX.

Longley, Mark, ed. Testing & Completing. 2nd ed. (Rotary Drilling Ser.: Unit II, Lesson 5). (Illus.). 72p. (C). 1983. pap. text ed. 14.00 (*0-88698-120-4*, 2.20520) PETEX.

Longley, Mark, ed. see Skinner, David.

Longley, Michael. Gorse Fires. LC 91-72021. 52p. 1991. 11.95 (*0-916390-49-7*); pap. 6.95 (*0-916390-48-9*) Wake Forest.

— No Continuing City, Poems Nineteen Sixty-Three to Nineteen Sixty-Eight. LC 72-84906. 1969. 14.95 (*0-8023-1248-9*) Dufour.

— Poems, Nineteen Sixty-Three to Nineteen Eighty-Three. LC 87-50675. 206p. 1987. pap. 8.95 (*0-916390-28-4*) Wake Forest.

Longley, Michael, intro. The Selected Poems of Louis MacNeice. LC 89-51504. 160p. 1990. 15.95 (*0-916390-39-X*); pap. 9.95 (*0-916390-38-1*) Wake Forest.

***Longley, Paul & Clarke, Graham, eds.** GIS for Businesss & Service Planning. LC 95-8670. 1995. write for info. (*0-470-23510-1*) Longman.

Longley, Paul, jt. auth. see Batty, Michael.

Longley, Ronald S. Sir Francis Hincks: A Study of Canadian Politics, Railways, & Finance in the Nineteenth Century. Bruchey, Stuart, ed. LC 80-1326. (Railroads Ser.). 1981. reprint ed. lib. bdg. 44.95 (*0-405-13800-8*) Ayer.

Longley, William R., et al. Analytic Geometry & Calculus. LC 60-3940. 616p. reprint ed. pap. 175.60 (*0-8357-5446-4*, 2055267) Bks Demand.

Longman. Composing Drama for Stage & Screen. 1986. text ed. 37.25 (*0-205-08737-X*, H87372) Allyn.

— Handbook Recon East Europe - Soviet Union 1990. 1991. 115.00 (*0-582-08502-0*, 101440, Pub. by Longman Grp UK) Gale.

— Science Dictionary. 136p. 1983. 39.95 (*0-8288-2096-1*, F34210) Fr & Eur.

Longman, C. J. & Walrond, H. Archery: The Badminton Library of Sports & Pastimes. Duck of Beaufort, ed. (Legends of the Longbow Ser.: Vol. 1). (Illus.). 540p. (YA). (gr. 10 up). 1992. reprint ed. 39.95 (*1-56416-087-4*) Derrydale Pr.

Longman, David. The Instant Guide to Successful Houseplants. (Illus.). 1980. 17.95 (*0-686-65926-0*, Times Bks) Random.

Longman, Debbie G. & Atkinson, Rhonda H. C. L. A. S. S. - College Learning & Study Skills. 3rd ed. Baxter, ed. LC 92-30204. 450p. (C). 1993. pap. text ed. 31.50 (*0-314-01231-1*) West Pub.

— Study Methods & Reading Techniques (SMART) Baxter, ed. LC 93-23612. 400p. (C). 1993. pap. text ed. 30.50 (0-314-02804-8) West Pub.

Longman, Debbie G., jt. auth. see Atkinson, Rhonda H.

Longman, Donald R. Distribution Cost Analysis. Assael, Henry, ed. LC 78-235. (Century of Marketing Ser.). 1979. reprint ed. lib. bdg. 25.95 (0-405-11167-3) Ayer.

Longman, George F. The Analysis of Detergents & Detergent Products. LC 74-4649. (Illus.). 649p. reprint ed. pap. 180.00 (0-8357-8797-4, 2033619) Bks Demand.

Longman, Inc. Staff. Longman Dictionary of American English: A Dictionary for Learners of English. 792p. (Orig.). (C). 1983. pap. text ed. 25.24 (0-582-90611-3, 75187); pap. text ed. 15.95 (0-582-79797-7, 75051) Longman.

Longman, K. A. Vegetative Propagation of Trees in the 1980s. 1980. 75.00 (0-85074-055-X) St Mut.

Longman, Kenneth A. Tropical Forest & Its Environment. 2nd ed. (Tropical Ecology Ser.). 347p. (Orig.). 1987. text ed. 79.95 (0-470-20742-6) Halsted Pr.

Longman, Kenneth A. & Jenik, I. J. Tropical Forest & Its Environment. LC 73-85681. (Illus.). 160p. (Orig.). 1974. pap. text ed. 11.95 (0-582-44045-9) Longman.

Longman, Mark W. Carbonate Diagenesis As a Control on Stratigraphic Traps: With Examples from the Williston Basin. (Education Course Note Ser.: No. 21). 166p. reprint ed. pap. 47.40 (0-7837-3974-5, 2043803) Bks Demand.

Longman, Mark W., et al, eds. Rocky Mountain Carbonate Reservoirs. (Core Workshop Notes Ser.: No. 7). 482p. 1985. pap. 42.00 (0-918985-55-2) SEPM.

Longman, Philip. The Coming War Between the Generations. (Illus.). 304p. 1987. text ed. 17.95 (0-317-57600-3) HM.

Longman, Robin, ed. TIA International Travel News Directory. (Illus.). 98p. (Orig.). 1988. pap. 140.00 (0-685-23260-3) Travel Ind Assoc.

Longman Staff. Longman Dictionary of English Idioms. (YA). 1979. pap. text ed. 25.95 (0-582-05863-5) Longman.

— Longman Handy Learner's Dictionary. (YA). (gr. 9-12). 1988. pap. text ed. 11.95 (0-582-96413-X, 78324) Longman.

— Longman Handy Learner's Dictionary of American English. 512p. 1992. pap. text ed. 10.95 (0-582-09483-6) Addison-Wesley.

— Western European Political Parties: A Comprehensive Guide. 550p. 1989. 180.00 (0-582-00113-7) Longman.

Longman, Stanley V. Remus Tales. 40p. (Orig.). (J). 1990. Playscript. pap. 5.00 (0-87602-293-X) Anchorage.

Longman, Tremper, III. Fictional Akkadian Autobiography: A Generic & Comparative Study. LC 90-20204. xi, 274p. 1991. 29.50 (0-931464-41-2) Eisenbrauns.

— How to Read the Psalms. LC 88-8835. 166p. (Orig.). 1988. pap. 11.99 (0-87784-941-2, 941) InterVarsity.

— Literary Approaches to Biblical Interpretation. (Foundations of Contemporary Interpretation Ser.). 192p. 1987. 17.99 (0-310-40941-1, 11503P) Zondervan.

***Longman, Tremper, 3rd.** Old Testament Commentary Survey. 2nd ed. LC 95-12250. 176p. 1995. pap. 10.99 (0-8010-2024-7) Baker Bk.

***Longman, Tremper, III & Reid, Daniel.** God Is a Warrior. 256p. 1995. pap. 16.99 (0-310-49461-3) Zondervan.

Longman, Tremper, III, jt. auth. see Allender, Dan.

Longman, Tremper, III, jt. auth. see Dillard, Raymond B.

Longman, Tremper, III, jt. ed. see Ryken, Leland.

Longman, W. Tokens of the Eighteenth Century, Connected with Booksellers & Bookmaker: Authors, Printers, Publishers, Engravers & Paper Makers. (Illus.). 1970. reprint ed. 35.00 (1-55888-237-5) Omnigraphics Inc.

***Longmeadow.** Robert's Rule Order. 1994. write for info. (0-517-11917-X) Random Hse Value.

Longmeadow Press. Fantastic Animals: The Marvels of Animal Behavior. 1994. 24.98 (0-681-45376-1) Longmeadow Pr.

Longmeadow Press Editors. Castles. 128p. 1993. 14.98 (0-681-41807-9) Longmeadow Pr.

***Longmeadow Press Staff.** Names for Boys - Names for Girls. 1994. pap. 5.95 (0-681-00431-2) Longmeadow Pr.

— Pregnancy, Birth & Bonding: A Guide for the Mother-to-Be. 1993. pap. 4.95 (0-681-40450-7) Longmeadow Pr.

— Pressed Flowers. 1994. pap. 10.95 (0-681-40956-8) Longmeadow Pr.

— ST Captains Log Book. 1993. 6.95 (0-681-41378-6) Longmeadow Pr.

— ST Ships Log Book. 1993. 6.95 (0-681-41379-4) Longmeadow Pr.

***Longmeadow Staff.** Christmas Cookbook: Over 150 Festive Recipes. 1994. 9.98 (0-681-45459-8) Longmeadow Pr.

Longmeyer, Carole M. An American Mystery: Script. (Lost Colony Collection). (Orig.). (J). (gr. 3-12). 1994. pap. 24.95 (0-935326-50-2) Gallopade Pub Group.

— Clemson Football Mystery. (Sportsmystery Ser.). (Illus.). (Orig.). (J). (gr. 3 up). 1994. lib. bdg. 24.95 (1-55609-164-8); pap. 14.95 (0-935326-28-6) Gallopade Pub Group.

— Deadly Duke Football Mystery. (Sportsmystery Ser.). (Illus.). (Orig.). (J). (gr. 3 up). 1994. pap. 14.95 (0-935326-31-6) Gallopade Pub Group.

— Georgia Tech Football Mystery. (Sportsmystery Ser.). (Illus.). (Orig.). (J). (gr. 3 up). 1994. pap. 14.95 (0-935326-30-8) Gallopade Pub Group.

— The Lost Colony Activity Book. (Lost Colony Collection). (Illus.). (Orig.). (J). (gr. 3 up). 1994. pap. 14.95 (0-935326-41-3) Gallopade Pub Group.

— The Lost Colony Storybook. (Lost Colony Collection). (Illus.). (J). (gr. 4 up). 1994. pap. 14.95 (0-935326-38-3) Gallopade Pub Group.

— Maryland Football Mystery. (Sportsmystery Ser.). (Illus.). 80p. (Orig.). (J). (gr. 3 up). 1994. pap. 14.95 (0-935326-32-4) Gallopade Pub Group.

— NC State Football Mystery. (Sportsmystery Ser.). (Illus.). (Orig.). (J). (gr. 3 up). 1994. pap. 14.95 (0-935326-33-2) Gallopade Pub Group.

— Next Time Say Where You're Going. (Lost Colony Collection). (Illus.). (Orig.). (gr. 4-9). 1994. pap. 14.95 (0-935326-42-1) Gallopade Pub Group.

— North Carolina Football Mystery. (Sportsmystery Ser.). (Illus.). (Orig.). (J). (gr. 3 up). 1994. pap. 14.95 (0-935326-29-4) Gallopade Pub Group.

— Virginia Football Mystery. (Sportsmystery Ser.). (Illus.). 80p. (Orig.). (J). (gr. 3 up). 1994. pap. 24.95 (0-935326-35-9) Gallopade Pub Group.

— Wake Forest Football Mystery. (Sportsmystery Ser.). (Illus.). (Orig.). (J). (gr. 3 up). 1994. pap. 14.95 (0-935326-34-0) Gallopade Pub Group.

— What Did You Sayeth? (Lost Colony Collection). (Illus.). (Orig.). (J). (gr. 4 up). 1994. pap. 14.95 (0-935326-45-6) Gallopade Pub Group.

Longmeyer, Carole M., ed. Croatoan. (Lost Colony Collection). (Illus.). 76p. (gr. 4-12). 1994. pap. 14.95 (0-935326-36-7) Gallopade Pub Group.

Longmeyer, Carole M., ed. see Long, Evelyn.

Longmire, Karen V., ed. see European World Tourism Institute Staff.

Longmire, Linda, jt. ed. see Cernic, David.

Longmire, Linda A., jt. auth. see Hickey, James E., Jr.

Longmire, R. A. Soviet Relations in South East Asia. 280p. 1989. 65.00 (0-7103-0343-2, A3918) Routledge Chapman & Hall.

Longmire, W. P., Jr. & Tompkins, R. K. Manual of Liver Surgery. (Comprehensive Manuals of Surgical Specialties Ser.). (Illus.). 267p. 1981. 142.00 (0-387-90212-0) Spr-Verlag.

Longmore, D. B., jt. auth. see Mohiaddin, R. H.

Longmore, Paul K. The Invention of George Washington. 1988. 42.50 (0-520-06272-8) U CA Pr.

Longmuir, Ian S., ed. Oxygen Transport to Tissue, No. VIII. LC 86-15125. (Advances in Experimental Medicine & Biology Ser.: Vol. 200). 670p. 1986. 125.00 (0-306-42379-0, Plenum Pr) Plenum.

Longmuir, John, ed. see Jamieson, John.

Longnecker, et al. Small Business Management. 9th ed. (C). 1994. text ed. 58.95 (0-538-83045-X, GG70IA) S-W Pub.

Longnecker, O. M., Jr., jt. auth. see Reed, L. C.

Longnon, Auguste. Polytyque de l'Abbaye de Saint-Germain-des-Pres, 2 vols. 852p. reprint ed. write for info. (0-318-71374-8, Pub. by Georg Olms GW) Lubrecht & Cramer.

Longo, Cranni, jt. auth. see Brambilla, Roberto.

Longo, Daniel R. & Bohr, Deborah, eds. Quantitative Methods in Quality Management: A Guide for Practitioners. LC 90-14398. 150p. 1991. 46.95 (1-55648-060-1, 169102) AHPI.

Longo, Daniel R., et al. Integrated Quality Assessment: A Model for Concurrent Review. LC 88-34999. 217p. (Orig.). 1989. pap. 49.50 (1-55648-028-8, 169100) AHPI.

Longo, G., ed. Information Theory: New Trends & Open Problems. (International Centre for Mechanical Sciences Ser.: No. 219). (Illus.). 1976. pap. 35.00 (3-211-81378-0) Spr-Verlag.

— Secure Digital Communications. (CISM International Centre for Mechanical Sciences Ser.: No. 279). (Illus.). v, 332p. 1984. pap. 46.00 (0-387-81784-0) Spr-Verlag.

Longo, G. & Hartmenn, C. R., eds. Algebraic Coding Theory & Application. (CISM Courses & Lectures Ser.: Vol. 258). (Illus.). 529p. 1980. pap. 68.00 (0-387-81544-9) Spr-Verlag.

Longo, G. & Picinbono, Bernard, eds. Time & Frequency Representation of Signals & Systems. (CISM Courses & Lectures Ser.: Vol. 309). (Illus.). vii, 175p. 1989. pap. 37.00 (0-387-82143-0) Spr-Verlag.

Longo, G., jt. ed. see Davisson, L. D.

Longo, G., et al, eds. Geometries, Codes & Cryptography. (CISM International Centre for Mechanical Sciences Ser.: Vol. 313). (Illus.). v, 227p. 1990. pap. 47.00 (0-387-82205-4) Spr-Verlag.

Longo, Gianni, jt. auth. see Brambilla, Roberto.

Longo, Giuseppe & De Vaucouleurs, Antoinette. A General Catalogue of Photoelectric Magnitudes & Colors in the UBV System of 3,578 Galaxies Brighter than the 16th V-Magnitude 1936-1982. LC 83-50257. (Monographs in Astronomy: No. 3). 214p. (Orig.). 1983. pap. 12.00 (0-9603796-2-2) U of Tex Dept Astron.

— Supplement to the General Catalogue of Photoelectric Magnitudes & Colors of Galaxies in the U, B, V System. LC 85-51711. (Monographs in Astronomy: No. 3A). 126p. (Orig.). 1985. pap. write for info. (0-9603796-4-9) U of Tex Dept Astron.

Longo, Giuseppe, jt. auth. see Asperti, Andrea.

Longo, Giuseppe, jt. auth. see De Vaucouleurs, Antoinette.

Longo, L. D., jt. ed. see Eskes, T. K.

Longo, Linda. Troll Jokes & Riddles. LC 92-22571. (Illus.). 48p. (J). (gr. 1-7). 1992. pap. 1.95 (0-8167-2940-9) Troll Assocs.

Longo, Lucas. Carl Sandburg: Poet & Historian. Rahmas, D. Steve, ed. LC 73-185665. (Outstanding Personalities Ser.: No. 9). 32p. (YA). (gr. 7-12). 1972. lib. bdg. 4.95 (0-87157-509-4) SamHar Pr.

— O. Henry, Short Story Writer. Rahmas, Sigurd C., ed. (Outstanding Personalities Ser.: No. 88). 32p. (gr. 7-12). 1982. 4.95 (0-87157-588-4) SamHar Pr.

Longo, Michael J. Physics Laboratory Experiments, 1990. (Illus.). 244p. 1990. student ed 7.50 (0-9621002-2-6) ML Pub MI.

Longo, Mildred S. Picture Postcard Views of Rhode Island Lighthouses & Beacons, Together with a Brief History of Lifesaving Stations. LC 90-60938. (Illus.). 100p. (Orig.). 1990. pap. 12.95 (0-917012-93-3) RI Pubns Soc.

Longo, Nancy. Predominantly Fish: New Interpretations for Cooking Fish & Shellfish. LC 87-82252. (Illus.). 128p. 1987. pap. 9.95 (0-9619112-0-4) Fissurelle.

Longo, Peter J., jt. auth. see Miewald, Robert D.

Longo, V. G., jt. auth. see Mikhelson, M.

Longobardi, Cesare. Land Reclamation in Italy. 1976. lib. bdg. 34.95 (0-8490-2127-8) Gordon Pr.

— Land-Reclamation in Italy: Rural Revival in the Building of a Nation. LC 78-180410. (Illus.). reprint ed. 27.50 (0-404-56134-9) AMS Pr.

Longobardi, Giuseppe, jt. auth. see Giorgi, Alessandra.

Longon, Auguste, ed. see Villon, Francois.

Longoni, J. C. Four Patients of Dr. Deibler: A Study in Anarchy. 232p. 1970. 25.00 (0-8464-0422-2) Beekman Pubs.

Longree, Karla & Armbruster, Gertrude. Quantity Food Sanitation. 4th ed. 452p. 1987. text ed. 59.95 (0-471-81902-6) Wiley.

Longree, Karla & Blaker, Gertrude G. Sanitary Techniques in Food Service. 2nd ed. LC 81-3047. 271p. (C). 1982. pap. write for info. (0-02-371550-2) Macmillan.

Longres, John. Human Behavior in the Social Environment. 2nd ed. LC 93-84980. 620p. 1995. pap. text ed. 43.50 (0-87581-379-8) Peacock Pubs.

***Longridge.** Cutty Sark Ship & Model. 1984. pap. text ed. 12.95 (0-87021-833-6) Naval Inst Pr.

Longridge, C. Nepean. The Anatomy of Nelson's Ships. LC 80-84981. (Illus.). 283p. 1980. 45.00 (0-87021-077-7) Naval Inst Pr.

Longrigg, James. Greek Rational Medicine: Philosophy & Medicine from Alcmaeon to the Alexandrians. LC 92-28865. (Illus.). 288p. 1993. 59.95 (0-415-02594-X, B0350) Routledge.

Longrigg, Stephen. Iraq Nineteen Hundred to Nineteen Fifty. (Arab Background Ser.). 1968. 18.00 (0-86685-020-1) Intl Bk Ctr.

— Syria & Lebanon under French Mandate, 1968. (Arab Background Ser.). 1967. 18.00 (0-86685-021-X) Intl Bk Ctr.

Longsdorf, George F., jt. auth. see Shumaker, Walter A.

Longsdorf, Robert, Jr. RVing America's Backroads: California. LC 86-50522. 1989. 15.95 (0-934798-11-7) TL Enterprises.

Longshaw, Robin, tr. see Selden, George.

Longshoe, Shirley. Careers without College: Office. 96p. (Orig.). (YA). 1994. pap. 7.95 (1-56079-353-8) Petersons Guides.

Longshore, George F. Tog Docs: Managing the Search for Physician Leaders. LC 92-75187. 129p. (Orig.). (C). 1993. pap. text ed. 32.00 (0-924674-20-2) Am Coll Phys Execs.

***Longshore, Martha.** Hearts of Gold. 1994. pap. 4.50 (0-06-108292-9, Harp PBks) HarpC.

Longshore, Randolph E., jt. ed. see Baars, Jan W.

Longsoldier, Tilda, jt. auth. see St. Pierre, Mark.

Longstaff, Alan & Revest, Patricia, eds. Protocols in Molecular Neurobiology. LC 92-30701. (Methods in Molecular Biology Ser.: Vol. 13). (Illus.). 408p. 1992. spiral bd. 59.50 (0-89603-199-3) Humana.

***Longstaff, Patricia H.** Information Theory As a Basis for Rationalizing Regulation of the Communications Industry. (Illus.). 44p. (Orig.). 1994. pap. text ed. write for info. (1-879716-08-9, P94-4) Ctr Info Policy.

Longstaff, Patricia H. & Finnegan, John R., Sr. Mass Communication Law in Minnesota. (State Law Ser.). 86p. (C). 1992. text ed. 7.95 (0-913507-23-7) New Forums.

Longstaff, Roberta & Mann, Jim. The Diabetics' Cookbook. write for info. (0-318-59667-9) S&S Trade.

Longstaff, Thomas R. Evidence of Conflation in Mark? A Study in the Synoptic Problem. LC 76-40001. (Society of Biblical Literature. Dissertation Ser.: No. 28). 255p. reprint ed. pap. 72.70 (0-7837-5430-2, 2045195) Bks Demand.

Longstaff, Thomas R. & Thomas, Page A., eds. Synoptic Problem: A Bibliography, 1716-1988. LC 88-21575. 264p. 1988. 35.00 (0-86554-321-6, MUP/H274) Mercer Univ Pr.

Longstaff, W., jt. auth. see Argyros, S.

Longston, Irma. WordPerfect: A Simple, Easy Approach. 4th ed. LC 90-84103. (Illus.). 300p. (C). 1990. teacher ed write for info. (0-9627715-1-1); pap. text ed. write for info. (0-9627715-0-3) Accurate Pub Co.

Longstreet, A. B. Georgia Scenes: Characters, Incidents, Etc. in the First Half Century of the Republic. 12.00 (0-8446-0777-0) Peter Smith.

***Longstreet, A. G.** Georgia Scenes: Characters, Incidents, Etc., in the First Half Century of the Republic. (Illus.). 252p. 1992. 30.00 (0-88322-004-0) Beehive GA.

Longstreet, Augustus B. Georgia Scenes. (Southern Classics Ser.). 330p. 1992. reprint ed. pap. 10.95 (1-879941-06-6) J S Sanders.

Longstreet, David H. Software Maintenance & Computers. 400p. 1990. 9.95 (0-8186-8898-X, 898) IEEE Comp Soc.

Longstreet, H. D. Lee & Longstreet at High Tide: Gettysburg in the Light of the Official Records. 1904. 31.00 (0-527-58200-X) Periodicals Srv.

Longstreet, Helen D. Lee & Longstreet at High Tide: Gettysburg in the Light of the Official Records. (Illus.). 360p. 1989. reprint ed. 30.00 (0-916107-92-2) Broadfoot.

Longstreet, James. From Manassas to Appomattox. (Illus.). 760p. 1992. reprint ed. pap. 17.95 (0-306-80464-6) Da Capo.

— From Manassas to Appomattox: Memoirs of the Civil War in America. Robertson, James I., Jr., ed. LC 60-10046. (Indiana University Civil War Centennial Ser.). (Illus.). 1968. reprint ed. 63.00 (0-527-58220-4) Periodicals Srv.

Longstreet, John J. CWL: From Manassas to Appomattox. 700p. 1995. 12.98 (0-8317-1334-8) Smithmark.

Longstreet Press Staff. Century of Heroes: One Hundred Years of Ole Miss Football. LC 92-84005. (Illus.). 192p. 1993. 29.95 (1-56352-072-9) Longstreet Pr Inc.

***Longstreet, Roxanne.** Cold Kiss. 256p. 1995. mass mkt. 4.50 (0-8217-4812-2) Windsor NY.

— Red Angel. 352p. 1994. mass mkt. 4.50 (0-8217-4532-8) Zebra.

— Storm Riders. Reummler, John, ed. (Shadow World Ser.). (Illus.). 300p. (Orig.). (C). 1990. pap. 5.95 (1-55806-138-X, 6200) Iron Crown Ent Inc.

— The Undead. 320p. 1993. mass mkt. 4.50 (0-8217-4068-7) Zebra.

Longstreet, Roy W. Viewpoints of a Commodity Trader. 160p. 1986. reprint ed. 14.95 (0-934380-14-7) Traders Pr.

Longstreet, Stephen. A Century on Wheels, the Story of Studebaker: A History, 1852-1952. LC 70-100238. (Illus.). 121p. 1970. reprint ed. text ed. 35.00 (0-8371-3978-3, LOCW, Greenwood Pr) Greenwood.

— Dance in Art. (Master Draughtsman Ser.). 1968. 10.95 (0-87505-042-5); pap. 4.95 (0-87505-195-2) Borden.

— Magic Trumpets: The Story of Jazz for Young People. (Illus.). (Orig.). (YA). (gr. 7 up). 1989. pap. 16.95 (0-913705-42-X) Zephyr Pr AZ.

— More Drawings of Delacroix. (Master Draughtsman Ser.). (Illus.). 48p. (Orig.). 1970. 10.95 (0-87505-055-7); pap. 4.95 (0-87505-208-8) Borden.

— More Drawings of Rembrandt. (Master Draughtsman Ser.). 48p. 1970. 10.95 (0-87505-054-9); pap. 4.95 (0-87505-207-X) Borden.

— The Pedlocks. LC 87-81548. 408p. 1987. reprint ed. pap. 8.95 (1-55611-047-2, Primus Lib Contemp) D I Fine.

— The Pembroke Colors. 400p. 1982. reprint ed. pap. 3.50 (0-8439-1127-1) Dorchester Pub Co.

— Storm Watch. 1981. pap. 2.50 (0-8439-0882-3) Dorchester Pub Co.

— Storyville to Harlem: Fifty Years in the Jazz Scene. 211p. (C). 1986. 29.95 (0-8135-1174-7) Rutgers U Pr.

— Straw Boss. 1981. pap. 2.95 (0-8439-0980-3, LB980) Dorchester Pub Co.

— War Cries on Horseback. reprint ed. lib. bdg. 24.95 (0-89190-143-4, Rivercity Pr) Amereon Ltd.

Longstreet, Stephen, comment. Jazz - The Chicago Scene: The Art of Stephen Longstreet. (Illus.). 30p. (Orig.). 1989. pap. 3.00 (0-943056-11-X) Univ Chi Lib.

Longstreet, Stephen, ed. Animal in Art. (Master Draughtsman Ser.). (Illus.). (Orig.). 1966. 10.95 (0-87505-040-9); pap. 4.95 (0-87505-193-6) Borden.

— Child in Art. (Master Draughtsman Ser.). (Illus.). (Orig.). 1966. 10.95 (0-87505-041-7); pap. 4.95 (0-87505-194-4) Borden.

— Darwings of Augustus John. (Master Draughtsman Ser.). 1967. 10.95 (0-614-06576-3) Borden.

— Drawings of Augustus John. (Master Draughtsman Ser.). 1967. pap. 4.95 (0-87505-167-7) Borden.

— Drawings of Dali. (Master Draughtsman Ser.). (Illus.). 1964. pap. 4.95 (0-87505-155-3) Borden.

— The Drawings of Matisse. 48p. 1973. 10.95 (0-87505-021-2); pap. 4.95 (0-87505-174-X) Borden.

— Drawings of Pontormo. (Master Draughtsman Ser.). 1966. pap. 4.95 (0-87505-203-7) Borden.

— Drawings of Tintoretto. (Master Draughtsman Ser.). (Illus.). (Orig.). 1967. 10.95 (0-87505-036-0); pap. 4.95 (0-87505-189-8) Borden.

— Drawings of Toulouse-Lautrec. (Master Draughtsman Ser.). (Illus.). 1966. 10.95 (0-87505-019-0); pap. 4.95 (0-87505-172-3) Borden.

— Drawings of Winslow Homer. (Master Draughtsman Ser.). (Illus.). 1970. pap. 4.95 (0-87505-165-0) Borden.

— Figure in Art. (Master Draughtsman Ser.). (Illus.). (Orig.). 1968. 10.95 (0-87505-043-3); pap. 4.95 (0-87505-196-0) Borden.

— Horse in Art. (Master Draughtsman Ser.). (Illus.). (Orig.). (J). (ps). 1965. pap. 4.95 (0-87505-198-7) Borden.

— Portrait in Art. (Master Draughtsman Ser.). (Illus.). (Orig.). 1965. pap. 4.95 (0-87505-199-5) Borden.

— Self Portraits of Great Artists. (Master Draughtsman Ser.). (Illus.). 1973. pap. 4.95 (0-87505-201-0) Borden.

— Tree in Art. (Master Draughtsman Ser.). (Illus.). (Orig.). 1966. 10.95 (0-87505-047-6); pap. 4.95 (0-87505-200-2) Borden.

Longstreet, Stephen, jt. auth. see Carmichael, Hoagy.

Longstreet, Stephen, ed. see Cezanne, Paul.

Longstreet, Stephen, ed. see Daumier, Honore.

Longstreet, Stephen, ed. see Degas, Hilaire.

Longstreet, Stephen, ed. see Durer, Albrecht.

Longstreet, Stephen, ed. see Fuseli, Henry.

Longstreet, Stephen, ed. see Gauguin, Paul.

Longstreet, Stephen, ed. see Ingres, Jean A.

Longstreet, Stephen, ed. see Kollwitz.

Longstreet, Stephen, ed. see Modigliani.

Longstreet, Stephen, ed. see Picasso, Pablo.

Longstreet, Stephen, ed. see Poussin, Nicolas.

Longstreet, Stephen, ed. see Raphael.

Longstreet, Stephen, ed. see Renoir, Pierre A.

Longstreet, Stephen, ed. see Rodin, Auguste.

Longstreet, Stephen, ed. see Romney, George.

Longstreet, Stephen, ed. see Rubens, Peter P.

Longstreet, Stephen, ed. see Stern, Jossi.

Longstreet, Stephen, ed. see Van Gogh, Vincent.

Longstreet, Stephen, ed. see Van Rijn Rembrandt, Hermansz.

Longstreet, Stephen, ed. see Von Menzel, Adolph F.

Longstreet, Stephen, ed. see Watteau.

Longstreet, Wilma S. & Shane, Harold G. Curriculum for a New Millennium. LC 92-31356. 1992. text ed. 57.00 (0-205-13966-3) Allyn.

Longstreth, Bevis. Modern Investment Management & the Prudent Man Rule. LC 86-16294. 224p. 1987. 49.95 (0-19-504196-8) OUP.

An Asterisk (*) at the beginning of an entry indicates that the title is appearing in BIP for the first time.

Longstreth, Billie J., et al. Tangled Emotions. 357p. 1989. 12.95 (*0-317-99837-4*); pap. 4.95 (*0-317-99838-2*) Shamrock Pubns.

Longstreth, Richard, ed. Studies in the History of Art: The Mall in Washington, 1791-1991. (Symposium Papers XIV: Vol. 30). (Illus.). 1991. pap. 39.95 (*0-89468-138-9*, U Pr of New Eng) Natl Gallery Art.

Longstreth, W. Thacher. Main Line Wasp. 1990. 21.95 (*0-393-02780-5*) Norton.

Longsworth, Elizabeth K., ed. Anatomy of a Start-Up: Why Some New Businesses Succeed & Others Fail. 456p. (Orig.). 1991. 24.95 (*0-9626146-8-8*); pap. 16.95 (*0-9626146-6-1*) Inc Pub MA.

Longsworth, Polly. The World of Emily Dickinson. 1990. 35.00 (*0-393-02892-5*) Norton.

Longsworth, Robert. The Cornish Ordinalia: Religion & Dramaturgy. LC 67-22869. 185p. reprint ed. pap. 52.80 (*0-7837-5935-5*, 2045734) Bks Demand.

Longton, R. E. Biology of Polar Bryophytes & Lichens. (Studies in Polar Research). (Illus.). 280p. 1988. 120.00 (*0-521-25015-3*) Cambridge U Pr.

Longuet-Higgins, H. & Christopher, H. Mental Processes: Studies in Cognitive Science. (Explorations in Cognitive Science Ser.). 508p. 1987. 50.00 (*0-262-12119-0*) MIT Pr.

Longus. 'SDaphnis et Chloe Suivi d'Histoire Veritable de Lucien. (FRE.). 1991. pap. 8.95 (*0-7859-4010-3*) Fr & Eur.

— The Story of Daphnis & Chloe. Connor, W. R., ed. LC 78-18586. (Greek Texts & Commentaries Ser.). (Illus.). 1979. reprint ed. lib. bdg. 21.95 (*0-405-11428-1*) Ayer.

Longver, Phyllis O. & Oesterlin, Pauline J. A Surname Guide to Massachusetts Town Histories. 440p. (Orig.). 1993. pap. text ed. 26.50 (*1-55613-854-7*) Heritage Bk.

Longwell, Alicia G., jt. auth. see Pisano, Ronald G.

Longwell, Dennis, jt. auth. see Meisner, Sanford.

Longwith, John. Provident: A Centennial History. (Illus.). 192p. 1986. 9.95 (*0-9617768-0-3*) Provident Life.

— Since Before the Yellow Fever: A History of Union Planters Bank. LC 94-60749. (Illus.). 224p. 1994. 19.95 (*0-944897-02-9*) Magic Chef.

Longwith, John C. Castle on a Cliff: A History of Baylor School. (Illus.). 216p. 1994. 24.95 (*0-944897-03-7*) Magic Chef.

— Spark of Enterprise: A History of Dixie Foundry - Magic Chef, Inc. LC 87-91291. (Illus.). 192p. 1988. 16.95 (*0-944897-00-2*) Magic Chef.

— Spark of Enterprise: A History of Dixie Foundry - Magic Chef, Inc. deluxe ed. LC 87-91291. (Illus.). 192p. 1988. ring bd. 29.95 (*0-944897-01-0*) Magic Chef.

Longworth, Alice R. Crowded Hours. Baxter, Annette K., ed. LC 79-8799. (Signal Lives Ser.). (Illus.). 1980. reprint ed. lib. bdg. 41.95 (*0-405-12846-0*) Ayer.

Longworth, I. H. Prehistoric Britain. (British Museum Paperbacks Ser.). (Illus.). 72p. 1986. 10.95 (*0-674-70025-2*) HUP.

***Longworth, J. W. & Brown, C. G.** Agribusiness Reforms in China: The Case of Wool. 280p. 1995. 70.00x (*0-85198-951-9*) CAB Intl.

Longworth, J. W. & Williamson, G. J. China's Pastoral Region: Sheep & Wool, Minority Nationalities, Rangeland Degradation & Sustainable Development. 370p. 1994. text ed. 85.50 (*0-85198-890-3*) CAB Intl.

Longworth, James W., et al, eds. International Congress on Photobiology 9th: Proceedings. LC 85-3379. 298p. 1985. text ed. 69.50 (*0-275-91318-X*, C1318, Praeger Pubs) Greenwood.

— Photobiology 1984. LC 85-604. 202p. 1985. text ed. 59.95 (*0-275-90189-0*, C0189, Praeger Pubs) Greenwood.

Longworth, John W. Beef in Japan: Politics, Production, Marketing & Trade. LC 83-14792. (Illus.). 327p. 1984. 49.95 (*0-7022-1965-7*, Pub. by Univ Queensland Pr AT) Intl Spec Bk.

Longworth, John W., ed. China's Rural Development Miracle. 1989. pap. 34.95 (*0-7022-2264-X*, Pub. by Univ Queensland Pr AT) Intl Spec Bk.

Longworth, Maria T. Teresina in America, 2 vols. in 1. LC 73-13158. (Foreign Travelers in America, 1810-1935 Ser.). 734p. 1974. reprint ed. 57.95 (*0-405-05478-5*) Ayer.

Longworth, Philip. Making of Eastern Europe. 1994. pap. write for info. (*0-312-12042-7*) St Martin.

Longy-Miquelle, Renee. Principles of Musical Theory. 1925. 9.50 (*0-911318-06-2*) E C Schirmer.

Longyear, Barry B. The Change. Ryan, Kevin, ed. (Alien Nation Ser.: No. 4). 320p. (Orig.). 1994. mass mkt. 5.50 (*0-671-73602-7*) PB.

— The Homecoming. (Millennium Series, A Byron Preiss Book). (Illus.). 224p. (YA). 1989. 15.95 (*0-8027-6863-6*) Walker & Co.

— Science Fiction Writer's Workshop-1: An Introduction to Fiction Mechanics. 168p. 1980. pap. 9.50 (*0-913896-18-7*) Owlswick Pr.

— Sea of Glass. 384p. 1988. pap. 3.50 (*0-380-70055-7*) Avon.

— Slag Like Me. Ryan, Kevin, ed. (Alien Nation Ser.: No. 5). 320p. (Orig.). 1994. mass mkt. 5.50 (*0-671-79514-7*) PB.

— St. Mary Blue. 1988. pap. 9.95 (*0-916595-05-6*) SteelDragon Pr.

Longyear, Edmund J. Longyear: The Descendants of Jacob Longyear of Ulster County, New York. 622p. 1992. reprint ed. lib. bdg. 99.00 (*0-8328-2392-9*); reprint ed. pap. 89.00 (*0-8328-2393-7*) Higginson Bk Co.

Longyear, J. M., 3rd. Archaeological Investigations in El Salvador. (HU PMM Ser.: Vol. 9, No. 2). 1972. reprint ed. 20.00 (*0-527-01173-8*) Periodicals Srv.

Longyear, John M. Copan Ceramics: A Study of Southeastern Maya Pottery. LC 77-11503. (Carnegie Institution of Washington. Publications: No. 597). reprint ed. 28.50 (*0-404-16267-3*) AMS Pr.

— Landlooker in the Upper Peninsula of Michigan. LC 60-53288. 80p. 1983. reprint ed. 8.95 (*0-938746-06-5*) Marquette Cnty.

Longyear, Rey M. Nineteenth Century Romanticism in Music. 3rd ed. (Illus.). 384p. (C). 1987. pap. text ed. 34.00 (*0-13-622697-3*) P-H.

Lonidier, Fred. Blueprint for a Strike: A Fragmentary Capsule History of the Ironworkers & Other Unions at NASSCO; Excerpts from the photo-text installation, BLUEPRINT FOR A STRIKE, Good News at NASSCO, Labor Link TV 26A&B. (Illus.). 32p. (Orig.). 1992. pap. 8.00 (*0-930495-16-0*) San Fran Art Inst.

Lonidier, Lynn. Clitoris Lost. 1989. pap. 11.95 (*0-317-04319-6*) Man-Root.

Lonie, Ian & Pisano, Raff. Local Government Litigation in Victoria. 69p. 1990. 40.00 (*1-875263-06-3*, Blckstone AT) W W Gaunt.

Lonier, Terri. Working Solo: The Real Guide to Freedom & Financial Success with Your Own Business. LC 93-84901. (Illus.). 400p. (Orig.). 1994. pap. 14.95 (*1-883282-40-3*) Portico Pr.

— Working Solo Sourcebook: Essential Resources for Independent Entrepreneurs. LC 94-67631. 320p. (Orig.). 1995. 24.95 (*1-883282-50-0*) Portico Pr.

— Working Solo Sourcebook: Essential Resources for Independent Entrepreneurs. LC 94-67631. (Illus.). 320p. (Orig.). 1994. pap. 14.95 (*1-883282-60-8*) Portico Pr.

***Lonigan, Loretta & Zatz, Carol.** Junior Seniors. 1995. 9.95 (*0-8062-5173-5*) Carlton.

Lonigan, Paul R. Early Irish Church. rev. ed. (Illus.). 90p. (C). 1988. pap. 7.95 (*0-9614753-2-3*) Celt Heritage Pr.

Lonik, Larry J. The Healthy Taste of Honey: Bee People's Recipes, Anecdotes & Lore. Campbell, Jean, ed. LC 80-27794. (Orig.). 1981. pap. 5.95 (*0-89865-020-8*) Donning Co.

Lonn, Ella. Desertion During the Civil War. (History - United States Ser.). 251p. 1992. reprint ed. lib. bdg. 79.00 (*0-7812-6180-5*) Rprt Serv.

— Foreigners in the Union Army & Navy. LC 74-90548. 725p. 1970. reprint ed. text ed. 35.00 (*0-8371-2248-1*, LOFU, Greenwood Pr) Greenwood.

Lonn, Oystein. Tom Reber's Last Retreat. McDuff, David, tr. 176p. (NOR.). 1992. 19.95 (*0-7145-2933-8*) M Boyars Pubs.

Lonnberg, Allan. Self & Savagery on the California Frontier: A Study of the Digger Stereotype. (Illus.). 98p. 1980. reprint ed. pap. text ed. 10.00 (*1-55567-048-2*) Coyote Press.

Lonnborg, Barbara, ed. see Hyland, Terry L. & Reilly, Hugh J.

Lonnborg, Barbara A., ed. Boys Town: A Photographic History. LC 92-18878. 144p. 1992. 29.95 (*0-938510-37-1*, 19-001); pap. 19.95 (*0-938510-31-2*, 19-002) Boys Town Pr.

Lonner, Walter J. & Berry, John W., eds. Field Methods in Cross-Cultural Research. LC 85-18360. (Cross-Cultural Research & Methodology Ser.: No. 8). 368p. (Orig.). reprint ed. pap. 104.90 (*0-7837-6587-8*, 2046152) Bks Demand.

Lonner, Walter J. & Malpass, Roy S., eds. Readings in Psychology & Culture. LC 93-14050. 1993. pap. text ed. write for info. (*0-205-14899-9*) Allyn.

Lonner, Walter J., jt. ed. see Berry, J. W.

Lonner, Walter J., ed. see International Association for Cross-Cultural Psychology.

Lonnerdal, Bo, ed. Iron Metabolism in Infants. 176p. 1989. 132.00 (*0-8493-5433-1*, RJ128) CRC Pr.

Lonnerdal, Bo, jt. auth. see Picciano, Mary F.

Lonngren. Introduction to Physical Electronics. (Engineering Science Ser.). 350p. (C). 1988. text ed. write for info. (*0-205-11141-6*, H11414); write for info. (*0-318-62208-4*, H11422) P-H.

Lonngren, Karl E., jt. auth. see Hirose, Akira.

Lonning, Per. Creation - An Ecumenical Challenge: Reflections Issuing from a Study by the Institute for Ecumenical Research, Strasbourg. LC 89-35703. viii, 272p. (C). 1989. 31.95 (*0-86554-356-9*, MUP/H285) Mercer Univ Pr.

Lonnquist, Lynne E., jt. auth. see Weiss, Gregory L.

Lonnrot, Elias, ed. The Kalevala: Poems of the Kaleva District. Magoun, Francis P., Jr., tr. 448p. 1990. pap. 15.50 (*0-674-50010-5*) HUP.

Lonnroth, Mans, et al. Energy in Transition: A Report on Energy Policy & Future Options. LC 78-68827. (Illus.). 197p. reprint ed. pap. 56.20 (*0-685-23974-8*, 2031538) Bks Demand.

Lono, Luz P., ed. see Ozaeta, Pablo.

Lonoff de Cuevas, Sue. The College Reader: Linking Reading to Writing. LC 92-15837. (C). 1992. 19.00 (*0-673-18726-8*) HarpCollege.

Lonoff, Sue. Wilkie Collins & His Victorian Readers: A Study in the Rhetoric of Authorship. LC 79-8835. (Studies in the Nineteenth Century: No. 2). (Illus.). 1982. 34.50 (*0-404-18044-2*) AMS Pr.

Lonon, James L. Tall Tales of the Rails: On the Carolina, Clinchfield & Ohio Railway. Mintz, James W., ed. (Illus.). 216p. 1989. 19.95 (*0-932807-50-X*) Overmountain Pr.

Lons, Veronica. Egyptian Mythology: The Library of the World's Myths & Legends. LC 83-71478. (Illus.). 144p. 1990. pap. 10.95 (*0-87226-298-7*) P Bedrick Bks.

Lonsdale. Free Oxygen Radicals & Disease. 1989. pap. 4.95 (*0-87983-451-X*) Keats.

Lonsdale, Alan, jt. auth. see Abbott, Jacqui.

***Lonsdale, Allison B.** Teaching Translation from Spanish to English: Worlds Beyond Words. 288p. 1995. pap. 30.00 (*0-7766-0399-X*) Paul & Co Pubs.

Lonsdale, Bernard J. & Mackintosh, Helen K. Children Experience Literature. 1973. text ed. 11.25 (*0-394-30368-7*) Random.

Lonsdale, Chris. Straights: Raw Materials for Animal Feed Compounders & Farmers. 92p. (Orig.). 1988. pap. text ed. 25.00 (*0-948617-15-2*) Scholium Intl.

Lonsdale, D., tr. see Butin, Heinz.

Lonsdale, David. Eyes to See, Ears to Hear. LC 91-13247. 184p. 1991. reprint ed. pap. 10.95 (*0-8294-0721-9*) Loyola Univ Pr.

— Listening to the Music of the Spirit: The Art of Discernment. LC 93-71539. 176p. (Orig.). 1993. pap. 7.95 (*0-87793-507-6*) Ave Maria.

Lonsdale, Derrick. A Nutritionist's Guide to the Clinical Use of Vitamin B-1. (Illus.). 214p. 1988. pap. 14.95 (*0-943685-02-8*) Life Sci Pr.

— Why I Left Orthodox Medicine: Healing for the 21st Century. 176p. (Orig.). 1994. pap. 10.95 (*1-878901-98-2*) Hampton Roads Pub Co.

***Lonsdale, Ellias.** Inside Planets. (Inside Astrology Ser.: Vol. 1). (Illus.). 350p. (Orig.). (C). 1995. pap. 16.95 (*1-55643-203-8*) North Atlantic.

Lonsdale, John, ed. South Africa in Question? LC 87-29396. 244p. (Orig.). 1988. pap. 12.50 (*0-435-08023-7*) Heinemann.

Lonsdale, John, jt. auth. see Berman, Bruce.

Lonsdale, Kathleen, jt. ed. see Kasper, John S.

Lonsdale, Roger, ed. Dryden to Johnson. LC 86-13995. (New History of Literature Ser.). 456p. 1987. 39.50 (*0-87226-128-X*) P Bedrick Bks.

— Dryden to Johnson. (Penguin History of Literature Ser.). 464p. 1994. 11.95 (*0-14-017754-X*, Penguin Bks) Viking Penguin.

— Eighteenth-Century Women Poets: An Oxford Anthology. 608p. 1990. reprint ed. pap. 12.95 (*0-19-282775-8*) OUP.

— The New Oxford Book of Eighteenth Century Verse. LC 83-17477. (Oxford Books of Verse). 1985. 29.95 (*0-19-214122-8*) OUP.

— The New Oxford Book of Eighteenth-Century Verse. 912p. 1989. pap. 16.95 (*0-19-282054-0*) OUP.

Lonsdale, S., et al. Invalidity Benefit: A Survey of Recipients. 70p. 1993. pap. 20.00 (*0-11-762087-4*, HM20874, Pub. by HMSO UK) UNIPUB.

Lonsdale, Steven H. Dance & Ritual Play in Greek Religion. LC 93-2787. (Ancient Society & History Ser.). (Illus.). 368p. (C). 1993. text ed. 39.95 (*0-8018-4594-7*) Johns Hopkins.

Lonsdale, Susan. Women & Disability: The Experience of Physical Disability among Women. LC 90-31332. 200p. 1990. text ed. 29.95 (*0-312-04613-8*) St Martin.

— Work & Inequality. LC 84-12235. (Social Policy in Modern Britain Ser.). 263p. reprint ed. pap. 75.00 (*0-7837-1603-6*, 2041895) Bks Demand.

Lonsdale, Susan, et al. Long-Term Psychiatric Patients: A Study in Community Care. 1980. 15.00 (*0-317-05802-9*, Pub. by Natl Inst Soc Work) St Mut.

Lonsdale, William, ed. Star Rhythms. 2nd ed. (Io Ser.: No. 27). (Illus.). 180p. 1982. pap. 8.95 (*0-938190-00-8*) North Atlantic.

Lonsdorf, Nancy, et al. A Woman's Best Medicine: Health, Happiness, & Long Life Through Ayur-Veda. LC 94-8619. 1995. 14.95 (*0-87477-785-2*, J P T-Putnam) Putnam Pub Group.

Lonse, Kris, ed. see Nielson, Norm.

Lonsinger, Nancy L. Around the Stove in Roscoe's General Store - 1866. (Illus.). 48p. (Orig.). 1976. pap. 2.00 (*1-880443-00-7*) Roscoe Village.

Lonstein, Albert I. & Marino, Vito. The Revised Compleat Sinatra. rev. ed. LC 79-88307. (Illus.). 702p. 1980. 49.95 (*0-87990-000-8*) Lonstein Pubns.

Lont, Cynthia & Decker, Warren. Senior Seminar in Theories of Communicative Interaction. 404p. (C). 1993. per. 39.95 (*0-8403-8609-5*) Kendall-Hunt.

***Lont, Cynthia M.** Women & Media: Content, Careers, & Criticism. LC 94-36309. 1995. pap. 26.95 (*0-534-24732-6*) Intl Thomson.

Lont, Cynthia M. & Freidley, Sheryl A., eds. Beyond Boundaries: Sex & Gender Diversity in Communication. LC 88-24414. 368p. (C). Date not set. lib. bdg. 73.50 (*0-913969-21-4*, G Mason Univ Pr); pap. 33.00 (*0-913969-33-8*) Univ Pub Assocs.

***Lontai, E.** Unification of Law in the Field of International Industrial Property. 230p. 1994. 105.00 (*963-05-6741-5*, Pub. by Akad Kiado HU) St Mut.

Lontie, Rene, ed. Copper Proteins & Copper Enzymes, Vol. I. 256p. 1984. 168.00 (*0-8493-6470-1*, QP552) CRC Pr.

— Copper Proteins & Copper Enzymes, Vol. II. 304p. 1984. 191.00 (*0-8493-6471-X*, QP552) CRC Pr.

— Copper Proteins & Copper Enzymes, Vol. III. 272p. 1984. 168.00 (*0-8493-6472-8*, QP552, CRC Reprint) Franklin.

Loo & Sun. Proceedings of International Symposium on Composite Materials & Structures. 1986. 150.00 (*0-318-23254-5*) T-C Pubns CA.

Loo, C. T., jt. contrib. see Yamanaka.

Loo, Chalsa. Chinatown: Most Time, Hard Time. LC 91-27984. 384p. 1991. text ed. 59.95 (*0-275-93893-X*, C3893, Praeger Pubs) Greenwood.

Loo, Chalsa M. Crowding & Behavior. LC 74-8362. 246p. 1974. 29.50 (*0-8422-5180-4*); pap. text ed. 6.95 (*0-8422-0415-6*) Irvington.

Loo, Francis K., ed. A Guide to Effective Property Management in Hong Kong. 200p. (C). 1991. pap. text ed. 45.00 (*0-685-65782-5*, Pub. by Hong Kong U Pr HK) St Mut.

Loo, Francis T., ed. see Failure Prevention & Reliability Conference Staff.

Loo, Oliver, ed. Contemporary Architectural Art Glass Studios: Glass by Fischer. (Illus.). 60p. (Orig.). 1994. pap. write for info. (*0-9641371-0-0*) C&R Loo.

Loo, Ronald J. He Kalana Kakau Ki Hoalu Helu Ekahi: A Slack Key Notebook, No. 1. 57p. 1984. pap. 30.00 (*1-885332-01-7*) P Nahenahe.

— He Kalana Kakau Ki Ho'alu Helu 'Ekolu: A Slack Key Notebook, No. 3. 80p. 1995. pap. 31.00 (*1-885332-04-1*) P Nahenahe.

— He Kalana Kakau Ki Hoalu Helu Elua: A Slack Key Notebook, No. 2. 76p. 1992. pap. 30.00 (*1-885332-02-5*) P Nahenahe.

— Logic - the Worksheet: A Study Guide for Chapters 1, 3, 8, 9 of Copi's Introduction to Logic (7th) 2nd ed. 114p. (C). 1986. student ed 10.75 (*1-885332-03-3*) P Nahenahe.

Loo, Tina. Making Law, Order, & Authority in British Columbia, 1821-1871. (Social History of Canada Ser.). (Illus.). 352p. (C). 1994. 45.00 (*0-8020-2961-2*); pap. 18.95 (*0-8020-7784-6*) U of Toronto Pr.

Loo, Yew C. & Cusens, Anthony R. The Finite-Strip Method in Bridge Engineering. (Viewpoint Publication Ser.). (Illus.). 1979. pap. text ed. 45.00 (*0-7210-1041-5*, Pub. by C & CA UK) Scholium Intl.

Looby, Christopher & Schlesinger, Arthur M., Jr. Benjamin Franklin. (World Leaders - Past & Present Ser.). (Illus.). 112p. (J). (gr. 5 up). 1990. 17.95 (*1-55546-808-X*) Chelsea Hse.

Looby, George P., jt. auth. see Thomas, Stephen.

Loofbourow, John. Thackeray & Form of Fiction. LC 75-42172. 224p. 1976. reprint ed. 45.00 (*0-87752-177-8*) Gordian.

Looff, Carolyn. Business & Economics Funding Guide. Bitting, Christina, ed. 134p. (Orig.). (C). 1987. lib. bdg. 34.75 (*0-88044-087-2*); pap. text ed. 17.75 (*0-88044-088-0*) AASCU Press.

Looijenga, E. J. Isolated Singular Points on Complete Intersections. LC 82-9707. (London Mathematical Society Lecture Note Ser.: No. 77). 200p. 1984. pap. 37.95 (*0-521-28674-3*) Cambridge U Pr.

Look, Burt. Spreadsheet Geomechanics: An Introduction. (Illus.). 256p. (C). 1994. 55.00 (*90-5410-151-2*); pap. text ed. 28.50 (*90-5410-152-0*, Pub. by A A Balkema NE) Ashgate Pub Co.

Look, David C. Electrical Characterization of GAAS Materials & Devices. (Design & Measurement in Electronic Engineering Ser.). 280p. 1989. 175.00 (*0-471-91702-8*) Wiley.

— Electrical Characterization of GAAS Materials & Devices. (Design & Measurement in Electronic Engineering Ser.). 280p. 1992. pap. text ed. 59.95 (*0-471-93573-5*) Wiley.

Look Magazine Staff, ed. Movie Lot to Beachhead: The Motion Picture Goes to War & Prepares for the Future. LC 79-6696. 1980. reprint ed. lib. bdg. 22.95 (*0-405-12935-1*) Ayer.

Look, Margaret K. At Home in Pittsburgh. LC 88-72337. (Illus.). 128p. (Orig.). 1989. pap. 4.95 (*0-916383-75-X*) Aegina Pr.

— At Home on The Workhouse Farm. (Illus.). 132p. (Orig.). (YA). (gr. 7 up). 1986. pap. 6.95 (*0-9616922-0-0*) M K Look.

— Courtney: Master Oarsman - Champion Coach. (Illus.). 168p. 1989. pap. 9.95 (*1-55787-044-6*, NY55032) Hrt of the Lakes.

Look, Travis, jt. auth. see McCarty, Diane.

Lookadoo, et al. Natural Gas Regulations Handbook. 2nd ed. Orig. Title: Fundamentals of Natural Gas Regulations. 152p. 1988. pap. 45.00 (*0-86587-493-X*) Gov Insts.

Looker, Earle. The White House Gang. 18.95 (*0-89190-546-4*, Am Repr) Amereon Ltd.

Looker, James M., jt. auth. see Painter, Mark P.

Looker, Thomas. The Sound & the Story: NPR & the Art of Radio. (Richard Todd Book). 256p. 1995. 24.95 (*0-395-67439-5*) HM.

Lookingbill, Donald P. & Marks, James G., Jr. Principles of Dermatology. 2nd ed. LC 92-48750. (Illus.). 384p. 1993. pap. text ed. 47.50 (*0-7216-4290-X*) Saunders.

***Lookingbill, Len.** From the Horse's Mouth Vol. 1: The Horseman's Guide to Equine Dental Health & Aging. 139p. Date not set. text ed. write for info. (*0-9644682-0-4*) Diamond L Pub.

Lookofsky, Joseph M. Consequential Damages in Comparative Context: From Breach of Promise to Monetary Remedy in the American, Scandinavian & International Law of Contracts & Sales. 300p. 1989. pap. 137.50x (*87-574-5510-4*, Pub. by Almqv & Wiksell SW) Coronet Bks.

— Transnational Litigation & Commercial Arbitration. A Comparative Analysis of American, European & International Law. 792p. (Orig.). 1992. pap. 280.00x (*87-574-5990-8*, Pub. by Almqv & Wiksell SW) Coronet Bks.

— Transnational Litigation & Commercial Arbitration under American, European & International Law. 400p. 1991. 95.00 (*0-929179-66-8*) Transnatl Juris Pubns.

Lookstein, Haskel. Were We Our Brothers' Keepers? The Public Response of Jews to the Holocaust, 1938-1944. (Illus.). 288p. 1985. 18.95 (*0-87677-148-7*) Hartmore.

Looman, Janice E., jt. auth. see Herz, David A.

***Loomans, Diane.** The Lovables. (Illus.). 12p. (J). (ps). 1994. bds. 7.95 (*0-915811-58-8*) H J Kramer Inc.

— The Lovables in the Kingdom of Self-Esteem. Carleton, Nancy, ed. LC 90-52633. (Illus.). 32p. (J). (ps-5). 1991. 14.95 (*0-915811-25-1*) H J Kramer Inc.

Loomans, Diane & Kolberg, Karen J. The Laughing Classroom: Everyone's Guide to Teaching with Humor & Play. LC 92-23351. (Illus.). 228p. (C). 1993. 14.95 (*0-915811-44-8*) H J Kramer Inc.

Loomans, Diane & Loomans, Julia. Full Esteem Ahead: One Hundred Ways to Build Self-Esteem in Children & Adults. Carleton, Nancy, ed. 360p. (Orig.). (J). 1994. pap. 14.95 (*0-915811-57-X*) H J Kramer Inc.

Loomans, Diane, et al. Positively Mother Goose. Kramer, Linda, ed. LC 90-52634. (Illus.). 32p. (J). (ps-2). 1991. 14.95 (*0-915811-24-3*) H J Kramer Inc.

Loomans, Julia, jt. auth. see Loomans, Diane.
Loomba, Ania. Gender, Race, Renaissance Drama. (Oxford India Paperbacks Ser.). 188p. 1992. pap. 6.95 (*0-19-563004-1*) OUP.
Loomer, Bradley M. & Strege, Maxine G. Useful Spelling: Levels 2-8. (J). (gr. 2-8). 1990. write for info. (*1-878712-03-9*) Useful Lrn.
***Loomes, Brian.** Antique British Clocks: A Buyer's Guide. (Illus.). 224p. Date not set. 35.00 (*0-7090-4611-1*, Pub. by R Hale Ltd UK) Antique Collect.
— British Clocks Illustrated. (Illus.). 272p. Date not set. 45.00 (*0-7090-4547-6*, Hale-Parkwest) Parkwest Pubns.
— The Concise Guide to British Clocks. (Illus.). 192p. 1992. pap. 22.95 (*0-7126-5187-X*, Pub. by Barrie & Jenkins) Trafalgar.
— The Concise Guide to Tracing Your Ancestry. 192p. 1993. pap. 22.95 (*0-7126-9877-9*, Pub. by Barrie & Jenkins) Trafalgar.
— Early Clockmakers of Great Britain. 589p. 1981. 59.50 (*0-7198-0200-8*, Pub. by NAG Press UK) Antique Collect.
— Painted Dial Clocks. (Illus.). 350p. 1995. 59.50 (*1-85149-183-X*) Antique Collect.
Loomes, Graham, jt. ed. see Hey, John D.
Loomes, Martin, jt. auth. see Woodcock, Jim.
Loomes, Martin J., jt. ed. see Johnson, J. H.
Loomes, Martin J., jt. auth. see Woodcock, Jim.
Loomie, Albert J. English Polemics at the Spanish Court: Joseph Creswell's "Letter to the Ambassador from England": The English & Spanish Texts of 1606. 176p. (C). 1993. 25.00 (*0-8232-1446-X*) Fordham.
— The Spanish Elizabethans: The English Exiles at the Court of Philip II. LC 63-14407. 293p. reprint ed. pap. 83.60 (*0-7837-0453-4*, 2040776) Bks Demand.
Loomie, Albert J., ed. see Finet, John.
Loomie, Christine. We're Going on a Trip. LC 93-17592. (Illus.). 48p. (J). (ps up). 1994. 15.00 (*0-688-10172-0*); lib. bdg. 14.93 (*0-688-10173-9*) Morrow Jr Bks.
Loomis, Albertine. For Whom Are the Stars? LC 76-16778. 248p. 1976. 10.95 (*0-8248-0416-3*) UH Pr.
Loomis, Andrew. Figures in Action. (How to Draw & Paint Ser.). (Illus.). 32p. (Orig.). 1989. pap. 5.95 (*1-56010-009-5*, HT191) W Foster Pub.
— Heads, No. 2. (How to Draw & Paint Ser.). (Illus.). 32p. (Orig.). 1989. pap. 5.95 (*1-56010-010-9*, HT197) W Foster Pub.
Loomis, Arthur K. The Techniques of Estimating School Equipment Costs. LC 70-177010. (Columbia University. Teachers College. Contributions to Education Ser.: No. 208). reprint ed. 22.50 (*0-404-55208-0*) AMS Pr.
Loomis, Bardett A., jt. auth. see Cigler, Allan J.
Loomis, Bob & Kadash, Kathy. Reining: The Art of Performance in Horses. (Illus.). 240p. 1990. write for info. (*0-9625898-8-8*) EquiMedia.
Loomis, Burdett. Time, Politics, & Policies: A Legislative Year. LC 93-29050. (Studies in Government & Public Policy). 200p. 1994. 29.95 (*0-7006-0621-1*); pap. 12.95 (*0-7006-0622-X*) U Pr of KS.
Loomis, Burdett, jt. auth. see Cigler, Allan.
Loomis, Burdett A., jt. auth. see Cigler, Allen J.
Loomis, Charles B. Cheerful Americans. LC 73-86150. (Short Story Index Reprint Ser.). 1977. 21.95 (*0-8369-3054-1*) Ayer.
— Four-Masted Cat-Boat & Other Truthful Tales. LC 73-110206. (Short Story Index Reprint Ser.). 1977. 19.95 (*0-8369-3357-5*) Ayer.
— More Cheerful Americans. LC 72-101817. (Short Story Index Reprint Ser.). 1977. 20.95 (*0-8369-3205-6*) Ayer.
Loomis, Chauncey C. Weird & Tragic Shores: The Story of Charles Francis Hall, Explorer. LC 90-21280. (Illus.). xii, 403p. 1991. reprint ed. pap. 12.95 (*0-8032-7937-X*) U of Nebr Pr.
Loomis, Christine. At the Laundromat. LC 93-10884. (Illus.). (J). 1993. 14.95 (*0-590-72830-X*); pap. 4.95 (*0-590-49488-0*) Scholastic Inc.
— At the Library. LC 93-10882. (Illus.). (J). 1994. 14.95 (*0-590-72831-8*); pap. 4.95 (*0-590-49489-9*) Scholastic Inc.
— At the Mall. (Illus.). (J). 1994. 14.95 (*0-590-72832-6*); pap. 4.95 (*0-590-49490-2*) Scholastic Inc.
— The Hippo Hop. LC 94-31308. (Illus.). 1995. write for info. (*0-395-69702-6*) Ticknor & Flds Bks Yng Read.
— In the Diner. (Illus.). 32p. (J). (ps-2). 1994. 14.95 (*0-590-46716-6*, Scholastic Hardcover) Scholastic Inc.
— My New Baby-Sitter. LC 90-38527. (Illus.). 48p. (J). (ps up). 1991. lib. bdg. 13.88 (*0-688-09626-3*) Morrow Jr Bks.
— One Cow Coughs: A Counting Book for the Sick & Miserable. LC 93-1836. (Illus.). 32p. (J). (ps-2). 1994. 14.95 (*0-395-67899-4*) Ticknor & Flds Bks Yng Read.
— Rush Hour. LC 94-47192. (Illus.). (J). 1996. write for info. (*0-395-69129-X*) Ticknor & Flds Bks Yng Read.
Loomis, Darlene. Growing Together with Guys, Gals & Animal Pals. (Illus.). (Orig.). 1977. pap. 2.00 (*0-686-36276-4*) Drain Enterprise.
— He Touched Me. (Illus.). 62p. (Orig.). 1977. pap. 3.00 (*0-686-36275-6*) Drain Enterprise.
— Joint Heirs in Christ. (Illus.). (Orig.). 1977. pap. 2.00 (*0-686-36277-2*) Drain Enterprise.
— On Fire for God. (Illus.). 53p. (Orig.). 1976. 2.00 (*0-686-36274-8*) Drain Enterprise.
— Those Who Won't & Those Who Will. (Illus.). 12p. (Orig.). 1977. pap. 1.00 (*0-686-36278-0*) Drain Enterprise.
Loomis, David. Combat Zoning: Military Land Use Planning in Nevada. LC 92-2838. (Illus.). 168p. (C). 1993. 24.95 (*0-87417-187-3*) U of Nev Pr.
Loomis, E. The Descendants (by the Female Branches) of Joseph Loomis, Who Came from Braintree, England in 1638, & Settled in Windsor, Connecticut, in 1639, 2 vols. in 1, Vol. 1. 1132p. 1989. reprint ed. lib. bdg. 159.00 (*0-8328-0785-0*); reprint ed. pap. 149.00 (*0-8328-0786-9*) Higginson Bk Co.
Loomis, Edward. Superstrings: Poems. (Orig.). 1994. pap. 8.95 (*0-963943-0-4*) Grafx Bks.
Loomis, Elias. The Recent Progress of Astronomy: Especially in the United States. Cohen, I. Bernard, ed. LC 79-7972. (Three Centuries of Science in America Ser.). 1980. reprint ed. lib. bdg. 23.95 (*0-405-12554-2*) Ayer.
Loomis, Ernest. Practical Occultism. 73p. 1959. reprint ed. spiral bd. 5.50 (*0-7873-0569-3*) Mokelumne.
Loomis, Evarts G. Amy: A Search for the Treasure Within. LC 85-73540. (Illus.). 144p. (Orig.). 1986. pap. 5.50 (*0-87516-564-8*) DeVorss.
Loomis, Evarts G., comp. To Self Be True: The Search Within. 144p. (Orig.). 1991. pap. 8.00 (*0-9630266-0-7*) Friendly Hills.
Loomis, F. A., jt. auth. see Rowland, Mary C.
Loomis, Farnsworth W. God Within. (Illus.). 1968. 7.95 (*0-8079-0122-9*) October.
Loomis, George A., Jr., jt. auth. see Caswell, Lucy S.
Loomis, J. Paul. Campfires in the Rain. 202p. 1979. 15.00 (*0-317-59458-3*) G K Westgard.
— Up Saskatchewan Way: An Anthology of Short Stories. (Illus.). 152p. 1985. 15.00 (*0-317-59459-1*) G K Westgard.
Loomis, James P., ed. High Speed Commercial Flight: From Inquiry to Action. LC 88-35013. (Proceedings of the Second High Speed Commercial Flight Symposium Ser.). 224p. 1989. 37.50 (*0-935470-49-2*) Battelle.
— High Speed Commercial Flight - the Coming Era: Proceedings of the First High Speed Commercial Flight Symposium, Oct. 1986. LC 86-32153. (Illus.). 288p. 1987. 27.50 (*0-935470-37-9*) Battelle.
Loomis, Jeffrey B. Dayspring in Darkness: Sacrament in Hopkins. LC 87-47819. 224p. 1988. 36.50 (*0-8387-5138-5*) Bucknell U Pr.
***Loomis, Jim.** All Aboard! The Complete Guide to North American Train Travel. LC 95-3849. 1995. pap. write for info. (*0-7615-0000-6*) Prima Pub.
Loomis, John B. Integrated Public Lands Management: Principles & Applications to National Forests, Parks, Wildlife Refuges, & BLM Lands. LC 93-17218. 474p. 1993. 50.00 (*0-231-08006-9*) Col U Pr.
Loomis, Julia. Monarch Notes on Virgil's Aeneid & Other Works. (Orig.). (C). pap. 4.25 (*0-671-00509-X*, Arco Test) P-H Gen Ref & Trav.
Loomis, Laura H. & Loomis, Roger S., eds. Medieval Romances. LC 57-11169. (Modern Library College Editions). (C). 1965. pap. text ed. write for info. (*0-07-553650-1*, 30970) McGraw.
Loomis, Louise R., jt. auth. see Shotwell, James T.
Loomis, Lynn H. Calculus. LC 81-14937. (Mathematics Ser.). (Illus.). 1000p. 1982. student ed write for info. (*0-201-05046-3*) Addison-Wesley.
— Calculus. 3rd ed. LC 81-14937. (Mathematics Ser.). (Illus.). 1000p. (C). 1982. text ed. 73.25 (*0-201-05045-5*) Addison-Wesley.
— The Lattice Theoretic Background of the Dimension Theory of Operator Algebras. LC 52-42839. (Memoirs Ser.: No. 1/18). 36p. 1972. 17.00 (*0-8218-1218-1*, MEMO 1/18) Am Math.
— The Lattice Theoretic Background of the Dimension Theory of Operator Algebras. (Memoirs of the American Mathematical Society Ser.: No. 18). 42p. reprint ed. pap. 25.00 (*0-7837-5925-8*, 2045724) Bks Demand.
Loomis, Lynne, ed. see Malmuth, Mason.
Loomis, Lynne, jt. auth. see Malmuth, Mason.
Loomis, Lynne, ed. see Malmuth, Mason.
Loomis, Lynne, ed. see Sklansky, David & Malmuth, Mason.
Loomis, Lynne, ed. see Sklansky, David, et al.
Loomis, Lynne, ed. see Zee, Ray.
Loomis, M. Clarifying the Economics of War & Peace: Why the United States Must Fight in Iraq & the Middle East. 1991. lib. bdg. 75.00 (*0-8490-4060-4*) Gordon Pr.
Loomis, M. E., et al. The Loomis - Wood Model: Applying Theory to Nursing Education, Research, & Practice. (Illus.). 192p. (Orig.). (C). 1992. pap. text ed. 25.95 (*0-88737-540-5*) Natl League Nurse.
***Loomis, Mary.** Object Databases: The Essentials. LC 94-26970. 256p. 1995. pap. 25.95 (*0-201-56341-X*) Addison-Wesley.
Loomis, Mary E. Dancing the Wheel of Psychological Types. (Illus.). 128p. (Orig.). 1991. pap. 14.95 (*0-933029-49-7*) Chiron Pubns.
— The Database Book. 475p. (C). 1987. text ed. write for info. (*0-02-371760-2*) Macmillan.
— Her Father's Daughter. 120p. (Orig.). 1995. pap. 14.95 (*0-933029-88-8*) Chiron Pubns.
Loomis, Mildred. Clarifying the Economics of Peace. 1971. 250.00 (*0-87700-142-1*) Revisionist Pr.
Loomis, Mildred J. Alternative Americas. LC 81-19775. (Universe Bks.). 175p. 1982. 5.00 (*0-87663-375-0*); pap. 3.00 (*0-87663-567-2*) Schalkenbach.
Loomis, Noel. Bonanza. large type ed. 1976. 12.00 (*0-85456-421-7*) Ulverscroft.
Loomis, Patricia. Signposts. Muller, Kathleen, ed. (Illus.). 97p. 1982. 19.95 (*0-914139-06-1*) San Jose His Mus Assn.
— Signposts II. (American Places Ser.). (Illus.). 104p. 1985. lib. bdg. 20.95 (*0-914139-02-9*) San Jose His Mus Assn.
Loomis, R. S. & Connor, D. J. Crop Ecology: Productivity & Management in Agricultural Systems. (Illus.). 600p. (C). 1992. 105.00 (*0-521-38379-X*); pap. 39.95 (*0-521-38776-0*) Cambridge U Pr.
Loomis, Rich. Starweb Rulebook. 1988. 2.00 (*0-940244-76-4*) Flying Buffalo.
Loomis, Richard M., tr. Dafydd ap Gwilym: The Poems. LC 81-16968. (Medieval & Renaissance Texts & Studies: Vol. 9). (Illus.). 352p. 1982. 18.00 (*0-86698-015-6*) MRTS.
Loomis, Richard M. & Johnston, Dafydd, trs. Medieval Welsh Poems: An Anthology. (Pegasus Paperbooks Ser.). 240p. 1992. pap. 7.00 (*0-86698-102-0*, P8) MRTS.
Loomis, Rick. Buffalo Castle. (Illus.). 1982. 3.00 (*0-940244-01-2*) Flying Buffalo.
— Heroic Fantasy Rulebook. 1982. 2.00 (*0-940244-77-2*) Flying Buffalo.
— Starweb - Heroic Fantasy Set. 1988. 5.00 (*0-940244-79-9*) Flying Buffalo.
Loomis, Rick, ed. see Arneson, Dave.
Loomis, Rick, ed. see O'Connor, Paul.
Loomis, Rick, ed. see Stackpole, Mike & Wykle, Debora.
Loomis, Roger S. Celtic Myth & Arthurian Romance. LC 67-31638. (Arthurian Legend & Literature Ser.: No. 1). 1969. reprint ed. lib. bdg. 75.00 (*0-8383-0586-5*) M S G Haskell Hse.
— Celtic Myth & Athurian Romance. (Illus.). 372p. 1995. pap. 36.50x (*0-09-473350-3*, Pub. by Constable Pubs UK) Trans-Atl Phila.
— The Grail: From Celtic Myth to Christian Symbol. (Illus.). 304p. 1991. pap. text ed. 12.95 (*0-691-02075-2*) Princeton U Pr.
Loomis, Roger S. & Wells, Henry W., eds. Representative Medieval & Tudor Plays. LC 77-111109. (Play Anthology Reprint Ser.). 1977. 24.95 (*0-8369-8202-9*) Ayer.
Loomis, Roger S., jt. ed. see Loomis, Laura H.
***Loomis, Ruth.** Keeping the Forest Alive: A Guide to the Video "Thinking Like a Forest" 35p. 1993. pap. 4.95 (*0-919970-10-9*); vhs 30.00 (*0-919970-09-5*) All About Us.
Loomis, Sabra. Rosetree. LC 88-31561. 72p. (Orig.). 1989. pap. 9.95 (*0-914086-85-5*) Alicejamesbooks.
Loomis, Samuel L. Modern Cities & Their Religious Problems. LC 73-112558. (Rise of Urban America Ser.). 1976. reprint ed. 25.95 (*0-405-02464-9*) Ayer.
Loomis, Stanley. Paris in the Terror: June, Seventeen Ninety-Three to July, Seventeen Ninety-Four. (Reprints Ser.). 415p. 1990. reprint ed. 17.95 (*0-88029-401-9*) Dorset Pr.
Loomis, Susan H. Farmhouse Cookbook. LC 91-50390. (Illus.). 528p. (Orig.). 1991. 22.95 (*1-56305-125-7*, 3125); pap. 14.95 (*0-89480-772-2*, 1772) Workman Pub.
— The Great American Seafood Cookbook. LC 87-40644. (Illus.). 320p. 1988. pap. 12.95 (*0-89480-578-9*, 1578) Workman Pub.
Loomis, Susn H. Clambakes & Fish Fries. LC 94-2420. 1994. 19.95 (*1-56305-671-2*); pap. 10.95 (*1-56305-295-4*) Workman Pub.
Loomis, Terrence. Pacific Migrant Labour, Class & Racism in New Zealand: Fresh off the Boat. (Research in Ethnic Relations Ser.). 255p. 1990. text ed. 59.95 (*1-85628-048-9*, Pub. by Avebury Pub UK) Ashgate Pub Co.
Loomis, W. Farnsworth, jt. ed. see Lenhoff, Howard M.
Loomis, William F. Four Billion Years: An Essay on the Evolution of Genes & Organisms. LC 88-1848. (Illus.). 286p. (Orig.). 1988. pap. text ed. 26.95 (*0-87893-476-6*) Sinauer Assocs.
Loomis, William F., ed. Genetic Regulation of Development. 1987. text ed. 159.95 (*0-471-63335-6*) Wiley.
***Loon, Joan, et al.** The Lunettes. (Illus.). 16p. (J). (gr. 1-4). 1984. 25.00 (*1-56611-503-5*); pap. 18.00 (*1-56611-504-3*) Jonas.
***Loonan, Elizabeth.** Love Your Cat. 93p. 1994. write for info. (*1-57215-006-8*) World Pubns.
Loone, Eero. Marxism & the Contemporary Philosophy of History: A Soviet View. 320p. 1990. 59.95 (*0-86091-235-3*, Pub. by Verso UK) Routledge Chapman & Hall.
Looney, Ben E. Beau Sejour: Watercolors of Louisiana Plantation Country. 1972. 13.95 (*0-87511-073-8*) Claitors.
— Drawings of the Vieux Carre. 1976. 3.95 (*0-614-06325-6*) Claitors.
— Watercolors of Dixie. 1974. 13.95 (*0-87511-075-4*) Claitors.
Looney, Carl. Random Signal Analysis: Self Study Course Package. (Illus.). 1989. student ed, disk 498.00 (*0-87942-460-5*, HL0401-0) Inst Electrical.
Looney, Douglas S. & Yaeger, Don. Under the Tarnished Dome: How Notre Dame Sold Its Soul for Football Glory. (Illus.). 320p. 1993. 23.00 (*0-671-86950-7*) S&S Trade.
Looney, J. Anna, jt. auth. see Scheps, Walter.
Looney, J. Jefferson & Woodward, Ruth L. Princetonians, 1791-1794: A Biographical Dictionary. (Illus.). 586p. 1991. text ed. 65.00 (*0-691-04772-3*) Princeton U Pr.
Looney, J. W. Business Management for Farmers. LC 80-67888. (Illus.). 739p. 1983. 42.00 (*0-932250-11-4*) Red Wing Busn.
Looney, J. W. & Uchtmann, Donald L. Agricultural Law: Principles & Cases. 2nd ed. LC 93-1644. 1993. text ed. write for info. (*0-07-038720-6*) McGraw.
Looney, J. W., jt. auth. see Uchtmann, Donald L.
***Looney, John.** Alternative to Violence Workbook. rev. ed. Bender, Danene M., ed. (Illus.). 372p. (C). 1995. student ed 25.00x (*0-9619819-4-6*) Peace Grows.
— The Alternatives to Violence Workbook. 2nd ed. Bender, Danene & Smith, Waring, eds. (Illus.). 440p. 1987. teacher ed 19.90 (*0-9619819-3-8*) Peace Grows.
— Alternatives to Violence Workbook: A Course in Solving Conflict Peaceably for Happier Relationships, Safer Communities, a More Peaceful World. Bender, Danene & Smith, Waring, eds. (Illus.). 278p. (Orig.). (YA). (gr. 9 up). 1986. ring bd. 12.95 (*0-9619819-1-1*) Peace Grows.
Looney, John & Bender, Danene. The Media's Social Responsibility. (Illus.). 92p. (Orig.). 1986. pap. 4.00 (*0-9619819-0-3*) Peace Grows.
Looney, John G. Chronic Mental Illness in Children & Adolescents. LC 87-1472. 284p. 1987. text ed. 38.50 (*0-88048-236-2*, 0-88048-236-2) Am Psychiatric.
Looney, Kim, jt. auth. see Looney, Michael D.
Looney, Louisa P. Tennessee Sketches. (Short Story Index Reprint Ser.). 1977. reprint ed. 23.95 (*0-8369-4020-2*) Ayer.
***Looney, Michael D. & Looney, Kim.** Southern Tailgating: Game Day Recipes & Traditions. LC 94-23210. (Illus.). 168p. (Orig.). 1994. pap. 12.95 (*0-9630700-9-6*, 641.5'78...dc20) Vision AL.
Looney, Ralph. Haunted Highways: The Ghost Towns of New Mexico. LC 68-65623. (Illus.). 220p. 1979. reprint ed. pap. 17.95 (*0-8263-0506-7*) U of NM Pr.
— O'Keeffe & Me. (Illus.). 192p. 1995. 39.95 (*0-87081-406-0*) Univ Pr Colo.
Looney, Robert. Economic Development in Saudi Arabia: Consequences of the Oil Price Decline. (Contemporary Studies in Economic & Financial Analysis: Vol. 66). 289p. 1990. 73.25 (*1-55938-153-1*) Jai Pr.
Looney, Robert E. Development Alternatives of Mexico: Beyond the 1980's. LC 82-11288. 286p. 1982. text ed. 49.95 (*0-275-90850-X*, C0850, Praeger Pubs) Greenwood.
— Economic Origins of the Iranian Revolution. LC 82-384. (Policy Studies on International Development). (Illus.). 320p. 1982. 80.00 (*0-08-025950-2*, L115, Pergamon Pr) Elsevier.
— Economic Policy-Making in Mexico: Factors Underlying the 1982 Crisis. LC 84-28739. (Duke Press Policy Studies). xviii, 309p. (C). 1985. text ed. 48.00 (*0-8223-0557-7*) Duke.
— The Economics of Third World Defense Expenditures. LC 95-1539. (Contemporary Studies in Economic & Financial Analysis: Vol. 72). 1995. write for info. (*1-55938-386-0*) Jai Pr.
— Industrial Development & Diversification of the Arabian Gulf Economics. LC 94-824. (Contemporary Studies in Economic & Financial Analysis: Vol. 70). 1994. 73.25 (*1-55938-384-4*) Jai Pr.
— Manpower Policies & Development in the Persian Gulf Region. LC 93-14137. 216p. 1994. text ed. 55.00 (*0-275-94217-1*, C4217, Praeger Pubs) Greenwood.
— Third-World Military Expenditure & Arms Production. LC 88-4465. 242p. 1988. text ed. 59.95 (*0-312-02034-1*) St Martin.
Looney, Robert E. & Winterford, David. Economic Causes & Consequences of Defense Expenditures in the Middle East & South Asia. 224p. (C). 1994. pap. text ed. 38.50 (*0-8133-8442-7*) Westview.
Looney, Robert F. Old Philadelphia in Early Photographs; 1839-1914: Two Hundred & Fifteen Prints from the Collection of the Free Library of Philadelphia. LC 75-41688. (Illus.). 256p. (Orig.). 1976. pap. 13.95 (*0-486-23345-6*) Dover.
Looney, Robert F., ed. Thirty-Two Picture Postcards of Old Philadelphia. (Postcard Ser.). (Illus.). (Orig.). 1977. pap. 3.50 (*0-486-23421-5*) Dover.
Looney, Sandra, jt. ed. see Huseboe, Arthur R.
Looney, Sandra, et al, eds. The Prairie Frontier. (Illus.). 166p. (Orig.). 1984. pap. text ed. 6.00 (*0-9604816-1-3*) Nordland Her Found.
Loong-Hoe, Tan. The State & Economic Distribution in Malaysia. 96p. (Orig.). 1982. pap. text ed. 10.00 (*9971-902-44-3*, Pub. by Inst SE Asian Studies SI) Ashgate Pub Co.
Loong-Hoe, Tan, jt. ed. see Selmer, Jan.
Loontjens, Lois. Talking to Children - Talking to Parents about Sexual Assault. 80p. 1984. spiral bd. 10.95 (*0-941816-14-1*) ETR Assocs.
Loontjer, Jacqueline L. The Teacher's Guide: Fifty-Two Devotions for the Christian Teacher. LC 93-2986. 1993. write for info. (*0-570-04611-4*) Concordia.
Loop, James, jt. auth. see Zaloga, Steven J.
Loope, Lloyd L., jt. auth. see Medeiros, Arthur C.
Looper, Robert B., et al. The Cheniere Caminada Story: A Commemorative of the Hurricane of 1893. Gorman, Carolyn P., ed. (Illus.). 80p. (Orig.). 1993. pap. 10.00 (*0-9621724-8-0*) Blue Heron LA.
Looper, Stan H. & Scott, Cynthia M. When Anxiety Attacks: What the Health Care Community Does Not Know about Anxiety Attacks. 152p. (Orig.). (C). 1993. 11.95 (*0-943629-08-X*) Swan Pub.
Looper, Travis. Byron & the Bible: A Compendium of Biblical Usage in the Poetry of Lord Byron. LC 78-1518. 330p. 1978. 27.50 (*0-8108-1123-5*) Scarecrow.
Loor, F. & Roelants, G. E., eds. B & T Cells in Immune Recognition. LC 76-26913. (Illus.). 538p. reprint ed. pap. 153.40 (*0-8357-5935-0*, 2030511) Bks Demand.
Loori, John D. Two Arrows Meeting in Mid-Air: The Zen Koan. LC 94-7737. (Library of Enlightenment). 288p. (Orig.). 1994. pap. 16.95 (*0-8048-3012-6*) C E Tuttle.
Loori, John D., jt. auth. see Maezumi, Hakuyu T.
Loory, Stuart, et al. CNN Reports: Seven Days That Shook the World: The Collapse of Soviet Communism. (Illus.). 256p. 1991. 29.95 (*1-878685-11-2*); pap. text ed. 19.95 (*1-878685-12-0*) Turner Pub GA.
***Loos.** Research Methods in Experimental Psychology. (C). 1995. text ed. 41.00 (*0-673-99481-3*) HarpCollege.
Loos, Amandus W., ed. Nature of Man. LC 69-18930. (Essay Index Reprint Ser.). 1977. 17.95 (*0-8369-1042-7*) Ayer.

An Asterisk (*) at the beginning of an entry indicates that the title is appearing in BIP for the first time.

— Religious Faith & World Culture. LC 71-128270. (Essay Index Reprint Ser.). 1977. 23.95 (*0-8369-1976-9*) Ayer.

Loos, Anita. But Gentlemen Marry Brunettes. 96p. 1994. 7.95 (*0-14-018488-0*, Penguin Classics) Viking Penguin.

— Gentlemen Prefer Blondes. 1994. lib. bdg. 21.95x (*1-56849-512-9*) Buccaneer Bks.

— Gentlemen Prefer Blondes. 1958. 5.00 (*0-87129-412-5*, G13) Dramatic Pub.

— Gentlemen Prefer Blondes. 160p. 1994. 8.95 (*0-14-018487-2*, Penguin Classics) Viking Penguin.

— Gentlemen Prefer Blondes, but Gentlemen Marry Brunettes. (Illus.). 480p. 1989. pap. 9.95 (*0-14-011788-1*, Penguin Bks) Viking Penguin.

— Les Hommes Prefer les Blondes. (FRE.). 1982. pap. 10.95 (*0-7859-4171-1*) Fr & Eur.

— Mais Ils Epousent les Brunes. 192p. (FRE.). 1982. pap. 8.95 (*0-7859-4172-X*, 2070373967) Fr & Eur.

Loos, Dorothy S., tr. Alfonsina Storni: Anthology of Poems. (Illus.). 200p. (Orig.). (SPA.). 1986. pap. 5.95 (*0-915597-31-4*) Amana Bks.

Loos, Dorothy S., tr. see De Queiroz, Rachel.

Loos, Eugene E. Phonology of Capanahua & Its Grammatical Basis. (Publications in Linguistics & Related Fields: No. 20). 233p. 1969. fiche 12.00 (*0-88312-422-X*) Summer Instit Ling.

Loos, F. J. The Franks. 1982. lib. bdg. 75.00 (*0-87700-385-8*) Revisionist Pr.

***Loos, Frank M.** Research Foundations for Psychology & the Behavioral Sciences. LC 94-31484. (C). 1995. 41.00 (*0-06-044088-0*) HarpCollege.

***Loos, Gregory P.** Field Guide for International Health Project Planners & Managers. 80p. 1995. pap. 14.95 (*1-85756-159-7*) Paul & Co Pubs.

Loos, Sigrun, jt. auth. see Breicha, Otto.

Loose, Frances F. Decimals & Percentages. (Illus.). 100p. (gr. 4-6). 1977. 10.00 (*0-87879-803-X*, Ann Arbor Div) Acad Therapy.

— Fractions: Teacher's Guide. 56p. 1973. 5.00 (*0-87879-797-1*, Ann Arbor Div) Acad Therapy.

— Fractions, Book 1: Reusable Edition. (J). (gr. 4). 1973. student ed 10.00 (*0-87879-795-5*, Ann Arbor Div) Acad Therapy.

— Fractions, Book 2: Reusable Edition. (J). (gr. 4-6). 1973. student ed 10.00 (*0-87879-796-3*, Ann Arbor Div) Acad Therapy.

— Metrics: Reusable Edition. (gr. 9-12). 1975. student ed 6.50 (*0-87879-801-3*, Ann Arbor Div) Acad Therapy.

— Metrics: Teacher's Guide. (Illus.). 1975. 1.00 (*0-87879-802-1*, Ann Arbor Div) Acad Therapy.

Loose, Gerhard. Ernst Junger. LC 74-4150. (Twayne's World Authors Ser.). 143p. (C). 1974. lib. bdg. 17.95 (*0-8057-2479-6*) Irvington.

***Loose, John W.** Lancaster: The Heritage of Lancaster. 1978. 14.95 (*0-89781-001-5*) Preferred Mktg.

— The Military Market Basket. Walker, Joseph E., ed. LC 76-21211. (Lancaster County During the American Revolution Ser.). (Illus.). 64p. 1976. pap. 5.00 (*0-915010-09-7*) Sutter House.

Loose, Katherine R. House of Yost. 1993. reprint ed. lib. bdg. 89.00 (*0-7812-5485-X*) Rprt Serv.

Loose Leaf Reference Services Staff. Clinical Dentistry, 5 vols. Hardin, ed. 1988. ring bd. 395.00 (*0-06-148003-7*) Lippincott.

— Clinical Dentistry, 5 vols. rev. ed. Hardin, ed. 1988. 60.00 (*0-686-86014-4*) Lippincott.

— Clinical Dermatology, 4 vols. Demis, D. Joseph et al, eds. ring bd. 450.00 (*0-06-148004-5*) Lippincott.

— Clinical Dermatology, 4 vols. rev. ed. Demis, D. Joseph et al, eds. 75.00 (*0-686-86015-2*) Lippincott.

— Duane's Clinical Ophthalmology, 5 vols. & index. Tasman, William et al, eds. (Illus.). 80.00 (*0-685-71848-4*) Lippincott.

— Duane's Clinical Ophthalmology, 5 vols. & index, Set. Tasman, William et al, eds. (Illus.). ring bd. 495.00 (*0-06-148007-X*) Lippincott.

— Otolaryngology, 5 vols. English, Gerald M., ed. ring bd. 525.00 (*0-06-148010-X*); 85.00 (*0-686-86019-5*) Lippincott.

Loose Leaf Reference Services Staff, et al. Gynecology & Obstetrics: Loose Leaf: New Page Service, 6 vols. Buchsbaum, Herbert J. et al, eds. 80.00 (*0-686-86017-9*) Lippincott.

— Gynecology & Obstetrics: Loose Leaf: New Page Service, 6 vols., Set. Buchsbaum, Herbert J. et al, eds. ring bd. 495.00 (*0-06-148008-8*) Lippincott.

Loose, Peter. Loose on Liquidators: The Role of the Liquidator in a Voluntary Winding-up. xxiii, 216p. 1972. text ed. 6.75 (*0-85308-023-2*, Pub. by Jordan & Sons) Rothman.

***Looseley, David L.** The Politics of Fun: Cultural Policy & Debate in Contemporary France. 256p. 1995. 49.95 (*1-85973-013-2*) Berg Pubs.

Loosen, Peter T., jt. ed. see Nemeroff, Charles B.

Loosigian, Allan M. Stock Index Futures: Buying & Selling the Market Averages. LC 84-24473. 288p. 1985. 34.95 (*0-201-10267-6*) Addison-Wesley.

Loosley, Ernest. When the Church Was Young. LC 88-63264. 92p. (Orig.). 1989. pap. 7.95 (*0-940232-32-4*) Seedsowers.

***Loosmore, Judy.** Reflections on Relaxation. (Life Line Ser.). (Illus.). 158p. (Orig.). 1994. pap. 16.95 (*1-55059-081-2*) Temeron Bks.

Lootens, Douglas J., ed. see Symposium on Environmental Management for the 1990's Staff.

Loots, P. C. Engineering & Construction. 466p. 1985. 78.00 (*0-7021-1563-0*, Pub. by Juta SA) W W Gaunt.

Loovis, E. Michael & Ersing, Walter F. Assessing & Programming Gross Motor Development for Children. 2nd ed. 1979. pap. text ed. 10.95 (*0-89917-495-7*) Tichenor Pub.

Looy, Mark, jt. auth. see Sterling, Robert M.

Looye, Johanna & Uphoff, Norman. Local Institutional Development for Non-Agricultural Enterprise. (Special Series on Local Institutional Development: No. 6). 46p. (Orig.). (C). 1985. pap. text ed. 7.50 (*0-86731-113-4*) Cornell CIS RDC.

Looze, D. P., jt. auth. see Freudenberg, J. S.

Lopata, Edwin L. Local Aid to Railroads in Missouri. Bruchey, Stuart, ed. LC 80-1327. (Railroads Ser.). (Illus.). 1981. reprint ed. lib. bdg. 18.95 (*0-405-13801-6*) Ayer.

Lopata, Helen. Circles & Settings: Role Changes of American Women. (SUNY Series in Gender & Society). 325p. 1994. 59.50 (*0-7914-1767-0*); pap. 19.95 (*0-7914-1768-9*) State U NY Pr.

Lopata, Helena Z. City Women, Vol. 2. LC 84-15933. 576p. 1985. text ed. 75.00 (*0-275-90190-4*, C01902, Praeger Pubs) Greenwood.

— Occupation: Housewife. LC 80-23658. (Illus.). xvi, 387p. 1980. reprint ed. text ed. 65.00 (*0-313-22697-0*, LOOH, Greenwood Pr) Greenwood.

— Widowhood in an American City. 369p. 1973. pap. text ed. 21.95 (*0-87073-091-6*) Transaction Pubs.

Lopata, Helena Z., ed. Current Research on Occupations & Professions, Vol. 4. 1988. 73.25 (*0-89232-561-5*) Jai Pr.

— Research in the Interweave of Social Roles, Vol. 1. 325p. 1980. Women & Men. lib. bdg. 73.25 (*0-89232-066-4*) Jai Pr.

— Widows, Vol. I: The Middle East, Asia, & the Pacific. LC 87-5410. xiii, 258p. (C). 1987. 48.00 (*0-8223-0680-8*); pap. 20.95 (*0-8223-0768-5*) Duke.

— Widows, Vol. II: North America. LC 87-5410. xii, 313p. (C). 1987. lib. bdg. 48.00 (*0-8223-0724-3*); pap. text ed. 20.95 (*0-8223-0770-7*) Duke.

Lopata, Helena Z. & Erdmans, Mary. Polish Americans. LC 92-41516. 376p. (C). 1993. text ed. 37.95 (*1-56000-100-3*) Transaction Pubs.

Lopata, Helena Z. & Maines, David R., eds. Research in the Interweave of Social Roles: Friendship, Vol. 2. 289p. 1981. 73.25 (*0-89232-191-1*) Jai Pr.

Lopata, Helena Z. & Pleck, Joseph H., eds. Jobs & Families. (Current Research on Occupations & Professions Ser.: Vol. 3). 329p. 1983. 73.25 (*0-89232-304-3*) Jai Pr.

Lopata, Helena Z., et al. City Women in America: Work, Jobs, Occupations, Careers. LC 84-15933. 316p. 1984. text ed. 33.95 (*0-275-91218-3*, C12181, Praeger Pubs) Greenwood.

***Lopate.** Art of the Personal Essay: An Anthology from the Classical Era to the Present. 1995. pap. (*0-385-42339-X*, Anchor NY) Doubleday.

Lopate, Carol. Education & Culture in Brooklyn: A History of Ten Institutions. LC 78-65790. (Brooklyn Rediscovery Booklet Ser.). (Illus.). 63p. 1979. pap. 3.00 (*0-933250-01-0*) Bklyn Educ.

— Women in Medicine. LC 68-19526. (Josiah Macy Foundation Ser.). (Illus.). 204p. 1968. 32.50x (*0-8018-0391-8*) Johns Hopkins.

LoPate, Philip, intro. The Ordering Mirror: Readers & Contexts. LC 93-2065. 288p. 1993. 30.00 (*0-8232-1515-6*) Fordham.

Lopate, Phillip. Bachelorhood: Tales of the Metropolis. 1989. pap. 8.95 (*0-671-67681-4*) S&S Trade.

Lopate, Phillip, ed. Journal of a Living Experiment. LC 79-19199. 239p. (Orig.). 1979. pap. 13.95 (*0-915924-09-9*) Tchrs & Writers Coll.

Lopate, Phillip, intro. & sel. The Art of the Personal Essay: An Anthology from the Classical Era to the Present. LC 93-29708. 1994. 30.00 (*0-385-42298-9*, Anchor NY) Doubleday.

Lopategui, Miren, text. Presents: A Gift Record Book. (Illus.). 142p. 1991. 14.95 (*0-948751-03-7*) Interlink Pub.

Lopater, Sanford, jt. auth. see Hahn, John F.

Lopatin, A. K., jt. auth. see Mitropolsky, Yu. A.

Lopatin, B. A. Conductometry & Oscillometry. 304p. 1970. text ed. 70.00 (*0-7065-1085-2*, Pub. by Keter Pub IS) Coronet Bks.

Lopatin, Judy. Modern Romances. LC 86-7711. 256p. 1986. 15.95 (*0-932511-02-3*); pap. 7.95 (*0-932511-03-1*) Fiction Coll.

Lopatin, Robert, jt. auth. see Kusnet, Jack.

Lopato, Marina, jt. auth. see Von Habsburg, Geza K.

Lopatov, V. Soviet Union & Africa. 192p. (C). 1987. 30.00 (*0-685-31632-7*, Pub. by Collets UK) Pro-Am Music.

Lopatto, Paul. Religion & the Presidential Election. LC 84-26281. (American Political Parties & Elections Ser.). 192p. 1985. text ed. 49.95 (*0-275-90138-6*, C0138, Praeger Pubs) Greenwood.

Lope de Vega. Fuente Ovejuna. Eigenauer, John D., ed. 71p. (SPA.). 1987. pap. text ed. 11.95 (*0-9625734-0-X*) Darien Pub.

Lope, Julia I. Diccionario Juridico. 4th ed. 320p. (SPA.). 1990. pap. 45.00 (*0-7859-5899-1*, 8431500549) Fr & Eur.

Loper, David E., ed. Structure & Dynamics of Partially Solidified Systems. (C). 1987. lib. bdg. 184.00 (*90-247-3500-9*) Kluwer Ac.

Loper, L., ed. see AIDS Foundation Dayton Staff & Volunteers.

Loper, Neal, jt. intro. see Todd, Arnold R., III.

Loper, Orla E. & Tedsen, Edgar. Direct Current Fundamentals. 3rd ed. 386p. 1986. teacher ed 12.00 (*0-8273-2236-4*); text ed. 34.95 (*0-8273-2235-6*) Delmar.

— Direct Current Fundamentals. 4th ed. 516p. 1991. 34.95 (*0-8273-4146-6*); teacher ed 12.00 (*0-8273-4148-2*); pap. 29.95 (*0-8273-4147-4*) Delmar.

Loper, Orla E. & Tedson, Edgar. Direct Current Fundamentals. LC 94-10135. 1995. 34.95 (*0-8273-6572-1*) Delmar.

— Direct Current Fundamentals. 1995. pap. write for info. (*0-8273-6573-X*) Delmar.

Lopes. English in Portugal 1367-1387. Lomax, ed. (Hispanic Classics Ser.). 1988. 55.00 (*0-85668-341-8*, Pub. by Aris & Phillips UK); pap. 25.00 (*0-85668-342-6*, Pub. by Aris & Phillips UK) David Brown.

Lopes, Albert R. Bom Dia! One-Minute Dialogues in Portugese. (C). 1980. reprint ed. pap. text ed. 4.95 (*0-89197-520-9*) Irvington.

Lopes, Albert R. & Yarbro, J. D. Bonjour: One Minute Dialogues in French. (FRE.). (C). 1947. reprint ed. pap. text ed. 2.95 (*0-89197-521-7*) Irvington.

***Lopes Cardozo, Nathan T.** Between Silence & Speech: Essays on Jewish Thought. LC 94-37611. 264p. 1995. pap. 25.00 (*1-56821-336-0*) Aronson.

— The Infinite Chain: Torah, Masorah & man. 191p. 1989. 12.95 (*0-944070-15-9*) Targum Pr.

***Lopes, Clifton.** Was Man Created to Die? 1995. 13.95 (*0-8062-5227-8*) Carlton.

Lopes Da Silva, F. H., jt. ed. see Pfurtscheller, G.

Lopes Da Silva, Jose, ed. Ajustamento e Crescimento na Actual Conjuntura Economica Mundial. xii, 200p. 1985. pap. 10.00 (*0-939934-47-7*) Intl Monetary.

***Lopes, Damian.** Transentence. 28p. (Orig.). 1994. pap. 3.00 (*1-57141-005-8*) Runaway Spoon.

— Unclear Family. 24p. (Orig.). 1992. pap. 3.00 (*0-926935-65-8*) Runaway Spoon.

Lopes, Duarte. A Report of the Kingdome of Congo, Gathered by P. Pigafetta. Hartwell, A., tr. LC 75-25675. (English Experience Ser.: No. 260). 1970. reprint ed. 65.00 (*90-221-0260-2*) Walter J Johnson.

Lopes, Henri. Laughing Cry: An African Cock & Bull Story. Moore, Gerald, tr. (Readers International Ser.). 260p. (C). 1987. 16.95 (*0-930523-32-6*); pap. 8.95 (*0-930523-33-4*) Readers Intl.

— Tribaliks: Contemporary Congolese Stories. Leskes, Andrea, tr. (African Writers Ser.). Orig. Title: Tribaliques. 112p. (Orig.). (C). 1987. pap. 8.95 (*0-435-90762-X*) Heinemann.

Lopes, J. Leite. Gauge Field Theories: An Introduction. (Illus.). 450p. 1983. text ed. 206.00 (*0-08-026501-4*, Pub. by Pergamon Repr UK) Franklin.

Lopes, Jose L. & Paty, Michel, eds. Quantum Mechanics, a Half Century Later. (Episteme Ser.: No. 5). 1977. lib. bdg. 103.00 (*90-277-0784-7*) Kluwer Ac.

***Lopes, Jose M.** Foregrounded Description in Prose Fiction: Five Cross-Literary Studies. (Theory - Culture Ser.). 216p. (C). 1995. 45.00 (*0-8020-0727-9*) U of Toronto Pr.

Lopes, L. J. Lectures on Symmetries. (Documents on Modern Physics Ser.). 182p. 1969. text ed. 190.00 (*0-677-02250-6*) Gordon & Breach.

Lopes, Marlene, jt. auth. see Lobban, Richard.

Lopes, Michael. Mr. & Mrs. Mephistopheles & Son. 44p. 1975. pap. 2.50 (*0-913218-42-1*) Dustbooks.

***Lopes, S. Ivan.** Domestic Violence: The Downfall of Human Society. 1995. 11.95 (*0-533-11441-1*) Vantage.

Lopeshinskaya, Elena. Martyr Bishop Confessors under Communism. (RUS.). pap. 5.00 (*0-89981-055-1*) Eastern Orthodox.

***Lopez.** Aviation. 1995. 27.50 (*0-02-860006-1*); pap. 18.00 (*0-02-860041-X*) Macmillan.

— Economic Sanctions: Panacea or Peace-Building in a Post-Cold War World? Cortright, ed. (C). 1995. pap. text ed. 19.95 (*0-8133-8909-7*) Westview.

— Guia Rapida Windows - Spanish Guide to Microsoft Windows. (FRE.). 1990. 12.95 (*0-7859-3717-X*, 842831781X) Fr & Eur.

Lopez, A. Noether-Lefschetz Theory & the Picard Group of Projective Surfaces. LC 90-19299. (MEMO Ser.: Vol. 89/438). 100p. 1991. pap. text ed. 20.00 (*0-8218-2500-3*, MEMO 89/438) Am Math.

Lopez, Adalberto. The Revolt of the Communeros, 1721-1735: A Study in the Colonial History of Paraguay. 214p. 1976. 34.95 (*0-87073-124-6*) Transaction Pubs.

Lopez, Adalberto, ed. The Puerto Ricans: Their History, Culture & Society. 490p. 1981. pap. text ed. 19.95 (*0-87073-845-3*) Schenkman Bks Inc.

Lopez-Adorno, Pedro. Vias Teoricas a Altazor de Vincete Huidobro. (American University Studies: Romance Languages & Literature: Ser. II, Vol. 33). 263p. 1987. text ed. 39.95 (*0-8204-0250-8*) P Lang Pubs.

Lopez, Adriana F., tr. see Pepper, Margot.

Lopez, Alan. Reality Construction in an Eastern Mystical Cult. LC 92-16320. (Cults & Nonconventional Religious Groups Ser.). 280p. 1992. 68.00 (*0-8153-0772-1*) Garland.

***Lopez, Alan D., et al, eds.** Adult Mortality in Developed Countries: From Description to Explanation. (International Studies in Demography). (Illus.). 414p. 1995. text ed. 70.00 (*0-19-823329-9*) OUP.

Lopez, Albert C., tr. see Ray, C. A.

Lopez, Alberto, tr. see Edge, Findley B.

Lopez, Alfredo. Dona Licha's Island: Modern Colonialism in Puerto Rico. LC 87-15646. 200p. (Orig.). 1987. 30.00 (*0-89608-258-X*); pap. 12.00 (*0-89608-257-1*) South End Pr.

— Turn Around Once, & Keep Running. 180p. (Orig.). 1990. pap. 8.00 (*0-685-26446-7*) Atabex Collection.

Lopez, Alfredo R., jt. ed. see Garcia, Francisco M.

Lopez, Alfredo R., jt. ed. see Garcia, Francisco.

***Lopez, Alonzo.** Celebration. (J). (gr. k-2). 1993. audio 8.95 (*0-7608-0484-2*) Sundance Pub.

— Celebration. (J). (gr. k-2). 1993. pap. 4.95 (*0-88741-878-3*) Sundance Pub.

— Celebration. (J). (gr. k-2). 1993. 21.95 (*0-88741-897-X*) Sundance Pub.

***Lopez, Ana.** The Mysterious Gymnast. 1995. 8.95 (*0-8062-5063-1*) Carlton.

Lopez, Andrew. Natural Pest Control: Alternatives to Chemicals for the Home & Garden. (Illus.). 200p. 1994. pap. 19.95 (*1-885489-07-2*) Invisible Grdner.

***Lopez, Angelo, illus.** Canto Latino: Spanish Songs for Children. (Orig.). (J). (gr. k-5). 1995. audio 5.95 (*0-9638395-0-0*) Bi-Lateral Pr.

— Canto Latino: Spanish Songs for Children. 36p. (Orig.). (J). (gr. k-5). 1995. audio, pap. text ed. 12.95 (*0-9638395-1-9*) Bi-Lateral Pr.

Lopez, Anthony. Complete Course in Canning, Set, Vols. 1, 2 & 3. rev. ed. LC 46-19487. (Illus.). (Orig.). 1987. Set. pap. text ed. 100.00 (*0-930027-10-8*) CTI Pubns.

— Complete Course in Canning, Set, Vols. 1, 2 & 3. 12th rev. ed. LC 46-19487. (Illus.). (Orig.). 1987. Set. text ed. 125.00 (*0-930027-06-X*) CTI Pubns.

— Complete Course in Canning, Vols. 1, 2 & 3. rev. ed. LC 46-19487. (Illus.). (Orig.). 1987. Bk. I. text ed. 50.00 (*0-930027-07-8*); Bk. II. text ed. 50.00 (*0-930027-08-6*); Bk. III. text ed. 50.00 (*0-930027-09-4*) CTI Pubns.

***Lopez, Antoinette S., ed. & intro.** Criminal Justice & Latino Communities. LC 94-36051. (Latinos in the United States Ser.: Vol. 3). 312p. 1994. 60.00 (*0-8153-1772-7*) Garland.

***Lopez, Antoinette S., ed.** Historical Themes & Identity: Mestizaje & Labels. LC 94-24661. (Latinos in the United States Ser.: Vol. 1). (Illus.). 568p. 1995. 85.00 (*0-8153-1769-7*) Garland.

— Land Grants, Housing & Political Power. LC 94-36779. (Latinos in the United States Ser.: No. 6). 400p. 1994. 75.00 (*0-8153-1800-6*) Garland.

— Latina Issues: Fragments of Historia(elle) (Herstory) LC 94-34157. (Latinos in the United States Ser.: Vol. 2). (Illus.). 456p. 1995. 75.00 (*0-8153-1771-9*) Garland.

— Latino Employment, Labor Organizations, & Immigration. LC 94-33597. (Latinos in the United States Ser.: Vol. 4). 1994. 75.00 (*0-8153-1773-5*) Garland.

— Latino Language & Education: Communication & the Dream Deferred. LC 94-36776. (Latinos in the United States Ser.: Vol. 5). (Illus.). 440p. 1995. reprint ed. 75.00 (*0-8153-1774-3*) Garland.

Lopez, Arcadia. Los Animales del Parque. (Illus.). (J). (gr. k-2). 1973. pap. 2.00 (*0-913632-06-6*) All Things Pr.

— Barrio Teacher. LC 92-6876. 96p. (Orig.). (YA). (gr. 6-12). 1992. pap. text ed. 9.50 (*1-55885-051-1*) Arte Publico.

Lopez, Arcadia & Smith, John. El Parque Paquete. (Illus.). (J). (gr. k-2). 1976. teacher ed, pap. 86.50 (*0-913632-09-0*) All Things Pr.

Lopez-Arias, Julio. Peculiaridades Estilisticas de Fernao Lopes. LC 93-23087. (Iberica Ser.: Vol. 10). 210p. (C). 1994. text ed. 47.95 (*0-8204-2251-7*) P Lang Pubs.

Lopez Austin, Alfredo. The Myths of Opossum: Pathways of Mesoamerican Mythology. Ortiz De Montellano, Bernard R. & Ortiz De Montellano, Thelma, trs. LC 92-27258. 434p. 1993. 39.95x (*0-8263-1394-9*) U of NM Pr.

Lopez Austin, Alfredo L. The Human Body & Ideology: Concepts of the Ancient Nahuas, 2 vols. Ortiz De Montellano, Thelma & Ortiz De Montellano, Bernard R., trs. LC 87-10691. (Illus.). 832p. (SPA.). 1988. text ed. 65.00 (*0-87480-260-1*) U of Utah Pr.

Lopez-Baison. Guia Rapida Serie Assistant de IBM: Spanish Guide to IBM Computers. 2nd ed. (SPA.). 1991. write for info. (*0-7859-3691-2*, 8428317275) Fr & Eur.

— Guia Rapida Symphony, Hoya de Calculo: Spanish Guide to "Lotus Symphony" 2nd ed. (SPA.). 1991. write for info. (*0-7859-3696-3*, 8428317623) Fr & Eur.

— Guia Rapida Symphony, Utilidades, Tratamiento de Textos: Spanish Guide to "Lotus Symphony, Utilities & Text Processing" 2nd ed. (SPA.). 1991. write for info. (*0-7859-3695-5*, 8428317615) Fr & Eur.

Lopez-Baralt, Luce. Islam in Spanish Literature: From the Middle Ages to the Present. Hurley, Andrew, tr. LC 91-34243. xvii, 323p. 1992. 83.00 (*90-04-09460-1*) E J Brill.

Lopez-Baralt, Mercedes. La Gestacion De Fortunata y Jacinta: Galdos y la Novela Como Re-Escritura. 225p. (Orig.). (SPA.). (C). 1992. pap. text ed. 9.95 (*0-929157-17-6*) Ediciones Huracan.

Lopez, Barry. Arctic Dreams. 1987. mass mkt. 6.99 (*0-553-26396-X*) Bantam.

— Crow & Weasel. LC 90-31500. (Illus.). 64p. (J). (gr. 5 up). 1990. 16.95 (*0-86547-439-7*, North Pt Pr) FS&G.

— Crow & Weasel. LC 92-54858. 1993. pap. 12.00 (*0-06-097528-8*, PL) HarpC.

— Field Notes: The Grace Note of the Canyon Wren. LC 94-2144. 1994. 20.00 (*0-679-43453-4*) Knopf.

— Field Notes: The Grace Note of the Canyon Wren. 176p. 1995. reprint ed. pap. 9.00 (*0-380-72482-0*) Avon.

— Giving Birth to Thunder, Sleeping with His Daughter. 192p. 1990. pap. 7.95 (*0-380-71111-7*) Avon.

— The Rediscovery of North America. LC 92-50087. 1992. 8.00 (*0-679-74099-6*, Vin) Random.

— The Rediscovery of North America. LC 90-24487. 64p. 1991. 15.00 (*0-8131-1742-9*) U Pr of Ky.

— Winter Count. 128p. 1993. pap. 8.00 (*0-380-71937-1*) Avon.

Lopez, Barry, jt. auth. see Beath, Mary.

Lopez, Barry H. Arctic Dreams: Imagination & Desire in a Northern Landscape. (Illus.). 496p. 1986. text ed. 22.95 (*0-684-18578-4*, Scribners) S&S Trade.

— Crossing Open Ground. 1989. pap. 9.00 (*0-679-72183-5*, Vin) Random.

— Crossing Open Ground. 1988. write for info. (*0-333-46943-7*, Scribners) S&S Trade.

— Desert Notes: Reflections in the Eye of a Raven. LC 76-6099. (Illus.). 96p. 1976. 6.95 (*0-8362-0661-4*) Andrews & McMeel.

— Desert Notes: Reflections in the Eye of the Raven. 96p. 1981. pap. 7.95 (*0-380-53819-9*) Avon.

— Desert Notes--Reflections in the Eye of a Raven. Bd. with River Notes--The Dance of Herons 144p. 1990. Set pap. 7.95 (*0-380-71110-9*) Avon.

— Giving Birth to Thunder, Sleeping with His Daughter. 208p. 1990. pap. 7.95 (*0-380-54551-9*) Avon.

L

— Giving Birth to Thunder, Sleeping with His Daughter: Coyote Builds North America. LC 77-17395. 1978. 8.95 (0-8362-0726-2) Andrews & McMeel.
— Of Wolves & Men. 1994. 24.75 (0-8446-6727-7) Peter Smith.
— Of Wolves & Men. LC 78-6070. (Illus.). 320p. 1979. pap. 17.00 (0-684-16322-5, Scribners) S&S Trade.
— River Notes: The Dance of Herons. LC 79-17192. 1979. 6.95 (0-8362-6106-2) Andrews & McMeel.
— River Notes: The Dance of the Herons. 96p. 1990. pap. 7.95 (0-380-52514-3) Avon.
— Winter Count. 128p. 1982. mass mkt. 4.95 (0-380-58107-8, Bard) Avon.
Lopez, Benito M., Jr., intro. Catholic Education: New Partnerships in the Service of the Church. (Current Issues in Catholic Higher Education Ser.: Vol. 14, No. 1). 46p. (Orig.). 1993. pap. text ed. 6.00 (1-55833-127-1) Natl Cath Educ.
Lopez-Berestein, Gabriel & Klostergaard, Jim, eds. Mononuclear Phagocytes in Cell Biology. 1992. 161.00 (0-8493-4706-8, QR185) CRC Pr.
Lopez-Bustos, Francisco, tr. see Jackins, Harvey.
Lopez, C., jt. ed. see Ades, E. W.
Lopez, C., jt. auth. see Gonzalez-Arroyo, A.
Lopez, C. M., jt. auth. see McGowen, M. K.
Lopez-Cajun, C. S., jt. auth. see Angeles, J.
Lopez, Carlos & Roizman, Bernard, eds. Human Herpesvirus Infections: Pathogenesis, Diagnosis, & Treatment. 320p. 1986. text ed. 79.00 (0-88167-235-1) Raven.
Lopez, Carlos, jt. ed. see Roizman, Bernard.
Lopez, Carlos, jt. ed. see Rouse, Barry T.
Lopez, Carlos, et al, eds. Immunobiology & Prophylaxis of Human Herpesvirus Infections. (Advances in Experimental Medicine & Biology Ser.: Vol. 278). (Illus.). 310p. 1990. 85.00 (0-306-43696-5, Plenum Pr) Plenum.
***Lopez, Carlos E.** Investigaciones Arqueologicas en el Magdalena Medio, Cuenca del Rio Carare (Departamento de Santander) (Illus.). 126p. (SPA.). 1991. pap. 8.50 (1-877812-27-7) UPLAAP.
Lopez-Casasnovas, G. & Van Eimeren, W., eds. Incentives in Health Systems: Health Systems Research. (Illus.). 224p. 1991. pap. 89.00 (0-387-53933-6) Spr-Verlag.
Lopez-Casero Olmedo, Francisco & Hierneis, Otto. Spanisch fur Kaufleute: Spanish Business Correspondence guide. 10th ed. 455p. (GER & SPA.). 1981. reprint ed. 49.95 (0-7859-5673-5, 3468403402) Fr & Eur.
Lopez Castellon, Enrique, ed. see Platon.
Lopez, Cecilia L. Alexander Pope: An Annotated Bibliography, 1945-1967. LC 78-99213. 164p. reprint ed. pap. 46.80 (0-8357-5302-6, 2007585) Bks Demand.
Lopez-Chiclana, Margarita, tr. see Ramirez, Rafael E.
Lopez, Christian J. Malocclusion: Subject Analysis & Research Index with Bibliography. LC 88-47593. 150p. 1988. 44.50 (0-88164-629-6); pap. 39.50 (0-88164-630-X) ABBE Pubs Assn.
Lopez-Claros, Augusto. The Search for Efficiency in the Adjustment Process: Spain in the 1980s. (Occasional Paper Ser.: No. 57). 43p. 1988. pap. 7.50 (1-55775-009-2) Intl Monetary.
Lopez, Claude A. Mon Cher Papa, Franklin & the Ladies of Paris. LC 66-12507. 418p. reprint ed. pap. 119.20 (0-8357-8230-1, 2033806) Bks Demand.
Lopez, Claude-Anne. Mon Cher Papa: Franklin & the Ladies of Paris. 424p. (C). 1990. reprint ed. text ed. 45.00 (0-300-04800-9); reprint ed. pap. 18.00 (0-300-04758-4) Yale U Pr.
Lopez, Claude-Anne & Herbert, Eugenia W. The Private Franklin: The Man & His Family. (Illus.). 400p. 1985. reprint ed. pap. 9.95 (0-393-30227-X) Norton.
Lopez-Corvo, Raphael E. Self-Envy: Therapy & the Divided Internal World. LC 94-7733. 248p. 1995. 30.00 (1-56821-252-6) Aronson.
Lopez, Cruz, jt. auth. see Tejera, Gomez.
Lopez, Daniel. Films by Genre: Seven Hundred Seventy-Five Categories, Styles, Trends & Movements Defined, with a Filmography for Each. LC 92-56661. 519p. 1993. lib. bdg. 45.00 (0-89950-780-8) McFarland & Co.
***Lopez, Daniel S., Jr.** Religions of India in Practice. LC 94-34695. (Princeton Readings in Religion Ser.). 1995. pap. 19.95 (0-691-04324-8) Princeton U Pr.
Lopez de Ayala, Pero. Coronica de Enrique Three. Wilkins, Constance L. & Wilkins, Heanon M., eds. (Spanish Ser.: No. 74). xxvi, 136p. 1992. 20.00 (0-940639-77-7) Hispanic Seminary.
Lopez de Gomara, Francisco. Cortes: The Life of the Conqueror of Mexico by His Secretary, Francisco Lopez de Gomara. Simpson, Lesley B., ed. & tr. by. LC 64-13474. 1964. pap. 14.00 (0-520-00493-0) U CA Pr.
***Lopez de Mariscal, Blanca.** The Harvest Birds: Los Pajaros de la Cosecha. LC 94-40016. (Illus.). (J). 1995. 14.95 (0-89239-131-6) Childrens Book Pr.
***Lopez de Martinez, Adelaida, ed.** A Ricardo Gullon: Sus Discipulos. (Homenajes de Aldeeu Ser.). (Illus.). 320p. (SPA.). (C). 1995. pap. 35.00 (0-9626630-3-4) Spanish Profs Amer.
Lopez De Maya, E. La Iglesia Del Dios Vivo: The Church of the Living God. (SPA.). 3.25 (84-7228-720-3, 360300, Pub. by Edit Clie SP) TSELF.
Lopez De Thorogood, Lucy, tr. see Robson, Ernest.
Lopez de Ubeda, Francisco, see Andrea Perez, pseud..
Lopez de Zuazo Algar, Antonio. Dictionary of Journalism: Diccionario del Periodismo. 5th ed. 256p. (SPA.). 1990. pap. 35.00 (0-7859-4921-6) Fr & Eur.
Lopez, Diana C. Graduate Education at Tennessee: An Historical Perspective. LC 90-37520. (Illus.). 325p. 1990. 19.95 (0-9625933-0-3) Univ TN Grad Schl.
Lopez, Diane. Teaching Children: A Curriculum Guide to What Children Need to Know at Each Grade Level Through Sixth Grade. LC 87-71895. 299p. 1988. pap. 12.99 (0-89107-489-9) Crossway Bks.
Lopez, Don, ed. see Dalai Lama.
***Lopez, Donald, ed.** Flight. LC 95-12949. (Discoveries Ser.). (Illus.). 64p. (J). (gr. 4-7). 1995. write for info. (0-7835-4761-7) Time-Life.
***Lopez, Donald S.** Fighter Pilot's Heaven. LC 94-21061. 1995. write for info. (1-56098-457-0) Smithsonian.
Lopez, Donald S., Jr. The Heart Sutra Explained: Indian & Tibetan Commentaries. LC 87-6479. (SUNY Series in Buddhist Studies). 230p. 1987. 59.50 (0-88706-589-9); pap. 19.95 (0-88706-590-2) State U NY Pr.
— A Study of Svatantrika. LC 86-14636. 490p. (Orig.). (C). 1987. lib. bdg. 35.00 (0-937938-20-3); pap. 19.95 (0-937938-19-X) Snow Lion Pubns.
***Lopez, Donald S., Jr., ed.** Buddhism in Practice. LC 94-48201. (Princeton Readings in Religion Ser.). 1995. write for info. (0-691-04442-2); pap. write for info. (0-691-04441-4) Princeton U Pr.
— Buddhist Hermeneutics. LC 87-30175. (Studies in East Asian Buddhism: No. 6). 320p. 1988. text ed. 35.00 (0-8248-1161-5) UH Pr.
— Buddhist Hermeneutics. (Studies in East Asian Buddhism: No. 6). 308p. (C). 1992. reprint ed. pap. text ed. 15.95 (0-8248-1447-9) UH Pr.
***Lopez, Donald S., ed.** Curators of the Buddha: The Study of Buddhism under Colonialism. 1995. lib. bdg. 45.95 (0-226-49308-3) U Ch Pr.
— Curators of the Buddha: The Study of Buddhism under Colonialism. 1995. pap. text ed. 16.95 (0-226-49309-1) U Ch Pr.
***Lopez, Donald S., Jr., ed.** Religions of India in Practice. LC 94-34695. (Princeton Readings in Religion Ser.). 1995. 59.50 (0-691-04325-6) Princeton U Pr.
Lopez, Donald S. & Lopez, Donald S. National Air & Space Museum: A Visit in Pictures. LC 88-36586. (Illus.). 64p. 1990. 6.98 (0-87474-710-4) Smithsonian.
Lopez, Donald S., Jr. & Rockefeller, Stephen C., eds. The Christ & the Bodhisattva. LC 86-14356. (Buddhist Studies). 274p. (C). 1987. 59.50 (0-88706-401-9); pap. 19.95 (0-88706-402-7) State U NY Pr.
Lopez, Donald S., jt. ed. see Boyne, Walter J.
Lopez, Donald S., Jr., tr. see Loma, Dalai.
Lopez, Donald S., jt. auth. see Lopez, Donald S.
Lopez Eire, Antonio, ed. see Homero.
Lopez, Ellen R. Through Different Colored Glasses: The World as Seen Through the Left & Right Hemispheres of the Brain. (Illus.). 60p. 1989. pap. write for info. (0-318-64915-2) McDonald & Hezlep.
Lopez, Estela R. El Teatro de Max Aub. LC 76-46372. (UPREX, Teatro y Cine Ser.: No. 52). 200p. (Orig.). 1976. pap. text ed. 1.50 (0-8477-0052-6) U of PR Pr.
***Lopez Estrada, Francisco, ed.** Historia Etiopica de Los Amores de Teagenes y Cariclea. Mena, Fernando de, tr. 430p. (SPA.). 1968. pap. 100.00 (0-614-00216-8) Elliots Bks.
Lopez Estrada, Francisco & Keller, John E. Antonio de Villegas' "El Abencerraje" (Studies in Comparative Literature: No. 33). (C). 1964. pap. 5.95 (0-8078-7033-1) U of NC Pr.
Lopez Estrada, Francisco, ed. see Bequer, Gustavo A.
Lopez, F. Solano & Lopez, Gabriel S. Ana. Thompson, Kim, tr. (Illus.). 120p. 1991. 12.95 (1-56097-066-9) Fantagraph Bks.
Lopez, F. Solano, jt. auth. see Barreiro.
***Lopez, Frances B.** Psychology of Anxiety, Worry & Troublesome Problems: Index of New Information with Authors & Subjects. rev. ed. LC 94-24769. 157p. 1994. 49.50 (0-7883-0370-8); pap. 44.50 (0-7883-0371-6) ABBE Pubs Assn.
Lopez, Gabriel S., jt. auth. see Lopez, F. Solano.
Lopez, Gary. Air Pollution. (Images Ser.). (J). (gr. 5 up). 1992. lib. bdg. 16.95 (0-88682-427-3) Creative Ed.
— Air Pollution. (J). (gr. 4-7). 1993. 15.95 (1-56846-050-3) Creative Ed.
— Sharks. (Nature Books Ser.). 32p. (J). (gr. 2-6). 1991. 22.79 (0-89565-705-8) Childs World.
Lopez-Gaston, Jose R., tr. see Caponnetto, Antonio.
Lopez-Gaston, Rosa M., tr. see Caponnetto, Antonio.
Lopez, George A., ed. Morals & Might: Ethics & the Use of Force in Modern International Affairs. 288p. (C). 1995. text ed. 55.00 (0-8133-8726-4) Westview.
Lopez, George A. & Stohl, Michael, eds. Dependence, Development, & State Repression. LC 87-32258. (Contributions in Political Science Ser.: No. 209). 286p. 1989. text ed. 59.95 (0-313-25298-X, LDV/, Greenwood Pr) Greenwood.
— Liberalization & Redemocratization in Latin America. LC 87-272. (Contributions in Political Science Ser.: No. 178). 288p. 1987. text ed. 59.95 (0-313-25299-8, LLB/, Greenwood Pr) Greenwood.
Lopez, George A., jt. auth. see Garrigan, Timothy B.
Lopez, George A., jt. ed. see Stohl, Michael.
Lopez, George A., et al. Testing Theories of State Violence, State Terror, & Repression. (Series on State Violence, Terrorism & Human Rights). 265p. (C). 1929. pap. text ed. 31.00 (0-8133-7525-8) Westview.
Lopez, Gerald P. Rebellious Lawyering: One Chicano's View of Progressive Law Practice. 433p. 1992. text ed. 58.00 (0-8133-8560-1) Westview.
— Rebellious Lawyering: One Chicano's View of Progressive Law Practice. 433p. (C). 1992. pap. text ed. 22.95 (0-8133-8561-X) Westview.
Lopez, Gilbert T., ed. Technical Book Buyer's Guide. 2nd ed. (Illus.). 400p. (Orig.). 1991. pap. text ed. 14.95 (1-880072-00-9) Utd Techbook.
Lopez, Gilbert T. & Cloney, Tom. Technical Book Buyer's Guide. 2nd ed. (Illus.). 370p. (Orig.). 1994. pap. text ed. 19.95 (1-880072-01-7) Utd Techbook.
Lopez Gonzalez, Julio. El Ensayo y Su Ensenanza: Dos Ejemplos Puertorriquenos. LC 80-17712. (Coleccion Mente y Palabra). 153p. 1980. 6.00 (0-8477-0568-4); pap. 5.00 (0-8477-0569-2) U of PR Pr.
Lopez, Heladio R. La Sindicalizacion de Trabajadores Agricolas en Mexico: La Experiencia de la Confederacion Nacional Campesina (CNC) (Research Report Ser.: No. 26). 16p. (Orig.). (C). 1981. pap. 5.00 (0-935391-25-8, RR-26) UCSD Ctr US-Mex.
Lopez-Hernandez, F. J., jt. auth. see Santamaria, A.
Lopez Hernandez, Marcela, ed. Textos y Concordancias del Libro de los Olios, MS2262: Salamanca, Universitaria. (Medieval Spanish Medical Texts Ser.: No. 28). 8p. (SPA.). 1989. 10.00 (0-940639-38-6) Hispanic Seminary.
***Lopez, Ian F.** White by Law: The Legal Construction of Race. (Critical America Ser.). 240p. 1995. 24.95 (0-8147-5099-0) NYU Pr.
Lopez-Ibor, J., ed. International College of Psychosomatic Medicine Madrid, October 1989, Selected Papers from the 10th World Congress: Journal: Psychotherapy & Psychosomatics, Vol. 52, No. 1-3, 1989. (Illus.). 172p. 1990. pap. 99.25 (3-8055-5273-4) S Karger.
Lopez, Ivette & Garcia, Dwight. Cantos y Rimas. (Lecturas Faciles). 68p. (SPA.). 1983. pap. text ed. 3.75 (0-88345-524-2, 21282) Prentice ESL.
— Cantos y Rimas. 1987. pap. text ed. 7.00 (0-13-113507-4) Prentice ESL.
Lopez, J. A. La Tecnica. (SPA.). 7.95 (84-241-5628-5) E Torres & Sons.
Lopez, J. L. & Nanopoulos, D. V. Recent Advances in the Superworld: Proceedings of the International Workshop. 396p. 1994. text ed. 106.00 (981-02-1730-7) World Scientific Pub.
Lopez, John, jt. auth. see Hall, George.
Lopez, Jorge M. & Ross, Kenneth A. Sidon Sets. (Lecture Notes in Pure & Applied Mathematics Ser.: Vol. 13). 208p. 1975. 99.75 (0-8247-6289-4) Dekker.
Lopez, Jorge M., tr. see Stenmark, Jean K., et al.
Lopez, Julio C., ed. see De Hostos, Eugenio M.
Lopez, Kathleen, jt. auth. see Jones, Patricia.
Lopez, Ken & Chaney, Bev. Robert Stone: A Bibliography, 1960-1992. (Illus.). 120p. 1992. 40.00 (0-9632898-0-2) Numinous Pr.
— Robert Stone: A Bibliography, 1960-1992. limited ed. (Illus.). 120p. 1992. 125.00 (0-9632898-1-0) Numinous Pr.
Lopez, Kerry, ed. see Heynes, Michael & Miller, Anne.
Lopez, Luce B. San Juan de la Cruz & el Islam: Estudio Sobre las Filiaciones Semiticas de su Literatura. 1986. 13.00 (968-12-0294-5) U of PR Pr.
Lopez, M. Elena, et al. Paths to School Readiness: An In-Depth Look at Three Early Childhood Programs. LC 93-79081. 126p. (Orig.). 1993. pap. text ed. 10.95 (0-9630627-2-7) Harvard Fam.
Lopez, Manuel D. Chinese Drama: An Annotated Bibliography of Commentary, Criticism, & Plays in English Translation. annot. ed. LC 91-15902. 535p. 1991. 57.50 (0-8108-2347-0) Scarecrow.
— New York: A Guide to Information & Reference Sources. LC 80-18634. x, 317p. 1980. 27.50 (0-8108-1326-2) Scarecrow.
— New York: A Guide to Information & Reference Sources, 1979-1986. LC 87-16531. 384p. 1987. 37.50 (0-8108-2018-8) Scarecrow.
Lopez, Manuel D., ed. Catalog of the Polish Room Collection: Lockwood Memorial Library, State University of New York at Buffalo, 2 vols., Set. LC 83-81936. 1983. lib. bdg. 195.00 (0-89941-288-2, 302970) W S Hein.
Lopez, Marcela, ed. Text & Concordance of Biblioteca Universitaria, Salamanca, MS2262: Doctor Gomez de Salamanca, Propiedades del Romero. (Medieval Spanish Medical Texts Ser.: No. 21). 6p. (SPA.). 1987. 10.00 (0-940639-17-3) Hispanic Seminary.
Lopez, Maria J., jt. auth. see Miranda, Julia.
Lopez, Maria M. & Zuniga Burmester, Ricardo. Perspectivas Criticas de la Psicologia Social. LC 85-1053. viii, 450p. 1988. pap. 16.00 (0-8477-2909-5) U of PR Pr.
Lopez-Medina, Silvia. Cantora: A Novel. LC 91-43406. 317p. 1992. 19.95 (0-8263-1375-2) U of NM Pr.
Lopez-Medina, Sylvia. Cantora: A Novel. 320p. 1993. pap. 10.00 (0-345-38166-1, One World) Ballantine.
Lopez Mendizabal, Isaak. Diccionario Vasco-Castellano. 6th ed. 452p. 1976. 49.95 (0-8288-5624-9, S50439) Fr & Eur.
Lopez, Mercedes, photos. Cuba Is My Home. LC 92-17725. (My Home Country Ser.). (Illus.). (J). 1992. lib. bdg. 18.60 (0-8368-0848-7) Gareth Stevens Inc.
Lopez, Michael. Emerson & Power. LC 94-10716. Date not set. 32.00 (0-87580-196-X) N Ill U Pr.
***Lopez, Michael J.** Retail Store Planning & Design Manual. 2nd ed. (NRF Publishing Program Ser.). 1995. text ed. 100.00 (0-471-07629-5) Wiley.
Lopez-Morales, Humberto, ed. Corrientes Actuales en la Dialectologia del Caribe Hispanico: Actas de un Simposio. LC 77-12823. 247p. 1978. pap. 6.00 (0-8477-3186-3) U of PR Pr.
Lopez-Morillas, Consuelo. The Qur'an in Sixteenth-Century Spain: Six Morisco Versions of Sura 79. (Serie A: Monografias, LXXXII). (Illus.). 102p. (C). 1982. 63.00 (0-7293-0121-4, Pub. by Tamesis Bks Ltd UK) Boydell & Brewer.
Lopez-Morillas, Frances M., tr. see Cela, Camilo J.
Lopez-Morillas, Frances M., tr. see Delibes, Miguel.
Lopez-Morillas, Frances M., tr. see Gaite, Carmen M.
Lopez-Morillas, Frances M., tr. see Galdos, Benito P.
Lopez-Morillas, Frances M., tr. see Marias, Julian.
Lopez-Morillas, Frances M., tr. see Pupo-Walker, Enrique, ed.
Lopez-Morillas, Frances M., tr. see Savater, Fernando.
Lopez-Morillas, Frances M., tr. see Weckmann, Luis.
Lopez-Morillas, Juan. The Krausist Movement & Ideological Change in Spain: 1854-1874. (Iberian & Latin American Studies). (Illus.). 180p. 1981. 69.95 (0-521-23256-2) Cambridge U Pr.
Lopez, N. C. King Pancho & the First Clock. LC 63-16396. (Illus.). 32p. (J). (gr. 2-7). 1967. lib. bdg. 9.95 (0-87783-020-7); digital audio 7.94 (0-685-03701-0) Oddo.
— King Pancho & the First Clock. deluxe ed. LC 63-16396. (Illus.). 32p. (J). (gr. 2-7). 1967. pap. 3.94 (0-87783-098-3) Oddo.
Lopez, Nancy & Wade, Ton. Nancy Lopez's The Complete Golfer. (Illus.). 240p. 1989. reprint ed. pap. 14.95 (0-8092-4711-9) Contemp Bks.
Lopez, Nancy, tr. see Torruellas, Luz M. & Vazquez, Jose L.
Lopez, Norbert. Cuento Del Rey Pancho y el Primer Reloj. LC 70-108730. (Illus.). 32p. (J). (gr. 2-7). 1970. lib. bdg. 9.95 (0-87783-010-X); audio 7.94 (0-685-03700-2) Oddo.
— Cuento Del Rey Pancho y el Primer Reloj. deluxe ed. LC 70-108730. (Illus.). 32p. (J). (gr. 2-7). 1970. pap. 3.94 (0-87783-104-1) Oddo.
Lopez, Orlando R. El Penon de las Animas. (Romance Real Ser.). 192p. (Orig.). pap. 1.50 (0-88025-007-0) Roca Pub.
Lopez, P. Fernando. Mami! Cuanto te Quiero! LC 83-80417. (Coleccion Espejo de Paciencia Ser.). (Illus.). 91p. (Orig.). (SPA.). 1983. pap. 6.00 (0-89729-329-0) Ediciones.
Lopez-Pedraza, Rafael. Hermes & His Children. 208p. 1995. pap. 17.95 (3-85630-518-1, Pub. by Daimon Verlag SZ) Atrium Pubs.
Lopez-Pereira. New Carbohydrate Diet Counter. 1985. pap. 2.00 (0-87980-107-7) Wilshire.
Lopez, Peter, tr. see Bellegarde, Ida R.
Lopez Pinero, Jose M. The Historical Origins of the Concept of Neurosis. Berrios, D., tr. LC 82-19858. 107p. 1983. 54.95 (0-521-24972-4) Cambridge U Pr.
***Lopez, R. J., ed.** Maple V: Mathematics & its Application. LC 94-29119. 234p. 1994. 36.50 (0-8176-3791-5) Birkhauser.
Lopez, Ralph I., ed. Adolescent Medicine: Topics, Vol. 2. LC 76-17896. (Illus.). 232p. 1980. text ed. 45.00 (0-88331-107-0) Luce.
***Lopez, Raymond & Aguilar, Miriam E.** The Business Tool: A Business Start-up & Reference Guide. (Illus.). 221p. (Orig.). 1994. pap. 42.00 (0-9643887-3-1) West Comm Tech.
— The Business Tool: A Business Start-up & Reference Guide. (Illus.). 246p. (Orig.). 1994. pap. 21.00 (0-9643887-1-5) West Comm Tech.
— La Herramienta de Negocios: Una Guia de Referencia Para Comenzar Su Negocio. (Illus.). 246p. (Orig.). (SPA.). 1994. pap. 42.00 (0-9643887-2-3) West Comm Tech.
— La Herramienta de Negocios: Una Guia de Referencia para Comenzar Su Negocio. (Illus.). 270p. (Orig.). (SPA.). 1994. pap. 21.00 (0-9643887-0-7) West Comm Tech.
Lopez-Rey, Jose. Velazquez: The Complete Paintings. limited ed. (Illus.). 536p. 1988. 175.00 (1-55660-013-5) A Wofsy Fine Arts.
Lopez-Rey, Manual. Guide to United Nations Criminal Policy. 200p. 1985. text ed. 59.95 (0-566-05070-6) Ashgate Pub Co.
Lopez-Rey, Manuel, et al. Extension, Carateristicas y Tendencias de la Criminalidad en Puerto Rico, 1964-1970. 2nd ed. (Centro de Investigaciones Sociales Ser.). 322p. 1975. reprint ed. pap. text ed. 5.00 (0-8477-2480-8) U of PR Pr.
Lopez, Rick. Hard Boil. (Racket Squad Ser.: No. 2). (Illus.). 24p. 1986. 2.50 (0-940381-05-2) Kangaroo Ct Pub.
Lopez, Rick, ed. see Eschweiler, Chuck.
Lopez, Rick, ed. see Moffeit, Tony.
Lopez, Rick, ed. see Sherman, Lonnie.
Lopez, Rick, jt. ed. see Sherman, Lonnie.
Lopez, Rigoberto A. & Polopolus, Leo C., eds. Vegetable Markets in the Western Hemisphere. LC 90-21777. (Illus.). 266p. 1992. text ed. 32.95 (0-8138-1052-3) Iowa St U Pr.
***Lopez, Robert J.** Maple via Calculus: Tutorial Approach. LC 94-28246. xiii, 166p. 1994. pap. 24.50 (0-8176-3771-0) Birkhauser.
Lopez, Robert S. The Birth of Europe. LC 66-23414. (Illus.). 448p. 1966. pap. 12.95 (0-87131-132-1) M Evans.
— Byzantium & the World Around It: Economic & Institutional Relations. (Collected Studies: No. CS85). (Illus.). 318p. (C). 1978. reprint ed. lib. bdg. 95.00 (0-86078-030-9, Pub. by Variorum UK) Ashgate Pub Co.
— The Commercial Revolution of the Middle Ages, 950-1350. LC 75-35453. (Illus.). 204p. 1976. pap. 16.95 (0-521-29046-5) Cambridge U Pr.
— The Shape of Medieval Monetary History. (Collected Studies: No. CS247). (Illus.). 330p. (C). 1986. reprint ed. lib. bdg. 89.95 (0-86078-195-X, Pub. by Variorum UK) Ashgate Pub Co.
— Three Ages of the Italian Renaissance. LC 75-94759. 137p. reprint ed. 39.10 (0-8357-9819-4, 2011465) Bks Demand.
Lopez-Roman, Juan E. La Obra Literaria de Vicente Pales Matos. LC 83-17123. (Coleccion Mente y Palabra). 293p. (Orig.). (SPA.). 1984. pap. 8.00 (0-8477-0587-0) U of PR Pr.
Lopez, Ron, ed. see Waller, Wanda W.
Lopez-Rubio, Jose. La Otra Orilla: Comedia en Tres Actos. Pasquariello, Anthony M. & Falconieri, John V., eds. LC 58-12829. (SPA.). 1977. reprint ed. pap. text ed. 7.95 (0-89197-324-9) Irvington.

An Asterisk (*) at the beginning of an entry indicates that the title is appearing in BIP for the first time.

— Venda en los Ojos. Holt, Marion P., ed. LC 66-21587. (Orig.). (SPA.). 1966. pap. text ed. 5.95 (*0-89197-464-4*) Irvington.

Lopez, Ruth K. A Child's Garden Diary: Coloring & Activity Book. (Illus.). 56p. (Orig.). (J). (gr. k-6). 1992. pap. 5.95 (*0-9627463-4-7*) Gardens Growing People.

Lopez, Salvador P., jt. auth. see Edades, Jean G.

***Lopez, Sandra.** Clearcut. limited ed. Trusky, Tom, ed. (Hemingway Western Studies Ser.). (Illus.). 3p. (Orig.). 1994. 14.95 (*0-932129-23-4*) Heming W Studies.

Lopez Sastre, Gerardo, ed. see Hume, David.

Lopez, Silvia L., jt. auth. see Canclini, Nestor G.

Lopez, Silvia L., tr. see Canclini, Nestor G.

Lopez, Silvia L., et al, eds. Critical Practices in Post-Franco Spain. LC 94-1236. (Hispanic Issues Ser.: Vol. 11). 1994. text ed. 49.95 (*0-8166-2473-9*) U of Minn Pr.

— Critical Practices in Post-Franco Spain. LC 94-1236. (Hispanic Issues Ser.: Vol. 11). 1994. pap. text ed. 19.95 (*0-8166-2474-7*) U of Minn Pr.

Lopez-Solar, Joyce, jt. auth. see Burchard, Elizabeth.

Lopez-Soto, Edwin. Trying to Cope with Continuing Disability Review Regulations. 30p. 1986. pap. 3.25 (*0-685-44379-5*, 40,963) NCLS Inc.

Lopez Soto, Vicente. Dictionary of Authors, Works & Personalities of Greek Literature: Diccionario de Autores, Obras y Personajes de la Literatura Griega. 316p. (SPA.). 1984. pap. 12.50 (*0-8288-1577-1*, S60272) Fr & Eur.

***Lopez, Steve.** Land of Giants. LC 95-9628. 240p. (Orig.). 1995. pap. 10.00 (*0-940159-30-9*) Camino Bks.

— Third & Indiana. 320p. 1995. 10.95 (*0-14-023945-6*, Penguin Bks) Viking Penguin.

— Third & Indiana: A Novel. LC 93-49815. 320p. 1994. 21.95 (*0-670-85676-2*, Viking) Viking Penguin.

Lopez Suria, Violeta. Antologia Poetica. 262p. (C). 1970. 3.50 (*0-8477-3207-X*) U of PR Pr.

Lopez, Tele P., ed. see De Andrade, Mario.

Lopez, Tiffany A. Growing up Chicana-O: An Anthology. LC 93-28195. 1993. 20.00 (*0-688-11467-9*) Morrow.

***Lopez, Tiffany A., ed.** Growing Up Chicana-O. 272p. 1995. pap. 11.00 (*0-380-72419-7*) Avon.

Lopez, Tom. Exploring Idaho's Mountains: A Guide for Climbers, Hiking & Scramblers. LC 90-6679. (Illus.). 300p. (Orig.). 1990. pap. 16.95 (*0-89886-235-3*) Mountaineers.

Lopez, Tony. The Poetry of W. S. Graham. 240p. 1989. 45.00 (*0-85224-587-4*, Pub. by Edinburgh U Pr UK) Col U Pr.

— The Poetry of W. S. Graham. 176p. 1990. pap. text ed. 15.00 (*0-85224-588-2*, Pub. by Edinburgh U Pr UK) Col U Pr.

Lopez, Ulises M. & Warrin, George E. Mechanical Drawing. (C). 1984. write for info. (*0-8359-4314-3*, Reston) P-H.

Lopez-Valdez, Jeanne, ed. see Friedenberg, Joan E., et al.

Lopez-Vasquez, Alfredo R., ed. see De Claramonte, Andres.

Lopez, Victor D. Business Law: An Introduction. LC 92-28448. 400p. (C). 1992. text ed. 34.95 (*0-256-12389-6*) Irwin.

Lopez, Victor D. & Ansley, Kenneth J. Free & User Supported Software for the IBM PC: A Resource Guide for Libraries & Individuals. LC 89-43656. 224p. 1990. pap. 22.50x (*0-89950-499-X*) McFarland & Co.

Lopez-Vidriero, M. L., jt. ed. see Revenga, Luis.

Lopez-Vidriero, M. T., et al, eds. Host Defense & the Role of Surfactant in the Lung, Amsterdam, September 1987. Lung Defensive System: Damages & Treatment, Milan, September 1987: Journal: Respiration, Vol. 55, Supplement 1. (Illus.). 100p. 1989. pap. 28.00 (*3-8055-5071-5*) S Karger.

Lopez Vigil, Maria. Don Lito of El Salvador. Palumbo, Eugene, tr. LC 89-48225. 1990. pap. 11.95 (*0-88344-669-3*) Orbis Bks.

Lopez y Fuentes, Gregorio. El Indio. Brenner, Anita, tr. LC 61-17563. (Illus.). 144p. 1961. pap. text ed. 11.95 (*0-8044-6429-4*, F Ungar Bks) Continuum.

Lopez y Rivas, Gilberto. The Chicanos: Life & Struggles of the Mexican Minority in the United States, with Readings. Martinez, Elizabeth, ed. & tr. by. LC 73-8056. 192p. reprint ed. pap. 54.80 (*0-8357-6053-7*, 2034340) Bks Demand.

LoPiccolo Jennett, Vickie & Hagen, Paula. A Prayer Companion for Moms. LC 93-19670. (Illus.). 104p. (Orig.). (C). 1993. pap. 6.95 (*0-89390-265-9*) Resource Pubns.

LoPiccolo, Joseph & LoPiccolo, Leslie, eds. Handbook of Sex Therapy. LC 77-18818. (Perspectives in Sexuality Ser.). (Illus.). 552p. 1978. 55.00 (*0-306-31074-0*, Plenum Pr) Plenum.

LoPiccolo, Leslie, jt. ed. see LoPiccolo, Joseph.

Lopinot, Alvin C., jt. auth. see Winterringer, Glen S.

Lopinski, Maciej, et al. Konspira: Solidarity Underground. Cave, Jane, tr. (Illus.). 261p. 1990. 30.00 (*0-520-06131-4*) U CA Pr.

LoPinto, Roslyn. A Guide to Centering: The Harmonious Response to Life. 72p. (Orig.). 1986. pap. 6.95 (*0-9619018-0-2*) Artistech.

— A Spiritual Concept: The Real Nature of Things. 86p. (Orig.). 1988. pap. 6.95 (*0-9619018-1-0*) Artistech.

Lopos, George J., jt. ed. see Holt, Margaret E.

Lopos, George J., et al, eds. Peterson's Guide to Certificate Programs at American Colleges & Universities. LC 88-43018. 351p. (Orig.). 1988. pap. 35.95 (*0-87866-741-5*) Petersons Guides.

Lopreato, Joseph. Human Nature & Biocultural Evolution. LC 84-402. (Illus.). 350p. 1984. text ed. 34.95 (*0-04-573017-2*) Routledge Chapman & Hall.

LoPreato, Joseph, jt. auth. see Jackson, Eugene.

Loprest, Pamela & Gates, Michael. State-Level Data Book on Health Care Access & Financing. LC 93-14692. (Illus.). 190p. (Orig.). (C). 1993. pap. text ed. 35.00 (*0-87766-597-4*) Urban Inst.

***LoPresti, Angeline S.** A Place for Zero. (J). 1995. 7.95 (*0-533-11196-X*) Vantage.

Lopresti, James. Penance: A Reform Proposal. 27p. 1987. 3.00 (*0-8146-1932-0*) Liturgical Pr.

LoPresti, Joan. Calendar Capers: A Child's School Year in Celebration. LC 90-36812. (Illus.). 32p. (J). (gr. k-3). 1990. lib. bdg. 18.60 (*0-8368-0428-7*) Gareth Stevens Inc.

Lopresti, Robert, ed. see Benchley, Robert.

Lopresti, Robert, ed. see Thurber, James.

***LoPresto, James C.** Space-Time: Fabric of the Universe. LC 94-78959. (Illus.). 258p. 1995. pap. 29.95 (*0-910042-72-1*) Allegheny.

LoPresto, R. L., et al. Reference Checking Handbook. 3rd rev. ed. 37p. (C). 1993. pap. 20.00 (*0-939900-61-0*) Soc Human Resc Mgmt.

***Loprete.** Iberoamerica: Historia de su Civilizacion y Cultural. 3rd ed. (Illus.). 464p. (C). 1994. text ed. write for info. (*0-13-323445-2*) P-H.

***Loprieno, Antonio.** Ancient Egyptian: A Linguistic Introduction. 304p. (C). Date not set. write for info. (*0-521-44384-9*); pap. write for info. (*0-521-44849-2*) Cambridge U Pr.

***Loprieno, Nicola.** Alternative Methodologies for the Safety Evaluation of Chemicals in the Cosmetic Industry. Hollinger, Mannfred, ed. LC 95-2335. (Basic & Clinical Aspects Ser.). 304p. 1995. 149.95 (*0-8493-8546-6*, 8546) CRC Pr.

Lopriore, Lanfranco, jt. auth. see Lazzerini, Beatrice.

Lopshire, Robert. I Want to Be Somebody New. LC 85-43098. (Illus.). 48p. (J). (gr. k-3). 1986. 7.99 (*0-394-87616-4*); lib. bdg. 7.99 (*0-394-97616-9*) Beginner.

— Put Me in the Zoo. LC 60-13494. (Illus.). 72p. (J). (gr. 1-2). 1960. 7.99 (*0-394-80017-6*) Beginner.

— Put Me in the Zoo. LC 60-13494. (Illus.). 72p. (J). (gr. 1-2). 1966. lib. bdg. 9.99 (*0-394-90017-0*) Beginner.

Lopsinger, Lutz W. & Michler, Ralf, eds. Salvador Dali: The Catalogue Raisonne of Etchings & Mixed-Media Prints, 1924-1980. (Illus.). 262p. 1993. 120.00 (*3-7913-1279-0*, Pub. by Prestel) TeNeues.

Lopsinger, Lutz W., jt. ed. see Michler, Ralf.

***Loptson, Peter.** Theories of Human Nature. 220p. 1995. pap. 19.95 (*1-55111-061-X*) Broadview Pr.

Lopucki. Strategies for Creditors in Bankruptcy Proceedings. 2nd ed. 1991. 145.00 (*0-316-53228-2*) Little.

LoPucki, Lynn M. Player's Manual for the Debtor Creditor Game. (Legal Exercise Ser.). 123p. 1985. pap. text ed. 16.50 (*0-314-89510-8*) West Pub.

LoPucki, Lynn M. & Reilly, Ann T., eds. Law & Business Directory of Bankruptcy Attorneys 1988. 1988. 125.00 (*0-318-36198-1*) P-H.

Lopukhin, Yu. M. Physiochemical Aspects of Medicine Reviews, Vol. 1. 450p. 1987. text ed. 310.00 (*3-7186-0316-0*) Gordon & Breach.

Lopukhin, Yu M., et al, eds. Cholesterosis - Membrane Cholesterol: Theoretical & Clinical Aspects. (Physicochemical Biology Reviews Supplement Ser.: Soviet Scientific Reviews, Sect. D). 382p. 1984. text ed. 319.00 (*3-7186-0159-1*) Gordon & Breach.

Lopuszanzki, J. Introduction to Symmetry & Supersymmetry in Quantum Field Theory. 388p. (C). 1990. text ed. 86.00 (*9971-5-0160-0*); pap. text ed. 40.00 (*9971-5-0161-9*) World Scientific Pub.

Loqinov, V. & Obuchov, V. Helenie. (Illus.). 46p. (Orig.). (RUS.). 1990. 9.00 (*1-878445-50-2*) Antiquary CT.

Loque, Rufino E. The Fragrance of Tina & Other Stories. v, 82p. (Orig.). (C). 1992. pap. 6.75 (*971-10-0439-9*, Pub. by New Day Pub PH) Cellar.

Lora, Eduardo, jt. auth. see Fleischer, Lowell.

Lora, Guillermo. A History of the Bolivian Labour Movement, 1848-1971. LC 76-22988. (Cambridge Latin American Studies: no. 27). 418p. reprint ed. pap. 119.20 (*0-317-28407-X*, 2022458) Bks Demand.

Lora, Ronald. Conservative Minds in America. Van Tassel, David D., ed. LC 79-14219. 274p. 1980. reprint ed. text ed. 35.00 (*0-313-21468-9*, LOCM, Greenwood Pr) Greenwood.

Lorac, E. C. Murder by Matchlight. 160p. 1988. reprint ed. pap. 5.95 (*0-486-25577-8*) Dover.

Loraditch, Andrew, ed. see Lords, Damien.

Lorain, Jean-Michel, jt. auth. see Lorain, Michel.

Lorain, Michel & Lorain, Jean-Michel. Bouquet de Bourgogne: Seasonal Recipes from La Cote St. Jacques, Joigny. (Illus.). 96p. 1994. 16.95 (*1-85793-396-6*, Pub. by Pavilion UK) Trafalgar.

Loraine, John A. Sex & the Population Crisis. LC 85-24774. 213p. 1986. reprint ed. text ed. 55.00 (*0-313-22505-2*, LOSP, Greenwood Pr) Greenwood.

Loraine, R. K. Construction Management in Developing Countries. 171p. 1992. text ed. 78.00 (*0-7277-1651-4*) Am Soc Civil Eng.

Loram, Ian C. & Phelps, Leland R., eds. Aus Unserer Zeit. 4th ed. (GER.). (C). 1988. pap. text ed. 19.95 (*0-393-95614-8*) Norton.

***Loran.** Sports Vision. 1995. write for info. (*0-7506-1578-8*, Focal) Buttrwrth-Heinemann.

Loran, Erle. Cezanne's Composition: Analysis of His Form with Diagrams & Photographs of His Motifs. 3rd ed. (Illus.). 1963. pap. 17.00 (*0-520-05459-8*) U CA Pr.

Lorand, Laszlo, jt. ed. see Colowick, Sidney P.

Lorand, Laszlo, jt. ed. see Najjar, Victor A.

Lorand, Laszlo, et al, eds. Methods in Enzymology, Vol. 223: Proteolytic Enzymes in Coagulation, Fibrinolysis, & Complement Activation, Pt. B: Complement Activation, Fibrinolysis, & Nonmammalian Blood Coagulation Factors & Inhibitors. (Illus.). 433p. 1993. text ed. 69.00 (*0-12-182124-2*) Acad Pr.

— Proteolytic Enzymes in Coagulation, Fibrinolysis, & Complement Activation. (Methods in Enzymology Ser.: Vol. 222). (Illus.). 613p. 1993. text ed. 95.00 (*0-12-182123-4*) Acad Pr.

Lorand Olazagasti, Adelaida. El Indio en la Narrativa Guatemalteca. 280p. (C). 1968. pap. 3.25 (*0-8477-3138-3*) U of PR Pr.

Lorand, Sandor, ed. Psychoanalysis Today. (Medical War Bks.). 420p. reprint ed. pap. 119.70 (*0-317-12975-9*, 2010688) Bks Demand.

L'Orange, H. P. Apotheosis in Ancient Portraiture. (Illus.). 156p. 1982. reprint ed. lib. bdg. 55.00 (*0-89241-149-X*) Caratzas.

— Art Forms & Civic Life in the Late Roman Empire. (Illus.). 1965. pap. 12.95 (*0-691-00305-X*) Princeton U Pr.

— Likeness & Icon: Selected Studies in Classical & Early Medieval Art. 344p. (Orig.). 1973. pap. 67.50 (*87-7492-062-6*, Pub. by Odense Universitets Forlag DK) Coronet Bks.

— Studies on the Iconography of Cosmic Kingship in the Ancient World. (Illus.). 206p. 1982. reprint ed. lib. bdg. 55.00 (*0-89241-150-3*) Caratzas.

L'Orange, Hans P. & Von Gerkan, Arnim. Der Spaetantike Bildschmuck des Konstantinsbogen: Text Vol. & Vol. with Plates. (Studien zur Spaetantiken Kunstgeschichte: Vol. 10). (Illus.). 238p. (C). 1978. reprint ed. 542.35 (*3-11-002249-4*) De Gruyter.

Lorange, Peter, ed. Strategic Planning & Control: Issues in the Strategy Process. (Corporate Strategy, Organization, & Change Ser.). 256p. 1993. 39.95 (*1-55786-103-X*) Blackwell Pubs.

— Strategic Planning Process. (International Library Management). 400p. 1994. 127.95 (*1-85521-350-8*, Pub. by Dartmth Pub UK) Ashgate Pub Co.

Lorange, Peter, jt. ed. see Contractor, Farok J.

Lorange, Peter, et al. Strategic Control. 1986p. (C). 1986. pap. text ed. 35.50 (*0-314-85258-1*) West Pub.

Lorange, Peter, et al, eds. Implementing Strategic Processes: Learning, Adaptation, & Innovation. LC 92-20359. 1993. 44.95 (*0-631-18565-8*) Blackwell Pubs.

Loranger, Alexina, jt. tr. see Notovitch, Nicolas.

Loranger, Richard. The Orange Book. (Illus.). (Orig.). 1990. pap. 5.00 (*0-9628018-0-1*) Intl Review CO.

Lorant, John H. The Role of Capital: Improving Innovations in American Manufacturing During the 1920's. LC 75-2588. (Dissertations in American Economic History Ser.). (Illus.). 1975. 34.95 (*0-405-07207-4*) Ayer.

Lorant, Stefan. The Glorious Burden: The American Presidency. LC 76-48760. (Illus.). 1976. 19.95 (*0-918058-00-7*) Authors Edn MA.

— Pittsburgh: The Story of an American City. enl. ed. LC 75-24970. (Illus.). 736p. 1988. 24.95 (*0-685-92012-7*) Authors Edn MA.

Loranth, Alice N., ed. Catalog of Folklore, Folklife & Folk Songs, 3 vols., Set. 2nd ed. 1978. lib. bdg. 280.00 (*0-8161-0249-X*, Hall Library) G K Hall.

Loras College Sesquicentennial Committee Staff. Look at Loras One Hundred & Fiftieth Celebration. Farrington, Anthony, ed. (Illus.). 100p. 1989. 39.95 (*0-936875-04-6*) Loras Coll Pr.

***Loraux, Nicole.** Children of Athena: Anthenian Ideas about Citizenship & the Division Between the Sexes. 1994. pap. 16.95 (*0-691-03762-0*) Princeton U Pr.

— The Children of Athena: Athenian Ideas about Citizenship & the Division Between the Sexes. Levine, Caroline, tr. (Illus.). 320p. 1993. text ed. 39.50 (*0-691-03272-6*) Princeton U Pr.

— The Experiences of Tiresias: The Feminine & the Greek Man. Wissing, Paula, tr. LC 94-36789. 1995. write for info. (*0-691-02985-7*) Princeton U Pr.

— Mothers in Mourning. Glassman, Deborah, tr. (New Ancient World Ser.). 128p. 1992. 39.50 (*0-415-90506-0*, A6475, Routledge NY); pap. 13.95 (*0-415-90507-9*, A6479, Routledge NY) Routledge.

— Tragic Ways of Killing a Woman. Forster, Anthony, tr. LC 87-390. 112p. 1987. 23.00 (*0-674-90225-4*) HUP.

— Tragic Ways of Killing a Woman. 112p. (C). 1991. pap. 12.50 (*0-674-90226-2*) HUP.

Lorayne, Harry. Harry Lorayne's Page-a-Minute Memory Book. 176p. 1986. pap. 3.95 (*0-345-33475-2*) Ballantine.

— How to Develop a Super-Power Memory. 192p. 1974. pap. 4.95 (*0-451-16149-1*, Sig); pap. 4.99 (*0-451-16036-3*, AE2941, Sig) NAL-Dutton.

— How to Develop a Super Power Memory - More Money, Higher Grades & More Friends. 218p. (YA). (gr. 9 up). 1995. reprint ed. 17.95 (*0-8119-0181-5*) LIFETIME.

— Memory Makes Money. 256p. 1988. 16.95 (*0-316-53267-3*) Little.

— Remembering People: The Key to Success. 1995. pap. 14.95 (*0-8128-8557-0*, Scrbrough Hse) Madison Bks UPA.

— Secrets of Mind Power. rev. ed. 240p. (YA). 1995. 17.95 (*0-8119-0756-2*) LIFETIME.

— Secrets of Mind Power: How to Organize & Develop the Hidden Powers of Your Mind. rev. ed. 228p. 1995. 17.95 (*0-8119-0666-3*) LIFETIME.

— Super Memory Super Student, Vol. 1. 1990. pap. 12.95 (*0-316-53268-1*) Little.

Lorayne, Harry & Lucas, Jerry. The Memory Book. (Reprints Ser.). 237p. 1989. reprint ed. 19.95 (*0-88029-322-5*) Dorset Pr.

Lorayne, Harry, jt. auth. see Lucas, Jerry.

Lorbeer, Floyd I. Philosophy of Light: An Introductory Treatise. 259p. 1981. pap. 20.00 (*0-89540-102-9*, SB-102) Sun Pub.

Lorbeer, George C. Science Activities for Children, Vol. II. 416p. (C). 1993. spiral bd. write for info. (*0-697-14691-X*) Brown & Benchmark.

Lorbeer, George C. & Nelson, Leslie W. Science Activities for Children, 2 vols., Set, Vols. I & II. 9th ed. 320p. (C). 1992. Set. pap. text ed. write for info. (*0-697-14687-1*) Brown & Benchmark.

— Science Activities for Children, Vol. I. 9th ed. 448p. (C). 1992. spiral bd. write for info. (*0-697-10416-8*) Brown & Benchmark.

Lorber, Catharine C. Amphipolis: The Civic Coinage in Silver & Gold. 196p. 1990. 87.50 (*0-9626987-0-9*) Numismatic Fine Arts.

***Lorber, Jakob.** Earth & Moon. Hanswille, Gerhard, tr. (Illus.). 200p. (Orig.). 1994. pap. text ed. 19.95 (*1-885928-01-7*) Merkur Pubng.

— The Lord's Book of Life & Health. Hanswille, Gerhard, tr. 265p. (Orig.). 1994. pap. 24.95 (*1-885928-00-9*) Merkur Pubng.

— The Lord's Sermons. Ozols, Violet & Von Koerber, Hildegard, trs. LC 80-50280. (Jakob Lorber Ser.). 256p. 1981. 12.95 (*0-934616-06-X*) Valkyrie Pub Hse.

— Spiritual View of Life. 364p. 1981. pap. 15.00 (*0-934616-15-9*) Valkyrie Pub Hse.

— The Three Days Scene at the Temple in Jerusalem. 2nd ed. Nordewin, Dr. & Von Koerber, Hildegard, trs. LC 82-83492. 116p. 1981. pap. 10.00 (*0-934616-10-8*) Valkyrie Pub Hse.

Lorber, Judith. Paradoxes of Gender. LC 93-23459. 448p. 1994. 35.00 (*0-300-05807-1*) Yale U Pr.

— Women Physicians: Careers, Status & Power. 250p. 1985. 25.00 (*0-422-79040-0*, NO. 9071); pap. 12.95 (*0-422-79050-8*, NO. 9103) Routledge Chapman & Hall.

Lorber, Judith & Farrell, Susan A., eds. The Social Construction of Gender. (Illus.). 400p. (C). 1990. text ed. 48.00 (*0-8039-3956-6*); pap. text ed. 22.95 (*0-8039-3957-4*) Sage.

Lorber, Judith, jt. ed. see Freidson, Eliot.

Lorber, Michael A. & Pierce, Walter. Objectives, Methods & Evaluation for Secondary Teaching. 3rd ed. 304p. (C). 1989. pap. text ed. write for info. (*0-13-629163-5*) P-H.

Lorber, Robert, jt. auth. see Blanchard, Kenneth.

Lorber, Robert, jt. auth. see Khadem, Riaz.

Lorber, Ruth, ed. see Radin, William G.

Lorberg, A. Otahki, Trail of Tears Princess. 1967. pap. 1.00 (*0-911208-13-5*) Ramfre.

Lorbiecki, Marybeth. Of Things Natural, Wild, & Free: A Story about Aldo Leopold. LC 92-44049. (Creative Minds Ser.). (Illus.). (J). (gr. 3-6). 1993. 15.95 (*0-87614-797-X*, Carolrhoda) Lerner Group.

Lorbiecki, Marybeth & Lowery, Linda. Earthwise at Play: A Guide to the Care & Feeding of Your Planet. LC 92-9870. (Illus.). (J). (gr. 1-4). 1993. 19.95 (*0-87614-729-5*, Carolrhoda) Lerner Group.

Lorbiecki, Marybeth, jt. auth. see Lowery, Linda.

Lorblanchet, Michel, ed. Rock Art in the Old World. (C). 1992. 78.00 (*0-685-66244-6*, Pub. by UBS Pubs Dist II) S Asia.

LORC Staff. Your New Life in the United States. 215p. (CAM, CHI, LAO, SPA & VIE.). 1984. pap. 5.00 (*0-685-16936-7*) Ctr Appl Ling.

Lorca. Gypsy Ballads. Harard, ed. (Hispanic Classics Ser.). 1990. 49.95 (*0-85668-490-2*, Pub. by Aris & Phillips UK); pap. 22.00 (*0-85668-491-0*, Pub. by Aris & Phillips UK) David Brown.

Lorca, Federico G. Blood Wedding; Yerma. Hughes, Langston & Merwin, W. S., trs. LC 93-51498. (TCG Translations Ser.: Vol. 5). 160p. 1994. 24.95 (*1-55936-079-8*); pap. 12.95 (*1-55936-080-1*) Theatre Comm.

— Bodas de Sangre. 4th ed. 232p. 1989. pap. 11.95 (*0-7859-5200-4*) Fr & Eur.

— Bodas de Sangre. 5th ed. 176p. (SPA.). 1989. pap. 8.95 (*0-7859-4977-1*) Fr & Eur.

— La Casa de Bernarda Alba. 15th ed. 194p. (SPA.). 1990. pap. 10.95 (*0-318-65030-4*, S30339) Fr & Eur.

— A Concordance to the Plays & Poems of Federico Garcia Lorca. Smith, Philip H. & Pollin, Alice M., eds. LC 73-20817. (Cornell Concordances Ser.). 1216p. 1975. 95.00 (*0-8014-0808-3*) Cornell U Pr.

— The Cricket Sings. Kirkland, Will, tr. LC 80-15560. (Illus.). 64p. (Orig.). 1980. pap. 6.95 (*0-8112-0734-X*, NDP506) New Directions.

— Deep Song & Other Prose. Maurer, Christopher, ed. LC 80-394. 1980. 5.95 (*0-8112-0764-1*) New Directions.

— Five Plays: Comedies & Tragicomedies. O'Connell, Richard L. & Graham-Lujan, James, trs. 1964. write for info. (*0-685-01695-1*, NDP232) New Directions.

— Five Plays: Comedies & Tragicomedies. O'Connell, Richard L. & Graham-Lujan, James, trs. Incl. Shoemaker's Prodigious Wife. LC 63-13642. 1964. (*0-318-54652-3*); Don Perlimplin. LC 63-13642. 1964. (*0-318-54653-1*); Dona Rosita the Spinster. LC 63-13642. 1964. (*0-318-54654-X*); Billy-Club Puppets. LC 63-13642. 1964. (*0-318-54655-8*); LC 63-13642. 1964. Set pap. 9.95 (*0-8112-0090-6*) New Directions.

— Lorca: Plays Three. Edwards, Gwynne & Livings, Henry, trs. 224p. 1993. pap. 11.95 (*0-413-65240-8*, A0630, Pub. by Methuen UK) Heinemann.

— Poema del Cante Jondo; Romancero Gitano. 12th ed. 320p. (SPA.). 1989. pap. 10.95 (*0-7859-4980-1*) Fr & Eur.

— Poeta En Nueva York. 8th ed. 184p. (SPA.). 1990. pap. 10.95 (*0-7859-4981-X*) Fr & Eur.

— The Public & Play Without a Title: Two Posthumous Plays. Bauer, Carlos, tr. LC 83-12117. 96p. (Orig.). 1983. 8.95 (*0-8112-0880-X*) New Directions.

— Selected Letters. Gershator, David, tr. LC 83-4006. 172p. (Orig.). 1984. 15.00 (*0-8112-0872-9*); pap. 6.95 (*0-8112-0873-7*, NDP557) New Directions.

— Selected Poems. Maurer, Christopher, ed. 320p. (ENG & SPA.). Date not set. pap. 13.00 (*0-374-52352-5*) FS&G.

— Selected Poems. Allen, Donald M., ed. LC 54-9872. (ENG & SPA.). 1962. pap. 9.95 (*0-8112-0091-4*, NDP114) New Directions.

— Songs & Ballads. (Essential Poets Ser.: No. 53). 66p. 1993. pap. 10.00 (*0-920717-65-9*) Guernica Editions.

— Three Plays: Blood Wedding; Yerma; The House of Bernarda Alba. Dewell, Michael & Zapata, Carmen, trs. (Illus.). 192p. 1993. pap. 16.00 (*0-374-52332-0*) FS&G.

— Yerma. 4th ed. 196p. (SPA.). 1990. pap. 13.95 (*0-7859-4978-X*) Fr & Eur.

— La Zapatera Prodigiosa. 13th ed. 184p. (SPA.). 1990. pap. write for info. (*0-7859-4976-3*) Fr & Eur.

Lorca, Federico G., et al. Spike Magazine: The Air of Hell Does Not Permit Hymns. Daniel, Darin, ed. Curtis, Walt, tr. (Spike Magazine Ser.: No. 4). (Illus.). 96p. (Orig.). 1994. pap. 8.00 (*1-885089-00-7*) Cityful Pr.

Lorca, Francisco G. In the Green Morning: Memories of Federico. Maurer, Christopher, tr. LC 85-28509. 256p. 1986. 23.50 (*0-8112-0969-5*); pap. 12.95 (*0-8112-0970-9*, NDP610) New Directions.

Lorca, Garcia. Bodas de Sangre. 172p. (SPA.). 1987. 11.95 (*0-8288-7011-X*) Fr & Eur.

— Dona Rosita la Soltera. 230p. (SPA.). 1982. 9.95 (*0-8288-7149-3*, S8989) Fr & Eur.

— Mariana Pineda. 109p. (SPA.). 1969. 6.25 (*0-8288-7147-7*) Fr & Eur.

— Mariana Pineda. 230p. (SPA.). 1984. 10.50 (*0-8288-7013-6*, S8991) Fr & Eur.

Lorch, Edgar R. Spectral Theory. LC 62-9824. (University Texts in the Mathematical Sciences). 170p. reprint ed. pap. 48.50 (*0-317-08657-X*, 2051947) Bks Demand.

Lorch, Frederick W. The Trouble Begins at Eight: Mark Twain's Lecture Tours. LC 68-17493. (Illus.). 391p. reprint ed. pap. 111.50 (*0-685-20389-1*, 2030318) Bks Demand.

Lorch, Janet. From Foal to Full-Grown. (Illus.). 192p. 1993. 29.95 (*0-7153-9976-4*, Pub. by David & Charles UK) Trafalgar.

Lorch, Jay W., jt. auth. see Lawrence, Paul R.

Lorch, Jennifer, jt. ed. see Bassnett, Susan.

Lorch, Maristella, jt. auth. see Grassi, Ernesto.

Lorch, Maristella, tr. see Valla, Lorenzo.

Lorch, Natanel, ed. Major Knesset Debates 1948-1981, Vol. II. 360p. (C). 1991. lib. bdg. 62.50 (*0-8191-8343-1*) U Pr of Amer.

Lorch, Netanel. One Long War. 1976. 8.00 (*0-685-82597-3*) Herzl Pr.

— Shield of Zion: The Israel Defense Forces. (Illus.). 144p. 1992. 34.95 (*0-943231-47-7*) Howell Pr VA.

Lorch, Netanel, ed. Major Knesset Debates, 1948-1981, Vol. 1: Peoples Council & Provisional Council of State, 1948-1949. 364p. (C). 1992. lib. bdg. 62.50 (*0-8191-8342-3*) U Pr of Amer.

— Major Knesset Debates, 1948-1981, Vol. 2: The Constituent Assembly - First Knesset (1949-1951) 369p. (C). 1991. lib. bdg. 52.50 (*0-685-50244-9*) U Pr of Amer.

— Major Knesset Debates, 1948-1981, Vol. 3: Second Knesset (1951-1955), Third Knesset (1955-1959) 432p. (C). 1992. lib. bdg. 57.50 (*0-8191-8344-X*) U Pr of Amer.

— Major Knesset Debates, 1948-1981, Vol. 4: Fourth Knesset (1959-1961), Fifth Knesset (1961-1965), Sixth Knesset (1965-1969) 574p. (C). 1992. lib. bdg. 84.50 (*0-8191-8345-8*) U Pr of Amer.

— Major Knesset Debates, 1948-1981, Vol. 5: Seventh Knesset (1969-1973), Eighth Knesset (1974-1977) 405p. (C). 1991. lib. bdg. 65.00 (*0-8191-8346-6*) U Pr of Amer.

— Major Knesset Debates, 1948-1981, Vol. 6: Ninth Knesset (1977-1981) 445p. (C). 1992. lib. bdg. 67.50 (*0-8191-8347-4*) U Pr of Amer.

Lorch, Netaniel. Israel's War of Independence, 1947-1949. 2nd ed. Orig. Title: Edge of the Sword. (Illus.). 1969. 15.00 (*0-87677-011-1*) Hartmore.

Lorch, Robert. Public Administration. 314p. 1977. pap. text ed. 35.50 (*0-8299-0144-2*) West Pub.

***Lorch, Robert F. & O'Brien, Edward J., eds.** Sources of Coherence in Reading. 416p. 1994. pap. 39.95 (*0-8058-1637-2*) L Erlbaum Assocs.

— Sources of Coherence in Reading. 416p. 1994. text ed. 89.95 (*0-8058-1339-X*) L Erlbaum Assocs.

Lorch, Robert S. Colorado's Government: Structure, Politics, Administration, & Policy. 5th ed. (Illus.). 352p. 1991. 34.95 (*0-87081-245-9*); pap. 19.95 (*0-87081-220-3*) Univ Pr Colo.

— Democratic Process & Administrative Law. rev. ed. LC 69-10420. (Waynebooks Ser.: No. 39). 263p. 1969. pap. 14.95 (*0-8143-1513-5*) Wayne St U Pr.

— State & Local Politics: The Great Entanglement. 5th ed. LC 94-17182. 448p. 1994. text ed. write for info. (*0-13-109117-4*) P-H.

Lorch, Sue. Basic Writing: A Practical Approach. 2nd ed. (C). 1987. pap. text ed. 21.50 (*0-673-39278-3*) HarpCollege.

Lorch, Walter. Competition Vehicles Choice Construction Maintenance. 74p. 1990. 66.00 (*0-85131-529-1*, Pub. by J A Allen & Co UK) St Mut.

Lorcher, Adolf. Das Fremde und das Eigene in Ciceros Buchern De Finibus Bonorum et Malorum und der Academica. vii, 327p. 1975. reprint ed. write for info. (*3-487-05609-7*, Pub. by Georg Olms GW) Lubrecht & Cramer.

***Lorcin, Patricia.** Imperial Identities: Stereotyping, Prejudice, & Race in Colonial Algeria. (Society & Culture in the Modern Middle East Ser.). 252p. 1995. text ed. 59.50 (*1-85043-909-5*) St Martin.

***Lord.** Celebrity Top 10 Things to-do Lists: The Secret Habits of the Big Stars. 1995. mass mkt. 4.99 (*1-56171-362-7*, S P I Bks) Sure Sellers.

— Garbage! The Trashiest Book. (J). 1993. pap. 2.75 (*0-590-46024-2*) Scholastic Inc.

— One Hundred One Thanksgiving Knock-Knocks, Jokes, & Riddles. (J). 1993. pap. 1.95 (*0-590-47163-5*) Scholastic Inc.

Lord Acton. Essays in Religion, Politics, & Morality, Vol. 3: Selected Writings of Lord Acton. LC 85-4522. 776p. 1988. 20.00 (*0-86597-050-5*); pap. 7.50 (*0-86597-051-3*) Liberty Fund.

Lord, Albert B. Epic Singers & Oral Tradition. LC 90-55888. (Myth & Poetics Ser.). 280p. 1991. 39.95 (*0-8014-2472-0*); pap. 15.95 (*0-8014-9717-5*) Cornell U Pr.

— The Singer of Tales. (Studies in Comparative Literature: No. 24). 319p. (C). 1981. pap. 15.95 (*0-674-80881-9*) HUP.

— The Singer Resumes the Tale. Lord, Mary L., ed. (Myth & Poetics Ser.). 336p. 1995. 39.95x (*0-8014-3103-4*) Cornell U Pr.

Lord, Albert B., ed. Harvard Dissertations in Folklore & Oral Tradition, 16 vols., Set. 1991. 1,205.00 (*0-8153-0206-1*) Garland.

Lord, Albert B. & Bynum, David E., eds. Serbo-Croatian Heroic Songs: Bijelo Polje: Three Texts from Avdo Mededovic, Vol. 3. (Milman Parry Collection, Texts & Translation Ser.: No. 4). (Illus.). 383p. 1980. 25.00 (*0-674-80166-0*) HUP.

Lord, Albert B., ed. see Beissinger, Margaret H.

Lord, Albert B., ed. see Doan, James E.

Lord, Albert B., ed. see Fisher, Laura G.

Lord, Albert B., ed. see Goldman, Kenneth A.

Lord, Albert B., ed. see Kolsti, John.

Lord, Albert B., ed. see Luethans, Tod N.

Lord, Albert B., ed. see Mills, Margaret A.

Lord, Albert B., ed. see Parry, Millman.

Lord, Albert B., ed. see Smith, Mary C.

Lord, Allyn, jt. ed. see O'Reilly, Priscilla.

Lord, Allyn, et al. Steal This Handbook! A Template for Creating a Museum's Emergency Preparedness Plan. LC 94-92256. 240p. (Orig.). 1994. pap. 25.00 (*0-9621348-1-3*) SERA LA.

Lord, Arthur E., Jr. & Koerner, Robert M. Detection of Subsurface Hazardous Waste Containers by Nondestructive Techniques. LC 89-22800. (Pollution Technology Review Ser.: No. 172). (Illus.). 83p. 1990. 39.00 (*0-8155-1224-4*) Noyes.

Lord, Arthur R. The Principles of Politics. LC 70-179637. (Select Bibliographies Reprint Ser.). 1977. reprint ed. 23.95 (*0-8369-6658-9*) Ayer.

Lord Baden-Powell. Lessons from the Varsity of Life. (Illus.). 320p. (YA). 1992. pap. 17.95 (*0-9632054-7-1*) Stevens Pub.

— Rovering to Success: A Guide for Young Manhood. (Illus.). 247p. (Orig.). (YA). 1992. pap. 16.95 (*0-9632054-3-9*) Stevens Pub.

— Scouting Round the World. (Illus.). 200p. 1992. pap. 16.95 (*0-9632054-6-3*) Stevens Pub.

Lord, Benjamin. America's Wealthiest People: Their Philanthropic & Nonprofit Affiliations. 78p. 1984. pap. 57.50 (*0-914756-57-5*) Taft Group.

Lord, Bette B. In the Year of the Boar & Jackie Robinson. LC 83-48440. (Illus.). 176p. (J). (gr. 3-7). 1984. lib. bdg. 14.89 (*0-06-024004-0*) HarpC Child Bks.

— Legacies: A Chinese Mosaic. 1990. 19.95 (*0-394-58325-6*) Knopf.

— Legacies: A Chinese Mosaic. large type ed. (General Ser.). 375p. 1991. 20.95 (*0-8161-5065-6*, Large Print Bks) Hall.

— Spring Moon. 1982. mass mkt. 4.95 (*0-380-59923-6*) Avon.

— Spring Moon. 1990. mass mkt. 5.99 (*0-06-100105-8*, Harp PBks) HarpC.

***Lord Bette Bao.** Legacies. 1991. pap. 5.99 (*0-517-07929-1*) Random.

Lord, Betty B. In the Year of the Boar & Jackie Robinson. LC 83-48440. (Trophy Bk.). (Illus.). 176p. (J). (gr. 3-7). 1986. pap. 3.95 (*0-06-440175-8*, Trophy) HarpC Child Bks.

Lord Blake, intro. Ireland after the Union: Proceedings of the Second Joint Meeting of the Royal Irish Academy & the British Academy, London, 1986. 134p. 1990. pap. 19.95 (*0-19-726074-8*) OUP.

Lord, Bob & Lord, Penny. Este Es Mi Cuerpo, Esta Es Mi Sangre: Milagros de la Eucaristia. Valls, Aminta et al, trs. (Illus.). 205p. (Orig.). (SPA.). 1987. pap. 8.95 (*0-926143-03-4*) Journeys Faith.

— The Many Faces of Mary: A Love Story. (Illus.). 242p. (Orig.). 1987. 12.95 (*0-926143-06-9*); pap. 8.95 (*0-926143-07-7*) Journeys Faith.

— Martyrs - They Died for Christ. 320p. (Orig.). 1993. pap. 12.95 (*0-926143-14-X*) Journeys Faith.

— The Rosary: The Life of Jesus & Mary. 192p. 1993. 12.95 (*0-926143-12-3*) Journeys Faith.

— Saints & Other Powerful Men in the Church. (Illus.). 528p. 1990. pap. 14.95 (*0-926143-09-3*) Journeys Faith.

— Saints & Other Powerful Women in the Church. (Illus.). 400p. (Orig.). 1989. pap. 12.95 (*0-926143-08-5*) Journeys Faith.

— Scandal of the Cross & Its Triumph. rev. ed. 320p. 1992. reprint ed. pap. 12.95 (*0-926143-15-8*) Journeys Faith.

— This is My Body, This is My Blood: Miracles of the Eucharist. (Illus.). 192p. (Orig.). 1986. 12.95 (*0-926143-01-8*); pap. 8.95 (*0-926143-02-6*) Journeys Faith.

— We Came Back to Jesus. (Illus.). 205p. (Orig.). 1988. 12.95 (*0-926143-04-2*); pap. 8.95 (*0-926143-05-0*) Journeys Faith.

Lord, Bob, jt. auth. see Lord, Penny.

Lord, Brian I., et al, eds. Stem Cells & Tissue Homeostasis. LC 77-80844. (Symposium of the British Society for Cell Biology Ser.: No. 2). 376p. reprint ed. pap. 107.20 (*0-685-15671-0*, 2027336) Bks Demand.

Lord Byron. Lord Byron. (Poets Ser.). 146p. 1993. 5.95 (*0-7117-0440-6*, Pub. by Jarrold Pub UK) Seven Hills Bk.

Lord, C. C. Lord: History of the Descendants of Nathan Lord of Ancient Kittery, Maine. Lord, G. E., ed. (Illus.). 218p. 1993. reprint ed. lib. bdg. 43.00 (*0-8328-3707-5*); reprint ed. pap. 33.00 (*0-8328-3708-3*) Higginson Bk Co.

Lord, C. E. Lord. (Illus.). 263p. 1991. reprint ed. lib. bdg. 52.00 (*0-8328-2025-3*); reprint ed. pap. 42.00 (*0-8328-2026-1*) Higginson Bk Co.

Lord, Carnes. Education & Culture in the Political Thought of Aristotle. LC 81-15272. 232p. 1982. 34.95 (*0-8014-1412-1*) Cornell U Pr.

— Presidential Management of National Security. 320p. 1988. text ed. 29.95 (*0-02-919341-9*) Free Pr.

— Strategy & Governmental Organization. (Special Issue of Comparative Strategy Ser.: Vol. 6, No. 3). 127p. 1987. pap. 18.00 (*0-8448-1532-2*) Taylor & Francis.

Lord, Carnes & O'Connor, David, eds. Essays on the Foundations of Aristotelian Political Science. LC 90-37112. 380p. 1991. 45.00 (*0-520-06711-8*) U CA Pr.

Lord, Carnes, tr. see Aristotle.

Lord, Carnes, tr. see Tasso, Torquato.

Lord, Carol. Historical Change in Serial Verb Construction. LC 93-12679. (Typological Studies in Language (TSL): No. 26). 275p. 1993. 71.00x (*1-55619-416-1*); pap. 24.95 (*1-55619-417-X*) Benjamins North Am.

***Lord, Catherine.** Pervert. (Illus.). 48p. (Orig.). 1995. pap. 16.50 (*1-884355-01-3*) U CA Fine Arts.

Lord Chalmers. Further Dialogues of the Buddha, 2 vols., Set. (C). 1988. reprint ed. text ed. 54.00 (*81-7030-139-4*) S Asia.

Lord Chesterfield. Lord Chesterfield's Letters. (World's Classics Ser.). 416p. 1993. pap. 12.95 (*0-19-282864-9*) OUP.

Lord, Christopher. British Entry to the European Community under the Heath Government of 1970-74. 194p. 1993. 59.95 (*1-85521-336-2*, Pub. by Dartmth Pub UK) Ashgate Pub Co.

Lord, Clifford L., ed. Presidential & Executive Orders: 1862-1938, 2 vols., Nos. 1-1830 list & index. 1985. reprint ed. lib. bdg. 95.00 (*0-89941-451-6*, 201640) W S Hein.

Lord, Clifford L., jt. auth. see Turnbull, Archibald D.

***Lord Cockfield.** The European Union: Creating the Single Market. 1994. pap. text ed. 14.95 (*0-471-95207-9*) Wiley.

Lord Cooper. The Scottish Legal Tradition. 4th ed. Meston, Michael C., ed. 36p. 1986. 22.00 (*0-85411-023-2*, Pub. by Saltire Soc) St Mut.

Lord, David, ed. Management Consulting, 1990: The State of the Profession. 130p. (Orig.). 1990. pap. text ed. 74.00 (*0-916654-65-6*) Kennedy Pubns.

Lord, Del. Gem of a Jam. LC 92-11183. 1992. lib. bdg. 12.95 (*1-56239-167-4*) Abdo & Dghtrs.

Lord, Del & Ullman, Elwood. Busy Buddies. LC 92-11185. 1992. lib. bdg. 12.94 (*1-56239-164-X*) Abdo & Dghtrs.

***Lord, Diana.** The Silver Dolphin. 448p. 1995. pap. 4.99 (*0-8217-5040-2*) Zebra.

Lord, Donald C. John F. Kennedy: The Politics of Confrontation & Conciliation. 1977. 19.95 (*0-8120-5134-3*) Barron.

Lord, Douglas R. Spacelab: An International Success Story. LC 86-17979. (NASA SP Ser.: No. 487). (Illus.). 570p. 1987. 33.00 (*0-16-004220-8*, S/N 033-000-01012-5) USGPO.

Lord Dufferin. Letters from High Latitudes. (Illus.). 228p. 1989. reprint ed. pap. 16.50 (*0-85036-387-X*, Pub. by Seafarer Bks UK) Sheridan.

Lord, E. Manual of Cotton Spinning: The Characteristics of Raw Cotton, Vol. 2, Pt. 1. 333p. 1971. 60.00 (*0-686-63772-0*) St Mut.

Lord, E. & Bernicer, G. Plant Reproduction: From Floral Induction Pollination. (C). 1991. text ed. 150.00 (*81-7233-006-5*, Pub. by Scientific Pubs II) St Mut.

Lord, E. A. & Wilson, C. B. The Mathematical Description of Shape & Form. LC 83-26685. (Mathematics & Its Applications Ser.: 1-176). 323p. 1986. text ed. 63.95 (*0-470-20043-X*) P-H.

Lord, Eileen, jt. auth. see Lord, Luther.

Lord, Eleanor L. Industrial Experiments in the British Colonies of North America. LC 78-64262. (Johns Hopkins University. Studies in the Social Sciences. Thirtieth Ser. 1912: 17). reprint ed. 13.00 (*0-404-61365-9*) AMS Pr.

Lord, Eliot, et al. The Italian in America. LC 71-130557. (Select Bibliographies Reprint Ser.). 1977. reprint ed. 20.95 (*0-8369-5530-7*) Ayer.

Lord, Elizabeth M. & Bernier, Georges, eds. Plant Reproduction: From Floral Induction to Pollination. LC 89-80454. 250p. 1989. pap. text ed. 25.00 (*0-943088-14-3*) Am Soc of Plan.

Lord, Elliot. Comstock Mining & Miners. (Illus.). 451p. 1958. 40.00 (*0-913814-07-5*) Nevada Pubns.

Lord, Ernest E. & Willis, J. H. Shrubs & Trees for Australian Gardens. 6th ed. (Illus.). 440p. 1995. 65.00 (*0-85091-250-4*, Pub. by Lothian Pub AT) Seven Hills Bk.

Lord, F. Townley. Acts of the Apostles: Missionary Message of the New Testament. 119p. 1946. 4.50 (*0-87921-003-6*) Attic Pr.

Lord, Frances. Christian Science Healing, Its Principles & Practice. 471p. 1972. reprint ed. spiral bd. 16.50 (*0-7873-0570-7*) Mokelumne.

Lord, Francis A. They Fought for the Union. LC 81-6579. (Illus.). x, 375p. 1981. reprint ed. text ed. 89.50 (*0-313-22740-3*, LOTF, Greenwood Pr) Greenwood.

Lord, Francis A., jt. auth. see Wise, Arthur.

Lord, Frederic M. Applications of Item Response Theory to Practical Testing Problems. LC 79-24186. (Illus.). 288p. 1980. text ed. 69.95 (*0-89859-006-X*) L Erlbaum Assocs.

Lord, G. E., ed. see Lord, C. C.

Lord, Gardner. Systems Analysis of Imagery. (C). 1992. text ed. 21.00 (*0-913412-64-3*) Brandon Hse.

Lord, George D. Heroic Mockery: Variations on Epic Themes from Homer to Joyce. LC 76-13930. 162p. 1977. 27.50 (*0-87413-117-0*) U Delaware Pr.

— Poems on Affairs of State: Augustan Satirical Verse, 1660-1714, Vol. 7, 1704-1714. Ellis, Frank H., ed. LC 63-7938. reprint ed. pap. 180.00 (*0-7837-2363-6*, 2022020) Bks Demand.

Lord, George D., ed. Poems on Affairs of State: Augustan Satirical Verse 1660-1714, Vol. 1, 1669-1678. (Illus.). 1963. 65.00 (*0-300-00726-4*) Yale U Pr.

Lord, George D., jt. ed. see Mack, Maynard.

***Lord, Gillian.** What's Wrong with My Hormones. 3rd rev. ed. 286p. 1994. pap. text ed. 15.95 (*1-883619-10-6*) D Ford Pubns.

Lord, Glenn, ed. see Howard, Robert E.

Lord, Gordon, jt. ed. see Harvey, John.

Lord, Guy. The French Budgetary Process. LC 70-186113. (Illus.). 233p. reprint ed. pap. 66.50 (*0-685-23975-6*, 2031539) Bks Demand.

Lord, H. D. Memorial of the Family of Morse. (Illus.). 556p. 1989. reprint ed. lib. bdg. 93.00 (*0-8328-0886-5*); reprint ed. pap. 85.00 (*0-8328-0887-3*) Higginson Bk Co.

Lord, Harold W., et al. Noise Control for Engineers. LC 87-22611. 448p. (C). 1987. reprint ed. lib. bdg. 49.50 (*0-89464-255-3*) Krieger.

Lord Hervey, jt. auth. see Scriblerus.

Lord Irwin. Indian Problems: Speeches of Lord Irwin. 396p. 1987. 20.00 (*81-212-0068-7*, Pub. by Gian Publng Hse II) S Asia.

Lord, Israel S. At the Extremity of Civilization: A Meticulously Descriptive Diary of an Illinois Physician's Journey in 1849 along the Oregon Trail to the Goldmines & Cholera of California, Thence in Two Years to Return by Boat Via Panama. Liles, Necia D., ed. (Illus.). 441p. 1995. lib. bdg. 45.00 (*0-7864-0000-5*) McFarland & Co.

Lord, J. The Jews in India & the Far East. 1976. lib. bdg. 39.95 (*0-8490-2104-9*) Gordon Pr.

Lord, J. Dennis. Spatial Perspectives on School Desegregation & Busing. Natoli, Salvatore J., ed. LC 76-57034. (Resource Papers for College Geography). (Illus.). 1977. pap. text ed. 10.00 (*0-89291-124-7*) Assn Am Geographers.

Lord, James. A Giacometti Portrait. (Illus.). 117p. 1980. pap. 9.00 (*0-374-51573-5*) FS&G.

— Making Memoirs. (Illus.). 19p. Date not set. 125.00 (*0-9640399-5-8*) Elysium Pr.

— Making Memoirs. (Illus.). 19p. 1995. 45.00 (*0-9640399-4-X*) Elysium Pr.

— Picasso & Dora: A Memoir. 1993. 35.00 (*0-374-23208-3*) FS&G.

— Picasso & Dora: A Personal Memoir. LC 94-23057. (Illus.). 352p. 1994. pap. 16.95 (*0-88064-162-2*) Fromm Intl Pub.

— Sam Szafran: Recent Works. (Illus.). 1987. 10.00 (*0-936827-05-X*) C Bernard Gallery Ltd.

— Six Exceptional Women. LC 93-42384. 1994. 27.50 (*0-374-26553-4*) FS&G.

Lord, James G. Building Your Case: The Step-by-Step System that Shows How the Most Successful Volunteers Raise Money. 1984. sl. 125.00 (*0-939120-04-6*) Third Sector.

— Philanthropy & Marketing: New Strategies for Fund Raising. LC 81-50197. 203p. (C). 1981. lib. bdg. 47.50 (*0-939120-00-3*); ring bd. 47.50 (*0-939120-01-1*) Third Sector.

— The Raising of Money: Thirty-Five Essentials (Accompanied by a Guide for the Professional) LC 84-50377. 128p. 1984. 34.50 (*0-939120-02-X*) Third Sector.

Lord, James H. The Jews in India & the Far East. LC 70-97292. 120p. 1977. reprint ed. text ed. 35.00 (*0-8371-2615-0*, LOJI, Greenwood Pr) Greenwood.

Lord, Janet D. When a Baby Suddenly Dies: Cot Death - the Impact & Effects. 291p. (Orig.). 1994. pap. 11.95 (*0-85572-162-6*, Pub. by Hill Content Pubng AT) Seven Hills Bk.

Lord, Janice H. Beyond Sympathy: What to Say & Do for Someone Suffering an Injury, Illness or Loss. 2nd ed. 192p. (C). 1990. reprint ed. lib. bdg. 31.00x (*0-8095-5904-8*) Borgo Pr.

— Beyond Sympathy: What to Say & Do for Someone Suffering an Injury, Illness or Loss. 2nd ed. Wheeler, Eugene D., ed. LC 88-61044. 192p. 1989. pap. 11.95 (*0-934793-21-2*) Pathfinder CA.

— No Time for Goodbyes. 4th ed. Wheeler, Eugene D., ed. LC 91-31702. (Illus.). 192p. 1995. pap. 11.95 (*0-934793-40-9*) Pathfinder CA.

— No Time for Goodbyes: Coping with Sorrow, Anger & Injustice after a Tragic Death. 4th ed. 192p. 1991. reprint ed. lib. bdg. 31.00x (*0-8095-5901-3*) Borgo Pr.

Lord, John. Capital & Steam Power: 1750-1800. 2nd ed. 253p. 1966. 32.00 (*0-7146-1339-8*, Pub. by F Cass Pubs UK) Intl Spec Bk.

— Energy Eighty-Seven. rev. ed. 56p. 1986. pap. 1.50 (*0-934653-08-9*) Enterprise Educ.

— Energy in the United States. rev. ed. (Teaching about Energy Ser.: Pt. 6). 120p. 1986. pap. 6.50 (*0-934653-14-3*) Enterprise Educ.

— Hazardous Wastes from Homes. 36p. (Orig.). 1986. pap. 2.75 (*0-934653-07-0*) Enterprise Educ.

— Infection, the Immune System, & AIDS. (Illus.). 56p. (Orig.). (YA). (gr. 11-12). 1989. pap. 4.95 (*0-934653-18-6*) Enterprise Educ.

— Sizes: The Illustrated Encyclopedia. LC 94-25381. (Illus.). 1995. pap. 15.00 (*0-06-273228-5*, PL) HarpC.

Lord, John & Braaten, Glenn. Energy Flows in Nature. rev. ed. (Teaching about Energy Ser.: Pt. 2). (Illus.). 136p. 1986. pap. 6.70 (*0-934653-12-7*) Enterprise Educ.

An Asterisk (*) at the beginning of an entry indicates that the title is appearing in BIP for the first time.

— Energy Fundamentals. rev. ed. (Teaching about Energy Ser.: Pt. 1). 200p. 1986. pap. 11.90 (*0-934653-11-9*) Enterprise Educ.

Lord, John & Wilson, Darlene. Energy Economics. rev. ed. (Teaching about Energy Ser.: Pt. 7). 136p. 1986. pap. 6.60 (*0-934653-15-1*) Enterprise Educ.

Lord, John, jt. auth. see Wilson, George.

Lord, John, et al. Teaching about Energy: Nineteen Eighty-Four to Nineteen Eighty-Five Supplement. (Energy Eighty Ser.). 280p. 1985. pap. 10.00 (*0-934653-05-4*) Enterprise Educ.

Lord, John V. Mr. Mead & His Garden. LC 74-20766. (Illus.). (J). (gr. k-3). 1975. lib. bdg. 6.95 (*0-395-20278-7*) HM.

Lord, John V. & Burroway, Janet. The Giant Jam Sandwich. LC 72-13578. (Illus.). 32p. (J). (gr. k-3). 1975. 16.95 (*0-395-16033-2*) HM.

— The Giant Jam Sandwich. LC 72-13578. (Illus.). 32p. (J). (gr. k-3). 1987. pap. 4.95 (*0-395-44237-0*) HM.

— The Giant Jam Sandwich. (Book & Cassette Favorites Ser.). (Illus.). (J). 1990. 7.95 (*0-395-53966-8*) HM.

Lord, Jonathan T., ed. The Physician Leader's Guide. 200p. 1992. pap. text ed. 39.00 (*0-915963-10-8*) Bader Assoc Inc.

Lord, Joni. The Bachelorette Party Book. (Illus.). 80p. (Orig.). 1986. pap. 6.95 (*0-916799-13-1*) Hollow Glen.

Lord, Kenniston W. The Data Center Disaster Consultant. 2nd ed. LC 81-52826. 223p. reprint ed. pap. 63.60 (*0-8357-6085-5*, 2034330) Bks Demand.

Lord, Kenniston W., Jr., jt. auth. see Lyon, Lockwood.

***Lord Killanin & Duignan, Michael.** The Shell Guide to Ireland. rev. ed. (Illus.). 340p. 1995. pap. 20.00 (*0-7171-2310-3*, Pub. by Gill & MacMill IE) Irish Bks Media.

Lord, Lilia. Exotic Vegetable Cuisine of LA: Nutritional Content of Exotic Vegetables. (Illus.). 654p. (Orig.). 1992. pap. 24.99 (*0-9633575-0-6*) L Lord.

Lord, Linda A. & Ramsdell, Marcia. Guide to Florida Environmental Issues & Information. rev. ed. LC 92-75965. 366p. 1993. pap. 29.95 (*0-913207-06-3*) FL Conser Fnd.

Lord, Lindsay. Nautical Etiquette & Customs. 2nd rev. ed. LC 86-47716. (Illus.). 128p. 1987. pap. 8.95 (*0-87033-356-9*) Cornell Maritime.

Lord, Lisa. Success in Reading & Writing: Grade 3. 2nd ed. (Illus.). 288p. 1991. 27.95 (*0-673-36003-2*) GdYrBks.

— Success in Reading & Writing: Grade 6. 2nd ed. (Illus.). 288p. 1991. 27.95 (*0-673-36006-7*) GdYrBks.

Lord, Louis E. Aristophanes: His Plays & His Influence. LC 63-10302. (Our Debt to Greece & Rome Ser.). reprint ed. 38.50 (*0-8154-0140-X*) Cooper Sq.

Lord, Louis E., tr. see Poliziano, Angelo.

Lord, Luther & Lord, Eileen. How to Communicate in Sobriety. LC 77-94793. (Illus.). 114p. (Orig.). 1978. pap. 9.00 (*0-89486-046-1*, 1086A) Hazelden.

***Lord, M. G.** Forever Barbie. 1995. pap. 12.50 (*0-380-72049-3*) Avon.

— Forever Barbie: The Unauthorized Biography of a Real Doll. LC 94-18272. 1994. 25.00 (*0-688-12296-5*) Morrow.

— Prig Tales. 192p. (Orig.). 1990. mass mkt. 6.95 (*0-380-76004-5*) Avon.

Lord, M. P., jt. auth. see James, Arthur M.

Lord, Marjorie F. Civil War Collector's Encyclopedia, Vol. V. 230p. 1989. lib. bdg. 35.00 (*0-916492-05-2*) Lord Americana.

Lord, Mark, jt. auth. see Hodgson, Michael.

Lord, Mary, ed. see Porter, Hal.

Lord, Mary L., ed. see Lord, Albert B.

Lord, Montague J. Imperfect Competition & International Commodity Trade: Theory, Dynamics & Policy Modelling. (Illus.). 488p. 1991. 89.00 (*0-19-828347-4*) OUP.

***Lord Montague of Beaulieu.** The Brighton Run. (C). 1989. pap. 25.00x (*0-7478-0099-5*, Pub. by Shire UK) St Mut.

Lord Moran. The Anatomy of Courage. 224p. 1987. pap. 9.95 (*0-89529-283-1*) Avery Pub.

Lord, Nancy. The Compass Inside Ourselves: Short Stories. 1984. 7.95 (*0-914221-03-5*); pap. 5.95 (*0-914221-01-9*) Fireweed Pr AK.

— Darkened Waters: A Review of the History, Science, & Technology Associated with the Exxon Valdez Oil Spill & Cleanup. (Illus.). 61p. (Orig.). (C). 1992. pap. 5.00 (*0-9619026-0-4*) Homer Soc.

— Survival. LC 90-27025. 161p. (Orig.). 1991. pap. 10.95 (*0-918273-84-6*) Coffee Hse.

Lord, Nogah. Raise Your Vibration with Nutrition & Fasting. LC 91-27781. (Illus.). 80p. (Orig.). 1991. pap. 8.95 (*0-931892-68-6*) B Dolphin Pub.

Lord of Host Books Staff, ed. see Sartin, Michael K.

Lord of Ronaldshay. Lands of the Thunderbolt. 3rd ed. (Illus.). 352p. 1987. reprint ed. 19.95 (*0-9617066-7-8*); reprint ed. pap. 12.95 (*0-9617066-6-X*) Snow Lion-SLG Bks.

Lord, P., jt. auth. see Maekawa, Z.

Lord, Penny & Lord, Bob. Heavenly Army of Angels. (Illus.). 256p. (Orig.). 1991. pap. 12.95 (*0-926143-10-7*) Journeys Faith.

Lord, Penny, jt. auth. see Lord, Bob.

***Lord, Peter.** Changing Wales Vol. II: The Aesthetics of Relevance. 1992. pap. 21.00 (*0-86383-897-9*, Pub. by Gomer Pr UK) St Mut.

— Hearing God. 240p. 1988. pap. 9.99 (*0-8010-5650-0*) Baker Bk.

— Keeping the Doors Open: What to Do When Your Child Wanders from God. LC 91-44900. 192p. 1992. pap. 8.99 (*0-8007-9198-3*) Chosen Bks.

— The Nine Hundred Fifty-Nine Plan. 2nd ed. 160p. 1988. pap. 8.99 (*0-8010-5647-0*) Baker Bk.

— Soul Care. 248p. 1990. 14.99 (*0-8010-5665-9*); pap. 9.99 (*0-8010-5661-6*) Baker Bk.

— Turkeys & Eagles. 104p. 1987. pap. 7.95 (*0-940232-40-5*) Seedsowers.

— The Twenty-Nine & Fifty-Nine Plan: The Revised Plan. 1989. pap. 9.99 (*0-8010-5653-5*) Baker Bk.

Lord, Peter & Templeton, Duncan. Architecture of Sound: Planning & Designing Auditoria. (Illus.). 176p. 1986. text ed. 79.95 (*0-85139-726-3*) Buttrwrth-Heinemann.

Lord, Philip L., Jr. War Over Walloomscolck: Land Use & Settlement Pattern on the Bennington Battlefield-1777. (Bulletin Ser.: No. 473). (Illus.). 190p. (Orig.). (C). 1989. pap. text ed. 15.00 (*1-55557-186-7*) NYS Museum.

Lord, R. Ronstadt's Financials Professional Planning & Budgeting Software & Documentation. 50p. (Orig.). 1989. pap. 99.00 (*0-930204-20-4*) Lord Pub.

Lord Raglan. Jocasta's Crime: An Anthropological Study. LC 90-40113. xiv, 215p. 1991. reprint ed. lib. bdg. 35.00 (*0-86527-401-0*) Fertig.

Lord Reay, jt. auth. see Archer, Peter.

Lord, Richard. The Nonprofit Problem Solver: A Management Guide. LC 88-32188. 165p. 1989. text ed. 49.95 (*0-275-93125-0*, C3125, Praeger Pubs) Greenwood.

Lord, Richard A. Williston on Contracts, 28 vols., Vol. 1. 4th ed. 1990. 2,100.00 (*0-686-14488-0*) Lawyers Cooperative.

***Lord, Richard A. & Lewis, Charles C.** North Carolina Security Interests. 450p. 1985. 40.00 (*0-614-05931-3*) Michie Butterworth.

***Lord, Robert.** The Words We Use. 128p. 1994. 16.95 (*1-871082-44-7*) Paul & Co Pubs.

Lord, Robert, ed. Hong Kong Language Papers. LC 79-106833. 256p. reprint ed. pap. 73.00 (*0-8357-2743-2*, 2039852) Bks Demand.

Lord, Robert, tr. see Dianin, Sergei A.

Lord, Robert F. Downeast Depots: Maine Railroad Stations in the Steam Era. (Illus.). 176p. 1986. ring bd. 17.95 (*0-9617353-0-9*) R F Lord.

Lord, Robert G. & Maher, Karen J. Leadership & Information Processing: Linking Perceptions & Performance. LC 93-13076. (People & Organizations Ser.). 352p. 1993. reprint ed. pap. 18.95 (*0-415-09901-3*, B2571) Routledge.

Lord, Robert H. Second Partition of Poland. LC 73-101268. 1970. reprint ed. 38.45 (*0-404-04009-8*) AMS Pr.

Lord, Robert H., jt. auth. see Coolidge, Harold J.

Lord, Robert W. Running Conventions, Conferences, & Meetings. LC 80-69704. 104p. reprint ed. pap. 29.70 (*0-317-20407-6*, 2023503) Bks Demand.

Lord, Russell. Behold Our Land. LC 74-2395. (FDR & the Era of the New Deal Ser.). 309p. 1974. reprint ed. lib. bdg. 39.50 (*0-306-70593-1*) Da Capo.

— The Henry Wallaces of Iowa. LC 76-167843. (FDR & the Era of the New Deal Ser.). (Illus.). 615p. 1971. reprint ed. lib. bdg. 69.50 (*0-306-70325-4*) Da Capo.

— Men of Earth. McCurry, Dan C. & Rubenstein, Richard E., eds. LC 74-30642. (American Farmers & the Rise of Agribusiness Ser.). 1975. reprint ed. 33.95 (*0-405-06812-3*) Ayer.

— To Hold This Soil. LC 78-171385. (FDR & the Era of the New Deal Ser.). (Illus.). 124p. 1972. reprint ed. lib. bdg. 22.50 (*0-306-70384-X*) Da Capo.

Lord, Russell, ed. Voices from the Fields. LC 78-76945. (Granger Index Reprint Ser.). 1977. 18.95 (*0-8369-6026-2*) Ayer.

Lord, Russell, ed. see Wallace, Henry A.

***Lord, Sandra S.** Discover Houston Downtown. (Discover Houston Ser.). (Illus.). 32p. (Orig.). 1994. pap. 5.00 (*0-9638792-1-9*) CitiWalks Pr.

Lord, Shirley. My Sister's Keeper. LC 93-22939. 1993. 22.00 (*0-517-58271-6*, Crown) Crown Pub Group.

Lord, Shirley A. Social Welfare & the Feminization of Poverty. LC 92-33245. (Children of Poverty Ser.). 112p. 1993. 36.00 (*0-8153-1119-2*) Garland.

Lord-Smith, Peter J. & Dobson, John. Avoiding Claims in Building Contracts. (Architecture Legal Ser.). 181p. 1994. pap. 49.95 (*0-7506-1728-4*) Buttrwrth-Heinemann.

Lord Stanley of Alderley, tr. see Alvares, Francisco.

Lord, Stuart M., jt. auth. see Ferguson, David G.

Lord, Suzanne. Drug Enforcement Agents. LC 89-1343. (At Risk Ser.). (Illus.). 48p. (J). (gr. 5-6). 1989. text ed. 11.95 (*0-89686-428-6*, Crstwood Hse) Silver Burdett Pr.

— Heathcliffs Halloween. 1989. pap. 1.95 (*0-8167-1560-2*) Troll Assocs.

— The Labrador Retriever. LC 90-34198. (Top Dog Ser.). (Illus.). 48p. (J). (gr. 4-5). 1990. text ed. 12.95 (*0-89686-526-6*, Crstwood Hse) Silver Burdett Pr.

— Radio-Controlled Model Airplanes. LC 88-7109. (Super-Charged Ser.). (Illus.). 48p. (J). (gr. 5-6). 1988. text ed. 11.95 (*0-89686-378-6*, Crstwood Hse) Silver Burdett Pr.

— Superstitions. LC 89-70867. (Incredible Histories Ser.). (Illus.). 48p. (J). (gr. 5-6). 1990. lib. bdg. 11.95 (*0-89686-512-6*, Crstwood Hse) Silver Burdett Pr.

Lord, Suzanne & Metzger, Jon. The West Virginia One-Day Trip Book: More Than 150 Jaunts in the Magic Mountain State. LC 93-16659. (Illus.). 304p. (Orig.). 1993. pap. 11.95 (*0-939009-70-6*) EPM Pubns.

Lord, Thomas F. Decent Housing: A Promise to Keep. 176p. 1976. boxed 22.95 (*0-87073-491-1*) Transaction Pubs.

Lord, Thomas R. More Stories of Lake George: Fact & Fancy. 218p. 1994. pap. 18.75 (*0-9640267-0-8*) Pinelands Pr.

— Stories of Lake George: Fact & Fancy. 204p. 1986. pap. 18.75 (*0-9640267-1-6*) Pinelands Pr.

Lord, Todd, 3rd, ed. The Designment Review. LC 85-63787. (Residential Design & Market Trends Ser.). 40p. (Orig.). pap. 8.00 (*0-936909-00-5*) Northwest Home.

Lord, Todd, ed. Designment Review '89. LC 86-657614. (Pacific Rim Edition Ser.). (Illus.). 40p. (Orig.). (JPN.). (C). 1988. pap. 8.00 (*0-936909-06-4*) Northwest Home.

Lord, Todd, ed. see Northwest Home Designing, Inc. Staff.

Lord, Todd, ed. see Northwest Home Designing Inc. Staff.

Lord, Tom. The Jazz Discography, Vol. 1: A-Bank. 608p. (Orig.). 1992. pap. 65.00 (*1-881993-00-0*) Cadence Jazz.

— The Jazz Discography, Vol. 2: Ban-Bou. 608p. (Orig.). 1992. pap. 65.00 (*1-881993-01-9*) Cadence Jazz.

— The Jazz Discography, Vol. 3: Bou-Cath. 608p. (Orig.). 1992. pap. 65.00 (*1-881993-02-7*) Cadence Jazz.

— The Jazz Discography, Vol. 4: Cath-Da. 608p. (Orig.). 1993. pap. 65.00 (*1-881993-03-5*) Cadence Jazz.

— The Jazz Discography, Vol. 5: Da-Dz. 608p. (Orig.). 1993. pap. 65.00 (*1-881993-04-3*) Cadence Jazz.

— The Jazz Discography, Vol. 6: Dz-Fis. 608p. (Orig.). 1993. pap. 65.00 (*1-881993-05-1*) Cadence Jazz.

— The Jazz Discography, Vol. 7: Fis-Go. 608p. (Orig.). 1993. pap. 65.00 (*1-881993-06-X*) Cadence Jazz.

— The Jazz Discography, Vol. 8: Go-Ha. 608p. (Orig.). 1994. pap. 65.00 (*1-881993-07-8*) Cadence Jazz.

— The Jazz Discography, Vol. 9: Har-Ho. 608p. (Orig.). 1994. pap. 65.00 (*1-881993-08-6*) Cadence Jazz.

— The Jazz Discography, Vol. 10: Ho-Je. 608p. (Orig.). 1994. pap. 65.00 (*1-881993-09-4*) Cadence Jazz.

— The Jazz Discography, Vol. 11: Je-Jo. 608p. (Orig.). Date not set. pap. 65.00 (*1-881993-10-8*) Cadence Jazz.

— The Jazz Discography, Vol. 12. 608p. (Orig.). Date not set. pap. 50.00 (*1-881993-11-6*) Cadence Jazz.

— The Jazz Discography, Vol. 13. 608p. (Orig.). Date not set. pap. 50.00 (*1-881993-12-4*) Cadence Jazz.

***Lord, Tony.** Best Borders. (Illus.). 144p. 1995. 30.00 (*0-670-85407-7*, Viking) Viking Penguin.

Lord, Trevor. Amazing Bikes. LC 92-911. (Eyewitness Juniors Ser.). (Illus.). 32p. (Orig.). (J). (gr. 1-5). 1992. lib. bdg. 9.99 (*0-679-92772-7*); pap. 7.99 (*0-679-82772-2*) Knopf Bks Yng Read.

— Amazing Cars. LC 91-53138. (Eyewitness Juniors Ser.). (Illus.). 32p. (Orig.). (J). (gr. 1-5). 1992. lib. bdg. 9.99 (*0-679-92766-2*); pap. 6.95 (*0-679-82766-8*) Knopf Bks Yng Read.

Lord, Vicki. Fun with Alkyds & Oils. 72p. (Orig.). 1990. pap. 14.95 (*0-943295-14-9*) Graphics Plus FL.

Lord, Vivian. Summer Kingdom. 1983. pap. 3.50 (*0-449-12476-2*) Fawcett.

Lord, Walter. The Dawn's Early Light. LC 93-43700. (Maryland Paperback Bookshelf Ser.). 400p. 1994. pap. 14.95 (*0-8018-4864-4*) Johns Hopkins.

— Day of Infamy. (Illus.). (J). (gr. 9 up). 1991. reprint ed. 15.00 (*0-03-027620-9*) Adm Nimitz Foun.

— History of the Five Hundred Eighth Parachute Infantry. (Airborne Ser.: No. 2). (Illus.). 120p. 1990. reprint ed. 32.50 (*0-89839-002-8*) Battery Pr.

— Incredible Victory: The Battle of Midway. LC 67-13687. (Illus.). 368p. 1993. pap. 13.00 (*0-06-092360-1*, PL) HarpC.

— The Night Lives On. 1987. pap. 4.50 (*0-515-09250-9*) Jove Pubns.

— Night Lives On. 1976. 20.95 (*0-8488-0568-2*) Amereon Ltd.

— A Night to Remember. (Henry Holt Classics Library). 224p. 1991. 30.00 (*0-8050-1733-X*) H Holt & Co.

— A Night to Remember. 1976. 21.95 (*0-8488-0056-7*) Amereon Ltd.

— A Night to Remember. (YA). (gr. 6-12). 1983. mass mkt. 4.99 (*0-553-27827-4*) Bantam.

— A Night to Remember. large type ed. 1976. 12.00 (*0-85456-444-6*) Ulverscroft.

— A Night to Remember. 300p. 1991. reprint ed. lib. bdg. 21.95x (*0-89966-794-5*) Buccaneer Bks.

— A Time to Stand. LC 78-8708. (Illus.). 271p. 1978. reprint ed. pap. 7.95 (*0-8032-7902-7*, Bison Books) U of Nebr Pr.

Lord, Walter, ed. see Ungermann, Kenneth A.

Lord, Walton J. Chinese Paintings & Mounted Rocks: Exhibition Catalogue. (Illus.). 28p. 1979. pap. 2.00 (*0-911209-14-X*) Palmer Mus Art.

Lord, Wayne, Sr. Our Dhammapada. 112p. (Orig.). 1993. pap. 14.95 (*0-9636577-0-4*) Trego-Hill.

***Lord Wedderburn, et al, eds.** Labour Law in the Post-Industrial Era: Essays in Honour of Hugo Sinzheimer. 160p. 1994. text ed. 39.95 (*1-85521-644-2*, Pub. by Dartmth Pub UK) Ashgate Pub Co.

Lord, Wendy. Big Mouth. Reck, Sue, ed. LC 94-1799. (Tabitha Ser.: Vol. 3). 112p. (J). (gr. 3-6). 1994. pap. 4.99 (*0-7814-0084-8*, Chariot Bks) Chariot Family.

— Gorilla on the Midway. LC 93-1051. (Tabitha Sarah Bigbee Book Ser.). (J). 1994. pap. 4.99 (*0-7814-0892-X*, Chariot Bks) Chariot Family.

— Pickle Stew. LC 93-19018. (Tabitha Sarah Bigbee Book Ser.). (J). 1994. pap. 4.49 (*0-7814-0886-5*, Chariot Bks) Chariot Family.

Lord, Wendy, et al. Shepherds & Shoppers. Johns, Helen, ed. LC 92-72129. (Illus.). 56p. (Orig.). 1992. pap. 6.95 (*0-916035-49-2*) Evangel Indiana.

Lord Wharncliffe, ed. see Montagu, Mary W.

Lord, William, ed. Electromagnetic Methods of Nondestructive Testing, Vol. 3. (Nondestructive Testing Monographs & Tracts). 392p. 1985. pap. text ed. 233.00 (*2-88124-020-8*) Gordon & Breach.

Lord, William B. Freaks of Fashion: The Corset & the Crinoline (1868) LC 93-18739. (Illus.). 240p. 1993. pap. 21.95 (*0-914046-18-7*) R L Shep.

Lord, William B. & Wallace, Mary G., eds. Indian Water Rights & Water Resources Management. (Technical Publication Ser.: No. 89-2). (Illus.). 188p. (Orig.). 1989. pap. 35.00 (*1-882132-06-8*) Am Water Resources.

Lord, William B., ed. see Symposium on Indian Water Rights & Water Resources Management Staff.

Lord, William G. Blue Ridge Parkway Guide: Grandfather Mountain to Great Smoky Mountain National Park. LC 92-28238. (Illus.). 1992. reprint ed. 5.95 (*0-89732-119-7*) Menasha Ridge.

— Blue Ridge Parkway Guide: Rockfish Gap to Grandfather Mountain 0.0 - 291.9 miles. LC 92-28237. (Illus.). 1992. reprint ed. 5.95 (*0-89732-118-9*) Menasha Ridge.

— The Complete Guide to the Blue Ridge Parkway, Vol. I. rev. ed. (Illus.). 160p. 1990. pap. 2.95 (*0-915992-38-8*) Eastern Acorn.

— The Complete Guide to the Blue Ridge Parkway, Vol. II. rev. ed. (Illus.). 160p. 1990. pap. 2.95 (*0-915992-39-6*) Eastern Acorn.

Lord, William H. Stagecraft One: Your Introduction to Backstage Work. LC 78-112693. (Illus.). 126p. (C). 1979. pap. 9.95 (*0-9606320-1-8*); student ed 3.00 (*0-9606320-2-6*) W H Lord.

— Stagecraft One: A Complete Guide to Backstage Work. 2nd ed. Zapel, Arthur L., ed. LC 90-26462. (Illus.). 160p. (C). 1991. reprint ed. pap. text ed. 12.95 (*0-916260-76-3*, B116) Meriwether Pub.

Lord, William S., comp. Best Short Poems of the Nineteenth Century: Being the Twenty-Five Best Short Poems As Selected by Ballot by Competent Critics. LC 76-152152. (Granger Index Reprint Ser.). 1977. reprint ed. 13.95 (*0-8369-6261-3*) Ayer.

— This Is for You. LC 78-121926. (Granger Index Reprint Ser.). 1977. 19.95 (*0-8369-6167-6*) Ayer.

***Lord Woolf of Barnes & Jowell, Jeffrey.** De Smith, Woolf & Jowell: Judicial Review of Administrative Action. 5th ed. 1994. 176.00 (*0-420-46620-7*, Pub. by Sweet & Maxwll) W W Gaunt.

Lordahl, Daniel S. Modern Statistics for Behavioral Sciences. LC 83-17569. 380p. (Orig.). 1984. reprint ed. lib. bdg. 32.95 (*0-89874-680-9*) Krieger.

Lordahl, Jo Ann. Reconnecting the Healing Circle: One Woman's Journey Toward High Level Wellness. LC 93-481. 192p. (Orig.). 1993. pap. 9.95 (*0-929895-10-X*) Maupin Hse.

Lorde, Audre. The Black Unicorn. 1978. pap. 8.95 (*0-393-04516-1*) Norton.

— The Black Unicorn: Poems. 136p. 1995. pap. 9.00 (*0-393-31237-2*) Norton.

— A Burst of Light. LC 88-3924. 134p. (Orig.). 1988. lib. bdg. 18.95 (*0-932379-40-0*); pap. 8.95 (*0-932379-39-7*) Firebrand Bks.

— The Cancer Journals. 2nd ed. LC 80-53110. 77p. 1980. pap. 7.00 (*1-879960-26-5*) Aunt Lute Bks.

— From a Land Where Other People Live. LC 73-82075. (YA). (gr. 12 up). 1973. pap. 5.00 (*0-910296-97-9*) Broadside Pr.

— I am Your Sister: Black Women Organizing Across Sexualities. (Freedom Organizing Pamphlet Ser.). 12p. (Orig.). (C). 1986. pap. 3.50 (*0-913175-07-2*) Kitchen Table.

— The Marvelous Arithmetics of Distance. LC 92-40859. 96p. 1993. 18.95 (*0-393-03513-1*) Norton.

— Marvelous Arithmetics of Distance. 1994. pap. 8.95 (*0-393-31170-8*) Norton.

— Need: A Chorale for Black Woman Voices. (Freedom Organizing Pamphlet Ser.). 20p. 1990. pap. 3.50 (*0-913175-22-6*) Kitchen Table.

— Our Dead Behind Us: Poems. LC 85-29646. 1986. pap. 7.95 (*0-393-30327-6*) Norton.

— Our Dead Behind Us: Poems. 88p. 1994. pap. 9.00 (*0-393-31238-0*) Norton.

— Sister Outsider: Essays & Speeches. LC 84-1844. (Feminist Ser.). 192p. 1984. 22.95 (*0-89594-142-2*); pap. 10.95 (*0-89594-141-4*) Crossing Pr.

— Undersong: Chosen Poems Old & New. rev. ed. 224p. 1992. 19.95 (*0-393-03395-3*) Norton.

— Undersong: Chosen Poems Old & New. rev. ed. 224p. 1992. pap. 9.95 (*0-393-30975-4*) Norton.

— Uses of the Erotic: The Erotic As Power. (Out & Out Pamphlet Ser.). 1978. pap. 3.00 (*0-918314-09-7*) Crossing Pr.

— Zami: A New Spelling of My Name. LC 82-15086. (Feminist Ser.). 256p. 1983. 23.95 (*0-89594-123-6*, C1983); pap. 10.95 (*0-89594-122-8*) Crossing Pr.

Lorde, Audre & Woo, Merle. Apartheid U. S. A. & Our Common Enemy, Our Common Cause: Freedom Organizing in the Eighties. (Freedom Organizing Pamphlet Ser.). 28p. (Orig.). (C). 1986. pap. 3.50 (*0-913175-06-4*) Kitchen Table.

Lorden, G., ed. Jack Carl Kiefer: Introduction to Statistical Inference. (Texts in Statistics Ser.). (Illus.). xii, 360p. 1987. 49.80 (*0-387-96420-7*) Spr-Verlag.

Lordon. Crown Law. 784p. 1991. 110.00 (*0-409-89386-2*) Butterworth Legal Pubs.

— Crown Law-Tort. 94p. 1991. pap. 13.00 (*0-409-90628-X*) Butterworth Legal Pubs.

— Crown Property. 76p. 1991. pap. 12.00 (*0-409-90626-3*) Butterworth Legal Pubs.

Lordon, Randye. Brotherly Love. 272p. 1993. 18.95 (*0-312-09254-7*) St Martin.

— Brotherly Love. 272p. 1994. pap. 9.95 (*0-312-10947-4*, Stonewall Inn) St Martin.

— Sister's Keeper. 272p. 1994. 20.95 (*0-312-11336-6*) St Martin.

***Lords, Bill.** Wonder Woman: The Contest. Kahan, B., ed. (Illus.). 120p. 1995. pap. 9.95 (*1-56389-194-8*) DC Comics.

***Lords, Damien.** The American Dream: A Damien Lords Story. Loraditch, Andrew, ed. 198p. (Orig.). 1995. pap. write for info. (*1-885591-89-6*) Morris Pubng.

Lore, A. G. Essays on the Periphery of the Quijote. Lathrop, Thomas et al, eds. (Documentacion Cervantina Ser.: No. 10). 124p. 1991. pap. 8.50 (*0-936388-47-1*) Juan de la Cuesta.

Lore, John M. An Atlas of Head & Neck Surgery. 3rd ed. (Illus.). 1219p. 1988. text ed. 172.00 (*0-7216-5816-4*) Saunders.

Lore-Kelly, Christin. Caring Community: A Design for Ministry. LC 83-22188. (C). 1983. 12.95 (*0-8294-0423-6*) Loyola Univ Pr.

Lore, Lily, tr. see Kollontai, Aleksandra M.

An Asterisk (*) at the beginning of an entry indicates that the title is appearing in BIP for the first time.

Loreau, Max. Dubuffet's Complete Work, 38 vols., Set. (Illus.). 6000p. (FRE.). 1986. pap. 2,200.00 (*1-55660-163-8*) A Wofsy Fine Arts.

Loredano, Giovanni. Life of Adam. LC 67-26617. 1967. reprint ed. 50.00 (*0-8201-1031-0*) Schol Facsimiles.

Loredo, Betsy. Avalanche in the Alps. LC 93-11175. (Explorers Club Ser.). (Illus.). 80p. (Orig.). (J). (gr. 4-6). 1993. lib. bdg. 12.95 (*1-881889-12-2*) Silver Moon.

— Faraway Families. (Family Ties Ser.). (Illus.). 64p. (J). (ps-4). 1995. lib. bdg. 12.95 (*1-881889-61-0*) Silver Moon.

— Mystery on the Mississippi. (Explorers Club Ser.). (Illus.). 80p. (J). (gr. 4-6). 1994. lib. bdg. 12.95 (*1-881889-35-1*) Silver Moon.

— Storm at the Shore. LC 93-16455. (Explorers Club Ser.). (Illus.). 64p. (Orig.). (J). (gr. 4-6). 1993. lib. bdg. 12.95 (*1-881889-10-6*) Silver Moon.

Loredo, Miguel A. De la Necesidad y Del Amor: (Poesia, 1967-1979) LC 88-80054. (Coleccion Espejo de Paciencia Ser.). (Illus.). 160p. (Orig.). (SPA.). 1990. pap. 15.00 (*0-89729-475-0*) Ediciones.

— Despues del Silencio: Entrevistas al Padre Franciscano Fray Miguel Angel Loredo, O.F.M. por Nicolas Perez Diez-Arguelles. 2nd ed. LC 89-84404. (Coleccion Cuba y Sus Jueces Ser.). (Illus.). 215p. (SPA.). 1989. reprint ed. pap. 15.00 (*0-89729-537-4*) Ediciones.

Loreen, Wendy. Easy Games for Early Learners. Milliken, Linda, ed. (Illus.). 64p. 1993. teacher ed 6.95 (*0-685-65659-4*) Edupress.

Lorel, Claire. Lord Brandsley's Bride. 224p. 1981. pap. 1.50 (*0-449-50200-7*, Coventry) Fawcett.

Lorell, Beverly H., jt. ed. see Grossman, William.

Lorell, K. R., ed. see IFAC Symposium on Automatic Control in Aerospace Staff.

Lorelli, John. To Foreign Shores: U. S. Amphibious Operations in World War II. LC 94-32014. (Illus.). 392p. 1995. 38.95 (*1-55750-520-9*) Naval Inst Pr.

***Lorelli, Mike.** Traveling Again, Dad? LC 95-60604. (Illus.). 32p. (J). 1995. 17.95 (*0-9646302-0-6*) Awesome Bks.

Loren & MacLean Marine & Offshore Publications Staff. Inert Gas Systems Maintenance. (C). 1987. 70.00 (*0-685-33849-5*, Pub. by Lorne & MacLean Marine) St Mut.

***Loren, Karl.** Four Roads to Ruin: Your Health in the Twenty-First Century. (Illus.). 400p. (Orig.). 1995. 19.95 (*1-882537-06-8*) Bigelow Charter.

— Life Flow One: The Solution for Heart Disease. (Illus.). 300p. 1994. write for info. (*1-882537-02-5*) Bigelow Charter.

— Life Flow One: The Solution for Heart Disease. rev. ed. (Illus.). 400p. 1995. pap. 19.95 (*1-882537-05-X*) Bigelow Charter.

— Trust, Taxes & Freedom. 475p. 1991. 195.00 (*1-882537-00-9*) Bigelow Charter.

Loren, Mary E. Meeting the Forgiving Jesus: Leader's Guide. 48p. 1984. pap. 2.95 (*0-89243-225-X*) Liguori Pubns.

***Loren, Michael L.** What Counts: Based on Ben Franklin's 13 Virtues. 150p. (Orig.). 1994. pap. 7.95 (*0-9641930-0-0*) Overland Park.

Lorence, David H. & Vaughan, Reginald E. Annotated Bibliography of Mascarene Plant Life: Including the Useful & Ornamental Plants of the Region, Covering the Period 1609-1990. 280p. (C). 1992. 29.95 (*0-915809-15-X*) Natl Trop Bot.

Lorence, James J. Gerald J. Boileau & the Progressive-Farmer-Labor Alliance: Politics of the New Deal. (Illus.). 344p. 1994. text ed. 44.95 (*0-8262-0918-1*) U of Mo Pr.

Lorence-Kot, Bogna. Child Rearing & Reform: A Study of the Nobility in Eighteenth-Century Poland. LC 84-25203. (Contributions in Family Studies: No. 9). (Illus.). ix, 170p. 1985. text ed. 49.95 (*0-313-24500-2*, LCR/, Greenwood Pr) Greenwood.

Lorene, Karen. Buying Antique Jewelry: Skipping the Mistakes. (Illus.). 164p. (Orig.). 1987. pap. 19.95 (*0-9618302-0-4*) Lorene Pubns.

Lorens, M. K. Sorrowheart. (Winston Marlowe Sherman Mystery Ser.). 1994. pap. 4.99 (*0-553-29441-5*) Bantam.

***Lorensen, Leonard.** Accounting for Liabilities. fac. ed. LC 91-41025. (Accounting Research Monograph: No. 4). 189p. 1992. pap. 53.90 (*0-7837-8235-7*, 2047999) Bks Demand.

— Illustrations of Accounting for Certain Investments in Debt & Equity Securities: A Survey of the Application of FASB Statement No. 112. LC 95-13038. (Financial Report Survey Ser.). 1995. write for info. (*0-87051-165-3*) Am Inst CPA.

— Illustrations of Accounting for Costs to Comply with Governmental Regulations to Protect the Environment: A Survey of the Application of FASB Statement No. 5. LC 93-25788. (Financial Report Survey Ser.). 1993. 26.50 (*0-87051-136-X*) Am Inst CPA.

— Illustrations of Accounting for Income Taxes: A Survey of the Application of FASB Statement No. 109. LC 93-9571. (Financial Report Survey Ser.). 1993. 26.50 (*0-87051-130-0*) Am Inst CPA.

— Illustrations of Accounting for Postretirement Benefits Other Than Pensions: A Survey of the Application of FASB Statement No. 106. LC 93-23269. 1993. 26.50 (*0-87051-141-6*) Am Inst CPA.

— Illustrations of Disclosures about Fair Value of Financial Instruments: A Survey of the Application of FASB Statement No. 107. LC 94-19447. 1994. write for info. (*0-87051-155-6*) Am Inst CPA.

— Illustrations of Financial Reporting by Entities in Reorganization under the Bankruptcy Code: A Survey of the Application of AICPA SOP 90-7. LC 94-2153. (Financial Report Survey Ser.). 1994. 26.50 (*0-87051-049-5*) Am Inst CPA.

— Illustrations of Pro Forma Financial Statements That Reflect Subsequent Events. fac. ed. LC 91-16949. (Financial Report Survey Ser.: No. 44). 92p. 1991. reprint ed. pap. 26.30 (*0-7837-8226-8*, 2047986) Bks Demand.

— Illustrations of Reporting the Results of Operations: A Survey of the Application of APB Opinion 30. rev. ed. LC 92-11043. (Financial Report Survey Ser.). 1992. 26.50 (*0-87051-121-1*) Am Inst CPA.

— Illustrations of Reporting the Results of Operations: A Survey of the Recent Application of APB Opinion 30. fac. ed. LC 92-11043. (Financial Report Survey Ser.: No. 47). 118p. 1992. reprint ed. pap. 33.70 (*0-7837-8219-5*, 2047979) Bks Demand.

— Illustrations of the Disclosure by Financial Institutions of Certain Information about Debt Securities Held as Assets: A Survey of the Application of SOP 90-11. LC 92-21816. (Financial Report Survey Ser.). 1992. 26.50 (*0-87051-122-X*) Am Inst CPA.

— Illustrations of the Disclosure by Financial Institutions of Certain Information about Debt Securities Held As Assets: A Survey of the Application of SOP 90-11. fac. ed. LC 92-21816. (Financial Report Survey Ser.: No. 48). 117p. 1992. reprint ed. pap. 33.40 (*0-7837-8225-X*, 2047985) Bks Demand.

— Illustrations of the Disclosure of Information about Financial Instruments with Off-Balance Sheet Risk & Financial Instruments with Concentrations of Credit Risk: A Survey of the Application of FASB Statement, No. 105. LC 92-12974. (Financial Report Survey Ser.: No. V). 1992. 26.50 (*0-87051-120-3*) Am Inst CPA.

— Illustrations of the Disclosure of Information about Financial Instruments with Off-Balance-Sheet Risk & Financial Instruments with Concentrations of Credit Risk: A Survey of the Application of FASB Statement No. 105. fac. ed. LC 92-12974. (Financial Report Survey Ser.: No. 46). 121p. 1992. reprint ed. pap. 34.50 (*0-7837-8227-6*, 2047987) Bks Demand.

***Lorensen, Leonard & American Institute of Certified Public Accountants Staff.** Illustrations of Accounting for Postemployment Benefits: A Survey of the Application of FASB Statement No. 112. LC 95-195. (Financial Report Survey Ser.). 1995. write for info. (*0-87051-163-7*) Am Inst CPA.

Lorensen, Leonard, ed. see American Institute of Certified Public Accountants Staff.

Lorensen, Leonard, jt. auth. see Clark, Hal G.

Lorente de No, Raphael. The Primary Acoustic Nuclei. (Illus.). 189p. 1981. text ed. 83.00 (*0-89004-318-3*) Raven.

Lorente, Maria A. Palynology & Palynofacies of the Upper Tertiary in Venezuela. (Dissertations Botanicae Ser.: Vol. 99). (Illus.). 1986. pap. text ed. 84.00 (*3-443-64011-7*) Lubrecht & Cramer.

Lorente, Mariano J., tr. see Aranha, Jose P.

Lorente, Mariano J., jt. auth. see Blasco-Ibanez, Vincenti.

Lorents, D. C., et al, eds. Electronic & Atomic Collisions: Invited Papers of the XIVth International Conference on the Physics of Electronic & Atomic Collisions, Palo Alto, CA, 21-30 July 1985. 820p. 1986. 200.00 (*0-444-86998-0*) Elsevier.

Lorentz, jt. auth. see Dietl.

Lorentz, Elizabeth, jt. auth. see Sarason, Seymour B.

Lorentz, Friedrich, et al. The Cassubian Civilization. LC 77-87520. 456p. 1983. reprint ed. 62.50 (*0-404-16603-2*) AMS Pr.

Lorentz, G., jt. ed. see Falcke, F. K.

Lorentz, G. G. Bernstein Polynomials. LC 55-527. (Mathematical Expositions Ser.: No. 8). 140p. reprint ed. pap. 39.90 (*0-8357-7144-X*, 2051966) Bks Demand.

Lorentz, George G. Approximation of Functions. 2nd ed. LC 66-13296. ix, 184p. (C). 1985. text ed. 16.95 (*0-8284-0322-8*) Chelsea Pub.

— Bernstein Polynomials. 2nd ed. x, 132p. 1985. text ed. 14.95 (*0-8284-0323-6*) Chelsea Pub.

Lorentz, George G., jt. auth. see DeVore, Ronald A.

Lorentz, George G., et al. Birkhoff Interpolation. (Encyclopedia of Mathematics & Its Applications Ser.: No. 19). 1984. 64.95 (*0-521-30239-0*) Cambridge U Pr.

***Lorentz, John H.** Historical Dictionary of Iran. LC 94-45843. (Asian Historical Dictionaries Ser.: No. 16). 1995. write for info. (*0-8108-2994-0*) Scarecrow.

Lorentz, Moses L. How to Prepare for the National Teacher Examination (NTE) Common Examinations. 1980. pap. text ed. 5.95 (*0-07-038745-1*) McGraw.

Lorentz, Pare. FDR's Moviemaker: Memoirs & Scripts. LC 91-38493. (Illus.). 256p. (C). 1992. 29.95 (*0-87417-186-5*) U of Nev Pr.

— Lorentz on Film: Movies 1927 to 1941. LC 86-40090. 1986. reprint ed. pap. 12.95 (*0-8061-2017-7*) U of Okla Pr.

Lorentz, Richard J. Recursive Algorithms. LC 93-9056. (Computations Sciences Ser.). 200p. 1993. 45.00 (*0-89391-913-6*); 24.50 (*1-56750-037-4*) Ablex Pub.

Lorentz, Rudolph A. Multivariate Birkhoff Interpolation. LC 92-27388. ix, 192p. 1992. pap. 39.00 (*0-387-55870-5*); pap. 35.00 (*3-540-55870-5*) Spr-Verlag.

Lorentzen, Bob. The Glove Box Guide: Mendocino Coast: Lodging, Eateries, Sights, History, Activities, & More. (Glove Box Guides Ser.). (Illus.). 224p. (Orig.). 1995. pap. 11.00 (*0-939431-09-2*) Bored Feet Pubns.

— Hiker's Hip Pocket Guide to Sonoma County. (Hiker's Hip Pocket Ser.). (Illus.). 208p. (Orig.). 1992. pap. 12.95 (*0-939431-07-6*) Bored Feet Pubns.

— The Hiker's Hip Pocket Guide to Sonoma County. (Hiker's Hip Pocket Guides Ser.). (Illus.). 224p. (Orig.). 1995. pap. 14.00 (*0-939431-12-2*) Bored Feet Pubns.

— The Hiker's Hip Pocket Guide to the Humboldt Coast: Including Redwood National Park, King Range - Lost Coast, Del Norte Coast, Lake Earl State Park, Humboldt Bay, Redwood State Parks, Patrick's Point & Other Natural Areas. 2nd ed. (Hiker's Hip Pocket Guide Ser.). (Illus.). 224p. 1993. pap. 11.95 (*0-939431-08-4*) Bored Feet Pubns.

— The Hiker's Hip Pocket Guide to the Mendocino Coast. 2nd ed. (Hiker's Hip Pocket Ser.). (Illus.). 192p. (Orig.). 1992. pap. 11.95 (*0-939431-03-3*) Bored Feet Pubns.

— The Hiker's Hip Pocket Guide to the Mendocino Highlands: Including Yolla-Bolly-Middle Eel Wilderness, Snow Mountain Wilderness, Mendocino National Forest, Clear Lake State Parks, Cow Mountain Recreation Area & Other Natural Areas. LC 92-23637. (Hiker's Hip Pocket Guide Ser.). (Illus.). 240p. (Orig.). 1992. pap. 13.95 (*0-939431-05-X*) Bored Feet Pubns.

— Hiker's Hip Pocket Guides Boxed Gift Set. (Illus.). 1990. 33.00 (*0-939431-04-1*) Bored Feet Pubns.

***Lorentzen, Bob & Petersen, Liz.** Mendocino Coast Bike Rides: For Mountain Bikers & Road Cyclists. 96p. (Orig.). 1995. pap. 9.00 (*0-939431-11-4*) Bored Feet Pubns.

***Lorentzen, Jochen.** Opening Up Hungary to the World Market: External Constraints & Opportunities. LC 94-32257. 212p. 1995. 69.95 (*0-312-12408-2*) St Martin.

Lorentzen, Karen M. & Neal, Robert D., eds. Health Education, Principles, Preparation & Practice. (Illus.). 124p. 1990. 18.75 (*0-87527-473-0*) Green.

Lorentzen, Karen M. & Roemer, Linda. Health Services Administration Handbook. 128p. 1988. 19.50 (*0-87527-353-X*) Green.

Lorentzen, Lisa & Waadeland, Haakon. Continued Fractions with Applications. LC 92-8592. (Studies in Computational Mathematics: Vol. 3). 1992. write for info. (*0-444-89265-6*, North Holland) Elsevier.

Lorentzen, R. J., jt. ed. see Flamm, W. G.

Lorentzen, Robin. Women in the Sanctuary Movement. 240p. 1991. 34.95 (*0-87722-768-3*) Temple U Pr.

Lorentzen, Sandra, jt. ed. see Breisacher, E. H.

***Lorentzi, Jakob & Nilsson, Magnus.** Spin-Off, Dual-Use & Conversion: Fashion or Reality? 51p. (Orig.). (C). 1994. pap. text ed. 35.00 (*0-7881-1381-X*) Diane Pub.

Lorentzon, Betsy. Life on the Edge of the Slashings. LC 93-85761. Date not set. pap. write for info. (*0-9637996-0-6*) Shinglemill.

Lorenz, A. A. Stochastic Automata. 340p. 1974. text ed. 82.00 (*0-7065-1379-7*, Pub. by Keter Pub IS) Coronet Bks.

Lorenz, Albert. Trace. LC 92-46409. (Illus.). 304p. 1993. pap. 35.00 (*0-8230-0172-5*, Whitney Lib) Watsn-Guptill.

Lorenz, Albert & Salzman, Stanley. Drawing in Color: Rendering Techniques for Architects & Illustrators. (Illus.). 256p. 1991. 45.00 (*0-8230-1384-7*, Whitney Lib) Watsn-Guptill.

Lorenz, Alfred, jt. auth. see Vivian, John H.

Lorenz, August O., ed. see Plautus.

Lorenz, Charlotte, jt. auth. see Umbreit, Paul.

Lorenz, Christopher. The Design Dimension: The New Competitive Weapon for Business. 1990. pap. 18.95 (*0-631-17748-5*) Blackwell Pubs.

Lorenz, Christopher & Leslie, Nicholas. The Financial Times on Management. (Financial Times Management Ser.). 224p. 1992. 75.00x (*0-273-60006-0*, Pub. by Pitman Pubng UK) St Mut.

Lorenz, Clare. Women in Architecture. LC 90-52973. (Illus.). 144p. 1990. 29.95 (*0-8478-1277-4*) Rizzoli Intl.

Lorenz, Dagmar C. Verfolgung Bis Zum Massenmord: Holocaust-Diskurse in Deutscher Sprache Aus der Sicht der Verfolgten. LC 91-37352. (German Life & Civilization Ser.: Vol. 11). 451p. (GER.). (C). 1993. text ed. 66.95 (*0-8204-1751-3*) P Lang Pubs.

Lorenz, Dagmar C. & Weinberger, Gabriele, eds. Insiders & Outsiders: Jewish & Gentile Culture in Germany & Austria. LC 93-46000. 378p. 1994. pap. text ed. 44.95 (*0-8143-2497-5*) Wayne St U Pr.

Lorenz, Delores R., jt. auth. see Breitenfeldt, Dorvan H.

Lorenz, Diane C., jt. auth. see Veblen, Thomas T.

Lorenz, E. St. Anthony's Guide to ASC Payment Groups. 200p. (C). Date not set. ring bd. write for info. (*1-56329-132-0*) St Anthony Pub.

— St. Anthony's ICD-9-CM Code Book, 3 vols. 387p. (C). Date not set. ring bd. 139.00 (*1-56329-130-4*) St Anthony Pub.

— St. Anthony's ICD-9-CM Code Book, 3 vols. annot. ed. (Illus.). 400p. (C). 1993. ring bd. 195.00 (*1-56329-101-0*, IAD) St Anthony Pub.

— St. Anthony's B-W ICD-9-CM for Nursing Home & Hospice, 3 vols. 350p. (Orig.). (C). 1993. pap. 107.00 (*1-56329-165-7*) St Anthony Pub.

— St. Anthony's Clinical Reference to Diagnostic Coding: ADX. (Illus.). 300p. (C). 1993. ring bd. 95.00 (*1-56329-115-0*) St Anthony Pub.

— St. Anthony's Clinical Reference to OB-GYN, '93-94: ATOB. (Illus.). 300p. (C). 1993. ring bd. 159.00 (*1-56329-125-8*) St Anthony Pub.

— St. Anthony's Color-Coded ICD-9-CM Codebook, '94, 3 vols. 247p. (C). 1993. pap. 69.95 (*1-56329-164-9*) St Anthony Pub.

— St. Anthony's DRG Optimizer. 175p. (Orig.). (C). 1993. 99.00 (*1-56329-197-5*) St Anthony Pub.

— St. Anthony's DRG Working Guidebook. 135p. (Orig.). (C). 1993. 69.00 (*1-56329-171-1*) St Anthony Pub.

— St. Anthony's HCFA 1500 Editor. 150p. (C). 1993. ring bd. 129.00 (*1-56329-134-7*) St Anthony Pub.

— St. Anthony's HCPCS Level II Code Book. 175p. (C). 1994. pap. 29.95 (*1-56329-169-X*); spiral bd. 75.00 (*1-56329-170-3*) St Anthony Pub.

— St. Anthony's HCPCS Reference Manual for Outpatient Services. 350p. (C). 1992. ring bd. 329.00 (*1-56329-133-9*) St Anthony Pub.

— St. Anthony's ICD-9-CM Annotated Code Book for Physicians, 2 vols. (Illus.). 285p. (C). 1993. ring bd. 180.00 (*1-56329-100-2*, PAB) St Anthony Pub.

— St. Anthony's ICD-9-CM Code Book for AMA, '94, 2 vols. 300p. (Orig.). 1993. pap. 20.00 (*1-56329-167-3*) St Anthony Pub.

— St. Anthony's ICD-9-CM Code Book for Outpatient Services, 3 vols. 278p. (C). 1993. ring bd. 139.00 (*1-56329-136-3*) St Anthony Pub.

— St. Anthony's ICD-9-CM Code Book for Physicians. 250p. (C). 1994. ring bd. 129.00 (*1-56329-131-2*) St Anthony Pub.

— St. Anthony's ICD-9-CM Code Book for Physicians - B-W. 185p. (Orig.). (C). 1993. pap. 39.95 (*1-56329-168-1*) St Anthony Pub.

— St. Anthony's ICD-9-CM Code Book, '94, 3 vols. 300p. (Orig.). (C). 1993. pap. 49.95 (*1-56329-166-5*); pap. 59.95 (*1-56329-163-0*) St Anthony Pub.

— St. Anthony's Medicare Coverage Manual. 147p. 1991. ring bd. 129.00 (*1-56329-135-5*) St Anthony Pub.

— St. Anthony's Medicare Payment Guide for Orthopaedics. 187p. (C). 1993. ring bd. 138.00 (*1-56329-157-6*) St Anthony Pub.

— St. Anthony's Medicare Payment Guide to Cardiology. 188p. (C). 1993. ring bd. 197.00 (*1-56329-156-8*) St Anthony Pub.

— St. Anthony's Medicare Secondary Payer - Billing & Reimbursement Guide. 200p. (C). 1994. ring bd. 149.00 (*1-56329-181-9*) St Anthony Pub.

— St. Anthony's Reimbursement Guide to Radiology Services, 1992. 340p. (C). 1992. ring bd. 177.00 (*1-56329-093-6*, SRA) St Anthony Pub.

— St. Anthony's Three-in-One Code Book for Cardiology. 1993. ring bd. 125.00 (*1-56329-106-1*, SCR) St Anthony Pub.

— St. Anthony's Three-in-One Code Book for OB-GYN. 147p. (C). 1993. 139.00 (*1-56329-119-3*) St Anthony Pub.

— St. Anthony's Three-in-One Code Book for Orthopaedics. 140p. (C). 1993. ring bd. 149.00 (*1-56329-120-7*) St Anthony Pub.

— St. Anthony's Three-in-One Code Book for Physical. 250p. 1993. ring bd. 175.00 (*1-56329-144-4*) St Anthony Pub.

— St. Anthony's UB-92 Editor, '93. 200p. (C). 1992. ring bd. 195.00 (*1-56329-114-2*) St Anthony Pub.

Lorenz, E., jt. auth. see Dietl, C. E.

Lorenz, Edward N. The Essence of Chaos. LC 93-1835. (Jessie & John Danz Lecture Ser.). (Illus.). 200p. 1993. 19.95 (*0-295-97270-X*) U of Wash Pr.

Lorenz, Hans-Walter. Nonlinear Dynamical Economics & Chaotic. (Lecture Notes in Economics & Mathematical Systems Ser.: Vol. 334). xii, 248p. 1989. pap. 28.60 (*0-387-51413-9*) Spr-Verlag.

— Nonlinear Dynamical Economics & Chaotic Motion. 2nd enl. rev. ed. LC 93-5233. 1993. 98.00 (*0-387-56881-6*); write for info. (*3-540-56881-6*) Spr-Verlag.

Lorenz, Hans-Walter, jt. auth. see Gabisch, G.

Lorenz, Herb. Damfino. 1992. 21.95 (*0-9633256-0-4*) Prairie House.

Lorenz, Jens, jt. ed. see Gartner, Uta.

Lorenz, Jens, jt. auth. see Kreiss, Heinz-Otto.

Lorenz, Joseph P. Egypt & the Arabs: Foreign Policy & the Search for National Identity. 184p. 1990. text ed. 57.00 (*0-8133-7593-2*) Westview.

Lorenz, K., ed. Konstruktionen Versus Positionen. Beitraege zur wissenschaftstheoretischen Diskussion zum 60: Geburtstag von Paul Lorensen, 2 vols., Set. (C). 1978. 288.50 (*3-11-006655-6*) De Gruyter.

Lorenz, Klaus & Kulp, Karel, eds. Handbook of Cereal Science & Technology. (Food Science & Technology Ser.: Vol. 41). 896p. 1991. 250.00 (*0-8247-8358-1*) Dekker.

Lorenz, Konrad. Behind the Mirror: A Search for a Natural History of Human Knowledge. Taylor, Ronald, tr. LC 78-6031. (Helen & Kurt Wolff Bk.). (Illus.). 1978. pap. 7.95 (*0-15-611776-2*, Harvest Bks) HarBrace.

— Behind the Mirror: A Search for a Natural History of Human Knowledge. 19.00 (*0-8446-6212-7*) Peter Smith.

— Evolution & Modification of Behavior. LC 65-24436. vi, 122p. 1986. reprint ed. pap. text ed. 9.95 (*0-226-49334-2*, Midway Reprint) U Ch Pr.

— The Foundations of Ethology. (Illus.). 380p. 1981. 58.00 (*0-387-81623-2*) Spr-Verlag.

— King Solomon's Ring. 216p. (J). (gr. 7). 1991. pap. 3.99 (*0-451-62831-4*, AE3229, Sig) NAL-Dutton.

— The Natural Science of the Human Species: An Introduction to Comparative Behavioral Research: the "Russian Manuscript", 1944-1948. Cranach, Agnes von, ed. Martin, Robert D., tr. LC 94-48788. (ENG & GER.). 1995. 35.00 (*0-262-12190-5*) MIT Pr.

— On Aggression. 20.75 (*0-8446-6213-5*) Peter Smith.

— On Aggression. Wilson, Marjorie K., tr. LC 74-5306. (Helen & Kurt Wolff Bk.). (Illus.). 306p. 1974. reprint ed. pap. 9.95 (*0-15-668741-0*, Harvest Bks) HarBrace.

— On Life & Living. 1991. pap. 9.95 (*0-312-05937-X*) St Martin.

— The Waning of Humaneness. 1987. 17.95 (*0-316-53291-6*) Little.

Lorenz, Konrad Z. Man Meets Dog. Wilson, Marjorie K., tr. (Illus.). 256p. 1994. reprint ed. pap. 12.00 (*1-56836-051-7*) Kodansha.

***Lorenz, Lee.** Art of the New Yorker, 1925-1995. 1995. 40.00 (*0-679-43679-0*) Knopf.

— Real Dogs Don't Eat Leftovers: A Guide to All That Is Truly Canine. (Illus.). 1983. write for info. (*0-318-57555-8*) S&S Trade.

— A Weekend in the City. (Illus.). 32p. (J). (gr. k-3). 1991. 15.95 (*0-945912-15-3*) Pippin Pr.

An Asterisk (*) at the beginning of an entry indicates that the title is appearing in BIP for the first time.

Lorenz, Lee, illus. Driving Me Crazy: Fun on Wheels Jokes. 40p. (J). (gr. 2-5). 1989. 13.95 (0-945912-05-6) Pippin Pr.

Lorenz, Lincoln. John Paul Jones, Fighter for Freedom & Glory. 1943. 52.00 (0-527-58400-2) Periodicals Srv.

Lorenz, Lori L, et al. Windows 3 Companion. 1990. pap. 27.95 (0-936767-19-7) Microsoft.

Lorenz, Lori L., et al. Windows 3.1 Companion. 2nd ed. 544p. 1992. pap. 27.95 (1-55615-372-4) Microsoft.

Lorenz, Marian, jt. auth. see Moose, Allan.

Lorenz, Marita. Marita: One Woman's Extraordinary Tale of Love & Espionage from Castro to Kennedy. 1993. 22.95 (1-56025-055-0) Thunders Mouth.

Lorenz, Mark. Object-Oriented Software Development: A Practical Guide. LC 92-18566. 250p. 1992. text ed. 41.00 (0-13-726928-5) Brady Compu Bks.

— Object-Oriented Software Metrics. 146p. 1994. text ed. 36.00 (0-13-179292-X) P-H.

— Rapid Software Development with Smalltalk. (Advances in Object Technology Ser.: Vol. 7). (Illus.). 200p. (Orig.). 1995. pap. 24.00 (1-884842-12-7) SIGS Bks.

Lorenz, Melinda. Contemporary Collage: Extensions. (Illus.). 32p. 1983. 4.00 (0-915478-47-1) Galleries Coll.

— The Denver Boulder Show. (Illus.). 20p. 1984. 4.00 (0-915478-50-1) Galleries Coll.

Lorenz, Michael D. & Cornelius, Larry M., eds. Small Animal Diagnosis. 2nd ed. LC 92-46032. 651p. 1993. pap. 49.50 (0-397-51200-7) Lippincott.

Lorenz, Michael D., jt. auth. see Oliver, John E., Jr.

Lorenz, Michael D., et al. Small Animal Medical Therapeutics. (Illus.). 656p. 1991. pap. 49.50 (0-397-50994-4) Lippincott.

Lorenz, Oscar A. & Maynard, Donald N. Knott's Handbook for Vegetable Growers. 3rd ed. LC 87-25224. 456p. 1988. pap. text ed. 64.95 (0-471-85240-6) Wiley.

Lorenz, R., et al, eds. Advances in Neurosurgery: Intracerebral Hemorrhages Hydrocephalus Malresorptivus Peripheral Nerves, Vol. 21. (Illus.). 360p. 1993. pap. 79.00 (0-387-56304-0) Spr-Verlag.

Lorenz, Richard. Imogen Cunningham: Ideas Without End: A Life in Photographs. LC 93-67. (Illus.). 1993. 35.00 (0-8118-0390-2); pap. 22.95 (0-8118-0357-0) Chronicle Bks.

— Landscape Images: Recent Photographs by Linda Connor, Judy Fiskin & Ruth Thorne-Thomsen. (Illus.). 40p. 1980. pap. 4.50 (0-934418-08-X) Mus Contemp Art.

Lorenz, Richard, jt. ed. see Rule, Amy.

Lorenz, Richardo, et al, eds. Scores & Recordings at the Indiana University Latin American Music Center. LC 94-945. 1994. 75.00 (0-253-33273-7) Ind U Pr.

Lorenz, Rita, jt. auth. see Adolph, A. L.

Lorenz, Rita, jt. auth. see Adolph, L.

Lorenz, T., tr. see Paulsen, Friedrich.

Lorenz, Theodore, tr. see Paulsen, Friedrich.

Lorenz, Walter. Social Work in a Changing Europe. LC 93-3483. 1994. write for info. (0-415-07807-5) Routledge.

Lorenz, William & Gilbertie, James. EWOT: Economic Way of Thinking. 3rd ed. 1991. pap. 37.75 (1-56226-090-1) CT Pub.

Lorenza, Olga. Vida y Obra de Una Maestra. LC 90-84146. (Coleccion Caniqui Ser.). 93p. (Orig.). (SPA.). 1990. pap. 9.95 (0-89729-574-9) Ediciones.

Lorenzana, Ronald, tr. see Dale, Ralph A.

Lorenzani, Shirley. Candida: A Twentieth Century Disease. LC 85-81549. (Pivot Original Health Bks.). 176p. (Orig.). 1986. pap. 4.95 (0-87983-375-0) Keats.

Lorenzani, Shirley S. Dietary Fiber. (Good Health Guide Ser.). 32p. (Orig.). 1988. pap. 1.95 (0-87983-479-X) Keats.

Lorenzano, Luis, jt. auth. see Dabat, Alejandro.

Lorenzatos, Zissimos. The Lost Center & Other Essays in Greek Poetry. Cicellis, Kay, tr. LC 79-3221. (Princeton Essays in Literature Ser.). 211p. reprint ed. pap. 60.20 (0-8357-4283-0, 2037082) Bks Demand.

Lorenzen. Of Swedish Ways. 1992. pap. 11.00 (0-06-092384-9) HarpC.

Lorenzen, Anna L. Tiger. (Illus.). 22p. (Orig.). (J). (gr. 1-2). 1989. pap. text ed. 2.95 (0-9626133-0-4) ALL Ventura Pub.

Lorenzen, Betty. Dental Assistant Techniques. LC 74-18674. (Allied Health Ser.). 1976. pap. write for info. (0-672-61395-6) Macmillan.

Lorenzen, D., et al, eds. Hazardous & Industrial Solid Waste Testing & Disposal, Vol. 6. LC 86-25944. (Special Technical Publication Ser.: No. 933). (Illus.). 470p. 1986. text ed. 63.00 (0-8031-0931-8, 04-933000-16) ASTM.

Lorenzen, David. Kapalikas & the Kalamukhas: Two Lost Saivite Sects. (C). 1991. reprint ed. 14.00 (81-208-0708-1, Pub. by Motilal Banarsidass II) S Asia.

Lorenzen, David N. Kabir Legends & Ananta-Das's Kabir Parachai: With a Translation of the Kabir Parachai Prepared in Collaboration with Jagdish Kumar & Uma Thukral & with an Edition of the Niranjani Revision of This Work. LC 90-30135. (SUNY Series in Hindu Studies). 282p. 1991. 59.50 (0-7914-0461-7); pap. 19.95 (0-7914-0462-5) State U NY Pr.

— The Kapalikas & Kalamukhas: Two Lost Saivite Sects. LC 70-138509. 228p. reprint ed. pap. 65.00 (0-685-23976-4, 2031540) Bks Demand.

— Praises to a Formless God: Nirguni Texts from North India. (SUNY Series in Religious Studies). 240p. 1996. pap. text ed. 16.95x (0-7914-2806-0) State U NY Pr.

— Praises to a Formless God: Nirguni Texts from North India. (SUNY Series in Religious Studies). 240p. (C). 1996. 49.50x (0-7914-2805-2) State U NY Pr.

Lorenzen, David N., ed. Bhakti Religion in North India: Community Identity & Political Action. LC 93-41538. (SUNY Series in Religious Studies). 304p. (C). 1994. 59.50 (0-7914-2025-6); pap. 19.95 (0-7914-2026-4) State U NY Pr.

Lorenzen, Emme I. Momentous Days: An Account in Poetry & Prose of a Family in Early Walnut Creek, California. (Illus.). 64p. (Orig.). 1990. pap. text ed. 12.00 (0-9627282-0-9) TYIL Pr.

Lorenzen, H. & Weissner, W. Intracellular & Intercellular Regulation & in Algae & Symbionts. (Illus.). 320p. 1981. pap. text ed. 56.00 (3-437-30368-6) Lubrecht & Cramer.

Lorenzen, H., jt. ed. see Eschrich, W.

Lorenzen, Paul. Constructive Philosophy. Pavlovic, Karl R., tr. LC 86-25003. 304p. 1987. lib. bdg. 32.50 (0-87023-564-8) U of Mass Pr.

Lorenzen, Paul, jt. auth. see Kamlah, Wilhelm.

Lorenzen, Thomas J. & Anderson, Virgil L. Design of Experiments: A No-Name Approach. LC 93-2095. (Statistics: Vol. 139). 432p. 1993. 65.00 (0-8247-9077-4) Dekker.

***Lorenzen, Thorwald.** Resurrection & Discipleship. 225p. (Orig.). 1995. pap. 21.95 (1-57075-042-4) Orbis Bks.

Lorenzetti, Michael, jt. ed. see Preas, Bryan.

Lorenzetti, R., jt. auth. see Lancini, G.

Lorenzi, Nancy M. & Riley, Robert T. Organizational Aspects of Health Informatics: Preparing for Technological Change. LC 94-19977. (Computers in Health Care Ser.). 1994. 45.00 (0-387-94226-2) Spr-Verlag.

Lorenzi, Peter, jt. auth. see Sims, Henry P., Jr.

Lorenzin, Tom & Sechler, Tim. One Thousand Plus: The Amateur Astronomer's Field Guide to Deep Sky Observing. (Illus.). 168p. 1987. write for info. (0-912081-06-6) Delmar Co.

Lorenzini, Jean. Medical Phrase Index. 2nd ed. 960p. 1989. 45.00 (0-87489-539-1) Med Economics.

Lorenzini, Jean A., ed. Medical Phrase Index. 2nd ed. 948p. (C). 1989. text ed. 45.00 (1-878487-26-4) Practice Mgmt Info.

Lorenzini, Jean A. & Lorenzini-Ley, Laura. Medical Phrase Index: A One-Step Reference to the Terminology of Medicine. 3rd ed. Rogers, Gregg & Swanson, Kathryn, eds. LC 93-42123. 1300p. 1994. 49.95 (1-878487-58-2, ME052) Practice Mgmt Info.

Lorenzini-Ley, Laura, jt. auth. see Lorenzini, Jean A.

Lorenzo. The Relaxation Sensation: The Number One Success Factor in Life. (Illus.). 128p. (Orig.). 1981. pap. 9.95 (0-941122-00-X) Prema Bks.

Lorenzo, ed. see Taine, Hippolyte A.

***Lorenzo, Carol L.** Nervous Dancer. LC 94-13062. (Flannery O'Connor Award for Short Fiction Ser.). 184p. 1995. 22.95 (0-8203-1704-7) U of Ga Pr.

Lorenzo, Jack M. The Leaves of Life & How to Change Your Mind about Growth, Love, Life, & Living. 90p. 1993. pap. write for info. (0-9636299-0-5) INCOM Pub Div.

Lorenzo, Jake. Cold Surveillance: The Jake Lorenzo Wine Columns. (Orig.). 1993. pap. 9.95 (0-9637438-4-8) Wine Patrol Pr.

Lorenzo, Javier, jt. auth. see Hartman, Patricia A.

Lorenzo, Luciano G. & Varey, J. E., eds. Teatro y Vida Teatral del Siglo de Oro a Traves de las Fuentes Documentales. (Serie A: Monagrafias: No. 145). (C). 1992. pap. text ed. 53.00 (1-85566-007-5, Pub. by Tamesis Bks Ltd UK) Boydell & Brewer.

Lorenzo, Orestes. Vuelo Hacia el Amanecer: El Vuelo de Orestes Lorenzo. 320p. (SPA.). 1994. 22.95 (0-312-10009-4) St Martin.

— Wings of the Morning: The Flights of Orestes Lorenzo. 320p. 1993. 22.95 (0-312-10008-6) St Martin.

— Wings of the Morning Vol. 1. 1995. mass mkt. 5.99 (0-312-95317-8) St Martin.

Lorenzo-Rivero, Luis, ed. see De Larra, Mariano J.

Lorenzo-Rivero, Luis, ed. see Dove, Richard.

***Lorenzo, Robert & Clark, Nate, Jr.** Bessemer & Lake Erie RR in Color. (Illus.). 128p. 1994. 49.95 (1-878887-34-3) Morning NJ.

Lorenzoni & Clark, eds. Applied Cost Engineering. 2nd exp. rev. ed. (Cost Engineering Ser.: Vol. 8). 368p. 1985. 65.00 (0-8247-7264-4) Dekker.

Lorenzoni, A. B., jt. auth. see Clark, Forrest D.

Loret, Pierre. The Story of the Mass: From the Last Supper to the Present Day. LC 82-83984. 144p. 1982. pap. 6.95 (0-89243-171-7) Liguori Pubns.

Loret, Victor. La Flore Pharaonique. 2nd ed. 145p. 1975. reprint ed. write for info. (3-487-05576-7, Pub. by Georg Olms GW) Lubrecht & Cramer.

Loretan, Joseph O. Teaching the Disadvantaged: New Curriculum Approaches. LC 66-15325. (Illus.). 256p. reprint ed. 73.00 (0-8357-9610-8, 2016939) Bks Demand.

Loreto, Luigi. Un Epoca di Buon Senso: Decisione, Consens e Stato a Roma Tra il 326 e il 264 a.C. 268p. (ITA.). 1993. pap. 44.00 (90-256-1059-5, Pub. by A M Hakkert NE) Benjamins North Am.

Loreto, Remo A. The TI 99-4A in Bits & Bytes. Wartman, Robert, ed. (Illus.). (Orig.). 1983. pap. 14.99 (0-914209-01-9) R A Loreto.

Lorette, Lineaus H. Communitarianism: A Prospectus for Revolution. Scales, Nancy, ed. 65p. (Orig.). 1990. pap. 10.00 (0-932225-01-2) Comm Pr.

— Medicine Ball Exercise Cycles. (Illus.). 99p. 1984. 16.95 (0-932225-00-4) Comm Pr.

Lorette, Richard. Cases in the Management of Information Systems & Information Technology. 592p. (C). 1990. pap. text ed. 45.95 (0-256-07122-5) Irwin.

Loretto, M. H. Electron Beam Analysis of Materials. 2nd ed. LC 93-32187. 1993. write for info. (0-412-47790-4, Chap & Hall NY) Chapman & Hall.

Loretto, M. H., ed. Dislocations & Properties of Real Materials. 382p. 1985. pap. text ed. 62.00 (0-904357-74-0, Pub. by Inst Materials UK) Ashgate Pub Co.

Loretz, Oswald. Die Konigspsalmen: Die Altorientalisch-Kanaanaische Konigstradition in Judischer Sicht, Teil 1: Psalm 20, 21, 72, 101, 144. (Ugaritisch-Biblische Literatur Ser.: Vol. 6). vii, 261p. (GER.). 1988. text ed. 52.00 (3-927120-01-4, Pub. by UGARIT GW) Eisenbrauns.

— Leberschau, Sundenbock, Asasel in Ugarit und Israel: Leberschau und Jahwestatue in Psalm 27, Psalm 74. (Ugaritisch-Biblische Literatur Ser.: Vol. 3). 138p. 1985. text ed. 30.00 (3-88733-061-7, Pub. by UGARIT GW) Eisenbrauns.

— Der Prolog des Jesaja-Buches (1: 1 - 2: 5) Ugaritlogische und Kolometrische Studien Zum Jesaja-Buch, Band I. (Ugaritisch-Biblische Literatur Ser.: Vol. 1). 171p. (GER.). 1984. text ed. 33.00 (3-88733-054-4, Pub. by UGARIT GW) Eisenbrauns.

— Regenritual und Jahwetag im Joelbuch: Kanaanaischer Hintergrund, Kolometrie, Aufbau und Symbolik Eines Prophetenbuches. (Ugaritisch-Biblische Literatur Ser.: Vol. 4). 189p. (GER.). 1986. text ed. 40.00 (3-88733-068-4, Pub. by UGARIT GW) Eisenbrauns.

— Ugarit-Texte und Thronbesteigungspsalmen: Die Metamorphose des Regenspenders Baal-Jahwe (Ps. 24: 7-10; 29; 47; 93; 95-100; Sowie Ps. 77: 17-20; 114) (Ugaritisch-Biblische Literatur Ser.: Vol. 7). xiv, 550p. (GER.). 1988. text ed. 60.00 (3-927120-04-9, Pub. by UGARIT GW) Eisenbrauns.

Loretz, Oswald & Kottseiper, Ingo. Colometry in Ugaritic & Biblical Poetry: Introduction, Illustrations & Topical Bibliography. (Ugaritisch-Biblische Literatur Ser.: Vol. 5). 166p. 1987. text ed. 33.00 (3-88733-074-9, Pub. by UGARIT GW) Eisenbrauns.

Loretz, Oswald, jt. auth. see Dietrich, Manfried.

Loretz, Oswald, jt. ed. see Dietrich, Manfried.

Lorey, Daniel. The Wildman, the Earth & the Stars. (Orig.). 1994. pap. 13.95 (1-878980-13-0) Delphi IL.

Lorey, David E. The Rise of the Professions in Twentieth-Century Mexico: University Graduates & Occupational Change since 1929. LC 92-15245. (Cycles & Trends Research Ser.: Vol. 2). 1992. 17.95 (0-87903-254-5) UCLA Lat Am Ctr.

— The Rise of the Professions in Twentieth-Century Mexico: University Graduates & Occupational Change Since 1929. 2nd ed. (Cycles & Trends Research Ser.: Vol. 2). 1994. 21.95 (0-87903-257-X) UCLA Lat Am Ctr.

— The University System & Economic Development in Mexico since 1929. LC 93-20289. 288p. (C). 1993. 39.50 (0-8047-2124-6) Stanford U Pr.

Lorey, David E., ed. United States - Mexico Border Statistics since 1900. 512p. (C). 1993. pap. 35.00 (0-87903-251-0) UCLA Lat Am Ctr.

— United States-Mexico Border Statistics since 1900: 1990 Update. LC 93-24225. (Statistical Abstract of Latin America Supplement Ser.: Vol. 13). 1993. 32.50 (0-87903-256-1) UCLA Lat Am Ctr.

Lorey, Dean & Rizzo, Fran. The Adventurer's Guide to Laser Play. 256p. 1987. pap. 3.50 (0-8217-2229-8) Zebra.

Lorge, Antonio, ed. Cuba: What's Next. 32p. (C). 1992. pap. 10.95 (0-935501-50-9) U Miami N-S Ctr.

Lorge, Irving. Influence of Regularly Interpolated Time Intervals Upon Subsequent Learning. LC 73-177011. (Columbia University. Teachers College. Contributions to Education Ser.: No. 438). reprint ed. 22.50 (0-404-55438-5) AMS Pr.

Lorge, Irving, jt. auth. see Brunner, Edmund D.

Lorho, Bernard, ed. Methods & Tools for Compiler Construction: An Advanced Course. LC 84-45239. 406p. reprint ed. pap. 115.80 (0-317-55471-9, 2029221) Bks Demand.

Loria, Achille. The Economic Foundations of Society. 1972. 250.00 (0-87968-305-8) Gordon Pr.

— Karl Marx. 1976. 300.00 (0-87968-304-X) Gordon Pr.

Loria, E. A., ed. Superalloy 718-Metallurgy & Applications. LC 89-60884. (Illus.). 710p. 1989. 41.00 (0-87339-097-0, 352) Minerals Metals.

— Superalloy 718, 625 & Various Derivatives. (Illus.). 800p. 1991. 35.00 (0-87339-173-X, 410) Minerals Metals.

***Loria, E. A. & International Symposium on Superalloys 718, 625, 706 & Various Derivatives Staff, eds.** Superalloys 718, 625, 706 & Various Derivatives: Proceedings of the International Symposium on Superalloys 718, 625, 706 & Various Derivatives Sponsored by the Minerals, Metals & Materials Society & Consponsored by ASM International & National Association of Corrrosion Engineers, held June 26-29, 1994. 969p. 1994. 170.00 (0-87339-235-3) Minerals Metals.

Loria, Edward A., ed. see International Symposium on the Metallurgy & Applications of Superalloy Seven Hundred Eighteen Staff.

***Loria, Stefano.** Picasso. (Masters of Art Ser.). (Illus.). 64p. 1995. lib. bdg. 19.95 (0-87226-318-5) P Bedrick Bks.

Loria, Wilson, tr. see Coutinho, Edilberto.

Lorian, D. D. The Adventures of Zeb-Roo & Weeboo. 16p. (J). (gr. k-3). 1994. pap. 6.00 (0-8059-3585-1) Dorrance.

Lorian, Nicole. A Birthday Present for Mama: A Step Two Book. LC 83-26849. (Step into Reading Bks.). (Illus.). (J). (ps-2). 1984. pap. 3.50 (0-394-86755-6) Random Bks Yng Read.

Lorian, Victor. Antibiotics in Laboratory Medicine. 3rd ed. (Illus.). 1268p. 1991. 185.00 (0-683-05168-7) Williams & Wilkins.

Lorian, Victor, jt. auth. see Silletti, Roger.

Loriaux, Michael. France after Hegemony: International Change & Financial Reform. LC 90-55721. (Cornell Studies in Political Economy). (Illus.). 304p. 1991. 36.50 (0-8014-2483-6) Cornell U Pr.

Loriaux, Michael, jt. ed. see Woo-Cumings, Meredith.

Lorich, Sonja. The Unwomanly Woman in Bernard Shaw's Drama & Her Social & Political Background. 166p. (Orig.). 1973. pap. text ed. 28.00x (91-554-0081-7, Pub. by Almqv & Wiksell SW) Coronet Bks.

Lorie, James H., et al. The Stock Market: Theories & Evidence. 2nd ed. 192p. (C). 1984. pap. text ed. 36.95 (0-256-01917-7) Irwin.

***Lorie, Peter.** The Millennium Planner: Your Personal Guide to the Year 2000. (Illus.). 128p. 1995. 24.95 (0-670-85682-7, Viking Studio) Studio Bks.

— Revelation: The Prophecies, the Apocalypse, & Beyond. LC 93-49383. 1995. 22.50 (0-671-88872-2) S&S Trade.

— Superstitions. (Illus.). 256p. 1992. 22.50 (0-671-78183-9) S&S Trade.

Lorie, Peter & Greene, Liz. Nostradamus: The Millennium & Beyond--the Prophecies to 2016. LC 92-43628. (Illus.). 224p. 1993. 20.00 (0-671-79698-4) S&S Trade.

***Lorie, Peter & Mascetti, Manuela D.** Nostradamus: Prophecies for Women. LC 94-45227. 1995. write for info. (0-671-89656-3) S&S Trade.

Lorie, Peter, jt. auth. see Hewitt, V. J.

Lorie, R. SQL & Its Applications. 1990. text ed. 48.00 (0-13-837956-4) P-H.

Loriedo, Camillo & Vella, Gaspare. Paradox & the Family System. LC 91-29684. 240p. 1992. 28.95 (0-87630-635-0) Brunner-Mazel.

***Loriferne, Bernard.** Analog-Digital & Digital-Analog Conversion. fac. ed. 206p. 1983. reprint ed. pap. 58.80 (0-7837-8287-X, 2049069) Bks Demand.

Lorig, et al. Living a Healthy Life with Chronic Conditions: Self-Management of Heart Disease, Arthritis, Strokes, Diabetes, Asthma, Bronchitis, Emphysema, & Others. 280p. 1994. pap. 14.95 (0-923521-28-3) Bull Pub.

Lorig, Kate. Arthritis Helpbook. 3rd ed. 1990. pap. 12.45 (0-201-52403-1) Addison-Wesley.

— Patient Education: A Practical Approach. 176p. 1991. pap. 22.95 (0-8151-5607-3) Mosby Yr Bk.

***Lorig, Kate & Fries, James F.** The Arthritis Helpbook: A Tested Self-Management Program for Coping with Your Arthritis & Fibromyalgia. 4th ed. 288p. 1995. pap. 13.46 (0-201-40963-1) Addison-Wesley.

***Loriggio, Francesco, ed.** Social Pluralism & Literary History: The Literature of Italian Immigration. (Essay Ser.: No. 22). 300p. 1995. 20.00 (1-55071-018-4) Guernica Editions.

Loriggio, Francesco, tr. see Campanile, Achille.

Loriggio, Francesco, jt. ed. see Sbrocchi, Leonard G.

Lorimer, A. R. & Hillis, W. S. Cardiovascular Disease. (Treatment in Clinical Medicine Ser.). (Illus.). 300p. 1985. pap. 43.00 (0-387-15426-4) Spr-Verlag.

Lorimer, A. R. & Shepherd, J. Preventive Cardiology. (Illus.). 253p. 1992. 80.00 (0-632-02746-0) Blackwell Sci.

Lorimer, D. L & Lorimer, E. D. Persian Tales. LC 78-63210. (Folktale Ser.). (Illus.). reprint ed. 30.00 (0-685-00405-8) AMS Pr.

Lorimer, David, ed. The Circle of Sacred Dance: Peter Deunov's Paneurythmy. (Illus.). 160p. 1991. pap. 14.95 (1-85230-207-0) Element MA.

— Prophet for Our Times: The Life & Teachings of Peter Deunov. 208p. 1991. pap. 14.95 (1-85230-211-9) Element MA.

Lorimer, Donald L., ed. Neale's Common Foot Disorders: Diagnosis & Management, a General Clinical Guide. 4th ed. LC 92-48834. (Illus.). 404p. 1993. pap. text ed. 42.95 (0-443-04470-8) Churchill.

Lorimer, E. D., jt. auth. see Lorimer, D. L.

Lorimer, E. O., tr. see Carcopino, Jerome.

Lorimer, Eric R. The First Deposit Guide to Starting a New Business: How & Where to Begin. (Illus.). (Orig.). 1992. student ed, pap. 15.00 (0-9635134-0-0) Frst Deposit NCCB.

Lorimer, Frank. Culture & Human Fertility: A Study of the Relation of Cultural Conditions to Fertility in Non-Industrial & Transitional Societies. LC 78-90549. 510p. 1970. reprint ed. text ed. 75.00 (0-8371-2152-3, LOHF, Greenwood Pr) Greenwood.

— The Population of the Soviet Union: History & Prospects. LC 76-29424. reprint ed. 37.50 (0-404-15339-9) AMS Pr.

Lorimer, G. W., jt. ed. see Bennett, M. J.

***Lorimer, George.** Letters from a Self-Made Merchant to His Son. 260p. 1995. 16.95 (0-89526-475-7) Regnery Pub.

Lorimer, George, et al, eds. Advances in Protein Chemistry: Accessory Folding Proteins, Vol. 44. (Illus.). 218p. 1993. text ed. 59.00 (0-12-034244-8) Acad Pr.

Lorimer, Graeme & Lorimer, Sarah. Men Are Like Street Cars. LC 78-122730. (Short Story Index Reprint Ser.). (Illus.). 1977. 18.95 (0-8369-3563-2) Ayer.

Lorimer, Iris, jt. auth. see Walker, Gladys.

Lorimer, J. G. Gazetteer of the Persian Gulf, Oman & Central Arabia, 1908-1915, 9 vols. 4900p. (C). 1987. 4,900.00 (1-85207-030-7, Pub. by Archive Res Ltd UK) St Mut.

Lorimer, J. W., jt. ed. see Cohen-Adad, R.

Lorimer, James. The Institutes of Law: A Treatise of the Principles of Jurisprudence, As Determined by Nature. LC 94-75657. 485p. (C). 1994. reprint ed. 98.00 (1-56169-086-4) W W Gaunt.

Lorimer, James J., et al. The Legal Environment of Insurance, 2 vols., Vol. 1. 4th ed. LC 93-71085. 342p. (C). 1993. text ed. 26.00 (0-89463-064-4) Am Inst FCPCU.

Lorimer, John G. Gazetteer of the Persian Gulf, Oman & Central Arabia, 8 vols. (Illus.). 4968p. 995.00 (0-7165-2350-7, Pub. by Irish Acad Pr IE) Intl Spec Bk.

Lorimer, Lawrence. El Arca de Noe. (Spanish Translations Picturebacks Ser.). (Illus.). 32p. (SPA.). (J). (ps-3). 1993. pap. 2.25 (0-394-85129-3) Random Bks Yng Read.

L

Lorimer, P. The Special Theory of Relativity for Mathematics Students. 112p. 1990. text ed. 36.00 (*981-02-0254-7*) World Scientific Pub.

— The Special Theory of Relativity for Mathematics Students. 112p. (C). 1990. 28.00 (*0-317-03851-6*); pap. text ed. 21.00 (*981-02-0255-5*) World Scientific Pub.

Lorimer, Robert, jt. auth. see Ackroyd, Neil.

Lorimer, Rowland & Scanell, Paddy. Mass Communications: A Comparative Introduction. LC 94-19057. 1994. text ed. 19.95 (*0-7190-3947-9*, Pub. by Manchester Univ Pr UK) St Martin.

Lorimer, Rowland M. The Nation in the Schools: Wanted, a Canadian Education. LC 84-215816. (Research in Education Ser.: No. 11). (Illus.). 131p. reprint ed. pap. 37.40 (*0-7837-0555-7*, 2040896) Bks Demand.

Lorimer, Sarah, jt. auth. see Lorimer, Graeme.

Lorimer, Thomas H. Why Not? Why is Premarital Sex Wrong? 142p. 1988. pap. 5.99 (*0-89957-645-1*) AMG Pubs.

Lorin, Amii, pseud. The Best of Joan Hohl: The Tawny Gold Man - Morning Rose, Evening Savage. 382p. 1989. reprint ed. pap. 3.95 (*0-8439-2738-0*) Dorchester Pub Co.

Lorin, Amii. Breeze off the Ocean - Morgan Wade's Woman, 2 vols. in 1. 384p. 1994. mass mkt., pap. text ed. 4.99 (*0-505-51977-1*) Dorchester Pub Co.

— Come Home to Love. 320p. 1992. pap. 3.99 (*0-8439-3317-8*) Dorchester Pub Co.

— Come Home to Love. 320p. 1995. mass mkt. 4.99 (*0-8439-3852-8*) Dorchester Pub Co.

— The Game Is Played. 192p. 1994. pap. 3.99 (*0-8439-3562-6*) Dorchester Pub Co.

— Morning Rose, Evening Savage. 192p. 1994. mass mkt., pap. text ed. 3.99 (*0-8439-3643-6*) Dorchester Pub Co.

— Night Striker. 288p. 1991. reprint ed. pap. 3.99 (*0-8439-3187-6*) Dorchester Pub Co.

— Power & Seduction. 192p. 1995. mass mkt. 3.99 (*0-8439-3736-X*) Dorchester Pub Co.

— Snowbound Weekend; Gambler's Love, 2 bks. in 1. 368p. 1994. pap. 4.99 (*0-505-51935-6*, Love Spell) Dorchester Pub Co.

— The Tawny Gold Man. 256p. 1993. pap. 4.99 (*0-505-51919-4*, Love Spell) Dorchester Pub Co.

— While the Fire Rages. 288p. 1992. reprint ed. pap. 3.99 (*0-8439-3369-0*) Dorchester Pub Co.

Lorin, Amii, pseud. While the Fire Rages - The Game Is Played. 480p. 1989. pap. 3.95 (*0-8439-2842-5*) Dorchester Pub Co.

Lorin, Elisabeth, jt. auth. see King-Hammond, Leslie.

Lorin, Harold. Aspects of Distributed Computer Systems. 2nd ed. 1988. text ed. 69.95 (*0-471-62589-2*) Wiley.

— Introduction to Computer Architecture & Organization. 2nd ed. 359p. 1989. text ed. 54.95 (*0-471-61404-1*, Wiley-Interscience) Wiley.

— Sorting & Sort Systems. (Illus.). 480p. 1975. write for info. (*0-201-14453-0*) Addison-Wesley.

Lorin, Harold & Deitel, Harvey M. Operating Systems. LC 80-10625. (Computer Science: Systems Programming (IBM) Ser.). (Illus.). 480p. (C). 1981. text ed. 41.95 (*0-201-14464-6*) Addison-Wesley.

Lorin, Martin. Appleton & Lange's Review of Pediatrics. 5th ed. 265p. 1993. pap. 26.95 (*0-8385-0057-9*, A0057-8) Appleton & Lange.

Lorinc, John M., ed. see Galova-Lorinc, Sylvia & Hoferka, Stephen R., Jr.

Lorinczy, A. Crystal Growth. 932p. 1992. text ed. 266.00 (*0-87849-545-2*, Pub. by Trans Tech SZ) LPS Dist Ctr.

Loring, Andrew. Rhymers' Lexicon. 928p. 1995. reprint ed. 51.00 (*1-55888-218-9*) Omnigraphics Inc.

Loring, Ann & Kaye, Evelyn. Write & Sell Your TV Drama! LC 84-72315. 100p. (Orig.). 1984. pap. 19.95 (*0-9613963-0-X*) Alek Pub.

Loring, D. W., et al. Amobarbital Effects & Lateralized Brain Function: The Wada Test. King, D. W., ed. xiii, 138p. 1991. 55.00 (*0-387-97738-4*) Spr-Verlag.

Loring, Denis W., ed. Monographs on Varieties of United States Large Cents, 1795-1803. LC 75-39497. (Illus.). 248p. 1976. 40.00 (*0-88000-075-9*) Quarterman.

Loring, Emilie. As Long As I Live. 1976. 19.95 (*0-88411-366-3*, Aeonian Pr) Amereon Ltd.

— Beckoning Trails. 1976. reprint ed. lib. bdg. 19.95 (*0-88411-351-5*, Aeonian Pr) Amereon Ltd.

— Behind the Cloud. reprint ed. lib. bdg. 17.95 (*0-88411-367-1*, Aeonian Pr) Amereon Ltd.

— Beyond the Sound of Guns. reprint ed. lib. bdg. 21.95 (*0-88411-361-2*, Aeonian Pr) Amereon Ltd.

— Bright Skies. 1976. reprint ed. lib. bdg. 20.95 (*0-88411-352-3*, Aeonian Pr) Amereon Ltd.

— A Candle in Her Heart. 1976. reprint ed. lib. bdg. 20.95 (*0-88411-353-1*, Aeonian Pr) Amereon Ltd.

— A Certain Crossroad. reprint ed. lib. bdg. 20.95 (*0-88411-375-2*, Aeonian Pr) Amereon Ltd.

— Fair Tomorrow. reprint ed. 19.95 (*0-88411-368-X*, Aeonian Pr) Amereon Ltd.

— Follow Your Heart. 1976. reprint ed. lib. bdg. 21.95 (*0-88411-354-X*, Aeonian Pr) Amereon Ltd.

— For All Your Life. 1976. reprint ed. lib. bdg. 20.95 (*0-88411-355-8*, Aeonian Pr) Amereon Ltd.

— Forsaking All Others. 276p. reprint ed. lib. bdg. 18.95 (*0-88411-382-5*, Aeonian Pr) Amereon Ltd.

— Gay Courage. reprint ed. lib. bdg. 22.95 (*0-88411-369-8*, Aeonian Pr) Amereon Ltd.

— Here Comes the Sun. reprint ed. lib. bdg. 21.95 (*0-88411-376-0*, Aeonian Pr) Amereon Ltd.

— Hilltops Clear. reprint ed. lib. bdg. 22.95 (*0-88411-377-9*, Aeonian Pr) Amereon Ltd.

— I Take This Man. reprint ed. lib. bdg. 16.95 (*0-88411-370-1*, Aeonian Pr) Amereon Ltd.

— In Times Like This. 1976. reprint ed. lib. bdg. 20.95 (*0-88411-356-6*, Aeonian Pr) Amereon Ltd.

— It's a Great World. 308p. reprint ed. lib. bdg. 19.95 (*0-88411-383-3*, Aeonian Pr) Amereon Ltd.

— Keepers of the Faith. 1976. reprint ed. lib. bdg. 20.95 (*0-88411-357-4*, Aeonian Pr) Amereon Ltd.

— A Key to Many Doors. 1976. reprint ed. lib. bdg. 20.95 (*0-88411-358-2*, Aeonian Pr) Amereon Ltd.

— Lighted Windows. reprint ed. lib. bdg. 22.95 (*0-88411-378-7*, Aeonian Pr) Amereon Ltd.

— Look to the Stars. reprint ed. lib. bdg. 19.95 (*0-88411-371-X*, Aeonian Pr) Amereon Ltd.

— Love Came by Laughing. 18.95 (*0-89190-128-0*, Am Repr) Amereon Ltd.

— My Dearest Love. 1976. reprint ed. lib. bdg. 19.95 (*0-88411-359-0*, Aeonian Pr) Amereon Ltd.

— No Time for Love. large type ed. 1977. 21.95 (*0-85456-538-8*) Ulverscroft.

— Rainbow at Dusk. 1976. reprint ed. lib. bdg. 22.95 (*0-88411-360-4*, Aeonian Pr) Amereon Ltd.

— The Solitary Horseman. reprint ed. lib. bdg. 18.95 (*0-88411-379-5*, Aeonian Pr) Amereon Ltd.

— Stars in Your Eyes. 1976. reprint ed. lib. bdg. 20.95 (*0-88411-362-0*, 362, Aeonian Pr) Amereon Ltd.

— Swift Water. reprint ed. lib. bdg. 23.95 (*0-88411-380-9*, Aeonian Pr) Amereon Ltd.

— There Is Always Love. 1976. reprint ed. lib. bdg. 20.95 (*0-88411-363-9*, Aeonian Pr) Amereon Ltd.

— Throw Wide the Door. reprint ed. lib. bdg. 19.95 (*0-88411-372-8*, Aeonian Pr) Amereon Ltd.

— The Trail of Conflict. reprint ed. lib. bdg. 19.95 (*0-88411-381-7*, Aeonian Pr) Amereon Ltd.

— Uncharted Seas. reprint ed. lib. bdg. 22.95 (*0-88411-373-6*, Aeonian Pr) Amereon Ltd.

— We Ride the Gale. reprint ed. lib. bdg. 22.95 (*0-88411-374-4*, Aeonian Pr) Amereon Ltd.

— When Hearts Are Light Again. 1976. reprint ed. lib. bdg. 21.95 (*0-88411-365-5*, Aeonian Pr) Amereon Ltd.

— Where Beauty Dwells. 1976. reprint ed. lib. bdg. 22.95 (*0-88411-364-7*, Aeonian Pr) Amereon Ltd.

Loring, Gloria. Gloria Lorings Guide to Health & Beauty. (Illus.). 128p. (Orig.). 1985. pap. write for info. (*0-932565-00-X*) Camex.

— Parenting a Diabetic Child: A Practical, Empathetic Guide to Help You & Your Child Live with Diabetes. 240p. 1991. 19.95 (*0-929923-33-2*) Lowell Hse.

— Parenting a Diabetic Child: A Practical, Empathetic Guide to Help You & Your Child Live with Diabetes. 192p. 1993. pap. 12.95 (*1-56565-001-8*) Lowell Hse.

Loring, H. H., ed. see Cannon, Thomas H.

Loring, Honey & Birch, Jeremy. You're on... Teaching Assertiveness & Communication Skills. (Illus.). 85p. (Orig.). 1984. pap. 10.95 (*0-9613102-0-0*) StressPress.

Loring, Honey & Harris, John. The Big Good Wolf. (Illus.). 28p. (J). (ps-6). 1990. pap. text ed. 2.75 (*0-9626566-0-7*) Gone Dogs.

Loring, Jewell. Indialantic, Florida: Then, Now, & Tomorrow. Coburn, Alan, ed. 96p. (Orig.). 1993. pap. 14.95 (*0-9636857-0-8*) Twn Indialantic.

Loring, Marianne, tr. see Drigalski, Dorte V.

Loring, Marti T. Emotional Abuse. LC 94-10293. 1994. text ed. 29.95 (*0-02-919343-5*) Free Pr.

Loring, Murray. Bees & the Law. LC 80-66362. 128p. (C). 1981. 8.96 (*0-915698-07-2*) Dadant & Sons.

Loring, Murray, jt. auth. see Favre, David S.

Loring, Patricia. Spiritual Discernment & the Use of Clearness Committees among Friends. LC 92-62676. 32p. (Orig.). 1992. pap. 3.00 (*0-87574-305-6*) Pendle Hill.

Loring, Tamara, ed. see Bach, Johann S.

Loring, William C. An American Romantic-Realist Abroad: Templeton Strong & His Music. LC 94-19028. (Composers of North America Ser.: No. 4). 1995. write for info. (*0-8108-2766-2*) Scarecrow.

Lorio, Kathryn V., jt. auth. see Swaim, Frederick W., Jr.

Lorio, Penny S. Expenses. Hines, Brenda K., ed. LC 90-64052. 192p. (Orig.). 1991. pap. 8.95 (*0-9628595-0-8*) Paradigm San Diego.

Lorion, Raymond P., ed. Protecting the Children: Strategies for Optimizing Emotional & Behavioral Development. LC 89-28933. (Prevention in Human Services Ser.: Vol. 7, No. 1). (Illus.). 275p. 1990. text ed. 39.95 (*0-86656-970-7*) Haworth Pr.

Loris, Michelle C. Innocence, Loss, & Recovery in the Art of Joan Didion. (American University Studies: English Language & Literature: Ser. IV, Vol. 74). 164p. (C). 1989. text ed. 22.95 (*0-8204-0661-9*) P Lang Pubs.

Loriston-Clarke, Jennie. Lungeing & Long Reining. (Illus.). 95p. 1994. 34.95 (*1-872082-14-9*, Pub. by Kenilworth Pr UK) Half Halt Pr.

— The Young Horse: Breaking & Training. (Illus.). 192p. 1995. 29.95 (*1-57076-023-3*, Trafalgar Sq Pub) Trafalgar.

Lorit, Sergius C. Frances Cabrini. rev. ed. Hearne, Jerry, tr. 136p. 1988. pap. 6.95 (*0-911782-63-X*) New City.

— Francoise Cabrini. (FRE.). 1989. reprint ed. pap. 5.00 (*0-9619397-1-0*) MSSH.

Loriuar, Andrea. Horoscopo De Pasion. Creative Publishing Concepts Staff, ed. (Orig.). (SPA.). 1990. pap. write for info. (*0-944499-83-X*) Editorial Amer.

Lorkovic, Tanja, tr. see Pecujlit, Miroslav.

***Lorkowski, Tom.** Dr. Nim & the Strange Quest. LC 94-62188. (Dr. Nim Ser.: Vol. 2). (Illus.). 25p. (J). (gr. 4-6). 1995. 11.95 (*0-914127-63-2*, L02T) Univ Class.

***Lorkowski, Tommy.** Dr. Nim & the Nombex. LC 94-60703. 30p. (Orig.). (J). (gr. 4 up). 1994. pap. 10.95 (*0-914127-20-9*) Univ Class.

Lorler, Marie L. Shamanic Healing Within the Medicine Wheel. LC 89-7393. 266p. 1989. pap. 16.95 (*0-914732-23-4*) Bro Life Inc.

Lorman, Alba, tr. see Neumann, Eckhard.

Lorme, Anna. A Traitor's Daughter. Bononno, Robert, tr. LC 91-39756. (French Expressions Ser.). 208p. 1993. 18.95 (*0-8419-1294-7*) Holmes & Meier.

Lormier, E. O., tr. see Beljame, Alexandre.

Lormor, Becky, ed. see King, Janie M.

Lorne & MacLean & Offshore Publications Staff. Guia de Operacoes Helicoptero Navio-Tanque: Guide to Helicopter-Ship Operations. (POR.). (C). 1987. 150.00 (*0-685-33865-7*, Pub. by Lorne & MacLean Marine) St Mut.

Lorne & MacLean Marine & Offshore Publications Staff. Chemical Tankers. (C). 1987. 75.00 (*0-685-33869-X*, Pub. by Lorne & MacLean Marine) St Mut.

— COW-IGS Conference Papers & Proceedings. (C). 1987. 150.00 (*0-685-33861-4*, Pub. by Lorne & MacLean Marine) St Mut.

— Cow-IGS Manual. (C). 1987. 250.00 (*0-685-33857-6*, Pub. by Lorne & MacLean Marine) St Mut.

— Dry Dock Planning Manual. (C). 1987. 495.00 (*0-685-33852-5*, Pub. by Lorne & MacLean Marine) St Mut.

— English-Portuguese Marine Engineering Glossary. (C). 1987. 220.00 (*0-685-33858-4*, Pub. by Lorne & MacLean Marine) St Mut.

— Gas Tankers. (C). 1987. 120.00 (*0-685-33871-1*, Pub. by Lorne & MacLean Marine) St Mut.

— Inert Gas Systems Manual. (C). 1987. 180.00 (*0-685-33860-6*, Pub. by Lorne & MacLean Marine) St Mut.

— International Manual of Maritime Safety. (C). 1987. 350.00 (*0-685-33856-8*, Pub. by Lorne & MacLean Marine) St Mut.

— L & M Maritime Correspondence Course Guide. (C). 1987. 150.00 (*0-685-33867-3*, Pub. by Lorne & MacLean Marine) St Mut.

— L & M Training Resources Manual. (C). 1987. 150.00 (*0-685-33866-5*, Pub. by Lorne & MacLean Marine) St Mut.

— Manual de Controle de Incendio de Burques. (SPA.). (C). 1987. 150.00 (*0-685-33864-9*, Pub. by Lorne & MacLean Marine) St Mut.

— Manual de Instrucciones - Sistema de Gas Inerte. (SPA.). (C). 1987. 600.00 (*0-685-33850-9*, Pub. by Lorne & MacLean Marine) St Mut.

— Manual Internacional de Seguranca Maritima. (POR.). (C). 1987. 250.00 (*0-685-33855-X*, Pub. by Lorne & MacLean Marine) St Mut.

— Offshore Fire-Fighting Manual. (C). 1987. 400.00 (*0-685-33853-3*, Pub. by Lorne & MacLean Marine) St Mut.

— Oil Tankers. (C). 1987. 100.00 (*0-685-33870-3*, Pub. by Lorne & MacLean Marine) St Mut.

— Operacion y Seguridad en Burques Tanqueros: Tanker Safety Manual. (SPA.). (C). 1987. 395.00 (*0-685-33863-0*, Pub. by Lorne & MacLean Marine) St Mut.

— Peabody Holmes Inert Gas System Manual. (C). 1987. 140.00 (*0-685-33862-2*, Pub. by Lorne & MacLean Marine) St Mut.

— Ship Squat Manual. (C). 1987. 300.00 (*0-685-33851-7*, Pub. by Lorne & MacLean Marine) St Mut.

— Shipowners Guide to Yard Repairs. (C). 1987. 195.00 (*0-685-33859-2*, Pub. by Lorne & MacLean Marine) St Mut.

— S.O.S. (Ships Operational Safety) Manual. (C). 1987. 300.00 (*0-685-33854-1*, Pub. by Lorne & MacLean Marine) St Mut.

— Steering Gear Systems. (C). 1987. 75.00 (*0-685-33868-1*, Pub. by Lorne & MacLean Marine) St Mut.

— Survival Techniques. (C). 1985. 75.00 (*0-685-33872-X*, Pub. by Lorne & MacLean Marine) St Mut.

Lorne & MacLean Marine Staff, ed. Coal Fired Ships, 3 vols. 1987. 210.00 (*0-317-43652-X*, Pub. by Lorne & MacLean Marine) St Mut.

— Guia de Operacoes Helicoptero Navio-Tanque. (POR.). 1985. 90.00 (*0-317-43661-9*, Pub. by Lorne & MacLean Marine) St Mut.

— Marginal Oilfield & Tanker Conversion '85. 1985. 500.00 (*0-317-43658-9*, Pub. by Lorne & MacLean Marine) St Mut.

— Offshore Safety Procedures Manual. 1987. 600.00 (*0-317-43643-0*, Pub. by Lorne & MacLean Marine) St Mut.

— Peabody Homes Inert Gas System. 1985. 95.00 (*0-317-43648-1*, Pub. by Lorne & MacLean Marine) St Mut.

— Ships Fire-Fighting Manual. 1987. 235.00 (*0-317-43641-4*, Pub. by Lorne & MacLean Marine) St Mut.

Lorne, David. The Last Prisoner. 288p. (Orig.). 1991. mass mkt. 4.50 (*0-380-76287-0*) Avon.

Lorne, Simon M. Acquisitions & Mergers: Negotiated & Contested Transactions, 4 vols., Set. LC 85-4103. (Securities Law Ser.). 1985. ring bd. 445.00 (*0-87632-462-6*) Clark Boardman Callaghan.

— Securities Law Considerations Affecting Employee Benefits Plans. (Corporate Practice Ser.: No. 44). 1985. 92.00 (*0-317-55348-8*) BNA.

Lornell, Christopher. Introducing American Folk Music. 272p. (C). 1993. pap. text ed. write for info. (*0-697-13383-4*) Brown & Benchmark.

***Lornell, Kip.** Happy in the Service of the Lord: African-American Sacred Vocal Harmony Quartets in Memphis. 2nd ed. LC 94-18735. (Illus.). 288p. (C). 1995. pap. 19.95x (*0-87049-877-0*) U of Tenn Pr.

— Virginia's Blues, Gospel, & Country Records, 1902-1943. LC 89-5613. 248p. 1989. 27.00 (*0-8131-1658-9*) U Pr of Ky.

Lornell, Kip, jt. auth. see Wolfe, Charles.

Lorning, Patrick & Johnson, Joy. Lucy Lettuce. (Illus.). 16p. 1994. pap. 5.95 (*1-56123-072-3*) Centering Corp.

Loroch, Kim J. Vessel Voyage Data Analysis: A Comparative Study. LC 65-20766. (Illus.). 160p. reprint ed. 45.60 (*0-8357-9075-4*, 2016601) Bks Demand.

Lorona, Lionel V. Bibliography of Latin American & Caribbean Bibliographies, 1989-1990. (Bibliography & Reference Ser.: No. 27). viii, 48p. (Orig.). 1990. pap. 17.50 (*0-917617-27-4*) SALALM.

— Bibliography of Latin American & Caribbean Bibliographies, 1990-1991. (Bibliography & Reference Ser.: No. 30). 125p. 1992. pap. 21.50 (*0-917617-29-0*) SALALM.

Lorona, Lionel V., comp. Bibliography of Latin American & Caribbean Bibliographies, Annual Report, 1991-1992. (Bibliography & Reference Ser.: No. 31). 59p. (Orig.). 1992. pap. 20.00 (*0-917617-34-7*) SALALM.

Lorona, Lionel V., ed. A Bibliography of Latin American & Caribbean Bibliographies, 1985-1989, Supplement No. 5: Social Sciences & Humanities. 330p. 1993. 39.50 (*0-8108-2702-6*) Scarecrow.

— Bibliography of Latin American & Caribbean Bibliographies, 1987-1988. (Bibliography & Reference Ser.: No. 23). (Orig.). 1988. pap. 15.00 (*0-917617-20-7*) SALALM.

— Bibliography of Latin American & Caribbean Bibliographies, 1988-1989. (Bibliography & Reference Ser.: No. 25). 1989. 17.50 (*0-917617-23-1*) SALALM.

— A Bibliography of Latin American Bibliographies, 1980-1984: Social Sciences & Humanities, Supplement to Arthur E. Gropp's a Bibliography of Latin American Bibliographies, No. 4. LC 86-22093. 239p. 1987. 29.50 (*0-8108-1941-4*) Scarecrow.

Lorona, Luisa, ed. see Bonta, Vanna.

***Lorquin, Bertrand.** Maillol. LC 94-61693. (Illus.). 200p. 1995. 40.00 (*0-500-97417-9*) Thames Hudson.

Lorr, David & Garshnek, Victoria, eds. Working in Orbit & Beyond: The Challenges for Space Medicine. LC 57-43769. (Science & Technology Ser.: Vol. 72). (Illus.). 188p. 1989. lib. bdg. 45.00 (*0-87703-295-5*, Pub. by Am Astro Soc); pap. text ed. 35.00 (*0-87703-296-3*, Pub. by Am Astro Soc) Univelt Inc.

Lorr, M. Explorations in Typing Psychotics. LC 66-24021. 1966. 109.00 (*0-08-011888-7*, Pub. by Pergamon Repr UK) Franklin.

Lorr, M. & Lkett, C. Syndromes of Psychosis. LC 63-19266. 1963. 120.00 (*0-08-010416-9*, Pub. by Pergamon Repr UK) Franklin.

Lorr, Maurice. Cluster Analysis for Social Scientists. LC 82-49283. (Jossey-Bass Social & Behavioral Science Ser.). (Illus.). 251p. reprint ed. pap. 71.60 (*0-8357-4905-3*, 2037835) Bks Demand.

Lorr, Maurice, jt. ed. see Strack, Stephen.

Lorr, Regina E. Miracles in the Kitchen: Delicious & Nutritious Replacements for Junk Foods. LC 91-60773. 304p. (Orig.). 1992. pap. 12.95 (*0-914711-09-1*) Rishis Inst.

Lorr, Regina E. & Crary, Robert W. The Path of Light. LC 83-71354. 192p. (Orig.). 1983. pap. 8.95 (*0-87516-520-6*) DeVorss.

THE PATH OF LIGHT is a Metaphysical classic. It contains many of the highest Spiritual Truths as well as the basic principles of the Teachings of Metaphysics. We have received many letters, unsolicited testimonies from all parts of the world as well as phone calls, telling us how the Sacred Truths explained in this book helped them MASTER & overcome seemingly insurmountable obstacles. In one case, a young man gratefully explained how the Truths of this Spiritual Philosophy saved him from committing suicide. These Teachings of Metaphysical Truths will help you achieve the greatest Goal on earth...SELF-MASTERY. Self-Mastery is attained by CONSCIOUSLY living the Spiritual Laws of body, mind, soul, & Spirit as explained in this text. You will learn to attain heaven right here on earth. By learning & applying these Sacred Truths, you will advance gradually into Cosmic (Christ) Consciousness & achieve an abundance of all good things. God's Will is that everyone on earth learn to Master the negative in themselves & become close to the God Self within, thus attaining the highest Spiritual Contact & acquiring the Spiritual/material blessings of Peace, Harmony, Happiness, Love, Success, & Abundance of Supply. Contact Publisher, DeVorss & Co., P.O. Box 550, Marina del Ray, CA 90294-0550; 800-843-5743. ***Publisher Provided Annotation.***

Lorrah, Jean. Metamorphosis. (Star Trek: The Next Generation Ser.). 416p. 1990. mass mkt. 5.99 (*0-671-68402-7*) PB.

— Metamorphosis. braille ed. 541p. 1992. Braille. vinyl bd. 43.28 (*1-56956-283-0*, BR8250) W A T Braille.

— Survivors. Stern, Dave, ed. (Star Trek: The Next Generation Ser.: No. 4). (Orig.). 1991. mass mkt. 5.50 (*0-671-74290-6*) PB.

— The Vulcan Academy Murders. (Star Trek Ser.: No. 20). (Orig.). 1991. mass mkt. 4.95 (*0-671-74283-3*) PB.

An Asterisk (*) at the beginning of an entry indicates that the title is appearing in BIP for the first time.

Lorrain. Electromagnetism. 2nd ed. LC 89-23822. (C). 1995. pap. text ed. write for info. (*0-7167-2096-5*) W H Freeman.
— Lushai Grammar & Dictionary. 346p. (ENG.). 1984. 24. 95 (*0-7859-7514-4*) Fr & Eur.
Lorrain, J. H. Lushai Grammar & Dictionary. 346p. 1984. reprint ed. 24.00 (*0-88431-060-4*) IBD Ltd.
Lorrain, Jacques, et al, eds. Comprehensive Management of the Menopause. LC 93-3255. (Clinical Perspectives in Obstetrics & Gynecology Ser.). 1993. 79.00 (*0-387-97972-7*) Spr-Verlag.
Lorrain, Jean. Monsieur De Phocas. (Dedalus European Fiction Ser.). 320p. 1993. pap. 14.95 (*0-7818-0210-5*) Hippocrene Bks.
Lorrain, Paul, et al. Electromagnetic Fields & Waves. 3rd ed. LC 86-31803. (Physics Ser.). (Illus.). 754p. (C). 1995. text ed. write for info. (*0-7167-1823-5*) W H Freeman.
Lorrain, R. D., jt. auth. see Douglas, Ian.
Lorrain-Smith, R. An Economic Analysis of Silvicultural Options for Broadleaved Woodlands, Vol. II. 1982. 42. 00 (*0-85074-042-8*) St Mut.
Lorrain-Smith, Roy. Computers in Forestry: Use of Spreadsheets. LC 93-3425. (Forestry Ser.: Vol. 1). 192p. 1993. text ed. 59.95 (*0-471-93961-7*) Wiley.

Lorraine, Genece. Primal Play. 136p. (Orig.). 1995. pap. 14.95 (*1-886992-00-2*) Thoth Publ. According to the ancient mystical teachings, we all have the capacity for consciously inducing & maximizing the experience of ecstasy. This book journeys you beyond the realm of limitations into a multidimensional world of fantasy where spirit is free in primal play. Now, you can take a tantalizing adventure that will awaken your imagination & enhance your relationship through the erotic mind. PRIMAL PLAY is a collection of tasteful, erotic poems about the imagination & romantic journeys. APRICOT CREAM TO SOOTHE YOUR MOST SENSUAL DREAMS. LUSCIOUS APPETITE FILLED WITH THE SWEETNESS OF A SUCCULENT KISS. SUMMER DAYS IN HEAT BURN MY SOUL IN PASSIONATE FANTASIES OF YOU. SOFT NIGHTS OF FRUITFUL LOVE TOUCHES MY TONGUE WITH THE EXOTIC TASTE OF YOUR ORGASMIC PLEASURES. TOGETHER, WE SAVOR THE ORCHARD OF SEXUAL JUICES--SWEET JUICE OF LOVE. Author Genece Lorraine states, "For centuries sexy images have provoked our thoughts as a way to express our understanding of human sexuality. In fact, the most accepted form of sexual expression throughout history has been through art & writing. Each poem in this special collection is filled with subtle visual images giving a fresh new perspective on sexuality." Call or write for information to order, Thoth Publishing, 8635 W. Sahara, Suite 544, Las Vegas, NV 89117. (702) 368-2451.** ***Publisher Provided Annotation.

Lorraine, Miranda, jt. auth. see Kursinski, Anne.
Lorraine, Tamsin E. Gender, Identity & the Production of Meaning. 227p. (C). 1991. pap. text ed. 19.95 (*0-8133-7878-8*) Westview.
Lorrance, Arleen. Born of Love. (Illus.). 200p. (Orig.). 1981. pap. 14.95 (*0-916192-16-4*) L P Pubns.
— Images. LC 85-23118. 83p. 1985. 8.95 (*0-916192-39-3*) L P Pubns.
— India Through Eyes of Love. (Illus.). (Orig.). 1982. pap. 7.95 (*0-916192-18-0*) L P Pubns.
— The Love Project. rev. ed. LC 78-15162. (Illus.). 103p. 1978. pap. 6.95 (*0-916192-14-8*) L P Pubns.
— Musings for Meditation. LC 76-14783. (Illus.). 180p. (Orig.). 1976. pap. 7.95 (*0-916192-03-2*) L P Pubns.
— Why Me? How to Heal What's Hurting You. LC 77-88151. 186p. 1982. 11.95 (*0-916192-19-9*) L P Pubns.
Lorrance, Arleen & Pike, Diane K. The Love Project Way. 216p. (Orig.). 1980. pap. 10.95 (*0-916192-15-6*) L P Pubns.
Lorriman, John & Kenjo, Takashi. Japan's Winning Margins: Management, Training, & Education. (Illus.). 232p. 1994. 24.95 (*0-19-856374-4*) OUP.
***Lorriman, John, et al.** Upside down Management: The Only Way to Win. LC 95-16851. 1995. pap. write for info. (*0-07-709067-5*) McGraw.
***Lorrimer, Claire.** Connie's Daughter. 1995. lib. bdg. 22.00 (*0-7278-4731-7*) Severn Hse.
— Last Year's Nightingale. large type ed. 752p. 1993. 23.95 (*0-7089-8708-7*, Charnwood) Ulverscroft.
— The Secret of Quarry House. large type ed. 1991. 21.95 (*0-7089-2539-1*) Ulverscroft.
— Secret of Quarry House. 1994. reprint ed. lib. bdg. 19.00 (*0-7278-4649-3*) Severn Hse.
— The Silver Link. large type ed. (Charnwood Large Print Ser.). 736p. 1995. 25.95 (*0-7089-8815-6*, Charnwood) Ulverscroft.
— Variations: Collected Short Stories. large type ed. (General Ser.). 368p. 1993. 21.95 (*0-7089-2880-3*) Ulverscroft.
— A Voice in the Dark. large type ed. 1991. 21.95 (*0-7089-2410-7*) Ulverscroft.
Lorrimer, Clarie. Relentless Storm. 1994. 19.00 (*0-7278-4580-2*) Severn Hse.
Lorsch, Jay W., ed. Handbook of Organizational Behavior. (Illus.). 544p. (C). 1986. text ed. 91.00 (*0-13-380650-2*) P-H.
Lorsch, Jay W. & MacIver, Elizabeth. Pawns & Potentates: The Reality of America's Corporate Boards. 1989. text ed. 24.95 (*0-07-103252-5*) McGraw.
Lorsch, Jay W., jt. auth. see Donaldson, Gordon A.
Lorsch, Jay W., jt. auth. see Lawrence, Paul R.
Lorsch, Susan E. Where Nature Ends: The Designation of Landscape in Arnold, Swinburne, Hardy, Conrad & Woolf. LC 81-72056. 240p. 1983. 26.50 (*0-8386-3162-2*) Fairleigh Dickinson.
Lorsch, Susan E., jt. ed. see Keener, Frederick M.
Lortat-Jacob, Bernard. Sardinian Chronicles. Fagan, Teresa L., tr. LC 94-10766. (Chicago Studies in Ethnomusicology). 120p. 1994. pap. text ed. 19.95 (*0-226-49341-5*) U Ch Pr.
— Sardinian Chronicles. Fagan, Teresa L., tr. LC 94-10766. (Chicago Studies in Ethnomusicology). 120p. 1995. lib. bdg. 47.50 (*0-226-49340-7*) U Ch Pr.
Lorthioir, Pascal. Commercial Estimator for Europe: L'Estimatif Commercial Bauschatzpreise Fur Gewerbliche Bauten. 265p. 1993. write for info. (*1-56842-007-2*); disk write for info. (*1-56842-009-9*) Marshall & Swift.
— Residential Estimator for Europe: L'Estimatif Residentiel Bauschatzpreise Fur Eigenheime. 172p. 1993. write for info. (*1-56842-006-4*); disk write for info. (*1-56842-010-2*) Marshall & Swift.
Lortie, Dan C. Schoolteacher: A Sociological Study. LC 74-11428. 1977. reprint ed. pap. text ed. 12.95 (*0-226-49354-7*, P748) U Ch Pr.
Lortie, Jeanne M., ed. Spun Yarns. 1986. lib. bdg. 7.00 (*0-936773-00-6*) Priory Bks.
Lortie, Jeanne M., jt. auth. see Weygant, Noemi.
Lorton, David. The Juridical Terminology for International Relations in Egyptian Texts through Dyn. XVIII. LC 73-8114. (Johns Hopkins Near Eastern Studies). 208p. reprint ed. pap. 59.30 (*0-685-15522-6*, 2026327) Bks Demand.
Lorton, Elizabeth, ed. see Blanc, Iris.
Lorton, John W. & Walley, Bertha L. The Administrator's Handbook for Child Care Education. LC 86-15204. 160p. 1987. pap. 12.95 (*0-89334-094-4*) Humanics Ltd.
Lorton, Mary B. Workjobs II: Number Activities for Early Childhood. 1978. spiral bd. 17.50 (*0-201-04302-5*) Addison-Wesley.
Lorton, Paul, Jr., jt. auth. see Muscat, Eugene J.
Lorton, Sherry. Merchant's Edge: A Guide to Grain Marketing. 2nd ed. 330p. 1994. pap. 22.00 (*0-87563-487-7*) Stipes.
Lorton, Sherry & White, Don. Profit on the Farm: A Marketing Guide to Help the Farmer Sell Better. 132p. (Orig.). (C). 1994. pap. text ed. 14.95 (*0-87563-501-6*) Stipes.
Lortz, Joseph. Francis, the Incomparable Saint. LC 85-82307. (Franciscan Pathways Ser.). 1986. 6.00 (*0-318-35490-X*) Franciscan Inst.
Lortz, Richard. Bereavements. 22.00 (*0-932966-08-X*) Permanent Pr.
— Dracula's Children. 208p. 1982. 22.00 (*0-932966-15-2*) Permanent Pr.
— Lovers Living, Lovers Dead. 224p. 22.00 (*0-933256-28-0*); pap. 16.00 (*0-933256-29-9*) Second Chance.
— The Valdepenas. LC 79-66114. 224p. 1984. 5.95 (*0-933256-49-3*); pap. 22.00 (*0-933256-06-X*) Second Chance.
Lortzing, F., ed. see Zeller, Eduard.
Lorusso, Andy. The Pierogie Diet: One Hundred One Fun Ways to Use & Enjoy Pierogies. (Illus.). 55p. (Orig.). 1989. pap. 2.95 (*0-317-93014-1*) Happy Heart.
Lorusso, Edward N., ed. see McAlmon, Robert.
Lorusso, Julia & Glick, Joel. Healing Stoned: The Therapeutic Use of Gems & Minerals. 2nd ed. 1985. reprint ed. pap. 12.95 (*0-914732-05-6*) Bro Life Inc.
— Stratagems. 108p. (Orig.). 1985. pap. 7.95 (*0-914732-15-3*) Bro Life Inc.
Lorwin, Lewis L. American Federation of Labor. LC 70-174559. (Library of American Labor History). 1972. reprint ed. 49.50 (*0-678-00880-9*) Kelley.
— International Labor Movement: History, Policies, Outlooks. LC 73-13404. 366p. 1973. reprint ed. text ed. 65.00 (*0-8371-7060-5*, LOLM, Greenwood Pr) Greenwood.
— Labor & Internationalism. (Brookings Institution Reprint Ser.). reprint ed. lib. bdg. 29.50 (*0-697-00164-4*) Irvington.
— Youth Work Programs: Problems & Policies, Vol. No. 3. LC 74-1694. (Children & Youth Ser.). 212p. 1974. reprint ed. 23.95 (*0-405-05970-1*) Ayer.
Lorwin, Lewis L. & Flexner, Jean A. American Federation of Labor. LC 70-126699. 1970. reprint ed. 15.00 (*0-404-04027-6*) AMS Pr.
— Syndicalism in France, by Louis Levine. LC 76-127443. (Columbia University. Studies in the Social Sciences: No. 116). reprint ed. 22.50 (*0-404-51116-3*) AMS Pr.
Lorwin, Louis, see Louis Levine, pseud..
Lorwin, Val R. French Labor Movement. LC 54-7062. (Wertheim Publications in Industrial Relations). 365p. 1954. 22.50 (*0-674-32200-2*) HUP.
Lory, Hillis. Japan's Military Masters: The Army in Japanese Life. LC 72-9367. 256p. 1973. reprint ed. text ed. 35.00 (*0-8371-6581-4*, LOMM, Greenwood Pr) Greenwood.
***Los, Adolph.** The Beauty of God & His Creation. 170p. (Orig.). 1994. pap. write for info. (*1-885591-18-7*) Morris Pubng.
Los Alamos Scientific Laboratory Public Relations Staff. Los Alamos, Beginning of An Era: 1943-1945. LC 92-8820. (Illus.). 64p. 1986. pap. 4.00 (*0-941232-07-7*) Los Alamos Hist Soc.
Los Angeles Children's Museum Staff. Color Your Way Through L. A. Polsky, Carol, ed. U. S.-Japan Cross Culture Center & La, Opinion Editors, trs. (Illus.). 56p. (Orig.). (ENG, JPN & SPA.). (J). (gr. k up). 1983. 3.95 (*0-914953-00-1*) Los Angeles.
Los Angeles Commission on Assaults Against Women Staff. Surviving Sexual Assault. (Illus.). 64p. 1992. pap. 4.99 (*0-312-92796-7*); pap. 134.73 (*0-312-92798-3*) Congdon & Weed.
— Surviving Sexual Assault. 96p. 1991. reprint ed. pap. 6.95 (*0-86553-219-2*) Congdon & Weed.
Los Angeles County Bar Association, Litigation Section Staff, et al, eds. California Practice Handbook: Depositions. LC 92-29942. 1992. write for info. (*0-8205-1782-8*) Bender.
— California Practice Handbook: General Discovery Principles. LC 92-2455. 1992. write for info. (*0-8205-1784-4*) Bender.
Los Angeles County Schools Ser. Audio Worksheets, 4 vol. set. (Auditory Skills Instructional Planning System Ser.: 3rd Component). (Illus.). 356p. 1980. ring bd. 380.00 (*0-943292-13-1*) Foreworks.
Los Angeles County Schools Staff. Audio Worksheets, Vol. 1. (Illus.). 1980. 95.00 (*0-943292-09-3*) Foreworks.
— Audio Worksheets, Vol. 2. (Illus.). 1980. 95.00 (*0-943292-10-7*) Foreworks.
— Audio Worksheets, Vol. 3. (Illus.). 1980. 95.00 (*0-943292-11-5*) Foreworks.
— Audio Worksheets, Vol. 4. (Illus.). 1980. 95.00 (*0-943292-12-3*) Foreworks.
— Auditory Skills Curriculum. LC 79-52375. (Auditory Skills Instructional Planning System Ser.: 1st Component). 329p. 1979. ring bd. 50.00 (*0-943292-07-7*) Foreworks.
— Auditory Skills Instructional Planning System, 4 Components. (Illus.). 1979. ring bd. 555.00 (*0-943292-06-9*) Foreworks.
Los Angeles Police Department Staff. Law Enforcement in Los Angeles: Los Angeles Police Department Annual Report, 1924. LC 74-3831. (Criminal Justice in America Ser.). 1974. reprint ed. 24.95 (*0-405-06151-X*) Ayer.
Los Angeles Public Library Staff. Catalog of the Police Library of the Los Angeles Public Library, 2 vols., Set. 1972. lib. bdg. 220.00 (*0-8161-0964-8*, Hall Library) G K Hall.
— Catalog of the Police Library of the Los Angeles Public Library, First Supplement. (Library Catalogs). 1980. lib. bdg. 255.00 (*0-8161-0328-3*, Hall Library) G K Hall.
— Index to the Stories of Guy de Maupassant. 1970. lib. bdg. 75.00 (*0-8161-0513-8*, Hall Library) G K Hall.
Los Angeles Times Editors. Nominating a President: The Process & the Press. LC 80-13824. 168p. 1980. 38.50 (*0-275-90509-8*, C0509, Praeger Pubs); pap. 14.95 (*0-03-057858-2*, Praeger Pubs) Greenwood.
Los Angeles Times Food Editors. The Los Angeles Times California Cookbook. Balsley, Betsy, ed. (Illus.). 528p. 1983. pap. 14.95 (*0-452-25448-5*, Plume) NAL-Dutton.
Los Angeles Times Staff. The San Francisco Bay Earthquake 1989: Portraits of Tragedy & Courage. Turner, Craig, ed. (Illus.). 96p. (Orig.). 1989. pap. 10.95 (*0-9619095-1-X*) LA Times.
— Understanding the Riots: Los Angeles & the Aftermath of the Rodney King Verdict. 1992. pap. 14.95 (*0-9619095-9-5*) LA Times.
— Witness to War: Images from the Persian War. 1991. pap. 16.95 (*0-9619095-6-0*) LA Times.
Los Angeles Unified School District Staff. Drafting. LC 77-73291. 64p. (gr. 7-9). 1978. pap. text ed. 5.76 (*0-02-820320-8*) Glencoe.
— Electricity. LC 77-73243. 96p. (gr. 7-9). 1978. pap. text ed. 6.48 (*0-02-820300-3*) Glencoe.
— General Industrial Education. LC 77-73280. 552p. (gr. 7-9). 1978. text ed. 30.64 (*0-02-820350-X*) Glencoe.
— Getting a Job. (Project Get That Job Ser.). (Illus.). 48p. (Orig.). (YA). (gr. 7-12). 1990. student ed 4.95 (*1-56119-093-4*); teacher ed 1.95 (*1-56119-094-2*) Educ Pr MD.
— Getting a Job, Set. (Project Get That Job Ser.). (Illus.). 48p. (Orig.). (YA). (gr. 7-12). 1990. student ed, teacher ed 44.95 (*1-56119-095-0*) Educ Pr MD.
— Graphic Arts. LC 77-73302. 128p. (gr. 7-9). 1978. pap. text ed. 5.32 (*0-02-820340-2*) Glencoe.
— Metalworking. LC 77-73297. 96p. (gr. 7-9). 1978. pap. text ed. 7.04 (*0-02-820290-2*) Glencoe.
— Starting Your New Job. (Project Get That Job Ser.). (Illus.). 48p. (Orig.). (YA). (gr. 7-12). 1990. student ed 4.95 (*1-56119-096-9*); teacher ed 1.95 (*1-56119-097-7*) Educ Pr MD.
— Starting Your New Job, Set. (Project Get That Job Ser.). (Illus.). 48p. (Orig.). (YA). (gr. 7-12). 1990. student ed, teacher ed 44.95 (*1-56119-098-5*) Educ Pr MD.
— Woodworking. LC 77-73286. 96p. (gr. 7-9). 1978. pap. text ed. 5.32 (*0-02-820400-X*) Glencoe.
— Working with Others. (Project Get That Job Ser.). (Illus.). 48p. (Orig.). (YA). (gr. 7-12). 1990. student ed 4.95 (*1-56119-090-X*); teacher ed 1.95 (*1-56119-091-8*) Educ Pr MD.
— Working with Others, Set. (Project Get That Job Ser.). (Illus.). 48p. (Orig.). (YA). (gr. 7-12). 1990. 44.95 (*1-56119-092-6*) Educ Pr MD.
— You & Your Attitude. (Project Get That Job Ser.). (Illus.). 48p. (Orig.). (YA). (gr. 7-12). 1990. student ed 4.95 (*1-56119-087-X*); teacher ed 1.95 (*1-56119-088-8*) Educ Pr MD.
— You & Your Attitude, Set. (Project Get That Job Ser.). (Illus.). 48p. (Orig.). (YA). (gr. 7-12). 1990. 44.95 (*1-56119-089-6*) Educ Pr MD.
Los Angeles Unified School District Staff, et al. FORE Language. Bagai, Eric & Bagai, Judith, eds. (System FORE Ser.: Vol. 2). (Illus.). 452p. 1977. student ed 25. 00 (*0-943292-02-6*) Foreworks.
— FORE Mathematics. rev. ed. Bagai, Eric & Bagai, Judith, eds. (System FORE Ser.: Vol. 4). (Illus.). 232p. 1977. 15.00 (*0-943292-04-2*) Foreworks.
— FORE Reading. Bagai, Eric & Bagai, Judith, eds. (System FORE Ser.: Vol. 3). (Illus.). 305p. 1977. student ed 28. 00 (*0-943292-03-4*) Foreworks.
Los, Maria. Communist Ideology, Law & Crime: A Comparative View of the U. S. S. R. & Poland. 320p. 1988. text ed. 39.95 (*0-312-15281-7*) St Martin.
Losa, Edith F., ed. ATA '92: "Frontiers" - Proceedings of the 33rd Annual Conference of the American Translators Association, November 4-8, 1992. 399p. 1992. pap. 50. 00 (*0-938734-68-7*) Learned Info.
— Keystones of Communication: Proceedings of the 34th Annual American Translators Association Conference. 392p. 1993. 50.00 (*0-938734-77-6*) Learned Info.
Losano, Wayne, jt. auth. see Gould, Jay.
LoSardo, Mary M. & Rossi, Norma M. At the Service Quality Frontier: A Handbook for Managers, Consultants, & Other Pioneers. LC 92-33879. 123p. 1993. pap. 19.95 (*0-87389-209-7*) ASQC Qual Pr.
Loscalzo, Craig A. Preaching Sermons That Connect: Effective Communication Through Identification. LC 92-34517. (Illus.). 165p. (Orig.). 1993. pap. 10.99 (*0-8308-1343-8*, 1343) InterVarsity.
Loscalzo, J. & Mendelson, M. E. Atrial Fibrillation. 1994. 45.00 (*0-86542-100-5*) Blackwell Sci.
Loscalzo, J. & Schafer, A. Thrombosis & Hemorrhage. 1993. 225.00 (*0-86542-263-X*) Blackwell Sci.
Loscalzo, Joseph, jt. auth. see Jenkins, Jon L.
Loscalzo, Joseph, et al, eds. Vascular Medicine: A Textbook of Vascular Biology & Diseases. LC 92-23658. 1992. 149.95 (*0-316-53317-3*) Little.
Loscalzo, William A. Cash Flow Forecasting. (Illus.). 192p. 1982. text ed. 45.00 (*0-07-038746-X*) McGraw.
Loscell, David M. & Jensen, Cary M. Bridging the Gap Between Nonprofit & For-Profit Board Members. (Nonprofit Governance Ser.: No. 13). 14p. (Orig.). (C). 1992. pap. text ed. 10.00 (*0-925299-20-0*) Natl Ctr Nonprofit.
Loscerbo, J. Being in Technology: A Study of the Philosophy of Martin Heidegger. (Phaenomenologica Ser.: No. 82). 200p. 1981. lib. bdg. 112.50 (*90-247-2411-2*) Kluwer Ac.
Losch, August. The Economics of Location. 2nd rev. ed. Woglom, William H. & Stolpher, Wolfgang F., trs. LC 52-9268. 548p. reprint ed. pap. 156.20 (*0-8357-8110-0*, 2033807) Bks Demand.
Losch, Naomi, tr. see Casil, Kathleen L.
Losch, Naomi N., tr. see Casil, Kathleen L.
Losch, Rainer. Funktionelle Voraussetzungen der Adaptiven Nischenbesetzung in der Evolution der Makaronesischen Semperviven. (Dissertationes Botanicae Ser.: Vol. 146). (Illus.). 482p. (GER.). 1990. pap. text ed. 120.00 (*3-443-64058-3*, Pub. by Gebruder Borntraeger GW) Lubrecht & Cramer.
Loschcke, V., jt. ed. see Woehrmann, K.
Losche, Norbert. Cosmic Tarot. 36p. 1988. 16.00 (*0-88079-395-3*) US Games Syst.
Losco, Joseph & Williams, Leonard. Political Theory: Classic Writings, Contemporary Views. LC 90-71614. 736p. (C). 1991. pap. text ed. 33.00 (*0-312-04693-6*) St Martin.
Lose, M. Phyllis. Blessed Are the Brood Mares. (Illus.). 1978. 22.95 (*0-02-575250-2*) Macmillan.
— Blessed Are the Brood Mares. 2nd ed. (Illus.). 256p. 1991. 27.50 (*0-87605-848-9*) Howell Bk.
— Blessed Are the Foals. (Illus.). 224p. 1987. text ed. 26.00 (*0-02-575230-8*) Macmillan.
— Keep Your Horse Healthy: Advice from a Veterinarian. 22.45 (*0-685-43064-2*) S&S Trade.
***Lose, Patrick.** Fun & Fancy Jackets & Vests: Folk Art Using No-Sew Applique. LC 95-6. (Illus.). 144p. 1995. 24.95 (*0-8069-1298-7*, Chapelle) Sterling.
— Patrick Lose's Whimsical Cross-Stitch. LC 94-42099. (Illus.). 144p. 1995. 24.95 (*0-8069-1292-8*, Chapelle) Sterling.
— Patrick Lose's Whimsical Sheatshirts. LC 95-16328. (Illus.). 144p. 1995. 24.95 (*0-8069-3179-5*, Chapelle) Sterling.
— Whimsical Woodcrafts to Make & Paint. LC 95-11545. (Illus.). 144p. 1995. 24.95 (*0-8069-1395-9*, Chapelle) Sterling.
Loseby, Paul H. Employment Security: Balancing Human & Economic Considerations. LC 92-1132. 192p. 1992. text ed. 42.95 (*0-89930-692-6*, LYT/, Quorum Bks) Greenwood.
Losee, John. A Historical Introduction to the Philosophy of Science. 3rd enl. rev. ed. LC 93-22328. (Illus.). 336p. 1993. 15.95 (*0-19-289247-9*) OUP.
— Philosophy of Science & Historical Enquiry. LC 86-23550. 152p. 1987. 45.00 (*0-19-824946-2*) OUP.
— Religious Language & Complementarity. 280p. (C). 1991. lib. bdg. 46.50 (*0-8191-8371-7*) U Pr of Amer.

An Asterisk (*) at the beginning of an entry indicates that the title is appearing in BIP for the first time.

L

Losee, Michael. The Cellular Telephone Installation Handbook. Mandelstein, Paul & Mandelstein, Cornelia, eds. (Illus.). 352p. (C). 1988. text ed. 49.95 (*0-930633-05-9*) Quantum Pub.

Losee, R. E. DOC: Memoirs of a Rocky Mountain Physician. (Illus.). 240p. 1994. 22.95 (*1-55821-323-6*) Lyons & Burford.

Losee, Rex, jt. auth. see McIntyre, Robert L.

***Losee, Rita.** The Waist Management Playbook. 160p. 1994. per., pap. text ed. 19.97 (*0-8403-9917-0*) Kendall-Hunt.

Losee, Robert M., Jr. The Science of Information: Measurement & Applications. (Library & Information Science Ser.). 293p. 1990. text ed. 49.00 (*0-12-455771-6*) Acad Pr.

Losee, Robert M., Jr. & Worley, Karen A. Research & Evaluation for Information Professionals. (Library & Information Science Ser.). (Illus.). 239p. 1993. text ed. 45.00 (*0-12-455770-8*) Acad Pr.

Loseff, Lev. Chudesnyi Desant. LC 85-8721. 160p. 1985. pap. 9.00 (*0-938920-50-2*) Hermitage.

Loseff, Lev & Polukhina, Valentina, eds. Brodsky's Poetics & Aesthetics. LC 89-70322. 240p. 1990. text ed. 45.00 (*0-312-04511-5*) St Martin.

Loseff, Lev & Scherr, Barry, eds. A Sense of Place Tsarskoe Selo & Its Poets: Papers from the Dartmouth Conference Dedicated to the Centennial of Anna Akhmatova, 1989. (Illus.). 368p. (Orig.). 1993. pap. 22.95 (*0-89357-239-X*) Slavica.

Loseke, Donileen, jt. ed. see Gelles, Richard J.

Loseke, Donileen R. The Battered Woman & Shelters: The Social Construction of Wife Abuse. (SUNY Series in Deviance & Social Control). 216p. (C). 1992. 59.50 (*0-7914-0831-0*); pap. 19.95 (*0-7914-0832-9*) State U NY Pr.

Losel, Freidrich, et al, eds. Psychology & Law: International Perspectives. LC 92-30454. xxviii, 557p. 1992. lib. bdg. 144.65 (*3-11-013725-9*) De Gruyter.

Losel, Friedrich, jt. ed. see Brambring, Michael.

Losel, Friedrich, jt. ed. see Hurrelmann, Klaus.

Loselle, Andrea, tr. see Restany, Pierre.

Losen, Joyce G., jt. auth. see Losen, Stuart M.

Losen, Stuart M. & Losen, Joyce G. The Special Education Team. 242p. 1984. text ed. 36.95 (*0-205-08203-3*, H82035) Allyn.

Loser, Eva, ed. Conflict Resolution & Democratization in Panama. (Significant Issues Ser.). 1992. pap. text ed. 9.95 (*0-89206-183-9*) CSI Studies.

Loser, Eva, jt. auth. see Fauriol, Georges A.

Loser, Eva, jt. ed. see Fauriol, Georges A.

Loserth, Johann. Wiclif & Hus. Evans, M. J., tr. LC 78-63198. (Heresies of the Early Christian & Medieval Era Ser.: Second Ser.). 1979. reprint ed. 48.00 (*0-404-16236-3*) AMS Pr.

Losev, Lev, ed. see Eremin, Mikhail.

Losev, S. A. Gasdynamic Laser. (Chemical Physics Ser.: Vol. 12). (Illus.). 300p. 1981. 57.00 (*0-387-10503-4*) Spr-Verlag.

Losey, Ralph, jt. auth. see Keyserling, Arnold.

***Losgton, Anne.** Dagger's Point. 272p. (Orig.). 1995. pap. text ed. 4.99 (*0-441-00134-3*) Ace Bks.

***Losh, John B. Who's Who in Luxury Real Estate, Vol. VIII. 8th rev. ed. Burns, Emily E., ed. 350p. 1995. 19.95 (*1-886020-00-0*) Whos Who Lux Real Est.**

John Brian Losh publishes the eighth edition of WHO'S WHO IN LUXURY REAL ESTATE which updates & expands the previous editions to include more of the finest independent luxury brokerage houses in the world. First published in 1987, this attractive 350-page hard-bound book accented in gold leaf, is a directory which includes Manhattan, San Francisco, Palm Beach, Paris, Hong Kong, the Caribbean, etc. An excellent reference for anyone interested in buying or selling their home, investing in real estate, or as an industry resource for real estate professionals. Over twenty foreign countries & virtually every state are represented in this latest edition. Inclusion is by invitation only, & each selected entry is recognized as a leader in the marketing of distinctive & luxury properties, committed to high performance, professionalism, & quality service. The publisher, John Brian Losh, is himself the owner of the oldest real estate brokerage in Seattle, & is a consultant for firms all over the United States. This directory is the only one of its kind & is limited to the top 500 luxury real estate brokers in the world. To order, contact the publisher at 2110 Western Ave., Seattle, WA 98121; call 800-488-4066. ***Publisher Provided Annotation.***

— Who's Who in Luxury Real Estate Vol. rev. ed. Burns, Emily E., ed. 279p. 1992. 19.95 (*1-886020-03-5*) Whos Who Lux Real Est.

— Who's Who in Luxury Real Estate Vol. rev. ed. Burns, Emily E., ed. 311p. 1993. 19.95 (*1-886020-02-7*) Whos Who Lux Real Est.

— Who's Who in Luxury Real Estate Vol. rev. ed. Burns, Emily E., ed. 336p. 1994. 19.95 (*1-886020-01-9*) Whos Who Lux Real Est.

Loshak, David. Munch. 112p. 1994. 14.98 (*0-8317-6118-0*) Smithmark.

***Loshin, H. David.** High-Performance Computing Demystified. (Illus.). 320p. 1994. pap. 34.95 (*0-12-455825-9*, AP Prof) Acad Pr.

***Loshin, Peter.** Electronic Commerce: On Line Ordering & Digital Cash. (Illus.). 300p. (Orig.). 1995. pap. 35.95 (*1-886801-08-8*) Chrles River Media.

— TCP/IP for Everyone. (Illus.). 350p. 1995. pap. write for info. (*0-12-455827-5*) Acad Pr.

Loshitzky, Yosefa. The Radical Faces of Godard & Bertolucci. LC 94-30602. (Contemporary Film & Television Ser.). (Illus.). 288p. 1994. text ed. 44.95 (*0-8143-2446-0*) Wayne St U Pr.

— The Radical Faces of Godard & Bertolucci. LC 94-30602. (Contemporary Film & Television Ser.). (Illus.). 288p. 1995. pap. text ed. 18.95 (*0-8143-2447-9*) Wayne St U Pr.

Loshor, J. K., tr. see Ilyushin, A. A. & Lenskii, V. S.

Losick, R. & Chamberlin, M., eds. RNA Polymerase. LC 76-17182. (Cold Spring Harbor Monograph Ser.). 909p. reprint ed. pap. 180.00 (*0-7837-6443-X*, 2046443) Bks Demand.

Losick, Richard & Shapiro, Lucy, eds. Microbial Development. LC 84-9599. (Monograph Ser.: Vol. 16). 303p. 1984. 60.00 (*0-87969-172-7*); pap. 35.00 (*0-87969-173-5*) Cold Spring Harbor.

Losique, Serge. Dictionnaire Etymologique des Noms de Pays et de Peuples: Eymological Dictionary of People's & Place Names. 243p. (FRE.). 1971. pap. 35.00 (*0-8288-6453-5*, F-135990) Fr & Eur.

Losito, Linda. The Ant on the Ground. LC 89-4460. (Animal Habitats Ser.). (Illus.). 32p. (J). (gr. 4-6). 1989. lib. bdg. 17.27 (*0-8368-0111-3*) Gareth Stevens Inc.

— Discovering Damselflies & Dragonflies. Caulkins, Janet, ed. LC 87-71047. (Illus.). 48p. (J). (gr. k-6). 1988. lib. bdg. 12.40 (*0-531-18168-5*, Bookwright Pr) Watts.

Losito, Linda, jt. auth. see Harrison, Virginia.

Losito, Linda, et al. Birds: Aerial Hunters. (Encyclopedia of the Animal World Ser.). (Illus.). 96p. (YA). 1989. 17.95 (*0-8160-1963-0*) Facts on File.

— Birds: The Plant- & Seed-Eaters. (Encyclopedia of the Animal World Ser.). (Illus.). 96p. (YA). 1989. 17.95 (*0-8160-1964-9*) Facts on File.

— Fish. (Encyclopedia of the Animal World Ser.). (Illus.). 96p. (YA). 1989. 17.95 (*0-8160-1966-5*) Facts on File.

— Insects & Spiders. (Encyclopedia of the Animal World Ser.). (Illus.). 96p. (YA). 1989. 17.95 (*0-8160-1967-3*) Facts on File.

— Mammals: Small Plant-Eaters. (Encyclopedia of the Animal World Ser.). (Illus.). 96p. (YA). 1988. 17.95 (*0-8160-1958-4*) Facts on File.

— Pets & Farm Animals. (Encyclopedia of the Animal World Ser.). (Illus.). 300p. (YA). (gr. 4-9). 1990. 17.95 (*0-8160-1969-X*) Facts on File.

— Simple Animals. (Encyclopedia of the Animal World Ser.). (Illus.). 96p. (YA). 1989. 17.95 (*0-8160-1968-1*) Facts on File.

***Loski, Diana.** The Boy on the Bus. (Illus.). 30p. (Orig.). (J). (ps-5). 1994. pap. 6.99 (*1-885101-02-3*) Writers Pr Srv.

— The Boy on the Bus, 35 bks., Large Class Set. (Illus.). (Orig.). (J). (gr. k-5). Date not set. pap. 244.65 (*1-885101-26-0*) Writers Pr Srv.

— The Boy on the Bus, 10 bks., Resource Room Set. (Illus.). (Orig.). (J). (gr. k-5). Date not set. pap. 69.90 (*1-885101-24-4*) Writers Pr Srv.

— The Boy on the Bus, 25 bks., Small Class Set. (Illus.). (Orig.). (J). (gr. k-5). Date not set. pap. 174.75 (*1-885101-25-2*) Writers Pr Srv.

— Zack Attacks. Kolsen, Wendy S., ed. (Illus.). 108p. (Orig.). (J). (gr. 3-8). 1995. pap. 3.50 (*1-885101-10-4*) Writers Pr Srv.

***Loski, Diana & Sniffen, Linda.** Dinosaur Hill. (Illus.). (Orig.). (J). (gr. 3-8). 1995. pap. 3.75 (*1-885101-16-3*) Writers Pr Srv.

Loskill, R., jt. ed. see Nagel, Roland.

Loskutov, A. Yu, jt. auth. see Mikhailov, A. S.

Losleben, Paul, ed. Advanced Research in VLSI: Proceedings of the Stanford Conference, 1987. 350p. 1987. 47.50x (*0-262-12121-2*) MIT Pr.

Losman. Heart Transplantation. 1991. write for info. (*0-8151-5620-0*, Yr Bk Med Pubs) Mosby Yr Bk.

Losman, Donald L. & Liang, Shu-Jan. The Promise of American Industry: An Alternative Assessment of Problems & Prospects. LC 89-24329. 296p. 1990. text ed. 55.00 (*0-89930-508-3*, LAB/, Quorum Bks) Greenwood.

***Losness, Howard.** Once I Was Lost. 170p. 1995. pap. 7.95 (*1-56901-697-6*) NW Pub.

Losoncy, Larry. What God Has Joined Together: Making Your Marriage Better. 156p. 1986. pap. text ed. 12.99 (*1-56322-018-0*) V Hensley.

***Losoncy, Lewis E.** The Motivating Team Leader. 256p. 1995. 14.95 (*1-884015-82-4*) St Lucie Pr.

— Salon Psychology: How to Succeed with People & Be a Positive Person. LC 87-63500. (Illus.). 242p. (Orig.). 1988. pap. text ed. 19.95 (*0-9619951-0-6*) Matrix Univ Pr.

Losoncy, Lewis E., jt. auth. see Scoleri, Donald W.

***Losonczy, H. & David, M., eds.** Trends in Haemostasis 1995. 200p. 1995. pap. 30.00 (*963-05-6844-6*, Pub. by A K HU) Intl Spec Bk.

Losonsky, Joyce, jt. auth. see Losonsky, Terry.

Losonsky, Michael, jt. ed. see Geirsson, Heimir.

Losonsky, Michael, tr. see Reich, Klaus.

***Losonsky, Terry & Losonsky, Joyce.** McDonald's Happy Meal Toys - Around the World. (Illus.). 224p. 1995. pap. 24.95 (*0-88740-835-4*) Schiffer.

— McDonald's Happy Meal Toys - In the U. S. A. LC 95-9054. (Illus.). 224p. (Orig.). 1995. pap. 24.95 (*0-88740-853-2*) Schiffer.

Losordo, Thomas M., jt. ed. see Timmons, Michael B.

Losq, Christine. Understanding Division. (Whole Math Project Ser.). (Illus.). 188p. 1993. teacher ed, spiral bd. 29.95 (*1-56892-000-8*) CSL Assocs.

Loss, Archie K. Joyce's Visible Art: The Work of Joyce & the Visual Arts. LC 84-2657. (Studies in Modern Literature: No. 38). (Illus.). 140p. reprint ed. pap. 39.90 (*0-8357-1576-0*, 2070595) Bks Demand.

— Of Human Bondage: Coming of Age in the Novel. (Masterwork Studies: No. 40). 128p. 1989. text ed. 21.95 (*0-8057-8067-X*, Twayne); pap. 12.95 (*0-8057-8112-9*, Twayne) Macmillan.

Loss, F. J., jt. ed. see Newman, J. C., Jr.

Loss, F. J., jt. ed. see Wessel, E. T.

Loss, Louis. Commentary on the Uniform Securities Act. 1977. 45.00 (*0-316-53326-2*) Little.

— Federal Securities Code: Official Draft, 2 vols., Set. LC 80-81036. 1160p. 1980. 90.00 (*0-686-63062-9*, 5069) Am Law Inst.

— Fundamental Set. 2nd ed. 1988. 145.00 (*0-316-53346-7*) Little.

— Fundamentals of Securities Regulation. 1302p. 1983. 75.00 (*0-316-53332-7*); student ed 50.00 (*0-316-53328-9*) Little.

— Fundamentals of Securities Regulation. 2nd ed. 1400p. 1987. 145.00 (*0-316-53335-1*) Little.

— Fundamentals of Securities Regulation: 1984 Supplement, Student Edition. 100p. (C). 1984. pap. 12.00 (*0-316-53330-0*) Little.

— Securities Register, Vol. 2. 3rd ed. 1988. 147.50 (*0-316-53338-6*) Little.

— Securities Register, Vol. 4. 3rd ed. 1989. 147.50 (*0-316-53347-5*) Little.

— Securities Register, Vol. 5. 3rd ed. 1990. 147.50 (*0-316-53348-3*) Little.

— Securities Register, Vol. 6. 3rd ed. 1990. 147.50 (*0-316-53360-2*) Little.

— Securities Register, Vol. 7. 3rd ed. 1991. 147.50 (*0-316-53375-0*) Little.

— Securities Regulation, Vol. 1. 3rd ed. 1988. 147.50 (*0-316-53337-8*) Little.

— Securities Regulation, Vol. 3. 3rd ed. 1988. 147.50 (*0-316-53339-4*) Little.

— Securities Regulation Complete Set. 3rd ed. 1989. 1,495.00 (*0-316-53343-2*) Little.

Loss, Louis & Seligman, Joel. Securities Regulation, 3 vols., Set. 3rd ed. 1800p. 1988. 240.00 (*0-318-36123-X*) Little.

Loss, Richard. The Modern Theory of Presidential Power: Alexander Hamilton & the Corwin Thesis. LC 89-27372. (Contributions in Political Science Ser.: No. 253). 192p. 1990. text ed. 49.95 (*0-313-26751-0*, LPW/, Greenwood Pr) Greenwood.

Loss, Richard, ed. see Corwin, Edward S.

Loss, Richard, ed. see Von Gentz, Friedrich.

***Losse, Bobb.** Reading Company Frieght Cars Vol. I: Covered Hopper Cars. 56p. (Orig.). 1995. pap. 24.95 (*1-882559-01-0*) D Carol Pubns.

Losse, Debra N. Sampling the Book: Renaissance Prologues & the French Conteurs. LC 92-55052. 1994. write for info. (*0-8387-5244-6*) Bucknell U Pr.

Losse, Peter & Griffiths, Michael, eds. Loose on Liquidators: The Role of a Liquidator in a Voluntary Winding-Up. 400p. (C). 1989. 200.00 (*0-685-44906-8*) St Mut.

Losseff, Nicky. The Best Concords: Polyphonic Music in Thirteenth-Century Britain. LC 93-45595. (Outstanding Dissertations in Music from British Universities Ser.). 328p. 1994. 72.00 (*0-8153-1710-7*) Garland.

Lossing, B. J. Matthew Brady's Illustrated History of the Civil War with 737 Brady Photographs. (Illus.). 1988. 15.99 (*0-517-22519-0*) Random Hse Value.

— Pictorial Field Book of the Revolution, 2 vols., Set. 1993. reprint ed. lib. bdg. 150.00 (*0-7812-5112-5*) Rprt Serv.

— Pictorial Field Book of the War of Eighteen Twelve. 108p. 1993. reprint ed. lib. bdg. 119.00 (*0-7812-5113-3*) Rprt Serv.

Lossing, Benjamin J., ed. Diary of George Washington from Seventeen Eighty-Nine to Seventeen Ninety-One. 246p. 1978. reprint ed. 22.50 (*0-87928-102-2*) Corner Hse.

Lossing, Benson. Pictorial Field Book of the Revolution. 1973. 69.95 (*0-8490-0834-4*) Gordon Pr.

— Pictorial History of Civil War, 3 vols. 1973. 300.00 (*0-8490-0835-2*) Gordon Pr.

Lossing, Benson J. Empire State: A Compendious History of the Commonwealth of New York. LC 68-57492. (Illus.). 1968. reprint ed. 25.00 (*0-87152-050-8*) Reprint.

— Harper's Encyclopaedia of United States History, from 458 A. D. to 1905: With Special Contributions Covering Every Phase of American History & Development by Eminent Authorities, 10 vols., Set. (Illus.). 1995. 420.00 (*1-55888-989-2*) Omnigraphics Inc.

— The Hudson: From the Wilderness to the Sea. (Illus.). 484p. 1972. 39.50 (*0-912274-22-0*) Picton Pr.

— The Hudson from the Wilderness to the Sea. (Illus.). 490p. reprint ed. pap. 29.50 (*1-55613-645-5*) Heritage Bk.

— The Life & Times of Philip Schuyler, 2 vols., Set. LC 78-167944. (Era of the American Revolution Ser.). 1052p. 1973. reprint ed. lib. bdg. 95.00 (*0-306-70533-8*) Da Capo.

— Matthew Brady's Illustrated History of the Civil War: 1861-65 & the Causes That Led up to the Great Conflict. (Illus.). 1994. 24.99 (*0-517-11979-X*) Random Hse Value.

— Pictorial Field-Book of the Revolution or Illustrations, by Pen & Pencil, of the History, Biography, Scenery, Relics & Traditions of the War for Independence, 2 Vols. LC 72-85457. (Select Bibliographies Reprint Ser.). 1977. 90.95 (*0-8369-5029-1*) Ayer.

Lossing, Benson J., ed. see Washington, George.

Lossing, Larry D., ed. see Pope John Center.

Losskaia, Veronique. Marina Tsvetaeva v Zhizni: Neizdannye Vospominaniia Sovremennikov. LC 88-32032. (Russian Ser.). (Illus.). 332p. (Orig.). 1989. pap. 15.00 (*1-55779-011-6*) Hermitage.

Lossky, Andrew. Louis XIV & the French Monarchy. LC 93-39313. 312p. (C). 1994. text ed. 59.00 (*0-8135-2081-9*) Rutgers U Pr.

Lossky, Andrew, ed. Seventeenth Century. LC 67-10426. (Orig.). 1967. pap. text ed. 14.95 (*0-02-919400-8*) Free Pr.

Lossky, Nicholas. Lancelot Andrewes, the Preacher (1555-1626) The Origins of the Mystical Theology of the Church of England. Louth, Andrew, tr. 392p. 1991. 89.00 (*0-19-826185-3*) OUP.

Lossky, Nicholas O. History of Russian Philosophy. 416p. (Orig.). 1969. reprint ed. text ed. 50.00 (*0-8236-2340-8*); reprint ed. pap. text ed. 24.95 (*0-8236-8074-6*, 22340) Intl Univs Pr.

Lossky, Vladimir. In the Image & Likeness of God. LC 76-383878. 232p. 1974. pap. 11.95 (*0-913836-13-3*) St Vladimirs.

— The Mystical Theology of the Eastern Church. LC 76-25448. Orig. Title: Essai sur la Theologie Mystique de l'Eglise d'Orient. 252p. 1976. reprint ed. pap. 12.95 (*0-913836-31-1*) St Vladimirs.

— Orthodox Theology: An Introduction. LC 78-1853. 137p. 1978. pap. 8.95 (*0-913836-43-5*) St Vladimirs.

— The Vision of God. 139p. 1963. 8.95 (*0-913836-19-2*) St Vladimirs.

Lossky, Vladimir & Ouspensky, Leonid. The Meaning of Icons. rev. ed. Palmer, G. E. & Kadloubovsky, E., trs. LC 82-22979. (Illus.). 224p. (C). 1982. reprint ed. text ed. 49.95 (*0-913836-77-X*); reprint ed. pap. 39.95 (*0-913836-99-0*) St Vladimirs.

Losson, Christopher. Tennessee's Forgotten Warriors: Frank Cheatham & His Confederate Division. LC 89-33944. (Illus.). 368p. 1990. 28.95 (*0-87049-615-8*) U of Tenn Pr.

Lost Moose Collective Staff, ed. Another Lost Whole Moose Catalogue: A Yukon Way of Knowledge, Vol. II. (Illus.). 160p. 1991. pap. 19.95 (*0-9694612-0-8*, Pub. by Lost Moose CN) Firefly Bks Ltd.

Lostracco & Wilkerson. Analyzing Short Stories. 2nd ed. 208p. (C). 1992. pap. text ed. 11.96 (*0-8403-8012-7*) Kendall-Hunt.

Lostritto, Donald. Jai Alai Wagering to Win: The Complete Book for Jai Alai Wagering. LC 84-73514. (Illus.). 197p. 1985. pap. 14.95 (*0-932227-00-7*) Fair Haven Pr.

***Losyk, Bob.** Managing a Changing Workforce: Achieving Outstanding Service with Today's Employees. 182p. 1996. 24.95 (*0-9647393-4-8*) Workplace Trends Pub.

Lotan, jt. ed. see Hong.

Lotchin, Roger W. Fortress California, 1910-1961: From Warfare to Welfare. (Illus.). 440p. 1992. 55.00 (*0-19-504779-6*) OUP.

Lotchin, Roger W., ed. The Martial Metropolis: U. S. Cities in War & Peace, 1900-1970. LC 83-21250. 288p. 1984. text ed. 55.00 (*0-275-91219-1*, C1219, Praeger Pubs) Greenwood.

Lote, Christopher J. Principles of Renal Physiology. 3rd ed. LC 93-35421. 1993. write for info. (*0-412-55520-4*, Chap & Hall NY) Chapman & Hall.

***Lotery, Fran & Melchiorre, Sherry.** Live Inside Out, Not Upside Down: Dynamic New Method of Self-Therapy Release Your Inner Strength, Confidence & Self Knowledge. (Illus.). 160p. 1996. write for info. (*0-9647103-5-8*) Bronze Pubng.

— Live Inside Out Not Upside Down: Dynamic New Method of Self-Therapy Release Your Inner Strength, Confidence & Self-Knowledge. 160p. 1975. write for info. (*0-614-06986-6*) Bronze Pubng.

Lotfi, Nasser. The Sword in the Sand: A Treatise on the Muslim Tradition & Its Challenge to the Christian World. Kearns, Marsha, ed. 104p. (Orig.). 1991. pap. write for info. (*1-878353-14-4*) Silent Partners.

Lotfi, Vahid & Pegels, C. Carl. Decision Support Systems for Production & Operations Management for Use with IBM PC. 2nd ed. 368p. (C). 1991. pap. text ed. 28.95 (*0-256-09349-0*, 18-2255-02) Irwin.

— Decision Support Systems for Production & Operations Management for Use with IBM PC. 2nd ed. 368p. (C). 1994. pap. text ed. 28.95 (*0-256-09350-4*, 18-3362-02) Irwin.

Lotfi, Vahid & Pegels, Carl C. Decision Support Systems for Management Science: 3.5 Inch Version & 5.25 Inch Version. 2nd ed. 400p. (C). 1992. text ed., 3.5 hd 28.95 (*0-256-09276-1*); text ed., 5.25 hd 28.95 (*0-256-09413-6*) Irwin.

Loth, Bernard & Michel, Albert. Dictionnaire de Theologie Catholique, Tables Generales: De Raison a Stolz: Dictionary of Catholic Theology, 3 vols., Set. (FRE.). 1970. 995.00 (*0-8288-6519-1*, M-6379) Fr & Eur.

***Loth, Calder, ed.** Virginia Landmarks of Black History: Sites on the Virginia Landmarks Register & the National Register of Historic Places. LC 94-32817. (Carter G. Woodson Institute Series in Black). (Illus.). 224p. (C). 1995. text ed. 40.00 (*0-8139-1600-3*); pap. 18.95 (*0-8139-1601-1*) U Pr of Va.

Loth, David. Swope of G. E. The Story of Gerard Swope & General Electric in American Business. LC 75-41769. (Companies & Men: Business Enterprises in America Ser.). 1976. reprint ed. 33.95 (*0-405-08084-0*) Ayer.

An Asterisk (*) at the beginning of an entry indicates that the title is appearing in BIP for the first time.

Loth, David G. Chief Justice: John Marshall & the Growth of the Republic. LC 77-94588. (Illus.). 395p. 1970. reprint ed. text ed. 75.00 (*0-8371-2450-6*, LOJM, Greenwood Pr) Greenwood.

Loth, John F. Beginner's Scales & Chords for Piano. 1993. 4.95 (*1-56222-267-8*, 94586) Mel Bay.

— Student's Basic Exercises for Piano, Vol. 1. 1993. 4.95 (*1-56222-268-6*, 94587) Mel Bay.

— Student's Basic Exercises for Piano, Vol. 2. 1993. 4.95 (*1-56222-269-4*, 94634) Mel Bay.

Loth, Lipgens, ed. Documents on the History of European Integration, Vol. 4: Transnational Organizations of the Political Parties & Pressure Groups in the Struggle for European Union, 1945-1950. (European University Institute Ser.: No. 1-4). xx, 650p. (C). 1990. fiche, lib. bdg. 229.25 (*3-11-011965-X*) De Gruyter.

Loth, Paul E. Teaching Adults with Confidence. 48p. 1984. pap. 4.25 (*0-910566-43-7*) Evang Trg Assn.

Loth, Richard. How To Profit from Reading Annual Reports. 176p. (Orig.). 1992. pap. 19.95 (*0-7931-0240-5*, 560848) Dearborn Finan.

Loth, Richard B. The Annual Report Glossary: An Easy-to-Understand Guidebook for Shareholders. LC 89-155320. 174p. 1988. ring bd. 26.00 (*0-924399-00-7*) FIPS Partners Inc.

Loth, Stanislaw. Crumbs of Life. 1993. 9.95 (*0-8062-4685-5*) Carlton.

Loth, Timothy S., ed. Orthopaedic Board Review. LC 92-22708. 625p. 1992. pap. 39.95 (*0-8016-2740-0*) Mosby Yr Bk.

Loth, Wilfried, jt. ed. see Lipgens, Walter.

Lothane, Zvi. In Defense of Schreber: Soul Murder & Psychiatry. 552p. 1992. text ed. 59.95 (*0-88163-103-5*) Analytic Pr.

***Lothario.** The Forbidden Apple. 30p. 1994. 7.95 (*0-9636309-1-1*) Lothario.

— A Simplified Existence. Pitts, Teresa A., ed. 17p. (Orig.). 1992. 7.95 (*0-9636309-0-3*, TXU514949) Lothario.

Lotharius, Alana. Numerology Cards: Expand Your Knowledge of Yesterday, Today & Tomorrow. (Illus.). 106p. (Orig.). 1991. 7.95 (*0-9629732-0-3*) Quintile.

— Numerology Cards & Guide. (Illus.). 106p. 1991. 23.95 (*0-9629732-2-X*) Quintile.

— Numerology: Enrich Your Life Through Numbers: Numerology Can Guide You in Your Search for the Answers, Vol. I. 120p. 1992. text ed. 24.95 (*0-9629732-9-7*) Quintile.

Lothe, Jakob. Conrad's Narrative Method. (Illus.). 328p. 1991. pap. 22.00 (*0-19-812255-1*) OUP.

Lothe, Jens, jt. auth. see Hirth, John P.

Lother, H., et al, eds. Vectors As Tools for the Study of Normal & Abnormal Growth & Differentiation. (NATO ASI Series H: Vol. 34). viii, 475p. 1989. 167.00 (*0-387-50419-2*) Spr-Verlag.

Lothers, John E. Design in Structural Steel. 3rd ed. LC 71-160254. (Civil Engineering & Engineering Mechanics Ser.). (Illus.). 1972. 38.95 (*0-685-03824-6*) P-H.

Lothes, Robert N., et al. Radar Vulnerabilty to Jamming. (Artech House Radar Library). 130p. 1990. text ed. 66.00 (*0-89006-388-5*) Artech Hse.

Lothian, Andrew. Lothian: Petronius - the Book. 1988. pap. 23.00 (*0-406-10396-8*) Butterworth Legal Pubs.

Lothian, J. M., ed. see Shakespeare, William.

Lothian, John M., ed. see Smith, Adam.

Lothian, Lord. Lord Lothian Versus Lord Lothian. 1991. lib. bdg. 76.00 (*0-8490-4420-0*) Gordon Pr.

Lothioir, Pascal. The Digest of Building Contract Awards: The Hard Facts - Comparables on Actual Project Listings. 383p. 1993. write for info. (*1-56842-003-X*) Marshall & Swift.

Lothrop, Eaton S., Jr. A Century of Cameras. rev. ed. LC 73-88444. (Illus.). 196p. 1982. pap. 24.00 (*0-87100-163-2*, 2163) Morgan.

Lothrop, Eleanor B. Throw Me a Bone: What Happens When You Marry an Archaeologist. (American Biography Ser.). 234p. 1991. reprint ed. lib. bdg. 69.00 (*0-7812-8251-9*) Rprt Serv.

Lothrop, Francis B. George Chinnery Seventeen Seventy-Four to Eighteen Fifty-Two & Other Artists of the Chinese Scene. (Illus.). 1967. pap. 3.00 (*0-87577-020-7*, Peabody Museum) Peabody Essex Mus.

Lothrop, Gloria R. A Guide to Historical Outings in Southern California. LC 91-73513. 144p. (Orig.). 1991. pap. 9.95 (*0-685-61090-X*) Hist Soc So CA.

— Pomona: A Centennial History. 1988. 29.95 (*0-89781-263-8*, 5304) Preferred Mktg.

Lothrop, Gloria R., jt. auth. see Jensen, Joan M.

Lothrop, Gloria R., jt. ed. see Nunis, Doyce B., Jr.

Lothrop, K. S., et al. Cocle: An Archaeological Study of Central Panama, 2 vols., 1. (HU PMM Ser.). 1972. reprint ed. 90.00 (*0-527-01169-X*) Periodicals Srv.

— Cocle: An Archaeological Study of Central Panama, 2 vols., 2. (HU PMM Ser.). 1972. reprint ed. 110.00 (*0-527-01170-3*) Periodicals Srv.

Lothrop, S. K. Inca Treasure As Depicted by Spanish Historians. (Frederick Webb Hodge Publications: No. 2). (Illus.). 1964. reprint ed. 5.00 (*0-916561-24-0*) Southwest Mus.

— Metals from the Cenote of Sacrifice. (Harvard University Peabody Museum of Archaeology & Ethnology Papers: Vol. 10, No. 2). 1974. reprint ed. 30.00 (*0-527-01177-0*) Periodicals Srv.

Lothrop, Samuel K. Atitlan: An Archaeological Study of Ancient Remains on the Borders of Lake Atitlan, Guatemala. LC 77-11509. (Carnegie Institution of Washington. Publications: No. 444). reprint ed. 22.00 (*0-404-16268-1*) AMS Pr.

— Indians of the Parana Delta, Argentina. LC 76-44751. (Anthropology Ser.). (Illus.). reprint ed. 34.00 (*0-404-15867-6*) AMS Pr.

— The Indians of Tierra Del Fuego. LC 76-44752. reprint ed. 27.50 (*0-404-15868-4*) AMS Pr.

— Pre-Columbian Designs from Panama: 591 Illustrations of Cocle Pottery. LC 75-17177. (Pictorial Archive Ser.). (Illus.). 112p. (Orig.). 1976. pap. 6.95 (*0-486-23232-8*) Dover.

— Pre-Columbian Designs from Panama: 591 Illustrations of Cocle Pottery. (Orig.). 14.00 (*0-8446-5508-2*) Peter Smith.

— Tulum: An Archaeological Study of the East Coast of Yucaton. 1976. lib. bdg. 69.95 (*0-8490-2779-9*) Gordon Pr.

— Zacualpa: A Study of Ancient Quiche Artifacts. LC 77-11508. (Carnegie Institution of Washington. Publications: No. 472). 1977. reprint ed. 20.00 (*0-404-16269-X*) AMS Pr.

Lothrop, Samuel K., et al. Essays in Pre-Columbian Art & Archaeology. LC 61-18531. 507p. reprint ed. pap. 144.50 (*0-7837-4116-2*, 2057939) Bks Demand.

Lothrop, T. J. The Nicholas White Family, 1643-1900. (Illus.). 493p. 1989. reprint ed. lib. bdg. 82.00 (*0-8328-1252-8*); reprint ed. pap. 74.00 (*0-8328-1253-6*) Higginson Bk Co.

Lothrop, Thorton K. William Henry Seward. Morse, John T., Jr., ed. LC 77-128959. (American Statesmen Ser.: No. 27). reprint ed. 37.50 (*0-404-50877-4*) AMS Pr.

Loti, Pierre. Aziyade. 182p. 1988. pap. 12.95 (*0-7103-0316-5*, Pub. by Kegan Paul Intl UK) Routledge Chapman & Hall.

— Aziyade. (Folio Ser.: No. 2058). (FRE.). 1990. pap. 12.95 (*2-07-038147-1*) Schoenhof.

— The Desert. Minn, Jay P., tr. LC 93-10090. 164p. (ENG.). 1993. reprint ed. pap. 14.95 (*0-87480-427-2*) U of Utah Pr.

— Japan: Madam Chrysanthemum. Ensor, Laura, tr. (Pacific Basin Bks.). (Illus.). 336p. (Orig.). 1985. pap. 19.95 (*0-7103-0138-3*, Pub. by Kegan Paul Intl UK) Routledge Chapman & Hall.

— Pecheur d'Islande. (Folio Ser.: No. 1982). 338p. (FRE.). 1988. pap. 9.95 (*2-07-038070-X*) Schoenhof.

Loti, Pierre, pseud. Pecheur d'Islande. (Coll. Bleue). 21.50 (*0-685-34265-4*) Fr & Eur.

Loti, Pierre. Ramuntcho. (Folio Ser.: No. 2120). (FRE.). pap. 9.95 (*2-07-038214-1*) Schoenhof.

— Roman d'un Spahi. (Folio Ser.: No. 2393). (FRE.). pap. 10.95 (*2-07-038531-0*) Schoenhof.

— Tahiti: The Marriage of Loti. Bell, Clara, tr. 217p. 1987. pap. 19.95 (*0-7103-0231-2*, 02312, Pub. by Kegan Paul Intl UK) Routledge Chapman & Hall.

Lotito, Barbara, tr. see Alba, Victor.

Lotito, Floyd A. Wisdom, Age & Grace: An Inspirational Guide to Staying Young at Heart. LC 93-7075. 64p. 1993. pap. 3.95 (*0-8091-3388-1*) Paulist Pr.

Lotito, Michael, jt. auth. see Pimentel, Richard.

Lotka, Alfred J., jt. auth. see Dublin, Louis I.

Lotke, Paul A., ed. Knee Arthroplasty. LC 93-42856. (Master Techniques in Orthopaedic Surgery Ser.). (Illus.). 400p. 1995. 189.00 (*0-7817-0032-9*) Raven.

— Postoperative Infections in Orthopaedic Surgery: Prevention & Treatment. 80p. 1992. 30.00 (*0-89203-099-2*) Amer Acad Ortho Surg.

Lotman, Iu M. Lektsii po Struktural'noe Poetike: Vvedenie, Teoriia Stikha. LC 68-10643. (Brown University Slavic Reprint Ser.: 5). 203p. reprint ed. pap. 57.90 (*0-685-15996-5*, 2008979) Bks Demand.

***Lotman, Jeff.** Animation Art: Illustrated Guide to Animation Art at Auction. (Illus.). 420p. 1995. 125.00 (*0-88740-763-3*) Schiffer.

Lotman, Ju M. & Uspenskij, B. A. Semiotics of Russian Culture. Shukman, Ann, ed. (Michigan Slavic Contributions Ser.: No. 11). 356p. 1984. pap. 15.00 (*0-930042-56-5*) Mich Slavic Pubns.

Lotman, Yuri. Universe of the Mind: A Semiotic Theory of Culture. Shukman, Ann, tr. LC 90-39870. (Second World Ser.). 300p. 1991. 45.00 (*0-253-33608-2*) Ind U Pr.

Lotocki, Borys. Borys' Odyssey. Chang, M., ed. (Illus.). 1993. 23.95 (*0-938103-03-2*) ZZYZX Pub.

Lotring, Alfred H. Reason & Nature: A Taxonomy of the Abstract & Natural Sciences. McKinney, Aubrey R., ed. (Adventures in Science Ser.). (Illus.). 208p. 1989. 24.95 (*0-914587-06-4*) Helix Pr.

Lotringer, Sylvere, ed. see Mueller, Heiner.

Lotschert, William & Beese, Gerhard. The Collins Guide to Tropical Plants. (Illus.). 256p. 1989. 24.95 (*0-685-44551-8*) Viking Penguin.

Lotspeich, Henry C. Classical Mythology in the Poetry of Edmund Spenser. LC 65-28856. (Princeton Studies in English: No. 9). 126p. 1965. reprint ed. 40.00 (*0-87752-064-X*) Gordian.

Lotspeich-Steininger, Cheryl A. & Stiene-Martin, E. Anne. Clinical Hematology: Principles, Procedures, Correlations. (Illus.). 800p. 1991. text ed. 49.95 (*0-397-54806-0*) Lippincott.

Lotspeich-Steininger, Cheryl A., et al. Clinical Hematology: Principles, Procedures, Correlations. LC 65-9558. (Illus.). 720p. 1991. 49.95 (*0-397-50790-9*, Lippincott Medical) Lippincott.

Lott. A Teacher's Stories: Reflections on High School Writers. LC 93-43816. 218p. (J). 1994. pap. text ed. 17.50 (*0-86709-331-5*) Boynton Cook Pubs.

Lott, Arnold S. Brave Ship, Brave Men. (Bluejacket Paperback Ser.). 1994. pap. 12.95 (*1-55750-523-3*) Naval Inst Pr.

Lott, Arnold S. & Sumrall, Robert F. Pearl Harbor Attack. (Illus.). 32p. 1992. reprint ed. pap. 2.95 (*0-9631388-1-2*) AZ Mem Mus.

Lott, Arnold S. & Sumrall, Robert F., eds. Ships Data 1. (Illus.). 32p. 1982. 3.00 (*0-915268-07-8*) USS North Car.

Lott, Bernard, ed. The Tempest. (New Swan Shakespeare Ser.). 1989. pap. 2.95 (*0-582-74500-4*, TG7013) Longman.

Lott, Bernard, ed. see Shakespeare, William.

Lott, Bernice. Women's Lives: Themes & Variations in Gender Learning. LC 86-26886. 367p. (C). 1987. pap. 27.95 (*0-534-07440-5*) Brooks-Cole.

— Women's Lives: Themes & Variations in Gender Learning. 2nd ed. 1994. pap. 27.95 (*0-534-15954-0*) Brooks-Cole.

***Lott, Bernice & Maluso, Diane, eds.** The Social Psychology of Interpersonal Discrimination. LC 95-2851. 1995. write for info. (*1-57230-021-3*) Guilford Pr.

Lott, Bret. A Dream of Old Leaves. Rosenman, Jane, ed. 144p. 1991. reprint ed. pap. 6.95 (*0-671-69344-1*, WSP) PB.

— Jewel. large type ed. LC 92-6987. 685p. 1992. reprint ed. bds. 20.95 (*1-56054-398-1*) Thorndike Pr.

— Jewel. large type ed. 685p. 1993. pap. 13.95 (*1-56054-930-0*) Thorndike Pr.

— Jewel. Rosenman, Jane, ed. 368p. 1992. reprint ed. pap. 9.00 (*0-671-74039-3*, WSP) PB.

— The Man Who Owned Vermont. 224p. 1988. mass mkt. 5.95 (*0-671-64587-0*, WSP) PB.

— Reed's Beach. Rosenman, Jane, ed. 352p. 1994. reprint ed. pap. 10.00 (*0-671-79239-3*, WSP) PB.

— A Stranger's House. 272p. 1990. pap. 7.95 (*0-671-68328-4*, WSP) PB.

Lott, Catherine S. How To Land a Better Job. 1989. pap. 7.95 (*0-8442-6675-2*, VGM Career Bks) NTC Pub Grp.

Lott, Catherine S. & Lott, Oscar C. How to Land a Better Job. 3rd ed. LC 93-46211. 144p. 1994. pap. 8.95 (*0-8442-4174-1*, VGM Career Bks) NTC Pub Grp.

Lott, Clarinda H. Domestic Animals. (Fanfare Ser.). 1982. pap. 2.00 (*0-932616-10-0*) New Poets Chestnut Hills.

Lott, Clarinda H., jt. auth. see De Ford, Sara.

Lott, Clarinda H., jt. auth. see DeFord, Sara.

Lott, Clarinda H., ed. see Dove, Jennifer.

Lott, Clarinda H., ed. see Dowell, Lynne.

Lott, Clarinda H., ed. see Menaker, Donald.

Lott, Clarinda H., ed. see Sherrill, Jan M.

Lott, Clarinda H., ed. see Wallace, Laura.

Lott, D. J., et al, eds. Studies in Osteoarthrosis: Pathogensis, Intervention, Assessment. 1987. text ed. 150.00 (*0-471-91336-7*) Wiley.

Lott, Dale F. Intraspecific Variation in the Social Systems of Wild Vertebrates. (Studies in Behavioural Biology: No. 2). (Illus.). 230p. (C). 1991. 47.95 (*0-521-37024-8*) Cambridge U Pr.

Lott, Davis N. Presidents Speak: The Inaugural Addresses of the American Presidents, from Washinton to Clinton. 1994. 35.00 (*0-8050-3305-X*) H Holt & Co.

Lott, Deborah A., jt. ed. see Hadorn, David C.

Lott, Eric. Blackface Minstrelsy & the American Working Class. LC 92-41071. (Race & American Culture Ser.). 1993. 35.00 (*0-19-507832-2*) OUP.

— Love & Theft: Blackface Minstrelsy & the American Working Class. (Race & American Culture Ser.). (Illus.). 328p. 1995. pap. 14.95 (*0-19-509641-X*) OUP.

Lott, Ira & McCoy, Ernest. Down's Syndrome: Today's Health Care Issues. 212p. 1992. text ed. 69.95 (*0-471-56181-9*, Wiley-Liss); pap. text ed. 34.95 (*0-471-56184-3*, Wiley-Liss) Wiley.

Lott, James E. Practical Protocol: A Guide to International Courtesies. LC 73-75393. (Illus.). 208p. reprint ed. pap. 59.30 (*0-685-23788-5*, 2032875) Bks Demand.

Lott, Johnny W., jt. auth. see Billstein, Rick.

***Lott, Judy W., et al.** Neonatal Infection: Assessment, Diagnosis, & Management. (Illus.). 215p. (Orig.). 1994. pap. text ed. 24.95 (*0-9622975-5-0*) NICU INK.

Lott, Lee. The Legend of Lucky Lee Lott & His Hell Drivers. (Illus.). 128p. 1994. pap. 14.95 (*0-87938-858-7*) Motorbooks Intl.

Lott, Lynn & Allen, Jane. Teaching Parenting. 81p. 1988. 40.00 (*1-882023-03-X*) Prctcl Pr.

Lott, Lynn & Intner, Riki. The Family That Works Together: Turning Family Chores from Drudgery to Fun. LC 93-48112. 1994. write for info. (*1-55958-523-4*) Prima Pub.

Lott, Lynn, jt. auth. see Nelsen, Jane.

Lott, Lynn, jt. auth. see Nelson, Jane.

Lott, Lynn, et al. The Family That Works Together... Whose Job Is It? (Illus.). 65p. 1988. pap. 9.95 (*1-882023-00-5*) Prctcl Pr.

Lott, Mary. Mixed Messages. Graves, Helen, ed. LC 88-50119. 64p. 1988. 7.95 (*1-55523-143-8*) Winston-Derek.

Lott, Oscar C., jt. auth. see Lott, Catherine S.

Lott-Penny, Lynn & West, Dru. Together & Liking It. 64p. (Orig.). 1988. pap. 7.95 (*1-882023-01-3*) Prctcl Pr.

Lott, R. E., ed. Juan Valera: Pepita Jimenez. 1974. 94.00 (*0-08-017918-5*, Pub. by Pergamon Repr UK) Franklin.

Lott, Richard W. Auditing the Data Processing Function. LC 79-54841. 222p. reprint ed. pap. 63.30 (*0-8357-5874-5*, 2023588) Bks Demand.

Lott, Rick. The Apple Pickers' Children. (Texas Review Southern & Southwestern Poets Breakthrough Ser.). 64p. 1993. pap. 6.95 (*1-881515-02-8*) TX Review Pr.

— Digging for Shark Teeth. 1984. pap. 5.00 (*0-938078-19-4*) Anhinga Pr.

Lott, Robert E. Siglo de Oro Tradition & Modern Adolescent Psychology in Pepita Jimenez. LC 75-172751. (Catholic University of America. Studies in Romance Languages & Literatures: No. 58). reprint ed. 34.00 (*0-404-50358-6*) AMS Pr.

***Lott, Ronnie.** The Official Book of Super Bowl XXIX: The Golden State of Football. Hyman, Laurence J. & Rochmis, Jon, eds. LC 95-60136. (Official Books of the Super Bowl: No. 1). (Illus.). 144p. (Orig.). 1995. pap. 19.95 (*0-942627-25-3*) Woodford Pub.

— Total Impact: Straight Talk from Football's Hardest Hitter. 1991. 19.50 (*0-385-42055-2*) Doubleday.

Lott, Sandra W., et al, eds. Global Perspectives on Teaching Literature: Shared Visions & Distinctive Visions. LC 93-4917. 410p. 1993. 32.95 (*0-8141-1854-2*) NCTE.

***Lott, Thaddeus & Harasim, Paul.** No Excuses: Every Child Can Learn. (Illus.). 248p. 1996. 19.95 (*1-56796-120-7*) WRS Group.

Lott, Thomas C., see Tom Carl, pseud..

Lott, William F. & Ray, Subhash C. Applied Econometrics. 450p. (C). 1992. pap. text ed. 27.00 (*0-15-502907-X*) Dryden Pr.

Lotta, Raymond, aft. & intro. Maoist Economics & the Revolutionary Road to Communism: The Shanghai Textbook. LC 94-94131. 346p. (Orig.). (C). 1994. pap. text ed. 15.00 (*0-916650-41-3*) Banner Pr.

Lotta, Raymond, ed. And Mao Makes Five: Mao Tsetung's Last Great Battle. LC 78-70431. (Illus.). 1978. 15.00 (*0-916650-09-X*); pap. 5.95 (*0-916650-08-1*) Banner Pr.

Lotta, Raymond & Shannon, Frank. America in Decline: An Analysis of the Developments Toward War & Revolution, in the U. S. & Worldwide in the 1980's, Vol 1. LC 83-22294. (Illus.). 278p. (Orig.). (C). 1984. 21.95 (*0-916650-12-X*); pap. 11.95 (*0-916650-13-8*) Banner Pr.

Lotta, Raymond & Szymanski, Albert. The Soviet Union: Socialist or Social-Imperialist? Pt. II: The Question Is Joined. LC 83-17746. 90p. (Orig.). 1983. pap. 4.95 (*0-89851-067-8*) RCP Pubns.

Lotte, Fernand. Dictionnaire Biographique des Personnages Fictifs de la Comedie Humaine: Dictionnaire des Personnages Fictifs Anonymes. 96p. (FRE.). 1952. 18.95 (*0-7859-5129-6*) Fr & Eur.

Lotter, Andre. Palaeooekologische und Palaeolimnologische Studie des Rotsees bei Luzern. (Dissertationes Botanicae Ser.: Vol. 124). (Illus.). 188p. (GER.). 1988. spiral bd. 72.00 (*3-443-64036-2*) Lubrecht & Cramer.

Lotter, Bruno. Manufacturing Assembly Handbook. (Illus.). 395p. 1990. text ed. 179.00 (*0-408-03561-7*) Buttrwrth-Heinemann.

Lotter, Donald W. Earthscore: Your Personal Environmental Audit & Guide. (Illus.). 119p. (Orig.). (YA). (gr. 10 up). 1993. pap. 8.95 (*0-9629069-4-8*) Morn Sun Pr.

Lotter, M. N. Universal & Extrasensory Perception by the Percipients. 1993. 14.95 (*0-533-10564-1*) Vantage.

Lotterhand, Jason C. Thursday Night Tarot. 1989. pap. 14.95 (*0-87877-147-6*) Newcastle Pub.

Lotterman, Andrew. Specific Techniques for the Psychotherapy of Schizophrenic Patients. 172p. 1995. text ed. 35.00 (*0-8236-6130-X*) Intl Univs Pr.

Lottery Player's Magazine Staff, ed. It Couldn't Happen to a Nicer Fella' Lottery & Casino Winners We Have Known. 96p. 1988. pap. 9.95 (*0-936918-11-X*) Intergalactic NJ.

Lottich, Kenneth, jt. auth. see Roucek, Joseph S.

Lottinville, Savoie. The Rhetoric of History. LC 75-19418. 272p. 1976. pap. 12.95 (*0-8061-2190-4*) U of Okla Pr.

Lottinville, Savoie, ed. see Hyde, George E.

Lottman, Herbert. Flaubert: A Biography. LC 90-2801. 396p. 1990. reprint ed. pap. 11.95 (*0-88064-120-7*) Fromm Intl Pub.

— The Left Bank. LC 91-28879. 319p. 1991. reprint ed. pap. 14.95 (*0-9622874-4-X*) Halo Bks.

Lottman, Herbert R. Flaubert: A Biography. 1989. 24.95 (*0-316-53342-4*) Little.

— The French Rothschilds: The Great Banking Dynasty Through Two Turbulent Centuries. 1995. 30.00 (*0-517-59229-0*, Crown) Crown Pub Group.

Lotto, Jill C., jt. auth. see Rosaw, Jerome M.

Lotto, Linda S. Building Basic Skills: Results from Vocational Education. 41p. 1983. 4.25 (*0-318-22048-2*, RD237) Ctr Educ Trng Employ.

Lottridge, Celia B. One Watermelon Seed. (Illus.). 24p. (J). (ps up). 1990. reprint ed. pap. 6.95 (*0-19-540735-0*) OUP.

— Ten Small Tales. LC 92-2878. (Illus.). 64p. (J). (gr. k-4). 1994. lib. bdg. 15.95 (*0-689-50568-X*, McElderry) S&S Childrens.

— Ticket to Canada. LC 95-10697. (Illus.). (J). 1995. write for info. (*0-382-39144-6*); lib. bdg. write for info. (*0-382-39145-4*); pap. write for info. (*0-382-39146-2*) Silver Burdett Pr.

— The Wind Wagon. LC 94-39398. (Illus.). (J). 1994. 10.95 (*0-382-24928-3*); lib. bdg. 12.95 (*0-382-24927-5*); pap. 4.95 (*0-382-24929-1*) Silver Burdett Pr.

***Lotts, Scott J. & Barnes-Rothmeier, Vicki.** Golf for Beginners: The Official Survival Guide. 100p. 1994. pap. 10.99 (*0-9645700-0-9*) Mulligans Pr.

Lottspeich, F., et al, eds. High Performance Liquid Chromatography in Protein & Peptide Chemistry. (Illus.). 1982. 123.10 (*3-11-008542-9*) De Gruyter.

Lotus Bks. Staff. The Lotus Guide to 1-2-3 Advanced Macro Commands. LC 86-32213. 1987. pap. 23.95 (*0-201-16822-7*) Addison-Wesley.

Lotus Development Corporation Staff. The Lotus Guide to Learning Symphony: Release 2.0. rev. ed. (Lotus Bks.). 1988. pap. 22.95 (*0-201-16699-2*) Addison-Wesley.

— Lotus Guide to Learning 1-2-3: Up to & Including Release 2.2. 1989. pap. 22.95 (*0-201-52320-5*) Addison-Wesley.

— The Lotus Guide to Learning 1-2-3 Macros. 1986. pap. 19.18 (*0-201-16821-9*) Addison-Wesley.

— Lotus Worksheet File Formats: Essential Data File Facts about 1-2-3-, Symphony, & Jazz. write for info. (*0-318-60208-3*) Addison-Wesley.

Lotus Staff. Lotus File Formats for 1-2-3, Symphony & Jazz. 1986. pap. 19.95 (*0-201-16824-3*) Addison-Wesley.

Lotveit. Chinese Communism, 1931-1934: Grass Roots History in Modern China. (C). 1979. pap. 29.95 (*0-7007-0065-X*, Pub. by Curzon Pr UK) Humanities.

Lotz, Aileen R. Birding Around the World. (Science Editions Ser.). 1988. pap. text ed. 10.95 (*0-471-62092-0*) Wiley.

— Birding Around the World: A Guide to Observing Birds Everywhere You Travel. 1987. pap. 10.95 (*0-396-09024-9*) WC Stone PMA.

Lotz, Arthur. Das Feuerwerk. 178p. write for info. (*3-283-00010-7*, Pub. by Georg Olms GW) Lubrecht & Cramer.

Lotz, Jan, jt. auth. see Hawthorne, Luanda.

Lotz, Jim. Nova Scotia. LC 91-951128. (Discover Canada Ser.). (Illus.). 144p. (J). (gr. 4 up). 1992. lib. bdg. 20.55 (*0-516-06613-7*) Childrens.

— Railways of Canada. 1988. 14.99 (*0-517-68235-4*) Random Hse Value.

Lotz, John. Script, Grammar, & the Hungarian Writing System. LC 74-167265. (Hungarian-English Contrastive Linguistics Project, Working Papers: No. 2). 61p. reprint ed. pap. 25.00 (*0-8357-3344-0*, 2039574) Bks Demand.

Lotz, Karen E. Can't Sit Still. LC 92-28853. (Illus.). 48p. (J). (ps-3). 1993. 13.99 (*0-525-45066-1*, DCB) Dutton Child Bks.

— Snowsong Whistling. LC 92-47117. (Illus.). 32p. (J). (ps-2). 1993. 14.99 (*0-525-45145-5*, DCB) Dutton Child Bks.

Lotz, Philip H., ed. Distinguished American Jews. LC 78-111842. (Essay Index Reprint Ser.). 1977. 17.95 (*0-8369-1671-9*) Ayer.

— Founders of Christian Movements. LC 71-111843. (Essay Index Reprint Ser.). 1977. 19.95 (*0-8369-1672-7*) Ayer.

— Rising above Color. LC 78-152190. (Essay Index Reprints - Creative Personalities Ser.: Vol. 5). 1977. reprint ed. 15.95 (*0-8369-2605-6*) Ayer.

— Unused Alibis, Creative Personalities, Vol. 7. LC 79-126322. (Biography Index Reprint Ser.). 1977. 17.95 (*0-8369-8028-X*) Ayer.

Lotz, Ranier E., jt. ed. see Heier, Uli.

Lotz, Robert, ed. Inter-Noise 86: Proceedings of the International Conference on Noise Control, Massachusetts Institute of Technology, Cambridge, MA, July 21-23, 1986, 2 vols., Vols. 1 & 2. (Inter-Noise Ser.). 1986. Set, Vol. 1, xxxv, 796 pp., Vol. 2, xxxv, 676 pp. 75.00 (*0-931784-15-8*) Noise Control.

— Noise-Con 83: Proceedings - National Conference on Noise Control Engineering 1983. 512p. 1983. 42.00 (*0-931784-08-5*) Noise Control.

Lotz, Roy E. Crime & the American Press. LC 91-4623. (Praeger Series in Political Communication). 192p. 1991. text ed. 42.95 (*0-275-94012-8*, C4012, Praeger Pubs) Greenwood.

Lotz, Walther. Die Deutsche Staatsfinanz-Wirtschaft im Kriege. (Wirtschafts-Und Sozialgeschichte des Weltkrieges (Osterreichische Und Ungarische Serie)). (GER.). 1927. 100.00 (*0-317-27438-4*) Elliots Bks.

Lotz, Wolfgang. Studies in Italian Renaissance Architecture. LC 76-44833. (Illus.). 256p. 1976. pap. 15.00 (*0-262-62036-7*) MIT Pr.

Lotze, Barbara, intro. Making Contributions: An Historical Overview of Women's Role in Physics. (Occasional Publications). 123p. (Orig.). 1984. pap. text ed. 10.00 (*0-917853-09-1*, OP52) Am Assn Physics.

Lotze, Detlef & Hample, Franz. Metary Eleutheron Kai Doulon & Die Lakesdaemonischen Perickon, 2 vols. in one. Vlastos, Gregory, ed. LC 78-14616. (Morals & Law in Ancient Greece Ser.). 1979. reprint ed. lib. bdg. 17.95 (*0-405-11591-1*) Ayer.

Lotze, Hermann. Microcosmus: An Essay Concerning Man & His Relation to the World, 2 vols, Set. Hamilton, Elizabeth & Jones, E. E., trs. LC 76-169769. (Select Bibliographies Reprint Ser.). 1977. reprint ed. 84.95 (*0-8369-5989-2*) Ayer.

— Outlines of Aesthetics. 1973. 59.95 (*0-8490-0790-9*) Gordon Pr.

— Outlines of Psychology. LC 73-2974. (Classics in Psychology Ser.). 1978. reprint ed. 16.95 (*0-405-05147-6*) Ayer.

— Outlines of Psychology, Vol. 6. Ladd, George T., tr. Bd. with Textbook of Psychology & the Study of Psychology. LC 77-72191. LC 77-72191. (Contributions to the History of Psychology Ser.: Vol. 6, Pt. A, Orientations). 492p. 1977. reprint ed. Set text ed. 75.00 (*0-313-26930-0*, U6930, Greenwood Pr) Greenwood.

Lotze, Wilhelm, tr. see Busch, Wilhelm, et al.

Lotzgar, Elaine, ed. see Gounaris, John, et al.

Lotzkar, Elaine, et al. Dining In - with the Great Chefs of Seattle. (Dining in with the Great Chefs Ser.). 186p. (Orig.). 1985. pap. 8.95 (*0-89716-145-9*) P B Pubng.

Lotzova. NK Cell Medicated Cytotoxicology: Receptors, Signaling & Mechanics. 1992. 225.00 (*0-8493-6267-9*, QR188) CRC Pr.

Lotzova, E., ed. Potential of Gene Therapy in Cancer: Journal: Natural Immunity, Vol. 13, Nos. 2-3, 1994. (Illus.). 104p. 1994. pap. 37.75 (*3-8055-5956-9*) S Karger.

Lotzova, E., et al, eds. International Natural Killer Cell Workshop, 8th, & First Meeting of the Society for Natural Immunity, St. Petersburg Beach, October 1992: Abstracts. (Journal: Natural Immunity: Vol. 11, No. 5, 1992). 80p. 1992. pap. 37.75 (*3-8055-5690-X*) S Karger.

Lotzova, Eva, ed. Natural Immunity & Biological Response International Symposium, Honolulu, Nov. 1985. (Journal: Natural Immunity & Cell Growth Regulation: Vol. 4, No. 5, 1985). 64p. 1985. pap. 25.75 (*3-8055-4243-7*) S Karger.

— Natural Immunity, Cancer & Biological Response Modification. (Illus.). xii, 324p. 1986. 176.00 (*3-8055-4412-X*) S Karger.

— Natural Killer Cells: Their Definition, Functions, Lineage & Regulation. (Journal: Natural Immunity: Vol. 12, Nos. 4-5, 1993). (Illus.). 128p. 1993. pap. 37.00 (*3-8055-5875-9*) S Karger.

Lotzova, Eva & Herberman, Ronald B., eds. Immunobiology of Natural Killer Cells, Vol. II. 272p. 1986. 138.00 (*0-8493-6543-0*, QR185, CRC Reprint) Franklin.

— Immunobiology of Natural Killer Cells: Assays for NK Cell Cytotoxicity; Their Values & Pitfalls, Vol. I. 256p. 1986. 168.00 (*0-8493-6542-2*, QR185) CRC Pr.

— Interleukin-2 & Killer Cells in Cancer. (Illus.). 791p. 1989. 240.00 (*0-8493-5388-2*, RC271) CRC Pr.

Lotzova, Eva & Sredni, B., eds. Future Trends in Research on AIDS, Cancer & Therapies. (Journal: Natural Immunity & Cell Growth Regulation: Vol. 7, No. 3, 1988). (Illus.). 68p. 1988. pap. 31.25 (*3-8055-4859-1*) S Karger.

Lotzova, Eva, et al, eds. International Symposium on AIDS & Cancer, Sao Paulo, Brazil, August 1988: Natural Immunity & Cell Growth Regulation Journal, Vol. 9, No. 3, 1990. (Illus.). 108p. 1990. pap. 62.50 (*3-8055-5225-4*) S Karger.

— International Workshop on Natural Killer Cells: 7th, Stockholm (Lidingo), June 1991 - Journal: Natural Immunity & Cell Growth Regulation, Vol. 10, No. 3, 1991. 68p. 1991. pap. 35.25 (*3-8055-5447-8*) S Karger.

***Lotzsch, Ronald.** Duden Taschenbucher: Jiddisches Woerterbuch. 2nd ed. 204p. (GER & YID.). 1992. 29.95 (*0-7859-8676-6*, 341106241x) Fr & Eur.

***Lou Guan Zhong.** Romance of the Three Kingdoms, Set, Vols. 1-2. 1276p. 1985. reprint ed. text ed. 34.50 (*0-614-06497-X*) Heian Intl.

Lou, Hans C. Developmental Neurology. (Illus.). 305p. 1982. text ed. 75.50 (*0-89004-700-6*) Raven.

Lou, Herbert H. Juvenile Courts in the United States. LC 77-169394. (Family in America Ser.). 297p. 1977. reprint ed. 20.95 (*0-405-03871-2*) Ayer.

Lou, Nils. The Art of Firing. 120p. 1995. pap. text ed. 30.00 (*0-9638064-0-8*) Clay Pacific.

Lou, Sue, et al. Get Ready! Get Set! Worship! (Illus.). 125p. 1992. ring bd. 25.00 (*0-9632053-0-7*) Sharing Tree.

— Get Ready! Get Set! Worship! Adapted for Use by United Methodist Church by Donna Strieb. (Illus.). 124p. 1994. ring bd. 25.00 (*0-9632053-1-5*) Sharing Tree.

Lou Tsu-K'uang. Personal Legends of Formosa I. (Asian Folklore & Social Life Monographs: No. 10). (CHI.). 1970. 14.00 (*0-89986-013-3*) Oriental Bk Store.

— Personal Legends of Formosa II. (Asian Folklore & Social Life Monographs: No. 66). 190p. (CHI.). 1975. 14.00 (*0-89986-061-3*) Oriental Bk Store.

Lou, Y. K., ed. see American Society of Mechanical Engineers Staff.

Louapre, Albert C., jt. ed. see Campion, Donald R.

Louasmaa, O. V. Experimental Principles & Methods Below 1k. 1974. text ed. 161.00 (*0-12-455950-6*) Acad Pr.

Louat, Frederic, et al. Welfare Implications of Female Headship in Jamaican Households. LC 93-21834. (Living Standards Measurement Study Working Paper Ser.: No. 96). 92p. 1993. 7.95 (*0-8213-2384-9*, 12384) World Bank.

Loubat, Joseph F. Gustavus Fox's Mission to Russia in 1866. LC 70-115559. (Russia Observed, Series I). 1970. reprint ed. 26.95 (*0-405-03045-2*) Ayer.

Loubere, Leo A. Louis Blanc: His Life & His Contribution to the Rise of French Jacobin-Socialism. LC 80-23424. (Northwestern University Studies in History: No.1). xii, 256p. 1980. reprint ed. text ed. 59.75 (*0-313-22690-3*, LOBL) Greenwood.

— Nineteenth-Century Europe: the Revolution of Life. LC 93-4487. 1993. pap. text ed. 23.00 (*0-13-221086-X*) P-H.

— Radicalism in Mediterranean France: Its Rise & Decline, 1848-1914. LC 73-171180. 258p. 1974. 64.50 (*0-87395-094-1*) State U NY Pr.

— The Red & the White: The History of Wine in France & Italy in the Nineteenth Century. LC 78-2304. (Illus.). 401p. 1978. 19.50 (*0-87395-370-3*) State U NY Pr.

— The Wine Revolution in France: The Twentieth Century. (Illus.). 331p. (C). 1990. text ed. 39.50 (*0-691-05592-0*) Princeton U Pr.

Louberge, Henri, ed. Risk, Information & Insurance. (C). 1990. lib. bdg. 64.00 (*0-7923-9041-5*, Pub. by Graham & Trotman UK) Kluwer Ac.

Loubert, Steven. The Snowmen of Berencia. Ingram, tr. 320p. 1995. pap. 9.95 (*1-56901-265-2*) NW Pub.

Loubet, Beth, et al. Privateer Playtesters' Guide. (Illus.). 96p. (Orig.). 1994. pap. 14.95 (*0-929373-16-2*) Origin Syst.

Loubet, Bruno. Cuisine Courante. (Illus.). 160p. 1992. 39.95 (*1-85165-652-9*, Pub. by Pavilion UK) Trafalgar.

— Cuisine Courante. (Illus.). 160p. 1995. 29.95 (*1-85145-819-0*, Pub. by Pavilion UK) Trafalgar.

Loubet del Bayle, Jean-Louis. Introduction to the Methods of Social Sciences. Johari, J. C., ed. 280p. (C). 1989. text ed. 27.95 (*81-207-0837-7*, Pub. by Sterling Pubs II) Apt Bks.

Loubier, Christiane. English - French Vocabulary of Editing & Binding. 56p. (ENG & FRE.). 1987. pap. 29.95 (*0-8288-9401-9*) Fr & Eur.

Loubriel, G. M., ed. Optically Activated Switching II. 1992. 62.00 (*0-8194-0778-X*, 1632) SPIE.

Loubser, A. Casebook on the Law of Partnership, Company Law & Insolvency Law - Vonnisbundel oor die Vennootskapsreg, Maatskappyereg en Insolvensiereg. 264p. 1992. pap. write for info. (*0-7021-2782-5*, Pub. by Juta SA) W W Gaunt.

Loubser, J. A. A Critical Review of Racial Theology in South Africa. LC 90-19168. (Texts & Studies in Religion: Vol. 53). (Illus.). 224p. 1990. reprint ed. lib. bdg. 89.95 (*0-7734-9794-3*) E Mellen.

Loucas, Penelope, ed. NW Crafts, 1988: A Northwest Competition, July 8-August 28, 1988. (Illus.). 12p. (Orig.). 1988. pap. 1.00 (*0-924335-05-X*) Tacoma Art Mus.

Loucas, Penelope, ed. see Crouse, Gloria E.

Loucas, Penelope, ed. see McBride, Delbert J.

Louch, Mary, tr. see Claparede, Edouard.

Louchheim, Katie, ed. The Making of the New Deal: The Insiders Speak. (Illus.). 392p. 1984. pap. text ed. 9.95 (*0-674-54346-7*) HUP.

Louck, J. D. & Metropolis, N. Symbolic Dynamics of Trapezoidal Maps. (Mathematics & Its Applications Main Ser.). 1986. lib. bdg. 112.00 (*90-277-2197-1*) Kluwer Ac.

Loucks, Daniel P. & Da Costa, J. R., eds. Decision Support Systems: Water Resources Planning. (NATO ASI Series G: Ecological Sciences: Vol. 26). xvi, 600p. 1991. 203.00 (*0-387-53097-5*) Spr-Verlag.

Loucks, Henry L. The Great Conspiracy of the House of Morgan & How to Defeat It. McCurry, Dan C. & Rubenstein, Richard E., eds. LC 74-30643. (American Farmers & the Rise of Agribusiness Ser.). 1975. reprint ed. 29.95 (*0-405-06813-1*) Ayer.

Loucks-Horsley, Susan & Hergert, Leslie F. An Action Guide to School Improvement. LC 85-70038. 82p. 1985. pap. text ed. 5.00 (*0-87120-130-5*, 611-85360) Assn Supervision.

Loucks-Horsley, Susan, et al. Elementary School Science for the Nineties. 166p. 1990. pap. 13.95 (*0-87120-176-3*, 611-90119) Assn Supervision.

Loucks, James M., ed. see Browning, Robert.

Loucks, Jennifer. Angry at Death & Other Poems. 1993. 8.95 (*0-533-10392-4*) Vantage.

Loucks, Kenneth. Training Entrepreneurs for Small Business Creation: Lessons from Experience. (Management Development Ser.: No. 26). xi, 137p. (Orig.). 1990. pap. 18.00 (*92-2-106343-7*) Intl Labour Office.

Loucks, R. G., jt. ed. see Bebout, D. G.

Loucks, Richard. Arthur Shepherd: American Composer. LC 79-22143. (Illus.). 1980. lib. bdg. 19.95 (*0-8425-1706-5*) BYU Scholarly.

Loucks, Robert G. & Sarg, J. Frederick, eds. Carbonate Sequence Stratigraphy Recent Developments & Applications. (AAPG Memoir Ser.: No. 57). (Illus.). vi, 545p. 1993. 78.00 (*0-89181-336-5*) AAPG.

Loucks, Robert G., jt. ed. see Halley, Robert B.

Loucks, Sandra, jt. auth. see Burstein, Alvin G.

Loucopoulos & Karakostas. Advanced Requirements Analysis & Specifications. 1995. text ed. 40.00 (*0-07-707464-5*) McGraw.

Loucopoulos, P., ed. see International Conference on Entity-Relationship Approach Staff.

Loucopoulos, Peri & Zicari, Roberto. Conceptual Modeling, Databases, & CASE: An Integrated View of Information Systems Development. 576p. 1992. text ed. 65.00 (*0-471-55462-6*) Wiley.

Loucopoulos, Peri, et al, eds. Advanced Information Systems Engineering: Proceedings of the Fourth International Conference, CAiSE 1992, Manchester, U. K., May 12-15, 1992. LC 92-16718. (Lecture Notes in Computer Science Ser.: Vol. 593). xi, 650p. 1992. pap. 85.00 (*0-387-55481-5*) Spr-Verlag.

***Loucopoulos, Pericles & Karakostas, Vassilios.** Software Requirements Engineering. LC 94-39117. (International Series in Software Engineering). 1995. pap. text ed. 40.00 (*0-07-707843-8*) McGraw.

Loud, G. H., jt. ed. see Wood, Ian.

Loud, Grover C. Evangelized America. LC 70-169770. (Select Bibliographies Reprint Ser.). 1977. reprint ed. 30.95 (*0-8369-5990-6*) Ayer.

Loud, John F., ed. see Andric, Ivo.

Loud, John F., tr. see Andric, Ivo.

Loud, Llewellyn L. & Harrington, M. R. Lovelock Cave. (University of California Publications in Social Welfare: Vol. 25(1)). (Illus.). viii, 183p. (C). reprint ed. pap. 20.00 (*1-55567-026-1*) Coyote Press.

Loud, Patricia C. The Art Museums of Louis I. Kahn. LC 89-51072. (Illus.). 304p. (Orig.). (C). 1989. text ed. 63.00 (*0-8223-0989-0*); pap. 32.00 (*0-8223-0998-X*) Duke.

Loud, Warren S. Periodic Solution of Perturbed Second-Order Autonomous Equations. (Memoirs of the American Mathematical Society Ser.: No. 47). 141p. reprint ed. pap. 40.20 (*0-7837-1632-X*, 2041925) Bks Demand.

— Periodic Solutions of X Double Prime Plus C Times X Plus G of (X) Equals F of T. LC 52-42839. (Memoirs Ser.: No. 1/31). 58p. 1978. reprint ed. pap. 16.00 (*0-8218-1231-9*, MEMO 1/31) Am Math.

— Periodic solutions of x" Plus cx' Plus g(x) Equals ef(t) fac. ed. (Memoirs of the American Mathematical Society Ser.: No. 31). 60p. 1994. pap. 25.00 (*0-7837-7552-0*, 2047305) Bks Demand.

Louda, Jiri. Lines of Succession. 2nd ed. 308p. 1992. text ed. 65.00 (*0-02-897255-4*) Macmillan.

Louden. Programming Languages: Principles & Practice. 608p. 1993. pap. 55.95 (*0-534-93277-0*) PWS Pubs.

Louden-Brown, P. The White Star Line. 1990. 59.00 (*0-9516038-2-5*, Pub. by Ship Pictorial Pubng UK) St Mut.

Louden, Jennifer. The Couple's Comfort Book: A Creative Guide for Renewing Passion, Pleasure & Commitment. LC 93-20733. 336p. 1994. pap. 15.00 (*0-06-250853-9*) Harper SF.

— A Little Book of Sensual Comfort. LC 93-46348. (Little Book of Wisdom Ser.). 96p. 1994. pap. 8.00 (*0-06-251112-2*) Harper SF.

— The Pregnant Woman's Comfort Book: A Self-Nurturing Guide to Your Emotional Well-Being During Pregnancy & Early Motherhood. LC 94-47638. 1995. pap. 14.00 (*0-06-251165-3*) Harper SF.

— The Woman's Comfort Book: A Self-Nurturing Guide for Restoring Balance in Your Life. LC 91-55316. 224p. 1992. pap. 14.00 (*0-06-250531-9*) Harper SF.

Louden, Keith E., jt. ed. see Wright, James A.

Louden, Robert B. Morality & Moral Theory: A Reappraisal & Reaffirmation. 256p. 1992. 49.95 (*0-19-507145-X*); pap. 18.95 (*0-19-507292-8*) OUP.

Louden, William. Understanding Teaching: Continuity & Change in Teachers' Knowledge. 224p. (C). 1991. text ed. 39.95 (*0-8077-3102-1*); pap. text ed. 17.95 (*0-8077-3101-3*) Tchrs Coll.

Louder, Dean R., ed. The Heart of French Canada: Quebec & Ontario. LC 92-11924. (Touring North America Ser.). (Illus.). 150p. 1992. 25.00 (*0-8135-1888-1*); pap. 9.95 (*0-8135-1889-X*) Rutgers U Pr.

Louder, Dean R. & Waddell, Eric, eds. French America: Mobility, Identity, & Minority Experience Across the Continent. Philip, Franklin, tr. LC 92-7982. (Illus.). 344p. (C). 1992. text ed. 42.50 (*0-8071-1669-6*); pap. text ed. 16.95 (*0-8071-1776-5*) La State U Pr.

Louderback, Joseph G., III, jt. auth. see Dominiak, Geraldine F.

Louderback, Joseph G., III, jt. auth. see Hirsch, Maurice L., Jr.

Louderback, Joseph G., III, et al. Survey of Accounting. Fenton, ed. LC 92-24023. 700p. (C). 1993. text ed. 60.25 (*0-314-01041-6*) West Pub.

Loudis, Leonard A., et al. Skiing Out of Your Mind: The Psychology of Peak Performance. Singer, Kenneth M., ed. LC 85-18210. (Illus.). 256p. (Orig.). 1986. pap. 16.95 (*0-88011-268-9*, PLOU0268) Human Kinetics.

Loudiyi, Dounia & Meares, Alison. Women in Conservation: Tools for Analysis & a Framework for Action. 153p. (C). 1993. pap. text ed. 20.00 (*2-8317-0196-1*, Pub. by IUCN SZ) Island Pr.

Loudon, A. G., ed. see Hill, Hilson C.

Loudon, Archibald. Selection of Some of the Most Interesting Narratives of Outrages Committed by the Indians in Their Wars with the White People, 2 Vols. in 1. LC 76-106124. (First American Frontier Ser.). 1971. reprint ed. 49.95 (*0-405-02866-0*) Ayer.

Loudon, Archibald & Lyman, Phineas. General Orders of 1757 Issued by the Earl of Loudoun & Phineas Lyman in the Campaign Against the French. LC 71-126241. (Select Bibliographies Reprint Ser.). 1977. reprint ed. 17.95 (*0-8369-5468-8*) Ayer.

Loudon, Betty. Nebraska History Magazine, 1959-1979: Index-Guide. LC 84-62608. 274p. 1985. pap. 7.00 (*0-318-17819-2*) Nebraska Hist.

Loudon, David L. & Della Bitta, Albert J. Consumer Behavior: Concepts & Applications. 3rd ed. 1988. text ed. write for info. (*0-07-038764-8*) McGraw.

Loudon, David L. & Della Britta, Albert J. Consumer Behavior: Concepts & Applications. 4th ed. LC 92-27875. 1993. text ed. write for info. (*0-07-038767-2*) McGraw.

Loudon, David L., jt. auth. see Stevens, Robert E.

Loudon, G. Marc. Organic Chemistry. LC 83-7075. (Chemistry Ser.). 1150p. 1984. text ed. write for info. (*0-201-14438-7*); student ed write for info. (*0-201-14436-0*); trans. write for info. (*0-201-14442-5*) Addison-Wesley.

— Organic Chemistry. 3rd ed. 1994. 94.25 (*0-8053-6550-8*) Benjamin-Cummings.

***Loudon, Irvine.** Childbed Fever: A Documentary History. LC 94-33390. (Diseases, Epidemics, & Medicine Ser.: Vol. 2). (Illus.). 288p. 1995. 43.00 (*0-8153-1079-X*, SS868) Garland.

— Medical Care & the General Practitioner, 1750-1850. LC 86-14172. 354p. (C). 1987. 69.00 (*0-19-822793-0*) OUP.

Loudon, J. C. Encyclopedia of Plants, Vols. 1 & 2. (C). 1988. text ed. 200.00 (*0-685-44244-6*, Scientific) St Mut.

Loudon, J. H. James Scott & William Scott, Bookbinders. (Illus.). 1980. 65.00 (*0-89679-003-7*) Moretus Pr.

Loudon, Jame W., jt. auth. see Loudon, Jane W.

Loudon, Jane W. The Mummy! A Tale of the Twenty-Second Century. LC 87-60458. 500p. 1988. reprint ed. 30.00 (*0-915431-03-3*); reprint ed. pap. 19.95 (*0-915431-04-1*) N American Archives.

Loudon, Jane W. & Loudon, Jame W. The Mummy! Or a Tale of the Twenty-Second Century. abr. ed. LC 94-12992. 1994. 42.50 (*0-472-09574-9*, Ann Arbor Bks) U of Mich Pr.

— The Mummy! Or a Tale of the Twenty-Second Century. abr. ed. LC 94-12992. 400p. 1994. pap. text ed. 17.95 (*0-472-06574-2*) U of Mich Pr.

Loudon, Jim. The Oneonta Roundhouse. 100p. 1993. pap. 17.95 (*0-9641119-0-X*) LRHS.

Loudon, Marc. Organic Chemistry. 2nd ed. (Illus.). 1300p. (C). 1988. text ed. 70.95 (*0-8053-6643-1*); student ed, pap. text ed. 24.75 (*0-8053-6644-X*); trans. 100.00 (*0-8053-6645-8*) Benjamin-Cummings.

— Organic Chemistry. 3rd ed. (C). 1995. text ed. 72.25 (*0-8053-6650-4*) Benjamin-Cummings.

Loudon, Mary. Unveiled: Nuns Talking. 290p. 1993. pap. 14.95 (*0-87243-201-7*) Templegate.

Loudon, Nancy B., ed. Handbook of Family Planning. 2nd ed. (Illus.). 472p. 1991. pap. text ed. 54.00 (*0-443-03964-X*) Churchill.

Loudon, Penny, jt. auth. see Wilkins, Robert.

Loudon, Rodney. The Quantum Theory of Light. 2nd ed. (Illus.). 1983. pap. 35.00 (*0-19-851155-8*) OUP.

Loudon, Rodney & Knight, P. L., eds. Squeezed Light: Special Issue of Journal of Modern Optics, Vol 34: 6/7. 310p. 1987. 51.00 (*0-85066-922-7*) Taylor & Francis.

Loudon, Rodney, jt. ed. see Agranovich, V. M.

Loudon, Rodney, jt. auth. see Barber, D. J.

Loudon, T. V. Computer Methods in Geology. 1979. text ed. 131.00 (*0-12-456950-1*) Acad Pr.

Loudy, Adlai. God's Eonian Purpose. 11.00 (*0-910424-56-X*); pap. 8.00 (*0-685-42097-3*) Concordant.

Loudy, Aldai. The Gospel of Our Salvation. 122p. 1973. text ed. 4.00 (*0-910424-60-8*) Concordant.

Loue, Sana. Immigration Law & Health: Patients & Providers. LC 93-11171. (Immigration Law Ser.). 1993. ring bd. 125.00 (*0-87632-920-2*) Clark Boardman Callaghan.

An Asterisk (*) at the beginning of an entry indicates that the title is appearing in BIP for the first time.

Louell, Margaret A. Fateful Journey. large type ed. (Linford Romance Library). 272p. 1992. pap. 14.95 (*0-7089-7283-7*, Trailtree Bookshop) Ulverscroft.

Louf, Andre. The Cistercian Way. (Cistercian Studies: No. 76). pap. 7.95 (*0-87907-976-2*) Cistercian Pubns.

— Teach Us to Pray: A Cowley Classic. LC 92-5949. 115p. 1992. pap. 8.95 (*1-56101-058-8*) Cowley Pubns.

— Tuning in to Grace the Quest for God. Vriend, John, tr. (Cistercian Studies). 300p. 1992. write for info. (*0-87907-729-8*); pap. write for info. (*0-87907-929-0*) Cistercian Pubns.

Louganis, Greg, jt. auth. see Marcus, Eric.

Lougee, George E., Jr. Durham, My Hometown. LC 90-84231. (Illus.). 272p. 1990. pap. 12.95 (*0-89089-436-1*) Carolina Acad Pr.

Lough, Don, contrib. Trumpet of the Lord. 1987. 8.50 (*0-685-68366-4*, MB-571) Lillenas.

***Lough, Francis.** Politics & Philosophy in the Early Novels of Ramon J. Sender, 1930-1936. LC 95-19531. (Hispanic Literature Ser.: Vol. 28). 228p. 1996. text ed. 89.95 (*0-7734-8897-9*) E Mellen.

Lough, George, jt. auth. see Sanford, John.

Lough, Glenn D. Now & Long Ago. (Illus.). 720p. (C). 1994. reprint ed. 35.00 (*0-87012-513-3*) McClain.

Lough, J., ed. see Diderot, Denis.

Lough, John. An Introduction to Eighteenth Century France. LC 60-2946. 397p. reprint ed. pap. 113.20 (*0-317-09444-0*, 2003670) Bks Demand.

Lough, John & Lough, Muriel. An Introduction to Nineteenth Century France. LC 79-305880. 360p. reprint ed. pap. 102.60 (*0-7837-4029-8*, 2043858) Bks Demand.

Lough, John & Merson, Elizabeth. John Graham Lough: A Northumbrian Sculptor. 96p. 1987. 39.00 (*0-85115-480-8*) Boydell & Brewer.

Lough, Mark, ed. see Perkins Coie Product Liability Practice Group Staff & Gerrard, Keith.

Lough, Muriel, jt. auth. see Lough, John.

Lough, Tom, ed. see Barrowman, Tom, et al.

Lough, W. J., ed. Chiral Liquid Chromatography. (Illus.). 256p. 1989. 112.00 (*0-412-01741-5*, A2081, Chap & Hall NY) Chapman & Hall.

Lough, W. J. & Wainer, I. W., eds. High Performance Liquid Chromatography: Fundamental Principles & Practice. 256p. 1992. 49.95 (*0-7514-0076-9*, A6878, Pub. by Blackie Acad & Prof UK) Routledge Chapman & Hall.

Lough, W. John, ed. see Riley, Christopher M.

Lough, William H. High-Level Consumption: Its Behavior; Its Consequences. LC 75-39258. (Getting & Spending: the Consumer's Dilemma Ser.). (Illus.). 1976. reprint ed. 29.95 (*0-405-08031-X*) Ayer.

Loughary, Jack & Ripley, Theresa. Working It Out Together: A Guide for Dual Career Couples. 167p. 1987. pap. 12.95 (*0-685-19247-4*) United Learn.

Loughary, John W. Uncle Jack among the English. (Illus.). 60p. (Orig.). 1984. pap. 3.95 (*0-915671-00-X*) United Learn.

Loughary, John W. & Ripley, Theresa M. Helping Others Help Themselves: A Guide to Counseling Skills. (Illus.). 218p. 1979. pap. text ed. write for info. (*0-07-038756-7*) McGraw.

Loughborough, J. N. The Great Second Advent Movement: Its Rise & Progress. LC 71-38453. (Religion in America, Ser. 2). 502p. 1977. reprint ed. 35.95 (*0-405-04073-3*) Ayer.

***Loughborough, Jas. M.** My Cave Life in Vicksburg with Letters of Trial & Travel. LC 75-46574. 196p. 1988. reprint ed. 21.00 (*0-87152-217-9*) Reprint.

Loughborough, John N. The Great Second Advent Movement. 1992. pap. 14.00 (*0-9633711-1-8*) Advent Pioneer Lib.

Loughborough, Mary A. My Cave Life in Vicksburg. 212p. 1989. reprint ed. 25.00 (*0-916107-65-5*) Broadfoot.

***Lougheed.** Grammar Skills Builder. (Regents Prep Series for the TOEFL Test). (Illus.). 192p. 1994. pap. text ed. 9.50 (*0-13-100637-1*) P-H.

— Listening Skills Builder. (Regents Prep Series for the TOEFL Test). (Illus.). 80p. 1994. pap. text ed. 7.95 (*0-13-100645-2*) P-H.

— Vocabulary & Reading Skills Builder. (Regents Prep Series for the TOEFL Test). (Illus.). 80p. 1994. pap. text ed. 7.95 (*0-13-100660-6*) P-H.

Lougheed, A. L., jt. auth. see Kenwood, A. G.

***Lougheed, Lin.** How to Prepare for the TOEIC: Test of English for International Communication. 1995. student ed, pap. 12.95 (*0-8120-1057-4*) Barron.

Lougheed, Linford. Four Practice Tests for the TOEFL. 128p. 1994. pap. text ed. 11.95 (*0-13-870015-X*) P-H.

— Listening Between the Lines: A Cultural Approach. (Illus.). (C). 1985. text ed. 14.89 (*0-201-14093-4*) Addison-Wesley.

— On Target for TOEIC. (A-W Japan Ser.). (Illus.). 224p. (C). 1989. text ed. 21.27 (*0-201-18263-7*) Addison-Wesley.

— Prentice Hall Prep Series for the Toefl Test: Listening Skills Builder. 1994. student ed, pap. 27.25 (*0-13-187790-9*) P-H.

— Prentice Hall Regents Prep Series for the Toefl Test: 4 Practice Tests. 1994. pap. 29.95 (*0-13-187717-8*) P-H.

— Prentice Hall TOEFL Prep Book. 448p. 1986. pap. text ed. 10.75 (*0-13-696600-4*) P-H.

— Regents Prentice Hall TOEFL Prep Book. 2nd ed. 432p. 1992. pap. text ed. write for info. (*0-13-714072-X*) P-H.

— Regents Prentice Hall Toefl Prep Book. 2nd ed. 1994. pap. 16.25 (*0-13-782632-X*) P-H.

Lougheed, Victor. Vehicles of the Air: A Popular Exposition of Modern Aeronautics with Working Drawings. LC 75-169427. (Literature & History of Aviation Ser.). 1972. reprint ed. 48.95 (*0-405-03770-8*) Ayer.

Loughery, John. Alias S. S. Van Dine. 320p. 1992. text ed. 24.00 (*0-684-19358-2*, Scribners) S&S Trade.

— John Sloan. (YA). (gr. 6 up). 1995. 37.50 (*0-8050-2878-1*) H Holt & Co.

Loughery, John, intro. First Sightings: Contemporary Stories of American Youth. 320p. 1993. 29.95 (*0-89255-186-0*); pap. 11.95 (*0-89255-187-9*) Persea Bks.

— Into the Widening World: International Coming-of-Age Stories. 288p. (Orig.). 1995. pap. 11.95 (*0-89255-204-2*) Persea Bks.

Loughhead, R. E., jt. auth. see Bray, R. J.

Loughlan, J., ed. Aerospace Structures. 212p. 1990. reprint ed. 90.00 (*1-85166-522-6*) Elsevier.

Loughlin, C. Sensors for Industrial Inspection. 1992. lib. bdg. 208.00 (*0-7923-2046-8*) Kluwer Ac.

Loughlin, Caroline & Anderson, Catherine. Forest Park. 304p. 1993. pap. 19.95 (*0-9638298-0-7*) Jr Leag St Louis.

Loughlin, Catherine E. & Suina, Joseph H. The Learning Environment: An Instructional Strategy. LC 81-23353. (Illus.). (C). 1982. pap. text ed. 18.95 (*0-8077-2714-8*) Tchrs Coll.

Loughlin, Gerald M. & Eigen, Howard. Pediatric Lung Disease: Diagnosis & Management. LC 93-1902. (Illus.). 862p. 1994. 125.00 (*0-683-05190-3*) Williams & Wilkins.

***Loughlin, James.** Ulster Unionism & British National Identity Since 1885. LC 95-3881. 1995. write for info. (*0-86187-845-0*, Pub. by Pinter Pubs UK) St Martin.

***Loughlin, John & Nazey, Sonia, eds.** The End of the French Uniley State: 10 Years of Regionalization 1982-1992. 164p. 1995. 29.50 (*0-7146-4643-1*, Pub. by F Cass Pubs UK); pap. 19.50 (*0-7146-4164-2*, Pub. by F Cass Pubs UK) Intl Spec Bk.

Loughlin, Julia, jt. auth. see Glassner, Barry.

Loughlin, Kathleen A. Women's Perceptions of Transformative Learning Experiences Within Consciousness-Raising. LC 93-32039. 426p. 1993. text ed. 109.95 (*0-7734-2252-8*, Mellen Univ Pr) E Mellen.

Loughlin, Laurie. Catmas Carols. LC 92-34649. (Illus.). 48p. 1993. 6.95 (*0-8118-0237-X*) Chronicle Bks.

— Hanukcats: Cat Parodies of Traditional Jewish Songs. LC 94-1393. (Illus.). 48p. 1994. 6.95 (*0-8118-0798-3*) Chronicle Bks.

Loughlin, M. A. Muscle Biopsy: Techniques. (Illus.). 256p. 1993. 80.00 (*0-7506-1406-4*) Buttrwrth-Heinemann.

Loughlin, Martin. Public Law & Political Theory. LC 92-5647. 288p. 1992. 59.00 (*0-19-876267-4*); pap. 24.95 (*0-19-876268-2*) OUP.

Loughlin, Nancy, jt. auth. see Gelb, Eric.

Loughlin, Peter J. Land Use Planning & Zoning. LC 93-11259. (New Hampshire Practice Ser.: Vol. 15). 600p. 1993. boxed 70.00 (*1-56257-361-6*) Michie Butterworth.

— Land Use Planning & Zoning, 2 vols., Set. (NH Practice Ser.: Vols. 1 & 1A). 920p. 1991. ring bd. 140.00 (*0-88063-703-X*) Butterworth Legal Pubs.

— Local Government Law, Set. (New Hampshire Practice Ser.: Vols. 13 & 14). 1500p. 1994. boxed 140.00 (*0-614-05922-4*) Michie Butterworth.

— Municipal Finance & Taxation. (New Hampshire Municipal Practice Ser.: Vol. 2). 880p. 1991. ring bd. 70.00 (*0-88063-704-8*) Butterworth Legal Pubs.

— Municipal Finance & Taxation. LC 93-33897. (New Hampshire Practice Ser.: Vol. 16). 860p. 1993. boxed 70.00 (*1-56257-362-4*) Michie Butterworth.

— New Hampshire Local Government Law, 1990-93. suppl. ed. 1993. ring bd. 34.50 (*0-614-03165-6*) Butterworth Legal Pubs.

— New Hampshire Local Government Law, 1990-93, Set. (NH Practice Ser.). 1500p. 1990. 130.00 (*0-88063-654-8*) Butterworth Legal Pubs.

— New Hampshire Municipal Practice Series, 4 vols., Set. ring bd. 225.00 (*0-88063-780-3*) Butterworth Legal Pubs.

— Public Health, Safety & Highways. (New Hampshire Municipal Practice Ser.: Vol. 3). 590p. 1991. ring bd. 70.00 (*0-88063-705-6*) Butterworth Legal Pubs.

Loughlin, Richard L. Prayer Conditioned: Faith-Lifting Poems with Helpful Comments & Notes. (Illus.). 96p. (Orig.). 1993. pap. 9.95 (*1-55605-232-4*) Wyndhall Pr.

— Verses Vice Verses. LC 80-81692. 120p. 1981. 9.95 (*0-911906-18-5*); pap. 5.95 (*0-911906-19-3*) Harian Creative Bks.

Loughlin, Sandra E. & Fallon, James H., eds. Neurotrophic Factors. (Illus.). 607p. 1992. text ed. 99.00 (*0-12-455830-5*) Acad Pr.

Loughlin, Sean, ed. Southern European Studies Guide: Critical Guide to the Academic Literature. 256p. 1994. lib. bdg. 70.00 (*0-86291-786-7*) Bowker-Saur.

Loughlin, Thomas R., ed. Marine Mammals & the "Exxon Valdez" (Illus.). 395p. 1994. text ed. 49.95 (*0-12-456160-8*) Acad Pr.

Loughman, B. C., jt. ed. see Gabelman, W. H.

Loughman, B. C., et al. Structural & Functional Aspects of Transport in Roots. (Developments in Plant & Soil Sciences Ser.). (C). 1900. pap. text ed. write for info. (*0-7923-0061-0*) Kluwer Ac.

Loughman, Michael. Learning to Rock Climb. LC 80-28639. (Outdoor Activities Guides Ser.). (Illus.). 192p. 1981. pap. 14.00 (*0-87156-281-2*) Sierra.

Loughmiller, Campbell & Loughmiller, Lynn. Texas Wildflowers: A Field Guide. (Illus.). 287p. 1984. 27.95 (*0-292-78059-1*); pap. 12.95 (*0-292-78060-5*) U of Tex Pr.

Loughmiller, Campbell & Loughmiller, Lynn, eds. Big Thicket Legacy. LC 76-46329. (Illus.). 253p. 1977. pap. 14.95 (*0-292-70733-9*) U of Tex Pr.

— Big Thicket Legacy. fac. ed. LC 76-46329. (Illus.). 254p. 1994. pap. 72.40 (*0-7837-7641-1*, 2047394) Bks Demand.

Loughmiller, Lynn, jt. auth. see Loughmiller, Campbell.

Loughmiller, Lynn, jt. ed. see Loughmiller, Campbell.

Loughney, Katharine, ed. Three Decades of Television: A Catalog of Television Programs Acquired by the Library of Congress, 1949-1979. LC 86-20098. 688p. 51.00 (*0-8444-0544-2*, 030-000-00185-1) Lib Congress.

— Three Decades of Television: A Catalog of Television Programs Acquired by the Library of Congress, 1949-1979. LC 86-20098. (Illus.). 716p. 1989. text ed. 51.00 (*0-16-003989-4*, S/N 030-000-00185-1) USGPO.

Loughney, Katherine. Film, Television, & Video Periodicals: A Comprehensive Annotated List. LC 90-14071. 448p. 1990. 50.00 (*0-8240-0647-X*) Garland.

Loughran, Charles S. Negotiating a Labor Contract: A Management Handbook. 2nd ed. LC 92-280. 590p. 1992. text ed. 58.00 (*0-87179-745-3*, HD6483) BNA.

Loughran, David K. Federico Garcia Lorca: The Poetry of Limits. (Serie A: Monografias, LXXIII). (Illus.). 219p. (C). 1978. 45.00 (*0-7293-0063-3*, Pub. by Tamesis Bks Ltd UK) Boydell & Brewer.

Loughran, Elizabeth L., jt. ed. see Reed, Horace B.

Loughran, Katheryne S., et al, eds. Somalia in Word & Image. LC 85-45470. (Illus.). 176p. 1986. pap. 25.00 (*0-253-20376-7*, MB-376) Ind U Pr.

Loughrey, Bryan, jt. ed. see Holderness, Graham.

Loughrey, Bryan, ed. see Middleton, Thomas.

Loughrey, Leo C., jt. auth. see Hegler, Jean.

Loughrey, Pat, intro. The People of Ireland. (Illus.). 200p. 1988. 35.00 (*0-86281-210-0*, Pub. by Appletree Pr IE) Irish Bks Media.

Loughrey, Patrick, ed. The People of Ireland. (Illus.). 208p. (C). 1989. 25.00 (*0-941533-55-7*) New Amsterdam Bks.

Loughridge, B. Which Dictionary? A Consumer's Guide to Selected English Dictionaries, Thesaurus, 1994 Edition. 1994p. 1994. 60.00 (*1-85604-110-7*, LAP1107) UNIPUB.

Loughrin, Judy. The Taste of Time, 1842-1992: One Hundred Fifty Years of Good Cooking Made Easy for Today's Kitchens. Patterson, Ce C., ed. LC 92-81893. (Illus.). 224p. (Orig.). 1992. pap. text ed. 14.95 (*0-9632981-2-7*) Lucky Canyon.

Lougy, Cameran, jt. auth. see Aaron, Henry J.

Lougy, Robert. Martin Chuzzlewit: An Annotated Bibliography. LC 89-23263. (Dickens Bibliographies Ser.: Vol. 10). 320p. 1990. 47.00 (*0-8240-4608-0*, H01083) Garland.

Lougy, Robert E. Charles Robert Maturin. 89p. 1975. 8.50 (*0-8387-7941-7*); pap. 1.95 (*0-8387-7986-7*) Bucknell U Pr.

Louhija, A., ed. see International Congress on Internal Medicine Staff.

Louhija, A., ed. see Paavo Nurmi Symposium Staff.

Loui, Shirley M. Murasaki's Genji & Proust's Recherche: A Comparative Study. LC 90-33212. (Studies in Comparative Literature: Vol. 8). 248p. 1991. lib. bdg. 89.95 (*0-88946-424-3*) E Mellen.

Louie, Ai-Ling. Yeh Shen: A Cinderella Story from China. (Illus.). 32p. (J). (ps-2). 1990. 14.95 (*0-399-20900-X*, Philomel Bks) Putnam Pub Group.

***Louie, Andrea.** Moon Cakes: A Novel. LC 94-48115. 288p. 1995. 21.00 (*0-345-38554-3*) Ballantine.

Louie, David W. Pangs of Love. (Contemporary Fiction Ser.). 240p. 1992. pap. 9.95 (*0-452-26888-5*, Plume) NAL-Dutton.

Louie, Elaine. New York City Man. 240p. (Orig.). 1989. pap. 8.95 (*0-446-38708-8*) Warner Bks.

— New York City Woman. 240p. (Orig.). 1989. pap. 8.95 (*0-446-38706-1*) Warner Bks.

Louie Gee Group Staff. Understanding Compressed Air Contamination & Coalescing Filters. (Illus.). 89p. (Orig.). Date not set. pap. 19.95 (*0-9631731-0-3*) Dico Pubns.

Louie, Kam. Between Fact & Fiction: Essays on Post-Mao Chinese Literature & Society. 150p. (C). 1990. pap. text ed. 18.00 (*0-9590735-6-6*, Pub. by Wild Peony Pty AT) UH Pr.

Louie, Kam, intro. Strange Tales from Strange Lands: Stories by Zheng Wanlong. (Cornell East Asia Ser.: No. 66). 147p. (Orig.). (C). 1993. 18.00 (*0-939657-85-6*); pap. 10.00 (*0-939657-66-X*) Cornell East Asia Pgm.

Louie, Reagan. Towards a Truer Life: Photographs of China, 1980-1990. (Illus.). 96p. 1991. 35.00 (*0-89381-465-2*) Aperture.

Louie, Reagan, photos. Toward a Truer Life. 96p. 1991. pap. 19.95 (*0-89381-477-6*) Frnds Photography.

Louis, jt. auth. see Shapiro.

Louis, Adrian C. Among the Dog Eaters. 91p. (Orig.). 1992. pap. 9.95 (*0-931122-69-4*) West End.

— Ancient Acid Flashing Back: Poems of the Sixties. LC 94-32912. 1994. 12.95 (*0-9636829-3-8*); pap. 9.95 (*0-9636829-4-6*) Mother Road.

— Blood Thirsty Savages. 109p. 1994. 18.95 (*1-56809-010-2*); pap. 12.50 (*1-56809-011-0*) Time Being Bks.

— Fire Water World. 69p. (Orig.). 1989. pap. 6.95 (*0-931122-51-1*) West End.

— Skins. 304p. 1995. 23.00 (*0-517-79958-8*, Crown) Crown Pub Group.

— Vortex of Indian Fevers. LC 94-45837. 1995. write for info. (*0-8101-5017-4*); pap. write for info. (*0-8101-5042-5*) TriQuarterly.

***Louis, Adrian C., et al.** Days of Obsidian, Days of Grace: Selected Poetry & Prose by Four Native American Writers. 152p. 1994. pap. 13.95 (*0-9641986-0-6*) Poetry Harbor.

Louis, Anne E., ed. Handbook of Difficult Diagnosis. 777p. 1990. pap. text ed. 33.95 (*0-443-08677-X*) Churchill.

Louis, Anthony. Horary Astrology: The History & Practice of Astro-Divination. LC 90-46436. 592p. (Orig.). 1991. pap. 18.95 (*0-87542-394-9*) Llewellyn Pubns.

***Louis, Cynthia B.** Jailhouse Key: Prevention vs. Conviction. (Juvenile Law Ser.). (Illus.). 113p. (Orig.). Date not set. pap. 9.95 (*0-9644630-0-8*) C B Louis.

Louis, Daphne R., jt. auth. see Johnson, Terry D.

Louis, David. Two Thousand Two Hundred & One Fascinating Facts, 2 vols. in 1. 1988. 9.99 (*0-517-39574-6*) Random Hse Value.

***Louis, Diana F. & Marinos, June.** Prospero's Kitchen: Mediterranean Cooking of the Ionian Islands from Corfu to Kythera. LC 94-49418. (Illus.). 1995. 21.95 (*0-87131-782-6*) M Evans.

Louis, Dorothy. How Lilacs Came to Rochester, Set. 1982. pap. write for info. (*0-9609624-3-3*); lp write for info. (*0-9609624-4-1*) Bookworm Rochester NY.

— My Father, the Chef. (Illus.). 148p. (Orig.). 1978. pap. 15.00 (*0-9609624-0-9*) Bookworm Rochester NY.

Louis, Edwin & Cole, Nancy C. The Unique Woman. 180p. 1991. pap. 7.95 (*1-56292-010-3*, HH010) Honor Bks OK.

Louis, Frances. Swift's Anatomy of Misunderstanding: A Study of Swift's Epistemological Imagination in "A Tale of a Tub" & "Gulliver's Travels" 220p. 1981. 52.50 (*0-389-20074-3*, 06804) B&N Imports.

Louis, J., jt. auth. see Louis, V.

Louis, Jean-Victor. From EMS to Monetary Union. 76p. 1990. pap. 10.00 (*92-826-0067-X*, CB-58-90-231-EN-C) UNIPUB.

Louis, Jennifer M., jt. auth. see Louis, Victor E.

Louis, Joseph. Madelaine. 1987. pap. 2.95 (*0-317-54101-3*) Bantam.

Louis, K. S., jt. auth. see Rosenblum, S.

***Louis, Karen S. & Kruse, Sharon D.** Professionalism & Community: Perspectives on Reforming Urban Schools. (Illus.). 272p. 1995. 49.95 (*0-8039-6252-5*); pap. 24.95 (*0-8039-6253-3*) Corwin Pr.

Louis, Karen S. & Miles, Matthew B. Improving the Urban High School: What Works & Why. 360p. (C). 1990. text ed. 44.95 (*0-8077-3022-X*); pap. text ed. 22.95 (*0-8077-3021-1*) Tchrs Coll.

Louis, Karen S. & Sieber, Sam D., eds. Bureaucracy & the Dispersed Organization: The Educational Extension Agent Experiment. LC 78-31623. (Modern Sociology Ser.). 272p. 1979. 39.50 (*0-89391-018-X*) Ablex Pub.

Louis, Karen S., jt. ed. see Murphy, Joseph.

Louis, Lisa. Butterflies of the Night: Mama-sans, Geisha, Strippers, & the Japanese Men They Serve. 224p. (C). 1992. 19.95 (*0-8348-0249-X*, Tengu Bks) Weatherhill.

Louis, M., jt. auth. see Hobson, G. D.

Louis, Margot K. Swinburne & His Gods: The Roots & Growth of an Agnostic Poetry. 256p. (C). 1990. text ed. 47.95 (*0-7735-0715-9*, Pub. by McGill CN) U of Toronto Pr.

Louis, Margot K., jt. auth. see Blank, Kim G.

Louis, Mary-Ben. Dark Windows. 288p. 1991. pap. 3.95 (*0-8217-3416-4*) Zebra.

— Sing Me to Sleep. 288p. 1993. mass mkt. 4.50 (*0-8217-4405-4*) Zebra.

Louis, Murray. Murray Louis on Dance. LC 92-6468. 1992. 19.95 (*1-55652-147-2*) A cappella Bks.

Louis-Napoleon, Geoffroy-Chateau & Geoffroy-Chateau, Louis-Napoleon. Napoleon & the Conquest of the World: A Fictional Account of Napoleon's Escape from Russia, Invasion of England, & Conquest of Asia & America. LC 94-72170. (Illus.). 440p. 1994. reprint ed. lib. bdg. 39.95 (*0-9642115-3-X*) Campaign Press.

Louis Of Granada. Summa of the Christian Life, 3 vols., 1. Aumann, Jordan, tr. LC 79-65716. 1979. reprint ed. write for info. (*0-89555-118-7*) TAN Bks Pubs.

— Summa of the Christian Life, 3 vols., 2. Aumann, Jordan, tr. LC 79-65716. 1979. reprint ed. write for info. (*0-89555-119-5*) TAN Bks Pubs.

— Summa of the Christian Life, 3 vols., 3. Aumann, Jordan, tr. LC 79-65716. 1979. reprint ed. write for info. (*0-89555-120-9*) TAN Bks Pubs.

— Summa of the Christian Life, 3 vols., Set. Aumann, Jordan, tr. LC 79-65716. 1979. reprint ed. pap. 36.00 (*0-89555-121-7*) TAN Bks Pubs.

Louis, R. Surgery of the Spine: Surgical Anatomy & Operative Approaches. (Illus.). 328p. 1983. 233.00 (*0-387-11412-2*) Spr-Verlag.

Louis, R. & Weidner, A., eds. Cervical Spine, No. II. (Illus.). 304p. 1990. 91.00 (*0-387-82151-1*, 3624) Spr-Verlag.

Louis, Raymond. Labour Co-Operatives: Retrospect & Prospects. vi, 162p. 1983. 28.00 (*92-2-103011-3*); pap. 20.00 (*92-2-103012-1*) Intl Labour Office.

Louis, Rene, jt. auth. see Chretien de Troyes.

Louis, Rita, tr. see Shaw, Lucy.

Louis, Roger W., jt. ed. see Gifford, Prosser.

***Louis, S., ed.** Fourth Golden West International Conference on Intelligent Systems. (Conference Proceedings Ser.). (C). 1995. write for info. (*1-880843-12-9*) Int Soc Comp App.

***Louis, Sang B., pseud.** Anyabwile. (Illus.). 374p. 1995. pap. 14.95 (*0-9645582-0-3*) R L Jackson.

Louis, V. Information Moscow. 178p. (C). 1991. 75.00 (*0-89771-897-6*, Pub. by Collets) St Mut.

Louis, V. & Louis, J. Complete Guide to the Soviet Union: New York St. Martin's Press, 1980. (Illus.). 378p. (C). 1980. 115.00 (*0-685-32379-X*) St Mut.

Louis, Victor E. & Louis, Jennifer M. Louis Motorists' Guide to the Soviet Union. 2nd ed. LC 85-21830. (Illus.). 625p. 1987. 105.00 (*0-08-031817-7*, Pergamon Pr); pap. 69.00 (*0-08-031816-9*, Pergamon Pr) Elsevier.

— Sport in the Soviet Union. 2nd ed. 74.00 (*0-08-024506-4*, Pub. by Pergamon Repr UK) Franklin.

Louis, W. Roger, jt. ed. see Livingston, William S.

Louis, William R. The British Empire in the Middle East, 1945-1951: Arab Nationalism, the United States, & Postwar Imperialism. (Illus.). 820p. 1986. pap. 35.00 (*0-19-822960-7*) OUP.

— Imperialism at Bay: The United States & the Decolonization of the British Empire, 1941-1945. 595p. 1987. reprint ed. pap. 32.50 (*0-19-822972-0*) OUP.

L

— In the Name of God, Go! Leo Amery & the British Empire in the Age of Churchill. 192p. 1992. 19.95 (*0-393-03393-7*) Norton.

Louis, William R. & Bull, Hedley, eds. The Special Relationship: Anglo-American Relations since 1945. 432p. 1987. reprint ed. 69.00 (*0-19-822925-9*) OUP.

— The Special Relationship: Anglo-American Relations since 1945. 432p. 1989. reprint ed. pap. 27.00 (*0-19-820183-4*) OUP.

Louis, William R. & Owen, Roger, eds. Suez Nineteen Fifty-Six: The Crisis & Its Consequences. (Illus.). 448p. 1991. reprint ed. pap. 29.95 (*0-19-820241-5*) OUP.

Louis, William R., jt. ed. see Bill, James A.

Louis, William R., jt. ed. see Blake, Robert.

Louis, William R., jt. auth. see Gifford, Prosser.

Louis, Wm. R., jt. auth. see Gifford, Prosser.

Louis, Wm. Roger & Stookey, Robert W., eds. The End of the Palestine Mandate. (Center for Middle Eastern Studies, Modern Middle East Ser.: No. 12). (Illus.). 197p. (C). 1986. reprint ed. text ed. 20.00 (*0-292-72052-1*); reprint ed. pap. 10.95 (*0-292-72063-7*) U of Tex Pr.

Louise Hsi Kuo, jt. auth. see Yuan Hsi Kuo.

***Louise, Jay D.** How to Have an Affair' & Never Get Caught! LC 94-74957. (Illus.). 128p. 1995. 17.95 (*0-9644789-0-0*, Roxan Bks) DeBergerac Pub.

Louise Lone Dog. Strange Journey: The Vision Life of a Psychic Indian Woman. Powell, Patricia, ed. (Illus.). 105p. 1990. reprint ed. pap. 8.95 (*0-87961-207-X*) Naturegraph.

Louise, Virginia, jt. auth. see Draper, Linda.

Louisell & Descamps. Developing a Teaching Style. (C). 1991. text ed. 46.50 (*0-06-044109-7*) HarpCollege.

Louisell, et al. Principles of Evidence & Proof. 3rd ed. 1977. text ed. 32.00 (*0-88277-424-7*) Foundation Pr.

Louisell, David W. Evidence: Adaptable to Courses Utilizing Materials by Louisell. 5th ed. 273p. write for info. (*0-318-62084-7*) HarBrace.

Louisell, David W. & Louisell, Williams H. Medical Malpractice, 4 vols. 1960. Updates. ring bd. write for info. (*0-8205-1370-9*) Bender.

Louisell, David W. & Mueller, Christopher B. Federal Evidence, 5 vols. LC 76-46689. 1985. 395.00 (*0-686-22901-0*) Lawyers Cooperative.

Louisell, David W., et al. Pleading & Procedure - State & Federal, 1993 Supplement to Cases & Materials. 6th ed. (University Casebook Ser.). 339p. Date not set. pap. text ed. 11.95 (*1-56662-106-2*) Foundation Pr.

Louisell, William H. Quantum Statistical Properties of Radiation. (Classics Library). 1990. pap. text ed. 44.95 (*0-471-52365-8*) Wiley.

Louisell, Williams H., jt. auth. see Louisell, David W.

Louisi, Gary. Dashiell Hammett & Raymond Chandler in Paperback. 100p. 1994. pap. 15.00 (*0-936071-36-2*) Gryphon Pubns.

Louisiana Appellate Court Handbook Committee. Louisiana Appellate Practice Handbook. LC 86-81536. 1986. 115.00 (*0-318-21801-1*) Lawyers Cooperative.

— Louisiana Appellate Practice Handbook: Supplement, 1992. suppl. ed. LC 86-81536. 1992. 52.50 (*0-317-04348-X*) Lawyers Cooperative.

Louisiana Commission des Avoyelles. Avoyelles: Crossroads of Louisiana Where All Cultures Meet. Woolfolk, Doug, ed. (Illus.). 224p. 1981. 29.95 (*0-86518-021-0*) Moran Pub Corp.

Louisiana District Judges Staff. Judges of Louisiana. 1972. 6.00 (*0-685-27203-6*) Claitors.

Louisiana Pen Women Staff. Louisiana Leaders. 1970. 12.50 (*0-87511-067-3*) Claitors.

— Vignettes of Louisiana History. 12.50 (*0-87511-068-1*) Claitors.

Louisiana Restaurant Association Staff. Chef's Secrets from Great Restaurants in Louisiana. 1989. 16.95 (*0-88289-639-3*) Pelican.

Louisiana School Students. Ascending. (Illus.). 302p. (Orig.). (J). (gr. 1-12). Date not set. pap. 25.00 (*1-882913-00-0*) Thornton LA.

***Louisiana State Bar Association Staff.** Louisiana Formulary, 2 vols., Set. 3rd annot. ed. 1970. 35.00 (*0-614-05886-4*) Michie Butterworth.

Louisiana State Staff. Civil Code of the State of Louisiana: By Authority. LC 74-19620. reprint ed. 94.50 (*0-404-12456-9*) AMS Pr.

Louisville Division of Fire Staff. Louisville Division of Fire History Book. LC 88-51134. 112p. 1988. 40.00 (*0-938021-69-9*) Turner Pub KY.

***Louisville's Young Playwrights Staff.** In Sight. 1986. 5.00 (*0-87129-578-4*) Dramatic Pub.

***Louizos, Dianna.** The Greater Northern California Road Map, Eatery Guide, & Cookbook. Paxton, Vicki, ed. 52p. (Orig.). 1994. pap. 11.00 (*0-9643901-0-8*) J Levy Ctr.

Louka, Elli. Overcoming National Barriers to International Waste Trade: A New Perspective on the Transnational Movement of Hazardous & Radioactive Materials. (International Environmental Law & Policy Ser.). 240p. (C). 1994. lib. bdg. 87.00 (*0-7923-2850-7*) Kluwer Ac.

***Loukaides, Loukes G.** Essays on the Developing Law of Human Rights. LC 94-23941. (International Studies in Human Rights: Vol. 39). 1995. lib. bdg. 96.00 (*0-7923-3276-8*, Pub. by M Nijhoff) Kluwer Ac.

Loukakis, Angelo. For the Patriarch. 191p. 1982. pap. 13.95 (*0-7022-1600-3*) Intl Spec Bk.

— Vernacular Dreams. LC 85-14088. 228p. 1986. pap. 14.95 (*0-7022-2025-6*, Pub. by Univ Queensland Pr AT) Intl Spec Bk.

Loukashevitch, Claudia. Sejatel. (Illus.). 462p. 1966. 20.00 (*0-317-30416-X*); pap. 15.00 (*0-317-30417-8*) Holy Trinity.

Loukes, Harold. Readiness for Religion. LC 63-11818. (Orig.). 1963. pap. 3.00 (*0-87574-126-6*) Pendle Hill.

Loukianoff, Gregoire. Poeme Heroique sur le Bataille de Qadech (1288 Av.J.C.) 24p. (Orig.). (FRE.). (C). reprint ed. pap. 8.50 (*0-933175-18-3*) Van Siclen Bks.

***Loukides, Mike.** GNU Programming Tools. 250p. 1995. pap. text ed. 39.95 (*1-56592-112-7*) OReilly & Assocs.

— System Performance Tuning. (Nutshell Handbook Ser.). 336p. (Orig.). 1990. pap. 24.95 (*0-937175-60-9*) OReilly & Assocs.

— UNIX for FORTRAN Programmers. 264p. 1990. 24.95 (*0-937175-51-X*) OReilly & Assocs.

Loukides, Mike, ed. see Bolinger, Don & Bronson, Tan.

Loukides, Mike, ed. see Dowd, Kevin.

Loukides, Mike, ed. see DuBois, Paul.

Loukides, Mike, ed. see Gilly, Daniel.

Loukides, Mike, ed. see Hunt, Craig.

Loukides, Mike, ed. see Kerrigan, James F.

Loukides, Mike, ed. see Krol, Ed.

Loukides, Mike, ed. see Radin, Dave.

Loukides, Mike, ed. see Rosenblatt, Bill.

Loukides, Mike, ed. see Welles & Bartok.

Loukides, Paul & Fuller, Linda, eds. Beyond the Stars Four: Locales in American Popular Film. LC 89-82334. 280p. (C). 1993. 39.95 (*0-87972-588-5*); pap. 18.95 (*0-87972-589-3*) Bowling Green Univ.

Loukides, Paul & Fuller, Linda K. Beyond the Stars Two: Plot Conventions in American Popular Film. LC 89-82334. 225p. (C). 1991. lib. bdg. 39.95 (*0-87972-517-6*); pap. text ed. 18.95 (*0-87972-518-4*) Bowling Green Univ.

Loukides, Paul & Fuller, Linda K., eds. Beyond the Stars: Stock Characters in American Popular Culture. LC 89-82334. (Illus.). 245p. (C). 1990. lib. bdg. 40.95 (*0-87972-479-X*); pap. 19.95 (*0-87972-480-3*) Bowling Green Univ.

— Beyond the Three: The Material World in American Popular Film. LC 89-82334. 245p. 1993. 35.95 (*0-87972-622-9*); pap. 13.95 (*0-87972-623-7*) Bowling Green Univ.

Loukomsky. Memoirs of the Russian Revolution. 1976. lib. bdg. 59.95 (*0-8490-2225-8*) Gordon Pr.

Loukopoulos, Dimitris, ed. Prenatal Diagnosis of Thalassemia & the Hemoglobinopathies. 272p. 1988. 151.00 (*0-8493-5972-4*, RJ416, CRC Reprint) Franklin.

Loukopoulos, Dimitris, jt. ed. see Bartsocas, Christos S.

Loukopoulos, Louisa D., ed. see Andronicos, Manolis, et al.

Loulan, Jo Ann. The Lesbian Erotic Dance: Butch, Femme, Androgyny, & Other Rhythms. LC 90-10177. 304p. (Orig.). 1990. pap. 12.95 (*0-933216-76-9*) Spinsters Ink.

— Lesbian Passion: Loving Ourselves & Each Other. LC 87-60781. 325p. (Orig.). 1987. pap. 12.95 (*0-933216-29-7*) Spinsters Ink.

— Lesbian Sex. LC 84-52008. (Illus.). 320p. (Orig.). 1984. pap. 12.95 (*0-933216-13-0*) Spinsters Ink.

Loulides, Mike, ed. see Harrison, Mark.

Loulie. Elements or Principles of Music. Cohen, Albert, ed. (Musical Theorists in Translation Ser.: Vol. 6). 1966. lib. bdg. 34.00 (*0-912024-26-7*) Inst Mediaeval Mus.

Loulis, John K. Greece under Papandreou: NATO's Ambivalent Partner. (C). 1985. 35.00 (*0-907967-50-7*, Pub. by Inst Euro Def & Strat UK) St Mut.

Loumaye, Jacqueline. Chagall: My Sad & Joyous Village. Goodman, John, tr. LC 93-39109. (Art for Children Ser.). (Illus.). 64p. (J). (gr. 3 up). 1994. lib. bdg. 14.95 (*0-7910-2807-0*) Chelsea Hse.

— Degas: The Painted Gesture. LC 93-33682. (Art for Children Ser.). (Illus.). 64p. (J). (gr. 3 up). 1994. lib. bdg. 14.95 (*0-7910-2809-7*) Chelsea Hse.

— The Tale of the Kite. (Child's World Library). (Illus.). 32p. (J). (gr. 3-5). 1991. lib. bdg. 18.50 (*0-89565-759-7*) Childs World.

— Van Gogh: The Touch of Yellow. (Art for Children Ser.). (Illus.). 64p. (J). (gr. 3 up). 1994. lib. bdg. 14.95 (*0-7910-2817-8*) Chelsea Hse.

Loumiet, James R. & Jungbauer, William G. Train Accident Reconstruction & FELA & Railroad Litigation. (Illus.). 560p. 1994. text ed. 79.00 (*0-88450-096-9*, 0969) Lawyers & Judges.

— Train Accident Reconstruction & FELA & Railroad Litigation. 2nd ed. (Illus.). 760p. 1995. text ed. 99.00 (*0-913875-18-X*, 0969) Lawyers & Judges.

Loumiet, Robin & Levack, Nancy. Independent Living: A Curriculum with Adaptations for Students with Visual Impairments. 600p. 1991. pap. 35.00 (*1-880366-00-2*) Texas Schl BVI.

— Independent Living: A Curriculum with Adaptations for Students with Visual Impairments, 1. 2nd ed. LC 93-6746. 1993. pap. write for info. (*1-880366-07-X*) Texas Schl BVI.

— Independent Living: A Curriculum with Adaptations for Students with Visual Impairments, 2. 2nd ed. LC 93-6746. 1993. pap. write for info. (*1-880366-08-8*) Texas Schl BVI.

— Independent Living: A Curriculum with Adaptations for Students with Visual Impairments, 3. 2nd ed. LC 93-6746. 1993. pap. write for info. (*1-880366-09-6*) Texas Schl BVI.

— Independent Living: A Curriculum with Adaptations for Students with Visual Impairments, Set. 2nd ed. LC 93-6746. 1993. pap. 50.00 (*1-880366-06-1*) Texas Schl BVI.

Lound, Karen, jt. auth. see Flynn, Tom.

Lounesto, Pertti, jt. ed. see Ablamowicz, Rafal.

Lounesto, Pertti, ed. see Riesz, Marcel.

Lounibos, L. P. Phytotelmata: Terrestrial Plants As Hosts of Aquatic Insect Communities. Frank, J. H., ed. 304p. 1983. pap. text ed. 24.95 (*0-937548-05-7*) Plexus Pub.

Lounibos, L. Phil, et al, eds. Ecology of Mosquitoes: Proceedings of a Workshop. LC 85-80456. (Illus.). 580p. 1985. 15.00 (*0-9615224-0-2*) Fla Med Entom.

Lounsberry, Barbara. The Art of Fact: Contemporary Artists of Nonfiction. LC 89-17222. (Contributions to the Study of World Literature Ser.: No. 53). 232p. 1990. text ed. 55.00 (*0-313-26893-2*, LCB/, Greenwood Pr) Greenwood.

— The Writer in You: A Writing Process Reader. (C). 1991. text ed. 27.50 (*0-06-044118-6*) HarpCollege.

Lounsberry, Barbara, jt. auth. see Talese, Gay.

Lounsbury, Charles. Pictures in the Fire. (Illus.). 48p. 1993. 18.95 (*0-9621131-9-0*) Blue Lantern Studio.

Lounsbury, Floyd G. Oneida Verb Morphology. LC 76-49736. (Yale University Publications in Anthropology Reprints Ser.: No. 48). 111p. 1976. pap. 20.00x (*0-87536-528-0*) HRAFP.

Lounsbury, John F. & Aldrich, Frank T. Introduction to Geographic Field Methods & Techniques. 2nd ed. 224p. (C). 1986. pap. write for info. (*0-675-20509-3*, Merrill Pub Co) Macmillan.

Lounsbury, John F. & Ogden, Lawrence. Earth Science. 3rd ed. LC 78-21130. 523p. reprint ed. pap. 149.10 (*0-317-28121-6*, 2022505) Bks Demand.

Lounsbury, John H. As I See It. 102p. (Orig.). 1991. pap. text ed. 14.00 (*1-56090-058-X*) Natl Middle Schl.

Lounsbury, John H., ed. Connecting the Curriculum Through Interdisciplinary Instruction. 168p. (Orig.). 1992. pap. text ed. 22.00 (*1-56090-071-7*) Natl Middle Schl.

Lounsbury, John H. & Johnston, J. Howard. Life in the Three Sixth Grades. 144p. (Orig.). 1988. pap. text ed. 11.00 (*0-88210-212-5*) Natl Assn Principals.

Lounsbury, John H., ed. see Hoff, Joseph W.

Lounsbury, Myron O. The Origins of American Film Criticisms, 1909-1939. LC 72-556. (Dissertations on Film Ser.). 560p. 1974. reprint ed. 31.95 (*0-405-04099-7*) Ayer.

Lounsbury, Patricia F., jt. auth. see Crow, Marjorie.

Lounsbury, Patricia S. Cardiac Rhythm Disorders: A Nursing Process Approach. 393p. 1992. pap. 29.95 (*0-8016-6576-0*) Mosby Yr Bk.

***Lounsbury, Richard C., ed.** Louisa S. McCord: Political & Social Essays. (Illus.). 608p. (C). 1995. text ed. 45.00 (*0-8139-1570-8*) U Pr of Va.

Lounsbury, T. R. Shakespeare & Voltaire. 1973. 59.95 (*0-8490-1033-0*) Gordon Pr.

Lounsbury, Thomas R. Early Literary Career of Robert Browning. LC 68-760. (Studies in Browning: No. 4). 1969. reprint ed. lib. bdg. 75.00 (*0-8383-0587-3*) M S G Haskell Hse.

— History of the English Language. 1972. 59.95 (*0-8490-0353-9*) Gordon Pr.

— James Fenimore Cooper. (BCL1-PS American Literature Ser.). 306p. 1992. reprint ed. lib. bdg. 89.00 (*0-7812-6694-7*) Rprt Serv.

— Pro-Slavery Overthrown & the True Principles of Abolitionism Declared. 1977. 16.95 (*0-8369-9169-9*, 9044) Ayer.

— Shakespeare & Voltaire. LC 72-172753. reprint ed. 18.45 (*0-404-04029-2*) AMS Pr.

— Shakespeare & Voltaire. LC 68-20237. 1972. reprint ed. 24.95 (*0-405-08754-3*, Pub. by Blom Pubns UK) Ayer.

— Text of Shakespeare. LC 74-130240. reprint ed. 29.50 (*0-404-04035-7*) AMS Pr.

Lounsbury, Warren C. Theatre Backstage from A to Z. rev. ed. LC 89-14715. (Illus.). 242p. 1989. pap. 22.50 (*0-295-96828-1*) U of Wash Pr.

Lounsbury, Warren C., jt. auth. see Boulanger, Norman C.

Loup Garou Press, Inc. Staff, ed. My Life Story: The LGP Autobiography System. 250p. 1988. student ed, ring bd. 35.00 (*0-921860-1-5*) Loup Garou Pr Inc.

Loup, Jacques. Can the Third World Survive? LC 82-9945. 264p. 1983. text ed. 38.50x (*0-8018-2765-5*) Johns Hopkins.

Loupy, Andre & Tchoubar, Bianca. Salt Effects in Organic & Organometallic Chemistry. 322p. 1992. lib. bdg. 125.00 (*0-89573-954-2*) VCH Pubs.

Lourdeaux, Lee. Italian & Irish Filmmakers in America: Ford, Capra, Coppola & Scorsese. (Illus.). 288p. 1990. 39.95 (*0-87722-697-0*) Temple U Pr.

— Italian & Irish Filmmakers in America: Ford, Capra, Coppola, & Scorsese. (Illus.). 288p. (Orig.). 1993. pap. 16.95 (*1-56639-087-7*) Temple U Pr.

— Italian & Irish Filmmakers in America: Ford, Capra, Coppola & Scorsese. 1993. reprint ed. pap. 14.95 (*1-55639-087-4*) Educ Tech IL.

Lourekas, Peter, jt. auth. see Weinmann, Elaine.

Lourey, Michael. Just Say Yes! Steele, M. B., ed. (Illus.). 248p. (Orig.). 1989. pap. 8.95 (*0-939497-17-4*) Promise Pub.

Louric, Michelle, comp. Christmas: An Illustrated Treasury. (Courage Illustrated Treasuries Ser.). (Illus.). 48p. 1994. 6.98 (*1-56138-437-2*) Running Pr.

— Love Letters: An Illustrated Treasury. (Courage Illustrated Treasuries Ser.). (Illus.). 48p. 1994. 6.98 (*1-56138-436-4*) Running Pr.

Lourie. Hunting the Devil. 1994. mass mkt. 5.99 (*0-06-109221-5*, Harp PBks) HarpC.

Lourie, Arthur. Sergei Koussevitsky & His Epoch. LC 78-121287. reprint ed. 17.50 (*0-404-04036-5*) AMS Pr.

— Sergei Koussevitzky & His Epoch. Pring, S. W., tr. LC 78-94276. (Select Bibliographies Reprint Ser.). 1977. 26.95 (*0-8369-5050-X*) Ayer.

Lourie, Dick. Anima. 1977. pap. 5.00 (*0-914610-09-0*) Hanging Loose.

Lourie, Dick & Pawlak, Mark. Smart Like Me: High School Age Writers 1966-1988. 200p. 1988. pap. 10.00 (*0-914610-58-9*); boxed 20.00 (*0-914610-57-0*) Hanging Loose.

Lourie, Elena. Crusade & Colonization: Muslims, Christians & Jews under the Crown of Aragon. (Collected Studies: No. 317). 350p. 1990. text ed. 89.95 (*0-86078-266-2*, Pub. by Variorum UK) Ashgate Pub Co.

Lourie, Iven, jt. auth. see Gold, E. J.

Lourie, Iven, ed. see Sams, Margaret, et al.

Lourie, J. A., jt. auth. see Weiner, J. S.

Lourie, John, et al. Essentials of Accident & Emergency Care. (Illus.). 132p. 1987. pap. 22.00 (*0-443-03903-8*) Churchill.

Lourie, Margaret & Conklin, Nancy. A Host of Tongues: Language Communities in the United States. 272p. (C). 1983. 27.95 (*0-02-906390-6*); pap. 16.95 (*0-02-906500-3*) Free Pr.

Lourie, Peter. Amazon: A Young Reader's Look at the Last Frontier. LC 90-85720. (Illus.). 48p. (J). (gr. 3-7). 1991. 17.95 (*1-878093-00-2*) Boyds Mills Pr.

— Everglades: Buffalo Tiger & the River of Grass. LC 92-73989. (Illus.). 48p. (J). (gr. 3 up). 1994. 17.95 (*1-878093-91-6*) Boyds Mills Pr.

— Hudson River: An Adventure from the Mountains to the Sea. LC 91-72870. (Illus.). 48p. (J). (gr. 3-7). 1992. 15.95 (*1-878093-01-0*) Boyds Mills Pr.

— River of Mountains: A Canoe Journey down the Hudson. (Illus.). 280p. 1995. 29.95 (*0-8156-0315-0*) Syracuse U Pr.

— Sweat of the Sun, Tears of the Moon: A Chronicle of an Incan Treasure. 320p. 1991. text ed. 19.95 (*0-689-12111-3*, Atheneum S&S) S&S Trade.

— Yukon River: An Adventure to the Gold Fields of the Klondike. (Illus.). 48p. (J). (gr. 3-7). 1992. lib. bdg. 15.95 (*1-878093-90-8*) Boyds Mills Pr.

Lourie, Richard. First Loyalty. LC 84-25169. 448p. 1985. 17.95 (*0-15-131287-7*) HarBrace.

— Predicting Russia's Future: How 1,000 Years of History Are Shaping the 1990s. Rukeyser, William S. & Kiser, Anthony C., eds. LC 91-65098. (Larger Agenda Ser.). (Illus.). 86p. 1991. 11.95 (*0-9624745-9-2*) Whittle Comns.

— Zero Gravity. 1987. 16.95 (*0-15-199984-8*) HarBrace.

Lourie, Richard, tr. see Czarnecka, Ewa & Fiut, Aleksander.

Lourie, Richard, tr. see Grynberg, Henry K.

Lourie, Richard, tr. see Hertz, Aleksander.

Lourie, Richard, tr. see Konwicki, Tadeusz.

Lourie, Richard, tr. see Korczak, Janusz.

Lourie, Richard, tr. see Milosz, Czeslaw.

Lourie, Richard, tr. see Sakharov, Andrei D.

Lourie, Richard, tr. see Shulevitz, Uri.

Lourie, Richard, tr. see Voinovich, Vladimir.

Lourie, Richard, tr. see Wat, Aleksander.

Lourtie, Isabel M., jt. ed. see Moura, Josee M.

Loury, Glenn C. One by One from the Inside Out: Essays & Reviews on Race & Responsibility in America. LC 94-46593. 332p. 1995. 25.00 (*0-02-919441-5*) Free Pr.

Lousada, Patricia. Game Cookery. (Illus.). 224p. 1991. pap. 22.95 (*0-7195-4774-1*, Pub. by John Murray UK) Trafalgar.

— Great American Baking Book. (Illus.). 256p. 1995. 19.98 (*0-8317-3971-1*) Smithmark.

Lousberg, Arlene L. You & Me - Me & You: A Kid's Own Life Story. (Illus.). 40p. (Orig.). (J). (gr. 3-9). 1990. pap. 9.95 (*0-9625397-1-6*) Memories In Print.

Louscher, David J. & Salomone, Michael D., eds. Marketing Security Assistance New Perspectives on Arms Sales. LC 85-45947. 256p. 1987. text ed. 45.00 (*0-669-12606-3*) Free Pr.

Louscher, David J., jt. ed. see Kennedy, Charles H.

Loushine, Robert, jt. auth. see Bellizzi, Ralph.

Lousin, Ann & Klein, Carter H. Law of Sales under the U. C. C. write for info. (*0-318-59314-9*) Little.

Loustau & Dillon. Linear Geometry with Computer Graphics. (Pure & Applied Mathematics Ser.: Vol. 62). 458p. 1993. disk 59.75 (*0-8247-8898-2*) Dekker.

Loustaunau, Philippe, jt. auth. see Adams, William W.

Loutfi, Martha F. Rural Women: Unequal Partners in Development. (WEP Study Ser.). (Illus.). 80p. 1987. pap. 12.00 (*92-2-102389-3*) Intl Labour Office.

Loutfi, Martine A., jt. auth. see Gillain, Anne.

Louth, Andrew. Denys the Areopagite. (Outstanding Christian Thinkers Ser.). 145p. 1989. pap. 9.95 (*0-8192-1485-X*) Morehouse Pub.

— Discerning the Mystery: An Essay on the Nature of Theology. 168p. 1990. reprint ed. pap. 19.95 (*0-19-826196-9*) OUP.

— The Origins of the Christian Mystical Tradition: From Plato to Denys. (C). 1983. pap. text ed. 19.95 (*0-19-826668-5*) OUP.

Louth, Andrew, tr. see Lossky, Nicholas.

Louth, Andrew, tr. see Von Balthasar, Hans U.

Louthan, Andrea S. & Louthan, Howard. Staying Faithful. (Christian Character Bible Studies). 64p. (Orig.). 1992. pap. 4.99 (*0-8308-1146-X*, 1146) InterVarsity.

Louthan, Doniphan. The Poetry of John Donne: A Study in Explication. LC 75-40927. 193p. 1976. reprint ed. text ed. 49.75 (*0-8371-8693-5*, LOPJ, Greenwood Pr) Greenwood.

Louthan, Howard, jt. auth. see Louthan, Andrea S.

Louthan, M. R., Jr., jt. auth. see Brooks, C. R.

Louthan, Robert. Shrunken Planets. LC 79-54883. 64p. 1980. pap. 9.95 (*0-914086-28-6*) Alicejamesbooks.

Loutner, Darrell, ed. see Gage, Terry.

Louttit, C. M. Handbook of Psychological Literature. 1972. 59.95 (*0-8490-0281-8*) Gordon Pr.

Loutzenhiser, jt. auth. see Epstein.

Loutzenhiser, Rodger, ed. Calcium Antagonists & the Kidney. LC 89-83347. (Illus.). 304p. 1991. text ed. 48.00 (*0-932883-20-6*) Hanley & Belfus.

Louv, Richard. Childhood's Future. 1992. pap. 11.00 (*0-385-42390-X*, Anchor NY) Doubleday.

— FatherLove. Regan, Judith, ed. 288p. 1994. reprint ed. pap. 10.00 (*0-671-79421-3*) PB.

— One Hundred Things You Can Do for Our Children's Future. LC 93-3774. 1994. 10.00 (*0-385-46878-4*, Anchor NY) Doubleday.

Louvar, Joseph F., jt. auth. see Crowl, Daniel A.

An Asterisk (*) at the beginning of an entry indicates that the title is appearing in BIP for the first time.

Louvau, Gordon E. & Jackson, Marjorie E. Computers in Accountants' Offices. (Accounting Ser.). (Illus.). 132p. 1982. text ed. 44.95 (*0-534-97967-X*) Van Nos Reinhold.

Louveau, Alain, jt. auth. see Kechris, Alexander S.

Louver Gallery New York Staff & Cameron, Dan. Inconsolable: An Exhibition about Painting. (Illus.). 40p. 1990. 15.00 (*0-9624271-3-6*) Louver Gallery.

— Tony Bevan. (Illus.). 80p. 1991. pap. write for info. (*0-9624271-4-4*) Louver Gallery.

L'Ouverture, Toussaint. Toussaint L'Ouverture: A Biography & Autobiography. LC 77-152924. (Black Heritage Library Collection). 1977. 32.95 (*0-8369-8768-3*) Ayer.

Louviere, Elton J. & Louviere, Pat. Images of Louisiana. LC 88-81862. (Illus.). 120p. 1988. 45.00 (*0-9620814-0-X*) Louviere Fine Arts.

Louviere, Jordon J. Analyzing Decision-Making: Metric Conjoint Analysis. (Quantitative Applications in the Social Sciences Ser.: Vol. 67). 96p. (C). 1988. pap. text ed. 9.95 (*0-8039-2757-6*) Sage.

Louviere, Pat. Louisiana Backroads & Bayous. (Illus.). 128p. 1992. ring bd. 50.00 (*0-9620814-3-4*); vinyl bd. 60.00 (*0-9620814-2-6*) Louviere Fine Arts.

— Louisiana Backroads & Bayous. deluxe ed. (Illus.). 128p. 1992. ring bd. 200.00 (*0-9620814-1-8*) Louviere Fine Arts.

Louviere, Pat, jt. auth. see Louviere, Elton J.

Louvish, David, tr. see Fraisse, R.

Louvish, David, ed. see Orevkov, V. P.

Louvish, Misha, tr. see Lipshitz, Arye.

***Louvish, Simon.** It's a Gift. (BFI Film Classics Ser.). 1994. pap. 9.95 (*0-85170-472-7*) Ind U Pr.

— The Resurrections. LC 94-10509. 252p. 1994. 18.95 (*1-56858-014-2*) FWEW.

— The Silencer. LC 92-24536. (Emerging Voices: New International Fiction Ser.). 264p. (Orig.). 1993. 29.95 (*1-56656-116-7*); pap. 10.95 (*1-56656-108-6*) Interlink Pub.

Louvre, Alf & Walsh, Jeffrey. Tell Me Lies about Vietnam: Cultural Battles for the Meaning of the War. 224p. 1989. 90.00 (*0-335-15594-4*, Open Univ Pr); pap. 34.00 (*0-335-15593-6*, Open Univ Pr) Taylor & Francis.

***Louw, Bill.** The Atlas of Languages. LC 95-15336. 1996. write for info. (*0-8160-3388-9*) Facts on File.

Louw, Eric & Duffy, Neil. Managing Computer Viruses. (Illus.). 189p. 1992. pap. 22.50 (*0-19-853974-6*) OUP.

Louw, Gideon N. Ecology of Desert Organisms. 240p. 1986. pap. text ed. 37.95 (*0-470-20532-6*) Halsted Pr.

— Physiological Animal Ecology. 288p. (Orig.). 1993. pap. text ed. 54.95 (*0-470-21866-5*) Halsted Pr.

— Physiological Animal Ecology. 288p. (Orig.). 1993. pap. 49.95 (*0-582-05922-4*, Pub. by Longman UK) Longman.

Louw, Gideon N. & Seely, M. K. Ecology of Desert Organisms. LC 81-6027. (Tropical Ecology Ser.). (Illus.). 240p. (C). 1982. pap. text ed. 32.95 (*0-582-44393-8*) Wiley.

Louw, J. P. Semantics of New Testament Greek. (Semeia Studies). 1982. pap. 19.95 (*0-89130-693-5*, 06 06 11) Scholars Pr GA.

Louw, J. P. & Nida, Eugene. Lexical Semantics of the Greek New Testament. (Society of Biblical Literature Resources for Biblical Study). 188p. (C). 1992. pap. 29.95 (*1-55540-578-9*, 060325) Scholars Pr GA.

Louw, Lente-Louise, jt. ed. see Griggs, Lewis B.

Louw-Potgieter, J. Afrikaner Dissidents: A Social Psychological Study of Identity & Dissent. 148p. 1988. 79.00 (*1-85359-012-6*, Pub. by Multilingual Matters UK); pap. 29.00 (*1-85359-011-8*, Pub. by Multilingual Matters UK) Taylor & Francis.

Louwrier, K., et al, eds. European Geothermal Update. (C). 1989. lib. bdg. 211.50 (*0-7923-0198-6*) Kluwer Ac.

Loux, John W. & Coffin, Chris. An Easy Course in Using the HP-28S. (Easy Course Ser.). 320p. 1988. pap. 13.00 (*0-931011-18-3*) Grapevine Pubns.

Loux, John W., jt. auth. see Coffin, Chris.

Loux, Michael J. Primary Ousia: An Essay on Aristotle's Metaphysics Z & H. LC 90-25775. 288p. 1991. 41.95 (*0-8014-2598-0*) Cornell U Pr.

Loux, Michael J., intro. The Possible & the Actual: Readings in the Metaphysics of Modality. LC 79-7618. 336p. 1979. pap. 14.95 (*0-8014-9178-9*) Cornell U Pr.

Louys, Pierre. Aphrodite, Moeurs Antiques. LC 75-41182. (FRE.). reprint ed. 30.00 (*0-404-14795-X*) AMS Pr.

— The Collected Tales. LC 70-160941. (Short Story Index Reprint Ser.). (Illus.). 1977. reprint ed. 22.95 (*0-8369-3920-4*) Ayer.

— The Songs of Bilitis. (Illus.). 192p. 1988. reprint ed. pap. 4.95 (*0-486-25670-7*) Dover.

— Two Erotic Tales by Pierre Louys: Aphrodite & The Songs of Bilitis. Kavka, Dorothy, ed. Harrison, Mary H., tr. 320p. (Orig.). 1994. pap. 18.00 (*1-879260-24-7*) Evanston Pub.

Louzecky, D. & Flannery, R. The Good Life: Personal & Public Choices. xiv, 258p. (Orig.). (C). 1989. lib. bdg. 35.00 (*0-917930-95-9*); pap. text ed. 12.00 (*0-917930-55-X*) Ridgeview.

Lovaas, Maggie, jt. auth. see Kramer, Felix.

Lovaas, O. Ivar. The Autistic Child: Language Development Through Behavior Modification. LC 76-5890. (Illus.). 256p. 1984. pap. text ed. 16.95 (*0-8290-1003-3*) Irvington.

— The Autistic Child: Language Development Through Behavior Modification. LC 76-5890. (Illus.). 256p. (C). 1986. reprint ed. text ed. 29.95 (*0-8290-0253-7*) Irvington.

— Teaching Developmentally Disabled Children: The Me Book. LC 80-26047. 264p. 1981. pap. 32.00 (*0-936104-78-3*, 1213) PRO-ED.

Lovaas, O. Ivar, et al. Autistic Behaviors: Experimental Analysis & Treatment Applications. 450p. 1990. text ed. 39.50 (*0-8290-2467-0*) Irvington.

— Problems of Autistic Behavior: Experimental Analysis of Autism, Vol. 1. 300p. text ed. write for info. (*0-8290-0740-7*) Irvington.

Lovag, Z., jt. auth. see Kovacs, E.

Lovallo, Lee T. Anton Bruckner: A Discography. LC 86-46229. (Reference Books in Music: No. 6). xviii, 200p. 1991. 33.00 (*0-914913-05-0*) Fallen Leaf.

Lovalvo, Jim. Book of Mormon Reflections. Van Treese, James B., ed. 395p. 1993. 14.95 (*1-880416-34-4*) NW Pub.

Lovas, Emily, ed. see Lokvam, Marian, et al.

Lovas, John C., jt. auth. see Fryer, Thomas W., Jr.

Lovas, Paula M., jt. ed. see Abramson, Marcia.

***Lovasik.** My First Prayerbook. (J). 2.95 (*0-89942-205-5*) Catholic Bk Pub.

Lovasik, L. G. My Picture Prayer Book. (J). (ps-3). 4.75 (*0-89942-134-2*) Catholic Bk Pub.

Lovasik, Lawrence. St. Joseph New American Catechism. (Illus.). 1978. 3.00 (*0-89942-253-5*, 253/05) Catholic Bk Pub.

Lovasik, Lawrence G. The Angels: God's Messengers & Our Helpers. (Saint Joseph Picture Bks.). (Illus.). 1978. 0.95 (*0-89942-281-0*, 281) Catholic Bk Pub.

— Clean Love in Courtship. 1974. reprint ed. pap. 2.50 (*0-89555-095-4*) TAN Bks Pubs.

— Concise Church History: St. Joseph Edition. (Orig.). 1989. pap. 5.95 (*0-89942-262-4*) Catholic Bk Pub.

— God Loves Us All. (Saint Joseph Picture Bks.). (Illus.). 1978. 0.95 (*0-89942-282-9*, 282) Catholic Bk Pub.

— Good St. Joseph. (Saint Joseph Picture Bks.). (Illus.). 1978. 0.95 (*0-89942-283-7*, 283) Catholic Bk Pub.

— The Holy Rosary. (Saint Joseph Picture Bks.). (Illus.). 1978. 0.95 (*0-89942-284-5*, 284) Catholic Bk Pub.

— I Believe in God: The Apostles' Creed. (Saint Joseph Picture Bks.). (Illus.). 1984. 0.95 (*0-89942-276-4*, 276) Catholic Bk Pub.

— The Lord Jesus. (Illus.). 1980. 3.95 (*0-89942-419-8*, 419/22) Catholic Bk Pub.

— Mary My Mother. rev. ed. (Saint Joseph Picture Bks.). (Illus.). 1978. 0.95 (*0-89942-280-2*, 280) Catholic Bk Pub.

— Meditations on the Rosary. LC 82-72204. (Living Meditation & Prayerbook Ser.). (Illus.). 270p. (Orig.). 1985. pap. text ed. 5.00 (*0-932406-09-2*) AFC.

— The Miracles of Jesus. (Saint Joseph Picture Bks.). 1978. 0.95 (*0-89942-279-9*, 279) Catholic Bk Pub.

— My Picture Missal. (Saint Joseph Picture Bks.). (Illus.). 1978. 0.95 (*0-89942-275-6*, 275) Catholic Bk Pub.

— Picture Book of Saints. (Illus.). 1988. 4.95 (*0-89942-235-7*, 235-22) Catholic Bk Pub.

— The Seven Sacraments. (Saint Joseph Picture Bks.). (Illus.). (J). (gr. 1-6). 1978. 0.95 (*0-89942-278-0*, 278) Catholic Bk Pub.

— St. Joseph First Children's Bible. (J). (ps-3). 1983. 4.95 (*0-89942-135-0*) Catholic Bk Pub.

— The Ten Commandments. (Saint Joseph Picture Bks.). (Illus.). (J). (gr. 1-6). 1978. 0.95 (*0-89942-287-X*, 287) Catholic Bk Pub.

— Treasury of Novenas. 352p. 1986. pap. 4.95 (*0-89942-345-0*, 345/22) Catholic Bk Pub.

— What Catholics Believe. (Illus.). 1977. pap. 4.00 (*0-89555-027-X*) TAN Bks Pubs.

Lovasy, Ernst. Dictionnaire des Termes d'Anatomie, d'Embryologie et d'Histologie. 624p. (FRE.). 1954. 65.00 (*0-8288-6871-9*, M-6380) Fr & Eur.

Lovasz, L. Combinatorial Problems & Exercises. 2nd ed. 636p. 1993. 157.25 (*0-444-81504-X*, North Holland) Elsevier.

Lovasz, L. & Plummer, M. D. Matching Theory. 544p. 1986. 75.00 (*0-444-87916-1*, North Holland) Elsevier.

Lovasz, L. & Recski, A., eds. Matroid Theory. (Colloquia Mathematica Societatis Janos Bolyai Ser.: 40). 440p. 1986. 107.75 (*0-444-87580-8*, North Holland) Elsevier.

Lovasz, L. & Szemeredi, E., eds. Theory of Algorithms. (Colloquia Mathematica Societatis Janos Bolyai Ser.: Vol. 44). 430p. 1986. 97.50 (*0-444-87760-6*) Elsevier.

Lovasz, Laszlo. An Algorithmic Theory of Numbers, Graphs, & Convexity. LC 86-61532. (CBMS-NSF Regional Conference Ser.: No. 50). v, 91p. 1986. pap. 18.25 (*0-89871-203-3*) Soc Indus-Appl Math.

Lovato, Charles. Life Under the Sun. Hausman, Gerald, ed. LC 81-23189. (Illus.). 48p. 1982. 35.00 (*0-86534-010-2*) Sunstone Pr.

Lovatt, Carol J., ed. Proceedings of the Second World Avocado Congress: The Shape of Things to Come. (Illus.). 730p. 1992. 75.00 (*0-9634770-0-5*) U CA Bot & Plant.

Lovatt, Edwin A., jt. auth. see Herail, Rene J.

Lovberg, Ralph H., jt. auth. see Glasstone, Samuel.

Love. Atlas of Breast Surgery. (Illus.). 1995. text ed. 95.00 (*0-397-50946-4*) Lippincott.

— Love. 100p. 1982. pap. 4.75 (*0-9608692-0-4*) Love.

— Take Action. 1994. pap. 5.99 (*0-517-13492-6*) Random Hse Value.

— Taking Control: Historical Adventure. 1990. 5.00 (*0-614-04740-4*) Royal Fireworks.

Love, ed. Yellowstone & Grand Teton National Parks & the Middle Rocky Mountains. (IGC Field Trip Guidebooks Ser.). 104p. 1989. 21.00 (*0-87590-668-0*, T328) Am Geophysical.

Love, jt. ed. see Abbott.

Love, A. Cytotaxonimical Atlas of the Pteridophyta, Vol. 3. (Cytotaxonomical Atlases Ser.: Vol. 3). 1977. 98.00 (*3-7682-1103-7*) Lubrecht & Cramer.

Love, A. & Love, D. Cytotaxonomical Atlas of the Arctic Flora. (Cytotaxonimical Atlases Ser.: Vol. 2). (Illus.). 598p. 1975. lib. bdg. 130.00 (*3-7682-0976-8*) Lubrecht & Cramer.

— Cytotaxonomical Atlas of the Slovenian Flora. (Cytotaxonimical Atlases Ser.: Vol. 1). (Illus.). 1242p. 1974. lib. bdg. 130.00 (*3-7682-0932-6*) Lubrecht & Cramer.

— North Atlantic Biota & Their History: Symposium, University of Iceland, July, 1962. LC 62-22038. 1963. 184.00 (*0-08-009944-0*, Pub. by Pergamon Repr UK) Franklin.

— Plant Chromosomes. 1975. 25.00 (*3-7682-0966-0*) Lubrecht & Cramer.

Love, A., jt. auth. see Bailin, D.

Love, Anami & Bradford, Anita J. Field Trips & Assemblies: A Guide to Exciting Education in Northern California. (Orig.). 1991. pap. 19.95 (*0-9627649-3-0*) Trumpetvine.

Love, Ann. The Prince Who Wrote a Letter. LC 92-27587. (J). 1992. 11.95 (*0-85953-398-0*, Pub. by Childs Play UK); pap. write for info. (*0-85953-399-9*, Pub. by Childs Play UK) Childs Play.

Love, Ann & Drake, Jane. Take Action. LC 92-30412. (J). 1993. pap. 7.95 (*0-688-12465-8*, Pub. by Beech Tree Bks) Morrow.

— Take Action: An Environmental Book for Kids. LC 92-30412. (Illus.). 96p. (J). (gr. 3 up). 1993. reprint ed. lib. bdg. 13.93 (*0-688-12464-X*, Tambourine Bks) Morrow.

Love, Ann, jt. auth. see Drake, Jane.

Love, Arnold J. Internal Evaluation: Building Organizations from Within. (Applied Social Research Methods Ser.: Vol. 24). (Illus.). 160p. 1991. 37.00 (*0-8039-3200-6*); pap. 16.95 (*0-8039-3201-4*) Sage.

Love, Augustus E. Treatise on the Mathematical Theory of Elasticity. 4th ed. (Illus.). 1927. pap. text ed. 14.95 (*0-486-60174-9*) Dover.

Love, Barbara. Re-Evaluation Counseling: A Component in Higher Education. 1987. pap. 2.00 (*0-685-47589-1*) Rational Isl.

Love, Barbara & Froidevaux, Frances L., eds. Lady's Choice: Ethel Waxham's Journals & Letters, 1905-1910. LC 92-36499. (Illus.). 416p. 1993. 29.95 (*0-8263-1393-0*) U of NM Pr.

Love, Bill R. The Core Gospel. LC 91-76128. 319p. 1992. pap. 14.95 (*0-89112-151-X*) Abilene Christ U.

Love, Bobby, II. The Penguin. (Illus.). (Orig.). 1991. write for info. (*1-879460-50-5*) A Love Memorial.

Love, Brenda. The Encyclopedia of Unusual Sex Practices. LC 92-16420. 1992. 29.95 (*0-942637-64-X*) Barricade Bks.

— Encyclopedia of Unusual Sex Practices. 1994. pap. 22.00 (*1-56980-011-1*) Barricade Bks.

Love, Bruce. Enterprise Information Technologies: Designing the Competitive Company. LC 92-40887. 1993. text ed. 39.95 (*0-442-00955-0*) Van Nos Reinhold.

— The Paris Codex: Handbook for a Maya Priest. LC 93-13028. (Illus.). 176p. (C). 1994. text ed. 37.50 (*0-292-74674-1*) U of Tex Pr.

Love, C. & Tinervia, Joseph. Commercial Correspondence: For Students of English As a Second Language. 2nd ed. 1980. text ed. 8.97 (*0-07-038785-0*) McGraw.

Love, C., jt. auth. see Scott, V.

***Love, C. E. & Clari, M.** Collins Italian Dictionary College Edition. 745p. (ENG & ITA.). (C). 1990. write for info. (*0-7859-7406-7*, 0062755064) Fr & Eur.

Love, Carol S. Leisure & Aging: A Practical & Theoretical Guide. 88p. (C). 1994. per. 15.25 (*0-8403-9425-X*) Kendall-Hunt.

***Love, Catherine E.** Collins-Mondadori Gem Italian Dictionary. 629p. (ENG & ITA.). 1992. write for info. (*0-7859-7415-6*, 004700473) Fr & Eur.

— Larousse Dictionnaire Compact Francais-Anglais, Anglias-Francais. 1184p. (ENG & FRE.). 1993. vinyl bd. 49.95 (*0-7859-7123-8*, 2034016319) Fr & Eur.

Love, Cathleen T. & Weis, Susan F. Communicating the Contributions of Home Economics Education. 1985. 4.00 (*0-911365-25-7*, A261-08466) Home Econ Educ.

Love, Charles. Designing to Help People Get Where They're Going. 238p. 1992. 49.95 (*0-685-60212-5*) McGraw.

Love, Charley. Being a Happy Millionaire: How to Do It. 227p. (Orig.). 1993. pap. text ed. 9.95 (*1-883978-01-7*, Loveseed Pr) Loveseed Revel.

— The Happiest Millionaire: A Novel of Transformation. 112p. (Orig.). 1993. pap. 9.95 (*1-883978-00-9*, Loveseed Pr) Loveseed Revel.

Love, Clyde E. Bridge Squeezes Complete; or, Winning End Play Strategy. LC 68-25410. (Illus.). 1968. pap. 4.95 (*0-486-21968-2*) Dover.

Love County Heritage Commission, ed. The History of Love County, Oklahoma. 371p. 1983. 50.00 (*0-88107-006-8*) Curtis Media.

Love, D., jt. auth. see Love, A.

***Love, D. Anne.** Bess's Log Cabin Quilt. (Illus.). 88p. (J). (gr. 2-6). 1995. 14.95 (*0-8234-1178-8*) Holiday.

— Dakota Spring. LC 94-46354. (Illus.). 144p. (J). 1995. pap. 14.95 (*0-8234-1189-3*) Holiday.

Love, Daphne & Love, Sid. Flower Arranging from the Garden. (Wisley Handbooks Ser.). (Illus.). 64p. 1992. pap. 5.95 (*0-304-32021-8*, Pub. by Cassell UK) Sterling.

Love, David. The Leadership Passion: A Psychology of Ideology. LC 76-45481. (Jossey-Bass Behavioral Science Ser.). 269p. reprint ed. pap. 76.70 (*0-685-16189-7*, 2027761) Bks Demand.

Love, David, jt. auth. see Freedman, David.

Love, Doris, jt. auth. see Aleksandrova, Vera.

Love, Doris, tr. see Andre, Edouard F.

Love, Douglas. Be Kind to Your Mother (Earth) (Illus.). 64p. (J). (gr. 3 up). 1994. pap. 3.50 (*0-694-00654-8*, Festival) HarpC Child Bks.

— Blame It on the Wolf. (Illus.). 48p. (J). (gr. 3 up). 1994. pap. 3.50 (*0-694-00653-X*, Festival) HarpC Child Bks.

— Holiday in the Rain Forest: Theater Kit. (Illus.). (J). (gr. 5 up). 1993. 14.95 (*0-694-00561-4*, Festival) HarpC Child Bks.

— Imagination Station: 99 Games to Spark Your Imagination. 202p. (J). (gr. 1 up). 1995. 10.95 (*0-694-00682-3*, Festival) HarpC Child Bks.

— Kabuki Gift: Theater Kit. (Illus.). 32p. (J). (gr. 5 up). 1993. 14.95 (*0-694-00562-2*, Festival) HarpC Child Bks.

— The Little House Christmas Theater Kit. (Illus.). (J). (gr. 3-7). 1995. 12.95 (*0-694-00681-5*, Festival) HarpC Child Bks.

— So You Want to Be a Star. (Illus.). 32p. (J). (gr. 5 up). 1993. 18.95 (*0-694-00428-6*, Festival) HarpC Child Bks.

Love, Douglas E. Martyr. LC 90-90401. (Orig.). 1990. pap. 5.00 (*0-9628240-0-3*) D E Love.

Love, Douglas O.. Minimum Cost of Living in Nebraska, Vol. I-II. 1986. 20.00 (*0-317-46859-6*) Bur Busn Res U Nebr.

Love, Douglas O. & Deichert, Jerome A. Locating Financial Branch Facilities: A Guide to Techniques & Literature. (Nebraska Economic & Business Report Ser.: No. 34). 1983. 10.00 (*0-318-02060-2*) Bur Busn Res U Nebr.

Love, E. L. World Textile Trade: An International Perspective. 52p. 1978. 39.00 (*0-686-63809-3*) St Mut.

— World Textile Trade: An International Perspective. (C). 1978. pap. text ed. 70.00 (*0-685-46392-3*, Pub. by Textile Institue UK) St Mut.

Love, E. M. Dress Up. 368p. (Orig.). 1992. pap. 4.50 (*0-8439-3258-9*) Dorchester Pub Co.

Love, Edgar J., jt. ed. see Miller, Max J.

Love, Edmond. The Twenty-Seventh Infantry Division in the World War II. (Divisional Ser.: No. 21). (Illus.). 677p. 1982. reprint ed. 32.50 (*0-89839-056-7*) Battery Pr.

Love, Edmund G. Hanging On: Or How to Get Through a Depression & Enjoy Life. LC 87-18897. (Great Lakes Bks.). 285p. 1987. reprint ed. 28.50 (*0-8143-1931-9*); reprint ed. pap. 15.95 (*0-8143-1932-7*) Wayne St U Pr.

— The Hourglass: A History of the 7th Infantry Division in World War II. (Divisional Ser.). (Illus.). 496p. 1988. reprint ed. 32.50 (*0-89839-118-0*) Battery Pr.

— The Situation in Flushing. LC 87-17769. (Great Lakes Bks.). 261p. 1987. reprint ed. 29.95 (*0-8143-1916-5*); reprint ed. pap. 15.95 (*0-8143-1917-3*) Wayne St U Pr.

— Small Bequest. LC 87-16202. (Great Lakes Bks.). 238p. 1987. 28.50 (*0-8143-1925-4*); pap. 13.95 (*0-8143-1926-2*) Wayne St U Pr.

Love, Frank. Hell's Outpost: A History of Old Fort Yuma. LC 92-60166. (Publication Ser.). (Illus.). 63p. (Orig.). 1992. pap. 6.95 (*0-9632228-0-5*) Yuma Crossing.

— Mining Camps & Ghost Towns: Along the Lower Colorado in Arizona & California. LC 73-86960. (Great West & Indian Ser.: Vol. 42). (Illus.). 240p. 24.95 (*0-87026-031-6*) Westernlore.

Love, Frederick R. Nietzsche's Saint Peter: Genesis & Cultivation of an Illusion. (Monographien und Texte zur Nietzscge-Forschung Ser.: Vol. 5). xvi, 296p. (C). 1981. 80.00 (*3-11-007875-9*) De Gruyter.

— Young Nietzsche & the Wagnerian Experience. LC 63-63585. (North Carolina. University. Studies in the Germanic Languages & Literatures: No. 39). reprint ed. 27.00 (*0-404-50939-8*) AMS Pr.

Love, G., jt. auth. see Scott, V. D.

Love, G. B., jt. ed. see Irwin, Walter.

Love, Gilly. The A-Z of Cut Flowers: Fresh & Dried. (Illus.). 192p. 1994. 22.95 (*0-670-85226-0*, Viking) Viking Penguin.

Love, Glen A. Babbitt: An American Life. LC 92-27096. (Masterwork Studies: No. 105). 105p. 1993. text ed. 21.95 (*0-8057-9440-9*, Twayne); pap. 12.95 (*0-8057-8562-0*, Twayne) Macmillan.

— Don Berry. LC 78-52564. (Western Writers Ser.: No. 35). 46p. 1978. pap. 3.95 (*0-88430-059-5*) Boise St U W Writ Ser.

— New Americans: The Westerner & the Modern Experience in the American Novel. LC 80-65717. 288p. 1982. 36.50 (*0-8387-5011-7*) Bucknell U Pr.

Love, Glen A., ed. The World Begins Here: An Anthology of Oregon Short Fiction. LC 92-43642. (Oregon Literature Ser.: Vol. 1). (Illus.). 320p. (Orig.). (YA). 1993. text ed. 35.95 (*0-87071-369-8*); pap. 21.95 (*0-87071-370-1*) Oreg St U Pr.

Love, Glen A., jt. ed. see Bingham, Edwin R.

Love, Hallie. A Is for Alligator. (Special Studies). (Illus.). 64p. (J). (gr. 1 up). 1993. 15.95 (*1-879244-02-0*) Windom Bks.

— Romantic Santa Fe. (Romantic Guide Ser.). (Illus.). 296p. (Orig.). 1993. pap. 10.95 (*1-879244-46-2*) Windom Bks.

Love, Harold. The Golden Age of Australian Opera: W. S. Lyster & His Companies, 1861-1880. (C). 1990. 59.00 (*0-86819-051-9*, Pub. by Currency Pr AT) St Mut.

— James Edward Neild: Victorian Virtuoso. 1989. 39.95 (*0-522-84384-0*) Intl Spec Bk.

— Scribal Publication in Seventeenth-Century England. (Illus.). 392p. 1993. 65.00 (*0-19-811219-X*) OUP.

Love, Harold, intro. Poeta De Tristibus: or The Poet's Complaint: A Poem in Four Canto's. LC 92-24287. (Augustan Reprints Ser.: No. 149 (1971)). reprint ed. 12.00 (*0-404-70149-3*, PR3291) AMS Pr.

Love, Harold, ed. see Southerne, Thomas.

***Love, Harold D.** Assessment of Intelligence & Development of Infants & Young Children: With Specialized Measures. 138p. 1991. pap. 19.95 (*0-398-06246-3*) C C Thomas.

— Assessment of Intelligence & Development of Infants & Young Children: With Specialized Measures. 138p. (C). 1991. text ed. 34.95x (*0-398-05676-5*) C C Thomas.

— Psychological Evaluation of Exceptional Children. (Illus.). 132p. 1985. 29.95x (*0-398-05045-7*) C C Thomas.

— Psychological Evaluation of Exceptional Children. (Illus.). 132p. 1985. pap. 15.95 (*0-398-06247-1*) C C Thomas.

***Love, Harold D. & Litton, Freddie W.** Teaching Reading to Disabled & Handicapped Learners. LC 94-3917. (Illus.). 260p. 1994. pap. 30.95 (*0-398-06248-X*) C C Thomas.

— Teaching Reading to Disabled & Handicapped Learners. LC 94-3917. (Illus.). 260p. (C). 1994. text ed. 51.95 (*0-398-05909-8*) C C Thomas.

Love, Henry D. Vestiges of Old Madras, 4 Vols. in 3, 1. reprint ed. write for info. (*0-404-04061-6*) AMS Pr.

— Vestiges of Old Madras, 4 Vols. in 3, 2. reprint ed. write for info. (*0-404-04062-4*) AMS Pr.

— Vestiges of Old Madras, 4 Vols. in 3, 3. reprint ed. write for info. (*0-404-04063-2*) AMS Pr.

— Vestiges of Old Madras, 4 Vols. in 3, Set. reprint ed. 127.50 (*0-404-04060-8*) AMS Pr.

Love, J. D. & Reed, John C. Creation of Teton Landscape: The Geologic Story of Grand Teton National Park. U. S. G. S. Staff, ed. (Illus.). 120p. reprint ed. pap. 8.95 (*0-931895-08-1*) Grand Teton NHA.

Love, J. Richard. Liberating Leaders from the Superman Syndrome. 254p. (C). Date not set. lib. bdg. 32.50 (*0-8191-9241-4*) U Pr of Amer.

Love, J. W. Autologous Tissue Heart Valves. (Medical Intelligence Unit Ser.). 128p. 1993. 89.95 (*1-879702-52-5*) R G Landes.

Love, Jack & Phil, D., eds. Cardiac Surgery in Patients with Chronic Renal Disease. LC 81-70202. (Illus.). 208p. 1982. 26.00 (*0-87993-169-8*) Futura Pub.

Love-Jackson, Marcia. Waitressing: Inside Tips for Better Tips. rev. ed. (Illus.). 44p. 1994. pap. 4.95 (*0-9614315-0-4*) Love-Jackson.

Love, James. Horse Racing, Pick Six & Pick Nine: The Complete Lotto Handbook. 1991. pap. 4.95 (*0-941271-15-3*) L S I Pub.

Love, James H., jt. auth. see Ashcroft, Brian.

Love, James K. Deafmutism. 1976. 250.00 (*0-87968-303-1*) Gordon Pr.

Love, Janice. The United States Anti-Apartheid Movement: Local Activism in Global Politics. LC 85-3564. 316p. 1985. text ed. 59.95 (*0-275-90139-4*, C0139, Praeger Pubs) Greenwood.

Love, John & Watson, Jeff. The Golden Eagle. 1989. pap. 25.00 (*0-7478-0091-X*, Pub. by Shire UK) St Mut.

Love, John A. Sea Otters. LC 92-53032. (Illus.). 160p. (Orig.). 1992. pap. 12.95 (*1-55591-123-4*) Fulcrum Pub.

***Love, John F.** McDonald's: Behind the Arches. LC 95-11540. 1995. write for info. (*0-553-34759-4*) Bantam.

Love, John R. Antiquity & Capitalism: Max Weber & the Sociological Foundations of Roman Civilization. 352p. (C). 1991. text ed. 49.95 (*0-415-04750-1*, A5188) Routledge.

Love, Joseph L. Rio Grande do Sul & Brazilian Regionalism, 1882-1930. LC 71-130829. (Illus.). xvi, 320p. 1971. 42.50 (*0-8047-0759-6*) Stanford U Pr.

— Sao Paulo in the Brazilian Federation, 1889-1937. LC 78-66177. (Illus.). xvii, 398p. 1980. 49.50 (*0-8047-0991-2*) Stanford U Pr.

Love, Joseph L. & Jacobsen, Nils, eds. Guiding the Invisible Hand: Economic Liberalism & the State in Latin American History. LC 88-11985. (Illus.). 232p. 1988. text ed. 47.95 (*0-275-92945-0*, C2945, Praeger Pubs) Greenwood.

Love, Joseph L., jt. ed. see Byars, Robert S.

Love, Karen, ed. see Rose, Tui.

Love, Ken & Love, Ruth. A Guide to the Trails of Badger Creek. rev. ed. (Illus.). (Orig.). 1980. pap. 4.95 (*0-913140-38-4*) Signpost Bk Pub.

Love, L. Carl. Principles of Metallurgy. (C). 1985. teacher ed write for info. (*0-8359-5673-3*, Reston) P-H.

Love, Laurie M. Using ClarisWorks. 1992. pap. 24.95 (*0-201-57017-3*) Addison-Wesley.

— Using ClarisWorks 2.0 for the Macintosh. 2nd ed. 1993. pap. 24.95 (*0-201-62629-2*) Addison-Wesley.

Love, Lilly C., ed. see Love, Norman, Jr.

Love, Louise. The Complete Book of Pizza. (Illus.). 100p. (Orig.). 1983. pap. 6.00 (*0-930528-03-4*) Sassafras Pr.

Love, Lucille T., et al, eds. Remembering Margaret Mitchell: Author of Gone with the Wind. (Illus.). 212p. 1992. 29.95 (*0-9634245-0-5*) E Ross Pubs.

Love, Mabel R. The Love Clan: The Family of Daniel Love & Sarah McColl. (Illus.). 192p. (Orig.). 1992. pap. 20.00 (*0-9632429-0-3*) Love Pubs.

— Mc Carroll: The Family of Simon Mc Carroll & Ann Cosky Glenn of County Derry, Ulster, Ireland to America 1775-1993. (Illus.). 278p. (Orig.). 1993. 38.00 (*0-9632429-1-1*) Love Pubs.

Love, Marianne. Pocket Girdles: And Other Confessions of a Northwest Farmgirl. Sullivan, Noelle, ed. LC 94-76285. (Illus.). 224p. (Orig.). 1994. pap. 9.95 (*1-56044-293-X*) Falcon Pr MT.

Love, Marla. Twenty Decoding Games. (J). (gr. 2-6). 1982. pap. 12.99 (*0-8224-5801-2*) Fearon Teach Aids.

— Twenty Reading Comprehension Games. (Makemaster Bk.). (J). (gr. 4-6). 1977. pap. 9.99 (*0-8224-5800-4*) Fearon Teach Aids.

— Twenty Word Structure Games. (J). (gr. 2-6). 1983. pap. 12.99 (*0-8224-5802-0*) Fearon Teach Aids.

Love, Marsha L. The Vitamin Parade. LC 89-51346. (Illus.). 44p. (J). (gr. k-3). 1989. 5.95 (*1-55523-264-7*) Winston-Derek.

Love, Mary. The Best of Mary Love. (Orig.). 1993. pap. text ed. 4.95 (*1-56333-099-7*) Masquerade.

— Mastering Mary Sue. (Orig.). 1995. pap. text ed. 5.95 (*1-56333-351-1*) Masquerade.

***Love, Michael C.** Better Takeoffs & Landings. LC 95-13583. 1995. write for info. (*0-07-038805-9*); pap. write for info. (*0-07-038806-7*) TAB Bks.

Love, Myra N. Christa Wolf: Literature & the Conscience of History. LC 91-17401. (DDR-Studien - East German Studies: Vol. 6). 202p. (C). 1992. text ed. 42.95 (*0-8204-1651-7*) P Lang Pubs.

Love, Nancy S. Dogmas & Dreams: Political Ideologies in the Modern World. LC 90-19909. (Chatham House Studies in Political Thinking). 576p. (C). 1991. pap. text ed. 29.95x (*0-934540-84-5*) Chatham Hse Pubs.

— Marx, Nietzsche, & Modernity. 224p. 1988. text ed. 40.50 (*0-231-06238-9*) Col U Pr.

***Love, Nat.** The Life & Adventures of Nat Love. (Blacks in the American West Ser.). 184p. 1995. pap. 9.00 (*0-8032-7955-8*, Bison Books) U of Nebr Pr.

— Life & Adventures of Nat Love, Better Known in the Cattle Country As Deadwood Dick. LC 68-29007. (American Negro: His History & Literature, Ser. No. 1). 1968. reprint ed. 25.95 (*0-405-01827-4*) Ayer.

— The Life & Adventures of Nat Love, Better Known in the Cattle Country As Deadwood Dick, by Himself. (American Biography Ser.). 162p. 1991. reprint ed. lib. bdg. 59.00 (*0-7812-8252-7*) Rprt Serv.

Love, Nigel. Generative Phonology: A Case Study from French. (Lingvisticae Investigationes Supplementa Ser.: Vol. 4). viii, 241p. 1981. 62.00x (*90-272-3113-3*) Benjamins North Am.

Love, Nigel, ed. The Foundations of Linguistic Theory: Selected Writing by Roy Harris. 273p. 1989. 65.00 (*0-415-03613-5*, A3469) Routledge.

Love, Norman, Jr. Norman's Letters. Love, Lilly C., ed. 312p. 1995. pap. 15.95 (*0-8059-3516-9*) Dorrance.

Love, Patricia. Emotional Incest Syndrome: What to Do When a Parent's Love Rules Your Life. 1991. pap. 11.95 (*0-553-35275-X*) Bantam.

Love, Patricia & Robinson, Jo. Hot Monogamy: Essential Steps to More Passionate, Intimate Lovemaking. LC 93-31491. 352p. 1994. 21.95 (*0-525-93649-1*, Dutton) NAL-Dutton.

— Hot Monogamy: Essential Steps to More Passionate, Intimate Lovemaking. 320p. 1995. pap. 10.95 (*0-452-27366-8*, Plume) NAL-Dutton.

Love, Paul, ed. Michigan State University Art Collection. (Illus.). 45p. (Orig.). 1966. pap. 2.50 (*1-879147-00-9*) Kresge Art Mus.

Love, Paula M. Will Rogers Book. 1972. 11.95 (*0-87244-030-3*) Texian.

***Love, Penelope.** Castle of Eyes. (Fiction Bks.). 236p. (Orig.). (YA). 1993. pap. 14.95 (*1-56882-005-4*, 6000) Chaosium.

Love, Penelope, et al. Terror Australis: Cthulhu down Under. Willis, Lynn & Petersen, Sandy, eds. (Call of Cthulhu Roleplaying Game System Ser.). (Illus.). 136p. (Orig.). (YA). (gr. 12 up). 1987. pap. 17.95 (*0-933635-40-0*, 2319) Chaosium.

Love, Peter. Labour & the Money Power: Australian Labour Populism 1890-1950. (Illus.). xii, 240p. (Orig.). 1984. pap. text ed. 17.50 (*0-522-84266-6*) Intl Spec Bk.

Love, Presley. Rock Lyrics Quiz Book. LC 93-46589. 1994. write for info. (*0-8065-1527-9*, Citadel Pr) Carol Pub Group.

Love, R. F., et al. Facilities Location: Models & Methods. (Publications in Operations Research Ser.: Vol. 7). 382p. 1988. 45.00 (*0-685-19998-3*, North Holland) Elsevier.

— Facilities Location: Models & Methods. 384p. 1988. 51.95 (*0-444-01031-9*) Elsevier.

Love, R. M. The Chemical Biology of Fishes: Vol. 2, Advances 1968-1977. 1980. text ed. 248.00 (*0-12-455852-6*) Acad Pr.

***Love, R. R., et al, eds.** Manual of Clinical Oncology: UICC International Union Against Cancer. 6th ed. 802p. 1994. pap. 49.00 (*0-387-58193-6*) Spr-Verlag.

Love, Ralph N., jt. ed. see Goodman, Louis J.

Love, Rik. Love's Post Journal. abr. ed. 130p. 1995. pap. 8.95 (*1-56901-482-5*) NW Pub.

Love, Robert. Chic Simple Tools. 1994. 12.50 (*0-679-43223-X*) Knopf.

— How to Start Your Own School. LC 72-90275. 176p. 1975. reprint ed. pap. 1.95 (*0-916054-01-2*) Green Hill.

Love, Robert A. Federal Financing. LC 68-58605. (Columbia University. Studies in the Social Sciences: No. 337). reprint ed. 21.00 (*0-404-51337-9*) AMS Pr.

Love, Robert W., Jr. History of the U. S. Navy, Vol. 2. LC 91-27510. (Illus.). 912p. 1992. 39.95 (*0-8117-1863-8*) Stackpole.

— History of the U. S. Navy: 1775-1941. LC 91-27510. (Illus.). 752p. 1992. 39.95 (*0-8117-1862-X*) Stackpole.

Love, Robert W., Jr., ed. Pearl Harbor Revisited. (Franklin & Eleanor Roosevelt Institute Series on Diplomatic & Economic History). 320p. 1994. text ed. 45.00 (*0-312-09593-7*) St Martin.

Love, Robert W., Jr. & Major, John, eds. The Year of D-Day: The Nineteen Forty-Four Diary of Admiral Sir Bertram Ramsay, RN. (Illus.). 208p. 1994. 25.00 (*0-85958-622-7*, Pub. by Hull Univ Pr UK) Paul & Co Pubs.

Love, Robertus. The Rise & Fall of Jesse James. LC 89-24965. xxiv, 446p. (YA). 1990. reprint ed. pap. 11.95 (*0-8032-7932-9*, Bison Books) U of Nebr Pr.

Love, Robin M. Probably More Than You Want to Know about the Fishes of the Pacific Coast. LC 91-90108. (Illus.). 224p. (Orig.). 1991. pap. 12.95 (*0-9628725-4-7*) Really Big Pr.

Love, Rosaleen, ed. Darwin & Social Darwinism. 69p. (C). 1982. 38.00 (*0-86828-132-8*, Pub. by Deakin Univ AT) St Mut.

***Love, Rosalind C., ed. & tr.** Three Eleventh-Century Anglo-Latin Saints' Lives: Vita S. Birini, Vita et Miracula S. Kenelmi, & Vita S. Rummoldi. (Oxford Medieval Texts Ser.). 340p. 1995. 65.00 (*0-19-820524-4*) OUP.

Love, Russell J. & Webb, Wanda G., eds. Neurology for the Speech-Language Pathologist. 2nd ed. (Illus.). 309p. 1991. pap. text ed. 32.95 (*0-7506-9076-3*) Buttrwrth-Heinemann.

Love, Ruth, jt. auth. see Love, Ken.

Love, Sid, jt. auth. see Love, Daphne.

Love, Steve. Florida Facts & Fiction. (Illus.). (Orig.). 1984. pap. 4.95 (*0-9613239-0-6*) S F Love.

Love, Susan M. Dr. Susan Love's Breast Book. 1991. pap. 15.38 (*0-201-57097-1*) Addison-Wesley.

***Love, Susan M. & Lindsey, Karen.** Dr. Susan Love's Breast Book. 2nd rev. ed. (Illus.). 608p. 1995. pap. 16.35 (*0-201-40835-X*) Addison-Wesley.

Love, Sydney F. Achieving Problem Free Project Management. 1989. text ed. 64.95 (*0-471-63522-7*) Wiley.

— Mastery & Management of Time. (Illus.). 1978. 14.95 (*0-13-559971-7*, Busn) P-H.

Love, Sydney S. Planning & Creating Successful Engineered Designs. rev. ed. (Illus.). 292p. 1986. 40.00 (*0-912907-00-2*) Adv Prof Dev.

Love, T. W. Construction Manual: Concrete & Formwork. (Illus.). 178p. 1973. pap. 17.75 (*0-910460-03-5*) Craftsman.

— Construction Manual: Finish Carpentry. LC 74-12339. (Illus.). 1974. pap. 15.25 (*0-910460-08-6*) Craftsman.

— Stair Builders Handbook. LC 74-4298. (Illus.). 1974. pap. 15.50 (*0-910460-07-8*) Craftsman.

***Love, Terry.** A-RA-5 "Mini" in Action. (Mini in Action Ser.). (Illus.). 50p. 1995. pap. 5.95 (*0-89747-334-5*) Squad Sig Pubns.

— A-37 - T-37 Dragonfly in Action. (Aircraft in Action Ser.). (Illus.). 50p. 1991. pap. 8.95 (*0-89747-239-X*, 1114) Squad Sig Pubns.

***Love, Thomas A.** Scheduling Residential Construction for Builders & Remodelers. LC 94-41539. (Illus.). 128p. (Orig.). 1995. pap. write for info. (*0-86718-401-9*) Home Builder.

Love, Tom. Object Lessons. 1993. pap. text ed. 29.00 (*0-13-472432-1*) P-H.

— Object Lessons: Lessons Learned in Object-Oriented Development Projects. Wiener, Richard S., ed. & intro. by. LC 93-84410. (Advances in Object Technology Ser.: Vol. 1). (Illus.). 266p. (Orig.). (C). 1993. pap. 29.00 (*0-9627477-3-4*) SIGS Bks.

***Love, Val.** Cat Sweaters & Cushions: To Knit by Hand or Machine. (Illus.). 16p. (Orig.). 1994. pap. 12.00 (*1-886828-01-6*) Dovetail Desgn.

— Christmas Tree Decorations: To Knit by Hand or Machine. (Illus.). 16p. (Orig.). 1987. pap. 8.50 (*1-886828-03-2*) Dovetail Desgn.

— Holiday Decorations: To Knit by Hand or Machine. (Illus.). 24p. 1992. pap. 11.50 (*1-886828-02-4*) Dovetail Desgn.

— Pocket Pals: To Knit by Hand or Machine. (Illus.). 32p. 1995. pap. 12.50 (*1-886828-00-8*) Dovetail Desgn.

— Story Book Afghans & Toys. (Illus.). (Orig.). 1990. pap. 10.00 (*1-886828-05-9*) Dovetail Desgn.

— Story Book Sweaters: To Knit by Hand or Machine. (Illus.). 16p. (Orig.). 1988. pap. 10.00 (*1-886828-04-0*) Dovetail Desgn.

Love, Vicky. Childless Is Not Less. LC 84-20464. 144p. (Orig.). 1984. pap. 8.99 (*0-87123-449-1*) Bethany Hse.

— Cuando los Ninos No Llegan. Ward, Rhode F., tr. 224p. (SPA.). (C). 1988. pap. 4.95 (*0-88113-263-2*) Edit Betania.

Love, W. W. Disposal Systems. LC 83-161604. (Mud Equipment Manual Ser.: No. 11). 58p. (Orig.). 1982. pap. 19.00 (*0-87201-623-4*) Gulf Pub.

Love, Warner & Lattman, Eaton, eds. Biophysical Applications of Crystallographic Techniques. (Transactions of the American Crystallographic Association Ser.: Vol. 9). 140p. 1973. pap. 25.00 (*0-686-60380-X*) Polycrystal Bk Serv.

Love, William. The Fundamentals of Murder. 1991. 18.95 (*1-55611-233-5*) D I Fine.

Love, William D. Colonial History of Hartford (Conn.) (Illus.). 368p. 1993. reprint ed. lib. bdg. 42.00 (*0-8328-3130-1*) Higginson Bk Co.

Love, William D. & Honig, Lucille J. Options & Perspectives: A Sourcebook of Innovative Foreign Language Programs in Action, K-12. LC 73-78994. 381p. reprint ed. pap. 108.60 (*0-685-15358-4*, 2026553) Bks Demand.

Love, William F. Bishop's Revenge: A Bishop Regan & Davey Goldman Myster. LC 92-54462. 1993. 20.00 (*1-55611-351-X*) D I Fine.

— Bloody Ten. 1992. 19.95 (*1-55611-275-0*) D I Fine.

— The Chartreuse Clue. 1990. 18.95 (*1-55611-211-4*) D I Fine.

— The Chartreuse Clue. 352p. 1991. reprint ed. pap. 5.50 (*0-451-40273-1*, Onyx) NAL-Dutton.

— Murder at St. Stephen's: A Bishop Regan & Davey Goldman Mystery. LC 93-72587. 288p. 1994. 21.00 (*1-55611-387-0*) D I Fine.

— The Ruby-Red Clue. Orig. Title: The Fundamentals of Murder. 288p. 1992. pap. 4.99 (*0-451-40329-0*, Onyx) NAL-Dutton.

Loveall, Jaquelyn. Phila Campbell: A Story of Nineteen Hundred Nine. 120p. 1994. 14.95 (*1-878208-39-X*) Guild Pr IN.

Lovece & Okamoto. Atomic Age, No. 1. 48p. 1990. 4.50 (*0-87135-709-7*) Marvel Entmnt.

— Atomic Age, No. 2. 48p. 1990. 4.50 (*0-87135-710-0*) Marvel Entmnt.

— Atomic Age, No. 3. 48p. 1991. 4.50 (*0-87135-711-9*) Marvel Entmnt.

— Atomic Age, No. 4. 48p. 1991. 4.50 (*0-87135-712-7*) Marvel Entmnt.

Lovece, Frank, jt. auth. see Edelstein, Andrew J.

Lovece, Joseph A. & Benson-Walker, Gwen E., eds. Military Robotics Sourcebook, 1991-1992 Edition, 3 sections. rev. ed. (Illus.). 400p. 1991. 700.00 (*0-9623132-1-1*); 325.00 (*0-685-72471-9*); 325.00 (*0-685-72472-7*); 325.00 (*0-685-72473-5*) L & B Ltd.

***Lovechild.** Gag. (Orig.). 1995. mass mkt., pap. 6.95 (*1-56333-369-4*) Masquerade.

Lovecraft, H. P. At the Mountains of Madness. (Illus.). 1990. 120.00 (*0-937986-69-0*) D M Grant.

— At the Mountains of Madness & Other Novels. rev. ed. Joshi, S. T., ed. LC 85-1254. (Collected Lovecraft Fiction Ser.: Vol. 2). (Illus.). 458p. 1985. reprint ed. 19.95 (*0-87054-038-6*) Arkham.

— At the Mountains of Madness & Other Tales of Terror. 1985. mass mkt. 4.95 (*0-345-32945-7*, Del Rey) Ballantine.

— The Best of H. P. Lovecraft: Bloodcurdling Tales of Horror & the Macabre. 304p. 1987. pap. 10.00 (*0-345-35080-4*) Ballantine.

— The Case of Charles Dexter Ward. 128p. (Orig.). 1987. mass mkt. 4.95 (*0-345-35490-7*) Ballantine.

— Commonplace Book. Schultz, David E., ed. 116p. (Orig.). 1987. pap. 9.95 (*0-940884-05-4*) Necronomicon.

— Dagon & Other Macabre Tales. rev. ed. Joshi, S. T., ed. LC 86-14105. (Collected Lovecraft Fiction Ser.: Vol. 3). (Illus.). 475p. 1987. 19.95 (*0-87054-039-4*) Arkham.

— The Doom That Came to Sarnath. 224p. 1991. mass mkt. 4.95 (*0-345-33105-2*, Del Rey) Ballantine.

— The Dream-Quest of Unknown Kadath. 1986. mass mkt. 4.95 (*0-345-33779-4*, Del Rey) Ballantine.

— The Dunwich Horror & Others. rev. ed. Joshi, S. T., ed. LC 84-14478. (Collected Lovecraft Fiction Ser.: Vol. 1). (Illus.). 433p. 1985. reprint ed. 19.95 (*0-87054-037-8*) Arkham.

— The Fantastic Poetry. Joshi, S. T., ed. (Illus.). 64p. (Orig.). 1990. pap. 7.95 (*0-940884-30-5*) Necronomicon.

— First Writings: The Pawtuxet Valley Gleaner. 32p. (Orig.). 1986. pap. 3.95 (*0-940884-13-5*) Necronomicon.

— Four Prose Poems. (Illus.). (Orig.). 1987. pap. 2.50 (*0-940884-10-0*) Necronomicon.

— The Fungi from Yuggoth. 2.50 (*0-686-31236-8*) Necronomicon.

— The H. P. Lovecraft Christmas Book. Michaud, Susan, ed. (Illus.). 12p. (Orig.). 1984. pap. 1.50 (*0-940884-22-4*) Necronomicon.

— Herbert West Reanimator. 35p. (Orig.). 1985. pap. 3.50 (*0-318-04714-4*) Necronomicon.

— History of the Necronomicon. 12p. (Orig.). 1984. pap. 1.50 (*0-318-04715-2*) Necronomicon.

— The Horror in the Museum & Other Revisions. enl. rev. ed. Joshi, S. T., ed. LC 88-7921. (Collected Lovecraft Fiction Ser.: Vol. 4). 464p. 1989. reprint ed. 19.95 (*0-87054-040-8*) Arkham.

— Juvenilia, Eighteen Ninety-Seven to Nineteen Hundred Five. 46p. (Orig.). 1984. pap. 4.95 (*0-318-04717-9*) Necronomicon.

— Lurking Fear & Other Stories. 1985. mass mkt. 4.99 (*0-345-32604-0*) Ballantine.

— Miscellaneous Writings. Joshi, S. T., ed. & intro. by. LC 94-27323. (Illus.). xiv, 570p. 1995. 29.95 (*0-87054-168-4*) Arkham.

— The Night Ocean. (Illus.). (Orig.). 1986. pap. 2.50 (*0-940884-16-X*) Necronomicon.

— Re-Animator: Tales of Herbert West. Jones, Steven, ed. (Illus.). 48p. 1991. pap. 4.95 (*1-56398-027-4*) Malibu Graphics.

— Selected Letters, Vol. 4. Derleth, August & Turner, James, eds. LC 75-44846. (Illus.). 424p. 1976. 12.50 (*0-87054-035-1*) Arkham.

— Selected Letters, Vol. 5. Derleth, August & Turner, James, eds. LC 75-44847. (Illus.). 400p. 1976. 12.50 (*0-87054-036-X*) Arkham.

— Selected Letters One. 1965. 10.00 (*0-87054-034-3*) Arkham.

— Selected Letters Two. 1968. 10.00 (*0-87054-029-7*) Arkham.

— Something about Cats, & Other Pieces. Derleth, August W., ed. LC 79-156681. (Essay Index Reprint Ser.). 1977. reprint ed. 24.95 (*0-8369-2410-X*) Ayer.

— Supernatural Horror in Literature. Bleiler, E. F., ed. 1973. reprint ed. pap. 3.95 (*0-486-20105-8*) Dover.

— The Tomb & Other Tales. 1986. mass mkt. 4.99 (*0-345-33661-5*) Ballantine.

— The Vivisector. 14p. (Orig.). 1990. pap. 2.50 (*0-940884-29-1*) Necronomicon.

— A Winter Wish. Collins, Tom, ed. & intro. by. LC 76-58618. (Illus.). 1977. 10.00 (*0-918372-00-3*) Whispers.

Lovecraft, H. P. & Derleth, August. The Lurker at the Threshold. 192p. 1988. pap. 3.50 (*0-88184-408-X*) Carroll & Graf.

— The Watchers Out of Time. 272p. 1991. pap. 4.95 (*0-88184-769-0*) Carroll & Graf.

— The Watchers Out of Time & Others. LC 73-88394. 1974. 15.95 (*0-87054-033-5*) Arkham.

Lovecraft, H. P. & Green, Sonia H. European Glimpses. 20p. (Orig.). 1988. pap. 2.50 (*0-940884-18-6*) Necronomicon.

Lovecraft, H. P., et al. Tales of the Cthulhu Mythos. LC 87-17503. (Illus.). 525p. 1990. 24.95 (*0-87054-159-5*) Arkham.

***Lovecraft, Howard P.** The Dream Cycle of H. P. Lovecraft: Dreams of Terror & Death. LC 95-15061. 1995. 10.00 (*0-345-38421-0*) Ballantine.

Lovecy, Ian. Automating Library Procedures: A Survivor's Handbook. LC 84-221628. (Illus.). 255p. reprint ed. pap. 72.70 (*0-7837-7014-6*, 2046828) Bks Demand.

Loveday, A. Britain & World Trade. LC 76-37894. (Select Bibliographies Reprint Ser.). 1977. reprint ed. 19.95 (*0-8369-6731-3*) Ayer.

— History & Economics of Indian Famines. 1986. reprint ed. 18.50 (*0-8364-1611-2*, Pub. by Usha II) S Asia.

Loveday, Alexander. Reflections on International Administration. LC 74-9168. 334p. 1974. reprint ed. text ed. 69.50 (*0-8371-7618-2*, LOIA, Greenwood Pr) Greenwood.

Loveday, Alexander, ed. Images of Empire. (JSOT Supplement Ser.: No. 122). 320p. (C). 1991. 35.00 (*1-85075-312-1*, Pub. by Sheffield Acad UK) CUP Services.

Loveday, Amos J., Jr. The Rise & Decline of the American Cut Nail Industry: A Study of the Interrelationships of Technology, Business Organization, & Management Techniques. LC 83-5542. (Contributions in Economics & Economic History Ser.: No. 53). (Illus.). xx, 160p. 1983. text ed. 47.95 (*0-313-23918-5*, LAC/) Greenwood.

Loveday, Anthony J. & Gattermann, Gunter, eds. University Libraries in Developing Countries: Structure & Function in Regard to Information Transfer for Science & Technology. (IFLA Publication Ser.: Vol. 33). 183p. 1985. lib. bdg. 25.00 (*3-598-20397-7*) K G Saur.

Loveday, George. Electronics Sourcebook for Engineers. 300p. (C). 1986. pap. text ed. 160.00 (*0-273-02667-4*, Pub. by Pitman Pubng UK) St Mut.

— Microprocessor Sourcebook. 256p. (C). 1986. pap. text ed. 120.00 (*0-273-02154-0*, Pub. by Pitman Pubng UK) St Mut.

Loveday, George, ed. Practical Interface Circuits for Micros. 192p. (C). 1984. pap. text ed. 110.00 (*0-273-01998-8*, Pub. by Pitman Pubng UK) St Mut.

Loveday, George, jt. ed. see Brighouse, Brian.

Loveday, George C. & Seidman, Arthur H. Troubleshooting Solid State Circuits. LC 80-21954. 110p. 1981. pap. text ed. 14.95 (*0-471-08371-2*) P-H.

Loveday, Helen. Chinese Bronzes. (Illus.). 48p. 1995. pap. 6.95 (*1-85444-003-9*, 003-9, Pub. by Ashmolean Mus UK) A Schwartz & Co.

Loveday, John. Davies' Medical Terminology: A Guide to Current Usage. 5th ed. 384p. 1991. pap. 34.95 (*0-7506-0175-2*) Buttrwrth-Heinemann.

— Halo. LC 93-35930. 1994. write for info. (*0-15-100070-0*) HarBrace.

— Halo. 1994. pap. 9.95 (*0-15-600113-6*) HarBrace.

Loveday, Leo. Explorations in Japanese Sociolinguistics. LC 86-26369. (Pragmatics & Beyond Ser.: Vol. VII, 1). xi, 153p. (Orig.). 1986. text ed. 53.00x (*1-55619-000-X*) Benjamins North Am.

Loveday, M. S., jt. auth. see Gould, D.

Loveday, Peggy L., ed. Zipp Kode Directory. 96p. (Orig.). 1989. pap. 6.95 (*0-9622861-0-9*) Zipp-Kode Co Inc.

Loveday, Peter. Parliament, Factions & Parties. 1966. 29.95 (*0-522-83659-3*) Intl Spec Bk.

Loveday, Robert. First Course in Statistics. 1970. pap. 9.95 (*0-521-05601-2*) Cambridge U Pr.

— Practical Statistics & Probability. 256p. 1974. pap. 10.95 (*0-521-20291-4*) Cambridge U Pr.

— Statistics: A Second Course in Statistics. 2nd ed. LC 74-96095. (Illus.). 1970. pap. 14.95 (*0-521-07234-4*) Cambridge U Pr.

Loveglo, Beau. Why Panic? Eat Organic!! Discover the Healing & Life-Nurturing Properties of Organically Grown Food. (Illus.). 80p. (Orig.). (C). 1989. lib. bdg. write for info. (*0-318-66088-1*); pap. 6.95 (*0-9624054-0-X*) Loveglo & Comfort.

***Lovegren, Sylvia.** Fashionable Food. (Illus.). 1995. 25.00 (*0-02-575705-9*) Macmillan.

— Fashionable Food. LC 94-5371. (Illus.). 1995. 25.00 (*0-02-575059-3*) Macmillan.

Lovegrove, A. Judicial Decision Making, Sentencing Policy & Numerical Guidance. (Research in Criminology Ser.). (Illus.). 310p. 1988. 114.00 (*0-387-96764-8*) Spr-Verlag.

Lovegrove, Deryck W. Established Church, Sectarian People: Itinerancy & the Transformation of English Dissent, 1780-1830. 300p. 1988. 69.95 (*0-521-34457-3*) Cambridge U Pr.

Lovegrove, G., et al, eds. Women into Computing: Selected Papers 1988-1990. (Workshops in Computing Ser.). (Illus.). 448p. 1991. pap. 59.00 (*0-387-19648-X*) Spr-Verlag.

Lovegrove, Roger. Collins Field Notebook of British Birds. 1987. 21.95 (*0-317-54060-2*) Viking Penguin.

***Lovejoy.** China Dome. 1995. mass mkt. 5.99 (*0-7860-0111-9*, Pinnacle NY) Windsor NY.

Lovejoy, Addison. The Baseball Song Book. 24p. (YA). (gr. 8 up). 1971. 1.95 (*0-87884-015-X*) Unicorn Ent.

Lovejoy, Ann. The American Mixed Border: Gardens for All Seasons. LC 92-27309. 240p. 1993. text ed. 35.00 (*0-02-575580-3*) Macmillan.

— The Border in Bloom: A Northwest Garden Through the Seasons. LC 90-32901. (Illus.). 262p. (Orig.). 1990. pap. 14.95 (*0-912365-26-9*) Sasquatch Bks.

— Eight Items or Less Cookbook: Fine Food in a Hurry. LC 88-4513. (Illus.). 254p. 1991. pap. 11.95 (*0-912365-43-9*) Sasquatch Bks.

— Farther Along the Garden Path. LC 95-11939. (Illus.). 1995. write for info. (*0-02-575585-4*) Macmillan.

— Fragrant Gardens. (Cascadia Gardening Ser.). (Illus.). 112p. (Orig.). 1995. pap. 10.95 (*1-57061-026-6*) Sasquatch Bks.

— Seasonal Bulbs. (Cascadia Gardening Ser.). (Illus.). 112p. (Orig.). 1995. pap. 10.95 (*1-57061-027-4*) Sasquatch Bks.

— The Year in Bloom: Gardening for All Seasons in the Pacific Northwest. LC 87-60480. (Illus.). 264p. 1987. pap. 11.95 (*0-912365-11-0*) Sasquatch Bks.

Lovejoy, Ann, ed. Perennials: Toward Continuous Bloom. (New Voices from American Gardens Ser.). 304p. 1991. pap. 17.95 (*0-913643-06-8*) Capabilitys.

Lovejoy, Ann, intro. Three Years in Bloom: A Garden-Keeper's Journal. (Illus.). 158p. 1988. 14.95 (*0-912365-17-X*) Sasquatch Bks.

Lovejoy, Arthur O. Essays in the History of Ideas. LC 78-17473. 359p. 1978. reprint ed. text ed. 35.00 (*0-313-20504-3*, LOEH, Greenwood Pr) Greenwood.

— Great Chain of Being: A Study of the History of an Idea. LC 36-14264. (William James Lectures). 382p. 1936. pap. text ed. 13.95 (*0-674-36153-9*) HUP.

— The Reason, the Understanding, & Time. LC 61-8177. 224p. reprint ed. pap. 63.90 (*0-317-20645-1*, 2024135) Bks Demand.

— Reflections on Human Nature. LC 61-15700. 281p. 1961. reprint ed. pap. 13.95x (*0-8018-0395-0*) Johns Hopkins.

— Three Studies in Current Philosophical Questions. LC 75-3249. reprint ed. write for info. (*0-404-59237-6*) AMS Pr.

Lovejoy, Bahija, jt. auth. see Cohen, Barbara.

Lovejoy, Carol. Living in Two Worlds. Oakes, Sandy, ed. 180p. (Orig.). 1992. pap. 12.95 (*0-9633137-6-2*) Golden Globe.

Lovejoy, D. J. Magnetic Particle Inspection. (Illus.). 256p. 1992. pap. 45.00 (*0-412-44750-9*, A4971) Chapman & Hall.

— Penetrant Testing: A Practical Guide. (Illus.). 256p. 1991. pap. 45.00 (*0-412-38700-X*, A6121) Chapman & Hall.

Lovejoy, David S. The Glorious Revolution in America. LC 86-22482. 423p. 1987. pap. 25.00 (*0-8195-6177-0*, Wesleyan Univ Pr) U Pr of New Eng.

— Religious Enthusiasm in the New World: Heresy to Revolution. 295p. 1985. 37.00 (*0-674-75864-1*) HUP.

— Rhode Island Politics & the American Revolution, 1760-1776. LC 58-10478. (Brown University Studies: Vol. 23). 266p. reprint ed. pap. 75.90 (*0-685-44066-4*, 2030025) Bks Demand.

Lovejoy Derek & Patrners Staff & Davis Langdon & Everest Staff, eds. Spon's Landscape & External Works Price Book 1992. 11th ed. 240p. 1991. write for info. (*0-419-17390-0*, E & FN Spon) Routledge Chapman & Hall.

Lovejoy, Eddie. Better Born Lucky Than Rich. (C). 1989. 39.00 (*0-86303-322-9*) St Mut.

Lovejoy, Eunice G. Library Service to People with Disabilities: Ten Case Studies. (Professional Librarian Ser.). 176p. 1989. text ed. 32.50 (*0-8161-1922-8*, Hall Reference); pap. 24.50 (*0-8161-1923-6*, Hall Reference) Macmillan.

Lovejoy, Evelyn M. History of Royalton, Vermont with Family Genealogies, 1769-1911. (Illus.). 1146p. 1992. reprint ed. lib. bdg. 100.00 (*0-8328-2257-4*) Higginson Bk Co.

Lovejoy, I. Psyche-Therapy: How to Master Your Mind(s) & Emotions. 250p. (Orig.). 1991. pap. 19.95 (*0-9601978-7-7*) Health Res Las Vegas.

Lovejoy, Jack. Outworld Cats. 352p. (Orig.). 1994. mass mkt. 4.99 (*0-88677-596-5*) DAW Bks.

Lovejoy, Joseph C. & Lovejoy, Owen. Memoir of the Rev. Elijah P. Lovejoy. LC 72-117882. (Select Bibliographies Reprint Ser.). 1977. reprint ed. 34.95 (*0-8369-5335-5*) Ayer.

— Memoir of the Reverend Elijah P. Lovejoy. LC 72-90183. (Mass Violence in America Ser.). 1969. reprint ed. 32.95 (*0-405-01323-X*) Ayer.

Lovejoy, Kim B., jt. auth. see Davis, Kenneth W.

Lovejoy, Margot. The Book of Plagues: Panic, Blame, Indifference. 48p. 1993. pap. 28.00 (*0-9637531-0-X*) M Lovejoy.

— Paradoxic Mutations. 28p. 1993. pap. 18.00 (*0-9637531-1-8*) M Lovejoy.

— Postmodern Currents: Art & Artists in the Age of Electronic Media. 1992. pap. text ed. 33.40 (*0-13-681164-7*) P-H.

Lovejoy, Margot, et al. Off the Shelf & On-line: Computers Move the Book Arts into Twenty-First Century Design. (Illus.). 56p. pap. 10.00 (*1-879832-04-6*) MN Ctr Book Arts.

Lovejoy, Mary I., comp. Poetry of the Seasons. LC 71-98083. (Granger Index Reprint Ser.). 1977. 23.95 (*0-8369-6082-3*) Ayer.

Lovejoy, Mary I., ed. Nature in Verse. LC 78-73490. (Granger Poetry Library). (Illus.). 1979. reprint ed. 24.50 (*0-89609-116-3*) Roth Pub Inc.

Lovejoy, Owen, jt. auth. see Lovejoy, Joseph C.

Lovejoy, Pamela. Fish On a Dish. (Illus.). 11p. (Orig.). (J). (ps-2). 1994. pap. write for info. (*1-880038-17-X*) Learn-Abouts.

— If I Were An Astronaut. (Illus.). 14p. (Orig.). (J). (ps-2). 1994. pap. write for info. (*1-880038-18-8*) Learn-Abouts.

— Rainbow Children. (Illus.). 7p. (Orig.). (J). 1994. pap. text ed. write for info. (*1-880038-19-6*) Learn-Abouts.

***Lovejoy, Paul & Rogers, Nicholas, eds.** Unfree Labour in the Development of the Atlantic World. 1994. pap. 20.00 (*0-7146-4152-9*, Pub. by F Cass Pubs UK) Intl Spec Bk.

Lovejoy, Paul E. Transformations in Slavery: A History of Slavery in Africa. LC 82-1284. (African Studies: No. 36). (Illus.). 336p. 1983. pap. 22.95 (*0-521-28646-8*) Cambridge U Pr.

Lovejoy, Paul E., ed. Africans in Bondage: Studies in Slavery & the Slave Trade. LC 86-40556. 378p. 1986. pap. text ed. 16.00 (*0-299-97020-5*) U of Wis Pr.

— Africans in Bondage; Studies in Slavery & the Slave Trade: Essays in Honor of Philip D. Curtin on the Occasion of the Twenty-Fifth Anniversary of African Studies at the University of Wisconsin. LC 86-24611. (Illus.). 390p. reprint ed. pap. 111.20 (*0-7837-7025-1*, 2046840) Bks Demand.

— The Ideology of Slavery in Africa. LC 81-9240. (Sage Series on African Modernization & Development: No. 6). 311p. reprint ed. pap. 88.70 (*0-8357-8492-4*, 2034766) Bks Demand.

Lovejoy, Paul E. & Falola, Toyin. Africa: The Legacy of Slavery & Colonialism in the Modern World. (C). 1929. text ed. 35.00 (*0-8133-0441-5*); pap. text ed. 16.95 (*0-8133-0442-3*) Westview.

Lovejoy, Paul E. & Falola, Toyin, eds. Pawnship in Africa. 200p. (C). 1994. text ed. 49.95 (*0-8133-8457-5*) Westview.

Lovejoy, Paul E. & Hogendorn, Jan S. Slow Death for Slavery: The Course of Abolition in Northern Nigeria, 1897- 1936. (African Studies: No. 76). (Illus.). 408p. (C). 1993. 74.95 (*0-521-37469-3*); pap. 19.95 (*0-521-44702-X*) Cambridge U Pr.

***Lovejoy, Paul E. & Rogers, Nicholas, eds.** Unfree Labour in the Development of the Atlantic World. LC 94-31528. (Studies in Slave & Post-Slave Societies & Cultures). 1994. 35.00 (*0-7146-4579-6*, Pub. by F Cass Pubs UK) Intl Spec Bk.

Lovejoy, Paul E., jt. ed. see Coquery-Vidrovitch, Catherine.

Lovejoy, S., jt. auth. see Schertzer, D.

Lovejoy, S., jt. ed. see Schertzer, D.

Lovejoy, Sharon. Hollyhock Days: Garden Adventures for the Young at Heart. Ligon, Lindon, ed. (Illus.). 1994. pap. 14.95 (*0-934026-90-4*) Interweave.

— Hollyhock Days: Garden Adventures for the Young at Heart. Ligon, Lindon, ed. (Illus.). 1994. 24.95 (*1-883010-01-2*) Interweave.

— Sunflower Houses. 1995. pap. 14.95 (*1-883010-00-4*) Interweave.

— Sunflower Houses: Garden Discoveries for Children of All Ages. LC 91-29880. (Illus.). 144p. 1991. 19.95 (*0-934026-70-X*) Interweave.

Lovejoy, Sharon, jt. auth. see Blose, Nora.

Lovejoy, Stephen B. & Napier, Ted L., eds. Conserving Soil: Insights from Socioeconomic Research. LC 86-1752. 155p. 1986. text ed. 9.00 (*0-935734-12-0*) Soil & Water Conserv.

Lovejoy, Stephen B., jt. ed. see Braden, John B.

Lovejoy, Surya. Getting Results: A Systematic Approach. 300p. 1993. 59.95 (*0-566-07326-9*, Pub. by Gower UK) Ashgate Pub Co.

Lovejoy, Surya, jt. auth. see De Haas, Paul.

Lovejoy, Thomas E., jt. auth. see Peters, Robert L.

Lovejoy, Thomas E., jt. ed. see Primack, Richard B.

Lovejoy, W., jt. auth. see Garfield, Paul.

Lovejoy, Wallace F. Methods of Estimating Reserves of Crude Oil, Natural Gas, & Natural Gas Liquids. LC 65-24790. 182p. reprint ed. pap. 51.90 (*0-317-26470-2*, 2023805) Bks Demand.

Lovejoy, Wallace F. & Homan, Paul T. Economic Aspects of Oil Conservation Regulation. (Resources for the Future Ser.). 310p. 1967. 22.50 (*0-8018-0397-7*) Johns Hopkins.

— Economic Aspects of Oil Conservation Regulation. LC 67-20283. 295p. 1967. 22.50 (*0-685-11640-9*) Resources Future.

Lovejoy, William. Delta Blue. 1991. mass mkt. 4.50 (*0-8217-3540-3*) Zebra.

— Phantom Strike. 384p. 1993. mass mkt. 4.50 (*0-8217-4392-9*) Zebra.

— Rip Cord. 288p. (Orig.). 1992. mass mkt. 3.99 (*0-380-76447-4*) Avon.

— Seaghost. 256p. (Orig.). 1991. mass mkt. 3.99 (*0-380-76577-2*) Avon.

— White Night. 560p. 1994. mass mkt. 4.50 (*0-8217-4587-5*) Zebra.

Lovejoy, William B. Alpha Kat. 384p. 1992. mass mkt. 4.50 (*0-8217-3958-1*) Zebra.

Lovejoy, William H. Black Sky. 1990. mass mkt. 4.50 (*0-8217-3236-6*) Zebra.

— China Dome. 544p. 1995. pap. 5.99 (*0-8217-0111-8*) Zebra.

— Cold Front. 1990. mass mkt. 4.50 (*0-8217-3041-X*) Zebra.

— Delta Green. 384p. 1993. mass mkt. 4.50 (*0-8217-4131-4*) Zebra.

— Ultra Deep. 1992. mass mkt. 4.50 (*0-8217-3694-9*) Zebra.

Lovekin, David. Technique, Discourse, & Consciousness: An Introduction to the Philosophy of Jacques Ellul. LC 89-85467. 256p. 1991. 42.50 (*0-934223-01-7*) Lehigh Univ Pr.

***Lovel, Hugh.** A Biodynamic Farm. LC 93-74953. 192p. 1994. 15.00 (*0-911311-45-9*) Halcyon Hse.

Lovel, Nina B. You're over the Hill, Honey. 18p. 1991. 10.95 (*0-685-71232-X*) About You.

Lovel, Nina B. & Thwaites, Beth. Nadines Guide to Love. 18p. (J). (ps-2). 1992. 10.95 (*1-879680-12-2*) About You.

Lovelace. Neuromuscular Disease. 400p. 1993. 44.95 (*0-8151-5623-5*, Yr Bk Med Pubs) Mosby Yr Bk.

Lovelace, Austin C. The Organist & Hymn Playing. rev. ed. LC 81-80265. (Illus.). 61p. 1981. reprint ed. pap. 7.95 (*0-916642-16-X*) Hope Pub.

Lovelace, Austin C. & Rice, William C. Music & Worship in the Church. rev. ed. LC 76-13524. reprint ed. pap. 15.95 (*0-317-09866-7*, 2020266) Bks Demand.

Lovelace, Carey, tr. see Bernadac, Marie-Laure & Du Bouchet, Paule.

Lovelace, Daniel D. China & People's War in Thailand, 1964-1969. LC 72-184630. (China Research Monographs: No. 8). 101p. reprint ed. pap. 28.80 (*0-317-08371-6*, 2004586) Bks Demand.

Lovelace, Delos, jt. auth. see Lovelace, Maud.

Lovelace, E. A., ed. Aging & Cognition: Mental Processes, Self-Awareness & Interventions. (Advances in Psychology Ser.: No. 72). 452p. 1991. 137.25 (*0-444-88367-3*, North Holland) Elsevier.

Lovelace, Earl. A Brief Conversion & Other Stories. (Caribbean Writers Ser.). 141p. (Orig.). (C). 1988. pap. 7.50 (*0-435-98882-4*, 98882) Heinemann.

— The Schoolmaster. (Caribbean Writers Ser.). xvii, 171p. (C). 1983. reprint ed. pap. 7.95 (*0-435-98550-7*) Heinemann.

Lovelace, Earl & Thorpe, Marjorie. The Wine of Astonishment. (Caribbean Writers Ser.). xiv, 146p. (C). 1986. reprint ed. pap. 9.95 (*0-435-98880-8*) Heinemann.

Lovelace, Jeff. Mount Mitchell: Its Railroad & Toll Road. (Illus.). 96p. 1994. pap. 9.95 (*0-932807-84-4*) Overmountain Pr.

Lovelace, Linda & McGrady, Mike. Linda Lovelace: Out of Bondage. 1986. 14.95 (*0-8184-0386-1*) Carol Pub Group.

— Ordeal. 1987. mass mkt. 4.99 (*0-425-10439-7*) Berkley Pub.

— Ordeal. 1980. 10.00 (*0-8065-0687-3*, Citadel Pr) Carol Pub Group.

— Out of Bondage. 224p. 1986. 14.95 (*0-8065-0992-9*, Citadel Pr) Carol Pub Group.

Lovelace, Maud & Lovelace, Delos. Gentlemen from England. LC 93-9412. 361p. 1993. reprint ed. pap. 12.95 (*0-87351-287-1*, Borealis Book) Minn Hist.

Lovelace, Maud H. Betsy & Joe. LC 48-8096. (Illus.). 256p. (YA). (gr. 5 up). 1948. 14.95 (*0-690-13378-2*, Crowell Jr Bks) HarpC Child Bks.

— Betsy & Joe. LC 48-8096. (Trophy Bk.). (Illus.). 288p. (J). (gr. 4-7). 1995. pap. 4.95 (*0-06-440546-X*, Trophy) HarpC Child Bks.

— Betsy & Tacy Go Downtown. LC 43-51264. (Illus.). 192p. (J). (gr. 2-5). 1966. lib. bdg. 14.89 (*0-690-13450-9*, Crowell Jr Bks) HarpC Child Bks.

— Betsy & Tacy Go Downtown. LC 43-51264. (Trophy Bk.). (Illus.). 192p. (J). (gr. 2-5). 1979. pap. 3.95 (*0-06-440098-0*, Trophy) HarpC Child Bks.

— Betsy & Tacy Go over the Big Hill. LC 42-23557. (Illus.). 176p. (J). (gr. 2-5). 1966. lib. bdg. 14.89 (*0-690-13521-1*, Crowell Jr Bks) HarpC Child Bks.

— Betsy & Tacy Go over the Big Hill. LC 42-23557. (Trophy Bk.). (Illus.). 176p. (J). (gr. 2-5). 1979. pap. 3.95 (*0-06-440099-9*, Trophy) HarpC Child Bks.

— Betsy in Spite of Herself. LC 46-11995. (Trophy Bk.). (Illus.). 288p. (J). (gr. 4-7). 1980. pap. 3.95 (*0-06-440111-1*, Trophy) HarpC Child Bks.

— Betsy-Tacy. LC 40-30965. (Illus.). 128p. (J). (gr. 2-5). 1966. lib. bdg. 14.89 (*0-690-13805-9*, Crowell Jr Bks) HarpC Child Bks.

— Betsy-Tacy. LC 40-30965. (Trophy Bk.). (Illus.). 128p. (J). (gr. 2-5). 1979. pap. 3.95 (*0-06-440096-4*, Trophy) HarpC Child Bks.

— Betsy-Tacy. LC 40-30965. (Illus.). 128p. (J). (gr. 2-5). 1994. 9.95 (*0-06-024415-1*) HarpC Child Bks.

— Betsy-Tacy & Tib. LC 41-18714. (Illus.). 144p. (J). (gr. 2-5). 1966. lib. bdg. 14.89 (*0-690-13876-8*, Crowell Jr Bks) HarpC Child Bks.

— Betsy-Tacy & Tib. LC 41-18714. (Trophy Bk.). (Illus.). 144p. (J). (gr. 2-5). 1979. pap. 3.95 (*0-06-440097-2*, Trophy) HarpC Child Bks.

— Betsy-Tacy & Tib. (Illus.). 144p. (J). (gr. 2-5). 1994. 9.95 (*0-06-024416-X*) HarpC Child Bks.

— The Betsy-Tacy Treasury. LC 94-25063. (Illus.). (J). (gr. 1-8). 1994. 5.50 (*0-06-024919-6*) HarpC.

— Betsy Was a Junior: A Betsy - Tacy High School Story. LC 46-11995. (Illus.). 248p. (YA). (gr. 5 up). 1947. 14.95 (*0-690-13946-2*) HarpC Child Bks.

— Betsy Was a Junior: A Betsy - Tacy High School Story. LC 46-11995. (Trophy Bk.). (Illus.). 288p. (J). (gr. 4-7). 1995. pap. 4.95 (*0-06-440547-8*, Trophy) HarpC Child Bks.

— Betsy's Wedding. LC 55-11108. (Illus.). 241p. (J). (gr. 5 up). 1955. 14.95 (*0-690-13733-8*, Crowell Jr Bks) HarpC Child Bks.

— Carney's House Party. 1976. 20.95 (*0-8488-1084-8*) Amereon Ltd.

— Early Candlelight. LC 91-38314. 322p. 1992. reprint ed. pap. 12.95 (*0-87351-269-3*, Borealis Book) Minn Hist.

— Emily of Deep Valley. 1976. 22.95 (*0-8488-1085-6*) Amereon Ltd.

— Heaven to Betsy. LC 45-9806. (Trophy Bk.). (Illus.). 288p. (J). (gr. 4-7). 1980. pap. 3.95 (*0-06-440110-3*, Trophy) HarpC Child Bks.

— The Trees Kneel at Christmas. LC 94-10512. (J). 1994. lib. bdg. 15.93 (*1-56239-999-3*) Abdo & Dghtrs.

— Winona's Pony Cart. 1976. 16.95 (*0-8488-1420-7*) Amereon Ltd.

— Winona's Pony Cart. 120p. 1986. reprint ed. lib. bdg. 17.95 (*0-89966-566-7*) Buccaneer Bks.

Lovelace, Merline. Bits & Pieces. 224p. (Orig.). 1993. pap. 2.95 (*1-56597-041-1*, Kismet) Meteor Pub.

— The Cowboy & the Cossack. (Intimate Moments Ser.). 1995. mass mkt. 3.75 (*0-373-07657-6*, 1-07657-9) Silhouette.

— His Lady's Ransom. (Historical Ser.). 1995. mass mkt. 4.50 (*0-373-28875-1*, 1-28875-2) Harlequin Bks.

— Maggie & Her Colonel. (Great Escapes Ser.). 1994. pap. 1.99 (*0-373-83273-7*, 1-83273-2) Harlequin Bks.

— Night of the Jaguar. (IM Extra, Code Name: Danger) (Intimate Moments Ser.). 1995. mass mkt. 3.75 (*0-373-07637-1*, 1-07637-1) Silhouette.

— Somewhere in Time. (Intimate Moments Ser.). 1994. mass mkt. 3.50 (*0-373-07593-6*, 1-07593-6) Harlequin Bks.

— Sweet Song of Love. (Historical Ser.). 1994. mass mkt. 3.99 (*0-373-28830-1*, 1-28830-7) Harlequin Bks.

— Undercover Man. 1995. mass mkt. 3.75 (*0-373-07669-X*, 1-07669-4) Silhouette.

Lovelace, Richard. Poems, 2 vols., Set. Wilkinson, C. H., ed. (BCL1-PR English Literature Ser.). 1992. reprint ed. lib. bdg. 150.00 (*0-7812-7369-2*) Rprt Serv.

Lovelace, Richard F. Dynamics of Spiritual Life. LC 78-24757. 1979. pap. 19.99 (*0-87784-626-X*, 626) InterVarsity.

Lovelace, Richard H. Mr. Taft's School: The First Century. (Illus.). 208p. 1989. 20.00 (*0-685-44853-3*) Taft Schl.

Lovelace, Richard T. Stress Master. 1990. pap. text ed. 14.95 (*0-471-51725-9*) Wiley.

Lovelady, J., ed. see Gimbel, Cheryl & Maners, Wendelin.

Lovelady, J., ed. see Schriner, Christian.

Lovelady, Janet. Aladdin Literature Mini-Unit. (Illus.). 32p. (J). (gr. 3-5). 1990. student ed 4.95 (*1-56096-016-7*) Mari.

— Annie & the Old One Literature Mini-Unit. (Illus.). 32p. (J). (gr. 3-5). 1990. student ed 4.95 (*1-56096-018-3*) Mari.

— Big Bad Bruce Literature Mini-Unit. (Illus.). 32p. (J). (gr. 2-4). 1989. student ed 4.95 (*1-56096-001-9*) Mari.

— Bread & Jam for Frances Literature Mini-Unit. (Illus.). 32p. (J). (gr. 2-4). 1989. student ed 4.95 (*1-56096-002-7*) Mari.

An Asterisk (*) at the beginning of an entry indicates that the title is appearing in BIP for the first time.

— Bremen-Town Musicians Literature Mini-Unit. (Illus.). 32p. (J). (gr. 2-4). 1989. student ed 4.95 (1-56096-004-3) Mari.
— The Drinking Gourd Literature Mini-Unit. (Illus.). 32p. (J). (gr. 3-5). 1990. student ed 4.95 (1-56096-019-1) Mari.
— Hill of Fire Literature Mini Unit. (Illus.). 32p. (J). (gr. 2-4). 1989. student ed 4.95 (1-56096-005-1) Mari.
— The Hundred Dresses Literature Mini-Unit. (Illus.). 32p. (J). (gr. 3-5). 1990. student ed 4.95 (1-56096-014-0) Mari.
— The Little House Literature Mini-Unit. (Illus.). 32p. (J). (gr. 2-4). 1989. student ed 4.95 (1-56096-000-0) Mari.
— Long Way to a New Land Literature Mini-Unit. (Illus.). 32p. (J). (gr. 3-5). 1990. student ed 4.95 (1-56096-013-2) Mari.
— Make Way for Ducklings Literature Mini-Unit. (Illus.). 32p. (J). (gr. 2-4). 1989. student ed 4.95 (1-56096-006-X) Mari.
— Miss Rumphius Literature Mini-Unit. (Illus.). 32p. (J). (gr. 2-4). 1989. student ed 4.95 (1-56096-003-5) Mari.
— Sam, Bangs & Moonshine Literature Mini-Unit. (Illus.). 32p. (J). (gr. 3-5). 1990. student ed 4.95 (1-56096-012-4) Mari.
— Shoeshine Girl Literature Mini-Unit. (Illus.). 32p. (J). (gr. 3-5). 1990. student ed 4.95 (1-56096-017-5) Mari.
— Song of the Swallows Literature Mini-Unit. (Illus.). 32p. (J). (gr. 2-4). 1989. student ed 4.95 (1-56096-007-8) Mari.
— Stone Soup Literature Mini-Unit. (Illus.). 32p. (J). (gr. 2-4). 1989. student ed 4.95 (1-56096-008-6) Mari.
— Strega Nona Literature Mini-Unit. (Illus.). 32p. (J). (gr. 2-4). 1989. student ed 4.95 (1-56096-009-4) Mari.
— The Ugly Duckling Literature Mini-Unit. (Illus.). 32p. (J). (gr. 3-5). 1990. student ed 4.95 (1-56096-015-9) Mari.
— Velveteen Rabbit Literature Mini-Unit. (Illus.). 32p. (J). (gr. 3-5). 1990. student ed 4.95 (1-56096-011-6) Mari.
— Wagon Wheels Literature Mini-Unit. (Illus.). 32p. (J). (gr. 3-5). 1990. student ed 4.95 (1-56096-010-8) Mari.
Lovelady, Janet, ed. see Drew, Naomi.
Lovelady, Janet, ed. see Fox, C. Lynn.
Lovelady, Janet, ed. see Kehayan, V. Alex.
Lovelady, Janet, ed. see McDaniel, Sandy & Bielen, Peggy.
Lovelady, Janet, ed. see Sevaly, Karen & Truax, Harry.
Loveland, Anne C. Lillian Smith, a Southerner Confronting the South. LC 86-10641. (Southern Biography Ser.). xii, 298p. 1986. text ed. 32.50 (0-8071-1343-3) La State U Pr.
— Southern Evangelicals & the Social Order, 1800-1860. LC 80-11200. xiv, 354p. 1980. pap. text ed. 14.95x (0-8071-0783-2) La State U Pr.
Loveland, Cherylon, jt. auth. see Rutherford, Clarice.
Loveland Comm. Staff. Discover Animals. (J). 1992. 4.49 (1-55513-910-8, Chariot Bks) Chariot Family.
— Discover Colors. (J). 1992. 4.49 (1-55513-916-7, Chariot Bks) Chariot Family.
— Discover Families. (J). 1992. 4.49 (1-55513-911-6, Chariot Bks) Chariot Family.
— Discover Sizes & Shapes. (J). 1992. 4.49 (1-55513-909-4, Chariot Bks) Chariot Family.
Loveland, D. W., ed. see Kruse, Robert, et al.
Loveland, D. W., ed. see Marek, V. W. & Truszczynski, M.
Loveland, D. W., ed. see Michalewicz, Zbigniew.
Loveland, D. W., ed. see Navinchandra, D.
Loveland, D. W., ed. see Peng, Y. & Reggia, J. A.
Loveland, Donald, jt. ed. see Bledsoe, W. W.
Loveland, G., jt. auth. see Loveland, J. B.
Loveland, Genevra K., jt. auth. see Aikman, Alex.
***Loveland, Ian.** Housing the Homeless: Administrative Law & Process. (Oxford Socio-Legal Studies). 288p. 1995. text ed. 65.00 (0-19-825876-3) OUP.
***Loveland, Ian, ed.** Frontiers of Criminality. (Modern Legal Studies). 1994. pap. 31.00 (0-421-52630-0) W W Gaunt.
Loveland, J. B. & Loveland, G. Genealogy of the Loveland Family in the United States, 1635 to 1892, Containing the Descendants of Thomas Loveland of Wethersfield, Now Glastonbury, Connecticut. (Illus.). 838p. 1989. reprint ed. lib. bdg. 133.50 (0-8328-0787-7); reprint ed. pap. 125.50 (0-8328-0788-5) Higginson Bk Co.
Loveland, Karen, jt. ed. see Adey, Walter H.
Loveland, Kay, jt. auth. see Bouch, Stephen.
Loveland, Kay, jt. auth. see Russillo, Fred.
Loveland, Kenneth, et al. Off the Beaten Track: Switzerland. LC 93-4065. (Illus.). 285p. (Orig.). 1993. pap. 14.95 (1-56440-300-9) Globe Pequot.
Loveland, Nicole. Boogins Gets a Basket. (Illus.). 32p. (J). (ps-2). 1984. lib. bdg. 4.95 (0-917107-00-4) Cat-Tales Pr.
— Boogins' Rainy Day. (Illus.). (J). (ps-3). 1985. lib. bdg. 5.95 (0-917107-02-0) Cat-Tales Pr.
Loveland, Peter J., jt. ed. see Rounsevell, Mark D.
Loveland, Roger P. Photomicrography: A Comprehensive Treatise, 2 vols., Set. LC 80-12428. 1070p. 1981. reprint ed. lib. bdg. 99.50 (0-89874-392-3) Krieger.
Loveland, Walter D., jt. auth. see Seaborg, Glenn T.
Loveless, Ganelle, jt. auth. see Bullock, Waneta B.
Loveless, James M., jt. ed. see Kinser, Katherine A.
Loveless, Joan P. The Century Book: A Family Record. 224p. 1993. pap. 19.95 (0-9637654-0-X) Century Pr NM.
— Three Weavers. LC 91-26721. (Illus.). 228p. 1992. 24.95 (0-8263-1318-3) U of NM Pr.
Loveless, Liz. One, Two, Buckle My Shoe. LC 92-40947. (Illus.). 32p. (J). (ps). 1993. 13.95 (1-56282-477-5); lib. bdg. 13.89 (1-56282-478-3) Hyprn Child.
Loveless, Thomas L. Selling Your Own Real Estate: Secrets from a Realtor. LC 92-81723. 194p. (Orig.). 1992. pap. 28.95 (0-9633103-0-5) TRuth Pub.
Lovelich, Henry. The History of the Holy Grail, Pts. 1 & 5. Furnivall, F. J., ed. (EETS, ES Ser.: Nos. 20, 24,). 1969. reprint ed. Pts. 1 & 2. 45.00 (0-527-00234-8) Periodicals Srv.
— Merlin, Pt. 1. Kock, E. A., ed. (EETS, ES Ser.: Nos. 93, 112). 1974. reprint ed. 34.00 (0-527-00184-8) Periodicals Srv.
— Merlin, Pt. 2. Kock, E. A., ed. (EETS, ES Ser.: Nos. 93, 112). 1974. reprint ed. 18.00 (0-527-00185-6) Periodicals Srv.
— Merlin, a Middle-English Metrical Version of a French Romance, Pt. III. (EETS. OS Ser.: No. 185). 1974. reprint ed. 44.00 (0-527-00183-X) Periodicals Srv.
Lovell. The Handbook of Photography. 3rd ed. 1993. teacher ed 14.00 (0-8273-5597-1) Delmar.
Lovell, A. Anarchist Cinema. 1974. 250.00 (0-87968-189-6) Gordon Pr.
Lovell, Alred C. Man's Relation to the Universe. LC 75-14096. 124p. reprint ed. pap. 35.40 (0-317-07757-0, 2055542) Bks Demand.
Lovell, Ann. Flying Time. large type ed. 1990. 21.95 (0-7089-2213-9) Ulverscroft.
***Lovell, Arnold, ed.** Evangelism in the Reformed Tradition. 160p. (Orig.). 1990. pap. 5.00 (1-885121-02-4) CTS Press.
Lovell, Bernard. Echoes of War: The Story of H2S Radar. (Illus.). 312p. 1991. 39.00 (0-85274-317-3) IOP Pub.
— Emerging Cosmology Convergence Series. 1981. text ed. 32.50 (0-231-05304-5, 1) Col U Pr.
— The Jodrell Bank Telescopes. (Illus.). 292p. 1985. 19.95 (0-19-858178-5) OUP.
— Voice of the Universe: Building the Jodrell Bank Telescope. rev. ed. LC 87-9322. 336p. 1987. text ed. 55.00 (0-275-92678-8, C2678, Praeger Pubs); pap. text ed. 14.95 (0-275-92679-6, B2679, Praeger Pubs) Greenwood.
Lovell, Bernard & Bank, Jodrell. Emerging Cosmology. Anshen, Ruth N., ed. LC 84-17954. (Convergence Ser.). 208p. 1984. pap. text ed. 12.95 (0-275-91790-8, B1790, Praeger Pubs) Greenwood.
Lovell, Bernard & Smith, F. Graham. Pathways to the Universe. (Illus.). 244p. 1989. 32.95 (0-521-32004-6) Cambridge U Pr.
Lovell, C. A., jt. ed. see Gulledge, Thomas R., Jr.
Lovell, C. R. Plants & the Skin. (Illus.). 240p. 1993. 89.95 (0-632-02562-X) Blackwell Sci.
Lovell, C. W. & Wiltshire, Richard L., eds. Engineering Aspects of Soil Erosion, Dispersive Clays & Loess. 176p. 1987. 20.00 (0-87262-590-7) Am Soc Civil Eng.
Lovell, C. W., jt. ed. see Khera, Raj P.
Lovell, Catherine H. Breaking the Cycle of Poverty: The BRAC Strategy. LC 92-5270. (Library of Management for Development). (Illus.). x, 205p. 1992. 29.00 (1-56549-005-3); pap. 21.95 (1-56549-004-5) Kumarian Pr.
Lovell, Charles, ed. Paul Horiuchi: Master of the Collage, November 20, 1987-January 17, 1988. (Illus.). 16p. (Orig.). 1987. pap. 5.00 (0-924335-04-1) Tacoma Art Mus.
***Lovell, Charles & Hester, Erwin, eds.** Minnie Evans: Artist. (Illus.). 72p. (Orig.). 1993. pap. 24.50 (0-9636759-0-7) East Carolin Mus.
Lovell, Charles, ed. see Gaston, Diana.
Lovell, Charles, ed. see Kegley, Dale.
Lovell, Charles M. Randy Hayes: Women & Men, August 13-September 13, 1987. (Illus.). 11p. (Orig.). 1987. pap. 1.00 (0-924335-03-3) Tacoma Art Mus.
Lovell, Charles M., intro. Martin of Tours Collection: The Art of St. Martin's Abbey, October 9-November 16, 1986. (Illus.). 23p. (Orig.). 1986. pap. 1.00 (0-924335-02-5) Tacoma Art Mus.
Lovell, D. J., ed. Optical Anecdotes. 148p. 1981. 20.00 (0-89252-353-0) SPIE.
Lovell, David W. From Marx to Lenin: An Evaluation of Marx's Responsibility for Soviet Authoritarianism. LC 83-26276. 1984. 49.95 (0-521-26188-0) Cambridge U Pr.
— Marx's Proletariat: The Making of a Myth. 320p. (C). 1988. lib. bdg. 52.50 (0-415-00116-1) Routledge.
Lovell, Douglas D. & Martin, Robert S. Subdivision Analysis. 120p. 1993. 25.00 (0-922154-11-2) Appraisal Inst.
Lovell, Edith H. Benjamin Bonneville: Soldier of the American Frontier. 228p. 1992. 18.98 (0-88290-438-8) Horizon Utah.
Lovell, Eleanor C. & Hall, Ruth M. Index to Handicrafts, Modelmaking & Workshop Projects. (Useful Reference Ser. of Library Bks.: Vol. 57). 1936. lib. bdg. 14.00 (0-87305-057-6) Faxon.
— Index to Handicrafts, Modelmaking & Workshop Projects, Suppl. 1. (Useful Reference Ser. of Library Bks.: Vol. 70). 1943. lib. bdg. 14.00 (0-87305-070-3) Faxon.
— Index to Handicrafts, Modelmaking & Workshop Projects, Suppl. 2. (Useful Reference Ser. of Library Bks.: Vol. 79). 1950. lib. bdg. 14.00 (0-87305-079-7) Faxon.
Lovell, Elizabeth R. Four Little Boys. LC 93-93975. 232p. (Orig.). 1994. pap. 9.00 (1-56002-351-1, Univ Edtns) Aegina Pr.
Lovell, George & Widdicombe, Catherine. Churches & Communities. 222p. 1990. pap. 40.00 (0-85532-387-6, Pub. by Srch Pr UK) St Mut.
***Lovell, Glenville.** Fire in the Canes. 272p. 1995. 22.00 (1-56947-044-8) Soho Press.
Lovell, James B. Anastasia: The Lost Princess. LC 91-7807. (Illus.). 528p. 1991. 24.95 (0-89526-536-2) Regnery Pub.
— Anastasia: The Lost Princess. (Illus.). 528p. 1995. pap. 15.95 (0-312-11133-9) St Martin.
Lovell, Jim & Kluger, Jeffrey. Lost Moon: The Perilous Voyage of Apollo 13. (Illus.). 384p. 1994. 22.95 (0-395-67029-2) HM.
Lovell, John C. Stevedores & Dockers: A Study of Trade Unionism in the Port of London, 1870-1914. LC 74-99263. (Illus.). 1969. 37.50 (0-678-07003-2) Kelley.
Lovell, John P. & Kronenberg, Philip S., eds. New Civil Military Relations. LC 72-94547. (Social Policy Ser.). 352p. 1974. 39.95 (0-87855-075-5); pap. 18.95 (0-87855-571-4) Transaction Pubs.
Lovell, M., jt. ed. see Chikan, A.
Lovell, Margaret. Fateful Journey. large type ed. (Linford Romance Library). 304p. 1992. pap. 14.95 (0-7089-7293-4, Trailtree Bookshop) Ulverscroft.
— Stranger in the Village. large type ed. (Linford Romance Library). 272p. 1994. pap. 14.95 (0-7089-7526-7, Linford) Ulverscroft.
— Teacher on the Wards. large type ed. (Linford Romance Library). 272p. 1993. pap. 14.95 (0-7089-7471-6, Trailtree Bookshop) Ulverscroft.
Lovell, Margaretta M. Venice: The American View 1860-1920. LC 84-81857. (Illus.). 174p. 1984. pap. 19.95 (0-88401-044-9) Fine Arts Mus.
— Venice: The American View, 1860-1920. LC 84-81857. (Illus.). 170p. 1984. pap. 19.95 (0-295-96288-7) U of Wash Pr.
— A Visitable Past: Views of Venice by American Artists, 1860-1915. (Illus.). 250p. 1988. 39.95 (0-226-49412-8) U Ch Pr.
Lovell, Mark R., jt. auth. see Franzen, Michael D.
Lovell, Mary S. Cast No Shadow: The Life of Betty Pack, the American Spy Who Changed the Course of World War II. LC 91-52625. (Illus.). 288p. 1992. 24.50 (0-394-57556-3) Pantheon.
— Rebel Heart: The Scandalous Life of Jane Digby. (Illus.). 384p. 1995. 25.00 (0-393-03895-5) Norton.
— The Sound of Wings: The Life of Amelia Earhart. (Illus.). 448p. 1991. pap. 12.95 (0-312-05160-3) St Martin.
— Straight on Till Morning. (Illus.). 440p. 1991. mass mkt. 5.99 (0-312-92515-8) St Martin.
— Straight on Till Morning: The Biography of Beryl Markham. (Illus.). 432p. 1988. pap. 10.95 (0-312-01895-9) St Martin.
Lovell, Michael, jt. auth. see Howell, Paul.
Lovell, Nancy C. Patterns of Injury & Illness in Great Apes: A Skeletal Analysis. LC 89-600389. (Illus.). 288p. 1990. 42.00 (0-87474-678-7) Smithsonian.
Lovell, Percy & Marcham, William, eds. Parish of St. Pancras, Pt. 1. LC 76-37851. (London County Council. Survey of London Ser.: No. 17). reprint ed. 84.50 (0-404-51667-X) AMS Pr.
— Parish of St. Pancras, Pt. 2. LC 70-37855. (London County Council. Survey of London Ser.: No. 19). reprint ed. 84.50 (0-404-51669-6) AMS Pr.
Lovell, R. I. The Struggle for South Africa, 1875-1899: A Study of Economic Imperialism. xv, 438p. 1995. reprint ed. lib. bdg. 52.00x (0-86527-362-6) Fertig.
Lovell, Richard. Churchills Doctor: A Biography of Lord Moran. (Illus.). 480p. 1993. 49.00 (1-85070-485-6) Prthnon Pub.
Lovell, Richard T. Nutrition & Feeding of Fish. (Illus.). 224p. (C). 1988. text ed. 52.95 (0-442-25927-1) Chapman & Hall.
Lovell, Rick, jt. auth. see Stojkovic, Stan.
Lovell, Robert. Probability Activities. 308p. (YA). (gr. 9-12). 1993. pap. 18.95 (1-55953-067-7) Key Curr Pr.
Lovell, Ronald. Free-Lancing: A Guide to Writing for Magazines & Other Markets. 356p. (Orig.). (C). 1993. pap. text ed. 18.95 (0-88133-752-8) Waveland Pr.
Lovell, Ronald P., et al. Handbook of Photography. 2nd ed. LC 86-23985. 288p. (C). 1987. spiral bd. 29.95 (0-8273-2789-7) Delmar.
Lovell, Ronald P. Reporting Public Affairs: Problems & Solutions. 2nd ed. (Illus.). 506p. 1993. pap. text ed. 24.95 (0-88133-696-3) Waveland Pr.
Lovell, Ronald P., et al. Handbook of Photography. 3rd ed. 337p. 1993. pap. text ed. 29.95 (0-8273-5279-4) Delmar.
— Two Centuries of Shadow Catchers: A Compact History of Photography. LC 94-8518. 1994. write for info. (0-8273-6457-1) Delmar.
Lovell, Sandra, jt. auth. see Lister, Marcie.
Lovell, Sarah, ed. see Trotsky, Leon.
Lovell, Sherry, jt. auth. see Hickman, Mina.
Lovell, Terry. British Feminist Thought: A Reader. 256p. (C). 1990. pap. text ed. 19.95 (0-631-16915-6) Blackwell Pubs.
— Consuming Fiction. (Questions for Feminism Ser.). 188p. 1987. text ed. 44.95 (0-86091-173-X, Pub. by Verso UK); pap. text ed. 14.95 (0-86091-885-8, Pub. by Verso UK) Routledge Chapman & Hall.
***Lovell, Terry, ed.** Feminist Cultural Studies. LC 95-11856. (International Library of Studies in Media & Culture: Vol. 1). 1995. write for info. (1-85278-767-8, Pub. by E Elgar Pub UK) Ashgate Pub Co.
Lovell-Troy, Larry & Eickmann, Paul. Course Design for College Teachers. LC 91-31295. (Illus.). 179p. (Orig.). 1992. pap. 21.95 (0-87778-239-3) Educ Tech Pubns.
Lovell-Troy, Lawrence A., ed. The Social Basis Ethnic Enterprise: Greeks in the Pizza Business. LC 90-42045. (European Immigrants & American Society Ser.). 264p. 1990. reprint ed. 20.00 (0-8240-7426-2) Garland.
Lovell, W. George. Conquest & Survival in Colonial Guatemala: A Historical Geography of the Cuchumatan Highlands, 1500-1821. rev. ed. (Illus.). 312p. 1992. pap. 22.95 (0-7735-0903-8, Pub. by McGill CN) U of Toronto Pr.
— Conquista y Cambio Cultural: La Sierra de Los Cuchumatanes De Guatemala, 1500-1821. LC 90-82409. (Monograph Ser.: No. 6). (Illus.). 288p. (SPA.). 1990. pap. 16.50 (0-910443-08-4) CIRMA.
***Lovell, W. George & Lutz, Christopher H.** Demography & Empire: A Guide to the Population History of Spanish Central America, 1500-1821. LC 94-24614. (Dellplain Latin American Studies). (C). 1994. text ed. 49.95 (0-8133-8865-1) Westview.
Lovell, W. George, jt. ed. see Cook, Noble D.
Lovell, William. Understanding Value Added Tax (VAT) (NatWest Business Handbook Ser.). 176p. (Orig.). (C). 1991. pap. 36.00x (0-273-03622-X, Pub. by Pitman Pubng UK) St Mut.
Lovelock, Christopher H. Managing Services: Marketing, Operations & Human Resources. 2nd ed. 496p. 1992. text ed. 70.00 (0-13-544701-1) P-H.
— Product Plus: Product Plus Service Equal Competitive Advantage. 224p. 1994. text ed. 24.95 (0-07-038798-2) McGraw.
— Services Marketing. 2nd ed. 576p. 1991. text ed. 70.00 (0-13-807066-0) P-H.
Lovelock, Christopher H. & Weinberg, Charles B. Marketing Challenges: Cases & Exercises. 3rd ed. 1993. text ed. write for info. (0-07-038802-4) McGraw.
— Public & Nonprofit Marketing. 2nd ed. 526p. (C). 1989. text ed. 47.50 (0-89426-134-7); Teaching notes. text ed. 47.50 (0-89426-135-5) Boyd & Fraser.
— Public & Nonprofit Marketing: Readings & Cases. 380p. (C). 1990. pap. text ed. 37.50 (0-89426-145-2); Teaching notes. pap. text ed. 37.50 (0-89426-148-7) Boyd & Fraser.
Lovelock, Christopher H. & Weinberg, Charles B., eds. Marketing Challenges: Cases & Exercises. 3rd ed. LC 92-38991. (Marketing Ser.). 1993. write for info. (0-07-911577-2) McGraw.
Lovelock, Christopher H., et al. Marketing Public Transit: A Strategic Approach. LC 87-11583. (Public & Nonprofit Sector Marketing Ser.). 238p. 1987. text ed. 52.95 (0-275-92499-8, C2499, Praeger Pubs) Greenwood.
Lovelock, D. W., ed. Plant Pathogens. (Society of Applied Bacteriology Technical Ser.). 1979. text ed. 88.00 (0-12-457050-X) Acad Pr.
Lovelock, D. W., jt. ed. see Board, R. G.
Lovelock, D. W., jt. ed. see Gilbert, R. J.
Lovelock, David. Tensors Differential Forms. 1989. pap. 9.95 (0-486-65840-6) Dover.
Lovelock, Harold J., jt. auth. see Ambrose, Paul V.
Lovelock, Harry, jt. auth. see Ambrose, Paul.
Lovelock, James. Ages of Gaia. 272p. 1994. pap. 12.00 (0-393-31239-9) Norton.
Lovelock, James E. The Ages of Gaia: A Biography of Our Living Earth. (Illus.). 1988. 16.95 (0-393-02583-7) Norton.
— Gaia: A New Look at Life on Earth. (Illus.). 176p. 1987. pap. 9.95 (0-19-286030-5) OUP.
— Healing Gaia: A New Prescription for the Living Planet. (Illus.). 192p. 1991. 25.00 (0-517-57848-4, Harmony) Crown Pub Group.
***Lovelock, Robin.** Visual Impairment: Social Support: Recent Research in Context. 309p. 1995. 59.95 (1-85628-391-7, Pub. by Avebury Pub UK) Ashgate Pub Co.
Lovelock, Robin & Powell, Jackie. Disability - Britain in Europe: An Evaluation of U. K. Participation in the HELIOS Programme (1988-1991) LC 94-19937. 264p. 1994. 59.95 (1-85628-646-0, Pub. by Avebury Pub UK) Ashgate Pub Co.
Lovelock, Robin, jt. auth. see Powell, Jacie.
Lovelock, Yann, ed. Building Jerusalem. (C). 1988. 25.00 (0-904524-48-5, Pub. by Rivelin Grapheme Pr) St Mut.
Loveman, Amy, et al, eds. Varied Harvest. LC 73-134109. (Essay Index Reprint Ser.). 1977. 23.95 (0-8369-1981-5) Ayer.
Loveman, Aurelia. Lace. Brenner, Carla, ed. (Illus.). 24p. (Orig.). 1988. pap. text ed. 4.00 (0-911886-36-2) Walters Art.
Loveman, Brian. Chile: The Legacy of Hispanic Capitalism. 2nd ed. (Latin American Histories Ser.). (Illus.). 464p. 1988. pap. 19.95 (0-19-505219-6) OUP.
— The Constitution of Tyranny: Regimes of Exception in Spanish America. (Latin American Ser.). 496p. 1994. pap. 19.95 (0-8229-5536-9) U of Pittsburgh Pr.
— The Constitution of Tyranny: Regimes of Exception in Spanish America. (Latin American Ser.). 496p. (C). 1994. text ed. 49.95 (0-8229-3766-2) U of Pittsburgh Pr.
Loveman, Brian, ed. see Guevara, Che.
Loveman, Gary W., jt. auth. see Johnson, Simon.
***Loven, Deborah.** The Great New York Dog Book. 1995. pap. 13.00 (0-06-095092-7, PL) HarpC.
Loven, Galen D. Succession Planning for Closely Held Businesses. 123p. 1993. pap. 19.95 (1-883480-00-0) Brkthgh Pubns.
— Winning Without Selling: Practice Building Handbook for Accountants. 3rd ed. 96p. 1993. 34.50 (1-883480-01-9) Brkthgh Pubns.
Loven, Juanita, ed. Wonderful Wisconsin Recipes. 160p. 1991. spiral bd. 5.50 (0-941016-79-X) Penfield.
Loven, Sven. Origins of the Tainan Culture, West Indies. LC 76-44753. (Taino Indians of Hispaniola & Eastern Cuba Ser.). (Illus.). reprint ed. 72.50 (0-404-15948-6) AMS Pr.
Lovenberg, Walter & Levine, R. A., eds. Unconjugated Pterins in Neurobiology: Basic & Clinical Aspects. LC 86-23177. (Topics in Neurochemistry & Neuropharmacology Ser.: Vol. 1). 250p. 1987. 99.00 (0-85066-370-9) Taylor & Francis.
Lovendahl, Shari, ed. see Schilling, Vivian.
Lovendale, Mark, ed. see Meinig, George E.
Lovenduski, Joni. Women & European Politics: Contemporary Feminism & Public Policy. LC 85-16501. (Illus.). 336p. 1986. lib. bdg. 17.95 (0-87023-507-9) U of Mass Pr.
Lovenduski, Joni & Norris, Pippa, eds. Gender & Party Politics. (Illus.). 288p. (C). 1994. text ed. 62.00 (0-8039-8659-9); pap. text ed. 22.95 (0-8039-8660-2) Sage.
Lovenduski, Joni & Randall, Vicky. Contemporary Feminist Politics: Women & Power in Britain. LC 92-41371. 1993. pap. 19.95 (0-19-878069-9) OUP.
Lovenduski, Joni, jt. auth. see Norris, Pippa.

An Asterisk (*) at the beginning of an entry indicates that the title is appearing in BIP for the first time.

Lovenheim, Barbara. Beating the Marriage Odds: When You Are Smart, Single, & over Thirty-Five. LC 90-37647. 256p. 1990. 17.95 (0-688-08426-5) Morrow.
Lovenheim, Peter. Mediate, Don't Litigate. 304p. 1990. text ed. 19.95 (0-07-038832-6) McGraw.
— Mediate, Don't Litigate: How to Resolve Disputes Quickly, Privately, & Inexpensively Without Going to Court. 1991. pap. text ed. 12.95 (0-07-038841-5) McGraw.
Lovenheim, Peter, jt. ed. see Katz, David A.
Loventhal, Milton & McDowell, Jennifer. Ronnie Goose Rhymes for Grown-Ups. LC 84-60716. (Mother Goose Rhymes for Grown-ups Ser.). 1984. 10.95 (0-930142-07-1) Merlin Pr.
Lover of Philalethes, tr. see Von Rosenroth, Knorr.
Lover, Samuel. Rory O'More: A National Romance, 3 vols. in 2, Set. LC 79-8423. 1979. reprint ed. 84.50 (0-404-61991-6) AMS Pr.
Loverance, Rowena. Ancient Greece. (See Through History Ser.). (Illus.). 48p. (J). (gr. 3-7). 1993. 14.99 (0-670-84754-2) Viking Child Bks.
— The Anglo-Saxons. (Fact Finders Ser.). (Illus.). 48p. (Orig.). (YA). (gr. 7 up). 1992. pap. 7.50 (0-563-35001-6, BBC-Parkwest) Parkwest Pubns.
— Byzantium. LC 88-539. (Illus.). 72p. (Orig.). 1988. pap. 11.50 (0-674-08972-3) HUP.
*__Loveridge & Cummings.__ Nursing Management: Principles & Practices. 300p. 1995. 49.00 (0-8342-0620-X) Aspen Pub.
Loveridge, J. W., jt. auth. see Hughes, H. G.
Loveridge, Raymond. Collective Bargaining by National Employees in the United Kingdom. LC 78-634399. (Comparative Studies in Public Employment Labor Relations Ser.). 1971. 10.00 (0-87736-015-4); pap. 5.00 (0-87736-016-2) U of Mich Inst Labor.
— Incorporating Excellence: Strategic Routes to Technological Change. 240p. 1993. 79.95 (0-415-05947-X, A7674) Routledge.
Loveridge, Raymond & Pitt, Martin, eds. The Strategic Management of Technological Innovation. 1990. text ed. 112.95 (0-471-92499-7) Wiley.
Loveridge, Raymond & Pitt, Martyn, eds. The Strategic Management of Technological Innovation. 404p. 1992. pap. text ed. 43.50 (0-471-93465-8) Wiley.
Loveridge, Raymond & Starkey, Ken, eds. Continuity & Crisis in the NHS. 224p. 1992. 95.00 (0-335-15620-7, Open Univ Pr); pap. 36.00 (0-335-15599-5, Open Univ Pr) Taylor & Francis.
Lovering, David G. Molten Salt Techniques, Vol. 1. Gale, Robert J., ed. LC 83-9582. (Illus.). 290p. 1983. 85.00 (0-306-41307-8, Plenum Pr) Plenum.
Lovering, David G., ed. Fuel Cells: Grove Anniversary Symposium, '89: Proceedings of the Grove Anniversary Symposium of 18-21 Sept. 1989, Royal Institution, London. 280p. 1990. 117.00 (1-85166-816-0) Elsevier.
— Molten Salt Technology. LC 82-14982. 550p. 1982. 105.00 (0-306-41076-1, Plenum Pr) Plenum.
Lovering, David G. & Gale, Robert J., eds. Molten Salt Techniques, Vol. 2. LC 83-9582. 276p. 1984. 85.00 (0-306-41549-6, Plenum Pr) Plenum.
— Molten Salt Techniques, Vol. 3. LC 83-9582. (Illus.). 368p. 1987. 95.00 (0-306-42504-1, Plenum Pr) Plenum.
Lovering, David G., jt. ed. see Gale, Robert J.
Lovering, David G., jt. ed. see Inman, Douglas.
Lovering, Frances K. Island Ebb & Flow: A Pioneer's Journal of Life on Waldron Island. LC 85-4841. 211p. 1985. pap. 8.95 (0-931317-02-9) Masterwrks Inc.
Lovering, John F. & Prescott, Victor. Last of Lands-Antarctica. 1979. pap. 19.95 (0-522-84142-2) Intl Spec Bk.
Lovering, Joseph P. S. Weir Mitchell. LC 76-125256. (Twayne's United States Authors Ser.). 1971. lib. bdg. 17.95 (0-89197-984-0); pap. text ed. 9.95 (0-8290-0002-X) Irvington.
Lovering, Martin. History of the Town of Holland, Mass. (Illus.). 745p. 1989. reprint ed. lib. bdg. 75.00 (0-8328-0832-6, MA0058) Higginson Bk Co.
*__Lovering, Robert.__ Out of the Darkness: Coping with Disability. 148p. (Orig.). 1993. pap. 7.95 (0-614-05342-0) ARCS Inc.
— Out of the Ordinary: A Digest on Disability. LC 85-71798. 260148p. (Orig.). 1985. 14.95 (0-9615213-0-9) ARCS Inc.
Lovering, Thomas S. & Stoll, W. M. Rock Alteration as a Guide to Ore East Tintic District, Utah. LC 50-6493. (Economic Geology, Monograph Ser.: No. 1). 102p. reprint ed. pap. 29.10 (0-317-27607-7, 2014764) Bks Demand.
Lovern, John D. Pathways to Reality: Erickson-Inspired Treatment Approaches to Chemical Dependency. LC 91-13541. 240p. 1991. 28.95 (0-87630-633-4) Brunner-Mazel.
Lovers of the Stinking Rose Staff & Harris, Lloyd J. The Book of Garlic. (Illus.). 286p. 1979. pap. 14.42 (0-201-11687-1) Addison-Wesley.
Loverseed, Helga. Brampton: An Illustrated History. LC 87-6254. 304p. 1987. 29.95 (0-89781-207-7) Preferred Mktg.
— Burlington: An Illustrated History. Powell, Lane, ed. (Illus.). 192p. 1988. 29.95 (0-89781-241-7) Preferred Mktg.
Loverseed, Helga, ed. see Pratson, Frederick.
Loves, June. The Grasshopper. LC 92-34263. (Voyages Ser.). (Illus.). (J). 1993. 4.25 (0-383-03626-7) SRA Schl Grp.
— I Know That. LC 92-34262. (Voyages Ser.). (Illus.). (J). 1993. 4.25 (0-383-03633-X) SRA Schl Grp.
— This Is the Book That I Borrowed. LC 92-31955. (Voyages Ser.). (Illus.). (J). 1993. 4.25 (0-383-03598-8) SRA Schl Grp.
Lovesey, E. J. Contemporary Ergonomics, 1990. 1990. 90.00 (0-85066-851-4) Taylor & Francis.
Lovesey, E. J., ed. Contemporary Ergonomics, Nineteen Ninety-One: Ergonomics-Design for Performance. 503p. 1991. pap. 85.00 (0-7484-0007-9, Pub. by Tay Francis Ltd UK) Taylor & Francis.
— Contemporary Ergonomics, 1992: Ergonomics for Industry. 576p. 1992. 90.00 (0-7484-0030-3, Pub. by Tay Francis Ltd UK) Taylor & Francis.
— Contemporary Ergonomics 1993: Ergonomics for Industry. 511p. 1993. pap. 95.00 (0-7484-0070-2) Taylor & Francis.
Lovesey, Nenia. Creative Design in Needlepoint Lace. (Illus.). 144p. 1983. 22.75 (0-7134-4141-0) Branford.
— Punto Tagliato Lace. (Illus.). 1986. 12.75 (0-85219-632-6) Branford.
— Venetian Gros Point Lace. (Illus.). 75p. 1986. 12.75 (0-85219-631-8, Pub. by Dryad Pr UK) Branford.
*__Lovesey, Peter.__ Abracadaver. 224p. 1994. 16.95 (0-7451-8645-9, Black Dagger) Chivers N Amer.
— Bertie & the Crime of Passion. 256p. 1995. 19.95 (0-89296-550-9) Mysterious Pr.
— Bertie & the Crime of Passion. 240p. 1995. mass mkt. 5.50 (0-446-40368-7, Mysterious Paperbk) Warner Bks.
— Bertie & the Crime of Passion. large type ed. LC 95-5405. (Large Print Book Ser.). 1995. pap. 20.95 (1-56895-099-3) Wheeler Pub.
— Bertie & the Seven Bodies. 208p. 1990. 16.95 (0-89296-399-9) Mysterious Pr.
— Bertie & the Seven Bodies. large type ed. LC 90-40509. 398p. 1990. reprint ed. lib. bdg. 19.95 (1-56054-038-9) Thorndike Pr.
— Bertie & the Tinman. 1988. 15.95 (0-89296-196-1) Mysterious Pr.
— Butchers & Other Stories of Crime. LC 87-42706. 208p. 1987. 15.95 (0-89296-195-3) Mysterious Pr.
— Butchers & Other Stories of Crime. LC 87-7718. 208p. 1988. pap. 9.95 (0-89296-960-1) Mysterious Pr.
— Diamond Solitaire. 352p. 1993. 18.95 (0-89296-535-5) Mysterious Pr.
— Diamond Solitaire. 336p. 1994. mass mkt. 5.50 (0-446-40347-4, Mysterious Paperbk) Warner Bks.
— Diamond Solitaire. large type ed. LC 93-35504. 1993. 20.95 (0-7862-0076-6) Thorndike Pr.
— The Last Detective. large type ed. LC 91-34644. 653p. 1992. reprint ed. bds. 19.95 (1-56054-288-8) Thorndike Pr.
— On the Edge. 208p. 1989. 16.95 (0-89296-363-8) Mysterious Pr.
— On the Edge. large type ed. (General Ser.). 312p. 1990. lib. bdg. 18.95 (0-8161-4858-9) G K Hall.
— The Summons. 1995. write for info. (0-89296-551-7) Mysterious Pr.
— Swing, Swing Together. 1976. 19.95 (0-89190-093-4, Am Repr) Amereon Ltd.
Lovesey, Stephen W. Theory of Neutron Scattering from Condensed Matter, Vol. 1. (International Series of Monographs on Physics). (Illus.). 1986. pap. 35.00 (0-19-852028-X) OUP.
— Theory of Neutron Scattering from Condensed Matter, Vol. 2. (International Series of Monographs on Physics). (Illus.). 1986. pap. 32.50 (0-19-852029-8) OUP.
Lovesey, Stephen W., jt. auth. see Balcar, Ewald.
Lovesey, Stephen W., et al, eds. Magnetic Excitations & Fluctuations. (Solid-State Sciences Ser.: Vol. 54). (Illus.). 240p. 1984. 63.00 (0-387-13789-0) Spr-Verlag.
*__Lovett.__ Learning to Listen: Positive Approaches & People with Difficult Behavior. 224p. 1995. pap. 23.00 (1-55766-164-2) P H Brookes.
— Transdisciplinary Play-Based Assessment: A Functional Approach to Working with Young Children. rev. ed. LC 89-70795. 224p. (Orig.). 1995. pap. 23.00 (1-55766-162-6, 1626) P H Brookes.
Lovett, A. W. Early Habsburg Spain, Fifteen Seventeen to Fifteen Ninety-Eight. (Illus.). 300p. 1986. pap. 23.00 (0-19-822138-X) OUP.
Lovett, Ann. Palimpsest. LC 90-70210. (Illus.). 48p. (Orig.). 1990. pap. 16.95 (0-89822-064-5) Visual Studies.
*__Lovett, Anne B.__ Career Prescription: How to Stop Sabotaging Your Career & Put It on a Winning Track. 1994. pap. text ed. 14.00 (0-13-303322-8) P-H.
Lovett, Bernard G. The Card Player. LC 84-61984. 250p. (Orig.). 1984. pap. 8.00 (0-9613960-0-8) Nike Pr.
Lovett, Brian, ed. Wisconsin Hunting: A Comprehensive Guide to Wisconsin's Public Hunting Lands. LC 93-77542. (Illus.). 208p. (Orig.). 1993. pap. 16.95 (0-87341-249-4) Krause Pubns.
Lovett, C. Academics & Career Change. write for info. (0-275-90016-9, C0016, Praeger Pubs) Greenwood.
Lovett, C. S. C. S. Lovett: Maranatha Man. (Illus.). 1978. pap. 2.95 (0-938148-02-8) Prsnl Christianity.
— Census Manual. 1961. pap. 2.95 (0-938148-18-4) Prsnl Christianity.
— The Compassionate Side of Divorce. 1975. pap. 7.45 (0-938148-08-7) Prsnl Christianity.
— Dealing with the Devil. 1967. pap. 7.45 (0-938148-05-2) Prsnl Christianity.
— Death: Graduation to Glory. 1974. pap. 6.25 (0-938148-20-6) Prsnl Christianity.
— Dynamic Truths for the Spirit-Filled Life. 1973. pap. 7.95 (0-938148-13-3) Prsnl Christianity.
— Help Lord-The Devil Wants Me Fat! (Illus.). (Orig.). 1977. pap. 8.45 (0-938148-33-8) Prsnl Christianity.
— It's Your Turn to Be Blessed. (Illus.). 128p. (Orig.). 1985. pap. 6.95 (0-938148-39-7) Prsnl Christianity.
— Jesus Is Coming-Get Ready Christian. 1969. pap. 6.95 (0-938148-04-4) Prsnl Christianity.
— Jesus Wants You Well. 1973. pap. 8.45 (0-938148-29-X) Prsnl Christianity.
— Jogging with Jesus. (Illus.). 1978. pap. 5.45 (0-938148-34-6) Prsnl Christianity.
— Latest Word on the Last Days. (Illus.). (Orig.). 1980. pap. 8.95 (0-938148-00-1) Prsnl Christianity.
— Let Your Spirit Soar (365 Inspirational Flights) (Illus.). 560p. 1994. pap. 19.95 (0-938148-47-8) Prsnl Christianity.
— Longing to Be Loved. 1982. pap. 7.95 (0-938148-36-2) Prsnl Christianity.
— Lovett's Lights on Acts. 1972. pap. 8.95 (0-938148-28-1) Prsnl Christianity.
— Lovett's Lights on Galatians, Ephesians, Philippians, Colossians, 1 & 2 Thessalonians. 1970. pap. 7.95 (0-938148-25-7) Prsnl Christianity.
— Lovett's Lights on Hebrews. 1976. pap. 8.45 (0-938148-32-X) Prsnl Christianity.
— Lovett's Lights on John. 1970. pap. 8.45 (0-938148-24-9) Prsnl Christianity.
— Lovett's Lights on Revelation. (Illus.). 352p. 1992. pap. 12.95 (0-938148-44-3) Prsnl Christianity.
— Lovett's Lights on Romans. 1975. pap. 8.95 (0-938148-30-3) Prsnl Christianity.
— Lovett's Lights on the Sermon on the Mount. 176p. (Orig.). 1985. pap. 7.45 (0-938148-40-0) Prsnl Christianity.
— Now Anyone Can...Teach Revelation. (Illus.). 128p. 1993. teacher ed, pap. 5.95 (0-938148-46-X) Prsnl Christianity.
— The One Hundred Percent Christian. 1970. pap. 6.95 (0-938148-07-9) Prsnl Christianity.
— Operation Manhunt Made Easy. 1961. 4.95 (0-938148-17-6) Prsnl Christianity.
— Soul-Winning Made Easy. 1978. pap. 6.25 (0-938148-10-9) Prsnl Christianity.
— Teach Dynamic Truths. 1973. teacher ed, pap. 7.95 (0-938148-14-1) Prsnl Christianity.
— Teach Soul-Winning. 1962. teacher ed, pap. 4.95 (0-938148-12-5) Prsnl Christianity.
— Teach Them about Satan. 1970. teacher ed, pap. 7.45 (0-938148-26-5) Prsnl Christianity.
— Teach Witnessing. 1966. teacher ed, pap. 7.95 (0-938148-09-5) Prsnl Christianity.
— The Thrill of Faith. 1960. pap. 4.95 (0-938148-21-4) Prsnl Christianity.
— Unequally Yoked Wives. 1968. pap. 7.45 (0-938148-22-2) Prsnl Christianity.
— Visitation Made Easy. 1959. pap. 4.95 (0-938148-15-X) Prsnl Christianity.
— What to Do When Your Friends Reject Christ. 1966. pap. 6.25 (0-938148-06-0) Prsnl Christianity.
— What's a Parent to Do? 1971. pap. 8.45 (0-938148-27-3) Prsnl Christianity.
— Witnessing Made Easy. 1964. pap. 7.95 (0-938148-01-X) Prsnl Christianity.
Lovett, Charles C. Alice on Stage: A History of the Early Theatrical Productions of Alice in Wonderland. 356p. 1989. text ed. 65.00 (0-313-27681-1, LVS/, Greenwood Pr) Greenwood.
Lovett, Charles C. & Lovett, Stephanie B. Lewis Carroll's Alice: An Annotated Checklist of the Lovett Collection, 1965-1986. 565p. 1989. text ed. 89.50 (0-313-27682-X, LLR/) Greenwood.
Lovett, Charles C., jt. auth. see Lovett, Robert W.
Lovett, Clara M. The Democratic Movement In Italy, Eighteen Thirty to Eighteen Seventy-Six. LC 81-6403. 295p. 1982. 39.95 (0-674-19645-7) HUP.
Lovett, Clara M., jt. ed. see Berkin, Carol R.
Lovett, D. Demonstrating Science with Soap Films. (Illus.). 200p. 1994. 80.00 (0-7503-0270-4); pap. 35.00 (0-7503-0269-0) IOP Pub.
Lovett, D. R. Tensor Properties of Crystals. LC 88-34757. (Illus.). 152p. reprint ed. pap. 43.40 (0-7837-3927-3, 2057917) Bks Demand.
Lovett, David. Tensor Properties of Crystals. (Illus.). 160p. 1989. pap. 26.90 (0-85274-031-X) IOP Pub.
Lovett-Doust, Jon & Lovett-Doust, Lesley, eds. Plant Reproductive Ecology: Patterns & Strategies. (Illus.). 352p. (C). 1990. pap. text ed. 24.95 (0-19-506394-5) OUP.
Lovett-Doust, Lesley, jt. ed. see Lovett-Doust, Jon.
Lovett, Gabriel. The Duke of Rivas. LC 77-5136. (Twayne's World Authors Ser.). 191p. (C). 1977. lib. bdg. 17.95 (0-8057-6289-2) Irvington.
Lovett, Gabriel H. Romantic Spain: Voices from Within, Views from Without. (American University Studies: Romance Languages & Literature: Ser. II, Vol. 74). 247p. (C). 1989. text ed. 43.95 (0-8204-0605-8) P Lang Pubs.
Lovett, Gabriel H., jt. auth. see Martin, Michael R.
Lovett, H. A. Canada & the Grand Trunk, 1829-1924. Bruchey, Stuart, ed. LC 80-1328. (Railroads Ser.). 1981. reprint ed. lib. bdg. 24.95 (0-405-13802-4) Ayer.
Lovett, H. Verney. History of the Indian Nationalist Movement. 3rd ed. LC 79-94540. 1969. reprint ed. lib. bdg. 39.50 (0-678-05100-3) Kelley.
Lovett, Herbert. Cognitive Counseling & Persons with Special Needs: Adapting Behavioral Approaches to the Social Context. LC 85-3495. 160p. 1985. pap. text ed. 19.95 (0-275-91651-0, B1651, Praeger Pubs) Greenwood.
Lovett, James E. Nuclear Materials: Accountability Management Safeguards. LC 74-78611. (ANS Monographs). 310p. 1974. 27.90 (0-89448-001-4, 300007) Am Nuclear Soc.
Lovett, Jennifer G. A Romance with Realism: The Art of Jean-Baptiste Carpeaux. LC 89-60886. (Illus.). 48p. 1989. pap. 12.95 (0-931102-26-X) S & F Clark Art.
Lovett, Jim D., jt. auth. see Branton, James L.
Lovett, Jim D., jt. ed. see Branton, James L.
Lovett, Jon C. & Wasser, Samuel K., eds. Biogeography & Ecology of the Rain Forests of Eastern Africa. (Illus.). 390p. (C). 1993. 120.00 (0-521-43083-6) Cambridge U Pr.
Lovett, Lisetta, jt. auth. see Seedhouse, David.
Lovett, Marc, jt. auth. see Munk, Robert J.
Lovett, Martha, jt. auth. see Partin, Ronald.
*__Lovett, Maurice.__ Brewing & Breweries. (C). 1989. pap. 25.00x (0-85263-568-0, Pub. by Shire UK) St Mut.
Lovett, Richard. Tamate. (SPA.). 4.25 (84-7228-320-8, 220864, Pub. by Edit Clie SP) TSELF.
Lovett, Richard A. The Essential Touring Cyclist: A Complete Course for the Bicycle Traveler. 1994. pap. text ed. 15.95 (0-07-038849-0) McGraw.
— Freewheelin' A Solo Journey Across America. 256p. 1992. 19.95 (0-87742-352-0, 60349) Intl Marine.
— Freewheelin' A Solo Journey Across America. 1992. 19.95 (0-07-038844-X) McGraw.
Lovett, Robert M. History of the Novel in England. 1988. reprint ed. lib. bdg. 59.00 (0-7812-0768-1) Rprt Serv.
— Preface to Fiction: A Discussion of Great Modern Novels. LC 68-16948. (Essay Index Reprint Ser.). 1977. 17.95 (0-8369-0625-X) Ayer.
Lovett, Robert M. & Hughes, Helen S. History of the Novel in England. (Illus.). 1971. reprint ed. 69.00 (0-403-00752-6) Scholarly.
Lovett, Robert W. & Lovett, Charles C. Robinson Crusoe: A Bibliographical Checklist of English Language Editions (1719-1979) LC 87-28952. (Bibliographies & Indexes in World Literature Ser.: No. 30). 352p. 1991. text ed. 59.95 (0-313-27695-1, LRS/, Greenwood Pr) Greenwood.
*__Lovett, Sarah.__ Dangerous Attachments. 1995. 22.00 (0-679-43559-X, Villard Bks) Random.
— Extremely Weird Bats. (Extremely Weird Ser.). (Illus.). 48p. (J). Date not set. 14.95 (1-56261-165-8) John Muir.
— Extremely Weird Birds. (Extremely Weird Ser.). (Illus.). 48p. (J). Date not set. 14.95 (1-56261-166-6) John Muir.
— Extremely Weird Birds. (J). (gr. 3 up). 1992. pap. 9.95 (1-56261-040-6) John Muir.
— Extremely Weird Endangered Species. (Extremely Weird Ser.). (Illus.). 48p. (Orig.). (J). (gr. 3 up). 1992. pap. 9.95 (1-56261-042-2) John Muir.
— Extremely Weird Endangered Species. (Extremely Weird Ser.). (Illus.). 48p. (J). Date not set. write for info. (1-56261-167-4) John Muir.
— Extremely Weird Fish. (Extremely Weird Ser.). (Illus.). 48p. (Orig.). (J). (gr. 3 up). 1992. pap. 9.95 (1-56261-041-4) John Muir.
— Extremely Weird Fishes. (Extremely Weird Ser.). (Illus.). 48p. (J). Date not set. 14.95 (1-56261-168-2) John Muir.
— Extremely Weird Frogs. (Extremely Weird Ser.). (Illus.). 48p. (J). Date not set. 14.95 (1-56261-169-0) John Muir.
— Extremely Weird Insects. LC 92-20098. (Extremely Weird Ser.). (Illus.). 48p. (J). (gr. 3 up). Date not set. pap. 9.95 (1-56261-076-7) John Muir.
— Extremely Weird Insects. (Extremely Weird Ser.). (Illus.). 48p. (J). Date not set. 14.95 (1-56261-170-4) John Muir.
— Extremely Weird Mammals. (Extremely Weird Ser.). (Illus.). 48p. (Orig.). (J). (gr. 3 up). 1993. pap. 9.95 (1-56261-107-0) John Muir.
— Extremely Weird Mammals. (Extremely Weird Ser.). (Illus.). 48p. (J). Date not set. 14.95 (1-56261-171-2) John Muir.
— Extremely Weird Micro Monsters. (Extremely Weird Ser.). (Illus.). 48p. (Orig.). (J). (gr. 3 up). 1993. pap. 9.95 (1-56261-120-8) John Muir.
— Extremely Weird Micro Monsters. (Extremely Weird Ser.). (Illus.). 48p. (J). Date not set. 14.95 (1-56261-172-0) John Muir.
— Extremely Weird Primates. (Extremely Weird Ser.). (Illus.). 48p. (Orig.). (J). (gr. 3 up). 1991. pap. 9.95 (1-56261-018-X) John Muir.
— Extremely Weird Primates. (Extremely Weird Ser.). (Illus.). 48p. (J). Date not set. 14.95 (1-56261-173-9) John Muir.
— Extremely Weird Reptiles. (Extremely Weird Ser.). (Illus.). 48p. (Orig.). (J). (gr. 3 up). 1991. pap. 9.95 (1-56261-036-8) John Muir.
— Extremely Weird Reptiles. (Extremely Weird Ser.). (Illus.). 48p. (J). Date not set. 14.95 (1-56261-174-7) John Muir.
— Extremely Weird Sea Creatures. LC 92-18383. (Extremely Weird Ser.). (Illus.). 48p. (Orig.). (J). (gr. 3 up). Date not set. pap. 9.95 (1-56261-077-5) John Muir.
— Extremely Weird Sea Creatures. (Extremely Weird Ser.). (Illus.). 48p. (J). Date not set. 14.95 (1-56261-175-5) John Muir.
— Extremely Weird Snakes. (Extremely Weird Ser.). (Illus.). 48p. (Orig.). (J). (gr. 3 up). 1993. pap. 9.95 (1-56261-108-9) John Muir.
— Extremely Weird Snakes. (Extremely Weird Ser.). (Illus.). 48p. (J). Date not set. 14.95 (1-56261-176-3) John Muir.
— Extremely Weird Spiders. (Extremely Weird Ser.). (Illus.). 48p. (J). Date not set. 14.95 (1-56261-177-1) John Muir.
— Kidding Around London: A Young Person's Guide to the City. (Illus.). 64p. (Orig.). (J). (gr. 3 up). 1989. pap. 9.95 (0-945465-24-6) John Muir.
— Kidding Around New York City: A Young Person's Guide. 2nd ed. (Kidding Around Travel Ser.). (Illus.). 64p. (J). (gr. 3 up). 1993. pap. 9.95 (1-56261-095-3) John Muir.
— Kidding Around the Hawaiian Islands: A Young Person's Guide to the Islands. (Illus.). 64p. (Orig.). (J). (gr. 3 up). 1990. pap. 9.95 (0-945465-37-8) John Muir.
— Kidding Around the National Parks of the Southwest: A Young Person's Guide. (Kidding Around Travel Ser.). (Illus.). 108p. (Orig.). (J). (gr. 3 up). 1990. pap. 12.95 (0-945465-72-6) John Muir.
— Unique Arizona: A Guide to the State's Quirks, Charisma, & Character. (Illus.). 112p. (Orig.). 1994. pap. 10.95 (1-56261-178-X) John Muir.
— Unique California: A Guide to the State's Quirks, Charisma, & Character. (Illus.). 112p. (Orig.). 1994. pap. 10.95 (1-56261-179-8) John Muir.
— Unique Colorado: A Guide to the State's Quirks, Charisma, & Character. (Unique Travel Ser.). (Illus.). 108p. (Orig.). 1993. pap. 10.95 (1-56261-103-8) John Muir.

— Unique Florida: A Guide to the State's Quirks, Charisma & Character. (Unique Travel Ser.). (Illus.). 108p. (Orig.). 1993. pap. 10.95 (*1-56261-104-6*) John Muir.
— Unique New England: A Guide to the Region's Quirks, Charisma, & Character. (Unique Travel Ser.). 112p. (Orig.). 1994. pap. 10.95 (*1-56261-146-1*) John Muir.
— Unique New Mexico: A Guide to the State's Quirks, Charisma & Character. (Unique Travel Ser.). (Illus.). 108p. (Orig.). 1993. pap. 10.95 (*1-56261-102-X*) John Muir.
— Unique Texas: A Guide to the State's Quirks, Charisma, & Character. LC 93-30384. (Unique Travel Ser.). 112p. (Orig.). 1994. pap. 10.95 (*1-56261-145-3*) John Muir.
Lovett, Sarah, text. Extremely Weird Bats. (Extremely Weird Ser.). (Illus.). 48p. (J). (gr. 3 up). 1991. 9.95 (*1-56261-008-2*) John Muir.
— Extremely Weird Frogs. (Extremely Weird Ser.). (Illus.). 48p. (J). (gr. 3 up). 1991. 9.95 (*1-56261-006-6*) John Muir.
— Extremely Weird Spiders. (Extremely Weird Ser.). (Illus.). 48p. (J). (gr. 3 up). 1991. 9.95 (*1-56261-007-4*) John Muir.
Lovett School Mothers Club Staff, ed. Cook & Love It. (Illus.). 287p. (Orig.). reprint ed. pap. 9.50 (*0-9610846-0-X*) Lovett Sch.
Lovett, Stephanie B., jt. auth. see Lovett, Charles C.
Lovett, Steven R. California Partnership Handbook, 2 vols. 2nd rev. ed. 520p. 1984. pap. text ed. 51.50 (*0-89074-090-9*) Lega Bks.
Lovett, Steven R., jt. auth. see Faber, Stuart J.
Lovett, T. Adult Education, Community Development & the Working Class. 176p. (C). 1982. text ed. 60.00 (*0-685-44259-4*, Pub. by Univ Nottingham UK) St Mut.
Lovett, Terrin, ed. Computer Economics Sourcebook: The Up-to-Date Financial Guide to DP Equipment Acquisition & Control of DP Expenses, 3 vols. annuals 900p. 1991. 1,495.00 (*0-945052-00-6*) Computer Econ.
— Computer Systems & Peripherals Residual Value Forecast: Multivendor Edition. (Illus.). 700p. 1995. 3, 450.00 (*0-945052-25-1*) Computer Econ.
— Seven-Year Residual Value Forecasts for IBM Systems & Peripherals. 325p. 1991. ring bd. 1,495.00 (*0-685-51621-0*) Computer Econ.
Lovett, Tom, ed. Adult Education, Community Development & the Working Class. (C). 1982. 35.00 (*0-902031-84-8*, Pub. by Univ Nottingham UK) St Mut.
Lovett, Verney. History of the Indian Nationalist Movement. 303p. 1968. 32.00 (*0-7146-2016-5*, Pub. by F Cass Pubs UK) Intl Spec Bk.
Lovett, William A. Banking & Financial Institutions Law in a Nutshell. 3rd ed. LC 92-18870. (Nutshell Ser.). 470p. (C). 1992. pap. text ed. 18.00 (*0-314-00929-9*) West Pub.
— World Trade Rivalry: Trade Equity & Competing Industrial Policies. LC 85-40388. 304p. 1987. text ed. 45.00 (*0-669-11027-2*) Free Pr.
*__Lovettovett, Sarah.__ Kidding Around London: A Family Guide to the City. 2nd ed. LC 94-44634. (Illus.). 1995. 9.95 (*1-56261-224-7*) John Muir.
Lovewell, Mark, jt. auth. see Russell, Eric P.
*__Lovey, Jane.__ Supporting Special Educational Needs in Secondary School Classrooms. (Roehampton Teaching Studies Ser.). 160p. 1995. pap. 24.95 (*1-85346-339-6*, Pub. by D Fulton UK) Taylor & Francis.
— Teaching Troubled & Troublesome Adolescents. 128p. 1992. pap. 24.95 (*1-85346-194-6*, Pub. by D Fulton UK) Taylor & Francis.
Lovgren, Florence N. Ringo Lake School. LC 92-62006. 168p. 1993. pap. 9.00 (*1-56002-238-8*, Univ Edtns) Aegina Pr.
Lovgren, Hakan, jt. ed. see Kleberg, Lars.
Lovi & Tirion. Men, Monsters & the Modern Universe. 1989. 24.95 (*0-943396-24-7*) Willmann-Bell.
*__Lovi, George.__ Sky & Telescope Monthly Star Charts: 24 All-Sky Charts for Star Watchers Worldwide. 68p. 1994. pap. 24.95 (*0-933346-69-7*) Sky Pub.
Lovi, Steve, photos. Christmas Tales: Celebrated Authors on the Magic of the Season. LC 92-54066. (Illus.). 96p. 1992. 14.95 (*0-670-83810-1*, Viking Studio) Studio Bks.
Lovibond, P. & Wilson, P., eds. Clinical & Abnormal Psychology, Vol. 9: Proceedings of the 24th International Congress of Psychology of the International Union of Psychological Science, Sydney, Australia, Aug. 28-Sept. 2, 1988. 504p. 1990. 107.75 (*0-444-88527-7*, North Holland) Elsevier.
Lovibond, S. Conditioning & Enuresis. LC 63-22192. 1964. 94.00 (*0-08-010449-5*, Pub. by Pergamon Repr UK) Franklin.
Lovie, A. D., et al. New Developments in Statistics for Psychology & the Social Sciences. 256p. 1991. 55.00 (*1-85433-017-9*, A5028, Pub. by British Psy Soc UK) Routledge.
Lovie, A. D. & Mosteller, Frederick, eds. New Developments in Statistics for Psychology & Social Sciences. 200p. 1986. 57.50 (*0-901715-46-8*, 1020, Pub. by British Psy Soc UK) Routledge.
Lovie-Kitchin, Jan E. & Bowman, Kenneth J. Senile Macular Degeneration. (Illus.). 1985. text ed. 37.95 (*0-409-90007-9*) Buttrwrth-Heinemann.
Lovik, Craig. Theodore Bump: What's in Your Trunk. Incl. You're Late for Church. 1985. 6.95 (*0-570-04124-4*, 56-1535); (Theodore Bump Ser.). (Illus.). 32p. (J). (gr. 6-8). 1985. 6.95 (*0-570-04123-6*, 56-1534) Concordia.
Lovik, Craig J. The Exodus. (Arch Bks.). (Illus.). 24p. (J). (gr. k-4). 1987. pap. 1.99 (*0-570-09001-6*, 59-1429) Concordia.
Lovil, Thomas M., jt. auth. see Young, Michael B.
Lovill, J. E., jt. ed. see McCormick, M. P.
Lovin-Boyd, Stacy, jt. auth. see Jackson, Janet.
Lovin, Hugh T. Labor in the West. (Illus.). 88p. 1986. pap. text ed. 15.00 (*0-89745-090-6*) Sunflower U Pr.
*__Lovin, Robin W.__ Reinhold Niebuhr & Christian Realism. 263p. (C). 1995. 54.95 (*0-521-44363-6*); pap. 16.95 (*0-521-47932-0*) Cambridge U Pr.
Lovin, Robin W. & Reynolds, Frank E., eds. Cosmogony & Ethical Order: New Studies in Comparative Ethics. LC 85-1159. viii, 448p. 1985. lib. bdg. 55.00 (*0-226-49416-0*) U Ch Pr.
Loving, Jerome. Emerson, Whitman, & the American Muse. LC 82-1868. xii, 220p. 1982. 29.95 (*0-8078-1523-3*) U of NC Pr.
— Emily Dickinson: The Poet of the Second Story. (Cambridge Studies in American Literature & Culture: No. 20). 144p. 1987. 44.95 (*0-521-32781-4*) Cambridge U Pr.
— Lost in the Customhouse: Authorship in the American Renaissance. LC 92-33051. 268p. 1993. text ed. 36.95 (*0-87745-404-3*) U of Iowa Pr.
Loving, Jerome, ed. see Norris, Frank.
Loving, Jerome M., ed. see Whitman, George.
Loving, Nancy J. Along the Rim: A Road Guide to the South Rim of Grand Canyon. (Illus.). 56p. (Orig.). 1981. pap. 4.95 (*0-938216-13-9*) GCNHA.
Loving, Nancy L. Veterinary Manual for the Performance Horse. Wagoner, Don, ed. (Illus.). 608p. (C). 1993. text ed. 75.00 (*0-935842-06-3*) Equine Res.
Loving, Neal V. Loving's Love: A Black American's Experience in Aviation. LC 93-24418. (History of Aviation Ser.). (Illus.). 304p. 1994. 29.95 (*1-56098-342-6*) Smithsonian.
Lovinger, David M., jt. ed. see Dunwiddie, Thomas V.
Lovinger, King F., comp. The Federal Government Subject Guide. LC 86-43179. 149p. 1987. lib. bdg. 28.50x (*0-89950-238-5*) McFarland & Co.
Lovinger, Robert J. Religion & Counseling: The Psychological Impact of Religious Belief. 176p. 1990. 17. 95 (*0-8245-1339-8*) Crossroad NY.
— Working with Religious Issues in Therapy. LC 84-6198. 328p. 1995. reprint ed. pap. 35.00 (*1-56821-236-4*) Aronson.
Lovinggood, Penman. Famous Modern Negro Musicians. LC 77-22215. (Music Reprint Ser.). (Illus.). 1978. reprint ed. lib. bdg. 19.50 (*0-306-77523-9*) Da Capo.
Lovingood, Paul & Reiman, Robert. Emerging Patterns in the Southern Highlands: Agriculture, Vol. II. Crutchfield, Malinda, ed. (Emerging Patterns in the Southern Highlands Ser.). (Illus.). 163p. (Orig.). (C). 1987. pap. text ed. 6.95 (*0-913239-46-1*) Appalach Consortium.
— Emerging Patterns in the Southern Highlands: Health Care, Vol. III. Buxton, Barry, ed. (Emerging Patterns in the Southern Highlands Ser.). (Illus.). 270p. (Orig.). (C). 1987. pap. text ed. 6.95 (*0-614-06599-2*) Appalach Consortium.
— Emerging Patterns in the Southern Highlands: A Reference Atlas: Introduction, Vol. I. (Emerging Patterns in the Southern Highlands Ser.). (Illus.). 93p. (Orig.). (C). 1985. reprint ed. pap. text ed. 6.95 (*0-913239-36-4*) Appalach Consortium.
Lovingood, Paul, et al. Emerging Patterns in the Southern Highlands: Business Patterns, Vol. IV. (Illus.). 326p. (Orig.). pap. 11.95 (*0-685-57186-6*) Appalach Consortium.
Lovingood, Sut, ed. see Lifshin, Lyn, et al.
*__Lovink, H. J. & Pine, L. A.__ The Hydrocarbon Chemistry of FCC Naphtha Formation: Symposium, Division of Petroleum Chemistry, American Chemical Society, Miami, 1989. (Illus.). 256p. (C). 1990. text ed. 108.00 (*2-7108-0588-X*) Technip.
Lovino, Vin. Overtime. 1991. pap. 6.95 (*0-930753-06-2*) Spect Ln Pr.
Lovins, Amory B. Openpit Mining. (Earth Island Ser.). 1973. pap. 1.75 (*0-85644-020-5*) Friends of Earth.
Lovins, Amory B., et al. Energy Unbound: A Fable for America's Future. LC 85-8199. (Illus.). 400p. 1986. 17. 95 (*0-87156-820-9*) Sierra.
Lovis, F. B., ed. Remote Education & Informatives - Teleteaching: Proceedings of the IFIP TC3 International Conference, Budapest, Hungary, 20-25 Oct., 1986. 254p. 1988. 64.00 (*0-444-70418-3*, North Holland) Elsevier.
Lovis, F. B. & Tagg, E. D., eds. Computers in Education: Proceedings of the IFIP TC3 1st European Conf., Lausanne, Switzerland, 24-29 July 1988. 690p. 1988. 115.50 (*0-444-70483-3*, North Holland) Elsevier.
— Informatics & Teacher Training: Proceedings of the IFIP WG 3.1 Working Conference, Birmingham, U. K., July 16-20, 1984. 254p. 1984. 46.25 (*0-444-87639-1*, North Holland) Elsevier.
— Informatics Education for All Students at University Level. 226p. 1984. 43.75 (*0-444-86807-0*, North Holland) Elsevier.
Lovis, F. B., jt. auth. see Johnson, David C.
Lovis, William, ed. see Anderson, Margaret U., et al.
Lovis, William A., ed. see Cleland, Nancy N., et al.
Loviscek, Anthony L., et al. West Virginia Input-Output Study 1975: Modeling a Regional Economy. 37p. 1979. pap. 10.00 (*0-930284-01-1*) West Va U Pr.
*__Lovisi, Gary.__ Extreme Measures. 1995. pap. write for info. (*0-614-06210-1*) Gryphon Pubns.
— The Gargoyle. (Illus.). 56p. (Orig.). 1988. 5.00 (*0-936071-12-5*) Gryphon Pubns.
— The Nemesis. (Illus.). 56p. (Orig.). 1988. 4.00 (*0-936071-10-9*) Gryphon Pubns.
— Relics of Sherlock Holmes. 48p. (Orig.). 1987. pap. 3.00 (*0-936071-05-2*) Gryphon Pubns.
— Relics of Sherlock Holmes. 2nd ed. (Illus.). 52p. (Orig.). 1989. reprint ed. 4.00 (*0-936071-16-8*) Gryphon Pubns.
— The Saga of Filster Stein. (Illus.). 52p. (Orig.). 1988. 4.00 (*0-936071-07-9*) Gryphon Pubns.
— Science Fiction Detective Tales: A Brief Overview of Futuristic Detective Fiction in Paperback. (Illus.). 107p. (Orig.). 1986. pap. 7.95 (*0-936071-01-X*) Gryphon Pubns.
Lovisi, Gary & Arnone, Terry. The Woman in the Dugout. 100p. (Orig.). 1992. pap. 9.95 (*0-936071-29-X*) Gryphon Pubns.
*__Lovisi, Gary & Reasoner, James.__ Minesweeper & Terran Girls Make Wonderful Wives. (Gryphon Double Novel Ser.: No. 8). 1995. per. 9.95 (*0-936071-40-0*) Gryphon Pubns.
Lovisi, Gary, jt. auth. see Black, Mike.
Lovisi, Gary, ed. see Corrick, James A.
Lovisi, Gary, jt. auth. see Corrick, James A.
Lovisi, Gary, ed. see Dolphin, Jack & Fitzgerald, Ted.
Lovisi, Gary, ed. see Kuttner, Henry.
Lovisi, Gary, jt. auth. see Smith, P.
Lovisi, Gary, ed. see Vaughan, Ralph E.
Lovisone, C. The Disco Hustle. (Ballroom Dance Ser.). 1986. lib. bdg. 79.95 (*0-8490-3316-0*) Gordon Pr.
— The Disco Hustle. (Ballroom Dance Ser.). 1985. lib. bdg. 74.00 (*0-87700-819-1*) Revisionist Pr.
Lovitky, Slonim, jt. auth. see Sheiman, Deborah.
*__Lovitt.__ Batman & the Ninja. (J). 1995. pap. text ed. 2.50 (*0-307-12837-7*, Golden Pr) Western Pub.
*__Lovitt, Charles & Lowe.__ Chance & Data Investigation, Vol. 1. 220p. 1994. pap. text ed. 32.50 (*1-86366-137-9*) Heinemann.
Lovitt, Chip. Michael Jordan. (J). (gr. 4-7). 1993. pap. 3.50 (*0-590-46094-3*) Scholastic Inc.
— Rock On! The Great Rock & Roll Activity Book. (J). (gr. 5-7). 1990. pap. 2.50 (*0-590-42973-6*) Scholastic Inc.
— Ultimate Disney Joke Book. LC 94-71693. (Illus.). 64p. (J). (gr. 1-4). 1995. pap. 3.50 (*0-7868-4022-6*) Disney Pr.
Lovitt, Harriet B., jt. auth. see Lovitt, William.
Lovitt, Thomas C. Introduction to Learning Disabilities. 528p. 1989. teacher ed write for info. (*0-318-63904-1*, H19508) Allyn.
— Preventing School Dropouts: Tactics for At-Risk, Remedial, & Mildly Handicapped Adolescents. LC 90-27493. 509p. 1991. pap. text ed. 36.00 (*0-89079-454-5*, 1998) PRO-ED.
— Tactics for Teaching. 333p. (C). 1984. pap. write for info. (*0-675-20133-0*, Merrill Pub Co) Macmillan.
— Tactics for Teaching. 2nd ed. (Illus.). 368p. (C). 1994. pap. text ed. write for info. (*0-02-371813-7*, Merrill Pub Co) Macmillan.
Lovitt, Thomas C., jt. auth. see Goodlad, John I.
Lovitt, Tom, et al. Translating Research into Practice (TRIP) Learning Strategies. (Illus.). 190p. 1992. 129.00 (*0-944584-63-2*) Sopris.
— Translating Research into Practice (TRIP) Teaching Strategies. (Illus.). 160p. 1992. 129.00 (*0-944584-59-4*) Sopris.
*__Lovitt, William & Lovitt, Harriet B.__ Modern Technology in the Heideggerian Perspective. LC 95-1886. (Problems in Contemporary Philosophy Ser.: Vol. 17a). 1995. write for info. (*0-88946-345-X*) E Mellen.
— Modern Technology in the Heideggerian Perspective. LC 95-1886. (Problems in Contemporary Philosophy Ser.: Vol. 17b). 1995. write for info. (*0-88946-269-0*) E Mellen.
Lovitt, William, tr. see Heidegger, Martin.
Lovka, Bob, ed. see Bobrick, Sam & Stein, Julie.
Lovleva, L. Tretyakov Gallery-Moscow: Russian & Soviet Painting. (C). 1986. 350.00 (*0-685-22620-4*, Pub. by Collets UK) Pro-Am Music.
Lovold, S. & Mullin, B., eds. Narrow Gap Semiconductors: Proceedings of the NATO Workshop, 25-27 June 1991, Oslo, Norway. (Illus.). 144p. 1992. 90.00 (*0-7503-0158-9*) IOP Pub.
Lovoll, Odd S. A Century of Urban Life: The Norwegians in Chicago Before 1930. (Illus.). 367p. 1988. 29.95 (*0-87732-075-6*) Norwegian-Am Hist Assn.
— A Folk Epic: The Bygdelag in America. LC 74-18430. (Illus.). 342p. reprint ed. pap. 97.50 (*0-317-58782-X*, 2029665) Bks Demand.
— The Promise of America: A History of the Norwegian-American People. LC 83-27350. (Illus.). 248p. 1984. pap. 16.95 (*0-8166-1334-6*) U of Minn Pr.
Lovoll, Odd S., ed. Cultural Pluralism versus Assimilation: The Views of Waldemar Ager. (Topical Studies: Vol. 2). 236p. 1977. 10.00 (*0-87732-059-4*) Norwegian-Am Hist Assn.
— Norwegian-American Studies. 402p. Vol. 29, 1983. 12.00 (*0-87732-068-3*) Norwegian-Am Hist Assn.
— Norwegian-American Studies, Vol. 31. (Illus.). 346p. 1986. 15.00 (*0-87732-072-1*) Norwegian-Am Hist Assn.
— Norwegian-American Studies, Vol. 32. (Illus.). 297p. 1989. 15.00 (*0-87732-076-4*) Norwegian-Am Hist Assn.
— Norwegian-American Studies, Vol. 33. (Studies & Records). 370p. 1992. 15.00 (*0-87732-080-2*) Norwegian-Am Hist Assn.
Lovoll, Odd S., intro. Nordics in America: The Future of Their Past. (Special Publications). (Illus.). 228p. 1993. 20.00 (*0-87732-081-0*) Norwegian-Am Hist Assn.
Lovoll, Odd S. & Bjork, Kenneth O. The Norwegian-American Historical Association, 1925-1975. 72p. 1975. 5.00 (*0-87732-056-X*) Norwegian-Am Hist Assn.
Lovoll, Odd S., ed. see Chrislock, Carl.
Lovoll, Odd S., jt. auth. see Clausen, C. A.
Lovoll, Odd S., ed. see Gieske, Millard & Keillor, Steven.
Lovoll, Odd S., jt. auth. see Leiren, Terje I.
Lovoll, Odd S., ed. see Naess, Harald & Stafford, Kate.
Lovoll, Odd S., jt. auth. see Soike, Lowell J.
Lovoos, Janice & McClelland, Gordon. Phil Dike. (Illus.). 64p. 1989. 27.50 (*0-914589-03-2*) Hillcrest Pr.
Lovorn, Janie, jt. auth. see Lovorn, Tom.
Lovorn, Tom. How to Build a Praying Church. Spear, Cindy G. & Johnson, Tamara, eds. 63p. (Orig.). 1992. pap. 1.99 (*0-941005-85-2*); ring bd. 59.95 (*0-941005-49-6*) Chrch Grwth VA.
Lovorn, Tom & Lovorn, Janie. How to Grow a Caring Church. Spear, Cindy G., ed. 103p. 1991. pap. 1.99 (*0-941005-33-X*); ring bd. 59.95 (*0-941005-34-8*) Chrch Grwth VA.
Lovret, Fredrick J. The Way & the Power: Secrets of Japanese Strategy. (Illus.). 328p. 1987. pap. 16.95 (*0-87364-409-3*) Paladin Pr.
*__Lovric.__ Countryside, Illustrated Treasuries. (Illus.). 1995. 6.98 (*1-56138-524-7*) Courage Bks.
— Roses, Illustrated Treasuries. (Illus.). 1995. 6.98 (*1-56138-550-6*) Courage Bks.
Lovric, Michele. Horses: An Illustrated Treasury. LC 93-72694. (Courage Illustrated Treasuries Ser.). (Illus.). 48p. 1994. 6.98 (*1-56138-373-2*) Courage Bks.
Lovric, Michelle. Flowers: An Illustrated Treasury. LC 92-50181. (Courage Illustrated Treasuries Ser.). 48p. 1992. 6.98 (*1-56138-174-8*) Courage Bks.
— Friends: An Illustrated Treasury. LC 92-54933. (Courage Illustrated Treasuries Ser.). (Illus.). 48p. 1993. 6.98 (*1-56138-273-6*) Courage Bks.
— Mothers: An Illustrated Treasury. LC 92-55009. (Courage Illustrated Treasuries Ser.). (Illus.). 48p. 1993. 6.98 (*1-56138-272-8*) Courage Bks.
Lovric, Michelle, ed. Birds. LC 92-50182. (Illustrated Treasury Ser.). (Illus.). 48p. 1992. 6.98 (*1-56138-173-X*) Courage Bks.
— Love Letters: An Anthology of Passion. (Illus.). 40p. (C). 1995. 19.95 (*1-56924-857-5*) Shoot Star NY.
— Seasons: An Illustrated Treasury. LC 93-70583. (Courage Illustrated Treasuries Ser.). (Illus.). 48p. 1993. 6.98 (*1-56138-326-0*) Courage Bks.
— Women: An Illustrated Treasury. LC 93-70582. (Illus.). 48p. 1993. 6.98 (*1-56138-327-9*) Courage Bks.
*__Lovric, Michelle & Philo, Maggie.__ Victorian Christmas. (Illus.). 48p. 1995. 17.95 (*0-614-07368-5*) Stewart Tabori & Chang.
Lovrich, Frank M. The Social System of a Rural Yugoslav-American Community-Oysterville. LC 79-155329. 1963. pap. 8.00 (*0-88247-119-8*) Ragusan Pr.
Lovrich, Nicholas P. Yugoslavs & Italians in San Pedro: Political Culture & Civic Involvement. LC 77-75809. 173p. 1977. pap. 10.00 (*0-918660-01-7*) Ragusan Pr.
Lovrinic, Jean H., jt. auth. see Durrant, John D.
Lovtrup, Soren. Darwinism: The Refutation of a Myth. 480p. 1987. lib. bdg. 85.00 (*0-7099-4153-6*, Pub. by Croom Helm UK) Routledge Chapman & Hall.
Lovy, Charles W., see Klemens Diez, pseud..
Low, A. M., jt. auth. see Haugum, J.
Low, A. W. & Clift, V. A. Encyclopedia of Black America. 1981. text ed. 130.00 (*0-07-038834-2*) McGraw.
*__Low, Abraham A.__ Manage Your Fears, Manage Your Anger, a Psychiatrist Speaks. 472p. 1995. 18.00 (*0-915005-05-0*) Willett Pub Co.
— Mental Health Through Will-Training. 336p. (C). 1984. reprint ed. text ed. 12.95 (*0-915005-01-8*) Willett Pub Co.
— Mental Illness, Stigma & Self-Help: The Founding of Recovery, Inc. 174p. 1991. reprint ed. 12.95 (*0-915005-04-2*) Willett Pub Co.
— Peace Versus Power in the Family: Domestic Discord & Emotional Distress. 197p. 1984. reprint ed. 12.95 (*0-915005-03-4*) Willett Pub Co.
Low, Alaine M. British Commercial Banking & Commonwealth Development: An International Survey. 320p. 1988. lib. bdg. 42.00 (*0-415-01945-1*) Routledge.
Low, Albert. Butterfly's Dream: In Search of the Spiritual Roots of Zen. 160p. 1993. pap. 14.95 (*0-8048-1822-3*) C E Tuttle.
— An Invitation to Practice Zen. 152p. 1989. pap. 9.95 (*0-8048-1598-4*) C E Tuttle.
— The Iron Cow of Zen. 240p. (Orig.). 1991. pap. 9.95 (*0-8048-1669-7*) C E Tuttle.
— The Iron Cow of Zen. LC 85-40413. 226p. (Orig.). 1985. pap. 6.50 (*0-8356-0598-1*, Quest) Theos Pub Hse.
— The World: a Gateway: Koan Commentaries for Self Study. LC 94-46614. 320p. (Orig.). 1995. pap. 16.95 (*0-8048-3046-0*) C E Tuttle.
— Zen & Creative Management. 256p. 1993. pap. 12.95 (*0-8048-1883-5*) C E Tuttle.
*__Low, Alfred D.__ The Anschluss Movement, 1931-1938. 512p. 1985. 43.50 (*0-88033-078-3*) East Eur Quarterly.
— The Sino-Soviet Confrontation since Mao Zedong: Dispute, Detente, or Conflict. (Social Science Monograph Ser.). 400p. 1987. text ed. 54.00 (*0-88033-958-6*, Columbia Univ Schl of Library) East Eur Quarterly.
— The Sino-Soviet Dispute: An Analysis of the Polemics. LC 74-2949. 364p. 1976. 39.50 (*0-8386-1479-5*) Fairleigh Dickinson.
— Soviet Jewry & Soviet Policy. (East European Monographs). 272p. 1990. text ed. 35.00 (*0-88033-178-X*) Col U Pr.
Low, Alfred M. America at Home. LC 73-13142. (Foreign Travelers in America, 1810-1935 Ser.). (Illus.). 278p. 1974. reprint ed. 21.95 (*0-405-05465-3*) Ayer.
Low, Alice. The Family Read-Aloud Holiday Treasury. (Illus.). 1991. 19.95 (*0-316-53368-8*) Little.
— The Macmillan Book of Greek Gods & Heroes. LC 85-7170. (Illus.). 192p. (J). (gr. 2-6). 1985. text ed. 16.95 (*0-02-761390-9*, Mac Bks Young Read) S&S Childrens.
— The Macmillan Book of Greek Gods & Heroes. LC 94-3198. (Illus.). 192p. (J). (gr. 3-7). 1994. pap. 12.95 (*0-689-71874-8*, Aladdin Paperbacks) S&S Childrens.
— The Popcorn Shop. LC 92-21423. (Hello Reader! Ser.). (Illus.). (J). 1994. 2.95 (*0-590-47121-X*) Scholastic Inc.

An Asterisk (*) at the beginning of an entry indicates that the title is appearing in BIP for the first time.

L

— The Witch Who Was Afraid of Witches. LC 78-5856. (Trophy Picture Bk.). (Illus.). 40p. (J). (gr. k-3). 1990. reprint ed. pap. 4.95 (*0-06-443234-3*, Trophy) HarpC Child Bks.

Low, Alice, ed. Spooky Stories for a Dark & Stormy Night. LC 93-33638. (Illus.). 128p. (J). (gr. 3 up). 1994. 19.95 (*0-7868-0012-7*); lib. bdg. 19.89 (*0-7868-2008-X*) Hyprn Child.

Low, Allan. Agricultural Development in Southern Africa: Farm Household-Economics & the Food Crisis. 218p. 1989. pap. text ed. 22.50 (*0-435-08027-X*, 08027) Heinemann.

Low-Altitude Wind Shear & Its Hazard to Aviation Committee Staff & National Research Council Staff. Low-Altitude Wind Shear & Its Hazard to Aviation. 112p. 1983. pap. text ed. 14.95 (*0-309-03432-9*) Natl Acad Pr.

Low, Angus, jt. auth. see Durant, Stuart.

Low, Anthony. Augustine Baker. LC 74-99527. (Twayne's English Authors Ser.). 170p. (C). 1970. lib. bdg. 17.95 (*0-8290-1759-3*) Irvington.

— The Georgic Revolution. LC 84-26520. (Illus.). 368p. 1985. text ed. 49.50 (*0-691-06643-4*) Princeton U Pr.

— The Reinvention of Love: Poetry, Politics, & Culture from Sidney to Milton. LC 93-18184. 240p. (C). 1993. 47.95 (*0-521-45030-6*) Cambridge U Pr.

Low, Archibald R. Normal Elliptic Functions: A Normalized Form of Weierstrass's Elliptic Functions. LC 55-37289. 32p. reprint ed. pap. 25.00 (*0-318-34719-9*, 2031927) Bks Demand.

Low, Barbara, tr. see Freud, Anna.

Low, Barbara B., contrib. Leasing Sourcebook, 1994: The Directory of the U. S. Capital Equipment Leasing Industry, No. 1045-2508. 352p. 1994. pap. 135.00 (*0-936857-05-6*) Bibliotec Systems & Pub.

Low, Barbara B., intro. Leasing Sourcebook, 1992-93: The Directory of the U. S. Capital Equipment Leasing Industry. 340p. 1992. pap. text ed. 135.00 (*0-936857-04-8*) Bibliotec Systems & Pub.

— Leasing Sourcebook, 1995-96: The Directory of the U. S. Capital Equipment Leasing Industry. 360p. 1995. pap. 135.00 (*0-936857-07-2*) Bibliotec Systems & Pub.

***Low-Beer, F. H.** Questions of Judgment: Determining What's Right. LC 95-8726. 245p. 1995. 29.95 (*0-87975-960-7*) Prometheus Bks.

Low, Benjamin R. Seth Low. LC 70-137256. reprint ed. 11. 50 (*0-404-04037-3*) AMS Pr.

— Seth Low. (BCL1 - United States Local History Ser.). 92p. 1991. reprint ed. lib. bdg. 59.00 (*0-7812-6276-3*) Rprt Serv.

Low, Betty-Bright P. France Views America, 1765-1815: An Exhibition to Commemorate the Bicentenary of French Assistance in the American War of Independence. LC 78-104642. (Illus.). 80p. reprint ed. pap. 25.00 (*0-8357-3127-8*, 2039388) Bks Demand.

Low, Brian & Withers, Graeme, eds. Developments in School & Public Assessment. (C). 1992. 65.00 (*0-86431-070-6*, Pub. by Aust Coun Educ Res AT) St Mut.

Low, C. M., jt. auth. see Ley, S. V.

Low, Colin, et al. Participation in Services for the Handicapped: Two Contrasting Models-Discussion Paper. 1979. 22.00 (*0-317-05799-5*, Pub. by Natl Inst Soc Work) St Mut.

Low, D. A. Eclipse of Empire. 272p. (C). 1991. 69.95 (*0-521-38329-3*) Cambridge U Pr.

— Eclipse of Empire. 400p. (C). 1993. pap. 18.95 (*0-521-45754-8*) Cambridge U Pr.

Low, D. A., ed. Constitutional Heads & Political Crises: Commonwealth Episodes, 1945-85. LC 88-10116. 550p. 1988. text ed. 65.00 (*0-312-02113-5*) St Martin.

Low, D. M., ed. see Gibbon, Edward.

Low, D. M., tr. see Ginzburg, Natalia.

Low, David H., tr. Ballads of Marco Kraljevic. LC 69-10123. (Illus.). 196p. 1968. reprint ed. text ed. 38.50 (*0-8371-0151-4*, LOMK, Greenwood Pr) Greenwood.

Low, Denise. Spring Geese & Other Poems. (Illus.). 84p. 1984. pap. 4.00 (*0-89338-024-5*) U of KS Mus Nat Hist.

— Starwater. (Illus.). 64p. (Orig.). 1988. per. 6.00 (*0-685-30038-2*) Cottonwood KS.

— Touching the Sky. 132p. 1994. pap. 16.50 (*0-9632475-8-1*) Penthe Pub.

— Tulip Elegies: An Alchemy of Writing. LC 92-85531. 70p. 1993. pap. 10.00 (*0-9632475-0-6*) Penthe Pub.

Low, Donald, ed. see Burns, Robert.

Low, Donald A. Lion Rampant: Essays in the Study of British Imperialism. (Studies in Commonwealth Politics & History: No. 1). 232p. 1973. 35.00 (*0-7146-2986-3*, Pub. by F Cass Pubs UK) Intl Spec Bk.

Low, Donald A., ed. see Byron, George G. B.

Low, Douglas, jt. auth. see Bray, David K.

Low, Douglas B. The Existential Dialectic of Marx & Merleau-Ponty. (American University Studies: Philosophy: Ser. V, Vol. 33). 260p. (C). 1987. text ed. 36.00 (*0-8204-0435-7*) P Lang Pubs.

Low, Erick. Fulton County Law Library Observations & Recommendations: A Technical Assistance Report. 82p. 1991. 5.00 (*0-685-50614-2*, SERO, T/A-509) Natl Ctr St Courts.

— New Hampshire State Law Library, Observations & Recommendations: A Technical Assistance Report. 156p. 1992. 9.50 (*0-685-55344-2*, NERO,T/A563) Natl Ctr St Courts.

— Overview of the Utah State Law Library - Technical Assistance Report. 155p. 1989. 9.50 (*0-685-38102-1*, WRO, T/A-510) Natl Ctr St Courts.

— Prince William County Law Library, Observations & Recommendations: Technical Assistance Final Report. 108p. 1992. 6.50 (*0-685-55340-X*, SERO,T/A510) Natl Ctr St Courts.

Low, Erick & James, Jim. Overview of the Arkansas Supreme Court Library: Technical Assistance Report. 74p. 1990. 4.50 (*0-685-38103-X*, MWRO-003) Natl Ctr St Courts.

Low, F. Symmetries & Elementary Particles. (Documents on Modern Physics Ser.). 112p. (Orig.). (C). 1967. text ed. 96.00 (*0-677-01750-2*) Gordon & Breach.

Low, Francis. Struggle for Asia. LC 79-167379. (Essay Index Reprint Ser.). 1977. reprint ed. 20.95 (*0-8369-2699-4*) Ayer.

***Low, Gail C.** White Skins/Black Masks: Representation, Colonialism & Cultural Cross-Dressing. LC 95-8889. 1996. write for info. (*0-415-08147-5*) Routledge.

Low, Hugh. Sarawak: Its Inhabitants & Productions. (Illus.). 416p. 1968. reprint ed. 35.00 (*0-7146-2017-3*, Pub. by F Cass Pubs UK) Intl Spec Bk.

Low, It- Meng, jt. ed. see Shi, Xing Sheng.

Low, J. O., jt. auth. see Warner, W. Lloyd.

Low, Jeanie W. China Connection: Finding Ancestral Roots for Chinese in America. 2nd rev. ed. LC 93-91747. (Illus.). 65p. 1994. per., pap. 11.95 (*0-9638835-1-8*) JWC Low.

Low, Jennie. Chopsticks, Cleaver & Wok: Homestyle Chinese Cooking. LC 87-11655. (Illus.). 160p. (Orig.). 1987. pap. 9.95 (*0-87701-421-3*) Chronicle Bks.

Low, John & Reed, Ann. Electrotherapy Explained. 260p. 1990. pap. text ed. 39.95 (*0-7506-0049-7*) Buttrwrth-Heinemann.

— Electrotherapy Explained: Principles & Practice. 2nd ed. 320p. 1995. pap. write for info. (*0-7506-0972-9*) Buttrwrth-Heinemann.

— Physical Principles Explained. 2nd ed. LC 93-33995. 208p. 1993. pap. 24.95 (*0-7506-0748-3*) Buttrwrth-Heinemann.

Low, John, jt. auth. see MacDonald, Ian.

Low, John J., tr. see Morgan, G. Campbell.

Low, John L. F. G. Tait - A Record. rev. ed. (Illus.). 250p. 1989. text ed. 28.00 (*0-940889-21-8*) Classics Golf.

Low, Joseph. A Mad Wet Hen & Other Riddles. LC 76-44329. (Illus.). 56p. (J). (gr. 3 up). 1992. pap. 3.95 (*0-688-11511-X*, Mulberry) Morrow.

— Mice Twice. LC 85-26768. (Illus.). 32p. (J). (ps-3). 1986. reprint ed. pap. 4.95 (*0-689-71060-7*, Aladdin Paperbacks) S&S Childrens.

Low, K. Brooks, ed. The Recombination of Genetic Material. 506p. 1988. text ed. 112.00 (*0-12-456270-1*) Acad Pr.

Low, Kathleen. Legislative Reference Services & Sources. LC 93-39408. 104p. 1994. lib. bdg. 29.95 (*1-56024-891-2*) Haworth Pr.

Low, Linda, et al, eds. Regional Outlook: Southeast Asia 1992-93. 82p. 1992. pap. 32.50 (*981-3016-18-3*, Pub. by Inst SE Asian Studies SI) Ashgate Pub Co.

Low, Linda, jt. auth. see Toh Mun Heng.

Low, Lisa E. & Harding, Anthony J., eds. Milton, the Metaphysicals, & Romanticism. LC 93-41033. 277p. (C). 1995. 54.95 (*0-521-44414-4*) Cambridge U Pr.

Low, Lyman. Hard Times Tokens. (Illus.). 1984. reprint ed. lib. bdg. 20.00 (*0-915262-16-9*) S J Durst.

Low, Lyman H. Observations on the Practice of Counterfeiting Coins & Medals. 1979. reprint ed. pap. 2.00 (*0-915262-25-8*) S J Durst.

Low, Marie A. Dust Bowl Diary. LC 84-3672. (Illus.). x, 188p. 1984. pap. 8.95 (*0-8032-7913-2*) U of Nebr Pr.

***Low, Martha.** Thresholds in Reading. 224p. 1995. pap. 17. 95 (*0-8384-5336-8*) Heinle & Heinle.

Low, Mary. A Voice in Three Mirrors: Poems. 48p. 1983. pap. 12.00 (*0-941194-21-3*) Black Swan Pr.

— Where the Wolf Sings. (Illus.). 64p. (Orig.). 1994. pap. 12. 00 (*0-614-06074-5*) Black Swan Pr.

Low, N. P. & Power, J. M. Policy Systems in An Australian Metropolitan Region: Political & Economic Determinants of Change in Victoria, Vols. 22 & 23. (Illus.). 70p. 1984. pap. 22.00 (*0-08-032329-4*, Pergamon Pr) Elsevier.

Low, Niels L., jt. ed. see Downey, John A.

***Low, Patrick.** Preshipment Inspection Services. LC 94-49060. (World Bank Discussion Paper Ser.: No. 278). 176p. 1995. 10.95 (*0-8213-3185-X*, 13185) World Bank.

— Trading Free: The GATT & U. S. Trade Policy. LC 93-12630. 310p. (C). 1993. 24.95 (*0-87078-352-1*); pap. 14. 95 (*0-87078-351-3*) TCFP-PPP.

Low, Patrick, ed. International Trade & the Environment. LC 92-13718. (Discussion Paper Ser.: Vol. 159). 376p. 1992. pap. 21.95 (*0-8213-2115-3*, 12115) World Bank.

Low, Peter & Jeffries, John. Civil Rights Actions: Section 1983 & Related Statutes. (University Casebook Ser.). 290p. 1993. pap. text ed. 11.50 (*1-56662-107-0*) Foundation Pr.

— Federal Courts & the Law of Federal-State Relations, 1993 Supplement. 2nd ed. (University Casebks.). 366p. 1993. pap. text ed. 11.95 (*1-56662-108-9*) Foundation Pr.

Low, Peter W. Criminal Law. rev. ed. (Black Letter Ser.). 443p. 1993. reprint ed. pap. text ed. 24.50 (*0-314-73494-5*) West Pub.

Low, Peter W. & Jeffries, John C., Jr. Civil Rights Actions: Section 1983 & Related Statutes. (University Casebook Ser.). 773p. 1988. text ed. 35.95 (*0-88277-635-5*) Foundation Pr.

— Civil Rights Actions: Section 1983 & Related Statutes. 2nd ed. LC 94-7715. (University Casebook Ser.). 953p. 1994. text ed. 42.50 (*1-56662-149-6*) Foundation Pr.

— Federal Courts & the Law of Federal-State Relations. 2nd ed. (University Casebook Ser.). 1243p. 1990. reprint ed. text ed. 40.50 (*0-88277-708-4*) Foundation Pr.

— Federal Courts & the Law of Federal-State Relations. 3rd ed. (University Casebook Ser.). 1341p. (C). 1994. text ed. 47.50 (*1-56662-160-7*) Foundation Pr.

Low, Peter W., et al. Criminal Law: Cases & Materials. 2nd ed. (University Casebook Ser.). 1089p. 1990. reprint ed. text ed. 40.95 (*0-88277-325-9*) Foundation Pr.

— Trial of John W. Hinckley, Jr.,; A Case Study in the Insanity Defense. (University Casebook Ser.). 137p. 1986. pap. text ed. 9.95 (*0-88277-333-X*) Foundation Pr.

Low, Phillip A. Clinical Autonomic Disorders: Evaluation & Management. LC 92-49907. 600p. 1992. 190.00 (*0-316-53390-4*) Little.

Low, Rachael. Film Making in Nineteen Thirties Britain. (Illus.). 384p. 1985. 39.95 (*0-04-791042-9*) Routledge Chapman & Hall.

Low, Robert. La Pasionaria: The Spanish Firebrand. (Illus.). 224p. 1993. 39.95 (*0-09-174572-1*, Pub. by Hutchnson UK) Trafalgar.

Low, Robert, ed. see Eyster, Pat.

Low, Robert J. Bottom Line Basics: Understand & Control Business Finances. Pinkham, Linda, ed. (Successful Business Library). 325p. (Orig.). 1994. pap. 19.95 (*1-55571-330-0*); ring bd. 39.95 (*1-55571-329-7*) Oasis Pr OR.

Low, Roderick, et al. Writing User Documentation: A Practical Guide for Those Who Want to Be Read. LC 93-25427. 1993. pap. text ed. 30.00 (*0-13-336835-1*) P-H Gen Ref & Trav.

Low, Rodolfo. Victory over Migraine: The Breakthrough Study That Explains What Causes It & How It Can Be Completely Prevented Through Diet. LC 86-7708. 208p. 1989. pap. 7.95 (*0-8050-0927-2*, Owl) H Holt & Co.

Low, Rosemary. Cockatoos in Aviculture. (Illus.). 160p. 1994. 24.95 (*0-7137-2322-X*, Pub. by Blandford Pr UK) Sterling.

— The Complete Book of Macaws. 144p. 1990. 18.95 (*0-8120-6073-3*) Barron.

— The Complete Book of Parrots. 144p. 1989. 18.95 (*0-8120-5971-9*) Barron.

— Hand-Rearing Parrots & Other Birds. (Illus.). 144p. 1991. pap. 17.95 (*0-7137-2254-1*, Pub. by Blandford Pr UK) Sterling.

— Lories & Lorikeets. (Illus.). 180p. 1990. pap. 19.95 (*0-86622-142-5*, PS-773) TFH Pubns.

— Parrots: Their Care & Breeding. 3rd rev. ed. (Illus.). 400p. 1992. 95.00 (*0-7137-2203-7*, Pub. by Blandford Pr UK) Sterling.

— Parrots in Aviculture: A Photo Reference Guide. (Illus.). 288p. 1992. 50.00 (*1-895270-11-1*) Silvio Mattacchione.

Low, Royston. Acupuncture in Gynaecology & Obstetrics. 1990. 14.95 (*0-7225-2108-1*) Thorsons SF.

Low, Ruth H. & Valls, Lito, eds. St. John Backtime. LC 80-68089. (Illus.). 96p. (Orig.). 1985. pap. 14.95 (*0-9614355-0-X*) Eden Hill Pr.

Low, Setha M. & Chambers, Erve. Housing, Culture, & Design: A Comparative Perspective. 440p. 1989. pap. text ed. 34.95x (*0-8122-1271-1*) U of Pa Pr.

Low, Setha M., jt. ed. see Altman, Irwin.

Low, Setha M., jt. ed. see Davis, Dona L.

Low, Setha M., jt. auth. see Johnston, Francis E.

Low, Shirley P., jt. auth. see Alderson, William T.

Low, Sidney & Sanders, Lloyd C. History of England During the Reign of Victoria, 1837-1907. LC 68-25247. (British History Ser.: No. 30). (Illus.). 1969. reprint ed. lib. bdg. 57.95 (*0-8383-0267-X*) M S G Haskell Hse.

Low, Sidney J. & Sanders, Lloyd C. History of England During the Reign of Victoria, 1837-1901. LC 74-5630. (Political History of England Ser.: No. 12). reprint ed. 45.00 (*0-404-50782-4*) AMS Pr.

Low, Theodore L. The Educational Philosophy & Practice of Art Museums in the United States. LC 77-177012. (Columbia University. Teachers College. Contributions to Education Ser.: No. 942). reprint ed. 22.50 (*0-404-55942-5*) AMS Pr.

***Low, Tom A., ed.** One Furrow at a Time: The Autobiography of Dave Low. (Illus.). 160p. 1995. 25.00 (*1-887301-00-3*) Palmetto Bookworks.

Low, Trevor. Gymnastics: Floor, Vault, Beam & Bar. (Skills of the Game Ser.). (Illus.). 128p. Date not set. pap. 15. 95 (*1-85223-752-X*, Pub. by Crowood Pr UK) Trafalgar.

Low, Victor. The Unimpressible Race: A Century of Educational Struggle by the Chinese in San Francisco. 236p. 1982. 15.50 (*0-934788-04-9*); pap. 9.95 (*0-934788-03-0*) E-W Pub Co.

Low, Victor N. Three Nigerian Emirates: A Study in Oral History. LC 74-176163. 328p. reprint ed. pap. 93.50 (*0-317-27770-7*, 2015424) Bks Demand.

Low, W. Augustus & Clift, Virgil A. Encyclopedia of Black America. (Quality Paperbacks Ser.). (Illus.). 941p. (C). 1984. reprint ed. pap. 35.00 (*0-306-80221-X*) Da Capo.

Low, Wendy, ed. see Drury, Finvola.

Low, Werner. Acerbic Amusings. (WEP Poetry Ser.: No. 1). 1978. pap. 1.00 (*0-917976-03-7*, White Ewe Pr) Thunder Baas Pr.

— Low Wit. LC 81-69718. 79p. (Orig.). 1982. pap. 3.95 (*0-917976-15-0*, White Ewe Pr) Thunder Baas Pr.

— Rime & Punishment. (Poetry Ser.: No. 2). (Illus.). (Orig.). 1989. pap. 3.00 (*0-938823-02-7*) Pogment Pr.

Lowalewski, Stephen A., jt. ed. see Fish, Suzanne K.

Lowance, Mason I., Jr. The Language of Canaan: Metaphor & Symbol in New England from the Puritans to the Transcendentalists. LC 79-21179. 345p. 1980. 32.00 (*0-674-50949-8*) HUP.

Lowance, Mason I., et al, eds. The Stowe Debate: Rhetorics in Uncle Tom's Cabin. LC 94-12254. 328p. (C). 1994. lib. bdg. 45.00 (*0-87023-951-1*); pap. 17.95 (*0-87023-952-X*) U of Mass Pr.

Lowbury, E. J. Control of Hospital Infection. 3rd ed. 1992. 99.95 (*0-442-31669-0*) Chapman & Hall.

Lowden, J. Alexander, jt. ed. see Callahan, John W.

Lowden, John. Illuminated Prophet Books: A Study of Byzantine Manuscripts of the Major & Minor Prophets. LC 86-43164. (Illus.). 176p. 1989. 50.00 (*0-271-00604-8*) Pa St U Pr.

— The Octateuchs: A Study of Illustrated Byzantine Manuscripts. (Illus.). 246p. 1992. text ed. 49.50 (*0-271-00771-0*) Pa St U Pr.

Lowden, John L. Silent Wings at War: Combat Gliders in World War II. LC 91-17898. (Illus.). 246p. 1992. 24.95 (*1-56098-121-0*) Smithsonian.

Lowden, M. Dancing to Learn, Learning to Dance. 1989. 70. 00 (*1-85000-618-0*); pap. 33.00 (*1-85000-619-9*) Taylor & Francis.

***Lowden, R. A., et al, eds.** Ceramic Matrix Composites - Advanced High-Temperature Structural Materials: 1994 MRS Fall Meeting, Boston, MA, Vol. 365. (MRS Symposium Proceedings Ser.). 1995. 67.00 (*1-55899-266-9*, 365K4) Materials Res.

Lowden, Stephanie G. Emily's Sadhappy Season. Johnson, Joy, ed. (Illus.). 24p. (J). (gr. 2-6). 1993. pap. 4.95 (*0-685-72223-6*) Centering Corp.

Lowder, Dwayne. In a Southern Tradition (Just Another Paradox) Sheridan, Helen, ed. (Illus.). 20p. (Orig.). 1982. pap. 6.00 (*0-933742-05-3*) Kalamazoo Inst Arts.

Lowder, Hughston E. The Silent Service: U. S. Submarines in World War II. LC 87-90657. 504p. (C). 1987. 24.95 (*0-9619189-0-X*) Silent Serv Bks.

Lowder, James. Crusade. LC 89-51890. (Forgotten Realms Empires Trilogy Bks.: Bk. 3). 320p. (Orig.). 1991. pap. 4.95 (*0-88038-908-7*) TSR Inc.

— Jungles of Chult. (Advanced Dungeons & Dragons, Second Edition; Al-Qadim Ser.). (Illus.). 1993. pap. 9.95 (*1-56076-605-0*) TSR Inc.

— Knight of the Black Rose. LC 90-71507. (Ravenloft Ser.: Bk. 2). 320p. (Orig.). 1991. pap. 4.95 (*1-56076-156-3*) TSR Inc.

— The Prince of Lies. 388p. (Orig.). 1993. pap. 5.95 (*1-56076-626-3*) TSR Inc.

— Realms of Infamy. (Forgotten Realms Ser.). 1994. pap. 4.95 (*1-56076-911-4*) TSR Inc.

— The Ring of Winter. (Harpers Ser.). 320p. (Orig.). 1992. pap. 4.95 (*1-56076-330-2*) TSR Inc.

— Screaming Tower. (Ebonacht Trilogy Ser.). 320p. (Orig.). Date not set. pap. 4.95 (*1-56076-915-7*) TSR Inc.

Lowder, Josef G. The Time Investment Register. (What in the World Are You Doing with Your Life Ser.: No. 2). 32p. 1986. pap. 1.50 (*0-935597-02-6*, 8507-02); disk 29. 95 (*0-935597-03-4*) Comm Architects.

— The Ultimate Purpose & Fundamental Principles of Life. LC 85-701. (What in the World Are You Doing with Your Life Ser.: No. 1). 72p. 9.95 (*0-935597-00-X*); pap. 3.95 (*0-935597-01-8*); disk 9.95 (*0-935597-04-2*) Comm Architects.

Lowder, Stella. The Geography of Third World Cities. LC 86-17366. 304p. 1986. 58.50 (*0-389-20671-7*, N8228) B&N Imports.

Lowder, Stella, jt. ed. see Morris, Arthur.

Lowder, W. M., et al. International Symposium in the Natural Radiation Environment Tutorial Sessions, 5th. (EUR Ser.: No. 14411). 287p. 1993. pap. 45.00 (*92-826-5604-7*, CG-NA-14411-EN-C, Pub. by Europ Com) UNIPUB.

Lowder, Wayne M., ed. The Natural Radiation Environment: International Symposium on the Natural Radiation Environment, 1963 Houston, Texas. LC 64-12256. (Rice University Semicentennial Publications). 1083p. pap. 180.00 (*0-8357-8963-2*, 2056765) Bks Demand.

Lowdermilk, Karen, ed. see Michael, Linda.

Lowdermilk, Walter C. Palestine: Land of Promise. rev. ed. LC 68-23308. (Illus.). 244p. 1968. reprint ed. text ed. 38. 50 (*0-8371-2616-9*, LOPL, Greenwood Pr) Greenwood.

Lowdermilk, Will H. History of Cumberland, (Maryland) LC 79-173260. (Illus.). 496p. 1976. reprint ed. 27.50 (*0-8063-7983-9*) Regional.

***Lowdin, P.** International Journal of Quantum Symposium. 28th ed. 1994. text ed. 150.00 (*0-471-12125-8*) Wiley.

Lowdin, Per-Olov. Quantum Biology & Quantum Pharmacology: Quantum Biology Symposium Proceedings, No. 18. 18th ed. 248p. 1991. pap. text ed. 155.00 (*0-471-57348-5*) Wiley.

— Quantum Chemistry, Solid-State Theory, & Molecular Dynamics: Quantum Chemistry Symposium, No. 25. 752p. 1991. pap. text ed. 120.00 (*0-471-57349-3*) Wiley.

Lowdin, Per-Olov, ed. Advances in Quantum Chemistry, Vol. 17. (Serial Publication Ser.). 1985. text ed. 189.00 (*0-12-034817-9*) Acad Pr.

— Advances in Quantum Chemistry, Vol. 18. (Serial Publication Ser.). 1986. text ed. 176.00 (*0-12-034818-7*) Acad Pr.

— Advances in Quantum Chemistry, Vol. 25. 320p. 1994. text ed. 79.00 (*0-12-034825-X*) Acad Pr.

— International Journal of Quantum Chemistry. 1989. pap. text ed. 69.95 (*0-471-50837-3*) Wiley.

— International Journal of Quantum Chemistry: Quantum Biology Symposium, No. 17. 1991. pap. text ed. 84.95 (*0-471-54598-8*) Wiley.

— International Journal of Quantum Chemistry - Quantum Biology Symposium Proceedings, No. 21. 21th ed. 1994. pap. text ed. 100.00 (*0-471-12016-2*) Wiley.

— Quantum Biology Symposium, 20. 20th ed. 1993. pap. text ed. 175.00 (*0-471-02504-6*) Wiley.

— Quantum Chemistry, Solid-State Theory, & Molecular Dynamics, 27. 27th ed. (Quantum Chemistry Symposium Ser.). 1993. pap. text ed. 173.00 (*0-471-02505-4*) Wiley.

Lowdin, Per-Olov & Pullman, Bernard, eds. New Horizons of Quantum Chemistry. 1982. lib. bdg. 145.50 (*90-277-1526-2*) Kluwer Ac.

Lowdin, Per-Olov, ed. see Trickey, Samuel B.

Lowdin, Per-Olov, et al, eds. Advances in Quantum Chemistry, Vol. 19. (Serial Publication Ser.). 365p. 1988. text ed. 134.00 (*0-12-034819-5*) Acad Pr.

— Advances in Quantum Chemistry, Vol. 20. (Serial Publication Ser.). 453p. 1989. text ed. 128.00 (*0-12-034820-9*) Acad Pr.
— Advances in Quantum Chemistry, Vol. 22. (Illus.). 385p. 1991. text ed. 94.00 (*0-12-034822-5*) Acad Pr.
— Advances in Quantum Chemistry, Vol. 23. (Illus.). 363p. 1992. text ed. 85.00 (*0-12-034823-3*) Acad Pr.
— Advances in Quantum Chemistry, Vol. 24. (Illus.). 298p. 1992. text ed. 75.00 (*0-12-034824-1*) Acad Pr.
Lowdon, Eric. Practical Transformer Design Handbook. 2nd ed. 1988. 41.95 (*0-07-156844-1*) McGraw.
— Practical Transformer Design Handbook. 2nd ed. (Illus.). 400p. 1989. 39.95 (*0-8306-3212-3*, TAB/TPR) TAB Bks.
***Lowe.** Creativity & Problem Solving: The McGraw-Hill One-Day Workshop. 1995. text ed. 99.95 (*0-07-912091-1*) McGraw.
— Empowerment: The McGraw-Hill One-Day Workshop. 1995. text ed. 99.95 (*0-07-912093-8*) McGraw.
— Illustrated Textbook of Diagnostic Histopathology. (Illus.). 1991. write for info. (*0-8151-5588-3*, Yr Bk Med Pubs) Mosby Yr Bk.
Lowe & Jeffrey. Surgical Pathology Techniques. 144p. 1990. 69.50 (*1-55664-297-0*) Mosby Yr Bk.
Lowe & Shaath. Sunscreens: Development, Evaluation, & Regulatory Aspects. (Cosmetic Science & Technology Ser.: Vol. 10). 672p. 1990. 190.00 (*0-8247-8265-8*) Dekker.
Lowe, jt. auth. see Barlow.
Lowe, jt. auth. see Lovitt, Charles.
Lowe, A. L. & Perry, G. W., eds. Zirconium in the Nuclear Industry: Third Conference - STP 633. 690p. 1977. 55. 50 (*0-8031-0756-0*, 04-633000-35) ASTM.
Lowe, A. V., jt. auth. see Churchill, R. R.
Lowe, Adolph. Essays in Political Economics: Public Control in a Democratic Society. Oakley, Allen, ed. 258p. 1991. pap. text ed. 18.50 (*0-8147-6173-9*) NYU Pr.
— Has Freedom a Future? LC 87-29943. (Convergence Ser.). 184p. 1988. text ed. 49.95 (*0-275-92937-X*, C2937, Praeger Pubs); pap. text ed. 12.95 (*0-275-92938-8*, B2938, Praeger Pubs) Greenwood.
Lowe, Albert G., jt. auth. see Stewart, Martha A.
***Lowe, Anthony M.** 300 Years in Eastern Virginia: Descendants of Arthur Jones (1630-1692) LC 95-1161. 1995. write for info. (*0-89865-934-5*) Donning Co.
Lowe, B. J. Author's Handbook. 4th ed. 48p. (Orig.). 1992. pap. 10.00 (*0-88415-050-X*) Gulf Pub.
***Lowe, Barry.** Media Mythologies. 1995. pap. 19.95 (*0-614-01955-9*, Pub. by New South Wales Univ Pr AT) Intl Spec Bk.
Lowe, Bia. Wild Ride. 1995. 20.00 (*0-06-019053-1*, HarpT) HarpC.
Lowe, Brett W. Clever Advertising: Getting the Most from Your Advertising Dollar. 152p. 1993. pap. 16.95 (*1-875680-06-3*, Pub. by Busn & Prof Pubng AT) Pubs Dist MI.
***Lowe, C. & Oldring, P. K.** Test Methods for UV & EB Curable Systems. (Illus.). 214p. 1994. text ed. 100.00 (*0-947798-47-1*) Scholium Intl.
Lowe, C., jt. auth. see Layne, C. E.
Lowe, C. Fergus, et al, eds. Behavior Analysis & Contemporary Psychology. 288p. 1986. text ed. 59.95 (*0-86377-025-8*) L Erlbaum Assocs.
Lowe, C. J. Salisbury & the Mediterranean, 1886-1896. 20. 00 (*0-89979-072-0*) British Am Bks.
Lowe, C. Marshall. Value Orientations in Counseling & Psychotherapy: The Meanings of Mental Health. 2nd ed. LC 76-25957. 1976. pap. text ed. 19.50 (*0-910328-09-9*) Sulzburger & Graham Pub.
Lowe, C. V., jt. auth. see Goodwin, Astly J.
Lowe, C. W. Industrial Statistics, Vol. 2. 1970. 32.00 (*0-8464-0512-1*) Beekman Pubs.
Lowe, Carl. The Civil War Remembered. LC 94-8757. 1994. write for info. (*1-56799-107-6*, Friedman-Fairfax) M Friedman Pub Grp Inc.
— The Complete Vitamin Book. 320p. (Orig.). 1994. pap. text ed. 5.99 (*0-425-14365-1*) Berkley Pub.
— Juice Power. 208p. (Orig.). 1992. pap. 4.50 (*0-425-13606-X*) Berkley Pub.
Lowe, Carl & Philip Lief Group Staff. Toxic Food: What You Need to Know to Feed Your Family Safely. 128p. 1990. pap. 3.95 (*0-380-76001-0*) Avon.
Lowe, Carl, jt. auth. see Fuentes, Robert.
Lowe, Carol, jt. ed. see Lugo, Ariel E.
Lowe, Celia, jt. auth. see Ottmann, Klaus.
Lowe, Charles. Alexander the Third of Russia. LC 72-4219. (Select Bibliographies Reprint Ser.). 1977. reprint ed. 23. 95 (*0-8369-6889-1*) Ayer.
Lowe, Charles H. Arizona's Natural Environment: Landscapes & Habitats. (Illus.). 144p. reprint ed. pap. 41.10 (*0-7837-5049-8*, 2044727) Bks Demand.
Lowe, Charles H., ed. see Cockrun, E. Lendell, et al.
Lowe, Christopher R. & Dean, P. D. Affinity Chromatography. LC 73-17598. 284p. reprint ed. pap. 81.00 (*0-8357-5219-4*, 2023997) Bks Demand.
Lowe, Chuan-Hua. Facing Labor Issues in China. LC 75-32322. (Studies in Chinese History & Civilization). 220p. 1977. reprint ed. text ed. 55.00 (*0-313-26972-6*, U6972, Greenwood Pr) Greenwood.
Lowe, Claude E. A Chronological Cyclopedia of Musicians & Musical Events from A. D. 320 to 1896. 1976. lib. bdg. 75.00 (*0-8490-1623-1*) Gordon Pr.
Lowe, Claudia J. Guide to Reference & Bibliography for Theatre Research. 2nd ed. 149p. 1980. pap. 20.00 (*0-88215-049-9*) Friends Ohio St U Lib.
Lowe-Clay, Carol. Country Suppers: From Uphill Farm. (Illus.). 160p. 1993. pap. 10.95 (*0-913589-74-8*) Williamson Pub Co.
Lowe, Cylvia Archer. Words of Wisdom from the Masters. 2nd ed. 120p. 1981. reprint ed. pap. 8.95 (*0-9606080-0-1*) Book Dept.

Lowe, D. The Transport & Distribution Manager's Guide to 1992. 206p. (C). 1989. 180.00 (*0-685-39893-5*, Inst Pur & Supply) St Mut.
Lowe, D. & Fox, H., eds. Advances in Gynaecological Pathology. (Illus.). 384p. 1992. text ed. 110.00 (*0-443-04377-9*) Churchill.
Lowe, D. Armstrong. Guide to International Recommendations on Names & Symbols for Quantities & on Units of Measurement. (Progress in Standardization: No. 2). 1975. pap. 14.40 (*92-4-068521-9*) World Health.
Lowe, D. G., ed. Histopathology Reporting. 208p. 1993. pap. 45.00 (*0-412-43040-1*) Chapman & Hall.
Lowe, Darla. Story of Adoption: Why Do I Look Different? LC 87-46273. (Illus.). (Orig.). (J). (gr. 3-6). 1987. pap. 4.95 (*0-9606090-2-4*) EastWest Pr.
Lowe, David. Lost Chicago. 1993. 16.99 (*0-517-46888-3*) Random Hse Value.
— Perceptual Organization & Visual Recognition. 176p. (C). 1995. lib. bdg. 82.00 (*0-89838-172-X*) Kluwer Ac.
— The Transport Manager's & Operator's Handbook, 1993. 23th ed. pap. text ed. write for info. (*0-7494-0772-7*, Pub. by Kogan Page Educ UK) Taylor & Francis.
Lowe, David, ed. The Great Chicago Fire in Eyewitness Accounts & Sixty-Three Contemporary Photographs & Illustrations. LC 78-73518. (Illus.). 87p. 1979. reprint ed. pap. 6.95 (*0-486-23771-0*) Dover.
Lowe, David & Richards, Jack. The Lace Heritage: A Guide to Nottingham Lace. (C). 1988. 60.00 (*0-685-30217-2*, Pub. by Lace Centre UK) St Mut.
Lowe, David & Watters, Annette. Legal Research for Educators. LC 83-63361. 48p. 1984. pap. 4.00 (*0-87367-790-0*) Phi Delta Kappa.
Lowe, David, jt. ed. see Beacham, Walton.
Lowe, David, jt. auth. see Darian-Smith, Kate.
Lowe, David, tr. see Dostoyevsky, Fyodor.
Lowe, David, ed. see Dostoyevsky, Fyodor.
Lowe, David, jt. auth. see Richard, Jack.
Lowe, David, tr. see Trifonov, Yury.
Lowe, David, et al, eds. Official World Wildlife Fund Guide to Endangered Species of North America, 2 vols., Set. LC 89-29757. (Illus.). 1258p. 1990. lib. bdg. 195.00 (*0-933833-17-2*) Beacham Pub.
Lowe, David A., ed. Critical Essays on Ivan Turgenev. (Critical Essays Ser.). 176p. 1988. text ed. 45.00 (*0-8161-8842-4*) G K Hall.
Lowe, David A., ed. see Dostoyevsky, Fyodor.
***Lowe, David J.** ENDOR & EPR of Metalloproteins. (Molecular Biology Intelligence Unit Ser.). 167p. 1995. write for info. (*1-57059-198-9*) R G Landes.
Lowe, Deborah, et al. Product Tampering: a Worldwide Problem: A Crisis Communications Tool for Newsrooms & Corporations. Ramsey, Doug & Warner, John, eds. (Illus.). 28p. 1993. pap. 7.95 (*0-910755-00-0*) Foun Am Comm.
Lowe, Diane & Davidson, Mike. One Hundred Best Balti Curries: Authentic Dishes from the Baltihouses. (Illus.). 160p. 1994. pap. 19.95 (*1-85793-221-8*, Pub. by Pavilion UK) Trafalgar.
Lowe, Don & Lowe, Roberta. Fifty Hiking Trails: Portland & Northwest Oregon. Bullard, Oral, ed. (Illus.). 128p. (Orig.). 1986. pa[illegible] (*0-911518-70-3*) Touchstone Oregon.
— The John Muir T[illegible] 75-28572. (Illus.). (Orig.). 1982. pap. 7.95 (*0-8700[illegible]*) Caxton.
— Sixty Hiking Trails, Central Oregon Cascades. Worcester, Thomas K., ed. (Illus.). 128p. (Orig.). 12.95 (*0-911518-51-7*) Touchstone Oregon.
— 35 Hiking Trails Columbia River Gorge. (Illus.). 96p. 1995. pap. 15.95 (*1-57188-010-0*) F Amato Pubns.
— Thirty Five Hiking Trails, Columbia River Gorge. 2nd ed. Bullard, Oral, ed. (Illus.). 80p. (Orig.). 1988. pap. 7.95 (*0-911518-77-0*) Touchstone Oregon.
— Thirty-Four Mountain Bike Routes, Northern Oregon Cascades. Bullard, Oral, ed. (Illus.). 80p. (Orig.). 1991. pap. 9.95 (*0-911518-82-7*) Touchstone Oregon.
Lowe, Donald M., jt. auth. see Balrow, Tani E.
Lowe, Donald R., jt. ed. see Graham, Stephan A.
***Lowe, Doug.** Approach 3 for Windows for Dummies. 1994. pap. 19.99 (*1-56884-233-3*) IDG Bks.
— CICS for the COBOL Programmer: An Advanced Course, Pt. 2. 2nd ed. LC 92-17814. 352p. 1992. 31.00 (*0-911625-67-4*) M Murach & Assoc.
— CICS for the COBOL Programmer: An Introductory Course, Pt. 1. 2nd ed. LC 92-17814. 409p. 1992. 31.00 (*0-911625-60-7*) M Murach & Assoc.
— The CICS Programmer's Desk Reference. 2nd ed. LC 92-38014. 507p. 1992. pap. 36.50 (*0-911625-68-2*) M Murach & Assoc.
— Client Server Computing for Dummies. 1995. pap. 22.99 (*1-56884-329-1*) IDG Bks.
— DOS Utilities. LC 80-84103. (Illus.). 185p. 1981. pap. 17. 50 (*0-911625-11-9*) M Murach & Assoc.
— The Least You Need to Know about DOS. 2nd ed. LC 93-17025. (Illus.). 290p. 1993. pap. 20.00 (*0-911625-76-3*) M Murach & Assoc.
— Microsoft Guide to DoubleSpace. 1993. pap. 14.95 (*1-55615-625-1*) Microsoft.
— More Word for Windows 6 for Dummies. 1994. pap. 19. 95 (*1-56884-165-5*) IDG Bks.
— MVS JCL. 2nd ed. LC 94-37779. 496p. 1994. pap. 34.50 (*0-911625-85-2*) M Murach & Assoc.
— MVS TSO Pt. 1: Concepts & ISPF. 2nd ed. LC 90-19907. 467p. 1991. pap. 31.00 (*0-911625-56-9*) M Murach & Assoc.
— MVS TSO Pt. 2: Commands & Procedures. 2nd ed. LC 90-19907. 450p. 1991. pap. 31.00 (*0-911625-57-7*) M Murach & Assoc.
— Networking for Dummies. (For Dummies Ser.). (Illus.). 350p. 1994. pap. 19.95 (*1-56884-079-9*) IDG Bks.

— The Only DOS Book You'll Ever Need. 2nd ed. LC 93-859. (Illus.). 610p. (Orig.). 1993. pap. 27.50 (*0-911625-71-2*) M Murach & Assoc.
— PowerPoint 4 for Windows for Dummies. 1994. pap. 16. 95 (*1-56884-161-2*) IDG Bks.
— QR - Memory Management for Dummies: Quick Reference. 1995. pap. 9.99 (*1-56884-362-3*) IDG Bks.
— QR-Microsoft Office 4 for Windows for Dummies. 1994. pap. 9.99 (*1-56884-958-3*) IDG Bks.
— VSAM: AMS & Application Programming. LC 86-60204. 260p. 1986. pap. 27.50 (*0-911625-33-X*) M Murach & Assoc.
— VSAM for the COBOL Programmer. 2nd ed. LC 88-60035. 187p. 1991. pap. 17.50 (*0-911625-45-3*) M Murach & Assoc.
— Word 6 for Windows for Dummies 101. 1995. pap. 24.99 (*1-56884-628-2*) IDG Bks.
Lowe, Duncan. Growing Alpines in Raised Beds Troughs & Tufa. (Illus.). 136p. 1992. 39.95 (*0-7134-7018-6*, Pub. by Batsford UK) Trafalgar.
Lowe, E. A., et al, eds. The Bobbio Missal. (Henry Bradshaw Society Ser.: No. 58, 61). (Illus.). 380p. (C). 1991. reprint ed. text ed. 90.00 (*1-870252-00-4*) Boydell & Brewer.
Lowe, E. J. Kinds of Being: A Study of Individuation, Identity & the Logic of Sortal Terms. 224p. 1989. pap. text ed. 47.95 (*0-631-16703-X*) Blackwell Pubs.
— Locke on Human Understanding. LC 94-43131. (Philosophical Guidebooks Ser.). 234p. 1995. 45.00x (*0-415-10090-9*, B7016); pap. 9.95 (*0-415-10091-7*, B7020) Routledge.
***Lowe, Ed.** Not As I Do: A Father's Report. 208p. 1995. pap. 9.95 (*0-8362-7045-2*) Andrews & McMeel.
Lowe, Ed, Jr., jt. auth. see Siegel, Stanley.
Lowe, Ed
***Lowe, Edward.** Hail Entrepreneur! An Encyclopedia of Basic Survival Skills. (Illus.). 206p. 1994. text ed. 24.00 (*0-8059-3659-9*) Dorrance.
Lowe, Elizabeth. The City in Brazilian Literature. LC 80-66823. 360p. 1982. 34.50 (*0-8386-3009-X*) Fairleigh Dickinson.
Lowe, Elizabeth, tr. see Lispector, Clarice.
Lowe, Ernest, jt. auth. see Arsham, Gary.
Lowe-Evans, Mary. Crimes Against Fecundity: Joyce & Population Control. (Irish Studies). 160p. 1989. text ed. 29.95x (*0-8156-2460-3*) Syracuse U Pr.
— Frankenstein: Mary Shelley's Wedding Guest. LC 92-41553. (Masterwork Studies: No. 126). 112p. 1993. text ed. 21.95 (*0-8057-8376-8*, Pub. by Royal Botanic Garden UK); pap. 12.95 (*0-8057-8597-3*, Pub. by Royal Botanic Garden UK) Macmillan.
Lowe, Felix C. John Ross. (Raintree-Rivilo American Indian Stories Ser.). (Illus.). 32p. (J). (gr. 3-6). 1990. lib. bdg. 19.97 (*0-8172-3407-1*); pap. 4.95 (*0-8114-4093-1*) Raintree Steck-V.
Lowe, Fonda, jt. ed. see Schopmeyer, Betty B.
Lowe, G. The Cysteine Proteinases. 1976. pap. 15.50 (*0-08-020471-6*, Pergamon Pr) Elsevier.
Lowe, G. D., et al. Fibrinogen 2: Biochemistry, Physiology & Clinical Relevance. (International Congress Ser.: Vol. 745). 1987. 92.50 (*0-444-80940-6*) Elsevier.
Lowe, Geoff, et al. Adolescent Drinking & Family Life. LC 93-19119. 1993. text ed. 38.00 (*3-7186-5413-X*); pap. text ed. 22.00 (*3-7186-5414-8*) Gordon & Breach.
Lowe, George L. B. G., Vol. 1: The Little Drummer Girl Who Drums for the Sun. (Illus.). 21p. (Orig.). (J). (ps). 1988. lib. bdg. 5.00 (*0-685-22681-6*) G L Lowe.
— Ninety Thousand Ninety-Nine: Environs of Infinity. LC 81-90003. 105p. (Orig.). 1981. pap. 4.95 (*0-686-30362-8*) G L Lowe.
Lowe, Gordon D., ed. Clinical Blood Rheology. 1988. write for info. (*0-318-62927-5*) CRC Pr.
— Clinical Blood Rheology, Vol. I. 224p. 1988. 177.00 (*0-8493-4598-7*, RB45) CRC Pr.
— Clinical Blood Rheology, Vol. II. 240p. 1988. 146.00 (*0-8493-4599-5*, RB45, CRC Reprint) Franklin.
Lowe, Graeme J., intro. Institution of Engineers, National Conference, 1990: Government, Engineering & the Nation. (Illus.). 233p. (Orig.). 1990. pap. 57.75 (*0-85825-497-2*, Pub. by Inst Engrs Aust-EA Bks AT) Accents Pubns.
Lowe, Graham, jt. ed. see Ashton, David.
Lowe, Graham S. Women in the Administrative Revolution: The Feminization of Clerical Work. 1987. 37.50 (*0-8020-2657-5*); pap. 18.95 (*0-8020-6686-0*) U of Toronto Pr.
Lowe, H. Y. The Adventures of Wu: The Life Cycle of a Peking Man. LC 82-48568. (Illus.). 512p. 1983. reprint ed. 55.00 (*0-691-06552-7*); reprint ed. pap. 15.95 (*0-691-01400-0*) Princeton U Pr.
Lowe, Harold, jt. auth. see McDonald, Anthony C.
Lowe, Harry J. & Ernst, Edward A. The Quantitative Practice of Anesthesia: Use of Closed Circuit. LC 80-21803. (Illus.). 249p. reprint ed. pap. 71.00 (*0-317-58237-2*, 2056386) Bks Demand.
Lowe, Heinz-Dietrich. The Tsars & the Jews: Reform, Reaction, & Antisemitism in Imperial Russia, 1772-1917 (Antisemitismus und Reaktion Are Utopie. LC 92-25147. (ENG & GER.). 1993. text ed. 68.00 (*3-7186-5289-7*) Gordon & Breach.
Lowe, Ian. Etchings of Wilfred Fairclugh: A Catalogue Raisonne. 112p. 1990. text ed. 93.95 (*0-85967-846-6*, Pub. by Scolar Pr UK) Ashgate Pub Co.
— Etchings of Wilfred Fairclugh: A Catalogue Raisonne. limited ed. 112p. 1990. 275.00 (*0-85967-849-0*, Pub. by Scolar Pr UK) Ashgate Pub Co.
— Our Universities Are Turning Us into the Ignorant Country. Date not set. pap. 5.00 (*0-86840-126-9*, Pub. by New South Wales Univ Pr AT) Intl Spec Bk.
Lowe, Ian, ed. Working Drawings: 1895-1938. (Illus.). 1968. pap. 1.50 (*0-89073-034-2*) Boston Public Lib.

Lowe, J. C. Reconstructing Quaternary Environments. 352p. (C). 1986. pap. text ed. 49.95 (*0-470-20533-4*) Halsted Pr.
Lowe, J. F., jt. auth. see Atkins, M. H.
Lowe, J. F., jt. auth. see Lowe, M.
Lowe, J. F., et al. Total Environmental Control: The Economics of Cross-Media Pollution Transfers. LC 82-9827. (Illus.). 134p. 1982. pap. 63.00 (*0-08-026276-7*, Pub. by Pergamon Repr UK) Franklin.
Lowe, J. J., jt. ed. see Gray, J. M.
Lowe, J. J., et al, eds. Studies in the Lateglacial of North-West Europe: Including Papers Presented at a Symposium of the Quaternary Research Association Held at University College London, January 1979. (Illus.). 215p. 1980. 88.00 (*0-08-024001-1*, Pub. by Pergamon Repr UK) Franklin.
Lowe, Jacqueline, et al. Worth Keeping: An Architectural History of Sutter & Yuba Counties, California. 168p. (Orig.). (C). 1990. pap. 18.00 (*0-9625659-0-3*) Comm Mem Mus Sutter Cnty.
Lowe, Jacques. JFK Remembered. LC 93-4181. 1993. 37.50 (*0-679-42399-0*) Random.
— Looking at Photographs - People. LC 94-26280. (Illus.). (J). (gr. 1 up). 1995. 14.95 (*0-8118-0446-1*) Chronicle Bks.
Lowe, Jacques, comp. Looking at Photographs - Animals. LC 94-10109. (J). 1995. 13.95 (*0-8118-0418-6*) Chronicle Bks.
Lowe, James. Creative Process of James Agee. LC 93-44684. (Southern Literary Studies). (Illus.). 200p. 1994. text ed. 27.50 (*0-8071-1896-6*) La State U Pr.
Lowe, James L. Lincoln Postcard Catalog. LC 73-83549. (Illus.). 144p. 1973. reprint ed. pap. 5.95 (*0-913782-05-X*) Deltiologists Am.
— Washington Postcard Catalog. LC 74-30734. (Illus.). 128p. 1986. pap. 5.95 (*0-913782-06-8*) Deltiologists Am.
Lowe, James L. & Papell, Ben, eds. Detroit Publishing Company Collector's Guide. LC 75-4127. (Illus.). 288p. 1975. pap. 12.95 (*0-913782-07-6*) Deltiologists Am.
Lowe, James N. Chemistry, Industry & the Environment. 352p. (C). 1993. pap. 40.23 (*0-697-17087-X*) Wm C Brown Pubs.
Lowe, James T. The Philosophy of Air Power. LC 84-5254. 474p. (Orig.). (C). 1984. lib. bdg. 62.00 (*0-8191-3953-X*); pap. text ed. 34.00 (*0-8191-3954-8*) U Pr of Amer.
Lowe, Jane I., jt. ed. see Austin, Michael J.
Lowe, Janet. Benjamin Graham on Value Investing. 1994. 22.95 (*0-7931-0702-4*, 560885-01) Dearborn Finan.
— The Secret Empire: How Twenty-Five Multi-Nationals Rule the World. 335p. 1992. 27.50 (*1-55623-513-5*) Irwin Prof Pubng.
Lowe, Janet, jt. auth. see Weiss, Geraldine.
Lowe, Janet C. Keys to Investing in International Stocks. 1992. pap. 4.95 (*0-8120-4759-1*) Barron.
Lowe, Jennifer, ed. see Braider, Jackson.
Lowe, Jim. Mountain Boys Are Free: Portrait of Ned Guthrie, the Musicians' Abraham Lincoln. (Illus.). 160p. (Orig.). 1993. pap. write for info. (*0-9635197-0-0*) J G Lowe.
Lowe, Jimmy. Jesse Stuart: the Boy from the Dark Hills: A Boyography. Herndon, Jerry A. & Charles, Chuck D., eds. LC 90-62199. (Jesse Stuart Foundation Juvenile Ser.). (Illus.). 79p. (YA). (gr. 4-12). 1990. pap. text ed. 15.00 (*0-945084-19-6*) J Stuart Found.
Lowe, John. The Great Powers, Imperialism, & the German Problem, 1865-1925. LC 93-36394. (Illus.). 272p. 1994. 59.95x (*0-415-10443-2*, B3737, Routledge NY); pap. 16. 95 (*0-415-10444-0*, B3741, Routledge NY) Routledge.
— Jump at the Sun: Zora Neale Hurston's Cosmic Comedy. LC 94-10586. 1994. write for info. (*0-252-02110-X*) U of Ill Pr.
***Lowe, John, ed.** Conversations with Ernest Gaines. (Literary Conversations Ser.). 240p. 1995. text ed. 37.50 (*0-87805-782-X*) U Pr of Miss.
— Conversations with Ernest Gaines. (Literary Conversations Ser.). 240p. 1995. pap. 15.95 (*0-87805-783-8*) U Pr of Miss.
Lowe, John, jt. auth. see George, Steve.
Lowe, John B., jt. auth. see LaPolla, Randy J.
Lowe, John C. Spasm: Why Your Body Is Painfully Tight & How You Can Loosen It for Good. (Illus.). 175p. (Orig.). 1983. pap. text ed. 15.00 (*0-914609-00-9*) McDowell Pub Co.
Lowe, John P. Quantum Chemistry. 2nd ed. (Illus.). 711p. 1993. text ed. 59.95 (*0-12-457555-2*) Acad Pr.
Lowe, John S. Oil & Gas Law in a Nutshell. 2nd ed. (Nutshell Ser.). 465p. (C). 1993. reprint ed. pap. text ed. 18.50 (*0-314-39781-7*) West Pub.
— Oil & Gas Law in a Nutshell. 3rd ed. (Nutshell Ser.). 444p. (C). Date not set. pap. text ed. write for info. (*0-314-06415-X*) West Pub.
Lowe, Joseph. A New Most Excellent Dancing Master: The Journal of Joseph Lowe's Visits to Balmoral & Windsor (1852-1860) to Teach Dance to the Family of Queen Victoria. Thomas, Allan, ed. LC 92-13521. (Dance & Music Ser.: No. 5). 150p. 1992. lib. bdg. 32.00 (*0-945193-30-0*) Pendragon NY.
— Present State of England in Regard to Agriculture, Trade & Finance. 2nd ed. LC 66-21682. (Reprints of Economic Classics Ser.). 1967. reprint ed. 57.50 (*0-678-00320-3*) Kelley.
***Lowe, Joseph D.** A Catalog of the Official Gazeteers of China in the University of Washington (Seattle) expanded rev. ed. (Illus.). xiv, 121p. 1994. pap. 25.00 (*0-930325-31-1*) Lowe Pub.
— The Changing Scenes of the United States Defense: Essays on National Security. LC 90-91734. (Illus.). xiv, 186p. 1982. reprint ed. pap. 36.00 (*0-9605506-5-8*) Lowe Pub.

An Asterisk (*) at the beginning of an entry indicates that the title is appearing in BIP for the first time.

— China's Cultural Development: From the Earliest Dynasties to the Present Day. LC 90-91679. (Illus.). xxiv, 565p. 1994. text ed. 90.00 (*0-930325-15-X*) Lowe Pub.

— China's Foreign Relations Conducted by the Warlords: 1916-1928. LC 88-91012. (Illus.). xii, 52p. 1991. 15.00 (*0-930325-05-2*) Lowe Pub.

— Chinese Language for Beginners with Exercises in Writing & Speaking. LC 90-91682. (Illus.). xxviii, 660p. 1994. text ed. 108.00 (*0-930325-01-X*) Lowe Pub.

— The Concept & Practice of International Law During the Period of the Warring States: 403-221 B.C. LC 88-91011. (Illus.). xi, 42p. 1994. 16.00 (*0-930325-04-4*) Lowe Pub.

— Dictionary of Diplomatic, International Law, International Relations Terms. limited ed. LC 92-90084. (Illus.). 800p. (CHI & ENG.). 1994. pap. 130.00 (*0-930325-22-2*) Lowe Pub.

— Dictionary of Military Law: Chinese-English, English-Chinese. LC 83-83213. (Illus.). xiv, 775p. 1994. 130.00 (*0-9605506-6-6*) Lowe Pub.

— Dictionary of Military Law, Chinese & English. 750p. (CHI & ENG.). 1987. 175.00 (*0-8288-0973-9*, M8721) Fr & Eur.

— Dictionary of Military Terms & Military Intelligence Phrases: Chinese-English & English-Chinese. limited ed. LC 88-91316. (Illus.). 725p. (CHI & ENG.). 1994. 130.00 (*0-930325-11-7*) Lowe Pub.

— Dictionary of Political Terms: Chinese-English, English-Chinese. LC 80-85163. (Illus.). 1250p. (CHI & ENG.). 1994. 160.00 (*0-9605506-0-7*) Lowe Pub.

— How the Two Chinas (PRC & ROC) Have Been Governed? (Illus.). xxiii, 225p. 1994. pap. 38.00 (*0-930325-32-X*) Lowe Pub.

— International Relations in Ancient China. LC 88-91010. (Illus.). xii, 42p. 1994. pap. 16.00 (*0-930325-03-6*) Lowe Pub.

— International System of the Warring States in Ancient China: 403-221 B.C. (Illus.). xxviii, 270p. 1994. pap. 45.00 (*0-930325-29-X*) Lowe Pub.

— Li Ssu's Contributions to the Founding of China's First Empire. LC 88-91009. (Illus.). xii, 42p. 1994. pap. 16.00 (*0-930325-02-8*) Lowe Pub.

— Major Problems in China's Foreign Relations Since 1840. (Illus.). xxxii, 180p. 1994. pap. 35.00 (*0-930325-30-3*) Lowe Pub.

— Map Collection of Geopolitical & Strategic Maps: A Set of 10 Raised Relief Topographic Maps (Approx. 24" x 36") Covering the Entire Region of Japan, etc. Bilingual with Commentaries. limited ed. (Illus.). 35p. 1994. 240.00 (*0-930325-23-0*) Lowe Pub.

— Map Collection of Geopolitical & Strategic Maps: A Set of 13 Raised Relief Topographic Maps (Approx. 24" x 36") on Europe Covering Austria, Belgium, Germany, Greece, Hungary, Ireland, Italy, Russia, etc. with Commentaries. limited ed. (Illus.). 38p. 1994. 300.00 (*0-930325-26-5*) Lowe Pub.

— Map Collection of Geopolitical & Strategic Maps: A Set of 16 Raised Relief Topographic Maps (Approx. 24" x 36") Covering the Entire Region of Vietnam (S & N), Burma, Indo-China, Indonesia, Malaysia, Singapore, etc. with Commentaries. limited ed. (Illus.). 41p. 1994. 370.00 (*0-930325-25-7*) Lowe Pub.

— Map Collection of Geopolitical & Strategic Maps: A Set of 2 Raised Relief Topographic Maps. (Illus.). 27p. 1994. 40.00 (*0-930325-18-4*) Lowe Pub.

— Map Collection of Geopolitical & Strategic Maps: A Set of 2 Raised Relief Topographic Maps. limited ed. (Illus.). 27p. 1994. 50.00 (*0-930325-24-9*) Lowe Pub.

— Map Collection of Geopolitical & Strategic Maps: A Set of 20 Raised Relief Topographic Maps. (Illus.). 98p. Date not set. 580.00 (*0-930325-28-1*) Lowe Pub.

— Map Collection of Geopolitical & Strategic Maps: A Set of 3 Raised Relief Topographic Maps (Approx. 24" x 36"0 Covering the Entire Region of North Africa with Commentaries. limited ed. (Illus.). 28p. 1994. 80.00 (*0-930325-20-6*) Lowe Pub.

— Map Collection of Geopolitical & Strategic Maps: A Set of 4 Raised Relief Topograhic Maps. (Illus.). 36p. 1994. 80.00 (*0-930325-27-3*) Lowe Pub.

— Map Collection of Geopolitical & Strategic Maps: A Set of 4 Raised Relief Topographic Maps (Approx. 24" x 36") Covering the Hawaiian Islands with Commentaries. limited ed. (Illus.). 36p. 1994. 105.00 (*0-614-06298-5*) Lowe Pub.

— Map Collection of Geopolitical & Strategic Maps: A Set of 7 Relief Topographic Maps (Approx. 24" x 36") Covering the Entire Middle East, with Commentaries. limited ed. (Illus.). 32p. 1994. 170.00 (*0-930325-19-2*) Lowe Pub.

— Map Collection of Geopolitical & Strategic Maps: A Set of 8 Raised Relief Topographic Maps (Approx. 24" x 36") on China (PRC, i. e. the Chinese Communist Regime on the Mainland China) Bilingual with Commentaries. limited ed. (Illus.). 33p. 1994. 195.00 (*0-930325-21-4*) Lowe Pub.

— Map Collection of Geopolitical & Strategic Maps: 5 Raised Relief Topographic Maps. (Illus.). 30p. 1994. 100.00 (*0-930325-17-6*) Lowe Pub.

— Map Collection on Asian Studies: 187 Maps Specially Designed for Briefing & Lecturing. LC 88-91060. (Illus.). xvi, 395p. 1994. 90.00 (*0-930325-08-7*) Lowe Pub.

— Map Collection on International Relations: 221 Maps Specially Designed for Briefing & Lecturing. LC 88-91061. (Illus.). xviii, 465p. 1994. 100.00 (*0-930325-09-5*) Lowe Pub.

— The North Atlantic Treaty Organization vs. the Warsaw Pact Military Alliance - a Geopolitical Struggle: Essays on National Security. LC 89-91186. (Illus.). 325p. 1994. 66.00 (*0-930325-13-3*) Lowe Pub.

— The Role Played by the American Political Scientists in the Supreme Command for the Allied Powers: The Purge Program: Why & How Japan Invaded China & the United States, & Why & How Japan Was Defeated & Occupied. LC 90-91738. (Illus.). xii, 201p. 1982. reprint ed. pap. 36.00 (*0-9605506-3-1*) Lowe Pub.

— The Role Played by the Ch'in Army: With Emphasis on Political & Legal Aspects. LC 90-91739. (Illus.). iii, 24p. 1976. reprint ed. pap. 16.00 (*0-9605506-7-4*) Lowe Pub.

— The Sino-American Foreign Policy & Relations since World War II. LC 88-91014. (Illus.). xii, 125p. 1994. pap. 30.00 (*0-930325-07-9*) Lowe Pub.

— Sino-Japanese Relations since 1894. LC 89-91187. (Illus.). xxxii, 375p. 1994. 80.00 (*0-930325-14-1*) Lowe Pub.

— The Sino-Soviet Relations: Nineteen Seventeen to Nineteen Forty-Nine; with Emphasis on the Early Period. LC 88-91013. (Illus.). xiv, 55p. 1994. pap. 22.00 (*0-930325-06-0*) Lowe Pub.

— Spy System of Soviet Russia: From Their Very Beginning to the Present Day. LC 90-91681. (Illus.). xxvi, 560p. 1994. text ed. 90.00 (*0-930325-16-8*) Lowe Pub.

— A Study on the Library Resources at the Military Institutions in Japan, the United States, England, France, Belgium, the Netherlands, Germany, & Switzerland. LC 90-91743. iii, 28p. 1973. reprint ed. pap. 10.00 (*0-9605506-1-5*) Lowe Pub.

— The Superpower Triumvirs - The United States Faces China & Russia since World War II: Their Geopolitical Intentions & Military Capabilities: Essays on National Security. LC 89-91185. (Illus.). xxv, 325p. 1994. 75.00 (*0-930325-12-5*) Lowe Pub.

— The Traditional Chinese Legal Thought: The Pre-Ch'in Period. LC 84-80994. (Illus.). 101p. 1984. pap. 30.00 (*0-9605506-8-2*) Lowe Pub.

— Translation & Interpretation in Principle & Practice: From English into Chinese & from Chinese into English. LC 88-90988. (Illus.). xviii, 475p. 1994. 90.00 (*0-930325-00-1*) Lowe Pub.

— The Yellow River Valley: A Geopolitical Appraisal. LC 90-91744. (Illus.). vii, 46p. 1982. reprint ed. pap. 20.00 (*0-9605506-4-X*) Lowe Pub.

Lowe, Julian & Crawford, Hick. Innovation & Technology Transfer for the Growing Firm: Text & Cases. LC 84-11180. 1984. text ed. 103.00 (*0-08-030228-9*, Pub. by Pergamon Repr UK) Franklin.

Lowe, K. C., ed. Blood Substitutes: Preparation Physiology & Medical Applications. LC 88-8358. (Ellis Horwood Series in Biomedicine). 187p. 1988. lib. bdg. 140.00 (*0-89573-578-4*) VCH Pubs.

Lowe, K. J. Church & Politics in Renaissance Italy: The Life & Career of Cardinal Francesco Soderini, 1453-1524. LC 92-33576. (Studies in Italian History & Culture). (Illus.). 308p. (C). 1993. 59.95 (*0-521-42103-9*) Cambridge U Pr.

Lowe, K. J., jt. ed. see Dean, Trevor.

Lowe, Kenneth S., ed. Michigan Out-of-Doors: An Almanac in Pictures, Prose, & Poetry. (Illus.). 156p. 1991. 34.95 (*0-933112-15-7*) Mich United Conserv.

Lowe, L. & Woodroffe, W. Consumer Law & Practice. 425p. (C). 1985. 180.00 (*0-685-39831-5*, Inst Pur & Supply) St Mut.

Lowe, L. F. & De Montreuil, Gerbert. Gerard de Nevers, a Study of the Prose Version of the Roman de la Violette ou, Gerat de Nevers. (Elliot Monographs in Romance Languages: Vol. 22). 1928. 20.00 (*0-527-02616-6*) Periodicals Srv.

Lowe, Larry. Applied Exercises for Fundamentals of Public Speaking. 2nd ed. 160p. (C). 1994. per., pap. text ed. 20.95 (*0-8403-9246-X*) Kendall-Hunt.

Lowe, Larry V. Applied Exercises for Fundamentals of Public Speaking. 2nd ed. 160p. 1992. 19.95 (*0-8403-8186-7*) Kendall-Hunt.

Lowe, Lisa. Critical Terrains: French & British Orientalisms. LC 91-55058. 232p. 1991. 34.50 (*0-8014-2579-4*) Cornell U Pr.

— Critical Terrains: French & British Orientalisms. 232p. 1994. pap. 12.95 (*0-8014-8195-3*) Cornell U Pr.

Lowe, M. & Lowe, J. F. Teaching Foreign Languages to Adults: A Symposium. LC 65-21905. 1965. 80.00 (*0-08-010971-3*, Pub. by Pergamon Repr UK) Franklin.

Lowe, M. J., et al. Elliott - The South African Notary. 6th ed. 411p. 1987. 72.00 (*0-7021-1980-6*, Pub. by Juta SA) W W Gaunt.

Lowe, Malcolm G. The Mulready Advertisements. (Illus.). lib. bdg. 45.00 (*0-911451-00-5*) Mulready Res.

Lowe, Malcolm V. Bombers. (Modern Military Techniques Ser.). (Illus.). 48p. (J). (gr. 5 up). 1987. pap. 4.95 (*0-8225-9541-9*, Lerner Publctns) Lerner Group.

— Bombers. (Modern Military Techniques Ser.). (Illus.). 48p. (YA). (gr. 5 up). 1987. lib. bdg. 14.95 (*0-8225-1381-1*, Lerner Publctns) Lerner Group.

— Fighters. LC 84-7941. (Modern Military Techniques Ser.). (Illus.). 48p. (J). (gr. 5 up). 1985. pap. 4.95 (*0-8225-9506-0*, Lerner Publctns) Lerner Group.

— Fighters. LC 84-7941. (Modern Military Techniques Ser.). (Illus.). 48p. (YA). (gr. 5 up). 1985. lib. bdg. 14.95 (*0-8225-1376-5*, Lerner Publctns) Lerner Group.

Lowe, Marcia D. Alternatives to the Automobile. 70p. (Orig.). 1990. pap. 5.00 (*0-916468-99-2*) Worldwatch Inst.

— The Bicycle: Vehicle for a Small Planet. (Orig.). (C). 1989. pap. write for info. (*0-916468-91-7*) Worldwatch Inst.

— Shaping Cities: The Environmental & Human Dimensions. 70p. (Orig.). 1991. pap. 5.00 (*1-878071-06-8*) Worldwatch Inst.

Lowe, Marian & Hubbard, Ruth. Woman's Nature: Rationalizations of Inequality. (Athene Ser.). 140p. 1983. text ed. 50.00 (*0-08-030143-6*, Pergamon Pr); pap. text ed. 19.95 (*0-08-030142-8*, Pergamon Pr) Elsevier.

— Woman's Nature: Rationalizations of Inequality. LC 83-4066. (Athene Ser.). (Illus.). 169p. 1983. reprint ed. pap. 48.20 (*0-7837-6797-8*, 2046629) Bks Demand.

Lowe, Marjorie. Jess. large type ed. 464p. 1985. 15.95 (*0-7089-1380-6*) Ulverscroft.

Lowe, Mark, ed. see Buttram, Nora.

Lowe, Mark, jt. auth. see Franklin, Denise.

***Lowe, Mary E.** How to Prepare for the ExCet - Examination for the Certification of Educators in Texas. 1995. student ed., pap. 12.95 (*0-8120-1774-9*) Barron.

Lowe, Maurice. The Sculpture of Maurice Lowe: Selected Works, 1956-1990. LC 91-60772. (Illus.). 110p. (Orig.). 1991. pap. text ed. 24.95 (*0-9629150-0-9*, U of Pa Pr) M Lowe.

Lowe-McConnell, R. H. Ecological Studies in Tropical Fish Communities. (Cambridge Tropical Biology Ser.). 300p. 1987. pap. 29.95 (*0-521-28064-8*) Cambridge U Pr.

Lowe-McConnell, R. H., jt. ed. see Le Cren, E. D.

Lowe-McConnell, R. H., et al. Symposium on Resource Use & Conservation of the African Great Lakes, Bujumbara, 1989. (International Association of Theoretical & Applied Limnology Communications Ser.: No. 23). (Illus.). 128p. 1992. pap. text ed. 44.30 (*3-510-52023-8*, Pub. by E Schweizerbartsche GW) Lubrecht & Cramer.

Lowe, Melissa, ed. see White, Tonee.

Lowe, Michael, et al. Early Childhood Teacher's Activities Handbook: A Resource Recipe for Early Childhood Learning Programs. 160p. 1981. pap. 9.95 (*0-685-03848-3*) P-H.

Lowe, Michael. Everyday Life in Early Imperial China. (Dorset Press Reprints Ser.). (Illus.). 256p. 1988. 16.95 (*0-88029-177-X*) Dorset Pr.

Lowe, Michelle, jt. auth. see Gregson, Nicky.

Lowe, Morgan. Risque Rhymes Naughty Poetry. 1994. pap. 20.00 (*0-685-72626-6*) Moonlite Pubng.

Lowe, N. & Hensby, C., eds. Nonsteroidal Anti-Inflammatory Drugs. (Pharmacology & the Skin Ser.: Vol. 2). (Illus.). x, 158p. 1989. 119.25 (*3-8055-4898-2*) S Karger.

Lowe, N. J., jt. ed. see Maibach, H. I.

Lowe, Nicholas. Physician's Guide to Sunscreens. 232p. 1991. 75.00 (*0-8247-8496-0*) Dekker.

***Lowe, Nicholas & Marks, Ronald.** Retinoids: A Clinician's Guide. 1995. 75.00 (*0-614-06222-5*); 75.00 (*0-614-07390-1*, M Dunitz) Scovill Paterson.

Lowe, Nicholas J. Managing Your Psoriasis. 1993. 17.95 (*0-942361-84-9*); pap. 10.95 (*0-942361-83-0*) MasterMedia Ltd.

Lowe, Nicholas J., ed. Practical Psoriasis Therapy. 2nd ed. LC 92-49243. 311p. 1992. pap. 63.00 (*0-8016-7181-7*) Mosby Yr Bk.

Lowe, Nicholas J., ed. see Leppard, Barbara & Ashton, Richard.

***Lowe, Nigel & Suffrin, Brenda.** Law of Contempt. 3rd ed. 562p. 1995. boxed write for info. (*0-406-02677-7*, UK) Butterworth Legal Pubs.

Lowe, P. Responding to Adolescent Needs: A Pastoral Care Approach. Mittler, Peter, ed. (Special Needs in Ordinary Schools Ser.). 192p. 1988. pap. text ed. 22.50 (*0-304-31453-6*) Cassell.

Lowe, Paul G. The Experiment Is Over. 272p. (Orig.). 1989. pap. 11.95 (*0-924239-00-X*) Roxmillion Pubns.

Lowe, Paula C. CarePooling: How to Get the Help You Need to Care for the Ones You Love. LC 93-26746. 320p. (Orig.). 1993. pap. 14.95 (*1-881052-16-8*) Berrett-Koehler.

***Lowe, Paula C. & Ferraro, Richard F.** Dolphin KidKit, Set. (Dolphin KidKit Ser.). 30p. (J). (ps-3). 1994. audio, pap. 16.00 (*1-886476-00-4*) BigEye.

— Dolphin KidKit: Discovery Edition, Set. (Dolphin KidKit Ser.). 50p. (J). (gr. 2-7). 1994. audio, pap. 16.00 (*1-886476-01-2*) BigEye.

Lowe, Percival G. Five Years a Dragoon ('49-'54) And Other Adventures on the Great Plains. LC 65-11223. (Illus.). 384p. 1991. pap. 14.95 (*0-8061-1089-9*) U of Okla Pr.

Lowe, Peter. Animal Powered Systems: An Alternative Approach to Agricultural Mechanization. (GATE Ser.). (Illus.). 60p. 1986. pap. 12.00 (*3-528-02023-7*, Pub. by Vieweg & Sohn GW) Ballen Bkslr.

— Britain in the Far East: A Survey from 1819 to the Present. LC 79-42619. 272p. reprint ed. pap. 77.60 (*0-8357-6044-8*, 2034486) Bks Demand.

— The Origins of the Korean War. (Origins of Modern Wars Ser.). 256p. (Orig.). (C). 1986. pap. text ed. 21.95 (*0-582-49278-5*, 73560) Longman.

— Western Interactions with Japan: Expansion, the Armed Forces & Readjustment, 1859-1956. (C). 1990. pap. 25.00 (*0-904404-84-6*, Pub. by Paul Norbury Pubns UK) Humanities.

Lowe, Peter, jt. ed. see Fraser, T. G.

Lowe, Phil. Presentation Skills: Trainer's Guide. LC 94-13299. (McGraw-Hill One-Day Workshop Ser.). 1994. text ed. 99.95 (*0-07-038852-0*) McGraw.

Lowe, Phil & Lewis, Ralph. Management Development Beyond the Fringe: A Practical Guide to Alternative Approaches. 192p. (Orig.). 1994. pap. text ed. 32.95 (*0-89397-397-1*) Nichols Pub.

Lowe-Porter, H. T., tr. see Mann, Thomas.

Lowe-Porter, Helen T., tr. see Frank, Bruno.

Lowe-Porter, Helen T., tr. see Mann, Thomas.

Lowe, R. W. A Bibliographical Account of English Theatrical Literature from Earliest Times to the Present Day. 1972. 59.95 (*0-87968-735-5*) Gordon Pr.

Lowe, R. W., ed. see Cibber, Colley.

Lowe, R. W., ed. see Doran, John.

Lowe, Ric. Successful Instructional Diagrams. (Educational & Training Technology Ser.). 160p. 1993. pap. 32.00 (*0-7494-0711-5*, Pub. by Kogan Page Educ UK) Taylor & Francis.

Lowe, Richard. Republicans & Reconstruction in Virginia, 1856-1870. (C). 1991. text ed. 35.00 (*0-8139-1306-3*) U Pr of Va.

Lowe, Richard C. & Bearup, George F. Michigan Revocable Grantor Trusts. LC 90-85064. 1991. ring bd. 95.00 (*0-685-47729-0*) U MI Law CLE.

— Michigan Revocable Grantor Trusts. suppl. ed. LC 90-85064. 1992. 40.00 (*0-685-58921-8*, 92-010) U MI Law CLE.

— Michigan Revocable Grantor Trusts. suppl. ed. LC 90-85064. 1993. disk 55.00 (*0-685-58922-6*, 93-012) U MI Law CLE.

Lowe, Richard G. & Campbell, Randolph B. Planters & Plain Folk: Agriculture in Antebellum Texas. LC 85-27844. 240p. 1987. 22.50 (*0-87074-212-4*) SMU Press.

Lowe, Robert. Judicial Workload Allocation: Study of the Monroe County (IN) Unified Circuit Court. 62p. 1992. 4.00 (*0-685-64937-7*, NERO-264) Natl Ctr St Courts.

Lowe, Robert & Adams, Lorraine. Michigan Community Dispute Resolution Program, Supreme Court of Michigan, State Court Administrative Office. 55p. 1989. 3.00 (*0-685-34854-7*, NERO-237) Natl Ctr St Courts.

Lowe, Robert & Steelman, David. A Literature Search & Analysis of Evaluations of Alternative Court Reporting Technologies. 159p. 1988. 10.00 (*0-685-33605-0*, NERO-225) Natl Ctr St Courts.

Lowe, Robert & Walker, Linda. Assessment of the Massachusetts Motor Vehicle Tort Litigation Case Evaluation Program. 61p. 1992. 4.00 (*0-685-55349-3*, NERO255) Natl Ctr St Courts.

Lowe, Robert, jt. auth. see Adams, Lorraine.

Lowe, Robert, ed. see Hazlitt, William.

Lowe, Robert, jt. auth. see Levy, Jill.

Lowe, Robert, et al. Brockton District Court Automation Requirements Analysis. 138p. 1989. 8.00 (*0-685-33609-3*, NERO-231) Natl Ctr St Courts.

— Dayton (OH) Municipal Court Automation Requirements Analysis. 202p. 1990. 12.00 (*0-685-38113-7*, NERO-241) Natl Ctr St Courts.

— Middlesex Multi-Door Courthouse Evaluation Project: Final Report. 272p. 1992. 16.50 (*0-685-64932-6*, NERO-262) Natl Ctr St Courts.

Lowe, Robert C. Louisiana Divorce. LC 83-82099. (Louisiana Practice Systems Library). 1984. ring bd. 120.00 (*0-317-00651-7*) Lawyers Cooperative.

— Louisiana Divorce. suppl. ed. LC 83-82099. (Louisiana Practice Systems Library). 1993. Suppl. 1993. 70.00 (*0-317-03231-3*) Lawyers Cooperative.

— State Public Welfare Legislation. LC 75-165602. (Research Monograph Ser.: Vol. 20). 1971. reprint ed. lib. bdg. 49.50 (*0-306-70352-1*) Da Capo.

Lowe, Robert E. West of the Scioto. (Illus.). 210p. (Orig.). 1993. pap. text ed. write for info. (*1-878455-05-2*) Markas Pub.

Lowe, Robert G. My Own Two Feet. Hill, Thelma L., ed. 110p. (Orig.). 1994. pap. text ed. 10.00 (*1-878455-10-9*) Markas Pub.

Lowe, Robert J. ALPHA (Assessment Link Between Phonology & Articulation) Test. 1986. 54.95 (*1-55999-011-2*) LinguiSystems.

— ALPHA Test (Assessment Link Between Phonology & Articulation) 1986. 36.00 (*1-55999-012-0*) LinguiSystems.

— Phonology: Applications to Assessment & Intervention. (Illus.). 272p. 1994. 32.00 (*0-683-05205-5*) Williams & Wilkins.

— Speech Language Pathology & Related Professions in the Schools. 250p. (C). 1992. text ed. 48.00 (*0-205-13499-8*) Allyn.

— Workbook for the Identification of Phonological Processes. Blosser, Jean, ed. 58p. (C). 1989. pap. text ed. 13.00 (*0-89079-468-5*, 3458) PRO-ED.

Lowe, Robert J., ed. Speech-Language Pathology & Related Professions. 304p. Date not set. write for info. (*0-318-71715-8*) Allyn.

Lowe, Robert W. Thomas Betterton. LC 77-144652. reprint ed. 16.45 (*0-404-04038-1*) AMS Pr.

Lowe, Roberta, jt. auth. see Lowe, Don.

Lowe, Ronnie W. Man's Greatest Questions. 1993. pap. 6.50 (*0-89137-132-X*) Quality Pubns.

Lowe, Roy. Education in the Post-War Years: A Social History, 1945-1964. 224p. (C). 1988. lib. bdg. 55.00 (*0-415-00592-2*) Routledge.

Lowe, Roy, ed. The Changing Primary School, Vol. 16. (Contemporary Analysis in Education Ser.). 200p. 1987. 65.00 (*1-85000-188-X*, Falmer Pr); pap. 33.00 (*1-85000-189-8*, Falmer Pr) Taylor & Francis.

— The Changing Secondary School. 240p. 1989. 65.00 (*1-85000-555-9*, Falmer Pr); pap. 33.00 (*1-85000-556-7*, Falmer Pr) Taylor & Francis.

— Education & the Second World War: Studies in Schooling & Social Change. 224p. 1992. 80.00 (*0-7507-0054-8*, Falmer Pr); pap. 29.00 (*0-7507-0055-6*, Falmer Pr) Taylor & Francis.

Lowe, Roy W., jt. auth. see Bayer, Range D.

***Lowe, Ruby H.** Lili'uokalani. (Intermediate Reading Program Ser.). (Illus.). 111p. (Orig.). (J). (gr. 3-7). 1993. pap. 7.95 (*0-87366-018-8*) Kamehameha Schools.

— O Lili'uokalani. Pau, Hannah H., ed. Walk, Kamoa'elehua, tr. (Illus.). 111p. (Orig.). (HAW.). (YA). (gr. 7-12). 1994. pap. 7.95 (*0-87336-027-3*) Kamehameha Schools.

Lowe, S. & Ince, A. Taking Over. large type ed. 1990. 21.95 (*0-7089-2307-0*) Ulverscroft.

Lowe, Sarah M. Frida Kahlo. (Women Artists Ser.). (Illus.). 128p. (Orig.). 1991. pap. 14.95 (*0-87663-607-5*) Universe.

***Lowe, Sarah M. & Philadelphia Museum of Art Staff.** Tina Modotti: Photographer. LC 95-889. 1995. write for info. (*0-8109-4280-1*) Abrams.

Lowe, Sarah M., jt. auth. see Millstein, Barbara H.

Lowe, Scott. Mo Tzu's Religious Blueprint for a Chinese Utopia: The Will & the Way. LC 92-4366. 200p. 1992. lib. bdg. 79.95 (*0-7734-9490-1*) E Mellen.

Lowe, Shirley & Ince, Angela. Shaping Up. 256p. 1992. 24.95 (*0-340-52830-3*, Pub. by H & S UK) Trafalgar.

— Swapping. 240p. 1988. 17.95 (*0-316-53381-5*) Little.

Lowe, Sigmund. Seventy Steps Toward Wisdom. 2nd ed. 95p. 1981. pap. 3.50 (*0-87516-050-6*) DeVorss.

Lowe, Stephen. Divine Gossip & Tibetan Inroads. (Methuen New Theatrescripts Ser.). 136p. (Orig.). (C). 1989. pap. 9.95 (*0-413-61220-1*, A0371, Pub. by Methuen UK) Heinemann.

— The Kid on the Sandlot: Congress & Professional Sports, 1910-1992. LC 94-79195. 1995. 34.95 (*0-87972-675-X*); pap. 15.95 (*0-87972-676-8*) Bowling Green Univ.

— Touched. (Methuen Modern Plays Ser.). 80p. (C). 1989. reprint ed. pap. 8.95 (*0-413-61210-4*, A0372, Pub. by Methuen UK) Heinemann.

Lowe, Stephen, ed. Peace Plays. (Methuen Theatrescripts Ser.). 135p. 1988. pap. 8.95 (*0-413-56000-7*, A0206, Pub. by Methuen UK) Heinemann.

Lowe, Stephen, jt. auth. see Robinson, J. F.

Lowe, Stephen, ed. see Stayton, Richard, et al.

Lowe, Steve, ed. see Columbus, Christopher.

Lowe, Stuart. Urban Social Movements: The City after Castells. LC 85-22301. 240p. 1986. text ed. 32.50 (*0-312-83470-5*) St Martin.

Lowe, Stuart & Hughes, David, eds. A New Century of Social Housing. 1991. text ed. 59.00 (*0-7185-1353-3*, Pub. by Pinter Pubs UK) St Martin.

Lowe, Sue D. Stieglitz: A Memoir-Biography. (Illus.). 419p. 1983. 25.50 (*0-374-26990-4*) FS&G.

Lowe, Sue D., et al. Ten Minutes Ahead of the Rest of the World. 2nd rev. ed. LC 81-81534. (Illus.). 308p. 1988. reprint ed. 30.00 (*0-9607742-0-3*) Milford Hist Soc.

Lowe, Sue J., jt. auth. see Graham, John.

Lowe, T. Physics for TEC Level: Level Eleven. (C). 1983. text ed. 80.00 (*0-85950-315-1*, Pub. by S Thornes Pubs UK) St Mut.

Lowe, T., et al, eds. Modeling the Deformation of Crystalline Solids. (Illus.). 650p. 1991. 142.00 (*0-87339-136-5*, 431) Minerals Metals.

Lowe, T. L. & Rounce, J. F. Calculations for A-Level Physics. 352p. (C). 1988. pap. 79.00 (*0-85950-144-2*, Pub. by S Thornes Pubs UK) St Mut.

— Calculations for A-Level Physics. 2nd ed. 452p. (C). 1994. pap. 33.00x (*0-7478-1452-X*, Pub. by S Thornes Pubs UK) St Mut.

Lowe, Ted. Snooker. (EP Sports Ser.). (Illus.). 1977. 6.95 (*0-7158-0585-1*) Charles River Bks.

Lowe, Terry C., ed. see Minerals, Metals & Materials Society Staff.

Lowe, Thomas. Adoptive Masonry. 6.00 (*0-685-19462-0*) Powner.

Lowe, Truman. Streams: Catalogue for the Exhibition. (Illus.). 24p. (Orig.). 1991. pap. write for info. (*0-9621886-1-1*) Univ Wl Art Gal.

***Lowe, Vaughan & Fitzmaurice, Malgosia, eds.** Fifty Years of the International Court of Justice: Essays in Honour of Sir Robert Jennings. (Illus.). 400p. (C). 1995. write for info. (*0-521-55093-9*) Cambridge U Pr.

Lowe, Vaughan, jt. ed. see Warbrick, Colin.

Lowe, Vicki & Howell, Lou. How Do We Know They Know? Alternative Assessments in Home Economics. 1994. 8.00 (*0-911365-35-4*, A261-08484) Home Econ Educ.

Lowe, Victor. Alfred North Whitehead: The Man & His Work, Vol. II; 1910-1917. 1990. 39.95 (*0-8018-3960-2*) Johns Hopkins.

— Alfred North Whitehead: The Man & His Work, Vol. 1: 1861-1910. LC 84-15467. 392p. 1985. 39.95 (*0-8018-2488-5*) Johns Hopkins.

Lowe, Victor, et al. Whitehead & the Modern World: Science, Metaphysics, & Civilization. LC 72-5738. (Essay Index Reprint Ser.). 1977. reprint ed. 18.95 (*0-8369-7281-3*) Ayer.

Lowe, Virginia, jt. auth. see Bliss, Pamela.

Lowe, W. D. Herodotus: The Wars of Greece & Persia. (Illus.). (C). 1984. reprint ed. pap. 10.00 (*0-86516-054-6*) Bolchazy-Carducci.

Lowe, W. D. & Freeman, C. E., eds. Rome & Her Kings: Extracts from Livy I. (Textbook Ser.). 110p. 1981. pap. text ed. 10.00 (*0-86516-000-7*) Bolchazy-Carducci.

Lowe, W. J. The Irish in Mid-Victorian Lancashire: The Shaping of a Working-Class Community. (American University Studies: History: Ser. IX, Vol. 77). 234p. (C). 1989. text ed. 46.50 (*0-8204-0999-5*) P Lang Pubs.

Lowe, Walter. Evil & the Unconscious. LC 82-19147. (American Academy of Religion, Studies in Religion). 142p. (C). 1983. 24.95 (*0-89130-600-5*, 01 00 30) Scholars Pr GA.

— Theology & Difference: The Wound of Reason. LC 92-26531. (Indiana Series in the Philosophy of Religion). 224p. 1993. 29.95 (*0-253-33611-2*) Ind U Pr.

Lowe, William C. Blessings of Liberty: Safeguarding Civil Rights. LC 92-9756. (Human Rights Ser.). (YA). 1992. 22.60 (*0-86593-173-9*); 16.95 (*0-685-59325-8*) Rourke Corp.

Lowell & Stokes, Joseph. Introduction to Linear Algebra. 464p. (C). 1991. pap. text ed. 13.50 (*0-15-601527-7*) HB Coll Pubs.

Lowell, Abbott L. Public Opinion in War & Peace. LC 73-14167. (Perspectives in Social Inquiry Ser.). 320p. 1974. reprint ed. 21.95 (*0-405-05512-9*) Ayer.

— What a University President Has Learned. LC 77-93355. (Essay Index Reprint Ser.). 1977. 18.95 (*0-8369-1303-5*) Ayer.

Lowell, Amy. Can Grande's Castle. LC 71-131771. 232p. 1918. reprint ed. 29.00 (*0-403-00658-9*) Scholarly.

— A Critical Fable. LC 78-64043. (Des Imagistes: Literature of the Imagist Movement Ser.). 112p. reprint ed. 17.50 (*0-404-17126-5*) AMS Pr.

— A Dome of Many-Coloured Glass. LC 78-64044. (Des Imagistes: Literature of the Imagist Movement Ser.). 152p. reprint ed. 20.00 (*0-404-17127-3*) AMS Pr.

— John Keats, 2 vols., Set. (BCL1-PR English Literature Ser.). 1992. reprint ed. lib. bdg. 150.00 (*0-7812-7573-3*) Rprt Serv.

— Pictures of the Floating World. LC 78-64045. (Des Imagistes: Literature of the Imagist Movement Ser.). reprint ed. 24.50 (*0-404-17128-1*) AMS Pr.

— Poetry & Poets. LC 77-162298. 1971. reprint ed. 25.00 (*0-8196-0274-4*) Biblo.

— Selected Poems. 1988. reprint ed. lib. bdg. 49.00 (*0-7812-0518-2*) Rprt Serv.

— Selected Poems. 1971. reprint ed. 49.00 (*0-403-00657-0*) Scholarly.

— Six French Poets: Studies in Contemporary Literature. LC 67-28737. (Essay Index Reprint Ser.). 1977. 22.95 (*0-8369-0626-8*) Ayer.

— Sword Blades & Poppy Seed. LC 78-64046. (Des Imagistes: Literature of the Imagist Movement Ser.). 256p. reprint ed. 27.50 (*0-404-17129-X*) AMS Pr.

— Tendencies in American Poetry. LC 68-54171. (Studies in Poetry: No. 38). 1969. reprint ed. lib. bdg. 75.00 (*0-8383-0588-1*) M S G Haskell Hse.

— Tendencies in Modern American Poetry. (BCL1-PS American Literature Ser.). 349p. 1992. reprint ed. lib. bdg. 89.00 (*0-7812-6629-7*) Rprt Serv.

Lowell, Anne. Change of He. (Sorority Girls Ser.: No. 7). 1987. pap. 2.50 (*0-449-13213-7*) Fawcett.

— Winner Takes. (Sorority Girls Ser.: No. 6). 1986. pap. 2.50 (*0-449-13009-6*) Fawcett.

Lowell, Anne, jt. auth. see Hunter.

Lowell, Bruce K. Dr. Bruce Lowell's Fat Percentage Finder: The New, Easy-to-Use System for Measuring the Fat in Your Diet. 192p. (Orig.). 1991. pap. 9.00 (*0-399-51653-0*, Perigree Bks) Berkley Pub.

***Lowell, Bruce L.** Body Signals. LC 95-9673. 1995. 25.00 (*0-06-270111-8*, HarpT) HarpC.

Lowell, Cym H., jt. auth. see Weistart, John C.

Lowell, D. R. The Historic Genealogy of the Lowells of America from 1639-1899. (Illus.). 878p. 1989. reprint ed. lib. bdg. 138.50 (*0-8328-0789-3*); reprint ed. pap. 130.50 (*0-8328-0790-7*) Higginson Bk Co.

Lowell, Edgar L. & Stoner, Marguerite. Play It by Ear! 1963. reprint ed. spiral bd. 9.00 (*0-9606312-0-8*) John Tracy Clinic.

Lowell, Edward J. Eve of the French Revolution. LC 72-1016. reprint ed. 42.50 (*0-404-07145-7*) AMS Pr.

— The Hessians & the Other German Auxiliaries of Great Britain in the Revolutionary War. (Illus.). 328p. 1995. reprint ed. lib. bdg. 42.00 (*0-8328-4495-0*) Higginson Bk Co.

— Hessians in the Revolutionary War. (Illus.). 328p. 1970. reprint ed. 24.00 (*0-87928-012-3*) Corner Hse.

Lowell, Elizabeth. Chain Lightning. 1993. mass mkt. 4.50 (*0-373-48278-7*) Harlequin Bks.

— Dark Fire. 1994. mass mkt. 4.50 (*0-373-48291-4*, 5-48291-4) Silhouette.

— Enchanted. 400p. (Orig.). 1994. mass mkt. 5.99 (*0-380-77257-4*) Avon.

— Enchanted. large type ed. LC 94-14259. 1995. 21.95 (*0-7862-0223-8*) Thorndike Pr.

— Fever. 1993. mass mkt. 4.50 (*0-373-48277-9*) Silhouette.

— Fire & Rain. 1994. mass mkt. 4.50 (*0-373-48299-X*, 5-48299-7) Silhouette.

— Forbidden. 400p. (Orig.). 1993. mass mkt. 5.99 (*0-380-76954-9*) Avon.

— Forbidden. large type ed. LC 93-42109. (Orig.). 1994. 21.95 (*0-7862-0144-4*) Thorndike Pr.

— Forget Me Not. 368p. (Orig.). 1994. mass mkt. 5.50 (*0-380-76759-7*) Avon.

— Forget Me Not. large type ed. LC 95-13695. 440p. 1995. 22.95 (*0-7862-0467-2*, Large Print Bks) Thorndike Pr.

— Granite Man. 1995. pap. 4.99 (*1-55166-015-6*, Mira Bks) Harlequin Bks.

— Granite Man. (Silhouette Desire Ser.: No. 625). 1991. pap. 2.75 (*0-373-05625-7*) Silhouette.

— Love Song for a Raven. 1993. mass mkt. 4.50 (*0-373-48276-0*, 5-48276-5) Silhouette.

— Lover in the Rough. 320p. 1994. mass mkt. 4.99 (*0-380-76760-0*) Avon.

— Only His. 400p. (Orig.). 1995. mass mkt. 5.99 (*0-380-76338-9*) Avon.

— Only Love. (Only Ser.). 416p. (Orig.). 1995. mass mkt. 5.99 (*0-380-77256-6*) Avon.

— Only Mine. 400p. (Orig.). 1995. mass mkt. 5.99 (*0-380-76339-7*) Avon.

— Only You. 384p. (Orig.). 1995. mass mkt. 5.99 (*0-380-76340-0*) Avon.

— Outlaw. 1994. mass mkt. 4.50 (*0-373-48304-X*, 5-48304-5) Silhouette.

— Outlaw. 1994. mass mkt. 4.99 (*1-55166-006-7*, 1-66066-7, Mira Bks) Harlequin Bks.

— A Sweet Wind, Wild Wind. 1992. mass mkt. 4.50 (*0-373-48258-2*, 5-48258-3) Harlequin Bks.

— Tell Me No Lies. (Best of the Best Ser.: No. 250). 1992. mass mkt. 4.99 (*0-373-48250-7*) Harlequin Bks.

— Too Hot to Handle. 1992. mass mkt. 3.99 (*0-373-48249-3*, 5-48249-2) Harlequin Bks.

— Untamed. 416p. (Orig.). 1993. mass mkt. 5.99 (*0-380-76953-0*) Avon.

— Untamed. large type ed. LC 93-13230. (Orig.). 1993. 21.95 (*1-56054-757-X*) Thorndike Pr.

— Warrior. 1995. mass mkt. 4.99 (*1-55166-032-6*, 1-66032-3, Mira Bks) Harlequin Bks.

Lowell Family Foundation Staff. The Lowell Family Cookbook, 1990. Gallion, Sue L., ed. 164p. 1990. spiral bd. 15.00 (*0-932845-42-8*) Lowell Pr.

Lowell, Francis C. Joan of Arc. 1977. 22.95 (*0-8369-7117-5*, 7951) Ayer.

Lowell, H. Bret & Rudnick, Lewis G. Investigate Before Investing: Guidance for Prospective Franchises. 32p. 1992. 5.00 (*0-317-66115-9*) Intl Franchise Assn.

Lowell, James. Essays, Poems & Letters. (BCL1-PS American Literature Ser.). 424p. 1993. reprint ed. lib. bdg. 99.00 (*0-7812-6985-7*) Rprt Serv.

— How to Survive in the Real World: Financial Independence for the Recent Grad. LC 94-23396. (Illus.). 272p. (Orig.). 1995. 10.95 (*0-14-023873-5*, Penguin Bks) Viking Penguin.

— James Russell Lowell: Representative Selections. (BCL1-PS American Literature Ser.). 498p. 1993. reprint ed. lib. bdg. 99.00 (*0-7812-6986-5*) Rprt Serv.

Lowell, James D. Structural Styles in Petroleum Exploration. LC 84-62622. 460p. 1985. 45.00 (*0-930972-08-2*) Oil & Gas.

Lowell, James Russell. Among My Books. LC 75-126666. 1970. reprint ed. 11.50 (*0-404-04039-X*) AMS Pr.

— Among My Books. (BCL1-PS American Literature Ser.). 380p. 1992. reprint ed. lib. bdg. 89.00 (*0-7812-0053-9*) Rprt Serv.

— Among My Books. 1870. reprint ed. 9.00 (*0-403-00032-7*) Scholarly.

— Bigelow Papers. LC 71-107179. 1970. reprint ed. 15.00 (*0-403-00235-4*) Scholarly.

— The Biglow Papers: First Series. (BCL1-PS American Literature Ser.). 198p. 1992. reprint ed. lib. bdg. 69.00 (*0-7812-6786-2*) Rprt Serv.

— The Biglow Papers: Second Series. (BCL1-PS American Literature Ser.). 564p. 1992. reprint ed. lib. bdg. 99.00 (*0-7812-6787-0*) Rprt Serv.

— Biglow Papers, 1st Series. Wilbur, Homer, ed. LC 75-93775. reprint ed. 24.50 (*0-404-04055-1*) AMS Pr.

— Biglow Papers, 2nd Series. Wilbur, Homer, ed. LC 76-37650. reprint ed. 32.00 (*0-404-04056-X*) AMS Pr.

— The Complete Poetical Works. (BCL1-PS American Literature Ser.). 492p. 1992. reprint ed. lib. bdg. 99.00 (*0-7812-6784-6*) Rprt Serv.

— Complete Writings, 16 vols., Set. Norton, Charles E., ed. LC 74-181949. reprint ed. write for info. (*0-404-04070-5*) AMS Pr.

— Complete Writings, 16 vols., Set. (BCL1-PS American Literature Ser.). 1992. reprint ed. lib. bdg. 1,440.00 (*0-7812-6783-8*) Rprt Serv.

— Conversations on Some of the Old Poets. 1977. 18.95 (*0-8369-7226-0*, 8025) Ayer.

— Fable for Critics. LC 72-6895. (Essay Index Reprint Ser.). 1977. reprint ed. 17.95 (*0-8369-7244-9*) Ayer.

— Latest Literary Essays & Addresses. (Essay Index Reprint Ser.). 1977. reprint ed. 19.95 (*0-518-10184-3*) Ayer.

— Letters of James R. Lowell, 2 Vols, 1. Norton, Charles E., ed. LC 76-172754. 1894. write for info. (*0-404-00081-9*) AMS Pr.

— Letters of James R. Lowell, 2 Vols, 2. Norton, Charles E., ed. LC 76-172754. 1894. write for info. (*0-404-00082-7*) AMS Pr.

— Letters of James R. Lowell, 2 Vols, Set. Norton, Charles E., ed. LC 76-172754. 1894. 67.50 (*0-404-00080-0*) AMS Pr.

— Literary Criticism of James Russell Lowell. Smith, Herbert F., ed. LC 69-10408. 290p. reprint ed. pap. 82.70 (*0-7837-6016-7*, 2045828) Bks Demand.

— Literary Essays, 2 vols, Set. LC 72-5803. (Essay Index Reprint Ser.). 1977. reprint ed. 49.95 (*0-8369-2998-5*) Ayer.

— My Study Windows. LC 70-126664. reprint ed. 11.25 (*0-404-04057-8*) AMS Pr.

— My Study Windows. (BCL1-PS American Literature Ser.). 433p. 1992. reprint ed. lib. bdg. 99.00 (*0-7812-6788-9*) Rprt Serv.

— The Old English Dramatists. 1977. text ed. 12.95 (*0-8369-8166-9*, 8306) Ayer.

Lowell, James Russell, ed. The Pioneer. LC 47-30458. 1947. reprint ed. lib. bdg. 50.00 (*0-8201-1215-1*) Schol Facsimiles.

***Lowell, Jax P.** Against the Grain: The Slightly Eccentric Guide to Living Well Without Gluten or Wheat. LC 94-39985. 320p. 1995. 22.50 (*0-8050-3624-5*) H Holt & Co.

— Mothers. 336p. 1995. 22.95 (*0-312-13126-7*) St Martin.

Lowell, Josephine S. Public Relief & Private Charity. LC 76-137176. (Poverty U. S. A. Historical Record Ser.). 1975. reprint ed. 16.95 (*0-405-03115-7*) Ayer.

Lowell, Julia & Yager, Loren. Pricing & Markets: U. S. & Japanese Responses to Currency Fluctuations. LC 94-16352. 1994. write for info. (*0-8330-1540-0*, MR-438-CAPP) Rand Corp.

Lowell, Julie C. Prehistoric Households at Turkey Creek Pueblo, Arizona. LC 90-48539. (Anthropological Papers: No. 54). (Illus.). 110p. (Orig.). 1991. pap. 21.95 (*0-8165-1238-8*) U of Ariz Pr.

Lowell, Laurel. Pluto. 105p. 1979. 7.00 (*0-317-66041-1*, L1296-014) Am Fed Astrologers.

Lowell, Lindsay & Papademetriou, Demetrios, eds. Immigration & U. S. Integration Policy Reforms. (Orig.). 1992. pap. 12.00 (*0-944285-29-5*) Pol Studies.

Lowell, Melissa. Breaking the Ice. (Silver Blades Ser.: No. 1). (J). 1993. pap. 3.50 (*0-553-48134-7*) Bantam.

— Center Ice. (Silver Blades Ser.: No. 10). (J). (gr. 4-7). 1995. mass mkt. 3.50 (*0-553-48313-7*) Bantam.

— Competition. (Silver Blades Ser.: No. 3). (J). (gr. 4-7). 1994. pap. 3.50 (*0-553-48136-3*, Skylark) Bantam.

— Going for the Gold. (Silver Blades Ser.: No. 4). (J). (gr. 4-7). 1994. pap. 3.50 (*0-553-48137-1*, Skylark) Bantam.

— The Ice Princess. (Silver Blades Ser.: No. 7). (J). (gr. 4-7). 1995. pap. 3.50 (*0-553-48289-0*) Bantam.

— In the Spotlight. (Silver Blades Ser.: No. 2). (J). 1993. 3.50 (*0-553-48135-5*) Bantam.

— The Perfect Pair. (Silver Blades Ser.: No. 5). (J). (gr. 4-7). 1994. pap. 3.50 (*0-553-48194-0*) Dell.

— Rumors at the Rink. (Silver Blades Ser.: No. 8). (J). (gr. 4-7). 1995. 3.50 (*0-553-48293-9*) Bantam.

— Skating Camp. (Silver Blades Ser.: No. 6). (J). (gr. 4-7). 1994. pap. 3.50 (*0-553-48198-3*) Dell.

— Spring Break. (Silver Blades Ser.: No. 9). (J). (gr. 4-7). 1995. pap. 3.50 (*0-553-48309-9*) Bantam.

Lowell, Michele. Your Purebred Kitten. 1995. 27.50 (*0-8050-3268-1*); pap. 12.95 (*0-8050-3269-X*) H Holt & Co.

— Your Purebred Puppy: A Buyer's Guide. 288p. 1991. pap. 10.95 (*0-8050-1892-1*, Owl) H Holt & Co.

Lowell, Michelle. Your Pet Bird: A Buyer's Guide. 224p. 1994. 27.50 (*0-8050-2325-9*); pap. 15.95 (*0-8050-2326-7*) H Holt & Co.

Lowell, Percival. Occult Japan. 1972. 250.00 (*0-8490-0750-X*) Gordon Pr.

— Occult Japan. (Illus.). 400p. 1990. pap. 12.95 (*0-89281-306-7*) Inner Tradit.

Lowell, Robert. The Collected Prose. 350p. 1987. 25.00 (*0-374-12625-9*); pap. 14.95 (*0-374-52267-7*) FS&G.

— Day by Day. LC 77-6799. 138p. 1977. 12.95 (*0-374-13525-8*) FS&G.

— Day by Day. LC 77-6799. 138p. 1978. pap. 9.00 (*0-374-51471-2*) FS&G.

— For Lizzie & Harriet. 48p. 1975. pap. 3.45 (*0-374-51291-4*) FS&G.

— Imitations. enl. rev. ed. 149p. 1995. pap. 11.00 (*0-374-50260-9*, Noonday) FS&G.

— Life Studies & for the Union Dead. 72p. 1967. pap. 8.00 (*0-374-50628-0*) FS&G.

— Lord Weary's Castle & The Mills of the Kavanaughs, 2 vols. in one. 120p. 1968. reprint ed. pap. 3.95 (*0-15-653500-9*, Harvest Bks) HarBrace.

— Notebook. 265p. 1995. pap. 12.00 (*0-374-50460-1*, Noonday) FS&G.

— Notebook. 265p. 1995. pap. 12.00 (*0-374-50947-6*, Noonday) FS&G.

— Selected Poems. LC 76-2000. 320p. 1977. pap. 14.00 (*0-374-51400-3*) FS&G.

Lowell, Robert T. The New Priest in Conception Bay, 2 vols. reprint ed. Vol. 1, 317p. write for info. (*0-318-53718-4*); reprint ed. Vol. 2, 345p. write for info. (*0-318-53719-2*) Irvington.

— The New Priest in Conception Bay, 2 vols., Set. LC 72-104520. reprint ed. lib. bdg. 37.00 (*0-8398-1173-X*) Irvington.

Lowell, Ross. Matters of Light & Depth: Creating Memorable Images for Video, Film & Stills Through Lighting. (Illus.). 224p. (Orig.). 1994. 28.95 (*1-879174-04-9*) Broad St Bks.

— Matters of Light & Depth: Creating Memorable Images for Video, Film, & Stills Through Lighting. Moran, Ed, ed. (Illus.). 224p. (Orig.). (C). 1992. pap. 28.95 (*1-879174-03-0*) Broad St Bks.

Lowell, S. & Shields, J. E. Powder Surface Area & Porosity. 3rd ed. (Powder Technology Ser.). (Illus.). 250p. 1991. 95.00 (*0-412-39690-4*, A5566) Chapman & Hall.

Lowell, Susan. Ganado Red: A Novella & Stories. LC 87-63531. (National Fiction Prize Ser.). 152p. (Orig.). 1988. pap. 9.95 (*0-915943-26-3*) Milkweed Ed.

— I Am Lavina Cumming. LC 93-24155. (Illus.). 184p. (YA). (gr. 8-12). 1993. 14.95 (*0-915943-39-5*); pap. 6.95 (*0-915943-77-8*) Milkweed Ed.

— The Three Little Javelinas. LC 92-14232. (Illus.). 32p. (J). (ps up). 1992. 14.95 (*0-87358-542-9*) Northland AZ.

— The Tortoise & the Jackrabbit. (Illus.). 32p. (J). (ps up). 1994. 14.95 (*0-87358-586-0*) Northland AZ.

Lowell, Waverly, ed. Architecture Records in the San Francisco Bay Area: A Guide to Research. LC 89-16904. (Reference Library of the Humanities). 370p. 1988. lib. bdg. 54.00 (*0-8240-6614-6*) Garland.

Lowen, Alexander. Betrayal of the Body. 288p. 1969. pap. 6.95 (*0-02-077300-5*, Collier S&S) S&S Trade.

— Bioenergetics. 1976. pap. 10.00 (*0-14-004322-5*, Penguin Bks) Viking Penguin.

— Depression & the Body. 1993. pap. 12.00 (*0-14-019465-7*, Arkana) Viking Penguin.

— Fear of Life. 274p. 1981. pap. 6.95 (*0-02-077330-7*) Macmillan.

— Joy: The Surrender to the Body & to Life. 320p. 1995. pap. 12.95 (*0-14-019493-2*, Penguin Bks) Viking Penguin.

— Language of the Body. 416p. 1971. pap. 6.95 (*0-02-077310-2*, Pub. by Gebrueder Borntraeger GW) Macmillan.

— Love & Orgasm: A Revolutionary Guide to Sexual Fulfillment. (Illus.). 303p. 1975. pap. 7.00 (*0-02-077320-X*, Collier S&S) S&S Trade.

— Love, Sex, & Your Heart. 240p. 1994. 11.95 (*0-14-019478-9*, Arkana) Viking Penguin.

— Narcissism. 1984. 13.95 (*0-02-575890-X*) Macmillan.

— Narcissism: Denial of the True Self. 288p. 1985. pap. 8.00 (*0-02-077290-4*, Collier S&S) S&S Trade.

— Pleasure: A Creative Approach to Life. 256p. 1994. 11.95 (*0-14-019477-0*, Arkana) Viking Penguin.

— Spirituality of the Body. 224p. 1990. text ed. 18.95 (*0-02-575871-3*) Macmillan.

Lowen-Colebunders. Function Classes of Cauchy Continuous Maps. (Pure & Applied Mathematics Ser.: Vol. 123). 192p. 1989. 140.00 (*0-8247-7992-4*) Dekker.

Lowen, Irwin, jt. auth. see Jackson, Don.

Lowen, R., ed. Fuzzy Logic: State of the Art. (Theory & Decision Library: No. D). 600p. (C). 1993. lib. bdg. 186.50 (*0-7923-2324-6*) Kluwer Ac.

Lowen, Tirzah. Peter Hall Directs Anthony & Cleopatra. LC 90-36644. (Illus.). 208p. 1991. pap. 16.95 (*0-87910-147-4*) Limelight Edns.

Lowenberg, Anton D., jt. auth. see Kaempfer, William H.

An Asterisk (*) at the beginning of an entry indicates that the title is appearing in BIP for the first time.

Lowenberg, B. & Hagenbeek, A., eds. Minimal Residual Disease in Acute Leukemia. (Developments in Oncology Ser.). 382p. 1984. lib. bdg. 140.00 (*0-89838-630-6*) Kluwer Ac.

Lowenberg, Carlton. Emily Dickinson's Textbooks. Lowenberg, Territa A. & Brown, Carla L., eds. (Illus.). 119p. (Orig.). 1986. 22.50 (*0-9617374-1-7*); pap. 12.75 (*0-9617374-0-9*) Carlton Lowenberg.

— Musicians Wrestle Everywhere: Emily Dickinson & Music. LC 92-9923. (Reference Books in Music: No. 19). xxviii, 210p. 1992. 39.50 (*0-914913-20-4*) Fallen Leaf.

Lowenberg-DeBoer, James. The Microeconomic Roots of the Farm Crisis. LC 86-21202. 185p. 1986. text ed. 55.00 (*0-275-92226-X*, C2226, Praeger Pubs) Greenwood.

Lowenberg, Heather. Unicorns & Other Fabulous Creatures. (Tattoo Tales Ser.). (Illus.). 24p. (Orig.). (J). (ps-3). 1994. pap. 4.99 (*0-679-86437-7*) Random Bks Yng Read.

Lowenberg, June S. Caring & Responsibility: The Crossroads of Holistic Practice & Traditional Medicine. LC 88-15067. (Studies in Health, Illness, & Caregiving). (Illus.). 306p. (C). 1989. text ed. 38.95 (*0-8122-8174-8*); pap. 17.95 (*0-8122-1408-0*) U of Pa Pr.

Lowenberg, Miriam E., et al. Food & Man. 2nd ed. LC 73-15800. (Illus.). 470p. reprint ed. pap. 134.00 (*0-7837-3491-3*, 2057824) Bks Demand.

— Food & People. 3rd ed. LC 78-19172. 382p. (C). 1979. write for info. (*0-02-371850-1*) Macmillan.

Lowenberg, Peter H., ed. see Georgetown University Round Table Meeting on Language & Linguistics Staff.

Lowenberg, Susan. C. S. Lewis: A Reference Guide, 1972-1988. LC 92-42316. (Reference Guide to Literature Ser.). 320p. 1993. text ed. 55.00 (*0-8161-1846-9*) G K Hall.

Lowenberg, Territa A., ed. see Lowenberg, Carlton.

Lowenfeld. Conflict of Laws. 1984. write for info. (*0-8205-0131-X*, 234); Supplement 1990. write for info. (*0-8205-0132-8*) Bender.

Lowenfeld & Tillinghast. International Economic Law, Pt. I: International Private Trade. 2nd ed. 1988. Pt. I, 1988, International Private Trade. write for info. (*0-8205-0601-X*, 554) Bender.

— International Economic Law, Pt. II: International Private Investment. 2nd ed. 1982. Pt. II, 1982, International Private Investment. write for info. (*0-8205-0606-0*) Bender.

— International Economic Law, Pt. III: Trade Controls for Political Ends. 2nd ed. 1983. Pt. III, 1983, Trade Controls for Political Ends. write for info. (*0-8205-0611-7*) Bender.

— International Economic Law, Pt. IV: The International Monetary System. 2nd ed. 1984. Pt. IV, 1984, The International Monetary System. write for info. (*0-8205-0616-8*) Bender.

— International Economic Law, Pt. V: Tax Aspects of International Transaction. 2nd ed. 1984. Pt. V, 1984, Tax Aspects of International Transaction. write for info. (*0-8205-0621-4*) Bender.

— International Economic Law, Pt. VI: Public Controls on International Trade. 2nd ed. 1983. Pt. VI, 1983, Public Controls on International Trade. write for info. (*0-8205-0626-5*) Bender.

Lowenfeld, Andreas F. Conflict of Laws: Documentary Materials; Federal, State & International. LC 86-61284. 1986. write for info. (*0-8205-1286-9*) Bender.

— International Litigation & Arbitration. (American Casebook Ser.). 1000p. (C). 1992. text ed. 50.00 (*0-314-01188-9*) West Pub.

— International Litigation & Arbitration: Teacher's Manual & Supplemental Litigation. (American Casebook Ser.). 530p. 1993. pap. text ed. write for info. (*0-314-02297-X*) West Pub.

— International Litigation & Arbitration, Selected Treaties, Statutes & Rules. (American Casebook Ser.). 180p. (C). 1992. pap. text ed. 16.00 (*0-314-01201-X*) West Pub.

Lowenfeld, Berthold. Berthold Lowenfeld on Blindness & Blind People. LC 81-3520. 254p. 1981. pap. 21.95 (*0-89128-101-0*) Am Foun Blind.

— Our Blind Children: Growing & Learning with Them. 3rd ed. (Illus.). 260p. 1977. 34.95x (*0-398-02200-3*) C C Thomas.

— Our Blind Children: Growing & Learning with Them. 3rd ed. (Illus.). 260p. 1977. pap. 19.95 (*0-398-06249-8*) C C Thomas.

Lowenfeld, Margaret. Play in Childhood. (Classics in Developmental Medicine Ser.: No. 6). (Illus.). 242p. (C). 1991. 15.95 (*0-521-41331-1*, Pub. by Mc Keith Pr UK) Cambridge U Pr.

Lowenfeld, Viktor. The Nature of Creative Activity. 2nd ed. LC 65-7654. 272p. 1959. reprint ed. 69.00 (*0-686-01428-6*) Somerset Pub.

— The Nature of Creative Activity. 1988. reprint ed. lib. bdg. 69.00 (*0-7812-0376-7*) Rprt Serv.

— Viktor Lowenfeld Speaks on Art & Creativity. National Art Education Association Staff, ed. 64p. (C). 1964. pap. 10.00 (*0-937652-26-1*, 061-02244) Natl Art Ed.

Lowenfeld, Viktor & Brittain, W. Lambert. Creative & Mental Growth. 8th ed. 402p. (C). 1987. write for info. (*0-02-372110-3*) Macmillan.

Lowenfels, Lewis D., jt. auth. see Bromberg, Alan R.

Lowenfels, Walter. Walt Whitman's Civil War. (Quality Paperbacks Ser.). (Illus.). 368p. 1989. pap. 13.95 (*0-306-80355-0*) Da Capo.

Lowenfels, Walter, et al. The Life of Fraenkel's Death: A Biographical Inquest. LC 71-11331. (Illus.). 102p. reprint ed. pap. 29.10 (*0-685-24156-4*, 2033030) Bks Demand.

Lowenfish, Lee. The Imperfect Diamond: A History of Baseball's Labor Wars. rev. ed. (Quality Paperbacks Ser.). (Illus.). 298p. 1991. pap. 14.95 (*0-306-80430-1*) Da Capo.

Lowenfish, Lee, jt. auth. see Major League Baseball Training Staff.

Lowenfish, Lee, jt. auth. see Seaver, Tom.

Lowengrub, M., jt. auth. see Sneddon, Ian.

Lowenhardt, John. Decision-Making in Soviet Politics. 1981. text ed. 32.50 (*0-312-19013-1*) St Martin.

— The Reincarnation of Russia: Struggling with the Legacy of Communism, 1990-1994. LC 94-38510. 256p. 1995. lib. bdg. 42.50 (*0-8223-1606-4*); pap. text ed. 15.95 (*0-8223-1623-4*) Duke.

Lowenhardt, John, et al. The Rise & Fall of the Soviet Politburo. LC 91-29623. 256p. 1992. text ed. 39.95 (*0-312-04784-3*) St Martin.

Lowenhaupt, Cecile K., jt. auth. see Baer, J. A.

Lowenheim, F., ed. Guide to the Selection & Use of Electroplated & Related Finishes- STP 785. 69p. 1982. pap. 18.00 (*0-8031-0749-8*, 04-785000-04) ASTM.

Lowenheim, Frederick A., ed. Modern Electroplating. 3rd ed. LC 73-20458. (Electrochemical Society Ser.). (Illus.). 801p. 1974. text ed. 145.00 (*0-471-54968-1*) Wiley.

Lowenkamp, William & McCall, Vicki B. The Country Poet: On the Road Again. (Illus.). 64p. (Orig.). 1984. pap. 6.00 (*0-913667-00-5*) Lowenkamp Pub.

Lowenkopf, Anne N., intro. Memories of Some of Anne's Friends. 125p. (Orig.). 1992. pap. 12.95 (*0-9633753-2-6*) Two Down Pr.

Lowenkopf, E. L., jt. ed. see Klebanow, S.

Lowenkopf, Shelly. Secrets of Successful Fiction Writing: A Guide to Techniques & Approaches the Professionals Take for Granted. (Santa Barbara Writers Conference Shop Talk Ser.: Bk. I). 152p. (Orig.). (C). 1991. pap. text ed. 9.95 (*1-880093-00-6*) Charters W.

Lowenkopf, Shelly, ed. see Conrad, Barnaby.

Lowens, Irving. Bibliography of Songsters Printed in America Before 1821. LC 75-5021. 1976. 25.00 (*0-912296-05-4*, U Pr of Va) Am Antiquarian.

— Haydn in America. LC 79-92140. (Bibliographies in American Music Ser.: No. 5). x, 134p. 1980. 11.50 (*0-911772-99-5*) Info Coord.

Lowens, Irving, pref. Lectures on the History & Art of Music: The Louis Charles Elson Memorial Lectures at the Library of Congress 1946-1965. LC 68-55319. (Music Ser.). 1968. reprint ed. lib. bdg. 32.50 (*0-306-71193-1*) Da Capo.

Lowenstam, Heinz A. Biostratigraphic Studies of the Niagaran Inter-Reef Formations of Northeastern Illinois. (Scientific Papers: Vol. IV). (Illus.). 146p. 1948. 3.00 (*0-89792-093-7*); pap. 2.00 (*0-89792-005-8*) Ill St Museum.

Lowenstam, Heinz A. & Weiner, Stephen. On Biomineralization. (Illus.). 336p. 1989. 59.95 (*0-19-504977-2*) OUP.

Lowenstam, Steven. The Scepter & the Spear: Studies on Forms of Repetition in the Homeric Poems. LC 93-19243. (Greek Studies: Interdisciplinary Approaches). 280p. (C). 1992. text ed. 62.50 (*0-8476-7772-9*); pap. text ed. 27.50 (*0-8476-7790-7*) Rowman.

Lowenstein, et al. New Jersey Environmental Law Handbook. 3rd ed. (State Environmental Law Ser.). 464p. 1993. pap. 79.00 (*0-86587-329-1*) Gov Insts.

Lowenstein, Amy C., ed. Middle East: Abstracts & Index, 1978, Vol. 1. 1979. 250.00 (*0-318-50002-7*) Northumberland Pr.

— Middle East: Abstracts & Index, 1979, Vol. 2. 1979. 250.00 (*0-318-50003-5*) Northumberland Pr.

— Middle East: Abstracts & Index, 1980, Vol. 3. 1980. 250.00 (*0-318-50004-3*) Northumberland Pr.

— Middle East: Abstracts & Index, 1981, Vol. 4. 1981. pap. 250.00 (*0-934565-00-7*) Northumberland Pr.

— Middle East: Abstracts & Index, 1982, Vol. 5. 1986. 250.00 (*0-318-49998-3*) Northumberland Pr.

— Middle East: Abstracts & Index, 1983, Vol. 6. 1988. 250.00 (*0-318-49999-1*) Northumberland Pr.

— Middle East: Abstracts & Index, 1984, Vol. 7. 1989. 250.00 (*0-318-50000-0*) Northumberland Pr.

— Middle East: Abstracts & Index, 1985, Vol. 8. 1990. 250.00 (*0-318-50001-9*) Northumberland Pr.

Lowenstein, Bill. Hunting in Michigan: The Early 80's. Arnold, David A., ed. 192p. 1981. pap. 6.95 (*0-941912-24-8*) Mich Nat Res.

Lowenstein, Christina, see B. B. Calhoun, pseud..

***Lowenstein, Daniel H.** Election Law: Cases & Materials. 730p. (C). 1995. text ed. write for info. (*0-89089-848-0*) Carolina Acad Pr.

Lowenstein, Eleanor. Bibliography of American Cookery Books 1742-1860. 132p. 1972. 18.00 (*0-912296-02-X*, U Pr of Va) Am Antiquarian.

Lowenstein, Jerome. Acid & Bases: A Guide to Understanding Acid-Base Disorders. (Illus.). 168p. 1993. 35.00 (*0-19-507572-2*); pap. 14.95 (*0-19-507573-0*) OUP.

Lowenstein, John M., ed. Citric Acid Cycle: Control & Compartmentation. LC 77-82152. 386p. reprint ed. pap. 110.10 (*0-685-15983-3*, 2027081) Bks Demand.

Lowenstein, K. L. The Manufacturing Technology of Continuous Glass Fibres. 3rd rev. ed. LC 92-39909. (Glass Science & Technology Ser.: Vol. 13). 1993. write for info. (*0-444-89346-6*) Elsevier.

Lowenstein, Karl. Political Power & the Governmental Process. LC 65-8901. (Chicago University Charles R. Walgreen Foundation for the Study of American Institutions, Lecture Ser.). 474p. reprint ed. pap. 135.10 (*0-317-09811-X*, 2020109) Bks Demand.

Lowenstein, Louis. Sense & Nonsense in Corporate Finance: An Antidote to Conventional Thinking about LOBs Capital Budgeting Divident Policy & Creating Shareholder Value. (Illus.). 272p. 1992. pap. 12.45 (*0-201-63223-3*) Addison-Wesley.

— Whats Wrong with Wall Street. 1989. pap. 10.53 (*0-201-51796-5*) Addison-Wesley.

— What's Wrong with Wall Street: Short-Term Gain & the Absentee Shareholder. 1988. 17.26 (*0-201-17169-4*) Addison-Wesley.

Lowenstein, M. Z., ed. Energy Applications of Biomass: Proceedings of the National Meeting on Biomass R & D for Energy Application 1-3 October, 1984 Arlington, Virginia. ix, 325p. 1985. 79.25 (*0-85334-409-4*, Pub. by Elsevier Applied Sci UK) Elsevier.

***Lowenstein, Michael W.** Customer Retention. 1994. 25.00 (*0-87389-257-7*) ASQC Qual Pr.

***Lowenstein, Roger.** Buffett: The Making of an American Capitalist. LC 95-8494. 512p. 1995. 27.50 (*0-679-41584-X*) Random.

Lowenstein, S. Lawyers, Legal Education, & Development: An Examination of the Process of Reform in Chile. x, 310p. 1970. pap. 7.50 (*0-8377-0803-6*) Rothman.

Lowenstein, Sharon R. Token Refuge: The Story of the Jewish Refugee Shelter at Oswego, 1944-1946. LC 85-42542. (Modern Jewish Experience Ser.). (Illus.). 256p. 1986. 29.95 (*0-253-36023-4*) Ind U Pr.

Lowenstein, Steven. The Jews of Oregon, 1850-1950. (Illus.). 236p. 1988. 29.95 (*0-9619786-0-0*); pap. 19.95 (*0-9619786-1-9*) JHS Oregon.

— The Jews of Oregon, 1850-1950. limited ed. (Illus.). 236p. 1988. 100.00 (*0-9619786-2-7*) JHS Oregon.

Lowenstein, Steven, et al. The Extramural Sanctuary of Demeter & Persephone at Cyrene, Libya, Final Reports, Vol. III. White, Donald, ed. (University Museum Monographs: No. 66). (Illus.). xi, 156p. 1987. text ed. 55.00 (*0-934718-77-6*) U PA Mus Pubns.

Lowenstein, Steven M. The Berlin Jewish Community: Enlightenment, Family, & Crisis, 1770-1830. LC 92-39884. (Studies in Jewish History). (Illus.). 320p. 1994. 49.95 (*0-19-508326-1*) OUP.

— Frankfurt on the Hudson: The German Jewish Community of Washington Heights, 1933-1983, Its Structure & Culture. LC 88-20520. (Illus.). 347p. 1989. pap. 19.95 (*0-8143-2385-5*) Wayne St U Pr.

— The Mechanics of Change: Essays in the Social History of German Jewry. (Brown Judaic Studies). 246p. (C). 1992. 59.95 (*1-55540-701-3*, 140246) Scholars Pr GA.

Lowenstein, Tom. Ancient Land: Sacred Whale. (Ancient Land Ser.). 1994. 20.00 (*0-374-10497-2*) FS&G.

— Ancient Land: Sacred Whale: The Inuit Hunt & Its Rituals. 192p. 1995. pap. 11.00 (*0-86547-488-5*, North Pt Pr) FS&G.

Lowenstein, Tom, jt tr. see Omnik, Tukummiq C.

Lowenthal, ed. see Herzl, Theodor.

Lowenthal, A. Agar Gel Electrophoresis in Neurology. 1964. pap. 22.00 (*0-444-40377-9*) Elsevier.

Lowenthal, A. & Raus, J., eds. Cellular & Humoral Components of Cerebrospinal Fluid in Multiple Sclerosis. (NATO ASI Series A, Life Sciences: Vol. 129). (Illus.). 538p. 1987. 135.00 (*0-306-42578-5*, Plenum Pr) Plenum.

Lowenthal, Abraham F. Brazil & the United States. LC 86-81679. (Headline Ser.: No. 279). 64p. (Orig.). (C). 1986. pap. 5.95 (*0-87124-109-9*) Foreign Policy.

Lowenthal, Abraham F. The Dominican Intervention. 246p. (C). 1994. reprint ed. pap. text ed. 14.95x (*0-8018-4755-9*) Johns Hopkins.

Lowenthal, Abraham F. Partners in Conflict: The United States & Latin America in the 1990s. rev. ed. 272p. 1990. text ed. 41.00x (*0-8018-4061-9*); pap. text ed. 13.95 (*0-8018-4059-7*) Johns Hopkins.

Lowenthal, Abraham F., ed. Exporting Democracy: Case Studies. LC 90-24062. 312p. 1991. pap. text ed. 13.95 (*0-8018-4133-X*) Johns Hopkins.

— Exporting Democracy: Themes & Issues. LC 90-24061. 288p. 1991. pap. text ed. 13.95 (*0-8018-4132-1*) Johns Hopkins.

— Latin America & Caribbean Contemporary Record 1985-1986, Vol. V. (Latin America & Caribbean Contemporary Record Ser.). (Illus.). 1000p. (C). 1987. 380.00 (*0-8419-1123-1*) Holmes & Meier.

— Latin America & Caribbean Contemporary Record 1986-1987, Vol. VI. (Latin American & Caribbean Contemporary Record Ser.). 1000p. 1988. 380.00 (*0-8419-1170-3*) Holmes & Meier.

— The Peruvian Experiment: Continuity & Change under Military Rule. LC 75-2998. 502p. reprint ed. pap. 143.10 (*0-8357-6254-8*, 2034656) Bks Demand.

Lowenthal, Abraham F. & Burgess, Katrina, eds. The California-Mexico Connection. LC 92-45247. 392p. 1993. 45.00 (*0-8047-2188-2*); pap. 16.95 (*0-8047-2187-4*) Stanford U Pr.

Lowenthal, Abraham F. & Fitch, J. Samuel, eds. Armies & Politics in Latin America. 2nd ed. LC 86-14918. 300p. (C). 1986. 45.00 (*0-8419-0913-X*); pap. 24.50 (*0-8419-0916-4*) Holmes & Meier.

Lowenthal, Abraham F. & Starr, Pamela K. The United States & the Cuban Revolution, 1958-1960. (Pew Case Studies in International Affairs). 50p. (C). 1994. pap. text ed. 2.50 (*1-56927-328-6*) Geo U Inst Dplmcy.

Lowenthal, Abraham F. & Treverton, Gregory F., eds. Latin America in a New World. LC 93-47321. (Inter-American Dialogue Bks.). (C). 1994. pap. text ed. 19.95 (*0-8133-8671-3*) Westview.

— Latin America in a New World. LC 93-47321. (Inter-American Dialogue Bks.). (C). 1994. text ed. 63.00 (*0-8133-8670-5*) Westview.

Lowenthal, Anne W. Joachim Wtewael: Mars & Venus Surprised by Vulcan. LC 94-17632. (Getty Museum Studies on Art). 94p. 1995. 15.95 (*0-89236-304-5*) J P Getty Trust.

Lowenthal, Cynthia. Lady Mary Wortley Montagu & the Eighteenth-Century Familiar Letter. LC 92-41757. 264p. 1994. 40.00 (*0-8203-1545-1*) U of Ga Pr.

Lowenthal, D., jt. ed. see Gathercole, P.

Lowenthal, D., jt. ed. see Penning-Roswell, Edmund C.

Lowenthal, David. The Past Is a Foreign Country. LC 85-10990. (Illus.). 516p. 1986. 54.95 (*0-521-22415-2*) Cambridge U Pr.

— The Past Is a Foreign Country. LC 85-10990. (Illus.). 516p. 1988. pap. 22.95 (*0-521-29480-0*) Cambridge U Pr.

— The West Indies Federation. LC 76-21682. (American Geographical Society; Research Ser.: No. 23). (Illus.). 142p. 1976. reprint ed. text ed. 49.75 (*0-8371-9005-3*, LOWI, Greenwood Pr) Greenwood.

Lowenthal, David, ed. Environmental Perception & Behavior. LC 66-29233. (Research Papers Ser.: No. 109). 88p. 1967. pap. 12.00 (*0-89065-018-7*) U Chicago Comm Geo.

— Environmental Perception & Behavior. LC 66-29233. (University of Chicago, Department of Geography, Research Paper Ser.: No. 109). 96p. reprint ed. pap. 27.40 (*0-7837-0391-0*, 2040712) Bks Demand.

Lowenthal, David & Riel, Marquita. Environmental Structures: Semantic & Experiental Components. (Publications in Environmental Perception: Report 8). 48p. 1972. 6.00 (*0-318-12730-X*) Am Geographical.

Lowenthal, David, ed. see Marsh, George P.

Lowenthal, David T., ed. Geriatric Cardiology. LC 70-6558. (Illus.). 263p. 1992. text ed. 70.00 (*0-8036-5653-X*) Davis Co.

Lowenthal, F. & Vandamme, Fernand, eds. Pragmatics & Education. 352p. 1986. 75.00 (*0-306-42374-X*, Plenum Pr) Plenum.

Lowenthal, Jeffrey N. Reengineering the Organization: A Step-by-Step Approach to Corporate Revitalization. LC 93-44774. 1994. write for info. (*0-87389-258-5*) ASQC Qual Pr.

Lowenthal, Larry. Iron Mine Railroads of New Jersey. (Illus.). 145p. 1981. 17.95 (*0-686-36238-1*); pap. 12.95 (*0-686-99308-X*) Tri-State Rail.

Lowenthal, Leo. Critical Theory & Frankfurt Theorists: Correspondence, Speeches, & Origins. (Communication & Society Ser.: Vol. 4). 236p. 1989. 34.95x (*0-88738-224-X*) Transaction Pubs.

— False Prophets: Studies on Authoritarianism Communication in Society, Vol. 3. 400p. 1986. 37.95 (*0-88738-136-7*) Transaction Pubs.

— Literature & Mass Culture. (Communication & Society Ser.: Vol. 1). 338p. 1984. 39.95 (*0-87855-489-0*) Transaction Pubs.

— Literature & the Image of Man. LC 78-134110. (Essay Index Reprint Ser.). 1980. 21.95 (*0-8369-1982-3*) Ayer.

— Literature & the Image of Man, Vol. 2. (Communication & Society Ser.). 224p. (C). 1985. 39.95x (*0-88738-057-3*) Transaction Pubs.

— Literature, Popular Culture & Society. LC 61-13532. (Paperbounds Ser.: No. PB-4). 1968. reprint ed. pap. 8.95 (*0-87015-166-5*) Pacific Bks.

— An Unmastered Past: The Autobiographical Reflections of Leo Lowenthal. LC 86-24942. (Illus.). 240p. 1987. 35.00 (*0-520-05638-8*) U CA Pr.

Lowenthal, Marjorie F. Lives in Distress: The Paths of the Elderly to the Psychiatric Ward. Stein, Leon, ed. LC 79-8675. (Growing Old Ser.). 1980. reprint ed. lib. bdg. 28.95 (*0-405-12791-X*) Ayer.

Lowenthal, Marjorie F., et al. Aging & Mental Disorder in San Francisco: A Social Psychiatric Study. LC 67-13168. (Langley Porter Institute Studies of Aging). (Illus.). 361p. reprint ed. pap. 102.90 (*0-8357-4906-1*, 2037836) Bks Demand.

— Four Stages of Life. LC 74-27911. (Jossey-Bass Behavioral Science Ser.). 318p. reprint ed. pap. 90.70 (*0-685-20949-0*, 2056561) Bks Demand.

Lowenthal, Mark M. U. S. Intelligence: Evolution & Anatomy. 2nd ed. Laqueur, Walter & Spitler, Donna R., eds. LC 92-15913. (Washington Papers: No. 157). 178p. 1992. text ed. 47.95 (*0-275-94435-2*, C4435); pap. text ed. 16.95 (*0-275-94434-4*, B4434) Greenwood.

— The U. S. Intelligence Community: An Annotated Bibliography. LC 94-10298. (Organizations & Interest Groups Ser.: Vol. 11). 224p. 1994. 34.00 (*0-8153-1423-X*, H1765) Garland.

Lowenthal, Martin & Short, Lar. Opening the Heart of Compassion: Transform Suffering Through Buddhist Psychology & Practice. (Illus.). 192p. 1993. pap. 12.95 (*0-8048-1985-8*) C E Tuttle.

Lowenthal, Marvin. A World Passed By: Great Cities in Jewish Diaspora History. LC 90-30824. (Illus.). 560p. (C). 1990. reprint ed. 34.50 (*0-934710-19-8*) J Simon.

Lowenthal, Marvin, tr. see Gluckel.

Lowenthal, Marvin, jt. auth. see Monaghan, Frank.

Lowenthal, Michael, ed. The Badboy Erotic Library, Vol. I. (Orig.). 1994. pap. text ed. 4.95 (*1-56333-190-X*) Masquerade.

— The Badboy Erotic Library, Vol. II. (Orig.). 1994. pap. text ed. 4.95 (*1-56333-211-6*) Masquerade.

— The Best of the Badboys. (Orig.). 1995. pap. 12.95 (*1-56333-233-7*) Masquerade.

Lowenthal, Michael, ed. see Preston, John.

Lowenthal, Michael, jt ed. see Preston, John.

Lowenthal, Richard. Social Change & Cultural Crisis. LC 84-4964. (European Perspectives Ser.). 224p. 1984. text ed. 35.50 (*0-231-05644-3*) Col U Pr.

Lowenthal, Richard, ed. see Borkenau, Franz.

Lowenthal, Werner. Pharmaceutical Calculations: A Self-Instructional Text. rev. ed. LC 74-9564. 460p. 1985. reprint ed. pap. 25.50 (*0-88275-573-0*) Krieger.

Lowenthal, Wolfe. Gateway to the Miraculous: Further Explorations in the Tao of Cheng Man-ch'ing. LC 93-39498. (Illus.). 124p. (Orig.). (C). 1994. pap. 12.95 (*1-883319-13-7*) Frog CA.

— There Are No Secrets: Professor Cheng Man Ch'ing & His Ta Chi Chuan. 1991. pap. 12.95 (*1-55643-112-0*) North Atlantic.

Lower, A. R., jt. ed. see Innis, Harold A.

Lower, Anne R. Centennial History of Sheltering Arms Hospital. (Illus.). 96p. 1989. lib. bdg. 20.00 (*0-9623370-0-5*); pap. write for info. (*0-9623370-1-3*) Sheltering Arms.
— Sheltering Arms Hospital: One Hundred Years of Caring. (Illus.). 100p. (Orig.). 1989. lib. bdg. 20.00 (*0-685-26159-X*); pap. (*0-318-65239-0*) Sheltering Arms.
Lower, Arthur R. Canadians in the Making: A Social History of Canada. LC 81-4142. (Illus.). xxiv, 475p. 1981. reprint ed. text ed. 89.50 (*0-313-23037-4*, LOCAN, Greenwood Pr) Greenwood.
Lower, Dorothy M., jt. ed. see Filby, P. William.
Lower, J. L. Lower: Some Account of the Lower Family in America, Principally of the Descendants of Adam Lower, Who Settled in Williamsport, PA in 1779. (Illus.). 144p. 1993. reprint ed. lib. bdg. 35.00 (*0-8328-3709-1*); reprint ed. pap. 25.00 (*0-8328-3710-5*) Higginson Bk Co.
Lower, Joyce Q. & Grix, Henry M. Michigan Estate Planning, Will Drafting & Estate Administration Forms, 2 vols. 1989. disk write for info. (*0-318-71302-0*) Butterworth Legal Pubs.
— Michigan Estate Planning, Will Drafting & Estate Administration Forms, 2 vols. suppl. ed. 1993. 80.00 (*0-685-74622-4*) Butterworth Legal Pubs.
— Michigan Estate Planning, Will Drafting & Estate Administration Forms, 2 vols., Set. 970p. 1994. disk, ring bd. 219.00 (*0-8342-0087-2*) Michie Butterworth.
Lower, Lucy, tr. see Taeko, Kono.
Lower, Lucy B., jt. ed. see Moore, Cornelia N.
Lower, M. A. English Surnames. 1972. 59.95 (*0-8490-0119-6*) Gordon Pr.
Lower, Mark A. Contributions to Literature: Historical, Antiquarian, & Metrical. LC 72-4578. (Essay Index Reprint Ser.). 1977. reprint ed. 23.95 (*0-8369-2959-4*) Ayer.
Lower, Richard C. A Bloc of One: The Political Career of Hiram W. Johnson. LC 93-6975. (C). 1993. 45.00 (*0-8047-2081-9*) Stanford U Pr.
Loweree, jt. auth. see Kimmons.
Lowerre, George F. Critical Reading: Workbook B: Reusable Edition. 70p. (J). (gr. 3-8). 1973. student ed 10.00 (*0-87879-720-3*, Ann Arbor Div) Acad Therapy.
— Critical Reading: Workbook C: Reusable Edition. 78p. (J). (gr. 3-8). 1973. student ed 10.00 (*0-87879-721-1*, Ann Arbor Div) Acad Therapy.
Lowerre, George F. & Scandura, Alice M. Critical Reading: Workbook A: Reusable Edition. 54p. (J). (gr. 3-8). 1973. 10.00 (*0-87879-719-X*, Ann Arbor Div); teacher ed 5.00 (*0-87879-723-8*, Ann Arbor Div) Acad Therapy.
Lowerre, George F. & Scandure, Alice M. Critical Reading: Workbook D: Reusable Edition. 68p. (J). (gr. 3-8). 1973. student ed 10.00 (*0-87879-722-X*, Ann Arbor Div) Acad Therapy.
Lowerre, Susan. Under the Neem Tree. LC 90-53323. 256p. 1991. 22.00 (*1-877946-03-6*) Permanent Pr.
— Under the Neem Tree. LC 92-43188. 264p. (C). 1993. pap. 12.95 (*0-295-97273-4*) U of Wash Pr.
Lowers, James K. Candide Notes. 1965. pap. 3.95 (*0-8220-0283-3*) Cliffs.
— Hamlet Notes. 1971. pap. 3.95 (*0-8220-0018-0*) Cliffs.
— King Henry IV, Pt. I Notes. 1971. pap. 3.95 (*0-8220-0023-7*) Cliffs.
— King Henry IV, Pt. II Notes. 1982. pap. 3.95 (*0-8220-0026-1*) Cliffs.
— King Lear Notes. 1968. pap. 4.25 (*0-8220-0041-5*) Cliffs.
— Pygmalion Notes & Arms & the Man Notes. (Orig.). 1981. pap. 3.95 (*0-8220-1103-4*) Cliffs.
— Richard III Notes. 1966. pap. 3.95 (*0-8220-0071-7*) Cliffs.
— Shakespeares Sonnets Notes. 1965. pap. 3.75 (*0-8220-0077-6*) Cliffs.
— Troilus & Cressida Notes. 1982. pap. 4.50 (*0-8220-0091-1*) Cliffs.
Lowerson, John. Sport & the English Middle Classes, 1870-1914. (International Studies in the History of Sport). (Illus.). 304p. (C). 1993. text ed. 69.95 (*0-7190-3777-8*, Pub. by Manchester Univ Pr UK) St Martin.
— Sport & the English Middle Classes, 1870-1914. (International Studies in the History of Sport). 320p. 1995. text ed. 24.95 (*0-7190-4651-3*, Pub. by Manchester Univ Pr UK) St Martin.
Lowery. The Reforming Kings: Cult & Society in First Temple Judah. (JSOT Supplement Ser.). 240p. (C). 1991. 25.00 (*1-85075-318-0*, Pub. by Sheffield Acad UK) CUP Services.
Lowery, A. J., jt. auth. see Turner, Capstan.
Lowery, Angi, ed. see Chorlton, David, et al.
***Lowery, Charles D.** James Barbour, A Jeffersonian Republican. LC 83-3453. 334p. 1984. pap. 95.20 (*0-7837-8392-2*, 2059203) Bks Demand.
Lowery, Charles D. & Marszalek, John F., eds. Encyclopedia of African-American Civil Rights: From Emancipation to the Present. LC 91-27814. 672p. 1992. text ed. 59.95 (*0-313-25011-1*, LDR/, Greenwood Pr) Greenwood.
Lowery, Craig, jt. auth. see Dowdy, Larry.
Lowery, Daniel. Following Christ: A Handbook of Catholic Moral Teaching. LC 82-84373. 160p. 1982. pap. 5.95 (*0-89243-173-3*) Liguori Pubns.
Lowery, Daniel L. Catholic Answers to Contemporary Questions. LC 91-62106. 80p. (Orig.). 1991. pap. text ed. 2.95 (*0-89243-410-4*) Liguori Pubns.
— Catholic Beliefs, Laws, Practices: Twenty-Six Questions & Answers. 64p. 1984. pap. 2.95 (*0-89243-213-6*) Liguori Pubns.
— Day by Day Through Lent: Reflections, Prayers, Practices. LC 83-82033. 142p. 1983. pap. 3.95 (*0-89243-194-6*) Liguori Pubns.
Lowery, Dave. Advanced Model Railroads. LC 93-70585. (Illus.). 80p. 1993. 12.98 (*1-56138-223-X*) Courage Bks.
Lowery, David, jt. auth. see Berry, William.
Lowery, Fred. Whistling in the Dark: The Story of Fred Lowery, the Blind Whistler. LC 83-4085. (Illus.). 416p. 1983. 25.00 (*0-88289-298-3*) Pelican.
Lowery, George H., Jr. Louisiana Birds. 3rd ed. LC 74-77662. (Illus.). xxx, 651p. 1974. 29.95 (*0-8071-0087-0*) La State U Pr.
— Mammals of Louisiana & Its Adjacent Waters. LC 73-89662. (Illus.). xxiv, 565p. 1974. 29.95 (*0-8071-0609-7*) La State U Pr.
Lowery, Gwen. Managing Projects with Microsoft Project: Version 4.0 for Windows & the Macintosh. 3rd ed. 304p. 1994. pap. 24.95 (*0-442-01768-5*) Van Nos Reinhold.
— Managing Projects with Microsoft Project for Windows. LC 90-12592. 1990. pap. 25.95 (*0-442-00411-7*) Van Nos Reinhold.
Lowery, Joanne. Coming to This. LC 90-2779. 80p. (Orig.). 1990. pap. 7.50 (*0-931832-50-0*) Fithian Pr.
— Corinth. LC 90-70445. 59p. (Orig.). 1991. pap. 7.00 (*1-56002-102-0*) Aegina Pr.
Lowery, Joanne & Anton, Debra. Christmas Gatherings: An American Celebration. Slack, Steve, ed. (Illus.). 118p. 1991. 19.95 (*0-944493-05-X*) Sampler Pubns.
Lowery, John. The Professional Pilot. LC 82-17207. (Illus.). 248p. (C). 1982. pap. 17.95 (*0-8138-1410-3*) Iowa St U Pr.
Lowery, Lawrence & Verbeeck, Carol. Explorations in Earth Science. 1987. pap. 6.99 (*0-8224-2315-4*) Fearon Teach Aids.
— Explorations in Life Science. (J). (gr. 1-3). 1987. pap. 6.99 (*0-8224-2314-6*) Fearon Teach Aids.
— Explorations in Physical Science. (J). (gr. 1-3). 1987. pap. 6.99 (*0-8224-2316-2*) Fearon Teach Aids.
Lowery, Linda. Earth Day. (Holiday on My Own Ser.). (Illus.). 48p. (J). (gr. k-3). 1991. lib. bdg. 15.95 (*0-87614-662-0*, Carolrhoda) Lerner Group.
— Earth Day. (J). (gr. k-3). 1992. pap. 5.95 (*0-87614-560-8*, Carolrhoda) Lerner Group.
— Earth Day. (Illus.). (J). (gr. 2-4). 1993. audio 22.95 (*0-87499-303-2*); audio, pap. 14.95 (*0-87499-302-4*) Live Oak Media.
— Earth Day, 4 bks., Set. (Illus.). (J). (gr. 2-4). 1993. audio, pap. 33.95 (*0-87499-304-0*) Live Oak Media.
— Earthwise at Home. (J). (gr. 1-4). 1992. 19.95 (*0-87614-730-9*, Carolrhoda) Lerner Group.
— Earthwise at Home: A Guide to the Care & Feeding of Your Planet. (J). (ps-3). 1992. pap. 7.95 (*0-87614-585-3*, Carolrhoda) Lerner Group.
— Earthwise at Play: A Guide to the Care & Feeding of Your Planet. (J). (gr. 1-4). 1992. pap. 7.95 (*0-87614-586-1*, Carolrhoda) Lerner Group.
— Georgia O'Keefe. LC 94-25413. (On My Own Bks.). (J). 1995. write for info. (*0-87614-860-7*, Carolrhoda) Lerner Group.
— Laurie Tells. LC 93-9786. (J). (gr. 4 up). 1994. 18.95 (*0-87614-790-2*, Carolrhoda) Lerner Group.
— Martin Luther King Day. (Carolrhoda On My Own Bks.). (Illus.). 56p. (J). (gr. k-3). 1987. lib. bdg. 15.95 (*0-87614-299-4*, Carolrhoda) Lerner Group.
— Martin Luther King Day. (Illus.). (J). (gr. 3-5). 1987. audio 19.95 (*0-87499-071-8*); audio, pap. 12.95 (*0-87499-070-X*); audio 27.95 (*0-87499-072-6*) Live Oak Media.
— Martin Luther King Day. (Holiday on My Own Bks.). (Illus.). 56p. (J). (gr. k-3). 1987. reprint ed. pap. 5.95 (*0-87614-468-7*, Lerner Publctns) Lerner Group.
— Somebody Somewhere Knows My Name. LC 94-49538. (Illus.). 1995. write for info. (*0-87614-946-8*, Carolrhoda) Lerner Group.
— Twist with a Burger, Jitter with a Bug. LC 93-38236. (Illus.). 32p. (J). 1994. 14.95 (*0-395-67022-5*) Ticknor & Fields.
— Wilma Mankiller. LC 95-12203. (On My Own Bks.). (Illus.). (J). 1996. write for info. (*0-87614-880-1*, Carolrhoda) Lerner Group.
***Lowery, Linda & Botts, Betty.** Earthwise Teaching Guide. (J). (gr. 1-4). 1994. 19.95 (*0-87614-461-X*) Lerner Group.
Lowery, Linda & Lorbiecki, Marybeth. Earthwise at School: A Guide to the Care & Feeding of Your Planet. LC 92-11221. (J). (gr. 1-4). 1993. lib. bdg. 19.95 (*0-87614-731-7*, Carolrhoda) Lerner Group.
— Earthwise at School: A Guide to the Care & Feeding of Your Planet. LC 92-11221. (J). (ps-3). 1993. pap. write for info. (*0-87614-587-X*, Carolrhoda) Lerner Group.
Lowery, Linda, jt. auth. see Lorbiecki, Marybeth.
Lowery, Marilyn. How to Write Romance Novels. 1982. 12.95 (*0-89256-224-2*, Rawson Assocs) Macmillan.
Lowery, Mildred. In the Shadows of the Big Thicket. 120p. Date not set. 16.95 (*1-878096-27-3*) Best E TX Pubs.
Lowery, Mimi, jt. auth. see Brown, Tracey.
Lowery, Missy. Not Just Another Day: Families, Grief, & Special Days. (Orig.). 1992. pap. 2.60 (*1-56123-055-3*) Centering Corp.
Lowery, Richard H. Revelation: Hope for the World in Troubled Times. LC 93-45777. (Covenant Bible Study Ser.). 1994. pap. 4.95 (*0-87178-739-3*) Brethren.
Lowery, Robert, ed. see Nathan, George J.
Lowery, Robert G. Sean O'Casey's Autobiographies: An Annotated Index. LC 83-826. xxxi, 487p. 1983. text ed. 65.00 (*0-313-23765-4*, LYS/, Greenwood Pr) Greenwood.
Lowery, Robert G., ed. A Whirlwind in Dublin: The Plough & the Stars Riots. LC 83-22652. (Contributions to Drama & Theatre Studies: No. 11). xiii, 121p. 1984. text ed. 29.95 (*0-313-23764-6*, LOW/, Greenwood Pr) Greenwood.
Lowery, Roger C. & Cody, Sue A. Political Science: Illustrated Search Strategy & Sources. (Library Research Guides Ser.: No. 12). 224p. 1993. pap. 25.00 (*0-87650-290-7*) Pierian.
***Lowery, Ruth A.** The Banner Book. 96p. 1995. pap. 15.95 (*0-8019-8641-9*) Chilton.
Lowery, Shearon A. & DeFleur, Melvin L. Milestones in Mass Communication Research. 2nd ed. (Illus.). 472p. (C). 1988. text ed. 47.95 (*0-8013-0039-8*, 75702); pap. text ed. 29.50 (*0-8013-0038-X*, 75702) Longman.
— Milestones in Mass Communication Research: Media Effects. 3rd ed. LC 94-3707. 432p. (C). 1995. pap. text ed. 30.95 (*0-8013-1437-2*) Longman.
Lowery, T. L., ed. El Don del Espiritu Santo. 80p. (SPA.). 1978. pap. 3.95 (*0-87148-307-6*) Pathway Pr.
Lowery, William R., et al. College Admissions Counseling. LC 82-48086. (Jossey-Bass Series in Higher Education). 652p. reprint ed. pap. 180.00 (*0-7837-0181-0*, 2040477) Bks Demand.
Lowes, Bryan, jt. auth. see Pass, Christopher.
***Lowes, Bryan, et al.** Understanding Companies & Markets. 350p. 1994. pap. write for info. (*0-631-19718-4*) Blackwell Pubs.
Lowes, F. J., et al, eds. Geomagnetism & Palaeomagnetism. (C). 1988. lib. bdg. 136.50 (*0-7923-0084-X*) Kluwer Ac.
Lowes, John L. Art of Geoffrey Chaucer. LC 70-114910. (Select Bibliographies Reprint Ser.). 1930. 6.00 (*0-8369-5315-0*) Ayer.
— Convention & Revolt in Poetry. 1972. 59.95 (*0-87968-943-9*) Gordon Pr.
— Geoffrey Chaucer. LC 83-45446. reprint ed. 26.00 (*0-404-20161-X*) AMS Pr.
— The Road to Xanadu: A Study in the Ways of the Imagination. LC 85-42661. 656p. 1986. 80.00x (*0-691-06645-0*); pap. 21.95x (*0-691-01421-3*) Princeton U Pr.
— The Road to Xanadu; a Study in the Ways of the Imagination. (BCL1-PR English Literature Ser.). 639p. 1992. reprint ed. lib. bdg. 109.00 (*0-7812-7501-6*) Rprt Serv.
Lowes, Peter D. The Genesis of International Narcotics Control. Grob, Gerald N., ed. LC 80-1267. (Additionn in America Ser.). 1981. reprint ed. lib. bdg. 23.95 (*0-405-13605-6*) Ayer.
Lowesdale School Children. Sarah Snail. LC 92-27084. (Voyages Ser.). (Illus.). (J). 1993. 3.75 (*0-383-03592-9*) SRA Schl Grp.
Loweth, Garth S., ed. see Davis, Robert E.
Lowett, Garth E., ed. see Berg, Charles M.
Lowett, Garth S., ed. see Karimi, A. M.
Lowett, Garth S., ed. see Pryluck, Calvin.
Lowett, Garth S., ed. see Shain, Russell E.
Lowett, Garth S., ed. see Stuart, Frederic.
Lowett, Garth S., ed. see Wead, George.
Lowey, Iklana & Inserm. The Polish School of Philosophy of Medicine: From Tytus Chalubinski (1820-1889) to Ludwick Fleck (1896-1961) (Philosophy & Medicine Ser.). 304p. 1990. lib. bdg. 89.00 (*0-7923-0958-8*) Kluwer Ac.
Lowhagen, Torsten, jt. auth. see Stanley, Michael W.
***Lowi, Miriam R.** Water & Power: The Politics of a Scarce Resource in the Jordan River Basin. (Middle East Library: No. 31). (Illus.). 320p. (C). Date not set. pap. write for info. (*0-521-55836-0*) Cambridge U Pr.
— Water & Power: The Politics of a Scarce Resource in the Jordan River Basin. LC 92-38277. (Middle East Library: No. 31). (Illus.). 276p. (C). 1993. 54.95 (*0-521-43164-6*) Cambridge U Pr.
Lowi, Theodore. The Intelligent Person's Guide to Political Corruption. 1981. 1.00 (*1-55614-053-3*) U of SD Gov Res Bur.
Lowi, Theodore J. The End of Liberalism: The Second Republic of the United States. (Illus.). (C). 1979. pap. text ed. 14.95 (*0-393-09000-0*) Norton.
— The End of the Republican Era. LC 94-31038. (Julia J. Rothbaum Distinguished Lecture Ser.: Vol. 5). (Illus.). 296p. 1995. 22.95 (*0-8061-2701-5*) U of Okla Pr.
— The Personal President: Power Invested, Promise Unfulfilled. LC 84-45804. 240p. 1985. 32.95 (*0-8014-1798-8*); pap. 12.95 (*0-8014-9426-5*) Cornell U Pr.
Lowi, Theodore J. & Ginsberg, Benjamin. American Government: Freedom & Power. (Illus.). (C). 1989. pap. text ed. 32.95 (*0-393-96020-X*) Norton.
— American Government: Freedom & Power. (Illus.). (C). 1990. text ed. 39.95 (*0-393-95699-7*) Norton.
— American Government: Freedom & Power. LC 93-14452. (Illus.). (C). 1994. pap. text ed. 14.95 (*0-393-96492-2*) Norton.
— American Government: Freedom & Power. LC 93-14452. (Illus.). (C). 1994. pap. text ed. write for info. (*0-393-96493-0*) Norton.
— American Government: Freedom & Power. (Illus.). (C). 1994. pap. text ed. 13.95 (*0-393-96494-9*) Norton.
— American Government: Freedom & Power. 2nd ed. LC 92-38847. (C). Date not set. pap. text ed. write for info. (*0-393-96406-X*) Norton.
— American Government: Freedom & Power. 3rd ed. LC 93-14452. (Illus.). (C). 1994. pap. text ed. 39.95 (*0-393-96465-5*) Norton.
— American Government: Freedom & Power. 3rd ed. (Illus.). (C). 1994. pap. text ed. 29.95 (*0-393-96473-6*) Norton.
— American Government: Freedom & Power. 6th ed. (Illus.). (C). 1994. pap. text ed. write for info. (*0-393-96495-7*) Norton.
— Embattled Democracy: Politics & Policy in the Clinton Era. LC 95-3403. (C). 1995. pap. text ed. 10.95 (*0-393-96197-4*) Norton.
— Poliscide: Big Government, Big Science, Lilliputian Politics. LC 89-25001. 330p. (C). 1990. reprint ed. pap. text ed. 24.50 (*0-8191-7654-0*) U Pr of Amer.
Lowi, Theodore J. & Stone, Alan, eds. Nationalizing Government: Public Policies in America. LC 78-19848. (Illus.). 455p. reprint ed. pap. 129.70 (*0-8357-8493-2*, 2034767) Bks Demand.
Lowi, Theodore J., et al. Analyzing American Government. (Orig.). (C). 1994. pap. text ed. 11.95 (*0-393-96496-5*) Norton.
Lowic, Lawrence. The Architectural Heritage of St. Louis 1803-1891. LC 81-71595. (Illus.). 160p. 1982. pap. 10.00 (*0-936316-02-0*) Wash U Gallery.
Lowic, Nicholas. Coinage & History of the Islamic World. Cribb, Joe, ed. (Collected Studies: No. CS311). 352p. 1990. text ed. 87.50 (*0-86078-259-X*, Pub. by Variorum UK) Ashgate Pub Co.
Lowick, Nicholas. Islamic Coins & Trade in the Medieval World. Cribb, Joe, ed. (Collected Studies: No. 318). 300p. 1990. text ed. 87.50 (*0-86078-267-0*, Pub. by Variorum UK) Ashgate Pub Co.
Lowie, R. H. Notes on Hopi Clans. LC 74-7984. (Anthropological Papers of the American Museum of Natural History: Vol. 30, Pt. 6). 12.95 (*0-404-11873-9*) AMS Pr.
Lowie, Robert H. The Assiniboine. LC 74-7978. reprint ed. 22.45 (*0-404-11868-2*) AMS Pr.
— The Crow Indians. LC 35-9409. (Illus.). 350p. 1982. reprint ed. pap. 9.95 (*0-8290-0409-2*) Irvington.
— The Crow Indians. LC 82-20103. (Illus.). xxii, 350p. 1983. reprint ed. pap. 12.00 (*0-8032-7909-4*, Bison Books) U of Nebr Pr.
— Hidatsa Texts. LC 74-7979. reprint ed. 11.50 (*0-404-11870-4*) AMS Pr.
— Indians of the Plains. LC 81-21813. xxvi, 223p. 1982. reprint ed. pap. 8.95 (*0-8032-7907-8*) U of Nebr Pr.
— The Material Culture of the Crow Indians. LC 74-7980. reprint ed. 11.50 (*0-404-11869-0*) AMS Pr.
— Myths & Traditions of the Crow Indians. LC 93-3734. xxviii, 308p. (C). 1993. pap. 9.95 (*0-8032-7944-2*, Bison Books) U of Nebr Pr.
— Myths & Traditions of the Crow Indians. LC 74-7981. reprint ed. 24.00 (*0-404-11872-0*) AMS Pr.
— The Northern Shoshone. LC 74-7983. reprint ed. 16.00 (*0-404-11871-2*) AMS Pr.
— Notes on the Social Organizations & Customs of the Mandan, Hidatsa, & Crow Indians. LC 74-7985. 1976. reprint ed. 13.45 (*0-404-11874-7*) AMS Pr.
— The Religion of the Crow Indians. LC 74-7986. reprint ed. 15.00 (*0-404-11876-3*) AMS Pr.
— Robert H. Lowie, Ethnologist: A Personal Record. LC 59-8762. (Illus.). 311p. reprint ed. pap. 64.50 (*0-685-20504-5*, 2029955) Bks Demand.
— Social Life of the Crow Indians. LC 74-7987. reprint ed. 11.50 (*0-404-11875-5*) AMS Pr.
— The Sun Dance of the Crow Indians. LC 76-43771. (AMNH. Anthropological Papers: Vol. 16, Pt. 1). 1977. reprint ed. 12.50 (*0-404-15624-X*) AMS Pr.
— The Tobacco Society of the Crow Indians. LC 74-7988. reprint ed. 13.45 (*0-404-11878-X*) AMS Pr.
Lowie, Robert H., tr. see Nimuendaju, Curt.
Lowie, Robert H., ed. see Nimuendaju, Curt.
Lowin, Joseph. Cynthia Ozick. 208p. 1988. text ed. 21.95 (*0-8057-7526-9*, TUSAS 545, Twayne) Macmillan.
— Hebrewspeak: An Insider's Guide to the Way Jews Think. LC 94-46454. 240p. 1995. 29.95 (*1-56821-418-9*) Aronson.
Lowinger, Armand. Methodology of Pierre Duhem. reprint ed. 10.00 (*0-404-04058-6*) AMS Pr.
***Lowinger, Thomas C. & Hinman, George W., eds.** Nuclear Power at the Crossroads: Challenges & Prospects for the Twenty-First Century. LC 93-81259. (Illus.). 218p. 1994. 24.00 (*0-918714-42-7*) Intl Res Ctr Energy.
Lowinsky, Edward E. Music in the Culture of the Renaissance & Other Essays, 2 vols. (Illus.). 1000p. 1989. lib. bdg. 250.00 (*0-226-49478-0*) U Ch Pr.
— Tonality & Atonality in Sixteenth-Century Music. (Music Reprint Ser.). 1989. 25.00 (*0-306-76299-4*) Da Capo.
Lowinsky, Edward E., ed. Medici Codex of Fifteen Eighteen, Vol. 1: Historical Introduction & Commentary. LC 67-13810. (Monuments of Renaissance Music Ser.: Vols. 1, 2 & 3). 1968. Vol. 1, Historical Introduction & Commentary. lib. bdg. 100.00 (*0-226-49480-2*) U Ch Pr.
— Medici Codex of Fifteen Eighteen, Vol. 2: Transcription. LC 67-13810. (Monuments of Renaissance Music Ser.: Vols. 1, 2 & 3). 1968. Vol. 2, Transcription. lib. bdg. 100.00 (*0-226-49481-0*) U Ch Pr.
— Medici Codex of Fifteen Eighteen, Vol. 3: Facsimile Edition. LC 67-13810. (Monuments of Renaissance Music Ser.: Vols. 1, 2 & 3). 1968. Vol. 3, Facsimile Edition. lib. bdg. 100.00 (*0-226-49482-9*) U Ch Pr.
Lowinsky, Naomi R. Stories from the Motherline: Reclaiming the Mother-Daughter Bond, Finding Our Feminine Souls. 256p. 1992. 19.95 (*0-87477-680-5*) J P Tarcher.
Lowinson, Joyce, et al. Substance Abuse: A Comprehensive Textbook. 2nd ed. (Illus.). 1136p. 1992. text ed. 140.00 (*0-683-05211-X*) Williams & Wilkins.
Lowinson, Joyce H. & Stimmel, Barry, eds. Conceptual Issues in Alcoholism & Substance Abuse. LC 84-3762. (Advances in Alcohol & Substance Abuse Ser.: Vol. 3, No. 3). 102p. 1984. text ed. 39.95 (*0-86656-316-4*) Haworth Pr.
Lowis, George W., comp. Sociodemographic Factors in the Epidemiology of Multiple Sclerosis: An Annotated Bibliography. LC 90-14016. (Bibliographies & Indexes in Medical Studies: No. 5). 256p. 1991. text ed. 59.95 (*0-313-26838-X*, LSY/, Greenwood Pr) Greenwood.
***Lowis, Peter.** South Africa, Free at Last. LC 95-12096. (Hot Off the Press Ser.). (J). 1996. write for info. (*0-8172-4175-2*) Raintree Steck-V.
Lowit, Roxanne, photos. Moments: Roxanne Lowit Photographs. LC 93-11115. (Illus.). 1993. 45.00 (*0-86565-145-0*) Vendome.

An Asterisk (*) at the beginning of an entry indicates that the title is appearing in BIP for the first time.

Lowith, Karl. From Hegel to Nietzsche. 1991. text ed. 63.00 (*0-231-07498-0*) Col U Pr.
— From Hegel to Nietzsche: The Revolution in Nineteenth Century Thought. 1991. pap. text ed. 16.50 (*0-231-07499-9*) Col U Pr.
— Martin Heidegger & European Nihilism. Wolin, Richard, ed. Steiner, Gary, tr. LC 94-48411. (European Perspectives Ser.). 1995. write for info. (*0-231-08406-4*) Col U Pr.
— Max Weber & Karl Marx. LC 93-18705. (Classics in Sociology Ser.). (ENG.). 1993. write for info. (*0-415-09381-3*) Routledge.
— Meaning in History: The Theological Implications of the Philosophy of History. LC 57-7900. 1957. pap. text ed. 11.95 (*0-226-49555-8*, P16) U Ch Pr.
— My Life in Germany Before & after 1933: A Report. King, Elizabeth, tr. LC 93-43772. (Illus.). 192p. 1994. 32.95 (*0-252-02121-5*); pap. 14.95 (*0-252-06409-7*) U of Ill Pr.
Lowitt, Richard. Bronson M. Cutting: Progressive Politician. LC 92-15345. (Illus.). 7432p. 1992. 55.00x (*0-8263-1347-7*) U of NM Pr.
— George W. Norris: The Making of a Progressive, 1861 to 1912. LC 79-18826. (Illus.). 341p. 1980. reprint ed. text ed. 65.00 (*0-313-22103-0*, LOGN, Greenwood Pr) Greenwood.
— George W. Norris: The Persistence of a Progressive, 1913-1933. LC 76-147923. (Illus.). 605p. 1971. 44.95 (*0-252-00176-1*) U of Ill Pr.
— The New Deal & the West. LC 93-15538. 1993. 14.95 (*0-8061-2557-8*) U of Okla Pr.
***Lowitt, Richard, ed.** Politics in the Postwar American West. LC 94-43095. (Illus.). 416p. 1995. 49.50x (*0-8061-2711-2*); pap. 19.95x (*0-8061-2741-4*) U of Okla Pr.
Lowitt, Richard, ed. see Garst, Roswell.
Lowitz, Barry B., jt. ed. see Casciato, Dennis A.
***Lowitz, Leza & Aoyama, Miyuki, eds.** Other Side River: Free Verse. Aoyama, Miyuki, tr. (Rock Spring Collection of Japanese Literature). (Illus.). 256p. (Orig.). 1995. pap. 14.00 (*1-880656-16-7*) Stone Bridge Pr.
Lowitz, Leza, et al, eds. A Long Rainy Season: Haiku & Tanka, Vol. 1. LC 94-28749. (Contemporary Japanese Women's Poetry Ser.: Vol. 1). 200p. (Orig.). 1994. pap. 12.00 (*1-880656-15-9*) Stone Bridge Pr.
Lowman, Al. Peter Mansbendel: A Swiss Woodcarver in Texas. (Illus.). 44p. pap. 2.38 (*0-933164-21-1*) U of Tex Inst Tex Culture.
— Printing Arts in Texas. (Illus.). 109p. 1981. 25.00 (*0-686-73811-X*, PA2-16-7528) Jenkins.
Lowman, Al, jt. intro. see Lee, Amy F.
Lowman, Evelyn. Arts & Crafts for the Elderly: A Resource Book for Activity Directors in Healthcare Facilities. LC 91-24182. (Illus.). 232p. 1992. 28.95 (*0-8261-7860-X*) Springer Pub.
Lowman, Guy S., Jr., jt. auth. see Kurath, Hans.
Lowman, Gwen, jt. ed. see Cater, Erlet.
Lowman, J., et al, eds. Transcarceration: Essays in the Sociology of Social Control. (Cambridge Studies in Criminology). 370p. 1987. text ed. 68.95 (*0-566-05106-0*, Pub. by Avebury Pub UK) Ashgate Pub Co.
Lowman, John & MacLean, Brian D., eds. Realist Criminology: Crime Control & Policing in the 1990s. LC 92-95006. 370p. 1992. pap. 24.95 (*0-8020-7702-1*) U of Toronto Pr.
Lowman, Joseph. Mastering the Techniques of Teaching. LC 83-49265. (Higher & Adult Education Ser.). 264p. 1990. pap. 22.00x (*1-55542-221-7*) Jossey-Bass.
— Mastering the Techniques of Teaching. 2nd ed. LC 95-12476. (Higher & Adult Education Ser.). 1995. 29.95 (*0-7879-0127-X*) Jossey-Bass.
— Mastering the Techniques of Teaching. LC 83-49265. (Jossey-Bass Higher Education Ser.). 267p. reprint ed. pap. 76.10 (*0-7837-2517-5*, 2042676) Bks Demand.
— Supershrink II: 3.5" 119p. (C). 1990. pap. text ed. 22.75 (*0-15-584764-3*) HB Coll Pubs.
— Supershrink II: 5.25" 119p. (C). 1990. pap. text ed. 22.75 (*0-15-584763-5*) HarBrace.
Lowman, Kathleen D., jt. ed. see Benjamin, Ludy T., Jr.
Lowman, Kaye. Of Cradles & Careers: A Guide to Reshaping Your Job to Include a Baby in Your Life. LC 84-80085. (Illus.). 300p. 1984. pap. 7.95 (*0-912500-14-X*) La Leche.
Lowman, Kaye & Kaszonyi, Kay. Especially for You. (Illus.). 1985. 1.50 (*0-912500-28-X*) La Leche.
***Lowman, Margaret D. & Nadkarni, Nalini M., eds.** Forest Canopies. (Physiological Ecology Ser.). (Illus.). 576p. 1995. text ed. 69.95 (*0-12-457650-8*) Acad Pr.
Lowman, Robert G., et al. Experimental Introductory Chemistry: Organic & Biochemistry. (Illus.). 84p. 1983. pap. text ed. 5.95x (*0-89641-125-7*) American Pr.
— Experimental Introductory Chemistry in 2 Pts. (Illus.). 274p. 1981. pap. text ed. 13.95x (*0-89641-096-X*) American Pr.
Lowman, Rodney L. The Clinical Practice of Career Assessment: Abilities, Interests, & Personality. (Illus.). 333p. (C). 1991. 37.50 (*1-55798-106-X*); pap. 19.50 (*1-55798-119-1*) Am Psychol.
— Counseling & Psychotherapy of Work Dysfunctions. (Illus.). 348p. 1993. text ed. 39.95 (*1-55798-204-X*); pap. text ed. 24.95 (*1-55798-205-8*) Am Psychol.
— Pre-Employment Screening for Psychopathology: A Guide to Professional Practice. Smith, Harold H., Jr., ed. LC 88-43546. (Practitioner's Resource Ser.). 86p. 1989. pap. 14.70 (*0-943158-34-6*, PESPB) Pro Resource.
Lowman, Rodney L. & Resnick, Robert J., eds. The Mental Health Professional's Guide to Managed Care. 197p. 1994. pap. text ed. 24.95 (*1-55798-232-5*) Am Psychol.
***Lowman, Zelvin D.** A Voice in the Desert: A History of First Presbyterian Church, Las Vegas, Nevada. (Illus.). 168p. 1992. 19.95 (*1-881576-03-5*) Providence Hse.
Lowmiller, Cathie, jt. auth. see Mike, Jan M.
Lowmiller, Cathie, jt. auth. see Mike, Jan.
Lown, Bella. Memories of My Life: A Personal History of a Lithuanian Shtetl. Joseph, Teresa, ed. LC 91-52907. 224p. 1991. 19.75 (*0-934710-27-9*) J Simon.
Lown, David, jt. auth. see Lown, Patricia T.
Lown, J. W., ed. Anthracycline & Anthracenedione-Based Anticancer Agents. (Bioactive Molecules Ser.: No. 6). 738p. 1989. 225.75 (*0-444-87275-2*) Elsevier.
Lown, Judy. Women & Industrialisation: Gender & Work in the Nineteenth Century. (Feminist Perspectives Ser.). 256p. (C). 1990. text ed. 44.95 (*0-8166-1846-1*) U of Minn Pr.
***Lown, Patricia T. & Lown, David.** Tout Paris: The Source Guide to the Art of French Decoration. (Illus.). 410p. 1994. 39.00 (*0-9643256-0-8*) Tout Paris-Palancar.
— Treasures of France: A Tout Paris Guide. (Illus.). 540p. 1996. 29.00 (*0-9643256-2-4*, Tout Paris) Tout Paris-Palancar.
Lown, Rebecca. Inner Dictates. 1992. 44.00 (*0-932526-39-X*) Nexus Pr.
Lown, Wilford F. The Church Bored. LC 88-63247. 140p. (Orig.). 1989. pap. 4.95 (*0-89900-327-3*) College Pr Pub.
Lowndes, Belloc. Lodger. 1976. 22.95 (*0-8488-0180-6*) Amereon Ltd.
Lowndes, L. & Rudolf, R. Law of General Average. (C). 1975. 800.00 (*0-685-32750-7*, Pub. by Witherby & Co UK) St Mut.
Lowndes, Leil. How to Talk to Anybody about Anything: Breaking the Ice with Everyone from Accountants to Zen Buddhists. 208p. 1993. pap. 9.95 (*0-8065-1458-2*, Citadel Pr) Carol Pub Group.
— Shopping the Insider's Way. 192p. 1985. pap. 5.95 (*0-8065-0939-2*, Citadel Pr) Carol Pub Group.
Lowndes, Marie A. The End of Her Honeymoon. LC 75-32763. (Literature of Mystery & Detection Ser.). 1976. reprint ed. 20.95 (*0-405-07884-6*) Ayer.
— Some Men & Women. LC 75-150549. (Short Story Index Reprint Ser.). 1977. reprint ed. 23.95 (*0-8369-3846-1*) Ayer.
— Studies in Love & in Terror. LC 74-167462. (Short Story Index Reprint Ser.). 1977. reprint ed. 21.95 (*0-8369-3988-3*) Ayer.
***Lowndes, Marie B.** The Lodger. Marcus, Laura, ed. (Oxford Popular Fiction Ser.). 224p. 1995. pap. 7.95 (*0-19-282371-X*) OUP.
— The Lodger. 224p. 1988. reprint ed. pap. 5.95 (*0-89733-299-7*) Academy Chi Pubs.
Lowndes, Robert A. Orchids for Doc: The Literary Adventures & Autobiography of Robert A. W. "Doc" Lowndes. LC 93-332. (Borgo Bioviews Ser.: No. 7). 144p. Date not set. lib. bdg. write for info. (*0-89370-344-3*); pap. write for info. (*0-89370-444-X*) Borgo Pr.
Lowndes, Robert A., jt. auth. see Ashley, Mike.
Lowndes, Rosemary, jt. auth. see Kailer, Claude.
Lowndes, William. The Royal Crescent in Bath: A Fragment of English Life. 96p. 1988. 60.00 (*0-905459-34-2*, Pub. by Redcliffe Pr Ltd) St Mut.
— The Theatre Royal at Bath. 1988. 39.00 (*0-317-20314-2*, Pub. by Redcliffe Pr Ltd) St Mut.
Lowndes, William, jt. auth. see Hardy, Paul.
Lownes, Millicent G. Entrepreneurially Yours: A Compilation of Articles about Starting & Managing a Small Business. Deming, Lynne, ed. 50p. (Orig.). 1990. pap. 5.95 (*0-943267-13-7*) Busn Your Own.
— The Purple Rose Within: A Woman's Basic Guide for Developing a Business Plan. Deming, Lynne, ed. 70p. (Orig.). 1989. pap. 9.95 (*0-943267-14-5*) Busn Your Own.
Lownes, Victor. The Day the Bunny Died. (Illus.). 224p. 1983. 14.95 (*0-8184-0340-3*) Carol Pub Group.
Lowney, Frank, ed. see Kujichagulia, Phavia.
Lowney, Kathleen S. Passport to Heaven: Gender Roles in the Unification Church. LC 92-20892. (Cults & Nonconventional Religious Groups Ser.). 248p. 1992. 74.00 (*0-8153-0775-6*) Garland.
Lowney, Roger G. Mentor Teachers: The California Model. LC 86-61750. (Fastback Ser.: No. 247). 50p. (Orig.). 1986. pap. 1.25 (*0-87367-247-X*) Phi Delta Kappa.
Lownie, Andrew, jt. ed. see Jeffreys-Jones, Rhodri.
Lownsbery, Eloise. Saints & Rebels. LC 72-156682. (Essay Index Reprint Ser.). 1977. reprint ed. 24.95 (*0-8369-2322-7*) Ayer.
Lowood, Henry. Patriotism, Profit & Promotion in the German Enlightenment: The Economic & Scientific Societies, 1760-1815. rev. ed. LC 91-27131. (Modern European History Ser.: No. 2). 464p. 1991. 90.00 (*0-8153-0677-6*) Garland.
Lowood, Henry E., jt. comp. see Rider, Robin E.
Lowrance, Richard, et al, eds. Agricultural Ecosystems: Unifying Concepts. LC 83-23504. (Wiley-Interscience Publication Ser.). 245p. reprint ed. pap. 69.90 (*0-7837-2400-4*, 2040085) Bks Demand.
Lowrance, William W. Modern Science & Human Values. 250p. 1986. pap. 15.95 (*0-19-504211-5*) OUP.
Lowrey, Alvin L. Lowrey's International Trumpet Discography, 2 vols., Set. LC 89-23960. 1677p. 1990. 150.00 (*0-938100-79-3*) Camden Hse.
Lowrey, Ernest, jt. auth. see Echols, William.
Lowrey, Janette S. The Poky Little Puppy. (Golden Sturdy Shape Bks.). (Illus.). 14p. (J). (ps-00). 1992. bds. write for info. (*0-307-12333-2*, 12333, Golden Pr) Western Pub.
— The Poky Little Puppy. (Big Golden Book Ser.). (Illus.). 24p. (J). (ps-00). 1992. reprint ed. write for info. (*0-307-10394-3*, 10394, Golden Bks) Western Pub.
***Lowrey, Joan, ed.** German Research Association Surname Book, Vol. I. 338p. (Orig.). 1990. pap. text ed. write for info. (*0-9626271-0-0*) German Res Assn.
Lowrey, Joan, jt. auth. see Przecha, Donna.
Lowrey, John, ed. Architectural Heritage III: Mackintosh & His Contemporaries. (Architectural Heritage Ser.). (Illus.). 128p. 1992. text ed. 49.00 (*0-685-57098-3*, Pub. by Edinburgh U Pr UK); pap. 20.00 (*0-7486-0382-4*, Pub. by Edinburgh U Pr UK) Col U Pr.
Lowrey, Lawrence. Secrets of Winning at Casino Roulette. 32p. 1988. pap. 6.95 (*0-934650-15-2*) Sunnyside.
Lowrey, Nathan, jt. auth. see Boynton, Mia.
Lowrey, Robert E., jt. ed. see Grimshaw, James A., Jr.
Lowrey, Robert S., jt. auth. see Cullison, Arthur E.
Lowrey, Wilson H. Radio in Rural Guatemala: Three Case Studies. (Illus.). 150p. (Orig.). (C). 1990. pap. text ed. 5.95 (*0-943089-01-8*) U GA CFIMCTR.
Lowrie, Alan. Carnivorous Plants of Australia, Vol. 2. (Illus.). 272p. 1990. 38.50 (*0-85564-299-8*, Pub. by Univ of West Aust Pr AT); pap. 27.50 (*0-85564-300-5*, Pub. by Univ of West Aust Pr AT) Intl Spec Bk.
Lowrie, Allen. Carnivorous Plants of Australia, Vol. 1. (Illus.). 226p. 1987. 38.50 (*0-85564-253-X*, Pub. by Univ of West Aust Pr AT) Intl Spec Bk.
— Seismic Stratigraphy & Hydrocarbon Traps: Louisiana Onshore & Offshore. LC 94-35381. (Course Notes Ser.). 1995. 30.00 (*1-56080-025-9*) Soc Expl Geophys.
Lowrie, D. L. Como Empezar y Terminar Bien Su Ministerio - A Glad Beginning - a Gracious Ending. Morales, Edgar O., tr. 112p. (Orig.). (SPA.). 1991. pap. 3.95 (*0-311-42088-5*) Casa Bautista.
Lowrie, Ernest B. The Shape of the Puritan Mind: The Thought of Samuel Willard. LC 74-76650. 267p. reprint ed. pap. 76.10 (*0-8357-8319-7*, 2033808) Bks Demand.
Lowrie, Jean E. & Nagakura, Mieko, eds. School Libraries: International Developments. 2nd ed. LC 91-10920. (Illus.). 403p. 1991. 42.50 (*0-8108-2390-X*) Scarecrow.
***Lowrie, Paul & Nicholaus, Bret.** The Conversation Piece: 200 Creative & Thought-Provoking Questions. rev. ed. LC 94-65462. 64p. 1994. pap. 3.95 (*0-9634251-1-0*) Questmarc Pub.
Lowrie, Samuel H. Culture Conflict in Texas, 1821-1835. LC 32-34638. (Columbia University. Studies in the Social Sciences: No. 376). reprint ed. 12.50 (*0-404-51376-X*) AMS Pr.
— Culture Conflict in Texas, 1821-1835. 1993. reprint ed. lib. bdg. 75.00 (*0-7812-5943-6*) Rprt Serv.
Lowrie, Walter. Kierkegaard, 2 vols., Set. 28.50 (*0-8446-0778-9*) Peter Smith.
— Land Claims in the Eastern District of the Orleans Territory: Communicated to the House of Representatives, Jan. 9, 1812. 160p. 1985. reprint ed. pap. 27.50 (*0-89308-582-0*) Southern Hist Pr.
— Short Life of Kierkegaard. 1942. pap. 14.95x (*0-691-01957-6*) Princeton U Pr.
Lowrie, Walter, tr. see Kierkegaard, Soren.
Lowringer, Gene. Bluegrass Fiddle. LC 73-92395. (Illus.). 1974. pap. 12.95 (*0-8256-0150-9*, 000150, Oak) Music Sales.
***Lowry.** Anastasia Krupnik. 1995. mass mkt. 1.99 (*0-440-21955-8*) Dell.
Lowry, Barbara, jt. auth. see Vogel, J. Thomas.
Lowry, Bates. Building a National Image: Architectural Drawings for the American Democracy, 1789-1912. (Illus.). 1986. 75.00 (*0-8027-0873-0*) Walker & Co.
— Looking for Leonardo: Naive & Folk Art Objects Found in America by Bates & Isabel Lowry. LC 93-22167. (Illus.). 128p. (Orig.). 1994. pap. 24.95 (*0-87745-441-8*) U of Iowa Pr.
— Renaissance Architecture. LC 61-13691. (Great Ages of World Architecture Ser.). (Illus.). 127p. 1962. pap. 9.95 (*0-8076-0335-X*) Braziller.
Lowry, Beverly. Crossed Over. 1992. pap. 21.50 (*0-679-41184-4*) McKay.
— Crossed Over: The True Story of the Houston Pickax Murders. 304p. 1994. mass mkt. 5.99 (*0-446-36510-6*) Warner Bks.
— The Track of Real Desire. LC 93-34755. 1994. 21.00 (*0-679-42939-5*) Knopf.
Lowry, Charles W. The First Theologians. 200p. (Orig.). (C). 1986. pap. 7.95 (*0-89526-804-3*) Regnery Pub.
— To Pray or Not to Pray: A Handbook for Study of Recent Supreme Court Decisions & American Church-State Doctrine. enl. ed. LC 68-8899. 260p. 1969. 22.95 (*0-87419-013-4*) Cherokee.
— William Temple: An Archbishop for All Seasons. LC 81-43869. 170p. (Orig.). 1982. pap. text ed. 17.00 (*0-8191-2356-0*) U Pr of Amer.
Lowry, Dan. Dark & Cruel War. (Illus.). 450p. 1993. 29.50 (*0-7818-0168-0*) Hippocrene Bks.
***Lowry, Dave.** Autumn Lightning: The Education of an American Samurai. (Illus.). 194p. 1995. pap. 13.00 (*1-57062-115-2*) Shambhala Pubns.
— Bokken: Art of the Japanese Sword. Lee, Mike, ed. LC 85-63391. (Weapons Ser.). 192p. 1985. pap. 11.95 (*0-89750-104-7*, 443) Ohara Pubns.
— Sword & Brush: The Spirit of the Martial Arts. LC 95-5653. (Illus.). 144p. (Orig.). 1995. pap. 14.00 (*1-57062-112-8*) Shambhala Pubns.
Lowry, Dave & Lee, Mike. Jo: Art of the Japanese Short Staff. LC 87-42877. (Weapons Ser.). 192p. 1987. pap. 14.95 (*0-89750-116-0*, 455) Ohara Pubns.
Lowry, David. The Prophetic Element in the Church: As Conceived in the Theology of Karl Rahner. 258p. (C). 1990. lib. bdg. 5.50 (*0-8191-7857-8*) U Pr of Amer.
Lowry, Don. The Fate of the Country: The Civil War from June-September, 1864. (Illus.). 555p. 1992. 27.50 (*0-7818-0064-1*) Hippocrene Bks.
— No Turning Back: The Beginning of the End of the Civil War May-June 1864. 576p. 1991. 27.50 (*0-87052-010-5*) Hippocrene Bks.
Lowry, Edward. The Filmology Movement & Film Study in France. Kirkpatrick, Diane, ed. LC 84-24099. (Studies in Cinema: No. 33). 225p. reprint ed. pap. 64.20 (*0-8357-1630-9*, 2070458) Bks Demand.
Lowry, Edward G. Washington Close-ups. LC 70-142656. (Essay Index Reprint Ser.). 1977. 23.95 (*0-8369-2057-0*) Ayer.
Lowry, Eugene. The Homiletical Plot: The Sermon As Narrative Art Form. LC 79-92074. 100p. (Orig.). 1983. pap. 10.99 (*0-8042-1652-5*, John Knox) Westminster John Knox.
Lowry, Eugene L. How to Preach a Parable: Designs for Narrative Sermons. LC 89-191. 176p. 1989. pap. 12.95 (*0-687-17924-6*) Abingdon.
— Living with the Lectionary: Preaching the Revised Common Lectionary. 128p. (Orig.). 1992. pap. 9.95 (*0-687-17921-1*) Abingdon.
Lowry, George, et al. Lab Experiments in General Chemistry. 1992. 22.00 (*0-88252-146-2*) Paladin Hse.
Lowry, George G., ed. Markov Chains & Monte Carlo Calculations in Polymer Science. LC 70-84777. (Monographs in Macromolecular Chemistry). 338p. reprint ed. pap. 96.40 (*0-317-08367-8*, 2055048) Bks Demand.
Lowry, George G. & Lowry, Robert C. Handbook of Hazard Communication & OSHA Requirements. LC 85-6982. (Illus.). 148p. 1985. 59.95 (*0-87371-022-3*, T55) Lewis Pubs.
— Lowrys' Handbook of Right-to-Know & Emergency Planning. (Illus.). 421p. 1988. 99.95 (*0-87371-112-2*, KF370) Lewis Pubs.
Lowry, George S. Autographs: Identification & Price Guide. (Illus.). 496p. (Orig.). 1994. pap. 15.00 (*0-380-77234-5*, Confident Collect) Avon.
Lowry, Glenn D. & Nemazee, Susan. A Jeweler's Eye: Islamic Arts of the Book from the Vever Collection. (Illus.). 240p. 1989. pap. 26.95 (*0-685-44108-3*) U of Wash Pr.
Lowry, Glenn D., jt. auth. see Lentz, Thomas W.
Lowry, Glenn D., et al. A Jeweler's Eye: Islamic Arts of the Book from the Vever Collection, Set. deluxe ed. (Illus.). 448p. 1988. Boxed set. boxed 125.00 (*0-295-96681-5*) U of Wash Pr.
Lowry, Glenn R. Systems Development Through the AD - Cycle: Using the Techniques & Tools of the 90's. 592p. (C). 1995. write for info. (*0-697-20225-9*) Bus & Educ Tech.
— Systems Development Through the AD - Cycle: Using the Techniques & Tools of the 90's. 224p. (C). 1995. student ed, pap. write for info. (*0-697-20240-2*); student ed, pap. write for info. (*0-697-20241-0*) Bus & Educ Tech.
Lowry, H. G. How the Nation Was Won: America's Untold Story 1630-1754. (Illus.). 1988. pap. 14.95 (*0-943235-01-4*) Exec Intel Review.
Lowry, Heath W. The Islamization & Turkification of the City of Trabzon, c. 1486-1583. LC 93-24121. 236p. Date not set. 29.95 (*0-87850-102-9*) Darwin Pr.
Lowry II, Porter P., jt. auth. see Lowry, William P.
***Lowry, Ira S.** Development Regulation & Housing Affordability. 180p. 1992. pap. text ed. 42.95 (*0-87420-729-0*) Urban Land.
Lowry, J., et al, eds. Plants Fed to Village Ruminants in Indonesia: Notes on 136 Species, Their Composition & Significance in Village Farming Systems. 60p. (C). 1992. text ed. 60.00 (*1-86320-071-1*, Pub. by ACIAR) St Mut.
Lowry, James. Doc Source International. 1991. 95.00 (*0-316-53404-8*) Little.
Lowry, James & Weinrich. Business in Today's World. 13th ed. (C). 1994. text ed. 31.95 (*0-538-82806-4*, GB75MA) S-W Pub.
Lowry, James & Weinrich, Bernard. Business in Today's World. 812p. (C). 1989. pap. text ed. write for info. (*0-538-80255-3*, BGB75LA) S-W Pub.
Lowry, James K. Soft Bottom Macrobenthic Community of Arthur Harbor, Antarctica: Paper 1 in Biology of the Antarctic Seas V. Pawson, David L., ed. LC 75-22056. (Antarctic Research Ser.: Vol. 23). (Illus.). 20p. 1975. pap. 5.20 (*0-87590-123-9*) Am Geophysical.
Lowry, James W. Haskins Genealogy: The Descendants of Jonas Haskins (1788-1837) LC 92-97185. (Illus.). 350p. 1992. text ed. 26.95 (*1-883453-04-6*) Deutsche Buchhandlung.
— In the Whale's Belly & Other Martyr Stories. (Illus.). (YA). (gr. 7 up). 1981. pap. 4.70 (*0-87813-513-8*) Christian Light.
— North America Is the Lord's. (Christian Day School Ser.). (J). (gr. 5). 1980. 21.25x (*0-87813-916-8*) Christian Light.
***Lowry, Jan M.** The Worm Whistle. (Illus.). (J). (gr. 2). 1994. pap. text ed. 12.95 (*1-881116-36-0*) Black Forrest Pr.

is embarrassed about his seemingly insignificant life & decides to see it firsthand. Little does he know what dangers lurk outside! Wally learns many lessons regarding life, other creatures & their importance in the chain of life & the impact of his own existence. The story stresses such important topics as fairness, sharing, kindness, safety & especially of concern today, recycling & the environment. It also includes themes relating to family life & self worth. A great book for young readers, but has something for everyone (even adults). To order, send $12.95 plus 7% tax (CA only) & $3.50 (1st copy, $.50 each additional copy) shipping to: Jan M. Lowry, 55 E. Emerson St., Chula Vista, CA 91911. (Personalization available if requested in writing). ***Publisher Provided Annotation.***

Lowry, John, jt. auth. see Oughton, David.

Lowry, Linda. Inside Colorado: An Artist's View of Colorado Interiors. Publishing Group Staff, ed. (Illus.). 64p. 1993. 24.50 (*0-9635461-0-4*) Trails End Edit.

Lowry, Lois. All about Sam. (Illus.). 144p. (J). (gr. k-6). 1989. pap. 3.50 (*0-440-40221-2*, YB) Dell.

— All about Sam. (Illus.). 144p. (J). (gr. 1-5). 1988. 13.95 (*0-395-48662-9*) HM.

— Anastasia. (J). write for info. (*0-318-60131-1*) HM.

— Anastasia, Absolutely. LC 95-9710. (J). 1995. 13.95 (*0-395-74521-7*) HM.

— Anastasia Again! 160p. (J). (gr. 4-7). 1982. pap. 3.50 (*0-440-40009-0*, YB) Dell.

— Anastasia Again! (Illus.). 160p. (J). (gr. 3-6). 1981. 14.95 (*0-395-31147-0*) HM.

— Anastasia & Her Chosen Career. 192p. (J). (gr. 3-7). 1987. 13.95 (*0-395-42506-9*) HM.

— Anastasia, Ask Your Analyst. 128p. (J). (gr. 4-6). 1992. pap. 3.50 (*0-440-40289-1*, YB) Dell.

— Anastasia, Ask Your Analyst. LC 83-26687. 128p. (J). (gr. 3-6). 1984. 13.95 (*0-395-36011-0*, 5-90388) HM.

— Anastasia at This Address. 144p. (J). (gr. 4-7). 1992. pap. 3.50 (*0-440-40652-8*, YB) Dell.

— Anastasia at This Address. LC 90-48308. 112p. (J). (gr. 3-7). 1991. 13.95 (*0-395-56263-5*) HM.

— Anastasia at This Address. large type ed. (J). (gr. 1-8). 1994. 16.95 (*0-7451-2087-3*, Galaxy Child Lrg Print) Chivers N Amer.

— Anastasia at Your Service. 160p. (J). (gr. 3-6). 1984. pap. 3.50 (*0-440-40290-5*, YB) Dell.

— Anastasia at Your Service. LC 82-9231. (Illus.). 160p. (J). (gr. 3-6). 1982. 14.95 (*0-395-32865-9*) HM.

— Anastasia Has the Answers. (J). (gr. k-6). 1987. pap. 3.50 (*0-440-40087-2*, YB) Dell.

— Anastasia Has the Answers. (J). (gr. 5 up). 1986. 14.95 (*0-395-41795-3*) HM.

— Anastasia Krupnik. (J). (gr. 4-7). 1984. pap. 3.50 (*0-440-40852-0*) Dell.

— Anastasia Krupnik. 160p. (J). (gr. 3-6). 1979. 14.95 (*0-395-28629-8*) HM.

— Anastasia on Her Own. 144p. (J). (gr. 2-6). 1986. pap. 3.50 (*0-440-40291-3*, YB) Dell.

— Anastasia on Her Own. LC 84-22432. 131p. (J). (gr. 5-7). 1985. 14.95 (*0-395-38133-9*) HM.

— Attaboy, Sam! (J). (gr. 4-7). 1993. pap. 3.50 (*0-440-40816-4*) Dell.

— Attaboy, Sam! (Illus.). 128p. (J). (gr. 2-6). 1992. 14.95 (*0-395-61588-7*) HM.

— Autumn Street. 192p. (J). (gr. 4-7). 1986. pap. 3.50 (*0-440-40344-8*, YB) Dell.

— Autumn Street. 160p. (J). (gr. 5 up). 1980. 14.95 (*0-395-27812-0*) HM.

— Find a Stranger, Say Good-Bye. (J). 1990. pap. 3.50 (*0-440-20541-7*, LFL) Dell.

— Find a Stranger, Say Good-Bye. LC 78-1024. 192p. (J). (gr. 5 up). 1978. 16.95 (*0-395-26459-6*) HM.

— The Giver. 1994. mass mkt. 4.50 (*0-440-21907-8*, LFL) Dell.

— The Giver. LC 92-15034. 208p. (J). (gr. 7-9). 1993. 14.95 (*0-395-64566-2*) HM.

— The Giver. large type ed. LC 93-21002. (Teen Scene Ser.). (YA). (gr. 9-12). 1993. 15.95 (*0-7862-0055-3*) Thorndike Pr.

— Number the Stars. 1990. mass mkt. 3.99 (*0-440-40327-8*, YB) Dell.

— Number the Stars. LC 88-37134. 160p. (J). (gr. 4-7). 1989. 14.95 (*0-395-51060-0*) HM.

— The One Hundredth Thing about Caroline. 160p. (J). (gr. k-6). 1985. pap. 3.50 (*0-440-46625-3*, YB) Dell.

— The One Hundredth Thing about Caroline. 160p. (J). (gr. 3-6). 1983. 14.95 (*0-395-34829-3*) HM.

— Rabble Starkey. (J). (gr. k-6). 1988. pap. 3.50 (*0-440-40056-2*, YB) Dell.

— Rabble Starkey. (J). (gr. 5 up). 1987. 13.95 (*0-395-43607-9*) HM.

— Rabble Starkey. large type ed. 1989. 14.95 (*0-8161-4776-0*, Large Print Bks) Hall.

— A Summer to Die. (Illus.). (J). (gr. 3-7). 1977. 14.95 (*0-395-25338-1*) HM.

— Summer to Die. (YA). 1984. pap. 3.99 (*0-440-21917-5*) Bantam.

— Switcharound. 1985. 14.95 (*0-395-39536-4*) HM.

— Taking Care of Terrific. 176p. (J). (gr. 4-7). 1984. pap. 3.99 (*0-440-48494-4*, YB) Dell.

— Taking Care of Terrific. LC 82-23331. 160p. (J). (gr. 5 up). 1983. 14.95 (*0-395-34070-5*) HM.

— Us & Uncle Fraud. LC 84-12783. 192p. (J). (gr. 5-9). 1984. 10.95 (*0-395-36633-X*) HM.

— Your Move, J. P.! 128p. (J). (gr. 3-7). 1990. 13.95 (*0-395-53639-1*) HM.

— Your Move, J. P. (J). (gr. 4-7). 1991. pap. 3.50 (*0-440-40497-5*) Dell.

Lowry, Macia D. Preservation & Conservation in Small Libraries. (LAMA Small Libraries Publications: No. 5). 16p. 1989. pap. text ed. 5.00 (*0-8389-5718-8*) ALA.

Lowry, Malcolm. Au-Dessous de Volcan. (FRE.). 1973. pap. 17.95 (*0-7859-4004-9*) Fr & Eur.

— Hear Us O Lord from Heaven Thy Dwelling Place. 288p. 1986. pap. 9.95 (*0-88184-281-8*) Carroll & Graf.

— Selected Poems. (Pocket Poets Ser.: No. 17). (Orig.). 1962. pap. 3.95 (*0-87286-030-2*, PP17) City Lights.

— Sursum Corda! The Collected Letters of Malcolm Lowry, 1926-1946, Vol. I. Grace, Sherrill E., ed. (Illus.). 736p. (C). 1995. 49.95 (*0-8020-0748-1*) U of Toronto Pr.

— Under the Volcano. 1984. pap. 11.95 (*0-452-25595-3*, Plume) NAL-Dutton.

Lowry, Malcolm, jt. auth. see Aiken, Conrad.

Lowry, Martin. Power, Print & Profit: Nicholas Jenson & the Rise of Venetian Publishing in Renaissance Europe. 300p. (C). 1991. text ed. 74.95 (*0-631-17394-3*) Blackwell Pubs.

Lowry, Michael & McCartney, Robert, eds. Automating Software Design. 394p. 1991. pap. 35.00x (*0-262-62080-4*) MIT Pr.

Lowry, Michael R. Major Depression: Prevention & Treatment. 136p. 1984. 15.00 (*0-87527-186-3*) Green.

Lowry, Montecue J. The Forge of West German Rearmament: Theodor Blank & the Amt Blank. LC 89-12894. (American University Studies: History: Ser. IX, Vol. 83). 358p. 1990. text ed. 56.50 (*0-8204-1157-4*) P Lang Pubs.

— Glasnost: Deception, Desperation, Dialectics. LC 90-48821. (American University Studies: History: Ser. IX, Vol. 103). 263p. (C). 1990. text ed. 46.95 (*0-8204-1522-7*) P Lang Pubs.

Lowry, Oliver H., jt. ed. see Passonneau, Janet V.

Lowry, Peter, comp. The Good Money Guide to the Social Investment Community, 1985. 33p. (Orig.). 1985. pap. 5.00 (*0-933609-02-7*) Good Money Pubns.

Lowry, Philip J. Green Cathedrals: An Anecdotal, Pictorial, & Statistical Celebration of Major League & Negro League Ballparks. (Illus.). 256p. 1992. 23.99 (*0-201-56777-6*) Addison-Wesley.

— Green Cathedrals: The Ultimate Celebration of All 27 Major League, Negro League Ballparks Past & Present. (Illus.). 304p. 1993. pap. 15.34 (*0-201-62229-7*) Addison-Wesley.

Lowry, Porter P., jt. auth. see Lowry, William P.

Lowry, Richard. The Architecture of Chance: An Introduction to the Logic & Arithmetic of Probability. (Illus.). 192p. (C). 1989. pap. text ed. 15.95 (*0-19-505608-6*) OUP.

— The Evolution of Psychological Theory: A Critical History of Concepts & Presuppositions. 2nd ed. 256p. 1982. text ed. 47.95 (*0-202-25134-9*); pap. text ed. 26.95 (*0-202-25135-7*) Aldine de Gruyter.

Lowry, Ritchie P. Good Money: A Guide to Profitable Social Investing in the '90s. 224p. 1993. pap. 9.95 (*0-393-30951-7*) Norton.

— Good Money: Profitable Social Investing in the '90s. 1991. 19.95 (*0-393-02966-2*) Norton.

— Is the Peaceful Atom a Good Investment? 52p. (Orig.). 1983. spiral bd. 1.75 (*0-933609-03-5*) Good Money Pubns.

— Socially Responsible Stock Guide (With Supplement Insert, "How to Screen Traditional Investments for Social Factors") 48p. (Orig.). 1985. spiral bd. 2.50 (*0-933609-01-9*) Good Money Pubns.

Lowry, Robert. Nothing but the Blood. (Illus.). (J). (gr. k-6). 2.99 (*3-901170-09-X*) CEF Press.

— The Violent Wedding. LC 76-110831. 255p. 1971. reprint ed. text ed. 55.00 (*0-8371-2566-9*, LOVW, Greenwood Pr) Greenwood.

Lowry, Robert & McCardle, William H. History of Mississippi from the Discovery of the Great River by Hernando De Soto. LC 70-172755. reprint ed. 37.50 (*0-404-04610-X*) AMS Pr.

— A History of Mississippi from the Discovery of the Great River by Hernando Desoto Including the Earliest Settlement Made by the French under Iberville to the Death of Jefferson Davis. LC 78-2335. 1978. reprint ed. 30.00 (*0-87152-265-9*) Reprint.

Lowry, Robert C., jt. auth. see Lowry, George G.

Lowry, Robert W. & Dickman, David. Professional Pool & Spa Technicians' Guide to pH, Alkalinity, Water Testing, & Water Balance. 64p. 1988. pap. 6.95 (*0-685-29431-5*) Serv Industry Pubns.

Lowry, Robert W., ed. see Taylor, Charlie.

Lowry, Robin P. & Takeuchi, Takumi. The Th1-Th2 Paradigm & Transplantation Tolerance: Exploring the Microcosm of Transplantation-Of What Is Past, Passing, & to Come. (Medical Intelligence Unit Ser.). 118p. 1994. 89.95 (*1-57059-108-3*, LN9108) R G Landes.

Lowry, S. Todd. The Archaeology of Economic Ideas. LC 87-15507. (Illus.). xviii, 366p. (C). 1988. lib. bdg. 57.00 (*0-8223-0774-X*) Duke.

Lowry, S. Todd, ed. Perspectives on the History of Economic Thought, Vol. VIII. 288p. 1992. 79.95 (*1-85278-448-2*, Pub. by E Elgar Pub UK) Ashgate Pub Co.

Lowry, Shannon. Natives of the Far North: Alaska's Vanishing Culture in the Eye of Edward Sheriff Curtis. (Illus.). 160p. 1994. 29.95 (*0-8117-1102-1*) Stackpole.

Lowry, Shannon & Schultz, Jeff. Northern Lights: Tales of Alaska's Lighthouses & Their Keepers. LC 91-46367. (Illus.). 128p. 1992. 29.95 (*0-8117-0954-X*) Stackpole.

Lowry, Shirley. Familiar Mysteries: The Truth in Myth. LC 80-27792. (Illus.). 1982. 35.00 (*0-19-502925-9*) OUP.

Lowry, Susan. Illustrated Encyclopedia of Mammals. 1993. 12.98 (*1-55521-880-6*) Bk Sales Inc.

Lowry, Terry. September Blood: The Battle of Carnifex Ferry. LC 85-60320. (Illus.). 168p. (Orig.). 1985. pap. 9.95 (*0-933126-59-X*) Pictorial Hist.

— Twenty-Sixth Battalion Virginia Infantry. (Virginia Regimental Histories Ser.). (Illus.). 167p. 1992. 19.95 (*1-56190-028-1*) H E Howard.

Lowry, Terry D. Twenty-Second Virginia Infantry. (Virginia Regimental Histories Ser.). (Illus.). 216p. 1988. 19.95 (*0-930919-55-6*) H E Howard.

Lowry, Thea S. Petaluma's Poultry Pioneers: Recall the Heyday of Chicken Ranching. (Illus.). 128p. (Orig.). 1993. pap. 10.95 (*0-9610116-0-2*) Manifold Pr.

Lowry, Thea S., jt. ed. see Petersen, Laura M.

Lowry, Thomas H. & Richardson, Kathleen S. Mechanism & Theory in Organic Chemistry. 3rd ed. (C). 1990. text ed. 84.00 (*0-06-044084-8*) HarpCollege.

Lowry, Thomas P. The Clitoris. LC 73-704. (Illus.). 304p. 1976. 22.50 (*0-87527-112-X*) Green.

— The Story the Soldiers Wouldn't Tell: Sex in the Civil War. (Illus.). 240p. 1994. 19.95 (*0-8117-1515-9*) Stackpole.

***Lowry, Thomas P. & Wellham, W. G.** The Attack on Taranto: Blueprint for Pearl Harbor. (Illus.). 224p. 1995. 22.95 (*0-8117-1726-7*) Stackpole.

Lowry, Todd, ed. The Beatles Fake Book. 176p. 1987. pap. 25.00 (*0-88188-757-9*, 00240069) H Leonard.

Lowry, W. McNeil, ed. The Arts & Public Policy in the U. S. LC 84-17686. 1984. reprint ed. 7.95 (*0-13-047689-7*) Am Assembly.

— The Performing Arts in American Society. LC 78-1404. (American Assembly Guides Ser.). 1978. 10.95 (*0-13-657155-7*); pap. 4.95 (*0-13-657148-4*) Am Assembly.

Lowry, William B., jt. auth. see Bischof, Larry.

Lowry, William P. Atmospheric Ecology for Designers & Planners. LC 88-90598. (Illus.). 435p. (Orig.). (C). 1988. pap. 35.25x (*1-882002-07-5*) Peavine Pubns.

— Atmospheric Ecology for Designers & Planners. LC 88-90598. (Illus.). 435p. (Orig.). 1991. 48.75 (*1-882002-08-3*) Peavine Pubns.

— Atmospheric Ecology for Designers & Planners. (Illus.). 448p. (Orig.). 1991. text ed. 54.95 (*0-442-00751-5*) Van Nos Reinhold.

Lowry, William P. & Lowry II, Porter P. Fundamentals of Biometeorology Vol. 1: Interactions of Organisms & the Atmosphere - The Physical Environment. LC 89-90922. (Illus.). 310p. (Orig.). (C). 1989. Vol. 1: Physical Environment. pap. 32.50 (*1-882002-03-2*) Peavine Pubns.

***Lowry, William P. & Lowry, Porter P.** Fundamentals of Biometeorology: Interactions of Organisms & the Atmosphere - the Physical Environment, 2 vols., Set, Vols. 1-2. (Illus.). 650p. 1995. pap. 66.00 (*1-882002-05-9*) Peavine Pubns.

— Fundamentals of Biometeorology Vol. 2: Interactions of Organisms & the Atmosphere - The Biological Environment, Vol. 2. LC 95-67346. (Illus.). 340p. 1995. pap. 36.00 (*1-882002-04-0*) Peavine Pubns.

Lowry, William R. The Capacity for Wonder: Preserving National Parks. 380p. (C). 1994. 28.95 (*0-8157-5298-9*) Brookings.

— The Dimensions of Federalism: State Governments & Pollution Control Policies. LC 91-13582. (Illus.). 181p. 1991. text ed. 32.95 (*0-8223-1162-3*) Duke.

Lowsley, B. A Glossary of Berkshire Words & Phrases. (English Dialect Society Publications Ser.: No. 56). 1969. reprint ed. pap. 20.00 (*0-8115-0477-8*) Periodicals Srv.

Lowson, Linda M. California Real Estate Register. 2nd ed. 1991. ring bd. 195.00 (*0-944354-01-7*); disk 425.00 (*0-317-94093-7*) Global Infonet.

— Who's Who in Southern California Real Estate. 285p. 1988. pap. text ed. 79.00 (*0-944354-00-9*) Global Infonet.

Lowstuter, Clude C. & Robertson, David P. Network Your Way to a New Job...Fast. 1994. text ed. 24.95 (*0-07-038882-2*); pap. text ed. 14.95 (*0-07-038883-0*) McGraw.

Lowstuter, Clyde C. & Robertson, David P. In Search of the Perfect Job. 1992. pap. text ed. 14.95 (*0-07-038881-4*) McGraw.

— In Search of the Perfect Job. 1992. text ed. 24.95 (*0-07-038880-6*) McGraw.

Lowth, Robert. Lectures on the Sacred Poetry of the Hebrews, 2 vols., Set. Gregory, G., tr. (Anglistica & Americana Ser.: No. 43). 935p. 1969. reprint ed. 180.70 (*0-685-25147-0*, 05102488, Pub. by Georg Olms GW) Lubrecht & Cramer.

— A Short Introduction to English Grammar. LC 79-4675. (American Linguistics Ser.). 1979. reprint ed. lib. bdg. 50.00 (*0-8201-1332-8*) Schol Facsimiles.

Lowther, David A. & Silvester, Peter P. Computer Aided Design in Magnetics. (Illus.). 324p. 1985. 99.50 (*0-387-15756-5*) Spr-Verlag.

Lowther, David A., jt. auth. see Silvester, Peter P.

Lowther, E. H., jt. auth. see Bates, R. S.

***Lowther, George.** The Adventures of Superman. LC 94-43029. (Illus.). 228p. (YA). (gr. 5 up). 1995. 16.95 (*1-55709-228-1*) Applewood.

Lowther, Gerald, jt. auth. see Bier, Norman.

Lowther, Gerald E. & Snyder, Christopher. Contact Lenses: Procedures & Techniques. 2nd ed. 432p. 1992. 65.00 (*0-7506-9187-5*) Buttrwrth-Heinemann.

Lowther, Malcolm, jt. auth. see Shaw, Kathleen M.

Lowther, Richard, jt. auth. see Robinson, Lynne.

Lowy, Albert, jt. ed. see Society of Hebrew Literature Staff.

Lowy, Aranka I. The Story of Aranka Ickovic Lowy: The Ugly Duckling (Non-Fiction Autobiography with Reference to WW II in Europe) 2nd ed. LC 81-90799. (Illus.). 264p. (Orig.). 1988. pap. 8.25 (*0-317-99842-0*) Lowy Pub.

Lowy, Bernard. Tremellales. LC 79-26289. (Flora Neotropica Monograph Ser.: No. 6S). 18p. (Orig.). 1980. pap. 4.50 (*0-89327-220-5*) NY Botanical.

— Tremellales. LC 76-130518. (Flora Neotropica Monograph Ser.: No. 6). (Illus.). 153p. (Orig.). 1987. reprint ed. pap. text ed. write for info. (*0-89327-321-X*) NY Botanical.

Lowy, David C. Pencil Drawings by David X: One Hundred & One Amusing, Artistic & Entertaining Drawings of Pencils. LC 79-88698. (Illus.). 1979. pap. 3.25 (*0-9602940-0-7*) Lowy Pub.

Lowy, Lance. Handball Handbook: Strategies & Techniques. 2nd ed. (Illus.). 143p. 1991. pap. text ed. 7.95x (*0-89641-207-5*) American Pr.

Lowy, Louis. The Function of Social Work in a Changing Society: A Continuum of Practice. 1976. text ed. 10.00 (*0-89182-004-3*); pap. 4.25 (*0-89182-005-1*) Charles River Bks.

— Social Work with the Aging: The Challenge & Promise of the Later Years. 2nd ed. 435p. (C). 1991. reprint ed. pap. text ed. 21.95 (*0-88133-614-9*) Waveland Pr.

Lowy, Louis & O'Connor, Darlene. Why Education in the Later Years? LC 82-47966. 288p. 1986. text ed. 35.00 (*0-669-05721-5*) Free Pr.

Lowy, Martin. High Rollers: Inside the Savings & Loan Debacle. LC 91-8344. 328p. 1991. text ed. 24.95 (*0-275-93988-X*, C3988, Praeger Pubs) Greenwood.

Lowy, Michael. On a Changing World: Essays in Political Philosophy, from Karl Marx to Walter Benjamin. LC 92-11652. (Revolutionary Studies). 176p. (C). 1992. text ed. 45.00 (*0-391-03718-8*) Humanities.

— Redemption & Utopia - Jewish Libertarian Thought in Central Europe: A Study in Elective Affinity. Heaney, Hope, tr. LC 89-51763. 282p. (C). 1992. 35.00 (*0-8047-1776-1*) Stanford U Pr.

— The Theory of Revolution in the Young Marx. 1995. pap. 16.50 (*1-899438-20-3*, Pub. by Porcupine Bks UK) Humanities.

Lowy, Michael, ed. Marxism in Latin America from 1909 to the Present: An Anthology. Pearlman, Michael, tr. LC 92-3708. (Revolutionary Studies). 344p. (C). 1992. text ed. 55.00 (*0-391-03755-2*) Humanities.

Loxdale, Hugh D. & Hollander, J. Den. Electrophoretic Studies on Agricultural Pests. (Systematics Association Special Volume Ser.: Vol. 39). (Illus.). 512p. 1990. 125.00 (*0-19-857710-9*) OUP.

Loxley, John, jt. ed. see Campbell, Bonnie K.

Loxton, Cathy, jt. auth. see Bartley, Paula.

***Loxton, H.** Cats. (Spotter's Guide Ser.). (Illus.). 64p. (YA). (gr. 4 up). 1995. pap. 4.95 (*0-7460-2151-8*, Usborne) EDC.

Loxton, Howard. Guide to Cats of the World. 1991. 5.98 (*1-55521-603-X*) Bk Sales Inc.

— Illustrated Cat. (Illus.). 1994. 12.98 (*0-7858-0179-0*) Bk Sales Inc.

— Illustrated Dog. (Illus.). 1994. 12.98 (*0-7858-0178-2*) Bk Sales Inc.

— Illustrated Horse. (Illus.). 1994. 12.98 (*0-7858-0180-4*) Bk Sales Inc.

— Noble Cat. 1994. 29.99 (*0-517-02325-3*) Random Hse Value.

— Theater. LC 89-11533. (Arts Ser.). (Illus.). 48p. (J). (gr. 6-11). 1990. lib. bdg. 11.95 (*0-8114-2359-X*) Raintree Steck-V.

Loxton, Howard, jt. auth. see Harrison, Colin.

Loxton, J. H. & Van der Poorten, A. J., eds. Diophantine Analysis: Proceedings at the Number Theory Section of the 1985 Australian Mathematical Society Convention. (London Mathematical Society Lecture Note Ser.: No. 109). 200p. 1986. pap. 34.95 (*0-521-33923-5*) Cambridge U Pr.

Loxton, Margaret, illus. Provence. LC 93-5084. (Robert Stewart Book Ser.). 64p. 1993. text ed. 14.00 (*0-684-19664-6*, Scribners); pap. 12.95 (*0-685-66884-3*, Scribners) S&S Trade.

Loxton, R. & Pope, P., eds. Instrumentation: A Reader. 290p. 1986. 30.00 (*0-335-15097-7*, Open Univ Pr) Taylor & Francis.

Loy, D. Gareth, jt. ed. see Todd, Peter.

***Loy, David.** Lack & Transcendence: The Problem of Death & Life in Psychotherapy, Existentialism, & Buddhism. 196p. (C). 1995. text ed. 45.00 (*0-391-03860-5*) Humanities.

Loy, J. D., et al. The Behavior of Gonadectomized Rhesus Monkeys. (Contributions to Primatology Ser.: Vol. 20). (Illus.). viii, 144p. 1983. 53.00 (*3-8055-3795-6*) S Karger.

Loy, James & Peters, Calvin B., eds. Understanding Behavior: What Primate Studies Tell Us about Human Behavior. (Illus.). 280p. 1991. 49.95 (*0-19-506020-2*) OUP.

Loy, James D., jt. ed. see Campbell, Bernard G.

Loy, John W., jt. ed. see Ingham, Alan G.

Loy, John W., et al. Sport, Culture & Society: A Reader on the Sociology of Sport. 2nd rev. ed. LC 81-3692. (Illus.). 385p. reprint ed. pap. 109.80 (*0-8357-7649-2*, 2056975) Bks Demand.

Loy, Joy A., ed. see Murdock, Michael D.

Loy, Mina. Insel. LC 91-29061. 196p. (Orig.). 1991. 20.00 (*0-87685-854-X*); 30.00 (*0-87685-855-8*); pap. 11.00 (*0-87685-853-1*) Black Sparrow.

— The Last Lunar Baedeker: The Poems of Mina Loy. 1982. 25.00 (*0-912330-46-5*, Inland Bk) Jargon Soc.

Loy, Myrna. Poetry's Promise: A Stigma Attached to Being Born. 60p. (Orig.). 1992. write for info. (*0-9632388-0-9*) M Loy.

An Asterisk (*) at the beginning of an entry indicates that the title is appearing in BIP for the first time.

Loy, Myrna & Davis, James K. Myrna Loy: On Being & Becoming. 1988. pap. 9.95 (1-55611-101-0, Primus Lib Contemp) D I Fine.

Loy, Nicholas J. An Engineer's Guide to FIR Digital Filters. LC 87-1352. (Illus.). 256p. 1987. text ed. 54.00 (0-13-278011-9) P-H.

Loya, John F. Gifts from the Poor. LC 88-62115. 128p. 1989. pap. 6.95 (1-55523-184-5) Winston-Derek.

***Loyacono, Laura.** Transforming Education Through the Arts. 38p. 1995. 12.00 (1-55516-221-5, 2111) Natl Conf State Legis.

***Loyacono, Laura L.** Reinventing the Wheel: A Design for Student Achievement in the 21st Century. 96p. 1992. 25.00 (1-55516-220-7, 2110) Natl Conf State Legis.

Loyalka, Sudarshan K., jt. auth. see Williams, M. M.

***Loyd, Gerald.** Preachers Are People Too! 266p. (Orig.). 1994. pap. 9.99 (1-56043-817-7) Destiny Image.

Loyd, Lewis C. The Origins of Some Anglo-Norman Families. xvi, 140p. 1992. 17.50 (0-8063-0649-1, 3450) Genealog Pub.

Loyd, Richard E. Electrical Raceways & Other Wiring Methods. 18p. 1993. teacher ed 12.00 (0-8273-5494-0) Delmar.

— Electrical Raceways & Other Wiring Methods Design Manual. 1,993th ed. LC 92-40582. 223p. 1993. pap. text ed. 19.95 (0-8273-5493-2) Delmar.

— Journeyman Electrician's Exam Preparation Book. 283p. 1994. pap. 22.95 (0-8273-5725-7) Delmar.

— Master Electrician's Exam Preparation Book. 305p. 1994. pap. 35.95 (0-8273-5852-0) Delmar.

Loyd, Roger, ed. see Grimes, Lewis H.

Loyd, S. Building Services for Swimming Pools: An Annotated Bibliography. 1992. 100.00 (0-86022-325-6, Pub. by Build Servs Info Assn UK) St Mut.

— Building Services Maintenance. 1990. 60.00 (0-86022-264-0, Pub. by Build Servs Info Assn UK) St Mut.

— Combined Heat & Power: An Annotated Bibliography. 1990. 60.00 (0-86022-247-0, Pub. by Build Servs Info Assn UK) St Mut.

— Fire Dampers. (C). 1994. 115.00x (0-86022-368-X, Pub. by Build Servs Info Assn UK) St Mut.

— Information Sources in Building Services. 1993. 40.00 (0-86022-344-2, Pub. by Build Servs Info Assn UK) St Mut.

— Ventilation System Hygiene. 6th ed. (C). 1993. 110.00x (0-86022-377-9, Pub. by Build Servs Info Assn UK) St Mut.

— Ventilation System Hygiene: A Review. 1993. 100.00 (0-86022-356-6, Pub. by Build Servs Info Assn UK) St Mut.

Loyd, S., ed. Commissioning Building Services: An Annotated Bibliography. (C). 1987. 110.00 (0-86022-149-0, Pub. by Build Servs Info Assn UK) St Mut.

— Smoke Control in Buildings: An Annotated Bibliography. (C). 1988. 105.00 (0-86022-221-7, Pub. by Build Servs Info Assn UK) St Mut.

Loyd, S. & Jerdin, D. Coordination of Building Services. (C). 1983. 60.00 (0-86022-156-3, Pub. by Build Servs Info Assn UK) St Mut.

Loyd, S. R. Building Services Maintenance. (C). 1987. 135.00 (0-86022-129-6, Pub. by Build Servs Info Assn UK) St Mut.

— The Heat Pump. (C). 1981. 75.00 (0-86022-099-0, Pub. by Build Servs Info Assn UK) St Mut.

— Heat Recovery from Buildings. (C). 1984. 63.00 (0-86022-151-2, Pub. by Build Servs Info Assn UK) St Mut.

— Software for Building Services: A Selection Guide. 1993. 120.00 (0-86022-354-X, Pub. by Build Servs Info Assn UK) St Mut.

Loyd, Sam. Best Mathematical Puzzles of Sam Loyd. Gardner, Martin, ed. 1959. pap. 4.50 (0-486-20498-7) Dover.

— Eighth Book of Tan: Seven Hundred Tangrams. LC 68-19895. 1968. reprint ed. pap. 4.50 (0-486-22011-7) Dover.

— More Mathematical Puzzles of Sam Loyd. pap. 4.50 (0-486-20709-9) Dover.

Loyd, William H. The Early Courts of Pennsylvania. (University of Pennsylvania Law School Ser.: No. 2). vii, 287p. 1986. reprint ed. 27.50 (0-8377-0875-3) Rothman.

Loydell, Rupert. Distances. LC 93-13724. 1993. pap. 4.00 (0-940895-12-9) Cornerstone IL.

Loye, David. The Knowable Future: A Psychology of Forecasting & Prophecy. LC 77-26713. 218p. reprint ed. pap. 62.20 (0-317-26298-X, 2025180) Bks Demand.

Loye, David, jt. auth. see Eisler, Riane.

Loye, J. E. & Zuk, M., eds. Bird - Parasite Interactions: Ecology, Evolution & Behavior. (Oxford Ornithology Ser.: No. 2). (Illus.). 424p. 1991. 69.95 (0-19-857738-9) OUP.

Loye, J. F., Jr., et al. Lam Son 719: The South Vietnamese Incursion into Laos. 166p. 1993. reprint ed. pap. 20.00 (0-923135-54-5) Dalley Bk Service.

Loyen, Frances. The Thames & Hudson Manual of Silversmithing: The Constructional Processes. (Illus.). 1980. pap. 10.95 (0-500-68021-3) Thames Hudson.

***Loyn.** Vikings in Britain. 1995. pap. (0-631-18712-X) Blackwell Pubs.

Loyn, H. R. Anglo-Saxon England & the Norman Conquest. 2nd ed. (Social & Economic History of England Ser.). 432p. (C). 1991. text ed. 57.95 (0-582-07297-2, 78873); pap. text ed. 31.50 (0-582-07296-4, 78874) Longman.

— The Governance of Anglo-Saxon England, 500-1087. (Governance of England Ser.). xviii, 222p. 1984. 32.50 (0-8047-1217-4) Stanford U Pr.

Loyn, H. R., ed. The Middle Ages: A Concise Encyclopaedia. LC 88-50254. (Illus.). 352p. 1991. pap. 24.95 (0-500-27645-5) Thames Hudson.

Loynes, R. M., jt. auth. see Anderson, C. W.

Loyning, Yngve, jt. ed. see Mostofsky, David I.

Loyola, Mary. The American Occupation of New Mexico, 1821-1852. Cortes, Carlos E., ed. LC 76-1281. (Chicano Heritage Ser.). 1977. reprint ed. 15.95 (0-405-09512-0) Ayer.

Loyola, R. Veinte Enemigos Del Matrimonio (Twenty Enemies of Marriage) (SPA.). Date not set. 2.49 (1-56063-106-6, 498070) Editorial Unilit.

Loyola, Rodolfo. Anecdotas, Sonrisas y Poemas: Anectdotes, Smiles & Poems. (SPA.). 5.00 (84-7645-476-7, 223572, Pub. by Edit Clie SP) TSELF.

— Bocadillos Para el Alma: Tidbits for the Soul. (SPA.). 4.00 (84-7228-306-2, 220113, Pub. by Edit Clie SP) TSELF.

— Dejad Que el Amor Presida (Let Love Preside) (SPA.). 1993. 6.99 (1-56063-437-5, 498579) Editorial Unilit.

— Manantial en la Ciudad: Streams in the City. (SPA.). 7.50 (84-7645-344-2, 223477, Pub. by Edit Clie SP) TSELF.

— Milagro de la Reproduccion: Miracle of Evangelism. (SPA.). 3.25 (84-7228-284-8, 220590, Pub. by Edit Clie SP) TSELF.

Loyrette, Henri. Degas: The Man & His Art. Paris, I. Mark, tr. (Discoveries Ser.). (Illus.). 192p. 1993. pap. 12.95 (0-8109-2897-3) Abrams.

Loyrette, Henri, jt. auth. see Tinterow, Gary.

Loyseau, Charles. A Treatise of Orders & Plain Dignities. Lloyd, Howell A., ed. (Cambridge Texts in the History of Political Thought Ser.). 288p. (C). 1994. 59.95 (0-521-40519-X) Cambridge U Pr.

— A Treatise of Orders & Plain Dignities. Lloyd, Howell A., ed. (Cambridge Texts in the History of Political Thought Ser.). 288p. (C). 1994. pap. 22.95 (0-521-45624-X) Cambridge U Pr.

Loyst, Ken, ed. see Hanauer, Eric.

Loyst, Ken, ed. see McPeak, Ronald H., et al.

Loyst, Ken, et al. Dive Computers: A Consumer's Guide to History, Theory & Performance. 191p. (Orig.). 1991. pap. text ed. 12.95 (0-922769-09-5) Watersport Pub.

— Night Diving: A Consumer's Guide to the Specialty of Night Diving. 1992. pap. 12.95 (0-922769-33-8) Watersport Pub.

Loza, Steven. Barrio Rhythm: Mexican American Music in Los Angeles. (Illus.). 392p. (C). 1993. 44.95 (0-252-01902-4); pap. 18.95 (0-252-06288-4) U of Ill Pr.

Lozac'h, N., et al. Forty Years of Heterocyclic Sulfur Chemistry; The Chemistry of 1,2-Dithiins. Senning, A., ed. (Sulfer Report Ser.: Vol. 9, No. 3). 108p. 1989. pap. text ed. 125.00 (3-7186-4994-2) Gordon & Breach.

Lozada, Hector R. & Polonsky, Michael J., eds. Environmental Issues in the Curricula of International Business: The Green Imperative. LC 93-39142. (Journal of Teaching in International Business: Vol. 5, Nos. 1-2). (Illus.). 186p. 1993. lib. bdg. 29.95 (1-56024-467-4) Haworth Pr.

Lozano, Anthony G. & Zayas-Bazan, Eduardo, eds. Del Amor a la Revolucion. 225p. (C). 1975. pap. text ed. 10.95 (0-393-09283-6) Norton.

Lozano-Ascencio, Fernando. Bringing It Back Home: Remittances to Mexico from Migrant Workers in the U. S. (Monograph Ser.: No. 37). 77p. 1993. pap. 10.95 (1-878367-11-0, MN-37) UCSD Ctr US-Mex.

Lozano, Beverly. The Invisible Work Force: How Outside & Home-Based Workers Improve Corporate Performance. 200p. 1989. text ed. 27.95 (0-02-919442-3) Free Pr.

Lozano, Carlos, tr. see Alegria, Fernando.

Lozano-Diaz, Nora O., jt. ed. see Baxter, Anne.

Lozano, Eduardo E. Community Design & the Culture of Cities: The Crossroad & the Wall. (Illus.). 300p. (C). 1990. 79.95 (0-521-38067-7); pap. 29.95 (0-521-38979-8) Cambridge U Pr.

Lozano, Fernando. American Painting. (Illus.). 64p. 1991. 32.00 (1-56721-008-2) Twnty-Fifth Cent Pr.

— Contemporary Painting. (Illus.). 64p. 1991. 32.00 (1-56721-007-4) Twnty-Fifth Cent Pr.

— European Painting. (Illus.). 64p. 1991. 32.00 (1-56721-006-6) Twnty-Fifth Cent Pr.

— Latin American Painting. (Illus.). 64p. 1991. 32.00 (1-56721-005-8) Twnty-Fifth Cent Pr.

— Modern - Impressionist Painting, Vol. 1. (Illus.). 64p. 1991. 32.00 (1-56721-009-0) Twnty-Fifth Cent Pr.

— Modern - Impressionist Painting, Vol. 2. (Illus.). 64p. 1991. 32.00 (1-56721-010-4) Twnty-Fifth Cent Pr.

— Modern - Impressionist Painting, Vol. 3. (Illus.). 64p. 1991. 32.00 (1-56721-011-2) Twnty-Fifth Cent Pr.

— Modern - Impressionist Painting, Vol. 4. (Illus.). 64p. 1991. 32.00 (1-56721-012-0) Twnty-Fifth Cent Pr.

— World Travelogue. (Illus.). 64p. 1991. 32.00 (1-56721-004-X) Twnty-Fifth Cent Pr.

Lozano Irueste, Jose M. Diccionario Bilingue de Economia y Empresa: Bilingual Spanish-English, English-Spanish Economics, 10 vols., Set. 1991. pap. write for info. (0-7859-5991-2, 8436806441) Fr & Eur.

— Diccionario Bilingue de Economia y Empresa, Vol. 1: Bilingual Spanish-English, English-Spanish Economics. 128p. 1991. pap. write for info. (0-7859-5981-5, 8436806344) Fr & Eur.

— Diccionario Bilingue de Economia y Empresa, Vol. 10: Bilingual Spanish-English, English-Spanish Economics. 128p. 1991. pap. write for info. (0-7859-5990-4, 8436806433) Fr & Eur.

— Diccionario Bilingue de Economia y Empresa, Vol. 2: Bilingual Spanish-English, English-Spanish Economics. 128p. 1991. pap. write for info. (0-7859-5982-3, 8436806352) Fr & Eur.

— Diccionario Bilingue de Economia y Empresa, Vol. 3: Bilingual Spanish-English, English-Spanish Economics. 128p. 1991. pap. write for info. (0-7859-5983-1, 8436806360) Fr & Eur.

— Diccionario Bilingue de Economia y Empresa, Vol. 5: Bilingual Spanish-English, English-Spanish Economics. 128p. 1991. pap. write for info. (0-7859-5985-8, 8436806387) Fr & Eur.

— Diccionario Bilingue de Economia y Empresa, Vol. 6: Bilingual Spanish-English, English-Spanish Economics. 128p. 1991. pap. write for info. (0-7859-5986-6, 8436806395) Fr & Eur.

— Diccionario Bilingue de Economia y Empresa, Vol. 7: Bilingual Spanish-English, English-Spanish Economics. 128p. 1991. pap. write for info. (0-7859-5987-4, 8436806409) Fr & Eur.

— Diccionario Bilingue de Economia y Empresa, Vol. 8: Bilingual Spanish-English, English-Spanish Economics. 128p. 1991. pap. write for info. (0-7859-5988-2, 8436806417) Fr & Eur.

— Diccionario Bilingue de Economia y Empresa, Vol. 9: Bilingual Spanish-English, English-Spanish Economics. 128p. 1991. pap. write for info. (0-7859-5989-0, 8436806425) Fr & Eur.

Lozano, Joaquin R. Una Poetica De la Oscuridad: La Recepcion Critica de las Soledades en el Siglo XVII. (Series A: Monagarafias: No. 155). 192p. (SPA.). (C). 1994. text ed. 63.00 (1-85566-026-1, Pub. by Tamesis Bks Ltd UK) Boydell & Brewer.

Lozano, Lidia, tr. see Garcia Canclini, Nestor.

Lozano, Lidia, tr. see Semo, Enrique.

Lozano Lopez, Gracia, ed. Texto y Concordancia de las Leyes de Toro: Seccion de Pergaminos, Archivo de la Real Chancilleria de Valladolid. (Spanish Legal Texts Ser.: No. 9). 8p. 1990. 10.00 (0-685-50754-8) Hispanic Seminary.

Lozano-Lopez, Gracia, ed. Texto y Concordancias de Libro de las Donas, Escorial MS. h.III.20. (Spanish Ser.: No. 67). 20p. 1992. 10.00 (0-940639-63-7) Hispanic Seminary.

Lozano, M., jt. auth. see Madurga, G.

Lozano, M., et al, eds. Nuclear Astrophysics. (Research Reports in Physics). (Illus.). 350p. 1989. pap. 66.00 (0-387-50751-5) Spr-Verlag.

Lozano Marcos, Miguel A., ed. see Miro, Gabriel.

Lozano Marcos, Miguel A., ed. see Perez De Ayala, Ramon.

Lozano-Perez, Tomas, et al. Handey: A Robot Task Planner. (Artificial Intelligence - Bobrow, Brady & Davis Ser.). (Illus.). 256p. 1992. 42.50 (0-262-12172-7) MIT Pr.

— The Robotics Review, 1988. Khatib, Oussama & Craig, John J., eds. 200p. 1989. 44.00 (0-262-11135-7) MIT Pr.

Lozano, Robert G. Understanding Your Automobile. (Illus.). 43p. (Orig.). 1984. 24.95 (0-934049-02-5); pap. 8.95 (0-934049-01-7) Handy Bk Co.

Lozano, Roberto, tr. see Schreuder, Sally A.

Lozano, Ruben R. Viva Tejas: The Story of the Tejanos, the Mexican-Born Patriots of the Texas Revolution. (Illus.). 82p. (Orig.). 1991. pap. 8.95 (0-943260-02-7) Alamo Pr TX.

Lozano, Salvador, tr. see LaRouche, Lyndon H., Jr.

Lozanov, G. Suggestology & Outlines of Suggestopedy. (Psychic Studies: Vol. 2). 380p. 1978. text ed. 45.00 (0-677-30940-6) Gordon & Breach.

Lozanov, G. & Gateva, E. The Foreign Language Teacher's Suggestopedic Manual. 416p. 1988. text ed. 71.00 (0-677-21660-2); pap. 41.00 (0-685-50152-3); pap. text ed. 33.00 (0-677-21750-1) Gordon & Breach.

Lozansky, Edward & Sakharov, Andrei D., eds. Andrei Sakharov & Peace. 325p. 1985. pap. 8.95 (0-380-89819-5) Avon.

Lozet, J. & Mathieu, C. French-English Dictionary of Earth Science with English-French Index. 2nd ed. 384p. (ENG & FRE.). 1990. pap. 160.00 (2-85206-617-3, Pub. by Tech Doc FR) IBD Ltd.

Lozet, Jean. French - English Dictionary of Earth Science: Bilingual Earth Sciences Dictionary. 2nd rev. ed. 278p. (ENG & FRE.). 1990. 175.00 (0-8288-4008-3, F12660) Fr & Eur.

Lozet, Jean & Mathieu, Clement. Dictionary of Soil Science. 2nd enl. rev. ed. 358p. (FRE.). (C). 1991. text ed. 95.00 (90-5410-201-2, Pub. by A A Balkema NE) Ashgate Pub Co.

— French & English Dictionary of Earth Science: Dictionnaire de Science du Sol. 2nd ed. 270p. (ENG & FRE.). 1990. pap. 175.00 (0-8288-2290-5, F12660) Fr & Eur.

Lozier, G. Gregory, jt. ed. see Teeter, Deborah J.

Lozina-Lozinski, L. K. Studies in Cryobiology. 270p. 1974. text ed. 70.50 (0-7065-1403-3, Pub. by Keter Pub IS) Coronet Bks.

Lozina-Lozinskij, A. Trottuar: Tpottyar. 65p. (Orig.). 1990. reprint ed. 12.00 (1-878445-54-5) Antiquary CT.

Lozinskaya, Tatjana A. Supernovae & Stellar Wind. Damashek, Marc, tr. (Translation Ser.). (Illus.). 352p. 1990. 120.00 (0-88318-659-4) Am Inst Physics.

Lozinskii, M. Industrial Applications of Induction Heating. LC 66-17266. 1969. 281.00 (0-08-011586-1, Pub. by Pergamon Repr UK) Franklin.

Lozinskii, M. & Herdan, L. High Temperature Metallography. 1961. 211.00 (0-08-009417-1, Pub. by Pergamon Repr UK) Franklin.

Lozner, Ruth. Scratchboard for Illustration. (Illus.). 144p. 1990. 29.95 (0-8230-4662-1, Watsn-Guptill) Watsn-Guptill.

Lozo, F. E., et al. Symposium on Edwards Limestone in Central Texas. (Publication Ser.: PUB 5905). (Illus.). 235p. 1959. 5.00 (0-318-03309-7) Bur Econ Geology.

Lozoff & Braswell. Inner Corrections: Finding Peace & Peace Making. 210p. 1989. pap. 14.95 (0-932930-85-9) Anderson Pub Co.

Lozoff, Bo. Just Another Spiritual Book. (Illus.). 384p. (Orig.). 1991. pap. 12.00 (0-9614444-5-2) Human Kind Found.

— Lineage & Other Stories. 120p. (Orig.). 1989. pap. 7.00 (0-9614444-1-X) Human Kind Found.

— Todos Estamos Encarcelados. Dialogos International Staff, ed. Beas, Ricardo, tr. (Illus.). 336p. (Orig.). (SPA.). 1989. pap. 10.00 (0-9614444-3-6) Human Kind Found.

— We're All Doing Time. LC 84-62787. (Illus.). 336p. (Orig.). (C). 1985. pap. 10.00 (0-9614444-0-1) Human Kind Found.

Lozoraitis, Jean. LOUDcracks-softHEARTS. LC 79-63806. (Illus.). 86p. 1979. 12.00 (0-89608-070-6); pap. 3.75 (0-89608-069-2) South End Pr.

Lozovan, Eugen, ed. see Munteanu, Basil.

Lozovskaya, Elena R., jt. auth. see Hartl, Daniel L.

Lozowick, Lee. Acting God. LC 80-85142. 64p. 1980. pap. 3.95 (0-934252-05-X) Hohm Pr.

— The Alchemy of Love & Sex. 298p. (C). 1995. pap. 16.95 (0-934252-58-0) Hohm Pr.

— The Cheating Buddha. LC 80-80802. 144p. 1980. pap. 7.95 (0-934252-03-3) Hohm Pr.

— In the Fire. LC 78-54139. 264p. 1978. pap. 9.95 (0-89556-002-X) Hohm Pr.

— Laughter of the Stones. 140p. 1984. pap. 9.95 (0-934252-00-9) Hohm Pr.

— Living God Blues. 168p. 1984. pap. 9.95 (0-934252-09-2) Hohm Pr.

— The Only Grace Is Loving God. LC 82-81992. 108p. 1982. pap. 5.95 (0-934252-07-6) Hohm Pr.

— Yoga of Enlightenment: Book of Unenlightenment. LC 80-85141. 250p. 1980. pap. 9.95 (0-934252-06-8) Hohm Pr.

Lozowick, Louis. William Gropper. (Illus.). 200p. 1983. 40.00 (0-87982-033-0) Art Alliance.

— William Gropper. LC 80-67118. (Illus.). 240p. 1983. 40.00 (0-8453-4730-6, Cornwall Bks) Assoc Univ Prs.

Lozoya, Jorge A., ed. Asia & the New International Economic Order. LC 80-25758. (Policy Studies on the New International Economic Order). 1981. 52.00 (0-08-025116-1, Pergamon Pr) Elsevier.

— International Trade, Industrialization & the New International Economic Order. (Policy Studies). 1981. 52.00 (0-08-025120-X, Pergamon Pr) Elsevier.

— The Social & Cultural Issues of the New International Economic Order. (Policy Studies). 1981. 52.00 (0-08-025123-4, Pergamon Pr) Elsevier.

Lozoya, Jorge A. & Estevez, Jaime, eds. Latin America & the New International Economic Order. LC 79-27384. (Policy Studies on the New International Economic Order). 112p. 1980. 44.00 (0-08-025118-8, Pergamon Pr) Elsevier.

Lozuk, Larry. Understanding & Using Microsoft Word for Windows. Leyh, ed. 300p. (C). 1992. spiral bd. 26.75 (0-314-93443-X) West Pub.

Lozuk, Larry & Ketcham, Emily M. Understanding & Using Microsoft Word for Windows 2.0. Leyh, ed. LC 93-1658. (Microcomputing Ser.). 384p. (C). 1993. pap. text ed. 26.75 (0-314-02473-5) West Pub.

Lozynsky, Artem. The Letters of Dr. Richard Maurice Bucke to Walt Whitman. LC 77-58. 317p. reprint ed. 90.40 (0-8357-9829-1, 2015539) Bks Demand.

Lozzi, Larsen K. Medical Studies of Saliva: Index of Modern Authors & Subjects with Guide for Rapid Research. LC 90-56295. 160p. 1991. 44.50 (1-55914-366-5); pap. 39.50 (1-55914-367-3) ABBE Pubs Assn.

Lpoez-Pedraza, Rafael. Cultural Anxiety. 117p. 1995. pap. 15.00 (3-85630-520-3, Pub. by Daimon Verlag SZ) Atrium Pubs.

LRP Publications Staff. Illinois Public Employee Reporter. write for info. (0-934753-02-4) LRP Pubns.

— Indiana Public Employee Reporter. text ed. write for info. (0-934753-05-9) LRP Pubns.

— Labor Arbitration Information System (LAIS) text ed. 475.00 (0-934753-12-1) LRP Pubns.

— Labor Arbitration Information Systems: Indexes-Tables. write for info. (0-934753-11-3) LRP Pubns.

— National Public Employee Reporter. text ed. write for info. (0-934753-10-5) LRP Pubns.

— National Public Employment Reporter: Tables. text ed. write for info. (0-934753-09-1) LRP Pubns.

— New Jersey Public Employee Reporter. text ed. write for info. (0-934753-07-5) LRP Pubns.

— New Jersey Public Employee Reporter, Vol. 12. 1987. write for info. (0-934753-15-6) LRP Pubns.

— NLRB Advice Memorandum Reporter. text ed. 510.00 (0-934753-08-3) LRP Pubns.

— Ohio Public Employee Reporter. text ed. write for info. (0-934753-03-2) LRP Pubns.

— Pennsylvania Public Employee Reporter. text ed. write for info. (0-934753-04-0) LRP Pubns.

— Public Employee Reporter for California. text ed. write for info. (0-934753-01-6) LRP Pubns.

LRP Publications Staff, ed. Federal Labor Relations Reporter: 1986. 1987. 685.00 (0-934753-23-7) LRP Pubns.

— Federal Merit Systems Reporter: 1986. 1987. 685.00 (0-934753-24-5) LRP Pubns.

— Federal Pay Benefits Reporter: 1986. 1987. 470.00 (0-934753-25-3) LRP Pubns.

— Florida Public Employee Reporter, Vol. 2. text ed. 640.00 (0-934753-06-7) LRP Pubns.

— Florida Public Employee Reporter, Vol. 12. 1987. write for info. (0-934753-16-4) LRP Pubns.

— Illinois Public Employee Reporter, Vol. 2. 1987. write for info. (0-934753-21-0) LRP Pubns.

— Indiana Public Employee Reporter, Vol. II. 1987. write for info. (0-934753-17-2) LRP Pubns.

— Labor Abritration Information System, Vol. 13. 1987. write for info. (0-934753-27-X) LRP Pubns.

— Labor Arbitration Index: 1987 Edition. text ed. write for info. (0-934753-29-6) LRP Pubns.

— National Public Employee Reporter, Vol. 9. 1987. write for info. (0-934753-13-X) LRP Pubns.

An Asterisk (*) at the beginning of an entry indicates that the title is appearing in BIP for the first time.

— New York Workers' Compensation Law Reporter, Vol. 1. 1987. text ed. write for info. (0-934753-22-9) LRP Pubns.

— NLRB Advice Memorandum Reporter, Vol. 14. 1987. text ed. write for info. (0-934753-26-1) LRP Pubns.

— Official Decisions, Opinions & Related Matters of the Public Employment Relations Board of the State of New York, Vol. 19. 1987. text ed. write for info. (0-934753-19-9) LRP Pubns.

— Ohio Public Employee Reporter, Vol. 3. 1987. text ed. write for info. (0-934753-20-2) LRP Pubns.

— Pennsylvania Public Employee Reporter, Vol. 17. 1987. text ed. write for info. (0-934753-14-8) LRP Pubns.

— Public Employee Reporter for California, Vol. 10. 1987. text ed. write for info. (0-934753-18-0) LRP Pubns.

Lstiburek, Joseph, jt. auth. see Carmody, John.

LTA Staff. Beauty of Seattle. (Illus.). 1993. 19.95 (1-55988-348-0); pap. 9.95 (1-55988-349-9) LTA Pub.

— Images of Pennsylvania. 1990. pap. 6.95 (1-55988-219-0) LTA Pub.

— Images of Seattle. (Illus.). 1993. pap. 6.95 (1-55988-350-2) LTA Pub.

LTV Corporation Staff, jt. auth. see American Political Network, Inc. Staff.

Lu & Antoniou. Two-Dimensional Digital Filters. LC 92-18745. (Electrical Engineering & Electronics Ser.: Vol. 80). 416p. 1992. 125.00 (0-8247-8434-0) Dekker.

Lu, Albert K., jt. auth. see Roberts, Gordon W.

Lu, Cary. The Apple Macintosh Book. 4th ed. 528p. 1992. pap. 24.95 (1-55615-278-7) Microsoft.

— Official e.World Guide. 1994. 29.95 (1-56830-090-5) Hayden.

Lu, Chao & Czanderna, A. W., eds. Applications of Piezoelectric Quartz Crystal Microbalances. (Methods & Phenomena Ser.: No. 7). 394p. 1984. 151.50 (0-444-42277-3, I-072-84) Elsevier.

Lu, Chih. The Sino-Indian Border Dispute: A Legal Study. LC 85-12713. (Contributions in Political Science Ser.: No. 139). 153p. 1986. text ed. 45.00 (0-313-25024-3, LSI/, Greenwood Pr) Greenwood.

Lu, David J., tr. see Japan Management Association Staff, ed.

Lu, Diane & Zung, Michael, eds. Access Asia: Guide to Specialists & Their Current Research. 100p. 1991. pap. text ed. 50.00 (0-9631625-0-0) Nat Bur Asian.

— AccessAsia: A Guide to Specialists & Current Research. 1,992th ed. 180p. 1992. 75.00 (0-9631625-1-9) Nat Bur Asian.

Lu, Donald & Weiss, Thomas G. International Negotiations on the Code of Conduct for Transnational Corporations. (Pew Case Studies in International Affairs). 50p. (C). 1994. pap. text ed. 2.50 (1-56927-117-8) Geo U Inst Dplmcy.

Lu, Fei-Pai. T. S. Eliot: The Dialectical Structure of His Theory of Poetry. LC 66-13877. 182p. reprint ed. pap. 51.90 (0-317-28152-6, 2024098) Bks Demand.

Lu, Frank C. Basic Toxicology: Fundamentals, Target Organs & Risk Assessment. 2nd ed. 376p. 1990. 79.00 (0-89116-894-X); pap. 42.00 (1-56032-080-X) Hemisp Pub.

Lu, Grant, jt. ed. see Aggarwal, Ishwar D.

Lu, H., et al, eds. Query Processing in Parallel Relationship Database Systems. LC 93-45665. 392p. 1994. text ed. 60.00 (0-8186-5452-X, 5452) IEEE Comp Soc.

Lu, H. J. & Ooi, B. C. GIS: Technology & Application. 500p. 1993. text ed. 121.00 (981-02-1445-6) World Scientific Pub.

Lu, Henry C. Chinese Foods for Longevity. LC 90-40723. 192p. (Orig.). 1990. pap. 9.95 (0-8069-5830-8) Sterling.

— Chinese Herbal Cures. LC 93-43376. (Illus.). 160p. 1994. pap. 9.95 (0-8069-0762-2) Sterling.

— The Chinese System of Food Cures: Prevention & Remedies. LC 86-5678. (Illus.). 192p. (Orig.). 1986. pap. 9.95 (0-8069-6308-5) Sterling.

— Chinese System of Natural Cures. LC 94-13706. 160p. 1994. pap. 9.95 (0-8069-0616-2) Sterling.

Lu, Hshun. The Complete Stories of Lu Xun. Xianyi, Yang & Yang, Gladys, trs. LC 81-47585. 305p. reprint ed. pap. 88.10 (0-685-23889-X, 2056708) Bks Demand.

Lu Hsun, pseud. A Brief History of Chinese Fiction. Yang, Hsien-yi & Yang, Gladys, trs. LC 73-870. (China Studies: from Confucius to Mao Ser.). (Illus.). 462p. 1990. reprint ed. 42.00 (0-88355-065-2) Hyperion Conn.

Lu Hsun. Selected Stories of Lu Hsun. 3rd ed. Yang, Gladys & Hsien-Yi, trs. (Illus.). 255p. (C). 1978. pap. 11.95 (0-917056-71-X, Pub. by Foreign Lang Pr CH) Cheng & Tsui.

— The True Story of Ah Q. 5th ed. Yang, Hsien-Yi & Yang, Gladys, trs. LC 89-81931. (C & T Asian Literature Ser.). 68p. (Orig.). (C). 1990. pap. 3.95 (0-917056-93-0) Cheng & Tsui.

Lu Huang, Jane & Wurmbrand, Michael, trs. The Primordial Breath: An Ancient Chinese Way of Prolonging Life Through Breath Control, Vol. I. 170p. (C). 1987. 22.50 (0-944558-00-3) Original Bks.

Lu, J. K. Boundary Value Problems for Analytic Functions. (Series in Pure Mathematics: No. 16). 450p. 1994. text ed. 74.00 (981-02-1020-5) World Scientific Pub.

— Complex Variable Methods in Plane Elasticity. (Series in Pure Mathematics). 300p. 1995. text ed. 61.00 (981-02-2093-6) World Scientific Pub.

Lu, J. L. The Missing Patient. 1978. pap. 2.75 (0-9601768-0-2) J L Lu.

Lu, John H. Mandarin Chinese, Vol. 1. LC 89-183898. 119p. (C). 1989. Price for individuals. audio, pap. 24.95 (0-9626654-0-1) East Oak Hse.

Lu, L., jt. ed. see Gardner, G. H.

Lu, Li. Moving the Mountain: My Life in China. 1990. 21.95 (0-399-13545-6) Putnam Pub Group.

Lu, Monica M., jt. auth. see Mayer, Barbara.

Lu, P., jt. ed. see Opella, S. J.

Lu, Phillip, jt. ed. see Davis Philip, A. G.

Lu, Quincey, jt. auth. see Wong, Vivien.

Lu, R. Q. New Approaches to Knowledge Acquisition. 360p. 1994. text ed. 58.00 (981-02-1316-6) World Scientific Pub.

Lu, S. C., jt. auth. see Wilhelm, R.

Lu, Sheldon H. From Historicity to Fictionality: The Chinese Poetics of Narrative. LC 93-31744. 1994. 40.00 (0-8047-2319-2) Stanford U Pr.

***Lu, Sheng-Yen.** Dharma Talks by a Living Buddha. Chow, Janny, tr. LC 94-36517. 1994. pap. 10.00 (1-881493-05-9) Purple Lotus Soc.

— Encounters with the World of Spirits. Chow, Janny, tr. LC 95-8839. 1995. write for info. (1-881493-03-2) Purple Lotus Soc.

— The Mystical Experiences of True Buddha Disciples. rev. ed. Ho, Siong-Chow et al, trs. 192p. 1993. pap. 10.00 (1-881493-01-6) Purple Lotus Soc.

***Lu, T., et al, eds.** Low-Dielectric Constant Materials - Synthesis & Applications in Microelectronics. (Symposium Proceedings Ser.: Vol. 381). 1995. text ed. 83.00 (1-55899-284-7) Materials Res.

Lu, T. M., et al. Diffraction from Rough Surfaces & Growth Fronts. 240p. 1993. text ed. 48.00 (981-02-1536-3) World Scientific Pub.

Lu, Tonglin, ed. Gender & Sexuality in Twentieth-Century Chinese Literature & Society. LC 92-6365. (SUNY Series in Feminist Criticism & Theory). 204p. (C). 1993. 59.50 (0-7914-1371-3); pap. 19.95 (0-7914-1372-1) State U NY Pr.

Lu, Wei, jt. ed. see Andrieu, Jean-Marie.

Lu Xun. Diary of a Madman & Other Stories. Lyell, William A., tr. LC 90-36785. (Illus.). 432p. 1990. text ed. 40.00 (0-8248-1278-6); pap. 18.95 (0-8248-1317-0) UH Pr.

— Selected Writings of Lu Xun, 4 vols. (Studies in Chinese Literature). 1990. lib. bdg. 750.00 (0-8490-4058-2) Gordon Pr.

Lu, Y., ed. Palaeontologia Cathayana, Vol. 5. 334p. 1990. 96.00 (0-387-52145-3) Spr-Verlag.

Lu, Y. P., jt. auth. see Sun, C. T.

Lu, Yong-Zai & Williams, Theodore J. Modelling, Estimation, & Control of the Soaking Pit: An Example of the Development & Application of Some Modern Control Techniques to Industrial Processes. LC 83-101. (Illus.). 482p. reprint ed. pap. 137.40 (0-8357-2998-2, 2039266) Bks Demand.

Lu, Yu, jt. auth. see Randjbar-Daemi, S.

Lu, Yuan, jt. ed. see Child, John.

Lu, Z. W., ed. Mathematical Logic for Computer Science. (Series in Computer Science: Vol. 13). 260p. (C). 1989. text ed. 60.00 (9971-5-0251-8) World Scientific Pub.

Luallin, Meryl D., jt. auth. see Sullivan, Kevin W.

Luard, E. Human Rights & Foreign Policy. LC 80-41774. 32p. 1981. pap. 23.00 (0-08-027405-6, Pub. by Pergamon Repr UK) Franklin.

Luard, Evan. The Balance of Power: The System of International Relations, 1648-1815. 340p. 1992. text ed. 59.95 (0-312-06208-7) St Martin.

— The Blunted Sword: The Erosion of Military Power in Modern World Politics. 194p. (C). 1989. 25.00 (0-941533-48-4) New Amsterdam Bks.

— Conflict & Peace in the Modern International System: A Study of the Principles of International Order. LC 87-27977. 318p. (C). 1988. 64.50 (0-88706-696-8); pap. 21.95 (0-88706-697-6) State U NY Pr.

— The Economic Relationships among States: A Further Study in International Sociology. LC 83-3293. 328p. 1984. text ed. 32.50 (0-312-23514-3) St Martin.

— Globalization of Politics. 208p. 1990. 45.00 (0-8147-5047-8) NYU Pr.

— International Society. 288p. (C). 1990. text ed. 25.00 (0-941533-80-8) New Amsterdam Bks.

— The Management of the World Economy. LC 82-23109. 290p. 1983. text ed. 35.00 (0-312-50950-2) St Martin.

— The United Nations: How It Works & What It Does. 2nd ed. Heater, Derek & Williamson, Pauline, eds. LC 93-15601. 1994. pap. 12.95 (0-312-10060-4) St Martin.

— War in International Society. LC 87-8175. 472p. 1987. 45.00 (0-300-04016-4) Yale U Pr.

Luard, Evan, intro. & sel. Basic Texts in International Relations: The Evolution of Ideas about International Society. LC 91-10832. 300p. (C). 1992. text ed. 49.95 (0-312-06506-X); pap. 19.95 (0-312-06511-6) St Martin.

Luard, Henry R., ed. Annales Monastici, 5 vols., Set. Incl. Vol. 1. De Margam. 1972. (0-8115-1088-3); Vol. 2. De Wintonia. 1972. (0-8115-1085-9); Vol. 3. De Dunstaplia. 1972. (0-8115-1086-7); Vol. 4. De Oseneia. 1972. (0-8115-1087-5); Vol. 5. Index & Glossary. 1972. (0-318-58898-6); (Rolls Ser.: No. 36). 1972. reprint ed. 225.00 (0-8115-1084-0) Periodicals Srv.

— Bartholomaeus de Cotton, Historia Anglicana (499-1298) Necnon Ejusdem Liber de Archiepiscopis et Episcopis Angliae. (Rolls Ser.: No. 16). 1972. reprint ed. 45.00 (0-8115-1021-2) Periodicals Srv.

— Flores Historiarum per Matthaeum Westmonasteriensem Collecti, 3 vols., Set. Incl. Vol. 1. Creation-1066. 1972. (0-8115-1173-1); Vol. 2. 1066-1264. 1972. (0-8115-1174-X); Vol. 3. 1265-1326. 1972. (0-318-58921-4); (Rolls Ser.: No. 95). 1972. reprint ed. 240.00 (0-8115-1172-3) Periodicals Srv.

— Lives of Edward the Confessor. (Rolls Ser.: No. 3). 1969. reprint ed. 45.00 (0-8115-1003-4) Periodicals Srv.

— Roberti Grosseteste Episcopi Quondam Lincolniensis Epistolae. (Rolls Ser.: No. 25). 1974. reprint ed. 45.00 (0-8115-1041-7) Periodicals Srv.

Luard, Lowes D. Horses & Movement. Beckett, Oliver, ed. (Illus.). 144p. 1990. 110.00 (0-85131-445-7, Pub. by J A Allen & Co UK) St Mut.

Luard, Nicholas. Himalaya. 400p. 1993. 24.95 (0-7126-3006-6, Pub. by Century UK) Trafalgar.

— Himalaya. large type ed. 640p. 1994. 26.95 (0-7089-8774-5, Trail West Pubs) Ulverscroft.

***Lubach.** Recovery of Love. Date not set. 14.95 (0-8245-1189-1) Crossroad NY.

Lubach, Peter. Harry & the Singing Fish. LC 91-73824. (Illus.). 32p. (J). (gr. k-4). 1992. lib. bdg. 12.89 (1-56282-159-8) Hyprn Child.

Lubala, R. T., jt. ed. see Kampunzu, A. B.

Luban, David. Just War & Human Rights. 66p. 1980. 1.50 (0-318-17326-3) IPPP.

— Lawyers & Justice: An Ethical Study. 1988. 60.00 (0-317-05209-8); pap. 17.95 (0-317-05210-1) IPPP.

— Lawyers & Justice: An Ethical Study. 464p. 1988. 69.50 (0-691-07784-3); pap. 18.95 (0-691-02290-9) Princeton U Pr.

— Legal Modernism. (Law, Meaning, & Violence Ser.). 400p. (C). 1993. text ed. 49.50x (0-472-10380-6) U of Mich Pr.

— Paternalism & the Legal Profession. 1981. 1.50 (0-318-33307-4) IPPP.

***Luban, David, ed.** The Ethics of Lawyers. LC 94-30377. (The International Library of Essays in Law & Theory, Areas Ser.: Vol. 25). 1994. 150.00 (0-8147-5066-4) NYU Pr.

— The Good Lawyer: Lawyer's Roles & Lawyers' Ethics. 1984. 60.00 (0-317-05528-3); pap. 27.25 (0-317-05225-X) IPPP.

Luban, David, jt. auth. see Rhode, Deborah L.

Luban, David J. & Rhode, Deborah L. Legal Ethics: Cases & Materials. (University Casebook Ser.). 1040p. (C). 1991. text ed. 42.95 (0-88277-939-7) Foundation Pr.

Luban, David J., jt. auth. see Rhode, Deborah L.

Luban, Marianne. The Samaritan Treasure. LC 90-2690. 221p. (Orig.). 1990. pap. 9.95 (0-918273-79-X) Coffee Hse.

Luban, Naomi L., ed. Transfusion Therapy in Infants & Children. LC 90-4280. (Series in Contemporary Medicine & Public Health). (Illus.). 288p. 1990. text ed. 65.00 (0-8018-4028-7) Johns Hopkins.

Luban-Plozza, B., et al. Psychosomatic Disorders in General Practice. 3rd enl. rev. ed. Blythe, G., tr. (Illus.). 296p. 1992. pap. 49.00 (0-387-54556-5) Spr-Verlag.

Luban, Ruth J. Keeping the Fire from Burnout to Balance. 175p. Date not set. lib. bdg. 15.00 (0-9641741-0-3) ChoicePoints.

***Lubar, David.** It's Not a Bug It's a Feature: Computer Wit & Wisdom. 1995. pap. 9.95 (0-201-48304-1) Addison-Wesley.

Lubar, Robert S. Antoni Tapies. LC 93-83249. (Illus.). 64p. (Orig.). 1993. pap. write for info. (1-878283-28-6) PaceWildenstein.

Lubar, Steven. InfoCulture: The Smithsonian Book of the Inventions of the Information Age. LC 93-4815. 1994. 34.45 (0-395-57042-5) HM.

Lubar, Steven & Kingery, W. David, eds. History from Things: Essays on Material Culture. LC 92-20535. (Illus.). 352p. (C). 1993. text ed. 49.00 (1-56098-204-7) Smithsonian.

Lubar, Steven, jt. auth. see Hindle, Brooke.

Lubaroff, Martin I. & Altman, Paul M. Limited Partnerships: A Practitioner's Guide under Delaware Law, 2 vols. 1270p. 1992. ring bd. 225.00 (0-13-110222-2) Aspen Law.

Lubarsky, David A., jt. auth. see Gallagher, Christopher J.

Lubarsky, Jared. Noble Heritage: Five Centuries of Portraits from the Hosokawa Family. LC 92-12047. (Illus.). 112p. (Orig.). 1992. pap. 19.95 (1-56098-209-8) Smithsonian.

Lubarsky, Sandra B. Tolerance & Transformation: Jewish Approaches to Religious Pluralism. (Jewish Perspectives Ser.: No. 4). 150p. 1990. 25.00 (0-87820-504-7) Hebrew Union Coll Pr.

***Lubarsky, Sandra B. & Griffin, David R., eds.** Jewish Theology & Process Thought. (SUNY Series in Constructive Postmodern Thought). 384p. (C). 1996. text ed. 64.50x (0-7914-2809-5) State U NY Pr.

— Jewish Theology & Process Thought. (SUNY Series in Constructive Postmodern Thought). 384p. (C). 1996. pap. 21.95x (0-7914-2810-9) State U NY Pr.

Lubarsky, Steve, et al. How to Improve Your Racquetball. 1980. pap. 5.00 (0-87980-374-6) Wilshire.

Lubavitch Women's Organization Staff. The Spice & Spirit of Kosher-Jewish Cooking. Blau, Esther, ed. LC 77-72116. (Illus.). 1977. 16.95 (0-930178-01-7) Lubavitch Women.

Lubbe, G. & Murray, C. Farlam & Hathaway: Contract - Cases, Commentary & Materials. 3rd ed. 825p. 1988. write for info. (0-7021-2172-X, Pub. by Juta SA); pap. 60.00 (0-7021-2173-8, Pub. by Juta SA) W W Gaunt.

Lubbe, Klaus. Deutsche Seitengewehre und Bajonette, 1740-1945. (Illus.). 279p. (GER.). 1991. pap. 32.00 (3-926598-48-4) Johnson Ref Bks.

Lubbeke, Isolde. Early German Painting in the Thyssen-Bornemisza Collection, 1350-1530. (Illus.). 432p. 1991. 250.00 (0-85667-376-5) Sothebys Pubns.

Lubben-Dunkelaar, Marrianne, jt. auth. see Long, Andrew F.

Lubben, R. T. Just-in-Time Manufacturing: An Elegant Solution. 352p. 1988. text ed. 55.00 (0-07-038911-X) McGraw.

Lubbers, Darcy, jt. ed. see Landgarten, Helen B.

Lubbers, Frank. El Lissitzky, 1890-1941. 1991. pap. 55.00 (0-500-97393-8) Thames Hudson.

Lubbers, Ronald J., jt. auth. see Rogers, Stuart C.

Lubbers, Ruud. Europe, a Continent of Traditions. (William & Mary Lecture: No. 1). 20p. (C). 1994. pap. 7.95 (0-521-46708-X) Cambridge U Pr.

Lubbig, H., jt. ed. see Koch, H.

Lubbig, Heinz, jt. ed. see Hahlbohm, Hans-Dieter.

Lubbock, Alfred B. The Opium Clippers. LC 75-36235. reprint ed. 47.50 (0-404-14483-7) AMS Pr.

Lubbock, Basil. The Arctic Whalers. (C). 1987. 138.00 (0-85174-107-X, Pub. by Brwn Son Ferg) St Mut.

— The Blackwall Frigates. (C). 1987. 114.00 (0-85174-108-8, Pub. by Brwn Son Ferg) St Mut.

— The China Clippers. (C). 1987. 126.00 (0-85174-109-6, Pub. by Brwn Son Ferg) St Mut.

— The Colonial Clippers. (C). 1987. 126.00 (0-85174-110-X, Pub. by Brwn Son Ferg) St Mut.

— Coolie Ships & Oil Sailers. (C). 1987. 125.00 (0-85174-111-8, Pub. by Brwn Son Ferg) St Mut.

— The Down Easters. (C). 1987. 114.00 (0-85174-112-6, Pub. by Brwn Son Ferg) St Mut.

— The Down Easters: American Deep-Water Sailing Ships, 1869-1929. 384p. 1987. reprint ed. pap. 8.95 (0-486-25338-4) Dover.

— The Last of the Windjammers, Vol. I. (C). 1987. 126.00 (0-85174-113-4, Pub. by Brwn Son Ferg) St Mut.

— The Last of the Windjammers, Vol. II. (C). 1987. 126.00 (0-85174-114-2, Pub. by Brwn Son Ferg) St Mut.

— The Log of the Cutty Sark. (C). 1987. 145.00 (0-85174-115-0, Pub. by Brwn Son Ferg) St Mut.

— The Nitrate Clippers. (C). 1987. 125.00 (0-85174-116-9, Pub. by Brwn Son Ferg) St Mut.

— The Nitrate Clippers: History of Sailing Ships & Trade Along the West Coast of South America. 1979. lib. bdg. 75.00 (0-8490-2978-3) Gordon Pr.

— The Opium Clippers. (C). 1987. 114.00 (0-85174-241-6, Pub. by Brwn Son Ferg) St Mut.

— Round the Horn Before the Mast. (C). 1987. 102.00 (0-85174-506-7, Pub. by Brwn Son Ferg) St Mut.

— The Western Ocean Packets. (C). 1987. 120.00 (0-85174-118-5, Pub. by Brwn Son Ferg) St Mut.

— The Western Ocean Packets. (Illus.). 192p. 1988. reprint ed. pap. 5.95 (0-486-25684-7) Dover.

Lubbock, John. Pre-Historic Times. LC 74-169771. (Select Bibliographies Reprint Ser.). 1977. reprint ed. 42.95 (0-8369-5991-4) Ayer.

— Scientific Lectures. LC 72-4522. (Essay Index Reprint Ser.). 1977. reprint ed. 20.95 (0-8369-2960-8) Ayer.

— The Uses of Life. LC 72-4585. (Essay Index Reprint Ser.). 1977. reprint ed. 23.95 (0-8369-2961-6) Ayer.

— Wild Flowering Plants Relation to Insects. 194p. 1989. 100.00 (81-7041-178-5, Pub. by Scientific Pubs II) St Mut.

***Lubbock, Jules.** The Tyranny of Taste: A Study of British Public Policy on Design Architecture & Town Planning Since 1550. LC 94-26853. 1995. write for info. (0-300-05889-6) Yale U Pr.

Lubbock, Jules, jt. auth. see Crinson, Mark.

Lubbock, Percy. Earlham. LC 74-11936. (Illus.). 254p. 1974. reprint ed. text ed. 59.75 (0-8371-7722-7, LUEA, Greenwood Pr) Greenwood.

— Elizabeth Barrett Browning in Her Letters. LC 75-148814. reprint ed. 21.45 (0-404-08879-1) AMS Pr.

Lubbock, Roger, jt. auth. see Keen, Alan.

Lubcker, Donna H. Sameer's Journey. (Illus.). 40p. (Orig.). (J). (gr. 3-5). 1992. pap. 10.00 (0-9633803-3-8) Jasmine Studios.

Lube, E. L., tr. see Bagdasarov, K. S., ed.

Lubec, G. Noninvasive Diagnosis of Kidney Disease. (Continuing Education Ser.: Vol. 3). (Illus.). xii, 368p. 1983. 78.50 (3-8055-3051-X) S Karger.

— Renal Immunology. (Contributions to Nephrology Ser.: Vol. 35). (Illus.). vi, 194p. 1983. pap. 77.75 (3-8055-3587-2) S Karger.

Lubec, G., ed. The Glomerular Basement Membrane. (Illus.). vii, 434p. 1981. 125.00 (3-8055-2952-X) S Karger.

Lubeck, Maria-Garza & Salinas, Ana M. Mexican Celebrations. 54p. (J). (gr. k-12). 1987. pap. text ed. 3.95 (0-86728-019-0) U TX Inst Lat Am Stud.

Lubeck, Mary B., ed. see McCutcheon, Hildreth V.

Lubeck, Paul M. Islam & Urban Labor in Northern Nigeria: The Making of a Muslim Working Class. (African Studies: No. 52). (Illus.). 368p. 1987. 79.95 (0-521-30942-5) Cambridge U Pr.

Lubeck, Sally. Sandbox Society: Early Education in Black & White America - An Ethnographic Comparison. LC 85-10422. 160p. 1985. 25.00 (1-85000-051-4, Falmer Pr) Taylor & Francis.

Lubeck, Sally, jt. ed. see Swadener, Beth B.

Lubeck, Scott, ed. see Carleton, Don E.

Lubeck, Scott, tr. see Turner, Ellen S. & Hester, Thomas R.

Lubeck, Walter. Complete Reiki Handbook. 256p. (Orig.). 1994. pap. 14.95 (0-941524-87-6) Lotus Light.

— Reiki - For First Aid: Reiki Treatment As Accompanying Therapy for over 40 Illnesses. With a Supplement on Nutrition. 160p. (Orig.). 1995. pap. 14.95 (0-914955-26-8) Lotus Pr WI.

Lubecki, John. The End of Cancer. 2nd ed. (Illus.). 198p. reprint ed. write for info. (1-884030-00-9) Better Hlth Bks.

Lubell, David L. The Cath Lab: An Introduction. 2nd ed. LC 92-48998. (Illus.). 143p. 1993. pap. text ed. 29.95 (0-8121-1675-5) Williams & Wilkins.

Lubell, Ellen B., jt. auth. see Wynne, Mary E.

Lubell, Harold, jt. auth. see Organisation for Economic Cooperation.

Lubell, Myron S. The Significance of Organizational Conflict on the Legislative Evolution of the Accounting Profession in the United States. Brief, Richard P., ed. LC 80-1515. (Dimensions of Accounting Theory & Practice Ser.). 1980. lib. bdg. 49.95 (0-405-13494-0) Ayer.

Lubell, Samuel. The Future of American Politics. LC 83-22872. viii, 285p. 1984. reprint ed. text ed. 41.50 (0-313-24377-8, LFAP, Greenwood Pr) Greenwood.

Lubell, Winifred M. The Metamorphosis of Baubo: Myths of Woman's Sexual Energy. LC 93-42729. (Illus.). 215p. (C). 1994. 29.95 (0-8265-1251-8); pap. 15.95 (0-8265-1252-6) Vanderbilt U Pr.

An Asterisk (*) at the beginning of an entry indicates that the title is appearing in BIP for the first time.

Lubenow, Gerald C., ed. California Votes - the Nineteen Ninety Governor's Race: An Inside Look at the Candidates & Their Campaigns by the People Who Managed Them. LC 91-29441. 240p. (Orig.). (C). 1991. pap. 15.95 (*0-87772-329-X*) UCB IGS.

Lubenow, Marvin L. Bones of Contention: A Creationist Assessment of the Human Fossils. LC 92-20925. (Illus.). 272p. 1992. pap. 12.99 (*0-8010-5677-2*) Baker Bk.

Lubens, Herman & Kiley, John C. Perish the Thought: The Stress Connection. 129p. (Orig.). 1995. pap. 14.95 (*0-9633198-4-1*) Jason Pr.

***Lubensky, Sophia.** Random House Russian-English Dictionary of Idioms. 1995. 75.00 (*0-679-40580-1*) Random.

Lubensky, T. C., jt. auth. see Chaikin, P. M.

Luber. Joan Miro: A Retrospective. 1991. pap. 29.50 (*0-89207-062-5*) S R Guggenheim.

— The World at Your Keyboard: An Alternative Guide to Global Computer Networking. 1993. pap. 15.95 (*1-897766-00-9*, Pub. by Jon Pubng UK) InBook.

Luber, Alan. Solving Business Problems with MRP II. (Enterprise Integration Ser.). (Illus.). 300p. 1990. text ed. 35.95 (*1-55558-058-0*, Digital DEC) Buttrwrth-Heinemann.

***Luber, Alan D.** Solving Business Problems with MRP II. 2nd ed. 350p. 1995. 34.95 (*1-55558-132-3*, Digital DEC) Buttrwrth-Heinemann.

Luber, B. Abruestungsatlas. Chancen und Risiken Des Amerikanischen Truppenabzugs Aus Der BRD. (Anstoesse Zur Friedensarbeit Ser.). 98p. (GER.). 1990. pap. 17.50 (*3-487-09377-4*, Pub. by Georg Olms GW) Lubrecht & Cramer.

Luber, Burkhard. When Trees Become the Enemy - Wenn Baume die Gegner Sind: Military Use of Defoliants - Militarische Verwendung von Entlaubungsmitteln. (Anstoesse Zur Friedensarbeit Ser.: Vol. 2). 136p. 1990. 11.57 (*0-685-66491-0*, Pub. by Georg Olms GW) Lubrecht & Cramer.

— When Trees Become the Enemy (Wenn Baeume Die Gegner Sind), Military Use of Defoliants. 128p. (ENG & GER.). 1990. pap. text ed. 13.50 (*3-487-09372-3*, Pub. by Georg Olms GW) Lubrecht & Cramer.

Luber, Philip. Forgive Us Our Sins. (Boston Mysteries Ser.). 1994. mass mkt. 5.99 (*0-449-14849-1*) Fawcett.

Luber, R. F., ed. Partial Hospitalization: A Current Perspective. LC 78-31915. (Illus.). 222p. 1979. 39.50 (*0-306-40201-7*, Plenum Pr) Plenum.

Luber, Raymond F. & Anderson, Carol, eds. Family Intervention with Psychiatric Patients. 169p. 1983. 33.95 (*0-89885-031-2*) Human Sci Pr.

Lubeski, Lori. Dissuasion Crowds the Slow Worker. LC 88-90557. 56p. 1988. 6.50 (*0-929022-01-7*) O Bks.

Lubet, Steven. Beyond Reproach: Ethical Restrictions on the Extrajudicial Activities of State & Federal Judges. LC 84-45429. 66p. (Orig.). 1984. pap. 6.95 (*0-938870-35-1*, 8578) Am Judicature.

— Vending Operator, Inc. v. Nita Department of Transportation. 131p. 1989. 10.00 (*1-55681-190-X*, FBA0190); teacher ed 5.00 (*1-55681-191-8*, FBA0191) Natl Inst Trial Ad.

Lubet, Steven & Rosenbaum, Judith. Financial Disclosure by Judges: Functional Analysis & Critique. LC 89-84613. 128p. (Orig.). 1989. pap. 12.95 (*0-938870-43-2*) Am Judicature.

Lubetkin, Barry & Oumano, Elena. Bailing Out: The Sane Way to Get Out of a Doomed Relationship & Survive with Hope & Self-Respect. 240p. 1993. pap. 11.00 (*0-671-86901-9*, Fireside) S&S Trade.

— Why Do I Need You to Leave Me in Order to Like Myself? How to Stop Your Need for Approval from Destroying Your Relationship with Your Life. LC 92-15335. 1992. 14.95 (*0-681-41457-X*) Longmeadow Pr.

Lubetkin, Daniel I. Basic Estate Administration (1992) (Illus.). 270p. pap. 35.00 (*0-685-09818-4*) NJ Inst CLE.

Lubetkin, John. Union College's Class of 1868: The Unique Experiences of Some Average Americans. (Illus.). 305p. 1995. 27.50 (*0-9645347-0-3*) J Lubetkin. The Civil War. The Industrial Revolution. The winning of the West. Union College's Class of 1868 was at the heart of these & other turning points in U.S. history. After reading the Class' long- forgotten "History," printed in 1919, author John Lubetkin, a Union graduate, became intrigued on discovering the book failed to state that a classmate who had won the Medal of Honor later had it revoked by an Act of Congress. And what a fascinating class it was! Numerous members were Civil War veterans: two fought at Little Round Top; one was captured & sent to Andersonville & the real-life, often dramatic & frequently moving stories of others are recounted. Another Class member was the impetuous George Westinghouse, whose legendary battles with Commodore Vanderbilt, Thomas Edison & J.P. Morgan are documented against the backdrop of laissez-faire 19th century capitalism. The class also included a "tenderfoot" engineer who became an Indian fighter, a pro-temperance minister whose first pastorate was in rough-&-tumble, Abeline, Kansas & others whose stories (whether painful or humorous) detail the Class members' frequently turbulent fortunes in the decades that followed. To order: John Lubetkin, c/o Mid-Atlantic DVPT, Suite 750, 5335 Wisconsin Ave., NW, Washington, DC 20015. (202) 364-3511.** ***Publisher Provided Annotation.

Lubetkin, Wendy. Deng Xiaoping. (World Leaders - Past & Present Ser.). (Illus.). 112p. (J). (gr. 5 up). 1988. 17.95 (*1-55546-830-6*) Chelsea Hse.

— George Marshall. (World Leaders - Past & Present Ser.). (Illus.). (YA). (gr. 5 up). 1990. 17.95 (*1-55546-843-8*) Chelsea Hse.

Lubheid, Colm. John Climacus, The Ladder of Divine Ascent. (Classics of Western Spirituality Ser.). 224p. 1982. pap. 15.95 (*0-8091-2330-4*) Paulist Pr.

Lubian, Arias, jt. auth. see Lubian, Rafael.

Lubian, Rafael & Lubian, Arias. En la Revolucion de Marti. (Illus.). 86p. (Orig.). (SPA.). 1984. pap. 6.95 (*0-89729-354-1*) Ediciones.

Lubian y Arias, Rafael. Episodios de las Guerras por la Independencia de Cuba. (Illus.). 78p. (Orig.). (SPA.). 1985. pap. 6.95 (*0-89729-358-4*) Ediciones.

Lubic, R. & Hawes, G. Environmental Hazards During Pregnancy. Orig. Title: Childbearing: A Book of Choices. 4p. 1988. reprint ed. write for info. (*0-318-63409-0*) Maternity Ctr.

Lubic, Ruth W. & Hawes, Giene R. Childbearing: A Book of Choices. (Illus.). 326p. 1987. 18.95 (*0-318-37618-0*) Maternity Ctr.

Lubich, Chiara. A Call to Love. Hearne, Jerry, tr. 166p. 1989. pap. 8.95 (*0-911782-67-2*) New City.

— Diary Sixty-Four to Sixty-Five. 184p. 1987. 6.95 (*0-911782-55-9*) New City.

— From Scripture to Life. 128p. 1991. 6.95 (*0-911782-83-4*) New City.

— The Love That Comes from God: Reflections on the Family. New City Press Editorial Staff, tr. (Spirituality of Unity Ser.). 96p. 1995. pap. 6.95 (*1-56548-030-9*) New City.

— On the Holy Journey. Hearne, Jerry, tr. 160p. (Orig.). 1988. pap. 6.95 (*0-911782-60-5*) New City.

— Stars & Tears. LC 85-72399. 153p. 1986. pap. 6.95 (*0-911782-54-0*) New City.

— Unity & Jesus Forsaken. LC 85-72397. 105p. 1985. pap. 4.95 (*0-911782-53-2*) New City.

— When Our Love Is Charity. New City Press Editorial Staff, ed. 152p. 1991. 8.95 (*0-911782-93-1*) New City.

***Lubich, Hannes P.** Towards a CSCW Framework for Scientific Cooperation in Europe. LC 94-46548. (Lecture Notes in Computer Sciences: Vol. 889). 1995. write for info. (*3-540-58844-2*) Spr-Verlag.

Lubick, Diana C., jt. auth. see Wallace, Andrew.

Lubin, Aasta S. Managing Success: High Echelon Careers & Motherhood. LC 86-19274. 192p. 1987. text ed. 37.00 (*0-231-06142-0*) Col U Pr.

Lubin, Alice W., et al, eds. Family Therapy: A Bibliography. LC 88-18682. 470p. 1988. text ed. 79.50 (*0-313-26172-5*, LFT/, Greenwood Pr) Greenwood.

Lubin, Bernard. Comprehensive Index of Group Psychotherapy Writings. (American Group Psychotherapy Association Monographs: No. 2). (C). 1987. text ed. 70.00 (*0-8236-1045-4*) Intl Univs Pr.

Lubin, Bernard, jt. auth. see Hanson, Philip G.

Lubin, Bernard, jt. auth. see O'Connor, William B.

Lubin, Bernard, et al, eds. Organizational Change: Sourcebook I: Cases in Organizational Development. 1984. pap. text ed. 19.95 (*0-88390-150-1*) L Erlbaum Assocs.

Lubin, Bertram, ed. see New York Academy of Sciences Staff.

Lubin, Carl K. Language Disturbance & Intellectual Functioning: A Comparison of the Performance of Hemiplegic Patients with Aphasia & Hemiplegic Patients Without Aphasia in Non-Verbal Tasks of Intellectual Functioning. LC 68-17904. (Janua Linguarum, Series Minor: No. 48). (Orig.). 1969. pap. text ed. 24.65 (*3-10-800093-4*) Mouton.

Lubin, Carol R. & Winslow, Anne. Social Justice for Women: The International Labor Organization & Women. LC 90-2003. (Duke Press Policy Studies). 348p. (C). 1991. text ed. 48.00 (*0-8223-1062-7*) Duke.

Lubin, David M. Picturing a Nation: Art & Social Change in Nineteenth-Century America. LC 93-19392. (Illus.). 584p. 1994. 45.00 (*0-300-05732-6*) Yale U Pr.

LuBin, Deanna R. Monster Mother. Fosten, Tom, tr. (Illus.). (J). (ps-9). 1991. lib. bdg. write for info. (*0-318-67146-8*); audio write for info. (*0-318-67147-6*) Lubin Pr.

Lubin, Ernest. The Piano Duet. LC 76-10328. (Quality Paperbacks Ser.). 1976. pap. 5.95 (*0-306-80045-4*) Da Capo.

— A Start at the Piano. LC 78-110975. (Orig.). (J). (gr. 5-8). 1977. pap. 9.95 (*0-8256-2149-6*) Music Sales.

Lubin, George. Handbook of Composites. 1982. text ed. 115.00 (*0-442-24897-0*) Chapman & Hall.

Lubin, George, ed. Handbook of Composites. 796p. 1982. 90.00 (*0-686-48234-4*, 0202) T-C Pubns CA.

Lubin, Georges, ed. see Sand, George.

Lubin, Georges, ed. see Sand, George, pseud.

Lubin, Georges, ed. see Sand, George.

Lubin, Gilbert. The Master Race: Jewish Blood. St. John, Charlotte, ed. LC 92-43704. 224p. 1994. 19.95 (*0-89896-492-X*) Larksdale.

Lubin, J., tr. see Merli, Giorgio.

Lubin, Jean. Train up a Child. 1994. pap. 14.99 (*1-56507-217-0*) Harvest Hse.

LuBin, L., ed. see Foster, Tom.

Lubin, Leonard, illus. My Little Book of Mother Goose Rhymes. (Golden Little Look-Look Book Ser.). 24p. (J). (ps-00). 1992. pap. write for info. (*0-307-11756-1*, 11756, Golden Bks) Western Pub.

Lubin, Martin, ed. Public Policy, Canada, & the United States. 164p. (Orig.). 1986. pap. 12.00 (*0-918592-89-5*) Pol Studies.

Lubin, Maurice A., jt. auth. see Saint-Louis, Carlos.

Lubin, Michael F., et al, eds. Medical Management of the Surgical Patient. 2nd ed. 707p. 1988. pap. text ed. 80.00 (*0-409-95168-4*) Buttrwrth-Heinemann.

Lubin, Michael F., et al. Medical Management of the Surgical Patient. (Illus.). 700p. 1995. 69.50 (*0-397-51318-6*) Lippincott.

Lubin, Nancy. Labour & Nationality in Soviet Central Asia. LC 83-26913. 275p. 1984. text ed. 47.50 (*0-691-07674-X*) Princeton U Pr.

Lubin, Rose. Call It What You Will. 22p. 1987. pap. 5.95 (*0-943454-07-7*) Jotarian.

Lubin, Yevgeny. Drevo Shizni: Poems. 1984. 3.95 (*0-685-22659-X*) RWCPH.

— In the Core: Three Novels about Yakov Bolotov. (Illus.). 424p. 1989. 23.95 (*0-929924-00-2*); pap. 19.95 (*0-685-24999-9*) RWCPH.

— On Shel na Svijaz: A Novel. 1980. 5.00 (*0-685-44306-X*) RWCPH.

— The Russian Triptych. 2nd ed. 230p. (ENG.). 1989. write for info. (*0-929924-06-1*); pap. 7.95 (*0-929924-07-X*) RWCPH.

— Russkii Triptich: A Novel & Stories. 1982. 7.95 (*0-685-22656-5*) RWCPH.

Lubiner, Elaine D. Learning about Languages: Upper Elementary Through First Year High School. 91p. (SPA.). (YA). 1992. teacher ed 22.60 (*0-8442-9371-7*, Natl Textbk); pap. text ed. 10.60 (*0-8442-9370-9*, Natl Textbk) NTC Pub Grp.

Lubiniecki. Large-Scale Mammalian Cell Culture Technology. (Bioprocess Technology Ser.: Vol. 10). 656p. 1990. 190.00 (*0-8247-8327-1*) Dekker.

Lubiniecki, A. S., jt. ed. see Brown, F.

Lubiniecki, Anthony S. & Vargo, Susan A., eds. Regulatory Practice for Biopharmaceutical Production. LC 94-7457. 1994. text ed. 110.95 (*0-471-04900-X*, Wiley-Liss) Wiley.

Lubinski. Dementia & Communication. 336p. (C). 1990. 55.00 (*1-55664-202-4*) Mosby Yr Bk.

Lubinski, Arthur. Developments in Petroleum Engineering, Vol. 1: Stability of Tubulars - Deviation Control. Miska, Stefan, ed. 464p. 1987. Vol. 1: Stabiltiy of Tubulars-Devition Control. 57.00 (*0-87201-038-4*) Gulf Pub.

— Developments in Petroleum Engineering, Vol. 2: Offshore Drilling, Strength of Tubulars, Drilling Practices & Reservoir Characterization. Miska, Stefan, ed. (Illus.). 408p. 1988. 59.00 (*0-87201-171-1*) Gulf Pub.

***Lubinski, David & Dawis, Rene, eds.** Assessing Individual Differences in Human Behavior: New Concepts, Methods, & Findings. LC 95-11998. 400p. (C). 1995. text ed. 49.95 (*0-89106-072-3*) Davies-Black.

***Lubinski, Rosemary, ed.** Dementia & Communication. (Illus.). 320p. (C). 1995. pap. text ed. 45.00 (*1-56593-084-3*, 1138) Singular Publishing.

Lubinski, Rosemary, ed. see Frattali, Carol.

Lubinsky, D. S. & Saff, Edward B. Strong Asymptotics for Extremal Polynomials Associated with Weights on IR. (Lecture Notes in Mathematics Ser.: Vol. 1305). vii, 153p. 1988. pap. 32.30 (*0-387-18958-0*) Spr-Verlag.

Lubinsky, D. S., jt. auth. see Levin, A. L.

Lubis, Mochtar. Indonesia: Land under the Rainbow. (Illus.). 236p. 1991. pap. 22.00 (*0-19-588977-0*) OUP.

Lubitz, Petra, jt. auth. see Lubitz, Wolfgang.

Lubitz, Wolfgang, ed. Trotsky Bibliography. 2nd rev. ed. xxxi, 612p. 1988. lib. bdg. 82.00 (*3-598-10754-4*) K G Saur.

***Lubitz, Wolfgang & Lubitz, Petra.** Trotskyist Serials Bibliography: With Locations & Indices. 475p. 1993. 128.00 (*3-598-11157-6*) K G Saur.

Lubitz, Wolfgang, jt. auth. see Kriste, Burkhard.

Lubke, Kraus, jt. ed. see Schroder, Eberhard.

Lubker, Detlev L. & Schroder, Hans. Lexikon der Schleswig-Holstein-Lauenburgischen und Eutinischen Schriftsteller Von 1796 Bis 1828, Vols. 1-2. xxxvii, 904p. 1983. write for info. (*0-318-71926-6*, Pub. by Georg Olms GW) Lubrecht & Cramer.

Lubkin, Gregory. A Renaissance Court: Milan under Galeazzo Maria Sforza. LC 93-17529. 1994. 47.00 (*0-520-08146-3*) U CA Pr.

Lubkin, Ilene M. Chronic Illness. 2nd ed. 480p. 1990. boxed 43.75 (*0-86720-430-3*) Jones & Bartlett.

***Lubkin, Ilene Morof.** Chronic Illness: Impact & Interventions. 3rd ed. LC 94-37265. (Series in Nursing). 1994. 43.75 (*0-86720-712-4*) Jones & Bartlett.

Lubkin, James L., ed. The Teaching of Elementary Problem Solving in Engineering & Related Fields. 198p. 1980. 10.00 (*0-318-13172-2*) Am Soc Eng Ed.

Lubliner, Jacob. Plasticity Theory. 500p. (C). 1990. write for info. (*0-02-372161-8*) Macmillan.

Lubliner, Murray. International Brand Packaging Awards. (Illus.). 160p. 1993. 34.99 (*1-56496-059-5*, 30544) Rockport Pubs.

Lubman, David & Wetherill, Ewart A., eds. Acoustics of Worship Spaces. LC 85-70273. 91p. 1985. 20.00 (*0-88318-466-4*) Acoustical Soc Am.

Lubman, David M., ed. Lasers & Mass Spectrometry. (Oxford Series on Optical Sciences). (Illus.). 560p. 1990. 75.00 (*0-19-505929-8*) OUP.

Luboff, Pat & Luboff, Pete. Eighty-Eight Songwriting Wrongs & How to Right Them. 144p. 1992. pap. 17.95 (*0-89879-508-7*) Writers Digest.

Luboff, Pete, jt. auth. see Luboff, Pat.

Luborsky, Lester. Principles of Psychoanalytic Psychotherapy: A Manual for Supportive-Expressive Treatment. LC 83-54377. 292p. 1984. text ed. 35.00 (*0-465-06328-4*) Basic.

Luborsky, Peter, tr. see Lindenberg, Christoph.

Luborsky, Peter, tr. see Wolff, Otto, et al.

Lubot, Eugene. Liberalism in an Illiberal Age: New Culture Liberals in Republican China, 1919-1937. LC 81-13409. (Contributions in Intercultural & Comparative Studies: No. 5). xi, 194p. 1982. text ed. 49.95 (*0-313-23256-3*, LUL/, Greenwood Pr) Greenwood.

Lubotsky, Alexander & Magid, Andy R. Varieties of Representations of Finitely Generated Groups. LC 85-21444. (MEMO Ser.: No. 58/336). 117p. 1985. pap. 18.00 (*0-8218-2337-X*, MEMO 58/336) Am Math.

Lubotsky, Terry L. Expressions of the Heart: A Healing Process for Love Loss, Vol. 1. (Illus.). 130p. (Orig.). 1993. pap. 13.95 (*0-9635513-0-2*) Express FL.

***Lubotzky, Alexander.** Discrete Groups, Expanding Graphs & Invariant Measures. Rogawski, Jonathan D., ed. LC 94-21726. (Progress in Mathematics Ser.: Vol. 125). 208p. 1994. 49.50 (*0-8176-5075-X*) Birkhauser.

Lubov, Don. East End Illustrated. 3rd ed. 55p. 1988. pap. 11.95 (*0-939820-05-6*) Lindon Ent.

— The East End Illustrated, Vol. 3. (Illus.). 55p. 1988. pap. write for info. (*0-939820-06-4*) Lindon Ent.

— The East End Illustrated, Vols. 1 & 2. 55p. 1980. pap. 9.95 (*0-686-31007-1*) Lindon Ent.

— Hyperspace, an Illustrated Introduction to the Fourth Dimension. 72p. 1983. pap. text ed. write for info. (*0-939820-02-1*) Lindon Ent.

— Suffolk Illustrated. 55p. 1984. pap. write for info. (*0-939820-03-X*) Lindon Ent.

***Lubove.** Twentieth-Century Pittsburgh Vol. 2: The Post-Steel Era. 1995. pap. text ed. write for info. (*0-8229-5566-0*) U of Pittsburgh Pr.

Lubove, ed. Pittsburgh. LC 76-3119. (Documentary History of American Cities Ser.). (C). 1976. reprint ed. pap. 6.95 (*0-531-05590-6*) Wiener Pubs Inc.

Lubove, Roy. The Professional Altruist: The Emergence of Social Work As a Career, 1880-1930. LC 65-12786. (Publication of the Center for the Study of the History of Liberty in America, Harvard University Ser.). 299p. reprint ed. pap. 85.30 (*0-7837-4117-0*, 2057940) Bks Demand.

— The Progressives & the Slums. LC 74-4843. (Illus.). 284p. 1974. reprint ed. text ed. 59.75 (*0-8371-7487-2*, LUPS, Greenwood Pr) Greenwood.

— The Struggle for Social Security, 1900-1935. LC 85-40854. (Series in Policy & Institutional Studies). 304p. 1986. reprint ed. pap. 14.95 (*0-8229-5379-X*) U of Pittsburgh Pr.

— Twentieth Century Pittsburgh Vol. 1: Government, Business & Change. rev. ed. (Illus.). 256p. (C). 1994. pap. 19.95 (*0-8229-5551-2*) U of Pittsburgh Pr.

— The Urban Community: Housing & Planning in the Progressive Era. LC 81-6328. (American Historical Sources: Research & Interpretation Ser.). ix, 148p. 1981. reprint ed. text ed. 49.75 (*0-313-22731-4*, LUUC, Greenwood Pr) Greenwood.

***Lubow.** Reporter Who Would King. 1994. pap. 6.99 (*0-517-13513-2*) Random.

Lubow, Allen. Bar Code Pro. 72p. 1991. pap. text ed. 149.95 (*1-880773-00-7*); disk 450.00 (*0-685-59076-3*) Synex.

— Label Press: Label Printing Software Tamed. (Illus.). 188p. (Orig.). 1994. pap. text ed. write for info. (*1-880773-19-8*) Synex.

— MacEnvelop Professional: Reference Manual. 192p. 1992. disk, pap. text ed. 250.00 (*1-880773-06-6*) Synex.

— Macenvelope. 131p. 1990. pap. text ed. write for info. (*1-880773-05-8*) Synex.

— MacEnvelope: Update Reference Manual. 88p. 1991. disk, pap. text ed. 79.95 (*1-880773-04-X*) Synex.

— Macenvelope Plus. 176p. 1990. pap. text ed. write for info. (*1-880773-03-1*) Synex.

— Macphonebook. 56p. 1990. pap. text ed. write for info. (*1-880773-01-5*) Synex.

Lubow, Allen, et al. Barron's Computer Study Program for the SAT. rev. ed. 1989. Apple version. disk write for info. (*0-8120-7597-8*); IBM PC version. disk write for info. (*0-318-64979-9*); Apple version, incl. 6 double-sided disks. write for info. (*0-8120-7598-6*) Barron.

— Barron's Computer Study Program for the SAT. 2nd rev. ed. 1989. 49.95 (*0-318-64978-0*) Barron.

Lubow, Arthur. The Reporter Who Would Be King: A Biography of Richard Harding Davis. (Illus.). 448p. 1992. text ed. 25.00 (*0-684-19404-X*, Scribners) S&S Trade.

Lubow, Joseph, ed. see Mayall, Donald.

Lubow, Joseph M. Reaching for Answers: Bill Belton's Story. (Illus.). 240p. (Orig.). 1995. pap. 9.95 (*0-89407-093-2*) Strawberry Hill.

Lubow, R. E. Latent Inhibition & Conditioned Attention Theory. (Problems in the Behavioral Sciences Ser.). (Illus.). (C). 1989. 64.95 (*0-521-36307-1*) Cambridge U Pr.

Lubs, H. A., ed. Chemistry of Synthetic Dyes & Pigments. LC 64-7905. (A C S Ser.: No. 127). 750p. 1971. reprint ed. 69.50 (*0-88275-039-9*) Krieger.

Lubs, Herbert A. & De La Cruz, Felix F., eds. Genetic Counseling. LC 76-52601. 616p. 1977. 97.50 (*0-89004-150-4*) Raven.

Lubulwa, A. S. The Implications of Regulatory Failure for Rail & Road Industries. 157p. 1990. text ed. 59.95 (*1-85628-128-0*, Pub. by Avebury Pub UK) Ashgate Pub Co.

Luby, Barry J. & Finke, Wayne H., eds. Anthology of Contemporary Latin American Literature: 1960 to 1984. 320p. 1986. 48.50 (*0-8386-3255-6*) Fairleigh Dickinson.

Luby, James J., jt. ed. see Dale, Adam.

An Asterisk (*) at the beginning of an entry indicates that the title is appearing in BIP for the first time.

Luby, James P. James Luby, Journalist. (American Newspapermen 1790-1933 Ser.). 135p. 1974. reprint ed. 20.00 (*0-8464-0014-6*) Beekman Pubs.

Luby, Michael. Pseudo-Randomness & Applications. (Computer Science Notes Ser.). 110p. 1992. text ed. 15.95 (*0-691-02546-0*) Princeton U Pr.

Luby, Sue. Hatha Yoga for Total Health: Handbook of Practical Programs. (Illus.). 1977. pap. 16.95 (*0-13-384123-5*) P-H.

Luc, D. T. Theory of Vector Optimization. (Lecture Notes in Economics & Mathematical Systems Ser.: Vol. 319). viii, 173p. 1988. pap. 30.70 (*0-387-50541-5*) Spr-Verlag.

Luc, Laura A. & Beattie, Michele. Long-Term Care Policies & Procedures: A Self-Care Approach. LC 92-48193. 174p. 1993. pap. 49.00 (*0-8342-0320-0*, 20320) Aspen Pub.

Luc, M., et al, eds. Plant Parasitic Nematodes in Subtropical & Tropical Agriculture. 648p. 1990. text ed. 121.00 (*0-85198-630-7*) CAB Intl.

Luca, Cornelius. Foreign Exchange Markets Handbook. 1994. 65.00 (*0-13-293424-8*) P-H.

Luca, Susan. Of Mice. (Illus.). 1970. pap. 9.00 (*0-912020-16-4*) Turtles Quill.

Lucadamo, Rhonda, jt. auth. see Dean, Theresa M.

Lucadamo, Rhonda, jt. auth. see Dean, Theresa.

Lucadano, Theresa A. Reclamation. Sherman, Alana, ed. (Chapbooks Fourth Ser.). 20p. 1991. pap. 4.95 (*0-939689-13-8*) Alms Hse Pr.

***Lucado.** Finding Courage to Overcome Your Past. 1995. pap. text ed. (*0-8499-3658-6*) Word Inc.

— He Still Moves Stones. 1994. (*0-8499-5072-4*) Word Inc.

— Heaven: Gods Highest Hope. 1995. pap. text ed. (*0-8499-3657-8*) Word Pub.

— How to Study the Bible. 1995. pap. text ed. (*0-8499-5104-6*) Word Pub.

— Stronger in the Broken Places. 1995. pap. text ed. (*0-8499-5103-8*) Word Inc.

— When God Whispers Your Name: Mini Book. 1995. (*0-8499-5108-9*) Word Pub.

Lucado, Max. And the Angels Were Silent: The Final Week of Jesus. LC 92-20146. 261p. 1992. 16.99 (*0-88070-487-X*, Multnomah Bks) Questar Pubs.

— And the Angels Were Silent: The Final Week of Jesus. LC 92-20146. 1995. pap. 11.99 (*0-88070-727-5*) Questar Pubs.

— And the Angels Were Silent: The Final Weeks of Jesus. large type ed. LC 93-24027. (EasyRead Type Ser.). 286p. 1993. reprint ed. pap. 11.95 (*0-8027-2675-5*) Walker & Co.

— The Applause of Heaven. 192p. 1990. write for info. (*0-8499-0727-6*) Word Inc.

— The Applause of Heaven. abr. ed. LC 93-19146. 1993. 4.99 (*0-8499-5032-5*) Word Pub.

— The Children of the King. LC 94-15160. (Illus.). 32p. (J). (gr. 3-6). 1994. 12.99 (*0-89107-823-1*) Crossway Bks.

— The Crippled Lamb. LC 94-19865. (Illus.). (J). 1994. 12.99 (*0-8499-1005-6*) Word Inc.

— Everyone Needs a Miracle: He Still Moves Stones. 1993. 17.99 (*0-8499-0864-7*) Word Inc.

— The Final Week of Jesus: Excerpts from And The Angels Were Silent. 128p. 1994. 17.99 (*0-88070-630-9*, Multnomah Bks) Questar Pubs.

— God Came Near. large type ed. Date not set. pap. 12.95 (*0-8027-2693-3*) Walker & Co.

— God Came Near: Chronicles of the Christ. 208p. 1993. 14.99 (*0-88070-610-4*, Multnomah Bks); pap. 10.99 (*0-88070-574-4*, Multnomah Bks) Questar Pubs.

— In the Eye of the Storm. 1991. 15.99 (*0-8499-0890-6*) Word Inc.

— In the Eye of the Storm. 1994. 4.99 (*0-8499-5090-2*) Word Inc.

— Just in Case You Ever Wonder. 32p. (J). (ps-2). 1992. 12.99 (*0-8499-0978-3*) Word Inc.

— No Wonder They Call Him Savior. large type ed. (Large Print Inspirational Ser.). 1987. pap. 9.95 (*0-8027-2579-1*) Walker & Co.

— No Wonder They Call Him the Savior: Chronicles of the Cross. LC 85-31026. 208p. 1993. 14.99 (*0-88070-611-2*, Multnomah Bks); pap. 10.99 (*0-88070-576-0*, Multnomah Bks) Questar Pubs.

— On the Anvil. 140p. 1994. 14.99 (*0-8423-4568-X*) Tyndale.

— Six Hours One Friday. 1994. 14.99 (*0-88070-709-7*, Multnomah Bks) Questar Pubs.

— Six Hours One Friday: Anchoring to the Power of the Cross. LC 89-9429. 233p. 1989. 14.99 (*0-88070-314-8*, Multnomah Bks) Questar Pubs.

— Six Hours One Friday: Anchoring to the Power of the Cross. 1993. pap. 10.99 (*0-88070-551-5*, Multnomah Bks) Questar Pubs.

— The Song of the King. LC 95-12970. (Illus.). 32p. (J). (gr. 2-6). 1995. 12.99 (*0-89107-827-4*) Crossway Bks.

— Tell Me the Secrets. LC 93-25957. (Illus.). 48p. 1993. 15.99 (*0-89107-730-8*) Crossway Bks.

— Tell Me the Story. LC 92-26963. (Illus.). 48p. 1992. 15.99 (*0-89107-679-4*) Crossway Bks.

— When God Whispers Your Name. LC 94-17302. 1994. write for info. (*0-8499-1099-4*) Word Inc.

— Y Los Angeles Guardaron Silencio: La Ultima Semana De Jesus. 1993. pap. 7.99 (*1-56063-396-4*, 498546) Editorial Unilit.

***Lucado, Max, ed.** The Inspirational Study Bible: Life Lessons from God's Inspired Word. LC 95-2380. 1995. text ed. 34.99 (*0-8499-5061-9*) Word Inc.

— The Inspirational Study Bible: Life Lessons from God's Inspired Word. deluxe ed. LC 95-2380. 1995. write for info. (*0-8499-5098-8*) Word Inc.

— The Inspirational Study Bible: Life Lessons from the Inspired Word of God. LC 95-3100. 1995. 34.99 (*0-8499-5123-2*); 54.99 (*0-8499-5124-0*) Word Inc.

Lucaire. Celebrity Setbacks. 1993. pap. 10.00 (*0-671-85031-8*) P-H Gen Ref & Trav.

Lucaites, John L. & Bernabo, Lawrance M. Great Speakers & Speeches. 2nd ed. 384p. 1991. per. 28.95 (*0-8403-7149-7*) Kendall-Hunt.

Lucaites, John L., jt. ed. see Calloway-Thomas, Carolyn.

Lucaites, John L., jt. auth. see Condit, Celeste M.

Lucal, Jane B. Estate Planning - a View from the Bench: The Beginner's Guide to the Basics. 480p. 1994. pap. 22.95 (*0-9640191-0-8*) Pro Pubng.

Lucan. Civil War. (Loeb Classical Library: No. 220). 658p. 1928. 18.95 (*0-674-99242-3*) HUP.

— Civil War. Braund, Susan H., ed. & tr. by. (World's Classics Ser.). (Illus.). 384p. 1993. pap. 9.95 (*0-19-282994-7*) OUP.

— Civil War VIII. Mayer, ed. (Classical Texts Ser.). 1981. 49.95 (*0-85668-155-5*, Pub. by Aris & Phillips UK); pap. 24.95 (*0-85668-176-8*, Pub. by Aris & Phillips UK) David Brown.

— De Bello Civili: Bk. II. Fantham, Elaine, ed. (Cambridge Greek & Latin Classics Ser.). (Illus.). 256p. (C). 1992. pap. 22.95 (*0-521-42241-8*) Cambridge U Pr.

— De Bello Civili: Bk. II. Fantham, Elaine, ed. (Cambridge Greek & Latin Classics Ser.). (Illus.). 256p. (C). 1992. 59.95 (*0-521-41010-X*) Cambridge U Pr.

— M. Annael Lucani De Bello Civili, Liber I. Connor, W. R. & Getty, R. J., eds. LC 78-67133. (Latin Texts & Commentaries Ser.). (ENG & LAT.). 1979. reprint ed. lib. bdg. 22.95 (*0-405-11603-9*) Ayer.

— Pharsalia. Joyce, Jane W., tr. (Masters of Latin Literature Ser.). 368p. 1993. 38.95 (*0-8014-2907-2*); pap. 17.95 (*0-8014-8137-6*) Cornell U Pr.

Lucan, Jacques. Rem Koolhaas-OMA: Architecture 1970-1990. (Illus.). 175p. (Orig.). (FRE.). 1991. pap. 29.95 (*1-878271-55-5*) Princeton Arch.

Lucanio, Patrick. Them or Us: Archetypal Interpretations of Fifties Alien Invasion Films. LC 86-43049. (Illus.). 206p. 1987. 29.95 (*0-253-35871-X*) Ind U Pr.

Lucanus, Ocellus. Neue Philologische Untersuchungen, Heft 1. xxix, 161p. 1966. write for info. (*3-296-14750-0*, Pub. by Georg Olms GW) Lubrecht & Cramer.

Lucardie, Paul, jt. ed. see Dobson, Andrew.

Lucarella, Dario, ed. Tex for Scientific Documentation of the First European Conference Como, Italy. 224p. 1986. pap. write for info. (*0-201-13399-7*) Addison-Wesley.

Lucas. Greer's Ocular Pathology. 4th ed. 1989. 195.00 (*0-632-01513-6*) Blackwell Sci.

— Jews in the Fourth Century. 1992. write for info. (*0-85668-586-0*, Pub. by Aris & Phillips UK); pap. write for info. (*0-85668-572-0*, Pub. by Aris & Phillips UK) David Brown.

Lucas, ed. New Materials for Optical Waveguides. 152p. 1987. 43.00 (*0-89252-834-6*, 799) SPIE.

Lucas, A. E. Ozark Almanac. 1986. pap. 8.00 (*0-8309-0443-3*) Independence Pr.

Lucas, Alan. Australia Cruising Guide. (Illus.). 1994. 39.95 (*0-85288-246-7*, Pub. by Imray Laurie Norie & Wilson UK) Bluewater Bks.

— Cruising in Tropical Waters & Coral. 240p. (Orig.). 1987. text ed. 18.95 (*0-87742-954-5*) Intl Marine.

— Illustrated Encyclopedia of Boating. LC 78-9809. (Illus.). 1980. 3.89 (*0-684-15900-7*, Scribners) S&S Trade.

— Red Sea & Indian Ocean Cruising Guide. 190p. (C). 1985. 160.00 (*0-85288-096-0*, Pub. by Imray Laurie Norie & Wilson UK) St Mut.

Lucas, Alice. Cambodians in America: Courageous People from a Troubled Country. (New Faces of Liberty Background Essays Ser.). (Illus.). 25p. 1993. pap. text ed. 5.00 (*0-936434-70-8*) SF Study Ctr.

— How the Farmer Tricked the Evil Demon. Tan, Samol, tr. (Illus.). 32p. (J). (gr. 1-5). 1994. 14.95 (*1-879600-20-X*) Pac Asia Pr.

— How the Farmer Tricked the Evil Demon. Nguyen, Anh, tr. (Illus.). 32p. (ENG & VIE.). (J). (gr. 1-5). 1994. 15.95 (*1-879600-23-4*) Pac Asia Pr.

— How the Farmer Tricked the Evil Demon. Sivongsay, Vandy, tr. (Illus.). 32p. (ENG & LAO.). (J). (gr. 1-5). 1994. 15.95 (*1-879600-24-2*) Pac Asia Pr.

— How the Farmer Tricked the Evil Demon: (English/Hmong Edition) Xiong, Ia, tr. (Illus.). 32p. (MUL.). (J). (gr. 1-5). 1994. 15.95 (*1-879600-25-0*) Pac Asia Pr.

— How the Farmer Tricked the Evil Demon: (Khmer/English Edition) Tan, Samol, tr. (Illus.). 32p. (MUL.). (J). (gr. 1-5). 1994. 15.95 (*1-879600-21-8*) Pac Asia Pr.

— Voices of Liberty. (Illus.). 1990. Complete Package incls. 3 story bks., 3 tchr. discussion guides & 3 audio tapes. audio, pap. text ed. 40.00 (*0-936434-49-X*, Pub. by Zellerbach Fam Fund) SF Study Ctr.

Lucas, Alice, ed. see Northup, Solomon.

Lucas, Anelissa. Chinese Medical Modernization: Comparative Policy Continuities 1930's-1980's. LC 81-23361. 190p. 1982. text ed. 45.00 (*0-275-90851-8*, C0851, Praeger Pubs) Greenwood.

Lucas, Angela. Women in the Middle Ages: Religion, Marriage & Letters. LC 82-42578. 215p. 1984. 11.95 (*0-312-88744-2*) St Martin.

Lucas, Ann F. Strengthening Departmental Leadership: A Team-Building Guide for Chairs in Colleges & Universities. LC 94-21302. (Higher & Adult Education Ser.). 346p. 1994. 30.95 (*0-7879-0012-5*) Jossey-Bass.

Lucas, Ann F., ed. The Department Chairperson's Role in Enhancing College Teaching. LC 85-644763. (New Directions for Teaching & Learning Ser.: No. TL 37). 1989. 16.95 (*1-55542-878-9*) Jossey-Bass.

Lucas, Anthony J., jt. auth. see Marco, Gayle J.

Lucas, Anton. One Soul, One Struggle. (Illus.). 224p. 1991. pap. text ed. 24.95 (*0-04-442249-0*, Pub. by Allen Unwin AT) Paul & Co Pubs.

Lucas, Arthur, jt. ed. see Black, Paul.

Lucas, Barbara. Little People's Mother Goose. LC 87-27261. (J). 1988. 5.99 (*0-517-65860-7*) Random Hse Value.

Lucas, Barbara, tr. see Lindgren, Astrid.

Lucas, Barbara A. & Freedman, Stephen, eds. Technology Choice & Change in Developing Countries: Internal & External Constraints. (Illus.). 155p. 1983. 70.00 (*0-907567-32-0*, Tycooly Pub); pap. 40.00 (*0-907567-33-9*, Tycooly Pub) Weidner & Sons.

Lucas, Barbara M. Snowed In. LC 92-39081. (Illus.). 32p. (J). (ps-3). 1993. text ed. 14.95 (*0-02-761465-4*, Bradbury S&S) S&S Childrens.

Lucas, Caroline. Writing for Women: The Example of Woman As Reader in Elizabethan Romance. (Gender in Writing Ser.). 160p. 1990. 90.00 (*0-335-09018-4*); pap. 32.00 (*0-335-09017-6*) Taylor & Francis.

Lucas, Ceil, ed. Sign Language Research: Theoretical Issues. LC 89-28131. (Illus.). 384p. (C). 1990. 49.95 (*0-930323-58-0*) Gallaudet Univ Pr.

— Sociolinguistics in Deaf Communities. (Sociolinguistics in Deaf Communities Ser.: Vol. 1). 280p. 1995. text ed. 39.95 (*1-56368-036-X*) Gallaudet Univ Pr.

— The Sociolinguistics of the Deaf Community. 307p. 1989. text ed. 54.95 (*0-12-458045-9*) Acad Pr.

Lucas, Ceil & Borders, Denise G. Language Diversity & Classroom Discourse. LC 93-37619. (Language & Educational Processes Ser.). 1993. 39.95 (*0-89391-969-1*); pap. 22.50 (*1-56750-076-5*) Ablex Pub.

Lucas, Ceil & Valli, Clayton. Language Contact in the American Deaf Community. (Illus.). 161p. 1992. text ed. 34.50 (*0-12-458040-8*) Acad Pr.

Lucas, Ceil, jt. auth. see Valli, Clayton.

Lucas, Celia. Prisoners of Santo Tomas. (Battle Standards Ser.). (Illus.). 220p. (C). 1989. reprint ed. lib. bdg. 25.00x (*0-8095-7543-4*) Borgo Pr.

Lucas, Charles, ed. The Pitcairn Island Register Book. LC 75-3444. (Illus.). reprint ed. 22.50 (*0-404-14447-0*) AMS Pr.

Lucas, Charles, illus. Handbook of Printing Processes. LC 92-73936. 225p. (Orig.). (C). 1994. pap. text ed. 55.00 (*0-88362-164-9*) Graphic Arts Tech Found.

Lucas, Charles, ed. see Lee, Douglas.

Lucas, Charles, ed. see Nitobe, Inazo.

Lucas, Christine A., jt. auth. see Lucas, John F.

Lucas, Christopher, ed. see Ricalton, James.

Lucas, Christopher J. American Higher Education: A History. LC 94-17001. 1994. text ed. 39.95 (*0-312-12294-2*) St Martin.

Lucas, Christopher J., ed. see Richalton, James.

Lucas, Claudia, tr. see Renirkens, Clement.

Lucas, Colin, ed. The French Revolution & the Creation of Modern Political Culture, Vol. 2: The Political Culture of the French Revolution. 500p. 1988. 170.00 (*0-08-034259-0*, Pergamon Pr) Elsevier.

— Rewriting the French Revolution: The Andrew Browning Lectures, 1989. 224p. 1991. 55.00 (*0-19-821976-8*) OUP.

Lucas, Colleen. The Bible-Sermon Companion. Date not set. pap. text ed. write for info. (*0-9634547-0-6*) Lucas Assocs.

***Lucas, Craig.** Craig Lucas: Collected Works. 1995. pap. 14.95 (*1-880399-17-2*) Smith & Kraus.

— Missing Persons. Date not set. 5.95 (*0-8222-1474-1*) Dramatists Play.

— Missing Persons. 1995. pap. 4.75 (*0-614-07221-2*) Dramatists Play.

— Prelude to a Kiss. 96p. 1991. pap. 8.00 (*0-452-26567-3*, Plume) NAL-Dutton.

— Prelude to a Kiss. 1992. pap. 7.95 (*0-452-25390-X*, Plume) NAL-Dutton.

— Reckless. 1985. pap. 4.75 (*0-8222-0937-3*) Dramatists Play.

— Reckless & Blue Window: Two Plays. LC 89-4413. 128p. 1989. pap. 9.95 (*0-930452-95-X*) Theatre Comm.

— Three Postcards. 1988. pap. 4.75 (*0-8222-1142-4*) Dramatists Play.

Lucas, D. & Gorman, M. Dione Lucas Book of French Cooking. 1986. 14.98 (*0-685-16789-5*, 615347) Random Hse Value.

Lucas, D. A., et al. Near Miss Reporting As a Safety Tool. (Illus.). 250p. 1991. 67.95 (*0-7506-1178-2*) Buttrwrth-Heinemann.

Lucas, Daniel B. Nicaragua: War of the Filibusters... 2194p. 1986. reprint ed. 25.00 (*0-913129-10-0*) La Tienda.

Lucas, Daryl. Children. (Famous Bible People Ser.). (Illus.). 18p. (J). (gr. 2). 1992. 7.99 (*0-8423-1013-4*) Tyndale.

— Choice Adventures, No. 2: The Smithsonian Connection. (J). (gr. 3-7). 1991. lib. bdg. 4.99 (*0-8423-5026-8*) Tyndale.

— Heroes. (Famous Bible People Ser.). (Illus.). 18p. (J). (gr. 2). 1992. 7.99 (*0-8423-1009-6*) Tyndale.

— Heroines. (Famous Bible People Ser.). (Illus.). 18p. (J). (gr. 2). 1992. 7.99 (*0-8423-1012-6*) Tyndale.

— Prophets. (Famous Bible People Ser.). (Illus.). (J). (gr. 2). 1992. 8.99 (*0-8423-1011-8*) Tyndale.

Lucas, David. First Science Dictionary: English with Arabic Glossary. 1986. 12.00 (*0-86685-077-5*) Intl Bk Ctr.

Lucas, David O. & Meinke, William. Zinsser Microbiology. 256p. 1990. student ed, pap. text ed. 15.50 (*0-8385-9980-X*, A9980-2) Appleton & Lange.

Lucas, David W., jt. auth. see LeBeau, Charles.

Lucas, Dennis. Rodeo Harpsicord. (Sundown Ser.). 22p. 1991. pap. 5.00 (*1-879969-01-7*) Catskill Reading.

— Thirteen Ways of Looking at a Crow. 32p. (Orig.). 1992. pap. 9.00 (*1-880516-05-5*) Left Hand Bks.

Lucas, DeWitt B. Handwriting & Character Analysis. 64p. 1922. reprint ed. 5.95 (*0-7873-0571-5*) Mokelumne.

Lucas, Dione, jt. auth. see Klapthor, Margaret.

Lucas, Dolores D. Emily Dickinson & Riddle. LC 73-76428. 151p. 1969. 15.00 (*0-87580-011-4*) N Ill U Pr.

Lucas, Don. The Father of American Tattooing: Franklin Paul Rogers. (Illus.). 96p. 1990. lib. bdg. 30.00 (*0-916638-78-2*) Meyerbooks.

Lucas-Dubreton, Jean. Restoration & the July Monarchy. LC 29-16694. (National History of France Ser.: No. 8). reprint ed. 45.00 (*0-404-50798-0*) AMS Pr.

Lucas, E. F. Seneca & Elizabethan Tragedy. 1973. 250.00 (*0-87968-047-4*) Gordon Pr.

Lucas, E. V. Life of Charles Lamb. 1972. 59.95 (*0-8490-0528-0*) Gordon Pr.

— Life of Charles Lamb, 2 vols. in 1. 5th rev. ed. LC 68-59324. reprint ed. 124.50 (*0-404-04059-4*) AMS Pr.

Lucas, E. V., ed. see Lamb, Charles & Lamb, Mary.

Lucas, Edward V. Adventures & Misgivings. LC 78-105027. (Essay Index Reprint Ser.). 1977. 18.95 (*0-8369-1523-2*) Ayer.

— All of a Piece: New Essays. LC 68-22923. (Essay Index Reprint Ser.). 1977. reprint ed. 19.95 (*0-8369-0627-6*) Ayer.

— Another Book of Verses for Children. LC 73-37017. (Granger Index Reprint Ser.). (Illus.). 1977. reprint ed. 29.95 (*0-8369-6316-4*) Ayer.

— Boswell of Bagdad. LC 79-107722. (Essay Index Reprint Ser.). 1977. 20.95 (*0-8369-1579-8*) Ayer.

— Cloud & Silver. LC 73-156685. (Essay Index Reprint Ser.). 1977. reprint ed. 19.95 (*0-8369-2411-8*) Ayer.

— The Colvins & Their Friends. (BCL1-PR English Literature Ser.). 365p. 1992. reprint ed. lib. bdg. 89.00 (*0-7812-7505-9*) Rprt Serv.

— Encounters & Diversions. LC 70-156684. (Essay Index Reprint Ser.). 1977. reprint ed. 20.95 (*0-8369-2560-2*) Ayer.

— English Leaves. LC 73-99709. (Essay Index Reprint Ser.). 1977. 21.95 (*0-8369-1361-2*) Ayer.

— Fireside & Sunshine. LC 68-8480. (Essay Index Reprint Ser.). 1977. 19.95 (*0-8369-0628-4*) Ayer.

— The Friendly Town: A Little Book for the Urbane. LC 70-152153. (Granger Index Reprint Ser.). 1977. reprint ed. 24.95 (*0-8369-6262-1*) Ayer.

— Fronded Isle, & Other Essays. LC 68-29225. (Essay Index Reprint Ser.). 1977. reprint ed. 18.95 (*0-8369-0629-2*) Ayer.

— Giving & Receiving. LC 73-142657. (Essay Index Reprint Ser.). 1977. 19.95 (*0-8369-2058-9*) Ayer.

— Lemon Verbena & Other Essays. LC 76-84320. (Essay Index Reprint Ser.). 1977. 18.95 (*0-8369-1090-7*) Ayer.

— The Life of Charles Lamb, 2 vols., Set. (BCL1-PR English Literature Ser.). 1992. reprint ed. lib. bdg. 150.00 (*0-7812-7586-5*) Rprt Serv.

— Loiterer's Harvest. LC 77-142658. (Essay Index Reprint Ser.). 1977. 20.95 (*0-8369-2059-7*) Ayer.

— Luck of the Year. LC 76-90657. (Essay Index Reprint Ser.). 1977. 19.95 (*0-8369-1224-1*) Ayer.

— Only the Other Day: A Volume of Essays. LC 67-28756. (Essay Index Reprint Ser.). 1977. 19.95 (*0-8369-0630-6*) Ayer.

— Phantom Journal & Other Essays & Diversions. LC 75-111844. (Essay Index Reprint Ser.). 1977. 20.95 (*0-8369-1615-8*) Ayer.

— Pleasure Trove. LC 68-57329. (Essay Index Reprint Ser.). 1977. 19.95 (*0-8369-0631-4*) Ayer.

— Reading, Writing & Remembering: A Literary Record. (Illus.). 1971. reprint ed. 24.00 (*0-403-01076-4*) Scholarly.

— Saunterer's Rewards. LC 75-128271. (Essay Index Reprint Ser.). 1977. 19.95 (*0-8369-1887-8*) Ayer.

— Selected Essays. Wethered, H. N., ed. LC 78-59029. 1979. reprint ed. 21.75 (*0-88355-702-9*) Hyperion Conn.

— Specially Selected. LC 77-117891. (Essay Index Reprint Ser.). 1977. 19.95 (*0-8369-1673-5*) Ayer.

— Turning Things over. LC 72-107723. (Essay Index Reprint Ser.). 1977. 19.95 (*0-8369-1524-0*) Ayer.

— Urbanities. LC 79-128272. (Essay Index Reprint Ser.). 1977. 19.95 (*0-8369-1888-6*) Ayer.

— Vermeer the Magical. LC 79-37352. (Select Bibliographies Reprint Ser.). (Illus.). 1977. reprint ed. 16.95 (*0-8369-6699-6*) Ayer.

— Visibility Good. LC 68-54356. (Essay Index Reprint Ser.). 1977. 18.95 (*0-8369-0632-2*) Ayer.

Lucas, Edward V., comp. Book of Verses for Children. LC 71-121927. (Granger Index Reprint Ser.). 1977. 20.95 (*0-8369-6168-4*) Ayer.

— Open Road. 7th ed. LC 75-121928. (Granger Index Reprint Ser.). 1977. 19.95 (*0-8369-6169-2*) Ayer.

Lucas, Edward V., jt. auth. see Graves, C. L.

Lucas, Eileen. Acid Rain. LC 91-3879. (Saving Planet Earth Ser.). 128p. (J). (gr. 4-8). 1991. lib. bdg. 20.55 (*0-516-05503-8*) Childrens.

— The Cherokees: People of the Southeast. LC 92-40874. (Native Americans Ser.). (Illus.). 64p. (J). (gr. 4-6). 1993. lib. bdg. 15.40 (*1-56294-312-X*) Millbrook Pr.

— The European Invasion. LC 95-5426. (Native Central & South American Cultures Ser.). (J). 1995. write for info. (*0-86625-556-7*) Rourke Pubns.

— Everglades. LC 94-26278. (J). (gr. 1 up). 1995. lib. bdg. write for info. (*0-8114-6373-7*) Raintree Steck-V.

— Jane Goodall: Friend of the Chimps. (J). (gr. 4-7). 1992. pap. 5.00 (*0-395-63570-5*) HM.

— Jane Goodall: Friend of the Chimps. LC 91-18060. (Gateway Biographies Ser.). (Illus.). 48p. (J). (gr. 2-4). 1992. lib. bdg. 13.40 (*1-56294-135-6*); pap. 5.95 (*1-56294-796-6*) Millbrook Pr.

— The Mind at Work: How to Make It Work Better for You. LC 92-34663. (Illus.). 96p. (YA). (gr. 7 up). 1993. lib. bdg. 15.90 (*1-56294-300-6*) Millbrook Pr.

— Naturalists, Conservationists & Environmentalists. (American Profiles Ser.). (Illus.). 128p. (YA). (gr. 4-11). 1994. 16.95 (*0-8160-2919-9*) Facts on File.

— The Ojibwas: People of the Northern Forests. LC 93-18640. (Native Americans Ser.). (Illus.). 64p. (J). (gr. 4-6). 1994. lib. bdg. 15.40 (*1-56294-313-8*) Millbrook Pr.

— Peace on the Playground: Nonviolent Ways of Problem-Solving. LC 91-12099. (First Bks.). (Illus.). 64p. (J). (gr. 5-8). 1991. lib. bdg. 13.93 (*0-531-20047-7*) Watts.

An Asterisk (*) at the beginning of an entry indicates that the title is appearing in BIP for the first time.

— Trade. LC 95-7292. (Native Latin American Cultures Ser.). (J). 1995. write for info. (*0-86625-555-9*) Rourke Pubns.

— Water: A Resource in Crisis. LC 91-36137. (Saving Planet Earth Ser.). 128p. (J). (gr. 4-8). 1991. lib. bdg. 20.55 (*0-516-05509-7*) Childrens.

Lucas, Elizabeth. Calligraphy: The Art of Beautiful Writing. (Illus.). 1984. pap. 18.50 (*0-13-112269-X*) P-H.

— Inspirations. Anderson, Mac, ed. 78p. (Orig.). 1990. pap. 7.95 (*0-931089-94-8*) Great Quotations.

— Thinking of You. Anderson, Mac, ed. 78p. (Orig.). 1990. pap. 7.95 (*0-931089-87-5*) Great Quotations.

Lucas, Elizabeth, ed. Nurses & Health Care. 1976. 24.95 (*0-8464-0679-9*) Beekman Pubs.

Lucas, Enver, jt. auth. see Dubin, Marc.

Lucas, F. L. Euripides & His Influence. 1972. 59.95 (*0-8490-0138-2*) Gordon Pr.

— Seneca & Elizabethan Tragedy. LC 68-1142. (Studies in Comparative Literature: No. 35). 1969. reprint ed. lib. bdg. 75.00 (*0-8383-0668-3*) M S G Haskell Hse.

Lucas, F. L., ed. see Webster, John.

Lucas, Frances. Cathy IV. LC 91-43339. (Orig.). 1992. pap. 8.95 (*0-934678-41-3*) New Victoria Pubs.

— Dark Horse. LC 89-13407. 196p. (Orig.). 1989. pap. 8.95 (*0-934678-21-9*) New Victoria Pubs.

— If Looks Could Kill. 190p. (Orig.). 1995. pap. 9.95 (*0-934678-63-4*) New Victoria Pubs.

Lucas, Frank L. Authors Dead & Living. LC 68-29226. (Essay Index Reprint Ser.). 1977. reprint ed. 20.95 (*0-8369-0633-0*) Ayer.

— The Decline & Fall of the Romantic Ideal. LC 75-30007. 1976. reprint ed. 24.50 (*0-404-14013-0*) AMS Pr.

— Drama of Checkhov, Synge, Yeats & Pirandello. 2nd ed. LC 76-18824. 452p. 1976. reprint ed. 50.00 (*0-87753-062-9*) Phaeton.

— Studies French & English. LC 69-17583. (Essay Index Reprint Ser.). 1977. 21.95 (*0-8369-0084-7*) Ayer.

— Woman Clothed with the Sun, & Other Stories. LC 71-122731. (Short Story Index Reprint Ser.). 1977. 20.95 (*0-8369-3564-0*) Ayer.

Lucas, Franz D. & Heitmann, Margret. Stadt des Glaubens. (Wissenschaftliche Abhandlungen des Salomon Ludwig Steinheim-Instituts fur Deutsch-Judische Geschichte Ser.: Bd. 3). viii, 583p. (GER.). 1992. write for info. (*3-487-09495-9*, Pub. by Georg Olms GW) Lubrecht & Cramer.

Lucas, G. B., jt. ed. see Shew, H. D.

Lucas, G. E., jt. ed. see Corwin, W. R.

Lucas, G. G. Road Vehicle Performance. (Transportation Studies: Vol. 7). 218p. 1986. text ed. 95.00 (*0-677-21400-6*) Gordon & Breach.

***Lucas, George.** Classic Star Wars: A New Hope. 272p. 1995. 16.00 (*0-345-40077-1*, Del Rey) Ballantine.

— Lucas vs the Green Machine: Landmark Supreme Court Property Rights Decision by the Man Who Won It Against the Odds. 320p. Date not set. pap. text ed. 16.95 (*1-57090-011-6*) Alexander Bks.

— The Star Wars: From the Adventures of Luke Skywalker. LC 77-88169. 1986. mass mkt. 4.99 (*0-345-34146-5*, Del Rey) Ballantine.

***Lucas, George & Claremont, Chris.** Shadow Moon. LC 95-3613. 1995. pap. 22.50 (*0-553-09596-X*) Bantam.

Lucas, George, jt. auth. see Kasdan, Lawrence.

Lucas, George, et al. The Star Wars Trilogy: Stars Wars; The Empire Strikes Back; Return of the Jedi, 3 vols. in 1. 1993. mass mkt. 5.99 (*0-345-38438-5*, Del Rey) Ballantine.

***Lucas, George A.** The Diary of George A. Lucas: An America Art Agent in Paris, Vol. 1. LC 77-85561. (Illus.). 209p. Date not set. reprint ed. pap. 59.60 (*0-7837-9415-0*, 2060171) Bks Demand.

— The Diary of George A. Lucas: An America Art Agent in Paris, Vol. 2. LC 77-85561. (Illus.). 979p. Date not set. reprint ed. pap. 180.00 (*0-7837-9416-9*, 2060171) Bks Demand.

***Lucas, George B.** Every Other Day: Letters from the Pacific. LC 95-8682. (Illus.). 328p. 1995. 29.95 (*1-55750-528-4*) Naval Inst Pr.

Lucas, George B., et al. Introduction to Plant Diseases: Identification & Management. 2nd ed. (Illus.). 368p. 1992. pap. 42.95 (*0-442-00578-4*) Chapman & Hall.

Lucas, George F. American Drop-Shippers Directory. 15th ed. 32p. 1986. pap. text ed. 7.00 (*0-911652-00-0*) Wrld Wide Trade.

— Importers Confidential Drop-Ship Directory. 16p. 1985. pap. text ed. 5.00 (*0-911652-01-9*) Wrld Wide Trade.

Lucas, George R., Jr. The Rehabilitation of Whitehead: An Analytic & Historical Assessment of Process Philosophy. LC 88-22607. (SUNY Series in Philosophy). 261p. 1989. 59.50 (*0-88706-988-6*); pap. 19.95 (*0-88706-989-4*) State U NY Pr.

Lucas, George R. Two Views of Freedom in Process Thought. LC 79-12287. (American Academy of Religion. Dissertation Ser.: No. 28). 186p. reprint ed. pap. 53.10 (*0-7837-5415-9*, 2045179) Bks Demand.

Lucas, George R., Jr., ed. Hegel & Whitehead: Contemporary Perspectives on Systematic Philosophy. LC 85-9745. (SUNY Series in Hegelian Studies in Philosophy). 325p. 1986. 59.50 (*0-88706-144-3*); pap. 19.95 (*0-88706-143-5*) State U NY Pr.

Lucas, H. J. Rock 'n Roll Is Here to Stay. 138p. 1983. 40.00 (*0-901976-82-2*, Pub. by United Writers Pubns UK) St Mut.

Lucas, H. M., tr. see Ehrenberg, Richard.

Lucas, H. M., tr. see Knapp, Georg F.

Lucas, Harry. Pensions & Industrial Relations: A Practical Guide for All Involved in Pensions. LC 77-30221. 1977. 88.00 (*0-08-021947-0*, Pub. by Pergamon Repr UK) Franklin.

Lucas, Henry, Jr. Information Systems Concepts for Management. 5th ed. 1994. text ed. write for info. (*0-07-038995-0*) McGraw.

Lucas, Henry C., Jr. The Analysis, Design & Implementation of Information Systems. 4th ed. 1992. text ed. write for info. (*0-07-038933-0*) McGraw.

— Implementation: The Key to Successful Information Systems. LC 80-27009. 224p. 1981. text ed. 53.50 (*0-231-04434-8*) Col U Pr.

— Information Systems Concepts for Management. 4th ed. 1990. teacher ed 18.95 (*0-07-836100-1*); pap. text ed. write for info. (*0-07-038971-3*) McGraw.

— Managing Information Services. Stewart, Charles E., Jr., ed. 719p. (C). 1989. text ed. write for info. (*0-02-372231-2*) Macmillan.

— The T-Form Organization. (Management Ser.). 1995. 28.95 (*0-7879-0167-9*) Jossey-Bass.

Lucas, Henry C. Why Information Systems Fail. LC 74-18395. (Illus.). 141p. reprint ed. pap. 40.20 (*0-317-10726-7*, 2021970) Bks Demand.

Lucas, Henry C., Jr., et al. Information Systems Implementation: Testing a Structural Model. (Computer Based Systems in Information Management Ser.: Vol. 4). 160p. 1990. text ed. 29.50 (*0-89391-665-X*) Ablex Pub.

Lucas, Henry S. The Renaissance & the Reformation. LC 83-45665. reprint ed. 67.50 (*0-404-19815-5*) AMS Pr.

Lucas, I., ed. see Comparative Pathology of the Heart Symposium Staff.

Lucas, Ian. Impertinent Decorum: Gay Theatrical Maneuvers. (Sexual Politics Ser.). 224p. 1994. pap. 15.95 (*0-304-32797-2*, Pub. by Cassell Pubng UK) InBook.

— Impertinent Decorum: Gay Theatrical Maneuvers. (Sexual Politics Ser.). 224p. 1994. 55.00 (*0-304-32795-6*, Pub. by Cassell Pubng UK) InBook.

Lucas, J. & Moynihan, C. T., eds. Halide Glasses. (Material Science Forum Ser.: Vols. 5/6). 840p. (C). 1985. pap. text ed. 196.00 (*0-87849-540-1*, Pub. by Trans Tech GW) LPS Dist Ctr.

Lucas, J. D., et al, eds. Phytophthora. (British Mycological Society Symposium Ser.: No. 17). 480p. (C). 1991. 125.00 (*0-521-40080-5*) Cambridge U Pr.

Lucas, J. R. Responsibility. LC 92-30980. (Illus.). 288p. 1993. 49.95 (*0-19-824008-2*) OUP.

— Responsibility. (Illus.). 306p. 1995. pap. 21.00 (*0-19-823578-X*) OUP.

Lucas, J. S., jt. auth. see Copland, J. W.

Lucas, James. Battle Group! German Kampfgruppen Action of World War Two. (Illus.). 224p. 1994. 24.95 (*1-85409-176-X*) Sterling.

— The Last Year of the German Army, May 1944 - May 1945. (Illus.). 192p. 1995. 24.95 (*1-85409-194-8*) Sterling.

Lucas, James & Von Habsburg, Otto. The Fighting Troops of the Austro-Hungarian Army 1868-1914. 256p. (C). 1991. 150.00 (*0-946771-04-9*, Pub. by Spellmount UK) St Mut.

Lucas, James S. & Barker, James. The Battle of Normandy: Falaise Gap. LC 78-17771. 176p. 1978. 24.50 (*0-8419-0418-9*) Holmes & Meier.

Lucas, Janice. Long Sun. 266p. 1994. 22.00 (*1-56947-013-8*) Soho Press.

Lucas, Jay H., jt. auth. see Woods, James D.

Lucas, Jeff. Pass, Set, Crush: Volleyball Illustrated. 2nd ed. (Illus.). 167p. (Orig.). 1988. 19.95 (*0-317-66788-2*); pap. 12.95 (*0-317-66789-0*) Euclid NW Pubns.

— Pass, Set, Crush: Volleyball Illustrated. 3rd rev. ed. (Illus.). 432p. (Orig.). 1993. pap. 19.95 (*0-9615088-6-8*) Euclid NW Pubns.

Lucas, Jerri M. Lessons from Esther. 1993. pap. 6.25 (*0-89137-459-0*) Quality Pubns.

Lucas, Jerri M., ed. Planning a Future. 1987. pap. 5.95 (*0-89137-816-2*) Quality Pubns.

Lucas, Jerry. Becoming a Mental Math Wizard. LC 91-19472. (Illus.). 192p. (Orig.). (YA). (gr. 12 up). 1991. pap. 8.95 (*1-55870-216-4*) Shoe Tree Pr.

— Great Unsolved Mysteries of Science: From the End of the Dinosaurs to Interstellar Travel & Life on Other Planets. (Illus.). 192p. (Orig.). (YA). (gr. 7 up). 1993. pap. 9.95 (*1-55870-291-1*) Betterway Bks.

Lucas, Jerry & Lorayne, Harry. The Memory Book. 208p. 1986. mass mkt. 4.95 (*0-345-33758-1*) Ballantine.

Lucas, Jerry, jt. auth. see Lorayne, Harry.

Lucas, Jo D. Admiralty: Cases & Materials On. 3rd ed. (University Casebook Ser.). 1146p. 1986. text ed. 41.95 (*0-88277-352-6*) Foundation Pr.

— Admiralty, 1991 Statute: Rule & Case Supplement for Use with Cases & Materials On. 3rd ed. (University Casebook Ser.). 408p. (C). 1991. pap. text ed. 14.00 (*0-88277-940-0*) Foundation Pr.

Lucas, Jocelyn. Pedigree Dog Breeding for Pleasure & Profit. 1992. lib. bdg. 79.95 (*0-8490-5239-4*) Gordon Pr.

Lucas, Joel M. Woman's Desk Reference: From HEO to CEO, Any Woman Can. 70p. (Orig.). 1994. pap. write for info. (*0-9640378-1-5*) Merrill & Merritt.

Lucas, John. Charles Dickens: The Major Novels. LC 92-20181. (Critical Studies). 1993. pap. 9.95 (*0-14-077252-9*, Penguin Bks) Viking Penguin.

— D. H. Lawrence: Selected Poetry & Non-Fictional Prose. (English Texts Ser.). 288p. 1991. pap. 12.95 (*0-415-01429-8*, A6137) Routledge.

— England & Englishness: Ideas of Nationhood in English Poetry, 1688-1900. LC 89-51574. 237p. (C). 1990. text ed. 28.95x (*0-87745-275-X*) U of Iowa Pr.

— John Clare. 1990. 40.00 (*0-7463-0724-1*, Pub. by Northcote UK); pap. 21.00 (*0-7463-0729-2*, Pub. by Northcote UK) St Mut.

— Katy Keene: Hollywood Priemer PD's. 1994. 5.95 (*0-87588-428-8*, 4743) Hobby Hse.

— Katy Keene's Swimsuit Paperdolls. 24p. 1995. 5.95 (*0-87588-437-7*) Hobby Hse.

— Low-Water Gardening: Creating & Running the Ideal Garden with Less Water. (Illus.). 176p. 1993. pap. 16.95 (*0-460-86151-4*) Trafalgar.

— Modern English Poetry from Hardy to Hughes: A Critical Survey. LC 86-3529. 224p. 1986. 54.00 (*0-389-20629-6*, N8187) B&N Imports.

— Romantic to Modern Literature: Essays & Ideas of Culture 1750-1900. LC 82-6842. 240p. (C). 1982. text ed. 58.50 (*0-389-20311-4*, N7148) B&N Imports.

— Tables. 432p. 1991. mass mkt. 5.99 (*0-312-92596-4*) St Martin.

Lucas, John & Engelman, Jeanne. Luke's Way. (Good Lives Ser.). 56p. 1994. pap. 4.95 (*1-56838-029-1*) Hazelden.

Lucas, John & Moriarty, Joe. Winning a Day at a Time. 225p. 1994. 19.95 (*1-56838-028-3*) Hazelden.

Lucas, John, tr. see Fell, Christine, ed. & tr.

Lucas, John A. Future of the Olympic Games. LC 91-46818. (Illus.). 248p. 1992. text ed. 32.00 (*0-87322-357-8*, BLUC0357) Human Kinetics.

Lucas, John F. Introduction to Abstract Mathematics. 2nd ed. (Illus.). 382p. 1990. teacher ed write for info. (*0-912675-74-8*); text ed. 42.95 (*0-912675-73-X*) Ardsley.

Lucas, John F. & Lucas, Christine A. A Guided Tour of the TI-85 Graphics Programmable Calculator with Emphasis on Calculus. 117p. 1992. pap. text ed. 18.95 (*1-880157-10-1*) Ardsley.

Lucas, John R. & Hodgson, P. E. Spacetime & Electromagnetism. 328p. 1990. pap. 29.95 (*0-19-852038-7*) OUP.

Lucas, John T. & Gurman, Richard. Truth in Advertising: An AMA Research Report. LC 72-79980. (AMA Research Report Ser.). 40p. reprint ed. pap. 25.00 (*0-317-28460-6*, 2051309) Bks Demand.

Lucas, John W., ed. Heat Transfer & Spacecraft Thermal Control. LC 70-147076. (PAAS Ser.: Vol. 24). (Illus.). 427p. 1971. 54.95 (*0-262-12042-9*) AIAA.

— Thermal Characteristics of the Moon. LC 79-39803. (PAAS Ser.: Vol. 28). (Illus.). 340p. 1972. 43.95 (*0-262-12058-5*) AIAA.

Lucas, K. Applied Statistical Thermodynamics. (Illus.). xvii, 514p. 1991. 198.00 (*0-387-52007-4*) Spr-Verlag.

Lucas, Kenneth W., Sr. Federal Law Enforcement Badges. 391p. 1991. 65.00 (*0-9630225-0-4*); pap. 35.00 (*0-9630225-1-2*) K W Lucas.

Lucas, Kevin A. & Clarke, Herbert. Corrosion of Aluminum-Based Metal Matrix Composites. LC 93-26513. 140p. 1993. text ed. 59.95 (*0-471-94189-1*) Wiley.

***Lucas, Laddie.** Malta: The Thorn in Rommel's Side. large type ed. 1994. 25.95 (*0-7089-3169-3*) Ulverscroft.

Lucas, Lawrence E. & Wright, Bruce M. Black Priest, White Church: Catholics & Racism. LC 88-71876. 280p. (C). 1989. 29.95 (*0-86543-108-6*); pap. 9.95 (*0-86543-109-4*) Africa World.

***Lucas, Leanne.** Addie & the Movie Mystery. (Addie McCormick Adventures Ser.: Bk. 8). (J). 1995. mass mkt. 3.99 (*1-56507-348-7*) Harvest Hse.

— Addie McCormick & the Chicago Surprise. (Addie McCormick Adventure Ser.: Bk. 4). (J). 1993. mass mkt. 3.99 (*1-56507-082-8*) Harvest Hse.

— Addie McCormick & the Mystery of the Missing Scrapbook. LC 92-10569. (Addie McCormick Adventure Ser.: Bk. 2). 1992. mass mkt. 3.99 (*1-56507-063-1*) Harvest Hse.

— Addie McCormick & the Mystery of the Skeleton Key. (Addie McCormick Adventure Ser.: Bk. 5). (J). (gr. 4-7). 1993. mass mkt. 3.99 (*1-56507-147-6*) Harvest Hse.

— Addie McCormick & the Secret of the Scarlet Box. 1994. mass mkt. 3.99 (*1-56507-230-8*) Harvest Hse.

— Addie McCormick & the Stolen Statue. (Addie McCormick Adventure Ser.: Bk. 3). (YA). (gr. 4 up). 1993. mass mkt. 3.99 (*1-56507-080-1*) Harvest Hse.

— Addie McCormick & the Stranger in the Attic. LC 92-2234. (Addie McCormick Adventure Ser.: Bk. 1). 1992. mass mkt. 3.99 (*1-56507-052-6*) Harvest Hse.

Lucas, Leanne C. Addie McCormick & the Computer Pirate. LC 93-32203. (Addie McCormick Adventure Ser.: Bk. 6). (Orig.). (J). (gr. 5 up). 1994. mass mkt. 3.99 (*1-56507-165-4*) Harvest Hse.

Lucas, Linda, ed. Library Service to Developmentally Disabled Children & Adults. 61p. 10.00 (*0-8389-6538-5*); 9.00 (*0-318-12141-7*) ASCLA.

Lucas, Lois. Plants of Old Hawaii. LC 82-72199. (Illus.). 112p. (Orig.). 1982. pap. 7.95 (*0-935848-11-8*) Bess Pr.

***Lucas, Luzanne.** A Sweet Breath of Life. 160p. 1995. 17.95 (*0-9645269-6-4*) Desirata Pr.

Lucas, Lydia A., comp. Manuscripts Collections of the Minnesota Historical Society Guide, No. 3. LC 35-27911. 189p. 1977. pap. 7.00 (*0-87351-120-4*) Minn Hist.

Lucas, Lynn, jt. auth. see Stokes, P. Burton.

Lucas, Marc, tr. see Renirkens, Clement.

Lucas, Maria E. Forged under the Sun - Forjada bajo el Sol: The Life of Maria Elena Lucas. LC 92-46311. (Illus.). 224p. 1993. text ed. 37.50 (*0-472-09432-7*); pap. 13.95 (*0-472-06432-0*) U of Mich Pr.

Lucas, Marilyn, jt. auth. see Jenkins, Jeanne B.

Lucas, Marion B. & Wright, George C. A History of Blacks in Kentucky, Set. LC 92-24574. 1992. 50.00 (*0-916968-23-5*) Kentucky Hist.

— A History of Blacks in Kentucky, Vol. 1: From Slavery to Segregation, 1760-1891. LC 92-24574. 1992. Volume 1. From Slavery to Segregation, 1760-1891. 29.95 (*0-916968-20-0*) Kentucky Hist.

— A History of Blacks in Kentucky, 2 vols., Vol. 2: In Pursuit of Equality, 1890-1980. LC 92-24574. 1992. Volume 2. In Pursuit of Equality, 1890-1980. 29.95 (*0-685-60096-3*) Kentucky Hist.

Lucas, Mark. Southern Vision of Andrew Lytle. LC 86-21076. (Southern Literary Studies). 192p. 1987. text ed. 29.95 (*0-8071-1338-7*) La State U Pr.

Lucas, Mark, ed. Home Voices: A Sampler of Southern Writing. LC 90-24521. 64p. 1991. pap. text ed. 4.50 (*0-8131-0906-X*) U Pr of Ky.

Lucas, Mayo. Matters of the Heart. 368p. 1988. pap. 3.95 (*0-380-75537-8*) Avon.

Lucas, Michael R. The Western Alliance after INF: Redefining U. S. Policy Toward Europe & the Soviet Union. LC 89-38359. 266p. 1989. lib. bdg. 35.00 (*1-55587-159-3*) Lynne Rienner.

Lucas, Michel, jt. auth. see Gardan, Yvon.

Lucas, N. J. Local Energy Centres. (Illus.). 261p. 1978. 63.00 (*0-85334-782-4*, Pub. by Elsevier Applied Sci UK) Elsevier.

***Lucas, Nathaniel.** Poetry on Life Collection. 1994. 12.95 (*0-533-10906-X*) Vantage.

Lucas, Noah, jt. ed. see Troen, Selwyn I.

Lucas, Oliver W. The Design of Forest Landscapes. (Illus.). 384p. 1991. 175.00 (*0-19-854280-1*) OUP.

Lucas, P. B., jt. auth. see Johnson, J. E.

Lucas, P. G., tr. see Martin, Gottfried.

Lucas, P. H. Protected Landscapes: A Guide for Policy Makers & Planners. (World Conservation Union (IUCN) Ser.). 208p. (C). 1992. 59.95 (*0-412-45530-7*, A7054) Chapman & Hall.

Lucas, Patricia, ed. Junior High Council: Foundation for Leadership. 32p. (Orig.). (gr. 6-9). 1982. pap. text ed. 7.00 (*0-88210-121-8*) Natl Assn Principals.

Lucas, Patricia, ed. see Ferguson, James.

Lucas, Patricia, ed. see Reum, Earl.

Lucas, Patty L. The Land of Tears Is a Secret Place. 88p. 1992. student ed 12.95 (*0-9632065-0-8*) Agape Acad Pr.

Lucas, Paul D. Modern Construction Accounting Methods & Controls. LC 83-22897. 252p. 1984. 39.95 (*0-13-590241-X*, Busn) P-H.

***Lucas, Paul H., comp.** Dictionary of Hawaiian Legal Land-Terms. LC 95-12500. 1995. write for info. (*0-8248-1636-6*) UH Pr.

Lucas, Paul J. The C Plus Plus Programmer's Handbook. 1992. pap. text ed. 32.00 (*0-13-118233-1*) P-H.

Lucas, Paul R. American Odyssey, Sixteen Seven to Seventeen Eighty-Nine. (Illus.). 336p. (C). 1983. pap. text ed. write for info. (*0-13-028233-2*) P-H.

— Valley of Discord: Church & Society along the Connecticut River, 1636-1725. LC 75-22520. 291p. reprint ed. pap. 83.00 (*0-7837-6205-4*, 2045926) Bks Demand.

Lucas, Philip C. The Odyssey of a New Religion: The Holy Order of MANS from New Age to Orthodoxy. LC 94-12587. (Religion in North America Ser.). 1995. 39.95 (*0-253-33612-0*) Ind U Pr.

Lucas, Phillip, jt. auth. see Melton, J. Gordon.

Lucas, R., et al, eds. Birth & Infancy of Stars: Proceedings of the Les Houches Summer School, Session XLI, 8 August-2 September 1983, Vol. 41. 846p. 1985. 233.50 (*0-444-86917-4*, North Holland) Elsevier.

Lucas, R. B., jt. auth. see Thackray, A. C.

Lucas, R. C. The Message of Colossians & Philemon. Motyer, J. A. & Stott, John R., eds. LC 79-3635. (Bible Speaks Today Ser.). 1984. pap. 12.99 (*0-87784-284-1*, 284) InterVarsity.

Lucas, R. D. & Eveson, John W. Atlas of Oral Pathology. (Current Histopathology Ser.). 1985. lib. bdg. 234.50 (*0-85200-328-5*) Kluwer Ac.

Lucas, Randolph. Illustrated Encyclopedia of Minerals & Rocks. 1993. 12.98 (*1-55521-877-6*) Bk Sales Inc.

Lucas, Rex A. Minetown, Milltown, Railtown: Life in Canadian Communities of Single Industry. LC 70-166934. 450p. reprint ed. pap. 128.30 (*0-8357-4158-3*, 2036932) Bks Demand.

Lucas, Richard B. Charles August Lindberg Sr. A Case Study of Congressional Insurgency, 1906-1912. (Studia Historica Upsaliensia: No. 61). (Illus.). 194p. (Orig.). 1974. pap. 25.00x (*91-554-0214-3*, Pub. by Uppsala Univ Acta Univ Uppsaliensis SW) Coronet Bks.

Lucas, Richard E., comp. Index to the New Atlas & Directory of Grand Traverse County, Michigan, 1895. 110p. 1988. pap. 9.00 (*0-940133-18-0*) Kinseeker Pubns.

Lucas, Richard H. & McCoy, K. Byron. The Winning Edge: Effective Communication & Persuasion Techniques for Lawyers. (Trial Practice Library Ser.). 224p. 1993. text ed. 108.00 (*0-471-59544-6*) Wiley.

Lucas, Richard M. Herbal Health Secrets from Europe & Around the World. LC 83-556. 226p. 1983. 21.95 (*0-13-387423-0*, Parker Publishing Co); pap. 5.95 (*0-318-00000-8*, Parker Publishing Co) P-H.

— Magic Herbs for Arthritis, Rheumatism & Related Ailments. LC 80-22346. 248p. 1981. 14.95 (*0-13-543900-0*, Parker Publishing Co); 4.95 (*0-685-03916-1*, Parker Publishing Co) P-H.

— Miracle Medicine Herbs. 224p. 1990. Parker edition. 24.95 (*0-13-585142-4*, Busn); Reward edition. pap. 9.95 (*0-13-585134-3*, Busn) P-H.

— Secrets of the Chinese Herbalists. rev. ed. 252p. 1986. reprint ed. pap. text ed. 10.95 (*0-13-798174-0*) P-H.

— Secrets of the Chinese Herbalists. rev. ed. 252p. 1987. reprint ed. 21.95 (*0-13-797879-0*) P-H.

***Lucas, Rob.** Mastering Prolog. 224p. 1995. pap. 39.95 (*1-85728-400-3*, Pub. by UCL Pr UK) Taylor & Francis.

Lucas, Robert A. The Grants World Inside Out. (Illus.). 192p. 1992. 21.95 (*0-252-01862-1*) U of Ill Pr.

Lucas, Robert C., jt. auth. see Shechter, Mordechai.

Lucas, Robert E., Jr. Models of Business Cycles. 128p. 1989. pap. 21.95 (*0-631-14791-8*) Blackwell Pubs.

— Studies in Business-Cycle Theory. 312p. (C). 1981. pap. 19.95 (*0-262-62044-8*) MIT Pr.

Lucas, Robert E., Jr. & Sargent, Thomas J., eds. Rational Expectations & Econometric Practice, 2 vols., 1. LC 80-24602. 776p. (C). 1981. pap. text ed. 15.95 (*0-8166-0917-9*) U of Minn Pr.

— Rational Expectations & Econometric Practice, 2 vols., 2. LC 80-24602. 776p. (C). 1981. pap. text ed. 15.95 (*0-8166-1071-1*) U of Minn Pr.

Lucas, Robert E., Jr., jt. auth. see Stokey, Nancy L.

Lucas, Robert W. Coaching Skills: A Guide for Supervisors. LC 93-44766. (Business Skills Express Ser.). 112p. 1994. 10.00 (*0-7863-0220-8*) Irwin Prof Pubng.

— Effective Interpersonal Relationships. LC 93-48220. (Business Skills Express Ser.). 120p. 1994. pap. 10.00 (*0-7863-0255-0*) Irwin Prof Pubng.

— Training Skills for Supervisors. LC 94-4999. (Business Skills Express Ser.). 112p. 1994. 10.00 (*0-7863-0313-1*) Irwin Prof Pubng.

***Lucas, Robin.** Stepmothers. 140p. 1995. pap. 16.95 (*0-7022-2644-0*, Pub. by Univ Queensland Pr AT) Intl Spec Bk.

Lucas, Robin & Forster, Clare, eds. Wilder Shores: Women's Travel Stories of Australia & Beyond. (Orig.). 1992. pap. 15.95 (*0-7022-2477-4*, Pub. by Univ Queensland Pr AT) Intl Spec Bk.

***Lucas, Roger S.** The Bellevue - Stratford Hotel. 66p. 1994. pap. 9.00 (*1-887287-02-7*) Res Rev Pubns.

— Boldt Castle - Heart Island. 4th ed. (Illus.). 60p. 1995. reprint ed. 9.00 (*1-887287-00-0*) Res Rev Pubns.

— Boldt's Boats. 2nd rev. ed. 62p. 1995. 9.00 (*1-887287-01-9*) Res Rev Pubns.

— The Waldorf-Astoria Hotel. 60p. 1996. pap. 9.00 (*1-887287-03-5*) Res Rev Pubns.

— Wellesley Island Farms. 60p. 1996. pap. 9.00 (*1-887287-04-3*) Res Rev Pubns.

Lucas, Ronald J. Pension Planning Within a Major Company. 1979. 54.00 (*0-08-024045-3*, Pub. by Pergamon Repr UK) Franklin.

***Lucas, Rosemary.** Managing Employee Relations in the Hotel & Catering Industry. LC 95-2056. (Illus.). 1995. pap. 23.95 (*0-304-32897-9*) Cassell.

***Lucas, Rosemary E.** Managing Employee Relations in the Hotel & Catering Industry. LC 95-2056. (Illus.). 256p. 1995. 60.00 (*0-304-32910-X*) Cassell.

Lucas, Rowland. The Voice of a Nation? 233p. (C). 1990. text ed. 59.00 (*0-85088-745-3*, Pub. by Gomer Pr UK) St Mut.

***Lucas, Ruta.** The Blushing Detectives. (Illus.). (Orig.). Date not set. 9.95 (*0-916897-21-4*) Andrew Mtn Pr.

Lucas, S. E., Jr. Dodson - Dotson, Lucas, Pyles, Rochester & Allied Families. (Illus.). 239p. 1993. reprint ed. lib. bdg. 47.50 (*0-8328-3663-X*); reprint ed. pap. 37.50 (*0-8328-3664-8*) Higginson Bk Co.

— Powell Family of Norfolk & Elizabeth City Cos. Virginia & Their Descendants, with Notes & Data on Collateral Families of Bush, Beckwith, Bowles, Cargill & Others. 305p. 1992. reprint ed. lib. bdg. 56.00 (*0-8328-2460-7*); reprint ed. pap. 46.00 (*0-8328-2461-5*) Higginson Bk Co.

Lucas, S. Emmett, Jr., ed. Quakers in South Carolina, Wateree & Bush River, Cane Creek, Piney Grove & Charleston Meetings. (Illus.). 150p. 1991. reprint ed. pap. 25.00 (*0-89308-450-6*, SC 90) Southern Hist Pr.

Lucas, Sally. Twin Monkeys. (Illus.). 32p. (J). (ps-2). Date not set. 11.95 (*1-56065-156-3*) Capstone Pr.

***Lucas, Scott & Kreinberg, Luke.** The Book of Goals: Achievements, Plans, & Dreams of a Lifetime. 125p. 1994. pap. text ed. 14.95 (*0-9642856-0-6*) First Step CA.

Lucas, Sidney. The Quaker Message. (C). 1948. pap. 3.00 (*0-87574-040-5*) Pendle Hill.

Lucas, Silas, Jr. & Holcomb, Brent. Marriage & Death Notices from Raleigh, N.C. Newspapers, 1796-1826. 168p. 1978. reprint ed. 20.00 (*0-89308-046-2*) Southern Hist Pr.

Lucas, Silas E., Jr. Eighteen Hundred Seven Land Lottery of Georgia. rev. ed. (Illus.). 1987. 27.50 (*0-89308-599-5*) Southern Hist Pr.

— The Eighteen Thirty-Two Gold Lottery of Georgia. rev. ed. (Illus.). 568p. 1987. 42.50 (*0-89308-638-X*, GA 28) Southern Hist Pr.

— The Fourth or 1821 Land Lotteries of Georgia. rev. ed. 262p. 1986. 32.50 (*0-89308-586-3*, GA 66) Southern Hist Pr.

— History of the Powell Families of Virginia & the South: An Encyclopedia. 604p. 1982. reprint ed. 40.00 (*0-89308-027-6*) Southern Hist Pr.

— Marriages from Early Tennessee Newspapers, 1794-1851. 1981. reprint ed. 37.50 (*0-89308-092-6*) Southern Hist Pr.

— Some Georgia County Records, Vol. 3. 368p. 1990. reprint ed. 40.00 (*0-89308-058-6*, GA 33) Southern Hist Pr.

— Some Georgia County Records, Vol. 4. 430p. 1990. 40.00 (*0-89308-685-1*, GA 92) Southern Hist Pr.

— Some Georgia County Records, Vol. 5. 326p. 1990. 40.00 (*0-89308-686-X*, GA 93) Southern Hist Pr.

— Third or Eighteen-Twenty Land Lotteries of Georgia. rev. ed. (Seven Land Lotteries of Georgia & Other Land Records Ser.). 382p. 1986. reprint ed. 35.00 (*0-89308-585-5*, GA 26) Southern Hist Pr.

Lucas, Silas E., Jr., ed. Thirty-Five Thousand Tennessee Marriage Records & Bonds, 3 vols. 1981. Vol. 1, (a-f), 604pp. write for info. (*0-89308-223-6*); Vol. 2, (g-n), 610pp. write for info. (*0-89308-224-4*); Vol. 3, (o-z), 580pp. write for info. (*0-89308-225-2*) Southern Hist Pr.

— Thirty-Five Thousand Tennessee Marriage Records & Bonds, 3 vols., Set. 1981. 135.00 (*0-89308-226-0*) Southern Hist Pr.

Lucas, Silas E., Jr. & Davis, Robert S., Jr., eds. The Georgia Land Lottery Papers, 1805-1914. 366p. 1979. 37.50 (*0-89308-156-6*, GA 30) Southern Hist Pr.

Lucas, Silas E., Jr. & Sheffield, Ella E., eds. The Hawkins County Minutes of the Court of Common Pleas, 1822-1825, & Fragment for the Period, November 1827-August 1828. 176p. 1983. pap. 21.50 (*0-89308-347-X*) Southern Hist Pr.

Lucas, Silas E., Jr. & Wilson, Caroline P. Records of Effingham County, Georgia. 410p. 1976. 30.00 (*0-89308-019-5*) Southern Hist Pr.

Lucas, Silas E., Jr., jt. auth. see Holcomb, Brent.

Lucas, Silas E., Jr., jt. ed. see Sheffield, Ella L.

Lucas, Silas E., Jr., jt. auth. see Williams, Sherman.

Lucas, Spencer G. Dinosaurs: The Textbook. 320p. (C). 1993. pap. write for info. (*0-697-14429-1*) Wm C Brown Pubs.

Lucas, Stephen E. The Art of Public Speaking. (Orig.). 1993. Videotape, Student speeches. vhs write for info. (*0-07-038980-2*) McGraw.

— The Art of Public Speaking. 2nd ed. 416p. (Orig.). (C). 1985. pap. text ed. 13.00 (*0-685-10323-4*) Random.

— The Art of Public Speaking. 3rd ed. (Illus.). 432p. (Orig.). (C). 1989. pap. text ed. write for info. (*0-318-63109-1*) Random.

— The Art of Public Speaking. 4th ed. (Orig.). 1990. Videotape, Wellesley College Commencement, 1990. vhs write for info. (*0-07-038991-8*) McGraw.

— The Art of Public Speaking. 4th ed. (Orig.). 1992. Pamphlet, Teaching Public Speaking. pap. text ed. write for info. (*0-07-038987-X*) McGraw.

— The Art of Public Speaking. 4th ed. (Orig.). 1992. text ed. write for info. (*0-07-038978-0*) McGraw.

— The Art of Public Speaking. 4th ed. (Orig.). 1992. Selections from The Speech Communication Teacher. pap. text ed. write for info. (*0-07-038988-8*) McGraw.

— The Art of Public Speaking. 4th ed. (Orig.). 1993. Commencement 1993, speeches by Hillary Rodham Clinton & Colin Powell. pap. text ed. write for info. (*0-07-039014-2*) McGraw.

— The Art of Public Speaking. 4th suppl. ed. (Orig.). 1992. National issues supplement, The Boundaries of Free Speech. pap. text ed. write for info. (*0-07-041736-9*) McGraw.

— The Art of Public Speaking. 5th ed. LC 94-30496. 1994. write for info. (*0-07-039015-0*) McGraw.

Lucas, T. M. Chyrology for the Deaf: Reading, Spelling & Ciphering by the Fingers. 1972. 250.00 (*0-87968-054-7*) Gordon Pr.

***Lucas, Teacia E.** Solomon's Instruction of Things Hateful to God. LC 95-94287. 50p. (YA). Date not set. write for info. (*0-9646486-0-1*) TDE Lucas.

Lucas, Thomas E. Elder Olson. Bowman, Sylvia E., ed. LC 70-125817. (Twayne's United States Authors Ser.). 195p. (C). 1972. lib. bdg. 17.95 (*0-8290-1705-4*) Irvington.

Lucas, Thomas J. Zulus & the British Frontiers. LC 73-78579. 371p. 1969. reprint ed. text ed. 38.50 (*0-8371-1413-6*, LUZ&, Greenwood Pr) Greenwood.

Lucas, Tim. Throat Sprockets. LC 94-6051. 1994. 9.95 (*0-385-31290-3*, Delta) Dell.

— The Video Watchdog Book. (Illus.). 416p. (Orig.). 1992. pap. 19.95 (*0-9633756-0-1*) Video Watchdog.

Lucas, Tim, jt. auth. see Johnson, Todd.

Lucas, Virginia H. & Barbe, Walter B. Resource Book for the Special Education Teacher. (Illus.). 1982. 34.95 (*0-88309-117-8*) Zaner-Bloser.

Lucas, W. F., ed. Modules in Applied Mathematics: Differential Equation Models, Vol. 1. (Illus.). 400p. 1991. 49.50 (*0-387-90695-9*) Spr-Verlag.

— Modules in Applied Mathematics, Vol. 2: Political & Related Models. (Illus.). 396p. 1982. 49.50 (*0-387-90696-7*) Spr-Verlag.

— Modules in Applied Mathematics, Vol. 4: Life Science Models. (Illus.). 366p. 1983. 49.00 (*0-387-90739-4*) Spr-Verlag.

Lucas, W. F., et al, eds. Modules in Applied Mathematics, Vol. 3: Discrete & System Models. (Illus.). 353p. 1983. 49.00 (*0-387-90724-6*) Spr-Verlag.

***Lucas, William F.** Fair Voting: Weighted Voting for Unequali Constituencies. (Hi Map Ser.: No. 19). (Illus.). 60p. Date not set. pap. text ed. 11.99 (*0-614-05308-0*, 5619) COMAP Inc.

Lucas, William F., ed. Game Theory & Its Applications. LC 81-12914. (Proceedings of Symposia in Applied Mathematics Ser.: Vol. 24). 136p. 1983. reprint ed. pap. 22.00 (*0-8218-0025-6*, PSAPM-24) Am Math.

Lucas, William J. & Berry, Joseph A., eds. Inorganic Carbon Uptake by Aquatic Photosynthetic Organisms. 512p. 1985. pap. text ed. 20.00 (*0-943088-05-4*) Am Soc of Plan.

Lucas, Winafred B. Regression Therapy: A Handbook for Professionals, 2 vols., Set. 1175p. 1993. 49.50 (*1-882530-00-4*) Deep Forest Pr.

— Regression Therapy: A Handbook for Professionals, 2 vols., Vol. I. 1175p. 1993. write for info. (*1-882530-01-2*) Deep Forest Pr.

— Regression Therapy: A Handbook for Professionals, 2 vols., Vol. II. 1175p. 1993. write for info. (*1-882530-02-0*) Deep Forest Pr.

Lucas, Winafred B., ed. see Blake, Doron W.

Lucas, Winafred B., ed. see Cunningham, Janet.

Lucas, Zoe. Wild Horses of Sable Island. (True Adventure Bks.). (Illus.). 36p. (J). (gr. 2 up). 1992. pap. 4.95 (*0-919872-73-5*, Pub. by Greey dePencier CN) Firefly Bks Ltd.

Lucash, Frank S., ed. Justice & Equality Here & Now. LC 85-19465. 176p. 1986. 32.50 (*0-8014-1807-0*); pap. 11.95 (*0-8014-9350-1*) Cornell U Pr.

Lucassen, Jan, jt. ed. see Davids, Karel.

Lucatt, Edward. Rovings in the Pacific, from 1837 to 1849, 2 vols. in 1. LC 75-35203. reprint ed. 72.50 (*0-404-14280-X*) AMS Pr.

Lucca, Carmen D. Brushstrokes & Landscapes (from My Pen) Pinceladas y Paisajes (de Mi Pluma) Ediciones Mairena Staff, ed. LC 89-92209. (Illus.). 130p. (Orig.). (ENG & SPA.). 1990. pap. 7.00 (*0-9623968-0-X*) Poets Refuge.

Lucca, Carmen D., ed. see De Burgos, Julia.

Lucca, Don A., jt. ed. see Wright, Roger N.

Luccarelli, Luigi, tr. see Goytisolo, Juan.

Luccarelli, Vincent, Jr. Job Revisited. LC 93-60359. 40p. (YA). (gr. 5 up). 1994. pap. 5.95 (*1-55523-616-2*) Winston-Derek.

***Lucchese, Jean.** Alphabet for Young ECKists. 26p. 1995. 6.00 (*1-57043-104-3*) ECKANKAR.

Lucchesi, Benedict R., et al, eds. Clinical Pharmacology of Antiarrhythmic Therapy. (Perspectives in Cardiovascular Research Ser.: Vol. 10). (Illus.). 296p. 1984. text ed. 114.00 (*0-89004-966-1*) Raven.

— Clinical Pharmacology of Antiarrhythmic Therapy. LC 84-1931. (Perspectives in Cardiovascular Research Ser.: No. 10). (Illus.). Date not set. reprint ed. pap. 83.00 (*0-7837-9564-5*, 2060313) Bks Demand.

Lucchesi, Bruno. Modeling the Head in Clay. (Illus.). 160p. 1979. 27.50 (*0-8230-3098-9*, Watsn-Guptill) Watsn-Guptill.

— Terracotta: The Technique of Fired Clay Sculpture. (Illus.). 160p. 1977. 24.95 (*0-8230-5320-2*, Watsn-Guptill) Watsn-Guptill.

Lucchesi, D. C. The Secrets of the Flying Saucers from Khabaram Khoom. 75p. 1985. reprint ed. spiral bd. 14.25 (*0-7873-0572-3*) Mokelumne.

Lucchesi, Joachim, jt. auth. see Shull, Ronald K.

Lucchesi, M. Dizionario Medico Ragionato Inglese-Italiano: Regionato English-Italian Medical Dictionary. 1489p. (ENG & ITA.). 1978. 150.00 (*0-8288-5206-5*, M9353) Fr & Eur.

***Lucchetti, Roberto, ed.** Recent Developments in Well-Posed Variational Problems. (Mathematics & Its Applications Ser.). 276p. (C). 1995. lib. bdg. 145.00 (*0-7923-3576-7*) Kluwer Ac.

Lucchin, Francesco, jt. auth. see Coles, Peter.

***Lucci, Franco R.** Sedimentographica: Photographic Atlas of Sedimentary Structures. 2nd ed. LC 94-24952. 1995. write for info. (*0-231-10018-3*) Col U Pr.

Lucci, Robert & Orlandini, Paolo. Product Design Models. (Illus.). 272p. 1990. text ed. 49.95 (*0-442-20654-2*) Van Nos Reinhold.

Lucci, Samuel J. Common Cents. 1985. write for info. (*0-9613870-0-9*) McClain.

Luccio, F., jt. ed. see Bertolazzi, P.

Luccioni, Jean. La Pensee Politique De Platon. Mayer, J. P., ed. LC 78-67365. (European Political Thought Ser.). (FRE.). 1980. reprint ed. lib. bdg. 28.95 (*0-405-11715-9*) Ayer.

Luccock, Halford E. American Mirror: Social, Ethical & Religious Aspects of American Literature, 1930-1940. LC 75-156806. 300p. 1971. reprint ed. lib. bdg. 60.50 (*0-8154-0385-2*) Cooper Sq.

— Contemporary American Literature & Religion. LC 73-111471. 1970. reprint ed. 20.50 (*0-404-00607-8*) AMS Pr.

Luccock, John. Notes on Rio De Janeiro & the Southern Parts of Brazil. 1976. lib. bdg. 134.95 (*0-8490-2359-9*) Gordon Pr.

Luccock, Robert E. Basic Bible Commentary, Vol. 17: Matthew. Deming, Lynne M., ed. LC 94-10965. 160p. (Orig.). 1994. pap. 4.95 (*0-687-02636-9*) Abingdon.

— On Becoming the Best We Can Be. LC 91-26975. 208p. (Orig.). 1991. pap. 12.95 (*0-8298-0911-2*) Pilgrim OH.

***Luce.** Now or Never: How We Can Save Our Public Schools. 1995. pap. text ed. 9.95 (*0-87833-109-3*) Taylor Pub.

Luce, A. Fishing & Thinking. 1993. text ed. 16.95 (*0-07-038994-2*) McGraw.

Luce, A. A. Fishing & Thinking. LC 93-15049. 1993. write for info. (*0-87742-400-4*, Ragged Mntn) Intl Marine.

— Fishing & Thinking. 1993. 16.95 (*0-87742-421-7*) Intl Marine.

Luce, A. A., ed. see Berkeley, George.

Luce, Allena, ed. Popular & Traditional Songs of Puerto Rico, Cuba, Mexico & Spain. (Latin American Music Ser.). 1979. lib. bdg. 59.95 (*0-8490-2985-6*) Gordon Pr.

Luce, Bob. Lifelines. (Illus.). 48p. 1994. 8.50 (*0-8378-6948-X*) Gibson.

Luce, Bryan R., jt. auth. see Warner, Kenneth E.

***Luce, Carol D.** Night Passage. 432p. 1995. mass mkt. 4.99 (*0-8217-4966-8*) Windsor NY.

— Night Prey. 1992. mass mkt. 4.99 (*0-8217-3661-2*) Zebra.

— Night Stalker. 1990. mass mkt. 4.99 (*0-8217-4245-0*) Zebra.

— Skin Deep. 1990. mass mkt. 4.50 (*1-55817-398-6*, Pinnacle NY) Windsor NY.

Luce, Celia, jt. auth. see Luce, Willard.

Luce, Clare Booth. Slam the Door Softly. 1970. pap. 2.75 (*0-8222-1039-8*) Dramatists Play.

Luce, Clare Booth, ed. Saints for Now. LC 93-78817. 300p. 1993. 12.95 (*0-89870-476-6*) Ignatius Pr.

Luce, Clare Boothe. Stuffed Shirts. LC 77-163043. (Short Story Index Reprint Ser.). 1977. reprint ed. 24.95 (*0-8369-3957-3*) Ayer.

Luce, Dianne C., anno. As I Lay Dying. (William Faulkner Annotations to Novels Ser.). 150p. 1990. 15.00 (*0-8240-4233-6*) Garland.

Luce, Dianne C., jt. ed. see Arnold, Edwin T.

Luce, Don & Rumpf, Roger. Martial Law in Taiwan. LC 85-241172. (Illus.). 50p. 1985. pap. 5.00 (*0-317-40849-6*) Asia Resource.

Luce, Don, jt. ed. see Sun-ai, Lee.

Luce, Donald T. Francis Lee Jaques: Artist-Naturalist. (Illus.). (C). 1982. pap. 13.95 (*0-8166-1146-7*) U of Minn Pr.

Luce, Donald T., intro. Wildlife Art in America: February 26 - May 15, 1994. (Illus.). 104p. (Orig.). 1994. pap. 15.00 (*1-884879-00-4*) UMN J F B Mus.

Luce, Gay G. Biological Rhythms in Human & Animal Physiology. Orig. Title: Biological Rhythms in Psychiatry & Medicine. 1971. reprint ed. pap. text ed. 6.95 (*0-486-22586-0*) Dover.

— Longer Life, More Joy: Techniques for Enhancing Health, Happiness & Inner Vision. 1992. pap. 12.95 (*0-87877-171-9*) Newcastle Pub.

Luce, Gordon H. Old Burma-Early Pagan, 3 Vols., Set. 1969. 120.00 (*0-686-92654-4*) J J Augustin.

***Luce, Gregory M., ed.** Defending the Hospital Under EMTALA. 50p. 1995. 30.00 (*0-614-05613-6*) Natl Health Lawyers.

Luce, J. V. Introduction to Greek Philosophy. LC 91-75043. 176p. 1992. pap. 16.95 (*0-500-27655-2*) Thames Hudson.

Luce, James, Jr., ed. Roman History, 43 vols., Set. 1975. 1,787.00 (*0-405-07177-9*) Ayer.

Luce, Janet, et al, eds. Service-Learning: An Annotated Bibliography for Linking Public Service with the Curriculum. 81p. (Orig.). 1988. pap. text ed. 15.00 (*0-937883-07-7*) NSEE.

Luce, John M. & Pierson, David J. Critical Care. (Illus.). 648p. 1988. pap. text ed. 37.50 (*0-7216-1711-5*) Saunders.

Luce, John M., jt. ed. see Fallat, Robert J.

Luce, John M., et al. Intensive Respiratory Care. 2nd ed. LC 92-48898. (Illus.). 400p. 1993. pap. text ed. 24.50 (*0-7216-4270-5*) Saunders.

Luce, Larry. The Single Cook's Book: One Hundred & Six Unusual Recipes for One-Person Servings. (Illus.). 1976. pap. 4.00 (*0-686-16919-0*) Other Bks.

Luce, Louise F. The Spanish-Speaking World: An Anthology of Cross-Cultural Perspectives. 400p. 1991. pap. 21.25 (*0-8442-7161-6*, Natl Textbk) NTC Pub Grp.

Luce, Louise F. & Smith, Elise, eds. Toward Internationalism: Readings in Cross-Cultural Communication. 2nd ed. 293p. 1986. pap. 22.95 (*0-8384-2689-1*, Newbury) Heinle & Heinle.

Luce, Morton. Handbook to the Works of William Shakespeare. 2nd rev. ed. LC 73-172756. reprint ed. 22.00 (*0-404-04064-0*) AMS Pr.

Luce, R. Duncan. Games & Decisions. 1989. pap. 12.95 (*0-486-65943-7*) Dover.

— Response Times: Their Role in Inferring Elementary Mental Organization. (Oxford Psychology Ser.: No. 8). (Illus.). 576p. 1986. 75.00 (*0-19-503642-5*) OUP.

— Response Times: Their Role in Inferring Elementary Mental Organization. (Oxford Psychology Ser.: No. 8). (Illus.). 584p. 1991. reprint ed. pap. 45.00 (*0-19-507001-1*) OUP.

— Sound & Hearing. 344p. 1992. text ed. 69.95 (*0-8058-1251-2*); pap. 32.50 (*0-8058-1389-6*); cd-rom 49.95 (*0-8058-1450-7*); cd-rom 19.95 (*1-56321-116-5*) L Erlbaum Assocs.

Luce, R. Duncan, et al, eds. Foundations of Measurement Vol. 3: Representations, Axiomatization, & Invariance. 356p. 1990. text ed. 92.00 (*0-12-425403-9*) Acad Pr.

— Geometric Representations of Perceptual Phenomena: Papers in Honor of Tarow Indow on His 70th Birthday. 376p. 1995. text ed. 79.95 (*0-8058-1686-0*) L Erlbaum Assocs.

— Leading Edges in Social & Behavioral Science. LC 89-24186. 720p. 1990. 59.95 (*0-87154-560-8*) Russell Sage.

***Luce, Ralph W.** The Doomsday Rock. 200p. Date not set. pap. 8.95 (*0-7610-0259-6*) NW Pub.

Luce, Robert. Legislative Assemblies. LC 73-5617. (American Constitutional & Legal History Ser). 692p. 1974. reprint ed. lib. bdg. 75.00 (*0-306-70583-4*) Da Capo.

— Legislative Principles. LC 77-148083. (American Constitutional & Legal History Ser). 1971. reprint ed. lib. bdg. 69.50 (*0-306-70144-8*) Da Capo.

— Legislative Problems. LC 76-152834. (American Constitutional & Legal History Ser). 1971. reprint ed. lib. bdg. 75.00 (*0-306-70153-7*) Da Capo.

— Legislative Procedure. LC 72-6113. (American Constitutional & Legal History Ser). 640p. 1973. reprint ed. lib. bdg. 69.50 (*0-306-70522-2*) Da Capo.

Luce, Robert B. Marriage: A Treasury of Words to Live By. (Illus.). 1992. 8.50 (*0-8378-2501-6*) Gibson.

Luce, Robert D. Individual Choice Behavior: A Theoretical Analysis. LC 78-25881. (Illus.). 153p. 1979. reprint ed. text ed. 35.00 (*0-313-20778-X*, LUIC, Greenwood Pr) Greenwood.

Luce, Robert D., ed. Developments in Mathematical Psychology: Information, Learning & Tracking. LC 80-14533. (Illus.). 294p. 1980. reprint ed. text ed. 59.75 (*0-313-22464-1*, LUDM, Greenwood Pr) Greenwood.

***Luce, Ron.** 56 Days Ablaze. 1995. pap. 7.99 (*0-88419-385-3*, Creation Hse) Strang Comms Co.

— Handling the Hard Stuff. LC 94-69835. 176p. (Orig.). 1995. pap. 9.95 (*0-89221-280-2*) New Leaf.

— Inspire the Fire. 1994. pap. 8.99 (*0-88419-370-5*, Creation Hse) Strang Comms Co.

Luce, S. Introduction to Composite Technology. 40p. 1988. pap. text ed. 9.50 (*0-87263-322-5*) SME.

Luce, Simeon. Histoire de Bertrand Du Gueselin et de Son Epoque. LC 78-63505. reprint ed. 37.50 (*0-404-17154-0*) AMS Pr.

Luce, Stanford L. Celine & His Critics: Scandals & Paradox. (Stanford French & Italian Studies: Vol. 44). 224p. 1986. pap. 46.50 (*0-915838-59-1*) Anma Libri.

Luce, Stephen B. Corpus Vasorum Antiquorum, Fasc. 1. (Illus.). 1933. 5.00 (*0-911517-16-2*) Mus of Art RI.

Luce, Stephen C. & Christian, Walter P. How to Reduce Autistic & Severely Maladaptive Behaviors. (Teaching the Autistic Ser.). 39p. 1981. pap. 8.00 (*0-89079-053-1*, 1032) PRO-ED.

Luce, T. J. & Woodman, A. J., eds. Tacitus & the Tacitean Tradition. LC 92-25050. (Magie Classical Publications). 240p. (C). 1993. text ed. 37.50 (*0-691-06988-3*) Princeton U Pr.

Luce, T. James, ed. Ancient Writers: Greece & Rome, 2 Vols., Vol. 2. LC 82-50612. 1184p. 1982. text ed. 180.00 (*0-684-16595-3*, Scribners) S&S Trade.

An Asterisk (*) at the beginning of an entry indicates that the title is appearing in BIP for the first time.

Luce, Thom. Architecture & Operating Systems. 384p. (C). 1989. text ed. write for info. (*0-394-39194-2*) Knopf.
— Using VP-Expert in Business. 1992. pap. text ed. write for info. (*0-07-038984-5*) McGraw.

Luce, Thom, jt. auth. see Hankins, Tom.

Luce, Thom, jt. auth. see Hawkins, Tom.

Luce, Thomas F., jt. auth. see Summers, Anita A.

Luce, Thomas G. Genetics with a Computer. pap. 16.95 (*0-87567-076-8*) Entelek.

***Luce, Tom.** Now or Never: How We Can Save Our Public Schools. 1995. 15.95 (*0-87833-108-5*) Taylor Pub.

Luce, Torrey J. Livy: The Composition of His History. LC 77-72126. 351p. reprint ed. pap. 100.10 (*0-685-44418-X*, 2032634) Bks Demand.

Luce, Willard & Luce, Celia. Jim Bridger: Man of the Mountains. (Discovery Biographies Ser.). (Illus.). 80p. (J). (gr. 2-6). 1991. reprint ed. lib. bdg. 12.95 (*0-7910-1454-1*) Chelsea Hse.

Luce, William. Lillian. 1986. pap. 4.75 (*0-8222-0666-8*) Dramatists Play.

Lucelle, Larry, jt. ed. see LaBianca, Oystein.

Luceno, James. A Fearful Symmetry. 272p. 1989. pap. 3.95 (*0-345-35957-7*, Del Rey) Ballantine.
— The Mata Hari Affair. (Young Indiana Jones Chronicles Ser.: Bk. 1). (J). (gr. 4-6). 1992. mass mkt. 4.99 (*0-345-38009-6*) Ballantine.

Lucente, Carla E., pref. The French Revolution, Literature & the Arts: Proceedings of the Western Pennsylvania Symposium on World Literatures: 1989. LC 90-81724. (Humanities Ser.: No. 4). 72p. (Orig.). (C). 1991. pap. 10.95 (*0-929914-07-4*) Eadmer Pr.
— The Western Pennsylvania Symposium on World Literatures, 1974-1991: Selected Proceedings, a Retrospective. LC 92-54567. (Humanities Ser.: No. 6). (Illus.). 266p. (C). 1992. text ed. 40.00 (*0-929914-13-9*) Eadmer Pr.

Lucente, Frank E. & Sobol, Steven M., eds. Essentials of Otolaryngology. 3rd ed. LC 92-48778. 608p. 1993. pap. 34.00 (*0-88167-996-8*) Raven.

***Lucente, Frank E., et al.** Diseases of the External Ear. 3rd ed. (Illus.). 352p. 1995. text ed. 89.00 (*0-7216-5667-6*) Saunders.

Lucente, Gregory L. Beautiful Fables: Self-Consciousness in Italian Narrative from Manzoni to Calvino. LC 86-7373. 384p. 1987. text ed. 55.00 (*0-8018-3331-0*) Johns Hopkins.
— The Narrative of Realism & Myth: Verga, Lawrence, Faulkner & Pavese. LC 81-2084. 208p. 1981. text ed. 26. 50 (*0-8018-2609-8*) Johns Hopkins.

Lucentini, jt. auth. see Fruttero.

Lucentini, Franco, jt. auth. see Fruttero, Carlo.

Lucero, ed. Acousto-Optic, Electro-Optic, & Magneto-Optic Devices & Applications. 186p. 1987. 43.00 (*0-89252-788-9*, 753) SPIE.

Lucero, Al. Maria's Real Margarita Book: How to Make the Perfect Margarita. LC 94-8404. 1994. 14.95 (*0-685-74710-7*) Ten Speed Pr.
— Maria's Real Margarita Book: How to Make the Perfect Margarita. 1994. pap. 14.95 (*0-89815-631-9*) Ten Speed Pr.

***Lucero, Donald L.** Adobe Kingdom No. 1: New Mexico 1598 - 1958 As Experienced by the Families Lucero De Gadsy y Baca. Simmo, Charlene G. & Vera, Mary O., eds. (Illus.). 275p. (Orig.). 1995. pap. text ed. write for info. (*0-9628974-3-4*) El Escrito.

Lucero, Faustina H. Little Indians' ABC. LC 73-87800. (Illus.). 32p. (J). (gr. k-2). 1974. lib. bdg. 9.95 (*0-87783-129-7*) Oddo.
— Little Indians' ABC. deluxe ed. LC 73-87800. (Illus.). 32p. (J). (gr. k-2). 1974. pap. 3.94 (*0-87783-130-0*) Oddo.

***Lucero, Roberto A.** Sangre Del Monte. 192p. (Orig.). 1994. pap. 12.95 (*0-9642480-3-4*) Mrningstar Bks.

Lucero, Ruth, tr. see Winter, Gerald A.

***Lucero, Teresa.** Beyond Courage. 1994. pap. text ed. 13.95 (*1-881116-42-5*) Black Forrest Pr.

Lucero-White, et al. Hispano Culture of New Mexico: An Original Anthology. Cortes, Carlos E., ed. & intro. by. LC 76-5929. (Chicano Heritage Ser.). (Illus.). 1977. 23. 95 (*0-405-09537-6*) Ayer.

Lucertini, M., jt. ed. see Ausiello, G.

Luces, Jose R. A Color Atlas of Foot Disorders. (Illus.). 152p. 1990. Monograph. 149.00 (*0-87993-369-0*) Futura Pub.

Lucey, Beryl. Twenty Centuries in Sedlescombe. 523p. 1984. 40.00 (*0-7212-0548-8*, Pub. by Regency Press) St Mut.

Lucey, Clare, jt. ed. see Reder, Peter.

Lucey, Donna M. Photographing Montana 1894-1928: The Life & Work of Evelyn Cameron. 1990. 59.50 (*0-394-54036-0*) Knopf.

Lucey, Jean. Insuring & Managing the Professional Risk. Date not set. 39.50 (*1-56461-122-1*, 46250) Rough Notes.

Lucey, Jerold F., jt. auth. see Dickerman, Joseph D.

Lucey, Kenneth G., ed. On Knowing & the Known: Introductory Readings in Epistemology. 450p. 1991. 22. 95 (*0-87975-699-3*) Prometheus Bks.
— What Is God? The Selected Essays of Richard LaCroix. LC 93-20193. 200p. (C). 1993. Alk. paper. 35.95x (*0-87975-739-6*) Prometheus Bks.

Lucey, M. N. A Sailor View of Live Yeshu. 759p. (C). 1989. text ed. 75.00 (*1-872795-55-2*, Pub. by Pentland Pr UK) St Mut.

Lucey, M. R., et al, eds. Liver Transplantation & the Alcoholic Patient. (Illus.). 150p. (C). 1994. 49.95 (*0-521-43332-0*) Cambridge U Pr.

***Lucey, Michael.** Gide's Bent: Writing, Sexuality, Politics. (Ideologies of Desire Ser.). (Illus.). 288p. 1995. 39.95 (*0-19-508086-6*); pap. 16.95 (*0-19-508087-4*) OUP.

Lucey, Michael, jt. ed. see Neuberger, James.

Lucey, Rose M. Roots & Wings: Dreamers & Doers of the Christian Family Movement. 135p. (Orig.). (C). 1987. pap. 7.95 (*0-89390-113-X*) Resource Pubns.

***Lucfigh, Betty A.** Chem TV: Organic Chem IBM Version 2.0. (Chemistry Ser.). Date not set. disk 495.00 (*0-86720-904-6*) Jones & Bartlett.

Luch, Bill. Steelhead Drift Fishing. (Illus.). 94p. (Orig.). 1976. pap. 7.95 (*0-936608-00-5*) F Amato Pubns.

Lucha-Burns, Carol. Musical Notes: A Practical Guide to Staffing & Staging Standards of the American Musical Theatre. LC 85-10017. 598p. 1986. text ed. 79.50 (*0-313-24648-3*, BMN/, Greenwood Pr) Greenwood.

Luchaire, Achille. Social France at the Time of Philip Augustus. 1976. lib. bdg. 59.95 (*0-8490-2617-2*) Gordon Pr.

Luchessi, M. Italian-English - English-Italian Medical Dictionary. 1456p. 1987. 154.00 (*88-7078-037-6*) IBD Ltd.

***Luchetti.** I Do: Love, Courtship & Marriage. Date not set. write for info. (*0-517-88449-6*) Random Hse Value.
— I Do: Love, Coutship & Marriage. Date not set. write for info. (*0-517-70158-8*) Random Hse Value.

Luchetti, Cathy. Home on the Range: A Culinary History of the American West. LC 92-50546. 1993. 25.00 (*0-679-74484-3*, Villard Bks) Random.
— I Do! Courtship, Love, & Marriage on the American Frontier : a Glimpse at America's Romantic Past Through Photographs, Diaries, & Journals, 1715-1915. LC 94-30128. 1996. write for info. (*0-679-42321-4*, Villard Bks) Random.
— Medicine Women. Date not set. write for info. (*0-517-59848-5*) Crown Pub Group.
— Under God's Spell. 1989. 27.95 (*0-15-192799-5*) HarBrace.
— Women of the West. LC 92-13653. (Library of the American West). 1992. pap. 22.00 (*0-517-59162-6*, Orion Bks) Crown Pub Group.

Luchetti, Emily. Stars' Desserts. LC 90-56386. (Illus.). 288p. 1991. 27.50 (*0-06-016688-6*, HarpT) HarpC.
— Stars Desserts. LC 90-56386. (Illus.). 272p. 1993. reprint ed. pap. 18.00 (*0-06-092218-4*, PL) HarpC.

***Luchi, Larry R.** Luchi No-Code Technician Class License Guide. 160p. 1995. ring bd. 22.95 (*0-936653-62-0*) Tiare Pubns.
— Luchi's Advanced Class License Guide. 150p. 1995. ring bd. 22.95 (*0-936653-66-3*) Tiare Pubns.
— Luchi's Novice Class License Guide. 1995. ring bd. 19.95 (*0-936653-63-9*) Tiare Pubns.

Luchinat, Christina A., ed. The Chapel of the Magi: The Frescoes of Benozzo Gozzoli. LC 94-60292. (Illus.). 388p. 1994. 100.00 (*0-500-23691-7*) Thames Hudson.

Luchinat, Claudio, jt. auth. see Bertini, Ivano.

***Luchinat, Cristina A.** Benozzo Gozzoli. Evans, Christopher, tr. (Library of Great Masters). (Illus.). 80p. (Orig.). 1995. pap. 12.99 (*1-878351-47-8*) Riverside NY.

Luchini, P. & Motz, H. Undulators & Free-Electron Lasers. (International Series of Monographs on Physics: No. 79). (Illus.). 336p. 1990. 85.00 (*0-19-852019-0*) OUP.

Luchins, Abraham S. & Luchins, Edith H. Wertheimer's Seminars Revisited: Problem Solving & Thinking, 3 vols., Vol. 1. (Illus.). 439p. reprint ed. pap. 114.20 (*0-8357-4204-0*, 2036983) Bks Demand.
— Wertheimer's Seminars Revisited: Problem Solving & Thinking, 3 vols., Vol. 2. (Illus.). 430p. reprint ed. pap. 122.60 (*0-8357-4205-9*) Bks Demand.
— Wertheimer's Seminars Revisited: Problem Solving & Thinking, 3 vols., Vol. 3. (Illus.). 445p. reprint ed. pap. 126.90 (*0-8357-4206-7*) Bks Demand.

Luchins, Edith H., jt. auth. see Luchins, Abraham S.

Luchner, K., et al, eds. Teaching Modern Physics. 500p. (C). 1989. text ed. 55.00 (*9971-5-0923-7*); pap. text ed. 33.00 (*9971-5-0960-1*) World Scientific Pub.

Luchnig, L. J., jt. auth. see Luschnig, C. A.

Luchok, John, ed. see Brown, Clifford W. & Brown, Clifford W.

***Luchs, Alison.** Tullio Lombardo & Ideal Portrait Sculpture in Renaissance Italy, 1490-1530. (Illus.). 336p. (C). Date not set. write for info. (*0-521-47075-7*) Cambridge U Pr.

Luchs, Alison, ed. Studies in the History of Art: Italian Plaquettes, Vol. 22. LC 72-600309. (Illus.). 310p. (Orig.). 1989. pap. 20.00 (*0-89468-114-1*, U Pr of New Eng) Natl Gallery Art.
— Western Decorative Arts. (Collections of the National Gallery of Art Systematic Catalogue). (Illus.). 350p. (C). 1994. 160.00 (*0-521-47068-4*) Cambridge U Pr.

Luchs, Alison, tr. see Wackernagel, Martin.

Luchs, Alvin S. Torchbearers of the Middle Ages. LC 77-160924. (Biography Index Reprint Ser.). (Illus.). 1977. reprint ed. 18.95 (*0-8369-8087-5*) Ayer.

Luchs, Kathleen, jt. ed. see Goold, Michael.

Luchs, Kathleen S., jt. auth. see Campbell, Andrew.

Luchsinger, Arlene E., jt. auth. see Jones, Samuel B.

Luchsinger, Arlene E., jt. auth. see Miner, John B.

Luchsinger, Vincent P., jt. auth. see Vroman, H. William.

Lucht, Irmgard. In This Night... LC 92-54620. (Illus.). 32p. (J). (ps-3). 1993. 13.95 (*1-56282-408-2*) Hyprn Child.
— The Red Poppy. large type ed. LC 94-15057. (Illus.). 32p. (J). (ps-3). 1995. 13.95 (*0-7868-0055-0*) Hyprn Child.
— The Red Poppy. large type ed. LC 94-15057. (Illus.). 32p. (J). (ps-3). 1995. lib. bdg. 13.89 (*0-7868-2043-8*) Hyprn Child.

Lucht, John. Executive Job-Changing Workbook. 640p. 1994. pap. 29.95 (*0-942785-22-3*) H Holt & Co.

Lucht, John, rev. The Rites of Passage at One Hundred Thousand Dollars Plus: The Insider's Lifetime Guide to Executive Job-Changing & Faster Career Progress. rev. ed. 640p. 1993. 29.95 (*0-942785-21-5*) H Holt & Co.

Luchterhand, Elmer & Sydiaha, Daniel. Choice in Human Affairs: An Application to Aging-Accident-Illness Problems. 1966. pap. 15.95x (*0-8084-0075-4*) NCUP.

Luchterhand, Kubet. Early Archaic Projectile Points & Hunting Patterns in the Lower Illinois Valley. (Reports of Investigations Ser.: No. 19). (Illus.). 67p. 1974. reprint ed. pap. 3.50 (*0-89792-043-0*) Ill St Museum.

Lucia, Alexander, jt. auth. see Harvey, Eric.

Lucia, Alfredo C., ed. Advances in Structural Reliability. 1987. lib. bdg. 101.50 (*90-277-2429-6*) Kluwer Ac.

Lucia, Ellis. Tillamook Burn Country: A Pictorial History. LC 83-18164. (Illus.). (Orig.). 1983. pap. 14.95 (*0-87004-296-3*) Caxton.

Lucia, Ellis, jt. auth. see Hanley, Mike.

Lucia, F. J., et al. Characterization of a Karsted, High-Energy, Ramp-Margin Carbonate Reservoir: Taylor-Link West San Andres Unit, Pecos County, Texas. (Illus.). 46p. 1992. pap. 3.50 (*0-317-05175-X*, RI 208) Bur Econ Geology.
— Characterization of a Karsted, High-Energy Ramp-Margin Carbonate Reservoir: Taylor-Lynd West San Andres Unit, Pecos County, Texas. (Report of Investigations Ser.: RI 208). (Illus.). 46p. 1992. 3.50 (*0-317-05186-5*) Bur Econ Geology.

Lucia, Salvatore P. Wine & Your Well Being. 160p. 1980. reprint ed. 9.95 (*0-932664-08-3*) Wine Appreciation.

Lucia, Tina. Releasing: The Key to Physical Manifestation, No. 1. Craig, Linda, ed. (Releasing Ser.). (Illus.). 30p. 1988. pap. 6.95 (*0-317-91334-4*) T Lucia.
— Releasing Through Numerology, No. 3. Craig, Linda, ed. (Releasing Ser.). 150p. 1988. 12.95 (*0-317-91330-1*); pap. 9.95 (*0-317-91331-X*) T Lucia.
— Releasing Through Tarot, No. 2. Craig, Linda, ed. (Releasing Ser.). 150p. 1988. 19.95 (*0-317-91332-8*); pap. 9.95 (*0-317-91333-6*) T Lucia.

Lucia, Victor O. Modern Gnathological Concepts-Updated. (Illus.). 1983. text ed. 180.00 (*0-86715-105-6*) Quint Pub Co.
— Treatment of the Edentulous Patient. LC 85-30060. (Illus.). 1986. text ed. 140.00 (*0-86715-122-6*, 1226) Quint Pub Co.

***Luciak, Ilja A.** The Sandinista Legacy: Lessons from a Political Economy in Transition. LC 95-6520. (Illus.). 248p. 1995. lib. bdg. 49.95 (*0-8130-1369-0*) U Press Fla.

Lucian. Dialogues, 1. (Loeb Classical Library: No. 14, 54, 130, 162, 302, 430-432). 486p. 1913. text ed. 18.95 (*0-674-99015-3*) HUP.
— Dialogues, 2. (Loeb Classical Library: No. 14, 54, 130, 162, 302, 430-432). 530p. 1915. text ed. 18.95 (*0-674-99060-9*) HUP.
— Dialogues, 3. (Loeb Classical Library: No. 14, 54, 130, 162, 302, 430-432). 498p. 1921. text ed. 18.95 (*0-674-99144-3*) HUP.
— Dialogues, 4. (Loeb Classical Library: No. 14, 54, 130, 162, 302, 430-432). 430p. 1925. text ed. 18.95 (*0-674-99179-6*) HUP.
— Dialogues, 5. (Loeb Classical Library: No. 14, 54, 130, 162, 302, 430-432). 548p. 1936. text ed. 18.95 (*0-674-99333-0*) HUP.
— Dialogues, 6. (Loeb Classical Library: No. 14, 54, 130, 162, 302, 430-432). 280p. 1959. text ed. 18.95 (*0-674-99474-4*) HUP.
— Dialogues, 7. (Loeb Classical Library: No. 14, 54, 130, 162, 302, 430-432). 488p. 1961. text ed. 18.95 (*0-674-99475-2*) HUP.
— Dialogues, 8. (Loeb Classical Library: No. 14, 54, 130, 162, 302, 430-432). 544p. 1967. text ed. 18.95 (*0-674-99476-0*) HUP.
— Opera: Tomus IV: Libelli 69-86. MacLeod, M. D., ed. (Classical Texts Ser.). 544p. 1987. 49.95 (*0-19-814596-9*) OUP.
— Opera: Tomus One, Libelli 1-25. MacLeod, M. D., ed. (Oxford Classical Texts Ser.). (C). 1972. text ed. 38.00 (*0-19-814656-6*) OUP.
— Opera: Tomus Two, Libelli 26-43. Macleod, M. D., ed. (Oxford Classical Texts Ser.). (C). 1975. text ed. 38.00 (*0-19-814580-2*) OUP.
— Opera Tomus III: Libelli 44-68. Macleod, M. D., ed. (Oxford Classical Texts Ser.). (C). 1980. text ed. 48.00 (*0-19-814592-6*) OUP.
— Selected Works. Reardon, B. P., tr. LC 64-16706. (Orig.). 1965. pap. 5.65 (*0-672-60385-3*, LLA161, Bobbs) Macmillan.
— A Selection. McLeod, M. C., ed. (Classical Texts Ser.). 320p. (C). 1991. text ed. 49.95 (*0-85668-415-5*, Pub. by Aris & Phillips UK); pap. text ed. 28.00 (*0-85668-416-3*, Pub. by Aris & Phillips UK) David Brown.

Lucian, Justin. Systematic Desensitization: Student Guide. 1976. pap. text ed. 5.95 (*0-89420-000-3*, 480011); audio 37.80 (*0-89420-186-7*, 480000) Natl Book.

Luciani, Giacomo. The Oil Companies & the Arab World: The Structure of the International Oil Industry in the 1980's. LC 83-42536. 208p. 1984. text ed. 29.95 (*0-312-58276-5*) St Martin.

Luciani, Giacomo, ed. The Arab State. 1989. 45.00 (*0-520-06432-1*); pap. 14.00 (*0-520-06434-8*) U CA Pr.
— Migration Policies in Europe & the United States. LC 93-23464. 172p. (C). 1993. lib. bdg. 85.00 (*0-7923-2537-0*) Kluwer Ac.

Luciani, Giacomo & Salame, Ghassan, eds. Nation, State & Integration in the Arab World, 4 vols., Set. 300p. 1988. lib. bdg. 192.50 (*0-317-64358-4*, Pub. by Croom Helm UK) Routledge Chapman & Hall.

Luciani, Giacomo, jt. auth. see Bebuawu, Gazen.

Luciani, Giacomo, ed. see Salame, Ghassan.

Luciani, Giacomo, et al, eds. Nation, State & Integration in the Arab World, Vol. 4: The Politics of Arab Integration. 300p. 1987. lib. bdg. 57.50 (*0-7099-4148-X*, Pub. by Croom Helm UK) Routledge Chapman & Hall.

Luciani, S., jt. auth. see Santi, R.

Luciani, V. Two Hundred One Italian Verbs. 1984. pap. 7.95 (*0-8120-0228-8*) Barron.

Luciani, Vincent. A Brief History of Italian Literature. (C). 1967. 12.95 (*0-913298-09-3*) S F Vanni.
— A Concise History of the Italian Theatre. (C). 1961. pap. 5.95 (*0-913298-10-7*) S F Vanni.
— Italian Idioms with Proverbs. (C). 1981. pap. 8.95 (*0-913298-15-8*) S F Vanni.

Luciani, Vincent, ed. Betti: Corruzione Al Palazzo di Giustizia. (C). 1980. pap. 8.95 (*0-913298-20-4*) S F Vanni.
— Bracco: Il Piccolo Santo. (C). 1961. pap. 7.95 (*0-913298-23-9*) S F Vanni.
— Giacosa: Come le Foglie. (C). 1979. pap. 7.95 (*0-913298-22-0*) S F Vanni.
— Goldoni: La Locandiera. (C). 1991. pap. 8.95x (*0-913298-18-2*) S F Vanni.
— Goldoni: Le Smanie per la Villeggiatura. (C). 1961. pap. 7.95 (*0-913298-17-4*) S F Vanni.
— Machiavelli: La Mandragola. (C). 1979. pap. 7.95 (*0-913298-19-0*) S F Vanni.

Luciani, Vincent & Colaneri, John. Italian Verbs. (Verbs Ser.). 350p. 1990. pap. 5.95 (*0-8120-4313-8*) Barron.

Luciani, Vincent, jt. auth. see Colaneri, John.

Luciani, Vincent, tr. see De Beaumarchais, Pierre-Augustin C.

Luciano, Antony, ed. Italy: A Culinary Journey. (Culinary Journey Ser.). 272p. 1991. 45.00 (*0-00-215960-0*) Collins SF.

Luciano, Dale, tr. see Abuli, Sanchez.

Luciano, Dorothy S., jt. auth. see Vander, Arthur J.

Luciano, Lenore B., jt. auth. see Bondurant-Utz, Judith A.

Luciano, Lisa, jt. auth. see Altmann, Patricia.

Luciano, Patrick. With Fire & Sword: Italian Spectacles on American Screens, 1958-1968. LC 93-43344. 1994. 67. 50 (*0-8108-2816-2*) Scarecrow.

Luciano, Ralph, jt. auth. see Stevens, Rikki.

Lucic, Karen. Charles Sheeler & the Cult of the Machine. 167p. 1991. pap. 18.95 (*0-674-11111-7*) HUP.
— Charles Sheeler & the Cult of the Machine. 167p. (C). 1991. 38.00 (*0-674-11110-9*) HUP.

Lucid, Daniel P., ed. Soviet Semiotics: An Anthology. LC 77-4543. (Illus.). 1978. text ed. 35.00 (*0-8018-1980-6*) Johns Hopkins.
— Soviet Semiotics: An Anthology. LC 77-4543. 272p. 1988. reprint ed. pap. text ed. 14.95 (*0-8018-3656-5*) Johns Hopkins.

Lucid, Joanne, ed. For Those We Love: A Spiritual Perspective on AIDS. 2nd enl. ed. (Illus.). 96p. (Orig.). 1990. pap. 7.50 (*1-879035-01-4*) AIDS Ministry.

Lucie C.Phillips, jt. auth. see Clark, Andrew F.

Lucie, Doug. Fashion. (Methuen Theatrescripts Ser.). 48p. 1988. pap. 8.95 (*0-413-17200-7*, A0087, Pub. by Methuen UK) Heinemann.
— Fashion, Progress, Hard Feelings & Doing the Business. (Methuen Modern Plays Ser.). 282p. (Orig.). 1991. pap. 15.95 (*0-413-65090-1*, AO557, Pub. by Methuen UK) Heinemann.
— Grace. 1993. 5.95 (*1-85459-245-9*, G55) Dramatic Pub.
— Progress. 1985. pap. 4.75 (*0-8222-0920-9*) Dramatists Play.
— Progress & Hard Feelings. 86p. (Orig.). 1988. pap. 8.95 (*0-413-57760-0*, A0229) Heinemann.

***Lucie-Smith.** Life Class: The Academic Male Nude 1820-1920. Date not set. per. 25.00 (*0-85449-103-1*, Pub. by Gay Mens Pr UK) InBook.

Lucie-Smith, E. The Liverpool Scene. (Illus.). 11.25 (*0-8446-2495-0*) Peter Smith.

Lucie-Smith, Edward. American Art Now. LC 85-60441. (Illus.). 160p. 1985. 24.95 (*0-688-05884-1*) Morrow.
— American Realism. LC 93-48535. 1994. write for info. (*0-8109-1941-9*) Abrams.
— Art & Civilization. LC 92-17099. (Illus.). 560p. 1993. 60. 00 (*0-8109-1924-9*) Abrams.
— Art & Civilization. 560p. (C). 1992. pap. text ed. write for info. (*0-13-046558-5*) P-H.
— Art in the Seventies. (Illus.). 128p. 1980. 45.00 (*0-8014-1328-1*); pap. 19.95 (*0-8014-9194-0*) Cornell U Pr.
— Art Today. (Illus.). 500p. (C). 1995. 59.95 (*0-7148-3201-4*, Pub. by Phaidon Press UK) Chronicle Bks.
— Fletcher Benton. (Illus.). 358p. 1990. 49.50 (*0-8109-3110-9*) Abrams.
— Furniture: A Concise History. (World of Art Ser.). (Illus.). 216p. 1985. pap. 12.95 (*0-500-20172-2*) Thames Hudson.
— Furniture: A Concise History. (World of Art Ser.). (Illus.). 216p. 1985. 19.95 (*0-500-18173-X*) Thames Hudson.
— Impressionist Women. 1993. 19.98 (*0-89660-039-4*, Artabras) Abbeville Pr.
— John Kirby: The Company of Strangers. (Illus.). 120p. 1995. 29.95 (*1-85158-625-3*, Pub. by Mnstream UK) Trafalgar.
— Latin American Art in the Twentieth Century. LC 92-70861. (World of Art Ser.). (Illus.). 216p. 1993. pap. 12. 95 (*0-500-20260-5*) Thames Hudson.
— Masterpieces of Time: Long-Case Clocks & Fine Furniture by Wendell Castle. (Illus.). 20p. (Orig.). 1985. pap. 5.00 (*0-915577-07-0*) Taft Museum.
— Movements in Art since 1945. rev. ed. LC 83-51503. (World of Art Ser.). (Illus.). 288p. (C). 1985. pap. 12.95 (*0-500-20197-8*) Thames Hudson.
— Movements in Art since 1945: Issues & Concepts. rev. ed. LC 94-61061. (World of Art Ser.). (Illus.). 304p. 1995. pap. 14.95 (*0-500-20282-6*) Thames Hudson.
— Race, Sex, & Gender in Contemporary Art: The Rise of Minority Culture. LC 93-29218. 1994. 39.95 (*0-8109-3767-0*) Abrams.
— Sexuality in Western Art. rev. ed. LC 90-71871. (World of Art Ser.). (Illus.). 288p. 1991. pap. 14.95 (*0-500-20252-4*) Thames Hudson.
— Symbolist Art. (World of Art Ser.). (Illus.). 216p. 1985. pap. 14.95 (*0-500-20125-0*) Thames Hudson.

An Asterisk (*) at the beginning of an entry indicates that the title is appearing in BIP for the first time.

— The Thames & Hudson Dictionary Art Terms. LC 83-51331. (World of Art Ser.). (Illus.). 208p. 1988. pap. 12.95 (*0-500-20222-2*) Thames Hudson.

— Thinking about Art. 237p. 1968. 15.95 (*0-7145-0552-8*) Dufour.

— Toulouse-Lautrec. (Color Library Ser.). (Illus.). 128p. (C). 1994. reprint ed. pap. 14.95 (*0-7148-2761-4*, Pub. by Phaidon Press UK) Chronicle Bks.

— Toulouse-Lautrec. (Color Library). (Illus.). 128p. (C). 1994. reprint ed. 19.95 (*0-7148-3232-4*, Pub. by Phaidon Press UK) Chronicle Bks.

Lucie-Smith, Edward, ed. The Faber Book of Art Anecdotes. 512p. 1993. 29.95 (*0-571-14382-2*) Faber & Faber.

Lucie-Smith, Edward, tr. & intro. Impressionist & Post-Impressionist Masterpieces at the Musee d'Orsay. LC 86-50216. (Illus.). 208p. 1987. pap. 14.95 (*0-500-27426-6*) Thames Hudson.

***Lucie-Smith, Edward & Frink, Elisabeth.** Frink: A Portrait. (Illus.). 138p. 1995. 34.95 (*0-7475-1572-7*, Pub. by Bloomsbury Pub Ltd UK) Trafalgar.

Lucie-Smith, Edward, et al. Albert Paley: Sculptural Adornment. (Renwick Contemporary American Craft Ser.). (Illus.). 80p. 1992. pap. 15.95 (*0-295-97152-5*) U of Wash Pr.

Lucien, Michele. Welcome to My World. 50p. (J). (ps-00). 1993. pap. text ed. write for info. (*0-9639678-0-0*) Write For You.

Lucier, ed. Thermal Infrared Sensing for Diagnostics & Controls: Thermosense, No. 10. 1988. 45.00 (*0-89252-969-5*, 934) SPIE.

Lucier, A. A. & Haines, S. G., eds. Mechanisms of Forest Response to Acidic Deposition. 232p. 1990. 69.00 (*0-387-97205-6*) Spr-Verlag.

***Lucier, Alvin.** Chambers: nterviews with the Composer by Douglas Simon. fac. ed. LC 79-24870. 187p. 1980. reprint ed. pap. 53.30 (*0-7837-8197-0*, 2047902) Bks Demand.

Lucier, Richard L. The International Political Economy of Coffee: From Juan Valdez to Yank's Diner. LC 87-38477. (Illus.). 341p. 1988. text ed. 55.00 (*0-275-92898-5*, C2898, Praeger Pubs) Greenwood.

Lucille, Helene. Le Parle Express Basic French. 82p. 1993. audio 95.00 (*1-882874-25-0*) Truespeech.

Lucio, J. L. & Zepeda, A., eds. Particles & Fields - Fourth Mexican School. 500p. (C). 1992. text ed. 130.00 (*981-02-0666-6*) World Scientific Pub.

Lucio, J. L., et al, eds. Mexican School of Particles & Fields. LC 86-81187. (AIP Conference Proceedings Ser.: No. 143). 267p. 1986. lib. bdg. 60.00 (*0-88318-342-0*) Am Inst Physics.

***Luciom, S. L. & Vargas, M., eds.** Fifth Mexican School of Particles & Fields. (AIP Conference Proceedings Ser.: No. 317). 416p. 1994. text ed. 135.00x (*1-56396-378-7*) Am Inst Physics.

Luciuk, Lubomyr Y. Ukrainians in the Making: Their Kingston Story. (Builders of Canada Ser.: No. 1). (Illus.). 1980. 16.50 (*0-919642-91-8*) Limestone Pr.

Luciuk, Lubomyr Y. & Kordan, Bohdan S. Anglo-American Perspectives on the Ukrainian Question, 1938 to 1958. Pierce, Richard A., ed. (Studies in East European Nationalisms: No. 1). 1987. 20.00 (*0-919642-26-8*) Limestone Pr.

— Creating a Landscape: A Geography of Ukrainians in Canada. (Illus.). 72p. 1989. 40.00 (*0-8020-5823-X*) U of Toronto Pr.

Luciuk, Lubomyr Y., jt. auth. see Kordan, Bohdan S.

Lucius, J. E., et al. Properties & Hazards of One Hundred Eight Selected Substances. 554p. (Orig.). (C). 1993. pap. text ed. 95.00 (*1-56806-361-X*) Diane Pub.

Luciw & Steimer. HIV Detection by Genetic Engineering Methods. 312p. 1989. 140.00 (*0-8247-7900-2*) Dekker.

Luciw, Iurii. Vplyvy davnikh filosofiv i Ottsvi tserkvy na tvorchist' Hryhora Skovorody. limited ed. 32p. (UKR.). 1982. 1.50 (*0-686-48389-8*) Slavia Lib.

Luciw, Jurij A. Building Slavic Collections. 63p. 1980. pap. text ed. 3.75 (*0-686-63318-0*) Slavia Lib.

— Sviatoslav the Conqueror: Emperor of Rus'-Ukraine. 1985. 30.00 (*0-317-12226-6*) Slavia Lib.

Luciw, W. O., ed. Ukrainian Culture at Pennsylvania State University: Papers, Articles & Synopses of Lectures. (Illus.). 256p. 1980. 30.00 (*0-686-63321-0*) Slavia Lib.

Luciw, Wasyl. Ahapius Honcharenko & the Alaska Hearald: The Editor's Life & an Analysis of His Newspaper. LC 65-923. pap. text ed. 10.00 (*0-918884-10-1*) Slavia Lib.

— Album ex libres medicorum. (Illus.). 31p. 1961. 25.00 (*0-918884-09-8*) Slavia Lib.

— Church Fraternities in Ukraine. 63p. (Orig.). (UKR.). 1980. pap. text ed. 3.50 (*0-686-63319-9*) Slavia Lib.

— Het'man Ivan Mazepa. LC 59-19855. (UKR.). 1954. text ed. 12.00 (*0-685-89027-9*) Slavia Lib.

— I Slava, I Hordist' (Shkil'na Biblioteka Ser.). (UKR.). 1969. pap. text ed. 10.00 (*0-685-89028-7*) Slavia Lib.

— Mandrivka U Viky. (Shkil'na Biblioteka Ser.). (UKR.). 1970. pap. text ed. 10.00 (*0-685-89030-9*) Slavia Lib.

— Pedahohichna Pratsia D-Ra Ivana Franka. (Ob'ednania Ukrains'kykh Pedahohiv U Kanadi Ser.). (UKR.). 1956. pap. text ed. 1.50 (*0-918884-06-3*) Slavia Lib.

— Pedahohichna Pratsia Tarasa Shevchenka. (Ob'ednania Ukrains'kykh Pedahohiv U Kanadi Ser.). (UKR.). 1959. pap. text ed. 1.50 (*0-918884-07-1*) Slavia Lib.

— Slovo Pedahoha. LC 75-541045. (Shkil'na Biblioteka Ser.). (UKR.). 1971. pap. text ed. 15.00 (*0-918884-01-2*) Slavia Lib.

— Tserkovni Bratsva v Ukraini. 1976. pap. 3.50 (*0-317-12225-8*) Slavia Lib.

— Tvortsi Netlinnoi Krasy. (UKR.). 1972. pap. text ed. 10.00 (*0-918884-05-5*) Slavia Lib.

Luciw, Wasyl, ed. Literaturna Boikivshchyna: Antologiia. LC 72-209437. (Illus.). (UKR.). 1969. text ed. 25.00 (*0-918884-00-4*) Slavia Lib.

Luciw, Wasyl O. Ukrainians & the Polish Revolt of Eighteen Sixty-Three. rev. ed. 100p. (Orig.). 1980. pap. text ed. 8.00 (*0-686-63322-9*) Slavia Lib.

— Vykhovannia I Navchannia, Zbirka Stattei I Lektsii. 175p. (UKR.). 1986. pap. 10.00 (*0-317-47658-0*) Slavia Lib.

— Z moroku vikiv na svitlo nashykh dniv, lektsii dopovidi rozvidky. 200p. (UKR.). 1986. pap. 20.00 (*0-317-47660-2*) Slavia Lib.

Luck, Edward C., ed. Arms Control, the Multilateral Alternative: The Multilateral Alternative. (UNA-USA Book Ser.). (Illus.). 250p. 1983. pap. 22.50x (*0-8147-5006-0*) NYU Pr.

Luck, Erich. The Compact Dictionary of Food Technology. 443p. (ENG & GER.). 1985. 150.00 (*0-8288-0843-0*, M8221) Fr & Eur.

— Dictionary of Food, Nutrition & Cookery. 392p. (ENG & GER.). 1983. 175.00 (*0-8288-0842-2*, M15385) Fr & Eur.

— Food Technology Dictionary English-German-French-Spanish. 680p. (ENG, FRE & GER.). 1991. text ed. 128.00 (*3-86022-010-1*) IBD Ltd.

— Viersprachiges Woerterbuch der Lebensmitteltechnologie: English-German-Spanish-French. 655p. (ENG, FRE & GER.). 1992. 295.00 (*0-7859-7051-7*) Fr & Eur.

Luck, G. C. The Bible Book by Book: An Introduction to Bible Synthesis. 1955. pap. text ed. 4.99 (*0-8024-0045-0*) Moody.

Luck, Georg. Arcana Mundi: Magic & the Occult in the Greek & Roman Worlds. LC 84-28852. 416p. (Orig.). 1985. pap. text ed. 15.95 (*0-8018-2548-2*) Johns Hopkins.

Luck, J. M., et al, eds. Number Theory & Physics. (Proceedings in Physics Ser.: Vol. 47). (Illus.). xiii, 311p. 1990. 68.00 (*0-387-52129-1*) Spr-Verlag.

Luck, J. Murray. History of Switzerland: From Before the Beginnings to the Days of the Present. LC 85-50338. (Illus.). 887p. 1985. 36.00 (*0-930664-06-X*) SPOSS.

Luck, J. Murray, comp. Excitement & Fascination of Science, Vol. 1. 1965. text ed. 25.00 (*0-8243-1602-9*) Annual Reviews.

Luck, Jeff, jt. auth. see Levine, Arnold S.

Luck, Kai von & Marburger, Heinz, eds. Management & Processing of Complex Data Structures: Third Workshop on Information Systems & Artificial Intelligence, Hamburg, Germany, February 28-March 2, 1994: Proceedings. LC 94-1559. (Lecture Notes in Computer Science Ser.: Vol. 777). v, 220p. 1994. pap. text ed. 35.00 (*0-387-57802-1*) Spr-Verlag.

Luck, Kenneth. Drugs & Ships. 60p. 1992. 75.00 (*1-85609-005-1*, Pub. by Witherby & Co UK) St Mut.

Luck, Martha S. Instant Secretary's Handbook. LC 72-76551. (Instant Ser.). 320p. 1992. 6.95 (*0-911744-11-8*) Career Pub IL.

Luck, Oliver W. Music Is Math. (Illus.). (Orig.). (YA). (gr. 4-12). 1987. pap. 7.00 (*0-9626686-0-5*) Owl Pub CA.

Luck, Penny, ed. see Daly, Edward A.

Luck, W. A. Transformation Groups & Algebraic K-Theory. (Lecture Notes in Mathematics Ser.: Vol. 1408). xii, 443p. 1989. pap. 55.70 (*0-387-51846-0*) Spr-Verlag.

Luck, W. E., jt. auth. see Kates, E. J.

Luck, Wilbert H. Journey to Honey Hill. 99p. 1985. pap. text ed. write for info. (*0-9626979-0-7*) Wiluk Pr.

Lucka, Emil. Eros: The Development of the Sex Relation Through the Ages. Schleussner, Ellic, tr. & intro. by. LC 72-9661. reprint ed. 42.50 (*0-404-57472-6*) AMS Pr.

Luckasson, Ruth, jt. auth. see Smith, Deborah D.

Luckasson, Ruth A., et al. Mental Retardation: Definition, Classification & Systems of Support. 9th ed. 189p. 1992. 65.00 (*0-940898-30-6*); Wkbk. student ed 22.95 (*0-685-62554-0*) Am Assn Mental.
MENTAL RETARDATION: DEFINITION, CLASSIFICATION, & SYSTEMS OF SUPPORTS, 9th Edition, presents a revolutionary new definition that will change the way you think about people with mental retardation. The new definition focuses on how the whole person functions within the context of their environment. A multidimensional approach using intelligence, adaptive behavior, health, environmental, & emotional considerations gives you a complete picture of each individual. A companion workbook helps you operationalize the new definition with easy-to-use forms & sample case studies. An essential reference. *Publisher Provided Annotation.*

—Mental Retardation: Definition, Classification & Systems of Support, Set. 9th ed. 189p. 1992. 79.00 (*0-685-62555-9*) Am Assn Mental.
MENTAL RETARDATION: DEFINITION, CLASSIFICATION, & SYSTEMS OF SUPPORTS, 9th Edition, presents a revolutionary new definition that will change the way you think about people with mental retardation. The new definition focuses on how the whole person functions within the context of their environment. A multidimensional approach using intelligence, adaptive behavior, health, environmental, & emotional considerations gives you a complete picture of each individual. A companion workbook helps you operationalize the new definition with easy-to-use forms & sample case studies. An essential reference. *Publisher Provided Annotation.*

Luckay, Tom, ed. see Toman, Jim & Cook, Dan.

Lucke, Bernd. Price Stabilization on World Agricultural Markets: An Application to the World Market for Sugar. LC 92-31169. (Lecture Notes in Economics & Mathematical Systems Ser.: Vol. 393). 1992. 55.00 (*0-387-56099-8*) Spr-Verlag.

Lucke, Eva M. & Poetzsch, Eleonore, eds. Biotechnology Directory of Eastern Europe. LC 92-44738. 1993. 152.35 (*3-11-013674-0*) De Gruyter.

Lucke, K. & Laqua, H. Silicone Oil in the Treatment of Complicated Retinal Detachments: Techniques, Results, & Complications. (Illus.). xix, 161p. 1990. 64.00 (*0-387-53035-5*) Spr-Verlag.

Lucke, Margaret. A Relative Stranger. 320p. 1991. 19.95 (*0-312-06307-5*) St Martin.

Lucke, Peggy. Outdoor Storage. Snow, Diane, ed. LC 83-62654. (Illus.). 96p. (Orig.). 1984. pap. 9.95 (*0-89721-022-0*) Ortho Info.

Lucke, Peggy, jt. auth. see Bergquist, Craig.

Luckenbach, R., ed. Beilstein: Centennial Index - Generalregister. 4th ed. (Handbook of Organic Chemistry Ser.: Vol. 28, Pts. 3-6). 1991. 642.00 (*0-685-74382-9*) Spr-Verlag.

— Beilstein: Centennial Index - Generalregister, Vol. 28, Pt. 3: Benzol-Bz. 4th ed. (Handbook of Organic Chemistry Ser.: Vol. 28, Pts. 3-6). iv, 1483p. 1991. 684.00 (*0-387-54082-2*) Spr-Verlag.

— Beilstein: Centennial Index - Generalregister, Vol. 28, Pt. 4: D-F. (Handbook of Organic Chemistry Ser.: Vol. 28, Pts. 3-6). 1600p. 1991. 684.00 (*0-387-54085-7*) Spr-Verlag.

— Beilstein: Centennial Index - Generalregister, Vol. 28, Pt. 6: G-I. 4th ed. (Handbook of Organic Chemistry Ser.: Vol. 28, Pts. 3-6). 1600p. 1991. 684.00 (*0-387-54086-5*) Spr-Verlag.

— Beilstein: Compound-Name Index for Vols. 20-22: E-Pq. 4th ed. (Handbook of Organic Chemistry: Supplementary Ser.). iv, 976p. 1992. 1,149.00 (*0-387-54625-1*) Spr-Verlag.

— Beilstein: Compound-Name Index for Vols. 20-22: Pr-Z. 4th ed. (Handbook of Organic Chemistry: Supplementary Ser.). 1000p. 1992. 1,163.00 (*0-387-54626-X*) Spr-Verlag.

— Beilstein Handbook of Organic Chemistry: Formula Index for Vols. 20-22. 4th ed. (Supplementary Series 5). iv, 859p. 1993. 945.00 (*0-387-56103-X*) Spr-Verlag.

— Beilstein Handbook of Organic Chemistry: Heterocyclic Compounds. 4th ed. (Fifth Supplementary Ser.: Vol. 26, Pt. I). lxxxvi, 772p. 1993. 2,400.00 (*0-387-56118-8*) Spr-Verlag.

— Beilstein, Handbook of Organic Chemistry, Vol. 28, Pt. 1: Centennial Index - Generalregister, General Compound-Name Index - General-Sachregister. 4th ed. 1600p. 1991. 684.00 (*0-387-54047-4*) Spr-Verlag.

— Formula Index for Vols. 20-22, Subvol. 2: Collective Indexes. (Beilstein Handbook of Organic Chemistry Ser.: 5th Suppl.). iv, 992p. 1993. 1,133.00 (*0-387-56101-3*) Spr-Verlag.

— Formula Index to Supplementary Series Five to the Handbook of Organic Chemistry: Volumes 20-22. iv, 1050p. 1993. 1,226.00 (*0-387-56102-1*) Spr-Verlag.

— Heterocyclic Compounds. (Beilstein Handbook of Organic Chemistry Ser.: 5th Suppl.: Vol. 24, Pt. 4). (Illus.). xxii, 824p. 1992. 2,065.00 (*0-387-55110-7*) Spr-Verlag.

— Heterocyclic Compounds. (Beilstein Handbook of Organic Chemistry Ser.: 5th Suppl.: Vol. 24, Pt. 5). (Illus.). 785p. 1992. 1,549.00 (*0-387-55134-4*) Spr-Verlag.

— Heterocyclic Compounds. (Handbook of Organic Chemistry, Supplementary Ser. 5: Vol. 25, Pt. 14). xxii, 815p. 1993. 2,219.00 (*0-387-56113-7*) Spr-Verlag.

— Heterocyclic Compounds. 4th ed. (Beilstein Handbook of Organic Chemistry Ser.: 5th Suppl.: Vol. 22, Pt. 13). 960p. 1991. 2,226.00 (*0-387-53167-X*) Spr-Verlag.

— Heterocyclic Compounds. 4th ed. (Beilstein Handbook of Organic Chemistry Ser.: 5th Suppl.: Vol. 23, Pt. 5). 675p. 1991. 1,549.00 (*0-387-53758-9*) Spr-Verlag.

— Heterocyclic Compounds. 4th ed. (Beilstein Handbook of Organic Chemistry Ser.: 5th Suppl.: Vol. 23, Pt. 4). 745p. 1991. 1,717.00 (*0-387-53670-1*) Spr-Verlag.

— Heterocyclic Compounds. 4th ed. (Beilstein Handbook of Organic Chemistry Ser.: 5th Suppl.: Vol. 25, Pt. 8). xxii, 785p. 1993. 2,171.00 (*0-387-56107-2*) Spr-Verlag.

— Heterocyclic Compounds. 4th ed. (Beilstein Handbook of Organic Chemistry Ser.: 5th Suppl.: Vol. 25, Pt. 10). 760p. 1993. 2,089.00 (*0-387-56109-9*) Spr-Verlag.

— Heterocyclic Compounds. 4th ed. (Beilstein Handbook of Organic Chemistry Ser.: 5th Suppl.: Vol. 25, Pt. 11). 800p. 1993. 2,194.00 (*0-387-56110-2*) Spr-Verlag.

— Heterocyclic Compounds. 4th ed. (Beilstein Handbook of Organic Chemistry Ser.: 5th Suppl.: Vol. 25, Pt. 13). 700p. 1993. 1,861.00 (*0-387-56112-9*) Spr-Verlag.

— Heterocyclic Compounds, 2 pts., Pt. 10. 4th ed. (Beilstein Handbook of Organic Chemistry Ser.: 5th Suppl.: Vol. 23). 770p. 1991. 1,859.00 (*0-387-54163-2*) Spr-Verlag.

— Heterocyclic Compounds, 2 pts., Pt. 11. 4th ed. (Beilstein Handbook of Organic Chemistry Ser.: 5th Suppl.: Vol. 23). 980p. 1991. 1,717.00 (*0-387-54164-0*) Spr-Verlag.

— Heterocyclic Compounds, 2 vols., Vol. 24, Pt. 7. 4th ed. (Beilstein Handbook of Organic Chemistry Ser.: 5th Suppl.). xxii, 774p. 1992. 2,047.00 (*0-387-55219-7*) Spr-Verlag.

— Heterocyclic Compounds, 2 vols., Vol. 24, Pt. 8. 4th ed. (Beilstein Handbook of Organic Chemistry Ser.: 5th Suppl.). 720p. 1992. 2,303.00 (*0-387-55334-7*) Spr-Verlag.

— Heterocyclic Compounds, Vol. 25, Pt. 1. cxxxvi, 564p. 1992. 1,846.00 (*0-387-55575-7*) Spr-Verlag.

— Heterocyclic Compounds, Vol. 25, Pt. 2. 770p. 1992. 1,572.00 (*0-387-55576-5*) Spr-Verlag.

Luckenbach, R. & Beilstein-Institut fur Literature der Organischen Chemie Staff, eds. Formula Index for Volumes Seventeen to Nineteen, Pt. 3. 4th ed. (Beilstein Collective Indexes Ser.). 1005p. 1991. 1,143.00 (*0-387-52585-8*) Spr-Verlag.

— Formula Index for Volumes Seventeen to Nineteen, Pt. 4. 4th ed. (Beilstein Collective Indexes Ser.). 965p. 1991. 1,097.00 (*0-387-52586-6*) Spr-Verlag.

— Formula Index for Volumes Seventeen to Nineteen, Set, Pts. 1-4. 4th ed. (Beilstein Collective Indexes Ser.). 3960p. 1991. 4,740.00 (*0-387-52587-4*) Spr-Verlag.

Luckenbach, R., ed. see Beilstein-Institut fur Literatur der Organischen Chemie.

Luckenbach, R., ed. see Beilstein-Institut fur Literature der Organischen Chemie.

Luckenbach, R., jt. ed. see Beilstein-Institut fur Literature der Organischen Chemie Staff.

Luckenbach-Sawyers, Phyllis, jt. auth. see Henry, Frances L.

Luckenbill, Daniel D. The Annals of Sennacherib. LC 78-72760. (Ancient Mesopotamian Texts & Studies). reprint ed. 37.50 (*0-404-18206-2*) AMS Pr.

Luckenbill, David F. & Best, Joel. Organizing Deviance. (Illus.). 272p. (C). 1982. pap. text ed. write for info. (*0-13-641605-5*) P-H.

Luckenbill, David F., jt. auth. see Best, Joel.

Lucker, Amy E., jt. ed. see Barnett, Patricia J.

Lucker, G. William, et al, eds. Psychological Aspects of Facial Form: Proceedings of a Sponsored Symposium Honoring Professor Robert E. Moyers, Held February 29 & March 1, 1980, in Ann Arbor, MI. LC 83-132873. (Craniofacial Growth Monograph Ser.: No. 11). (Illus.). 233p. reprint ed. pap. 66.50 (*0-8357-7560-7*, 2052324) Bks Demand.

***Lucker, Raymond A., et al, eds.** The People's Catechism: Catholic Faith for Adults. 224p. (Orig.). 1995. pap. 14.95 (*0-8245-1466-1*) Crossroad NY.

Luckert, Karl W. Egyptian Light & Hebrew Fire: Theological & Philosophical Roots of Christendom in Evolutionary Perspective. LC 91-11980. (SUNY Series in Religious Studies). 347p. 1991. 64.50 (*0-7914-0967-8*); pap. 21.95 (*0-7914-0968-6*) State U NY Pr.

— The Navajo Hunter Tradition. fac. ed. Cook, John et al, trs. LC 75-9142. (Illus.). 247p. reprint ed. pap. 70.40 (*0-7837-6963-6*, 2046913) Bks Demand.

— Navajo Mountain & Rainbow Bridge Religion. Goossen, Irvy W. & Bilagody, Harry, Jr., trs. LC 77-153661. (American Tribal Religions Ser.: No. 1). 165p. reprint ed. pap. 47.10 (*0-8357-7771-5*, 2036131) Bks Demand.

Luckert, Karl W., ed. see Haile, Berard & Goossen, Irvy W.

Luckert, Karl W., ed. see Haile, Berard.

Luckert, Karl W., jt. auth. see Li, Shujiang.

Luckert, Yelena. Soviet Jewish History, 1917-1991: An Annotated Bibliography. LC 92-1682. 296p. 1992. 44.00 (*0-8240-2583-0*, SS611) Garland.

Luckett, Essie P. Leaves of Truth. 217p. 1990. 10.00 (*0-533-08922-0*) Vantage.

Luckett, P., ed. Reproductive Biology of the Primates. (Contributions to Primatology Ser.: Vol. 3). 284p. 1974. pap. 103.25 (*3-8055-1671-1*) S Karger.

Luckett, Perry D. Charles A. Lindbergh: A Bio-Bibliography. LC 86-3165. (Popular Culture Bio-Bibliographies Ser.). 159p. 1986. text ed. 42.95 (*0-313-23098-6*, LCL/, Greenwood Pr) Greenwood.

Luckett, Pete, jt. auth. see Robinson, Kathleen.

Luckett, Richard. Handel's Messiah: A Celebration. LC 93-22069. 1993. 22.95 (*0-15-138437-1*) HarBrace.

Luckey. Depression-Era Glassware. 3rd ed. 220p. 1993. pap. 22.95 (*0-89689-104-6*) Bks Americana.

— Hummel Figurines & Plates. 10th ed. 384p. 1993. pap. 22.95 (*0-89689-100-3*) Bks Americana.

Luckey, Carl. Antique Bird Decoys. 2nd ed. 224p. 1992. 22.95 (*0-89689-078-3*) Bks Americana.

***Luckey, Carl F.** Identification & Value Guide to Old Fishing Lures & Tackle. 4th ed. 472p. 1995. pap. 22.95 (*0-89689-117-8*, 1215) Americana.

Luckey, E. Z., jt. auth. see Arnold, L. W.

Luckey, Hugh A. & Kubli, Fred, Jr., eds. Titanium Alloys in Surgical Implants - STP 796. LC 84-72888. 295p. 1983. text ed. 37.50 (*0-8031-0241-0*, 04-796000-54) ASTM.

Luckey, Laura C., jt. auth. see Giese, Lucretia.

Luckey, T. D. Hormesis with Ionizing Radiation. 232p. 1980. 124.95 (*0-8493-5841-8*, QP82, CRC Reprint) Franklin.

— Radiation Hormesis. (Illus.). 336p. 1991. 167.00 (*0-8493-6159-1*, QC) CRC Pr.

Luckey, T. D., jt. auth. see Venugopal, B.

Luckey, William A. Bad Company. 176p. (Orig.). 1991. pap. 3.95 (*0-449-14714-2*, GM) Fawcett.

— The Death of Joe Gilead. 192p. 1987. mass mkt. 3.99 (*0-345-34991-1*) Ballantine.

— Flags over Texas. (Illus.). 352p. 1991. mass mkt. 4.95 (*0-345-36190-3*) Ballantine.

— Long Ride to Nowhere. 176p. (Orig.). 1987. mass mkt. 3.99 (*0-345-34568-1*) Ballantine.

***Luckham, Claire.** The Choice. 1995. 5.00 (*0-87129-482-6*, C89) Dramatic Pub.

An Asterisk (*) at the beginning of an entry indicates that the title is appearing in BIP for the first time.

Luckham, David C. Programming with Specifications: An Introduction to ANNA: A Language for Specifying Ada Programs. (Texts & Monographs in Computer Science). (Illus.). 440p. 1990. text ed. 55.00 (*0-387-97254-4*) Spr-Verlag.

Luckham, R., ed. Studies of Law in Social Change & Development: Law & Social Enquiry-Case Studies of Research. 1981. 20.00 (*91-7106-181-9*); pap. 12.00 (*91-7106-178-9*) Intl Ctr Law.

Luckham, Robin. The Nigerian Military: A Sociological Analysis of Authority & Revolt, 1960-67. LC 73-152643. (African Studies Ser.: No. 4). 390p. reprint ed. pap. 111.20 (*0-685-20560-6*, 2030607) Bks Demand.

Luckhardt, C. G. & Aue, M. A., trs. Last Writings on the Philosophy of Psychology, Vol. II: The Inner & the Outer. 240p. (ENG & GER.). 1992. write for info. (*0-318-68386-5*) Blackwell Pubs.

Luckhardt, C. G., tr. see Wittgenstein, Ludwig.

***Luckhardt, C. Grant & Bechtel, William.** How to Do Things with Logic. 376p. 1994. student ed, pap. 27.50 (*0-8058-1665-8*) L Erlbaum Assocs.

— How to Do Things with Logic. 104p. 1994. student ed 13.50 (*0-8058-0077-8*); text ed. 59.95 (*0-8058-0075-1*); pap. 22.50 (*0-8058-0076-X*) L Erlbaum Assocs.

Luckhardt, C. J., tr. see Wittgenstein, Ludwig.

Luckhardt, H. Extensional Goedel Functional Interpretation: A Consistency Proof of Classical Analysis. LC 72-96046. (Lecture Notes in Mathematics Ser.: Vol. 306). 161p. 1973. pap. 27.00 (*0-387-06119-3*) Spr-Verlag.

***Luckhardt, Ulrich.** David Hockney Paintings. Melia, Paul, ed. (Illus.). 200p. 1994. 55.00 (*3-7913-1381-9*) TeNeues.

Luckhardt, Ulrich, ed. Lyonel Feininger. (Illus.). 188p. 1989. 60.00 (*3-7913-1022-4*, Pub. by Prestel) TeNeues.

Luckhurst, G. R. & Veracini, C. A., eds. The Molecular Dynamics of Liquid Crystals: Proceedings of the NATO Advanced Study Institute, Il Ciocco, Barga, Italy, September 11-23, 1989. LC 94-7985. (NATO ASI Series C: Mathematical & Physical Sciences: Vol. 431). 624p. (C). 1994. lib. bdg. 222.00 (*0-7923-2809-4*) Kluwer Ac.

Luckie, Anita, ed. see Wynn, Mychal.

Luckie, P. T., ed. Industrial Practice of Fine Coal Cleaning. LC 88-63132. (Illus.). 392p. 1988. pap. 45.00 (*0-87335-078-2*, 782) SMM&E Inc.

Luckiesh, M. Visual Illusions: Their Causes, Characteristics & Applications. (Illus.). 18.75 (*0-8446-0780-0*) Peter Smith.

Luckiesh, Matthew. Visual Illusions: Their Causes, Characteristics & Applications. (Illus.). 252p. 1965. pap. 5.95 (*0-486-21530-X*) Dover.

Luckin, Richard W. Dining on Rails: An Encyclopedia of Railroad China. rev. ed. (Illus.). 392p. (C). reprint ed. pap. 48.70 (*0-9626362-0-7*) RK Pub.

— Mimbres to Mimbreno. (Illus.). 88p. 22.45 (*0-685-59605-2*) RK Pub.

— Teapot Treasury. (Illus.). 152p. 24.95 (*0-685-59604-4*) RK Pub.

Lucking, Richard C. Mathematics for Management. LC 80-40127. (Illus.). 340p. reprint ed. pap. 96.90 (*0-7837-6388-3*, 2046101) Bks Demand.

Luckingham, Bradford. Epidemic in the Southwest. (Southwestern Studies: No. 72). (Illus.). 84p. 1984. pap. 10.00 (*0-87404-148-1*) Tex Western.

— Minorities in Phoenix: A Profile of Mexican American, Chinese American, & African American Communities, 1860-1992. LC 94-8103. 270p. 1994. 35.00 (*0-8165-1457-7*) U of Ariz Pr.

— Phoenix: The History of a Southwestern Metropolis. LC 88-26171. 316p. 1989. 15.95 (*0-8165-1087-3*) U of Ariz Pr.

Luckman, A. Dick, ed. see Sloan, Tod.

***Luckman, Sidney.** Luckman at Quarterback. (American Autobiography Ser.). 233p. 1995. reprint ed. lib. bdg. 79.00 (*0-7812-8582-8*) Rprt Serv.

Luckmann, Joan. Your Health. 650p. (C). 1990. pap. text ed. write for info. (*0-13-977166-2*) P-H.

Luckmann, Joan & Sorensen, Karen C. Medical-Surgical Nursing: A Psychophysiologic Approach. 3rd ed. (Illus.). 2160p. 1987. teacher ed write for info. (*0-03-013659-8*); Software avail. write for info. (*0-318-62262-9*); write for info. (*0-03-013697-0*) Saunders.

Luckmann, Thomas. The Sociology of Language. LC 74-19085. (Studies in Sociology). 79p. 1975. pap. 3.00 (*0-672-61262-3*, Bobbs) Macmillan.

Luckmann, Thomas, jt. ed. see Beckford, James A.

Luckmann, Thomas, jt. auth. see Berger, Peter L.

Luckmann, Thomas, jt. auth. see Schutz, Alfred.

Luckmann, William H., jt. auth. see Metcalf, Robert L.

Luckmann, William H., jt. ed. see Metcalf, Robert L.

Luckner. Migration Processes in Soil & Groundwater Zone. 1991. 89.95 (*0-87371-302-8*, TC176) Lewis Pubs.

Luckner, John, jt. auth. see Luetke-Stahlman, Barbara.

Luckner, M. Secondary Metabolism in Microorganisms, Plants & Animals. 400p. 1990. 125.00 (*0-387-50287-4*) Spr-Verlag.

— Secondary Metabolism in Microorganisms, Plants & Animals. 2nd rev. ed. (Illus.). 570p. 1984. 93.50 (*0-387-12771-2*) Spr-Verlag.

Luckner, M., jt. ed. see Schreiber, K.

Luckow, James. The Technical Drawing Workbook. (Illus.). 208p. (C). 1994. pap. text ed. 21.50 (*0-201-62330-7*) Addison-Wesley.

Luckow, Melissa. Monograph of Desmanthus (Leguminosae-Mimosoideae) Anderson, Christiane, ed. (Systematic Botany Monographs: Vol. 38). (Illus.). 166p. 1993. pap. 20.00 (*0-912861-38-X*) Am Soc Plant.

Luckstead, Eugene & Greydanus, Donald E. Medical Care of the Adolescent Athlete. 384p. 1990. text ed. 42.95 (*0-87489-584-7*) Med Economics.

Luckstead, Eugene F. & Greydanus, Donald E. Medical Care of the Adolescent Athlete. (Illus.). 250p. 1993. pap. 45.95 (*1-878487-18-3*) Practice Mgmt Info.

Luckstead, Ingrid, jt. auth. see Harris, Carolyn.

Luckstone, Harold, Jr. & Holliday, Richard W. Werbel Approved Course for Rental Vehicle Companies & Their Franchisees. 64p. 1991. pap. text ed. 19.95 (*0-317-04251-3*) Werbel Pub.

Lucky, Robert. Lucky Strikes ... Again. LC 92-30769. (Illus.). 296p. (C). 1993. 32.95 (*0-7803-0433-0*, PC03301) Inst Electrical.

— Silicon Dreams: Information, Man, & Machine. 1991. pap. 13.95 (*0-312-05517-X*) St Martin.

Lucky, Robert W. Lucky Strikes...Again, 6 bks., Set. write for info. (*0-7803-1018-7*) Inst Electrical.

Lucky, William A. High Line Rider. 1985. pap. 2.50 (*0-8217-1615-8*) Zebra.

Luckyj, Christina. A Winter's Snake: Dramatic Form in the Tragedies of John Webster. LC 88-38689. 208p. 1989. 27.50 (*0-8203-1144-8*) U of Ga Pr.

Luckyj, G., jt. auth. see Kulish, Panteleimon.

***Luckyj, George S.** Discordant Voices: The Non-Russian Soviet Literature 1952-1973. 160p. 1995. lib. bdg. 27.00 (*0-8095-4935-2*) Borgo Pr.

— Literary Politics in the Soviet Ukraine, 1917-1934. rev. ed. LC 90-3499. (Studies of the Harriman Institute). 367p. (C). 1990. reprint ed. lib. bdg. 39.50 (*0-8223-1081-3*); reprint ed. pap. text ed. 21.95 (*0-8223-1099-6*) Duke.

— Literary Politics in the Soviet Ukraine 1917-1934. LC 75-165645. (Select Bibliographies Reprint Ser.). 1977. reprint ed. 24.95 (*0-8369-5954-X*) Ayer.

— Panteleimon Kulish: A Sketch of His Life & Times. (East European Monographs: No. 127). 229p. 1983. text ed. 42.00 (*0-88033-016-3*) East Eur Quarterly.

— Ukrainian Literature in the Twentieth Century: A Reader's Guide. 136p. (Orig.). 1992. 40.00 (*0-8020-5019-0*); pap. 18.95 (*0-8020-6003-X*) U of Toronto Pr.

Luckyj, George S., ed. Shevchenko & the Critics, Eighteen Sixty-One to Nineteen Eighty. 1981. pap. 11.95 (*0-8020-6377-2*) U of Toronto Pr.

— Shevchenko & the Critics, 1861-1980. Ferguson, Dolly & Yurkevich, Sophia, trs. LC 81-192007. 536p. reprint ed. pap. 152.80 (*0-8357-4731-X*, 2037647) Bks Demand.

Luckyj, George S., tr. see Sverstiuk, Ievhen.

Luckyj, George S., tr. see Zaitsev, Pavlo.

Luclaire, Ed. The Celebrity Almanac. 288p. 1991. pap. 10.00 (*0-13-122367-4*) P-H Gen Ref & Trav.

***Lucock, John & Peak, Robin, eds.** Workouts in Modern Economics. 3rd ed. LC 94-42567. 1994. write for info. (*0-582-25938-X*, Pub. by Longman UK) Longman.

Lucotte, Gerald & Baneyx, Francois. Introduction to Molecular Cloning Techniques. LC 93-22418. 298p. 1993. 49.00 (*1-56081-613-9*) VCH Pubs.

Lucovsky, G. & Pantelides, S. T., eds. SiO2 & Its Interfaces. (Symposium Proceedings Ser.: Vol. 105). 1988. text ed. 46.00 (*0-931837-73-1*) Materials Res.

Lucovsky, G., ed. see American Institute of Physics.

Lucovsky, G., jt. ed. see Joannopoulos, J. D.

Lucovsky, G., et al, eds. Characterization of Plasma-Enhanced CVD Processes: Materials Research Society Symposium Proceedings, Vol. 165. 1990. text ed. 36.00 (*1-55899-053-4*) Materials Res.

Lucovsky, Gerald, ed. see Brillson, L. J.

Lucovsky, Gerald, jt. ed. see Rubloff, Gary.

Lucretius. De Rerum Natura. 2nd ed. Bailey, Cyril, ed. (Oxford Classical Texts Ser.). 1922. 19.95 (*0-19-814624-8*) OUP.

— De Rerum Natura, Bk. 3. Kenney, Edwin J., ed. (Cambridge Greek & Latin Classics Ser.). 1977. pap. 21.95 (*0-521-29177-1*) Cambridge U Pr.

— De Rerum Natura, No. VI. Godwin, ed. 1991. 49.95 (*0-85668-499-6*, Pub. by Aris & Phillips UK); pap. 24.95 (*0-85668-500-3*, Pub. by Aris & Phillips UK) David Brown.

— De Rerum Natura: The Latin Text of Lucretius. Leonard, William E. & Smith, Stanley B., eds. (Illus.). 896p. 1942. text ed. 29.50 (*0-299-00362-0*) U of Wis Pr.

— De Rerum Natura IV. Godwin, ed. (Classical Texts Ser.). 1987. 49.95 (*0-85668-308-6*, Pub. by Aris & Phillips UK); pap. 19.95 (*0-85668-309-4*, Pub. by Aris & Phillips UK) David Brown.

— Lucretius: The Way Things Are: The De Rerum Natura of Titus Lucretius Carus. Humphries, Rolfe, tr. LC 68-27349. (Greek & Latin Classics Ser.). 256p. 1968. reprint ed. pap. 7.95 (*0-253-20125-X*, MB-125) Ind U Pr.

— The Nature of Things. Copley, F. O., tr. (C). 1977. pap. text ed. 8.95 (*0-393-09094-9*) Norton.

— On the Nature of the Universe. Lathan, Ronald E., tr. (Classics Ser.). (Orig.). 1951. pap. 10.95 (*0-14-044018-6*, Penguin Classics) Viking Penguin.

— On the Nature of the Universe. Latham, R. E., tr. 320p. 1994. 11.95 (*0-14-044610-9*, Penguin Classics) Viking Penguin.

— On the Nature of Things. 1976. 18.95 (*0-8488-0824-X*) Amereon Ltd.

— On the Nature of Things. (Loeb Classical Library: No. 181). 664p. 1924. text ed. 18.95 (*0-674-99200-8*) HUP.

— On the Nature of Things-De Rerum Natura. Esolen, Anthony M., ed. 336p. 1994. text ed. 35.95x (*0-8018-5054-1*); pap. 14.95 (*0-8018-5055-X*) Johns Hopkins.

— Selections. Benfield, G. E. & Reeves, R. C., eds. 1967. 11.95 (*0-19-831768-9*) OUP.

Lucuham, Robin, jt. ed. see Austin, Dennis.

Lucwig, Friedrich. Repertorium Organorum Recentioris et Motetorum Vetustissimi Stili, 4 vols., Set. 1972. reprint ed. write for info. (*3-487-04197-9*, Pub. by Georg Olms GW) Lubrecht & Cramer.

Lucy, J. A. The Plasma Membrane. 2nd ed. Head, J. J., ed. LC 77-75589. (Carolina Biology Readers Ser.: No. 81). (Illus.). 16p. (gr. 10 up). 1979. pap. 2.75 (*0-89278-281-1*, 45-9681) Carolina Biological.

Lucy, John A. Grammatical Categories & Cognition: A Case Study of the Linguistic Relativity Hypothesis. (Studies in the Social & Cultural Foundations of Language: No. 13). 250p. (C). 1992. 59.95 (*0-521-38419-2*) Cambridge U Pr.

— Language Diversity & Thought: A Reformulation of the Linguistic Relativity Hypothesis. (Studies in the Social & Cultural Foundations of Language: No. 12). 300p. (C). 1992. 64.95 (*0-521-38418-4*); pap. 24.95 (*0-521-38797-3*) Cambridge U Pr.

Lucy, John A., ed. Reflexive Language: Reported Speech & Metapragmatics. (Illus.). 408p. (C). 1993. 74.95 (*0-521-35164-2*) Cambridge U Pr.

Lucy, Margaret. Shakespeare & the Supernatural. LC 70-144653. reprint ed. 6.50 (*0-404-04065-9*) AMS Pr.

Lucy, Matthew I. The Duke of Alandriai. Van Treese, James B., ed. 588p. 1994. pap. 12.95 (*1-56901-057-9*) NW Pub.

Lucy, Reda, pseud. The Lord's Prayer for Children. (Illus.). 24p. (Orig.). (J). (ps-3). 1981. pap. 2.25 (*0-87516-437-4*) DeVorss.

Lucy, Sean, ed. Irish Poets in English. 1972. pap. 7.95 (*0-85342-301-6*) Dufour.

Lucy, William. Close to Power: Setting Priorities with City Officials. LC 87-71119. 289p. (Orig.). (C). 1988. lib. bdg. 44.95 (*0-685-18627-X*); pap. 26.95 (*0-918286-49-2*) Planners Pr.

Lucyk, Blaine. Advanced Topics in DB2. (Illus.). 400p. (C). 1993. text ed. 47.50 (*0-201-57652-X*) Addison-Wesley.

Luczak, Holger, et al, eds. Work with Display Units '92: Selected Proceedings of the Third International Scientific Conference on Work with Display Units, Berlin, Germany, September 1-4, 1992. LC 93-19702. 549p. 1993. 137.25 (*0-444-89759-3*, North Holland) Elsevier.

Luczak, James E. Rats. (Orig.). 1992. pap. 2.50 (*0-87129-169-X*, R52) Dramatic Pub.

— Some Rain. (Illus.). 60p. (Orig.). 1983. pap. 4.95 (*0-88145-001-4*) Broadway Play.

Luczak, Raymond, ed. Eyes of Desire: A Deaf Gay & Lesbian Reader. LC 93-1324. (Illus.). 260p. (Orig.). 1993. pap. 9.95 (*1-55583-204-0*) Alyson Pubns.

Luczyc-Wyhowska, Jose, jt. auth. see Hull, Alastair.

Ludanyi, Andrew, jt. ed. see Joo, Rudolf.

Ludanyi, Julianna N. Advanced Hungarian 2. (Illus.). 123p. (Orig.) (HUN.). (C). 1988. teacher ed, pap. 8.00 (*0-87415-127-9*, 52A); student ed, pap. text ed. 16.00 (*0-87415-126-0*, 52); audio 5.00 (*0-87415-128-7*, 52B) OSU Foreign Lang.

Ludanyi, Julianna N., jt. auth. see Pereszlenyi-Pinter, Martha.

Ludbrook, John & Marshall, Vernon C. Clinical Science for Surgeons. 2nd ed. (Illus.). 754p. 1989. text ed. 165.00 (*0-409-49454-2*) Buttrwrth-Heinemann.

Ludd, Steven O., jt. ed. see Reichert, William O.

Ludden, David. Peasant History in South India. LC 85-42692. (Illus.). 360p. 1985. 59.50x (*0-691-05456-8*) Princeton U Pr.

***Ludden, David, ed.** Agricultural Production & Indian History. (Oxford in India Readings Ser.). 400p. 1995. 29.95 (*0-19-563268-0*) OUP.

Ludden, LaVerne. Directory of Franchise Opportunities: A Handbook for Assisting Entrepreneur - Franchise Investors with the Sources for Public - Private Aid. 300p. (Orig.). 1994. pap. 14.95 (*1-57112-062-9*, PA2054, Park Avenue) JIST Works.

— Franchise Opportunity Handbook. 2nd ed. 1995. pap. 16.95 (*1-57112-073-4*) JIST Works.

Ludden, LaVerne & Ludden, Marsha. Job Savvy Instructor's Guide: How to Be a Success at Work. Hall, Sara, ed. 112p. 1993. pap. 12.95 (*0-942784-80-4*, JSTM) JIST Works.

Ludden, LaVerne & Maitlen, Bonnie. Mind Your Own Business: Getting Started As an Entrepreneur. LC 93-6007. 224p. 1994. pap. 9.95 (*1-56370-083-2*, MYOB) JIST Works.

Ludden, LaVerne L. Back to School: A College Primer for Adults. 232p. (Orig.). 1995. pap. 14.95 (*1-57112-070-X*, P070X, Park Avenue) JIST Works.

Ludden, Marsha. Effective Communication Skills: Essential Tools for Success in Work, Social & Personal Situations. Hall, Sara, ed. (Living Skills Ser.). (Illus.). 138p. 1992. pap. 7.95 (*1-56370-038-7*, ECS) JIST Works.

Ludden, Marsha, jt. auth. see Ludden, LaVerne.

Ludden, Mary C., tr. see Honore, Jean.

Luddington, J. Starting to Collect Silver. (Illus.). 1984. 49.50 (*0-907462-48-0*) Antique Collect.

Luddington, Stephen. Aircraft Maintenance Regulations. 120p. 1991. 49.95 (*0-7506-0043-8*) Buttrwrth-Heinemann.

***Luddy, Maria.** Women & Philanthropy in Nineteenth-Century Ireland. 272p. (C). 1995. 64.95 (*0-521-47433-7*); pap. 27.95 (*0-521-48361-1*) Cambridge U Pr.

Luddy, Maria & Murphy, Cliona. Women Surviving: Studies in Irish Women's History in 19th-20th Century. 224p. 1990. pap. 18.95 (*1-85371-064-4*, Pub. by Poolbeg Pr IE) Dufour.

Luddy, Maria, jt. auth. see Cullen, Mary.

Ludecke, Dieter K. & Tolis, George, eds. Growth Hormone, Growth Factors, & Acromegaly. (Progress in Endocrine Research & Therapy Ser.: Vol. 3). (Illus.). 304p. 1987. text ed. 72.00 (*0-88167-299-8*) Raven.

Ludecke, Dieter K., et al. ACTH, Cushing's Syndrome, & Other Hypercortisolemic States. (Progress in Endocrine Research & Therapy Ser.: Vol. 5). 352p. 1990. 110.50 (*0-88167-718-3*) Raven.

Ludecke, Kurt G. I Knew Hitler: The Story of a Nazi Who Escaped the Blood Purge. LC 78-63687. (Studies in Fascism: Ideology & Practice). (Illus.). 848p. reprint ed. 74.00 (*0-404-16904-X*) AMS Pr.

Ludeke, Kenneth L., jt. auth. see Day, Arden D.

Ludeke, Paul & Swebeck, Brad. Enterprise Bargaining: A Practical Approach. 160p. pap. 33.00 (*1-86287-079-9*, Pub. by Federation Pr AU) W W Gaunt.

Ludel. Jeep Owners Bible. 1992. pap. 29.95 (*0-8376-0154-1*) Bentley.

Ludel, Leonard. How to Cut a Diamond. LC 86-223110. (Illus.). 250p. 1985. 47.50 (*0-9617615-0-4*) L Ludel.

***Ludel, Moses.** Ford-F Series Pickup Owner's Bible: A Hands-on Guide to Getting the Most from Your F-Series Pickup. LC 94-35251. (Ford F-Ser.). 1994. 29.95 (*0-8376-0152-5*) Bentley.

***Ludell, M.** Chevrolet C-K Pick up Owners. 1995. 29.95 (*0-8376-0157-6*) Bentley.

Ludema, K. C., ed. see International Conference on Wear of Materials Staff.

Ludema, Kenneth C. & Bayer, Raymond G., eds. Tribological Modeling for Mechanical Designers. LC 91-8238. (Special Technical Publication Ser.: No. STP 1105). (Illus.). 195p. 1991. text ed. 76.00 (*0-8031-1412-5*, 04-011050-27) ASTM.

Ludema, Kenneth C., jt. auth. see Dorinson, A.

Ludema, Kenneth C., et al. Manufacturing Engineering: Economics & Processes. (Illus.). 608p. 1987. text ed. 86.00 (*0-13-555582-5*) P-H.

Ludema, Kenneth C., et al, eds. Wear of Materials: Proceedings, 9th International Conference, San Francisco, USA, April 1993. xxiv, 1170p. 1993. 357.25 (*0-444-81471-X*) Elsevier.

Ludeman, Kate & Henderson, Louise. Do-It-Yourself Allergy Analysis Handbook. 154p. 1990. reprint ed. pap. 10.95 (*0-87983-542-7*) Keats.

Ludeman, Lonnie C. Fundamentals of Digital Signal Processing. 352p. 1986. Net. text ed. write for info. (*0-471-60363-5*) Wiley.

Ludeman, Robert A. Introduction to Electronic Devices & Circuits. 576p. (C). 1989. text ed. 55.00 (*0-03-009538-7*) SCP.

Ludena, Eduardo V., jt. auth. see Kryachko, Eugene S.

Ludendorff, Erich Von. The General Staff & Its Problems, 2 vols., Set. Holt, F. A., tr. LC 79-165646. (Select Bibliographies Reprint Ser.). 1977. reprint ed. 51.95 (*0-8369-5955-8*) Ayer.

— Ludendorff's Own Story, 2 vols., Set. LC 72-165647. (Select Bibliographies Reprint Ser.). 1977. reprint ed. 60.95 (*0-8369-5956-6*) Ayer.

Luder, Hope E. Women & Quakerism. LC 74-82914. 36p. (Orig.). 1974. pap. 3.00 (*0-87574-196-7*) Pendle Hill.

***Luder, Ian & Mock, Patricia.** Tax & Remuneration Strategies. 275p. 1994. boxed 154.00 (*0-406-02801-X*, UK) Butterworth Legal Pubs.

Luderer, Albert A. & Weetal, Howard H., eds. The Human Oncogenic Viruses. LC 86-7518. (Illus.). 304p. 1986. 69.50 (*0-89603-088-1*) Humana.

Luderer, Albert A. & Weetall, Howard H., eds. Clinical Cellular Immunology. LC 81-83307. (Contemporary Immunology Ser.). (Illus.). 416p. 1982. 89.50 (*0-89603-011-3*) Humana.

***Luderer, William, ed.** Making Global Connections in the Middle School: Lessons on the Environment, Development & Equity. 87p. (Orig.). 1994. pap. text ed. 12.00 (*0-928630-02-1*) Global Learning.

***Luderitz, Berndt.** History of the Disorders of Cardiac Rhythm. LC 94-26949. (Illus.). 184p. (GER.). 1994. 75.00 (*0-87993-606-1*) Futura Pub.

Luderitz, Berndt & Saksena, Sanjeev, eds. Interventional Electrophysiology. (Illus.). 592p. 1991. 95.00 (*0-87993-507-3*) Futura Pub.

Luderitz, Berndt, jt. ed. see Saksena, Sanjeev.

Luderitz, P., jt. auth. see Elster, P.

Luders, Hans, ed. Advanced Evoked Potentials. (Topics in Neurosurgery Ser.). (C). 1989. lib. bdg. 104.00 (*0-89838-963-1*) Kluwer Ac.

Luders, Hans & Lesser, R. P., eds. Epilepsy: Electroclinical Syndromes. (Clinical Medicine & the Nervous System Ser.). (Illus.). 420p. 1987. 131.00 (*0-387-16205-4*) Spr-Verlag.

Luders, Hans O. Epilepsy Surgery. 880p. 1992. 142.00 (*0-88167-821-X*) Raven.

***Luders, Lesa.** Lady God. 200p. (Orig.). 1995. pap. 9.95 (*0-934678-59-6*) New Victoria Pubs.

Luders, Rolf, jt. auth. see Hachette, Dominique.

Ludes, B., jt. auth. see Mangin, P.

Ludes, Peter. Bibliographie zur Entwicklung des Fernsehens - Bibliography on the Development of Television: Fernsehsysteme & Programmgeschichte in den U. S. A., Gro Britannien & der Bundesrepublik Deutschland - Television Systems & Programme Development in the U. S. A., Gr. Britain & FRG. 241p. (GER.). 1990. lib. bdg. 45.00 (*3-598-10973-3*) K G Saur.

Ludford, G., ed. Reacting Flows: Combustion & Chemical Reactors, 2 pts., Pt. I. LC 86-1088. (Lectures in Applied Mathematics: Vol. 24). 512p. 1986. text ed. 64.00 (*0-8218-1127-4*, LAM-24.1) Am Math.

— Reacting Flows: Combustion & Chemical Reactors, 2 pts., Pt. II. LC 86-1088. (Lectures in Applied Mathematics: Vol. 24). 536p. 1986. text ed. 64.00 (*0-8218-1128-2*, LAM-24.2) Am Math.

— Reacting Flows: Combustion & Chemical Reactors, 2 pts., Set. LC 86-1088. (Lectures in Applied Mathematics: Vol. 24). 1048p. 1986. text ed. 107.00 (*0-8218-1124-X*, LAM-24) Am Math.

Ludford, G. S., ed. Reacting Flows: Combustion & Chemical Reactors. 160p. 1986. 46.25 (*0-444-87014-8*, North Holland) Elsevier.

Ludford, G. S., jt. auth. see Buckmaster, J. D.

Ludgate, John, tr. see Boccaccio, Giovanni.

Ludgate, Katherine E.

Ludi, Maria A. & Hull, Nancy. Balance Your Act: A Book for Adults with Diabetes. rev. ed. LC 83-16009. (Illus.). 96p. (Orig.). 1993. reprint ed. pap. text ed. 4.75 (*0-939838-14-1*) Pritchett & Hull.

Ludi, Maria A. & Hull, Nancy R. Mantenga el Equilibrio: Un Libro para Adultos con Diabetes. Hoffman, Faye, ed. De La Vega, Olimpia, tr. (Illus.). 96p. (Orig.). 1991. pap. text ed. 5.25 (*0-939838-31-1*) Pritchett & Hull.

Ludicke, F. Intercomparison of Flatness Measurements, No. 14059. 80p. 1992. pap. 13.00 (*92-826-3986-X*, CD-NA-14059-EN-C, Pub. by Europ Com) UNIPUB.

Ludier, Carol. Little Mermaid: What's under the Sea? (J). (ps-3). 1993. 9.95 (*0-307-06077-2*, Golden Pr) Western Pub.

Ludin, H. P., ed. Electromyography. LC 93-36498. (Handbook of Electroencephalography & Clinical Neurophysiology, Revised Ser.: Vol. 5). 1993. 287.50 (*0-444-81256-3*) Elsevier.

Ludin, Irwin, jt. auth. see Kliem, Ralph L.

Ludin, Irwin S., jt. auth. see Kliem, Ralph L.

Ludington, Aileen. Salvation in the Killing Field. 192p. 1991. pap. 4.99 (*0-685-54254-8*) Pacific Pr Pub Assn.

***Ludington, Aileen & Diehl, Hans.** Dynamic Living. rev. ed. LC 95-7074. Orig. Title: Lifestyle Capsules. 1995. write for info. (*0-8280-0942-2*) Review & Herald.

Ludington, Townsend, ed. The Fourteenth Chronicle: Letters & Diaries of John Dos Passos. LC 72-94006. (Illus.). 662p. 1973. 15.00 (*0-87645-073-7*) Harvard Common Pr.

Ludins, George H. Seamanship for New Skippers. (Illus.). 1980. pap. 5.95 (*0-916224-54-6*) Banyan Bks.

Ludium, David. The American Weather Book. (Illus.). 296p. 1989. reprint ed. pap. 20.00 (*0-933876-97-1*) Am Meteorological.

Ludke, Jill B., jt. auth. see Cresanta, Judy.

Ludkovsky, G., ed. see Metallurgical Society Staff.

Ludlam, jt. auth. see Wilson-Ludlum.

Ludlam, Christopher A., ed. Clinical Haematology. (Illus.). 496p. 1990. pap. text ed. 59.00 (*0-443-03834-1*) Churchill.

Ludlam, F. H. Clouds & Storms: The Behavior & Effect of Water in the Atmosphere. LC 77-22281. (Illus.). 1980. 65.00 (*0-271-00515-7*) Pa St U Pr.

Ludlam, Harry, jt. auth. see Lund, Paul.

Ludlam, Mae R., ed. see Goode, John H.

Ludlow, Angela. The Fun at Christmas Book. (Illus.). 32p. (J). (gr. 4-8). 1991. pap. 5.99 (*0-7459-1877-8*) Lion USA.

Ludlow, Barbara L. & Sobsey, Richard. The School's Role in Educating Severely Handicapped Students. LC 84-61199. (Fastback Ser.: No. 213). 50p. (Orig.). 1984. pap. 1.25 (*0-87367-213-5*) Phi Delta Kappa.

Ludlow, Charles. Brisbane's River. 64p. (C). 1990. 90.00 (*0-86439-016-5*, Pub. by Boolarong Pubns AT) St Mut.

Ludlow, Daniel H. A Companion to Your Study of the Book of Mormon. LC 76-27139. 396p. 1976. 12.95 (*0-87747-610-1*) Deseret Bk.

— A Companion to Your Study of the Doctrine & Covenants, 2 vols. LC 78-64752. 1978. Vol. 2, 390 p. write for info. (*0-87747-729-9*) Deseret Bk.

— Companion to Your Study of the New Testament: The Four Gospels. 454p. 1982. 13.95 (*0-87747-945-3*) Deseret Bk.

— A Companion to Your Study of the Old Testament. LC 80-28088. 437p. 1981. 15.95 (*0-87747-853-8*) Deseret Bk.

Ludlow, Daniel H., comp. Latter-Day Prophets Speak. 9.95 (*0-88494-012-8*) Bookcraft Inc.

***Ludlow, Daniel H., ed.** Church History: Selections from the Encyclopedia of Mormonism. (Orig.). 1995. pap. write for info. (*0-87579-924-8*) Deseret Bk.

— Encyclopedia of Mormonism. 2480p. (C). 1991. text ed. 360.00 (*0-02-904040-X*) Macmillan.

— Jesus Christ & His Gospel: Selections from the Encyclopedia of Mormonism. LC 94-68130. (Orig.). 1994. pap. 16.95 (*0-87579-922-1*) Deseret Bk.

— Priesthood & Church Organization: Selections from the Encyclopedia of Mormonism. (Orig.). 1995. pap. 16.95 (*0-87579-926-4*) Deseret Bk.

— Scriptures of the Church: Selections from the Encyclopedia of Mormonism. (Orig.). 1995. pap. 18.95 (*0-87579-923-X*) Deseret Bk.

Ludlow, Edmund. The Memoirs of Edmund Ludlow, Lieutenant-General of the Horse in the Army of the Commonwealth of England, 1625-1672, 2 vols., Set. Firth, C. H., ed. LC 75-31098. (Illus.). reprint ed. 95.00 (*0-404-13520-X*) AMS Pr.

Ludlow, Helen W., jt. auth. see Armstrong, Mary F.

Ludlow, James M. The Age of the Crusades. 1977. lib. bdg. 59.95 (*0-8490-1405-0*) Gordon Pr.

Ludlow, John M. Popular Epics of the Middle Ages of the Norse-German & Carlovingian Cycles, 2 vols. 1976. lib. bdg. 200.00 (*0-8490-2455-2*) Gordon Pr.

— Woman's Work in the Church. LC 75-33300. 1976. reprint ed. 24.95 (*0-89201-007-X*) Zenger Pub.

Ludlow, John M. & Jones, Lloyd. Progress of the Working Classes, 1832-1867. LC 72-77050. (Reprints of Economic Classics Ser.). 1973. reprint ed. 39.50 (*0-678-00909-0*) Kelley.

Ludlow, John W. & Skuse, Gary R. Tumor Suppressors: Involvement in Human Diseases, Viral Protein Interactions, & Growth Regulation. (Molecular Biology Intelligence Unit Ser.). 103p. 1994. 89.95 (*1-57059-105-9*, LN9105) R G Landes.

Ludlow, Louis. Hell or Heaven. 1973. 59.95 (*0-8490-0291-5*) Gordon Pr.

Ludlow, Nicholas H. The Development Bank Business Market: What the MDBs Lend For, Why They Lend for It, & How Much They Lend, Including a Lending Scenario for the Year 2000. LC 93-71061. (Illus.). 460p. 1993. 383.00 (*0-943781-03-5*) Develop Bank.

— A Practical Guide to the Development Bank Business: How to Identify It, Market to It, & Win It. LC 88-71941. (Illus.). 312p. 1988. pap. text ed. 191.00 (*0-943781-00-0*) Develop Bank.

Ludlow, Nicholas H., jt. auth. see Kelleher, John J.

Ludlow, Nicholas H., et al. Financing Urban Transport - Sources & Techniques: Vol. I North America. (Illus.). 341p. (C). 1987. pap. 93.00 (*0-943781-04-3*) Develop Bank.

Ludlow, Noah M. Dramatic Life As I Found It. LC 66-16759. 1972. reprint ed. 30.95 (*0-405-08755-1*, Pub. by Blom Pubns UK) Ayer.

Ludlow, Patricia D., illus. Dear Santa. LC 93-28618. (J). 1993. 11.95 (*0-85953-778-1*) Childs Play.

Ludlow, Peter, ed. Europe & North America in the 1990s: Papers Presented to CEPS Annual Conference, 1991. (CEPS Papers). 92p. 1992. pap. 17.00 (*1-85753-062-4*, Pub. by Brasseys UK) Brasseys Inc.

Ludlow, Peter, intro. Europe & the Mediterranean. 272p. 1994. 56.00 (*1-85753-059-4*, Pub. by Brasseys UK) Brasseys Inc.

Ludlow, Peter & Gros, Daniel. Setting European Community Priorities. 154p. 1994. 25.00 (*0-08-041314-5*) Elsevier.

Ludlow, Peter, jt. ed. see Beakley, Brian.

Ludlow, Peter, ed. see Centre for European Policy Studies Staff.

Ludlow, Ron. Essence of Recruitment & Selection. 1991. 53.33 (*0-13-284704-3*) P-H.

Ludlow, Rose B. Total Health & Food Power. LC 85-29594. (Illus.). 240p. (Orig.). 1986. pap. 7.95 (*0-88007-158-3*) Woodbridge Pr.

Ludlow, Victor L. Isaiah: Prophet, Seer, & Poet. LC 82-1444. (Illus.). 578p. 1982. 18.95 (*0-87747-884-8*) Deseret Bk.

— Principles & Practices of the Restored Gospel. LC 92-29955. ix, 656p. 1992. 21.95 (*0-87579-649-4*) Deseret Bk.

— Unlocking the Old Testament. LC 81-68266. (Illus.). 239p. 1981. 11.95 (*0-87747-873-2*) Deseret Bk.

Ludlow, W. James. The Road to Wealth: How to Improve Your Investing, Saving & Spending Skills for Worry-Free Living & Retirement. LC 93-90503. 144p. (Orig.). 1994. pap. 16.95 (*0-9635781-0-3*) Applewood Pub.

Ludlow, William L. The Story of Bible Translation. 1990. 14.95 (*0-533-08494-6*) Vantage.

— What It Means to Be a Christian. LC 85-73080. 1986. pap. 8.95 (*0-8158-0434-2*) Chris Mass.

***Ludlum, Anne.** Kate & Isabel. Date not set. write for info. (*0-87129-591-1*, K24) Dramatic Pub.

Ludlum, David. The Audubon Society Field Guide to North American Weather. LC 91-52707. (Audubon Field Guide Ser.). (Illus.). 640p. 1991. 19.00 (*0-679-40851-7*) Knopf.

— The Nantucket Weather Book. Farlow, Lesley, ed. (Illus.). 195p. (Orig.). 1986. pap. text ed. 17.95 (*0-9607340-4-X*) Nantucket Hist Assn.

Ludlum, David M. Early American Tornados, 1586-1870. (History of American Weather-Historical Monograph Ser.). (Illus.). 219p. 1970. 20.00 (*0-933876-32-7*) Am Meteorological.

— Early American Winters, 1604-1820: The History of American Weather. (History of American Weather - Historical Monograph Ser.). (Illus.). 283p. 1966. 20.00 (*0-933876-23-8*) Am Meteorological.

— Early American Winters, 1821-1870, Vol. II. (History of American Weather - Historical Monograph Ser.). (Illus.). 255p. 1968. 20.00 (*0-933876-24-6*) Am Meteorological.

— The New Jersey Weather Book. 250p. 1983. 35.00 (*0-8135-0915-7*); pap. 14.95 (*0-8135-0940-8*) Rutgers U Pr.

— Social Ferment in Vermont, Seventeen Ninety-One to Eighteen Fifty. LC 39-22998. reprint ed. 24.50 (*0-404-04066-7*) AMS Pr.

***Ludlum, Robert.** The Apocalypse Watch. LC 95-1860. 1995. 24.95 (*0-553-09993-0*) Bantam.

— The Aquitaine Progression. 704p. 1985. mass mkt. 6.99 (*0-553-26256-4*) Bantam.

— The Aquitaine Progression. LC 83-19078. 752p. 1984. 17.95 (*0-394-53674-6*) Random.

— The Bourne Identity. 544p. (Orig.). 1984. mass mkt. 6.99 (*0-553-26011-1*) Bantam.

— Bourne Identity. 1987. pap. 16.99 (*0-553-45053-0*) Bantam.

— The Bourne Supremacy. 656p. 1987. mass mkt. 6.99 (*0-553-26322-6*) Bantam.

— The Bourne Ultimatum. 1990. 21.95 (*0-394-58408-2*) Random.

— Bourne Ultimatum. 1991. mass mkt. 6.99 (*0-553-28773-7*) Bantam.

— The Bourne Ultimatum. large type ed. 1312p. 1990. 24.45 (*0-679-40043-5*) Random.

— The Chancellor Manuscript. 448p. 1984. mass mkt. 6.99 (*0-553-26094-4*) Bantam.

— The Gemini Contenders. 1989. mass mkt. 6.99 (*0-553-28209-3*) Bantam.

— The Holcroft Covenant. 512p. (Orig.). 1984. mass mkt. 6.99 (*0-553-26019-7*) Bantam.

— The Icarus Agenda. 1989. mass mkt. 6.99 (*0-553-27800-2*) Bantam.

— The Icarus Agenda. LC 87-28624. 688p. 1988. 19.95 (*0-394-54397-1*) Random.

— The Matarese Circle. 544p. 1983. mass mkt. 6.99 (*0-553-25899-0*) Bantam.

— The Matlock Paper. 1989. mass mkt. 6.99 (*0-553-27960-2*) Bantam.

— Osterman Weekend. 1984. mass mkt. 6.99 (*0-553-26430-3*) Bantam.

— The Osterman Weekend. limited ed. LC 90-38523. 336p. 1991. 75.00 (*0-922890-50-1*) Armchair Detective.

— The Osterman Weekend. LC 90-38523. 336p. 1991. reprint ed. 19.95 (*0-922890-48-X*); reprint ed. 25.00 (*0-922890-49-8*) Armchair Detective.

— The Parsifal Mosaic. 1983. mass mkt. 6.99 (*0-553-25270-4*) Bantam.

— The Parsifal Mosaic. 1982. 15.95 (*0-394-52111-0*) Random.

— Rhineman Exchange. 1989. mass mkt. 6.99 (*0-553-28063-5*) Bantam.

— The Rhinemann Exchange. large type ed. 672p. 1983. 23.95 (*0-7089-8100-3*, Trail West Pubs) Ulverscroft.

— The Rhinemann Exchange. 464p. 1991. reprint ed. lib. bdg. 31.95 (*0-89966-778-3*) Buccaneer Bks.

— The Road to Gandolfo. 1992. mass mkt. 6.99 (*0-553-27109-1*) Bantam.

— The Road to Omaha. 1993. mass mkt. 6.99 (*0-553-56044-1*) Bantam.

— The Road to Omaha. 1992. 23.95 (*0-394-57329-3*) Random.

— Road to Omaha. 1992. 6.99 (*0-517-11695-2*) Random Hse Value.

— The Road to Omaha. large type ed. 1992. 26.00 (*0-679-41016-3*) Random.

— Scarlatti Inheritance. 1982. mass mkt. 6.99 (*0-553-27146-6*) Bantam.

— The Scarlatti Inheritance. limited ed. LC 90-38021. 368p. 1990. reprint ed. 75.00 (*0-922890-47-1*) Armchair Detective.

— The Scarlatti Inheritance. LC 90-38021. 368p. 1990. reprint ed. 19.95 (*0-922890-45-5*); reprint ed. 25.00 (*0-922890-46-3*) Armchair Detective.

— Scorpio Illusion. 1994. mass mkt. 6.99 (*0-553-56603-2*) Bantam.

— The Scorpio Illusion. large type ed. 1993. pap. 29.95 (*0-385-47039-8*, Bantam LT) BDD LT Grp.

— Three Complete Novels: The Holcroft Covenant, The Matarese Circle, The Bourne Identity. LC 93-34510. 1994. 11.99 (*0-517-10118-1*, Pub. by Wings Bks) Random Hse Value.

— Trevayne. 1992. mass mkt. 6.99 (*0-553-28179-8*) Bantam.

Ludman, Allan. Laboratory Exercises in Physical Geology. 240p. (C). 1992. spiral bd. write for info. (*0-697-14706-1*) Wm C Brown Pubs.

Ludman, Dianne M. Hugh Stubbins & His Associates: The First Fifty Years. LC 86-61773. (Illus.). 152p. (Orig.). 1986. write for info. (*0-9617416-0-0*); pap. 20.00 (*0-9617416-1-9*) Stubbins Assocs.

Ludman, Harold. ABC of Otolaryngology. (Illus.). 58p. 1993. pap. text ed. 18.00 (*0-7279-0765-4*, BMJ Pubng Grp) Amer Coll Phys.

Ludman, Joan. Prints by Fairfield Porter: From the Lauris & Daniel J. Mason Collection. (Illus.). 8p. 1982. 4.00 (*0-685-70930-2*) Gal Assn NY.

Ludman, Joan, jt. auth. see Mason, Lauris.

Ludman, Mark D. & Wyndbrandt, James. The Encyclopedia of Genetic Disorders & Birth Defects. (Illus.). 360p. 1990. 45.00 (*0-8160-1926-6*) Facts on File.

Ludmer, Joyce P. Carlo Pedretti: A Bibliography of His Work on Leonardo Da Vinci & the Renaissance, 1944-1984. In Celebration of His Twenty Five Years at the University of California, Los Angeles. (Illus.). 144p. (Orig.). 1987. pap. write for info. (*0-9617550-0-8*) E Belt Lib.

Ludmer, Larry. The Great American Wilderness: Touring America's National Parks. (Illus.). 300p. (Orig.). 1993. pap. 11.95 (*1-55650-567-1*) Hunter NJ.

Ludmer, Larry H. Arizona, Utah & Colorado: A Touring Guide. (Illus.). 256p. (Orig.). 1994. pap. 11.95 (*1-55650-656-2*) Hunter NJ.

Ludmerer, Kenneth M. Genetics & American Society: A Historical Appraisal. LC 72-4227. 238p. reprint ed. pap. 67.90 (*0-8357-8143-7*, 2034153) Bks Demand.

— Learning to Heal: The Development of American Medical Education. 359p. 1995. reprint ed. pap. text ed. 16.95x (*0-8018-5258-7*) Johns Hopkins.

Ludomirsky, Achi & Huhta, James C., eds. Color Doppler of Congenital Heart Disease in the Child & Adult. (Illus.). 128p. 1987. 75.00 (*0-87993-295-3*); sl. 200.00 (*0-317-55990-7*); sl. 150.00 (*0-87993-301-1*) Futura Pub.

Ludovici, A. Nietzsche & Art. LC 72-148824. (Studies in German Literature: No. 13). 1971. reprint ed. lib. bdg. 75.00 (*0-8383-1229-2*) M S G Haskell Hse.

Ludovici, A. M. Creation or Recreation. 1973. 99.95 (*0-87968-957-9*) Gordon Pr.

— A Defence of Conservatism. 1972. 59.95 (*0-8490-0014-9*) Gordon Pr.

— Lysistrata: Woman's Future or Future Woman. 1973. 99.95 (*0-8490-0569-8*) Gordon Pr.

— The Secret of Laughter. 1972. 79.95 (*0-8490-1011-X*) Gordon Pr.

— Specious Origins of Liberalism. 1972. 59.95 (*0-8490-1106-X*) Gordon Pr.

— Who Is to Be Master of the World? an Introduction to the Philosophy of Friedrich Nietzsche. 1972. 99.95 (*0-8490-1295-3*) Gordon Pr.

Ludovici, A. M., tr. see Lichtenberger, Henri.

Ludovici, Anthony. The Sanctity of Private Property. 1977. lib. bdg. 59.95 (*0-8490-2566-4*) Gordon Pr.

Ludowyk, E. F. The Story of Ceylon. 1986. reprint ed. 28.50 (*81-7013-020-4*, Pub. by Navrang) S Asia.

Ludowyk, Evelyn F. Understanding Shakespeare. LC 62-6756. 284p. reprint ed. pap. 81.00 (*0-317-20599-4*, 2024489) Bks Demand.

Luds, Peter, jt. auth. see Apel, Max.

Ludtke, Alf. Police & State in Nineteenth-Century Prussia. Burgess, Pete, tr. (Illus.). 320p. (C). 1990. 69.95 (*0-521-30164-5*) Cambridge U Pr.

***Ludtke, Alf, ed.** The History of Everyday Life: Reconstructing Historical Experiences & Ways of Life. Templer, William, tr. LC 94-35512. 1995. 49.50 (*0-691-05693-5*); pap. 18.95 (*0-691-00892-2*) Princeton U Pr.

Ludtke, David A., jt. auth. see Kelley, Donald H.

Ludtke, Hartwig. The Bryggen Papers, Bryggen Pottery: Introduction & Pingsdorf Ware, No. 1. (Supplementary Ser.: No. 4). (Illus.). 128p. (Orig.). 1989. pap. 59.50x (*82-00-02796-1*, Pub. by Almqv & Wiksell SW) Coronet Bks.

Ludtke, Jean E. Atlantic Peeks: An Ethnographic Guide to the Portuguese-Speaking Islands. LC 87-70196. 1989. 24.95 (*0-8158-0441-5*) Chris Mass.

***Luduena, Richard F.** Learning Biochemistry: One Hundred Case Oriented Problems. LC 94-43218. 1995. pap. text ed. 24.95 (*0-471-01887-2*) Wiley.

Ludvigsen, Karl. Corvette: America's Star-Spangled Sports Car, Complete History. 3rd ed. LC 72-85847. (Illus.). 324p. 1978. 49.95 (*0-915038-06-4*, 3-AQ-0006) Auto Quarterly.

— Gurney's Eagles. (Illus.). 136p. 1992. 24.95 (*0-87938-651-7*) Motorbooks Intl.

Ludvigsen, Karl, ed. The Best of Corvette News. LC 76-20955. 656p. 1976. 39.95 (*0-915038-07-2*, 3-AQ-0011) Auto Quarterly.

— Porsche: Excellence Was Expected. LC 77-83507. 888p. 1977. 89.95 (*0-915038-09-9*, 3-AQ-0014) Auto Quarterly.

Ludvigsen, Karl & Frere, Paul. Opel: Wheels to the World. 2nd ed. LC 79-88372. (Illus.). 112p. 1979. 19.95 (*0-915038-16-1*, 3-AQ-0026) Auto Quarterly.

Ludvigson, Gary. Bedtime Teaching Tales for Kids: A Parent's Storybook. LC 88-27148. 224p. (Orig.). 1989. pap. 9.95 (*0-938179-18-7*) Mills Sanderson.

Ludvigson, Susan. The Beautiful Moon of No Shadow. Poems. LC 86-21073. 50p. 1987. text ed. 13.95 (*0-8071-1378-6*) La State U Pr.

— Everything Winged Must Be Dreaming. Poems. LC 93-10738. 64p. 1993. text ed. 15.95 (*0-8071-1836-2*); pap. 8.95 (*0-8071-1837-0*) La State U Pr.

— Northern Lights: Poems. fac. ed. LC 81-6039. 79p. 1981. reprint ed. pap. 25.00 (*0-7837-7805-8*, 2047561) Bks Demand.

— The Swimmer. Poems. LC 83-25593. 53p. 1984. 13.95 (*0-8071-1155-4*); pap. 6.95 (*0-8071-1172-4*) La State U Pr.

— To Find the Gold. LC 89-28159. 80p. 1990. text ed. 14.95 (*0-8071-1599-1*); pap. 7.95 (*0-8071-1600-9*) La State U Pr.

***Ludvik, Catherine.** Hanuman: In the Ramayana of Valmiki & the Ramacaritamanasa of Tulasi Dasa. (C). 1994. text ed. 14.00 (*81-208-1122-4*, Pub. by Motilal Banarsidass II) S Asia.

Ludvik, M. & Mohyla, O. Czechoslovakia-Prague Guide. (Illus.). 282p. (C). 1989. pap. 100.00 (*0-569-09232-9*, Pub. by Collets) St Mut.

Ludwich, A., ed. Scholia in Homeri Odysseae A 1-309. iv, 120p. 1966. reprint ed. write for info. (*0-318-71024-2*, Pub. by Georg Olms GW) Lubrecht & Cramer.

Ludwich, Arthur. Aristarchs Homerische Textkritik, 2 vols., Set. viii, 1409p. 1971. reprint ed. write for info. (*3-487-04082-4*, Pub. by Georg Olms GW) Lubrecht & Cramer.

Ludwickson, John, jt. auth. see O'Shea, John.

Ludwig, Allan I. Graven Images: New England Stonecarving & Its Symbols, 1650-1815. LC 66-14665. (Illus.). 514p. (Orig.). reprint ed. pap. 146.50 (*0-685-20342-5*, 2029783) Bks Demand.

Ludwig, Armin K., et al. Radial Freeways & the Growth of Office Space in Central Cities. 417p. (Orig.). 1977. pap. 25.00 (*1-55719-008-9*) U NE CPAR.

***Ludwig, Arnold M.** The Price of Greatness: Resolving the Creativity & Madness Controversy. 1995. lib. bdg. 26.95 (*0-89862-839-3*) Guilford Pubns.

— Principles of Clinical Psychiatry. 2nd ed. 672p. 1985. text ed. 60.00 (*0-02-919350-8*) Free Pr.

— Understanding the Alcoholic's Mind: The Nature of Craving & How to Control It. (Illus.). 240p. 1987. reprint ed. 21.95 (*0-19-504878-4*) OUP.

— Understanding the Alcoholic's Mind: The Nature of Craving & How to Control It. (Illus.). 240p. 1989. reprint ed. pap. 10.95 (*0-19-505918-2*) OUP.

***Ludwig, Art.** Create an Oasis with Greywater: Your Complete Guide to Managing Greywater in the Landscape. 2nd expanded rev. ed. 49p. 1994. pap. 7.00 (*0-9643433-0-4*) Oasis Biocomp.

— Living with Nature: Integrating Human Culture, Technology, & Economics with Nature. 49p. 1990. pap. 5.00 (*0-9643433-1-2*) Oasis Biocomp.

Ludwig, Arwin K., et al. The Impact of Rural Nebraska Industrial Development on the Migration of Rural Youth. 150p. (Orig.). 1978. pap. 9.00 (*1-55719-007-0*) U NE CPAR.

Ludwig, Charles. At Pentecost. 1992. pap. 6.95 (*0-87162-603-9*, D8151) Warner Pr.

— At the Cross. 1990. pap. 5.95 (*0-87162-596-2*, D1379) Warner Pr.

— At the Tomb. 1990. per. 6.95 (*0-87162-514-8*, D8150) Warner Pr.

— Defender of the Faith. LC 88-22116. 240p. (Orig.). (C). 1988. pap. 7.99 (*0-87123-999-X*) Bethany Hse.

— A Foot in Two Cultures. 1992. 7.95 (*0-87162-620-9*, D8152) Warner Pr.

— George Frideric Handel: Composer of The Messiah. (Sower Ser.). (Illus.). (J). (gr. 3-6). 1987. pap. 6.95 (*0-88062-048-X*) Mott Media.

— Jason Lee. (Sower Ser.). (J). (gr. 3-6). 1992. pap. 6.95 (*0-88062-161-3*) Mott Media.

An Asterisk (*) at the beginning of an entry indicates that the title is appearing in BIP for the first time.

— Ludwig's Handbook of New Testament Cities & Rulers. LC 83-71619. 244p. (Orig.). 1983. pap. 6.95 (*0-89636-111-X*) Accent CO.
— Ludwig's Handbook of Old Testament Rulers & Cities. LC 84-70426. 244p. (Orig.). 1990. pap. 6.95 (*0-89636-130-6*) Accent CO.
— Michael Faraday, Father of Electronics. 1988. ring bd. 7.95 (*0-8361-3479-6*) Herald Pr.
— Mother of An Army. LC 86-33439. 240p. (Orig.). 1987. pap. 7.99 (*0-87123-924-8*) Bethany Hse.
— Queen of the Reformation. LC 86-11754. 224p. 1986. pap. 7.99 (*0-87123-652-4*) Bethany Hse.
— Spinning Shoes. 1989. pap. 6.96 (*0-87162-582-2*, D7225) Warner Pr.
— Stonewall Jackson: Loved in the South Admired in the North. (Sower Ser.). (Illus.). (J). (gr. 3-6). 1989. pap. 6.95 (*0-88062-157-5*) Mott Media.
— Susanna Wesley. LC 84-60314. (Sower Ser.). 195p. (J). (gr. 3-6). 1984. pap. 6.95 (*0-88062-110-9*) Mott Media.
— The Wright Brothers: They Gave Us Wings. (Sower Ser.). (Illus.). (J). (gr. 3-6). 1985. write for info. (*0-88062-142-7*); pap. 6.95 (*0-88062-141-9*) Mott Media.

Ludwig, Cleo R. I Am What I Am ... & Here's Why! (Illus.). 216p. 1986. write for info. (*0-318-60702-6*) Vimach Assocs.

Ludwig, Coy. Maxfield Parrish. (Illus.). 14.98 (*0-517-15265-7*) Random Hse Value.
— Maxfield Parrish. LC 73-5691. (Illus.). 220p. reprint ed. 39.95 (*0-88740-527-4*) Schiffer.

Ludwig, D. Stochastic Population Theories. (Lecture Notes in Biomathematics Ser.: Vol. 3). 1978. reprint ed. pap. 22.00 (*0-387-07010-9*) Spr-Verlag.

Ludwig, D. & Cooke, K. L., eds. Epidemiology. LC 75-22944. (SIAM-SIMS Conference Ser.: No. 2). xi, 164p. 1975. pap. text ed. 28.00 (*0-89871-031-6*) Soc Indus-Appl Math.

Ludwig, Dale. Blood Secrets. 304p. 1993. mass mkt. 4.50 (*1-55817-695-0*, Pinnacle NY) Windsor NY.

Ludwig, David J. Renewing the Family Spirit. 1989. 7.99 (*0-570-04527-4*) Concordia.

Ludwig, Dean C., ed. Business & Society in a Changing World Order. LC 93-18882. 312p. 1993. text ed. 99.95 (*0-7734-9267-4*) E Mellen.

Ludwig, Dean C. & Paul, Karen, eds. Contemporary Issues in the Business Environment. LC 92-16202. 264p. 1992. lib. bdg. 89.95 (*0-7734-9543-6*) E Mellen.

Ludwig, Delton, ed. see Goff, Bruce.

Ludwig, Dorene. But It Was Just a Joke ... ! Theater Scenes & Monologues for Eliminating Sexual Harassment: A Performance Manual & Workshop Guide. 170p. 1991. student ed 17.50 (*0-89215-170-6*) U Cal LA Indus Rel.

Ludwig, Emil. Cleopatra - Story of a Queen. (African Studies). 221p. reprint ed. 25.00 (*0-938818-92-9*) ECA Assoc.
— Defender of Democracy: Masaryk of Czechoslovakia. LC 70-135814. (Eastern Europe Collection Ser.). 1971. reprint ed. 20.95 (*0-405-02756-7*) Ayer.
— The Germans: Double History of a Nation. LC 78-63688. (Studies in Fascism: Ideology & Practice). (Illus.). 560p. reprint ed. 45.00 (*0-404-16951-1*) AMS Pr.
— Nine Etched from Life. LC 70-90658. (Essay Index Reprint Ser.). 1977. 26.95 (*0-8369-1225-X*) Ayer.
— Of Life & Love. LC 72-128273. (Essay Index Reprint Ser.). 1977. 20.95 (*0-8369-1984-X*) Ayer.
— Three Portraits: Hitler, Mussolini, Stalin. LC 78-63689. (Studies in Fascism: Ideology & Practice). 128p. reprint ed. 19.50 (*0-404-16905-8*) AMS Pr.
— Wilhelm Hohenzollern: The Last of the Kaisers. LC 74-100815. (Illus.). reprint ed. 31.25 (*0-404-04067-5*) AMS Pr.

Ludwig, Ernest. Applied Process Design for Chemical & Petrochemical Plants, 3 vols., Vol. 2: 1979. 2nd ed. LC 76-40867. 308p. Vol. 2. 1979, 2nd Ed., 308p. 49.00 (*0-87201-753-2*) Gulf Pub.
— Applied Process Design for Chemical & Petrochemical Plants, 3 vols., Vol. 3: 1983. 2nd ed. LC 76-40867. 506p. Vol. 3. 1983, 2nd., 506p. 75.00 (*0-87201-754-0*) Gulf Pub.
— Applied Process Design for Chemicals & Petrochemical Plants, Vol. 1. 3rd ed. 480p. 1994. 150.00 (*0-88415-025-9*) Gulf Pub.
— The Visit of Teshoo Lama to Peking. LC 78-70096. reprint ed. 18.50 (*0-404-17345-4*) AMS Pr.

***Ludwig, Ernest E.** Applied Process Design for Chemical & Petrochemical Plants Vol. 1. 2nd ed. LC 76-40867. (Illus.). 379p. 1977. pap. 108.10 (*0-7837-8352-3*, 2049142) Bks Demand.
— Applied Project Engineering & Management for the Process Industries. 2nd ed. 582p. 1988. 49.95 (*0-87201-045-7*) Gulf Pub.
— Applied Project Management for the Process Industries. LC 72-93694. (Illus.). 381p. reprint ed. pap. 108.60 (*0-8357-5687-4*, 2051872) Bks Demand.

Ludwig, Frank, jt. ed. see McHardy, John.

Ludwig, Frederic C., ed. Life Span Extension: Consequences & Open Questions. 176p. 1991. 34.95 (*0-8261-7450-7*) Springer Pub.

Ludwig, Fredrich. Repertorium Organorum Recentioris et Motetorum Vetustissimi Stili, Band I, 2: Handschriften in Mensuralnotation. (Wissenschaftliche Abhandlungen-Musicological Studies: Vol. 26). 350p. (GER.). 1979. lib. bdg. 134.00 (*0-912024-37-2*) Inst Mediaeval Mus.

Ludwig, Friedrich. Repertorium Organorum Recentioris et Motetorum Vetustissimi Stili, Katalog. Dittmer, Luther, ed. (Wissenschaftliche Abhandlungen-Musicological Studies: Vol. 17). 128p. (GER.). 1971. lib. bdg. 54.00 (*0-912024-87-9*) Inst Mediaeval Mus.

Ludwig, G. An Axiomatic Basis for Quantum Mechanics, Vol. 1. (Illus.). 240p. 1985. 89.00 (*0-387-13773-4*) Spr-Verlag.
— Foundations of Quantum Mechanics I. (Texts & Monographs in Physics). (Illus.). 426p. 1983. 94.00 (*0-387-11683-4*) Spr-Verlag.
— Foundations of Quantum Mechanics II. Hein, C., tr. (Texts & Monographs in Physics). (Illus.). 430p. 1985. 147.00 (*0-387-13009-8*) Spr-Verlag.
— Wave Mechanics. 1968. 99.00 (*0-08-012302-3*, Pub. by Pergamon Repr UK) Franklin.

Ludwig, G., jt. ed. see Weidner, W.

Ludwig, Garth. How to Study & Understand the Bible. (Orig.). 1991. pap. 5.99 (*0-570-09747-9*) Concordia.

***Ludwig, Gerd & Steimer, Christine.** The Bernese & Other Mountain Dogs: Bernese, Greater Swiss, Appenzellers, & Entlebuchers: Everything about Purchase, Care, Nutrition, Breeding, Behavior, & Training. Crawford, Elizabeth D., tr. LC 94-49012. (Complete Pet Owner's Manual Ser.). (Illus.). 1995. write for info. (*0-8120-9135-3*) Barron.

Ludwig, Glenn E. Walking to, Walking with, Walking Through: Sermons for Lent, Holy Week, & Easter - Gospel. LC 93-51081. (Orig.). 1994. pap. write for info. (*0-7880-0005-5*) CSS OH.

Ludwig, Glenn E. & Smothers, Rodney T. Homiletic Meditations, Vol. 2: Lent Through Ascension of Our Lord, First Reading & Gospel, Cycle C. LC 94-207. (Orig.). 1994. pap. write for info. (*0-7880-0055-1*) CSS OH.

Ludwig, Hans E., ed. Mycoses of the Female Genitals: Current Diagnostics & Therapy. 1989. pap. text ed. 49.95 (*0-471-56510-5*) Wiley.

Ludwig, Hans E., jt. ed. see Steffen, C.

Ludwig, Herbert. Computer Applications & Techniques in Clinical Medicine. LC 73-20100. (Wiley Biomedical-Health Publication Ser.). 330p. reprint ed. pap. 94.10 (*0-317-09245-6*, 2007144) Bks Demand.

Ludwig, Herbert R., jt. auth. see Leitch, Jay A.

Ludwig, Irene, comp. Directory of Camps for Blind & Visually Impaired Children, Youths, & Adults. 34p. 1989. 15.95 (*0-89128-159-2*) Am Foun Blind.

Ludwig, Irene, et al. Creative Recreation for Blind & Visually Impaired Adults. large type ed. LC 88-3471. 56p. (Orig.). 1988. pap. text ed. 15.95 (*0-89128-154-1*) Am Foun Blind.

Ludwig, J. Liver Biopsy Diagnoses & Reports. (Illus.). x, 158p. 1984. 46.50 (*3-8055-3841-3*) S Karger.

Ludwig, James, jt. auth. see Huberman, Jeffrey.

Ludwig, Jean, jt. auth. see Leptin, Horst.

Ludwig, John A. & Reynolds, James F. Statistical Ecology: A Primer on Methods & Computing. LC 87-26348. 352p. 1988. text ed. 64.95 (*0-471-83235-9*) Wiley.

Ludwig, Jurgen. Liver Biopsy Interpretation: A Manual of Diagnostic Tables. 248p. 1992. 75.00 (*0-89189-347-4*) Am Soc Clinical.

Ludwig, Jurgen & Ishak, Kamal G., eds. Diseases of the Liver & Bile Ducts: Proceedings of the Fifty Fourth Annual Anatomic Pathology Slide Seminar of the ASCP. LC 89-17874. 133p. 1989. 35.00 (*0-89189-294-X*, D50-1-055-00) Am Soc Clinical.

Ludwig, K. S. & Hartels, H., eds. Progress in Comparative Placentology. (Illus.). 1973. 32.00 (*3-8055-1365-8*) S Karger.

***Ludwig, Knoll.** Lexikon der Praktischen Psychologie. 488p. (GER.). 1993. 29.95 (*0-7859-8543-3*, 3893501657) Fr & Eur.

Ludwig, Lyndell. The Little White Dragon. (Illus.). 23p. (YA). (gr. 5 up). 1989. pap. 4.95 (*0-9621782-0-9*) Star Dust Bks.

Ludwig, Mark. Computer Viruses, Artificial Life & Evolution. 384p. 1993. pap. 22.95 (*0-929408-07-1*) Amer Eagle Pubns Inc.

—The Giant Black Book of Computer Viruses. (Illus.). 400p. 1995. pap. 39.95 (*0-929408-10-1*) Amer Eagle Pubns Inc. This definitive work on computer viruses discusses the techniques modern viruses use to propagate, evade anti-virus software, cause damage, & compromise system security. Unlike most works on the subject, THE GIANT BLACK BOOK doesn't stop short of giving the reader what he needs to fully understand the subject. It is a technical work which contains complete, fully-functional commented code and explanations of more than 200 computer viruses & 3 anti-virus programs, alone with detailed discussions of stealth technology, polymorphism, evolutionary viruses & good viruses. The book discusseS viruses for DOS, Windows, OS/2, Unix systems, & more. Also see related listings: Mark Ludwig, COMPUTER VIRUSES, ARTIFICIAL LIFE & EVOLUTION (ISBN 0-929408-07-1), an in depth discussion of whether computer viruses are alive, & the implications of evolutionary reproduction in the world of viruses. Mark Ludwig, THE MILITARY USE OF COMPUTER VIRUSES (ISBN 0-929408-11-X). George Smith, THE VIRUS CREATION LABS (ISBN 0-929408-09-8) a popular inside account of the computer virus subculture. Call American Eagle Publications at (800) 719-4957 for a catalog of books & software related to computer viruses, computer security & cryptography, or write P.O. Box 1507, Show Low, AZ 85901. ***Publisher Provided Annotation.***

— The Little Black Book of Computer Viruses: Technical Aspects. 192p. (Orig.). 1991. pap. 14.95 (*0-929408-02-0*) Amer Eagle Pubns Inc.
— The Military Use of Computer Viruses. 250p. 1996. pap. 22.95 (*0-929408-11-X*) Amer Eagle Pubns Inc.

Ludwig, Mary S. Understanding Interest Rate Swaps. LC 92-39058. 1993. text ed. 42.95 (*0-07-039020-7*) McGraw.
— Your Dream Vacation Home. 224p. 1991. pap. 14.95 (*0-8306-8687-8*, 3687, Liberty Hall Pr) TAB Bks.

Ludwig, Myles. Hawaii Style: Living in Hawaii. (Illus.). 160p. 1994. 35.00 (*0-685-66713-8*) Inter-Pac Media.
— Kauai in the Eye of Iniki. (Illus.). 72p. (Orig.). 1992. 25.00 (*1-882709-00-4*); pap. 17.95 (*1-882709-01-2*) Inter-Pac Media.

Ludwig, Nohl. Life of Haydn. 195p. 1990. reprint ed. lib. bdg. 59.00 (*0-685-35205-6*, 10,068) Rprt Serv.

Ludwig, Otto, jt. ed. see Gunther, Hartmut.

Ludwig, Patsy, jt. auth. see Flores, Norma P.

Ludwig, R. A., jt. ed. see Taylor, Roy L.

Ludwig, R. G. & Almeida, S. A., eds. Marine Disposal of Wastewater: Proceedings of An IAWPRC Specialised Seminar Held at Rio de Janeiro, Brazil, 25-27 August 1986. LC 82-645900. (Water Science & Technology Ser.: No. 18). (Illus.). 240p. 1987. pap. 52.00 (*0-08-035581-1*, Pergamon Pr) Elsevier.

Ludwig, Raymond H. Illustrated Handbook of Electronic Tables, Symbols, Measurements & Values. 2nd ed. LC 83-17620. 415p. 1986. 34.95 (*0-13-450494-1*, Busn); 22.95 (*0-685-07964-3*, Busn) P-H.

Ludwig, Richard, ed. see McGuire, Bill & Wheeler, Leslie.

Ludwig, Richard M., ed. Dr. Panofsky & Mr. Tarkington: An Exchange of Letters, 1938-1946. LC 74-10252. (Illus.). 151p. 1974. 25.00 (*0-87811-019-4*) Princeton Lib.

Ludwig, Richard M. & Nault, Clifford A., Jr., eds. Annals of American Literature, 1602-1983. (Oxford Paperback Reference Ser.). (Illus.). 352p. 1989. pap. 14.95 (*0-19-505919-0*) OUP.

Ludwig, Richard M., jt. auth. see Jones, H. Mumford.

Ludwig, Richard M., jt. auth. see Jones, Howard M.

***Ludwig, Robert.** Reconstructing Catholicism for a New Generation. 192p. (Orig.). 1995. pap. 15.95 (*0-8245-1462-9*) Crossroad NY.

Ludwig, Robert A., jt. ed. see Carlson, Jeffrey.

Ludwig, Rosemarie. Thoughts in Solitude: A Guide to Your Inner Journey. 120p. (Orig.). 1993. pap. 17.95 (*1-879046-01-6*) Jacaranda AZ.

Ludwig, Stephen, ed. Pediatric Emergencies. (Clinics in Emergency Medicine Ser.: Vol. 7). (Illus.). 266p. 1985. text ed. 39.00 (*0-443-08303-7*) Churchill.

Ludwig, Stephen & Kornberg, Allan E., eds. Child Abuse: A Medical Reference. 2nd ed. (Illus.). 563p. 1992. text ed. 64.95 (*0-443-08722-9*) Churchill.

Ludwig, Stephen, jt. ed. see Fleisher, Gary R.

Ludwig, Susan & Steinberg, Janice. Petite Style: The Ultimate Fashion Guide for Women 5'4" & Under. 194p. 1989. pap. 20.00 (*0-452-26262-3*, Plume) NAL-Dutton.

Ludwig, Theodore. The Sacred Paths: Understanding the Religions of the World. 2nd ed. (Illus.). 560p. (C). 1995. text ed. write for info. (*0-02-372175-8*) Macmillan.

Ludwig, Theodore M. The Sacred Paths: Understanding the Religions of the World. 576p. (C). 1989. text ed. write for info. (*0-02-372170-7*) Macmillan.
— The Sacred Paths of the East. (Illus.). 320p. (Orig.). (C). 1992. pap. write for info. (*0-02-372163-4*) Macmillan.
— The Sacred Paths of the West. LC 93-5914. (Illus.). 272p. (Orig.). (C). 1994. pap. write for info. (*0-02-372181-2*, Maxwell Macmillan) Macmillan.

***Ludwig, Timothy.** The Flower & the Caterpillar: A Program about Accepting Differences for Students in Grades One Through Four. 16p. (J). (gr. 1-4). 1991. 4.95 (*1-884063-22-5*) Mar Co Prods.

***Ludwig, Timothy G.** The Name-Game: A Program About Inappropriate Behavior for Students in Grades One Through Four. 32p. (J). (gr. 1-4). 1991. 6.95 (*1-884063-21-7*) Mar Co Prods.
— Terry's Temper: A Program about Anger for Students in Grades One Through Four. 316p. (J). (gr. 1-4). 1991. 4.95 (*1-988406-32-3*) Mar Co Prods.

Ludwig, W. D. Recent Developments in Lattice Theory. (Tracts in Modern Physics Ser.: Vol. 43). (Illus.). 1967. 79.00 (*0-387-03982-1*) Spr-Verlag.

Ludwig, W. D. & Falter, C. Symmetries in Physics. (Solid-State Sciences Ser.: Vol. 64). (Illus.). 470p. 1988. 66.00 (*0-387-18021-4*) Spr-Verlag.

Ludwig, W. D. & Thiel, E., eds. Recent Advances in Cell Biology of Acute Leukemia: Impact on Clinical Diagnosis & Therapy. LC 93-16157. (Recent Results in Cancer Research Ser.: Vol. 131). 1993. 150.00 (*0-387-56417-9*) Spr-Verlag.

Ludwig, Warren. Old Noah's Elephants. LC 90-35379. (Whitebird Bks.). (Illus.). 32p. (J). (ps-3). 1991. 14.95 (*0-399-22256-1*, Putnam) Putnam Pub Group.

Ludwig, William B. & Roach, Lee S. Studies on the Animal Ecology of the Hocking River Basin: The Bottom Invertebrates of the Hocking River & the Plankton of the Hocking River. (Bulletin Ser.: No. 26). 1932. 2.00 (*0-86727-025-X*) Ohio Bio Survey.

Ludwigson, John, ed. Hazardous Materials Spills Conference, 1986. LC 86-80397. 565p. 1986. pap. text ed. 74.00 (*0-86587-131-0*) Gov Insts.

Ludwigson, Susan. Ludwigson: Selected Poems. 160p. (Orig.). Date not set. pap. 13.95 (*0-7145-4187-7*) Riverrun NY.

Ludwikowski, Rett R. Continuity & Change in Poland: Conservatism in Polish Political Thought. LC 90-25001. 313p. 1991. text ed. 39.95 (*0-8132-0743-6*) Cath U Pr.

Ludwikowski, Rett R. & Fox, William F. The Beginning of the Constitutional Era. LC 92-34679. 331p. 1993. 49.95 (*0-8132-0776-2*) Cath U Pr.

Ludwikowski, Rett R., jt. ed. see Thompson, Kenneth W.

Ludwin, William G., jt. ed. see Worthley, John A.

Ludy, Andrew. Condominium Ownership: A Buyer's Guide. LC 83-102592. (Illus.). 128p. (Orig.). 1982. pap. 7.95 (*0-943912-00-8*) Landing Pr.
— Diet Diary: The Culinary Companion for a New You! (Illus.). 193p. (Orig.). 1984. pap. 4.95 (*0-943912-01-6*) Landing Pr.

Ludy, Claude E. The End of the Age: A Commentary on the Revelation. LC 89-92157. (Illus.). 125p. (Orig.). (YA). 1989. pap. 7.00 (*0-9625164-1-4*) C E Ludy.
— The Vile & the Holy: A Commentary on the Book of Daniel. LC 77-94874. (Illus.). 100p. (Orig.). (YA). 1978. pap. 5.00 (*0-9625164-0-6*) C E Ludy.

Ludyk, Gunter. Stability of Time-Variant Discrete-Time Systems. (Advances in Control Systems & Signal Processing Ser.: Vol. 5). (Illus.). x, 148p. 1985. pap. 34.00 (*3-528-08911-3*, Pub. by Vieweg & Sohn GW) Ballen Bkslr.

Ludz, Peter C. The German Democratic Republic from the Sixties to the Seventies: A Socio-Political Analysis. (Harvard University. Center for International Affairs. Occasional Papers in International Affairs: No. 26). reprint ed. 11.50 (*0-404-54626-9*) AMS Pr.

Lue-Hing, Cecil, et al, eds. Municipal Sewage Sludge Management, Vol. 4: Processing, Utilization & Disposal. LC 92-53520. (Water Quality Management Library). 830p. 1992. text ed. 95.00 (*0-87762-930-7*) Technomic.

Luebbe, Herrmann, ed. Wozu Philosophie? Stellungnahmen eines Arbeitskreises. (C). 1978. 29.25 (*3-11-007513-X*) De Gruyter.

***Luebbe, Weyma, ed.** Kausalitaet und Zurechnung: Ueber Verantwortung in Komplexen Kulturellen Prozessen. (Philosophie und Wissenschaft Ser.: Bd. 5). 320p. (GER.). (C). 1994. pap. text ed. 44.65 (*3-11-014398-4*) De Gruyter.

***Luebben, Craig.** Crack Climbing. (How to Rock Climb Ser.). (Illus.). 48p. 1995. pap. 5.95 (*0-934641-69-2*) Chockstone Pr.

***Luebben, Craig & Ferguson, Duncan.** Ice Climbing. (Illus.). 160p. 1995. pap. 11.95 (*0-934641-90-0*) Chockstone Pr.

Luebben, Tom. Historical Background of the Santa Ana Pueblo. (Treaty Manuscripts Ser.: No. 13). 25p. 8.50 (*0-944253-35-0*) Inst Dev Indian Law.

Luebberman, Mimi, jt. ed. see Bennett, Julienne.

Luebberman, Mimi, jt. auth. see Brennan, Georgeanne.

Luebbermann, Mimi. Climbing Vines: Simple Secrets for Glorious Gardens, Indoors & Out. LC 94-13127. 1995. 12.95 (*0-8118-0723-1*) Chronicle Bks.
— Coping with Miscarriage: A Simple, Reassuring Guide to Emotional & Physical Healing. 1994. pap. 9.95 (*1-55958-503-X*) Prima Pub.
— Pay Dirt: How to Raise & Sell Specialty Herbs & Vegetables for Serious Cash. LC 92-39923. 275p. (Orig.). 1993. pap. 12.95 (*1-55958-287-1*) Prima Pub.
— Terrific Tomatoes: Simple Secrets for Glorious Gardens, Indoors & Out. LC 93-6088. (Illus.). 96p. 1994. pap. 12.95 (*0-8118-0551-4*) Chronicle Bks.

Luebbermann, Mimi, jt. auth. see Brennan, Georgeanne.

Luebbers, David J. Bicycle Bibliography Nineteen Fifty to Nineteen Seventy-Two, Pt. 1. (Bicycle Bibliographies Ser.: No. 5). (Illus.). 96p. 1977. pap. 5.00 (*0-9607406-5-1*) D Luebbers.
— Bicycle Bibliography Nineteen Seventy-Six. (Bicycle Bibliographies Ser.: No. 4). (Illus.). 106p. 1977. pap. 5.00 (*0-9607406-4-3*) D Luebbers.
— Bicycle Resource Guide 1981. (Bicycle Bibliographies Ser.: No. 8). (Illus.). 136p. (Orig.). 1981. pap. 5.00 (*0-9607406-0-0*) D Luebbers.

Luebbers, Raymond J., jt. auth. see Kunz, Karl S.

Luebbert, Gregory M. Comparative Democracy: Policymaking & Governing Coalitions in Europe & Israel. 352p. 1986. text ed. 42.00 (*0-231-06298-2*) Col U Pr.
— Liberalism, Fascism, or Social Democracy: Social Classes & the Political Origins of Regimes in Interwar Europe. 432p. 1991. 49.95 (*0-19-506610-3*); pap. 22.00 (*0-19-506611-1*) OUP.

Luebbert, Peggy P. Laboratory Safety & Infection Control. (NLM Ser.: No. WA485). 1990. vhs 125.00 (*0-89189-303-2*) Am Soc Clinical.
— OSHA's Bloodborne Pathogens Standard: Compliance in Clinical Laboratory. 1992. vhs 135.00 (*0-89189-349-0*) Am Soc Clinical.

Luebbig, H., jt. ed. see Hahlbohm, H. D.

Luebering, Carol. The Forgiving Family: First Steps to Reconciliation. 84p. (Orig.). 1983. pap. text ed. 3.95 (*0-86716-027-6*) St Anthony Mess Pr.
— Ministers of the Lord's Presence: Reflection & Prayer for Liturgical Ministers. 58p. 1990. Eucharistic Ministers Ed. 2.95 (*0-86716-105-1*) St Anthony Mess Pr.
— Ministers of the Lord's Presence: Reflections & Prayer for Liturgical Ministers. 48p. 1990. Lectors Ed. 2.95 (*0-86716-905-2*) St Anthony Mess Pr.
— Ministers of the Lord's Presence: Reflections & Prayer for Liturgical Ministers, Ushers' - Greeters' Edition. 46p. 1990. 2.95 (*0-86716-605-3*) St Anthony Mess Pr.
— Open Your Hearts: Prayer Exercises for Engaged & Newly Married Couples. 56p. 1992. 3.50 (*0-86716-162-0*) St Anthony Mess Pr.
— What Do You Ask for Your Child? 64p. (Orig.). 1980. pap. 1.95 (*0-912228-64-4*) St Anthony Mess Pr.

— Your Child's Confirmation: Reflections for Parents on the Sacrament of Christian Identity. 1987. pap. 1.95 (0-86716-076-4) St Anthony Mess Pr.
— Your Child's First Communion: A Look at Your Dreams. 32p. (Orig.). 1984. pap. 1.95 (0-86716-035-7) St Anthony Mess Pr.
*Luebke, Barbara & Reilly, Mary E. Women's Studies Graduates: The First Generation. (Athene Ser.). 240p. (C). 1994. text ed. 44.00x (0-8077-6275-X); pap. text ed. 21.95x (0-8077-6274-1) Tchrs Coll.
Luebke, Frederick C. Germans in Brazil: A Comparative History of Cultural Conflict During World War I. LC 86-27371. (Illus.). 272p. 1987. text ed. 37.50 (0-8071-1347-6) La State U Pr.
— Germans in the New World: Essays in the History of Immigration. (Statue of Liberty-Ellis Island Centennial Ser.). 224p. 1990. 24.95 (0-252-01680-7) U of Ill Pr.
— A Harmony of the Arts: The Nebraska State Capitol. (C). 1990. pap. 19.95 (0-8032-7931-0, Bison Books) U of Nebr Pr.
— Immigrants & Politics: The Germans of Nebraska, 1880-1900. LC 69-15924. (Illus.). 234p. reprint ed. pap. 66.70 (0-7837-6018-3, 2045830) Bks Demand.
— Nebraska: An Illustrated History. (Illus.). 384p. 1995. 35.00 (0-8032-2902-X) U of Nebr Pr.
Luebke, Frederick C., ed. Ethnic Voters & the Election of Lincoln. LC 72-139370. 260p. reprint ed. pap. 74.10 (0-7837-6017-5, 2045829) Bks Demand.
— Ethnicity on the Great Plains. LC 79-17743. (Illus.). xxxiv, 237p. 1980. 25.00 (0-8032-2855-4) U of Nebr Pr.
— A Harmony of the Arts: The Nebraska State Capitol. LC 89-4773. (Great Plains Photography Ser.). (Illus.). x, 122p. 1990. 40.00 (0-8032-2887-2) U of Nebr Pr.
Luebke, Frederick C., jt. ed. see Blouet, Brian W.
Luebke, Frederick C., jt. ed. see Faulkner, Virginia.
Luebke-Hill, Barbara, ed. Painting Animals Step by Step. (Illus.). 144p. 1993. 27.95 (0-89134-459-4, 30462) North Light Bks.
Luebke, Paul. Tar Heel Politics: Myths & Realities. LC 89-14677. xiv, 238p. (C). 1990. pap. 12.95 (0-8078-4271-0) U of NC Pr.
Luebke, William R. Astronomy: A Student Study Guide. 196p. (C). 1993. pap. text ed., spiral bd. 19.95 (0-8403-9126-9) Kendall-Hunt.
Luebking, Sandra, jt. auth. see Szucs, Loretto.
Lueck, E. Antimicrobial Food Additives: Characteristics, Uses, Effects. (Illus.). 280p. 1980. 62.00 (0-387-10056-3) Spr-Verlag.
Luecke. The Phone Book. 1992. pap. 16.95 (0-7906-1028-0, Prompt Pubns) H W Sams.
Luecke, Barbara. Feeding the Frontier Army, 1775-1865. (Illus.). 120p. 1989. 9.95 (0-9621020-1-6) Grenadier Pubns.
Luecke, Barbara K. & Luecke, John C. The Snellings: Minnesota's First First Family. (Illus.). 250p. (Orig.). 1992. pap. 15.00 (0-9621020-3-2) Grenadier Pubns.
Luecke, David. Evangelical Style Lutheran Substance. (Orig.). 1988. pap. 8.95 (0-570-04496-0, 12-3109) Concordia.
Luecke, David S. New Designs for Church Leadership. 176p. (Orig.). 1990. pap. 11.95 (0-570-04544-4, 12-3148) Concordia.
Luecke, Editha L. Factors Related to Children's Participation in Certain Types of Home Activities. LC 70-177013. (Columbia University. Teachers College. Contributions to Education Ser.: No. 839). reprint ed. 22.50 (0-404-55839-9) AMS Pr.
Luecke, Gerald, ed. see Fulton, Stanley R. & Rawlins, John C.
Luecke, Gerald, ed. see West, Gordon & Maia, Fred.
Luecke, Gerald, ed. see West, Gordon.
Luecke, John. Dreams, Disaster, Demise: The Milwaukee Road in Minnesota. (Illus.). 230p. (C). 1988. 39.95 (0-9621020-0-8) Grenadier Pubns.
— The Great Northern in Minnesota: The Foundations of an Empire. (Illus.). 300p. 1995. 49.95 (0-9621020-4-0) Grenadier Pubns.
Luecke, John C. The Chicago Northwestern in Minnesota. (Illus.). 250p. (C). 1990. 39.95 (0-9621020-2-4) Grenadier Pubns.
Luecke, John C., jt. auth. see Luecke, Barbara K.
Luecke, Richard, ed. A New Dawn in Guatemala: Toward a Worldwide Health Vision. (Illus.). 264p. (Orig.). (C). 1993. pap. text ed. 11.95 (0-88133-734-X) Waveland Pr.
*Luecke, Richard A. Scuttle Your Ships Before Advancing: And Other Lessons from History on Leadership & Change for Today's Managers. (Illus.). 224p. 1995. pap. 10.95 (0-19-509642-8) OUP.
— Scuttle Your Ships Before Advancing: Lessons from History on Leadership & Change for Today's Managers. (Illus.). 240p. 1993. 19.95 (0-19-508408-X) OUP.
Lueckenotte. Pocket Guide to Gerontologic Assessment. (Illus.). 304p. 1990. spiral bd. 19.95 (0-8016-3332-X) Mosby Yr Bk.
— Pocket Guide to Gerontologic Assessment, No. 2. 310p. 1994. write for info. (0-08-151778-5); spiral bd. 18.95 (0-8016-7785-8) Mosby Yr Bk.
— Textbook of Gerontologic Nursing. 864p. 1995. pap. 42.95 (0-8016-7414-X) Mosby Yr Bk.
Luecking, Evelyn M., jt. auth. see Sumption, Merle R.
Luecking, Robert. Foliicolous Lichens: A Contribution to the Knowledge of the Lichen Flora of the Costa Rica (C. A.) (Nova Hedwigia Beiheft Ser.: No. 104). (Illus.). 180p. 1992. pap. 112.20 (3-443-51026-4, Pub. by Cramer-Borntraeger GW) Lubrecht & Cramer.
Luedde, Marie-Elisabeth. Die Rezeption, Interretation & Transformation Biblischer Motiv & Mythen in der DDR-Literatur & Ihre Bedeutung fuer die Theologie. (Arbeiten zur Praktischen Theologie Ser.: Bd 4). vi, 178p. (GER.). (C). 1993. lib. bdg. 90.80 (3-11-013773-9) De Gruyter.
Luedeking, Leila & Edmonds, Michael. Leonard Woolf: A Bibliography. (Illus.). 310p. 1992. 78.00 (0-938768-41-7) Oak Knoll.
Lueder, Dianne & Webb, Sally. Administrator's Guide to Library Building Maintenance. LC 92-5566. 290p. (C). 1992. pap. text ed. 45.00 (0-8389-3409-9) ALA.
Lueder, Rani, ed. The Ergonomics Payoff: Designing the Electronic Office. (Illus.). 388p. 1986. 28.50 (0-9629901-0-8) Humanics ErgoSysts.
Lueders, Edward. Carl Van Vechten. (Twayne's United States Authors Ser.). 1964. pap. 13.95x (0-8084-0070-3, T74) NCUP.
Lueders, Edward, ed. Writing Natural History: Dialogues with Authors. LC 89-4764. (Illus.). 144p. 1989. 11.95 (0-87480-323-3) U of Utah Pr.
*Lueders, Edward & Koriyama, Naoshi, trs. Like Underground Water: Modern Japanese Poetry. 350p. (Orig.). 1995. 30.00 (1-55659-102-0) Copper Canyon.
— Like Underground Water: Modern Japanese Poetry. 350p. (Orig.). 1995. pap. 15.00 (1-55659-103-9) Copper Canyon.
Lueders, Edward G. The Wake of the General Bliss. LC 88-20687. 196p. reprint ed. pap. 55.90 (0-7837-5533-3, 2045306) Bks Demand.
Lueders, V., jt. ed. see Moeller, P.
*Luedke, John, et al, contribs. Remains to Be Seen. (Illus.). 72p. 1983. pap. 18.95 (0-932718-15-9) Kohler Arts.
Luedtke, Barbara E. An Archaeologist's Guide to Chert & Flint. LC 92-46805. (Archaeological Research Tools Ser.: No. 7). (Illus.). 176p. (C). 1992. 18.75 (0-917956-75-3) UCLA Arch.
Luedtke, Gerhard, ed. Kuerschners Deutscher Literatur-kalender Nekrolog 1901-1935. 976p. (C). 1973. reprint ed. 119.25 (3-11-004432-3) De Gruyter.
Luedtke, Helmut, ed. Kommunikationstheoretische Grundlagen des Sprachwandels. (Grundlagen der Kommunikation Ser.). 280p. (C). 1979. text ed. 84.60 (3-11-007271-8) De Gruyter.
Luedtke, Luther S. Nathaniel Hawthorne & the Romance of the Orient. LC 88-46018. (Illus.). 304p. 1989. 29.95 (0-253-33613-9) Ind U Pr.
Luedtke, Luther S., ed. Making America: The Society & Culture of the United States. LC 91-50786. (Illus.). xii, 570p. (C). 1992. 37.50 (0-8078-2030-X); pap. 16.95 (0-8078-4370-9) U of NC Pr.
Luedtke, Ralph D., jt. ed. see Kanenberg, Cyndee.
Luedtke, Robert, jt. auth. see Bodian, Nat G.
*Lueg. The Next Threat: Western Perceptions of Islam. Hippler, ed. (Transnational Institute Ser.). (C). 1995. pap. text ed. 16.95 (0-7453-0953-4, Pub. by Pluto Pr UK) Westview.
Lueg, Andrea, jt. ed. see Hippler, Jochen.
Lueger, Robert J. Assessing Quality in Outpatient Psychotherapy: Implications for Designing & Selecting Cost-Efficient Mental Health Care Benefits. LC 93-77662. 75p. (Orig.). 1993. pap. 37.00 (0-89154-463-1) Intl Found Employ.
Luehe, Bill, jt. auth. see Ehrgott, Richard H.
Luehe, F. William & Ehrgott, Richard H. Clinical Teaching & Supervision. rev. ed. (Illus.). 243p. 1976. pap. text ed. 13.00 (0-943141-00-1) Key Pubns CA.
— Target Teaching. 4th ed. (Illus.). 102p. 1984. pap. text ed. 7.95 (0-943141-01-X) Key Pubns CA.
Luehe, F. William, jt. auth. see Ehrgott, Richard H.
*Luehlfing, Michael S. The Development of the Second Partner Review in Audit Engagements. 20p. 1991. pap. text ed. 19.50 (0-933179-05-7) Bus Account Pubns.
— Minimizing the Impact of Alternative Recording Methods on the Consolidation Process - "Conversion to Complete Equity" 21p. 1995. pap. text ed. 19.50 (0-933179-09-X) Bus Account Pubns.
Luehrman, Timothy A., jt. ed. see Kester, W. Carl.
Luehrmann, Arthur. Computer Literacy: A Hands-on-Approach, Apple Version. 248p. 1985. teacher ed 32.00 (0-07-049246-8); student ed 9.80 (0-07-049245-X) McGraw.
— Computer Literacy: A Hands-on-Approach, Apple Version. rev. ed. 400p. 1985. Rev., 400pp. text ed. 30.88 (0-07-049242-5) McGraw.
— Computer Literacy: A Hands-On-Approach, TRS-80 Version. Hague, Nola J., ed. 256p. 1985. teacher ed 32.00 (0-07-049251-4); student ed 9.80 (0-07-049250-6); text ed. 30.88 (0-07-049247-6) McGraw.
— Introduction to Computer Applications: Apple Version. 104p. 1985. teacher ed 26.88 (0-07-049244-1); text ed. 15.56 (0-07-049243-3) McGraw.
— Introduction to Computer Applications: TRS-80. 160p. 1986. text ed. 15.56 (0-07-049248-4) McGraw.
Luehrmann, Arthur & Peckham, Herbert. Appleworks Date Bases: A Hands-On Guide. LC 87-11734. (Illus.). 166p. (Orig.). (YA). (gr. 7-12). 1987. pap. text ed. 11.95 (0-941681-03-3) Computer Lit Pr.
— Appleworks Spreadsheets: A Hands-On Guide. LC 87-11745. (Illus.). 160p. (Orig.). (YA). (gr. 7-12). 1987. pap. text ed. 11.95 (0-941681-05-X) Computer Lit Pr.
— Appleworks Word Processing: A Hands-On Guide. LC 87-836. (Illus.). 152p. (Orig.). (YA). (gr. 7-12). 1987. pap. text ed. 11.95 (0-941681-01-7) Computer Lit Pr.
— AppleWorks 3 Word Processing. (Illus.). 176p. 1991. teacher ed, pap. 24.95 (0-941681-36-X) Computer Lit Pr.
— AppleWorks 3 Word Processing. LC 91-17736. (Illus.). 176p. (YA). (gr. 7-12). 1991. pap. text ed. 12.95 (0-941681-29-7) Computer Lit Pr.
— Hands-on Appleworks: A Guide to Word Processing, Data Bases & Spreadsheets, 3 bks., Set. LC 87-836. (Illus.). 478p. (Orig.). (YA). (gr. 7-12). 1987. pap. text ed. 23.95 (0-941681-07-6) Computer Lit Pr.
— Hands-on AppleWorks 3. LC 91-3607. (Illus.). 416p. 1991. text ed. 30.95 (0-941681-28-9); spiral bd. 23.95 (0-941681-27-0) Computer Lit Pr.
— Hands-On ClarisWorks: Mac Version 2.0. 2nd ed. LC 93-25634. (Illus.). 544p. (YA). (gr. 7 up). 1993. text ed. 30.95 (0-941681-61-0); Spiralbound. spiral bd. 23.95 (0-941681-60-2) Computer Lit Pr.
Luehrmann, Arthur & Peckham, Herbert D. Computer Literacy: A Hands-on Approach. 1985. Apple II. 32.52 (0-07-049186-0); TRS-80. 32.12 (0-07-049191-7); Apple II. student ed 11.04 (0-07-049187-9); TRS-80. student ed 11.04 (0-07-049188-7) McGraw.
— Computer Literacy Survival Kit: For the Apple II, IIe Family of Computers. 384p. 1984. pap. text ed. 29.95 (0-07-049206-9, BYTE Bks) McGraw.
— Hands-on Pascal: For the IBM Personal Computer. (Personal Programmimg Ser.). 448p. 1984. pap. text ed. write for info. (0-07-049176-3) McGraw.
*Luehrs, John. Flexibility & Waiver Authority for Health Care Reform: A Primer for States. Glass, Karen, ed. 94p. (Orig.). 1992. pap. text ed. 20.00 (1-55877-172-7) Natl Governor.
Luehrs, John, jt. auth. see McCloskey, Amanda H.
Luehrs, John, jt. auth. see Phillips, Stephen.
Luehrsen, Thomas, ed. see Sumeria Staff.
Lueke, Ada, jt. auth. see Musladin, Judith M.
Lueker, Erwin. Companion Dictionary of the Bible. 192p. 1985. pap. 7.99 (0-570-03947-9, 12-2880) Concordia.
Lueker, Erwin L., ed. Lutheran Cyclopedia: A Concise In-Home Reference for the Christian Family. 856p. 1987. 24.95 (0-570-03255-5, 15-2163) Concordia.
Lueker, G. S., jt. auth. see Coffman, E. G.
Lueking, Dean. From Ashes to Holy Wind. 1989. pap. 7.90 (1-55673-127-2, 9852) CSS OH.
Luel, Steven & Marcus, Paul. Psychoanalytic Reflections on the Holocaust: Selected Essays. 1985. 25.00 (0-88125-041-4) Ktav.
Luellen, Valentina. One Love. large type ed. 1994. 18.95 (0-263-13977-8, Pub. by Mills & Boon Ltd UK) Chivers N Amer.
Luelsdorff, P. Soviet Contributions to the Sociology of Language. 1977. pap. text ed. 40.00 (90-279-7613-9) Mouton.
Luelsdorff, Philip. Constraints on Error Variables in Grammar: Bilingual Misspelling Orthographies. LC 85-30823. vii, 442p. 1986. 118.00x (0-915027-73-9); pap. 27.95x (0-915027-74-7) Benjamins North Am.
— Developmental Orthography. LC 91-7333. xii, 258p. 1991. 89.00x (90-272-2065-4) Benjamins North Am.
Luelsdorff, Philip A. A Segmental Phonology of Black English. LC 72-94483. (Janua Linguarum, Ser.: No. 191). (Illus.). 102p. (Orig.). 1975. pap. text ed. 22.00 (90-279-3047-3) Mouton.
*Luelsdorff, Philip A., ed. Prague School of Structural & Functional Linguistics: A Short Introduction. LC 94-31089. (Linguistic & Literary Studies in Eastern Europe: No. 41). 1994. lib. bdg. 95.00x (1-55619-266-5) Benjamins North Am.
Luelsdorff, Philip A., et al, eds. Praguiana 1945-1990. LC 93-44739. (Linguistic & Literary Studies in Eastern Europe: No. 40). 250p. 1994. 75.00 (0-685-70948-5) Benjamins North Am.
Luelsdorff, Phillip A., ed. Orthography & Phonology. LC 87-9361. xi, 238p. (C). 1987. 74.00x (90-272-2039-5) Benjamins North Am.
Luenberger, David G. Introduction to Dynamic Systems: Theory, Models & Applications. LC 78-12366. 446p. 1979. Net. text ed. write for info. (0-471-02594-1) Wiley.
— Microeconomic Theory. 1995. text ed. 54.00 (0-07-049313-8) McGraw.
— Optimization by Vector Space Methods. (Decision & Control Ser.). 326p. 1969. text ed. 94.95 (0-471-55359-X) Wiley.
Lueneburg, H., ed. Translation Planes. 256p. 1980. 69.00 (0-387-09614-0) Spr-Verlag.
Luening, et al. Contemporary Etudes & Solos for the Violoncello. LC 90-70867. 35.00 (0-685-65729-9) Am String Tchrs.
Luening, R. A., et al. Farm Management Handbook. 7th ed. (Illus.). 607p. 1991. 35.95 (0-8134-2872-6); teacher ed 6.95 (0-8134-2873-4); text ed. 26.95 (0-685-47684-7) Interstate.
*Luenn. Mother Earth Spanish. (Illus.). (J). 1996. 15.00 (0-689-80000-2, Atheneum Bks Young) S&S Childrens.
Luenn, Nancy. The Dragon Kite. LC 81-11709. (Illus.). 12p. (J). (ps-3). 1983. pap. 5.95 (0-15-224197-3, Voyager Bks) HarBrace.
— Goldclimbers. LC 90-589. 192p. (YA). (gr. 7 up). 1991. text ed. 14.95 (0-689-31585-6, Atheneum Bks Young) S&S Childrens.
— Mother Earth. LC 90-19134. (Illus.). 32p. (J). (ps-3). 1992. text ed. 14.95 (0-689-31668-2, Atheneum Bks Young) S&S Childrens.
— Mother Earth. (Illus.). (J). (ps-3). 1995. pap. 4.95 (0-689-80164-5, Aladdin Paperbacks) S&S Childrens.
— Nessa's Fish. LC 89-10548. (Illus.). 32p. (J). (gr. k-3). 1990. text ed. 14.95 (0-689-31477-9, Atheneum Bks Young) S&S Childrens.
— Nessa's Fish. (One World Friends & Neighbors Ser.). (Illus.). (J). (gr. k-4). 1993. 13.95 (0-685-64812-5); audio 11.00 (1-882869-81-8) Varsity Read Servs.
— Nessa's Story (El Cuento de Nessa) Ada, Alma F., tr. LC 93-34814. (Illus.). 32p. (ENG & SPA.). (J). (ps-3). 1994. text ed. 14.95 (0-689-31782-4, Atheneum Bks Young); text ed. 14.95 (0-689-31919-3, Atheneum Bks Young) S&S Childrens.
— La Pesca de Nessa. (J). (ps-3). 1994. 15.95 (0-689-31977-0, Atheneum S&S) S&S Trade.
— Song for the Ancient Forest. LC 91-17187. (Illus.). 32p. (J). (gr. k-3). 1993. text ed. 14.95 (0-689-31719-0, Atheneum Bks Young) S&S Childrens.
— Squish! A Wetland Walk. LC 93-22628. (Illus.). 32p. (J). 1994. text ed. 14.95 (0-689-31842-1, Atheneum Bks Young) S&S Childrens.
— Unicorn Crossing. LC 87-995. (Illus.). 64p. (J). (gr. 2-5). 1987. lib. bdg. 12.95 (0-689-31384-5, Atheneum S&S) S&S Trade.
— Unicorn Crossing. 64p. (J). (gr. 2-9). 1988. reprint ed. pap. 2.50 (0-8167-1321-9) Troll Assocs.
Luenn, Nancy, ed. A Horse's Tale: Ten Adventures in One Hundred Years. LC 88-61152. (Illus.). 96p. (Orig.). (J). (gr. 2-6). 1988. lib. bdg. 16.95 (0-943990-51-3); pap. 7.95 (0-943990-50-5) Parenting Pr.
Luepke, Niels-Peter, ed. see International Workshop on Monitoring Environmental Materials & Specimen Banking Staff.
Luepker, Russell V., jt. ed. see Higgins, Millicent W.
Luepnitz, Deborah A. The Family Interpreted: Feminist Theory in Clinical Practice. LC 88-47761. 352p. 1992. reprint ed. pap. 15.00 (0-465-02351-7) Basic.
Lueptow, Lloyd B. Adolescent Sex Roles & Social Change. LC 83-7842. (Illus.). 352p. 1984. text ed. 52.00 (0-231-05712-1) Col U Pr.
*Luer, Carlyle A. Icones Pleurolthallidinarum XI: Lepantnes Subgenus Brachycladium & Pleurothallis Subgenera Aenigma, Elongatia, & Kraenzlinella. (Monographs in Systematic Botany from the Missouri Botanical Garden: No. 52). (Illus.). (Orig.). 1994. pap. 21.00 (0-915279-29-0) Miss Botan.
— Icones Pleurothallidinarum IX: Systematics of Myoxanthus: Addenda to Platystele, Pleurothallus Subgenus Scopula & Scaphosepalum (Orchidaceae) (Monographs in Systematic Botany from the Missouri Botanical Garden: No. 44). (Illus.). 128p. 1992. pap. 15.00 (0-685-70548-X) Miss Botan.
— Native Orchids of the United States & Canada. LC 75-905. (Illus.). 363p. 1975. 38.00 (0-89327-015-6) NY Botanical.
*Luer, Carlyle A. & Escobar, Rodrigo R. Thesaurus Dracularum Five: Eine Monographie der Galtung Dracula - A Monograph of the Genus Dracula. Hamer, Fritz, tr. (Thesaurus Draculanum Ser.). (Illus.). 62p. (Orig.). (GER.). 1992. pap. 46.50 (0-614-04648-3) Miss Botan.
— Thesaurus Draculanum Four: Eine Monographie der Galtung Dracula - A Monograph of the Genus Dracula. Hamer, Fritz, tr. (Thesaurus Draculanum Ser.). (Illus.). 62p. (Orig.). (GER.). 1991. pap. 44.50 (0-614-04647-5) Miss Botan.
— Thesaurus Draculanum Seven: Eine Monographie der Galtung Dracula - A Monograph of the Genus Dracula. Hamer, Fritz, tr. (Thesaurus Draculanum Ser.). (Illus.). v, 78p. (Orig.). (GER.). 1994. pap. 57.00 (0-915279-28-2) Miss Botan.
— Thesaurus Draculanum Six: Eine Monographie der Galtung Dracula - A Monograph of the Genus Dracula. Hamer, Fritz, tr. (Thesaurus Draculanum Ser.). (Illus.). 64p. (Orig.). (GER.). 1993. pap. 46.50 (0-614-04649-1) Miss Botan.
— Thesaurus Draculanum Three: Eine Monographie der Galtung Dracula - A Monograph of the Genus Dracula. Hamer, Fritz, tr. (Thesaurus Draculanum Ser.). (Illus.). 66p. (Orig.). (GER.). 1990. pap. text ed. 41.50 (0-614-04646-7) Miss Botan.
— Thesaurus Draculanum Two: Eine Monographie der Galtung Dracula - A Monograph of the Genus Dracula. Hamer, Fritz, tr. (Thesaurus Draculanum Ser.). (Illus.). 62p. (Orig.). (GER.). 1989. pap. 41.50 (0-614-04645-9) Miss Botan.
Luer, Carlyle A., ed. see Chase, Mark W.
Luer, Carlyle A., ed. see Cribb, Phillip J. & Bell, Sandra.
Luer, Carlyle A., ed. see Stewart, Joyce.
Luer, Carlyle A., ed. see Wood, Jeffrey J., et al.
Luer, Carlyle A., ed. see Wood, Jeffrey J.
*Luer, Carlyle S. & Escobar, Rodrigo R. Thesaurus Draculanum One: Eine Monographie der Gattung Dracula - A Monograph of the Genus Dracula. Hamer, Fritz, tr. (Thesaurus Draculanum Ser.). (Illus.). 62p. (Orig.). (GER.). 1988. pap. 41.50 (0-614-04644-0) Miss Botan.
Luer, G., et al, eds. Eye Movement Research: Physiological & Psychological Aspects, Vol. 2. LC 88-16032. 392p. (C). 1988. text ed. 79.00 (0-88937-020-6) Hogrefe & Huber Pubs.
Lueras, Leonard, ed. Kanyaku: A Hundred Years of Japanese Life in Hawaii. (Illus.). 160p. 1985. 19.95 (0-9615045-0-1) Kanyaku Imin JV.
Luere, Jean. Playwright vs.Director: Authorial Intentions & Performance Interpretations. Vol. 54. 1994. write for info. (0-318-72318-2, Greenwood Pr) Greenwood.
Luere, Jeane & Berger, Sidney, eds. Playwright vs. Director: Authorial Intentions & Performance Interpretations. LC 93-44134. (Contributions in Drama & Theatre Studies: No. 54). 200p. 1994. text ed. 55.00 (0-313-28679-5, Greenwood Pr) Greenwood.
Luerkens, David W. Theory & Application of Morphological Analysis: Fine Particles & Surfaces. Beddow, John K., ed. (Fine Particle Science & Technology Ser.). 336p. 1991. 110.00 (0-8493-6777-8, TA418) CRC Pr.
Luescher, T. F. Endothelial Vasoactive Substances & Cardiovascular Disease. (Illus.). xiv, 134p. 1988. 119.25 (3-8055-4675-0) S Karger.
Luessen, Lawrence H., jt. ed. see Kunhardt, Erich E.
Luessen, Lawrence H., jt. ed. see Proud, Joseph M.
Luessen, Lawrence H., jt. ed. see Thompson, James E.
*Luessenhop. Risky Business: An Insider's Account of the Collapse of Lloyd's of London. 1995. 25.00 (0-684-19739-1, Scribners) S&S Trade.
Lueth, Shirley. Bubble, Bubble, Toil & Trouble. 264p. 1993. reprint ed. pap. 7.95 (0-937911-03-8) Lueth Hse Pub.
— I Didn't Plan to Be a Witch. 238p. 1988. reprint ed. pap. 7.95 (0-937911-02-X) Lueth Hse Pub.

An Asterisk (*) at the beginning of an entry indicates that the title is appearing in BIP for the first time.

— Prayer & Peanut Butter. (Illus.). 147p. (Orig.). 1986. reprint ed. pap. 7.95 (0-937911-01-1) Lueth Hse Pub.

— Prayer & Peanut Butter: Talking Book. (Illus.). 147p. 1983. pap. 4.85 (0-8300-2129-9) Aurora News Reg.

— Watch Out! I'm Peeking in Your Window! 140p. (Orig.). 1986. pap. 7.95 (0-937911-00-3) Lueth Hse Pub.

Luethans, Tod N. Gormont et Isembart: The Epic As Seen in the Light of the Oral Theory. Lord, Albert B., ed. LC 90-2973. (Harvard Dissertations in Folklore & Oral Literature Ser.). 249p. 1990. reprint ed. lib. bdg. 59.00 (0-8240-2787-6) Garland.

***Luetje, Carolyn & Marcrander, Meg.** Face to Face with God in Your Home: Guiding Children & Youth in Prayer. LC 94-48475. 1995. write for info. (0-8066-2767-0, Augsburg) Augsburg Fortress.

Luetke, Frederick. Voyage Around the World, 1826-1829, Vol. 1: To Russian America & Siberia. Pierce, Richard A., ed. Marshall, Renee, tr. (Alaska History Ser.: No. 29). (Illus.). 1986. 26.50 (0-919642-97-7) Limestone Pr.

Luetke-Stahlman, Barbara & Luckner, John. Effectively Educating Students with Hearing Impairments. 384p. (Orig.). (C). 1991. pap. text ed. 40.95 (0-8013-0317-6, 78085) Longman.

Luetscher, George D. Early Political Machinery in the United States. LC 70-155356. (Studies in American History & Government). 1971. reprint ed. lib. bdg. 27.50 (0-306-70187-1) Da Capo.

Luetschg, J., ed. Neuropaediatrie III, III. (Paediatrische Fortbildungskurse fuer die Praxis Ser.: Vol. 60). (Illus.). xii, 92p. 1986. pap. 43.25 (3-8055-4232-1) S Karger.

Luettge, U. & Higinbotham, N. Transport in Plants. (Illus.). 1979. 81.00 (0-387-90383-6) Spr-Verlag.

Luettig, G. W., ed. Recent Technologies of the Uses of Peat: Reports of the International Symposium. (Illus.). 223p. 1983. pap. text ed. 61.95 (3-510-65115-4) Lubrecht & Cramer.

Luettig, G. W., jt. ed. see Arndt, Peter.

Luetzeler, Heinrich. Dictionary of Art: Bildwoerterbuch der Kunst. 3rd ed. 448p. (GER.). 1980. pap. 45.00 (0-8288-1422-8, M7310) Fr & Eur.

Luetzelschwab, John. Household Energy Use & Conservation: How to Prepare an Energy Budget. LC 79-16895. (Illus.). 1980. 35.95 (0-88229-476-8) Nelson-Hall.

Luey, Beth. Handbook for Academic Authors. rev. ed. (Illus.). 240p. (C). 1990. pap. 15.95 (0-521-39646-8) Cambridge U Pr.

— Handbook for Academic Authors. rev. ed. (Illus.). 240p. (C). 1990. 34.95 (0-521-39494-5) Cambridge U Pr.

— Handbook for Academic Authors. 3rd ed. (Illus.). 256p. (C). 1995. pap. 14.95 (0-521-49892-9) Cambridge U Pr.

— Handbook for Academic Authors. 3rd ed. (Illus.). 256p. (C). 1995. 34.95 (0-521-49549-0) Cambridge U Pr.

Luey, Beth, jt. ed. see Kobrak, Fred.

Luey, Beth, jt. ed. see Park, Karin R.

Luey, Beth E. Editing Documents & Texts: An Annotated Bibliography. LC 89-14552. 304p. 1990. 19.95 (0-945612-13-3) Madison Hse.

Luezak, James E. Come & Gone. 1992. pap. 5.45 (0-87129-187-8, C55) Dramatic Pub.

Lufburrow, Bill. The Most Honest People. LC 80-69253. (Illus.). (Orig.). 1980. pap. 4.95 (0-918464-23-4) D Armstrong.

Luff, Alan. Welsh Hymns & Their Tunes. LC 90-81524. 255p. (Orig.). (C). 1990. 14.95 (0-916642-42-9) Hope Pub.

Luff, David. Bulldog: The Bristol Bulldog Fighter. LC 88-60697. (Illus.). 188p. 1988. 29.95 (0-87474-648-5) Smithsonian.

Luff, Martin L. The Carabidae, Coleoptera, Larvae of Fennoscandia & Denmark. LC 93-3419. (Fauna Entomologica Scandinavica Ser.: Vol. 27). (Illus.). 187p. 1993. 54.50 (90-04-09836-4) E J Brill.

Luff, Moe. United States Postal Slogan Cancel Catalog. rev. ed. LC 68-2266. 128p. 1977. pap. text ed. 5.75 (0-9600162-0-1) M Luff.

Luff, Paul, et al, eds. Computers & Conversation. (Computers & People Ser.). 284p. 1990. text ed. 61.00 (0-12-459560-X) Acad Pr.

***Luff, Rosemary & Rowley-Conwy, Peter, eds.** Whither Environmental Archaeology? (Oxbow Monographs in Archaeology: No. 38). (Illus.). 224p. (Orig.). 1994. pap. 57.60 (0-946897-69-7, Pub. by Oxbow Bks UK) David Brown.

Luff, Rosemary M. Animal Remains in Archaeology. 1989. pap. 25.00 (0-85263-633-4, Pub. by Shire UK) St Mut.

Luffman, George, et al. Business Policy: An Analytical Introduction. 2nd ed. 208p. (Orig.). (C). 1991. pap. text ed. 24.95 (0-631-18195-4) Blackwell Pubs.

Luffman, George A. & Reed, Richard. The Strategy & Performance of British Industry, 1970-80. LC 84-17716. 360p. 1985. text ed. 39.95 (0-312-76469-3) St Martin.

Luffman, George A., jt. auth. see Newbould, Gerald D.

Lufkin. Magnetic Resonance Imaging Manual. 336p. 1989. pap. 39.95 (0-8151-5593-X, Yr Bk Med Pubs) Mosby Yr Bk.

Lufkin & Hanafee. Magnetic Resonance Imaging of the Head & Neck. 300p. 124.95 (0-8016-3064-9) Mosby Yr Bk.

Lufkin, Alan, ed. California's Salmon & Steelhead: The Struggle to Restore an Imperiled Resource. (Illus.). 288p. 1991. 28.00 (0-520-07029-1) U CA Pr.

Lufkin, Robert B. & Hanafee, William N. MRI of the Head & Neck. (MRI Teaching File Ser.). 253p. 1991. 70.00 (0-88167-704-3) Raven.

— Pocket Atlas of Head & Neck MRI Anatomy. (Illus.). 83p. 1989. pap. 15.95 (0-88167-498-2) Raven.

Lufkin, Robert B., et al, eds. The Raven MRI Teaching File, 10 vols., Set. 1991. 700.00 (0-7817-0204-6, RA004) Raven.

Luft & Tsuo. Hydrogenated Amorphous Silicon Alloy Deposition Processes. LC 93-18931. (Applied Physics Ser.: Vol. 1). 344p. 1993. 125.00 (0-8247-9146-0) Dekker.

Luft, C. P., jt. auth. see Fernandes, F.

Luft, Carl F. Understanding & Trading Futures: A Hands-on Study Guide for Investors & Traders. rev. ed. 1994. pap. 22.95 (1-55738-570-X) Probus Pub Co.

Luft, Carl F. & Sheiner, Richard K. Listed Stock Options: The Hands-On Study Guide for Investors & Traders. rev. ed. 1993. pap. 24.95 (1-55738-520-3) Probus Pub Co.

Luft, David S. Robert Musil & the Crisis of European Culture, 1880-1942. LC 78-66008. 336p. 1980. pap. 13.00 (0-520-05328-1) U CA Pr.

Luft, David S., ed. see Musil, Robert.

Luft, David S., tr. see Musil, Robert.

Luft, David S., ed. see Musil, Robert.

Luft, David S., tr. see Musil, Robert.

Luft, Edward D. The Naturalized Jews of the Grand Duchy of Posen in 1834-35. LC 87-15881. (Brown Judaic Studies). 211p. 1987. 34.95 (1-55540-137-6, 14-50-04) Scholars Pr GA.

Luft, Eric, ed. & tr. Hegel, Hinrichs & Schleiermacher on Feeling & Reason in Religion: The Texts of Their 1821-1822 Debate. LC 87-5550. (Studies in German Thought & History: Volume 3). 544p. 1984. lib. bdg. 119.95 (0-88946-352-2) E Mellen.

Luft, Harold S. Health Maintenance Organizations: Dimensions of Performance. 468p. 1986. pap. 21.95 (0-88738-681-4) Transaction Pubs.

***Luft, Harold S., ed.** HMOs & the Elderly. 1994. write for info. (1-56793-021-2) Health Admin Pr.

Luft, Harold S., et al. Hospital Volume, Physician Volume, & Patient Outcomes: Assessing the Evidence. LC 90-4003. 406p. (Orig.). 1990. pap. text ed. 37.00 (0-910701-46-6, 0896) Health Admin Pr.

Luft, Herbert A., jt. auth. see Burnham, Robert, Jr.

Luft, Joseph. Group Processes: An Introduction to Group Dynamics. 3rd ed. LC 83-62828. 237p. 1984. pap. 24.95 (0-87484-542-4) Mayfield Pub.

Luft, Kathleen, tr. see Hertle, Bernd, et al.

Luft, Roger L. & Schoen, Janice L. Index to Doctoral Dissertations in Business Education, Supplement, 1980-1985. 3rd ed. 26p. (C). 1986. pap. text ed. 8.00 (0-685-50913-3) Delta Pi Epsilon.

Luft, Rolf, jt. ed. see Levine, R.

***Luft, S. & Smith, M.** Nursing in General Practice. 272p. 1994. 37.50 (1-56593-187-4, 0502) Singular Publishing.

Luft, Werner, ed. Photovoltaic Safety. LC 88-42854. (AIP Conference Proceedings Ser.: No. 166). 264p. 1988. lib. bdg. 60.00 (0-88318-366-8) Am Inst Physics.

Luftig, Richard L. Assessment of Learners with Special Needs: Concepts & Applications. 576p. 1988. text ed. 45.00 (0-205-11733-3, H1733-8) Allyn.

— Assessment of Learners with Special Needs: Concepts & Applications. 576p. 1989. teacher ed write for info. (0-318-63879-7, H17346) Allyn.

— Teaching the Mentally Retarded Student. 1986. text ed. 46.00 (0-205-10262-X, H02629) Allyn.

***Luftig, Victor.** Seeing Together: Friendship Between the Sexes in English Writing from Mill to Woolf. 320p. 1995. pap. 15.95 (0-8047-2591-8) Stanford U Pr.

— Seeing Together: Friendship Between the Sexes in English Writing from Mill to Woolf. LC 92-44199. 320p. (C). 1995. 45.00x (0-8047-2168-8) Stanford U Pr.

***Luftman, Jerry N.** Competing in the Information Age: Strategic Alignment in Practice. (Illus.). 368p. 1996. 30.00 (0-19-509016-0) OUP.

Lug, Sieglinde, tr. see Schwaiger, Brigitte.

***Lugalla, Joe.** Crisis, Urbanization, & Urban Poverty in Tanzania: A Study of Urban Poverty & Survival Politics. (Illus.). 248p. (C). 1995. lib. bdg. 44.50 (0-8191-9741-6) U Pr of Amer.

— Poverty & Adjustments in Tangible World. (Bremen African Studies). (C). 1995. pap. text ed. 22.95 (3-8258-2007-6) Westview.

Lugan, A. Fray Luis De Leon. 159p. 1924. 1.00 (0-318-14268-6) Hispanic Inst.

Lugard, Frederick J. Political Memoranda: Revision of Instructions to Political Officers on Subjects Chiefly Political & Administrative, 1913-1918. 3rd rev. ed. 480p. 1970. 42.50 (0-7146-1693-1, Pub. by F Cass Pubs UK) Intl Spec Bk.

Lugardon, B., jt. auth. see Tryon, Alice F.

Lugaresi, Elio, jt. ed. see Andermann, Frederick.

Lugbill, Ann, jt. auth. see Helmer, James B.

Lugenbeel, Barbara. Virginia Samdahl: Reiki Master Healer. (Illus.). 137p. 1984. pap. 12.95 (0-915133-05-9) Gindi Pr.

Lugenbeel, Gerald, Jr. A Game of Marbles. LC 88-50834. 235p. 1989. pap. 10.95 (1-55523-161-6) Winston-Derek.

Luger, George F. Cognitive Science: The Science of Intelligent Systems. (Illus.). 666p. 1994. boxed 49.95 (0-12-459570-7) Acad Pr.

***Luger, George F., ed.** Computation & Intelligence: Collected Readings. (AAAI Press Ser.). (Illus.). 650p. (C). 1995. pap. 35.00x (0-262-62101-0) MIT Pr.

Luger, George F. & Stubblefield, William A. Artificial Intelligence: Structures & Strategies for Complex Problem-Solving. 2nd ed. 784p. (C). 1993. text ed. 60.25 (0-8053-4780-1) Benjamin-Cummings.

Luger, H. J., jt. ed. see Vermeer, P. A.

Luger, Jack. Ask Me No Questions, I'll Tell You No Lies: How to Survive Being Interviewed, Interrogated, Questioned, Quizzed, Sweated, Grilled... LC 91-61943. 184p. 1991. pap. 16.95 (1-55950-072-7, 58072) Loompanics.

— The Big Book of Secret Hiding Places. (Illus.). 136p. (Orig.). 1987. pap. 14.95 (0-915179-66-0, 10048) Loompanics.

— Code Making & Code Breaking. LC 90-6021. (Illus.). 128p. (Orig.). 1990. pap. 10.95 (1-55950-034-4, 10052) Loompanics.

— Counterfeit ID Made Easy. LC 90-60515. (Illus.). 144p. 1990. pap. 14.95 (0-915179-90-3, 61111) Loompanics.

— How to Use Mail Drops for Privacy & Profit. LC 87-83527. 120p. 1988. pap. 12.50 (0-915179-75-X, 61092) Loompanics.

— Improvised Weapons in American Prisons. LC 84-52482. (Illus.). (Orig.). 1985. pap. 8.00 (0-915179-26-1) Loompanics.

— Snitch: A Handbook for Informers. LC 91-62782. 152p. (Orig.). 1991. pap. 16.95 (1-55950-076-X, 40072) Loompanics.

Luger, Michael I. & Goldstein, Harvey A. Technology in the Garden: Research Parks & Regional Economic Development. LC 91-50255. (Illus.). xxii, 242p. (C). 1991. 45.00 (0-8078-2000-8); pap. 14.95 (0-8078-4345-8) U of NC Pr.

Luger, Peter. Modern X-Ray Analysis on Single Crystals. 312p. 1980. 77.70 (3-11-006830-3) De Gruyter.

Luger, Thomas A. & Schwarz, Thomas, eds. Epidermal Growth Factors & Cytokines. LC 93-27742. (Basic & Clinical Dermatology Ser.: Vol. 10). 504p. 1994. 180.00 (0-8247-9102-9) Dekker.

Lugg, George W., ed. see Burroughs, John.

Luggen, Bill. Flexible Manufacturing Cells & Systems. 448p. 1990. text ed. 70.00 (0-13-321738-8) P-H.

Luggen, William W. Fundamentals of Computer Numerical Control. 3rd ed. LC 93-30141. 336p. 1994. text ed. 36.95 (0-8273-6496-2) Delmar.

— Fundamentals of Numerical Control. 2nd ed. (Illus.). 256p. 1984. teacher ed 12.00 (0-8273-3140-1); text ed. 36.95 (0-8273-3139-8) Delmar.

Lugger, Phyllis, ed. Asteroids to Quasars: A Symposium for the 60th Birthday of William Liller. 280p. (C). 1991. 69.95 (0-521-35231-2) Cambridge U Pr.

Lugi, Lucia, jt. auth. see Berzins, Valdis.

Lugiato, L. A., jt. ed. see Pike, E. R.

Luginbuhl, Christian B. & Skiff, Brian A. Observing Handbook & Catalogue of Deep-Sky Objects. (Illus.). 450p. (C). 1990. 49.95 (0-521-25665-8) Cambridge U Pr.

Luginbuhl, Martha, jt. auth. see Emerson, Haven.

Luginsky, Y. N., et al, eds. Dictionary of Electrical Engineering: English, German, French, Dutch, Russian. (C). 1987. lib. bdg. 124.50 (90-201-1910-9) Kluwer Ac.

Lugli, P., jt. auth. see Jacobini, C.

Lugn, Alvin L. Sedimentation in the Mississippi River Between Davenport, Iowa, & Cairo, Illinois. LC 28-14418. (Augustana College Library Publication Ser.: No. 11). 104p. 1927. pap. 1.00 (0-910182-08-6) Augustana Coll.

***Lugo, Ariel E. & Lowe, Carol, eds.** Tropical Forests: Management & Ecology. LC 94-23823. (Ecological Studies: Vol. 112). 1995. write for info. (0-387-94320-X) Spr-Verlag.

Lugo, Ariel E., jt. ed. see Wisniewski, Joe.

Lugo, Ariel E., et al, eds. Ecological Development in the Humid Tropics: Guidelines for Planners. (Illus.). 362p. 1988. per. 19.50 (0-933595-20-4) Winrock Intl.

— Forested Wetlands: Ecosystems of the World, No. 15. 504p. 1990. 205.75 (0-444-42812-7) Elsevier.

Lugo de Kaplan, Sarah. Manual Ilustrado de Laboratorio Para Botanica. 2nd ed. 145p. (C). 1990. 19.95 (1-881375-10-2) Libreria Univ.

— Manual Ilustrado de Laboratorio Para Curso Basico de Biologia. 124p. (C). 1980. 19.95 (1-881375-09-9) Libreria Univ.

Lugo, Elena. Etica Medica. 173p. (C). 1984. pap. text ed. 19.95 (1-881375-13-7) Libreria Univ.

— Etica Profesional Para la Ingenieria. 263p. (C). 1985. pap. text ed. 19.95 (1-881375-12-9) Libreria Univ.

Lugo-Guernelli, A., et al. Manuel de Gramatica Comercial. 204p. (ENG & SPA.). 1976. pap. 14.95 (0-8288-5741-5, S50369) Fr & Eur.

Lugo-Guernelli, Adelaida. Hostos y la Literatura. 19p. 1988. pap. 3.00 (0-685-51573-7) U of PR Pr.

Lugo, Herminio L., intro. Primer Simposio sobre Ecologia Islena-First Symposium on Island Ecological Systems: Papers of the Symposium Held at Inter American University, Oct. 28, 1983. 160p. (Orig.). (ENG & SPA.). (C). 1984. pap. text ed. 5.95 (0-913480-62-2) Inter Am U Pr.

Lugo, James. Living Psychology Handbook. 50p. (C). 1990. pap. text ed. 14.75 (0-929655-98-2) CT Pub.

— Living Psychology Instructor's Manual: Instructor's Manual. (C). 1990. pap. text ed. write for info. (1-56226-025-1) CT Pub.

Lugo, James, jt. auth. see Arcie, Eve M.

Lugo, James, jt. auth. see Dixon, Lugenia.

Lugo, James, jt. auth. see Till, Robert.

Lugo, James O. Living Psychology: A Lifespan Approach. 4th ed. (C). 1991. pap. text ed. 41.95 (1-56226-039-1) CT Pub.

Lugo, Jorge. The Complete Guide to Car Noises. 64p. (Orig.). 1983. pap. 2.95 (0-9611794-0-6) EXPIM Co.

Lugo, Luis E., ed. Religion, Public Life, & the American Polity. LC 93-38721. 320p. 1994. text ed. 39.00 (0-87049-830-4) U of Tenn Pr.

***Lugo, Margarita.** Fun, Sun & Mexico: The Spanish Phrasebook. (Illus.). 220p. (Orig.). 1994. per., pap. 9.95 (0-9643536-4-4) Type Team.

Lugo, Marta. Dominican Republic Guidebook. 1989. pap. 15.95 (0-932030-29-7) Eurasia Pr NY.

Lugo, Roberto, jt. ed. see Catala, Rafael.

Lugoe. The Beginning & Now: Cosmology & Cosmogany for Intellectuals & Philistines. 1993. 11.95 (0-533-10679-6) Vantage.

Lugones, Nestor, jt. ed. see Ramos-Garcia, Luis A.

Lugosi, L. & Hennessen, W., eds. BCG Vaccines & Tuberculins Part A & B. (Developments in Biological Standardization Ser.: Vol. 58). (Illus.). xviii, 782p. 1987. pap. 224.00 (3-8055-4279-8) S Karger.

Lugowski, Clemens. Form, Individuality, & the Novel: An Analysis of Narrative Structure in Early German Prose. Halliday, John D., tr. LC 90-70302. 234p. 1990. 29.95 (0-8061-2312-5) U of Okla Pr.

Lugt, Frits. Les Marques de Collections de Dessins & d'Estampes. LC 75-21068. (Illus.). 608p. (FRE.). 1975. reprint ed. 125.00 (0-915346-08-7) A Wofsy Fine Arts.

— Les Marques de Collections de Dessins et d'Estampes: Supplement. (Illus.). 476p. (FRE.). 1988. reprint ed. 125.00 (1-55660-023-2) A Wofsy Fine Arts.

***Lugt, Hans J.** Vortex Flow in Nature & Technology. 316p. (C). 1994. lib. bdg. 64.50 (0-89464-916-7) Krieger.

Lugtenberg, B. J., ed. Signal Molecules in Plants & Plant-Microbe Interactions. (NATO ASI Series H: Vol. 36). (Illus.). 448p. 1990. 153.00 (0-387-50381-1) Spr-Verlag.

Lugton, Robert C. American Topics. 2nd ed. (Illus.). 272p. (C). 1985. pap. text ed. 18.95 (0-13-029588-4) P-H.

Luh, Bor S., ed. Rice, 2 vols., Set. 2nd enl. rev. ed. (Illus.). 1024p. 1991. 189.95 (0-442-00735-3) Chapman & Hall.

— Rice, 2 vols., Vol. I. enl. rev. ed. (Illus.). 1024p. 1991. text ed. 110.00 (0-442-00484-2) Chapman & Hall.

— Rice, 2 vols., Vol. II. enl. rev. ed. (Illus.). 1024p. 1991. text ed. 110.00 (0-442-00485-0) Chapman & Hall.

Luh, Bor S., jt. ed. see Woodroof, Jasper G.

Luh, Chih Wei. On Chinese Poetry. 1972. lib. bdg. 79.95 (0-87968-540-9) Krishna Pr.

Luhan, Mabel D. Edge of Taos Desert: An Escape to Reality. Rudnick, Lois P., ed. LC 86-25283. 353p. 1987. reprint ed. pap. 15.95 (0-8263-0971-2) U of NM Pr.

— Lorenzo in Taos. 1988. reprint ed. lib. bdg. 79.00 (0-7812-0464-X) Rprt Serv.

— Winter in Taos. (Illus.). 264p. reprint ed. 14.95 (0-686-38775-9) Las Palomas.

***Luhan, Mabel D., et al.** A History of Having a Great Many Times Not Continued to be Friends: The Correspondence Between Mabel Dodge & Gertrude Stein, 1911-1934. LC 95-4345. (Illus.). 292p. 1996. 29.95 (0-8263-1640-9) U of NM Pr.

— Three Fates in Taos. (Literary Ser.). (Illus.). 228p. 1997. 35.00 (0-933806-10-8) Black Swan CT.

Luhan, Mabel G. Lorenzo in Taos. LC 78-145147. 352p. 1932. reprint ed. 59.00 (0-403-01077-2) Scholarly.

Luhman, John C. A Taxonomic Revision of Nearctic Endasys Foerster 1868 (Hymenoptera: Ichneumonidae, Gelinae) LC 89-20636. (Publications in Entomology: Vol. 109). (Illus.). 198p. 1991. pap. 30.00 (0-520-09757-2) U CA Pr.

Luhman, Reid. The Sociological Outlook. 3rd ed. (Illus.). 525p. (C). 1992. pap. text ed. 30.75 (0-939693-25-9) Collegiate Pr.

Luhmann, Barbara, ed. see Bell, G. V.

Luhmann, Douglas, ed. see Bell, G. V.

Luhmann, J. G., et al, eds. Venus & Mars: Atmospheres, Ionospheres, & Solar Wind Interactions. (Geophysical Monograph Ser.: Vol. 66). (Illus.). 448p. 1992. 59.00 (0-87590-032-1) Am Geophysical.

Luhmann, Niklas. Ecological Communication. Bednarz, John, Jr., tr. LC 89-4843. 200p. 1989. 34.95 (0-226-49651-1) U Ch Pr.

— Essays in Self-Realization. 320p. 1990. text ed. 44.00 (0-231-06368-7) Col U Pr.

— Love As Passion: The Codification of Intimacy. Gaines, Jeremy & Jones, Doris L., trs. LC 86-14929. 256p. 1987. 37.00 (0-674-53923-0) HUP.

— Political Theory in the Welfare State. vi, 239p. (C). 1990. lib. bdg. 46.95x (3-11-011932-3) De Gruyter.

— Religious Dogmatics & the Evolution of Societies. Beyer, Peter, tr. LC 84-8976. (Studies in Religion & Society: Vol. 9). 192p. 1984. lib. bdg. 79.95 (0-88946-866-4) E Mellen.

— Risk: A Sociological Theory. (Communication & Social Order Ser.). 249p. 1993. lib. bdg. 49.95 (0-202-30443-4) Aldine de Gruyter.

— Social Systems. Bednarz, John, Jr. & Baecker, Dirk, trs. (Writing Science Ser.). 570p. Date not set. 24.95 (0-8047-2625-6) Stanford U Pr.

— Social Systems. Bednarz, John, Jr. & Baecker, Dirk, trs. LC 94-46175. (Writing Science Ser.). 570p. (GER.). 1995. 65.00x (0-8047-1993-4) Stanford U Pr.

— A Sociological Theory of Law. King-Utz, Elizabeth & Albrow, Martin, trs. 448p. 1985. 59.95 (0-7100-9747-6, RKP) Routledge.

— Soziologie des Risikos. 252p. 1993. pap. 37.70 (3-11-012939-6) De Gruyter.

— Trust & Power: Two Works. Burns, Tom & Poggi, Gianfranco, eds. Davis, Howard et al, trs. LC 79-40579. 228p. reprint ed. pap. 65.00 (0-685-20594-0, 2030528) Bks Demand.

Luhn, Rebecca. Buying Your First Franchise: The Least You Need to Know. Gerould, Philip, ed. (Small Business & Entrepreneurship Ser.). 175p. (Orig.). 1994. pap. 15.95 (1-56052-190-2) Crisp Pubns.

— Employee Benefits with Cost Control. Crisp, Michael G., ed. LC 91-76244. (Fifty-Minute Ser.). 90p. (Orig.). 1992. pap. 9.95 (1-56052-133-3) Crisp Pubns.

— Managing Anger. Crisp, Michael G., ed. LC 91-76242. (Fifty-Minute Ser.). (Illus.). 90p. (Orig.). 1992. pap. 9.95 (1-56052-114-7) Crisp Pubns.

Luhn, Rebecca H. Managing Anger. (Orig.). pap. text ed. write for info. (0-7494-0834-0, Pub. by Kogan Page Educ UK) Taylor & Francis.

Luhr, James F. & Simkin, Tom. Paricutin: The Volcano Born in a Mexican Cornfield. LC 93-77812. (Illus.). 456p. (Orig.). 1993. 50.00 (0-945005-14-8); pap. 25.00 (0-945005-11-3) Geoscience Pr.

An Asterisk (*) at the beginning of an entry indicates that the title is appearing in BIP for the first time.

Luhr, Overton. Physics Tells Why: An Explanation of Some Common Physical Phenomena. 2nd ed. LC 51-30387. (Illus.). 397p. reprint ed. pap. 113.20 (*0-317-09229-4*, 2012363) Bks Demand.

Luhr, William. Raymond Chandler & Film. 2nd ed. 224p. (C). 1991. reprint ed. pap. 16.95 (*0-8130-1091-8*) U Press Fla.

Luhr, William, ed. World Cinema since Nineteen Forty-Five. 1987. 59.50 (*0-8044-3078-0*, F Ungar Bks) Continuum.

Luhr, William & Lehman, Peter. Returning to the Scene: Blake Edwards, Vol. 2. LC 80-28440. (Illus.). 320p. (C). 1989. 29.95 (*0-8214-0917-4*); pap. 14.95 (*0-8214-0918-2*) Ohio U Pr.

Luhr, William, ed. see Huston, John.

Luhr, William, jt. auth. see Lehman, Peter.

Luhrmann, Baz. Strictly Ballroom. 1993. pap. 22.00 (*0-86819-359-3*, Pub. by Currency Pr AT) St Mut.

Luhrmann, Dieter. An Itinerary for New Testament Study. LC 89-5024. 144p. 1989. pap. 9.95 (*0-334-02076-X*) TPI PA.

Luhrmann, T. M. Persuasions of the Witch's Craft: Ritual Magic in Contemporary England. LC 88-33382. (Illus.). 416p. 1989. 32.00 (*0-674-66323-3*) HUP.

— Persuasions of the Witch's Craft: Ritual Magic in Contemporary England. (Illus.). 416p. 1991. pap. text ed. 14.95 (*0-674-66324-1*, LUHPEX) HUP.

Luhrs, Dietrich. Untersuchungen Zu Den Athetesen Aristarchs in der Ilias und Zu Ihrer Behandlung Im Corpus der Exegetischen. Bd. 11. Date not set. write for info. (*0-318-70715-2*, Pub. by Georg Olms GW) Lubrecht & Cramer.

— Untersuchungen Zu Den Athetesen Aristarchs in der Ilias und Zu Ihrer Behandlung Im Corpus der Exegetischen Scholien. (Beitrage Zur Altertumswissenschaft Ser.: Bd. 11). xviii, 286p. (GER.). 1992. write for info. (*3-487-09629-3*, Pub. by Georg Olms GW) Lubrecht & Cramer.

Luhrs, Kathleen, ed. see Caldwell, John & Roque, Oswaldo R.

Luhrs, Ruth J. Kidding Around San Diego: A Young Person's Guide to the City. (Illus.). 64p. (Orig.). (J). (gr. 3 up). 1991. pap. 9.95 (*1-56261-010-4*) John Muir.

Lui, jt. auth. see Chen.

Lui, Anthony T., ed. Magnetotail Physics. LC 86-27614. (Johns Hopkins Studies in Earth & Planetary Sciences Ser.). (Illus.). 404p. 1987. text ed. 70.00 (*0-8018-3496-1*) Johns Hopkins.

Lui, B. The Gasteromycetes of China. (Nova Hedwigia Beiheft Ser.: No. 76). (Illus.). 240p. 1984. lib. bdg. 78.00 (*3-7682-5476-3*) Lubrecht & Cramer.

Lui, Cheng & Evett, Jack B. Soil Properties: Testing, Measurement, & Evaluation. 2nd ed. 320p. 1990. pap. text ed. 53.00 (*0-13-815051-6*) P-H.

Lui, E. M., jt. auth. see Chen, W. F.

Lui, G. P., jt. auth. see Whidborne, J. F.

Lui-Ma, Amy, ed. see Yun, Hsing.

Luibheid, Colm, ed. Pseudo Dionysius: The Complete Works. (Classics of Western Spirituality Ser.: Vol. 54). 336p. 1987. pap. 16.95 (*0-8091-2838-1*) Paulist Pr.

Luibheid, Colm, tr. see Cassian, John.

Luiggi, Alice H. Sixty-Five Valiants. LC 65-28692. (Illus.). 213p. reprint ed. pap. 60.80 (*0-7837-4930-9*, 2044596) Bks Demand.

Luiggi, Sadi O. Introduccion a las Cooperativas de Ahorro y Credito. Bauza, Carmen M., ed. (Cooperatives Ser.). 268p. (Orig.). (SPA.). 1990. 12.00 (*0-934885-02-8*) Edit Nosotros.

*__Luijkx, G. C.__ Hydrothermal Conversion of Carbohydrates & Related Compounds. 128p. (Orig.). 1994. pap. 52.50x (*90-407-1002-3*, Pub. by Delft U Pr NE) Coronet Bks.

Luijpen, W. A. & Koren, H. J. First Introduction to Existential Phenomenology. LC 79-75975. 243p. 1969. pap. text ed. 14.50 (*0-8207-0110-6*) Duquesne.

Luijten, Ger. Hollstein's Dutch & Flemish Etchings, Engravings & Woodcuts 1450-1700: Maarten Van Heemskerck, Pt. 1. rev. ed. (New Hollstein Ser.). 246p. 1993. 310.00 (*90-72658-25-6*, Pub. by K V Poll) IBD Ltd.

Luijten, Ger & Meij, A. W., eds. From the Pisanello to Cezanne: Master Drawings from the Museum Boymans-van Beuningen, Rotterdam. (Illus.). 230p. (C). 1990. 115.00 (*0-521-40105-4*) Cambridge U Pr.

Luijters, Guus. Marilyn Monroe: In Her Own Words. (Illus.). 96p. 1991. pap. 15.95 (*0-7119-2302-7*, OP46010) Omnibus NY.

Luikov, A. & Harrison, P. Heat & Mass Transfer in Capillary Porous Bodies. LC 64-23679. 1966. 219.00 (*0-08-010832-6*, Pub. by Pergamon Repr UK) Franklin.

Luikov, A. & Mikhailov, Y. Theory of Energy & Mass Transfer. 126.00 (*0-08-010127-5*, Pub. by Pergamon Repr UK) Franklin.

Luine, Jerome. Science Mysteries. 80p. (J). 1994. pap. 4.95 (*1-56565-173-1*) Lowell Hse Juvenile.

*__Luine, Victoria & Harding, Cheryl F., eds.__ Hormonal Restructuring of the Adult Brain: Basic & Clinical Perspectives, 743. LC 94-24685. (Annals Ser.: Vol. 743). 1994. write for info. (*0-89766-919-3*); pap. text ed. 75.00 (*0-89766-920-7*) NY Acad Sci.

*__Luinenberg & Osborne.__ The Little Green Book: Quotations on the Environment. Date not set. per. 3.95 (*0-88978-225-3*, Pub. by Arsenal Pulp CN) InBook.

*__Luinenburg & Osborne.__ The Little Grey Flannel Book: Quotations on Men. Date not set. per. 3.95 (*0-88978-239-3*, Pub. by Arsenal Pulp CN) InBook.

— The Little Pink Book: Quotations on Women. Date not set. per. 3.95 (*0-88978-226-1*, Pub. by Arsenal Pulp CN) InBook.

Luis Borges, Jorge. Hacedor. 158p. (SPA.). 1981. 10.00 (*0-8288-8559-1*) Fr & Eur.

Luis, Carlos M. Transito De la Mirada. (Illus.). 266p. (Orig.). 1991. pap. 12.00 (*0-917049-56-X*) Saeta.

Luis, Jose, ed. see Cowman, Charles E.

Luis Vives, Juan. Dialogos, No. 128. 153p. (SPA.). 1959. write for info. (*0-8288-8580-X*) Fr & Eur.

Luis, William. Literary Bondage: Slavery in Cuban Narrative. LC 89-37603. (Texas Pan American Ser.). 326p. 1990. text ed. 40.00 (*0-292-72463-2*) U of Tex Pr.

Luis, William, ed. Voices from Under: Black Narrative in Latin America & the Caribbean. LC 83-22792. (Contributions in Afro-American & African Studies: No. 76). xii, 263p. 1984. text ed. 55.00 (*0-313-23826-X*, LUV/, Greenwood Pr) Greenwood.

Luisada, Aldo A. Pulmonary Edema in Man & Animals. LC 71-96988. (Illus.). 168p. 1970. 12.75 (*0-87527-050-6*) Green.

— The Sounds of the Diseased Heart. LC 74-176171. (Illus.). 416p. 1973. text ed. 27.60 (*0-87527-113-8*) Green.

— The Sounds of the Normal Heart. LC 78-176172. (Illus.). 280p. 1972. 27.60 (*0-87527-051-4*) Green.

Luisada, Aldo A. & Portaluppi, Francesco. The Heart Sounds: New Facts & Their Clinical Implications. LC 81-19240. 256p. 1982. text ed. 59.95 (*0-275-91372-4*, C1372, Praeger Pubs) Greenwood.

Luisada, Aldo A. & Sainani, Gurmukh S. A Primer of Cardiac Diagnosis: The Physical & Technical Study of the Cardiac Patient. LC 68-20943. (Illus.). 262p. 1968. 12.75 (*0-87527-049-2*) Green.

Luise, Marco, jt. ed. see De Denzi, Riccardo.

Luiselli, Cassio. The Route to Food Self-Sufficiency in Mexico: Interactions with the U. S. Food System. Del Castillo, Sandra, tr. (Monograph Ser.: No. 17). 64p. (Orig.) (C). 1985. pap. 7.50 (*0-935391-68-1*, MN-17) UCSD Ctr US-Mex.

— The Sistema Alimentario Mexicano (SAM) Elements of a Program of Accelerated Production of Basic Foodstuffs in Mexico. Sweet, David, tr. (Research Report Ser.: No. 22). 24p. (Orig.). (C). 1982. pap. 5.00 (*0-935391-21-5*, RR-22) UCSD Ctr US-Mex.

Luiselli, Cassio, jt. ed. see Glade, William.

Luiselli, J. K., ed. Behavioral Medicine & Developmental Disabilities. (Disorders of Human Learning, Behavior, & Communication Ser.). (Illus.). 235p. 1989. 68.00 (*0-387-96875-X*) Spr-Verlag.

Luiselli, J. K., et al, eds. Self-Injurious Behavior: Analysis, Assessment & Treatment. (Disorders of Human Learning, Behavior, & Communication Ser.). (Illus.). x, 393p. 1991. 65.00 (*0-387-97580-2*) Spr-Verlag.

Luisi, Billie. Overlook Guide to Smallscale Goatkeeping. LC 85-8910. (Orig.). 1985. reprint ed. pap. 8.95 (*0-87951-230-X*) Overlook Pr.

Luisi, P. L. & Straub, B. E., eds. Reverse Micelles: Biological & Technological Relevance of Amphiphilic Structures in Apolar Media. 364p. 1984. 85.00 (*0-306-41620-4*, Plenum Pr) Plenum.

Luisi, T., jt. ed. see Flamm, J.

Luisigi, W. Planning Human Activities on Protected Natural Ecosystems. (Dissertationes Botanicae Ser.: No. 48). (Illus.). 1979. pap. 24.00 (*3-7682-1214-9*) Lubrecht & Cramer.

Luisotti, Theresa, ed. see Mahurin, Matt.

Luitel, S. Women in Development. (C). 1992. 21.00 (*0-7855-0221-1*, Pub. by Ratna Pustak Bhandar) St Mut.

Luithlen, Lutz. Office Development & Capital Accumulation in the UK. 296p. 1994. 59.95 (*1-85628-627-4*, Pub. by Avebury Pub UK) Ashgate Pub Co.

Luithui, Luingam. Nagaland File: A Question of Human Rights. 1985. 21.00 (*0-8364-1358-X*, Pub. by Lancer II) S Asia.

Luitjters, Guus & Timmer, Gerard. Sexbomb: The Life & Death of Jane Mansfield. Pachter, Josh, tr. (Illus.). 164p. 1988. pap. 12.95 (*0-8065-1049-8*, Citadel Pr) Carol Pub Group.

Luizzi, Vincent. A Case for Legal Ethics: Legal Ethics As a Source for a Universal Ethic. (SUNY Series in Ethical Theory). 176p. (C). 1993. 59.50 (*0-7914-1271-7*); pap. 19.95 (*0-7914-1272-5*) State U NY Pr.

Lujan, Leonardo L. The Offerings of the Templo Mayor of Tenochtitlan. Ortiz De Montellano, Bernard R. & Ortiz De Montellano, Thelma, trs. (Illus.). 480p. 1994. 39.95 (*0-87081-318-8*) Univ Pr Colo.

Lujan, Nestor. Diccionari Lujan De Gastronomie Catalana. 2nd ed. 192p. 1990. pap. 34.95 (*0-7859-6401-0*, 8486491347) Fr & Eur.

Lujan, Nestor & Lujan, Tin. Spain - a Cookbook. (Illus.). 160p. 1993. 29.95 (*3-576-80017-4*, Pub. by GeoCenter Intl UK) Seven Hills Bk.

Lujan, Pedro, jt. auth. see Ingberman, Jeanette.

Lujan, Tin, jt. auth. see Lujan, Nestor.

Lujaniand, Rosa E., et al, eds. The Kidnapped Saint & Other Stories. 2nd ed. LC 91-22338. 208p. 1991. reprint ed. pap. 11.95 (*1-55652-115-4*) L Hill Bks.

Luk, ed. Advanced Algorithms & Architectures for Signal Processing, No. II. 255p. 1987. 51.00 (*0-89252-861-3*, 826) SPIE.

Luk, Bernard H., ed. Eastern Asia: History & Social Sciences. LC 92-39880. (Contacts Between Cultures Ser.: Vol. 4). 668p. 1993. text ed. 129.95 (*0-7734-9206-2*) E Mellen.

Luk, Bernard H. & Steben, Barry D., eds. Eastern Asia: Humanities. LC 92-39880. (Contacts Between Cultures Ser.: Vol. 3). 640p. 1993. text ed. 129.95 (*0-7734-9204-6*) E Mellen.

Luk, Charles. Ch'an & Zen Teaching, Vol. 1. LC 93-17161. 256p. (Orig.). 1993. 12.95 (*0-87728-795-3*) Weiser.

— Ch'an & Zen Teaching, Vol. 2. 256p. (Orig.). 1993. pap. 12.95 (*0-87728-797-X*) Weiser.

— Ch'an & Zen Teaching, Vol. 3. 304p. (Orig.). 1993. pap. 14.95 (*0-87728-798-8*) Weiser.

— Secrets of Chinese Meditation. (Illus.). 240p. 1969. pap. 12.50 (*0-87728-066-5*) Weiser.

— Taoist Yoga. 224p. 1985. pap. 9.95 (*0-87728-067-3*) Weiser.

Luk, F. T. Advanced Signal Processing Algorithms, Architectures, & Implementations, Vol. 1348. 1990. 77.00 (*0-8194-0409-8*) SPIE.

— Advanced Signal Processing Algorithms, Architectures, & Implementations Two. 1992. 70.00 (*0-8194-0694-5*, 1566) SPIE.

Luk, F. T., ed. Advanced Algorithms & Architectures for Signal Processing III. 1988. 59.00 (*0-8194-0010-6*, 975) SPIE.

Luk, Franklin T., ed. Advanced Algorithms & Architectures for Signal Processing IV. 508p. 1989. 70.00 (*0-8194-0188-9*, VOL. 1152) SPIE.

Luk, Ivan. Microsoft Windows Sound System Book. Date not set. pap. 24.95 (*0-07-882015-4*) Osborne-McGraw.

Luk, Michael Y. The Origins of Chinese Bolshevism: An Ideology in the Making, 1921-1928. (South-East Asian Historical Monographs). (Illus.). 376p. 1990. 32.50 (*0-19-584209-X*) OUP.

Luk Ming. Cantonese for Foreigners. 1984. audio 29.95 (*962-14-0069-4*, CAFOFO) China Bks.

Luk, Shiu-Hung & Whitney, Joseph, eds. Megaproject: A Case Study of China's Three Gorges Project. LC 91-22964. (Chinese Environment & Development Ser.). 248p. (C). 1992. 57.95 (*0-87332-733-0*) M E Sharpe.

Luk, V. K., jt. ed. see Chen, E. P.

*__Luk, Y. F.__ Hong Kong's Economic & Financial Future. (Significant Issues Ser.). (C). 1995. pap. text ed. 14.95 (*0-89206-306-8*) CSI Studies.

Lukac, Louis, et al. Comparison of Twelve Technical Trading Systems. 72p. 1990. pap. text ed. 25.00 (*0-934380-18-X*) Traders Pr.

*__Lukac, P.__ Plasticity of Metals & Alloys: ISPMA-6. (Key Engineering Materials Ser.: Vols. 97-98). (Illus.). 526p. (C). 1995. text ed. 170.00 (*0-87849-687-4*, Pub. by Trans Tech SZ) LPS Dist Ctr.

Lukac, P., ed. Plasticity of Metals & Alloys, 5: Proc. of the Fifth Internat. Symp., 27-31 August 1990, Prague, Czechoslovakia. 200p. 1991. 144.50 (*1-85166-817-9*) Elsevier.

Lukacher, Maryline. Maternal Fictions: Stendhal, Sand, Rachilde, and Bataille. LC 93-38693. 192p. 1994. lib. bdg. 35.00 (*0-8223-1432-0*); pap. text ed. 15.95 (*0-8223-1436-3*) Duke.

Lukacher, Ned. Daemonic Figures: Shakespeare & the Question of Conscience. (Illus.). 240p. 1994. 37.50 (*0-8014-3052-6*); pap. 15.95 (*0-8014-8223-2*) Cornell U Pr.

— Primal Scenes: Literature, Philosophy, Psychoanalysis. LC 85-25513. 368p. (C). 1986. 41.95 (*0-8014-1886-0*); pap. 15.95 (*0-8014-9486-9*) Cornell U Pr.

Lukacher, Ned, tr. see Derrida, Jacques.

Lukacher, Ned, tr. see Roustang, Francois.

*__Lukacs.__ Meaning of Contemporary Realism. 1979. text ed. 19.95 (*0-85036-069-2*, Pub. by Merlin Pr UK) Humanities.

Lukacs, B., jt. auth. see Diosi, L.

Lukacs, E. Developments in Characteristic Function Theory. (Charles Griffin Book Ser.). 190p. 1987. reprint ed. 35.00 (*0-19-520577-4*) OUP.

Lukacs, E. & Laha, R. G. Applications of Charateristics Functions. (J). 1964. 17.95 (*0-85264-086-2*) Lubrecht & Cramer.

*__Lukacs, G.__ Georg Lukacs: Versuche zu Einer Ethik. Mezei, Gy. I., ed. 246p. (GER.). 1994. pap. 32.00 (*963-05-6656-7*, Pub. by A K HU) Intl Spec Bk.

Lukacs, Gabor. Le Roman Historique. (FRE.). 1977. pap. 28.95 (*0-7859-3036-1*) Fr & Eur.

Lukacs, Gabor, ed. Recent Progress in the Chemical Synthesis of Antibiotics & Related Microbial Products, Vol. 2. LC 93-2183. (Illus.). 980p. 1993. 240.00 (*0-387-56754-2*) Spr-Verlag.

Lukacs, Gabor & Ohno, M., eds. Recent Progress in the Chemical Synthesis of Antibiotics. 816p. 1990. 212.00 (*0-387-52444-4*) Spr-Verlag.

*__Lukacs, Georg.__ The Destruction of Reason. (C). 1952. text ed. 49.95 (*0-85036-247-4*, Pub. by Merlin Pr UK) Humanities.

— Essays on Thomas Mann. Mitchell, Stanley, tr. (C). 1995. pap. 18.50 (*0-85036-238-5*, Pub. by Merlin Pr UK) Humanities.

— Georg Lukacs: Selected Correspondence, 1902-1920. Marcus, Judith & Tar, Zoltan, eds. Tar, Zoltan, tr. LC 85-19027. (Illus.). 256p. 1986. text ed. 38.50 (*0-231-05968-X*) Col U Pr.

— German Realists in the Nineteenth Century. Gaines, Jeremy & Keast, Paul, trs. (Illus.). 350p. 1992. 37.50 (*0-262-12171-9*) MIT Pr.

— Goethe & His Age. Anchor, Robert, tr. 260p. (C). 1979. pap. 19.95 (*0-85036-071-4*, Pub. by Merlin Pr UK) Humanities.

— Goethe & His Age. Anchor, Robert, tr. 1978. reprint ed. 35.00 (*0-86527-256-5*) Fertig.

— History & Class Consciousness. Livingstone, Rodney, tr. 1971. reprint ed. pap. 14.50 (*0-262-62020-0*) MIT Pr.

— Lenin: A Study on the Unity of His Thought. Jacobs, Nicholas, tr. 1971. pap. 5.95x (*0-262-62024-3*) MIT Pr.

— The Meaning of Contemporary Realism. 137p. (C). 1979. pap. 19.95 (*0-85036-250-4*, Pub. by Merlin Pr UK) Humanities.

— Ontology of Social Being Vol. 1: Hegel. (C). 1982. pap. 8.95 (*0-85036-226-1*, Pub. by Merlin Pr UK) Humanities.

— Ontology of Social Being Vol. 2: Marx. (C). 1982. pap. 9.95 (*0-85036-227-X*, Pub. by Merlin Pr UK) Humanities.

— Ontology of Social Being Vol. 3: Labour. (C). 1980. pap. 9.95 (*0-85036-255-5*, Pub. by Merlin Pr UK) Humanities.

— The Process of Democratization. Bernhardt, Susanne & Levine, Norman, trs. LC 90-47554. (SUNY Series in Contemporary Continental Philosophy). 189p. (C). 1991. 59.50 (*0-7914-0761-6*); pap. 19.95 (*0-7914-0762-4*) State U NY Pr.

— Record of a Life: An Autobiographical Sketch. Livingstone, Rodney, tr. 204p. 1983. pap. text ed. 14.95 (*0-86091-771-1*, Pub. by Verso UK) Routledge Chapman & Hall.

— Reviews & Articles: From Die Rote Fahne. Palmer, Peter, tr. (C). 1978. pap. 7.50 (*0-85036-281-4*, Pub. by Merlin Pr UK) Humanities.

— Theory of the Novel. Bostock, Anna, tr. 1971. pap. 11.95 (*0-262-62027-8*) MIT Pr.

— The Theory of the Novel. Bostock, Anna, tr. (C). 1971. pap. 15.00 (*0-85036-236-9*, Pub. by Merlin Pr UK) Humanities.

— Writer & Critic: And Other Essays. Kahn, Arthur, tr. (C). 1995. pap. 17.50 (*0-85036-128-1*, Pub. by Merlin Pr UK) Humanities.

Lukacs, George. The Historical Novel. Mitchell, Hannah & Mitchell, Stanley, trs. LC 82-24772. 363p. 1983. reprint ed. pap. 12.00x (*0-8032-7910-8*, Bison Books) U of Nebr Pr.

Lukacs, Janos, jt. auth. see Burawoy, Michael.

Lukacs, John. Budapest, Nineteen Hundred: A Historical Portrait of a City & Its Culture. (Illus.). 1990. pap. 10.95 (*0-8021-3250-2*) Grove-Atltic.

— Destinations Past: Traveling Through History with John Lukacs. LC 93-45629. 240p. 1994. 26.95 (*0-8262-0956-4*) U of Mo Pr.

— Duel: May 10-July 31, 1940: The Eighty-Day Struggle Between Churchill & Hitler. 1992. pap. 10.95 (*0-395-61863-0*) HM.

— Historical Consciousness: The Remembered Past. rev. ed. 420p. 1994. pap. 21.95 (*1-56000-732-X*) Transaction Pubs.

— Immigration & Migration: A Historical Perspective. 20p. 1986. pap. 2.00 (*0-936247-05-3*) Amer Immigration.

— Philadelphia: Patricians & Philistines 1900-1950. (Illus.). 368p. 1981. 17.50 (*0-374-23161-3*) FS&G.

Lukacs, John R., ed. The People of South East Asia: Biological Anthropology of India, Pakistan & Nepal. 458p. 1984. 95.00 (*0-306-41407-4*, Plenum Pr) Plenum.

Lukacs, Jozset & Tokei, Ference. Philosophy & Culture: Studies from Hungary Published on the Occasion of the 17th World Congress of Philosophy. 368p. 1983. 67.50 (*0-317-53780-6*, Pub. by Collets UK) Pro-Am Music.

*__Lukacs, K.__ Hungarian-Slovak Pocket Dictionary. 576p. 1988. 15.00x (*963-205-219-6*, Pub. by Akad Kiado HU) St Mut.

*__Lukacs, Lajos.__ Chapters on the Hungarian Political Emigration, 1849-1867. (Studia Historica Academiae Scientarium Hungaricae Ser.: No. 196). 160p. 1995. 24.00 (*963-05-6838-1*, Pub. by A K HU) Intl Spec Bk.

Lukacs, Yehuda, ed. The Israeli-Palestinian Conflict: A Documentary Record. 2nd ed. 567p. (C). 1991. 84.95 (*0-521-37561-4*) Cambridge U Pr.

— The Israeli-Palestinian Conflict: A Documentary Record. 2nd ed. 567p. (C). 1992. pap. 29.95 (*0-521-37597-5*) Cambridge U Pr.

Lukaczer, Moses. The Federal Buy Indian Program: Promise Versus Performance. LC 75-32667. 126p. 1976. 9.00 (*0-87881-034-X*); pap. 7.00 (*0-87881-035-8*) Mojave Bks.

Lukanic, Steven A., ed. Film Actors Guide. 512p. 1992. 49.95 (*0-943728-38-X*) Lone Eagle Pub.

*__Lukas.__ Ambush. 4.99 (*0-679-87025-3*) Random.

Lukas, Cynthia K. Center Stage Summer. 157p. (Orig.). (YA). (gr. 8-12). 1988. pap. 4.95 (*0-938961-02-0*, Stamp Out Sheep Pr) Sq One Pubs.

Lukas, Elisabeth. Meaning in Suffering: Comfort in Crisis Through Logotherapy. Fabry, Joseph, tr. 160p. (Orig.). 1986. pap. 7.95 (*0-917867-05-X*) Inst Logo.

— Meaningful Living. LC 83-20235. 140p. 1984. pap. 8.95 (*0-317-16582-8*) Inst Logo.

Lukas, George. Home Brewmastery. 112p. 1991. pap. text ed. 7.95 (*0-9631242-1-8*) Yerba Buena.

Lukas, J. Anthony. Common Ground: A Turbulent Decade in the Lives of Three American Families. LC 85-127. 672p. 1985. 19.95 (*0-394-41150-1*) Knopf.

— Common Ground: A Turbulent Decade in the Lives of Three American Families. LC 86-40132. 784p. 1986. pap. 15.00 (*0-394-74616-3*, Vin) Random.

Lukas, Johannes. A Study of the Kanuri Language, Grammar & Vocabulary. LC 38-24176. 271p. 1937. reprint ed. pap. 77.60 (*0-8357-3017-4*, 2057103) Bks Demand.

Lukas, Jurgen, jt. auth. see Eiden, Heribert.

Lukas, Karen. The Educational System of the Former German Democratic Republic. 80p. (Orig.). 1991. pap. 20.00 (*0-910054-94-0*) Am Assn Coll Registrars.

Lukas, Karen, jt. auth. see Dickey, Karlene N.

Lukas, Karen H. Austria: A Study of the Educational System of Austria & a Guide to the Academic Placement of Students in Educational Institutions of the United States. LC 87-980. (World Education Ser.). (Illus.). 178p. reprint ed. pap. 50.80 (*0-8357-3114-6*, 2039371) Bks Demand.

Lukas, Noah. The Stinky Book. LC 92-22701. (Illus.). 24p. (J). (ps up). 1993. 7.99 (*0-679-83619-5*) Random Bks Yng Read.

— Tiny Trolls' ABC. LC 92-62940. (Mini-Storybooks Ser.). (Illus.). 24p. (Orig.). (J). (ps-00). 1993. pap. 1.50 (*0-679-84797-9*) Random Bks Yng Read.

— Tiny Trolls' 1, 2, 3. LC 92-62939. (Mini-Storybooks Ser.). (Illus.). 24p. (Orig.). (J). (ps-00). 1993. pap. 1.50 (*0-679-84792-8*) Random Bks Yng Read.

An Asterisk (*) at the beginning of an entry indicates that the title is appearing in BIP for the first time.

Lukas, Noah, jt. auth. see Ross, Katharine.

Lukas, P. & Polak, J., eds. Basic Mechanisms in Fatigue of Materials: Proceedings of the International Colloquium, Brno, Czechoslovakia, 12-14 April, 1988. (Materials Science Monographs: 46). 450p. 1988. 166.75 (*0-444-98926-9*) Elsevier.

Lukas, Richard C. Bitter Legacy: Polish-American Relations in the Wake of World War II. LC 82-1972. (Illus.). 200p. 1982. 22.00 (*0-8131-1460-8*) U Pr of Ky.

— Did the Children Cry? Hitler's War Against Jewish & Polish Children, 1939-1945. (Illus.). 320p. 1994. 22.50 (*0-7818-0242-3*) Hippocrene Bks.

— Eagles East: The Army Air Forces & the Soviet Union, 1941-1945. LC 78-126957. 266p. reprint ed. pap. 75.90 (*0-7837-4949-X*, 2044615) Bks Demand.

— Forgotten Holocaust. 1990. pap. 9.95 (*0-87052-632-4*) Hippocrene Bks.

— The Strange Allies: The United States & Poland, 1941-1945. LC 77-8585. 240p. reprint ed. 68.40 (*0-685-16069-6*, 2027566) Bks Demand.

Lukas, Richard C., ed. Out of the Inferno: Poles Remember the Holocaust. LC 89-5646. 224p. 1989. 25.00 (*0-8131-1692-9*) U Pr of Ky.

Lukas, Scott E. Amphetamines: Danger in the Fast Lane. (Encyclopedia of Psychoactive Drugs - Compact Paperback Library). (Illus.). 32p. (YA). (gr. 5 up). 1991. pap. 4.49 (*0-7910-0003-6*) Chelsea Hse.

— Amphetamines: Danger in the Fast Lane. (Encyclopedia of Psychoactive Drugs Ser.: No. 1). (Illus.). (YA). (gr. 5 up). 1992. lib. bdg. 19.95 (*0-685-54573-3*) Chelsea Hse.

— Steroids. LC 93-38524. (Drug Library Ser.). (Illus.). 112p. (J). (gr. 6 up). 1994. lib. bdg. 17.95 (*0-89490-471-X*) Enslow Pubs.

Lukas, Susan. Where to Start & What to Ask: The Assessment Handbook. 220p. (C). 1992. 22.94 (*0-393-70148-4*) Norton.

— Where to Start & What to Ask: The Assessment Handbook. 220p. (C). 1993. pap. 14.95 (*0-393-70152-2*) Norton.

Lukas, Viktor. Guide to Organ Music. Wyburd, Anne, tr. LC 89-30795. (Illus.). 272p. 1989. 22.95 (*0-931340-10-1*, Amadeus Pr) Timber.

Lukasevich, Ann. Favorites, Friendships, Food & Fantasy: Literature-Based Thematic Units for Early Primary. 1993. pap. 24.95 (*0-201-81844-2*) Addison-Wesley.

— Food & Fantasy, Vol. 2: Literature-Based Thematic Units for Early Primary. (J). (ps-3). 1993. pap. 18.95 (*0-201-49037-4*) Addison-Wesley.

Lukashevich, Stephen. Ivan Aksakov, 1823-1886: A Study in Russian Thought & Politics. LC 65-22050. (Historical Monographs: No. 57). 203p. 1965. 15.00 (*0-674-46975-5*) HUP.

— N. F. Federov (Eighteen Twenty-Eight to Nineteen Hundred Three) A Study in Russian Eupsychian & Utopian Thought. LC 75-29731. 316p. 1977. 39.50 (*0-87413-113-8*) U Delaware Pr.

— Thus Spake Master Chuang: A Structural Exegesis of Taoist Philosophy. (American University Studies: Philosophy: Ser. V, Vol. 25). 170p. (C). 1987. text ed. 35.00 (*0-8204-0390-3*) P Lang Pubs.

Lukasiewicz, J. Elements of Mathematical Logic. 2nd ed. (International Series on Pure & Applied Mathematics: Vol. 31). 1964. 56.00 (*0-08-010393-6*, Pub. by Pergamon Repr UK) Franklin.

Lukasiewicz, Julius & Bogdonoff, Seymour. Experimental Methods of Hypersonics. 2nd ed. LC 72-90377. 1996. write for info. (*0-89464-846-2*) Krieger.

Lukasiewicz, Michael A., ed. see Symposium on Industrial Combustion Technologies Staff.

Lukasiewicz, S. Local Loads in Plates & Shells, No. 4. (Mechanics of Surface Structures Ser.). 596p. 1979. lib. bdg. 183.00 (*90-286-0047-7*) Kluwer Ac.

Lukaszewicz, Joseph. Girys I Biruta: Poemat Z Dawnych Czasow Litewskich. 1964. 2.75 (*0-685-09284-4*) Endurance.

Lukaszewski, David. Little Ms. Rosey & Friends. (J). 1993. 7.75 (*0-8062-4622-7*) Carlton.

***Lukaszewski, James E.** Building Quality Community Relationships: A Planning Model to Gain & Maintain Public Consent. 59p. 1995. pap. 40.00 (*1-883291-11-9*) Lukaszewski.

— Communication Standards: The Principles & Protocols for Standard-Setting Individual & Corporate Communication. 8p. Date not set. pap. 20.00 (*1-883291-12-7*) Lukaszewski.

— Coping with Activist Intrusions & Threats. 9p. 1995. pap. 20.00 (*1-883291-13-5*) Lukaszewski.

— Executive Action Corporate Crisis Communication Model Plan. 100p. Date not set. student ed 60.00 (*1-883291-09-7*) Lukaszewski.

— Executive Action Crisis Management Anthology: 1992 Edition. LC 91-90776. 100p. 1992. student ed 50.00 (*1-883291-01-1*) Lukaszewski.

— Executive Action Crisis Management Workbook. LC 93-91384. 120p. 1993. student ed 50.00 (*1-883291-05-4*); vhs 40.00 (*1-883291-04-6*) Lukaszewski.

— Executive Action Emergency Media Relations Guide. LC 93-91383. 116p. 1993. student ed 60.00 (*1-883291-06-2*) Lukaszewski.

— Executive Action Managing Litigation Visibility: A Strategic Planning Guide. 100p. Date not set. student ed 60.00 (*1-883291-08-9*) Lukaszewski.

— Exxon Valdez: The Great Crisis Management Paradox. 27p. 1995. pap. 20.00 (*1-883291-14-3*) Lukaszewski.

— Influencing Public Attitudes: Strategies That Reduce the Media's Power. Fisher, Audrey, ed. (Illus.). 64p. (Orig.). 1992. pap. text ed. 14.95 (*0-913869-03-1*) Issue Action Pubns.

— The Peppermill Public Hearing: A Communication Skill-Building Simulation Exercise. 12p. 1995. pap. 30.00 (*1-883291-15-1*) Lukaszewski.

— Surviving "60 Minutes" & the Other News Magazine Shows. 16p. 1995. pap. 40.00 (*1-883291-16-X*) Lukaszewski.

— The Tactical Ingenuity Pyramid & Thinker's Manual. 12p. 1990. pap. 10.00 (*1-883291-00-3*) Lukaszewski.

Lukawecki. Applied Calculus. 1983. Student's Solution Manual. student ed, pap. text ed. write for info. (*0-07-029314-7*) McGraw.

Lukawecki, jt. auth. see Feiner.

Luke. Complete Luke Multi-Pesticide Residue Method. 1994. write for info. (*0-8493-7993-8*) CRC Pr.

— Jesus & His First Followers: The True Story. 180p. (Orig.). 1989. pap. 4.99 (*0-8010-5654-3*) Baker Bk.

Luke, Allan. Literacy, Textbooks & Ideology: Postwar Literacy Instruction & the Mythology of Dick & Jane. 200p. 1988. 85.00 (*1-85000-318-1*, Falmer Pr); pap. 33.00 (*1-85000-319-X*, Falmer Pr) Taylor & Francis.

Luke, Allan & Gilbert, Pam, eds. Literacy in Contexts: Australian Perspectives & Issues. 144p. (Orig.). 1993. pap. text ed. 14.95 (*1-86373-340-X*, Pub. by Allen Unwin AT) Paul & Co Pubs.

Luke, Allan, jt. ed. see Baker, Carolyn D.

Luke, Allan, jt. ed. see Baldauf, Richard B.

Luke, Allan, ed. see Edelsky, Carole.

Luke, B. & Keith, Louis G. Principles & Practice of Maternal Nutrition. (Illus.). 250p. 1992. 39.00 (*1-85070-324-8*) Prthnon Pub.

***Luke, Barbara.** Every Pregnant Woman's Guide to Preventing Premature Birth: A Program for Reducing the Sixty Proven Risks That Can Lead to Prematurity. LC 95-12213. 1995. 23.00 (*0-8129-2472-X*, Times Bks) Random.

Luke, Barbara, et al. Clinical Maternal-Fetal Nutrition. LC 92-48905. (Illus.). 368p. 1993. 79.95 (*0-316-53614-8*) Little.

Luke, Carmen. Constructing the Child Viewer: A History of the American Discourse on Television & Children, 1950-1980. LC 90-7354. 344p. 1990. text ed. 59.95 (*0-275-93516-7*, C3516, Praeger Pubs) Greenwood.

— Pedagogy, Printing, & Protestantism: The Discourse on Childhood. LC 88-13924. (Philosophy of Education Ser.). 171p. (C). 1989. 64.50 (*0-7914-0002-6*); pap. 21.95 (*0-7914-0003-4*) State U NY Pr.

Luke, Carmen & Gore, Jennifer, eds. Feminisms & Critical Pedagogy. 224p. 1992. 49.95 (*0-415-90533-8*, A6754, Routledge NY); pap. 14.95 (*0-415-90534-6*, A6758, Routledge NY) Routledge.

Luke, Carmen, jt. ed. see Manley-Casimir, Michael E.

Luke, Cheryl M. & Swafford, Ann J. Word Processing Communication Skills. 136p. (C). 1988. pap. text ed. 15.50 (*0-15-596660-X*) Dryden Pr.

Luke, Christopher. Unfinished Business. LC 93-10692. 352p. 1993. 22.95 (*1-56790-000-3*, 93-010692) Cool Hand Comms.

Luke, David, tr. Goethe: Selected Verse. 367p. 1982. pap. 10.95 (*0-14-042074-6*, Penguin Classics) Viking Penguin.

Luke, David, tr. see Goethe, Johann Wolfgang Von.

Luke, David, tr. see Grimm, Jacob & Grimm, Wilhelm K.

Luke, David, tr. see Mann, Thomas.

Luke, David, tr. see Von Kleist, Heinrich.

Luke, David F. Labour & Parastatal Politics in Sierra Leone: A Study of African Working-Class Ambivalence. (Dalhousie African Studies). (Illus.). 306p. (Orig.). (C). 1984. lib. bdg. 52.00 (*0-8191-3957-2*); pap. text ed. 25.50 (*0-8191-3958-0*) U Pr of Amer.

Luke, Elmer, ed. Monkey Brain Sushi: New Tastes in Japanese Fiction. (Japan's Modern Writers Ser.). (Illus.). 312p. 1993. pap. 10.00 (*4-7700-1688-3*) Kodansha.

Luke, Elmer, ed. see Kennedy, Rick.

Luke, Elmer, ed. see Murakami, Haruki.

Luke, Elmer, ed. see Shimada, Masahiko.

Luke, Elmer, ed. see Zielinski, Robert & Holloway, Nigel.

Luke, F. D., tr. see Goethe, Johann Wolfgang Von.

Luke, Harry C. In the Margin of History. LC 67-26755. (Essay Index Reprint Ser.). 1977. 23.95 (*0-8369-0634-9*) Ayer.

Luke, heather. Easy Upholstery: Step by Step. 192p. 1994. pap. 24.95 (*0-8019-8630-3*) Chilton.

Luke, Helen. Woman: Earth & Spirit. 112p. 1984. pap. 9.95 (*0-8245-0633-2*) Crossroad NY.

Luke, Helen M. Dark Wood to White Rose: Journey & Transformation in Dante's Divine Comedy. 1989. 19.95 (*0-930407-15-6*) Parabola Bks.

— Dark Wood to White Rose: Journey & Transformation in Dante's "Divine Comedy" 1993. pap. 14.95 (*0-930407-28-8*) Parabola Bks.

— Kaleidoscope: The Way of Woman & Other Essays. 1992. 17.95 (*0-930407-24-5*) Parabola Bks.

— Kaleidoscope: The Way of Woman & Other Essays. 1993. pap. 14.95 (*0-930407-29-6*) Parabola Bks.

— Life of the Spirit in Women: A Jungian Approach. LC 79-91960. (C). 1980. pap. 3.00 (*0-87574-230-0*) Pendle Hill.

— Old Age: Journey into Simplicity. (Illus.). 128p. 1987. 12.95 (*0-930407-04-0*); pap. 7.95 (*0-930407-05-9*) Parabola Bks.

— The Way of Woman: Awakening the Perennial Feminine. LC 95-15929. 1995. write for info. (*0-385-47850-X*) Doubleday.

Luke, High, Jr., ed. see Shelley, Mary Wollstonecraft.

Luke, Hugh J., ed. see Swinburne, Algernon C.

Luke, Igumen, ed. see Anatoly, Elder.

Luke, Jeff. A Preliminary Study of the Homeless in Omaha-Douglas County. 43p. (Orig.). 1986. pap. 3.50 (*1-55719-020-8*) U NE CPAR.

Luke, Jeff, et al. Health Care for the Poor in Omaha-Douglas County: Problems & Policy Options. 136p. (Orig.). 1985. pap. 9.50 (*1-55719-108-5*) U NE CPAR.

Luke, Jeffrey S. & Webb, Vincent J., eds. Nebraska Policy Choices, 1986. (Illus.). 240p. (Orig.). 1986. pap. 9.95 (*1-55719-000-3*) U NE CPAR.

Luke, Jeffrey S., et al. Managing Economic Development: A Guide to State & Local Leadership Strategies. LC 87-46347. (Public Administration Ser.). 296p. 1988. 36.95 (*1-55542-092-3*) Jossey-Bass.

Luke, Kang K. Utterance Particles in Cantonese Conversations. LC 90-31714. (Pragmatics & Beyond New Ser.: Vol. 9). xvi, 329p. 1990. 76.00x (*1-55619-275-4*) Benjamins North Am.

***Luke, Mary.** The Nine Days Queen. 1994. reprint ed. lib. bdg. 32.95x (*1-56849-526-9*) Buccaneer Bks.

Luke, Peter. Mad Pomegranate & the Praying Mantis: An Andalusian Adventure. 238p. 1984. 25.00 (*0-86140-200-6*, Pub. by Colin Smythe Ltd UK) Dufour.

Luke, Peter, ed. Enter Certain Players: Edwards - MacLiammoir & the Gate, 1928-1978. (Illus.). 104p. 1978. pap. 9.95 (*0-318-40002-2*, Pub. by Colin Smythe Ltd UK) Dufour.

— Enter Certain Players: Edwards, Mac Liammoir & the Gate 1928-1978. (Illus.). 1978. pap. 12.95 (*0-85105-345-9*, Pub. by Dolmen Pr IE) Dufour.

Luke, Peter, tr. see Garcia Lorca, Federico.

Luke, Robert A., ed. see Ulmer, Curtis.

Luke, Susan. Awsome Family Nights. Date not set. pap. 7.95 (*1-55503-689-9*, 01111639) Covenant Comms.

— Fantastic Family Nights. LC 92-75978. 1991. pap. 6.95 (*1-55503-520-5*, 01111175) Covenant Comms.

— Little Talks for Little People. Date not set. pap. 7.95 (*1-55503-654-6*, 01111507) Covenant Comms.

— Log Cabin Logic: Creating Success Where You Are with What You Have. 150p. 1995. pap. 12.50 (*0-9646034-0-3*) Luke Communs.

Luke, Timothy W. Ideology & Soviet Industrialization. LC 84-12812. (Contributions in Political Science Ser.: No. 120). xi, 283p. 1985. text ed. 59.95 (*0-313-23831-6*, LIS/, Greenwood Pr) Greenwood.

— Screens of Power: Ideology, Domination, & Resistance in Informational Society. LC 88-37528. 280p. 1989. 34.95 (*0-252-01629-7*); pap. 14.95 (*0-252-06154-3*) U of Ill Pr.

— Shows of Force: Power, Politics, & Ideology in Art Exhibitions. LC 91-20018. 264p. 1992. lib. bdg. 39.95 (*0-8223-1188-7*); pap. 16.95 (*0-8223-1123-2*) Duke.

— Social Theory & Modernity: Critique, Dissent, & Revolution. 280p. (C). 1990. text ed. 49.95 (*0-8039-3860-8*); pap. text ed. 24.00 (*0-8039-3861-6*) Sage.

Luke, Y. L., et al. Index to Mathematics of Computation, 1943-1969. 461p. 1972. 47.00 (*0-8218-4000-2*, MCOMIN-1) Am Math.

Luke, Yudell L. Special Functions & Their Approximations, 2 Vols, 1. LC 68-23498. (Mathematics in Science & Engineering Ser.: Vol. 53). 1969. text ed. 121.00 (*0-12-459901-X*) Acad Pr.

— Special Functions & Their Approximations, 2 Vols, 2. LC 68-23498. (Mathematics in Science & Engineering Ser.: Vol. 53). 1969. text ed. 136.00 (*0-12-459902-8*) Acad Pr.

Lukefahr, Oscar. A Catholic Guide to the Bible. LC 92-82795. 208p. (Orig.). 1992. pap. text ed. 5.95 (*0-89243-477-5*) Liguori Pubns.

— A Catholic Guide to the Bible Workbook. 62p. (Orig.). 1992. pap. text ed. 2.95 (*0-89243-478-3*) Liguori Pubns.

— Morning Star: Christ's Mother & Ours. 208p. 1995. pap. 7.95 (*0-89243-766-9*); student ed, pap. 2.95 (*0-89243-767-7*) Liguori Pubns.

— The Privilege of Being Catholic. 208p. (Orig.). 1993. pap. 5.95 (*0-89243-563-1*); student ed, pap. 2.95 (*0-89243-564-X*) Liguori Pubns.

— We Believe...Workbook. 64p. (Orig.). 1995. pap. 2.95 (*0-89243-539-9*) Liguori Pubns.

***Lukefahr, Oscar C.** We Believe... A Survey of the Catholic Faith. LC 90-60495. 224p. (Orig.). 1995. pap. 7.95 (*0-89243-536-4*) Liguori Pubns.

Lukehart, Peter M., jt. ed. see Smyth, Craig H.

Lukehart, S., jt. auth. see Hook, E.

***Lukei, Reese, ed.** The American Discovery Trail Explorer's Guide. (Illus.). 128p. (Orig.). 1995. pap. 14.95 (*1-55566-135-1*) Johnson Bks.

Lukeman, Alex. What Your Dreams Can Teach You. LC 90-45793. 288p. 1990. pap. 12.95 (*0-87542-475-9*) Llewellyn Pubns.

Lukeman, Brenda S. & Lukeman, Noah T. Journey Through Illness & Beyond. LC 94-66317. 160p. (C). 1995. pap. 9.95 (*0-9641416-0-4*) Steppstone Pr. A powerful tool for creating emotional health during illness & loss offers simple, practical guidelines and exercises. Written by a psychologist who has worked for years with the seriously ill, friends, families & staff, it includes a complete program which helps us communicate effectively, understand feelings, deal with loss & parting & find the courage to move on. Finally, an easy-to- read, hands-on-guide. "Dr.Brenda Shoshanna Lukeman's words are wonderful." Marianne Williamson, best-selling author. "..wisdom, tears, smiles, consoling hands & spiritual guidance. The most important work I have read in the last years. & the most beautiful one, too." Judge Amnon Carmi, Editor-in-Chief of Medicine and Law, Haifa Israel. "This is by far the most practical, profound, wise & tender book on illness, loss & emotional healing that I have ever read. A life giving book." Dr. Jana Klenburg. "I have recently begun leading a health program for persons with and concerned about AIDS. Your book has been extremely helpful. A masterpiece." Dr. Peter Hendrickson, Author of Alive and Well: A Path for Living in the Time of HIV. Order from Steppingstones Press, PO BOX 220-249, Great Neck, NY, 11022. Tel. 1-800-879-4214.** ***Publisher Provided Annotation.

— Journey Through Illness & Beyond. rev. ed. LC 94-66317. 160p. (C). 1995. 14.95 (*0-9641416-1-2*) Steppstone Pr. A powerful tool for creating emotional health during illness & loss offers simple, practical guidelines & exercises. Written by a psychologist who has worked for years with the seriously ill, friends, families & staff, it includes a complete program which helps us communicate effectively, understand feelings, deal with loss & parting & find the courage to move on. Finally, an easy-to-read, hands-on-guide. NABE best book of the year in "Health" category. "Dr. Brenda Shoshanna Lukeman's words are wonderful." - Marianne Williamson, best-selling author. "..wisdom, tears, smiles, consoling hands & spiritual guidance. The most important work I have read in the last years. & the most beautiful one, too." - Judge Amnon Carmi, Editor-in-Chief of Medicine & Law, Haifa Israel. "This is by far the most practical, profound, wise & tender book on illness, loss & emotional healing that I have ever read. A life giving book." - Dr. Jana Klenburg. "I have recently begun leading a health program for persons with & concerned about AIDS. Your book has been extremely helpful. A masterpiece." - Dr. Peter Hendrickson, Author of Alive & Well: A Path for Living in the Time of HIV. Order from Steppingstones Press, PO BOX 220-249, Great Neck, NY, 11022. Tel. 1-800-879-4214. ***Publisher Provided Annotation.***

Lukeman, Chester M. Schools - Progress, Activities & Trends: Index of New Information with Authors, Subjects & Bibliography. 180p. 1993. 49.50 (*1-55914-808-X*); pap. 39.50 (*1-55914-809-8*) ABBE Pubs Assn.

Lukeman, Noah T., jt. auth. see Lukeman, Brenda S.

Luken, James O. Directing Ecological Succession. 192p. 1990. 77.50 (*0-412-34450-5*, A5005) Chapman & Hall.

Lukenbill, Stewart. Youth Literature: An Interdisciplinary, Annotated Guide to North American Dissertation Research, 1930-1985. LC 87-38077. 482p. 1988. 77.00 (*0-8240-8498-5*) Garland.

Lukenbill, W. Bernard. AIDS & HIV Programs & Services for Libraries. 160p. 1994. lib. bdg. 32.00 (*1-56308-175-X*) Libs Unl.

Lukens, C. Randolph. Reflections. LC 91-67926. 64p. 1993. pap. 8.00 (*1-56002-190-X*, Univ Edtns) Aegina Pr.

Lukens, James P. Heart Thoughts. 1994. 8.95 (*0-533-10881-0*) Vantage.

Lukens, Michael B. Conflict & Community: New Studies in Thomistic Thought. LC 89-34167. 204p. (C). 1992. text ed. 39.95 (*0-8204-1204-X*) P Lang Pubs.

Lukens, Nancy & Rosenberg, Dorothy, eds. Daughters of Eve: Women's Writing from the German Democratic Republic. LC 92-31238. (European Women Writers Ser.). xi, 332p. 1993. 40.00 (*0-8032-2892-9*); pap. 14.95 (*0-8032-7942-6*) U of Nebr Pr.

Lukens, Rebecca J. A Critical Handbook of Children's Literature. 4th ed. (C). 1989. pap. text ed. 16.25 (*0-673-38773-9*) HarpCollege.

Lukens, Rebecca J. & Cline, eds. Critical Handbook of Children's Literature. 5th ed. LC 93-42826. 352p. (C). 1994. text ed. 17.25 (*0-673-46937-9*) HarpCollege.

— Critical Handbook of Young Adult & Children's Literature. 5th ed. (C). 1994. text ed. 20.00 (*0-06-501108-2*) HarpCollege.

Lukens, Sheila, jt. auth. see Rosso, Julee.

Luker & Adelsberger. Intelligent Simulation Environments. 166p. 1986. 40.00 (*0-685-67786-9*, SS17-1) Soc Computer Sim.

Luker & Brirtwistle. AI & Simulation. 100p. 1987. 40.00 (*0-685-66775-8*, SS18-3) Soc Computer Sim.

Luker, Benjamin F. Use of the Infinitive Instead of a Finite Verb in French. LC 16-16932. (Columbia University. Studies in Romance Philology & Literature: No. 18). reprint ed. 14.50 (*0-404-50618-6*) AMS Pr.

Luker, Karen A. & Orr, Jean. Health Visiting: Towards Community Health Nursing. 2nd ed. (Illus.). 272p. 1992. pap. 32.95 (*0-632-03324-X*) Blackwell Sci.

Luker, Kristin. Abortion & the Politics of Motherhood. LC 83-47849. (California Series on Social Choice & Political Economy: Vol. 3). 350p. (C). 1984. pap. 30.00 (0-520-04314-6); pap. 14.00 (0-520-05597-7) U CA Pr.

— Taking Chances: Abortion & the Decision Not to Contracept. LC 74-22965. 200p. 1975. pap. 11.00 (0-520-03594-1) U CA Pr.

Luker, Nicholas, ed. An Anthology of Russian Neo-Realism: The "Znanie" School of Maxim Gorky. LC 81-12758. (Illus.). 283p. 1982. pap. 15.95 (0-88233-422-0) Ardis Pubs.

— From Furmanov to Sholokhov: An Anthology of the Classics of Socialist Realism. (Illus.). (C). 1988. pap. text ed. 17.95 (0-87501-037-7) Ardis Pubs.

Luker, Ralph. A Southern Tradition in Theology & Social Criticism, 1830-1930. LC 84-8954. (Studies in American Religion: Vol. 11). 468p. 1984. lib. bdg. 109.95 (0-88946-655-6) E Mellen.

Luker, Ralph E. The Social Gospel in Black & White: American Racial Reform, 1885-1912. LC 91-50257. (Studies in Religion). (Illus.). xvi, 446p. (C). 1991. 45.00 (0-8078-1978-6) U of NC Pr.

Luker, Ralph E., ed. see Ovington, Mary W.

Lukert, Barbara P., jt. auth. see Overton, Meredith H.

Lukes, Bonnie L. How to Be a Reasonably Thin Teenage Girl (Without Starving, Losing Your Friends, or Running Away from Home) LC 86-3347. (Illus.). 96p. (YA). (gr. 6 up). 1986. text ed. 13.95 (0-689-31269-5, Aladdin Paperbacks) S&S Childrens.

Lukes, Dahlard L. Differential Equation: Classical to Controlled. (Mathematics in Science and Engineering Ser.). 1982. text ed. 91.00 (0-12-459980-X) Acad Pr.

Lukes, Igor, jt. auth. see Ra'anan, Uri.

Lukes, Igor, jt. ed. see Ra'anan, Uri.

Lukes, J., et al. Fine Topology Methods in Real Analysis & Potential Theory. (Lecture Notes in Mathematics Ser.: Vol. 1189). x, 472p. 1986. pap. 53.00 (0-387-16474-X) Spr-Verlag.

Lukes, Steven. Emile Durkheim: His Life & Work: A Historical & Critical Study. LC 85-50791. x, 676p. 1985. reprint ed. 62.50 (0-8047-1282-4); reprint ed. pap. 19.95 (0-8047-1283-2) Stanford U Pr.

— Essays in Social Theory. LC 77-8505. 1977. text ed. 40.50 (0-231-04450-X) Col U Pr.

— Essays in Social Thought. (Modern Revivals in Sociology Ser.). 238p. 1994. 59.95 (0-7512-0315-7, Pub. by Gregg Revivals UK) Ashgate Pub Co.

— Marxism & Morality. (Marxist Introductions Ser.). 163p. 1985. 36.00 (0-19-876101-5) OUP.

— Marxism & Morality. (Marxist Introductions Ser.). 163p. 1987. pap. 16.95 (0-19-282074-5) OUP.

— Moral Conflict & Politics. 336p. 1991. 69.00 (0-19-827536-6, 1675) OUP.

— Power: A Radical Review. 4th ed. 64p. (C). 1974. pap. 12.50 (0-333-16672-8, Pub. by Macmillan UK) Humanities.

Lukes, Steven, ed. Power. LC 86-8511. (Readings in Social & Political Theory Ser.). 256p. 1986. 45.00x (0-8147-5030-3); pap. 17.50x (0-8147-5031-1) NYU Pr.

Lukes, Steven, jt. ed. see Hollis, Martin.

Lukes, Timothy J. The Flight into Inwardness: Herbert Marcuse & Liberatory Aesthetics. LC 83-40508. 184p. 1985. 32.50 (0-941664-04-X) Susquehanna U Pr.

Lukes, Timothy J., jt. ed. see Bokina, John.

Lukevics, E. & Ignatovich, L. M. Organosilicon & Organogermanium Derivatives of Furan, Vol. 12. (Chemistry Reviews Ser.: SSR Sec. B, Vol. 12, Pt. 3). 88p. 1988. pap. text ed. 65.00 (3-7186-4854-7) Gordon & Breach.

Lukevics, E., et al. Thiophene Derivatives of Group IV B Elements. (Sulfur Report Ser.: Vol. 2, No. 5). 38p. 1982. pap. text ed. 76.00 (3-7186-0133-8) Gordon & Breach.

***Lukey, Joan.** A Fiduciary Duty. 378p. 1994. pap. 9.95 (1-56901-577-5) NW Pub.

Lukezic, Joyce & Schwarz, Ted. False Arrest: The Joyce Lukezic Story. LC 89-63990. 342p. 1990. 21.95 (0-88282-050-8) New Horizon NJ.

Lukhaup, D., jt. auth. see Junge, H. D.

***Lukhaup, Dieter.** Dictionary of Environmental Protection: French-German, German-French. 500p. (FRE & GER.). 1993. 250.00 (0-7859-8418-6, 3527282432) Fr & Eur.

— Parat Dictionary of Environmental Protection: English-German, German-English. 532p. (ENG & GER.). 1992. 225.00 (0-7859-6956-X) Fr & Eur.

Lukic, Marie. Pasquale's Gift. LC 93-29002. (Voyages Ser.). (Illus.). (J). 1994. 4.25 (0-383-03768-9) SRA Schl Grp.

***Lukic, Reneo & Lynch, Allan.** Europe from the Balkans to the Urals: The Disintegration of Yugoslavia & the USSR & World Politics. (SIPRI Publication Ser.). (Illus.). 368p. 1995. 49.95 (0-19-829200-7) OUP.

Lukic, Sveta. Contemporary Yugoslav Literature: Sociopolitical Approach. Robinson, Gertrude J., ed. Triandis, Pola, tr. LC 77-166116. 296p. reprint ed. pap. 84.40 (0-317-09655-9, 2020864) Bks Demand.

Lukierski, J., jt. ed. see Jancewicz, B.

Lukin. The Big Carrot Vegetarian Cookbook: From the Kitchen of Big Carrot Natural Food Mart. (NFS Canada). Date not set. pap. 14.95 (0-929005-05-8, Pub. by Second Story Pr CN) InBook.

Lukin, Anne. On the Road to Vegetarian Cooking: Easy Meals for Everyone. Date not set. pap. 14.95 (0-929005-28-7, Pub. by Second Story Pr CN) InBook.

Lukin, James, ed. Turning Lathes: A Guide to Turning, Screw Cutting, Metal Spinning & Ornamental Turning. (Illus.). 432p. 1994. reprint ed. pap. 24.95 (1-879335-49-2) Astragal Pr.

Lukin, James & Hilscher, Hilary, eds. Alaska's Arctic. (Illus.). 160p. 1991. 39.95 (1-55868-044-6) Gr Arts Ctr Pub.

***Lukin, Vladimir P.** Atmospheric Adaptive Optics. Schippnick, Paul F., tr. LC 95-12082. 1995. write for info. (0-8194-1871-4) SPIE.

Lukinich, Imre. History of Hungary in Biographical Sketches. LC 68-20314. (Essay Index Reprint Ser.). 1977. 19.95 (0-8369-0635-7) Ayer.

Lukins, Sheila. Sheila Lukins All Around the World Cookbook. LC 94-2421. 1994. 27.95 (1-56305-636-4); pap. 18.95 (1-56305-237-7) Workman Pub.

Lukins, Sheila, jt. auth. see Rosso, Julee.

Lukitsh, Joanne. Julia Margaret Cameron: Her Work & Career. (Illus.). 103p. (Orig.). 1986. pap. 15.00 (0-935398-13-9) G Eastman Hse.

***Lukitz, Libra.** Iraq: The Search for National Indentity. 224p. 1995. 31.50 (0-7146-4550-8, Pub. by F Cass Pubs UK); pap. 18.50 (0-7146-4128-6, Pub. by F Cass Pubs UK) Intl Spec Bk.

Lukka, Orpena, ed. see Orpana, V.

***Lukken, Miriam W.** Read This Book Before Your Child Starts School. (Illus.). 240p. 1994. pap. 16.95 (0-614-02262-2) C C Thomas.

— Read This Book Before Your Child Starts School. (Illus.). 240p. (C). 1994. text ed. 31.95 (0-398-05916-0) C C Thomas.

Lukman, Mphahlele K. The Critical Issues of Skin Colour: A Treatise on the Sociological, Economic & Political Reality of Blacks in a White Society. 300p. 1985. text ed. 19.95 (0-9602660-0-3) M Lukman.

Lukoff, Fred. English for Koreans. (English for Foreigners Ser.). xvi, 480p. (ENG & KOR.). 1980. student ed, audio 100.00 (0-87950-611-3) Spoken Lang Serv.

— English for Koreans. (English for Foreigners Ser.). xvi, 480p. (ENG & KOR.). 1980. reprint ed. pap. 15.00 (0-87950-306-8); reprint ed. audio 85.00 (0-87950-610-5) Spoken Lang Serv.

— Spoken Korean. LC 73-17223. (Spoken Language Ser.). 370p. (gr. 9-12). 1975. audio 70.00 (0-87950-155-3) Spoken Lang Serv.

— Spoken Korean, Bk. 1. LC 73-17223. (Spoken Language Ser.). 370p. (gr. 9-12). 1975. audio 80.00 (0-87950-156-1) Spoken Lang Serv.

— Spoken Korean, Bk, 1, Units 1-12. LC 73-17223. (Spoken Language Ser.). 370p. (gr. 9-12). 1975. pap. 10.00 (0-87950-150-2) Spoken Lang Serv.

— Spoken Korean, Bk. 2, Units 13-30. LC 73-17223. (Spoken Language Ser.). 305p. (gr. 9-12). 1975. pap. 15.00 (0-87950-151-0) Spoken Lang Serv.

Lukoff, Irving F. & Whiteman, Martin. The Social Sources of Adjustment to Blindness. LC 73-84034. (American Foundation for the Blind Research Ser.: No. 21). 301p. reprint ed. pap. 85.80 (0-7837-2759-3, 2043142) Bks Demand.

Lukoff, Irving F., et al. Attitudes Toward Blind Persons. LC 72-82239. 80p. reprint ed. pap. 25.00 (0-7837-5187-7, 2044921) Bks Demand.

Lukomski-Borowiak-Dunkelberg. Zum Arabischen Pferd. (Documenta Hippologica Ser.). (Illus.). 78p. 1979. reprint ed. write for info. (3-487-08192-X, Pub. by Georg Olms GW) Lubrecht & Cramer.

Lukomskii, A. S. Memoirs of the Russian Revolution. Vitali, tr. LC 74-10078. (Russian Studies: Perspectives on the Revolution). (Illus.). 255p. 1974. reprint ed. 25.85 (0-88355-186-1) Hyperion Conn.

Lukonin, Vladimir G., jt. auth. see Dandamaev, Muhammad A.

Lukose, Ani. Labour Movements & Agrarian Relations. (C). 1991. 23.00 (81-7033-100-5, Pub. by Rawat II) S Asia.

Lukowski, Jerzy T. Liberty's Folly: The Polish-Lithuanian Commonwealth in the Eighteenth Century, 1697-1795. 272p. 1991. 87.50 (0-415-03228-8, A4716) Routledge.

Lukowski, Susan, jt. ed. see Grayson, Cary T., Jr.

Luks, Allan & Barbato, Joseph. You Are What You Drink: The Authoritative Report on What Alcohol Does to Your Mind, Body & Longevity. 1989. pap. 7.95 (0-679-72364-1, Vin) Random.

— You Are What You Drink: The Authoritative Report on What Alcohol Does to Your Mind, Body & Longevity. 1989. pap. 7.95 (0-318-41620-4, Villard Bks) Random.

Luksic, et al. Differential Geometry: The Interface Between Pure & Applied Mathematics. LC 87-30648. (CONM Ser.: Vol. 68). 273p. 1991. pap. text ed. 37.00 (0-8218-5075-X, CONM-68) Am Math.

Luk'yanov, A. & Teplov, I. Tables of Coulomb Wave Functions: Whittaker Functions. LC 63-20585. (Mathematical Tables Ser.: Vol. 24). 1965. 110.00 (0-08-010128-3, Pub. by Pergamon Repr UK) Franklin.

Lula, R., ed. Toughness of Ferritic Stainless Steels, Vol. STP 706. 348p. 1978. 32.50 (0-8031-0792-7, 04-706000-02) ASTM.

Lula, R. A., ed. High Manganese High Nitrogen Austenitic Steels: Proceedings. LC 93-72311. 231p. 1993. 76.00 (0-87170-482-X) ASM.

Lula, R. A., ed. see American Society for Metals Staff.

Lula, R. A., ed. see Conference on Manganese Containing Stainless Steels Staff.

Lulat, Y. G. U. S. Relations with South Africa: An Annotated Bibliography, Vol. 1: Books, Documents, Reports, & Monographs. 468p. (C). 1991. pap. text ed. 64.00 (0-8133-7138-4) Westview.

Lulat, Y. G-M. The Academic Impact of Foreign Graduate Students: Perceptions of Faculty. LC 94-6859. 205p. 1995. lib. bdg. 39.90 (0-944265-13-8, Cerebrum Bks) Librosmondiale.

— The Academic Impact of Foreign Graduate Students: Perceptions of Faculty. 205p. 1995. pap. text ed. 29.90 (0-944265-16-2, Cerebrum Bks) Librosmondiale.

— Analyzing U. S. Relations with South Africa: Past, Present & Future. LC 90-38974. 1024p. (C). 1996. lib. bdg. write for info. (0-944265-08-1); pap. text ed. write for info. (0-944265-07-3) Librosmondiale.

— Comparative Politics: Toward the Year 2000 & Beyond-An Analytical Survey & Bibliographic Guide. LC 87-32056. 224p. 1988. lib. bdg. 27.90 (0-944265-00-6) Librosmondiale.

— Librarians & the Selection of Publications from Small Presses: Implications for Intellectual Freedom. LC 94-7608. 176p. 1995. lib. bdg. 39.90 (0-944265-14-6, Cerebrum Bks) Librosmondiale.

— Librarians & the Selection of Publications from Small Presses: Implications for Intellectual Freedom. 176p. 1995. pap. text ed. 29.90 (0-944265-15-4, Cerebrum Bks) Librosmondiale.

Lulat, Y. G-M. & Pappas, James G. Perspectives on Blacks in Cinema: An Introductory Text on Select Topics. LC 93-11628. 708p. 1996. lib. bdg. 55.50 (0-944265-11-1, Cerebrum Bks); pap. text ed. 45.50 (0-944265-12-X, Cerebrum Bks) Librosmondiale.

Lulat, Y. G-M, et al. Governmental & Institutional Policies on Foreign Students: Analysis, Evaluation, & Bibliography. LC 86-17559. (Special Studies in Comparative Education: No. 16). (Illus.). 114p. 1986. pap. text ed. 10.00 (0-937033-05-7) SUNY GSE Pubns.

Lulchak, L., jt. auth. see Kolesnikova, A.

***Lulek, T., et al.** Symmetry & Structural Properties of Condensed Matter: Proceedings of the 3rd International School on Theoretical Physics. 524p. 1995. text ed. 109.00 (981-02-2059-6) World Scientific Pub.

Lulek, T., et al, eds. Symmetry & Structural Properties of Condensed Matter. 440p. (C). 1991. text ed. 137.00 (981-02-0422-1) World Scientific Pub.

Lulic, Margaret A. Who We Could Be at Work. 245p. 1994. 19.95 (0-9638526-3-9) Blue Edge Pub.

Lull, David J. The Spirit in Galatia: Paul's Interpretation of Pneuma As Divine Power. LC 79-26094. (Society of Biblical Literature. Dissertation Ser.: No. 49). 254p. reprint ed. pap. 72.40 (0-7837-5443-4, 2045208) Bks Demand.

Lull, H., jt. auth. see Sopper, W.

Lull, Howard W., jt. auth. see Reifsynder, William E.

Lull, James. China Turned On: Television, Reform & Resistance. (Illus.). 208p. 1991. 49.95 (0-415-05215-7, A6221); pap. 16.95 (0-415-05216-5, A6225) Routledge.

— Inside Family Viewing: Ethnographic Research on Television's Audiences. 208p. 1991. 49.95 (0-415-04414-6, A4310, Comedia); pap. 17.95 (0-415-04997-0, A4314, Comedia) Routledge.

— Media, Communication, Culture: A Global Approach. 1995. 39.50 (0-231-10264-X); pap. write for info. (0-231-10265-8) Col U Pr.

Lull, James, ed. Popular Music & Communication. 2nd ed. (Focus Editions Ser.: Vol. 89). 334p. (C). 1991. text ed. 49.95 (0-8039-3916-7); pap. text ed. 24.95 (0-8039-3917-5) Sage.

— World Families Watch Television. LC 88-9658. (Communication & Human Values Ser.). (Illus.). 264p. 1988. pap. 75.30 (0-7837-8965-3, 2049746) Bks Demand.

Lull, Janis. The Metaphysical Poets: A Chronology. LC 93-8212. (Reference Ser.). 240p. 1994. text ed. 45.00 (0-8161-7251-X, Hall Reference) Macmillan.

— The Poem in Time: Reading George Herbert's Revisions of The Church. LC 88-40586. (Illus.). 168p. 1990. 32.50 (0-87413-357-2) U Delaware Pr.

Lull, Ramon, pseud. The Art of Contemplation. Peers, Allison, tr. 1976. lib. bdg. 250.00 (0-8490-1451-4) Gordon Pr.

Lull, Ramon. Blanquerna. (Dedalus European Classics Ser.). 550p. 1987. pap. 14.95 (0-87052-376-7, Pub. by Dedalus Bks UK) Hippocrene Bks.

— The Order of Chivalry. Ellis, F. S., ed. Caxton, William, tr. LC 79-8368. reprint ed. 45.00 (0-404-18352-2) AMS Pr.

Lull, Ramon & Caxton, William. The Book of the Order of Chivalry. 118p. 1991. 24.95 (0-9633100-0-3) START Grp.

Lull, Richard S. The Sauropod Dinosaur Barosaurus Marsh. (Connecticut Academy of Arts & Sciences Ser., Trans.: Vol. 6). 1919. pap. 150.00 (0-685-22867-3) Elliots Bks.

Lull, Timothy F., ed. Martin Luther's Basic Theological Writings. LC 89-34201. 752p. (Orig.). 1989. pap. 25.00 (0-8006-2327-4, 1-2327, Fortress Pr) Augsburg Fortress.

Lull, Timothy F., jt. ed. see Nickle, Keith F.

Lulling, Darrel R. Communist Military of the Vietnam War. LC 80-83872. (Illus.). 1980. pap. 14.95 (0-912958-10-3); spiral bd. 8.95 (0-912958-09-X) MCN Pr.

Lullmann, Heinz, et al. Pocket Atlas of Pharmacology. LC 92-48531. (Flexibook Ser.). (Illus.). 374p. (ENG & GER.). 1993. pap. text ed. 27.00 (0-86577-455-2) Thieme Med Pubs.

Lully, Jean-Baptiste. Alceste. De Lajarte, Theodore D., ed. (Chefs-d'oeuvre classiques de l'opera francaise Ser.: Vol. 16). (Illus.). 314p. (FRE.). 1970. reprint ed. pap. 35.00 (0-8450-1116-2) Broude.

— Armide. De Lajarte, Theodore D., ed. (Chefs-d'oeuvre classiques de l'opera francaise Ser.: Vol. 17). (Illus.). 338p. (FRE.). 1970. reprint ed. pap. 35.00 (0-8450-1117-0) Broude.

— Atys. De Lajarte, Theodore D., ed. (Chefs-d'oeuvre classiques de l'opera francaise Ser.: Vol. 18). (Illus.). 362p. (FRE.). 1970. reprint ed. pap. 37.50 (0-8450-1118-9) Broude.

— Bellerophon. De Lajarte, Theodore, ed. (Chefs-d'oeuvre classiques de l'opera francaise Ser.: Vol. 19). (Illus.). 318p. (FRE.). 1970. reprint ed. pap. 35.00 (0-8450-1119-7) Broude.

— Cadmus et Hermione. De Lajarte, Theodore, ed. (Chefs-d'oeuvre classiques de l'opera francaise Ser.: Vol. 20). (Illus.). 274p. (FRE.). 1970. reprint ed. pap. 32.50 (0-8450-1120-0) Broude.

— Isis. De Lajarte, Theodore, ed. (Chefs-d'oeuvre classiques de l'opera francaise Ser.: Vol. 21). (Illus.). 398p. (FRE.). 1970. reprint ed. pap. 40.00 (0-8450-1121-9) Broude.

— Oeuvres Completes de Jean-Baptiste Lully, 11 vols., Set. Prunieres, Henry, ed. Incl. Ballets, 1654-1657. 1966. pap. 95.00 (0-8450-1261-4); Ballets, 1658-1660 Tome 2. 1966. pap. 95.00 (0-8450-1262-2); Comedies-Ballets, 1664-1665 Tome 1. 1966. pap. 85.00 (0-8450-1263-0); Comedies-Ballets, 1666-1668 Tome 2. 1966. pap. 85.00 (0-8450-1264-9); Comedies-Ballets, 1669-1670 Tome 3. 1966. pap. 85.00 (0-8450-1265-7); Motets, 1664 Tome 1: Miserere Mei Deus. 1966. pap. 85.00 (0-8450-1266-5); Motets, 1668-1677 Tome 2: Plaude, Laetare, Gallia; Te Deum Laudamus; Dies Irae; Dies Illa. 1966. pap. 85.00 (0-8450-1267-3); Operas Tome 1: Cadmus et Hermione. 1966. pap. 125.00 (0-8450-1269-X); Operas Tome 2: Alceste. 1966. pap. 125.00 (0-8450-1270-3); Operas, 1684 Tome 3: Amadis. 1966. pap. 125.00 (0-8450-1271-1); (Illus.). 1972. reprint ed. Set pap. 880.00 (0-8450-1260-6) Broude.

— Persee. De Lajarte, Theodore, ed. (Chefs-d'oeuvre classiques de l'opera francaise Ser.: Vol. 22). (Illus.). 354p. (FRE.). 1970. reprint ed. pap. 35.00 (0-8450-1122-7) Broude.

— Phaeton. De Lajarte, Theodore, ed. (Chefs-d'oeuvre classiques de l'opera francaise Ser.: Vol. 23). (Illus.). 346p. (FRE.). 1970. reprint ed. pap. 35.00 (0-8450-1123-5) Broude.

— Proserpine. De Lajarte, Theodore, ed. (Chefs-d'oeuvre classiques de l'opera francaise Ser.: Vol. 24). (Illus.). 376p. (FRE.). 1970. reprint ed. pap. 37.50 (0-8450-1124-3) Broude.

— Psyche. De Lajarte, Theodore, ed. (Chefs-d'oeuvre classiques de l'opera francaise Ser.: Vol. 25). (Illus.). 256p. 1970. reprint ed. pap. 32.50 (0-8450-1125-1) Broude.

— Thesee. De Lajarte, Theodore, ed. (Chefs-d'oeuvre classiques de l'opera francaise Ser.: Vol. 26). (Illus.). 262p. (FRE.). 1970. reprint ed. pap. 35.00 (0-8450-1126-X) Broude.

Lully, Raymond. The Hermetic Mercuries of Raymond Lully. 1984. reprint ed. pap. 3.95 (0-916411-36-2) Holmes Pub.

Lully, Raymond, see Ramon Lull, pseud..

Luloff, A. E. & Steahr, Thomas E. Rural Population Growth in New England. 92p. 1987. pap. 5.00 (0-9609010-2-7) NE Regional Ctr.

Luloff, A. E., jt. ed. see Steahr, Thomas E.

Lulofs, Roxane S. Conflict - From Theory to Action. LC 93-32038. 1993. pap. text ed. 30.00 (0-89787-352-1) Gorsuch Scarisbrick.

— Persuasion: Contexts, People & Messages. (Illus.). 300p. (Orig.). (C). 1991. pap. text ed. 35.00 (0-89787-343-2) Gorsuch Scarisbrick.

Lulofs, Timothy J. & Ostrom, Hans. Leigh Hunt: A Reference Guide. (Reference Guides to Literature Ser.). 1985. lib. bdg. 55.00 (0-8161-8385-6, Hall Reference) Macmillan.

Lulow, Kalia, jt. auth. see Jackson, Carole.

Lulu Huang Chang. From Confucius to Kublai Khan: Music & Poetics Through the Centuries. (Wissenschaftliche Abhandlungen-Musicological Studies: Vol. 58). xxi, 184p. 1992. lib. bdg. 120.00 (0-931902-75-4) Inst Mediaeval Mus.

Lum, Ada. Luke: Good News of Hope & Joy. (LifeGuide Bible Studies). 112p. (Orig.). 1992. pap. 4.99 (0-8308-1005-6) InterVarsity.

Lum, Arlene, ed. Sailing for the Sun: Chinese in Hawaii, 1789-1989. (Illus.). 200p. 1990. 39.95 (0-8248-1313-8) UH Pr.

***Lum, Bernice.** More Steps to Heaven. (Illus.). 28p. 1993. 6.00 (1-872819-06-0, Pub. by Tuppy Owens UK) AK Pr Dist.

— Twelve Steps to Heaven: My First Impression of Sex. (Illus.). 78p. (Orig.). Date not set. 6.00 (1-872819-00-1, Pub. by Tuppy Owens UK) AK Pr Dist.

Lum, Cal, ed. see Kratz, Karl.

Lum, Darrell. The Golden Slipper: A Vietnamese Legend. LC 93-33588. (Legends of the World Ser.). (Illus.). 32p. (J). (gr. 2-5). 1994. lib. bdg. 11.89 (0-8167-3405-4); pap. text ed. 3.95 (0-8167-3406-2) Troll Assocs.

Lum, Darrell, jt. ed. see Chock, Eric.

Lum, Darrell, ed. see Kono, Juliet S.

Lum, Darrell, ed. see Lum, Wing T.

Lum, Darrell, ed. see Morales, Rodney.

Lum, Darrell H. Pass On, No Pass Back. LC 90-85158. 128p. (Orig.). 1990. pap. 8.00 (0-910043-19-1) Bamboo Ridge Pr.

— Sun. 76p. 1980. 5.00 (0-910043-02-7) Bamboo Ridge Pr.

Lum, Darrell H., ed. see Chock, Erick.

Lum, Doman. Social Work Practice & People of Color: A Process-Stage Approach. 2nd ed. 336p. (C). 1992. pap. 30.95 (0-534-17040-4) Brooks-Cole.

— Social Work Practice & People of Color: A Process-Stage Approach. 3rd ed. LC 95-2871. 1996. pap. 30.95 (0-534-33854-2) Brooks-Cole.

Lum, Dyer D. Concise History of the Great Trial of the Chicago Anarchists in 1886. LC 75-90181. (Mass Violence in America Ser.). 1973. reprint ed. 24.95 (0-405-01324-8) Ayer.

— The Mormon Question in Its Economic Aspects. 1973. lib. bdg. 59.95 (0-8490-0672-4) Gordon Pr.

Lum, Dyer D. & DeCleyre, V. In Memoriam, Chicago, Nov. 11, 1887. 1973. 59.95 (0-8490-0390-3) Gordon Pr.

Lum, Edward H. Lum: Genealogy of the Lum Family. 270p. 1993. reprint ed. lib. bdg. 52.50 (0-8328-3711-3); reprint ed. pap. 42.50 (0-8328-3712-1) Higginson Bk Co.

Lum, Henry, jt. ed. see Heer, Ewald.

Lum, Peter. Growth of Civilization in East Asia. LC 73-77311. (Illus.). (J). (gr. 8 up). 1969. 33.95 (0-87599-144-0) S G Phillips.

An Asterisk (*) at the beginning of an entry indicates that the title is appearing in BIP for the first time.

— Six Centuries in East Asia: China, Japan & Korea from the 14th Century to 1912. LC 72-12582. (Illus.). 288p. 1973. 33.95 (*0-87599-183-1*) S G Phillips.

Lum, Ray J. The Rebus Escape. LC 91-76970. 64p. (Orig.). (J). (gr. 3-5). 1992. pap. 5.95 (*0-943864-63-1*) Davenport.

Lum, Shelly. True & Tried Recipes. Herr, Ethel et al, eds. (Illus.). 200p. (Orig.). Date not set. pap. 14.95 (*0-941201-06-6*) INNPRO.

Lum, Wing T. Expounding the Doubtful Points. Chock, Eric & Lum, Darrell, eds. LC 87-72145. 108p. (Orig.). (C). 1987. pap. 6.00 (*0-910043-14-0*) Bamboo Ridge Pr.

Lumans, Valdis O. Himmler's Auxiliaries: The Volkdeutsche Mittelstelle & the German National Minorities of Europe, 1933-1945. LC 92-24080. xiv, 336p. (C). 1993. 39.95 (*0-8078-2066-0*) U of NC Pr.

Lumb, Philip D., ed. Complications in Critical Care Medicine. (Illus.). 576p. 1987. 75.00 (*0-8151-5652-9*, ZGD-1, Yr Bk Med Pubs) Mosby Yr Bk.

Lumb, R. D. Australian Constitutionalism. 1983. Australia. pap. 44.00 (*0-409-49300-7*) Butterworth Legal Pubs.

— The Constitution of the Commonwealth of Australia Annotated. 4th ed. 1986. Australia. 85.00 (*0-409-49128-4*); Australia. pap. 69.00 (*0-409-49129-2*) Butterworth Legal Pubs.

— Constitutions of the Australian States. 5th rev. ed. 1991. pap. 29.95 (*0-7022-2218-6*, Pub. by Univ Queensland Pr AT) Intl Spec Bk.

Lumbala, Francois K., jt. ed. see Chauvet, Louis.

Lumbala, Kabasele & Power, David N., eds. The Specter of Mass Death. (Concilium Ser.). 1993. write for info. (*0-88344-871-8*) Orbis Bks.

Lumbert, Lindy H. Dear Diary. 119p. (J). (gr. 4-10). 1981. pap. 4.25 (*0-943280-00-1*) Blossom Bks.

— The Two Minute Philosopher. 19.00 (*0-943280-01-X*); pap. 8.50 (*0-943280-02-8*) Blossom Bks.

Lumbley, Joe. Informix Database Administrator's: Survival Guide. 320p. 1994. pap. text ed. 36.00 (*0-13-124314-4*) P-H.

— The Informix Database Administrator's Survival Guide. 1994. pap. text ed. 27.00 (*0-685-70700-8*) P-H.

***Lumbra, Elaine.** More Hoosier Cooking. LC 82-47959. 1994. pap. 13.95 (*0-253-20917-X*) Ind U Pr.

Lumbra, Elaine, ed. The Hoosier Cookbook. LC 75-31420. (Illus.). 344p. 1976. 18.95 (*0-253-13865-5*) Ind U Pr.

— The Hoosier Cookbook. LC 75-31420. 1994. pap. 17.95 (*0-253-20916-1*) Ind U Pr.

— More Hoosier Cooking. LC 82-47959. (Illus.). 256p. 1982. 12.95 (*0-253-15430-8*) Ind U Pr.

Lumbreras, Luis G. The Peoples & Cultures of Ancient Peru. LC 74-2104. (Illus.). 248p. 1974. pap. 17.95 (*0-87474-151-3*) Smithsonian.

Lumbroso, G. Researchers sur l'Economie Politique de l'Egypte sous les Lagides. 4121p. reprint ed. text ed. 67.50 (*0-685-13378-8*) Coronet Bks.

Lumbsch, H. T., jt. ed. see Feige, G. B.

Lumby, E. W., ed. Policy & Operations in the Mediterranean: Nineteen Twelve to Nineteen Fourteen. 1986. 80.00 (*0-317-44210-4*) St Mut.

Lumby, E. W., jt. ed. see Smith, David B.

Lumby, Edmond W. The Transfer of Power in India: Nineteen Forty-Five to Nineteen Forty-Seven. LC 79-1634. 1981. reprint ed. 25.75 (*0-88355-938-2*) Hyperion Conn.

Lumby, J. R. & McKnight, G. H., eds. King Horn, Floritz & Blauncheflur, Etc. (EETS, OS Ser.: No. 14). 1969. reprint ed. 27.00 (*0-8115-3345-X*) Periodicals Srv.

Lumby, Joseph R. Ratis Raving, & Other Moral & Religious Pieces. (EETS, OS Ser.: No. 43). 1974. reprint ed. 28.00 (*0-527-00038-8*) Periodicals Srv.

Lumby, Joseph R., ed. Chronicon Henrici Knighton: Vel Cnitthon, Monachi Leycestrensis, 2 vols., Set. (Rolls Ser.: No. 92). 1972. reprint ed. 160.00 (*0-8115-1169-3*) Periodicals Srv.

Lumby, Joseph R., jt. ed. see Babington, Churchill.

Lumby, Judy. Nursing: Reflecting on an Evolving Practice. (C). 1991. pap. 33.00 (*0-7300-1263-8*, NPR300, Pub. by Deakin Univ AT) St Mut.

Lumby, S. P. Investment Appraisal & Financing Decisions. 4th ed. (Accounting & Finance Ser.). 544p. (C). 1990. pap. text ed. 45.00 (*0-412-41070-2*) Chapman & Hall.

Lumer, Gunter, jt. ed. see Clement, Philippe.

Lumer, Hyman. Israel Today: War or Peace? 1970. pap. 0.45 (*0-87898-061-X*) New Outlook.

— Jewish Defense League: A New Face for Reaction. 1971. pap. 0.35 (*0-87898-072-5*) New Outlook.

— Middle East Crisis. 1967. pap. 0.25 (*0-87898-023-7*) New Outlook.

— What Happened in Poland. 1969. pap. 0.35 (*0-87898-035-0*) New Outlook.

— Which Way Israel? 1966. pap. 0.20 (*0-87898-010-5*) New Outlook.

***Lumer, Mark & Ireton, Donna.** Federal Acquisition Streamlining Act of 1994 Vol. 2: Synopsis & Implications, Set. 210p. (Orig.). 1994. pap. 59.95 (*0-940343-63-0*); pap. write for info. (*0-940343-65-7*) Natl Contract Mgmt.

Lumer, Wilfred. Small Business at the Crossroad. Bruchey, Stuart & Carosso, Vincent P., eds. LC 78-18967. (Small Business Enterprise in America Ser.). (Illus.). 1979. reprint ed. lib. bdg. 15.95 (*0-405-11471-0*) Ayer.

Lumet, L., jt. auth. see Keim, A.

***Lumet, Sidney.** Making Movies. LC 94-34449. 1995. 23.00 (*0-679-43709-6*) Knopf.

Lumgair, Irene. Wave Action. (How to Draw & Paint Ser.). (Illus.). 32p. (Orig.). 1995. pap. 5.95 (*1-56010-143-1*, HT244) W Foster Pub.

Lumholtz, Carl. A Nation of Shamans. 2nd ed. Finson, Bruce, ed. (Shamanic Library: No. 1). (Illus.). 236p. 1989. reprint ed. pap. 20.00 (*0-943907-01-2*) Bruce Finson.

— New Trails in Mexico. LC 90-30449. (Southwest Center Ser.). 410p. 1990. reprint ed. pap. 18.95 (*0-8165-1175-6*) U of Ariz Pr.

— Unknown Mexico, 2 vols. 1973. 500.00 (*0-8490-1249-X*) Gordon Pr.

— Unknown Mexico: Explorations in the Sierra Madre & Other Regions, 1890-1898, 2 vols. 1987. reprint ed. pap. 15.95 (*0-685-17651-7*) Dover.

— Unknown Mexico: Explorations in the Sierra Madre & Other Regions, 1890-1898, 2 vols., Vol. 1. 576p. 1987. reprint ed. pap. 15.95 (*0-486-25364-3*) Dover.

— Unknown Mexico: Explorations in the Sierra Madre & Other Regions, 1890-1898, 2 vols., Vol. 2. 544p. 1987. reprint ed. pap. 15.95 (*0-486-25413-5*) Dover.

Lumholtz, Carl, jt. auth. see De la Cruz, Pablo.

Lumholtz, Karl S. Through Central Borneo: An Account of Two Years' Travel in the Land of the Head-Hunters Between the Years 1913 & 1917, 2 vols., Set. LC 77-87504. (Illus.). reprint ed. 53.00 (*0-404-16760-8*) AMS Pr.

— Unknown Mexico: A Record of Five Years' Exploration among the Tribes of the Western Sierra Madre, in the Tierra Caliente of Tepic & Jalisco, & Among the Tarascos of Michoacan, 2 vols, Set. LC 72-5010. (Antiquities of the New World Ser.: Vol. 15). (Illus.). reprint ed. 105.00 (*0-404-57315-0*) AMS Pr.

Lumholtz, Ludvig L. A Slice of Life. 220p. (C). 1989. text ed. 65.00 (*1-872795-51-X*, Pub. by Pentland Pr UK) St Mut.

Lumiansky, Robert M. Malory's Originality: A Critical Study of Le Morte Darthur. LC 78-19255. 1979. 28.95 (*0-405-10612-2*) Ayer.

Lumiansky, Robert M. & Mills, David. The Chester Mystery Cycle: Essays & Documents. LC 82-1838. 347p. reprint ed. pap. 98.90 (*0-7837-3769-6*, 2043586) Bks Demand.

Lumiansky, Robert M. & Mills, David, eds. The Chester Mystery Cycle: Vol. II: Commentary & Glossary. (Early English Text Society Ser.: No. 8). 550p. 1986. 39.95 (*0-19-722408-3*) OUP.

Lumiansky, Robert M., ed. see Malory, Thomas.

Lumicao-Lora, Maria L. Gaddang Literature. 152p. (Orig.). 1984. pap. 8.50 (*971-10-0174-8*, Pub. by New Day Pub PH) Cellar.

Lumiere, Cornel. Feeling Younger Longer. Brand, Eileen, ed. LC 72-76846. 224p. 1973. 7.95 (*0-8184-0032-3*) Carol Pub Group.

Luminet, Jean-Pierre. Black Holes. (Illus.). 300p. (C). 1992. 59.95 (*0-521-40029-5*); pap. 19.95 (*0-521-40906-3*) Cambridge U Pr.

Lumiste, V. & Peetre, J. Edgar Krahn: A Centenary Volume (1894-1961) LC 94-76402. 196p. 1994. pap. 53.00 (*90-5199-168-1*) IOS Press.

Lumley. Essentials of Experimental Surgery. 1990. 155.00 (*0-407-01395-4*) Buttrwrth-Heinemann.

— MCQ's in Anatomy. 2nd ed. 272p. 1988. pap. 26.00 (*0-443-03574-1*) Churchill.

Lumley, Benjamin. Reminiscences of the Opera. LC 76-15185. (Music Reprint Ser.). 448p. 1976. reprint ed. 55.00 (*0-306-70842-6*) Da Capo.

Lumley, Brian. Blood Brothers. 576p. 1993. mass mkt. 5.99 (*0-8125-2061-0*) Tor Bks.

— Bloodwars. 512p. 1994. 23.95 (*0-312-85679-2*) Tor Bks.

— Bloodwars. 1995. mass mkt. 6.99 (*0-8125-3628-2*) Tor Bks.

— Brian Lumley. 1990. Boxed set. 13.85 (*0-8125-2858-1*) Tor Bks.

— The Burrowers Beneath. limited ed. (Illus.). 192p. 1988. reprint ed. 22.50 (*0-932445-30-6*) Ganley Pub.

— Clock of Dreams. deluxe limited ed. LC 91-75683. (Illus.). 1994. reprint ed. boxed 42.50 (*0-932445-52-7*) Ganley Pub.

— Clock of Dreams. LC 91-75683. (Illus.). 1994. reprint ed. 26.50 (*0-932445-51-9*) Ganley Pub.

— The Compleat Crow. LC 86-81094. (Illus.). 192p. 1987. 21.00 (*0-932445-22-5*); pap. 7.50 (*0-932445-21-7*) Ganley Pub.

— The Compleat Khash, Vol. I: Never a Backward Glance. LC 90-81729. (Illus.). 1991. 25.00 (*0-932445-43-8*); 40.00 (*0-932445-44-6*) Ganley Pub.

— Deadspawn. (Necroscope Ser.: No. V). (Orig.). 1991. mass mkt. 5.99 (*0-8125-0835-1*) Tor Bks.

— Deadspeak. (Necroscope Ser.: No. 4). 1992. mass mkt. 5.99 (*0-8125-3032-2*) Tor Bks.

— Demogorgon. 1992. mass mkt. 4.99 (*0-8125-1199-9*) Tor Bks.

— Elysia: The Coming of Cthulhu. LC 88-81853. (Illus.). 192p. 1989. 25.00 (*0-932445-33-0*); pap. 8.50 (*0-932445-32-2*) Ganley Pub.

— Fruiting Bodies & Other Fungi. 288p. 1993. 18.95 (*0-312-85458-7*) Tor Bks.

— Hero of Dreams. LC 85-80774. (Illus.). 192p. 1986. 21.00 (*0-932445-18-7*); pap. 7.50 (*0-932445-17-9*) Ganley Pub.

— Hero of Dreams. 256p. 1993. mass mkt. 4.99 (*0-8125-2419-5*) Tor Bks.

— House of Doors. 1990. mass mkt. 4.99 (*0-8125-0832-7*) Tor Bks.

— Iced on Aran. 256p. (Orig.). 1994. mass mkt. 4.99 (*0-8125-2422-5*) Tor Bks.

— Iced on Aran: And Other Dream Quests. deluxe ed. LC 91-75679. (Illus.). 184p. 1992. boxed 40.00 (*0-932445-48-9*) Ganley Pub.

— Iced on Aran: And Other Dream Quests. LC 91-75679. (Illus.). 184p. 1992. reprint ed. 25.00 (*0-932445-47-0*) Ganley Pub.

— The Last Aerie. 480p. 1993. 22.95 (*0-312-85358-0*) Tor Bks.

— The Last Aerie. 832p. 1994. mass mkt. 5.99 (*0-8125-2062-9*) Tor Bks.

— Mad Moon of Dreams. LC 87-82043. (Illus.). 192p. 1987. 21.00 (*0-932445-28-4*); pap. 7.50 (*0-932445-27-6*) Ganley Pub.

— Mad Moon of Dreams. 256p. 1994. mass mkt. 4.99 (*0-8125-2421-7*) Tor Bks.

— Necroscope: The Lost Years. 1992. mass mkt. 5.99 (*0-8125-2137-4*) Tor Bks.

— Necroscope: The Lost Years. 384p. 1994. 23.95 (*0-312-85787-X*) Tor Bks.

— Psychamok. 512p. (Orig.). 1993. mass mkt. 5.99 (*0-8125-2032-7*) Tor Bks.

— Psychomech. 448p. (Orig.). 1992. mass mkt. 5.99 (*0-8125-2023-8*) Tor Bks.

— Psychosphere. 448p. (Orig.). 1992. mass mkt. 5.99 (*0-8125-2030-0*) Tor Bks.

— Ship of Dreams. LC 86-81017. (Illus.). 192p. 1986. 21.00 (*0-932445-25-X*); pap. 7.50 (*0-932445-24-1*) Ganley Pub.

— Ship of Dreams. 256p. 1994. mass mkt. 4.99 (*0-8125-2420-9*) Tor Bks.

— The Source: Necroscope III. 1989. mass mkt. 4.95 (*0-8125-2127-7*) Tor Bks.

— Spawn of the Winds. deluxe ed. LC 95-77334. (Illus.). 1995. boxed 42.50 (*0-932445-60-8*) Ganley Pub.

— Spawn of the Winds. LC 95-77334. (Illus.). 1995. reprint ed. 26.50 (*0-932445-59-4*) Ganley Pub.

— Transition of Titus Crow. rev. ed. LC 88-81855. 192p. 1992. reprint ed. 25.00 (*0-932445-45-4*); reprint ed. 40.00 (*0-932445-46-2*) Ganley Pub.

— Vamphyri. 1989. mass mkt. 5.99 (*0-8125-2126-9*) Tor Bks.

Lumley, Dan & Bailey, Gerald D. Planning for Technology: A Guidebook for School Administrators. LC 92-596. 1995. 24.95x (*0-590-49221-7*, 10283L86 1993) Scholastic Inc.

Lumley, Dan, jt. auth. see Bailey, Gerald D.

Lumley, Dan, jt. auth. see Fagen, Carol.

Lumley, Frederick H. Measurement in Radio. LC 71-161164. (History of Broadcasting Ser.). 1977. reprint ed. 28.95 (*0-405-03576-4*) Ayer.

Lumley, J. L. & Van Dyke, M., eds. Annual Review of Fluid Mechanics, Vol. 19. (Illus.). 1987. text ed. 40.00 (*0-8243-0719-4*) Annual Reviews.

— Annual Review of Fluid Mechanics, Vol. 21. (Illus.). 1989. text ed. 40.00 (*0-8243-0721-6*) Annual Reviews.

— Annual Review of Fluid Mechanics, Vol. 22. 1990. text ed. 40.00 (*0-8243-0722-4*) Annual Reviews.

— Annual Review of Fluid Mechanics, Vol. 23. 1991. text ed. 40.00 (*0-8243-0723-2*) Annual Reviews.

— Annual Review of Fluid Mechanics, Vol. 24. 1992. text ed. 44.00 (*0-8243-0724-0*) Annual Reviews.

***Lumley, J. S. & Benjimen, W.** Research: Some Ground Rules. (Illus.). 256p. 1995. 70.00 (*0-19-854823-0*); pap. 33.50 (*0-19-854822-2*) OUP.

Lumley, J. S. P., et al. Essential Anatomy & Some Clinical Applications. 5th ed. LC 94-18967. Date not set. write for info. (*0-443-04808-8*) Churchill.

Lumley, James E. How to Get a Mortgage in Twenty-Four Hours. 3rd ed. LC 93-26682. 1994. text ed. 42.50 (*0-471-59937-9*); pap. text ed. 14.95 (*0-471-59938-7*) Wiley.

— Real Estate Psychology: The Dynamics of Successful Selling. LC 81-10473. (Real Estate For Professional Practitioners Ser.). 245p. reprint ed. pap. 69.90 (*0-7837-3454-9*, 2057780) Bks Demand.

— Top Dollar for Your Property. LC 87-36863. 1988. pap. text ed. 12.95 (*0-471-63610-X*) Wiley.

Lumley, John. A Color Atlas of Vascular Surgery. 256p. 1987. 92.50 (*0-683-05248-9*) Williams & Wilkins.

Lumley, John L. Annual Review of Fluid Mechanics, Vol. 26. Van Dyke, Milton, ed. (Illus.). 1994. text ed. 47.00 (*0-8243-0726-7*) Annual Reviews.

— Stochastic Tools in Turbulence. (Applied Mathematics & Mechanics Ser.: Vol. 12). 1970. text ed. 107.00 (*0-12-460050-6*) Acad Pr.

Lumley, John L. & Van Dyke, M., eds. Annual Review of Fluid Mechanics, Vol. 20. (Illus.). 1988. text ed. 40.00 (*0-8243-0720-8*) Annual Reviews.

***Lumley, John L. & Van Dyke, Milton, eds.** Annual Review of Fluid Mechanics. (Illus.). 550p. 1995. lib. bdg. 47.00 (*0-8243-0727-5*) Annual Reviews.

— Annual Review of Fluid Mechanics, Vol. 25. (Illus.). 1993. text ed. 44.00 (*0-8243-0725-9*) Annual Reviews.

Lumley, John L., jt. auth. see Tennekes, Hendrik.

Lumley, John L., et al, eds. Wither Turbulence? Turbulence at the Crossroads: Proceedings of a Workshop Held at Cornell University, Ithaca, New York, March 22-24, 1989. (Lecture Notes in Physics Ser.: Vol. 357). iv, 525p. 1990. 70.00 (*0-387-52535-1*) Spr-Verlag.

Lumley, John S. Surface Anatomy: The Anatomical Basis of Clinical Examination. (Illus.). 104p. 1990. pap. text ed. 21.95 (*0-443-04084-2*) Churchill.

Lumley, Judith, jt. ed. see Chamberlain, Geoffrey.

Lumley, Katherine W. District of Columbia: In Words & Pictures. LC 80-39645. (Young People's Stories of Our States Ser.). (Illus.). 48p. (J). (gr. 2-5). 1981. lib. bdg. 17.27 (*0-516-03951-2*) Childrens.

Lumley, Kathryn W. Monkeys & Apes. LC 82-12779. (New True Bks.). (Illus.). (J). (gr. k-4). 1982. lib. bdg. 12.90 (*0-516-01633-4*); pap. 4.95 (*0-516-41633-2*) Childrens.

Lumley, Kay. I Can Be an Animal Doctor. LC 85-12802. (I Can Be Bks.). 32p. (J). (gr. k-3). 1985. lib. bdg. 11.85 (*0-516-01836-1*); pap. 3.95 (*0-516-41836-X*) Childrens.

Lumley, Robert. States of Emergency: Social Movements in Italy from 1969 to 1978. 320p. 1990. 60.00 (*0-86091-254-X*, A3749); pap. 18.95 (*0-86091-969-2*, A3753) Routledge Chapman & Hall.

Lumley, Robert, jt. ed. see Baranski, Zygmunt G.

Lumley, Robert, ed. see Eco, Umberto.

Lumley, Robert, tr. see Passerini, Luisa.

Lumley, William, tr. see Chavannes, Henry.

Lummis, Adair T., jt. auth. see Haddad, Yvonne Y.

Lummis, Charles. Letters from the Southwest. Byrkit, James W., ed. LC 88-27793. 309p. 1989. 35.00 (*0-8165-1039-3*) U of Ariz Pr.

Lummis, Charles F. King of the Broncos, & Other Stories of New Mexico. LC 73-125231. (Short Story Index Reprint Ser.). 1977. 19.95 (*0-8369-3598-5*) Ayer.

— The Man Who Married the Moon & Other Pueblo Indian Folk Stories. LC 74-7989. (Illus.). reprint ed. 19.45 (*0-404-11877-1*) AMS Pr.

— My Friend Will. 1972. 5.00 (*0-87516-161-8*) DeVorss.

— New Mexico David, & Other Stories, & Sketches of the South-West. LC 76-90586. (Short Story Index Reprint Ser.). 1977. 19.95 (*0-8369-3069-X*) Ayer.

— Pueblo Indian Folk-Stories. LC 91-40614. (Illus.). xxx, 257p. 1992. reprint ed. pap. 8.95 (*0-8032-7938-8*, Bison Books) U of Nebr Pr.

— Some Strange Corners of Our Country. LC 88-26703. 270p. 1989. reprint ed. pap. 14.95 (*0-8165-0852-6*) U of Ariz Pr.

— A Tramp Across the Continent. LC 81-16194. xxvi, 270p. 1982. reprint ed. pap. 8.95 (*0-8032-7908-6*, Bison Books) U of Nebr Pr.

Lummis, Dayton. High Lonesome: The Vanishing American West. 1993. pap. 9.95 (*1-879395-24-X*) CA Classics Bks.

Lummis, Suzanne. Falling Short of Heaven. (Illus.). 32p. (Orig.). 1990. pap. 5.00 (*0-938631-12-8*) Pennywhistle Pr.

— Idiosyncrasies. 66p. (Orig.). 1989. 7.95 (*0-9622847-0-X*) Red Wind Bks.

Lummis, Suzanne, ed. Spreading the Word. 1993. 7.00 (*0-9622847-7-7*) Red Wind Bks.

Lummis, Suzanne, jt. ed. see Webb, Charles H.

Lummis, Trevor. The Labour Aristocracy, 1851-1914. LC 94-6771. 1994. 59.95 (*1-85928-049-8*, Pub. by Scolar Pr UK) Ashgate Pub Co.

— Listening to History: The Authenticity of Oral Evidence. 175p. 1988. 48.50 (*0-389-20779-9*, N8338) B&N Imports.

— Occupation & Society: The East Anglian Fisherman 1880-1914. (Illus.). 224p. 1985. 49.95 (*0-521-26602-5*) Cambridge U Pr.

Lummus, James L. & Azar, J. J. Drilling Fluids Optimization: A Practical Field Approach. 294p. (C). 1986. 69.95 (*0-87814-306-8*, P4385) PennWell Bks.

Lummus, James L., jt. auth. see Azar, J. J.

Lumpkin. Physical Education: A Contemporary Introduction. 1993. write for info. (*0-8016-7821-8*); 31.95 (*0-8016-7822-6*) Mosby Yr Bk.

— Physical Education: A Contemporary Introduction. 2nd ed. (Illus.). 336p. (C). 1989. 32.95 (*0-8016-3264-1*) Mosby Yr Bk.

Lumpkin, et al. Sport Ethics. LC 94-12858. 288p. 1994. pap. 29.95 (*0-8016-7731-9*) Mosby Yr Bk.

Lumpkin, Angela. A Guide to the Literature of Tennis. LC 85-9941. xiv, 238p. 1985. text ed. 42.95 (*0-313-24492-8*, LUT/, Greenwood Pr) Greenwood.

— Women's Tennis: A Historical Documentary. LC 79-57328. 200p. 1981. 15.00 (*0-87875-189-0*) Whitston Pub.

Lumpkin, Angela, ed. see Stoll, Sharon K. & Beller, Jennifer M.

Lumpkin, Beatrice. Senefer: A Young Genius in Old Egypt. LC 92-71026. (Young Reader's Ser.). (Illus.). 32p. (J). (gr. 2-5). 1992. 16.95 (*0-86543-244-9*); pap. 8.95 (*0-86543-245-7*) Africa World.

— Senefer & Hatshepsut. LC 91-75349. (Young Reader's Ser.). (Illus.). 64p. 1995. reprint ed. 24.95 (*0-86543-272-4*); reprint ed. pap. 9.95 (*0-86543-273-2*) Africa World.

Lumpkin, Beatrice, tr. see Gerdes, Paulus.

***Lumpkin, Beryl, ed. & photos.** The Kudzu Crypt, Dark Visions to Haunt & Entwine You. (Illus.). 1989. pap. 7.95 (*0-9622568-3-8*) Earthside Pubns.

Lumpkin, Beryl, ed. see Thompson, Naomi J.

Lumpkin, Beryl O. From Vines to Vessels. 2nd ed. (Illus.). 124p. 1987. reprint ed. pap. 9.95 (*0-932807-25-9*) Overmountain Pr.

— Something Gentle: Quiet Words for Hurried Times. (Illus.). 60p. (Orig.). 1988. pap. text ed. 3.95 (*0-9622568-0-3*) Earthside Pubns.

Lumpkin, Beryl O., ed. see Sisson, Patricia H.

Lumpkin, Betty S., jt. auth. see Sorrow, Barbara H.

***Lumpkin, Grace.** To Make My Bread. LC 95-3561. (Radical Novel Reconsidered Ser.). 1995. write for info. (*0-252-06501-8*) U of Ill Pr.

— The Wedding: A Novel. LC 75-28481. (Lost American Fiction Ser.). 325p. 1976. reprint ed. 8.95 (*0-8093-0767-7*) S Ill U Pr.

Lumpkin, James R., et al. Direct Marketing, Direct Selling, & the Mature Consumer: A Research Study. LC 88-18519. 240p. 1989. text ed. 55.00 (*0-89930-298-X*, LDT/, Quorum Bks) Greenwood.

Lumpkin, John, ed. see Cochran, Mike.

Lumpkin, Katharine D. The Making of a Southerner. LC 91-26583. (Brown Thrasher Bks.). 280p. 1991. reprint ed. pap. 14.95 (*0-8203-1385-8*) U of Ga Pr.

Lumpkin, Susan. Big Cats. LC 92-26838. (Great Creatures of the World Ser.). (Illus.). 72p. (YA). (gr. 6-9). 1993. 17.95 (*0-8160-2847-8*) Facts on File.

— Small Cats. LC 92-26837. (Great Creatures of the World Ser.). (Illus.). 72p. (YA). (gr. 6-9). 1993. 17.95 (*0-8160-2848-6*) Facts on File.

Lumpkin, Susan & Weinberg, Susan. Animals of the National Zoological Park Coloring Book. (Illus.). 24p. (Orig.). (J). (ps-4). 1989. pap. 3.95 (*0-9622062-1-0*) Friends Natl Zoo.

Lumpkin, Susan, jt. auth. see Greenberg, Russell.

Lumpkin, Susan, ed. see Roberson, Mary-Russell.

Lumpkin, Susan, jt. ed. see Seidensticker, John.

Lumpkin, T. & McClary, D. Azuki Bean: Botany, Production & Uses. 280p. 1994. 59.50 (*0-85198-765-6*) CAB Intl.
Lumpkin, William L. Baptist Confessions of Faith. (Illus.). 1959. 23.00 (*0-8170-0016-X*) Judson.
Lumpkin, William L. & Butterfield, Lyman. Colonial Baptists & Southern Revivals: An Original Anthology. Gaustad, Edwin S., ed. LC 79-52585. (Baptist Tradition Ser.). 1980. lib. bdg. 28.95 (*0-405-12452-X*) Ayer.
Lumpkin, Wilson. Removal of the Cherokee Indians from Georgia. LC 79-90182. (Mass Violence in America Ser.). 1977. reprint ed. 50.95 (*0-405-01325-6*) Ayer.
Lumpkins, Debbie B., ed. see Smothers, Thelma W.
Lumpkins, William. La Casa Adobe. 2nd rev. ed. LC 86-71415. (Illus.). 64p. 1987. reprint ed. pap. 11.95 (*0-941270-34-3*) Ancient City Pr.
Lumpuy, Luis B., tr. see Robertson, John M.
Lumsdaine, David H. Moral Vision in International Politics: The Foreign Aid Regime, 1949-1989. LC 92-18508. (Illus.). 416p. (C). 1993. text ed. 52.50 (*0-691-07887-4*); pap. text ed. 16.95 (*0-691-02767-6*) Princeton U Pr.
***Lumsdaine, Edward & Lumsdaine, Monika.** Creative Problem Solving: Thinking Skills for a Changing World. 489p. 1994. pap. 35.95 (*0-07-039091-6*) McGraw.
Lumsdaine, Monika, jt. auth. see Lumsdaine, Edward.
***Lumsden.** Collector's Guide to the Waffen-SS. 1995. pap. (*0-7818-0357-8*) Hippocrene Bks.
Lumsden, jt. auth. see Martin.
Lumsden, Alec, jt. auth. see Thetford, Owen.
Lumsden, Barry & Stewart, G. Bryan. Directory of Community College Graduate-Level Courses on Two-Year Institutions. 1992. pap. 10.00 (*0-87117-246-1*) Am Assn Comm Coll.
Lumsden, Barry D., jt. auth. see Alexander-Mott, LeeAnn.
Lumsden, Charles J. & Wilson, Edward O. Genes, Mind, Culture: The Coevolutionary Process. LC 80-26543. (Illus.). 442p. 1981. 37.50 (*0-674-34475-8*) HUP.
— Promethean Fire: Reflections on the Origin of Mind. (Illus.). 224p. 1983. 26.00 (*0-674-71445-8*) HUP.
— Promethean Fire: Reflections on the Origin of Mind. 224p. 1984. pap. text ed. 10.95 (*0-674-71446-6*) HUP.
Lumsden, D. Barry, ed. The Older Adult As Learner: Aspects of Educational Gerontology. 250p. 1985. pap. 42.00 (*0-89116-211-9*) Taylor & Francis.
Lumsden, D. Barry, jt. auth. see Sherron.
Lumsden, Donald, jt. auth. see Lumsden, Gay.
Lumsden, E. S. Art of Etching. (Illus.). 1924. pap. 7.50 (*0-486-20049-3*) Dover.
— Art of Etching. (Illus.). 19.25 (*0-8446-2497-7*) Peter Smith.
Lumsden, Ennis, jt. auth. see Boylston.
Lumsden, Gay & Lumsden, Donald. Communicating in Groups & Teams: Sharing Leadership. 410p. (C). 1993. pap. 28.95 (*0-534-19068-5*) Intl Thomson.
Lumsden, George I., ed. Geology & the Environment in Western Europe: A Coordinated Statement by the Western European Geological Survey. (Illus.). 340p. 1994. reprint ed. pap. 45.00 (*0-19-854870-2*) OUP.
Lumsden, George J. Building a Winning Sales Force. 300p. 1986. ring bd. 159.95 (*0-85013-157-X*) Dartnell Corp.
— Getting up to Speed: One Hundred Fifteen Tips for the New or Future Manager. LC 92-23822. 192p. 1992. pap. 17.95 (*0-8144-7789-5*) AMACOM.
— How to Succeed in Middle Management. LC 82-71323. 256p. reprint ed. pap. 73.00 (*0-317-19942-0*, 2023565) Bks Demand.
— Impact Management: Personal Power Strategies for Success. LC 79-11632. 158p. reprint ed. pap. 45.10 (*0-317-26947-X*, 2023586) Bks Demand.
Lumsden, Glenn, jt. auth. see De Vries, David.
***Lumsden, Ian.** Machos, Maricones, & Gays: Cuba & Homosexuality. 288p. (Orig.). (C). 1995. lib. bdg. 39.95 (*1-56639-370-1*); pap. text ed. 16.95 (*1-56639-371-X*) Temple U Pr.
Lumsden, Ian, ed. Close the Forty-Ninth Parallel Etc. The Americanization of Canada. LC 79-477171. 343p. reprint ed. pap. 97.80 (*0-8357-6385-4*, 2023645) Bks Demand.
Lumsden, M. S. Affirmations: Poems in Scots & English. (Illus.). 76p. 1990. text ed. 19.00 (*0-08-040929-6*, Pub. by Aberdeen U Pr) Macmillan.
Lumsden, Michael. Existential Sentences: Their Structure & Meaning. 208p. 1988. lib. bdg. 59.95 (*0-7099-4114-5*) Routledge Chapman & Hall.
Lumsden, P. J., et al, eds. Physiology, Growth, & Development of Plants in Culture. LC 93-20900. 430p. (C). 1994. lib. bdg. 199.00 (*0-7923-2516-8*) Kluwer Ac.
Lumsden, R. D., jt. ed. see Whipps, J. M.
Lumsden, Robert D. & Vaughn, James L., eds. Pest Management: Biologically Based Technologies: Proceedings of the Beltsville Symposium XVIII, Agricultural Research Service, U. S. Department of Agriculture, Beltsville, Maryland, May 2-6, 1993. LC 93-26355. 1993. 109.95 (*0-8412-2726-8*) Am Chemical.
Lumsden, Robin. The Allgemeine SS. (Men-at-Arms Ser.). (Illus.). 48p. 1993. pap. 11.95 (*1-85532-358-3*, 9237, Pub. by Osprey UK) Stackpole.
— The Black Corps: A Collector's Guide to the History & Regalia of the SS. (Illus.). 176p. (Orig.). 1992. pap. 19.95 (*0-7818-0112-5*) Hippocrene Bks.
Lumsden, Sharon L. Green Byways: Garden Discoveries In the Great Lakes States. LC 93-78515. (Illus.). 317p. 1993. pap. 19.95 (*0-9636467-0-2*) Lime Tree Pubns.
Lumsden, W. H. & Evans, D. A., eds. Biology of the Kinetoplastida, Vol. 2. 1979. text ed. 248.00 (*0-12-460202-9*) Acad Pr.
Lumsden, W. H., et al, eds. Advances in Parasitology, Vol. 18. (Serial Publication Ser.). 1980. text ed. 187.00 (*0-12-031718-4*) Acad Pr.
— Advances in Parasitology, Vol. 19. (Serial Publication Ser.). 224p. 1982. text ed. 187.00 (*0-12-031719-2*) Acad Pr.
— Advances in Parasitology, Vol. 20. (Serial Publication Ser.). 1982. text ed. 187.00 (*0-12-031720-6*) Acad Pr.
Lumsdon, Les. The U. K. Cycling Guide 1994. (Illus.). 250p. (Orig.). 1994. pap. 27.50 (*1-85058-386-2*, Pub. by Sigma Press UK) Coronet Bks.
***Lumsedn.** Detecting the Fakes: A Collector's Guide to Third Reich Militaria. 1991. pap. (*0-7818-0324-1*) Hippocrene Bks.
Lumumba-Kasongo, Tukumbi. Political Re-Mapping of Africa: Transnational Ideology & the Redefinition of Africa in World Politics. LC 93-30867. 170p. (C). 1993. lib. bdg. 32.50 (*0-8191-9299-6*) U Pr of Amer.
Lumumba-Kasongo, Tukumbi. Nationalistic Ideologies: Their Policy Implications & the Struggle for Democracy in African Politics. LC 91-27345. (African Studies: Vol. 23). 148p. 1991. lib. bdg. 69.95 (*0-7734-9696-3*) E Mellen.
Lumumba-Kasongo, Tukumbi, jt. ed. see Kennett, David.
Lun, Anthony W., tr. see Yan, L. & Shiran, Du.
Lun, Hrvoje. Revolucija I Sloboda. 1978. pap. 16.00 (*0-9602138-1-3*) Plamen Pub.
Lun, Marc A. Poems of Euphoria, Melancholy, & Madness. 1993. 8.95 (*0-533-10557-9*) Vantage.
Luna, Claire. Ebony Blood. Van Treese, James B., ed. 120p. 1994. pap. 7.95 (*1-56901-153-2*) NW Pub.
Luna, David. Ultimate Fitness. LC 88-61234. (Illus.). 152p. (Orig.). 1989. pap. 16.95 (*0-915677-38-5*) Roundtable Pub.
Luna, Guillermo A. Hacia una Administracion Eficaz. 144p. (SPA.). 1985. 3.95 (*0-88113-114-8*) Edit Betania.
***Luna Imaging, Inc.** Frank Lloyd Wright: Presentation & Conceptual Drawings. (Illus.). 1995. cd-rom 1,500.00 (*0-19-509576-6*) OUP.
***Luna, James G.** Youth of the 80s, Vol. 22. 152p. (Orig.). 1994. pap. text ed. 10.95 (*0-9641606-0-9*) Easy Break.
Luna, Jerry, jt. auth. see Jenks, Bill.
Luna, Larry. The New Polish Joke Book. 1977. pap. 1.25 (*0-8439-0440-2*) Dorchester Pub Co.
Luna-Lawhn, Juanita, tr. see Torres, Olga B.
Luna, Lee G., jt. auth. see Thompson, Samuel W.
Luna, Luis E. & Amaringo, Pablo. Ayahuasca Visions: The Religious Iconography of a Peruvian Shaman. (Illus.). 160p. 1991. 60.00 (*1-55643-064-7*) North Atlantic.
Luna, Margaret A. Aspects of Grief. 100p. 1991. 12.95 (*0-9630974-2-3*) M A Luna.
Luna, O. Personalidad Transformada (Transformed Personality) (SPA.). Date not set. 1.99 (*1-56063-454-5*, 498158) Editorial Unilit.
Luna, P. Understanding Type for Desktop Publishing. (Illus.). 144p. 1992. 44.95 (*0-685-54900-3*) Van Nos Reinhold.
***Luna, Paul.** Understanding Type for Desktop Publishing. 136p. 1992. 29.95 (*0-948905-76-X*) Chapman & Hall.
Luna, R. K. Plantation Forestry in India. 509p. 1989. 300.00 (*81-7089-141-8*, Pub. by Intl Bk Distr II) St Mut.
— Plantation Forestry in India. 509p. (C). 1989. 595.00 (*0-685-61467-0*, Pub. by Intl Bk Distr II); text ed. 595.00 (*0-685-52010-2*, Pub. by Intl Bk Distr II) St Mut.
***Luna, Rachel N.** The Animals' Nutcracker Ballet. 28p. (J). (ps-3). 1995. pap. write for info. (*1-886551-03-0*) R N Luna.
— Muffy's Day at the Park. 20p. (J). (ps-3). 1995. pap. write for info. (*1-886551-02-2*) R N Luna.
— Nutcracker Magic. 20p. (J). (ps-3). 1995. pap. write for info. (*1-886551-04-9*) R N Luna.
— The Thank You God Book. 10p. (J). (ps). 1994. pap. 7.95 (*1-886551-00-6*) R N Luna.
— Where Is Muffy Hiding? 10p. (J). (ps). 1994. pap. 7.95 (*1-886551-01-4*) R N Luna.
Luna, Roger M., tr. see Desramaut, Francis.
Luna, Rose Mary, tr. see Miller, Billie M.
Lunan-Ferguson, Ira. Don't Marry That Woman: Or, How to Get & Hold a Husband. LC 73-92689. 456p. 1973. 12.95 (*0-685-03126-8*) Lunan-Ferguson.
— G. Wash Carter, White. LC 74-81532. 1969. 7.95 (*0-685-03129-2*) Lunan-Ferguson.
— I Dug Graves at Night, to Attend College by Day, Vol. 1. LC 67-31239. (Illus.). 1968. 12.95 (*0-685-03130-6*) Lunan-Ferguson.
— I Dug Graves at Night, to Attend College by Day, Vol. 2. LC 67-31239. (Illus.). 1970. 12.95 (*0-911724-06-0*) Lunan-Ferguson.
— I Dug Graves at Night, to Attend College by Day, Vol. 3. LC 67-31239. 1970. 10.95 (*0-911724-07-9*) Lunan-Ferguson.
— Lectures in Black Studies. LC 72-83316. (C). 1972. text ed. 10.95 (*0-911724-12-5*) Lunan-Ferguson.
— Our Two Ocean Voyages: The Orient & the Mediterranean. LC 68-31071. 319p. 1968. 9.95 (*0-685-03131-4*) Lunan-Ferguson.
— Twenty-Five Good Reasons Why Men Should Marry: With a Marriage Manual for Husbands on How to Treat a Wife. LC 76-2990. 1976. 9.95 (*0-685-03132-2*) Lunan-Ferguson.
— Which One of You Is Interracial? & Other Stories. LC 78-79431. 1969. 6.95 (*0-685-03133-0*) Lunan-Ferguson.
Lunar & Planetary Institute, ed. see Lunar & Planetary Institute Staff.
Lunar & Planetary Institute Staff. Proceedings of the Lunar & Planetary Science Conference, 12th, Houston, Texas, March 16-20, 1981. Lunar & Planetary Institute, ed. (Geochimica & Cosmochimica Acta Ser.: No. 16). (Illus.). 2000p. 1982. 235.00 (*0-08-028074-9*, Pergamon Pr) Elsevier.
Lunar & Planetary Institute Staff, comp. Proceedings: Eleventh Lunar & Planetary Science Conference, Houston, Texas, March 17-21, 1980, 3 vols, Set. (Geochimica & Cosmochimica Acta Ser.: Suppl. 14). 3000p. 1981. 265.00 (*0-08-026314-3*, Pergamon Pr) Elsevier.
Lunar & Planetary Institute Staff, ed. Proceedings of the Conference on Multi-Ring Basins, Houston, Texas. 300p. 1981. 47.00 (*0-08-028045-5*, Pergamon Pr) Elsevier.
Lunar & Planetary Science Conference Staff. Proceedings of the Lunar & Planetary Science Conference, 10th, Houston, Texas, March 19-23, 1979, 3 vols. LC 79-22554. (Illus.). 3200p. 1980. 400.00 (*0-08-025128-5*, Pergamon Pr) Elsevier.
— Proceedings of the Lunar & Planetary Science Conference, 9th, Houston, Texas, 1978, 3 vols., Set. (Geochimica & Cosmochimica Acta Ser.: Suppl. 10). 1979. 450.00 (*0-08-022966-2*, Pergamon Pr) Elsevier.
Lunar Science Conference, 8th, Houston, 1977. Proceedings, 3 Vols. (Lunar Science Ser.: No. 8). (Illus.). 1977. 1,646.00 (*0-08-022052-5*, Pub. by Pergamon Repr UK) Franklin.
Lunar Science Institute Staff & Criswell, D. Proceedings Third Lunar Science Conference, Houston 1-72: Physical Properties. Vol. 3. 1972. write for info. (*0-318-69664-9*, Pub. by Pergamon Repr UK) Franklin.
Lunar Science Institute Staff & Levinson, A. A. Journal of Geochemical Society & Meteoritical Society Supp 2, 3 vols., Set. LC 78-165075. 1971. 1,137.00 (*0-08-020602-6*, Pub. by Pergamon Repr UK) Franklin.
***Lunardi, Alessandra.** Analytic Semigroups & Optimal Regularity in Parabolic Problems. LC 94-47600. (Progress in Nonlinear Differential Equations & Their Applications Ser.: Vol. 16). 1995. 98.00 (*0-8176-5172-1*) Birkhauser.
Lunardi, Egidio & Nugent, Robert, trs. Giovanni Pascoli: Convivial Poems, Vol. VIII. (Lake Erie College Studies). 1979. pap. 12.50 (*0-935518-02-9*) Lake Erie Col Pr.
— Giovanni Pascoli: Convivial Poems, Part II, Vol. IX. (Lake Erie College Studies). 1981. pap. 7.50 (*0-935518-03-7*) Lake Erie Col Pr.
Lunardini, Christine. What Every American Should Know about Women's History: Two Hundred Events That Shaped Our Destiny. 1994. 16.00 (*1-55850-417-6*) Adams Pubng.
Lunardini, Christine A. American Peace Movement in the Twentieth Century. (Clio Companions Ser.). 269p. 1994. lib. bdg. 55.00 (*0-87436-714-X*) ABC-CLIO.
— From Equal Suffrage to Equal Rights: Alice Paul & the National Woman's Party, 1910-1928. (American Social Experience Ser.: No. 5). 250p. 1988. 55.00x (*0-8147-5022-2*); pap. 18.50 (*0-8147-5038-9*) NYU Pr.
— Women's Rights. (Social Issues in American History Ser.). (Illus.). 256p. 1995. pap. 29.95 (*0-89774-872-7*) Oryx Pr.
Lunardini, V. J. Heat Transfer with Freezing & Thawing. (Developments in Geotechnical Engineering Ser.: No. 65). 450p. 1991. 151.50 (*0-444-88905-1*) Elsevier.
Lunati, Rinaldo. Book Selection: Principles & Practice. Marulli, Luciana, tr. LC 75-23498. 174p. 1975. 20.00 (*0-8108-0846-3*) Scarecrow.
Lunau, F. W., jt. ed. see Leslie, G. B.
Lunbeck, C. J. Child Care in Omaha, Pt. 1: Facilities. (Illus.). 33p. (Orig.). 1971. pap. 3.00 (*1-55719-073-9*) U NE CPAR.
— CUA Census Report, No. 3: Indian Population in Douglas County. 23p. (Orig.). 1972. pap. 2.50 (*1-55719-054-2*) U NE CPAR.
Lunbeck, Elizabeth. The Psychiatric Persuasion: Knowledge, Gender, & Power in Modern America. LC 93-43818. (C). 1994. 29.95 (*0-691-04804-5*) Princeton U Pr.
Lunc, M., ed. International Astronautical Congress: Proceedings, 20th, Argentina, 1969. 1972. 406.00 (*0-08-016841-8*, Pub. by Pergamon Repr UK) Franklin.
Lunc, M. & Contensou, P. Astrodynamics & Astrionics: Proceedings of the Nineteenth International Astronautical Congress, New York, 1968. LC 58-23647. (International Astronautical Congress Ser.: Vol. 2). 1970. 248.00 (*0-08-006930-4*, Pub. by Pergamon Repr UK) Franklin.
— Bioastronautics: Proceedings of the Nineteenth International Astronautical Congress, New York, 1968. LC 58-23647. (International Astronautical Congress Ser.: Vol. 4). 1970. 128.00 (*0-08-006932-0*, Pub. by Pergamon Repr UK) Franklin.
— Proceedings of the Nineteenth International Astronautical Congress, New York, 1968, 4 vols., Set. LC 58-23647. 1970. 846.00 (*0-08-006933-9*, Pub. by Pergamon Repr UK) Franklin.
— Propulsion Re-Entry Physics: Proceedings of the Nineteenth International Astronautical Congress, New York, 1968. LC 58-23647. (International Astronautical Congress Ser.: Vol. 3). 1970. 239.00 (*0-08-006931-2*, Pub. by Pergamon Repr UK) Franklin.
— Spacecraft Systems: Proceedings of the Nineteenth International Astronautical Congress, New York, 1968. LC 58-23647. (International Astronautical Congress Ser.: Vol. 1). 1970. 233.00 (*0-08-006929-0*, Pub. by Pergamon Repr UK) Franklin.
Lunceford, Alvin M., Jr. Taliaferro County, Georgia: Records & Notes. LC 85-20994. (Illus.). 704p. 1987. 45.00 (*0-87152-414-7*) Reprint.
Lunch, Lydia. Incriminating Evidence: The Collected Writings of Lydia Lunch. 1992. pap. 12.95 (*0-86719-380-8*) Last Gasp.
Lunch, Richard L., jt. ed. see Lynch, Richard L.
Lunch, William M. The Nationalization of American Politics. (C). 1987. 38.00 (*0-520-05661-2*); pap. 14.00 (*0-520-06613-8*) U CA Pr.
Lunchbox, Deacon, see Tim Ruttenber, pseud..
***Lund.** Critical Essays on Daniel Defoe. 1997. 42.00 (*0-7838-0007-X*) G K Hall.
Lund, jt. ed. see Heldman.
Lund, A. & Shiotani, M. Radical Ionic Systems Properties in Condensed Physics. (Topics in Molecular Organization & Engineering Ser.). 488p. 1991. lib. bdg. 164.00 (*0-7923-0988-X*) Kluwer Ac.
***Lund, Adrienne F.** An Amish Potpourri Cookbook. (Illus.). 170p. (Orig.). 1991. pap. 12.95 (*1-886645-02-7*) Jupiter Press.
— The Amish Recipe Sampler. 65p. (Orig.). 1982. pap. 4.95 (*1-886645-00-0*) Jupiter Press.
— Katie's Dream. (Illus.). 30p. (Orig.). (J). (gr. k-5). 1987. pap. 5.95 (*1-886645-03-5*) Jupiter Press.
— Plain & Fancy Amish Cookie Recipes. (Illus.). 69p. (Orig.). 1993. pap. 6.95 (*1-886645-01-9*) Jupiter Press.
***Lund, Anders & Rhodes, Christopher, eds.** Radicals on Surfaces. LC 94-31444. (Topics in Molecular Organization & Engineering Ser.: 13). 260p. (C). 1995. lib. bdg. 154.00 (*0-7923-3108-7*) Kluwer Ac.
Lund, Ann. Dining in Style. 250p. 1992. spiral bd. write for info. (*0-9634750-0-2*) A Lund.
Lund, Barbara, ed. see Grossman, Peter J.
Lund, Birger, jt. ed. see Danneskiold-Samsoe, Bente.
***Lund, Bonnie.** Business Communication That Really Works! Technology for Business. Engel, Peter H., ed. (Office Depot's Small Business Solutions Ser.). (Illus.). 128p. (Orig.). 1995. pap. 13.95 (*1-886111-24-3*) Affinity CA.
***Lund, Bonnie & Office Depot Staff.** Business Communication That Really Works. Knudsen, Anne, ed. (Small Business Solutions Ser.). (Orig.). 1995. pap. 13.95 (*0-8442-2997-0*, NTC Busn Bks) NTC Pub Grp.
Lund, C. A. Coastal & Deep Sea Navigation for Yachtsmen. (C). 1987. 35.00 (*0-85174-119-3*, Pub. by Brwn Son Ferg) St Mut.
— Compasses in Small Craft. (C). 1987. 40.00 (*0-85174-453-2*, Pub. by Brwn Son Ferg) St Mut.
— The Handling of Motor Craft. (C). 1987. 25.00 (*0-85174-121-5*, Pub. by Brwn Son Ferg) St Mut.
Lund, Candida, comp. Praymates. 1994. Encore Edition. pap. 13.95 (*0-88347-278-3*) Thomas More.
Lund, Candida, ed. God & Me. (Orig.). 1988. pap. 12.95 (*0-88347-222-8*) Thomas More.
Lund, Carol A. A Journey with Jesus. (Illus.). 214p. (Orig.). 1982. pap. 4.95 (*0-9608418-0-6*) MasterSon Pub.
Lund, Caroline, jt. auth. see Cannon, James P.
Lund, Carolyn. Bronchopulmonary Dysplasia: Strategies for Total Patient Care. 260p. 1990. text ed. 19.95 (*0-9622975-2-6*) NICU INK.
Lund, Carsten. The Power of Interaction. (ACM Distinguished Dissertation, 1991 Ser.). (Illus.). 125p. 1992. 25.00 (*0-262-12170-0*) MIT Pr.
Lund, Charles. Dot Paper Geometry: With or Without a Geoboard. (Illus.). 84p. (J). (gr. 4-8). 1980. pap. text ed. 9.95 (*0-914040-87-1*) Cuisenaire.
— Tricks of the Trade with Cards. Laycock, Mary, ed. (J). (gr. 2-9). 1978. pap. text ed. 7.95 (*0-918932-57-2*) Activity Resources.
Lund, Charles & Andersen, Edwin D. Computer Graphing Experiments, 3 vols., Set. 1982. write for info. (*0-201-23480-7*) Addison-Wesley.
— Computer Graphing Experiments, 4 vols., Vol. 1. 1982. write for info. (*0-201-23465-3*) Addison-Wesley.
— Computer Graphing Experiments, 4 vols., Vol. 2. 1982. write for info. (*0-201-23470-X*) Addison-Wesley.
— Computer Graphing Experiments, 4 vols., Vol. 3. 1982. write for info. (*0-201-23475-0*) Addison-Wesley.
Lund, Charles & Smart, Margaret. Focus on Calculator Math. (Illus.). (J). (gr. 4-12). 1979. pap. text ed. 8.50 (*0-918932-66-1*) Activity Resources.
Lund, Coby, et al. Who Lives in the Igloo? (Illus.). 52p. (Orig.). (J). (gr. 4-9). 1984. 6.95 (*0-88047-046-1*, 8402) DOK Pubs.
Lund, D. & Oksendal, B., eds. Stochastic Models & Option Values: Applications to Resources, Environment & Investment Problems. (Contributions to Economic Analysis Ser.: No. 200). 302p. 1991. 69.00 (*0-444-88630-3*, North Holland) Elsevier.
Lund, Dale. All about Tarantulas. (Illus.). 1977. 9.95 (*0-87666-909-7*, PS-749) TFH Pubns.
Lund, Dale A., ed. Older Bereaved Spouses. 196p. 1989. 55.00 (*0-89116-803-6*); pap. 26.00 (*1-56032-240-3*) Hemisp Pub.
Lund, Daulatram, et al, eds. Pricing Policies & Strategies: An Annotated Bibliography. LC 82-809. (Bibliography Ser.). 110p. (Orig.). 1982. pap. text ed. 6.00 (*0-87757-157-0*) Am Mktg.
Lund, David, jt. auth. see Lund, Lauren.
Lund, David H. Death & Consciousness. LC 84-43211. 204p. 1985. lib. bdg. 27.50x (*0-89950-140-0*) McFarland & Co.
— Perception, Mind & Personal Identity: A Critique of Materialism. LC 94-25527. 286p. (Orig.). (C). reprint ed. lib. bdg. 47.50 (*0-8191-9615-0*); reprint ed. pap. text ed. 28.50 (*0-8191-9616-9*) U Pr of Amer.
Lund, Deborah S. Ambiguity As Narrative Strategy in the Prose of C. F. Meyer. (Studies in Nineteenth-Century German Literature: Vol. 6). 212p. (C). 1990. text ed. 45.95 (*0-8204-1279-1*) P Lang Pubs.
Lund-Dillon, Karen. Finding Karen: The Journey Through Sadness. (Illus.). 164p. (Orig.). Date not set. pap. 14.95 (*0-9642000-0-7*) K Lund-Dillon.
Lund, Doniver A. Gustavus Adolphus College: Celebrating One Hundred Twenty-Five Years. LC 87-61257. (Illus.). 117p. 1987. 29.95 (*0-685-19540-6*) Primarius Ltd.
Lund, Doris. Eric. LC 88-45954. 272p. 1989. reprint ed. mass mkt. 6.00 (*0-06-080925-6*, P 925, PL) HarpC.
Lund, Duane. Our Historic Upper Mississippi. 1991. 8.95 (*0-934860-73-4*) Adventure Pubns.
— Sauces, Seasonings & Marinades for Fish & Wild Game. 1991. 8.95 (*0-934860-74-2*) Adventure Pubns.

An Asterisk (*) at the beginning of an entry indicates that the title is appearing in BIP for the first time.

Lund, Duane R. Andrew the Youngest Lumberjack. 1990. 8.95 (*0-934860-62-9*) Adventure Pubns.
— A Beginner's Guide to Hunting & Trapping Secrets. 1988. 8.95 (*0-934860-52-1*) Adventure Pubns.
— Camp Cooking. 198p. 1991. 8.95 (*0-934860-05-X*) Adventure Pubns.
— Early Native American Recpies. 1989. 8.95 (*0-934860-57-2*) Adventure Pubns.
— Fishing & Hunting Stories. 1992. 8.95 (*0-934860-95-5*) Adventure Pubns.
— Gourmet Freshwater Fish Recipes. 1993. 8.95 (*0-934860-09-2*) Adventure Pubns.
— A Kid's Guide to Fishing Secrets. 1984. 8.95 (*0-934860-37-8*) Adventure Pubns.
— Lake of the Woods II. 1984. 8.95 (*0-934860-36-X*) Adventure Pubns.
— Lake of the Woods, Yesterday & Today. 1976. 8.95 (*0-934860-03-3*) Adventure Pubns.
— Nature's Bounty for Your Table. 1982. 8.95 (*0-934860-20-3*) Adventure Pubns.
— The North Shore of Lake Superior Yesterday & Today. 1993. pap. 8.95 (*0-934860-01-7*) Adventure Pubns.
— One Hundred & One Favorite Wild Rice Recipes. 1983. pap. 8.95 (*0-934860-24-6*) Adventure Pubns.
— One Hundred & One Mushroom Recipes. 1985. 6.95 (*0-934860-43-2*) Adventure Pubns.
— One Hundred One Favorite Freshwater Fish Recipes. 1979. 8.95 (*0-934860-11-4*) Adventure Pubns.
— One Hundred One Ways to Add to Your Income. 1993. 8.95 (*0-934860-10-6*) Adventure Pubns.
— Our Historic Boundary Waters. 1980. 8.95 (*0-934860-13-0*) Adventure Pubns.
— Scandinavian Cookbook. 1992. pap. 8.95 (*0-934860-88-2*) Adventure Pubns.
— Tales of Four Lakes. 1977. 8.95 (*0-934860-04-1*) Adventure Pubns.
— White Indian Boy. 1981. 7.95 (*0-934860-17-3*) Adventure Pubns.
— The Youngest Voyageur. 1985. 7.95 (*0-934860-41-6*) Adventure Pubns.
Lund, Duane R. & Finch, Lewis W. Lessons in Leadership: Mostly Learned the Hard Way. 96p. (Orig.). (C). 1987. pap. 8.95 (*0-934860-47-5*) Adventure Pubns.
Lund, E. Cien Bosquejos Ilustrados: 100 Illustrated Sermon Outlines. (SPA.). 5.95 (*84-7645-468-6*, 223340, Pub. by Edit Clie SP) TSELF.
Lund, Eloise E., ed. see Lund, Harry C.
Lund, Enrique. Bosquejos Para Reuniones Oracion: Sermon Outlines for Prayer. (SPA.). 6.95 (*84-7645-040-0*, 223110, Pub. by Edit Clie SP) TSELF.
— Comentario Epistola a los Galatas: Galatians-A Practical. (SPA.). 3.95 (*84-7645-028-1*, 223097, Pub. by Edit Clie SP) TSELF.
— Epistola a los Filipenses: Paul's Letter to the Philippians. (SPA.). 3.95 (*84-7645-060-5*, 223119, Pub. by Edit Clie SP) TSELF.
Lund, Eric. Alternatives to Lumber & Plywood in Home Construction. (Illus.). 61p. (Orig.). (C). 1994. pap. text ed. 45.00 (*0-7881-0264-8*) Diane Pub.
Lund, Fred B. Greek Medicine. LC 75-23668. (Clio Medica Ser.: 18). (Illus.). reprint ed. 20.00 (*0-404-58918-9*) AMS Pr.
Lund, Gary, illus. Life: Before, During & After. (Celebration of Discovery Ser.: Vol. II). 192p. (Orig.). 1988. pap. 12. 95 (*0-938283-01-4*) Spirit Speaks.
Lund, Gene J., tr. see Fagerberg, Holsten.
Lund, Gerald. Three Adventure Novels: One in Thine Hand; Leverage Point; The Alliance, 3 bks., Set. LC 94-71451. 875p. 1994. 15.95 (*0-87579-861-6*) Deseret Bk.
Lund, Gerald N. The Coming of the Lord. 9.95 (*0-88494-229-5*) Bookcraft Inc.
— The Freedom Factor. LC 87-15548. 295p. 1995. pap. 6.95 (*0-87579-961-2*) Deseret Bk.
— Jesus Christ, Key to the Plan of Salvation. LC 90-48801. viii, 196p. 1991. 12.95 (*0-87579-421-1*) Deseret Bk.
— Work & the Glory: A Season of Joy, Vol. 5. 1994. 17.95 (*0-88494-960-5*) Bookcraft Inc.
— The Work & the Glory: Pillar of Light. 14.95 (*0-88494-770-X*) Bookcraft Inc.
— The Work & the Glory: Truth Will Prevail, Vol. 3. 1992. 15.95 (*0-88494-853-6*) Bookcraft Inc.
— The Work & the Glory, Vol. 2: Like a Fire Is Burning. 1991. 15.95 (*0-88494-801-3*) Bookcraft Inc.
— The Work & the Glory, Vol. 4: Thy Gold to Refine. 1993. 16.95 (*0-88494-893-5*) Bookcraft Inc.
Lund, Hans. Text As Picture: Studies in the Literary Transformation of Pictures. (Illus.). 228p. 1992. lib. bdg. 89.95 (*0-7734-9449-9*) E Mellen.
Lund, Harry C. Michigan Wildflowers in Color. Lund, Eloise E., ed. (Illus.). 120p. (Orig.). 1985. pap. 10.95 (*0-685-10417-6*) H C Lund.
— Michigan Wildflowers in Color. 120p. (Orig.). 1991. reprint ed. pap. 16.95 (*0-9614818-0-3*) Northmont Pub.
Lund, Helen S. Lysimachus: A Study in Early Hellenistic Kingship. LC 92-2796. 256p. 1992. 69.95 (*0-415-07061-9*, A7939) Routledge.
Lund, Henning & Baizer, Manuel M., eds. Organic Electrochemistry: An Introduction & a Guide. 3rd ed. 1568p. 1991. 255.00 (*0-8247-8154-6*) Dekker.
Lund, Henning, jt. ed. see Bard, Allan J.
Lund, Herbert F. Recycling Handbook. LC 92-18267. 1992. text ed. 87.50 (*0-07-039096-7*) McGraw.
Lund, Ingeborg, tr. see Behrend, William.
Lund, J. Survey of the Users of the Large Installations Plan, No. EUR 14461. 100p. 1992. pap. 15.00 (*92-826-4379-4*, CG-NA-14461-EN-C, Pub. by Europ Com) UNIPUB.
Lund, J. A., jt. ed. see Chaklader, A. C.
Lund, J. W., tr. see Korshikov, O. A.
Lund, James R. & Heidkamp, Mary. Moving Faith into Action: A Facilitator's Guide for Creating Parish Social Ministry Organizations. 192p. 1990. pap. 9.95 (*0-8091-3157-9*) Paulist Pr.
Lund, Jennifer S. Sensory Processing in the Mammalian Brain: Neural Substrates & Experimental Strategies. (Illus.). 384p. 1988. 49.95 (*0-19-504554-8*) OUP.
***Lund, Jens.** Flatheads & Spooneys: Fishing for a Living in the Ohio River Valley. (Ohio River Valley Ser.). (Illus.). 216p. 1995. 24.95 (*0-8131-1927-8*) U Pr of Ky.
***Lund, Jens, intro.** Contact: A Directory of Ethnic Organizations in Washington State. 3rd ed. (Illus.). 1995. pap. 20.00 (*0-9627942-1-X*) Ethnic Herit.
Lund, Jens & Simpson, Elizabeth, eds. Folk Arts of Washington State: A Survey of Contemporary Folk Arts & Artists in the State of Washington. LC 89-16696. (Illus.). 103p. (Orig.). (C). 1989. pap. 14.95 (*0-9623539-0-6*, U of Wash Pr) WA St Folklife Coun.
Lund, Jillian. Way Out West Lives a Coyote Named Frank. LC 91-46011. (Illus.). 32p. (J). (ps-2). 1993. 14.99 (*0-525-44982-5*, DCB) Dutton Child Bks.
Lund, JoAnna M. Best of Healthy Exchanges Food Newsletter. (Illus.). 180p. (Orig.). 1993. 11.50 (*0-9635632-1-1*) Hlthy Exchange.
— Health Wagon Journal. (Illus.). 175p. 1994. 14.95 (*0-9635632-4-6*) Hlthy Exchange.
— Healthy Exchanges Cookbook. 1995. 16.95 (*0-399-14065-4*) Putnam Pub Group.
— Notes of Encouragement. (Illus.). 32p. Date not set. 4.95 (*0-9635632-3-8*) Hlthy Exchange.
Lund, John. Auditing Local Union Financial Records: A Guide for Local Union Trustees. LC 92-27352. (ILR Bulletin Ser.: No. 67). 96p. 1992. pap. 9.95 (*0-87546-194-8*) ILR Pr.
Lund, John & Berg, Ruth. Project Air Force Analysis of the Air War in the Gulf: An Assessment of Strategic Airlift Operational Efficiency. LC 93-3532. 1993. 10.00 (*0-8330-1351-3*, R-4269/4) Rand Corp.
Lund, John & Bowers, Kenneth. Sinc Methods for Quadrature & Differential Equations. LC 92-12139. (Miscellaneous Bks.: No. 32). x, 304p. 1992. 45.00 (*0-89871-298-X*) Soc Indus-Appl Math.
Lund, John, jt. auth. see Bowers, Kenneth L.
Lund, John, jt. ed. see Bowers, Kenneth L.
Lund, John W. More Southern Oregon Cross Country Ski Trails. (Illus.). 138p. (Orig.). (C). 1990. pap. 8.95 (*0-9619389-2-7*) J W Lund.
— Southern Oregon Cross Country Ski Trails. (Illus.). 222p. (Orig.). 1987. pap. 9.95 (*0-9619389-1-9*) J W Lund.
Lund, John W., jt. ed. see Haworth, Elizabeth Y.
Lund, John W., jt. auth. see Lecklider, G. Robert.
***Lund, Kristin.** Dogs in Marin: A Reference Guide for Marin County Dog Owners. 200p. 1994. pap. 9.95 (*0-9643445-0-5*) Lundehund Pr.
Lund, Lauren. Bunny: A Storybook for Children Who Have a Parent with Multiple Personalities. (Illus.). 36p. (Orig.). (J). 1993. pap. text ed. 5.95 (*0-9637149-1-0*) Soft Words.
Lund, Lauren & Lund, David. Many Minds: Information for People Who Have Multiple Personalities. (Illus.). 34p. (Orig.). 1993. pap. 4.95 (*0-9637149-0-2*) Soft Words.
Lund, Linda O., jt. auth. see Hulme, Ashley.
***Lund, Lynn S.** Piano Hymn Favorites: Songs of Eternal Faith, Songs of Everlasting Joy, Songs of Inspiration, 3 bks., Set. 1994. pap. 25.98 (*0-88290-492-2*) Horizon Utah.
— Songs of Eternal Faith: Artistic Piano Arrangements of Best-Loved Hymns. LC 81-80954. 56p. (Orig.). 1982. pap. 8.98 (*0-88290-184-2*, 2901) Horizon Utah.
— Songs of Everlasting Joy: Artistic Piano Arrangements of Best-Loved Hymns. 1980. 8.98 (*0-88290-155-9*) Horizon Utah.
— Songs of Inspiration: Artistic Piano Arrangements of New Latter-Day Saint Hymns. 40p. 1986. pap. text ed. 8.98 (*0-88290-276-8*) Horizon Utah.
Lund, Margaret. Privatization & Employee Ownership: The International Experience. 41p. (Orig.). (C). 1992. pap. text ed. 15.00 (*0-926902-21-0*) NCEO.
Lund, Michael. America's Continuing Story: An Introduction to Serial Fiction, 1850-1900. LC 92-18953. 228p. (C). 1992. text ed. 29.95 (*0-8143-2401-0*) Wayne St U Pr.
— Reading Thackeray. LC 88-1295. 174p. 1988. 24.95 (*0-8143-1987-4*) Wayne St U Pr.
— Reading Thackeray. 174p. (C). 1992. pap. text ed. 15.95 (*0-8143-1988-2*) Wayne St U Pr.
Lund, Michael, jt. auth. see Hughes, Linda K.
Lund, Michael S., jt. ed. see Salamon, Lester M.
Lund, Morten. The Real Skiers' Dictionary. 1984. Calender. write for info. (*0-318-57465-9*, Fireside) S&S Trade.
Lund, Morten, ed. see Pfeifer, Friedl.
Lund, Nancy, jt. auth. see Gullard, Pamela.
Lund, Nancy J. & Duchan, Judith F. Assessing Children's Language in Naturalistic Contexts. 3rd ed. 384p. 1992. text ed. write for info. (*0-13-051905-7*) P-H.
Lund, Nils W. Chiasmus in the New Testament: A Study in the Form & Function of Chiastic Structures. LC 92-35. 464p. 1992. reprint ed. pap. 14.95 (*0-943575-92-3*) Hendrickson MA.
***Lund, Orval.** Take Paradise. 1989. 2.50 (*0-941127-05-2*) Dacotah Terr Pr.
Lund, Patsy H. Understanding & Using Application Software, Vol. 4. Leyh, ed. 718p. (C). 1990. pap. text ed. 46.00 (*0-314-66777-6*) West Pub.
Lund, Patsy H. & Hayden, Barbara A. Understanding & Using Displaywrite 3 & 4. 204p. (C). 1988. pap. text ed. 26.75 (*0-314-78996-0*) West Pub.
Lund, Patsy H., et al. Understanding & Using WordPerfect. LC 86-26727. (Microcomputing Ser.). 227p. (C). 1987. pap. text ed. 26.75 (*0-314-30122-4*); teacher ed. pap. text ed. write for info. (*0-314-35883-8*) West Pub.
Lund, Paul & Ludlam, Harry. Atlantic Jeopardy: PQ17 Convoy to Hell, Trawlers Go to War, & Night of the U-Boats, 3 vols. in 1. 720p. 1995. 29.95 (*0-572-01577-1*, Pub. by Foulsham UK) Atrium Pubs.
Lund, Phillip. Sales Reports, Records & Systems. (Illus.). 128p. 22.95 (*0-8464-0812-0*) Beekman Pubs.
Lund, Preben. Generation of Precision Artwork for Printed Circuit Boards. LC 77-12388. 371p. reprint ed. pap. 105. 80 (*0-317-29703-1*, 2024007) Bks Demand.
Lund, Ragnhild, jt. auth. see Lie, Merete.
Lund, Raymond D. Development & Plasticity of the Brain: An Introduction. (Illus.). 1978. pap. text ed. 19.95 (*0-19-502308-0*) OUP.
Lund, Reinhard, jt. ed. see Pedersen, Peder J.
Lund, Robert. Pig Tale. 8p. 1994. pap. 5.00 (*0-941543-07-2*) Sun Dog Pr.
Lund, Robert A. Taming the HP 3000, Vol. 1: Over 101 Ways to Monitor, Manage, & Maximize System Performance on the Hewlett-Packard 3000. LC 87-92025. 142p. (Orig.). (C). 1990. pap. text ed. 49.95 (*0-945325-01-0*) Perf Pr OR.
— Taming the HP 3000, Vol. 2: The Theory & Practice of Successful Performance Management for Hewlett-Packard HP 3000 Computer Systems. LC 87-92025. 282p. (C). 1992. text ed. 99.95 (*0-945325-02-9*); pap. text ed. 79.95 (*0-945325-03-7*) Perf Pr OR.
Lund, Robert T., et al. Designed to Work: People & Production Systems. 224p. 1993. text ed. 56.00 (*0-13-203944-3*) P-H.
Lund, Roger D. Restoration & Early Eighteenth-Century English Literature, 1660-1740: A Selected Bibliography of Resource Materials. LC 79-87585. (Selected Bibliographies in Language & Literature Ser.: No. 1). 42p. (Orig.). 1980. pap. 10.00 (*0-87352-950-2*, SB1) Modern Lang.
***Lund, Roger D., ed.** The Margins of Orthodoxy: Heterodox Writing & Cultural Response, 1660-1750. 330p. (C). 1995. write for info. (*0-521-47177-X*) Cambridge U Pr.
Lund, Shirley & Foster, Julia A. Variant Versions of Targumic Traditions Within Codex Neofiti 1. LC 77-5389. (Society of Biblical Literature. Aramaic Studies: No. 2). 186p. reprint ed. pap. 53.10 (*0-7837-5457-4*, 2045222) Bks Demand.
Lund, Sophie, tr. see Bunin, Ivan.
Lund, Steven. James Joyce: Letters, Manuscripts & Photographs at Southern Illinois University. LC 82-50414. 170p. 1983. 18.50 (*0-87875-253-6*) Whitston Pub.
Lund, Thomas A. American Wildlife Law. LC 78-68829. 1980. 35.00 (*0-520-03883-5*) U CA Pr.
Lund, Valarie, jt. auth. see Maran, Arnold.
***Lund, Valerie J.** Let's Make Banners. 10p. (Orig.). 1994. pap. text ed. 14.95 (*0-9622405-2-4*) Creative Recovery.
— Let's Make Seasonal Windsocks. (Illus.). 70p. (Orig.). 1992. pap. text ed. 10.95 (*0-9622405-1-6*) V J Lund.
— Let's Make Windsocks. rev. ed. (Illus.). 70p. (C). 1989. pap. text ed. 10.95 (*0-9622405-0-8*) V J Lund.
Lund, Valerie J., jt. ed. see Harrison, Donald.
Lundahl, Craig R. A Collection of Near-Death Research Readings. LC 82-14134. 272p. (C). 1982. 32.95 (*0-88229-640-X*) Nelson-Hall.
***Lundahl, Craig R. & Widdison, Harold A.** The Eternal Journey: What Near-Death Experiences Reveal about Life & Death. 1995. write for info. (*0-88290-537-6*) Horizon Utah.
Lundahl, G. D. & Lundahl, Ruth C. Divorce: How You Can Survive & Thrive in Spite of It. Achziger, John, ed. 156p. (Orig.). 1989. pap. write for info. (*0-318-64644-7*) How Pub CA.
Lundahl, Mats. Apartheid in Theory & Practice: An Economic Analysis. 375p. (C). 1992. pap. text ed. 34.85 (*0-8133-8447-8*) Westview.
— Incentives & Agriculture in East Africa. 224p. (C). 1991. text ed. 65.00 (*0-415-03736-0*, A4817) Routledge.
— Politics or Markets? Essays on Haitian Underdevelopment. 480p. 1992. 99.95 (*0-415-04347-6*, A6816) Routledge.
Lundahl, Mats, ed. The Primary Sector in Economic Development. LC 84-24807. 384p. 1985. text ed. 45.00 (*0-312-64418-3*) St Martin.
Lundahl, Mats & Wadensjo, Eskil. Unequal Treatment: A Study in the Neoclassical Theory of Discrimination. 336p. 1985. 55.00x (*0-8147-5012-5*) NYU Pr.
Lundahl, Mats, jt. ed. see Blomstrom, Magnus.
Lundahl, Ruth C., jt. auth. see Lundahl, G. D.
Lundbaek, Knud. Joseph De Premare, 1666-1736, S. J. Chinese Philology & Figurism. (Acta Jutlandica LXVI: 2, Humanities Ser.: No. 65). (Illus.). 228p. (Orig.). 1991. pap. 52.50 (*87-7288-344-8*, Pub. by Aarhus Univ Pr DK) Coronet Bks.
— T. S. Bayer, 1649-1738: Pioneer Sinologist. (Scandinavian Institute of Asian Studies Monograph: No. 54). (Illus.). 256p. (C). 1986. pap. 29.95 (*0-7007-0189-3*, Pub. by Curzon Pr UK) Humanities.
Lundbeck, J., jt. auth. see Sahrhage, D.
Lundberg, Arne & Alatalo, Rauno V. The Pied Flycatcher. (Illus.). 267p. 1992. text ed. 39.95 (*0-85661-072-0*, 784672) Acad Pr.
Lundberg, Carol W. The Secret Life. LC 93-33743. 68p. 1993. pap. 12.95 (*0-7734-2801-1*, Mellen Poetry Pr) E Mellen.
Lundberg, Craig, ed. Consultation Education: A Special Issue of Consultation: An International Journal. 66p. 1987. 14.95 (*0-89885-368-0*) Human Sci Pr.
Lundberg, Dag B., jt. auth. see Mueller, Robert A.
Lundberg, David W. Government by the People: What You Can Do for America. LC 79-65905. 1979. 10.95 (*0-934762-00-7*); pap. 7.95 (*0-934762-01-5*) Voice of Liberty.
Lundberg, Donald E. The Hotel & Restaurant Business. 5th ed. LC 79-207. (Illus.). 464p. (C). 1989. pap. 44.95 (*0-442-20505-8*); 20.95 (*0-442-31914-2*) Van Nos Reinhold.
— The Hotel & Restaurant Business. 6th ed. LC 92-28353. (Illus.). 416p. 1994. text ed. 38.95 (*0-442-01246-2*) Van Nos Reinhold.
— International Travel & Tourism. 2nd ed. 480p. 1993. Net. text ed. write for info. (*0-471-53146-4*) Wiley.
— Tourist Business. 6th ed. 1990. pap. 39.95 (*0-442-23376-0*) Van Nos Reinhold.
Lundberg, Donald E. & Walker, John R. The Restaurant: From Concept to Operation. 2nd ed. 400p. 1993. text ed. write for info. (*0-471-57883-5*) Wiley.
Lundberg, Donald E., et al. Tourism Economics. LC 94-20598. 1995. text ed. write for info. (*0-471-57884-3*) Wiley.
Lundberg, Elaine & Thurston, Cheryl M. If They're Laughing, They're Not Killing Each Other: Ideas for Using Humor Effectively in the Classroom - Even If You're Not Funny Yourself. 96p. 1992. 10.95 (*1-877673-14-5*, IF) Cottonwood Pr.
Lundberg, Emma O. & Lenrott, Katherine F. Illegitimacy As a Child-Welfare Problem. LC 74-1713. (Children & Youth Ser.: Pts. 1 & 2). 1974. 41.95 (*0-405-05972-8*) Ayer.
Lundberg, Erik. Instability & Economic Growth. LC 68-13917. (Studies in Comparative Economics: No. 8). (Illus.). 449p. reprint ed. pap. 128.00 (*0-317-09709-1*, 2022016) Bks Demand.
— Study in the Theory of Economic Expansion. (Reprints of Economic Classics Ser.). 1964. reprint ed. 35.00 (*0-678-00046-8*) Kelley.
Lundberg, Ferdinand. Cracks in the Constitution. 1980. 15. 00 (*0-8184-0279-2*) Carol Pub Group.
— Imperial Hearst. LC 73-125704. (American Journalists Ser.). 1971. reprint ed. 25.95 (*0-405-01685-9*) Ayer.
— The Myth of Democracy. 1989. 11.95 (*0-8184-0500-7*) Carol Pub Group.
— The Natural Depravity of Mankind: Observations on the Human Condition. LC 93-40407. 1994. 15.95 (*1-56980-003-0*) Barricade Bks.
— Politicians & Other Scoundrels. LC 92-17314. 1992. pap. 7.95 (*0-942637-72-0*) Barricade Bks.
— Politicians & Other Scoundrels. 160p. 1988. reprint ed. pap. 6.95 (*0-8184-0483-3*) Carol Pub Group.
— The Rich & Super-Rich. 820p. reprint ed. pap. 14.95 (*0-8184-0486-8*) Carol Pub Group.
— Rich & the Super-Rich. Brand, Eileen, ed. LC 67-10015. 1968. 15.00 (*0-8184-0069-2*) Carol Pub Group.
— The Rockefeller Syndrome. LC 75-23031. 1975. 12.50 (*0-8184-0215-6*) Carol Pub Group.
— Scoundrels All. LC 68-18764. 1968. 3.95 (*0-8184-0072-2*) Carol Pub Group.
— The Treason of the People. LC 73-19114. 370p. 1974. reprint ed. text ed. 69.50 (*0-8371-7307-8*, LUTP, Greenwood Pr) Greenwood.
Lundberg, George. Some Neglected Aspects of the 'Minorities' Problem. 1994. lib. bdg. 250.00 (*0-8490-5666-7*) Gordon Pr.
Lundberg, George A. Can Science Save Us? 2nd ed. LC 79-16792. 150p. 1979. reprint ed. text ed. 49.75 (*0-313-21299-6*, LUCS, Greenwood Pr) Greenwood.
— Foundations of Sociology. LC 79-9742. (Illus.). 179p. 1979. reprint ed. text ed. 38.50 (*0-313-21264-3*, LUFS, Greenwood Pr) Greenwood.
— Some Neglected Aspects of the Minorities Problems. 1982. lib. bdg. 59.00 (*0-87700-411-0*) Revisionist Pr.
Lundberg, Gertrude W., comp. Cook County Illinois 1850 Federal Census: Not Including the City of Chicago. 1987. pap. 20.00 (*1-881125-11-4*) Chi Geneal Soc.
Lundberg, Joy S. Book of Mormon Summer. (J). (gr. 5-8). 1991. 6.95 (*0-915029-00-6*) Cherished Bks.
Lundberg, Lars, jt. ed. see Fagerberg, Jan.
Lundberg, Louise, ed. see Williams, Selver B.
Lundberg, Margaret J. The Incomplete Adult. LC 74-67. (Illus.). 245p. 1974. text ed. 55.00 (*0-8371-7362-0*, LUA/, Greenwood Pr) Greenwood.
Lundberg, Paul. The Book of Shiatsu. (Illus.). 128p. (Orig.). 1992. pap. 14.95 (*0-671-74488-7*, Fireside) S&S Trade.
Lundberg, W., jt. auth. see Holman, R. J.
Lundbergh, Holger, tr. see Donner, Jorn.
Lundblad, J. Nathaniel Hawthorne & the Tradition of Gothic Romance. LC 65-15898. (Studies in Hawthorne: No. 15). 1969. reprint ed. lib. bdg. 75.00 (*0-8383-0589-X*) M S G Haskell Hse.
Lundblad, Jane. Nathaniel Hawthorne & European Literary Tradition. (BCL1-PS American Literature Ser.). 196p. 1993. reprint ed. lib. bdg. 69.00 (*0-7812-6965-2*) Rprt Serv.
Lundblad, Roger L. Chemical Reagents for Protein Modification. 2nd ed. (Illus.). 376p. 1991. 167.00 (*0-8493-5097-2*, QP551) CRC Pr.
— Techniques in Protein Modification. LC 94-11646. 304p. 1994. 49.95 (*0-8493-2606-0*, 2606) CRC Pr.
Lundblad, Roger L. & Noyes, Claudia M. Chemical Reagents for Protein Modification, Vol. I. 192p. 1984. 144.00 (*0-8493-5086-7*, TP453) CRC Pr.
— Chemical Reagents for Protein Modification, Vol. II. 184p. 1984. 144.00 (*0-8493-5087-5*) CRC Pr.
Lundbom, Jack R. The Early Career of the Prophet Jeremiah. LC 93-5511. 128p. 1993. text ed. 59.95 (*0-7734-2372-9*, Mellen Biblical Pr) E Mellen.
— Jeremiah: A Study in Ancient Hebrew Rhetoric. LC 75-15732. (Society of Biblical Literature. Dissertation Ser.: No. 18). 209p. reprint ed. 59.60 (*0-8357-9574-8*, 2017520) Bks Demand.
Lundborg, Goran. Nerve Injury & Repair. (Illus.). 256p. 1988. text ed. 135.00 (*0-443-03528-8*) Churchill.
Lundborg, Louis B. The Art of Being an Executive. 275p. 1981. 19.95 (*0-02-919300-1*) Free Pr.

L

Lundborg, Per. The Economics of Export Embargoes. 128p. 1987. 55.00 (0-7099-4151-X, Pub. by Croom Helm UK) Routledge Chapman & Hall.

Lunde, Anders S. Whirligigs in Silhouette. (Illus.). 128p. 1989. 19.95 (0-86675-013-4); pap. 14.95 (0-86675-014-2) KC Pub.

*Lunde, David. Blues for Port City. 24p. (Orig.). 1995. pap. 5.00x (0-932412-07-6) Mayapple Pr.

— Calibrations. LC 79-16512. 1980. 8.00 (0-931588-07-3); pap. 3.50 (0-931588-08-1) Allegany Mtn Pr.

— Heart Transplants & Other Misapproppriations. LC 93-36484. 64p. 1993. pap. 12.95 (0-7734-0008-7, Mellen Poetry Pr) E Mellen.

Lunde, Erik S. & Noverr, Douglas A., eds. Film History. LC 88-17395. (Selected Course Outlines in Popular Culture Ser.). 300p. (Orig.). (C). 1989. pap. text ed. 16.95 (1-55876-002-4) Wiener Pubs Inc.

Lunde, Gregory J. Colligation: Covering Law & Colligation: Two Theories of Historical Explanation for Decision Making Applications. 1994. 16.95 (0-533-11032-7) Vantage.

*Lunde, Joyce P., ed. Reshaping Curricula: Revitalization Programs at Three Land Grant Universities. 350p. (C). 1995. text ed. 34.95 (1-882982-09-6) Anker Pub.

Lunde, Karl. John Day. (Illus.). 96p. 1985. 30.00 (0-932169-00-7) Tenth Ave Edit.

Lunde, Ken. Understanding Japanese Information Processing. Mui, Peter & Reilly, Tim, eds. (Illus.). 470p. (Orig.). 1993. pap. 29.95 (1-56592-043-0) OReilly & Assocs.

Lunde, Linda, ed. see Bernzen, George.

Lunde, Norman. You Unlimited. LC 65-23608. 1985. reprint ed. pap. 7.95 (0-87516-249-5) DeVorss.

Lunde, Paul & Wintle, Justin. A Dictionary of Arabic & Islamic Proverbs. 200p. 1984. 19.95 (0-7102-0179-6, RKP) Routledge.

Lunde, Paul, tr. see Masudi.

Lunde, Paul D. Great Restraint. LC 85-73100. 478p. (Orig.). 1986. 19.95 (0-935689-07-9); pap. 12.95 (0-935689-16-8) CRI Pubns.

Lundeberg, Philip K. Samuel Colt's Submarine Battery: The Secret & the Enigma. LC 74-7322. (Smithsonian Studies in History & Technology: No. 29). (Illus.). 96p. reprint ed. pap. 27.40 (0-317-09446-7, 2004227) Bks Demand.

Lundeen & Hawkins. Foot & Ankle Arthroscopy. 325p. 1994. 95.00 (0-8016-6928-6) Mosby Yr Bk.

Lundeen, Gerald, jt. auth. see Tenopir, Carol.

Lundeen, Gerald W., jt. auth. see Davis, Charles H.

*Lundeen, Howard K., et al. The Tenant Retention Solution: A Revolutionary Approach to Commercial Real Estate Management. LC 95-11791. (Illus.). 238p. 1995. text ed. 41.95 (1-57203-008-9, 742) Inst Real Estate.

Lundeen, Joel W., ed. Luther's Works-Index, Vol. 55. LC 86-45197. 512p. 1986. 30.00 (0-8006-0355-9, 1-355, Fortress Pr) Augsburg Fortress.

Lundeen, Lyman T. Risk & Rhetoric in Religion: Whitehead's Theory of Language & the Discourse of Faith. LC 71-171501. 288p. reprint ed. pap. 82.10 (0-685-15360-6, 2026868) Bks Demand.

Lundeen, Richard O. Manual of Ankle & Foot Arthroscopy. (Manuals in Podiatric Surgery Ser.). (Illus.). 121p. (Orig.). 1992. pap. text ed. 38.00 (0-443-08694-X) Churchill.

Lundegaard, Graham. Keeping Marine Fish: An Aquarium Guide. rev. ed. (Illus.). 96p. 1991. pap. 9.95 (0-7137-2251-7, Pub. by Blandford Pr UK) Sterling.

Lundegradh, H. Environment & Plants Development. 1330p. 1981. reprint ed. 200.00 (0-685-21854-6, Pub. by Intl Bk Distr II) St Mut.

Lundegren, Herberta M., jt. auth. see Farrell, Patricia.

Lundell, Cyrus L. The Vegetation of Peten. LC 77-11507. (Carnegie Institution of Washington. Publications: No. 478). reprint ed. 35.00 (0-404-16270-3) AMS Pr.

Lundell, In-Gyeong K. Bridging the Gaps: Contextualization among Korean Churches in America. LC 94-20468. (Asian Thought & Culture: Vol. 18). 168p. (C). 1995. text ed. 38.95 (0-8204-2541-9) P Lang Pubs.

Lundell, Kerth, et al. Criterion Test of Basic Skills. (J). (gr. 1 up). 1974. pap. 55.00 (0-87879-154-X) Acad Therapy.

Lundell, Margaretta. The Land of Colors. LC 84-81410. (Poke & Look Bks.). (Illus.). 24p. (J). (ps-00). 1989. 9.95 (0-448-21028-2, G&D) Putnam Pub Group.

Lundell, Margo. Bedtime for Baby. (J). (ps). 1994. 2.25 (0-307-06065-9, Golden Pr) Western Pub.

— Disney Babies A to Z. (Golden Sturdy Shape Bks.). (Illus.). 14p. (J). (ps-00). 1989. write for info. (0-307-12317-0, Golden Bks) Western Pub.

— A Girl Named Helen Keller. (Hello Reader! Ser.: Level 4). (Illus.). (J). 1995. write for info. (0-590-47963-6, Cartwheel) Scholastic Inc.

— My Book of Funny Valentines. (Read with Me Paperback Ser.). (Illus.). 32p. (J). (ps-3). 1993. pap. 2.50 (0-590-44187-6) Scholastic Inc.

— The Wee Mouse Who Was Afraid of the Dark. (All Aboard Bks.). (Illus.). 32p. (J). 1991. pap. 1.95 (0-448-40060-X, Platt & Munk Pubs) Putnam Pub Group.

— What Does Baby See? (Poke & Look Book Ser.). (Illus.). 24p. (J). (ps-00). 1990. bds. 9.95 (0-448-19098-2, G&D) Putnam Pub Group.

— Woody, Be Good! A First Book of Manners. (Illus.). 24p. (J). (ps-2). 1988. 3.95 (0-448-09288-3, G&D) Putnam Pub Group.

Lundell, Torborg. Fairy Tale Mothers. (American University Studies: Germanic Languages & Literature: Ser. I, Vol. 82). 304p. (C). 1989. text ed. 53.95 (0-8204-0980-4) P Lang Pubs.

Lunden, Keith M. Chapter Thirteen Bankruptcy, Vol. 3. 2nd ed. LC 94-11918. 1994. Set. text ed. 308.00 (0-471-00130-9) Wiley.

Lunden, Richard. Risk-Needs Assessment & Parole Outcome in Massachusetts: An Evaluation Study. (Illus.). 65p. (Orig.). (C). 1993. pap. text ed. 35.00 (1-56806-902-2) Diane Pub.

Lunden, Rolf. Business & Religion in the American 1920s. LC 87-17597. (Contributions in American Studies: No. 91). (Illus.). 220p. 1988. text ed. 55.00 (0-313-25151-7, LBU/, Greenwood Pr) Greenwood.

— The Inevitable Question: The Antithetic Pattern of Theodore Dreiser's Thought & Art. 186p. (Orig.). 1973. pap. text ed. 21.50x (91-554-0084-1) Coronet Bks.

Lunden, Rolf & Asard, Erik, eds. Networks of Americanization: Aspects of the American Influence in Sweden. (Studia Anglistica Upsaliensia Ser.: No. 79). 182p. (Orig.). 1992. pap. 46.00x (91-554-2981-5, Pub. by Almqv & Wiksell SW) Coronet Bks.

Lunden, Walter A. Crimes & Criminals. LC 66-21643. 353p. reprint ed. pap. 100.70 (0-317-28205-0, 2022766) Bks Demand.

Lundergardh, H., ed. Environment & Plant Development. (C). 1981. text ed. 275.00 (0-89771-580-2, Pub. by Intl Bk Distr II) St Mut.

Lunderquist, Anders, jt. ed. see Pettersson, Holger.

*Lundervold, Duane A. & Lewin, Lewis M. Behavior Analysis & Therapy in Nursing Homes. (Illus.). 178p. 1992. pap. 29.95 (0-398-06250-1) C C Thomas.

— Behavior Analysis & Therapy in Nursing Homes. (Illus.). 178p. (C). 1992. text ed. 44.95x (0-398-05807-5) C C Thomas.

Lundestad, Geir. America, Scandinavia, & the Cold War: 1945-1949. LC 80-73048. 416p. 1980. text ed. 53.50 (0-231-04974-9) Col U Pr.

Lundgaard, Kris, jt. auth. see Bailey, T. E.

Lundgreen-Nielsen, Kay. The Polish Problem at the Paris Peace Conference: A Study of the Great Powers & the Poles, 1918-1919. (Odense Studies in History & Social Sciences: No. 59). 603p. (Orig.). 1979. pap. 42.50 (87-7492-261-0, Pub. by Odense Universitets Forlag DK) Coronet Bks.

Lundgren, Anders. Technological Innovation & Network Evolution. LC 94-10897. 304p. 1995. 69.95x (0-415-08219-6, B4764, Routledge NY) Routledge.

Lundgren, Anna, ed. see Evans, David.

Lundgren, Anna, ed. see Wilson, Sarah.

Lundgren, Chuck, ed. S-36 Power Tools: Tips & Techniques from "News 3x - 400" 768p. (Orig.). 1991. pap. 89.00 (0-9628743-0-2) Duke Commns Intl.

Lundgren, Dale A., ed. see Aerosol Measurement Workshop Staff.

Lundgren, Dale A., et al. Airborne Pollutants: Characteristics & Detection. (Air Pollution Ser.: Vol. 7). 153p. (C). 1974. text ed. 24.00 (0-8422-7158-9) Irvington.

*Lundgren, Eva. Feminist Theory & Violent Empiricism. 459p. 1995. boxed, pap. 59.95 (1-85628-541-3, Pub. by Avebury Pub UK) Ashgate Pub Co.

*Lundgren-Gothlin, Eva. Sex & Existence: Simon de Beauvoir's "the Second Sex" 240p. (C). 1995. text ed. 90.00 (0-485-11469-0, Pub. by Athlone Pr UK) Humanities.

Lundgren, Jane. Acute Neuroscience Nursing: Concepts & Care. 400p. (C). 1986. 52.50 (0-86720-355-2) Jones & Bartlett.

Lundgren, Laura, tr. see Von Sacher-Masoch, Leopold.

Lundgren, Lawrence. Environmental Geology. (Illus.). 528p. (C). 1986. text ed. write for info. (0-13-283300-X) P-H.

Lundgren, Mary B. We Sing the City. LC 93-34860. (Illus.). (J). 1994. write for info. (0-395-68188-X, Clarion Bks) HM.

Lundgren, Regina E. Risk Communications: A Handbook for Communicating Environmental, Safety, & Health Risks. LC 93-31903. (C). 1994. pap. text ed. 29.95 (0-935470-76-X) Battelle.

Lundgren, Shirley & Young, Woody. One Hundred Plus Desserts & Appetizers. (Illus.). 96p. 1992. pap. 9.95 (0-939513-63-3) Joy Pub SJC.

Lundgren, Stefan, jt. auth. see Carlsson, Olle.

Lundgren, Terry D. & Garrett, Norman A. Advanced Microcomputer Applications. 800p. (C). 1994. pap. write for info. (0-02-372681-4) Macmillan.

Lundgren, Ulf P. Between Education & Schooling: Outline of a Diachronic Curriculum Theory. 73p. (C). 1991. pap. 48.00x (0-7300-1242-5, ECS802, Pub. by Deakin Univ AT) St Mut.

— Frame Factors & the Teaching Process: A Contribution to Curriculum Theory & Theory on Teaching. (Goteborg Studies in Educational Sciences: No. 8). 378p. (Orig.). 1972. pap. 67.50x (0-317-65794-1) Coronet Bks.

Lundgvist, Lars & Persson, Lars O. Visions & Strategies in European Integration: A Northern European Perspective. LC 93-1585. 1993. 98.00 (0-387-56615-5) Spr-Verlag.

*Lundh, Lennart. H-34 Choctaw in Action. (Aircraft in Action Ser.). (Illus.). 50p. 1994. pap. 8.95 (0-89747-319-1) Squad Sig Pubns.

Lundholm, Andrew S. Circuit Simulation & Optimization Using Matrix Analysis. LC 92-23513. (Six Sigma Research Institute Ser.). 1993. pap. write for info. (0-201-63427-9) Addison-Wesley.

Lundin, Anne & Cubberley, Carol. Teaching Children's Literature: A Resource Guide, with a Directory of Courses. 256p. 1994. lib. bdg. 42.50 (0-89950-990-8) McFarland & Co.

Lundin, Anne H., jt. ed. see Lundin, Edward.

Lundin, C. E., jt. ed. see Nachman, Joseph F.

Lundin, Carl G., jt. auth. see Zilinskas, Raymond A.

Lundin, Edward & Lundin, Anne H., eds. Contemporary Religious Ideas: Bibliographic Essays. (Illus.). 250p. 1995. lib. bdg. 37.50 (0-87287-679-9) Libs Unl.

Lundin, Jon W. Rockford: An Illustrated History. 1989. 27.95 (0-89781-305-7) Preferred Mktg.

Lundin, Kathleen, jt. auth. see Lundin, William.

Lundin, Keith M. Chapter Thirteen Bankruptcy: 1991 Supplement, 2 vols., Set. 1272p. 1991. ring bd. 105.00 (0-471-55811-7) Wiley.

— Chapter 13 Practice Guide, Vol. 1. LC 95-1656. 1995. write for info. (0-471-12265-3) Wiley.

— Chapter 13 Practice Guide, Vol. 2. LC 95-1656. 1995. 235.00 (0-471-11754-4); 117.50 (0-471-12264-5) Wiley.

Lundin, Lena. On Building-Related Causes of Sick Building Syndrome. (Illus.). 314p. (Orig.). 1992. pap. 52.50x (91-22-01466-7, Pub. by Almqv & Wiksell SW) Coronet Bks.

Lundin, Norman, et al. Drawing: At the Henry. LC 80-17746. (Illus.). 56p. 1980. 5.95 (0-935558-06-3) Henry Art.

*Lundin, Rickard, et al, eds. The Freja Mission. LC 94-46544. 1995. lib. bdg. 96.00 (0-7923-3317-9) Kluwer Ac.

*Lundin, Robert. Agency Compensation: A Guidebook. 1995. pap. 37.50 (1-56318-018-9) Assn Natl Advertisers.

Lundin, Robert W. Alfred Adler's Basic Concepts & Implications. LC 88-71464. 166p. (Orig.). 1989. pap. text ed. 17.95 (0-915202-83-2) Accel Devel.

— An Objective Psychology of Music. 3rd ed. LC 83-22209. 352p. (C). 1986. 33.50 (0-89874-712-0) Krieger.

— Personality: A Behavioral Analysis. 2nd ed. LC 86-7432. 496p. 1986. reprint ed. text ed. 42.50 (0-89874-958-1) Krieger.

— Theories & Systems of Psychology. 3rd ed. LC 84-81195. 400p. (C). 1985. text ed. 29.00 (0-669-06744-X); teacher ed 2.00 (0-669-09444-7) Heath.

— Theories & Systems of Psychology. 4th ed. LC 90-81474. 411p. (C). 1991. pap. text ed. 29.00 (0-669-20881-7); Test item file. 2.00 (0-669-20882-5) Heath.

Lundin, Roger. The Culture of Interpretation: A Christian Encounter with Postmodern Critical Theory. LC 93-6750. 280p. (Orig.). (C). 1993. pap. 19.99 (0-8028-0636-8) Eerdmans.

Lundin, Roger & Gallagher, Susan. Literature Through the Eyes of Faith. LC 88-45684. (Christian College Coalition Ser.). 192p. 1989. pap. text ed. 11.00 (0-06-065318-3) Harper SF.

Lundin, Roger & Noll, Mark A., eds. Voices from the Heart: Four Centuries of American Piety. LC 87-441. 414p. reprint ed. pap. 118.00 (0-7837-3183-3, 2042787) Bks Demand.

Lundin, S. J., ed. Verification of Dual-Use Chemicals under the Chemical Weapons Convention: The Use of Thiodiglycol. (SIPRI Chemical & Biological Warfare Studies: No. 13). (Illus.). 150p. 1992. pap. 35.00 (0-19-829156-6) OUP.

— Views on Possible Verification Measures for the Biological Weapons Convention. (SIPRI Chemical & Biological Warfare Studies: No. 12). 144p. 1991. pap. 35.00 (0-19-829142-6, 12316) OUP.

Lundin, William & Lundin, Kathleen. Building Positive Relationships at Work, 2 vols. 1993. ring bd. 95.00 (0-87425-243-1) Human Res Dev Pr.

— The Healing Manager: How to Build Quality Relationships & Productive Cultures at Work. LC 93-2704. 268p. 1993. 27.95 (1-881052-13-3) Berrett-Koehler.

Lundkvist, Artur. Journeys in Dream & Imagination. Weissmann, Ann B. & Planck, Annika, trs. 129p. 1991. 17.95 (0-941423-67-0) FWEW.

— The Talking Tree: Poems in Prose. Wormuth, Diana, tr. 240p. 1982. 9.95 (0-8425-2099-6) BYU Scholarly.

Lundlin, Vernard E. At the Bend in the River Mankato: An Illustrated History. 128p. 1990. 25.95 (0-89781-339-1) Preferred Mktg.

Lundman, Richard J. Prevention & Control of Juvenile Delinquency. 2nd ed. (Illus.). 204p. (C). 1993. pap. text ed. 16.95 (0-19-506407-0) OUP.

Lundman, Richard J., jt. auth. see Ermann, M. David.

Lundon, Ace. The Closets Are Empty...the Dining Room's Full: An Autobiographical Legacy. 384p. 1993. 24.95 (0-9635670-4-7) Ponderosa NV.

Lundquist, Eric G. Salvage of Water Damaged Books, Documents, Micrographic & Magnetic Media. 144p. (Orig.). 1986. pap. 12.95 (0-9616850-0-X) Doc Reprocessors.

Lundquist, James. Jack London: Adventures, Ideas & Fiction. (Literature & Life Ser.). 224p. (C). 1987. 19.95 (0-8044-2566-3, F Ungar Bks) Continuum.

— Sinclair Lewis. LC 72-76774. (Literature & Life Ser.). 160p. (C). 1987. reprint ed. 19.95 (0-8044-2562-0, F Ungar Bks) Continuum.

— Theodore Dreiser. LC 73-84600. (Literature & Life Ser.). 159p. (C). 1974. 19.95 (0-8044-2563-9, F Ungar Bks) Continuum.

*Lundquist, Joegil K. English from the Roots Up: Help for Reading, Writing, Spelling & S. A. T. Scores, Vol. I. 125p. 1989. pap. 19.95 (0-9643210-3-3); 12.95 (0-9643210-8-4) Lit Unltd.

Lundquist, John M. The Temple. LC 92-62138. (Art & Imagination Ser.). (Illus.). 96p. 1993. pap. 15.95 (0-500-81040-0) Thames Hudson.

Lundquist, John M. & Ricks, Stephen D., eds. By Study & Also by Faith Vol. 1: Essays in Honor of Hugh W. Nibley. LC 89-77960. 704p. 1990. 21.95 (0-87579-339-8) Deseret Bk.

— By Study & Also by Faith Vol. 2: Essays in Honor of Hugh W. Nibley. LC 89-77960. 676p. 1990. 21.95 (0-87579-340-1) Deseret Bk.

Lundquist, L., et al. Spatial Energy Analysis: Models for Strategic Decisions in an Urban & Regional Context. 398p. 1989. text ed. 69.95 (0-566-05580-5, Pub. by Avebury Pub UK) Ashgate Pub Co.

Lundquist, Lennart. The Party & the Masses: Lenin's Model for the Bolshevik Revolution. LC 82-8505. 336p. 1982. lib. bdg. 40.00 (0-941320-03-0) Transnatl Pubs.

Lundquist, Lynn. On-Line Electrical Troubleshooting. 240p. 1989. text ed. 44.00 (0-07-039110-6) McGraw.

Lundquist, N., jt. auth. see Ahlberg, A. W.

Lundquist, Robert. Before-the-Rain. 44p. (Orig.). 1985. pap. 9.95 (0-939952-05-X) Moving Parts.

Lundquist, Suzanne. The Trickster: A Transformation Archetype. LC 90-29311. 128p. 1991. lib. bdg. 59.95 (0-7734-9958-X) E Mellen.

*Lundqvist, J. & Clausen, T. Jonch, eds. Putting Dublin-Agenda 21 into Practice, Lessons & New Approaches in Water & Land Management: Special Session VIII IWRA World Congress, Cairo, Nov. 21-25, 1995. 101p. 1995. 25.00 (0-614-06674-3) Intl Water Resc.

Lundqvist, Jan, et al, eds. Strategies for River Basin Management: Environmental Integration of Land & Water in a River Basin. LC 85-18293. 1985. lib. bdg. 129.50 (90-277-2111-4) Kluwer Ac.

Lundqvist, L. J. Dislodging the Welfare State? Housing a Privatisation in Four European Nations. 160p. (Orig.). 1992. pap. 42.50 (90-6275-771-5, Pub. by Delft U Pr NE) Coronet Bks.

Lundqvist, Lennart J. The Hare & the Tortoise: Clean Air Policy in the United States and Sweden. 248p. 1980. 29.95x (0-472-09310-X) U of Mich Pr.

— Housing Policy & Ternures in Sweden. 191p. 1988. text ed. 63.95 (0-566-05620-8, Pub. by Avebury Pub UK) Ashgate Pub Co.

Lundqvist, S. O., ed. Nobel Lectures in Physics 1971-1980. 600p. (C). 1992. text ed. 97.00 (981-02-0726-3); pap. text ed. 48.00 (981-02-0727-1) World Scientific Pub.

Lundqvist, S. O. & Cerdeira, H. A., eds. Frontiers in Physics: High Technology & Mathematics. 328p. (C). 1990. pap. 36.00 (981-02-0173-7) World Scientific Pub.

Lundqvist, S. O. & March, Norman H., eds. Theory of the Inhomogeneous Electron Gas. (Physics of Solids & Liquids Ser.). 426p. 1983. 105.00 (0-306-41207-1, Plenum Pr) Plenum.

Lundqvist, S. O. & Nilsson, N. R., eds. Nobel Symposium '73, Physics of Low-Dimensional Systems. 168p. (C). 1989. text ed. 81.00 (9971-5-0971-7); pap. text ed. 36.00 (9971-5-0972-5) World Scientific Pub.

Lundqvist, S. O., et al, eds. High Temperature Superconductivity: Proceedings of the Adriatic Research Conference. (Progress in High Temperature Super Conductivity Ser.: Vol. 1). 532p. (C). 1987. pap. 58.00 (9971-5-0400-6) World Scientific Pub.

— Path Summation: Achievements & Goals. 536p. (C). 1988. pap. 48.00 (9971-5-0700-5) World Scientific Pub.

— Towards the Theoretical Understanding of High Temperature Superconductors: ICTP, Trieste, Italy, June 20-July 29, 1988. (Progress in High Temperature Superconductivity: Vol. XIV). 808p. 1988. pap. 53.00 (9971-5-0640-8) World Scientific Pub.

Lundsager, Soren, jt. auth. see Tuve, Merle A.

Lundsgaard-Hansen, P., ed. Surgical Hemotherapy. (Bibliotheca Haematologica Ser.: No. 46). (Illus.). viii, 252p. 1980. pap. 72.00 (3-8055-0361-X) S Karger.

Lundsgaard-Hansen, P. & Blauhut, B., eds. Albumin & Systematic Circulation. (Current Studies in Hematology & Blood Transfusion: No. 53). (Illus.). xiv, 234p. 1986. 141.75 (3-8055-4367-0) S Karger.

Lundst, jt. auth. see Tway.

Lundsted, Betty. Astrological Insights into Personality. 368p. (Orig.). 1980. pap. 14.95 (0-917086-22-8) ACS Pubns.

— Planetary Cycles. LC 84-51107. (Illus.). 192p. (Orig.). 1984. pap. 12.95 (0-87728-630-2) Weiser.

— Transits: The Time of Your Life. 176p. 1980. pap. 8.95 (0-87728-503-9) Weiser.

Lundstedt, Sven B. Telecommunication, Values & the Public Interest. Dervin, Brenda, ed. LC 90-999. (Communication & Information Science Ser.). 320p. (C). 1990. text ed. 59.50 (0-89391-693-5); pap. text ed. 29.50 (0-89391-733-8) Ablex Pub.

Lundsteen, C. & Piper, J., eds. Automation of Cytogenetics. (Illus.). 335p. 1989. 90.00 (0-387-51105-9, 2914) Spr-Verlag.

Lundsteen, Sara. Children Learn to Communicate: Language Arts Through Creative Problem Solving. LC 75-19324. (Illus.). 1976. Ideas into practice companion guide. write for info. (0-13-449231-5) P-H.

— Language Arts: A Problem-Solving Approach. 608p. (C). 1989. text ed. 50.50 (0-06-044094-5) HarpCollege.

Lundstrohm, Torsten, jt. auth. see Aronsson, Bertil.

Lundstrom, Boyce. Advanced Fusing Techniques Glass Fusing Book Two. Lundstrom, Kathleen, ed. LC 83-50657. 144p. (Orig.). 1989. pap. 40.00 (0-9612282-1-0) Vitreous Pubns.

— Glass Casting & Moldmaking: Glass Fusing, Bk. III. Lundstrom, Kathleen, ed. LC 83-50657. 144p. (Orig.). 1989. pap. 40.00 (0-9612282-2-9) Vitreous Pubns.

— Kiln Firing Glass Bk. 1: Glass Fusing. 2nd ed. Salmonson, Lola, ed. LC 94-60542. (Illus.). 144p. 1994. pap. 30.00 (0-9612282-3-7) Vitreous Pubns.

Lundstrom, David E. A Few Good Men from UNIVAC. (History of Computing Ser.). 300p. 1990. reprint ed. pap. 14.00x (0-262-62075-8) MIT Pr.

Lundstrom, Johan. The History of the Sodefors Anchorworks 1791. Hedin, Lars-Erik, tr. (Kress Library of Business & Economics Publication: No. 21). (Illus.). 1970. pap. 9.95 (0-678-09915-4, Kress Lib Business) Kelley.

Lundstrom, John. The First Team: Pacific Naval Air Combat from Pearl Harbor to Midway. LC 84-9822. (Illus.). 547p. 1984. 38.95 (0-87021-189-7) Naval Inst Pr.

— The First Team & the Guadalcanal Campaign: Naval Fighter Combat from August to November 1942. LC 93-8184. 550p. 1993. 44.95 (1-55750-526-8) Naval Inst Pr.

Lundstrom, Kathleen, ed. see Lundstrom, Boyce.

Lundstrom, Lowell. Heaven's Answer for the Home. rev. ed. 142p. 1985. reprint ed. pap. 2.99 (0-938220-16-0) Whitaker Hse.

An Asterisk (*) at the beginning of an entry indicates that the title is appearing in BIP for the first time.

L

— How You Can Pray with Power & Get Results. 272p. 1984. pap. text ed. 5.99 (*0-88368-151-X*) Whitaker Hse.

Lundstrom, Mark S. Fundamentals of Carrier Transport. Vol. IX. (Illus.). 288p. (C). 1990. text ed. write for info. (*0-318-66312-0*) Addison-Wesley.

— Fundamentals of Carrier Transport, Vol. X. (Modular Series on Solid State Devices). (Illus.). 228p. (C). 1990. text ed. 58.25 (*0-201-18436-2*) Addison-Wesley.

Lundstrom, Rinda F. William Poel's Hamlets: The Director as Critic. LC 84-22. (Theater & Dramatic Studies: No. 20). (Illus.). 204p. reprint ed. pap. 58.20 (*0-8357-1547-7*, 2070489) Bks Demand.

Lundt, Henry, jt. auth. see Israel, John.

Lundwall, N. B. Lectures on Faith. pap. 2.95 (*0-88494-442-5*) Bookcraft Inc.

— Temples of the Most High. deluxe ed. 1993. Collector's ed. write for info. (*0-88494-875-7*) Bookcraft Inc.

Lundy, Alan. Diagnosing & Treating Mental Illness. (Psychological Disorders & Their Treatment Ser.). (Illus.). 136p. (YA). (gr. 6-12). 1990. 18.95 (*0-7910-0047-8*) Chelsea Hse.

***Lundy, Arthel.** Curse of Wallingford. 480p. 1995. pap. 12. 95 (*1-56901-629-1*) NW Pub.

Lundy, Benjamin. The Life, Travels & Opinions of Benjamin Lundy. (American Biography Ser.). 316p. 1991. reprint ed. lib. bdg. 79.00 (*0-7812-8253-5*) Rprt Serv.

— The Life Travels & Opinions of Benjamin Lundy: Including His Journeys to Texas. Earle, Thomas, ed. Bd. with War in Texas (1836) LC 76-136302. 57p. LC 76-136302. 316p. 1971. reprint ed. Set lib. bdg. 45.00 (*0-678-00809-4*) Kelley.

Lundy, Bob. Relief Carving with Bob Lundy. LC 92-60641. (Illus.). 96p. 1992. pap. 14.95 (*0-88740-439-1*) Schiffer.

Lundy, Daniel, ed. see Brown, Gene.

***Lundy, Derek.** Scott Turow. Date not set. pap. 9.95 (*1-55022-234-1*) InBook.

Lundy, Desmond. Hand Made Table Wines. LC 86-82244. (Illus.). 144p. 1986. pap. 15.00 (*0-9690131-1-6*) Fermenthaus.

— Leisure Winemaking. (Illus.). 223p. 1978. 14.95 (*0-920490-06-9*) Temeron Bks.

— No Sour Grapes: Introduction to Wine Making. LC 87-80544. (Illus.). 48p. 1987. pap. 5.00 (*0-9690131-3-2*) Fermenthaus.

Lundy, James. TEAMS, Together Each Achieves More Success. 1994. pap. 14.95 (*0-85013-228-2*) Dartnell Corp.

Lundy, James L. Lead, Follow, or Get Out of the Way: Invaluable Insights into Leadership Style. rev. ed. Padgett, JoAnn, ed. LC 92-51085. (Illus.). 94p. 1993. pap. 9.95 (*0-89384-224-9*) Pfeiffer & Co.

Lundy, Jeremy. Fantasy Football Preview, 1993. 208p. (Orig.). 1993. pap. 14.95 (*0-917939-08-5*) Sang Froid.

Lundy, Jim. Lead, Follow, Or Get Out of Way. 1991. pap. 4.50 (*0-425-12492-4*) Berkley Pub.

— T.E.A.M.S: Together Each Achieves More Success. 230p. 1992. 19.95 (*0-85013-207-X*, TE7607) Dartnell Corp.

Lundy, John P. Monumental Christianity: The Art & Symbolism of the Primitive Church. 1977. lib. bdg. 59.95 (*0-8490-2278-9*) Gordon Pr.

Lundy, Joseph E., ed. The Journal of Taxation of Exempt Organizations. 150.00 (*0-685-69581-6*, EOTJ) Warren Gorham & Lamont.

***Lundy, Katherine C.** Sidewalk Talk: A Naturalistic Study of Street Kids. rev. ed. LC 94-42201. (Children of Poverty Ser.). 242p. 1995. 55.00 (*0-8153-2014-0*) Garland.

Lundy, Kathryn R. Women View Librarianship: Nine Perspectives. LC 80-23611. (ACRL Publications in Librarianship: No. 41). 108p. reprint ed. pap. 30.80 (*0-7837-5951-7*, 2045751) Bks Demand.

***Lundy, Marta & Younger, Beverly, eds.** Empowering Women in the Workplace: Perspectives, Innovations, & Techniques for Helping Professionals. LC 94-43715. (Employee Assistance Quarterly Ser.). (Illus.). 228p. 1995. pap. text ed. 14.95 (*1-56023-062-2*) Haworth Pr.

— Women in the Workplace & Employee Assistance Programs: Perspectives, Innovations, & Techniques for Helping Professionals. 144p. 1994. 39.95 (*1-56024-674-X*) Haworth Pr.

Lundy, Mike. Baby Farm. 256p. 1987. 15.95 (*0-8184-0408-6*) Carol Pub Group.

— Raven. 224p. 1985. 15.95 (*0-8184-0377-2*) Carol Pub Group.

Lundy, Richard. You Can Say That Again: Cultivating New Life in Time-Worn Christian Sayings. (Illus.). 72p. 1980. pap. 2.95 (*0-89505-051-X*, 21038) Tabor Pub.

***Lundy, Robert.** Henry Pardin. 210p. 1995. pap. 8.95 (*1-56901-837-5*) NW Pub.

Lundy, Robert E. Carving the Historic Western Face. LC 87-73231. 112p. (Orig.). 1988. pap. 34.95 (*0-9619094-0-4*) BJ Enterprises.

— Carving the Historic Western Face. LC 87-73231. (Illus.). 160p. (Orig.). 1991. pap. 14.95 (*0-88740-321-2*) Schiffer.

***Lundy, Ronni.** The Festive Table: Stories & Recipes for Renewing Celebrations. LC 95-6751. 1995. write for info. (*0-374-24902-4*, North Pt Pr) FS&G.

— The Festive Table: Stories & Recipes for Renewing Celebrations. 356p. Date not set. 25.00 (*0-374-47492-3*) FS&G.

— Shuck Beans, Stack Cakes, & Honest Fried Chicken: The Heart & Soul of Southern Country. LC 91-18142. 364p. 1991. 24.95 (*0-87113-517-5*) Grove-Atltic.

— Shuck Beans, Stack Cakes, & Honest Fried Chicken: The Heart & Soul of Southern Country Kitchens. (Illus.). 400p. 1994. pap. 15.00 (*0-87113-600-7*) Grove-Atltic.

Lune, Denis. Cloud & Silver Lining. 1985. pap. 3.95 (*9971-972-28-X*) OMF Bks.

Luneau, Andre, ed. see Leskov, Saltykov & Leskov, Chtchedri.

Luneburg, H. Kombinatorik. (Elemente der Mathematik Vom Hoeheren Standpunkt Aus Ser.: Band 6). 108p. (GER.). 1980. pap. 22.00 (*0-8176-0548-7*) Birkhauser.

— Vorlesungen uber Zalentheorie. (Elemente der Mathematik Vom Hoeheren Standpunkt Aus Ser.: Vol. 8). 108p. (GER.). 1980. pap. 24.00 (*0-8176-0932-6*) Birkhauser.

Lunel, Armand. Nicolo-Peccavi ou l'Affaire Dreyfus a Carpentras. (FRE.). 1976. pap. 10.95 (*0-7859-4064-2*) Fr & Eur.

Lunel, Sjoerd M., jt. auth. see Hale, Jack K.

Lunelli, Aldo, ed. Curae Ennianae Ultimae in Editionem Alteram Impensae. 84p. (Orig.). (GER & ITA.). 1989. pap. 15.00 (*90-256-0956-2*, Pub. by A M Hakkert NE) Benjamins North Am.

Lunenburg, Fred C. & Ornstein, Allan C. Educational Administration: Concepts & Practices. 557p. (C). 1991. text ed. 51.95 (*0-534-14850-6*) Intl Thomson.

Lunenburg, Frederick C. The Principalship: Concepts & Applications. 352p. (C). 1994. text ed. write for info. (*0-02-372391-2*) Macmillan.

Lunenfeld, B., ed. Basic Science of GnRH Analogues, Vol. 2. (Advances in the Study of GnRH Analogues Ser.). (Illus.). 200p. (C). 1992. text ed. 70.00 (*1-85070-326-4*) Prthnon Pub.

— Current Status of GnRH Analogues, Vol. 1. (Advances in the Study of GnRH Analogues Ser.). (Illus.). 100p. (C). 1991. text ed. 55.00 (*1-85070-325-6*) Prthnon Pub.

— FSH Alone in Ovulation Induction. (Illus.). 70p. 1992. pap. text ed. 28.00 (*1-85070-439-2*) Prthnon Pub.

— GnRH Analogues & Cancer, Vol. 4. (Advances in the Study of GnRH Analogues Ser.). (Illus.). 200p. 1992. text ed. 70.00 (*1-85070-328-0*) Prthnon Pub.

— GnRH Analogues in Obstetrics & Gynecology, Vol. 3. (Advances in the Study of GnRH Analogues Ser.). (Illus.). 200p. (C). 1992. text ed. 70.00 (*1-85070-327-2*) Prthnon Pub.

Lunenfeld, B., jt. ed. see Vickers, B. H.

Lunenfeld, B., jt. ed. see Vickery, B. H.

Lunenfeld, B., et al. Diagnosis & Treatment of Functional Infertility. 1993. 65.00 (*3-89412-129-7*) Blackwell Sci.

Lunenfeld, Bruno, jt. ed. see Insler, Vaclav.

Lunenfeld, Marvin. College Basics: How to Start Right & Finish Strong. 144p. (C). 1993. per., pap. text ed. 12.95 (*0-8403-8655-9*) Kendall-Hunt.

— Keepers of the City: The Corregidores of Isabella of Castile, 1474-1504. (Cambridge Iberian & Latin American Studies). (Illus.). 288p. 1987. 74.95 (*0-521-32930-2*) Cambridge U Pr.

Lunenfeld, Marvin, ed. Fourteen Ninety-Two: Discovery, Invasion, Encounter: Sources & Interpretations. LC 90-80531. (Sources in Modern History Ser.). 355p. (C). 1990. pap. text ed. write for info. (*0-669-21115-X*); Instr. 's handbk. teacher ed write for info. (*0-669-29426-8*) Heath.

Lunenfeld, Marvin & Lunenfeld, Peter. College Basics: How to Start Right & Finish Strong. 2nd ed. LC 91-90353. (Illus.). 144p. 1992. pap. 12.95 (*0-9629783-1-0*) Semester Pr.

Lunenfeld, Marvin & Lunenfeld, Peter B. College Basics: How to Start Right & Finish Strong. 2nd ed. LC 91-90353. (Illus.). 144p. 1991. pap. 11.95 (*0-9629783-0-2*) Semester Pr.

Lunenfeld, Peter, jt. auth. see Lunenfeld, Marvin.

Lunenfeld, Peter B., jt. auth. see Lunenfeld, Marvin.

Luner, Philip, ed. Paper Preservation: Current Issues & Recent Developments. 150p. 1990. 88.00 (*0-89852-500-4*, 0101R175) TAPPI.

— Paper Preservation: Current Issues & Recent Developments. LC 90-46550. 160p. reprint ed. pap. 43. 20 (*0-8357-2957-5*, 2039219) Bks Demand.

Lunet De Lajonquiere, Etienne E. Ethnographie du Tonkin Septentrional. LC 77-87043. reprint ed. 49.50 (*0-404-16836-1*) AMS Pr.

Lunetta, Vincent N. & Novick, Shimshon. Inquiring & Problem Solving in the Physical Sciences: A Sourcebook. 224p. (C). 1982. per. 35.95 (*0-8403-2631-9*) Kendall-Hunt.

Luney, Percy R., Jr. & Yakahashi, Kazuyuki, eds. Japanese Constitutional Law. 330p. (C). 1993. text ed. 67.50 (*0-86008-497-3*, Pub. by U of Tokyo JA) Col U Pr.

Lung & French. Water Quality Modeling, Vol. 3: Applications to Estuaries. 1993. 139.95 (*0-8493-6973-8*, TD370) CRC Pr.

***Lung, Haha.** Ninja Craft. (Illus.). 136p. (Orig.). 1995. pap. 14.00 (*0-939427-84-2*) Alpha Pubns OH.

***Lung, Hoang N.** Strategy & Tactics. 1994. pap. text ed. 15. 00 (*0-923135-27-8*) Dalley Bk Service.

Lung, James & Hinsdale, C. E. Oaths of Office for the Use of City, County & State Officials in North Carolina. 42p. 1975. 3.00 (*1-56011-121-6*) Institute Government.

Lung, Kung-Sun. Works. Perleberg, Max, tr. LC 73-884. (China Studies: from Confucius to Mao Ser.). xxiii, 160p. 1990. reprint ed. 23.50 (*0-88355-077-6*) Hyperion Conn.

Lung Kwan-Hai. A Social Survey of the Kuting District of Taipei City. (Asian Folklore & Social Life Monographs: No. 65). 200p. (CHI.). 1975. 14.00 (*0-89986-060-5*) Oriental Bk Store.

— Trends of Urbanization in Taiwan, 2 vols. in one. (Asian Folklore & Social Life Monographs: Nos. 39-40). (CHI.). 1972. 17.00 (*0-89986-039-7*) Oriental Bk Store.

Lungago. Santa Stories. rev. ed. 1989. write for info. (*0-930061-26-8*) Interspace Bks.

Lunger, Harold L., ed. Facing War-Waging Peace: Findings of the American Church Study Conferences, 1940-60. 420p. 1988. pap. 18.95 (*0-377-00186-4*) Friendship Pr.

Lunger, Sheila. The Pacific Rim Region Teacher's Guide. LC 88-31038. (Illus.). 49p. 1988. pap. 6.60 (*0-89490-241-5*) Enslow Pubs.

Lungies, N. J., jt. auth. see Hayes, M.

Lungstrom, Virgil. Angler's Journal: For Freshwater Fishing. 120p. 1993. pap. 7.95 (*1-883607-02-7*) Prairie Ldr.

— Angler's Journal: For Ice Fishing. 120p. 1993. pap. 7.95 (*1-883607-03-5*) Prairie Ldr.

— Camper's Journal. 120p. 1993. pap. 7.95 (*1-883607-06-X*) Prairie Ldr.

— Deer Hunter's Journal. 120p. 1993. pap. 7.95 (*1-883607-00-0*) Prairie Ldr.

— Travel Journal: For Motorhome & RV Owners. 120p. 1993. pap. 7.95 (*1-883607-01-9*) Prairie Ldr.

— Upland Game Hunter's Journal. 120p. 1993. pap. 7.95 (*1-883607-05-1*) Prairie Ldr.

— Waterfowler's Journal. 120p. 1993. pap. 7.95 (*1-883607-04-3*) Prairie Ldr.

Lungu, Dov B. Romania & the Great Powers, 1933-1940. LC 89-1553. 294p. 1989. lib. bdg. 52.50 (*0-8223-0915-7*) Duke.

Lungu, N., et al. A Guide to the Music of the Eastern Orthodox Church. Orig. Title: Gramatica Muzicii Psaltice. (Illus.). 180p. (Orig.). 1984. pap. 15.00 (*0-917651-00-6*) Holy Cross Orthodox.

Lungwangwa, Geoffrey. Zambia in the 1990's. Sumaili, Fanuel K., ed. 182p. 1991. pap. text ed. 10.95 (*9966-835-13-X*) Prof World Peace.

Lungwitz, Anton. A Textbook of Horseshoeing for Horseshoers & Veterinarians. Adams, John W., tr. LC 66-28443. (Illus.). 216p. 1966. 19.95 (*0-87071-308-6*) Oreg St U Pr.

Lungwitz, Hans. Psychology & Cognitive Therapy of the Neuroses. rev. ed. Becker, Reinhold, ed. MacLean, Norman, tr. LC 93-17037. (Illus.). 200p. 1993. 41.00 (*0-8176-2866-5*) Birkhauser.

Lunin, Joseph, jt. auth. see New Jersey Institute for Continuing Legal Education Staff.

Lunin, Lois F. Multimedia in the Information Industry. Cunningham, Ann M. & Wicks, Wendy, eds. (Report Series, 1992: No. 4). 160p. (Orig.). (C). 1992. pap. 100. 00 (*0-942308-37-9*) NFAIS.

Lunine, Leo R. How to Research, Write, & Package Administrative Manuals. LC 84-45785. 320p. 1985. 75. 00 (*0-8144-5805-X*) AMACOM.

Luning, Klaus, et al. Seaweed Biogeography & Ecophysiology. 1990. text ed. 99.95 (*0-471-62434-9*) Wiley.

Luning Prak, Niels. The Language of Architecture: A Contribution to Architectural Theory. (Illus.). 1968. 44. 65 (*90-279-6394-0*) Mouton.

Lunis, Ben C., jt. auth. see Lienau, Paul J.

Lunis, Natalie, ed. see Berger, Melvin.

Lunis, Natalie, ed. see White, Nancy.

Lunman, Larry, jt. auth. see Stewart, Jim.

Lunn & Decesaris. Investigacion de Gramatica. 1992. pap. 33.95 (*0-8384-2348-5*); teacher ed, pap. 33.95 (*0-8384-2349-3*) Heinle & Heinle.

Lunn, A. D. & McNeil, D. Computer Interactive Data Analysis. 350p. 1992. pap. 110.00 (*0-471-93114-4*) Wiley.

Lunn, Arnold. Roman Converts. (Essay Index Reprint Ser.). 275p. 1982. reprint ed. lib. bdg. 17.00 (*0-8290-0482-3*) Irvington.

Lunn, Arnold H. The Revolt Against Reason. LC 72-108396. xiv, 273p. 1971. reprint ed. text ed. 49.75 (*0-8371-3819-1*, LURA, Greenwood Pr) Greenwood.

— Roman Converts. LC 67-22102. (Essay Index Reprint Ser.). 1977. 20.95 (*0-8369-0636-5*) Ayer.

— Switzerland in English Prose & Poetry. 1976. lib. bdg. 59. 95 (*0-8490-2720-9*) Gordon Pr.

Lunn, Carolyn. Bobby's Zoo. LC 88-36865. (Rookie Reader Ser.). (Illus.). 32p. (J). (ps-2). 1989. lib. bdg. 10.35 (*0-516-02089-7*); pap. 2.95 (*0-516-42089-5*) Childrens.

— Bobby's Zoo Big Book. (Rookie Readers Big Bks.). (Illus.). 32p. (J). (ps-2). 1991. lib. bdg. 22.95 (*0-516-49501-1*) Childrens.

— A Buzz Is Part of a Bee. LC 89-25434. (Rookie Reader Ser.). (Illus.). 32p. (J). (ps-2). 1990. lib. bdg. 10.35 (*0-516-02062-5*); pap. 2.95 (*0-516-42062-3*) Childrens.

— Joy ... Anyway! 191p. 1992. pap. 9.95 (*0-8341-1441-0*) Beacon Hill.

— Un Murmullo Es Silencioso: A Whisper Is Quiet. LC 88-11968. (Rookie Reader Big Bks.). (Illus.). 32p. (SPA.). (J). (ps-2). 1991. lib. bdg. 10.35 (*0-516-32087-4*); pap. 2.95 (*0-516-52087-3*) Childrens.

— Spiders & Webs. LC 89-34665. (Rookie Reader Ser.). (Illus.). 32p. (J). (ps-2). 1989. lib. bdg. 12.35 (*0-516-02093-5*); pap. 2.95 (*0-516-42093-3*) Childrens.

— A Whisper Is Quiet. LC 88-11968. (Rookie Reader Ser.). (Illus.). 32p. (J). (ps-2). 1988. lib. bdg. 10.35 (*0-516-02087-0*); pap. 2.95 (*0-516-42087-9*) Childrens.

Lunn, David. The English Benedictines 1540-1688: From Reformation to Revolution. 296p. 1990. 59.00 (*0-86012-095-3*, Pub. by Srch Pr UK) St Mut.

Lunn, Eugene. Marxism & Modernism: An Historical Study of Lukacs, Brecht, Benjamin, & Adorno. LC 81-23169. 344p. 1982. pap. 14.00 (*0-520-05330-3*) U CA Pr.

— Prophet of Community: The Romantic Socialism of Gustav Landauer. 434p. 1973. 35.00 (*0-88286-136-0*); write for info. (*0-88286-213-8*) C H Kerr.

Lunn, George & Sansone, Erci B. Destruction of Hazardous Chemicals in the Laboratory. 1990. text ed. 89.95 (*0-471-51063-7*) Wiley.

Lunn, George & Sansone, Eric B. Destruction of Hazardous Chemicals in the Laboratory. 2nd ed. LC 93-35634. 1994. text ed. 79.95 (*0-471-57399-X*) Wiley.

Lunn, Harry H., Jr. Milton Avery, Prints, Nineteen Thirty-Three to Nineteen Fifty-Five. 99p. 1973. pap. 30.00 (*1-55660-121-2*) A Wofsy Fine Arts.

— Milton Avery Prints, 1933-1955: With an Original Etching. (Illus.). 99p. 1973. boxed 400.00 (*1-55660-159-X*) A Wofsy Fine Arts.

***Lunn, Hugh.** Head over Heels: Hugh Lunn's 60s Sequel to Over the Top with Jim. 312p. 1995. pap. 14.95 (*0-7022-2864-8*, Pub. by Univ Queensland Pr AT) Intl Spec Bk.

— More over the Top with Jim Stories. (Fred & Olive's Blessed Lino Collection). 184p. 1995. pap. 14.95 (*0-7022-2863-X*, Pub. by Univ Queensland Pr AT) Intl Spec Bk.

— Over the Top with Jim. 1989. pap. 14.95 (*0-7022-2255-0*) Intl Spec Bk.

— The Over the Top with Jim Album. (Illus.). 200p. 1995. pap. 34.95 (*0-7022-2563-0*, Pub. by Univ Queensland Pr AT) Intl Spec Bk.

— Spies Like Us. 1995. pap. 16.95 (*0-7022-2757-9*, Pub. by Univ Queensland Pr AT) Intl Spec Bk.

— Vietnam: A Reporter's War. LC 85-40967. (Illus.). 272p. 1987. 18.95 (*0-8128-3088-1*, Scrbrough Hse) Madison Bks UPA.

— Vietnam: A Reporter's War. (Illus.). 283p. 1989. reprint ed. pap. 14.95 (*0-7022-2018-3*, Pub. by Univ Queensland Pr AT) Intl Spec Bk.

Lunn, Hugh K., ed. see Inge, William R.

Lunn, J. A. & Waldron, H. A., eds. Concerning the Careers. 155p. 1991. pap. text ed. 39.95 (*0-7506-0022-5*) Buttrwrth-Heinemann.

Lunn, J. N. Lecture Notes on Anaesthetics. 4th ed. (Lecture Notes Ser.). (Illus.). 149p. 1991. pap. 32.95 (*0-632-03192-1*) Blackwell Sci.

Lunn, Janet. Amos's Sweater. (J). (ps-3). 1991. 12.95 (*0-88899-074-X*, Pub. by Groundwood-Douglas & McIntyre CN) Firefly Bks Ltd.

— Double Spell. (Novels Ser.). 144p. (J). (gr. 3-7). 1986. pap. 3.95 (*0-14-031858-5*, Puffin) Puffin Bks.

— Duck Cakes for Sale. (Illus.). 32p. (J). (ps-2). 1991. 13.95 (*0-88899-094-4*, Pub. by Groundwood-Douglas & McIntyre CN); pap. 4.95 (*0-88899-157-6*, Pub. by Groundwood-Douglas & McIntyre CN) Firefly Bks Ltd.

— One Hundred Shining Candles. LC 90-8892. (Illus.). 32p. (J). (gr. 2-4). 1991. text ed. 13.95 (*0-684-19280-2*, C Scribner Sons Young) S&S Childrens.

— The Root Cellar. 230p. (J). (gr. 7 up). 1985. pap. 3.99 (*0-14-031835-6*, Puffin) Puffin Bks.

— The Root Cellar. LC 83-3246. 256p. (YA). (gr. 5 up). 1983. text ed. 14.95 (*0-684-17855-9*, C Scribner Sons Young) S&S Childrens.

Lunn, Jon. Consumer & Commercial Collection Deskbook. LC 85-2470. 400p. 1985. 65.00 (*0-87624-097-X*, Inst Busn Plan) P-H.

Lunn, Kenneth. A Social History of British Labour, 1870-1970. 224p. 1993. pap. 19.95 (*0-7131-6478-6*, A3400, Pub. by E Arnold UK) Routledge Chapman & Hall.

Lunn, Kenneth, ed. Hosts, Immigrants & Minorities: Historical Responses to Newcomers in British Society 1870-1914. 1980. text ed. 28.00 (*0-312-39238-9*) St Martin.

— Race & Labour in Twentieth-Century Britain. 192p. 1986. 32.00 (*0-7146-3238-4*, Pub. by F Cass Pubs UK); pap. 17.50 (*0-7146-4052-2*, Pub. by F Cass Pubs UK) Intl Spec Bk.

Lunn, Kenneth, jt. ed. see Kushner, Tony.

Lunn, Mary. A First Course in Mechanics. (Illus.). 208p. 1991. pap. 29.95 (*0-19-853433-7*) OUP.

Lunn, Terry & Neff, Susan A. MRP: Integrating Material Requirement Planning & Modern Business. (APICS Ser.). (Illus.). 275p. 1992. 45.00 (*1-55623-656-5*) Irwin Prof Pubng.

Lunneborg, C. E. & Abbott, R. D. Elementary Multivariate Analysis for the Behavioral Sciences: Applications of Basic Structure. 432p. 1983. 56.00 (*0-444-00753-9*, North Holland) Elsevier.

Lunneborg, Clifford E. Modeling Experimental & Observational Data. 505p. 1994. text ed. 52.95 (*0-534-21426-6*) Intl Thomson.

Lunneborg, Patricia. O U Women: Undoing Educational Obstacles. (Cassell Education Ser.). 160p. 1994. 55.00 (*0-304-33161-9*); pap. 16.95 (*0-304-33163-5*) Cassell.

Lunneborg, Patricia W. Abortion: A Positive Decision. LC 91-27946. 232p. 1992. text ed. 19.95 (*0-89789-243-7*, H243, Bergin & Garvey) Greenwood.

— Women Changing Work. LC 89-25673. (Contributions in Women's Studies: No. 112). 256p. 1990. text ed. 55.00 (*0-313-26843-6*, LWD/, Bergin & Garvey); pap. text ed. 12.95 (*0-89789-214-3*, G214, Bergin & Garvey) Greenwood.

— Women Police Officers - Current Career Profile. 222p. 1989. pap. 29.95 (*0-398-06251-X*) C C Thomas.

— Women Police Officers - Current Career Profile. 222p. (C). 1989. text ed. 45.95 (*0-398-05623-4*) C C Thomas.

Lunney, D. & Grigg, G., eds. Kangaroo Harvesting & the Conservation of Arid & Semi-Arid Lands. 72p. (C). 1988. text ed. 39.00 (*0-7855-0033-2*, Pub. by Surrey Beatty & Sons AT) St Mut.

Lunney, Daniel, ed. Conservation of Australia's Forest Fauna. 416p. (C). 1992. text ed. 175.00 (*0-9599951-5-3*, Pub. by Surrey Beatty & Sons AT) St Mut.

— Zoology in Court. 100p. (C). 1992. text ed. 120.00 (*0-9599951-7-X*, Pub. by Surrey Beatty & Sons AT) St Mut.

Lunny, William J. The Jesus Option. LC 93-28023. 224p. (Orig.). 1994. pap. 12.95 (*0-8091-3445-4*) Paulist Pr.

Luns, Joseph M. The Western Alliance: Its Future & Its Implications for Asia. (Singapore Lecture Ser.). 40p. 1985. pap. text ed. 10.00 (*9971-902-96-6*, Pub. by Inst SE Asian Studies SI) Ashgate Pub Co.

Lunsford, Alyce. A Carousel of Poetry. LC 85-50265. 94p. 1985. 7.95 (*0-938232-81-9*, Baker & Taylor) Winston-Derek.

Lunsford, Andrea & Connors, Robert J. St. Martin's Handbook. 2nd annot. ed. 848p. (C). 1992. teacher ed write for info. (*0-318-68814-X*) St Martin.

L

***Lunsford, Andrea & Ruszkiewicz, John.** The Presence of Others: Readings for Critical Thinking & Writing. 688p. 1994. pap. text ed. 17.50 (*0-312-05677-X*) St Martin.

Lunsford, Andrea, jt. auth. see Altick, Richard.

Lunsford, Andrea, jt. auth. see Ede, Lisa.

Lunsford, Andrea, et al, eds. The Future of Doctoral Studies in English. LC 89-36166. xii, 179p. 1989. text ed. 32.00 (*0-87352-184-6*, W420C); pap. text ed. 15.50 (*0-87352-185-4*, W420P) Modern Lang.

***Lunsford, Andrea A., ed.** Reclaiming Rhetorica: Women in the Rhetorical Tradition. LC 95-3298. (Series in Composition, Literary, & Culture). 1995. write for info. (*0-8229-3872-3*); pap. text ed. write for info. (*0-8229-5553-9*) U of Pittsburgh Pr.

Lunsford, Andrea A., et al, eds. The Right to Literacy. LC 90-33855. iv, 306p. 1990. text ed. 37.50 (*0-87352-197-8*, W430C); pap. text ed. 19.75 (*0-87352-198-6*, W430P) Modern Lang.

***Lunsford, Andrea & Connors, Robert.** The St. Martin's Handbook. 3rd ed. 944p. (C). 1995. pap. 23.94 (*0-312-10212-7*) St Martin.

Lunsford, Charlou, jt. auth. see Beck, Susan P.

Lunsford, Dade L. Stereotactic Radiosurgery Update. (C). 1992. text ed. 128.00 (*0-13-050139-5*) P-H.

Lunsford, E. Michael. Application Development with Quattro. 1993. pap. 40.00 (*0-679-79155-8*) Random.

***Lunsford, E Michael.** Classic 1-2-3 Macros. 3rd ed. 1995. pap. text ed. 24.95 (*0-471-06398-3*) Wiley.

Lunsford, E. Michael. Lotus 1-2-3 for Windows: Wiley Command Reference. 1992. pap. text ed. 10.95 (*0-471-56942-9*) Wiley.

Lunsford, James R., et al, eds. The Birmingham Dining Guide. (Illus.). 80p. 1991. pap. 3.95 (*0-9624032-1-0*) Best Times Inc.

Lunsford, L. D., et al, eds. Proceedings of the Meeting of the American Society for Stereotactic & Functional Neurosurgery, Pittsburgh, PA, June 1991, Pt. 1: Journal: Stereotactic & Functional Neurosurgery, Vol. 58, Nos. 1-4, 1992. (Illus.). vi, 214p. 1992. pap. 144.00 (*3-8055-5684-5*) S Karger.

— Proceedings of the Meeting of the American Society for Stereotactic & Functional Neurosurgery, Pittsburgh, PA, June 1991, Pt. 2: Journal: Stereotactic & Functional Neurosurgery, Vol. 59, Nos. 1-4, 1992. (Illus.). vi, 210p. 1992. pap. 144.00 (*3-8055-5688-8*) S Karger.

Lunsford, L. Dade, ed. Modern Stereotactic Neurosurgery. (C). 1988. lib. bdg. 207.00 (*0-89838-950-X*) Kluwer Ac.

Lunsford, Michael. Fully Powered Quattro Pro for Windows. (Illus.). (Orig.). 1992. pap. 39.95 (*0-13-334061-9*) Brady Compu Bks.

— Macros, Menus & Miracles for Lotus 1-2-3. 2nd ed. 1990. pap. text ed. 24.95 (*0-471-52432-8*) Wiley.

— PC Magazine Guide to 1-2-3 for Windows. (Guide to... Ser.). 643p. (Orig.). 1991. pap. 27.95 (*1-56276-021-1*) Ziff-Davis.

Lunsford, Ron, jt. auth. see Straub, Richard.

Lunsford, Ronald F., jt. auth. see Haley, Michael C.

Lunsford, Ronald F., jt. ed. see Moran, Michael G.

Lunstedt, Sven B. & Moss, Thomas H., eds. Managing Innovation & Change. (C). 1989. lib. bdg. 102.00 (*0-7923-0079-3*) Kluwer Ac.

Lunstroth, Claudia, ed. Adobe Anthology. 78p. 1993. pap. 5.00 (*0-9639737-0-3*) Adobe Bkstore.

— Adobe Anthology Vol. 2. (Illus.). 84p. (Orig.). 1994. pap. 7.50 (*0-9639737-1-1*) Adobe Bkstore.

Lunstrum, John P. & Taylor, Bob L. Teaching Reading in the Social Studies. LC 78-17205. 98p. reprint ed. pap. 28.00 (*0-8357-2628-2*, 2040116) Bks Demand.

Lunt, Anthony. Apollo Versus the Echomaker: A Langian Approach to Psychotherapy Dreams & Shamanism. 1990. pap. 12.95 (*1-85230-153-8*, Pub. by Element Bks UK) Element MA.

Lunt, Bob. The Man Without a Mate Cookbook: The Successful Lifestyle Cookbook for the Unmarried Man. LC 91-66424. (Successful Life Alone Cookbook Ser.). (Illus.). 135p. 1991. 17.95 (*0-9630296-3-0*) SKM Pub.

Lunt, Dolly S. A Woman's Wartime Journal: An Account of Sherman's Devastation of a Southern Plantation. LC 88-20209. 64p. 1990. reprint ed. pap. 5.95 (*0-87797-149-8*) Cherokee.

Lunt, Dudley C. Taylors Gut: In the Delaware State. (Illus.). 320p. 1986. reprint ed. pap. 8.95 (*0-912608-30-7*) Mid Atlantic.

Lunt, Dudley C., ed. see Thoreau, Henry David.

Lunt, Edward C. Key to the Publications of the United States Census, 1790-1887. LC 75-38138. (Demography Ser.). 1976. reprint ed. 15.95 (*0-405-07991-5*) Ayer.

Lunt, G. G. & Olsen, R. W., eds. Comparative Invertebrate Neurochemistry. LC 87-27446. (Illus.). 300p. 1988. 57.50 (*0-8014-2177-2*) Cornell U Pr.

Lunt, George G., ed. Neurotox 'Eighty-Eight - Molecular Basis of Drug & Pesticide Action: Proceedings of the Neurotox '88, Nottingham UK, 10-15 April, 1988. (International Congress Ser.: No.832). 596p. 1989. 205.25 (*0-444-81034-X*, Excerpta Medica) Elsevier.

Lunt, Horace G. Fundamentals of Russian. rev. ed. xiv, 402p. (C). 1982. reprint ed. pap. 19.95 (*0-89357-097-4*) Slavica.

— Old Church Slavonic Grammar. rev. ed. (Slavistic Printings & Reprintings Ser.: No. 3). 1974. text ed. 66.15 (*90-279-3362-6*) Mouton.

Lunt, Horace G., jt. ed. see Altbauer, Moshe.

Lunt, Horace G., et al, eds. Harvard Slavic Studies, Vol. 5. LC 52-12516. viii, 166p. 1970. text ed. 18.00 (*0-674-37804-0*) HUP.

Lunt, Ingrid, jt. auth. see Evans, Jennifer.

***Lunt, Ingrid, et al.** Working Together: Inter-School Collaboration for Special Needs. 144p. 1994. pap. 18.95x (*1-85346-301-9*, Pub. by D Fulton UK) Taylor & Francis.

Lunt, Lawrence K., frwd. Leave Me My Spirit: An American's Story of Fourteen Years in Castro's Prisons. (Illus.). 288p. 1990. 19.95 (*0-918080-58-4*) Affil Writers America.

Lunt, Paul S., jt. auth. see Warner, William L.

Lunt, Peter, jt. auth. see Livingstone, Sonia M.

Lunt, Peter K. & Livingstone, Sonia M. Mass Consumption & Personal Identity: Everyday Economic Experience. 192p. 1992. 90.00 (*0-335-09672-7*, Open Univ Pr); pap. 32.00 (*0-335-09671-9*, Open Univ Pr) Taylor & Francis.

Lunt, Richard. Law & Order vs. the Miners: West Virginia, 1907-1933. 182p. reprint ed. pap. 12.95 (*0-9627486-2-5*) Applchin Eds.

Lunt, Richard D. The High Ministry of Government: The Political Career of Frank Murphy. LC 65-10195. (Illus.). 264p. reprint ed. pap. 75.30 (*0-7837-3603-7*, 2043468) Bks Demand.

Lunt, T. F., ed. Research Directions in Database Security. (Illus.). 288p. 1992. pap. 49.50 (*0-387-97736-8*) Spr-Verlag.

Lunt, T. S. A History of the Lunt Family in America. (Illus.). 306p. 1989. reprint ed. lib. bdg. 54.00 (*0-8328-0791-5*); reprint ed. pap. 46.00 (*0-8328-0792-3*) Higginson Bk Co.

Lunt, W. E. Financial Relations of the Papacy with England to 1327. (Medieval Academy Bks.: No. 33). 1967. reprint ed. 45.00 (*0-910956-13-8*) Medieval Acad.

— Financial Relations of the Papacy with England, 1327-1534. LC 62-19287. (Medieval Academy Bks.: No. 74). 1962. 45.00 (*0-910956-48-0*) Medieval Acad.

Lunt, William E. Accounts Rendered by Papal Collectors in England, 1317-1378. LC 67-19647. (American Philosophical Society, Memoirs Ser.: Vol. 70). 633p. reprint ed. pap. 180.00 (*0-8357-5073-6*, 2019712) Bks Demand.

Luntley, Michael. Language, Logic & Experience: The Care for Anti-Realism. 1988. pap. 17.95 (*0-8126-9062-1*) Open Court.

— The Meaning of Socialism. 214p. (C). 1990. 34.95 (*0-8126-9113-X*); pap. 16.95 (*0-8126-9114-8*) Open Court.

— Reason, Truth & Self: The Postmodern Reconditioned. LC 95-14748. 1995. write for info. (*0-415-11852-2*); pap. write for info. (*0-415-11853-0*) Routledge.

Lunts, G., jt. auth. see Volkovskii, L.

Lunts, Lev. Things in Revolt. Kern, Gary, tr. & intro. by. Date not set. 29.95 (*0-88233-924-9*) Ardis Pubs.

Lunts, Valery, jt. auth. see Bernstein, Joseph.

***Luntta, Karl.** Caribbean Handbook: The Virgin, Leeward, & Windward Islands. (Moon Travel Handbooks Ser.). (Illus.). 330p. 1995. pap. 16.95 (*1-56691-027-7*) Moon Pubns CA.

— Jamaica Handbook. 2nd ed. LC 93-29905. (Illus.). 220p. (Orig.). 1993. pap. 14.95 (*1-56691-012-9*) Moon Pubns CA.

Luntz, H. Assessment of Damages for Personal Injury & Death. 3rd ed. 1990. Australia. 94.00 (*0-409-49544-1*) Butterworth Legal Pubs.

Luntz, M. H. & Harrison, R. Glaucoma Surgery. 228p. 1994. text ed. 159.00 (*981-02-1418-9*) World Scientific Pub.

Luntz, Maurice H., ed. see Harrison, Raymond.

Luntzel, James R., Jr. Leningrad Diary: One Surprise after Another in the U.S.S.R. LC 91-90331. (Illus.). 180p. (Orig.). 1991. pap. 8.00 (*0-9629878-0-8*) Luntzel Enterp.

Lunze, Jan. Feedback Control of Large Scale Systems. 350p. 1992. text ed. 54.00 (*0-13-318353-X*) P-H.

Lunzer, E. A. Child Development at Primary School: A Report of the Educational Research Workshop Held in Madrid, 24-27 September 1985. 162p. 1987. pap. 15.00 (*0-317-91053-1*, Pub. by Swets Pub Serv NE) Taylor & Francis.

***Luo, D. J., et al.** Bifurcation Theory & Methods of Dynamical Systems. (Advanced Series in Dynamical Systems). 400p. 1995. text ed. 86.00 (*981-02-2094-4*) World Scientific Pub.

Luo, D. J. & Teng, L. B. Theory of Dynamical Systems. (Advanced Series in Dynamical Systems). 280p. 1993. text ed. 61.00 (*981-02-1268-2*) World Scientific Pub.

Luo, F., jt. auth. see Freedman, M.

Luo Guan-Zhong. Au Bord de l'Eau, Vol. 1. (FRE.). 1978. lib. bdg. 95.00 (*0-8288-3522-5*, F120800) Fr & Eur.

— Au Bord de l'Eau, Vol. 2. (FRE.). 1978. lib. bdg. 89.98 (*0-8288-3523-3*, M5576) Fr & Eur.

Luo Guan-Zhong, jt. auth. see Shi Nai-An.

Luo, J., jt. ed. see Reijns, G. L.

Luo, J., jt. auth. see Wu, Dan-Di.

***Luo, Jenn-Ching.** Parallel Computations on Windows NT. LC 94-93901. 281p. (C). 1995. pap. 25.00 (*0-9644361-0-8*); pap. text ed. 49.00 (*0-614-03971-1*) Paral Integ.

Luo, Ren C. & Kay, Michael G., eds. Multisensor Integration & Fusion for Intelligent Machines & Systems. LC 93-45356. (Computer Engineering & Computer Science Ser.). 696p. 1995. 85.00 (*0-89391-863-6*) Ablex Pub.

Luo, Shijun, jt. auth. see Pai, Shih-I.

Luo, Wei. A Pathfinder to U. S. Export Control Laws & Regulations. LC 94-18558. (Legal Research Guides Ser.: Vol. 18). xiv, 110p. 1994. 35.00x (*0-89941-889-9*, 308320) W S Hein.

Luobriel, Marta B., tr. see Resnik, Hank, et al.

Luoma, Bill. My Trip to New York City. 1994. pap. 5.00 (*0-935724-65-6*) Figures.

Luoma, Jon R. The Air Around Us: An Air Pollution Primer. (Illus.). 20p. (YA). (gr. 5 up). 1989. 9.95 (*0-935577-10-6*) Acid Rain Found.

Luoma, Jon R. & Joyner, Kimberly C. Air Pollution & Forest Decline: Is There a Link? (USDA Forest Service Agriculture Information Bulletin Ser.: No. 595). (Illus.). 20p. 1990. write for info. (*0-935577-23-8*) Acid Rain Found.

Luoma, Robert C. Music Mode & Words in Lasso's Last Works. LC 87-28228. (Studies in the History & Interpretation of Music: Vol. 11). 200p. 1988. lib. bdg. 79.95 (*0-88946-435-9*) E Mellen.

Luoma, Robert G., tr. see Barbier, Patrick.

Luoma, William. God So Loved the World. 1986. pap. 4.15 (*0-89536-788-2*, 6806) CSS OH.

— Honest to Goodness. (Orig.). 1988. pap. 6.25 (*1-55673-061-6*, 8858) CSS OH.

Luomala, K. Ethnobotany of the Gilbert Islands. (BMB Ser.). 1972. reprint ed. 25.00 (*0-527-02321-3*) Periodicals Srv.

— Maui-Of-A-Thousand-Tricks: His Oceanic & European Biographers. (BMB Ser.: No. 198). 1969. reprint ed. 45.00 (*0-527-02306-X*) Periodicals Srv.

— Oceanic, American Indian, & African Myths of Snaring the Sun. (BMB Ser.: No. 168). 1974. reprint ed. 15.00 (*0-527-02276-4*) Periodicals Srv.

Luomala, K., et al. Specialized Studies in Polynesian Anthropology. (BMB Ser.). 1974. reprint ed. 20.00 (*0-527-02301-9*) Periodicals Srv.

Luomala, Katharine. Voices on the Wind: Polynesian Myths & Chants. (Illus.). 209p. 1986. reprint ed. pap. 15.95 (*0-930897-83-8*) Bishop Mus.

Luong, Hy V. Discursive Practices & Linguistic Meanings: The Vietnamese System of Person Reference. LC 90-31711. (Pragmatics & Beyond New Ser.: Vol. 11). x, 213p. 1990. 59.00x (*1-55619-277-0*) Benjamins North Am.

— Revolution in the Village: Tradition & Transformation in North Vietnam, 1925-1988. LC 91-40031. (Illus.). 286p. (C). 1992. lib. bdg. 38.00 (*0-8248-1382-0*); pap. text ed. 16.95 (*0-8248-1399-5*) UH Pr.

Luong Si Hang. Baby Tam Talking to You, Vol. II. Vuong Thanh Son & Messick, William, eds. Nguyen, Xuan-Mai, tr. 96p. 1994. pap. 6.00 (*0-9633690-3-2*) Vo Vi Frndship.

— Practical Method of Vovi Esoteric Science. rev. ed. Nguyen, Mai et al, eds. Vinh, Hoang, tr. (Illus.). 104p. 1994. pap. 5.00 (*0-9633690-4-0*) Vo Vi Frndship.

— Die Praktische Methode der Vovi Kontemplation. Nguyen, Mai et al, eds. Hua Bach Mai, tr. (Illus.). 76p. (Orig.). (GER.). 1993. pap. 5.00 (*0-9633690-2-4*) Vo Vi Frndship.

***Luong, Tuoc V., et al.** Internationalization: Developing Software for Global Markets. Date not set. pap. text ed. 29.95 (*0-471-07661-9*) Wiley.

Luongo, Anthony P. Josette (and Family) Coping with Manic Depression. 86p. (Orig.). 1993. pap. 8.00 (*1-56002-139-X*, Univ Edtns) Aegina Pr.

Luongo, Giuseppe, jt. ed. see Kilburn, Christopher J.

Luongo, John. The Adventure of Faith: When Religion Is Just the Beginning. LC 92-15128. 176p. 1992. pap. 5.95 (*0-8091-3313-X*) Paulist Pr.

Luongo, Kenneth N. & Wander, W. Thomas, eds. The Search for Security in Space. LC 88-47928. (Cornell Studies in Security Affairs). 304p. 1989. 39.95 (*0-8014-2145-4*); pap. 14.95 (*0-8014-9482-6*) Cornell U Pr.

Luongo, Kenneth N., jt. ed. see Wander, W. Thomas.

Luongo, Pino & Raives, Barbara. Fish Talk: Recipes from Le Madri, Coco Pazzo, & Sapore di Mare. LC 93-31297. 1994. 20.00 (*0-517-59352-1*, C P Pubs) Crown Pub Group.

Luongo, Pino, et al. A Tuscan in the Kitchen: Recipes & Tales from My Home. (Illus.). 1988. 24.95 (*0-517-56916-7*, C P Pubs) Crown Pub Group.

Luonsi, A. A. & Rantala, P. K. Forest Industry Wastewaters - Biological Treatment: First Volume of the Proceedings of an IAWPRC Symposium Held in Tampere, Finland, 9-12 June 1987. LC 82-645900. (Water Science & Technology Ser.: No. 20-1). (Illus.). 296p. 1988. pap. 61.00 (*0-08-036630-9*, Pergamon Pr) Elsevier.

Luonsi, A. A., jt. ed. see Rantala, P. K.

Luopa, Michael. A Spiritual Primer on Abortion: A Simple Handbook for the Spiritual Truth about Abortion. 32p. 1994. pap. 4.95 (*0-9640549-0-6*) Ruby Ray Pubng.

Luorie, Richard, tr. see Szczpiorski, Andrzej.

Lupack, Alan, ed. Arthurian Drama: An Anthology. LC 90-20122. 358p. 1991. 48.00 (*0-8240-3424-4*, 90-20122) Garland.

— Lancelot of the Lake & Sir Tristrem. 1994. pap. 12.00 (*1-879288-50-8*) Medieval Inst.

— Modern Arthurian Literature: An Anthology of English & American Arthuriana from the Renaissance to the Present. LC 91-46442. 502p. 1992. 75.00 (*0-8153-0055-7*, H#1420); pap. 18.95 (*0-8153-0843-4*) Garland.

— Three Middle English Charlemagne Romances. (TEAMS Middle English Text Ser.). 1990. pap. 6.95 (*0-918720-44-3*) Medieval Inst.

Lupack, Barbara, ed. Take Two: Adpting the Contemporary American Novel to Film. LC 93-72985. (Illus.). 191p. (C). 1994. text ed. 45.95 (*0-87972-641-5*); pap. text ed. 18.95 (*0-87972-642-3*) Bowling Green Univ.

***Lupack, Barbara T.** Insanity As Redemption in Contemporary American Fiction: Inmates Running the Asylum. LC 94-29265. 256p. (C). 1995. lib. bdg. 39.95 (*0-8130-1331-3*) U Press Fla.

Lupandin, K. K., jt. auth. see Rabinowitch, Z. E.

Lupart, jt. ed. see McKeough, A.

Lupart, Judy L., jt. auth. see Fry, Prem S.

Lupas, L. & Rhodes, E. Scriptures of the World: 1992. (Illus.). 145p. 1993. pap. text ed. 2.95 (*0-8267-0304-6*, 105176) Untd Bible Soc.

Lupas, Liana. Phonologie du Grec Attique. (Janua Linguarum, Series Practica: No. 164). 186p. (Orig.). (FRE.). 1972. pap. 49.25 (*90-279-2325-6*) Mouton.

Lupdag, Anselmo. In Search of Filipino Leadership. vii, 131p. (Orig.). (C). 1984. pap. 10.75 (*971-10-0122-5*, Pub. by New Day Pub PH) Cellar.

Luper, Albert T., jt. auth. see Gleason, Harold.

Luper, Albert T., jt. auth. see Helm, Eugene.

Luper-Foy, Steven. Problems of International Justice. LC 87-13570. 314p. 1988. text ed. 51.50 (*0-8133-0392-3*) Westview.

Luper-Foy, Steven, ed. The Possibility of Knowledge: Nozick & His Critics. 352p. 1987. 65.00 (*0-8476-7446-0*); pap. 24.00 (*0-8476-7447-9*) Rowman.

Luper-Foy, Steven & Brown, Curtis. The Moral Life. 460p. (C). 1992. pap. text ed. 28.00 (*0-03-033969-3*) HB Coll Pubs.

Luper-Foy, Steven & Brown, Curtis, eds. Drugs, Morality, & the Law. LC 93-48114. (Studies in Applied Ethics: Vol. 3). 392p. 1994. 55.00 (*0-8153-0485-4*, SS666) Garland.

Luper, Gregory L. Teletheory: Grammatology in the Age of Video. 256p. 1989. 45.00 (*0-415-90120-0*, A3232, Routledge NY); pap. 14.95 (*0-415-90121-9*, A3236, Routledge NY) Routledge.

Lupertz, Markus. Manner Ohne Fraune - Parsifal. 1994. pap. 30.00 (*1-881616-31-2*) Dist Art Pubs.

Lupetin. Magnetic Resonance Imaging of the Chest. 1991. write for info. (*0-8151-5666-9*, Yr Bk Med Pubs) Mosby Yr Bk.

Lupfer, E. A. Ornate Pictorial Calligraphy: Instructions & over 150 Examples. (Lettering, Calligraphy, Typography Ser.). (Illus.). 80p. 1982. pap. 4.50 (*0-486-21957-7*) Dover.

Lupi, Sam, II. Destruction of Success. 320p. 1994. 20.95 (*0-8059-3551-7*) Dorrance.

Lupia, Charles. Two Times in the Stream. 100p. 1993. pap. 5.00 (*0-9637558-0-3*) Celnote Pr.

Lupiano, Vincent & Sayes, Ken. It Was a Very Good Year: A Cultural History of the United States from 1776 to the Present. 1994. pap. 15.00 (*1-55850-419-2*) Adams Pubng.

Lupica, Mike. Extra Credits: A Peter Finley Mystery. LC 87-29611. 250p. 1988. 15.95 (*0-394-55458-2*, Villard Bks) Random.

— Jump. LC 94-20609. 1995. 22.00 (*0-679-40334-5*, Villard Bks) Random.

Lupin, M. S., et al. Briquetting: Alternative Process for Urea Supergranules. LC 83-18396. (Technical Bulletin Ser.: No. T-26). (Illus.). 20p. (Orig.). 1983. pap. 4.00 (*0-88090-046-6*) Intl Fertilizer.

Lupinacci, Lucille A. The Schools of Griswold, Connecticut in Historical Perspective. (Connecticut Educational History Ser.). 16p. 1987. 2.00 (*0-318-32532-2*) I N Thut World Educ Ctr.

***Lupini, Valerie.** There Goes the Neighborhood. 128p. (YA). 1995. pap. 7.95 (*0-88995-128-4*, Pub. by Red Deer CN) BookWorld Dist.

Lupinski, John H. & Moore, Robert S., eds. Polymeric Materials for Electronics Packaging & Interconnection. (ACS Symposium Ser.: No. 407). 512p. 1989. 99.95 (*0-8412-1679-7*) Am Chemical.

Lupis, C. P. Chemical Thermodynamics of Materials. LC 93-9743. 1983. pap. text ed. 79.00 (*0-13-050238-3*) P-H.

Lupis, Claude H. Chemical Thermodynamics of Materials. 608p. 1983. pap. 60.00 (*0-444-00779-2*) P-H.

Lupis, Ivo F. Medu Nasim Narodom U Americi. LC 71-155327. 1971. reprint ed. 8.00 (*0-88247-053-1*) Ragusan Pr.

Lupis, James. Handbook of Warehouse & Distribution Management Forms & Reports. 1991. 69.95 (*0-13-369968-4*, Busn) P-H.

Lupo, et al, eds. DARPA Neural Network Study. LC 88-31655. (Illus.). 625p. (C). 1988. text ed. 49.95 (*0-916159-17-5*) AFCEA Intl Pr.

Lupo, Ann. Being Me & Drug Free Kid-Pak. rev. ed. Fox, Greg, ed. (Life-Skill Builder Educational Ser.). (Illus.). 16p. (J). (gr. k-3). 1991. pap. text ed. 3.95 (*1-56230-135-7*); audio, pap. text ed. 4.95 (*1-56230-125-X*) Syndistar.

— Healthy Bodies Don't Need Drugs Kid-Pak. rev. ed. Fox, Greg, ed. (Life-Skill Builder Educational Ser.). (Illus.). 20p. (J). (gr. 3-5). 1991. pap. text ed. 3.95 (*1-56230-138-1*); pap. text ed. 4.95 (*1-56230-128-4*) Syndistar.

— Red the Firedog's How to Plan for a Safe Escape Kid-Pak. rev. ed. Fox, Greg, ed. (Life-Skill Builder Educational Ser.). (Illus.). 20p. (J). (ps-3). 1991. pap. text ed. 3.95 (*1-56230-137-3*); audio 4.95 (*1-56230-134-9*) Syndistar.

Lupo, Ann, ed. see Bosco, James.

Lupo, Margaret. Southern Cooking from Mary Mac's Tea Room. LC 93-38488. 320p. 1993. reprint ed. pap. 14.95 (*0-87797-257-5*) Cherokee.

Lupo, Maxine V. How to Master a Great Golf Swing. 1992. pap. 13.95 (*0-8092-4032-7*) Contemp Bks.

Lupo, Raphael V. & Tanguay, Donna M. What Corporate & General Practitioners Should Know about Intellectual Property Litigation. LC 91-71727. 242p. 1991. text ed. 85.00 (*0-8318-0576-5*, B576) Am Law Inst.

Lupoff, Richard. Stroka Prospekt. Disch, Thomas M., ed. LC 82-19269. (Singularities Ser.). (Illus.). 45p. (Orig.). 1982. pap. 10.00 (*0-915124-73-4*, Toothpaste) Coffee Hse.

Lupoff, Richard A. The Bessie Blue Killer: A Hobart LIndsey - Marvia Plum Mystery. 304p. 1994. 20.95 (*0-312-10425-1*) St Martin.

— The Forever City. (Millennium Science Fiction Ser.). (Illus.). (YA). (gr. 7-12). 1988. 15.95 (*0-8027-6742-7*) Walker & Co.

— Gryphon Double: The Digital Wristwatch of Philip K. Dick & Hyperprism, No. 7. 1994. per. 9.95 (*0-936071-25-7*) Gryphon Pubns.

— Lovecraft's Book. LC 84-24290. (Illus.). 272p. 1985. 15.95 (*0-87054-151-X*) Arkham.

An Asterisk (*) at the beginning of an entry indicates that the title is appearing in BIP for the first time.

— The Sepia Siren Killer. (Hobart Lidsey-Mariva Plum Mystery Ser.). 304p. 1994. 20.95 (*0-312-11332-3*) St Martin.

Lupold, Harry F. & Haddad, Gladys, eds. Ohio's Western Reserve: A Regional Reader. LC 88-691. 290p. 1988. pap. 15.00 (*0-87338-372-9*) Kent St U Pr.

***Lupold, John S.** Chattahoochee Valley Sources & Resources: An Annotated Bibliography Vol. II: The Georgia Counties. 736p. 1994. 31.00 (*0-945477-07-4*) Hist Chattahoochee.

Lupold, John S., comp. Chattahoochee Valley Sources & Resources--an Annotated Bibliography: The Alabama Counties, Vol. 1. 497p. 1988. lib. bdg. 19.95 (*0-945477-06-6*) Hist Chattahoochee.

Lupovici, Zaharia. Good Cholesterol, Bad Cholesterol, & the Most Discussed Cholesterol: HDL. 1993. pap. 10.95 (*0-533-10342-8*) Vantage.

Lupowski & Assouline. Jane & Johnny Love Math. 1992. pap. 10.00 (*0-89824-539-7*) Trillium Pr.

Luppi, Diana, jt. auth. see Jho, Zoev.

Luppinacci. Fifty-Two Ways to Shrink Your Grocer. pap. 6.95 (*1-56530-108-0*) Summit TX.

Luprecht, Mark. What People Call Pessimism: Sigmund Freud, Arthur Schnitzler & Nineteenth-Century Controversy at the University of Vienna Medical School. (Studies in Austrian Literature, Culture, & Thought). 172p. 1990. pap. 23.00 (*0-929497-28-7*) Ariadne CA.

Lupsewicz, Veronica A. Misty the Manatee. Weinberger, Jane, ed. (Illus.). 46p. (J). (ps-4). 1993. pap. 9.95 (*0-932433-96-0*) Windswept Hse.

Lupson, J. P., ed. Everyday German Idioms. 128p. (C). 1987. 50.00 (*0-85950-185-X*, Pub. by S Thornes Pubs UK) St Mut.

Lupson, P. Echt Deutsch: German Reading Materials from Authentic Sources. (C). 1987. 50.00 (*0-85950-700-9*, Pub. by S Thornes Pubs UK) St Mut.

Lupson, Peter. Guide to German Idioms. 120p. pap. 6.95 (*0-8442-2501-0*, Natl Textbk) NTC Pub Grp.

— Schreiben Ohne Leiden! (C). 1985. 12.95 (*0-85950-248-1*, Pub. by S Thornes UK) Dufour.

Lupson, Peter & Aufderstrasse, H. Los Geht's, Stage 2. (C). 1988. pap. 16.95 (*0-85950-725-4*, Pub. by S Thornes UK); teacher ed, pap. 19.95 (*0-85950-726-2*, Pub. by S Thornes UK); audio 22.00 (*0-85950-727-0*, Pub. by S Thornes UK); Minimum order 10 cassettes. audio 85.00 (*0-85950-914-1*, Pub. by S Thornes UK) Dufour.

— Los Geht's, Stage 3. (C). 1989. pap. 17.95 (*0-85950-833-1*, Pub. by S Thornes UK); teacher ed, pap. 19.95 (*0-85950-834-X*, Pub. by S Thornes UK); Minimum order 10 cassettes. audio 85.00 (*0-7487-0103-6*, Pub. by S Thornes UK); disk 22.00 (*0-85950-835-8*, Pub. by S Thornes UK) Dufour.

Lupson, Peter & Pelissier, Michael. Everyday French Idioms. 128p. (C). 1986. 65.00 (*0-85950-552-9*, Pub. by S Thornes Pubs UK) St Mut.

Lupson, Peter & Pelissier, Michel. Guide to French Idioms. 128p. 1987. pap. 6.95 (*0-8442-1502-3*, Natl Textbk) NTC Pub Grp.

Lupson, Peter, et al. Los Geht's, Stage 1. (C). 1986. teacher ed 16.95 (*0-85950-509-X*, Pub. by S Thornes UK); pap. 16.95 (*0-85950-508-1*, Pub. by S Thornes UK); audio 22.00 (*0-85950-510-3*, Pub. by S Thornes UK) Dufour.

— Working with German Cassette, No. 1. 1989. 32.00 (*0-85950-840-4*, Pub. by S Thornes UK) Dufour.

— Working with German Coursebook, No. 1. 154p. 1989. pap. 18.95 (*0-85950-838-2*, Pub. by S Thornes UK) Dufour.

— Working with German, Level 2: Coursebook. 1990. pap. 25.00 (*0-7487-0147-8*); pap. 35.00 (*0-7487-0148-6*) Dufour.

Lupton. Theirs Is the Kingdom. 1989. pap. 10.00 (*0-06-065307-8*, PL) HarpC.

Lupton, Charles T. Oil & Gas in the Olympic Peninsula. (Shorey Prospecting Ser.). 60p. reprint ed. pap. 4.95 (*0-8466-0055-2*, S55) Shorey.

Lupton, D., tr. see Jacobus, Verheiden.

***Lupton, David W. & Lupton, Dorothy R.** Lancaster Platt Lupton Vol. 1: The Legacy of a Fur Trader. (Road to Delhi). (Illus.). 124p. (Orig.). 1994. pap. 11.50 (*0-9644165-1-4*) S Platte Valley.

***Lupton, Deborah.** The Imperative of Health: Public Health & the Regulated Body. 192p. (C). 1995. 65.00 (*0-8039-7935-5*); pap. 21.95 (*0-8039-7936-3*) Sage.

— Medicine As Culture: Illness, Disease & the Body in Western Societies. 256p. (C). 1994. text ed. 65.00 (*0-8039-8924-5*); pap. text ed. 21.95 (*0-8039-8925-3*) Sage.

— Moral Threats & Dangerous Desires: AIDS in the News Media. (Social Aspects of AIDS Ser.). 208p. 1994. 75.00 (*0-7484-0179-2*, Pub. by Tay Francis Ltd UK); pap. 27.00 (*0-7484-0180-6*, Pub. by Tay Francis Ltd UK) Taylor & Francis.

Lupton, Donald. London & the Countrey Carbonadoed & Quartered into Several Characters. LC 77-7413. (English Experience Ser.: No. 879). 1977. reprint ed. lib. bdg. 11.50 (*90-221-0879-1*) Walter J Johnson.

Lupton, Dorothy R., jt. auth. see Lupton, David W.

Lupton, E., jt. ed. see Schofield, Philip F.

Lupton, Ellen. Mechanical Brides: Women & Machines from Home to Office. Aakre, Nancy, ed. LC 93-22169. (Illus.). 64p. (Orig.). 1993. pap. 19.95 (*1-878271-97-0*) Princeton Arch.

***Lupton, Ellen & Cohen, Elaine L.** Letters from the Avant-Garde: Modern Graphic Design. (Illus.). 128p. (Orig.). 1995. pap. 24.95 (*1-56898-052-3*) Princeton Arch.

***Lupton, Ellen & Miller, J. Abbott.** Design - Writing - Research: Essays on Graphic Design & Typography. (Illus.). 208p. 1995. 45.00 (*1-56898-047-7*) Princeton Arch.

— The Process of Elimination: The Bathroom, the Kitchen, & the Aesthetics of Waste. (Illus.). 80p. (Orig.). 1992. pap. 19.95 (*0-938437-42-9*) MIT List Visual Arts.

Lupton, Ellen & Miller, J. Abbott, eds. The ABCs of Triangle, Square, Circle: The Bauhaus & Design Theory. (Illus.). 64p. (Orig.). 1991. pap. 21.95 (*1-878271-42-3*) Princeton Arch.

Lupton, F. G. Wheat Breeding & Its Scientific Basis. 580p. 1987. lib. bdg. 145.00 (*0-412-24470-5*) Chapman & Hall.

***Lupton, Gillian & Najman, Jake, eds.** Sociology of Health & Illness. 2nd ed. 420p. 1995. 69.95 (*0-7329-2800-1*); pap. 34.95 (*0-7329-2799-4*) Paul & Co Pubs.

Lupton, Gillian, et al. Society & Gender: An Introduction to Sociology. 368p. 1994. 69.95 (*0-7329-1303-9*, Pub. by Macmill Educ AT); pap. 34.95 (*0-7329-1302-0*, Pub. by Macmill Educ AT) Paul & Co Pubs.

Lupton, Hugh R. Whence? Where? Whither? & Occasional Verse. 120p. 1984. 40.00 (*0-7212-0678-6*, Pub. by Regency Press) St Mut.

Lupton, Julia R. & Reinhard, Kenneth. After Oedipus: Shakespeare in Psychoanalysis. LC 92-54975. (Illus.). 288p. 1993. 37.50 (*0-8014-2407-0*); pap. 14.95 (*0-8014-9687-X*) Cornell U Pr.

Lupton, Mary J. Menstruation & Psychoanalysis. LC 92-39667. 240p. 1993. 34.95 (*0-252-02012-X*); pap. 14.95 (*0-252-06315-5*) U of Ill Pr.

Lupton, Robert. Statistics in Theory & Practice. LC 92-36396. (Illus.). 128p. (C). 1993. text ed. 24.95 (*0-691-07429-1*) Princeton U Pr.

Lupton, Robert D. Theirs Is the Kingdom. 1989. write for info. (*0-318-65615-9*) Harper SF.

Lupton, T. On the Shop Floor: Two Studies of Workshop Organization & Output. LC 62-22099. (International Series of Monographs on Solid State Physics: Vol. 2). 1963. 91.00 (*0-08-009764-2*, Pub. by Pergamon Repr UK) Franklin.

Lupton, T., ed. Human Factors in Manufacturing: Proceedings of the International Conference on Human Factors in Manufacturing, Stratford-upon-Avon, 3rd, November 4-6, 1986. (Illus.). ix, 409p. 1987. 119.00 (*0-387-16333-6*) Spr-Verlag.

— Human Factors in Manufacturing: Proceedings of the International Conference, 1st, London, U. K., April 3-5, 1984. 400p. 1984. 107.75 (*0-444-87517-4*, North Holland) Elsevier.

Lupton, Thomas. All for Money. LC 79-133700. (Tudor Facsimile Texts. Old English Plays Ser.: No. 51). reprint ed. 49.50 (*0-404-53351-5*) AMS Pr.

Lupton, Tom. Industrial Behaviour & Personnel Management. 96p. (C). 1978. 35.00 (*0-85292-164-0*) St Mut.

Lupton, Tom & Tanner, Ian. Achieving Change: A Systematic Approach. 100p. 1987. text ed. 39.95 (*0-566-02526-4*, Pub. by Gower UK) Ashgate Pub Co.

Lupul, Manoly R. The Roman Catholic Church & the North-West School Question: A Study in Church-State Relations in Western Canada, 1875-1905. LC 73-89844. 304p. reprint ed. pap. 86.70 (*0-8357-3646-6*, 2036373) Bks Demand.

Lupulescu, Aurel. Hormones & Carcinogenesis. LC 82-15110. 366p. 1983. text ed. 75.00 (*0-275-91402-X*, C1402, Praeger Pubs) Greenwood.

— Hormones & Vitamins in Cancer Treatment. (Illus.). 336p. 1990. 190.00 (*0-8493-5973-2*, 5973) CRC Pr.

Lupus, Bernhard. Der Sprachgebrauch Des Cornelius Nepos. vii, 224p. 1972. reprint ed. write for info. (*3-487-04508-7*, Pub. by Georg Olms GW) Lubrecht & Cramer.

Luque, A. & Araujo, G. L., eds. Physical Limitations to Photovoltaic Energy Conversion. (Illus.). 192p. 1990. 86.00 (*0-7503-0030-2*) IOP Pub.

Luque, A. & Palz, W., eds. Photovoltaic Concentration: A Special Issue of International Journal of Solar Energy. 80p. 1988. pap. text ed. 65.00 (*3-7186-4861-X*) Gordon & Breach.

Luque, A., et al, eds. Tenth E. C. Photovoltaic Solar Energy Conference. 1490p. (C). 1991. lib. bdg. 309.00 (*0-7923-1389-5*) Kluwer Ac.

Luque, Antonio. Solar Cells & Optics for Photovoltaic Concentration. (Optics & Optoelectronics Ser.). (Illus.). 552p. 1989. 181.00 (*0-85274-106-5*) IOP Pub.

Luque de Castro, M. D., jt. auth. see Valcarcel, M.

Luque De Sanchez, Maria D. Ocupacion Norteamericana y La Ley Foraker: Como Reaccionaron los Puertorriquenos. LC 77-10859. 197p. 1986. pap. 7.00 (*0-8477-0851-9*) U of PR Pr.

Luque, E., ed. Mini & Microcomputers & Their Applications - MIMI '85: Proceedings, ISMM Symposium, Sant Feliu de Guixols, Spain, June 25-28, 1985. 518p. 1985. 108.00 (*0-88986-121-8*, 077) Acta Pr.

— Mini & Microcomputers & Their Applications - Mimi '88: Proceedings of ISMM Symposium, Sant Feliu de Guixols, Spain, June 27-30, 1988. 680p. 1988. 125.00 (*84-7488-121-8*, 148) Acta Pr.

***Luque Faxardo, Francisco de.** Fiel Desengano Contra La Ociosidad y Los Juegos, 2 vols. Riquer, Martin de, ed. 529p. (SPA.). 1968. pap. 200.00 (*0-614-00215-X*) Elliots Bks.

Luqueer, Frederick L. Hegel As Educator. LC 03-12359. reprint ed. 14.50 (*0-404-04068-3*) AMS Pr.

Luquet, F. M., jt. auth. see Boudier, J. F.

Luquire, Jerry, ed. see Kempf, Michael J.

Luquire, Wilson. Coordinating Cooperative Collection Development: A National Perspective. LC 85-24847. (Resource Sharing & Information Networks Ser.: Vol. 2, Nos. 3-4). 253p. 1986. text ed. 49.95 (*0-86656-543-4*) Haworth Pr.

Luquire, Wilson, ed. Experiences of Library Network Administrators: Paper Based on the Symposium "From Our Past! Toward 2000" LC 84-22428. (Resource Sharing & Information Networks Ser.: Vol. 2, Nos. 1-2). 131p. 1985. text ed. 39.95 (*0-86656-388-1*) Haworth Pr.

— Library Networking: Current Problems & Future Prospects. LC 83-18474. (Resource Sharing & Information Networks Ser.: Vol. 1, Nos. 1-2). 140p. 1983. text ed. 39.95 (*0-86656-270-2*) Haworth Pr.

Luraghi, Silvia. Old Hittite Sentence Structure. (Croom Helm Linguistic Ser.). 224p. 1990. 72.50 (*0-415-04735-8*, A4540) Routledge.

Lurati, O. Parole Nuovo. 1991. 49.95 (*0-8288-3918-2*, F112072) Fr & Eur.

Luray, Martin. The Sailing Doctor: The Essential Shipboard Companion. 1992. 27.00 (*0-679-40911-4*, Villard Bks) Random.

Lurcat, F., jt. ed. see Levy, Maurice.

Lurdang, Laurence & Robbins, Ceila D. Every Bite a Delight & Other Slogans. 1992. pap. 15.95 (*0-8103-9423-5*) Visible Ink Pr.

Luria. Kitve Ari: Hebrew Text, 18 vols., Set. 1985. write for info. (*0-943688-16-7*) Res Ctr Kabbalah.

Luria, A. R. Basic Problems of Neurolinguistics. Haigh, Basil, tr. (Janua Linguarum, Series Major: No. 73). 1976. text ed. 107.70 (*90-279-3205-0*) Mouton.

— The Mind of a Mnemonist: A Little Book about a Vast Memory. LC 86-31847. 160p. 1987. pap. 11.00 (*0-674-57622-5*) HUP.

— Traumatic Aphasia: Its Syndromes, Psychology & Treatment. Bowden, Douglas, tr. LC 68-17903. (Janua Linguarum, Ser. Major: No. 5). 1970. text ed. 101.55 (*90-279-0717-X*) Mouton.

Luria, A. R., jt. auth. see Vygotsky, L. S.

Luria, Aleksandr R. Cognitive Development. 180p. 1982. pap. 12.00 (*0-674-13732-9*) HUP.

— Higher Cortical Functions in Man. 2nd ed. LC 77-20421. 656p. 1980. 49.50 (*0-306-10966-2*, Consultants) Plenum.

— The Making of Mind: A Personal Account of Soviet Psychology. Cole, Michael & Cole, Sheila, eds. (Illus.). 234p. (C). 1979. 26.00 (*0-674-54326-2*) HUP.

— The Making of Mind: A Personal Account of Soviet Psychology. Cole, Michael & Cole, Sheila, eds. 234p. 1986. pap. 15.50 (*0-674-54327-0*) HUP.

— The Man with a Shattered World: The History of a Brain Wound. LC 86-31866. 168p. 1987. pap. 11.95 (*0-674-54625-3*) HUP.

— The Mind of a Mnemonist: A Little Book about a Vast Memory. LC 86-33487. 160p. 1987. pap. text ed. 7.95 (*0-317-59999-2*) HUP.

— Neuropsychological Studies in Aphasia. (Neurolinguistics Ser.: Vol. 6). 184p. 1977. 30.00 (*90-265-0244-3*, Pub. by Swets Pub Serv NE) Taylor & Francis.

— The Working Brain. Haigh, B., tr. LC 72-95540. 408p. 1976. pap. text ed. 17.00 (*0-465-09208-X*) Basic.

Luria, Aleksandr R. & Haigh, B. Restoration of Function after Brain Injury. LC 63-10016. 1963. 118.00 (*0-08-010130-5*, Pub. by Pergamon Repr UK) Franklin.

Luria, Aleksandr R. & Robinson, W. Mentally Retarded Child: Essays Study Peculiarities Higher Nerve Function Choligophren. LC 63-10015. 1963. 88.00 (*0-08-010131-3*, Pub. by Pergamon Repr UK) Franklin.

Luria, Aleksandr R. & Tizard, J. Role of Speech in Regulation of Normal & Abnormal Behavior. LC 60-9965. 1961. 68.00 (*0-08-009495-3*, Pub. by Pergamon Repr UK) Franklin.

Luria, Daniel. Beyond Free Trade & Protectionism: The Public Interest in a U. S. Auto Policy. 30p. 1990. 10.00 (*0-944826-08-3*) Economic Policy Inst.

Luria, Edward M., jt. ed. see Loebbecke, James K.

Luria, Emile. Tornado Weather. LC 93-13597. 64p. 1993. pap. 12.95 (*0-7734-2763-5*, Mellen Poetry Pr) E Mellen.

Luria, Isaac. Gates of Reincarnation. 200p. (HEB.). 1985. pap. write for info. (*0-943688-49-3*) Res Ctr Kabbalah.

— Tzadik Yesod Olam. 124p. 1960. write for info. (*0-943688-21-3*) Res Ctr Kabbalah.

Luria, Keith P. Territories of Grace: Cultural Change in the Seventeenth-Century Diocese of Grenoble. LC 90-38259. (Studies on the History of Society & Culture: No. 11). (Illus.). 275p. 1991. 40.00 (*0-520-06810-6*) U CA Pr.

Luria, Maxwell, tr. see Benamozegh, Elijah.

Luria, Maxwell S. & Hoffman, Richard L., eds. Middle English Lyrics. (Critical Editions Ser.). (Illus.). (C). 1974. pap. text ed. 10.95 (*0-393-09338-7*) Norton.

Luria, Mazwell, tr. see Benamozegh, Elijah.

Luria, R. Issac. Bet Shaar Hakavonot. (HEB.). 1983. write for info. (*0-924457-48-1*) Res Ctr Kabbalah.

Luria, Salvador E., et al. A View of Life. 1981. teacher ed 10.75 (*0-8053-6649-0*); teacher ed, text ed. 10.75 (*0-8053-6648-2*) Benjamin-Cummings.

Luria-Sukenick, Lynn. Houdini Houdini. (CSU Poetry Ser.: No. X). 55p. 1982. pap. 4.50 (*0-914946-29-3*) Cleveland St Univ Poetry Ctr.

Luria, Zella, et al. Human Sexuality. LC 85-22629. 752p. 1987. Net. text ed. write for info. (*0-471-88653-X*) Wiley.

Lurie & Wittwer. High-Performance Liquid Chromatography in Forensic Chemistry. (Chromatographic Science Ser.: Vol. 24). 456p. 1983. 175.00 (*0-8247-1756-2*) Dekker.

Lurie, A. I. Non-Linear Theory of Elasticity. (Applied Mathematics & Mechanics Ser.: No. 36). 618p. 1990. 168.75 (*0-444-87439-9*, North Holland) Elsevier.

Lurie, Abraham & Rosenberg, Gary, eds. Social Work Administration in Health Care. LC 84-799. 310p. 1984. text ed. 49.95 (*0-917724-42-9*); pap. 39.95 (*0-86656-314-8*) Haworth Pr.

Lurie, Abraham, et al, eds. Social Work with Groups in Health Settings. LC 82-18151. 124p. 1982. pap. 7.95 (*0-88202-137-0*) Watson Pub Intl.

Lurie, Alison. Clever Gretchen & Other Forgotten Folktales. LC 78-22512. (Illus.). 128p. (J). (gr. 4-6). 1980. lib. bdg. 13.89 (*0-690-03944-1*, Crowell Jr Bks) HarpC Child Bks.

— Don't Tell the Grown-Ups: Why Kids Love the Books They Do. 256p. 1991. reprint ed. pap. 9.95 (*0-380-71402-7*) Avon.

— Foreign Affairs. 1990. pap. 10.00 (*0-380-70990-2*) Avon.

— Foreign Affairs. LC 84-42657. 320p. 1984. 15.95 (*0-394-54076-X*) Random.

— Imaginary Friends. 288p. 1986. mass mkt. 4.50 (*0-380-70073-5*) Avon.

— Imaginary Friends. 1991. pap. 8.95 (*0-380-71136-2*) Avon.

— Love & Friendship. 304p. 1993. pap. 9.00 (*0-380-71945-2*) Avon.

— Nowhere City. 336p. 1986. mass mkt. 4.50 (*0-380-70070-0*) Avon.

— The Nowhere City. 336p. 1992. pap. 9.00 (*0-380-71936-3*) Avon.

— Only Children. 272p. 1990. pap. 7.95 (*0-380-70875-2*) Avon.

— The Truth about Lorin Jones. 336p. 1990. pap. 9.00 (*0-380-70807-8*) Avon.

— The War Between the Tates. 1991. pap. 8.95 (*0-380-71135-4*) Avon.

— The War Between the Tates. LC 73-3991. 1974. 16.95 (*0-394-46201-7*) Random.

— Women & Ghosts. LC 93-46332. 1994. 21.00 (*0-385-47392-3*) Doubleday.

— Women & Ghosts. 1995. pap. 9.00 (*0-380-72501-0*) Avon.

— Women & Ghosts. large type ed. LC 94-48925. 1995. write for info. (*0-7862-0415-X*) Thorndike Pr.

Lurie, Alison, ed. The Oxford Book of Modern Fairy Tales. LC 92-28007. 480p. 1993. 25.00 (*0-19-214218-6*) OUP.

— The Oxford Book of Modern Fairy Tales. 480p. 1994. reprint ed. pap. 13.95 (*0-19-282385-X*) OUP.

Lurie, Ann T., et al. European Paintings of the Sixteenth, Seventeenth, & Eighteenth Centuries: The Cleveland Museum of Art Catalogue of Paintings, Pt. 3. LC 81-3961. (Illus.). 542p. 1982. 40.00 (*0-910386-66-8*) Cleveland Mus Art.

Lurie, Boris J. Feedback Maximization. 290p. (C). 1986. text ed. 29.00 (*0-89006-200-5*) Artech Hse.

Lurie, David H. Pacto, el Holocausto & la Semana 70: Covenant, the Holocaust & the 70th Week. (SPA.). 4.95 (*84-7645-446-5*, 223455, Pub. by Edit Clie SP) TSELF.

Lurie, Edward. Louis Agassiz: A Life in Science. LC 88-45392. 496p. 1988. reprint ed. pap. text ed. 15.95 (*0-8018-3743-X*) Johns Hopkins.

Lurie, Elinor E. & Swan, James H., eds. Serving the Mentally Ill Elderly: Problems & Perspectives. 272p. 1987. text ed. 37.95 (*0-669-14113-5*) Free Pr.

***Lurie, Elinore E., et al.** Longitudinal Retirement History Study: Student Workbook. (Gerontology Research Toolkit Ser.). 168p. (Orig.). 1994. student ed, pap. text ed. 49.00x (*0-8018-5045-2*) Johns Hopkins.

— Longitudinal Study of Aging: Student Workbook. (Gerontology Research Toolkit Ser.). 182p. (Orig.). 1994. student ed, pap. text ed. 49.00x (*0-8018-5043-6*) Johns Hopkins.

— National Long Term Care Survey: Student Workbook. (Gerontology Research Toolkit Ser.). 206p. (Orig.). 1994. student ed, pap. text ed. 49.00x (*0-8018-5041-X*) Johns Hopkins.

Lurie, Hannah R. The Edge of an Era. Buckalew, Jean, ed. LC 73-76165. 82p. 1974. student ed 3.00 (*0-685-41240-7*); pap. 3.00 (*0-9600728-1-0*) H R Lurie.

— The Edge of an Era. 3rd ed. Buckalew, Jean & Ferson, Jean, eds. 74p. 1983. pap. 3.00 (*0-686-79368-4*) H R Lurie.

Lurie, Hannah R., et al, eds. The Mystic Muse. LC 76-20284. 1976. pap. 3.00 (*0-9600728-2-9*) H R Lurie.

***Lurie, Hugh J.** Practical Management of Emotional Problems in Medicine. enl. rev. ed. LC 81-40019. 272p. 1982. pap. 77.60 (*0-7837-8357-4*, 2049147) Bks Demand.

Lurie, J. B., ed. The Twentieth AIPR Workshop: Computer Vision Applications - Meeting the Challenges, Oct. 1991, McLean, VA. 1992. write for info. (*0-8194-0765-8*, 1623) SPIE.

Lurie, Joe & Miller, Jonathan. A Foreign Student's Selected Guide to Financial Assistance for Study & Research in the U. S. 1983. pap. 22.50 (*0-88461-010-1*) Adelphi Univ.

***Lurie, Jon.** Fundamental Snowboarding. LC 95-11721. (Illus.). (J). 1995. write for info. (*0-8225-3457-6*, Lerner Publctns) Lerner Group.

Lurie, Jonathan. Arming Military Justice, Vol. I: The Origins of the United States Court of Military Appeals, 1775-1950. (Illus.). 280p. 1992. text ed. 45.00 (*0-691-06944-1*) Princeton U Pr.

— The Chicago Board of Trade, 1859-1905: The Dynamics of Self-Regulation. LC 78-20881. (Illus.). 250p. 1979. 24.95 (*0-252-00732-8*) U of Ill Pr.

— The Constitution & Economic Change. LC 88-71596. (Bicentennial Essays on the Constitution Ser.). 52p. 1988. pap. 7.00 (*0-87229-041-7*) Am Hist Assn.

Lurie, Joseph. Directory of Financial Aid for American Undergraduates Interested in Overseas Study & Travel. 1981. pap. 9.00 (*0-88461-007-1*) Adelphi Univ.

Lurie, K. A. Applied Optimal Control Theory of Distributed Systems. (Mathematical Concepts & Methods in Science & Engineering Ser.: Vol. 43). (Illus.). 540p. 1993. 110.00 (*0-306-43993-X*, Plenum Pr) Plenum.

Lurie, Leonard. Senator Pothole: The Unauthorized Biography of Al D'Amato. LC 93-47232. 1994. 21.95 (*1-55972-227-4*, Birch Ln Pr) Carol Pub Group.

An Asterisk (*) at the beginning of an entry indicates that the title is appearing in BIP for the first time.

L

Lurie, Max B. Resistance to Tuberculosis: Experimental Studies in Native & Acquired Defense Mechanisms. LC 64-25055. (Commonwealth Fund Publications). (Illus.). 410p. 1965. 37.00 (*0-674-76516-8*) HUP.

Lurie, Maxine N., ed. A New Jersey Anthology. LC 94-2821. 485p. (Orig.). (C). 1994. pap. 18.95 (*0-911020-29-2*) NJ Hist Soc.

Lurie, Maxine N. & Walroth, Joanne R., eds. The Minutes of the Board of Proprietors of the Eastern Division of New Jersey from 1764 to 1794, Vol. IV. LC 84-42826. xlii, 522p. 1985. 30.00 (*0-911020-11-X*) NJ Hist Soc.

Lurie, Morris. Snow Jobs. 143p. (C). 1990. 45.00 (*0-685-52919-3*, Pub. by Pascoe Pub AT) St Mut.

Lurie, Morris, et al. Jewish Writing from Down Under: Australia & New Zealand. Kalechofsky, Roberta & Kalechofsky, Robert, eds. LC 84-1098. (Echad: a Whole Global Anthology Ser.: No. 4). 304p. (Orig.). 1984. pap. 12.95 (*0-916288-16-1*) Micah Pubns.

Lurie, Nancy O. North American Indian Lives. (Illus.). 72p. (Orig.). (C). 1991. reprint ed. pap. text ed. 6.95 (*0-88133-549-5*) Waveland Pr.

— Wisconsin Indians. (Illus.). 66p. 1987. 3.00 (*0-87020-252-9*) State Hist Soc Wis.

Lurie, Nancy O., ed. Mountain Wolf Woman, Sister of Crashing Thunder: The Autobiography of a Winnebago Indian. (Illus.). 1961. pap. 14.95 (*0-472-06109-7*, 109, Ann Arbor Bks) U of Mich Pr.

Lurie, Nancy O., jt. ed. see Leacock, Eleanor B.

Lurie, Patty. A Guide to the Impressionist Landscape: Day Trips from Paris to Sites of Great Nineteenth-Century Paintings. (Illus.). 136p. 1990. pap. 18.95 (*0-8212-1796-8*) Bulfinch Pr.

***Lurie, Rod.** Once upon a Time in Hollywood: Moviemaking, Con Games, & Murder in Glitter City. 416p. 1995. 25.00 (*0-679-43522-0*) Pantheon.

Lurie, Susan. Ghostwriter Detective Guide: Tools & Tricks of the Trade. (J). (ps-3). 1992. pap. 3.50 (*0-553-48069-3*) Bantam.

— Rally! (J). (gr. 7-10). 1993. pap. 3.50 (*0-553-48092-8*) Bantam.

Lurie, Toby. The Beach at Cleone. 80p. 1983. pap. 4.95 (*0-930090-20-9*) Applezaba.

— Cliff House Poems. (Orig.). 1992. pap. 6.50 (*0-945349-04-1*) Journeys Into Language.

— Duets. LC 95-11880. 72p. 1995. pap. 12.95 (*0-7734-2727-9*, Mellen Poetry Pr) E Mellen.

— The Haight Street Blues. (Orig.). 1988. pap. 4.95 (*0-945349-00-9*) Journeys Into Language.

— New Forms New Spaces. 94p. (Orig.). 1971. reprint ed. pap. 5.95 (*0-945349-03-3*) Journeys Into Language.

— Quartets. LC 90-32741. (Poetry Ser.: Vol. 8). 84p. 1990. lib. bdg. 24.95 (*0-88946-883-4*) E Mellen.

— Quintets. LC 92-30599. (Poetry Ser.: Vol. 20). 76p. 1993. text ed. 24.95 (*0-7734-9515-0*); pap. 12.95 (*0-685-62281-9*) E Mellen.

***Lurier, Harold.** The Emergence of the Western World. 288p. (C). 1994. per., pap. text ed. 31.95 (*0-8403-9963-4*) Kendall-Hunt.

***Lurigio, Arthur & Bensinger, Gad, eds.** Drugs & Community Corrections. 104p. (C). Date not set. lib. bdg. 15.00 (*0-942854-19-5*) Loyola U Crim.

Lurigio, Arthur J., jt. ed. see Bensinger, Gad J.

Lurigio, Arthur J., jt. auth. see Lewis, Dan A.

Lurigio, Arthur J., et al, eds. Victims of Crime: Problems, Policies, & Programs. (Criminal Justice System Annuals Ser.). (Illus.). 320p. (C). 1990. text ed. 49.95 (*0-8039-3369-X*); pap. text ed. 24.00 (*0-8039-3370-3*) Sage.

Lurin, Ely S. Radio & Wireless Telecommunications Equipment & Services - U. S. Markets & Opportunities: 1992-1997 Analysis. (Illus.). 237p. 1993. pap. text ed. 1,900.00 (*1-878218-36-0*) World Info Tech.

— Telecommunications Test Equipment - U. S. Markets & Opportunities: 1991-1996 Analysis. (Illus.). 220p. 1992. pap. text ed. 1,900.00 (*1-878218-26-3*) World Info Tech.

— Telecommunications Test Equipment - U.S. Markets & Opportunities: 1993-1998 Analysis & Forecasts. 250p. 1994. pap. text ed. 1,900.00 (*1-878218-47-6*) World Info Tech.

Lurker, Manfred. Dictionary of Biblical Terms & Symbols: Woerterbuch Biblischer Bilder und Symbole. 4th ed. 505p. (GER.). 1990. 75.00 (*0-8288-2308-1*, M7046) Fr & Eur.

— Dictionary of Gods & Goddesses, Devils & Demons. 460p. 1987. 45.00 (*0-415-03943-6*, 08774, RKP); pap. 15.95 (*0-415-03944-4*, 11066, RKP) Routledge.

— Dictionary of Gods & Goddesses, Devils & Demons. LC 86-21911. 451p. (C). 1987. 45.00 (*0-7102-0877-4*, RKP); pap. 15.95 (*0-7102-1106-6*, RKP) Routledge.

— Gods & Symbols of Ancient Egypt: An Illustrated Dictionary. (Illus.). 142p. 1984. pap. 14.95 (*0-500-27253-0*) Thames Hudson.

— Woerterbuch der Symbolik. 5th ed. 871p. (GER.). 1991. 49.95 (*0-7859-8409-7*, 3520464055) Fr & Eur.

Lurkis, Alexander. The Power Brink: Con Edison, A Centennial of Electricity. (Illus.). 207p. (Orig.). (C). 1982. 13.95 (*0-9609492-1-6*); pap. 9.95 (*0-9609492-0-8*) ICARE Pr.

Lurry-Wright, Jerome W. Custom & Conflict on a Bahamian Out-Island. LC 86-31785. (Orig.). (C). 1987. pap. text ed. 21.00 (*0-8191-6098-9*) U Pr of Amer.

Lurtsema, Robert J. A Pocket Full of Verse. (Illus.). 240p. 1991. pap. 12.95 (*0-940160-50-1*) Parnassus Imprints.

Lury, Celia. Cultural Rights: Technology, Legality, & Personality. LC 92-37656. (International Library of Sociology). 1993. write for info. (*0-415-03155-9*, Routledge NY); pap. write for info. (*0-415-09578-6*, Routledge NY) Routledge.

Lury, D. A., jt. auth. see Casley, D. J.

Luryi, Yuri I. Soviet Family Law. LC 80-83797. vi, 93p. 1980. lib. bdg. 34.00 (*0-89941-062-6*, 300890) W S Hein.

Lusane, Clarence. African Americans at the Crossroads: The Restructuring of Black Leadership & the 1992 Elections. 160p. (Orig.). 1993. 40.00 (*0-89608-469-8*); pap. text ed. 16.00 (*0-89608-468-X*) South End Pr.

— Pipe Dream Blues: Racism & the War on Drugs. 234p. 1991. 30.00 (*0-89608-411-6*); pap. 14.00 (*0-89608-410-8*) South End Pr.

— The Struggle for Equal Education. (African-American Experience Ser.). (Illus.). 160p. (YA). (gr. 7-12). 1992. lib. bdg. 14.98 (*0-531-11121-0*) Watts.

Lusanna, L., ed. New Trends in Particle Theory: Proceedings of the 9th Johns Hopkins Workshop on Current Problems in Particle Theory, Firenze, Italy, June 5-7, 1985. 184p. 1985. 46.00 (*9971-5-0044-2*) World Scientific Pub.

Lusardi, James P. & Schlueter, June. Reading Shakespeare in Performance: King Lear. LC 89-46412. (Illus.). 248p. 1991. 37.50 (*0-8386-3394-3*) Fairleigh Dickinson.

Lusas, E. W., et al, eds. Food Uses of Whole Oil & Protein Seeds. 410p. 1989. 90.00 (*0-935315-23-3*) AOCS Pr.

Lusby, Keith S., jt. auth. see Neumann, A. L.

***Lusch & Wehinger.** North American Endangered & Protected Species. Flint, Mark, ed. LC 94-77816. (Illus.). 180p. (C). 1995. 500.00 (*1-885743-00-9*) Internat Wildlife.

Lusch, Ed. American Bass Angling Guide. (Illus.). 128p. 1990. pap. 15.95 (*0-936608-94-3*) F Amato Pubns.

— Comprehensive Guide to Western Gamefish. (Illus.). 125p. 1985. pap. 14.95 (*0-936608-38-2*) F Amato Pubns.

***Lusch, Robert & Zizzo, Deborah.** Competing for Customers: How Wholesaler-Distributors Can Meet the Power Retailer Challenge. 123p. 1995. pap. 130.00 (*0-614-06918-1*) Natl Assn Wholesale Dists.

Lusch, Robert F. & Darden, William R., eds. Retail Patronage Theory Proceedings. 1981. 17.00 (*0-931880-02-5*) U OK Ctr Econ.

Lusch, Robert F. & Zinszer, Paul H., eds. Contemporary Issues in Marketing Channels. 187p. 1979. 12.00 (*0-931880-00-9*) U OK Ctr Econ.

Lusch, Robert F., jt. auth. see Constantin, James A.

Lusch, Robert F., jt. ed. see Harvey, Michael G.

Lusch, Robert F., et al. Retail Management. 704p. (C). 1990. text ed. write for info. (*0-538-80294-4*, SF62AA) S-W Pub.

— Retail Marketing. 2nd ed. LC 92-2394. 1993. text ed. 58.95 (*0-538-82697-5*) S-W Pub.

Lusch, Robert F., et al, eds. AMA Educators' Proceedings, No. 51. LC 85-11077. 403p. (Orig.). 1985. pap. text ed. 37.00 (*0-87757-178-3*) Am Mktg.

Luschei, Glenna. Back into My Body. LC 74-10804. (Illus.). 1974. pap. 3.00 (*0-914476-30-0*) Thorp Springs.

— Matriarch Selected Poems (1968-1992) LC 92-80450. 96p. (Orig.). 1992. pap. 10.95 (*0-912292-98-9*) The Smith.

Luschen, Gunther & Sage, George, eds. Handbook of Social Science of Sport. 700p. 1981. text ed. 32.00 (*0-87563-191-6*) Stipes.

Luschen, Gunther, tr. see Schmalenbach, Herman.

Luscher, E. & Coufal, H., eds. Liquid & Amorphous Metals: Mechanics of Plastic Solids. (NATO-Advanced Study Institute Ser.). 672p. 1980. lib. bdg. 162.50 (*90-286-0680-7*) Kluwer Ac.

Luscher, E., et al, eds. Amorphous & Liquid Materials. 1987. lib. bdg. 154.50 (*90-247-3411-8*) Kluwer Ac.

Luscher, Keith F. Advertise! An Assessment of Fundamentals for Small Business. LC 90-91596. (Illus.). 140p. (Orig.). 1991. pap. 14.95 (*0-9625977-9-1*) K & L Pubns.

— Promotional Publishing: Turn Wary Prospects into Trusting Clients by Packaging Your Knowledge, Experience & Expertise. LC 94-78028. 40p. (Orig.). 1994. pap. 4.75 (*0-9625977-0-8*) K & L Pubns.

Luscher, Kurt K., et al. Early Child Care in Switzerland. (International Monographs on Early Child Care). (Illus.). 134p. 1973. text ed. 86.00 (*0-677-04930-7*) Gordon & Breach.

Luscher, Martin, ed. Phase & Caste Determination in Insects - Endocrine Aspects: Proceedings of the International Congress of Entomology, 15th, Washington, D.C., 1976. 1976. 64.00 (*0-08-021256-5*, Pub. by Pergamon Repr UK) Franklin.

Luscher, N. Decubitus Ulcers of the Pelvic Region: Diagnostics & Surgical Therapy. (Illus.). 160p. 1992. text ed. 113.00 (*0-88937-049-4*) Hogrefe & Huber Pubs.

Luscher, Robert M. John Updike: A Study of the Short Fiction. (Twayne's Studies in Short Fiction). 170p. 1993. text ed. 23.95 (*0-8057-0850-2*, Pub. by Royal Botanic Garden UK) Macmillan.

Luscher, T., et al, eds. Coronary Artery Graft Disease: Mechanism & Prevention. LC 94-16135. 1994. 99.00 (*0-387-57438-7*) Spr-Verlag.

Luscher, T. F. & Kaplan, N. M., eds. Renovascular & Renal Parenchymatous Hypertension. (Illus.). 560p. 1992. 239.00 (*0-387-53324-9*) Spr-Verlag.

Luscher, Thomas F., ed. see Ganten, Detlev & Kurokowa, Kiyoshi.

Luscher, Thomas F., jt. ed. see Vanhoutte, Paul M.

Luschnig, C. A. An Introduction to Ancient Greek. LC 86-17427. 406p. (C). 1976. pap. text ed. write for info. (*0-13-033739-0*) P-H.

— Introduction to Ancient Greek. 1984. 19.95 (*0-684-14710-6*, Scribners) S&S Trade.

— Time Holds the Mirror: A Study of Knowledge in Euripides' Hippolytus. (Mnemosyne Ser.: Supplement 102). 1988. pap. 27.50 (*90-04-08601-3*) E J Brill.

Luschnig, C. A. & Luchnig, L. J. Etymidion II: A Student's Workbook for Vocabulary Building. 2nd ed. 246p. (C). Date not set. pap. text ed. 37.50 (*0-8191-9387-9*) U Pr of Amer.

Luschnig, C. A. & Luschnig, L. J. Etyma: An Introduction to Vocabulary-Building from Latin & Greek. LC 82-45038. 346p. (Orig.). 1982. pap. text ed. 26.00 (*0-8191-2571-7*) U Pr of Amer.

— Etymidion: A Students's Workbook for Vocabulary Building from Latin & Greek. 184p. (Orig.). 1985. student ed 22.50 (*0-8191-4838-5*) U Pr of Amer.

Luschnig, L. J., jt. auth. see Luschnig, C. A.

Luscomb, Sally C. The Collector's Encyclopedia of Buttons. LC 67-27049. (Illus.). 256p. 1993. 24.95 (*0-88740-500-2*) Schiffer.

Luscombe, D. E., ed. see Abelard, Peter.

Luscombe, D. E., ed. see Knowles, David.

Luscombe, D. K., jt. ed. see Ellis, G. P.

Luscombe, Martyn. MRP II: Integrating the Business. (Illus.). 240p. 1993. 49.00 (*0-7506-1626-1*) Buttrwrth-Heinemann.

Luse, Marv. Bitmapped Graphics Programming in C Plus Plus. LC 92-38363. 1993. pap. 37.95 (*0-201-63209-8*) Addison-Wesley.

Lusebrink, Amy L. Celtic Borders, Alphabets, & Motifs. LC 93-10729. (Pictorial Archive Ser.). 1993. pap. write for info. (*0-486-27688-0*) Dover.

Lusebrink, V. B. Imagery & Visual Expression in Therapy. LC 90-6901. (Emotions, Personality, & Psychotherapy Ser.). (Illus.). 300p. 1990. 42.50 (*0-306-43453-9*, Plenum Pr) Plenum.

Lush, Jay L. Animal Breeding Plans. 451p. reprint ed. pap. 128.60 (*0-7837-1249-9*, 2041386) Bks Demand.

Lush, Jean. Emotional Phases of a Woman's Life. LC 86-33931. 1990. pap. 8.99 (*0-8007-5377-1*) Revell.

Lush, Jean & Rushford, Patricia. Emotional Phases of a Woman's Life. LC 86-33931. 1987. 12.99 (*0-8007-1529-2*) Revell.

Lush, Jean & Vredevelt, Pam. Women & Stress: A Practical Approach to Managing Tension. LC 92-11494. 1992. 14.99 (*0-8007-1675-2*) Revell.

Lush, Jean & Vredevelt, Pamela. Mothers & Sons: Raising Boys to Be Men. LC 88-18210. 224p. 1994. reprint ed. 13.99 (*0-8007-1602-7*); reprint ed. pap. 7.99 (*0-8007-5503-0*) Revell.

Lush, Minnie & Sirota, David. California Real Estate Finance. 3rd ed. LC 94-5784. 1994. pap. 36.95 (*0-7931-1043-2*, Real Estate Ed) Dearborn Finan.

Lush, Nicholas. Australia: Cadogan Guides. LC 87-32998. (Illus.). 484p. (Orig.). 1988. pap. 14.95 (*0-87106-796-X*) Globe Pequot.

Lushbough, Martin & Hood, Loretta L. Vitamins & Minerals. 1983. pap. 2.00 (*0-933904-09-6*) Gold Quill Pubs CA.

Lusher, J., jt. auth. see Novozhilov, V.

Lusher, Jeanne M., et al, eds. Factor VIII - vWF & Platelet Formation & Function in Health & Disease: A Tribute to Marion I. Barnhart. (Annals Ser.: Vol. 509). 223p. 1987. 56.00 (*0-89766-414-0*) NY Acad Sci.

Lusher, T., jt. auth. see Bolotin, V. V.

Lushing, Peter, ed. see Ezon, Jack S. & Dweck, Jeffrey S.

Lushington, Laura, jt. auth. see Halliday, Sonia.

Lushington, Laura, jt. photos see Halliday, Sonia.

Lushington, Nolan & Mills, Willis N., Jr. Libraries Designed for Users: A Planning Handbook. LC 80-24928. (Illus.). 289p. 1980. 39.50 (*0-208-01892-1*, Lib Prof Pubns) Shoe String.

Lushington, Nolan A. & Kusack, James M. The Design & Evaluation of Public Library Buildings. LC 91-8009. (Illus.). 250p. (C). 1991. lib. bdg. 39.50 (*0-208-02300-3*, Lib Prof Pubns) Shoe String.

Lusht, Kenneth M. Real Estate Mathematics - Fundamentals & Applications. 2nd ed. 1986. text ed. write for info. (*0-538-19680-7*, S68) S-W Pub.

Lusin, Natalia. Barron's Russian Grammar. 250p. (RUS.). 1992. pap., vinyl bd. 5.95 (*0-8120-4902-0*) Barron.

Lusis, A. J., jt. ed. see Sparkes, R. S.

Lusis, A. J., et al, eds. Molecular Genetics of Coronary Artery Disease: Candidate Genes & Processes in Atherosclerosis. (Monographs in Human Genetics: Vol. 14). (Illus.). xviii, 454p. 1992. 256.00 (*3-8055-5558-X*) S Karger.

Lusis, A. S. Chess: An Annotated Bibliography, 1969-1988. 350p. 1991. text ed. 100.00 (*0-7201-2079-9*, Mansell Pub) Cassell.

Lusk, David T. Within the Halls of Pilate. 1983. pap. 4.95 (*0-89137-538-4*) Quality Pubns.

Lusk, Diane & McPherson, Bruce. Nothing but the Best: Making Day Care Work for You & Your Child. 288p. 1992. pap. 12.00 (*0-688-09547-X*, Quill) Morrow.

Lusk, Dorothy T. Redactive. 64p. 1991. pap. 8.95 (*0-88922-279-7*) SPD-Small Pr Dist.

Lusk, Ewing L. & Overbeek, R., eds. Ninth International Conference on Automated Deduction. (Lecture Notes in Computer Science Ser.: Vol. 310). 775p. 1988. pap. 79.00 (*0-387-19343-X*) Spr-Verlag.

Lusk, Ewing L. & Overbeek, Ross A., eds. Logic Programming: Proceedings of the North American Conference 1989. (Logic Programming - Research Reports & Notes). 1000p. 1989. pap. 85.00x (*0-262-62064-2*) MIT Pr.

Lusk, Ewing L., et al. Portable Programs for Parallel Processors. (C). 1987. pap. text ed. 27.00 (*0-03-014404-3*) SCP.

Lusk, Graham. Nutrition. LC 75-23660. (Clio Medica Ser.: No. 10). (Illus.). reprint ed. 13.00 (*0-404-58910-3*) AMS Pr.

Lusk, Harold, jt. auth. see French, William.

Lusk, Julie T. Thirty Scripts for Relaxation, Imagery & Inner Healing. 192p. (Orig.). 1992. pap. 19.95 (*0-938586-69-6*) Whole Person.

— Thirty Scripts for Relaxation, Imagery & Inner Healing, Vol. 2. LC 92-80231. 192p. (Orig.). 1993. pap. 19.95 (*0-938586-76-9*) Whole Person.

***Lusk, Martha L.** If Butterflies Return. 220p. (Orig.). 1995. pap. 8.95 (*0-7610-0157-3*) NW Pub.

Lusk, Rodney P. Pediatric Sinusitis. 160p. 1992. 131.50 (*0-88167-894-5*, 2386) Raven.

Lusk, Wilma J. Cat's Paws & Morning Glories. 61p. (Orig.). 1985. pap. 4.95 (*0-942424-00-X*) W Anglia Pubns.

Luskacovas, Marketa, et al. Aperture, Issue 92. (Fine Photography Ser.). (Illus.). 80p. 1983. pap. 18.50 (*0-89381-128-9*) Aperture.

Luske, Bruce. Mirrors of Madness: Patroling the Psychic Border. (Social Problems & Social Issues Ser.). 143p. (Orig.). 1990. lib. bdg. 44.95 (*0-202-30422-1*); pap. 21.95 (*0-202-30423-X*) Aldine de Gruyter.

Luskey, Judith L., jt. auth. see Fleming, Paula R.

Luski, Sarah W. Cien Poesias de Sarah Wekselbaum Luski. LC 80-69466. (Coleccion Espejo de Paciencia Ser.). (Illus.). 267p. (Orig.). (SPA.). 1981. pap. 14.95 (*0-89729-272-3*) Ediciones.

Luskin, Donald L., ed. Portfolio Insurance: A Guide to Dynamic Hedging. 1988. text ed. 85.00 (*0-471-85849-8*) Wiley.

Lusky, Louis. Our Nine Tribunes. LC 92-28482. 232p. 1993. text ed. 49.95 (*0-275-94463-8*, C4463, Praeger Pubs) Greenwood.

Lusnikov, Aleksey. Soviet Thin Film Technology: From Research to Production. Nobel, Erika D., ed. (Illus.). 130p. (Orig.). 1987. pap. text ed. 75.00 (*1-55831-002-9*) Delphic Associates.

Luss, Dan & Weekman, Vern W., Jr., eds. Chemical Reaction Engineering Reviews: Houston. LC 78-8477. (ACS Symposium Ser.: No. 72). 1978. 36.95 (*0-8412-0432-2*) Am Chemical.

Luss, Dan, jt. ed. see Weekman, Vern W., Jr.

***Lussert, Anneliese.** The Christmas Visitor. Lanning, Rosemary, tr. LC 95-1642. (Illus.). (J). 1995. 14.95 (*1-55858-449-8*); lib. bdg. write for info. (*1-55858-450-1*) North-South Bks NYC.

Lusseyran, Jacques. And There Was Light. Cameron, Elizabeth R., tr. 320p. 1987. reprint ed. pap. text ed. 10.95 (*0-930407-03-2*) Parabola Bks.

— The Blind in Society & Blindness, a New Seeing of the World. Winkler, Dorothea, tr. 32p. (gr. 7-12). 1978. pap. 1.50 (*0-913098-11-6*) Myrin Institute.

Lussier, Donald E. How to Get the "L" Out of Learning: The Job Search Book That Shows You How to Turn Your Degree into Dollars. 148p. (C). 1991. pap. 12.95 (*0-9628723-0-X*) Premium Pr.

Lussier, Frances M., jt. auth. see Pinkston, Elizabeth.

Lussier, Mark & Heninger, S. K., eds. Perspective As a Problem in the Art, History & Literature of Early Modern England. LC 92-8707. (Illus.). 152p. 1992. lib. bdg. 69.95 (*0-7734-9620-3*) E Mellen.

Lussier, Robert N. Human Relations in Organizations: A Skill-Building Approach. 2nd ed. LC 92-20313. 592p. (C). 1992. text ed. 51.95 (*0-256-10532-4*) Irwin.

— Human Relations in Organizations: A Skill-Building Approach. 3rd ed. LC 95-4180. 576p. (C). 1995. 51.95 (*0-256-16207-7*) Irwin.

— Supervision: A Skill Building Approach. 528p. (C). 1989. pap. text ed. 45.95 (*0-256-06502-0*) Irwin.

— Supervision: A Skill-Building Approach. 2nd ed. LC 93-10673. 624p. (C). 1993. Acid-free paper. pap. text ed. 49.95 (*0-256-09050-5*) Irwin.

Lussier, Virginia L., jt. ed. see Wheeler, Kenneth W.

Lusson, Michelle. Creative Wellness: The Power of the Personality to Heal Self. rev. ed. LC 94-2787. 360p. 1994. pap. 11.95 (*0-9637891-2-0*) Printed Voice.

Lusson, Michelle, jt. auth. see Mella, Dorothee L.

Lussu, Emilio. An Autobiographical Account by a Leading Sardinian Republican Politician of Resistance to Fascism in Sardinia from 1918-1930: Marcia su Roma e Dintorni (The March on Rome & Thereabouts) Davis, Roy W., tr. LC 92-15142. 224p. 1992. lib. bdg. 89.95 (*0-7734-9558-4*) E Mellen.

— Enter Mussolini: Observations & Adventures of an Anti-Fascist. Rawson, Marion, tr. LC 78-63690. (Studies in Fascism: Ideology & Practice). reprint ed. 28.50 (*0-404-16952-X*) AMS Pr.

Lust, et al. New Mime in North America. (Mime Journal Ser.). (Illus.). 183p. (Orig.). 1982. pap. text ed. 12.00 (*0-9611066-8-9*) Pomona Coll.

Lust, Barbara, ed. Studies in the Acquisition of Anaphora. (C). 1987. lib. bdg. 117.00 (*1-55608-022-0*); pap. text ed. 24.00 (*0-317-67682-2*) Kluwer Ac.

— Studies in the Acquisition of Anaphoria. 1986. lib. bdg. 123.00 (*90-277-2121-1*) Kluwer Ac.

— Studies in the Acquisition of Anaphoria. 1986. pap. text ed. 47.50 (*90-277-2122-X*) Kluwer Ac.

Lust, Barbara, et al, eds. Syntactic Theory & First Language Acquisition: Cross-Linguistic Perspectives, 2 vols., Set. 1994. text ed. 125.00 (*0-8058-1575-9*) L Erlbaum Assocs.

— Syntactic Theory & First Language Acquisition Vol. 1: Cross-Linguistic Perspectives--Heads, Projections & Learnability. 376p. 1994. text ed. 79.95 (*0-8058-1351-9*) L Erlbaum Assocs.

— Syntactic Theory & First Language Acquisition Vol. 2: Cross-Linguistic Perspectives--Binding, Dependences & Learnability. 568p. 1994. text ed. 99.95 (*0-8058-1350-0*) L Erlbaum Assocs.

Lust, Benedict. About Herbs: Nature's Medicine. 1983. pap. 2.95 (*0-87904-045-9*) Lust.

— About Prostate Trouble. 1983. pap. 2.95 (*0-87904-042-4*) Lust.

— Kneipp Herbs: Regeneration thru Herbal Juices. (Illus.). 1968. pap. 0.75 (*0-87904-009-2*) Lust.

— Only Nature Cures. 1983. pap. 5.95 (*0-87904-014-9*) Lust.

— Superbath: The Blood Washing Method. (Illus.). 1982. pap. 2.00 (*0-87904-027-0*) Lust.

An Asterisk (*) at the beginning of an entry indicates that the title is appearing in BIP for the first time.

— Zone Therapy: Regeneration through Nerve Pressure. (Illus.). 1980. pap. 3.95 (*0-87904-038-6*) Lust.

Lust, D. & Theisen, S. Lectures on String Theory. (Lecture Notes in Physics Ser.: Vol. 346). vii, 346p. 1989. 43.00 (*0-387-51882-7*) Spr-Verlag.

***Lust, Herbert, 3rd.** Alexandera Finds Out. (Illus.). 32p. (J). 1995. pap. 8.00 (*0-8059-3607-6*) Dorrance.

Lust, Herbert. Violence & Defiance. LC 83-81847. 184p. (Orig.). 1984. 12.95 (*0-930794-91-5*); pap. 5.95 (*0-930794-90-7*) Station Hill Pr.

Lust, Herbert C. Giacometti (Alberto) The Complete Graphics. rev. ed. (Illus.). 240p. 1991. 150.00 (*1-55660-093-3*) A Wofsy Fine Arts.

Lust, John. Western Books on China Published up to 1850. (Illus.). 352p. 1987. 67.50 (*1-870076-02-8*, Pub. by Bamboo Pub UK) Antique Collect.

Lust, John, ed. The Herb Book. 672p. 1983. mass mkt. 6.99 (*0-553-26770-1*) Bantam.

Lust, John & Tierra, Michael. The Natural Remedy Bible: Everyone's Guide to the Natural of Healing. McCarthy, Paul, ed. 448p. 1990. reprint ed. pap. 6.99 (*0-671-66127-2*) PB.

Lust, John, jt. auth. see Scott, Cyril.

Lust, John B. About Diabetes & the Diet. pap. 2.95 (*0-87904-046-7*) Lust.

— About Raw Juices. 1982. pap. 2.95 (*0-87904-047-5*) Lust.

— The Complete Massage Book. (Illus.). 1982. 15.95 (*0-87904-021-1*) Lust.

— Drink Your Troubles Away: Raw Juice Therapy. LC 66-28198. 1981. pap. 4.95 (*0-87904-006-8*) Lust.

— The Herb Book. LC 74-75368. (Illus.). 640p. 1974. 19.95 (*0-87904-007-6*); pap. 5.95 (*0-685-57752-X*) Lust.

— Kneipp's My Water Cure. 1978. 15.95 (*0-87904-022-X*) Lust.

— Lust for Living. 1982. 12.95 (*0-87904-036-X*) Lust.

— Raw Juice Therapy. 1982. 5.95 (*0-87904-026-2*) Lust.

— The Royal Jelly Miracle. 1981. pap. 1.95 (*0-87904-023-8*) Lust.

Lust, Patricia, comp. American Vocal Chamber Music, 1945-1980: An Annotated Bibliography. LC 84-25212. (Music Reference Collection Ser.: No. 4). (Illus.). xvi, 273p. 1985. text ed. 49.95 (*0-313-24599-1*, LUC/, Greenwood Pr) Greenwood.

Lust, Peter. The Last Seal Pup: The Story of Canada's Seal Hunt. LC 67-21282. 152p. reprint ed. pap. 43.40 (*0-317-28424-X*, 2022309) Bks Demand.

— Two Germanies. LC 66-23304. 237p. reprint ed. pap. 67.60 (*0-8357-6441-9*, 2035812) Bks Demand.

***Lustbader.** Floating City. (Illus.). (J). 1995. mass mkt. 5.99 (*0-671-86809-8*) PB.

Lustbader, Eric. Black Blade. 1994. mass mkt. 5.99 (*0-449-22287-X*, Crest) Fawcett.

— The Kaisho. Zion, Claire, ed. 576p. 1994. reprint ed. pap. 6.50 (*0-671-86807-1*, Pocket Star Bks) PB.

— Second Skin: A Nicholas Linnear Novel. Zion, Claire, ed. 464p. 1995. 22.00 (*0-671-86810-1*) PB.

Lustbader, Eric V. Angel Eyes. 1992. mass mkt. 5.99 (*0-449-21852-X*, Crest) Fawcett.

— Beneath an Opal Moon: Book Four of the Sunset Warrior Cycle. 272p. 1990. pap. 3.95 (*0-449-21649-7*, Crest) Fawcett.

— Dai-San. (Sunset Warrior Cycle Ser.: Bk. 3). 256p. 1989. pap. 5.99 (*0-449-21648-9*, Crest) Fawcett.

— French Kiss. 510p. 1989. mass mkt. 5.95 (*0-449-21849-X*, Crest) Fawcett.

— White Ninja. 1991. mass mkt. 5.95 (*0-449-21851-1*, Crest) Fawcett.

Lustbader, Joyce W., et al. Glycoprotein Hormone. LC 93-33014. 1994. 125.00 (*0-387-94165-7*) Spr-Verlag.

Lustbader, Wendy. Counting on Kindness: An Exploration of Dependency. 160p. 1991. text ed. 18.95 (*0-02-919515-2*) Free Pr.

Lustbader, Wendy & Hooyman, Nancy R. Taking Care of Aging Family Members: A Practical Guide. enl. rev. ed. LC 93-24322. 322p. 1993. pap. 14.95 (*0-02-919518-7*) Free Pr.

— Taking Care of Aging Family Members: A Practical Guide. 2nd enl. rev. ed. LC 93-24322. 322p. 1993. text ed. 22.95 (*0-02-919517-9*) Free Pr.

Lustburg, Lynn, ed. see Morgan, Diane, et al.

Lusted, David, ed. The Media Studies Book: A Guide for Teachers. (Comedia Bk.). 242p. 1990. text ed. 45.00 (*0-415-01461-1*); pap. text ed. 14.95 (*0-415-01460-3*) Routledge.

Luster, Bill, photos. University of Kentucky - Then & Now. (Illus.). 112p. 1993. 39.95 (*1-56469-004-0*) Harmony Hse Pub LO.

Luster-Gillis, Melodye, ed. see Hermann, Richard L. & Sutherland, Linda P.

Luster, Helen. Crystal, Bk. VII. 1980. pap. 5.00 (*0-686-28713-4*) Man-Root.

— I(EE) Book of Rose. 1988. 2.50 (*0-318-41317-5*) Man-Root.

Luster, Robert E. The Amelioration of the Slaves in the British Empire, 1790-1833. LC 92-27278. (American University Studies: History: Ser. IX, Vol. 134). 1994. write for info. (*0-8204-2068-9*) P Lang Pubs.

Luster, Tom & Okagaki, Lynn, eds. Parenting: An Ecological Perspective. 272p. 1992. text ed. 59.95 (*0-8058-0792-6*); pap. 29.95 (*0-8058-0857-4*) L Erlbaum Assocs.

***Lusterbader, Eric.** Batman: The Last Angel. O'Neil, D., ed. 96p. 1994. pap. 12.95 (*1-56389-156-5*) DC Comics.

Lusterman, Seymour. The Organization & Staffing of Corporate Public Affairs. (Report Ser.: No. 894). (Illus.). v, 31p. (Orig.). 1987. pap. text ed. 60.00 (*0-8237-0336-3*) Conference Bd.

Lusternik, L. A. & Sobolev, V. J. Elements of Functional Analysis. (Russian Monographs). (Illus.). 428p. 1962. text ed. 162.00 (*0-677-20270-9*) Gordon & Breach.

Lustgarten, Edgar. One More Unfortunate. LC 80-17167. 202p. 1980. 18.95 (*0-8398-2651-6*) Boulevard.

Lustgarten, K. Complete Guide to Touch Dancing. (Ballroom Dance Ser.). 1986. lib. bdg. 79.95 (*0-8490-3315-2*) Gordon Pr.

— Complete Guide to Touch Dancing. (Ballroom Dance Ser.). 1985. lib. bdg. 69.95 (*0-87700-818-3*) Revisionist Pr.

Lustgarten, Kevin & Gutmann, Steve. Now Hiring! Outdoor Jobs: The Insider's Guide to Gaining Seasonal & Year-round Employment in America's National Parks & Forests. Veith, Elliot, ed. (Illus.). 320p. (Orig.). (C). 1993. pap. 17.95 (*1-881199-50-9*, Perpetual Pr) Progress Media.

Lustgarten, Laurence & Leigh, Ian. In from the Cold: National Security & Parliamentary Democracy. 550p. 1994. 38.00 (*0-19-825234-X*) OUP.

Lustgarten, Steven. Productivity & Prices: The Consequences of Industrial Concentration. LC 83-17133. (AEI Studies: No. 392). (Illus.). 62p. reprint ed. pap. 25.00 (*0-8357-4526-0*, 2037390) Bks Demand.

Lustick, Ian. Arabs in the Jewish State: Israel's Control of a National Minority. LC 79-22311. (Modern Middle East Ser.: No. 6). (Illus.). 399p. reprint ed. pap. 113.80 (*0-7837-1105-0*, 2041634) Bks Demand.

— Israel & Jordan: The Implications of an Adversarial Partnership. LC 78-620041. (Policy Papers in International Affairs Ser.: No. 6). (Illus.). 1978. pap. 2.00 (*0-87725-506-7*) U of Cal IAS.

— State-Building Failure in British Ireland & French Algeria. LC 85-19763. (Research Ser.: No. 63). x, 109p. 1985. pap. 8.95 (*0-87725-163-0*) U of Cal IAS.

Lustick, Ian, ed. The Conflict with the Arabs in Israeli Politics & Society. LC 93-51015. (Arab-Israeli Relations Ser.: Vol. 7). 384p. 1994. 62.00 (*0-8153-1587-2*) Garland.

Lustick, Ian, intro. From War to War: Israel vs. the Arabs, 1948-1967. LC 93-50084. (Arab-Israeli Relations Ser.: Vol. 3). 336p. 1994. 56.00 (*0-8153-1583-X*) Garland.

Lustick, Ian S. For the Land & the Lord: Jewish Fundamentalism in Israel. 256p. 1988. pap. 11.95 (*0-87609-036-6*) Coun Foreign.

— Unsettled States, Disputed Lands: Britain & Ireland, France & Algeria, Israel & the West Bank/Gaza. (Wilder House Series in Politics, History, & Culture). (Illus.). 592p. 1993. 37.50 (*0-8014-2840-8*) Cornell U Pr.

— Unsettled States, Disputed Lands: Britain & Ireland, France & Algeria, Israel & the West Bank/Gaza. (Wilder House Ser.). (Illus.). 592p. 1995. pap. 19.95x (*0-8014-8088-4*) Cornell U Pr.

Lustick, Ian S., ed. Arab-Israeli Relations: Historical Background & Origins of the Conflict. LC 93-50089. 424p. 1994. reprint ed. 66.00 (*0-8153-1581-3*) Garland.

— Arab-Israeli Relations in World Politics, Vol. 10. LC 93-49876. 360p. 1994. reprint ed. 59.00 (*0-8153-1590-2*) Garland.

— Books on Israel, Vol. I. LC 87-26763. 111p. (C). 1988. 49.50 (*0-88706-776-X*); pap. 16.95 (*0-88706-777-8*) State U NY Pr.

— The Conflict with Israel in Arab Politics & Society. LC 93-50083. (Arab-Israeli Relations Ser.: Vol. 8). 408p. 1994. reprint ed. 64.00 (*0-8153-1588-0*) Garland.

— Economic, Legal, & Demographic Dimensions of Arab-Israeli Relations. LC 93-49091. (Arab-Israeli Relations Ser.: Vol. 6). 368p. 1994. reprint ed. 60.00 (*0-8153-1586-4*) Garland.

— From Wars Toward Peace in the Arab-Israeli Conflict, 1969-1993. LC 93-48175. (Arab-Israeli Relations Ser.: Vol. 4). (Illus.). 376p. 1994. reprint ed. 61.00 (*0-8153-1584-8*) Garland.

— Palestinians under Israeli Rule. LC 93-51256. (Arab-Israeli Relations Ser.: Vol. 9). 352p. 1994. reprint ed. 58.00 (*0-8153-1589-9*) Garland.

— Religion, Culture, & Psychology in Arab-Israeli Relations. LC 93-48221. (Arab-Israeli Relations Ser.: Vol. 5). (Illus.). 416p. 1994. reprint ed. 68.00 (*0-8153-1585-6*) Garland.

— Triumph & Catastrophe: The War of 1948, Israeli Independence, & the Refugee Problem. LC 93-50088. (Arab-Israeli Relations Ser.: Vol. 2). (Illus.). 384p. 1994. reprint ed. 62.00 (*0-8153-1582-1*) Garland.

Lustick, Ian S. & Rubin, Barry, eds. Critical Essays on Israeli Society, Politics, & Culture: Books on Israel, Vol. II. LC 90-10055. (SUNY Series in Israeli Studies). 205p. 1991. 49.50 (*0-7914-0646-6*); pap. 16.95 (*0-7914-0647-4*) State U NY Pr.

Lustick, Sheldon I., jt. ed. see Aspey, Wayne P.

***Lustig.** Children of the Holocaust. 1995. pap. text ed. (*0-8101-1279-5*) Northwestern U Pr.

Lustig, Arnold. Darkness Casts No Shadow. 173p. 1985. pap. 9.95 (*0-8101-0704-X*) Northwestern U Pr.

Lustig, Arnost. Diamonds of the Night. rev. ed. 287p. 1986. reprint ed. pap. 15.95 (*0-8101-0706-6*) Northwestern U Pr.

— Dita Saxova. 320p. 1994. 49.95 (*0-8101-1131-4*); pap. 17.95 (*0-8101-1132-2*) Northwestern U Pr.

— Indecent Dreams. Urwin-Levit, Iris et al, trs. 159p. 1990. pap. 9.95 (*0-8101-0909-3*) Northwestern U Pr.

— Night & Hope. Theiner, George, tr. 219p. 1985. reprint ed. pap. 9.95 (*0-8101-0702-3*) Northwestern U Pr.

— A Prayer for Katerina Horovitzova. Nemcova, Jeanne, tr. LC 84-25593. 176p. 1987. 15.95 (*0-87951-998-3*); pap. 9.95 (*0-87951-223-7*) Overlook Pr.

— Street of Lost Brothers. 207p. (Orig.). 1990. 32.95 (*0-8101-0959-X*); pap. 12.95 (*0-8101-0960-3*) Northwestern U Pr.

Lustig, B. Andrew, ed. Bioethics Yearbook Vol. 1: Theological Developments in Bioethics, 1988-1990. 232p. (C). 1991. lib. bdg. 119.50 (*0-7923-1280-5*) Kluwer Ac.

— Bioethics Yearbook Vol. 2: Regional Developments in Bioethics: 1989-1991. 448p. (C). 1992. lib. bdg. 175.00 (*0-7923-1893-5*) Kluwer Ac.

Lustig, B. Andrew, jt. ed. see Campbell, Courtney S.

Lustig, David A., jt. auth. see Silverman, Marvin.

Lustig, David C. Railroads. 1990. 17.99 (*0-517-68849-2*) Random Hse Value.

Lustig, Esther, jt. auth. see Lustig, Michael.

***Lustig, Irma S., ed.** Boswell: Citizen of the World, Man of Letters. 288p. 1995. text ed. 37.50 (*0-8131-1910-3*) U Pr of Ky.

Lustig, Joel W., ed. The National Directory of Corporate Distress Specialists: A Comprehensive Guide to Firms & Professionals Providing Services in Bankruptcies, Workouts, Turnarounds & Distressed Investments. 720p. 1992. 99.00 (*0-9630173-0-6*) Lustig Data Res.

Lustig, Loretta, illus. The Pop-Up Book of the Circus. LC 78-68789. (Pop-Up Bks.: No. 37). (J). (ps-3). 1979. 8.99 (*0-394-84134-4*) Random Bks Yng Read.

— The Pop-up Book of Trucks. LC 73-19318. (Pop-Up Bks.). (J). (ps-2). 1974. 8.99 (*0-394-82826-7*) Random Bks Yng Read.

— The Three Billy Goats Gruff. (Children's Classics Ser.). (J). 1991. 6.95 (*0-8362-4913-5*) Andrews & McMeel.

Lustig, Mary L. Privilege & Prerogative: New York's Provincial Elite, 1710-1776. LC 93-51010. (C). 1994. write for info. (*0-8386-3554-7*) Fairleigh Dickinson.

— Robert Hunter, Sixteen Sixty-Six to Seventeen Thirty-Four: New York's Augustan Statesman. LC 83-4750. (New York State Bks.). (Illus.). 312p. 1983. text ed. 39.95x (*0-8156-2296-1*) Syracuse U Pr.

Lustig, Mary L., jt. ed. see Prince, Carl E.

Lustig, Mary L., et al, eds. The Papers of William Livingston: Guide to the Microfilm Edition. 205p. 1986. 20.00 (*0-8357-0723-7*) Univ Microfilms.

Lustig, Michael & Lustig, Esther. Willy Whyner, Cloud Designer. LC 93-21957. (Illus.). 40p. (J). (gr. k up). 1994. text ed. 14.95 (*0-02-761365-8*, Four Winds Pr) S&S Childrens.

***Lustig, Myron W. & Koester, Jolena.** Intercultural Competence: Interpersonal Communication Across Cultures. 2nd ed. LC 94-45056. (C). 1995. write for info. (*0-673-99710-3*) HarpCollege.

Lustig, Myron W. & Koester, Jolene. Intercultural Competence: Interpersonal Communication Across Cultures. LC 92-18628. (C). 1992. 32.00 (*0-06-044129-1*) HarpCollege.

Lustig, Nora. Mexico: The Remaking of an Economy. 224p. (C). 1992. 28.95 (*0-8157-5314-4*); pap. 11.95 (*0-8157-5313-6*) Brookings.

Lustig, Nora, ed. Coping with Austerity: Poverty & Inequality in Latin America. 350p. (C). Date not set. 39.95 (*0-8157-5318-7*); pap. 18.95 (*0-8157-5317-9*) Brookings.

Lustig, Nora, et al, eds. North American Free Trade: Assessing the Impact. 288p. (C). 1992. 31.95 (*0-8157-5316-0*); pap. 12.95 (*0-8157-5315-2*) Brookings.

Lustig, R. J. Corporate Liberalism: The Origins of Modern American Political Theory, 1890-1920. LC 81-16376. 350p. (C). 1982. pap. 15.00 (*0-520-05894-1*) U CA Pr.

Lustig, Roger, tr. see Dahlhaus, Carl.

Lustig, T. J. Henry James & the Ghostly. 341p. (C). 1995. 54.95 (*0-521-45378-X*) Cambridge U Pr.

Lustig, Theodore S., jt. auth. see Bledsoe, John D.

Lustig, Tim, ed. see James, Henry.

Lustiger, Jean-Marie. Dare to Live. 164p. (C). 1990. 49.00 (*0-85439-276-9*, Pub. by St Paul Pubns UK) St Mut.

— The Lord's Prayer. Balinski, Rebecca H., tr. LC 87-62880. 159p. (Orig.). 1988. 9.95 (*0-87973-497-3*, 497); pap. 3.95 (*0-87973-493-0*, 493) Our Sunday Visitor.

Lustiger, Jean-Marie C. Dare to Live. 192p. 1988. 15.95 (*0-8245-0873-4*) Crossroad NY.

Lustigman, Michael M. Kindness of Truth & the Art of Reading Ashes. (American University Studies: History: Ser. IX, Vol. 38). 146p. (C). 1988. text ed. 27.50 (*0-8204-0672-4*) P Lang Pubs.

Lustman, Francois. Managing Computer Projects. 400p. (C). 1987. text ed. 33.33 (*0-317-60112-1*) P-H.

***Lustrup, Karen.** Pluto: Transforming the New You. 1995. pap. 10.00 (*0-86690-448-4*) Am Fed Astrologers.

Lusty, ed. Handbook of Nucleobase Complexes, Vol. I. 1990. 130.95 (*0-8493-3281-8*, QP625) CRC Pr.

Lusty, James R., et al. Handbook of Nucleobase Complexes: Transition Metal Complexes of the Naturally Occurring Nucleobases & Their Derivatives, Vol. II. (Illus.). 512p. 1991. 212.95 (*0-8493-3282-6*, QP625) CRC Pr.

Lusty, Tim & Diskett, Pat. Selective Feeding Programmes. 96p. (C). 1984. pap. text ed. 21.00 (*0-85598-094-X*, Pub. by Oxfam Pubns UK) St Mut.

Lusty, Tim, jt. auth. see Shears, Paul.

Lustzig, George. Introduction to Quantum Groups. LC 93-7800. (Progress in Mathematics Ser.: Vol. 110). xii, 346p. 1994. Acid-free paper. 49.50 (*0-8176-3712-5*) Birkhauser.

Luszcz, M. & Nettelbeck, T., eds. Psychological Development: Perspectives Across the Life-Span, Vol. 7: Proceedings of the 24th International Congress of Psychology of the International Union of Psychological Science, Sydney, Australia, Aug. 28-Sept. 2, 1988. 380p. 1990. 89.75 (*0-444-88525-0*, North Holland) Elsevier.

Luszki. Psych Yourself to Better Tennis. 1978. pap. 2.00 (*0-87980-246-4*) Wilshire.

Luszki, Walter A. A Rape of Justice: MacArthur & the New Guinea Hangings. 196p. (C). 1991. 24.95 (*0-8191-8348-2*) Madison Bks UPA.

Lusztig, George. Characters of Reductive Groups Over a Finite Field. LC 83-43083. (Annals of Mathematics Studies: Vol. 107). 495p. 1984. 69.50 (*0-691-08350-9*); pap. 29.95 (*0-691-08351-7*) Princeton U Pr.

— The Discrete Series Representations of the General Linear Groups Over a Finite Field. (Annals of Mathematics Studies: Vol. 1). 150p. 1974. 19.95 (*0-691-08154-9*) Princeton U Pr.

— Introduction to Quantum Groups. LC 93-7800. (Progress in Mathematics Ser.: Vol. 110). 341p. 1993. 49.50 (*3-7643-3712-5*) Birkhauser.

— Representations of Finite Chevalley Groups. LC 78-24068. (CBMS Regional Conference Series in Mathematics: Vol. 39). 48p. 1990. reprint ed. 19.00 (*0-8218-1689-6*, CBMS/39C) Am Math.

Lutemaker, Einar, pseud., ed. Scientiae Draconis Project Book. (Illus.). (Orig.). 1989. pap. 2.00 (*0-685-34696-X*) Rose & Nefr Pr.

Luten, Robert C., ed. Problems in Pediatric Emergency Medicine. (Contemporary Issues in Emergency Medicine Ser.: Vol. 1). (Illus.). 296p. 1988. text ed. 43.50 (*0-443-08579-X*) Churchill.

Luten, Susan B. California Civil Litigation. 2nd ed. Hannan, ed. LC 92-24750. 420p. (C). 1993. pap. text ed. 35.50 (*0-314-01031-9*) West Pub.

Lutenegger, Benedict, tr. see Rios, Eduardo E.

***Luter, A. Boyd & Davis, Barry C.** God Behind the Seen: Expositions of the Books of Ruth & Esther. (Expositor's Guide to the Historical Bks.). 352p. (Orig.). 1995. pap. 16.99 (*0-8010-9000-8*) Baker Bk.

Luter, Boyd. Looking Back, Moving On. LC 92-42570. 192p. (Orig.). 1993. pap. 10.00 (*0-89109-720-1*) NavPress.

Luter, Boyd & McReynolds, Kathy. Truthful Living: What Christianity Really Teaches about Recovery. LC 94-29018. 200p. (Orig.). 1994. pap. 10.99 (*0-8010-5692-6*) Baker Bk.

Luter, James, Jr., jt. auth. see Modisett, Noah F.

Luter, James G. Pronunciation of Standard American English. 131p. (Orig.). (C). 1988. pap. text ed. 10.50 (*0-939085-00-3*) Garrett.

Luterbacher, Urs, jt. ed. see Intriligator, Michael D.

Luterman, David. Counseling Parents of Hearing-Impaired Children. 1979. text ed. 15.00 (*0-316-53750-0*, Little Med Div) Little.

— Counseling the Communicatively Disordered & Their Families. 2nd ed. LC 90-45168. 187p. (C). 1991. pap. text ed. 25.00 (*0-89079-414-6*, 1585) PRO-ED.

— In the Shadows: Living & Coping with a Loved Ones Chronic Illness. 1995. pap. write for info. (*0-9644862-0-2*) Jade Pr.

Luterman, David M. & Ross, Mark. When Your Child Is Deaf: A Guide for Parents. LC 91-3239. (Illus.). 182p. 1991. pap. text ed. 19.95 (*0-912752-27-0*) York Pr.

Lutes, Chris. Lo Que Dicen los Adolescentes-Drogas-Alcohol (What Teenagers Are Saying about Drugs & Alcohol) (SPA.). 1992. 6.99 (*1-56063-088-4*, 490236) Editorial Unilit.

Lutes, Della T. The Country Kitchen. (American Biography Ser.). 264p. 1991. reprint ed. lib. bdg. 69.00 (*0-7812-8254-3*) Rprt Serv.

— The Country Kitchen. LC 92-26831. (Great Lakes Bks.). 269p. (C). 1992. reprint ed. pap. text ed. 14.95 (*0-8143-2438-X*, Great Lks Bks) Wayne St U Pr.

Lutes, Loren D. & Niedzwecki, John M., eds. Engineering Mechanics: Proceedings of the Ninth Conference. LC 92-8712. 1112p. 1992. pap. text ed. 89.00 (*0-87262-867-1*) Am Soc Civil Eng.

Lutes, Margaret D., ed. Excerpts from the Diaries of Rev. Robert Dilworth & Blacksmith Dilworth. 11p. 1989. pap. 5.00 (*0-933227-73-6*) Closson Pr.

Lutes, W. John. Cunningham Gambit. 236p. (Orig.). 1990. pap. 12.95 (*0-945470-00-2*) Chess Ent Inc.

***Luteyn, J., et al.** Ericaceae Pt. 2. (Flora Neotropica Monograph Ser.: No. 66). (Illus.). 1995. 85.00 (*0-614-02539-7*); pap. 85.00 (*0-89327-389-9*) NY Botanical.

Luteyn, James, jt. ed. see Balslev, Henrik.

Luteyn, James L. Ericaceae: Cavendishia, Pt. 1. LC 82-24611. (Flora Neotropica Monograph Ser.: No. 35). (Illus.). 290p. (Orig.). 1983. pap. 41.00 (*0-89327-247-7*) NY Botanical.

— A Revision of the Mexican-Central American Species of Cavendishia (Vacciniaceae) LC 66-6394. (Memoirs Ser.: Vol. 28, No. 3). (Illus.). 138p. 1976. pap. 19.00 (*0-89327-011-3*) NY Botanical.

Luteyn, James L. & O'Brien, Mary E., eds. Contributions Toward a Classification of Rhododendron. LC 79-27378. (Illus.). 330p. 1980. pap. 22.00 (*0-89327-221-3*) NY Botanical.

Lutfalla, Michel, jt. auth. see Patat, Jean-Pierre.

Lutfiyya, Abdulla H. Readings in Arab Middle Eastern Societies & Cultures. Churchill, Charles W., ed. LC 69-19116. (Orig.). 1970. pap. text ed. 38.50 (*90-279-1062-6*) Mouton.

Lutfiyya, M. Nawal. The Social Construction of Context Through Play. 238p. (Orig.). 1987. lib. bdg. 46.00 (*0-8191-6134-9*); pap. text ed. 23.00 (*0-8191-6135-7*) U Pr of Amer.

Lutfiyya, Zana M., ed. see Taylor, Steven J., et al.

Lutfy, Michael. Hot Wheels Race Team. (Play Set Ser.). (Illus.). 24p. (J). (gr. 1 up). 1993. 7.95 (*0-8431-3472-0*, Troubador) Price Stern.

Lutfy, Michael, ed. see Edwards, John.

Lutgendorf, Philip. The Life of a Text: Performing the "Ramcaritmanas of Tulsidas" (Illus.). 450p. 1990. 48.00 (*0-520-06690-1*) U CA Pr.

Lutgendorf, Philip & James, Shirley M. The Parts of Speech. LC 77-730079. (Illus.). (J). (gr. 7-9). 1976. student ed, digital audio 219.00 (*0-89290-118-7*, A134-SATC) Soc for Visual.

Lutgens, Frederick K. Essentials of Geology. 4th ed. (Illus.). 464p. (C). 1992. pap. write for info. (*0-02-372830-2*) Macmillan.

Lutgens, Frederick K. & Tarbuck, Edward J. The Atmosphere: An Introduction to Meteorology. 6th ed. LC 94-18573. 1994. text ed. write for info. (*0-13-350612-6*) P-H.

— Essentials of Geology. 5th ed. LC 94-26725. (Illus.). 464p. (C). 1994. pap. text ed. write for info. (*0-02-372840-X*, Merrill Pub Co) Macmillan.

Lutgens, Frederick K., jt. auth. see Tarbuck, Edward J.

Luth, Hans. Surfaces & Interfaces of Solids. LC 92-28267. (Surface Sciences Ser.: Vol. 15). 1993. 89.00 (*0-387-52681-1*) Spr-Verlag.

— Surfaces & Interfaces of Solids. 2nd ed. LC 93-32523. (Illus.). 500p. 1993. 64.50 (*0-387-56840-9*) Spr-Verlag.

Luth, Hans, jt. auth. see Ibach, Harald.

Luth, Paul. Woerterbuch zur Medizinischen Soziologie. 408p. (GER.). 1980. 79.95 (*0-8288-2362-6*, M15305) Fr & Eur.

Luth, Sophie A. The Special Princess. (Illus.). 36p. (J). 1990. 5.95 (*0-9626153-0-7*) Luth & Assocs.

Luthans, Fred. Organizational Behavior. 4th ed. LC 84-17189. (Management Ser.). 704p. 1985. Instr's. man. teacher ed write for info. (*0-07-039150-5*) McGraw.

— Organizational Behavior. 6th ed. 1992. text ed. write for info. (*0-07-039166-1*) McGraw.

— Organizational Behavior. 7th ed. 1994. text ed. 46.50 (*0-07-039180-7*) McGraw.

Luthans, Fred & Hodgetts, Richard M. Business. 2nd ed. LC 91-11117. 651p. (C). 1992. text ed. 50.00 (*0-03-054624-9*) Dryden Pr.

— Business. 2nd ed. 864p. 1993. pap. text ed. 29.50 (*0-03-097378-3*) Dryden Pr.

— Social Issues in Business: Strategy & Public Policy Perspectives. 6th rev. ed. 672p. (C). 1990. text ed. write for info. (*0-02-372971-6*) Macmillan.

Luthans, Fred, jt. auth. see Hodgetts, Richard M.

***Luthardt, Klaus.** When Love Had a Face. LC 90-62547. 1995. write for info. (*0-943512-31-X*) Linwood Pub.

Luther, jt. auth. see Lewis.

Luther, Arch C. Authoring Interactive Multimedia. (Illus.). 298p. 1994. cd-rom, pap. 49.95 (*0-12-460430-7*, AP Prof) Acad Pr.

— Digital Video in the PC Environment. 2nd ed. 370p. 1991. pap. text ed. 29.95 (*0-07-039179-3*) McGraw.

— Digital Video in the PC Environment: Featuring DVI Technology. 2nd ed. (Illus.). 370p. (C). 1991. text ed. 29.95 (*0-07-039176-9*); pap. text ed. 32.95 (*0-07-039177-7*) McGraw.

— Using Digital Video. (Illus.). 320p. 1994. pap. text ed. 34.95 (*0-12-460432-3*, AP Prof) Acad Pr.

Luther, Bernard J., jt. auth. see Bois, Thomas J., II.

Luther, Bertha K., jt. auth. see Luther, Leslie L.

Luther Bible Society Revision Committee Staff, tr. see Giessler, Phillip B., ed.

Luther, Brenda, jt. auth. see Lewis, Joanna.

Luther-Davies, B., tr. see Basov, N. G., et al.

Luther, Donald J. Preparing for Marriage: A Guide for Christian Couples. 72p. 1992. pap. 5.99 (*0-8066-2569-4*, 9-2569) Augsburg Fortress.

Luther, Edward T. Our Restless Earth: The Geologic Regions of Tennessee. LC 77-21433. (Tennessee Three Star Ser.). (Illus.). 106p. 1977. pap. 4.95 (*0-87049-230-6*) U of Tenn Pr.

Luther, Ernest W. Ethiopia Today. LC 58-7842. 171p. reprint ed. pap. 48.80 (*0-317-11033-0*, 2000573) Bks Demand.

***Luther-Heyeckhaus, Freda.** Songs - In Memoriam. 42p. 1995. spiral bd. 34.95 (*0-9615847-2-6*) Marwolf Pub.

Luther, Johannes. Die Titeleinfassungen der Reformationszeit, 3 pts. in 1. 20p. 1973. reprint ed. write for info. (*3-487-04662-8*, Pub. by Georg Olms GW) Lubrecht & Cramer.

Luther, Judith. For the Working Artist: A Survival Guide for Performing, Visual & Media Artists Who Choose to Manage Their Own Careers. 2nd rev. ed. 338p. 1991. pap. 30.00 (*0-685-39993-1*) NNAP.

Luther, Kem. Cottonwood Roots. LC 92-44167. (Illus.). xii, 152p. 1993. 20.00 (*0-8032-2906-2*) U of Nebr Pr.

Luther, Kurt R. & Muller, Wolfgang C., eds. Politics in Austria: Still a Case for Consociationalism. 232p. 1992. text ed. 29.50 (*0-7146-3461-1*, Pub. by F Cass Pubs UK) Intl Spec Bk.

Luther, Leslie L. & Luther, Bertha K. A Complete Name Index of the Biographical Review of Cayuga County, NY: 1894. 1977. 10.50 (*0-932334-00-8*, NY06009) Hrt of the Lakes.

Luther, Luana, ed. see Abney, Don.

Luther, Luana, ed. see Ackerman, Lowell.

Luther, Luana, ed. see Bennett, William A.

Luther, Luana, ed. see Craige, Patricia V.

Luther, Luana, ed. see Daniels, Julie.

Luther, Luana, ed. see Grossman, Alvin.

Luther, Luana, ed. see Grossman, Alvin & Grossman, Beverly.

Luther, Luana, ed. see Martin, Nancy A.

Luther, Luana, ed. see McDaniel, Jack & McDaniel, Colleen.

Luther, Luana, ed. see Palika, Liz.

Luther, Luana, ed. see Ross, Nina P.

Luther, Luana, ed. see Smith, Sally Ann.

Luther, Luana, ed. see Strand, Rod & Strand, Patti.

Luther, Luana, ed. see Van Goron Kline, David & Hoffman, Patricia B.

Luther, Luana, ed. see White, Joseph J.

***Luther, Martin.** Basic Luther. LC 95-60058. 1995. pap. 12.95 (*0-87243-213-0*) Templegate.

— Christian Liberty. Grimm, Harold J., ed. Lambert, W. A., tr. 1943. pap. 3.50 (*0-8006-0182-3*, 1-182, Fortress Pr) Augsburg Fortress.

— Commentary on Galatians. LC 78-59151. 408p. 1987. pap. 14.99 (*0-8254-3124-7*) Kregel.

— Commentary on Galatians: Modern-English Edition. 416p. 1994. 21.99 (*0-8007-1702-3*) Revell.

— Commentary on Peter & Jude. LC 82-4652. 304p. 1982. pap. 10.99 (*0-8254-3147-6*) Kregel.

— Commentary on Romans. Mueller, J. Theodore, tr. LC 76-12077. Orig. Title: Commentary on the Epistle to the Romans. 224p. 1976. pap. 10.99 (*0-8254-3119-0*) Kregel.

— Daily Readings from Luther's Writings. LC 93-14902. 336p. 1993. pap. 19.99 (*0-8066-2639-9*, 9-2639) Augsburg Fortress.

— Daily Readings with Martin Luther. Atkinson, James, ed. 1987. pap. 4.95 (*0-87243-157-6*) Templegate.

— Day by Day We Magnify Thee. LC 82-2481. 448p. 1982. pap. 16.00 (*0-8006-1637-5*, 1-1637, Fortress Pr) Augsburg Fortress.

— The Essential Luther: A Reader on Scripture, Redemption, & Society. Robbins, Jerry K., ed. LC 91-30764. 112p. (Orig.). 1991. pap. 6.99 (*0-8010-7759-1*) Baker Bk.

— The Jews & Their Lies. 1982. lib. bdg. 250.00 (*0-87700-378-5*) Revisionist Pr.

— Luther's Large Catechism. 106p. text ed. 12.00 (*0-8006-0885-2*, 1-885, Fortress Pr) Augsburg Fortress.

— Luther's Ninety-Five Theses. Jacobs, C. M., tr. 1957. pap. 2.50 (*0-8006-1265-5*, 1-1265, Fortress Pr) Augsburg Fortress.

— Luthers Werke, 4 vols., Set. 1920p. (GER.). 1982. pap. 113.85 (*3-11-008942-4*) De Gruyter.

— Luther's Works, Vol. 12 Psalms. LC 55-9893. 1955. 19.95 (*0-570-06412-0*, 15-1754) Concordia.

— Luther's Works, Vol. 14 Selected Psalms 3. LC 55-9893. 1958. 19.95 (*0-570-06414-7*, 15-1756) Concordia.

— Luther's Works, Vol. 17. Bouman, Herbert J., tr. LC 55-9893. 1972. 19.95 (*0-570-06417-1*, 15-1759) Concordia.

— Luther's Works, Vol. 28. LC 55-9893. 1973. 19.95 (*0-570-06428-7*, 15-1770) Concordia.

— Luther's Works: Catholic Epistles, Vol. 30. Pelikan, Jaroslav, ed. LC 55-9893. 1967. 19.95 (*0-570-06430-9*, 15-1772) Concordia.

— Luther's Works: Lectures on Romans Glosses & Scholia, Vol. 25. LC 55-9893. (Luther's Works). 1972. 19.95 (*0-570-06425-2*, 15-1767) Concordia.

— Luther's Works: Selected Psalms 2, Vol. 13. Pelikan, Jaroslav, ed. LC 55-9893. 1956. 19.95 (*0-570-06413-9*, 15-1755) Concordia.

— Martin Luther: Selections from His Writings. Dillenberger, John, ed. LC 61-9503. 1958. mass mkt. 10.95 (*0-385-09876-6*, Anchor NY) Doubleday.

— Schmalkald Articles. 1994. pap. 4.00 (*0-8006-2661-3*, Fortress Pr) Augsburg Fortress.

— Sermons of Martin Luther, 8 vols. Lenker, John N., ed. 1992. reprint ed. 175.00 (*0-8010-5626-8*) Baker Bk.

— Small Catechism in Contemporary English. LC 15-6732. 32p. 1960. pap. 0.80 (*0-8066-0324-0*, 15-6732, Augsburg); pap. 8.80 (*0-685-00588-7*, Augsburg); pap. 63.00 (*0-685-00589-5*, Augsburg); pap. 0.75 (*0-685-73179-0*, 15-6733, Augsburg) Augsburg Fortress.

— The Table Talk of Martin Luther. Kepler, Thomas S., ed. Hazlitt, William, tr. 368p. 1995. reprint ed. pap. 14.99 (*0-8010-5205-X*) Baker Bk.

— Theologia Germanica. 240p. 1992. reprint ed. pap. 19.95 (*1-56459-012-7*) Kessinger Pub.

— Three Treatises. rev. ed. LC 73-114753. 320p. 1970. pap. 10.00 (*0-8006-1639-1*, 1-1639, Fortress Pr) Augsburg Fortress.

Luther, Martin, jt. auth. see Erasmus, Desiderius.

Luther, Martin E. The Compasses of God: Science & Human Destiny. 144p. (Orig.). 1991. 14.95 (*0-9615847-1-8*) Marwolf Pub.

— The Free Market - Your Stake in Its Future. LC 85-90462. 160p. (Orig.). (C). 1986. pap. 9.95 (*0-9615847-0-X*) Marwolf Pub.

— The Infinite Voyage: A Metaphysical Odyssey. 200p. (Orig.). 1995. pap. 17.95 (*0-9615847-3-4*) Marwolf Pub.

Luther, Norman Y., et al. Consistent Correction of Census & Vital Registration Data for Thailand, 1960-80. LC 86-32807. (Papers of the East-West Population Institute: No. 103). (Illus.). viii, 39p. (Orig.). 1986. pap. 3.00 (*0-86638-089-2*) EW Ctr HI.

Luther, Rebekah S. The Yoda Family. (Illus.). 16p. (J). (gr. 3). 1994. 7.95 (*0-8059-3486-3*) Dorrance.

Luther, Sara F. The United States & the Direct Broadcast Satellite: The Politics of International Broadcasting in Space. (Illus.). 238p. 1988. 49.95 (*0-19-505138-6*) OUP.

Luther, Sara F., et al. Diverse Perspectives on Marxist Philosophy: East & West. LC 94-25057. (Contributions in Philosophy Ser.: Vol. 53). 158p. 1995. text ed. 55.00 (*0-313-29396-1*, Greenwood Pr) Greenwood.

Luther Standing Bear. My Indian Boyhood. LC 88-12222. (Illus.). viii, 200p. 1988. reprint ed. pap. 8.00 (*0-8032-9186-8*) U of Nebr Pr.

Luther, Walter. Darlehen im Konkurs. 144p. 1990. pap. 36.00 (*3-7890-1938-0*, Pub. by Nomos Verlags GW) Intl Bk Import.

Luther, William M. How to Develop a Business Plan in Fifteen Days. LC 86-47854. 255p. reprint ed. pap. 72.70 (*0-7837-7062-6*, 2046874) Bks Demand.

— The Marketing Plan: How to Prepare & Implement It. LC 92-17618. 208p. 1992. 17.95 (*0-8144-7805-0*) AMACOM.

— The Start-up Business Plan. 240p. 1991. pap. 14.00 (*0-13-842543-4*, J K Lasser) P-H Gen Ref & Trav.

Lutheran Church in America Task Group for Long-Range Planning. Theology: An Assessment of Current Trends Report. LC 68-55757. 174p. reprint ed. pap. 49.60 (*0-685-15423-8*, 2026880) Bks Demand.

Lutheran Episcopal Dialogue III Staff. Implications of the Gospel. 128p. (Orig.). 1988. pap. 5.95 (*0-88028-089-1*) Forward Movement.

Lutheran Historical Conference Staff, jt. auth. see Concordia Historical Institute Staff.

Lutheran Research Society Staff. The Sedition Case of Nineteen Forty-Four. 1979. lib. bdg. 59.95 (*0-8490-3005-6*) Gordon Pr.

Lutherer, Lorenz O. & Simon, Margaret S. Targeted: The Anatomy of an Animal Rights Attack. LC 92-32505. (C). 1993. 22.95 (*0-8061-2492-X*) U of Okla Pr.

Luthert, Joanna M. & Robinson, Lorraine. The Royal Marsden Hospital Manual of Multidisciplinary Standards of Care. (Illus.). 512p. 1993. pap. 26.95 (*0-632-03386-X*) Blackwell Sci.

Luthi, J. J. Dictionnaire General de la Francophonie. 390p. (FRE.). 1986. 95.00 (*0-8288-1944-0*, F59710) Fr & Eur.

Luthi, Max. The European Folktale: Form & Nature. Niles, John D., tr. LC 85-45990. (Folklore Studies in Translation). 196p. 1986. pap. 7.95 (*0-253-20393-7*, MB-393) Ind U Pr.

— The Fairytale As Art Form & Portrait of Man. Erickson, Jon S., tr. LC 83-48897. (Folklore Studies in Translation). 222p. 1985. 24.95 (*0-253-32099-2*); pap. 7.95 (*0-253-20420-8*, MB-420) Ind U Pr.

— Once upon a Time: On the Nature of Fairy Tales. Chadeayne, Lee & Gottwald, Paul, trs. LC 76-6992. 192p. 1976. reprint ed. pap. 7.95 (*0-253-20203-5*, MB-203) Ind U Pr.

Luthin, jt. auth. see Marino, M. A.

Luthin, James N. Drainage Engineering. rev. ed. LC 77-9299. (Illus.). 288p. 1978. 29.50 (*0-88275-578-1*) Krieger.

Lutholtz, M. William. Grand Dragon: D. C. Stephenson & the Ku Klux Klan in Indiana. LC 90-20132. (Illus.). 392p. 1991. 25.50 (*1-55753-010-6*) Purdue U Pr.

— Grand Dragon: D. C. Stephenson & the Ku Klux Klan in Indiana. (Illus.). 392p. 1993. reprint ed. pap. 14.95 (*1-55753-046-7*) Purdue U Pr.

Luthor. Jane Goodall Jr. (J). Date not set. lib. bdg. write for info. (*0-8050-2272-4*) H Holt & Co.

Luthra, H. L. Tales from Kalidasa. 136p. (C). 1989. 60.00 (*81-209-0228-9*, Pub. by Pitambar Pub II); pap. 35.00 (*81-209-0037-5*, Pub. by Pitambar Pub II) St Mut.

Luthra, Nirupama, jt. auth. see Mahajan, Amar J.

Luthra, Nirupamja, jt. auth. see Mahajan, Amar J.

Luthy, Melvin J. Phonological & Lexical Aspects of Colloquial Finnish. (Uralic & Altaic Ser.: No. 119). 93p. 1973. pap. text ed. 22.70 (*90-279-2686-7*) Mouton.

— Phonological & Lexical Aspects of Colloquial Finnish, Vol. 119. (Uralic & Altaic Ser.). x, 94p. 1973. pap. text ed. 11.00 (*0-87750-173-4*) Res Inst Inner Asian Studies.

Luthy, W., jt. auth. see Weber, H. P.

Luti, J. Mary. Teresa of Avila's Way. (Way of the Christian Mystics Ser.). 208p. (Orig.). 1991. pap. text ed. 14.95 (*0-8146-5548-3*) Liturgical Pr.

***Lutjen-Drecoll, E., ed.** Basic Aspects of Glaucoma Research No. 3. 1993. pap. text ed. 69.95 (*0-471-02519-4*) Wiley.

Lutjen-Drecoll, E., et al. Basic Aspects of Glaucoma Research No. 2: Functional Morphology of the Vasculature in the Anterior Eye Segment. 1991. pap. text ed. 69.00 (*0-471-56088-X*) Wiley.

Lutjens, Louette R. Callista Roy: An Adaptation Model. (Notes on Nursing Theories Ser.: Vol. 3). (Illus.). 68p. (C). 1991. 18.95 (*0-8039-4577-9*); pap. 8.95 (*0-8039-4228-1*) Sage.

— Martha Rogers: The Science of Unitary Human Beings. (Notes on Nursing Theories Ser.: Vol. 1). (Illus.). 40p. (C). 1991. 18.95 (*0-8039-4578-7*); pap. 8.95 (*0-8039-4229-X*) Sage.

***Lutkehaus, Nancy & Roscoe, Paul B., eds.** Gender Rituals: Female "Initiation" in Papua New Guinea. LC 94-39869. 288p. 1995. 59.95x (*0-415-91106-0*, B4820, Routledge NY) Routledge.

Lutkehaus, Nancy, jt. auth. see Mead, Margaret.

Lutkehaus, Nancy, et al. Sepik Heritage: Tradition & Change in Papua New Guinea. LC 90-80282. (Illus.). 688p. 1990. lib. bdg. 75.00 (*0-89089-322-5*) Carolina Acad Pr.

Lutkehaus, Nancy C. Zaria's Fire: Representations of Gender Power & Change in Manam Society. (C). 1994. write for info. (*0-318-72267-4*) Carolina Acad Pr.

***Lutkehaus, Nancy C. & Roscoe, Paul B., eds.** Gender Rituals: Female "Initiation" in Papua New Guinea. LC 94-39869. 288p. 1995. pap. 18.95 (*0-415-91107-9*, B4824, Routledge NY) Routledge.

Lutkenhuff, Steven D., jt. ed. see Mehlman, M. A.

Lutkepohl, Helmut. Forecasting Aggregated Vector ARMA Processes. (Lecture Notes in Economics & Mathematical Systems Ser.: Vol. 284). x, 323p. 1987. pap. 44.80 (*0-387-17208-4*) Spr-Verlag.

— Introduction to Multiple Time Series Analysis. 552p. 1991. pap. text ed. 59.00 (*0-387-53194-7*) Spr-Verlag.

— Introduction to Multiple Time Series Analysis. 2nd ed. LC 93-28356. (Illus.). xxi, 545p. 1993. pap. write for info. (*3-540-56940-5*); pap. 49.00 (*0-387-56940-5*) Spr-Verlag.

Lutker, Eric, jt. auth. see Wand, Carl.

Lutkin, Peter C. Music in the Church. LC 72-135722. reprint ed. 21.45 (*0-404-04069-1*) AMS Pr.

Lutkus, Anthony D., jt. ed. see Baird, John C.

Lutman, Frank C. Rhodesian Ridgebacks. (Illus.). 160p. 1989. lib. bdg. 11.95 (*0-86622-595-1*, KW159) TFH Pubns.

Lutman, M. E. & Haggard, M. P., eds. Hearing Science & Hearing Disorders. 1983. text ed. 82.00 (*0-12-460440-4*) Acad Pr.

Lutman, Richard A. Crowsfield. LC 93-94026. 136p. (Orig.). 1994. pap. 8.00 (*1-56002-363-5*, Univ Edtns) Aegina Pr.

Luton, Harry H. The Log-Jam. Williams, S. Bradford, Jr., ed. LC 94-2677. 161p. 1994. 12.95 (*0-9608522-4-7*) Copper Orchid.

Luton, Mildred. Christmas Time in the Mountains. (Illus.). 44p. (Orig.). (J). (gr. 1-6). 1981. pap. 5.00 (*0-87516-434-X*) DeVorss.

Lutoslawski, Wincenty. The Origin & Growth of Plato's Logic: With an Account of Plato's Style & of the Chronology of His Writings. xviii, 547p. 1983. reprint ed. 89.70 (*3-487-07336-6*, Pub. by Georg Olms GW) Lubrecht & Cramer.

— The Origin & Growth of Plato's Logic: With an Account of Plato's Style & the Chronology of His Writings. (Classical Studies Ser.). reprint ed. lib. bdg. 59.00 (*0-697-00041-9*) Irvington.

Lutoslawski, Witold, ed. see Rosen, Judith.

Lutovich, Diane, jt. auth. see Chan, Janis F.

Lutrell, Claude, et al. Arthurian Literature, Vol. III. Barber, Richard, ed. 224p. 1983. 63.00 (*0-85991-149-7*) Boydell & Brewer.

Lutrin, Carl E. & Settle, Allen K. American Public Administration: Concepts & Cases. 3rd ed. (Illus.). 544p. (C). 1985. text ed. write for info. (*0-13-028705-9*) P-H.

— American Public Administration: Concepts & Cases. 4th ed. Jucha, ed. 522p. (C). 1992. text ed. 53.75 (*0-314-91349-1*) West Pub.

Luts, Jack & Peterson, Pete. The Complete Guide to Painting Your Home. (Illus.). 160p. (Orig.). 1989. pap. 14.95 (*1-55870-119-2*) Betterway Bks.

***Lutske, Harvey.** The Book of Jewish Customs. 400p. 1995. pap. 24.95 (*1-56821-608-4*) Aronson.

— The Book of Jewish Customs. LC 86-22362. 400p. 1987. reprint ed. 30.00 (*0-87668-916-0*) Aronson.

— History in Their Hands: A Book of Jewish Autographs. LC 94-19626. 1995. write for info. (*1-56821-290-9*) Aronson.

Lutskevich, N. Museum of Western & Oriental Art: Odessa. (Illus.). 180p. (C). 1985. text ed. 70.00 (*0-685-40291-6*, Pub. by Collets) St Mut.

Luttbeg. Comparing the States & Communities. (C). 1991. text ed. 45.00 (*0-673-46184-X*) HarpCollege.

Luttbeg, Norman R. & Gant, Michael M. American Electoral Behavior: 1952-1992. LC 94-66866. 248p. 1994. pap. text ed. 28.00 (*0-87581-386-0*) Peacock Pubs.

Luttbeg, Norman R. & Zeigler, Harmon. Attitude Consensus & Conflict in an Interest Group: An Assessment of Cohesion. (Reprint Series in Social Sciences). (C). 1993. reprint ed. pap. text ed. 1.00 (*0-8290-3351-3*, PS-395) Irvington.

Luttenberger, David N., jt. contrib. see Smith, Nancy D.

Lutter. Atlas of Adult Foot & Ankle Surgery. 450p. 1994. 135.00 (*0-8016-6280-X*) Mosby Yr Bk.

***Lutter, Lowell D., et al, eds.** Orthopaedic Knowledge Update: Foot & Ankle. LC 94-77974. (Illus.). 324p. 1994. 110.00 (*0-89203-112-3*) Amer Acad Ortho Surg.

Lutter, Marcus, ed. Die Grundung einer Tochtergesellschaft im Ausland. 359p. (GER.). 1983. 98.50 (*3-11-008787-1*) De Gruyter.

Lutter, Tiiu J., ed. see Gilkes, Lolita W.

Lutterjohann, Martin. IQ Tests for Children. LC 77-1520. 192p. pap. 4.95 (*0-8128-2271-4*, Scrbrough Hse) Madison Bks UPA.

— IQ Tests for School Children: How to Test Your Child's Intelligence. (Illus.). 1980. pap. 5.95 (*0-8128-6026-8*, Scrbrough Hse) Madison Bks UPA.

Lutterman, Kenneth G., jt. auth. see Alvarez, Rodolfo.

***Lutterman, LaVonne.** How to Make & Repair Leather Doll Bodies. Shields, Kim, ed. 64p. (Orig.). 1995. pap. 14.95 (*1-879825-17-1*) Jones Publish.

Lutterodt, Sarah A. & Grafinger, Deborah J. Developing Objective Test Items I. (Self-paced Instructor Training Mod. Ser.). (Illus.). 56p. (Orig.). 1985. pap. text ed. 16.50 (*0-87683-687-2*) GP Pub.

— How to Write Learning Objectives. (Instructor Training Ser.). (Illus.). 40p. (Orig.). 1985. pap. text ed. 16.50 (*0-317-38598-4*) GP Pub.

— Measurement & Evaluation: Basic Concepts. (Instructor Training Ser.). (Illus.). 40p. (Orig.). 1985. pap. text ed. 16.50 (*0-87683-686-4*) GP Pub.

Luttgau, Hans-Christoph. Membrane Control of Cellular Activity. (Progress in Zoology-Fortschritte der Zoologie: Vol. 33). 462p. 1987. text ed. 180.00 (*0-89574-229-2*, Pub. by Gustav Fischer Verlag) VCH Pubs.

Luttge, U., ed. Vascular Plants As Epiphytes. (Ecological Studies: Vol. 76). (Illus.). 280p. 1989. 139.00 (*0-387-50796-5*) Spr-Verlag.

Luttgens, Kathryn, et al. Kinesiology: Scientific Basis of Human Motion. 8th ed. 704p. (C). 1992. boxed write for info. (*0-697-11632-8*) Brown & Benchmark.

Luttger, Hans & Jeschek, Hans H., eds. Festschrift fuer Eduard Dreher zum 70. Geburtstag. (C). 1977. 253.85 (*3-11-005988-6*) De Gruyter.

Luttig, John C. Journal of a Fur Trading Expedition on the Upper Missouri, 1812-1813. (Illus.). 1964. reprint ed. 17.50 (*0-87266-019-2*) Argosy.

***Luttikhuizen, Frances.** The World of Science & Technology: A Theme-Based, Study-Skills Approach. 200p. 1994. pap. text ed. 15.95x (*0-472-08269-8*) U of Mich Pr.

Luttikhuizen, Gerard P. The Revelation of Elchasai: Investigations into the Evidence for a Mesopotamian Jewish Apocalypse of the Second Century & Its Reception by Judeo-Christian Propagandists. 263p. 1985. lib. bdg. 72.50 (*3-16-144935-5*, Pub. by J C B Mohr GW) Coronet Bks.

Luttinger, Abigail. Good Evening & Other Poems. 1979. pap. 12.50 (*0-686-25781-2*) Penumbra Press.

Luttmann, Gail. Raising Milk Goats Successfully. Griffith, Roger, ed. LC 86-26694. (Illus.). 176p. (Orig.). 1986. pap. 9.95 (*0-913589-24-1*) Williamson Pub Co.

Luttmann, Gail, jt. auth. see Luttmann, Rick.

Luttmann, Rick & Luttmann, Gail. Chickens in Your Backyard. LC 76-14357. 168p. 1976. pap. 9.95 (*0-87857-125-6*, 13-488-1) Rodale Pr Inc.

Lutton, Thomas, jt. auth. see Gordon, Patrice L.

Lutton, Wayne. The Myth of Open Borders. 47p. 1988. pap. 3.00 (*0-936247-09-6*) Amer Immigration.

An Asterisk (*) at the beginning of an entry indicates that the title is appearing in BIP for the first time.

Lutton, Wayne & Tanton, John. The Immigration Invasion. 192p. (Orig.). 1994. pap. 4.95 (*1-881780-01-5*) Social Contract.

Lutton, Wayne, jt. auth. see Stacy, Palmer.

Luttrell, Anthony. The Hospitallers of Rhodes & Their Mediterranean World. (Collected Studies: Vol. CS360). 352p. 1992. 95.00 (*0-86078-307-3*, Pub. by Variorum UK) Ashgate Pub Co.

Luttrell, Barbara. Mirabeau. LC 90-39621. 317p. (C). 1991. 35.00 (*0-8093-1705-2*) S Ill U Pr.

Luttrell, Chuck, illus. Everything's Going Wrong. 74p. (Orig.). (J). (gr. 3-6). 1986. pap. 6.95 (*0-9617609-0-7*) Shade Tree NV.

Luttrell, Claude, ed. see De Troyes, Chretien.

Luttrell, Clifton B. The High Cost of Farm Welfare. LC 88-34439. 149p. 1989. pap. 3.00 (*0-932790-71-2*) Cato Inst.

Luttrell, Ida. Be Nice to Marilyn. LC 91-25879. (Illus.). 32p. (J). (ps-3). 1992. text ed. 13.95 (*0-689-31716-6*, Atheneum Bks Young) S&S Childrens.

— The Bear Next Door. LC 90-4153. (I Can Read Bk.). (Illus.). 64p. (J). (gr. k-3). 1991. lib. bdg. 11.89 (*0-06-024024-5*) HarpC Child Bks.

— Mattie's Little Possum Pet. LC 91-47709. (Illus.). 40p. (J). (ps-3). 1993. text ed. 14.95 (*0-689-31786-7*, Atheneum Bks Young) S&S Childrens.

— Milo's Toothache. LC 91-24315. (Easy-to-Read Ser.). (Illus.). 40p. (J). (ps-3). 1992. 11.00 (*0-8037-1034-8*); lib. bdg. 10.89 (*0-8037-1035-6*) Dial Bks Young.

— The Star Counters. LC 93-20342. (Illus.). 32p. (J). 1994. 15.00 (*0-688-12149-7*, Tambourine Bks); lib. bdg. 14.93 (*0-688-12150-0*, Tambourine Bks) Morrow.

— Three Good Blankets. LC 89-36353. (Illus.). 32p. (J). (ps-2). 1990. lib. bdg. 13.95 (*0-689-31586-4*, Atheneum Bks Young) S&S Childrens.

Luttrell, Jean. Arizona Strip: Christmas on the Homestead & Other Stories. (Illus.). 40p. (Orig.). 1988. pap. 4.25 (*0-9617609-1-5*) Shade Tree NV.

— Winning Isn't Everything. (Dave Owens Adventures Ser.). (Illus.). 76p. (Orig.). (J). (gr. 3-5). 1990. pap. 6.95 (*0-9617609-2-3*) Shade Tree NV.

Luttrell, Julia, jt. auth. see Radwanski, George.

Luttrell, Narcissus. A Brief Historical Relation of State Affairs from September 1678 to April 1714, 6 vols., Set. Straka, Gerald M., ed. LC 72-83165. (English Studies Ser.). 1972. reprint ed. lib. bdg. 324.00 (*0-8420-1423-3*) Scholarly Res Inc.

Luttrell, Susan E. Love Was Born at Christmas. (Orig.). (J). (gr. k-4). 1981. pap. 3.40 (*0-89536-483-2*, 1234) CSS OH.

Luttrell, Wanda. Home on Stoney Creek. LC 93-47084. (J). (gr. 4 up). 1994. write for info. (*0-7814-0901-2*) Chariot Family.

— Reunion in Kentucky. (Illus.). (J). (gr. 4-7). 1994. 5.99 (*0-7814-0907-1*) Chariot Family.

— Reunion in Kentucky. LC 94-31114. (Illus.). (J). 1995. write for info. (*0-7814-0236-0*, Chariot Bks) Chariot Family.

— Stranger in Williamsburg. LC 94-20574. 1995. write for info. (*0-7814-0902-0*, Chariot Bks) Chariot Family.

Luttrell, William L. Post-Capitalist Industrialization: Planning Economic Independence in Tanzania. LC 86-9452. (Illus.). 208p. 1986. text ed. 55.00 (*0-275-92310-X*, C2310, Praeger Pubs) Greenwood.

Lutts, Ralph H. The Nature Fakers: Wildlife, Science & Sentiment. LC 89-29521. (Illus.). 255p. 1990. 22.95 (*1-55591-054-8*) Fulcrum Pub.

Luttwak, Edward N. Coup d'Etat: A Practical Handbook. 215p. 1979. pap. text ed. 14.95 (*0-674-17547-6*) HUP.

Luttwak, Edward N. Endangered American Dream. 1994. pap. 14.00 (*0-671-89667-9*, Touchstone Bks) S&S Trade.

— The Endangered American Dream: How to Stop the United States from Becoming a Third World Country & How to Win the Geo-Economic Struggle for Industrial Supremacy. 320p. 1993. 24.00 (*0-671-86963-9*) S&S Trade.

— The Grand Strategy of the Roman Empire: From the First Century A. D. to the Third. LC 76-17232. (Illus.). 272p. 1977. pap. 14.95x (*0-8018-2158-4*) Johns Hopkins.

— The Political Uses of Sea Power. LC 74-8219. (Washington Center of Foreign Policy Research. Studies in International Affairs: No. 23). 90p. reprint ed. pap. 25.70 (*0-685-15480-7*, 2026324) Bks Demand.

— Strategy: The Logic of War & Peace. 296p. 1990. pap. text ed. 10.95 (*0-674-83996-X*) HUP.

— Strategy & History: Collected Essays. 225p. (C). 1985. 32.95x (*0-88738-065-4*) Transaction Pubs.

— Strategy & Politics: Collected Essays. LC 79-65224. 328p. 1980. pap. 21.95 (*0-87855-904-3*) Transaction Pubs.

Luttwak, Edward N. & Horowitz, Daniel. The Israeli Army, 1948 to 1973, Vol. 1. 408p. 1983. text ed. 40.00 (*0-89011-585-0*) Abt Bks.

Lutwack, Leonard. Birds in Literature. LC 93-30647. 304p. (C). 1994. lib. bdg. 29.95 (*0-8130-1254-6*) U Press Fla.

— The Role of Place in Literature. LC 83-24264. 304p. 1984. 39.95x (*0-8156-2305-4*) Syracuse U Pr.

Lutwack, Ralph & Morrison, Andrew, eds. Silicon Material Preparation & Economical Wafering Methods. LC 84-5968. (Illus.). 586p. 1984. 54.00 (*0-8155-0990-1*) Noyes.

Lutwak-Mann, C., jt. auth. see Mann, T.

***Lutwick.** Tuberculosis: A Clinical Handbook. 1994. pap. (*0-412-60740-9*) Chapman & Hall.

Lutwiniak, William. Scrabble Crossword Puzzle Book, No. 4. 1988. pap. 4.95 (*0-02-688817-3*) Macmillan.

— Washington Post Sunday Crossword Puzzles, Vol. 3. 1992. pap. 8.00 (*0-8129-2109-7*, Times Bks) Random.

Lutwiniak, William & Mackaye, William R., eds. The Washington Post Sunday Crossword Puzzles, Vol. 1. 64p. 1991. pap. 7.50 (*0-8129-1933-5*, Times Bks) Random.

— The Washington Post Sunday Crossword Puzzles, Vol. 2. 64p. 1991. pap. 7.50 (*0-8129-1934-3*, Times Bks) Random.

Luty, F., ed. Proceedings of the International Conference on Defects in Insulating Crystals: A Special Issue of Crystal Lattice Defects & Amorphous Materials, Vol. 1. 280p. 1979. text ed. 135.00 (*3-7186-0009-9*) Gordon & Breach.

— Proceedings of the International Conference on Defects in Insulating Crystals: A Special Issue of Crystal Lattice Defects & Amorphous Materials, Vol. 2. 282p. 1980. text ed. 173.00 (*3-7186-0035-8*) Gordon & Breach.

— Proceedings of the International Conference on Defects in Insulating Crystals: A Special Issue of Crystal Lattice Defects & Amorphous Materials, Vol. 3. 263p. 1981. text ed. 154.00 (*3-7186-0066-8*) Gordon & Breach.

— Proceedings of the International Conference on Defects in Insulating Crystals: A Special Issue of Crystal Lattice Defects & Amorphous Materials, Vol. 4. 244p. 1982. text ed. 154.00 (*3-7186-0119-2*) Gordon & Breach.

Lutyens, Elizabeth, jt. auth. see Levine, Robert.

Lutyens, Mary. Krishnamurti: The Open Door. 1991. pap. 7.95 (*0-380-70971-6*) Avon.

— Krishnamurti: The Years of Awakening. 1991. pap. 9.95 (*0-380-71113-3*) Avon.

— Krishnamurti: The Years of Fulfillment. 264p. 1991. pap. 8.95 (*0-380-71112-5*, Discus) Avon.

Lutyens, Mary, ed. see Krishnamurti, Jiddu.

***Lutyens, Sally.** A Pocket Full of Wry. Weinberger, Jane, ed. (Illus.). 84p. (Orig.). 1995. pap. 9.95 (*1-883650-14-3*) Windswept Hse.

Lutyk, Carol B., ed. Discover America. (Illus.). 336p. (YA). 1989. 26.95 (*0-87044-804-8*); 36.95 (*0-87044-805-6*); lib. bdg. 39.95 (*0-87044-806-4*) Natl Geog.

— Our World's Heritage. 312p. 1987. 21.95 (*0-87044-696-7*); text ed. 21.95 (*0-87044-698-3*); lib. bdg. 23.95 (*0-87044-697-5*) Natl Geog.

***Lutz.** Abnormal Psychology: Update with DSM-IV. 2nd ed. (C). 1994. student ed, text ed. 14.00 (*0-673-46910-7*) HarpCollege.

— Surviving Hypoxia: Mechanisms of Control & Adaptation. 1993. 105.00 (*0-8493-4226-0*, RB150) CRC Pr.

— Topics Clinical Cardiology: Complications of Interventional Procedures. 1995. write for info. (*0-89640-260-6*) Igaku-Shoin.

Lutz & Otrio, eds. Optical Systems for Space Applications. 291p. 1987. 57.00 (*0-89252-845-1*, 810) SPIE.

Lutz, A. M., jt. ed. see Nguyen-Khac, U.

Lutz, Albert, jt. auth. see Brinker, Helmut.

Lutz, Alma. Emma Willard: Daughter of Democracy. LC 75-37635. 1976. reprint ed. 18.95 (*0-89201-018-5*) Zenger Pub.

— Emma Willard: Pioneer Educator of American Women. LC 83-18567. viii, 143p. 1984. reprint ed. text ed. 38.50 (*0-313-24254-2*, LUEW, Greenwood Pr) Greenwood.

— Susan B. Anthony: Rebel, Crusader, Humanitarian. LC 75-37764. 1976. reprint ed. 19.95 (*0-89201-017-7*) Zenger Pub.

Lutz, Arthur, jt. auth. see Lutz, Martha.

Lutz, Bertha & Lutz, Gualter. Brazilian Species of "Hyla" LC 70-39502. (Illus.). 286p. 1973. 25.00 (*0-292-70704-5*) U of Tex Pr.

Lutz, C., ed. see Joannes, S. E.

Lutz, Carl F. How to Develop, Conduct & Use Pay-Benefit Surveys. 211p. 1986. ring bd. 125.00 (*0-916506-22-3*) Abbott Langer Assocs.

Lutz, Carroll A. & Przytulski, Karen. Nutrition, Diet Therapy. (Illus.). 750p. (C). 1994. pap. text ed. 29.95 (*0-8036-5681-5*) Davis Co.

Lutz, Catherine A. Unnatural Emotions: Every Day Sentiments on a Micronesian Atoll & Their Challenge to Western Theory. (Illus.). 280p. 1988. lib. bdg. 35.00 (*0-226-49721-6*); pap. text ed. 13.95 (*0-226-49722-4*) U Ch Pr.

Lutz, Catherine A. & Abu-Lughod, Lila, eds. Language & the Politics of Emotion. (Studies in Emotion & Social Interaction). (Illus.). 215p. (C). 1990. 49.95 (*0-521-38204-1*); pap. 16.95 (*0-521-38868-6*) Cambridge U Pr.

Lutz, Catherine A. & Collins, Jane L. Reading National Geographic. LC 92-40698. (Illus.). 312p. (C). 1993. pap. 19.95 (*0-226-49724-0*) U Ch Pr.

***Lutz, Charles P.** Loving Neighbors Far & Near: U. S. Lutherans Respond to a Hungry World. LC 94-24888. 1994. pap. 9.99 (*0-8066-2761-1*, 10-27611, Augsburg) Augsburg Fortress.

— Surprising Gift: The Story of Holden Village, Church Renewal Center. (Illus.). 144p. (Orig.). 1987. pap. 6.00 (*0-9618617-0-3*) Holden Village.

Lutz, Christian. West Europa Auf Dem Weg in die Informationsgesellschaft. 148p. (Orig.). (GER.). 1984. pap. text ed. 20.00 (*0-685-09491-X*) Interbk Inc.

Lutz, Christopher H. Historia Sociodemografica de Santiago de Guatemala, 1541-1773. LC 82-73081. (CIRMA Serie Monografica: No. 2). 499p. 1982. pap. 14.50 (*0-910443-02-5*) CIRMA.

— Santiago de Guatemala, 1541-1773: City, Caste, & the Colonial Experience. (Illus.). 304p. 1994. 37.95 (*0-8061-2597-7*) U of Okla Pr.

Lutz, Christopher H., jt. auth. see Lovell, W. George.

Lutz, Cora E. Dunchad: Glossae in Martianum. (American Philological Association Philological Monographs). 1982. 15.95 (*0-89130-705-2*, 40-00-12) Scholars Pr GA.

Lutz, Dick & Lutz, J. Marie. Komodo, the Living Dragon. LC 94-44423. (Illus.). 192p. 1991. pap. 10.95 (*0-931625-21-1*) DIMI Pr.

— Komodo, the Living Dragon. rev. ed. LC 94-44423. (Illus.). 260p. 1995. pap. 14.95 (*0-931625-27-0*) DIMI Pr.

Lutz, Dick, ed. see Henderson, John L. & Henderson, Lilli I.

Lutz, Dieter S. Towards a Methodology of Military Force Comparison. 255p. 1986. pap. 38.50 (*3-7890-0915-6*, Pub. by Nomos Verlags GW) Intl Bk Import.

Lutz, Donald S. The Origins of American Constitutionalism. LC 88-6415. 178p. 1988. pap. text ed. 12.95 (*0-8071-1506-1*) La State U Pr.

— A Preface to American Political Theory. LC 92-11700. (American Political Thought Ser.). xii, 188p. 1992. 27.50 (*0-7006-0545-2*); pap. 12.95 (*0-7006-0546-0*) U Pr of KS.

Lutz, Donald S. & Warren, Jack D. A Covenanted People: The Religious Tradition & the Origins of American Constitutionalism. (Illus.). 104p. 1987. pap. 30.00 (*0-916617-27-0*) J C Brown.

Lutz, Donald S., jt. auth. see Hyneman, Charles S.

Lutz, E. A. Some Problems & Alternatives in Developing Federal Block Grants: To States for Public Welfare Purposes. LC 77-74945. (American Federalism-the Urban Dimension Ser.). (Illus.). 1978. lib. bdg. 33.95 (*0-405-10493-6*) Ayer.

Lutz, E. G. Animated Cartoons. 1976. lib. bdg. 150.00 (*0-8490-1433-6*) Gordon Pr.

Lutz, Edwin G. Motion-Picture Cameraman. LC 76-169332. (Literature of Cinema, Ser. 2). (Illus.). 264p. 1978. reprint ed. 18.95 (*0-405-03899-2*) Ayer.

Lutz, Ellen L., jt. auth. see Randall, Glenn R.

Lutz, Ellen L., et al, eds. New Directions in Human Rights. LC 88-29984. 260p. (C). 1989. text ed. 42.95x (*0-8122-8128-4*) U of Pa Pr.

Lutz, Ernst, ed. Toward Improved Accounting for the Environment. LC 93-13831. 334p. 1993. 32.95 (*0-8213-2436-5*, 12436) World Bank.

Lutz, Ernst, et al, eds. Economic & Institutional Analyses of Soil Conservation Projects in Central America & the Caribbean. LC 93-45505. (Environment Paper Ser.: Vol. 8). 218p. 1994. write for info. (*0-8213-2741-0*) World Bank.

Lutz, Francis E. Richmond in World War II. 1951. 7.50 (*0-87517-026-9*) Dietz.

Lutz, Frank & Merz, Carol. The Politics of School-Community Relations. 224p. (C). 1992. text ed. 40.00 (*0-8077-3162-5*); pap. text ed. 19.95 (*0-8077-3161-7*) Tchrs Coll.

Lutz, Frank W. & Ferrante, Reynolds. Emergent Practices in the Continuing Education of School Administrators. 48p. (Orig.). (C). 1972. pap. text ed. 1.25 (*1-55996-114-7*, W113) Univ Council Educ Admin.

Lutz, Friedrich A. Corporate Cash Balances, 1914-43: Manufacturing & Trade. (Financial Research Program III: Studies in Business Financing: No. 8). 148p. 1945. reprint ed. 38.50 (*0-87014-136-8*); reprint ed. mic. film 20.00 (*0-685-61257-0*) Natl Bur Econ Res.

Lutz, Friedrich A. & Lutz, Vera C. Theory of Investment of the Firm. LC 69-13978. 253p. 1970. reprint ed. text ed. 59.75 (*0-8371-1108-0*, LUTI, Greenwood Pr) Greenwood.

Lutz, Giles A. The Echo. 160p. 1981. pap. 1.75 (*0-345-29100-X*) Ballantine.

— Forked Tongue. 160p. 1981. pap. 1.75 (*0-345-29220-0*) Ballantine.

— The Great Railroad War. 176p. 1982. pap. 3.50 (*0-345-29879-9*) Ballantine.

— Killer's Trail. 160p. 1981. pap. 1.75 (*0-345-29441-6*) Ballantine.

— Man Hunt. 1981. pap. 1.75 (*0-345-29218-9*) Ballantine.

— Outcast Gun. 1985. pap. 2.25 (*0-449-12987-X*) Fawcett.

— Relentless Gun. 144p. 1981. pap. 1.75 (*0-449-13996-4*, GM) Fawcett.

— Thieves' Brand. 1982. pap. 2.25 (*0-345-30254-0*) Ballantine.

Lutz, Gualter, jt. auth. see Lutz, Bertha.

Lutz, H., ed. Cultures D'Organes D'Invertebres. 280p. 1969. text ed. 255.00 (*0-677-50100-5*) Gordon & Breach.

— Invertebrate Organ Cultures. (Documents in Biology Ser.: Vol. 2). 264p. (C). 1970. text ed. 207.00 (*0-677-30100-6*); pap. text ed. 99.00 (*0-677-30105-7*) Gordon & Breach.

Lutz, H. & Demling, L., eds. Diagnostic Imaging Methods in Hepatology. 1984. lib. bdg. 148.00 (*0-85200-807-4*) Kluwer Ac.

Lutz, H. & Meudt, R. Manual of Ultrasound. (Illus.). 160p. 1983. pap. 60.00 (*0-387-12377-6*) Spr-Verlag.

Lutz, Henry F. Early Babylonian Letters from Larsa. LC 78-63531. (Yale Oriental Series: Babylonian Texts: No. 2). (Illus.). reprint ed. 34.50 (*0-404-60252-5*) AMS Pr.

— The Intensifying Conjunction in Egyptian. LC 36-1182. (University of California Publications in Social Welfare: Vol. 10, No. 4). 8p. reprint ed. pap. 25.00 (*0-317-10216-8*, 2021475) Bks Demand.

— Real Estate Transactions from Kish. LC 32-813. (University of California Publications in Social Welfare: Vol. 10, No. 3). 32p. reprint ed. pap. 25.00 (*0-317-10207-9*, 2021474) Bks Demand.

— The Unidentified Sign. LC 72-995. (University of California Publications in Social Welfare: Vol. 10, No. 2). 4p. reprint ed. pap. 25.00 (*0-317-10202-8*, 2021473) Bks Demand.

— An Uruk Document of the Time of Cambyses. (University of California Publications in Social Welfare: Vol. 10, No. 8). 10p. reprint ed. pap. 25.00 (*0-317-10219-2*, 2021479) Bks Demand.

Lutz, J. Marie, jt. auth. see Lutz, Dick.

Lutz, James M. Protectionism: An Annotated Bibliography with Analytical Introductions. LC 88-15273. (Resources on Contemporary Issues Ser.: No. 2). 215p. 1988. pap. 40.00 (*0-87650-249-4*) Pierian.

Lutz, James M. & Kihl, Young W. World Trade Issues: Regime, Structure & Policy. LC 84-15986. 288p. 1985. text ed. 55.00 (*0-275-90127-0*, C0127, Praeger Pubs) Greenwood.

Lutz, Jeanne, ed. Georgia Attorney's - Secretary's Handbook, 1992-93. rev. ed. (Attorney's-Secretary's Handbooks Ser.). 520p. 1992. ring bd. 59.00 (*0-927573-26-1*) Mariposa Pub.

— Ohio Attorney's-Secretary's Handbook, 1993. 5th rev. ed. (Attorney's-Secretary's Handbooks Ser.). 580p. 1992. ring bd. 59.00 (*0-927573-28-8*) Mariposa Pub.

Lutz, Jeanne & Walburg, Jean, eds. Ohio Attorney's-Secretary's Handbook, 1991-1992. (Attorney's-Secretary's Handbooks Ser.). 1991. ring bd. 59.00 (*0-927573-23-7*) Mariposa Pub.

Lutz, Jeanne, ed. see Walburg, Jean M.

Lutz, Jeanne, jt. ed. see Walburg, Jean.

Lutz, Jerre, et al. Hurst's the Heart: PreTest Self-Assessment & Review. 8th ed. (Pretest Specialty Level Ser.). 304p. 1995. pap. 39.95 (*0-07-052011-9*) Hlth Prof Div.

Lutz, Jerre F. Heart: Pretest Self-Assessment & Review. 7th ed. (Pretest Specialty Level Ser.). 1990. pap. text ed. 39.95 (*0-07-051000-8*) Hlth Prof Div.

Lutz, Jerry. Pitchman's Melody: Shaw About Shakespeare. LC 72-3529. 175p. 1974. 18.00 (*0-8387-1247-9*) Bucknell U Pr.

Lutz, Jessie G. Chinese Politics & Christian Missions. LC 87-72450. (Church & the World Ser., The West & the Wider World Ser.). xviii, 440p. 1988. 48.85 (*0-940121-05-0*) Cross Cultural Pubns.

Lutz, John. Bloodfire. (Fred Carver Mystery Ser.). 224p. 1992. reprint ed. mass mkt. 3.99 (*0-380-71446-9*) Avon.

— Burn. LC 94-32187. (Henry Holt Mystery Ser.). 1995. 22.50 (*0-8050-3480-3*) H Holt & Co.

— Burning Evidence: A Mystery Jigsaw Puzzle. (BePuzzled Ser.). (Orig.). (C). 1993. 20.00 (*0-922242-53-4*) Lombard Mktg.

— Buyer Beware. (Mystery Scene Book Ser.). 192p. 1992. pap. 3.95 (*0-88184-840-9*) Carroll & Graf.

— Double Cross. (BePuzzled Ser.). 4p. (Orig.). (J). 1989. pap. 19.95 (*0-922242-14-3*) Lombard Mktg.

— Feline Frenzy. (Illus.). 6p. (C). 1991. 20.00 (*0-922242-22-4*) Lombard Mktg.

— Flame. 272p. 1991. pap. 3.95 (*0-380-71070-6*) Avon.

— Flowers from a Stranger: A Mystery Jigsaw Puzzle Thriller. (BePuzzled Ser.). (Orig.). (YA). (gr. 7 up). 1994. 20.00 (*0-922242-69-0*) Bepuzzled.

— Grounds for Murder: A Mystery Jigsaw Puzzle Thriller. (Bepuzzled Ser.). (Orig.). (YA). (gr. 7 up). 1995. 20.00 (*0-922242-74-7*) Bepuzzled.

— Hot. 256p. 1993. mass mkt. 4.99 (*0-380-71447-7*) Avon.

— Introduction to Learning & Memory. 1994. text ed. 43.95 (*0-534-22266-8*) Brooks-Cole.

— Kiss. 272p. 1990. pap. 3.95 (*0-380-70934-1*) Avon.

— Scorcher. 256p. 1988. pap. 3.95 (*0-380-70526-5*) Avon.

— Scorcher. 272p. 1995. pap. 5.95 (*0-8050-3829-9*, Owl) H Holt & Co.

— Single White Female. Rubenstein, Julie, ed. 288p. 1992. reprint ed. mass mkt. 4.99 (*0-671-74500-X*) PB.

— Thicker Than Blood: A Novel of Suspense Featuring Private Investigator Nudger. 272p. 1993. 19.95 (*0-312-09922-3*, Pub. by Thomas Dunne Bks) St Martin.

— Torch. LC 93-28431. (Henry Holt Mystery Ser.). 1994. 22.00 (*0-8050-2610-X*) H Holt & Co.

— Tropical Heat. 256p. 1987. pap. 3.95 (*0-380-70309-2*) Avon.

— Tropical Heat. 252p. 1995. pap. 5.95 (*0-8050-3828-0*, Owl) H Holt & Co.

— The Truth of the Matter. LC 87-72700. 176p. 1988. reprint ed. pap. 4.95 (*0-88739-090-0*, Blk Lizard) Creat Arts Bk.

Lutz, John T. & Dunkelberger, David L. Impact Modifiers for PVC: The History & Practice. (Society of Plastics Engineers Monographs: No. 1262). 216p. 1991. text ed. 72.95 (*0-471-52764-5*) Wiley.

Lutz, Katia B. Finance & Accounting: Lectures & Vocabulary in French. 1992. pap. text ed. 10.95 (*0-07-056810-3*) McGraw.

Lutz, Katia B., jt. auth. see Schmitt, Conrad J.

Lutz, Lorry, jt. auth. see Foster, Robert L.

Lutz, Marcetta R., et al. Arvada, Just Between You & Me: 1904-1941. LC 82-71574. (Dual Ser.). (Illus.). 207p. 1985. 17.50 (*0-9615540-0-2*) Arvada Hist.

Lutz, Mark & Lux, Kenneth. Humanistic Economics: The New Challenge. LC 88-7324. 352p. (Orig.). 1988. 28.50 (*0-942850-10-6*); pap. 15.50 (*0-942850-06-8*) Intermediate Tech.

Lutz, Mark, jt. ed. see Diwan, Romesh.

Lutz, Mark A., ed. Social Economics: Retrospect & Prospect. (C). 1989. lib. bdg. 73.50 (*0-7923-9004-0*) Kluwer Ac.

Lutz, Martha & Lutz, Arthur. Woodville Long Ago. 68p. (J). (gr. 3-7). 1986. pap. write for info. (*0-318-61400-6*) Vimach Assocs.

Lutz, Pamela B., jt. ed. see Holdzkom, David.

Lutz, Peter L. & Nilsson, G oran E. The Brain Without Oxygen: Causes of Failure & Mechanisms for Survival. LC 94-16812. (Neuroscience Intelligence Unit Ser.). 1994. 89.95 (*1-57059-187-3*) R G Landes.

Lutz, Peter L. & Nilsson, Goran. The Brain Without Oxygen-Causes of Failure: Mechanisms for Survival. (Medical Intelligence Unit Ser.). 118p. 1994. 89.95 (*1-879702-96-7*, LN0296) R G Landes.

Lutz, R., jt. ed. see Brinberg, D.

Lutz, Ralph H. The German Revolution, Nineteen Eighteen to Nineteen Nineteen. LC 68-54283. (Stanford University. Stanford Studies in Language & Literature: Vol. 1, Pt. 1). reprint ed. 20.00 (*0-404-50961-4*) AMS Pr.

Lutz, Raymond P. Finance, Economics & Accounting: A Handbook for Managers & Engineers. 1400p. 1986. text ed. write for info. (*0-471-07822-0*, Wiley-Interscience) Wiley.

L

Lutz, Richard, ed. Advances in Consumer Research: Proceedings of the 1985 Conference, Vol. 13. 1986. 29.00 (*0-915552-17-5*) Assn Consumer Res.

Lutz, Richard A. Mussel Culture & Harvest: A North American Perspective. (Developments in Aquaculture & Fisheries Science Ser.: Vol. 7). 350p. 1980. 120.00 (*0-444-41866-0*) Elsevier.

Lutz, Richard A., jt. ed. see Kennish, M. J.

Lutz, Richard A., jt. ed. see Rhoads, Donald C.

Lutz, Richard J., jt. ed. see Houston, Michael J.

Lutz, Richard L. Feel Better! Live Longer! Relax. LC 88-10872. 144p. 1988. pap. 9.95 (*0-931625-18-1*) DIMI Pr.

Lutz, Robert E., jt. ed. see Handl, Gunther.

Lutz, Robert R. & Taylor, Bruce T. Surviving in Ministry: Navigating the Pitfalls, Experiencing the Renewals. 1990. pap. 11.95 (*0-8091-3156-0*) Paulist Pr.

Lutz, Ronald J. Applied Sketching & Technical Drawing. (Illus.). 224p. 1991. text ed. 29.28 (*0-87006-764-8*) Goodheart.

Lutz, Susan, jt. auth. see Mott, Steve.

Lutz, Tim. Gem Hunter's Kit. (Discovery Kit Ser.). (Illus.). 64p. (Orig.). (J). (gr. 3 up). 1990. 17.95 (*0-89471-828-2*) Running Pr.

Lutz, Tom. American Nervousness, 1903: An Anecdotal History. LC 90-55737. (Illus.). 366p. 1991. 36.95 (*0-8014-2581-6*) Cornell U Pr.

— American Nervousness, 1903: An Anecdotal History. LC 90-55737. (Illus.). 344p. 1993. pap. 14.95 (*0-8014-9901-1*) Cornell U Pr.

Lutz, Vera C. Italy: A Study in Economic Development. LC 75-3738. (Illus.). 342p. 1975. reprint ed. text ed. 75.00 (*0-8371-8055-4*, LUIT, Greenwood Pr) Greenwood.

Lutz, Vera C., jt. auth. see Lutz, Friedrich A.

***Lutz, Vicki J.** Forever & Always. 300p. (Orig.). 1995. pap. 8.95 (*1-56901-824-3*) NW Pub.

Lutz, William, jt. auth. see Brent, Harry.

Lutz, William D. The Cambridge Thesaurus of American English. LC 93-31878. 500p. (C). 1994. 16.95 (*0-521-41427-X*) Cambridge U Pr.

— Double-Speak: Rom Revenue Enhancement to Terminal Living How Government, Business, Advertisers & Others Use the Language to Deceive You. 1990. 8.95 (*0-00-003850-4*, PL) HarpC.

Lutz, William D. & Brent, Harry. The Critical Reader. 528p. (C). 1990. pap. text ed. 28.00 (*0-06-044111-9*) HarpCollege.

Lutz, William D., jt. auth. see Brent, Harry.

Lutz, Wolfgang. Distributional Aspects of Human Fertility. (Studies in Population). 200p. 1989. text ed. 66.00 (*0-12-460470-6*) Acad Pr.

— Future Population World. 1995. 29.95 (*1-85383-239-1*, Pub. by Erthscan Pubns UK) Island Pr.

Lutz, Wolfgang, ed. Future Demographic Trends in Europe & North America: What Can We Assume Today? (Studies in Population). (Illus.). 585p. 1991. text ed. 127.00 (*0-12-460445-5*) Acad Pr.

— Population-Development-Environment: Understanding Their Interactions in Mauritius. LC 94-26937. 1994. 115.00 (*0-387-58301-7*); write for info. (*3-540-58301-7*) Spr-Verlag.

Lutz, Wolfgang, et al, eds. Demographic Trends & Patterns in the Soviet Union Before 1991. (Illus.). 496p. 1993. 150.00 (*0-415-10194-8*, B2448) Routledge.

Lutze, L., ed. see Narain, I.

Lutze, Lothar. Drama in Contemporary South Asia: Varieties & Settings. (South Asian Digest of Regional Writing Ser.: No. 10). 86p. (Orig.). 1984. pap. 32.50x (*3-515-04207-5*) Coronet Bks.

— Hindi Writing in Post-Colonial India: A Study in the Aesthetics of Literary Production. (South Asian Studies: No. 16). 239p. 1986. text ed. 39.00 (*3-515-04763-8*) Coronet Bks.

— Hindi Writings in Post-Colonial India. 1985. 27.00 (*0-8364-1422-5*, Pub. by Manohar II) S Asia.

Lutze, W., ed. Scientific Basis for Nuclear Waste Management XII, Vol. 127. (Materials Research Society Symposium Proceedings Ser.). 1989. text ed. 55.00 (*0-931837-97-9*) Materials Res.

Lutze, W. & Ewing, R. C., eds. Radioactive Waste Forms for the Future. 712p. 1989. 241.00 (*0-444-87104-7*, North Holland) Elsevier.

Lutzeier, Elizabeth. The Coldest Winter. LC 91-7159. 160p. (YA). (gr. 5-9). 1991. 13.95 (*0-8234-0899-X*) Holiday.

— The Wall. LC 92-52712. 160p. (J). (gr. 5-9). 1992. 14.95 (*0-8234-0987-2*) Holiday.

Lutzeier, Elizabeth, tr. see Nissen, Hans J.

***Lutzeler, Paul M.** Europe after Maastricht: American & European Perspectives. 1994. 27.95 (*0-8264-0783-8*) Continuum.

***Lutzeler, Paul M., ed.** After Maastricht: American & European Perspectives. LC 94-33658. 320p. (C). 1994. 29.95 (*1-57181-020-X*) Berghahn Bks.

Lutzen, J. Joseph Liouville, 1809-1882. (Studies in the History of Mathematics & Physical Sciences: Vol. 15). (Illus.). 824p. 1990. 98.00 (*0-387-97180-7*) Spr-Verlag.

Lutzen, Karl F. & Stevens, Mark. Homebrew Favorites: A Coast-to-Coast Collection of over 240 Beer & Ale Recipes. LC 93-33377. (Illus.). 256p. 1994. pap. 12.95 (*0-88266-613-4*, Storey Pub) Storey Comm Inc.

Lutzer. Living with Your Passions. 1983. 8.99 (*0-88207-294-3*, Victor Books) SP Pubns.

Lutzer, Erwin. Chiseled by the Master's Hand. 144p. (Orig.). 1993. pap. 7.99 (*1-56476-059-6*, Victor Books) SP Pubns.

— Coming to Grips with God's Discipline of Believers. (Salt & Light Pocket Guides Ser.). pap. 3.50 (*0-8024-3547-5*) Moody.

— Coming to Grips with Heaven. (Salt & Light Pocket Guides Ser.). pap. 3.50 (*0-8024-3541-6*) Moody.

— Coming to Grips with Hell. (Salt & Light Pocket Guides Ser.). pap. 3.50 (*0-8024-3542-4*) Moody.

— Coming to Grips with Homosexuality. (Salt & Light Pocket Guides Ser.). pap. 3.50 (*0-8024-3548-3*) Moody.

— Coming to Grips with Marital Conflict. (Salt & Light Pocket Guides Ser.). 1991. pap. 3.50 (*0-8024-3503-3*) Moody.

— Coming to Grips with Satan's Plan for Your Life. (Salt & Light Pocket Guides Ser.). pap. 3.50 (*0-8024-3544-0*) Moody.

— Coming to Grips with the Antichrist's New Age Roots. (Salt & Light Pocket Guides Ser.). pap. 3.50 (*0-8024-3546-7*) Moody.

— Coming to Grips with the Role of Europe in Prophecy. (Salt & Light Pocket Guides Ser.). pap. 3.50 (*0-8024-3545-9*) Moody.

— Coming to Grips with Unanswered Prayer. (Salt & Light Pocket Guides Ser.). pap. 3.50 (*0-8024-3543-2*) Moody.

— Coming to Grips with Your Sexual Past. (Salt & Light Pocket Guides Ser.). pap. 3.50 (*0-8024-3504-1*) Moody.

— Fracaso: Una Puerta Abierta Al Exito: Failure: Back Door to Success. (SPA.). 4.95 (*84-7228-493-X*, 220416, Pub. by Edit Clie SP) TSELF.

— Getting Closer to God. 180p. (Orig.). 1994. pap. 8.99 (*1-56476-119-3*, Victor Books) SP Pubns.

— Growing Through Conflict. (Life in Perspective Ser.). (Orig.). 1992. pap. 1.60 (*0-89693-063-7*, Victor Books) SP Pubns.

— How to Say No to a Stubborn Habit. 2nd ed. 1994. pap. 8.99 (*1-56476-331-5*, Victor Books) SP Pubns.

— Keeping Your Dream Alive. (Life in Perspective Ser.). 156p. 1991. student ed. pap. 1.60 (*0-89693-811-5*); teacher ed, pap. 1.20 (*0-89693-812-3*) SP Pubns.

— Overcoming the Grasshopper Complex. (Life in Perspective Ser.). 1991. teacher ed. pap. 5.99 (*0-89693-827-1*) SP Pubns.

— Will America Be Given Another Chance? A Message of Hope in Today's Spiritual Crisis. 1993. pap. 2.99 (*0-8024-9369-6*) Moody.

Lutzer, Erwin, jt. auth. see Van Stone, Doris.

Lutzer, Erwin W. Christ among Other Gods. 1994. 12.99 (*0-8024-1648-9*) Moody.

— Coming to Grips with Death & Dying. (Salt & Light Pocket Guides Ser.). 1992. pap. 3.50 (*0-8024-3585-8*) Moody.

— Coming to Grips with Your Role in the Workplace. (Salt & Light Pocket Guides Ser.). 1992. 3.50 (*0-8024-3586-6*) Moody.

— Failure: The Backdoor to Success. 138p. (Orig.). 1975. pap. 7.99 (*0-8024-2593-3*) Moody.

— How in This World Can I Be Holy? 173p. 1974. pap. 7.99 (*0-8024-3676-5*) Moody.

— How to Say No to a Stubborn Habit. LC 79-64039. 143p. 1979. pap. 7.99 (*0-88207-787-2*, Victor Books) SP Pubns.

— Managing Your Emotions. 180p. 1983. pap. 8.99 (*0-88207-386-9*, Victor Books) SP Pubns.

— Matters of Life & Death. pap. 8.99 (*0-8024-5292-2*) Moody.

— Twelve Myths Americans Believe. (Orig.). 1993. pap. 8.99 (*0-8024-9017-4*) Moody.

— Where Do We Go From Here? 2.99 (*0-8024-9399-8*) Moody.

— Why Are We the Enemy? 2.99 (*0-8024-9367-X*) Moody.

Lutzer, Erwin W. & Van Stone, Doris. Dorie: The Girl Nobody Loved. 1981. pap. 7.99 (*0-8024-2275-6*) Moody.

Lutzin, Sidney G., ed. Managing Municipal Leisure Services. LC 80-17378. (Municipal Management Ser.). 271p. 1980. pap. text ed. 21.00 (*0-87326-023-6*) Intl City-Cnty Mgt.

Lutzker, John R. & Campbell, Randy. Ecobehavioral Family Interventions in Development Disabilities. LC 94-3954. 1994. pap. 18.95 (*0-534-24396-7*) Brooks-Cole.

Lutzker, Marilyn. Criminal Justice Research in Libraries: Strategies & Resources. LC 85-17765. (Illus.). 183p. 1986. text ed. 55.00 (*0-313-24490-1*, LCJ/, Greenwood Pr) Greenwood.

— Multiculturalism in the College Curriculum: A Handbook of Strategies & Resources for Faculty. LC 94-37880. (Greenwood Educators' Reference Collection Ser.). 160p. 1995. text ed. 49.95 (*0-313-28918-2*, Greenwood Pr) Greenwood.

— Research Projects for College Students: What to Write Across the Curriculum. LC 87-37549. 152p. 1988. text ed. 42.95 (*0-313-25149-5*, LRW/, Greenwood Pr) Greenwood.

Lutzow, C. The Story of Prague. 1976. lib. bdg. 59.95 (*0-8490-2688-1*) Gordon Pr.

Lutzow, F. H. The Story of Prague. (Mediaeval Towns Ser.: Vol. 12). 1974. reprint ed. pap. 30.00 (*0-8115-0854-4*) Periodicals Srv.

Lutzow, Franz. Lectures on the Historians of Bohemia. LC 72-173174. 1972. reprint ed. 18.95 (*0-405-08756-X*, Pub. by Blom Pubns UK) Ayer.

— The Life & Times of Master John Hus. LC 77-84728. (Illus.). reprint ed. 40.00 (*0-404-16128-6*) AMS Pr.

Luukkanen, Eino. Fighter over Finland: The Memorirs of a Fighter Pilot. Gilbert, James B. & Green, William, eds. Salo, Mauno A., tr. LC 79-7282. (Flight: Its First Seventy-Five Years Ser.). (Illus.). 1980. reprint ed. lib. bdg. 30.95 (*0-405-12191-1*) Ayer.

Luurila, Olavi J. Sauna & the Heart: Arrhythmias & Other Cardiovascular Responses During Finnish Sauna & Exercise Testing in Healthy Men & Post-Myocardial Infarction Patients. 60p. 1980. pap. 12.50 (*951-99256-6-X*) Sauna Soc.

Luv, Bud E. You Oughta Be Me: How to be a Lounge Singer & Live Like One. (Illus.). 256p. (Orig.). 1993. pap. 10.95 (*0-312-09947-9*) St Martin.

Luvaas, Jay. The Military Legacy of the Civil War: The European Inheritance. LC 88-27800. (Modern War Studies). (Illus.). xxx, 258p. 1988. pap. 12.95 (*0-7006-0379-4*) U Pr of KS.

Luvaas, Jay, ed. Dear Miss Em: General Eichelberger's War in the Pacific, 1942-1945. LC 71-176429. (Contributions in Military History Ser.: No. 2). 322p. 1972. text ed. 55.00 (*0-8371-6278-5*, LDM/, Greenwood Pr) Greenwood.

***Luvaas, Jay & Nelson, Harold W., eds.** The U. S. Army War College Guide to the Battles of Chancellorsville & Fredericksburg. (U. S. Army War College Guides to Civil War Battles Ser.). (Illus.). 382p. 1988. 22.50x (*0-7006-0568-1*) U Pr of KS.

Luvaas, Jay, ed. see Henderson, George F.

Luvaas, Tanha. Notes from My Inner Child: I'm Always Here. 86p. 1993. pap. 8.95 (*1-882591-10-0*) Nataraj Pub.

Luvaas, William. Going Under. LC 94-14231. 352p. 1994. 22.95 (*0-399-13968-0*, Putnam) Putnam Pub Group.

Luvera, Paul N., Jr. Attorney's Guidebook of Trial Forms & Techniques for Successful Handling of Personal Injury Cases. 1979. 89.50 (*0-13-050294-4*) Exec Reports.

Luvera, Paul N. How to Prepare & Try a Plaintiff's Soft Tissue Neck Injury Case: A Practice Primer for Preparing & Trying a Plaintiff's "Whiplash" Case. (Illus.). xii, 346p. write for info. (*0-318-57762-3*) P N Luvera.

Luvera, Paul N., jt. auth. see Trine, William A.

***Luvmour & Luvmour.** Everyone Wins! Date not set. 34.95 (*1-55092-010-3*) New Soc Pubs.

Luvmour, jt. auth. see Luvmour.

Luvmour, Josette & Luvmour, Sambhava. Natural Learning Rhythms: How & When Children Learn. LC 93-33182. 1993. pap. 12.95 (*0-89087-699-1*) Celestial Arts.

Luvmour, Jusette, jt. auth. see Luvmour, Sambhaua.

Luvmour, Sambhaua & Luvmour, Jusette. Everyone Wins! 112p. (Orig.). 1990. lib. bdg. 34.95 (*0-86571-189-5*); pap. 8.95 (*0-86571-190-9*) New Soc Pubs.

Luvmour, Sambhava, jt. auth. see Luvmour, Josette.

Lux, Claudia. Das Bibliothekswesen der Volksrepublik China. (Bibliothekspraxis Ser.: No. 26). (Illus.). 119p. (GER.). 1986. lib. bdg. 19.00 (*3-598-21127-9*) K G Saur.

Lux, David S. Patronage & Royal Science in Seventeenth-Century France: The Academie De Physique in Caen. LC 89-1002. 256p. 1989. 34.95 (*0-8014-2334-1*) Cornell U Pr.

Lux, Harm. Francesca Woodman: Photography. (Illus.). 1994. pap. 25.00 (*1-881616-13-4*) Dist Art Pubs.

Lux, Ivan & Koblinger, Laszlo. Monte Carlo Particle Transport Methods: Neutron & Photon Calculations. 448p. 1991. 104.00 (*0-8493-6074-9*, QC793) CRC Pr.

Lux, J. Richard & Pieters, Richard S. Basic Exercises in Algebra & Trigonometry. 1979. 8.48 (*0-8013-0068-1*); pap. text ed. 8.22 (*0-88334-122-0*, 76096) Longman.

Lux, Jonathan, jt. auth. see Fisher, Christopher.

Lux, K., jt. auth. see Hiss, G.

Lux, Kenneth, jt. auth. see Lutz, Mark.

Lux, Thomas. The Drowned River. 68p. (C). 1993. reprint ed. pap. 7.00 (*0-938566-60-1*) Adastra Pr.

— The Drowned River: New Poems. 80p. 1990. pap. 8.95 (*0-685-29459-5*) HM.

— Half Promised Land. LC 94-70469. (Classic Contemporaries Ser.). 100p. 1994. reprint ed. pap. 11.95 (*0-88748-205-8*) Carnegie-Mellon.

— Massachusetts: Ten Poems. 15p. (C). 1981. pap. 3.00 (*0-913219-32-0*) Pym-Rand Pr.

— Massachusetts: Ten Poems. deluxe ed. 15p. (C). 1981. 10.00 (*0-913219-33-9*) Pym-Rand Pr.

— Split Horizon. LC 93-46333. 1994. 18.95 (*0-395-70098-1*) HM.

— Split Horizon. LC 93-46333. 1995. pap. 9.95 (*0-395-70097-3*) HM.

— Sunday. LC 88-63541. (Classic Contemporaries Ser.). 1989. pap. 10.95 (*0-88748-089-6*) Carnegie-Mellon.

— Tarantulas on the Lifebuoy. 22p. 1983. pap. 2.50 (*0-9604740-4-8*) Ampersand RI.

Lux, Thomas, ed. see Winner, Robert.

Luxbacher, Joe. Soccer: Winning Techniques. 2nd ed. (Illus.). 162p. (Orig.). 1992. pap. 10.95 (*0-945483-11-2*) E Bowers Pub.

Luxbacher, Joseph A. Soccer: Steps to Success. LC 90-35489. (Steps to Success Activity Ser.). (Illus.). 176p. (Orig.). (C). 1991. pap. text ed. 14.95x (*0-88011-391-X*, PLUX0391) Human Kinetics.

— Soccer Practice Games. LC 94-12525. 160p. 1955. pap. 13.95 (*0-87322-554-6*, PLUX0554) Human Kinetics.

— Teaching Soccer: Steps to Success. LC 90-28870. (Steps to Success Activity Ser.). (Illus.). 188p. (Orig.). 1991. pap. 19.95x (*0-88011-392-8*, PLUX0392) Human Kinetics.

Luxbacher, Joseph A. & Klein, Gene. The Soccer Goalkeeper. 2nd ed. LC 93-6290. 176p. 1993. pap. 14.95 (*0-87322-397-7*, PLUX0397) Human Kinetics.

Luxemburg, Rosa. Letters to Karl & Luise Kautsky, 1896-1918. 1974. 250.00 (*0-87968-190-X*) Gordon Pr.

— The National Question: Selected Writings by Rosa Luxemburg. Davis, Horace B., ed. LC 74-2148. 318p. 1976. reprint ed. pap. 90.70 (*0-7837-3913-3*, 2043761) Bks Demand.

— Reform or Revolution. 1973. 250.00 (*0-87968-069-5*) Gordon Pr.

— Reform or Revolution. Integer, tr. LC 73-79783. 79p. 1988. reprint ed. lib. bdg. 30.00 (*0-87348-302-2*); reprint ed. pap. 9.95 (*0-87348-303-0*) Pathfinder NY.

— Russian Revolution, & Leninism or Marxism? 1961. pap. 12.95 (*0-472-06057-0*, 57, Ann Arbor Bks) U of Mich Pr.

— The Russian Revolution, & Leninism or Marxism? LC 80-24374. (Ann Arbor Paperbacks for the Study of Communism & Marxism). 109p. 1981. reprint ed. text ed. 38.50 (*0-313-22429-3*, LURR, Greenwood Pr) Greenwood.

— Selected Political Writings of Rosa Luxemburg. Howard, Dick, ed. LC 75-142991. 448p. 1971. reprint ed. pap. 12.00 (*0-85345-197-4*) Monthly Rev.

— Theory & Practice. Wolff, David, tr. (Illus.). 67p. (Orig.). 1980. pap. 2.00 (*0-914441-22-1*) News & Letters.

Luxemburg, Rosa & Bukharin, Nikolai I. The Accumulation of Capital - An Anti-Critique & Imperialism & the Accumulation of Capital. Wichmann, Rudolf, tr. LC 72-81768. 299p. reprint ed. pap. 85.30 (*0-8357-6001-4*, 2034339) Bks Demand.

Luxemburg, W. A. & Zaanen, A. C. Riesz Spaces. (Mathematical Library: Vol. 1). 514p. 1972. 118.00 (*0-444-10129-2*, North Holland) Elsevier.

Luxemburg, W. A., jt. ed. see Huijsmans, C. B.

Luxenberg, Larry. Walking the Appalachian Trail. (Illus.). 256p. 1994. pap. 16.95 (*0-8117-3095-6*) Stackpole.

Luxenburg, Joan. Probation Casework: The Convergence of Theory with Practice. (Illus.). 174p. (Orig.). (C). 1983. pap. text ed. 21.00 (*0-8191-3271-3*) U Pr of Amer.

Luxenburg, Norman. Europe since World War II: The Big Change. enl. rev. ed. LC 78-26092. (Illus.). 330p. 1979. 18.95 (*0-8093-0911-4*) S Ill U Pr.

Luxenburg, Norman, ed. see Skrjabina, Elena.

Luxenburg, Norman, tr. see Skrjabina, Elena.

Luxford, Michael. Children with Special Needs. (Rudolf Steiner's Ideas in Practice Ser.). (Illus.). 128p. (Orig.). 1994. pap. 9.95 (*0-88010-381-7*) Anthroposophic.

Luxiang, Wang, jt. auth. see Xiaokang, Su.

Luxmoore, A. R., ed. Optical Transducers & Techniques in Engineering Measurement. (Illus.). 1983. 90.00 (*0-85334-203-2*, Pub. by Elsevier Applied Sci UK) Elsevier.

Luxmoore, Charles F. English Saltglazed Earthenware. (Illus.). 95.00 (*0-685-53309-3*) Ars Ceramica.

Luxmoore, Jonathan. The Helsinki Agreement: Dialogue or Delusion? (C). 1990. 35.00 (*0-907967-76-0*, Pub. by Inst Euro Def & Strat UK) St Mut.

Luxmoore, R. A., ed. A Directory of Crocodilian Farming Operation. 2nd ed. 352p. 1992. 30.00 (*2-8317-0078-7*, Pub. by IUCN SZ) Island Pr.

Luxmoore, R. J., jt. ed. see Zelazny, Lucian W.

Luxon, James T. & Parker, David E. Industrial Lasers & Their Applications, No. 209. (Illus.). 248p. (C). 1985. text ed. 66.00 (*0-13-461369-4*) P-H.

Luxon, S. G., jt. auth. see Collings, A. J.

***Luxon, Thomas H.** Literal Figures: Puritan Allegory & the Reformation Crisis in Representation. LC 94-30412. 1995. 28.00 (*0-226-49785-2*) U Ch Pr.

Luxton, Brian C. Old Barry in Photographs. (C). 1989. 75.00 (*0-900807-25-3*, Pub. by D Brown & Sons Ltd UK) St Mut.

Luxton, Elsie. The Technique of Honiton Lace. (Illus.). 168p. 1979. 13.50 (*0-8231-5051-8*) Robin & Russ.

Luxton, Elsie & Fukuyama, Yusai. Flowers in Honiton Lace. (Illus.). 125p. 1993. 39.95 (*0-7134-6314-7*, Pub. by Batsford UK) Trafalgar.

Luxton, Peter. Charity Fund-Raising & the Public Interest: An Anglo-American Legal Perspective. 321p. 1990. text ed. 59.95 (*1-85628-016-0*, Pub. by Avebury Pub UK) Ashgate Pub Co.

Luxton, Peter & Wilkie, Margaret. Commercial Property, 1993-94. (Legal Practice Course Guides Ser.). 225p. 1994. pap. 34.00 (*1-85431-351-7*, Pub. by Blackstone Pr UK) W W Gaunt.

Luy, J. F. & Russer, P. Silicon-Based Millimeter-Wave Devices: Series in Electronics & Photonics. LC 94-12946. 1994. 69.00 (*0-387-58047-6*) Spr-Verlag.

Luyben, William L. Process Modeling, Simulation & Control. 2nd ed. (Chemical Engineering Ser.). 896p. 1990. text ed. write for info. (*0-07-039159-9*) McGraw.

Luyben, William L., ed. Practical Distillation Control. LC 92-10642. 1992. text ed. 89.95 (*0-442-00601-2*) Chapman & Hall.

Luyendijk. Cerebral Circulation. (Progress in Brain Research Ser.: Vol. 30). 1968. 56.50 (*0-444-40691-3*) Elsevier.

Luyet, Ron, jt. auth. see Pastor, Marion.

Luyken, Jan. Vonken der Liefde Jesu. xvi, 232p. (GER.). 1982. reprint ed. write for info. (*3-487-06955-5*, Pub. by Georg Olms GW) Lubrecht & Cramer.

Luyten, Meredith. Prayerwheels. Kaplan, Peter, ed. LC 76-14544. 1976. 3.00 (*0-915176-14-9*) Pourboire.

Luyters, Mary. Years of Awakening. 1991. pap. 9.95 (*0-380-00734-7*) Avon.

Luz, Consuelo. Open Air. 32p. write for info. (*0-938631-32-2*) Pennywhistle Pr.

Luz, Ehud. Parallels Meet: Religion & Nationalism in the Early Zionist Movement 1882-1904. 392p. 1988. 29.95 (*0-8276-0297-9*) JPS Phila.

Luz, George A., jt. ed. see De Pauw, John W.

Luz, Ulrich. Matthew in History: Interpretation, Influence, & Effects. LC 94-8912. 1994. pap. 9.00 (*0-8006-2833-0*, Fortress Pr) Augsburg Fortress.

— Matthew One - Seven: A Continental Commentary. Linss, Wilhelm C., tr. LC 92-23792. 416p. 1992. text ed. 42.00 (*0-8006-9600-X*, 1-9600, Fortress Pr) Augsburg Fortress.

— The Theology of the Gospel of Matthew. Robinson, J. Bradford, tr. (New Testament Theology Ser.). 180p. (C). 1992. 44.95 (*0-521-43433-5*); pap. 12.95 (*0-521-43576-5*) Cambridge U Pr.

Luz Villanueva, Alma. Weeping Woman: La Llorona & Other Stories. LC 93-29735. 168p. 1994. 14.00 (*0-927534-38-X*) Biling Rev-Pr.

Luza, Radomir V. The Resistance in Austria, 1938-1945. LC 83-6714. 383p. reprint ed. pap. 109.20 (*0-7837-2936-7*, 2057518) Bks Demand.

Luzadder, Warren J. & Duff, Jon M. The Fundamentals of Engineering Drawing: With an Introduction to Interactive Computer Graphics for Design & Production. 11th ed. 752p. 1992. text ed. 73.00 (*0-13-335050-9*) P-H.

— Introduction to Engineering Drawing: The Foundations of Engineering Design & Computer Aided Drafting. 2nd ed. 384p. 1992. pap. text ed. 45.00 (*0-13-480849-5*) P-H.

An Asterisk (*) at the beginning of an entry indicates that the title is appearing in BIP for the first time.

L

Luzatto, Moshe C. Derech HaShem: The Way of G-D. Kaplan, Aryeh, tr. 1978. 16.95 (*0-87306-136-5*); pap. 13.95 (*0-685-01627-7*) Feldheim.

Luzbetak, Louis J. The Church & Cultures: New Perspectives in Missiological Anthropology. rev. ed. LC 89-2880. (American Society of Missiology Ser.). 384p. 1989. pap. 21.95 (*0-88344-625-1*) Orbis Bks.

Luzeng, Song, tr. see Mao, Li, ed.

*__Luzi, Marina.__ The Story of Baby Jesus. Daughters of St. Paul Staff, tr. (Illus.). (J). (ps). Date not set. 12.95 (*0-8198-6972-4*) Pauline Bks.

Luzi, Mario. After Many Years. (C). 1990. 26.00 (*0-948268-77-8*, Pub. by Dedalus Pr IE); pap. 18.00 (*0-948268-76-X*, Pub. by Dedalus Pr IE) St Mut.

— For the Baptism of Our Fragments. (Essential Poets Ser.: No. 46). 190p. 1993. pap. 13.00 (*0-920717-55-1*) Guernica Editions.

— In the Dark Body of Metamorphosis & Other Poems. Salomon, I. L., tr. 110p. 1975. 6.95 (*0-393-04391-6*); pap. 2.50 (*0-393-04403-3*) Norton.

Luzier, J. Michael, jt. auth. see Brandes, Donald H., Jr.

*__Luzietti, Eugene A., et al.__ Shallow Deformation Along the Crittenden County Fault Zone Near the Southeastern Margin of the Reelfoot Rift, Northeastern Arkansas. (Investigations of the New Madrid Seismic Zone & Professional Paper Ser.). 1996. write for info. (*0-615-00333-8*) US Geol Survey.

Luzikov, Valentin N. Mitochondrial Biogenesis & Breakdown. Galkin, Alexander V., tr. LC 84-12157. 378p. 1985. 95.00 (*0-306-10979-4*, Consultants) Plenum.

*__Luzio, Eduardo.__ The Microcomputer Industry in Brazil: The Case of a Protected High Technology Industry. LC 94-36640. 1995. text ed. write for info. (*0-275-94923-0*, Praeger Pubs) Greenwood.

Luzio, J. P. & Thompson, R. J. Macromolecular Aspects of Medical Biochemistry. (Illus.). (C). 1990. 79.95 (*0-521-26083-3*); pap. 29.95 (*0-521-27828-7*) Cambridge U Pr.

Luzmeier, Tom & Taylor, Jesse. Making Your Living from the Stockmarket: A How-to Book for the Novice Investor. 184p. (Orig.). Date not set. pap. 24.95 (*0-9639975-0-5*) Blue Walrus.

*__Luzsa, G.__ X-Ray Anatomy of the Vascular System. 388p. (C). 1975. 75.00x (*963-05-0060-4*, Pub. by Akad Kiado HU) St Mut.

Luzwick, Dierdre. The Surrealist's Bible. LC 75-44001. (Illus.). 128p. 1976. 20.00 (*0-8246-0206-4*) Jonathan David.

Luzzato. The Path of the Just-Mesilath Yesharim. 1982. 16.95 (*0-87306-114-4*); pap. 12.95 (*0-87306-115-2*) Feldheim.

Luzzatti, G., et al. Xeromammography. 240p. 1980. 229.75 (*0-444-90167-1*, Excerpta Medica) Elsevier.

Luzzatti, M. Nautics an English Reader. 275p. 1976. pap. text ed. 49.95 (*0-8288-5744-X*, M9295) Fr & Eur.

*__Luzzatto, Moses H.__ The Path of the Upright: Mesillat Yesharim. Kaplan, Mordecai M., tr. LC 94-40542. 504p. 1995. 35.00 (*1-56821-427-8*) Aronson.

Luzzatto, Moshe C. Daat Tevnoth: The Knowing Heart. Silverstein, Shraga, tr. (Torah Classics Library). 357p. 1982. 16.95 (*0-87306-194-2*) Feldheim.

— General Principles of Kabbalah. 288p. 1970. write for info. (*0-943688-07-8*); pap. write for info. (*0-943688-31-0*) Res Ctr Kabbalah.

— General Principles of Kabbalah. 224p. (ITA.). 1992. pap. write for info. (*0-318-70259-2*) Res Ctr Kabbalah.

— The Path of the Just. Feldman, Yaakov, tr. 1996. write for info. (*1-56821-596-7*) Aronson.

— Ways of Reason: Guide to Talmudic Reasoning & Logic. 1992. 22.95 (*0-87306-495-X*) Feldheim.

*__Luzzi, D. E., et al, eds.__ Beam-Solid Interactions for Materials Synthesis & Characterization: 1994 MRS Fall Meeting, Boston, MA, Vol. 354. (MRS Symposium Proceedings Ser.). 1995. 75.00 (*1-55899-255-3*, 354K4) Materials Res.

LVA Basic Reading Task Force Staff. Basic Reading Tutor Training Workshop. Lawson, V. K., ed. 1981. Guidebook, slides, cassettes. student ed. audio 550.00 (*0-930713-42-7*); audio 2.25 (*0-930713-55-9*); 2.75 (*0-318-41707-3*) Lit Vol Am.

LVIS, Cookbook Committee Staff. The East Hampton LVIS Centennial Cookbook: Celebrating the 100th Anniversary of the Ladies' Village Improvement Society of East Hampton, Long Island. 304p. Date not set. 21.95 (*0-9641759-0-8*) Ladies Village.

L'vov-Anokhin, B. Galina Ulanova. 350p. (RUS.). 1984. 42.00 (*0-317-42742-3*, Pub. by Collets UK) St Mut.

Lvov, Arkady A., ed. see Vysotskii, Vladimir.

Lvov, D. K., ed. see Balandin, I. G., et al.

Lvov, D. K., ed. see Frolov, A. V., et al.

Lvov, D. K., jt. auth. see Zhdanov, V. M.

Lvov, Dmitri K., jt. ed. see Mahy, Brian W.

L'vov, M. R. Dictionary of Antonyms of the Russian Language. 400p. (C). 1978. 35.00 (*0-317-92414-1*, Pub. by Collets UK) Pro-Am Music.

Lvov, N., jt. auth. see Davats, V.

*__L'Vov, V. S. & Fuchssteiner, B., eds.__ Wave Turbulence under Parametric Excitation. LC 94-25113. (Nonlinear Dynamics Ser.). 352p. 1994. 99.00 (*0-387-51991-2*) Spr-Verlag.

Lvov, Yurij, jt. auth. see Eaton, Joseph W.

L'Vovich, M. I. World Water Resources & Their Future. LC 79-67029. (Illus.). 416p. 1979. 34.00 (*0-87590-224-3*) Am Geophysical.

Lwanga, S. K. & Cho-Yook Tye, eds. Teaching Health Statistics: Twenty Lesson & Seminar Outlines. 243p. 1987. pap. 23.40 (*92-4-156090-8*) World Health.

Lwin, T., jt. auth. see Maritz, J. S.

*__Ly, Holly.__ Piano Playing. (You Can Do It! Ser.). (Illus.). 52p. (Orig.). (J). (ps up). Date not set. pap. 12.95 (*1-56530-071-8*) Summit TX.

Ly, Judith, jt. auth. see Lewins, Frank.

Ly, Singko & Comber, Leon, eds. Modern Malaysian Chinese Stories. 1967. pap. 5.50 (*0-435-00230-9*, 00230) Heinemann.

Ly, Tran D. American Clocks: Price Guide Up-Date, 1995, Vol. 1. 16p. 1995. pap. 5.00 (*0-930163-52-4*) Arlington Bk.

— American Clocks, Vol. 1: A Guide to Identification & Prices. (Illus.). 320p. 1989. pap. 39.50 (*0-930163-39-7*) Arlington Bk.

— American Clocks, Vol. 2: Price Guide Up-Date, 1993. 12p. 1993. pap. 5.00 (*0-930163-54-0*) Arlington Bk.

— American Clocks, Vol. 2: With a Special Section on Self-Winding Clocks. (Illus.). 336p. 1991. 39.50 (*0-930163-44-3*); pap. 30.00 (*0-685-60151-X*) Arlington Bk.

— Ansonia Clocks: History, Identification & Price Guide. (Illus.). 304p. 1989. 35.00 (*0-930163-32-X*); pap. 25.00 (*0-685-25237-X*) Arlington Bk.

— Ansonia Clocks: Price Guide Up-Date 1992. (Illus.). 16p. pap. 5.00 (*0-930163-56-7*) Arlington Bk.

— Longcase Clocks & Standing Regulators, Pt. 1: Machine Made Clocks. (Illus.). 1994. 69.50 (*0-930163-60-5*) Arlington Bk.

— Seth Thomas Clocks & Movements: A Guide to Identification & Prices. (Illus.). 260p. (Orig.). 1985. pap. 25.00 (*0-930163-26-5*) Arlington Bk.

— Ulysse Nardin Chronometers, Pocket Watches & Wrist Watches with 1988 Price Guide. (Illus.). 20p. 1988. pap. 4.95 (*0-930163-66-4*) Arlington Bk.

— Waterbury Clocks: History, Identification, & Price Guide. (Illus.). 304p. 1989. 39.50 (*0-930163-40-0*); pap. 25.00 (*0-685-60153-6*) Arlington Bk.

— Waterbury Clocks: Price Guide Up-Date, 1992. (Illus.). 12p. 1992. pap. 5.00 (*0-930163-69-9*) Arlington Bk.

— Welch Clocks. (Illus.). 304p. 1992. 39.50 (*0-930163-38-9*); pap. 32.95 (*0-685-60154-4*) Arlington Bk.

— Welch Clocks: Price Guide Up-Date, 1992. 8p. 1992. pap. 5.00 (*0-930163-64-8*) Arlington Bk.

Ly, Tran D., tr. Calendar Clocks. (Illus.). 360p. 1993. 39.50 (*0-930163-43-5*) Arlington Bk.

Ly, Xeng, tr. see Leyman, Jean.

Lyakhovich, L. S. Thermochemical Treatment of Metals & Alloys. 1986. 36.00 (*81-205-0049-0*, Pub. by Oxford IBH II) S Asia.

Lyakhovich, L. S., et al. Multicomponent Diffusion Coatings. Gupt, K. M., tr. (Illus.). 304p. (C). 1987. 18.00 (*81-7087-014-3*, Pub. by Oxford IBH II) S Asia.

Lyal, Fox. And I Alone. 150p. 1985. 12.00 (*0-88107-025-4*) Curtis Media.

Lyal, Richard, jt. auth. see Farmer, Paul.

Lyall, ed. Diwans of Abid Ibn Al-Abras of Asad & Amir Ibn At-Tufail of Amir Ibn Sa Sa Ah. (Gibb Memorial Ser.: Vol. 21). 1980. reprint ed. 45.00 (*0-906094-13-5*, Pub. by Aris & Phillips UK) David Brown.

Lyall, A. Tennyson. LC 76-53034. (Studies in Tennyson: No. 27). 1977. lib. bdg. 42.95 (*0-8383-2164-X*) M S G Haskell Hse.

Lyall, Alfred C. History of India from the Close of the Seventeenth Century to the Present Time. LC 72-14391. (History of India Ser.: No. 8). reprint ed. 90.00 (*0-404-09008-7*) AMS Pr.

— The Rise & Expansion of the British Dominion in India. 5th ed. (Illus.). reprint ed. text ed. 28.50 (*0-685-13409-1*) Coronet Bks.

— The Rise & Expansion of the British Dominion in India. LC 67-24585. 1968. reprint ed. 48.00 (*0-86527-172-0*) Fertig.

— Studies in Literature & History. LC 68-29227. (Essay Index Reprint Ser.). 1977. reprint ed. 23.95 (*0-8369-0637-3*) Ayer.

— Warren Hastings. LC 73-140364. (Select Bibliographies Reprint Ser.). 1977. reprint ed. 20.95 (*0-8369-5607-9*) Ayer.

Lyall, Bob. The Tokens, Checks, Metallic Tickets, Passes, & Tallies of the British Caribbean & Bermuda. Schenkman, David E., ed. (Illus.). 210p. 1989. text ed. 30.00 (*0-918492-08-4*) TAMS.

Lyall, Charles J. Translations of Ancient Arabian Poetry. LC 79-2872. 200p. 1987. reprint ed. 22.00 (*0-8305-0042-1*) Hyperion Conn.

*__Lyall, David.__ Counselling in the Pastoral & Spiritual Context. LC 94-26387. (Counselling in Context Ser.). 1994. write for info. (*0-335-19163-0*); pap. write for info. (*0-335-19162-2*, Open Univ Pr) Taylor & Francis.

Lyall, Elizabeth, ed. see Walley, Susan.

Lyall, Fiona & El Haj, A. J., eds. Biomechanics & Cells. LC 93-42046. (Society for Experimental Biology Seminar Ser.: No. 54). (Illus.). 400p. (C). 1994. 74.95 (*0-521-45454-9*) Cambridge U Pr.

Lyall, Francis. Law & Space Telecommunications. 1989. text ed. 99.95 (*1-85521-039-8*, Pub. by Dartmth Pub UK) Ashgate Pub Co.

— Of Presbyters & Kings: Church & State in the Law of Scotland. 220p. 1980. 27.00 (*0-08-025715-1*, Pergamon Pr) Elsevier.

Lyall, Gavin. The Crocus List. large type ed. 512p. 1986. 23.95 (*0-7089-8327-8*, Charnwood) Ulverscroft.

— Judas Country. large type ed. 1977. 15.95 (*0-7089-0069-0*) Ulverscroft.

— Uncle Target. large type ed. 487p. 1989. 17.95 (*0-7089-1945-6*) Ulverscroft.

— Venus with Pistol. large type ed. 1975. 12.00 (*0-85456-370-9*) Ulverscroft.

*__Lyall, John & Anisfeld, Michael.__ GMP Auditing by Mail. 200p. 1995. 189.00 (*0-935184-66-X*) Interpharm.

Lyall, Katharine C. Microeconomic Issues of the Seventies: Exercises in Applied Price Theory. 2nd ed. (C). 1990. 14.00 (*0-06-044116-X*) HarpCollege.

Lyall, Katharine C., jt. auth. see Rossi, Peter H.

Lyall, Leslie, ed. The Phoenix Rises: The Phenomenal Growth of Eight Chinese Churches. 145p. (Orig.). 1992. pap. 5.95 (*981-3009-04-7*) OMF Bks.

Lyall, Leslie T. God Reigns in China. 1985. pap. 6.95 (*0-340-36199-9*) OMF Bks.

Lyall, R. J. Ane Resonyng of Ane Scottis & Inglis Merchand Betuix Rowand & Lionis: William Lamb (c. 1494 - c. 1550) Ane Resonyng. 250p. 1985. text ed. 35.00 (*0-08-030386-2*, Pergamon Pr); pap. text ed. 18.50 (*0-08-028485-X*, Pergamon Pr) Elsevier.

Lyall, Robert. Travels in Russia, the Krimea, the Caucasus & Georgia. LC 74-115560. (Russia Observed Ser., No. 1). 1970. reprint ed. 52.95 (*0-405-03046-0*) Ayer.

Lyall, Sutherland. Imagination Headquarters: London 1990 Herron Associates. (Architecture in Detail Ser.). (Illus.). 60p. (C). 1993. pap. 29.95 (*0-7148-2764-9*, Pub. by Phaidon Press UK) Chronicle Bks.

Lyapunov, A. M. The General Problem of the Stability of Motion. Fuller, A. T., ed. & tr. by. (Control Theory & Applications Ser.). 280p. 1992. 65.00 (*0-7484-0062-1*, Pub. by Tay Francis Ltd UK) Taylor & Francis.

Lyas, Colin, tr. see Croce, Benedetto.

Lyaskovskaya, Y., jt. auth. see Emanuel, N. M.

*__Lyback, Johanna R.__ Indian Legends. (Long Ago Ser.). (Illus.). 279p. (J). (gr. 3 up). 1994. pap. 7.95 (*1-877976-15-6*, 406-0012) Tipi Pr.

Lybarger, Jeffrey A., et al, eds. Priority Health Conditions: An Integrated Strategy to Evaluate the Relationship Between Illness & Exposure to Hazardous Substances. 214p. (Orig.). (C). 1994. pap. text ed. 65.00 (*0-7881-0530-2*) Diane Pub.

Lybecj, J. A. & Henrekson, M., eds. Explaining the Growth of Government. (Contributions to Economic Analysis Ser.: No. 171). 396p. 1988. 84.75 (*0-444-70426-4*, North Holland) Elsevier.

Lyberg, M. D., ed. Source Book for Energy Auditors, 2 vols., Set. 694p. (Orig.). 1987. pap. 170.00x (*91-540-4763-3*) Coronet Bks.

Lybrand, jt. auth. see Cooper.

Lybrand, jt. auth. see Coopers.

Lybrand, Fred. Heavenly Citizenship. 140p. (Orig.). 1993. pap. 7.99 (*1-56043-785-5*) Destiny Image.

*__Lybrand International Tax Network Staff & Coopers.__ Nineteen Ninety-four International Tax Summaries: A Guide for Planning & Decisions. 1994. text ed. 105.00 (*0-471-30908-7*) Wiley.

Lybrand, L., jt. auth. see Coopers, C.

Lybrand, R. E., Jr. Holy Communion Is... Sherer, Michael L., ed. LC 86-28345. (Orig.). 1987. pap. 6.85 (*0-89536-853-6*, 7812) CSS OH.

Lybrand, William A., jt. ed. see Lipkin, Mack.

Lybrand, William A., et al. A Study on Evaluation of Driver Education. LC 75-121262. 225p. 1968. 19.00 (*0-403-04515-0*) Scholarly.

Lybyer, Albert H. The Government of the Ottoman Empire in the Time of Suleiman the Magnificent. LC 75-41305. reprint ed. 18.00 (*0-404-14681-3*) AMS Pr.

Lybyer, J. M. David Copperfield Notes. 1980. pap. 3.75 (*0-8220-0364-3*) Cliffs.

— Lord Jim Notes. 1986. pap. 4.25 (*0-8220-0762-2*) Cliffs.

— Our Town Notes. 1990. pap. 3.75 (*0-8220-0967-6*) Cliffs.

— Poe's Short Stories: Notes. 70p. (Orig.). (C). 1981. pap. text ed. 3.50 (*0-8220-1046-1*) Cliffs.

— Red Badge of Courage Notes. 1982. pap. 3.75 (*0-8220-1120-4*) Cliffs.

— Uncle Tom's Cabin Notes. 70p. 1984. pap. text ed. 3.75 (*0-8220-1313-4*) Cliffs.

*__Lycan, William G.__ Consciousness. (Illus.). 184p. 1995. pap. text ed. 14.95 (*0-262-62096-0*, Bradford Bks) MIT Pr.

— Judgment & Justification. (Cambridge Studies in Philosophy). 280p. 1988. pap. 19.95 (*0-521-33580-9*) Cambridge U Pr.

— Logical Form in Natural Language. 360p. 1986. 37.50 (*0-262-12108-5*, Bradford Bks); pap. 12.50 (*0-262-62053-7*, Bradford Bks) MIT Pr.

— Mind & Cognition. 340p. 1989. pap. text ed. 21.95 (*0-631-16763-3*) Blackwell Pubs.

— Modality & Meaning. (Studies in Linguistics & Philosophy). 334p. (C). 1994. lib. bdg. 105.00 (*0-7923-3006-4*) Kluwer Ac.

— Modality & Meaning. (Studies in Linguistics & Philosophy). 334p. (C). 1995. pap. text ed. 49.50 (*0-7923-3007-2*) Kluwer Ac.

Lycett, G. W., jt. ed. see Ginerson, D.

*__Lychack, William.__ England. LC 95-10109. (Games People Play Ser.). (J). 1995. write for info. (*0-516-04436-2*) Childrens.

Lychak, M., jt. auth. see Kuntzevich, V. M.

Lyche, T., jt. auth. see Goldman, R. N.

Lyche, Tom & Schumaker, Larry L., eds. Mathematical Methods in Computer Aided Geometric Design. (Perspectives in Computing Ser.). 500p. 1989. text ed. 66.00 (*0-12-460515-X*) Acad Pr.

— Mathematical Methods in Computer Aided Geometric Design II. (Illus.). 626p. 1992. text ed. 69.95 (*0-12-460510-9*) Acad Pr.

*__Lycholat, Tony.__ The Complete Book of Stretching. (Illus.). 96p. 1995. pap. 15.95 (*1-85223-917-4*, Pub. by Crowood Pr UK) Trafalgar.

Lyck, Lise, ed. Denmark & EC Membership Evaluated. LC 92-30749. (EC Membership Evaluated Ser.). 1992. text ed. 49.95 (*0-312-09081-1*, Pub. by Pinter Pubs UK) St Martin.

Lycophron. Alexandra. 427p. 1973. reprint ed. write for info. (*3-487-04686-5*, Pub. by Georg Olms GW) Lubrecht & Cramer.

— Alexandra, Vol. I. Scheer, Eduard, ed. xxxii, 148p. 1958. write for info. (*3-296-14501-X*, Pub. by Georg Olms GW) Lubrecht & Cramer.

— Alexandra, Vol. II. Scheer, Eduard, ed. lxiv, 398p. 1958. write for info. (*3-296-14502-8*, Pub. by Georg Olms GW) Lubrecht & Cramer.

— The Alexandra of Lycophron. Connor, W. R., ed. LC 78-18587. (Greek Texts & Commentaries Ser.). (Illus.). (ENG & GRE.). 1979. reprint ed. lib. bdg. 21.95 (*0-405-11429-X*) Ayer.

Lycos, Kimon. Plato on Justice & Power: Reading Book I of Plato's Republic. LC 86-19166. (SUNY Series in Philosophy). 201p. 1987. 64.50 (*0-88706-415-9*); pap. 21.95 (*0-88706-416-7*) State U NY Pr.

Lyczkowski, R. W., ed. see American Society of Mechanical Engineers Staff.

Lyda, Hap C. History of Biblical Judaism: An Introductory Study of the Bible. 3rd ed. LC 93-39503. 1994. write for info. (*0-9630629-2-1*) Twenty Fst Century.

Lyda, Hap C. & Wendling, Dennis J. History of Biblical Judaism: An Introductory Study of the Bible. 2nd ed. (C). 1991. pap. text ed. 18.00 (*0-9630629-0-5*) Twenty Fst Century.

Lydall, H. F. Trade & Employment: A Study of the Effects of Trade Expansion on Employment in Developing & Developed Countries (WEP Study) x, 140p. 1975. 22.00 (*92-2-101240-9*); pap. 14.00 (*92-2-101239-5*) Intl Labour Office.

Lydall, Harold F. Yugoslav Socialism: Theory & Practice. (Illus.). 302p. 1987. pap. 21.00 (*0-19-828583-3*) OUP.

Lydamore, Margaret, tr. see Hamman, Adalbert.

*__Lyday, Cookie.__ Country Ribbon Crafts: Delightful Projects Using Easy Techniques. LC 94-35542. (Illus.). 144p. 1995. 24.95 (*0-8069-0990-0*, Chapelle) Sterling.

Lyday, L., jt. auth. see Dauster, F.

Lyday, Richard W., jt. auth. see Wheeler, Donald J.

*__Lyddon, Eileen.__ Door Through Darkness: John of the Cross & Mysticism in Everyday Life. 176p. (Orig.). 1995. pap. 9.95 (*1-56548-037-6*) New City.

Lyddon, Jan W., jt. ed. see Layzell, Daniel T.

Lydecker, Beatrice. Stories the Animals Tell Me. LC 79-1777. (Illus.). 1979. 22.00i (*0-06-065316-7*) Harper SF.

Lydecker, Beatrice C. Stories Animals Tell Me. (Illus.). 160p. 1988. reprint ed. pap. 7.95 (*0-317-93280-2*) B Lydecker.

Lydecki, Richard G. Physical Therapy & Health Sciences: Medical Analysis Index with Research Bibliography. LC 88-47603. 150p. 1988. 37.50 (*0-88164-358-0*); pap. 34.50 (*0-88164-359-9*) ABBE Pubs Assn.

Lydeen, Lottie F. Child Abuse: Medical & Scientific Guide for Reference & Research. LC 83-46098. 150p. 1987. 39.50 (*0-88164-128-6*); pap. 34.50 (*0-88164-129-4*) ABBE Pubs Assn.

— Child Abuse II: Medical Analysis Index with Research Bibliography. LC 85-47845. 150p. 1987. 39.50 (*0-88164-754-3*); pap. 34.50 (*0-88164-755-1*) ABBE Pubs Assn.

— Emotions & Moods: Medical & Psychological Subject Analysis with Bibliography. LC 84-45992. 150p. 1987. 39.50 (*0-88164-306-8*); pap. 34.50 (*0-88164-307-6*) ABBE Pubs Assn.

— Human Concepts of Self in Life, Love & Work: Index of New Information with Authors, Subjects & Bibliography. 180p. 1993. 49.50 (*1-55914-790-3*); pap. 39.50 (*1-55914-791-1*) ABBE Pubs Assn.

— Incest - Acts, Myths & Facts: Index of Modern Authors & Subjects with Guide for Rapid Research. LC 90-56269. 200p. 1991. 44.50 (*1-55914-312-6*); pap. 39.50 (*1-55914-313-4*) ABBE Pubs Assn.

— Learning Disorders: Psychology & Medical Aspects with Reference Bibliography. LC 85-48092. 150p. 1987. 44.50 (*0-88164-456-0*); pap. 39.50 (*0-88164-457-9*) ABBE Pubs Assn.

— Psychology of Attachment & Bonding: Index of Modern Information. LC 88-47600. 150p. 1988. 44.50 (*0-88164-790-X*); pap. 39.50 (*0-88164-791-8*) ABBE Pubs Assn.

— Sexual Abuse of Children: Index of Modern Information. LC 88-47967. 150p. 1990. 44.50 (*1-55914-038-0*); pap. 39.50 (*1-55914-039-9*) ABBE Pubs Assn.

Lydekker, Richard, jt. auth. see Flower, William H.

Lyden, Fremont & Legters, Lyman H., eds. Native Americans & Public Policy. (Orig.). 1988. pap. 12.00 (*0-944285-02-3*) Pol Studies.

Lyden, Fremont J. & Legters, Lyman H., eds. Native Americans & Public Policy. LC 91-25998. (Series in Policy & Institutional Studies). (Illus.). 336p. (Orig.). 1992. 49.95 (*0-8229-3699-2*) U of Pittsburgh Pr.

Lyden, Fremont J. & Miller, Ernest G. Public Budgeting: Program Planning & Implementation. 4th ed. (Illus.). 384p. (C). 1982. pap. text ed. write for info. (*0-13-737403-8*) P-H.

Lyden, Fremont J., jt. ed. see Legters, Lyman H.

Lyden, Fremont J., et al. Training of Good Physicians: Critical Factors in Career Choices. LC 68-21977. (Commonwealth Fund Publications). 262p. 1968. 32.00 (*0-674-90285-8*) HUP.

Lyden, John, ed. Enduring Issues in Religion. (Enduring Issues Ser.). 312p. (C). 1995. lib. bdg. 19.95 (*1-56510-260-6*, 2606); pap. text ed. 11.55 (*1-56510-259-2*, 2592) Greenhaven.

Lyden, John P., jt. auth. see Arnold, William D.

Lydenberg, Harry M. & Archer, John. The Care & Repair of Books. 4th rev. ed. LC 60-11980. 128p. reprint ed. pap. 36.50 (*0-317-10303-2*, 2013679) Bks Demand.

Lydenberg, Robin. Word Cultures: Radical Theory & Practice in William S. Burroughs' Fiction. LC 86-30719. 224p. 1987. 24.95 (*0-252-01413-8*) U of Ill Pr.

Lydenberg, Robin, jt. ed. see Skerl, Jennie.

Lydenberg, Steve. Bankrolling Ballots Update, 1980. 200p. 1981. 2.95 (*0-87871-016-7*) CEP.

— CEP's First Decade. 61p. 1980. 3.00 (*0-318-35437-3*) CEP.

— Minding the Corporate Conscience, 1980: Annual Meeting Roundup. 49p. 1980. 3.00 (*0-318-35439-X*) CEP.

— Weapons for the World Update: The U. S. Corporate Role in International Arms Transfer. 72p. 1977. 2.00 (*0-318-35442-X*) CEP.

Lyders, Josette A. Journal & Newsletter Editing. (Illus.). 200p. 1993. lib. bdg. 35.00 (*0-87287-917-8*) Libs Unl.

Lyders, Richard, jt. auth. see Fingerman, Joel.

Lydersen, Aksel L. & Dahlo, Ingrid. Dictionary of Chemical Engineering: English, German, Spanish, French. LC 92-12716. 250p. (ENG, FRE, GER & SPA.). 1992. pap. text ed. 79.95 (*0-471-93392-9*) Wiley.

***Lydersen, Bjorn K., ed.** Large Scale Cell Culture Technology. 1993. text ed. 74.95 (*0-471-03732-X*) Wiley.

Lyderson, Bjorn K., ed. see Nelson, Kim L.

Lydgate, J., tr. see De Deguileville, Guillaume.

Lydgate, John. Assembly of Gods, or, the Accord of Reason & Sensuality in the Fear of Death. LC 77-136399. (University of Chicago Studies in English: No. 1). 1970. reprint ed. 24.50 (*0-404-50261-X*) AMS Pr.

— Here Endeth the Book of the Lyf of Our Lady. LC 73-38207. (English Experience Ser.: No. 473). 192p. 1972. reprint ed. 75.00 (*90-221-0473-7*) Walter J Johnson.

— Lydgate's Minor Poems: The Two Nightingale Poems. Glauning, Otto, ed. (EETS, ES Ser.: No. 80). 1969. reprint ed. 26.00 (*0-527-00282-8*) Periodicals Srv.

— Lydgate's Siege of Thebes, Pt. 2. Erdmann, Axel, ed. (EETS, ES Ser.: No. 125). 1969. reprint ed. 32.00 (*0-527-00311-5*) Periodicals Srv.

— Lydgate's Temple of Glass. Schick, J., ed. (EETS, ES Ser.: No. 60). 1969. reprint ed. 42.00 (*0-527-00263-1*) Periodicals Srv.

— Lydgate's Troy Book, Pt. 1. Bergen, Henry, ed. (EETS, ES Ser.: Nos. 97, 103, 106, 126). 1969. reprint ed. 42.00 (*0-527-00298-4*) Periodicals Srv.

— Lydgate's Troy Book, Pt. 4. Bergen, Henry, ed. (EETS, ES Ser.: Nos. 97, 103, 106, 126). 1969. reprint ed. 60.00 (*0-527-00300-X*) Periodicals Srv.

— Lydgate's Troy Book, Pts. 2-3. Bergen, Henry, ed. (EETS, ES Ser.: Nos. 97, 103, 106, 126). 1969. reprint ed. 55.00 (*0-527-00299-2*) Periodicals Srv.

— Minor Poems of John Lydgate. (BCL1-PR English Literature Ser.). 1992. reprint ed. lib. bdg. write for info. (*0-7812-7185-1*) Rprt Serv.

— The Minor Poems of John Lydgate, Pt. I. MacCracken, H., ed. (EETS, OS Ser.: Nos. 107 & 192). 1974. reprint ed. 28.00 (*0-527-00308-5*) Periodicals Srv.

— The Minor Poems of John Lydgate, Pt. II. MacCracken, H., ed. (EETS, OS Ser.: Nos. 107 & 192). 1974. reprint ed. 26.00 (*0-527-00193-7*) Periodicals Srv.

Lydgate, Tony. The Art of Making Elegant Wood Boxes: Award Winning Designs. LC 92-38556. (Illus.). 144p. 1993. pap. 16.95 (*0-8069-8838-X*) Sterling.

— Award-Winning Boxes: Design & Techniques. LC 94-48062. 1994. write for info. (*0-8069-8841-X*, Chapelle) Sterling.

Lydiard. Running the Lydiard War. 1978. 12.95 (*0-02-499720-X*) Macmillan.

Lydiard, Arthur & Gilmour, Garth. Running the Lydiard Way. LC 78-360. (Illus.). 241p. 1978. 12.95 (*0-89037-096-6*) Anderson World.

Lydiard, Teri. The British Columbia Bicycling Guide. (Illus.). 76p. (Orig.). 1984. pap. 9.95 (*0-9691693-0-2*) Gordon Soules Bk.

Lydiate, Liz, ed. Professional Practice in Design Consultancy: A Design Business Association Guide. (Illus.). 208p. (C). 1992. pap. 40.95x (*0-85072-304-3*, Pub. by Design Council Bks UK) Ashgate Pub Co.

Lydic, Ralph & Biebuyck, Julian F., eds. Clinical Physiology of Sleep. (Clinical Physiology Series - An American Physiological Society Book). (Illus.). 253p. 1988. 49.00 (*0-19-520780-7*) OUP.

Lydick, Patty. Matter of Independence. abr. ed. 170p. 1995. pap. 7.95 (*1-56901-425-6*) NW Pub.

Lydolph, P. E. Climates of the Soviet Union. (World Survey of Climatology Ser.: Vol. 7). 444p. 1977. 174.50 (*0-444-41516-5*) Elsevier.

Lydolph, Paul E. Geography of the USSR. 5th ed. LC 89-63699. (Illus.). 447p. (C). 1990. text ed. 37.50 (*0-9624933-0-9*) Misty Val Pub.

— Weather & Climate. LC 84-18080. (Illus.). 230p. (C). 1985. 41.50 (*0-86598-120-5*, R3924) Rowman.

Lydon, F. D. Concrete Mix Design. 2nd ed. (Illus.). xii, 196p. 1983. 63.00 (*0-85334-162-1*, I-358-82, Pub. by Elsevier Applied Sci UK) Elsevier.

Lydon, F. D., ed. Developments in Concrete Technology, Vol. 1. (Illus.). 325p. 1979. 79.25 (*0-85334-855-3*, Pub. by Elsevier Applied Sci UK) Elsevier.

Lydon, John, et al. Rotten: No Irish, No Blacks, No Dogs. (Illus.). 384p. 1994. 22.95 (*0-312-09903-7*) St Martin.

Lydon, Kerry R. A Birthday for Blue. Levine, Abby, ed. LC 88-21697. (Illus.). 32p. (J). (gr. k-3). 1989. 13.95 (*0-8075-0774-1*) A Whitman.

***Lydon, Mary.** Skirting the Issue: Essays in Literary Theory. LC 94-27062. 1995. 48.00 (*0-299-14460-7*); pap. 24.95 (*0-299-14464-X*) U of Wis Pr.

Lydon, Michael. Rock Folk. 1990. pap. 9.95 (*0-8065-1206-7*, Citadel Pr) Carol Pub Group.

— Writing & Life. LC 95-13843. 112p. (C). 1995. pap. 9.95 (*0-87451-730-3*) U Pr of New Eng.

Lydon, Michael & Mandel, Ellen. Boogie Lightning: How Music Became Electric. (Illus.). 1980. pap. 6.95 (*0-306-80123-X*) Da Capo.

Lydon, Peter, jt. ed. see Rogers, Peter.

Lydon, Sandy. Chinese Gold: The Chinese in the Monterey Bay Region. LC 84-72699. (Illus.). 550p. (C). 1985. 29.95 (*0-932319-00-9*); pap. text ed. 24.95 (*0-932319-01-7*) Capitola Bk.

Lydon, Susan G. Take the Long Way Home: Memoirs of a Survivor. LC 92-56400. 320p. 1993. 22.00 (*0-06-250550-5*) Harper SF.

— Take the Long Way Home: Memoirs of a Survivor. LC 92-56400. 336p. 1994. reprint ed. pap. 12.00 (*0-06-250723-0*) Harper SF.

Lydon, William T. & McGraw, M. Loretta. Concept Development for Visually Handicapped Children: A Resource Guide for Teachers & Other Professionals Working in Educational Settings. rev. ed. 80p. 1973. pap. 12.95 (*0-89128-018-9*) Am Foun Blind.

Lydtin, H. & Trenkwalder, P. Calcium Antagonists. (Illus.). 272p. 1989. 70.00 (*0-387-51372-8*, 3257) Spr-Verlag.

Lydtin, Hans, ed. see International Conference on Chemical Vapor Deposition Staff.

Lye, Edward, ed. see Junius, Franciscus.

Lye, Keith. Coasts. Furstinger, Nancy, ed. (Our World Ser.). (Illus.). 48p. (J). (gr. 5-8). 1989. lib. bdg. 12.95 (*0-382-09790-4*) Silver Burdett Pr.

— The Complete Atlas of the World. LC 94-19316. (J). 1994. lib. bdg. 31.36 (*0-8114-5804-0*) Raintree Steck-V.

— Deserts. (Our World Ser.). (Illus.). 48p. (J). (gr. 5-8). 1987. lib. bdg. 12.95 (*0-382-09501-4*) Silver Burdett Pr.

— The Earth. (Young Readers' Nature Library). (Illus.). 64p. (J). (gr. 4-6). 1991. lib. bdg. 15.40 (*1-56294-025-2*) Millbrook Pr.

— The Earth in Three Dimensions: An Atlas & Pop-up Globe of the World. (Illus.). 40p. (J). (gr. 3 up). 1995. pap. 17.95 (*0-8037-1739-3*) Dial Bks Young.

— Earthquakes. LC 92-31816. (First Starts Ser.). (Illus.). 32p. (J). (gr. 2-3). 1992. lib. bdg. 19.97 (*0-8114-3409-5*) Raintree Steck-V.

— Mountains. LC 92-31815. (First Starts Ser.). (Illus.). 32p. (J). (gr. 2-3). 1992. lib. bdg. 19.97 (*0-8114-3410-9*) Raintree Steck-V.

— Mountains. (Natural World Ser.). 1992. 24.99 (*0-517-07694-2*) Random Hse Value.

— Mountains. (Our World Ser.). (Illus.). 48p. (J). (gr. 5-8). 1987. lib. bdg. 12.95 (*0-382-09498-0*) Silver Burdett Pr.

— Our Planet the Earth. LC 79-2346. (Lerner Question & Answer Bks.). (Illus.). (J). (gr. 3-6). 1980. lib. bdg. 13.50 (*0-8225-1182-7*, Lerner Publctns); pap. 4.95 (*0-8225-9510-9*, Lerner Publctns) Lerner Group.

— Passport to Germany. LC 93-26680. (Passport to...Ser.). (Illus.). 48p. (J). (gr. 5-8). 1994. lib. bdg. 14.77 (*0-531-14296-5*) Watts.

— Passport to Spain. rev. ed. LC 93-21186. (Illus.). 48p. (J). (gr. 5-8). 1994. lib. bdg. 14.77 (*0-531-14294-9*) Watts.

— Rocks & Minerals. LC 92-31817. (First Starts Ser.). (Illus.). 32p. (J). (gr. 2-3). 1992. lib. bdg. 19.97 (*0-8114-3411-7*) Raintree Steck-V.

— Rocks & Minerals. (J). (ps-3). 1994. 4.95 (*0-8114-6441-5*) Raintree Steck-V.

— Rocks, Minerals & Fossils. (Our World Ser.). (Illus.). 48p. (J). (gr. 5-8). 1991. lib. bdg. 12.95 (*0-382-24226-2*) Silver Burdett Pr.

— Volcanoes. LC 92-32016. (First Starts Ser.). (Illus.). 32p. (J). (gr. 2-3). 1992. lib. bdg. 19.97 (*0-8114-3412-5*) Raintree Steck-V.

— The World Today. (World of Science Ser.). (Illus.). 64p. (YA). 1985. 12.95 (*0-8160-1072-2*) Facts on File.

Lye, Keith, jt. auth. see Dempsey, Michael W.

Lye, Keith, jt. auth. see Mason, Antony.

Lye, M. D. Acute Geriatric Medicine. LC 85-12727. (Modern Geriatric Medicine Ser.). 1985. lib. bdg. 78.00 (*0-85200-801-5*) Kluwer Ac.

Lyell, Andrew. It's Really Quite Safe! Observation Post Officer. 162p. (C). 1987. 84.00 (*0-948251-06-9*, Pub. by Picton UK) St Mut.

Lyell, Anne M., ed. NONQUITT, A Summer Album: 1872-1985. LC 87-71240. (Illus.). 288p. (C). 1987. 35.00 (*0-9618732-0-5*) Barekneed Pubs.

Lyell, Charles. Geological Evidence of the Antiquity of Man. 4th ed. LC 72-1728. (Illus.). reprint ed. 47.50 (*0-404-08138-X*) AMS Pr.

— Life, Letters & Journals, 2 vols., Vol. I. Lyell, Katharine M., ed. LC 72-1728. (Darwin Ser.). (Illus.). 488p. (C). 1983. reprint ed. 94.50 (*0-404-08156-8*) AMS Pr.

— Life, Letters & Journals, 2 vols., Vol. 2, 504 pgs. Lyell, Katharine M., ed. (Illus.). (C). 1983. reprint ed. Vol. II, 504 pgs. write for info. (*0-318-57959-6*) AMS Pr.

— Principles of Geology, 3 vols., Set. (Illus.). 1970. reprint ed. text ed. 100.00 (*3-7682-0685-8*) Lubrecht & Cramer.

— Principles of Geology, Vol. 1. LC 90-11008. (Illus.). 576p. 1990. lib. bdg. 39.95 (*0-226-49793-3*); pap. text ed. 17.95 (*0-226-49794-1*) U Ch Pr.

— Principles of Geology, Vol. 3. LC 90-11008. (Illus.). 580p. 1991. pap. text ed. 17.95 (*0-226-49799-2*) U Ch Pr.

— Principles of Geology, Vol. 3. LC 90-11008. (Illus.). 580p. 1991. lib. bdg. 39.95 (*0-226-49798-4*) U Ch Pr.

— Principles of Geology, Vol. 2: An Inquiry How Far the Former Changes of the Earth's Surface Are Referable to Causes Now in Operation. (Illus.). 352p. 1991. lib. bdg. 35.00 (*0-226-49796-8*); pap. text ed. 15.95 (*0-226-49797-6*) U Ch Pr.

— A Second Visit to North America, 2 vols., Set. (BCL1 - U. S. History Ser.). 1991. reprint ed. lib. bdg. 150.00 (*0-7812-6012-4*) Rprt Serv.

— Sir Charles Lyell's Scientific Journals on the Species Question. Wilson, Leonard G., ed. LC 77-99848. (Yale Studies in the History of Science & Medicine: No. 5). (Illus.). 636p. reprint ed. pap. 180.00 (*0-8357-8322-7*, 2033922) Bks Demand.

— Travels in North America, the Years, 1841-2: Geological Observations on the United States, Canada & Nova Scotia, 2 vols. in one. Albritton, Claude C., Jr., ed. LC 77-6525. (History of Geology Ser.). (Illus.). 1978. reprint ed. lib. bdg. 44.95 (*0-405-10447-2*) Ayer.

Lyell, Charles B. Second Visit to North America, 2 vols., Set. 1855. 79.00 (*0-403-00357-1*) Scholarly.

Lyell, Denis D. Memories of an African Hunter. (Illus.). 288p. 1987. 15.95 (*0-312-00155-X*) St Martin.

Lyell, Katharine M., ed. see Lyell, Charles.

Lyell, William A., tr. see Lu Xun.

Lyell, William J., Jr., comp. A Lu Hsun Reader. 1976. 14.95 (*0-88710-046-5*) Yale Far Eastern Pubns.

Lyerly. Surgical Intensive Care. 2nd ed. 1988. 22.50 (*0-8151-5670-7*, Yr Bk Med Pubs) Mosby Yr Bk.

Lyerly, Elaine M., jt. auth. see Neely, Cynthia H.

Lyerly, H. Kim, jt. ed. see Sabiston, David C., Jr.

Lyford, Carrie. Iroquois: Their Arts & Crafts. (Illus.). 100p. 1989. pap. 9.95 (*0-88839-135-8*) Hancock House.

Lyford, Carrie A. Iroquois Crafts. (Illus.). 100p. 1982. reprint ed. pap. 5.95 (*0-936984-02-3*) Schneider Pubs.

— Ojibwa Crafts. (Illus.). 216p. 1982. reprint ed. pap. 8.95 (*0-936984-01-5*) Schneider Pubs.

— Quill & Beadwork of the Western Sioux. (Illus.). 116p. 1979. reprint ed. pap. 9.95 (*0-933472-00-5*) Johnson Bks.

— Quill & Beadwork of the Western Sioux. (Illus.). 116p. 1984. reprint ed. pap. 6.95 (*0-936984-08-2*) Schneider Pubs.

***Lyftogt, Kenneth, ed.** Left for Dixie: The Civil War Diary of John Rath. 100p. 1991. pap. 6.95 (*0-931209-51-X*) Mid Prairie Bks.

Lyftogt, Kenneth L. From Blue Mills to Columbia: Cedar Falls & the Civil War. LC 93-24495. 1993. 23.95 (*0-8138-1399-9*) Iowa St U Pr.

Lygidakis, N. J. & Tytgat, G. N., eds. Hepatobiliary & Pancreatic Malignancies. (Illus.). 472p. 1989. text ed. 165.00 (*0-86577-327-0*) Thieme Med Pubs.

Lygidakis, N. T., et al, eds. Pitfalls & Complications in the Diagnosis & Management of Hepatobiliary & Pancreatic Diseases. LC 93-11759. 1993. 259.00 (*0-86577-487-0*) Thieme Med Pubs.

Lygre, David G. General, Organic, & Biological Chemistry. LC 94-8083. 1995. text ed. 58.95 (*0-534-24252-9*) Brooks-Cole.

Lygre, David G., jt. auth. see Miller, G. Tyler, Jr.

Lyina, T. Masterworks of Russian Painting from Soviet Museums. (Illus.). 295p. (C). 1989. text ed. 350.00 (*0-569-09218-3*, Pub. by Collets) St Mut.

Lyiubarskii, Yu, tr. see Feldman, G. M.

Lyke, Evelyn M. Assessing for Nursing Diagnoses: A Human Needs Approach. (Illus.). 222p. 1991. pap. 15.50 (*0-397-54819-2*) Lippincott.

Lyke, J., et al. Keyboard Musicianship, Bk. 1: Group Piano for Adults. 6th ed. (Orig.). 1993. spiral bd. 23.80 (*0-87563-444-3*) Stipes.

— Keyboard Musicianship, Bk. 2: Group Piano for Adults. 6th ed. 1994. spiral bd. 26.80 (*0-87563-504-0*) Stipes.

Lyke, James. Ensemble Music for Group Piano, 1. 1976. 12.40 (*0-87563-120-7*) Stipes.

— Ensemble Music for Group Piano, 2. 1976. 14.80 (*0-87563-128-2*) Stipes.

Lyke, James & Enoch, Yvonne. Creative Piano Teaching. 2nd ed. 1987. text ed. 24.80 (*0-87563-297-1*) Stipes.

Lyke, James, et al. Keyboard Fundamentals. 180p. 1991. pap. text ed. 21.80x (*0-87563-368-4*) Stipes.

Lyke, James P. What We Have Seen & Heard: A Pastoral Letter on Evangelization from the Black Bishops of the United States. 40p. (Orig.). 1984. pap. text ed. 1.95 (*0-86716-040-3*) St Anthony Mess Pr.

Lyke, Jim & Kocour, Mike. Irving Berlin Melodies for Student & Teacher: The Bass Clef Book. 23p. (C). 1992. pap. text ed. 4.00 (*0-87563-398-6*) Stipes.

— Irving Berlin Melodies for Student & Teacher: The Treble Clef Book. 23p. (C). 1992. pap. text ed. 4.00 (*0-87563-399-4*) Stipes.

Lyke, William L. & Hoban, Thomas J., eds. Coastal Water Resources. LC 88-70648. (Technical Publication Ser.: No. 88-1). (Illus.). 874p. (Orig.). 1988. pap. 59.00 (*1-882132-02-5*) Am Water Resources.

Lyke, William L., ed. see National Symposium on the Future Availability of Ground Water Resources Staff.

Lykes, Aimee, tr. see Zong Pu.

Lykes, Brinton M., jt. ed. see Stewart, Abigail J.

***Lykes, Dorothy R.** Cobalt Blue. (Illus.). 64p. 1995. 20.00 (*0-933313-24-1*); pap. 12.95 (*0-933313-25-X*) SUN Gemini Pr.

— Cobalt Blue. deluxe limited ed. (Illus.). 64p. 1995. 30.00 (*0-933313-23-3*) SUN Gemini Pr.

Lykiard, Alexis. Catkin. 60p. 1985. 21.00 (*0-947612-08-4*, Pub. by Rivelin Grapheme Pr) St Mut.

Lykiard, Alexis, tr. see Jarry, Alfred.

Lykins, Benjamin W., Jr., jt. auth. see Clark, Robert M.

Lykins, Benjamin W., Jr., et al. Point-of-Use - Point-of-Entry. 200p. 1991. 64.95 (*0-87371-354-0*, TD433) Lewis Pubs.

Lykke, Erik, ed. Achieving Environmental Goals: The Concept & Practice of Environmental Performance Review. 1992. 72.95 (*1-85293-263-5*, TD153) CRC Pr.

— Achieving Environmental Goals: The Concept & Practice of Environmental Performance Review. LC 09-224768. 1994. text ed. 74.95 (*0-471-94709-1*) Wiley.

***Lykken, David T.** The Antisocial Personalities. 272p. 1995. text ed. 49.95 (*0-8058-1941-X*); pap. text ed. 24.50 (*0-8058-1974-6*) L Erlbaum Assocs.

Lyklema, J. Fundamentals of Interface & Colloid Science. (Illus.). 744p. 1991. text ed. 105.00 (*0-12-460525-7*) Acad Pr.

Lykos, Peter, ed. Computer Modeling of Matter. LC 78-25828. (ACS Symposium Ser.: No. 86). 1978. 32.95 (*0-8412-0463-2*) Am Chemical.

Lykos, Peter & Shavitt, Isaiah, eds. Supercomputers in Chemistry. LC 81-17630. (ACS Symposium Ser.: No. 173). 1981. 38.95 (*0-8412-0666-X*) Am Chemical.

Lykov, A. V. Heat & Mass Transfer in Technological Processes. 272p. 1971. text ed. 69.00 (*0-7065-1240-5*, Pub. by Keter Pub IS) Coronet Bks.

Lyle, Alexandra. All Her Dreams. 448p. 1993. mass mkt. 4.99 (*1-55817-703-5*, Pinnacle NY) Windsor NY.

— Keepsakes. 1991. mass mkt. 4.95 (*1-55817-539-3*, Pinnacle NY) Windsor NY.

— Stolen Dreams. 1990. mass mkt. 4.95 (*1-55817-396-X*, Pinnacle NY) Windsor NY.

Lyle, Anna C. Poetic Justice: A Memoir of My Father Roy Campbell. 156p. 1986. 100.00 (*0-930126-17-3*) Typographeum.

Lyle, Anthony C. Antiques & Their Values. Incl. Americana. 1983. 5.95 (*0-698-11239-3*); Clocks & Watches. 1983. 5.95 (*0-698-11238-5*); Kitchenware. 1983. 5.95 (*0-698-11237-7*); Militaria. 1983. 5.95 (*0-698-11236-9*); 1983. write for info. (*0-318-56979-5*, Coward) Putnam Pub Group.

Lyle, Barbara S., jt. auth. see Dunn, Joseph W., Jr.

Lyle, C., et al, eds. Women Artists of the World. LC 83-63369. (Illus.). 166p. 1984. pap. 12.50 (*0-9602476-4-5*) Midmarch Arts-WAN.

Lyle, David. The Book of Masonry Stoves: Rediscovering an Old Way of Warming. LC 83-3897. (Illus.). 224p. (Orig.). 1994. pap. 24.95 (*0-931790-57-3*) Brick Hse Pub.

Lyle, Dorothy S. Modern Textiles. 2nd ed. LC 81-11574. 513p. (C). 1982. write for info. (*0-02-372880-9*) Macmillan.

Lyle, Dorothy S. & Brinkley, Jeanne. Contemporary Clothing. 1983. text ed. 19.60 (*0-02-663140-7*) Bennett IL.

Lyle, E. S., Jr. Surface Mine Reclamation Manual. 299p. 1986. 66.50 (*0-444-01014-9*) P-H.

Lyle, Elizabeth. Cassy. large type ed. 512p. 1982. 15.95 (*0-7089-0862-4*) Ulverscroft.

Lyle, Emily B., jt. auth. see Shuldham-Shaw, Patrick.

Lyle, Emily B., jt. ed. see Shuldham-Shaw, Patrick.

Lyle, F., ed. Environmentally Induced Cracking: The Interaction Between Mechanisms & Design. LC 88-62410. (Illus.). 161p. 1988. 10.00 (*0-915567-36-9*) NACE Intl.

Lyle, Garry. Cyprus. (Let's Visit Places & Peoples of the World Ser.). (Illus.). 96p. (J). (gr. 5 up). 1988. 14.95 (*0-222-00942-X*) Chelsea Hse.

— Pacific Islands. (Let's Visit Places & Peoples of the World Ser.). (Illus.). 96p. (J). (gr. 5 up). 1988. 14.95 (*0-222-01034-7*) Chelsea Hse.

Lyle, Guy R. Beyond My Expectation: A Personal Chronicle. LC 81-5071. 244p. 1981. 20.00 (*0-8108-1426-9*) Scarecrow.

Lyle, Jack & McLeod, Douglas. Communication, Media & Change. LC 92-19127. 264p. (C). 1993. pap. text ed. 25.95 (*0-87484-935-7*) Mayfield Pub.

Lyle, James & Torras, Hoyt. The Managed Care Handbook: A Comprehensive Guide to Preparing Your Practice for the Managed Care Revolution. Davis, James B., ed. 180p. 1994. pap. 49.95 (*1-57066-002-6*) Practice Mgmt Info.

Lyle, James & Torres, Art. Physicians Fee Guide 1993. rev. ed. 350p. 1993. pap. 99.95 (*1-878487-66-3*) Practice Mgmt Info.

Lyle, James R., jt. auth. see Torras, Hoyt W.

Lyle, Jane. The Key to the Tarot. (Illus.). 1994. 10.00 (*0-06-251133-5*) Harper SF.

— The Lovers' Tarot: For Affairs of the Heart. (Illus.). 144p. 1992. 27.50 (*0-312-08258-4*, Pub. by Thomas Dunne Bks) St Martin.

— A Miscellany of Women's Wisdom. LC 93-83522. (Miscellany Ser.). (Illus.). 96p. 1993. 14.95 (*1-56138-313-9*) Running Pr.

— Secrets of the Zodiac. 64p. 1994. 10.00 (*0-06-251130-0*) Harper SF.

Lyle, Jean K., ed. see Donn, Elizabeth R.

Lyle, Jim. SBus: TELOS: The Electronic Library of Science. LC 92-18701. (Illus.). ix, 351p. 1992. 44.95 (*0-387-97862-3*) Spr-Verlag.

Lyle, John T. Regenerative Design for Sustainable Development. 1994. text ed. 54.95 (*0-471-55582-7*) Wiley.

Lyle, Katie L. The Man Who Wanted Seven Wives. 160p. 1986. 14.95 (*0-912697-35-0*) Algonquin Bks.

— Scalded to Death by the Steam: Authentic Stories of Railroad Disasters & the Ballads That Were Written about Them. (Illus.). 212p. 1983. 22.50 (*0-912697-01-6*) Algonquin Bks.

— Scalded to Death by the Steam: Authentic Stories of Railroad Disasters & the Ballads That Were Written about Them. LC 88-830. (Illus.). 240p. 1988. pap. text ed. 11.95 (*0-945575-01-7*) Algonquin Bks.

— The Wild Berry Book: Romance. Recipes & Remedies. LC 93-48078. (Camp & Cottage Ser.). (Illus.). 144p. 1994. pap. 16.95 (*1-55971-221-X*) NorthWord.

Lyle, Linda & Doty, Howard. Legal Transcription. 450p. 1994. teacher ed 8.00 (*1-56118-672-4*); pap. text ed. 20.95 (*1-56118-671-6*); audio 150.00 (*1-56118-673-2*) Paradigm MN.

Lyle, M. C. Nourse: James Nourse & His Descendants. (Illus.). 167p. 1991. reprint ed. lib. bdg. 32.50 (*0-8328-1822-4*); reprint ed. pap. 22.50 (*0-8328-1823-2*) Higginson Bk Co.

Lyle, Marjorie. The English Heritage Book of Canterbury. (Illus.). 136p. 1994. pap. 34.95 (*0-7134-7315-0*, Pub. by Batsford UK) Trafalgar.

Lyle, Rob. Mistral. 1953. 49.50 (*0-686-50050-4*) Elliots Bks.

Lyle, Royster, Jr., jt. auth. see Crawford, Barbara.

Lyle, Tony, jt. auth. see Sargent, Michael.

Lyle, Watson. Camille Saint-Saens: His Life & Art. 210p. 1990. reprint ed. lib. bdg. 69.00 (*0-7812-9083-X*) Rprt Serv.

— Rachmaninoff. LC 74-24140. 1976. reprint ed. 19.00 (*0-404-13003-8*) AMS Pr.

Lyles, jt. auth. see Staab, Angela S.

Lyles, Anne. British Watercolours: The Great Age, 1750-1880. Wilton, Andrew, ed. (Illus.). 340p. 1993. 70.00 (*3-7913-1254-5*, Pub. by Prestel) TeNeues.

Lyles, Charlise. Do I Dare Disturb the Universe? From Projects to Prep School. LC 93-46456. 200p. 1994. 22.95 (*0-571-19836-8*) Faber & Faber.

Lyles, J. B. The Preacher's Outline & Sermon Bible: Genesis, Vol. 1. LC 92-75229. 1992. text ed. 29.95 (*0-945863-34-9*) Ldrship Minist Wrldwide.

— The Preacher's Outline & Sermon Bible Vol. 1: Matthew. (KOR.). 1994. text ed. 29.95 (*0-945863-80-2*) Ldrship Minist Wrldwide.

— The Preacher's Outline & Sermon Bible Vol. 1: Matthew. (SPA.). 1995. text ed. 29.95 (*0-945863-65-9*) Ldrship Minist Wrldwide.

— The Preacher's Outline & Sermon Bible Vol. 2: Genesis. 1994. text ed. 29.95 (*0-945863-35-7*) Ldrship Minist Wrldwide.

— The Preacher's Outline & Sermon Bible Vol. 2: Matthew. (KOR.). 1994. text ed. 29.95 (*0-945863-81-0*) Ldrship Minist Wrldwide.

— The Preacher's Outline & Sermon Bible Vol. 2: Matthew. (SPA.). 1995. text ed. 29.95 (*0-945863-66-7*) Ldrship Minist Wrldwide.

— The Preacher's Outline & Sermon Bible Vol. 3: Mark. (KOR.). 1994. text ed. 29.95 (*0-945863-82-9*) Ldrship Minist Wrldwide.

— The Preacher's Outline & Sermon Bible Vol. 4: Luke. (KOR.). 1994. text ed. 29.95 (*0-945863-83-7*) Ldrship Minist Wrldwide.

— The Preacher's Outline & Sermon Bible Vol. 5: John. (KOR.). 1994. text ed. 29.95 (*0-945863-84-5*) Ldrship Minist Wrldwide.

— The Preacher's Outline & Sermon Bible Vol. 7: Romans. (SPA.). 1995. text ed. 29.95 (*0-945863-71-3*) Ldrship Minist Wrldwide.

— The Preacher's Outline & Sermon Bible Vol. 7: Romans. (RUS.). 1995. text ed. 5.00 (*0-945863-56-X*) Ldrship Minist Wrldwide.

— The Preacher's Outline & Sermon Bible Vol. 9: Galatians, Ephesians, Phillipians, Colossians. (RUS.). 1995. text ed. 5.00 (*0-945863-58-6*) Ldrship Minist Wrldwide.

— Preacher's Outline & Sermon Bible, Vol. 1: Matthew. LC 91-70855. 1991. text ed. 29.95 (*0-945863-17-9*) Ldrship Minist Wrldwide.

— Preacher's Outline & Sermon Bible, Vol. 10: I & II Thessalonians, I & II Timothy, Titus, Philemon. LC 91-70855. 1991. text ed. 29.95 (*0-945863-26-8*) Ldrship Minist Wrldwide.

— Preacher's Outline & Sermon Bible, Vol. 11: Hebrews & James. LC 91-70855. 1991. text ed. 29.95 (*0-945863-27-6*) Ldrship Minist Wrldwide.

— Preacher's Outline & Sermon Bible, Vol. 12: I & II Peter, I, II, III John, Jude. LC 91-70855. 1991. text ed. 29.95 (*0-945863-28-4*) Ldrship Minist Wrldwide.

— Preacher's Outline & Sermon Bible, Vol. 13: Revelation. LC 91-70855. 1991. text ed. 29.95 (*0-945863-29-2*) Ldrship Minist Wrldwide.

— Preacher's Outline & Sermon Bible, Vol. 14: Master Index. LC 91-70855. 1991. text ed. 29.95 (*0-945863-30-6*) Ldrship Minist Wrldwide.

— Preacher's Outline & Sermon Bible, Vol. 2: Matthew. LC 91-70855. 1991. text ed. 29.95 (*0-945863-18-7*) Ldrship Minist Wrldwide.

— Preacher's Outline & Sermon Bible, Vol. 3: Mark. LC 91-70855. 1991. text ed. 29.95 (*0-945863-19-5*) Ldrship Minist Wrldwide.

— Preacher's Outline & Sermon Bible, Vol. 4: Luke. LC 91-70855. 1991. text ed. 29.95 (*0-945863-20-9*) Ldrship Minist Wrldwide.

— Preacher's Outline & Sermon Bible, Vol. 5: John. LC 91-70855. 1991. text ed. 29.95 (*0-945863-21-7*) Ldrship Minist Wrldwide.

— Preacher's Outline & Sermon Bible, Vol. 6: Acts. LC 91-70855. 1991. text ed. 29.95 (*0-945863-22-5*) Ldrship Minist Wrldwide.

— Preacher's Outline & Sermon Bible, Vol. 7: Romans. LC 91-70855. 1991. text ed. 29.95 (*0-945863-23-3*) Ldrship Minist Wrldwide.

— Preacher's Outline & Sermon Bible, Vol. 8: First & Second Corinthians. LC 91-70855. 1991. text ed. 29.95 (*0-945863-24-1*) Ldrship Minist Wrldwide.

— Preacher's Outline & Sermon Bible, Vol. 9: Galatians, Ephesians, Philippians, Colossians. LC 91-70855. 1991. text ed. 29.95 (*0-945863-25-X*) Ldrship Minist Wrldwide.

— What the Bible Says to the Minister: The Minister's Personal Handbook. 400p. (Orig.). (C). 1992. pap. 14.95 (*0-945863-33-0*) Ldrship Minist Wrldwide.

— What the Bible Says...to the Minister: The Minister's Personal Handbook. (SPA.). 1995. pap. text ed. 9.95 (*0-945863-79-9*) Ldrship Minist Wrldwide.

Lyles, Jean. Ducks & Geese. 48p. 1987. pap. 6.50 (*1-56770-172-8*) S Scheewe Pubns.

Lyles, Kevin. Vietnam: U. S. Uniforms in Colour Photographs. (Europa Militaria Ser.). (Illus.). 96p. 1992. pap. 19.95 (*1-872004-52-0*, Pub. by Windrow & Green UK) Motorbooks Intl.

Lyles, Lois, jt. auth. see Mc Clean, Vernon.

Lyles, Peggy. Red Leaves in the Air. 20p. 1979. pap. 2.00 (*0-913719-37-4*) High-Coo Pr.

Lyles, Richard I. & Joiner, Carl. Supervision in the Health Care Organizations. LC 85-17799. 245p. 1986. text ed. 31.95 (*0-8273-4294-2*) Delmar.

Lyles, William H. Putting Dell on the Map: A History of the Dell Paperbacks. LC 83-1661. (Contributions to the Study of Popular Culture Ser.: No. 5). xxiv, 178p. 1983. text ed. 49.95 (*0-313-23667-4*, LPD/, Greenwood Pr) Greenwood.

Lyles, William H., comp. Dell Paperbacks, Nineteen Forty-Two to Mid-Nineteen Sixty-Two: A Catalog-Index. LC 82-25505. (Illus.). xxxv, 471p. 1983. text ed. 75.00 (*0-313-23668-2*, LYE/, Greenwood Pr) Greenwood.

Lyly, John. Campaspe & Sappho & Phao. Hunter, George K. et al, eds. LC 90-13563. (Revels Plays Ser.). (Illus.). 352p. 1992. text ed. 59.95 (*0-7190-1550-2*, Pub. by Manchester Univ Pr UK) St Martin.

— Complete Works of John Lyly, 3 vols., Set. (BCL1-PR English Literature Ser.). 1992. reprint ed. lib. bdg. 225.00 (*0-7812-7212-2*) Rprt Serv.

— Euphues: The Anatomy of Wit: Euphues & His England. (BCL1-PR English Literature Ser.). 473p. 1992. reprint ed. lib. bdg. 99.00 (*0-7812-7213-0*) Rprt Serv.

— Euphues, the Anatomy of Wit. Arber, Edward, ed. reprint ed. pap. 25.00 (*0-87556-213-2*) Saifer.

— Gallathea & Midas. Lancashire, Anne B., ed. LC 69-11445. (Regents Renaissance Drama Ser.). 206p. reprint ed. pap. 58.80 (*0-7837-6465-0*, 2046469) Bks Demand.

Lyman. Biochemistry. (Applied Science Review Ser.). 1993. 11.95 (*0-87434-572-3*) Springhouse Pub.

— Civil War Quotations. 1995. pap. text ed. 11.95 (*0-938289-45-4*) Combined Bks.

Lyman, et al. Clinical, Instruction & Supervision for Accountability. 2nd ed. 176p. 1987. per. 24.95 (*0-8403-4418-X*) Kendall-Hunt.

Lyman, Amy R. Personnel Decisions in the Family Farm Business. 64p. 1993. 6.00 (*1-879906-13-9*, 3357) ANR Pubns CA.

Lyman, B. A Psychology of Food: More Than a Matter of Taste. (Illus.). 144p. (Orig.). 1988. pap. 16.95 (*0-442-25939-5*) Chapman & Hall.

Lyman, C. E., et al. Scanning Electron Microscopy, X-Ray Microanalysis & Analytical Electricity: A Laboratory Workbook. (Illus.). 420p. 1990. spiral bd. 32.50 (*0-306-43591-8*, Plenum Pr) Plenum.

Lyman, Charles, et al. Hibernation & Torpor in Mammals & Birds. (Physiological Ecology Ser.). 317p. 1982. text ed. 91.00 (*0-12-460420-X*) Acad Pr.

Lyman, Charles P. & Lynch, David W. The Massachusetts Society for Promoting Agriculture: 1942-1992. (Illus.). 128p. 1992. 20.00 (*0-938864-16-5*) Ipswich Pr.

Lyman, Chester S. Around the Horn to the Sandwich Islands & California 1845-1850. (American Biography Ser.). 328p. 1991. reprint ed. lib. bdg. 79.00 (*0-7812-8255-1*) Rprt Serv.

— Around the Horn to the Sandwich Islands & California 1845-50. Teggart, Frederick J., ed. LC 70-152992. (Select Bibliographies Reprint Ser.). 1977. reprint ed. 25.95 (*0-8369-5744-X*) Ayer.

Lyman, Clara, jt. ed. see Core, Lucy.

Lyman, Darius, Jr. Leaven for Doughfaces: Parables Touching Slavery. LC 78-146266. (Black Heritage Library Collection). 1977. 28.95 (*0-8369-8741-1*) Ayer.

Lyman, Darryl. Civil War Wordbook: Including Sayings, Phrases, & Expletives. 240p. 1993. pap. 11.95 (*0-938289-25-X*, 7305) Combined Bks.

— The Dictionary of Animal Words & Phrases. enl. rev. ed. LC 94-10106. Orig. Title: The Animal Things We Say. 1994. 19.95 (*0-8246-0378-8*) Jonathan David.

— Great Jews in Music. 500p. 1986. 24.95 (*0-8246-0315-X*) Jonathan David.

— Great Jews on Stage & Screen. 288p. 1987. 19.95 (*0-8246-0328-1*) Jonathan David.

— Jewish Comedy Catalog. 320p. 1989. 19.95 (*0-8246-0339-7*) Jonathan David.

Lyman, Dean B. Last Lutanist & Other Poems. LC 73-144722. (Yale Series of Younger Poets: No. 15). reprint ed. 18.00 (*0-404-53815-0*) AMS Pr.

***Lyman, E. Leo.** San Bernardino: The Rise & Fall of a California Community. 1995. 24.95 (*1-56085-067-1*) Signature Bks.

Lyman, E. R., ed. see Wong, Theodore R.

Lyman, Ed, Jr. Daily Praise. 308p. 1990. 8.99 (*1-56043-701-4*) Destiny Image.

Lyman, Edna. Story Telling: What to Tell & How to Tell It. 1971. reprint ed. 50.00 (*1-55888-230-8*) Omnigraphics Inc.

Lyman, Edward L. Political Deliverance: The Mormon Quest for Utah Statehood. LC 85-1204. (Illus.). 352p. 1986. 22.95 (*0-252-01239-9*) U of Ill Pr.

Lyman, George D. Ralston's Ring: California Plunders the Comstock Lode. 1992. reprint ed. lib. bdg. 75.00 (*0-7812-5062-5*) Rprt Serv.

Lyman, Henry. Bluefishing. (Illus.). 160p. (Orig.). 1987. pap. 10.95 (*0-941130-58-4*) Lyons & Burford.

Lyman, Henry & Woolner, Frank. Bottom Fishing. (Illus.). 120p. 1988. pap. 10.95 (*0-941130-63-0*) Lyons & Burford.

Lyman, Henry, tr. see Rannit, Aleksis.

Lyman, Henry, jt. auth. see Woolner, Frank.

Lyman, Howard B. Test Scores & What They Mean. 4th ed. (Illus.). 204p. (C). 1986. pap. text ed. write for info. (*0-13-903832-9*) P-H.

— Test Scores & What They Mean. 5th ed. 1990. pap. text ed. 33.00 (*0-13-904178-8*) P-H.

Lyman, Irene P. Dark Isle of Love. large type ed. (Linford Romance Library). 320p. 1986. pap. 11.95 (*0-7089-6233-5*, Linford) Ulverscroft.

Lyman, J. Rebecca. Christology & Cosmology: Models of Divine Activity in Origen, Eusebius, & Athanasius. LC 92-32481. (Oxford Theological Monographs). (C). 1993. 42.00 (*0-19-826745-2*, Clarendon Pr) OUP.

Lyman, Jane W. & Palmer, Glenn R. Recycling of NdFeB Magnet Scrap. 1993. write for info. (*0-318-71697-6*) US Interior.

Lyman, June. Don't Take Away My Passport. LC 92-11035. 274p. 1992. 14.95 (*0-931541-27-1*) Mancorp Pub.

Lyman, Karen A. Day in, Day Out with Alzheimer's: Stress in Caregiving Relationships. LC 93-9157. (Health, Society, & Policy Ser.). 256p. 1993. 44.95 (*1-56639-098-2*); pap. 18.95 (*1-56639-097-4*) Temple U Pr.

Lyman, Kennie, ed. see Bigon, Maria, et al.

Lyman, Kennie, ed. see Cippriani, Curzio & Borelli, Alessando.

Lyman, Lawrence & Foyle, Harvey C. Cooperative Grouping for Interactive Learning: Students, Teachers, & Administrators. 96p. 1990. 11.95 (*0-8106-1842-7*) NEA.

Lyman, Lawrence, et al. Cooperative Learning in the Elementary Classroom. LC 93-4125. (Developments in Classroom Instruction Ser.). 160p. 1993. 14.95 (*0-8106-3042-7*, NEA Prof Lib) NEA.

Lyman, M. Practical Aspects of Drug Enforcement: Procedures & Administration. (Practical Aspects of Criminal & Forensic Investigations Ser.). iix, 450p. 1989. 49.50 (*0-444-01455-1*) CRC Pr.

Lyman, M. A. Lydia. Jones, M. L., ed. 140p. (Orig.). 1994. pap. 9.95 (*1-882270-14-2*) Old Rugged Cross.

Lyman, Mary E. Death & the Christian Answer. LC 60-9784. (C). 1960. pap. 3.00 (*0-87574-107-X*) Pendle Hill.

Lyman, Michael D. Criminal Investigation: The Art & the Science. 464p. 1993. text ed. 66.00 (*0-13-151929-8*) P-H.

— Narcotics & Crime Control. (Illus.). 206p. 1987. 42.95 (*0-398-05347-2*) C C Thomas.

— Narcotics & Crime Control. (Illus.). 206p. 1987. pap. 25.95 (*0-398-06252-8*) C C Thomas.

— Practical Drug Enforcement: Procedures & Administration. LC 93-19071. 1992. 52.00 (*0-8493-9514-3*, HV8079) CRC Pr.

Lyman, Michael D. & Potter, Gary W. Drugs in Society: Causes, Concepts & Control. LC 90-84732. 423p. (C). 1991. pap. text ed. 28.95 (*0-87084-548-9*) Anderson Pub Co.

Lyman, Nanci A. Paul Bunyan. LC 79-66320. (Illus.). 48p. (J). (gr. 3-6). 1980. lib. bdg. 9.89 (*0-89375-310-6*); pap. 3.50 (*0-89375-309-2*) Troll Assocs.

— Pecos Bill. LC 79-66319. (Illus.). 48p. (J). (gr. 3-6). 1980. lib. bdg. 9.89 (*0-89375-308-4*); pap. 3.50 (*0-89375-307-6*) Troll Assocs.

Lyman, Patricia. Beads & Cabochons: How to Create Fashion Earrings & Jewelry. Knight, Denise, ed. LC 90-86227. (Illus.). 92p. (Orig.). 1992. per., pap. 9.95 (*0-943604-32-X*) Eagles View.

Lyman, Paul D. National Directory for the Service of Civil Process. 587p. (Orig.). 1990. pap. 49.95 (*1-878337-24-6*) Knowles Law.

Lyman, Payson W. History of Easthampton, Its Settlement & Growth: With a Genealogical Record of Its Original Families. vi, 209p. 1985. reprint ed. 20.00 (*0-917890-58-2*) Heritage Bk.

Lyman, Phineas, jt. auth. see Loudon, Archibald.

Lyman, Princeton N., jt. auth. see Cole, David C.

***Lyman, R. D. & Hembree-Kigin, T. L.** Mental Health Interventions with Preschool Children. (Issues in Clinical Child Psychology Ser.: 1). (Illus.). 290p. (C). 1994. 45.00 (*0-306-44860-2*, Plenum Pr) Plenum.

Lyman, R. D., et al, eds. Residential & Inpatient Treatment of Children & Adolescents. (Illus.). 390p. 1989. 62.50 (*0-306-43161-0*, Plenum Pr) Plenum.

Lyman, R. Lee. Prehistory of the Oregon Coast: The Effects of Excavation Strategies & Assemblage Size on Archaeological Inquiry. (Illus.). 391p. 1991. text ed. 66.00 (*0-12-460415-3*) Acad Pr.

— Vertebrate Taphonomy. LC 93-28675. (Manuals in Archaeology Ser.). (Illus.). 576p. (C). 1994. 84.95 (*0-521-45215-5*); pap. 34.95 (*0-521-45840-4*) Cambridge U Pr.

Lyman, Ralph. Binding & Finishing. Groff, Pamela, ed. LC 92-85317. (Illus.). 200p. 1993. text ed. 55.00 (*0-88362-163-0*) Graphic Arts Tech Found.

Lyman, Samuel & Marshall, Atwood. Bastogne: The Story of the First Eight Days. LC 79-18262. reprint ed. 19.95 (*0-89201-060-6*) Zenger Pub.

Lyman, Stanford M. Civilization: Contents, Discontents, Malcontents & Other Essays in Social Theory. LC 89-20221. 352p. 1990. 30.00 (*1-55728-136-X*) U of Ark Pr.

— Color, Culture, Civilization: Race & Minority Issues in American Society. LC 93-17539. 408p. 1994. 44.95 (*0-252-02048-0*) U of Ill Pr.

— Color, Culture, Civilization: Race & Minority Issues in American Society. 408p. (C). 1995. pap. 19.95 (*0-252-06475-5*) U of Ill Pr.

— Militarism, Imperialism, & Racial Accommodation: An Analysis & Interpretation of the Early Writings of Robert E. Park. 360p. 1992. 30.00 (*1-55728-219-6*) U of Ark Pr.

— NATO & Germany: A Study in the Sociology of Supranational Relations. LC 95-12243. (Illus.). 384p. 1995. 36.00 (*1-55728-389-3*) U of Ark Pr.

— The Seven Deadly Sins: Society & Evil. rev. ed. LC 88-82176. 368p. 1989. pap. text ed. 18.95 (*0-930390-81-4*) Gen Hall.

— The Seven Deadly Sins: Society & Evil. 2nd rev. ed. LC 88-82176. 368p. 1989. text ed. 35.95 (*0-930390-82-2*) Gen Hall.

Lyman, Stanford M. & Scott, Marvin B. A Sociology of the Absurd. 2nd ed. LC 89-80378. 256p. 1989. text ed. 35.95 (*0-930390-86-5*); pap. text ed. 15.95 (*0-930390-85-7*) Gen Hall.

Lyman, Stanford M. & Vidich, Arthur J. Social Order & the Public Philosophy: An Analysis & Interpretation of the Work of Herbert Blumer. LC 87-30257. 396p. (C). 1988. 35.00 (*0-938626-87-6*) U of Ark Pr.

Lyman, Stanford M., jt. auth. see Vidich, Arthur J.

Lyman, Stanford M., et al, eds. Social Movements: Critiques, Concepts, Case Studies. (Main Trends of the Modern World Ser.). 340p. 1994. 50.00 (*0-8147-5085-0*); pap. 17.50 (*0-8147-5086-9*) NYU Pr.

Lyman, Stanley D. Wounded Knee, 1973: A Personal Account. O'Neil, Floyd A. et al, eds. LC 90-12653. (Illus.). xxxx, 196p. 1991. 33.00 (*0-8032-2889-9*) U of Nebr Pr.

***Lyman, Stephen, illus. & photos.** Into the Wilderness: An Artist's Journey. LC 95-15654. 1995. boxed write for info. (*0-86713-029-6*) Greenw Pr Ltd.

Lyman, Taylor, ed. see American Society for Metals Staff.

Lyman, Theodore. Meade's Headquarters Eighteen Sixty-Three to Eighteen Sixty-Five: Letters of Colonel Theodore Lyman from the Wilderness to Appomattox. Agassiz, George R., ed. LC 71-137381. (Select Bibliographies Reprint Ser.). 1977. reprint ed. 32.95 (*0-8369-5582-X*) Ayer.

— Meade's Headquarters, 1863-1865: Letters of Colonel Theodore Lyman from the Wilderness to Appomattox. (American Biography Ser.). 371p. 1991. reprint ed. lib. bdg. 79.00 (*0-7812-8256-X*) Rprt Serv.

— With Grant & Meade from the Wilderness to Appomattox. LC 93-45368. (Illus.). xxiv, 371p. 1994. pap. 13.95 (*0-8032-7935-3*, Bison Books) U of Nebr Pr.

Lyman, Theodore R., jt. auth. see Gardiner, John A.

Lyman, Thomas A. Dictionary of Mong Njua: A Miao (Meo) Language of Southeast Asia. LC 72-94484. (Janua Linguarum, Ser. Practica: No. 123). (Illus.). 403p. (Orig.). (MON.). 1974. pap. text ed. 100.00 (*90-279-2696-4*) Mouton.

Lyman, Thomas W. & Smartt, Daniel. French Romanesque Sculpture: An Annotated Bibliography. 464p. 1987. lib. bdg. 50.00 (*0-8161-8330-9*, Hall Reference) Macmillan.

Lyman, Warren J., et al. Handbook of Chemical Property Estimation Methods: Environmental Behavior of Organic Compounds. 960p. 1990. reprint ed. 49.95 (*0-8412-1761-0*) Am Chemical.

Lyman, William D. & Rubinstein, Arye, eds. Pediatric AIDS: Clinical, Pathologic, & Basic Science Perspectives. LC 93-37011. (Annals Ser.: Vol. 693). 1993. write for info. (*0-89766-791-3*); pap. write for info. (*0-89766-792-1*) NY Acad Sci.

Lymbery, A. J., jt. ed. see Thompson, R. C.

Lympany, Moura & Strickland, Margot. Moura Lympany: Her Autobiography. (Illus.). 186p. 1991. 40.00 (*0-7206-0824-4*, Pub. by P Owen Ltd UK) Dufour.

Lyn. Raw Opals. 60p. (Orig.). 1987. pap. 7.95 (*0-89807-251-4*) Illuminati.

***Lyn, Craig.** The Macintosh 3D Professional. (Illus.). 600p. (Orig.). 1995. pap. 39.95 (*1-886801-17-7*) Chrles River Media.

Lyn, Judy. The Sun Always Rises. 77p. 1990. pap. 9.95 (*0-9638550-0-X*) Judy Lyn.

Lynam, Joss, ed. Best Irish Walks. (Illus.). 175p. (Orig.). 1994. pap. 15.95 (*0-7171-2144-5*, Pub. by Gill & MacMill IE) Irish Bks Media.

Lynam, Shevawn. Humanity Dick Martin: "King of Connemara," Seventeen Fifty-Four to Eighteen Thirty-Four. (Illus.). 300p. 1989. reprint ed. pap. 13.95 (*0-946640-36-X*, Pub. by Lilliput Pr Ltd IE) Irish Bks Media.

Lynas, Wendy. Communication in the Education of Deaf Children. 100p. (Orig.). (C). 1994. pap. text ed. 32.50 (*1-56593-373-7*, 0750) Singular Publishing.

***Lynaugh, Joan E., ed.** Nursing History Review: Official Journal of the American Association for the History of Nursing, Vol. 4. (Illus.). 224p. 1996. pap. text ed. 36.00 (*0-8122-1453-6*) U of Pa Pr.

— Nursing History Review Vol. 2: Official Journal of the American Association for the History of Nursing. (Illus.). 208p. 1993. pap. text ed. 35.00 (*0-8122-1451-X*) U of Pa Pr.

— Nursing History Review Vol. 3: Official Journal of the American Association for the History of Nursing. (Illus.). 312p. 1994. pap. text ed. 35.00 (*0-8122-1452-8*) U of Pa Pr.

Lynberg, Michael. The Path with Heart. 96p. 1989. pap. 7.95 (*0-449-90452-0*, Columbine) Fawcett.

Lynberg, Michael, comp. Winning! Great Coaches & Athletes Share Their Secrets of Success. LC 92-40069. 1993. 6.99 (*0-385-47017-7*) Doubleday.

***Lynch.** Emergency Nursing: Forensics, Protocols, Policies & Guidelines. 250p. 1995. 145.00 (*0-8342-0666-8*) Aspen Pub.

— Images Never Seen Before. Date not set. pap. 15.95 (*0-06-092219-2*) HarpC.

— Management Accounting. 1006p. (Orig.). 1986. 45.00 (*0-685-67007-4*, 5476) Commerce.

— Management Accounting Study Guide. 224p. 1986. 12.50 (*0-685-67008-2*, 5447) Commerce.

— Organization Theory & Management. (Public Administration & Public Policy Ser.: Vol. 20). 280p. 1983. 55.00 (*0-8247-7021-8*) Dekker.

Lynch, ed. Cancer Genetics in Women, 2 vols., Set. 1987. 220.00 (*0-8493-5180-4*, RC281, CRC Reprint) Franklin.

— Hereditary Malignant Melanoma. 1991. 223.00 (*0-8493-6051-X*, RC280, CRC Reprint) Franklin.

Lynch & Pickett. General & Oral Pathology for the Dental Hygienist. (Illus.). 500p. 1991. 35.00 (*0-8016-3101-7*) Mosby Yr Bk.

Lynch & Warfel, eds. Enjoy. (Illus.). 304p. 1981. spiral bd. 10.00 (*0-9607538-0-X*) Womens Com Buffalo.

Lynch, jt. auth. see Banks.

Lynch, jt. auth. see Rabin.

Lynch, A. J. Mineral Crushing & Grinding Circuits: Their Simulation, Design & Control. (Developments in Mineral Processing Ser.: Vol. 1). 342p. 1977. 97.50 (*0-444-41528-9*) Elsevier.

An Asterisk (*) at the beginning of an entry indicates that the title is appearing in BIP for the first time.

Lynch, A. J., et al. Mineral & Coal Flotation Circuits: Their Simulation & Control. (Developments in Mineral Processing Ser.: Vol. 3). 292p. 1981. 92.50 (*0-444-41919-5*) Elsevier.

Lynch, Acklyn. Nightmare Overhanging Darkly: Essays on Black Culture & Resistance. rev. ed. 1993. reprint ed. pap. 14.95 (*0-88378-142-5*) Third World.

Lynch, Alfred F., jt. auth. see Newman, Pamela.

Lynch, Allan, jt. auth. see Lukic, Reneo.

Lynch, Allen. The Cold War Is over - Again. 208p. 1992. text ed. 49.00 (*0-8133-1470-4*) Westview.

— The Cold War Is over - Again. 208p. (C). 1992. pap. text ed. 19.95 (*0-8133-1471-2*) Westview.

— Gorbachev's International Outlook, Vol. 9: Intellectual Origins & Political Consequences. 72p. (C). 1989. pap. text ed. 14.85 (*0-8133-7795-1*) Westview.

— The Soviet Breakup & U. S. Foreign Policy. Hoepli, Nancy L., ed. LC 92-71574. (Headline Ser.: No. 297). (Illus.). 72p. (Orig.). 1992. pap. 5.95 (*0-87124-146-3*) Foreign Policy.

— The Soviet Study of International Relations. (Soviet & East European Studies). 224p. (C). 1989. pap. 19.95 (*0-521-36763-8*) Cambridge U Pr.

Lynch, Allen C. & Thompson, Kenneth W., eds. Soviet & Post-Soviet Russia in a World of Change. LC 93-35876. (Miller Center Series on a World in Change: Vol. 5). 238p. (Orig.). 1994. lib. bdg. 52.00 (*0-8191-8705-4*, Pub. by White Miller Center); pap. text ed. 21.50 (*0-8191-8706-2*, Pub. by White Miller Center) U Pr of Amer.

Lynch, Amy. Nashville. LC 90-41611. (Downtown America Ser.). (Illus.). 60p. (J). (gr. 3 up). 1991. text ed. 13.95 (*0-87518-453-7*, Dillon Silver Burdett) Silver Burdett Pr.

Lynch, Annette. Redesigning School Health Services. LC 82-12178. (Illus.). 351p. 1983. 45.95 (*0-89885-102-5*) Human Sci Pr.

Lynch, Audry. With Steinbeck in the Sea of Cortez: A Memoir of the Steinbeck - Ricketts Expedition. (Illus.). 96p. (Orig.). 1991. pap. 7.95 (*0-944627-56-0*) Sand River Pr.

Lynch, Barbara S. & Bonnie, Richard J., eds. Growing up Tobacco Free: Preventing Nicotine Addiction in Children & Youths. 320p. (Orig.). (C). 1994. pap. 24.95 (*0-309-05129-0*) Natl Acad Pr.

Lynch, Barry. The BBC Diet: The Easiest, Healthiest Diet Ever. 178p. 1992. pap. 5.95 (*0-563-20689-6*, BBC-Parkwest) Parkwest Pubns.

Lynch, Barry, ed. Ada: Experiences & Prospects: Proceedings of the Ada-Europe International Conference, Dublin, 1990. (Ada Companion Ser.). (Illus.). 300p. (C). 1990. 74.95 (*0-521-39522-4*) Cambridge U Pr.

Lynch, Bernard. A Priest on Trial. (Illus.). 198p. 1994. 29.95 (*0-7475-1036-9*, Pub. by Bloomsbury Pub Ltd UK) Trafalgar.

Lynch, Beverly, ed. Academic Library in Transition: Planning for the 1990s. 400p. (Orig.). (C). 1989. pap. text ed. 39.95 (*1-55570-043-8*) Neal-Schuman.

Lynch, Beverly P., ed. Management Strategies for Libraries: A Basic Reader. LC 85-5668. 682p. 1985. pap. text ed. 37.50 (*0-918212-86-3*) Neal-Schuman.

Lynch, Brian. Voices from the Nettle-Way. 60p. 1990. pap. 10.95 (*1-85186-055-X*) Dufour.

Lynch, Brian, jt. auth. see Tobin, Robert.

***Lynch, Brian K.** Language Program Evaluation: Theory & Practice. (Cambridge Applied Linguistics Ser.). (Illus.). 192p. (C). 1995. write for info. (*0-521-48191-0*); pap. write for info. (*0-521-48438-3*) Cambridge U Pr.

Lynch-Brown, C., ed. International Children's Literature: A Special Issue of the Journal of Early Child Development & Care. 80p. 1989. pap. text ed. 78.00 (*0-677-25910-7*) Gordon & Breach.

Lynch-Brown, Carol & Tomlinson, Carl M. Essentials of Children's Literature. LC 92-28378. 1992. pap. text ed. 30.00 (*0-205-13937-X*) Allyn.

Lynch, Carl, III, ed. Clinical Cardiac Electrophysiology: Perioperative Considerations. (Illus.). 300p. 1994. 49.95 (*0-397-51405-0*) Lippincott.

Lynch, Carmen, jt. auth. see Blinder, Martin.

Lynch, Charles T., ed. Handbook of Materials Science. Incl. Vol. I. General Properties. 760p. 1974. 141.95 (*0-87819-231-X*, TA403); Vol. II. Metals, Composites & Refractory Materials. 448p. 1975. 120.95 (*0-87819-232-8*); Vol. III. Nonmetallic Materials & Applications. 642p. 1975. 120.95 (*0-87819-233-6*, TA403); write for info. (*0-318-51462-1*) CRC Pr.

— Practical Handbook of Materials Science. 736p. 1989. 73.95 (*0-8493-3702-X*, TA403) CRC Pr.

***Lynch, Chris.** Blue-Eyed Son. LC 94-18728. (J). 1995. lib. bdg. 13.89 (*0-06-025397-5*) HarpC.

— Gypsy Davey. LC 94-2674. 160p. (YA). (gr. 7 up). 1994. 14.00 (*0-06-023586-1*); lib. bdg. 13.89 (*0-06-023587-X*) HarpC Child Bks.

— Iceman. LC 93-7776. 160p. (YA). (gr. 7 up). 1994. 15.00 (*0-06-023340-0*); lib. bdg. 14.89 (*0-06-023341-9*) HarpC Child Bks.

— Shadow Boxer. LC 92-47490. 224p. (J). (gr. 5 up). 1993. 14.95 (*0-06-023027-4*); lib. bdg. 14.89 (*0-06-023028-2*) HarpC Child Bks.

— Shadow Boxer. LC 92-47490. 224p. (YA). (gr. 5 up). 1995. pap. 3.95 (*0-06-447112-8*, Trophy) HarpC Child Bks.

— Walk. LC 94-48235. (Illus.). 192p. (YA). (gr. 6 up). 1995. 14.95 (*0-06-023584-5*); lib. bdg. 14.89 (*0-06-023585-3*) HarpC Child Bks.

Lynch, Chris, comp. National Directory of Post Card Deck Media. 1988. 39.95 (*0-87280-160-8*, 3362, Asher-Gallant) Caddylak Systs.

Lynch, Cyprian J. A Poor Man's Legacy: An Anthology of Franciscan Poverty. 1989. 37.50 (*0-317-02684-4*) Franciscan Inst.

Lynch, D. O., ed. Studies of Law in Social Change & Development: Legal Roles in Columbia, No. 4. 1981. 14.00 (*91-7106-180-0*); pap. 7.00 (*91-7106-177-0*) Intl Ctr Law.

***Lynch, Dan.** SNA Internetworking Handbook. 1995. 59.00 (*0-13-127168-7*) P-H.

Lynch, Daniel. Brennan's Point. 526p. 1988. 18.95 (*0-945167-03-2*) British Amer Pub.

— Deadly Earnest. 464p. 1986. pap. 3.95 (*0-8217-1909-2*) Zebra.

— Deathly Pale. 448p. 1988. pap. 3.95 (*0-8217-2379-0*) Zebra.

— Native & Naturalized Woody Plants of Austin & the Hill Country. Mosely, Jane, ed. LC 80-53737. (Illus.). 180p. (Orig.). 1981. pap. 7.95 (*0-938472-00-3*) St Edwards Univ.

— Yellow: A Novel. LC 92-17332. 211p. 1992. 19.95 (*0-8027-1226-6*) Walker & Co.

Lynch, Daniel C. Ventry. 1990. 16.95 (*1-55972-049-2*, Birch Ln Pr) Carol Pub Group.

Lynch, Daniel C. & Rose, Marshall T. Internet System Handbook. (Illus.). 900p. (C). 1993. text ed. 61.25 (*0-201-56741-5*) Addison-Wesley.

***Lynch, Daniel R. & Davies, Alan M., eds.** Quantitative Skill Assessment for Coastal Ocean Models. LC 95-9943. (Coastal & Estuarine Studies). 1995. write for info. (*0-87590-261-8*) Am Geophysical.

Lynch, David. Images. LC 94-2543. 192p. 1994. 40.00 (*0-7868-6060-X*) Hyperion.

Lynch, David K. & Livingston, William. Color & Light in Nature. LC 93-46711. (Illus.). 288p. (C). 1995. 69.95 (*0-521-43431-9*); pap. 29.95 (*0-521-46836-1*) Cambridge U Pr.

Lynch, David W., jt. auth. see Lyman, Charles P.

Lynch, Dell R. Bright Orbits. 110p. 1974. 7.95 (*0-87881-019-6*) Mojave Bks.

Lynch, Denis T. Boss Tweed: Story of a Grim Generation. LC 73-19157. (Politics & People Ser.). (Illus.). 448p. 1974. reprint ed. 34.95 (*0-405-05879-9*) Ayer.

— Boss Tweed: The Story of a Grim Generation. (BCL1 - United States Local History Ser.). 433p. 1991. reprint ed. lib. bdg. 99.00 (*0-7812-6277-1*) Rprt Serv.

Lynch, Don & Thompson, David. Battleborn Nevada: Its People, History & Stories. Bean, James H., ed. LC 93-79470. (Illus.). 360p. (YA). (gr. 6 up). 1994. 31.00 (*0-913205-20-6*) Grace Dangberg.

Lynch, Don, ed. see Adams, Randy L. & Sodaro, Craig.

Lynch, Don, ed. see Sanger, David.

Lynch, Dudley. Your Dolphin High-Performance Business Brain - An Operator's Manual: 21st Century Thinking Skills for Ambitious People under Challenge or under Fire. (Illus.). 260p. 1993. pap. 25.00 (*0-945822-04-9*) Brain Technologies.

Lynch, Dudley & Kordis, Paul L. DolphinThink: The Workbook: Mastering the Skills You Need to Get Tough, Get Free, Get Focused & Get Going As a New Kind of Winner. (Illus.). 122p. (Orig.). 1989. pap. 24.95 (*0-945822-02-2*) Brain Technologies.

— Strategy of the Dolphin: Scoring a Win in a Chaotic World. 288p. 1990. pap. 12.00 (*0-449-90529-2*, ExPress) Fawcett.

***Lynch, Dudley & Neenan, David.** Evergreen: Playing a Continuous Comeback Business Game. 208p. 1995. 25.00 (*0-945822-05-7*) Brain Technologies.

Lynch, Edith M. Decades: Lifestyle Changes in Career Expectations. LC 80-65703. 154p. reprint ed. pap. 43.90 (*0-317-26955-0*, 2023579) Bks Demand.

Lynch, Edmund C. Views of an Early Bird. Eakin, Ed, ed. (Illus.). 304p. 1990. 19.95 (*0-89015-730-8*) Sunbelt Media.

Lynch, Edmund C., jt. ed. see Lynch, Peggy Z.

Lynch, Edward A. Latin America's Christian Democratic Parties: A Political Economy. LC 92-23069. 224p. 1992. text ed. 45.00 (*0-275-94464-6*, C4464, Praeger Pubs) Greenwood.

— Religion & Politics in Latin America: Liberation Theology & Christian Democracy. LC 90-48694. 216p. 1991. text ed. 49.95 (*0-275-93774-7*, C3774, Praeger Pubs) Greenwood.

Lynch, Eleanor, jt. auth. see Hanson, Marci.

Lynch, Eleanor W. & Hanson, Marci J., eds. Developing Cross-Cultural Competence: A Guide for Working with Young Children & Their Families. 405p. (Orig.). (C). 1992. reprint ed. pap. text ed. 32.00 (*1-55766-086-7*) P H Brookes.

Lynch, Eleanor W. & Lewis, Rena B. Exceptional Children & Adults: An Introduction to Special Education. (C). 1987. text ed. 51.00 (*0-673-15903-5*) HarpCollege.

Lynch, Eleanor W., jt. auth. see Hanson, Marci J.

***Lynch, Elizabeth.** Dear Deceiver. 272p. (Orig.). 1995. mass mkt. 3.99 (*0-380-78046-1*) Avon.

Lynch, Elizabeth C. Lynch Record, Containing Biographical Sketches of Men of the Name Lynch, 16th-20th Century, Together with Information Regarding the Origin of the Name. 154p. 1993. reprint ed. lib. bdg. 35.00 (*0-8328-3149-2*); reprint ed. pap. 25.00 (*0-8328-3150-6*) Higginson Bk Co.

Lynch, Ella F. Educating the Child at Home. 1972. 59.95 (*0-8490-0086-6*) Gordon Pr.

Lynch, F. D. Clozentropy: A Technique for Studying Audience Response to Films. LC 77-22911. (Illus.). 1978. lib. bdg. 11.95 (*0-405-10754-4*) Ayer.

***Lynch, Frances.** Draw the Line: A Sexual Harassment-Free Workplace. Doyle, Kathleen, ed. (Successful Business Library). 250p. (Orig.). 1995. pap. 17.95 (*1-55571-370-X*) Oasis Pr OR.

Lynch, Francis T. Garnishing. LC 87-8714. 1987. pap. 14.95 (*0-89586-476-2*, HP Books) Berkley Pub.

Lynch-Fraser, Diane. Life's Little Miseries: Helping Your Child with the Disasters of Everyday Life: For Parents & Teachers of Children Ages 3-12. LC 92-12816. 224p. 1992. text ed. 19.95 (*0-02-919323-0*) Free Pr.

Lynch-Fraser, Diane & Morris-Tigerman, Ellen. Baby Signals. 1987. 17.95 (*0-8027-0982-6*) Walker & Co.

Lynch-Fraser, Diane & Tiegerman, Ellenmorris. Baby Signals: The Break-Through Parenting Guide for the '90s. 176p. 1991. mass mkt. 3.99 (*0-312-92456-9*) St Martin.

Lynch, Frederick R. Invisible Victims: White Males & the Crisis of Affirmative Action. LC 89-1899. (Contributions in Sociology Ser.: No. 80). 253p. 1989. text ed. 55.00 (*0-313-26496-1*, LYN, Greenwood Pr) Greenwood.

— Invisible Victims: White Males & the Crisis of Affirmative Action. LC 91-15288. (Illus.). 256p. 1991. pap. text ed. 16.95 (*0-275-94102-7*, B4102, Praeger Pubs) Greenwood.

Lynch, Gary. Synapses, Circuits, & the Beginnings of Memory. (Cognitive Neuroscience Ser.). (Illus.). 152p. (C). 1986. 25.00 (*0-262-12114-X*, Bradford Bks) MIT Pr.

Lynch, George. Desktop Publishing Word for Windows. 1993. pap. 8.95 (*1-56243-112-9*) DDC Pub.

— OS-2 Version 2. 1993. pap. 8.95 (*1-56243-091-2*) DDC Pub.

— OS 2 2.1: IBM PC. 1993. pap. 8.95 (*1-56243-119-6*) DDC Pub.

— QR - Word - Windows for Dummies. (Illus.). 176p. 1993. pap. 8.95 (*1-56884-029-2*) IDG Bks.

— QR - Word for Windows 6 for Dummies. (Quick Reference Ser.). (Illus.). 176p. 1994. pap. 8.95 (*1-56884-095-0*) IDG Bks.

***Lynch, George & Lynch, Helen.** ClarisWorks Step-by-Step: Macintosh Version 3.0. LC 94-48501. (Illus.). 140p. (YA). (gr. 7 up). 1995. spiral bd. 15.95 (*0-941681-86-6*) Computer Lit Pr.

— ClarisWorks Step-by-Step: Windows Version 3.0. LC 94-48501. (Illus.). 416p. (YA). (gr. 7 up). 1995. teacher ed 9.95 (*0-941681-93-9*); spiral bd. 15.95 (*0-941681-92-0*) Computer Lit Pr.

— Microsoft Works Step-by-Step: Macintosh Version 4.0. LC 94-46423. (Illus.). 139p. 1995. teacher ed, pap. 9.95 (*0-941681-81-5*) Computer Lit Pr.

— Microsoft Works Step-by-Step: Macintosh Version 4.0. LC 94-46423. (Illus.). 139p. (YA). (gr. 7 up). 1995. spiral bd. 15.95 (*0-941681-80-7*) Computer Lit Pr.

— Microsoft Works Step-by-Step: Windows Version 3.0: Word Processing, Databases, Spreadsheets, Graphics. LC 94-26895. (Illus.). 124p. (YA). (gr. 7 up). 1994. teacher ed, pap. 9.95 (*0-941681-75-0*); spiral bd. 15.95 (*0-941681-74-2*) Computer Lit Pr.

Lynch, George C. Canaries. (Colorguide Ser.). 1982. pap. 6.95 (*0-940842-10-6*) South Group.

***Lynch, Gerald.** Kisbey: A Story Cycle. 220p. 1995. lib. bdg. 37.00 (*0-8095-4560-8*) Borgo Pr.

— One's Company. 200p. 1995. 27.00 (*0-8095-4572-1*) Borgo Pr.

— Roughnecks, Drillers, & Tool Pushers: Thirty-three Years in the Oil Fields. (Personal Narratives of the West Ser.). (Illus.). 278p. 1987. 24.95 (*0-292-71553-6*) U of Tex Pr.

— Roughnecks, Drillers, & Tool Pushers: Thirty-Three Years in the Oil Fields. LC 87-13857. (Personal Narratives of the West Ser.). (Illus.). 278p. 1991. reprint ed. pap. 12.95 (*0-292-77052-9*) U of Tex Pr.

— Stephen Leacock: Humour & Humanity. 216p. (C). 1988. text ed. 44.95 (*0-7735-0652-7*, Pub. by McGill CN) U of Toronto Pr.

Lynch, Gerald, ed. & intro. Bliss Carman: A Reappraisal. 208p. 1990. pap. 21.00 (*0-7766-0286-1*, Pub. by Univ Ottawa Pr CN) Paul & Co Pubs.

Lynch, Gerald J., jt. auth. see Barron, John M.

Lynch, Gerald J., jt. ed. see Horwich, George.

Lynch, Gerard. Gauged Brickwork: A Technical Handbook. 150p. 1990. text ed. 61.95 (*0-566-09057-0*, Pub. by Gower UK) Ashgate Pub Co.

Lynch, Gloria E., ed. see Thibodaux Service League Members Staff.

Lynch, H. Toledo: The Story of an Old Spanish Capital. (Mediaeval Towns Ser.: Vol. 5). 1974. reprint ed. pap. 30.00 (*0-8115-0847-1*) Periodicals Srv.

Lynch, H. F. Armenia: Travels & Studies, 2 vols., Set. 1990. reprint ed. 70.00 (*0-86685-461-4*) Intl Bk Ctr.

Lynch, Hannah. George Meredith. LC 73-128572. (Studies in George Meredith: No. 21). 1972. reprint ed. lib. bdg. 57.95 (*0-8383-0906-2*) M S G Haskell Hse.

Lynch, Helen, jt. auth. see Lynch, George.

Lynch, Henry T. & Takeshi Hirayama, eds. Genetic Epidemiology of Cancer. 336p. 1989. 228.00 (*0-8493-6756-5*, RC268) CRC Pr.

Lynch, Henry T. & Tautu, P., eds. Recent Progress in the Genetic Epidemiology of Cancer. (Illus.). 160p. 1991. pap. 64.00 (*0-387-53022-3*) Spr-Verlag.

Lynch, J. Bragg's Hunch. (Bragg Ser.: No. 1). 1982. pap. 2.25 (*0-449-14449-6*) Fawcett.

Lynch, J., et al. The Behaviour of Sheep. 220p. (Orig.). 1992. pap. text ed. 38.00 (*0-85198-787-7*) CAB Intl.

Lynch, J. M. The Rhizosphere. (Environmental & Applied Microbiology Ser.). 1990. text ed. 229.95 (*0-471-92548-9*) Wiley.

Lynch, James. Education for Citizenship in a Multicultural Society. 144p. 1992. pap. text ed. 19.95 (*0-304-31929-5*) Cassell.

— Multicultural Education: A Global Approach. 220p. 1989. 29.00 (*1-85000-557-5*, Falmer Pr) Taylor & Francis.

— Multicultural Education: Principles & Practice. (Education Bks.). 256p. (C). 1986. text ed. 37.50 (*0-7102-0411-6*, RKP); pap. text ed. 19.95 (*0-7102-0768-9*, RKP) Routledge.

— Provision for Children with Special Educational Needs in the Asia Region. LC 94-34138. (Technical Paper: No. 261). 1994. write for info. (*0-8213-3036-5*) World Bank.

Lynch, James, et al, eds. Cultural Diversity & the Schools, 4 vols., Set. 1992. 336.00 (*0-7507-0149-8*, Falmer Pr) Taylor & Francis.

— Education for Cultural Diversity: Convergence & Divergence. (Cultural Diversity & the Schools Ser.: Vol. 1). 500p. 1992. 99.00 (*1-85000-989-9*, Falmer Pr) Taylor & Francis.

— Equity or Excellence? Education & Cultural Reproduction. (Cultural Diversity & the Schools Ser.: Vol. 3). 500p. 1992. 99.00 (*1-85000-993-7*, Falmer Pr) Taylor & Francis.

— Human Rights, Education, & Global Responsibilities. (Cultural Diversity & the Schools Ser.: Vol. 4). 400p. 1992. 99.00 (*1-85000-995-3*, Falmer Pr) Taylor & Francis.

— Prejudice, Polemic or Progress? (Cultural Diversity & the Schools Ser.: Vol. 2). 500p. 1992. 99.00 (*1-85000-991-0*, Falmer Pr) Taylor & Francis.

Lynch, James A. & Tasch, Edward B. Food Production & Public Policy in Developing Countries: Case Studies. LC 83-2155. 376p. 1983. text ed. 65.00 (*0-275-91038-5*, C1038, Praeger Pubs) Greenwood.

Lynch, James B., Jr. The Custis Chronicles: The Years of Migration. LC 92-62069. (Illus.). 288p. 1993. 32.50 (*0-929539-70-2*) Picton Pr.

Lynch, James D. Kemper County Vindicated, & a Peep at Radical Rule in Mississippi. LC 70-91663. 416p. 1970. reprint ed. text ed. 38.50 (*0-8371-2069-1*, LYK&, Negro U Pr) Greenwood.

Lynch, James J. Ethical Banking: The Cutting Edge of Service Quality. 176p. 1991. text ed. 49.95 (*0-312-06201-X*) St Martin.

— Henry Fielding & the Heliodoran Novel: Romance, Epic & Fielding's New Province of Writing. LC 85-27402. 128p. 1986. 28.50 (*0-8386-3268-8*) Fairleigh Dickinson.

— Sustaining Quality Advantages in Financial Services. (C). 1994. 175.00x (*0-7478-1828-2*, Pub. by S Thornes Pubs UK) St Mut.

Lynch, James J., jt. auth. see Evans, Bertrand.

Lynch, James M., jt. ed. see Hokkanen, Heikki M.T.

***Lynch, James P. & Bell, Anita W.** Dr. Lynch's Holistic Self-Health Program: Three Months to Total Well-Being. 256p. 1995. pap. 11.95 (*0-452-27150-9*, Plume) NAL-Dutton.

Lynch, James R. Checkmate. Choppin, Hazel & Frost, Anne, eds. 150p. 1991. text ed. write for info. (*0-318-68542-6*) Frost Pub.

Lynch, Jeffrey. Computerized Fuel Injection - Engine Control: GM. 352p. 1991. 10.00 (*0-8273-4526-7*); text ed. 25.95 (*0-8273-4525-9*) Delmar.

Lynch, Jeremiah, jt. auth. see Lipton, Sydney.

Lynch, Jerry. Living Beyond Limits: The Zen of Self-Empowerment. LC 88-60869. 222p. (Orig.). 1988. pap. 10.95 (*0-913299-50-2*) Stillpoint.

— The Total Runner: A Complete Mind-Body Guide to Optimal Performance. (Illus.). 224p. 1987. 21.95 (*0-13-925678-4*); pap. 10.95 (*0-13-925660-1*) P-H.

Lynch, Jerry, jt. auth. see Huang, Al Chung-liang.

Lynch, J.M., jt. ed. see Bazin, M.J.

Lynch, Joe. The VHF How to Book: A Guide for All Amateurs. (Illus.). 136p. (Orig.). 1994. pap. 15.95 (*0-943016-07-X*) CQ Commns Inc.

Lynch, John. Bourbon Spain: Seventeen Hundred to Eighteen Hundred Eight. (History of Spain Ser.). (Illus.). 400p. (C). 1989. text ed. 59.95 (*0-631-14576-1*) Blackwell Pubs.

— Bourbon Spain: 1700-1808. 1994. pap. 21.95 (*0-631-19245-X*) Blackwell Pubs.

— Caudillos in Spanish America, 1800-1850. (Illus.). 420p. 1992. 76.00 (*0-19-821135-X*) OUP.

— Hispanic World in Crisis & Change: 1598-1700. 1994. pap. 21.95 (*0-631-19397-9*) Blackwell Pubs.

— Max Beerbohm in Perspective. LC 73-21682. (English Biography Ser.: No. 31). 1974. lib. bdg. 53.95 (*0-8383-1788-X*) M S G Haskell Hse.

— Spain 1516-1598: From Nation State to World Empire. (History of Spain Ser.). (Illus.). 432p. (C). 1992. text ed. 59.95 (*0-631-17696-9*) Blackwell Pubs.

— Spain 1516-1598: From Nation State to World Empire. 1994. pap. 21.95 (*0-631-19398-7*) Blackwell Pubs.

— The Spanish-American Revolutions 1808-1826. (C). 1986. pap. text ed. 13.95 (*0-393-95537-0*) Norton.

— Spanish Colonial Administration, 1782-1810: The Intendant System in the Viceroyalty of the Rio De la Plata. LC 69-13979. 335p. 1969. reprint ed. text ed. 65.00 (*0-8371-0546-3*, LYSC, Greenwood Pr) Greenwood.

— The TNT Hollywood Birthday Book. 1993. 10.95 (*1-878685-39-2*) Turner Pub GA.

— Troubled Journey: Sermons for Pentecost, Middle Third - Gospel. LC 94-999. (Orig.). 1994. pap. write for info. (*0-7880-0015-2*) CSS OH.

Lynch, John, ed. Latin American Revolutions, 1808-1826: Old & New World Origins. LC 94-16521. Date not set. pap. write for info. (*0-8061-2663-9*) U of Okla Pr.

— Latin American Revolutions, 1808-1826: Old & New World Origins. LC 94-16521. 409p. 1994. 24.95 (*0-8061-2661-2*) U of Okla Pr.

— Plant Closures & Community Recovery. 208p. (Orig.). 1990. pap. 39.50 (*0-317-04839-2*) Natl Coun Econ Dev.

Lynch, John, ed. see Reilly, Bernard F.

***Lynch, John A., Jr. & Bourne, Richard W.** Modern Maryland Civil Procedure. 1166p. 1993. 95.00 (*1-55834-077-7*) Michie Butterworth.

Lynch, John D. Leptodactylid Frogs of the Genus Eleutherodactylus from the Andes of Southern Ecuador. (Miscellaneous Publications: No. 66). 62p. 1979. pap. 3.25 (*0-686-80375-2*) U of KS Mus Nat Hist.

— Leptodactylid Frogs of the Genus Eleutherodactylus in the Andes of Northern Ecuador & Adjacent Colombia. (Miscellaneous Publications: No. 72). 46p. 1981. 2.75 (*0-317-04880-5*) U of KS Mus Nat Hist.

— New Species of Frogs (Leptodactylidae Eleutherodactylus) from the Pacific Versant of Ecuador. (Occasional Papers: No. 55). 33p. 1976. pap. 1.00 (0-686-80372-8) U of KS Mus Nat Hist.

— A Re-Assessment of the Telmatobiine Leptodactylid Frogs of Patagonia. (Occasional Papers: No. 72). 57p. 1978. pap. 1.00 (0-686-80373-6) U of KS Mus Nat Hist.

— A Review of the Andean Leptodactylid Frog Genus Phrynopus. (Occasional Papers: No. 35). 51p. 1975. pap. 1.00 (0-686-80370-1) U of KS Mus Nat Hist.

— A Review of the Broad-Headed Eleutherodactyline Frogs of South America (Leptodactylidae) (Occasional Papers: No. 38). 46p. 1975. pap. 1.00 (0-686-80371-X) U of KS Mus Nat Hist.

Lynch, John D. & Duellman, William E. The Eleutherodactylus of the Amazonian Slopes of the Ecuadorian Andes: (Anura: Lepodactylidae) (Miscellaneous Publications: No. 69). 86p. 1980. 4.75 (0-317-04879-1) U of KS Mus Nat Hist.

— A Review of the Centrolenid Frogs of Ecuador, with Descriptions of New Species. (Occasional Papers: No. 16). (Illus.). 66p. 1973. 1.00 (0-317-04877-5) U of KS Mus Nat Hist.

Lynch, John E. The Theory of Knowledge of Vital Du Four. (Philosophy Ser.). 1972. 17.00 (0-686-11546-5) Franciscan Inst.

Lynch, John F., jt. auth. see Bellomo, Charles.

Lynch, John G. Prophets' Bread. 1989. pap. 7.10 (1-55673-131-0, 9856) CSS OH.

Lynch, John J., jt. auth. see Joseph, Lou.

Lynch, John M. Real Estate Tax Abatement Practice & Procedure. LC 92-81121. 162p. 1992. pap. 45.00 (0-944490-45-X) Mass CLE.

Lynch, John R. Facts of Reconstruction. LC 68-29009. (American Negro: His History & Literature, Ser. 1). 1969. reprint ed. 30.95 (0-405-01828-2) Ayer.

Lynch, John W. Bernadette: The Only Witness. LC 81-1725. 1981. 5.00 (0-8198-1104-1); pap. 4.00 (0-8198-1105-X) Pauline Bks.

— A Woman Wrapped in Silence. 288p. 1976. pap. 9.95 (0-8091-1905-6) Paulist Pr.

Lynch, Joseph H. Godparents & Kinship in Early Medieval Europe. LC 85-43297. (Illus.). 368p. 1986. text ed. 59.50 (0-691-05466-5) Princeton U Pr.

— The Medieval Church: A Brief History. 400p. (C). 1993. pap. text ed. 28.50 (0-582-49467-2, 79361) Longman.

— Simoniacal Entry into Religious Life, 1000 to 1260: A Social, Economic, & Legal Study. LC 76-22670. (Illus.). 286p. 1976. 39.50 (0-8142-0222-5) Ohio St U Pr.

Lynch, Joseph P. & DeRemee, Richard. Immunologically Mediated Pulmonary Diseases. (Illus.). 547p. 1991. text ed. 95.00 (0-397-51051-9) Lippincott.

Lynch, Juliann. Just Thinking. 1993. pap. 7.95 (0-533-10350-9) Vantage.

Lynch, K., jt. auth. see Willigan, Dennis J.

Lynch, K. A., ed. see Jaworski, Ron, et al.

Lynch, Katherine A. Family, Class, & Ideology: In Early Industrial France: Social Policy & the Working-Class Family, 1825-1848. LC 88-40198. 352p. (C). 1988. text ed. 39.50 (0-299-11790-1); pap. text ed. 18.75 (0-299-11794-4) U of Wis Pr.

Lynch, Kathleen M. Jacob Tonson, Kit-Cat Publisher. LC 77-111046. 256p. reprint ed. pap. 73.00 (0-317-10254-0, 2022218) Bks Demand.

— Roger Boyle, First Earl of Orrery. LC 65-17348. 328p. reprint ed. pap. 93.50 (0-317-29904-2, 2021780) Bks Demand.

— The Social Mode of Restoration Comedy. LC 65-23483. 1926. 18.00 (0-8196-0164-0) Biblo.

— The Social Mode of Restoration Comedy. (BCL1-PR English Literature Ser.). 242p. 1992. reprint ed. lib. bdg. 79.00 (0-7812-7109-6) Rprt Serv.

Lynch, Kathryn L. The High Medieval Dream Vision: Poetry, Philosophy, & Literary Form. LC 87-18042. 280p. 1988. 37.50 (0-8047-1275-1) Stanford U Pr.

Lynch, Kermit. Adventures on the Wine Route: A Wine Buyer's Tour of France. (Illus.). 288p. 1988. 19.95 (0-374-10092-6) FS&G.

— Adventures on the Wine Route: A Wine Buyer's Tour of France. (Illus.). 1990. pap. 14.00 (0-374-52266-9, Noonday) FS&G.

Lynch, Kevin. City Sense & City Design: Writings & Projects of Kevin Lynch. Banerjee, Tribib et al, eds. (Illus.). 850p. 1990. 65.00x (0-262-12143-3) MIT Pr.

— City Sense & City Design: Writings & Projects of Kevin Lynch. (Illus.). 872p. 1995. pap. text ed. 29.95 (0-262-62095-2) MIT Pr.

— Good City Form. 528p. 1984. reprint ed. pap. 17.95x (0-262-62046-4) MIT Pr.

— Image of the City. (Illus.). 1960. pap. 9.95 (0-262-62001-4, 11) MIT Pr.

— Wasting Away. LC 90-45553. (Illus.). 256p. 1991. 30.00 (0-87156-675-3) Sierra.

— What Time Is This Place? LC 72-7059. 1972. pap. 15.95 (0-262-62032-4) MIT Pr.

Lynch, Kevin & Hack, Gary. Site Planning. 3rd ed. (Illus.). 450p. (C). 1984. 50.00 (0-262-12106-9) MIT Pr.

Lynch, Kevin, jt. auth. see Hession, Joseph.

Lynch, Kevin A. Managing the Sense of a Region. 152p. 1976. pap. 11.95 (0-262-62035-9) MIT Pr.

Lynch, Kilian. The Scapular of Carmel. 2nd rev. ed. 48p. 1973. 1.95 (0-911988-11-4) AMI Pr.

Lynch, Kilian F. The Sacrament of Confirmation in the Early - Middle Scholastic Period: Texts, Vol. 1. (Theology Ser.). 1957. 17.00 (0-686-11589-9) Franciscan Inst.

Lynch, Kilian F., ed. John de la Rochelle: Eleven Marian Sermons. (Text Ser.). 1961. 7.00 (0-686-11557-0) Franciscan Inst.

Lynch, Kristin. Iron Butterfly. LC 93-93781. 104p. 1994. pap. 7.00 (1-56002-316-3, Univ Edtns) Aegina Pr.

Lynch, L. Jules Verne. (Twayne's World Authors Ser.). 160p. 1992. text ed. 22.95 (0-8057-8278-8, Pub. by Royal Botanic Garden UK) Macmillan.

Lynch, L. R. Educational Approaches to High Level Wellness: An Annotated Bibliography. 1982. pap. 3.95 (0-685-06384-4) R Bernard.

Lynch, L. Riddick. The Complete Guide to Selected Health & Health-Related Careers. Chatman, Urella et al, eds. (Illus.). (Orig.). 1980. pap. 10.45 (0-685-04204-9) R Bernard.

Lynch, L. Riddick, ed. Cross-Cultural Approach to Health Behavior. LC 73-84199. 364p. 1975. 38.50 (0-8386-7439-9); pap. 17.95 (0-8386-1377-2) Fairleigh Dickinson.

Lynch, Larry. Set Dances of Ireland: Tradition & Evolution. (Illus.). 316p. (Orig.). 1989. 25.00 (0-9623366-0-2) Seadna Bks.

Lynch, Larry & Lynch, Renee. A Wisconsin Town & Country Christmas. LC 87-83382. (Illus.). 80p. (Orig.). 1987. pap. 4.95 (0-945309-00-7) Hedgerow Pr.

Lynch, Laura B. Poetry to Read Alone at Night. Cook, Janice E., ed. (Illus.). 20p. (Orig.). 1982. pap. 4.95 (0-943190-00-2) Artefact Co.

Lynch, Lawrence L. Dangerous Ground: The Rival Detectives. LC 75-32764. (Literature of Mystery & Detection Ser.). (Illus.). 1976. reprint ed. 39.95 (0-405-07885-4) Ayer.

Lynch, Lawrence W. Eighteenth Century French Novelists & the Novel. 3rd ed. LC 79-88359. 190p. 1979. 17.95 (0-917786-16-5) Summa Pubns.

— The Marquis de Sade. (World Authors Ser.: No. 724). 178p. 1984. lib. bdg. 19.95 (0-8057-6571-9, Twayne) Macmillan.

Lynch, Lee. Cactus Love. 240p. 1994. pap. 9.95 (1-56280-071-X) Naiad Pr.

— Home in Your Hands. 240p. 1986. pap. 7.95 (0-930044-80-0) Naiad Pr.

— Morton River Valley. 320p. 1992. pap. 9.95 (1-56280-016-7) Naiad Pr.

— Old Dyke Tales. 224p. (Orig.). 1984. pap. 8.95 (0-930044-51-7) Naiad Pr.

— The Swashbuckler. 288p. (Orig.). 1985. pap. 8.95 (0-930044-66-5) Naiad Pr.

— That Old Studebaker. 272p. (Orig.). 1991. pap. 9.95 (0-941483-82-7) Naiad Pr.

— Toothpick House. LC 83-4093. 264p. (Orig.). 1983. pap. 7.95 (0-930044-45-2) Naiad Pr.

Lynch, Linda. The Nutrition Mission: A Nutrition Education Unit for Grades 1-3. Myers, Elaine, ed. (Illus.). 16p. (Orig.). 1994. teacher ed 16.20 (0-944943-49-7, 22749-0) Current Inc.

Lynch, Lisa M., ed. Training & the Private Sector: International Comparisons. LC 93-46425. (National Bureau of Economic Research Comparative Labor Markets Ser.). (C). 1994. 47.00 (0-226-49810-7) U Ch Pr.

Lynch, M. & Roberts, J. C. The Consequences of Child Abuse. 1982. text ed. 84.00 (0-12-460570-2) Acad Pr.

Lynch, M. Elizabeth, jt. auth. see Webb-Vignery, June.

***Lynch, M. Nadine.** Business Plus Strategy Equals Success: Business Plannign Made Easier. (Illus.). 203p. (Orig.). Date not set. pap. 19.95 (0-9645674-0-7) MNL Pub.

Lynch, Malcolm. The Dartmoor Yankee. 174p. (Orig.). 1993. 19.95 (0-907018-68-8, Pub. by Tabb Hse Pubs UK); pap. 11.95 (0-907018-98-X, Pub. by Tabb Hse Pubs UK) Seven Hills Bk.

Lynch, Malcolm A., ed. Burket's Oral Medicine. 8th ed. (Illus.). 875p. 1983. text ed. 55.00 (0-397-52106-5, 65-07131, Lippincott Medical) Lippincott.

Lynch, Malcolm A., et al, eds. Burket's Oral Medicine. 9th ed. (Illus.). 816p. 1994. 75.00 (0-397-51242-2) Lippincott.

Lynch, Margaret. Business of Insurance: An Introduction. 5th ed. 36p. 1993. pap. text ed. 2.50 (1-879143-16-X) Health Ins Assn Am.

Lynch, Margaret, ed. Health Insurance Terminology: A Glossary of Health Insurance Terms. 112p. 1992. pap. text ed. write for info. (1-879143-13-5) Health Ins Assn Am.

Lynch, Marietta & Perry, Patricia. No More Monkeys: A Photographic Version of the Children's Finger Game. (Orig.). (J). (ps-3). pap. 2.95 (0-9610962-0-9) M Lynch.

Lynch, Martha. Reminiscences of Adams, Jay & Randolph Cos., Ind., 1896. 363p. 1979. 19.00 (0-686-27819-4) Bookmark.

Lynch, Martha E., jt. auth. see Goldman, Ronald.

Lynch, Mary & Grisogono, Vivian. Strokes & Head Injuries: A Guide for Patients, Families, Friends, & Carers. (Illus.). 160p. 1992. pap. 19.95 (0-7195-4697-4, Pub. by John Murray UK) Trafalgar.

Lynch, Mary J. Libraries in an Information Society: A Statistical Summary. 32p. 1987. pap. 5.00 (0-8389-7145-8) ALA.

— Non-Tax Sources of Revenue for Public Libraries. 1988. 5.00 (0-8389-7253-5) ALA.

Lynch, Mary J., ed. Academic Libraries: Research Perspectives. LC 90-32120. (ACRL Publications in Librarianship: No. 47). 279p. reprint ed. pap. 79.60 (0-7837-5906-1, 2045704) Bks Demand.

Lynch, Mary J., jt. auth. see Drake, Sandra L.

Lynch, Mary J., et al. ALA Survey of Librarian Salaries, 1991. 63p. reprint ed. pap. 25.00 (0-7837-5913-4, 2045712) Bks Demand.

Lynch, Mary Jo & Eckard, Helen M., eds. Library Data Collection Handbook. LC 82-147483. 236p. reprint ed. pap. 67.30 (0-317-26561-X, 2023948) Bks Demand.

Lynch, Mary Jo, et al. ALA Survey of Librarian Salaries, 1994. 57p. 1994. pap. text ed. 45.00 (0-8389-7719-7) ALA.

Lynch, Mary L. On Your Own: Professional Growth Through Independent Nursing Practice. LC 81-19702. 250p. 1983. boxed, text ed. 33.75 (0-8185-0507-9) Jones & Bartlett.

Lynch, Michael. Art & Artifact in Laboratory Science: A Study of Shop Work & Shop Talk in a Laboratory. (Studies in Ethnomethodology). (Illus.). 180p. 1985. 45.00 (0-7100-9753-0, RKP) Routledge.

— Computer Numerical Control Accessory Devices. LC 93-8902. 1993. text ed. 53.00 (0-07-039226-9) McGraw.

— Computer Numerical Control Advanced Techniques. 1992. text ed., disk 75.00 (0-07-039224-2) McGraw.

— Computer Numerical Controls for Machining. 416p. 1992. text ed. 60.00 (0-07-039223-4) McGraw.

— Edinburgh & the Reformation. (Modern Revivals in History Ser.). 432p. 1993. 69.95 (0-7512-0203-7, Pub. by Gregg Revivals UK) Ashgate Pub Co.

— How Oil Rigs Are Made. (How It Is Made Ser.). (Illus.). 32p. (YA). (gr. 7 up). 1986. 12.95 (0-8160-0041-7) Facts on File.

— Scientific Practice & Ordinary Action: Ethnomethodology & Social Studies of Science. (Illus.). 350p. (C). 1994. 54.95 (0-521-43152-2) Cambridge U Pr.

— These Waves of Dying Friends. Kenny, Maurice & Gosciak, J. G., eds. (Illus.). 80p. (Orig.). 1988. pap. 5.00 (0-936556-19-6) Contact Two.

Lynch, Michael & Woolgar, Steve, eds. Representation in Scientific Practice. 320p. 1990. pap. 20.00 (0-262-62076-6) MIT Pr.

Lynch, Michael F. Creative Revolt: A Study of Wright, Ellison, & Dostoevsky. (American University Studies: American Literature: Ser. XXIV, Vol. 12). 200p. (C). 1989. text ed. 42.95 (0-8204-1018-7) P Lang Pubs.

Lynch, Michel A. Microprogrammed State Machine Design. 1993. 49.95 (0-8493-4464-6, QA76) CRC Pr.

Lynch, Miriam. A Regency Rose. 1980. pap. 1.75 (0-449-50031-4, Coventry) Fawcett.

— Time to Kill. (Mystery Puzzler Ser.: No. 15). (Illus.). (Orig.). 1979. pap. 1.95 (0-89083-435-0) Zebra.

Lynch, N. Timothy & Vasudevan, Sridhar V., eds. Persistent Pain: Psychosocial Assessment & Intervention. (Current Management of Pain Ser.). (C). 1988. lib. bdg. 94.00 (0-89838-363-3) Kluwer Ac.

***Lynch, Nancy.** Distributed Algorithms. 1995. 54.95 (1-55860-348-4) Morgan Kaufmann.

Lynch, Nancy, et al. Atomic Transactions. 500p. (C). 1993. text ed. 54.95 (1-55860-104-X) Morgan Kaufmann.

Lynch, Niel M. The Penny Pincher's Supplement to the Guide-Books of Europe. 1978. pap. 2.95 (0-87881-076-5) Mojave Bks.

Lynch, Otto E. Finding Gold in the Desert: The Art of Dry Washing. Fessler, Diane M., ed. (Illus.). 40p. 1994. pap. 4.95 (0-935810-53-6) Primer Pubs.

Lynch, Owen M. The Politics of Untouchability: Social Mobility & Social Change in a City of India. LC 76-87148. (Illus.). 251p. 1969. text ed. 42.00 (0-231-03230-7) Col U Pr.

Lynch, Owen M., ed. Divine Passions: The Social Construction of Emotion in India. 340p. 1990. 45.00 (0-520-06647-2) U CA Pr.

Lynch, P. J., jt. illus. see Lawrence, John.

***Lynch, P. T. & Davey, M. R., eds.** Electrical Manipulation of Cells. LC 95-10508. 1995. write for info. (0-412-03001-2) Chapman & Hall.

Lynch, Patricia. Back of Beyond. 180p. (J). (gr. 4 up). 1993. pap. 8.95 (1-85371-206-X, Pub. by Poolbeg Pr IE) Dufour.

— Brogeen & the Green Shoes. 208p. 1989. pap. 6.95 (1-85371-051-2, Pub. by Poolbeg Pr IE) Dufour.

— Brogeen & the Princess of Sheen. (J). (gr. 1 up). 1986. pap. 11.95 (0-85105-905-8, Pub. by Colin Smythe Ltd UK) Dufour.

— Brogeen Follows the Magic Flute. 191p. (J). (ps-8). 1988. pap. 6.95 (1-85371-022-9, Pub. by Poolbeg Pr IE) Dufour.

— Life Cycles, Money Cycles: Using Your Intuition for Personal Power & Financial Success. 288p. 1992. text ed. 19.95 (0-471-53998-8) Wiley.

— Sally from Cork. 1990. pap. 8.95 (1-85371-070-9, Pub. by Poolbeg Pr IE) Dufour.

— Tales of Irish Enchantment. (Illus.). 108p. (J). 1986. pap. 8.95 (0-85342-790-9, Pub. by Mercier Pr IE) Dufour.

— Turf-cutter's Donkey. 1984. 22.00 (0-85105-900-7, Pub. by Colin Smythe Ltd UK) Dufour.

— Turf Cutter's Donkey. 243p. (J). (ps-8). 1988. pap. 6.95 (1-85371-016-4, Pub. by Poolbeg Pr IE) Dufour.

Lynch, Patricia A. Christianity. (World Religions Ser.). (Illus.). 128p. (YA). (gr. 7-12). 1991. 17.95 (0-8160-2441-3) Facts on File.

Lynch, Patrick, tr. see Ott, Ludwig.

Lynch, Patrick J., ed. see Andersen, Hans Christian.

Lynch, Patrick J., jt. auth. see Jaffe, C. Carl.

Lynch, Patrick J., jt. auth. see Proctor, Noble S.

Lynch, Patti. Gourmet Inspirations: The Art of Healthy Cooking. (Illus.). 170p. 1993. pap. 12.95 (0-9620469-1-4) Sweet Inspirations.

— Kids' Stuffin's: Good & Healthy Snacks for Kids to Make & Eat. (Illus.). (J). 1995. pap. 15.95 (0-9620469-2-2) Sweet Inspirations.

— Sweet Inspirations: A Sugar Free Dessert Cookbook. 4th ed. (Illus.). 150p. 1992. reprint ed. pap. 12.95 (0-9620469-0-6) Sweet Inspirations.

Lynch, Peggy Z. & Lynch, Edmund C., eds. The Many-Eyed Landscapes. (Illus.). 88p. 1991. lib. bdg. 10.95 (1-878149-05-9) Counterpoint Pub.

Lynch, Peter. Dermatology. 2nd ed. (House Officer Ser.). 320p. 1986. pap. 20.00 (0-683-05251-9) Williams & Wilkins.

Lynch, Peter & Rothchild, John. Beating the Street: The Best-Selling Author of One Up on Wall Street Shows You How to Pick Winning Stocks & Mutual Funds. 320p. 1993. 23.00 (0-671-75915-9) S&S Trade.

— Beating the Street: The Best-Selling Author of (One up on Wall Street) Shows You How to Pick Winning Stocks & Mutual Funds. 1994. pap. 12.50 (0-671-89163-4, Fireside) S&S Trade.

— Learn to Earn: An Introduction to the Basics of Investing. 1995. pap. 12.50 (0-684-81163-4, Fireside) S&S Trade.

— One up on Wall Street: How to Use What You Already Know to Make Money in the Market. 1989. 19.95 (0-318-41474-0) S&S Trade.

— One up on Wall Street: How to Use What You Already Know to Make Money in the Market. 320p. 1990. pap. 12.95 (0-14-012792-5, Penguin Bks) Viking Penguin.

Lynch, Peter J. Dermatology. 3rd ed. LC 92-48556. (House Officer Ser.). 434p. 1994. 20.00 (0-683-05252-7) Williams & Wilkins.

— Genital Dermatology. LC 94-19068. 292p. 1994. 135.00 (0-443-08885-3) Churchill.

Lynch, Peter J., jt. auth. see Dahl, Mark V.

Lynch, Peter J., jt. ed. see Sams, W. Mitchell, Jr.

***Lynch, Philip F.** Downhole Operations. LC 81-4254. (Primer in Drilling & Production Equipment Ser.: No. 3). (Illus.). 128p. (Orig.). 1981. reprint ed. pap. 36.50 (0-7837-8147-4, 2047955) Bks Demand.

— Rig Equipment. fac. ed. LC 80-24533. (His a Primer in Drilling & Production Equipment: No. 2). (Illus.). 142p. Date not set. pap. 40.50 (0-7837-7426-5, 2047221) Bks Demand.

***Lynch, Priscilla & Laraja, Taryn.** Stories of the States Activity Book. (Illus.). 64p. 1995. pap. 6.95 (1-881889-83-1) Silver Moon.

Lynch, R. G., ed. FC Receptors Symposium: Journal: Immunologic Research, Vol. 11, Nos. 3-4, 1992. (Illus.). iv, 144p. 1992. pap. 32.00 (3-8055-5695-0) S Karger.

Lynch, R. L. & Plessman, C. K. Financial Services. 2nd ed. 1989. write for info. (0-07-039205-6); pap. write for info. (0-07-039204-8) McGraw.

Lynch, Ransom V. & Ostberg, Donald R. Calculus: A First Course. LC 82-23300. 704p. (C). 1983. reprint ed. text ed. 49.50 (0-89874-597-7) Krieger.

Lynch, Ransom V., et al. Calculus, with Computer Applications. LC 72-86514. 975p. reprint ed. pap. 180.00 (0-8357-7972-6, 2055979) Bks Demand.

***Lynch, Realing.** Inside Convent Walls. 96p. (Orig.). 1994. pap. 12.95 (0-614-01904-4) Rudi Pub.

***Lynch, Realino.** Inside Convent Walls. LC 94-41306. 1994. 12.95 (0-945213-18-2) Rudi Pub.

Lynch, Regina H. A History of Navajo Clans. 10.00 (0-936008-27-X) Rough Rock Pr.

Lynch, Renee, jt. auth. see Lynch, Larry.

Lynch, Richard. European Marketing: A Strategic Guide to the New Opportunities. 300p. 1993. text ed. 35.00 (1-55623-757-X) Irwin Prof Pubng.

— Getting out of Your Own Way. Abbott, Helen, ed. 112p. (Orig.). 1989. pap. 7.95 (0-933445-02-4) Abbott Pr WA.

— Health & Spiritual Healing. 148p. 1992. pap. 12.00 (0-89540-146-0, SB-146) Sun Pub.

— Know Thyself. rev. ed. LC 89-50840. 1989. 9.95 (0-87159-077-8) Unity Bks.

— LEAD! How Public & Nonprofit Managers Can Bring Out the Best in Themselves & Their Organizations. LC 92-1708. (Nonprofit Sector-Public Administration Ser.). 232p. 1992. 25.95 (1-55542-494-5) Jossey-Bass.

— Precision Management: How to Build & Manage the Winning Organization. 2nd ed. 243p. (Orig.). 1988. reprint ed. pap. 8.95 (0-685-25390-2) Abbott Pr WA.

— The Secret of Health. rev. ed. 1989. 6.95 (0-87159-143-X) Unity Bks.

Lynch, Richard, jt. ed. see Leibovitz, Maury.

Lynch, Richard C., comp. Broadway on Record: A Directory of New York Cast Recordings of Musical Shows, 1931-1986. LC 87-11822. (Discographies Ser.: No. 28). 357p. 1987. text ed. 45.00 (0-313-25523-7, LBR/, Greenwood Pr) Greenwood.

— Movie Musicals on Record: A Directory of Recordings of Motion Picture Musicals, 1927-1987. LC 89-2137. (Discographies Ser.: No. 32). 455p. 1989. text ed. 55.00 (0-313-26540-2, LMV/, Greenwood Pr) Greenwood.

Lynch, Richard C., ed. TV & Studio Cast Musicals on Record: A Discography of Television Musicals & Studio Recordings of Stage & Film Musicals. LC 90-40205. (Discographies Ser.: No. 38). 352p. 1990. text ed. 55.00 (0-313-27324-3, LTV, Greenwood Pr) Greenwood.

Lynch, Richard L. Marketing Education: A Future Perspective. 86p. 1983. 8.75 (0-318-22150-0, SN37) Ctr Educ Trng Employ.

— Marketing Your Business Education Program. 64p. 1986. pap. text ed. 6.95 (0-07-039199-8) McGraw.

Lynch, Richard L. & Cross, Kelvin F. Measure Up! Yardsticks for Continuous Improvement. 250p. (C). 1991. text ed. 39.95 (1-55786-099-8) Blackwell Pubs.

— Measure Up! Yardsticks for Continuous Improvement. 2nd ed. LC 95-1580. 1995. 17.95 (1-55786-718-6) Blackwell Pubs.

Lynch, Richard L. & Lunch, Richard L., eds. Food Marketing. (Career Competencies in Marketing Ser.). (Illus.). 1979. text ed. 12.04 (0-07-051483-6) McGraw.

Lynch, Richard L., jt. auth. see Crawford, Lucy.

Lynch, Richard L., ed. see Mathisen, Marilyn.

Lynch, Richard L., ed. see Smith, William O.

Lynch, Richard L., ed. see Vorndran, Barbara S. & Litchfield, Carolyn.

Lynch, Richard L., ed. see Wray, Ralph.

Lynch, Richard L., et al. Introduction to Marketing Casebook. 1984. pap. text ed. 11.95 (0-07-039192-0) McGraw.

Lynch, Rick, jt. auth. see McCurley, Steve.

Lynch, Rick, jt. auth. see Vineyard, Sue.

Lynch, Robert E., jt. auth. see Birkhoff, Garrett.
Lynch, Robert F., jt. auth. see Werner, Thomas J.
Lynch, Robert N., jt. ed. see Poggie, John J., Jr.
Lynch, Robert P. Business Alliances Guide: The Hidden Competitive Weapon. LC 92-15341. 352p. 1993. text ed. 29.95 (0-471-57030-3) Wiley.
— Practical Guide to Joint Ventures & Corporate Alliances: How to Form How to Organize How to Operate. 1989. text ed. 84.95 (0-471-62456-X) Wiley.
Lynch, Roberta, jt. auth. see Bensman, David.
Lynch, Ronald C. The Police Manager. 3rd ed. 320p. 1986. text ed. write for info. (0-07-554818-6) McGraw.
Lynch, Ronald G. The Police Manager. 4th rev. ed. LC 94-70022. 265p. (C). 1994. pap. text ed. write for info. (0-87084-707-4) Anderson Pub Co.
Lynch, S., jt. auth. see Brown, Ray.
Lynch, Sarah, jt. auth. see CFNPP Staff.
Lynch, Shelly. Living for Today, Planning for Tomorrow. 1989. 13.95 (0-89066-176-6) World Wide Pubs.
Lynch, Stacy C. Classical Music for Beginners. 1994. pap. 9.95 (0-86316-162-6) Writers & Readers.
***Lynch, Sylvia D.** Aristocracy's Outlaw: The Doc Holliday Story. (Illus.). 332p. 1995. 29.95x (0-9645781-0-7, Iris Press); pap. 24.00x (0-9645781-1-5, Iris Press) Tenn Iris Pr.
Lynch, Ted, ed. see International SAMPE Technical Conference Staff, et al.
Lynch, Ted, ed. see International SAMPE Technical Conference Staff.
Lynch, Thomas D. Federal Budget & Financial Management Reform. LC 90-20711. 232p. 1991. text ed. 49.95 (0-89930-538-5, LFF/, Quorum Bks) Greenwood.
— Public Budgeting in America. 4th ed. LC 94-519. 400p. 1994. text ed. write for info. (0-13-735846-6) P-H.
Lynch, Thomas D. & Martin, Lawrence L., eds. Handbook of Comparative Public Budgeting & Financial Management. LC 92-36823. (Public Administration & Public Policy Ser.: Vol. 50). 328p. 1993. 140.00 (0-8247-8773-0) Dekker.
Lynch, Thomas J. Data Compression Techniques & Applications. (Illus.). 352p. 1985. text ed. 69.95 (0-534-03418-7) Van Nos Reinhold.
Lynch, Tim, ed. see Morin, William J.
Lynch, V. E. Trails to Successful Trapping. 170p. 1935. pap. 4.00 (0-936622-23-7) A R Harding Pub.
Lynch, Vincent. American Jukebox: The Classic Years. (Illus.). 120p. (Orig.). 1990. 29.95 (0-87701-722-0); pap. 16.95 (0-87701-678-X) Chronicle Bks.
***Lynch, Vincent J., et al, eds.** The Changing Face of Aids: Implications for Social Work Practice. LC 92-42902. 288p. 1995. pap. text ed. 18.95 (0-86569-260-2, Auburn Hse) Greenwood.
— The Expanding Face of AIDS: Implications for Social Work Practice. LC 92-42902. 248p. 1993. text ed. 55.00 (0-86569-205-X, T205, Auburn Hse) Greenwood.
Lynch, W. O. Fifty Years of Party Warfare (1789-1837) 12.75 (0-8446-1293-6) Peter Smith.
Lynch, Wayne. Bears: Monarchs of the Northern Wilderness. LC 93-666. (Illus.). 256p. 1993. 40.00 (0-89886-372-4) Mountaineers.
Lynch, William, jt. ed. see Kearsley, Greg.
Lynch, William F. Approach to the Metaphysics of Plato Through the Parmenides. LC 68-23310. 255p. 1968. reprint ed. text ed. 55.00 (0-8371-4833-2, LYMP, Greenwood Pr) Greenwood.
— Images of Hope: Imagination as Healer of the Hopeless. LC 73-20418. (C). 1987. reprint ed. pap. text ed. 12.95 (0-268-00537-0) U of Notre Dame Pr.
— Narrative of the United States' Expedition to the River Jordan & the Dead Sea. Davis, Moshe, ed. LC 77-70719. (America & the Holy Land Ser.). (Illus.). 1977. reprint ed. lib. bdg. 50.95 (0-405-10264-X) Ayer.
Lynchard, Danny. Sure to Endure. 43p. 1983. pap. 1.95 (0-88144-043-4) Christian Pub.
***Lynchard, Percy L.** Shine. 200p. 1995. pap. 7.95 (1-56901-786-7) NW Pub.
Lynchburg College Faculty Staff, ed. The Nature of Man: Series One, Volume I. LC 82-45158. (Classical Selections on Great Issues, Symposium Readings Ser.). 480p. (Orig.). (C). 1982. pap. text ed. 14.75 (0-8191-2463-X) U Pr of Amer.
Lynchburg College Staff. Lynchburg College Symposium Readings, Vol. I: Tyranny & Freedom. LC 93-26942. 408p. (Orig.). 1993. lib. bdg. 45.00 (0-8191-9323-2); pap. 19.95 (0-8191-9284-8) U Pr of Amer.
— Lynchburg College Symposium Readings, Vol. II: War & Peace. 366p. (Orig.). (C). 1993. lib. bdg. 45.00 (0-8191-9324-0); pap. text ed. 19.95 (0-685-71325-3) U Pr of Amer.
Lynd, Alice & Lynd, Staughton, eds. Rank & File: Personal Histories by Working-Class Organizers. 320p. (YA). (gr. 9-12). 1988. reprint ed. pap. 10.00 (0-85345-752-2) Monthly Rev.
Lynd, Alice, jt. ed. see Lynd, Staughton.
Lynd, Helen M. England in the Eighteen-Eighties: Toward a Social Basis for Freedom. 518p. 1984. 44.95 (0-88738-004-2) Transaction Pubs.
Lynd, Helen M., jt. auth. see Lynd, Robert S.
Lynd, Louise. Creative Fund Raising. LC 87-60658. 94p. 1987. pap. 9.95 (0-9618773-0-8) PC Ltd.
Lynd, Robert. Dr. Johnson & Company. LC 73-21749. (English Biography Ser.: No. 31). 1974. lib. bdg. 49.95 (0-8383-1836-3) M S G Haskell Hse.
— Peal of Bells. LC 75-131772. 1971. reprint ed. 16.00 (0-403-00659-7) Scholarly.
Lynd, Robert S. Art of Letters. LC 71-152191. (Essay Index Reprint Ser.). 1977. reprint ed. 19.95 (0-8369-2239-5) Ayer.
— Blue Lion, & Other Essays. LC 68-55848. (Essay Index Reprint Ser.). 1977. 19.95 (0-8369-0638-1) Ayer.
— Books & Authors. LC 73-90659. (Essay Index Reprint Ser.). 1977. 19.95 (0-8369-1209-8) Ayer.
— Books & Writers. LC 71-105028. (Essay Index Reprint Ser.). 1977. 29.95 (0-8369-1525-9) Ayer.
— Knowledge for What? The Place of Social Science in American Culture. LC 86-7795. 287p. 1986. reprint ed. pap. 19.95 (0-8195-6170-3, Wesleyan Univ Pr) U Pr of New Eng.
— Money-Box. LC 70-84321. (Essay Index Reprint Ser.). 1977. 18.95 (0-8369-1091-5) Ayer.
— Old & New Masters. LC 79-111845. (Essay Index Reprint Ser.). 1977. 20.95 (0-8369-1616-6) Ayer.
— Passion of Labour. LC 73-76909. (Essay Index Reprint Ser.). 1977. 19.95 (0-8369-0025-1) Ayer.
— Peal of Bells. LC 78-90660. (Essay Index Reprint Ser.). 1977. 20.95 (0-8369-1226-8) Ayer.
— Solomon in All His Glory. LC 72-86769. (Essay Index Reprint Ser.). 1977. 21.95 (0-8369-1420-1) Ayer.
Lynd, Robert S. & Lynd, Helen M. Middletown. 550p. 1959. pap. 13.95 (0-15-659550-8, Harvest Bks) HarBrace.
— Middletown in Transition: A Study in Cultural Conflicts. LC 37-27243. 604p. 1982. pap. 9.95 (0-15-659551-6, Harvest Bks) HarBrace.
Lynd, Starghton, intro. On Third World Legs: An Autobiography. 96p. (Orig.). 1992. pap. 10.00 (0-88286-211-1) C H Kerr.
Lynd, Staughton. Class Conflict, Slavery & the United States Constitution: Ten Essays. LC 80-18219. xiii, 288p. 1980. reprint ed. text ed. 55.00 (0-313-22672-5, LYCC, Greenwood Pr) Greenwood.
— Fight Against Shutdowns: Youngstown's Fight Against Steelmill Closings. LC 82-60169. 256p. (Orig.). 1982. pap. 10.95 (0-917300-14-9) Singlejack Bks.
— The Fight Against Shutdowns: Youngstown's Steel Mill Closings. 244p. 1992. reprint ed. pap. 10.00 (0-88286-217-0) C H Kerr.
— Intellectual Origins of American Radicalism. 192p. 1982. pap. 10.95 (0-674-45780-3) HUP.
— Labor Law for the Rank-&-Filer. 64p. (Orig.). 1994. pap. 10.00 (0-88286-222-7) C H Kerr.
— Labor Law for the Rank & Filer. rev. ed. LC 77-95429. 1982. pap. 2.95 (0-917300-04-1) Singlejack Bks.
— Labor Law for the Rank & Filer. 2nd ed. 72p. 2.50 (0-317-06691-9) Indus Workers World.
***Lynd, Staughton & Lynd, Alice, eds.** Nonviolence in America: A Documentary History. rev. ed. LC 94-41973. 600p. 1995. pap. 24.95 (1-57075-010-6) Orbis Bks.
— Nonviolence in America: A Documentary History. rev. ed. LC 94-41973. 600p. 1995. 44.95 (1-57075-013-0) Orbis Bks.
Lynd, Staughton, jt. ed. see Lynd, Alice.
Lynd, Staughton, et al. Homeland: Oral Histories of Palestine & Palestinians. LC 93-8075. 1994. 35.00 (1-56656-133-7, Olive Branch Pr); pap. 14.95 (1-56656-132-9, Olive Branch Pr) Interlink Pub.
Lynd, Sylvia. Mulberry Bush. LC 78-142886. (Short Story Index Reprint Ser.). 1977. 19.95 (0-8369-3751-1) Ayer.
Lyndall, Terri M., jt. auth. see Lynton, Jonathan S.
Lynde, Eleanor. Daylight in the Canyon: The Memoirs of Eleanor Lynde. 2nd ed. (Illus.). 231p. reprint ed. pap. text ed. write for info. (0-9639967-0-3) Daylght MT.
Lynde, Francis. Cripple Creek, Nineteen Hundred. Jones, William R., ed. (Illus.). 20p. 1976. reprint ed. pap. 3.95 (0-89646-001-0) Vistabooks.
— The Grafters. LC 68-20017. (Americans in Fiction Ser.). 408p. reprint ed. lib. bdg. 27.50 (0-8398-1177-2); reprint ed. pap. text ed. 4.95 (0-89197-774-0) Irvington.
Lynde, Rob, jt. auth. see Curtin, Dave.
***Lynde, Stan.** The Bodacious Kid. Prezeau, Jael, ed. LC 95-68395. (Illus.). 352p. 1996. 29.00 (1-886370-10-9) Cttnwd Pub.
— Grass Roots. 2nd rev. ed. LC 91-77329. (Illus.). 152p. 1993. pap. 13.00 (0-9626999-4-2) Cttnwd Pub.
— Latigo, Book One: 1979-1980. LC 91-77330. (Illus.). 88p. (Orig.). 1991. pap. 9.95 (0-9626999-3-4) Cttnwd Pub.
— Latigo, Book Two: 1980-1981. LC 91-77330. (Illus.). 72p. (Orig.). 1992. pap. 9.95 (0-9626999-7-7) Cttnwd Pub.
— Latigo, Book 3 Bk. 3: 1981-1983. LC 94-72092. (Illus.). 168p. (Orig.). 1994. pap. 18.95 (0-9626999-9-3) Cttnwd Pub.
— A Month of Sundays: The Best of Rick O'Shay & Hipshot. 2nd ed. LC 92-72285. (Illus.). 64p. (Orig.). 1993. reprint ed. pap. 15.00 (0-9626999-8-5) Cttnwd Pub.
— Rick O'Shay & Hipshot: The Price of Fame, Bk. One. LC 92-72288. (Illus.). 32p. (Orig.). 1992. pap. 4.95 (0-9626999-5-0) Cttnwd Pub.
— Rick O'Shay & Hipshot: The Price of Fame, Bk. Two. LC 92-72288. (Illus.). 32p. (Orig.). 1992. pap. 4.95 (0-9626999-6-9) Cttnwd Pub.
— Rick O'Shay, Hipshot, & Me . . . a Memoir by Stan Lynde: Includes 10 Complete Stories from the Daily Comic Strip 1959-1977. 2nd ed. Gold, Mike, ed. LC 90-82941. (Illus.). 264p. 1990. reprint ed. pap. 18.95 (0-9626999-0-X) Cttnwd Pub.
— Rick O'Shay, the Dailies: 1959-1960, No. 1. LC 94-69453. (Illus.). 168p. (Orig.). 1994. pap. 18.95 (1-886370-00-1) Cttnwd Pub.
— Rick O'Shay, the Dailies: 1961-1962, No. 2. LC 95-68475. 160p. 1995. pap. 20.00 (1-886370-01-X) Cttnwd Pub.
— Stan Lynde's Pardners, Bk. 1: The Bonding. LC 90-84936. (Illus.). 40p. (Orig.). (J). (gr. 3 up). 1990. pap. 4.95 (0-9626999-1-8) Cttnwd Pub.
— Stan Lynde's Pardners, Book Two: The Legacy. LC 90-84936. (Illus.). 48p. (Orig.). 1992. pap. 4.95 (0-9626999-2-6) Cttnwd Pub.
Lynden-Bell, D., ed. Cosmical Magnetism: Proceedings of the NATO Advanced Research Workshop, Cambridge, England, July 5-9, 1993. LC 94-668. (NATO Advanced Study Institutes Series C, Mathematical & Physical Sciences: Vol. 422). 228p. (C). 1994. lib. bdg. 89.00 (0-7923-2730-6) Kluwer Ac.
Lynden-Bell, D. & Gilmore, Gerry, eds. Baryonic Dark Matter. (C). 1990. lib. bdg. 102.50 (0-7923-0699-6) Kluwer Ac.
Lyndon, Donlyn. The City Observed - Boston. 1982. pap. 7.95 (0-394-74894-8) Random.
Lyndon, Donlyn & Moore, Charles W. Chambers for a Memory Palace. (Illus.). 182p. 1994. 29.95x (0-262-12182-4, October Bk) MIT Pr.
***Lyndon, John.** Rotten: No Irish, No Blacks, No Dogs. 1995. pap. 14.00 (0-312-11883-X) St Martin.
Lyndon, Robert. Plant Development: The Cellular Basis. (Topics in Plant Physiology Ser.: No. 3). (Illus.). 220p. (C). 1990. text ed. 75.00 (0-04-581032-X); pap. text ed. 24.95 (0-04-581033-8) Routledge Chapman & Hall.
Lynds, Beverly T., ed. Dark Nebulae, Globules, & Protostars. LC 73-152040. 160p. reprint ed. pap. 45.60 (0-318-35032-7, 2030981) Bks Demand.
***Lynds, Dennis.** Talking to the World: And Other Stories. 176p. (Orig.). 1995. 18.95 (1-880284-10-3) J Daniel.
— Why Girls Ride Sidesaddle. LC 79-50801. (Illus.). 115p. (C). 1980. pap. 12.50 (0-913204-13-7) December Pr.
Lynds, Sheila, ed. see Hanson, A. E.
Lyne, Andrew & Graham-Smith, Francis. Pulsar Astronomy. (Cambridge Astrophysics Ser.: No. 16). (Illus.). (C). 1990. 79.95 (0-521-32681-8) Cambridge U Pr.
Lyne, Clare, ed. Leisure Travel & Tourism. 344p. (Orig.). 1989. pap. 35.00 (0-931202-15-9) Inst Cert Trav Agts.
Lyne, Deborah J., ed. see Finkel, Madelon L.
Lyne, Debra J., ed. see Rothman, Howard.
Lyne, G. M. Personae Comicae. (C). 1982. pap. text ed. 39.00 (0-900269-11-1, Pub. by Old Vicarage UK) St Mut.
— Personae Comicae. 48p. reprint ed. 5.00 (0-86516-031-7) Bolchazy-Carducci.
***Lyne, Patricia M. & Grange, J. M.** Collins & Lyne's Microbiological Methods. 7th ed. LC 94-21648. 1995. pap. 59.95 (0-7506-0653-3) Buttrwrth-Heinemann.
Lyne, R. N. Zanzibar in Contemporary Times. 384p. 1987. 270.00 (1-85077-173-1, Darf Pubs Ltd) St Mut.
Lyne, R. O. Further Voices in Virgil's Aeneid. 320p. 1987. 69.00 (0-19-814461-X) OUP.
— Further Voices in Virgil's Aeneid. 264p. 1992. pap. 26.00 (0-19-814092-4) OUP.
— Words & the Poet: Characteristic Techniques of Style in Vergil's Aeneid. 224p. 1990. 49.95 (0-19-814896-8) OUP.
Lyne, R. O., ed. see Catullus, Gaius V.
***Lyne, R.O.A.M.** Horace: Public Poet & Private Self. LC 94-43759. 1995. write for info. (0-300-06322-9) Yale U Pr.
Lyne, Sandy. The Lion & the Boy. (Illus.). 48p. (J). (gr. 4-7). 1988. 12.95 (0-933905-04-1); pap. 9.95 (0-933905-15-7) Claycomb Pr.
Lyne, William R. Space Aliens from the Pentagon: Flying Saucers Are Man-Made Electrical Machines. (Illus.). 250p. 1993. pap. 24.95 (0-9637467-0-7) Creatopia Prods.
— Space Aliens from the Pentagon: Flying Saucers Are Man-Made Electrical Machines. 2nd expanded rev. ed. (Illus.). 250p. 1995. pap. 24.95 (0-9637467-1-5) Creatopia Prods.
Lyneis, Margaret M. The Main Ridge Community at Lost City: Virgin Anasazi Architecture, Ceramics, & Burials. LC 92-53608. (Anthropological Papers: No. 117). (Illus.). 120p. 1992. 25.00 (0-87480-411-6) U of Utah Pr.
Lynes, Barbara B. Georgia O'Keeffe. LC 92-40051. (Rizzoli Art Ser.). (Illus.). 24p. (Orig.). 1993. 7.95 (0-8478-1650-8) Rizzoli Intl.
— O'Keefe, Stieglitz & the Critics, 1916 to 1929. LC 90-48860. (Illus.). 392p. 1991. pap. 14.95 (0-226-49824-7) U Ch Pr.
Lynes, Carlos, Jr., ed. see Camus, Albert.
Lynes, Carlos, Jr., ed. see Proust, Marcel.
Lynes, J. A. & Pritchard, D. C., eds. Developments in Lighting, Vols. 1 & 2. 1982. Vol. 1, 1978. 68.50 (0-85334-774-3, Pub. by Elsevier Applied Sci UK); Vol. 2, 1982. 74.00 (0-85334-985-1, Pub. by Elsevier Applied Sci UK) Elsevier.
Lynes, Martha A. The Twining Family of Nova Scotia, Descendants of Reverend William Twining. 35.00 (0-9616631-0-3); pap. 25.00 (0-9616631-1-1) M A Lynes.
Lynes, Russell. The Art-Makers: An Informal History of Painting, Sculpture & Architecture in 19th Century America. 1983. 18.25 (0-8446-5930-4) Peter Smith.
— The Art Makers: An Informal History of Painting, Sculpture, & Architecture in 19th Century America. (Illus.). xii, 514p. 1982. reprint ed. pap. 10.95 (0-486-24239-0) Dover.
— The Tastemakers. LC 82-25116. (Illus.). xiv, 362p. (C). 1983. reprint ed. text ed. 67.50 (0-313-23843-X, LYTA, Greenwood Pr) Greenwood.
— The Tastemakers: The Development of American Popular Taste. (Illus.). 384p. 1980. reprint ed. pap. 8.95 (0-486-23993-4) Dover.
Lynes, Tony. The Unemployment Assistance Board: The Origins of Supplementary Benefit. 448p. 1986. 42.00 (0-415-02458-7) Routledge.
Lyness, James. Multiple Choice Questions in Preparation for the AP Computer Science ("A" & "AB") Examination. 2nd ed. 69p. 1989. student ed 15.95 (1-878621-18-1) D & S Mktg Syst.
***Lyness, Stephanie.** Steam Machine Cuisine. LC 95-2328. 1995. write for info. (0-688-13814-4) Hearst Bks.
Lyness, Stephanie, tr. see Maniere, Jacques.
Lyng, Mervin J., et al. Career Mathematics: Industry & the Trades. 1977. text ed. 42.36 (0-395-24552-4); teacher ed, text ed. 55.32 (0-395-24553-2) HM.
Lyng, Merwin J. Dancing Curves: A Dynamic Demonstration of Geometric Principles. LC 78-2781. (Illus.). 16p. 1978. pap. 6.50 (0-87353-124-8) NCTM.
Lyng, Merwin J., et al. Applied Technical Mathematics. LC 77-76423. 880p. (C). 1991. text ed. write for info. (0-697-08543-0) Wm C Brown Pubs.
— Applied Technical Mathematics. LC 77-76423. (Illus.). 496p. 1983. reprint ed. text ed. 33.95x (0-88133-073-6) Waveland Pr.
— Applied Technical Mathematics with Calculus. 1168p. (C). 1991. text ed. write for info. (0-697-05970-7) Wm C Brown Pubs.
Lyng, Stephen. Holistic Health & Biomedical Medicine: A Countersystem Analysis. LC 89-11531. (SUNY Series in the Political Economy of Health Care). 268p. 1990. 64.50 (0-7914-0255-X); pap. 21.95 (0-7914-0256-8) State U NY Pr.
Lyngaae-Jorgensen, J., jt. ed. see Sondergaard, K.
***Lyngbye, Jorgen.** Twins: A Unique World Scenario. 1995. 10.95 (0-533-11247-8) Vantage.
Lyngdoh, Mary P. The Festival in the History & Culture of the Khasi. 1991. text ed. 30.00 (0-7069-5615-X, Pub. by Vikas II) S Asia.
Lynge, B., jt. auth. see Wainio, E. A., pseud.
Lynge, Finn. Arctic Wars, Animal Rights, Endangered Peoples. Stenbaek, Marianne, tr. LC 92-1516. (Arctic Visions Ser.). (Illus.). 134p. 1993. 16.95 (0-87451-588-2) U Pr of New Eng.
Lyngheim, Linda. California Mission Projects & Activities. LC 93-79027. (California Junior Heritage Ser.). (Illus.). 54p. (Orig.). (J). (gr. 3-6). 1993. pap. 8.95 (0-915369-05-2) Langtry Pubns.
— Gold Rush Adventure. LC 87-82679. (California Junior Heritage Ser.). (Illus.). 96p. (J). (gr. 3-6). 1988. 12.95 (0-915369-03-6); pap. 9.95 (0-915369-02-8) Langtry Pubns.
— The Indians & the California Missions. rev. ed. LC 84-80543. (California Junior Heritage Ser.). (Illus.). 160p. (J). (gr. 4-6). 1990. 14.95 (0-915369-04-4); pap. 10.95 (0-915369-00-1) Langtry Pubns.
Lyngheim, Linda, et al. Father Junipero Serra, the Traveling Missionary. LC 85-82131. (Illus.). 64p. (J). (gr. 3-5). 1986. 12.95 (0-915369-01-X) Langtry Pubns.
Lyngheim, Lynda, jt. auth. see Scagnetti, Jack.
Lyngstad, Alexandra & Lyngstad, Sverre. Ivan Goncharov. 184p. 1971. 49.50 (0-685-63210-5) Elliots Bks.
Lyngstad, Alexandra H. Dostoevskij & Schiller. 1975. pap. text ed. 32.35 (3-10-800094-2) Mouton.
Lyngstad, Sverre. Jonas Lie. LC 76-50007. (Twayne's World Authors Ser.). 223p. (C). 1977. lib. bdg. 17.95 (0-8057-6274-4) Irvington.
— Sigurd Hoel's Fiction: Cultural Criticism & Tragic Vision. LC 83-26470. (Contributions to the Study of World Literature Ser.: No. 6). xvi, 198p. 1984. text ed. 49.95 (0-313-24343-3, LSH/, Greenwood Pr) Greenwood.
Lyngstad, Sverre, tr. see Askildsen, Kjell.
Lyngstad, Sverre, tr. see Faldbakken, Knut.
Lyngstad, Sverre, tr. see Hoel, Sigurd.
Lyngstad, Sverre, jt. auth. see Lyngstad, Alexandra.
Lyngstad, Sverre, et al, eds. Norway: Annual Volume Review of National Literatures. 240p. 1983. pap. 23.00 (0-918680-17-4) Bagehot Council.
Lynip, Ryllis G., jt. auth. see Garrick, David.
Lynk, Miles V. The Black Troopers. LC 70-153875. reprint ed. 15.00 (0-404-00196-3) AMS Pr.
Lynk, William M. Dinner Theatre: A Survey & Directory. LC 92-36607. 160p. 1993. text ed. 49.95 (0-313-28442-3, LDE, Greenwood Pr) Greenwood.
Lynn. Texts & Contexts: Writing about Literature. (C). 1993. text ed. 21.00 (0-06-500099-4) HarpCollege.
— To See a Stranger. (Black Dagger Crime Ser.). 16.50 (0-86220-787-8, C1027, Black Dagger) Chivers N Amer.
Lynn, Andrew J. Small Business Tax Guide: Guide to Small Business Tax. (Illus.). (Orig.). 1992. pap. 24.95 (1-877983-04-7) Data-Lynn Bk.
— Starting a Small Business Handbook: How to Start & Operate Your Own Small Business. 2nd rev. ed. (Illus.). 190p. (Orig.). 1992. pap. 24.95 (1-877983-05-5) Data-Lynn Bk.
Lynn, Ann. Beautiful Dreamer. (Historical Ser.). 1994. mass mkt. 3.99 (0-373-28834-4, 1-28834-9) Harlequin Bks.
— Midnight Safari. 1991. mass mkt. 4.25 (0-8217-3550-0) Zebra.
— Passion's Chase. 384p. 1992. mass mkt. 4.25 (0-8217-3862-3) Zebra.
— Slave of My Heart. 1990. mass mkt. 4.25 (0-8217-2884-9) Zebra.
Lynn-Ann, ed. see Valenti, Vince & Jaeger, Jag.
Lynn, Arthur D., Jr., ed. see Taxation, Resources & Economic Development Committee.
Lynn, Arthur D., Jr., ed. see Taxation, Resources & Economic Development Committee Staff.
Lynn, B. W. & Verzegnassi, C., eds. Tests of Electroweak Theories, Polarized Processes & Other Phenomena: Proceedings of the 2nd ICTP Conference on Tests of Electroweak Physics, Trieste, Italy, June 1985. 476p. 1987. pap. 51.00 (9971-5-0305-0) World Scientific Pub.
Lynn, B. W. & Wheater, J. F., eds. Radiative Corrections in SU (2) L X U (1) Proceedings of the Workshop on Radiative Corrections in SU (2) O X U (1), Miramore, Trieste, Italy, June 6-8. 340p. 1984. 55.00 (9971-966-26-3); pap. 33.00 (9971-966-28-X) World Scientific Pub.
Lynn-Barnes, Diana. Celebrity Parenting: Famous Parents Share Personal Stories. 240p. (Orig.). 1992. pap. 12.95 (0-9633286-3-8) F Charles Pubns.
Lynn, Barry. Polluting the Censorship Debate: A Summary & Critique of the Final Report of the Attorney General's Commission on Pornography. 188p. 1986. 5.00 (0-86566-040-9) ACLU DC.

An Asterisk (*) at the beginning of an entry indicates that the title is appearing in BIP for the first time.

*Lynn, Barry, et al, eds. The Right to Religious Liberty: The Basic ACLU Guide to Religious Rights. LC 94-13635. (ACLU Handbook Ser.). 176p. (C). 1995. pap. 7.95 (0-8093-1967-5) S Ill U Pr.
— The Right to Religious Liberty: The Basic ACLU Guide to Religious Rights. rev. ed. LC 94-13635. (ACLU Handbook Ser.). 176p. (C). 1995. 29.95 (0-8093-1966-7) S Ill U Pr.
Lynn, Caroline. Kentucky Wildlife Viewing Guide. (Falcon Guides Ser.). 80p. (Orig.). 1994. pap. 8.95 (1-56044-304-9) Falcon Pr MT.
Lynn, Catherine. Wallpaper in America: From the Seventeenth Century to World War I. (Illus.). 1980. 45.00 (0-393-01448-7) Norton.
Lynn, Cathy, ed. Expressions. 32p. (Orig.). 1984. pap. write for info. (0-318-57742-9) Myriad.
Lynn Chao, Yenshew, intro. Card Catalog of the Rubel Asiatic Research Collection: Harvard University Fine Arts Library, 7 Vols. 3680p. 1989. lib. bdg. 2,010.00 (0-86291-852-9) U Pubns Amer.
Lynn, Claire. A Cave Is a Deep Dark Hole. 48p. (J). (gr. 1-4). 1978. pap. 1.00 (0-89323-012-X, 100) Bible Memory.
— Esther, Queen of Persia. 63p. 1981. pap. 1.00 (0-89323-019-7) Bible Memory.
Lynn, Claire, jt. auth. see Ellis, Joyce.
Lynn, Claire, ed. see Philips, Martha & Hadden, Mary.
Lynn, Conrad. There Is a Fountain: The Autobiography of Conrad Lynn. rev. ed. LC 92-29965. 270p. 1993. pap. 11.95 (1-55652-166-9) L Hill Bks.
— There Is a Fountain: The Autobiography of Conrad Lynn. 2nd rev. ed. LC 92-29965. 270p. 1993. 27.00 (1-55652-165-0) L Hill Bks.
Lynn, Daryl, et al. Evident Progress. 60p. (Orig.). (YA). 1991. pap. 2.25 (0-89323-046-4) Bible Memory.
Lynn, David. High School Talk Sheets. 112p. 1987. pap. 10.99 (0-310-20931-5, 13262P) Zondervan.
— Junior High Talk Sheets. 112p. 1988. pap. 10.99 (0-310-20941-2, 13263P) Zondervan.
— More High School Talksheets: Fifty All-New Creative Discussions for High School Youth Groups. 112p. (YA). 1992. pap. 10.99 (0-310-57491-9) Zondervan.
— More Junior High Talksheets: Fifty All-New Creative Discussions for Junior High Youth Groups. 112p. (YA). 1992. pap. 10.99 (0-310-57481-1) Zondervan.
— More Zingers. (J). 1990. pap. 9.99 (0-310-52521-7) Zondervan.
— Parent Ministry Talksheets: Creative Discussions That Get Parents Talking to Each Other & to Their Teens. 112p. 1992. pap. 9.99 (0-310-57501-X) Zondervan.
— Zingers: Twenty-five Real-Life Character Builder. 64p. 1990. pap. 8.99 (0-310-52511-X) Zondervan.
Lynn, David & Lynn, Kathy. Fourth to Sixth Grade Talksheets: 25 Creative, Easy-to-Use Discussions for Upper Elementary Students. 64p. 1993. pap. 8.99 (0-310-37491-X) Zondervan.
— Great Games for Kids. 128p. 1990. pap. 10.99 (0-310-52541-1) Zondervan.
— More Zingers for First to Third Graders. 64p. (J). (gr. 1-3). 1993. Saddle stitch. pap. 9.99 (0-310-37231-3) Zondervan.
— Zingers for First to Third Graders: 12 Real-Life Character Builders. 64p. (J). (gr. 1-3). 1993. Saddle stitch. pap. 7.99 (0-310-37221-6) Zondervan.
Lynn, David & Lynn, Kathy, eds. Great Fundraising Ideas for Youth Groups. 208p. 1993. pap. 12.99 (0-310-67171-X) Zondervan.
Lynn, David & Yaconelli, Mike. Grow for It Journal. 116p. (Orig.). 1985. pap. 8.95 (0-910125-06-6) Youth Special.
Lynn, David, jt. auth. see Reynolds, Randy.
Lynn, David, jt. ed. see Yaconelli, Mike.
Lynn, David H. The Hero's Tale: Narration in the Early Modern Novel. LC 88-826. 160p. 1989. text ed. 35.00 (0-312-01621-2) St Martin.
Lynn, Edward S., jt. auth. see Thompson, Joan W.
Lynn, Elizabeth & Horner, Matina. Babe Didrikson Zaharias. (American Women of Achievement Ser.). (Illus.). 112p. (J). (gr. 5 up). 1989. lib. bdg. 17.95 (1-55546-684-2) Chelsea Hse.
Lynn, Gary S. Breaking Through Bureaucracy: How Corporate Entrepreneurs Create, Protect & Commercialize. 1993. 18.95 (1-55738-521-1) Probus Pub Co.
— From Concept to Market. 1989. text ed. 55.00 (0-471-50126-3); pap. text ed. 22.95 (0-471-50125-5) Wiley.
Lynn, Hugh. Head over Heels. (Orig.). 1993. pap. 14.95 (0-7022-2530-4, Pub. by Univ Queensland Pr AT) Intl Spec Bk.
*Lynn, Irene & Wills, Loan L. School Lessons, Work Lessons: Recruiting & Sustaining Employer Involvement in School-to-Work Programs. 100p. 1994. 12.00 (0-937846-48-1) Inst Educ Lead.
Lynn, J. W., jt. auth. see Sen Gupta, D. P.
Lynn, J. W., et al, eds. High-Temperature Superconductivity. (Graduate Texts in Contemporary Physics Ser.). xv, 403p. 1990. text ed. 49.00 (0-387-96770-2) Spr-Verlag.
Lynn, Jack M. Bio-Finishing: The Manual. (Illus.). 205p. (C). 1987. pap. 75.00 (0-9618586-0-5) Five Star Assocs.
Lynn, James, tr. see Schlaffer, Heinz.
Lynn, James, ed. see Von La Roche, Sophie.
Lynn, Jermyn Chi-Mung. Political Parties in China. LC 75-42523. (Studies in Chinese Government & Law). 255p. 1975. reprint ed. text ed. 55.00 (0-313-26961-0, U6961, Greenwood Pr) Greenwood.
Lynn, Joanne. By No Extraordinary Means. 1986. 35.00 (0-253-31287-6) Ind U Pr.
Lynn, Joanne, ed. By No Extraordinary Means: The Choice to Forgo Life-Sustaining Food & Water. LC 85-45781. (Medical Ethics Ser.). 323p. 1986. 35.00 (0-253-33659-7); pap. 16.95 (0-253-20517-4, MB-517) Ind U Pr.
Lynn, John & Bloom, Stephen. Surgical Endocrinology. (Illus.). 576p. 1993. 295.00 (0-7506-1390-4) Buttrwrth-Heinemann.
Lynn, John A. Bayonets of the Republic: Motivation & Tactics in the Army of Revolutionary France, 1791-94. LC 83-9093. 368p. 1984. 29.95 (0-252-01091-4) U of Ill Pr.
Lynn, John A., ed. Feeding Mars: Logistics in Modern Warfare from the Middle Ages to the Present. LC 92-27652. (History & Warfare Ser.). 326p. 1993. text ed. 47.00 (0-8133-1716-9) Westview.
— Feeding Mars: Logistics in Western Warfare from the Middle Ages to the Present. (C). 1994. pap. text ed. 21.95 (0-8133-1865-3) Westview.
— Tools of War: Instruments, Ideas, & Institutions of Warfare, 1445-1871. fac. ed. LC 89-4887. 276p. 1990. reprint ed. pap. 78.70 (0-7837-8077-X, 2047830) Bks Demand.
Lynn-Jones, Sean M., ed. The Cold War & After: Prospects for Peace. 2nd ed. (Illus.). 400p. 1993. pap. 18.00 (0-262-62088-X) MIT Pr.
Lynn-Jones, Sean M. & Miller, Steven E., eds. America's Strategy in a Changing World. (International Security Reader Ser.). (Illus.). 410p. 1993. 18.00x (0-262-62085-5) MIT Pr.
— Global Dangers: Changing Dimensions of International Security. LC 94-24037. (International Security Readers Ser.). 1995. 15.95 (0-262-62097-9) MIT Pr.
Lynn-Jones, Sean M., ed. see Van Evera, Stephen, et al.
Lynn-Jones, Sean M., et al, eds. Nuclear Diplomacy & Crisis Management: An International Security Reader. 410p. 1990. pap. 15.95 (0-262-62078-2) MIT Pr.
— Soviet Military Policy: An International Security Reader. 350p. (Orig.). 1989. pap. 14.95 (0-262-62066-9) MIT Pr.
*Lynn, Judith. Feminist Sex Slave. (Orig.). 1994. pap. 20.00 (0-9645883-9-0) Estrum Pr.
Lynn, Kathy, jt. auth. see Lynn, David.
Lynn, Kathy, jt. ed. see Lynn, David.
Lynn, Kenneth S. The Air-Line to Seattle: Studies in Literary & Historical Writing about America. LC 83-13459. 240p. 1984. pap. text ed. 8.95 (0-226-49833-6) U Ch Pr.
— A Divided People. LC 76-25779. (Contributions in American Studies: No. 30). 113p. 1977. text ed. 42.95 (0-8371-9271-4, LYD/, Greenwood Pr) Greenwood.
— Hemingway. (Illus.). 702p. 1995. pap. 18.95 (0-674-38732-5, LYNHEX) HUP.
— Mark Twain & Southwestern Humor. LC 70-176135. (Illus.). 300p. 1972. reprint ed. text ed. 59.75 (0-8371-6270-X, LMTPB, Greenwood Pr) Greenwood.
Lynn, Kenneth S., ed. Houghton Books in Literature. Incl. Designs for Reading: Level I, 4 bks. Price per book. pap. 6.76 (0-685-73344-0); Short Stories. pap. 16.00 (0-395-02780-2); pap. 16.00 (0-395-02784-5); Nonfiction Prose. pap. 19.08 (0-395-02794-2); write for info. (0-318-53415-0) HM.
Lynn, Kenneth S. & Levin, David, eds. Huckleberry Finn: Text, Sources & Criticism. (Harbrace Sourcebooks Ser.). 218p. (Orig.). (C). 1961. pap. text ed. 17.50 (0-15-539490-8) HB Coll Pubs.
Lynn, Kristie & Pelton, Robert W. The Early American Cookbook. LC 83-81148. (Illus.). 176p. (Orig.). 1983. pap. 8.95 (0-89709-199-X) Liberty Pub.
Lynn, L. Cancer Treatment & Care. 1990. pap. 30.00 (0-7463-0581-8, Pub. by Northcote UK) St Mut.
Lynn, Laurel. Chasing Rainbows: A Search for Family Ties. 16072p. (Orig.). 1992. pap. 9.95 (0-934896-19-4) Adopt Aware Pr.
Lynn, Laurence E., Jr., jt. intro. see Joseph, Lawrence B.
*Lynn, Lawrence. How to Invest Today: A Beginner's Guide to the World of Investments. LC 95-10838. 1995. write for info. (0-8050-3733-0) H Holt & Co.
Lynn, Lawrence, jt. auth. see Cross, Warren D., Jr.
Lynn, Lawrence E., Jr. Managing Public Policy. (C). 1987. pap. text ed. 17.00 (0-673-39461-1) HarpCollege.
— The State & Human Services: Organizational Change in a Political Context. 1980. 27.50 (0-262-12084-4) MIT Pr.
Lynn, Leonard H. & McKeown, Timothy J. Organizing Business: Trade Associations in America & Japan. LC 87-17468. (AEI Studies: No. 459). 214p. (Orig.). (C). 1988. lib. bdg. 21.75 (0-8447-3629-5, Am Enterprise) U Pr of Amer.
*Lynn, Les. Environmental Biology. 160p. (C). 1995. pap. text ed., ring bd. 32.50 (0-7872-0974-0) Kendall-Hunt.
Lynn, Les M. Environmental Biology Laboratory Manual. 124p. (C). 1994. spiral bd. 24.95 (0-8403-9459-4) Kendall-Hunt.
Lynn, Leslie. The Duke's Deceit. (Orig.). 1993. mass mkt. 3.99 (0-449-21969-0) Fawcett.
— The Rake's Redemption. 256p. 1989. pap. 3.50 (0-449-21692-6, Crest) Fawcett.
— Rake's Redemption. 1989. pap. 3.50 (0-449-14572-7) Fawcett.
*Lynn, Less. Intro to Environmental Biology. 48p. (C). 1995. student ed, pap. text ed. 10.00 (0-7872-1072-2) Kendall-Hunt.
Lynn, Loretta & Vecsey, George. Selected from Coal Miner's Daughter. abr. ed. Literacy Volunteers of New York City Staff, ed. (Writers' Voices Ser.). 64p. (Orig.). 1990. pap. text ed. 3.50 (0-929631-11-0, Signal Hill) New Readers.
*Lynn, Mac. Churches of Christ in the United States, 1994. 750p. 1994. pap. 14.95 (1-885836-00-7) Morrison & Phillips.
Lynn, Mark, jt. auth. see Pope, Dan.
Lynn, Martha D. The Clay Art of Adrian Saxe. LC 93-5654. (Illus.). 160p. 1994. 29.95 (0-500-09238-9) Thames Hudson.
— Clay Today: Contemporary Ceramists & Their Work. LC 89-13731. (Illus.). 240p. 1990. 24.95 (0-87701-756-5) Chronicle Bks.
Lynn, Mary, ed. see Red, James.
Lynn, Mary C., ed. An Eyewitness Account of the American Revolution & New England Life: The Journal of J. F. Wasmus, German Company Surgeon, 1776-1783. Doblin, Helga, tr. LC 90-3631. (Contributions in Military Studies: No. 106). 344p. 1990. text ed. 59.95 (0-313-27355-3, WEH/, Greenwood Pr) Greenwood.
Lynn, Mary C., jt. tr. see Doblin, Helga.
Lynn, Mary E. The Tavera Legacy. 448p. 1994. 24.95 (0-312-93136-0) Forge NYC.
Lynn, N. M., jt. auth. see Gates, P. J.
Lynn, Naomi B., ed. United Nations Decade for Women World Conference. LC 84-4559. (Women & Politics Ser.: Vol. 4, No. 1). 93p. 1984. text ed. 32.95 (0-86656-150-1) Haworth Pr.
— Women, Politics & the Constitution. LC 90-37948. (Women & Politics Ser.: Vol. 10, No. 2). 161p. 1990. pap. text ed. 14.95 (0-918393-75-2) Harrington Pk.
— Women, Politics & the Constitution. LC 90-37948. (Women & Politics Ser.: Vol. 10, No. 2). 161p. 1990. text ed. 29.95 (1-56024-029-6) Haworth Pr.
Lynn, Naomi B. & McClure, Arthur F. The Fulbright Premise: Senator J. William Fulbright's Views on Presidential Power. LC 72-14248. 224p. 1973. 20.00 (0-8387-1358-0) Bucknell U Pr.
Lynn, Naomi B. & Wildavsky, Aaron, eds. Public Administration: The State of the Discipline. LC 89-29690. 560p. (Orig.). 1990. pap. text ed. 34.95x (0-934540-62-4) Chatham Hse Pubs.
Lynn, Patricia. Everything about Him. 224p. (Orig.). 1993. pap. 2.95 (1-56597-106-X, Kismet) Meteor Pub.
Lynn, Patricia, tr. see Kraay, Robert & Kiefer, Jan, eds.
*Lynn, Paul & Fuerst, Wolfgang. Introductory Digital Signal Processing with Computer Application. rev. ed. 1994. pap. text ed. 54.95 (0-471-94374-6) Wiley.
Lynn, Paul A. Electronic Signals & Systems. 347p. (C). 1987. text ed. 50.00 (0-333-39163-2, Pub. by Macmill Press UK); pap. 32.50 (0-333-39164-0, Pub. by Macmill Press UK) Scholium Intl.
— An Introduction to the Analysis & Processing of Signals. 3rd ed. 263p. (C). 1989. 42.00 (0-89116-981-4) Hemisp Pub.
— Radar Systems. (Illus.). 144p. 1989. text ed. 17.98 (0-442-23684-0) Chapman & Hall.
Lynn, R. Attention, Arousal & the Orientation Reaction. 1966. 60.00 (0-08-011524-1, Pub. by Pergamon Repr UK) Franklin.
Lynn, R., ed. Dimensions of Personality: Essays in Honour of H. J. Eysenck. (Illus.). 490p. 1981. 162.00 (0-08-024294-4, Pub. by Pergamon Repr UK) Franklin.
Lynn, Richard. Entrepreneur. 176p. 1973. 25.00 (0-8464-1319-1) Beekman Pubs.
Lynn, Richard, et al. Shortcut Through Adventureland, Vol. II: Infocom. write for info. (0-318-58218-X) P-H.
Lynn, Richard J., tr. The Classic of Changes: A New Translation of the I Ching As Interpreted by Wang Bi. LC 93-43999. (Translations from the Asian Classics Ser.). 688p. (C). 1994. 19.95 (0-231-08294-0) Col U Pr.
Lynn, Richard J., jt. ed. see Liu, James J.
Lynn, Richardson R. Appellate Litigation. 2nd ed. 450p. 1993. 74.95 (1-880921-02-2); pap. 54.95 (1-880921-00-6) Austin & Winfield.
Lynn, Richardson R., jt. auth. see Cody, W. J.
Lynn, Robert, jt. auth. see Sindel, Stan.
Lynn, Robert E., ed. Chicorel Abstracts to Reading & Learning Disabilities. 1,983th ed. (Chicorel Index Ser.: Vol. 19). 325p. 1984. text ed. 125.00 (0-934598-85-1) Am Lib Pub Co.
— Chicorel Abstracts to Reading & Learning Disabilities, 1981. (Chicorel Index Ser.: Vol. 19). 490p. 1983. 125.00 (0-934598-83-5) Am Lib Pub Co.
— Chicorel Abstracts to Reading & Learning Disabilities, 1982. (Chicorel Index Ser.: Vol. 19). 424p. 1984. 125.00 (0-934598-84-3) Am Lib Pub Co.
Lynn, Robert H. All the Kings Men Notes. 1982. pap. 3.75 (0-8220-0146-2) Cliffs.
Lynn, Robert J. Introduction to Estate Planning in a Nutshell. 4th ed. (Nutshell Ser.). 340p. 1992. pap. text ed. 15.00 (0-314-00809-8) West Pub.
Lynn, Russel I., jt. auth. see Fischer, Dennis A.
Lynn, Ruth. Ester: The Story of a Small Ghost. Wagner, R. M., ed. LC 81-69693. (Illus.). 28p. (J). (gr. 5 up). 1981. 12.95 (0-941674-00-2) Woodcock Pr.

Lynn, Ruth N., ed. Fantasy Literature for Children & Young Adults: An Annotated Bibliography. 4th rev. ed. LC 94-42529. 1150p. (J). (gr. 3-12). 1995. 52.00 (0-8352-3456-8) Bowker. "A highly recommended work for all levels of school, public, & academic libraries..."--VOICE OF YOUTH ADVOCATES. "...a valuable resource that should be on the desk of every librarian who works with children..."--BOOKLIST. "Excellent not only for the generous number of books included but also for its recommendation system & extensive cross-referencing."--SCHOOL LIBRARY JOURNAL. Fully revised & updated, & drawing on distinguished review sources, this fourth edition of Bowker's classic guide includes more than 4,800 fantasy novels & story collections for children & young adults in grades 3-12. Each annotated title entry includes extensive bibliographic references, along with reading level, major awards won, recommendation symbols, & review citations. New to this edition: * Numbered entries that make access to titles easier. * 1,500 new fantasy novels & collections. * 4,000 new books, articles, & dissertations added to the extensive research guide. * 5 new reviewing sources in addition to the 24 used in previous editions. * Recommendation symbols denote books of superior & outstanding quality. * Expanded subject index that includes topical headings on fantasy worlds & imaginary beings as well as historical periods & series titles. *Publisher Provided Annotation.*

Lynn, Sandra. I Must Hold These Strangers. Oliphant, David, ed. (Illus.). 1980. pap. 5.00 (0-933384-04-1) Prickly Pear.
Lynn, Sandra, jt. auth. see Fenker, Richard, Jr.
Lynn, Sara. Clothes. (Aladdin Board Bks.). (Illus.). 14p. (J). (ps). 1986. pap. 2.95 (0-689-71095-X, Aladdin Paperbacks) S&S Childrens.
— I Can Make It! Dress Up. (J). (ps-3). 1994. mass mkt. 4.99 (0-553-37260-2) Bantam.
— I Can Make It! Fun Food. (ICMI Ser.: No. 1). (J). (ps-3). 1994. mass mkt. 4.99 (0-553-37259-9) Bantam.
— Noises: Huxley & Friends. 1990. 3.50 (0-517-02004-1) Random Hse Value.
— Play with Paper. (J). (ps-2). 1992. 18.95 (0-87614-754-6, Carolrhoda) Lerner Group.
— Toys. (Aladdin Board Bks.). (Illus.). 14p. (J). (ps). 1986. bds. 2.95 (0-689-71096-8, Aladdin Paperbacks) S&S Childrens.
Lynn, Sara & James, Diane. Play with Paint. (Play with Crafts Ser.). (Illus.). 24p. (J). (ps-2). 1993. 18.95 (0-87614-755-4, Carolrhoda) Lerner Group.
— Rain & Shine. LC 93-36420. (Play & Discover Ser.). (Illus.). 32p. (J). (ps-2). 1994. 14.95 (1-56847-142-4) Thomson Lrning.
— What We Eat. LC 93-35627. (Play & Discover Ser.). (Illus.). 32p. (J). (ps-2). 1994. 14.95 (1-56847-141-6) Thomson Lrning.
Lynn, Sara, jt. auth. see James, Diane.
Lynn, Sarah, jt. auth. see English, Laura M.
*Lynn, Sheryl. Dark Knight. (Intrigue Ser.). 1995. mass mkt. 3.50 (0-373-22331-5, 1-22331-2) Harlequin Bks.
— Dark Star. (Intrigue Ser.). 1995. mass mkt. 3.50 (0-373-22336-6, 1-22336-1) Harlequin Bks.
— Deadly Devotion. (Intrigue Ser.). 1993. pap. 2.89 (0-373-22223-8, 1-22223-1) Harlequin Bks.
— Ladykiller. (Intrigue Ser.). 1995. pap. 2.99 (0-373-22306-4, 1-22306-4) Harlequin Bks.
— Simon Says. (Intrigue Ser.). 1994. mass mkt. 2.99 (0-373-22258-0, 1-22258-7) Harlequin Bks.
Lynn, Sheryl, jt. ed. see Rimanelli, Marco.
Lynn, Stacey, ed. see Davis, Carolyn O.
Lynn, Steven. Samuel Johnson after Deconstruction: Rhetoric & "The Rambler" LC 91-4951. 208p. (C). 1992. 24.95 (0-8093-1770-2) S Ill U Pr.
Lynn, Steven J. & Rhue, Judith W. Dissociation: Clinical, Research & Theoretical Perspectives. 477p. 1994. lib. bdg. 40.00 (0-89862-186-0) Guilford Pr.
Lynn, Steven J. & Rhue, Judith W., eds. Theories of Hypnosis: Current Models & Perspectives. LC 91-28531. (Guilford Clinical & Experimental Hypnosis Ser.). 634p. 1991. lib. bdg. 55.00 (0-89862-343-X) Guilford Pr.
*Lynn, Stuart. Preservation & Access Technology: A Structured Glossary of Technical Terms. 68p. 1990. pap. 5.00 (1-887334-03-3) Comm Preserv & Access.
Lynn, Susan. Progressive Women in Conservative Times: Racial Justice, Peace, & Feminism, 1945-1960s. LC 92-7978. 220p. (C). 1993. text ed. 40.00 (0-8135-1867-9); pap. text ed. 15.00 (0-8135-1868-7) Rutgers U Pr.
Lynn, Terri. Uncommon Stock. (Superromance Ser.). 1993. mass mkt. 3.39 (0-373-70534-4, 1-70534-2) Harlequin Bks.
— Valentine's Summer. (Superromance Ser.). 1993. mass mkt. 3.50 (0-373-70555-7, 1-70555-7) Harlequin Bks.
Lynn, Theodore A. Introductory Musicianship: A Workbook. 3rd ed. 272p. (C). 1988. pap. text ed. 24.00 (0-15-543553-1) HB Coll Pubs.
— Introductory Musicianship: A Workbook. 4th ed. 300p. (C). 1992. pap. text ed. 25.50 (0-15-543555-8) HB Coll Pubs.
*Lynn, Theodore S. & Bloomfield, Micah. Real Estate Investment Trust. 1088p. Date not set. 145.00 (0-7913-1932-6) Warren Gorham & Lamont.
Lynn, Theodore S., et al. Real Estate Limited Partnerships. 3rd ed. LC 09-28277. (Real Estate Practice Library). 522p. 1991. text ed. 138.00 (0-471-52022-5) Wiley.
Lynn, Tim & Lynn, Tom. Making Marvelous Wood Toys. LC 88-15947. (Illus.). 136p. (Orig.). 1988. pap. 10.95 (0-8069-6744-7) Sterling.
— Making Toy Trains in Wood. LC 90-9978. (Illus.). 136p. (Orig.). (YA). (gr. 10-12). 1990. pap. 10.95 (0-8069-6989-X) Sterling.
Lynn, Tom, jt. auth. see Lynn, Tim.

L

Lynn, Vera, et al. Unsung Heroines: The Women Who Won the War. large type ed. 222p. 1993. 22.95 (*1-85089-596-1*, Pub. by ISIS UK) Transaction Pubs.

Lynn, Wayne B. Dare to Dream. pap. 6.95 (*0-88494-826-9*) Bookcraft Inc.

Lynn, William S., ed. Inflammatory Cells & Lung Disease. 120p. 1983. 98.00 (*0-8493-5792-6*, RC771, CRC Reprint) Franklin.

Lynne, Alma. Alma Lynne's Country Cross-Stitch. 1990. 24.95 (*0-8487-1014-2*) Oxmoor Hse.

Lynne, Erica. Angora: A Handbook for Spinners. LC 92-367. (Illus.). 120p. (Orig.). 1992. pap. 14.95 (*0-934026-75-0*) Interweave.

Lynne, Heather. Golden Girl. large type ed. (Linford Romance Library). 1993. pap. 14.95 (*0-685-67906-3*, Linford) Ulverscroft.

Lynne, James B. Rogue Diamond. large type ed. 534p. 1982. 23.95 (*0-7089-8044-9*, Trail West Pubs) Ulverscroft.

***Lynne, Mary.** Galaxy of Scents: The Ancient Art of Perfume Making. 291p. 1994. pap. 29.95 (*1-56459-458-0*) Kessinger Pub.

Lynne, Terry, jt. auth. see Graham.

***Lynne, Victoria.** Captured. 384p. (Orig.). 1995. mass mkt. 4.99 (*0-380-78044-5*) Avon.

***Lynnford, Janet.** Pirate's Rose. 384p. (Orig.). 1995. mass mkt. 4.99 (*0-451-40597-8*, Topaz) NAL-Dutton.

Lynnlee, J. L. All That Glitters. LC 86-61197. (Illus.). 128p. 1986. pap. 9.95 (*0-88740-069-8*) Schiffer.

— All That Glitters. rev. ed. LC 86-61197. (Illus.). 128p. 1993. pap. 12.95 (*0-88740-504-5*) Schiffer.

— Purrrfection: The Cat. LC 90-61743. (Illus.). 96p. (Orig.). 1990. pap. 16.95 (*0-88740-269-0*) Schiffer.

Lynnworth, Lawrence C. Ultrasonic Measurements for Process Control: Theory, Techniques, Applications. 694p. 1989. text ed. 132.00 (*0-12-460585-0*) Acad Pr.

Lynott, Bob. The Weather Tomorrow: Why Can't They Get It Right? LC 86-83330. 190p. (Orig.). 1987. pap. 10.00 (*0-9618077-0-9*) Gadfly Pr.

***Lynott, Mark J. & Wylie, Alison, eds.** Ethics in American Archaeology: Challenges for the 1990s. 100p. 1995. pap. 7.00 (*0-932839-12-6*) Soc Am Arch.

Lynott, Robert E. How Weather Works, & Why. LC 93-81357. (Illus.). 144p. (C). 1994. pap. text ed. 19.00 (*0-9618077-1-7*) Gadfly Pr.

Lynskey, Edward C. The Tree Surgeon's Gift. 1990. 22.50 (*0-916379-75-2*) Scripta.

Lynskey, Marie. Creative Calligraphy. (Illus.). 192p. (Orig.). 1984. pap. 12.95 (*0-7225-1509-X*) Thorsons SF.

Lynton, Ernest A. The Missing Connection Between Business & the Universities. (ACE-Oryx Series on Higher Education). (Illus.). 192p. 1984. 27.95 (*0-02-919280-3*, ACE-Oryx) Oryx Pr.

Lynton, Ernest A. & Elman, Sandra E. New Priorities for the University: Meeting Society's Needs for Applied Knowledge & Competent Individuals. LC 86-27729. (Higher & Adult Education Ser.). 216p. 1987. 29.95x (*1-55542-029-X*) Jossey-Bass.

Lynton, H. R. My Dear Nawab Saheb. (Illus.). 308p. 1991. 35.00 (*0-86311-168-8*, Pub. by Orient Longman Ltd II) Apt Bks.

***Lynton, Jonathan.** Ballentine's Legal Dictionary & Thesaurus. LC 94-33514. 768p. 1994. 32.95 (*0-8273-6526-8*) Delmar.

Lynton, Jonathan, et al. Law Office Management for Paralegals. 1991. text ed. 36.95 (*0-8273-4865-7*) Delmar.

Lynton, Jonathan S. Ballentine's Thesaurus for Legal Research & Writing. LC 93-13825. (Paralegal Ser.). 401p. 1994. pap. text ed. 19.95 (*0-8273-6208-0*) Delmar.

Lynton, Jonathan S. & Lyndall, Terri M. Legal Ethics & Professional Responsibility. LC 92-36136. (Illus.). 392p. 1994. pap. text ed. 26.95 (*0-8273-5504-1*) Delmar.

— Legal Ethics & Professional Responsibility: Instructor's Guide. 34p. 1994. 12.00 (*0-8273-5506-8*) Delmar.

***Lynton, Linda & Singh, Sanjay.** The Sari: History, Pattern, Style, Technique. LC 95-1590. 1995. write for info. (*0-8109-4461-8*) Abrams.

***Lynton, Mark.** Accidental Journey: A Cambridge Internee's Memoir of World War II. 352p. 1995. 23.95 (*0-87951-577-5*) Overlook Pr.

Lynton, Norbert. Ben Nicholson. (Illus.). 472p. (C). 1993. reprint ed. 125.00 (*0-7148-2813-0*, Pub. by Phaidon Press UK) Chronicle Bks.

— Henry Moore: The Human Dimension. (Illus.). 160p. 1991. pap. 35.00 (*0-906909-04-X*, Pub. by Lund Humphries UK) Antique Collect.

— The Story of Modern Art. 2nd ed. 400p. (C). 1989. pap. text ed. write for info. (*0-13-849860-1*) P-H.

— Victor Pasmore: Paintings & Graphics 1980-92. (Illus.). 156p. (C). 1992. 95.00 (*0-85331-606-6*, Pub. by Lund Humphries UK) Antique Collect.

***Lynton, Rolf P. & Pareek, Udai.** Training for Development. 2nd fac. ed. LC 89-7989. (Kumarian Press Library of Management for Development). (Illus.). 364p. 1994. pap. 103.80 (*0-7837-7584-9*, 2047337) Bks Demand.

Lynton, Rolf P. & Pareek, Udai, eds. Facilitating Development: Readings for Trainers, Consultants, & Policy-Makers. LC 92-17104. 1992. 38.50 (*0-8039-9417-6*) Sage.

Lynwander. Gear Drive Systems: Design & Application. (Mechanical Engineering Ser.: Vol. 20). 432p. 1983. 110.00 (*0-8247-1896-8*) Dekker.

Lynx, David & Martin, Alvin. Setting the Stage & the House That Jack Built. LC 92-70719. (Illus.). 16p. (Orig.). (C). 1992. pap. 5.95 (*1-880269-08-2*) D H Sheehan.

Lynx, David, jt. ed. see Munns, Frank.

Lynx, Lajoya & Savage, Temptra. Unfaithful Devotion. 176p. 1994. write for info. (*1-56167-134-7*) Noble Hse MD.

Lyon. Advanced Remote Sensing 1994. 1995. write for info. (*0-87371-891-7*) Lewis Pubs.

— Chic Simple: Paint. 1995. (*0-679-43217-5*) Knopf.

— Wetland Identification & Delineation. 1993. 59.95 (*0-87371-590-X*, QH104) Lewis Pubs.

Lyon, ed. French Short Stories. 1966. pap. 11.95 (*0-14-002385-2*, Penguin Bks) Viking Penguin.

Lyon, ed. see De Molina.

Lyon, ed. see Valle-Inclan.

Lyon, A. B., et al. Lyon Memorial: Massachusetts Families, Including Descendants of the Immigrant William Lyon of Roxbury, Peter & George of Dorchester, with an Introduction Treating the English Ancestry of the American Families. (Illus.). 491p. 1989. reprint ed. lib. bdg. 81.50 (*0-8328-0795-8*); reprint ed. pap. 73.50 (*0-8328-0796-6*) Higginson Bk Co.

Lyon, A. J. Dealing with Data. LC 76-92111. 1970. text ed. 172.00 (*0-08-006398-5*, Pub. by Pergamon Repr UK) Franklin.

Lyon, Adrian, jt. auth. see Lyon, C. M.

***Lyon, Albert.** There's a Dollar on the Drum Head. 230p. (Orig.). Date not set. pap. 8.95 (*0-7610-0188-3*) NW Pub.

Lyon, Albert L. The Smallest Principality. LC 90-70571. 238p. 1990. 8.95 (*1-55523-349-X*) Winston-Derek.

Lyon, Brenda L. Nursing Practice: An Exemplification of the Statutory Definition. 24p. (Orig.). (C). 1983. pap. text ed. 2.25 (*0-912919-01-9*, B200) Pathway AL.

Lyon, Bryce, ed. High Middle Ages, One Thousand to Thirteen Hundred. LC 64-21207. (Orig.). 1964. pap. 16.95 (*0-02-919480-6*) Free Pr.

Lyon, Bryce, tr. see Ganshof, Francois L.

Lyon, Bryce D. Medieval Finance: A Comparison of Financial Institutions in Northwestern Europe. LC 67-19657. 100p. reprint ed. 28.50 (*0-685-15738-5*, 2027516) Bks Demand.

Lyon, Bryce D., ed. see Stephenson, C.

Lyon, Buck. The Crow Horse. large type ed. (Linford Western Library). 320p. 1993. pap. 14.95 (*0-7089-7361-2*, Trailtree Bookshop) Ulverscroft.

Lyon, C. M. Lyon: The Law Relating to Children. 265p. 1993. 65.00 (*0-406-01653-4*, U.K.) Butterworth Legal Pubs.

Lyon, C. M. & De Cruz, Stephen. Lyon & de Cruz: Parents, Children & the Law. 1992. pap. 36.00 (*0-406-50800-3*) Butterworth Legal Pubs.

Lyon, C. M. & Lyon, Adrian. Butterworths Family Law Handbook. 1991. pap. 48.00 (*0-406-60980-2*, U.K.) Butterworth Legal Pubs.

Lyon, Carol B. Darling, I'm Still Alive & Recovering from Love. 38p. (Orig.). 1993. pap. 3.95 (*1-879559-07-2*) Galaxy WV.

Lyon, Charleen C. The Tale of Halley's Comet: An Educational Coloring Book. (Illus.). 32p. (Orig.). (J). (gr. 3-6). 1985. pap. 2.95 (*0-9614973-0-0*) Niota Pr.

Lyon, Christina M., jt. auth. see Freeman, Michael D.

Lyon, Christopher. International Dictionary of Films & Filmmakers, 5 vols. Incl. Vol. III. Actors & Actresses. 650p. 1986. 60.00 (*0-912289-08-2*); Set. 250.00 (*0-685-06728-9*) St James Pr.

Lyon, Clyde. Early Part of This Century in What Is Now the Land Between the Lakes: or, 1913 to 1929 in What Is Now the Land Between the Lakes. 228p. 1994. pap. 9.95 (*0-9640691-0-5*) Country Life.

Lyon, D., et al, eds. Guidelines for Sensory Analysis in Food Product Development & Quality Control. 160p. 1992. 48.95 (*0-442-31553-8*) Chapman & Hall.

Lyon, Danny. I Like to Eat Right on the Dirt: A Child's Journey Back in Space & Time. Wolff, Daniel, ed. LC 89-91769. (Illus.). 56p. (Orig.). 1989. spiral bd. 35.00 (*0-9620992-2-8*) Bleak Beauty Bks.

— Memories of the Southern Civil Rights Movement. LC 92-5961. (Lyndhurst Series on the South, Published for the Duke University Center for Documentary Studies). (Illus.). vii, 185p. (C). 1992. 39.95 (*0-8078-2054-7*); pap. 19.95 (*0-8078-4386-5*) U of NC Pr.

— Merci Gonaives: A Photgrapher's Account of Haiti & the February Revolution. (Illus.). 64p. 1994. pap. 19.95 (*1-881616-28-2*) Dist Art Pubs.

— Merci Gonaives: A Photographer's Account of Haiti & the February Revolution. LC 87-73298. (Illus.). 64p. (Orig.). (C). 1988. pap. 20.00 (*0-9620992-0-1*) Bleak Beauty Bks.

— Pictures from the New World. deluxe limited ed. 144p. 1987. 600.00 (*0-89381-082-7*) Aperture.

Lyon, David. The Biggest Truck. LC 87-22640. (Illus.). 32p. (J). (ps-3). 1988. 13.95 (*0-688-05513-3*); lib. bdg. 13.88 (*0-688-05514-1*) Lothrop.

— The Crumbly Coast. LC 93-41083. (J). 1995. 14.95 (*0-385-32079-5*) Doubleday.

— The Electronic Eye: The Rise of Surveillance Society. LC 93-35598. (C). 1994. text ed. 44.95 (*0-8166-2513-1*); pap. 16.95 (*0-8166-2515-8*) U of Minn Pr.

— The Information Society: Issues & Illusions. (Illus.). 200p. 1988. text ed. 39.95 (*0-7456-0260-6*); pap. text ed. write for info. (*0-7456-0369-6*) Blackwell Pubs.

— Postmodernity. (Concepts in Social Thought Ser.). 112p. 1994. text ed. 39.95x (*0-8166-2612-X*) U of Minn Pr.

— Postmodernity. (Concepts in Social Thought Ser.). 112p. 1994. pap. text ed. 13.95x (*0-8166-2613-8*) U of Minn Pr.

— The Runaway Duck. LC 84-5677. (Illus.). 32p. (J). (ps-1). 1985. 15.93 (*0-688-04002-0*); lib. bdg. 16.00 (*0-688-04003-9*) Lothrop.

— The Runaway Duck. LC 84-5677. (Illus.). 32p. (J). (ps up). 1987. reprint ed. pap. 3.95 (*0-688-07334-4*, Mulberry) Morrow.

— The Silicon Society. LC 86-194046. (London Lectures in Contemporary Christianity: 1979). 127p. (Orig.). reprint ed. pap. 36.20 (*0-685-23726-5*, 2032740) Bks Demand.

— The Sound of Horns. LC 82-24968. 63p. 1984. pap. 4.95 (*0-934332-38-X*) LEpervier Pr.

Lyon, Dorothy M. The Wheel of Life. 1989. 67.00 (*0-7223-2167-8*, Pub. by A H S Ltd UK) St Mut.

Lyon, Edmund. The Lyon Phonetic Manual. 1973. 59.95 (*0-8490-0566-3*) Gordon Pr.

Lyon, Edward E. Earth Science-Physical Geography: Review Through Programmed Learning. (C). 1986. pap. text ed. 18.95 (*0-89917-476-0*) Tichenor Pub.

Lyon, Edward E. & Dillon, Lowell I. Indiana: The American Heartland. (C). 1986. reprint ed. pap. text ed. 15.95 (*0-89917-475-2*) Tichenor Pub.

***Lyon, Elizabeth C.** Nonfiction Book Proposals Anybody Can Write: How to Get a Contract & Advance Before You Write Your Book. 272p. (Orig.). 1995. pap. 14.95 (*0-936085-31-2*) Blue Heron.

Lyon, Eugene. The Enterprise of Florida: Pedro Menendez de Aviles & the Spanish Conquest of 1565-1568. LC 76-29612. (Illus.). 1976. pap. 22.95 (*0-8130-0777-1*) U Press Fla.

— Motherlode! Concluding the Seventeen Year Search for the Atocha. (Florida Classics Ser.). (Illus.). (Orig.). 1989. pap. 15.95 (*0-912451-21-1*) Florida Classics.

— Motherlode! Concluding the Seventeen Year Search for the Atocha. (Illus.). (Orig.). 1995. 15.95 (*0-912451-20-3*) Florida Classics.

Lyon, Eugene, ed. Pedro Menendez De Aviles. LC 94-10710. (Spanish Borderlands Sourcebooks Ser.: Vol. 24). (Illus.). 640p. 1994. 62.00 (*0-8240-2099-5*) Garland.

Lyon, F. H., tr. see Von Blixen-Finecke, Bror.

Lyon, Francis D. Twists of Fate. 256p. (Orig.). 1993. pap. 14.95 (*1-879260-10-7*) Evanston Pub.

Lyon, G., ed. Virus Infection & the Developing Nervous System. (C). 1988. lib. bdg. 88.00 (*0-7462-0053-6*) Kluwer Ac.

Lyon, G. F. A Narrative of Travels in Northern Africa. 400p. 1985. 350.00 (*1-85077-032-8*, Darf Pubs Ltd) St Mut.

— Narrative of Travels in Northern Africa in the Years 1818, 1819 & 1820. 383p. 1966. reprint ed. 45.00 (*0-7146-1830-6*, Pub. by F Cass Pubs UK) Intl Spec Bk.

***Lyon, G. Reid & Krasnegor, Norman A.** Attention, Memory, & Executive Function. LC 95-2540. 432p. 1995. boxed 43.00 (*1-55766-198-7*) P H Brookes.

Lyon, G. Reid, et al, eds. Better Understanding Learning Disabilities: New Views from Research & Their Implications for Education & Public Policies. 304p. (C). 1993. boxed 35.00 (*1-55766-116-2*) P H Brookes.

***Lyon, George E.** Catalpa: Poems by George Ella Lyon. 62p. (Orig.). 1993. pap. 9.95 (*0-9636545-2-7*) Wind Pubns.

— Cecil's Story. LC 90-7775. (Illus.). 32p. (J). (gr. k-2). 1995. pap. text ed. 5.95 (*0-531-07063-8*) Orchard Bks Watts.

— Choices. LC 89-38082. 64p. 1989. pap. 4.50 (*0-8131-0900-0*) U Pr of Ky.

— Five Live Bongos. (Illus.). 40p. (J). (ps-3). 1994. 15.95 (*0-590-46654-2*, Scholastic Hardcover) Scholastic Inc.

— A Regular Rolling Noah. LC 90-39984. (Illus.). 32p. (J). (gr. k-3). 1991. reprint ed. pap. 4.95 (*0-689-71449-1*, Aladdin Paperbacks) S&S Childrens.

Lyon, George-Ella. A B Cedar: An Alphabet of Trees. LC 88-22797. (Illus.). 32p. (J). (ps-1). 1989. 14.95 (*0-531-05795-X*); lib. bdg. 14.99 (*0-531-08395-0*) Orchard Bks Watts.

— Basket. LC 89-71011. (Illus.). 32p. (J). (ps-2). 1990. 15.95 (*0-531-05886-7*); lib. bdg. 15.99 (*0-531-08486-8*) Orchard Bks Watts.

— Borrowed Children. 1990. mass mkt. 3.99 (*0-553-28380-4*) Bantam.

— Borrowed Children. LC 87-22700. 160p. (J). (gr. 5-7). 1988. 15.95 (*0-531-05751-8*); lib. bdg. 15.99 (*0-531-08351-9*) Orchard Bks Watts.

— Cecil's Story. LC 90-7775. (Illus.). 32p. (J). (gr. k-2). 1991. 15.95 (*0-531-05912-X*); lib. bdg. 15.99 (*0-531-08512-0*) Orchard Bks Watts.

— Come a Tide. LC 89-35650. (Illus.). 32p. (J). (ps-2). 1990. 15.95 (*0-531-05854-9*); lib. bdg. 15.99 (*0-531-08454-X*) Orchard Bks Watts.

— Come a Tide. LC 89-35650. (Illus.). 32p. (J). (ps-2). 1993. pap. 5.95 (*0-531-07036-0*) Orchard Bks Watts.

— Dreamplace. LC 92-25102. (Illus.). 32p. (J). (ps-2). 1993. 15.95 (*0-531-05466-7*); lib. bdg. 15.99 (*0-531-08616-X*) Orchard Bks Watts.

— Father Time & the Day Boxes. LC 93-25201. (Illus.). 32p. (J). (gr. k-3). 1994. reprint ed. pap. 4.95 (*0-689-71792-X*, Aladdin Paperbacks) S&S Childrens.

— Here & Then. LC 94-6921. 128p. (J). (gr. 5-7). 1994. 14.95 (*0-531-06866-8*); lib. bdg. 14.99 (*0-531-08716-6*) Orchard Bks Watts.

— Mama Is a Miner. LC 93-49398. (Illus.). 32p. (J). (gr. k-3). 1994. 15.95 (*0-531-06853-6*); lib. bdg. 15.99 (*0-531-08703-4*) Orchard Bks Watts.

— The Outside Inn. LC 90-14285. (Illus.). 32p. (J). (ps-1). 1991. 14.95 (*0-531-05936-7*); 14.99 (*0-531-08536-8*) Orchard Bks Watts.

— Together. LC 89-2892. (Illus.). 32p. (J). (ps-1). 1989. 14.95 (*0-531-05831-X*); lib. bdg. 14.99 (*0-531-08431-0*) Orchard Bks Watts.

Lyon, George Ella. Together. LC 89-2892. (Illus.). 32p. (J). (ps-1). 1994. pap. 5.95 (*0-531-07047-6*) Orchard Bks Watts.

Lyon, George-Ella. Who Came Down That Road? LC 91-20742. (Illus.). 32p. (J). (ps-2). 1992. 15.95 (*0-531-05987-1*); lib. bdg. 15.99 (*0-531-08587-2*) Orchard Bks Watts.

Lyon, H., ed. Theory & Strategy in Histochemistry: A Guide to the Selection & Understanding of Techniques. (Illus.). xviii, 591p. 1991. 89.00 (*0-387-19311-1*) Spr-Verlag.

Lyon, H. P. Nearing Retirement: A Study of Late Working Lives. 160p. 1986. text ed. 63.95 (*0-566-05233-4*, Pub. by Avebury Pub UK) Ashgate Pub Co.

Lyon, Harris M. Graphics. LC 72-4458. (Short Story Index Reprint Ser.). 1977. reprint ed. 23.95 (*0-8369-4182-9*) Ayer.

Lyon, Hastings & Block, Herman. Edward Coke, Oracle of the Law. (Illus.). viii, 385p. 1992. reprint ed. lib. bdg. 47.50 (*0-8377-2413-9*) Rothman.

Lyon, Howard, jt. auth. see Johnson, Warren T.

Lyon, Hugh. Modern Warships. (New Illustrated Guide Ser.). (Illus.). 1992. 5.98 (*0-8317-5053-7*) Smithmark.

Lyon, Isaac. Recollections of an Old Cartman: Old New York Street Life. (Illus.). 114p. 1983. reprint ed. 17.50 (*0-9608788-4-X*) NY Bound.

Lyon, J. Noel & Atkey, Ronald G., eds. Canadian Constitutional Law in a Modern Perspective. LC 78-18165. 1403p. reprint ed. pap. 180.00 (*0-8357-7993-9*, 2014276) Bks Demand.

Lyon, Jack, ed. see Harrison, Conrad B.

Lyon, James. Urania: A Choice Collection of Psalm-Tunes, Anthems & Hymns. LC 69-11667. (Music Reprint Ser.). 198p. 1974. reprint ed. lib. bdg. 37.50 (*0-306-71198-2*) Da Capo.

Lyon, James & Wheeler, Tony. Bali & Lombok: A Travel Survival Kit. 5th ed. (Illus.). 376p. 1994. pap. 14.95 (*0-86442-215-6*) Lonely Planet.

Lyon, James K. Bertolt Brecht & Rudyard Kipling: A Marxist's Imperialist. LC 73-94231. (Studies in General & Comparative Literature: No. 3). 138p. 1975. pap. text ed. 50.70 (*90-279-3411-8*) Mouton.

— Bertolt Brecht in America. LC 80-7543. (Illus.). 440p. (Orig.). 1980. reprint ed. pap. 16.95x (*0-691-01394-2*) Princeton U Pr.

***Lyon, James K. & Breuer, Hans-Peter, eds.** Brecht Unbound. LC 95-1992. 1995. write for info. (*0-87413-537-0*) U Delaware Pr.

Lyon, James K. & Inglis, Craig, eds. Benn Gottfried: Konkordanz Zur Lyrik Gottfried Benns. (Alpha-Omega, Reihe D Ser.). 524p. 1971. write for info. (*3-487-04037-9*, Pub. by Georg Olms GW) Lubrecht & Cramer.

Lyon, Jeff & Gorner, Peter. Altered Fates: The Genetic Re-Engineering of Human Life. 800p. 1995. 27.50 (*0-393-03596-4*) Norton.

Lyon-Jenness, Cheryl, comp. From the Homestead Kitchen. (Illus.). 233p. 1982. pap. 10.00 (*0-939294-12-5*, TX-715-F7) Beech Leaf.

Lyon, Jim, jt. auth. see McDowell, Judith A.

Lyon, John. The Merchant of Venice. LC 88-16466. 192p. 1988. lib. bdg. 20.95 (*0-8057-8708-9*, Twayne); pap. 13.95 (*0-8057-8712-7*, Twayne) Macmillan.

— Teares for the Death of Alexander, Earle of Dunfermeling, Lord Chancellar of Scotland. LC 79-172760. (Bannatyne Club, Edinburgh. Publications: No. 4). reprint ed. 14.50 (*0-404-52704-3*) AMS Pr.

— The Theatre of Valle-Inclan. LC 83-7368. (Cambridge Iberian & Latin American Studies). 241p. reprint ed. pap. 68.70 (*0-317-55473-5*, 2029222) Bks Demand.

***Lyon, John, ed. & intro.** The Sacred Fount. 240p. 1995. 10.95 (*0-14-043350-3*, Penguin Classics) Viking Penguin.

Lyon, John & Sloan, Philip. From Natural History to the History of Nature: Readings from Buffon & His Critics. LC 81-1320. 432p. 1981. text ed. 26.95 (*0-268-00955-4*) U of Notre Dame Pr.

Lyon, John, ed. see Conrad, Joseph.

Lyon, John, tr. see Duhem, Pierre.

Lyon, John F. & Lee, Siu-Lam. Laboratory Manual for Life Science I. 100p. (C). 1994. spiral bd. 14.95 (*0-8403-9563-9*) Kendall-Hunt.

***Lyon, John G. & McCarthy, Jack, eds.** Wetland & Environmental Applications of GIS. LC 95-10772. (Mapping Sciences Ser.). 368p. 1995. 69.95 (*0-87371-897-6*, L897) Lewis Pubs.

Lyon, John H. Study of the New Metamorphosis. LC 20-3786. reprint ed. 19.75 (*0-404-04087-X*) AMS Pr.

Lyon, Jonathan, jt. auth. see Horwich, Robert H.

Lyon, Kenneth S., jt. auth. see Sedjo, Roger A.

Lyon, Larry. The Community in Urban Society. 320p. (C). 1989. text ed. 24.95 (*0-669-21416-7*) Free Pr.

Lyon, Larry, jt. ed. see Warren, Roland L.

Lyon, Larry J. The Community in Urban Society. 320p. 1986. 37.95 (*0-87722-459-5*) Temple U Pr.

Lyon, Leverett, et al. The National Recovery Administration. LC 71-171386. (FDR & the Era of the New Deal Ser.). 1972. reprint ed. lib. bdg. 95.00 (*0-306-70385-8*) Da Capo.

Lyon, Leverett S. Hand-to-Mouth Buying: A Study in the Organization, Planning & Stabilization of Trade. LC 75-39259. (Getting & Spending: the Consumer's Dilemma Ser.). (Illus.). 1976. reprint ed. 41.95 (*0-405-08032-8*) Ayer.

— Salesman in Marketing Strategy. Assael, Henry, ed. LC 78-240. (Century of Marketing Ser.). 1979. reprint ed. lib. bdg. 36.95 (*0-405-11183-5*) Ayer.

Lyon, Leverett S., et al. Government & Economic Life: Development & Current Issues of American Public Policy, 2 vols., Set. LC 78-16476. (Institute of Economics of Brookings Institution Publication: No. 79). 1978. reprint ed. text ed. 95.00 (*0-313-20601-5*, LYGE) Greenwood.

— Government & Economic Life: Development & Current Issues of American Public Policy, 2 vols., Vol. 1. LC 78-16476. (Institute of Economics of Brookings Institution Publication: No. 79). 1978. reprint ed. text ed. 55.00 (*0-313-20600-7*, LYGE1) Greenwood.

— Government & Economic Life: Development & Current Issues of American Public Policy, 2 vols., Vol. 2. LC 78-16476. (Institute of Economics of Brookings Institution Publication: No. 79). 1978. reprint ed. text ed. 55.00 (*0-313-20599-X*, LYGE2) Greenwood.

Lyon, Lockwood. IMS vs. Expert's Guide: A Complete Guide to Compliance with OSHA. 1990. text ed. 44.95 (*0-442-23977-7*) Van Nos Reinhold.

An Asterisk (*) at the beginning of an entry indicates that the title is appearing in BIP for the first time.

— Migrating to DB2. 1991. 44.95 (0-89435-381-0) Wiley.
— Migrating to DB2. 254p. 1993. text ed. 49.95 (0-471-58180-1) Wiley.
— MIS Manager's Appraisal Guide: Practical Guidelines & Forms for Evaluating & Appraising Your MIS Staff. 1994. text ed. 39.95 (0-07-039272-2) McGraw.

Lyon, Lockwood & Lord, Kenniston W., Jr. CDP Review Manual. 5th ed. 800p. 1991. pap. 59.95 (0-442-00726-4) Van Nos Reinhold.

Lyon, Lucy, jt. auth. see Dewey, Jennifer.

Lyon, Marcus W., Jr. Mammals of Indiana. LC 73-17829. (Natural Sciences in America Ser.). (Illus.). 388p. 1974. reprint ed. 33.95 (0-405-05747-4) Ayer.

Lyon, Mary, tr. see Ganshof, Francois L.

Lyon, Mary F. & Southern, E. M., eds. The Prevention & Avoidance of Genetic Disease. (Philosophical Transactions of the Royal Society, Series B: Vol. 319). (Illus.). 157p. 1988. reprint ed. text ed. 92.50 (0-85403-352-1) Scholium Intl.

***Lyon, Mary F., et al, eds.** Genetic Variants & Strains of the Laboratory Mouse, 2 vols. 3rd ed. (Illus.). 2000p. 1995. 270.00 (0-19-854869-9) OUP.

Lyon, Melanie. Terror on Cape Cod. Van Treese, James B., ed. 320p. 1994. pap. 8.95 (1-56901-043-9) NW Pub.

Lyon, Melvin E. Symbol & Idea in Henry Adams. LC 67-20597. 338p. reprint ed. pap. 96.40 (0-7837-6019-1, 2045831) Bks Demand.

Lyon, Michael C. The Light & Other Poems. 1992. 12.95 (0-533-10003-8) Vantage.

Lyon, Nancy. The Mystery of Stonehenge. LC 77-10044. (Great Unsolved Mysteries Ser.). (Illus.). 48p. (J). (gr. 4 up). 1983. reprint ed. lib. bdg. 21.36 (0-8172-1049-0) Raintree Steck-V.

Lyon, P. C. & Alpern, B., eds. Coal: Classification, Coalification, Mineralogy, Trace-Element Chemistry, & Oil & Gas Potential. 600p. 1990. 172.00 (0-444-88011-9) Elsevier.

Lyon, Pamela & Parsons, Michael. We Are Staying: The Alyawarre Struggle for Land at Lake Nash. 240p. (C). 1990. 60.00 (0-7316-7458-8, Pub. by Pascoe Pub AT) St Mut.

Lyon, Patricia. Native South Americans: Ethnology of the Least Known Continent. (Illus.). 433p. (C). 1985. reprint ed. pap. text ed. 15.95 (0-88133-133-3) Waveland Pr.

Lyon, Patricia J., tr. see Gasparini, Graziano & Margolies, Luise.

Lyon, Peter, ed. Britain & Canada. (Studies in Commonwealth Politics & History: No. 4). 191p. 1976. 35.00 (0-7146-3052-7, Pub. by F Cass Pubs UK) Intl Spec Bk.

Lyon, Phyllis, jt. auth. see Martin, Del.

Lyon, R. H., jt. ed. see Elishakoff, I.

Lyon, Reid, ed. Frames of Reference for the Assessment of Learning Disabilities: New Views on Measurement Issues. 672p. 1994. pap. 55.00 (1-55766-138-3) P H Brookes.

Lyon, Richard H. Machinery Noise & Diagnostics. (Illus.). 299p. 1987. pap. 62.95 (0-7506-9330-4) Buttrwrth-Heinemann.

***Lyon, Richard H. & DeJong, Richard G.** Theory & Application of Statistical Energy Analysis. 2nd ed. 265p. 1994. 89.95 (0-7506-9111-5) Buttrwrth-Heinemann.

***Lyon, Richards.** Vine & Wine '95. (Yearly Datebook Journals Ser.). 162p. (Orig.). (C). Date not set. pap. text ed. 14.95 (0-9616004-6-2) Stonecrest Pr.
— Vine to Wine. LC 85-62333. (Illus.). 120p. (Orig.). 1985. pap. 9.95 (0-9616004-0-3) Stonecrest Pr.

Lyon, Rick. Bell Eight. (New Poets of America Ser.). 1994. pap. 12.50 (1-880238-09-8) BOA Edns.

***Lyon, Robert, ed.** Rivers of Dreams: Fly Fishing Stories. 192p. (Orig.). 1992. pap. 12.95 (0-920501-74-5) Orca Bk Pubs.

***Lyon, Robert L. & Rosenauer, Johnnie L.** How to Prepare for the Texas Real Estate Exam. 5th rev. ed. 207p. (C). 1994. pap. 21.95 (0-7931-0785-7, 1970-0305, Real Estate Ed) Dearborn Finan.

Lyon, Rod, ed. Everyday Cornish. (C). 1989. pap. 45.00 (0-907566-82-0, Pub. by Dyllansow Truran UK) St Mut.

Lyon, Rod & Pengilly, John. Notes on Spoken Cornish. (C). 1989. 30.00 (1-85022-034-4, Pub. by Dyllansow Truran UK) St Mut.

Lyon, Ron. Beyond Belief: Bizarre Facts & Incredible Legends from All over the World. 1994. pap. 12.00 (0-679-74883-0, Villard Bks) Random.
— Writing an ISO 9000 Quality Manual: Practical Guidelines. (C). 1994. 150.00x (0-946655-89-8, Pub. by S Thornes Pubs UK) St Mut.

Lyon, Roy B. Bosquejos Utiles para Laicos. (Illus.). 96p. (SPA.). 1990. reprint ed. pap. 3.50 (0-311-42401-5) Casa Bautista.

Lyon, Shirley A., tr. see Lazard, Gilbert.

Lyon, Sue, comp. Science in Action: The Living World. LC 92-36322. (Guide to Projects & Experiments Ser.). (J). (gr. 4-9). 1993. write for info. (0-86307-938-5) Marshall Cavendish.
— Science in Action: The World of Numbers. LC 92-36323. (J). (gr. 4-9). 1993. write for info. (0-86307-939-3) Marshall Cavendish.

Lyon, Sue, comp. & rev. Science in Action: Experiments in Physics. LC 92-34427. (Guide to Projects & Experiments Ser.). (J). 1993. write for info. (0-86307-342-5) Marshall Cavendish.
— Science in Action: Fun with Chemistry. rev. ed. LC 92-36324. (J). (gr. 4-9). 1993. write for info. (0-86307-340-9) Marshall Cavendish.
— Science in Action: Projects in Physics. LC 92-36325. (Guide to Projects & Experiments Ser.). (J). (gr. 4-9). 1993. write for info. (0-86307-341-7) Marshall Cavendish.

Lyon, Sue, comp. Science in Action: Light & Sound: Light & Sound. LC 92-36326. (Guide to Projects & Experiments Ser.). (J). (gr. 4-9). 1993. write for info. (0-86307-937-7) Marshall Cavendish.

Lyon, T. Edgar. John Lyon: The Life of a Pioneer Poet. (Specialized Monograph Ser.: Vol. 6). 14.95 (0-88494-708-4) Bookcraft Inc.

***Lyon, Thomas & Williams, Terry T., eds.** Great & Peculiar Beauty: A Utah Reader, 2. LC 95-13281. (Illus.). 500p. 1995. boxed 40.00 (0-87905-691-6) Gibbs Smith Pub.

Lyon, Thomas E., Jr. Juan Godoy. LC 73-161825. (Twayne's World Authors Ser.). 161p. (C). 1972. lib. bdg. 17.95 (0-8290-1732-1) Irvington.

Lyon, Thomas J. The Incomperable Lande: A Book of American Nature Writing. 1989. 29.95 (0-395-48313-1) HM.
— John Muir. LC 72-619587. (Western Writers Ser.: No. 3). (Illus.). 48p. (Orig.). (C). 1972. pap. 3.95 (0-88430-002-1) Boise St U W Writ Ser.

Lyon, Thomas J., ed. This Incomperable Lande: A Book of American Nature Writing. (Illus.). 512p. 1991. pap. 15. 95 (0-14-014441-2) Viking Penguin.

Lyon, Thomas J., intro. This Incomparable Land: A Book of American Nature Writing. 1989. 29.95 (0-395-48312-3) HM.

Lyon, Thomas J., ed. see Bass, Rick, et al.

Lyon, Thomas J., ed. see Western Literature Association Staff.

Lyon, Thomas J., et al. Places, Shadows, Dancing People. LC 71-632230. (Utah State University, Monograph Ser.: Vol. 17, No. 1). 70p. reprint ed. pap. 25.00 (0-8357-6264-5, 2034607) Bks Demand.

Lyon, Todd. Chic Simple Desk. 1994. 12.50 (0-679-43220-5) Knopf.

***Lyon, Tolbert J.** Lyon Hunts & Humor: True Life Hunting & Adventure Stories. LC 90-37549. 1990. pap. 12.95 (0-86534-148-6) Sunstone Pr.

Lyon, Victor L. Our Endangered Atmosphere: Global Warming & the Ozone Layer. McCuen, Gary E., ed. (Ideas in Conflict Ser.). (Illus.). 133p. 1987. lib. bdg. 12. 95 (0-86596-063-1) G E M.

Lyon, Wanda S. & Sutton, Cynthia E. Osteoporosis: How to Make Your Bones Last a Lifetime. 1993. pap. 10.99 (1-56943-005-5, Tribune) Contemp Bks.

Lyon, Wanda S., jt. auth. see Sutton, Cynthia E.

Lyon, Wendy. A Mother's Dilemma. 123p. 1993. 8.95 (1-878526-44-8) Pineapple MI.

Lyon, William F., jt. auth. see Davidson, Ralph H.

Lyon, William F., jt. auth. see Sherman, M. L.

Lyon, William H. Those Old Yellow Dog Days: Frontier Journalism in Arizona, 1859-1912. LC 93-49523. (Illus.). 272p. 1994. 29.95 (0-910037-32-9) AZ Hist Soc.

Lyon, William H., ed. Journalism in the West. (Illus.). 108p. 1980. pap. text ed. 15.00 (0-89745-008-6) Sunflower U Pr.

Lyon, William S., jt. auth. see Elk, Wallace B.

Lyonga, Lynne N., ed. see Ngeyi, Stanley-Pierre.

Lyongrun, Arnold. Masterpieces of Art Nouveau Stained Glass Design. (Illus.). 32p. 1989. pap. 6.95 (0-486-25953-6) Dover.

Lyonhardt, Lawrence & Howells, John. Russians & Others: Conversations with Twelve Soviet Citizens about Change. LC 91-52747. 128p. 1991. lib. bdg. 23.95x (0-89950-632-1) McFarland & Co.

Lyonnet, P. Tools of Total Quality: An Introduction to Statistical Process Control. (Illus.). 184p. 1991. 42.95 (0-412-37690-3) Chapman & Hall.

Lyonnet, Stanislas & Sabarin, Leopold. Sin, Redemption & Sacrifice: A Biblical & Patristic Study. (Analecta Biblica Ser.: Vol. 48). 1971. pap. 27.00 (88-7653-048-7, Pub. by Biblical Inst Pr IT) Loyola Univ Pr.

Lyons. Castles Burning. 1981. pap. 2.50 (0-671-41864-5) PB.
— Principles of Air Pollution Meteorology. 1990. 49.95 (0-8493-7106-6, QC) CRC Pr.
— Raw Head, Bloody Bones. (Illus.). (J). 1996. 3.95 (0-689-80306-0, Aladdin Paperbacks) S&S Childrens.

Lyons, ed. A Transect Through the New England Appalachians. (IGC Field Trip Guidebooks Ser.). 72p. 1989. 21.00 (0-87590-607-9, T162) Am Geophysical.

Lyons & Petrucelli. Medicine: An Illustrated History. (Illus.). 618p. 1987. pap. 49.98 (0-8109-8080-0, Abradale Pr) Abrams.

Lyons, A. B., jt. ed. see Miller, R. B.

Lyons, Alan S. Winning in the Options Market: A Streetwise Trader Shows You How to Outsmart the Pros. 1994. 42.50 (1-55738-431-2) Probus Pub Co.

Lyons, Albert. Abergavenny Nine Hundred: A Pictorial Celebration. (C). 1989. 70.00 (1-870402-55-3, Pub. by D Brown & Sons Ltd UK) St Mut.

Lyons, Albert C. Old Abergavenny in Photographs. (C). 1989. 59.00 (0-900807-56-3, Pub. by D Brown & Sons Ltd UK) St Mut.

Lyons, Albert M. Fifty-Fifty: A Blend of Old & New. LC 73-178445. (Short Story Index Reprint Ser.). 1977. reprint ed. 23.95 (0-8369-4046-6) Ayer.

Lyons, Anne. Values for Your Son, Your Daughter, & Yourself. 52p. 1993. pap. 12.95 (0-9638076-0-9) Fulton Freeman Pubs.

Lyons, Anne K. Anthony Trollope: An Annotated Bibliography of Periodical Works by & about Him in the United States & Great Britain to 1900. 175p. 1985. 25. 00 (0-913283-04-5) Penkevill.

Lyons, Art. Writing: Word Processing Strategies. LC 93-27990. 1993. pap. text ed. 18.80 (0-13-042912-0) P-H.

Lyons, Art & Lyons, Vicki. Writing Word Processing Strategies: Microsoft Word for Windows. LC 93-38756. 224p. 1994. pap. text ed. 18.80 (0-13-606054-4) P-H.
— Writing Word Processing Strategies: WordPerfect 6.0. LC 94-5829. 224p. 1994. pap. text ed. 17.80 (0-13-606062-5) P-H.

Lyons, Art & Seraydarian, Patricia E. Paradigm Reference Manual. 304p. (C). 1993. student ed 6.40 (1-56118-372-5); pap. text ed. 14.95 (1-56118-370-9); teacher ed, pap. text ed. 8.00 (1-56118-371-7) Paradigm MN.

Lyons, Art, jt. auth. see McLean, Gary.

Lyons, Arthur. False Pretenses. 240p. 1994. 18.95 (0-89296-220-8) Mysterious Pr.
— False Pretenses. 224p. 1995. mass mkt. 5.50 (0-446-40422-5, Mysterious Paperbk) Warner Bks.
— Other People's Money. 1989. 17.95 (0-89296-218-6) Mysterious Pr.

Lyons, Arthur & Truzzi, Marcello. The Blue Sense: Psychic Detectives & Crime. 1991. 19.95 (0-89296-426-X) Mysterious Pr.

Lyons, B. Me & My World: Teacher's Guide. (Graphic Learning Integrated Social Studies Ser.). 200p. (gr. k). 1993. 95.00 (0-87746-364-6) Graphic Learning.

Lyons, Barbara. The Brook. LC 75-42444. 1976. 10.00 (0-914916-10-6); pap. 1.95 (0-914916-15-7) Ku Paa.

Lyons, Barbara, jt. ed. see Rowland, Diane.

Lyons, Benita M. Scratch Cooking. 154p. (Orig.). 1990. pap. 12.95 (0-9616911-6-6) M F Sohn Pubns.

Lyons, Beth. Asian American: Minoru Yasui. (Graphic Learning Multicultural Literature Program Ser.). (Illus.). (ENG & SPA.). (J). (gr. k-5). 1994. 39.00 (0-87746-416-2) Graphic Learning.
— Federal Control of Business: Antitrust Laws. rev. ed. LC 72-84857. (Antitrust Ser.). 1972. Revised annually with supplement. 135.00 (0-685-59804-7) Clark Boardman Callaghan.
— Florida Studies Program: Teacher's Guide. (Illus.). 24p. 1983. teacher ed 10.00 (0-943068-30-4) Graphic Learning.
— New Jersey Studies Program: Activity Manual. Combs, Eunice A., ed. (Illus.). 200p. (gr. 4). 1983. 95.00 (0-943068-58-4) Graphic Learning.
— New Jersey Studies Program: Teacher's Guide. 2nd ed. Combs, Eunice A., ed. 28p. (gr. 4). 1983. teacher ed 10. 00 (0-943068-57-6) Graphic Learning.

Lyons, Beth, ret. African American: Harriet Tubman. (Graphic Learning Multicultural Literature Program Ser.). (Illus.). (ENG & SPA.). (J). (gr. k-5). 1994. 39.00 (0-87746-401-4) Graphic Learning.
— African American: The Name of the Tree. (Graphic Learning Multicultural Literature Program Ser.). (Illus.). (ENG & SPA.). (J). (gr. k-5). 1994. 39.00 (0-87746-410-3) Graphic Learning.
— Native American: When Coyote Stole Fire. (Graphic Learning Multicultural Literature Program Ser.). (Illus.). (ENG & SPA.). (J). (gr. k-5). 1994. 39.00 (0-87746-440-5) Graphic Learning.

Lyons, Blythe & Janes, Missy. Choosing the Right School for Your Child: A Guide to Selected Elementary Schools in the Washington Area. 344p. (Orig.). 1990. pap. 14.95 (0-8191-7682-6) Madison Bks UPA.

Lyons, Bonnie G., jt. auth. see Stuth, Jerry W.

Lyons, Bridget G., ed. Chimes at Midnight. (Films in Print Ser.). (Illus.). 225p. (Orig.). (C). 1988. text ed. 40.00 (0-8135-1338-3); pap. text ed. 15.00 (0-8135-1339-1) Rutgers U Pr.

Lyons, Carol, et al. Partners in Learning: Teachers & Children in Reading Recovery. (Language & Literacy Ser.). 256p. (C). 1993. text ed. 39.00 (0-8077-3298-2); pap. text ed. 18.95 (0-8077-3297-4) Tchrs Coll.

Lyons, Cathie. Journey Toward Wholeness. 1987. pap. 4.95 (0-377-00171-6) Friendship Pr.

Lyons, Champ, Jr. Alabama Practice Series, 2 vols. 2nd ed. 1250p. 1986. 120.00 (0-317-52097-0) West Pub.

Lyons, Charles, ed. see Robinson, Marcus S.

Lyons, Charles H., et al. Education for What? British Policy Versus Local Initiative. (Foreign & Comparative Studies Program, Eastern Africa Ser.: No. 13). 100p. 1973. pap. 3.00 (0-915984-10-5) Syracuse U Foreign Comp.

Lyons, Charles R. Critical Essays on Henrik Ibsen. (Critical Essays on World Literature Ser.). 264p. 1987. text ed. 45.00 (0-8161-8835-1) G K Hall.
— Hedda Gabler: Gender, Role & the World. Lecker, Robert, ed. (Twayne's Masterwork Studies). 168p. 1990. text ed. 21.95 (0-8057-9417-4, MWS 62, Pub. by Royal Botanic Garden UK); pap. 7.95 (0-8057-8141-2, MWS 62, Twayne) Macmillan.
— Samuel Beckett. King, Bruce & King, Adele, eds. (Modern Dramatists Ser.). 209p. 1990. pap. 13.95 (0-333-29466-1) St Martin.
— Shakespeare & the Ambiguity of Love's Triumph. (Studies in English Literature: No. 68). 213p. 1971. text ed. 56. 00 (90-279-1751-5) Mouton.

Lyons, Christine, jt. auth. see Schaefer, Dan.

Lyons, Dan, jt. auth. see Benson, Jann.

Lyons, Daniel. The Last Good Man. LC 93-3464. 176p. (Orig.). (C). 1993. 19.95x (0-87023-865-5) U of Mass Pr.
— The Last Good Man. LC 93-3464. (Associated Writing Programs Award for Short Fiction Ser.). 176p. (Orig.). 1995. pap. 12.95 (0-87023-978-3) U of Mass Pr.

Lyons, Daniel, tr. see Bosco, John.

Lyons, David. Ethics & the Rule of Law. LC 83-7687. 229p. 1984. pap. 16.95 (0-521-27712-4) Cambridge U Pr.
— In the Interest of the Governed: A Study in Bentham's Philosophy of Utility & Law. rev. ed. 176p. 1991. 45.00 (0-19-823964-5) OUP.
— Moral Aspects of Legal Theory: Essays on Law, Justice, & Political Responsibility. LC 92-28985. 208p. (C). 1993. 54.95 (0-521-43244-8); pap. 16.95 (0-521-43835-7) Cambridge U Pr.
— Rights, Welfare, & Mill's Moral Theory. 224p. 1994. 38. 00 (0-19-508217-6); pap. 17.95 (0-19-508218-4) OUP.

Lyons, David B. Lute, Vihuela, Guitar to Eighteen Hundred: A Bibliography. LC 78-6302. (Detroit Studies in Music Bibliography: No. 40). 214p. 1978. 20.00 (0-911772-93-6) Info Coord.

***Lyons, Deborah.** Edward Hopper: A Journal of His Work. (Illus.). 128p. 1995. pap. 14.95 (0-393-31330-1) Norton.

Lyons, Deboral, tr. see Berard, Claude, et al.

***Lyons, Deborha, et al.** Edward Hopper & the American Imagination. (Illus.). 272p. 1995. 39.95 (0-393-03814-9) Norton.

Lyons, Dianne J. & Satterfield, Archie. Washington Handbook. 4th ed. LC 94-6902. 430p. 1994. 15.95 (1-56691-055-2) Moon Pubns CA.

Lyons, Donald. Independant Visions: A Critical Introduction to Recent Independent American Film. (Illus.). 352p. (Orig.). 1994. pap. 12.00 (0-345-38249-8, Ballantine Trade) Ballantine.

Lyons, Edward, ed. see Jurado, Eunice S.

Lyons, Edward A. Practical Color Atlas of Sectional Anatomy: Chest, Abdomen, & Pelvis. 319p. 1990. 62.00 (0-88167-550-4) Raven.

Lyons, Elizabeth & Peters, Heather. Buddhism: History & Diversity of a Great Tradition. (Illus.). 64p. 1985. pap. 9.95 (0-934718-76-8) U PA Mus Pubns.

Lyons, Elizabeth G., jt. auth. see Lyons, Richard A.

Lyons, Emily B. How to Use Your Power of Visualization. (Lyons Visualization Ser.). (Illus.). 145p. (Orig.). 1980. pap. 6.95 (0-9604374-0-1) Lyons Visual.

***Lyons, Enda.** Jesus: Self-Portrait by God. LC 95-12265. 208p. (Orig.). 1995. 9.95 (0-8091-3583-3) Paulist Pr.

***Lyons, Eric R.** Black Art of Windows Game Programming. 600p. Date not set. cd-rom, pap. 34.95 (1-878739-95-6) Waite Group Pr.

Lyons, Ernest. Last Cracker Barrel. LC 75-7562. (Florida Classics Ser.). 201p. (Orig.). 1976. pap. 6.95 (0-912451-02-5) Florida Classics.
— My Florida. LC 69-14559. (Florida Classics Ser.). (Illus.). 136p. 1977. reprint ed. pap. 5.95 (0-912451-01-7) Florida Classics.

Lyons, Eugene. Assignment in Utopia. 290p. (C). 1990. pap. 24.95 (0-88738-856-6) Transaction Pubs.
— Assignment in Utopia. LC 76-110271. 658p. 1971. reprint ed. text ed. 85.00 (0-8371-4497-3, LYAU, Greenwood Pr) Greenwood.
— Life & Death of Sacco & Vanzetti. LC 74-107414. (Civil Liberties in American History Ser.). 1970. reprint ed. lib. bdg. 27.50 (0-306-71888-X) Da Capo.
— Red Decade: The Stalinist Penetration of America. 1980. reprint ed. lib. bdg. 75.00 (0-87700-313-0) Revisionist Pr.

Lyons, Eugene, ed. Six Soviet Plays. LC 68-8937. 468p. 1968. reprint ed. text ed. 65.00 (0-8371-0154-9, LYSP, Greenwood Pr) Greenwood.

Lyons, Evanthia, jt. ed. see Breakwell, Glynis M.

Lyons, F. S., ed. see Trollope, Anthony.

Lyons, Francis S. John Dillon: A Biography. LC 68-8594. 544p. reprint ed. pap. 155.10 (0-317-09551-X, 2020112) Bks Demand.

Lyons, Gail G. & Harlan, Donald L. Buyer Agency: Your Competitive Edge in Real Estate. 2nd ed. LC 93-13458. 1993. pap. 24.95 (0-7931-0717-2, 197803, Real Estate Ed) Dearborn Finan.

Lyons, Gene. The Higher Illiteracy: Essays on Bureaucracy, Propaganda, & Self-Delusion. LC 87-34013. 278p. (Orig.). 1988. 22.95 (1-55728-003-7); pap. 12.95 (1-55728-004-5) U of Ark Pr.
— Widow's Web. 1994. mass mkt. 5.99 (0-8041-1268-1) Ivy Books.
— Widow's Web. (Illus.). 352p. 1993. 23.00 (0-671-64185-9) S&S Trade.

***Lyons, Gene & Harper's Magazine Staff.** The Great Whitewater Hoax: On the Waywardness of the Media & the Foolishness of the New York Times. LC 94-47455. 1995. write for info. (1-879957-24-8, Franklin Sq Pr) Harpers Mag Found.

Lyons, Gene M. The Uneasy Partnership: Social Science & the Federal Government in the Twentieth Century. LC 72-93761. 394p. 1969. 39.95 (0-87154-561-6) Russell Sage.

Lyons, Gene M. & Lambert, Richard D. Social Science & the Federal Government. LC 76-148005. (Annals of the American Academy of Political & Social Science Ser.: No. 394). 1971. 27.00 (0-87761-137-8); pap. 18.00 (0-87761-136-X) Am Acad Pol Soc Sci.

Lyons, Gene M. & Masland, John W. Education & Military Leadership: A Study of the R. O. T. C. LC 75-18401. (Illus.). 283p. 1975. reprint ed. text ed. 59.75 (0-8371-8335-9, LYED, Greenwood Pr) Greenwood.

***Lyons, Gene M. & Mastanduno, Michael, eds.** Beyond Westphalia? State Sovereignty & International Invention. LC 94-32440. 360p. 1994. text ed. 48.50x (0-8018-4953-5); pap. text ed. 16.95x (0-8018-4954-3) Johns Hopkins.

Lyons, Genevieve. The Last Inheritor. 480p. 1988. pap. 3.95 (1-55817-064-2, Pinnacle NY) Windsor NY.
— The Palucci Vendetta. large type ed. 625p. 1993. 21.95 (0-7505-0510-9, Pub. by Magna Print Bks) Ulverscroft.
— Summer in Dranmore. large type ed. 261p. 1994. 19.95 (0-7505-0599-0, Pub. by Magna Print Bks) Ulverscroft.

Lyons, George. Holiness in Everyday Life. 48p. 1992. pap. 3.50 (0-8341-1432-1) Beacon Hill.
— Pauline Autobiography: Toward a New Understanding. (Society of Biblical Literature Dissertation Ser.). 1985. pap. 22.95 (0-89130-765-6, 06-01-73) Scholars Pr GA.

Lyons, Gracie. Constructive Criticism: A Handbook. (Illus.). 72p. (Orig.). 1988. reprint ed. pap. 6.95 (0-914728-62-8) Wingbow Pr.

Lyons, Graham. Duets for Teacher & Pupil, 2 bks., Bk. 1. Date not set. pap. 5.95 (0-685-69022-9, Chester Music) Music Sales.
— Duets for Teacher & Pupil, 2 bks., Bk. 2. Date not set. pap. 5.95 (0-685-69021-0, Chester Music) Music Sales.
— Duets for Teacher & Pupil, Bks. 1 & 2. Date not set. pap. 11.90 (0-685-69020-2, Chester Music) Music Sales.

L

— Take up the Clarinet, Bk. 1. Date not set. pap. 6.95 (*0-7119-1940-2*, Chester Music) Music Sales.

— Take up the Clarinet, Bk. 2. Date not set. pap. 6.95 (*0-685-69164-0*, Chester Music) Music Sales.

— Take up the Flute, 2 bks. Date not set. pap. 6.95 (*0-685-74679-8*, Chester Music) Music Sales.

Lyons, Graham, ed. The Russian Version of the Second World War: The History of the War As Taught to Soviet Schoolchildren. Vanston, Marjorie, tr. LC 82-24236. (Illus.). 168p. reprint ed. pap. 47.90 (*0-7837-1572-2*, 2041864) Bks Demand.

Lyons Graphic Designs Staff, ed. see Perry, Kate.

Lyons, H. P. Praying Our Prayers. 1976. 4.95 (*0-8199-0598-4*, Frncscn Herld) Franciscan Pr.

Lyons, Harold, jt. auth. see Bolch, Ben W.

Lyons, Harold D. The Final Prophet. Graves, Helen, ed. LC 86-40282. 288p. 1987. 12.95 (*1-55523-035-0*) Winston-Derek.

Lyons, Harold D., Jr., ed. see Bailey, D'Army.

Lyons, Harriet, ed. see Roth, Joan.

Lyons, Henry G. Royal Society, Sixteen Sixty to Nineteen Forty: A History of Its Administration under Its Charters. LC 69-10124. (Illus.). 354p. 1968. reprint ed. text ed. 35.00 (*0-8371-0155-7*, LYRS, Greenwood Pr) Greenwood.

Lyons, Ivan, jt. auth. see Lyons, Nan.

Lyons, J. B. Oliver St. John Gogarty. (Irish Writers Ser.). 89p. 1976. 8.50 (*0-8387-1359-9*); pap. 1.95 (*0-8387-1397-1*) Bucknell U Pr.

Lyons, James, jt. auth. see Howard, John T., Jr.

Lyons, James R., ed. The Intellectual Legacy of Paul Tillich. LC 68-63714. (Slaughter Foundation Lectures: 1966). 119p. reprint ed. pap. 34.00 (*0-685-15631-1*, 2027636) Bks Demand.

Lyons, Janes E., ed. Winning Strategies & Techniques for Civil Litigators. 350p. 1992. 95.00 (*0-685-69515-8*) PLI.

Lyons, Jerry L. & Askland, Carl L., Jr. Lyon's Encyclopedia of Valves. rev. ed. LC 92-4490. 302p. (C). 1993. reprint ed. lib. bdg. 45.25 (*0-89464-734-2*) Krieger.

Lyons, Jim. How to Find Buried Treasure. rev. ed. (Illus.). 42p. 1986. reprint ed. pap. 7.95 (*0-9616231-0-1*) Jim Lyons.

Lyons, Joan. My Mother's Book. (Illus.). 48p. (Orig.). 1993. pap. 10.00 (*0-89822-104-8*) Visual Studies.

Lyons, Joan, intro. Artists' Books: A Critical Anthology & Sourcebook. 3rd ed. LC 85-3180. (Research, Fine Arts Ser.). (Illus.). 274p. (C). 1993. reprint ed. pap. text ed. 119.95 (*0-89822-041-6*, N74333A75) Visual Studies.

Lyons, Jodi & Stevenson, Lanelle. P. O. P. S. Principles of Pop Singing. 320p. 1990. audio 32.00 (*0-02-871971-9*) Schirmer Bks.

Lyons, John. Guts: Advertising from the Inside Out. LC 86-47816. 324p. 1989. pap. 16.95 (*0-8144-7721-6*) AMACOM.

— Introduction to Theoretical Linguistics. (Illus.). (Orig.). (C). 1968. pap. 32.95 (*0-521-09510-7*) Cambridge U Pr.

— Language & Linguistics. LC 80-42002. (Illus.). 280p. (C). 1981. pap. 19.95 (*0-521-29775-3*) Cambridge U Pr.

— Linguistic Semantics: An Introduction. 432p. (C). 1995. write for info. (*0-521-43302-9*); pap. write for info. (*0-521-43877-2*) Cambridge U Pr.

— Lyons on Horses. 1991. 27.50 (*0-385-41398-X*) Doubleday.

— Natural Language & Universal Grammar: Essays in Linguistic Theory. 416p. (C). 1991. 64.95 (*0-521-24696-2*) Cambridge U Pr.

— Semantics One. LC 76-40838. (Illus.). 1977. pap. 29.95 (*0-521-29165-8*) Cambridge U Pr.

— Semantics Two. LC 76-40838. (Illus.). 1977. 89.95 (*0-521-21560-9*); pap. 29.95 (*0-521-29186-0*) Cambridge U Pr.

Lyons, John, tr. see Cardenal, Ernesto.

Lyons, John, ed. see De Lafayette, Madame.

Lyons, John A. Historical Sketches of Parish of St. Bernard of Clairvaux on Casey Creek, Kentucky. (Illus.). 1979. pap. 5.00 (*0-934906-02-5*) R J Liederbach.

Lyons, John D. Exemplum: The Rhetoric of Example in Early Modern France & Italy. 352p. 1990. text ed. 45.00 (*0-691-06782-1*) Princeton U Pr.

— The Listening Voice: An Essay on the Rhetoric of Saint-Amant. LC 82-82429. (French Forum Monographs: No. 40). 138p. (Orig.). 1982. pap. 10.95 (*0-917058-39-9*) French Forum.

Lyons, John D. & McKinley, Mary B., eds. Critical Tales: New Studies of the Heptameron & Early Modern Culture. LC 93-26575. 296p. (C). 1994. text ed. 36.95 (*0-8122-3206-2*) U of Pa Pr.

Lyons, John D. & Nichols, Stephen G., Jr., eds. Mimesis: From Mirror to Method, Augustine to Descartes. LC 82-40340. (Illus.). 287p. 1982. 35.00 (*0-87451-244-1*) U Pr of New Eng.

Lyons, John D. & Vickers, Nancy J., eds. The Dialectic of Discovery: Essays on the Teaching & Interpretation of Literature Presented to Lawrence E. Harvey. LC 83-81598. (French Forum Monographs: No. 50). 192p. (Orig.). 1984. pap. 17.95 (*0-917058-50-X*) French Forum.

Lyons, John O. The Invention of the Self: The Hinge of Consciousness in the Eighteenth Century. LC 77-27103. (Illus.). 277p. 1978. 19.95 (*0-8093-0815-0*) S Ill U Pr.

Lyons, John S., jt. ed. see Hultmand, Cheryl I.

Lyons, John W. The Chemistry & Uses of Fire Retardants. LC 84-11213. 478p. (C). 1987. reprint ed. lib. bdg. 64.00 (*0-89874-767-8*) Krieger.

— Fire. LC 85-2185. (Scientific American Library). (Illus.). 170p. 1995. text ed. write for info. (*0-7167-5010-4*) W H Freeman.

Lyons, Joseph. Clare Booth Luce. (American Women of Achievement Ser.). (Illus.). 112p. (YA). (gr. 5 up). 1989. lib. bdg. 17.95 (*1-55546-665-6*) Chelsea Hse.

— Ecology of the Body: Styles of Behavior in Human Life. LC 87-9080. 339p. (C). 1987. lib. bdg. 41.95 (*0-8223-0710-3*) Duke.

Lyons, Joy M. Mammoth Cave: The Story Behind the Scenery. LC 91-60037. (Illus.). 48p. 1991. 6.95 (*0-88714-050-5*) KC Pubns.

Lyons, Kelly A., jt. auth. see Akl, Selim G.

Lyons, Kenneth P. Cardiovascular Nuclear Medicine. (Illus.). 334p. 1988. boxed 99.95 (*0-8385-1052-3*, A1052-8) Appleton & Lange.

Lyons, Kim. In Padua. 32p. 1991. pap. 4.00 (*0-685-56987-X*) St Lazaire.

Lyons, L. & Stenning, S. Managing Staff in Schools. (C). 1989. 140.00 (*0-09-159620-3*, Pub. by S Thornes Pubs UK) St Mut.

Lyons, Lael, jt. auth. see Thompson, Charles C.

Lyons, Laura. Lyons' Guide to the Career Jungle: Workplace Ethics. LC 89-91730. (Orig.). 1989. pap. 12.95 (*0-9623216-0-5*) Odenwald Pr.

Lyons, Laurence, jt. auth. see Birchall, David.

Lyons, Lawrence, jt. auth. see Gutmann, Felix.

Lyons, Lawrence W. Dan Quayle Meets the Last Judgement: Why It Happened. LC 90-85362. 238p. (Orig.). 1992. pap. 11.88 (*0-942121-33-3*) Grammar Pub.

— The Language Crystal: The Complete Solution to Civilization's Oldest Puzzle. LC 87-80516. (Illus.). 510p. (Orig.). 1988. pap. 14.76 (*0-942121-18-X*) Grammar Pub.

Lyons, Len. The Commodore 64 Connection. 256p. 1985. pap. write for info. (*0-201-17631-9*) Addison-Wesley.

— Jazz Portraits: The Lives & Music of the Jazz Masters. LC 88-8929. (Illus.). 610p. 1990. reprint ed. pap. 14.95 (*0-688-10002-3*, Quill) Morrow.

— The One Hundred One Best Jazz Albums: A History of Jazz on Records. LC 80-20735. 1980. pap. 15.45 (*0-688-08720-5*, Quill) Morrow.

Lyons, Leonard S. The Great Jazz Pianists. (Quality Paperbacks Ser.). (Illus.). 320p. 1989. reprint ed. pap. 12.95 (*0-306-80343-7*) Da Capo.

Lyons, Letitia M. Francis Norbet Blanchet & the Founding of the Oregon Missions (1838-1848) LC 73-3585. (Catholic University of America. Studies in Romance Languages & Literatures: No. 31). reprint ed. 28.00 (*0-404-57781-4*) AMS Pr.

Lyons, Linda B. A Handbook fo the Pension Building: Home of the National Building Museum. 2nd ed. LC 93-27937. 1993. pap. write for info. (*0-9619752-2-9*) Natl Bldg Mus.

Lyons, Lisa, ed. see Arlen, Alice.

Lyons, Lisa, ed. see Perry, Katy.

Lyons, Lona, ed. see Treadgold, Richard.

***Lyons, Lorenzo.** Makua Laiana: Story of Lorenzo Lyons. (American Autobiography Ser.). 278p. 1995. reprint ed. lib. bdg. 79.00 (*0-7812-8583-6*) Rprt Serv.

***Lyons, Louis.** All You Wanted to Know about Mathematics but Were Afraid to Ask Vol. 1: Mathematics Applied to Science. (Illus.). 240p. (C). 1995. write for info. (*0-521-43465-3*); pap. write for info. (*0-521-43600-1*) Cambridge U Pr.

— A Practical Guide to Data Analysis for Physical Science Students. (Illus.). 112p. (C). 1991. 34.95 (*0-521-41415-6*); pap. 14.95 (*0-521-42463-1*) Cambridge U Pr.

***Lyons, M., ed.** Electroactive Polymer Electrochemistry: Fundamentals, Pt. 1. (Illus.). 483p. (C). 1995. 110.00 (*0-306-44792-4*, Plenum Pr) Plenum.

***Lyons, M. C.** The Arabian Epic: Heroic & Oral Storytelling. (University of Cambridge Oriental Publications Ser.: 52). (C). 1995. write for info. (*0-521-48354-9*) Cambridge U Pr.

— The Arabian Epic: Heroic & Oral Storytelling Vol. 1: Introduction. (University of Cambridge Oriental Publications: 49). 192p. (C). 1995. write for info. (*0-521-47428-0*) Cambridge U Pr.

— The Arabian Epic: Heroic & Oral Storytelling Vol. 2: Analysis. (University of Cambridge Oriental Publications Ser.: 49). 500p. (C). 1995. write for info. (*0-521-47449-3*) Cambridge U Pr.

— The Arabian Epic: Heroic & Oral Storytelling Vol. 3: Texts. (University of Cambridge Oriental Publications Ser.: 49). 500p. (C). 1995. write for info. (*0-521-47450-7*) Cambridge U Pr.

Lyons, M. T. & Johnson, A. Preparing the Winning Bid. 352p. 1992. 60.00 (*0-85314-377-3*, Pub. by Tolley Pubng UK) St Mut.

Lyons, Malcom C. & Jackson, D. E. Saladin: The Politics of the Holy War. LC 79-13078. (Cambridge University Oriental Publicstions: No. 30). (Illus.). 400p. 1985. pap. 24.95 (*0-521-31739-8*) Cambridge U Pr.

Lyons, Mark. The Good Parishioner. 1983. 1.95 (*0-8199-0830-4*, Frncscn Herld) Franciscan Pr.

Lyons, Mark E. Selected Poems. (YA). 1992. 7.95 (*0-533-09578-6*) Vantage.

Lyons, Mark J. Background for Belief. 74p. (Orig.). 1990. pap. 1.95 (*0-8199-0957-2*, Frncscn Herld) Franciscan Pr.

***Lyons, Marty.** Napoleon Bonaparte & the Legacy of the French Revolution Vol. 1. 1994. pap. 17.95 (*0-312-12123-7*) St Martin.

Lyons, Mary. The Butter Tree. (J). 1995. 13.95 (*0-8050-2673-8*) H Holt & Co.

— Keeping Secrets. (J). 1995. 15.95 (*0-8050-3065-4*) H Holt & Co.

— Love Is the Key. (Presents Ser.). 1994. mass mkt. 2.99 (*0-373-11633-0*, 1-11633-4) Harlequin Bks.

— Love Is the Key. large type ed. 1993. 17.95 (*0-263-13407-5*, Pub. by Mills & Boon Ltd UK) Chivers N Amer.

— No Surrender. large type ed. 215p. 1992. 21.95 (*0-7505-0313-0*, Pub. by Magna Print Bks) Ulverscroft.

— Silver Lady. 1993. mass mkt. 2.99 (*0-373-11610-1*, 1-11610-2) Harlequin Bks.

— The Yuletide Bride. 1995. pap. 3.25 (*0-373-11781-7*, 1-11781-1) Harlequin Bks.

Lyons, Mary D. Poetry in the Latin Class. 9p. (Orig.). 1991. spiral bd. 1.35 (*0-939507-15-3*, B16) Amer Classical.

Lyons, Mary E. Deep Blues: Bill Trayler, Self-Taught Artist. LC 93-23736. (J). 1994. text ed. 15.95 (*0-684-19458-9*, Scribners) S&S Trade.

— Letters from a Slave Girl: The Story of Harriet Jacobs. LC 91-45778. (Illus.). 160p. (YA). (gr. 7 up). 1992. text ed. 14.95 (*0-684-19446-5*, C Scribner Sons Young) S&S Childrens.

— Master of Mahogany: The Story of Tom Day, Free Black Cabinetmaker. LC 93-37900. (J). 1994. text ed. 15.95 (*0-684-19675-1*, Scribners) S&S Trade.

— Painting Dreams: Minnie Evans, Visionary Artist. LC 95-3994. (J). 1995. write for info. (*0-395-72032-X*) Ticknor & Flds Bks Yng Read.

— Sorrow's Kitchen: The Life & Folklore of Zora Neale Hurston. LC 90-8058. (Illus.). 160p. (YA). (gr. 7 up). 1990. text ed. 14.95 (*0-684-19198-9*, C Scribner Sons Young) S&S Childrens.

— Sorrow's Kitchen: The Life & Folklore of Zora Neale Hurston. LC 90-30600. (Great Achievers Ser.). (Illus.). 160p. (YA). (gr. 7 up). 1993. pap. 5.95 (*0-02-044445-1*, Collier Bks Young) S&S Childrens.

— Starting Home: The Story of Horace Pippin, Painter. LC 92-26990. (African-American Artists & Artisans Ser.). (Illus.). 48p. (J). (gr. 3-6). 1993. text ed. 15.95 (*0-684-19534-8*, C Scribner Sons Young) S&S Childrens.

— Stitching Stars: The Story Quilts of Harriet Powers. LC 92-38561. (African-American Artists & Artisans Ser.). (Illus.). 48p. (J). (gr. 3-6). 1993. text ed. 15.95 (*0-684-19576-3*, C Scribner Sons Young) S&S Childrens.

Lyons, Mary E., sel. Raw Head, Bloody Bones: African-American Tales of the Supernatural. LC 91-10690. (Illus.). 96p. (J). (gr. 5 up). 1991. text ed. 13.95 (*0-684-19333-7*, C Scribner Sons Young) S&S Childrens.

Lyons, Maryanne, jt. ed. see Corro, Ann.

Lyons, Maryinez. A Colonial Disease: A Social History of Sleeping Sickness in Northern Zaire, 1900-1940. (History of Medicine Ser.). (Illus.). 338p. (C). 1992. 79.95 (*0-521-40350-2*) Cambridge U Pr.

Lyons, Matthew. The Grassroots Network: Radical Nonviolence in the Federal Republic of Germany, 1972-1985. (Western Societies Papers). 70p. 1989. 11.95 (*0-8014-9640-3*) Cornell U Pr.

Lyons, Matthew N. Rose Kohn Goldsen Papers: A Descriptive Guide. (Illus.). 32p. 1992. pap. text ed. write for info. (*0-935995-02-1*) Cornell Manu.

Lyons, Matthew N., jt. auth. see Berlet, Chip.

Lyons, Melinda, ed. see Kennedy, Jan.

Lyons, Melvin K. The Care & Feeding of Dirt Archaeologists. x, 76p. 1978. pap. text ed. 5.95 (*0-685-66562-3*) Am Sch Orient Res.

— The Care & Feeding of Dirt Archaeologists: A Manual of Sanitation, Hygiene, & Medicine for Archaeological Field Expeditions in the Near East. x, 76p. 1978. pap. text ed. 5.95 (*0-317-04130-4*) Am Schls Oriental.

Lyons, Michael, jt. auth. see Alexander, James A.

Lyons, Michael J. World War I: A Short History. LC 93-19794. 1993. pap. text ed. write for info. (*0-13-953514-4*) P-H.

— World War Two: A Short History. 2nd ed. LC 93-14685. 1993. pap. text ed. write for info. (*0-13-501156-6*) P-H.

Lyons, Morgan, et al. Key Organizational Issues in Intergenerational Mentoring. 71p. 1993. 10.00 (*0-86510-067-5*) Natl Inst Work.

***Lyons, Nan.** Fielding's London Agenda. Knoles, Kathy, ed. (Travel Guides Ser.). (Illus.). 256p. (Orig.). 1995. pap. 12.95 (*1-56952-039-9*) Fielding Wrldwide.

— Fielding's New York Agenda. Knoles, Kathy, ed. (Travel Guides Ser.). (Illus.). 256p. (Orig.). 1995. pap. 12.95 (*1-56952-044-5*) Fielding Wrldwide.

— Fielding's Paris Agenda. Knoles, Kathy, ed. (Travel Guides Ser.). (Illus.). 256p. (Orig.). 1995. pap. 12.95 (*1-56952-045-3*) Fielding Wrldwide.

— Someone Is Killing the Great Chefs of America, Vol. 1. 1993. 19.95 (*0-316-54023-4*) Little.

Lyons, Nan & Lyons, Ivan. Champagne Blues. 1980. pap. 2.25 (*0-449-24317-6*, Crest) Fawcett.

— Imperial Taste. (Illus.). 184p. 1991. 27.95 (*4-7700-1513-5*) Kodansha.

— Someone Is Killing the Great Chefs of Europe. LC 75-45140. 240p. 1990. 19.95 (*0-15-183760-0*) HarBrace.

Lyons, Nathan. Notations in Passing. 1974. 23.95 (*0-262-12067-4*); pap. 10.95 (*0-262-62028-6*) MIT Pr.

— Verbal Landscape-Dinosaur Sat Down. (Illus.). 1987. pap. 10.00 (*0-939784-16-5*) CEPA Gall.

Lyons, Nathan, ed. see Denison, Herbert.

Lyons, Nathan, ed. see Story, Alfred T.

Lyons, Nene W. The Healing Touch. 80p. (C). 1988. pap. 35.00 (*0-7212-0743-X*, Pub. by Regency Press) St Mut.

Lyons, Nick. Confessions of a Fly-Fishing Addict. 1989. pap. 10.00 (*0-671-67653-9*, Fireside) S&S Trade.

— The Seasonable Angler: The Adventures & Misadventures of an Angling Addict. 1988. pap. 6.95 (*0-318-36077-2*, Fireside) S&S Trade.

— Spring Creek. LC 92-13026. (Illus.). 169p. 1992. 20.00 (*0-87113-525-6*) Grove-Atltic.

Lyons, Oren, et al. Exiled in the Land of the Free: Democracy, Indian Nations, & the U. S. Constitution. LC 91-72479. 336p. (C). 1992. 24.95 (*0-940666-15-4*) Clear Light.

— Exiled in the Land of the Free: Democracy, Indian Nations & the U.S. Constitution. LC 91-72479. (Illus.). 427p. (C). 1994. pap. 14.95 (*0-940666-50-2*) Clear Light.

Lyons, P., et al. Involving Parents: A Handbook for Participation in Schools. 248p. 1984. pap. 12.95 (*0-931114-19-5*) High-Scope.

Lyons, P. C. & Alpern, B., eds. Peat & Coal: Origin, Facies, & Depositional Models. 800p. 1990. 197.50 (*0-444-88012-7*) Elsevier.

Lyons, Pat & Burgard, Debby. Great Shape: The First Fitness Guide for Large Women. rev. ed. (Illus.). 300p. 1990. pap. 14.95 (*0-923521-01-1*) Bull Pub.

Lyons, Patrick J. Applying Expert System Technology to Business. 269p. (C). 1994. pap. 27.95 (*0-534-20538-0*); disk, 5.25 hd 36.95 (*0-534-20540-2*); disk 36.95 (*0-534-20541-0*) Boyd & Fraser.

Lyons, Paul. Class of '66: Living in Suburban Middle America. LC 93-50899. 272p. (C). 1994. text ed. 44.95 (*1-56639-213-6*); pap. text ed. 16.95 (*1-56639-214-4*) Temple U Pr.

— Going for Broke. 204p. 1991. 17.95 (*0-945575-45-9*) Algonquin Bks.

— Table Legs. LC 89-25840. 160p. (C). 1989. 15.95 (*0-941533-42-5*) New Amsterdam Bks.

— Thirty-Five Lesson Formats: A Sourcebook of Instructional Alternatives. LC 91-45289. 160p. (Orig.). 1992. pap. 24.95 (*0-87778-244-X*) Educ Tech Pubns.

Lyons, Paul C. & Brownlow, Arthur H., eds. Studies in New England Geology: A Memoir in Honor of C. Wroe Wolfe. LC 75-30494. (Geological Society of America, Memoir Ser.: No. 146). (Illus.). 410p. reprint ed. pap. 116.90 (*0-8357-3149-9*, 2039412) Bks Demand.

Lyons, Paul C. & Rice, Charles L., eds. Paleoenvironmental & Tectonic Controls in Coal-Forming Basins of the United States. (Special Paper Ser.: No. 210). (Illus.). 208p. 1987. pap. 5.00 (*0-8137-2210-1*) Geol Soc.

***Lyons, Paul C., et al, eds.** Historical Perspective of Early Twentieth Century Carboniferous Paleobotany in North America: In Memory of William Culp Darrah. LC 95-15891. (Memoir Ser.: No. 185). (Illus.). 1995. write for info. (*0-8137-1185-1*) Geol Soc.

Lyons, Paul J. Managing Contributed Funds & Assets: The Tax-Exempt Financial Planning Manual. LC 85-24991. 350p. 1985. 135.00 (*0-914756-27-3*, 600009) Taft Group.

Lyons, Paul R., et al. The Management Field Experience. (Illus.). 100p. (Orig.). (C). 1983. pap. text ed. 15.00 (*0-8191-3403-1*) U Pr of Amer.

Lyons, Pauline D., jt. auth. see Marzano, Kathryn M.

***Lyons, Pete.** Can-Am History. (Illus.). 256p. 1995. 39.95 (*0-7603-0017-8*) Motorbooks Intl.

Lyons, Pete, jt. auth. see Consumer Guide Auto Editors.

Lyons, Phyllis I. The Saga of Dazai Osamu: A Critical Study with Translations. LC 83-42542. (Illus.). 432p. 1985. 47.50 (*0-8047-1197-6*) Stanford U Pr.

Lyons, Ponsonby, jt. ed. see Hart, William.

Lyons, Rex & Lyons, Rose. Holly Hill Inn Cookbook. (Illus.). 248p. 1989. pap. 11.95 (*0-9621134-0-9*) Cider Pr KY.

***Lyons, Richard.** Enough to Be a Woman. 68p. 1994. 7.50 (*1-881604-01-2*) Scopcraeft.

— Fable for a North Window. 160p. 1995. 8.00 (*1-881604-18-7*) Scopcraeft.

— Men & Tin Kettles. LC 71-179814. (New Poetry Ser.). reprint ed. 16.00 (*0-404-56014-8*) AMS Pr.

— These Modern Nights: Poems. LC 87-26355. 80p. (Orig.). 1988. pap. 10.95 (*0-8262-0672-7*) U of Mo Pr.

— A Wilderness of Faith & Love: Contemporary Fiction Ser. LC 87-73429. 130p. (Orig.). 1988. pap. 7.95 (*0-935306-42-0*) Barnwood Pr.

Lyons, Richard, ed. see Chambers, George.

Lyons, Richard, jt. auth. see Gorenstein, Daniel.

Lyons, Richard, et al. Schooling to Working: Exploring the Connections. LC 90-40764. (American University Studies: Vol. 30). 200p. (C). 1991. text ed. 34.95 (*0-8204-1344-5*) P Lang Pubs.

Lyons, Richard A. & Lyons, Elizabeth G. Making Miniature Furniture. 240p. 1988. pap. 14.95 (*0-13-547258-X*) P-H.

Lyons, Robert, ed. Autobiography: A Reader for Writers. 2nd ed. (C). 1984. pap. 18.95 (*0-19-503401-5*) OUP.

— My Darling Clementine: John Ford, Director. LC 83-26883. (Films in Print Ser.). (C). 1984. pap. text ed. 15.00 (*0-8135-1051-1*) Rutgers U Pr.

Lyons, Robert E. The Conquest of Mexico by Hernan Cortez, 1518-1521: Selected Translations & a Portfolio of Etchings. (Illus.). 16p. (Orig.). 1987. 785.00 (*0-943435-00-5*) Cartographer Ink.

Lyons, Robert J. Michelangelo Antonioni's Neo-Realism: A World View. LC 75-21433. (Dissertations on Film Ser.). 1976. lib. bdg. 19.95 (*0-405-07618-5*) Ayer.

Lyons, Roderick. How Progression Is Recorded. (Orig.). 1991. pap. text ed. 10.50 (*0-913412-55-4*) Brandon Hse.

Lyons, Rose, jt. auth. see Lyons, Rex.

Lyons, Ruth, jt. ed. see Gold, Charlotte.

Lyons, S. L. Exterior Lighting for Industry & Security. (Illus.). xiv, 320p. 1980. 84.75 (*0-85334-879-0*, Pub. by Elsevier Applied Sci UK) Elsevier.

***Lyons, Stanely & Beigel, Renate.** Carpet & Floorcoverings for Your Home. 1995. 8.95 (*1-899163-09-3*) Cimino Pub Grp.

Lyons, Stanley. Emergency Lighting: For Industrial, Commercial & Residential Premises. (Illus.). 192p. 1992. 54.95 (*0-7506-0806-4*) Buttrwrth-Heinemann.

— Lighting for Industry & Security: A Handbook for Providers & Users of Lighting. LC 92-10329. (Illus.). 320p. 1993. 115.00 (*0-7506-1084-0*) Buttrwrth-Heinemann.

— Security of Premises: A Manual for Managers. (Illus.). 132p. 1988. text ed. 29.95 (*0-408-01367-2*) Buttrwrth-Heinemann.

***Lyons, Steve.** The Bicyclist's Guide to Northwest Connecticut. 271p. (Orig.). 1995. pap. 14.95 (*0-9632585-6-7*) Freewheel Pub.

— The Bicyclist's Guide to the Southern Berkshires. 272p. 1993. pap. 14.95 (*0-9632585-5-9*) Freewheel Pub.

— Steve Lyons: Psycho Analysis. (Illus.). 275p. 1995. 22.95 (*1-57167-013-0*) Sagamore Pub.

***Lyons, Steven A.** HomeBuyer: The Book & Software Home Buying Kit. (Illus.). 136p. (Orig.). 1995. pap. 27.95 (*0-9618084-3-8*) Stratosphere Pub.

Lyons, T. P. Personnel Function in a Changing Environment. (Times Management Library). 1971. 22.95 (*0-8464-0709-4*); pap. 9.95 (*0-8464-0710-8*) Beekman Pubs.

Lyons, Therese, tr. see Riffaterre, Michael.

Lyons, Thomas & Nee, Victor, eds. The Economic Transformation of South China: Reform & Development in the Post-Mao Era. No. 70. 298p. (C). 1994. lib. bdg. 25.00 (*0-939657-82-1*) Cornell East Asia Pgm.

— The Economic Transformation of South China: Reform & Development in the Post-Mao Era, No. 70. 298p. (C). 1994. pap. 17.00 (*0-939657-70-8*) Cornell East Asia Pgm.

Lyons, Thomas P. Economic Integration & Planning in Maoist China. 440p. 1987. text ed. 61.00 (*0-231-06542-6*) Col U Pr.

— Poverty & Growth in a South China County: Anxi, Fujian, 1949-1992. (Cornell East Asia Ser.: No. 72). (Illus.). 174p. (Orig.). 1994. lib. bdg. 18.00 (*0-939657-81-3*, 72); pap. text ed. 11.00 (*0-939657-72-4*, 72) Cornell East Asia Pgm.

Lyons, Thomas P. & Wang Yan. Planning & Finance in China's Economic Reforms. (Cornell East Asia Ser.: No. 46). 57p. (Orig.). (C). 1988. pap. 7.00 (*0-939657-46-5*) Cornell East Asia Pgm.

Lyons, Thomas S. & Hamlin, Roger E. Creating an Economic Development Action Plan: A Guide for Development Professionals. LC 90-38845. 224p. 1990. text ed. 49.95 (*0-275-93648-1*, C3648, Praeger Pubs) Greenwood.

Lyons, Thomas T., ed. The President: Preacher, Teacher, Salesman-Selected Presidential Speeches, 1933-1983. LC 84-51315. (Illus.). 206p. (Orig.). (C). 1985. pap. text ed. 11.95 (*0-9608014-4-8*) World Eagle.

Lyons, Tim. Astrology Beyond Ego. LC 86-40123. 204p. (Orig.). 1986. pap. 6.95 (*0-8356-0612-0*, Quest) Theos Pub Hse.

Lyons, Timothy J. The Silent Partner: The History of the American Film Manufacturing Company 1910-1921, Vol. 7. LC 73-21590. 266p. 1974. 18.95 (*0-405-04872-6*) Ayer.

Lyons, Tom W. The Pelican & After: A Novel about Emotional Disturbance. LC 83-3283. 268p. 1983. 14.95 (*0-9609506-0-5*) Prescott Durrell & Co.

Lyons, V. & Ziegler, C. Business Desktop Publishing Applications: Job-Based Tasks. 200p. (C). 1994. teacher ed write for info. (*1-56118-399-7*); disk, pap. text ed. 15.95 (*1-56118-398-9*); 3.5 hd, pap. text ed. 15.95 (*1-56118-400-4*) Paradigm MN.

Lyons, Vicki, jt. auth. see Lyons, Art.

***Lyons, Vonnie.** Keikilani, the Kona Nightingale. (Illus.). 32p. (J). (ps-6). 1994. lib. bdg. 8.95 (*0-9643512-0-X*) Mouse Pubng.

Lyons, W. Practical Petroleum Engineer, Vol. 1. 6th ed. 1996. write for info. (*0-87201-718-4*) Gulf Pub.

— Practical Petroleum Engineer, Vol. 2. 6th ed. 1996. write for info. (*0-88415-643-5*) Gulf Pub.

Lyons, W. E. The Politics of City-County Merger: The Lexington-Fayette County Experience. LC 77-73706. 192p. 1978. 21.00 (*0-8131-1363-6*) U Pr of Ky.

Lyons, W. E., et al. Politics of Dissatisfaction: Citizens, Services, & Urban Institutions. LC 91-35287. (Bureaucracies, Public Administration, & Public Policy Ser.). 248p. 1992. pap. text ed. 20.95 (*1-56324-378-4*) M E Sharpe.

Lyons, W. F. Brigadier-General Thomas Francis Meagher: His Political & Military Career; with Selections from His Speeches & Writings. LC 04-24937. (Illus.). 1975. reprint ed. 17.50 (*0-89097-005-X*) Archer Edns.

***Lyons, William.** Approaches to Intentionality. 304p. 1995. 49.95 (*0-19-823526-7*) OUP.

— The Disappearance of Introspection. 216p. 1988. 25.00 (*0-262-12115-8*, Bradford Bks); pap. 10.95 (*0-262-62062-6*, Bradford Bks) MIT Pr.

***Lyons, William, ed.** Modern Philosophy of Mind. 336p. (Orig.). 1995. pap. 7.50 (*0-460-87558-2*, Everyman's Classic Lib) C E Tuttle.

Lyons, William, ed. see Elder, Crawford.

Lyons, William, jt. auth. see Hopkins, Anne H.

***Lyons, William, et al.** American Government: Politics & Political Culture. LC 94-38187. 650p. 1995. text ed. 56.00 (*0-314-04558-9*) West Pub.

Lyons, William C., et al. Well Construction Engineering. 250p. 1993. boxed 64.00 (*0-13-953423-7*) P-H.

Lyons, William H, jt. auth. see Duncan, Richard F.

Lyons, William H.

Lyotard, Jean F. The Postmodern Explained. Pefanis, Julian & Thomas, Morgan, eds. Barry, Don et al, trs. LC 92-10408. 104p. (C). 1992. text ed. 29.95 (*0-8166-2210-8*); pap. 11.95 (*0-8166-2211-6*) U of Minn Pr.

Lyotard, Jean-Francois. The Differend: Phrases in Dispute. Van Den Abbeele, Georges, tr. LC 88-4780. (Theory & History of Literature Ser.: Vol. 46). 224p. (Orig.). 1989. text ed. 39.95 (*0-8166-1610-8*); pap. 14.95 (*0-8166-1611-6*) U of Minn Pr.

— Duchamp's Transformers. McLeod, Ian, tr. (Illus.). 200p. (C). 1990. 55.00 (*0-932499-63-5*) Lapis Pr.

— Heidegger & "the Jews" Michel, Andreas & Roberts, Mark S., trs. 144p. (C). 1990. pap. text ed. 12.95 (*0-8166-1857-7*) U of Minn Pr.

— The Inhuman: Reflections on Time. Bennington, Geoffrey & Bowlby, Rachel, trs. LC 91-66838. 224p. (C). 1992. 39.50 (*0-8047-2006-1*); pap. 11.95 (*0-8047-2008-8*) Stanford U Pr.

— Lessons on the Analytic of the Sublime. LC 93-10683. 208p. (C). 1993. 37.50 (*0-8047-2241-2*); pap. 14.95 (*0-8047-2242-0*) Stanford U Pr.

— The Libidinal Economy. Grant, Iain H., tr. LC 91-32761. (Theories of Contemporary Culture Ser.). 1993. text ed. 49.95 (*0-253-33614-7*); pap. text ed. 17.95 (*0-253-20728-2*, MB-728) Ind U Pr.

— Pacific Wall. Lindsay, Cecile, tr. (Illus.). 70p. 1990. 37.50 (*0-932499-64-3*) Lapis Pr.

— Peregrinations: Law, Form, Event. (Wellek Library Lectures). 128p. 1988. text ed. 27.50 (*0-231-06670-8*) Col U Pr.

— Phenomenology. (SUNY Series in Contemporary Continental Philosophy). 153p. 1991. 59.50 (*0-7914-0805-1*); pap. 19.95 (*0-7914-0806-X*) State U NY Pr.

— Political Writings. Readings, Bill & Geiman, Kevin P., trs. 380p. (C). 1993. text ed. 49.95 (*0-8166-2043-1*); pap. text ed. 18.95 (*0-8166-2045-8*) U of Minn Pr.

— The Post-Modern Condition: A Report on Knowledge. Bennington, Geoff & Massumi, Brian, trs. LC 83-14717. (Theory & History of Literature Ser.: Vol. 10). 131p. (C). 1984. pap. 12.95 (*0-8166-1173-4*) U of Minn Pr.

— Sam Francis, Lesson of Darkness. Bennington, Geoffrey, tr. (Illus.). 100p. 1993. 60.00 (*0-932499-70-8*) Lapis Pr.

— Toward the Postmodern. Harvey, Robert & Roberts, Mark S., eds. LC 92-719. (Philosophy & Literary Theory Ser.). 280p. (C). 1995. pap. 17.50 (*0-391-03890-7*) Humanities.

Lyotard, Jean-Francois & Thebaud, Jean-Loup. Just Gaming. Massumi, Brian, tr. LC 85-1109. (Theory & History of Literature Ser.: Vol. 20). vi, 129p. 1985. pap. text ed. 12.95 (*0-8166-1277-3*) U of Minn Pr.

***Lyovin, Anatole V.** An Introduction to the Languages of the World. (Illus.). 416p. 1995. 49.95 (*0-19-508115-3*); pap. text ed. 24.95 (*0-19-508116-1*) OUP.

Lyovin, Valentina V., tr. see St. Theophan the Recluse.

Lyovina, Valentina V., tr. see Kavelin, Archimandrite L.

Lypny, Gregory J., jt. auth. see Burger, Albert E.

Lypyns'kyi, Viacheslav. Ukraina na Perelomi, 1657-1659: Zamitky do Istorii Ukrains'koho Derzhavnoho Budivnyctva v XVII-im Stolittiu. (Viacheslav Lypyns'kyi, Tvory Ser.: Vol. 3). 400p. 1992. text ed. 39.95 (*0-9631165-0-9*) WKL East Europ.

Lyr, Guyette. La Fuite end Douce. (FRE.). 1979. pap. 10.95 (*0-7859-4121-5*) Fr & Eur.

— L' Herbe des Fous. (FRE.). 1982. pap. 10.95 (*0-7859-4170-3*) Fr & Eur.

Lyra, F., tr. see Dzielska, Maria.

Lyrand, L., jt. auth. see Coopers, C.

Lyre, Larry. Deja Vu...with...Flippance...& Flippance. 174p. (C). 1989. 39.95 (*0-7212-0774-X*, Pub. by Regency Press) St Mut.

Lyren, Delon, jt. auth. see Hickman, Jane W.

Lyric Opera of Chicago Staff. The Lyric Opera Companion. 448p. (Orig.). 1991. pap. 14.95 (*0-8362-6218-2*) Andrews & McMeel.

Lysaght, M. J., jt. ed. see Gurland, H. J.

Lysaght, M. J., et al, eds. Disputed Issues in Renal Failure Therapy. (Contributions to Nephrology Ser.: Vol. 44). (Illus.). xii, 294p. 1984. 78.50 (*3-8055-3938-X*) S Karger.

Lysaght, Sean. Noah's Irish Art. (C). 1990. 30.00 (*0-948268-63-8*, Pub. by Dedalus Pr IE); pap. 15.00 (*0-948268-62-X*, Pub. by Dedalus Pr IE) St Mut.

Lysaght, Sidney R. Reading of Life. LC 70-142659. (Essay Index Reprint Ser.). 1977. 20.95 (*0-8369-2060-0*) Ayer.

Lysaght, Thomas A., comp. A Selection of Ancient Slav Literary Monuments. 184p. (ENG & RUS.). 1982. 195.00 (*0-317-40872-0*, Pub. by Collets UK) Pro-Am Music.

Lysak, Robert L., ed. Auroral Plasma Dynamics. LC 93-43462. (Geophysical Monograph Ser.: No. 80). 1993. 57.00 (*0-87590-039-9*) Am Geophysical.

***Lysakowski, Rich & Gregg, Charles E., eds.** Computerized Chemical Data Standards: Databases, Data Interchange, & Information Systems, STP 1214. LC 94-31856. (Special Technical Publication Ser.: Vol. 1214). (Illus.). 175p. 1994. text ed. 53.00 (*0-8031-1876-7*, 04-012140-63) ASTM.

Lysanov, Y. P., jt. auth. see Brekhovskikh, L. M.

***Lysaught, Brian.** Eye of the Beholder. LC 95-10830. 1995. 22.00 (*0-684-80078-0*) S&S Trade.

Lysaught, Jerome P. Action in Affirmation: Towards an Unambiguous Profession of Nursing. (Illus.). 224p. 1980. text ed. 28.95 (*0-07-039271-4*) McGraw.

Lysek, G., jt. auth. see Kloidt, M.

***Lysen.** Quick Reference to Clinical Dietetics. 350p. 1995. 36.00 (*0-8342-0629-3*) Aspen Pub.

Lysenko, V. On the Way to Knowledge: Man, the Earth, Outer Space, Acceleration. 266p. (C). 1988. 30.00 (*0-685-36905-6*, Pub. by Collets) St Mut.

Lysiak, Lynne D., jt. ed. see Baker, Barry B.

Lysias. Ausgewahlt Reden, 2 vols. in 1. viii, 310p. 1963. write for info. (*3-296-14510-9*, Pub. by Georg Olms GW) Lubrecht & Cramer.

— Lysia Epitaphios, Pts. I & II. Connor, W. R., ed. LC 78-18608. (Greek Texts & Commentaries Ser.). 1979. reprint ed. lib. bdg. 21.95 (*0-405-11448-6*) Ayer.

— Orationes. Hude, Karl, ed. (Oxford Classical Texts Ser.). (GRE.). 1979. reprint ed. text ed. 24.95 (*0-19-814538-1*) OUP.

— Orations. (Loeb Classical Library: No. 244). 734p. 1930. 18.95 (*0-674-99269-5*) HUP.

— Selected Speeches. Carey, Christopher, ed. (Cambridge Greek & Latin Classics Ser.). 232p. (C). 1990. 59.95 (*0-521-26435-9*); pap. 21.95 (*0-521-26988-1*) Cambridge U Pr.

***Lysik, David, ed.** At Home with the Word 1994. (Illus.). 160p. (Orig.). 1995. pap. 6.00 (*1-56854-069-8*, AHW96) Liturgy Tr Pubns.

— At Home with the Word 1995. (Illus.). 160p. (Orig.). 1994. pap. 6.00 (*1-56854-034-5*, AHW95) Liturgy Tr Pubns.

Lysing, Henry, pseud. Secret Writing: An Introduction to Cryptograms, Ciphers, & Codes. LC 74-75261. 128p. 1974. reprint ed. pap. 3.95 (*0-486-23062-7*) Dover.

Lyskowski, Roman, ed. see Miami Herald Staff & El Nuevo Herald Staff.

Lysman, Frederick D. Being Public. 4th ed. 30p. Date not set. pap. text ed. 15.00 (*0-936093-37-4*) Packard Pr Fin.

Lysne, D. K., jt. ed. see Broch, E.

Lysne, Mary. New Testament Match Up. (Illus.). 32p. (J). 1991. pap. 1.99 (*0-87403-876-6*, 25-02506) Standard Pub.

— Old Testament Match Up. (Illus.). 32p. (J). 1991. pap. 1.99 (*0-87403-875-8*, 25-02505) Standard Pub.

— Read the Pictures: Fun from the New Testament, Bk. 1. (Illus.). 32p. (J). (gr. k-3). 1991. pap. 1.99 (*0-87403-879-0*, 23-02509) Standard Pub.

— Read the Pictures: Fun from the Old Testament, Bk. 1. (Illus.). 32p. (J). (gr. k-3). 1991. pap. 1.99 (*0-87403-877-4*, 23-02507) Standard Pub.

— Read the Pictures: More Fun from the New Testament, Bk. 2. (Illus.). 32p. (J). (gr. k-3). 1991. pap. 1.99 (*0-87403-880-4*, 23-02510) Standard Pub.

— Read the Pictures: More Fun from the Old Testament, Bk. 2. (Illus.). 32p. (J). (gr. k-3). 1991. pap. 1.99 (*0-87403-878-2*, 23-02508) Standard Pub.

Lysne, Mary E. Come & See. Gambill, Henrietta, ed. (Bible Hero Rebus Bks.). (Illus.). 24p. (J). (ps-3). 1993. student ed 2.39 (*0-7847-0104-0*, 23-02584) Standard Pub.

— Mary & Elizabeth. Gambill, Henrietta, ed. (Bible Hero Rebus Bks.). (Illus.). 24p. (J). (ps-3). 1993. student ed 2.39 (*0-7847-0101-6*, 23-02581) Standard Pub.

— Parables of Jesus. Gambill, Henrietta, ed. (Bible Hero Rebus Bks.). (Illus.). 24p. (J). (ps-3). 1993. student ed 2.39 (*0-7847-0102-4*, 23-02582) Standard Pub.

— Paul. Gambill, Henrietta, ed. (Bible Hero Rebus Bks.). (Illus.). 24p. (J). (ps-3). 1993. student ed 2.39 (*0-7847-0106-7*, 23-02586) Standard Pub.

— Peter. Gambill, Henrietta, ed. (Bible Hero Rebus Bks.). (Illus.). 24p. (J). (ps-3). 1993. student ed 2.39 (*0-7847-0105-9*, 23-02585) Standard Pub.

— What Happened? Gambill, Henrietta, ed. (Bible Hero Rebus Bks.). (Illus.). 24p. (J). (ps-3). 1993. student ed 2.39 (*0-7847-0103-2*, 23-02583) Standard Pub.

***Lysne, Robin H.** Dancing up the Moon: A Woman's Guide to Creating Traditions That Bring Sacredness to Daily Life. 256p. (Orig.). 1995. pap. 12.95 (*0-943233-85-2*) Conari Press.

— Dancing up the Moon: A Woman's Guide to Creating Traditions That Bring Sacredness to Daily Life. 256p. 1995. lib. bdg. 33.00 (*0-8095-5890-4*) Borgo Pr.

Lyson, Thomas A. Two Sides of the Sunbelt: The Growing Divergence Between the Rural & Urban South. LC 88-31928. 163p. 1989. text ed. 49.95 (*0-275-93201-X*, C3201, Praeger Pubs) Greenwood.

Lyson, Thomas A. & Falk, William W., eds. Forgotten Places: Uneven Development in Rural America. LC 92-43847. (Rural America Ser.). 298p. 1993. 35.00 (*0-7006-0592-4*); pap. 14.95 (*0-7006-0593-2*) U Pr of KS.

Lyson, Thomas A., jt. auth. see Falk, William W.

Lysons, C. K. Purchasing. 2nd ed. 240p. 1989. pap. 26.50 (*0-7121-1748-2*, Pub. by Pitman Pub Ltd UK) Trans-Atl Phila.

— Purchasing Handbook. 211p. (C). 1989. 130.00 (*0-685-39933-8*, Inst Pur & Supply) St Mut.

Lysons, Kenneth. Earning Money in Retirement. (C). 1991. 50.00 (*0-86242-103-9*, Pub. by Age Concern Eng UK) St Mut.

— Hearing Impairments & Business Administration. (Special Needs & Business Administration Ser.). 78p. 1992. pap. 36.00 (*1-85302-196-2*, Pub. by J Kingsley Pubs UK) Taylor & Francis.

— Learning Difficulties & Business Administration. (Special Needs & Business Administration Ser.). 76p. 1993. pap. 36.00 (*1-85302-198-9*, Pub. by J Kingsley Pubs UK) Taylor & Francis.

— Visual Impairments & Business Administration. (Special Needs & Business Administration Ser.). 76p. 1993. pap. 36.00 (*1-85302-197-0*, Pub. by J Kingsley Pubs UK) Taylor & Francis.

— Your Hearing Loss & How to Cope with It. rev. ed. 200p. 1995. pap. 21.00x (*1-85302-214-4*, Pub. by J Kingsley Pubs UK) Taylor & Francis.

Lyssiotis, Peter. Three Cheers for Civilization. 96p. (C). 1990. 120.00 (*0-685-52924-X*, Pub. by Pascoe Pub AT) St Mut.

Lyssiotis, Peter, jt. auth. see Couani, Anna.

Lystad, Mary. At Home in America: As Seen Through Its Books for Children. (Illus.). 154p. 1984. 18.95 (*0-87073-378-8*); pap. 13.25 (*0-87073-379-6*) Schenkman Bks Inc.

— From Dr. Mather to Dr. Seuss: Two Hundred Years of American Books for Children. (Illus.). 276p. 1980. pap. text ed. 19.95 (*0-87073-210-2*) Schenkman Bks Inc.

— Violence in the Home: Interdisciplinary Perspectives. LC 85-25450. 360p. 1986. 34.95 (*0-87630-416-1*) Brunner-Mazel.

Lystad, Mary, ed. Mental Health Response to Mass Emergencies: Theory & Practice. LC 88-5025. (Psychosocial Stress Ser.: No. 12). 454p. 1988. 51.95 (*0-87630-514-1*) Brunner-Mazel.

Lystad, Mary, ed. see National Institute of Mental Health Staff.

***Lyster, Mimi E.** Child Custody: Building Agreements That Work. (Illus.). 275p. 1995. pap. 24.95 (*0-87337-283-2*) Nolo Pr.

Lyster, Simon. International Wildlife Law. 493p. (C). 1985. 46.00 (*0-906496-46-2*, Pub. by Grotius Pubns UK); pap. 23.00 (*0-906496-22-5*, Pub. by Grotius Pubns UK) St Mut.

Lysternik, L. & Brown, D. Ten Decimal Tables Logarithms Complex Cartesian Polar Coordination: Tables of Functions. LC 63-18926. 60.00 (*0-08-010132-1*, Pub. by Pergamon Repr UK) Franklin.

Lystra, Helen P., ed. Kitchen Sampler, a Heritage Cookbook. (Illus.). 192p. (Orig.). 1982. pap. 6.95 (*0-9608642-0-2*) UMCD.

Lystra, Karen. Searching the Heart: Women, Men, & Romantic Love in Nineteenth-Century America. 352p. 1992. pap. 17.95 (*0-19-507476-9*) OUP.

— Searching the Heart: Women, Men, & Romantic Love in Nineteenth Century America, 1830-1900. 352p. 1989. 30.00 (*0-19-505817-8*) OUP.

***Lysymy, Paul.** Groud Zero. 470p. 1996. pap. 9.95 (*0-7610-0496-3*) NW Pub.

***Lytch, William E.** The Cradle of Texas Presbyterianism: Memorial Presbyterian Church, San Augustine, Texas. (Illus.). 224p. 1993. 19.95 (*1-881576-19-1*) Providence Hse.

Lytel, Robert B. & Botterbusch, Karl F. Physical Demands Job Analysis: A New Approach. (Illus.). 166p. (Orig.). 1981. pap. 20.50 (*0-916671-34-8*) Material Dev.

Lyth, Isabel M. Containing Anxiety in Institutions: Selected Essays, Vol. 1. 269p. 1988. pap. 27.00 (*1-85343-001-3*) Col U Pr.

— The Dynamics of the Social, Vol. 2: Selected Essays. 279p. 1989. 60.00 (*1-85343-051-X*); pap. 19.50 (*1-85343-052-8*) Col U Pr.

Lyth, Peter, tr. see Schmidt, Elfriede.

Lyth, Peter J. Inflation & the Merchant Economy: The Hamburg Mittelstand, 1914-1924. LC 89-18118. 212p. 1990. 59.95 (*0-85496-592-0*) Berg Pubs.

Lythe, S. G. Economy of Scotland in Its European Setting: 1550-1625. LC 75-31475. 277p. 1977. reprint ed. text ed. 38.50 (*0-8371-8533-5*, LYES, Greenwood Pr) Greenwood.

Lythgoe, Dennis L. Let'em Holler: A Political Biography of J. Bracken Lee. LC 82-60039. (Illus.). xii, 343p. 1982. 17.50 (*0-913738-33-6*) Utah St Hist Soc.

Lythgoe, Gillian, jt. auth. see Lythgoe, John N.

Lythgoe, John N. & Lythgoe, Gillian. Fishes of the Sea: The North Atlantic & Mediterranean. (Illus.). 272p. 1992. 40.00x (*0-262-12162-X*) MIT Pr.

Lytinen, Kalle & Tahvananinen, Veli-Pekka, eds. Next Generation CASE Tools. LC 91-59042. (Studies in Computer & Communications Systems: Vol. 3). 240p. 1992. pap. 70.00 (*90-5199-076-6*, Pub. by IOS Pr NE) IOS Press.

Lytle, Andrew. At the Moon's Inn: A Novel about the De Soto Expedition. (Library of Alabama Classics). 400p. (Orig.). 1990. pap. 18.95 (*0-8173-0511-4*) Univ South Pr.

— Kristin: A Reading by Andrew Lytle. LC 92-7255. 112p. 1992. text ed. 17.95 (*0-8262-0847-9*) U of Mo Pr.

— The Long Night. LC 88-12101. (Library of Alabama Classics). 336p. 1988. reprint ed. pap. 14.50 (*0-8173-0415-0*) U of Ala Pr.

— Southerners & Europeans: Essays in a Time of Disorder. LC 87-24169. (Library of Southern Civilization). xix, 308p. 1988. text ed. 37.50 (*0-8071-1420-0*) La State U Pr.

— Stories: Alchemy & Others. 192p. 1984. pap. 9.95 (*0-918769-00-0*) Univ South Pr.

— Velvet Horn. 370p. 1987. pap. 10.95 (*0-918769-03-5*) Univ South Pr.

Lytle, Andrew N. Bedford Forrest & His Critter Company. 402p. (Orig.). 1984. reprint ed. 60.00 (*0-918450-16-0*) C Elder.

— Bedford Forrest & His Critter Company. (Southern Classics Ser.). 405p. (Orig.). 1992. reprint ed. pap. 12.95 (*1-879941-09-0*) J S Sanders.

— Wake for the Living. (Southern Classics Ser.). 308p. 1992. reprint ed. pap. 10.95 (*1-879941-10-4*) J S Sanders.

Lytle, Andrews. Reflections of a Ghost. deluxe limited ed. 35.00 (*0-686-78139-2*) New London Pr.

Lytle, Arthur. Beating Tantra at Its Own Game: Spiritual Sexuality. LC 89-81551. 200p. (Orig.). 1990. pap. 12.95 (*0-941404-89-7*) New Falcon Pubns.

— A Spiritual Psychology for the Aquarian Age. LC 91-68304. 192p. (Orig.). 1992. pap. 12.95 (*1-56184-052-1*) New Falcon Pubns.

Lytle, Arthur C. So You Want to Be a Channel. 2nd ed. LC 87-83572. (Orig.). 1988. pap. 12.95 (*1-56184-106-4*) New Falcon Pubns.

Lytle, C., jt. auth. see Cortner, Richard C.

Lytle, Charles & Wodsedalek, J. E. General Zoology Laboratory Guide: Complete. 10th ed. 336p. (C). 1987. spiral bd. write for info. (*0-697-05139-0*); Short Version, 272p. spiral bd. write for info. (*0-697-05140-4*) Wm C Brown Pubs.

— General Zoology Laboratory Guide: Short Version. 11th ed. 368p. (C). 1990. Complete version, 368p. spiral bd. write for info. (*0-697-05209-5*) Wm C Brown Pubs.

— General Zoology Laboratory Guide: Short Version. 11th ed. 288p. (C). 1991. spiral bd. write for info. (*0-697-05210-9*) Wm C Brown Pubs.

— General Zoology Laboratory Guide, Complete Version. 12th ed. 368p. (C). 1995. spiral bd. write for info. (*0-697-13669-8*) Wm C Brown Pubs.

Lytle, Clifford M. The Warren Court & Its Critics. LC 66-28788. 149p. reprint ed. pap. 42.50 (*0-317-28216-6*, 2022756) Bks Demand.

Lytle, Clifford M., jt. auth. see Deloria, Vine, Jr.

Lytle, Clyde F., ed. Leaves of Gold. 14.99 (*0-915720-74-4*); 14.99 (*0-915720-86-8*) Brownlow Pub Co.

— Leaves of Gold. deluxe ed. 19.99 (*0-915720-84-1*) Brownlow Pub Co.

Lytle, Eldon G. A Grammar of Subordinate Structures in English. (Janua Linguarum, Series Practica: No. 175). 1974. pap. text ed. 26.00 (*90-279-2630-1*) Mouton.

Lytle, Elizabeth S. Careers As an Electrician. LC 93-12776. (YA). 1993. 14.95 (*0-8239-1513-1*) Rosen Group.

An Asterisk (*) at the beginning of an entry indicates that the title is appearing in BIP for the first time.

— Careers in Plumbing, Heating, & Cooling. LC 94-13577. (YA). 1995. 14.95 (*0-8239-2052-6*) Rosen Group.
— Exploring Careers in the Construction Industry. Rosen, Ruth, ed. (Careers in Depth Ser.). (YA). (gr. 7-12). 1992. lib. bdg. 14.95 (*0-8239-1405-4*) Rosen Group.
Lytle, Guy F., ed. Reform & Authority in the Medieval & Reformation Church. LC 79-17380. 351p. reprint ed. pap. 100.10 (*0-685-17824-2*, 2029496) Bks Demand.
Lytle, Guy F. & Orgel, Stephen, eds. Patronage in the Renaissance. LC 81-47143. (Folger Institute Essays Ser.). (Illus.). 405p. reprint ed. pap. 115.50 (*0-8357-4199-0*, 2036977) Bks Demand.
Lytle, Horace. Point! 2nd ed. (Fifty Greatest Bks.). (Illus.). 200p. 1992. reprint ed. 40.00 (*1-56416-036-X*) Derrydale Pr.
***Lytle, John F.** What Do Your Customers Really Want? Here's a Sure-Fire Way to Find Out. 1994. pap. 19.95 (*1-55738-829-6*) Probus Pub Co.
Lytle, Joyce, ed. see Anderson, Alex.
Lytle, Joyce, ed. see Porcella, Yvonne.
Lytle, Joyce, ed. see Sienkiewicz, Elly.
Lytle, Joyce E., ed. see Laury, Jean R.
Lytle, Joyce E., ed. see Pace, Kathy.
Lytle, Joyce E., ed. see Sienkiewicz, Elly.
Lytle, Joyce E., ed. see Wells, Jean.
Lytle, Joyce E., ed. see Wolfrom, Joen.
Lytle, L. D., jt. ed. see Jacoby, J. H.
Lytle, Mark H. The Origins of the Iranian-American Alliance 1941-1953. 254p. 1987. 49.50 (*0-8419-1060-X*) Holmes & Meier.
Lytle, Mark H., jt. auth. see Davidson, James W.
Lytle, Milton S. History of Huntingdon County, Pennsylvania: From the Earliest Times to the Centennial Anniversary of American Independence. (Illus.). 361p. 1992. reprint ed. lib. bdg. 39.50 (*0-8328-1416-4*) Higginson Bk Co.
Lytle, Richard A., jt. auth. see Kircher, Harry B.
***Lytle, Robert A.** Mackinac Passage: A Summer Adventure. (Illus.). 184p. 1995. pap. 10.95 (*1-882376-11-0*) Thunder Bay Pr.
Lytle, Robert J. Live Free, Don't Become a Corporate Mule. (Illus.). 200p. (Orig.). 1990. pap. text ed. 15.95 (*0-9626082-0-3*) Tana Starr Pub.
Lytle, Stewart. Iron City. 400p. (Orig.). Date not set. 19.00 (*1-884363-03-2*) Odenwald Pr.
Lytle, Susan L. & Wolfe, Marcie. Adult Literacy Education: Program Evaluation & Learner Assessment. 1989. 8.75 (*0-317-03008-6*, IN338) Ctr Educ Trng Employ.
Lytle, Susan L., jt. ed. see Cochran-Smith, Marilyn.
Lytle, William S., jt. auth. see Wagner, Walter R.
Lytle, William S., et al. A Summary of Oil & Gas Developments in Pennsylvania: 1955 to 1959. (Mineral Resource Report Ser.: No. 45). (Illus.). 133p. 1984. reprint ed. pap. 15.15 (*0-8182-0036-7*) Commonweal PA.
Lyttle, Bradford. The Chicago Anti-Vietnam War Movement. (Illus.). 173p. (Orig.). 1988. pap. text ed. 4.95 (*0-9620611-0-7*) Midwest Pacifist Ctr.
— You Come with Naked Hands: The Story of the San Francisco to Moscow March for Peace. LC 66-1279. (Illus.). 289p. 1966. 25.00 (*0-934676-08-9*) Greenlf Bks.
Lyttle, C. R., jt. ed. see Strauss, Jerome F., III.
Lyttle, Richard B. Ernest Hemingway: The Life & the Legend. LC 91-11218. (Illus.). 224p. (YA). (gr. 7 up). 1992. text ed. 15.95 (*0-689-31670-4*, Atheneum Bks Young) S&S Childrens.
— Land Beyond the River: Europe in the Age of Migration. LC 85-28758. (Illus.). 192p. (YA). (gr. 5 up). 1986. text ed. 15.95 (*0-689-31199-0*, Atheneum Bks Young) S&S Childrens.
— Mark Twain - The Man & His Adventure. LC 93-11247. 192p. (YA). (gr. 7 up). 1994. text ed. 15.95 (*0-689-31712-3*, Atheneum Bks Young) S&S Childrens.
— Pablo Picasso: The Man & the Image. LC 89-6561. (Illus.). 256p. (YA). (gr. 7 up). 1989. text ed. 15.95 (*0-689-31393-4*, Atheneum Bks Young) S&S Childrens.
Lyttle, Thomas, comp. Psychedelics. LC 93-19655. 1993. 14.95 (*0-9623032-2-4*) Barricade Bks.
Lyttle, Thomas, et al. Psychedelic Monographs & Essays, 6 vols. rev. ed. (Psychedelic Monographs & Essays Ser.). (Illus.). 325p. (Orig.). 1992. Per vol. pap. 17.98 (*1-880332-00-0*) PM&E Pub.
— Psychedelic Monographs & Essays, 6 vols., 4. rev. ed. (Psychedelic Monographs & Essays Ser.). (Illus.). 325p. (Orig.). 1992. write for info. (*1-880332-02-7*) PM&E Pub.
— Psychedelic Monographs & Essays, 6 vols., 5. rev. ed. (Psychedelic Monographs & Essays Ser.). (Illus.). 325p. (Orig.). 1992. write for info. (*1-880332-03-5*) PM&E Pub.
— Psychedelic Monographs & Essays, 6 vols., 6. rev. ed. (Psychedelic Monographs & Essays Ser.). (Illus.). 325p. (Orig.). 1992. write for info. (*1-880332-04-3*) PM&E Pub.
— Psychedelic Monographs & Essays, 6 vols., Vols. 1-3. rev. ed. (Psychedelic Monographs & Essays Ser.). (Illus.). 325p. (Orig.). 1992. write for info. (*1-880332-01-9*) PM&E Pub.
Lyttleton, David, jt. auth. see McDonald, Ian.
Lyttleton, Raymond A. The Earth & Its Mountains. LC 82-13701. (Illus.). 232p. reprint ed. pap. 66.20 (*0-8357-3079-4*, 2039336) Bks Demand.
Lytton. Advances in Urology, Vol. 2. 272p. 1989. 64.95 (*0-8151-5669-3*, Yr Bk Med Pubs) Mosby Yr Bk.
— Advances in Urology, Vol. 3. 232p. 1990. 64.95 (*0-8151-5667-7*, Yr Bk Med Pubs) Mosby Yr Bk.
— Advances in Urology, Vol. 4. 220p. 1991. 69.95 (*0-8151-5692-8*, Yr Bk Med Pubs) Mosby Yr Bk.
— Advances in Urology, Vol. 5. 262p. 1992. 69.95 (*0-8151-5693-6*) Mosby Yr Bk.
— Advances in Urology, Vol. 8. 240p. 1995. 69.95 (*0-8151-5696-0*, Yr Bk Med Pubs) Mosby Yr Bk.
Lytton, ed. see Royal Society of Literature, United Kingdom Staff.
Lytton, et al. Advances in Urology, Vol. 6. 288p. 1993. 69.95 (*0-8151-5694-4*, Yr Bk Med Pubs) Mosby Yr Bk.
— Advances in Urology, Vol. 7. 300p. 1994. 69.95 (*0-8151-5695-2*, Yr Bk Med Pubs) Mosby Yr Bk.
Lytton, Bart & Bulwer, Edward. Zanoni. 398p. 1970. reprint ed. spiral bd. 13.75 (*0-7873-0573-1*) Mokelumne.
Lytton, Constance. Prisons & Prisoners. 1989. pap. 10.95 (*0-86068-682-5*) Random.
— Prisons & Prisoners: Experiences of a Suffragette. 1977. reprint ed. 25.00 (*0-7158-1154-1*) Charles River Bks.
Lytton, Edward B. Alice: or the Mysteries. 437p. 1972. reprint ed. spiral bd. 11.00 (*0-7873-1112-X*) Mokelumne.
— The Caxtons, a Family Picture, 3 vols., Set. (BCL1-PR English Literature Ser.). 1992. reprint ed. lib. bdg. 225.00 (*0-7812-7590-3*) Rprt Serv.
— The Coming Race. 144p. 1967. reprint ed. spiral bd. 5.50 (*0-7873-0574-X*) Mokelumne.
— Pelham; or, The Adventures of a Gentleman. LC 77-88085. 512p. reprint ed. pap. 146.00 (*0-8357-7934-3*, 2057007) Bks Demand.
— Rienzi: The Last of the Rome Tribune. LC 70-145150. 1971. reprint ed. 69.00 (*0-403-01079-9*) Scholarly.
— Rienzi, the Last of the Roman Tribunes, 2 vols. in 1. (BCL1-PR English Literature Ser.). 1992. reprint ed. lib. bdg. 99.00 (*0-7812-7591-1*) Rprt Serv.
— Strange Story. 499p. 1971. reprint ed. spiral bd. 13.20 (*0-7873-1094-8*) Mokelumne.
— A Strange Story & the Haunted & the Haunters: Or the House & the Brain. 500p. 1992. reprint ed. pap. text ed. 35.00 (*1-56459-000-3*) Kessinger Pub.
Lytton, Edward G. My Novel, or Varieties in English Life, 4 vols. in 2, Set. LC 79-8160. reprint ed. 84.50 (*0-404-62003-5*) AMS Pr.
— What Will He Do with It?, 4 vols. in 2, Set. LC 79-8161. reprint ed. 84.50 (*0-404-62008-6*) AMS Pr.
Lytton, H., jt. auth. see Grusec, J. E.
Lytton, Henry. The Secrets of a Savoyard. LC 80-17086. (Music Reprint Ser.). 1980. reprint ed. 29.50 (*0-306-76048-7*) Da Capo.
Lytton, Robert L., et al. Development & Validation of Performance Prediction Models & Specifications for Asphalt Binders & Paving Mixes. 500p. (Orig.). (C). 1993. pap. text ed. 20.00 (*0-309-05617-9*, SHRP-A-357) SHRP.
***Lyu, Michael R.** McGraw-Hill Software Reliability Engineering Handbook. 1995. text ed. 69.50 (*0-07-039400-8*) McGraw.
***Lyu, Michael R., ed.** Software Fault Tolerance. (Trends in Software Ser.). 1995. pap. text ed. 44.95 (*0-471-95068-8*) Wiley.
Lyubarev, A. E., jt. ed. see Kurganov, B. I.
Lyubarskii, G. & Dedijer, S. Application of Group Theory in Physics. LC 59-15292. 1960. 157.00 (*0-08-009335-3*, Pub. by Pergamon Repr UK) Franklin.
Lyubarskii, Yu I., tr. see Govorov, N. V.
Lyubich, Y. I. Functional Analysis One: Linear Functional Analysis. Nikol'skij, N. K. & Gamkrelidze, R. V., eds. Tweddle, I., tr. (Encyclopaedia of Mathematical Sciences Ser.: Vol. 19). xi, 278p. 1992. 79.00 (*0-387-50584-9*) Spr-Verlag.
— Introduction to the Theory of Banach Representations of Groups. (Operator Theory Ser.: No. 30). 232p. 1988. 124.00 (*0-8176-2207-1*) Birkhauser.
— Mathematical Structures in Population Genetics. Akin, E. & Levin, S. A., eds. (Biomathematics Ser.: Vol. 22). (Illus.). x, 373p. 1992. 139.00 (*0-387-53337-0*) Spr-Verlag.
Lyubich, Y. I., jt. auth. see Belitskii, G. R.
Lyubimov, D. V., et al. Universal Scenarios of Transitions to Chaos Via Homoclinic Bifurations, Vol. 8. (SSR: Mathematical Physics Review Ser., Section C: Vol. 8, Pt. 4). 80p. 1989. pap. text ed. 53.00 (*3-7186-4867-9*) Gordon & Breach.
Lyuboshitz, N. A., jt. auth. see Volkov, M. V.
Lyubutin, I. S., jt. auth. see Kagan, Yu. M.
Lyubutin, I. S., jt. ed. see Kagan, Yu M.
Lyuksyutov, Igor, et al. Two-Dimensional Crystals. (Illus.). 423p. 1992. text ed. 105.00 (*0-12-460590-7*) Acad Pr.
Lyusternik, L. & Chervonenkis, O. Handbook for Computing Elementary Functions. LC 64-22370. (International Series Mono on Pure & Applied Mathematics: Vol. 76). 1965. 108.00 (*0-08-010844-X*, Pub. by Pergamon Repr UK) Franklin.
Lyusternik, L. & Collins, P. Shortest Paths Variational Problems: Survey of Recent East European Mathematical Literature. LC 64-14145. (Popular Lectures in Mathematics: Vol. 13). 1964. 45.00 (*0-08-010647-1*, Pub. by Pergamon Repr UK) Franklin.
Lyusternik, L. & Yanpol'skii, A. Mathematical Analysis: Functions Limits Series Continued Fractions. LC 63-19330. (International Series of Monographs on Pure & Applied Mathematics: Vol. 69). 1965. 172.00 (*0-08-010133-X*, Pub. by Pergamon Repr UK) Franklin.
Lyuu, Yuh-Dauh. Information Dispersal & Parallel Computation. (International Series on Parallel Computation: No. 3). 220p. (C). 1993. 42.95 (*0-521-43226-X*) Cambridge U Pr.
Lyvely & Farmer. Abortion Eve. (On Abortion Ser.). (Illus.). 1973. 1.25 (*0-918440-01-7*) Nanny Goat.
— Pandora's Box. (Women's Humor Ser.). (Illus.). 1973. 1.25 (*0-918440-02-5*) Nanny Goat.
— Tits & Clits, No. 4. (Women's Humor Ser.). (Illus.). 1977. 1.25 (*0-918440-05-X*) Nanny Goat.
Lyvely, jt. auth. see Farmer.
Lyzinski, Stan. Creating Access Applications. 1994. pap. 49.95 (*1-56529-636-2*) Que.
Lyzlova & Stefanv. Phosphagen Kinases. 1990. 179.00 (*0-8493-6467-1*, QP606) CRC Pr.

M

M. Cartoons by M. (Illus.). 64p. 1992. pap. 12.00 (*0-9635101-0-X*) A V A Pr.
M, pseud. The Condensed Gospel of Sri Ramakrishna. 1979. pap. 5.95 (*0-87481-489-8*) Vedanta Pr.
M. The International Directory of Names Men Call Their... (Illus.). 80p. (Orig.). 1989. pap. 5.95 (*0-9621447-3-8*) Little Sam.
— Lord God of Truth Within. 1976. reprint ed. 15.00 (*0-911662-56-1*) Yoga.
— The Sensuous Man. 1972. mass mkt. 4.99 (*0-440-17916-5*) Dell.
— Sensuous Man. 6.00 (*0-8184-0076-5*) Carol Pub Group.
M & Abhedananda, Swami. Ramakrishna Kathamrita: Memoirs of Ramakrishna. Orig. Title: Gospel of Ramakrishna. 266p. 1988. 6.95 (*0-87481-654-8*, Pub. by Rama Ved Math II) Vedanta Pr.
***M. A. C. C. Team Staff.** Bilingual Rite of Baptism. 47p. (SPA.). 1991. write for info. (*0-614-04879-6*) Mex Am Cult.
— Cantos Para Pedir Posadas y Otras Canciones de Navidad. 24p. (SPA.). 1982. write for info. (*0-614-04893-1*) Mex Am Cult.
— Celebremos la Cuaresma y la Pascua. (Illus.). 8p. (SPA.). 1980. write for info. (*0-614-04887-7*) Mex Am Cult.
— Celebremos la Cuaresma y la Semana Santa. 82p. (SPA.). 1982. write for info. (*0-614-04895-8*) Mex Am Cult.
— Expresiones de Fe de los Hispanos en el Sur Oeste. 68p. (SPA.). 1994. write for info. (*0-614-04885-0*) Mex Am Cult.
— Faith Expressions of Hispanics in the Southwest. 64p. 1977. write for info. (*0-614-04884-2*) Mex Am Cult.
— The Family Novena of Guadalupe. 50p. (SPA.). Date not set. write for info. (*0-614-04898-2*) Mex Am Cult.
— Fronteras. 469p. 1983. write for info. (*0-614-04897-4*) Mex Am Cult.
— Guia Practica para Ayudar a Sacerdotes a Celebrar la Misa en Espanol. 16p. (SPA.). Date not set. audio write for info. (*0-614-04882-6*) Mex Am Cult.
— La Historia de la Virgen de Guadalupe. 11p. (SPA.). 1980. write for info. (*0-614-04889-3*) Mex Am Cult.
— The Image of Our Lady of Guadalupe. (Illus.). 4p. 1977. write for info. (*0-614-04894-X*) Mex Am Cult.
— M. A. C. C. en Fiesta. 96p. (SPA.). 1982. write for info. (*0-614-04891-5*) Mex Am Cult.
— Manual Para Comunidades Eclesiales De Base. 36p. (SPA.). 1991. write for info. (*0-614-04890-7*) Mex Am Cult.
— Matrimony in Christ, the New Rite. 20p. (SPA.). 1970. write for info. (*0-614-04880-X*) Mex Am Cult.
— Ojo de Dios. 6p. Date not set. write for info. (*0-614-04896-6*) Mex Am Cult.
— Oraciones Del Corazon, Prayers of the Heart. 34p. (SPA.). 1992. write for info. (*0-614-04892-3*) Mex Am Cult.
— Pastoral Care of the Sick. 205p. (SPA.). 1986. write for info. (*0-614-04883-4*) Mex Am Cult.
— Que es Ser Catolico? About Being Catholic. (Illus.). 36p. (SPA.). 1976. write for info. (*0-614-04901-6*) Mex Am Cult.
— R. I. C. A. Rito Para Iniciar los Cristianos Adultos. (Illus.). 68p. (SPA.). 1989. write for info. (*0-614-04886-9*) Mex Am Cult.
— Religious Celebration of the Quinceanera. 50p. (SPA.). 1980. write for info. (*0-614-04881-8*) Mex Am Cult.
— The Story of Our Lady of Guadalupe. 11p. 1978. write for info. (*0-614-04888-5*) Mex Am Cult.
M. Abdul Hamid Siddiqi, tr. see Sunnah.
M. Bruce Corp. Staff. Zzaap! Taming ESD, RFI, & EMI. 236p. 1990. text ed. 44.95 (*0-12-189930-6*) Acad Pr.
M. D. Anderson Symposia on Fundamental Cancer Research Staff. Genes, Chromosomes, & Neoplasia: M. D. Anderson Annual Symposia on Fundamental Cancer Research, 33rd. Arrighi, Frances E. et al, eds. 550p. 1981. 147.00 (*0-89004-532-1*) Raven.
***M. Dutta.** Economics, Econometrics & the Link: Essays in Honor of Lawrence R. Klein. LC 94-34470. (Contributions to Economic Analysis Ser.: Vol. 226). 1994. write for info. (*0-444-81787-5*) Elsevier.
***M. E. R.** Mary Jones & Her Bible. (Victorian Children's Classics Ser.). 96p. 1985. pap. 4.95 (*1-85030-012-7*) Bridge Pub.
M. Garvelmann, Donald, ed. see Herz, Henri.
M. H. Publications Staff. As You Like It. 170p. 1990. 95.00 (*1-872680-11-9*, Pub. by M H Pubns UK) St Mut.
— The Comedie of Errors. 138p. 1990. 95.00 (*1-872680-13-5*, Pub. by M H Pubns UK) St Mut.
— The Life & Death of King Richard the Second. 1990. 95.00 (*1-872680-16-X*, Pub. by M H Pubns UK) St Mut.
— The Life of Henry the Fifth. 242p. 1990. 95.00 (*1-872680-07-0*, Pub. by M H Pubns UK) St Mut.
— Measure for Measure. 1990. 95.00 (*1-872680-15-1*, Pub. by M H Pubns UK) St Mut.
— A Midsommer Nights Dreame. 166p. 1990. 95.00 (*1-872680-00-3*, Pub. by M H Pubns UK) St Mut.
— Much Ado about Nothing. 196p. 1990. 95.00 (*1-872680-04-6*, Pub. by M H Pubns UK) St Mut.
— The Tempest. 165p. 1990. 95.00 (*1-872680-08-9*, Pub. by M H Pubns UK) St Mut.
— The Tragedie of Anthonie, & Cleopatra. 300p. 1990. 95.00 (*1-872680-06-2*, Pub. by M H Pubns UK) St Mut.
— The Tragedie of Hamlet, Prince of Denmarke. 272p. 1990. 95.00 (*1-872680-01-1*, Pub. by M H Pubns UK) St Mut.
— The Tragedie of Julius Caesar. 280p. 1990. 95.00 (*1-872680-09-7*, Pub. by M H Pubns UK) St Mut.
— The Tragedie of King Lear. 225p. 1990. 95.00 (*1-872680-10-0*, Pub. by M H Pubns UK) St Mut.
— The Tragedie of Macbeth. 207p. 1990. 95.00 (*1-872680-12-7*, Pub. by M H Pubns UK) St Mut.
— The Tragedie of Romeo & Juliet. 238p. 1990. 95.00 (*1-872680-05-4*, Pub. by M H Pubns UK) St Mut.
— The Tragedie of Troylus & Cressida. 1990. 95.00 (*1-872680-17-8*, Pub. by M H Pubns UK) St Mut.
— The Tragedy of Richard the Third. 277p. 1990. 95.00 (*1-872680-03-8*, Pub. by M H Pubns UK) St Mut.
— Twelfe Night: or What You Will. 191p. 1990. 95.00 (*1-872680-02-X*, Pub. by M H Pubns UK) St Mut.
***M. J., Neale, ed.** Component Failures. Maintenance & Repair. LC 94-32562. (Tribology Handbook). 1995. write for info. (*0-615-00175-0*) Buttrwrth-Heinemann.
M. J. Studios Staff, illus. Daffy Dinosaurs Sticker Pad. 32p. (Orig.). (J). (gr. k-6). 1993. pap. 2.95 (*1-879424-48-7*) Nickel Pr.
— Dress up Sticker Pad. 32p. (J). (gr. k-6). 1993. reprint ed. pap. 2.95 (*1-879424-17-7*) Nickel Pr.
— Monster Madness Sticker Pad. 32p. (J). (gr. k-6). 1993. pap. 2.95 (*1-879424-56-8*) Nickel Pr.
— Wacky Animals Sticker Pad. 32p. (J). (gr. k-6). 1993. reprint ed. pap. 2.95 (*1-879424-30-4*) Nickel Pr.
M, Joseph L. Hellas. 1994. 15.95 (*0-8062-4828-9*) Carlton.
M. K. Graphic & Design Editorial Dept. Staff, ed. see Donaldson, Peter.
M. K. Graphic Staff, ed. see Kozak, Donald.
M, Mary. How to Have a No-Hands Orgasm: Having Orgasms Through Intercourse. 133p. (Orig.). 1986. pap. 7.16 (*0-9618974-0-6*) Books NY.
M., Mary. Mental Illness Heal Yourself. LC 93-73310. (Heal Yourself Ser.). (Illus.). 125p. (Orig.). 1994. pap. 14.95 (*0-9636781-9-1*) BBCS.
M, Mike, jt. auth. see K, Dave.
M, Nectario. Juan Colon, Alias Cristobal Colon, Alias Christopher Columbus, Was a Spanish Jew. Josephson, E., ed. 1985. lib. bdg. 79.95 (*0-87700-867-1*) Revisionist Pr.
M. Tayyib Bakhsh Budayuni, tr. see Allama Shibli Numani.
M-USA Business Systems, Inc. Staff. Understanding Computer Accounting. (VideoNotes Ser.). (Illus.). (Orig.). 1988. pap. text ed. 9.95 (*0-929978-02-1*) M-USA Busn Systs.
— Understanding Computer Project Management. (VideoNotes Ser.). (Illus.). (Orig.). 1988. pap. text ed. 9.95 (*0-929978-04-8*) M-USA Busn Systs.
— Understanding Lotus 1-2-3. (VideoNotes Ser.). (Illus.). (Orig.). 1988. pap. text ed. 9.95 (*0-929978-01-3*) M-USA Busn Systs.
M-USA Business Systems, Inc. Staff, ed. Understanding MS-DOS. (VideoNotes Ser.). (Illus.). (Orig.). 1988. pap. 9.95 (*0-929978-00-5*) M-USA Busn Systs.
M-USA Video Staff. Lotus 1-2-3 Version 2.3. (LogicNotes Ser.). 1991. vhs write for info. (*0-929978-57-9*) M-USA Busn Systs.
— MS-DOS 5.0. (LogicNotes Ser.). 1991. vhs write for info. (*0-929978-60-9*) M-USA Busn Systs.
— One-Two-Three for Kids, Set. (LogicNotes Ser.). (Illus.). (Orig.). 1991. pap. text ed., vhs write for info. (*0-929978-53-6*) M-USA Busn Systs.
— Using IBM Displaywrite 5. (LogicNotes Ser.). (Illus.). (Orig.). 1991. pap. text ed. write for info. (*0-929978-32-3*) M-USA Busn Systs.
— Using Microsoft's Word for DOS 5.0. (LogicNotes Ser.). (Illus.). (Orig.). 1991. pap. text ed. write for info. (*0-929978-63-3*) M-USA Busn Systs.
— Word Perfect for Windows. (LogicNotes Ser.). 1991. write for info. (*0-929978-52-8*) M-USA Busn Systs.
Ma & Rittner. Modern Organic Elemental Analysis. 512p. 1979. 190.00 (*0-8247-6786-1*) Dekker.
Ma, Alan W., jt. ed. see Fisher, Theresa A.
Ma, Benjamin. Nuclear Reactor Materials & Applications. 1982. text ed. 69.95 (*0-442-22559-8*) Chapman & Hall.
Ma, C. Y., jt. ed. see Harwalker, V. R.
Ma Chengyuan. Ancient Chinese Bronzes. Shih, Hsio-Yen, ed. (Illus.). 224p. 1986. 75.00 (*0-19-583795-9*) OUP.
Ma Cindy, jt. auth. see Edwards, Franklin.
***Ma, D. C., ed.** Sloshing, Fluid-Structure Interaction & Structural Response due to Shock & Impact Loads 1994: Proceedings of the Pressure Vessels & Piping Conference, Minneapolis, MN, 1994. LC 94-71745. (PVP Ser.: Vol. 272). 233p. 1994. pap. 60.00 (*0-7918-1195-6*) ASME.
Ma, D. C., jt. ed. see Au-Yang, M. K.
Ma Deva Sarito, ed. see Osho Rajneesh.
Ma Deva Sarito, ed. see Rajneesh, Osho.
Ma Dhyan Sagar, ed. see Osho Rajneesh.
Ma Dhyan Yogini, ed. see Zorba the Buddha Rajneesh Restaurants Staff.
Ma, Dong M., jt. auth. see Liveson, Jay A.
Ma, E., jt. ed. see Cence, R. J.
Ma, Ho-t'ien. Chinese Agent in Mongolia. De Francis, John, tr. LC 49-11857. 231p. reprint ed. pap. 65.90 (*0-317-08380-5*, 2003913) Bks Demand.
Ma, Jing-heng. At Middle Age: A Learning Guide for Students of Advanced Chinese. 2nd ed. 262p. (C). 1991. spiral bd. 18.00 (*0-89264-103-7*) Ctr Chinese Studies.
Ma, Jing-Heng. A Great Wall: A Learning Guide. 264p. (CHI.). (C). 1990. pap. text ed. 18.00 (*0-89264-092-8*) Ctr Chinese Studies.
Ma, Jing-heng. Strange Friends: A Learning Guide for Students of Intermediate Chinese. 2nd ed. 224p. (C). 1991. spiral bd. 18.00 (*0-89264-102-9*) Ctr Chinese Studies.
— The True Story of Ah-Q: A Learning Guide. 230p. 1992. spiral bd. 18.00 (*0-89264-105-3*) Ctr Chinese Studies.

An Asterisk (*) at the beginning of an entry indicates that the title is appearing in BIP for the first time.

Ma, Kee M. Chinese American Food Practices, Customs, & Holidays. (Ethnic & Regional Food Practices Ser.). 36p. 1990. ring bd. 5.75 (*0-88091-077-1*, 0868) Am Dietetic Assn.

Ma, L. Eve. Revolutionaries, Monarchists, & Chinatowns: Chinese Politics in the Americas & the 1911 Revolution. LC 89-28021. (Illus.). 248p. 1990. text ed. 28.00 (*0-8248-1239-5*) UH Pr.

Ma, M. T. Theory & Application of Antenna Arrays. LC 73-15615. 429p. pap. 122.30 (*0-317-09841-1*, 2022491) Bks Demand.

***Ma, Marina & Rallo, John A.** My Son, Yo-Yo: A Biography of the Early Years of Yo-Yo Ma. (Illus.). 150p. 1995. pap. 39.50x (*962-201-640-5*, Pub. by Chinese Univ HK) Coronet Bks.

Ma P. Karima, ed. see Rajneesh, Osho.

Ma Prem Lisa, ed. see Osho Rajneesh.

Ma Prem Mangla, ed. see Osho.

Ma Prem Taranga, ed. see Osho Rajneesh.

Ma Renu, ed. see Dass, B. Hari.

Ma, S. Marshall, ed. Effects of Deterioration on Safety & Reliability of Structures. (Sessions Proceedings Ser.). 49p. 1986. 11.00 (*0-87262-519-2*) Am Soc Civil Eng.

Ma, Shang-Keng. Modern Theory of Critical Phenomena. LC 76-8386. (Frontiers in Physics Ser.: Vol. 46). (Illus.). (C). 1976. pap. 44.95 (*0-8053-6671-7*, Adv Bk Prog) Addison-Wesley.

— Statistical Mechanics. 576p. 1985. text ed. 67.00 (*9971-966-06-9*); pap. text ed. 53.00 (*9971-966-07-7*) World Scientific Pub.

Ma Shivam Suvarna, ed. see Osho Rajneesh.

Ma Shivan Suvarna, ed. see Osho Rajneesh.

Ma, T. P. & Dressendorfer, Paul V. Radiation Effects in MOS Devices & Circuits. 1989. text ed. 138.00 (*0-471-84893-X*) Wiley.

Ma, T. S. & Hassan, S. S. Organic Analysis Using Ion-Selective Electrodes, 1. (Analysis of Organic Materials Ser.). 1982. text ed. 139.00 (*0-12-462901-6*) Acad Pr.

— Organic Analysis Using Ion-Selective Electrodes, 2. (Analysis of Organic Materials Ser.). 1982. text ed. 146.00 (*0-12-462902-4*) Acad Pr.

Ma, Tom. Chinese Fables & Wisdom: Insights for Better Living. 126p. 1995. pap. 16.95 (*0-89876-211-1*) Gardner Pr.

***Ma, Tsoy-Wo.** Classical Analysis on Normed Spaces. LC 94-44467. 376p. 1995. text ed. 74.00 (*981-02-2137-1*) World Scientific Pub.

Ma, Tsu S. & Horak, V. Microscale Manipulations in Chemistry. LC 75-20093. (Chemical Analysis Ser.: Vol. 44). 504p. reprint ed. pap. 143.70 (*0-317-09305-3*, 2022487) Bks Demand.

Ma, Tsu-Sheng. Quantitative Analysis of Organic Mixtures: General Principles, Pt. 1. LC 78-23202. 384p. reprint ed. pap. 109.50 (*0-317-08874-2*, 2055601) Bks Demand.

Ma, Wei-Yi. A Bibliography of Chinese-Language Materials on the People's Communes. LC 82-14617. (Michigan Monographs in Chinese Studies: No. 44). xxviii, 301p. (C). 1982. pap. text ed. 11.00 (*0-89264-044-8*) Ctr Chinese Studies.

Ma, Wen-Hwan. American Policy Toward China. LC 73-111743. (American Imperialism: Viewpoints of United States Foreign Policy, 1898-1941 Ser.). 1977. reprint ed. 25.95 (*0-405-02037-6*) Ayer.

***Ma, Wenhai, illus.** Older Brother, Younger Brother: A Korean Folktale. LC 94-43046. 32p. (J). 1995. 14.99 (*0-670-85645-2*, Viking) Viking Penguin.

***Ma Wong, Angi.** Night of the Red Moon. LC 94-68680. (Illus.). 96p. (YA). (gr. 4 up). 1994. text ed. 6.00 (*0-9635906-1-8*) Pacific Herit.

Ma, X. W. Introduction to Theoretical Computer Science. 120p. (C). 1990. text ed. 36.00 (*981-02-0193-1*) World Scientific Pub.

Ma, Y. W. & Lau, Joseph S., eds. Traditional Chinese Stories: Themes & Variations. LC 86-71550. (C & T Asian Literature Ser.). 632p. (C). 1986. reprint ed. pap. text ed. 22.95 (*0-88727-071-9*) Cheng & Tsui.

Ma Yin-Ch'u. Finances of the City of New York. LC 68-56669. (Columbia University, Studies in the Social Sciences: No. 149). reprint ed. 29.50 (*0-404-51149-X*) AMS Pr.

Ma, Z., et al. Earthquake Prediction. (Illus.). 344p. 1990. 64.00 (*0-387-50271-8*) Spr-Verlag.

Ma, Z. Q. Yang-Baxter Equation & Quantum Enveloping Algebras. 328p. 1993. text ed. 86.00 (*981-02-1383-2*) World Scientific Pub.

Ma, Zhi-Ming, jt. auth. see Rockner, Michael.

Maack, Mary N. & Passet, Joanne. Aspirations & Mentoring in an Academic Environment: Women Faculty in Library & Information Science. LC 93-16200. (Contributions in Librarianship & Information Science Ser.: No. 75). 232p. 1994. Alk. paper. text ed. 49.95 (*0-313-27836-9*, MRL, Greenwood Pr) Greenwood.

Maag, Edith B., ed. Scenes from the Classics. 64p. 1987. pap. 5.95 (*0-9611792-5-2*) Dramaline Pubns.

Maag, Marilyn, et al. Anderson's Ohio Probate Practice & Procedure, 3 vols., Set. 2074p. 1990. text ed. 350.00 (*0-87084-019-3*) Anderson Pub Co.

Maag, Marilyn J. The Simple Will in Ohio. (Anderson's Ohio Practice Manual Ser.). 1991. pap. write for info. (*0-87084-550-0*) Anderson Pub Co.

Maaler, Josua. Die Teutsch Spraach. xvi, 1072p. (GER.). 1971. reprint ed. write for info. (*0-318-70473-0*, Pub. by Georg Olms GW) Lubrecht & Cramer.

Maaloe, S. Principles of Igneous Petrology. (Illus.). 415p. 1985. 135.00 (*0-387-13520-0*) Spr-Verlag.

Maalouf, Amin. Crusades Through Arab Eyes. 1989. pap. 16.00 (*0-8052-0898-4*) Schocken.

— The First Century after Beatrice. Blair, Dorothy S., tr. 192p. 1995. 18.50 (*0-8076-1373-8*) Braziller.

— Leo Africanus. 360p. 1991. reprint ed. pap. 14.95 (*1-56131-022-0*) New Amsterdam Bks.

— The Rock of Tanios. Blair, Dorothy S., tr. 256p. 1994. 18.50 (*0-8076-1365-7*) Braziller.

— Samarkand. Harris, Russell, tr. 256p. 1992. 24.95 (*0-7043-2741-4*, Pub. by Quartet UK) Interlink Pub.

***Maalouf, Jean.** Bold Prayers from the Heart. (Illus.). 100p. (Orig.). 1995. text ed. 16.95 (*1-55612-773-1*); pap. 9.95 (*1-55612-850-9*) Sheed & Ward MO.

Maamiry, Al. Economics in Islam. (C). 1987. 17.50 (*0-8364-2135-3*, Pub. by Lancer II) S Asia.

Maan, Bashir. The New Scots. 200p. (C). 1989. pap. text ed. 40.00 (*0-85976-357-9*, Pub. by J Donald) St Mut.

Maan, H. S. Scientific Reviews on Arid Zone Research, 5 vols., 4. (C). 1991. 350.00 (*0-685-60029-7*, Pub. by Scientific Pubs II) St Mut.

— Scientific Reviews on Arid Zone Research, 5 vols., Set, Vols. 1-6. (C). 1991. Set. write for info. (*81-85046-06-9*, Pub. by Scientific Pubs II) St Mut.

— Scientific Reviews on Arid Zone Research, 5 vols., Vols. 1-3 & 5-6. (C). 1991. Vols. 1-3 & Vols. 5-6. 250.00 (*0-685-74447-7*, Pub. by Scientific Pubs II) St Mut.

***Maanen, John Van.** Representation in Ethnography: In Other Wor(l)ds. 240p. 1995. text ed. 42.00 (*0-8039-7162-1*); pap. text ed. 19.95 (*0-8039-7163-X*) Sage.

Ma'ani, Baharieh R. Asiyih Khanum: The Most Exalted Leaf Entitled Navvab. 96p. 1993. 11.95 (*0-85398-353-4*, Pub. by G Ronald England UK) Bahai.

***Maar, Paul.** Home Sweet Home. (Illus.). 32p. 1995. pap. 5.95 (*1-55037-382-X*, Pub. by Annick CN) Firefly Bks Ltd.

— Home Sweet Home. (Illus.). 32p. 1995. lib. bdg. 15.95 (*1-55037-383-8*, Pub. by Annick CN) Firefly Bks Ltd.

Maaranen, Steven A., jt. ed. see Taylor, William J., Jr.

***Maarbjerg, John P.** Scandinavia in the European World-Economy, Ca. 1570-1625: Some Local Evidence of Economic Integration. (American University Studies, Series IX: Vol. 169). 320p. (C). 1995. text ed. 49.95 (*0-8204-2532-X*) P Lang Pubs.

Maarse, F. J. The Study of Handwriting Movement: Peripheral Models & Signal Processing Techniques. 160p. 1987. pap. 14.80 (*90-265-0812-3*, Pub. by Swets Pub Serv NE) Taylor & Francis.

Maarse, F. J., et al. Computers in Psychology: Methods, Instrumentation, & Psychodiagnostics. 220p. 1988. pap. 44.00 (*90-265-0896-4*, Pub. by Swets Pub Serv NE) Taylor & Francis.

***Maarse, F. J., et al, eds.** Computers in Psychology: Applications, Methods & Instrumentation. (Computers in Psychology Ser.: Vol. 5). 286p. 1995. 73.00 (*90-265-1415-8*, Pub. by Swets Pub Serv NE) Taylor & Francis.

— Computers in Psychology: Tools for Experimental & Applied Psychology. LC 92-49200. 260p. 1992. 57.00 (*90-265-1268-6*, Pub. by Swets Pub Serv NE) Taylor & Francis.

Maarse, H. & Belz, R. Isolation, Separation & Identification of Volatile Compounds in Aroma Research. 1982. lib. bdg. 121.50 (*90-277-1432-0*) Kluwer Ac.

Maarse, H. & Van der Heij, D. G., eds. Trends in Flavour Research: Proceedings of the 7th Weurman Flavour Research Symposium, Noordwijkerhout, The Netherlands, 15-18 June, 1993. LC 93-50139. (Developments in Food Science Ser.: No. 35). 1994. write for info. (*0-444-81587-2*) Elsevier.

Maarse, Henk, ed. Volatile Compounds in Foods & Beverages. (Food Science & Technology Ser.: Vol. 44). 784p. 1991. 195.00 (*0-8247-8390-5*) Dekker.

Maarsingh, B. Numbers: A Practical Commentary. LC 86-29263. (Text & Interpretation Ser.). 128p. reprint ed. pap. 36.50 (*0-7837-3189-2*, 2042793) Bks Demand.

Maarten van Bemmelen, Peter. Issues in Biblical Inspiration: Sanday & Warfield. (Andrews University Seminary Doctoral Dissertation Ser.: Vol. 13). 430p. (Orig.). 1988. pap. 19.99 (*0-943872-49-9*) Andrews Univ Pr.

Maartens, Maretha. Paper Bird: A Novel of South Africa. 144p. (J). (gr. 4-9). 1991. 13.95 (*0-395-56490-5*, Clarion Bks) HM.

Maas, David E. The Return of the Massachusetts Loyalists. (Outstanding Studies in Early American History). 596p. 1989. reprint ed. 35.00 (*0-8240-6189-6*) Garland.

Maas, David F. The Images of Order. (American University Studies: Language: Ser. XIV, Vol. 15). 262p. (C). 1988. text ed. 37.50 (*0-8204-0680-5*) P Lang Pubs.

***Maas, David R.** North American Game Animals. (Hunting & Fishing Library). 128p. 1995. 19.95 (*0-86573-048-2*) Cy De Cosse.

Maas, Elaine H. The Jews of Houston: An Ethnographic Study. LC 89-45444. (Immigrant Communities & Ethnic Minorities in the U. S. & Canada Ser.: No. 66). 1989. 52.50 (*0-404-19476-1*) AMS Pr.

Maas, Erich, ed. see Palermo, Blinky.

Maas, Ernestus, ed. see Aratus of Soli.

Maas, Ernst. De Biographis Graecis Questiones Selectae Scripsit Maas. Heft 3. 169p. Date not set. write for info. (*0-318-70971-6*, Pub. by Georg Olms GW) Lubrecht & Cramer.

— Philologische Untersuchungen, Heft 3: De Biographis Graecis Questiones Selectae. 169p. write for info. (*0-318-70817-5*, Pub. by Georg Olms GW) Lubrecht & Cramer.

Maas, Ernst, ed. Commentariorum in Aratum Reliquiae. lxxi, 750p. 1958. write for info. (*3-296-11900-0*, Pub. by Georg Olms GW) Lubrecht & Cramer.

Maas, Gerhard, jt. auth. see Regitz, Manfred.

Maas, Henry. Letters of A. E. Housman. 1979. 25.00 (*0-8464-0090-1*) Beekman Pubs.

Maas, Henry, ed. see Dowson, Ernest.

Maas, Henry, tr. see Goldmann, Lucien.

Maas, Henry, et al, eds. Letters of Aubrey Beardsley. LC 68-11571. (Illus.). 472p. 1975. 65.00 (*0-8386-6884-4*) Fairleigh Dickinson.

Maas, Henry S. & Kuypers, Joseph A. From Thirty to Seventy. LC 74-6742. (Jossey-Bass Behavioral Science Ser.). 256p. reprint ed. pap. 73.00 (*0-7837-0182-9*, 2040478) Bks Demand.

Maas, J., ed. Medicinal Chemistry: Proceedings, Vol. IV. 350p. 1975. 79.50 (*0-444-41296-4*) Elsevier.

Maas, James B. & Kleiber, Douglas A. Directory of Teaching Innovations in Psychology. 610p. reprint ed. pap. 173.90 (*0-7837-0485-2*, 2040809) Bks Demand.

Maas, James W., jt. ed. see Davis, John M.

Maas, Jane. Better Brochures, Catalogs & Mailing Pieces. (Illus.). 128p. 1984. pap. 7.95 (*0-312-07731-9*) St Martin.

Maas, Jane & Maas, Michael. Christmas in Wales: A Homecoming. (Illus.). 112p. 1994. 16.95 (*0-312-11464-8*, Pub. by Thomas Dunne Bks) St Martin.

Maas, Jane, jt. auth. see Roman, Kenneth.

Maas, Jeremy. Holman Hunt & the Light of the World. 258p. 1987. pap. text ed. 21.95 (*0-7045-0568-1*, Pub. by Scolar Pr UK) Ashgate Pub Co.

Maas, Jim. DC - AC Fundamentals. 383p. 1992. student ed 15.95 (*1-881483-03-7*) HyperGraphics.

— F2A Buffalo in Action. (Aircraft in Action Ser.). (Illus.). 50p. 1987. pap. 8.95 (*0-89747-196-2*) Squad Sig Pubns.

— Industrial Electronics. (Illus.). 800p. (C). 1994. write for info. (*0-02-373023-4*, Merrill Pub Co) Macmillan.

Maas, John L., ed. Compendium of Strawberry Diseases. 159p. 1984. pap. 30.00 (*0-89054-054-3*) Am Phytopathol Soc.

Maas, Jonathon. Airport Humor. 120p. 1992. pap. 6.95 (*0-9632230-0-3*) Travelers Pub.

Maas, Judith, ed. see Gumpert, David E.

Maas, Martha & Snyder, Jane M. Stringed Instruments of Ancient Greece. LC 87-2103. 288p. (C). 1989. text ed. 47.00 (*0-300-03686-8*) Yale U Pr.

Maas, Meridean. Health Care Rationing: Dilemma & Paradox. Kelly, Kathleen, ed. Vol. 6. 1994. write for info. (*0-318-72368-9*) Mosby Yr Bk.

***Maas, Meridean & Kelly, Kathleen.** Health Care Work Redesign. (Series on Nursing Administration Ser.: 7). 256p. 1995. text ed. 39.95 (*0-8039-7164-8*) Sage.

Maas, Meridean, et al. Nursing Diagnosis & Interventions for the Elderly. McCormick, Mark, ed. 736p. (C). 1991. pap. text ed. 45.25 (*0-201-12679-6*) Addison-Wesley.

Maas, Michael. John Lydus & the Roman Past: Antiquarianism & Politics in the Age of Justinian. 240p. 1991. 49.95 (*0-415-06021-4*, A6166) Routledge.

Maas, Michael, jt. auth. see Maas, Jane.

Maas, P. & Westra, L. Y. Neotropical Plant Families: A Concise Guide to Families of Vascular Plants in the Neotropics. (Illus.). 300p. 1993. 45.00 (*1-878762-38-9*) Koeltz Sci Bks.

Maas, P. J. Flora of the Guianas: Series A: Phanerogams: Family 190-Strelitziaceae; 191-Heliconiaceae; 192-Musaceae; 193-Zingiberaceae; 194-Costaceae; 195-Cannaceae. Gorts Van Rijn, A. R., ed. (Illus.). 72p. 1985. pap. text ed. 50.00 (*3-87429-255-X*, 018912) Koeltz Sci Bks.

— Renealmia (Zingiberaceae-Zingiberoideae) Costoideae (Additions) (Zingiberaceae) LC 77-72241. (Flora Neotropica Monograph Ser.: No. 18). (Illus.). 218p. 1977. pap. 21.00 (*0-89327-192-6*) NY Botanical.

Maas, P. J. & Maas-van de Kamer, H. Flora of the Guianas: Series A: Phanerogams: Burmanniaceae, Fascicle 6: 206. Gorts Van Rijn, A. R., ed. (Illus.). 45p. 1989. pap. text ed. 39.00 (*3-87429-290-8*, 036458) Koeltz Sci Bks.

— Flora of the Guianas: Series A: Phanerogams: Triuridaceae, Fascicle 5: 174. Gorts Van Rijn, A. R., ed. (Illus.). 18p. 1989. pap. text ed. 33.00 (*3-87429-289-4*) Koeltz Sci Bks.

Maas, Paul, et al. Saprophytes Pro Parte. (Flora Neotropica Monograph Ser.: No. 40-42). (Illus.). (Orig.). 1986. pap. 49.50 (*0-89327-271-X*) NY Botanical.

— Saprophytes Pro Parte, Vol. 40: Triuridaceae. (Illus.). 55p. (Orig.). 1986. write for info. (*0-318-60171-0*) NY Botanical.

— Saprophytes Pro Parte, Vol. 41: Voyria & Voyriella. (Illus.). 93p. (Orig.). 1986. write for info. (*0-318-60172-9*) NY Botanical.

— Saprophytes Pro Parte, Vol. 42: Burmanniaceae. (Illus.). 189p. (Orig.). 1986. write for info. (*0-318-60173-7*) NY Botanical.

Maas, Paul J. Zingiberaceae: Costoideae. LC 76-180013. (Flora Neotropica Monograph Ser.: No. 8). (Illus.). 139p. (Orig.). 1972. pap. 13.95 (*0-89327-291-4*) NY Botanical.

Maas, Paul J. & Maas-van de Kamer, Hiltje. Haemodoraceae. (Flora Neotropica Monograph Ser.: No. 61). (Illus.). 44p. (Orig.). 1993. pap. text ed. 12.50 (*0-89327-380-5*) NY Botanical.

Maas, Peter. China White. 1994. 23.00 (*0-671-69417-0*) S&S Trade.

— China White. 320p. 1995. pap. 5.99 (*0-7860-0204-2*) Windsor NY.

— China White. large type ed. LC 95-5406. (Large Print Book Ser.). 1995. pap. write for info. (*1-56895-096-9*) Wheeler Pub.

— Father & Son. 1990. mass mkt. 5.50 (*0-06-100020-5*, Harp PBks) HarpC.

— Father & Son. large type ed. (General Ser.). 455p. 1990. lib. bdg. 19.95 (*0-8161-4891-0*) G K Hall.

— In a Child's Name. Rubenstein, Julie, ed. 352p. 1991. reprint ed. mass mkt. 5.99 (*0-671-74619-7*) PB.

— In a Child's Name: The Legacy of a Mother's Murder. (Illus.). 1990. 15.95 (*0-671-72627-7*) S&S Trade.

— Killer Spy: The Inside Story of the FBI's Pursuit & Capture of Aldrich Ames, America's Deadliest Spy. 1995. 21.95 (*0-446-51973-1*) Warner Bks.

— Killer Spy: The Inside Story of the FBI's Pursuit & Capture of Aldrich Ames, America's Deadliest Spy. 256p. 1996. mass mkt. 6.50 (*0-446-60279-5*) Warner Bks.

— Manhunt. LC 85-25762. 352p. 1986. 17.95 (*0-394-55293-8*) Random.

Maas, Robert W. Expat Investor's Working & Retiring Abroad. 250p. 1993. 30.00 (*0-85459-657-7*, Pub. by Tolley Pubng UK) St Mut.

— Tolley's Anti-Avoidance Provisions. 632p. 1992. 150.00 (*0-85459-519-8*, Pub. by Tolley Pubng UK) St Mut.

— Tolley's Property Taxes 1993-94. 460p. 1993. 80.00 (*0-85459-788-3*, Pub. by Tolley Pubng UK) St Mut.

— Tolley's Taxation of Employments. 352p. 1991. 90.00x (*0-85459-578-3*, Pub. by Tolley Pubng UK) St Mut.

— Tolley's Taxation of Employments. 352p. (C). 1994. 102.00x (*0-85459-904-5*) St Mut.

Maas, Robin, jt. auth. see O'Donnell, Gabriel.

Maas, Stephen A. C - NL: Linear & Nonlinear Microwave Circuit Analysis & Optimization Software & Users Manual. (Microwave Library). 100p. 1990. Incl. software. disk 550.00 (*0-89006-428-8*) Artech Hse.

— Microwave Mixers. 2nd ed. (Microwave Ser.). 500p. 1992. text ed. 76.00 (*0-89006-605-1*) Artech Hse.

— Nonlinear Microwave Circuits. (Microwave Library). 500p. 1988. text ed. 79.00 (*0-89006-251-X*) Artech Hse.

***Maas, Terry.** BlueWater Hunting & Freediving. LC 95-75143. 200p. 1995. 39.95 (*0-9644966-0-7*) BlueWtr Freedivers.

Maas, Utz & Van Reijen, Willem, eds. Geteilte Sprache: Festschrift fur Rainer Marten. vi, 349p. (GER.). 1988. 69.00 (*90-6032-314-9*, Pub. by B R Gruener NE) Benjamins North Am.

Maas-van de Kamer, H., jt. auth. see Maas, P. J.

Maas-van de Kamer, Hiltje, jt. auth. see Maas, Paul J.

Maas, Virginia. Niddy Noddy the Noodlemaker. (Color-A-Story Ser.). (Illus.). 12p. (J). (ps-2). 1981. pap. 2.75 (*0-933992-15-7*) Coffee Break.

Maas, Willard, jt. ed. see Van Ghent, Dorothy.

Maasdorp, Gavin & Whiteside, Alan, eds. Towards a Post-Apartheid Future: Political & Economic Relations in Southern Africa. LC 91-30440. 240p. 1992. text ed. 55.00 (*0-312-07496-4*) St Martin.

***Maasen, Sabine.** Biology As Society, Society As Biology: Metaphors. Mendelsohn, Everett et al, eds. LC 94-36251. (Sociology of the Sciences (Yearbook) Ser.). 364p. (C). 1995. lib. bdg. 160.00 (*0-7923-3174-5*) Kluwer Ac.

***Maasik, Sonia & Solomon, Jack.** Notes from the Promised Land. 384p. 1995. pap. text ed. 21.28 (*0-312-11495-8*) St Martin.

***Maasik, Sonia & Solomon, James F.** Signs of Life in the U. S. Readings on Popular Culture for Writers. 768p. 1994. pap. text ed. 18.00 (*0-312-09020-X*) St Martin.

Maaskant-Kleibrink, M. Settlement Excavations at Borgo Le Ferriere - Satricum, Vol. 1. (Illus.). viii, 356p. (C). 1987. 93.00 (*90-6980-013-6*, Pub. by Egbert Forsten NE) Benjamins North Am.

Maaskant-Kleibrink, M., ed. Papers on Mediterranean Archaeology. (Caelcvlvs: Images of Ancient Latin Culture Ser.: Vol. I). 172p. 1993. pap. 40.00 (*0-685-68014-2*, Pub. by Egbert Forsten NE) Benjamins North Am.

Maaskant-Kleibrink, Marianne. Catalogue of the Engraved Gems in the Royal Coin Cabinet, The Hague: The Greek, Etruscan & Roman Collections. (Illus.). 576p. 1978. text ed. 175.00 (*3-515-02919-2*) Coronet Bks.

— Settlement Excavations at Borgo le Ferriere (Satricum), Vol. 2: The Campaigns 1983, 1985, 1987. (Illus.). 384p. 1993. 130.00 (*90-6980-048-9*, Pub. by Egbert Forsten NE) Benjamins North Am.

Maasoumi, Esfandiar, ed. see Sargan, John D.

Maass & Hill. Gallery of Waterfowl & Upland Game Birds. (Illus.). 130p. 1983. 45.00 (*0-940143-37-2*) Safari Pr.

Maass, Arlene. That's Life. LC 93-8592. 1993. pap. 6.00 (*0-940895-14-5*) Cornerstone IL.

Maass, Arthur. Muddy Waters: The Army Engineers & the Nation's Rivers. LC 73-20238. (FDR & the Era of the New Deal Ser.). 306p. 1974. reprint ed. lib. bdg. 39.50 (*0-306-70607-5*) Da Capo.

Maass, Arthur & Anderson, Raymond L. And the Desert Shall Rejoice: Conflict, Growth, & Justice in Arid Environments. LC 85-24157. 456p. (C). 1986. reprint ed. lib. bdg. 38.50 (*0-89874-908-5*) Krieger.

— And the Desert Shall Rejoice, Part 2: A Simulation of Irrigation Systems. LC 86-20027. 56p. 1987. reprint ed. pap. 10.50 (*0-89874-978-6*) Krieger.

Maass, Bruno. The Organization of the German Air Force High Command & Higher Echelon Headquarters within the German Air Force. (USAF Historical Studies: No. 190). 247p. 1955. reprint ed. pap. 29.95 (*0-89126-151-6*) MA-AH Pub.

Maass, David & Hill, Gene. A Gallery of Waterfowl & Upland Birds. LC 78-61769. (Illus.). 1978. text ed. 44.95 (*0-8227-8019-4*) Petersen Pub.

***Maass, Eliezer.** Stand Firm: A Survival Guide for the New Jewish Believer. rev. ed. Anderson, Fran, ed. 202p. 1995. reprint ed. pap. 8.00 (*1-878678-02-7*) A M F Intl.

Maass, Ernst, ed. see Aratus.

Maass, John, tr. see Sekler, Eduard F.

Maass, Martin, ed. see Groner, Erich.

Maass, Michael. Die Geometrischen Dreifuesse. (Olympische Forschungen Ser.: Bd. X). (C). 1978. 153.85 (*3-11-006703-X*) De Gruyter.

Maass, Richard, et al. Supplier Certification: A Continuous Improvement Strategy. (Supplier Quality Ser.). (Illus.). 141p. (Orig.). 1990. pap. 26.50 (*0-87389-083-3*) ASQC Qual Pr.

Maass, Richard A., jt. auth. see Supplier-Customer Committee.

An Asterisk (*) at the beginning of an entry indicates that the title is appearing in BIP for the first time.

Maass, Robert. Fire Fighters. (Illus.). (J). 1992. 3.95 (0-590-41460-7) Scholastic Inc.

— Tugboat Life. (J). 1996. 15.95 (0-8050-3116-2) H Holt & Co.

— U. N. Ambassador: A Behind-the-Scenes Look at Madeleine Albright's World. (Illus.). 48p. (J). (gr. 2-6). 1995. 15.95 (0-8027-8355-4); lib. bdg. 16.85 (0-8027-8356-2) Walker & Co.

— When Autumn Comes. LC 90-32069. (Illus.). 32p. (J). (ps-2). 1990. 15.95 (0-8050-1259-1, Bks Young Read) H Holt & Co.

— When Autumn Comes. LC 90-32069. (Illus.). 32p. (J). (ps-2). 1992. pap. 5.95 (0-8050-2349-6, Owlet BYR) H Holt & Co.

— When Spring Comes. LC 93-29816. (J). 1994. 14.95 (0-8050-2085-3, Bks Young Read) H Holt & Co.

— When Summer Comes. LC 92-26955. (Illus.). 32p. (J). (gr. 1-3). 1993. 14.95 (0-8050-2087-X, Bks Young Read) H Holt & Co.

— When Winter Comes. LC 93-7146. (Illus.). 32p. (J). (gr. 1-3). 1993. 14.95 (0-8050-2086-1, Bks Young Read) H Holt & Co.

***Maassen, Bernhard & Whaite, Robin, eds.** In Vitro Diagnostic Medical Devices: Law & Practice in Five EU Member States. LC 94-3568. 140p. (C). 1994. lib. bdg. 87.00 (0-7923-2996-1) Kluwer Ac.

***Maassen, Henriette.** Female Labor Supply, Child Care & Marital Conflict: An Empirical Analysis. 225p. 1994. pap. 32.50 (90-5356-072-6) IBD Ltd.

Maassen, Pierce. Heavenly Comfort. 1959. pap. 0.55 (0-686-23473-1) Rose Pub MI.

— Motherhood. 1959. pap. 0.55 (0-686-23476-6) Rose Pub MI.

Maatman, Russell. The Bible, Natural Science, & Evolution. (Orig.). 1980. pap. 4.95 (0-932914-03-9) Dordt Coll Pr.

— The Impact of Evolutionary Theory: A Christian View. 318p. (Orig.). 1993. pap. 12.95 (0-932914-28-4) Dordt Coll Pr.

— The Unity in Creation. 143p. (Orig.). 1978. pap. 4.95 (0-932914-00-4) Dordt Coll Pr.

Maatz, R., et al. Intramedullary Nailing & Other Intermedullary Osteosyntheses. 230p. 1986. text ed. 121.00 (0-7216-1279-2) Saunders.

Maayo, Geraldine C. A Quality of Sadness: Ten Stories. 90p. (Orig.). 1987. pap. 6.75 (971-10-0312-0, Pub. by New Day Pub PH) Cellar.

Maaz, Hans J. Behind the Wall: The Inner Life of Communist Germany. Date not set. 27.50 (0-393-03364-3) Norton.

Maaz, Wolfgang. Lateinische Epigrammatik im Hohen Mittelalter. (Spolia Berolinensia Ser.: Bd. 2). viii, 306p. (GER.). 1992. write for info. (3-615-00075-7, Pub. by Georg Olms GW) Lubrecht & Cramer.

Mabandla, Oyama, jt. auth. see Ellis, Stephen.

Mabank Sesquicentennial Committee. History of Mabank Texas. (Illus.). 445p. 1987. 55.00 (0-88107-080-7) Curtis Media.

Mabbe, James, tr. see Aleman, Matheo.

Mabbe, James, tr. see De Rojas, Fernando.

Mabbe, James, tr. see De Rojas.

Mabberley, D. J. Jupiter Botanicus: Robert Brown of the British Museum. (Illus.). 500p. 1985. lib. bdg. 90.00 (3-7682-1408-7) Lubrecht & Cramer.

— The Plant Book: A Portable Dictionary of the Higher Plants. 700p. 1987. pap. 44.95 (0-521-34060-8) Cambridge U Pr.

— Tropical Rain Forest Ecology. 2nd ed. (Tertiary Level Biology Ser.). 200p. 1991. 87.50 (0-412-02881-6, A6375, Blackie & Son-Chapman NY); pap. 35.00 (0-412-02891-3, A6379, Blackie & Son-Chapman NY) Routledge Chapman & Hall.

Mabberley, D. J. & Placito, P. J. Algarve Plants & Landscapes: Passing Tradition & Ecological Change. LC 92-26904. (Illus.). 336p. 1993. 49.95 (0-19-858702-3) OUP.

***Mabberley, Julie.** Activity-Based Costing in Financial Institutions. 240p. 1993. 141.00 (0-273-03921-0, Pub. by Pitman Pubng UK) St Mut.

— The Price Waterhouse Guide to Activity-Based Costing for Financial Institutions. 1994. 75.00 (0-7863-0143-0) Irwin Prof Pubng.

***Mabbett, Andy.** Complete Guide to the Music of Pink Floyd. (Illus.). 150p. (Orig.). 1995. pap. 7.95 (0-7119-4301-X, OP 47735, Pub. by Omnibus Press UK) Omnibus NY.

Mabbett, Andy, jt. auth. see Mabbett, Miles.

Mabbett, Andy, jt. auth. see Miles.

***Mabbett, Deborah.** Trade, Employment, & Welfare: A Comparative Study of Trade & Labour Market Policies in Sweden & New Zealand, 1880-1980. (Illus.). 216p. 1995. 42.00 (0-19-828379-2) OUP.

Mabbett, Deborah, jt. auth. see Bolderson, Helen.

Mabbett, Ian & Chandler, David. The Khmers. (PeopleTalk Ser.). (Illus.). 288p. 1995. 34.95 (0-631-17582-2) Blackwell Pubs.

***Mabbett, Miles & Mabbett, Andy.** Pink Floyd: The Visual Documentary. rev. ed. Charlesworth, Chris, ed. (Illus.). Date not set. pap. text ed. 24.95 (0-7119-4109-2, OP 40583) Omnibus NY.

Mabbitt, J. H. The Health Services of Glamorgan. 232p. (C). 1989. 39.00 (0-9500789-5-6, Pub. by D Brown & Sons Ltd UK) St Mut.

Mabbott, Maureen C. Mabbott As Poe Scholar: The Early Years. Kadis, Averil J., ed. (Orig.). 1980. pap. 2.95 (0-910556-14-8) Enoch Pratt.

Mabbott, Thomas O., ed. see Poe, Edgar Allan.

Mabbs, F. E. & Collison, D. Electron Paramagnetic Resonance of d Transition Metal Compounds. LC 92-36527. (Studies in Inorganic Chemistry: Vol. 16). 1992. write for info. (0-444-89852-2) Elsevier.

Mabbutt, Anita, jt. auth. see Mabbutt, Bill.

Mabbutt, Bill & Mabbutt, Anita. North American Wild Game Cookbook. LC 82-73116. (Illus.). 216p. (Orig.). 1982. 9.95 (0-932722-03-2) Solstice Pr.

— North American Wild Game Cookbook. (Illus.). 212p. (Orig.). 1992. reprint ed. pap. 12.95 (0-9634334-0-7); reprint ed. spiral bd. 12.95 (0-9634334-1-5) B & A Mabbutt.

— Tastes of Idaho Cookbook. (Illus.). 139p. 1989. pap. 9.95 (0-932722-16-4) Solstice Pr.

Mabbutt, Bill, et al. North American Game Fish Cookbook. LC 83-50732. (Illus.). 192p. (Orig.). 1983. pap. 9.95 (0-932722-06-7) Solstice Pr.

Mabe, Edouard, jt. auth. see Shapiro, Bob.

Mabe, Joni. Joni Mabe's Museum Book. 1988. 25.00 (0-932526-18-7) Nexus Pr.

Mabee, Carleton. Black Education in New York State: From Colonial to Modern Times. (Illus.). 352p. 1979. 39.95x (0-8156-2209-0) Syracuse U Pr.

***Mabee, Carleton & Newhouse, Susan M.** Sojourner Truth: Slave, Prophet, Legend. LC 93-9370. (Illus.). 320p. 1995. pap. 16.95 (0-8147-5525-9) NYU Pr.

— Sojourner Truth: Slave, Prophet, Legend. LC 93-9370. (Illus.). 320p. (C). 1995. 45.00 (0-8147-5484-8) NYU Pr.

Mabee, Carleton H. A Guide to Croquet Court Planning, Building & Maintenance. Seughas, Richard, ed. (Illus.). 120p. (Orig.). 1991. pap. 45.00 (0-9630074-0-8) Bass Cove.

Mabee, Charles. Reading Sacred Texts Through American Eyes: Biblical Interpretation as Cultural Critique. LC 91-14356. (Studies in American Biblical Hermeneutics). 128p. (C). 1991. 24.95 (0-86554-385-2, H313); pap. text ed. 16.95 (0-86554-403-4, P95) Mercer Univ Pr.

— Reimagining America: A Theological Critique of the American Mythos & Biblical Hermeneutics. LC 84-27335. xvi, 156p. 1985. 15.95 (0-86554-148-5, MUP/H139) Mercer Univ Pr.

Mabee, Charles, ed. see Mercer, Calvin R.

***Maben, Laura.** Homework for Thinkers: A Year's Worth of Creative Assignments to Stimulate Critical Thinking. Britt, Leslie, ed. & intro. by. (Illus.). 64p. (Orig.). (J). (gr. 3-6). 1995. pap. text ed. 7.95 (0-86530-300-2, IP300-2) Incentive Pubns.

Maben, Manly. Vanport, Oregon: Life & Death of an Instant City. (Illus.). (Orig.). (C). 1987. pap. 15.95 (0-87595-118-X) Oregon Hist.

Maberly, Norman C. Mastering Speed Reading. 127p. (YA). (gr. 7 up). 1966. pap. 4.99 (0-451-16644-2, Sig) NAL-Dutton.

— Mastering Speed Reading. 127p. (YA). (gr. 9-12). 1989. pap. 3.50 (0-451-15511-4, Sig) NAL-Dutton.

Maberry, Grace W. & Smith, L. Barrett. It's Never Too Early: Helping Parents & Prospective Parents to Be Religious with Preschoolers. LC 87-51692. 80p. (Orig.). 1988. pap. 5.95 (0-88177-057-4, DR057) Discipleship Res.

Mabert, Vincent A. Cases in Manufacturing & Service System Management. 352p. (C). 1990. text ed. write for info. (0-13-116278-0) P-H.

Mabert, Vincent A. & Jacobs, F. Robert, eds. Integrated Production Systems: Design, Planning, Control, & Scheduling. 4th ed. 1991. 39.95 (0-89806-119-9) Ind Eng Mgmt Pr.

Mabery, D. L. Janet Jackson. (Entertainment World Ser.). (Illus.). 48p. (J). (gr. 4-9). 1988. pap. 13.50 (0-8225-1618-7, Lerner Publctns) Lerner Group.

Mabery, D L. Prince. (Entertainment World Ser.). (Illus.). 48p. (J). (gr. 4-9). 1985. lib. bdg. 13.50 (0-8225-1603-9, Lerner Publctns) Lerner Group.

Mabery, D. L. This Is Michael Jackson. LC 84-10043. (Entertainment World Ser.). (Illus.). 48p. (J). (gr. 4-9). 1984. lib. bdg. 13.50 (0-8225-1600-4, Lerner Publctns) Lerner Group.

Mabery, Marilyne V. El Malpais National Monument. Priehs, T. J. & Houk, Rose, eds. LC 90-60723. (Illus.). 16p. (Orig.). 1990. 2.95 (0-911408-89-4) SW Pks Mnmts.

— Right after Sundown: Teaching Stories of the Navajo. 1991. pap. 14.95 (0-912586-69-9) Navajo Coll Pr.

Mabey, Chris, jt. auth. see Thomson, Rosemary.

Mabey, Christopher. Graduates into Industry. 1986. text ed. 62.00 (0-566-00886-6) Ashgate Pub Co.

Mabey, Christopher & Iles, Paul, eds. Managing Learning. LC 94-17871. 288p. 1994. 65.00x (0-415-11983-9, C0111); pap. 19.95 (0-415-11984-7, C0461) Routledge.

Mabey, Christopher, et al. Strategic Human Resources Management. LC 93-9495. (Illus.). 450p. (C). 1995. 69.95 (0-631-18504-6); pap. 34.95 (0-631-18505-4) Blackwell Pubs.

***Mabey, Judith & Sorensen, Bernice.** Counselling for Young People. LC 94-41293. 160p. 1995. pap. 19.95 (0-335-19298-X, Open Univ Pr) Taylor & Francis.

Mabey, Richard. Home Country. large type ed. 250p. 1992. 11.47 (1-85089-580-5, Pub. by ISIS UK) Transaction Pubs.

— A Nature Journal. (Illus.). 152p. 1992. 24.95 (0-7011-3507-7, Pub. by Chatto & Windus UK) Trafalgar.

— Whistling in the Dark: In Pursuit of the Nightingale. (Illus.). 120p. 1995. 19.95 (1-85619-176-1, Sinclair-Stevenson) Trafalgar.

Mabey, Richard, ed. Class, a Symposium. (Great Society Ser.). 1967. 10.00 (0-218-51456-5) Dufour.

— The Oxford Book of Nature Writing. 272p. 1995. 25.00 (0-19-214172-4) OUP.

Mabey, Richard, intro. & notes. A Victorian Flora: The Flower Paintings of Caroline May. LC 90-7498. (Illus.). 192p. 1991. 35.00 (0-87951-412-4) Overlook Pr.

Mabey, Richard & McIntyre, Michael. The New Age Herbalist: How to Use Herbs for Healing, Nutrition, Body Care & Relaxation. LC 87-35019. (Illus.). 288p. 1988. 32.50 (0-02-577180-9, Collier S&S); pap. 21.00 (0-02-063350-5, Collier S&S) S&S Trade.

Mabey, Richard, ed. see White, Gilbert.

Mabie, C. W. Behold I Show You a Mystery. LC 80-82229. 150p. (Orig.). 1980. pap. 4.95 (0-9601416-5-0) J C Print.

Mabie, Caroline W., ed. see Wilson, J. Eugene.

Mabie, Grace. A Picture Book of Animal Opposites. LC 91-33596. (Picture Book of...Ser.). (Illus.). 24p. (J). (gr. 1-4). 1992. text ed. 9.59 (0-8167-2438-5); 2.50 (0-8167-2439-3) Troll Assocs.

— A Picture Book of Baby Animals. LC 92-26264. (Picture Book of...Ser.). (Illus.). 24p. (J). (gr. 1-4). 1992. lib. bdg. 9.59 (0-8167-2468-7); pap. text ed. 2.50 (0-8167-2469-5) Troll Assocs.

— A Picture Book of Night-Time Animals. LC 91-33597. (Picture Book of...Ser.). (Illus.). 24p. (J). (gr. 1-4). 1992. lib. bdg. 9.59 (0-8167-2432-6); pap. text ed. 2.50 (0-8167-2433-4) Troll Assocs.

— A Picture Book of Water Birds. LC 91-34129. (Picture Book of...Ser.). (Illus.). 24p. (J). (gr. 1-4). 1992. lib. bdg. 9.59 (0-8167-2436-9); pap. text ed. 2.50 (0-8167-2437-7) Troll Assocs.

Mabie, Grace, ed. see Baum, L. Frank.

Mabie, H. W. In the Forest of Arden. 34p. 1989. pap. 6.95 (0-912132-22-1) Dominion Pr.

Mabie, Hamilton H. & Reinholtz, Charles F. Mechanisms & Dynamics of Machinery. 4th ed. LC 86-11115. 644p. 1987. Net. text ed. write for info. (0-471-80237-9) Wiley.

Mabie, Hamilton W. American Ideals, Character & Life. LC 74-157965. (Essay Index Reprint Ser.). 1977. reprint ed. 23.95 (0-8369-2240-9) Ayer.

— Backgrounds of Literature. LC 72-111846. (Essay Index Reprint Ser.). 1977. 31.95 (0-8369-1617-4) Ayer.

— Essays in Lent. LC 69-18931. (Essay Index Reprint Ser.). 1977. 15.95 (0-8369-0046-4) Ayer.

— Essays in Literary Interpretation. LC 72-293. (Essay Index Reprint Ser.). 1977. reprint ed. 20.95 (0-8369-2802-4) Ayer.

— Fruits of the Spirit. LC 67-22103. (Essay Index Reprint Ser.). 1977. 20.95 (0-8369-0639-X) Ayer.

— Myths Every Child Should Know. 20.00 (0-8195-1235-4) Biblo.

— Writers of Knickerbocker New York. 121p. 1993. reprint ed. lib. bdg. 69.00 (0-7812-5278-4) Rprt Serv.

Mabie, Hamilton W., comp. Book of Old English Ballads. LC 79-121929. (Granger Index Reprint Ser.). 1977. 19.95 (0-8369-6170-6) Ayer.

— Book of Old English Love Songs. LC 73-121930. (Granger Index Reprint Ser.). 1977. 19.95 (0-8369-6171-4) Ayer.

Mabie, Margot C. Bioethics & the New Medical Technology. LC 92-22642. 176p. (YA). (gr. 7 up). 1993. text ed. 14.95 (0-689-31637-2, Atheneum Bks Young) S&S Childrens.

Mabileau, Albert, et al, eds. Local Politics & Participation in France & Britain. (Illus.). (C). 1990. 69.95 (0-521-34576-6) Cambridge U Pr.

Mabin, Alan, ed. Organisation & Economic Change. 220p. (Orig.). 1989. pap. text ed. 17.95 (0-86975-382-7, Pub. by Ravan Pr ZA) Ohio U Pr.

Mablekos, Carole M. Engineer's Guide to Business-Presentations That Work. (Illus.). 1991. 12.95 (0-7803-0305-9, HL0453-1) Inst Electrical.

Mablekos, Carole M., ed. Technical Writing & Communication. 174p. 1988. 510.00 (0-8412-1484-0, A3); teacher ed 39.00 (0-8412-1501-4) Am Chemical.

Mabley, Edward, jt. auth. see Howard, David.

Mabogunje, Akin L. The Development Process: A Spatial Perspective. LC 80-19939. 357p. 1980. 36.50 (0-8419-0659-9) Holmes & Meier.

— Perspective on Urban Land & Urban Management Policies in Sub-Saharan Africa. LC 92-43900. (Technical Paper Ser.: No. 196). 65p. 1993. 6.95 (0-8213-2355-5, 12355) World Bank.

Mabon, E., tr. see Godwin, Francis.

Mabon, George, comp. Caring in Homes Initiative: A Policies & Foundation Training. (C). 1991. 55.00 (0-7855-0083-9, Pub. by Natl Inst Soc Work) St Mut.

— Caring in Homes Initiative: An Induction Programme. (C). 1991. 35.00 (0-7855-0082-0, Pub. by Natl Inst Soc Work) St Mut.

***Mabourguet, Patrice.** Larousse Dictionnaire General. 1690p. (FRE.). 1993. 69.95 (0-7859-7124-6, 203320300X) Fr & Eur.

Mabro, Judy, jt. ed. see El-Solh, Camillia F.

Mabro, Robert, jt. auth. see Horsnell, Paul.

Mabrouk, Patricia A. Analytical Chemistry Lab Manual. (C). 1993. 13.80 (1-56870-088-1) RonJon Pub.

— Analytical Chemistry, No. One: Problem Solver. (C). 1993. 14.47 (1-56870-089-X) RonJon Pub.

Mabry, Bevars D. The Development of Labor Institutions in Thailand. LC 79-113663. (Cornell University, Southeast Asia Program, Data Paper Ser.: No. 112). 164p. reprint ed. pap. 46.80 (0-8357-6090-1, 2034595) Bks Demand.

Mabry, Donald J. The Mexican University & the State: Student Conflicts, 1910-1971. LC 81-48377. 344p. 1982. 24.75 (0-89096-128-X) Tex A&M Univ Pr.

Mabry, Donald J., ed. The Latin American Narcotics Trade & U. S. National Security. LC 89-12030. (Contributions in Political Science Ser.: No. 240). 216p. 1989. text ed. 55.00 (0-313-26786-3, MLJ/, Greenwood Pr) Greenwood.

Mabry, E. Scott. Triangle Power: A Source of Staying Power in Marriage. LC 94-65479. 210p. (Orig.). 1994. pap. 11.95 (0-9639732-0-7) St Croix Pubns.

Mabry, Eddie. Balthasar Hubmaier's Doctrine of the Church. 236p. Date not set. lib. bdg. 32.50 (0-8191-9472-7) U Pr of Amer.

Mabry, J. God As Nature Sees God. 1994. pap. 14.95 (1-85230-594-0) Element MA.

***Mabry, Jonathan B., et al.** Tucson at the Turn of the Century: The Archaeology of a City Block. (Illus.). 198p. (Orig.). 1994. pap. 15.00 (1-886398-14-3) Desert Archaeol.

Mabry, Linda A., jt. auth. see Moyer, Homer E., Jr.

***Mabry, Marcus.** White Bucks & Black-Eyed Peas: Coming of Age Black in White America. 304p. 1995. 23.00 (0-684-19669-7, Scribners) S&S Trade.

Mabry, Richard L. Skin Endpoint Titration. 2nd ed. LC 93-50108. (AAOA Monograph Ser.). (Illus.). 104p. 1994. text ed. 19.00 (0-86577-525-7) Thieme Med Pubs.

Mabry, Richard L., jt. auth. see King, Hueston C.

Mabry, Rodney H. & Ulbrich, Holley H. Introduction to Economic Principles. 1989. pap. text ed. write for info. (0-07-044797-7); Study guide. student ed, pap. text ed. write for info. (0-07-044803-5) McGraw.

Mabry, Steve, jt. auth. see McNabb, Bill.

Mabry, T. J., jt. ed. see Behnke, H. D.

Mabry, Tom J. & Wagenitz, G. W. Research Advances in the Compositae. (Plant Systematics & Evolution Ser.: Suppl. 4). (Illus.). 120p. 1990. 90.00 (0-387-82174-0) Spr-Verlag.

Mabry, William A. Negro in North Carolina Politics Since Reconstruction. LC 75-110130. (Duke University. Trinity College Historical Society. Historical Papers: No. 23). reprint ed. 30.00 (0-404-51773-0) AMS Pr.

Mabry, William E. The Wildness of Worship. 1994. pap. 4.95 (1-55673-826-9, 7997) CSS OH.

***Mabuchi, T., et al.** Geometry & Analysis on Complex Manifolds: Festschrift for S. Kobayashi's 60th Birthday. 260p. 1994. text ed. 74.00 (981-02-2067-7) World Scientific Pub.

Mabuchi, Toshiki & Mukai, Shigeru, eds. Einstein Metrics & Yang-Mills Connections. LC 93-18074. (Lecture Notes in Pure & Applied Mathematics Ser.: Vol. 145). 240p. 1993. 110.00 (0-8247-9069-3) Dekker.

Mac Adam, Alfred, tr. see Fuentes, Carlos.

Mac Adam, Alfred, tr. see Mendoza, Eduardo.

Mac Adam, Alfred, tr. see Vargas Llosa, Mario.

Mac A'Ghobhainn, Seamus, jt. auth. see Ellis, Peter B.

Mac an Ghaill, Mairtin. The Making of Men: Masculinities, Sexualities & Schooling. LC 93-37338. 1994. 79.00 (0-335-15782-3, Open Univ Pr); pap. 27.50 (0-335-15781-5, Open Univ Pr) Taylor & Francis.

***Mac Arthur, Margaret & Sharrow, Gregory.** The Vermont Heritage Songbook. 108p. 1994. 9.95 (0-916718-13-1) VT Folklife Ctr.

Mac Caskey, Michael, jt. auth. see Haas, Cathy.

Mac Cormack, Karen. Quirks & Quillets. (Illus.). 56p. (Orig.). 1990. pap. 8.00 (0-925904-04-X) Chax Pr.

***Mac Cragh, Esteban.** Nuevo Diccionario Ingles-Espanol y Espanol-Ingles: New Spanish-English & English-Spanish Dictionary. 5th ed. 1990. 29.95 (0-7859-5037-0) Fr & Eur.

Mac Curtain, Margaret & O'Corrain, Donncha, eds. Women in Irish Society: The Historical Dimension. LC 79-964. (Contributions in Women's Studies: No. 11). 125p. 1979. text ed. 38.50 (0-313-21254-6, MWI/, Greenwood Pr) Greenwood.

Mac Donald, Hugh, tr. see Debussy, Claude.

Mac Dougall, David S., ed. European Community Energy Law: Selected Topics. (International Energy & Resources Law & Policy Ser.). 304p. (C). 1994. lib. bdg. 110.00 (1-85333-962-8, Pub. by Graham & Trotman UK) Kluwer Ac.

***Mac Farlane, Muriel.** The Panic Attack, Anxiety & Phobia Solutions Handbook. Mills, L. E., ed. 288p. (Orig.). Date not set. pap. 12.95 (1-887053-00-X) United Res CA.

Mac, Freddy, pseud. How to Buy Gold & Silver for Half Price. (Illus.). 80p. (Orig.). 1984. pap. 10.00 (0-9614202-0-0) Golden Aloha.

Mac, Gerard. Pilgrims: A Novel of the Mayflower. 320p. 1994. 21.95 (0-312-11551-2) St Martin.

Mac Gillivray, H. T., ed. Digitised Optical Sky Surveys: Proceedings of the Conference on Digitised Optical Sky Surveys, Held in Edinburgh, Scotland, June 18-21, 1991. (Astrophysics & Space Science Library). 544p. (C). 1992. lib. bdg. 156.50 (0-7923-1642-8) Kluwer Ac.

Mac Gregor, Felipe E., ed. Coca & Cocaine: An Andean Perspective. LC 92-12282. (Contributions in Criminology & Penology Ser.: No. 37). 168p. 1993. text ed. 49.95 (0-313-28530-6, ACN/, Greenwood Pr) Greenwood.

***Mac Harg, Marcia L., ed.** International Survey of Investment Adviser Regulation. 368p. 1994. lib. bdg. 125.00 (1-85966-078-9, Pub. by Graham & Trotman UK) Kluwer Ac.

Mac Kay, James A. Enciclopedia Mundial Del Sello 1945-1975. 112p. (SPA.). 1976. 87.50 (0-8288-5670-2, S50553) Fr & Eur.

Mac Kay, Ross & Jones, David. Labour Markets in Distress: The Denial of Choice. 172p. 1989. text ed. 68.95 (0-566-05700-X, Pub. by Avebury Pub UK) Ashgate Pub Co.

Mac Kenzie, Robert. Setting Limits: How to Raise Responsible, Independent Children by Providing Reasonable Boundaries. (Illus.). 272p. (Orig.). 1992. pap. 10.95 (1-55958-220-0) Prima Pub.

Mac Lane, Jude. Heart Messages: From Archangel Michael & Jude Mac Lane. 75p. (Orig.). (C). 1989. pap. 8.00 (0-9622052-0-6) Turtle Prints.

Mac Lane, S. & Moerdijk, I. Sheaves in Geometry & Logic: A First Introduction to Topos Theory. (Universitext Ser.). (Illus.). 616p. 1994. pap. 55.00 (0-387-97710-4) Spr-Verlag.

An Asterisk (*) at the beginning of an entry indicates that the title is appearing in BIP for the first time.

***Mac Lane, Saunders.** Homology. LC 94-47666. 1995. write for info. (*3-540-58662-8*) Spr-Verlag.

Mac Lane, Saunders & Birkhoff, Garrett. Algebra. 3rd ed. xv, 630p. (C). 1987. text ed. 32.50 (*0-8284-0330-9*) Chelsea Pub.

Mac Laverty, Bernard. Andrew McAndrew. LC 92-52993. (Illus.). 80p. (J). (gr. k-3). 1993. 13.95 (*1-56402-173-4*) Candlewick Pr.

Mac Lean, Alistair & Bowser, Milton. What the Hell...? Glen, Jeffrey & Monconduit, Barbara, eds. (Illus.). 368p. 1991. reprint ed. lib. bdg. write for info. (*0-940178-18-4*) Sitare.

Mac Lean, Norman, tr. see Pischinger, Alfred.

Mac Low, Jackson. Forty-Two Merzgedichte in Memoriam Kurt Schwitters: February, 1987 - September, 1989. LC 94-2575. 1994. 14.95 (*0-88268-145-1*) Station Hill Pr.

— From Pearl Harbor Day to FDR's Birthday. LC 82-61709. 72p. 1982. pap. 5.95 (*0-940650-19-3*) Sun & Moon CA.

— Pieces O' Six. (Sun & Moon Classics Ser.: No. 17). 1989. pap. 11.95 (*1-55713-060-4*) Sun & Moon CA.

Mac Namara, Desmond. Picture Framing: A Practical Guide from Basic to Baroque. (Illus.). 128p. 1994. pap. 14.95 (*0-7153-0205-1*, Pub. by D & C Pub UK) Sterling.

Mac Orlan, Pierre. Le Chant de l'Equippage. (FRE.). 1979. pap. 10.95 (*0-7859-4112-6*) Fr & Eur.

— Chronique des Jours Desesperes Suivi de les Voisins. 148p. (FRE.). 1985. pap. 10.95 (*0-7859-4236-X*, 2070376915) Fr & Eur.

— Sous la Lumiere Froide. 224p. (FRE.). 1979. pap. 10.95 (*0-7859-4124-X*, 2070371530) Fr & Eur.

Mac Poilin, Aodan, ed. see Fiacc, Padraic.

***Mac Rebennack, John & Rummel, Jack.** Under a Hoodoo Moon: The Life of the Night Tripper. LC 95-2219. 1995. pap. 12.00 (*0-312-13197-6*) St Martin.

Mac Uistin, Liam. Post-Mortem. (Irish Play Ser.). 1977. pap. 2.50 (*0-912262-43-5*) Proscenium.

Macabre, J. B., jt. auth. see Guiley, Rosemary E.

Macadam. The Temples of Kawa, 2 vols., Set. (Griffith Institute Ser.). 75.00 (*0-900416-46-7*, Pub. by Aris & Phillips UK) David Brown.

MacAdam, A., tr. see Arenas, Reinaldo.

***MacAdam, A. I.** Statutes. 3rd ed. 360p. 1993. pap. 63.00 (*0-409-30504-9*, Austral) Butterworth Legal Pubs.

MacAdam, Alfred, tr. see Carpentier, Alejo.

MacAdam, Alfred, tr. see Fuentes, Carlos.

MacAdam, Alfred, tr. see Pessoa, Fernando.

MacAdam, Alfred J. Textual Confrontations: Comparative Readings in Latin American Literature. LC 86-24913. 216p. 1987. 19.95 (*0-226-49990-1*) U Ch Pr.

***Macadam, Alta.** Blue Guide: Rome & Environs. 5th ed. 1995. pap. 21.95 (*0-393-31259-3*, Norton Paperbks) Norton.

— Blue Guide: Sicily. 4th ed. 306p. 1993. pap. 19.95 (*0-393-31054-X*) Norton.

— Blue Guides: Northern Italy. 1991. pap. 25.95 (*0-393-30727-1*) Norton.

— Florence. 6th ed. (Blue Guide Ser.). (Illus.). 304p. 1995. pap. 17.95 (*0-393-31274-7*, Norton Paperbks) Norton.

— Tuscany. (Blue Guides Ser.). (Illus.). 416p. 1993. pap. 24.95 (*0-393-30970-3*) Norton.

— Umbria. (Blue Guides Ser.). (Illus.). 192p. 1993. pap. 18.95 (*0-393-30990-8*) Norton.

— Venice. 5th ed. (Blue Guide Ser.). 1994. pap. 17.95 (*0-393-31189-9*) Norton.

***MacAdam, Barbara J.** Looking for America: Prints of Rural Life from the 1930s & 1940s. LC 94-45118. (Illus.). 1994. write for info. (*0-944722-18-0*) Hood Mus Art.

MacAdam, D. L. Color Measurement. 2nd rev. ed. (Optical Sciences Ser.: Vol. 27). (Illus.). 256p. 1985. pap. 63.00 (*0-387-15573-2*) Spr-Verlag.

MacAdam, D. L., ed. see Agarwal, B. K.

MacAdam, D. L., ed. see Hanna, David C., et al.

MacAdam, David L., ed. Selected Papers on Colorimetry-Fundamentals. LC 93-10037. (Milestone Ser.: Vol. MS 77). 1993. write for info. (*0-8194-1296-1*); pap. write for info. (*0-8194-1295-3*) SPIE.

MacAdam, Don & Reynolds, Gail. Hockey Fitness: Year Round Conditioning on & off the Ice. LC 88-681. (Illus.). 152p. (Orig.). 1988. pap. 14.95x (*0-88011-314-6*, PMAC0314) Human Kinetics.

Macadam, Heather D., jt. auth. see Gelissen, Rena K.

***Macadam, John.** South West Coast Path: Padstow to Falmouth. (National Trail Guides Ser.). (Illus.). 168p. Date not set. pap. 19.95 (*1-85410-098-X*, London Bridge) Genl Dist Srvs.

MacAdam, Robert, jt. auth. see McIlvaine, Charles.

MacAdam, Robert K., jt. auth. see McIlvaine, Charles.

MacAdams, Lewis, Jr. The Poetry Room. LC 73-123978. 65p. 1970. 12.50 (*0-89366-104-X*) Ultramarine Pub.

MacAdams, Phoebe. Sunday. 100p. (Orig.). 1983. pap. 6.00 (*0-939180-20-0*) Tombouctou.

MacAdams, William. Ben Hecht: A Biography. LC 88-19046. (Illus.). 384p. 1990. 24.95 (*0-684-18980-1*, Scribners) S&S Trade.

— Ben Hecht: A Biography. LC 94-45636. 1995. pap. write for info. (*1-56980-028-6*) Barricade Bks.

Macafee, Caroline. Glasgow. (Varieties of English Around the World (VEAW) Text Ser.: No. 3). v, 167p. (Orig.). 1983. 38.00x (*90-272-4711-0*) Benjamins North Am.

— The Nuttis Schell: Essays on the Scots Language Presented to a J Aitken. 240p. 1987. text ed. 39.00 (*0-08-034530-1*, Pergamon Pr) Elsevier.

MacAfee, Helen, ed. see Yale Review Staff.

MacAfee, Norman, tr. see De Beauvoir, Simone, ed.

Macafee, Norman, tr. see Sartre, Jean-Paul.

***Macagba, Jonathan.** Go Figure Vol. 1. LC 94-70879. 120p. 1994. write for info. (*0-88108-140-X*) Art Dir.

— Go Figure Vol. 2. LC 94-73085. 120p. (Orig.). 1994. write for info. (*0-88108-123-X*) Art Dir.

Macagno, Eduardo R., jt. ed. see Shankland, Marty.

MacAgy, Jermayne & Sourian, Etienne. Out of This World. (Illus.). 1964. pap. 2.00 (*0-914412-23-X*) Inst for the Arts.

MacAlan, Peter. Fireball. large type ed. (Magna Adventure Suspense Ser.). 403p. 1992. 21.95 (*0-7505-0286-X*) Ulverscroft.

— The Windsor Protocol. 320p. 1992. 20.00 (*0-7278-4367-2*) Severn Hse.

Macalister, R. A. The Philistines: Their History & Civilization. (British Academy, London, Schweich Lectures on Biblical Archaeology Series, 1930). 1974. reprint ed. pap. 20.00 (*0-8115-1253-3*) Periodicals Srv.

Macalister, R. A., tr. Life of St. Finan. 1987. reprint ed. pap. 1.95 (*0-89979-035-6*) British Am Bks.

Macalister, Robert A. Ancient Ireland: A Study in the Lessons of Archeology & History. LC 72-83747. (Illus.). 1978. reprint ed. 26.95 (*0-405-08757-8*, Pub. by Blom Pubns UK) Ayer.

— The Archaeology of Ireland. rev. ed. LC 70-172160. (Illus.). 1972. reprint ed. 36.95 (*0-405-08758-6*, Pub. by Blom Pubns UK) Ayer.

— A Century of Excavation in Palestine. Davis, Moshe, ed. LC 77-70720. (America & the Holy Land Ser.). (Illus.). 1977. reprint ed. lib. bdg. 35.95 (*0-405-10265-8*) Ayer.

— Ireland in Pre-Celtic Times. LC 68-56469. (Illus.). 1972. reprint ed. 34.95 (*0-405-08759-4*, Pub. by Blom Pubns UK) Ayer.

MacAlister, Robert A. The Secret Languages of Ireland. LC 78-72637. (Celtic Language & Literature Ser.: Goidelic & Brythonic). reprint ed. 29.50 (*0-404-17566-X*) AMS Pr.

MacAllan, Andrew. Diamond Hard. 672p. 1992. pap. 11.95 (*0-7472-3513-9*, Pub. by Headline UK) Trafalgar.

— Speculator. 608p. 1994. pap. 13.95 (*0-7472-4181-3*, Pub. by Headline UK) Trafalgar.

MacAllister, Carol L. Windows to My Soul: Reflections of an "Inner" Traveler. (Illus.). 100p. (Orig.). 1990. pap. 6.95 (*0-9624856-0-8*) Handsome Bks.

MacAllister, Dawson & Kimmel, Tim. Student Relationships, Vol. 3. (J). (gr. 5-12). 1981. teacher ed, pap. 6.95 (*0-923417-19-2*) Shepherd Minst.

MacAllister, Joyce. Writing about Literature: Aims & Process. 320p. (C). 1987. pap. write for info. (*0-02-373030-7*) Macmillan.

MacAloon, John J. Brides of Victory: Nationalism & Gender in Olympic Ritual. 122p. 1994. 49.95 (*0-85496-718-4*) Berg Pubs.

— This Great Symbol: Pierre de Coubertin & the Origins of the Modern Olympic Games. LC 80-21898. (Illus.). xiv, 360p. (C). 1984. pap. text ed. 9.95 (*0-226-50001-2*) U Ch Pr.

MacAloon, John J., ed. General Education in the Social Sciences: Centennial Reflections on the College of the University of Chicago. LC 91-42118. (Centennial Publication Ser.). 296p. 1992. pap. text ed. 12.95 (*0-226-50003-9*) U Ch Pr.

— General Education in the Social Sciences: Centennial Reflections on the College of the University of Chicago. LC 91-42118. (Centennial Publication Ser.). 296p. 1992. lib. bdg. 42.00 (*0-226-50002-0*) U Ch Pr.

MacAlpin, Miles. Book of the Living: A Handbook of Self-Directed Consciousness. 1989. 6.25 (*0-913004-65-0*) Point Loma Pub.

Macalpine, Ida, jt. auth. see Hunter, Richard.

***MacAlpine, Loretta.** Inside KidVid: The Essential Parent's Guide to Video. LC 95-14876. (Illus.). 224p. 1995. pap. 9.95 (*0-14-017341-2*, Penguin Bks) Viking Penguin.

Macaluso, Donald G. The Financial Advantage of Multinational Firm During Tight Credit Periods in Host Countries. Bruchey, Stuart, ed. LC 80-582. (Multinational Corporations Ser.). 1981. lib. bdg. 19.95 (*0-405-13374-X*) Ayer.

Macaluso, Gregory J. Morris, Orange & King William Artillery. (Virginia Regimental Histories Ser.). (Illus.). 122p. 1991. 19.95 (*1-56190-011-7*) H E Howard.

***Macaluso, Pamela.** Christmas Wedding. 1995. pap. 3.25 (*0-373-05970-1*, 1-05970-8) Silhouette.

— Dream Wedding: (Just Married) (Desire Ser.). 1995. mass mkt. 3.25 (*0-373-05928-0*, 1-05928-6) Silhouette.

— Hometown Wedding. (Desire Ser.). 1994. mass mkt. 2.99 (*0-373-05897-7*, 1-05897-3) Silhouette.

— Remember My Love. 224p. (Orig.). 1990. pap. 2.75 (*1-878702-23-8*, Kismet) Meteor Pub.

— Rose among Thornes. 224p. (Orig.). 1993. pap. 2.95 (*1-56597-097-7*, Kismet) Meteor Pub.

— Yesterday's Fantasy. 224p. (Orig.). 1991. pap. 2.95 (*1-878702-63-7*, Kismet) Meteor Pub.

Macalypse The Younger. Principia Discordia: or How I Found Goddess & What I Did to Her When I Found Her. 1976. lib. bdg. 250.00 (*0-685-75085-X*) Revisionist Pr.

Macan, T. T. A Key to the Adults of the British Trichoptera. 1973. 35.00 (*0-900386-19-3*) St Mut.

— A Key to the British Fresh-& Brackish-Water Gastropods. 4th ed. 1977. 30.00 (*0-900386-30-4*) St Mut.

— A Key to the Nymphs of British Ephemeroptera. 3rd ed. 1979. 50.00 (*0-900386-35-5*) St Mut.

— A Revised Key to the British Water Bugs (Hempitera-Heteroptera) 2nd ed. 1976. 45.00 (*0-900386-07-X*) St Mut.

Macan, T. T., ed. Factors That Regulate the Sizes of Natural Populations in Fresh Water. (Communications of the International Association of Theoretical & Applied Limnology: No. 13). (Illus.). 211p. (Orig.). 1965. pap. text ed. 38.50 (*3-510-52013-0*, Pub. by E Schweizerbartsche GW) Lubrecht & Cramer.

Macan, Thomas T. Freshwater Ecology. 2nd ed. LC 75-300630. (Longman Text Ser.). (Illus.). 351p. reprint ed. pap. 100.10 (*0-8357-6121-5*, 2034507) Bks Demand.

Macandrew, Andrew, tr. see Frank, Joseph & Goldstein, David I., eds.

MacAndrew, Andrew, tr. see MacAndrew, Andrew R.

MacAndrew, Andrew R. Diary of a Madman & Other Stories. MacAndrew, Andrew, tr. 1961. pap. 4.95 (*0-451-52403-9*, CE1824, Sig Classics) NAL-Dutton.

MacAndrew, Andrew R., tr. see De Maupassant, Guy.

MacAndrew, Andrew R., tr. see Dostoyevsky, Fyodor.

MacAndrew, Andrew R., tr. see Gogol, Nikolai V.

MacAndrew, Elizabeth. The Gothic Tradition in Fiction. LC 79-9447. 303p. reprint ed. pap. 86.40 (*0-685-20374-3*, 2029829) Bks Demand.

MacAndrew, Hugh. Old Master Drawings from the National Gallery of Scotland. LC 90-5990. (Illus.). 192p. (Orig.). 1990. pap. 9.99 (*0-89468-151-6*) Natl Gallery Art.

MacAndrew, Marie-Christine, ed. see Zaleski, Eugene.

MacAndrew, Ronald, ed. see Patterson, William R.

MacAndrews, C., jt. auth. see Chia, L. S.

MacAndrews, Colin. Land Policy in Modern Indonesia: A Study of Land Issues in the New Order Period. LC 86-5144. (Lincoln Institute of Land Policy Book Ser.). (Illus.). 127p. reprint ed. pap. 36.20 (*0-7837-5764-6*, 2045427) Bks Demand.

MacAninch, Jack W., jt. auth. see Tanagho, Emil A.

Macann, Christopher E. Four Phenomenological Philosophers: Hesserl, Heidegger, Sartre, Merleau-Ponty. LC 93-16569. 1993. 49.00 (*0-415-07353-7*); pap. 25.00 (*0-415-07354-5*) Routledge.

— Presence & Coincidence: The Transformation of Transcendental into Ontological Phenomenology. 152p. (C). 1991. lib. bdg. 67.50 (*0-7923-0923-5*) Kluwer Ac.

Macann, Christopher E., ed. Martin Heidegger: Critical Assessments, 4 vol. set. LC 91-46751. 1472p. 1993. 600.00 (*0-415-04982-2*, A7593) Routledge.

MacAoidh, Aonghus. Manuscript of Dove, Vol. 1. 186p. 1992. pap. 34.00 (*0-685-62622-9*) A MacRaonuill.

— Manuscript of Dove, Vol. 2. 200p. 1992. pap. 36.00 (*0-685-62623-7*) A MacRaonuill.

— Manuscript of Dove, Vol. 3. 162p. 1992. pap. 30.00 (*0-685-66249-7*) A MacRaonuill.

MacAonghas, Pol. An Guth Aoibhneach. (C). 1989. 39.00 (*0-85411-054-2*, Pub. by Saltire Soc) St Mut.

MacAormick, Neil, jt. ed. see Amselek, Paul.

Macar, Francoise, et al, eds. Time, Action & Cognition Towards Bridging the Gap: Proceedings of the NATO Advanced Research Workshop, Held in St. Malo, France, 22-25 October, 1991. LC 92-10966. (NATO Advanced Study Institutes Series D, Behavioural & Social Sciences: No. 66). 432p. (C). 1992. lib. bdg. 144.00 (*0-7923-1783-1*) Kluwer Ac.

Macaranas, Natividad. Growing up in the Philippines. 1995. 11.95 (*0-8062-5120-4*) Carlton.

Macaraya, Batua A., jt. auth. see McKaughan, Howard P.

MacArdle, Donald W., tr. see Beethoven, Ludwig van.

Macardle, Dorothy. The Unforeseen. reprint ed. lib. bdg. 21.95 (*0-89190-113-2*, Rivercity Pr) Amereon Ltd.

— The Uninvited. adapted ed. 1979. pap. 4.75 (*0-8222-1196-3*) Dramatists Play.

— The Uninvited. 342p. 1976. reprint ed. lib. bdg. 23.95 (*0-89244-068-6*, Queens House) Amereon Ltd.

Macardle, Melanie T. Biotechnology: Index of Modern Information. LC 88-47996. 150p. 1990. 44.50 (*1-55914-230-8*); pap. 39.50 (*1-55914-231-6*) ABBE Pubs Assn.

— Lasers in Medicine, Science & Biology: Research & Reference Guidebook. LC 84-45167. 150p. 1985. 44.50 (*0-88164-168-5*); pap. 39.50 (*0-88164-169-3*) ABBE Pubs Assn.

Macaree, David. Daniel Defoe: His Political Writings & Literary Devices. LC 90-25038. (Studies in British Literature: Vol. 14). 164p. 1991. lib. bdg. 79.95 (*0-88946-590-8*) E Mellen.

Macaree, David, jt. auth. see MacAree, Mary.

MacAree, Mary & Macaree, David. One Hundred Three Hikes in Southwestern British Columbia. 4th ed. (Orig.). 1994. pap. 12.95 (*0-89886-395-3*) Mountaineers.

Macari, Patricia. Interlude of Widowhood. (Greeting Book Line Ser.). 32p. (Orig.). 1983. pap. 1.95 (*0-89622-200-4*) Twenty-Third.

Macario, Alberto J. & De Macario, Everly C., eds. Gene Probes for Bacteria. 515p. 1990. text ed. 128.00 (*0-12-463000-6*) Acad Pr.

— Monoclonal Antibodies Against Bacteria, Vol. 1. (C). 1985. text ed. 93.00 (*0-12-463001-4*) Acad Pr.

— Monoclonal Antibodies Against Bacteria, Vol. 2. 1986. text ed. 93.00 (*0-12-463002-2*) Acad Pr.

— Monoclonal Antibodies Against Bacteria, Vol. 3. 336p. 1986. text ed. 95.00 (*0-12-463003-0*) Acad Pr.

Macario, Raymond. Cellular Radio Principles & Design. 1993. text ed. 40.00 (*0-07-044301-7*) McGraw.

Macario, Raymond C. V., jt. ed. see Balston, D. M.

Macarius. Fifty Spiritual Homilies. 1974. reprint ed. 12.50 (*0-89981-035-7*) Eastern Orthodox.

***Macarius (St.) of Optina.** Spiritual Direction: Letters of Spiritual Advice & Comfort to Lay People Living in the World. large type ed. 1994. pap. 10.00 (*0-89981-307-0*) Eastern Orthodox.

Macarius The Elder Of Egypt. Macarii Anecdota. Marriott, G. L., ed. (Harvard Theological Studies: Vol. 5). 1918. pap. 15.00 (*0-527-01005-7*) Periodicals Srv.

Macaro, E. A. Radio France. 1985. pap. text ed. 9.63 (*0-582-35400-5*, 72218); audio 16.96 (*0-582-37684-X*, 72581) Longman.

Macarov, David. Certain Change. LC 90-27568. 185p. 1991. 21.95 (*0-87101-191-3*) Natl Assn Soc Wkrs.

— Incentives to Work. LC 71-110629. (Jossey-Bass Behavioral Science Ser.). 270p. reprint ed. 77.00 (*0-8357-9326-5*, 2013829) Bks Demand.

— The Structure of Social Welfare. 344p. 1995. text ed. 48.00 (*0-8039-4939-1*); pap. text ed. 24.95 (*0-8039-4940-5*) Sage.

Macarov, David, jt. auth. see Dixon, John.

MacArtain, Aonghus. Manuscript by Aonghus MacArtain. 105p. 1992. pap. 19.00 (*0-685-67869-5*) A MacRaonuill.

***MacArthur.** Vanishing Conscience. 1995. pap. text ed. (*0-8499-3678-0*) Word Inc.

MacArthur, A. Anton Rubinstein. 1971. 35.00 (*0-87968-650-2*) Gordon Pr.

MacArthur, Barbara. Canten Navidad. (Illus.). 15p. (Orig.). (ENG & SPA.). (J). (ps-12). 1993. audio, pap. 12.95 (*1-881120-09-0*) Frog Pr WI.

— Chantez Noel. (Illus.). 14p. (ENG & FRE.). (J). (ps-12). 1993. audio, pap. 12.95 (*1-881120-10-4*) Frog Pr WI.

— Sing, Dance, Laugh & Eat Cheeseburgers. (Illus.). 35p. (Orig.). (J). (ps-12). 1992. audio, pap. 17.95 (*1-881120-06-6*) Frog Pr WI.

— Sing, Dance, Laugh & Eat Quiche. rev. ed. (Illus.). 35p. (FRE.). (J). (ps-12). 1990. reprint ed. audio, pap. 14.95 (*1-881120-00-7*) Frog Pr WI.

— Sing, Dance, Laugh & Eat Quiche 2. (Illus.). 35p. (Orig.). (FRE.). (J). (ps-12). 1989. audio, pap. 14.95 (*1-881120-01-5*) Frog Pr WI.

— Sing, Dance, Laugh, & Eat Quiche 3. (Illus.). 35p. (Orig.). (ENG & FRE.). (J). (ps-12). 1992. audio, pap. 14.95 (*1-881120-07-4*) Frog Pr WI.

— Sing, Dance, Laugh & Eat Tacos. (Illus.). 35p. (Orig.). (ENG & SPA.). (J). (ps-12). 1990. audio, pap. 14.95 (*1-881120-04-X*) Frog Pr WI.

— Sing, Dance, Laugh & Eat Tacos 2. (Illus.). 36p. (Orig.). (ENG & SPA.). (J). (ps-12). 1991. audio, pap. 14.95 (*1-881120-05-8*) Frog Pr WI.

— Sing, Dance, Laugh & Eat Tacos 3. (Illus.). 35p. (SPA.). (J). (ps-12). 1993. audio, pap. 14.95 (*1-881120-13-9*) Frog Pr WI.

— Sing, Dance, Laugh & Learn German. (Illus.). 18p. (Orig.). (ENG & GER.). (J). (ps-8). 1993. audio, pap. 12.95 (*1-881120-11-2*) Frog Pr WI.

— Sing, Dance, Laugh & Learn Spanish. (Illus.). 18p. (Orig.). (ENG & SPA.). (J). (ps-8). 1993. audio, pap. 12.95 (*1-881120-08-2*) Frog Pr WI.

— Singen Weihnachten. (Illus.). 14p. (Orig.). (ENG & GER.). (J). (ps-12). 1993. audio, pap. 12.95 (*1-881120-12-0*) Frog Pr WI.

MacArthur, Blair. The Love Formula: A Unique Way to Evaluate Your Love Partner. 2nd ed. 287p. 1990. 15.95 (*0-944052-00-2*) Cayman Isle Ent.

MacArthur, Brian, ed. The Penguin Book of Twentieth-Century Speeches. 512p. 1994. 12.95 (*0-14-023234-6*, Penguin Bks) Viking Penguin.

MacArthur, Catherine. The Flight of the Dove. large type ed. 341p. 1982. 15.95 (*0-7089-0791-1*) Ulverscroft.

— George's Women. large type ed. 283p. 1980. 12.00 (*0-7089-0451-3*) Ulverscroft.

— It Was the Lark. large type ed. 1979. 12.00 (*0-7089-0370-3*) Ulverscroft.

MacArthur, D. A., jt. ed. see Ho, K. C.

MacArthur, David. Tasting It. (Illus.). 104p. (Orig.). 1984. pap. 9.95 (*0-9612674-0-2*) Wine Country.

MacArthur, Douglas. Reminiscences. (Quality Paperbacks Ser.). (Illus.). 1985. reprint ed. pap. 10.95 (*0-306-80254-6*) Da Capo.

MacArthur, Elizabeth, tr. see Serres, Michael.

MacArthur, Elizabeth J. Extravagant Narratives: Closure & Dynamics in the Epistolary Form. 299p. 1990. text ed. 35.00 (*0-691-06793-7*) Princeton U Pr.

MacArthur, John, Jr. Acts 1-12. (MacArthur New Testament Commentary Ser.). 1994. 19.99 (*0-8024-0759-5*) Moody.

***MacArthur, John.** Alone with God. 192p. 1995. pap. 9.99 (*1-56476-488-5*, 6-3488, Victor Books) SP Pubns.

MacArthur, John, Jr. Anxiety Attacked. LC 93-3721. (MacArthur Study Ser.). (Illus.). 192p. (Orig.). 1993. pap. 9.99 (*1-56476-128-2*, Victor Books) SP Pubns.

— The Believer's Armor. (John MacArthur's Bible Studies). 1986. pap. 6.99 (*0-8024-5092-X*) Moody.

Macarthur, John. Colossians-Philemon. 1992. 17.99 (*0-88469-236-1*) BMH Bks.

MacArthur, John. Different by Design. 192p. (Orig.). 1994. pap. 9.99 (*1-56476-247-5*, Victor Books) SP Pubns.

MacArthur, John, Jr. Faith Works. 276p. 1993. 17.99 (*0-8499-0841-8*) Word Inc.

MacArthur, John. The Family. 1982. pap. 7.99 (*0-8024-2524-0*) Moody.

MacArthur, John, Jr. First Corinthians. 1984. 19.99 (*0-88469-161-6*) BMH Bks.

MacArthur, John. First Love. LC 94-41137. (MacArthur Study Ser.). 208p. (Orig.). 1994. pap. 9.99 (*1-56476-334-X*, Victor Books) SP Pubns.

Macarthur, John, Jr. Found God's Will. 1977. pap. 2.99 (*0-88207-503-9*, Victor Books) SP Pubns.

MacArthur, John, Jr. The Fulfilled Family. (John MacArthur's Bible Studies). 146p. (Orig.). 1981. pap. 5.99 (*0-8024-5318-X*) Moody.

— Galatians. (MacArthur New Testament Commentary Ser.). 1987. 15.99 (*0-8024-0762-5*) Moody.

— God. (MacArthur Study Ser.). (Orig.). 1993. pap. 9.99 (*1-56476-071-5*, Victor Books) SP Pubns.

— God's High Calling for Women. (John MacArthur's Bible Studies). 1987. pap. 4.99 (*0-8024-5308-2*) Moody.

— Heaven: Selected Scriptures. (John MacArthur's Bible Studies). 5.99 (*0-8024-5383-X*) Moody.

MacArthur, John. Hebrews. (MacArthur New Testament Commentary Ser.). (Orig.). 19.99 (*0-8024-0753-6*) Moody.

MacArthur, John, Jr. How to Meet the Enemy. (MacArthur Study Ser.). (Orig.). 1992. pap. 9.99 (*1-56476-016-2*, Victor Books) SP Pubns.

— How to Study the Bible. (John MacArthur's Bible Studies). 1985. pap. 4.99 (*0-8024-5105-5*) Moody.

— Jesus' Pattern of Prayer. LC 81-3947. 200p. (C). 1981. 7.99 (*0-8024-4963-8*) Moody.

MacArthur, John. Keys to Spiritual Growth. rev. ed. LC 91-31245. 192p. 1991. reprint ed. pap. 7.99 (*0-8007-5396-8*) Revell.

MacArthur, John, Jr. Kingdom Living Here & Now. LC 79-25326. (C). 1980. pap. 7.99 (*0-8024-4561-6*) Moody.

MacArthur, John. MacArthur New Testament Commentary: Colossians & Philemon. 1992. 19.99 (*0-8024-0761-7*) Moody.

— MacArthur New Testament Commentary: Romans 9-16. 1994. 19.99 (*0-8024-0768-4*) Moody.

MacArthur, John, Jr. MacArthur New Testament Commentary Series, 9 bks., Set. 174.91 (*0-8024-7587-6*) Moody.

— The Master's Plan for the Church. 1991. pap. 9.99 (*0-8024-7841-7*) Moody.

— Matthew Eight-Fifteen. (MacArthur New Testament Commentary Ser.). 1986. text ed. 19.99 (*0-8024-0763-3*) Moody.

MacArthur, John. Matthew Twenty-Four to Twenty-Eight (MacArthur New Testament Commentary) (MacArthur New Testament Commentary Ser.). 1989. 19.99 (*0-8024-0765-X*) Moody.

MacArthur, John, Jr. Matthew 1-7. (MacArthur New Testament Commentary Ser.). 1985. text ed. 19.99 (*0-8024-0755-2*) Moody.

MacArthur, John. Matthew 16-23. (MacArthur New Testament Commentary Ser.). 1988. 19.99 (*0-8024-0764-1*) Moody.

MacArthur, John, Jr. Matthew 8-15. 1986. 19.99 (*0-88469-172-1*) BMH Bks.

MacArthur, John. Our Sufficiency in Christ. 1993. pap. 10.99 (*0-8499-3519-9*) Word Inc.

***MacArthur, John.** The Power of Suffering: LGI. (MacArthur Ser.: No. 7). 192p. 1995. pap. 8.99 (*1-56476-429-X*, 6-3429, Victor Books) SP Pubns.

MacArthur, John, Jr. Romans One-Eight. (MacArthur New Testament Commentary Ser.). 1991. 19.99 (*0-8024-0767-6*) Moody.

— Saved Without a Doubt. (MacArthur Study Ser.). (Orig.). 1992. pap. 9.99 (*1-56476-017-0*, Victor Books) SP Pubns.

— Signs of Christ's Return. (John MacArthur's Bible Studies). 1987. pap. 6.99 (*0-8024-5311-2*) Moody.

— Spiritual Gifts. (John MacArthur's Bible Studies). 1985. pap. 6.99 (*0-8024-5121-7*) Moody.

MacArthur, John. Spiritual Warfare: Fighting to Win. 75p. 1989. pap. 3.95 (*0-318-42572-6*) Word Grace.

MacArthur, John, Jr. True Worship. (John MacArthur's Bible Studies). 1985. pap. 4.99 (*0-8024-5108-X*) Moody.

— The Ultimate Priority. 1983. pap. 7.99 (*0-8024-0186-4*) Moody.

***MacArthur, John, Jr. & Master's Seminary Faculty.** Rediscovering Pastoral Ministry: Shaping Contemporary Ministry with Biblical Mandates. LC 95-6452. 1995. write for info. (*0-8499-1092-7*) Word Pub.

MacArthur, John, Jr., jt. auth. see Master's Seminary Faculty Staff.

***MacArthur, John, et al.** Justification by Faith Alone. 1995. pap. 12.95 (*1-877611-93-X*) Soli Deo Gloria.

MacArthur, John D. & Weiss, John. Agriculture, Projects & Development: Papers in Honour of David Edwards. 400p. 1994. 68.95 (*1-85628-647-9*, Pub. by Avebury Pub UK) Ashgate Pub Co.

MacArthur, John F., Jr. Ashamed of the Gospel: When the Church Becomes Like the World. LC 93-23849. 1993. 17.99 (*0-89107-729-4*) Crossway Bks.

Macarthur, John F. Charismatic Chaos: Signs & Wonders; Speaking in Tongues; Health, Wealth & Prosperity. 1993. pap. 5.99 (*0-310-57572-9*) Zondervan.

MacArthur, John F., Jr. Charismatic Chaos. rev. ed. Orig. Title: The Charismatics: A Doctrinal Perspective. 272p. 1992. 17.99 (*0-310-57570-2*) Zondervan.

Macarthur, John F. Christmas Celebrations. 1993. text ed. 4.99 (*0-310-96264-1*) Zondervan.

MacArthur, John F. Cuidado con los Falaces! Orig. Title: Beware the Pretenders. 102p. (SPA.). pap. 2.99 (*0-8254-1453-9*) Kregel.

MacArthur, John F., Jr. Drawing Near. LC 93-5469. 384p. 1993. 17.99 (*0-89107-758-8*) Crossway Bks.

— Ephesians. 1986. 18.99 (*0-88469-171-3*) BMH Bks.

— El Evangelio Segun Jesucristo - The Gospel According to Jesus: Que Significa Realmente el "Sigueme" de Cristo Jesus? - What Does Jesus Mean When He Says "Follow Me"? De Bustamante, Rafael C., tr. 256p. (Orig.). (SPA.). 1992. pap. 7.50 (*0-311-09138-5*) Casa Bautista.

— The Gospel According to Jesus: What Does Jesus Mean When He Says "Follow Me" exp. rev. ed. 320p. 1994. 13.99 (*0-310-39491-0*) Zondervan.

— Hebrews. (Orig.). 1983. 19.99 (*0-88469-155-1*) BMH Bks.

— Matthew One-Seven. 1985. 19.99 (*0-88469-168-3*) BMH Bks.

Macarthur, John F. Miracle of Christmas. 1993. text ed. 4.99 (*0-310-96263-3*) Zondervan.

MacArthur, John F., Jr. The Miracle of Christmas: God with Us. 144p. 1993. reprint ed. Printed caseside. 12.99 (*0-310-38580-6*); reprint ed. Two cassettes, 90 min. pap. 12.99 (*0-310-38588-1*) Zondervan.

— Reckless Faith: When the Church Loses It's Will to Discern. LC 94-39874. 256p. 1994. 17.99 (*0-89107-793-6*) Crossway Bks.

MacArthur, John F. Vanishing Conscience: Drawing the Line in a No-Fault, Guilt-Free World. 1994. 17.99 (*0-8499-0842-6*) Word Inc.

***MacArthur, John F. & Coleman, Robert E.** The Glory of Heaven: The Truths about Heaven, Angels & Eternal Life. LC 94-45708. 256p. 1995. 19.99 (*0-89107-849-5*) Crossway Bks.

MacArthur, John R. Second Front: Censorship & Propaganda in the Gulf War. 224p. 1992. 20.00 (*0-8090-8517-8*) Hill & Wang.

— Second Front: Censorship & Propaganda in the Gulf War. LC 93-19604. 1993. reprint ed. 10.00 (*0-520-08398-9*) U CA Pr.

MacArthur, Mairi. Iona. 1991. text ed. 35.00 (*0-7486-0214-3*, Pub. by Edinburgh U Pr UK) Col U Pr.

MacArthur, Mary, jt. auth. see Clark, LaVerne H.

MacArthur, Robert C. Room at the Mark: A History of the Development of Yachts, Yacht Clubs, Yacht Racing & the Racing Rules. (Illus.). 340p. 1990. 40.00 (*0-915953-03-X*) Yacht Owners.

MacArthur, Robert H. Geographical Ecology. LC 83-24477. 269p. 1984. pap. 19.95 (*0-691-02382-4*) Princeton U Pr.

MacArthur, Roger H. & Wilson, Edward O. Theory of Island Biogeography. (Monographs in Population Biology: Vol. 1). (Illus.). 1967. pap. 17.95x (*0-691-08050-X*) Princeton U Pr.

MacArthur, William J., Jr. Knoxville, Crossroads of the New South. LC 82-71491. (Illus.). 192p. 1982. 11.00 (*0-941199-06-1*) ETHS.

Macarthurm, John F. Introduction to Biblical Counseling. 1994. 24.99 (*0-8499-1093-5*) Word Inc.

Macartney, Carlile A. The Magyars in the Ninth Century. 1978. lib. bdg. 59.95 (*0-8490-2198-7*) Gordon Pr.

— The Magyars in the Ninth Century. LC 31-19298. 253p. reprint ed. pap. 72.20 (*0-317-20592-7*, 2024496) Bks Demand.

— The Medieval Hungarian Historians: A Critical & Analytical Guide. LC 53-7690. 206p. reprint ed. pap. 58.80 (*0-317-09533-1*, 2050792) Bks Demand.

Macartney, Clarence E. Chariots of Fire. 192p. 1994. pap. 9.99 (*0-8254-3274-X*) Kregel.

— Faith Once Delivered. 144p. 1995. pap. 9.99 (*0-8254-3281-2*) Kregel.

— Grant & His Generals. LC 75-142660. (Essay Index Reprint Ser.). 1977. 23.95 (*0-8369-2171-2*) Ayer.

— Great Women of the Bible. LC 91-21648. 208p. (Orig.). 1992. pap. 9.99 (*0-8254-3268-5*) Kregel.

— The Greatest Questions of the Bible & Life. LC 93-36683. 160p. 1995. pap. 9.99 (*0-8254-3273-1*) Kregel.

— The Greatest Texts of the Bible. LC 92-16136. 160p. 1992. reprint ed. pap. 9.99 (*0-8254-3266-9*) Kregel.

— The Greatest Words of the Bible & in Human Speech. LC 93-36682. 140p. 1995. pap. 9.99 (*0-8254-3271-5*) Kregel.

— He Chose Twelve. LC 92-23989. 160p. 1993. 9.99 (*0-8254-3270-7*) Kregel.

— Lincoln & His Generals. LC 70-124241. (Select Bibliographies Reprint Ser.). (Illus.). 1977. reprint ed. 18.95 (*0-8369-5429-7*) Ayer.

— The Parables of the Old Testament. 160p. 1995. pap. 9.99 (*0-8254-3278-2*) Kregel.

— Parallel Lives of the Old & New Testaments. LC 95-8799. 128p. 1995. pap. 9.99 (*0-8254-3280-4*) Kregel.

— Paul the Man: His Life & His Ministry. LC 92-16135. 176p. 1992. reprint ed. pap. 9.99 (*0-8254-3269-3*) Kregel.

— Six Kings of the American Pulpit. LC 75-152192. (Essay Index Reprint Ser.). 1977. reprint ed. 18.95 (*0-8369-2323-5*) Ayer.

— Strange Texts but Grand Truths. 192p. 1994. pap. 9.99 (*0-8254-3272-3*) Kregel.

— Twelve Great Questions about Christ. LC 92-23990. 160p. 1993. pap. 9.99 (*0-8254-3267-7*) Kregel.

Macartney, Clarence E., ed. Men Who Missed It. LC 76-128274. (Essay Index Reprint Ser.). 1977. 18.95 (*0-8369-1835-5*) Ayer.

Macartney, F. J., ed. Congenital Heart Disease. (Current Status of Clinical Cardiology Ser.). 1985. lib. bdg. 103.50 (*0-85200-719-1*) Kluwer Ac.

Macartney, John D., jt. auth. see Kozak, David C.

Macartney, W. J. Self-Determination in the Commonwealth. 128p. 1988. pap. text ed. 25.90 (*0-08-034525-5*, Pergamon Pr) Elsevier.

Macarulla, D. Diccionario Lexicon Ingles-Espanol, Espanol-Ingles. 384p. (ENG & SPA.). 1974. pap. 13.95 (*0-8288-5996-5*, S31391) Fr & Eur.

Macary, Leonce, jt. auth. see Crispin, M. Jackson.

Macasek, Fedor & Navratil, James D. Separation Chemistry. 500p. 1993. text ed. 91.00 (*0-13-807660-X*) P-H.

Macaskill, C. Against the Odds: Adopting Mentally Handicapped Children. (C). 1989. 60.00 (*0-903534-58-4*, Pub. by Brit Ag for Adopt & Fost UK) St Mut.

Macaskill, Catherine. Adopting or Fostering a Sexually Abused Child. 176p. 1992. pap. 34.95 (*0-7134-6760-6*, Pub. by Batsford UK) Trafalgar.

Macat, Andreas. Die Bergische Presse: Bibliographie und Standortnachweis der Zeitungen und Zeitungs-Ahnlichen Periodika Seit, 1769, Vol. 49. (Dortmunder Beitraige Zur Zeitungsforschung Ser.). 251p. (GER.). 1991. lib. bdg. 32.00 (*3-598-21310-7*) K G Saur.

Macaulay, Ambrose. William Crolly, Archbishop of Amargh 1835-49. 256p. 1994. 39.50 (*1-85182-147-3*, Pub. by Four Cts Pr IE) Intl Spec Bk.

***Macaulay, Catherine.** Letters on Education. LC 94-25055. 1995. 95.00 (*1-85477-184-1*, Mansell Pub) Cassell.

Macaulay, Craig. Dix Hommes et une Echelle. (J). (ps-3). 1993. pap. 5.95 (*1-55037-342-0*, Pub. by Annick CN) Firefly Bks Ltd.

Macaulay, David. BAAA. LC 85-2316. (Illus.). 64p. (J). (gr. 6 up). 1985. 13.95 (*0-395-38948-8*); pap. 4.95 (*0-395-39588-7*) HM.

— Black & White. (Illus.). 32p. (J). 1990. 14.95 (*0-395-52151-3*) HM.

— Castle. LC 77-7159. (Illus.). 80p. (J). (gr. 1 up). 1977. 16.95 (*0-395-25784-0*) HM.

— Castle. LC 77-7159. (Illus.). 80p. (J). (gr. 1 up). 1982. pap. 7.95 (*0-395-32920-5*) HM.

— Cathedral. (Illus.). (J). (gr. k up). 1981. pap. 7.95 (*0-395-31668-5*) HM.

— Cathedral: The Story of Its Construction. LC 73-6634. (Illus.). 80p. (J). (gr. 1-5). 1973. 16.95 (*0-395-17513-5*) HM.

— City: A Story of Roman Planning & Construction. (Illus.). 112p. (J). (gr. 6 up). 1974. 16.95 (*0-395-19492-X*) HM.

— City: A Story of Roman Planning & Construction. (Illus.). 112p. (J). (gr. 6 up). 1983. pap. 7.95 (*0-395-34922-2*) HM.

— Great Moments in Architecture. (Illus.). 128p. 1978. 22.95 (*0-395-25500-7*); pap. 11.95 (*0-395-26711-0*) HM.

— Mill. (Illus.). 128p. (J). (gr. 6 up). 1983. 16.95 (*0-395-34830-7*) HM.

— Mill. 128p. (J). (ps up). 1989. pap. 7.95 (*0-395-52019-3*, Sandpiper) HM.

— The Motel of the Mysteries. 1979. pap. 9.95 (*0-395-28425-2*) HM.

— Pyramid. (Illus.). 80p. (J). (gr. 7 up). 1975. 16.95 (*0-395-21407-6*) HM.

— Pyramid PA. (Illus.). (J). (gr. 5 up). 1982. pap. 7.95 (*0-395-32121-2*) HM.

— Ship. (J). (gr. 4-7). 1993. 19.95 (*0-395-52439-3*) HM.

— Short Cut. LC 95-2542. 1995. 15.95 (*0-395-52436-9*) HM.

— Unbuilding. (Illus.). (J). (gr. 3 up). 1980. 16.95 (*0-395-29457-6*) HM.

— Unbuilding. (J). (gr. k-3). 1987. pap. 7.95 (*0-395-45425-5*) HM.

— Unbuilding. LC 80-15491. (Sandpipers Ser.). (Illus.). 128p. (J). (gr. 5 up). 1987. pap. 6.95 (*0-395-45360-7*) HM.

— Underground. (Illus.). (J). (gr. 1 up). 1976. 16.95 (*0-395-24739-X*) HM.

— Underground. (Illus.). (J). (gr. 1 up). 1983. pap. 8.95 (*0-395-34065-9*) HM.

— The Way Things Work. (Illus.). 400p. (J). (ps up). 1988. 29.95 (*0-395-42857-2*) HM.

— Why the Chicken Crossed the Road. (Illus.). 32p. (J). (gr. 4-6). 1987. 13.95 (*0-395-44241-9*, Clarion Bks) HM.

— Why the Chicken Crossed the Road. (J). 1991. pap. 4.95 (*0-395-58411-6*) HM.

MacAulay, Donald, ed. The Celtic Languages. (Language Surveys Ser.). (Illus.). 415p. (C). 1993. 99.95 (*0-521-23127-2*) Cambridge U Pr.

MacAulay, Donald, et al, eds. Modern Scottish Gaelic Poems-Nua-Bhardach Ghaidhlig. LC 76-21270. 1977. 16.00 (*0-8112-0631-9*) New Directions.

Macaulay, E. J. The Soul of Cambria. rev. ed. LC 88-71795. (Illus.). 128p. 1989. reprint ed. pap. 6.00 (*0-934666-28-8*) Artisan Sales.

Macaulay, F. S. The Algebraic Theory of Modular Systems. (Mathematical Library). 144p. (C). 1994. pap. 19.95 (*0-521-45562-6*) Cambridge U Pr.

Macaulay, Frederick R. The Smoothing of Time Series. (General Ser.: No. 19). 172p. 1931. reprint ed. 44.80 (*0-87014-018-3*); reprint ed. mic. film 22.40 (*0-685-61151-5*) Natl Bur Econ Res.

— Some Theoretical Problems Suggested by the Movements of Interest Rates, Bond Yields & Stock Prices in the United States Since 1856. Bruchey, Stuart, ed. LC 80-1161. (Rise of Commercial Banking Ser.). (Illus.). 1981. reprint ed. lib. bdg. 33.95 (*0-405-13668-4*) Ayer.

— Some Theoretical Problems Suggested by the Movements of Interest Rates, Bond Yields & Stock Prices in the United States since 1856. (General Ser.: No. 33). 625p. 1938. reprint ed. 160.00 (*0-87014-032-9*) Natl Bur Econ Res.

Macaulay, G. C., ed. see Gower, John.

Macaulay, H. M., jt. auth. see Llewelyn-Davies, R.

Macaulay, Hugh H. Fringe Benefits & Their Federal Tax Treatment. LC 79-18950. (Columbia University. Studies in the Social Sciences: No. 600). reprint ed. 12.50 (*0-404-51600-9*) AMS Pr.

Macaulay, James. Glasgow School of Art, Glasgow 1897-1909: Charles Mackintosh. 1993. pap. 29.99 (*0-7148-2778-9*, Pub. by Phaidon Press UK) Chronicle Bks.

— Hill House: Helensburgh 1903 Charles Rennie MacKintosh. (Illus.). 60p. (C). 1994. pap. 29.95 (*0-7148-2780-0*, Pub. by Phaidon Press UK) Chronicle Bks.

Macaulay, Kenneth. Colony of Sierra Leone Vindicated from the Misrepresentations of Mr. MacQueen of Glasgow. 127p. 1968. reprint ed. 35.00 (*0-7146-1831-4*, Pub. by F Cass Pubs UK) Intl Spec Bk.

Macaulay, Linda, jt. ed. see Sutcliffe, Alistair G.

Macaulay, M. A. Introduction to Impact Engineering. 300p. 1987. 39.95 (*0-412-28930-X*, 1126) Chapman & Hall.

Macaulay, Neill. Dom Pedro: The Struggle for Liberty in Brazil & Portugal, 1798-1834. LC 86-16711. xiv, 362p. 1986. 41.95 (*0-8223-0681-6*) Duke.

— A Rebel in Cuba: An American's Memoir. 199p. 1991. 19.95 (*1-879915-00-6*); pap. 11.95 (*1-879915-01-4*) Affil Writers America.

— The Sandino Affair. LC 85-20430. (Illus.). 320p. 1985. reprint ed. pap. 16.95 (*0-8223-0696-4*) Duke.

Macaulay, Neill, jt. auth. see Bushnell, David.

***Macaulay, Peter.** Understanding ISDN. 400p. 1995. 29.99 (*0-614-04234-8*); 29.99 (*0-614-04235-6*) Sams.

Macaulay, R. S. Language, Social Class, & Education. 179p. 1978. 15.00 (*0-85224-320-0*, Pub. by Edinburgh U Pr UK) Col U Pr.

Macaulay, Richard, jt. auth. see Wald, Jerry.

Macaulay, Ronald K. Locating Dialect in Discourse: The Language of Honest Men & Bonnie Lassies in Ayr. (Oxford Studies in Sociolinguistics). 320p. 1991. 49.95 (*0-19-506559-X*) OUP.

Macaulay, Rose. Crewe Train. 319p. 1986. pap. 8.95 (*0-88184-201-X*) Carroll & Graf.

— Dangerous Ages. 270p. 1986. pap. 8.95 (*0-88184-226-5*) Carroll & Graf.

— Keeping Up Appearances. 256p. 1986. pap. 8.95 (*0-88184-290-7*) Carroll & Graf.

— Milton. LC 74-7050. (Studies in Milton: No. 22). 1974. lib. bdg. 75.00 (*0-8383-1911-4*) M S G Haskell Hse.

— Orphan Island. 1971. reprint ed. 39.00 (*0-403-01081-0*) Scholarly.

— Personal Pleasures. LC 79-152193. (Essay Index Reprint Ser.). 1977. 23.95 (*0-8369-2195-X*) Ayer.

— Personal Pleasures. 395p. 1990. reprint ed. pap. 9.95 (*0-88001-265-X*) Ecco Pr.

— The Shadow Flies. LC 70-145153. (Literature Ser.). 484p. 1972. reprint ed. 59.00 (*0-403-01082-9*) Scholarly.

MacAulay, Rose. Some Religious Elements in English Literature. (BCL1-PR English Literature Ser.). 160p. 1992. reprint ed. lib. bdg. 69.00 (*0-7812-7027-8*) Rprt Serv.

Macaulay, Rose. Some Religious Elements in English Literature. LC 72-158506. 160p. 1972. reprint ed. 13.00 (*0-403-01305-4*) Scholarly.

— Staying with Relations. 320p. 1987. pap. 9.50 (*0-88001-148-3*) Ecco Pr.

— The Towers of Trebizond. 277p. 1989. pap. 10.95 (*0-88184-454-3*) Carroll & Graf.

— The Towers of Trebizond. braille ed. 427p. 1991. vinyl bd. 34.16 (*1-56956-429-9*, BR8497) W A T Braille.

— The World My Wilderness. (Modern Classic Ser.). 254p. 1993. pap. 10.95 (*0-86068-340-0*, Pub. by Virago Pr UK) Trafalgar.

Macaulay, Stewart. Law & the Balance of Power: The Automobile Manufacturers & Their Dealers. LC 66-26503. 224p. 1966. 29.95 (*0-87154-574-8*) Russell Sage.

Macaulay, Susan S. For the Children's Sake: Foundations of Education for Home & School. LC 83-72043. 192p. 1984. pap. 8.99 (*0-89107-290-X*) Crossway Bks.

— How to Be Your Own Selfish Pig. LC 81-70769. (Illus.). (YA). 1982. pap. 9.99 (*0-89191-530-3*, Chariot Bks) Chariot Family.

Macaulay, Thomas. The History of England. Trevor-Roper, Hugh, ed. (English Library). 1979. pap. 10.95 (*0-14-043133-0*, Penguin Classics) Viking Penguin.

Macaulay, Thomas B. Essay on Frederic the Great. LC 73-137257. reprint ed. 14.00 (*0-404-04100-0*) AMS Pr.

— History of England from the Accession of James Second, 6 Vols, 1. Firth, C. H., ed. LC 14-14308. reprint ed. write for info. (*0-404-04111-6*) AMS Pr.

— History of England from the Accession of James Second, 6 Vols, 2. Firth, C. H., ed. LC 14-14308. reprint ed. write for info. (*0-404-04112-4*) AMS Pr.

— History of England from the Accession of James Second, 6 Vols, 3. Firth, C. H., ed. LC 14-14308. reprint ed. write for info. (*0-404-04113-2*) AMS Pr.

— History of England from the Accession of James Second, 6 Vols, 4. Firth, C. H., ed. LC 14-14308. reprint ed. write for info. (*0-404-04114-0*) AMS Pr.

— History of England from the Accession of James Second, 6 Vols, 5. Firth, C. H., ed. LC 14-14308. reprint ed. write for info. (*0-404-04115-9*) AMS Pr.

— History of England from the Accession of James Second, 6 Vols, 6. Firth, C. H., ed. LC 14-14308. reprint ed. write for info. (*0-404-04116-7*) AMS Pr.

— History of England from the Accession of James Second, 6 Vols, Set. Firth, C. H., ed. LC 14-14308. reprint ed. 425.00 (*0-404-04110-8*) AMS Pr.

— Milton. (BCL1-PR English Literature Ser.). 155p. 1992. reprint ed. lib. bdg. 69.00 (*0-7812-7386-2*) Rprt Serv.

— Napoleon & the Restoration of the Bourbons: The Complete Portion of Macaulay's Projected History of France from the Restoration of the Bourbons to the Accession of Louis Phillipe. LC 77-7107. 117p. 1977. text ed. 35.50 (*0-231-04376-7*) Col U Pr.

— Selected Letters. Pinney, Thomas, ed. LC 81-10016. 350p. 1983. 69.95 (*0-521-24009-3*) Cambridge U Pr.

— Speeches by Lord Macaulay, with His Minute on Indian Education. Young, G. M., ed. LC 76-29441. 1935. 28.00 (*0-404-15348-8*) AMS Pr.

— The Works of Lord Macaulay Complete: The Albany Edition, 12 vols., Set. LC 76-42708. reprint ed. 540.00 (*0-404-59480-8*) AMS Pr.

Macaulay, Tom. How to Hit Four Hundred: The Physical & Mental Fundamentals of Hitting a Baseball. rev. ed. LC 85-73344. (Illus.). 91p. 1987. pap. 7.95 (*0-935781-10-2*) Double Eagle.

Macaulay, Vincent A., jt. ed. see Buck, Brian.

Macauley, Ed, jt. auth. see Friedl, Francis.

Macauley, Molly K., et al. Using Economic Incentives to Regulate Toxic Substances. 140p. 1992. lib. bdg. 24.95 (*0-915707-65-9*) Resources Future.

***Macauley, Peter.** Implementing ISDN. (Illus.). 400p. (Orig.). 1995. pap. 35.00 (*0-672-30747-2*) Sams.

Macauley, Robie & Betcher, William. The Seven Basic Quarrels of Marriage: Recognize, Defuse, Negotiate, & Resolve Your Conflicts. 1993. mass mkt. 4.99 (*0-345-37649-8*) Ballantine.

Macauley, Robie & Lanning, George. Technique in Fiction. 288p. 1990. pap. 10.95 (*0-312-05168-9*) St Martin.

Macauley, Ronald K. The Social Art: Language & Its Uses. (Illus.). 256p. 1994. 25.00 (*0-19-508382-2*) OUP.

Macauliff, Dan, ed. Effective Technical Communications. 2nd ed. 1989. 11.50 (*0-536-57614-9*) Ginn Pr.

Macauliffe, M. A. The Sikhs: Their Religion, Gurus, Sacred Writings & Authors, 6 vols., Set. (C). 1988. 500.00 (*0-7855-0054-5*, Pub. by Print Hse II) St Mut.

MacAuliffe, Max A. The Sikh Religion, 6 vols. in 3. 1963. text ed. 125.00 (*0-685-13749-X*) Coronet Bks.

— The Sikh Religion: Its Gurus Sacred Writings & Authors, 3 vols., Set. 1990. reprint ed. 62.50 (*81-85395-94-2*, Pub. by Low Price II) S Asia.

MacAuslan, Janna, comp. A Catalog of Compositions for Guitar by Women Composers. LC 84-72460. 47p. (Orig.). 1984. pap. text ed. 5.00 (*0-9614170-0-5*) Dearhorse Pubns.

An Asterisk (*) at the beginning of an entry indicates that the title is appearing in BIP for the first time.

***MacAvery, Tristan A.** Divine Intervention, Set, 4 vols. 156p. (Orig.). 1993. 6.95 (1-883688-04-3) Starwolf Pr.
— Divine Intervention: Dies Irae, Pt. 4. 45p. (Orig.). 1993. 3.00 (1-883688-03-5) Starwolf Pr.
— Divine Intervention: Invocation, Pt. 1. 24p. (Orig.). 1993. 1.00 (1-883688-00-0) Starwolf Pr.
— Divine Intervention: Liturgy, Pt. 3. 50p. (Orig.). 1993. 3.00 (1-883688-02-7) Starwolf Pr.
— Divine Intervention: Procession, Pt. 2. 37p. (Orig.). 1993. 3.00 (1-883688-01-9) Starwolf Pr.
— Tristan's Two Cents (Plain) 128p. (Orig.). 1992. 3.95 (1-883688-05-1) Starwolf Pr.
Macavoy, Elizabeth. Marilyn Syndrome: Breaking Your Love Addiction Before It Breaks You. 1992. pap. 5.50 (1-56171-160-8) Sure Sellers.
Macavoy, Elizabeth & Israelson, Susan. Lovesick: The Marilyn Syndrome. LC 90-55017. 1991. 18.95 (1-55611-220-3) D I Fine.
MacAvoy, Paul W. Energy Policy: An Economic Analysis. (Illus.). (C). 1983. pap. text ed. 4.95 (0-393-95321-1) Norton.
— Industry Regulation & the Performance of the American Economy. (Orig.). (C). 1992. pap. text ed. 8.95 (0-393-96186-9) Norton.
— Industry Regulation & the Performance of the American Economy. 192p. (Orig.). 1992. 24.95 (0-393-03354-6) Norton.
— Price Formation in Natural Gas Fields. LC 76-43984. (Yale Studies in Economics: No. 14). (Illus.). 281p. 1977. reprint ed. text ed. 49.50 (0-8371-8981-0, MAPF, Greenwood Pr) Greenwood.
— Regulated Industries. (C). 1979. pap. text ed. 4.95 (0-393-95094-8) Norton.
MacAvoy, Paul W., jt. auth. see Carron, Andrew S.
MacAvoy, R. A. The Belly of the Wolf. LC 93-22924. 1994. 20.00 (0-688-09601-8) Morrow.
— King of the Dead, Bk. II: Lens of the World Trilogy. 288p. 1992. mass mkt. 4.50 (0-380-71017-X, AvoNova) Avon.
— Lens of the World. 288p. 1991. reprint ed. mass mkt. 4.99 (0-380-71016-1) Avon.
— Lens of the World Bk. 3: The Belly of the Wolf. 224p. 1995. mass mkt. 4.99 (0-380-71018-8, AvoNova) Avon.
MacBain, A. Etymological Dictionary of the Gaelic Language. 1991. lib. bdg. 45.00 (0-8288-3342-7, M12095) Fr & Eur.
MacBain, Alexander, ed. see Cameron, Alexander.
MacBain, William. De Sainte Katerine: An Anonymous Picard Version of the Life of St. Catherine of Alexandria. 232p. (C). 1987. text ed. 47.50 (0-8026-0010-7, G Mason Univ Pr) Univ Pub Assocs.
MacBean, Alasdair I. Export Instabilty & Economic Development. LC 67-1818. (Center for International Affairs Ser.). 367p. 1966. 34.50 (0-674-28600-6) HUP.
MacBean, Alasdair I. & Balasubramanyam, V. N. Meeting the Third World Challenge. LC 76-16702. (World Economic Issues Ser.). 1976. text ed. 29.95 (0-312-52850-7) St Martin.
MacBean, Alasdair I. & Nguyen, D. T. Commodity Policies: Problems & Prospects. 464p. 1987. lib. bdg. 95.00 (0-7099-1708-2, Pub. by Croom Helm UK) Routledge Chapman & Hall.
MacBean, Alasdair I. & Snowden, N. International Institutions in Trade & Finance. (Studies in Economics: No. 18). (Illus.). 272p. (C). 1981. pap. text ed. 18.95 (0-04-382033-6) Routledge Chapman & Hall.
Macbean, James R. Film & Revolution. LC 75-1936. 347p. reprint ed. pap. 98.90 (0-317-27834-7, 2056045) Bks Demand.
Macbeath, Alexander. Experiments in Living: A Study of the Nature & Foundation of Ethics or Morals in the Light of Recent Work in Social Anthropology. LC 77-27180. (Gifford Lectures: 1948-49). reprint ed. 28.00 (0-404-60503-6) AMS Pr.
MacBeath, John. Home from School: Its Current Relevance. (C). 1989. 30.00 (1-85098-225-2, Pub. by Jordanhill College UK) St Mut.
— Home from School: Speaking As a Parent. (C). 1989. lib. bdg. 60.00 (1-85098-233-3, Pub. by Jordanhill College UK) St Mut.
MacBeath, John, jt. auth. see Hough, Mike.
MacBeath, John, et al, eds. Home from School. (C). 1989. 180.00 (1-85098-107-8, Pub. by Jordanhill College UK) St Mut.
MacBeath, Murray. The Philosophy of Time. Le Poidevin, Robin, ed. LC 92-26125. (Readings in Philosophy Ser.). (Illus.). 240p. 1993. pap. 16.95 (0-19-823999-8) OUP.
MacBeth, A. & Ramsey, S. Emergency Reporting Requirements for Environmental Spills & Releases. 1989. ring bd. write for info. (0-13-834698-4) P-H.
Macbeth, Angus, et al. Reporting Requirements for Environmental Releases, 2 vols. 1264p. 1992. ring bd. 185.00 (0-13-010083-8) Aspen Law.
MacBeth, D. K. Advanced Manufacturing Strategy & Management. 180p. 1989. 79.00 (0-387-51113-X) Spr-Verlag.
MacBeth, D. K. & Southern, G., eds. Operations Management in Advanced Manufacture & Services. 300p. 1989. 99.00 (0-387-51009-5) Spr-Verlag.
Macbeth, Douglas K., et al. Partnership Sourcing: An Integrated Supply Chain Approach. (Financial Times Management Ser.). 240p. 1993. 135.00x (0-273-60208-X, Pub. by Pitman Pub Ltd UK) Trans-Atl Phila.
Macbeth, Fiona & Fine, Nic. Playing with Fire: Creative Conflict Resolution for Young Adults. (Illus.). 192p. 1995. pap. 19.95 (0-86571-306-5) New Soc Pubs.
— Playing with Fire: Creative Conflict Resolution for Young Adults. (Illus.). 192p. 1995. lib. bdg. 49.95 (0-86571-305-7) New Soc Pubs.
MacBeth, George, ed. The Penguin Book of Victorian Verse. 448p. 1986. pap. 10.95 (0-14-042110-6, Penguin Classics) Viking Penguin.
MacBeth, George & Booth, Martin, eds. The Book of Cats. (Illus.). 360p. 1992. reprint ed. pap. 19.95 (1-85224-163-2, Pub. by Bloodaxe Bks UK) Dufour.
Macbeth, Jessica. Centering: Finding the Place of Inner Power. 63p. 1995. audio 10.95 (0-946551-38-3, Pub. by Gateway Bks UK) Atrium Pubs.
— Letting Go: Breathing into Deep Peace. 93p. 1995. audio 12.95 (0-946551-72-3, Pub. by Gateway Bks UK) Atrium Pubs.
— Sun over Mountain: Using the Creative Imagination for Growth & Healing. (Illus.). 192p. (Orig.). 1995. pap. 13.95 (0-946551-67-7, Pub. by Gateway Bks UK) Atrium Pubs.
Macbeth, Norman. Darwin Retried: An Appeal to Reason. LC 73-160418. 1979. reprint ed. pap. 8.95 (0-87645-105-9) Gambit Inc Pubs.
— Darwinism: A Time for Funerals. (Broadside Editions Ser.). 32p. (C). 1985. reprint ed. pap. 2.95 (0-9609850-8-5) Rob Briggs.
Macbeth, Norman, tr. see Steiner, Rudolf.
***Macblis, Joseph & Forney, Kristine.** The Norton Recordings to Accompany the Norton Scores & the Enjoyment of Music: Standard. 7th ed. (Illus.). (C). 1995. pap. text ed. 45.95 (0-393-96683-6) Norton.
MacBrayne, jt. auth. see Picton Publishing Staff.
MacBrayne, Edna. Alida: An Erotic Novel. LC 81-80486. 180p. (Orig.). 1981. pap. 9.00 (0-939500-00-0) Parkhurst.
MacBrayne, Lewis & Ramsey, James P. One More Chance: An Experiment with Human Salvage. LC 73-156023. reprint ed. 24.00 (0-404-09124-5) AMS Pr.
Macbride, A. S. Speculative Masonry Its Mission, Its Evolution & Its Landmarks. 254p. 1986. reprint ed. pap. text ed. 7.50 (0-88053-040-5, M-89) Macoy Pub.
MacBride, Dexter, ed. Opportunities in Appraising-Valuation Sciences. (Illus.). 160p. 1980. 13.95 (0-8442-6659-0, VGM Career Bks); pap. 10.95 (0-8442-6660-4, VGM Career Bks) NTC Pub Grp.
MacBride, Dexter D. Power & Process, a Commentary on Eminent Domain & Condemnation. LC 70-77921. (ASA Monograph Ser.: No. 1). 1969. 5.00 (0-937828-10-6) Am Soc Appraisers.
MacBride, J. D. Handbook of Practical Shipbuilding. 1973. lib. bdg. 75.00 (0-8490-1932-X) Gordon Pr.
***MacBride, Maud G.** The Autobiography of Maud Gonne: A Servant of the Queen. rev. ed. Jeffares, A. Norman & White, Anna M., eds. LC 94-39713. 1995. lib. bdg. 32.00 (0-226-30251-2); pap. 14.95 (0-226-30252-0) U Ch Pr.
MacBride, Robert. Timesharing: What's in It for You. LC 76-10858. 26p. reprint ed. pap. 25.00 (0-317-08635-9, 2004617) Bks Demand.
***MacBride, Roger L.** In the Land of the Big Red Apple. LC 94-33646. (Illus.). 352p. (J). (gr. 3-7). 1995. 14.95 (0-06-024963-3); lib. bdg. 14.89 (0-06-024964-1) HarpC.
— Little Farm in the Ozarks. (Illus.). 256p. (J). (gr. 3-7). 1994. 14.95 (0-06-024245-0); lib. bdg. 14.89 (0-06-024246-9) HarpC Child Bks.
— Little Farm in the Ozarks. (Illus.). 256p. (J). (ps-2). 1994. pap. 3.95 (0-06-440510-9, Trophy) HarpC Child Bks.
— Little House on Rocky Ridge. LC 92-39132. (Illus.). 368p. (J). (gr. 3-7). 1993. 14.95 (0-06-020842-2); lib. bdg. 14.89 (0-06-020843-0); pap. 3.95 (0-06-440478-1, Trophy) HarpC Child Bks.
Macbride, Roger L. A New Dawn for America: The Libertarian Challenge. LC 76-174402. 111p. 1976. 5.95 (0-916054-03-9) Green Hill.
***MacBride, Roger L.** On the Other Side of the Hill. LC 95-14263. (Illus.). 256p. (J). (gr. 3-7). 1995. 14.95 (0-06-024967-6); lib. bdg. 14.89 (0-06-024968-4) HarpC Child Bks.
MacBride, Roger L., ed. see Wilder, Laura I.
MacBride, Sean, ed. Israel in Lebanon. 282p. 1983. pap. 19.00 (0-903729-96-2, Pub. by Ithaca UK) Evergreen Dist.
Maccabe, Arthur B. Computer Systems: Architecture, Organization, Programming. LC 92-27699. 792p. (C). 1993. text ed. 65.95 (0-256-11456-0) Irwin.
MacCabe, Colin. Tracking the Signifier: Theoretical Essays on Film, Linguistics, & Literature. LC 85-51114. 160p. 1985. text ed. 29.95 (0-8166-1460-1); pap. text ed. 13.95 (0-8166-1462-8) U of Minn Pr.
MacCabe, Colin, ed. High Theory-Low Culture: Analysing Popular Television & Films. LC 86-14261. 180p. 1986. pap. 11.95 (0-312-37230-2) St Martin.
— The Talking Cure: Essays in Psychoanalysis & Language. LC 79-28551. 243p. 1986. pap. 12.95 (0-312-78475-9) St Martin.
MacCabe, Colin, jt. auth. see Julien, Isaac.
***MacCabe, S. L., ed.** Seismic Engineering 1994: Proceedings of the Pressure Vessels & Piping Conference, 2 vol. LC 88-71134. (PVP Ser.: Vol. 275-1,275-2). 382p. 1994. pap. 115.00 (0-7918-1198-0) ASME.
Maccabee, Bruce, jt. auth. see Haines, Richard F.
***Maccabee, Paul.** John Dillinger Slept Here: A Crooks' Tour of Crime & Corruption in St. Paul, 1920-1936. LC 95-5236. 1995. 45.00 (0-87351-315-0); pap. 27.50 (0-87351-316-9) Minn Hist.
MacCaffrey, I., ed. see Milton, John.
MacCaffrey, Isabel G. Paradise Lost As "Myth" LC 59-9282. 229p. reprint ed. pap. 68.20 (0-7837-4169-3, 2059018) Bks Demand.
— Spenser's Allegory: The Anatomy of Imagination. LC 75-30197. 457p. reprint ed. pap. 130.30 (0-8357-3548-6, 2034296) Bks Demand.
MacCaffrey, James. History of the Catholic Church: From the Renaissance to the French Revolution, Vol. I. LC 75-130558. 419p. reprint ed. lib. bdg. 25.50 (0-8290-0463-7) Irvington.
— History of the Catholic Church: From the Renaissance to the French Revolution, Vol. II. LC 75-130558. 470p. reprint ed. lib. bdg. 25.50 (0-8290-0464-5) Irvington.
— History of the Catholic Church from the Renassaince to the French Revolution, 2 vols, 1. LC 75-130558. (Select Bibliographies Reprint Ser.). 1977. reprint ed. 29.95 (0-8369-9984-3) Ayer.
— History of the Catholic Church from the Renassaince to the French Revolution, 2 vols, 2. LC 75-130558. (Select Bibliographies Reprint Ser.). 1977. reprint ed. 29.95 (0-8369-9985-1) Ayer.
— History of the Catholic Church from the Renassaince to the French Revolution, 2 vols, Set. LC 75-130558. (Select Bibliographies Reprint Ser.). 1977. reprint ed. 58.95 (0-8369-5531-5) Ayer.
***MacCaffrey, Wallace.** Elizabeth I. 1994. pap. 19.95 (0-340-61455-2, B4719, Pub. by E Arnold UK) Routledge Chapman & Hall.
— Shaping of the Elizabethan Regime. 1994. pap. 18.95 (0-691-00767-5, 250) Princeton U Pr.
— Shaping of the Elizabethan Regime. LC 68-27409. 517p. reprint ed. pap. 147.40 (0-8357-9513-6, 2014636) Bks Demand.
MacCaffrey, Wallace T. Elizabeth I: War & Politics, 1588-1603. (Illus.). 552p. 1992. text ed. 75.00 (0-691-03188-6) Princeton U Pr.
— Elizabeth I & Religion. LC 93-3568. (Illus.). 512p. 1993. 35.00 (0-340-56167-X, B2317, Pub. by E Arnold UK); pap. 9.95 (0-415-07352-9, B2460, Pub. by E Arnold UK) Routledge Chapman & Hall.
— Elizabeth the First: War & Politics, 1588-1603. (C). 1994. pap. 18.95 (0-691-03651-9) Princeton U Pr.
— Exeter, Fifteen Forty to Sixteen Forty: The Growth of an English County Town. 2nd ed. (Historical Monographs: No. 35). (Illus.). 328p. 1973. 32.00 (0-674-27501-2) HUP.
— Queen Elizabeth & the Making of Policy, 1572-1588. LC 80-8564. 536p. 1981. pap. 18.95 (0-691-10112-4) Princeton U Pr.
MacCaig, Norman. Collected Poems. 456p. 1991. 39.95 (0-7011-3713-4, Pub. by Chatto & Windus UK) Trafalgar.
MacCall, Alec D. Dynamic Geography of Marine Fish Populations. 200p. 1990. text ed. 25.00 (0-295-96911-3); pap. 15.00 (0-295-96912-1) U of Wash Pr.
Maccall, William. Foreign Biographies, 2 vols, Set. LC 72-5617. (Essay Index Reprint Ser.). 1977. reprint ed. 39.95 (0-8369-2999-3) Ayer.
Maccalla, G., jt. ed. see Cercone, N. J.
MacCallum, Anne C. Pumpkin, Pumpkin! Lore, History, Outlandish Facts & Good Eating. LC 84-81831. (Illus.). 200p. (Orig.). 1986. pap. 8.95 (0-685-09560-6) Heather Foun.
MacCallum, Elizabeth P. The Nationalist Crusade in Syria. LC 79-2873. (Illus.). 299p. 1981. reprint ed. 26.25 (0-8305-0043-X) Hyperion Conn.
MacCallum, Gerald C., Jr. Legislative Intent & Other Essays on Politics, Law, & Morality. Singer, Marcus G. & Martin, Rex, eds. LC 93-841. 288p. (C). 1993. text ed. 43.00 (0-299-13860-7) U of Wis Pr.
MacCallum, Hugh. Milton & the Sons of God: The Divine Image in Milton's Epic Poetry. 335p. 1986. 40.00 (0-8020-5679-2) U of Toronto Pr.
MacCallum, Hugh, ed. see Woodhouse, Arthur S.
MacCallum, Iain. Pascal for the Apple. 1983. disk (0-318-57193-5) P-H.
— UCSD Pascal for the IBM PC. write for info. (0-318-59632-6) S&S Trade.
MacCallum, Ian. She Loved Gravity & Would Fall Down Exquisitely Anywhere. (Illus.). 32p. 1987. pap. 4.00 (0-907791-17-4) Synerg AZ.
MacCallum, J. R. & Vincent, C. A., eds. Polymer Electrolyte Reviews, Vol. 1. 356p. 1987. 79.25 (0-317-63617-0, Pub. by Elsevier Applied Sci UK) Elsevier.
— Polymer Electrolyte Reviews, Vol. 2. 344p. 1990. 99.00 (1-85166-348-7) Elsevier.
MacCallum, Malcolm A. General Relativity & Gravitation: Proceedings of the 11th International Conference on General Relativity & Gravitation. 500p. 1987. 59.95 (0-521-33296-6) Cambridge U Pr.
MacCallum, Malcolm A., ed. Galaxies, Axisymmetric Systems & Relativity. 300p. 1985. 69.95 (0-521-30812-7) Cambridge U Pr.
MacCallum, Malcolm A. & Wright, Francis J. Algebraic Computing with REDUCE. 320p. 1992. 59.95 (0-19-853444-2); pap. 29.95 (0-19-853443-4) OUP.
***MacCallum, Malcolm A., et al.** Algebraic Computing in General Relativity: Lecture Notes from the First Brazilian School on Computer Algebra, Vol. 2. Reboucas, Marcelo J. & Roque, Waldir L., eds. 400p. 1995. text ed. 63.00 (0-19-853646-1) OUP.
Maccallum, Mungo W. Tennyson's Idylls of the King & Arthurian Story from the Sixteenth Century. LC 73-154159. (Select Bibliographies Reprint Ser.). 1977. reprint ed. 26.95 (0-8369-5775-X) Ayer.
MacCallum, Reid. Imitation & Design: And Other Essays. Blissett, William, ed. LC 54-7922. 227p. reprint ed. pap. 64.70 (0-317-10442-X, 2016087) Bks Demand.
MacCallum, Spencer H. Art of Community. LC 78-112866. 118p. 1970. 10.00 (0-317-06383-9) Heather Foun.
MacCallum, Spencer H., ed. see Riegel, E. C.
MacCallum, William G. William Stewart Halsted, Surgeon. LC 30-31890. 263p. reprint ed. pap. 75.00 (0-317-28138-0, 2055744) Bks Demand.
MacCameron, Robert. Bananas, Labor, & Politics in Honduras: 1954-1963. LC 82-24946. (Foreign & Comparative Studies Program, Latin American Ser.: No. 5). (Illus.). (Orig.). (C). 1983. pap. text ed. 14.00 (0-915984-96-2) Syracuse U Foreign Comp.
MacCann, Donnarae, ed. Social Responsibility in Librarianship: Essays on Equality. LC 89-42965. 144p. 1989. pap. 21.95x (0-89950-457-4) McFarland & Co.
MacCann, Donnarae & Woodard, Gloria, eds. The Black American in Books for Children: Readings in Racism. 2nd ed. LC 85-10893. (Illus.). 310p. 1985. 29.50 (0-8108-1826-4) Scarecrow.
— Cultural Conformity in Books for Children: Further Readings in Racism. LC 77-22174. 215p. 1977. 22.50 (0-8108-1064-6) Scarecrow.
MacCann, Lydon. Casebook on Company Law. 1991. U.K. pap. 68.00 (1-85475-023-2) Butterworth Legal Pubs.
***MacCann, Lyndon.** Butterworths Ireland Companies Act. 1993. pap. text ed. 120.00 (1-85475-148-4, IE) Butterworth Legal Pubs.
— Company Secretarial Manual. 1994. pap. text ed. 99.00 (0-85475-238-2, IE) Butterworth Legal Pubs.
MacCann, Richard D. The First Film Makers. (American Movies: The First Thirty Years Ser.). (Illus.). 335p. 1989. 32.50 (0-8108-2229-6); pap. 15.00 (0-8108-2230-X) Scarecrow.
— The First Tycoons. LC 86-22064. (Illus.). 269p. 1987. 25.00 (0-8108-1949-X); pap. 14.00 (0-8108-1950-3) Scarecrow.
— Hollywood in Transition. LC 77-5314. 208p. 1977. reprint ed. text ed. 55.00 (0-8371-9616-7, MAHT, Greenwood Pr) Greenwood.
— A New Vice Presidency for a New Century. LC 91-76548. (Illus.). vi, 90p. (Orig.). 1991. pap. write for info. (0-934570-01-9) Image & Idea.
— The Silent Comedians. LC 93-11399. (American Movies: The First Thirty Years Ser.). (Illus.). 257p. 1993. 29.50 (0-8108-2725-5); pap. 16.50 (0-8108-2730-1) Scarecrow.
— The Stars Appear. LC 91-42748. (American Movies: The First Thirty Years Ser.: No. 3). (Illus.). 339p. 1992. 42.50 (0-8108-2527-9); pap. 22.50 (0-8108-2528-7) Scarecrow.
— To Save Us From Ourselves: The Vision of a Future President. 226p. (Orig.). 1994. pap. 19.95 (0-934570-02-7) Image & Idea.
MacCann, William. Two Thousand Miles' Ride Through the Argentine Provinces, 2 Vols, Set. LC 70-128433. reprint ed. 52.00 (0-404-04102-7) AMS Pr.
MacCannell, Dean. Empty Meeting Grounds: The Tourist Papers. 256p. 1992. 49.95 (0-415-05692-6, A6832); pap. 15.95 (0-415-05693-4, A6836) Routledge.
Maccannell, Dean. Tourist: A New Theory of the Leisure Class. 1989. pap. 9.56 (0-8052-0895-X) Schocken.
MacCannell, Dean & MacCannell, Juliet F. The Time of the Sign: A Semiotic Interpretation of Modern Culture. LC 81-47960. (Advances in Semiotics Ser.). 221p. reprint ed. pap. 63.90 (0-685-23890-3, 2056709) Bks Demand.
MacCannell, Juliet F. Figuring Lacan: Criticism & the Cultural Unconscious. LC 86-11217. (Critics of the Twentieth Century Ser.). 204p. reprint ed. pap. 58.20 (0-7837-6884-2, 2046714) Bks Demand.
— The Other Perspective in Gender & Culture: Rewriting Woman & the Symbolic. 1990. text ed. 37.50 (0-231-07256-2) Col U Pr.
— The Regime of the Brother: After the Patriarchy. (Opening Out Ser.). 208p. 1991. 49.95 (0-415-05434-6, A4766); pap. 15.95 (0-415-05435-4, A5613) Routledge.
MacCannell, Juliet F. & Zakarin, Laura, eds. Thinking Bodies. LC 93-34805. (Irvine Studies in the Humanities). 1994. 37.50 (0-8047-2306-0); pap. 13.95 (0-8047-2304-4) Stanford U Pr.
MacCannell, Juliet F., jt. auth. see MacCannell, Dean.
Maccari, Elisabetta, tr. see Johansen, Hanna.
Maccaro, James A. American Postcard Publishers, 1895-1945. (Illus.). 52p. (Orig.). 1986. pap. write for info. (0-930429-00-1) Bibliographic Pr.
Maccarone, Grace. Cars! Cars! Cars! LC 94-18389. (Story Corner Ser.). (Illus.). (J). 1995. 6.95 (0-590-47572-X) Scholastic Inc.
— The Classroom Pet. LC 95-13151. (Hello Reader! Level 1: First Grade Friends Ser.: Bk. 3). (Illus.). (J). 1995. write for info. (0-590-26264-5) Scholastic Inc.
— Ghost on the Hill. (J). 1990. pap. 2.75 (0-590-42978-7) Scholastic Inc.
— The Gym Day Winner. LC 95-10285. (Hello Reader! Level 1: First Grade Friends Ser.: Bk. 2). (Illus.). (J). 1996. write for info. (0-590-26263-7, Cartwheel) Scholastic Inc.
— The Haunting of Grade Three. 96p. (Orig.). (J). (gr. 2-5). 1987. pap. 2.75 (0-590-43868-9) Scholastic Inc.
— Itchy, Itchy Chickenpox. (Illus.). 32p. (J). 1992. pap. 2.95 (0-590-44948-6) Scholastic Inc.
— The Lunch Box Surprise. LC 95-10284. (Hello Reader! Level 1: First Grade Friends Ser.: Bk. 1). (Illus.). (J). 1995. write for info. (0-590-26267-X, Cartwheel) Scholastic Inc.
— Monster Math. LC 95-12133. (Hello Math Reader Level 1 Ser.). (Illus.). (J). 1995. write for info. (0-590-22712-2) Scholastic Inc.
— My Tooth Is about to Fall Out. LC 94-9772. (Hello Reader! Ser.). (J). (gr. 3-7). 1995. 2.95 (0-590-48376-5) Scholastic Inc.
— Oink! Moo! How Do You Do? LC 93-45962. (Illus.). (J). 1994. 6.95 (0-590-48161-4) Scholastic Inc.
— Oink Moo How Do You Do. (J). (ps). 1994. 6.95 (0-590-20655-9) Scholastic Inc.
— Pizza Party. LC 93-19732. (Hello Reader! Ser.). (Illus.). 48p. (J). (ps-4). 1994. pap. 2.95 (0-590-47563-0, Cartwheel) Scholastic Inc.
— Return of the Third-Grade Ghosthunters. (J). 1989. pap. 2.75 (0-590-41944-7) Scholastic Inc.
— The Silly Story of Goldilocks & the Three Squares. LC 95-13226. (Hello Math Reader Ser.: Level 2). (Illus.). (J). 1995. write for info. (0-590-54344-X, Cartwheel) Scholastic Inc.

An Asterisk (*) at the beginning of an entry indicates that the title is appearing in BIP for the first time.

— Soccer Game! LC 93-43742. (Illus.). (J). 1994. 2.95 (*0-590-48369-2*) Scholastic Inc.

— The Sword in the Stone. (Hello Reader! Ser.). (Illus.). (J). 1992. pap. 2.95 (*0-590-45527-3*, 043, Cartwheel) Scholastic Inc.

— "What Is That?" Said the Cat. LC 94-39100. (Hello Reader! Level 1 Ser.). (Illus.). (J). 1995. 2.95 (*0-590-25945-8*, Cartwheel) Scholastic Inc.

Maccarone, Grace & Chardiet, Bernice. Martin & the Tooth Fairy. (School Friends Ser.: No. 3). (Illus.). 32p. (J). 1991. pap. 2.50 (*0-590-43305-9*) Scholastic Inc.

Maccarone, Grace, jt. auth. see Chardiet, Bernice.

MacCarter, Jane S. New Mexico Wildlife Viewing Guide. LC 93-42965. (Watchable Wildlife Ser.). 96p. (Orig.). 1994. pap. 8.95 (*1-56044-213-1*) Falcon Pr MT.

MacCarthy, Alan W., Jr. How to Save Big Bucks on Your Pet's Veterinary Bills. 128p. 1992. pap. 14.95 (*1-882822-00-5*) First-Care.

MacCarthy, B., tr. see Oengus the Culdee.

MacCarthy, Bartholomew, ed. The Codex Palatino-Vaticanus. LC 78-72679. (Royal Irish Academy. Todd Lecture Ser.: Vol. 3). reprint ed. 35.00 (*0-404-60563-X*) AMS Pr.

MacCarthy, D., ed. Concentration & Drying of Foods: Proceedings of the Kellog Foundation Second International Food Research Symposium, University College, Cork, Republic of Ireland, 16-18 September 1985. 320p. 1986. 72.00 (*0-85334-442-6*) Elsevier.

MacCarthy, Daphne, jt. auth. see Bonar, Ann.

MacCarthy, Desmond. Court Theatre, 1904-1907: A Commentary & Criticism. Weintraub, Stanley, ed. LC 66-27969. (Books of the Theatre: No. 6). 182p. 1966. 10.95 (*0-87024-068-4*) U of Miami Pr.

Maccarthy, Desmond. Criticism. LC 78-97710. (Essay Index Reprint Ser.). 1977. 23.95 (*0-8369-1360-4*) Ayer.

MacCarthy, Desmond. Experience. LC 68-54357. (Essay Index Reprint Ser.). 1977. 21.95 (*0-8369-0640-3*) Ayer.

— Portraits. LC 72-5613. (Essay Index Reprint Ser.). 1977. reprint ed. 21.95 (*0-8369-7299-6*) Ayer.

***MacCarthy, Fiona.** William Morris. 1995. pap. 45.00 (*0-394-58531-3*) Knopf.

MacCarthy, Mary. Handicaps: Six Studies. LC 67-26756. (Essay Index Reprint Ser.). 1977. 18.95 (*0-8369-0642-X*) Ayer.

MacCarthy-Morrogh, Michael. The Munster Plantation: English Migration to the Southern Ireland, 1583-1641. (Illus.). 340p. 1986. 59.00 (*0-19-822952-6*) OUP.

MacCarthy, P., ed. Humic Substances in Soil & Crop Sciences: Selected Readings. 304p. 1990. 30.00 (*0-89118-104-0*) Soil Sci Soc Am.

MacCarthy, Patricia. Ocean Parade. (J). 1990. 11.95 (*0-8037-0780-0*) Dial Bks Young.

MacCarthy, Patrick, jt. ed. see Suffet, I. H.

MacCary, W. T. Childlike Achilles: Ontogeny & Phylogeny in the Iliad. LC 82-4458. 304p. 1982. text ed. 50.00 (*0-231-05504-8*) Col U Pr.

MacCary, W. Thomas. Childlike Achilles: Ontogeny & Phylogeny in the Iliad. LC 82-4458. 294p. reprint ed. pap. 83.80 (*0-7837-0422-4*, 2040745) Bks Demand.

— Friends & Lovers: The Phenomenology of Desire in Shakespearean Comedy. LC 84-17605. 276p. reprint ed. pap. 78.70 (*0-8357-3443-9*, 2039700) Bks Demand.

MacCasKey, Michael. Lawns & Ground Covers: How to Select, Grow & Enjoy. LC 81-82133. 160p. (Orig.). 1982. pap. 14.99 (*0-89586-099-6*) Price Stern.

MacCaskey, Michael, ed. Complete Guide to Basic Gardening. LC 85-80863. 240p. pap. 12.95 (*0-89586-325-1*) Price Stern.

MacCaskey, Michael & Stebbins, Robert L. Pruning: How to Guide for Gardeners. LC 82-83307. 160p. 1982. pap. 14.99 (*0-89586-188-7*) Price Stern.

MacCaskey, Michael, jt. auth. see Ray, Richard.

MacCaskill, Bridget. On the Swirl of the Tide. (Illus.). 176p. 1993. 29.95 (*0-224-03289-5*, Pub. by Jonathan Cape UK) Trafalgar.

— On the Swirl of the Tide. (Illus.). 224p. 1994. pap. 19.95 (*0-224-03668-8*, Pub. by Jonathan Cape UK) Trafalgar.

MacCauley, Nancy L. Diana: A Modern Metaphysical Fairy Tale. Teasdale, Carrie, ed. LC 85-73902. 320p. (Orig.). 1986. pap. 9.95 (*0-251-93702-X*) Another Way.

MacCharles, D. C. Trade among Multinationals: Intra-Industry Trade & National Competitiveness. 224p. 1987. lib. bdg. 65.00 (*0-7099-4618-X*, Pub. by Croom Helm UK) Routledge Chapman & Hall.

Macchi, C. & Guilbert, J. F. Teleinformatics: Data & Computer Communications. St. Quinton, J. M., tr. (Studies in Telecommunication: Vol. 3). 452p. 1985. 138.50 (*0-444-87507-7*, North Holland) Elsevier.

Macchi, G., et al, eds. Somatosensory Integration in the Thalamus: A Reevaluation Based on the New Methodological Approaches. 396p. 1983. 213.25 (*0-444-80485-4*, I-363-83) Elsevier.

Macchi, John W. & Kane, Art. Choosing the Right Cruise for You: The Bon Voyage Guide. LC 94-29665. (Illus.). 112p. 1994. pap. 9.95 (*0-942963-52-0*) Distinctive Pub.

***Macchi, O.** LMS Adaptive Processing with Applications in Transmission. 1995. text ed. 95.00 (*0-471-93403-8*) Wiley.

***Macchi, Vladimir.** Sansoni Woerterbuch der Italienischen und Deutschen Sprache. 2nd ed. 3178p. (GER & ITA.). 1989. 795.00 (*0-7859-8578-6*, 8838314535) Fr & Eur.

***Macchi, Vladimiro.** Collins-Sansoni Italian Dictionary. 3rd ed. 2277p. (ENG & ITA.). 1988. 50.00 (*0-7859-7399-0*, 0060178035) Fr & Eur.

— Harrap's Standard Italian Dictionary, Vol. 1: Italian-English A-L. 1991. 59.95 (*0-13-382540-X*) P-H.

— Harrap's Standard Italian Dictionary, Vol. 2: Italian-English M-Z. 1991. 59.95 (*0-13-382557-4*) P-H.

— Harrap's Standard Italian Dictionary, Vol. 3: English-Italian A-L. 1991. 59.95 (*0-13-382565-5*) P-H.

— Harrap's Standard Italian Dictionary, Vol. 4: English-Italian M-Z. 1991. pap. 59.95 (*0-13-382573-6*) P-H.

— Italian-German Dictionary: Woerterbuch Italienisch-Deutsch. 5th ed. 600p. (GER & ITA.). 1986. 17.95 (*0-8288-0374-9*, F42340) Fr & Eur.

— Langenscheidt Large German-Italian Dictionary: Langenscheidt Grosswoerterbuch Deutsch-Italienisch. 2nd ed. 938p. (GER & ITA.). 1984. 135.00 (*0-8288-0373-0*, F41300) Fr & Eur.

— Woerterbuch Italienisch-Deutsch, Deutsch-Italienisch. 1114p. (GER & ITA.). 1989. 29.95 (*0-7859-8442-9*, 3572037522) Fr & Eur.

Macchi, Vladimiro, ed. see Sansoni.

Macchia, Donald. Weightlifting & Bodybuilding: Total Fitness for Men & Women. 200p. 1987. pap. 20.95 (*0-8304-1183-6*) Nelson-Hall.

Macchia, Donald D., jt. auth. see Asterita, Mary F.

Macchia, Frank D. Spirituality & Social Liberation: The Message of the Blumhardts & the Light of Wuerttemberg Pietism. LC 93-27785. (Pietist & Wesleyan Studies: No. 4). 205p. 1993. 27.50 (*0-8108-2639-9*) Scarecrow.

Macchiavelli, Niccolo. The Arte of Warre, (Certain Waies of the Orderyng of Souldiours) Whitehorne, P., tr. LC 79-26097. (English Experience Ser.: No. 135). 1969. reprint ed. 85.00 (*90-221-0135-5*) Walter J Johnson.

Macchio, Ralph. X-Men Adventures, Vol. 2. 1994. pap. 4.95 (*0-7851-0028-8*) Marvel Entmnt.

— X-Men Adventures, Vol. III. 96p. 1994. pap. 5.95 (*0-7851-0044-X*) Marvel Entmnt.

— X-Men Adventures, Vol. 4. (Illus.). 96p. 1995. pap. 4.95 (*0-7851-0113-6*) Marvel Entmnt.

Macchio, William J., ed. Hurricane Andrew: Path of Destruction. 100p. (Orig.). Date not set. pap. 11.95 (*1-882526-00-7*) BD Pub.

MacCiarnain, Seamus, ed. see National Graves Association of Ireland Staff.

Macciocchi, Maria A. Daily Life in Revolutionary China. LC 72-81757. 512p. 1973. pap. 5.95 (*0-85345-282-2*) Monthly Rev.

Macciomei, Nancy R. & Ruben, Douglas H. Homebound Teaching: A Handbook for Educators. LC 89-42732. 215p. 1989. lib. bdg. 31.50x (*0-89950-381-0*) McFarland & Co.

Macciomei, Nancy R., jt. ed. see Douglas, Ruben H.

MacClancy, Jeremy. Consuming Culture. 256p. 1993. 23.00 (*0-8050-2578-2*) H Holt & Co.

— Consuming Culture: Why You Eat What You Eat. 1995. pap. 13.95 (*0-8050-3587-7*) H Holt & Co.

***MacCleery, Douglas.** American Forests: A History of Resiliency & Recovery. (Illus.). 58p. (Orig.). (C). (gr. 12 up). 1994. pap. text ed. 40.00 (*0-7881-0858-1*) Diane Pub.

MacCleery, Douglas W. American Forests: A History of Resiliency & Recovery. LC 92-29771. (Issues Ser.). (Illus.). 58p. (C). 1993. pap. 6.95 (*0-89030-048-8*) Forest Hist Soc.

MacClennan, Carole. Learning by Doing: Eighty Activities to Enrich Religion Classes for Young Children. LC 93-60026. (Illus.). 128p. (Orig.). 1993. pap. 14.95 (*0-89622-562-3*) Twenty-Third.

— When Jesus Was Young: Stories, Crafts, & Activities for Children. LC 91-65005. 80p. (Orig.). (gr. k-5). 1991. pap. 7.95 (*0-89622-485-6*, C58) Twenty-Third.

***MacClintock, Carol, ed. & tr.** Readings in the History of Music in Performance. LC 78-8511. (Illus.). 448p. 1994. text ed. 35.00 (*0-253-14495-7*) Ind U Pr.

— Readings in the History of Music in Performance. LC 78-8511. (Illus.). 448p. 1994. pap. 17.50 (*0-253-20285-X*) Ind U Pr.

MacClintock, Dorcas. Animals Observed: A Look at Animals in Art. LC 91-36795. (Illus.). 64p. (J). 1993. text ed. 18.95 (*0-684-19323-X*, C Scribner Sons Young) S&S Childrens.

— Red Pandas: A Natural History. LC 88-3528. (Illus.). 112p. (YA). (gr. 7 up). 1988. text ed. 14.95 (*0-684-18677-2*, C Scribner Sons Young) S&S Childrens.

MacCluer, Barbara I., jt. auth. see Cowen, Carl C., Jr.

MacCluer, C. R. Boundary Value Problems & Orthogonal Expansions: Physical Problems from a Sobolev Viewpoint. LC 94-20004. 368p. 1994. 64.95 (*0-7803-1071-3*, PC04226) Inst Electrical.

MacCluer, J. W., et al, eds. Genetic Analysis Workshop Seven: Issues in Gene Mapping & Detection of Major Genes Held at Bergamo Conference Center, Dayton, Ohio, October 1990. (Journal: Cytogenetics & Cell Genetics: Vol. 59, No. 2-3, 1992). (Illus.). 176p. 1992. pap. 57.75 (*3-8055-5578-4*) S Karger.

MacClure, Victor. She Stands Accused: Being a Series of Accounts of the Lives & Deeds of Notorious Women Murderesses. LC 74-10429. (Classics of Crime & Criminology Ser.). (Illus.). 239p. 1975. reprint ed. 15.40 (*0-88355-196-9*) Hyperion Conn.

Maccoby, Annie & Church, Jeff. Alien Equation. 47p. 1986. reprint ed. 3.45 (*0-87129-024-3*, A45) Dramatic Pub.

Maccoby, Eleanor E. Social Development: Psychological Growth & the Parent-Child Relationship. 436p. (C). 1980. pap. text ed. 24.00 (*0-15-581422-2*) HB Coll Pubs.

Maccoby, Eleanor E. & Jacklin, Carol N. The Psychology of Sex Differences, 2 vols., Vol. I. LC 73-94488. xv, 634p. 1974. pap. 16.95 (*0-8047-0974-2*) Stanford U Pr.

— The Psychology of Sex Differences, 2 vols., Vol. II. LC 73-94488. xv, 634p. 1974. pap. 10.95 (*0-8047-0975-0*) Stanford U Pr.

Maccoby, Eleanor E. & Mnookin, Robert H. Dividing the Child: Social & Legal Dilemmas of Custody. (Illus.). 369p. 1992. 45.00 (*0-674-21294-0*) HUP.

— Dividing the Child: Social & Legal Dilemmas of Custody. (Illus.). 369p. 1994. pap. text ed. 18.95 (*0-674-21295-9*, MACDIX) HUP.

Maccoby, Hyam. Paul & Hellenism. LC 90-44765. 256p. 1991. pap. 17.95 (*1-56338-014-5*) TPI PA.

— Revolution in Judaea: Jesus & the Jewish Resistance. LC 80-16752. 256p. 1980. 9.95 (*0-8008-6784-X*) Taplinger.

Maccoby, Hyam, ed. & tr. Judaism on Trial: Jewish-Christian Disputations in the Middle Ages. (Littman Library of Jewish Civilization). 246p. 1982. 39.95 (*0-19-710046-5*, Pub. by Littman Lib Jew UK) Bnai Brith Bk.

— Judaism on Trial: Jewish-Christian Disputations in the Middle Ages. 246p. 1994. reprint ed. pap. 19.95 (*1-874774-16-1*, Pub. by Littman Lib Jew UK) Bnai Brith Bk.

Maccoby, Hyam Z. Judas Iscariot & the Myth of Jewish Evil. 280p. 1992. text ed. 24.95 (*0-02-919555-1*) Free Pr.

— The Mythmaker. 256p. 1987. pap. 11.00 (*0-06-250585-8*) Harper SF.

***Maccoby, Michael.** Why Work? Motivating the New Workforce. 2nd ed. 285p. 1995. pap. 24.95 (*0-917917-05-7*) Miles River.

Maccoby, Michael, ed. Sweden at the Edge: Lessons for American & Swedish Managers. LC 90-44875. (Innovations in Organizations Ser.). 260p. (C). 1991. text ed. 32.95 (*0-8122-8153-5*) U of Pa Pr.

Maccoby, Michael, jt. ed. see Cortina, Mauricio.

MacCoby, Simon, ed. The English Radical Tradition, 1763-1914. LC 78-681. 236p. 1978. reprint ed. text ed. 59.75 (*0-313-20284-2*, MAER, Greenwood Pr) Greenwood.

MacColl, E. Kimbark & Stein, Harry H. Merchants, Money & Power: The Portland Establishment, 1843-1913. Stein, Harry H. & Brunsman, Philippa, eds. LC 88-24653. (Illus.). 550p. 1988. 29.95 (*0-9603408-3-1*); pap. 19.95 (*0-9603408-4-X*) Georgian Pr.

MacColl, Ewan. Folk Songs & Ballads of Scotland. (Illus.). 96p. 1965. pap. 9.95 (*0-8256-0057-X*, OK61341, Oak) Music Sales.

MacColl, Gail. The Book of Cards for Kids. LC 91-50962. (J). (ps-3). 1992. pap. 10.95 (*1-56305-240-7*) Workman Pub.

MacColl, Gail & Wallace, Carol McD. To Marry an English Lord: Or, How Anglomania Really Got Started. LC 85-40529. (Illus.). 416p. 1986. pap. 14.95 (*0-89480-939-3*, 939) Workman Pub.

MacColl, L. A., ed. see Applied Mathematics Symposium Staff.

MacColl, Linda, jt. ed. see Richards, Gillian.

***MacColl, Linda, et al, eds.** Dramatists Sourcebook: 1995-96 Edition. 300p. (Orig.). 1995. pap. 15.95 (*1-55936-111-5*) Theatre Comm.

Maccoll, R. & Guard-Friar, D. Phycobiliproteins. LC 85-32567. 1986. 191.00 (*0-8493-5525-7*) CRC Pr.

MacColla, Charles J. Breach of Promise: Its History & Social Considerations... ix, 93p. 1993. reprint ed. lib. bdg. 25.00 (*0-8377-2445-7*) Rothman.

MacCollium, David V. Construction Safety Planning. 352p. 1995. text ed. 49.95 (*0-442-01940-8*) Van Nos Reinhold.

MacCollum, David V. Crane Hazards & Their Prevention. LC 93-39816. (Illus.). 172p. (Orig.). 1993. pap. 34.95 (*0-939874-95-4*, 4348) ASSE.

MacCollum, David V., ed. Readings in Hazard Control & Hazardous Materials. 114p. 1985. 10.00 (*0-939874-70-9*) ASSE.

Maccombie, Turi. Realistic Dinosaurs Stickers. (Illus.). (J). (gr. k-3). 1994. pap. 1.00 (*0-486-28066-7*) Dover.

MacCombie, Turi, illus. My First Book of Animals from A to Z: More Than 150 Animals Every Child Should Know. LC 92-19284. (Cartwheel Learning Bookshelf Ser.). 64p. (J). (ps-2). 1994. 12.95 (*0-590-46305-5*, Cartwheel) Scholastic Inc.

— Velveteen Rabbit. (Fairy Tale Classics Ser.). 48p. (J). (ps-3). 1991. 9.95 (*0-88101-114-2*) Unicorn Pub.

— Velveteen Rabbit. (Pop-Out Ornament Book Ser.). 48p. (J). (ps-3). 1992. 12.95 (*0-88101-236-X*) Unicorn Pub.

MacConaill, M. A., jt. auth. see Basmajian, J. V.

Macconaill, P. A., jt. ed. see Rathmill, K.

MacConaill, P. A., et al, eds. Mechatronics & Robotics. (Advances in Design & Manufacturing Ser.: No. 1). 346p. 1991. 90.00 (*90-5199-057-X*, Pub. by IOS Pr NE) IOS Press.

***Maccone, Claudio.** Telecommunications, KLT & Relativity. Blade, Richard A., ed. (Textbooks in Science & Mathematics Ser.). (Illus.). x, 238p. (Orig.). (C). 1994. pap. 35.00 (*1-880930-04-8*) IPI Pr.

***MacConghail, Muiris.** The Blaskets: People & Literature. rev. ed. (Illus.). 176p. 1995. pap. 16.95 (*1-57098-033-0*) R Rinehart.

MacConnell, Anita. Instrument Makers to the World. (C). 1989. pap. 48.00 (*1-85072-096-7*, Pub. by W Sessions UK) St Mut.

MacConnell, James D. Dr. Mac, Planner for Schools: Memoirs of My First 80 Years. (Illus.). vi, 194p. 1988. 17.95 (*0-929558-00-6*) Johnson-Dole.

MacConnell, Marcia. Florida Motor Vehicle Liability Law Service, 1981. suppl. ed. 1994. ring bd. 45.00 (*0-685-14238-8*) Butterworth Legal Pubs.

— Florida Motor Vehicle Liability Law Service, 1981, 4 vols., Set. 2000p. 1995. ring bd. 280.00 (*0-409-26142-4*) Michie Butterworth.

— Florida Negligence Law Manual. suppl. ed. 1987. ring bd. 45.00 (*0-685-14241-8*) Butterworth Legal Pubs.

— Florida Negligence Law Manual, 2 vols., Set. 900p. 1995. ring bd. 160.00 (*0-409-26454-7*) Michie Butterworth.

— Florida Traffic & DUI Practice. suppl. ed. 1994. 47.00 (*0-318-59843-4*) Butterworth Legal Pubs.

— Florida Traffic & DUI Practice, 3 vols., Set. 1000p. 1995. ring bd. 270.00 (*0-409-26131-9*) Michie Butterworth.

Maccord, Howard A., Sr. The Archeological Society of Virginia: A Forty-Year History, No. 21. 66p. 1991. pap. 15.00 (*1-884626-07-6*) Archeolog Soc.

MacCord, Howard A., Sr. Falls Zone Archaeology in Virginia. 142p. 1985. pap. 16.00 (*1-884626-21-1*) Archeolog Soc.

— The Lewis Creek Mound Culture in Virginia. 92p. 1986. pap. 19.00 (*1-884626-20-3*) Archeolog Soc.

— Prehistory of the Gathright Dam Area, Virginia. 75p. 1986. pap. 19.00 (*1-884626-19-X*) Archeolog Soc.

Maccord, Howard A., Sr. & Buchanan, William T., Jr. The Crab Orchard Site, Tazewell County, Virginia, No. 8. 156p. 1980. pap. 9.00 (*1-884626-02-5*) Archeolog Soc.

MacCorkle, Douglas B. God's Special Secret: The Case Paul Argues in the Epistle to the Ephesians. (Illus.). 300p. (Orig.). 1994. pap. text ed. write for info. (*0-9639865-0-3*) MacCorkle Bible.

MacCorkle, Lyn. Cubans in the United States: A Bibliography for Research in the Social & Behavioral Science. LC 84-6675. (Bibliographies & Indexes in Sociology Ser.: No. 1). xiii, 227p. 1984. text ed. 55.00 (*0-313-24509-6*, MKC/, Greenwood Pr) Greenwood.

MacCorkle, Stuart A. American Policy of Recognition Toward Mexico. LC 72-131774. 1971. reprint ed. 9.00 (*0-403-00661-9*) Scholarly.

— American Policy of Recognition Towards Mexico. LC 70-155620. reprint ed. 11.50 (*0-404-04108-6*) AMS Pr.

MacCormac, Earl R. A Cognitive Theory of Metaphor. 264p. 1989. reprint ed. pap. 14.95x (*0-262-63124-5*) MIT Pr.

— Metaphor & Myth in Science & Religion. LC 75-23941. 187p. reprint ed. pap. 53.30 (*0-317-55477-8*, 2052207) Bks Demand.

MacCormac, John P. This Time for Keeps. LC 72-4584. (Essay Index Reprint Ser.). 1977. reprint ed. 20.95 (*0-8369-2962-4*) Ayer.

MacCormack, C. P., ed. Ethnography of Fertility & Birth. 1982. text ed. 99.00 (*0-12-463550-4*) Acad Pr.

MacCormack, Carol & Strathern, Marilyn, eds. Nature, Culture & Gender. (Illus.). 1980. pap. 19.95 (*0-521-28001-X*) Cambridge U Pr.

MacCormack, Dave & Michael, Toni. Algorithms for Personal Computing. (Essential Algorithms Ser.). (Illus.). 250p. (Orig.). 1985. pap. 14.95 (*0-931145-07-4*) Sandlight Pubns.

MacCormack, Ellen, jt. auth. see Janda, Louis.

***MacCormack, Geoffrey.** The Spirit of Traditional Chinese Law. LC 94-39610. (Spirit of the Laws Ser.). 1995. write for info. (*0-8203-1722-5*) U of Ga Pr.

— Traditional Chinese Penal Law. 1991. text ed. 69.00 (*0-7486-0211-9*, Pub. by Edinburgh U Pr UK) Col U Pr.

MacCormack, John R. Revolutionary Politics in the Long Parliament. LC 72-93952. 352p. 1973. 32.00 (*0-674-76775-6*) HUP.

MacCormack, Sabine. Art & Ceremony in Late Antiquity. (Transformation of the Classical Heritage Ser.: Vol. 1). (Illus.). 450p. 1981. pap. 16.00 (*0-520-06966-8*) U CA Pr.

— Religion in the Andes: Vision & Imagination in Early Colonial Peru. (Illus.). 531p. 1991. text ed. 59.50 (*0-691-09468-3*) Princeton U Pr.

— Religion in the Andes: Vision & Imagination in Early Colonial Peru. (Illus.). 506p. 1993. pap. text ed. 18.95 (*0-691-02106-6*) Princeton U Pr.

MacCormick, Alex. The Dried Flower Arranger. (Illus.). 144p. (Orig.). 1994. pap. 17.95 (*1-895565-32-4*) Firefly Bks Ltd.

— Papier Mache Style. 128p. 1995. pap. 15.95 (*0-8019-8755-5*) Chilton.

MacCormick, Austin H. The Education of Adult Prisoners. LC 73-38668. (Foundations of Criminal Justice Ser.). reprint ed. 32.50 (*0-404-09178-4*) AMS Pr.

***MacCormick, Carol P., ed.** Ethnography of Fertility & Birth. 2nd rev. ed. (Illus.). 283p. (C). 1994. pap. text ed. 11.95x (*0-88133-817-6*) Waveland Pr.

MacCormick, D. Neil & Summers, Robert S. Interpreting Statutes: A Comparative Study. (Applied Legal Philosophy Ser.). 567p. 1991. text ed. 69.95 (*1-85521-183-1*, Pub. by Dartmth Pub UK) Ashgate Pub Co.

MacCormick, D. Neil, jt. ed. see Aarnio, Aulis.

MacCormick, Neil. Enlightenment, Rights & Revolutions: Essays in Philosophy of Law & Social Philosophy. 396p. 1989. pap. text ed. 60.00 (*0-08-037734-3*, Pub. by Aberdeen U Pr) Macmillan.

— H. L. A. Hart. Twining, William, ed. LC 81-50790. (Jurists: Profiles in Legal Theory Ser.). 192p. 1981. 27.50 (*0-8047-1107-0*) Stanford U Pr.

— Legal Reasoning & Legal Theory. (Clarendon Law Ser.). 310p. 1994. pap. 24.95 (*0-19-876384-0*) OUP.

MacCormick, Neil & Birks, Peter B., eds. The Legal Mind: Essays for Tony Honore. 352p. 1986. 74.00 (*0-19-876196-1*) OUP.

MacCormick, Neil & Weinberger, Ota. An Institutional Theory of Law. 1986. lib. bdg. 85.50 (*90-277-2079-7*) Kluwer Ac.

MacCormick, Neil, tr. see Alexy, Robert W.

MacCormick, Neil, ed. see Wroblewski, Jerzy.

MacCormick, Neil, et al, eds. Conditions of Validity & Cognition in Modern Legal Thought: Proceedings of the 11th World Congress on Philosophy of Law & Social Philosophy Helsinki. 214p. (Orig.). 1985. pap. 44.00 (*3-515-04460-4*) Coronet Bks.

MacCorquodale, Patricia, jt. auth. see DeLamater, John.

MacCorquodale, Stuart W. Find Great Work When They're Not Hiring. 117p. (Orig.). 1992. pap. 12.50 (*0-9632806-0-0*) Intra-Syst Res.

MacCorquodale, Patricia L. Engineers & Economic Conversion: From the Military to the Marketplace. LC 92-40393. 1993. 34.50 (*0-387-94005-7*) Spr-Verlag.

MacCoull, Leslie S. Coptic Perspective on Late Antiquity. LC 92-41249. (Collected Studies: Vol. CS398). 256p. 1993. 82.50 (*0-86078-364-2*, Pub. by Variorum UK) Ashgate Pub Co.

An Asterisk (*) at the beginning of an entry indicates that the title is appearing in BIP for the first time.

MacCrach, E. Spanish-English - English-Spanish. 5th ed. 758p. 1990. 25.00 (84-261-0079-1) IBD Ltd.

MacCracken. U. S.-U. S. S. R. Report on Climate & Climate Change. 1990. 75.95 (0-87371-440-7, QC981) Lewis Pubs.

MacCracken, Calvin D. A Handbook for Inventors: How to Protect, Patent, Finance, Develop, Manufacture, & Market Your Ideas. (Illus.). 224p. 1983. text ed. 19.95 (0-684-17906-7, Scribners) S&S Trade.

MacCracken, H., ed. see Lydgate, John.

Maccracken, H. N., ed. Lydgate's Minor Poems, Pt. 1: Religious Poems. (EETS ES Ser.: Vol. 107). 1969. reprint ed. 28.00 (0-8115-3409-X) Periodicals Srv.

— Lydgate's Minor Poems, Pt. 2: Secular Poems. (EETS, OS Ser.: Vol. 192). 1969. reprint ed. 26.00 (0-8115-3380-8) Periodicals Srv.

MacCracken, Jim. Ohio Fishing Guide: Region Eight Northern Ohio. (Fishing Guides Ser.: Pt. 8). 62p. (Orig.). 1984. pap. 2.95 (0-685-22555-0) Recreational Guides.

— Ohio Fishing Guide: Region Eleven Northeast Central Ohio. (Fishing Guides Ser.: Pt. 11). 64p. (Orig.). 1986. pap. 2.95 (0-685-44291-8) Recreational Guides.

— Ohio Fishing Guide: Region Five Western Ohio. (Fishing Guides Ser.: Pt. 5). 66p. (Orig.). 1986. pap. 2.95 (0-685-44288-8) Recreational Guides.

— Ohio Fishing Guide: Region Four Southeast Ohio. (Fishing Guides Ser.: Pt. 4). 62p. (Orig.). 1983. pap. 2.95 (0-685-22551-8) Recreational Guides.

— Ohio Fishing Guide: Region Nine North Central Ohio. (Fishing Guides Ser.: Pt. 9). 64p. (Orig.). 1984. pap. 2.95 (0-685-44289-6) Recreational Guides.

— Ohio Fishing Guide: Region One Southwest Ohio. (Fishing Guides Ser.: Pt. 1). 78p. (Orig.). 1985. pap. 3.95 (0-685-22548-8) Recreational Guides.

— Ohio Fishing Guide: Region Seven Northwest Ohio. (Fishing Guides Ser.: Pt. 7). 80p. (Orig.). 1986. pap. 3.95 (0-685-22554-2) Recreational Guides.

— Ohio Fishing Guide: Region Six Eastern Ohio. (Fishing Guides Ser.: Pt. 6). 78p. (Orig.). 1984. pap. 3.95 (0-685-22553-4) Recreational Guides.

— Ohio Fishing Guide: Region Ten Northeast Ohio. (Fishing Guides Ser.: Pt. 10). 60p. (Orig.). 1984. pap. 2.95 (0-685-44290-X) Recreational Guides.

— Ohio Fishing Guide: Region Three Central Ohio. (Fishing Guides Ser.: Pt. 3). 72p. (Orig.). 1986. pap. 2.95 (0-685-22550-X) Recreational Guides.

— Ohio Fishing Guide: Region Twelve Lake Erie. (Fishing Guides Ser.: Pt. 12). 100p. (Orig.). 1985. pap. 4.95 (0-685-44292-6) Recreational Guides.

— Ohio Fishing Guide: Region Two Southern Ohio. (Fishing Guides Ser.: Pt. 2). 64p. (Orig.). 1985. pap. 2.95 (0-685-22549-6) Recreational Guides.

— Ohio Fishing Guide, Vol. 1: Northern Ohio. (Fishing Guides Ser.). 424p. (Orig.). 1986. pap. 18.95 (0-685-44293-4) Recreational Guides.

— Ohio Fishing Guide, Vol. 2: Southern Ohio. (Fishing Guides Ser.). 434p. (Orig.). 1986. pap. 17.95 (0-685-44294-2) Recreational Guides.

— Pennsylvania Fishing Guide: Region Four Armstrong County, Indiana County, Westmoreland County. (Fishing Guides Ser.). 70p. (Orig.). 1988. pap. 3.95 (0-685-44297-7) Recreational Guides.

— Pennsylvania Fishing Guide: Region One Allegheny County, Fayette County, Greene County, Washington County. (Fishing Guides Ser.). 66p. (Orig.). 1988. pap. 3.95 (0-685-44295-0) Recreational Guides.

— Pennsylvania Fishing Guide: Region 2 Beaver County, Butler County, Lawrence County, Mercer County. (Fishing Guides Ser.). 70p. (Orig.). 1988. pap. 3.95 (0-685-44296-9) Recreational Guides.

MacCracken, John H. College & Commonwealth, & Other Educational Papers & Addresses. LC 67-26757. (Essay Index Reprint Ser.). 1977. 21.95 (0-8369-0644-6) Ayer.

MacCracken, Mary. A Circle of Children. 224p. (YA). (gr. 9). 1975. pap. 3.95 (0-451-14763-4, Sig) NAL-Dutton.

— Lovey: A Very Special Child. 256p. 1977. pap. 3.50 (0-451-13364-1, Sig) NAL-Dutton.

— Turnabout Children. 256p. 1987. pap. 5.99 (0-451-15876-8, Sig) NAL-Dutton.

MacCracken, Thomas G., ed. see Baratz, Lewis R.

MacCracken, Thomas G., ed. see Chancey, Tina & Neely, Patricia A.

MacCready, Jean & Quade, Vicki. Two under the Covers. (Illus.). (Orig.). 1981. pap. 2.95 (0-9602604-1-2) V Quade.

MacCrimmon, Kenneth R. & Wehrung, Donald A. Taking Risks: The Management of Uncertainty. 384p. 1986. 27.95 (0-02-919560-8) Free Pr.

Maccrimmon, Kenneth R. & Wehrung, Donald A. Taking Risks: The Management of Uncertainty. (Illus.). 384p. 1988. pap. 14.95 (0-02-919563-2) Free Pr.

MacCrossan, Tadhg. The Sacred Cauldron: Secrets of the Druids. LC 90-27755. (Llewellyn's New World Magic Ser.). (Illus.). 304p. (Orig.). 1991. pap. 10.95 (0-87542-103-2) Llewellyn Pubns.

Maccubbin, Robert P., ed. Tis Nature's Fault: Unauthorized Sexuality During the Enlightenment. 270p. 1988. pap. 17.95 (0-521-34768-8) Cambridge U Pr.

Maccubbin, Robert P. & Hamilton-Phillips, M., eds. The Age of William Third & Mary Second: Power, Politics & Patronage, 1688-1702. (Illus.). (Orig.). 1988. pap. 26.95 (0-317-93141-5) Col Wm & Mary Eng Dept.

MacCuish & Flyn. Crofting Law. U.K. text ed. 112.00 (0-406-17912-3) Butterworth Legal Pubs.

MacCuish, Marianne R. Into Another Country: Poetry. LC 90-33838. 64p. (Orig.). 1990. pap. 7.50 (0-931832-59-4) Fithian Pr.

MacCullagh, Richard. The Irish Currach Folk. (Illus.). 191p. 1993. 38.00 (0-86327-341-6, Pub. by Wolfhound Pr IE) Dufour.

MacCulloch, Diarmaid. Groundwork of Christian History. (Groundwork Ser.). 320p. (C). 1987. pap. text ed. 19.95 (0-7162-0434-7, Epworth Pr) TPI PA.

— The Later Reformation in England, 1547-1603. LC 89-27571. 205p. 1990. text ed. 45.00 (0-312-04064-4) St Martin.

— Suffolk & the Tudors: Politics & Religion in an English County 1500-1600. (Illus.). 360p. 1987. text ed. 79.00 (0-19-822914-3) OUP.

MacCulloch, John A. The Celtic & Scandinavian Religions. LC 72-11739. 180p. 1973. reprint ed. text ed. 38.50 (0-8371-6705-1, MCSR, Greenwood Pr) Greenwood.

— Celtic Mythology & Slavic Mythology. Bd. with LC 63-19088. LC 63-19088. (Mythology of All Races Ser.: Vol. 3). (Illus.). 477p. reprint ed. 40.00 (0-8154-0142-6) Cooper Sq.

— Medieval Faith & Fable. 1977. 17.95 (0-8369-7118-3, 7952) Ayer.

Macculloch, M. J., jt. auth. see Feldman, M. P.

Macculluch, John A. The Harrowing of Hell: A Comparative Study of an Early Christian Doctrine. LC 79-8113. 1983. reprint ed. 33.50 (0-404-18426-X) AMS Pr.

MacCumaill, Finn. Fianaigecht. LC 78-72614. (Royal Irish Academy. Todd Lecture Ser.: Vol. 16). reprint ed. 17.00 (0-404-60576-1) AMS Pr.

MacCunn, John. Six Radical Thinkers: Bentham, J.S. Mill, Codden, Carlyle, Massine, T.H. Green. Mayer, J. P., ed. LC 78-67370. (European Political Thought Ser.). 1979. reprint ed. lib. bdg. 21.95 (0-405-11720-5) Ayer.

MacCurdy, Doug & Tully, Shawn. Sports Illustrated Tennis: Strokes for Success. LC 93-28170. (Illus.). 1993. pap. 12.95 (1-56800-006-5, Pub. by Sports Illus Bks) Natl Bk Netwk.

MacCurdy, G. G. Human Skulls from Gazelle Peninsula. (Anthropological Publications Ser.: Vol. 6 no.1). (Illus.). 21p. 1914. pap. 10.00 (0-686-24089-8) U PA Mus Pubns.

MacCurdy, George G. A Study of Chiriquian Antiquities. (Connecticut Academy of Arts & Sciences Ser., Trans.: Vol. 3). 1911. pap. 300.00 (0-685-22870-3) Elliots Bks.

MacCurdy, George G., ed. Early Man. LC 77-86770. (Essay Index Reprint Ser.). 1977. 30.95 (0-8369-1184-9) Ayer.

MacCurdy, Raymond R. Francisco de Rojas Zorrilla. LC 68-9514. (Twayne's World Authors Ser.). 1968. lib. bdg. 17.95 (0-8057-2770-1) Irvington.

MacCurdy, Raymond R., ed. Spanish Drama of the Golden Age. (SPA.). 1985. reprint ed. 49.50 (0-89197-985-9); reprint ed. pap. text ed. 24.95 (0-89197-986-7) Irvington.

MacCurdy, Tim. Caesar of Santa Fe: A Novel from History. LC 89-85379. 246p. (Orig.). 1993. pap. 11.95 (0-938513-07-9) Amador Pubs.

MacCurtain, Margaret & O'Dowd, Mary, eds. Women in Early Modern Ireland: 1500-1800. 1991. text ed. 50.00 (0-7486-0223-2, Pub. by Edinburgh U Pr UK) Col U Pr.

— Women in Early Modern Ireland 1500-1800. (Illus.). 240p. 1992. pap. 25.00 (0-7486-0241-0, Pub. by Edinburgh U Pr UK) Col U Pr.

MacCutchan, Philip. Corpse. large type ed. 317p. 1992. 21.95 (0-7505-0309-2) Ulverscroft.

Macdaid, et al. Myers-Briggs Type Indicator: Atlas of Type Tables. 2nd ed. LC 86-32635. 595p. 1987. 50.00 (0-935652-13-2) Ctr Applications Psych.

MacDaniels, L. H. Study of the Fe'i Banana & Its Distribution with Reference to Polynesian Migrations. (BMB Ser.: No. 190). 1947. 12.00 (0-527-02298-5) Periodicals Srv.

MacDari, Conor. The Bible: An Irish Book. 84p. 1973. spiral bd. 9.35 (0-7873-0576-6) Mokelumne.

— The Bible: An Irish Book of Pre-Roman Spiritual Culture. 102p. 1973. spiral bd. 9.35 (0-7873-0577-4) Mokelumne.

— Irish Wisdom Preserved in Bible & Pyramids. 235p. 1993. reprint ed. spiral bd. 9.35 (0-7873-0575-8) Mokelumne.

MacDermot, Brian, ed. The Catholic Question in Ireland & England 1798-1822: The Papers of Denys Scully. 776p. 1988. 95.00 (0-7165-2423-6, Pub. by Irish Acad Pr IE) Intl Spec Bk.

— The Irish Catholic Petition of Eighteen Hundred Five: The Diary of Denys Scully. 230p. (C). 1993. text ed. 39.50 (0-7165-2497-X, Pub. by Irish Acad Pr IE) Intl Spec Bk.

Macdermot, C. G., jt. auth. see Anderson, Norman E.

MacDermot, Niall & Fahlander, Inger. Report of Mission to Uruguay in April-May, 1974. 10p. reprint ed. pap. 25.00 (0-317-29849-6, 2051908) Bks Demand.

MacDermot, Violet. The Cult of the Seer in the Ancient Middle East: A Contribution to Current Research on Hallucinations Drawn from Coptic & Other Texts. LC 79-152047. 841p. reprint ed. pap. 180.00 (0-7837-4674-1, 2044420) Bks Demand.

MacDermott. Selecting Thermoplastics for Engineering Applications. (Plastics Engineering Ser.: Vol. 5). 184p. 1984. 99.75 (0-8247-7099-4) Dekker.

MacDermott, Barbara & Deglin, Judith H. Understanding Basic Pharmacology: Practical Approaches for Effective Application. 546p. (C). 1994. pap. text ed. 24.95 (0-8036-5714-5) Davis Co.

MacDermott, Lord. Protection from Power under English Law. (Hamlyn Lectures Legal Reprint Ser.). viii, 196p. 1986. reprint ed. lib. bdg. 25.00 (0-8377-2430-9) Rothman.

***MacDermott, Richard P.** Inflammatory Bowel Disease Esophagus. Tytgat, G. N., ed. (Current Opinion in Gastroenterology Ser.). (Illus.). 480p. (Orig.). 1994. pap. text ed. 39.95 (1-85922-609-4) Current Science.

MacDermott, Richard P. & Tytgat, G. N. Inflammatory Bowel Disease & Esophagus. (Current Opinion in Gastroenterology 1993 Ser.). (Illus.). 210p. (Orig.). 1993. pap. 39.95 (1-870485-89-0) Current Science.

MacDevitt, Margaret L., jt. auth. see Brault, Margaret A.

MacDhomhnuill, Domhnull. Manuscript by Domhnull MacDhomhnuill. 282p. 1992. pap. 51.00 (0-685-67870-9) A MacRaonuill.

MacDiarmid, Alan G. The Bond to Halogens & Halogenoids, Pt. 1. (Organometallic Compounds of the Group IV Elements Ser.: Vol. 2). (Illus.). 392p. reprint ed. pap. 111.80 (0-8357-7338-8, 2055068) Bks Demand.

MacDiarmid, Alan G., ed. Organometallic Compounds of the Group Four Elements, Vol. 1 Part 2: The Bond to Carbon. LC 68-11573. 275p. reprint ed. pap. 78.40 (0-685-15958-2, 2027831) Bks Demand.

— Organometallic Compounds of the Group Four Elements, Vol. 2, Pt. 2: The Bond of Halogens & Halogenoids. LC 68-11573. 248p. reprint ed. Vol. 2, Pt. 2-The Bond to Halogens & Halogenoids. pap. 70.70 (0-685-16077-7, 2027076) Bks Demand.

— Organometallic Compounds of the Group Four Elements, Vol. 1, Pt. 1: The Bond to Carbon. LC 68-11573. (Illus.). 619p. reprint ed. pap. 176.50 (0-685-23608-0, 2029002) Bks Demand.

MacDiarmid, Hugh. Aesthetics in Scotland. Bold, Alan, ed. LC 84-28469. (Illus.). 100p. 1985. 31.00 (0-389-20558-3, N8120) B&N Imports.

— Selected Poetry. Riach, Alan & Grieve, Michael, eds. LC 93-5312. 320p. 1993. 23.95 (0-8112-1248-3) New Directions.

Macdiarmid, Hugh, jt. auth. see Chiari, Joseph.

MacDiarmid, Hugh, et al. Seven Poets. 88p. 1989. 30.00 (0-906474-13-2, Pub. by Third Eye Centre UK) St Mut.

— Seven Poets. 1989. 85.00 (0-906474-14-0, Pub. by Third Eye Centre UK) St Mut.

MacDicken, Kenneth, jt. ed. see Taylor, David.

Macdicken, Kenneth G. & Vergara, Napoleon T., eds. Agroforestry: Classification & Management. 416p. 1990. text ed. 84.95 (0-471-83781-4) Wiley.

MacDodnald, Stuart. Technology & the Tyranny of Export Controls: Whisper Who Dares. 256p. 1990. text ed. 59.95 (0-312-04085-7) St Martin.

MacDonagh, Donagh. Warning to Conquerors. LC 68-26023. 1968. 12.95 (0-8023-1167-9) Dufour.

MacDonagh, Oliver. Early Victorian Government, 1830-1870. LC 76-57957. 242p. 1977. 34.95 (0-8419-0304-2) Holmes & Meier.

— The Emancipist: Daniel O'Connell, 1830-47, Vol. 2. 375p. 1989. text ed. 39.95 (0-312-03711-2) St Martin.

— Jane Austen: Real & Imagined Worlds. 240p. (C). 1993. reprint ed. pap. text ed. 13.00 (0-300-05449-1) Yale U Pr.

— A Pattern of Government Growth 1800-1860. (Modern Revivals in History Ser.). 370p. 1993. 67.95 (0-7512-0165-0, Pub. by Gregg Revivals UK) Ashgate Pub Co.

MacDonagh, Oliver, et al, eds. Irish Culture & Nationalism, 1750-1950. LC 81-21292. 1983. text ed. 32.50 (0-312-43595-9) St Martin.

MacDonagh, Sandra. Victorian Patchwork Patterns: Instructions & Full-Size Templates for 12 Quilts. (Illus.). 64p. (Orig.). 1988. pap. 4.50 (0-486-25543-3) Dover.

MacDonagh, Thomas. The Poetical Works of Thomas MacDonagh. LC 75-28822. reprint ed. 20.00 (0-404-13814-4) AMS Pr.

MacDonagh, Tom. My Green Age. 148p. 1986. pap. 8.95 (0-905169-76-X, Pub. by Poolbeg Pr IE) Dufour.

MacDonald. At the Back of the North Wind. 1986. lib. bdg. 9.49 (0-8167-2876-3); pap. 2.95 (0-8167-0470-8) Troll Assocs.

— Drugs, Drinking & Adolescence. 2nd ed. 264p. 1989. pap. 23.95 (0-8151-5993-5, Yr Bk Med Pubs) Mosby Yr Bk.

— Europe: A Tantalizing Romance. 1992. 52.00 (0-8191-8843-3); pap. 21.50 (0-8191-8844-1) U Pr of Amer.

— Hidden Markov & Other Models for Discrete-Valued Time. 1995. (0-412-55850-5) Chapman & Hall.

— Historic Warplanes. 1995. (0-7858-0337-8) Bk Sales Inc.

— Lakes, Lures & Lodges: An Angler's Guide to Western Canada. 1993. per. 14.95 (0-88801-176-8) InBook.

— Manual of Oncologic Therapeutics. 1995. write for info. (0-397-51394-1) Lippincott.

— Newar Art: Nepalese Art During the Malla Period. 1979. 55.00 (0-85668-056-7, Pub. by Aris & Phillips UK) David Brown.

— Ontogeny of the Immune System of the Gut. 1990. 133.00 (0-8493-6084-6, QR185) CRC Pr.

— Son of the Day & the Daughter of the Night. (J). Date not set. pap. 7.95 (0-671-75230-8, S&S Bks Young Read) S&S Childrens.

— Trout Tales & Salmon Stories. 1993. per. 14.95 (0-88982-121-6, Pub. by Oolichan Bks CN) InBook.

— Vancouver: A Visual History. (NFS Canada Ser.). Date not set. 43.00 (0-88922-311-4, Pub. by Talonbooks CN) InBook.

— Very Windy Day. 1994. 4.99 (0-517-13500-0) Random Hse Value.

MacDonald, ed. Advances in Resist Technology & Processing, No. V. 1988. 65.00 (0-89252-955-5, 920) SPIE.

***MacDonald & Acig.** Caught in the Act: The Feldberg Investigation. 1994. pap. 9.95 (1-897766-05-X, Pub. by Jon Pubng UK) InBook.

MacDonald, jt. auth. see Bohm.

MacDonald, jt. auth. see Brown.

MacDonald, ed. see European Nutritionists Staff.

MacDonald, jt. auth. see Fravel.

MacDonald, A. A., jt. ed. see Drijvers, J. W.

MacDonald, A. A., jt. ed. see Houwen, L. A.

***MacDonald, A. A., et al, eds.** The Renaissance in Scotland: Studies in Literature, Religion, History & Culture Offered to John Durkan. LC 94-26032. (Studies in Intellectual History: 54). 1994. 91.50 (90-04-10097-0) E J Brill.

MacDonald, A. F. Federal Aid: A Study of the American Subsidy System. (American Federalism-the Urban Dimension Ser.). (Illus.). 1978. reprint ed. lib. bdg. 29.95 (0-405-10494-4) Ayer.

MacDonald, A. G. Effects of High Pressure on Biological Systems. (Advances in Comparative & Environmental Physiology Ser.: Vol. 17). (Illus.). 260p. 1993. 189.00 (0-387-54845-9) Spr-Verlag.

MacDonald, A. H., ed. Quantum Hall Effect. (C). 1990. lib. bdg. 130.00 (0-7923-0537-X); pap. text ed. 64.00 (0-7923-0538-8) Kluwer Ac.

MacDonald, A. R. Prison Secrets: Things Seen, Suffered, & Recorded During Seven Years in Ludlow Street Jail. LC 70-90185. (Mass Violence in America Ser.). 1977. reprint ed. 17.95 (0-405-01327-2) Ayer.

MacDonald, Agnes, jt. auth. see MacDonald, Kenneth B.

MacDonald, Aileen A. The Figure of Merlin in Thirteenth Century French Romance. (Studies in Mediaeval Literature: Vol. 3). 260p. 1990. lib. bdg. 89.95 (0-88946-317-4) E Mellen.

MacDonald, Alan. The Family Easter Book. LC 92-36602. (Illus.). 96p. (J). 1993. 12.95 (0-7459-2349-6) Lion USA.

MacDonald, Alan & Stickley, Janet. The Family Christmas Book. (Illus.). 96p. 1992. 14.95 (0-7459-2032-2) Lion USA.

MacDonald, Alasdair A., jt. ed. see Aertsen, Henk.

Macdonald, Alastair, tr. see Malraux, Andre.

Macdonald, Alexander, ed. Letters to the Argyll Family from Elizabeth Queen of England, Mary Queen of Scots, & Others. LC 77-12765. (Maitland Club, Glasgow. Publications: No. 50). reprint ed. 12.50 (0-404-53031-1) AMS Pr.

— Papers Relative to the Royal Guard of Scottish Archers in France. LC 79-175588. (Maitland Club, Glasgow. Publications: No. 36). reprint ed. 11.50 (0-404-53007-9) AMS Pr.

— Reports on the State of Certain Parishes in Scotland. LC 79-175588. (Maitland Club, Glasgow. Publications: No. 34). reprint ed. 24.50 (0-404-53003-6) AMS Pr.

MacDonald, Alexander, ed. see Blackwood, Adam.

Macdonald, Alexander, ed. see James First King of England.

MacDonald, Alexander, ed. see Maitland Club Staff.

MacDonald, Alexander, ed. see Miles, Dorothy.

Macdonald, Alexander W. Essays on the Enthnology of Nepal & South Asia. 1984. 75.00 (0-7855-0224-6, Pub. by Ratna Pustak Bhandar) St Mut.

— Essays on the Enthnology of Nepal & South Asia, Vol. 2. 1987. 75.00 (0-7855-0225-4, Pub. by Ratna Pustak Bhandar) St Mut.

— Essays on the Ethnology of Nepal & South Asia. 1984. 75.00 (0-7855-0311-0, Pub. by Ratna Pustak Bhandar) St Mut.

Macdonald, Alexander W., ed. Essays on the Ethnology of Nepal & South Asia, Vol. I. 318p. (C). 1984. 125.00 (0-89771-119-X, Pub. by Ratna Pustak Bhandar) St Mut.

— Essays on the Ethnology of Nepal & South Asia, Vol. II. 147p. (C). 1987. 200.00 (0-89771-120-3, Pub. by Ratna Pustak Bhandar) St Mut.

Macdonald, Alexandra, ed. see Jackson, Mildred & Teague, Terri.

MacDonald, Alice J. The Macmillan College Workbook. 2nd ed. 480p. (C). 1991. pap. write for info. (0-02-373075-7) Macmillan.

Macdonald, Alister G. Physiological Aspects of Deep Sea Biology. LC 73-90652. (Physiological Society Monographs: No. 31). 464p. reprint ed. pap. 132.30 (0-318-34818-7, 2031685) Bks Demand.

Macdonald, Allan J. Berengar & the Reform of the Sacramental System. 444p. 1977. reprint ed. lib. bdg. 30.00 (0-915172-25-9) Richwood Pub.

— Hildebrand: A Life of Gregory the Seventh. (Great Medieval Churchmen Ser.). 254p. 1977. reprint ed. lib. bdg. 17.50 (0-915172-26-7) Richwood Pub.

— Lanfranc, a Study of His Life, Work & Writing. LC 80-2223. reprint ed. 37.50 (0-404-18768-4) AMS Pr.

***MacDonald, Amy.** Cousin Ruth's Tooth. LC 94-26426. (Illus.). (J). (gr. 1-8). write for info. (0-395-71253-X) HM.

— Let's Do It. LC 91-71836. (Let's Explore Board Bks.). (Illus.). 12p. (J). (ps). 1992. bds. 5.95 (1-56402-024-X) Candlewick Pr.

— Let's Go. LC 92-46095. (Illus.). 12p. (J). (ps up). 1994. 5.95 (1-56402-202-1) Candlewick Pr.

— Let's Make a Noise. LC 91-71837. (Let's Explore Board Bks.). (Illus.). 12p. (J). (ps). 1992. bds. 5.95 (1-56402-025-8) Candlewick Pr.

— Let's Play. LC 91-71838. (Let's Explore Board Bks.). (Illus.). 12p. (J). (ps). 1992. bds. 5.95 (1-56402-023-1) Candlewick Pr.

— Let's Try. LC 91-71839. (Let's Explore Board Bks.). (Illus.). 12p. (J). (ps). 1992. bds. 5.95 (1-56402-022-3) Candlewick Pr.

— Little Beaver & the Echo. (Illus.). 32p. (J). 1990. 14.95 (0-399-22203-0, Putnam) Putnam Pub Group.

— Little Lumpty. 12p. (J). (ps). 1994. 5.95 (1-56402-201-3) Candlewick Pr.

— Rachel Fister's Blister. (Illus.). 32p. (J). (ps-3). 1990. 13.95 (0-395-52152-1) HM.

— Rachel Fister's Blister. (Illus.). 32p. (J). (gr. k-3). 1993. pap. 4.95 (0-395-65744-X) HM.

MacDonald, Amy, et al. The Presumpscot River Watch Guide to the Presumpscot River: Its History, Ecology, & Recreational Uses. 80p. (Orig.). 1994. pap. 9.99 (0-9639872-0-8) Presumpscot River.

MacDonald, Andrew. Hunter. 259p. (Orig.). 1989. pap. 5.95 (0-937944-04-1) Natl Alliance.

Macdonald, Andrew. The Turner Diaries. 2nd ed. LC 80-82692. 216p. (Orig.). 1980. pap. 4.95 (0-937944-02-5) Natl Alliance.

M

An Asterisk (*) at the beginning of an entry indicates that the title is appearing in BIP for the first time.

MacDonald, Andrew S. Nowhere to Go but Down? 232p. 1989. text ed. 44.95 (*0-04-445408-2*); pap. text ed. 18.95 (*0-04-445305-1*) Routledge Chapman & Hall.

MacDonald, Andy. Don't Slip on the Soap: More Crazy Capers from the Best-Selling Author of Bread & Molasses. 177p. 1978. pap. 12.95 (*0-7737-1021-3*, Pub. by Stoddart Pubng CN) Genl Dist Srvs.

MacDonald, Angus & MacDonald, Patricia. Granite & Green: Above North-East Scotland. (Illus.). 168p. 1993. 34.95 (*1-85158-465-X*, Pub. by Mnstream UK) Trafalgar.

MacDonald, Angus A. The Spirit of Service: Recollections of a Pioneer. Macdonald, Eleanor J., ed. (Illus.). 131p. (Orig.). 1988. 20.00 (*0-9637172-0-0*) E J Macdonald.

Macdonald, Angus J. Structure & Architecture. LC 94-1101. (Illus.). 144p. 1994. pap. 29.95 (*0-7506-1798-5*, Butterwrth Archit) Buttrwrth-Heinemann.

MacDonald, Angus W. Building Your Own Earth-Tempered Home: A Construction Manual. (Illus.). 96p. (Orig.). 1984. pap. 11.95 (*0-938432-19-2*) Mother Earth.

MacDonald, Anne. Wickiup Walkingstick. (Illus.). 23p. (J). 1995. 6.95 (*0-88995-063-6*, Pub. by Red Deer CN) BookWorld Dist.

MacDonald, Anne L. Feminine Ingenuity: How Women Inventors Changed America. (Illus.). 544p. 1994. pap. 14.00 (*0-345-38314-1*, Ballantine Trade) Ballantine.

Macdonald, Anne L. No Idle Hands: The Social History of American Knitting. (Illus.). 512p. 1990. pap. 12.95 (*0-345-36253-5*, Ballantine Trade) Ballantine.

MacDonald, Arley R. Managers View Information. LC 89-19570. (Illus.). 96p. reprint ed. pap. 27.40 (*0-7837-6302-6*, 2046017) Bks Demand.

MacDonald, Arthur. Criminology. LC 75-156960. reprint ed. 34.50 (*0-404-09123-7*) AMS Pr.

MacDonald, Austin F. Government of the Argentine Republic. LC 71-180411. reprint ed. 34.00 (*0-404-56136-5*) AMS Pr.

Macdonald, Barbara & Rich, Cynthia. Look Me in the Eye: Old Women, Aging, & Ageism. 2nd ed. LC 91-36595. 192p. (Orig.). 1991. pap. 8.95 (*0-933216-87-4*) Spinsters Ink.

MacDonald, Barbara J., jt. ed. see Lawson, V. K.

MacDonald, Barrie. Broadcasting in the United Kingdom: A Guide to Information Sources. 2nd ed. 304p. 1993. text ed. 100.00 (*0-7201-2086-1*, Mansell Pub) Cassell.

MacDonald-Bayne, M. Beyond the Himalayas. 1973. 250.00 (*0-87968-063-6*) Gordon Pr.

MacDonald, Betty. Anybody Can Do Anything. 1993. reprint ed. lib. bdg. 27.95x (*1-56849-019-4*) Buccaneer Bks.

— The Egg & I. 21.95 (*0-89190-959-1*, Am Repr) Amereon Ltd.

— The Egg & I. 287p. 1991. reprint ed. lib. bdg. 23.00x (*0-8095-9103-0*) Borgo Pr.

— The Egg & I. 1993. reprint ed. lib. bdg. 27.95 (*1-56849-016-X*) Buccaneer Bks.

— The Egg & I. LC 87-45068. 288p. 1987. reprint ed. pap. 12.00 (*0-06-091428-9*, PL/1428, PL) HarpC.

— Hello, Mrs. Piggle-Wiggle. LC 57-5613. (Illus.). (J). (gr. k-3). 1957. 14.95 (*0-397-31715-8*, Lipp Jr Bks) HarpC Child Bks.

— Hello, Mrs. Piggle-Wiggle. LC 57-5613. (Trophy Bk.). (Illus.). (J). (gr. 1-3). 1985. pap. 3.95 (*0-06-440149-9*, Trophy) HarpC Child Bks.

— Mrs. Piggle-Wiggle. rev. ed. LC 47-1876. (Illus.). (J). (gr. k-3). 1957. 14.95 (*0-397-31712-3*, Lipp Jr Bks) HarpC Child Bks.

— Mrs. Piggle-Wiggle. rev. ed. LC 47-1876. (Trophy Bk.). (Illus.). 120p. (J). (gr. 1-3). 1985. pap. 3.95 (*0-06-440148-0*, Trophy) HarpC Child Bks.

— The Mrs. Piggle-Wiggle Treasury. LC 94-15040. (J). Date not set. 19.95 (*0-06-024812-2*); lib. bdg. 19.89 (*0-06-024813-0*) HarpC Child Bks.

— Mrs. Piggle-Wiggle's Farm. LC 54-7299. (Illus.). (J). (gr. k-3). 1954. 14.95 (*0-397-31713-1*, Lipp Jr Bks) HarpC Child Bks.

— Mrs. Piggle-Wiggle's Farm. LC 54-7299. (Trophy Bk.). (Illus.). 132p. (J). (gr. 1-3). 1985. pap. 3.95 (*0-06-440150-2*, Trophy) HarpC Child Bks.

— Mrs. Piggle-Wiggle's Magic. (J). 1976. 15.95 (*0-8488-1087-2*) Amereon Ltd.

— Mrs. Piggle-Wiggle's Magic. LC 49-11124. (Illus.). (J). (gr. k-3). 1957. 14.95 (*0-397-31714-X*, Lipp Jr Bks) HarpC Child Bks.

— Mrs. Piggle-Wiggle's Magic. LC 49-11124. (Trophy Bk.). (Illus.). 144p. (J). (gr. 1-3). 1985. pap. 3.95 (*0-06-440151-0*, Trophy) HarpC Child Bks.

— Nancy & Plum. (Orig.). 1993. reprint ed. lib. bdg. 27.95x (*1-56849-017-8*) Buccaneer Bks.

— Onions in the Stew. Dalzell, William, ed. 1984. 4.95 (*0-87129-383-8*, O16) Dramatic Pub.

— The Plague & I. 1993. reprint ed. lib. bdg. 27.95x (*1-56849-018-6*) Buccaneer Bks.

MacDonald, Bob & Grace, Eric. Wonderstruck. 96p. 1991. pap. 10.95 (*0-7737-5477-6*, Pub. by Stoddart Pubng CN) Genl Dist Srvs.

— Wonderstruck II. 96p. 1991. pap. 10.95 (*0-7737-5478-4*, Pub. by Stoddart Pubng CN) Genl Dist Srvs.

MacDonald, Bonney. Henry James's "Italian Hours" Revelatory & Resistant Impression. Litz, A. Walton, ed. LC 89-20128. (Studies in Modern Literature: No. 106). 146p. reprint ed. 41.40 (*0-8357-2025-X*, 2070733) Bks Demand.

MacDonald, Brian, ed. see Kendall, F. R.

Macdonald, Bruce. Practical Woody Plant Propagation for Nursery Growers, Vol. I. (Illus.). 660p. 1986. 59.95 (*0-88192-062-2*) Timber.

Macdonald, Bruce, jt. auth. see Mumford, Enid.

MacDonald, Bruce A., ed. see Metallurgical Society of AIME Staff.

MacDonald, Bruce K., ed. see Meyerowitz, Joel.

MacDonald, Byron J. Calligraphy: The Art of Lettering with the Broad Pen. pap. 5.95 (*0-8008-1182-8*) Taplinger.

MacDonald, C. Cicero: Pro Murena. 220p. 1982. reprint ed. 17.95 (*0-86292-010-8*, Pub. by Brstl Class Pr UK) Focus Info Gr.

MacDonald, C. A. The United States, Britain & Appeasement 1936-1939. LC 79-27121. 224p. 1981. text ed. 32.50 (*0-312-83313-X*) St Martin.

MacDonald, C. A., jt. auth. see Lanham, L. W.

MacDonald, Callum A. The Killing of SS Obergruppenfuhrer Reinhard Heydrich. 288p. 1989. text ed. 24.95 (*0-02-919561-6*) Free Pr.

— The Killing of SS Obergruppenfuhrer Reinhard Heydrich. (Illus.). 256p. 1990. reprint ed. pap. 9.95 (*0-02-034505-4*) Macmillan.

— Korea: The War Before Vietnam. LC 86-22943. 320p. 1987. text ed. 29.95 (*0-02-919621-3*) Free Pr.

— The Lost Battle: Crete 1941. 320p. 1993. text ed. 24.95 (*0-02-919625-6*) Free Pr.

***MacDonald, Cameron.** Could It Be Stress? Reflections on Psychosomatic Illness. 192p. (C). 1992. pap. 32.00x (*1-874640-10-6*, Pub. by Argyll Pubng UK) St Mut.

MacDonald, Caroline. Hostilities: Nine Bizarre Stories. LC 93-19019. 112p. (YA). (gr. 7 up). 1994. 13.95 (*0-590-46063-3*) Scholastic Inc.

— Secret Lives. (J). 1995. 15.00 (*0-671-51081-9*, S&S Bks Young Read) S&S Childrens.

— Speaking to Miranda. LC 91-47901. (Willa Perlman Bks.). 256p. (YA). (gr. 7 up). 1992. lib. bdg. 13.89 (*0-06-021103-2*) HarpC Child Bks.

***MacDonald, Carolyn A.** Advanced Concepts for Geriatric Nursing Assistants. LC 94-61648. (Illus.). 224p. 1994. pap. 28.95 (*0-910251-71-1*, ACG73) Venture Pub PA.

Macdonald, Charles. The Goals-Oriented Performance Appraisal Workshop, Set. 159p. 1990. ring bd. 99.95 (*0-87425-139-7*) Human Res Dev Pr.

MacDonald, Charles. Scotland's Gift - Golf. rev. ed. (Classics of Golf Ser.). (Illus.). 340p. 28.00 (*0-940889-07-2*) Classics Golf.

***MacDonald, Charles B.** Company Commander. 320p. 1984. 9.95 (*1-56865-044-2*, GuildAmerica) Dblday Bk Music.

— The Mighty Endeavor: The American War in Europe. (Illus.). 621p. 1992. reprint ed. pap. 16.95 (*0-306-80486-7*) Da Capo.

— United States Army in World War 2, European Theater of Operations: The Last Offensive. LC 71-183070. (Illus.). 532p. 1973. 25.50 (*0-16-001922-2*, S/N 008-029-00087-3) USGPO.

MacDonald, Charles G. Iran, Saudi Arabia, & the Law of the Sea: Political Interaction & Legal Development in the Persian Gulf. LC 79-6186. (Contributions in Political Science Ser.: No. 48). xv, 226p. 1980. text ed. 55.00 (*0-313-20768-2*, MLS/) Greenwood.

Macdonald, Charles R. The Marketing Audit Workbook. LC 81-7096. 446p. 1986. 49.95 (*0-87624-364-2*) P-H.

— MBO Can Work! How to Manage by Contract. (Illus.). 224p. 1982. text ed. 31.95 (*0-07-044331-9*) McGraw.

MacDonald, Charles R. Twenty-Four Ways to Greater Business Productivity: Master Checklists for Marketing, Advertising, Sales, Distribution & Customer Service. LC 81-7096. 446p. 1981. text ed. 49.50 (*0-87624-203-4*, Inst Busn Plan) P-H.

Macdonald, Christine. Lewis the Story of an Island. (C). 1992. text ed. 39.00 (*0-86152-804-2*, Pub. by Acair Ltd UK) St Mut.

MacDonald, Claire. Quick & Easy Desserts & Puddings. (Illus.). 130p. (Orig.). 1994. pap. 9.95 (*0-563-36443-2*, BBC-Parkwest) Parkwest Pubns.

MacDonald, Colin. Down to Earth: Life in the Highlands & Islands of Scotland. (Aberdeen University Press Bks.). (Illus.). 352p. 1991. pap. 17.90 (*0-08-041224-6*, Pub. by Aberdeen U Pr) Macmillan.

Macdonald, Cynthia. Living Wills: New & Selected Poems. LC 90-52737. 160p. 1992. pap. 12.00 (*0-679-74278-6*) Knopf.

MacDonald, Cynthia. Mind-Body Identity Theories. 256p. 1989. 45.00 (*0-415-03347-0*, A3659) Routledge.

Macdonald, Cynthia. Mind-Body Identity Theories. (Problems of Philosophy Series: Their Past & Present). 256p. 1992. pap. 16.95 (*0-415-07104-6*, A7024) Routledge.

MacDonald, Cynthia & MacDonald, Graham. Philosophy of Psychology: Debates on Psychological Explanation. 401p. 1995. 74.95 (*0-631-18541-0*); pap. 24.95 (*0-631-18542-9*) Blackwell Pubs.

***Macdonald, Cynthia & Macdonald, Graham, eds.** Connectionism: Debates on Psychological Exploration. (Illus.). 320p. (C). 1995. 59.95 (*0-631-19744-3*) Blackwell Pubs.

— Connectionism: Debates on Psychological Exploration. (Illus.). (C). 1995. pap. 24.95 (*0-631-19745-1*) Blackwell Pubs.

Macdonald, D. Sedimentation, Tectonics & Eustasy. 1991. pap. 125.00 (*0-632-03017-8*) Blackwell Sci.

Macdonald, D., jt. ed. see Amlaner, C.

MacDonald, D. B. The Development of Muslim Theology, Jurisprudence & Constitution Theory. 400p. 1985. 280.00 (*1-85077-066-2*, Darf Pubs Ltd) St Mut.

— The Religious Attitude & Life in Islam. 336p. 1985. 230.00 (*1-85077-050-6*, Darf Pubs Ltd) St Mut.

***MacDonald, D. J.** Factors Related to Laboratory Production & Evaluation of Berlinite Crystal. 1994. write for info. (*0-615-00091-6*) US Interior.

MacDonald, D. L. Poor Polidor: A Critical Biography of the Author of the Vampyre. 400p. 1991. 60.00 (*0-8020-2774-1*) U of Toronto Pr.

Macdonald, D. L. & Scherf, K. D., eds. Frankenstein: or The Modern Prometheus: Mary Shelley. 280p. 1994. pap. 7.95 (*1-55111-038-5*) Broadview Pr.

Macdonald, D. L., ed. see Polidori, John W.

MacDonald, D. M., ed. Immunodermatology. (Illus.). 304p. 1984. text ed. 95.00 (*0-407-00338-X*) Buttrwrth-Heinemann.

MacDonald, D. R. Eyestone. LC 87-83285. 1988. 15.95 (*0-916366-48-0*) Pushcart Pr.

***Macdonald, D. Ross.** Mercantile Law of Scotland. 1995. pap. text ed. write for info. (*0-406-10585-5*, UK) Butterworth Legal Pubs.

Macdonald, D. W., et al, eds. Chemical Signals in Vertebrates. (Illus.). 688p. 1991. 95.00 (*0-19-857731-1*) OUP.

MacDonald, Daniel. Radicalism of Shelley & Its Sources. LC 76-90369. 143p. (C). 1970. reprint ed. 40.00 (*0-87753-029-7*) Phaeton.

MacDonald, Dave & Patterson, Vicky. A Handbook of Drug Training: Learning About Drugs & Working with Drug Users. 240p. 1991. 35.00 (*0-415-06171-7*, A5428) Routledge.

MacDonald, David. Twenty Years in Tibet. (C). 1991. reprint ed. 36.00 (*81-85326-50-9*, Pub. by Vintage II) S Asia.

— The Velvet Claw: A Natural History of the Carnivores. (Illus.). 256p. 1993. 31.95 (*0-563-20844-9*, BBC-Parkwest) Parkwest Pubns.

MacDonald, David A., jt. auth. see Schmidt, Volkmar.

Macdonald, David S. Traveler Stamp Album. (Illus.). 272p. 1986. pap. 12.95 (*0-937458-42-2*) Harris & Co.

Macdonald, David S., ed. Adventurer II Stamp Album. (Illus.). 272p. 1986. pap. 6.95 (*0-937458-44-9*) Harris & Co.

— Canada Stamp Album. (Illus.). 416p. 1984. pap. 21.95 (*0-937458-08-2*) Harris & Co.

— U. S. Liberty Album. (Illus.). 416p. (J). (gr. 6 up). 1984. text ed. 18.95 (*0-937458-29-5*) Harris & Co.

— U. S. Plate Blocks, Vol. A. (Illus.). 480p. 1983. pap. text ed. 24.95 (*0-937458-18-X*) Harris & Co.

— U. S. Plate Blocks, Vol. B. (Illus.). 416p. 1984. reprint ed. pap. text ed. 24.95 (*0-937458-19-8*) Harris & Co.

MacDonald, David W. Rabies & Wildlife: A Biologist's Perspective. (Illus.). 1980. write for info. (*0-318-54886-0*) OUP.

Macdonald, David W., ed. The Encyclopedia of Mammals. (Illus.). 960p. 65.00 (*0-87196-871-1*) Facts on File.

MacDonald, David W., jt. ed. see Brown, Richard E.

MacDonald, Dennis R. Christianizing Homer: The Odyssey, Plato, & the Acts of Andrew. 384p. 1994. 45.00 (*0-19-508722-4*) OUP.

— The Legend & the Apostle: The Battle for Paul in Story & Canon. LC 82-21953. 144p. (Orig.). (C). 1983. pap. 11.99 (*0-664-24464-5*, Westminster) Westminster John Knox.

***MacDonald, Diane L.** Transgressive Corporeality: The Body, Poststructuralism & the Theological Imagination. LC 94-24727. 272p. 1995. text ed. 57.50x (*0-7914-2487-1*); pap. text ed. 18.95x (*0-7914-2488-X*) State U NY Pr.

Macdonald, Digby D., ed. Transient Techniques in Electrochemistry. LC 77-24603. 330p. 1977. 75.00 (*0-306-31010-4*, Plenum Pr) Plenum.

MacDonald, Donald. Christian Experience. 160p. 1988. 16.95 (*0-85151-527-4*) Banner of Truth.

— Diaries of Donald MacDonald. LC 72-77060. 233p. 1973. reprint ed. lib. bdg. 29.50 (*0-678-00914-7*) Kelley.

— A Geography of Modern Japan. 176p. (C). 1985. pap. 12.50 (*0-904404-43-9*, Pub. by Paul Norbury Pubns UK) Humanities.

Macdonald, Donald F. Fasti Ecclesiae Scoticanae. 530p. (C). 1988. text ed. 125.00 (*0-7152-0495-5*) St Mut.

— Fasti Ecclesiae, Vol. X: Scoticanae. 530p. (C). 1989. 150.00 (*0-685-60688-0*, Pub. by St Andrew UK) St Mut.

— Scotland's Shifting Population: 1770-1850. LC 78-15153. (Illus.). vii, 172p. 1979. reprint ed. lib. bdg. 29.50 (*0-87991-860-8*) Porcupine Pr.

Macdonald, Donald S. The Koreans: Contemporary Politics & Society. 2nd ed. (Illus.). 326p. (C). 1990. pap. text ed. 21.50 (*0-8133-0967-0*, MACKREP) Westview.

— The Koreans: Contemporary Politics & Society. 2nd ed. (Illus.). 326p. (C). 1990. text ed. 66.00 (*0-8133-0966-2*, MACKREH) Westview.

MacDonald, Donald S. U. S.-Korea Relations from Liberation to Self-Reliance: The Twenty-Year Record. 345p. (C). 1992. pap. text ed. 53.50 (*0-8133-8193-2*) Westview.

Macdonald, Dorothy, comp. Cumulative Index to American Book Collector. Date not set. 7.50 (*0-89679-008-8*) Moretus Pr.

MacDonald, Douglas. Spirals. (Offset Offshoot Ser.: No.4). 34p. 1979. pap. 10.00 (*0-317-06440-1*) Ommation Pr.

Macdonald, Douglas J. Adventures in Chaos: American Intervention for Reform in the Third World. 361p. 1992. 45.00 (*0-674-00577-5*) HUP.

MacDonald, Douglas M., jt. auth. see Edwards, James C.

MacDonald, Duncan & Sagendorph, Robb. Old-Time New England Cookbook. LC 92-47279. Orig. Title: Rain, Hail, & Baked Beans: A New England Seasonal Cookbook. (Illus.). 224p. 1993. reprint ed. pap. 5.95 (*0-486-27630-9*) Dover.

Macdonald, Duncan B. Aspects of Islam. LC 77-179530. (Select Bibliographies Reprint Ser.). 1980. reprint ed. 28.95 (*0-8369-6659-7*) Ayer.

— Religious Attitude & Life in Islam. LC 70-121277. reprint ed. 20.50 (*0-404-04125-6*) AMS Pr.

Macdonald, Dwight. Against the American Grain: Essays on the Effects of Mass Culture. LC 83-7665. (Quality Paperbacks Ser.). (Illus.). xvi, 429p. 1983. reprint ed. pap. 9.95 (*0-306-80205-8*) Da Capo.

MacDonald, Dwight. Discriminations: Essays & Afterthoughts. (Quality Paperbacks Ser.). (Illus.). 500p. 1985. reprint ed. pap. 11.95 (*0-306-80252-X*) Da Capo.

— On Movies. LC 81-9717. (Quality Paperbacks Ser.). 492p. 1981. reprint ed. pap. 11.95 (*0-306-80150-7*) Da Capo.

MacDonald, Dwight & Geng, Veronica, eds. Parodies: An Anthology from Chaucer to Beerbohm & after. (Quality Paperbacks Ser.). 600p. 1985. reprint ed. pap. 12.95 (*0-306-80239-2*) Da Capo.

Macdonald, Dwight & Sutton, Francis X. The Ford Foundation: The Men & the Millions. 212p. (Orig.). 1988. pap. 29.95 (*0-88738-748-9*) Transaction Pubs.

MacDonald, Dwight, tr. see Camus, Albert.

MacDonald, Dwight, ed. see Herzen, Alexander.

Macdonald, Dwight

Macdonald, E. K., et al. Control of Emissions of Volatile Organic Compounds from the Large Scale, No. EUR 13568. 96p. 1991. pap. 11.00 (*92-826-2867-1*, CD-NA-13568-EN-C) UNIPUB.

MacDonald, Edgar. James Branch Cabell & Richmond-in-Virginia. (Illus.). 373p. 1992. text ed. 42.00 (*0-685-62416-1*) U Pr of Miss.

— James Branch Cabell & Richmond-in-Virginia. LC 92-44966. (Illus.). 373p. (C). 1993. text ed. 39.95 (*0-87805-622-X*) U Pr of Miss.

MacDonald, Edgar E. & Inge, Tonette B. Ellen Glasgow: A Reference Guide. (Reference Guides to Literature Ser.). 328p. 1986. text ed. 50.00 (*0-8161-8218-3*, Hall Reference) Macmillan.

MacDonald, Edgar E., jt. ed. see Inge, M. Thomas.

MacDonald, Edgar E., ed. see Lazarus, Rachel M.

MacDonald, Eileen. Shoot the Women First: Inside the Secret World of Female Terrorists. LC 92-386. 1992. 19.50 (*0-679-41596-3*) Random.

Macdonald, Eleanor J., ed. see MacDonald, Angus A.

***MacDonald, Eleanor K.** A Window into History: Family Memory in Children's Literature. 208p. 1995. pap. 24.95 (*0-89774-879-4*, 2119) Oryx Pr.

***MacDonald, Elisabeth.** Voices on the Wind. 352p. (Orig.). 1994. mass mkt. 4.99 (*0-380-77376-7*) Avon.

MacDonald, Elizabeth. The Very Windy Day. LC 91-690. (Illus.). 40p. (J). (ps-3). 1992. 15.00 (*0-688-11044-4*, Tambourine Bks); lib. bdg. 14.93 (*0-688-11045-2*, Tambourine Bks) Morrow.

MacDonald, Elizabeth, jt. auth. see Koffman, Laurence.

Macdonald, Elspeth T. & Macdonald, J. B. Drug Treatment in the Elderly. LC 82-1913. (Wiley Series on Disease Management in the Elderly: No. 1). 259p. reprint ed. pap. 73.90 (*0-8357-8623-4*, 2035046) Bks Demand.

MacDonald, Erik. Theater at the Margins: Texts for a Post-Structured Stage. (Theater: Theory - Text - Performance Ser.). 184p. (C). 1993. text ed. 37.50 (*0-472-10311-3*) U of Mich Pr.

Macdonald, F. & Ford, C. H. Oncogenes & Tumor Suppressor Genes. (Medical Perspectives Ser.). 112p. (Orig.). 1991. pap. 46.50x (*1-872748-55-4*, Pub. by Bios Scientific UK) Coronet Bks.

MacDonald, Fiona. Ancient Egyptians. (Insights Ser.). (Illus.). 60p. (J). (gr. 4 up). 1993. 15.95 (*0-8120-6378-3*) Barron.

— Aztecs. (Insights Ser.). (Illus.). 60p. (J). (gr. 4 up). 1993. 15.95 (*0-8120-6377-5*) Barron.

— Cities: Citizens & Civilizations. LC 91-33498. (Timelines Ser.). (Illus.). 48p. (J). 1992. 13.95 (*0-531-15247-2*) Watts.

— Crime & Punishment. LC 95-10385. (Timelines Ser.). (Illus.). 48p. (J). (gr. 5-8). 1995. lib. bdg. 15.33 (*0-531-14368-6*); pap. 7.95 (*0-531-15280-4*) Watts.

Macdonald, Fiona. Explorers: Expeditions & Pioneers. LC 94-17370. (Timelines Ser.). (J). 1994. pap. 17.95 (*0-531-15718-0*) Watts.

MacDonald, Fiona. Explorers: Expeditions & Pioneers. LC 94-14040. (Timelines Ser.). (Illus.). 48p. (J). (gr. 5-8). 1994. lib. bdg. 14.98 (*0-531-14332-5*) Watts.

— Houses: Habitats & Home Life. (Timelines Ser.). (Illus.). 48p. (J). (gr. 5-8). 1994. lib. bdg. 14.98 (*0-531-14333-3*) Watts.

— Houses: Habitats & Home Life. LC 94-14040. (Timelines Ser.). 1994. pap. 7.95 (*0-531-15719-9*) Watts.

— How Would You Survive As an Ancient Greek? LC 95-3177. (How Would You Survive? Ser.). (Illus.). 48p. (J). (gr. 5-8). 1995. lib. bdg. 14.98 (*0-531-14342-2*) Watts.

— How Would You Survive as an Aztec? LC 94-28068. (How Would You Survive? Ser.). (Illus.). (J). lib. bdg. 14.98 (*0-531-14348-1*) Watts.

— How Would You Survive in the Middle Ages? LC 95-3176. (How Would You Survive? Ser.). (Illus.). 48p. (J). (gr. 5-8). 1995. lib. bdg. 14.98 (*0-531-14343-0*) Watts.

— Kings & Queens: Rulers & Despots. (Timelines Ser.). (Illus.). 48p. (J). (gr. 5-8). 1995. lib. bdg. 15.33 (*0-531-14369-4*) Watts.

— Kings & Queens: Rulers & Despots. (Timelines Ser.). (Illus.). 48p. (J). (gr. 5-8). 1995. pap. 7.95 (*0-531-15281-2*) Watts.

— A Medieval Castle. (Inside Story Ser.). (Illus.). 48p. (J). (gr. 5 up). 1990. 17.95 (*0-87226-340-1*) P Bedrick Bks.

Macdonald, Fiona. A Medieval Castle. (Inside Story Ser.). (Illus.). 48p. (J). (gr. 5 up). 1993. pap. 8.95 (*0-87226-258-8*) P Bedrick Bks.

— A Medieval Cathedral. (Inside Story Ser.). (Illus.). 48p. (J). (gr. 5 up). 1994. 17.95 (*0-87226-350-9*); pap. 8.95 (*0-87226-266-9*) P Bedrick Bks.

MacDonald, Fiona. The Middle Ages. (Illustrated History of the World Ser.). (Illus.). 80p. (J). (gr. 2-6). 1993. 17.95 (*0-8160-2788-9*) Facts on File.

— Plains Indians. (Insights Ser.). (Illus.). 60p. (J). (gr. 4 up). 1993. 15.95 (*0-8120-6376-7*) Barron.

Macdonald, Fiona. Rain Forest. LC 93-24449. (New View Ser.). (J). 1994. lib. bdg. 19.97 (*0-8114-9243-5*) Raintree Steck-V.

— A Roman Fort. LC 93-16397. (Inside Story Ser.). (Illus.). 48p. (J). (gr. 5 up). 1993. 17.95 (*0-87226-370-3*); pap. 8.95 (*0-87226-259-6*) P Bedrick Bks.

***MacDonald, Fiona.** Ships. (Worldwise Ser.). (Illus.). 48p. (J). (gr. 4-6). 1995. lib. bdg. 14.98 (*0-531-14379-1*) Watts.

An Asterisk (*) at the beginning of an entry indicates that the title is appearing in BIP for the first time.

— A Sixteenth Century Mosque. LC 94-20008. (Inside Story Ser.). (Illus.). 48p. (J). 1994. lib. bdg. 17.95 (*0-87226-310-X*) P Bedrick Bks.

— A Viking Town. LC 95-1845. (Inside Story Ser.). (Illus.). 48p. (YA). (gr. 5 up). 1995. lib. bdg. 18.95 (*0-87226-382-7*) P Bedrick Bks.

— Vikings. (Insights Ser.). (Illus.). 60p. (J). (gr. 4 up). 1993. 15.95 (*0-8120-6375-9*) Barron.

MacDonald, Fiona & Bergin, Mark. A Greek Temple. LC 92-10712. (Inside Story Ser.). (Illus.). 48p. (J). (gr. 5 up). 1992. 17.95 (*0-87226-361-4*) P Bedrick Bks.

***MacDonald, Fiona, et al.** A Samurai Castle. LC 95-2181. (Inside Story Ser.). (Illus.). 48p. (YA). (gr. 5 up). 1995. lib. bdg. 18.95 (*0-87226-381-9*) P Bedrick Bks.

MacDonald, Frank, jt. ed. see Sanderson, George.

Macdonald, Frederick. Bishop Stirling of the Falklands. 1976. lib. bdg. 59.95 (*0-8490-1509-X*) Gordon Pr.

Macdonald, G. The Little Island. (J). 1993. mass mkt. 4.99 (*0-440-40830-X*) Dell.

— The Silver Coinage of Crete: A Metrological Note. (Illus.). 29p. 1974. pap. 5.00 (*0-916710-13-0*) Obol Intl.

MacDonald, G. & Rutherford, Brian, eds. Accounts, Accounting & Accountability: Essays in Memory of Peter Bird. 240p. 1990. 57.50 (*0-412-02781-X*, A4461, Chap & Hall NY) Chapman & Hall.

MacDonald, G. J. & Sertorio, L., eds. Global Climate & Ecosystem Change. LC 90-47793. (NATO ASI Series B, Physics: Vol. 240). (Illus.). 240p. 1991. 75.00 (*0-306-43715-5*, Plenum Pr) Plenum.

MacDonald, Gail. A Step Farther & Higher. 288p. 1993. pap. 8.99 (*0-88070-599-X*, Multnomah Bks) Questar Pubs.

MacDonald, Gail & MacDonald, Gordon. Till the Heart Be Touched: Building Love in Marriage, Family & Friendship. LC 92-15967. 224p. 1992. 14.99 (*0-8007-1672-8*) Revell.

Macdonald, Gaynor, jt. ed. see Maher, John C.

MacDonald, George. Adela Cathcart. (George MacDonald Original Works: Series IV). 462p. 1994. reprint ed. 18.00 (*1-881084-23-X*) Johannesen.

— The Adventures of Ranald Bannerman. rev. ed. Phillips, Michael, ed. (George MacDonald Classics for Young Readers Ser.: Bk. 4). 192p. (J). (gr. 3 up). 1991. 10.99 (*1-55661-223-0*) Bethany Hse.

— Alec Forbes & His Friend Annie. Phillips, Michael R., ed. (George MacDonald Classics for Young Readers Ser.). 256p. (YA). (gr. 2-7). 1990. 10.99 (*1-55661-140-4*) Bethany Hse.

— Alec Forbes of Howglen. LC 87-82627. (Sunrise Centenary Editions Ser.: Vol. 1). 489p. 1988. 27.50 (*0-940652-50-1*) Sunrise Bks.

— Annals of a Quiet Neighbourhood. deluxe ed. 1992. 37.50 (*0-940652-60-9*) Sunrise Bks.

— Annals of a Quiet Neighbourhood. (George MacDonald Original Works: Series V). 600p. 1995. reprint ed. 20.00 (*1-881084-29-9*) Johannesen.

Macdonald, George. At the Back of the North Wind. LC 64-21758. (Airmont Classics Ser.). (Illus.). (YA). (gr. 5 up). 1966. pap. 1.50 (*0-8049-0100-7*, CL-100) Airmont.

MacDonald, George. At the Back of the North Wind. 7.99 (*1-55748-024-9*, Christian Lib) Barbour & Co.

— At the Back of the North Wind. LC 87-45455. (Illus.). 320p. (J). 1988. 18.95 (*0-87923-703-1*) Godine.

— At the Back of the North Wind. LC 88-63292. (Books of Wonder). (Illus.). 352p. (J). (gr. 5 up). 1989. 17.95 (*0-688-07808-7*) Morrow Jr Bks.

— At the Back of the North Wind. 352p. 1990. 12.99 (*0-517-69120-5*) Random Hse Value.

— At the Back of the North Wind. (Victorian Children's Classics Ser.). 370p. (YA). Date not set. pap. 4.95 (*0-88270-556-3*) Bridge Pub.

— At the Back of the North Wind. rev. ed. Phillips, Michael, ed. 176p. (J). (ps-2). 1991. 10.99 (*1-55661-196-X*) Bethany Hse.

— At the Back of the North Wind. (George MacDonald Original Works: Series II). (Illus.). 378p. (YA). 1992. reprint ed. 16.00 (*1-881084-07-8*) Johannesen.

— Baronet's Song. 1995. pap. 5.99 (*1-55661-580-9*) Bethany Hse.

— The Baronet's Song. abr. rev. ed. Phillips, Michael, ed. LC 83-6417. 208p. 1983. pap. 6.99 (*0-87123-291-X*) Bethany Hse.

— Castle Warlock. (George MacDonald Original Works: Series I). 379p. 1992. reprint ed. 16.00 (*1-881084-03-5*) Johannesen.

— The Christmas Stories of George MacDonald. LC 81-68187. (J). (gr. 3-7). 1981. 12.99 (*0-89191-491-9*, 54916, Chariot Bks) Chariot Family.

— The Curate's Awakening. Phillips, Michael R., ed. LC 85-18513. 224p. 1985. pap. 7.99 (*0-87123-838-1*) Bethany Hse.

— Curate's Awakening. 1993. pap. 5.99 (*1-55661-372-5*) Bethany Hse.

— A Daughter's Devotion. rev. ed. Phillips, Michael, ed. LC 88-19256. (George MacDonald Classics Ser.). 320p. (YA). (gr. 11 up). 1988. pap. 7.99 (*0-87123-906-X*) Bethany Hse.

— Diary of an Old Soul: Reflections for Each Day of the Year. LC 94-21982. 1994. pap. 8.99 (*0-8066-2734-4*, Augsburg) Augsburg Fortress.

— The Disciple & Other Poems. deluxe ed. 1989. 27.50 (*0-940652-87-0*) Sunrise Bks.

— Discovering the Character of God. Phillips, Michael R., ed. 320p. 1989. 17.99 (*1-55661-068-8*) Bethany Hse.

— Donal Grant. 1990. 47.50 (*0-940652-56-0*) Sunrise Bks.

— Donal Grant. (George MacDonald Original Works: Series I). 397p. 1992. reprint ed. 16.00 (*1-881084-02-7*) Johannesen.

— The Elect Lady. 1989. 26.50 (*0-940652-79-X*) Sunrise Bks.

— The Evolution of Coinage. viii, 148p. 1980. 20.00 (*0-916710-73-4*) Obol Intl.

— The Fantasy Stories of George Macdonald, 4 vols. 1980. pap. 23.90 (*0-8028-1858-7*) Eerdmans.

Macdonald, George. Fifty Years of Freethought, 2 vols, Set. 1974. lib. bdg. 400.00 (*0-8490-0161-7*) Gordon Pr.

MacDonald, George. Fisherman's Lady. 1993. pap. 5.99 (*1-55661-371-7*) Bethany Hse.

— The Fisherman's Lady. abr. rev. ed. Phillips, Michael, ed. LC 82-1322. 278p. 1982. pap. 7.99 (*0-87123-197-2*) Bethany Hse.

— Flashman & the Dragon. 1989. pap. 8.95 (*0-317-02805-7*) NAL-Dutton.

— Flight of the Shadow. (George MacDonald Original Works: Series IV). 337p. 1994. reprint ed. 16.00 (*1-881084-26-4*) Johannesen.

— The Gentlewoman's Choice. 2nd ed. Phillips, Mike, ed. LC 87-6556. 228p. 1987. pap. 6.99 (*0-87123-941-8*) Bethany Hse.

— George MacDonald Original Works, 5 vols., Series III. (Illus.). 354p. (YA). (gr. 5 up). 1993. reprint ed. Per volume, last 2 volumes with B&W illus. 32.00 (*1-881084-21-3*) Johannesen.

— George MacDonald Original Works, 6 vols., Set. (Illus.). 1992. reprint ed. 78.00 (*1-881084-06-X*) Johannesen.

— George MacDonald Original Works, 5 vols., Set. (Illus.). 1992. reprint ed. 65.00 (*1-881084-12-4*) Johannesen.

— George MacDonald Original Works, 5 vols., Set. (Illus.). (J). (gr. 5 up). 1993. reprint ed. 74.00 (*1-881084-18-3*) Johannesen.

— George MacDonald Original Works, 3 vols., Set. (Illus.). (YA). (gr. 5 up). 1993. reprint ed. Per volume, first 3 volumes with color plates. 60.00 (*1-881084-20-5*) Johannesen.

— George MacDonald Original Works, 6 vols., Set. (Illus.). 1994. reprint ed. 84.00 (*1-881084-28-0*) Johannesen.

— George MacDonald Original Works, 6 bks., Set, Series V. 1995. reprint ed. 90.00 (*1-881084-35-3*) Johannesen.

— Getting to Know Jesus. 160p. 1987. pap. 3.50 (*0-345-34307-7*, Ballantine Epiphany) Ballantine.

— Gold Coast, Past & Present: A Short Description of the Country & Its People. LC 70-94483. (Illus.). 352p. 1969. reprint ed. text ed. 35.00 (*0-8371-2370-4*, MGC&, Negro U Pr) Greenwood.

— The Golden Key. (Illus.). 1993. 17.25 (*0-8446-6661-0*) Peter Smith.

— The Golden Key. 2nd ed. LC 67-6087. (Illus.). 96p. (J). (gr. 1 up). 1984. 15.00 (*0-374-32706-8*); pap. 4.95 (*0-374-42590-6*) FS&G.

— Golden Key & Other Fantasy Stories. Sadler, Glenn G., ed. (Fantasy Stories of George MacDonald Ser.). 176p. 1980. pap. 6.99 (*0-8028-1859-5*) Eerdmans.

— The Gray Wolf & Other Fantasy Stories. Sadler, Glenn G., ed. (Fantasy Stories of George MacDonald Ser.). 200p. 1980. pap. 6.99 (*0-8028-1862-5*) Eerdmans.

— Guild Court, a London Story. (George MacDonald Original Works: Series II). 382p. 1992. reprint ed. 16.00 (*1-881084-10-8*) Johannesen.

— The Heart of George MacDonald: A One-Volume Collection of His Most Important Fiction, Essays, Sermons, Drama, Poetry, & Letters. Hein, Rolland, ed. (Wheaton Literary Ser.). 464p. 1994. 24.99 (*0-87788-371-8*) Shaw Pubs.

— A Hidden Life & Other Poems. 1989. 27.50 (*0-940652-86-2*) Sunrise Bks.

— The Highlander's Last Song. Phillips, Michael, ed. LC 86-11739. 250p. 1986. pap. 7.99 (*0-87123-658-3*) Bethany Hse.

— Home Again - The Elect Lady (Duplex) (George MacDonald Original Works: Series II). 373p. 1992. reprint ed. 16.00 (*1-881084-11-6*) Johannesen.

— The Hope of the Gospel. 1989. 24.50 (*0-940652-84-6*) Sunrise Bks.

— The Hope of the Gospel. fac. ed. (Sermons of George MacDonald Ser.: Vol. 5). 240p. (C). 1987. pap. 14.95 (*0-944724-00-0*) J J Flynn.

— The Lady's Confession. Phillips, Michael, ed. LC 86-8243. 250p. 1986. pap. 7.99 (*0-87123-881-0*) Bethany Hse.

— Lady's Confession. 1994. pap. 5.99 (*1-55661-452-7*) Bethany Hse.

Macdonald, George. The Laird's Inheritance. rev. ed. Phillips, Michael R., ed. LC 87-18434. 352p. 1987. pap. 7.99 (*0-87123-903-5*) Bethany Hse.

MacDonald, George. The Landlady's Master. Phillips, Michael R., ed. 208p. (Orig.). (YA). (gr. 11 up). 1989. pap. 7.99 (*0-87123-904-3*) Bethany Hse.

— The Landlady's Master. large type ed. Phillips, Michael R., ed. (Orig.). 1991. pap. 20.95 (*0-7927-1030-4*, CS0269, Curley Lrg Print) Chivers N Amer.

— Life Essential: The Hope of the Gospel. 2nd ed. Hein, Rolland, ed. LC 74-16732. (Wheaton Literary Ser.). 102p. 1978. pap. 6.99 (*0-87788-499-4*) Shaw Pubs.

— The Light Princess. LC 93-561. (Little Barefoot Bks.). (Illus.). 148p. (J). 1993. 6.00 (*1-56957-903-2*) Barefoot Bks.

— The Light Princess. rev. ed. LC 69-14981. (Illus.). 120p. (J). (gr. 1 up). 1969. 15.00 (*0-374-34455-8*) FS&G.

— The Light Princess. rev. ed. LC 69-14981. (Illus.). 120p. (J). (gr. 1 up). 1984. pap. 4.95 (*0-374-44458-7*) FS&G.

— The Light Princess & Other Fairy Tales. (George MacDonald Original Works: Series III). (Illus.). 305p. (J). (gr. 5 up). 1993. reprint ed. 16.00 (*1-881084-16-7*) Johannesen.

— The Light Princess & Other Fantasy Stories. Sadler, George G., ed. (Fantasy Stories of George MacDonald Ser.). 176p. 1980. pap. 6.99 (*0-8028-1861-7*) Eerdmans.

— Lilith. 1981. pap. 6.99 (*0-8028-6061-3*) Eerdmans.

— Lilith A & Lilith 1896: A Duplex. (George MacDonald Original Works: Series IV). 388p. 1994. reprint ed. 18.00 (*1-881084-27-2*) Johannesen.

— Little Daylight. LC 85-29769. (Illus.). 40p. (J). (gr. 2 up). 1988. 12.95 (*0-688-06300-4*); lib. bdg. 12.88 (*0-688-06301-2*) Morrow Jr Bks.

— The Lost Princess: A Double Story. Sadler, Glenn E., ed. (Illus.). 144p. (J). 1992. text ed. 21.99 (*0-8028-5070-7*) Eerdmans.

— The Maiden's Bequest. Phillips, Michael, ed. LC 85-4024. (Orig.). 1985. pap. 7.99 (*0-87123-823-3*) Bethany Hse.

— Malcolm. deluxe ed. 1988. 27.50 (*0-940652-53-6*) Sunrise Bks.

— Malcolm. (George MacDonald Original Works: Series V). 450p. 1995. reprint ed. 18.00 (*1-881084-31-0*) Johannesen.

— The Marquis of Lossie. 1994. 27.50 (*0-940652-54-4*) Sunrise Bks.

— Marquis of Lossie. (George MacDonald Original Works: Series V). 390p. 1995. reprint ed. 18.00 (*1-881084-32-9*) Johannesen.

— Marquis' Secret. Phillips, Michael, ed. LC 82-12949. 229p. 1986. 13.99 (*0-87123-914-0*) Bethany Hse.

— Marquis' Secret. 1994. pap. 5.99 (*1-55661-451-9*) Bethany Hse.

— The Marquis' Secret: Sequel to The Fisherman's Lady. 320p. 1983. reprint ed. pap. 7.99 (*0-87123-324-X*) Bethany Fellow.

— The Minister's Restoration. Phillips, Michael R., ed. LC 87-33813. (George MacDonald Classics Ser.). 208p. (Orig.). 1988. pap. 6.99 (*0-87123-905-1*) Bethany Hse.

— The Miracles of Our Lord. (Sermons of George MacDonald Ser.: Vol. 4). 280p. (C). 1987. reprint ed. pap. 14.95 (*0-317-89464-1*); reprint ed. write for info. (*0-944724-02-7*) J J Flynn.

— The Musician's Quest. Phillips, Michael, ed. LC 84-18508. 272p. 1984. reprint ed. pap. 8.99 (*0-87123-444-0*) Bethany Hse.

— Paul Faber, Surgeon. (George MacDonald Original Works: Series II). 396p. 1992. reprint ed. 16.00 (*1-881084-08-6*) Johannesen.

— The Peasant Girl's Dream. rev. ed. Phillips, Michael R., ed. LC 88-33336. (George MacDonald Classics Ser.). 224p. (YA). (gr. 11 up). 1989. pap. 7.99 (*1-55661-023-8*) Bethany Hse.

— Phantastes. 1981. pap. 7.99 (*0-8028-6060-5*) Eerdmans.

— Phantastes. (George MacDonald Original Works: Series IV). (Illus.). 324p. 1994. reprint ed. 18.00 (*1-881084-22-1*) Johannesen.

— The Portent & Other Stories. (George MacDonald Original Works: Series IV). 340p. 1994. reprint ed. 18.00 (*1-881084-24-8*) Johannesen.

— The Princess & Curdie. 306p. (J). 1989. reprint ed. lib. bdg. 26.95 (*0-89966-591-8*) Buccaneer Bks.

— The Princess & Curdie. (George MacDonald Original Works: Ser. III). (Illus.). 320p. (J). (gr. 5 up). 1993. reprint ed. 20.00 (*1-881084-15-9*) Johannesen.

— Princess & the Goblin. (Airmont Classics Ser.). (J). (gr. 3 up). 1967. pap. 1.50 (*0-8049-0156-2*, CL-156) Airmont.

— Princess & the Goblin. (J). (gr. 1-4). 1984. pap. 3.50 (*0-14-035029-2*, Puffin) Puffin Bks.

— The Princess & the Goblin. LC 93-11264. (Everyman's Library of Children's Classics). (J). (gr. 2 up). 1993. 12.95 (*0-679-42810-0*, Everymans Lib) Knopf.

— The Princess & the Goblin. LC 86-2532. (Books of Wonder). (Illus.). 208p. (J). (ps up). 1986. 20.00 (*0-688-06604-6*) Morrow Jr Bks.

Macdonald, George. The Princess & the Goblin. (J). (gr. 4-7). 1991. pap. 2.95 (*0-590-44025-X*) Scholastic Inc.

MacDonald, George. The Princess & the Goblin. (J). 1989. reprint ed. lib. bdg. 26.95 (*0-89966-598-5*) Buccaneer Bks.

— The Princess & the Goblin. (George MacDonald Original Works: Series III). (Illus.). 308p. (J). (gr. 5 up). 1993. reprint ed. 20.00 (*1-881084-14-0*) Johannesen.

— The Princess & the Goblin, The Princess & Curdie. (World's Classics Ser.). 400p. (J). 1990. pap. 6.95 (*0-19-282579-8*) OUP.

— Rampolli. (George MacDonald Original Works: Series V). 330p. 1995. reprint ed. 18.00 (*1-881084-34-5*) Johannesen.

— Ranald Bannerman's Boyhood. (George MacDonald Original Works: Vol. III). (Illus.). 335p. (J). (gr. 5 up). 1993. reprint ed. 20.00 (*1-881084-13-2*) Johannesen.

— Robert Falconer. 1990. 33.50 (*0-940652-52-8*) Sunrise Bks.

— A Rough Shaking. (George MacDonald Original Works: Series I). (Illus.). 384p. 1992. reprint ed. 16.00 (*1-881084-04-3*) Johannesen.

— Salted with Fire. deluxe ed. 1989. 26.50 (*0-940652-98-6*) Sunrise Bks.

— Seaboard Parish. (George MacDonald Original Works: Series V). 650p. 1995. reprint ed. 20.00 (*1-881084-30-2*) Johannesen.

— The Shepherd's Castle. 240p. (Orig.). 1995. mass mkt. 5.99 (*1-55661-633-3*) Bethany Hse.

— Sir Gibbie. 1989. 27.50 (*0-940652-55-2*) Sunrise Bks.

— Sir Gibbie. (George MacDonald Original Works: Series I). 390p. 1992. reprint ed. 16.00 (*1-881084-01-9*) Johannesen.

— The Son of the Day & the Daughter of the Night. LC 84-145155. (Illus.). 40p. (YA). (gr. 7-9). 1991. reprint ed. pap. 7.95 (*0-914676-45-8*, Green Tiger S&S) S&S Childrens.

— Stephen Archer & Other Tales. (George MacDonald Original Works: Series IV). 354p. 1994. reprint ed. 16.00 (*1-881084-25-6*) Johannesen.

— The Story of Little Christmas. abr. ed. (Illus.). 32p. (J). (gr. 2-6). 1995. 14.99 (*0-7814-0233-6*, Chariot Bks) Chariot Family.

— There & Back. (George MacDonald Original Works: Series I). 392p. 1992. reprint ed. 16.00 (*1-881084-05-1*) Johannesen.

— Thomas Wingfold, Curate. 1989. 29.50 (*0-940652-57-9*) Sunrise Bks.

— A Time to Grow. (Michael Phillips Ser.). 192p. (Orig.). 1991. pap. 6.99 (*1-55661-202-8*) Bethany Hse.

— A Time to Harvest. Phillips, Michael, ed. (George MacDonald Classic Devotionals Ser.: Bk. 2). 128p. (Orig.). 1991. pap. 6.99 (*1-55661-207-9*) Bethany Hse.

— The Tutor's First Love. Phillips, Mike, ed. LC 84-6481. 240p. 1984. reprint ed. pap. 7.99 (*0-87123-596-X*) Bethany Hse.

— Unspoken Sermons, Vol. 1. 1989. 24.50 (*0-940652-80-3*); pap. 9.95 (*0-940652-42-0*) Sunrise Bks.

— Unspoken Sermons, Vol. 2. 1989. 24.50 (*0-940652-81-1*); pap. 9.95 (*0-940652-43-9*) Sunrise Bks.

— Unspoken Sermons, Vol. 3. 1989. pap. 9.95 (*0-940652-44-7*) Sunrise Bks.

— Unspoken Sermons (Series One) The Sermons of George MacDonald. (C). 1987. reprint ed. pap. 14.95 (*0-944724-04-3*) J J Flynn.

— Unspoken Sermons (Series Three) The Sermons of George MacDonald. 250p. (C). 1987. reprint ed. pap. 14.95 (*0-944724-06-X*) J J Flynn.

— Unspoken Sermons (Series Two) The Sermons of George MacDonald. 250p. (C). 1987. reprint ed. pap. 14.95 (*0-944724-05-1*) J J Flynn.

— The Vicar's Daughter. (George MacDonald Original Works: Series II). 389p. 1992. reprint ed. 16.00 (*1-881084-09-4*) Johannesen.

— Wee Sir Gibbie of the Highlands. Phillips, Michael R., ed. (George MacDonald Classics for Young Readers Ser.). 240p. (J). (gr. 2-7). 1990. 10.99 (*1-55661-139-0*) Bethany Hse.

— What's Mine's Mine. 1994. write for info. (*0-940652-64-1*) Sunrise Bks.

— What's Mine's Mine. (George MacDonald Original Works: Series I). 387p. 1991. reprint ed. 16.00 (*1-881084-00-0*) Johannesen.

— The Wise Woman - Gutta Percha Willie, (Duplex) (George MacDonald Original Works: Ser. III). (Illus.). 354p. (J). (gr. 5 up). 1993. reprint ed. 16.00 (*1-881084-17-5*) Johannesen.

— Wise Woman & Other Fantasy Stories. Sadler, Glenn G., ed. (Fantasy Stories of George MacDonald Ser.). 176p. 1980. pap. 6.99 (*0-8028-1860-9*) Eerdmans.

MacDonald, George & Phillips, Michael. The Baron's Apprenticeship. LC 86-11734. 250p. 1986. pap. 7.99 (*0-87123-655-9*) Bethany Hse.

MacDonald, George & Phillips, Michael R. Knowing the Heart of God. 368p. 1990. 17.99 (*1-55661-131-5*) Bethany Hse.

— The Poet's Homecoming. 192p. 1990. pap. 7.99 (*1-55661-135-8*) Bethany Hse.

MacDonald, George & Phillips, Mike. The Shepherd's Castle. 288p. (Orig.). 1983. pap. 7.99 (*0-87123-579-X*) Bethany Hse.

MacDonald, George, ed. see Robinson, Andrew.

MacDonald, George, et al. Champions: The Super Hero Role Playing Game. rev. ed. (Illus.). 352p. (C). 1989. 32.00 (*1-55806-043-X*, 400) Hero Games.

— Fantasy Hero. (Hero System Ser.). (Illus.). 256p. (Orig.). (C). 1990. pap. 20.00 (*1-55806-102-9*, 502) Iron Crown Ent Inc.

— Hero System Rulesbook. (Hero System Ser.). (Illus.). 220p. (Orig.). (C). 1990. pap. 20.00 (*1-55806-094-4*, 500) Iron Crown Ent Inc.

Macdonald, George A. How Successful Lawyers Were Educated. Addressed to Students, to Those Who Expect to Become Students, & to Their Parents & Teachers. 168p. 1985. reprint ed. lib. bdg. 22.50 (*0-8377-0853-2*) Rothman.

Macdonald, George E. England's Antiphon. 1977. 18.95 (*0-8369-7227-9*, 8026) Ayer.

— Fifty Years of Freethought, Being the Story of the Truth Seeker with the Natural History of Its Third Editor, 2 vols. in 1. LC 76-161334. (Atheist Viewpoint Ser.). (Illus.). 1224p. 1972. reprint ed. 80.95 (*0-405-03793-7*) Ayer.

— Stephen Archer, & Other Tales. LC 79-152946. (Short Story Index Reprint Ser.). 1977. reprint ed. 23.95 (*0-8369-3805-4*) Ayer.

— Thumbscrew & Rack. rev. ed. (Illus.). 26p. 1991. reprint ed. 4.00 (*0-910309-68-X*, 5232) Am Atheist.

***MacDonald, George F.** Chiefs of the Sea & Sky: Haida Heritage Sites of the Queen Charlotte Islands. (Illus.). 96p. 1989. pap. 19.95 (*0-7748-0331-2*) U of Wash Pr.

— Haida Monumental Art: Villages of the Queen Charlotte Islands. LC 94-3977. (Illus.). 228p. 1994. pap. 39.95 (*0-295-97362-5*) U of Wash Pr.

— Kitwanga Fort Report. (Canadian Museum of Civlization Mercury Series-Canadian Ethnology Service). (Illus.). 250p. 1988. pap. text ed. 12.95 (*0-660-10777-5*, Pub. by CN Mus Civilization CN) U Ch Pr.

— Ninstints: Haida World Heritage Site. (Illus.). 64p. 1983. pap. 14.95 (*0-7748-0163-8*) U of Wash Pr.

MacDonald, George F. & Inglis, Richard I. The Dig: An Archaeological Reconstruction of a West Coast Village. (Canadian Prehistory Ser.). (Illus.). x, 90p. 1985. pap. text ed. 8.50 (*0-317-18868-2*, 56528-9, Pub. by Natl Mus Sci Tech CN) U Ch Pr.

MacDonald, George F., ed. see Barbeau, Marius & Beynon, William.

MacDonald, George W. Historical Papers on Modern Explosives. 1991. lib. bdg. 250.00 (*0-87700-977-5*) Revisionist Pr.

MacDonald, Gerald, ed. Vocabulario De Romance En Latin: Antonio De Nebrija. LC 72-96003. 214p. (LAT & SPA.). 1973. 19.95 (*0-87722-018-2*) Temple U Pr.

Macdonald, Geraldine M., jt. auth. see Hudson, Barbara L.

MacDonald, Glenn M., jt. auth. see Davies, James B.

M

*Macdonald, Glynn. Alexander Technique. (Headway Lifeguides Ser.). (Illus.). 94p. 1995. pap. 13.95 (0-340-59680-5, Pub. by Hodder & Stoughton Ltd UK) Trafalgar.

MacDonald, Gordon. The Effective Father. 256p. 1990. pap. 4.99 (0-8423-0669-2) Tyndale.

*Macdonald, Gordon. The Life God Blesses. LC 94-28151. 1994. 18.99 (0-8407-9155-0) Oliver-Nelson.

MacDonald, Gordon. Ponga Orden En Su Mundo Interior. Araujo, Juan S., tr. 176p. (SPA.). (C). 1989. pap. 4.95 (0-88113-246-2) Edit Betania.

— Rediscovering Yourself: How to Grasp the Opportunities of Mid-Life. 1987. pap. 7.99 (0-8007-1561-6) Revell.

— Restaurando Su Vida Deshecha (Rebuilding Your Broken World) (SPA.). 1993. 7.99 (1-56063-009-4, 498458) Editorial Unilit.

— Restoring Joy to Your Inner World. (Guidelines for Living Ser.). 1992. 10.98 (0-88486-059-0) Arrowood Pr.

Macdonald, Gordon & Hubbard, Douglass. Volcanoes of the National Parks in Hawaii. rev. ed. (Illus.). 64p. (C). 1989. pap. text ed. 5.95 (0-940295-01-6) HI Natural Hist.

MacDonald, Gordon, jt. ed. see Bunton, Robin.

MacDonald, Gordon, jt. auth. see MacDonald, Gail.

Macdonald, Gordon A., et al. Volcanoes in the Sea: The Geology of Hawaii. 2nd ed. LC 82-23685. (Illus.). 528p. 1983. 29.95 (0-8248-0832-0) UH Pr.

MacDonald, Grace E., comp. Check-List of Legislative Journals of States of the United States of America. LC 79-92126. (Legal Bibliographic & Research Reprint Ser.: Vol. 3). 274p. 1980. reprint ed. lib. bdg. 42.00 (0-89941-034-0, 300900) W S Hein.

MacDonald, Graham & Pettit, Philip. Semantics & the Social Sciences. 224p. (C). 1981. pap. 13.95 (0-7100-0784-1, RKP) Routledge.

MacDonald, Graham, jt. auth. see MacDonald, Cynthia.

Macdonald, Graham, jt. ed. see Macdonald, Cynthia.

Macdonald, Greville. Sanity of William Blake. (Studies in Blake: No. 3). 1970. reprint ed. pap. 24.95 (0-8383-0097-9) M S G Haskell Hse.

Macdonald, H. Malcolm, ed. The Intellectual in Politics. LC 66-29160. (Quarterly Ser.). 1966. 15.00 (0-87959-074-2) U of Tex H Ransom Ctr.

MacDonald, Hugh. Chung Lee Loves Lobsters. (Illus.). 24p. (J). (gr. k-3). 1992. lib. bdg. 14.95 (1-55037-217-3, Pub. by Annick CN); pap. 4.95 (1-55037-214-9, Pub. by Annick CN) Firefly Bks Ltd.

MacDonald, Hope. When Angels Appear. 128p. (Orig.). 1982. pap. 8.99 (0-310-28531-3, 10047P) Zondervan.

— When Angels Appear. (Orig.). 1994. 4.99 (0-310-96278-1) Zondervan.

Macdonald, Hugh. Portraits in Prose. LC 71-101830. (Biography Index Reprint Ser.). 1977. 30.95 (0-8369-8004-2) Ayer.

— The Soviet Challenge & the Structure of European Security. 272p. 1990. text ed. 69.95 (1-85278-002-9, Pub. by E Elgar Pub UK) Ashgate Pub Co.

MacDonald, Hugh, ed. see Gasgoinge, George & Etchells, Frederick.

MacDonald, I., ed. Effect of Carbohydrates on Lipid Metabolism. (Progress in Biochemical Pharmacology Ser.: Vol. 8). (Illus.). 1973. 115.25 (3-8055-1600-2) S Karger.

Macdonald, I., ed. Metabolic Effects of Dietary Carbohydrates. (Progress in Biochemical Pharmacology Ser.: Vol. 21). (Illus.). x, 274p. 1986. 171.25 (3-8055-4229-1) S Karger.

Macdonald, I. G. Symmetric Functions & Hall Polynomials. 2nd ed. (Mathematical Monographs). 400p. 1995. 82.00 (0-19-853489-2) OUP.

Macdonald, I. G., tr. see Dieudonne, Jean A.

Macdonald, I. G., jt. ed. see Pietrzik, K.

MacDonald, Iain, ed. Saint Brendan. (Celtic Studies). 62p. 1992. pap. 5.95 (0-86315-141-8, Pub. by Floris Books UK) Dufour.

— Saint Bride. 62p. 1992. pap. 5.95 (0-86315-142-6, Pub. by Floris Books UK) Dufour.

— Saint Columba. 62p. 1992. pap. 5.95 (0-86315-143-4, Pub. by Floris Books UK) Dufour.

— Saint Patrick. 62p. 1992. pap. 5.95 (0-86315-144-2, Pub. by Floris Books UK) Dufour.

MacDonald, Iain, ed. see Aelred of Rievaulx.

MacDonald, Iain, ed. see Jocelinus of Furness.

MacDonald, Iain, ed. see Robert of Orkney.

MacDonald, Iain, ed. see Turgot.

Macdonald, Iain A. Representing the Debtor in a Chapter 7 Business Bankruptcy, Pts. 1 & 2: Summer 1992 Action Guide, 2 pts., Set. Hagelstein, Marie & Johnson, Elizabeth M., eds. 213p. 1992. pap. 52.00 (0-88124-529-1, BU-11311) Cont Ed Bar-CA.

Macdonald, Ian. Introduction to Optimal Control. 2nd ed. LC 76-55807. 272p. 1979. 27.50 (0-88275-707-5) Krieger.

— Key Words German. 1989. pap. text ed. 9.48 (0-582-20349-X, 70715) Longman.

MacDonald, Ian. The Penguin French Newsreader. 272p. 1990. pap. 7.95 (0-14-011223-5, Penguin Bks) Viking Penguin.

Macdonald, Ian. Revolution in the Head: The Beatles' Records & the Sixties. 373p. 1994. 25.00 (0-8050-2780-7) H Holt & Co.

MacDonald, Ian & Hearle, David. Communication Skills for Rural Development. (Illus.). 119p. 1991. pap. 11.95 (0-237-50791-9, Pub. by Evans Bros Ltd UK) Trafalgar.

MacDonald, Ian & Low, John. Fruit & Vegetables. (Illus.). 137p. 1991. pap. 12.95 (0-237-50790-0, Pub. by Evans Bros Ltd UK) Trafalgar.

— Tropical Field Crops. (Illus.). 112p. 1991. pap. 13.95 (0-237-50792-7, Pub. by Evans Bros Ltd UK) Trafalgar.

*Macdonald, Ian A. & Blake, Nicholas J. Immigration Law & Practice. 4th ed. 702p. 1994. boxed 198.00 (0-406-02508-8, UK) Butterworth Legal Pubs.

Macdonald, Ian D. Alex. LC 85-2418. 32p. 1985. pap. 3.95 (0-936428-10-4) Polygonal Pub.

MacDonald, Ian D. The Theory of Groups. LC 88-578. 262p. (C). 1988. reprint ed. lib. bdg. 28.50 (0-89464-287-1) Krieger.

Macdonald, Ian R. Gabriel Miro: His Private Library & His Literary Blackground. (Serie A: Monagrafias, XLI). 250p. (Orig.). (C). 1975. pap. 46.00 (0-900411-91-0, Pub. by Tamesis Bks Ltd UK) Boydell & Brewer.

Macdonald, Isobel. A Family in Skye. 1985. 30.00 (0-86152-055-6, Pub. by Acair Ltd UK) St Mut.

MacDonald, J. Compleat Theory of Scots Highland Bagpipe: Manuscript of J. MacDonald. MacRaonuill, A., ed. (Illus.). 117p. 1992. pap. 20.00 (0-685-59540-4) A MacRaonuill.

MacDonald, J. & Renton, R. Abair: Pocket Gaelic-English-Gaelic Dictionary. 1990. pap. 19.95 (0-8288-3376-1, F132981) Fr & Eur.

Macdonald, J. A., ed. The Time Projection Chamber: AIP Conference Proceedings, TRIUMF, Vancover, 1983, No. 108. LC 83-83445. 264p. 1984. lib. bdg. 39.00 (0-88318-307-2) Am Inst Physics.

MacDonald, J. A., jt. auth. see Renton, R. W.

Macdonald, J. B., jt. auth. see Macdonald, Elspeth T.

MacDonald, J. E. The Barbados Journal, 1932. (Illus.). 144p. 1989. 15.95 (0-921254-03-2, Pub. by Penumbra Pr CN) U of Toronto Pr.

— Sketchbook, Nineteen Seventeen. Bishop, Hunter, ed. 134p. 1979. 9.95 (0-920806-07-4, Pub. by Penumbra Pr CN) U of Toronto Pr.

MacDonald, J. Fred. Blacks & White TV: African Americans in Television Since 1948. 2nd ed. (Communications Ser.). 350p. (C). 1992. pap. text ed. 20.95 (0-8304-1326-X) Nelson-Hall.

— Don't Touch That Dial! LC 79-87700. 408p. 1979. pap. 20.95 (0-88229-673-6); student ed write for info. (0-8304-1178-X) Nelson-Hall.

— One Nation under Television: The Rise & Decline of Network TV. 300p. 1993. pap. text ed. 20.95 (0-8304-1362-6) Nelson-Hall.

— Television & the Red Menace: The Video Road to Vietnam. LC 84-18302. 277p. 1985. text ed. 55.00 (0-275-90141-6, C0141, Praeger Pubs); pap. text ed. 19.95 (0-275-91807-6, B1807, Praeger Pubs) Greenwood.

— Who Shot the Sheriff? The Rise & Fall of the Television Western. LC 86-18230. 172p. 1986. text ed. 42.95 (0-275-92326-6, C2326, Praeger Pubs) Greenwood.

MacDonald, J. Fred, ed. Richard Durham's Destination Freedom: Scripts from Radio's Black Legacy, 1948-50. LC 88-35686. 280p. 1989. text ed. 59.95 (0-275-93138-2, C3138, Praeger Pubs) Greenwood.

Macdonald, J. Ross. Annotated Topical Guide to U. S. Income Tax Treaties: A Service, 6 vols. 6618p. 1988. ring bd. 790.00 (0-13-103037-X) Aspen Law.

— Impedance Spectroscopy Emphasizing Solid Materials & Systems. LC 86-32582. 448p. 1987. text ed. 89.95 (0-471-83122-0) Wiley.

MacDonald, Jack. Handbook of Radio Publicity & Promotion. LC 73-114020. 1970. 34.95 (0-8306-0213-5, 213AH) TAB Bks.

MacDonald, James. Food from the Far West: American Agriculture with Special Reference to Beef Production & Importation of Dead Meat from America to Great Britain. LC 72-89059. (Rural America Ser.). 1973. reprint ed. 31.00 (0-8420-1490-X) Scholarly Res Inc.

— Food from the Far West or, American Agriculture. 1980. lib. bdg. 69.95 (0-8490-3187-7) Gordon Pr.

— Religion & Myth. LC 74-82059. 240p. 1969. reprint ed. text ed. 35.00 (0-8371-1550-7, MAR&, Negro U Pr) Greenwood.

Macdonald, James, jt. auth. see Doyle, Debra.

MacDonald, James, jt. auth. see Kennedy, Sandra.

MacDonald, James, et al. Programming with Comal 1: Lab Pack 1. Schroeder, Bonnie, ed. (Illus.). teacher ed 19.95 (1-56177-131-7, TE403-1); student ed 9.95 (1-56177-125-2, 403-1); student ed, teacher ed 159.95 (1-56177-129-5, L403-1); disk 6.95 (0-685-45809-1, D403-1) CES Compu-Tech.

— Programming with Comal 1: Lab Pack 2. Schroeder, Bonnie, ed. (Illus.). student ed, teacher ed 159.95 (1-56177-130-9, L403-2); teacher ed 19.95 (0-685-45810-5, T403-2); student ed 9.95 (1-56177-126-0, 403-2); disk 6.95 (1-56177-128-7, D403-2) CES Compu-Tech.

MacDonald, James D. Becoming Partners with Children: From Play to Conversation. 304p. 1989. pap. 19.95 (1-55990-010-5) Special Pr TX.

MacDonald, James D. & Gillette, Yvonne. ECO--A Partnership Program. 1989. 149.00 (1-55990-009-1) Special Pr TX.

— ECO Sources: Resources for Building Communication Partnerships. 392p. 1989. ring bd. 49.95 (1-55990-012-1) Special Pr TX.

— Manual for ECO Scales of Early Interaction & Communication. 128p. 1989. pap. 19.95 (1-55990-013-X) Special Pr TX.

Macdonald, James D., jt. auth. see Doyle, Debra.

MacDonald, James D.

MacDonald, James D., ed. see Doyle, Debra.

MacDonald, James D., jt. auth. see Doyle, Debra.

MacDonald, James D., ed. see Doyle, Debra.

MacDonald, James M. The Life & Writings of St. John of the Cross. 1977. lib. bdg. 250.00 (0-8490-2164-2) Gordon Pr.

*MacDonald, Janet. The Ornamental Kitchen Garden. (Illus.). 144p. 1995. 24.95 (0-7153-0236-1, Pub. by D & C Pub UK) Sterling.

— Riding to Music. 95p. 1990. pap. 24.00 (0-85131-433-3, Pub. by J A Allen & Co UK) St Mut.

— Teaching Side-Saddle. 100p. (C). 1990. pap. 24.00 (0-85131-556-9, Pub. by J A Allen & Co UK) St Mut.

MacDonald, Janet W. Running a Stable As a Business. 112p. pap. 20.00 (0-87556-544-1) Saifer.

Macdonald, Janet W. Running a Stables as a Business. 112p. (C). 1990. pap. 21.00 (0-685-68110-6, Pub. by J A Allen & Co UK) St Mut.

— Running a Tack Shop As a Business. 112p. (C). 1990. pap. 21.00 (0-85131-425-2, Pub. by J A Allen & Co UK) St Mut.

MacDonald, Jennifer, jt. auth. see Waldrop, Rosmarie.

MacDonald, Jerry. Earth's First Steps: Tracking Life Before the Dinosaurs. LC 94-32303. (Illus.). 280p. 1994. 22.95 (1-55566-119-X) Johnson Bks.

*MacDonald, Joan B. The Holiness of Everyday Life. 1995. 14.95 (0-87579-938-8) Deseret Bk.

*MacDonald, John. Deep Blue Goodbye. 320p. 1995. mass mkt. 6.99 (0-449-22383-3) Fawcett.

— Gastrointestinal Oncology. Ahlgren, James, ed. (Illus.). 670p. 1992. text ed. 140.00 (0-397-51150-7) Lippincott.

Macdonald, John. Great Battles of World War II. LC 93-70592. (Illus.). 192p. 1993. reprint ed. 19.98 (1-56138-329-5) Courage Bks.

MacDonald, John. Memar Marqah: The Teaching of Marqah, 2 vols., Set. (C). 1963. 89.25 (3-11-005567-8) De Gruyter.

Macdonald, John. Samaritan Chronicle No. 2 (or, Sepher Ha-Yamim) from Joshua to Nebuchadnezzar. (Beiheft 107 zur Zeitschrift fuer die Alttestamentliche Wissenschaft Ser.). (C). 1969. 92.35 (3-11-002582-5) De Gruyter.

MacDonald, John. Seven. 18.95 (0-89190-775-0, Am Repr) Amereon Ltd.

— TQM: Does It Always Work? 1994. 150.00 (0-946655-77-4, Pub. by S Thornes Pubs UK) St Mut.

Macdonald, John & Piggot, John. Global Quality: The New Management Culture. rev. ed. Padgett, JoAnn, ed. LC 92-50993. (Illus.). 320p. 1993. 21.95 (0-89384-206-0) Pfeiffer & Co.

Macdonald, John, jt. auth. see Schiffer, Charles A.

MacDonald, John A. The Line of Sight. LC 93-80956. 112p. 1993. 12.00 (0-8233-0491-4) Golden Quill.

— Troublous Times in Canada: A History of the Fenian Raids of 1866 & 1870. 255p. (C). 1987. 91.00 (0-317-90438-8, Pub. by Picton UK) St Mut.

MacDonald, John D. Area of Suspicion. 208p. 1986. pap. 3.95 (0-449-13099-1, GM) Fawcett.

— Barrier Island. (Florida Mysteries Ser.). 272p. 1987. reprint ed. mass mkt. 5.99 (0-449-13179-3, GM) Fawcett.

— Bright Orange for the Shroud. LC 85-17697. (Travis McGee Mystery Ser.). 1987. mass mkt. 5.99 (0-449-13358-3, GM) Fawcett.

— Cape Fear. 1986. mass mkt. 5.99 (0-449-13190-4, GM) Fawcett.

— Cape Fear. 1994. reprint ed. lib. bdg. 27.95 (1-56849-304-5) Buccaneer Bks.

— Cinnamon Skin. 288p. 1986. mass mkt. 5.95 (0-449-12873-3, GM) Fawcett.

— Clemmie. 240p. 1982. pap. 2.50 (0-449-12359-6, GM) Fawcett.

— Condominium. 1985. mass mkt. 5.99 (0-449-20737-4, Crest) Fawcett.

— Czar Ferdinand & His People. LC 74-135815. (Eastern Europe Collection Ser.). 1971. reprint ed. 26.95 (0-405-02757-5) Ayer.

Macdonald, John D. Darker Than Amber. 1987. mass mkt. 5.99 (0-449-13339-7) Fawcett.

MacDonald, John D. A Deadly Shade of Gold. (Travis McGee Mystery Ser.). 288p. 1987. mass mkt. 4.95 (0-449-13313-3, GM) Fawcett.

— Deadly Welcome. 1985. pap. 2.95 (0-449-12890-3, GM) Fawcett.

— Death Trap. 256p. 1985. mass mkt. 4.95 (0-449-13017-7, GM) Fawcett.

— The Deceivers. 208p. 1981. pap. 3.95 (0-449-14016-4, GM) Fawcett.

— Deep Blue Goodbye. 1987. mass mkt. 4.95 (0-449-13252-8) Fawcett.

— Dreadful Lemon Sky. 1987. mass mkt. 5.99 (0-449-13404-0) Fawcett.

— Dress Her in Indigo. 192p. 1987. mass mkt. 5.99 (0-449-13293-5, GM) Fawcett.

— The Empty Copper Sea. 19.95 (0-89190-778-5, Am Repr) Amereon Ltd.

— Empty Copper Sea. 1987. mass mkt. 4.99 (0-449-13333-8) Fawcett.

— End of the Tiger & Other Stories. 192p. 1985. pap. 2.95 (0-449-12868-7, GM) Fawcett.

— A Flash of Green. 1984. mass mkt. 4.95 (0-449-12692-7, GM) Fawcett.

— Free Fall in Crimson. 1987. pap. 3.95 (0-449-13253-6) Fawcett.

— Girl in the Plain Brown Wrapper. 1988. mass mkt. 4.95 (0-449-13341-9) Fawcett.

— The Girl, the Gold Watch, & Everything. 1985. mass mkt. 5.99 (0-449-12769-9, GM) Fawcett.

— The Green Ripper. 19.95 (0-89190-779-3, Am Repr) Amereon Ltd.

— Green Ripper. 1987. mass mkt. 4.95 (0-449-13246-3) Fawcett.

— The House Guests. 192p. 1988. pap. 3.50 (0-449-13416-4, GM) Fawcett.

— John D. MacDonald: Five Complete Travis McGee Novels. 1991. 11.99 (0-517-05948-7) Random Hse Value.

— Judge Me Not. 17.95 (0-89190-776-9, Am Repr) Amereon Ltd.

— Key to the Suite. 1989. 17.95 (0-89296-393-X) Mysterious Pr.

— The Lonely Silver Rain. LC 85-9816. (Florida Mysteries Ser.). 288p. 1986. mass mkt. 5.95 (0-449-12509-2, GM) Fawcett.

— The Long Lavender Look. (Travis McGee Mystery Ser.). 1987. mass mkt. 4.95 (0-449-13334-6, GM) Fawcett.

— More Good Old Stuff. LC 84-47643. 288p. 1984. 15.95 (0-394-53898-6) Knopf.

— Nightmare in Pink. (Travis McGee Mystery Ser.). 144p. 1987. mass mkt. 4.95 (0-449-13312-5, GM) Fawcett.

— Nothing Can Go Wrong. 1987. pap. 3.95 (0-449-21574-1) Fawcett.

— On the Run. 1984. pap. 3.50 (0-449-12851-2) Fawcett.

— One Fearful Yellow Eye. 1987. mass mkt. 4.95 (0-449-13292-7) Fawcett.

— One Monday We Killed Them All. 1985. pap. 3.50 (0-449-12937-3) Fawcett.

— One More Sunday. 448p. 1985. mass mkt. 5.99 (0-449-20703-X, Crest) Fawcett.

— Pale Gray for Guilt. 1987. mass mkt. 4.95 (0-449-13331-1) Fawcett.

— Please Write for Details. 288p. 1986. mass mkt. 4.95 (0-449-12926-8, GM) Fawcett.

— Price of Murder. 1976. 16.95 (0-8488-0569-0) Amereon Ltd.

Macdonald, John D. Purple Place for Dying. 1987. mass mkt. 5.99 (0-449-13336-2) Fawcett.

— Quick Red Fox. 1987. mass mkt. 4.95 (0-449-13403-2) Fawcett.

MacDonald, John D. Reon Jungle. 1984. pap. 3.95 (0-449-12853-9) Fawcett.

— Scarlet Ruse. 1987. mass mkt. 4.95 (0-449-13247-1) Fawcett.

— Seven Ages. 1983. pap. 2.95 (0-449-13102-5) Fawcett.

— Slam the Big Door. 272p. 1987. mass mkt. 4.95 (0-449-13275-7, GM) Fawcett.

— Tan & Sandy Silence. 1987. mass mkt. 4.95 (0-449-13250-1) Fawcett.

— Turquoise Lament. 1987. mass mkt. 4.95 (0-449-13249-8) Fawcett.

— Two. 104p. 1983. pap. 2.50 (0-88184-011-4) Carroll & Graf.

— Wine of the Dreamers. 18.95 (0-89190-777-7, Am Repr) Amereon Ltd.

— You Live Once. 1981. pap. 1.95 (0-449-14050-4, GM) Fawcett.

MacDonald, John D., jt. auth. see Rowen, Dan.

MacDonald, John D., et al. Mystery for Christmas: And Other Stories. 256p. 1990. pap. 4.99 (0-451-16909-3, Sig) NAL-Dutton.

MacDonald, John J. Primary Health Care: Medicine in Its Place. LC 92-46103. (Library of Management for Development). (Illus.). viii, 196p. (C). 1993. pap. text ed. 21.95 (1-56549-024-X) Kumarian Pr.

*Macdonald, John M. The Murderer & His Victim. 2nd ed. 342p. 1986. pap. 32.95 (0-398-06254-4) C C Thomas.

— The Murderer & His Victim. 2nd ed. 342p. (C). 1986. 54.95x (0-398-05205-0) C C Thomas.

Macdonald, John M. & Haney, Thomas P. Criminal Investigation. LC 90-82052. 320p. (Orig.). (C). 1990. pap. text ed. 9.95 (0-9618230-1-1) Apache Pr.

*Macdonald, John M. & Kennedy, Jerry. Criminal Investigation of Drug Offenses: The Narcs' Manual. 422p. 1983. pap. 37.95 (0-398-06253-6) C C Thomas.

— Criminal Investigation of Drug Offenses: The Narcs' Manual. 422p. (C). 1983. 67.95x (0-398-04915-7) C C Thomas.

Macdonald, John M. & Michaud, David L. Criminal Interrogation. enl. rev. ed. LC 92-70604. Orig. Title: The Confession: Interrogation & Criminal Profiles for Police Officers. 232p. (C). 1992. pap. text ed. 9.95 (0-9618230-2-X) Apache Pr.

Macdonald, John S., ed. Gastrointestinal Oncology. (Cancer Treatment & Research Ser.). 1987. lib. bdg. 161.50 (0-89838-829-5) Kluwer Ac.

Macdonald, John S., ed. see Schiffer, Charles A.

MacDonald, Jon. Great Battlefields of the World. 200p. 1988. pap. 25.95 (0-02-044464-8, Pub. by Gebrueder Borntraeger GW) Macmillan.

— Great Battles of the Civil War. (Illus.). 1988. 19.95 (0-02-577300-3) Macmillan.

— Great Battles of the Civil War. 200p. 1992. pap. 22.95 (0-02-034554-2, Pub. by Gebrueder Borntraeger GW) Macmillan.

Macdonald, Joseph. Building Construction Codes, Specifications, & Regulations Sourcebook. 1992. text ed. 65.50 (0-07-044334-3) McGraw.

MacDonald, Judith B. Teaching & Parenting: Effects of the Dual Role. LC 93-44356. 160p. (C). 1994. lib. bdg. 26.50 (0-8191-9389-5) U Pr of Amer.

MacDonald, June F., ed. NABC Report Three, Agricultural Biotechnology at the Crossroads: Biological, Social & Institutional Concerns. 307p. (Orig.). 1992. pap. text ed. 5.00 (0-685-60015-7) Natl Agri Biotech.

— NABC Report 3, Agricultural Biotechnology at the Crossroads: Biological, Social & Institutional Concerns. 307p. 1991. pap. 7.00 (0-9630907-4-7) Natl Agri Biotech.

— NABC Report 4, Animal Biotechnology: Opportunities & Challenges. 181p. 1992. pap. 5.00 (0-9630907-2-0) Natl Agri Biotech.

— NABC Report 5, Agricultural Biotechnology: A Public Conversation about Risk. 135p. 1993. pap. 5.00 (0-9630907-3-9) Natl Agri Biotech.

— NABC Report 6, Agricultural Biotechnology & the Public Good. 213p. 1994. pap. 5.00 (0-9630907-5-5) Natl Agri Biotech.

Macdonald, K. Sociobiological Perspectives on Human Development. (Illus.). 450p. 1987. 64.00 (0-387-96581-5) Spr-Verlag.

An Asterisk (*) at the beginning of an entry indicates that the title is appearing in BIP for the first time.

MacDonald, K. B. Social & Personality Development: An Evolutionary Synthesis. (Perspectives in Developmental Psychology Ser.). (Illus.). 340p. 1988. 55.00 (*0-306-42891-1*, Plenum Pr) Plenum.

MacDonald, K. L. Small Gasoline Engines Student's Workbook. 2nd ed. 1973. pap. write for info. (*0-672-97632-3*) Macmillan.

Macdonald, Kate. The Anne of Green Gables Cookbook. (Illus.). 48p. (J). 1987. 12.95 (*0-19-540496-3*) OUP.

— Anne of Green Gables Cookbook. 1988. mass mkt. 4.95 (*0-7704-2258-6*) Bantam.

Macdonald, Kate, ed. see Buchan, John.

MacDonald, Kathleen. When Writers Write. 2nd ed. (Illus.). 320p. (C). 1987. pap. text ed. write for info. (*0-13-956509-4*) P-H.

***MacDonald, Kathryn & Morgan, Mar Lou.** The Farm & City Cookbook. 1995. pap. 14.95 (*0-929005-67-8*) InBook.

***MacDonald, Kathy, et al.** Counselling for Sexual Abuse: A Therapist's Guide to Working with Adults, Children & Families. 320p. 1995. 39.95 (*0-19-558315-9*) OUP.

MacDonald, Keith N. The Practice of Medicine among the Burmese. LC 77-87505. reprint ed. 35.00 (*0-404-16837-X*) AMS Pr.

MacDonald, Kenneth B. & MacDonald, Agnes. The Second Coming: Tough Questions Answered. 300p. (Orig.). (YA). 1991. pap. text ed. 9.95 (*0-9626490-0-7*) Revivals & Missions.

MacDonald, Kenneth D. On Fire with Selling: A Rich Analysis of Sales Experiences Mixed with Amazing Real-Life Stories. LC 94-30534. (Illus.). 80p. 1995. pap. 9.95 (*0-942963-54-7*) Distinctive Pub.

***MacDonald, Kenny.** Scottish Football Quotations. 244p. 1995. pap. 15.95 (*1-85158-643-1*, Pub. by Mnstream UK) Trafalgar.

Macdonald, Kevin. Emeric Pressburger: The Life & Death of a Screenwriter. (Illus.). 512p. 1994. 24.95 (*0-571-16853-1*) Faber & Faber.

— A People That Shall Dwell Alone: Judaism as an Evolutionary Group Strategy. LC 94-16446. (Human Evolution, Behavior & Intelligence Ser.). 320p. 1994. text ed. 57.95 (*0-275-94869-2*, Praeger Pubs) Greenwood.

MacDonald, Kevin, ed. Parent-Child Play: Descriptions & Implications. LC 92-20562. (SUNY Series, Children's Play in Society). 389p. (C). 1993. 59.50 (*0-7914-1463-9*); pap. 19.95 (*0-7914-1464-7*) State U NY Pr.

MacDonald, L. Ian. From Bourassa to Bourassa: A Pivotal Decade in Canadian History. LC 85-103559. (Illus.). 328p. reprint ed. pap. 93.50 (*0-8357-6438-9*, 2035809) Bks Demand.

MacDonald, L. W., jt. auth. see Heaton, Nigel.

MacDonald, Lachlan, jt. ed. see Gilmore, Elaine.

MacDonald, Lachlan P. The Guide to Whale Watching: The Grey Whale. (Illus.). 96p. (Orig.). 1990. pap. 4.95 (*0-936940-06-9*) Helm Pub.

— The Hunter & Other Stories. 1989. write for info. (*0-318-65384-2*) Pr MacDonald & Reinecke.

— Uncommon Guide to Carmel, Monterey & Big Sur. (Illus.). 1990. pap. 8.95 (*0-939919-03-6*) Bear Flag Bks.

— An Uncommon Guide to San Luis Obispo County California. 2nd rev. ed. LC 75-2794. (Illus.). 1990. pap. 8.95 (*0-939919-00-1*) Bear Flag Bks.

MacDonald, Lachlan P., ed. Channel X Short-Short Stories, Vol. 1, No. 1. (Illus.). 64p. 1990. pap. 6.95 (*1-877947-06-7*) Pr MacDonald & Reinecke.

MacDonald, Lachlan P., ed. see Angel, Myron.

MacDonald, Laura. A Case of Make-Believe. large type ed. 1994. 17.95 (*0-263-13844-5*, Pub. by Mills & Boon Ltd UK) Chivers N Amer.

— Love Changes Everything. large type ed. (Medical Romance Ser.). 1992. 16.95 (*0-263-13148-3*, Pub. by Mills & Boon Ltd UK) Chivers N Amer.

— Somebody to Love. large type ed. 1994. 17.95 (*0-263-13978-6*, Pub. by Mills & Boon Ltd UK) Chivers N Amer.

— Supporting Civil Society: The Political Role of Non-Governmental Organizations in Central America. LC 94-43333. (International Political Economy Ser.). 1995. write for info. (*0-312-12535-6*) St Martin.

— Waiting Game. large type ed. 1993. 17.95 (*0-263-13513-6*, Pub. by Mills & Boon Ltd UK) Chivers N Amer.

Macdonald, Laura A. Island Partner. large type ed. 246p. 1993. 21.95 (*0-7505-0574-5*, Pub. by Magna Print Bks) Ulverscroft.

Macdonald, Lawrence W. The Collected Works of Lawrence W. Macdonald. Shapiro, Abraham, ed. (Illus.). 299p. (C). 1992. lib. bdg. 15.00 (*0-943599-56-3*) OEPF.

— The Collected Works of Lawrence W. Macdonald, Set. Shapiro, Abraham, ed. (Illus.). 299p. (C). 1992. lib. bdg. write for info. (*0-943599-55-5*) OEPF.

— The Collected Works of Lawrence W. Macdonald, Vol. II. Schwartz, Ira & Shapiro, Abraham, eds. (Illus.). 350p. (C). 1992. lib. bdg. 18.00 (*0-943599-58-X*) OEPF.

MacDonald, Linda B., et al. Teaching Technologies in Libraries. (Professional Librarian Ser.). 198p. (C). 1990. text ed. 34.95 (*0-8161-1906-6*, Hall Reference); pap. 24.95 (*0-8161-1907-4*, Hall Reference) Macmillan.

MacDonald, Lindsay W. & Vince, John, eds. Interacting with Virtual Environments. 288p. 1994. text ed. 64.95 (*0-471-93941-2*) Wiley.

MacDonald, Lisa, ed. Jazz: The National Gallery Pocket Address Book. (Illus.). 144p. 1985. 7.95 (*0-939456-12-5*) Galison.

— Winterthur's Twelve Months of Flowers. (Illus.). 32p. 1985. 12.95 (*0-939456-11-7*) Galison.

MacDonald, Lorna. A Grammar of Tauya. (Grammar Library: No. 6). (Illus.). xiii, 385p. 1990. lib. bdg. 141.00 (*0-89925-760-7*) Mouton.

— A Grammar of Tauya. (Mouton Grammar Library: No. 6). (Illus.). xiii, 385p. (C). 1990. lib. bdg. 152.35 (*3-11-012673-7*) Mouton.

MacDonald, Lorne. Basic Circuit Analysis for Electronics Through Experimentation. 2nd ed. 352p. 1992. pap. 18.50 (*0-911908-21-8*) Tech Ed Pr.

— Basic Solid-State Electronic Circuit Analysis Through Experimentation. 3rd ed. 424p. 1992. pap. 23.50 (*0-911908-12-9*) Tech Ed Pr.

— Practical Analysis of Advanced Electronic Circuits Through Experimentation. 2nd ed. 384p. 1984. pap. 18.50 (*0-911908-18-8*) Tech Ed Pr.

— Practical Circuit Analysis of Amplifiers. 544p. 1994. pap. 25.00 (*0-911908-22-6*) Tech Ed Pr.

MacDonald, Lyn. The First Year of Fighting. 1988. 24.95 (*0-318-37460-9*, Atheneum S&S) S&S Trade.

— 1915: The Death of Innocence. LC 94-25654. 1995. 35.00 (*0-8050-3499-4*) H Holt & Co.

Macdonald, Lyn. The Roses of No Man's Land. 320p. 1989. pap. 13.95 (*0-689-70810-6*, Atheneum S&S) S&S Trade.

Macdonald, Malcolm. All Desires Known. 352p. 1993. 21.95 (*0-312-10415-4*) St Martin.

MacDonald, Malcolm. Brahms. 1990. text ed. 29.95 (*0-02-871393-1*) Schirmer Bks.

— Brahms. LC 90-8545. 490p. 1993. pap. 18.00 (*0-02-872851-3*) Schirmer Bks.

Macdonald, Malcolm. Dancing on Snowflakes. 384p. 1994. 21.95 (*0-312-11256-4*) St Martin.

***MacDonald, Malcolm.** For I Have Sinned. 384p. 1995. 22.95 (*0-312-13078-3*) St Martin.

— John Foulds & His Music: An Introduction. (Illus.). 162p. (Orig.). 1989. pap. 21.95 (*0-912483-02-4*) Pro-Am Music.

— Ronald Stevenson: A Musical Biography. 1990. 21.95 (*0-912483-62-8*) Pro-Am Music.

Macdonald, Malcolm. To the End of Her Days. 384p. 1994. 23.95 (*0-312-11080-4*) St Martin.

MacDonald, Malcolm, comp. Dmitri Shostakovich - a Complete Catalog. 1977. pap. text ed. 17.00 (*0-913932-39-6*) Boosey & Hawkes.

***MacDonald, Mandy & Gatehouse, Mike.** In the Mountains of Morazan: Portrait of a Returned Refugee Community in El Salvador. (Illus.). 220p. 1994. pap. 16.00 (*0-85345-957-6*, PB9576) Monthly Rev.

MacDonald, Margaret F. James McNeill Whistler: Watercolors, Pastels, & Drawings: A Catalogue Raisonne. LC 94-10253. (Illus.). 688p. 1995. 145.00 (*0-300-05987-6*) Yale U Pr.

— Whistler's Mother's Cook Book. 2nd ed. LC 94-67328. (Illus.). 144p. 1995. pap. 10.95 (*0-87654-108-2*) Pomegranate Calif.

MacDonald, Margaret F., jt. auth. see Dorment, Richard.

MacDonald, Margaret R. Bookplay: One Hundred-One Creative Themes to Share with Young Children. (Illus.). 260p. 1995. lib. bdg. 32.50 (*0-208-02280-5*, Lib Prof Pubns) Shoe String.

— Booksharing: One Hundred One Programs to Use with Preschoolers. LC 87-35777. (Illus.). 236p. 1988. lib. bdg. 32.50 (*0-208-02159-0*, Lib Prof Pubns) Shoe String.

Macdonald, Margaret R. Booksharing: One Hundred One Programs to Use with Preschoolers. LC 87-35777. (Illus.). 236p. 1991. pap. text ed. 19.50 (*0-208-02314-3*, Lib Prof Pubns) Shoe String.

MacDonald, Margaret R. Celebrate the World: Twenty Tellable Folktales for Multicultural Festivals. LC 94-6682. (Illus.). 225p. 1994. 40.00 (*0-8242-0862-5*) Wilson.

— Ghost Stories of the Pacific Northwest. (American Storytelling Ser.). 1995. 21.95 (*0-87483-436-8*); pap. 10.95 (*0-87483-437-6*) August Hse.

— Look Back & See: Twenty Lively Tales for Gentle Tellers. (Illus.). 178p. (Orig.). 1991. 35.00 (*0-8242-0810-2*) Wilson.

— The Old Woman Who Lived in a Vinegar Bottle. LC 94-46967. (Illus.). (J). (ps-2). 1995. 15.95 (*0-87483-415-5*) August Hse.

— A Parent's Guide to Storytelling. LC 95-3093. (J). 1995. 11.95 (*0-06-026295-8*, HarpT) HarpC.

— A Parent's Guide to Storytelling. 128p. 1995. pap. 11.95 (*0-06-446180-7*) HarpC.

— Scipio, Indiana: Threads from the Past. 417p. 1988. 24.95 (*0-87770-455-4*) Ye Galleon.

— Storyteller's Start-up Book: Finding, Learning, Performing, & Using Folktales. 215p. 1993. 23.95 (*0-87483-304-3*); pap. 13.95 (*0-87483-305-1*) August Hse.

— When the Lights Go Out. (Illus.). 176p. 1988. 35.00 (*0-8242-0770-X*); pap. 20.00 (*0-8242-0823-4*) Wilson.

MacDonald, Margaret R., ed. The Folklore of World Holidays. 600p. 1991. text ed. 95.00 (*0-8103-7577-X*, 003317) Gale.

— Tom Thumb. (Multicultural Folktale Ser.). 184p. 1993. pap. 23.50 (*0-89774-728-3*) Oryx Pr.

— Twenty Tellable Tales: Audience Participation for the Beginning Storyteller. LC 85-26565. 220p. 1986. 35.00 (*0-8242-0719-X*); pap. 20.00 (*0-8242-0822-6*) Wilson.

MacDonald, Margaret R., jt. auth. see Vathanaprida, Supaporn.

MacDonald, Margaret Y. The Pauline Churches: A Socio-Historical Study of Institutionalisation in the Pauline & Deutero-Pauline Writings. (Society for New Testament Studies Monographs: No. 60). 288p. 1988. 74.95 (*0-521-35337-8*) Cambridge U Pr.

Macdonald, Marianne. The Pirate Queen. (Illus.). 32p. (J). (ps-3). 1992. 12.95 (*0-8120-6288-4*); pap. 5.95 (*0-8120-4952-7*) Barron.

MacDonald, Marion & Rogers-Cordon, Sue. Action Plans: Eighty Student-Centered Language Activities. 1984. pap. 19.95 (*0-8384-2712-X*, Newbury) Heinle & Heinle.

Macdonald, Marion E. The Significance of Various Kinds of Preparation for the City-Elementary School Principalship in Pennsylvania with Implications for a Program for Preparing for the Elementary-School Principalship in. LC 77-177020. (Columbia University. Teachers College. Contributions to Education Ser.: No. 416). reprint ed. 22.50 (*0-404-55416-4*) AMS Pr.

Macdonald, Mary A. Hedgehog Bakes a Cake - Bank Street. (J). (ps-3). 1990. mass mkt. 3.99 (*0-553-34890-6*) Bantam.

Macdonald, Mary E. Federal Grants for Vocational Rehabilitation. Phillips, William R. & Rosenberg, Janet, eds. LC 79-6914. (Physically Handicapped in Society Ser.). 1980. reprint ed. lib. bdg. 44.95 (*0-405-13123-2*) Ayer.

MacDonald, Mary L. Literature & Society in the Canadas, 1817-1850. LC 92-11215. 368p. 1992. lib. bdg. 99.95 (*0-7734-9524-X*) E Mellen.

MacDonald, Mary N. Mararoko: A Study in Melanesian Religion. LC 90-35291. (American University Studies: Anthropology & Science: Ser. XI, Vol. 45). 592p. (C). 1990. text ed. 85.95 (*0-8204-1194-9*) P Lang Pubs.

MacDonald, Maryann. No Room for Francie No. 2: Lots of O'Learys. LC 94-8596. (J). 1995. lib. bdg. write for info. (*0-7868-2027-6*) Hyprn Child.

— No Room for Francie No. 2: Lots of O'Learys. LC 94-8596. 64p. (J). (gr. 2-5). 1995. 10.95 (*0-7868-0032-1*) Hyprn Child.

Macdonald, Maryann. The Pink Party. LC 93-20989. (Illus.). 40p. (J). (gr. k-3). 1994. 10.95 (*1-56282-620-4*); lib. bdg. 10.89 (*1-56282-621-2*) Hyprn Child.

MacDonald, Maryann. Rabbit's Birthday Kite. (J). (ps-3). 1991. pap. 3.50 (*0-553-34908-2*) Bantam.

Macdonald, Maryann. Rosie & the Poor Rabbits. LC 92-42766. (Illus.). 32p. (J). (ps-2). 1994. text ed. 13.95 (*0-689-31832-4*, Atheneum Bks Young) S&S Childrens.

— Rosie's Baby Tooth. LC 90-35923. (Illus.). 32p. (J). (ps-2). 1991. text ed. 12.95 (*0-689-31626-7*, Atheneum Bks Young) S&S Childrens.

— Sam's Worries. LC 91-71379. (Illus.). 32p. (J). (ps-3). 1991. 13.95 (*1-56282-081-8*); lib. bdg. 13.89 (*1-56282-082-6*) Hyprn Child.

— Sam's Worries. LC 91-71379. (Illus.). 32p. (J). (ps-2). 1994. pap. 4.95 (*1-56282-522-4*) Hyprn Ppbks.

MacDonald, Maryann. Secondhand Star. LC 93-31812. (Lots of O'Learys Ser.). (Illus.). 64p. (J). (gr. 2-5). 1994. 11.95 (*1-56282-616-6*); lib. bdg. 11.89 (*1-56282-617-4*) Hyprn Child.

MacDonald, Marylee, jt. auth. see Konzo, Seichi.

MacDonald, Mhairi G. Emergency Transport of the Perinatal Patient. 1989. 55.00 (*0-316-54198-2*) Little.

MacDonald, Mhairi G., jt. ed. see Fletcher, Mary Ann.

MacDonald, Mia. Reinventing Systems: Collaborations to Support Families. Harvard Family Research Project Staff, ed. 92p. 1994. pap. text ed. 7.50 (*0-9630627-3-5*) Harvard Fam.

***MacDonald, Michael & Benfield, Steve, eds.** Power Builder 4. 0: Secrets of the Power Builder Masters: Creating Mission Critical Applications in Power Builder 4. 0. (Power Engineering Ser.). (Illus.). 600p. 1995. pap. 49.95 (*1-886141-00-2*) SYS-Con Pubns.

MacDonald, Michael & Murphy, Terence R. Sleepless Souls: Suicide in Early Modern England. (Oxford Studies in Social History). (Illus.). 400p. 1991. 89.00 (*0-19-822919-4*) OUP.

— Sleepless Souls: Suicide in Early Modern England. (Oxford Studies in Social History). (Illus.). 400p. 1994. reprint ed. pap. 19.95 (*0-19-820450-7*) OUP.

MacDonald, Michael, ed. see Ackerman, David, et al.

MacDonald, Michael, ed. see Fisk, Colin, et al.

MacDonald, Michael, ed. see Jorden, Edward & Case, Mary G.

***MacDonald, Michael, et al.** Home of the Brave. (Cyberpunk Ser.). (Illus.). 144p. (Orig.). 1993. pap. 14.00 (*0-937279-36-6*, CP3221) R Talsorian.

— Operation: Rimfire. (Mekton Ser.). (Illus.). 104p. (Orig.). 1993. pap. 14.00 (*0-937279-37-4*, MK1501) R Talsorian.

Macdonald, Michael-Albion. Secret of Secrets: The Unwritten Mysteries of Esoteric Qabbalah. LC 86-81789. (Illus.). 96p. 1986. 20.00 (*0-935214-08-9*) Heptangle.

Macdonald, Michael-Albion, ed. see Bacon, Roger.

MacDonald, Michael G. & Meyer, Kathryn C. Health Care Law: A Practical Guide. 1985. Updates. ring bd. write for info. (*0-8205-1398-9*) Bender.

***MacDonald, Micheil.** Clans of Scotland. 1994. 19.98 (*0-7858-0108-1*) Bk Sales Inc.

***MacDonald, Mike, et al.** Mekton Z. (Mekton Ser.). (Illus.). 160p. (Orig.). 1995. pap. 20.00 (*0-937279-54-4*, MK1003) R Talsorian.

MacDonald, N. Biological Delay Systems: Linear Stability Theory. (Cambridge Studies in Mathematical Biology). (Illus.). 200p. 1989. 74.95 (*0-521-34084-5*) Cambridge U Pr.

— REDUCE for Physicists. (Illus.). 184p. 1994. 50.00 (*0-7503-0277-1*) IOP Pub.

— Time Lags in Biological Models. (Lecture Notes in Biomathematics Ser.: Vol. 27). (Illus.). 1978. pap. 23.00 (*0-387-09092-4*) Spr-Verlag.

MacDonald, Nancy. Homage to the Spanish Exiles: Voices from the Spanish Civil War. LC 86-10541. 358p. 1987. 28.95 (*0-89885-325-7*, Plenum Insight) Human Sci Pr.

MacDonald, Neil. The Andes: A Quest for Justice. 128p. (C). 1993. pap. text ed. 24.00 (*0-85598-200-4*, Pub. by Oxfam Pubns UK) St Mut.

— Brazil: A Mask Called Progress. 96p. (C). 1991. pap. text ed. 24.00 (*0-85598-091-5*, Pub. by Oxfam Pubns UK) St Mut.

— The Caribbean: Making Our Own Choices. (C). 1990. pap. text ed. 30.00 (*0-85598-086-9*, Pub. by Oxfam Pubns UK) St Mut.

— Central America: Options for the Poor. 78p. (C). 1988. pap. text ed. 35.00 (*0-85598-113-X*, Pub. by Oxfam Pubns UK) St Mut.

MacDonald, Norbert. Distant Neighbors: A Comparative History of Seattle & Vancouver. LC 86-30892. (Illus.). xxii, 291p. 1987. 30.00 (*0-8032-3111-3*) U of Nebr Pr.

MacDonald, Oliver, ed. Polish August: Documents from the Beginnings of the Polish Workers' Rebellion. (Illus.). 177p. 1982. pap. 2.00 (*0-939306-02-6*) Left Bank.

MacDonald, Pat, ed. see Auch, Mary J.

MacDonald, Pat, ed. see Beach, Lynn.

MacDonald, Pat, ed. see Bennett, Cherie.

MacDonald, Pat, ed. see Bennett, Cherrie.

MacDonald, Pat, ed. see Carris, Joan D.

MacDonald, Pat, ed. see Clayton, Ed.

MacDonald, Pat, ed. see Cohen, Daniel.

MacDonald, Pat, ed. see Coville, Bruce.

MacDonald, Pat, ed. see Cusick, Richie T.

MacDonald, Pat, ed. see Gibson, Jamie.

MacDonald, Pat, ed. see Gilson, Jamie.

MacDonald, Pat, ed. see Gondosch, Linda.

MacDonald, Pat, ed. see Gorman, S. S.

MacDonald, Pat, ed. see Haas, Dorothy.

MacDonald, Pat, ed. see Hermes, Patricia.

MacDonald, Pat, ed. see Hiser, Constance.

MacDonald, Pat, ed. see Hodgman, Ann.

MacDonald, Pat, ed. see Jackson, Alison.

MacDonald, Pat, ed. see Kehret, Peg.

MacDonald, Pat, ed. see Lewis, Linda.

MacDonald, Pat, ed. see Miller, Judi.

MacDonald, Pat, ed. see Murrow, Liza K.

MacDonald, Pat, ed. see Peel, John.

MacDonald, Pat, ed. see Pike, Christopher.

MacDonald, Pat, ed. see Poploff, Michelle.

MacDonald, Pat, ed. see Posner, Richard.

MacDonald, Pat, ed. see Ragz, M. M.

MacDonald, Pat, ed. see Ransom, Candice F.

MacDonald, Pat, ed. see Rubenstein, Gillian.

MacDonald, Pat, ed. see Rubinstein, Gillian.

MacDonald, Pat, ed. see Shirts, Morris A.

MacDonald, Pat, ed. see Siegal, Barbara & Seigel, Scott.

MacDonald, Pat, ed. see Siegal, Barbara & Siegel, Scott.

MacDonald, Pat, ed. see Smith, L. J.

MacDonald, Pat, ed. see Smith, L. T.

MacDonald, Pat, ed. see Smith, Lisa.

MacDonald, Pat, ed. see Specter, B. J.

MacDonald, Pat, ed. see Stine, R. L.

MacDonald, Pat, ed. see Thompson, Joan.

MacDonald, Pat, ed. see Wallace, Bill.

MacDonald, Patricia. Mother's Day. 384p. 1994. mass mkt. 5.99 (*0-446-60078-4*, Warner Vision) Warner Bks.

— Mother's Day. large type ed. LC 93-43971. 1994. 23.95 (*0-7927-1962-X*, Eagle Lrg Print); pap. write for info. (*0-7927-1961-1*, Eagle Lrg Print) Chivers N Amer.

— Secret Admirer. 352p. 1995. 21.95 (*0-446-51686-4*) Warner Bks.

— A Stranger in the House. large type ed. 464p. 1986. 23.95 (*0-7089-8365-0*, Trail West Pubs) Ulverscroft.

— The Unforgiven. large type ed. 416p. (Orig.). 1986. 23.95 (*0-7089-8375-8*, Trail West Pubs) Ulverscroft.

MacDonald, Patricia, ed. see Baker, Barbara.

MacDonald, Patricia, ed. see Beach, Lynn.

MacDonald, Patricia, ed. see Clifford, Eth.

MacDonald, Patricia, ed. see Cohen, Daniel.

MacDonald, Patricia, ed. see Coville, Bruce.

MacDonald, Patricia, ed. see Cusick, Richie T.

MacDonald, Patricia, ed. see Dillon, Barbara.

MacDonald, Patricia, ed. see Garden, Nancy.

MacDonald, Patricia, ed. see Gorman, S. S.

MacDonald, Patricia, ed. see Helldorfer, M. C.

MacDonald, Patricia, ed. see Hiser, Constance.

MacDonald, Patricia, ed. see Hollands, Judith.

MacDonald, Patricia, ed. see Kehret, Peg.

MacDonald, Patricia, ed. see Lawlor, Laurie.

MacDonald, Patricia, ed. see Leroe, Ellen.

MacDonald, Patricia, jt. auth. see MacDonald, Angus.

MacDonald, Patricia, ed. see Monsell, Mary E.

MacDonald, Patricia, ed. see Nash, Bruce & Zullo, Allan.

MacDonald, Patricia, ed. see Nelson, Peter.

MacDonald, Patricia, ed. see Pike, Christopher.

MacDonald, Patricia, ed. see Ragz, M. M.

MacDonald, Patricia, ed. see Siegal, Barbara & Siegal, Scott.

MacDonald, Patricia, jt. auth. see Sommer, Robin L.

MacDonald, Patricia, ed. see Stine, R. L.

MacDonald, Patricia, ed. see Wallace, Bill.

MacDonald, Patricia J. No Way Home. large type ed. 1991. 21.95 (*0-7089-2484-0*) Ulverscroft.

MacDonald, Patty V. Long Lost Recipes: Of Aunt Susan. (Illus.). 200p. 1989. 14.95 (*0-9624490-0-8*) Starr-Toof.

MacDonald, Patty V., ed. Spiced with Wit: Will Rogers' Tomfoolery More Aunt Susan Recipes. (Illus.). 220p. 1992. 15.95 (*0-9624490-1-6*) P V MacDonald.

MacDonald, Peter. Giap: The Victor in Vietnam. 352p. 1993. 25.00 (*0-393-03401-1*) Norton.

— The Last Warrior: Peter MacDonald & the Navajo Nation. (Library of the American Indian). 1993. 25.00 (*0-517-59323-8*, Orion Bks) Crown Pub Group.

— Special Forces: A History of the World's Elite Fighting Units. 1988. 12.98 (*1-55521-112-7*) Bk Sales Inc.

MacDonald, Philip. The Choice. 256p. 1994. 16.95 (*0-7451-8633-5*, Black Dagger) Chivers N Amer.

— List of Adrian Messenger. 1976. 18.95 (*0-8488-0570-4*) Amereon Ltd.

— The List of Adrian Messenger. 1993. reprint ed. lib. bdg. 16.95 (*1-56849-210-3*) Buccaneer Bks.

— The Rasp. 21.95 (*0-89190-094-2*, Am Repr) Amereon Ltd.

— The Rasp. 280p. 1984. pap. 3.50 (*0-88184-094-7*) Carroll & Graf.

An Asterisk (*) at the beginning of an entry indicates that the title is appearing in BIP for the first time.

— The Rasp. 1979. reprint ed. pap. 5.95 (*0-486-23864-4*) Dover.

MacDonald, Philip E., jt. ed. see Shah, Vikram N.

MacDonald, R. The International Law & Policy of Human Welfare. 708p. 1978. lib. bdg. 185.50 (*90-286-0808-7*) Kluwer Ac.

MacDonald, R. & Travis, C. Libraries & Special Collections on Latin America & the Caribbean: A Directory of European Resources. 2nd ed. LC 87-24114. (Institute of Latin American Studies Monographs). 256p. (C). 1988. text ed. 75.00 (*0-485-17714-5*, Pub. by Athlone Pr UK) Humanities.

Macdonald, R. E., jt. ed. see Campbell, R. E.

MacDonald, R. H. A Broadcast News Manual of Style. 202p. (C). 1987. pap. text ed. 25.50 (*0-582-99865-4*, 75290) Longman.

Macdonald, R. Heather, jt. auth. see Stover, Susan G.

Macdonald, R. S., jt. ed. see Djwa, Sandra.

MacDonald, Ranald. Ranald MacDonald: The Narrative of His Life, 1824-1894. 2nd ed. Lewis, William S. & Murakami, Naojiro, eds. (North Pacific Studies: No. 16). Orig. Title: Ranald MacDonald 1824-1894. (Illus.). 384p. 1990. reprint ed. 30.00 (*0-87595-229-1*) Oregon Hist.

M

MacDonald, Reby E. The Ghosts of Austwick Manor. LC 91-22122. 160p. (J). (gr. 3-7). 1991. reprint ed. pap. 3.95 (*0-689-71533-1*, Aladdin Paperbacks) S&S Childrens.

MacDonald, Robbyn. Victorian Embroidery. (Illus.). 128p. 1994. 24.95 (*1-86351-110-5*, Pub. by S Milner AT) Sterling.

Macdonald, Robert. Islands of the Pacific Rim & Their People. LC 94-7541. (People & Places Ser.). 48p. (J). (gr. 5-8). 1994. 15.95 (*1-56847-167-X*) Thomson Lrning.

— Maori. LC 93-35530. (Threatened Cultures Ser.). (Illus.). 48p. (J). (gr. 5-9). 1994. 16.95 (*1-56847-151-3*) Thomson Lrning.

— Transitions: Military Pathways to Civilian Careers. Rosen, Roger, ed. (Military Opportunities Ser.). (YA). (gr. 7 up). 1988. lib. bdg. 14.95 (*0-8239-0777-5*) Rosen Group.

MacDonald, Robert, ed. The Lay of the Land: The Golf Writings of Pat Ward-Thomas. (Illus.). 253p. 1990. 28.00 (*0-940889-29-3*) Classics Golf.

MacDonald, Robert & Coffield, Frank. Risky Business? Youth, Enterprise & Policy for the 1990s. 224p. 1991. 80.00 (*1-85000-897-3*, Falmer Pr); pap. 31.00 (*1-85000-898-1*, Falmer Pr) Taylor & Francis.

MacDonald, Robert, jt. contrib. see Boske, Leigh.

Macdonald, Robert, jt. ed. see Wind, Herbert W.

MacDonald, Robert A., ed. Text & Concordance of Especulo, Alfonso el Sabio, MS10.123: Biblioteca Nacional de Madrid. (Spanish Legal Texts Ser.: No. 3). 12p. (SPA.). 1989. 10.00 (*0-940639-37-8*) Hispanic Seminary.

MacDonald, Robert D. Chinchilla. (Phoenix Theatre Ser.). 1982. pap. 2.95 (*0-912262-73-7*) Proscenium.

MacDonald, Robert E. A Handbook of Basic Skills & Strategies for Beginning Teachers: Facing the Challenge of Teaching in Today's Schools. 256p. (Orig.). (C). 1991. pap. text ed. 36.95 (*0-8013-0608-6*, 78541) Longman.

MacDonald, Robert H. Sons of the Empire: The Frontier & the Boy Scout Movement 1890-1918. LC 93-93285. 258p. 1993. 35.00 (*0-8020-2843-8*) U of Toronto Pr.

Macdonald, Robert M. Collective Bargaining in the Automobile Industry: A Study of Wage Structure & Competitive Relations. LC 63-13967. (Yale Studies in Economics: No. 17). 424p. reprint ed. pap. 120.90 (*0-317-29276-5*, 2022017) Bks Demand.

Macdonald, Robert S. The Catherine. 356p. 1982. 12.95 (*0-89433-181-7*) Petrocelli.

Macdonald, Robert S., ed. The Darwin Sketchbook: Portraits of Golf's Greatest Players & Other Selections from Bernard Darwin's Writings, 1910-55. 2nd ed. (Illus.). 410p. 1992. lib. bdg. 28.00 (*0-685-65027-8*) Classics Golf.

Macdonald, Robert W. Exploring Careers in the Military Services. rev. ed. Rosen, Ruth, ed. (Military Opportunities Ser.). (Illus.). 190p. (YA). (gr. 7 up). 1991. 14.95 (*0-8239-1358-9*) Rosen Group.

MacDonald, Robert W. League of Arab States: A Study in the Dynamics of Regional Organization. 1965. pap. 17.95 (*0-691-00003-4*) Princeton U Pr.

MacDonald, Roger. Provence & the Cote d'Azur. 1989. pap. 16.95 (*0-8442-9938-3*, Passport Bks) NTC Pub Grp.

MacDonald, Ronald. A Broadcast News Manual of Style. 2nd ed. 384p. (C). 1994. pap. text ed. 14.95 (*0-8013-1110-1*, 79570) Longman.

— Floating Exchange Rates: Theories & Evidence. (Illus.). 260p. (C). 1988. text ed. 49.95 (*0-04-338134-0*); pap. text ed. 24.95 (*0-04-338135-9*) Routledge Chapman & Hall.

— From a Northern Window: A Personal Remembrance of George MacDonald. 1989. 11.95 (*0-940652-33-1*) Sunrise Bks.

— From a Northern Window: A Personal Remembrance of George MacDonald. 1989. 7.95 (*0-940652-30-7*) Sunrise Bks.

MacDonald, Ronald & Taylor, Mark P., eds. Exchange Rate Economics. (International Library of Critical Writings in Business History: Vol. 16). 1136p. 1992. text ed. 339.95 (*1-85278-409-1*, Pub. by E Elgar Pub UK) Ashgate Pub Co.

— Exchange Rates & Open Economy Macroeconomics. (Illus.). 288p. 1989. pap. text ed. 55.00 (*0-631-16238-0*) Blackwell Pubs.

MacDonald, Ronald, jt. auth. see Hallwood, Paul.

Macdonald, Ronald R. The Burial-Places of Memory: Epic Underworlds in Vergil, Dante, & Milton. LC 86-19216. 240p. 1987. 27.50 (*0-87023-558-3*) U of Mass Pr.

— William Shakespeare: The Comedies. (Twayne's English Authors Ser.: No. 489). 200p. (C). 1992. text ed. 22.95 (*0-8057-7010-0*, Pub. by Royal Botanic Garden UK) Macmillan.

Macdonald, Ronald S., ed. Essays in Honour of Wang Tieya. 960p. (C). 1994. lib. bdg. 228.00 (*0-7923-2469-2*) Kluwer Ac.

Macdonald, Ronald S. & Johnston, Douglas M., eds. The Structure & Process of International Law. 1983. lib. bdg. 292.00 (*90-247-2882-7*) Kluwer Ac.

Macdonald, Ronald S., et al, eds. Canadian Perspectives on International Law & Organization. LC 72-98024. 992p. reprint ed. pap. 180.00 (*0-317-27016-8*, 2023647) Bks Demand.

— The European System for the Protection of Human Rights. LC 93-26605. (International Studies on Human Rights). 968p. (C). 1993. lib. bdg. 185.00 (*0-7923-2431-5*) Kluwer Ac.

MacDonald, Rose. Taping Techniques: Principles & Practice. (Illus.). 263p. 1994. pap. 40.00 (*0-7506-0577-4*) Buttrwrth-Heinemann.

Macdonald, Ross. Archer in Jeopardy, 3 bks., Set. Incl. Doomsters. LC 79-63807. 1979. (*0-318-54004-5*); Instant Enemy. LC 79-63807. 1979. (*0-318-54005-3*); Zebra-Striped Hearse. LC 79-63807. 1979. (*0-318-54006-1*); LC 79-63807. 1979. 24.95 (*0-394-50804-1*) Knopf.

— Black Money: A Lew Archer Novel. large type ed. LC 95-7492. 1996. write for info. (*0-7862-0464-8*) Thorndike Pr.

— Blue City: A Lew Archer Novel. large type ed. LC 95-7491. 1996. write for info. (*0-7862-0463-X*) Thorndike Pr.

MacDonald, Ross. The Blue Hammer. 21.95 (*0-89190-095-0*, Am Repr) Amereon Ltd.

***Macdonald, Ross.** The Chill: A Lew Archer Novel. large type ed. LC 95-7490. 436p. 1995. 21.95 (*0-7862-0461-3*) Thorndike Pr.

— Find a Victim. large type ed. LC 95-2660. 335p. 1995. pap. 19.95 (*0-7862-0450-8*) Hall.

— Meet Me at the Morgue. large type ed. LC 95-7487. 1995. write for info. (*0-7862-0462-1*) Thorndike Pr.

— Self-Portrait: Ceaselessly into the Past. Sipper, Ralph B., ed. (Brownstone Mystery Guides Ser.: Vol. 13). iv, 131p. (Orig.). 1995. 27.00x (*0-941028-25-9*, Brownstone Bks); pap. 17.00x (*0-941028-26-7*, Brownstone Bks) Borgo Pr.

MacDonald, Ross. Sleeping Beauty. 21.95 (*0-89190-096-9*, Am Repr) Amereon Ltd.

***Macdonald, Ross.** The Three Roads. large type ed. LC 95-724. 1995. write for info. (*0-7862-0419-2*) Thorndike Pr.

MacDonald, Ross, jt. auth. see Molyneux, Bill.

MacDonald, Ross B. The Master Tutor: A Guidebook for Mor Effective Tutoring. (Illus.). 150p. (Orig.). (C). 1994. teacher ed. 64.95 (*0-935637-20-6*); student ed. 19.95 (*0-935637-19-2*); trans. 85.00 (*0-935637-21-4*) Cambridge Strat.

***MacDonald, Ruby.** Smooth Sailing. 512p. 1995. mass mkt. 4.99 (*0-8217-4971-4*) Windsor NY.

MacDonald, Ruth K. Beatrix Potter. (English Authors Ser.: No. 422). 168p. 1986. text ed. 21.95 (*0-8057-6917-X*, Twayne) Macmillan.

— Christian's Children: The Influence of John Bunyan's The Pilgrim's Progress on American Children's Literature. (American University Studies: American Literature: Ser. XXIV, Vol. 10). 208p. (C). 1989. text ed. 35.10 (*0-8204-1003-9*) P Lang Pubs.

— Dr. Seuss (Theodore Seuss Geisel) 208p. 1988. text ed. 21.95 (*0-8057-7524-2*, TUSAS NO. 54, Twayne) Macmillan.

— Literature for Children in England & America: 1646-1774. LC 81-52810. 193p. 1982. 15.00 (*0-87875-227-7*) Whitston Pub.

— Louisa May Alcott, No. 457. (United States Authors Ser.). 128p. 1983. text ed. 20.95 (*0-8057-7397-5*, Twayne) Macmillan.

***MacDonald, S. O. & Myhrman, Matts.** Build It with Bales: A Step-by-Step Guide to Straw-Bale Construction. 80p. 1994. write for info. (*0-9642821-0-0*) Inhabit Srvs.

MacDonald, Sandra. Ben of Colonial Newport. (Geronimo Pack Ser.). 8p. (J). (gr. k-2). 1993. pap. write for info. (*1-882563-08-5*) Lamont Bks.

— Birds at the Sanctuary. (Birds Pack Ser.). 8p. (J). (gr. k-2). 1993. pap. write for info. (*1-882563-03-4*) Lamont Bks.

Macdonald, Sandy. From the Ground Up: Training Manual for Pilots. 26th ed. (Illus.). 1991. pap. 25.95 (*0-9690054-8-2*) Aviation.

MacDonald, Scott. Avant-Garde Film: Motion Studies. LC 92-17446. (Cambridge Film Classics Ser.). (Illus.). 192p. (C). 1993. 47.95 (*0-521-38129-0*); pap. 13.95 (*0-521-38821-X*) Cambridge U Pr.

— A Critical Cinema: Interviews with Independent Filmmakers. 1988. 60.00 (*0-520-05800-3*); pap. 18.00 (*0-520-05801-1*) U CA Pr.

— Critical Cinema Two: Interviews with Independent Filmmakers. 1992. 48.00 (*0-520-07917-5*); pap. 18.00 (*0-520-07918-3*) U CA Pr.

Macdonald, Scott. Frames of Mind. (Illus.). 24p. 1986. pap. 1.00 (*0-915895-04-8*) Munson Williams.

MacDonald, Scott, ed. Being & Goodness: The Concept of Good in Metaphysics & Philosophical Theology. LC 90-55197. 336p. 1991. 46.95 (*0-8014-2312-0*); pap. 15.95 (*0-8014-9779-5*) Cornell U Pr.

— Screen Writings: Scripts & Texts from Independent Filmmakers. LC 92-30429. 1994. 45.00 (*0-520-08024-6*); pap. 20.00 (*0-520-08025-4*) U CA Pr.

Macdonald, Scott & Roman, Paul M., eds. Drug Testing in the Workplace. (Research Advances in Alcohol & Drug Problems: Vol. 11). (Illus.). 315p. (C). 1994. 85.00 (*0-306-44557-3*, Plenum Pr) Plenum.

Macdonald, Scott, jt. auth. see Coxeter, Harold.

MacDonald, Scott A. Complete Job Finder's Guide for the 90's: Marketing Yourself in the New Job Market. 230p. (Orig.). 1993. pap. 13.95 (*0-942710-84-3*) Impact VA.

MacDonald, Scott B. Dancing on a Volcano: The Latin American Drug Trade. LC 88-9950. 177p. 1988. text ed. 42.95 (*0-275-92752-0*, C2752, Praeger Pubs); pap. text ed. 15.95 (*0-275-93105-6*, B3105, Praeger Pubs) Greenwood.

— European Destiny, Atlantic Transformations: Portuguese Foreign Policy under the Second Republic, 1974-1992. LC 92-20671. 192p. (C). 1992. 39.95 (*1-56000-078-3*) Transaction Pubs.

— Mountain High, White Avalanche: Cocaine & Power in the Andean States & Panama. LC 88-39214. (Washington Papers: No. 137). (Illus.). 166p. 1989. text ed. 49.95 (*0-275-93234-6*, C3234, Praeger Pubs); pap. text ed. 11.95 (*0-275-93235-4*, B3235, Praeger Pubs) Greenwood.

— Trinidad & Tobago: Democracy & Development in the Caribbean. LC 86-539. 240p. 1986. text ed. 55.00 (*0-275-92004-6*, C2004, Praeger Pubs) Greenwood.

MacDonald, Scott B. & Fauriol, Georges A., eds. The Politics of the Caribbean Basin Sugar Trade. LC 90-20868. 176p. 1991. text ed. 49.95 (*0-275-93052-1*, C3052, Praeger Pubs) Greenwood.

MacDonald, Scott B. & Zagaris, Bruce, eds. International Handbook on Drug Control. LC 91-35118. 463p. 1992. text ed. 89.50 (*0-313-27375-8*, MHB/, Greenwood Pr) Greenwood.

MacDonald, Scott B., et al, eds. The Caribbean after Grenada: Revolution, Conflict, & Democracy. LC 88-11986. 304p. 1988. text ed. 65.00 (*0-275-92722-9*, C2722, Praeger Pubs) Greenwood.

— Latin American Debt in the 1990s: Lessons from the Past & Forecasts for the Future. LC 91-2244. 168p. 1991. text ed. 49.95 (*0-275-93903-0*, C3903, Praeger Pubs) Greenwood.

MacDonald, Sebastian K. Moral Theology & Suffering. LC 93-41341. (AUS VII: Vol. 171). 185p. (C). 1995. text ed. 39.95 (*0-8204-2371-8*) P Lang Pubs.

***MacDonald, Shari.** Sierra. 1995. pap. 8.99 (*0-88070-726-7*) Questar Pubs.

MacDonald, Sharman. All Things Nice. 80p. (Orig.). 1991. pap. 9.95 (*0-571-16429-3*) Faber & Faber.

— Shades. 96p. (Orig.). 1993. pap. 8.95 (*0-571-16884-1*) Faber & Faber.

— Sharman Macdonald Plays, No. 1. 384p. (Orig.). 1995. pap. 13.95 (*0-571-17621-6*) Faber & Faber.

— When I Was a Girl I Used to Scream & Shout; When We Were Women; The Brave. 256p. (Orig.). 1990. pap. 8.95 (*0-571-14348-2*) Faber & Faber.

MacDonald, Sharon. Inside European Identities. Ardener, Shirley et al, eds. LC 92-14740. (Ethnicity & Identity Ser.). 224p. 1993. 49.95 (*0-85496-723-0*); pap. 19.95 (*0-85496-888-1*) Berg Pubs.

— We Learn All about Community Helpers. (J). (ps-1). 1988. pap. 7.99 (*0-8224-4599-9*) Fearon Teach Aids.

— We Learn All about Dinosaurs. (J). (ps-1). 1988. pap. 7.99 (*0-8224-4595-6*) Fearon Teach Aids.

— We Learn All about Endangered Species. 1992. pap. 10.99 (*0-86653-944-1*) Fearon Teach Aids.

— We Learn All about Fall. (J). (ps-1). 1988. pap. 7.95 (*0-8224-4596-4*) Fearon Teach Aids.

— We Learn All about Farms. (J). (ps-1). 1988. pap. 7.99 (*0-8224-4594-8*) Fearon Teach Aids.

Macdonald, Sharon. We Learn All about Machines. 1991. 7.99 (*0-8224-4590-5*) Fearon Teach Aids.

MacDonald, Sharon. We Learn All about Protecting Our Environment. 1992. pap. 10.99 (*0-86653-942-5*) Fearon Teach Aids.

Macdonald, Sharon. We Learn All about Spring. 1991. 7.99 (*0-8224-4591-3*) Fearon Teach Aids.

MacDonald, Sharon. We Learn all about the Circus. (J). (ps-1). 1988. pap. 7.99 (*0-8224-4598-0*) Fearon Teach Aids.

— We Learn All about the Earth's Habitats. 1992. pap. 10.99 (*0-86653-943-3*) Fearon Teach Aids.

Macdonald, Sharon. We Learn All about Transportation. 1991. 7.99 (*0-8224-4592-1*) Fearon Teach Aids.

MacDonald, Sharon. We Learn All about Winter. (J). (ps-1). 1988. pap. 7.99 (*0-8224-4597-2*) Fearon Teach Aids.

Macdonald, Sharon, et al, eds. Images of Women in Peace & War: Cross-Cultural & Historical Perspectives. LC 87-40518. 256p. (C). 1988. text ed. 35.00 (*0-299-11760-X*); pap. text ed. 14.95 (*0-299-11764-2*) U of Wis Pr.

Macdonald, Shawn. The Darkness Within. 320p. 1993. mass mkt. 4.50 (*0-8217-4163-2*) Zebra.

Macdonald, Sheila & Mason, Chris. Otters: An Action Plan for Their Conservation. Foster-Turley, Pat et al, eds. (Illus.). 130p. (Orig.). 1991. pap. 22.00 (*2-8317-0013-2*, Pub. by IUCN SZ) Island Pr.

MacDonald, Simon, ed. see Buckmaster, Charles.

Macdonald, Stephen C. A German Revolution: Local Change & Continuity in Prussia, 1918-1920. LC 91-12411. (Modern European History Outstanding Studies & Dissertations). 376p. 1991. 76.00 (*0-8240-2544-X*) Garland.

MacDonald, Stephen L., intro. The Role of Natural Gas in Environmental Policy. LC 92-76046. 120p. (Orig.). 1993. pap. 16.50 (*0-87755-332-7*) Bureau Busn UT.

MacDonald, Susan P. Anthony Trollope. (Twayne's English Authors Ser.: No. 441). 167p. 1987. text ed. 21.95 (*0-8057-6945-5*, TEAS 441, Twayne) Macmillan.

— Professional Academic Writing in the Humanities & Social Sciences. LC 93-11093. 256p. (C). 1994. 29.95 (*0-8093-1930-6*) S Ill U Pr.

MacDonald, Suse. Alphabatics. LC 85-31429. (Illus.). 64p. (J). (ps up). 1986. text ed. 16.95 (*0-02-761520-0*, Bradbury S&S) S&S Childrens.

— Alphabatics. LC 91-38497. (Illus.). 56p. (J). (ps-1). 1992. reprint ed. pap. 6.95 (*0-689-71625-7*, Aladdin Paperbacks) S&S Childrens.

— Award Puzzles: The Caldecott Collection - Alphabatics. (Illus.). 1992. 6.95 (*0-938971-71-9*) JTG Nashville.

— Nanta's Lion: A Search-&-Find Adventure. LC 94-16634. (Illus.). 24p. 1995. 15.00 (*0-688-13125-5*) Morrow Jr Bks.

Macdonald, Suse. Puzzlers. LC 88-33392. (J). 1989. 13.89 (*0-8037-0690-1*); lib. bdg. 13.95 (*0-8037-0689-8*) Dial Bks Young.

MacDonald, Suse. Sea Shapes. LC 93-27957. 1994. 13.95 (*0-15-200027-5*) HarBrace.

MacDonald, T. C., ed. Immunology of Gastrointestinal Diseases. (Immunology & Medicine Ser.). (C). 1992. lib. bdg. 149.50 (*0-7923-8961-1*) Kluwer Ac.

MacDonald, T. C., et al, eds. Advances in Mucosal Immunology. (C). 1990. lib. bdg. 276.00 (*0-7462-0113-3*) Kluwer Ac.

MacDonald, Thoreau. Thoreau MacDonald's Notebooks. Flood, John, ed. 224p. 1980. 14.95 (*0-920806-05-8*, Pub. by Penumbra Pr CN) U of Toronto Pr.

MacDonald, Violet M., tr. see Vollard, Ambroise.

Macdonald, W. C. Elder-Character & Duties. 1993. pap. 22.00 (*0-7152-0658-3*) St Mut.

MacDonald, W. Colt. Destination Danger. large type ed. 1979. 21.95 (*0-7089-0389-4*) Ulverscroft.

MacDonald, W. S., ed. Roll of Graduates of the University of Aberdeen, 1956-1970: With Supplement 1860-1955. 1982. 70.00 (*0-08-028469-8*, Pergamon Pr) Elsevier.

MacDonald, W. Scott & Oden, Chester W., Jr. Moose: The Story of a Very Special Person. 2nd ed. 200p. (Orig.). (YA). (gr. 8 up). 1978. pap. 10.95 (*0-03-043936-1*) Brookline Bks.

***Macdonald, Webster.** Memoirs of a Maverick Lawyer. (Illus.). 237p. (Orig.). 1993. pap. 19.95 (*1-55059-068-5*) Temeron Bks.

MacDonald, Wilbert L. Pope & His Critics. LC 74-30369. (English Literature Ser.: No. 33). 1974. lib. bdg. 75.00 (*0-8383-1990-4*) M S G Haskell Hse.

MacDonald, William. The Architecture of the Roman Empire: An Urban Appraisal, Vol. 2. rev. ed. LC 81-16513. 320p. (C). 1988. reprint ed. pap. 25.00 (*0-300-03470-9*) Yale U Pr.

— Armageddon Soon? 1992. pap. 3.50 (*0-937396-89-3*) Walterick Pubs.

— Las Buenas Nuevas. Orig. Title: Good News. 96p. (SPA.). 1986. pap. 3.50 (*0-8254-1451-2*) Kregel.

— Christ Loved the Church. 1956. pap. 5.95 (*0-937396-09-5*) Walterick Pubs.

— Cual Es la Diferencia? Orig. Title: What Is the Difference?. 112p. (SPA.). 1981. pap. 3.99 (*0-8254-1450-4*) Kregel.

— Enjoying Ecclesiastes. 1988. pap. 5.00 (*0-937396-07-9*) Walterick Pubs.

— Enjoying the Proverbs. 1982. pap. 5.00 (*0-937396-23-0*) Walterick Pubs.

— Ephesians. 1988. pap. 5.00 (*0-937396-74-5*) Walterick Pubs.

— First Peter. 1988. pap. 5.00 (*0-937396-75-3*) Walterick Pubs.

Macdonald, William. George Washington: A Brief Biography. 2nd ed. LC 87-34823. (Illus.). 40p. 1987. pap. 2.00 (*0-931917-14-X*) Mt Vernon Ladies.

MacDonald, William. God's Answers to Man's Questions. 1958. pap. 2.50 (*0-937396-16-8*) Walterick Pubs.

— Grace of God. 1960. pap. 2.50 (*0-937396-18-4*) Walterick Pubs.

— Grasping for Shadows. 1972. pap. 2.50 (*0-937396-19-2*) Walterick Pubs.

— Greek Enchiridion: A Concise Handbook of Grammar for Translation & Exegesis. 198p. 1986. pap. 12.95 (*0-913573-18-3*) Hendrickson MA.

— Here's the Difference. 1975. pap. 5.00 (*0-937396-55-9*) Walterick Pubs.

— Jacksonian Democracy, 1829-37. LC 74-169921. reprint ed. 24.75 (*0-404-04126-4*) AMS Pr.

— Let Me Introduce You to the Bible. 1980. pap. 2.95 (*0-937396-22-2*) Walterick Pubs.

— Lord, Break Me. 1972. pap. 2.50 (*0-937396-24-9*) Walterick Pubs.

— Matthew: Behold Your King. 1988. pap. 8.50 (*0-937396-26-5*) Walterick Pubs.

— Old Testament Digest: Vol. 3, Job-Malachi. 1981. pap. 7.95 (*0-937396-29-X*) Walterick Pubs.

— Second Peter & Jude. 1988. pap. 5.00 (*0-937396-77-X*) Walterick Pubs.

— Seek Ye First. 1972. pap. 2.50 (*0-937396-38-9*) Walterick Pubs.

— Select Charters & Other Documents Illustrative of American History, 1606-1775. (Illus.). ix, 401p. 1992. reprint ed. 45.00 (*0-8377-2443-0*) Rothman.

— There's a Way Back to God. 1986. reprint ed. pap. 2.50 (*0-937396-42-7*) Walterick Pubs.

— Think of Your Future. 1956. pap. 2.50 (*0-937396-44-3*) Walterick Pubs.

— To What Should We Be Loyal. 1981. pap. 2.50 (*0-937396-47-8*) Walterick Pubs.

— True Discipleship. 1975. pap. 5.00 (*0-937396-50-8*) Walterick Pubs.

— Winning Souls the Bible Way. 1988. pap. 5.00 (*0-937396-56-7*) Walterick Pubs.

— Worlds Apart. 76p. (Orig.). 1993. pap. 4.95 (*1-882701-05-4*) Gospel Folio.

MacDonald, William, intro. Chester Michalik: Photographs. 32p. 1985. pap. 10.00 (*0-87391-035-4*) Smith Coll Mus Art.

MacDonald, William & Farstad, Arthur, eds. Believer's Bible Commentary New Testament. 1205p. 1989. 24.95 (*0-945681-00-3*) A & O Pr.

An Asterisk (*) at the beginning of an entry indicates that the title is appearing in BIP for the first time.

MacDonald, William & Hamel, Mike. Old Testament Digest: Gen-Deut., Vol. 1. 1981. pap. 7.95 (*0-937396-59-1*) Walterick Pubs.

— Old Testament Digest: Vol. 2, Joshua - Esther. 1982. pap. 7.95 (*0-937396-61-3*) Walterick Pubs.

MacDonald, William A., ed. The First One Hundred Fifty Years: A Pictorial History of Carroll County, MD. 1839-1987. (Illus.). 128p. (Orig.). 1986. pap. 15.00 (*0-9614125-1-8*) Hist Soc Carroll.

MacDonald, William B. Sketch of Coptic Grammar: Adapted for Self-Tuition. 1987. reprint ed. pap. 12.95 (*0-89979-047-X*) British Am Bks.

***MacDonald, William C.** The Mad Marshal. 1995. 15.95 (*0-7451-4624-4*) Chivers N Amer.

— Restless Guns. large type ed. LC 94-35253. 300p. 1995. pap. 15.95 (*0-7838-1148-9*) Hall.

Macdonald, William C. Stir up the Dust. 1994. lib. bdg. 15.95 (*0-7451-4602-3*, Gunsmoke) Chivers N Amer.

***MacDonald, William C.** Sunrise Guns. large type ed. LC 94-33672. 346p. 1995. pap. 15.95 (*0-7838-1151-9*, Large Print Bks) Hall.

Macdonald, William K. Digging for Gold: Papers on Archaeology for Profit. (Technical Reports: No. 5). 1976. pap. 2.00 (*0-932206-14-X*) U Mich Mus Anthro.

MacDonald, William K., jt. ed. see Hutterer, Karl L.

MacDonald, William L. The Architecture of the Roman Empire: An Introductory Study. rev. ed. LC 81-16513. (Publications in the History of Art: No. 17). (Illus.). 372p. 1982. pap. 25.00 (*0-300-02819-9*, Y-429) Yale U Pr.

— The Architecture of the Roman Empire: An Urban Appraisal, Vol. II. LC 81-16513. (History of Art Ser.: No. 35). 328p. 1986. 55.00 (*0-300-03456-3*) Yale U Pr.

— Early Christian & Byzantine Architecture. LC 62-7531. (Great Ages of World Architecture Ser.). 128p. 1963. pap. 10.95 (*0-8076-0338-4*) Braziller.

— The Pantheon: Design, Meaning, & Progeny. (Harvard Paperbacks Ser.). 160p. (C). 1981. pap. text ed. 10.95 (*0-674-65346-7*) HUP.

— Piranesi's Carceri: Sources of Invention. (Illus.). 18p. (Orig.). (C). 1979. pap. 6.95 (*1-880269-01-5*) D H Sheehan.

***MacDonald, William L. & Pinto, John A.** Hadrian's Villa & Its Legacy. LC 94-28183. 1995. 55.00 (*0-300-05381-9*) Yale U Pr.

Macdonald, William W. The Making of an English Revolutionary: The Early Parliamentary Career of John Pym. LC 80-65867. 208p. 1982. 32.50 (*0-8386-3018-9*) Fairleigh Dickinson.

Macdonell, A., jt. auth. see Martin, W.

***Macdonell, A. A.** India's Past: A Survey of Her Literature, Religions, Languages & Antiquities. (C). 1995. reprint ed. 28.00x (*81-206-0570-5*, Pub. by Asian Educ Servs II) S Asia.

Macdonell, Annie. Thomas Hardy. LC 77-148276. reprint ed. 19.45 (*0-404-08885-6*) AMS Pr.

Macdonell, Arthur. Sanskrit Grammar for Students. (C). Date not set. 12.50 (*81-208-0504-6*, Pub. by Motilal Banarsidass II); pap. 8.50 (*81-208-0505-4*, Pub. by Motilal Banarsidass II) S Asia.

***Macdonell, Arthur A.** Brhad Devata, 2 pts. (C). 1994. text ed. 44.00 (*81-208-1141-0*, Pub. by Motilal Banarsidass II) S Asia.

MacDonell, Arthur A. History of Sanskrit Literature. 472p. reprint ed. text ed. 34.00 (*0-685-13411-3*) Coronet Bks.

— History of Sanskrit Literature. LC 68-24966. (Studies in Comparative Literature: No. 35). 1969. reprint ed. lib. bdg. 75.00 (*0-8383-0211-4*) M S G Haskell Hse.

Macdonell, Arthur A. A Sanskrit Grammar for Students. 3rd ed. 284p. 1986. pap. 29.95 (*0-19-815466-6*) OUP.

MacDonell, Arthur A. Vedic Mythology. 1973. 300.00 (*0-87968-153-5*) Gordon Pr.

Macdonell, Arthur A. A Vedic Reader for Students. 296p. 1992. pap. 10.95 (*0-19-560038-X*) OUP.

— Vedic Reader for Students: Containing Thirty Hymns of the Rigveda in the Original Samhita & Pada Texts, with Transliteration, Translation, Explanatory Notes, Introduction, Vocabulary. (C). 1992. reprint ed. text ed. 14.00 (*81-208-1018-X*, Pub. by Motilal Banarsidass II) S Asia.

Macdonell, Diane. Theories of Discourse: An Introduction. 160p. 1986. pap. text ed. 21.95 (*0-631-14839-6*) Blackwell Pubs.

Macdonell, John. Historical Trials. Lee, R. W., ed. xvi, 234p. 1983. reprint ed. lib. bdg. 25.00 (*0-8377-0848-6*) Rothman.

MacDonnel, Anna. Margery Nahl: California Impressionist. (Illus.). 140p. 1994. 37.50 (*0-9640481-0-8*) M W Morse.

Macdonnel, Arthur A. The Brhad-Devata, Attributed to Saunaka: A Summary of the Deities & Myths of the RgVeda, Vols. 5-6. (Harvard Oriental Ser.). (C). 1965. 27.50 (*0-8364-2357-7*, Pub. by Motilal Banarsidass II) S Asia.

Macdonnell, Anna M. Ting Shao Kuang. (Illus.). 192p. 1989. text ed. 100.00 (*0-685-27816-6*) Segal Fine Art.

MacDonnell, Arthur. A History of Sanskrit Literature. vi, 406p. 1990. reprint ed. 16.00 (*81-208-0035-4*, Pub. by Motilal Banarsidass II) S Asia.

MacDonnell, Arthur A. Practical Sanskrit Dictionary: With Transliteration Accentuation & Etymological Analysis Throughout. (SAN.). 1924. 85.00 (*0-19-864303-9*) OUP.

MacDonnell, Colum. Tark & the Golden Tide. 1977. pap. 1.25 (*0-8439-0470-4*) Dorchester Pub Co.

***MacDonnell, Francis.** Insidious Foes: The Axis Fifth Column & the American Home Front. (Illus.). 256p. 1995. 35.00 (*0-19-509268-6*) OUP.

MacDonnell, J. E. Full Fathom Five. 1979. reprint ed. pap. 1.25 (*0-8439-0663-4*) Dorchester Pub Co.

Macdonnell, J. E. Mission Hopeless. 1979. reprint ed. pap. 1.25 (*0-8439-0670-7*) Dorchester Pub Co.

MacDonnell, John D. King Leopold Second: His Rule in Belgium & the Congo. (Illus.). 1970. reprint ed. 17.50 (*0-87266-041-9*) Argosy.

MacDonnell, Joseph. Jesuit Geometers: A Study of Fifty-Six Prominent Jesuit Geometers During the First Two Centuries of Jesuit History. LC 89-80568. (Studies on Jesuit Topics Series IV: No. 11). (Illus.). iv, 106p. 1989. pap. 8.00 (*0-912422-94-7*) Inst Jesuit.

MacDonnell, Julia. A Year of Favor: A Novel. LC 93-11432. 1994. 25.00 (*0-688-12546-8*) Morrow.

MacDonnell, Kenneth F. & Segal, Maurice S. Current Respiratory Care. 489p. 1977. pap. text ed. 15.95 (*0-316-54191-5*, Little Med Div) Little.

MacDonnell, Kenneth F., et al. Respiratory Intensive Care. 478p. 1987. 100.00 (*0-316-54193-1*) Little.

MacDonnell, Lawrence J. & Bates, Sarah F., eds. Natural Resources Policy & Law: Trends & Directions. LC 93-8388. 280p. 1993. text ed. 38.00 (*1-55963-245-3*); pap. 19.95 (*1-55963-246-1*) Island Pr.

MacDonnell, Margaret & Shaw, John, eds. Luirgean Eachainn Nill: Folktales from Cape Breton. 1985. 35.00 (*0-86152-086-6*, Pub. by Acair Ltd UK); pap. 25.00 (*0-317-54622-8*, Pub. by Acair Ltd UK) St Mut.

MacDonnell, Ray, jt. auth. see MacNamee, Brian.

MacDonogh, Giles. Brillat-Savarin: The Judge & His Stomach. LC 93-13879. 256p. 1993. 27.50 (*1-56663-028-2*) I R Dee.

Macdonogh, Giles. A Good German: Adam von Trott zu Solz. (Illus.). 358p. 1992. 25.00 (*0-87951-449-3*) Overlook Pr.

MacDonogh, Giles. A Good German: Adam von Trott Zu Solz. 368p. 1993. pap. 13.95 (*0-87951-496-5*) Overlook Pr.

— Prussia: The Perversion of an Idea. (Illus.). 456p. 1995. 34.95 (*1-85619-267-9*, Sinclair-Stevenson) Trafalgar.

MacDonogh, Steve. The Dingle Peninsula: History, Folklore & Archaeology. (Illus.). 256p. (Orig.). 1993. pap. 11.95 (*0-86322-159-9*, Pub. by Brandon Bk Pubs IE) Irish Bks Media.

MacDonogh, Steve, ed. see Carey, Peter, et al.

MacDonough, Glen, jt. auth. see Herbert, Victor.

MacDonough, R. MacDonough-Hackstaff Ancestry. (Illus.). 526p. 1989. reprint ed. lib. bdg. 87.00 (*0-8328-0846-6*); reprint ed. pap. 79.00 (*0-8328-0847-4*) Higginson Bk Co.

MacDorman, John, jt. auth. see Leary, Brian.

MacDougal. Cases in Maladjustment. (C). 1992. text ed. 16.00 (*0-673-46400-8*) HarpCollege.

***MacDougal, Dennis.** In the Best of Families: The Anatomy of a True Tragedy. 1995. mass mkt. write for info. (*0-446-60235-3*) Warner Bks.

MacDougal, John M. Revision of Passiflora Subgenus Decaloba Section Pseudodysosmia, Passifloraceae. Anderson, Christiane, ed. (Systematic Botany Monographs: Vol. 41). (Illus.). 146p. 1994. pap. 19.00 (*0-912861-41-X*) Am Soc Plant.

MacDougal-Kennedy, Nancy. Winter Reckoning. large type ed. (Romance Suspense Ser.). 432p. 1992. 21.95 (*0-7089-2773-4*) Ulverscroft.

***MacDougall.** James IV. 1995. pap. 29.95 (*0-85976-415-X*) Humanities.

MacDougall, A. Colin. Implementing Multiple Drug Therapy for Leprosy. 64p. (C). 1988. pap. text ed. 30.00 (*0-85598-092-3*, Pub. by Oxfam Pubns UK) St Mut.

MacDougall, Alan & Prytherch, Ray. Cooperative Training in Libraries. (Illus.). 1990. text ed. 69.95 (*0-566-05709-3*, Pub. by Gower UK) Ashgate Pub Co.

MacDougall, Alan F. & Chaney, Michael. Security & Crime Prevention in Libraries. 250p. 1992. 59.95 (*1-85742-014-4*, Pub. by Ashgate UK) Ashgate Pub Co.

MacDougall, Alan F. & Prytherch, Ray. Handbook of Library Co-Operation. 300p. 1991. text ed. 69.95 (*0-566-03627-4*, Pub. by Gower UK) Ashgate Pub Co.

MacDougall, Alice F. The Autobiography of a Business Woman. Baxter, Annette K., ed. LC 79-8800. (Signal Lives Ser.). (Illus.). 1980. reprint ed. lib. bdg. 26.95 (*0-405-12847-9*) Ayer.

***MacDougall, B. R., et al, eds.** Proceedings of the Symposium on Oxide Films on Metals & Alloys. LC 92-74173. (Proceedings Ser.: Vol. 92-22). 624p. 1992. 55.00 (*1-56677-023-8*) Electrochem Soc.

MacDougall, Curtis. Hoaxes. 2nd ed. 1982. pap. 7.95 (*0-486-20465-0*) Dover.

MacDougall, Curtis D. Reporters Report Reporters. LC 68-15283. (Illus.). 193p. reprint ed. pap. 55.10 (*0-685-20340-9*, 2029781) Bks Demand.

— Superstition & the Press. LC 83-61115. (Science & the Paranormal Ser.). 616p. 1983. 41.95 (*0-87975-211-4*); pap. 25.95 (*0-87975-212-2*) Prometheus Bks.

MacDougall, Curtis D. & Reid, Robert D. Interpretative Reporting. 9th ed. 782p. (C). 1987. pap. write for info. (*0-02-373140-0*) Macmillan.

MacDougall, Donald, ed. Scots & Scots' Descendants in America. 390p. 1992. reprint ed. pap. 29.95 (*0-685-60523-X*, 9105) Clearfield Co.

MacDougall, E. B., ed. Microcomputers in Landscape Architecture. 268p. 1983. 49.50 (*0-444-00771-7*) Elsevier.

MacDougall, Elisabeth B. Fountains, Statues, & Flowers: Studies in Italian Gardens of the Sixteenth & Seventeenth Centuries. LC 93-9546. (Illus.). 356p. 1994. 50.00x (*0-88402-216-1*) Dumbarton Oaks.

MacDougall, Elisabeth B., ed. Colloquium on the History of Landscape Architecture Vol. 5: Fons Sapientiae: Renaissance Garden Fountains. LC 78-55012. (Illus.). 212p. 1979. 25.00 (*0-88402-080-0*) Dumbarton Oaks.

— Medieval Gardens: Dumbarton Oaks Colloquium on the History of Landscape Architecture, No. 9. LC 85-29343. (Illus.). 352p. 1986. 35.00 (*0-88402-146-7*) Dumbarton Oaks.

— Studies in the History of Art: The Architectural Historian in America. (Symposium Papers XIX: Vol. 35). (Illus.). 316p. 1990. pap. 20.00 (*0-89468-139-7*) Natl Gallery Art.

MacDougall, Elisabeth B. & Jashemski, Wilhelmina F., eds. Ancient Roman Villa Gardens. LC 86-24255. (Dumbarton Oaks Colloquium on the History of Landscape Architecture Ser.: No. 10). (Illus.). 268p. 1987. 36.00 (*0-88402-162-9*, MAVG) Dumbarton Oaks.

— Colloquium on the History of Landscape Architecture Vol. 7: Ancient Roman Gardens. LC 81-4510. (Illus.). 212p. 1981. 22.00 (*0-88402-100-9*) Dumbarton Oaks.

MacDougall, Elisabeth B., jt. ed. see Tatum, George B.

***MacDougall, Elizabeth B.** Gardens of Naples. (Illus.). 208p. 1995. 55.00 (*0-935748-95-4*) Scala Books.

MacDougall, Hamilton C. Early New England Psalmody: An Historical Appreciation, 1620-1820. LC 79-87398. (Music Reprint Ser.). 1969. reprint ed. lib. bdg. 29.50 (*0-306-71542-2*) Da Capo.

MacDougall, Ian, ed. Voices from the Spanish Civil War: Personal Recollections of Scottish Volunteers. (Illus.). 369p. 1986. pap. 21.00 (*0-948275-19-7*) Dufour.

MacDougall, J. A., jt. ed. see Koerner, R. M.

MacDougall, J. Duncan, et al, eds. Physiological Testing of the High Performance Athlete. 2nd ed. LC 90-35488. 448p. (C). 1991. text ed. 44.00x (*0-87322-300-4*, BMAC0300) Human Kinetics.

MacDougall, James. Folk Tales & Fairy Lore in Gaelic & English: Collected from Oral Tradition. Dorsen, Richard M., ed. LC 77-70587. (International Folklore Ser.). 1977. reprint ed. lib. bdg. 28.95 (*0-405-10106-6*) Ayer.

MacDougall, James, ed. Folk & Hero Tales. LC 75-144456. (Waifs & Strays of Celtic Tradition: Argyllshire Ser.: No. 3). (Illus.). reprint ed. 35.00 (*0-404-53533-X*) AMS Pr.

MacDougall, Jean. Highland Postbag: Correspondence of Four MacDougal Chiefs 1715-1865. (Illus.). 304p. 1985. 22.50 (*0-85683-071-2*, Pub. by Shepheard-Walwyn Pubs UK) Paul & Co Pubs.

MacDougall, Jill, tr. see Micone, Marco.

MacDougall, John. Land or Religion? The Sardar & Kherwar Movements in Bihar, 1858-1895. 1986. 27.00 (*0-8364-1591-4*, Pub. by Manohar II) S Asia.

MacDougall, Margaret O. The Clan MacKay. (Johnston & Bacon Clan Histories Ser.). (Illus.). 32p. 1993. reprint ed. pap. 8.95 (*0-685-69984-6*, 9614) Clearfield Co.

MacDougall, Mary K. Se Sano Ahora! rev. ed. LC 93-61519. (SPA.). 1994. 12.95 (*0-87159-195-2*) Unity Bks.

MacDougall, Mary Katheine. Dear Me, I Love You. 176p. (Orig.). 1986. pap. 9.95 (*0-940175-00-2*) Now Comns.

MacDougall, Mary-Katherine. Black Jupiter. Gruver, Kate E., ed. (Illus.). 181p. (J). (gr. 5 up). 1983. 8.95 (*0-940175-01-0*) Now Comns.

MacDougall, Mary Katherine. Dear Friend, I Love You. 176p. (Orig.). 1986. pap. 9.95 (*0-87707-226-4*) Now Comns.

MacDougall, Mary-Katherine. Making Love Happen. Liepa, Alex, ed. 236p. 1980. 8.95 (*0-940175-02-9*) Now Comns.

MacDougall, Myron H. Simulating Computer Systems: Techniques & Tools. (Computer Systems Ser.). 290p. (C). 1987. 44.00 (*0-262-13229-X*) MIT Pr.

MacDougall, Norman. Scotland & War. 232p. 1991. text ed. 66.00 (*0-685-58963-3*) B&N Imports.

— Scotland & War. 220p. (C). 1993. 90.00x (*0-85976-248-3*) St Mut.

MacDougall, Norman, jt. ed. see Mason, Roger.

MacDougall, Pauleena M., jt. auth. see Chaney, Michael.

MacDougall, Peter R. & Friedlander, Jack, eds. Models for Conducting Institutional Research. LC 85-644753. (New Directions for Community Colleges Ser.: No. CC 72). 1990. 16.95 (*1-55542-804-5*) Jossey-Bass.

MacDougall, Philip. Phantoms of the High Seas. (Illus.). 192p. 1991. 19.95 (*0-7153-9834-2*, Pub. by D & C Pub UK) Sterling.

***MacDougall, Phillip.** Royal Dockyards. 1989. pap. 25.00 (*0-7478-0033-2*, Pub. by Shire UK) St Mut.

MacDougall, Ruth D. Snowy. 384p. 1993. 21.95 (*0-312-09913-4*) St Martin.

***MacDougall, Terry E., ed.** Political Leadership in Contemporary Japan, No. 1. xiv, 146p. 1982. pap. 7.00 (*0-939512-06-8*) U MI Japan.

MacDougall, William L. American Revolutionary: A Biography of General Alexander McDougall. LC 76-15324. (Contributions in American History Ser.: No. 57). (Illus.). 186p. 1977. text ed. 45.00 (*0-8371-9035-5*, MAR/, Greenwood Pr) Greenwood.

— The Search for Virginia Dare. (Illus.). 40p. (C). 1995. text ed. 19.50 (*0-930329-95-3*) KABEL Pubs.

MacDowall, D. W. Indian Numismatics, History, Art & Culture: Essays in Honour of Dr. Parmeshwari Lal Gupta, 2 vols., Set. (Agam Indological Ser.: No. 14). (C). 1992. 200.00 (*0-8364-2833-1*, Pub. by Agam Kala Prakashan) S Asia.

MacDowall, David W. The Western Coinages of Nero. LC 74-82869. (Numismatic Notes & Monographs: No. 161). (Illus.). 281p. (Orig.). 1979. pap. 40.00 (*0-89722-176-1*) Am Numismatic.

Macdowall, M. W., tr. see Franzos, Karl E.

***MacDowall, Simon.** Late Roman Cavalryman 236-565 AD. (Warrior Ser.). (Illus.). 64p. 1995. pap. 12.95 (*1-85532-567-5*, Pub. by Osprey UK) Stackpole.

— Late Roman Infantry, 236-565 A.D. (Warrior Ser.). (Illus.). 64p. 1994. pap. 12.95 (*1-85532-419-9*, 9608, Pub. by Osprey UK) Stackpole.

MacDowell, Betty, jt. auth. see Harley, Rachel B.

MacDowell Colony Staff. Medal Day at the MacDowell Colony. Dawes, Lyell & Carswell, Mary, eds. (Orig.). 1994. pap. 10.00 (*0-942389-08-5*) Cobblestone Pub.

MacDowell, D. M. Gorgias: Encomium of Helen. 48p. 1982. 10.95 (*0-86292-053-1*, Pub. by Brstl Class Pr UK) Focus Info Gr.

***MacDowell, Douglas M.** Aristophanes & Athens: An Introduction to the Plays. 350p. 1995. 56.00 (*0-19-872158-7*); pap. 19.95 (*0-19-872159-5*) OUP.

— The Law in Classical Athens. LC 78-54141. (Aspects of Greek & Roman Life Ser.). 280p. 1978. pap. 15.95 (*0-8014-9365-X*) Cornell U Pr.

MacDowell, Douglas M., ed. see Demosthenes.

MacDowell, Edward. Critical & Historical Essays. 2nd ed. LC 69-11289. 1969. reprint ed. lib. bdg. 37.50 (*0-306-71098-6*) Da Capo.

— Etudes & Technical Exercises for Piano. (Earlier American Music Ser.: No. 29). 140p. 1987. reprint ed. 27.50 (*0-306-77325-2*) Da Capo.

— Piano Pieces, (Opus 51, 55, 61, 62) LC 70-170391. (Earlier American Music Ser.: No. 8). 144p. 1972. reprint ed. lib. bdg. 32.50 (*0-306-77308-2*) Da Capo.

— Songs (Op. 40, 47, 56, 58, 60) LC 73-170392. (Earlier American Music Ser.). 1972. 23.50 (*0-685-45908-X*) Da Capo.

MacDowell, Edward A. Critical & Historical Essays: Lectures Delivered at Columbia University. 293p. 1990. reprint ed. lib. bdg. 69.00 (*0-7812-9014-7*) Rprt Serv.

MacDowell, Jeanne & Conley, Effie. Christmas at New England's Favorite Inns: A Sampler of Traditions, Love, & Recipes. 287p. 1992. pap. 14.95 (*0-930267-31-1*) Bergh Pub.

MacDowell, John F., jt. ed. see Boyd, David C.

MacDowell, Karin, jt. auth. see MacDowell, Robert.

MacDowell, L. D. Trip to Wonderful Alaska. 33p. reprint ed. pap. 2.95 (*0-8466-2063-4*, S63) Shorey.

MacDowell, Laurel S. Remember Kirkland Lake: The Gold-Miners' Strike of 1941-42. (State & Economic Life Ser.). 308p. 1983. 35.00 (*0-8020-5585-0*); pap. 14.95 (*0-8020-6457-4*) U of Toronto Pr.

— Remember Kirkland Lake: The History & Effects of the Kirkland Lake Gold Miners' Strike, 1941-42. LC 83-132702. (State & Economic Life Ser.: No. 5). (Illus.). 308p. reprint ed. pap. 87.80 (*0-8357-6386-2*, 2035741) Bks Demand.

MacDowell, Mark. A Comparative Study of Teachings of Don Juan & Madhyamaka Buddhism. xv, 116p. (C). 1991. reprint ed. 11.00 (*81-208-0162-8*, Pub. by Motilal Banarsidass II) S Asia.

MacDowell, Marsha. Stories in Thread. Fitzgerald, Ruth & Caltrider, Sue, eds. (Illus.). (Orig.). 1989. spiral bd. 20.00 (*0-944311-02-4*) MSU Museum.

***MacDowell, Marsha, ed.** African American Quiltmaking in Michigan. 375p. 1996. 45.00 (*0-87013-410-8*) Mich St U Pr.

MacDowell, Marsha & Fitzgerald, Ruth D. Michigan Quilts: One Hundred & Fifty Years of a Textile Tradition. LC 87-62538. (Illus.). 175p. (Orig.). (C). 1987. 34.95 (*0-944311-00-8*); pap. 24.95 (*0-944311-01-6*) MSU Museum.

MacDowell, Michael A. Public Understanding of Economic Policies: The Tax Cuts of 1962 & 1964. LC 77-14765. (Dissertations in American Economic History Ser.). 1978. 33.95 (*0-405-11048-0*) Ayer.

MacDowell, Robert & MacDowell, Karin. The Collector's Digest on German Character Dolls. (Illus.). 160p. (Orig.). 1981. pap. text ed. 9.95 (*0-87588-177-7*, 422) Hobby Hse.

Macduff, Nancy. Building Effective Volunteer Committees. Millgard, Janie, ed. (Illus.). 82p. (C). 1986. pap. 11.95 (*0-945795-01-7*) MBA Pub.

— Episodic Volunteer: Strategies to Develop an Effective Short-Term Volunteer Program. Millgard, Janie & Ricketts, Jennifer, eds. 24p. (C). 1991. pap. 6.95 (*0-945795-07-6*) MBA Pub.

— Slide Shows on a Shoe String. Millgard, Janie, ed. (Illus.). 54p. (C). 1986. pap. 7.95 (*0-945795-02-5*) MBA Pub.

— Volunteer Recruiting & Retention: A Marketing Approach. Millgard, Janie, ed. (Illus.). 196p. (C). 1985. pap. 24.95 (*0-945795-00-9*) MBA Pub.

Macduff, Nancy, ed. see Henson, Sarah & Larson, Bruce.

MacDugall, Elizabeth B., jt. ed. see Tatum, George B.

Mace. Trafalgar Square: Emblem of Empire. (C). 1976. pap. 22.50 (*0-85315-367-1*, Pub. by Lawrence & Wishart UK) Humanities.

Mace & Kowalczyk. Radiographic Pathology for Technologists. (Illus.). 288p. 1988. pap. text ed. 26.95 (*0-8016-3046-0*) Mosby Yr Bk.

— Radiographic Pathology for Technologists. 2nd ed. 400p. 1993. pap. 29.95 (*0-8016-7059-4*) Mosby Yr Bk.

Mace, A. C., jt. auth. see Carter, Howard.

Mace, Alice E., ed. see Ortho Books Editorial Staff.

Mace, Arthur C. & Winlock, Herbert E. The Tomb of Senebtisi at Lisht: Metropolitan Museum of Art Egyptian Expedition Publications, Vol. 1. LC 73-168408. (Metropolitan Museum of Art Publications in Reprint). (Illus.). 228p. 1973. reprint ed. 35.95 (*0-405-02241-7*) Ayer.

Mace, Aurelia G. The Aletheia. 2nd ed. (Illus.). 146p. 1992. reprint ed. 14.95 (*0-915836-23-8*) United Soc Shakers.

— The Aletheia: Spirit of Truth. 2nd ed. LC 72-2989. reprint ed. 28.00 (*0-404-10751-6*) AMS Pr.

Mace, Carroll E. Two Spanish-Quiche Dance Dramas of Rabinal, Vol. 3. 221p. 1970. pap. 7.00 (*0-912788-02-X*) Tulane Romance Lang.

***Mace, Chris J., ed.** The Art & Science of Assessment in Psychotherapy. LC 94-46785. 208p. 1995. 59.95x (*0-415-10538-2*, C0459); pap. 17.95 (*0-415-10539-0*, C0465) Routledge.

Mace, D. R., et al. Teaching of Human Sexuality in Schools for Health Professionals. (Public Health Papers: No. 57). 1974. pap. 2.00 (*92-4-130057-4*) World Health.

Mace, David & Mace, Vera. How to Have a Happy Marriage. 1987. reprint ed. pap. 8.95 (*0-687-17832-0*, Festival) Abingdon.

M

An Asterisk (*) at the beginning of an entry indicates that the title is appearing in BIP for the first time.

M

Mace, David R. A los Que Dios Ha Juntado En Matrimonio. 96p. 1986. reprint ed. pap. 3.50 (*0-311-40036-1*, Edit Mundo) Casa Bautista.

— Getting Ready for Marriage. LC 84-28320. 128p. 1985. reprint ed. pap. 6.95 (*0-687-14136-2*) Abingdon.

— Sexual Difficulties in Marriage. LC 72-75652. (Pocket Counsel Bks.). 64p. (Orig.). reprint ed. pap. 25.00 (*0-685-15400-9*, 2027178) Bks Demand.

Mace, David R., ed. Modern Marriage & the Clergy. LC 74-19593. (Special Issue of Pastoral Psychology Ser.). 84p. 1978. 16.95 (*0-87705-368-5*) Human Sci Pr.

Mace, Emden C. The Lord of Glory. 1986. pap. 5.99 (*0-88019-182-1*) Schmul Pub Co.

Mace, Evelyn. The Edgar Family: Ireland & the New World. 135p. (Orig.). 1990. pap. text ed. 20.00 (*0-9616632-1-9*) E Mace.

— Our Group Cookbook. 75p. (Orig.). 1986. pap. 6.00 (*0-9616632-0-0*) E Mace.

Mace, Gillian S., et al. The Bereaved Child: Analysis, Education, & Treatment - An Abstracted Bibliography. LC 81-8637. 292p. 1981. 95.00 (*0-306-65197-1*, IFI-Plenum) Plenum.

***Mace, Harvey F.** The Highs & Lows of Flying. Frisque, Tom, ed. (Illus.). 149p. 1994. pap. 19.95 (*0-9623080-5-6*) Aviation Usk.

Mace, Irving B. Mind of an Addict. 280p. (Orig.). 1993. pap. 14.95 (*0-914339-45-1*) P E Randall Pub.

Mace, James E. Communism & the Dilemmas of National Liberation: National Communism in Soviet Ukraine, 1918-1933. LC 83-4361. (Harvard Ukrainian Research Institute Monograph). 334p. 1990. 27.00 (*0-916458-09-1*) Harvard Ukrainian.

Mace, Jane. Talking about Literacy: Principles & Practices of Adult Literacy Education. 1992. 59.95 (*0-415-08044-4*, A9634); pap. 16.95 (*0-415-06655-7*, A9638) Routledge.

— Working with Words: Literacy Beyond School. (Chameleon Education Ser.). 144p. 1981. pap. 4.95 (*0-906495-15-6*) Writers & Readers.

***Mace, Jane, ed.** Literacy, Language & Community Publishing: Essays in Adult Education. LC 94-47982. 1995. write for info. (*1-85359-280-3*, Pub. by Multilingual Matters UK); pap. write for info. (*1-85359-279-X*, Pub. by Multilingual Matters UK) Taylor & Francis.

Mace, Jean. Home Fairy Tales. Booth, Mary L., tr. LC 78-74517. (Children's Literature Reprint Ser.). (Illus.). (J). (gr. 4-5). 1979. reprint ed. 24.75 (*0-8486-0220-X*) Roth Pub Inc.

Mace, John. Teach Yourself Persian, Modern. (Teach Yourself Ser.). 1992. 14.95 (*0-685-63252-0*) Fr & Eur.

Mace, M. E. & Bell, A. A., eds. Fungal Wilt Diseases of Plants. 1981. text ed. 139.00 (*0-12-464450-3*) Acad Pr.

Mace, Mary E. Memory Storage Patterns in Parallel Processing. (C). 1987. lib. bdg. 52.00 (*0-89838-239-4*) Kluwer Ac.

Mace, Myles L. Directors: Myth & Reality. 1986. pap. text ed. 14.95 (*0-07-103253-3*) McGraw.

Mace, Nancy L., ed. Dementia Care: Patient, Family, & Community. LC 89-8106. 416p. 1991. reprint ed. text ed. 50.00 (*0-8018-3859-2*); reprint ed. pap. text ed. 18.95 (*0-8018-4314-6*) Johns Hopkins.

Mace, Nancy L. & Rabins, Peter V. The Thirty-Six Hour Day: A Family Guide to Caring for Persons with Alzheimer's Disease, Related Dementing Illnesses & Memory Loss in Later Life. rev. ed. LC 90-49523. 352p. (Orig.). 1991. pap. 11.95 (*0-8018-4034-1*) Johns Hopkins.

— The Thirty-Six Hour Day: A Family Guide to Caring for Persons with Alzheimer's Disease, Related Dementing Illnesses & Memory Loss in Later Life. rev. ed. 448p. (Orig.). 1992. reprint ed. mass mkt. 6.50 (*0-446-36104-6*) Warner Bks.

— The Thirty-Six Hour Day: A Family Guide to Caring for Persons with Alzheimer's Disease, Related Dementing Illnesses & Memory Loss in Later Life. 2nd rev. ed. LC 90-49523. 352p. (Orig.). 1991. text ed. 38.95 (*0-8018-4033-3*) Johns Hopkins.

Mace, Nancy L., jt. auth. see Rabins, Peter.

Mace, O. Henry. Between the Rivers: A History of Early Calaveras County, California. 2nd ed. (Illus.). 159p. 1993. pap. 24.95 (*0-938121-05-7*) Cenotto Pubns.

— Collectors Guide to Early Photographs. 224p. 1990. pap. 16.95 (*0-87069-547-9*, Wallace-Hmestead) Chilton.

— The Collector's Guide to Victoriana. LC 90-50637. (Illus.). 248p. 1991. pap. text ed. 17.95 (*0-87069-576-2*) Chilton.

Mace, P. W. Visible Record Computers. 216p. 1974. 29.00 (*0-8464-0957-7*) Beekman Pubs.

Mace, Patrick B. The Silver Whistle. (Orig.). (J). (gr. k up). 1985. pap. 5.00 (*0-87602-250-6*) Anchorage.

Mace, Paul. The Paul Mace Guide to Utility Software. Gabriel, ed. 508p. 1990. pap. 24.95 (*0-13-654468-1*) P-H.

— Paul Mace's Tools for Windows. 1993. pap. 59.95 (*0-553-37123-1*) Bantam.

— Paul Mace's Tools for Windows. 1994. pap. 29.00 (*0-679-79123-X*) Random.

Mace, Shirley. Silhouette Collectibles: On Glass. (Illus.). 160p. 1992. 24.95 (*0-9633674-5-5*) Shadow Enter.

Mace, Vera, jt. auth. see Mace, David.

MacEacher, Douglad B. Don Juan Notes. 1970. pap. 4.50 (*0-8220-0411-9*) Cliffs.

— Keats & Shelley Notes. (Orig.). 1971. pap. 4.50 (*0-8220-0702-9*) Cliffs.

MacEachern, Diane. Enough Is Enough: The Hell-Raiser's Guide to Community Activism. 176p. (Orig.). 1994. pap. 10.00 (*0-380-77335-X*) Avon.

— Save Our Planet: Seven Hundred & Fifty Everyday Ways You Can Help Clean up the Earth. 1995. mass mkt. 10.95 (*0-440-50267-5*, Dell Trade Pbks) Dell.

***MacEachren, Alan.** How Maps Work: Issues in Representation, Visualization, & Design. 1994. write for info. (*0-08-986258-9*) Guilford Pr.

— How Maps Work: Issues in Representation, Visualization, & Design. 1995. lib. bdg. 42.00 (*0-89862-589-0*) Guilford Pr.

MacEachren, Alan M. Some Truth with Maps: A Primer on Symbolization & Design. Cromley, Robert & Cromley, Ellen, eds. (Resource Publications in Geography). (Illus.). 136p. (C). 1994. pap. 10.00 (*0-89291-214-6*) Assn Am Geographers.

— Visualization in Modern Cartography. LC 94-19075. (Modern Cartography Ser.: No. 2). 1994. pap. text ed. 47.00 (*0-08-042415-5*, Pergamon Pr) Elsevier.

MacEachren, Alan M., jt. ed. see Monmonier, Mark.

MacEachron, Judith. Tomorrow Is for Weeping. LC 79-63106. 1979. 8.95 (*0-914338-04-8*) Regmar Pub.

Macebuh, Stanley. James Baldwin: A Critical Study. LC 72-93679. 194p. 1973. 24.95 (*0-89388-064-7*) Okpaku Communications.

Maceda, Teresita G., ed. see Navarra, Marcel M.

Macedo, D., tr. see Freire, Paulo.

Macedo, Donaldo P. Literacies of Power: What Americans Are Not Allowed to Know. LC 94-3375. (Edge Ser.). (C). 1994. pap. text ed. 15.95 (*0-8133-2253-7*) Westview.

— Literacies of Power: What Americans Are Not Allowed to Know. LC 94-3375. (Edge Ser.). 1994. text ed. 49.95 (*0-8133-2252-9*) Westview.

Macedo, Donaldo P. & Koike, Dale A. Romance Linguistics: The Portuguese Context. LC 92-19868. 216p. 1992. text ed. 45.00 (*0-89789-297-6*, H297, Bergin & Garvey) Greenwood.

Macedo, Donaldo P., jt. auth. see Freire, Paulo.

Macedo, Donaldo P., tr. see Freire, Paulo.

Macedo, E. A. & Rasmussen, P. Liquid-Liquid Equilibrium Data Collection, Supplement 1: Tables, Diagrams & Model Parameters for Binary, Ternary & Quaternary Systems. (Dechema Chemistry Data Ser.: Vol. V, Pt. 4). (Illus.). 340p. 1987. text ed. 229.00 (*3-921567-73-4*, Pub. by Dechema GW) Scholium Intl.

Macedo, Helder, ed. Studies in Portuguese Literature & History in Honour of Luis de Sousa Rebelo. (Serie A: Monagrafias: No. 147). (Illus.). 208p. (POR.). (C). 1993. text ed. 63.00 (*1-85566-012-1*) Boydell & Brewer.

Macedo, Jorge. The Theoretical Basis of the Living System. LC 75-17399. (Illus.). 84p. 1979. 8.90 (*0-87527-158-8*) Green.

Macedo, Roberto B., jt. ed. see Willumsen, Maria J.

Macedo, Stephen. Liberal Virtues: Citizenship, Virtue, & Community in Liberal Constitutionalism. 320p. 1991. reprint ed. pap. 16.95 (*0-19-827872-1*) OUP.

Macedonia, Raymond, jt. auth. see Dunnigan, James.

Macek, A. Coal Research. 140p. 1977. pap. text ed. 205.00 (*0-677-40255-4*) Gordon & Breach.

Macek, Carl. Robotech Art 3. Reynolds, Kay, ed. (Robotech Ser.). (Illus.). 120p. (Orig.). 1988. pap. 12.95 (*0-89865-575-7*, Starblaze) Donning Co.

— Robotech Art 3. limited ed. Reynolds, Kay, ed. (Robotech Ser.). (Illus.). 120p. (Orig.). 1988. 40.00 (*0-89865-576-5*, Starblaze) Donning Co.

Macek, Josef. The Hussite Movement in Bohemia. Fried, Vilem & Milner, Ian, trs. LC 78-63207. (Heresies of the Early Christian & Medieval Era Ser.: Second Ser.). reprint ed. 39.50 (*0-404-16237-1*) AMS Pr.

Macek, K. Pharmaceutical Applications of Thin-Layer & Paper Chromatography. 743p. 1972. 172.00 (*0-444-40923-8*) Elsevier.

Macek, Vladko. In the Struggle for Freedom. LC 68-8182. (Illus.). 1968. 30.00 (*0-271-00069-4*) Pa St U Pr.

MacEllven, Douglass T. Legal Research Handbook. 440p. 1993. text ed. 75.00 (*0-409-91114-3*); pap. text ed. 34.95 (*0-409-91116-X*) Butterworth Legal Pubs.

MacElrevey, Daniel H. Shiphandling for the Mariner. 3rd ed. (Illus.). 352p. 1995. text ed. 35.00x (*0-87033-464-6*) Cornell Maritime.

***Macelroy.** Life Science & Space Research XXV: Natural & Artificial Ecosystems. (Advances in Space Research Ser.). 1994. pap. 165.00 (*0-08-042488-0*, Pergamon Pr) Elsevier.

MacElroy, R. D., et al, eds. Life Sciences & Space Research: Natural & Artificial Ecosystems, No. XXIII. (Advances in Space Research Ser.: No. 9). (Illus.). 196p. 1989. pap. 100.00 (*0-08-040150-3*, Pergamon Pr) Elsevier.

Macelwane, James B. When the Earth Quakes. LC 76-29402. reprint ed. 23.50 (*0-404-15340-2*) AMS Pr.

***Maceoin, Beth.** Homeopathy. 1994. pap. 8.99 (*0-06-104321-4*, Harp PBks) HarpC.

— Homoeopathy. (Headway Lifeguides Ser.). (Illus.). 127p. 1995. pap. 13.95 (*0-340-56578-0*, Pub. by Hodder & Stoughton Ltd UK) Trafalgar.

MacEoin, Denis. Rituals in Babism & Baha'ism. (Pembroke Persian Papers). 192p. 1995. text ed. 59.50 (*1-85043-654-1*, Pub. by I B Tauris UK) St Martin.

— The Sources for Early Babi Doctrine & History: A Survey. LC 91-43294. ix, 274p. 1992. 71.50 (*90-04-09462-8*) E J Brill.

MacEoin, G., et al, eds. Third International Conference on Minority Languages: Galway 1986: General Papers. 240p. 1987. 59.00 (*0-905028-78-3*, MM31, Pub. by Multilingual Matters UK) Taylor & Francis.

MacEoin, Gary. Unlikely Allies: The Christian-Socialist Convergence. 128p. (Orig.). 1990. pap. 10.95 (*0-8245-1046-1*) Crossroad NY.

Macer-Story, Eugenia. Angels of Time. 88p. 1984. 30.00 (*0-7212-0697-2*, Pub. by Regency Press) St Mut.

— Battles with Dragons: Certain Tales of Political Yoga. 180p. (Orig.). 1994. pap. 25.00 (*1-879980-03-7*) Magick Mirror.

— Gypsy Fair. 49p. 1990. 12.95 (*1-879980-00-2*) Magick Mirror.

— Legacy of Daedalus. 94p. 1995. pap. 6.00 (*1-879980-05-3*) Magick Mirror.

— The Strawberry Man & 27 Love Poems. 1992. 12.95 (*1-879980-01-0*) Magick Mirror.

Maceri, Domenico. Dalla Novellas Alla Commedia Pirandelliana. LC 90-26478. (American University Studies: Romance Languages & Literature: Ser. II, Vol. 165). 179p. (C). 1991. text ed. 34.95 (*0-8204-1483-2*) P Lang Pubs.

Maceri, Franco & Iazeolla, Giuseppe, eds. EUROSIM 'Ninety-Two Simulation Congress: Proceedings of the 1992 EUROSIM Conference, EUROSIM 92, Capri, Italy, 28 September-4 October 1992. LC 93-5658. 787p. 1993. 200.00 (*0-444-89331-8*, North Holland) Elsevier.

Maceri, Franco, jt. ed. see Del Piero, G.

Macesich, George. Commercial Banking & Regional Development in the United States, 1950-1960. LC 65-64030. (Florida State University Studies: No. 45). 178p. reprint ed. pap. 50.80 (*0-7837-4932-5*, 2044598) Bks Demand.

— The International Monetary Economy & the Third World. LC 81-7298. 314p. 1981. text ed. 69.50 (*0-275-90674-4*, C0674, Praeger Pubs) Greenwood.

— Monetarism: Theory & Policy. Zecher, J. Richard & Wilford, D. Sykes, eds. LC 82-19040. (Praeger Studies in International Monetary Economics & Finance). 270p. 1983. text ed. 55.00 (*0-275-91039-3*, C1039, Praeger Pubs) Greenwood.

— Monetary Policy & Rational Expectations. LC 86-20538. 164p. 1987. text ed. 49.95 (*0-275-92327-4*, C2327, Praeger Pubs) Greenwood.

— Monetary Reform & Cooperation Theory. LC 88-25883. 142p. 1989. text ed. 55.00 (*0-275-93109-9*, C3109, Praeger Pubs) Greenwood.

— Money & Democracy. LC 89-26540. 184p. 1990. text ed. 49.95 (*0-275-93480-2*, C3480, Greenwood Pr) Greenwood.

— The Politics of Monetarism: Its Historical & Institutional Development. (Illus.). 170p. 1984. 45.50 (*0-8476-7344-8*) Rowman.

— Reform & Market Democracy. LC 91-10179. 160p. 1991. text ed. 45.00 (*0-275-93989-8*, C3989, Praeger Pubs) Greenwood.

— Successor States & Cooperation Theory. LC 94-6377. 192p. 1994. text ed. 55.00 (*0-275-94936-2*, Praeger Pubs) Greenwood.

— World Banking & Finance: Cooperation Versus Conflict. LC 84-17908. 192p. 1984. text ed. 42.95 (*0-275-91220-5*, C1220, Praeger Pubs) Greenwood.

— World Debt & Stability. LC 90-37787. 128p. 1991. text ed. 49.95 (*0-275-93669-4*, C3669, Praeger Pubs) Greenwood.

Macesich, George, ed. Yugoslavia in the Age of Democracy: Essays on Economic & Political Reform. LC 91-34495. 250p. 1992. text ed. 49.95 (*0-275-94175-2*, C4175, Praeger Pubs) Greenwood.

Macesich, George & Dimitrejevic, Dimitrije. Monetary Reform in Former Socialist Economies. LC 94-25042. 146p. 1994. text ed. 49.95 (*0-275-95008-5*, Praeger Pubs) Greenwood.

Macesich, George & Tsai, Hui-Liang. Money in Economic Systems. Zecher, J. Richard & Wilford, D. Sykes, eds. LC 81-20977. (Studies in International Monetary Economics & Finances). 254p. 1982. text ed. 49.95 (*0-275-90852-6*, C0852, Praeger Pubs) Greenwood.

Macesich, George, jt. auth. see Dimitrijevic, Dimitrije.

Macesich, George, et al, eds. Essays on the Yugoslav Economic Model. LC 87-38474. 152p. 1989. text ed. 59.95 (*0-275-92670-2*, C2670, Praeger Pubs) Greenwood.

MacEslin, Diz. Mushrooms Mushrooms. 36p. (Orig.). 1982. pap. 2.75 (*0-940844-12-5*) Wellspring.

MacEwan, Arthur. Debt & Disorder: International Economic Instability & U. S. Imperial Decline. 144p. (C). 1989. 26.00 (*0-85345-795-6*); pap. 10.00 (*0-85345-796-4*) Monthly Rev.

— Revolution & Economic Development in Cuba: Moving Towards Socialism. LC 80-11130. 240p. 1981. text ed. 39.95 (*0-312-67980-7*) St Martin.

MacEwan, Arthur & Tabb, William K., eds. Instability & Change in the World Economy. 352p. (C). 1989. 36.00 (*0-85345-782-4*); pap. 18.00 (*0-85345-783-2*) Monthly Rev.

MacEwan, Bonnie, jt. ed. see Johnson, Peggy.

MacEwan, Elias J., tr. see Freytag, Gustav.

MacEwan, Grant. Heavy Horses: Highlights of Their History. (Illus.). 1991. reprint ed. 21.95 (*0-9622663-7-X*) Heart Prairie Pr.

MacEwan, Gwendolyn. Mermaids & Ikons: A Greek Summer. 110p. (Orig.). 1978. pap. 6.95 (*0-88784-062-0*, Pub. by Hse of Anansi Pr CN) Genl Dist Srvs.

— Poetry of Gwendolyn Macewan, Vol. 1: The Early Years. 1994. pap. 19.95 (*1-55096-019-9*, Pub. by Exile Edits CN) InBook.

— Poetry of Gwendolyn Macewan, Vol. 2: The Later Years. 1994. pap. 19.95 (*1-55096-076-8*, Pub. by Exile Edits CN) InBook.

MacEwan, Malcolm, jt. auth. see MacEwen, Ann.

MacEwen, Ann & MacEwan, Malcolm. National Parks: Conservation or Cosmetics. (Resource Management Ser.). 1982. pap. text ed. 24.95 (*0-04-719004-3*) Routledge Chapman & Hall.

MacEwen, Ann & MacEwen, Malcolm. Greenprints for the Countryside: The Story of Britain's National Parks. 304p. 1987. text ed. 65.00 (*0-04-719013-2*) Routledge Chapman & Hall.

MacEwen, E. Gregory, jt. auth. see Withrow, Stephen J.

MacEwen, G. Dean, et al, eds. Pediatric Fractures: A Practical Approach to Assessment & Treatment. LC 92-48218. (Illus.). 464p. 1993. 120.00 (*0-683-05310-8*) Williams & Wilkins.

MacEwen, Glenn H. Introduction to Computer Systems: Using the PDP-Eleven & Pascal. (Computer Science Ser.). (Illus.). 400p. 1980. text ed. write for info. (*0-07-044350-5*) McGraw.

MacEwen, Gwendolyn. Noman. 120p. 1985. pap. 4.95 (*0-7736-7086-6*, Pub. by Stoddart Pubng CN) Genl Dist Srvs.

***MacEwen, Gwendolyn, ed.** The T. E. Lawrence Poems. 80p. 1995. 27.00 (*0-8095-4588-8*) Borgo Pr.

MacEwen, Malcolm. The Greening of a Red. 306p. (C). 1991. text ed. 51.50 (*0-7453-0440-0*); pap. text ed. 21.00 (*0-7453-0441-9*) Westview.

MacEwen, Malcolm, jt. auth. see MacEwen, Ann.

MacEwen, Martin. Housing, Race & Law. 416p. (C). 1991. text ed. 95.00 (*0-415-00063-7*, A4887) Routledge.

— Tackling Racism in Europe: An Examination of Anti-Discrimination Law in Practice. 224p. 1995. 38.95 (*0-85496-857-1*); pap. 16.95 (*1-85973-047-7*) Berg Pubs.

MacEwen, Sally, ed. Views of Clytemnestra, Ancient & Modern. LC 89-28420. (Studies in Comparative Literature: Vol. 9). (Illus.). 154p. 1990. lib. bdg. 69.95 (*0-88946-627-0*) E Mellen.

MacEwen, Sally & Tarkow, Theodore A. Euripides: Iphigenia at Aulis. (Greek Commentaries Ser.). 120p. (Orig.). (C). 1989. pap. text ed. 7.00 (*0-929524-55-1*) Bryn Mawr Commentaries.

MacEwen, W. A. & Lewis, A. H. Encyclopedia of Nautical Knowledge. LC 53-9685. 626p. 1953. 38.50 (*0-87033-010-1*) Cornell Maritime.

MacEwen, William A., jt. auth. see Turpin, Edward A.

Macey, David. Lacan in Contexts. 320p. 1988. text ed. 55.00 (*0-86091-215-9*, Pub. by Verso UK); pap. text ed. 18.95 (*0-86091-942-0*, Pub. by Verso UK) Routledge Chapman & Hall.

— The Lives of Michel Foucault. 624p. 1994. 30.00 (*0-679-43074-1*) Pantheon.

— The Lives of Michel Foucault. 1995. 16.00 (*0-679-75792-9*, Vin) Random.

Macey, David, tr. see Camard, Florence.

Macey, David, tr. see Debray, Regis.

Macey, David, tr. see Lacoste, Yves.

Macey, David, tr. see Laplanche, Jean.

Macey, David, tr. see Lefort, Claude.

Macey, David, tr. see Lemaire, Anika.

Macey, David, tr. see Sapir, Jacques.

Macey, David, tr. see Touraine, Alain.

Macey, David, tr. see Whitford, Margaret, ed.

Macey, David A. Government & Peasant in Russia, 1861-1906: The Prehistory of the Stolypin Reforms. 1987. text ed. 32.00 (*0-87580-122-6*) N Ill U Pr.

Macey, Jonathan R. Insider Trading: Economics, Politics, & Policy. 85p. (C). 1991. pap. text ed. 9.75 (*0-8447-7010-8*, AEI Pr) Am Enterprise.

— Model Business Corporation Act. 530p. 1991. ring bd. 95.00 (*0-13-596628-0*) Aspen Law.

— Model Business Corporation Act, 4 vols., Set. annot. ed. 2892p. 1985. ring bd. 395.00 (*0-13-209107-0*) Aspen Law.

— Third Party Legal Opinions: Evaluation & Analysis. 332p. 1992. ring bd. 95.00 (*0-13-110470-5*) Aspen Law.

Macey, Jonathan R. & Miller, Geoffrey P. Costly Policies: State Regulation & Antitrust Exemption in Insurance Markets. 123p. 1993. 24.75 (*0-8447-3831-X*); pap. 9.75 (*0-8447-3830-1*) Am Enterprise.

Macey, Robert I., jt. auth. see Kapit, Wynn.

Macey, Samuel L. The Dynamics of Progress: Time, Method, & Measure. LC 89-31886. (Illus.). 272p. 1989. 35.00 (*0-8203-1159-6*) U of Ga Pr.

— Patriarchs of Time: Dualism in Saturn-Cronus, Father Time, the Watchmaker God & Father Christmas. LC 86-25115. (Illus.). 227p. 1987. 25.00 (*0-8203-0934-6*) U of Ga Pr.

— Time: A Bibliographic Guide. LC 91-25934. (Reference Books on Sociology & Science Ser.). 448p. 1991. 62.00 (*0-8153-0646-6*, H1506) Garland.

Macey, Samuel L., ed. Encyclopedia of Time. LC 93-43355. (Illus.). 728p. 1994. 95.00 (*0-8153-0615-6*, SS810) Garland.

Macey, Samuel L., intro. A Learned Dissertation on Dumpling; with a Word upon Pudding: And Pudding & Dumpling Burnt to Pot: or a Compleat Way to the Dissertation on Dumpling. LC 92-22731. (Augustan Reprints Ser.: No. 140 (1970)). reprint ed. 12.00 (*0-404-70140-X*, PR3291) AMS Pr.

Macey, Sheila. The Full Circle. 150p. 1984. 30.00 (*0-7212-0672-7*, Pub. by Regency Press) St Mut.

Macfadden, B. Natural Cure for Rupture. 1991. lib. bdg. 69.75 (*0-8490-4523-1*) Gordon Pr.

Macfadden, Barnarr. Natural Cure for Rupture. 125p. 1962. reprint ed. spiral bd. 6.60 (*0-7873-0578-2*) Mokelumne.

Macfadden, Bernar. The Walking Cure. (Illus.). 179p. 1984. reprint ed. pap. text ed. 15.00 (*0-87556-391-0*) Saifer.

MacFadden, Bruce J. Fossil Horses: Systematics, Paleobiology, & Evolution of the Family Equidae. (Illus.). 300p. (C). 1992. 74.95 (*0-521-34041-1*) Cambridge U Pr.

— Fossil Horses: Systematics, Paleobiology & Evolution of the Family Equidae. (Illus.). 384p. (C). 1994. pap. 29.95 (*0-521-47708-5*) Cambridge U Pr.

MacFadden, Bruce J., jt. ed. see Damuth, John D.

Macfadden, Clifford H. A Bibliography of Pacific Area Maps. LC 75-30119. (International Research Series of the Institute of Pacific Relations). 1976. reprint ed. 22.50 (*0-404-59542-1*) AMS Pr.

MacFadden, Fred R., ed. see Whibley, Charles.

MacFadyen, A. & Ford, E. David, eds. Advances in Ecological Research, Vol. 13. (Serial Publication Ser.). 1983. text ed. 127.00 (*0-12-013913-8*) Acad Pr.

An Asterisk (*) at the beginning of an entry indicates that the title is appearing in BIP for the first time.

MacFadyen, A. J. & MacFadyen, H. W., eds. Economic Psychology: Intersections in Theory & Application. 698p. 1986. 131.00 (*0-444-70072-2*, North Holland) Elsevier.

MacFadyen, H. W., jt. ed. see MacFadyen, A. J.

MacFadyen, John A. & Hurst, Barbara. Rhode Island Criminal Procedure, 1988-1991. 530p. 1993. ring bd. 125.00 (*0-88063-075-2*) Michie Butterworth.

— Rhode Island Criminal Procedure, 1988-1991. suppl. ed. 530p. 1993. 55.00 (*0-250-40700-0*) Butterworth Legal Pubs.

Macfadzean, Robert H. Surface-Based Air Defense Systems Analysis. (Radar Library). 460p. 1992. text ed. 95.00 (*0-89006-451-2*) Artech Hse.

Macfadzean, Robert H. & Johnson, James M. Surface-Based Air Defense System Analysis Software & User's Manual. (Radar Software Library). 300p. 1992. 200.00 (*0-89006-457-1*) Artech Hse.

MacFall, Russell P. Gem Hunter's Guide. 5th rev. ed. (Illus.). 336p. 1989. 7.99 (*0-517-68240-0*) Random Hse Value.

Macfarlan, Allan & Macfarlan, Paulette. Handbook of American Indian Games. (American Indians Ser.). 288p. 1985. reprint ed. pap. 6.95 (*0-486-24837-2*) Dover.

MacFarlan, Allan & MacFarlan, Paulette. Knotcraft: The Practical & Entertaining Art of Tying Knots. (Crafts Ser.). 186p. (J). (gr. 6-p). 1983. reprint ed. pap. 4.50 (*0-486-24515-2*) Dover.

Macfarlan, Allan A. Exploring the Outdoors with Indian Secrets. LC 82-5466. (Illus.). 224p. 1982. pap. 12.95 (*0-8117-2183-3*) Stackpole.

MacFarlan, Duncan. The Revivals of the Eighteenth Century. 312p. 1980. reprint ed. 16.00 (*0-939464-32-2*) Labyrinth Pr.

Macfarlan, Duncan. The Revivals of the Eighteenth Century, Particularly at Cambuslang: With Three Sermons by the Rev. George Whitefield. (Revival Library). (Illus.). 312p. (C). 1980. reprint ed. lib. bdg. 16.00 (*0-940033-14-3*) R O Roberts.

Macfarlan, Paulette, jt. auth. see Macfarlan, Allan.

MacFarlan, Paulette, jt. auth. see MacFarlan, Allan.

MacFarland, Charles S. The New Church & the New Germany: A Study of Church & State. LC 78-63691. (Studies in Fascism: Ideology & Practice). 224p. reprint ed. 28.00 (*0-404-16953-8*) AMS Pr.

MacFarland, Cynthia. Cows in the Parlor. LC 89-14972. (Illus.). 32p. (J). (ps-2). 1990. text ed. 14.95 (*0-689-31584-8*, Atheneum Bks Young) S&S Childrens.

MacFarland, David T. Contemporary Radio Programming Strategies. (CTS Broadcasting Ser.). 224p. 1990. pap. text ed. 22.50 (*0-8058-0665-2*) L Erlbaum Assocs.

— Development of the Top Forty Radio Format. Sterling, Christopher H., ed. LC 78-21726. (Dissertations in Broadcasting Ser.). (Illus.). 1980. lib. bdg. 48.95 (*0-405-11765-5*) Ayer.

MacFarland, David T., ed. Contemporary Radio Programming Strategies. 244p. (C). 1990. text ed. 49.95 (*0-8058-0664-4*) L Erlbaum Assocs.

MacFarland, Diane, ed. see Holbrook, Sally.

***MacFarland, E. Randolph.** Ground-Water Flow, Geochemistry & Effects of Agricultural Practices on Nitrogen Transport at Study Sites in the Piedmont & Coastal Plain Physiographic Provinces, Patuxent River Basin, Maryland. LC 95-16027. (Water-Supply Papers: Vol. 2449). 1996. write for info. (*0-615-00734-1*) US Geol Survey.

MacFarland, Elaine. Protestants First: Orangeism in Nineteenth-Century Scotland. (Illus.). 224p. 1990. 39.00 (*0-7486-0202-X*, Pub. by Edinburgh U Pr UK) Col U Pr.

MacFarland, Frank. Studies of Opisthobranchiate Mollusks of the Pacific Coast of North America. Kessell, Howard L., ed. (Memoirs of the California Academy of Sciences Ser.: No. 6). (Illus.). 546p. 1966. 25.00 (*0-940228-10-6*) Calif Acad Sci.

MacFarland, Gerald D. Malpractice in Health Occupations: Index of New Information. 150p. 1994. 44.50 (*0-7883-0050-4*); pap. 39.50 (*0-7883-0051-2*) ABBE Pubs Assn.

MacFarland, P. Kant's Concept of Teleology. 150p. 1971. 22.50 (*0-85224-070-8*, Pub. by Edinburgh U Pr UK) Col U Pr.

MacFarland, Paul. How to Build Frameshop Worktables, Fixtures & Jigs. (Illus.). 64p. 1991. 19.00 (*0-938655-36-1*) Columba Pub.

MacFarlane. Clinical Oral Microbiology. (Illus.). 284p. 1989. 49.95 (*0-7236-0934-9*, Pub. by John Wright UK) Buttrwrth-Heinemann.

MacFarlane, jt. auth. see Johnson.

Macfarlane, A. & Gurung, G. Gurungs of Nepal: A Guide to the Gurungs. 1992. 20.00 (*0-7855-0227-0*, Pub. by Ratna Pustak Bhandar) St Mut.

MacFarlane, A. A. Architectural Supervision on Site. (Illus.). iv, 189p. 1973. 47.00 (*0-85334-574-0*, Pub. by Elsevier Applied Sci UK) Elsevier.

MacFarlane, A. G., jt. auth. see De Silva, C. W.

MacFarlane, A. G., jt. auth. see Hung, Y. S.

Macfarlane, Aidan. The Psychology of Childbirth. (Developing Child Ser.). 160p. 1977. pap. text ed. 6.95 (*0-674-72106-3*) HUP.

Macfarlane, Aidan, et al. Child Health: The Screening Tests. (Practical Guides for General Practice Ser.: No. 11). (Illus.). 64p. 1989. pap. 12.95 (*0-19-261768-0*) OUP.

Macfarlane, Alan. A Guide to English Historical Records. LC 82-25102. 144p. reprint ed. pap. 41.10 (*0-685-16059-9*, 2027238) Bks Demand.

— Marriage & Love in England: Modes of Reproduction 1300-1840. 356p. 1987. pap. 15.95 (*0-631-15438-8*) Blackwell Pubs.

MacFarlane, Alan. The Origins of English Individualism: The Family, Property & Social Transition. 232p. 1989. pap. 22.95 (*0-631-12761-5*) Blackwell Pubs.

— Witchcraft in Tudor & Stuart England: A Regional & Comparative Study. (Illus.). 334p. (C). 1991. reprint ed. pap. text ed. 13.50x (*0-88133-532-0*) Waveland Pr.

Macfarlane, Alan, ed. see Josselin, Ralph.

Macfarlane, Alan, et al. Reconstructing Historical Communities. LC 77-24234. 1978. 13.95 (*0-521-21796-2*) Cambridge U Pr.

MacFarlane, Alistair G., ed. Frequency-Response Methods in Control Systems. LC 79-90572. 536p. 1979. pap. 39.95 (*0-685-55578-X*, PP01214) Inst Electrical.

MacFarlane, Brian. Australian Cinema. (Illus.). 304p. 1988. text ed. 37.50 (*0-231-06728-3*) Col U Pr.

***Macfarlane, Brian A.** MVS Capacity Planning for a Balanced System. LC 94-21735. (IBM Ser.). 1994. write for info. (*0-07-709053-5*) McGraw.

***MacFarlane, Bud, Jr.** Pierced by a Sword: A Chronicle of the Coming Tribulations. 624p. (Orig.). 1995. pap. write for info. (*0-9646316-0-1*) St Jude Media.

MacFarlane, Charles. The Chinese Revolution, with Details of the Habits, Manners & Customs of China & the Chinese. 1972. 59.95 (*0-87968-856-4*) Gordon Pr.

MacFarlane, D. & Shelton, M. Pastures in Vanuatu. (C). 1986. text ed. 36.00 (*0-949511-15-3*, Pub. by ACIAR) St Mut.

Macfarlane, Eleanor C., jt. auth. see Simic, Marjorie R.

MacFarlane, Ellen B. & Burstein, Patricia. Legwork: An Inspiring Journey Through a Chronic Illness. LC 94-11726. 1994. write for info. (*0-02-578001-8*) Macmillan.

Macfarlane, Eric. Education 16-19: In Transition. LC 92-24739. (Educational Management Ser.). 160p. 1992. 52.50 (*0-415-08085-1*, A9934, Routledge NY); pap. write for info. (*0-415-08086-X*, Routledge NY) Routledge.

Macfarlane, G. Layman's Dictionary of Law. 256p. 1984. pap. 10.00 (*0-08-039157-5*, Pergamon Pr) Elsevier.

Macfarlane, George T., jt. ed. see Gibson, Glenn R.

Macfarlane, Gwyn. Alexander Fleming: The Man & the Myth. LC 83-18358. (Illus.). 352p. 1984. 32.00 (*0-674-01490-1*) HUP.

MacFarlane, I. A., jt. auth. see Eyes, B.

MacFarlane, Ian. Automatic Control of Food Manufacturing Processes. (Illus.). 308p. 1983. 88.25 (*0-85334-200-8*, I-207-83, Pub. by Elsevier Applied Sci UK) Elsevier.

MacFarlane, Ivan C., ed. see National Research Council of Canada, Associate Committee on Geotechnical Research, Muskeg Subcommittee.

Macfarlane, J. T., et al. A Colour Atlas of Respiratory Infections. (Medical Atlas Ser.: No. 12). (Illus.). 150p. 1993. 123.50 (*0-412-38960-6*) Chapman & Hall.

MacFarlane, Jane. Catalogue of Films & Television Programmes on Architecture, Town Planning & the Environment. (C). 1988. 95.00 (*0-685-30243-1*, Pub. by Oxford Polytechnic UK) St Mut.

Macfarlane, Jean W. Studies in Child Guidance. (SRCD M: Vol. 3, No. 6). 1938. 23.00 (*0-527-01506-7*) Periodicals Srv.

Macfarlane, Joan G., jt. auth. see Bresnahan, Michaeline.

MacFarlane, Kee & Cunningham, Carolyn. Steps to Healthy Touching. (Illus.). 144p. (Orig.). (J). (gr. k-7). 1988. student ed 19.95 (*0-685-20041-8*, 1400) Kidsrights.

MacFarlane, Kee, et al. Sexual Abuse of Young Children: Evaluation & Treatment. LC 85-30539. 355p. 1988. pap. text ed. 19.95 (*0-89862-703-6*) Guilford Pr.

MacFarlane, L. W. Dr. Mac: The Man, His Land & His People. LC 85-79991. (Illus.). 466p. Date not set. 29.95 (*0-935615-00-8*) S Utah St Coll.

MacFarlane, Leslie J. Human Rights: Realities & Possibilities: Northern Ireland, the Republic of Ireland, Yugoslavia & Hungary. 256p. 1990. text ed. 55.00 (*0-312-04533-6*) St Martin.

— William Elphinstone & the Kingdom of Scotland 1431-1514: The Struggle for Order. (Illus.). 540p. 1985. text ed. 60.00 (*0-08-030408-7*, Pub. by Aberdeen U Pr) Macmillan.

Macfarlane, M. H., jt. ed. see Hwang, W-Y. P.

Macfarlane, Michael. Urology. 2nd ed. (House Officer Ser.). 304p. 1994. 20.00 (*0-683-05325-6*) Williams & Wilkins.

— Urology for the House Officer. (House Officer Ser.). (Illus.). 300p. (Orig.). (C). 1988. pap. 20.00 (*0-683-05324-8*) Williams & Wilkins.

MacFarlane, Nigel. A Paper Journey: Travels among the Village Papermakers of India & Nepal. limited ed. (Illus.). 90p. 1993. 240.00 (*0-938768-45-X*) Oak Knoll.

MacFarlane, P. W. & De Padva, F. Electrocardiology 92. 400p. 1993. text ed. 121.00 (*981-02-1387-5*) World Scientific Pub.

MacFarlane, P. W. & Rautarharju, P. Electrocardiology '93. 364p. 1994. text ed. 86.00 (*981-02-1793-5*) World Scientific Pub.

MacFarlane, P. W., jt. ed. see Ruttkay-Nedecky, I.

MacFarlane, P. W., jt. ed. see Wolf, H. K.

MacFarlane, Peter. Health Law: Commentary & Materials. 240p. 1993. pap. 39.00 (*1-86287-098-5*, Pub. by Federation Pr AU) W W Gaunt.

— Health Law: Commentary & Materials. 2nd ed. 250p. 1995. pap. 39.00 (*1-86287-162-0*, Pub. by Federation Pr AU) W W Gaunt.

Macfarlane, Peter W. & Lawrie, T. D., eds. Comprehensive Electrocardiology: Theory & Practice in Health & Disease, 3 vols., Set. LC 88-17891. (Illus.). 1900p. 1988. 715.00 (*0-08-035568-4*, Pergamon Pr) Elsevier.

Macfarlane, Peter W., et al. Twelve-Lead Vectorcardiography. (Illus.). 160p. 1994. pap. 49.95 (*0-7506-0778-5*) Buttrwrth-Heinemann.

Macfarlane, Quentin. Alison: A Father's Search for His Missing Daughter. (Illus.). 192p. 1994. pap. 17.95 (*1-85158-624-5*, Pub. by Mnstream UK) Trafalgar.

MacFarlane, Ruth B. Collecting & Preserving Plants. unabridged ed. LC 94-11884. (Illus.). 192p. 1994. pap. text ed. 5.95 (*0-486-28281-3*) Dover.

MacFarlane, S. Neil. Superpower Rivalry & Third World Radicalism: The Idea of National Liberation. LC 84-43081. 236p. (C). 1985. text ed. 34.50x (*0-8018-2671-3*) Johns Hopkins.

MacFarlane, S. Neil, jt. ed. see Cambell, Kurt M.

***MacFarlane, Sheryl.** Tides of Change: Faces of the Northwest Coast. (Illus.). 32p. (J). (gr. k-4). Date not set. 12.95 (*1-55143-040-1*) Orca Bk Pubs.

MacFarlane, T. W., jt. auth. see Samaranayake, L. P.

MacFarlane, W., jt. auth. see Keegan, H.

MacFarlane, W. N. Principles of Small Business Management. (Illus.). 1977. text ed. 38.25 (*0-07-044380-7*) McGraw.

MacFarlane, W. Norman. A Third of a Century in the World's Oldest Profession. 1992. pap. 9.95 (*1-55673-486-7*, 7936) CSS OH.

Macfarlene, R. M., jt. auth. see Kaplyanski, A. A.

MacFarquhar, Roderick. The Origins of the Cultural Revolution, Vol. 1: Contradictions among the People, 1956-1957. LC 73-15793. (Studies of the East Asian Institute). 439p. 1974. pap. 18.00 (*0-685-42093-0*) Col U Pr.

— The Origins of the Cultural Revolution, Vol. 1: Contradictions Among the People, 1956-1957. (Studies of the East Asian Institute). (Illus.). 470p. 1987. pap. text ed. 19.00 (*0-231-08385-8*, King's Crown Paperbacks) Col U Pr.

— The Origins of the Cultural Revolution, Vol. 2: The Great Leap Forward. LC 73-15194. (Studies of the East Asian Institute). 480p. 1983. text ed. 53.50 (*0-231-05716-4*) Col U Pr.

— The Origins of the Cultural Revolution, Vol. 2: The Great Leap Forward, 1958-1960. (Studies of the East Asian Institute). (Illus.). 439p. 1987. pap. text ed. 19.00 (*0-231-05717-2*) Col U Pr.

MacFarquhar, Roderick, ed. The Politics of China, 1949-1989. LC 92-39147. (Illus.). 528p. (C). 1994. 64.95 (*0-521-44247-8*); pap. 19.95 (*0-521-44762-3*) Cambridge U Pr.

MacFarquhar, Roderick & Fairbank, John K., eds. The Cambridge History of China Vol. 14: The People's Republic of China, Pt. 1: The Emergence of Revolutionary China, 1949-1965. LC 76-29852. (Illus.). 680p. 1987. 130.00 (*0-521-24336-X*) Cambridge U Pr.

— The Cambridge History of China Vol. 15: The People's Republic, Pt. 2: Revolutions Within the Chinese Revolution, 1966-1982. (Illus.). 1024p. (C). 1991. 135.00 (*0-521-24337-8*) Cambridge U Pr.

MacFarquhar, Roderick, et al, eds. The Secret Speeches of Chairman Mao: From the Hundred Flowers to the Great Leap Forward. (Contemporary China Ser.: No. 6). 400p. 1989. pap. 18.00 (*0-674-79673-X*) HUP.

MacFate, Robert P., jt. auth. see Levinson, Samuel A.

Macfayden, A. & Ford, E. D., eds. Advances in Ecological Research, Vol. 15. (Serial Publication Ser.). 448p. 1986. text ed. 127.00 (*0-12-013915-4*) Acad Pr.

— Advances in Ecological Research, Vol. 16. (Serial Publication Ser.). 300p. 1987. text ed. 108.00 (*0-12-013916-2*) Acad Pr.

Macfie, A. L. Atat Urk. LC 93-33763. (Profiles in Power Ser.). (C). 1994. text ed. 47.50 (*0-582-07862-8*) Longman.

— Atat Urk. LC 93-33763. (Profiles in Power Ser.). (C). 1995. pap. text ed. 17.95 (*0-582-07863-6*) Longman.

Macfie, Alec L. Theories of the Trade Cycle. LC 78-119544. (Reprints of Economic Classics Ser.). ix, 198p. 1971. reprint ed. lib. bdg. 29.50 (*0-678-00699-7*) Kelley.

***Macfie, Dan, ed.** The Investor's Guide to Measuring Share Performance. 256p. 1994. disk 135.00 (*0-273-60628-X*, Pub. by Pitman Pubng UK) St Mut.

Macfie, H. J., jt. auth. see McBride, R. L.

***Macfie, J. M.** Myths & Legends of India: An Introduction to the Study of Hinduism. (C). 1994. pap. 9.50 (*81-7167-131-4*, Pub. by Rupa II) S Asia.

Macfie, John. Parry Sound Logging Days. Hudson, Noel, ed. (Illus.). 208p. pap. 19.95 (*1-55046-055-2*, Pub. by Boston Mills Pr CN) Genl Dist Srvs.

Macfie, Matthew. Vancouver Island & British Columbia: Their History, Resources & Prospects. LC 72-9458. (Far Western Frontier Ser.). (Illus.). 600p. 1973. reprint ed. 41.95 (*0-405-04986-2*) Ayer.

MacGaffey, Janet, et al. The Real Economy of Zaire: The Contribution of Smuggling & Other Unofficial Activities to National Wealth. LC 91-3844. 192p. (Orig.). (C). 1991. text ed. 29.95 (*0-8122-3140-6*); pap. text ed. 19.95 (*0-8122-1365-3*) U of Pa Pr.

MacGaffey, Wyatt. Modern Kongo Prophets: Religion in a Plural Society. LC 82-48554. (African Systems of Thought Ser.). (Illus.). 298p. reprint ed. pap. 85.80 (*0-685-23906-3*, 2056729) Bks Demand.

MacGaffey, Wyatt, ed. & tr. Art & Healing of the Bakongo Commented by Themselves: Minkisi from the Laman Collection. LC 91-71122. (Illus.). 192p. 1991. 29.95 (*91-85344-24-9*) Ind U Pr.

MacGaffey, Wyatt & Barnett, Clifford R. Cuba: Its People, Its Society, Its Culture. LC 73-19296. (Survey of World Cultures: No. 10). (Illus.). 1962p. 1974. reprint ed. text ed. 35.00 (*0-8371-7319-1*, MCUB, Greenwood Pr) Greenwood.

MacGaffey, Wyatt & Harris, Michael D. Astonishment & Power: Kongo Minkisi - The Art of Renee Stout. (Illus.). 224p. (Orig.). 1993. pap. 34.95 (*1-56098-274-8*) Smithsonian.

MacGahan, J. A. Campaigning on the Oxus & the Fall of Khiva. LC 78-115561. (Russia Observed Ser.). 1970. reprint ed. 28.95 (*0-405-03047-9*) Ayer.

Macgee, Thomas D. Gallery of Irish Writers: The Irish Writers of the Seventeenth Century. Bd. with Poets & Dramatists of Ireland. LC 75-28823. LC 75-28823. reprint ed. 39.50 (*0-404-13815-2*) AMS Pr.

MacGeorge, Andrew. Old Glasgow: The Place & the People, from the Roman Occupation to the Eighteenth Century. (Illus.). 1977. reprint ed. 29.00 (*0-7158-1178-9*) Charles River Bks.

MacGibbon & Ross. Castellated & Domestic Architecture of Scotland. (C). 1986. 500.00 (*0-901824-18-6*, Pub. by Mercat Pr Bks UK) St Mut.

MacGibbon, Duncan A. The Canadian Grain Trade. LC 32-18135. 237p. reprint ed. pap. 67.60 (*0-8357-7996-3*, 2014307) Bks Demand.

MacGibbon, James, ed. see Smith, Stevie.

MacGibbon, Jean. I Meant to Marry Him. large type ed. 368p. 1986. 15.95 (*0-7089-1473-X*) Ulverscroft.

***MacGilchrist, Barbara, et al.** School Development Planning Matters: The Impact of Development Planning in Primary Schools. 288p. 1995. pap. 26.95x (*1-85396-267-8*, Pub. by Paul Chapman UK) Taylor & Francis.

MacGill-Callahan, Sheila. And Still the Turtle Watched. (J). (ps-3). 1991. 15.99 (*0-8037-0931-5*); lib. bdg. 14.89 (*0-8037-0932-3*) Dial Bks Young.

— The Children of Lir. LC 91-2712. (Illus.). 32p. (J). (ps-3). 1993. 14.99 (*0-8037-1121-2*); lib. bdg. 14.99 (*0-8037-1122-0*) Dial Bks Young.

— Finn Mac Cool & the Salmon of Knowledge. LC 93-43953. (J). 1995. write for info. (*0-8037-1537-4*); lib. bdg. write for info. (*0-8037-1538-2*) Dial Bks Young.

— How the Boats Got Their Sails. LC 93-45966. (J). 1995. write for info. (*0-8037-1541-2*); lib. bdg. write for info. (*0-8037-1542-0*) Dial Bks Young.

— The Seal Prince. LC 93-16248. (J). 1995. 15.99 (*0-8037-1486-6*); lib. bdg. 15.89 (*0-8037-1487-4*) Dial Bks Young.

— When Solomon Was King. LC 93-28058. (Illus.). (J). 1995. 15.99 (*0-8037-1589-7*); lib. bdg. 15.89 (*0-8037-1590-0*) Dial Bks Young.

MacGill, Elsie. My Mother the Judge. 248p. 1981. pap. 7.95 (*0-88778-210-8*, Pub. by Stoddart Pubng CN) Genl Dist Srvs.

MacGillavry, et al. International Tables for X-Ray Crystallography. (Mathematical Tables Ser.: Vol. I). 1983. lib. bdg. 85.00 (*90-277-1532-7*) Kluwer Ac.

MacGillivray, A. J. & Birnie, G. D., eds. Nuclear Structures: Isolation & Characterization. 224p. 1986. text ed. 87.95 (*0-407-00323-1*) Buttrwrth-Heinemann.

MacGillivray, Catherine A., tr. see Cixous, Helene.

MacGillivray, H. T., ed. Astronomy from Wide-Field Imaging: Proceedings of the 161st Symposium of the International Astronomical Union, Held in Potsdam, Germany, August 23-27, 1993. LC 94-12286. (International Astronomical Union Symposia Ser.). 792p. (C). 1994. lib. bdg. 215.50 (*0-7923-2878-7*); pap. text ed. 105.00 (*0-7923-2879-5*) Kluwer Ac.

***MacGillivray, Ian, ed.** Twinning & Twins. fac. ed. LC 88-14385. (Wiley Medical Publication Ser.). 331p. 1988. reprint ed. pap. 94.40 (*0-7837-8268-3*, 2049049) Bks Demand.

MacGillivray, James R. Keats: A Bibliography & Reference Guide. (Toronto University Dept. of English, Studies & Texts: No. 3). 292p. reprint ed. pap. 83.30 (*0-317-10742-9*, 2014308) Bks Demand.

MacGillivray, Lois. Decision-Related Research on the Organization of Service Delivery Systems in Metropolitan Areas: Fire Protection. LC 79-83819. 1979. write for info. (*0-89138-985-7*) ICPSR.

MacGillivray, W. R., et al, eds. Physics of Electronic & Atomic Collisions: Proceedings, of ICPEAC XVII Brisbane, 10-16 July 1991. 720p. 1992. 170.00 (*0-7503-0167-8*) IOP Pub.

— Physics of Electronic & Atomic Collisions Abstracts: Abstracts of XVII ICPEAC, Brisbane, 10-16 Julu 1991. 758p. 1992. 161.00 (*0-7503-0139-2*) IOP Pub.

MacGillivray, William. William MacGillivray. 160p. 1993. pap. 49.95 (*0-11-310044-2*, HM100442, Pub. by HMSO UK) UNIPUB.

MacGinitie, Harry D. The Eocene Green River Flora of Northwestern Colorado & Northeastern Utah. LC 73-626230. (University of California Publications in Social Welfare: Vol. 83). (Illus.). 210p. reprint ed. pap. 59.90 (*0-685-23527-0*, 2015003) Bks Demand.

MacGinitie, Walter H., ed. Assessment Problems in Reading. LC 73-84793. 107p. reprint ed. pap. 30.50 (*0-8357-5809-5*, 2026814) Bks Demand.

MacGinley, T. J. & Ang, T. C. Structural Steelwork: Design to Limit State Theory. (Illus.). 224p. (C). 1987. 52.95 (*0-408-03020-8*) Buttrwrth-Heinemann.

— Structural Steelwork: Design to Limit State Theory. 2nd ed. 400p. 1992. pap. 42.95 (*0-7506-0440-9*) Buttrwrth-Heinemann.

MacGlashan, M. E. Iran-U. S. Claims Tribunal Reports, Vols. 8-22. (C). 1992. text ed. 350.00 (*0-7855-0125-8*, Pub. by Grotius Pubns UK) St Mut.

MacGorman, J. W. The Gifts of the Spirit. LC 75-55191. 1992. pap. 5.99 (*0-8054-1385-5*) Broadman.

— The Layman's Bible Commentary: Romans, I Corinthians, Vol. 20. LC 79-51501. 1991. 8.99 (*0-8054-1190-9*) Broadman.

MacGowan, Christopher, ed. see Williams, William Carlos.

MacGowan, Kenneth & Hester, Joseph. Early Man in the New World. 11.50 (*0-8446-2501-9*) Peter Smith.

MacGowan, Kenneth & Jones, Robert E. Continental Stagecraft. LC 64-14711. (Illus.). 1972. 20.95 (*0-405-08765-9*, Pub. by Blom Pubns UK) Ayer.

MacGowan, Sandra, ed. see Faiola, Theodora & Pullen, Jo A.

MacGowan, Sandra F. & McGinty, Sarah M. Fifty College Admission Directors Speak to Parents. 192p. 1988. pap. 8.95 (*0-15-601595-1*) HarBrace.

MacGowan, Shane, et al. Poguetry: The Lyrics of Shane MacGowan. (Illus.). 96p. 1990. pap. 14.95 (*0-571-14198-6*) Faber & Faber.

An Asterisk (*) at the beginning of an entry indicates that the title is appearing in BIP for the first time.

Macgowen, Kenneth. A Primer of Playwriting. 2nd ed. LC 80-39768. 199p. 1981. reprint ed. text ed. 65.00 (*0-313-22896-5*, MACP, Greenwood Pr) Greenwood.

MacGrath, Harold. Man on the Box. LC 70-124776. reprint ed. 18.50 (*0-404-04130-2*) AMS Pr.

Macgrath, Harold. The Man on the Box. LC 78-145155. 361p. 1972. reprint ed. 16.00 (*0-403-01083-7*) Scholarly.

MacGreevy, Thomas. Collected Poems of Thomas MacGreevy. Schreibman, Susan, ed. 180p. 1992. text ed. 24.95 (*0-8132-0756-8*) Cath U Pr.

***MacGregor.** Magnificent Trickster. 1995. pap. 9.95 (*0-929929-01-2*) Atrium Pubs.

MacGregor, A. J. Fire & Light in the Western Triduarm. LC 92-9600. (Alcuin Club Collections: No. 71). 560p. 1992. 29.95 (*0-8146-2066-3*) Liturgical Pr.

— Graphics Simplified: How to Plan & Prepare Effective Charts, Graphs, Illustrations, & Other Visual Aids. LC 79-10358. 1979. pap. 9.95 (*0-8020-6363-2*) U of Toronto Pr.

MacGregor, A. R. Clinical Dental Prosthetics. 3rd ed. (Illus.). 351p. 1989. text ed. 180.00 (*0-7236-0911-X*, Pub. by John Wright UK) Buttrwrth-Heinemann.

MacGregor, A. R., jt. auth. see Watt, D. M.

***MacGregor, Arthur, ed.** Antiquities from Europe & the Near East - Collection of the Lord McAlpine. (Illus.). 142p. 1995. pap. 29.95 (*0-907849-70-9*, 709, Pub. by Ashmolean Mus UK) A Schwartz & Co.

— The Late King's Goods: Collections, Possessions, & Patronage of Charles I in the Light of the Commonwealth Sale Inventories. (Illus.). 432p. 1990. 175.00 (*0-19-920171-4*) OUP.

MacGregor, Barrie. Volleyball. (EP Sports Ser.). (Illus.). 1978. 8.95 (*0-685-42064-7*) Charles River Bks.

MacGregor, C., jt. ed. see Elazo-Ayala, Cast.

Macgregor, Charles. Directory of Feeds & Feed Ingredients. 2nd ed. 85p. (C). Date not set. pap. text ed. 7.00 (*0-932147-20-8*, Hoards Dairyman) Hoard & Sons Co.

Macgregor, Charles A. Directory of Feeds & Feed Ingredients. 2nd ed. LC 89-85192. 64p. (C). 1989. pap. text ed. 6.00 (*0-932147-07-0*) Hoard & Sons Co.

***MacGregor, Cynthia.** Creative Family Projects: Exciting & Practical Activities You Can Do Together. 240p. 1995. pap. 9.95 (*0-8065-1636-4*, Citadel Pr) Carol Pub Group.

— Free Family Fun (& Super Cheap) And Super Cheap. 176p. (Orig.). 1994. pap. text ed. 4.50 (*0-425-14367-8*) Berkley Pub.

— Mommy, There's Nothing to Do! 160p. (Orig.). 1993. pap. 4.50 (*0-425-13911-5*) Berkley Pub.

— Totally Terrific Family Games. 272p. (Orig.). 1995. pap. text ed. 4.99 (*0-425-14574-3*) Berkley Pub.

***MacGregor, D. J.** Naked in Death. 320p. (Orig.). 1995. pap. text ed. 5.99 (*0-425-14829-7*) Berkley Pub.

MacGregor, D. R. The Tea Clippers: Their History & Development, 1833-1875. enl. rev. ed. (Illus.). 1983. 50.00 (*0-85177-256-0*) Lloyds London Pr.

MacGregor, David. British & American Clippers: A Comparison of Their Design, Construction & Performance. (Illus.). 192p. 1993. 39.95 (*1-55750-084-3*) Naval Inst Pr.

— The Communist Ideal in Hegel & Marx. 320p. 1984. 40.00 (*0-8020-5616-4*); pap. 19.95 (*0-8020-6816-2*) U of Toronto Pr.

— Hegel, Marx, & the English State. 345p. 1992. pap. text ed. 51.50 (*0-8133-1221-3*) Westview.

MacGregor, David R. The Tea Clippers: Their History & Development 1833-1875. LC 82-61670. (Illus.). 255p. 1982. 34.95 (*0-87021-884-0*) Naval Inst Pr.

MacGregor, Doug. MacGregor's Editorial Cartoons: A Collection of Cartoons Published in the Norwich Bulletin. (Illus.). 192p. (Orig.). (YA). (gr. 6-8). 1988. pap. write for info. (*0-318-64007-4*) Norwich Bulletin.

MacGregor, Douglas. A Collection of MacGregor Editorial Cartoons from the Norwich Bulletin. LC 88-92529. 196p. (Orig.). (YA). (gr. 6-8). 1988. pap. text ed. 10.00 (*0-9621270-0-0*) Norwich Bulletin.

Macgregor, Douglas A. The Soviet-East German Military Alliance. (Illus.). (C). 1989. 54.95 (*0-521-36562-7*) Cambridge U Pr.

MacGregor, Douglas S. Florida Condominium Law Manual, 1987-1991, 3 vols., Set. 1200p. 1995. ring bd. 270.00 (*0-409-26137-8*) Michie Butterworth.

— Virginia Condominium Law, 1990-1991. 250p. 1991. ring bd. 50.00 (*0-409-26579-9*) Michie Butterworth.

MacGregor, Douglas S., jt. auth. see Brown, Barry.

Macgregor, Elaine. Cake Decorating. 1990. 5.00 (*0-517-03164-7*) Random Hse Value.

MacGregor, Elaine. Wedding Cakes: From Start to Finish. 1995. 19.95 (*0-285-63134-9*, Pub. by Souvenir UK) Atrium Pubs.

MacGregor, Elizabeth A. & Greenwood, C. T. Polymers in Nature. LC 79-41787. (Illus.). 399p. reprint ed. pap. 113.80 (*0-8357-3737-3*, 2036463) Bks Demand.

Macgregor, Forbes. Macgregor's Mixture. 144p. (C). 1989. 35.00 (*0-903065-15-0*, Pub. by G Wright Pub Ltd) St Mut.

— More MacGregor's Mixture. 144p. (C). 1989. 40.00 (*0-903065-42-8*, Pub. by G Wright Pub Ltd) St Mut.

— Scots Proverbs & Rhymes. 80p. (C). 1989. 30.00 (*0-903065-39-8*, Pub. by G Wright Pub Ltd) St Mut.

Macgregor, Forbes, ed. Famous Scots. 344p. (C). 1989. 49.00 (*0-903065-47-9*, Pub. by G Wright Pub Ltd) St Mut.

Macgregor, Frances C. After Plastic Surgery: Adaptation & Adjustment. LC 79-11808. (Praeger Special Studies). 160p. 1979. text ed. 45.00 (*0-275-90383-4*, C0383, Praeger Pubs) Greenwood.

MacGregor, G. Ethnology of Tokelau Islands. (BMB Ser.). 1972. reprint ed. 30.00 (*0-527-02254-3*) Periodicals Srv.

MacGregor, G. H. & Purdy, A. C. Jew & Greek: Tutors Unto Christ. 1972. 59.95 (*0-8490-0444-6*) Gordon Pr.

MacGregor, Geddes. Angels: Ministers of Grace. LC 87-11243. (Illus.). 230p. 1987. pap. 12.95 (*1-55778-001-3*) Paragon Hse.

— Apostles Extraordinary: A Celebration of Saints & Sinners. LC 85-22118. (Illus.). 168p. (Orig.). 1986. pap. 8.95 (*0-89407-065-7*) Strawberry Hill.

— Dictionary of Religion & Philosophy. 696p. 1989. 35.00 (*1-55778-019-6*) Paragon Hse.

— Dictionary of Religion & Philosophy. 696p. (C). 1991. reprint ed. pap. 19.95 (*1-55778-441-8*) Paragon Hse.

— Gnosis. LC 78-64908. 1979. 12.95 (*0-8356-0522-1*) Theos Pub Hse.

— The Gospels As a Mandala of Wisdom. 224p. (Orig.). 1982. pap. 6.50 (*0-8356-0554-X*, Quest) Theos Pub Hse.

— Images of Afterlife: Beliefs from Antiquity to Modern Times. (Illus.). 256p. 1992. 21.95 (*1-55778-396-9*) Paragon Hse.

— The Nicene Creed, Illumined by Modern Thought. LC 80-19348. 163p. reprint ed. pap. 46.50 (*0-317-20013-5*, 2023220) Bks Demand.

— Reincarnation in Christianity. (Orig.). 1989. pap. 9.95 (*0-8356-0501-9*, Quest) Theos Pub Hse.

— Scotland: An Intimate Portrait. 288p. 1990. pap. 10.95 (*0-395-56236-8*) HM.

MacGregor, Graham A. Current Advances in Ace Inhibition. 3rd ed. 1994. 98.00 (*4-89370-071-5*) Churchill.

MacGregor, Graham A. & Sever, Peter S., eds. Current Advances in Ace Inhibition. (Illus.). 320p. 1989. text ed. 72.00 (*0-443-04235-7*) Churchill.

— Current Advances in Ace Inhibition 2. (Illus.). 320p. 1991. text ed. write for info. (*0-443-04600-X*) Churchill.

Macgregor, H. C. An Introduction to Animal Cytogenetics. LC 93-13470. 1993. write for info. (*0-412-54600-0*) Chapman & Hall.

MacGregor-Hastie, Roy, ed. Anthology of Contemporary Romanian Poetry. 1969. 25.00 (*0-7206-0280-7*) Dufour.

MacGregor, Herbert C. Working with Animal Chromosomes. 2nd ed. 250p. 1988. pap. text ed. 126.95 (*0-471-92028-2*) Wiley.

MacGregor, I. J. & Doyle, A. T., eds. Nuclear & Particle Physics, 1993: Proceedings of the Conference Held in Glasgow, 30 March-1 April 1992. (Institute of Physics Conference Ser.: No. 133). (Illus.). 288p. 1993. 160.00 (*0-7503-0289-5*) IOP Pub.

MacGregor, J. J. Forest Economic Research at Oxford: 1945-1974. 1974. 32.00 (*0-686-45514-2*) St Mut.

MacGregor, James G. Reinforced Concrete: Mechanics & Design. 2nd ed. 832p. 1991. text ed. 87.00 (*0-13-770819-X*, 320601) P-H.

***MacGregor, Jean, ed.** Student Self-Evaluation: Fostering Reflective Learning. LC 85-644763. (New Directions for Teaching & Learning Ser.: No. 56). 123p. (Orig.). 1993. pap. 16.95 (*1-55542-683-2*) Jossey-Bass.

Macgregor, Jimmie. Along the Southern Upland Way. (Illus.). 86p. 1992. pap. 8.95 (*0-563-20870-8*, Pub. by BBC UK) Parkwest Pubns.

— In the Footsteps of Bonnie Prince Charlie. (Illus.). 88p. 1988. pap. 9.95 (*0-563-20654-3*, Pub. by BBC UK) Parkwest Pubns.

MacGregor, Jimmie. Jimmie MacGregor's Scotland. (Illus.). 192p. 1994. 29.95 (*0-563-36316-9*, BBC-Parkwest) Parkwest Pubns.

— MacGregor Across Scotland: A Long-Distance Walk from Montrose to Ardnamurchan. LC 92-80836. (Illus.). 96p. (Orig.). 1992. pap. 8.95 (*0-563-36187-5*, BBC-Parkwest) Parkwest Pubns.

MacGregor, John C. A Portfolio of Rose Hips. (Illus.). 20p. 1981. 35.00 (*0-936736-01-1*); pap. 25.00 (*0-936736-02-X*) Sweetbrier.

MacGregor, John M. The Discovery of the Art of the Insane. (Illus.). 512p. (C). 1992. text ed. 80.00 (*0-691-04071-0*, Spir Rsch Edit); pap. text ed. 29.95 (*0-691-00036-0*, Spir Rsch Edit) Princeton U Pr.

***MacGregor, Kerr & Porteous, Colin, eds.** North Sun '94: Solar Energy at High Latitudes. (Illus.). 460p. (Orig.). (C). 1994. pap. text ed. 70.00 (*1-873936-33-8*, Pub. by J & J Sci Pubs UK) Bks Intl VA.

MacGregor, Lorri. Coping with the Cults: Practical Insights for Concerned Christians. 160p. (Orig.). 1992. pap. 6.99 (*0-89081-940-8*) Harvest Hse.

— What You Need to Know about Jehovah's Witnesses. rev. ed. (Conversations with the Cults Ser.). 160p. 1992. pap. 5.99 (*0-89081-944-0*) Harvest Hse.

Macgregor, M., jt. auth. see Field, F.

MacGregor, Malcolm & Baldwin, Stanley C. Your Money Matters. LC 76-56123. 176p. 1977. pap. 7.99 (*0-87123-662-1*) Bethany Hse.

MacGregor, Malcolm & Baldwin, Stanley G. Tu y Tu Dinero. 160p. (SPA.). 1984. 3.95 (*0-88113-369-8*) Edit Betania.

MacGregor, Malcolm B. The Sources & Literature of Scottish Church History. LC 76-1125. 260p. 1977. reprint ed. lib. bdg. 20.00 (*0-915172-10-0*) Richwood Pub.

MacGregor, Malcolm H. The Enigmatic Electron. LC 92-31829. (Fundamental Theories of Physics Ser.: Vol. 49). 1992. lib. bdg. 96.00 (*0-7923-1982-6*) Kluwer Ac.

Macgregor, Margaret E., jt. ed. see Chase, Mary E.

***MacGregor Mathers, S. L.** Grimoire of Armadel. 88p. 1995. 17.50 (*0-87728-839-9*) Weiser.

— Key of Solomon the King. 160p. 1989. pap. 12.50 (*0-87728-698-1*) Weiser.

— The Tarot: A Short Treatise on Reading Cards. rev. ed. LC 71-17150. (Illus.). 96p. 1993. pap. 5.95 (*0-87728-754-6*) Weiser.

MacGregor, Miles. The Sunflower. Thatch, Nancy R., ed. (Books for Students by Students Ser.). (Illus.). 29p. (J). (gr. 3-6). 1994. lib. bdg. 14.95 (*0-933849-52-4*) Landmark Edns.

MacGregor, Miriam. Boss of Brightland. large type ed. 304p. 1993. 21.95 (*0-7505-0554-0*, Pub. by Magna Print Bks) Ulverscroft.

— Cat Cuts. (Illus.). 64p. (C). 1989. text ed. 35.00 (*1-85183-017-0*, Silent Bks) St Mut.

— The Glowing Dark. large type ed. 336p. 1987. 17.95 (*0-7089-1613-9*) Ulverscroft.

— The House At Lake Taupo. large type ed. 304p. 1987. 16.95 (*0-7089-1730-5*) Ulverscroft.

— Lord of the Lodge. large type ed. 285p. 1992. 21.95 (*0-7505-0315-7*, Pub. by Magna Print Bks) Ulverscroft.

Macgregor, Miriam. Master of Marshlands. large type ed. 288p. 1991. reprint ed. lib. bdg. 18.95 (*0-263-12718-4*, Pub. by Mills & Boon UK) Thorndike Pr.

MacGregor, Miriam. The Orchard King. 1993. pap. 2.89 (*0-373-03255-2*, 1-03255-6) Harlequin Bks.

Macgregor, Miriam. The Orchard King. large type ed. 1993. reprint ed. lib. bdg. 18.95 (*0-263-13182-3*, Pub. by Mills & Boon UK) Thorndike Pr.

— Riddell of Rivermoon. large type ed. 1990. lib. bdg. 18.95 (*0-263-12348-0*, Pub. by Mills & Boon UK) Thorndike Pr.

MacGregor, Miriam. A Sigh on the Breeze. large type ed. 336p. 1986. 21.95 (*0-7089-1423-3*) Ulverscroft.

Macgregor, Miriam. The Stairway to Destiny. large type ed. 303p. 1994. 18.95 (*0-7505-0661-X*) Ulverscroft.

MacGregor, Miriam. Winter at Whitecliffs. large type ed. (Magna Romance Ser.). 301p. 1992. 21.95 (*0-7505-0411-0*) Ulverscroft.

MacGregor, Molly. Mississippi Headwaters Guide Book: A Guide to the Natural, Cultural, Scenic, Scientific & Recreational Values of the Mississippi River's First 400 Miles. (Illus.). 88p. (Orig.). 1995. pap. 15.00 (*0-9645849-1-3*) MS Headwaters. MISSISSIPPI HEADWATERS GUIDE BOOK surveys the natural, cultural, scenic, scientific & recreational values of the Mississippi River's first 400 miles in northern Minnesota. The guide is illustrated by four-color maps depicting recreational sites, historical locations, unusual plants & animals; black & white photographs illustrate representative ecosystems & pencil drawings illuminate the text. The river's landscapes were created by glaciers 10, 000 years ago. The Mississippi Headwaters represents intersection of the boreal forest of the north, prairies of the west & hardwood hills of the south. Diversity of landscapes & vegetation produced a diversity of animal & plant life. Bald eagles, timber wolves, marsh birds, orchids & ferns endangered elsewhere in the country are abundant here. The location of lakes, tributaries & forests influenced how prehistoric & early Native American people used the river & its lands. Human use has been consistent over time: today's towns are located at prehistoric village sites. Today's highways were once trails used by nomadic people. People's use of the river has resulted in the mandate to protect the river's natural diversity. Maintenance of the river's natural landforms & vegetation is necessary to support continued use of the Mississippi River. To order: Mississippi Headwaters Board, P.O. Box 3000, Walker, MN 56484, (218) 547-7263.** ***Publisher Provided Annotation.

MacGregor, Morna. Early Celtic Art in North Britain: A Study of the Decorative Metalwork from the Third Century BC to the Third Century AD, 2 vols. Incl. Vol. 1. (Illus.). 240p. 1975. (*0-318-53483-5*); Vol. 2. (Illus.). 322p. 1975. (*0-318-53484-3*); 1975. Set text ed. 57.50 (*0-7185-1135-2*, Pub. by Leicester Univ Pr) St Martin.

MacGregor, Morris J. A Parish for the Federal City: St. Patrick's in Washington, 1794-1994. LC 93-49694. (Illus.). 463p. (C). 1994. 29.95 (*0-8132-0801-7*); pap. 19.95 (*0-8132-0802-5*) Cath U Pr.

MacGregor, Morris J., jt. ed. see Nalty, Bernard C.

MacGregor, Morris J., jt. auth. see Wright, Robert K.

MacGregor-Morris, Pamela. The History of the H. I. S. Eighteen Eighty-Five to Nineteen Eighty-Five: 100 Years of the Hunters' Improvement & National Light Horse Breeding Society. 277p. (C). 1988. 100.00 (*0-9509663-1-2*) St Mut.

MacGregor, Neil. A Victim of Anonymity. LC 93-60981. (Walter Neurath Memorial Lecture Ser.). (Illus.). 48p. 1994. 14.95 (*0-500-55026-3*) Thames Hudson.

MacGregor, Rob. Crystal Skull. 288p. (Orig.). 1991. mass mkt. 4.99 (*0-345-36159-8*) Ballantine.

— Indiana Jones & Genesis. 1992. pap. 4.99 (*0-553-29502-0*, Bantam Falcon) Bantam.

— Indiana Jones & the Dance of the Giants. 1991. mass mkt. 4.99 (*0-553-29035-5*) Bantam.

— Indiana Jones & the Interior World. 1992. mass mkt. 4.99 (*0-553-29966-2*) Bantam.

— Indiana Jones & the Last Crusade. 224p. 1989. mass mkt. 4.99 (*0-345-36161-X*) Ballantine.

— Indiana Jones & the Last Crusade. braille ed. 385p. 1992. Braille. vinyl bd. 30.80 (*1-56956-266-0*, BR7894) W A T Braille.

— Indiana Jones & the Seven Veils. 1991. 4.99 (*0-553-29334-6*) Bantam.

— Indiana Jones, No. 5: Unicorns Legacy. 1992. 4.99 (*0-553-29666-3*) Bantam.

— The Peril at Delphi. (Indiana Jones Ser.: No. 1). 1991. mass mkt. 4.99 (*0-553-28931-4*) Bantam.

— Prophecy Rock. LC 94-33163. (J). 1995. 15.00 (*0-689-80056-8*, S&S Bks Young Read) S&S Childrens.

MacGregor, Rob, jt. auth. see Grosso, Tony.

MacGregor, Rob R., jt. auth. see Rossman, Milton D.

MacGregor, Ronald J. Neural & Brain Modelling. (Neuroscience Perspectives Ser.). 643p. 1987. text ed. 140.00 (*0-12-464260-8*); pap. text ed. 60.00 (*0-12-464261-6*) Acad Pr.

— Theoretical Mechanics of Biological Neural Networks. (Neural Networks: Foundations to Applications Ser.). (Illus.). 377p. 1993. text ed. 49.95 (*0-12-464255-1*) Acad Pr.

***MacGregor, Roy.** Ottawa Senators. LC 93-48454. (NHL Today Ser.). (J). 1995. write for info. (*0-88682-682-9*) Creative Ed.

MacGregor, Roy, jt. auth. see Dryden, Ken.

MacGregor, Stewart. The Sinner. LC 72-95425. 256p. 1973. 7.95 (*0-87955-903-9*) O'Hara.

***MacGregor, Susanne, ed.** The Other City: People & Politics in New York & London. LC 94-24212. 304p. (C). 1995. text ed. 49.95 (*0-391-03852-4*); pap. 18.50 (*0-391-03885-0*) Humanities.

MacGregor, Susanne & Pimlott, Ben, eds. Tackling the Inner Cities: The Nineteen Eighties Reviewed, Prospects for the 1990s. (Illus.). 304p. 1990. 74.00 (*0-19-827737-7*) OUP.

MacGregor, Suzanne. Drugs & British Society: Responses to a Social Problem in the 1980s. 208p. 1989. 52.50 (*0-415-03064-1*) Routledge.

MacGregor, T. J. Blue Pearl. LC 93-49700. 384p. 1994. 21.95 (*0-7868-6061-8*) Hyperion.

— Dark Fields. 1986. mass mkt. 5.99 (*0-345-33756-5*) Ballantine.

— Death Flats. (Florida Mysteries Ser.). (Orig.). 1991. mass mkt. 4.99 (*0-345-35768-X*) Ballantine.

— Kill Flash. 1987. mass mkt. 4.99 (*0-345-33754-9*) Ballantine.

— Kin Dread. 320p. (Orig.). 1990. mass mkt. 4.95 (*0-345-35766-3*) Ballantine.

— Mistress of the Bones. LC 95-10123. 384p. 1995. 21.95 (*0-7868-6106-1*) Hyperion.

— On Ice. 1989. mass mkt. 4.99 (*0-345-35045-6*) Ballantine.

— Spree. (Florida Mysteries Ser.). (Orig.). 1992. mass mkt. 4.99 (*0-345-37346-4*) Ballantine.

— Storm Surge. LC 92-42516. 336p. 1993. 19.95 (*1-56282-789-8*) Hyperion.

MacGregor-Villarreal, Mary. Brazilian Folk Narrative Scholarship: A Critical Survey & Selective Annotated Bibliography. LC 94-20707. (Folklore Library: Vol. 8). 264p. 1994. reprint ed. 40.00 (*0-8153-1243-1*, H1683) Garland.

MacGregor, William B., tr. see Rouquette, Max.

MacGregory, Alastair R. & Lechner, Sybille K. Removable Partial Prosthodontics. LC 93-2006. (Case Oriented Manual of Treatment). 1993. write for info. (*0-7234-1960-4*) Mosby Yr Bk.

MacGreil, Michael. Prejudice & Tolerance in Ireland. LC 79-49275. 600p. 1980. text ed. 75.00 (*0-275-90515-2*, C0515, Praeger Pubs) Greenwood.

MacGrory, Yvonne. The Secret of the Ruby Ring. LC 93-35950. (Illus.). 192p. (Orig.). (J). (gr. 4-7). 1994. reprint ed. pap. 6.95 (*0-915943-92-1*) Milkweed Ed.

***MacGruer, Malcolm S.** Horse-Horse Tiger-Tiger. LC 94-77797. 352p. 1994. 22.00 (*0-9642624-0-1*) Mereside Hse.

MacGuigan, Mark R. Cases & Materials on Creditors' Rights. 2nd ed. LC 67-108724. (Illus.). 724p. reprint ed. pap. 180.00 (*0-8357-8058-9*, 2034064) Bks Demand.

MacGuire, James, jt. auth. see Buckley, Christopher.

MacGuire, James, jt. auth. see Fliegel, Sy.

MacGuire, M., jt. auth. see Fliegel, S. W.

MacGunnigle, Bruce C. Rhode Island Freemen, 1747-1755: A Census of Registered Voters. LC 76-55839. 49p. 1982. reprint ed. pap. 5.00 (*0-685-01895-4*) Genealog Pub.

Mach, Bogdan W. & Weslowski, Wlodzimierz. Social Mobility & Social Structure. 180p. 1987. text ed. 47.50 (*0-7100-9982-7*, RKP) Routledge.

Mach, E. P., jt. ed. see Djukanovic, V.

Mach, Elyse. Contemporary Class Piano. 3rd ed. 320p. (Orig.). (C). 1988. pap. text ed. 26.75 (*0-15-513481-7*, MACH3) HB Coll Pubs.

— Contemporary Class Piano, Vol. 1. 4th ed. 400p. (Orig.). (C). 1992. pap. text ed. 28.00 (*0-15-513483-3*) HB Coll Pubs.

— Great Contemporary Pianists Speak for Themselves. 1991. pap. 11.95 (*0-486-26695-8*) Dover.

Mach, Ernst. Principles of the Theory of Heat. 1986. lib. bdg. 194.50 (*90-277-2206-4*) Kluwer Ac.

— The Science of Mechanics. 6th ed. McCormack, T. J., tr. (Illus.). 666p. 1960. pap. 22.00 (*0-87548-202-3*) Open Court.

Mach III Plus Staff. Airliners in Colour. (C). 1993. pap. 59.00 (*0-9515462-4-4*, Mach III Plus) St Mut.

— European Air Arms 1993. (C). 1993. pap. 30.00 (*0-9515462-8-7*, Mach III Plus) St Mut.

— European Military Aircraft Directory 1993. (C). 1993. pap. 30.00 (*0-9515462-6-0*, Mach III Plus) St Mut.

An Asterisk (*) at the beginning of an entry indicates that the title is appearing in BIP for the first time.

— United Kingdom Air Arms 1993. (C). 1993. 30.00 (*0-9515462-7-9*, Mach III Plus) St Mut.

— United Kingdom Airfields. (C). 1993. pap. 35.00 (*0-685-72563-4*, Mach III Plus) St Mut.

— United States Military Aircraft Directory 1993. (C). 1993. pap. 55.00 (*0-9515462-5-2*, Mach III Plus) St Mut.

Mach III Plus Staff, ed. United States Air Force 1993. (C). 1993. pap. 30.00 (*0-9515462-9-5*, Mach III Plus) St Mut.

Mach, K. A., et al. Paradigm Keyboarding & Applications: A Mastery Approach for Microcomputers & Typewriters, Short Course. (C). 1990. 7.95 (*1-56118-155-2*); pap. text ed. 19.95 (*1-56118-154-4*); 10.45 (*1-56118-158-7*) Paradigm MN.

Mach, R., jt. ed. see Truhlik, E.

Mach, Rudolph. Catalogue of Arabic Manuscripts (Yahuda Section) in the Garrett Collection, Princeton University Library. LC 75-2999. (Illus.). 1976. 350.00x (*0-691-03908-9*) Princeton U Pr.

Mach, Rudolph & Ormsby, Eric L. Handlist of Arabic Manuscripts. LC 84-42613. (Near East Studies). 600p. 1985. text ed. 99.50 (*0-691-05429-0*) Princeton U Pr.

Mach, Zdzislaw. Symbols, Conflict, & Identity: Essays in Political Anthropology. LC 92-22553. (SUNY Series in Anthropological Studies of Contemporary Issues). 297p. (C). 1993. 59.50 (*0-7914-1465-5*); pap. 19.95 (*0-7914-1466-3*) State U NY Pr.

***Macha, Gary P.** Aircraft Wrecks in the Mountains & Deserts of California, 1908-1990. (Illus.). 150p. 1991. 17.95 (*0-9630073-0-0*) Aviat Arch Pr.

Machac, Kathy, jt. auth. see McWaid, Helen.

***Machado, Ana M.** Explorations into Latin America. LC 94-28624. (Illus.). (J). (gr. 4 up). 1995. 15.95 (*0-02-718084-0*, New Dscvry Bks); pap. 7.95 (*0-382-24971-2*, Dillon Silver Burdett) Silver Burdett Pr.

Machado, Antonio. Antonio Machado: Selected Poems. Trueblood, Alan S., ed. & tr. by. LC 81-13481. 332p. 1988. reprint ed. pap. 16.95 (*0-674-04066-X*) HUP.

— Canciones. Bly, Robert, tr. LC 80-27641. 15p. 1980. pap. 4.00 (*0-915124-46-7*) Coffee Hse.

— I Never Wanted Fame. Bly, Robert, tr. 1979. pap. 4.00 (*0-915408-19-8*) Ally Pr.

— I Never Wanted Fame. deluxe limited ed. Bly, Robert, tr. 1979. pap. 10.00 (*0-915408-20-1*) Ally Pr.

— The Landscape of Soria. Maloney, Dennis, tr. 1985. pap. 4.00 (*0-934834-57-1*) White Pine.

— Poesias Completas. Alvar, Manuel, ed. (Nueva Austral Ser.: Vol. 33). (SPA.). 1991. pap. text ed. 29.95x (*84-239-1833-5*) Elliots Bks.

— Selected Poems of Antonio Machado. Craige, Betty J., tr. & intro. by. LC 78-57504. 192p. 1978. text ed. 27.50 (*0-8071-0456-6*) La State U Pr.

— Times Alone: Selected Poems of Antonio Machado. Bly, Robert, tr. LC 83-6955. (Wesleyan Poetry in Translation Ser.). 187p. 1983. pap. 14.95 (*0-8195-6081-2*, Wesleyan Univ Pr) U Pr of New Eng.

Machado, Antonio A., jt. ed. see Solimeo, Gustavo.

Machado, Antonio A., et al. Our Lady at Fatima: Prophecies of Tragedy or Hope for America & the World? LC 85-70673. (Illus.). 128p. (Orig.). (J). (gr. 8). 1986. pap. 7.95 (*1-877905-10-0*) Am Soc Defense TFP.

Machado de Assis, Joaquim M. Counselor Ayres' Memorial. Caldwell, Helen, tr. LC 72-187876. 1973. pap. 11.00 (*0-520-04775-3*) U CA Pr.

— The Devil's Church & Other Stories. Schmitt, Jack & Ishimatsu, Lorie, trs. LC 76-53828. (Texas Pan American Ser.). (Illus.). 166p. (C). 1977. pap. 9.95 (*0-292-71542-0*) U of Tex Pr.

— Helena. Caldwell, Helen, tr. LC 83-17966. 197p. (C). 1984. 35.00 (*0-520-04812-1*); pap. 11.00 (*0-520-06025-3*) U CA Pr.

Machado, Diamantino P. The Structure of Portuguese Society: The Failure of Fascism. LC 91-9646. 240p. 1991. text ed. 55.00 (*0-275-93784-4*, C3784, Praeger Pubs) Greenwood.

***Machado, Ed.** One Tree Island. 264p. (J). (ps up). 1994. pap. 5.99 (*0-9642652-0-6*) Reef Pubng.

Machado, Eduardo. The Floating Island Plays. LC 91-25117. 232p. 1991. 24.95 (*1-55936-035-6*); pap. 13.95 (*1-55936-034-8*) Theatre Comm.

Machado, Jeanne M. Early Childhood Experiences in Language Arts. 4th ed. 416p. 1989. teacher ed 10.00 (*0-8273-3505-9*); pap. text ed. 27.95 (*0-8273-3504-0*) Delmar.

— Early Childhood Experiences in Language Arts: Emerging Literacy. 5th ed. LC 94-25760. (Illus.). 496p. 1994. 29.95 (*0-8273-5880-6*) Delmar.

Machado, Jeanne M. & Botnarescue, Helen M. Student Teaching: Early Childhood Practicum Guide. 2nd ed. LC 92-10647. 456p. 1993. pap. text ed. 27.95 (*0-8273-5242-5*) Delmar.

Machado, Jeanne M. & Meyer-Botnarescue, Helen. Instructor's Guide for Student Teaching: Early Childhood Practicum Guide. 2nd ed. 70p. 1993. 12.00 (*0-8273-5243-3*) Delmar.

Machado, Jeanne M. & Meyer, Helen C. Early Childhood Practicum Guide. LC 83-71047. (Illus.). 400p. 1984. teacher ed 10.00 (*0-8273-2081-7*); pap. text ed. 26.95 (*0-8273-2080-9*) Delmar.

Machado, Luis A. The Right to Be Intelligent. 85p. 1980. text ed. 38.00 (*0-08-025781-X*, CRC Reprint) Franklin.

Machado, M. Diccionario Tecnico de la Construccion, Edificacion y Obras Publicas Frances-Espanol y Espanol-Frances. 576p. (FRE & SPA.). 1969. 59.95 (*0-8288-6577-9*, S-50242) Fr & Eur.

Machado, M. A. & Narducci, L. M., eds. Optics in Four Dimensions-1980: ICO Ensenada. LC 80-70771. (AIP Conference Proceedings Ser.: No. 65). 745p. 1981. lib. bdg. 40.75 (*0-88318-164-9*) Am Inst Physics.

Machado, Manual. The Border, Its Culture. 1996. write for info. (*1-878610-50-3*) Red Crane Bks.

***Machado, Manuel.** Antologia. 11th ed. 152p. 1979. pap. 8.95 (*0-7859-5189-X*) Fr & Eur.

Machado, Manuel A. Barbarians of the North: Modern Chihuahua & the Mexican Political System. (Illus.). 224p. 1993. 19.95 (*0-89015-839-8*) Sunbelt Media.

Machado, Manuel A., Jr. Centaur of the North: Francisco Villa, the Mexican Revolutions, & Northern Mexico. Roberts, Melissa, ed. (Illus.). 288p. 1988. 17.95 (*0-89015-641-7*) Sunbelt Media.

Machado, Manuel A. An Industry in Crisis: Mexican-United States Cooperation in the Control of Foot & Mouth Disease. LC 68-64741. (University of California Publications in Social Welfare: Vol. 80). 110p. reprint ed. pap. 31.40 (*0-317-29077-0*, 2021439) Bks Demand.

Machado, Manuel A., Jr. Listen Chicano: An Informal History of the Mexican-American. LC 77-16650. (Illus.). 216p. 1978. 31.95 (*0-88229-258-7*) Nelson-Hall.

— The North Mexican Cattle Industry, 1910-1975: Ideology, Conflict & Change. LC 80-5515. (Illus.). 168p. 1981. 14.50x (*0-89096-104-2*) Tex A&M Univ Pr.

Machado, Manuel Y. Las Adelfas. La Lola Se Va a los Puertos. Chicharro Chamorro, Damaso, ed. (Nueva Austral Ser.: Vol. 271). (SPA.). 1993. pap. text ed. 34.95x (*84-239-7271-2*) Elliots Bks.

— Desdichas de la Fortuna O Julianillo Valcarcel. Juan de Manara. Chicharro Chamorro, Damaso, ed. (Nueva Austral Ser.: Vol. 236). (SPA.). 1991. pap. text ed. 24.95x (*84-239-7236-4*) Elliots Bks.

Machado, Mary K. How to Plan Children's Liturgies. rev. ed. LC 86-60892. 104p. (Orig.). 1989. pap. 9.95 (*0-89390-074-5*) Resource Pubns.

Machado, Rod. Rod Machado's Instrument Pilot's Survival Manual. rev. ed. 232p. (C). 1992. reprint ed. pap. text ed. 29.95 (*0-9631229-0-8*) Av Speak Bur.

***Machado, Rodolfo & El-Khoury, Rodolphe.** Monolithic Architecture. (Illus.). 168p. 1995. text ed. 60.00 (*3-7913-1609-5*) Pegasus.

Machado y Ruiz, Antonio. Solitudes, Galleries, & Other Poems. Predmore, Richard L., tr. LC 86-32758. ix, 237p. 1987. lib. bdg. 34.50 (*0-8223-0713-8*) Duke.

MacHaffie, Barbara J. Her Story: Women in Christian Tradition. LC 85-45494. 192p. 1986. pap. 13.00 (*0-8006-1893-9*, 1-1893, Fortress Pr) Augsburg Fortress.

MacHaffie, Barbara J., ed. Readings in Her Story: Women in Christian Tradition. LC 92-3693. 144p. (Orig.). 1992. pap. 15.00 (*0-8006-2575-7*, 1-2575, Fortress Pr) Augsburg Fortress.

MacHaffie, Ingeborg. Henry: The Heron. (Illus.). 55p. (Orig.). (J). (ps). 1988. lib. bdg. 7.95 (*0-9609374-3-9*) Skribent.

MacHaffie, Ingeborg N. Danish in Portland. (Illus.). 287p. (Orig.). 1982. 10.95 (*0-685-06962-1*); lib. bdg. 13.50 (*0-9609374-0-4*); pap. 8.95 (*0-686-40237-5*) Skribent.

MacHaffie, Ingeborg S. Historic Inns of Denmark. Nielsen, Margaret A., ed. (Illus.). 176p. (Orig.). 1988. pap. 9.50 (*0-9609374-4-7*) Skribent.

— To Teachers with Love. Nielsen, Margaret, ed. (Illus.). 90p. (Orig.). 1986. per. 5.95 (*0-9609374-2-0*) Skribent.

Machairas, Leontios. Recital Concerning the Sweet Land of Cyprus, 2 vols., Set. Dawkins, R. M., ed. LC 78-63351. (Crusades & Military Orders Ser.: Second Series). reprint ed. 92.50 (*0-404-17030-7*) AMS Pr.

MacHale, Des. Book of Corkman Jokes. 1990. pap. 4.95 (*0-85342-478-0*) Dufour.

— The Book of Irish Bull. 118p. 1991. reprint ed. pap. 10.95 (*0-85342-822-0*, Pub. by Mercier Pr IE) Dufour.

— Book of Kerryman Jokes. 1990. pap. 4.95 (*0-85342-466-7*) Dufour.

— Bumper Book of Kerryman Jokes. 1990. pap. 7.95 (*0-85342-666-X*) Dufour.

— Humorous Quotations. 221p. 1995. pap. 15.95 (*1-85635-076-2*, Pub. by Mercier Pr IE) Dufour.

— Irish Love & Marriage Jokes. 1991. pap. 4.95 (*0-85342-500-0*) Dufour.

— Last of the Kerryman Jokes. LC 89-81671. 96p. (Orig.). 1990. pap. 9.95 (*0-85342-897-2*, Pub. by Mercier Pr IE) Dufour.

— More Kerryman Jokes. 1992. pap. 5.95 (*1-85635-007-X*) Dufour.

— Mrs. Malaprop Lives. (Illus.). 88p. (Orig.). 1991. pap. 9.95 (*0-85342-966-9*, Pub. by Mercier Pr IE) Dufour.

— Official Kerryman Jokebook. 1990. pap. 4.95 (*0-85342-609-0*) Dufour.

— Worst Kerryman Jokes. 1990. pap. 4.95 (*0-85342-499-3*) Dufour.

MacHale, Des, jt. auth. see Sloane, Paul.

MacHale, Don. East of the Sun, West of the Moon. LC 91-15220. (We All Have Tales Ser.). (Illus.). 40p. (J). (gr. k up). 1992. pap. 14.95 (*0-88708-192-4*, Rabbit); audio 19.95 (*0-88708-193-2*, Rabbit) S&S Childrens.

Machalow, Robert. Using Lotus 1-2-3: A How-to-Do-It Manual for Library Applications. Katz, Bill, ed. (How-to-Do-It Ser.: No. 1). (Illus.). 166p. (Orig.). 1989. pap. text ed. 39.95 (*1-55570-033-0*) Neal-Schuman.

— Using Lotus 1-2-3 for Windows. LC 94-25790. (How to Do It Manual Ser.: No. 43). 1994. pap. 39.95 (*1-55570-187-6*) Neal-Schuman.

— Using Microsoft Excel: A How-to-Do-It Manual for Librarians. LC 90-21524. (How-to-Do-It Ser.). 238p. 1991. 39.95 (*1-55570-075-6*) Neal-Schuman.

— Using Microsoft Works: A How-to-Do-It Manual for Librarians. (How-to-Do-It Ser.). 276p. 1992. 39.95 (*1-55570-110-8*) Neal-Schuman.

Machamer, Gene. The Illustrated Black American Profiles. Sager, Linda C., ed. LC 90-82937. (Illus.). 192p. (Orig.). (YA). 1991. pap. 8.00 (*0-9627369-0-2*) Carlisle Pr.

— The Illustrated Hispanic American Profiles. Acevedo, Maria, ed. LC 93-91377. (Illus.). 176p. (Orig.). (YA). 1993. pap. 8.00 (*0-9627369-2-9*) Carlisle Pr.

— One Hundred One Uses for a Crooked Politician. LC 92-90220. (Illus.). 104p. (Orig.). 1992. pap. 6.95 (*0-9627369-1-0*) Carlisle Pr.

Machamer, Peter K. & Turnbull, Robert G., eds. Studies in Perception: Interrelations in the History of Philosophy & Science. LC 77-10857. (Illus.). 577p. 1978. 52.50 (*0-8142-0244-6*) Ohio St U Pr.

Machamer, Peter K., jt. ed. see Fine, Arthur I.

Machan Aal, Katharyn & Crooker, Barbara. Writing Home. LC 83-1715. (Orig.). 1983. pap. 4.50 (*0-935020-08-X*) Gehry Pr.

Machan, Tibor. Individuals & Their Rights. 282p. 1989. pap. 19.95 (*0-8126-9090-7*) Open Court.

Machan, Tibor, ed. Commerce & Morality: Alternative Essays in Business Ethics. 264p. 1988. 53.00 (*0-8476-7586-6*); pap. 25.00 (*0-8476-7587-4*) Rowman.

Machan, Tibor, jt. intro. see Spencer, Herbert.

Machan, Tibor R. Capitalism & Individualism: Reframing the Argument for a Free Society. LC 90-32882. 208p. 1990. text ed. 35.00 (*0-312-04766-5*) St Martin.

— Introduction to Philosophical Inquiries. 384p. 1985. reprint ed. pap. text ed. 29.00 (*0-8191-4967-5*) U Pr of Amer.

— Liberty & Culture: Essays on the Idea of a Free Society. 288p. 1989. 23.95 (*0-87975-524-5*) Prometheus Bks.

— The Moral Case for the Free Market Economy: A Philosophical Argument. LC 88-37917. (Problems in Contemporary Philosophy Ser.: Vol. 15). 140p. 1989. lib. bdg. 69.95 (*0-88946-343-3*) E Mellen.

— Private Rights, Public Illusions. LC 93-45616. 420p. (C). 1994. 34.95 (*1-56000-176-3*); pap. 19.95 (*1-56000-749-4*) Transaction Pubs.

Machan, Tibor R. & Johnson, M. Bruce, eds. Rights & Regulation: Ethical, Political, & Economic Issues. LC 83-11309. (Illus.). 309p. (C). 1983. pap. 14.95 (*0-936488-61-1*) PRIPP.

Machan, Tibor R. & Nelson, John O. A Dialogue Partly on Political Liberty. 82p. (Orig.). (C). 1989. pap. text ed. 13.50 (*0-8191-7736-9*) U Pr of Amer.

Machan, Tim W. Techniques of Translation: Chaucer's Boece. LC 85-524. 163p. (C). 1985. 29.95 (*0-937664-68-5*) Pilgrim Bks OK.

— Textual Criticism & Middle English Texts. LC 94-5441. 1994. text ed. 40.00 (*0-8139-1508-2*) U Pr of Va.

Machan, Tim W., ed. Medieval Literature: Texts & Interpretation. (Medieval & Renaissance Texts & Studies: Vol. 79). 208p. 1991. 20.00 (*0-86698-090-3*, MR79) MRTS.

Machan, Tim W. & Scott, Charles T., eds. English in Its Social Contexts: Essays in Historical Sociolinguistics. (Oxford Studies in Sociolinguistics). (Illus.). 320p. (C). 1992. 55.00 (*0-19-506499-2*); pap. text ed. 17.95 (*0-19-506500-X*) OUP.

Machan, Wayne & Bruggen, Bill. The Corvair, 1960-1969. LC 89-63378. (Authenticity Ser.). (Illus.). 128p. (Orig.). (YA). 1991. pap. 19.95 (*0-929758-07-2*) Beeman Jorgensen.

Machando, M. E., jt. ed. see Pick, M.

Machann, Clinton. The Essential Matthew Arnold: An Annotated Bibliography of Major Modern Studies. LC 92-36565. (Reference Ser.). 177p. 1993. text ed. 50.00 (*0-8161-9087-9*) G K Hall.

— Victorian Autobiography. 160p. (C). 1994. text ed. 37.50x (*0-472-10565-5*) U of Mich Pr.

Machann, Clinton & Burt, Forrest D., eds. Matthew Arnold in His Time & Ours: Centenary Essays. LC 87-25271. 220p. 1988. 30.00 (*0-8139-1173-7*) U Pr of Va.

Machann, Clinton & Clark, William B., eds. Katherine Anne Porter & Texas: An Uneasy Relationship. LC 89-20667. (Illus.). 216p. 1990. 29.50 (*0-89096-441-6*) Tex A&M Univ Pr.

Machann, Clinton & Mendl, James W. Krasna Amerika. (Illus.). 264p. 1983. 16.95 (*0-89015-391-4*) Sunbelt Media.

Machann, Clinton & Mendl, James W., Jr., eds. Czech Voices: Stories from Texas in the Amerikan Narodni Kalendar. LC 90-43294. (Centennial Series of the Association of Former Students: No. 39). 184p. 1991. 18.95 (*0-89096-471-8*) Tex A&M Univ Pr.

Machann, Clinton, jt. ed. see Burt, Forrest D.

Macharzina, Klaus & Staehle, Wolfgang H., eds. European Approaches to International Management. xiv, 386p. 1986. 74.95 (*3-11-009827-X*) De Gruyter.

— European Approaches to International Management. xiv, 386p. 1986. 64.95 (*0-89925-018-1*) De Gruyter.

MacHaster, Eve B. God Comforts His People. LC 95-835. (Story Bible Ser.: No. 7). (Illus.). 176p. (Orig.). (J). (gr. 3 up). 1985. pap. 5.95 (*0-8361-3393-5*) Herald Pr.

Machavelli, Niccolo. 91 Principe (De Principatibus) Richardson, Brian & Speight, Kathleen, eds. 153p. (ITA.). 1979. pap. 16.95x (*0-7190-0742-9*, Pub. by Manchester Univ Pr UK) St Martin.

Mache, Francois-Bernard. Music, Myth, & Nature, or, the Dolphins of Arion. rev. ed. Delaney, Susan, tr. LC 92-39112. (Contemporary Music Studies: Vol. 6). 1993. text ed. 70.00 (*3-7186-5321-4*); pap. text ed. 30.00 (*3-7186-5322-2*) Gordon & Breach.

Mache, R., et al, eds. The Translational Apparatus of Photosynthetic Organelles. (NATO ASI Series H: Cell Biology: Vol. 55). (Illus.). 241p. 1991. 109.00 (*0-387-51779-0*) Spr-Verlag.

Mache, Wolfgang W. Lexikon der Textkommunikation und Datenkommunikation: Lexicon of Text & Data Communication. 3rd ed. 580p. (GER.). 1993. 195.00 (*0-8288-1358-2*, M15282) Fr & Eur.

Macheath, Jean. Activity, Health & Fitness in Old Age. LC 83-40128. 224p. 1984. text ed. 45.00 (*0-312-00390-0*) St Martin.

Machedlover, Helene, jt. auth. see Connor, Billie M.

Machell, Carolyn, jt. auth. see Fielder, Ron.

Machell, Keith, jt. auth. see Potts, Kathryn H.

Machelon, Jean-Pierre, jt. auth. see De Lolme, J. L.

Machem, J. Gresham. The New Testament: An Introduction to Its History & Literature. 1976. 15.95 (*0-85151-449-9*) Banner of Truth.

Machen, Arthur. The Children of the Pool & Other Stories. Reginald, R. & Menville, Douglas, eds. LC 76-1366. (Supernatural & Occult Fiction Ser.). 1976. reprint ed. lib. bdg. 24.95 (*0-405-08424-2*) Ayer.

— Dreads & Drolls. LC 67-28757. (Essay Index Reprint Ser.). 1977. 28.95 (*0-8369-0648-9*) Ayer.

— Eleusinia & Beneath the Barley. 20p. (Orig.). 1988. pap. 2.95 (*0-940884-00-3*) Necronomicon.

— Great God Pan. LC 79-128737. (Short Story Index Reprint Ser.). 1977. 24.95 (*0-8369-3628-0*) Ayer.

— Guinevere & Lancelot & Others. Brooks, Cuyler W., Jr. & Shoemaker, Michael, eds. (Illus.). 50p. 1987. pap. 10.00 (*0-9603300-2-X*) Purple Mouth.

— The Hill of Dreams. 256p. 1986. reprint ed. pap. 6.95 (*0-486-24994-8*) Dover.

— House of Souls. LC 72-152947. (Short Story Index Reprint Ser.). 1977. reprint ed. 27.95 (*0-8369-3806-2*) Ayer.

Machen, Arthur, tr. see Casanova, Jacques.

Machen, Arthur, tr. see Marguerite D'Angouleme.

Machen, Arthur W., Jr. A Venerable Assembly: The History of Venable, Baetjer & Howard. 240p. 1991. write for info. (*0-9631294-0-6*) V B & H.

Machen, J. G. God Transcendent. 208p. 1982. pap. 9.95 (*0-85151-355-7*) Banner of Truth.

Machen, J. Gresham. Christianity & Liberalism. 1946. pap. 10.99 (*0-8028-1121-3*) Eerdmans.

— New Testament Greek for Beginners. (C). 1923. text ed. write for info. (*0-13-033747-1*) P-H.

— What Is Faith? 264p. 1991. pap. text ed. 9.95 (*0-85151-594-0*) Banner of Truth.

Machenzie, J. Lachlan & Todd, Richard, eds. In Other Words: Festschrift H. H. Meier. (Illus.). 346p. (C). 1989. pap. 76.95 (*90-6765-413-2*) Mouton.

Macher, E., jt. ed. see Klippel, K. F.

Macher, J. P. & Crocq, M. A., eds. New Prospects in Psychiatry: The Bio-Clinical Interface I: Edited Proceedings of the Bio-Clinical Interface Conferences, Held in Rouffach, France, Between 1989 and 1991. LC 92-49252. (Developments in Psychiatry Ser.: Vol. 9). 1992. write for info. (*0-444-89805-0*) Elsevier.

Macherauch, E. & Hauk, V., eds. Residual Stresses in Science & Technology: Proceedings of an International Conference, 1986, 2 vols., 1. 1050p. 1987. lib. bdg. write for info. (*3-88355-099-X*, Pub. by DGM Metallurgy Info GW) IR Pubns.

— Residual Stresses in Science & Technology: Proceedings of an International Conference, 1986, 2 vols., 2. 1050p. 1987. lib. bdg. write for info. (*3-88355-100-7*, Pub. by DGM Metallurgy Info GW) IR Pubns.

— Residual Stresses in Science & Technology: Proceedings of an International Conference, 1986, 2 vols., Set. 1050p. 1987. 142.00 (*0-685-18223-1*, Pub. by DGM Metallurgy Info GW) IR Pubns.

***Macherey, Pierre.** The Object of Literature. (Literature, Culture, Theory Ser.: No. 14). 240p. (C). 1995. 59.95 (*0-521-41955-7*); pap. 16.95 (*0-521-47678-X*) Cambridge U Pr.

— A Theory of Literary Production. Wall, Geoffrey, tr. 1978. pap. 15.95 (*0-7100-0087-1*) Routledge.

Maches, Richard W. Travel, Entertainment & Gifts. 150p. (Orig.). (C). 1993. pap. 79.00 (*1-878025-37-6*) Western Schls.

Macheski, Cecilia. Quilt Stories. LC 93-33292. 304p. 1994. 27.00 (*0-8131-1849-2*) U Pr of Ky.

Macheski, Cecilia, jt. ed. see Schofield, Mary A.

Macheski, Cecilia, jt. auth. see Schofield, Mary Anne.

Machesky, Jefry J., jt. auth. see Jordan, Eleanor W.

Machi, Antonio, tr. see De Finetti, Bruno.

journey...& we are all made the richer for it." UNDER THE RISING SUN contains photographs. Available from Wolfenden, P.O. Box 789, Miranda, CA 95553; 707-923- 2455. ***Publisher Provided Annotation.***

Machi, S., ed. Radiation Processing for Environmental Conservation. 202p. 1985. pap. 30.00 (*0-08-031435-X*, Pergamon Pr) Elsevier.

Machia, James Y., see J. Thomas, pseud..

Machiavel, Nicholas. Le Prince. 192p. (FRE.). 1986. pap. 10.95 (*0-7859-4477-X*, 204016653X) Fr & Eur.

Machiavelli, Niccolo. Art of War. rev. ed. Farneworth, Ellis, tr. LC 64-66078. (Orig.). (C). 1965. pap. write for info. (*0-672-60434-5*, LLA196, Bobbs) Macmillan.

— The Art of War. Farneworth, Ellis, tr. (Quality Paperbacks Ser.). 336p. 1990. reprint ed. pap. 12.95 (*0-306-80412-3*) Da Capo.

— The Art of War. Whitehorne, Peter, tr. Bd. with Prince. LC 73-172705. LC 73-172705. (Tudor Translations, First Ser.: No. 39). reprint ed. 115.00 (*0-404-51951-2*) AMS Pr.

— The Comedies of Machiavelli: The Woman from Andros, The Mandrake, Clizia. Sices, David & Atkinson, James B., eds. Atkinson, James B., tr. LC 84-40595. 416p. (ENG & ITA.). 1985. pap. 18.00 (*0-87451-330-8*) U Pr of New Eng.

— Discourses. Crick, Bernard, ed. (Classics Ser.). 1984. mass mkt. 8.95 (*0-14-044428-9*, Penguin Classics) Viking Penguin.

Machiavelli, Niccol'o. The First Decennale. LC 77-91630. 33p. reprint ed. pap. 25.00 (*0-7837-2293-1*, 2057381) Bks Demand.

Machiavelli, Niccolo. Florentine Histories. Banfield, Laura, tr. 412p. (C). 1990. text ed. 59.50 (*0-691-05521-1*); pap. text ed. 16.95 (*0-691-00863-9*) Princeton U Pr.

— Florentine History. Bedingfeld, T., tr. LC 73-172705. (Tudor Translations, First Ser.: No. 40). reprint ed. 45. 00 (*0-404-51952-0*) AMS Pr.

— History of Florence & of the Affairs of Italy. 17.75 (*0-8446-2503-5*) Peter Smith.

— The History, Political & Diplomatic Writings of Niccolo Machiavelli, 4 vols. 1981. 1,200.00 (*0-87968-405-4*) Gordon Pr.

— The Letters of Machiavelli: A Selection. Gilbert, Allan, ed. & tr. by. 252p. 1988. pap. text ed. 9.95 (*0-226-50041-1*) U Ch Pr.

— The Literary Works of Machiavelli: Mandragola, Clizia, a Dialogue on Language & Belfagor, with Selections from the Private Correspondence. Hale, John R., ed. LC 79-4216. 202p. 1979. reprint ed. text ed. 35.00 (*0-313-21248-1*, MALW) Greenwood.

— The Living Thoughts of Machiavelli. Sforza, Carlo, ed. LC 74-28758. (Illus.). 161p. 1975. reprint ed. text ed. 35. 00 (*0-8371-7923-8*, MALIT, Greenwood Pr) Greenwood.

— Machiavelli: The History of Florence & Other Selections. Rawson, Judith A., ed. 1970. 29.50 (*0-671-48364-1*) Irvington.

— Mandragola. Flaumenhaft, Mera J., tr. LC 80-54106. 64p. (C). 1981. pap. text ed. 4.50x (*0-917974-57-3*) Waveland Pr.

— The Mandrake. Shawn, Wallace, tr. 1978. pap. 4.75 (*0-8222-0728-1*) Dramatists Play.

— Oeuvres Completes. (FRE.). 1978. lib. bdg. 105.00 (*0-8288-3524-1*, F30070) Fr & Eur.

— Oeuvres Completes: La Mandragore, Le Prince, etc. 1664p. 42.95 (*0-686-56535-5*) Fr & Eur.

— Prince. (Airmont Classics Ser.). (J). (gr. 11 up). 1965. pap. 2.25 (*0-8049-0056-6*, CL-56) Airmont.

— Prince. 1952. pap. 3.50 (*0-451-62755-5*, Ment) NAL-Dutton.

— Prince. Bull, George, tr. (Classics Ser.). (YA). (gr. 9 up). 1961. pap. 4.50 (*0-14-044107-7*, Penguin Classics) Viking Penguin.

— The Prince. Price, Russell, ed. (Cambridge Texts in the History of Political Thought Ser.). 200p. 1988. pap. 7.95 (*0-521-34993-1*) Cambridge U Pr.

— The Prince. Price, Russell, ed. (Cambridge Texts in the History of Political Thought Ser.). 200p. 1989. 39.95 (*0-521-34240-6*) Cambridge U Pr.

— The Prince. 1992. 15.00 (*0-679-41044-9*) McKay.

— The Prince. Bergin, Thomas G., ed. & tr. by. (Crofts Classics Ser.). 96p. 1947. pap. text ed. write for info. (*0-88295-053-3*) Harlan Davidson.

— The Prince. Atkinson, James, ed. LC 75-15946. (Library of Liberal Arts: Vol. 172). 448p. 1976. pap. write for info. (*0-672-61244-5*) Macmillan.

— The Prince. Bondanella, Peter E. & Musa, Mark, trs. (World's Classics Paperback Ser.). 1984. pap. 3.50 (*0-19-281602-0*) OUP.

— The Prince. LC 86-70377. (Great Books in Philosophy). 90p. 1986. pap. text ed. 4.95 (*0-87975-344-7*) Prometheus Bks.

— The Prince. Wootton, David, tr. LC 94-44698. (Classics Ser.). 128p. (C). 1995. lib. bdg. 24.95x (*0-87220-317-4*); pap. text ed. 2.95x (*0-87220-316-6*) Hackett Pub.

— The Prince. Sonnino, Paul, tr. & intro. by. 128p. (C). 1995. text ed. 39.95 (*0-391-03939-3*) Humanities.

— The Prince. Sonnino, Paul, tr. & intro. by. 128p. (C). 1995. pap. 9.95 (*0-391-03940-7*) Humanities.

— The Prince. unabridged ed. 80p. 1992. reprint ed. pap. text ed. 1.00 (*0-486-27274-5*) Dover.

— The Prince. 2nd ed. Adams, Robert M., ed. & tr. by. (Critical Editions Ser.). (C). 1992. pap. text ed. 6.95 (*0-393-96220-2*) Norton.

— The Prince. Penman, Bruce, tr. & intro. by. 144p. 1994. reprint ed. pap. text ed. 2.95 (*0-460-87143-9*, Everyman's Classic Lib) C E Tuttle.

— The Prince. Thompson, Hill, tr. 186p. 1988. reprint ed. 19.95 (*0-88280-115-5*); reprint ed. pap. 12.95 (*0-88280-116-3*) ETC Pubns.

— The Prince. De Alvarez, Leo P., tr. (Illus.). 168p. (C). 1989. reprint ed. pap. text ed. 6.95 (*0-88133-444-8*) Waveland Pr.

— The Prince: A New Translation. Mansfield, Harvey C., Jr., tr. LC 85-2536. xxviii, 124p. 1985. pap. text ed. 6.95 (*0-226-50038-1*) U Ch Pr.

— The Prince: And Selected Discourses. Donno, Daniel, ed. 160p. (gr. 9-12). 1984. 2.95 (*0-553-21278-8*, Bantam Classics) Bantam.

— The Prince & Other Works. Gilbert, Alan H., ed. & tr. by. (University Classics Ser.). 332p. 1964. pap. 12.95 (*0-87532-101-1*) Hendricks House.

— Selected Political Writings. Wootton, David et al, eds. LC 94-21202. (Hackett Classics Ser.). 272p. (Orig.). (C). 1994. pap. text ed. 6.95x (*0-87220-247-X*) Hackett Pub.

— Selected Political Writings. Wootton, David et al, eds. LC 94-21202. (Hackett Classics Ser.). 272p. (Orig.). (C). 1994. lib. bdg. 34.95x (*0-87220-248-8*) Hackett Pub.

Machiavelli, Niccolo, et al. The Prince & Other Discourses. Ricci, Luigi, tr. Bd. with Discourses. (Modern Library College Editions). (C). 1950. Set pap. text ed. write for info. (*0-07-553577-7*, T25) McGraw.

Machiavelli, Nicolo. The Prince. 15.95 (*0-89190-547-2*, Am Repr) Amereon Ltd.

— The Prince. 1994. lib. bdg. 18.95x (*1-56849-500-5*) Buccaneer Bks.

Machida, Margo, et al. Asia - America: Identities in Contemporary Asian American Art. 128p. 1994. pap. 22. 00 (*1-56584-090-9*) New Press NY.

Machida, Robert. Eritrea: The Struggle for Independence. (Current Issues Ser.: No. 2). 100p. 1987. pap. 5.95 (*0-932415-24-5*) Red Sea Pr.

Machin, David. Statistical Tables for the Desk. 1987. 80.00 (*0-632-01275-7*) Blackwell Sci.

Machin, David, jt. auth. see Campbell, Michael J.

Machin, E., ed. National Communism in Western Europe: A Third Way for Socialism? LC 82-24945. 1983. pap. 13. 95 (*0-416-73440-5*, NO. 3854) Routledge Chapman & Hall.

Machin, E. Anthony, jt. auth. see Fife, Ian.

Machin, Henry. Diary of Henry Machyn. Nichols, John G., ed. (Camden Society, London. Publications, First Ser.: No. 42). reprint ed. 105.00 (*0-404-50142-7*) AMS Pr.

Machin, Howard. The Prefect in French Public Administration. LC 76-27185. (C). 1977. text ed. 29.95 (*0-312-63805-1*) St Martin.

Machin, Ian. Disraeli. LC 94-11277. (Profiles in Power Ser.). 208p. (C). 1995. text ed. 36.95 (*0-582-09806-8*, 76875, Pub. by Longman UK); pap. text ed. 14.95 (*0-582-09805-X*, 76874, Pub. by Longman UK) Longman.

Machin, James T. A Spiritual Guide for Life. 77p. (Orig.). 1993. pap. text ed. 4.95 (*0-9637794-1-9*) Machia.

Machin, S. J., jt. auth. see Pittilo, R. M.

Machinability Data Center Technical Staff, ed. Machining Data Handbook, 2 vols., Set. 3rd ed. LC 80-81480. (Illus.). 1980. 150.00 (*0-936974-00-1*) Metcut Res Assocs.

Machine-Vision Association of the Society of Manufacturing Engineers. Vision '87 Conference Proceedings. (Illus.). 981p. (Orig.). 1987. pap. 87.00 (*0-87263-278-4*) SME.

Machlas, Sally, jt. auth. see Field, Nancy.

Machle, Edward J. Nature & Heaven in the Xunzi: A Study of the Tian Lun. LC 92-31573. (Chinese Philosophy & Culture Ser.). 224p. (C). 1993. 59.50 (*0-7914-1553-8*); pap. 19.95 (*0-7914-1554-6*) State U NY Pr.

Machleder, Herbert I., ed. Vascular Disorders of the Upper Extremity. 2nd enl. rev. ed. (Illus.). 432p. 1989. 55.00 (*0-87993-347-X*) Futura Pub.

Machlin. Handbook of Vitamins. 2nd rev. ed. (Food Science & Technology Ser.: Vol. 40). 616p. 1990. 150.00 (*0-8247-8351-4*) Dekker.

Machlin, E. S. An Introduction to Aspects of Thermodynamics & Kinetics Relevant to Materials Science. (Illus.). 352p. (C). 1991. text ed. 65.00 (*1-878857-02-9*) Giro Pr.

— Materials Science in Microelectronics I: The Relationships Between Thin Film Processing & Structure. (Materials Science Ser.). (Illus.). 240p. (C). 1995. text ed. 65.00x (*1-878857-07-X*) Giro Pr.

Machlin, E. S., ed. see Metallurgical Society of AIME Staff.

Machlin, Edda S. The Classic Cuisine of the Italian Jews, No. I. rev. ed. (Illus.). 254p. 1993. 27.50 (*1-878857-05-3*); pap. 18.95 (*1-878857-06-1*) Giro Pr.

— The Classic Cuisine of the Italian Jews, No. II. (Illus.). 272p. 1992. 27.50 (*1-878857-03-7*) Giro Pr.

— In the Shadow of the Bell Tower: "Growing up As a Jew in Fascist Italy" (Illus.). 250p. 1995. 29.00 (*1-878857-08-8*) Giro Pr.

Machlin, Evangeline. Dialects for the Stage. LC 75-7880. 1975. 49.95 (*0-87830-040-6*, Theatre Arts Bks) Routledge Chapman & Hall.

— Speech for the Stage. LC 80-51639. 1980. 17.95 (*0-87830-120-8*, Theatre Arts Bks) Routledge Chapman & Hall.

— Speech for the Stage. 1992. pap. 14.95 (*0-87830-015-5*, Theatre Arts Bks) Routledge Chapman & Hall.

— Teaching Speech for the Stage: A Manual for Classroom Instruction. 1980. pap. 4.95 (*0-87830-573-4*, Theatre Arts Bks) Routledge Chapman & Hall.

Machlin, Jennifer L. & Young, Tomme R. Managing Environmental Risk: Real Estate & Business Transactions. LC 88-17497. (Environmental Law Ser.). 1988. ring bd. 145.00 (*0-87632-603-3*) Clark Boardman Callaghan.

Machlin, Jerome S. Tournament Bridge: An Uncensored Memoir. LC 84-223705. 121p. 1980. pap. 5.95 (*0-939460-06-8*) Devyn Pr.

Machlin, Lawrence J., ed. see New York Academy of Sciences Staff.

Machlin, Lawrence J., jt. ed. see Sauberlich, Howerde E.

Machlin, Milt. Joshua's Altar: The Dig at Mount Ebal. Ladenheim-Gil, Randy, ed. (Illus.). 320p. (C). 1991. 22. 95 (*0-688-08115-0*) Morrow.

— The Worldshakers. 1983. pap. 3.50 (*0-345-29676-1*) Ballantine.

Machlis, Gary E., ed. Interpretive Views: Opinions on Evaluating Interpretation. LC 86-61991. (Illus.). (Orig.). 1986. pap. 9.95 (*0-940091-15-1*) Natl Parks & Cons.

Machlis, Gary E. & Field, Donald R., eds. On Interpretation: Sociology for Interpreters of Natural & Cultural History. rev. ed. LC 92-3386. (Illus.). 320p. (C). 1992. pap. text ed. 19.95x (*0-87071-365-5*) Oreg St U Pr.

Machlis, Joseph. American Composers of Our Time. LC 88-31968. 237p. 1990. reprint ed. text ed. 59.75 (*0-313-22141-3*, MACT, Greenwood Pr) Greenwood.

— Introduction to Contemporary Music. 2nd ed. (Illus.). (C). 1979. text ed. 32.95 (*0-393-09026-4*) Norton.

— Lisa's Boy: A Novel. 416p. 1982. 13.95 (*0-393-01606-4*) Norton.

— Stefan in Love: A Novel. 240p. 1991. 19.95 (*0-393-03005-9*) Norton.

Machlis, Joseph & Forney, Kristine. The Enjoyment of Music. (C). 1990. Chronological ed. text ed. 43.95 (*0-393-95950-3*) Norton.

— The Enjoyment of Music. (C). 1990. Cassettes, 6. audio 44.95 (*0-393-99155-5*) Norton.

— The Enjoyment of Music. (C). 1990. LPs, 7. lp 44.95 (*0-393-99152-0*) Norton.

— The Enjoyment of Music. (C). 1990. pap. text ed. 11.95 (*0-393-95721-7*) Norton.

— The Enjoyment of Music. suppl. ed. (C). 1990. Supplementary recordings, 4 LPs. lp 22.50 (*0-393-99151-2*) Norton.

— The Enjoyment of Music. 6th ed. (C). 1990. text ed. 43. 95 (*0-393-95717-9*) Norton.

— The Enjoyment of Music, No. I. (C). 1990. Album I, 4 discs. disk, lp 40.00 (*0-393-99165-2*) Norton.

— The Enjoyment of Music, No. II. (C). 1990. Album II, 4 discs. disk, lp 40.00 (*0-393-99166-0*) Norton.

— The Enjoyment of Music: Shorter Version. (C). 1990. Instr's. guide. 45.00 (*0-393-99188-1*) Norton.

— The Enjoyment of Music: Shorter Version. (Illus.). (C). 1995. pap. text ed. 36.95 (*0-393-96682-8*); student ed, pap. text ed. 11.95 (*0-393-96684-4*); teacher ed, pap. text ed. write for info. (*0-393-96685-2*) Norton.

— The Enjoyment of Music, Shorter Chronological. (C). 1991. pap. text ed. 41.95 (*0-393-96116-8*) Norton.

— The Enjoyment of Music, Shorter Chronological. (C). 1991. pap. text ed. 4.95 (*0-393-96123-0*) Norton.

— The Enjoyment of Music, Shorter Chronological. (C). 1991. pap. text ed. write for info. (*0-393-96124-9*) Norton.

— The Enjoyment of Music, Shorter Chronological. 6th ed. (C). 1991. pap. text ed. 34.95 (*0-393-96070-6*) Norton.

— The Norton Recordings to Accompany the Norton Scores & the Enjoyment of Music: Standard. 6th ed. (C). 1995. 40.00x (*0-393-99208-X*) Norton.

***Machlis, Joseph & Forney, Kristine, eds.** The Enjoyment of Music: An Introduction to Perceptive Listening - Chronological. 7th ed. LC 94-28824. (Illus.). (C). 1995. text ed. 45.95 (*0-393-96643-7*) Norton.

Machlis, Joseph, jt. auth. see Forney, Kristine.

Machlis, Paul. Union Catalog of Letters to Clemens. LC 92-1225. (UC Publications in Catalogs & Bibliographies: Vol. 8). 407p. 1992. 60.00 (*0-520-09743-2*) U CA Pr.

Machlis, Paul, ed. Union Catalog of Clemens Letters. (UC Publications in Catalogs & Bibliographies: Vol. 1). 1986. 60.00 (*0-520-09688-6*) U CA Pr.

Machlis, Sally, jt. auth. see Field, Nancy.

Machlowitz, David S., ed. A Legal Guide to Working with Environmental Consultants. (Environmental Law Library). 520p. 1992. text ed. 128.00 (*0-471-56951-8*) Wiley.

Machlowitz, Marilyn. Advanced Career Strategies: Corporate Smarts for Women on the Way Up. 220p. 1984. 15.95 (*0-943066-04-2*) CareerTrack Pubns.

Machlup, Fritz. The Alignment of Foreign Exchange Rates. LC 72-169260. (Special Studies in International Economics & Development). 1972. 19.50 (*0-8290-0384-3*); pap. text ed. 9.95 (*0-89197-655-8*) Irvington.

— The Book Value of Monetary Gold. LC 72-38795. (Essays in International Finance Ser.: Vol. 91). 24p. reprint ed. pap. 25.00 (*0-8357-7344-2*, 2032315) Bks Demand.

— Economic Semantics. 2nd ed. 368p. (C). 1990. pap. 21.95 (*0-88738-836-1*) Transaction Pubs.

— The Economics of Sellers Competition, Vol. 2. 602p. 1952. 72.50 (*0-8018-0414-0*) Johns Hopkins.

— International Trade & the National Income Multiplier. LC 65-18335. (Reprints of Economic Classics Ser.). xvi, 237p. 1965. reprint ed. 29.50 (*0-678-00083-2*) Kelley.

— Knowledge: Its Creation, Distribution, & Economic Significance, Vol. II. LC 80-7544. (Branches of Learning Ser.). 176p. 1982. 37.50 (*0-691-04230-6*) Princeton U Pr.

— Knowledge: Its Creation, Distribution, & Economic Significance, Vol. III, The Economics of Information & Human Cap. LC 83-42588. 576p. 1984. 85.00 (*0-691-04233-0*) Princeton U Pr.

— Methodology of Economics & Other Social Sciences. (Economic Theory, Econometrics & Mathematical Economics Ser.). 1978. text ed. 99.00 (*0-12-464550-X*) Acad Pr.

— The Political Economy of Monopoly: Business, Labor, & Government Policies. LC 53-6338. 560p. reprint ed. pap. 159.60 (*0-8357-8274-3*, 2034121) Bks Demand.

— Remaking the International Monetary System: The Rio Agreement & Beyond. LC 68-31419. (Committee For Economic Development, CED Supplementary Papers: No. 24). 171p. reprint ed. pap. 48.80 (*0-317-19923-4*, 2023125) Bks Demand.

— Remaking the International Monetary System - the Rio Agreement & Beyond. LC 68-31419. 176p. 1968. pap. 3.00 (*0-87186-224-7*) Comm Econ Dev.

Machlup, Fritz & Leeson, Kenneth W. Information Through the Printed Word The Dissemination of Scholarly, Scientific, & Intellectual Knowledge. Incl. Vol. 1. Book Publishing. LC 78-19460. 320p. 1978. text ed. 65.00 (*0-275-90301-X*, C03011, Praeger Pubs); Vol. 2. Journals. LC 78-19460. 1978. text ed. 59.95 (*0-275-90302-8*, C03022, Praeger Pubs); Vol. 3. Libraries. LC 78-19460. 219p. 1978. text ed. 55.00 (*0-275-90303-6*, C03033, Praeger Pubs); Vol. 4. Book, Journals, & Bibliographic Services. LC 78-19460. 342p. 1980. text ed. 65.00 (*0-275-90516-0*, C05164, Praeger Pubs); LC 78-19460. 363p. 1978. write for info. (*0-318-55346-5*, Praeger Pubs) Greenwood.

Machlup, Fritz, et al, eds. International Mobility & Movement of Capital. (Universities-National Bureau Conference Ser.: No. 24). 719p. 1972. text ed. 160.00 (*0-87014-249-6*) Natl Bur Econ Res.

— International Mobility & Movement of Capital: A Conference of the Universities - National Bureau Committee for Economic Research. LC 76-188342. (Universities-National Burear Conference Ser.: No. 24). 719p. reprint ed. pap. 180.00 (*0-8357-3242-8*, 2057136) Bks Demand.

— Reflections on a Troubled World Economy. (Essays in Honor of Herbert Giersch Ser.). 350p. 1983. text ed. 39. 95 (*0-312-66741-8*) St Martin.

Machmer, Richard S. & Machmer, Rosemarie B. Just for Nice: Carving & Whittling Magic of Southeastern Pennsylvania. (Illus.). 88p. (C). 1991. text ed. 35.00 (*0-8122-3209-7*) U of Pa Pr.

Machmer, Rosemarie B., jt. auth. see Machmer, Richard S.

Machner, H. & Jahn, J., eds. Coincident Particle Emission from Continuum States in Nuclei (COPECOS) Proceedings of the Workshop on Coincident Particle Emission from Continuum States in Nucle (COPECOS), F R, Germany, June 1984. 642p. 1984. 121.00 (*9971-966-98-0*) World Scientific Pub.

Machnik, Joe & Harris, Paul. So You Want to Be a Goalkeeper: The No. 1 Handbook for Soccer Coaches & Players. (Illus.). 62p. 1980. pap. 6.95 (*0-916802-18-3*) Soccer for Am.

Macho, James & Cable, Greg. Everyone's Guide to Outpatient Surgery: The Easiest Source of Vital Information on the Fastest Growing Phenomenon in American Health Care. 304p. Date not set. 24.95 (*0-8362-2422-1*); pap. 14.95 (*0-8362-2421-3*) Andrews & McMeel.

Macho, Linda. Crocheting Ruffled Doilies. (Knitting, Crocheting, Tatting Ser.). (Illus.). 48p. (Orig.). 1983. pap. 2.95 (*0-486-24400-8*) Dover.

— Patterns for Quilting. 80p. 1984. pap. 4.95 (*0-486-24632-9*) Dover.

Macho, Linda, ed. Knitting Fashion Sweaters Forties. (Knitting, Crocheting, Tatting Ser.). (Illus.). 48p. (Orig.). 1983. pap. 2.95 (*0-486-24409-1*) Dover.

— Treasury of Pineapple Designs for Crocheting. (Illus.). 48p. (Orig.). 1983. pap. 2.95 (*0-486-24494-6*) Dover.

Macho, Linda, jt. auth. see Weiss, Rita.

Machobane, L. B. Government & Change in Lesotho, 1800-1966. 260p. 1990. text ed. 59.95 (*0-312-03680-9*) St Martin.

Machonis, Peter A. Histoire de la Langue: Du Latin a L'Ancien Francais. 290p. (Orig.). (C). 1990. lib. bdg. 46. 50 (*0-8191-7873-X*); pap. text ed. 25.00 (*0-8191-7874-8*) U Pr of Amer.

Machor, James L. Pastoral Cities: Urban Ideals & the Symbolic Landscape of America. LC 87-2171. (History of American Thought & Culture Ser.). 288p. (C). 1987. text ed. 45.00 (*0-299-11280-2*); pap. text ed. 14.95 (*0-299-11284-5*) U of Wis Pr.

Machor, James L., ed. Leaders in History: Nineteenth-Century American Literature & the Contexts of Response. LC 92-14471. 304p. 1993. pap. text ed. 15.95 (*0-8018-4437-1*) Johns Hopkins.

— Readers in History: Nineteenth-Century American Literature & the Contexts of Response. LC 92-14471. 304p. 1993. text ed. 45.00x (*0-8018-4436-3*) Johns Hopkins.

Machotka, Hana. Breathtaking Noses. LC 91-12252. (Illus.). 32p. (J). (gr. k up). 1992. 15.00 (*0-688-09526-7*); lib. bdg. 14.93 (*0-688-09527-5*) Morrow Jr Bks.

— Magic Ring: A Year With The Big Apple Circus. LC 87-28230. (Illus.). 80p. (J). (gr. 3 up). 1988. 13.95 (*0-688-07449-9*); pap. 8.95 (*0-688-08222-X*) Morrow Jr Bks.

— Outstanding Outsides. LC 92-19517. (Illus.). 32p. (J). (gr. k up). 1993. 15.00 (*0-688-11752-X*); lib. bdg. 14.93 (*0-688-11753-8*) Morrow Jr Bks.

— Pasta Factory. LC 92-4333. (Illus.). 32p. (J). (ps-3). 1992. 14.95 (*0-395-60197-5*) HM.

— Terrific Tails. LC 93-17687. (Illus.). 32p. (J). (gr. k up). 1994. 15.00 (*0-688-04562-6*); lib. bdg. 14.93 (*0-688-04563-4*) Morrow Jr Bks.

— What Do You Do at a Petting Zoo? LC 89-34478. (Illus.). 32p. (J). (gr. k up). 1990. lib. bdg. 13.88 (*0-688-08738-8*) Morrow Jr Bks.

— What Neat Feet! LC 90-40886. (Illus.). 32p. (J). (gr. k up). 1991. 13.95 (*0-688-09474-0*); lib. bdg. 13.88 (*0-688-09475-9*) Morrow Jr Bks.

An Asterisk (*) at the beginning of an entry indicates that the title is appearing in BIP for the first time.

Machotka, Pavel. The Nude: Perception & Personality. (Illus.). 352p. (C). 1979. text ed. 39.50 (*0-8290-0868-3*) Irvington.

Machotka, Pavel & Spiegel, John P. Articulate Body. (Illus.). 250p. 1982. 29.50 (*0-8290-0229-4*) Irvington.

— The Articulate Body. (Illus.). 250p. (C). 1985. reprint ed. pap. text ed. 18.95 (*0-8290-1662-7*) Irvington.

MacHovec, et al. The Aware Bears, Set. Downey, John & Cohen, Lois, eds. (Children's Personal Safety Ser.). (Illus.). (Orig.). (J). (gr. k-2). 1991. Set. pap. 39.50 (*0-89976-236-0*) Oceana Educ Comm.

MacHovec, Frank. Becoming Street Smart: How to Protect Yourself & Your Love Ones from Being Crime Victims. 1993. pap. 12.95 (*0-88282-081-8*) New Horizon NJ.

— Private Investigation: Methods & Materials. 134p. 1991. pap. 18.95 (*0-398-06258-7*) C C Thomas.

— Private Investigation: Methods & Materials. 134p. (C). 1991. text ed. 32.95x (*0-398-05749-4*) C C Thomas.

— Security Services, Security Science. 154p. 1992. pap. 19.95 (*0-398-06259-5*) C C Thomas.

— Security Services, Security Science. 154p. (C). 1992. text ed. 35.95x (*0-398-05811-3*) C C Thomas.

***MacHovec, Frank J.** Cults & Personality. 210p. 1989. pap. 29.95 (*0-398-06255-2*) C C Thomas.

— Cults & Personality. 210p. (C). 1989. text ed. 44.95x (*0-398-05607-2*) C C Thomas.

— The Expert Witness Survival Manual. 186p. 1987. pap. 25.95 (*0-398-06256-0*) C C Thomas.

— The Expert Witness Survival Manual. 186p. 1987. 42.95 (*0-398-05374-X*) C C Thomas.

— Hypnosis Complications: Prevention & Risk Management. 172p. 1986. pap. 19.95 (*0-398-06257-9*) C C Thomas.

— Hypnosis Complications: Prevention & Risk Management. 172p. (C). 1986. 35.95 (*0-398-05271-9*) C C Thomas.

— Interview & Interrogation: A Scientific Approach. 176p. (C). 1989. text ed. 44.95x (*0-398-05578-5*) C C Thomas.

***Machovec, Frank M.** Perfect Competition & the Transformation of Economics. LC 94-32765. (Foundations of the Market Economy Ser.). 360p. 1995. 84.95x (*0-415-11580-9*, C0028) Routledge.

Machovec, George S. Telecommunications & Networking Glossary. (LITA Guides Ser.: No. 3). 68p. 1990. pap. 12.50 (*0-8389-7476-7*) ALA.

— Telecommunications, Networking, & Internet Glossary. LC 93-31054. (LITA Monographs: Vol. 4). 124p. 1993. pap. 18.00 (*0-8389-7697-2*) Lib Info Tech.

***Machover.** CAD - CAM Handbook. 1995. 69.50 (*0-07-039375-3*) McGraw.

Machover, Carl. The C Handbook: CAD, CAM, CAE, CIM. (Computer Graphics Technology & Management Ser.). (Illus.). 400p. 1989. 44.50 (*0-8306-9398-X*, 3098) TAB Bks.

MacHover, Carl. The C4 Handbook: CAD, CAM, CAE, CIM. 1989. 44.50 (*0-07-155426-2*) McGraw.

Machover, Carl. The Economics of PC Graphics & Peripherals: An Audiocassette Briefing. 42.95 (*0-317-65608-2*) TBC Inc.

Machover, John M. Jewish State or Ghetto: Dangers of Palestine Partition. LC 75-10531. (Rise of Jewish Nationalism & the Middle East Ser.). 208p. 1976. reprint ed. 22.00 (*0-88355-364-3*) Hyperion Conn.

Machover, Karen. Personality Projection in the Drawing of the Human Figure: A Method of Personality Investigation. (Illus.). 192p. 1980. 31.95 (*0-398-01184-2*) C C Thomas.

— Personality Projection in the Drawing of the Human Figure: A Method of Personality Investigation. (Illus.). 192p. 1980. pap. 16.95 (*0-398-06260-9*) C C Thomas.

Machover, M., jt. auth. see Bell, J.

***Machover, Moshe.** Set Theory, Logic & Their Limitations. 256p. (C). 1995. write for info. (*0-521-47493-0*); pap. write for info. (*0-521-47998-3*) Cambridge U Pr.

Machover Reinisch, June, jt. ed. see Bancroft, John.

Machover, Tod. Musical Thought at Ircam. (Contemporary Music Review Ser.). 230p. 1984. pap. text ed. 30.00 (*3-7186-0272-5*) Gordon & Breach.

Machovich, R. & Owen, W. G., eds. Enzymology of Plasminogen Activation. (Journal: Enzymology: Vol. 40, No. 2-3, 1988). (Illus.). 116p. 1988. pap. 69.00 (*3-8055-4854-0*) S Karger.

Machovich, Raymond, ed. Blood Vessel Wall & Thrombosis, 2 vols., Vol. I: Hemostasis. 320p. 1988. Vol. I, Hemostasis, 320 pogs. 191.00 (*0-8493-5626-1*, RC694) CRC Pr.

— Blood Vessel Wall & Thrombosis, 2 vols., Vol. II: Thrombotic Processes in Atherogenesis. 280p. 1988. Vol. II, Thrombotic Processes in Atherogenesis, 280 pgs. 180.00 (*0-8493-5627-X*, RC694) CRC Pr.

Machovich, Raymund, ed. The Thrombin, 2 vols., Vol. I. 176p. 1984. 115.00 (*0-8493-6186-9*, QP93, CRC Reprint) Franklin.

— The Thrombin, 2 vols., Vol. II. 128p. 1984. 115.00 (*0-8493-6187-7*, QP93, CRC Reprint) Franklin.

Machowski, Barbara & Consumer Reports Books Editors. The Complete Book of Bathroom Design. (Illus.). 224p. (Orig.). 1993. pap. 18.95 (*0-89043-590-1*) Consumer Reports.

Machray, Robert. The Little Entente. LC 68-9665. 1970. reprint ed. 48.50 (*0-86527-118-6*) Fertig.

Macht, Joel. Poor Eaters: Helping Children Who Refuse to Eat. LC 89-26514. (Illus.). 328p. 1990. 19.95 (*0-306-43451-2*, Plenum Pr) Plenum.

Macht, Mary W. Introduction to Social Work & Social Welfare. 2nd ed. 480p. (C). 1991. write for info. (*0-675-21192-1*, Merrill Pub Co) Macmillan.

Macht, Norm. Babe Ruth. (Baseball Legends Ser.). (Illus.). 64p. (J). (gr. 3 up). 1991. lib. bdg. 14.95 (*0-7910-1189-5*) Chelsea Hse.

— Christy Mathewson. (Baseball Legends Ser.). (Illus.). 64p. (J). (gr. 3 up). 1991. lib. bdg. 14.95 (*0-7910-1182-8*) Chelsea Hse.

— Frank Robinson. (Baseball Legends Ser.). (Illus.). 64p. (J). (gr. 3 up). 1991. lib. bdg. 14.95 (*0-7910-1187-9*) Chelsea Hse.

— Jimmie Foxx. (Baseball Legends Ser.). (Illus.). 64p. (J). (gr. 3 up). 1991. lib. bdg. 14.95 (*0-7910-1175-5*) Chelsea Hse.

— Satchel Paige. (Baseball Legends Ser.). (Illus.). 64p. (J). (gr. 3 up). 1991. lib. bdg. 14.95 (*0-7910-1185-2*) Chelsea Hse.

Macht, Norman, jt. auth. see Barney, Rex.

Macht, Norman, jt. auth. see Bartell, Dick.

Macht, Norman L. Christopher Columbus: Explorer. (Junior World Biographies Ser.). (Illus.). 80p. (J). (gr. 3-6). 1992. lib. bdg. 14.95 (*0-7910-1752-4*) Chelsea Hse.

— Christopher Columbus: Explorer. (Junior World Biographies Ser.). (J). (gr. 3-6). 1992. pap. 4.95 (*0-7910-1953-5*) Chelsea Hse.

— Clarence Thomas. Huggins, Nathan I., ed. LC 94-44353. (Black Americans of Achievement Ser.). (Illus.). 144p. (YA). (gr. 5 up). 1995. 18.95 (*0-7910-1883-0*) Chelsea Hse.

— Clarence Thomas. Huggins, Nathan I., ed. LC 94-44353. (Black Americans of Achievement Ser.). (YA). (gr. 5 up). 1995. pap. write for info. (*0-7910-1912-8*) Chelsea Hse.

— Cy Young. (Baseball Legends Ser.). (Illus.). 64p. (J). (gr. 3 up). 1992. lib. bdg. 14.95 (*0-7910-1196-8*) Chelsea Hse.

— Jim Abbott: Baseball Star. LC 93-31838. (Great Achievers: Lives of the Physically Challenged Ser.). (Illus.). (J). 1994. 18.95 (*0-7910-2079-7*, Am Art Analog); pap. write for info. (*0-7910-2092-4*, Am Art Analog) Chelsea Hse.

— Lou Gehrig. (Baseball Legends Ser.). (Illus.). 64p. (J). (gr. 3 up). 1992. lib. bdg. 14.95 (*0-7910-1176-3*) Chelsea Hse.

— Reggie Jackson. LC 94-228. (Baseball Legends Ser.). (Illus.). 64p. (J). (gr. 3 up). 1994. lib. bdg. 14.95 (*0-7910-2169-6*) Chelsea Hse.

— Roberto Clemente: Baseball Great. LC 93-26178. (Junior Hispanics of Achievement Ser.). (Illus.). 80p. (J). (gr. 3-6). 1993. lib. bdg. 14.95 (*0-7910-1764-8*, Am Art Analog); pap. 4.95 (*0-7910-2541-1*, Am Art Analog) Chelsea Hse.

— Sandra Day O'Connor: Supreme Court Justice. (Junior World Biographies Ser.). (Illus.). 80p. (J). (gr. 3-6). 1992. lib. bdg. 14.95 (*0-7910-1756-7*) Chelsea Hse.

— Sojourner Truth: Crusader for Civil Rights. (Junior Black Americans of Achievement Ser.). (Illus.). 80p. (J). (gr. 3-6). 1993. lib. bdg. 14.95 (*0-7910-1754-0*, Am Art Analog); pap. 4.95 (*0-7910-1998-5*, Am Art Analog) Chelsea Hse.

— Tom Seaver. (Baseball Legends Ser.). (Illus.). 64p. (J). (gr. 3 up). 1994. lib. bdg. 14.95 (*0-7910-1951-9*, Am Art Analog) Chelsea Hse.

— Ty Cobb. (Baseball Legends Ser.). (Illus.). 64p. (J). (gr. 3 up). 1992. lib. bdg. 14.95 (*0-7910-1172-0*) Chelsea Hse.

Macht, Philip. Circles in the Sand. LC 84-90597. (Illus.). 64p. (YA). (gr. 7 up). 1985. 12.95 (*0-930339-00-2*) Maxrom Pr.

— Great Mountain. (Illus.). 30p. (Orig.). (J). 1991. pap. 15.00 (*0-930339-01-0*) Maxrom Pr.

— Pumpkin Art. (Illus.). 48p. (Orig.). 1991. pap. 20.00 (*0-930339-02-9*) Maxrom Pr.

— Wonderpup. (Illus.). 40p. (J). (gr. 4-6). 1992. 15.00 (*0-930339-03-7*) Maxrom Pr.

***Machtinger, John F.** How to Own a Gun & Stay Out of Jail: What You Need to Know about the Law if You Own a Gun or Are Thinking of Buying One - California, 1995. LC 94-96585. (Illus.). 176p. 1994. pap. 8.95 (*0-9642864-4-0*) Gun Law Pr.

Machugh, R. Modern Mexico. 1976. lib. bdg. 59.95 (*0-8490-2268-1*) Gordon Pr.

MacHuisdean, W. Hamish. The Great Law, Vol. 1: First Two Visits. 53p. 1993. reprint ed. spiral bd. 5.50 (*0-7873-0579-0*) Mokelumne.

Machulsky, E., jt. auth. see Topornin, B.

Machung, Anne, jt. auth. see Hochschild, Arlie.

Machutta, Stephen T., Sr. Acne? Try Nature's Remedy. LC 88-92625. 90p. (Orig.). (YA). (gr. 3-11). 1991. pap. 9.95 (*0-9621489-0-3*) New Begin Life.

Machwe, Prabhar, jt. ed. see Kumar, Shrawan.

Machwe, Prabhar, tr. see Kumar, Shrawan & Machwe, Prabhar, eds.

Machy, Patrick & Leserman, Lee. Liposomes in Cell Biology & Pharmacology. (Research in Ser.). 192p. 1987. 51.00 (*2-85598-327-4*) S M P F Inc.

Machynka, Josef. Eclectic Tarot. 96p. 1986. 22.00 (*0-88079-349-X*) US Games Syst.

Macian, jt. auth. see Long.

MacIan, Paula S. It Was the Year of the Scalping: Poems about Emotional Incest, Sexually Motivated Abuse, Mother-Daughter Incest, Father-Daughter Incest. LC 91-65735. 56p. (Orig.). 1991. 14.95 (*0-9629497-6-0*); pap. 6.95 (*0-9629497-4-4*) Still Wtrs Pr.

Maciariello, Joseph A. Management Control Systems. (Illus.). 720p. (C). 1984. text ed. write for info. (*0-318-57575-2*) P-H.

Maciariello, Joseph A. & Kirby, Calvin J. Management Control Systems: Using Adaptive Systems to Attain Control. 2nd ed. LC 93-29228. 1994. text ed. write for info. (*0-13-098146-X*) P-H.

Maciariello, Joseph A., jt. auth. see Asay, Lyal D.

Macias, Anna. Against All Odds: The Feminist Movement in Mexico to 1940. LC 81-6201. (Contributions in Women's Studies: No. 30). xv, 195p. 1982. text ed. 42.95 (*0-313-23028-5*, MAO/, Greenwood Pr) Greenwood.

Macias, Benjamin. One Hundred One Bible Riddles for All Ages. (Illus.). 112p. (Orig.). (J). (gr. 1 up). 1993. pap. 7.95 (*0-9638277-1-5*) Fam of God.

Macias, Edward S. & Hopke, Phillip K., eds. Atmospheric Aerosol: Source-Air Quality Relationships. LC 81-10960. (ACS Symposium Ser.: No. 167). 359p. 1981. 43.95 (*0-8412-0646-5*) Am Chemical.

Macias, José. Die Entwicklung des Bildjournalismus. (Kommunikation und Politik Ser.: Vol. 22). 360p. (GER.). 1990. pap. text ed. 37.00 (*3-598-20552-X*) K G Saur.

Macias-Lopez, Antonio. An Assessment of Agricultural Education in Mexico, Central America, & the Caribbean. (Studies in Technology & Social Change: No. 18). (Illus.). 133p. (Orig.). (C). 1990. pap. 12.00 (*0-945271-26-3*) ISU-TSCP.

Macias, Regina, ed. see Burrill, Richard.

Macias, Susan. First Mate. 224p. (Orig.). 1992. pap. 2.95 (*1-56597-006-3*, Kismet) Meteor Pub.

— Master of the Chase. 224p. (Orig.). 1993. pap. 2.95 (*1-56597-074-8*, Kismet) Meteor Pub.

— Sweet Escape. 304p. (Orig.). 1994. pap. 4.99 (*0-7865-0025-5*) Diamond.

— Tender Victory. 336p. (Orig.). 1993. mass mkt. 4.99 (*1-55773-862-9*) Diamond.

Maciaszek, Leszek. Data Base Design & Implementation. 350p. 1990. boxed 41.00 (*0-13-200015-6*) P-H.

Macie, Michelle, ed. see Damp, Dennis V.

Macie, Michelle, ed. see Wood, Patricia B.

Macieira, ed. Cancer & Aging. 1990. 121.00 (*0-8493-6878-2*, RC262) CRC Pr.

Macieira-Coelho, A. The Biology of Normal Proliferating Cells in Vitro Relevance for in vivo Aging. (Interdisciplinary Topics in Gerontology Ser.: Vol. 23). (Illus.). vi, 218p. 1987. 136.00 (*3-8055-4660-2*) S Karger.

Maciejowski, J. & Zieba, J. Genetic & Animal Breeding, Pt. A: Biological & Genetic Fndn. of Animal Breed. (Developments in Animal & Veterinary Science Ser.: Vol. 10). 1983. Pt. A, Biological & Genetic Foundation of Animal Breeding. 84.75 (*0-444-99696-6*) Elsevier.

— Genetic & Animal Breeding, Pt. B: Stock Improvement Methods. (Developments in Animal & Veterinary Science Ser.: Vol. 10). 1983. Pt. B, Stock Improvement Methods. 84.75 (*0-444-99732-6*, I-528-82) Elsevier.

— Genetic & Animal Breeding, 2 pts., Set. (Developments in Animal & Veterinary Science Ser.: Vol. 10). 1983. 115.00 (*0-444-99676-1*) Elsevier.

Maciejowski, J. M. The Modelling of Systems with Small Observation Sets. (Lecture Notes in Control & Information Sciences Ser.: Vol. 10). (Illus.). 1978. pap. 22.00 (*0-387-09004-5*) Spr-Verlag.

Maciejunes, Nannette & Roberts, Norma J., eds. A New Variety, Try One: De Scott Evans or S. S. David. LC 85-73103. (Illus.). 32p. 1985. pap. 5.00 (*0-918881-15-5*) Columbus Mus Art.

Maciejunes, Nannette V. Personal Mythologies: Columbus Painter Lucius Kutchin, 1901-1936. Roberts, Norma J. & Parsons, Merribell, eds. 33p. (Orig.). 1988. pap. 5.00 (*0-918881-21-8*) Columbus Mus Art.

Maciejunes, Nannette V., jt. auth. see Keny, James M.

Maciejunes, Nannette V., et al. The American Collections, Columbus Museum of Art. Roberts, Norma J., ed. LC 88-23774. (Illus.). 288p. (Orig.). 1988. 35.00 (*0-8109-1811-0*); pap. 22.50 (*0-918881-20-X*) Columbus Mus Art.

Maciel, David R. El Norte: The U. S.-Mexican Border in Contemporary Cinema. (Border Studies Ser.: No. 3). (Illus.). 95p. (Orig.). 1990. pap. 9.50 (*0-925613-03-7*) SDSU Inst Reg Studies.

***Maciel, Gary E., ed.** Nuclear Magnetic Resonance in Modern Technology: Proceedings of the NATO Advanced Study Institute, Sarigerme Park (Dalaman), Turkey, August 16-September 4, 1992. (NATO ASI, Series C, Mathematical & Physical Sciences: Vol. 447). 620p. (C). 1995. lib. bdg. 282.00 (*0-7923-3167-2*) Kluwer Ac.

***Maciel, Jairo.** A Traveller's Road. Sacchette, Reinaldo & Borges, Renato, eds. Kowarick, Margaret, tr. 135p. (Orig.). 1994. pap. write for info. (*0-9642230-0-7*) J Maciel.

Maciel, Marcel. Integral Formation of Catholic Priests. LC 92-7349. 215p. (Orig.). 1992. pap. 12.95 (*0-8189-0629-4*) Alba.

***Macierira-Coelho, Alvaro, ed.** Molecular Basis of Aging. 528p. 1995. 149.95 (*0-8493-4786-6*, 4786) CRC Pr.

Macierowski, Edward, tr. see Apollonius.

***Maciha, John.** Code 911: Emergency Procedures for Apartment Communities: A Guideline for Disaster Management. LC 94-74383. (Illus.). 240p. (Orig.). 1995. pap. 49.00 (*1-883422-33-7*) Adams-Blake.

Macijauskas, Aleksandras. My Lithuania. Mrazkova, Daniela & Remes, Vladimir, eds. LC 90-70291. (Illus.). 144p. 1991. 35.00 (*0-500-54132-9*) Thames Hudson.

Macillwain, Charles H., ed. see Wraxall, Peter.

MacIlwaine, Herbert, jt. auth. see Sharp, C. J.

MacIlwaine, Herbert C., jt. auth. see Sharp, Cecil J.

MacIlwaine, P. S., jt. auth. see Plumpton, C. A.

Macilwaine, P. S.

Macin, Enrique. Adan Se Despide. Dos Pasos, ed. (Palabra Nueva Ser.). (Orig.). (SPA.). 1988. pap. 12.00 (*0-9615403-3-8*) Dos Pasos Ed.

MacInaugh, Edmond A. Disguise Techniques: Fool All of the People Some of the Time. (Illus.). 88p. 1984. pap. 8.00 (*0-87364-307-0*) Paladin Pr.

MacInaugh, Edmund A. Disguise Techniques. (Illus.). 88p. 1988. reprint ed. pap. 5.95 (*0-8065-1098-6*, Citadel Pr) Carol Pub Group.

Macinko, George, jt. ed. see Platt, Rutherford H.

MacInnes, Allan. Charles the First & the Making of the Covenanting Movement, 1625-41. 120p. (C). 1991. text ed. 85.00 (*0-85976-295-5*) Humanities.

MacInnes, Charles M. Bristol: Gateway of Empire. LC 68-23841. (Illus.). 456p. 1968. reprint ed. 49.50 (*0-678-05609-9*) Kelley.

MacInnes, Colin. Les Blanc-Becs. (FRE.). 1985. pap. 13.95 (*0-7859-4218-1*) Fr & Eur.

— City of Spades. (Twentieth Century Classics Ser.). 256p. Date not set. pap. 10.95 (*0-7490-0116-X*, London Bridge) Genl Dist Srvs.

Macinnes, D., ed. Folk & Hero Tales. (Folk-Lore Society London Monographs: Vol. 25). (ENG & GAE.). 1972. reprint ed. pap. 45.00 (*0-8115-0511-1*) Periodicals Srv.

MacInnes, Duncan. Folk & Hero Tales. Nutt, Alfred, ed. LC 71-144455. (Waifs & Strays of Celtic Tradition: Argyllshire Ser.: No. 2). (Illus.). reprint ed. 45.00 (*0-404-53532-1*) AMS Pr.

MacInnes, Fiona. To Step among Wrack. (C). 1986. 35.00 (*0-907618-17-0*, Pub. by Orkney Pr UK) St Mut.

MacInnes, Hamish. The Price of Adventure: Mountain Rescue Stories from Four Continents. (Illus.). 192p. 1988. 15.95 (*0-89886-174-8*) Mountaineers.

MacInnes, Helen. Above Suspicion. LC 54-928. 1954. 24.95 (*0-15-102707-2*) HarBrace.

— Agent in Place. 23.95 (*0-89190-106-X*, Am Repr) Amereon Ltd.

— Assignment in Brittany. LC 42-17993. 1971. 24.95 (*0-15-109620-1*) HarBrace.

— Decision at Delphi. 1984. mass mkt. 4.95 (*0-449-20610-6*, Crest) Fawcett.

— Decision at Delphi. LC 60-15705. 1960. 24.95 (*0-15-124221-6*) HarBrace.

— The Double Image. 22.95 (*0-89190-105-1*, Am Repr) Amereon Ltd.

Macinnes, Helen. Helen Macinnes: Three Bestselling Novels of Terror & Suspense. 1993. 11.98 (*0-88365-814-3*) Galahad Bks.

MacInnes, Helen. Home Is the Hunter. 18.95 (*0-89190-102-7*, Am Repr) Amereon Ltd.

— Horizon. LC 46-3853. 1971. 24.95 (*0-15-142171-4*) HarBrace.

— Horizon. large type ed. LC 93-17775. 1993. bds. 19.95 (*1-56054-454-6*) Thorndike Pr.

— Horizon. large type ed. 1975. 12.00 (*0-85456-316-4*) Ulverscroft.

— I & My True Love. LC 52-13765. 1953. 24.95 (*0-15-143403-4*) HarBrace.

— I & My True Love. large type ed. LC 92-41149. 524p. 1993. reprint ed. bds. 20.95 (*1-56054-453-8*) Thorndike Pr.

— Neither Five nor Three. LC 51-1551. 1951. 24.95 (*0-15-165069-1*) HarBrace.

— North from Rome. LC 58-5922. 1958. 24.95 (*0-15-167001-3*) HarBrace.

— Pray for a Brave Heart. 1985. pap. 3.95 (*0-449-21013-8*, Crest) Fawcett.

— Pray for a Brave Heart. LC 55-5241. 1955. 24.95 (*0-15-173901-3*) HarBrace.

— Ride a Pale Horse. 384p. 1985. mass mkt. 5.99 (*0-449-20726-9*, Crest) Fawcett.

— Ride a Pale Horse. LC 84-9037. 352p. 1984. 15.95 (*0-15-177268-1*) HarBrace.

— The Salzburg Connection. large type ed. LC 92-23906. (All-Time Favorites Ser.). 698p. 1993. reprint ed. lib. bdg. 20.95 (*1-56054-455-4*) Thorndike Pr.

— The Snare of the Hunter. 22.95 (*0-89190-103-5*, Am Repr) Amereon Ltd.

— Triple Threat. 25.95 (*0-89190-104-3*, Am Repr) Amereon Ltd.

— While Still We Live. 448p. 1985. mass mkt. 5.95 (*0-449-20835-4*, Crest) Fawcett.

— While Still We Live. LC 44-2182. 1971. 24.95 (*0-15-196090-9*) HarBrace.

— While Still We Live. large type ed. LC 92-27926. 830p. 1992. reprint ed. lib. bdg. 20.95 (*1-56054-456-2*) Thorndike Pr.

MacInnes, Hugh. Turbochargers. LC 81-83821. (Illus.). 1976. pap. 14.95 (*0-89586-135-6*) Price Stern.

MacInnes, J. Watson. Guard Dogs: Alsatians, Boxers & Bull Mastiffs. 1992. lib. bdg. 88.00 (*0-8490-5232-7*) Gordon Pr.

MacInnes, John W. The Comical As Textual Practice in Les Fleurs du Mal. LC 87-14269. 165p. 1988. 22.95 (*0-8130-0866-2*) U Press Fla.

Macinnes, Lesley & Wickham-Jones, Caroline R., eds. All Natural Things: Archaeology & the Green Debate. (Oxbow Monographs in Archaeology: No. 21). (Illus.). 203p. 1992. pap. 31.50 (*0-946897-45-X*, Pub. by Oxbow Bks UK) David Brown.

MacInnes, M. J. Nature to Advantage Dress'd. spiral bd. 3.75 (*0-87018-043-6*) Ross.

MacInnes, Mairi. Elsewhere & Back: New & Selected Poems. 80p. 1993. pap. 13.95 (*1-85224-199-3*, Pub. by Bloodaxe Bks UK) Dufour.

— Herring, Oatmeal, Milk & Salt. (QRL Poetry Book Ser.: Vol. XXII). 20.00 (*0-614-06386-8*) Quarterly Rev.

— Herring, Oatmeal, Milk & Salt. (QRL Poetry Book Ser.: Vol. XXII). 1978. pap. 10.00 (*0-614-06387-6*) Quarterly Rev.

— House on the Ridge Road: Poems. LC 88-61638. 55p. (Orig.). 1988. pap. 7.95 (*0-937672-25-4*) Rowan Tree.

— Quondam Wives. Novel. LC 92-24432. 128p. 1993. 19.95 (*0-8071-1810-9*) La State U Pr.

MacInnes, Patricia. Last Night on Bikini. LC 94-17929. 1995. write for info. (*0-688-08001-4*) Morrow.

MacInnis. Ophthalmology Board Review of Optics & Refraction. 432p. 1993. 59.95 (*0-8016-7999-0*) Mosby Yr Bk.

— Religion in China Today: Policy & Practice. LC 89-38900. 450p. 1989. 39.95 (*0-88344-594-8*); pap. 19.95 (*0-88344-645-6*) Orbis Bks.

MacInnis, Donald, tr. see Zhufeng, Luo, ed.

MacInnis, Donald, et al. Focus on China: Values & Religion in China Today. 144p. (Orig.). (YA). (gr. 7-12). 1988. Grades 7-12. teacher ed 8.00 (*0-941395-01-4*) Maryknoll Miss.

An Asterisk (*) at the beginning of an entry indicates that the title is appearing in BIP for the first time.

M

*MacInnis, Frank. The Aging Game: Better to Wear Out Than Rust Out. 1994. pap. 14.95 (0-533-10956-6) Vantage.

MacInnis, Jamie. Practicing. 88p. (Orig.). 1980. pap. 5.00 (0-939180-13-8) Tombouctou.

MacInnis, Jeff & Rowland, Wade. Polar Passage. 224p. 1990. pap. 4.95 (0-8041-0650-9) Ivy Books.

MacInnis, Joseph. Titanic: In a New Light. LC 92-22682. 96p. 1992. pap. 16.95 (1-56566-021-8) Thomasson-Grant.

MacInnis, Joseph, ed. Saving the Oceans. 1992. 50.00 (1-55013-416-7) U of Toronto Pr.

MacInnes, John. Thatcherism at Work: Industrial Relations & Economic Change. 192p. 1987. 85.00 (0-335-15517-0, Open Univ Pr); pap. 29.00 (0-335-15516-2, Open Univ Pr) Taylor & Francis.

Macintire, Elizabeth J., tr. see Gad, Carl.

MacIntosh, Craig, jt. auth. see Howard, Greg.

Macintosh, Donald & Hawes, Michael. Sport & Canadian Diplomacy. 248p. 1994. 34.95 (0-7735-1161-X, Pub. by McGill CN) U of Toronto Pr.

Macintosh, Donald & Whitson, David. The Game Planners: Transforming Canada's Sport & System. 176p. (C). 1994. pap. text ed. 19.95 (0-7735-1211-X, Pub. by McGill CN) U of Toronto Pr.

— The Game Planners: Transforming Canada's Sport System. 128p. (C). 1990. 49.95 (0-7735-0758-2, Pub. by McGill CN) U of Toronto Pr.

Macintosh, Donald, et al. Sport & Politics in Canada: Federal Government Involvement since 1961. 210p. (C). 1987. pap. text ed. 22.95 (0-7735-0665-9, Pub. by McGill CN) U of Toronto Pr.

Macintosh, Douglas C. Theology As an Empirical Science. Gaustad, Edwin S., ed. LC 79-52601. (Baptist Tradition Ser.). 1980. reprint ed. lib. bdg. 25.95 (0-405-12466-X) Ayer.

***Macintosh, Duncan.** Chinese Blue & White Porcelain. 1994. 59.50 (1-85149-210-0) Antique Collect.

***Macintosh, Fiona.** Dying Acts: Death in Ancient Greek & Modern Irish Tragic Drama. 224p. 1994. 55.00 (0-312-12555-0) St Martin.

Macintosh, H. G., jt. auth. see Frith, D.

Macintosh, H. G., jt. ed. see Frith, D.

Macintosh, H. G., jt. auth. see Garforth, D.

Macintosh Inc. Staff. Stupid Mac Tricks. 1990. pap. 19.95 (0-201-57046-7) Addison-Wesley.

Macintosh, John. Life of Robert Burns. LC 78-144517. (Illus.). reprint ed. 22.95 (0-404-08519-9) AMS Pr.

***Macintosh, Norman B.** Management Accounting & Control Systems: Organisational & Behavioural Approach. LC 94-31614. 1994. pap. text ed. 39.95 (0-471-94411-4) Wiley.

— Management Accounting & Control Systems: Organisational & Behavioural Approach. LC 94-31614. 1995. text ed. 60.00 (0-471-94409-2) Wiley.

— Social Software of Accounting & Information Systems. LC 84-10447. 294p. 1985. text ed. 69.95 (0-471-90543-7) Wiley.

MacIntosh, Robert J. The Dawning of a Shipmaster. LC 87-47620. 230p. 1987. 21.50 (0-88164-530-3); pap. 15.50 (0-88164-531-1) ABBE Pubs Assn.

— The Valiant Association. LC 88-47632. 339p. 1988. 19.50 (0-88164-730-6); pap. 15.50 (0-88164-731-4) ABBE Pubs Assn.

***Macintosh, Sherwin, ed.** Songs of the Kingdom. 4th ed. 184p. 1994. ring bd. 3.50 (1-884553-46-X) Discipleshp.

MacIntrye, Iain. Vancouver Canucks. LC 93-48447. (NHL Today Ser.). 32p. (J). 1995. 14.95 (0-88682-690-X) Creative Ed.

MacIntyre. Proletarian Science: Marxism in Britain 1917-1933. (C). 1986. pap. 22.50 (0-85315-667-0, Pub. by Lawrence & Wishart UK) Humanities.

MacIntyre, A., et al. Logic Colloquium 1977. (Studies in Logic & the Foundations of Mathematics: Vol. 96). 312p. 1978. 82.00 (0-444-85178-X, North Holland) Elsevier.

MacIntyre, Alasdair. After Virtue: A Study in Moral Theory. 2nd ed. LC 83-40601. 320p. 1984. pap. text ed. 12.95 (0-268-00611-3) U of Notre Dame Pr.

— Against the Self-Images of the Age: Essays on Ideology & Philosophy. LC 78-1571. 1978. reprint ed. pap. text ed. 12.95 (0-268-00587-7) U of Notre Dame Pr.

— First Principles, Final Ends & Contemporary Philosophical Issues. LC 89-64321. (Aquinas Lectures). 1990. 10.00 (0-87462-157-7) Marquette.

— Free Rival Versions of Moral Enquiry: Encyclopaedia, Genealogy, & Tradition. LC 89-29275. 256p. (C). 1990. text ed. 24.95x (0-268-01871-5) U of Notre Dame Pr.

— Free Rival Versions of Moral Enquiry: Encyclopaedia, Genealogy, & Tradition. LC 89-29275. (C). 1991. pap. text ed. 12.95 (0-268-01877-4) U of Notre Dame Pr.

— Hume's Ethical Writings: Selections from David Hume. LC 79-1346. 1979. reprint ed. pap. text ed. 12.95 (0-268-01073-0) U of Notre Dame Pr.

— Marxism & Christianity. LC 83-40600. 143p. 1984. reprint ed. pap. text ed. 7.95 (0-268-01358-6) U of Notre Dame Pr.

Macintyre, Alasdair. Short History of Ethics. 288p. 1966. pap. 11.00 (0-02-087260-7, Collier S&S) S&S Trade.

MacIntyre, Alasdair. Whose Justice? Which Rationality? LC 87-40354. 432p. (C). 1989. text ed. 22.95 (0-268-01942-8); pap. text ed. 14.95 (0-268-01944-4) U of Notre Dame Pr.

MacIntyre, Alasdair & Ricoeur, Paul. The Religious Significance of Atheism. LC 68-28398. (Bampton Lectures in America: No. 18). 106p. reprint ed. pap. 30.30 (0-8357-4569-4, 2037479) Bks Demand.

MacIntyre, Alasdair, jt. ed. see Hauerwas, Stanley.

MacIntyre, Andrew. Business & Politics in Indonesia. 176p. 1991. pap. 24.95 (0-04-442330-6, Pub. by Allen & Unwin Aust Pty AT) Paul & Co Pubs.

MacIntyre, Andrew, ed. Business & Government in Industrializing Asia. LC 94-1663. 1994. write for info. (0-8014-8227-5) Cornell U Pr.

MacIntyre, Angus, jt. auth. see Picton Publishing Staff.

Macintyre, Ben. Forgotten Fatherland: The Search for Elisabeth Nietzsche. LC 92-9699. 1992. 22.00 (0-374-15759-6) FS&G.

MacIntyre, Ben. Forgotten Fatherland: The Search for Elisabeth Nietzsche. LC 92-56260. (Illus.). 272p. 1993. pap. 12.00 (0-06-097561-X, PL) HarpC.

MacIntyre, Bruce. Haydn: The Creation. (Monuments of Western Music Ser.). (Illus.). 1996. text ed. 35.00 (0-02-871375-3) Schirmer Bks.

MacIntyre, Bruce C. The Viennese Concerted Mass of the Early Classic Period. LC 85-20872. (Studies in Musicology: No. 89). (Illus.). 788p. reprint ed. pap. 180.00 (0-8357-1673-2, 2070609) Bks Demand.

MacIntyre, C. E., tr. Poems of Tristan Corbiere. (Illus.). 105p. 1989. 185.00 (0-933861-03-6) H Berliner.

— Poems of Tristan Corbiere. deluxe ed. (Illus.). 105p. 1989. 420.00 (0-933861-09-5) H Berliner.

MacIntyre, C. F., tr. French Symbolist Poetry. (C). 1958. pap. 11.00 (0-520-00784-0) U CA Pr.

MacIntyre, C. F., tr. see Goethe, Johann Wolfgang Von.

MacIntyre, C. F., tr. see Mallarme, Stephane.

MacIntyre, C. F., tr. see Rilke, Rainer M.

MacIntyre, C. F., tr. see Verlaine, Paul.

MacIntyre, D. E. & Gordon, J. L., eds. Platelets in Biology & Pathology, III. (Research Monographs in Cell & Tissue Physiology: Vol. 13). 628p. 1987. 231.50 (0-444-80820-5) Elsevier.

Macintyre DeLuca, Diane, ed. Essays on Creativity & Science. (Illus.). 308p. (Orig.). 1986. pap. 5.00 (0-9616581-0-X) Hawaii CTE.

MacIntyre, Donald G. Fighting Ships & Seamen. LC 78-2703. (Illus.). 192p. 1978. text ed. 49.75 (0-313-20357-1, MFSS, Greenwood Pr) Greenwood.

Macintyre, Edgar T. On Parade: A Manual for Drum Majors Modified British Style for Highland Scottish Pipe Bands & Other Marching Bands. 1994. pap. 13.95 (0-533-10915-9) Vantage.

Macintyre, F. Gwynplaine. The Woman Between the Worlds. 1994. pap. 12.95 (0-440-50327-2) Dell.

MacIntyre, Gordon. Accreditation of Teacher Education: The Story of CATE 1984-1989. 224p. 1991. 65.00 (1-85000-980-5, Falmer Pr); pap. 31.00 (1-85000-981-3, Falmer Pr) Taylor & Francis.

Macintyre, Ian G., jt. auth. see James, Noel P.

Macintyre, Ian G., jt. auth. see Miller, James A.

Macintyre, Ian G., jt. ed. see Ruetzler, Klaus.

Macintyre, Jane E., ed. Dictionary of Inorganic Compounds. (C). 1992. text ed. 3,995.00 (0-412-30120-2, A6962) Chapman & Hall.

— Dictionary of Organometallic Compounds: Fifth Supplement. 1125p. 1990. 895.00 (0-412-28180-5, A3821) Chapman & Hall.

— Dictionary of Organometallic Compounds: Fourth Supplement. (Illus.). 600p. 1988. 695.00 (0-412-28170-8, A1997) Chapman & Hall.

— Dictionary of Organometallic Compounds: Structure Index for Supplements 1-5. 208p. 1990. 275.00 (0-412-35680-5, A4395) Chapman & Hall.

— Dictionary of Organometallic Compounds: Third Supplement. 600p. 1988. text ed. 450.00 (0-412-26340-8) Chapman & Hall.

Macintyre, Lorn. Cruel in the Shadow. large type ed. 576p. 1982. 15.95 (0-7089-0867-5) Ulverscroft.

Macintyre, Martha & Jolly, Margatet, eds. Family & Gender in the Pacific: Domestic Contradictions & the Colonial Impact. (Illus.). 300p. 1989. 59.95 (0-521-34667-3) Cambridge U Pr.

Macintyre, Pamela, jt. auth. see Lees, Stella.

MacIntyre, Ross J., ed. Molecular Evolutionary Genetics. LC 85-19312. (Monographs in Evolutionary Biology). 632p. 1985. 120.00 (0-306-42042-2, Plenum Pr) Plenum.

Macintyre, Sally. Single & Pregnant: The Pregnancy Careers of Unmarried Women. LC 77-325. 1977. lib. bdg. 25.00 (0-88202-112-5) Watson Pub Intl.

Macintyre, Stuart. The Oxford History of Australia, Vol. 4: 1901-42, the Succeeding Age. (Illus.). 420p. 1993. reprint ed. pap. 19.95 (0-19-553518-9) OUP.

MacIntyre, Stuart F., ed. The Oxford History of Australia, Vol. IV: 1901-1942, 5 vols. LC 87-107443. (Illus.). 360p. 1987. 38.00 (0-19-554612-1) OUP.

MacIntyre, Tom. Fleurs-du Lit. (C). 1990. 25.00 (0-948268-84-0, Pub. by Dedalus Pr IE) St Mut.

— I Bailed Out at Ardee. (C). 1987. pap. 30.00 (0-948268-28-X, Pub. by Dedalus Pr IE) St Mut.

Macioci, R. Nikolas. Cafes of Childhood. 52p. (Orig.). 1992. pap. 6.95 (0-9627501-9-0) Event Horizon.

— Cafes of Childhood. 44p. (Orig.). 1991. pap. 7.00 (0-9628094-2-X) Pearl Edit.

***Maciocia, Giovanni.** Tongue Diagnosis in Chinese Medicine. rev. ed. LC 94-61961. (Illus.). 210p. (C). 1995. text ed. 45.00 (0-939616-19-X) Eastland.

Macionis, John J. Introduction to Sociology. (Illus.). 704p. (C). 1987. text ed. write for info. (0-13-497272-4) P-H.

— Society: The Basics. 2nd ed. LC 93-10848. 1993. pap. text ed. 23.50 (0-13-042730-6) P-H.

— Society: The Basics. 3rd annot. ed. LC 95-2839. 1995. teacher ed., pap. write for info. (0-13-437906-3) P-H.

— Society: The Basics. 3rd ed. LC 95-2839. 1995. pap. text ed. write for info. (0-13-435819-8) P-H.

— Sociology. 4th ed. 736p. (C). 1992. text ed. write for info. (0-13-818485-2) P-H.

MacIonis, John J. Sociology. 5th ed. LC 94-13021. 708p. 1994. text ed. 36.00 (0-13-101155-3) P-H.

Macionis, John J. Sociology Text. 2nd ed. 704p. (C). 1989. Incl. audio cassette. audio write for info. (0-13-823832-4) P-H.

Macionis, John J., ed. Seeing Ourselves: Classic, Contemporary, & Cross-Cultural Readings in Sociology. 3rd ed. LC 94-6822. 476p. 1994. pap. text ed. 18.00 (0-13-101130-8) P-H.

Maciora, Joseph G. The Maciora & Mik Families Genealogy: Historia Rodzin Mikow i Maciorow. LC 83-62000. (Illus.). 30p. (Orig.). 1983. pap. 7.00 (0-9613407-0-3) J G V Maciora.

MacIsaac, Daniel, jt. auth. see Shibata, Edward.

MacIsaac, Daniel L., jt. auth. see Shibata, Edward I.

Macisaac, Daniel L., jt. auth. see Shibata, Edward T.

MacIsaac, David, ed. The Defeat of the German Air Force: United States Strategic Bombing Survey, 10 vols. Incl. Vol. 1. LC 75-26396. 1976. (0-8240-2026-X); Vol. 2. LC 75-26396. 1976. (0-8240-2027-8); Vol. 3. LC 75-26396. 1976. (0-8240-2028-6); Vol. 4. LC 75-26396. 1976. (0-8240-2029-4); Vol. 5. LC 75-26396. 1976. (0-8240-2030-8); Vol. 6. LC 75-26396. 1976. (0-8240-2031-6); Vol. 7. LC 75-26396. 1976. (0-8240-2032-4); Vol. 8. LC 75-26396. 1976. (0-8240-2033-2); Vol. 9. LC 75-26396. 1976. (0-8240-2034-0); Vol. 10. LC 75-26396. 1976. (0-8240-2035-9); LC 75-26396. 1976. Set lib. bdg. 53.00 (0-685-01848-2) Garland.

MacIsaac, David S., jt. auth. see Rowe, Crayton E., Jr.

MacIsaac, Duncan, ed. see Campbell, John G.

MacIsaac, Maryellen. Handbook of IS Management. rev. suppl. ed. 1992. Supplemented annually; write for info. 54.95 (0-7913-0648-8) Warren Gorham & Lamont.

— Handbook of IS Management. 3rd rev. ed. 1991. per. 139.00 (0-87769-285-8) Warren Gorham & Lamont.

MacIsaac, Maryellen, jt. ed. see Gilhooley, Ian A.

MacIsaac, Robert, ed. see Traubel, Horace.

***MacIsaac, Ron & Champagne, Anne.** The Clayoquot Mass Trials: Defending the Rainforest. (Illus.). 224p. 1995. lib. bdg. 49.95 (0-86571-320-0) New Soc Pubs.

***MacIsaac, Ron & Champagne, Anne, eds.** Clayoquot Mass Trials: Defending the Rainforest. (Illus.). 224p. 1995. pap. 19.95 (0-86571-321-9) New Soc Pubs.

MacIsaac, Sharon. Freud & Original Sin. LC 73-92232. 176p. reprint ed. pap. 50.20 (0-317-10302-4, 2009042) Bks Demand.

Macisco, John J., Jr., jt. auth. see Powers, Mary G.

Macisco, John J., Jr., jt. ed. see Powers, Mary G.

Maciuba-Koppel, Darlene. Telemarketer's Handbook. LC 91-42682. 192p. 1992. pap. 12.95 (0-8069-8242-X) Sterling.

— Telemarketer's Handbook: Professional Tactics & Strategies for Instant Results. 192p. 1994. 33.00x (0-8095-7624-4) Borgo Pr.

Maciunas, Robert, ed. Interactive Image - Guided Neurosurgery. 200p. 1993. 90.00 (1-879284-15-4) Am Assn Neuro.

Maciuszko, Jerzy J. The Polish Short Story in English: A Guide & Critical Bibliography. LC 68-12253. 474p. reprint ed. pap. 135.10 (0-7837-3617-7, 2043483) Bks Demand.

MacIver, D. Chinese-English Dictionary: Hakka-Dialect. (CHI & ENG.). 1982. reprint ed. 45.00 (0-89986-344-2) Oriental Bk Store.

MacIver, Douglas J., jt. auth. see Epstein, Joyce L.

MacIver, Elizabeth, jt. auth. see Lorsch, Jay W.

MacIver, Ian. Urban Water Supply Alternatives: Perception & Choice in the Grand Basin, Ontario. LC 70-115926. (Research Papers Ser.: No. 126). 1970. pap. 12.00 (0-89065-033-0) U Chicago Comm Geo.

— Urban Water Supply Alternatives: Perception & Choice in the Grand Basin, Ontario. LC 70-115926. (University of Chicago, Department of Geography, Research Paper Ser.: No. 126). 193p. reprint ed. pap. 55.10 (0-7837-0402-X, 2040723) Bks Demand.

MacIver, Joyce. The Glimpse. LC 82-90994. 160p. 1983. 12.95 (0-87212-174-7) Libra.

MacIver, Mary. Pilgrim Souls. 1990. text ed. 28.00 (0-08-037978-8, Pergamon Pr) Elsevier.

MacIver, Mathew E. & Schreiber, Jan, eds. Planning with the Small Computer: An Applications Reader. LC 86-8462. (Lincoln Institute of Land Policy Book Ser.). 182p. reprint ed. pap. 51.90 (0-7837-3270-8, 2043289) Bks Demand.

MacIver-Neeb, Nancy D., ed. see White, Eric.

MacIver, R. M. Community: A Sociological Study. LC 70-172924. 1972. reprint ed. 24.95 (0-405-08766-7, Pub. by Blom Pubns UK) Ayer.

MacIver, R. M., ed. see Institute for Religious & Social Studies Staff.

MacIver, Robert. Robert M. MacIver on Community, Society & Power. Bramson, Leon, ed. LC 70-123374. (Heritage of Sociology Ser.). (C). 1970. lib. bdg. 20.00 (0-226-50047-0) U Ch Pr.

MacIver, Robert M. Academic Freedom in Our Time. LC 67-18441. 329p. 1967. reprint ed. 60.00 (0-87752-065-8) Gordian.

— Community: A Sociological Study Being an Attempt to Set Out the Fundamental Laws of Social Life. 446p. 1970. reprint ed. 30.00 (0-7146-1581-1, BHA-01581, Pub. by F Cass Pubs UK) Intl Spec Bk.

— Group Relations & Group Antagonisms. 11.25 (0-8446-1294-4) Peter Smith.

— The Nations & the United Nations. LC 74-7382. (National Studies on International Organization-Carnegie Endowment for International Peace). (Illus.). 186p. 1974. reprint ed. text ed. 49.75 (0-8371-7535-6, MANU) Greenwood.

— Social Causation. 11.25 (0-8446-2504-3) Peter Smith.

MacIvor, Iain. Edinburgh Castle. (Historic Scotland Ser.). (Illus.). 152p. 1994. pap. 29.95 (0-7134-7295-2, Pub. by Batsford UK) Trafalgar.

MacIvor, Virginia & LaForest, Sandra. Vibrations: Healing Through Color, Homeopathy & Radionics. 192p. 1979. pap. 9.95 (0-87728-393-1) Weiser.

Mack. EMT Certification Preparation & Review. (Illus.). 208p. 1990. 19.95 (0-8016-5853-5) Mosby Yr Bk.

— Essentials of Clinical Pediatric Dentistry. 1991. write for info. (0-8151-5715-0, Yr Bk Med Pubs) Mosby Yr Bk.

— Paul Cezanne. 1994. pap. 14.95 (1-56924-904-0) Marlowe & Co.

— Who Really Wrote the New Testament? Date not set. pap. 11.00 (0-06-065518-6, PL) HarpC.

Mack & Keal, eds. Security & Arms Control. 1989. 37.95 (0-04-335061-5, Pub. by Allen Unwin AT) Paul & Co Pubs.

Mack, Al. Calligraphy & Lettering, No. 2. (How to Draw & Paint Ser.). (Illus.). 32p. (Orig.). 1989. pap. 5.95 (1-56010-024-9, HT211) W Foster Pub.

Mack, Alice. Beyond Turmoil: A Guide to Renewal Through Deep Personal Change. 176p. 1992. pap. 12.95 (0-9632450-7-4) Connexions.

Mack, Alison. Dry All Night: The Picture Book Technique That Stops Bedwetting. (Illus.). 1990. pap. 14.95 (0-316-54225-3) Little.

— Toilet Learning: The Picture Book Technique for Children & Parents. 1983. pap. 10.95 (0-316-54237-7) Little.

Mack, Andrew, ed. Asian Flashpoint: Security & the Korean Peninsula. 175p. 1994. pap. 24.95 (1-86873-401-3, Pub. by Allen Unwin AT) Paul & Co Pubs.

— A Peaceful Ocean? Maritime Security in the Pacific in the Post-Cold War Era. 200p. 1994. pap. 24.95 (1-86373-593-3, Pub. by Allen Unwin AT) Paul & Co Pubs.

***Mack, Andrew & Ravenhill, John, eds.** Pacific Cooperation: Building Economic & Security Regimes in the Asia-Pacific Region. LC 94-40166. (C). 1995. text ed. 58.00 (0-8133-8917-8) Westview.

Mack, Anna E. For His Sake. LC 74-86800. (Granger Index Reprint Ser.). 1977. 15.95 (0-8369-6083-1) Ayer.

Mack, Anna E., comp. Because I Love You. LC 77-121931. (Granger Index Reprint Ser.). 1977. 19.95 (0-8369-6172-2) Ayer.

Mack, Arien, ed. Home: A Place in the World. LC 92-44279. (Illus.). 281p. 1993. 45.00 (0-8147-5483-X) NYU Pr.

— Home: A Place in the World. (Illus.). 281p. 1995. pap. 18.95 (0-8147-5526-7) NYU Pr.

— In Time of Plague: The History & Social Consequences of Lethal Epidemic Disease. 272p. (C). 1992. text ed. 45.00 (0-8147-5467-8); pap. 16.50 (0-8147-5485-6) NYU Pr.

Mack, Arthur C. Enjoying the Catskills. 1972. 5.95 (0-686-31391-7); pap. 4.95 (0-685-03754-1) Outdoor Pubns.

— The Palisades of the Hudson. (Illus.). 64p. 1982. reprint ed. pap. 5.95 (0-915850-05-2) Walking News Inc.

Mack, Beverly, jt. ed. see Coles, Catherine.

Mack, Budd. Undaunted Spirits. 1994. 16.95 (0-8062-4845-9) Carlton.

Mack, Burton L. The Lost Gospel: The Book of Q & Christian Origins. LC 92-53921. 288p. 1994. reprint ed. pap. 12.00 (0-06-065375-2) Harper SF.

— Myth of Innocence: Mark & Christian Origins. LC 86-45906. (Foundations & Facets Ser.). 448p. 1991. pap. 22.00 (0-8006-2549-8, 1-2549) Augsburg Fortress.

— Rhetoric & the New Testament. LC 89-36039. (Guides to Biblical Scholarship Ser.). 128p. (Orig.). 1989. pap. 9.00 (0-8006-2395-9, 1-2395) Augsburg Fortress.

— Who Really Wrote the New Testament? The Making of the Christian Myth. 1995. 22.00 (0-06-065517-8, HarpT) HarpC.

Mack, Burton L. & Robbins, Vernon K. Patterns of Persuasion in the Gospels. LC 89-3832. (Foundations & Facets: Literary Facets Ser.). 240p. 1989. pap. 19.95 (0-944344-08-9) Polebridge Pr.

Mack, C. Essentials of Statistics for Scientists & Technologists. LC 67-17769. 182p. 1967. 39.50 (0-306-30303-5, Plenum Pr); pap. 22.50 (0-306-20014-7, Plenum Pr) Plenum.

Mack, Charles R. Pienza: The Creation of a Renaissance City. LC 86-24269. (Illus.). 256p. 1987. 46.95 (0-8014-1699-X) Cornell U Pr.

Mack, Charles S. The Executive Handbook of Trade & Business Associations: How They Work & How To Make Them Work Effectively for You. LC 90-8957. 272p. 1990. text ed. 59.95 (0-89930-531-8, MEJ/, Quorum Bks) Greenwood.

— Lobbying & Government Relations: A Guide for Executives. LC 88-35730. 244p. 1989. text ed. 59.95 (0-89930-390-0, MGV/, Quorum Bks) Greenwood.

Mack, Charlie. Lesney's Matchbox Toys: Regular Wheel Years, 1947-1969. LC 92-60637. (Illus.). 144p. 1992. pap. 16.95 (0-88740-434-0) Schiffer.

— Lesney's Matchbox Toys: The Superfast Years, 1969-1982. LC 92-63103. (Illus.). 128p. (Orig.). 1993. pap. 16.95 (0-88740-463-4) Schiffer.

— Matchbox Toys: The Tyco Years 1993-1994. (Illus.). 144p. (Orig.). 1995. pap. 19.95 (0-88740-865-6) Schiffer.

— Matchbox Toys: The Universal Years, 1982-1992. (Illus.). 256p. 1993. pap. 19.95 (0-88740-550-9) Schiffer.

Mack, Charlotte W. & Feldt, Constance C. Spatial Reasoning with Soma Cube Activities. 79p. 1993. pap. 19.95 (0-939765-61-6, G157) Janson Pubns.

Mack, Chester. Punchdrunk Man Reader. LC 87-51416. (Illus.). 140p. 1988. 14.95 (0-9605630-1-6) Thistlerose.

Mack, Connie. Connie Mack's Baseball Book. 1976. 21.95 (0-8488-1591-2) Amereon Ltd.

— My Sixty-Six Years in the Big Leagues. 1976. 19.95 (0-8488-1587-4) Amereon Ltd.

Mack, Daniel. Making Rustic Furniture: The Tradition, Spirit & Technique with Dozens of Project Ideas. LC 91-45157. (Illus.). 164p. 1992. 24.95 (0-8069-8264-0) Sterling.

Mack, David, jt. auth. see Francis, Gary.

An Asterisk (*) at the beginning of an entry indicates that the title is appearing in BIP for the first time.

Mack, Dietrich. Senatsreden und Volksreden Bei Cicero. No. 2. v, 129p. 1967. reprint ed. write for info. (*0-318-71169-9*, Pub. by Georg Olms GW) Lubrecht & Cramer.

Mack, Donald R. The Unofficial IEEE Brainbuster Gamebook: Mental Workouts for the Technically Inclined. LC 92-4724. (Illus.). 144p. 1992. pap. 9.95 (*0-7803-0423-3*, PP0318-6) Inst Electrical.

Mack, Donald W. Lenin & the Russian Revolution. Reeves, Marjorie, ed. (Then & There Ser.). (Illus.). 104p. (Orig.). (gr. 7-12). 1970. pap. text ed. 8.76 (*0-582-20457-7*, 70766) Longman.

Mack, Dorothy. The Awakening Heart. 224p. 1993. pap. 3.99 (*0-451-17825-4*, Sig) NAL-Dutton.

— The Last Waltz. 1986. pap. 3.99 (*0-451-14156-3*, Sig) NAL-Dutton.

— The Lost Heir. (Signet Regency Romance Ser.). 224p. (Orig.). 1993. pap. 3.99 (*0-451-17638-3*, Sig) NAL-Dutton.

— A Prior Attachment. 224p. 1989. pap. 3.99 (*0-451-15964-0*, Sig) NAL-Dutton.

— The Steadfast Heart. 224p. 1988. pap. 3.99 (*0-451-15601-3*, Sig) NAL-Dutton.

— A Temporary Betrothal. (Regency Romance Ser.). 224p. (Orig.). 1995. mass mkt. 3.99 (*0-451-18469-6*, Sig) NAL-Dutton.

Mack, Douglas, ed. see Hogg, James.

Mack, Douglas S., ed. see Scott, Walter.

Mack, Edward C. Public Schools & British Opinion Since 1860: The Relationship Between Contemporary Ideas & the Evolution of an English Institution. LC 75-109777. 511p. 1971. reprint ed. text ed. 65.00 (*0-8371-4267-9*, MAPS, Greenwood Pr) Greenwood.

Mack, Eric, jt. auth. see Spencer, Herbert.

Mack, Faite. Resources for Educational Testing & Measurement. 352p. (Orig.). (C). 1994. pap. text ed. 19. 80 (*0-87563-489-3*) Stipes.

Mack, Frances, ed. Seinte Marherete. (EETS, OS Ser.: Vol. 193). 1974. reprint ed. 31.00 (*0-8115-3381-6*) Periodicals Srv.

Mack, Gerstle. Gustave Courbet: A Biography. (Quality Paperbacks Ser.). (Illus.). 494p. 1989. pap. 14.95 (*0-306-80375-5*) Da Capo.

Mack, Glenn. Adventures in Improvisation at the Keyboard. 64p. 1970. pap. text ed. 9.95 (*0-87487-076-3*) Summy-Birchard.

— Adventures in Modes & Keys. 32p. 1991. pap. text ed. 5.95 (*0-87487-625-7*) Summy-Birchard.

Mack, Grace C. My Special Book of Jewish Celebrations. (Illus.). 36p. (Orig.). (J). (ps-2). 1984. pap. 8.95 (*0-9602338-4-9*) Rockdale Ridge.

Mack, Hananel. The Aggadic Midrash Literature. 144p. 1989. pap. 12.00 (*0-317-05863-0*, Pub. by Israel Ministry Def IS) Gefen Bks.

Mack, Harold C., ed. see Symposium on the Physiology & Pathology of Human Reproduction (3rd: 1967, Detroit).

Mack, Jacqueline. Tales about Tails. (Illus.). 24p. (J). (ps-00). 1985. 10.95 (*0-88625-089-7*) Durkin Hayes Pub.

Mack, Jane, ed. see Meier, Paul.

Mack, Jim. Haleakala: The Story Behind the Scenery. rev. ed. LC 92-70431. (Illus.). 48p. 1992. pap. 6.95 (*0-88714-052-1*) KC Pubns.

Mack, Joanne, jt. auth. see Koeninger, Kay.

Mack, John. Emil Torday & the Art of the Congo, 1900-1909. 96p. 1991. pap. 17.50 (*0-295-97074-X*) U of Wash Pr.

— Malagasy Textiles. 1989. pap. 25.00 (*0-7478-0015-4*, Pub. by Shire UK) St Mut.

— Nightmares & Human Conflict. 288p. 1989. text ed. 50. 50 (*0-231-07102-7*); pap. text ed. 16.50 (*0-231-07103-5*) Col U Pr.

Mack, John, ed. Ethnic Jewelry. 1988. 49.50 (*0-8109-0891-3*) Abrams.

— Masks & the Art of Expression. LC 93-48524. 1994. write for info. (*0-8109-3641-0*) Abrams.

***Mack, John & Noonan, Joe.** The U. F. O. Abduction Phenomenon. 1995. 16.95 (*1-879323-35-4*) Atrium Pubs.

Mack, John, jt. auth. see McLeod, Malcolm.

***Mack, John E.** Abduction: Human Encounters with Aliens. 1995. mass mkt. 6.99 (*0-345-39300-7*) Ballantine.

— Abduction: Human Encounters with Aliens. LC 93-38116. (Illus.). 352p. 1994. text ed. 22.00 (*0-684-19539-9*, Scribners) S&S Trade.

— Abduction: Human Encounters with Aliens. large type ed. 1994. pap. 21.95 (*1-56895-082-9*) Wheeler Pub.

— A Prince of Our Disorder: The Life of T. E. Lawrence. (Illus.). 1978. 15.00 (*0-316-54232-6*) Little.

Mack, John E. & Ablon, Steven L., eds. The Development & Sustaining of Self-Esteem in Childhood. LC 83-22726. xiv. 304p. 1984. 42.50x (*0-8236-1255-4*) Intl Univs Pr.

Mack, John E. & Rogers, Rita S. The Alchemy of Survival: One Woman's Journey. (Radcliffe Biography Ser.). (Illus.). 1988. 17.26 (*0-201-12682-6*) Addison-Wesley.

— The Alchemy of Survival: One Woman's Journey. (Radcliffe Biography Ser.). (Illus.). 1989. pap. 13.41 (*0-201-51800-7*) Addison-Wesley.

Mack, Karen. The Magical Adventures of Sun Beams. (Illus.). 32p. (J). (ps-4). 1992. pap. 5.95 (*0-9631644-0-6*) Shooting Star.

Mack, Karin & Skjei, Eric. Overcoming Writing Blocks. 1980. 10.00 (*0-685-02301-X*); pap. 6.95 (*0-685-02302-8*) HM.

— Overcoming Writing Blocks. LC 78-55592. 1979. 7.95 (*0-87477-159-5*) J P Tarcher.

Mack, Ken E. & Newbold, Philip A. Health Care Sales: New Strategies for Improving Quality, Client Relations, & Revenue. LC 91-7084. (Health-Management Ser.). 264p. 1991. 32.95 (*1-55542-382-5*) Jossey-Bass.

Mack, Leo. Handicap a Winner at the Hounds: Quinelas Trifectas Daily Doubles. 99p. 1991. pap. text ed. 15.95 (*0-9630208-1-1*) Macks Bks.

— Handicap a Winning Bet at the Greyhounds. abr. ed. 103p. 1991. pap. text ed. 16.95 (*0-9630208-2-X*) Macks Bks.

— How to Win at the Greyhounds. 145p. 1990. pap. text ed. 20.00 (*0-9630208-0-3*) Macks Bks.

Mack, Lillian M., jt. auth. see Sulik, Stephen R.

***Mack, Lois.** Medical Terminology: A Method of Understanding. 176p. (C). 1994. pap. text ed., spiral bd. 22.00 (*0-8403-9946-4*) Kendall-Hunt.

***Mack, Lorrie.** The Art of Home Conversion: Transforming Uncommon Properties into Stylish Homes. (Illus.). 160p. 1995. pap. 17.95 (*0-304-34591-1*, Pub. by Cassell UK) Sterling.

— Conran's Living in Small Spaces. 1988. 29.95 (*0-316-54383-7*) Little.

— Making the Most of Work Spaces. LC 95-67264. (Illus.). 80p. 1995. 19.95 (*0-8478-1897-7*) Rizzoli Intl.

***Mack, Lorrie & Lodge, Diana.** Laura Ashley Decorating with Fabric: A Room-by-Room Guide to Home Decorating. (Illus.). 144p. 1995. 16.00 (*0-517-88229-9*) Random.

Mack, Lorrie, et al. Laura Ashley Guide to Country Decorating. 208p. 1993. 35.00 (*1-56282-745-6*) Hyperion.

— Laura Ashley Guide to Country Decorating. (Illus.). 208p. 1994. pap. 17.95 (*0-7868-8086-4*) Hyperion.

Mack, Maynard. Alexander Pope: A Life. LC 85-2941. (Illus.). 1986. 25.95 (*0-393-02208-0*) Norton.

— Alexander Pope: A Life. LC 85-2941. (Illus.). 1988. pap. 14.95 (*0-393-30529-5*) Norton.

— Alexander Pope: A Life. LC 85-40466. (Illus.). 976p. 1985. 40.00 (*0-300-03391-5*) Yale U Pr.

— Alexander Pope: A Life. LC 85-40466. (Illus.). 976p. 1988. pap. 22.00 (*0-300-04303-1*) Yale U Pr.

— Collected in Himself: Essays, Critical, Biographical & Bibliographical on Pope & Some of His Contemporaries. LC 79-57524. 576p. 1982. 70.00 (*0-87413-182-0*) U Delaware Pr.

— Everybody's Shakespeare: Reflections Chiefly on the Tragedies. LC 92-25122. xii, 279p. (C). 1993. 30.00 (*0-8032-3161-X*) U of Nebr Pr.

— Everybody's Shakespeare: Reflections Chiefly on the Tragedies. xii, 279p. 1993. reprint ed. pap. 12.00 (*0-8032-8214-1*, Bison Books) U of Nebr Pr.

— Killing the King: Three Studies in Shakespeare's Tragic Structure. LC 72-91301. (Yale Studies in English: No. 180). 220p. reprint ed. pap. 62.70 (*0-8357-8197-6*, 2033809) Bks Demand.

— The World of Alexander Pope. (Illus.). 70p. (Orig.). 1988. pap. 5.00 (*0-685-59700-8*) Yale Ctr Brit Art.

Mack, Maynard, ed. The Last & Greatest Art: Some Unpublished Poetical Manuscripts of Alexander Pope. LC 81-50304. 448p. 1984. 85.00 (*0-87413-183-9*) U Delaware Pr.

Mack, Maynard & Lord, George D., eds. Poetic Traditions of the English Renaissance. LC 82-1941. 336p. 1982. 40. 00 (*0-300-02785-0*) Yale U Pr.

Mack, Maynard, jt. auth. see Boynton, Robert W.

Mack, Maynard, ed. see Homer.

Mack, Maynard, ed. see Shakespeare, William.

Mack, Maynard, et al, eds. Norton Anthology of World Masterpieces. (C). 1987. teacher ed, pap. text ed. 2.95 (*0-393-95489-7*) Norton.

— Norton Anthology of World Masterpieces. 5th ed. (C). 1987. pap. text ed. 37.95 (*0-393-95486-2*) Norton.

— The Norton Anthology of World Masterpieces, I. 6th ed. (C). 1992. text ed. 41.95 (*0-393-96140-0*); pap. text ed. 37.95 (*0-393-96141-9*) Norton.

— The Norton Anthology of World Masterpieces, II. 6th ed. (C). 1992. text ed. 41.95 (*0-393-96142-7*); pap. text ed. 37.95 (*0-393-96143-5*) Norton.

— The Norton Anthology of World Masterpieces, Vol. 2. 6th expanded ed. (C). 1995. pap. text ed. 37.95 (*0-393-96348-9*) Norton.

— The Norton Anthology of World Masterpieces Vol. 1. 6th expanded ed. LC 94-42732. (C). 1995. pap. text ed. 37. 95 (*0-393-96346-2*) Norton.

— Teaching with the Norton Anthology of World Masterpieces. 6th expanded ed. (C). 1995. teacher ed, pap. text ed. write for info. (*0-393-96364-0*) Norton.

Mack, Michael & Taylor, Mark, eds. Fact Finder 1994: An Almanac of Christian Churches & Churches of Christ. 272p. (Orig.). 1994. pap. 16.99 (*0-7847-0238-1*, 30-88576) Standard Pub.

Mack, Michael, ed. see Johnson, Jan.

Mack, Michael, ed. see McCann, Mike.

Mack, Michael C., ed. see Cottrell, Jack.

Mack, Michael C., ed. see Odor, Kent & Ingmeier, Mark.

***Mack, Michael J.** Advanced Thoracoscopic Procedures. 1995. 135.00 (*0-942219-79-1*) Quality Med Pub.

Mack, Michael J., jt. auth. see Krasna, Mark J.

***Mack, Nancy, ed.** Country Cookies. 48p. Date not set. 4.98 (*0-89821-114-X*) Reiman Pubns.

— Words from the Heart. 48p. Date not set. 4.98 (*0-89821-113-1*) Reiman Pubns.

Mack, Nancy & Piepenbrink, Linda, eds. Taste of the Country Six. LC 93-84018. 100p. 1993. 9.98 (*0-89821-105-0*) Reiman Pubns.

Mack, Nathan A., jt. auth. see Mack, Wayne A.

Mack, Pamela E. Viewing the Earth: The Social Construction of the Landsat Satellite System. Bijker, Wiebe E. et al, eds. (Inside Technology Ser.). 280p. 1990. 30.00 (*0-262-13259-1*) MIT Pr.

Mack, Pauline B. & Urbach, C. Study of Institutional Children with Particular Reference to the Caloric Value As Well As Other Factors of the Dietary. (SRCD M: Vol. 13, No. 1). 1948. pap. 16.00 (*0-527-01543-1*) Periodicals Srv.

Mack, Pauline B., et al. Study of Two Levels of Bread Enrichment in Children's Diets. (SRCD M: Vol. 18, No. 2). 1953. pap. 15.00 (*0-527-01558-X*) Periodicals Srv.

Mack, Peter. Renaissance Argument: Valla & Agricola in the Traditions of Rhetoric & Dialectic. LC 93-26623. (Brill's Studies in Intellectual History: Vol. 43). xi, 395p. 1993. 97.25 (*90-04-09879-8*) E J Brill.

— Renaissance Rhetoric. LC 93-8119. 1993. text ed. 49.95 (*0-312-10184-8*) St Martin.

***Mack, Phyllis.** Visionary Women: Ecstatic Prophecy in Seventeenth-Century England. 1992. pap. 16.00 (*0-520-08937-5*) U CA Pr.

— Visionary Women: Ecstatic Prophecy in Seventeenth-Century England. 431p. (C). 1992. 40.00 (*0-520-07845-4*) U CA Pr.

Mack, Phyllis & Jacob, Margaret C., eds. Politics & Culture in Early Modern Europe: Essays in Honour of H. G. Koenigsberger. (Illus.). 319p. 1987. 69.95 (*0-521-30197-1*) Cambridge U Pr.

Mack, R. Russian-English Veterinary Dictionary. 104p. (Orig.). 1972. pap. text ed. 28.50 (*0-85198-255-7*) CAB Intl.

— Russian-English Veterinary Dictionary. 104p. (Orig.). (C). 1972. 50.00 (*0-89771-927-1*, Pub. by Collets) St Mut.

Mack, R. P. Coinage of Ancient Britain. 1975. 20.00 (*0-685-51540-0*) S J Durst.

Mack, Raymond W., ed. Changing South. LC 72-91467. 115p. 1970. 29.95x (*0-87855-060-7*); pap. 16.95x (*0-87855-557-9*) Transaction Pubs.

Mack, Raymond W. & Duster, Troy S. Patterns of Minority Relations. 60p. 0.75 (*0-686-74878-6*) ADL.

Mack, Richard, Jr. Bittersweet: Poems. LC 94-6754. Date not set. 10.95 (*0-944957-45-5*) Rivercross Pub.

Mack, Richard I., jt. auth. see Walters, Timothy R.

***Mack, Robert, ed.** Arabian Night's Entertainments. (World's Classics Ser.). 1300p. 1995. pap. 14.95 (*0-19-282832-0*) OUP.

Mack, Robert D. Appeal to Immediate Experience. LC 68-58803. (Essay Index Reprint Ser.). 1977. 17.95 (*0-8369-0085-5*) Ayer.

Mack, Robert L., jt. auth. see Nielsen, Jakob.

Mack, Robert W., jt. auth. see Healy, Martin R.

Mack, Roy. Dictionary for Veterinary Science & Biosciences. 324p. (ENG & GER.). 1987. pap. 85.00 (*0-8288-2385-5*, M4375) Fr & Eur.

— Dictionnaire des Termes Veterinaires et Animlaiers: French-English, English-French. 576p. (ENG & FRE.). 1991. 195.00 (*0-7859-8134-9*, 2863260863) Fr & Eur.

— Veterinary Dictionary: Russian-English. 104p. (ENG & RUS.). 1972. pap. 35.00 (*0-8288-6425-X*, M-9710) Fr & Eur.

Mack, Roy, ed. Dictionary of Animal Health Terminology: In English, French, Spanish, German, & Latin. LC 92-9212. 1992. write for info. (*0-444-88085-2*) Elsevier.

Mack, Roy, ed. see Office International des Epizooties Staff.

Mack, Ruth P. Consumption & Business Fluctuations: A Case Study of the Shoe, Leather, Hide Sequence. (Studies in Business Cycles: No. 7). 318p. 1956. reprint ed. 82.70 (*0-87014-090-6*); reprint ed. mic. film 41.40 (*0-685-61304-6*) Natl Bur Econ Res.

— Controlling Retailers. LC 77-76646. (Columbia University. Studies in the Social Sciences: No. 423). reprint ed. 34.00 (*0-404-51423-5*) AMS Pr.

— Factors Influencing Consumption: An Experimental Analysis of Shoe Buying. (Technical Papers: No. 10). 132p. 1954. reprint ed. 34.40 (*0-87014-416-2*); reprint ed. mic. film 20.00 (*0-685-61299-6*) Natl Bur Econ Res.

— Information, Expectations, & Inventory Fluctuation: A Study of Materials Stock on Hand & on Order. (Studies in Business Cycles: No. 16). 320p. 1967. reprint ed. 83. 20 (*0-87014-478-2*) Natl Bur Econ Res.

Mack, Sara. Ovid. (C). 1988. 13.00 (*0-300-04295-7*) Yale U Pr.

Mack, Scarlett. Good-Bye Diet Demon: You Can Become Sophisticated at Permanent Weight Control! LC 88-50008. 176p. 1989. pap. 14.95 (*0-945654-00-6*) Aroc Pub.

Mack-Smith, Denis. Cavour & Garibaldi Eighteen Sixty: A Study in Political Conflict. 480p. 1985. pap. 27.95 (*0-521-31637-5*) Cambridge U Pr.

— Garibaldi: A Great Life in Brief. LC 82-6271. (Great Lives In Brief Ser.). vii, 207p. 1982. reprint ed. text ed. 55.00 (*0-313-23618-6*, MSGA, Greenwood Pr) Greenwood.

Mack Smith, Denis. Italy: A Modern History. enl. rev. ed. LC 69-15851. (History of the Modern World Ser.). (Illus.). 1969. 29.95 (*0-472-07051-7*) U of Mich Pr.

Mack-Smith, Denis. Italy & Its Monarchy. 402p. (C). 1990. 40.00 (*0-300-04661-8*) Yale U Pr.

Mack Smith, Denis. Mazzini. LC 93-38313. (Illus.). 352p. 1994. 30.00 (*0-300-05884-5*) Yale U Pr.

Mack-Smith, Denis M. Italy & Its Monarchy. (Illus.). 413p. (C). 1992. reprint ed. pap. text ed. 20.00 (*0-300-05132-8*) Yale U Pr.

Mack, Stan. The King's Cat Is Coming. (Illus.). (J). (ps-1). 1976. lib. bdg. 4.99 (*0-394-93302-8*) Pantheon.

— Stan Mack's Out-Takes. LC 84-42756. (Illus.). 128p. 1985. 12.95 (*0-87951-986-X*); pap. 7.95 (*0-87951-997-5*) Overlook Pr.

— Stan Mack's Real Life American Revolution. LC 94-17808. (Illus.). 144p. (Orig.). 1994. pap. 10.00 (*0-380-77223-X*) Avon.

— Ten Bears in My Bed: A Goodnight Countdown. LC 74-151. (Illus.). 32p. (J). (ps-1). 1974. lib. bdg. 11.99 (*0-394-92902-0*) Pantheon.

Mack, Stan, jt. auth. see Bode, Janet.

Mack, Wayne. Fortaleciendo el Matrimonio. Orig. Title: Strengthening Your Marriage. 176p. (SPA.). 1992. pap. 6.99 (*0-8254-1454-7*) Kregel.

— Homework Manual for Biblical Living: Family & Marital Problems, Vol. 2. 1980. pap. 5.99 (*0-87552-357-9*) Presby & Reformed.

— Homework Manual for Biblical Living: Personal & Interpersonal Problems, Vol. 1. 1979. pap. 6.99 (*0-87552-356-0*) Presby & Reformed.

— The Saga of the Saints: An Illustrated History of the First 25 Seasons. LC 92-13809. 1992. 29.95 (*0-930892-18-6*) A Hardy & Assocs.

— Strengthening Your Marriage. (Christian Growth Ser.). 1977. pap. 6.99 (*0-87552-333-1*) Presby & Reformed.

Mack, Wayne A. Your Family, God's Way. 239p. 1991. pap. 7.99 (*0-87552-358-7*) Presby & Reformed.

Mack, Wayne A. & Mack, Nathan A. Preparing for Marriage God's Way: A Step-by-Step Guide for Marriage Readiness & After-the-Wedding Conflicts. 152p. 1986. pap. text ed. 12.99 (*1-56322-019-9*) V Hensley.

Mack, William P. Checkfire! LC 92-50363. 1992. 22.95 (*1-877853-17-8*) Nautical & Aviation.

— New Guinea. 320p. 1993. 22.95 (*1-877853-32-1*) Nautical & Aviation.

— Normandy. (Destroyer Ser.: Bk. 6). 250p. 1995. 22.95 (*1-877853-38-0*) Nautical & Aviation.

— Pursuit of the Seawolf. LC 91-22050. 419p. 1991. 22.95 (*1-877853-12-7*) Nautical & Aviation.

— Straits of Messina. LC 94-22931. 1994. 22.95 (*1-877853-34-8*) Nautical & Aviation.

Mack, William P. & Connell, Royal W. Naval Ceremonies, Customs, & Traditions. 5th ed. LC 79-92236. 386p. 1980. 27.95 (*0-87021-412-8*) Naval Inst Pr.

Mack, William P., Jr. & Konetzni, Albert H. Command at Sea. 4th ed. LC 81-85469. (Illus.). 519p. 1982. 22.95 (*0-87021-130-7*) Naval Inst Pr.

Mack, William P. & Mack, William P., Jr. South to Java. LC 87-24768. 460p. 1987. 22.95 (*0-933852-70-3*) Nautical & Aviation.

Mack, William P. & Paulsen, Thomas D. The Naval Officer's Guide. 10th ed. LC 90-22820. (Illus.). 528p. 1991. 24.95 (*0-87021-296-6*) Naval Inst Pr.

Mack, William P., Jr., jt. auth. see Mack, William P.

***Mack-Williams, Kibibi.** Food & Our History. LC 95-6590. (African American Life Ser.). (J). 1995. write for info. (*1-57103-033-6*) Rourke Pr.

— Malcolm X. LC 92-46767. (Biographies: Pioneers Ser.). (J). 1993. 19.93 (*0-86625-493-5*); 14.95 (*0-685-66548-8*) Rourke Pubns.

— People of Faith. LC 95-11444. (African American Life Ser.). (J). 1995. write for info. (*1-57103-031-X*) Rourke Pr.

Mack, Zella. California Paralegal's Guide, 2 vols., 1. 4th ed. 1993. write for info. (*0-250-47215-5*) Butterworth Legal Pubs.

— California Paralegal's Guide, 2 vols., 2. 4th ed. 1993. write for info. (*0-250-47216-3*) Butterworth Legal Pubs.

— California Paralegal's Guide, 2 vols., No. 1. 4th suppl. ed. 1988. Suppl. 1, 4/88. 32.50 (*0-685-66642-5*) Butterworth Legal Pubs.

— California Paralegal's Guide, 2 vols., No. 2. 4th suppl. ed. 1989. Suppl. 2, 4/89. 30.00 (*0-685-66643-3*) Butterworth Legal Pubs.

— California Paralegal's Guide, 2 vols., No. 3. 4th suppl. ed. 1990. Suppl. 3, 7/90. 36.50 (*0-685-66644-1*) Butterworth Legal Pubs.

— California Paralegal's Guide, 2 vols., No. 4. 4th suppl. ed. 1991. Suppl. 4, 4/91. 31.00 (*0-685-66645-X*) Butterworth Legal Pubs.

— California Paralegal's Guide, 2 vols., No. 5. 4th suppl. ed. 1992. Suppl. 5, 4/92. 36.50 (*1-55943-156-3*) Butterworth Legal Pubs.

— California Paralegal's Guide, 2 vols., Set. 4th ed. 1300p. 1993. ring bd. 110.00 (*0-250-47217-1*) Michie Butterworth.

Mackaay, E., jt. tr. see Haanappel, P. P.

Mackail, Denis G. Barrie: The Story of J. M. B. LC 73-37896. (Select Bibliographies Reprint Ser.). 1977. reprint ed. 37.95 (*0-8369-6734-8*) Ayer.

— How Amusing: & a Lot of Other Fables. LC 76-144160. (Short Story Index Reprint Ser.). 1977. reprint ed. 30.95 (*0-8369-3775-9*) Ayer.

— Tales from Greenery Street. LC 75-140335. (Short Story Index Reprint Ser.). 1977. 23.95 (*0-8369-3727-9*) Ayer.

Mackail, J. W. Lectures on Greek Poetry. LC 66-23520. 1910. 25.00 (*0-8196-0180-2*) Biblo.

— Lectures on Greek Poetry. 1972. 59.95 (*0-8490-0495-0*) Gordon Pr.

Mackail, John. Pope. 1972. 59.95 (*0-8490-0877-8*) Gordon Pr.

MacKail, John W. Approach to Shakespeare. LC 75-109655. (Select Bibliographies Reprint Ser.). 1977. 20.95 (*0-8369-5264-2*) Ayer.

Mackail, John W. Approach to Shakespeare. 2nd ed. LC 72-133815. reprint ed. 11.50 (*0-404-04131-0*) AMS Pr.

— Classical Studies. LC 68-16950. (Essay Index Reprint Ser.). 1977. 19.95 (*0-8369-0649-7*) Ayer.

— Lectures on Poetry. LC 67-23242. (Essay Index Reprint Ser.). 1977. 22.95 (*0-8369-0650-0*) Ayer.

— Life of William Morris, 2 vols. in 1. LC 68-57988. 1972. reprint ed. 36.95 (*0-405-08767-5*, Pub. by Blom Pubns UK) Ayer.

— Life of William Morris, 2 vols., Set. LC 79-118180. (English Biography Ser.: No. 31). 1970. reprint ed. lib. bdg. 79.95 (*0-8383-1070-2*) M S G Haskell Hse.

— Studies in Humanism. LC 73-84322. (Essay Index Reprint Ser.). 1977. 20.95 (*0-8369-1092-3*) Ayer.

— Studies of English Poets. LC 68-25604. (Essay Index Reprint Ser.). 1977. reprint ed. 20.95 (*0-8369-0651-9*) Ayer.

— William Morris & His Circle. LC 79-117585. (English Literature Ser.: No. 33). 1970. reprint ed. lib. bdg. 50.95 (*0-8383-1018-4*) M S G Haskell Hse.

Mackal, P. K. Psychological Theories of Aggression: A Social Psychologist's Reflection about Aggression. 216p. 1980. 64.00 (*0-444-85350-2*, North Holland) Elsevier.

Mackall, Dandi D. Christmas Gifts That Didn't Need Wrapping. LC 89-82553. (Illus.). 32p. (J). (ps-2). 1990. pap. 5.99 (*0-8066-2466-3*, 9-2466) Augsburg Fortress.

— Jesus Loves Me. LC 94-71206. (J). (ps-3). 1994. pap. 4.99 (*0-8066-2695-X*, 9-2695, Augsburg) Augsburg Fortress.

— Kids Are Still Saying the Darndest Things. LC 93-1715. 1993. 12.95 (*1-55958-352-5*) Prima Pub.

*__MacKall, Dandi D.__ Kids Are Still Saying the Darndest Things. 1994. pap. 7.95 (*1-55958-575-7*) Prima Pub.

Mackall, Dandi D. So I Can Read. (J). (ps-3). 1993. pap. 4.99 (*0-8066-2686-0*, Augsburg) Augsburg Fortress.

Mackall, Phyllis, ed. see Barkey, Tom.

Mackall, Phyllis, ed. see Crist, Terry M., Jr.

MacKall, Phyllis, ed. see Dalessandro, Gloria.

MacKall, Phyllis, ed. see Renner, Rick.

Mackan, Donald, tr. see Sehlin, Gunhild.

*__Mackay.__ Administration of Justice. (1993 Hamlyn Lecture Ser.). 1994. 28.00 (*0-421-52250-X*); text ed. 12.00 (*0-421-52260-7*) W W Gaunt.

— Prisms. 1986. pap. 3.95 (*0-449-21175-4*) Fawcett.

Mackay, et al. Tumors of the Lung. (Illus.). 432p. 1990. text ed. 79.50 (*0-7216-5807-5*) Saunders.

MacKay, A. Vitruvius Architect & Engineer. 88p. 1985. reprint ed. 12.50 (*0-86292-157-0*, Pub. by Brstl Class Pr UK) Focus Info Gr.

MacKay, A. L. A Dictionary of Scientific Quotations. (Illus.). 312p. 1991. 25.00 (*0-7503-0106-6*) IOP Pub.

Mackay, A. L., jt. auth. see Barrett, A. N.

Mackay, Agnes E. An Anatomy of Solitude: Towards a New Interpretation of the Sources of Creative Inspiration. 235p. 1982. 35.00 (*0-85335-229-1*, Pub. by Stuart Titles Ltd UK) St Mut.

— The Universal Self: A Study of Paul Valery. 263p. 1982. 45.00 (*0-85335-235-6*, Pub. by Stuart Titles Ltd UK) St Mut.

Mackay, Alexander. Western World: Or, Travels in the United States in 1846-47. LC 68-55900. 1970. reprint ed. text ed. 45.00 (*0-8371-0549-8*, MAWF, Greenwood Pr) Greenwood.

— Western World: Or, Travels in the United States in 1846-47, Vol. 2. LC 68-55900. 1970. reprint ed. text ed. 45.00 (*0-8371-0823-3*, MAWG, Greenwood Pr) Greenwood.

— Western World: Or, Travels in the United States in 1846-47, Vol. 3. LC 68-55900. 1970. reprint ed. text ed. 45.00 (*0-8371-0824-1*, MAWH, Greenwood Pr) Greenwood.

— The Western World; or, Travels in the United States in 1846-47, 3 vols. 2nd ed. LC 68-55900. (Illus.). 1970. reprint ed. text ed. 95.00 (*0-8371-2586-3*, MAWE, Greenwood Pr) Greenwood.

MacKay, Alfred F. Arrow's Theorem, the Paradox of Social Choice: A Case Study in the Philosophy of Economics. LC 79-26445. 152p. reprint ed. pap. 43.40 (*0-8357-5754-4*, 2056644) Bks Demand.

MacKay, Alfred F., ed. see Oberlin Colloquium in Philosophy Staff.

Mackay, Allen. Team up for Excellence. (Illus.). 220p. 1993. pap. 28.00 (*0-19-558268-3*) OUP.

MacKay, Angus. Brontes: Fact & Fiction. LC 70-148277. reprint ed. 16.00 (*0-404-08886-4*) AMS Pr.

— Society, Economy & Religion in Late Medieval Castile. (Collected Studies: No. CS261). (Illus.). 334p. (ENG & SPA.). (C). 1987. reprint ed. lib. bdg. 95.00 (*0-86078-209-3*, Pub. by Variorum UK) Ashgate Pub Co.

MacKay, Angus, jt. ed. see Bartlett, Robert.

Mackay, Angus, jt. ed. see Goodman, Anthony.

Mackay, Ann, jt. auth. see Mackay, Kenneth.

MacKay, Anne, ed. Wolf Girls at Vassar: Lesbian & Gay Experiences 1930-1990. 128p. 1992. pap. 10.95 (*0-9631911-0-1*) Ten Percent.

Mackay, Anthony. Journeys into Oxfordshire: A Collection of Ink Drawings. LC 93-39698. 1993. write for info. (*0-7509-0293-0*) A Sutton Pub.

*__MacKay, Brian.__ Hiking, Cycling, & Canoeing in Maryland: A Family Guide. LC 94-36543. (Illus.). 544p. 1994. text ed. 35.95x (*0-8018-5033-9*) Johns Hopkins.

*__MacKay, Brian & Glover, Sandra.__ Hiking, Cycling, & Canoeing in Maryland: A Family Guide. LC 94-36543. (Illus.). 544p. 1994. pap. 18.95x (*0-8018-5035-5*) Johns Hopkins.

Mackay, Bruce, jt. auth. see Bracken, R. Bruce.

MacKay, Carol H. Soliloquy in Nineteenth-Century Fiction. 208p. 1987. 48.00 (*0-389-20710-1*, N8268) B&N Imports.

MacKay, Carol H., ed. Dramatic Dickens. LC 88-26378. 192p. 1989. text ed. 45.00 (*0-312-02692-7*) St Martin.

*__Mackay, Charles.__ Extraordinary Pop Delusions. Date not set. 14.00 (*0-517-88433-X*) Random.

MacKay, Charles. Extraordinary Popular Delusions. 1976. 35.95 (*0-8488-1421-5*) Amereon Ltd.

Mackay, Charles. Extraordinary Popular Delusions & the Madness of Crowds. (Illus.). 752p. 1980. pap. 11.00 (*0-517-53919-5*, Harmony) Crown Pub Group.

— Extraordinary Popular Delusions & the Madness of Crowds. 1991. lib. bdg. 75.95 (*0-8490-4713-7*) Gordon Pr.

MacKay, Charles. Extraordinary Popular Delusions & the Madness of Crowds. 774p. 1986. reprint ed. lib. bdg. 36.95 (*0-89966-516-0*) Buccaneer Bks.

Mackay, Charles. Lost Beauties of the English Language. 268p. 1988. 16.95 (*0-317-67849-3*) Dorset Pr.

— Poetical Works of Charles Mackay. LC 70-144452. reprint ed. 25.00 (*0-404-08564-4*) AMS Pr.

Mackay, Charles, ed. Medora Leigh: A History & an Autobiography. LC 78-37700. reprint ed. 30.00 (*0-404-56759-2*) AMS Pr.

Mackay, Charles & LeBon, Gustav. Extraordinary Popular Delusions & the Madness of Crowds & The Crowd, A Study of the Popular Mind: Twin Classics of Crowd Psychology, 2 bks. abr. ed. 324p. (Orig.). 1993. reprint ed. pap. 19.95 (*0-934380-23-6*) Traders Pr.

MacKay, Charles K., jt. auth. see Inlander, Charles B.

MacKay, Claire. The Toronto Story. (Illus.). 112p. (Orig.). (J). (gr. 5 up). 1991. 34.95 (*1-55037-137-1*, Pub. by Annick CN); pap. 24.95 (*1-55037-135-5*, Pub. by Annick CN) Firefly Bks Ltd.

Mackay, Colin. The Song of the Forest. 240p. (Orig.). 1987. mass mkt. 5.95 (*0-345-34647-5*, Available Pr) Ballantine.

MacKay, Colin, ed. Electronic Packaging: Materials & Processes to Reduce Package Cycle Time & Improve Reliability. 264p. 1993. 107.00 (*0-87170-449-8*, 6292NR) ASM.

Mackay, Colin, jt. ed. see Ledingham, Iain M.

Mackay, Constance D. Plays of the Pioneers: A Book of Historical Pageant Plays. LC 76-40389. (One-Act Plays in Reprint Ser.). 1976. reprint ed. 17.75 (*0-8486-2005-4*) Roth Pub Inc.

Mackay, D. G. The Organization of Perception & Action. (Cognitive Science Ser.). (Illus.). xxii, 233p. 1987. pap. 41.00 (*0-387-96509-2*) Spr-Verlag.

Mackay, David. In the Wake of Cook: Exploration, Science & Empire 1780-1801. LC 85-40080. 240p. 1985. text ed. 39.95 (*0-312-41177-4*) St Martin.

— The Modern House: Designed by the World's Leading Architects. (Illus.). 160p. 1991. 29.95 (*0-8038-9276-4*) Archit CT.

*__Mackay, Donald, et al.__ Illustrated Handbook of Physical-Chemical Properties & Environmental Fate for Organic Chemicals Vol. 4: Oxygen, Nitrogen, & Sulfur-Containing Compounds. (Illus.). 500p. 1995. 99.50 (*1-56670-035-3*, L1035) Lewis Pubs.

Mackay, Donald. Multimedia Environmental Models: The Fugacity Approach. 260p. 1991. 64.95 (*0-87371-242-0*, TD196) Lewis Pubs.

MacKay, Donald, et al. Illustrated Handbook of Environmental Fate for Organic Chemicals, Vol. I: Monoaromatics, Clorobenzenes & PCBs. 1991. Vol. I: Monoaromatics, Chlorobenzenes & PCBs. 79.95 (*0-87371-513-6*, TD176) Lewis Pubs.

Mackay, Donald, et al. Illustrated Handbook of Environmental Fate for Organic Chemicals, Vol. II. 1991. 94.95 (*0-87371-583-7*) Lewis Pubs.

MacKay, Donald A. The Building of Manhattan: How Manhattan Was Built, Overground & Underground, from the Dutch Settlers to the Skyscaper. LC 87-45069. (Illus.). 160p. 1989. reprint ed. pap. 18.00 (*0-06-091603-6*, PL) HarpC.

MacKay, Donald M. Behind the Eye. MacKay, Valerie, ed. (Illus.). 288p. 1990. 24.95 (*0-631-17332-3*) Blackwell Pubs.

— Science & the Quest for Meaning. LC 81-17504. 87p. reprint ed. pap. 25.00 (*0-317-30150-0*, 2025333) Bks Demand.

MacKay, Douglas. Honourable Company. LC 73-124242. (Select Bibliographies Reprint Ser.). 1977. 25.95 (*0-8369-5430-0*) Ayer.

Mackay, Douglas. Pet Owner's Guide to the Yorkshire Terrier. (Illus.). 80p. 1994. 8.00 (*0-87605-993-0*) Howell Bk.

Mackay, E. J. Chanhu-Daro Excavations, 1935-1936. (American Folklore Society Memoirs Ser.: Vol. 20). 1972. reprint ed. 45.00 (*0-527-02694-8*) Periodicals Srv.

Mackay, Edith. Universal Typing. 3rd ed. 192p. 1988. 27.50 (*0-273-02706-9*, Pub. by Pitman Pub Ltd UK) Trans-Atl Phila.

— Universal Typing: Advanced. 2nd ed. 192p. 1990. pap. text ed. 23.50 (*0-273-02707-7*, Pub. by Pitman Pub Ltd UK) Trans-Atl Phila.

— Universal Typing: Study Key & Notes. 128p. (Orig.). 1988. pap. 17.95 (*0-273-02956-8*, Pub. by Pitman Pub Ltd UK) Trans-Atl Phila.

MacKay, Ernest J., et al. Further Excavations at Mohenjo-Daro: Being an Official Account of Archaeological Excavations at Mohenjo-Daro Carried out by the Government of India Between 1927 & 1931, 2 vols., Set. LC 77-87006. reprint ed. 127.00 (*0-404-16670-9*) AMS Pr.

MacKay, Ernest J. H. The Indus Civilization. LC 77-86434. (Illus.). 240p. 1983. reprint ed. 27.50 (*0-404-16673-3*) AMS Pr.

Mackay, G. A., jt. auth. see Lind, T.

Mackay, G. R., jt. ed. see Bradshaw, J. E.

Mackay, George L. From Far Formosa, the Island, Its People & Missions. (Illus.). 346p. reprint ed. 35.00 (*957-638-072-3*, HSE019, Pub. by SMC Pub CC) Oriental Bk Store.

Mackay, Gilbert. Sensori-Motor Development. (C). 1989. 40.00 (*1-85098-062-4*, Pub. by Jordanhill College UK) St Mut.

MacKay, Gilbert, ed. Weekenders: An Exploratory Study. (C). 1989. 45.00 (*1-85098-223-6*, Pub. by Jordanhill College UK) St Mut.

Mackay, Gilbert F. & Dunn, William R. Early Communicative Skills. 224p. 1989. 49.95 (*0-415-03204-0*); pap. 16.95 (*0-415-03205-9*) Routledge.

*__Mackay, H.__ Sharkproof. Date not set. pap. 5.98 (*0-8317-0044-0*) Smithmark.

MacKay, H. G. Story of Your Bible. 1985. pap. 3.50 (*0-937396-65-6*) Walterick Pubs.

Mackay, Harold. Christian Woman in God's Church & Family. 1988. pap. 3.50 (*0-937396-70-2*) Walterick Pubs.

— Coming of Christ. 1989. 3.50 (*0-937396-79-6*) Walterick Pubs.

— The Study of Your Bible. 1988. pap. 3.50 (*0-937396-68-0*) Walterick Pubs.

MacKay, Harold G. Morning in My Heart. (Illus.). 120p. (Orig.). 1993. pap. 5.95 (*1-882701-04-6*) Gospel Folio.

Mackay, Harvey. Beware the Naked Man Who Offers You His Shirt. 416p. 1991. mass mkt. 5.95 (*0-8041-0583-9*) Ivy Books.

MacKay, Harvey. Cuidade del Hombre Desnudo Que Te Ofrece Su Camisa. 1987. pap. text ed. 17.95 (*0-07-104030-7*) McGraw.

Mackay, Harvey. Harvey Mackay, 2 vols., Set. 1993. Boxed set. mass mkt. 11.90 (*0-8041-0898-6*) Ivy Books.

— The Harvey Mackay Rolodex Network Builder. 62p. 1993. pap. 8.95 (*0-9637967-0-4*) MacKay Envelope.

— Sharkproof: Get the Job You Want, Keep the Job You Love . . . in Today's Frenzied Job Market. 368p. 1994. pap. 9.00 (*0-88730-663-2*) Harper Busn.

— Swim with the Sharks Without Being Eaten Alive. 352p. 1989. mass mkt. 6.99 (*0-8041-0426-3*) Ivy Books.

— Swim with the Sharks Without Being Eaten Alive: Outsell, Outmanage, Outmotivate & Outnegotiate Your Competition. LC 87-24757. 224p. 1988. 20.00 (*0-688-07473-1*) Morrow.

Mackay, Helen G. Chill Hours. LC 77-178446. (Short Story Index Reprint Ser.). 1977. reprint ed. 19.95 (*0-8369-4047-4*) Ayer.

Mackay, Henry F. Followers in the Way. LC 71-93359. (Essay Index Reprint Ser.). 1977. 19.95 (*0-8369-1304-3*) Ayer.

MacKay, Hugh. Memoirs of the War Carried on in Scotland & Ireland. LC 70-172707. (Maitland Club, Glasgow. Publications: No. 22). reprint ed. 37.50 (*0-404-52755-8*) AMS Pr.

Mackay, Hughie & Beynon, John, eds. Understanding Technology in Education. 272p. 1991. 65.00 (*1-85000-887-6*, Falmer Pr); pap. 27.00 (*1-85000-888-4*, Falmer Pr) Taylor & Francis.

Mackay, Hughie, jt. auth. see Beynon, John.

Mackay, I. R., ed. Multidisciplinary Gerontology: A Structure for Research in Gerontology in a Developed Country. (Interdisciplinary Topics in Gerontology Ser.: Vol. 11). (Illus.). 1977. 49.00 (*3-8055-2679-2*) S Karger.

MacKay, I. S., ed. Rhinitis Mechanisms & Management. (Illus.). 230p. 1989. 38.00 (*1-85070-892-4*) Prthnon Pub.

*__Mackay, Ian.__ Appraisal Discussion. (C). 1992. pap. 18.00x (*0-85171-099-9*, Pub. by IPM Hse UK) St Mut.

— Choosing Staff: A Guide to Better Selection Interviewing. 72p. (C). 1991. pap. 21.00x (*0-85171-092-1*, Pub. by IPM Hse UK) St Mut.

— Expecting Answers? An Introduction to the Skills of Questioning & Listening. (C). 1989. pap. 30.00x (*0-614-03376-4*, Pub. by IPM Hse UK) St Mut.

— A Guide to Asking Questions. (C). 1980. pap. 18.00x (*0-85171-075-1*, Pub. by IPM Hse UK) St Mut.

— A Guide to Listening. (C). 1984. pap. 18.00x (*0-85171-080-8*, Pub. by IPM Hse UK) St Mut.

— A Guide to Managing Time. (C). 1990. pap. 60.00x (*0-85171-090-5*, Pub. by IPM Hse UK) St Mut.

— Handbook of Training Activities Interpersonal Skills. 253p. (C). 1992. ring bd. 285.00x (*0-85171-100-6*, Pub. by IPM Hse UK) St Mut.

— Phonetics & Speech Science: A Bilingual Dictionary--Dictionnaire Bilingue des Sciences de la Parole. (American University Studies: Linguistics: Ser. XIII, Vol. 10). 249p. (ENG & FRE.). (C). 1989. text ed. 37.95 (*0-8204-1036-5*) P Lang Pubs.

MacKay, Ian. Thirty-Five Checklists for Human Resource Development. (Illus.). 179p. 1989. text ed. 59.95 (*0-566-02823-9*, Pub. by Gower UK) Ashgate Pub Co.

MacKay, Ian R. Phonetics: The Science of Speech Production. 2nd ed. (Illus.). 336p. (C). 1991. pap. text ed. 46.00 (*0-205-13545-5*) Allyn.

Mackay, Ian R., jt. ed. see Rose, Noel R.

Mackay, Ian S., jt. ed. see Bull, T. R.

Mackay, James. Dictionary of Sculptors in Bronze. 416p. 1992. reprint ed. 69.50 (*1-85149-110-4*) Antique Collect.

— Guinness Book of Stamps: Facts & Feats. 224p. 1992. 19.95 (*1-55859-432-9*) Abbeville Pr.

Mackay, James A. Burnsiana. (C). 1988. 150.00 (*0-907526-35-7*, Alloway Pub) St Mut.

MacKay, James A. Kilmarnock. 204p. (C). 1989. text ed. 75.00 (*0-907526-52-7*, Alloway Pub) St Mut.

Mackay, James A., ed. The Complete Poetical Works of Robert Burns. 640p. 1993. 45.00 (*0-907526-64-0*, Alloway Pub) St Mut.

— The Complete Poetical Works of Robert Burns. deluxe ed. 640p. 1993. boxed 75.00 (*0-907526-62-4*, Alloway Pub) St Mut.

Mackay, Jeff. Windows Programming with Borland C. 1993. pap. text ed. 34.95 (*0-07-044596-6*) McGraw.

— Windows Programming with Borland C Plus Plus. LC 92-40040. 1993. pap. 34.95 (*0-8306-4319-2*, Windcrest) TAB Bks.

Mackay, John. Hibernian: The Complete Story. 250p. (C). 1989. text ed. 30.00 (*0-85976-321-8*, Pub. by J Donald) St Mut.

— Life of Lieutenant-General Hugh Mackay. LC 74-172708. (Bannatyne Club, Edinburgh. Publications: No. 53). reprint ed. 27.50 (*0-404-52763-9*) AMS Pr.

Mackay, John, jt. auth. see Erickson, Robert.

Mackay, John H. The Anarchists. LC 77-185840. 1972. reprint ed. lib. bdg. 250.00 (*0-87700-059-X*) Revisionist Pr.

— Max Stirner: His Life & Work. (Men & Movements in the History & Philosophy of Anarchism Ser.). 1978. lib. bdg. 75.00 (*0-87700-314-9*) Revisionist Pr.

MacKay, John R., II. New Jersey Business Corporations: Law & Practice, 3 vols., Set. LC 92-24970. 1460p. 1992. ring bd. 270.00 (*1-56257-288-1*) Michie Butterworth.

Mackay, Joy. Raindrops Keep Falling on My Tent. 20p. 1981. pap. 4.95 (*0-87603-060-6*) Am Camping.

Mackay, Judith, et al. The State of Health Atlas. LC 92-27298. 1993. pap. 16.00 (*0-671-79375-6*, Touchstone Bks) S&S Trade.

MacKay, Judy F. Tales of a Nuf in the Land of Doon. (Illus.). 84p. (Orig.). (J). (gr. 4-7). 1992. per. 9.95 (*1-882748-00-X*) MacKay-Langley.

MacKay, June, tr. see Jackins, Harvey.

Mackay, Kames A. Coins: Facts & Feats. (Illus.). 1992. 34.95 (*1-85264-025-1*, Pub. by Seaby UK) Trafalgar.

MacKay, Kathryn. Ontario. (Discover Canada Ser.). (Illus.). 144p. (J). (gr. 5-8). 1992. lib. bdg. 20.55 (*0-516-06614-5*) Childrens.

Mackay, Kenneth & Mackay, Ann. Introduction to Modern Inorganic Chemistry. 4th ed. 400p. 1989. text ed. 86.00 (*0-13-488487-6*) P-H.

Mackay, Kris. The Ultimate Love. 1994. 10.95 (*0-88494-926-5*) Bookcraft Inc.

Mackay, Kris, jt. auth. see Jones, Barbara B.

MacKay, Lesley. Nursing a Problem. 1989. 90.00 (*0-335-09902-5*, Open Univ Pr); pap. 32.00 (*0-335-09901-7*, Open Univ Pr) Taylor & Francis.

Mackay, Lesley & Torrington, Derek. The Changing Nature of Personnel Management. 160p. (C). 1986. 120.00 (*0-85292-377-5*) St Mut.

Mackay, Louis, tr. see Brantenberg, Gerd.

Mackay, M. Burns Lore of Dumfries & Galloway. (C). 1988. 75.00 (*0-907526-36-5*, Alloway Pub) St Mut.

— The Complete Letters of Robert Burns: Souvenir Edition. (C). 1988. 160.00 (*0-907526-32-2*, Alloway Pub) St Mut.

— Complete Works & Letters of Burns, 2 vols., Set. (C). 1988. 290.00 (*0-907526-33-0*, Alloway Pub) St Mut.

— The Complete Works of Robert Burns: Presentation Edition. (C). 1988. 350.00 (*0-907526-29-2*, Alloway Pub) St Mut.

— The Complete Works of Robert Burns: Souvenir Edition. (C). 1988. 110.00 (*0-907526-23-3*, Alloway Pub) St Mut.

Mackay, Marguerite, ed. see Benjamin, Linda W.

Mackay, Marguerite, ed. see Hill, Roger.

MacKay, Marguerite, ed. see Sage, Jewel R.

MacKay, Mary. The Strange Visitation of Josiah McNason: A Christmas Ghost Story. Reginald, R. & Menville, Douglas, eds. LC 75-46262. 1976. reprint ed. lib. bdg. 17.95 (*0-405-08120-0*) Ayer.

Mackay, Nancy & Pisano, Vivian M. Swim Bay Area: A Guide to Swimming Pools in the San Francisco Bay Area. (Illus.). 192p. (Orig.). 1988. pap. 8.95 (*0-943937-00-0*) Swimming Across West.

MacKay, Niall. Over the Hills to Georgian Bay. (Illus.). 136p. reprint ed. 19.95 (*0-317-05898-3*, Pub. by Boston Mills Pr CN) Genl Dist Srvs.

Mackay, Nigel. Motivation & Explanation: An Essay on Freud's Philosophy of Science. (Psychological Issues Monograph: No. 56). 260p. 1989. 35.00 (*0-8236-3474-4*) Intl Univs Pr.

Mackay, Noel. Go For the Gold in Real Estate Sales & Exchanges: A Mental & Physical Approach to Excellence in Real Estate Performance. 100p. (Orig.). 1986. pap. 13.95 (*0-9616070-0-9*) Mountain Pr CA.

MacKay, P. Computers Arabic Language. 1990. 116.00 (*0-89116-563-0*) Hemisp Pub.

Mackay, R. A., et al, eds. Superalloys Nineteen Ninety-Two. (Illus.). 974p. 1992. 150.00 (*0-87339-189-6*, 451) Minerals Metals.

Mackay, R. S. Bio-Medical Telemetry: Sensing & Transmitting Biological Information from Animals & Man. 2nd ed. 540p. 1993. 49.95 (*0-7803-1028-4*) Inst Electrical.

MacKay, R. S. Renormalization in Area-Preserving Maps. (Advanced Series in Nonlinear Dynamics). 324p. 1993. text ed. 61.00 (*981-02-1371-9*) World Scientific Pub.

MacKay, R. S. & Meiss, J. D. Hamiltonian Dynamical Systems: A Reprint Selection. (Illus.). 800p. 1987. 183.00 (*0-85274-205-3*) IOP Pub.

Mackay, R. S. & Meiss, J. D. Hamiltonian Dynamical Systems: A Reprint Selection. (Illus.). 800p. 1987. pap. 64.00 (*0-85274-216-9*) IOP Pub.

Mackay, R. Stuart. Medical Images & Displays: Comparisons of Nuclear Magnetic Resonance, Ultrasound, X-Rays & Other Modalities. 290p. (C). 1984. lib. bdg. 57.95 (*0-471-89617-9*) Krieger.

Mackay, Raymond A. & Texter, John, eds. Electrochemistry in Colloids & Dispersions. LC 92-11403. 546p. 1992. 115.00 (*1-56081-573-6*) VCH Pubs.

*__MacKay, Robert.__ Letters of Robert MacKay to His Wife. (American Autobiography Ser.). 325p. 1995. reprint ed. lib. bdg. 89.00 (*0-7812-8584-4*) Rprt Serv.

Mackay, Robert, jt. auth. see Thompson, Moira.

Mackay, Robert A., ed. Newfoundland: Economic, Diplomatic & Strategic Studies. LC 76-46180. reprint ed. 39.50 (*0-404-15366-6*) AMS Pr.

Mackay, Robert J., et al, eds. Public Choice & Regulation: A View from Inside the Federal Trade Commission. (Publication Ser.: No. 356). 363p. 1987. pap. 22.95 (*0-8179-8562-X*) Hoover Inst Pr.

MacKay-Robinson, Christina. Edd the Astronaut. (Illus.). 32p. (J). (gr. k-3). 1992. pap. 4.95 (*0-563-36062-3*, BBC-Parkwest) Parkwest Pubns.

— Edd's Ghost Story. (Illus.). 32p. (J). (gr. k-3). 1992. pap. 4.95 (*0-563-36063-1*, BBC-Parkwest) Parkwest Pubns.

MacKay-Robinson, Christina & Faulkner, Keith. Edd the Duck in Storyland. (Illus.). 32p. (J). (gr. k-3). 1992. 12.95 (*0-563-36046-1*, BBC-Parkwest) Parkwest Pubns.

Mackay, Roderick & Reynolds, William. Algonquin. (Illus.). 120p. 40.00 (*1-55046-088-9*, Pub. by Boston Mills Pr CN) Genl Dist Srvs.

MacKay, Ron. Hawker Sea Fury in Action. (Aircraft in Action Ser.). (Illus.). 50p. 1991. pap. 8.95 (*0-89747-267-5*, 1117) Squad Sig Pubns.

— Lancaster in Action. (Aircraft in Action Ser.). (Illus.). 50p. 1982. pap. 8.95 (*0-89747-130-X*, 1052) Squad Sig Pubns.

— 381st Bomb Group. (Groups - Squadrons Ser.). (Illus.). 64p. 1994. pap. 9.95 (*0-89747-314-0*) Squad Sig Pubns.

MacKay, Ronald & Allan, James. Bridging the Computer GAP 10-14. (C). 1989. 75.00 (*0-685-52506-6*, Pub. by Jordanhill College UK) St Mut.

An Asterisk (*) at the beginning of an entry indicates that the title is appearing in BIP for the first time.

Mackay, Ronald & Mountford, A. J., eds. English for Specific Purposes: A Case Study Approach. LC 78-319777. (Applied Linguistics & Language Study Ser.). 239p. reprint ed. pap. 68.20 (*0-317-09518-8*, 2020988) Bks Demand.

Mackay, Ronald W. Towards a United States of Europe. LC 75-31435. 160p. 1976. reprint ed. text ed. 59.75 (*0-8371-8509-2*, MATU, Greenwood Pr) Greenwood.

MacKay, Ruth, et al, eds. Empathy in the Helping Relationship. LC 89-11408. 208p. 1989. 25.95 (*0-8261-6140-5*) Springer Pub.

Mackay, S. E., jt. auth. see Trzeciak, John.

Mackay, Sheena. Dunedin. LC 93-15236. 296p. 1993. reprint ed. 21.95 (*1-55921-093-1*) Moyer Bell.

Mackay, Sheila. Bridge Across the Century. (C). 1989. 35.00 (*0-948473-00-2*) St Mut.

— Faces of Leith. (Illus.). (C). 1989. 30.00 (*0-948473-01-0*) St Mut.

— The Forth Bridge: A Picture History. (Illus.). 112p. (C). 1989. 100.00 (*0-948473-13-4*) St Mut.

Mackay, Shena. A Bowl of Cherries. 192p. 1992. 16.95 (*1-55921-070-2*) Moyer Bell.

— A Bowl of Cherries. 192p. 1994. pap. 9.95 (*1-55921-114-8*) Moyer Bell.

— Dreams of Dead Women's Handbags: Collected Stories. LC 94-15578. 480p. 1994. 24.95 (*1-55921-121-0*) Moyer Bell.

MacKay, Shena. Dunedin. 1994. pap. 5.95 (*1-55921-119-9*) Moyer Bell.

Mackay, Shena, ed. Such Devoted Sisters. 336p. 1994. reprint ed. 21.95 (*1-55921-110-5*) Moyer Bell.

MacKay, Susan E. Field Glossary of Agricultural Terms in French & English. Drenkhahn, Betty Jo, ed. LC 84-82622. (International Programs in Agriculture Ser.). 197p. (Orig.). 1985. pap. text ed. 4.00 (*0-9614109-0-6*) Intl Prog Agricult.

Mackay, T. F., jt. ed. see Hill, W. G.

Mackay, Thomas, ed. A Plea for Liberty. LC 81-80950. 565p. 1982. reprint ed. 20.00 (*0-913966-95-9*); reprint ed. pap. 7.00 (*0-913966-96-7*) Liberty Fund.

Mackay, Thomas & Nicholls, George. History of the English Poor Law, 3 vols., Set, Vols. 1-3. rev. ed. LC 66-19700. (Reprints of Economic Classics Ser.). 1967. reprint ed. 150.00 (*0-678-00277-0*) Kelley.

MacKay, Thomas W., jt. auth. see Hayes, Peter C.

MacKay, Valerie, ed. see MacKay, Donald M.

***MacKay, Virginia.** Northern Delights. (Illus.). 108p. 1994. pap. text ed. 8.00 (*1-885781-00-8*) Soapstone Pr.

***Mackay, W. P.** Grace & Truth: Under Twelve Different Aspects. Austin, Bobby W., ed. 288p. 1995. pap. write for info. (*0-9639640-4-6*) Grace Vision.

— La Gracia y la Verdad. Austin, Bobby W., ed. Arancibia, Rene, tr. 288p. 1995. pap. write for info. (*0-9639640-5-4*) Grace Vision.

Mackay, Wendy E., intro. Resources in Human-Computer Interaction. 1100p. 1990. text ed. 119.95 (*0-89791-373-6*, 219901) Assn Compu Machinery.

Mackay, William, ed. see Denby, Edwin.

MacKay, William M. & Conte, Mario. An Introduction to the Physics of Particle Accelerators. 250p. (C). 1991. text ed. 74.00 (*981-02-0812-X*); pap. text ed. 36.00 (*981-02-0813-8*) World Scientific Pub.

MacKaye, Arvia. The Battle for the Sunlight. 2nd ed. 62p. 1983. reprint ed. pap. 5.00 (*0-932776-07-8*) Adonis Pr.

MacKaye, Arvia, tr. see Steffen, Albert.

MacKaye Ege, Arvia. A Biography of Percy & Marion MacKaye. (Illus.). 730p. 1991. write for info. (*0-318-66785-1*) Kennebec River.

MacKaye, Maria E. The Abbess of Port Royal, & Other French Studies. 1977. 12.95 (*0-8369-7228-7*, 8027) Ayer.

MacKaye, Percy. Epoch: The Life of Steele MacKaye Genius of the Theatre, in Relation to His Time & Contemporaries, a Memoir, 2 vols., Set. LC 27-25140. reprint ed. 69.00 (*0-403-00077-7*) Scholarly.

— Epoch: The Life of Steele MacKaye, Genius of the Theatre, in Relation to His Times & Contemporaries, a Memoir, 2 vols., Set. (BCL1-PS American Literature Ser.). 1992. reprint ed. lib. bdg. 150.00 (*0-7812-6790-0*) Rprt Serv.

MacKaye, Percy & Torrence, Ridgely. Miami Poets: Percy MacKaye & Ridgely Torrence. Pratt, William, ed. (Keepsakes Ser.). (Illus.). 74p. (Orig.). 1988. pap. text ed. write for info. (*0-918761-02-6*) Miami U Pubns.

MacKaye, Percy, tr. see Steffen, Albert.

Mackaye, William R. Washington Post Sunday Crosswords, Vol. 4. 1994. pap. 8.00 (*0-8129-2396-0*, Times Bks) Random.

Mackaye, William R., jt. ed. see Lutwiniak, William.

Mackechnie, John. The Clan MacLean. (Johnston & Bacon Clan Histories Ser.). (Illus.). 32p. 1993. reprint ed. pap. 8.95 (*0-685-69987-0*, 9615) Clearfield Co.

Mackechnie, John, comp. Catalogue of Gaelic Manuscripts in Selected Libraries in Great Britain & Ireland, 2 vols, Set. 1973. lib. bdg. 265.00 (*0-8161-0832-3*, Hall Library) G K Hall.

MacKeen, Leslie A. Who Can Fix It? Thatch, Nancy R., ed. LC 89-31819. (Books for Students by Students Ser.). (Illus.). 26p. (J). (gr. k-3). 1989. lib. bdg. 14.95 (*0-933849-19-2*) Landmark Edns.

MacKeever, Frank C. Native & Naturalized Plants of Nantucket. Ahles, Harry E., ed. LC 68-19673. 160p. 1968. 22.50 (*0-87023-037-9*) U of Mass Pr.

MacKeever, Maggie. An Eligible Connection. 1980. pap. 1.75 (*0-449-50029-2*, Coventry) Fawcett.

— The Misses Millikin. 224p. (Orig.). 1980. pap. 1.75 (*0-449-50074-8*, Coventry) Fawcett.

Mackeever, Samuel A., ed. see Sutton, Charles.

MacKeigan, John M. & Cataldo, Peter A., eds. Intestinal Stomas: Principles, Techniques, & Management. LC 93-7281. 1993. 85.00 (*0-942219-40-6*) Quality Med Pub.

MacKeigan, John M. & Hillary, Kathleen M. Colon & Rectal Cancer. Grin, Oliver D. & Bouwman, Dorothy L., eds. (Patient Education Ser.). (Illus.). 30p. 1990. pap. text ed. 3.00 (*0-929689-44-5*) Ludann Co.

— Rectal Bleeding & Colon Polyps. Grin, Oliver D. & Bouwman, Dorothy L., eds. (Patient Education Ser.). (Illus.). 26p. 1990. pap. text ed. 3.00 (*0-929689-43-7*) Ludann Co.

MacKeith, Stephen, jt. auth. see Cohen, David C.

Mackell, Phyllis, ed. see Penn-Brown, Adelle.

***MacKellar, Robin.** God Has No Grandchildren. (Orig.). 1995. pap. 8.95 (*0-88270-726-4*) Bridge Pub.

Mackellar, Thompson, ed. see Martin, Joyce L.

***Mackellav, Colin.** Yamaha Racing Motorcycle Factory Production. (Illus.). 192p. 1995. 34.95 (*1-85223-920-4*, Pub. by Crowood UK) Motorbooks Intl.

MacKelvie, Charles F. & Handler, Marcia S. The Trustee's Guide to Board Duties, Responsibilities & Liabilities. LC 92-48301. 92p. 1993. 24.95 (*1-882198-15-8*) Hlthcare Fin Mgmt.

Macken, C. A. & Perelson, A. S. Branching Processes Applied to Cell Surface Aggregation Phenomena. (Lecture Notes in Biomathematics Ser.: Vol. 58). vii, 122p. 1985. pap. 28.20 (*0-387-15656-9*) Spr-Verlag.

— Stem Cell Proliferation & Differentiation. (Lecture Notes in Biomathematics Ser.: Vol. 76). viii, 113p. 1988. pap. 24.00 (*0-387-50183-5*) Spr-Verlag.

Macken, J. J. The Employment Revolution. iv, 138p. 1992. pap. 33.00 (*1-86287-099-3*, Pub. by Federation Pr AU) W W Gaunt.

Macken, J. J., et al. The Law of Employment. 3rd ed. xxxiv, 618p. 1990. pap. 59.50 (*0-455-20965-0*, Pub. by Law Bk Co) W W Gaunt.

Macken, James J. Award Restructuring. 165p. 1989. pap. 27.50 (*1-86287-028-4*, Pub. by Federation Pr AU) W W Gaunt.

Macken, John S. The Autonomy Theme in the Church Dogmatics: Karl Barth & His Critics. 244p. (C). 1990. 74.95 (*0-521-34626-6*) Cambridge U Pr.

Macken, Walter. The Bogman. 288p. 1994. reprint ed. pap. 11.95 (*0-86322-184-X*, Pub. by Brandon Bk Pubs IE) Irish Bks Media.

— Brown Lord of the Mountain. 284p. 1995. reprint ed. pap. 11.95 (*0-614-06646-8*, Pub. by Brandon Bk Pubs IE) Irish Bks Media.

— Flight of the Doves. LC 91-3922. (YA). 1992. pap. 14.00 (*0-671-73801-1*, S&S Bks Young Read) S&S Childrens.

— Island of the Great Yellow Ox. LC 90-22515. 192p. (YA). (gr. 5-9). 1991. pap. 14.00 (*0-671-73800-3*, S&S Bks Young Read) S&S Childrens.

— Island of the Great Yellow Ox. LC 90-22515. 192p. (J). (gr. 5-9). 1993. pap. 2.95 (*0-671-86689-3*, Half Moon Paper) S&S Childrens.

— Quench the Moon. 412p. 1995. pap. 11.95 (*0-86322-201-3*, Pub. by Brandon Bk Pubs IE) Irish Bks Media.

— Rain on the Wind. 288p. 1994. reprint ed. pap. 11.95 (*0-86322-185-8*, Pub. by Brandon Bk Pubs IE) Irish Bks Media.

Mackendrick, John, tr. see Buchner, Georg.

Mackendrick, Louis. Al Purdy & His Works. 56p. (C). 1990. pap. text ed. 9.95 (*1-55022-058-6*, Pub. by ECW Press CN) Genl Dist Srvs.

MacKendrick, Louis. Robert Harlow & His Works. (Canadian Author Studies). 57p. (C). 1989. pap. text ed. 9.95 (*0-920763-90-1*, Pub. by ECW Press CN) Genl Dist Srvs.

MacKendrick, Louis K. Some Other Reality: Alice Munro's Something I've Been Meaning to Tell You. (Canadian Fiction Studies: No. 25). 120p. (C). 1993. pap. text ed. 14.95 (*1-55022-129-9*, Pub. by ECW Press CN) Genl Dist Srvs.

MacKendrick, Louise. Passion's Thief. 1978. pap. 1.95 (*0-8439-0573-5*) Dorchester Pub Co.

MacKendrick, Paul. The Greek Stones Speak: The Story of Archaeology in Greek Lands. (Illus.). 576p. 1983. pap. 13.95 (*0-393-30111-7*) Norton.

— The Mute Stones Speak: The Story of Archaeology in Italy. (Illus.). 1983. pap. 14.95 (*0-393-30119-2*) Norton.

— The Philosophical Books of Cicero. LC 89-34979. 400p. 1989. text ed. 55.00 (*0-312-03623-X*) St Martin.

— The Roman Mind at Work. LC 80-13022. (Anvil Ser.). 192p. 1980. reprint ed. pap. text ed. 8.50 (*0-89874-200-5*) Krieger.

MacKendrick, Paul L. The Athenian Aristocracy, 399 to 31 B. C. LC 69-12728. (Martin Classical Lectures: No. 23). 120p. reprint ed. pap. 35.70 (*0-7837-2294-X*, 2057382) Bks Demand.

— The Dacian Stones Speak. LC 73-16210. (Illus.). 270p. reprint ed. pap. 77.00 (*0-7837-3753-X*, 2043570) Bks Demand.

— The North African Stones Speak. LC 79-18534. (Illus.). 456p. reprint ed. pap. 130.00 (*0-7837-6860-5*, 2046689) Bks Demand.

MacKendrick, Paul L & Howe, Herbert M, eds. Classics in Translation, 2 vols. Incl. Vol. 1. Greek Literature. 444p. 1959. 14.95 (*0-299-80895-5*); Vol. 2. Latin Literature. 452p. 1959. 14.95 (*0-299-80896-3*); 1959. write for info. (*0-318-56167-0*) U of Wis Pr.

Mackenfuss, Pam, jt. auth. see Abbott, Fran W.

MacKenna, B. R. & Callander, R. Illustrated Physiology. 5th ed. (Illus.). 352p. 1991. pap. text ed. 29.95 (*0-443-04095-8*) Churchill.

MacKenna, David W. Field Training for Medium & Small City Police Departments: A Program Planning Manual. 118p. (Orig.). 1985. pap. text ed. 10.00 (*0-936440-69-4*) U TX SUPA.

MacKenna, David W., ed. see Seminar on Grant Proposal Development Staff.

MacKenna, John. Clare: A Novel. 181p. 1994. pap. 13.95 (*0-85640-467-5*, Pub. by Blackstaff Pr IE) Dufour.

— The Fallen & Other Stories. 169p. 1993. pap. 15.95 (*0-85640-495-0*, Pub. by Blackstaff Pr IE) Dufour.

Mackenna, Robert W. As Shadows Lengthen: Later Essays. LC 67-26759. (Essay Index Reprint Ser.). 1977. 18.95 (*0-8369-0653-5*) Ayer.

MacKenna, Stephen, ed. see Plotinus.

MacKenna, Stephen, tr. see Plotinus.

Mackenna, Stephen, tr. see Turnbull, Grace R., ed.

Mackenney, Richard. The City-State, 1500-1700: Republican Liberty in an Age of Princely Power. LC 88-13075. (Studies in European History). (C). 1989. pap. 10.95 (*0-391-03598-3*) Humanities.

— Sixteenth Century Europe: Expansion & Conflict. 1993. pap. 18.95 (*0-312-06739-9*) St Martin.

Mackenroth, Donald R. HP 48SX Programming Examples. (Illus.). 224p. 1991. pap. text ed. 26.95 (*0-685-49803-4*) Addison-Wesley.

— Practical Examples for: HP48 Calculator. 1992. pap. 24.95 (*0-201-56325-8*) Addison-Wesley.

— The Waite Group's QBASIC Primer Plus. (Waite Group Ser.). 550p. (Orig.). 1991. pap. 24.95 (*0-672-22830-0*) Sams.

Mackenroth, Donald R. & Sands, Leo G. Illustrated Encyclopedia of Solid State Circuits & Applications. LC 84-23077. (Illus.). 353p. 1984. text ed. 32.95 (*0-13-450537-9*, Busn) P-H.

Mackensen, G., ed. see Ophthalmic Microsurgery Study Group Staff.

Mackensen, Lutz. Deutsches Woerterbuch. 1263p. (GER.). 1986. 69.95 (*0-8288-1978-5*, M7339) Fr & Eur.

— Ursprung der Woerter: Etymologisches Woerterbuch der Deutschen Sprache. 446p. (GER.). 1985. 49.95 (*0-7859-8406-2*, 3517008583) Fr & Eur.

MacKenthun, Carole. Biblical Bulletin Boards. (Helping Hand Ser.). 48p. (J). (gr. k-4). 1984. student ed 7.95 (*0-86653-197-1*, SS 814, Shining Star Pubns) Good Apple.

— Celebrate Summer. (Celebrate Ser.). (Illus.). 144p. (J). (gr. k-3). 1985. student ed 11.95 (*0-86653-265-X*, SS 837, Shining Star Pubns) Good Apple.

MacKenthun, Carole & Dwyer, Paulinus. Faith. (Fruit of the Spirit Ser.). (Illus.). 48p. (J). (gr. 2-7). 1986. student ed 7.95 (*0-86653-361-3*, SS 874, Shining Star Pubns) Good Apple.

— Gentleness. (Fruit of the Spirit Ser.). 48p. (J). (gr. 2 up). 1987. pap. 7.95 (*0-86653-395-8*, SS879, Shining Star Pubns) Good Apple.

— Goodness. (Fruit of the Spirit Ser.). (Illus.). 48p. (J). (gr. 2-7). 1986. student ed 7.95 (*0-86653-363-X*, SS 875, Shining Star Pubns) Good Apple.

— Joy. (Fruit of the Spirit Ser.). (Illus.). 48p. (J). (gr. 2-7). 1986. student ed 7.95 (*0-86653-360-5*, SS 873, Shining Star Pubns) Good Apple.

— Kindness. (Fruit of the Spirit Ser.). (Illus.). 48p. (J). (gr. 2 up). 1987. pap. 7.95 (*0-86653-379-6*, SS880, Shining Star Pubns) Good Apple.

— Love. (Fruit of the Spirit Ser.). (Illus.). 48p. (J). (gr. 2-7). 1986. student ed 7.95 (*0-86653-359-1*, SS 872, Shining Star Pubns) Good Apple.

— Patience. (Fruit of the Spirit Ser.). (Illus.). 48p. (J). (gr. 2-7). 1986. student ed 7.95 (*0-86653-364-8*, SS 876, Shining Star Pubns) Good Apple.

— Peace. (Fruit of the Spirit Ser.). (Illus.). 48p. (J). (gr. 2-7). 1986. student ed 7.95 (*0-86653-365-6*, SS 877, Shining Star Pubns) Good Apple.

— Self-Control. (Fruit of the Spirit Ser.). (Illus.). 48p. (J). (gr. 2 up). 1987. pap. 7.95 (*0-86653-396-6*, SS878, Shining Star Pubns) Good Apple.

***MacKenthun, Carole & Thoresen, Kathy.** One Hundred Best Ideas for Primary Language Arts. (One Hundred Best Ideas Ser.). 112p. (J). (gr. k-3). 1994. teacher ed, pap. 9.95 (*1-57310-001-3*) Teachng & Lrning Co.

MacKenthun, Kenneth M. & Bregman, Jacob I. Environmental Regulations Handbook. 344p. 1991. 69.95 (*0-87371-494-6*, KF3775) Lewis Pubs.

MacKenty, John E. Apportionment of Death Taxes. 1988. write for info. (*0-318-61708-0*) Am Coll Trust & Est.

MacKenzie. District Heating Thermal Generation & Distribution. LC 78-40890. 1979. 88.00 (*0-08-022711-2*, Pub. by Pergamon Repr UK) Franklin.

Mackenzie. A Theory of Group Structures, 2 vols, Vol. 2. 550p. 1976. Set. text ed. 123.00 (*0-677-05330-4*) Gordon & Breach.

MacKenzie, A. History of the Frasers of Lovat with Genealogy of the Principal Families of the Name; to Which Is Added Those of Dunballock & Phopacy. (Illus.). 761p. 1990. reprint ed. lib. bdg. 113.00 (*0-8328-1464-4*); reprint ed. pap. 105.00 (*0-8328-1465-2*) Higginson Bk Co.

— Munroe: History of the Munros of Fowlis, with Genealogies of the Principal Families of the Names, to Which Are Added Those of Lexington & New England. 632p. 1992. reprint ed. lib. bdg. 105.00 (*0-8328-2694-4*); reprint ed. pap. 95.00 (*0-8328-2695-2*) Higginson Bk Co.

MacKenzie, A. B., et al. Natural Decay Series Radionuclide Studies at the Needle's Eye Natural Analogue, No. EUR 13126. 62p. 1991. pap. 9.00 (*92-826-2347-5*, CD-NA-13126-EN-C, Pub. by Europ Com) UNIPUB.

MacKenzie, A. R., jt. auth. see Colbeck, I.

Mackenzie, Agnes M. David One: On the Declaration of Arbroath. 26p. 1985. 22.00 (*0-317-39135-6*, Pub. by Saltire Soc) St Mut.

— The Foundations of Scotland: From the Earliest Times to 1286. LC 75-41505. 316p. 1979. reprint ed. text ed. 59.75 (*0-8371-8703-6*, MAFN, Greenwood Pr) Greenwood.

— Robert Bruce, King of Scots. LC 78-128880. (Select Bibliographies Reprint Ser.). 1977. reprint ed. 24.95 (*0-8369-5500-5*) Ayer.

— The Scotland of Queen Mary & the Religious Wars, 1513-1638. LC 75-41506. (Illus.). 404p. 1976. reprint ed. text ed. 65.00 (*0-8371-8704-4*, MASQ, Greenwood Pr) Greenwood.

Mackenzie, Alastair, jt. auth. see Benson, Jeffrey.

Mackenzie, Alec. The Time Trap: The New Version of the 20-Year Classic on Time Management. 176p. 1991. pap. 14.95 (*0-8144-7760-7*) AMACOM.

Mackenzie, Alec, jt. auth. see Engstrom, Ted.

Mackenzie, Alexander. History of the Highland Clearances. 532p. (C). 1883. pap. 45.00 (*0-9505884-7-4*, Pub. by Mercat Pr Bks UK) St Mut.

— Mackenzie's Rock. (Shorey Historical Ser.). 39p. reprint ed. pap. 1.95 (*0-8466-0048-X*, S48) Shorey.

— Voyages from Montreal Through the Continent of North America to the Frozen & Pacific Oceans in 1789 & 1793, with an Account of the Rise & State of the Fur Trade, 2 vols. LC 72-2721. (American Explorers Ser.). reprint ed. 80.00 (*0-404-54912-8*) AMS Pr.

Mackenzie, Alexander S. First Man West. Sheppe, Walter, ed. LC 76-3568. (Illus.). 366p. 1976. reprint ed. text ed. 65.00 (*0-8371-8789-3*, SHFM, Greenwood Pr) Greenwood.

— The Life of Paul Jones. LC 70-160981. (Select Bibliographies Reprint Ser.). 1977. reprint ed. 23.95 (*0-8369-5849-7*) Ayer.

Mackenzie, Alison M. Adult Age Differences in Memory. (C). 1991. 35.00 (*1-85041-037-2*, Pub. by Univ Nottingham UK) St Mut.

Mackenzie, Alistair. Golf Architecture. rev. ed. 1988. 28.00 (*0-940889-16-1*) Classics Golf.

***Mackenzie, Alister.** The Spirit of St. Andrews. LC 95-2712. 1995. write for info. (*0-615-00484-9*) Sleeping Bear Software.

— The Spirit of St. Andrews. (Illus.). 300p. 1995. 24.95 (*1-886947-00-7*) Sleepng Bear.

Mackenzie, Anne, ed. see Nelson, Mary C.

Mackenzie, Barbara A. Shakespeare's Sonnets: Their Relation to His Life. LC 78-6965. reprint ed. 11.50 (*0-404-04135-3*) AMS Pr.

MacKenzie, C. El Amoroso Creador (The Caring Creator) (SPA.). Date not set. 9.99 (*1-56063-305-0*, 490445) Editorial Unilit.

Mackenzie, C. Ninos De la Biblia (Children of the Bible) (SPA.). Date not set. 9.99 (*1-56063-546-0*, 498748) Editorial Unilit.

— Nuestro Bebe (Our Baby Book) (SPA.). Date not set. 10.99 (*1-56063-613-0*, 494014) Editorial Unilit.

Mackenzie, Campbell, tr. see Bonnechose, Emile de.

MacKenzie, Carol. Whirr Pop Click Clang. LC 94-8525. (Illus.). (J). 1994. write for info. (*0-688-13292-8*, Tambourine Bks) Morrow.

— Whirr Pop Click Clang. limited ed. LC 94-8525. (Illus.). (J). 1994. Limited Ed. write for info. (*0-688-13293-6*, Tambourine Bks) Morrow.

MacKenzie, Catherine. Alexander Graham Bell: the Man Who Contracted Space. LC 77-150193. (Select Bibliographies Reprint Ser.). 1977. reprint ed. 33.95 (*0-8369-5706-7*) Ayer.

Mackenzie, Chalmers J. The Mackenzie--McNaughton Wartime Letters. Thistle, Mel, ed. LC 72-185741. 192p. reprint ed. pap. 54.80 (*0-317-09549-8*, 2014433) Bks Demand.

Mackenzie, Charles E. Coded-Character Sets: History & Development. LC 77-90165. (IBM Systems Programming Ser.). 1980. text ed. write for info. (*0-201-14460-3*) Addison-Wesley.

MacKenzie, Charles S. The Trinity & Culture. (American University Studies: Theology & Religion: Ser. VII, Vol. 34). 150p. (C). 1987. text ed. 25.95 (*0-8204-0492-6*) P Lang Pubs.

MacKenzie, Charlotte. Psychiatry for the Rich: A History of Ticehurst Private Asylum, 1792-1917. LC 92-49160. (Wellcome Institute Series in the History of Medicine). (Illus.). 248p. 1993. 74.50 (*0-415-08891-7*, A9941) Routledge.

MacKenzie, Christine L. & Iberall, Thea. The Grasping Hand. LC 93-47171. 482p. 1994. 142.75 (*0-444-81746-8*, North Holland) Elsevier.

Mackenzie, Clara C. Wolf Smeller: A Biography of John Fredson, Native Alaskan. LC 85-23011. (Alaskana Book Ser.: No. 41). (Illus.). 201p. (Orig.). 1986. 21.95 (*0-935094-10-5*); pap. 10.95 (*0-935094-11-3*) Alaska Pacific.

MacKenzie, Clyde L., Jr. Fisheries of Raritan Bay. LC 91-43031. (Illus.). 304p. (C). 1992. text ed. 45.00 (*0-8135-1839-3*); pap. text ed. 16.95 (*0-8135-1840-7*) Rutgers U Pr.

Mackenzie, Compton. Greek Memories. LC 86-13217. (Foreign Intelligence Book Ser.). 650p. 1987. text ed. 49.95 (*0-313-27006-6*, U7006, Greenwood Pr) Greenwood.

MacKenzie, Compton. Guy & Pauline. 1988. reprint ed. lib. bdg. 69.00 (*0-7812-0377-5*) Rprt Serv.

Mackenzie, Compton. Guy & Pauline. LC 71-145156. (Literature Ser.). 396p. 1972. reprint ed. 69.00 (*0-403-01084-5*) Scholarly.

— Literature in My Time. LC 67-28758. (Essay Index Reprint Ser.). 1977. 18.95 (*0-8369-0654-3*) Ayer.

— Realms of Silver. Wilkins, Mira, ed. LC 78-3934. (International Finance Ser.). (Illus.). 1979. reprint ed. lib. bdg. 35.95 (*0-405-11236-X*) Ayer.

— Sinister Street. (Twentieth-Century Classics Ser.). 832p. 1992. pap. 10.95 (*0-14-018475-9*, Penguin Classics) Viking Penguin.

MacKenzie, Craig, ed. see Head, Bessie.

Mackenzie, D. Califate of the West. 368p. 1987. 290.00 (*1-85077-163-4*, Darf Pubs Ltd) St Mut.

— Myths of Pre-Columbian America. 1972. 75.00 (*0-8490-0701-1*) Gordon Pr.

***Mackenzie, D. A.** Myths & Legends of India. (Illus.). 463p. 1989. pap. 19.50 (*9971-4-9126-5*) Heian Intl.

M

An Asterisk (*) at the beginning of an entry indicates that the title is appearing in BIP for the first time.

MacKenzie, D. N., jt. auth. see Blumhardt, J. F.

***MacKenzie, D. R. & Henry, Suzanne C., eds.** The Biosafety Results of Field Tests of Genetically Modified Plants & Microorganisms: Proceedings of an International Symposium, Kiawah Island Conference, Sponsored by ARI, November 27-30, 1990. 303p. Date not set. pap. 25.00 (0-614-04327-1) Agri Research Inst.

Mackenzie, David. Apis: The Congenial Conspirator. (East European Monographs: No. 265). 320p. 1989. text ed. 54.00 (0-88033-162-3) East Eur Quarterly.

MacKenzie, David. Arthur Irwin: A Biography. LC 93-93699. 323p. 1993. 45.00 (0-8020-2632-X) U of Toronto Pr.

— Canada & International Civil Aviation 1932-1948. 228p. 1989. text ed. 40.00 (0-8020-5828-0) U of Toronto Pr.

— Goat Husbandry. 5th ed. Goodwin, Ruth, ed. (Illus.). 384p. 1993. pap. 16.95 (0-571-16595-8) Faber & Faber.

— Ilija Garasnin. 1985. text ed. 59.00 (0-88033-073-2, 181) Col U Pr.

— Inside the Atlantic Triangle: Canada & the Entrance of Newfoundland into Confederation 1939-1949. 304p. 1986. text ed. 35.00 (0-8020-2587-0) U of Toronto Pr.

Mackenzie, David. A Manual of Manuscript Transcription for the Dictionary of the Old Spanish Language. 4th ed. Burrus, Victoria, ed. (Illus.). 182p. 1986. 25.00 (0-942260-73-2) Hispanic Seminary.

MacKenzie, David, et al. Still Married, Still Sober: Hope for Your Alcoholic Marriage. LC 91-21963. 180p. (Orig.). 1991. pap. 8.99 (0-8308-1376-4, 1376) InterVarsity.

Mackenzie, David & Curran, Michael W. A History of Russia, the Soviet Union, & Beyond. 4th ed. 912p. (C). 1993. text ed. 42.95 (0-534-17970-3) Intl Thomson.

MacKenzie, David & Curran, Michael W. A History of the Soviet Union. 2nd ed. 550p. (C). 1991. pap. 38.95 (0-534-14910-3) Intl Thomson.

MacKenzie, David, ed. see Denny, Steven.

MacKenzie, Dolly. Bargain Hunting in New Jersey: A Guide. (Illus.). 184p. (Orig.). 1988. pap. 7.95 (0-929211-00-6) Directories NJ.

MacKenzie, Donald. Inventing Accuracy: A Historical Sociology of Nuclear Missile Guidance. (Inside Technology Ser.). (Illus.). 500p. 1990. 37.50 (0-262-13258-3) MIT Pr.

— Inventing Accuracy: A Historical Sociology of Nuclear Missile Guidance. (Inside Technology Ser.). (Illus.). 480p. 1993. 20.00x (0-262-63147-4) MIT Pr.

— Knowing Machines: Essays on Technical Change. (Inside Technology Ser.). (Illus.). 360p. (C). 1995. 35.00 (0-262-13315-6) MIT Pr.

— Loose Cannon. LC 93-28769. 1994. write for info. (0-8161-5859-2) G K Hall.

— Loose Cannon: A John Raven Mystery. 160p. 1993. 17.95 (0-312-09863-4) St Martin.

Mackenzie, Donald. Raven Feathers His Nest. large type ed. 317p. 1982. 15.95 (0-7089-0787-3) Ulverscroft.

— Raven's Longest Night. large type ed. 336p. 1985. 15.95 (0-7089-1381-4) Ulverscroft.

— Statistics in Britain, Eighteen Sixty-Five to Nineteen Thirty: The Social Construction of Scientific Knowledge. 306p. 1980. 26.50 (0-85224-369-3, Pub. by Edinburgh U Pr UK) Col U Pr.

MacKenzie, Donald & Wajcman, Judy, eds. The Social Shaping of Technology. 336p. 1985. pap. 32.00 (0-335-15026-8, Open Univ Pr) Taylor & Francis.

Mackenzie, Donald, ed. see Kipling, Rudyard.

Mackenzie, Donald A. Buddhism in Pre-Christian Britain. 1977. lib. bdg. 59.95 (0-8490-1558-8) Gordon Pr.

MacKenzie, Donald A. Egyptian Myths & Legends. LC 94-14845. 1994. write for info. (0-517-11915-3, Pub. by Gramercy) Random Hse Value.

Mackenzie, Donald A. Myths of China & Japan. LC 93-46195. 1994. 9.99 (0-517-10163-7, Pub. by Gramercy) Random Hse Value.

— Otfrid Von Weissenburg: Narrator or Commentator. (Stanford University. Stanford Studies in Language & Literature: Vol. 6, Pt. 3). reprint ed. 18.00 (0-404-51812-5) AMS Pr.

— Statistics in Britain, Eighteen Sixty-Five to Nineteen Thirty: The Social Construction of Scientific Knowledge. 304p. 50.00 (0-685-04773-3, Pub. by Edinburgh U Pr UK) Col U Pr.

Mackenzie, Donald G. Planning Educational Facilities. LC 89-14610. 102p. (Orig.). (C). 1989. pap. text ed. 20.00 (0-8191-7480-7) U Pr of Amer.

MacKenzie, Donald R. & Kerst, Erna W. A Bibliographic Overview of Housing in Developing Countries: Annotated, Nos. 1225-1227. 1977. 12.50 (0-686-19686-4) CPL Biblios.

MacKenzie, Doris L. & Uchida, Craig, eds. Drugs & Crime: Evaluating Public Policy Initiatives. LC 93-35738. 316p. (C). 1994. text ed. 38.00 (0-8039-4456-X); pap. text ed. 18.95 (0-8039-4457-8) Sage.

MacKenzie, Doris L., et al, eds. Measuring Crime: Large-Scale, Long-Range Efforts. LC 89-30043. (SUNY Series in Critical Issues in Criminal Justice). 278p. 1989. 74.50 (0-7914-0144-8); pap. 24.95 (0-7914-0145-6) State U NY Pr.

Mackenzie, Dorothy. Design for the Environment. LC 91-8409. (Illus.). 176p. 1991. 35.00 (0-8478-1390-8) Rizzoli Intl.

MacKenzie, Drew, jt. auth. see Ritchie, Jean.

MacKenzie, E. T., jt. ed. see Seylaz, J.

MacKenzie, E. T., et al, eds. Neurotransmitters & the Cerebral Circulation. (L. E. R. S. Monograph Ser.: Vol. 2). (Illus.). 270p. 1984. text ed. 96.50 (0-88167-010-3) Raven.

Mackenzie, Fiona, jt. ed. see Taylor, D. R.

Mackenzie, Fred T. & MacKenzie, Judith A. Our Changing Planet: An Introduction to Earth System Science & Global Environmental Change. LC 94-10075. 387p. (C). 1994. pap. 34.67 (0-02-373653-4) Macmillan.

Mackenzie, Fred T., jt. ed. see Morse, J. W.

MacKenzie, Fred T., jt. auth. see Woodwell, George M.

MacKenzie, Frederick. British Fusilier in Revolutionary Boston. French, Allen, ed. LC 79-102237. (Select Bibliographies Reprint Ser.). 1977. 21.95 (0-8369-5122-0) Ayer.

— Diary of Frederick MacKenzie, 2 vols., 1. LC 67-29038. (Eyewitness Accounts of the American Revolution Ser., No. 1). 1968. reprint ed. 19.95 (0-405-01130-X) Ayer.

— Diary of Frederick MacKenzie, 2 vols., 2. LC 67-29038. (Eyewitness Accounts of the American Revolution Ser., No. 1). 1968. reprint ed. 19.95 (0-405-01131-8) Ayer.

— Diary of Frederick MacKenzie, 2 vols., Set. LC 67-29038. (Eyewitness Accounts of the American Revolution Ser., No. 1). 1968. reprint ed. 36.95 (0-405-01132-6) Ayer.

Mackenzie, G. Calvin. Government & Public Policy in America. 352p. 1986. 8.25 (0-685-10335-8) McGraw.

Mackenzie, G. Calvin, ed. The In-&-Outers: Presidential Appointees & Transient Government in Washington. LC 86-46281. 272p. 1987. text ed. 38.50x (0-8018-3441-4) Johns Hopkins.

MacKenzie, G. Calvin, jt. ed. see Cooper, Joseph.

Mackenzie, Gavin. The Aristocracy of Labor: The Position of Skilled Craftsmen in the American Class Structure. LC 73-80484. (Cambridge Studies in Sociology: Vol. 7). 218p. reprint ed. pap. 62.20 (0-8357-5732-3, 2027244) Bks Demand.

Mackenzie, George A., ed. see Muir, Alexander.

***Mackenzie, George H., et al.** Beam Instrumentation Workshop. (Conference Proceedings: No. 333). (Illus.). 608p. 1995. boxed 140.00 (1-56396-352-3) Am Inst Physics.

***Mackenzie, George N.** Colonial Families of the United States of America Vol. I: Main Families. (Illus.). 730p. 1995. reprint ed. 45.00 (0-8063-0223-2) Genealog Pub.

— Colonial Families of the United States of America Vol. II: Main Families. (Illus.). 941p. 1995. reprint ed. 50.00 (0-8063-0224-0) Genealog Pub.

— Colonial Families of the United States of America Vol. III: Main Families. (Illus.). 740p. 1995. reprint ed. 45.00 (0-8063-0225-9) Genealog Pub.

— Colonial Families of the United States of America Vol. IV: Main Families. (Illus.). 684p. 1995. reprint ed. 40.00 (0-8063-0226-7) Genealog Pub.

— Colonial Families of the United States of America Vol. V: Main Families. (Illus.). 719p. 1995. reprint ed. 40.00 (0-8063-0227-5) Genealog Pub.

— Colonial Families of the United States of America Vol. VI: Main Families. (Illus.). 600p. 1995. reprint ed. 40.00 (0-8063-0228-3) Genealog Pub.

— Colonial Families of the United States of America Vol. VII: Main Families. (Illus.). 605p. 1995. reprint ed. 40.00 (0-8063-0229-1) Genealog Pub.

Mackenzie, Georgena M. & Irby, A. P. Travels in the Slavonic Provinces of Turkey-In-Europe. LC 78-135816. (Eastern Europe Collection Ser.). 1971. reprint ed. 44.95 (0-405-02758-3) Ayer.

MacKenzie, Gordene O. Transgender Nation. LC 94-71363. (Illus.). 190p. (C). 1994. text ed. 41.95 (0-87972-596-6); pap. text ed. 14.95 (0-87972-597-4) Bowling Green Univ.

Mackenzie, Gordon, jt. ed. see Karekezi, Stephen.

Mackenzie-Grieve, Averil. Clara Novello, Eighteen Eighteen to Nineteen Eight. LC 79-24421. (Music Reprint Ser.). 1980. reprint ed. lib. bdg. 39.50 (0-306-76009-6) Da Capo.

— Last Years of the English Slave Trade, Liverpool 1705-1807. 331p. 1968. reprint ed. 35.00 (0-7146-1895-0, Pub. by F Cass Pubs UK) Intl Spec Bk.

Mackenzie, Harry & Polomski, Lothar, comps. One Night Stand Series, 1-1001. LC 91-7317. (Discographies Ser.: No. 44). 448p. 1991. text ed. 65.00 (0-313-27729-X, MKZ, Greenwood Pr) Greenwood.

Mackenzie, Harry, jt. auth. see Kiner, Larry F.

MacKenzie, Hector, ed. see International Trade Staff.

MacKenzie, Henry. An Account of the Life & Writings of John Home, Esq. LC 78-67532. reprint ed. 27.50 (0-404-17196-6) AMS Pr.

Mackenzie, Henry, ed. The Mirror & the Lounger. LC 78-67534. (Scottish Enlightenment Ser.). Orig. Title: The Mirrors, Nos. 1-110, the Lounger, Nos. 1-101. reprint ed. 32.50 (0-404-17675-5) AMS Pr.

Mackenzie, Hettie M. Hegel's Educational Theory & Practice. LC 79-122985. (Studies in Philosophy: No. 40). 1971. reprint ed. lib. bdg. 75.00 (0-8383-1118-0) M S G Haskell Hse.

MacKenzie, I. Scott. The Eight Thousand Fifty-One Microcontroller. 2nd ed. LC 94-8278. 384p. (C). 1994. write for info. (0-02-373660-7) Merrill.

— The Eighty Fifty-One Microprocessor. 2nd ed. (Illus.). 384p. 1994. write for info. (0-615-00147-5, Merrill Pub Co) Macmillan.

— The 8051 Microprocessor. 2nd ed. (Illus.). 384p. 1994. write for info. (0-615-00071-1, Merrill Pub Co) Macmillan.

— The 6800 Microprocessor. LC 94-32687. 578p. 1995. 66.00 (0-02-373654-2) P-H.

MacKenzie, Iain M., ed. Archaeological Theory: Progress or Posture? (Worldwide Archaeology Ser.). 192p. 1994. 51.95 (1-85628-710-6, Pub. by Avebury Pub UK) Ashgate Pub Co.

Mackenzie, Ian. British Prints: Dictionary & Price Guide. (Illus.). 360p. 1988. 89.50 (0-902028-96-0) Antique Collect.

MacKenzie, Ian, ed. see Radha, Sivananda.

Mackenzie, J. D. & Ulrich, D. R. Sol-Gel Optics, Vol. 1328. 1990. 70.00 (0-8194-0389-X) SPIE.

Mackenzie, J. S. & Van Halm, J. Innovation in the Information Chain: The Effects of Technological Development on the Provision of Scientific & Technical Information. 224p. 1989. 35.00 (0-415-03871-5, A3645) Routledge.

MacKenzie, James. The History of Health, & the Art of Preserving It. Kastenbaum, Robert, ed. LC 78-22208. (Aging & Old Age Ser.). 1979. reprint ed. lib. bdg. 37.95 (0-405-11822-8) Ayer.

Mackenzie, James J. Air Pollution's Toll on Forests. 1990. text ed. 45.00 (0-300-04569-7) Yale U Pr.

MacKenzie, James J. Breathing Easier: Taking Action on Climate Change, Air Pollution & Energy Insecurity. 24p. (Orig.). 1988. pap. text ed. 5.00 (0-915825-35-X) World Resources Inst.

— Electric & Hydrogen Vehicles: Transportation Technologies for the Twenty-First Century. large type ed. 75p. 1993. Large format. pap. 14.95 (0-915825-93-7, MAEHP) World Resources Inst.

MacKenzie, James J. & El-Ashry, Mohamed T. Air Pollution's Toll on Forests & Crops. 384p. (C). 1992. reprint ed. pap. text ed. 22.00 (0-300-05232-4) Yale U Pr.

— Ill Winds: Airborne Pollution's Toll on Trees & Crops. LC 88-51128. 84p. (Orig.). 1988. pap. text ed. 10.00 (0-915825-29-5) World Resources Inst.

MacKenzie, James J. & Walsh, Michael P. Driving Forces: Motor Vehicle Trends & Their Implications for Global Warming, Energy Strategies, & Transportation Planning. large type ed. 50p. 1990. Large format. pap. 14.95 (0-915825-61-9, MADFP) World Resources Inst.

MacKenzie, James J., et al. The Going Rate: What It Really Costs to Drive. large type ed. 32p. 1992. Large format. pap. 12.95 (0-915825-77-5, MACTP) World Resources Inst.

Mackenzie, Jean G. A Lexicon of the Fourteenth-Century Aragonese Manuscripts of Juan Fernandez de Heredia. (Dialect Ser.: No. 8). xlii, 234p. 1984. 35.00 (0-942260-48-1) Hispanic Seminary.

MacKenzie, Jeanne, ed. see Webb, Beatrice.

***MacKenzie, Jeff L.** Financial Engineering with Basic Trading: Customizing Yield-Enhancement. rev. ed. 1994. 55.00 (1-55738-802-4) Probus Pub Co.

Mackenzie, Jill W. The Golden Fairy. LC 90-70311. (Illus.). 44p. (J). (gr. 1-6). 1990. 6.95 (1-55523-336-8) Winston-Derek.

MacKenzie, John. Be Good to Yourself. (Illus.). 156p. 1981. pap. 9.95 (0-89496-026-1) Ross Bks.

Mackenzie, John. Dictionary of Bible. 976p. 1967. pap. 15.95 (0-02-087720-X) Macmillan.

— Orientalism: History, Theory, & the Arts. LC 94-43434. 1995. text ed. write for info. (0-7190-1861-7, Pub. by Manchester Univ Pr UK); text ed. write for info. (0-7190-4578-9, Pub. by Manchester Univ Pr UK) St Martin.

Mackenzie, John D. Ultrastructure Processing of Advanced Ceramics. LC 87-28574. 1988. text ed. 190.00 (0-471-62416-0) Wiley.

Mackenzie, John M. Diary, 1851. (C). 1992. text ed. 75.00 (0-86152-872-7, Pub. by Acair Ltd UK) St Mut.

MacKenzie, John M. The Empire of Nature: Hunting, Conservation & British Imperialism. (Studies in Imperialism). 320p. 1989. text ed. 62.50 (0-7190-2227-4, Pub. by Manchester Univ Pr UK) St Martin.

— Propaganda & Empire: The Manipulation of British Public Opinion, 1880-1960. LC 83-25325. (Illus.). 320p. (C). 1988. text ed. 19.95 (0-7190-1869-2, Pub. by Manchester Univ Pr UK) St Martin.

MacKenzie, John M., ed. Imperialism & Popular Culture. LC 85-13657. (Studies in Imperialism). (Illus.). 292p. 1989. reprint ed. text ed. 13.95 (0-7190-1868-4, Pub. by Manchester Univ Pr UK) St Martin.

Mackenzie, John M., ed. Popular Imperialism & the Military: 1850-1950. LC 91-17800. (Studies in Imperialism). 272p. 1992. text ed. 69.95 (0-7190-3358-6, Pub. by Manchester Univ Pr UK) St Martin.

MacKenzie, John M., ed. see Anderson, David, et al.

MacKenzie, John M., ed. see Bliss, Robert M.

MacKenzie, John M., jt. auth. see Richards, Jeffrey.

MacKenzie, John M., jt. ed. see Richards, Jeffrey.

Mackenzie, John P. Birds of Prey. LC 86-62790. (Birds of the World Ser.). (Illus.). 144p. 1986. 24.95 (1-55971-019-5) NorthWord.

MacKenzie, John P. Gamebirds. (Birds of the World Ser.: No. 4). (Illus.). 144p. 1989. 24.95 (1-55971-043-8, 0183) NorthWord.

Mackenzie, John P. Seabirds. (Birds of the World Ser.). (Illus.). 144p. 1987. 24.95 (0-942802-52-7) NorthWord.

— Song Birds. 1990. 24.95 (1-55971-091-8) NorthWord.

— Wading Birds. (Birds of the World Ser.). 1993. 24.95 (1-55013-279-2) U of Toronto Pr.

— Waterfowl. (Illus.). 144p. 1988. 24.95 (1-55971-018-7) NorthWord.

MacKenzie, John R. Organized Labor Education & Training Programs. 45p. 1984. 5.50 (0-318-22163-2, IN286) Ctr Educ Trng Employ.

MacKenzie, John W. Chronicle of the Kings of Scotland. LC 72-1037. (Maitland Club, Glasgow. Publications: No. 8). reprint ed. 18.00 (0-404-52935-6) AMS Pr.

Mackenzie, Josephine, ed. see Hall, Sharlot M.

MacKenzie, Joy. Bible Read-to-Me: ABC. LC 87-18337. 48p. (J). (ps-1). 1988. 9.99 (1-55513-861-6, Chariot Bks) Chariot Family.

— Bible Read-to-Me: 1-2-3. LC 87-18334. 48p. (J). (ps-1). 1988. 9.99 (1-55513-480-7, Chariot Bks) Chariot Family.

— The Big Book of Bible Crafts & Projects. (Illus.). 212p. (Orig.). (J). (ps-4). 1981. pap. 15.99 (0-310-70151-1, 14019P) Zondervan.

— Hunting for Bible Treasures: One Hundred One Games, Puzzles, Projects, Crafts, Experiments, & More. 1994. pap. 9.99 (0-310-59751-X) Zondervan.

MacKenzie, Joy & Hodges, Lynn. Keep 'Em Singing. 160p. 1994. pap. 11.99 (0-310-48221-6) Zondervan.

MacKenzie, Joy, jt. auth. see Forle, Imogene.

MacKenzie, Joy, jt. auth. see Forte, Imogene.

MacKenzie, Joy, et al. A Big Book of Bible Games & Puzzles. 192p. (J). (gr. 1-6). 1982. reprint ed. pap. 15.99 (0-310-70271-2, 14029P) Zondervan.

MacKenzie, Judith A., jt. auth. see Mackenzie, Fred T.

MacKenzie, Judith-Anne & Phillips, Mary. A Practical Approach to Land Law. 332p. (C). 1989. 160.00 (1-85431-046-1, Pub. by Blackstone Pr UK) St Mut.

— A Practical Approach to Land Law. 3rd ed. 332p. (C). 1991. text ed. 35.00 (1-85431-143-3, Pub. by Blackstone Pr UK) W W Gaunt.

— A Practical Approach to Land Law. 4th ed. 1993. 46.00 (1-85431-266-9, Pub. by Blackstone Pr UK) W W Gaunt.

— A Practical Approach to Land Law. 5th ed. 342p. 1994. text ed. 36.00 (1-85431-354-1, Pub. by Blackstone Pr UK) W W Gaunt.

MacKenzie, Julia, jt. auth. see Corey, D. Stephen.

Mackenzie, Julie. Horse Law. 1988. pap. 100.00 (0-7219-1130-7, Scientific) St Mut.

MacKenzie, K. & Dempster, J. Case Presentations in Otolaryngology. (Illus.). 180p. 1992. pap. 30.00 (0-7506-1356-4) Buttrwrth-Heinemann.

Mackenzie, K. A. A Theory of Group Structures, Vol. 1. xviii, 242p. 1976. text ed. 85.00 (0-677-05310-X) Gordon & Breach.

— A Theory of Group Structures, Vol. 2. xviii, 270p. 1976. text ed. 69.00 (0-677-05320-7) Gordon & Breach.

MacKenzie, K. Roy. Classics in Group Psychotherapy. LC 91-35412. 356p. 1992. lib. bdg. 45.00 (0-89862-799-0) Guilford Pr.

— Introduction to Time-Limited Group Psychotherapy. LC 89-17508. 400p. 1989. text ed. 40.00 (0-88048-168-4, 8168) Am Psychiatric.

***MacKenzie, K. Roy, ed.** Effective Use of Group Therapy in Managed Care. LC 94-3529. (Clinical Practice). 1994. boxed write for info. (0-88048-492-6) Am Psychiatric.

MacKenzie, K. Roy, jt. ed. see Bernard, Harold S.

MacKenzie, K. Roy, jt. ed. see Dies, Robert R.

MacKenzie, K. Roy, jt. auth. see Harper-Giuffre, Heather.

Mackenzie, Katherine. Wild Flowers of the Midwest. LC 75-44840. (Illus.). 1976. pap. 2.95 (0-912766-33-6) Tundra Bks.

MacKenzie, Katherine. Wild Flowers of the South. (Illus.). 1977. pap. 2.95 (0-912766-56-5) Tundra Bks.

Mackenzie-Kennedy, C. The Atlantic Blue Riband: Evolution of the Express Liner. 1993. 68.00 (1-85072-133-5, Pub. by W Sessions UK) St Mut.

Mackenzie, Kenneth. Turkey in Transition: The West's Neglected Ally. (C). 1984. 35.00 (0-907967-20-5, Pub. by Inst Euro Def & Strat UK) St Mut.

MacKenzie, Kenneth D. Organizational Design. Voigt, Melvin J., ed. LC 85-13454. (Communication & Information Science Ser.). 304p. 1986. text ed. 55.00 (0-89391-348-0); pap. 29.50 (0-685-73695-4) Ablex Pub.

— Practitioner's Guide for Improving an Organization. LC 95-94247. 159p. (Orig.). 1995. pap. text ed. 39.95 (0-9646185-0-8) Mackenzie & Co.

MacKenzie, Kenneth D., ed. see Jabes, Jak.

Mackenzie, Kenneth D., ed. see Kiesler, Sara B.

Mackenzie, Kenneth D., ed. see Pfeffer, Jeffrey.

Mackenzie, Kenneth D., ed. see Simmons, Richard E.

Mackenzie, Kenneth D., ed. see Tuggle, Francis D.

Mackenzie, Kenneth R. The Royal Masonic Cyclopaedia. 790p. 1994. pap. 49.95 (1-56459-420-3) Kessinger Pub.

Mackenzie, Kennety R., tr. see Mickiewicz, Adam.

***Mackenzie, Kirill.** The General Theory of Lie Groupoids & Lie Algebroids. (London Mathematical Society Lecture Note Ser.: No. 213). 300p. (C). 1995. pap. write for info. (0-521-49928-3) Cambridge U Pr.

Mackenzie, Leslie, ed. The Complete Directory for People with Chronic Illness, 1994. 600p. 1993. 135.00 (0-939300-56-7); pap. 125.00 (0-939300-55-9) Grey Hse Pub.

— Complete Directory for People with Disabilities. 800p. 1992. text ed. 125.00 (0-939300-19-2); pap. text ed. 99.95 (0-685-60585-X) Grey Hse Pub.

— The Complete Directory for People with Learning Disabilities, 1993. 800p. pap. 125.00 (0-939300-29-X); boxed write for info. (0-939300-24-9) Grey Hse Pub.

— The Directory of Business Information Resources: Associations, Newsletters, Magazines & Trade Shows. 1992. 135.00 (0-939300-11-7); pap. 120.00 (0-939300-15-X) Grey Hse Pub.

— The Directory of Business Information Resources, 1994. 887p. 1994. pap. 145.00 (0-939300-26-5) Grey Hse Pub.

— Directory of Business to Business Catalogs. 600p. 1992. pap. text ed. 110.00 (0-939300-16-8) Grey Hse Pub.

— The Encyclopedia of Education Information for Elementary & Secondary School Professionals. 563p. 1994. pap. 125.00 (0-939300-59-1) Grey Hse Pub.

MacKenzie, Lewis, tr. Autumn Wind: A Selection from the Poems of Issa. LC 83-48874. (Illus.). 126p. (C). 1984. pap. 8.00 (0-87011-657-6) Kodansha.

Mackenzie, Lord. Studies in Roman Law. Kirkpatrick, John, ed. LC 90-56337. 524p. 1991. reprint ed. lib. bdg. 83.00 (0-912004-88-6) W W Gaunt.

MacKenzie, Louis A., Jr. Pascal's Lettres Provinciales: The Motif & Practice of Fragmentation. LC 88-61122. 146p. (ENG & FRE.). 1988. lib. bdg. 24.95 (0-917786-63-7) Summa Pubns.

MacKenzie, Malcolm S. People Portraits. LC 88-72341. (Illus.). 96p. (Orig.). 1990. pap. 7.00 (0-916383-82-2) Aegina Pr.

— Selected Poems, 1981-1984. 103p. 1984. 4.95 (0-89697-180-5) Intl Univ Pr.

MacKenzie, Manfred. Communities of Honor & Love in Henry James. 247p. 1975. 26.00 (0-674-15160-7) HUP.

An Asterisk (*) at the beginning of an entry indicates that the title is appearing in BIP for the first time.

MacKenzie, Margaret & MacKenzie, Roderick. The Ultimate Guide to Toronto. (Illus.). 240p. 1992. pap. 11.95 (0-8118-0151-9) Chronicle Bks.

MacKenzie, Marilyn. Curing Terminal Niceness: Building Healthy Volunteer-Staff Relations. 1990. pap. 7.00 (0-911029-28-1) Heritage Arts.

MacKenzie, Marilyn. Dealing with Difficult Volunteers. (Volunteer Management Ser.). 1988. 7.00 (0-911029-11-7) Heritage Arts.

MacKenzie, Marilyn & Moore, Gail. Building Credibility with the Powers That Be. 1990. pap. 7.95 (0-911029-29-X) Heritage Arts.

— Group Member's Handbook. 1993. pap. 15.00 (0-911029-42-7) Heritage Arts.

MacKenzie, Marilyn, jt. auth. see Moore, Gail.

MacKenzie, Marlin M. Tennis: The Mind Game. 1991. mass mkt. 11.95 (0-440-50271-3) Dell.

MacKenzie, Marlin M. & Denlinger, Ken. Golf: The Mind Game. 1990. pap. 11.95 (0-440-50209-8, Dell Trade Pbks) Dell.

Mackenzie, Mary M. Plato on Punishment. LC 80-6065. 272p. 1981. pap. 14.00 (0-520-05624-8) U CA Pr.

***MacKenzie, Maxwell.** Abandonings: Photographs of Other Tail County, Minnesota. (Illus.). 64p. 1995. 22.95 (1-880216-34-5) Elliott & Clark.

MacKenzie, Melody K., ed. Native Hawaiian Rights Handbook. 336p. 1991. pap. text ed. 25.00 (0-8248-1374-X) UH Pr.

Mackenzie, Michael, tr. see Gelman, Alexander.

Mackenzie, Midge. Shoulder to Shoulder. 1988. pap. 15.95 (0-679-72131-2, Vin) Random.

Mackenzie, Mollie. Turkish Athens: The Forgotten Centuries, 1456-1832. 150p. 1991. 39.95 (0-86372-144-3, Pub. by Ithaca UK); pap. 25.00 (0-86372-143-5, Pub. by Ithaca UK) Paul & Co Pubs.

***Mackenzie, Morell.** Great Danes, Past & Present. deluxe ed. 257p. 1995. 30.00 (0-614-04538-X) Donald R Hoflin.

Mackenzie, Myrna. The Baby Wish. 1994. pap. 2.75 (0-373-19046-8, 1-19046-1, Pergamon Pr) Elsevier.

— The Daddy List. (Romance Ser.). 1995. mass mkt. 2.99 (0-373-19090-5, 1-19090-9) Silhouette.

***MacKenzie, Nancy.** Science & Technology Today. 560p. 1994. pap. text ed. 17.50 (0-312-09692-5) St Martin.

Mackenzie, Neil D. Ayyubid Cairo: A Topographical Study. (Illus.). 208p. 1992. text ed. 35.00 (977-424-275-0, Pub. by Am Univ Cairo Pr UA) Col U Pr.

MacKenzie, Norman, ed. see Wells, H. G.

MacKenzie, Norman H. The Escape from Elba: The Fall & Flight of Napoleon, 1814-1815. (Illus.). 1982. 30.00 (0-19-215863-5) OUP.

— A Reader's Guide to Gerard Manley Hopkins. LC 80-69275. 256p. (C). 1981. pap. 17.95 (0-8014-9221-1) Cornell U Pr.

Mackenzie, Norman H., ed. The Early Poetic Manuscripts & Notebooks of Gerard Manley Hopkins. LC 89-32239. 304p. 1989. 118.00 (0-8240-3898-3) Garland.

MacKenzie, Norman H., ed. see Hopkins, Gerard M.

MacKenzie, Norman H., ed. see Hopkins, Gerard Manley.

MacKenzie, Norman H., ed. see Webb, Beatrice.

MacKenzie, Patrick. Lawful Occasions. 1992. pap. 14.95 (1-85635-024-X) Dufour.

Mackenzie, Patrick T. The Problems of Philosophers: An Introduction. 314p. (C). 1989. pap. text ed. 21.95x (0-87975-486-9) Prometheus Bks.

MacKenzie, R. Alec. New Time Management Methods for You & Your Staff. 320p. 1990. ring bd. 91.50 (0-85013-168-5) Dartnell Corp.

MacKenzie, R. Alec. Sirach. LC 82-83725. (Old Testament Message Ser.: Vol. 19). 197p. 1983. pap. 10.95 (0-8146-5253-0) Liturgical Pr.

Mackenzie, R. Alec. Teamwork Through Time Management: New Time Management Methods for Everyone in Your Organization. 320p. 1991. pap. 22.95 (0-85013-182-0) Dartnell Corp.

— Time for Success: A Goal-Getter's Strategy. 192p. 1991. pap. text ed. 9.95 (0-07-044656-3) McGraw.

MacKenzie, R. Sheldon. The Isolated Jesus: Seven Messages for Good Friday or Lent. LC 93-39814. 68p. 1993. pap. 6.50 (1-55673-703-3) CSS OH.

MacKenzie, Ralph E., jt. auth. see Geisler, Norman L.

Mackenzie, Rob. David Livingstone: The Truth Behind the Legend. (Orig.). 1993. pap. 32.50 (0-85476-387-2) Trans-Atl Phila.

Mackenzie, Robert, jt. ed. see Stone, Peter B.

Mackenzie, Robert, jt. ed. see Stone, Peter.

Mackenzie, Robert E., jt. auth. see Auslander, Louis.

Mackenzie, Robert H. The Trafalgar Roll. 354p. 1989. 27.95 (0-87021-990-1) Naval Inst Pr.

MacKenzie, Roderick, jt. auth. see MacKenzie, Margaret.

MacKenzie, Roderick A. Faith & History in the Old Testament. LC 63-10585. 127p. reprint ed. pap. 36.20 (0-7837-4524-9, 2057519) Bks Demand.

MacKenzie, Ross. Brief Points: An Almanac for Parents & Friends of U. S. Naval Academy Midshipmen. LC 93-12792. (Illus.). 217p. 1993. pap. 14.95 (1-55750-565-9) Naval Inst Pr.

Mackenzie, Ross & Culbertson, Todd, eds. Eyewitness: Writings from the Ordeal of Communism. 492p. (C). 1992. lib. bdg. 27.95 (0-932088-77-5) Freedom Hse.

— Eyewitness: Writings from the Ordeal of Communism. LC 92-30861. (Focus on Issues Ser.: No. 15). 1992. pap. write for info. (0-932088-76-7) Freedom Hse.

***MacKenzie, S. P.** The Home Guard. (Illus.). 272p. 1995. 29.95 (0-19-820577-5) OUP.

— Politics & Military Morale: Current Affairs & Citizenship Education in the British Army 1914-1950. (Oxford Historical Monographs). 310p. 1992. 60.00 (0-19-820244-X) OUP.

MacKenzie, Samuel L. & Taylor, David C., eds. Seed Oils for the Future. LC 93-7118. 190p. 1993. 60.00 (0-935315-46-2) AOCS Pr.

MacKenzie, Scott B., jt. ed. see Childers, Terry L.

MacKenzie, Shea. Bread Machine Gourmet: Simple Recipes for Extraordinary Breads. LC 93-977. 320p. 1993. pap. 13.95 (0-89529-560-1) Avery Pub.

— The Garden of Earthly Delights Cookbook: Gourmet Vegetarian Cooking. LC 93-8339. 464p. 1993. pap. 14.95 (0-89529-530-X) Avery Pub.

— The Pizza Gourmet: Simple Recipes for Spectacular Pizzas. (Illus.). 260p. 1995. pap. 13.95 (0-89529-656-X) Avery Pub.

Mackenzie, Steve. Ambush. (Seals Ser.: No. 1). 192p. 1987. pap. 2.50 (0-380-75189-5) Avon.

— Fundamentals of Free Lungeing: An Introduction to Tackless Training. (Illus.). 98p. 1994. 20.95 (0-939481-35-9) Half Halt Pr.

— Seals, No. 10: Sniper. 1988. pap. 2.95 (0-380-75533-5) Avon.

MacKenzie, Steve. Seals, No. 11: Attack. 160p. 1989. pap. 2.95 (0-380-75582-3) Avon.

Mackenzie, Steve. Seals, No. 13: Crisis! 160p. (Orig.). 1989. pap. 2.95 (0-380-75771-0) Avon.

— Seals No. 4: Target. 192p. 1987. pap. 2.95 (0-380-75193-3) Avon.

— Seals, No. 7: Recon. 160p. 1988. pap. 2.95 (0-380-75529-7) Avon.

— Seals No. 8: Infiltrate. 160p. (Orig.). 1988. pap. 2.95 (0-380-75530-0) Avon.

— Seals No. 9: Assault! 160p. 1988. pap. 2.95 (0-380-75532-7) Avon.

MacKenzie, Steve. Stronghold. (Seals Ser.: No. 12). 160p. (Orig.). 1989. pap. 2.95 (0-380-75583-1) Avon.

Mackenzie, Steve. Treasure. (Seals Ser.: No. 14). 176p. 1989. pap. 2.95 (0-380-75772-9) Avon.

Mackenzie, Susan, jt. ed. see Gold, Charlotte.

Mackenzie, Suzanne. Visible Histories: Women & Environments in a Post-War British City. 240p. (C). 1990. text ed. 44.95 (0-7735-0712-4, Pub. by McGill CN) U of Toronto Pr.

Mackenzie, Suzanne, jt. ed. see Kobayashi, Audrey.

Mackenzie, W. J. Political Identity. LC 77-26851. 1978. text ed. 16.95 (0-312-62308-9) St Martin.

Mackenzie, W. Mackay. The Medieval Castle in Scotland. LC 75-174843. (Illus.). 1972. reprint ed. 24.95 (0-405-08769-1, Pub. by Blom Pubns UK) Ayer.

MacKenzie, W. Roy. Quest of the Ballad. LC 68-815. (Studies in Poetry: No. 38). 1969. reprint ed. lib. bdg. 75.00 (0-8383-0591-1) M S G Haskell Hse.

MacKenzie, W. S. & Adams, A. E. A Color Atlas of Rocks & Minerals in Thin Section. LC 93-6167. (Illus.). 1994. pap. text ed. 29.95 (0-470-23338-9) Wiley.

Mackenzie, W. S. & Guilford, C. Atlas of Rock-Forming Minerals in Thin Section. LC 79-27822. 98p. 1980. pap. text ed. 52.95 (0-470-26921-9) Halsted Pr.

MacKenzie, W. S., et al. Atlas of Igneous Rock & Their Textures. 148p. 1982. pap. text ed. 52.95 (0-470-27339-9) Halsted Pr.

MacKenzie, Warren. For Women Only: A Woman's Guide to Financial Security. rev. ed. LC 86-70681. (Financial & Business Services Ser.). 196p. 1987. pap. 5.95 (0-938125-03-6); pap. text ed. 5.50 (0-938125-04-4); 5.25 (0-938125-05-2) Crystal Rainbow.

Mackenzie, William. Practical Treatise on the Diseases of the Eye. deluxe ed. LC 78-31614. 732p. 1979. 49.50 (0-88275-947-7) Krieger.

— Practical Treatise on the Diseases of the Eye. LC 78-31614. 732p. 1979. reprint ed. 44.50 (0-88275-841-1) Krieger.

Mackenzie, William C. The Highlands & Isles of Scotland: A Historical Survey. LC 75-41183. reprint ed. 26.45 (0-404-14682-1) AMS Pr.

Mackenzie, William L. Eighteen Thirty-Seven: Revolution in the Canadas. 240p. Date not set. text ed. 8.95 (0-919600-22-0, Pub. by NC Press CN) U of Toronto Pr.

Mackenzie, William R. English Moralities from the Point of View of Allegory. LC 66-29466. 278p. 1966. reprint ed. 50.00 (0-87752-066-6) Gordian.

MacKenzie, William R. English Moralities from the Point of View of Allegory. LC 68-54172. (Studies in Drama: No. 39). 1969. reprint ed. lib. bdg. 59.95 (0-8383-0592-X) M S G Haskell Hse.

— English Moralities from the Point of View of Allegory. (BCL1-PR English Literature Ser.). 278p. 1992. reprint ed. lib. bdg. 79.00 (0-7812-7099-5) Rprt Serv.

MacKeown, P. K. & Newman, D. J. Computational Techniques in Physics. (Illus.). 240p. 1987. pap. 33.00 (0-85274-548-6); disk 52.00 (0-85274-429-3) IOP Pub.

Macker, John. The First Gangster. (Illus.). 28p. 1994. pap. 6.00 (0-9623013-2-9) Long Road Pr.

Mackereth, F. J., et al. Water Analysis: Some Revised Methods for Limnologists. 1978. 39.00 (0-900386-31-2) St Mut.

Mackerian, Gail. Dissolved Oxygen in the Chesapeake Bay: Processes & Effects. 6.95 (0-943676-26-6) MD Sea Grant Col.

Mackerle, M. The Boundary Element Reference Book. LC 87-72284. 350p. 1987. 77.00 (0-931215-67-6) Computational Mech MA.

Mackerness, Eric D. A Social History of English Music. LC 75-40994. (Illus.). 307p. 1976. reprint ed. text ed. 38.50 (0-8371-8705-2, MAHEM, Greenwood Pr) Greenwood.

Mackerness, M. Hazlitt: Spirit of the Age. 1990. pap. 24.00 (0-7463-0599-0, Pub. by Northcote UK) St Mut.

Mackerras, Colin. China's Minorities: Integration & Modernization in the Twentieth Century. LC 93-43882. (Illus.). 364p. (C). 1994. 79.00 (0-19-585988-X) OUP.

— The Chinese Theatre in Modern Times: From 1840 to the Present Day. LC 75-13827. (Illus.). 260p. 1975. 30.00x (0-87023-196-0) U of Mass Pr.

Mackerras, Colin, ed. Chinese Theater: From Its Origins to the Present Day. LC 83-6687. (Illus.). 228p. (C). 1989. reprint ed. pap. 14.95 (0-8248-1220-4) UH Pr.

Mackerras, Colin & Knight, Nick, eds. Marxism in Asia. LC 85-14591. 320p. 1985. text ed. 39.95 (0-312-51852-8) St Martin.

Mackerras, Colin & Yorke, Amanda. The Cambridge Handbook of Contemporary China. (Illus.). 280p. (C). 1992. pap. 22.95 (0-521-38755-8) Cambridge U Pr.

Mackerras, Colin, jt. auth. see Tung, Constantine.

Mackerras, Colin, et al. China since 1978: Reform, Modernisation & Socialism with Chinese Characteristics. LC 93-24509. 1994. text ed. 49.95 (0-312-10252-6); pap. write for info. (0-312-10306-9) St Martin.

MacKerron, Conrad. Tropical Deforestation. (Orig.). 1991. pap. 45.00 (0-931035-85-6) IRRC Inc DC.

MacKerron, D. K., jt. ed. see Haverkort, A. J.

Mackersey, Ian. Tom Rolt & the Cressy Years. 106p. (C). 1989. 45.00 (0-947712-01-1, Pub. by S A Baldwin UK) St Mut.

***Mackesey, Piers.** The British Victory in Egypt 1801: The End of Napoleon's Conquest. LC 94-26059. (Illus.). 304p. 1995. 79.95x (0-415-04064-7, B2238) Routledge.

Mackesy, Piers. Could the British Have Won the War of Independence? Billias, George A., ed. LC 76-41409. (Bland-Lee Lectures in History Ser.). 1976. pap. 1.00 (0-914206-08-7) Clark U Pr.

— The War for America, 1775-1783. LC 92-37789. xxx, 569p. (C). 1993. pap. 16.95 (0-8032-8192-7, Bison Books) U of Nebr Pr.

— The War in the Mediterranean, 1803 to 1810. LC 81-6457. (Illus.). xviii, 430p. 1981. reprint ed. text ed. 75.00 (0-313-22913-9, MAWM, Greenwood Pr) Greenwood.

Mackethan, Lucinda H. Daughters of Time: Creating Woman's Voice in Southern Story. LC 89-4824. (Brown Thrasher Bks.). 144p. 1992. pap. 10.95 (0-8203-1444-7) U of Ga Pr.

Mackett, M. & Williamson, J. Human Vaccines & Vaccination. (Medical Perspectives Ser.). 160p. (Orig.). 1994. pap. 52.50x (1-872748-77-5, Pub. by Bios Scientific UK) Coronet Bks.

Mackett, Muriel & Steele, Donald. Society & Education: Education Management for the 1980s & Beyond. 94p. (Orig.). (C). 1982. pap. text ed. 6.25 (1-55996-122-8, TF1) Univ Council Educ Admin.

Mackey. Horses at the Gate. Date not set. 22.00 (0-06-251068-1, HarpT); pap. 15.00 (0-06-251069-X, PL) HarpC.

— Year the Horses Came. Date not set. pap. 11.00 (0-06-250736-2, PL) HarpC.

Mackey, A. G. Jurisprudence of Freemasonry. 21.95 (0-685-22001-X) Wehman.

Mackey, Agnes E. The Universal Self: A Study of Paul Valery. LC 61-65142. 279p. reprint ed. pap. 79.60 (0-685-15380-0, 2026530) Bks Demand.

Mackey, Aidan, ed. Collected Works of G. K. Chesterton: Collected Poetry, Vol. X, Pt. 1. 565p. Date not set. 39.95 (0-89870-390-5); pap. 24.95 (0-89870-391-3) Ignatius Pr.

Mackey, Albert G. Encyclopedia of Free Masonry. 1046p. 1991. reprint ed. pap. 75.00 (1-56459-099-2) Kessinger Pub.

— Jurisprudence of Freemasonry. 17.00 (0-685-19480-9) Powner.

— A Lexicon of Freemasonry. 527p. 1994. reprint ed. pap. 39.95 (1-56459-463-7) Kessinger Pub.

— Mackey's Jurisprudence of Freemasonry. 406p. 1985. reprint ed. 13.95 (0-88053-026-X, M 073) Macoy Pub.

— Symbolism of Freemasonry. 17.00 (0-685-19504-X) Powner.

— Symbolism of Freemasonry: Its Science, Philosophy, Legends, Myths & Symbols. 375p. 1994. pap. 24.95 (1-56459-469-6) Kessinger Pub.

***Mackey, Arthur L.** Biblical Principles of Success: A Practical Guide for Living. 1993. pap. 8.00 (0-927936-47-X) Vincom Inc.

Mackey, Bertha. A Saloon Keeper's Daughter Saved. 15p. 1982. pap. 0.15 (0-686-36264-0); pap. 0.25 (0-686-37285-9) Faith Pub Hse.

Mackey, Betty. Garden Notes Through the Years: Four-Year Comparative Garden Diary. 116p. 1993. pap. 11.95 (0-9616338-4-0) B B Mackey Bks.

— The Plant Collector's Notebook. 140p. 1993. 7.95 (0-9616338-5-9) B B Mackey Bks.

Mackey, Betty, jt. auth. see Kite, Pat.

Mackey, Betty B. & Brandies, Monica M. A Cutting Garden for Florida. 2nd ed. (Illus.). 96p. (Orig.). 1992. pap. 8.95 (0-9616338-2-4) B B Mackey Bks.

Mackey, Betty B., jt. auth. see Halpin, Anne M.

Mackey, Betty B., et al. The Gardener's Home Companion. 608p. 1991. text ed. 31.00 (0-02-578035-2) Macmillan.

Mackey, Cleo. The Cowboy & Rodeo Evolution. (Illus.). 120p. 1980. reprint ed. 7.95 (0-9608176-0-3); reprint ed. pap. 5.95 (0-9608176-1-1) C Mackey.

Mackey, D., jt. auth. see Defilippo, J.

Mackey, D., jt. auth. see DeFillippo, J.

Mackey, Daphne, jt. auth. see Abraham, Paul.

Mackey, David. Multiple Family Housing. (Illus.). 1977. 32.50 (0-8038-0164-5) Archit CT.

Mackey, Donald R., jt. auth. see Jensen, Rue.

Mackey, Douglas A. D. H. Lawrence: The Poet Who Was Not Wrong. LC 84-291. (Milford Series: Popular Writers of Today: Vol. 42). 149p. (Orig.). 1986. lib. bdg. 27.00x (0-89370-171-8); pap. 17.00x (0-89370-271-4) Borgo Pr.

— The Dance of Consciousness: Enlightenment in Modern Literature. LC 94-27641. (I. O. Evans Studies in the Philosophy & Criticism of Literature: No. 16). 157p. 1994. lib. bdg. 27.00x (0-89370-305-2); pap. 17.00x (0-89370-405-9) Borgo Pr.

— Iris Murdoch: A Sea of Contingency. (Milford Series: Popular Writers of Today). 160p. Date not set. lib. bdg. write for info. (0-89370-185-8); pap. write for info. (0-89370-285-4) Borgo Pr.

— Philip K. Dick. (United States Authors Ser.). 168p. 1988. text ed. 21.95 (0-8057-7515-3, Twayne) Macmillan.

— The Rainbow Quest of Thomas Pynchon. rev. ed. LC 80-11219. (Milford Series: Popular Writers of Today: Popular Writers of Today: Vol. 28). 68p. 1989. lib. bdg. 20.00x (0-89370-142-4); pap. text ed. 10.00x (0-89370-242-0) Borgo Pr.

— The Work of Ian Watson: An Annotated Bibliography & Guide. Clarke, Boden, ed. LC 88-36646. (Bibliographies of Modern Authors Ser.: No. 18). 148p. (C). 1989. lib. bdg. 27.00x (0-8095-0512-6); pap. 17.00x (0-8095-1512-1) Borgo Pr.

***Mackey, Douglas A., ed.** The Corporate University Guide to Management Seminars. 900p. 1993. ring bd. 69.00 (0-8095-8400-X) Borgo Pr.

Mackey, Douglas A., jt. ed. see Gilius, Lawrence W.

Mackey, Douglas A., jt. auth. see Spayde, Sydney H.

Mackey, G. W. Theory of Unitary Group Representation. Kaplansky, Irving, ed. LC 76-17697. (Chicago Lectures in Mathematics Ser.). 1976. pap. text ed. 10.00 (0-226-50052-7) U Ch Pr.

Mackey, G. W., ed. The Scope & History of Commutative & Noncommutative Harmonic Analysis. LC 92-12857. (History of Mathematics Ser.: Vol. 5). 370p. 1992. 52.00 (0-8218-9903-1, HMATH/5C) Am Math.

Mackey, G. W., jt auth. see Segal, I. E.

Mackey, Henry B., tr. see De Sales, Francis.

Mackey, James P. Power & Christian Ethics. (New Studies in Christian Ethics: No. 3). 200p. (C). 1994. 59.95 (0-521-41595-0) Cambridge U Pr.

— The Religious Imagination. 256p. 1986. 17.50 (0-85224-512-2, Pub. by Edinburgh U Pr UK) Col U Pr.

Mackey, James P., ed. An Introduction to Celtic Christianity. 432p. 1993. pap. text ed. 29.95 (0-567-29507-9, Pub. by T & T Clark UK) Bks Intl VA.

***Mackey-Kallis.** Oliver Stone's America. (Film Studies). 1996. text ed. 68.95 (0-8133-2662-1) Westview.

***Mackey, Laura.** Math in the Garden. (Math Is Everywhere Ser.). (Illus.). 48p. 1994. teacher ed, pap. text ed. 6.45 (1-55799-320-3, EMC 092) Evan-Moor Corp.

— Math in the Kitchen. (Math Is Everywhere Ser.). (Illus.). 48p. 1994. teacher ed, pap. text ed. 6.45 (1-55799-327-0, EMC 099) Evan-Moor Corp.

Mackey, Louis H. Points of View: Readings of Kierkegaard. LC 85-22713. (Kierkegaard & Postmodernism Ser.). 240p. (Orig.). 1986. pap. 24.95 (0-8130-0824-7) U Press Fla.

Mackey, M. C. Time's Arrow: Origins of Thermodynamic Behavior. 2nd ed. (Illus.). 190p. 1993. write for info. (3-540-94093-6) Spr-Verlag.

— Time's Arrow: Origins of Thermodynamic Behavior. (Illus.). 192p. 1993. reprint ed. pap. 34.95 (0-387-94093-6) Spr-Verlag.

— Time's Arrow: The Origin of Thermodynamic Behavior. (Illus.). 150p. 1991. 49.00 (0-387-97702-3) Spr-Verlag.

Mackey, M. C., jt. ed. see Rensing, L.

Mackey, Margaret. Picture Books & the Making of Readers: A New Trajectory. (Concept Paper Ser.: No. 7). 33p. 1993. write for info. (0-8141-3556-0) NCTE.

Mackey, Margaret G. & Sooy, Louise P. Early California Costumes, 1769-1850. (Illus.). vii, 138p. 1932. 22.50 (0-8047-0994-7) Stanford U Pr.

Mackey, Marilynn. Secrets to Dating an Independent Woman. 96p. (Orig.). 1991. pap. text ed. 10.00 (0-9631497-0-9) Cent City Pub.

Mackey, Mary. The Dear Dance of Eros. LC 86-7612. (International Poetry Ser.: No. 2). 150p. (Orig.). 1987. pap. 7.95 (0-940242-17-6) Fjord Pr.

— The Year the Horses Came. 400p. 1995. mass mkt., pap. 5.99 (0-451-18298-7, Onyx) NAL-Dutton.

— The Year the Horses Came: A Novel. LC 92-56119. 512p. 1993. 22.00 (0-06-250735-4) Harper SF.

Mackey, Mary S. & Mackey, Maryette G. The Pronunciation of Ten Thousand Proper Names: Giving Geographical & Biographical Names, Names of Books, Works of Art, Characters in Fiction, Foreign Titles, Etc. LC 89-71138. xiii, 329p. 1993. reprint ed. lib. bdg. 48.00 (1-55888-918-3) Omnigraphics Inc.

Mackey, Maryette G., jt. auth. see Mackey, Mary S.

Mackey, Michael C., jt. auth. see Glass, Leon.

Mackey, Michael C., jt. auth. see Lasota, Andrzej.

Mackey, Nathaniel. Bedouin Hornbook. LC 86-1471. (From a Broken Bottle Traces of Perfume Still Emanate Ser.: No. 1). 216p. (Orig.). reprint ed. pap. 61.60 (0-7837-6485-5, 2046512) Bks Demand.

— Discrepant Engagement: Dissonance, Cross-Culturality, & Experimental Writing. LC 93-626. (Cambridge Studies in American Literature & Culture: No. 71). 336p. (C). 1993. 59.95 (0-521-44453-5) Cambridge U Pr.

— Djbot Baghostus's Run. (New American Fiction Ser.: No. 29). 208p. (Orig.). 1993. pap. 12.95 (1-55713-055-8) Sun & Moon CA.

— Eroding Witness. Poems. LC 85-1010. 112p. 1986. pap. 9.95 (0-252-01230-5) U of Ill Pr.

— School of UDHRA. 144p. (Orig.). 1993. pap. 9.95 (0-87286-278-X) City Lights.

— Song of the Andoumboulou: 18-20. (Illus.). 24p. (Orig.). 1994. pap. 66.00 (0-939952-16-5) Moving Parts.

Mackey, Nathaniel, jt. ed. see Lange, Art.

Mackey, Philip E. The Givers' Guide: Making Your Charity Dollars Count. LC 90-39943. 288p. (Orig.). 1990. pap. 14.95 (0-945774-11-7, HV914.M25) Catbird Pr.

Mackey, Philip E., jt. auth. see Hansen, Barbara.

***Mackey, R. Scott.** Barbary Baseball: The Pacific Coast League of the 1920s. 288p. 1995. pap. 25.95x (0-7864-0055-2) McFarland & Co.

An Asterisk (*) at the beginning of an entry indicates that the title is appearing in BIP for the first time.

*Mackey, Richard A. & O'Brien, Bernard A. Lasting Marriages: Men & Women Growing Together. LC 95-3336. 208p. 1995. text ed. 55.00 (0-275-95075-1, Praeger Pubs); pap. text ed. 17.95 (0-275-95076-X, Praeger Pubs) Greenwood.

Mackey, Richard T. Bowling. 5th rev. ed. LC 92-12893. 97p. (C). 1993. pap. text ed. 12.95 (1-55934-161-0) Mayfield Pub.

Mackey, Richard W. The Zabern Affair, 1913-1914. 268p. (C). 1991. lib. bdg. 43.00 (0-8191-8408-X) U Pr of Amer.

Mackey, Robert, jt. auth. see Mitcham, Carl.

Mackey, Robert, jt. ed. see Mitcham, Carl.

Mackey, Samson A. Mythological Astronomy of the Ancients Demonstrated, Pt. 1. Bd. with Pt. 2. Key to Urania. LC 73-84043. LC 73-84043. (Secret Doctrine Reference Ser.). 380p. 1973. reprint ed. 17.00 (0-913510-06-8) Wizards.

Mackey, Sandra. Better Than Gold & Silver. 1975. pap. 6.25 (0-89137-407-8) Quality Pubns.

— Lebanon: The Death of a Nation. 1991. pap. 12.95 (0-385-41381-5, Anchor NY) Doubleday.

— Passion & Politics: The Turbulent World of the Arabs. LC 93-45398. 464p. 1994. pap. 13.95 (0-452-27036-7, Plume) NAL-Dutton.

— The Saudis: Inside the Desert Kingdom. 448p. 1990. pap. 5.95 (0-451-17051-2, Sig) NAL-Dutton.

Mackey, Scott. Constitutional Amendment to Require a Balanced Federal Budget. (State Legislative Reports: Vol. 17, No. 11). 8p. 1992. pap. text ed. 5.00 (1-55516-283-5, 7302-1711) Natl Conf State Legis.

Mackey, Scott, jt. auth. see Snell, Ronald.

Mackey, Scott R. State & Local Tax Levels: Fiscal Year 1991. (Legislative Finance Papers: No. 80). 24p. 1992. pap. text ed. 25.00 (1-55516-080-8, 5101-80) Natl Conf State Legis.

— State-Local Tax Levels: Fiscal Year 1992. (Legislative Finance Paper Ser.: No. 92). 7p. 1994. 10.00 (1-55516-552-4, 5105-92) Natl Conf State Legis.

— State Programs to Assist Distressed Local Governments. (Legislative Finance Paper Ser.: No. 86). 37p. 1993. 15.00 (1-55516-083-2, 5101-86) Natl Conf State Legis.

— State Property Tax Relief Programs for Homeowners & Renters. (Legislative Finance Papers: No. 81). 21p. 1992. pap. text ed. 15.00 (1-55516-081-6, 5101-81) Natl Conf State Legis.

— State Tax Actions, 1994. (Legislative Finance Paper Ser.: No. ZZ). 56p. 1994. 35.00 (1-55516-001-8, 5101-ZZ) Natl Conf State Legis.

*Mackey, Scott R. & Carter, Karen. State Tax Policy & Senior Citizens. 2nd ed. 78p. 1994. 25.00 (1-55516-523-0, 5323) Natl Conf State Legis.

Mackey, Sylvia E. Echoes from the Prairie. (Illus.). 260p. (Orig.). 1992. pap. 14.95 (0-9632931-0-9) Kiitos Pub.

Mackey, T. S. & Prengaman, R. D., eds. Lead-Zinc, '90. (Illus.). 1140p. 1990. 52.00 (0-87339-111-X, 365) Minerals Metals.

Mackey, Tomas, tr. see Streett, R. Alan.

Mackey, Wade C. Fathering Behaviors: The Dynamics of the Man-Child Bond. LC 85-6599. (Perspectives in Developmental Psychology Ser.). 220p. 1985. 42.50 (0-306-41868-1, Plenum Pr) Plenum.

Mackey, William F. & Ornstein, Jacob, eds. Sociolinguistic Studies in Language Contact. (Trends in Linguistics, Studies & Monographs: No. 6). 1979. text ed. 65.40 (90-279-7866-2) Mouton.

Mackey, William F., jt. auth. see Beebe, Von N.

Mackey, William J., et al. Urbanism as Delinquency: Compromising the Agenda for Social Change. 184p. (C). 1993. pap. text ed. 25.50 (0-8191-9103-5) U Pr of Amer.

— Urbanism as Delinquency: Compromising the Agenda for Social Change. 184p. (C). 1993. lib. bdg. 49.50 (0-8191-9102-7) U Pr of Amer.

Macki, J. & Strauss, A. Introduction to Optimal Control Theory. (Undergraduate Texts in Mathematics Ser.). (Illus.). 165p. 1981. 42.00 (0-387-90624-X) Spr-Verlag.

MacKichan, Margaret & Ross, Robert. In the Kingdom of Grass. LC 91-34853. (Great Plains Photography Ser.). (Illus.). xii, 131p. 1992. 40.00 (0-8032-3159-8) U of Nebr Pr.

Mackichan, N. D. The GP & the Primary Health Care Team. (Illus.). 1976. text ed. 29.00 (0-8464-0453-2) Beekman Pubs.

*MacKie. Florida Contract Law. 1991. pap. 15.00 (0-409-27212-4) Michie Butterworth.

— Florida Evidence Rules & Cases. 1991. pap. 15.00 (0-409-27337-6) Michie Butterworth.

— Florida Real Property Manual. 1991. pap. 15.00 (1-56257-861-8) Michie Butterworth.

Mackie. Skin Cancer. 352p. 1989. 89.95 (0-8151-5716-9, Yr Bk Med Pubs) Mosby Yr Bk.

MacKie, et al. For Henry Kucera Studies in Slavic Philology & Computational Linguistics. (Papers in Slavic Philology Ser.: Vol. 6). 1992. 29.50 (0-930042-72-7) Mich Slavic Pubns.

Mackie, et al. Ghost Rider: Resurrected. (Illus.). 192p. 1991. pap. 12.95 (0-87135-803-4) Marvel Entmnt.

Mackie, A., jt. auth. see McAuliffe, C. A.

Mackie, Alastair. Ingaidherins: Selected Poems. 100p. 1987. pap. text ed. 13.75 (0-08-035071-2, Pub. by Aberdeen U Pr) Macmillan.

Mackie, Allan. Picture Book of Log Homes. 180p. 1989. 55.00 (0-920270-11-5, Pub. by Camden Hse CN) Firefly Bks Ltd.

Mackie, Allister. The Trade Unionist & the Tycoon. 224p. Date not set. 24.95 (1-85158-515-X, Pub. by Mnstream UK) Trafalgar.

Mackie, Alwynne. Art-Talk: Theory & Practice in Abstract Expressionism. (Illus.). 288p. 1989. text ed. 31.50 (0-231-06648-1) Col U Pr.

Mackie, B. Building with Logs. (Illus.). 96p. 1971. pap. 19.95 (0-920270-14-X) Firefly Bks Ltd.

— Log House Plans. (Illus.). 180p. 1979. pap. 19.95 (0-920270-30-1, Pub. by Camden Hse CN) Firefly Bks Ltd.

— Notches of All Kinds. (Illus.). 92p. 1983. pap. 15.95 (0-920270-24-7, Pub. by Camden Hse CN) Firefly Bks Ltd.

Mackie, B. Allan, et al. Log Span Tables: For Floor Joists, Beams & Roof Support Systems. (Illus.). 117p. (C). 1993. pap. 15.00 (0-9636902-0-5) CN Log Builders.

Mackie, Benita & Rompf, Shirley J. Building Sentences. 3rd ed. LC 94-16909. 384p. 1994. pap. text ed. write for info. (0-13-150138-0) P-H.

Mackie, Beverly J. Afrocentric Shopping Guide: Where to Find African-American Products in Houston & Surrounding Areas. 44p. (Orig.). 1994. pap. 6.95 (1-884509-05-3) Creat Info.

MacKie, Christine. Life & Food in the Caribbean. 190p. 1991. 18.95 (1-56131-029-8) New Amsterdam Bks.

Mackie, D. Undersea. (CHP Technology Ser.). (Illus.). 32p. (J). (gr. 4-9). 1987. pap. 5.95 (0-88625-156-7) Durkin Hayes Pub.

Mackie, Dan. Communications. (CHP Technology Ser.). (Illus.). 32p. (J). (gr. 4-9). 1987. pap. 5.95 (0-88625-135-4) Durkin Hayes Pub.

— Electricity. Goshorn, Bill, ed. (Technology Ser.). (Illus.). 32p. (J). (gr. 4). 1986. lib. bdg. 14.65 (0-88625-133-8); pap. 5.95 (0-685-30764-6) Durkin Hayes Pub.

— Flight. (Hayes Technology Ser.). (Illus.). 32p. (J). (gr. 5-9). 1985. pap. 5.95 (0-88625-112-5) Durkin Hayes Pub.

— I'd Die for You. 170p. 1995. lib. bdg. 33.00 (0-8095-4554-3) Borgo Pr.

— Space Tour. (Hayes Technology Ser.). (Illus.). 32p. (J). (gr. 5-9). 1985. pap. 5.95 (0-88625-103-6) Durkin Hayes Pub.

Mackie, David, jt. auth. see Mackie, Dean.

Mackie, Dean & Mackie, David. BASIC. (Let's Look At Ser.). (Illus.). 48p. (J). (gr. 1-5). 1985. pap. 3.95 (0-88625-085-4) Durkin Hayes Pub.

Mackie, Diane & Hamilton, David, eds. Affect, Cognition, & Stereotyping: Interactive Processes in Group Perception. (Illus.). 389p. 1993. text ed. 59.95 (0-12-464410-4) Acad Pr.

Mackie, Diane, jt. auth. see Smith, Elliott.

Mackie, Dianne. Affirmations for Adult Children. 1991. 6.95 (0-9622150-0-7) Aurora VA.

Mackie, Dustin & Decker, Douglas. Group & Ipa HMO's. LC 81-2096. 492p. 1981. text ed. 90.00 (0-89443-341-5) Aspen Pub.

Mackie, Fiona. The Status of Everyday Life: A Sociological Excavation of the Prevailing Framework of Perception. (International Library of Sociology). 288p. 1985. 49.95 (0-7102-0154-0, RKP) Routledge.

Mackie, G. N., jt. auth. see Slavin, K.

Mackie, Gerald L., jt. auth. see Claudi, Renata.

Mackie, Hank & Palermo, Phil. Basic Fingerstyle Guitar Method. 1993. 4.95 (0-87166-738-X, 93342) Mel Bay.

*Mackie, Howard. Gambit. (Illus.). 96p. 1995. pap. 12.95 (0-7851-0109-8) Marvel Entmnt.

Mackie, Howard, et al. Ghost Rider: Rise of the Midnight Sons. (Illus.). 1993. pap. 19.95 (0-87135-969-3) Marvel Entmnt.

Mackie, Ian A. Medical Contact Lens Practice. LC 93-3876. (Illus.). 360p. 1993. 99.95 (0-7506-0939-7) Buttrwrth-Heinemann.

Mackie, J. A., ed. Australia in the New World Order: Foreign Policy in the 1970s. LC 76-378596. 164p. reprint ed. pap. 46.80 (0-7837-1455-6, 2052431) Bks Demand.

— The Chinese in Indonesia: Five Essays. LC 76-139. 292p. 1976. text ed. 15.00 (0-8248-0449-X) UH Pr.

— The Chinese in Indonesia: Five Essays. LC 76-139. 295p. reprint ed. pap. 84.10 (0-317-26525-3, 2023971) Bks Demand.

Mackie, J. D. A History of Scotland. 416p. 1984. mass mkt. 5.95 (0-14-020671-X, Penguin Bks) Viking Penguin.

— History of Scotland. 300p. 1985. 16.95 (0-88029-040-4) Dorset Pr.

Mackie, J. L. Ethics: Inventing Right & Wrong. 1977. pap. 7.95 (0-14-021957-9, Penguin Bks) Viking Penguin.

Mackie, Joan, ed. see Mackie, John L.

Mackie, John D. Earlier Tudors, 1485-1558. (Oxford History of England Ser.). (Illus.). 1952. 59.00 (0-19-821706-4) OUP.

— The Earlier Tudors, 1485-1558. LC 93-30483. (Oxford History of England Ser.: Vol. VII). 732p. 1994. reprint ed. pap. 16.95 (0-19-285292-2) OUP.

Mackie, John L. The Cement of the Universe: A Study of Causation. (Clarendon Library of Logic & Philosophy). 1980. pap. 28.00 (0-19-824642-0) OUP.

— Logic & Knowledge: Selected Papers, Vol. 1. Mackie, Joan & Mackie, Penelope, eds. 1985. 59.00 (0-19-824679-X) OUP.

— The Miracle of Theism. 1983. pap. text ed. 19.95 (0-19-824682-X) OUP.

— Problems from Locke. (Illus.). (C). 1976. pap. text ed. 19.95 (0-19-875036-6) OUP.

Mackie, Joyce. Basic Ballet. 1980. mass mkt. 7.00 (0-14-046445-X, Penguin Bks) Viking Penguin.

Mackie, K. The Application of Learning Theory to Adult Teaching. (C). 1988. text ed. 40.00 (0-685-22143-1, Pub. by Univ Nottingham UK) St Mut.

Mackie, Karl. The Application of Learning Theory to Adult Teaching. (C). 1981. 35.00 (0-902031-88-0, Pub. by Univ Nottingham UK) St Mut.

Mackie, Karl, ed. A Handbook of Dispute Resolution: ADR in Action. 253p. (C). 1991. text ed. 49.95 (0-415-04124-4, A5590) Routledge.

*Mackie, Karl & Miles, David. Commercial Dispute Resolution: An ADR Practice Guide. 1994. boxed 121.00 (0-406-02011-6, UK) Butterworth Legal Pubs.

*Mackie, Keith. Golf at Saint Andrews. (Illus.). 192p. 1995. 45.00 (1-56554-129-4) Pelican.

Mackie, Keith, jt. auth. see Smith, Peter.

Mackie, Louise W. The Splendor of Turkish Weaving: An Exhibition of Silks & Carpets of the 13th-18th Centuries. (Illus.). 86p. 1973. 8.00 (0-87405-002-2) Textile Mus.

Mackie, Louise W. & Thompson, Jon, eds. Turkmen: Tribal Carpets & Traditions. LC 80-53159. (Illus.). 240p. 1980. 75.00 (0-87405-014-6) Textile Mus.

Mackie, Louise W., jt. auth. see Straka, Jerome A.

MacKie, Marie D., tr. see Prunieres, Henry.

Mackie, Mary. Castle Kintyle. large type ed. LC 94-3349. 263p. 1994. pap. 15.95 (0-8161-7452-0) Hall.

— The Clouded Land. 608p. 1995. pap. 10.95 (0-7472-4684-X, Pub. by Headline UK) Trafalgar.

— Cobwebs & Cream Teas. (Illus.). 176p. 1995. pap. 13.95 (0-575-05980-X, Pub. by V Gollancz UK) Trafalgar.

— Counterfeit Love. large type ed. (Linford Romance Library). 272p. 1992. pap. 14.95 (0-7089-7205-5, Trailtree Bookshop) Ulverscroft.

— Dry Rot & Daffodils. (Illus.). 192p. 1995. pap. 13.95 (0-575-05934-6, Pub. by V Gollancz UK) Trafalgar.

— Dry Rot & Daffodils: Life in a National Trust House. (Illus.). 185p. 1995. 34.95 (0-575-05754-8, Pub. by V Gollancz UK) Trafalgar.

— Falconer's Wood. large type ed. 304p. 1994. 20.95 (0-7089-3079-4) Ulverscroft.

— The Flower & the Storm. large type ed. (Linford Romance Library). 1991. pap. 13.95 (0-7089-7045-1) Ulverscroft.

— Into the Twilight. large type ed. (Linford Romance Library). 336p. 1994. pap. 14.95 (0-7089-7527-5, Linford) Ulverscroft.

— A Light in the Valley. large type ed. 1991. 21.95 (0-7089-2464-6) Ulverscroft.

— A Man Like Matthew. large type ed. (Linford Romance Library). 1991. pap. 13.95 (0-7089-7118-0) Ulverscroft.

— Nightflower. large type ed. 1990. pap. 12.95 (0-7089-6883-X, Linford) Ulverscroft.

— Sandringham Rose. 608p. 1994. pap. 13.95 (0-7472-4051-5, Pub. by Headline UK) Trafalgar.

— A Season for Singing. large type ed. LC 93-509. 1993. 19.95 (0-7927-1550-0, Curley Lrg Print) Chivers N Amer.

— Still Weeps the Willow. large type ed. (Linford Romance Library). 336p. 1992. pap. 14.95 (0-7089-7242-X, Trailtree Bookshop) Ulverscroft.

— Straw in the Wind. large type ed. LC 94-33451. 238p. 1995. pap. 15.95 (0-8161-7453-9, Large Print Bks) Hall.

— A Voice in the Fog. large type ed. (Romance Ser.). 288p. 1992. 21.95 (0-7089-2695-9) Ulverscroft.

— The Waiting Web. large type ed. (Linford Romance Library). 272p. 1992. pap. 14.95 (0-7089-7287-X, Trailtree Bookshop) Ulverscroft.

MacKie, Mary-Frances L. Avon Connecticut: An Historical Story. LC 88-5999. (Illus.). 336p. 1988. 22.50 (0-914659-33-2) Phoenix Pub.

Mackie, P., et al. British Transport Industry & the European Community. (Institute for Transport Studies: Vol. 3). 120p. 1987. text ed. 54.95 (0-566-05368-3, Pub. by Avebury Pub UK) Ashgate Pub Co.

Mackie, Penelope, ed. see Mackie, John L.

Mackie, Raymond K., et al. Guidebook to Organic Synthesis. 2nd ed. (Orig.). 1990. pap. text ed. 49.95 (0-470-21568-2) Halsted Pr.

Mackie, Richard. Take This Job & Sell It! The Recruiter's Handbook. LC 93-33890. (Illus.). 176p. (Orig.). 1994. pap. 24.95 (0-936609-30-3) QED Ft Bragg.

Mackie, Richard A. Beat the Devil: How to Get Government Regulators Off Your Back - Permanently! 288p. 1994. 29.95 (1-885372-01-9) Solution CA.

Mackie, Ron. A Wild Garden: The Monterey Peninsula. (Illus.). 1985. pap. 7.95 (0-910286-99-X) Boxwood.

Mackie, Rona M. Clinical Dermatology: An Illustrated Textbook. 3rd ed. (Illus.). 376p. 1991. 75.00 (0-19-261981-0); pap. 29.95 (0-19-261980-2) OUP.

— Healthy Skin: The Facts: Good Skin Care Throughout Life. (Facts Ser.). (Illus.). 160p. 1992. 18.95 (0-19-262246-3) OUP.

Mackie, Rona M., ed. Malignant Melanoma. (Pigment Cell Ser.: Vol. 6). (Illus.). viii, 204p. 1983. 111.25 (3-8055-3690-9) S Karger.

*Mackie, Sam. How to Form a Nonprofit Corporation in Florida. 3rd ed. 116p. 1994. pap. text ed. 19.95 (1-57248-004-1) Sphinx Pub FL.

*Mackie, Sam A. Florida Civil Procedure Guide. Stephens, Mark, ed. 606p. Date not set. write for info. (1-878337-46-7) Knowles Law.

Mackie, Stella. Portraits. (How to Draw & Paint Ser.). (Illus.). 32p. (Orig.). 1989. pap. 5.95 (1-56010-001-X, HT014) W Foster Pub.

Mackie, Thomas. Europe Votes Three. 2nd ed. (Parliamentary Research Services Ser.). 442p. 1990. text ed. 64.95 (0-900178-35-3, Pub. by Dartmth Pub UK) Ashgate Pub Co.

Mackie, Thomas T. & Rohds, Richard. International Almanac of Electoral History. 3rd ed. 511p. 1991. 99.00 (0-87187-575-6) Congr Quarterly.

Mackie, Thomas T. & Rose, Richard. International Almanac of Electoral History. LC 74-11577. 1974. 29.95 (0-02-919640-X) Free Pr.

Mackie, William. The Diary of a Canny Man 1818-1828: Adam Mackie, Farmer, Merchant & Innkeeper in Fyvie. (Aberdeen University Press Bks.). (Illus.). 96p. 1991. pap. 13.90 (0-08-041213-0, Pub. by Aberdeen U Pr) Macmillan.

MacKiernan, Elizabeth. Ancestors Maybe. (Burning Deck Fiction Ser.). 160p. (Orig.). 1993. pap. 8.00 (0-930901-81-9) Burning Deck.

— Ancestors Maybe. deluxe ed. (Burning Deck Fiction Ser.). 160p. (Orig.). 1993. pap. 15.00 (0-930901-82-7) Burning Deck.

Mackiewi, jt. auth. see Breborowicz.

Mackiewicz, Andrea. Guide to Building a Global Image. LC 93-6485. (Economist Intelligence Unit Ser.). 256p. 1993. text ed. 39.95 (0-07-009350-4) McGraw.

Mackiewicz, Andrzej, et al, eds. Acute Phase Proteins: Molecular Biology, Biochemistry, & Clinical Applications. 1993. 250.00 (0-8493-6913-4, RB131) CRC Pr.

Mackiewicz, Edward R., jt. auth. see Veal, Edward T.

Mackiewicz, S. Dostoievski. LC 73-21635. (Studies in Dostoyevsky: No. 86). 1974. lib. bdg. 75.00 (0-8383-1818-5) M S G Haskell Hse.

MacKillop, Andrew. Oil Crisis & Economic Adjustment: Case Studies of Six Developing Countries. Al-Shaikly, Salah, ed. LC 83-40158. 192p. 1984. text ed. 29.95 (0-312-58302-8) St Martin.

MacKillop, Ian. The British Ethical Societies. 224p. 1986. 69.95 (0-521-26672-6) Cambridge U Pr.

MacKillop, James. Fionn MacCumhaill: Celtic Myth in English Literature. LC 85-22116. (Irish Studies). 256p. (Orig.). 1986. pap. 15.00 (0-8156-2353-4); pap. text ed. 39.95x (0-8156-2344-5) Syracuse U Pr.

MacKillop, James & Woolfolk, Donna. Speaking of Words: A Language Reader. 3rd ed. LC 81-6734. 324p. (C). 1986. pap. text ed. 20.75 (0-03-003953-3) HB Coll Pubs.

MacKillop, James, jt. ed. see Murphy, Maureen O.

Mackin, Bill. Cowboy & Gunfighter Collectibles. rev. ed. LC 89-3416. 176p. 1993. pap. 20.00 (0-87842-244-7) Mountain Pr.

Mackin, Edward. The Nominative Case. 192p. 1991. 18.95 (0-8027-5780-4) Walker & Co.

Mackin, Elton E. Suddenly We Didn't Want to Die: Memoirs of a World War I Marine. LC 93-10485. 272p. 1993. 19.95 (0-89141-498-3) Presidio Pr.

Mackin, Rick. Chopper Cops, No. 1: Fire Storm. 1990. pap. 2.95 (1-55817-353-6, Pinnacle NY) Windsor NY.

— Gulf Attack. (Chopper Cops Ser.: No. 2). 1990. pap. 2.95 (1-55817-400-1, Pinnacle NY) Windsor NY.

— Recon Strike. (Chopper Cops Ser.: No. 3). 1991. pap. 3.50 (1-55817-480-X, Pinnacle NY) Windsor NY.

— Sky War. (Chopper Cops Ser.: No. 4). 1991. pap. 3.50 (1-55817-511-3, Pinnacle NY) Windsor NY.

Mackin, Ronald. A Short Course in Spoken English. 1975. pap. 5.95 (0-87789-137-0); audio 55.00 (0-87789-140-0) ELS Educ Servs.

Mackin, Theodore. Divorce & Remarriage. (Marriage in the Catholic Church Ser.: Vol. II). 688p. (Orig.). 1984. pap. 19.95 (0-8091-2585-4) Paulist Pr.

— The Marital Sacrament. (Marriage in the Catholic Church Ser.: Vol. 3). 1989. pap. 24.95 (0-8091-3055-6) Paulist Pr.

Mackinder, Halford J. Britain & the British Seas. LC 68-25248. (British History Ser.: No. 30). 1969. reprint ed. lib. bdg. 49.95 (0-8383-0212-2) M S G Haskell Hse.

— Democratic Ideas & Reality. LC 81-12797. xxiv, 278p. 1981. reprint ed. text ed. 65.00 (0-313-23150-8, MADM, Greenwood Pr) Greenwood.

— The First Ascent of Mount Kenya. LC 90-46888. (Illus.). 288p. (C). 1991. text ed. 39.95 (0-8214-0987-5) Ohio U Pr.

MacKinder, Hanford J. Britain & the British Seas. LC 69-13982. 377p. 1970. reprint ed. text ed. 65.00 (0-8371-2754-8, MABR, Greenwood Pr) Greenwood.

Mackinlay, John. Peacekeepers: An Assessment of Peacekeeping Operations at the Arab-Israel Interface. 208p. 1989. 29.95 (0-685-29202-9) Routledge Chapman & Hall.

Mackinlay, Leila. Broken Armour. large type ed. 346p. 1989. 17.95 (0-7089-1961-8) Ulverscroft.

— Echo of Applause. large type ed. 448p. 1986. 21.95 (0-7089-1515-9) Ulverscroft.

— Farewell to Sadness. large type ed. (Romance Ser.). 304p. 1992. 21.95 (0-7089-2729-7) Ulverscroft.

— Guilt's Pavilions. large type ed. (Romance Suspense Ser.). 416p. 1992. 21.95 (0-7089-2664-9) Ulverscroft.

— Midnight Is Mine. large type ed. 1991. 21.95 (0-7089-2540-5) Ulverscroft.

— No Room for Loneliness. large type ed. 1975. 21.95 (0-85456-344-X) Ulverscroft.

— Pilot's Point. large type ed. 464p. 1987. 16.95 (0-7089-1601-5) Ulverscroft.

— Restless Dream. large type ed. 1988. 15.95 (0-7089-1746-1) Ulverscroft.

— Spring Rainbow. large type ed. 384p. 1987. 16.95 (0-7089-1702-X) Ulverscroft.

— The Third Boat. large type ed. 1989. 17.95 (0-7089-2106-X) Ulverscroft.

— Uneasy Conquest. large type ed. 368p. 1987. 16.95 (0-7089-1643-0) Ulverscroft.

— Unwise Wanderer. large type ed. 432p. 1986. 21.95 (0-7089-1492-6) Ulverscroft.

— Vain Delights. large type ed. 400p. 1988. 21.95 (0-7089-1902-2) Ulverscroft.

Mackinlay, Sterling. Origin & Development of Light Opera. 1972. 59.95 (0-8490-0772-0) Gordon Pr.

Mackinley, Malcolm S. Garcia the Centenarian & His Times. LC 75-40206. (Music Reprint Ser.). 1975. reprint ed. lib. bdg. 42.50 (0-306-70671-7) Da Capo.

MacKinney, Archie A., Jr., ed. Pathophysiology of Blood. LC 83-26040. (Wiley Pathophysiology Ser.). (Illus.). 462p. (Orig.). reprint ed. pap. 131.70 (0-8357-4660-7, 2037590) Bks Demand.

MacKinney, Loren C. Early Medieval Medicine: With Special Reference to France & Charters. 1979. 25.95 (0-405-10613-0) Ayer.

MacKinney, Loren C., ed. see University of North Carolina, Division of the Humanities Staff.

M

An Asterisk (*) at the beginning of an entry indicates that the title is appearing in BIP for the first time.

MacKinnon. Introduction to Open Systems. (C). 1995. text ed. write for info. (*0-7167-8180-8*, Computer Sci Pr) W H Freeman.

MacKinnon, ed. Each Small Step: Breaking the Chains of Abuse & Addiction. (NFS Canada Ser.). Date not set. pap. 10.95 (*0-921881-17-7*, Pub. by Gynergy-Ragweed CN) InBook.

— Oil in the California Monterey Formation. (IGC Field Trip Guidebooks Ser.). 64p. 1989. 21.00 (*0-87590-600-1*, T311) Am Geophysical.

MacKinnon, Barbara. American Philosophy: An Historical Anthology. LC 84-2458. (SUNY Series in Philosophy). 688p. 1985. 59.50 (*0-87395-922-1*); pap. 19.95 (*0-87395-923-X*) State U NY Pr.

— Ethics: Theory & Contemporary Issues. LC 94-12192. 473p. 1995. pap. 31.95 (*0-534-20310-8*) Intl Thomson.

MacKinnon, Bernie. Meantime. (YA). 1992. pap. 4.95 (*0-395-61622-0*) HM.

Mackinnon, Bernie. Song for a Shadow. LC 90-39647. 320p. (YA). (gr. 7 up). 1991. 17.95 (*0-395-55419-5*) HM.

MacKinnon, Catharine A. Feminism Unmodified: Discourses on Life & Law. LC 86-25694. 328p. 1988. pap. text ed. 14.95 (*0-674-29874-8*) HUP.

— Feminism Unmodified: Discourses on Life & Law. LC 86-25694. 352p. 1987. reprint ed. 32.00 (*0-674-29873-X*) HUP.

— Only Words. LC 93-13600. 160p. 1993. text ed. 14.95 (*0-674-63933-2*) HUP.

— Sexual Harassment of Working Women: A Case of Sex Discrimination. LC 78-9645. (Fastback Ser.: No. 19). 1979. pap. 16.00 (*0-300-02299-9*) Yale U Pr.

— Toward a Feminist Theory of the State. LC 89-7540. 304p. 1989. text ed. 27.50 (*0-674-89645-9*) HUP.

— Toward a Feminist Theory of the State. 304p. (C). 1991. pap. text ed. 14.95 (*0-674-89646-7*) HUP.

***MacKinnon, Christy.** Silent Observer. (Awareness & Caring Ser.). (Illus.). 48p. (J). (gr. k-6). Date not set. lib. bdg. 17.95 (*1-56674-075-4*) Forest Hse.

MacKinnon, D. I., et al, eds. Brachiopods Through Time: Proceedings of the Second International Brachiopods Congress, University of Otago, Dunedin, New Zealand, 5-9 February 1990. 580p. (C). 1990. text ed. 105.00 (*90-6191-160-5*, Pub. by A A Balkema NE) Ashgate Pub Co.

MacKinnon, Debbie. Baby's First Year. LC 92-21830. 26p. (J). (ps). 1993. 11.95 (*0-8120-6334-1*) Barron.

— How Many? LC 91-46720. (Illus.). 24p. (J). (ps-00). 1993. 10.99 (*0-8037-1253-7*) Dial Bks Young.

— My First ABC. LC 92-11500. (Illus.). (J). (ps). 1992. 11.95 (*0-8120-6331-7*) Barron.

— My World of Words. LC 94-42967. (Illus.). (J). 1995. write for info. (*0-8120-6505-0*) Barron.

— My World of Words. LC 94-42966. (Illus.). (ENG & FRE.). (J). 1995. write for info. (*0-8120-6506-9*) Barron.

— My World of Words. LC 94-43792. (Illus.). (J). 1995. write for info. (*0-8120-6507-7*) Barron.

— The Seasons. (Illus.). 32p. (J). (ps). 1995. 12.95 (*0-8120-6422-4*) Barron.

— Things to Cuddle. (Learn-Along Board Bks.). (Illus.). (J). (ps up). 1994. pap. 2.99 (*0-553-09570-6*, Little Rooster) Bantam.

— Things to Eat. (Learn-Along Board Bks.). (Illus.). (J). (ps up). 1994. 2.99 (*0-553-09568-4*, Little Rooster) Bantam.

— Things to Wear. (Learn-Along Board Bks.). (Illus.). (J). (ps up). 1994. pap. 2.99 (*0-553-09569-2*, Little Rooster) Bantam.

— Things with Wheels. (Learn-Along Board Bks.). (Illus.). (J). (ps up). 1994. pap. 2.99 (*0-553-09571-4*, Little Rooster) Bantam.

— What Am I? LC 94-44393. (Illus.). (J). 1996. 10.99 (*0-8037-1826-8*) Dial Bks Young.

— What Color? (Illus.). 24p. (J). (ps-00). 1994. 10.99 (*0-8037-0909-9*) Dial Bks Young.

— What Noise? LC 92-43651. (Illus.). (J). (gr. 4 up). 1994. 10.99 (*0-8037-1510-2*) Dial Bks Young.

— What Shape? LC 91-34700. (Illus.). 24p. (J). (ps-00). 1992. 10.99 (*0-8037-1244-8*) Dial Bks Young.

— What Size. LC 93-40103. (J). 1995. 10.99 (*0-8037-1745-8*) Dial Bks Young.

MacKinnon, Debbie & Sieveking, Anthea. All about Me. LC 93-23143. (Illus.). 32p. (J). (ps). 1994. 11.95 (*0-8120-6348-1*) Barron.

Mackinnon, Donald. The Clan Ross. (Johnston & Bacon Clan Histories Ser.). (Illus.). 32p. 1993. reprint ed. pap. 8.95 (*0-685-69992-7*, 9616) Clearfield Co.

MacKinnon, Donald D. Fingon, Memoirs of Clan Fingon, with Family Tree. 246p. 1993. reprint ed. lib. bdg. 49.00 (*0-8328-3590-0*); reprint ed. pap. 39.00 (*0-8328-3591-9*) Higginson Bk Co.

MacKinnon, Donald W. In Search of Human Effectiveness: Identifying & Developing Creativity. LC 78-62345. 1978. pap. 13.95 (*0-930222-03-2*) Creat Educ Found.

MacKinnon, Flora I., ed. see More, Henry.

MacKinnon, G. E., jt. ed. see Waller, T. Gary.

Mackinnon, I. D. & Mumpton, F. A., eds. Electron - Optical Methods in Clay Science, No. 2. (CMS Workshop Lectures). (Illus.). 159p. (Orig.). (C). 1990. pap. text ed. 18.00 (*1-881208-02-8*) Clay Minerals.

***Mackinnon, J. P. & Shadbolt, S. H.** The South African Campaign, 1879. (Illus.). 384p. 1995. 50.00 (*1-85367-203-3*, Pub. by Greenhill Bks UK) Stackpole.

Mackinnon, James. Calvin & the Reformation. LC 83-45648. reprint ed. 37.50 (*0-404-19841-4*) AMS Pr.

— Luther & the Reformation, 4 vols., Set. LC 83-45648. reprint ed. 157.50 (*0-404-19857-0*) AMS Pr.

MacKinnon, James G., jt. auth. see Davidson, Russell.

MacKinnon, Jan, ed. see Smedley, Agnes.

MacKinnon, Janice R. & MacKinnon, Stephen R. Agnes Smedley: The Life & Times of an American Radical. 460p. (C). 1988. 32.00 (*0-520-05966-2*); pap. 14.00 (*0-520-06614-6*) U CA Pr.

MacKinnon, John, et al. A Field Guide to the Birds of Borneo, Sumatra, Java, & Bali, the Greater Sunda Islands. LC 92-30340. (Illus.). 692p. 1993. 85.00 (*0-19-854035-3*); pap. 39.95 (*0-19-854034-5*) OUP.

MacKinnon, John R. & Stuart, Simon N., eds. The Kouprey: An Action Plan for Its Conservation. (Illus.). 20p. (Orig.). 1988. pap. 7.00 (*2-88032-972-8*, Pub. by IUCN SZ) Island Pr.

MacKinnon, Kathy, et al, eds. Managing Protected Areas in the Tropics. (International Union for the Conservation of Nature & Natural Resources: A Belhaven Press Book Ser.). (Illus.). 320p. 1986. pap. 35.00 (*2-88032-808-X*, Pub. by IUCN SZ) Island Pr.

MacKinnon, Kenneth. Gaelic: A Past & Future Prospect. (C). 1989. 39.00 (*0-85411-047-X*, Pub. by Saltire Soc) St Mut.

— Greek Tragedy into Film. LC 86-13420. 256p. 1987. 36.50 (*0-8386-3301-3*) Fairleigh Dickinson.

— Hollywood's Small Towns: An Introduction to the American Small-Town Movie. LC 83-27113. 218p. 1984. 22.00 (*0-8108-1678-4*) Scarecrow.

— Misogyny in the Movies: The De Palma Question. LC 88-40607. (Illus.). 224p. 1990. 38.50 (*0-87413-376-9*) U Delaware Pr.

— The Politics of Popular Representation: Reagan, Thatcher, AIDS, & the Movies. LC 91-58581. 256p. 1992. 38.50 (*0-8386-3474-5*) Fairleigh Dickinson.

Mackinnon, Lachlan. Experimental Physics at Low Temperatures: An Introductory Survey. LC 65-14928. (Illus.). 282p. reprint ed. pap. 80.40 (*0-7837-3606-1*, 2043471) Bks Demand.

Mackinnon, Laurel T. Exercise & Immunology. LC 91-42289. (Current Issues in Exercise Science Ser.). (Illus.). 128p. (Orig.). 1992. pap. text ed. 18.00x (*0-87322-347-0*, BMAC0347) Human Kinetics.

MacKinnon, Lilias. Music by Heart. (Music Book Index Ser.). 141p. 1992. reprint ed. lib. bdg. 69.00 (*0-7812-9459-2*) Rprt Serv.

MacKinnon, Lillias. Music by Heart. LC 80-26551. xi, 141p. 1981. reprint ed. text ed. 45.00 (*0-313-22810-8*, MAMB, Greenwood Pr) Greenwood.

MacKinnon, Mary, jt. ed. see Grantham, George.

***MacKinnon, Mary H. & McIntyre, Moni.** Readings in Ecology & Feminist Theology. 356p. (Orig.). 1995. pap. 19.95 (*1-55612-762-6*) Sheed & Ward MO.

MacKinnon, Neil. This Unfriendly Soil: The Loyalist Experience in Nova Scotia, 1783-1791. 244p. (C). 1989. pap. text ed. 22.95 (*0-7735-0719-1*, Pub. by McGill CN) U of Toronto Pr.

MacKinnon, Neil J. Symbolic Interaction As Affect Control. LC 93-38563. (SUNY Series in the Sociology of Emotions). 245p. 1994. text ed. 64.50x (*0-7914-2041-8*); pap. text ed. 21.95x (*0-7914-2042-6*) State U NY Pr.

Mackinnon, Niall. The British Folk Scene: Musical Performance & Social Identity. LC 93-4036. (Popular Music in Britain Ser.). 224p. 1994. 90.00 (*0-335-09774-X*, Open Univ Pr); pap. 27.50 (*0-335-09773-1*, Open Univ Pr) Taylor & Francis.

MacKinnon, Pamela C. & Morris, John B. Oxford Textbook of Functional Anatomy. 2nd ed. LC 92-48317. (Oxford Medical Publications). (C). 1994. pap. 24.95 (*0-19-262195-5*) OUP.

— Oxford Textbook of Functional Anatomy, Vol. 2: Thorax & Abdomen. (Illus.). 144p. 1988. pap. 24.95 (*0-19-261518-1*) OUP.

Mackinnon, Pamela C. & Morris, John F. Oxford Textbook of Functional Anatomy, Vol. 3: Head & Neck. (Illus.). 164p. 1991. pap. 35.00 (*0-19-261519-X*) OUP.

MacKinnon, Richard M. World Place Location Learning System. 7th ed. LC 94-70456. 96p. (C). 1995. student ed 7.45 (*0-9618558-3-5*) A Hancock Coll.

Mackinnon, Roderick. Teach Yourself Gaelic. (Teach Yourself Ser.). 1979. 11.95 (*0-679-10217-5*) McKay.

— Teach Yourself Gaelic. (Teach Yourself Ser.). 1992. 15.95 (*0-8288-8333-5*) Fr & Eur.

MacKinnon, Roger A. & Michels, Robert. Psychiatric Interview in Clinical Practice. LC 70-151680. 1971. text ed. 43.95 (*0-7216-5973-X*) Saunders.

MacKinnon, Roger A. & Yudofsky, Stuart C. Principles of the Psychiatric Evaluation. (Illus.). 325p. 1991. text ed. 34.50 (*0-397-51064-0*) Lippincott.

MacKinnon, Stephen R. & Friesen, Oris. China Reporting: An Oral History of American Journalism in the 1930's & 1940's. 200p. (C). 1987. pap. 13.00 (*0-520-06967-6*) U CA Pr.

MacKinnon, Stephen R., jt. auth. see MacKinnon, Janice R.

MacKinnon, Steve, ed. see Smedley, Agnes.

Mackintosh. Damascus & Its People: Sketches of Modern Life in Syria. LC 77-87617. reprint ed. 25.00 (*0-404-16444-7*) AMS Pr.

Mackintosh, A. Symbolism & Art Nouveau. LC 77-76764. (Modern Movements in Art Ser.). 1978. reprint ed. pap. 3.50 (*0-8120-0882-0*) Barron.

Mackintosh, Alan. Case Presentation in Heart Disease. 176p. (C). 1985. pap. text ed. 27.95 (*0-407-00541-2*) Buttrwrth-Heinemann.

— Case Presentations in Heart Disease. 2nd ed. (Illus.). 224p. 1992. pap. 30.00 (*0-7506-1261-4*) Buttrwrth-Heinemann.

Mackintosh, Allan, ed. Advanced Telescope Making Techniques, Vol. 1: Optics. LC 86-18935. (Illus.). 320p. 1986. pap. text ed. 19.95 (*0-943396-11-5*) Willmann-Bell.

— Advanced Telescope Making Techniques, Vol. 2: Mechanical. LC 86-18935. (Illus.). 320p. 1986. pap. text ed. 19.95 (*0-943396-12-3*) Willmann-Bell.

Mackintosh, Barry. The National Park Service. (Know Your Government Ser.). (Illus.). 96p. (J). (gr. 5 up). 1988. lib. bdg. 14.95 (*1-55546-116-6*) Chelsea Hse.

Mackintosh, Barry, et al. National Park Service: The First 75 Years. (Illus.). 64p. (Orig.). 1990. pap. 5.95 (*0-915992-52-3*) Eastern Acorn.

Mackintosh, C. H. Genesis to Deuteronomy: Notes on the Pentateuch, 6 vols. in 1. LC 72-75082. 928p. 1972. 29.99 (*0-87213-617-5*) Loizeaux.

— The Mackintosh Treasury: Miscellaneous Writings of C. H. Mackintosh. rev. ed. LC 75-44323. 1976. 29.99 (*0-87213-609-4*) Loizeaux.

Mackintosh, Carlos H. La Oracion y los Cultos de Oracion. 2nd ed. Daniel, Roger P., ed. Bautista, Sara, tr. (Serie Diamante). (Illus.). 40p. (SPA.). 1982. pap. 0.85 (*0-942504-08-9*) Overcomer Pr.

— El Perdon de los Pecados. 2nd ed. Bennett, Gordon H., ed. Bautista, Sara, tr. (Serie Diamante). 36p. (SPA.). 1982. pap. 0.85 (*0-942504-02-X*) Overcomer Pr.

Mackintosh, David, jt. auth. see Gray, Nigel.

Mackintosh, Douglas R. The Economics of Airborne Emissions. LC 72-89646. (Special Studies in U. S. Economic, Social & Political Issues). 1973. 39.50 (*0-275-28668-1*) Irvington.

Mackintosh, Duncan R. A Further Collection of Chinese Lyrics, & Other Poems: Rendered into Verse by Alan Ayling from the Translations of the Chinese by Duncan Mackintosh in Collaboration with Ch'eng Hsi & T'ung Ping-cheng. LC 73-112602. (Illus.). 293p. reprint ed. pap. 83.60 (*0-7837-6195-3*, 2045917) Bks Demand.

***Mackintosh, Graham.** Into a Desert Place: A 3000 Mile Walk Around the Coast of Baja California. (Illus.). 336p. 1995. pap. 14.00 (*0-393-31289-5*, Norton Paperbks) Norton.

MacKintosh, Graham. Into a Desert Place: A 3000 Mile Walk Around the Coast of Baja California. 2nd rev. ed. LC 90-91690. (Illus.). 312p. 1990. reprint ed. 24.95 (*0-9626109-0-9*) Graham MacKintosh.

Mackintosh, Graham, ed. Oranges & Snowfields: Southern California at the Turn of the Century. (Illus.). 1978. pap. 5.95 (*0-915520-07-9*) R-E CA.

MacKintosh, H. R., ed. see Schleiermacher, Friedrich.

Mackintosh, Helen K., jt. auth. see Lonsdale, Bernard J.

Mackintosh, Ian. Architect, Actor & Audience. (Illus.). 208p. 1992. 49.95 (*0-415-03182-6*, A7956); pap. 14.95 (*0-415-03183-4*, A7960) Routledge.

Mackintosh, J. J. Birds of Darjeling & India. 226p. 1986. 135.00 (*81-7089-147-7*, Pub. by Intl Bk Distr II) St Mut.

Mackintosh, J. W. The Hunts & the Hunted. 237p. (C). 1989. text ed. 50.00 (*1-872795-67-6*, Pub. by Pentland Pr UK) St Mut.

Mackintosh, James. Memoirs of the Life of the Right Honorable Sir James Mackintosh, 2 Vols. reprint ed. write for info. (*0-318-50657-2*) AMS Pr.

— Memoirs of the Life of the Right Honorable Sir James Mackintosh, 2 Vols, 1. LC 76-172711. reprint ed. 21.00 (*0-404-07434-0*) AMS Pr.

— Memoirs of the Life of the Right Honorable Sir James Mackintosh, 2 Vols, 2. LC 76-172711. reprint ed. 21.00 (*0-404-07435-9*) AMS Pr.

— Memoirs of the Life of the Right Honorable Sir James Mackintosh, 2 Vols, Set. LC 76-172711. reprint ed. 40.00 (*0-404-07433-2*) AMS Pr.

— Roman Law in Modern Practice. xii, 202p. 1995. lib. bdg. 32.50 (*0-8377-2477-5*) Rothman.

— The Roman Law of Sale: With Modern Illustrations Digest XVII.1 & XIX.1 Translated with Notes & References to Cases & the Sale of Goods Act. 2nd enl. ed. LC 93-79722. (Illus.). 318p. 1994. reprint ed. 75.00 (*1-56169-080-5*) W W Gaunt.

— The Roman Law of Sale, Digest XVIII.I & XIX.1: With Notes & References to Cases & the Sale of Goods Bill. LC 93-79721. (Illus.). 292p. 1994. reprint ed. 70.00 (*1-56169-079-1*) W W Gaunt.

Mackintosh, John J. Scotland: From the Earliest Times to the Present Century. LC 75-39198. (Select Bibliographies Reprint Ser.). 1977. reprint ed. 29.95 (*0-8369-6800-X*) Ayer.

Mackintosh, L. J. Birds of Darjeeling & India. 226p. 1986. reprint ed. 175.00 (*81-7089-047-0*, Pub. by Intl Bk Distr II) St Mut.

Mackintosh, Maureen. Gender, Class & Rural Transition: Agribusiness & the Food Crisis in Senegal. LC 89-5836. 192p. (C). 1989. text ed. 55.00 (*0-86232-840-3*, Pub. by Zed Books UK); pap. 17.50 (*0-86232-841-1*, Pub. by Zed Books UK) Humanities.

Mackintosh, N. J. Psychology of Animal Learning. 1974. text ed. 115.00 (*0-12-464650-6*) Acad Pr.

***Mackintosh, N. J., ed.** Cyril Burt: Fraud or Framed? (Illus.). 160p. 1995. 24.95 (*0-19-852336-X*) OUP.

Mackintosh, N. K., ed. Animal Learning & Cognition. 2nd ed. (Handbook of Perception & Cognition Ser.). (Illus.). 379p. 1994. text ed. 59.95 (*0-12-161953-2*) Acad Pr.

MacKintosh, Paul, tr. see Chuya, Nakahara.

Mackintosh, Paul S., tr. see Oe, Kenzaburo.

Mackintosh, Robert. Silk. 1992. pap. 4.99 (*0-685-53101-5*) Pinnacle MO.

— Silk. 1992. mass mkt. 4.99 (*1-55817-579-2*, Pinnacle NY) Windsor NY.

Mackintosh, Robert, jt. auth. see Short, Bobby.

***Mackintosh, Robert H., Jr.** Selected Bibliography of County, City & Town History & Related Published Records in the South Carolina Archives Reference Library. 43p. 1994. pap. text ed. write for info. (*1-880067-27-7*) SC Dept of Arch & Hist.

Mackintosh, Sam. Passover Seder for Christian Families. LC 88-36529. 32p. 1986. pap. 3.50 (*0-89390-057-5*) Resource Pubns.

Mackintosh, Sherwin, ed. Songs of the Kingdom. 410p. 1992. ring bd. 8.00 (*1-884553-05-2*) Discipleshp.

— Songs of the Kingdom - Update. 24p. 1994. ring bd. 0.50 (*1-884553-47-8*) Discipleshp.

Mackintosh, William H. & Goliwas, Ruth M. The Stained Glass Coloring Book. (Illus.). 48p. (J). (ps-2). 1990. pap. 2.95 (*0-671-69477-4*, Litl Simon S&S) S&S Childrens.

Mackirdy, A. & Willis, W. N. The White Slave Market. 1972. 59.95 (*0-8490-1291-0*) Gordon Pr.

***Mackle, Christine.** Life & Food in the Caribbean. 190p. 1995. pap. 11.95 (*1-56131-064-6*) New Amsterdam Bks.

Macklem, Francesca. Tomorrow & Forever. 256p. (Orig.). 1984. pap. 2.75 (*0-8439-2155-2*) Dorchester Pub Co.

Macklem, P. T. & Permutt, S., eds. The Lung in Transition Between Health & Disease. (Lung Biology in Health & Disease Ser.: Vol. 12). 464p. 1979. 155.00 (*0-8247-7750-6*) Dekker.

Macklem, Peter T., ed. see Mead, Jere.

Macklem, Peter T., jt. ed. see Roussos, Charis.

Macklen, E. D. Thermistors. 226p. 1980. 150.00 (*0-901150-07-X*) St Mut.

Mackler, Tasha. Murder...by Category: A Subject Guide to Mystery Fiction. LC 91-37638. 484p. 1991. 52.50 (*0-8108-2463-9*) Scarecrow.

Mackley, Bush. Pizza & Pasta Cookbook. 1991. 12.99 (*0-517-06148-1*) Random Hse Value.

Mackley, George. Confessions of a Woodpecker. deluxe ed. 1981. 250.00 (*0-905418-92-1*, Pub. by Gresham Bks UK) St Mut.

— George Mackley: Wood Engraver. 136p. 1984. 110.00 (*0-905418-90-5*, Pub. by Gresham Bks UK) St Mut.

Mackley, George E. Wood Engraving. 128p. 1984. 90.00 (*0-905418-84-0*, Pub. by Gresham Bks UK) St Mut.

— Wood Engraving. 144p. 1985. 45.00 (*0-946095-18-3*, Pub. by Gresham Bks UK) St Mut.

Mackley, Lesley. Book of Afternoon Tea. 120p. 1992. pap. 12.00 (*1-55788-046-8*, HP Books) Berkley Pub.

— Book of Greek Cooking. (Illus.). 120p. (Orig.). 1993. pap. 10.95 (*1-55788-062-X*, HP Books) Berkley Pub.

Mackley, Leslie. The Book of Pasta. LC 87-8721. 120p. 1987. pap. 10.95 (*0-89586-641-2*) Price Stern.

— A Gourmet's Guide to Chocolate. (Gourmet's Guide to Ser.). (Illus.). 120p. 1990. pap. 11.00 (*0-89586-853-9*, HP Books) Berkley Pub.

— A Gourmet's Guide to Coffee & Tea. (Illus.). 120p. (Orig.). 1989. pap. 11.00 (*0-89586-804-0*) Price Stern.

Mackley, Lynne, ed. see Beale, E. M.

Macklin, ed. see Cervantes.

Macklin, Alys E., ed. Twenty-Nine Tales from the French. Herrick, Robert, tr. & intro. by. LC 72-157785. (Short Story Index Reprint Ser.). 1977. reprint ed. 21.95 (*0-8369-3897-6*) Ayer.

Macklin, Barbara J. Structural Stability & Culture Change in a Mexican-American Community. Cortes, Carlos E., ed. LC 76-1249. (Chicano Heritage Ser.). 1977. 25.95 (*0-405-09513-9*) Ayer.

Macklin, Charles. The Covent Garden Theatre. LC 93-20862. (Augustan Reprints Ser.: No. 116 (1965)). 1993. reprint ed. 12.00 (*0-404-70116-7*) AMS Pr.

— Four Comedies. (Illus.). 270p. 1968. 19.95 (*0-910278-40-7*) Boulevard.

— A Will & No Will: or A Bone for the Lawyers: And the New Play Criticized: or the Plague of Envy. LC 92-23648. (Augustan Reprints Ser.: Nos. 127-128 (1967)). reprint ed. 18.50 (*0-404-70127-2*, PR3543) AMS Pr.

***Macklin, Eleanor.** AIDS & Families. LC 89-32929. 1993. pap. 17.95 (*0-918393-60-4*) Harrington Pk.

Macklin, Elizabeth. A Woman Kneeling in the Big City. 96p. 1992. 18.95 (*0-393-03400-3*) Norton.

— A Woman Kneeling in the Big City. 96p. 1994. pap. 8.95 (*0-393-31105-8*) Norton.

***Macklin, F. Anthony.** Beyond Justice: Three Novellas. 164p. (Orig.). 1994. pap. 9.95 (*0-9601886-1-4*) Herculean Pr.

Macklin, Gerald. A Study of Theatrical Vision in Arthur Rimbaud's Illuminations. LC 93-32574. (Studies in French Literature: Vol. 16). 290p. 1993. 89.95 (*0-7734-9349-2*) E Mellen.

Macklin, John. World's Most Bone-Chilling "True" Ghost Stories. (Illus.). 96p. 1994. pap. 3.95 (*0-8069-0391-0*) Sterling.

— World's Strangest "True" Ghost Stories. LC 89-26125. (Illus.). 96p. (J). (gr. 4 up). 1991. pap. 3.95 (*0-8069-5785-9*) Sterling.

Macklin, John J. The Window & the Garden: The Modernist Fictions of Ramon Perez de Ayala. LC 87-62378. 206p. 1988. pap. 30.00 (*0-89295-053-6*) Society Sp & Sp-Am.

Macklin, Ken. Dr. Watchstop. (Illus.). 1989. 7.95 (*0-913035-85-8*) Eclipse Bks.

Macklin, Mark G., jt. ed. see Needham, Stuart.

Macklin, Michael. Agricultural Extension in India. LC 92-38463. (Technical Paper Ser.: No. 190). 37p. 1992. 6.95 (*0-8213-2291-5*, 12291) World Bank.

Macklin, Ronald R. The Logging Business Management Handbook. LC 82-83344. (Forest Industries Book Ser.). (Illus.). 176p. 1983. pap. 42.50 (*0-87930-146-5*) Miller Freeman.

Macklin, Ruth. Enemies of Patients. 272p. 1993. 25.00 (*0-19-507200-6*) OUP.

— Man, Mind & Morality: The Ethics of Behavior Control. 160p. 1982. pap. text ed. write for info. (*0-13-551127-5*) P-H.

— Mortal Choices: Ethical Dilemmas in Modern Medicine. 256p. 1988. 19.95 (*0-317-58080-9*); pap. 12.95 (*0-395-46847-7*) HM.

— Surrogates & Other Mothers: The Debates over Assisted Reproduction. LC 93-5988. 240p. 1994. 44.95 (*1-56639-179-2*); pap. 18.95 (*1-56639-180-6*) Temple U Pr.

Macklin, Ruth & Gaylin, Willard, eds. Mental Retardation & Sterilization: A Problem of Competency & Paternalism. LC 81-7393. (Hastings Center Series in Ethics). 274p. 1981. 39.50 (*0-306-40689-6*, Plenum Pr) Plenum.

Macklin, Ruth, jt. ed. see Gaylin, Willard.

Macklis, Leonard, ed. Annual Review of Plant Physiology, Vol. 17. 1966. text ed. 40.00 (*0-8243-0617-1*) Annual Reviews.

— Annual Review of Plant Physiology, Vol. 18. 1967. text ed. 40.00 (*0-8243-0618-X*) Annual Reviews.

— Annual Review of Plant Physiology, Vol. 19. 1968. text ed. 40.00 (*0-8243-0619-8*) Annual Reviews.

— Annual Review of Plant Physiology, Vol. 20. 1969. text ed. 40.00 (*0-8243-0620-1*) Annual Reviews.

— Annual Review of Plant Physiology, Vol. 21. 1970. text ed. 40.00 (*0-8243-0621-X*) Annual Reviews.

— Annual Review of Plant Physiology, Vol. 22. 1971. text ed. 40.00 (*0-8243-0622-8*) Annual Reviews.

— Annual Review of Plant Physiology, Vol. 23. 1972. text ed. 40.00 (*0-8243-0623-6*) Annual Reviews.

Macklis, Roger, et al. Introduction to Clinical Medicine: A Student-to-Student Manual. 3rd ed. LC 94-14222. 1994. 28.95 (*0-316-54243-1*) Little.

Macklis, Roger M. Introduction to Medicine ISE, No. 2. 1988. 15.95 (*0-316-54249-0*) Little.

— Macklis-Wash Package. 1984. 26.90 (*0-316-54248-2*) Little.

***Mackmin, David.** The Valuation & Sale of Residential Property. 2nd ed. 272p. 1994. pap. 29.95x (*0-415-09329-5*, B3723) Routledge.

Mackmin, David, jt. auth. see Baum, Andrew.

***Mackness, M.I. & Clerc, M., eds.** Esterases, Lipases, & Phospholipases: From Structure to Clinical Significance. (NATO ASI Series A, Life Sciences: 266). (Illus.). 1994. pap. text ed. 105.00 (*0-306-44802-5*, Plenum Pr) Plenum.

Mackness, Robin. Oradour: Massacre & Aftermath. large type ed. (Illus.). 1991. 21.95 (*0-7089-2503-0*) Ulverscroft.

***Macknight, Anthony D. & Leader, John P., eds.** Epithelial Ion & Water Transport. fac. ed. LC 80-5542. (Illus.). 392p. Date not set. pap. 111.80 (*0-7837-7209-2*, 2047090) Bks Demand.

MacKnight, C. C. Farthest Coast. 1969. 27.50 (*0-522-83916-9*) Intl Spec Bk.

— The Voyage to Marege' Macassan Trepangers in Northern Australia. (Illus.). 1976. 29.95 (*0-522-84088-4*) Intl Spec Bk.

Macknight, James, ed. see Drummond, John.

Macknight, Nancy, ed. see Sackville-West, Vita.

Macknight, Nigel. Modern Formula One Car: From Concept to Starting Grid. 1993. 29.95 (*0-87938-823-4*) Motorbooks Intl.

MacKnight, Nigel. Showroom Stock Race Car Preparation. (Illus.). 160p. 1992. pap. 24.95 (*0-87938-652-5*) Motorbooks Intl.

— Shuttle Three. 3rd ed. (Illus.). 116p. 1991. pap. 9.95 (*0-87938-553-7*) Motorbooks Intl.

Macknight, Nigel. Tomahawk Cruise Missile. (Mil-Tech Ser.). (Illus.). 96p. 1995. pap. 9.95 (*0-87938-717-3*) Motorbooks Intl.

MacKnight, Scott D., jt. auth. see Mudroch, Alena.

MacKnight, Scott D., jt. ed. see Mudroch, Alena.

MacKnight, William J., jt. auth. see Aklonis, John J.

Macko, S., jt. ed. see Engel, M.

Mackoff, Barbara. The Art of Self-Renewal: Balancing Pressure & Productivity on & off the Job. 176p. 1993. pap. 11.95 (*1-56565-037-9*) Lowell Hse.

— What Mona Lisa Knew: A Woman's Guide to Getting Ahead in Business by Lightening Up. 1991. reprint ed. pap. 9.95 (*0-929923-68-5*) Lowell Hse.

Mackowiak, Paula. Relief of Pain from Headaches & TMJ. LC 89-927914. (Illus.). 200p. (Orig.). 1989. pap. 11.95 (*0-9625508-2-5*) Solomon Bks.

Mackowiak, Philip A., ed. Fever: Basic Mechanisms & Management. 384p. 1991. 105.00 (*0-88167-719-1*) Raven.

Mackowski, Richard M. Jerusalem: City of Jesus: An Exploration of the Traditions, Writings, & Remains of the Holy City from the Time of Christ. LC 79-28093. 231p. reprint ed. pap. 65.90 (*0-317-30152-7*, 2025334) Bks Demand.

Mackrell, Alice. Coco Chanel. LC 91-40599. (Fashion Designers Ser.). (Illus.). 96p. (Orig.). 1993. pap. 25.95 (*0-8419-1301-3*) Holmes & Meier.

— Paul Poiret. LC 90-4086. (Illus.). 100p. (Orig.). (C). 1990. 39.95 (*0-8419-1279-3*); pap. 23.95 (*0-8419-1280-7*) Holmes & Meier.

Mackrell, Gerald. Thoughts for Religious. (C). 1988. 39.00 (*0-85439-234-3*, Pub. by St Paul Pubns UK) St Mut.

Mackrell, Judith. Out of Line: The Story of British New Dance. (Illus.). 160p. (Orig.). 1992. pap. 17.95 (*1-85273-038-2*, Pub. by Dance Bks UK) Princeton Bk Co.

Mackreth, Donald. Peterborough: History & Guide. (History & Guide Ser.). (Illus.). 128p. 1994. pap. 16.00 (*0-7509-0235-3*) A Sutton Pub.

Mackridge, Peter. A Descriptive Analysis of Standard Modern Greek. 308p. 1987. pap. 29.95 (*0-19-815854-8*) OUP.

— Dionysios Solomos. (Studies in Modern Greek). 114p. (Orig.). (C). 1989. lib. bdg. 25.00 (*0-89241-487-1*); pap. text ed. 16.00 (*0-89241-488-X*) Caratzas.

Mackridge, Peter, tr. see Prevelakis, Pandelis.

Mackrodt, jt. ed. see Catlow, C. R.

Macksey, Catherine C., tr. see Descombes, Vincent.

Macksey, Kenneth. For Want of a Nail: The Impact on War of Logistics & Communications. (Illus.). 203p. 1990. 42.00 (*0-08-036268-0*, Pub. by Brasseys UK) Brasseys Inc.

— Guderian: Panzer General. 254p. 1992. 35.00 (*1-85367-059-6*, 5517) Stackpole.

— Invasion: The German Invasion of England, July 1940. 256p. 1990. 35.00 (*1-85367-065-0*, 5535) Stackpole.

— Military Errors of World War Two. (Illus.). 256p. 1993. pap. 16.95 (*1-85409-199-9*) Sterling.

— The Penguin Encyclopedia of Weapons & Military Technology: From Prehistory to the Present Day. (Illus.). 416p. 1994. 29.95 (*0-670-84411-X*, H Hamilton) Viking Penguin.

— Tank vs. Tank. 1991. 12.99 (*0-517-06578-9*) Random Hse Value.

***Macksey, Kenneth, ed.** The Hitler Options: Alternate Decisions of World War II. LC 94-40997. 1995. 29.95 (*1-85367-192-4*, Pub. by Greenhill Bks UK) Stackpole.

Macksey, Richard & Donato, Eugenio, eds. The Language of Criticism & the Sciences of Man: The Structuralist Controversy. LC 78-95789. 367p. reprint ed. pap. 104.60 (*0-317-08981-1*, 2004197) Bks Demand.

— The Structuralist Controversy: The Languages of Criticism & the Sciences of Man. LC 78-95789. 365p. reprint ed. pap. 104.10 (*0-7837-3390-9*, 2043348) Bks Demand.

Macksey, Richard A., ed. Velocities of Change: Critical Essays from MLN. LC 72-12343. 397p. 1974. 45.00 (*0-8018-1494-4*); pap. 14.95 (*0-8018-1495-2*) Johns Hopkins.

MacKuen, Michael B. & Coombs, Steven L. More Than News: Media Power in Public Affairs. LC 81-183. (People & Communication Ser.: No. 12). (Illus.). 231p. reprint ed. pap. 65.90 (*0-8357-4767-0*, 2037704) Bks Demand.

Mackworth, Alan K., jt. ed. see Freuder, Eugene C.

Mackworth, Cecily. The Destiny of Isabelle Eberhardt. 228p. 1986. reprint ed. pap. 9.50 (*0-88001-118-1*) Ecco Pr.

Mackworth, Cecily, ed. Mirror for French Poetry, Eighteen Forty to Nineteen Forty. LC 71-76946. (Granger Index Reprint Ser.). 1977. 19.95 (*0-8369-6027-0*) Ayer.

***Mackworth-Praed, Ben.** Book of Kells. 1995. 10.00 (*0-06-251131-9*) Harper SF.

Mackworth-Praed, Humphrey. Conservation Pieces. 220p. (C). 1991. pap. text ed. 110.00 (*1-85341-046-2*, Pub. by Surrey Beatty & Sons AT) St Mut.

Macky, Peter W. Candles in the Dark: Modern Parables. 62p. (Orig.). 1986. pap. 4.00 (*0-936014-17-2*) Dawn Valley.

— The Centrality of Metaphors to Biblical Thought: A Method for Interpreting the Bible. LC 89-49023. (Studies in the Bible & Early Christianity: Vol. 19). 312p. 1990. lib. bdg. 99.95 (*0-88946-619-X*) E Mellen.

***MacLachlan.** Journey. Date not set. pap. write for info. (*0-09-910751-1*) Random Hse Value.

MacLachlan, Bonnie. The Age of Grace: Charis in Early Greek Poetry. LC 92-37031. (Illus.). 192p. (C). 1993. text ed. 29.95 (*0-691-06974-3*) Princeton U Pr.

Maclachlan, C., jt. ed. see Harvey, W. J.

***MacLachlan, Cheryl.** Bringing France Home. 1995. pap. 25.00 (*0-517-88165-9*) Crown Pub Group.

— Bringing France Home. 1995. 40.00 (*0-517-59806-X*) Crown Pub Group.

MacLachlan, Colin M. Anarchism & the Mexican Revolution: The Political Trials of Ricardo Flores Magon in the United States. LC 90-42212. 201p. 1991. 38.00 (*0-520-06928-5*); pap. 13.00 (*0-520-07117-4*) U CA Pr.

— Spain's Empire in the New World: The Role of Ideas in Institutional & Social Change. 215p. 1991. pap. 14.00 (*0-520-07410-6*) U CA Pr.

MacLachlan, Colin M. & Beezley, William H. El Gran Pueblo: A History of Greater Mexico. LC 93-30737. 496p. 1994. pap. text ed. 32.20 (*0-13-146010-2*) P-H.

— El Gran Pueblo, Vols. 1 & 2: A History of Greater Mexico, Vol. 1: 1821-1911. LC 93-5920. 240p. 1994. Vol. 1, 1821-1911. pap. text ed. write for info. (*0-13-146028-5*) P-H.

— El Gran Pueblo, Vols. 1 & 2: A History of Greater Mexico, Vol. 2: 1911-the Present. LC 93-5920. 304p. 1994. Vol. 2, 1911-the Present. pap. text ed. write for info. (*0-13-146036-6*) P-H.

MacLachlan, Colin M. & Rodriguez, Jaime E. The Forging of the Cosmic Race: A Reinterpretation of Colonial Mexico. LC 78-68836. (Illus.). 408p. 1980. pap. 15.00 (*0-520-04280-8*) U CA Pr.

Maclachlan, D. F., ed. see Sopcak, James E.

Maclachlan, Fiona C. Keynes' General Theory of Interest: A Reconsideration. LC 92-28826. (Foundations of the Market Economy Ser.). 208p. 1993. 49.95 (*0-415-07934-9*, A9856) Routledge.

Maclachlan, John M. & Floyd, Joe S., Jr. This Changing South. LC 56-12858. 166p. reprint ed. pap. 47.40 (*0-8357-6720-5*, 2035355) Bks Demand.

Maclachlan, John M., ed. see Southern Conference on Gerontology Staff.

MacLachlan, Patricia. All the Places to Love. LC 92-794. (Charlotte Zolotow Bk.). (Illus.). 32p. (J). (gr. 1 up). 1994. 15.00 (*0-06-021098-2*) HarpC Child Bks.

— All the Places to Love. LC 92-794. (Charlotte Zolotow Bk.). (Illus.). 32p. (J). (gr. 1 up). 1994. lib. bdg. 14.89 (*0-06-021099-0*) HarpC Child Bks.

— Arthur, for the Very First Time. LC 79-2007. (Illus.). 128p. (J). (gr. 4-7). 1980. lib. bdg. 14.89 (*0-06-024047-4*) HarpC Child Bks.

— Arthur, for the Very First Time. LC 79-2007. (Trophy Bk.). (Illus.). 128p. (J). (gr. 3-6). 1989. pap. 3.95 (*0-06-440288-6*, Trophy) HarpC Child Bks.

— Baby. LC 93-22117. (J). (gr. 1-8). 1993. 13.95 (*0-385-31133-8*) Delacorte.

— Cassie Binegar. LC 81-48641. (Charlotte Zolotow Bk.). 128p. (J). (gr. 3-7). 1982. lib. bdg. 13.89 (*0-06-024034-2*) HarpC Child Bks.

— Cassie Binegar. LC 81-48641. (Trophy Bk.). 128p. (J). (gr. 3-7). 1987. pap. 3.95 (*0-06-440195-2*, Trophy) HarpC Child Bks.

— The Facts & Fictions of Minna Pratt. LC 85-45388. (Charlotte Zolotow Bk.). 144p. (J). (gr. 3-7). 1988. 12.95 (*0-06-024114-4*); lib. bdg. 12.89 (*0-06-024117-9*) HarpC Child Bks.

— The Facts & Fictions of Minna Pratt. LC 85-45388. (Trophy Bk.). 144p. (J). (gr. 3-7). 1990. pap. 3.95 (*0-06-440265-7*, Trophy) HarpC Child Bks.

— Journey. (J). (gr. 4-7). 1993. pap. 3.50 (*0-440-40809-1*) Dell.

— Journey. 1991. pap. 13.95 (*0-385-30427-7*) Doubleday.

— Mama One, Mama Two. LC 81-47795. (Charlotte Zolotow Bk.). (Illus.). 32p. (J). (gr. 1-3). 1982. 13.00 (*0-06-024081-4*); lib. bdg. 14.89 (*0-06-024082-2*) HarpC Child Bks.

— Sarah, Plain & Tall. LC 83-49481. (Charlotte Zolotow Bk.). 64p. (J). (gr. 3-5). 1985. 12.95 (*0-06-024101-2*); lib. bdg. 12.89 (*0-06-024102-0*) HarpC Child Bks.

— Sarah, Plain & Tall. LC 83-49481. (Trophy Bk.). 64p. (J). (gr. 3 up). 1987. pap. 3.95 (*0-06-440205-3*, Trophy) HarpC Child Bks.

— Sarah, Plain & Tall. braille ed. 56p. (J). 1994. pap. 4.48 (*1-56956-561-9*, BR9531) W A T Braille.

— Sarah, Plain & Tall. large type ed. 64p. (J). (gr. 4-8). 1995. reprint ed. lib. bdg. 16.95 (*1-885885-12-1*, Cornerstone FL) Pages Inc FL.

— Seven Kisses in a Row. LC 82-47718. (Charlotte Zolotow Bk.). (Illus.). 64p. (J). (gr. 2-5). 1983. lib. bdg. 13.89 (*0-06-024084-9*) HarpC Child Bks.

— Seven Kisses in a Row. LC 82-47718. (Charlotte Zolotow Bk.). (Illus.). 64p. (J). (gr. 2-5). 1988. pap. 3.95 (*0-06-440231-2*, Trophy) HarpC Child Bks.

— The Sick Day. LC 78-11686. (Illus.). (J). (gr. k-3). 1979. 6.95 (*0-394-83876-9*) Pantheon.

— Skylark. LC 93-33211. 64p. (J). (gr. 3-5). 1994. 12.95 (*0-06-023328-1*); lib. bdg. 12.89 (*0-06-023333-8*) HarpC Child Bks.

— Three Names. LC 90-4444. (Charlotte Zolotow Bk.). (Illus.). 32p. (J). (gr. k-4). 1991. lib. bdg. 14.89 (*0-06-024036-9*) HarpC Child Bks.

— Three Names. LC 90-4444. (Illus.). 32p. (J). (gr. k-4). 1994. pap. 4.95 (*0-06-443360-9*, Trophy) HarpC Child Bks.

— Through Grandpa's Eyes. LC 79-2019. (Trophy Picture Bk.). (Illus.). 48p. (J). (gr. k-3). 1983. pap. 4.95 (*0-06-443041-3*, Trophy) HarpC Child Bks.

— Through Grandpa's Eyes. LC 79-2019. (Illus.). 48p. (J). (gr. 2-4). 1980. lib. bdg. 14.89 (*0-06-024043-1*) HarpC.

— Tomorrow's Wizard. LC 81-47733. (Charlotte Zolotow Bk.). (Illus.). 96p. (J). (gr. 3-6). 1982. lib. bdg. 13.89 (*0-06-024074-1*) HarpC Child Bks.

— Unclaimed Treasures. LC 83-47714. (Charlotte Zolotow Bk.). 128p. (J). (gr. 5-7). 1984. 14.00 (*0-06-024093-8*); lib. bdg. 14.89 (*0-06-024094-6*) HarpC Child Bks.

— Unclaimed Treasures. LC 83-47714. (Trophy Bk.). 128p. (J). (gr. 5-7). 1987. pap. 3.95 (*0-06-440189-8*, Trophy) HarpC Child Bks.

— What You Know First. LC 94-38341. (Joanna Cotler Books). (Illus.). 32p. (J). (gr. k up). 1995. 14.95 (*0-06-024413-5*); lib. bdg. 14.89 (*0-06-024414-3*) HarpC Child Bks.

Maclachlan, Simon, ed. Life after Big Bang. (C). 1988. lib. bdg. 56.50 (*0-86010-982-8*, Pub. by Graham & Trotman UK) Kluwer Ac.

Maclachlin, Cheryl. Bringing Italy Home. 1995. 40.00 (*0-517-59807-8*) Crown Pub Group.

Maclagan, David. Creation Myths: Man's Introduction to the World. (Art & Imagination Ser.). (Illus.). 1977. pap. 14.95 (*0-500-81010-9*) Thames Hudson.

MacLagan, Robert C., comp. The Games & Diversions of Argyleshire. (Folk-Lore Society London Monographs: Vol. 47). 1969. reprint ed. pap. 25.00 (*0-8115-0521-9*) Periodicals Srv.

Maclagen, Robert C., comp. Games & Diversions of Argyleshire. LC 75-34848. (Studies in Play & Games). (Illus.). 1976. reprint ed. 25.95 (*0-405-07927-3*) Ayer.

MacLain, M., ed. see Reider, Barbara.

MacLaine, Allan H. Robert Fergusson. LC 65-18225. (Twayne's English Authors Ser.). 178p. (C). 1965. lib. bdg. 17.95 (*0-8057-1192-9*) Irvington.

MacLaine, Shirley. Dance While You Can. 1992. mass mkt. 5.99 (*0-553-29786-4*) Bantam.

— Dance While You Can. large type ed. LC 92-34910. (General Ser.). 386p. 1993. pap. 16.95 (*0-8161-5638-7*) G K Hall.

— Dancing in the Light. 1986. mass mkt. 6.50 (*0-553-27557-7*) Bantam.

— Don't Fall off the Mountain. 1985. mass mkt. 5.99 (*0-553-27438-4*) Bantam.

— Going Within. 1989. 18.95 (*0-685-24546-2*) S&S Trade.

— Going Within: A Guide for Inner Transformation. 1990. mass mkt. 5.99 (*0-553-28331-6*) Bantam.

— It's All in the Playing. 1988. mass mkt. 5.99 (*0-553-27299-3*) Bantam.

— My Lucky Stars: A Hollywood Memoir. LC 94-49220. 1995. 22.95 (*0-553-09717-2*) Bantam.

— Out on a Limb. 1986. mass mkt. 5.99 (*0-553-27370-1*) Bantam.

— You Can Get There from Here. 224p. 1976. mass mkt. 5.99 (*0-553-26173-8*) Bantam.

— You Can Get There from Here. 249p. 1975. 17.95 (*0-393-07489-7*) Norton.

MacLane, Jack. Blood Dreams. 352p. 1989. pap. 3.95 (*0-8217-2680-3*) Zebra.

— Goodnight Moom. 352p. 1989. pap. 3.95 (*0-8217-2570-X*) Zebra.

Maclane, Jack. Just Before Dark. 1990. pap. 3.95 (*0-8217-3212-9*) Zebra.

MacLane, Jack. Keepers of the Beast. 352p. 1988. pap. 3.95 (*0-8217-2486-X*) Zebra.

Maclane, Jack. Rest in Peace. 1990. pap. 3.95 (*0-8217-2987-X*) Zebra.

MacLane, Mary. I, Mary MacLane: A Diary of Human Days. (American Biography Ser.). 317p. 1991. reprint ed. lib. bdg. 79.00 (*0-7812-8257-8*) Rprt Serv.

— The Story of Mary MacLane by Herself. (American Biography Ser.). 322p. 1991. reprint ed. lib. bdg. 79.00 (*0-7812-8258-6*) Rprt Serv.

— Tender Darkness: A Mary MacLane Anthology. Pruitt, Elisabeth A., ed. (Illus.). 208p. 1993. reprint ed. pap. 14.95 (*1-883304-01-6*) Abernathy & Brown.

MacLane, S. Categories for the Working Mathematician. LC 78-166080. (Graduate Texts in Mathematics Ser.: Vol. 5). 272p. 1994. 39.95 (*0-387-90035-7*) Spr-Verlag.

— Homology. (Grundlehren der Mathematischen Wissenschaften Ser.: Vol. 114). (Illus.). x, 422p. 1994. 89.00 (*0-387-03823-X*) Spr-Verlag.

MacLane, S. & Siefkes, D. J., eds. The Collected Works of J. Richard Buchi. (Illus.). 705p. 1989. 69.00 (*0-387-97064-9*, 3061) Spr-Verlag.

MacLane, Saunders. Selected Papers: Saunders MacLane. Kaplansky, Irving, ed. LC 79-10105. 1979. 79.00 (*0-387-90394-1*) Spr-Verlag.

Maclaran, Andrew. Dublin: The Shaping of a Capital. LC 92-43255. (World Cities Ser.). 242p. 1993. text ed. 49.95 (*0-470-22009-0*, Belhaven) Halsted Pr.

— Dublin: The Shaping of a Capital. (World Cities Ser.). 1993. text ed. 59.95 (*0-471-94711-3*) Wiley.

MacLaren. C & A: Maternal & Neonatal Nursing. 1993. 19.95 (*0-87434-576-6*) Springhouse Pub.

— Nurse's Clinical Guide to Maternity Care. 1991. 26.95 (*0-87434-397-6*) Springhouse Pub.

MacLaren, et al. Student Manual to Maternal, Neonatal & Women's Health Nursing. 1991. 14.95 (*0-87434-360-7*) Springhouse Pub.

MacLaren & Kenner. Essentials of Maternal & Neonatal Nursing. 1992. 34.95 (*0-87434-471-9*) Springhouse Pub.

— Instructor's Manual to Essentials of Material & Neonatal Nursing. 1992. write for info. (*0-87434-472-7*) Springhouse Pub.

Maclaren, Alexander. After the Resurrection. LC 91-21642. 160p. 1992. pap. 9.99 (*0-8254-3199-9*) Kregel.

— Best of Alexander Maclaren. Atkins, Gaius G., ed. LC 74-179733. (Biography Index Reprint Ser.). 1977. reprint ed. 17.95 (*0-8369-8101-4*) Ayer.

MacLaren, Alexander. Expositions of Holy Scripture, 17 vols, Set. 12830p. 1975. reprint ed. 495.00 (*0-8010-5967-4*) Baker Bk.

Maclaren, Alexander. Victory in Failure. Petersen, William J., ed. LC 79-88309. (Shepherd Illustrated Classics Ser.). (Illus.). 196p. (Orig.). pap. 5.95 (*0-8254-5311-9*) Kregel.

MacLaren, Angus, jt. auth. see Hammer, David L.

MacLaren, Catherine B. Fashion: Nineteen Hundred to Nineteen Seventy. LC 83-90107. (Illus.). 64p. 1985. 28.00 (*0-88014-063-1*) Mosaic Pr OH.

MacLaren, Dorothy. Esopus Hodie, Aesop Today, Vol. II. 68p. (Orig.). (LAT.). 1991. pap. text ed. 9.50 (*0-939507-25-0*, B21) Amer Classical.

MacLaren, Dorothy H. Esopus Hodie, Vol. 1: Aesop Today. 64p. (ENG & LAT.). (YA). (gr. 9-12). 9.50 (*0-939507-06-4*, B20) Amer Classical.

MacLaren, Ian. Beside the Bonnie Brier Bush. 1976. 21.95 (*0-8488-0290-X*) Amereon Ltd.

— Beside the Bonnie Brier Bush. 224p. 1992. reprint ed. lib. bdg. 16.95 (*0-89966-891-7*) Buccaneer Bks.

— Days of Auld Lang Syne. 1976. 21.95 (*0-8488-0291-8*) Amereon Ltd.

— Kate Carnegie. 1976. 21.95 (*0-8488-0292-6*) Amereon Ltd.

MacLaren, J. Gaelic Self-Taught. 1991. pap. 19.95 (*0-8288-3344-3*, M4217) Fr & Eur.

MacLaren, J. M., et al. Surface Crystallographic Information Service: A Handbook of Surface Structures. (C). 1987. pap. text ed. 80.50 (*90-277-2554-3*) Kluwer Ac.

MacLaren, James. Gaelic Self-Taught. (C). 1989. pap. 30.00 (*0-901771-20-1*, Pub. by Gairm Pubns UK) St Mut.

Maclaren, James. Gaelic Self Taught. 4th ed. 1992. pap. 24.50 (*0-901771-84-8*) Colton Bk.

— The Hitchhiker's Handbook. LC 95-75679. 152p. (Orig.). (YA). 1995. pap. 11.95 (*1-55950-125-1*, 17075) Loompanics.

MacLaren, Margaret. The MacLarens: A History of Clan Labhran. 153p. (C). 1989. text ed. 60.00 (*0-946270-10-4*, Pub. by Pentland Pr UK) St Mut.

MacLaren, Margaret, jt. auth. see Hills, P. J.

MacLaren, Neil. Dutch School, 2 vol. set. exp. rev. ed. (National Gallery Publications). (Illus.). 1990. text ed. 175.00 (*0-300-06137-4*) Yale U Pr.

— Spanish School. rev. ed. (National Gallery Publications). (Illus.). 1989. text ed. 25.00 (*0-300-06143-9*) Yale U Pr.

MacLaren-Ross, J. Doomsday Book. 1961. 11.95 (*0-8392-1027-2*) Astor-Honor.

Maclaren-Ross, J., tr. see Simenon, Georges.

MacLaren, Terrence F. Eckstrom's Licensing in Foreign & Domestic Operations: Joint Ventures, 3 vols., Set. LC 85-10934. (IP Ser.). 1985. ring bd. 425.00 (*0-87632-466-9*) Clark Boardman Callaghan.

MacLaren, Terrence F., ed. Worldwide Trade Secrets Law. LC 93-27434. (IP Ser.). 1993. ring bd. 425.00 (*0-87632-921-0*) Clark Boardman Callaghan.

Maclaren, W. A. Rubber, Tea & Cacao with Special Sections on Coffee, Spices & Tobacco. 1980. lib. bdg. 75.00 (*0-8490-3110-9*) Gordon Pr.

MacLauchlan, Andrew. New Classic Deserts. (Illus.). 288p. 1994. text ed. 39.95 (*0-442-01735-9*) Van Nos Reinhold.

MacLaughlin, Margaret L., jt. ed. see Cody, Michael J.

Maclauries. A Narrative or Journal of Voyages & Travels through the Northwest Continent in the Years 1789 & 1793. 93p. 1980. 14.95 (*0-87770-231-4*) Ye Galleon.

Maclaurin, Colin, ed. An Account of Sir Isaac Newton's Philosophical Discoveries. (Anglistica & Americana Ser.: No. 87). (Illus.). 440p. 1971. reprint ed. 83.20 (*3-487-04002-6*, Pub. by Georg Olms GW) Lubrecht & Cramer.

MacLaurin, Diane. The Magick Horn. Karcher, Pamela, ed. (Illus.). 75p. (Orig.). (YA). (gr. 6 up). 1993. pap. write for info. (*0-934549-01-X*) Laurin Hse.

***MacLaurin, Katherine B.** Death & Birth, Heaven & Earth. 470p. 1995. pap. 12.95 (*0-7610-0128-X*) NW Pub.

Maclaurin, W. Rupert. Invention & Innovation in the Radio Industry. LC 74-161146. (History of Broadcasting: Radio to Television Ser.). 1976. reprint ed. 25.95 (*0-405-03567-5*) Ayer.

MacLaury, Jean. Selected Federal & State Publications of Interest to Planning Librarians: List No. 4, No. 1151. 1976. 5.50 (*0-686-20413-1*) CPL Biblios.

— Selected Federal & State Publications of Interest to Planning Librarians: No. 8. 1977. 2.50 (*0-686-19123-4*, 1246) CPL Biblios.

— Selected Federal & State Publications of Interest to Planning Librarians: No. 9. 1977. 2.50 (*0-686-19104-8*, 1268) CPL Biblios.

— Selected Federal & State Publications of Interest to Planning Librarians, No. 1, No. 1092. 1976. 7.00 (*0-686-20404-2*) CPL Biblios.

— Selected Federal & State Publications of Interest to Planning Librarians, No. 2, No. 1115. 1976. 5.00 (*0-686-20405-0*) CPL Biblios.

— Selected Federal & State Publications of Interest to Planning Librarians, No. 5, No. 1174. 1976. 6.00 (*0-686-20417-4*) CPL Biblios.

***MacLaverty, Bernard.** Cal: A Novel. 160p. 1995. pap. 11.00 (*0-393-31332-8*, Norton Paperbks) Norton.

— Walking the Dog: And Other Stories. LC 94-36707. 208p. 1995. 20.00 (*0-393-03758-4*) Norton.

Maclay, Carol & Harrison, John. The Executive Secretary in Europe: International Administration & Secretarial Procedures. 400p. (Orig.). 1994. pap. 44.50 (*0-273-60311-6*, Pub. by Pitman Pub Ltd UK) Trans-Atl Phila.

***Maclay, Charlotte.** The Cowboy & the Belly Dancer. (American Romance Ser.). 1995. mass mkt. 3.50 (*0-373-16585-4*, 1-16585-1) Harlequin Bks.

— Elusive Treasure. (American Romance Ser.). 1993. mass mkt. 3.50 (*0-373-16503-X*, 1-16503-4) Harlequin Bks.

— A Ghostly Affair. (American Romance Ser.). 1993. mass mkt. 3.39 (*0-373-16488-2*, 1-16488-8) Harlequin Bks.

— How to Marry a Millionaire. (American Romance Ser.). 1995. pap. 3.50 (*0-373-16566-8*, 1-16566-1) Harlequin Bks.

— The Kidnapped Bride. 1994. mass mkt. 3.50 (*0-373-16537-4*, 1-16537-2) Harlequin Bks.

— Michael's Magic. (American Romance Ser.). 1994. mass mkt. 3.50 (*0-373-16532-3*, 1-16532-3) Harlequin Bks.

— The Villain's Lady. (American Romance Ser.). 1993. mass mkt. 3.39 (*0-373-16474-2*, 1-16474-8) Harlequin Bks.

Maclay, Edgar S. A History of American Privateers. LC 74-119937. (Select Bibliographies Reprint Ser.). 1977. reprint ed. 36.95 (*0-8369-5380-0*) Ayer.

***Maclay, Elise.** Bev Doolittle: New Magic. LC 95-15256. 1995. write for info. (*0-86713-026-1*) Greenw Pr Ltd.

— Green Winter: Celebrations of Later Life. 142p. 1995. pap. 8.95 (*0-8050-3805-1*, Owl) H Holt & Co.

— Green Winter: Celebrations of Old Age. 1977. 8.95 (*0-07-044617-2*) Readrs Digest Pr.

***Maclay, Elise, text.** Bev Doolittle. LC 95-15087. 1995. write for info. (*0-553-10104-8*) Bantam.

Maclay, John, intro. Voices from the Night. deluxe limited ed. LC 93-80782. 320p. 1994. 60.00 (*0-940776-29-4*) Maclay Assoc.

Maclay, John, ed. see Castle, Mort, et al.

Maclay, John, jt. auth. see Williamson, J. N.

Maclay, Sarah. Weeding the Duchess. 1979. pap. 5.00 (*0-686-71066-5*) Black Stone.

Maclay, William. The Journal of William Maclay: United States Senator from Pennsylvania, 1789-1791. (American Biography Ser.). 429p. 1991. reprint ed. lib. bdg. 89.00 (*0-7812-8259-4*) Rprt Serv.

Maclean. Compendium of Kaffir Laws & Customs. (Illus.). 171p. 1968. reprint ed. 37.50 (*0-7146-1907-8*, Pub. by F Cass Pubs UK) Intl Spec Bk.

— Lecture Notes on Clinical Investigation. 229p. 1991. 32.95 (*0-632-02907-2*) Blackwell Sci.

MacLean, Alair, jt. auth. see Rennie, Caroline.

MacLean, Alex, photos. Look at the Land: Aerial Reflections on America. LC 93-13555. (Illus.). 176p. 1993. 50.00 (*0-8478-1656-7*) Rizzoli Intl.

MacLean, Alistair. Athabasca. 288p. 1982. mass mkt. 4.95 (*0-449-20001-9*, Crest) Fawcett.

— Breakheart Pass. (Paperback Ser.). 184p. 1990. pap. 12.95 (*0-8161-4982-8*) G K Hall.

— Caravan to Vaccares. large type ed. 1972. 12.00 (*0-85456-099-8*) Ulverscroft.

— Circus. 22.95 (*0-89190-672-X*, Am Repr) Amereon Ltd.

— Fear Is the Key. 1976. 20.95 (*0-89190-171-X*) Amereon Ltd.

Maclean, Alistair. Floodgate. 320p. 1985. mass mkt. 4.95 (*0-449-20343-3*, Crest) Fawcett.

MacLean, Alistair. Force Ten from Navarone. large type ed. 1975. 12.00 (*0-85456-345-8*) Ulverscroft.

— Golden Gate. 1976. 19.95 (*0-8488-0571-2*) Amereon Ltd.

— Goodbye, California. 22.95 (*0-89190-671-1*, Am Repr) Amereon Ltd.

— The Guns of Navarone. 1987. mass mkt. 5.99 (*0-449-21472-9*, Expression) Fawcett.

— The Guns of Navarone. 1994. reprint ed. lib. bdg. 27.95 (*1-56849-306-1*) Buccaneer Bks.

— H. M. S. Ulysses. large type ed. 577p. 1980. 21.95 (*0-7089-0471-8*) Ulverscroft.

— Ice Station Zebra. 1984. mass mkt. 4.95 (*0-449-20576-2*, Crest) Fawcett.

Maclean, Alistair. A MacDonald for the Prince. 1985. 27.00 (*0-86152-002-5*, Pub. by Acair Ltd UK) St Mut.

MacLean, Alistair. Night Without End. reprint ed. lib. bdg. 19.95 (*0-89190-174-4*, Rivercity Pr) Amereon Ltd.

— Partisans. large type ed. 368p. 1983. 21.95 (*0-7089-1003-3*) Ulverscroft.

— Puppet on a Chain. reprint ed. lib. bdg. 19.95 (*0-89190-175-2*, Rivercity Pr) Amereon Ltd.

Maclean, Alistair. Red Alert. large type ed. 1993. pap. 16.95 (*0-7927-1254-4*, Paragon Lrg Print) Chivers N Amer.

MacLean, Alistair. Santorini. 1988. mass mkt. 4.95 (*0-449-20974-1*, Crest) Fawcett.

— The Satan Bug. large type ed. 1972. 21.95 (*0-85456-111-0*) Ulverscroft.

— The Satan Bug. 1994. reprint ed. lib. bdg. 27.95 (*1-56849-305-3*) Buccaneer Bks.

— Seawitch. 19.95 (*0-89190-673-8*, Am Repr) Amereon Ltd.

Maclean, Alistair. Seawitch. 1978. mass mkt. 4.95 (*0-449-21049-9*, Crest) Fawcett.

MacLean, Alistair. Secret Ways. 1976. 20.95 (*0-89190-172-8*) Amereon Ltd.

— South by Java Head. 1976. 21.95 (*0-89190-173-6*) Amereon Ltd.

— When Eight Bells Toll. large type ed. LC 93-19775. 1993. 20.95 (*0-7927-1666-3*, Eagle Lrg Print); pap. 18.95 (*0-7927-1665-5*, Eagle Lrg Print) Chivers N Amer.

— Where Eagles Dare. LC 94-6446. 1994. 20.95 (*0-7927-2058-X*, Eagle Lrg Print) Chivers N Amer.

— Where Eagles Dare. LC 94-6446. 1995. pap. 19.95 (*0-7927-2057-1*, Paragon Lrg Print) Chivers N Amer.

— Where Eagles Dare. 1987. mass mkt. 4.95 (*0-449-21581-4*) Fawcett.

***MacLean, Alistair & Bowser, M.** What the Hell...? Cole, Jean & Simons, Jeffrey, eds. (Illus.). 368p. 1991. lib. bdg. 20.00 (*0-614-06652-2*) Sitare.

MacLean, Alistair, ed. see Bowser, Milton.

MacLean, Alister, ed. see Bowser, M.

MacLean, Alister, ed. see Bowser, Milton.

MacLean, Alister, ed. see Haramilio, Alyce.

Maclean, Allan B., ed. Clinical Infection in Obstetrics & Gynecology. (Illus.). 400p. 1990. 95.00 (*0-632-02694-4*) Blackwell Sci.

***MacLean, Amanda.** Westward. 1995. pap. 8.99 (*0-88070-751-8*) Questar Pubs.

MacLean, Ana, jt. ed. see Weller, Marc.

MacLean, Angus. The Beginning of Time & Other Stories. (Illus.). 233p. (Orig.). 1984. 14.95 (*0-914598-67-8*); pap. 8.95 (*0-914598-68-6*) Bear Flag Bks.

— The Ghosts of Frank & Jesse James & Other Stories. (Illus.). 124p. (Orig.). 1987. 10.95 (*0-914598-72-4*); pap. 7.95 (*0-914598-73-2*) Bear Flag Bks.

— Legends of the California Bandidos. (Illus.). 256p. 1989. reprint ed. 12.50 (*0-939919-21-4*); reprint ed. pap. 8.95 (*0-939919-20-6*) Bear Flag Bks.

— The Wind in Both Ears. 2nd ed. 1987. pap. 6.00 (*0-933840-30-6*, Skinner Hse Bks) Unitarian Univ.

Maclean, Anne. The Elimination of Morality: Reflections on Utilitarianism & Bioethics. LC 93-20281. 232p. 1993. 49.95 (*0-415-01081-0*, B2368, Routledge NY); pap. 15.95 (*0-415-09538-7*, B2372, Routledge NY) Routledge.

MacLean, Annie M. Wage-Earning Women. LC 74-3962. (Women in America Ser.). (Illus.). 218p. 1974. reprint ed. 24.95 (*0-405-06111-0*) Ayer.

MacLean, Brian D., jt. ed. see Lowman, John.

MacLean, C., jt. auth. see Hilbers, C. W.

Maclean, C. D. Manual of the Administration of the Madras Presidency, 3 vols., Set, Vols. I-III. (C). 1987. reprint ed. Set. 168.50 (*0-8364-2415-8*, Pub. by Asian Educ Servs II) S Asia.

Maclean, Calum I. The Highlands. (Illus.). 224p. 1992. 34.95 (*1-85158-365-3*, Pub. by Mnstream UK) Trafalgar.

Maclean, Catherine H. Dorothy & William Wordsworth. LC 71-39678. (English Biography Ser.: No. 31). 1972. reprint ed. lib. bdg. 58.95 (*0-8383-1403-1*) M S G Haskell Hse.

Maclean, Catherine M. Dorothy Wordsworth: The Early Years. LC 77-124243. (Select Bibliographies Reprint Ser.). 1977. reprint ed. 25.95 (*0-8369-5431-9*) Ayer.

MacLean, Charles. Clan Almanac. (Illus.). 144p. 1990. 5.99 (*0-517-05415-9*) Random Hse Value.

— A Little Book of Clans & Tartans. (Illus.). 60p. 1995. 7.95 (*0-86281-547-9*, Pub. by Appletree Pr IE) Irish Bks Media.

— Pocket Whiskey Book: A Guide to Malt, Grain, Liquor & Leading Blended Whiskies. 192p. 1993. 12.95 (*1-85732-171-5*, Pub. by Reed Illust Books UK) Antique Collect.

— Romantic Scotland. (Illus.). 160p. 1995. 24.95 (*0-297-83252-2*) Trafalgar.

— Romantic Scotland. (Country Ser.). (Illus.). 160p. 1995. pap. 16.95 (*0-297-83472-X*, Pub. by Orion) Trafalgar.

— Scottish Toasts & Graces. (Illus.). 60p. 1994. 7.95 (*0-8118-0622-7*) Chronicle Bks.

Maclean, Charles & Sykes, Christopher S. Scottish Country: Living in Scotland's Private Houses. (Illus.). 240p. 1992. 45.00 (*0-517-58273-2*, C P Pubs) Crown Pub Group.

Maclean, Colin & Maclean, Moira, illus. Mother Goose Rhymes. LC 92-26443. 32p. (J). (ps-1). 1993. 9.95 (*1-85697-898-2*, Kingfisher LKC) LKC.

Maclean, Colin, jt. illus. see Maclean, Moira.

MacLean Craig, Jane, jt. auth. see Feder, Lewis M.

Maclean, D. M. Trusts & Powers. xx, 139p. 1989. 43.00 (*0-455-20910-3*, Pub. by Law Bk Co) W W Gaunt.

Maclean, Derryl N. Religion & Society in Arab Sind. LC 88-24064. (Monographs & Theoretical Studies in Sociology & Anthropology in Honour of Nels Anderson: Vol. 25). x, 191p. (Orig.). 1989. pap. text ed. 43.00 (*90-04-08551-3*) E J Brill.

Maclean, Donald, tr. see Reinckens, Sunnhild.

Maclean, Donald, tr. see Von Goethe, Johann W.

Maclean, Dorothy. To Hear the Angels Sing. 217p. (Orig.). 1983. pap. text ed. 7.00 (*0-936878-01-0*) Lorian Pr.

— To Hear the Angels Sing: An Odyssey of Co-creation with the Devic Kingdom. 218p. 1990. reprint ed. pap. 10.95 (*0-940262-37-1*) Lindisfarne Pr.

Maclean, Doug & Gould, Sue. The Helping Process: An Introduction. 224p. 1988. lib. bdg. 52.50 (*0-7099-4682-1*, Pub. by Croom Helm UK) Routledge Chapman & Hall.

MacLean, Douglas, ed. The Security Gamble: Deterrence Dilemmas in the Nuclear Age. 1984. pap. 22.75 (*0-317-05231-4*) IPPP.

— Values at Risk. 1986. 49.00 (*0-317-05233-0*); pap. 22.75 (*0-317-05529-1*) IPPP.

— Values at Risk. (Maryland Studies in Public Philosophy). 192p. (C). 1986. 49.00 (*0-8476-7414-2*); pap. 25.00 (*0-8476-7415-0*) Rowman.

MacLean, Douglas & Brown, Peter G., eds. Energy & the Future. 1983. 59.50 (*0-317-05527-5*); pap. 27.25 (*0-317-05223-3*) IPPP.

— Energy & the Future. LC 82-18609. (Illus.). 218p. (C). 1983. text ed. 65.00 (*0-8476-7149-6*, R7149) Rowman.

MacLean, Douglas & Mills, Claudia, eds. Liberalism Reconsidered. 1983. 55.75 (*0-317-05227-6*); pap. 24.00 (*0-317-05228-4*) IPPP.

— Liberalism Reconsidered. LC 83-8623. (Maryland Studies in Public Philosophy). 160p. (C). 1983. 55.75 (*0-8476-7279-4*); pap. 26.50 (*0-8476-7280-8*) Rowman.

MacLean, Edna A. Inupiallu Tannillu Uqalunisa Ilanich: Abridged Inupiaq & English Dictionary. (Illus.). xxii, 168p. (Orig.). (C). 1981. pap. 14.00 (*0-933769-19-9*) Alaska Native.

— North Slope Inupiaq Dialogues. 13p. (C). 1985. pap. 2.50 (*1-55500-014-2*) Alaska Native.

— North Slope Inupiaq Grammar: First Year. 3rd rev. ed. (Illus.). xii, 279p. 1986. pap. text ed. 18.00 (*1-55500-026-6*) Alaska Native.

— Quliaqtuat Mumiaksrat Ilisaqtuanun Savaaksriat. (Illus.). iv, 35p. (Orig.). (ESK.). (C). 1986. pap. 4.00 (*1-55500-027-4*) Alaska Native.

MacLean, Elizabeth K. Joseph E. Davies: Envoy to the Soviets. LC 91-44445. 264p. 1992. text ed. 47.95 (*0-275-93580-9*, C3580, Praeger Pubs) Greenwood.

***Maclean, Fitzroy.** Highlanders: A History of the Scottish Clans. (Illus.). 256p. 1995. 40.00 (*0-670-86644-X*, Viking Studio) Studio Bks.

— Scotland: A Concise History. rev. ed. LC 92-62136. (Illus.). 240p. 1993. pap. 15.95 (*0-500-27706-0*) Thames Hudson.

MacLean, Gary E. Documenting Quality for ISO 9000 & Other Industry Standards. LC 93-27743. 231p. 1993. pap. 24.95 (*0-87389-212-7*) ASQC Qual Pr.

MacLean, George. Suicide in Children & Adolescents. 144p. 1990. 22.00 (*0-920887-52-X*) Hogrefe & Huber Pubs.

MacLean, George & Rappen, Ulrich. Hermine Hug-Hellmuth: Her Life & Work. 320p. 1991. 39.95 (*0-415-90060-3*, A2408, Routledge NY) Routledge.

***Maclean, Gerald, ed.** Culture & Society in the Stuart Restoration: Literature, Drama, History. (Illus.). 288p. (C). 1995. 59.95 (*0-521-41605-1*) Cambridge U Pr.

— Culture & Society in the Stuart Restoration: Literature, Drama, History. (Illus.). 288p. (C). 1995. pap. 19.95 (*0-521-47566-X*) Cambridge U Pr.

Maclean, Gerald, jt. auth. see Landry, Donna.

Maclean, Gerald, ed. see Spivak, Gayatri C.

MacLean, Gerald M. Time's Witness: Historical Representation in English Poetry, 1603- 1660. LC 89-40532. (Illus.). 336p. (C). 1990. text ed. 40.00 (*0-299-12390-1*); pap. text ed. 17.50 (*0-299-12394-4*) U of Wis Pr.

Maclean, Gordon L. Ornithology for Africa. 1991. 45.00 (*0-86980-737-4*, Pub. by Univ Natal Pr SA); pap. 35.00 (*0-86980-771-4*, Pub. by Univ Natal Pr SA) Intl Spec Bk.

— Roberts Birds of Southern Africa. 600p. (C). 1988. 275.00 (*1-85368-037-0*, Pub. by New Holland Pubs UK) St Mut.

Maclean, Harry. Once Upon a Time: Did Eileen Franklin Suddenly Remember a 20 Year Old Murder? 1994. mass mkt. 5.99 (*0-440-21716-4*) Dell.

Maclean, Harry N. In Broad Daylight. 1990. mass mkt. 5.99 (*0-440-20509-3*) Dell.

MacLean, Harry N. Once upon a Time: A True Tale of Memory, Murder, & the Law. LC 92-53325. (Illus.). 512p. 1993. 22.50 (*0-06-016543-X*, HarpT) HarpC.

MacLean, Heather. Women's Experience of Breastfeeding. 208p. 1990. pap. 13.95 (*0-8020-6756-5*) U of Toronto Pr.

MacLean, Heather & Oram, Barbara. Living with Diabetes. xii, 154p. 1988. pap. 11.95 (*0-8020-6693-3*) U of Toronto Pr.

Maclean, Hector. Photography for Artists. LC 72-9218. (Literature of Photography Ser.). 1979. reprint ed. 15.95 (*0-405-04925-0*) Ayer.

MacLean, Helene. Pediatric Nutrition in Clinical Practice. (Illus.). 300p. 1984. write for info. (*0-318-58157-4*) Addison-Wesley.

MacLean, Helene, jt. auth. see Harris, Dena E.

Maclean, Hugh & Smythe, Emma. Yukon Lady: A Tale of Loyalty & Courage. (Illus.). 180p. 1985. pap. text ed. 11.95 (*0-88839-186-2*) Hancock House.

Maclean, Hugh, ed. see Jonson, Ben, et al.

MacLean, Hugh, ed. see Spenser, Edmund.

Maclean, Ian. Interpretation & Meaning in the Renaissance: The Case of Law. (Ideas in Context Ser.: No. 21). (Illus.). 232p. (C). 1992. 54.95 (*0-521-41546-2*) Cambridge U Pr.

— The Renaissance Notion of Woman: A Study in the Fortunes of Scholasticism & Medical Science in European Intellectual Life. LC 79-52837. (Cambridge Monographs in the History of Medicine). 119p. 1983. pap. 14.95 (*0-521-27436-2*) Cambridge U Pr.

Maclean, Ian, ed. see Moliere.

Maclean, Ian, et al, eds. The Political Responsibility of Intellectuals. 264p. (C). 1991. pap. 18.95 (*0-521-39859-2*) Cambridge U Pr.

MacLean, J. Elsevier's Dictionary of Building Construction: English - French. 390p. (ENG & FRE.). 1989. 225.00 (*0-8288-9283-0*) Fr & Eur.

— Elsevier's Dictionary of Building Construction: French - English. 346p. (ENG & FRE.). 1988. 225.00 (*0-8288-9282-2*, M801) Fr & Eur.

— Elsevier's Dictionary of Building Construction: French-English. 346p. 1988. 113.00 (*0-444-42931-X*) Elsevier.

Maclean, J. H. Elsevier's Dictionary of Building Construction: English-French. 390p. 1989. 113.00 (*0-444-42966-2*) Elsevier.

Maclean, J. L. & Temprosa, R. M. Bibliography on Indo-Pacific Red Tides. 1990. pap. text ed. 5.00 (*971-10-2259-1*, Pub. by ICLARM PH) Intl Spec Bk.

MacLean, J. L., jt. ed. see Hallegraeff, G. M.

MacLean, Jan. An Island Loving. large type ed. (Linford Romance Library). 416p. 1985. pap. 11.95 (*0-7089-6099-5*, Trailtree Bookshop) Ulverscroft.

Maclean, Jan. White Fire. large type ed. (Linford Romance Library). 368p. 1985. pap. 11.95 (*0-7089-6051-0*, Trailtree Bookshop) Ulverscroft.

Maclean, Janet R. Recreation & Leisure. 4th ed. 370p. (C). 1985. text ed. write for info. (*0-02-374370-0*) Macmillan.

Maclean, Joan. English in Basic Medical Science. (English in Focus Ser.). (Illus.). 1975. teacher ed 14.95 (*0-19-437503-X*); pap. text ed. 12.95 (*0-19-437515-3*) OUP.

MacLean, John. History of the College of New Jersey from Its Origin in 1746 to the Commencement of 1854, 2 Vols, Set. LC 74-89198. (American Education: Its Men, Institutions & Ideas, Ser. 1). 1970. reprint ed. 38.95 (*0-405-01435-X*) Ayer.

— Mac. 192p. 1989. reprint ed. pap. 2.95 (*0-380-70700-4*, Flare) Avon.

— When the Mountain Sings. LC 91-26720. 212p. (J). (gr. 5-9). 1992. 14.95 (*0-395-59917-2*) HM.

MacLean, John, ed. see Salisbury, Robert C.

Maclean, John, ed. see Totnes, George C.

MacLean, John C. A Rich Harvest: The History, Buildings, & People of Lincoln, Massachusetts. 680p. 1987. 30.00 (*0-944856-01-2*) Lincoln Hist Soc.

MacLean, John C. & Martin, Margaret M. Lincoln Libraries, 1789-1984. (Illus.). 112p. (Orig.). 1984. pap. 15.00 (*0-944856-06-3*) Lincoln Hist Soc.

MacLean, Kenneth. Blue Heron's Sky. 1991. pap. 10.00 (*0-941179-28-1*) Latitudes Pr.

MacLean, Loraine. Old Inverness in Pictures. 1978. 24.95 (*0-8464-0682-9*) Beekman Pubs.

Maclean, Magnus. Literature of the Highlands. LC 70-144492. reprint ed. 11.50 (*0-404-08595-4*) AMS Pr.

Maclean, Mairi. French Enterprise & the Challenge of the British Water Industry: Water Without Frontiers. 158p. 1991. text ed. 68.95 (*1-85628-100-0*, Pub. by Avebury Pub UK) Ashgate Pub Co.

Maclean, Mairi & Howorth, Jolyon, eds. Europeans on Europe: Transnational Visions of a New Continent. LC 91-24048. 220p. 1992. text ed. 69.95 (*0-312-06834-4*) St Martin.

MacLean, Margaret G. H., ed. Cultural Heritage in Asia & the Pacific: Proceedings of a Symposium Held in Honolulu, Hawaii, September 8-13, 1991. LC 93-25491. (Illus.). 131p. 1993. 25.00 (*0-89236-248-0*) J P Getty Trust.

MacLean, Marie. The Name of the Mother: Writing Illegitimacy. LC 93-34974. 272p. 1994. 69.95 (*0-415-10686-9*, B3802) Routledge.

Maclean, Marie & MacLean, Marie. Narrative As Performance: The Baudelairean Experiment. 220p. 1988. text ed. 49.95 (*0-415-00663-5*); pap. 14.95 (*0-415-00664-3*) Routledge.

MacLean, Marie, jt. auth. see Maclean, Marie.

MacLean, Mary M., ed. see Bowser, Milton.

Maclean, Mavis. Surviving Divorce: Women's Resources after Separation. 166p. 1991. text ed. 40.00 (*0-8147-5462-7*) NYU Pr.

Maclean, Mavis & Groves, Dulcie, eds. Women's Issues in Social Policy. 240p. 1990. 55.00 (*0-415-04121-X*, A5157); pap. 18.95 (*0-415-04122-8*, A5161) Routledge.

Maclean, Mavis & Kurczewski, Jacek, eds. Families, Politics, & the Law: Perspectives for East & West Europe. (Oxford Socio-Legal Studies). 336p. 1994. 55.00 (*0-19-825810-0*) OUP.

MacLean, Mavis, jt. ed. see Eekelaar, John.

Maclean, Moira & Maclean, Colin, illus. Little Red Riding Hood & Other Stories. LC 92-26448. (Nursery Library). 24p. (J). (ps-00). 1993. 5.95 (*1-85697-904-0*, Kingfisher LKC) LKC.

— Nursery Rhymes. LC 92-26446. (Nursery Library). 32p. (J). (ps-00). 1993. pap. 4.95 (*1-85697-905-9*, Kingfisher LKC) LKC.

— The Nursery Treasury: A Collection of Rhymes, Poems, Lullabies & Games. 128p. (J). 1988. pap. 18.95 (*0-385-24650-1*) Doubleday.

Maclean, Moira, jt. illus. see Maclean, Colin.

MacLean, Mrs. Alistair & Bowser, Milton. The Fire of Humiliation. (Illus.). 350p. 1992. 25.00 (*0-940178-49-4*) Sitare.

***MacLean, Murray.** New Hedges for the Countryside. (Illus.). 288p. 1992. text ed. 34.95 (*0-614-07151-8*, Pub. by Farming Pr UK) Diamond Farm Bk.

***MacLean, Nancy K.** Behind the Mask of Chivalry: The Making of the Second Ku Klux Klan. (Illus.). 336p. 1995. pap. 13.95 (*0-19-509836-6*) OUP.

— Behind the Mask of Chivalry: The Making of the Second Ku Klux Klan in a Georgia Town. LC 93-27548. 336p. 1994. 30.00 (*0-19-507234-0*) OUP.

MacLean, Neil, intro. Food for All Seasons: The New Scottish Cooking. 130p. (C). 1989. 110.00 (*0-948473-10-X*) St Mut.

MacLean, Norman. Genes & Gene Regulation. (New Studies in Biology). 144p. (Orig.). (C). 1992. pap. 14.95 (*0-521-42777-0*) Cambridge U Pr.

Maclean, Norman. Norman Maclean. McFarland, Ron & Nichols, Hugh, eds. LC 87-72517. (American Authors Ser.). 200p. 1988. pap. 12.95 (*0-917652-71-1*) Confluence Pr.

— Oxford Surveys on Eukaryotic Genes, Vol. 3: 1986. (Illus.). 250p. 1987. 45.00 (*0-19-854200-3*) OUP.

— Oxford Surveys on Eukaryotic Genes, Vol. 5: 1988. (Illus.). 296p. 1989. 50.00 (*0-19-854237-2*) OUP.

— Oxford Surveys on Eukaryotic Genes, Vol. 6: 1989. (Illus.). 202p. 1990. 65.00 (*0-19-854255-0*) OUP.

— A River Runs Through It. (Illus.). vi, 161p. 1989. 24.95 (*0-226-50060-8*) U Ch Pr.

— A River Runs Through It & Other Stories. LC 75-20895. 232p. 1976. 15.00 (*0-226-50055-1*) U Ch Pr.

— A River Runs Through It & Other Stories. LC 75-20895. 232p. 1979. pap. 9.95 (*0-226-50057-8*, P821) U Ch Pr.

MacLean, Norman. A River Runs Through It & Other Stories. Peters, Sally, ed. 256p. 1992. reprint ed. mass mkt. 5.99 (*0-671-77697-5*) PB.

Maclean, Norman. Young Men & Fire. LC 92-11890. (Illus.). 328p. 1992. 19.95 (*0-226-50061-6*) U Ch Pr.

— Young Men & Fire. LC 92-11890. (Illus.). xiv, 302p. 1993. pap. 10.95 (*0-226-50062-4*) U Ch Pr.

— Young Men & Fire. large type ed. LC 92-45046. (General Ser.). 1993. 20.95 (*0-8161-5734-0*, Large Print Bks) Hall.

MacLean, Norman, ed. Animals with Novel Genes. LC 94-11728. (Illus.). 295p. (C). 1995. 49.95 (*0-521-43256-1*) Cambridge U Pr.

Maclean, Norman, ed. Oxford Surveys on Eukaryotic Genes, Vol. 7. (Illus.). 184p. 1991. 72.00 (*0-19-854256-9*) OUP.

— Oxford Surveys on Eukaryotic Genes: 1987, Vol. 4. (Illus.). 250p. 1988. 45.00 (*0-19-854231-3*) OUP.

— Oxford Surveys on Eukaryotic Genes 1984, 2 vols., 1. 1985. 65.00 (*0-19-854157-0*) OUP.

— Oxford Surveys on Eukaryotic Genes 1984, 2 vols., 2. 1986. 65.00 (*0-19-854175-9*) OUP.

Maclean, Norman & Hall, Brian K. Cell Commitment & Differentiation. (Illus.). 256p. 1987. 79.95 (*0-521-30884-4*) Cambridge U Pr.

Maclean, Norman, tr. see Lungwitz, Hans.

MacLean, P. D. The Triune Brain in Evolution: Role in Paleocerebral Functions. LC 89-22899. (Illus.). 696p. 1990. 95.00 (*0-306-43168-8*, Plenum Pr) Plenum.

***Maclean, R.** Stalin's Nose. 1994. pap. 3.99 (*0-517-12879-9*) Random.

MacLean, R., jt. auth. see Matthews, P.

MaClean, Richard, jt. auth. see Penner, Peter.

MacLean, Robert M. European Community Law. 250p. (C). 1991. pap. 40.00 (*1-85352-787-4*, Pub. by HLT Pubns UK) St Mut.

— Narcissus & the Voyeur: Three Books & Two Films. (Approaches to Semiotics Ser.: No. 48). 1979. text ed. 60.00 (*90-279-7838-7*) Mouton.

MacLean, Robert M., ed. Public International Law. 316p. (C). 1990. pap. 40.00 (*1-85352-752-1*, Pub. by HLT Pubns UK) St Mut.

— Public International Law. 325p. (C). 1991. 90.00 (*1-85352-398-4*, Pub. by HLT Pubns UK) St Mut.

MacLean, Robert M. & Rossiter, Sean. Flying Cold: The Adventures of Russel Merrill, Pioneer Alaskan Aviator. Graydon, Don, ed. LC 94-27416. (Illus.). 192p. 1994. 34.95 (*0-945397-32-1*); pap. 24.95 (*0-945397-33-X*) Epicenter Pr.

MacLean, Rory. Stalin's Nose: Travels Around the Bloc. LC 92-21702. 1993. 19.95 (*0-316-54239-3*) Little.

MacLean, Roy. Stalin's Nose. large type ed. 1993. 39.95 (*0-7066-1002-4*, Pub. by Remploy Pr CN) St Mut.

MacLean, Roy, et al. Analysing Systems: Determining Requirements for Change & Development. LC 94-19590. 312p. 1994. pap. text ed. 48.00 (*0-13-301433-9*) P-H.

Maclean, Rupert, ed. Teacher's Career & Promotional Patterns: A Sociological Analysis. 284p. 1991. 55.00 (*0-685-50669-X*, Falmer Pr); pap. 25.00 (*0-685-50670-3*, Falmer Pr) Taylor & Francis.

Maclean, Rupert & McKenzie, Phillip. Australian Teachers Careers. (C). 1990. 75.00 (*0-86431-077-3*, Pub. by Aust Council Educ Res AT) St Mut.

MacLean, Sally-Beth. Chester Art: A Subject List of Extant & Lost Art Including Items Relevant to Early Drama. (Early Drama, Art & Music Reference Ser.: No. 3). 1982. 14.95 (*0-918720-20-6*); pap. 7.95 (*0-918720-21-4*) Medieval Inst.

MacLean, Sally-Beth, jt. ed. see Carpenter, Jennifer.

MacLean, Sorley, tr. see MacLean, Sorley, et al.

MacLean, Sorley, et al. Sorley Maclean Poems 1932-82. Gillis, Daniel, ed. MacLean, Sorley, tr. LC 87-2755. (Columban Celtic Ser.: Vol. 2). 180p. (Orig.). 1986. 12.95 (*0-941638-01-4*); pap. 8.95 (*0-941638-02-2*) Iona Phila.

Maclean, T. S. Principles of Antennas: Wire & Aperture. (Illus.). 275p. 1986. 105.00 (*0-521-30668-X*) Cambridge U Pr.

Maclean, T. S. & Wu, Z. Radiowave Propagation over Ground. LC 92-36063. 1993. write for info. (*0-412-42730-3*) Chapman & Hall.

Maclean, William A., jt. auth. see Waldo, Albert L.

Maclean, Williams. Computing in School. 200p. (C). 1987. 50.00 (*81-85017-35-2*, Pub. by Interprint II) St Mut.

Maclear, jt. auth. see Srivastava.

Maclear, Anne B. Early New England Towns. LC 08-18393. (Columbia University. Studies in the Social Sciences: No. 78). reprint ed. 17.50 (*0-404-51078-7*) AMS Pr.

Maclear, G. F. Canterbury: Its Rise, Ruin & Restoration. 1976. lib. bdg. 34.95 (*0-8490-1568-5*) Gordon Pr.

Maclear, George F. Apostles of Mediaeval Europe. LC 72-624. (Essay Index Reprint Ser.). 1977. reprint ed. 23.95 (*0-8369-2803-2*) Ayer.

***Maclear, J. F.** Church & State in the Modern Age: A Documentary History. 480p. 1995. text ed. 60.00 (*0-19-508681-3*) OUP.

MacLear, Michael. The Ten Thousand Day War: Vietnam 1945-1975. 384p. 1982. pap. 10.95 (*0-380-60970-3*) Avon.

MacLeary, A. National Taxation for Property Management & Valuation. 240p. 1990. pap. write for info. (*0-419-15320-9*, E & FN Spon) Routledge Chapman & Hall.

Macleay, Iain, jt. auth. see Scott, Andrew M.

MacLehose, Alexander, tr. see Vercors.

MacLehose, Christopher. Leopard Two: Turning the Page. 363p. (Orig.). 1994. pap. 14.00 (*0-00-272174-0*, Pub. by HarpC UK) HarpC.

***MacLehose, Christopher, ed.** Leopard III. 320p. 1995. pap. 15.00 (*0-00-271403-5*, Pub. by HarpC UK) HarpC.

Maclehose, Louisa S., tr. see Vasari, Giorgio.

Macleish, A., ed. see Frankfurter, Felix.

MacLeish, Andrew. Middle English Subject-Verb Cluster: A Quantitative Synchronic Description. LC 68-23809. (Janua Linguarum, Ser. Practica: No. 26). (Orig.). (C). 1969. pap. text ed. 73.10 (*90-279-0689-0*) Mouton.

MacLeish, Andrew & Reyerson, Kathryn L., eds. The Medieval Monastery. (Medieval Studies at Minnesota: Vol. 2). 1988. pap. text ed. 16.95 (*0-8166-2005-9*) U of Minn Pr.

MacLeish, Archibald. Champion of a Cause: Essays & Addresses on Librarianship. LC 70-150577. 262p. reprint ed. pap. 74.70 (*0-317-26595-4*, 2024191) Bks Demand.

— Freedom Is the Right to Choose. LC 72-142662. (Essay Index Reprint Ser.). 1977. 19.95 (*0-8369-2172-0*) Ayer.

— The Great American Fourth of July Parade. LC 74-24682. (Poetry Ser.). 51p. 1976. pap. 12.95 (*0-8229-5272-6*) U of Pittsburgh Pr.

— J.B. pap. 10.95 (*0-395-08353-2*, 4, SenEd) HM.

— Land of the Free. LC 77-9353. (Photography Ser.). (Illus.). 1977. reprint ed. lib. bdg. 25.00 (*0-306-77435-6*); reprint ed. pap. 7.95 (*0-306-80080-2*) Da Capo.

— New & Collected Poems: 1917-1984. 544p. 1985. pap. 16.95 (*0-395-39569-0*) HM.

— Nobodaddy. LC 74-1356. (Studies in Poetry: No. 38). 1974. lib. bdg. 75.00 (*0-8383-2034-1*) M S G Haskell Hse.

— Poetry & Opinion. LC 74-2189. (Studies in Poetry: No. 38). (C). 1974. lib. bdg. 75.00 (*0-8383-2043-0*) M S G Haskell Hse.

Macleish, Archibald. Three Short Plays. 1961. pap. 13.00 (*0-8222-0600-5*) Dramatists Play.

MacLeish, Archibald. Time to Act. LC 71-117820. (Essay Index Reprint Ser.). 1977. 20.95 (*0-8369-1713-8*) Ayer.

MacLeish, Rod. Crossing at Ivalo. 320p. 1992. reprint ed. mass mkt. 4.99 (*0-8217-3961-1*) Zebra.

Macleish, Roderick. The First Book of Eppe. 384p. 1981. pap. 2.95 (*0-449-24405-9*, Crest) Fawcett.

MacLeish, Roderick. Prince Ombra. 320p. 1994. pap. 12.95 (*0-312-89024-9*) Orb NYC.

MacLeish, William H. The Day Before America. LC 94-9504. 1994. 21.95 (*0-395-46882-5*) HM.

MacLellan, P., jt. ed. see Saucier, Gabriele.

MacLelland, Bruce. Prosperity Through Thought Force. 158p. 1994. pap. 12.00 (*0-89540-276-9*, SB-276) Sun Pub.

MacLelland, Jackie. High Heels. Tilton, Marquetta H., ed. (Illus.). 34p. (Orig.). 1992. pap. 6.50 (*0-942186-04-4*) Paperbacks Plus.

***MacLennan, Alastair H., et al, eds.** Progress in Relaxin Research: Proceedings of the 2nd International Congress on the Hormone Relaxin. LC 94-31284. 340p. 1995. text ed. 106.00 (*981-3049-02-2*) World Scientific Pub.

MacLennan, Andres, ed. see Barston, R. P.

MacLennan, Beryce W. & Dies, Kathryn R. Group Counseling & Psychotherapy with Adolescents. 2nd ed. LC 92-13564. 224p. 1992. text ed. 30.00 (*0-231-07834-X*); pap. text ed. 17.50 (*0-231-07835-8*) Col U Pr.

MacLennan, Beryce W. & Felsenfeld, Naomi. Group Counseling & Psychotherapy with Adolescents. LC 68-18998. 204p. reprint ed. pap. 59.30 (*0-8357-8669-2*, 2056825) Bks Demand.

MacLennan, Bruce J. Functional Programming: Practice & Theory. (Illus.). 416p. (C). 1990. text ed. 37.75 (*0-201-13744-5*) Addison-Wesley.

— Principles of Programming Languages. 2nd ed. 576p. (C). 1987. text ed. 61.25 (*0-03-005163-0*) SCP.

Maclennan, David, ed. A Pocket Book of Healing. (C). 1990. pap. 24.00 (*0-85305-220-4*, Pub. by J Arthur Ltd UK) St Mut.

MacLennan, David N. & Simmonds, E. John. Fisheries Acoustics. 344p. 1992. 79.95 (*0-442-31472-8*) Chapman & Hall.

Maclennan, Duncan. Housing Economics: An Applied Approach. LC 80-42053. (Illus.). 304p. reprint ed. pap. 86.70 (*0-7837-1588-9*, 2041880) Bks Demand.

Maclennan, Duncan & Gibb, Kenneth, eds. Housing Finance & Subsidies in Britain. LC 93-21587. 230p. 1993. 59.95 (*1-85628-423-9*, Pub. by Avebury Pub UK) Ashgate Pub Co.

Maclennan, Elizabeth. The Moon Belongs to Everyone: Making Theatre with 7: 84. 214p. (Orig.). 1990. pap. 20.95 (*0-413-64150-3*, A0478, Pub. by Methuen UK) Heinemann.

***MacLennan, George.** Anchanult. 352p. (C). 1993. pap. 32.00x (*1-874640-20-3*, Pub. by Argyll Pubng UK) St Mut.

— Lucid Interval: Subjective Writing & Madness in History. 232p. 1992. 38.50 (*0-8386-3505-9*) Fairleigh Dickinson.

MacLennan, J. M., tr. see Sukachev, V. & Dylis, N.

Maclennan, M. Gaelic-English - English-Gaelic: Scottish-Gaelic. 613p. 1992. reprint ed. pap. 41.00 (*1-873644-11-6*) IBD Ltd.

MacLennan, Malcolm. Gaelic Dictionary: Gaelic-English English-Gaelic. 632p. (ENG & GAE.). 1980. 38.00 (*0-08-025713-5*, Pergamon Pr); pap. 22.00 (*0-685-04003-8*, Pergamon Pr) Elsevier.

— Gaelic-English - English-Gaelic Dictionary: A Pronouncing & Etymological Dictionary of Scots Gaelic. 632p. 1991. pap. 25.00 (*0-08-025712-7*, Pub. by Aberdeen U Pr) Macmillan.

Maclennan, Malcolm. Gaelic-English, English-Gaelic Dictionary. 613p. (ENG & GAE.). 1991. reprint ed. 39.95 (*0-8288-7881-1*, F45412) Fr & Eur.

— Maclennan's Gaelic-English-English-Gaelic Dictionary: English-Gaelic Dictionary. 1985. 125.00 (*0-317-54667-8*, Pub. by Acair Ltd UK); pap. 80.00 (*0-685-17737-8*, Pub. by Acair Ltd UK) St Mut.

***MacLennan, Nigel.** Coaching & Mentoring. 200p. 1995. 42.95 (*0-566-07562-8*, Pub. by Gower Pub UK) Human Res Dev Pr.

— Opportunity Spotting: Creativity for Corporate Growth. (Illus.). 200p. 1994. 59.95 (*0-566-07497-4*, Pub. by Gower UK) Ashgate Pub Co.

MacLennan, Robert, jt. auth. see Overman, J. Andrew.

MacLennan, Robert, et al. Cancer Registration & Its Techniques. Davis, W., ed. LC 80-471857. (IARC Scientific Publications: No. 21). 248p. reprint ed. pap. 70.70 (*0-7837-3999-0*, 2043830) Bks Demand.

MacLennan, Robert S. Early Christian Texts on Jews & Judaism. (Brown Judaic Studies). 234p. 1990. 55.95 (*1-55540-414-6*) Scholars Pr GA.

MacLennan, Toby. One Walked Out of Two & Forgot It. LC 75-189887. 1972. 15.00 (*0-87110-083-5*) Ultramarine Pub.

MacLennan, W. J. Old Age: A Guide for Professional & Lay Carriers. 141p. (C). 1989. pap. 40.00 (*0-685-60680-5*, Pub. by St Andrew UK) St Mut.

— Old Age: A Guide for Professional & Lay Carriers. 141p. 1993. pap. 24.00 (*0-7152-0640-0*, Pub. by St Andrew UK) St Mut.

MacLennan, W. J., tr. Old Age: A Guide for Professional & Lay Careers. 141p. (C). 1991. pap. text ed. 50.00 (*86-15-30640-0*, Pub. by St Andrew UK) St Mut.

MacLennan, W. J. & Peden, N. R. Metabolic & Endocrine Problems in the Elderly. (Illus.). 210p. 1989. pap. 69.00 (*0-387-19541-6*) Spr-Verlag.

MacLennan, W. J., jt. auth. see Paterson, Colin R.

MacLeod. Analytical Modelling Structural Systems. 1990. pap. write for info. (*0-318-68283-4*) P-H.

— Brief Enchantment. large type ed. 1991. 17.95 (*0-7451-9993-3*, AH029, Atlantic Lrg Print); pap. 15.95 (*0-7927-0458-4*, AS065, Atlantic Lrg Print) Chivers N Amer.

— Cats: Homoeopathic Remedies. 1995. pap. 11.95 (*0-85207-190-6*) Atrium Pubs.

— Dogs: Homoeopathic Remedies. 1995. pap. 13.95 (*0-85207-218-X*) Atrium Pubs.

— Goats: Homoeopathic Remedies. 1995. pap. 19.95 (*0-85207-244-9*) Atrium Pubs.

***MacLeod & Mathews.** Cognitive Psychology & Emotional Disorders. 2nd ed. (Clinical Psychology Ser.). Date not set. pap. text ed. 39.95 (*0-471-94430-0*) Wiley.

Macleod, jt. auth. see Radde.

MacLeod, A. J., jt. ed. see Morton, I. D.

MacLeod, A. J., jt. ed. see Morton, J. D.

MacLeod, Alistair. The Lost Salt Gift of Blood: New & Selected Stories. LC 87-36439. 227p. (Orig.). 1988. pap. 11.95 (*0-86538-063-5*) Ontario Rev NJ.

MacLeod, Ann. Being Someone. LC 91-21475. 288p. (Orig.). 1991. pap. 9.95 (*0-933216-86-6*) Spinsters Ink.

MacLeod, Anne S. American Childhood: Essays on Children's Literature of the Nineteenth & Twentieth Centuries. LC 92-38269. 256p. 1994. 40.00 (*0-8203-1551-6*) U of Ga Pr.

MacLeod, Anne S. & Kidd, Jerry S., eds. Children's Literature: Selected Essays & Bibliographies. LC 77-620023. (Student Contribution Ser.: No. 9). 1977. pap. 9.75 (*0-911808-13-2*) U of Md Lib Serv.

MacLeod, Arlene. Accommodating Protest: Working Women, the New Veiling, & Change in Cairo. 240p. (C). 1993. text ed. 32.00 (*0-231-07280-5*); pap. 14.00 (*0-231-07281-3*) Col U Pr.

MacLeod, B. An Epigrapher's Annotated Index to Cholan & Yucatecan Verb Morphology. xi, 107p. 1987. 10.00 (*0-913134-28-7*) Mus Anthro MO.

MacLeod, Bruce A. Club Date Musicians: Playing the New York Party Circuit. LC 92-10010. (Illus.). 240p. (C). 1993. 29.95 (*0-252-01954-7*) U of Ill Pr.

Macleod-Brudenell, Iain, jt. auth. see Deshpande, Chris.

Macleod, C. W., ed. see Homer.

MacLeod, Caroline, ed. Parasitic Infections of Pregnancy & the Newborn. (Illus.). 300p. 1988. 65.00 (*0-19-261653-6*) OUP.

MacLeod, Charlotte. The Bilbao Looking Glass. 208p. 1984. pap. 3.50 (*0-380-67454-8*) Avon.

— Cirak's Daughter. LC 89-18343. 192p. (J). (gr. 7 up). 1990. pap. 3.95 (*0-02-044465-6*, Collier Bks Young) S&S Childrens.

— The Convivial Codfish. 224p. 1985. pap. 3.50 (*0-380-69865-X*) Avon.

— The Corpse in Oozak's Pond. 224p. 1988. mass mkt. 4.99 (*0-445-40683-6*, Mysterious Paperbk) Warner Bks.

Macleod, Charlotte. Curse of the Giant Hogweed. (Peter Shandy Ser.). 176p. 1986. pap. 3.50 (*0-380-70051-4*) Avon.

MacLeod, Charlotte. Family Vault. 240p. 1980. mass mkt. 4.50 (*0-380-49080-3*) Avon.

— The Gladstone Bag. 1990. 16.95 (*0-89296-370-0*) Mysterious Pr.

— The Gladstone Bag. 1991. mass mkt. 4.99 (*0-446-40002-5*, Mysterious Paperbk) Warner Bks.

— The Gladstone Bag. large type ed. LC 90-34616. 417p. 1990. lib. bdg. 19.95 (*1-56054-006-0*) Thorndike Pr.

— Grab Bag. 224p. 1986. pap. 3.50 (*0-380-75099-6*) Avon.

— Had She but Known: A Biography of Mary Roberts Rinehart. 352p. 1994. 21.95 (*0-89296-444-8*) Mysterious Pr.

— The Luck Runs Out. 192p. 1981. pap. 3.50 (*0-380-54171-8*) Avon.

— The Odd Job. 288p. 1995. 18.95 (*0-89296-571-1*) Mysterious Pr.

— The Odd Job. 1996. mass mkt. write for info. (*0-446-40397-0*, Mysterious Paperbk) Warner Bks.

— The Odd Job. large type ed. LC 95-2920. 352p. 1995. reprint ed. 20.95 (*0-7838-1374-0*) Hall.

— An Owl Too Many. 240p. 1992. mass mkt. 4.99 (*0-446-40101-3*, Mysterious Paperbk) Warner Bks.

— An Owl too Many. 1991. 17.95 (*0-89296-431-6*) Mysterious Pr.

— An Owl Too Many. large type ed. (General Ser.). 355p. 1991. text ed. 19.95 (*0-8161-5235-7*, Large Print Bks) Hall.

— The Palace Guard. 176p. 1982. mass mkt. 3.99 (*0-380-59857-4*) Avon.

— The Plain Old Man. 224p. 1986. mass mkt. 3.99 (*0-380-70148-0*) Avon.

— The Recycled Citizen. 272p. 1989. mass mkt. 4.99 (*0-445-40689-5*, Mysterious Paperbk) Warner Bks.

— The Recycled Citizen. large type ed. (General Ser.). 352p. 1989. 19.95 (*0-8161-4777-9*, Large Print Bks) Hall.

Macleod, Charlotte. Rest You Merry. (Armchair Detective Library). 224p. 1993. 20.00 (*1-56287-052-1*) Armchair Detective.

— Rest You Merry. limited ed. (Armchair Detective Library). 224p. 1993. 75.00 (*1-56287-051-3*) Armchair Detective.

MacLeod, Charlotte. Rest You Merry. 224p. 1980. reprint ed. mass mkt. 4.99 (*0-380-47530-8*) Avon.

— The Resurrection Man. 256p. 1992. 17.95 (*0-89296-443-X*) Mysterious Pr.

— The Resurrection Man. 256p. 1993. mass mkt. 4.99 (*0-446-40332-6*, Mysterious Paperbk) Warner Bks.

— The Resurrection Man: A Sarah Kelling & Max Bittersohn Mystery. large type ed. LC 92-16313. 386p. 1992. reprint ed. lib. bdg. 17.95 (*1-56054-457-0*) Thorndike Pr.

— The Silver Ghost: A Sarah Kelling Mystery. 224p. 1989. reprint ed. mass mkt. 4.99 (*0-445-40828-6*, Mysterious Paperbk) Warner Bks.

— Something in the Water. 272p. 1994. 18.95 (*0-89296-430-8*) Mysterious Pr.

— Something in the Water. 240p. 1995. mass mkt. 5.50 (*0-446-40446-2*, Mysterious Paperbk) Warner Bks.

— Something in the Water. large type ed. LC 94-6063. 364p. 1994. reprint ed. lib. bdg. 19.95 (*0-7862-0213-0*) Thorndike Pr.

— Something the Cat Dragged In. 208p. (Orig.). 1984. mass mkt. 3.99 (*0-380-69096-9*) Avon.

— Vane Pursuit. 224p. 1990. mass mkt. 5.50 (*0-445-40780-8*, Mysterious Paperbk) Warner Bks.

— The Withdrawing Room. 192p. 1982. mass mkt. 3.99 (*0-380-56473-4*) Avon.

— Wrack & Rune. 208p. 1983. mass mkt. 3.99 (*0-380-61911-3*) Avon.

MacLeod, Charlotte, comp. Christmas Stalkings. LC 91-10306. 272p. 1991. 17.95 (*0-89296-437-5*) Mysterious Pr.

— Christmas Stalkings. 272p. 1992. mass mkt. 5.50 (*0-446-40303-2*, Mysterious Paperbk) Warner Bks.

— Christmas Stalkings. 272p. 1993. mass mkt. 4.99 (*0-446-77820-6*, Mysterious Paperbk) Warner Bks.

— Mistletoe Mysteries. 256p. 1990. mass mkt. 5.50 (*0-445-40920-7*, Mysterious Paperbk) Warner Bks.

— Mistletoe Mysteries. 256p. 1993. mass mkt. 4.50 (*0-446-77819-2*, Mysterious Paperbk) Warner Bks.

MacLeod, Charlotte, ed. Mistletoe Mysteries. large type ed. (General Ser.). 341p. 1990. 19.95 (*0-8161-4992-5*, Large Print Bks) Hall.

MacLeod, Charlotte, sel. Christmas Stalkings: Tales of Yuletide Murder. large type ed. LC 93-16770. 1993. 21.95 (*0-8161-5576-3*) Hall.

Macleod, Charlotte, see Alisa Craig, pseud..

Macleod, Charlotte

MacLeod, Charlotte

MacLeod, D., ed. Intermittent High Intensity Exercise. 384p. 1992. 65.00 (*0-419-17860-0*, A9475, E & FN Spon) Chapman & Hall.

Macleod, D., et al, eds. Exercise: Benefits, Limits & Adaptations. 416p. 1987. pap. text ed. 27.50 (*0-419-14140-5*, E & FN Spon) Routledge Chapman & Hall.

MacLeod, Dan. Ergonomics: Management Issues & Strategies. (Illus.). 224p. 1995. pap. 39.95 (*0-442-01259-4*) Van Nos Reinhold.

MacLeod, David, jt. auth. see McKay, Sharon.

Macleod, David I. Building Character in the American Boy: The Boy Scouts, YMCA, & Their Forerunners, 1870-1920. LC 83-47763. 464p. 1983. text ed. 27.50 (*0-299-09400-6*) U of Wis Pr.

MacLeod, Dawn. Oasis of the North. 276p. (C). 1985. pap. 39.00 (*0-906664-02-0*, Pub. by Mercat Pr Bks UK) St Mut.

***MacLeod, Don.** The Internet Guide for the Legal Researcher: A How-To Guide to Locating & Retrieving Free & Fee-Based Information on the Internet. LC 94-4494. 1995. write for info. (*0-939486-34-2*) Infosources.

Macleod, Donald. The Humiliated & Exalted Lord: A Study of Philippians 2 & Christology. Duncan, J. Ligon, III, ed. 80p. (C). 1993. pap. text ed. 7.95 (*1-884416-03-9*) A Press.

Macleod, Donald A., jt. auth. see Hendrie, William F.

MacLeod, Douglas, jt. ed. see Moser, Mary A.

An Asterisk (*) at the beginning of an entry indicates that the title is appearing in BIP for the first time.

*__MacLeod, Elizabeth.__ Dinosaurs: The Fastest, the Fiercest, the Most Amazing. (Illus.). 32p. (J). (gr. 1-4). 1995. 11.99 (*0-670-86026-3*) Viking Child Bks.

Macleod, Finlay, ed. Togail Tir Marking Time. 160p. (C). 1992. text ed. 75.00 (*0-86152-842-5*, Pub. by Acair Ltd UK) St Mut.

Macleod, Fiona. Iona. 176p. 1990. pap. 10.95 (*0-86315-500-6*, 620, Pub. by Floris Books UK) Anthroposophic.

— The Sin-Eater. (H. P. Lovecraft's Favorite Horror Stories Ser.). 26p. (Orig.). 1985. pap. 2.00 (*0-318-04719-5*) Necronomicon.

MacLeod, Flora. Forming & Managing a Non-Profit Organization in Canada. 2nd ed. (Legal Ser.). 208p. (Orig.). 1991. Canadian Edition. 14.95 (*0-88908-962-0*) Self-Counsel Pr.

— Motivating & Managing Today's Volunteers: How to Build & Lead a Terrific Team. (Business Ser.). 1993. pap. 11.95 (*0-88908-275-8*) Self-Counsel Pr.

Macleod, Flora, ed. Parents & Schools: The Contemporary Challenge. 200p. 1989. 65.00 (*1-85000-498-6*, Falmer Pr); pap. 33.00 (*1-85000-499-4*, Falmer Pr) Taylor & Francis.

Macleod, G. Goats: Homoeopathic Remedies. 192p. (Orig.). Date not set. pap. 29.95 (*0-8464-4178-0*) Beekman Pubs.

MacLeod, G. The Treatment of Cattle by Homoeopathy. 160p. (Orig.). Date not set. pap. 26.95 (*0-8464-4303-1*) Beekman Pubs.

— Treatment of Horses by Homeopathy. rev. ed. 182p. 1993. pap. 26.95 (*0-8464-1284-5*) Beekman Pubs.

— A Veterinary Material Medical & Clincial Repertory. 208p. (Orig.). Date not set. pap. 26.95 (*0-8464-4309-0*) Beekman Pubs.

Macleod, Gael S., jt. auth. see Macleod, William M.

Macleod, George. Cats: Homoeopathic Remedies. 156p. (Orig.). 1990. pap. 19.95 (*0-8464-1335-3*) Beekman Pubs.

— Dogs: Homoeopathic Remedies. 156p. (Orig.). 1990. pap. 20.95 (*0-8464-1334-5*) Beekman Pubs.

Macleod, George, jt. auth. see Hawkins, M. Raymonde.

MacLeod, George F. The Whole Earth Shall Cry Glory. 1987. 35.00 (*0-947988-04-1*, Pub. by Wild Goose Pubns UK); pap. 21.00 (*0-947988-01-7*, Pub. by Wild Goose Pubns UK) St Mut.

MacLeod, Glen. Wallace Stevens & Modern Art: From the Armory Show to Abstract Expressionism. LC 92-25358. (C). 1993. text ed. 35.00 (*0-300-05360-6*) Yale U Pr.

MacLeod, Glen G. Wallace Stevens & Company: The Harmonium Years, 1913-1923. LC 83-3624. (Studies in Modern Literature: No. 3). 133p. reprint ed. pap. 38.00 (*0-8357-1405-5*, 2070504) Bks Demand.

Macleod, H. A. & Langenbeck, P., eds. In-Process Optical Measurements & Industrial Methods. 1990. 53.00 (*0-8194-0313-X*, VOL. 1266) SPIE.

*__MacLeod, Heather.__ City Birds. LC 95-12940. (Rookie Reader Ser.). (Illus.). (J). 1995. write for info. (*0-516-02028-5*) Childrens.

Macleod, I., jt. auth. see Brander, M.

Macleod, I. M. & Heher, A. D., eds. Software for Computer Control (SOCOCO 1988) Selected Papers from the Fifth IFAC-IFIP Symposium, Johannesburg, South Africa, 26-28 April, 1988. (IFAC Proceedings Ser.). (Illus.). 161p. 1989. 100.00 (*0-08-035724-5*) Elsevier.

MacLeod, Ian. Talks for Children. 108p. (C). 1992. pap. 39.00 (*0-685-60704-6*, Pub. by St Andrew UK) St Mut.

MacLeod, Ian, comp. More Talks for Children. 128p. (C). 1992. pap. 39.00 (*0-685-60705-4*, Pub. by St Andrew UK) St Mut.

— More Talks for Children. 128p. 1993. pap. 24.00 (*0-7152-0657-5*, Pub. by St Andrew UK) St Mut.

MacLeod, Ian, jt. auth. see Surtees, Beatrice.

MacLeod, Ian, jt. ed. see Surtees, Beatrice.

Macleod, Innes. Discovering Galloway. 288p. (C). 1989. pap. text ed. 26.00 (*0-85976-114-2*, Pub. by J Donald) St Mut.

MacLeod, Innes & Gilroy, Margaret. Discovering the River Clyde. 180p. (C). 1989. pap. text ed. 26.00 (*0-85976-333-1*, Pub. by J Donald) St Mut.

MacLeod, Iseabail, intro. Mrs. McLintock's Receipts for Cookery & Pastry-Work. 96p. 1986. pap. 3.90 (*0-08-034519-0*, Pub. by Aberdeen U Pr) Macmillan.

Macleod, Iseabail, et al. The Pocket Scots Dictionary. 320p. 1988. pap. 9.95 (*0-08-036581-7*, Pub. by Aberdeen U Pr) Macmillan.

Macleod, Iseabail, et al, eds. The Scots Thesaurus. (Illus.). 556p. 1991. 37.00 (*0-08-036582-5*, Pub. by Aberdeen U Pr); pap. 19.90 (*0-08-036583-3*, Pub. by Aberdeen U Pr) Macmillan.

— The Scots Thesaurus. deluxe ed. (Illus.). 556p. 1991. lib. bdg. 76.50 (*0-08-040926-1*, Pub. by Aberdeen U Pr) Macmillan.

Macleod, J. K. Consumer Sales Law. 1989. U.K. pap. 70.00 (*0-406-50388-5*) Butterworth Legal Pubs.

MacLeod, J. S. & Levitt, A. R. Taxation of Insurance Business. 3rd ed. 1992. 170.00 (*0-406-50882-8*, U.K.) Butterworth Legal Pubs.

MacLeod, Jalerie, ed. Search Inform. 4th ed. 1990. 65.00 (*0-914604-00-7*) UMI Louisville.

MacLeod, James. The Great Doctor Waddel: A Study of Moses Waddel, 1770-1840, As Teacher & Puritan. 194p. 1985. pap. 12.50 (*0-89308-546-4*) Southern Hist Pr.

MacLeod, Jay. Ain't No Makin' It: Leveled Aspirations in a Low-Income Neighborhood. 198p. (C). 1987. pap. text ed. 15.95 (*0-8133-7163-5*) Westview.

Macleod, Jay. Ain't No Makin' It: Leveled Aspirations in a Low-Income Neighborhood. 2nd rev. ed. 338p. (C). 1995. text ed. 55.00 (*0-8133-1514-X*); pap. text ed. 15.95 (*0-8133-1515-8*) Westview.

MacLeod, Jean S. A Handful of Shells. large type ed. 1993. 17.95 (*0-263-13456-3*, Pub. by Mills & Boon Ltd UK) Chivers N Amer.

Macleod, John. No Great Mischief If You Fall: The Highland Experience. (Illus.). 240p. 1994. 34.95 (*1-85158-540-0*, Pub. by Mnstream UK) Trafalgar.

— Some Favourite Books. 128p. 1989. pap. 4.50 (*0-85151-538-X*) Banner of Truth.

MacLeod, Joseph. Beauty & the Beast. LC 74-30346. (Studies in Comparative Literature: No. 35). 1974. lib. bdg. 53.95 (*0-8383-1884-3*) M S G Haskell Hse.

MacLeod, Kenneth, ed. see Martin, Stephen.

Macleod, M., jt. auth. see Wilkins, J.

Macleod, M. D., ed. see Lucian.

MacLeod, M. D.

Macleod, M. D.

MacLeod, M. D.

MacLeod, Malcolm. A Bridge Built Halfway: A History of Memorial University College, 1925-1950. 416p. (C). 1990. text ed. 44.95 (*0-7735-0761-2*, Pub. by McGill CN) U of Toronto Pr.

Macleod, Malcolm L. Concordance to the Poems of Robert Herrick. LC 76-92974. (Studies in Poetry: No. 38). 1970. reprint ed. lib. bdg. 75.00 (*0-8383-0991-7*) M S G Haskell Hse.

Macleod, Margaret A., ed. see Hargrave, Letitia M.

MacLeod, Marian B. Dancing Through Pentecost: Dance Language for Worship from Pentecost to Thanksgiving. Adams, Doug, ed. (Orig.). 1981. pap. 3.00 (*0-941500-23-3*) Sharing Co.

MacLeod, Michael. Thomas Hennell: Countryman, Artist, & Writer. (Illus.). 256p. (C). 1989. 69.95 (*0-521-33124-2*) Cambridge U Pr.

*__MacLeod, Milly.__ Art of Christmas Crafts. 1994. 15.99 (*0-517-12088-7*) Random Hse Value.

MacLeod, Murdo J., et al. Indian-Religious Relations in Colonial Spanish America. Ramirez, Susan E. et al, eds. LC 88-39611. (Foreign & Comparative Studies Program, Latin American Ser.: No. 9). (Illus.). (Orig.). (C). 1989. pap. text ed. 13.00 (*0-915984-32-6*) Syracuse U Foreign Comp.

MacLeod, Murdo J. & Wasserstrom, Robert, eds. Spaniards & Indians in Southeastern Mesoamerica: Essays on the History of Ethnic Relations. LC 82-23725. (Latin American Studies). (Illus.). xviii, 291p. 1983. 30.00 (*0-8032-3082-6*) U of Nebr Pr.

MacLeod, Neil. The Real Paradise: Flora & Fauna of the Gold Coast & Hinterland. 112p. (C). 1990. 60.00 (*0-86439-049-1*, Pub. by Boolarong Pubns AT) St Mut.

Macleod, Norman. German Lyric Poetry. LC 74-164696. reprint ed. 16.00 (*0-404-04138-8*) AMS Pr.

MaCleod, Norman. He Called Himself the Son of Man. 475p. (Orig.). 1993. pap. 12.95 (*1-882270-02-9*) Old Rugged Cross.

Macleod, Norman W. Selected Poems of Norman Macleod. 3rd ed. Trusky, Tom, ed. LC 75-21690. (Ahsahta Press Modern & Contemporary Poets of the West Ser.). 60p. 1975. pap. 6.95 (*0-916272-00-1*) Ahsahta Pr.

MacLeod, Olive. Chiefs & Cities of Central Africa: Across Lake Chad by Way of British, French, & German Territories. LC 78-161269. (Illus.). 408p. 1977. reprint ed. 36.95 (*0-8369-8828-0*) Ayer.

MacLeod, P. A Place to Work. (Down to Earth Ser.). (C). 1990. 23.00 (*0-09-138641-1*, Pub. by S Thornes Pubs UK) St Mut.

MacLeod, Paul K., jt. auth. see Field, Ben T.

Macleod, Pegi N. Daffodils in Winter. Murray, Joan, ed. 346p. 1984. 27.50 (*0-920806-48-1*, Pub. by Penumbra Pr CN) U of Toronto Pr.

MacLeod, R. & Friday, J. Archives of British Men of Science. 1972. 440.00 (*0-7201-0281-2*, Mansell Pub) Cassell.

MacLeod, R., jt. auth. see Brook, W.

MacLeod, R. C. MacLeod: A Short Sketch of Their Clan, History, Folk-Lore, Tales & Biographical Notices of Some Eminent Clansmen. 118p. 1992. reprint ed. lib. bdg. 29.00 (*0-8328-2680-4*); reprint ed. pap. 19.00 (*0-8328-2681-2*) Higginson Bk Co.

Macleod, R. C. The NWMP & Law Enforcement, Eighteen Seventy-Three to Nineteen Hundred Five. LC 76-3709. 230p. reprint ed. pap. 65.60 (*0-8357-8254-9*, 2034011) Bks Demand.

*__MacLeod, R. C. & Schneiderman, David, eds.__ Police Powers in Canada: The Evolution & Practice of Authority. 370p. 1994. 50.00 (*0-8020-2863-2*); pap. 24.95 (*0-8020-7362-X*) U of Toronto Pr.

MacLeod, R. D. & Dickinson, C. H. Root, Soil & Microbe Interactions. 200p. Date not set. pap. write for info. (*0-85198-737-0*) CAB Intl.

MacLeod, R. M., jt. ed. see Muller, E. E.

MacLeod, Robert. All Other Perils. large type ed. 1978. 15.95 (*0-7089-0138-7*) Ulverscroft.

— Ambush at Junction Rock. 1979. pap. 1.75 (*0-449-14303-1*, GM) Fawcett.

Macleod, Robert. Ambush at Junction Rock. large type ed. 1982. 15.95 (*0-7089-0855-1*) Ulverscroft.

MacLeod, Robert. The Appaloosa. 144p. 1980. pap. 1.95 (*0-449-13971-9*, GM) Fawcett.

— The Californio. 224p. 1981. pap. 1.75 (*0-449-14301-5*) Fawcett.

— The Californio. large type ed. 1992. pap. 19.95 (*0-7927-1181-5*, Curley Lrg Print) Chivers N Amer.

Macleod, Robert. The Californio. large type ed. 1980. 12.00 (*0-7089-0588-9*) Ulverscroft.

MacLeod, Robert. Dragonship. large type ed. 1978. 15.95 (*0-7089-0182-4*) Ulverscroft.

— A Killing in Malta. large type ed. 1979. 15.95 (*0-7089-0320-7*) Ulverscroft.

— A Legacy from Tenerife. large type ed. 1985. 15.95 (*0-7089-1351-2*) Ulverscroft.

— The Money Mountain. large type ed. 400p. 1988. 15.95 (*0-7089-1838-7*) Ulverscroft.

— The Muleskinner. large type ed. 1976. 15.95 (*0-85456-453-5*) Ulverscroft.

— Path of Ghosts. large type ed. 248p. 1980. 12.00 (*0-7089-0458-0*) Ulverscroft.

— A Property in Cyprus. large type ed. 1978. 15.95 (*0-7089-0092-5*) Ulverscroft.

Macleod, Robert. The Running Gun. 1980. pap. 1.75 (*0-449-14302-3*, GM) Fawcett.

MacLeod, Robert. The Running Gun. large type ed. 1992. pap. 17.95 (*0-7927-0861-X*, Curley Lrg Print) Chivers N Amer.

— Six Guns South. 1979. pap. 1.50 (*0-449-14235-3*, GM) Fawcett.

— A Witchdance in Bavaria. large type ed. 1977. 15.95 (*0-7089-0010-0*) Ulverscroft.

MacLeod, Robert B. The Persistent Problems of Psychology. LC 75-15636. 207p. 1975. pap. text ed. 19.50x (*0-8207-0254-4*) Duquesne.

MacLeod, Robert B., jt. frwd. see Ketchum, John D.

Macleod, Roderick, ed. see Ironside, Edmund.

MacLeod, Roy. Imperial Science under the Southern Cross. 1992. 39.95 (*0-522-84443-X*) Intl Spec Bk.

MacLeod, Roy, ed. The Commonwealth of Science: ANZAAS & the Scientific Enterprise in Australasia 1888-1988. (Illus.). 400p. 1988. 45.00 (*0-19-554683-0*) OUP.

— Government & Expertise: Specialists, Administrators & Professionals, 1860-1914. (Illus.). 370p. 1988. 79.95 (*0-521-30428-8*) Cambridge U Pr.

*__MacLeod, Roy & Kumar, Deepak, eds.__ Cultural Identity & Global Process. (Theory, Culture & Society Ser.: Vol. 31). 340p. (C). 1995. 32.00 (*0-8039-9237-8*) Sage.

Macleod, Roy & Lewis, Milton, eds. Disease, Medicine & Empire. 302p. (C). 1989. lib. bdg. 79.95 (*0-415-00685-6*) Routledge.

MacLeod, Roy & Rehbock, Philip F., eds. Nature in Its Createst Extent: Western Science in the Pacific. LC 87-30069. (Illus.). 288p. 1988. text ed. 34.00 (*0-8248-1120-8*) UH Pr.

MacLeod, Roy M. & Rehbock, Philip F., eds. Darwin's History: Evolutionary Theory & Natural History in the Pacific. LC 94-20341. 1994. write for info. (*0-8248-1613-7*) UH Pr.

*__MacLeod, Ruairidh H.__ Flora MacDonald: The Jacobite Heroine in Scotland & North America. (Illus.). 256p. 1995. pap. 18.95 (*0-85683-147-6*, Pub. by Shepheard-Walwyn Pubs UK) Paul & Co Pubs.

Macleod, S. & Giltinan, D. Child Care Law: A Summary of the Law in Scotland. (C). 1989. 50.00 (*0-903534-70-3*, Pub. by Brit Ag for Adopt & Fost UK) St Mut.

MacLeod, S. M. & Szefler, S. J., eds. Childhood Asthma & Sustained Release Theophylline: International Workshop, Whistler, Canada. 146p. 1986. 97.00 (*0-444-90450-6*) Elsevier.

MacLeod, V. & Thornberry, S., eds. Business Dateline Controlled Vocabulary. 1990. 25.00 (*0-914604-41-4*) UMI Louisville.

MacLeod, Wendy. Apocalyptic Butterflies. 1990. pap. 4.75 (*0-8222-0060-0*) Dramatists Play.

Macleod, Wendy. The Shallow End & The Lost Colony. 1992. 4.75 (*0-8222-1346-X*) Dramatists Play.

Macleod, William M. & Macleod, Gael S. M. I. N. D. over Weight: How to Stay Slim the Rest of Your Life. 126p. (Orig.). 1985. reprint ed. 10.95 (*0-934439-02-8*); reprint ed. pap. 9.95 (*0-934439-03-6*); reprint ed. 9.95 (*0-934439-04-4*); reprint ed. 19.95 (*0-934439-05-2*) W G M Pub.

MacLeoid, Tormod, et al. Invention of the Cremona Hoax Canntaireachd - Articulate Music Piobaireachd As Verbally Taught, 3 vols. in 1. MacRaonuill, A., tr. & intro. by. 96p. 1992. pap. 18.00 (*0-685-66248-9*) A MacRaonuill.

MacLeon, H. A. Thin-Film Optical Filters. 2nd ed. 1986. pap. 90.00 (*0-07-044694-6*) McGraw.

Macler, F. Contes Armeniens. LC 78-20139. (Collection de contes et de chansons populaires: Vol. 29). reprint ed. 21.50 (*0-404-60379-3*) AMS Pr.

— Contes syriaques. LC 78-20135. (Collection de contes et de chansons populaires: Vol. 26). reprint ed. 21.50 (*0-404-60376-9*) AMS Pr.

MacLer, Veronica, jt. auth. see Broch, Janice.

MacLiammoir, Michael. All for Hecuba. (Illus.). 25.95 (*0-8283-1137-4*) Branden Pub Co.

MacLiammoir, Michael & Boland, Eavan. W. B. Yeats. (Literary Lives Ser.). (Illus.). 1986. pap. 9.95 (*0-500-26022-2*) Thames Hudson.

MacLimore, Guy. Mekton Empire. Quintanar, Derek, ed. (Mekton Ser.). (Illus.). 120p. (C). 1990. pap. 14.00 (*0-937279-15-3*, MK1301) R Talsorian.

Maclin, A. P., et al, eds. Magnetic Phenomena. (Lecture Notes in Physics Ser.: Vol. 337). vi, 142p. 1989. 41.00 (*0-387-51428-7*) Spr-Verlag.

Maclin, Alice. Reference Guide to English. 2nd ed. 496p. (C). 1987. pap. text ed. 15.50 (*0-03-004193-7*) HB Coll Pubs.

Maclin, C. S., intro. United States Navy, Diving Manual, Vol. 1: Air Diving. rev. ed. (NAVSEA Ser.: No. 0994-LP-001-9010). (Illus.). 357p. 1985. student ed. 34.00 (*0-16-002059-X*, S/N 008-046-001) USGPO.

Macliver, C. & Thom, M. Family Talk: Picture Sheets for Children Whose Family Is Adopting or Fostering. (C). 1989. 39.00 (*0-903534-89-4*, Pub. by Brit Ag for Adopt & Fost UK) St Mut.

MacLochlainn, Alf. The Corpus in the Library & Other Stories. (Illus.). 170p. 1996. 19.95 (*1-56478-068-6*) Dalkey Arch.

— Out of Focus. LC 85-72481. 64p. 1985. 20.00 (*0-916583-12-0*); pap. 5.95 (*0-916583-13-9*) Dalkey Arch.

MacLochlainn, Alf, ed. see National Library of Ireland Staff.

Maclow, Jackson. Bloomsday. 112p. (Orig.). 1984. pap. 5.95 (*0-88268-008-0*) Station Hill Pr.

MacLow, Jackson. French Sonnets. (Illus.). 62p. 1989. pap. 5.00 (*0-87924-064-4*) Membrane Pr.

— Is That Wool Hat My Hat? 82p. (Orig.). 1983. pap. 5.00 (*0-87924-046-6*) Membrane Pr.

— The Pronouns: A Collection of Forty Dances for the Dancers-February 3rd to March 22nd 1964. LC 79-64919. 88p. 1979. pap. 4.45 (*0-930794-06-0*) Station Hill Pr.

— The Pronouns: A Collection of Forty Dances for the Dancers-February 3rd to March 22nd 1964. deluxe limited ed. LC 79-64919. 88p. 1979. boxed 50.00 (*0-930794-74-5*) Station Hill Pr.

— Representative Works, Nineteen Thirty-Eight-Nineteen Eighty-Five. LC 85-61392. 350p. (Orig.). 1985. 18.95 (*0-937804-19-3*); pap. 12.95 (*0-937804-18-5*) Segue NYC.

— Twenties. (Roof Bks.). 112p. 1991. pap. text ed. 8.95 (*0-937804-42-8*) Segue NYC.

— The Virginia Woolf Poems. 44p. 1985. pap. 5.00 (*0-930901-28-2*) Burning Deck.

— Words & Ends from E-Z. LC 89-80484. 96p. (Orig.). 1989. pap. 7.50 (*0-939691-03-5*) Avenue B.

— Words & Ends from E-Z. deluxe ed. LC 89-80484. 96p. (Orig.). 1989. 18.00 (*0-685-25266-3*) Avenue B.

Maclulich, T. D. Between Europe & America: The Canadian Tradition in Fiction. 266p. (C). 1988. text ed. 25.00 (*0-920763-96-0*, Pub. by ECW Press CN); pap. text ed. 15.00 (*0-920763-95-2*, Pub. by ECW Press CN) Genl Dist Srvs.

MacLulich, T. D. Hugh MacLennan. (World Authors Ser.: No. 708). 166p. 1983. text ed. 24.95 (*0-8057-6555-7*, Pub. by Royal Botanic Garden UK) Macmillan.

MacLure, Margaret, jt. ed. see French, Peter.

MacLure, Margaret, et al. Oracy Matters. 224p. 1988. pap. 29.00 (*0-335-15855-2*, Open Univ Pr) Taylor & Francis.

MacLure, Millar. Register of Sermons Preached at Paul's Cross 1534-1642. Boswell, Jackson C., ed. 100p. 1989. pap. 8.00 (*0-919473-48-2*, DH78, Pub. by Dovehouse CN) MRTS.

MacLure, Millar, ed. Marlowe: The Critical Heritage, Fifteen Eighty-Eight to Eighteen Ninety-Six. 1979. 69.50 (*0-7100-0245-9*, RKP) Routledge.

MacLure, Millar & Watt, F. W., eds. Essays in English Literature from The Renaissance to the Victorian Age: Presented to A. S. P. Woodhouse, 1964. LC 64-55295. 352p. reprint ed. pap. 100.40 (*0-685-15394-0*, 2026532) Bks Demand.

Maclure, Stuart & Davies, Peter, eds. Learning to Think: Thinking to Learn: Proceedings of the 1989 OECD Conference Organized by the Centre for Educational Research & Innovation. (Illus.). 320p. 1991. 96.00 (*0-08-040646-7*, Pergamon Pr); pap. 43.00 (*0-08-040657-2*, Pergamon Pr) Elsevier.

Maclure, W. Observations on the Geology of the United States of America. 1966. reprint ed. text ed. 44.00 (*0-934454-67-1*) Lubrecht & Cramer.

Maclure, William. Opinions on Various Subjects: Dedicated to the Industrious Producers, 3 vols. LC 68-18220. 1971. reprint ed. 150.00 (*0-678-00712-8*) Kelley.

MacLysaght, Edward. Irish Families: Their Names, Arms & Origins. (Illus.). 248p. 1985. 45.00 (*0-7165-2364-7*, Pub. by Irish Acad Pr IE) Intl Spec Bk.

— Irish Families - Their Names, Arms & Origins. (Illus.). 366p. 1994. reprint ed. lib. bdg. 39.50 (*0-8328-3879-9*) Higginson Bk Co.

— More Irish Families. 254p. 1983. 45.00 (*0-7165-0126-0*, Pub. by Irish Acad Pr IE) Intl Spec Bk.

— The Surnames of Ireland. 336p. 1985. pap. 9.50 (*0-7165-2366-3*, Pub. by Irish Acad Pr IE) Intl Spec Bk.

MacMahon. The Imagination of Jean Genet. 18.50 (*0-685-34133-X*) Fr & Eur.

MacMahon, A. W., et al. The Administration of Federal Work Relief. LC 73-167845. (FDR & the Era of the New Deal Ser.). 408p. 1971. reprint ed. lib. bdg. 49.50 (*0-306-70326-2*) Da Capo.

MacMahon, Alice T. Women & Hormones: An Essential Guide to Being Female. MacMahon, James R., ed. LC 90-81214. (Illus.). 208p. (Orig.). 1990. pap. 9.95 (*0-931128-03-X*) Family Pubns.

Macmahon, Arthur W. Memorandum on the Postwar International Information Program of the United States. LC 72-4673. (International Propaganda & Communications Ser.). 135p. 1972. reprint ed. 18.95 (*0-405-04757-6*) Ayer.

Macmahon, Arthur W. & Millett, John D. Federal Administrators: A Biographical Approach to the Problems of Departmental Administration. LC 70-181953. reprint ed. 31.00 (*0-404-04139-6*) AMS Pr.

MacMahon, Brian & Sugimura, Takashi, eds. Coffee & Health. LC 84-14199. (Banbury Report Ser.: Vol.17). 259p. 1984. 47.50 (*0-87969-217-0*) Cold Spring Harbor.

Macmahon, Brian, jt. ed. see Clark, Duncan W.

MacMahon, Bryan. The Honey Spike. 247p. 1993. reprint ed. pap. 11.95 (*1-85371-310-4*, Pub. by Poolbeg Pr IE) Dufour.

— The Master. (Illus.). 1994. 29.00 (*1-85371-222-1*, Pub. by Poolbeg Pr IE); pap. 9.95 (*1-85371-254-X*, Pub. by Poolbeg Pr IE) Dufour.

— Patsy-O. LC 89-51016. 128p. (Orig.). (J). (gr. 4-7). 1989. pap. 5.95 (*1-85371-036-9*, Pub. by Poolbeg Pr IE) Dufour.

— The Tallystick: And Other Stories. 256p. 1995. 5.25 hd 29.00 (*1-85371-338-4*, Pub. by Poolbeg Pr IE) Dufour.

MacMahon, Bryan, tr. see Sayers, Peig.

MacMahon, Candace W. Elizabeth Bishop: A Bibliography, 1927-1979. LC 79-13063. 247p. reprint ed. pap. 70.40 (*0-7837-2150-1*, 2042436) Bks Demand.

MacMahon, Darcie A., jt. auth. see Deagan, Kathleen A.

M

MacMahon, Desmond. Brass, Wood-Wind, & Strings: The Instruments of the Orchestra: Music Book Index. 101p. 1993. reprint ed. lib. bdg. 69.00 (0-7812-9705-2) Rprt Serv.

MacMahon, Edward B. & Curry, Leonard. Medical Cover-ups in the White House. LC 87-81241. 171p. 1987. 16.95 (0-918535-01-8) Farragut Pub.

Macmahon, Horace. Stereogram Book of Contours. LC 74-188860. 32p. (J). (gr. 1 up). 1972. spiral bd. 6.00 (0-8331-1705-X) Hubbard Sci.

MacMahon, James R., ed. see MacMahon, Alice T.

MacMahon, Percy A. Combinatory Analysis, 2 Vols. in 1. LC 59-10267. 49.50 (0-8284-1137-9) Chelsea Pub.

MacMahon, Percy A. & Andrews, George E., eds. Percy Alexander MacMahon: Collected Papers: Combinatorics, Vol. 1. LC 77-28962. (Mathematicians of Our Time Ser.). 1978. 125.00 (0-262-13121-8) MIT Pr.

— Percy Alexander MacMahon: Collected Papers, Vol. II: Number Theory, Invariants & Applications. (Mathematicians of Our Time Ser.: No. 24). (Illus.). 904p. 1986. 95.00 (0-262-13214-1) MIT Pr.

MacMahon, R. A., ed. An Aid to Paediatric Surgery. 2nd ed. (Illus.). 272p. (Orig.). 1991. pap. text ed. 33.00 (0-443-04185-7) Churchill.

MacManiman, Gen. Dry It-You'll Like It. 3rd ed. (Illus.). 80p. 1983. reprint ed. pap. 6.95 (0-9611998-0-6) MacManiman.

MacManus, Dermot. Middle Kingdom. 1979. pap. 6.95 (0-900675-82-9) Dufour.

— Middle Kingdom: The Faerie World of Ireland. (Illus.). 191p. 1973. 6.95 (0-317-65888-3, Pub. by Colin Smythe Ltd UK) Dufour.

MacManus, Diarmuid. Irish Earth Folk. (Illus.). 1959. 8.95 (0-8159-5814-5) Devin.

MacManus, Francis. Men Withering. 1988. pap. 7.95 (0-85342-115-3) Dufour.

Macmanus, Seumas. Dark Patrick. LC 70-178447. (Short Story Index Reprint Ser.). 1977. reprint ed. 15.95 (0-8369-4048-2) Ayer.

MacManus, Seumas. A Lad of the O'Friels. 19.95 (0-8159-6100-6) Devin.

— The Rocky Road to Dublin. 9.95 (0-8159-6712-8) Devin.

Macmanus, Seumas. The Story of the Irish Race. 1990. 14.99 (0-517-06408-1) Random Hse Value.

MacManus, Seumas. The Story of the Irish Race: A Popular History of Ireland. 41th rev. ed. 740p. 1990. 18.95 (0-8159-6827-2) Devin.

Macmanus, Seumas. Through the Turf Smoke. LC 72-81273. (Short Story Index Reprint Ser.). 1977. 20.95 (0-8369-3025-8) Ayer.

MacManus, Seumas, ed. Donegal Fairy Stories. (Illus.). xii, 256p. (J). (gr. 4-6). 1968. pap. 5.95 (0-486-21971-2) Dover.

MacManus, Susan A. Federal Aid to Houston. LC 82-74101. 59p. 1983. pap. 8.95 (0-8157-5425-6) Brookings.

— Revenue Patterns in U. S. Cities & Suburbs: A Comparative Analysis. LC 77-27499. (Praeger Special Studies). 228p. 1978. text ed. 55.00 (0-275-90304-4, C0304, Praeger Pubs) Greenwood.

MacManus, Susan A., et al. Governing: A Changing America. LC 83-21579. 646p. (C). 1984. teacher ed write for info. (0-02-374470-7); text ed. write for info. (0-02-374440-5); student ed write for info. (0-02-374450-2); write for info. (0-02-374460-X) Macmillan.

MacManus, Theodore. Advertising: Sword Arm of Business. 9.50 (0-8159-6832-9) Devin.

Macmartin, D. F. Thirty Years in Hell: Or, the Confessions of a Drug Fiend. Grob, Gerald N., ed. LC 80-1256. (Addiction in America Ser.). 1981. reprint ed. lib. bdg. 27.95 (0-405-13606-4) Ayer.

Macmaster, Eve. God Gives the Land: Stories of God & His People: Joshua. LC 83-182. (Story Bible Ser.: No. 3). (Illus.). 168p. (Orig.). (J). (ps-1). 1983. pap. 5.95 (0-8361-3332-3) Herald Pr.

MacMaster, Eve. God Rescues His People: Stories of God & His People: Exodus, Leviticus, Numbers & Deuteronomy. LC 82-2849. (Story Bible Ser.: No. 2). (Illus.). 176p. (Orig.). (J). (ps-1). 1982. pap. 5.95 (0-8361-1994-0) Herald Pr.

Macmaster, Eve. God's Chosen King: Stories of God & His People: I Samuel. LC 83-12736. (Story Bible Ser.: No. 4). (Illus.). 190p. (Orig.). (J). (gr. 5-6). 1983. pap. 5.95 (0-8361-3344-7) Herald Pr.

MacMaster, Eve. God's Family. LC 81-6551. (Story Bible Ser.: No. 1). (Illus.). 168p. (J). (gr. 3 up). 1981. pap. 5.95 (0-8361-1964-9) Herald Pr.

— God's Justice. LC 84-20514. (Story Bible Ser.: No. 6). (Illus.). 168p. (Orig.). (J). (ps-1). 1984. pap. 5.95 (0-8361-3381-1) Herald Pr.

— God's Wisdom & Power. LC 84-8974. (Story Bible Ser.: No. 5). (Illus.). 168p. (Orig.). (J). (gr. 3-8). 1984. pap. 5.95 (0-8361-3362-5) Herald Pr.

MacMaster, Eve B. God Builds His Church. LC 87-2875. (Story Bible Ser.: No. 10). (Illus.). 184p. (Orig.). (J). (gr. 3 up). 1987. pap. 5.95 (0-8361-3446-X) Herald Pr.

— God Sends His Son. LC 86-18342. (Story Bible Activity Ser.: No. 8). (Illus.). 160p. (Orig.). (J). (gr. 3-9). 1986. pap. 5.95 (0-8361-3420-6) Herald Pr.

— God's Suffering Servant. LC 86-19526. (Story Bible Activity Ser.: No. 9). (Illus.). 120p. (Orig.). (J). (gr. 3-9). 1987. pap. 5.95 (0-8361-3422-2) Herald Pr.

MacMaster, Neil. Spanish Fighters: An Oral History of War & Exile. 260p. 1991. text ed. 49.95 (0-312-04738-X) St Martin.

MacMaster, Richard K. History of Hardy County, WV, Seventeen Eighty-Six to Nineteen Eighty-Six. 338p. 1986. 35.00 (0-317-54414-4) Hardy Cnty Lib.

— Land, Piety & Peoplehood. LC 84-15790. (Mennonite Experience in America Ser.: Vol. 1). 344p. (Orig.). 1985. pap. 17.95 (0-8361-1261-X) Herald Pr.

MacMaster, Richard K. & Hiebert, Ray E. A Grateful Remembrance: The Story of Montgomery County, Maryland. 1976. 20.00 (0-686-63842-5) Montgomery Co Hist.

Macmaster, Richard K., jt. auth. see Copeland, Pamela C.

MacMaster, Richard K.

MacMaster, Richard K., et al. Conscience in Crisis. LC 78-27530. (Studies in Anabaptist & Mennonite History: No. 20). 528p. 1979. 19.95 (0-8361-1213-X) Herald Pr.

Macmath, Fiona. Blessings for Your Birthday. LC 91-71041. 24p. 1992. 4.50 (0-8066-2565-1, 9-2565) Augsburg Fortress.

— Blessings for Your Graduation. LC 91-71040. 24p. 1992. 4.50 (0-8066-2566-X, 9-2566) Augsburg Fortress.

— Blessings for Your Marriage. LC 91-71038. 24p. 1992. 4.50 (0-8066-2568-6, 9-2568) Augsburg Fortress.

— Blessings for Your New Baby. LC 91-71039. 24p. 1992. 4.50 (0-8066-2567-8, 9-2567) Augsburg Fortress.

MacMath, Fiona, ed. Flora: A Celebration of Plants, Flowers & the Human Spirit. 206p. (Orig.). (C). 1990. pap. 19.95 (0-7459-1840-9) Lion USA.

MacMathuna, Sean. Atheist: And Other Stories. 172p. 1988. 19.95 (0-86327-102-2, Pub. by Wolfhound Pr IE) Dufour.

— Atheist: And Other Stories. 172p. 1993. pap. 10.95 (0-86327-103-0, Pub. by Wolfhound Pr IE) Dufour.

MacMichael, D. B., jt. auth. see Reay, D. A.

Macmichael, H. A. History of the Arabs in Sudan, 2 vols., Set. 1967. reprint ed. 95.00 (0-7146-1041-0, Pub. by F Cass Pubs UK) Intl Spec Bk.

— Tribes of Northern & Central Kordofan. 260p. 1967. reprint ed. 47.50 (0-7146-1113-1, Pub. by F Cass Pubs UK) Intl Spec Bk.

MacMichael, William. Journal from Moscow to Constantinople in the Years 1817 & 1818. LC 71-135817. (Eastern Europe Collection Ser.). 1971. reprint ed. 21.95 (0-405-02759-1) Ayer.

MacMillan. Orbit of Darkness. 1991. 21.95 (0-15-170095-8) HarBrace.

Macmillan & Gilleasbuig. On Reflection: A Workable Relief. 90p. 1993. pap. 21.00 (0-7152-0683-4, Pub. by St Andrew UK) St Mut.

Macmillan, Bill, ed. Remodelling Geography. (Illus.). 320p. 1989. text ed. 59.95 (0-631-16099-X) Blackwell Pubs.

MacMillan, C. J. & Garrison, James W. A Logical Theory of Teaching: Erotetics & Intentionality. (C). 1988. lib. bdg. 90.00 (90-277-2813-5) Kluwer Ac.

MacMillan, Carrie, et al. Silenced Sextet: Six Nineteenth-Century Canadian Women Novelists. (Illus.). 240p. 1993. 42.95 (0-7735-0945-3, Pub. by McGill CN) U of Toronto Pr.

Macmillan, Daniel. Obesity. (Venture Bks.). (Illus.). (YA). (gr. 9-12). 1994. lib. bdg. 14.42 (0-531-11201-2) Watts.

MacMillan, Dianne & Freeman, Dorothy. My Best Friend Mee-Yung Kim: Meeting a Korean-American Family. Steltenpohl, Jane, ed. (My Best Friends Ser.). (Illus.). 48p. (J). (gr. 3-5). 1989. lib. bdg. 9.98 (0-671-65691-0, Julian Messner) Silver Burdett Pr.

MacMillan, Dianne M. Chinese New Year. LC 93-46183. (Best Holiday Books Ser.). (Illus.). 48p. (J). (gr. 1-4). 1994. lib. bdg. 15.95 (0-89490-500-7) Enslow Pubs.

— Easter. LC 92-18970. (Best Holiday Books Ser.). (Illus.). 48p. (J). (gr. 1-4). 1993. lib. bdg. 15.95 (0-89490-405-1) Enslow Pubs.

— Elephants: Our Last Land Giants. LC 92-35268. (J). (gr. 2-5). 1993. 19.95 (0-87614-770-8, Carolrhoda) Lerner Group.

— Jewish Holidays in the Fall. LC 92-30952. (Best Holiday Books Ser.). (Illus.). 48p. (J). (gr. 1-4). 1993. lib. bdg. 15.95 (0-89490-406-X) Enslow Pubs.

— Jewish Holidays in the Spring. LC 93-38637. (Best Holiday Books Ser.). (Illus.). 48p. (J). (gr. 1-4). 1994. lib. bdg. 15.95 (0-89490-503-1) Enslow Pubs.

— Martin Luther King, Jr. Day. LC 91-43097. (Best Holiday Books Ser.). (Illus.). 48p. (J). (gr. 1-4). 1992. lib. bdg. 15.95 (0-89490-382-9) Enslow Pubs.

— Ramadan & Id al-Fitr. LC 93-46185. (Best Holiday Books Ser.). (Illus.). 48p. (J). (gr. 1-4). 1994. lib. bdg. 15.95 (0-89490-502-3) Enslow Pubs.

— Tet: Vietnamese New Year. LC 93-46184. (Best Holiday Books Ser.). (Illus.). 48p. (J). (gr. 1-4). 1994. lib. bdg. 15.95 (0-89490-501-5) Enslow Pubs.

MacMillan, Dianne M., jt. auth. see Freeman, Dorothy R.

***Macmillan, Don.** John Deere Tractors Worldwide: A Century of Progress 1893-1993. LC 94-78879. 248p. 1994. 33.50 (0-929355-55-5); text ed. 29.50 (0-614-01765-3) Am Soc Ag Eng.

Macmillan, Don & Harrington, Roy. John Deere Tractors & Equipment, 1960-1990, Vol. 2. LC 88-71413. (Illus.). 400p. 37.50 (0-929355-19-9, H0190) Am Soc Ag Eng.

Macmillan, Don & Jones, Russell. John Deere Tractors & Equipment, Vol. One: 1837-1959. LC 88-71413. (Illus.). 400p. 1988. 36.00 (0-916150-95-X, H0388) Am Soc Ag Eng.

MacMillan, Donald L. Hidden Youth: Dropouts from Special Education. (Exceptional Children at Risk Ser.). 37p. 1991. 8.90 (0-86586-211-7, P354) Coun Exc Child.

Macmillan, Duncan. The Paintings of Steven Campbell: The Story So Far. (Illus.). 120p. 1994. 29.95 (1-85158-546-X, Pub. by Mnstream UK) Trafalgar.

— Scottish Art 1460-1990. (Illus.). 432p. 1992. 95.00 (1-85158-251-7, Pub. by Mnstream UK) Trafalgar.

MacMillan, Duncan. Symbols of Survival: The Art of Will MacLean. (Illus.). 120p. 1993. 34.95 (1-85158-419-6, Pub. by Mnstream UK) Trafalgar.

Macmillan Editorial Staff. The College Blue Book, 5 vols., Set. 20th ed. 1985. text ed. 185.00 (0-02-695830-9) Macmillan.

Macmillan Educational Company Staff. Collier's Encyclopedia, 1991, 24 vols., Set. 1991. text ed. 959.00 (0-02-942517-4) Macmillan.

— Macmillan Encyclopedia of Science, 12 vols., Set. (Illus.). 1184p. (J). 1991. text ed. 360.00 (0-02-941346-X) Macmillan.

Macmillan Educational Company Staff, ed. Merit Students Encyclopedia, 1991, 20 vols., Set. 1991. text ed. 579.00 (0-02-943752-0) Macmillan.

Macmillan, Ernest. Music in Canada. 1988. reprint ed. lib. bdg. 49.00 (0-7812-0198-5) Rprt Serv.

Macmillan, Ernest, ed. Music in Canada. LC 77-18206. 232p. 1955. reprint ed. 49.00 (0-403-01616-9) Scholarly.

***MacMillan, Gail & Strang, Alison.** The Nova Scotia Duck Tolling Retriever. (Illus.). 1995. write for info. (0-931866-73-1) Alpine Pubns.

***MacMillan, Gordon.** At the End of the Rainbow? Gold, Land, & People in the Brazilian Amazon. LC 95-139. (Methods & Cases in Conservation Science Ser.). 1995. write for info. (0-231-10354-9); pap. write for info. (0-231-10355-7) Col U Pr.

Macmillan, H. F. Handbook of Tropical Plants. 5th ed. 1989. 98.50 (81-7041-177-7, Pub. by Anmol II) S Asia.

— Tropical Planting & Gardening. 6th rev. ed. Enoch, I. & Russell, R. A., eds. 767p. 1991. 66.50 (967-99906-9-9) CAB Intl.

MacMillan, Harold. War Diaries: Politics & War in the Mediterranean, January 1943-May 1945. LC 84-50454. (Illus.). 800p. 1984. 29.95 (0-312-85566-4) St Martin.

MacMillan, Harriet L., jt. auth. see Dawson, David L.

MacMillan, Hugh. Africa & Empire: W. H. MacMillan, Historian & Social Critic. Marks, Shula, ed. (Commonwealth Papers: No. 25). 351p. 1989. text ed. 59.95 (0-566-05494-9, Pub. by Dartmth Pub UK) Ashgate Pub Co.

Macmillan, Hugh P. Law & Other Things. LC 76-152195. (Essay Index Reprint Ser.). 1977. 18.95 (0-8369-2196-8) Ayer.

— Roman Mosaics, or Studies in Rome & It's Neighbourhood. 1977. 18.95 (0-8369-7322-4, 8115) Ayer.

MacMillan, Ian, jt. ed. see Birley, Sue.

MacMillan, Ian C. & Jones, Patricia E. Strategy Formulation: Power & Politics. 2nd ed. LC 85-20389. (Strategic Management Ser.). (Illus.). 160p. (C). 1986. pap. text ed. 34.25 (0-314-85260-3) West Pub.

MacMillan, Ian C., jt. ed. see Birley, Sue.

MacMillan, Ian C., jt. auth. see Block, Zenas.

Macmillan, J., ed. Hormonal Regulation of Development I: Molcular Aspects of Plant Hormones. (Encyclopedia of Plant Physiology Ser.: Vol. 9). (Illus.). 681p. 1980. 207.00 (0-387-10161-6) Spr-Verlag.

MacMillan, J. A. Authority of the Believer. LC 80-68065. 96p. 1981. pap. 2.99 (0-87509-152-0) Chr Pubns.

MacMillan, Joan, jt. auth. see Lofas, Jeannette.

***MacMillan, John & Linklater, Andrew, eds.** Boundaries in Question: New Directions in International Relations. LC 95-3441. 1995. write for info. (1-85567-265-0, Pub. by Pinter Pubs UK); pap. write for info. (1-85567-266-9, Pub. by Pinter Pubs UK) St Martin.

MacMillan, John A. Encounter with Darkness. LC 80-67656. 116p. 1980. 2.99 (0-87509-287-X) Chr Pubns.

MacMillan, Joseph E. The MacMillan Index of Antique Coffee Mills. LC 94-20756. (Illus.). 1392p. 1995. 129.95 (0-87797-264-8) Cherokee.

Macmillan, Kathleen, tr. see Prezzolini, Giuseppe.

Macmillan, Katie, jt. ed. see Allen, Kristen.

MacMillan, Laurie. Santa Barbara Secrets & Sidetrips. (Illus.). 128p. (Orig.). 1991. pap. 8.95 (0-945092-17-2) EZ Nature.

Macmillan, M. Freud Evaluated: The Completed Arc. (Advances in Psychology Ser.: No. 75). 688p. 1991. 140.00 (0-444-88717-2, North Holland) Elsevier.

Macmillan, M. A., tr. see Von Bredow, Ilse.

Macmillan, Mary W., jt. auth. see King, James C.

MacMillan, N. H., jt. auth. see Kelly, A.

Macmillan, Neil A. & Creelman, C. Douglas. Detection Theory: A User's Guide. (Illus.). 435p. (C). 1991. 69.95 (0-521-36359-4) Cambridge U Pr.

***MacMillan, Norma.** Cook's Kitchen Bible. 256p. 1995. 19.98 (0-8317-4363-8) Smithmark.

— In a Shaker Kitchen: One Hundred of the Best Shaker Recipes. LC 94-41491. 1995. 25.00 (0-684-80110-8) S&S Trade.

— A Little New Orleans Cookbook. (Illus.). 1995. text ed. 7.95 (0-8118-0906-4) Chronicle Bks.

Macmillan, Norman. Into the Blue. LC 79-169430. (Literature & History of Aviation Ser.). 1972. reprint ed. 25.95 (0-405-03773-2) Ayer.

Macmillan, Pat. Hiring Excellence: Six Steps to Making Good People Decisions. LC 92-61233. 288p. 1992. 18.00 (0-89109-691-4) NavPress.

***Macmillan Publishing Company, Inc. Staff.** College Blue Book, 5 vols. Incl. College Blue Book Vol. 1. 25th ed. 1995. 50.00 (0-02-895026-7); College Blue Book Vol. 2. 25th ed. 1995. 50.00 (0-02-895027-5); College Blue Book Vol. 3. 25th ed. 1994. 50.00 (0-02-895028-3); College Blue Book Vol. 4. 25th ed. 1994. 50.00 (0-02-895029-1); College Blue Book Vol. 5. 25th ed. 1994. 50.00 (0-02-895143-3); 185.00 (0-02-895148-4) Macmillan.

— College Blue Book Vols. 1-3. 25th ed. 1995. 150.00 (0-02-895144-1) Macmillan.

— College Blue Book Vols. 1-3 & 5. 25th ed. 1994. 200.00 (0-02-895146-8) Macmillan.

— College Blue Book Vols. 1-4. 25th ed. 1994. 200.00 (0-02-895145-X) Macmillan.

Macmillan Publishing Company Staff. The College Blue Book. 23th ed. 1991. text ed. 200.00 (0-02-695981-X) Macmillan.

— Macmillan Dictionary. 1973. write for info. (0-02-195340-6) Macmillan.

— Macmillan Dictionary for Students. LC 84-3880. (Illus.). 1216p. (J). (gr. 6-12). 1984. text ed. 16.95 (0-02-761560-X, Mac Bks Young Read) S&S Childrens.

— Macmillan School Dictionary. 1974. write for info. (0-02-195310-4) Macmillan.

— Macmillan Very First Dictionary: A Magic World of Words. rev. ed. LC 82-22901. (Illus.). 280p. (J). (ps-2). 1983. 10.95 (0-02-761730-0) Macmillan.

MacMillan, Scott. At Sword's Point. (Knights of the Blood Ser.: No. 2). 352p. (Orig.). 1994. pap. 4.99 (0-451-45407-3, ROC) NAL-Dutton.

MacMillan, Scott, ed. Knights of the Blood. 352p. (Orig.). 1993. pap. 4.99 (0-451-45256-9, ROC) NAL-Dutton.

Macmillan Staff. The Baseball Encyclopedia: The Complete & Official Record of Major League Baseball. 8th ed. 2600p. 1990. text ed. 49.95 (0-02-579040-4) Macmillan.

— Baseball Encyclopedia Update, 1994. 224p. 1994. pap. 12.00 (0-02-022649-7, Collier S&S) S&S Trade.

— Macmillan Visual Dictionary, Multilingual Edition: English, French, Spanish, German. 1994. text ed. 60.00 (0-02-578115-4) Macmillan.

— Magic World of Words. 1977. 8.95 (0-02-578770-5) Macmillan.

— Scholar's Fellow Grant Loan. 1986. 44.00 (0-02-695790-6) Macmillan.

— Tabular Data. 20th ed. 1986. 44.00 (0-02-695760-4) Macmillan.

— Visual Dictionary, Four Languages. 928p. 1993. 60.00 (0-685-70478-5) Macmillan.

Macmillan Staff, et al. Macmillan Field Guides: Rocks & Minerals. (Illus.). 192p. 1985. pap. 12.95 (0-02-079640-4, Collier S&S) S&S Trade.

MacMillan, Susan, ed. see Bright, William.

Macmillan, William M. Bantu, Boer, & Briton: The Making of the South African Native Problem. LC 78-27446. (Illus.). 382p. 1979. reprint ed. text ed. 35.00 (0-313-20906-5, MABB, Greenwood Pr) Greenwood.

— The Road to Self-Rule: A Study in Colonial Evolution. LC 77-140365. (Select Bibliographies Reprint Ser.). 1977. reprint ed. 21.95 (0-8369-5608-7) Ayer.

— Warning from the West Indies. LC 73-160982. (Select Bibliographies Reprint Ser.). 1977. reprint ed. 25.95 (0-8369-5850-0) Ayer.

Macmillian, H. F. A Handbook for Tropical Planting & Gardening. 560p. 1984. 400.00 (81-85046-12-3, Scientific) St Mut.

MacMinn, Edwin. On the Frontier with Colonel Antes. 514p. 1991. lib. bdg. 35.00 (1-880484-01-3) Zebrowski Hist.

MacMinn, Strother, ed. Detroit Style: Automotive Form 1925-1950. (Illus.). 120p. 1985. pap. 9.95 (0-89558-113-2) Det Inst Arts.

MacMitchell, Melanie. Sacred Footsteps: A Traveler's Guide to Spiritual Places of Italy & France. (Illus.). 164p. (Orig.). 1991. pap. 9.95 (0-9629727-0-3) Opal Star Pr.

MacMorris, Gale C. The Kremlin Conspiracy: The Coup That Failed. 320p. (Orig.). 1992. 19.95 (0-9632078-4-9); pap. 14.95 (0-9632078-5-7) Charter.

MacMullen, Edith N. In the Cause of True Education: Henry Barnard & Nineteenth-Century School Reform. 368p. (C). 1991. text ed. 42.50 (0-300-04809-2) Yale U Pr.

MacMullen, Grace R. Pain: the Gift Nobody Wants. (Joyful Living Ser.). pap. 1.50 (0-912623-00-4) Joyful Woman.

MacMullen, Jerry, jt. auth. see McNairn, Jack.

MacMullen, Ramsay. Changes in the Roman Empire: Essays in the Ordinary. (Illus.). 444p. 1990. text ed. 44.50 (0-691-03601-2) Princeton U Pr.

— Christianizing the Roman Empire: A.D. 100-400. LC 84-3694. 200p. 1984. 27.00 (0-300-03216-1) Yale U Pr.

— Christianizing the Roman Empire: A.D. 100-400. LC 84-3694. 200p. 1986. pap. 14.00 (0-300-03642-6, Y-571) Yale U Pr.

— Constantine. (Classical Lives Ser.). 272p. 1987. pap. 14.95 (0-7099-4685-6, Pub. by Croom Helm UK) Routledge Chapman & Hall.

— Enemies of the Roman Order. 1992. pap. 17.95 (0-415-08621-3, A9752) Routledge.

— Enemies of the Roman Order: Treason, Unrest, & Alienation in the Empire. LC 66-18250. (Illus.). 380p. reprint ed. pap. 110.10 (0-7837-1717-2, 2057246) Bks Demand.

— Paganism in the Roman Empire. LC 80-54222. 384p. 1983. pap. text ed. 14.00 (0-300-02984-5) Yale U Pr.

— Roman Social Relations, 50 B. C to A. D. 284. LC 73-86909. 317p. 1981. pap. 14.00 (0-300-02702-8, Y-392) Yale U Pr.

— Soldier & Civilian in the Later Roman Empire. LC 63-7591. (Historical Monographs: No. 52). (Illus.). 224p. 1963. 15.00 (0-674-81690-0) HUP.

MacMullen, Ramsay & Lane, Eugene N., eds. Paganism & Christianity, 100-425 C.E. A Sourcebook. LC 92-3069. 224p. (Orig.). 1992. pap. 16.00 (0-8006-2647-8, 1-2647, Fortress Pr) Augsburg Fortress.

MacMullen, Ramsey. Corruption & the Decline of Rome. 331p. (C). 1990. reprint ed. pap. 15.00 (0-300-04799-1) Yale U Pr.

— Roman Government's Response to Crisis, A.D. 235-337. LC 76-43324. 320p. reprint ed. pap. 91.20 (0-8357-8311-1, 2033810) Bks Demand.

MacMunn, George F. Leadership Through the Ages. LC 68-16951. (Essay Index Reprint Ser.). 1977. 19.95 (0-8369-0657-8) Ayer.

Macmurray, John. Conditions of Freedom. LC 93-9222. 108p. (C). 1993. reprint ed. pap. 15.00 (0-391-03714-5) Humanities.

MacMurray, John. The Form of the Personal, 2 vols., Set. LC 77-27175. (Gifford Lectures: 1953-54). reprint ed. 37.50 (0-404-60550-8) AMS Pr.

An Asterisk (*) at the beginning of an entry indicates that the title is appearing in BIP for the first time.

Macmurray, John. Freedom in the Modern World. LC 91-32303. 200p. (C). 1992. pap. 15.00 (*0-391-03728-5*) Humanities.
— Interpreting the Universe. LC 93-20101. 112p. 1995. reprint ed. pap. 15.00 (*0-391-03818-4*) Humanities.
— Persons in Relation. LC 91-21420. 256p. (C). 1991. pap. 15.00 (*0-391-03716-1*) Humanities.
— Reason & Emotion. LC 91-32302. 200p. (C). 1992. pap. 15.00 (*0-391-03729-3*) Humanities.
— The Self As Agent. LC 91-21419. 232p. (C). 1991. pap. 15.95 (*0-391-03715-3*) Humanities.
Macmurray, John, ed. Some Makers of the Modern Spirit: A Symposium. LC 68-22926. (Essay Index Reprint Ser.). 1977. reprint ed. 18.95 (*0-8369-0658-6*) Ayer.
MacMurray, John V. How the Peace Was Lost: The Nineteen Thirty-Five Memorandum Developments Affecting American Policy in the Far East. Waldron, Arthur & Hessen, Robert, eds. (Publication Series: Archival Documentaries). 165p. 1992. 29.95 (*0-8179-9151-4*); pap. 16.95 (*0-8179-9152-2*) Hoover Inst Pr.
MacMurray, Robert R. Technological Change in the American Cotton Spinning Industry, 1790-1836. Bruchey, Stuart, ed. LC 76-39835. (Nineteen Seventy-Seven Dissertations Ser.). (Illus.). 1977. lib. bdg. 62.95 (*0-405-09915-0*) Ayer.
***Macnab.** J. Arthur Rank & the British Film Industry. (Cinema & Society Ser.). 1994. pap. 18.95 (*0-415-11711-9*, B4597) Routledge.
MacNab, Alan A., jt. auth. see Sherf, Arden F.
MacNab, F. A Ride in Morocco. 400p. 1985. 220.00 (*1-85077-071-9*, Darf Pubs Ltd) St Mut.
Macnab, Frances. Life after Loss. 1989. pap. 9.95 (*0-85574-879-6*, Pub. by E J Dwyer AT) Morehouse Pub.
***Macnab, Francis.** Brief Psychotherapy: An Integrative Approach in Clinical Practice. 1993. pap. text ed. 42.95 (*0-471-94078-X*) Wiley.
— The Thirty Vital Years: The Positive Experience of Ageing. LC 93-40291. 1994. pap. text ed. 36.95 (*0-471-94333-9*) Wiley.
MacNab, Geoffrey. J. Arthur Rank & the British Film Industry. LC 92-24832. (Cinema & Society Ser.). (Illus.). 800p. 1993. 49.95 (*0-415-07272-7*, B0137, Routledge NY) Routledge.
Macnab, Ian. Neck Ache & Shoulder Pain. (Illus.). 512p. 1994. 69.00 (*0-683-05354-X*) Williams & Wilkins.
Macnab, Ian & McCulloch, John A. Backache. 2nd ed. (Illus.). 448p. 1990. 60.00 (*0-683-05352-3*) Williams & Wilkins.
***Macnab, P. A.** Mull & Iona. (Pevensey Island Guides Ser.). (Illus.). 112p. 1995. pap. 14.95 (*0-907115-92-6*, Pub. by D & C Pub UK) Sterling.
— Tall Tales from an Island. 245p. 1989. 35.00 (*0-946487-07-3*, Pub. by Luath Pr UK) St Mut.
Macnab, Peter. Highways & Byways in Mull & Iona. (C). 1989. pap. 29.00 (*0-946487-16-2*, Pub. by Luath Pr UK) St Mut.
MacNabb, Elizabeth L. The Fractured Family: The Second Sex & Its (Dis) Connected Daughters. LC 92-34830. (Writing about Women Ser.: Vol. 5). 209p. (C). 1994. text ed. 46.95 (*0-8204-1881-1*) P Lang Pubs.
MacNaffie. Of Danish Ways. 1992. pap. 10.00 (*0-06-092318-0*) HarpC.
Macnaghten, Angus. Haunted Berkshire. 96p. 1987. pap. 30.00 (*0-905392-58-2*) St Mut.
MacNaghten, Hugh. Emile Coue: The Man & His Work. 52p. 1993. pap. 5.00 (*0-89540-230-0*, SB-230) Sun Pub.
MacNair, Donald J. The Challenge of the Eldership: A Handbook for the Elders of the Church. (Orig.). 1984. pap. text ed. 1.95 (*0-934688-12-5*) Great Comm Pubns.
— The Living Church: A Guide for Revitalization. (Illus.). 167p. (Orig.). 1980. pap. 5.95 (*0-934688-00-1*) Great Comm Pubns.
MacNair, Edward A., jt. auth. see Sauer, Charles H.
MacNair, Edward A., et al, eds. Winter Simulation Conference Proceedings: Washington, DC, 1989. 1140p. 1989. 130.00 (*0-911801-58-8*, WSC-89) Soc Computer Sim.
— WSC 1989: Winter Simulation Conference, 1989, Held in Washington, D.C., December 4-6, 1989. 1139p. 1989. pap. text ed. 95.00 (*0-685-33071-0*, 578890) Assn Compu Machinery.
MacNair, Harley F. Modern Chinese History. 1976. lib. bdg. 250.00 (*0-8490-2264-9*) Gordon Pr.
— The Real Conflict Between China & Japan: An Analysis of Opposing Ideologies. (Double-Page Reprint Ser.). 116p. reprint ed. pap. 33.10 (*0-317-29846-1*, 2020114) Bks Demand.
MacNair, Harley F., ed. China. LC 71-134111. (Essay Index Reprint Ser.). 1977. 39.95 (*0-8369-1987-4*) Ayer.
MacNair, Mary W. American Doctoral Dissertations. 1973. 250.00 (*0-87968-598-0*) Gordon Pr.
MacNair, Rachel, et al. Profile Feminism: Yesterday & Today. 380p. (Orig.). 1995. pap. 14.99 (*0-945819-62-5*) Sulzburger & Graham Pub.
MacNair, Ray & McKinney, Elizabeth. Assessment of Child & Adolescent Functioning: A Practitioner's Instrument for Assessing Clients. LC 83-26602. 75p. 1983. pap. 4.50 (*0-911847-02-2*) U GA Inst Community.
MacNair, William. Dictionary of Computer & Video Terms. (Illus.). 87p. (Orig.). 1987. lib. bdg. 49.95 (*0-941303-35-7*); pap. 14.50 (*0-941303-05-5*) Comput & Arts Pubns.
***MacNair, Wilmer.** Basic Thinking: On Beginning at the Beginning in Thinking about Social & Economic Problems. 360p. (C). 1995. lib. bdg. 49.00 (*0-614-03244-X*) U Pr of Amer.
— Basic Thinking: On Beginning at the Beginning in Thinking about Social & Economic Problems. LC 94-44029. 1995. write for info. (*0-8191-9840-4*); pap. write for info. (*0-8191-9841-2*) U Pr of Amer.
MacNally, John & Felix, Antonia. Ireland's Own John MacNally: A Life of Song. (Orig.). 1995. pap. 9.99 (*1-56171-233-7*, S P I Bks) Sure Sellers.
***MacNally, Ralph C.** Ecological Versatility & Community Ecology. (Cambridge Studies in Ecology). (Illus.). 400p. (C). 1992. write for info. (*0-521-40553-X*) Cambridge U Pr.
Macnamara, Angela. Ready Steady Grow! 1989. pap. 22.00 (*0-86217-166-0*, Pub. by Veritas IE) St Mut.
MacNamara, Desmond. The Book of Intrusions. LC 93-36126. 214p. 1994. 19.95 (*1-56478-041-4*) Dalkey Arch.
MacNamara, Donal E. & Karmen, Andrew, eds. Deviants: Victims or Victimizers. LC 83-17825. (Sage Annual Reviews of Studies in Deviance: No. 7). (Illus.). 256p. reprint ed. pap. 73.00 (*0-8357-4768-9*, 2037705) Bks Demand.
MacNamara, Donal E. & McCorkle, Llyod. Crime, Criminals & Corrections. LC 81-84361. 304p. 1982. lib. bdg. 17.00 (*0-89444-032-7*); pap. text ed. 15.00 (*0-89444-033-0*) John Jay Pr.
MacNamara, Donal E. & Sagarin, Edward. Sex, Crime, & the Law. LC 77-5231. 1978. pap. 16.95 (*0-02-919690-6*) Free Pr.
MacNamara, Donal E. & Stead, Philip J. New Dimensions in Transnational Crime. 154p. 1982. lib. bdg. 10.00 (*0-89444-035-7*) John Jay Pr.
MacNamara, Donal E., jt. auth. see Kelly, Robert J.
Macnamara, Ellen. The Etruscans. (British Museum Ser.). (Illus.). 72p. 1991. pap. 12.50 (*0-674-26907-1*, MACETX) HUP.
MacNamara, Ellen. Everyday Life of the Etruscans. 1987. 17.95 (*0-88029-126-5*) Dorset Pr.
MacNamara, John. A Border Dispute: The Place of Logic in Psychology. (Learning, Development & Conceptual Change Ser.). 200p. 1986. 25.00 (*0-262-13216-8*, Bradford Bks) MIT Pr.
MacNamara, John, ed. Language Learning & Thought. 1977. text ed. 51.00 (*0-12-464750-2*) Acad Pr.
MacNamara, John & Reyes, Gonzalo E. The Logical Foundations of Cognition. (Vancouver Studies in Cognitive Science). 400p. 1994. 49.95 (*0-19-509215-5*); pap. 24.95 (*0-19-509216-3*) OUP.
MacNamara, Mark, jt. auth. see Marshall, Richard.
Macnamara, Paul. Those Were the Days, My Friend: My Life in Hollywood with David O. Selznick & Others. LC 93-32129. (Filmmakers Ser.: No. 35). (Illus.). 207p. 1993. 27.50 (*0-8108-2694-1*) Scarecrow.
***MacNamara, Roger D.** Creating Abuse-Free Caregiving Environments for Children, the Disabled, & the Elderly: Preparing, Supervising, & Managing Caregivers for the Emotional Impact of Their Responsibilities. 270p. 1992. pap. 29.95 (*0-398-06261-7*) C C Thomas.
— Creating Abuse-Free Caregiving Environments for Children, the Disabled, & the Elderly: Preparing, Supervising, & Managing Caregivers for the Emotional Impact of Their Responsibilities. 270p. (C). 1992. text ed. 45.95x (*0-398-05761-3*) C C Thomas.
— Freedom from Abuse in Organized Care Settings for the Elderly & Handicapped: Lessons from Human Service Administration. 104p. 1988. pap. 19.95 (*0-398-06262-5*) C C Thomas.
— Freedom from Abuse in Organized Care Settings for the Elderly & Handicapped: Lessons from Human Service Administration. 104p. (C). 1988. text ed. 33.95x (*0-398-05493-2*) C C Thomas.
MacNamara, Vincent. Faith & Ethics: Recent Roman Catholicism. LC 85-5539. 261p. reprint ed. pap. 74.40 (*0-7837-6701-3*, 2046333) Bks Demand.
***MacNamee, Brian & MacDonnell, Ray.** The Marketing Casebase: Short Examples of Marketing Practice. LC 94-31229. 288p. 1995. pap. 19.95 (*0-415-10321-5*, C0029) Routledge.
MacNamee, Verda, illus. Verda: An Artist Sketches Europe, 1951. LC 90-70192. 100p. (Orig.). 1990. pap. 14.95 (*0-9625879-0-7*) Wilde Pr.
MacNaughten, Rick. Game of the Year. 1994. 7.95 (*0-8062-4901-3*) Carlton.
MacNaughton, Edgar. Elementary Steam Power Engineering. 3rd ed. LC 48-7834. 654p. reprint ed. pap. 180.00 (*0-317-07925-5*, 2055263) Bks Demand.
MacNaughton, Mary D. Art at Scripps: The Early Years. (Illus.). 48p. 1987. 6.00 (*0-915478-56-0*) Galleries Coll.
— Crossing the Line: Word & Image in Art, 1960-1990. (Illus.). 14p. 1990. 3.00 (*0-685-51609-1*) Galleries Coll.
— New California Printmaking: Selections from Northern & Southern California. (Illus.). 20p. 1987. 3.00 (*0-915478-55-2*) Galleries Coll.
MacNaughton, Mary D., jt. auth. see Alloway, Lawrence.
MacNaughton, Mary D., et al. Revolution in Clay: The Marer Collection of Contemporary Ceramics. (Ruth Chandler Williamson Gallery Ser.). (Illus.). 183p. 1994. pap. 30.00 (*0-295-97405-2*) U of Wash Pr.
MacNaughton, Robert D. Seventh Goswami: Biography of Bhaktivinode Thakur. (Lives of Vaisnava Acaryas Ser.: Vol. 2). (Illus.). 300p. (C). 1989. pap. 12.95 (*0-923519-02-5*) New Jaipur.
MacNaughton, Robert D., jt. auth. see Rupa Vitasa Dasa, pseud..
MacNaughton, Robert H., jt. auth. see Tracy, Saundra J.
***MacNaughton, Robin.** How to Seduce Any Man in the Zodiac. Todd, Rebecca, ed. 128p. 1995. mass mkt. 5.50 (*0-671-86803-9*) PB.
— Power Astrology: Make the Most of Your Sun Sign. 304p. 1990. mass mkt. 5.99 (*0-671-67181-2*) PB.
— Robin MacNaughton's Sun Sign Personality Guide. 1983. mass mkt. 6.99 (*0-553-27380-9*) Bantam.
Macnaughton, William R. Henry James: The Later Novels. (United States Authors Ser.: No. 521). 200p. 1987. text ed. 23.95 (*0-8057-7505-6*, TUSAS 521, Pub. by Royal Botanic Garden UK) Macmillan.
MacNaughton, William R. Mark Twain's Last Years As a Writer. LC 78-19846. 264p. reprint ed. pap. 75.30 (*0-7837-3201-5*, AU00429) Bks Demand.
MacNaughtton, Don. They Stood in the Door. 413p. 1985. 24.00 (*0-7223-1752-2*, Pub. by A H S Ltd UK) St Mut.
Macneacail, Aonghas. An Seachnadh: The Avoiding & Other Poems. (C). 1989. 39.00 (*0-86334-058-X*, Pub. by Saltire Soc) St Mut.
MacNeal. Finite Elements: Their Design & Performance. 552p. 1994. 125.00 (*0-8247-9162-2*) Dekker.
MacNeal, Donald L. The Flora of the Upper Cretaceous Woodbine Sand in Denton County, Texas. (Monograph: No. 10). (Illus.). 152p. (Orig.). 1958. pap. 6.00 (*0-910006-17-2*) Acad Nat Sci Phila.
MacNeal, Edward. Mathsemantics: Making Numbers Talk Sense. 320p. 1994. 22.95 (*0-670-85390-9*, Viking) Viking Penguin.
— Mathsemantics: Making Numbers Talk Sense. 320p. 1995. 12.95 (*0-14-023486-1*, Penguin Bks) Viking Penguin.
— The Semantics of Air Passenger Transportation. LC 80-85432. (Illus.). 132p. 1981. 19.95 (*0-9605682-0-4*) Norfolk Port.
MacNeal, Kenneth. Truth in Accounting. LC 74-75709. 1970. reprint ed. text ed. 20.00 (*0-914348-04-3*) Scholars Bk.
MacNeal, Richard H. Electric Circuit Analogies for Elastic Structures. LC 62-17465. (Airplane, Missile, & Spacecraft Structures Ser.: Vol. 2). 278p. reprint ed. pap. 79.30 (*0-317-09604-4*, 2007401) Bks Demand.
MacNealy, Mary S., jt. ed. see Kruez, Roger J.
MacNee, Marie J., jt. auth. see Stein, Gordon.
Macnee, Patrick. Blind in One Ear: The Avenger Returns. LC 89-32147. 304p. 1992. pap. 9.95 (*0-916515-85-0*) Mercury Hse Inc.
MacNeice, Corinna, jt. auth. see Dolphin, Johnny.
Macneice, Jill. Guide to National Monuments & Historic Sites. 1990. pap. 14.95 (*0-13-611682-5*) P-H.
MacNeice, Louis. Collected Poems. Dodds, E. R., ed. 593p. 1979. pap. 18.95 (*0-571-11353-2*) Faber & Faber.
Macneice, Louis. Modern Poetry: A Personal Essay. LC 77-95439. (Studies in Poetry: No. 38). (C). 1969. reprint ed. lib. bdg. 75.00 (*0-8383-0992-5*) M S G Haskell Hse.
MacNeice, Louis. The Poetry of W. B. Yeats. LC 79-17894. 242p. 1979. reprint ed. text ed. 38.50 (*0-313-22102-2*, MAPO, Greenwood Pr) Greenwood.
— Selected Plays of Louis MacNeice. Heuser, Alan & McDonald, Peter, eds. 430p. 1994. 55.00 (*0-19-811245-9*) OUP.
— Selected Prose of Louis MacNeice. Heuser, Alan, ed. 328p. 1990. 49.95 (*0-19-818525-1*) OUP.
— Varieties of Parable. LC 66-10036. (Clark Lectures, 1963). 165p. reprint ed. pap. 47.10 (*0-317-20590-0*, 2024498) Bks Demand.
Macneil. Nineteen Seventy-Eight Statutory Supplement to Contracts, Second Edition. 1978. pap. text ed. 10.75 (*0-88277-357-7*) Foundation Pr.
MacNeil, Duncan. By Command of the Viceroy. large type ed. 1979. 15.95 (*0-7089-0341-X*) Ulverscroft.
MacNeil, Heather. Without Consent: The Ethics of Disclosing Personal Information in Public Archives. LC 92-16754. (Society of American Archivists Ser.). 200p. 1992. 27.50 (*0-8108-2581-3*) Scarecrow.
MacNeil, Ian B. & Umphrey, Gary J., eds. Advances in the Statistical Sciences, Vol. II: Foundations of Statistical Inference, Vol. II. (C). 1986. lib. bdg. 99.50 (*90-277-2394-X*) Kluwer Ac.
— Advances in the Statistical Sciences, Vol. IV: Stochastic Hydrology. (C). 1986. lib. bdg. 84.50 (*90-277-2396-6*) Kluwer Ac.
— Advances in the Statistical Sciences, Vol. V: Biostatistics. (C). 1986. lib. bdg. 99.50 (*90-277-2397-4*) Kluwer Ac.
— Advances in the Statistical Sciences, Vol. VI: Actuarial Science. (C). 1986. lib. bdg. 92.00 (*90-277-2398-2*) Kluwer Ac.
Macneil, Ian R. American Arbitration Law: Reformation - Nationalization - Internationalization. 288p. 1992. 45.00 (*0-19-507062-3*) OUP.
MacNeil, Ian R. Contracts: Exchange Transactions & Relations, Cases & Materials. 2nd ed. (University Casebook Ser.). 1320p. 1978. reprint ed. text ed. 39.00 (*0-88277-432-8*) Foundation Pr.
Macneil, Ian R. The New Social Contract: An Inquiry into Modern Contractual Relations. LC 80-5395. 180p. reprint ed. pap. 51.30 (*0-7837-6218-6*, 2080220) Bks Demand.
MacNeil, Joe N. Tales until Dawn: The World of a Cape Breton Gaelic Story-Teller. Shaw, John W., ed. 460p. (ENG & GAE.). 1987. 70.00 (*0-7735-0559-8*, Pub. by McGill CN); pap. 22.95 (*0-7735-0560-1*, Pub. by McGill CN) U of Toronto Pr.
MacNeil, Madeline. You Can Teach Yourself Dulcimer. 1993. 9.95 (*0-87166-266-3*, 94304); audio 9.98 (*0-87166-322-8*, 94304); audio 18.95 (*0-87166-309-0*, 94304) Mel Bay.
***MacNeil, Neil.** Levon West. (Illus.). 16p. (Orig.). (C). 1968. pap. 6.00 (*0-943526-33-7*) Parrish Art.
MacNeil of Barra. MacNeil: The Clan MacNeil (Clann Niall) of Scotland. (Illus.). 227p. 1993. reprint ed. lib. bdg. 44.00 (*0-8328-3369-X*); reprint ed. pap. 34.00 (*0-8328-3370-3*) Higginson Bk Co.
MacNeil, Richard D., jt. auth. see Teague, Michael L.
MacNeil, Robert. Burden of Desire. 1993. mass mkt. 5.99 (*0-440-21509-9*) Dell.
— Eudora Welty: Seeing Black & White. LC 90-12640. 1990. pap. 9.95 (*0-87805-471-5*) U Pr of Miss.
— Wordstruck. 256p. 1990. pap. 10.95 (*0-14-010401-1*, Penguin Bks) Viking Penguin.
MacNeil, Sylvia. The Paris Collection: French Doll Fashions & Accessories. (Illus.). 192p. 1992. 24.95 (*0-87588-372-9*) Hobby Hse.
MacNeilage, P. F., ed. The Production of Speech. (Illus.). 302p. 1983. 73.00 (*0-387-90735-1*) Spr-Verlag.
MacNeill, Alastair. Alistair Maclean's Time of the Assassins. 1993. mass mkt. 5.99 (*0-06-104229-3*, Harp PBks) HarpC.
MacNeill, Alistair. Alistar MacLean's Red Alert. large type ed. 1992. 18.95 (*0-7927-1255-2*, E0036, Eagle Lrg Print) Chivers N Amer.
MacNeill, Carol. Teaching Orienteering. Renfrew, Tom & Ramsden, Jean, eds. (C). 1989. 200.00 (*1-85137-020-X*, Pub. by Jordanhill College UK) St Mut.
MacNeill, Debra J. Customer Service Excellence. LC 93-6. 112p. 1993. pap. 10.00 (*1-55623-969-6*) Irwin Prof Pubng.
— Customer Service Excellence. LC 94-72158. (Illus.). 93p. (Orig.). 1994. pap. 9.95 (*1-884926-26-6*) Amer Media.
MacNeill, Eoin. Celtic Ireland. 1972. 99.95 (*0-87968-824-6*) Gordon Pr.
Macneill, Hector. Poetical Works of Hector Macneill, 2 Vols, 1. LC 74-144453. reprint ed. 7.00 (*0-404-08566-0*) AMS Pr.
— Poetical Works of Hector Macneill, 2 Vols, 2. LC 74-144453. reprint ed. 7.00 (*0-404-08567-9*) AMS Pr.
— Poetical Works of Hector Macneill, 2 Vols, Set. LC 74-144453. reprint ed. 13.50 (*0-404-08565-2*) AMS Pr.
MacNeill, James H., jt. auth. see Roy, Robert H.
MacNeill, Jim, et al. Beyond Interdependence: The Meshing of the World's Economy & the Earth's Ecology. (Illus.). 192p. 1991. pap. 8.95 (*0-19-507126-3*) OUP.
— CIDA & Sustainable Development: How Canada's Aid Policies Can Support Sustainable Development in the Third World More Effectively. 110p. 1990. pap. text ed. 17.95 (*0-88645-097-7*, Pub. by Inst Res Pub CN) Ashgate Pub Co.
MacNeill, M. Everyday Gaelic. 1991. pap. 19.95 (*0-8288-3346-X*, F132984) Fr & Eur.
MacNeish, Jerry. The Definitive Nineteen Sixty-Seven to Nineteen Sixty-Eight Camaro Z-28 Book. (Illus.). 148p. 1990. pap. 21.95 (*0-9626399-0-7*) J MacNeish.
Macneish, R., et al. The Central Peruvian Prehistoric Interaction Sphere, Vol. 7. 1975. 10.00 (*0-939312-08-5*) Peabody Found.
MacNeish, R., et al. First Annual Report of the Belize Archaic Archaeological Reconnaissance. 1980. 10.00 (*0-939312-17-4*) Peabody Found.
MacNeish, R. S., jt. ed. see Byers, Douglas S.
MacNeish, Richard S. The Origins of Agriculture & Settled Life. LC 91-50304. (Illus.). 448p. (C). 1992. text ed. 75.00 (*0-8061-2364-8*) U of Okla Pr.
MacNeish, Richard S. & Johnson, Frederick, eds. The Prehistory of the Tehuacan Valley. Incl. Vol. 4. Chronology & Irrigation. 302p. 1972. 35.00 (*0-292-70155-1*); (Illus.). write for info. (*0-318-56145-X*) U of Tex Pr.
MacNeish, Richard S., jt. auth. see Wray, Donald E.
MacNeish, Richard S., et al. The Prehistory of the Ayacucho Basin, Peru: Nonceramic Artifacts, Vol. III. (Illus.). 360p. 1980. 49.50x (*0-472-02707-7*) U of Mich Pr.
— Prehistory of the Ayacucho Basin, Peru, Vol. II: Excavations & Chronology. LC 80-13960. (Illus.). 368p. (C). 1981. text ed. 49.50x (*0-472-04907-0*) U of Mich Pr.
— Prehistory of the Ayacucho Basin, Peru, Vol. IV: The Preceramic Way of Life. (Illus.). 312p. 1983. text ed. 49.50x (*0-472-04967-4*) U of Mich Pr.
MacNelly, jt. auth. see Shields-West.
MacNelly, Jeff. Athletic Shoe. 1991. pap. 6.95 (*0-312-04873-4*) St Martin.
— A Cigar Means Never Having to Say You're Sorry. 128p. (Orig.). 1989. pap. 5.95 (*0-312-02651-X*) St Martin.
— New Shoes. (Illus.). 330p. 1994. pap. 7.95 (*0-8092-3627-3*) Contemp Bks.
— Pluggers: Calm in the Face of Disaster. LC 95-8426. (Illus.). 160p. 1995. pap. 7.95 (*0-7868-8029-5*) Hyperion.
— Shake the Hand, Bite the Taco: A New Shoe Book. 128p. 1989. pap. 6.95 (*0-312-03931-X*) St Martin.
— Shoe Goes to Wrigley Field: How Many Next Years Do You Get in Baseball? (Illus.). 64p. (Orig.). 1988. pap. 5.95 (*0-933893-51-5*) Bonus Books.
Macnelly, Jeff. Too Old for Summer Camp & Too Young to Retire. (New Shoe Book Ser.). 128p. 1988. pap. 5.95 (*0-312-01822-3*) St Martin.
MacNicholas, John. James Joyce's Exiles: A Textual Companion. LC 78-67061. (Reference Library Ser.). 1979. lib. bdg. 46.00 (*0-8240-9781-5*) Garland.
MacNicholas, John, ed. Twentieth-Century American Dramatists, 2 vols., Set. (Dictionary of Literary Biography Ser.: Vol. 7). (Illus.). 848p. 1981. 238.00 (*0-8103-0928-9*) Gale.
MacNicol, Eona K. Lamp in the Night Wind: St. Columba Story. 256p. (C). 1988. 50.00 (*0-85335-006-X*, Pub. by Stuart Titles Ltd UK) St Mut.
Macnicol, Fred, tr. see Forrai, Katalin, et al.
Macnicol, Fred, tr. see Hegyi, Erzsebet.
Macnicol, Fred, tr. see Karpati, Janos.
MacNicol, Gregory. Desktop Computer Animation: A Guide to Low-Cost Computer Animation. (Illus.). 187p. 1992. 45.00 (*0-240-80065-6*, Focal) Buttrwrth-Heinemann.
***Macnicol, Malcolm F.** The Problem Knee. 2nd ed. LC 94-45158. 1995. write for info. (*0-7506-0487-5*) Buttrwrth-Heinemann.
MacNicoll, Murray G., ed. see Azevedo, Aluisio.
MacNicoll, Murray G., tr. see Azevedo, Aluisio.
MacNiece, Louis, tr. see Goethe, Johann Wolfgang Von.

M

***MacNish, C., et al, eds.** Logic in Artificial Intellegence, 838. (Lecture Notes in Artificial Intelligence Ser.). 413p. 1994. pap. text ed. 58.00 (*0-387-58332-7*) Spr-Verlag.

MacNiven, Don. Bradley's Moral Psychology. LC 87-1731. (Studies in the History of Philosophy: Vol. 3). 288p. 1987. lib. bdg. 89.95 (*0-88946-306-9*) E Mellen.

— Creative Morality: An Introduction to Theoretical & Practical Ethics. LC 92-30808. 256p. 1993. 49.95 (*0-415-00029-7*, B0414); pap. 17.95 (*0-415-00030-0*, B0418) Routledge.

— Moral Expertise: Studies in Practical Professional Ethics. 272p. 1990. 55.00 (*0-415-03576-7*, A3499) Routledge.

MacNiven, Ian S., ed. see Durrell, Lawrence & Miller, Henry.

Macnow, Glen. David Robinson: Star Center. LC 94-15647. (Sports Reports Ser.). (Illus.). 104p. (J). (gr. 4-10). 1994. lib. bdg. 17.95 (*0-89490-483-3*) Enslow Pubs.

— Sports Great Cal Ripken, Jr. LC 92-24158. (Sports Great Books Ser.). (Illus.). 64p. (J). (gr. 4-10). 1993. lib. bdg. 15.95 (*0-89490-387-X*) Enslow Pubs.

— Sports Great Charles Barkley. LC 91-45827. (Sports Great Books Ser.). (Illus.). 64p. (J). (gr. 4-10). 1992. lib. bdg. 15.95 (*0-89490-386-1*) Enslow Pubs.

— Sports Great Troy Aikman. LC 94-30537. (Sports Great Bks.). (Illus.). 64p. (J). (gr. 4-10). 1995. lib. bdg. 15.95 (*0-89490-593-7*) Enslow Pubs.

MacNulty, W. K. Freemasonry: A Journey Through Ritual & Symbol. LC 91-65320. (Art & Imagination Ser.). (Illus.). 96p. (Orig.). 1991. pap. 15.95 (*0-500-81037-0*) Thames Hudson.

MacNutt, F. A. Bartolome de las Casas. 1972. 59.95 (*0-87968-708-8*) Gordon Pr.

***MacNutt, Francis.** Deliverance from Evil Spirits: A Practical Manual. 2nd ed. LC 95-5150. 288p. (Orig.). 1995. pap. 11.99 (*0-8007-9232-7*) Chosen Bks.

— Healing. LC 74-81446. (Illus.). 336p. 1974. pap. 7.95 (*0-87793-074-0*) Ave Maria.

— Healing. 1990. mass mkt. 7.95 (*0-385-26664-2*) Doubleday.

— Healing. rev. ed. LC 88-71068. 1988. pap. 8.99 (*0-88419-217-2*, Creation Hse) Strang Comms Co.

Macnutt, Francis. Overcome By the Spirit. LC 90-44727. 1990. pap. 8.99 (*0-8007-9170-3*) Chosen Bks.

MacNutt, Francis. The Power to Heal. LC 77-77845. 256p. 1977. pap. 6.95 (*0-87793-133-X*) Ave Maria.

— The Prayer That Heals. LC 80-69770. 120p. (Orig.). 1981. pap. 3.95 (*0-87793-219-0*) Ave Maria.

Macnutt, Francis. Praying for Your Unborn Child. 1989. mass mkt. 9.00 (*0-385-23282-9*) Doubleday.

MacNutt, Francis A. Bartholome de las Casas: His Life, His Apostolate, & His Writings. LC 70-172712. reprint ed. 32.45 (*0-404-07146-5*) AMS Pr.

MacNutt, Francis A. & Greenway, John, intros. Fernando Cortes: His Five Letters of Relation to the Emperor Charles V of Spain, 2 vols. LC 77-1155. (Beautiful Rio Grande Classics Ser.). 895p. 1983. reprint ed. lib. bdg. 50.00 (*0-87380-125-3*) Rio Grande.

MacNutt, J. Scott. A Manual for Health Officers. Rosenkrantz, Barbara G., ed. LC 76-40634. (Public Health in America Ser.). (Illus.). 1977. reprint ed. lib. bdg. 54.95 (*0-405-09825-1*) Ayer.

MacNutt, Karen L. Ladies Legal Companion. (Illus.). 87p. (Orig.). 1993. pap. 8.95 (*0-9622534-1-3*) MacNutt Art Trust.

— A Sketch of Glenn G. MacNutt. (Illus.). 24p. 1989. 9.52 (*0-9622534-0-5*) MacNutt Art Trust.

MacNutt, William S. Days of Lorne: Impressions of a Governor-General. LC 77-16170. (Illus.). 272p. 1978. reprint ed. text ed. 59.75 (*0-313-20021-1*, MADL, Greenwood Pr) Greenwood.

Maco, David. Tractor: Iron Work Horse. Date not set. pap. 11.99 (*0-517-10350-8*) Random Hse Value.

Macoboy, Stirling. The Ultimate Rose Book: One Thousand Five Hundred Roses--Antique, Modern (Including Miniature), & Wild--All Shown in Color & Selected for Their Beauty, Fragrance, & Enduring Popularity. LC 93-10419. (Illus.). 1993. 49.50 (*0-8109-3920-7*) Abrams.

— What Flower Is That? 1988. 24.99 (*0-517-66998-6*) Random Hse Value.

— What Shrub Is That. 1989. 24.99 (*0-517-69211-2*) Random Hse Value.

Macomber. Season of Angels. 1993. mass mkt. 5.50 (*0-06-108184-1*, Harp PBks) HarpC.

— Someday Soon. 1995. mass mkt. 5.50 (*0-06-108309-7*, Harp PBks) HarpC.

Macomber, Beddie. First Comes Marriage. (Romance Ser.: No. 3113). 1991. pap. 2.75 (*0-373-03113-0*) Harlequin Bks.

***Macomber, Debbie.** All Things Considered. (Western Lovers Ser.). 1996. mass mkt. 3.99 (*0-373-88535-0*, 1-88535-9) Harlequin Bks.

— The Apartment. (To Mother with Love Ser.). 1993. pap. 4.99 (*0-685-61545-6*) Silhouette.

— Baby Blessed. 1994. mass mkt. 3.50 (*0-373-09895-2*, 1-09895-3) Harlequin Bks.

— The Bachelor Prince. 1994. pap. 2.75 (*0-373-91012-6*, 5-91012-0); pap. 2.75 (*0-373-19012-3*, 5-19012-9) Harlequin Bks.

— Borrowed Dreams. (Men Made in America Ser.). 1993. mass mkt. 3.59 (*0-373-45152-0*, 1-45152-5) Harlequin Bks.

— Bride on the Loose. large type ed. (Silhouette Romance Ser.). 1995. 18.95 (*0-373-59421-6*) Thorndike Pr.

— Bride Wanted from This Day Forward. 1993. mass mkt. 3.50 (*0-373-09836-7*, 5-09836-3) Silhouette.

— Brides for Brothers. 1995. mass mkt. 2.99 (*0-373-03379-6*, 1-03379-4) Harlequin Bks.

— The Courtship of Carol Sommars. large type ed. (Special Edition Ser.). 1993. 17.95 (*0-373-58805-4*, Silhouette Lrg Print); pap. 16.95 (*0-373-58905-0*, Silhouette Lrg Print) Chivers N Amer.

— Daddy's Little Helper. 1995. pap. 2.99 (*0-373-03387-7*, 1-03387-7) Harlequin Bks.

— Father's Day. (Romance Ser.: No. 3130). 1991. pap. 2.75 (*0-373-03130-0*) Harlequin Bks.

— The Forgetful Bride. (Romance Ser.: No. 166). 1991. pap. 2.79 (*0-373-03166-1*) Harlequin Bks.

— Groom Wanted: From This Day Forward. (Silhouette Special Edition Ser.). 1993. mass mkt. 3.50 (*0-373-09831-6*, 5-09831-4) Silhouette.

— Hasty Wedding. 1993. mass mkt. 3.39 (*0-373-09798-0*, 5-09798-5) Silhouette.

— Here Comes Trouble. (Romance Ser.: No. 3148). 1991. pap. 2.79 (*0-373-03148-3*) Harlequin Bks.

— Lone Star Lovin' (Romance Ser.). 1993. mass mkt. 2.99 (*0-373-03271-4*, 1-03271-3) Harlequin Bks.

— The Marriage Risk (Midnight Sons) 1995. mass mkt. 2.99 (*0-373-03383-4*) Harlequin Bks.

— Marriage Wanted: From This Day Forward. (Silhouette Special Edition Ser.). 1993. mass mkt. 3.50 (*0-373-09842-1*, 5-09842-1) Silhouette.

— Morning Comes Softly. 1993. mass mkt. 5.50 (*0-06-108063-2*, Harp PBks) HarpC.

— Navy Baby. large type ed. (Silhouette Special Edition Ser.). 1994. 17.95 (*0-373-58891-7*, Silhouette Lrg Print) Chivers N Amer.

— Navy Brat. large type ed. (Silhouette Special Edition Ser.). 1994. 17.95 (*0-373-58843-7*, Silhouette Lrg Print); pap. 16.95 (*0-373-58935-2*, Silhouette Lrg Print) Chivers N Amer.

— One Night. 1994. mass mkt. 5.50 (*0-06-108185-X*) HarpC.

— Promise Me Forever. 1995. pap. 4.99 (*1-55166-052-0*, 1-66052-1, Mira Bks) Harlequin Bks.

— Purrfect Love. 1994. mass mkt. 5.50 (*0-06-108129-9*, Harp PBks) HarpC.

— Rainy Day Kisses. (Romance Ser.: No. 3076). 1990. pap. 2.50 (*0-373-03076-2*) Harlequin Bks.

— Ready for Marriage. (Romance Ser.). 1994. mass mkt. 2.99 (*0-373-03307-9*, 1-03307-5) Harlequin Bks.

— Ready for Marriage. large type ed. 1995. pap. 18.95 (*0-7838-1176-4*, Large Print Bks) Hall.

— Ready for Romance. (Romance Ser.). 1993. mass mkt. 2.99 (*0-373-03288-9*, 1-03288-7) Harlequin Bks.

— Reflections of Yesterday. (Mira Bks.). 1995. mass mkt. 4.99 (*1-55166-070-9*, 1-66070-3, Mira Bks) Harlequin Bks.

— Same Time, Next Year. (Special Edition Ser.). 1995. pap. 3.75 (*0-373-09937-1*, 1-09937-3) Silhouette.

— Starlight. 1995. pap. 4.99 (*1-55166-021-0*, Mira Bks) Harlequin Bks.

— Stephanie. 1992. pap. 2.89 (*0-373-03239-0*, 1-03239-0) Harlequin Bks.

— Trouble with Angels. 1994. pap. 5.50 (*0-06-108308-9*, Harp PBks) HarpC.

— Wanted: Perfect Partner. (Yours Truly Ser.). 1995. mass mkt. 3.50 (*0-373-52001-8*, 1-52001-4) Silhouette.

***Macomber, Debbie, et al.** Three Mothers & a Cradle: Rock-a-Bye Baby; Cradle Song; Beginnings. (Silhouette Promo Ser.). 1995. mass mkt. 4.99 (*0-373-48335-X*, 1-48335-3) Harlequin Bks.

***Macomber, Debbin.** The Playboy & the Widow. 1996. mass mkt. 4.99 (*1-55166-080-6*, Mira Bks) Harlequin Bks.

Macomber, Frank, jt. auth. see Fleming, William.

Macomber, J. D., jt. ed. see Lippert, E.

Macomber, James D. The Dynamics of Spectroscopic Transitions: Illustrated by Magnetic Resonance & Laser Effects. LC 75-25852. (Wiley-Interscience Monographs in Chemical Physics). (Illus.). 358p. reprint ed. pap. 102.10 (*0-317-09275-8*, 2013078) Bks Demand.

Macomber, Roger S. NMR Spectroscopy. (College Outline Ser.). 220p. (C). 1988. pap. text ed. 13.50 (*0-15-601650-8*) HB Coll Pubs.

Macomber, William F. Project Numbers One to Three Hundred: A Catalogue of Ethiopian Manuscripts Microfilmed for the Ethiopian Manuscript Microfilm Library, Addis Ababa, & the Hill Monastic Manuscript Library, Collegeville, Vol. 1. (Illus.). ix, 355p. (Orig.). 1975. pap. 15.00 (*0-940250-51-9*) Hill Monastic.

— Project Numbers Seven Hundred One to Eleven Hundred: A Catalogue of Ethiopian Manuscripts Microfilmed for the Ethiopian Manuscript Microfilm Library, Addis Ababa, & the Hill Monastic Manuscript Library, Collegeville, Vol. 3. ix, 524p. (Orig.). 1978. pap. 30.50 (*0-8357-0303-7*) Hill Monastic.

— Project Numbers Three Hundred One to Seven Hundred: A Catalogue of Ethiopian Manuscripts Microfilmed for the Ethiopian Manuscript Microfilm Library, Addis Ababa, & the Hill Monastic Manuscript Library, Collegeville, Vol. 2. v, 524p. (Orig.). 1976. pap. 25.00 (*0-940250-52-7*) Hill Monastic.

Macomber, William F., jt. auth. see Haile, Getatchew.

Macombi, Turi, illus. Little Bunny's Magic Nose. (Golden Fuzzy Wuzzy Book Ser.). (J). (ps-2). 1991. 5.25 (*0-307-15701-6*, Golden Pr) Western Pub.

Macon, James. Little House on the Prairie: A Study Guide. (Novel-Ties Ser.). 1989. student ed, teacher ed 15.95 (*0-88122-051-5*) Lrn Links.

— Treasure Island: A Study Guide. (Novel-Ties Ser.). 1989. student ed, teacher ed 15.95 (*0-88122-060-4*) Lrn Links.

Macon, James H., et al. Responses to Literature, Grades K-8. 32p. 1990. pap. 4.50 (*0-87207-747-0*) Intl Reading.

***Macon, Larry L.** Discipling the African American Male. LC 94-61589. 133p. (YA). (gr. 6 up). 1995. per., pap. 10.95 (*1-55523-733-9*) Winston-Derek.

Macon, Myra, ed. School Library Media Services to the Handicapped. LC 81-4262. (Illus.). xii, 208p. 1982. text ed. 49.95 (*0-313-22684-9*, MAL/, Greenwood Pr) Greenwood.

***Macon Telegraph Staff, et al.** Deluge! The Flood of '94. Brown, Oby, ed. (Illus.). 96p. 1994. pap. 12.95 (*0-8362-8096-2*) Andrews & McMeel.

Maconchy, Elizabeth. Music for Woodwind & Brass. Date not set. pap. 21.95 (*0-685-69099-7*, Chester Music) Music Sales.

Maconie, Robin. The Concept of Music. (Illus.). 200p. 1991. 55.00 (*0-19-816215-4*) OUP.

— The Concept of Music. 200p. 1993. reprint ed. pap. 15.95 (*0-19-816388-6*) OUP.

— Stockhausen. LC 79-56837. (Illus.). 352p. 1981. pap. 20.00 (*0-7145-2706-8*) M Boyars Pubs.

— The Works of Karlheinz Stockhausen. 2nd ed. (Illus.). 336p. 1990. 74.00 (*0-19-315477-3*) OUP.

Macor, Alida. And Sew On... LC 82-91121. (Illus.). 56p. 1983. pap. 3.95 (*0-9610632-0-3*) Alida Macor.

Macorini, Edgardo, ed. The History of Science & Technology: A Narrative Chronology, 2 vols., Set. 960p. 1988. 160.00 (*0-87196-477-5*) Facts on File.

MacOrlan, Pierre. Le Bandera. (FRE.). 1972. pap. 8.95 (*0-7859-3994-6*) Fr & Eur.

— Le Quai des Brumes. (FRE.). 1972. pap. 8.95 (*0-7859-3985-7*) Fr & Eur.

Macosko, Christopher W. Rheology: Principles, Measurements, & Applications. LC 93-31652. (Advances in Interfacial Engineering Ser.). 1994. 95.00 (*1-56081-579-5*) VCH Pubs.

— RIM: Fundamentals of Reaction Injection Molding. 246p. (C). 1989. text ed. 49.95 (*1-56990-055-8*) Hanser-Gardner.

Macoupon County Homemakers Extension Association Staff. The Homemaker's Sampler. 350p. 1980. pap. 6.50 (*0-918544-45-9*) MCH.

Macourek, Chris. Heart to Heart: Low-Fat Cooking Made Easy. (Illus.). 200p. 1992. 11.95 (*0-9635418-0-3*) Chris Kitchen.

Macourek, Milos. Max & Sally & the Phenomenal Phone. Herrmann, Dagmar, tr. LC 88-33871. (Illus.). 82p. (J). (gr. 2-4). 1989. 16.95 (*0-922984-00-X*) Wellington IL.

Macovski, Albert. Medical Imaging Systems. (Illus.). 256p. 1983. text ed. 81.00 (*0-13-572685-9*) P-H.

Macovski, Michael. Dialogue & Literature: Apostrophe, Auditors, & the Collapse of Romantic Discourse. 250p. 1994. 38.00 (*0-19-506965-X*) OUP.

Macovski, Michael S., ed. Dialogue & Critical Discourse: Language, Culture, Critical Theory. LC 92-28231. 224p. 1995. 45.00 (*0-19-507063-1*); pap. 21.00 (*0-19-508124-2*) OUP.

Macoy, jt. auth. see Simons.

Macoy Publishing & Masonic Supply Co. Staff. Book of the Scarlet Line; Heroines of Jericho Ritual & Ceremonies. 152p. 1994. reprint ed. text ed. 7.95 (*0-88053-304-8*, S 077) Macoy Pub.

Macoy, Robert. Adoptive Rite. 8.50 (*0-685-19463-9*) Powner.

— The Adoptive Rite. rev. ed. 303p. 1994. reprint ed. text ed. 9.00 (*0-88053-300-5*, S 073) Macoy Pub.

— Amaranth Ritual. 6.50 (*0-685-19464-7*) Powner.

— Amaranth Ritual. 169p. 1994. reprint ed. text ed. 6.50 (*0-88053-301-3*, S 074) Macoy Pub.

— Christmas, Easter, Ascension & Burial Services for Knights Templar. rev. ed. 111p. 1978. pap. 4.60 (*0-88053-011-1*, M 036) Macoy Pub.

— Dictionary of Freemasonary. 704p. 1989. 9.99 (*0-517-69213-9*) Random Hse Value.

— General History, Cyclopedia & Dictionary of Freemasonry: Containing an Elaborate Account of the Rise & Progress of Freemasonry, & Its Kindred Associations, Ancient & Modern. Also, Definitions of the Technical Terms Used by the Fraternity. (Illus.). 710p. 1994. reprint ed. pap. 49.95 (*1-56459-428-9*) Kessinger Pub.

— Worshipful Master's Assistant. rev. ed. xiv, 253p. 1991. reprint ed. 17.95 (*0-88053-008-1*, M-026) Macoy Pub.

MacPhail. Family Therapy in the Community. (Illus.). 192p. 1988. pap. text ed. 29.95 (*0-433-00046-5*) Buttrwrth-Heinemann.

— Highland Papers Vol. 1. (Illus.). 368p. Date not set. pap. text ed. 25.00 (*1-55613-996-9*) Heritage Bk.

MacPhail, Elizabeth C. The Story of New San Diego & of Its Founder Alonzo E. Horton. 2nd rev. ed. LC 79-63134. (Illus.). 63p. 1979. pap. 8.95 (*0-918740-01-0*) San Diego Hist.

MacPhail, Elizabeth R. The Infuence of German Immigrants on the Growth of San Diego. (Illus.). 104p. 1986. 14.95 (*0-918740-05-3*) San Diego Hist.

MacPhail, Eric. Voyage to Rome in French Renaissance Literature. (Stanford French & Italian Studies: Vol. 68). 224p. 1991. pap. 46.50 (*0-915838-84-2*) Anma Libri.

MacPhail, Euan. Brain & Intelligence in Vertebrates. (Illus.). 1982. pap. 19.95 (*0-19-854551-7*) OUP.

Macphail, Euan M. The Neuroscience of Animal Intelligence: From the Seahare to the Seahorse. Terrace, Herbert S., ed. LC 92-31167. (Animal Intelligence Ser.). (Illus.). 506p. (C). 1992. text ed. 65.00 (*0-231-06144-7*) Col U Pr.

Macphail, I. M. The Crofters War. 250p. (C). 1992. text ed. 90.00 (*0-86152-860-3*, Pub. by Acair Ltd UK) St Mut.

MacPhail, I. M. A Short History of Dumbartonshire. 136p. (C). 1986. 45.00 (*0-907590-01-2*) St Mut.

***MacPhail, J. R.** Highland Papers, Vol. IV. 290p. 1994. reprint ed. pap. text ed. 25.00 (*0-7884-0220-X*) Heritage Bk.

***MacPhail, J. R., ed.** Highland Papers, Vol. III. 338p. (Orig.). 1995. pap. text ed. 25.00 (*0-7884-0186-6*) Heritage Bk.

— Highland Papers Vol. II. (Illus.). 375p. (Orig.). 1994. pap. text ed. 25.00 (*0-7884-0043-6*) Heritage Bk.

MacPhail, Jessica. Yesterday's Papers: The Rolling Stones in Print, 1963-1984. (Rock & Roll Reference Ser.: No. 19). (Illus.). 236p. 1986. 39.50 (*0-87650-209-5*) Popular Culture.

MacPhail, Lee. My Nine Innings: An Autobiography of 50 Years in Baseball. 1989. 21.95 (*0-88736-387-3*) Mecklermedia.

MacPhail, R. M. An Introduction to Santali, Pt. 1-2. 1983. reprint ed. 12.50 (*0-8364-1046-7*, Pub. by Mukhopadhyaya II) S Asia.

MacPhail, R. M., ed. Campbell's English-Santali Dictionary. 1984. 40.00 (*0-8364-1137-4*, Pub. by Mukhopadhyaya II) S Asia.

MacPhail, Ralph, Jr., ed. see Gilbert, W. S.

MacPhee, R. D. Auditory Regions of Primates & Eutherian Insectivores. (Contributions to Primatology Ser.: Vol. 18). (Illus.). xvi, 288p. 1981. pap. 53.00 (*3-8055-1963-X*) S Karger.

MacPhee, R. D., ed. Primates & Their Relatives in Phylogenetic Perspective. (Advances in Primatology Ser.). (Illus.). 370p. (C). 1993. 85.00 (*0-306-44422-4*, Plenum Pr) Plenum.

MacPhee, Tracey H. & DeBruyn, Robert L. School Promotion, Publicity & Public Relations...Nothing but Benefits. LC 87-60751. 320p. (Orig.). 1987. text ed. 29.95 (*0-914607-24-3*) Master Tchr.

Macpherson, ed. see Garcia Lorca, Federico.

Macpherson, A. K. The Atomic Mechanics of Solids, No. 2: Mechanics & Physics of Discrete Systems. 214p. 1991. 123.00 (*0-444-88374-6*, North Holland) Elsevier.

MacPherson, Andrew. International Telecommunication Standards Organizations. (Artech House Telecom Management Library). 240p. 1990. text ed. 66.00 (*0-89006-365-6*) Artech Hse.

MacPherson, Andrew & Raab, Charles. Governing Education: Policy Making in Scotland. 500p. 1988. 60.00 (*0-317-65657-0*, Pub. by Edinburgh U Pr UK) Col U Pr.

Macpherson, Angus. Landscapes Angus Macpherson. 1993. pap. write for info. (*0-9637700-0-4*) AM DSG Pr.

Macpherson, Ann, et al. Prophets One. Bright, Laurence, ed. LC 71-173033. (Scripture Discussion Commentary Ser.: Vol. 2). 214p. 1971. pap. text ed. 4.95 (*0-87946-001-6*, 212) ACTA Pubns.

MacPherson, Anne, jt. auth. see Schendel, Shirley.

MacPherson, Bryan. An International Criminal Court: Applying World Law to Individuals. (U. N. Reform Series Monograph: No. 10). 70p. 1992. pap. 5.00 (*1-881520-00-5*) Ctr U N Reform Educ.

***MacPherson, Bryan F.** World Court Enhancements to Advance the Rule of Law. (CURE Monograph Ser.: No. 13). 78p. (Orig.). 1994. pap. text ed. 5.00 (*1-881520-03-X*) Ctr U N Reform Educ.

Macpherson, C. B. Democracy in Alberta: Social Credit & the Party System. LC 54-4046. (Social Credit in Alberta Ser.). 1953. pap. 13.95 (*0-8020-6009-9*) U of Toronto Pr.

— Democratic Theory: Essays in Retrieval. (C). 1973. pap. 16.95 (*0-19-827189-1*) OUP.

— The Life & Times of Liberal Democracy. 1978. pap. text ed. 13.95 (*0-19-289106-5*) OUP.

— Real World of Democracy. 1972. pap. 9.95 (*0-19-501534-7*) OUP.

— The Rise & Fall of Economic Justice & Other Essays. 176p. 1987. reprint ed. pap. 14.95 (*0-19-285186-1*) OUP.

Macpherson, C. B., ed. Property: Mainstream & Critical Positions. LC 78-2311. (Controversy Ser.). 216p. 1978. pap. 15.95 (*0-8020-6336-5*) U of Toronto Pr.

Macpherson, C. B., jt. ed. see Crepeau, P. A.

Macpherson, C. B., ed. see Hobbes, Thomas.

Macpherson, C. B., ed. see Locke, John.

Macpherson, Charles. Memoirs of the Life & Travels of the Late Charles Macpherson, Esq. in Asia, Africa & America. 1977. 19.95 (*0-8369-9229-6*, 9083) Ayer.

Macpherson, Colin, jt. auth. see Pierce, Steven R.

Macpherson, Crawford B. Political Theory of Possessive Individualism: Hobbes to Locke. 1964. pap. 13.95 (*0-19-881084-9*) OUP.

Macpherson, Crawford B., ed. Property, Mainstream & Critical Positions. LC 78-2311. 217p. reprint ed. pap. 61.90 (*0-8357-8290-5*, 2034062) Bks Demand.

***Macpherson, David.** The Rapture Plot. 256p. (Orig.). 1995. pap. 12.95 (*0-9625220-2-3*) Millennium Three Pubs.

Macpherson, David A., jt. auth. see Hirsch, Barry T.

MacPherson, Donald W. April Fifteenth: The Most Pernicious Attack upon English Liberty. rev. ed. 210p. 1983. pap. 12.00 (*0-9617124-2-2*) Winning St Paul.

— Tax Fraud & Evasion: The War Stories. 250p. (Orig.). 1989. pap. 17.95 (*0-9617124-6-5*) Winning St Paul.

***Macpherson, Duncan.** Bullet Penetration: Modeling the Dynamics & the Incapacitation Resulting from Wound Trauma. LC 94-79577. (Illus.). 303p. 1994. 39.95 (*0-9643577-0-4*) Ballistic Pubns.

Macpherson, Duncan, et al. Luke. LC 71-173033. (Scripture Discussion Commentary Ser.: Vol. 8). 192p. 1971. pap. text ed. 4.95 (*0-87946-007-5*, 218) ACTA Pubns.

— Paul One. Bright, Laurence, ed. LC 71-173033. (Scripture Discussion Commentary Ser.: Vol. 10). 224p. 1972. pap. text ed. 4.95 (*0-87946-009-1*, 220) ACTA Pubns.

MacPherson, Earl & Schneider, Merylene. Memoirs: Earl MacPherson - The King of "Pin-up Art" (Illus.). 48p. (Orig.). 1991. pap. 9.95 (*0-941613-20-8*) Stabur Pr.

Macpherson, Gavin. Highway & Transportation Engineering & Planning. LC 93-28924. 385p. 1993. pap. text ed. 59.95 (*0-470-20003-0*) Halsted Pr.

***MacPherson, George.** Home-Grown Energy from Short-Rotation Coppice. (Illus.). 250p. (C). 1995. 32.95 (*0-85236-289-7*, Pub. by Farming Pr UK) Diamond Farm Bk.

MacPherson, Glenn J., jt. ed. see Marvin, Ursula B.

Macpherson, Gordon, ed. Black's Medical Dictionary. 656p. (C). 1992. text ed. 95.00 (*0-389-20989-9*) B&N Imports.

Macpherson, H. D., jt. auth. see Kaye, R. W.

An Asterisk (*) at the beginning of an entry indicates that the title is appearing in BIP for the first time.

Macpherson, Ian, ed. Juan Manuel Studies. (Serie A: Monagrafias, LX). 199p. (SPA.). (C). 1977. 45.00 (*0-7293-0024-2*, Pub. by Tamesis Bks Ltd UK) Boydell & Brewer.

MacPherson, Ian, ed. Western Canada. (Illus.). 80p. 1985. pap. text ed. 15.00 (*0-89745-064-7*) Sunflower U Pr.

MacPherson, J. Hope & Gabriel, C. J. Marine Molluscs of Victoria. 1962. 39.95 (*0-522-83665-8*) Intl Spec Bk.

Macpherson, James. Fragments of Ancient Poetry, Collected in the Highlands of Scotland, & Translated from the Galic or Erse Language. LC 92-1719. (Augustan Reprints Ser.: No. 122 (1966)). reprint ed. 12.00 (*0-404-70122-1*, PR3544) AMS Pr.

MacPherson, James. The Highlander: An Heroic Poem in Six Cantos. LC 78-67535. reprint ed. 17.50 (*0-404-17198-2*) AMS Pr.

— Poems of Ossian. (BCL1-PR English Literature Ser.). 298p. 1992. reprint ed. lib. bdg. 79.00 (*0-7812-7370-6*) Rprt Serv.

Macpherson, James. Poems of Ossian, 2 Vols, Set. LC 76-144459. reprint ed. 95.00 (*0-404-08697-7*) AMS Pr.

— Poems of Ossian in the Original Gaelic, 3 Vols, Set. M'Arthur, John, ed. LC 70-144460. reprint ed. 120.00 (*0-404-08730-2*) AMS Pr.

MacPherson, James, ed. see McGuire, Bill & Wheeler, Leslie.

Macpherson, James, ed. see Ossian.

MacPherson, James L., jt. ed. see Kasprisin, Duke O.

Macpherson, Jay. The Spirit of Solitude: Conventions & Continuities in Late Romance. LC 81-11462. (Illus.). 364p. 1982. 45.00 (*0-300-02632-3*) Yale U Pr.

MacPherson, Jay, tr. see Marmeladov, Yuri.

MacPherson, Jennifer B. To Attempt a Tower. LC 85-90339. 84p. (YA). (gr. 9-12). 1985. 16.95 (*0-9614849-0-X*); pap. 8.95 (*0-9614849-1-8*) MacPherson Pub.

***Macpherson, Kay.** When in Doubt, Do Both: The Times of My Life. (Illus.). 298p. 1994. 50.00 (*0-8020-0454-7*); pap. 18.95 (*0-8020-7473-1*) U of Toronto Pr.

MacPherson, Kenneth & Bryher, Winifred, eds. Close-up: A Magazine Devoted to the Art of Films, Set, Vols 1-10. LC 70-88572. (Contemporary Art Ser.). reprint ed. Set. 300.00 (*0-405-00732-9*) Ayer.

MacPherson, Malcolm C. In Cahoots: A Novel of Southern California, 1953. 1994. 21.00 (*0-679-42204-8*) Random.

Macpherson, Marion M., jt. auth. see Symonds, E. Malcolm.

MacPherson, Mary. Best of Ontario. 240p. 1994. pap. 19.95 (*1-55111-052-0*) Broadview Pr.

Macpherson, Michael C. The Psychology of Abuse. LC 83-62297. 125p. (Orig.). (C). 1985. pap. text ed. 16.95 (*0-88247-722-6*) R & E Pubs.

— Remembering. 224p. (Orig.). 1995. pap. 12.00 (*0-9642136-0-5*) Green Duck Pr.

MacPherson, Myra. Long Time Passing: Vietnam & the Haunted Generation. LC 93-11992. 1993. reprint ed. 15.95 (*0-385-47016-9*, Anchor NY) Doubleday.

Macpherson, Pat. Reflecting on Jane Eyre. (Heroines? Ser.). 96p. 1989. pap. 9.95 (*0-415-01787-4*) Routledge.

— Reflecting on The Bell Jar. (Heroines? Ser.). 128p. 1991. pap. 10.95 (*0-415-04393-X*, A5733) Routledge.

Macpherson, R., jt. auth. see Goresky, M.

MacPherson, R. D. Raoul Bott: Collected Papers, Vol. 2: Differential Operators (the 1960s) (Contemporary Mathematicians Ser.). (Illus.). xxxiii, 802p. 1994. 95.00 (*0-8176-3646-3*) Birkhauser.

MacPherson, R. D., ed. The Collected Works of Raoul Bott: Topology of Lie Groups - the 1950s, Vol. 1. (Contemporary Mathematicians Ser.). (Illus.). 450p. 1995. 95.00 (*0-8176-3613-7*) Birkhauser.

— Raoul Bott: Collected Papers. 485p. 1995. 95.00 (*0-8176-3647-1*) Spr-Verlag.

— Raoul Bott: Collected Papers. (Contemporary Mathematicians Ser.: Vol. 4). 484p. 1995. 95.00 (*0-8176-3648-X*) Spr-Verlag.

MacPherson, R. D., jt. auth. see Brylinski, Jean-Luc.

Macpherson, R. J., jt. ed. see Duignan, P. A.

Macpherson, R. J., jt. ed. see Martin, Yvonne M.

MacPherson, Robert, jt. auth. see Fulton, William.

MacPherson, Robert C. Automotive Collision Appraisal. (Illus.). 240p. (C). 1974. text ed. 32.95 (*0-07-044695-4*) McGraw.

— Collision Repair Guide. 1971. text ed. 32.95 (*0-07-044690-3*) McGraw.

MacPherson, Robert D., ed. Collected Works of Raoul Bott, Set. LC 93-36938. (Contemporary Mathematicians Ser.). 1993. write for info. (*0-8176-3701-X*); write for info. (*3-7643-3701-X*) Birkhauser.

***MacPherson, Selina.** Conquer the Night. 384p. (Orig.). 1995. mass mkt. 4.99 (*0-380-77252-3*) Avon.

— Embrace the Wild Dawn. 368p. (Orig.). 1994. mass mkt. 4.50 (*0-380-77251-5*) Avon.

— Forbidden Flame. 400p. (Orig.). 1993. mass mkt. 4.50 (*0-380-77250-7*) Avon.

— Rough & Tender. 384p. 1991. pap. 3.95 (*0-380-76322-2*) Avon.

MacPherson, Stewart. Social Policy in the Third World: The Social Dilemmas of Underdevelopment. LC 82-6837. 220p. (C). 1983. pap. text ed. 20.00 (*0-86598-090-X*, R3890) Rowman.

Macpherson, W. J., ed. The Industrialization of Japan. LC 93-43724. (Industrial Revolutions Ser.: No. 7). 1994. write for info. (*0-631-18074-5*) Blackwell Pubs.

MacPhillamy, Daizui, jt. ed. see Jiyu-Kennett, P. T.

MacPhillamy, Daizui, jt. auth. see Jiyu-Kennett, Roshi.

MacPike, Loralee, ed. There's Something I've Been Meaning to Tell You: An Anthology about Lesbians & Gay Men Coming Out to Their Children. 288p. 1989. 16.95 (*0-941483-54-1*); pap. 9.95 (*0-941483-44-4*) Naiad Pr.

MacQuarrie. Principles of Christian Theology. 1985. 24.00 (*0-684-14777-7*, Scribners) S&S Trade.

***MacQuarrie, Gordon.** Flyfishing with MacQuarrie. (Illus.). 256p. 1995. 19.50 (*1-57223-025-8*) Outlook Pubng.

— The Gordon MacQuarrie Treasury. Taylor, Zack, ed. 320p. 1995. 29.00 (*1-57223-032-0*, WCP) Outlook Pubng.

— The Gordon MacQuarrie Trilogy, 3 vols., Set. Taylor, Zack, ed. (Illus.). 630p. 1985. Slip cased set. boxed 49.00 (*1-55971-072-1*) Willow Creek Pr.

— The Gordon MacQuarrie Trilogy, Vol. 1: Stories of the Old Duck Hunters & Other Dr. Taylor, Zack, ed. (Illus.). 630p. 1985. write for info. (*0-318-59738-1*) Willow Creek Pr.

— The Gordon MacQuarrie Trilogy, Vol. 2: More Stories of the Old Duck Hunters. Taylor, Zack, ed. (Illus.). 630p. 1985. write for info. (*0-318-59739-X*) Willow Creek Pr.

— The Gordon MacQuarrie Trilogy, Vol. 3: The Last Stories of the Old Duck Hunters. Taylor, Zack, ed. (Illus.). 630p. 1985. write for info. (*0-318-59740-3*) Willow Creek Pr.

Macquarrie, Gordon. Last Stories of Old Duck Hunters. 1990. pap. 9.95 (*1-55971-053-5*) NorthWord.

MacQuarrie, Gordon. The Last Stories of the Old Duck Hunters. Taylor, Zack, ed. (Illus.). 204p. 1985. 17.50 (*0-932558-24-0*) Willow Creek Pr.

— A MacQuarrie Miscellany. (Illus.). 204p. 1987. 19.50 (*0-932558-38-0*) Willow Creek Pr.

Macquarrie, Gordon. More Stories of Old Duck Hunters. 1990. pap. 9.95 (*1-55971-052-7*) NorthWord.

MacQuarrie, Gordon. More Stories of the Old Duck Hunters. 198p. 1983. 17.50 (*0-932558-18-6*) Willow Creek Pr.

Macquarrie, Gordon. Stories of Old Duck Hunters. 1992. pap. 9.95 (*1-55971-051-9*) NorthWord.

MacQuarrie, Gordon. Stories of the Old Duck Hunters & Other Drivel. Taylor, Zack, ed. 228p. 1985. reprint ed. 17.50 (*0-932558-25-9*) Willow Creek Pr.

MacQuarrie, Heath. Red Tory Blues: A Political Memoir. 320p. 1992. 35.00 (*0-8020-5958-9*) U of Toronto Pr.

Macquarrie, John. The Concept of Peace. LC 90-34038. 96p. (Orig.). (C). 1990. pap. text ed. 7.95 (*0-334-02449-8*) TPI PA.

— An Existentialist Theology: A Comparison of Heidegger & Bultmann. LC 79-4604. 252p. 1979. reprint ed. text ed. 35.00 (*0-313-20795-X*, MAAE, Greenwood Pr) Greenwood.

— Heidegger & Christianity. 144p. (C). 1994. 19.95 (*0-8264-0694-7*) Continuum.

— Invitation to Faith. LC 95-6403. 1995. 7.95 (*0-8192-1642-9*) Morehouse Pub.

— Jesus Christ in Modern Thought. LC 90-31831. 512p. (C). 1991. pap. 23.95 (*0-334-02446-3*) TPI PA.

MacQuarrie, John. Mary for All Christians. 176p. (Orig.). 1991. pap. 10.99 (*0-8028-0543-4*) Eerdmans.

Macquarrie, John. Paths in Spirituality. 2nd ed. LC 93-8172. 176p. 1993. pap. 10.95 (*0-8192-1602-X*) Morehouse Pub.

— Principles of Christian Theology. 2nd ed. LC 76-23182. 544p. (C). 1977. pap. write for info. (*0-02-374510-X*, Scribners) S&S Trade.

— Twentieth Century Religious Thought. LC 81-9349. (C). 1981. pap. text ed. write for info. (*0-684-17334-4*, Scribners) S&S Trade.

— Twentieth-Century Religious Thought. rev. ed. LC 89-5026. 472p. 1989. pap. 19.95 (*0-334-01709-2*) TPI PA.

MacQuarrie, John & Macquarrie, John. Mystery & Truth. (Pere Marquette Lectures). 1970. 10.00 (*0-87462-518-1*) Marquette.

Macquarrie, John, jt. ed. see Childress, James F.

Macquarrie, John, jt. auth. see MacQuarrie, John.

MacQueen, Bruce. Plato's Republic in the Monographs of Sallust. 100p. pap. 12.95 (*0-86516-012-0*) Bolchazy-Carducci.

MacQueen, Bruce D. Myth, Rhetoric, & Fiction: A Reading of Longus's Daphnis & Chloe. xviii, 279p. 1991. 40.00 (*0-8032-3137-7*) U of Nebr Pr.

***MacQueen, Dave, ed.** Practical Applications of Functional Languages. (Trends in Software Ser.). Date not set. pap. text ed. 59.95 (*0-471-95144-7*) Wiley.

MacQueen, Hector L. Copyright, Competition & Industrial Design. (David Hume Papers: No. 14). 117p. 1990. pap. text ed. 14.00 (*0-08-037965-6*, Pub. by Aberdeen U Pr) Macmillan.

— MacQueen: Studying Scots Law. 170p. 1993. pap. 19.00 (*0-406-00013-1*, U.K.) Butterworth Legal Pubs.

MacQueen, Hector L., jt. ed. see Kiralfy, Albert.

MacQueen, Jack. Numerology: Theory & Outline of a Literary Mode. 163p. 1984. 14.00 (*0-85224-492-4*, Pub. by Edinburgh U Pr UK) Col U Pr.

MacQueen, John. Humanism in Renaissance Scotland. 224p. 1989. 45.00 (*0-7486-0111-2*, Pub. by Edinburgh U Pr UK) Col U Pr.

MacQueen, John & Scott, Tom, eds. The Oxford Book of Scottish Verse. 672p. 1989. reprint ed. pap. 14.95 (*0-19-282600-X*) OUP.

MacQueen, Megan, ed. see Mills, Kenneth G.

MacQueen, Peter. In Wildest Africa. 1909. 29.00 (*0-403-00353-9*) Scholarly.

Macqueen, R. W., jt. ed. see Hutchinson, R. W.

MacQueen, Roger W. & Leckie, Dale A., eds. Foreland Basins & Fold Belts. (AAPG Memoir Ser.: No. 55). (Illus.). x, 460p. 1992. 110.00 (*0-89181-334-9*) AAPG.

Macquet, Claire. Looking for Ammu. 232p. 1993. pap. 13.95 (*1-85381-393-1*, Pub. by Virago Pr UK) Trafalgar.

***MacQuitty, Jane.** Jane MacQuitty's Guide to Champagne & Sparkling Wines. 318p. 1993. pap. 14.95 (*1-85732-948-1*, Pub. by Reed Illust Books UK) Antique Collect.

MacQuitty, Miranda. Desert. LC 93-21068. (Eyewitness Bks.). (J). 1994. 16.00 (*0-679-86003-7*); lib. bdg. 16.99 (*0-679-96003-1*) Knopf Bks Yng Read.

— Shark. LC 92-4712. (Eyewitness Bks.). (Illus.). 64p. (J). 1992. 16.00 (*0-679-81683-6*); lib. bdg. 16.99 (*0-679-91683-0*) Knopf Bks Yng Read.

MacQuoid, Percy. A History of English Furniture, 2 vols. (Illus.). 1000p. 1987. The Age of Oak & the Age of Walnut. 89.50 (*0-685-73886-8*); The Age of Mahogany & the Age of Satinwood. 89.50 (*0-685-73887-6*) Antique Collect.

— A History of English Furniture, 2 vols., Set. (Illus.). 1000p. 1987. write for info. (*1-85149-052-3*) Antique Collect.

***Macrae.** Presenting Young Adult Fantasy. 1995. 26.95 (*0-8057-8220-6*, Twayne) Macmillan.

MacRae, Alasdair, ed. Shelley: Selected Poetry & Prose. (English Texts Ser.). 256p. 1991. pap. 11.95 (*0-415-01607-X*, A5370) Routledge.

Macrae, Alasdair D. F. W. B. Yeats: A Literary Life. LC 94-20524. (Literary Lives Ser.). 1994. write for info. (*0-312-12310-8*) St Martin.

Macrae, Alexander. Macrae: History of the Clan Macrae, with Genealogies. (Illus.). xxii, 442p. 1992. reprint ed. lib. bdg. 81.00 (*0-8328-2682-0*); reprint ed. pap. 71.00 (*0-8328-2683-9*) Higginson Bk Co.

MacRae, Allan A. The Gospel of Isaiah. LC 92-71421. 192p. 1992. pap. 6.95 (*0-944788-94-7*) IBRI.

— JEDP: Lectures on the Higher Criticism of the Pentateuch. LC 89-81338. 294p. 1994. pap. 9.95 (*0-944788-89-0*) IBRI.

MacRae-Campbell, Linda & McKisson, Micki. Endangered Species: Their Struggle to Survive. (Our Only Earth Ser.). 104p. (J). (gr. 4-12). 1990. 19.95 (*0-913705-54-3*) Zephyr Pr AZ.

Macrae-Campbell, Linda & McKisson, Micki. The Future of Our Tropical Rainforests. (Our Only Earth Ser.). 104p. (J). (gr. 4-12). 1990. pap. text ed. 19.95 (*0-913705-49-7*) Zephyr Pr AZ.

MacRae-Campbell, Linda & McKisson, Micki. Our Troubled Skies. (Our Only Earth Ser.). 104p. (J). (gr. 4-12). 1990. 19.95 (*0-913705-50-0*) Zephyr Pr AZ.

— War: The Global Battlefield. (Our Only Earth Ser.). 104p. (J). (gr. 4-12). 1990. 19.95 (*0-913705-51-9*) Zephyr Pr AZ.

MacRae-Campbell, Linda, jt. auth. see McKisson, Micki.

MacRae-Campbell, Linda, et al. The Ocean Crisis. (Our Only Earth Ser.). 104p. (J). (gr. 4-12). 1990. 19.95 (*0-913705-53-5*) Zephyr Pr AZ.

Macrae, Chris. World Class Brands. (C). 1991. text ed. 30.25 (*0-201-54407-5*) Addison-Wesley.

MacRae, David, tr. see Yaroshinskaya, Alla.

***MacRae, Diann.** Birder's Guide to Washington. LC 95-1573. (Illus.). 332p. 1995. 17.95 (*0-88415-126-3*) Gulf Pub.

MacRae, Donald L. Television Production: An Introduction. 2nd ed. (Illus.). 1982. pap. 17.95 (*0-458-93930-7*, 6508) Routledge Chapman & Hall.

MacRae, Donald L. & Hartleib, Carl J. Relating Styles Participant Kit. 1981. pap. text ed. 65.00 (*0-07-092327-2*) McGraw.

MacRae, Duncan, Jr. Policy Indicators: Links Between Social Science & Public Debate. LC 84-17294. (Urban & Regional Policy & Development Studies). xvi, 414p. 1985. 45.00 (*0-8078-1628-0*) U of NC Pr.

— The Social Function of Social Science. LC 75-32282. 376p. 1976. 45.00 (*0-300-01921-1*) Yale U Pr.

MaCrae, Duncan, Jr. & Wilde, James A. Policy Analysis for Public Decisions. 344p. 1985. reprint ed. pap. text ed. 25.50 (*0-8191-4835-0*) U Pr of Amer.

MacRae, Duncan, jt. auth. see Haskins, Ron.

MacRae, George W. The Epistle to the Hebrews. Karris, Robert J., ed. (Collegeville Bible Commentary - New Testament Ser.: No. 10). 64p. (C). 1983. pap. 3.95 (*0-8146-1310-1*) Liturgical Pr.

MacRae, George W., ed. see Conzelmann, Hans.

MacRae, George W., jt. auth. see Epp, Eldon J.

Macrae-Gibson, Gavin. The Secret Life of Buildings: An American Mythology for Modern Architecture. (Graham Foundation Architecture Ser.). 223p. 1988. 35.00 (*0-262-13203-6*) MIT Pr.

Macrae-Gibson, O. D., ed. The Old English Riming Poem. 74p. 1983. 45.00 (*0-85991-134-9*) Boydell & Brewer.

Macrae-Gibson, O. D., jt. auth. see Marples, N. J.

Macrae, James. With Lord Byron in the Sandwich Islands. 90p. 1972. reprint ed. pap. 3.95 (*0-912180-14-5*) Petroglyph.

Macrae, Janet. Therapeutic Touch: A Practical Guide. LC 87-45444. (Illus.). 112p. 1988. pap. 9.00 (*0-394-75588-X*) Knopf.

Macrae, Janet A., jt. ed. see Calabria, Michael D.

***Macrae, Joann, et al, eds.** War & Hunger: Rethinking International Responses to Complex Emergencies. LC 94-41463. (C). 1995. pap. 25.00 (*1-85649-292-3*, Pub. by Zed Books UK) Humanities.

Macrae, Mason. The Distant Hills. large type ed. (Linford Western Library). 352p. 1985. pap. 11.95 (*0-7089-6188-6*) Ulverscroft.

MacRae, Norma M. Canning & Preserving Without Sugar. 3rd ed. LC 92-21478. (Illus.). 240p. (Orig.). 1993. pap. 12.95 (*1-56440-163-4*) Globe Pequot.

Macrae, Norman. John von Neumann. Date not set. pap. 4.99 (*0-517-11261-2*) Random Hse Value.

Macrae, Robert. HPLC in Food Analysis. 502p. 1988. text ed. 109.00 (*0-12-464781-2*) Acad Pr.

Macrae, Robert, jt. auth. see Clarke, R. J.

Macrae, Robert, jt. ed. see Clarke, R. J.

Macrae, Robert, et al, eds. Encyclopedia of Food Science, Food Technology, & Nutrition, 8 vols., 1. LC 92-15557. (Illus.). 5500p. 1993. text ed. 275.00 (*0-12-226851-2*) Acad Pr.

— Encyclopedia of Food Science, Food Technology, & Nutrition, 8 vols., 2. LC 92-15557. (Illus.). 5500p. 1993. text ed. 275.00 (*0-12-226852-0*) Acad Pr.

— Encyclopedia of Food Science, Food Technology, & Nutrition, 8 vols., 3. LC 92-15557. (Illus.). 5500p. 1993. text ed. 275.00 (*0-12-226853-9*) Acad Pr.

— Encyclopedia of Food Science, Food Technology, & Nutrition, 8 vols., 4. LC 92-15557. (Illus.). 5500p. 1993. text ed. 275.00 (*0-12-226854-7*) Acad Pr.

— Encyclopedia of Food Science, Food Technology, & Nutrition, 8 vols., 5. LC 92-15557. (Illus.). 5500p. 1993. text ed. 275.00 (*0-12-226855-5*) Acad Pr.

— Encyclopedia of Food Science, Food Technology, & Nutrition, 8 vols., 6. LC 92-15557. (Illus.). 5500p. 1993. text ed. 275.00 (*0-12-226856-3*) Acad Pr.

— Encyclopedia of Food Science, Food Technology, & Nutrition, 8 vols., 7. LC 92-15557. (Illus.). 5500p. 1993. text ed. 275.00 (*0-12-226857-1*) Acad Pr.

— Encyclopedia of Food Science, Food Technology, & Nutrition, 8 vols., 8. LC 92-15557. (Illus.). 5500p. 1993. text ed. 275.00 (*0-12-226858-X*) Acad Pr.

— Encyclopedia of Food Science, Food Technology, & Nutrition, 8 vols., Set. LC 92-15557. (Illus.). 5500p. 1993. text ed. 2,100.00 (*0-12-226850-4*) Acad Pr.

MacRae, Sheila & Jeffers, H. Paul. Hollywood Mother of the Year: Sheila MacRae's Own Story. (Illus.). 256p. 1992. 18.95 (*1-55972-112-X*, Birch Ln Pr) Carol Pub Group.

MacRae, Thomas H., et al, eds. Biochemistry & Cell Biology of Artemia. 272p. 1988. 156.00 (*0-8493-4897-8*, QL444, CRC Reprint) Franklin.

MacRae, W. R. & Wildsmith, J. A., eds. Induced Hypotension. (Monographs in Anaesthesiology: Vol. 20). 352p. 1991. 217.50 (*0-444-81292-X*) Elsevier.

Macrakis, Kristie. Surviving the Swastika: Scientific Research in Nazi Germany. LC 93-19919. (Illus.). 256p. 1993. 39.95 (*0-19-507010-0*) OUP.

Macran, Henry S., ed. & tr. Harmonika Stoicheia - The Harmonics of Aristoxenus. 303p. 1990. reprint ed. 57.20 (*3-487-05254-7*, Pub. by Georg Olms GW) Lubrecht & Cramer.

Macrander, George, jt. auth. see Swaminathan, V. J.

MacRaois, Cormac. Battle below Giltspur. (Illus.). 1989. pap. 8.95 (*0-86327-198-7*, Pub. by Wolfhound Pr IE) Dufour.

— Dance of the Midnight Fire. 1990. pap. 8.95 (*0-86327-262-2*) Dufour.

— Dance of the Midnight Fire. LC 89-82284. (Illus.). 144p. (J). (gr. 4-8). 1990. 12.95 (*0-86327-241-X*, Pub. by Wolfhound Pr IE); pap. 8.95 (*0-685-33034-6*, Pub. by Wolfhound Pr IE) Dufour.

— It's Pin Bin Dim Dominilli! 15 Centimeters of Mischief! (Illus.). 174p. (J). 1994. pap. 7.95 (*0-86327-408-0*, Pub. by Wolfhound Pr IE) Dufour.

— Lightning over Giltspur. (Illus.). 139p. (J). (gr. 4-6). 1991. 14.95 (*0-86327-308-4*, Pub. by Wolfhound Pr IE) Dufour.

— Lightning over Giltspur. (Illus.). 144p. (J). (gr. 4-8). 1993. pap. 9.95 (*0-86327-332-7*, Pub. by Wolfhound Pr IE) Dufour.

MacRaonuill, A., ed. see MacDonald, J.

MacRaonuill, A., tr. see MacLeoid, Tormod, et al.

MacRaonuill, Alasdair. Eachdraidh a' Ciuil Mhoir: History of the Music Great. 380p. 1988. 69.00 (*0-9621754-0-4*); pap. 69.00 (*0-9621754-1-2*) A MacRaonuill.

MacRauch, Earl. Buckaroo Banzai. pap. 4.95 (*0-671-50574-2*) S&S Trade.

Macray, W. D., ed. Charters & Documents Illustrating the History of the Cathedral: City & Diocese of Salisbury in the 12th & 13th Centuries. (Rolls Ser.: No. 97). 1972. reprint ed. 80.00 (*0-8115-1176-6*) Periodicals Srv.

Macray, W. Dunn, ed. see Hyde, Edward.

Macray, William D., ed. Chronicon Abbatiae de Evesham Ad Annum 1418. (Rolls Ser.: No. 29). 1972. reprint ed. 45.00 (*0-8115-1057-3*) Periodicals Srv.

— Chronicon Abbatiae Rameseiensis. (Rolls Ser.: No. 83). 1972. reprint ed. 80.00 (*0-8115-1156-1*) Periodicals Srv.

***Macrea, Joanna & Zwi, Anthony, eds.** War & Hunger: Rethinking International Responses to Complex Emergencies. LC 94-41463. 256p. (C). 1995. text ed. 59.95 (*1-85649-291-5*, Pub. by Zed Books UK) Humanities.

Macready, Robert. The Reincarnation of Robert Macready. 336p. (Orig.). 1981. pap. 2.75 (*0-89083-703-1*) Zebra.

Macready, William C. Diaries of William Charles Macready, 2 vols., 1. Toynbee, William C., ed. LC 78-84519. 1972. 24.95 (*0-405-08773-X*, Pub. by Blom Pubns UK) Ayer.

— Diaries of William Charles Macready, 2 vols., 2. Toynbee, William C., ed. LC 78-84519. 1972. 24.95 (*0-405-08774-8*, Pub. by Blom Pubns UK) Ayer.

— Diaries of William Charles Macready, 2 vols., Set. Toynbee, William C., ed. LC 78-84519. 1972. 48.95 (*0-405-08772-1*, Pub. by Blom Pubns UK) Ayer.

Macridis, Roy C. Contemporary Political Ideologies. 5th ed. (C). 1991. text ed. 36.50 (*0-673-52165-6*) HarpCollege.

— Foreign Policy in World Politics. 8th ed. 432p. (C). 1991. pap. text ed. write for info. (*0-13-335084-3*) P-H.

— Greek Politics at a Crossroads: What Kind of Socialism? (Publication Ser.: No. 299). x, 72p. (Orig.). (C). 1984. pap. text ed. 3.98 (*0-8179-7992-1*) Hoover Inst Pr.

— Modern Political Systems: Europe. 5th ed. (Illus.). 576p. 1983. write for info. (*0-13-597195-0*) P-H.

Macridis, Roy C. & Brown, Bernard E. Comparative Politics: Notes & Readings. 7th ed. 600p. (C). 1990. pap. 29.95 (*0-534-12636-7*) Intl Thomson.

— The De Gaulle Republic: Quest for Unity. LC 76-7417. 400p. 1976. reprint ed. text ed. 55.00 (*0-8371-8848-2*, MADG, Greenwood Pr) Greenwood.

Macridis, Roy C. & Burg. Comparative Political Regimes. 2nd ed. (C). 1990. pap. text ed. 28.50 (*0-673-52035-8*) HarpCollege.

***Macrina, Francis L.** Scientific Integrity: An Introductory Text with Cases. LC 94-46226. 1995. write for info. (*1-55581-069-1*) Am Soc Microbio.

Macris, C. J., ed. see NATO Advanced Study Institute Staff.

Macris, George P. The Orthodox Church & the Ecumenical Movement During the Period 1920-1969. (Illus.). 196p. (Orig.). 1986. pap. 12.50 (*0-913026-74-3*) St Nectarios.

Macris, Georgia, ed. A Greek Feast: A Book of Greek Recipes. (Illus.). 150p. (Orig.). 1993. pap. text ed. 12.00 (*0-9638023-0-5*) Daugh of Penelope.

***Macris, Michael, ed.** ERISA & Benefits Law Journal. 1992. pap. 125.00 (*1-56257-322-5*) Michie Butterworth.

Macriss, R. A., et al. Physical & Thermodynamic Properties of Ammonia-Water Mixtures. (Research Bulletin Ser.: No. 34). iv, 42p. 1964. 5.00 (*0-317-56884-1*) Inst Gas Tech.

— Physical & Thermodynamic Properties of Ammonia-Water Mixtures. suppl. ed. (Research Bulletin Ser.: No. 34). iv, 42p. 1964. 3.50 (*0-317-56885-X*) Inst Gas Tech.

MacRitchie, David. Scottish Gypsies under the Stewarts. LC 75-3463. reprint ed. 14.50 (*0-404-16892-2*) AMS Pr.

MacRitchie, David, ed. Accounts of the Gypsies of India. LC 75-3461. (Illus.). reprint ed. 24.00 (*0-404-16893-0*) AMS Pr.

MacRitchie, Finlay. Chemistry at Interfaces. 283p. 1990. text ed. 69.00 (*0-12-464785-5*) Acad Pr.

MacRitchie, Finlay, jt. auth. see Bekes, Ferenc.

MacRitchie, James. HE: Chi Kung: Cultivating Personal Energy. (Health Essentials Ser.). (Illus.). 136p. 1993. pap. 9.95 (*1-85230-371-9*) Element MA.

Macro, Allen & Buxton, John. The Craft of Software Engineering. 400p. (C). 1987. pap. text ed. 29.25 (*0-201-18488-5*) Addison-Wesley.

Macro Systems, Inc. Staff. Social Skills on the Job Computer Software Manual. (Social Skills on the Job Ser.). 1989. pap. text ed. 7.95 (*0-88671-347-1*, 4704) Am Guidance.

— Social Skills on the Job Teacher's Guide. (Social Skills on the Job Ser.). 1989. teacher ed 9.95 (*0-88671-346-3*, 4703) Am Guidance.

MacRobbie, Bill. Add Spice to Your Travels. (Illus.). 196p. 1980. pap. 4.95 (*0-9605244-0-1*) B Sales.

— All Aboard, Set Sail, Let's Go. (Illus.). 216p. 1994. pap. 12.95 (*0-931541-39-5*) Mancorp Pub.

MacRobert, Alan M. Star-Hopping for Backyard Astronomers. LC 93-25106. (Illus.). 160p. 1993. 21.95 (*0-933346-68-9*) Sky Pub.

MacRobert, C. M., et al, eds. Oxford Slavonic Papers, New Series, Vol. XXV. (Illus.). 176p. 1993. 65.00 (*0-19-815670-7*) OUP.

— Oxford Slavonic Papers, New Series, Vol. XXVI (1993) (Illus.). 122p. 1994. 55.00 (*0-19-815671-5*) OUP.

— Oxford Slavonic Papers, New Series Vol. XXVII: (1994) (Illus.). 184p. 1995. 55.00 (*0-19-815672-3*) OUP.

MacRobert, Iain. The Black Roots & White Racism of Early Pentacostalism in the U. S. A. LC 87-35745. 176p. 1988. text ed. 39.95 (*0-312-01690-5*) St Martin.

Macrobert, T. M., ed. see Bromwich, T. J. I.

MacRoberts, Barbara R., jt. auth. see MacRoberts, Michael H.

MacRoberts, Michael H. & MacRoberts, Barbara R. Social Organization & Behavior of the Acorn Woodpecker in Central Coastal California. 115p. 1976. 7.50 (*0-943610-21-4*) Am Ornithologists.

Macromedia, Inc. Authorware Academic for Macintosh. 1994. pap. text ed. 112.50 (*0-13-289802-0*) P-H.

— Authorware Academic for Windows. 1994. pap. text ed. 113.00 (*0-13-289794-6*) P-H.

***Macrone, Michael.** Animalogies: A Fine Kettle of Fish & 277 Other Animal Expressions. LC 95-6739. (Illus.). 1995. write for info. (*0-385-47587-X*) Doubleday.

— Brush up Your Bible! LC 93-4350. (Illus.). 368p. 1993. 20.00 (*0-06-270024-3*, Harper Ref) HarpC.

— Brush up Your Bible. (Illus.). 384p. 1995. pap. 10.00 (*0-06-272020-1*) HarpC.

— Brush up Your Shakespeare! (Illus.). 256p. 1994. pap. 10.00 (*0-06-272018-X*, Harper Ref) HarpC.

— By Jove! Brush up Your Mythology. (Illus.). 256p. 1994. reprint ed. pap. 10.00 (*0-06-272019-8*, Harper Ref) HarpC.

— Eureka! What Archimedes Really Meant. LC 94-19424. (Illus.). 1994. 20.00 (*0-06-270096-0*, HarpT) HarpC.

— It's Greek to Me: Brush Up Your Classics. LC 91-55004. (Illus.). 256p. 1991. 17.00 (*0-06-270022-7*, Harper Ref) HarpC.

— It's Greek to Me! Brush up Your Classics. (Illus.). 256p. 1994. reprint ed. pap. 10.00 (*0-06-272044-9*, Harper Ref) HarpC.

Macrorie, Ken. The I-Search Paper. rev. ed. LC 88-10329. 359p. (C). 1988. pap. text ed. 19.50 (*0-86709-223-8*, 0223) Boynton Cook Pubs.

— Telling Writing. 4th ed. 300p. (YA). (gr. 10 up). 1985. pap. text ed. 17.50 (*0-86709-153-3*) Boynton Cook Pubs.

— Twenty Teachers. (Illus.). 272p. 1987. pap. 10.95 (*0-19-504982-9*) OUP.

— Writing to Be Read. 3rd rev. ed. LC 84-14922. 287p. (J). (gr. 9-12). 1984. pap. text ed. 17.50 (*0-86709-133-9*) Boynton Cook Pubs.

Macrory, Richard & Hollins, Steve. A Source Book of European Community Environmental Law. 90p. 1995. 45.00 (*0-19-825937-9*) OUP.

Macsai, John, et al. Housing. 2nd ed. LC 81-7584. 590p. 1982. text ed. 91.95 (*0-471-08126-4*, Wiley-Interscience) Wiley.

MacShane, Denis. International Labour & the Origins of the Cold War. 336p. 1992. 69.00 (*0-19-827366-5*) OUP.

— Solidarity. 1982. 37.50 (*0-85124-319-3*) Dufour.

— Solidarity: Poland's Independent Trade Union. LC 81-16515. 1982. 37.50 (*0-685-38820-4*, Pub. by Spkesman UK) Dufour.

— Solidarity: Poland's Independent Trade Union. 172p. 1987. 75.00 (*0-685-12449-5*, Bertrand Russell Soc); pap. 20.00 (*0-685-12450-9*, Bertrand Russell Soc) St Mut.

MacShane, Denis, et al. Power! Black Workers, Their Unions, & the Struggle for Freedom in South Africa. 195p. (Orig.). 1984. 30.00 (*0-89608-245-8*); pap. 8.00 (*0-89608-244-X*) South End Pr.

MacShane, Frank, ed. Ford Madox Ford: The Critical Heritage. (Critical Heritage Ser.). 1972. 69.50 (*0-7100-6957-X*, RKP) Routledge.

— Selected Letters of Raymond Chandler. LC 81-4852. 616p. 1981. text ed. 43.00 (*0-231-05080-1*) Col U Pr.

MacShane, Frank & Carlson, Lori, eds. Return Trip Tango & Other Stories from Abroad. (Columbia Collection). 320p. (C). 1992. text ed. 50.00 (*0-231-07992-3*); pap. 14.95 (*0-231-07993-1*) Col U Pr.

MacShane, Frank, ed. see Ford, Ford Madox.

MacShane, Frank, ed. see O'Hara, John.

Macsich, George. Economic Nationalism & Stability. LC 85-12342. 176p. 1985. text ed. 45.00 (*0-275-90215-3*, C0215, Praeger Pubs) Greenwood.

Macskasy, H., jt. auth. see Pal, G.

***MacSkimming, Roy.** Gordie: A Hockey Legend. (Illus.). 224p. 1995. pap. 9.95 (*1-55054-455-1*, Pub. by Doug & McIntyre CN) Sterling.

— Gordie: In Search of a Hockey Legend. (Illus.). 240p. 1994. 19.95 (*1-55054-159-5*, Pub. by Doug & McIntyre CN) Sterling.

Macsolis. Baile de Luna: Dance Moon. (Illus.). 25p. (SPA.). (J). (ps-2). 1991. 12.95 (*84-261-2583-2*) Donars.

MacStravic, R. Scott. Beyond Patient Satisfaction: Building Patient Loyalty. LC 91-7086. 279p. 1991. text ed. 42.00 (*0-910701-70-9*, 0905) Health Admin Pr.

MacStravic, Scott. Partnering: The Story of a Community Hospital. LC 92-32391. 151p. (Orig.). 1993. pap. text ed. 28.00 (*0-910701-92-X*, 0927) Health Admin Pr.

MacStravic, Sue, ed. see Ryder, Tracie R.

MacSween, Ann & Sharp, Mick. Prehistoric Scotland. (Illus.). 192p. (C). 1990. 30.00 (*0-941533-87-5*) New Amsterdam Bks.

MacSween, Morag. Anorectic Bodies: A Feminist & Sociological Perspective On Anorexia Nervosa. LC 93-7246. 1993. write for info. (*0-415-02846-9*) Routledge.

— Anorexic Bodies: A Feminist & Sociological Perspective on Anorexia Nervosa. LC 95-9185. 1996. write for info. (*0-415-02847-7*) Routledge.

MacSween, Robert, et al, eds. Pathology of the Liver. 2nd ed. (Illus.). 717p. 1987. 230.00 (*0-443-03049-9*) Churchill.

MacSween, Roderick N., jt. ed. see Anthony, Peter P.

***MacSween, Roderick N. M., et al, eds.** Pathology of the Liver. 3rd ed. LC 94-33377. 1994. write for info. (*0-443-04454-6*) Churchill.

MacSweeney, David. The Crazy Ape: Sanity, Madness, Your Brain & You. 244p. 1982. 25.00 (*0-7206-0565-2*, Pub. by P Owen Ltd UK) Dufour.

MacSweeney, J. E., jt. auth. see Morris, R. J.

Mactaggart, Ken. Discovering Caithness & Sutherland. 200p. (C). 1989. pap. text ed. 26.00 (*0-85976-376-5*, Pub. by J Donald) St Mut.

MacTavish, David, jt. auth. see Heron, Michal.

Mactavish, Sandy. For Struggling Golfers Only: A Simplified Swing Which Will Have You Scoring in the 80's. (Illus.). 64p. (Orig.). 1994. pap. 12.85 (*0-9641095-0-6*) Supreme Pubng.

MacThomais, Eamonn. Gur Cake & Coal Blocks. 160p. 1988. reprint ed. pap. 8.95 (*0-86278-096-9*, Pub. by OBrien Pr IE) Dufour.

— Janey Mack, Me Shirt Is Black. 160p. 1988. reprint ed. pap. 8.95 (*0-86278-070-5*, Pub. by OBrien Pr IE) Dufour.

— Labour & the Royal. 108p. 1979. 13.95 (*0-905140-56-7*, Pub. by OBrien Pr IE); pap. 7.95 (*0-86278-047-0*, Pub. by OBrien Pr IE) Dufour.

— Me Jewel & Darling Dublin. 144p. 1988. reprint ed. pap. 14.95 (*0-905140-88-5*, Pub. by OBrien Pr IE) Dufour.

MacThomais, R. Gaelic Learner's Handbook. 1991. pap. 10.95 (*0-8288-3347-8*, F132987) Fr & Eur.

Mactier, R. A. & Nolph, K. D., eds. Current Concepts of CAPD: Journal: Blood Purification, Vol. 7, No. 2-3, 1989. (Illus.). 120p. 1989. pap. 68.00 (*3-8055-5009-X*) S Karger.

Mactire, Sean P. Lyme Disease & Other Pest-Borne Illnesses. LC 91-40895. (Venture Bks.). (Illus.). 112p. (YA). (gr. 7-12). 1991. lib. bdg. 14.28 (*0-531-12523-8*) Watts.

— Malicious Intent: A Writer's Guide to How Criminals Think. 240p. (Orig.). 1995. pap. 16.99 (*0-89879-648-2*) Writers Digest.

— Victims of Domestic Violence: What to Look For, How to Help Them. 32p. (Orig.). 1988. pap. 3.95 (*0-945485-01-8*) Comm Intervention.

MacTurk, Robert H., ed. see Pdersen, Frank A., et al.

Macuch, Rudolf. Geschichte der und Neusyrischen Literatur. (C). 1976. 292.30 (*3-11-005959-2*) De Gruyter.

— Grammatik des Samaritanischen Hebraeisch. (Studia Samaritana: Band 1). (C). 1969. 280.75 (*3-11-000133-0*) De Gruyter.

— Handbook of Classical & Modern Mandaic. (C). 1965. 246.15 (*3-11-000261-2*) De Gruyter.

— Zur Sprache und Literatur der Mandaer: Mit Beitraegen von Kurt Rudolph & Eric Segelberg. (C). 1976. 192.30 (*3-11-004838-8*) De Gruyter.

Macuga, Linda. Harvest of Hope. 372p. 1994. pap. 9.95 (*1-56901-300-4*) NW Pub.

— United We Stand. Ingram, tr. 530p. 1995. pap. 12.95 (*1-56901-708-5*) NW Pub.

MacUistin, Liam. Celtic Magic Tales. (Illus.). 94p. (J). (gr. 3-7). 1994. pap. 7.95 (*0-86278-341-0*, Pub. by OBrien Pr IE) Dufour.

— The Tain: The Great Celtic Epic. LC 89-81775. (Illus.). 96p. 1990. 12.95 (*0-86278-204-X*, Pub. by OBrien Pr IE) Dufour.

— The Tain: The Great Celtic Epic. (Illus.). 93p. (J). (gr. 5-12). 1991. pap. 9.95 (*0-86278-238-4*, Pub. by OBrien Pr IE) Dufour.

Maculaitis, Jean D. Blue MAC (2-3) Test Administration Booklet. 96p. (C). 1991. pap. text ed. write for info. (*0-13-544073-4*) P-H.

— Green MAC BCT Test Administration Booklet. 112p. (C). 1991. pap. text ed. write for info. (*0-13-544081-5*) P-H.

— Maculaitis Assessment Batteries. 1982. BCT Sampler. 19.10 (*0-88084-079-X*); K-1 Sampler. 21.85 (*0-88084-088-9*); 34.50 (*0-88084-109-5*); 19.75 (*0-88084-108-7*) Alemany Pr.

— Maculaitis Assessment Batteries. (J). (gr. 2-3). 1982. Grades 2-3 Sampler. 33.70 (*0-88084-089-7*) Alemany Pr.

— Maculaitis Assessment Batteries. (J). (gr. 4-5). 1982. Grades 4-5 Sampler. 26.00 (*0-88084-094-3*) Alemany Pr.

— Maculaitis Assessment Batteries. (J). (gr. 6-8). 1982. Grades 6-8 Sampler. 26.00 (*0-88084-099-4*) Alemany Pr.

— Maculaitis Assessment Batteries. (YA). (gr. 9-12). 1982. Grades 9-12 Sampler. 43.90 (*0-88084-104-4*) Alemany Pr.

— Pink MAC (K-1) Test Administration Booklet. 96p. (C). 1991. pap. text ed. write for info. (*0-13-544099-8*) P-H.

Maculiffe, Max A. Sikh Religion, 6 vols., Set. 1270p. 1986. 400.00 (*0-317-52153-5*, Pub. by S Chand II) St Mut.

Macunovich, Janet. Easy Garden Design: Twelve Simple Steps to Creating Successful Gardens & Landscapes. Art, Pam, ed. LC 91-58926. (Illus.). 176p. 1992. pap. 14.95 (*0-88266-791-2*, Garden Way Pub) Storey Comm Inc.

Macur, Mary. Curious What You Might Find When You Go Out to Look for Elephants. LC 48-29. pap. 5.00 (*0-686-28865-3*) First Amend.

Macura, P. Dictionary of Botany, Vol. 2: General Terms. 744p. (ENG, FRE, GER & RUS.). 1982. 169.25 (*0-444-41977-2*) Elsevier.

— Elsevier's Dictionary of Botany, Vol. 1: Plant Names. LC 79-15558. 580p. 1979. 169.25 (*0-444-41787-7*) Elsevier.

— Elsevier's Dictionary of Botany, Vol. 1: Plant Names. 580p. 1979. 295.00 (*0-8288-9210-5*, M8804) Fr & Eur.

— Elsevier's Dictionary of Botany, Vol. 2: General Terms. 744p. 1982. 295.00 (*0-8288-9211-3*, M14277) Fr & Eur.

— Elsevier's Dictionary of Chemistry: Russian - English. 1000p. (ENG & RUS.). 1993. write for info. (*0-8288-9225-3*) Fr & Eur.

— Elsevier's Russian - English Dictionary. 3264p. (ENG & RUS.). 1990. 495.00 (*0-8288-9306-3*, F30420) Fr & Eur.

— Elsevier's Russian-English Dictionary. 3264p. 1990. 307.75 (*0-444-88467-X*) Elsevier.

Macura, Paul. Russian-English Botanical Dictionary. 678p. (ENG & RUS.). 1982. 49.95 (*0-89357-092-3*) Slavica.

— Russian-English Dictionary of Electrotechnology & Applied Sciences. LC 85-8653. 958p. 1986. reprint ed. lib. bdg. 95.50 (*0-89874-869-0*) Krieger.

Macurdy, G. H. Il Forrer: Vassal Queens & Portraits of Royal Greek Ladies on Coins. 230p. pap. 25.00 (*0-685-70633-8*) Ares.

***Macurdy, G. H. & Forrer, L.** Two Studies on Women in Antiquity: Vassal Queens & Some Contemporary Women in the Roman Empire - Portraits of Royal Ladies on Greek Coins. (Illus.). 1993. pap. 25.00 (*0-685-75722-6*) Ares.

Macurdy, Grace H. Chronology of the Extant Plays of Euripides. LC 68-9236. (Studies in Drama: No. 39). 1969. reprint ed. lib. bdg. 44.95 (*0-8383-0590-3*) M S G Haskell Hse.

— Hellenistic Queens. (Illus.). xv, 250p. 1985. reprint ed. pap. 20.00 (*0-89005-542-4*) Ares.

— Hellenistic Queens. LC 75-16848. (Johns Hopkins University Studies in Archaeology: No. 14). (Illus.). 250p. 1975. reprint ed. text ed. 35.00 (*0-8371-8271-9*, MAHQ, Greenwood Pr) Greenwood.

— Hellenistic Queens: A Study of Woman-Power in Macedonia, Seleucid Syria, & Ptolemaic Egypt. LC 75-41184. reprint ed. 17.50 (*0-404-14683-X*) AMS Pr.

— Troy & Paeonia: With Glimpses of Ancient Balkan History & Religion. xi, 259p. 1989. reprint ed. text ed. 50.00 (*0-89241-439-1*) Caratzas.

Macvannel, John A. The Educational Theories of Herbart & Froebel. LC 72-177043. (Columbia University. Teachers College. Contributions to Education Ser.: No. 4). reprint ed. 37.50 (*0-404-55004-5*) AMS Pr.

— Hegel's Doctrine of the Will. LC 03-12358. reprint ed. 27.50 (*0-404-04146-9*) AMS Pr.

***MacVeagh, Lincoln.** Ambassador MacVeagh Reports: Greece, 1933-1947. Iatrides, John O., ed. LC 79-19079. reprint ed. pap. 180.00 (*0-7837-9352-9*, 2060094) Bks Demand.

Macveagh, Rogers. The Transportation Act 1920. Bruchey, Stuart, ed. LC 80-1330. (Railroads Ser.). 1981. reprint ed. lib. bdg. 93.95 (*0-405-13804-0*) Ayer.

MacVean, Jean, ed. see Blackburn, Thomas.

Macvey, John W. Interstellar Travel. LC 77-8766. 272p. 1991. pap. 11.95 (*0-8128-8523-6*, Scrbrough Hse) Madison Bks UPA.

MacVicar, Duncan & Throne, Darwin. Managing High-Tech Start-Ups. (Illus.). 244p. 1992. 34.95 (*0-7506-9247-2*) Buttrwrth-Heinemann.

MacVicar, Thaddeus. Franciscan Spirituals & the Capuchin Reform. (History Ser.). 1987. 9.00 (*0-318-35492-6*) Franciscan Inst.

MacVittie, T. J., jt. ed. see Broerse, J. J.

MacWalter. ICH in Clinical Medicine. 128p. 1993. pap. 24.95 (*0-8151-5805-X*, Yr Bk Med Pubs) Mosby Yr Bk.

MacWeeney, Alen, ed. Book of Days Nineteen Ninety. (Illus.). 120p. 1989. 9.95 (*0-945618-03-4*) Dorsoduro Pr.

MacWethy, Lou D. The Book of Names Especially Relating to the Early Palatines & the First Settlers in the Mohawk Valley. (Illus.). 209p. 1985. 15.00 (*0-8063-0231-3*, 3620) Genealog Pub.

MacWhinney, ed. Hungarian Language Acquisition As an Exemplification of a General Model of Grammatical Development: The Crosslinguistic Study of Language. (Crosslinguistic Study of Language Acquisition Ser.). 80p. 1986. pap. 14.95 (*0-89859-850-8*) L Erlbaum Assocs.

MacWhinney, B. Mechanisms of Language Acquisition. (Carnegie-Mellon Symposium Ser.). 500p. (C). 1987. pap. 32.50 (*0-89859-973-3*) L Erlbaum Assocs.

***MacWhinney, Brian.** The Childes Project: Tools for Analyzing Talk. 2nd ed. 460p. 1995. text ed. 35.00 (*0-8058-2027-2*) L Erlbaum Assocs.

MacWhinney, Brian & Bates, Elizabeth, eds. The Cross-Linguistic Study of Sentence Processing. (Illus.). (C). 1990. 44.95 (*0-521-26196-1*) Cambridge U Pr.

MacWhinney, Brian, jt. ed. see Fletcher, Paul.

MacWhinney, Brian, jt. auth. see Higginson, Roy.

MacWhirter, P. J., ed. Everybird: A Guide to Bird Health. 176p. 1987. 38.00 (*0-909605-48-3*, Pub. by Inkata Pr AT) Intl Spec Bk.

***MacWilliams, Ed J.** The Apostates: A Biblical Study for Local Churches. 1995. ring bd. 12.95 (*1-878897-03-9*) Blueprint Revival.

— Ghana Diary: The Revival Begins. 1995. pap. 12.95 (*1-878897-04-7*) Blueprint Revival.

— The Last Days of God's Church: Is True Christianity Being Forgotten? 1995. pap. 9.95 (*0-926557-09-2*) Blueprint Revival.

— The New Rapture Scenario: It's Not Like Your Daddy Pictured It. 1995. pap. 7.95 (*1-878897-01-2*) Blueprint Revival.

— Without Natural Affection: Is Criminal Hardness Replacing Natural Feelings? 1995. pap. 7.95 (*1-878897-02-0*) Blueprint Revival.

MacWilliams, F. J. & Sloane, N. J. The Theory of Error Correcting Codes, 2 Pts. in 1 vol. (Mathematical Library: Vol. 16). 762p. 1978. 72.00 (*0-444-85193-3*, North Holland) Elsevier.

MacWillson, Alastair C. Hostage-Taking Terrorism: Incident-Response Strategy. LC 92-25749. 224p. 1992. text ed. 69.95 (*0-312-06784-4*) St Martin.

***MacWithey, Bill.** Cry Vengeance. 390p. Date not set. pap. 9.95 (*0-7610-0344-4*) NW Pub.

Macworld Editors & Borrell, Jerry. Mastering the World of QuickTime: Create Your Own Multimedia Videos on the Macintosh. LC 93-25273. 218p. 1993. pap. 19.00 (*0-679-74291-3*) Random.

Macy & Dow. Manual of Veterinary Medical Therapeutics. 500p. 1990. 35.00 (*0-8016-3232-3*) Mosby Yr Bk.

Macy, Dayna, jt. ed. see Halm, Meesha.

Macy, Eliot E. Captain's Daughters of Martha's Vineyard. LC 78-62650. (How We Lived Ser.: No. 1). 1979. 12.95 (*0-85699-141-4*); pap. 7.95 (*0-85699-142-2*) Chatham Pr.

Macy, Gary. The Banquet's Wisdom: A Short History of the Theologies of the Lord's Supper. LC 91-45240. 224p. 1992. pap. 12.95 (*0-8091-3309-1*) Paulist Pr.

Macy, Harry, Jr. & Mocete, Melissa, eds. Index to Baptismal Surnames: In the Reformed Churches of Claverack, Cortlandt, Fishkill, Gallatin, Gravesend, Hillsdale, Kaatsbaan, Kinderhook, Linlithgo, Phillipsburgh, Poughkeepsie, Red Hook - Old, Red Hook - Upper, Reyn Beeck, Rhinebeck Flatts & Rochester. 228p. 1991. 35.00 (*0-9628194-0-9*) Holland Soc NY.

Macy, Jesse. Anti-Slavery Crusade: A Chronicle of the Gathering Storm. (History - United States Ser.). 245p. 1992. reprint ed. lib. bdg. 79.00 (*0-7812-6154-6*) Rprt Serv.

— The English Constitution: A Commentary on Its Nature & Growth. xxiii, 534p. 1988. reprint ed. lib. bdg. 42.50 (*0-8377-2438-4*) Rothman.

— Party Organization & Machinery. LC 73-19159. (Politics & People Ser.). 336p. 1974. reprint ed. 25.95 (*0-405-05881-0*) Ayer.

— Political Parties in the United States, 1846-1861. LC 73-19160. (Politics & People Ser.). 344p. 1974. reprint ed. 26.95 (*0-405-05882-9*) Ayer.

***Macy, Joanna.** Dharma & Development: Religion As Resource in the Sarvodaya Self-Help Movement. fac. rev. ed. LC 85-236. (Illus.). 119p. 1994. pap. 34.00 (*0-7837-7573-3*, 2047326) Bks Demand.

— Mutual Causality in Buddhism & General Systems Theory: The Dharma of Natural Systems. LC 90-39937. (SUNY Series in Buddhist Studies). 254p. 1991. 59.50 (*0-7914-0636-9*); pap. 19.95 (*0-7914-0637-7*) State U NY Pr.

— World As Lover, World As Self. LC 91-681. 251p. (Orig.). 1991. pap. 15.00 (*0-938077-27-9*) Parallax Pr.

Macy, Joanna R. Despair & Personal Power in the Nuclear Age. 200p. 1983. lib. bdg. 39.95 (*0-86571-030-9*); pap. 16.95 (*0-86571-031-7*) New Soc Pubs.

Macy, Joanna R., jt. auth. see Robbins, John.

Macy, John. Edgar Allan Poe. LC 75-3089. (Studies in Poe: No. 23). 1975. lib. bdg. 75.00 (*0-8383-2090-2*) M S G Haskell Hse.

Macy, John A. The Spirit of American Literature. (BCL1-PS American Literature Ser.). 347p. 1992. reprint ed. lib. bdg. 89.00 (*0-7812-6604-1*) Rprt Serv.

Macy, Jon. Tropo, Vol. I. (Illus.). 132p. (Orig.). 1994. pap. 5.95 (*1-883611-04-0*) Blckbird Comics.

Macy, Jonathan R., jt. ed. see Brown, J. Robert, Jr.

***Macy, Marianne.** Working Sex. 320p. 1996. 22.00 (*0-7867-0249-4*) Carroll & Graf.

Macy, Mark, ed. Solutions for a Troubled World. LC 87-8859. (Peace Ser.: Vol. I). (Illus.). 314p. (Orig.). 1987. pap. 8.95 (*0-930705-03-2*) M H Macy & Co.

Macy, Mark, jt. auth. see Kubis, Pat.

An Asterisk (*) at the beginning of an entry indicates that the title is appearing in BIP for the first time.

***Macy, Obed & Macy, William C.** History of Nantucket, Being a Compendious Acct. of the First Settlement of the Island by the English, Together with the Rise & Progress of the Whale Fishery, & Other Historical Facts. 2nd ed. 313p. 1995. reprint ed. lib. bdg. 39.50 (*0-8328-4466-7*) Higginson Bk Co.

Macy, Robert B., jt. auth. see Pandya, Abhijit S.

Macy, S. J. Genealogy of the Macy Family, 1635-1868. (Illus.). 457p. 1989. reprint ed. lib. bdg. 76.50 (*0-8328-0848-2*); reprint ed. pap. 68.50 (*0-8328-0849-0*) Higginson Bk Co.

Macy, Sheryl. Two Romantic Trios: A Sextet of Extraordinary Musicians. 250p. 1991. per. 12.95 (*0-9627040-0-8*) Allegro OR.

Macy, Sue. A Whole New Ball Game: The Story of the All-American Girls Professional Baseball League. LC 92-31813. (Illus.). 160p. (YA). (gr. 7 up). 1993. 14.95 (*0-8050-1942-1*, Bks Young Read) H Holt & Co.

— A Whole New Ball Game: The Story of the All-American Girls Professional Baseball League. LC 94-46789. (J). 1995. 4.99 (*0-14-037423-X*) Puffin Bks.

Macy, William C., jt. auth. see Macy, Obed.

MacYoung, Marc. Cheap Shots, Ambushes, & Other Lessons: A Down & Dirty Book on Streetfighting & Survival. (Illus.). 264p. 1988. pap. 15.00 (*0-87364-496-4*) Paladin Pr.

— Fists, Wits, & a Wicked Right: Surviving on the Wild Side of the Street. (Illus.). 152p. 1991. pap. 14.00 (*0-87364-611-8*) Paladin Pr.

— Floor Fighting: Stompings, Maimings, & Other Things to Avoid When a Fight Goes to the Floor. (Illus.). 200p. 1993. pap. 19.00 (*0-87364-716-5*) Paladin Pr.

— Knives, Knife Fighting, & Related Hassles: How to Survive a Real Knife Fight. (Illus.). 128p. 1990. pap. 12.00 (*0-87364-544-8*) Paladin Pr.

— Street E&E: Evading, Escaping, & Other Ways to Save Your Ass When Things Get Ugly. (Illus.). 192p. 1993. pap. 16.00 (*0-87364-743-2*) Paladin Pr.

— Violence, Blunders, & Fractured Jaws. 344p. 1992. pap. 22.95 (*0-87364-671-1*) Paladin Pr.

MacYoung, Marc & Pfouts, Chris. Safe in the City: A Streetwise Guide to Avoid Being Robbed, Raped, Ripped off, Or Run Over. 312p. 1994. pap. 21.95 (*0-87364-775-0*) Paladin Pr.

MacYoung, Marc A. Pool Cues, Beer Bottles, & Baseball Bats: Animal's Guide to Improvised Weapons for Self-Defense & Survival. (Illus.). 152p. 1990. pap. 12.00 (*0-87364-545-6*) Paladin Pr.

***Maczak, Antoni.** Money, Prices & Power in Poland 16th-17th Centuries: A Comparative Approach. LC 94-43313. (Collected Studies Ser.: No. CS487). 320p. 1995. 89.95 (*0-86078-478-9*, Pub. by Variorum UK) Ashgate Pub Co.

— Travel in Early Modern Europe. Phillips, Ursula, tr. 368p. 1995. 54.95 (*0-7456-0840-X*) Blackwell Pubs.

Maczak, Antoni & Parker, William N., eds. Natural Resources in European History: A Conference Report. LC 78-24688. (RFF Research Paper Ser.: No. R-13). 238p. pap. 67.90 (*0-8357-4683-6*, 2037630) Bks Demand.

Maczka, Kathleen. Assessing Physically Disabled People at Home. Campling, Jo, ed. (Therapy in Practice Ser.: No. 12). 128p. 1990. pap. 23.00 (*0-412-32480-6*, A4417) Chapman & Hall.

Maczka, Rom & Elliott, Mark, eds. Christian - Marxist Studies in United States Higher Education: A Handbook of Syllabi. 233p. 1991. pap. 20.00 (*1-879089-06-8*) B Graham Ctr.

MacZura, Jason, jt. auth. see Scott, David.

Mad, Aztec. Baseball Sabermetric 1991. 1991. pap. 15.95 (*0-9625846-4-9*) Mad Aztec Pr.

***Mad Dog & Merrill Staff.** Festever Holiday Grilling: Turn Every Holiday Meal into a Fiesta. 2nd rev. ed. 56p. 1994. pap. 5.95 (*1-879432-11-0*) Explorers Guide Pub.

Mad Magazine Editors. Mad about the Buoy. Feldstein, Albert B., ed. (Mad Ser.: No. 53). 1986. mass mkt. 3.95 (*0-446-30506-5*) Warner Bks.

— The Wet & Wisdom of Mad. 192p. (Orig.). 1987. mass mkt. 3.99 (*0-446-34366-8*) Warner Bks.

Madach, Imre. The Tragedy of Man. 200p. 1989. text ed. 23.50 (*0-88033-169-0*) East Eur Quarterly.

— The Tragedy of Man. 1973. 300.00 (*0-8490-1225-2*) Gordon Pr.

Madachy, Joseph S. Madachy's Mathematical Recreations. LC 78-74116. (Illus.). 1979. pap. 4.95 (*0-486-23762-1*) Dover.

Madahil, Antonio Gomes da Rocha, tr. see Schaub-Koch, Emile.

Madaj, E. J., Jr., jt. auth. see Truce, W. E.

Madala. Inductive Learning Algorithms for Complex Systems Modeling. 1993. 79.95 (*0-8493-4438-7*) CRC Pr.

Madaliyar, C. Rasanayagam. Anciet Jaffna. (Illus.). 478p. 1986. reprint ed. 22.00 (*0-8364-1744-5*, Pub. by Manohar II) S Asia.

Madama, John. Desktop Publishing: The Art of Communication. (Media Workshop Ser.). (Illus.). 80p. (YA). (gr. 5 up). 1993. lib. bdg. 19.95 (*0-8225-2303-5*, Lerner Publctns) Lerner Group.

Madama, Vincent C. Proficiency Laboratory Manual to Accompany Pulmonary Function Testing & Cardiopulmonary Stress Testing. 95p. 1993. 15.95 (*0-8273-5558-0*) Delmar.

— Pulmonary Function Testing & Cardiopulmonary Stress Testing Transparency Masters. 126p. 1993. 18.00 (*0-8273-3864-3*) Delmar.

— Pulmonary Function Testing & Cardiovascular Stress Testing. LC 92-18604. 590p. 1993. pap. text ed. 29.95 (*0-8273-3863-5*) Delmar.

Madame d'Aulnoy's Collection Staff. Jack & the Beanstalk. (Creative's Collection of Fairy Tales). (Illus.). 32p. (J). (gr. 4 up). 1983. lib. bdg. 13.95 (*0-87191-947-8*) Creative Ed.

Madame de Villeneuve. Beauty & the Beast. (Creative's Collection of Fairy Tales). (Illus.). 48p. (J). (gr. 4 up). 1984. lib. bdg. 13.95 (*0-87191-946-X*) Creative Ed.

Madame Guyon. Madame Guyon. 382p. 1974. pap. 12.99 (*0-8024-5135-7*) Moody.

Madan, A., et al, eds. Amorphous Silicon Semiconductors Pure & Hydrogenated. (MRS Symposium Proceedings Ser.: Vol. 95). 1987. text ed. 52.00 (*0-931837-62-6*) Materials Res.

— Amorphous Silicon Technology. (Symposium Proceedings Ser.: Vol. 118). 1988. text ed. 45.00 (*0-931837-88-X*) Materials Res.

— Amorphous Silicon Technology - 1989: Materials Research Society Symposium Proceedings, Vol. 149. 1989. text ed. 54.00 (*1-55899-022-4*) Materials Res.

— Amorphous Silicon Technology - 1991: Materials Research Society Symposium Proceedings, Vol. 219. 1991. text ed. 72.00 (*1-55899-113-1*) Materials Res.

Madan, Arun & Shaw, Melvin P. The Physics & Applications of Amorphous Semiconductors. 545p. 1988. text ed. 105.00 (*0-12-464960-2*) Acad Pr.

Madan, Brij M. Engine Electrical Equipment - U. S. Markets & Opportunities: 1991-1996 Analysis. (Illus.). 220p. 1992. pap. text ed. 1,900.00 (*1-878218-27-1*) World Info Tech.

Madan, D. S., et al, eds. Computational & Numerical Techniques in Powder Metallurgy. (Illus.). 300p. 1993. 82.00 (*0-87339-201-9*, 470) Minerals Metals.

Madan, Falconer. Books in Manuscript. LC 68-25315. (Reference Ser.: No. 44). (Illus.). (C). 1972. reprint ed. lib. bdg. 39.95 (*0-8383-0213-0*) M S G Haskell Hse.

Madan, G. Swahili English Dictionary. 442p. (ENG & SWA.). 1992. 59.95 (*0-8288-8458-7*) Fr & Eur.

Madan, G., jt. auth. see Steere.

Madan, G. R. Indian Social Problems, 2 vols., Set. 505p. 1981. 24.95 (*0-318-36851-X*) Asia Bk Corp.

— India's Social Transformation: Problems of Welfare & Planning, Vol. II. 2nd enl. rev. ed. 324p. reprint ed. 15.95 (*0-317-39863-6*, Pub. by Allied Pubs II) Asia Bk Corp.

Madan, N. L. Indian Political System. 1989. 38.50 (*81-202-0246-5*, Pub. by Ajanta II) S Asia.

Madan, R. Chua's Circuit: A Paradigm for Chaos. 1088p. 1993. text ed. 213.00 (*981-02-1366-2*) World Scientific Pub.

Madan, Rabinder N., jt. ed. see Indo-U. S. Workshop on Parallel.

Madan, Raj, comp. Colored Minorities in Great Britain: A Comprehensive Bibliography, 1970-1977. LC 78-74656. 199p. 1979. text ed. 49.95 (*0-313-20705-4*, MCM/, Greenwood Pr) Greenwood.

Madan, S. N. Dictionary of Anthropology. 328p. 1989. 80.00 (*81-7041-163-7*, Pub. by Scientific Pubs II) St Mut.

Madan, T. N. Family & Kinship: A Study of the Pandits of Rural Kashmir. 2nd ed. (Illus.). 366p. 1990. 25.00 (*0-19-562138-7*) OUP.

Madan, T. N., ed. Religion in India. (Oxford in India Readings in Sociology & Social & Cultural Anthropology Ser.). 464p. 1993. reprint ed. pap. 12.95 (*0-19-563092-0*) OUP.

— Way of Life: King, Householder, Renouncer: Essays in Honour of Louis Dumont. (C). 1988. reprint ed. 31.00 (*81-208-0527-5*, Pub. by Motilal Banarsidass II) S Asia.

Madan, T. N., jt. ed. see Uberoi, Patricia.

Madan, Triloki N. Pathways: Approaches to the Study of Society in India. 255p. 1994. 26.00 (*0-19-563211-7*) OUP.

Madan, Triloki N., jt. ed. see Appell, George N.

Madancy, Joyce A., jt. auth. see Lampton, David M.

Madanes, Chloe. Metaphors & Paradoxes. 1990. audio 22.95 (*1-55542-301-9*) Jossey-Bass.

Madanes, Claudio, jt. auth. see Madanes, Cloe.

Madanes, Cloe. Behind the One-Way Mirror: Advances in the Practice of Strategic Therapy. LC 83-49266. (Social & Behavioral Science Ser.). 213p. 1984. 27.95x (*0-87589-599-9*) Jossey-Bass.

— Sex. Love, & Violence: Strategies for Transformation. (C). 1990. 25.95 (*0-393-70096-8*) Norton.

— Strategic Family Therapy. LC 80-26286. (Social & Behavioral Science Ser.). 270p. 1981. 29.95x (*0-87589-487-9*) Jossey-Bass.

— Strategic Family Therapy. LC 80-26286. (Social & Behavioral Science Ser.). 272p. 1991. pap. 16.95 (*1-55542-363-9*) Jossey-Bass.

Madanes, Cloe & Madanes, Claudio. The Secret Meaning of Money: How It Binds Together Families in Love, Envy, Compassion, or Anger. (Social Behavioral Sciences Ser.). 140p. 1994. boxed 24.00 (*1-55542-701-4*) Jossey-Bass.

***Madanes, Cloe, et al.** The Violence of Men: A Therapy of Social Action. LC 95-12239. (Social & Behavioral Studies). 1995. 26.95 (*0-7879-0117-2*) Jossey-Bass.

Madani, Johsen S. Impact of Hindu Culture on Muslims. 181p. (C). 1993. 75.00 (*81-85880-15-8*, Pub. by Print Hse II) St Mut.

Madansky, A. Prescriptions for Working Statisticians. (Texts in Statistics Ser.). (Illus.). 350p. 1988. 39.80 (*0-387-96627-7*) Spr-Verlag.

Madany, B. M. The Bible & Islam. 1989. 4.95 (*0-685-74119-2*) Chr Lit.

Madar, Z. & Odes, S. H. Dietary Fiber Research. (Progress in Biochemical Pharmacology Ser.: Vol. 24). (Illus.). viii, 148p. 1990. 107.25 (*3-8055-5043-X*) S Karger.

Madara, Edward, ed. see American Self-Help Clearinghouse Staff.

***Madaraka, Jelani M.** African Origins of Law & Justice: The Concept of Maat in Ancient Egypt. 45p. 1994. pap. write for info. (*1-884897-00-2*) Zamani Pr.

Madaras, Area & Madaras, Lynda. My Body, My Self: The What's Happening Workbook for Girls. (Illus.). 128p. (Orig.). (J). (gr. 3-10). 1993. 9.95 (*1-55704-150-4*) Newmarket.

Madaras, Area, jt. auth. see Madaras, Lynda.

Madaras, Lynda. Lynda Madaras Talks to Teens about AIDS: An Essential Guide for Parents, Teachers & Young People. LC 87-31567. (Illus.). 128p. (YA). (gr. 7 up). 1988. 14.95 (*1-55704-010-9*); pap. 6.95 (*1-55704-009-5*) Newmarket.

— Lynda Madaras Talks to Teens about AIDS: An Essential Guide for Parents, Teachers & Young People. rev. ed. (Illus.). 128p. (YA). (gr. 9-12). 1993. 16.95 (*1-55704-188-1*); pap. 7.95 (*1-55704-180-6*) Newmarket.

***Madaras, Lynda & Madaras, Area.** My Body, My Self, Workbook for Boys. (Illus.). 128p. (YA). 1995. pap. 9.95 (*1-55704-230-6*) Newmarket.

— My Feelings, My Self: Lynda Madaras' Growing-Up Guide for Girls. LC 86-23719. Orig. Title: Lynda Madaras' Growing-Up Guide for Girls. (Illus.). 160p. (J). (gr. 3-10). 1993. pap. 9.95 (*1-55704-157-1*) Newmarket.

— What's Happening to My Body? Book for Girls: A Growing Up Guide for Parents & Daughters. rev. ed. LC 87-28117. (Illus.). 304p. 1987. 16.95 (*1-55704-001-X*); pap. 10.95 (*0-937858-98-6*) Newmarket.

Madaras, Lynda & Patterson, Jane. Womancare: A Gynecological Guide to Your Body. 960p. 1983. pap. 15.00 (*0-380-87643-4*) Avon.

Madaras, Lynda & Saavedra, Dane. What's Happening to My Body? Book for Boys: A Growing Up Guide for Parents & Sons. rev. ed. LC 87-28116. (Illus.). 288p. 1991. pap. 10.95 (*0-937858-99-4*) Newmarket.

— What's Happening to My Body? Book for Boys: A Growing Up Guide for Parents & Sons. 2nd rev. ed. LC 87-28116. (Illus.). 288p. 1991. 16.95 (*1-55704-002-8*) Newmarket.

Madaras, Lynda, jt. auth. see Madaras, Area.

Madarassy, Andrea, jt. auth. see Pfeffermann, Guy P.

Madariaga, L. Thematic Dictionary of Literary Terms: Diccionario Tematico des Terminos Literarios. 572p. (SPA.). 1980. 29.95 (*0-8288-1578-X*, S39853) Fr & Eur.

Madariaga, Salvador de. Christopher Columbus: Being the Life of the Very Magnificent Lord Don Cristobal Colon. LC 79-16973. (Illus.). 534p. 1979. reprint ed. text ed. 95.00 (*0-313-22031-X*, MACB, Greenwood Pr) Greenwood.

— El Corazon de Piedra Verde, I. (Nueva Austral Ser.: Vol. 55). (SPA.). 1991. pap. text ed. 34.95x (*84-239-1855-6*) Elliots Bks.

— El Corazon de Piedra Verde, II. (Nueva Austral Ser.: Vol. 56). (SPA.). 1991. pap. text ed. 29.95x (*84-239-1864-5*) Elliots Bks.

— Don Quixote: An Introductory Essay in Psychology. LC 79-16911. 159p. 1980. reprint ed. text ed. 35.00 (*0-313-22011-5*, MADQ, Greenwood Pr) Greenwood.

— Hernan Cortes: Conqueror of Mexico. LC 79-2570. (Illus.). 554p. 1979. reprint ed. text ed. 41.50 (*0-313-22030-1*, MACM, Greenwood Pr) Greenwood.

Madaris, Don. Scrap-Paper Miracle. Butler, Cathy, ed. 85p. (Orig.). 1993. reprint ed. pap. text ed. 6.95 (*1-56309-022-8*, New Hope AL) Womans Mission Union.

Madaris, Don L. Little Donald Lee, Miss Etta G, & the Two Room Schoolhouse. (Illus.). 112p. (Orig.). 1991. pap. 7.95 (*0-943487-34-X*) Sevgo Pr.

Madaris, Don L., jt. auth. see Miller, Sarah W.

Madaro, Giancenzo, text. Alfa Romeo Duetto. (Illus.). 96p. 24.95 (*88-7911-063-2*, Pub. by Giorgio Nada Editore IT) Howell Pr VA.

***Madas, A., ed.** World Consumption of Wood Trends & Prognoses. 130p. (C). 1974. 23.00x (*963-05-0183-X*, Pub. by Akad Kiado HU) St Mut.

Madathanus, Hinricus. Parabola, a Rosicrucian Tale. 1992. pap. 7.00 (*1-56459-035-6*) Kessinger Pub.

Madaule, ed. see Claudel, Paul.

Madaule, Jacques. The Albigensian Crusade: An Historical Essay. Wall, Barbara, tr. LC 66-23621. 191p. reprint ed. pap. 54.50 (*0-7837-0455-0*, 2040778) Bks Demand.

Madaus, George F., ed. Evaluation Models: Viewpoints on Educational & Human Services Evaluation (Text Edition) (C). 1983. lib. bdg. 73.00 (*0-89838-123-1*) Kluwer Ac.

Madaus, George F. & Scriven, Michael S., eds. Evaluation Models: Viewpoints on Educational & Human Services Evaluation (Text Edition) 440p. (C). 1983. lib. bdg. 47.00 (*0-89838-132-0*) Kluwer Ac.

Madaus, George F. & Stufflebeam, Daniel, eds. Educational Evaluation: Classic Works of Ralph W. Tyler. (C). 1988. lib. bdg. 61.00 (*0-89838-273-4*) Kluwer Ac.

Madaus, George F., et al. Teach Them Well: An Introduction to Education. 529p. (C). 1990. text ed. 54.50 (*0-06-044186-0*) HarpCollege.

Madaus, Howard M., jt. auth. see Murphy, John M.

Madauss, Martyria. Jesus: A Portrait of Love. 1983. 6.50 (*3-87209-603-6*) Evang Sisterhood Mary.

— The Shield of Faith. 1974. 0.95 (*3-87209-659-1*) Evang Sisterhood Mary.

Madavan, Vijay. Cooking the Indian Way. (Easy Menu Ethnic Cookbooks Ser.). (Illus.). 52p. (J). (gr. 5 up). 1985. lib. bdg. 14.95 (*0-8225-0911-3*, Lerner Publctns) Lerner Group.

Maday, Bela C., jt. auth. see Hollos, Marida.

Maday, Michael, ed. see Cady, H. Emilie.

Maday, Michael, ed. see Fillmore, Charles.

Maday, Michael, ed. see Gatlin, Dana.

Maday, Michael, ed. see Unity School of Christianity Staff.

***Maday, Tom & Landers, Sam.** Great Chicago Stories. LC 94-60776. (Illus.). 224p. 1994. 40.00 (*0-9641703-0-2*) TwoPress Pubng.

Maday, Yvon, jt. ed. see Bernardi, Christine.

Maddala, G. S. Econometric Methods & Applications. (Economists of the Twentieth Century Ser.: Vol. 2). 1120p. 1994. text ed. 149.95 (*1-85278-804-6*, Pub. by E Elgar Pub UK) Ashgate Pub Co.

— Introduction to Econometrics. (Illus.). 656p. (C). 1992. teacher ed write for info. (*0-318-69329-1*) Macmillan.

— Introduction to Econometrics. 2nd ed. (Illus.). 656p. (C). 1992. text ed. write for info. (*0-02-374545-2*) Macmillan.

— Limited-Dependent & Qualitative Variables in Econometrics. LC 82-9554. (Econometric Society Monographs: No. 3). 416p. 1986. pap. 27.95 (*0-521-33825-5*) Cambridge U Pr.

Maddala, G. S., ed. The Econometrics of Panel Data, 2 vols., Set. (International Library of Critical Writings in Business History). 1000p. 1993. 324.95 (*1-85278-585-3*, Pub. by E Elgar Pub UK) Ashgate Pub Co.

***Maddala, G. S., et al.** Advances in Econometrics & Quantitative Economics. (Illus.). 352p. (C). 1995. write for info. (*1-55786-382-2*) Blackwell Pubs.

Maddala, G. S., et al, eds. Econometrics. LC 93-12857. (Handbook of Statistics Ser.: Vol. 11). 1993. 190.00 (*0-444-89577-9*, North Holland) Elsevier.

Maddams, W. F., jt. auth. see Bower, D. I.

Maddaus, William O. Water Conservation. 100p. 1987. pap. 26.50 (*0-89867-387-9*, 20238) Am Water Wks Assn.

Maddava, Karuna A. Peace Studies: Toward a Transformative Perspective. LC 94-12330. 198p. 1994. lib. bdg. 15.95 (*1-879528-10-X*) LEPS Pr.

Madden. Abdominal Wall Hernias. 368p. 1989. text ed. 125.00 (*0-7216-1288-1*) Saunders.

— Current Dermatologic Therapy. 2nd ed. 1991. text ed. 61.50 (*0-7216-1053-6*) Saunders.

— Fiction Tutor Nineteen Ninety-One. 200p. (C). 1991. pap. text ed. write for info. (*0-318-69146-9*) HB Coll Pubs.

— Small Business Start up Index 1991, Issue 3. 1991. 95.00 (*0-8103-7993-7*) Gale.

— Small Business Start up Index 1992 ISS 1, 2 Vols., Vol. 1. 3rd ed. 1995. 600.00 (*0-8103-8240-7*) Gale.

— Toxic Torts Deskbook. 1992. 75.00 (*0-87371-508-X*, KF1299) Lewis Pubs.

— Toxic Torts Liability. 1995. write for info. (*0-87371-507-1*) Lewis Pubs.

Madden, jt. auth. see Gass.

Madden, A. F. & Morris-Jones, W. H., eds. Australia & Britain: Studies in a Changing Relationship. (Studies in Commonwealth Politics & History: No. 8). (Illus.). 214p. 1983. 32.50 (*0-7146-3149-3*, Pub. by F Cass Pubs UK) Intl Spec Bk.

Madden, B., jt. ed. see Jeffrey, D. W.

Madden, Bill. Damned Yankees: A No-Holds-Barred Account of Life with Boss Steinbrenner. 1991. mass mkt. 5.95 (*0-446-36089-9*) Warner Bks.

— Gering High Athletics: A Sportswriter's View. 100p. 1994. write for info. (*0-9644166-0-3*) Sports Amer.

Madden, Bob. Nuclear Missiles & a Justification for a Crazy Life. 170p. (Orig.). 1982. pap. 2.50 (*0-9608256-0-6*) R Madden.

Madden, Carl H. Clash of Culture: Management & the Age of Changing Values. LC 72-88236. 132p. 1976. 5.00 (*0-685-03540-9*) Natl Planning.

Madden, Carl H., ed. The Case for the Multinational Corporation. LC 76-12863. (Special Studies). 234p. 1976. 45.00 (*0-275-90248-X*, C0248, Praeger Pubs) Greenwood.

***Madden, Carolyn G. & Myers, Cynthia L., eds.** Discourse & Performance of International Teaching Assistants. 252p. 1994. pap. 25.95 (*0-939791-52-8*) Tchrs Eng Spkrs.

Madden, Carolyn G. & Reinhart, Susan M. Pyramids: Structurally Based Tasks for E. S. L. Learners. (English As a Second Language Ser.). (Illus.). 80p. (C). 1987. pap. text ed. 12.95 (*0-472-08072-5*); 11.95 (*0-472-08073-3*) U of Mich Pr.

Madden, Cary T., jt. ed. see Whitmore, Frank C., Jr.

Madden, Charles F., ed. Talks with Authors. LC 68-10729. 256p. 1968. 5.85 (*0-8093-0300-0*) S Ill U Pr.

***Madden, Charles S., ed.** Proceedings of the Conference of the American Academy of Advertising, 1995. 1995. per., pap. text ed. 25.00 (*0-931030-18-8*) Am Acad Advert.

Madden, Charles S. & Cooper, Marjorie J. Introduction to Marketing. LC 91-55402. (Outline Ser.). (Illus.). 224p. (Orig.). (C). 1993. pap. 11.00 (*0-06-467130-5*, Harper Ref) HarpC.

Madden, Chris C. Baby Hints Handbook. (Illus.). 144p. (Orig.). 1982. pap. 3.95 (*0-941298-05-1*) M E Pinkham.

— Baby's First Helping. (Family Bk. Ser.). (Illus.). 159p. pap. 5.95 (*0-318-19492-9*) M E Pinkham.

— Baths. LC 95-12991. 1996. write for info. (*0-517-59938-4*, Clarkson Potter) Crown Bks Yng Read.

— Kitchens. LC 92-16444. (Illus.). 288p. 1993. 45.00 (*0-517-58160-4*, C P Pubs) Crown Pub Group.

Madden, Chris C. & Showhouse, Kips B. Rooms with a View: Two Decades of Outstanding American Interior Design. LC 92-35193. 1993. 45.00 (*0-86636-190-1*) PBC Intl Inc.

Madden, Christine W., ed. see Madden, Yvonne M.

Madden, David. Cain's Craft. LC 84-20215. 176p. 1985. 20.00 (*0-8108-1750-0*) Scarecrow.

— Eight Classic American Novels. 1592p. (C). 1989. pap. text ed. 28.00 (*0-15-520926-4*) HB Coll Pubs.

— James M. Cain. LC 86-72297. 200p. (C). 1987. 9.95 (*0-685-17324-0*) Carnegie-Mellon.

— James M. Cain. (Twayne's United States Authors Ser.). 1974. lib. bdg. 17.95 (*0-8057-0128-1*) Irvington.

— A Pocketful of Prose: Contemporary Short Fiction. 236p. (C). 1991. pap. text ed. write for info. (*0-318-69117-5*) HB Coll Pubs.

— A Pocketful of Prose: Contemporary Short Fiction. 230p. (C). 1992. pap. text ed. 10.00 (*0-03-054934-5*); 13.50 (*0-03-014289-X*) HB Coll Pubs.

— A Pocketful of Prose: Vintage Short Fiction. 288p. (C). 1992. pap. text ed. 10.00 (0-03-054937-X); disk write for info. (0-318-69139-6) HB Coll Pubs.

— A Primer of the Novel: For Readers & Writers. LC 79-21881. 466p. 1980. lib. bdg. 27.50 (0-8108-1265-7) Scarecrow.

— Revising Fiction. 1988. pap. 12.95 (0-452-26414-6, Plume) NAL-Dutton.

— Revising Fiction: A Handbook for Writers. 320p. 1988. pap. 8.95 (0-452-26088-4, Plume) NAL-Dutton.

— Wright Morris. (Twayne's United States Authors Ser.). 1964. pap. 13.95 (0-8084-0336-2, T71) NCUP.

Madden, David, ed. American Dreams, American Nightmares. LC 72-5512. (Arcturus Books Paperbacks). 271p. 1972. pap. 9.95 (0-8093-0600-X) S Ill U Pr.

— Proletarian Writers of the Thirties. LC 78-16323. (Arcturus Books Paperbacks). 320p. 1979. reprint ed. pap. 9.95 (0-8093-0895-9) S Ill U Pr.

— Tough Guy Writers of the Thirties. LC 68-10115. (Crosscurrents-Modern Critiques Ser.). 287p. 1968. 16.95 (0-8093-0287-X) S Ill U Pr.

— Tough Guy Writers of the Thirties. LC 78-24304. (Arcturus Books Paperbacks). 287p. 1979. reprint ed. pap. 10.95 (0-8093-0912-2) S Ill U Pr.

— The World of Fiction. LC 89-11088. 1200p. (C). 1989. pap. text ed. 25.50 (0-03-014292-X) HB Coll Pubs.

Madden, David & Bach, Peggy, eds. Classics of Civil War Fiction. LC 91-16947. 1991. 37.50 (0-87805-522-3); pap. 15.95 (0-87805-541-X) U Pr of Miss.

Madden, David & Powers, Richard. Writers' Revisions: An Annotated Bibliography of Articles & Books About Writers' Revisions & Their Comments on the Creative Process. LC 80-22942. 254p. 1981. 20.00 (0-8108-1375-0) Scarecrow.

Madden, David & Scott, Virgil, eds. Studies in the Short Story. 6th ed. LC 83-8590. 540p. (C). 1984. pap. text ed. 22.00 (0-03-063644-2) HB Coll Pubs.

***Madden, David W.** Critical Essays on Thomas Berger. (Critical Essays on American Literature Ser.). 1995. lib. bdg. 45.00x (0-7838-0029-0, Twayne) Macmillan.

— Understanding Paul West. LC 93-12537. (Understanding Contemporary British Literature Ser.). (C). 1993. 34.95 (0-87249-886-7) U of SC Pr.

Madden, Deirdre. Remembering Light & Stone. 192p. (Orig.). 1994. pap. 9.95 (0-571-16946-5) Faber & Faber.

Madden, Dodgson H. The Diary of Master William Silence. (BCL1-PR English Literature Ser.). 386p. 1992. reprint ed. lib. bdg. 89.00 (0-7812-7309-9) Rprt Serv.

— Diary of Master William Silence: A Study of Shakespeare & Elizabethan Sport. LC 71-95440. (Studies in Shakespeare: No. 24). 1970. reprint ed. lib. bdg. 61.95 (0-8383-0993-3) M S G Haskell Hse.

— Diary of Master William Silence: A Study of Shakespeare & of Elizabethan Sport. LC 78-89018. 386p. 1970. reprint ed. text ed. 65.00 (0-8371-2322-4, MAMS, Greenwood Pr) Greenwood.

Madden, Don. The Wartville Wizard. LC 92-22246. (Illus.). 32p. (J). (gr. k-3). 1993. reprint ed. pap. 4.95 (0-689-71667-2, Aladdin Paperbacks) S&S Childrens.

Madden, Donald L. & Holmes, James R. Management Accountants: Responding to Change. Barth, Claire, ed. 63p. (Orig.). 1990. pap. 13.95 (0-86641-185-2, 90246) Inst Mgmt Account.

Madden, Edward F. Carpe Diem. 204p. 1993. pap. text ed. 9.95 (0-86720-782-5) Jones & Bartlett.

Madden, Edward H. Civil Disobedience & Moral Law in Nineteenth-Century American Philosophy. LC 68-11043. 222p. 1970. pap. 9.00 (0-295-95070-6) U of Wash Pr.

— Philosophical Problems of Psychology. LC 72-11481. 149p. 1973. reprint ed. text ed. 38.50 (0-8371-6668-3, MAPH, Greenwood Pr) Greenwood.

Madden, Edward H. & Hamilton, James E. Freedom & Grace: The Life of Asa Mahan. LC 82-5724. (Studies in Evangelicalism: No. 3). 287p. 1982. 25.00 (0-8108-1555-9) Scarecrow.

Madden, Edward H., jt. auth. see Hare, Peter H.

Madden, F. W., jt. auth. see Herman, H. A.

Madden, Frederic. Syr Gawayne. 1972. 59.95 (0-8490-1171-X) Gordon Pr.

Madden, Frederic, ed. Matthaei Parisiensis, Monachi Sancti Albani, Historia Anglorum Sive, ut Vulgo Dicitur, Historia Minor, 3 vols., Set. (Rolls Ser.: No. 44). 1969. reprint ed. 155.00 (0-8115-1103-0) Periodicals Srv.

— Syr Gawayne: A Collection of Ancient Romance Poems by Scottish & English Authors. LC 71-144420. (Bannatyne Club. Edinburgh. Publications: No. 61). reprint ed. 49.50 (0-404-52772-8) AMS Pr.

Madden, Frederic, tr. see Layamon.

Madden, Frederic W. Coins of the Jews. (International Numismata Orientalia Ser.: Vol. II). (Illus.). viii, 1703p. 1976. reprint ed. write for info. (3-487-06006-X, Pub. by Georg Olms GW) Lubrecht & Cramer.

— History of Jewish Coinage & of Money in the Old & New Testaments. LC 66-26486. (Library of Biblical Studies). (Illus.). 1968. 39.50 (0-87068-082-X) Ktav.

***Madden, Frederick & Darwin, John.** The Dependent Empire: Colonies, Protectorates & Mandates Select Documents, Vol. 7. LC 84-21213. (Documents in Imperial History Ser.: Vol. 7). 912p. 1994. text ed. 125.00 (0-313-27318-9, Greenwood Pr) Greenwood.

Madden, Frederick & Darwin, John, eds. The Dominions & India Since 1900: Select Documents on the Constitutional History of the British Empire & Commonwealth, Vol. 6. LC 84-21213. 906p. 1993. text ed. 125.00 (0-313-27317-0, Greenwood Pr) Greenwood.

Madden, Frederick & Fieldhouse, David, eds. Advance & Retreat in Representative Self-Government, 1840-1900: Select Documents on the Constitutional History of the British Empire & Commonwealth. LC 84-21213. (Documents in Imperial History Ser.: Vol. 5, No. 5). 848p. 1991. text ed. 135.00 (0-313-27757-5, MNT/, Greenwood Pr) Greenwood.

— The Classical Period of the First British Empire, 1689-1783; The Foundations of a Colonial System of Government: Select Documents on the Constitutional History of the British Empire with Commonwealth, Vol. II. LC 84-21213. (Documents of Imperial History Ser.: No. 2). xxxvii, 628p. 1985. text ed. 105.00 (0-313-25176-2, MDL/) Greenwood.

— The Dependent Empire & Ireland, 1840-1900: Advance & Retreat in Representative Self-Government - Select Documents on the Constitutional History of the British Empire & Commonwealth, Vol. V. (Documents in Imperial History Ser.: No. 5). 864p. 1991. 95.00 (0-685-54256-4, MNT/, Greenwood Pr) Greenwood.

— The Empire of the Bretaignes, Eleven Seventy-Five to Sixteen Eighty-Eight: Foundations of a Colonial System of Government; Select Documents on the Constitutional History of the British Empire & Commonwealth, Vol. I. LC 84-21213. (Documents in Imperial History Ser.: No. 1). (Illus.). xxv, 669p. 1985. text ed. 105.00 (0-313-23897-9, MFI/) Greenwood.

— Imperial Reconstruction, 1763-1840: The Evolution of Alternative Systems of Colonial Government: Select Documents on the Constitutional History of the British Empire & Commonwealth, Vol. 3. LC 84-21213. (Documents in Imperial History Ser.: No. 3). 933p. 1987. text ed. 135.00 (0-313-25916-X, MRN/) Greenwood.

— Settler Self-Government, 1840-1900: Select Documents on the Constitutional History of the British Empire & Commonwealth. LC 84-21213. (Documents in Imperial History Ser.: No. 4). 864p. 1990. text ed. 115.00 (0-313-27326-X, MGO/) Greenwood.

Madden, Frederick, jt. ed. see Robinson, Kenneth.

Madden, Gerald P. Investment Analysis with Value Screen Plus. 96p. (C). 1991. pap. text ed. write for info. (0-13-488982-7) P-H.

Madden, Henry. Strasburg Tapes. write for info. (0-318-62725-6) Daedalus Act.

Madden, J. Patrick, et al. Beyond Pesticides: Biological Approaches to Pest Management in California. LC 92-61146. (Illus.). 220p. 1992. pap. 14.00 (1-879906-10-4, 3354) ANR Pubns CA.

Madden, James W. The Art of Throwing Weapons. LC 91-60071. (Illus.). 104p. (Orig.). 1991. pap. 8.95 (0-9628825-3-4) Patrick Las Vegas.

Madden, Janet & Blake, Sara M. Crosscurrents: Themes for Developing Writers. 400p. (C). 1992. teacher ed write for info. (0-03-055853-0); pap. text ed. 20.00 (0-03-055852-2) HB Coll Pubs.

— Emerging Voices: A Cross-Cultural Reader. 544p. (C). 1990. pap. text ed. 20.00 (0-03-028767-7) HB Coll Pubs.

— Emerging Voices: Reading in the American Experience. 2nd ed. 512p. (C). 1993. lib. bdg. write for info. (0-15-500303-8) HB Coll Pubs.

— Emerging Voices: Reading in the American Experience. 2nd ed. 512p. (C). 1993. pap. text ed. 2.75 (0-15-500729-7) HB Coll Pubs.

Madden, Janet, jt. auth. see Blake, Sara M.

Madden, Janet, jt. auth. see Eula, Michael J.

Madden, Janice F. & Stull, William J. Work, Wages, & Poverty: Income Distribution in Post-Industrial Philadelphia. LC 91-22426. 240p. (Orig.). (C). 1991. pap. text ed. 21.95 (0-8122-1348-3) U of Pa Pr.

Madden, Janice F., jt. auth. see Stull, William J.

Madden, Jennifer, et al. Children's Fiction Sourcebook. 200p. 1992. 43.95 (1-85742-022-5, Pub. by Ashgate UK) Ashgate Pub Co.

Madden, John, IV. Neurobiology of Learning, Emotion, & Affect. 368p. 1991. 133.00 (0-88167-807-4) Raven.

Madden, John. One Size Doesn't Fit All & Other Thoughts from the Road. 227p. 1991. 3.99 (0-517-03030-6) Random Hse Value.

Madden, John & Anderson, Dave. Hey, Wait a Minute: (I Wrote a Book!) 256p. 1985. mass mkt. 4.95 (0-345-32507-9) Ballantine.

— One Knee Equals Two Feet (& Everything Else You Need to Know about Football) LC 86-40099. 240p. 1986. 16.95 (0-394-55328-4, Villard Bks) Random.

— One Knee Equals Two Feet (And Everything Else You Need to Know about Football) 1988. mass mkt. 5.50 (0-515-09193-6) Jove Pubns.

— One Size Doesn't Fit All. 1989. pap. 5.50 (0-515-10146-X) Jove Pubns.

***Madden, John L.** Atlas of Techniques in Surgery, 2 vols. 2nd ed. Incl. Vol. 1. General & Abdominal Surgery. 2nd ed. (Illus.). 680p. 1969. boxed 98.00 (0-8385-0131-1, A0131-1); Vol. 2. Thoracic & Cardiovascular Surgery. (Illus.). 458p. 1969. boxed 98.00 (0-8385-0132-X, A0132-9); 180.00 (0-8385-0130-3) Appleton & Lange.

— Federal & State Lands in Louisiana. 1972. 25.00 (0-87511-078-9) Claitors.

Madden, John T. & Nadler, Marcus. International Money Markets. LC 68-23311. 548p. 1969. reprint ed. text ed. 45.50 (0-8371-0552-8, MAIM, Greenwood Pr) Greenwood.

Madden, Joseph P. A Documentary History of Yonkers, New York, No. Six: The Formative Years 1820-1852. (Illus.). 275p. (Orig.). 1992. pap. 24.00 (1-55613-572-6) Heritage Bk.

— A Documentary History of Yonkers, New York, Vol. 2, Pt. 1: The Unsettled Years, 1853-1860. 342p. 1994. pap. text ed. 28.50 (1-55613-930-6) Heritage Bk.

— A Documentary History of Yonkers, NY, Vol. 2, Pt. 2: The Dutch, the English & an Incorporated American Village, 1609-1860. 286p. (Orig.). 1994. pap. text ed. 25.50 (1-55613-946-2) Heritage Bk.

Madden, L., jt. auth. see Storey, Richard.

Madden, Lawrence J., ed. The Joseph Campbell Phenomenon: Implications for the Contemporary Church. 168p. (Orig.). 1992. pap. 10.95 (0-912405-89-9) Pastoral Pr.

Madden, Lionel. How to Find Out about the Victorian Period. LC 74-116777. 1970. 82.00 (0-08-015834-X, Pub. by Pergamon Repr UK) Franklin.

Madden, Lionel, ed. Robert Southey: The Critical Heritage. 1972. 69.50 (0-7100-7375-5, RKP) Routledge.

Madden, Lyn, jt. auth. see Levine, June.

Madden, Lynne R., jt. auth. see Forster, Jas. H.

Madden, M. Stuart, ed. see Boston, Gerald W.

Madden, M. Stuart, jt. auth. see Boston, Gerald W.

Madden, Maia, jt. ed. see Fifield, Donnali.

Madden, Margaret L., jt. auth. see Herda, D. J.

Madden, Mary. The Pagan Divinities & Their Worship As Depicted in the Work of St. Augustine. 1972. 59.95 (0-8490-0796-8) Gordon Pr.

Madden, Mary J. Thinward Bound: Medical Management & Weight Loss. Hoel, Donna, ed. LC 82-17679. (Illus.). 112p. 1982. pap. text ed. 11.50 (0-89303-228-X) P-H.

Madden, Meg, jt. auth. see Leblond, Richard E.

Madden, Michael, jt. auth. see Crouch, Tammy.

***Madden, Mickee.** Everlastin' 1995. pap. 5.99 (0-7860-0003-1, Pinnacle NY) Windsor NY.

***Madden, Micki.** Everlastin' 384p. 1995. pap. 5.99 (0-8217-0003-0) Zebra.

Madden, Moss, jt. ed. see Hewings, Geoffrey J.

Madden, Myron C. Blessing: Giving the Gift of Power. LC 88-2599. (Orig.). 1988. pap. 10.99 (0-8054-5056-4) Broadman.

Madden, Onyx. The Mysterious Chronicles of Oz or Tip & the Sawhorse of Oz. LC 83-73621. (Illus.). 240p. 1985. 14.95 (0-930422-34-1) Dennis-Landman.

Madden, P. J. Wigglesworth Standard. 242p. 1993. pap. 4.99 (0-88368-261-3) Whitaker Hse.

Madden, Patrick T. The Art of Falling. 30p. (Orig.). 1989. pap. text ed. write for info. (0-318-65571-3) Quest Pr.

Madden, Paul. Fidel Castro. LC 92-46482. (Biographies: World Leaders Ser.). (J). 1993. 19.93 (0-86625-479-X); 14.95 (0-685-67776-1) Rourke Pubns.

Madden, Richard & Clark, Stephen. And a Year Went By. (Illus.). 128p. 1994. pap. 22.00 (0-7509-0540-9) A Sutton Pub.

Madden, Richard C. Catholics in South Carolina: A Record. 428p. (Orig.). 1985. lib. bdg. 54.00 (0-8191-4457-6); pap. text ed. 29.00 (0-8191-4458-4) U Pr of Amer.

Madden, Richard R. Literary Life & Correspondence of the Countess of Blessington, 3 Vols, 1. reprint ed. write for info. (0-404-07721-8) AMS Pr.

— Literary Life & Correspondence of the Countess of Blessington, 3 Vols, 2. reprint ed. write for info. (0-404-07722-6) AMS Pr.

— Literary Life & Correspondence of the Countess of Blessington, 3 Vols, 3. reprint ed. write for info. (0-404-07723-4) AMS Pr.

— Literary Life & Correspondence of the Countess of Blessington, 3 Vols, Set. reprint ed. 210.00 (0-404-07720-X) AMS Pr.

Madden, Robert E. Tax Planning for Highly Compensated Individuals. 2nd ed. 816p. 1989. Supplemented semi-annually. 155.00 (0-7913-0210-5) Warren Gorham & Lamont.

— Tax Planning for Highly Compensated Individuals. 2nd suppl. ed. 816p. 1989. 45.75 (0-7913-0902-9); 48.50 (0-685-32298-X) Warren Gorham & Lamont.

Madden, Stuart M. Products Liability: 1985 Pocket Part. 130p. 1985. pap. text ed. write for info. (0-318-59390-4) West Pub.

Madden, T. O., Jr. We Were Always Free: The Maddens of Culpepper, Virginia, a 200-Year Family History. LC 92-50681. 1993. pap. 12.00 (0-679-74581-5, Vin) Random.

Madden, T. O., Jr. & Miller, Anne. We Were Always Free: The Story of the Maddens, a Free Negro Family of Virginia. (Illus.). 256p. 1992. 19.95 (0-393-03347-3) Norton.

***Madden, Tara R.** Romance on the Run: Five Minutes of Quality Sex for Busy Couples. 96p. 1995. 10.00 (0-8217-4885-8) Zebra.

Madden, Thomas A., et al. The Health Almanac. (Illus.). 368p. 1982. pap. text ed. 39.50 (0-89004-757-X) Raven.

***Madden, Wayne.** Implementing AS-400 Security: A Practical Guide to Implementing, Evaluating, & Auditing Your AS-400 Security Strategy. 2nd ed. 300p. 1995. pap. 69.00 (1-882419-20-0, Duke Pr) Duke Commns Intl.

— Starter Kit for the AS-400: Thirty-Three Fundamental Concepts. 2nd ed. 440p. 1994. pap. 89.00 (1-882419-09-X) Duke Commns Intl.

Madden, Wayne, jt. auth. see Yergin, Jonathan.

Madden, William. Hoosiers of Summer. 200p. 24.95 (1-878208-44-6) Guild Pr IN.

Madden, Yvonne M. Black Magic & Stolen Timber. Madden, Christine W., ed. 296p. 1993. text ed. 25.00 (0-9619080-0-9); pap. text ed. 20.00 (0-9619080-1-7) Vonnie Pub.

— Black Magic & Stolen Timber. Madden, Christine W., ed. 1995. digital audio 50.00 (0-9619080-2-5) Vonnie Pub.

Madderlake, et al. Flowers Rediscovered. rev. ed. LC 94-20401. (Illus.). 1994. pap. 24.95 (1-885183-03-8) Artisan Hse.

Madderlake, Pure, et al. Trade Secrets: Natural Flower Arranging. LC 92-29775. 1994. 40.00 (0-517-59332-7, C P Pubs) Crown Pub Group.

Maddern, Eric. Life Story. LC 87-73253. (Illus.). 32p. (J). (gr. 1 up). 1988. 11.95 (0-8120-5941-7) Barron.

— Rainbow Bird. (J). (gr. 4-8). 1993. 14.95 (0-316-54314-4) Little.

Maddern, Philippa C. Violence & Social Order: East Anglia 1422-1442. (Oxford Historical Monographs). (Illus.). 280p. 1992. 65.00 (0-19-820235-0) OUP.

Maddex, Diane, ed. Master Builders: A Guide to Famous American Architects. LC 85-16982. (Building Watchers Ser.). (Illus.). 204p. 1985. pap. 9.95 (0-685-10506-7) Preservation Pr.

Maddex, Diane, ed. see Stevenson, Katherine C. & Jandl, H. Ward.

***Maddex, Robert L.** Constitutions of the World. LC 95-11374. 1995. write for info. (0-87187-922-0) Congr Quarterly.

***Maddex, Robert L., Jr.** Constitutions of the World. 360p. 1995. 69.95 (0-87187-992-1) Congr Quarterly.

Maddi, Salvatore. Personality Theories: A Comparative Analysis. 5th ed. 749p. (C). 1989. text ed. 55.95 (0-534-10696-X) Brooks-Cole.

Maddicott, J. R. Simon de Montfort. LC 93-33224. (Illus.). 424p. (C). 1994. 69.95 (0-521-37493-6) Cambridge U Pr.

Maddieson, Ian, jt. auth. see Ladefoged, Peter.

Maddigan, Judi. Learn Bearmaking. (Illus.). 168p. (Orig.). 1988. pap. 15.95 (0-932086-13-6) Open Chain Pub.

— Soft Toys for Babies. Fanning, Robbie, ed. (Stitch & Enrich Ser.). (Illus.). 200p. (Orig.). 1991. pap. 17.95 (0-932086-29-2) Open Chain Pub.

Maddin, Robert, ed. The Beginning of the Use of Metals & Alloys. (Illus.). 480p. 1988. 65.00x (0-262-13232-X) MIT Pr.

Maddin, Robert, jt. auth. see Kimura, H.

Madding, ed. Thermal Infrared Sensing for Diagnostics & Control: Thermosense, No. 9. 274p. 1987. 57.00 (0-89252-815-X, 780) SPIE.

Maddison, A. C., jt. ed. see Rudgard, S. A.

Maddison, Angus. Dynamic Forces in Capitalist Development. (Illus.). 352p. 1991. pap. 24.95 (0-19-828398-9) OUP.

— Explaining the Economic Performance of Nations: Essays in Time & Space. (Economists of the Twentieth Century Ser.). 496p. 1995. 79.95 (1-85278-600-0, Pub. by E Elgar Pub UK) Ashgate Pub Co.

— Unemployment: The European Perspective. LC 81-21264. 220p. 1982. text ed. 29.95 (0-312-83261-3) St Martin.

Maddison, Angus, jt. auth. see OECD Staff.

Maddison, Angus, et al. The Political Economy of Poverty, Equity, & Growth: Brazil & Mexico. LC 92-15645. (World Bank Comparative Study Ser.). 264p. 1992. 27.95 (0-19-520874-9, 60874) OUP.

Maddison, Bernard H. Handbook of Timber Engineering Design. (Illus.). 83p. 1982. pap. text ed. 17.25 (0-9593488-1-6, Pub. by Univ of West Aust Pr AT) Intl Spec Bk.

Maddison, David, jt. auth. see Maddison, Wayne.

Maddison, Dorothy, jt. auth. see Sullivan, Gail.

***Maddison, Francis, et al.** Science, Tools, & Magic. (Nasser D. Khalili Collection of Islamic Art: Vol. XII). (Illus.). 320p. 1996. 260.00 (0-19-727610-5) OUP.

Maddison, Gordon R., jt. auth. see Van Alstyne, Judith S.

Maddison, John. Education in the Microelectronics Era. LC 99-943832. 208p. 1983. pap. 25.00 (0-335-10182-8, Open Univ Pr) Taylor & Francis.

— Felbrigg Hall. (Illus.). 96p. 1995. pap. 9.95 (0-7078-0220-2, Pub. by Natl Trust UK) Trafalgar.

— Information Technology & Education. 320p. 1982. 99.00 (0-335-10183-6, Open Univ Pr) Taylor & Francis.

Maddison, John, jt. auth. see National Trust Staff.

Maddison, Lowinger, jt. auth. see Holst, Imogen.

Maddison, P. J., et al, eds. Oxford Textbook of Rheumatology, 1. LC 92-48994. 1993. write for info. (0-19-262432-6) OUP.

— Oxford Textbook of Rheumatology, 2. LC 92-48994. 1993. write for info. (0-19-262343-5) OUP.

— Oxford Textbook of Rheumatology, Set. LC 92-48994. 1308p. 1993. 210.00 (0-19-262026-6) OUP.

Maddison, R. N. & Bhabuta, L. Information System Methodologies. LC 83-16684. (Monographs in Informatics). 138p. reprint ed. pap. 39.40 (0-685-23436-3, 2032679) Bks Demand.

Maddison, Ralph. Englands Looking In & Out: Presented to the High Court of Parliament Now Assembled. LC 76-57397. (English Experience Ser.: No. 813). 1977. reprint ed. lib. bdg. 5.00 (90-221-0813-9) Walter J Johnson.

Maddison, Wayne & Maddison, David. MacClade 3.0 User's Book: Interactive Analysis of Phylogeny & Character Evolution. (Illus.). 398p. (Orig.). (C). 1992. pap. text ed. 40.00 (0-87893-490-1); pap. text ed. 75.00 (0-87893-491-X) Sinauer Assocs.

Maddock. Drug Abuse: Guide for Pharmacists. 1987. pap. 12.00 (0-85369-190-8, Pub. by Pharmaceutical Pr UK) Rittenhouse.

Maddock, Cathy L. Creative Projects: Seasonal & Holiday Projects That Teach, Fall Through December, Vol. I. 1991. 14.95 (1-55691-071-1, 398) Learning Pubns.

— Creative Projects: Seasonal & Holiday Projects That Teach, January Through Summer, Vol. II. 1991. 14.95 (1-55691-039-8, 398) Learning Pubns.

Maddock, James W. & Hogan, Janice M. Families Before & after Perestroika: Russian & U. S. Perspectives. (Perspectives on Marriage & the Family Ser.). 240p. 1993. lib. bdg. 30.00 (0-89862-085-6) Guilford Pr.

***Maddock, James W. & Larson, Noel.** Child Sexual Abuse: An Ecological Approach to Treating Victims & Perpetrators. 400p. 1996. 40.00 (0-393-70211-1) Norton.

***Maddock, James W. & Larson, Noel R.** Incestuous Families: An Ecological Approach to Understanding & Treatment. 380p. (C). 1995. 40.00 (0-393-70193-X) Norton.

An Asterisk (*) at the beginning of an entry indicates that the title is appearing in BIP for the first time.

Maddock, James W., et al, eds. Human Sexuality & the Family. LC 83-13013. (Marriage & Family Review Ser.: Vol. 6, Nos. 3-4). 159p. 1984. text ed. 39.95 (*0-86656-159-5*) Haworth Pr.

Maddock, Jerome T., jt. ed. see Drancsak, Marina.

Maddock, John. History of Road Trains in the Northern Territory. (Illus.). 176p. 1993. reprint ed. pap. 21.95 (*0-86417-187-0*, Pub. by Kangaroo Pr AT) Seven Hills Bk.

— People Movers: A HIstory of the Private Bus Companies of Victoria. (Illus.). 214p. (Orig.). 1994. 39.95 (*0-86417-412-8*, Pub. by Kangaroo Pr AT) Seven Hills Bk.

Maddock, Kenneth, jt. ed. see Buchler, Ira R.

***Maddock, Linda, et al, eds.** Mechanics & Physiology of Animal Swimming. (Illus.). 260p. (C). 1995. 54.95 (*0-521-46078-6*) Cambridge U Pr.

Maddock, Nicholas & Wilson, Frank. Project Design for Agricultural Development. 236p. 1994. 54.95 (*1-85628-413-1*, Pub. by Avebury Pub UK) Ashgate Pub Co.

Maddock, R. T. The Political Economy of Soviet Defence Spending. LC 87-25075. 272p. 1988. text ed. 55.00 (*0-312-01579-8*) St Martin.

Maddocks, Eileen. Lives in Channel. 321p. (Orig.). 1989. pap. 10.95 (*0-9642074-0-0*) Journeys Maddocks.

Maddocks, Hugh C. Deep-Sky Name Index 2000.0. LC 90-84968. 125p. (Orig.). 1991. pap. 16.95 (*0-9628305-0-X*) Foxon-Maddocks.

— Generic Markup of Electronic Index Manuscripts. LC 88-10896. 1988. pap. text ed. 15.00 (*0-936547-04-9*) Am Soc Index.

Maddocks, Margaret. Fair Shines the Day. large type ed. (Ulverscroft Ser.). 464p. 1994. 21.95 (*0-7089-3026-3*) Ulverscroft.

— The Frozen Fountain. large type ed. 352p. 1994. 20.95 (*0-7089-3080-8*) Ulverscroft.

— November Tree. large type ed. 1989. 17.95 (*0-7089-2058-6*) Ulverscroft.

— Piper's Tune. large type ed. 384p. 1994. 20.95 (*0-7089-3097-2*) Ulverscroft.

— Remembered Spring. large type ed. (Ulverscroft Ser.). 400p. 1994. 21.95 (*0-7089-3062-X*) Ulverscroft.

— The Silver Answer. large type ed. 1990. 21.95 (*0-7089-2126-4*) Ulverscroft.

— Thea. large type ed. (Linford Romance Library). 304p. 1986. pap. 11.95 (*0-7089-6307-2*, Trailtree Bookshop) Ulverscroft.

— A View of the Sea. large type ed. (Linford Romance Library). 1990. pap. 12.95 (*0-7089-6884-8*) Ulverscroft.

Maddocks, Peter. Cartooning for Beginners. 1994. 8.98 (*0-7858-0090-5*) Bk Sales Inc.

Maddoux, Marlin. America Betrayed. Orig. Title: Humanism Exposed. 153p. 1984. pap. 6.99 (*0-910311-18-8*) Huntington Hse.

Maddow, Ben. Edward Weston: His Life. rev. ed. (Illus.). 288p. 1989. reprint ed. pap. 16.95 (*0-89381-369-9*) Aperture.

— Edward Weston: His Life & Photographs. deluxe limited rev. ed. (Illus.). 300p. 1979. 600.00 (*0-89381-045-2*) Aperture.

— A False Autobiography: Poems 1940-1990. 88p. 1991. 15.00 (*0-9629909-0-6*); pap. 9.00 (*0-9629909-1-4*) Other Shores Pr.

Maddox. D. H. Lawrence: The Married Man. LC 94-28960. 621p. 1994. 30.00 (*0-671-68712-3*) S&S Trade.

Maddox, A. J. The Work of a Magistrate. (C). 1980. pap. 58.00 (*0-7219-0561-7*, Scientific) St Mut.

Maddox, Beverly B., ed. see Stevens, Rose B.

Maddox, Brenda. Nora: A Biography of Nora Joyce. 1989. pap. 12.95 (*0-449-90410-5*, Columbine) Fawcett.

Maddox, Don. Karpov-Kasparov: The 1990 World Chess Championship. 1991. pap. 15.00 (*0-8129-1923-8*) Random.

— The Official ISRA Baseball Handbook: How to Beg, Borrow & Steal Your Way to a Pennant. (International Sports Replay Association Handbooks Ser.). (Illus.). 243p. (Orig.). 1994. pap. 16.95 (*1-883358-18-3*) R&D Pub NJ.

Maddox, Don, jt. auth. see Bisguier, Arthur.

Maddox, Don, jt. auth. see Henley, Ron.

Maddox, Don, ed. see Henley, Ron & Hodges, Paul.

Maddox, Don, ed. see Wolff, Patrick.

Maddox, Donald. The Arthurian Romances of Chretien de Troyes: Once & Future Fictions. (Cambridge Studies in Medieval Literature: No. 12). 220p. (C). 1991. 54.95 (*0-521-39450-3*) Cambridge U Pr.

— Semiotics of Deceit: Language, Drama, & Culture in Maistre Pierre Pathelin. LC 82-74491. (Illus.). 232p. 1984. 35.00 (*0-8387-5040-0*) Bucknell U Pr.

— Structure & Sacring: The Systematic Kingdom in Chretien's Erec et Enide. LC 77-93405. (French Forum Monographs: No. 8). 221p. (Orig.). 1978. pap. 10.95 (*0-917058-07-0*) French Forum.

Maddox, Donald & Sturm-Maddox, Sara, eds. Literary Aspects of Courtly Culture: Selected Papers from the Seventh Triennial Congress of the International Courtly Literature Society, University of Massachusetts, Amherst, USA, 27 July-1 August 1992. LC 94-6753. (Illus.). 320p. (C). 1994. text ed. 69.00 (*0-85991-406-2*, DS Brewer) Boydell & Brewer.

***Maddox, Everette.** American Waste. 92p. 1993. 10.00 (*0-614-05039-1*) Portals Pr.

— Bar Scotch. LC 87-63109. 57p. (Orig.). 1988. pap. 7.00 (*0-944100-01-5*) Pirogue Pub.

— The Everette Maddox Songbook. Cassin, Maxine, ed. (Journal Press Books: Louisiana Legacy). (Illus.). 80p. 1982. pap. 12.00 (*0-938498-02-9*) New Orleans Poetry.

Maddox, Everette, ed. see Maxine, Cassin.

Maddox, George, et al. Nature & Extent of Alcohol Problems among the Elderly. 332p. 1986. 36.95 (*0-8261-5480-8*) Springer Pub.

Maddox, George L., ed. The Domesticated Drug. 1970. 29.95x (*0-8084-0108-4*); pap. 24.95x (*0-8084-0109-2*) NCUP.

— The Encyclopedia of Aging. 928p. (C). 1987. 96.00 (*0-8261-4840-9*) Springer Pub.

Maddox, George L. & Busse, E. W., eds. Aging: The Universal Human Experience; Selected Papers from the XIIth Congress of the International Association of Gerontology. LC 87-26624. 688p. 1987. 75.00 (*0-8261-5490-5*) Springer Pub.

Maddox, George L. & Lawton, M. Powell, eds. Annual Review of Gerontology & Geriatrics, Vol. 8. 320p. 1988. 36.95 (*0-8261-6490-0*) Springer Pub.

— The Annual Review of Gerontology & Geriatrics, 1993. (Annual Review of Gerontology Ser.: Vol. 13). 280p. 1993. text ed. 46.00 (*0-8261-6495-1*) Springer Pub.

Maddox, George L. & McCall, Bevode C. Drinking among Teen-Agers. 1964. pap. 15.95x (*0-8084-0413-X*) NCUP.

— Drinking Among Teen-Agers. LC 64-63392. (Monograph Ser.: No. 4). 1964. 14.95 (*0-911290-31-1*) Rutgers Ctr Alcohol.

Maddox, George L., jt. ed. see Brody, Jacob.

Maddox, George L., jt. auth. see Busse, Ewald W.

Maddox, George L., jt. ed. see Eisdorfer, Carl.

Maddox, George L., jt. auth. see Lawton, M. Powell.

Maddox, Gregory, ed. African Nationalism & Revolution. LC 93-11080. (Articles on Colonialism & Nationalism in Africa Ser.: Vol. 4). (Illus.). 400p. 1993. 65.00 (*0-8153-1391-8*) Garland.

— The Colonial Epoch in Africa. LC 93-17822. (Articles on Colonialism & Nationalism in Africa Ser.: Vol. 2). 408p. 1993. 69.00 (*0-8153-1389-6*) Garland.

— Conquest & Resistance to Colonialism in Africa. LC 93-19790. (Articles on Colonialism & Nationalism in Africa Ser.: Vol. 1). 384p. 1993. 62.00 (*0-8153-1388-8*) Garland.

Maddox, Gregory, ed. see Mnyampala, Mathias.

***Maddox, Gregory, et al, eds.** Custodians of the Land: Environment & Hunger in Tanzanian History. (East African Studies). 320p. (C). 1995. text ed. 44.95 (*0-8214-1133-0*); pap. text ed. 19.95 (*0-8214-1134-9*) Ohio U Pr.

Maddox, Harry. How to Study. 1983. pap. 3.50 (*0-449-30011-0*, Prem) Fawcett.

***Maddox, Hugh.** Alabama Rules of Criminal Procedure, 2 vols., Set. 2nd suppl. ed. 1994. 130.00 (*0-87473-636-6*) Michie Butterworth.

Maddox, I. J. Elements of Functional Analysis. 2nd ed. 200p. 1989. pap. 27.95 (*0-521-35868-X*) Cambridge U Pr.

— Infinite Matrices of Operators. (Lecture Notes in Mathematics Ser.: Vol. 786). 122p. 1980. pap. 23.00 (*0-387-09764-3*) Spr-Verlag.

Maddox, Irene & Blakenship, Rosalyn, eds. Campfire Songs. 2nd ed. (East Woods Book Ser.). (Illus.). 192p. 1994. pap. 9.95 (*1-56440-372-6*) Globe Pequot.

Maddox, J., jt. auth. see Capers, Roberta M.

Maddox, J. L. The Medicine Man: A Sociological Study of the Character & Evolution of Shamanism. 1977. lib. bdg. 59.95 (*0-8490-2219-3*) Gordon Pr.

Maddox, John, jt. auth. see Beaton, Leonard.

Maddox, John L. The Medicine Man: A Sociological Study of the Character & Evolution of Shamanism. LC 75-23737. reprint ed. 45.00 (*0-404-13294-4*) AMS Pr.

Maddox, Karen. From Beneath the Surface. LC 90-82946. (Illus.). 74p. (Orig.). 1994. reprint ed. 10.00 (*0-9620375-6-7*) Faith Unlimited.

***Maddox, Kathleen B.** Collected Poems & One Essay. Orth, Jane, ed. (Illus.). 97p. 1995. pap. 6.00 (*1-885761-01-5*) Turner Geriatric.

Maddox, Kenneth W. An Unprejudiced Eye: The Drawings of Jasper F. Cropsey. LC 79-90970. (Illus.). 72p. (Orig.). 1979. pap. 5.00 (*0-943651-07-7*) Hudson Riv.

Maddox, Lucy. Removals: Nineteenth-Century American Literature & the Politics of Indian Affairs. 216p. 1991. 42.00 (*0-19-506931-5*) OUP.

Maddox, Muriel. Llantarnam. Smith, James C., Jr., ed. LC 91-38366. 416p. (Orig.). 1992. pap. 16.95 (*0-86534-173-7*) Sunstone Pr.

Maddox, Peggy. On the Edge: Health Crisis - Helping Yourself. LC 90-81973. (Illus.). 140p. 1991. pap. 9.95 (*0-944435-11-4*) Glenbridge Pub.

Maddox, R. N. Process Engineer's Absorption Pocket Handbook. LC 85-852. (Illus.). 90p. 1985. 19.00 (*0-87201-016-3*) Gulf Pub.

Maddox, Randy L. Responsible Grace: John Wesley's Practical Theology. (Kingswood Ser.). 400p. (Orig.). 1994. pap. 19.95 (*0-687-00334-2*) Abingdon.

— Toward an Ecumenical Fundamental Theology. LC 84-13838. (American Academy of Religion, Studies in Religion). 1984. 20.95 (*0-89130-771-0*, 01 01 47) Scholars Pr GA.

***Maddox, Rebecca J.** Inc. Your Dreams: For Any Woman Who Has Ever Considered Business Ownership. LC 95-1448. 1995. 22.95 (*0-670-85433-6*, Viking) Viking Penguin.

Maddox, Richard. El Castillo: The Politics of Tradition in an Andalusian Town. 1993. pap. 19.95 (*0-252-06339-2*) U of Ill Pr.

— El Castillo: The Politics of Tradition in an Andalusian Town. (Illus.). 368p. (C). 1993. 49.95 (*0-252-01946-6*) U of Ill Pr.

— DAT Technical Service Handbook. (Illus.). 256p. 1994. text ed. 49.95 (*0-442-01423-6*) Van Nos Reinhold.

***Maddox, Robert.** Annual Editions: American History, Vol. 2. annuals 13th rev. ed. (Illus.). 256p. (C). 1995. pap. text ed. 12.95x (*1-56134-345-5*) Dushkin Pub.

— Purpose of Luke-Acts. Riches, John, ed. 220p. 1982. 37.95 (*0-567-09312-3*, Pub. by T & T Clark UK) Bks Intl VA.

— The Purpose of Luke-Acts. 220p. 1995. pap. text ed. 24.95 (*0-567-29270-3*, Pub. by T & T Clark UK) Bks Intl VA.

Maddox, Robert C. Cross-Cultural Problems in International Business: The Role of the Cultural Integration Function. LC 92-43086. 160p. 1993. text ed. 45.00 (*0-89930-581-4*, MOK, Quorum Bks) Greenwood.

***Maddox, Robert J.** Annual Editions: American History, Vol. 1. annuals 13th rev. ed. (Illus.). 256p. (C). 1995. pap. text ed. 12.95x (*1-56134-344-7*) Dushkin Pub.

— The United States & World War II. 358p. (C). 1991. pap. text ed. 23.50 (*0-8133-0437-7*) Westview.

— The United States & World War II. 358p. (C). 1992. text ed. 67.00 (*0-8133-0436-9*) Westview.

Maddox, Robert L., Jr. Layman's Bible Book Commentary: Acts, Vol. 19. LC 78-67926. 1991. 8.99 (*0-8054-1189-5*) Broadman.

Maddox, Robert N., jt. auth. see Hines, Anthony L.

***Maddox, Ruth P.** Building SMU: 1915-1957. 1995. pap. 27.00 (*1-884363-07-5*) Odenwald Pr.

***Maddox, S. & Aragon-Salamanca, A.** Wide Field Spectroscopy & the Distant Universe: Proceedings of the 35th Herstmonceux Conference. 436p. 1995. text ed. 99.00 (*981-02-2031-6*) World Scientific Pub.

Maddox, S. J., ed. see Welding Institute Staff.

Maddox, Sam. The Quest for Cure: Restoring Function after Spinal Cord Injury. LC 92-50575. (Illus.). 200p. (Orig.). 1993. pap. 22.45 (*0-929819-03-9*) Paralyzed Vets.

— Spinal Network. Corbet, Barry, ed. 374p. 1991. pap. 27.95 (*0-943489-02-4*); spiral bd. 29.95 (*0-685-50434-4*) Spinal Network.

— Spinal Network. LC 87-12812. (Illus.). 374p. 1988. reprint ed. 39.95 (*0-943489-01-6*); reprint ed. pap. 24.94 (*0-943489-00-8*) Spinal Network.

Maddox, Sam, ed. Spinal Network. 2nd ed. LC 93-28422. 1993. 39.95 (*0-943489-03-2*); pap. 37.95 (*0-943489-04-0*) Spinal Network.

Maddox, Tom. Halo. 224p. 1992. mass mkt. 3.99 (*0-8125-1096-8*) Tor Bks.

Maddox, Tony. Fergus the Farmyard Dog. (Illus.). 28p. (J). 12.95 (*0-8120-6373-2*); pap. 4.95 (*0-8120-1763-3*) Barron.

— Fergus's Upside-Down Day. LC 94-16656. (J). 1994. write for info. (*0-8120-6471-2*); pap. write for info. (*0-8120-9074-8*) Barron.

Maddox, William. Profits in Building Spec Homes. (Illus.). 232p. (Orig.). 1994. pap. 27.25 (*0-934041-93-8*) Craftsman.

Maddox, William A. The Free School Idea in Virginia Before the Civil War: A Phase of Political & Social Evolution. LC 70-177045. (Columbia University. Teachers College. Contributions to Education Ser.: No. 93). reprint ed. 37.50 (*0-404-55093-2*) AMS Pr.

— Free School Idea in Virginia Before the Civil War: A Phase of Poltiical & Social Evolution. LC 75-89202. (American Education: Its Men, Institutions & Ideas, Ser. 1). 1978. reprint ed. 18.95 (*0-405-01436-8*) Ayer.

Maddren, Gerry. The Case of the Johannisberg Riesling. Chirich, Nancy, ed. LC 88-4326. 192p. 1988. 13.95 (*0-912761-15-6*) Cliffhanger Pr.

Maddrey, W., jt. ed. see Williams, R.

Maddrey, W. C. Transplantation of the Liver. 352p. 1988. boxed 83.00 (*0-8385-8999-5*, A8999-3) Appleton & Lange.

***Maddrey, Willis C. & Sorrell, Michael F.** Transplantation of the Liver. 2nd ed. LC 94-25108. (C). 1994. text ed. 135.00 (*0-8385-8990-1*, A8990-2) Appleton & Lange.

Maddron, Ernest. Love, Shame, & Honor. LC 93-34504. 204p. (Orig.). 1993. pap. text ed. 9.95 (*1-882185-15-3*) Crnrstone Pub.

— Lucky Shanty Town Girl. 360p. Date not set. pap. 9.95 (*0-7610-0249-9*) NW Pub.

Maddux, Bob, et al. The Dog That Went Too Fast. (Land of Pleasant Dreams Ser.). (Illus.). 26p. (J). (ps up). 1987. 7.95 (*1-55578-104-7*); audio (*0-318-61948-2*) Worlds Wonder.

Maddux, Cleborne D. Distance Education: A Selected Bibliography. Milheim, William D., ed. LC 92-24055. (Educational Technology Selected Bibliography Ser.: Vol. 7). 71p. (Orig.). 1992. 14.95 (*0-87778-249-0*) Educ Tech Pubns.

Maddux, Cleborne D., ed. Logo in the Schools. LC 85-8411. (Computers in the Schools Ser.: Vol. 2. Nos. 2-3). 305p. 1985. text ed. 49.95 (*0-86656-424-1*); pap. text ed. 19.95 (*0-86656-425-X*) Haworth Pr.

Maddux, Cleborne D., jt. auth. see Cummings, Rhoda W.

Maddux, Cleborne D., jt. auth. see Kass, Corrine E.

Maddux, Cleborne D., et al. Educational Computing: Learning with Tomorrow's Technologies. 384p. (C). 1992. pap. text ed. 42.00 (*0-205-13648-6*) Allyn.

Maddux, Dealy-Doe-Eyes. Flower Arrangements. (Illus.). 24p. 1983. 24.00 (*0-88014-065-8*) Mosaic Pr OH.

Maddux, Dorothy, jt. auth. see Maddux, Robert.

Maddux, J. E., et al, eds. Social Processes in Clinical & Counseling Psychology. (Illus.). 392p. 1987. 52.00 (*0-387-96533-5*) Spr-Verlag.

***Maddux, James E., ed.** Self-Efficacy, Adaptation, & Adjustment: Theory, Research, & Application. LC 95-3668. (Series in Social-Clinical Psychology). 390p. (C). 1995. 54.50 (*0-306-44875-0*, Plenum Pr) Plenum.

Maddux, Mike. MASM: Tips & Techniques for Unisys 1100 - 2200 Systems. Drolet, Michele, ed. 260p. 1990. 45.00 (*0-9627241-0-6*) PCI TX.

Maddux, Rachel. Communication: The Autobiography of Rachel Maddux, & Her Novella, Turnips Blood. Walker, Nancy A., ed. LC 91-7248. (Rachel Maddux Ser.). (Illus.). 240p. (C). 1991. 28.95 (*0-87049-699-9*) U of Tenn Pr.

— The Green Kingdom. LC 92-26664. (Rachel Maddux Ser.: Vol. 4). 576p. (C). 1993. 37.95 (*0-87049-780-4*) U of Tenn Pr.

— A Walk in the Spring Rain & The Orchard Children. LC 92-4980. 344p. 1992. 31.95 (*0-87049-757-X*) U of Tenn Pr.

— The Way Things Are: The Stories of Rachel Maddux. LC 91-40099. 296p. 1992. 28.95 (*0-87049-751-0*) U of Tenn Pr.

Maddux, Robert. Team Building: An Exercise in Leadership. 70p. (Orig.). 1988. 7.95 (*0-318-33263-9*, 116) Am Bartenders.

Maddux, Robert & Maddux, Dorothy. Ethics in Business. Crisp, Michael G., ed. LC 88-63799. (Fifty-Minute Ser.). (Illus.). 96p. (Orig.). 1989. pap. 9.95 (*0-931961-69-6*) Crisp Pubns.

Maddux, Robert, jt. auth. see Voorhees, Lynda.

Maddux, Robert B. Delegating for Results. Crisp, Mike, ed. LC 89-81246. (Fifty-Minute Ser.). (Illus.). (Orig.). 1990. pap. 9.95 (*1-56052-008-6*) Crisp Pubns.

— Effective Performance Appraisals. rev. ed. Gerould, Philip, ed. 65p. (Orig.). reprint ed. pap. 9.95 (*1-56052-196-1*) Crisp Pubns.

— Effective Performance Appraisals. rev. ed. Crisp, Michael G., ed. LC 85-73180. (Fifty-Minute Ser.). (Illus.). 80p. (Orig.). 1987. pap. 9.95 (*0-931961-11-4*) Crisp Pubns.

— Quality Interviewing. rev. ed. Gerould, W. Philip, ed. LC 93-7049. (Fifty-Minute Ser.). (Illus.). 100p. (Orig.). 1994. pap. 9.95 (*1-56052-262-3*) Crisp Pubns.

— Successful Negotiation. rev. ed. LC 85-73178. (Fifty-Minute Ser.). (Illus.). 80p. (Orig.). 1987. pap. 8.95 (*0-931961-09-2*) Crisp Pubns.

— Team Building: An Exercise in Leadership. rev. ed. Crisp, Michael G., ed. LC 91-77080. (Fifty-Minute Ser.). (Illus.). 80p. (Orig.). 1992. pap. 9.95 (*1-56052-118-X*) Crisp Pubns.

— Tworzenie Zespolu: Rozwijanie Umiejetnosci Zarzadzania. Grycz, Czeslaw J. & Salski, Andrzej, eds. Salski, Andrzej, tr. (Illus.). iv, 74p. (Orig.). (POL.). (C). 1991. pap. 7.95 (*1-56513-002-2*) W Poniecki Charit.

Maddux, Robert B., jt. auth. see Conrad, Pamela J.

Maddux, Vernon. John Hittson: Cattle King on the Texas & Colorado Frontier. (Illus.). 288p. 1994. 27.50 (*0-87081-353-6*) Univ Pr Colo.

Maddy, A. H. & Harris, James R., eds. Subcellular Biochemistry, Vol. 22: Membrane Biogenesis. (Illus.). 345p. (C). 1994. 95.00 (*0-306-44554-9*, Plenum Pr) Plenum.

Maddy, Olive. Maddy - Us Maddys: An Account of the Family in England & the Descendants of William Maddy of Fairfax of Fairfax County, Virginia, & James Maddy of Fairfax & Orange County. (Illus.). 280p. 1994. reprint ed. lib. bdg. 54.00 (*0-8328-4035-1*); reprint ed. pap. 44.00 (*0-8328-4036-X*) Higginson Bk Co.

Maddy, Penelope. Realism in Mathematics. 216p. 1992. pap. 19.95 (*0-19-824035-X*) OUP.

Maddy-Weitzman, Bruce. The Crystalization of the Arab State System: Inter-Arab Politics, 1945-1954. (Contemporary Issues in the Middle East Ser.). 400p. 1992. text ed. 39.95 (*0-8156-2575-8*); pap. text ed. 18.95 (*0-8156-2580-4*) Syracuse U Pr.

Made in the USA Foundation Staff. Made in the U. S. A. The Complete Guide to America's Finest Products. 4th ed. 334p. (Orig.). 1993. pap. 12.95 (*1-882605-01-2*) Natl Pr Bks.

Madeira, Louis C., comp. Annals of Music in Philadelphia & History of the Musical Fund Society. LC 78-169650. (Music Reprint Ser.). (Illus.). 234p. 1973. reprint ed. lib. bdg. 29.50 (*0-306-70260-6*) Da Capo.

Madej, Victor & Zaloga, Stefan. Polish Campaign of 1939. (Illus.). 195p. 1991. pap. 11.95 (*0-87052-013-X*) Hippocrene Bks.

Madeja, Stanley S., ed. Gifted & Talented in Art Education. (Illus.). 128p. (Orig.). (C). 1983. pap. text ed. 16.00 (*0-937652-00-8*) Natl Art Ed.

Madeja, W. Victor. Dictionary of German Military Terms, Abbreviations & Map Symbols. 146p. 1992. 18.00 (*0-941052-75-3*) Valor Pub.

— German Replacement Army. LC 84-80673. (Illus.). 184p. (Orig.). 1984. 16.00 (*0-941052-54-0*, 54) Valor Pub.

— Hitler's Dying Ground: Disintegration of the German Armed Forces in WW2. 4th ed. LC 84-80623. (Illus.). 212p. 1992. 16.00 (*0-685-42692-0*) Valor Pub.

— Italian Army Handbook, 1940-1944. LC 84-8059. (Illus.). 176p. (Orig.). 1984. 16.00 (*0-941052-60-5*) Valor Pub.

— U. S. Army Order of Battle: Pacific Divisions. 1984. 14.00 (*0-941052-72-9*); pap. 9.95 (*0-941052-19-2*) Valor Pub.

Madeja, W. Victor, ed. The German War Machine: German Weapons & Manpower. LC 84-80626. (Illus.). 180p. 1984. 14.00 (*0-941052-58-3*); pap. 14.00 (*0-941052-21-4*) Valor Pub.

— Hitler's Elite Guards: The Waffen SS & Parachutists Between Fascism & Genocide. LC 84-80623. (Illus.). 211p. 1992. 16.00 (*0-941052-55-9*) Valor Pub.

— Italian Army Order of Battle: 1940-1944. 3rd ed. (Illus.). 202p. 1990. 16.00 (*0-941052-59-1*) Valor Pub.

— Japanese Armed Forces Order of Battle, 1937-1945: Divisions. (Illus.). 1993. 14.00 (*0-941052-67-2*) Valor Pub.

— Japanese Mobilization & Pacific Campaign. LC 84-80624. (Illus.). 200p. 1985. 16.00 (*0-941052-69-9*); pap. 16.00 (*0-941052-27-3*) Valor Pub.

— The Motorization Myth. LC 84-8625. (Illus.). 176p. 1984. 14.00 (*0-941052-57-5*); pap. 14.00 (*0-941052-20-6*) Valor Pub.

— The Polish Second Corps & the Italian Campaign. LC 84-81892. (Illus.). 186p. 1984. 14.00 (*0-941052-51-6*); pap. 9.95 (*0-941052-34-6*) Valor Pub.

An Asterisk (*) at the beginning of an entry indicates that the title is appearing in BIP for the first time.

— Russo-German War: Autumn 1941. (Battle Situation - East Front Ser.). (Illus.). 80p. (Orig.). (GER.). 1988. pap. 12.95 (0-941052-82-6) Valor Pub.

— Russo-German War: Autumn 1944 to January 25 1945. (Battle Situation - East Front Ser.). (Illus.). 78p. (Orig.). (GER.). 1987. pap. 18.00 (0-941052-89-3) Valor Pub.

— Russo-German War: January 25 Through Spring 1945: The Last 100 Days, No. 35. 80p. (GER.). 1987. pap. 18.00 (0-941052-90-7) Valor Pub.

— Russo-German War: Small Unit Actions. 194p. 1986. 14.00 (0-941052-74-5); pap. 14.00 (0-941052-36-2) Valor Pub.

— Russo-German War: Summer-Autumn 1942. (Ost-Lage Ser.: No. 29). 80p. 1993. pap. 18.00 (0-941052-79-6) Valor Pub.

— Russo-German War: Summer-Autumn 1943. (Battle Situation - East Front Ser.). (Illus.). 100p. (Orig.). 1987. pap. text ed. 18.00 (0-941052-86-9, 31) Valor Pub.

— Russo-German War: Summer 1941 (Barbarossa) (Battle Situation - East Front Ser.). (Illus.). 130p. (Orig.). (GER.). 1992. pap. text ed. 18.00 (0-941052-76-1) Valor Pub.

— Russo-German War: Summer 1944. (Battle Situation - East Front Ser.). (Illus.). 80p. (Orig.). (GER.). 1992. pap. text ed. 18.00 (0-941052-88-5) Valor Pub.

— Russo-German War: Winter-Spring 1942. (Battle Situation - East Front Ser.). (Illus.). 80p. (Orig.). (GER.). 1993. pap. text ed. 18.00 (0-941052-78-8) Valor Pub.

— Russo-German War: Winter-Spring 1943. (Battle Situation - East Front Ser.). (Illus.). 80p. (Orig.). 1994. pap. text ed. 18.00 (0-941052-85-0) Valor Pub.

— Russo-German War: Winter-Spring 1944. (Battle Situation - East Front Ser.). (Illus.). 92p. (Orig.). (GER.). 1988. pap. text ed. 18.00 (0-941052-87-7) Valor Pub.

— Russo-German War - Balkans: November 1940 - November 1944. (Battle Situation - South East Front Ser.). (Illus.). 128p. 1989. pap. 18.00 (0-941052-91-5) Valor Pub.

— U. S. Army Order of Battle: Mediterranean & Europe 1942-1945. 190p. 1984. 14.00 (0-941052-70-2); pap. 14.00 (0-941052-26-5) Valor Pub.

Madeleine, Fredric. The Drug Controversy & the Rise of Antichrist. 2nd ed. 40p. (C). 1994. pap. 7.00 (0-9627423-3-3) Candlestick.

Madeleva, M. Grace. Chaucer's Nuns & Other Essays. reprint ed. 39.00 (0-403-04008-6) Somerset Pub.

— Pearl: A Study in Spiritual Dryness. LC 68-59311. 235p. (C). 1968. reprint ed. 45.00 (0-87753-025-4) Phaeton.

Madeley, J. Human Rights Begin with Breakfast. 34p. 1982. pap. 22.00 (0-08-028926-6, Pub. by Pergamon Repr UK) Franklin.

Madeley, John. Trade & the Poor: The Impact of International Trade on Developing Countries. LC 92-39846. 224p. 1993. text ed. 39.95 (0-312-09236-9) St Martin.

Madelin, Louis. Consulate & Empire, 2 Vols. No. 7. reprint ed. write for info. (0-318-50547-9) AMS Pr.

— Consulate & Empire, 2 Vols, 1. LC 34-10700. (National History of France Ser.: No. 7). reprint ed. 45.00 (0-404-50808-1) AMS Pr.

— Consulate & Empire, 2 Vols, 2. LC 34-10700. (National History of France Ser.: No. 7). reprint ed. 45.00 (0-404-50809-X) AMS Pr.

— Consulate & Empire, 2 Vols, Set. LC 34-10700. (National History of France Ser.: No. 7). reprint ed. 90.00 (0-404-50810-3) AMS Pr.

— Figures of the Revolution. Curtis, R., tr. LC 68-22221. (Essay Index Reprint Ser.). 1977. 21.95 (0-8369-0663-2) Ayer.

— French Revolution. LC 73-181954. (National History of France Ser.: No. 6). reprint ed. 45.00 (0-404-50796-4) AMS Pr.

Madeline, Fredric. The Drug Controversy & the Rise of Antichrist. (Orig.). (C). 1990. pap. 7.00 (0-9627423-0-9) Candlestick.

Madeline X. How to Become a Vampire in Six Easy Lessons. 1986. pap. 3.99 (0-9611944-3-X) Dracula Pr.

Madeling, O., ed. Semiconductors: Group IV-Elements & III-V-Compounds. (Data in Science & Technology Ser.). 200p. 1991. pap. 49.50 (0-387-53150-5) Spr-Verlag.

Madell, Geoffrey. The Identity of the Self. 145p. 1981. 15.00 (0-85224-422-3, Pub. by Edinburgh U Pr UK) Col U Pr.

— Mind & Materialism. 176p. 1988. 30.00 (0-85224-575-0, Pub. by Edinburgh U Pr UK) Col U Pr.

— Mind & Materialism. 160p. 1990. pap. text ed. 18.00 (0-85224-602-1, Pub. by Edinburgh U Pr UK) Col U Pr.

Madell, Tom, et al. Developing & Localizing International Software. LC 93-41466. (Hewlett-Packard Professional Books Ser.). 224p. 1994. pap. text ed. 34.80 (0-13-300674-3) P-H Gen Ref & Trav.

Madelung, M. Referaten des Fachausschusses Halbleiter, Berlin 1968. LC 64-51891. (Festkorper Probleme Ser.). (GER.). 1968. 136.00 (0-08-013109-3, Pub. by Pergamon Repr UK) Franklin.

Madelung, Margaret A., jt. auth. see Moayyad, Heshmat.

Madelung, O. Introduction to Solid-State Theory. LC 77-26263. (Solid-State Sciences Ser.: Vol. 2). (Illus.). 1988. 54.50 (0-387-08516-5) Spr-Verlag.

***Madelung, O., ed.** Phase Equilibria, Crystallographic Data & Values of Thermodynamic Properties of Binary Alloys. (Numerical Data & Functional Relationships in Science & Technology Ser.: Vol. 5). 385p. 1994. 1,263.00 (0-387-56073-4) Spr-Verlag.

— Semiconductors: Physics of Group IV Elements & IL-V Compounds. (Landolt-Boernstein Ser.: Group III, Vol. 17, Pt. a). (Illus.). 670p. 1981. 1,170.00 (0-387-10610-3) Spr-Verlag.

***Madelung, O. & Martienssen, W.** Theoretical Structures of Molecules, 22. (Atomic & Molecular Physics Ser.: 22). 160p. 1994. 469.00 (0-387-56332-6) Spr-Verlag.

Madelung, O. & Poerschke, R., eds. Semiconductors: Others Than Group IV Elements & III-V Compounds. LC 92-8630. (Data in Science & Technology Ser.). vii, 153p. 1992. Berlin. write for info. (3-540-55373-8); New York. 49.50 (0-387-55373-8) Spr-Verlag.

Madelung, O. & Voigt, H. H., eds. Lanolt-Boernstein Numerical Data & Functional Relationships in Science & Technology: Astronomy, Astrophysics & Space Research; Astronomy & Astrophysics; Methods, Constants, the Solar System, Group VI; Vol. 3; Subvol. A. 240p. 1993. 556.00 (0-387-56079-3) Spr-Verlag.

Madelung, O, ed. see Asmus, K. D. & Bonifacic, M.

Madelung, O., ed. see Albanese, G., et al.

Madelung, O., ed. see Burzo, E.

Madelung, O., ed. see Every, A. G. & McCurdy, A. K.

Madelung, O., ed. see Ferchmin, A. R., et al.

Madelung, O., ed. see Goldmann, A., et al.

Madelung, O., ed. see Predel, B.

Madelung, O., jt. ed. see Ullmaier, H.

Madelung, O., jt. ed. see Wijn, H. P.

Madelung, Wilferd. Religious Schools & Sects in Medieval Islam. (Collected Studies: No. CS213). 352p. (C). 1985. reprint ed. lib. bdg. 95.00 (0-86078-161-5, Pub. by Variorum UK) Ashgate Pub Co.

— Religious Trend in Early Islamic Iran. 1988. 30.00 (0-88706-700-X) Mazda Pubs.

Madelung, Wilfred. Political & Ethnic Movements in Medieval Islam. (Collected Studies: Vol. CS364). 352p. 1992. 95.00 (0-86078-310-3, Pub. by Variorum UK) Ashgate Pub Co.

***Mademoiselles Noires, Inc., Staff.** The Black Gourmet Cookbook. (Illus.). 80p. (Orig.). Date not set. spiral bd. 15.95 (0-9643335-0-3) Mmlle Noires.

Maden, Marc F. The Disposition of Reported Child Abuse. LC 79-93296. 130p. 1980. 12.95 (0-86548-016-8) R & E Pubs.

***Maden, Mary.** Flying High with the Wright Brothers: The Story of Their First Flight - a Dog's Tale. 20p. (J). (gr. 1-3). 1995. pap. 4.95 (0-9646970-0-9) Dog & Pony Enter.

— The Secret of Blackbeard's Treasure - a Pony's Tale. 20p. (J). (gr. 1-3). 1995. pap. 4.95 (0-9646970-1-7) Dog & Pony Enter.

Maden, Sue. Greetings from Jamestown, Rhode Island: Picture Post Card Views, 1900-1950. (Illus.). 152p. (Orig.). 1988. pap. 16.00 (0-9620875-0-5) West Ferry Pr.

***Maden, Tony, et al.** The Treatment & Security Needs of Special Hospital Patients. 150p. 1995. pap. text ed. 150.00 (1-56593-501-2, 1160) Singular Publishing.

Madenski, Melissa. In My Mother's Garden. LC 93-40112. (Illus.). (J). 1995. 15.95 (0-316-54326-8) Little.

Madenwald, Abbie M. Arctic Schoolteacher: Kulukak, Alaska, 1931-1933. LC 92-54129. (Western Frontier Library: Vol. 59). (Illus.). 224p. 1992. 21.95 (0-8061-2469-5) U of Okla Pr.

— Arctic Schoolteacher: Kulukak, Alaska, 1931-1933. LC 92-54129. (Western Frontier Library: Vol. 59). (Illus.). 224p. 1994. pap. 11.95 (0-8061-2611-6) U of Okla Pr.

***Madeo, Silvia A., et al.** Sommerfeld's Concepts of Taxation, 1995 Edition. 683p. (C). 1994. text ed. 49.75 (0-03-006833-9) Dryden Pr.

— Sommerfeld's Concepts of Taxation, 1995 Edition. 95th ed. 272p. (C). 1994. student ed, pap. text ed. 28.00 (0-03-006834-7) Dryden Pr.

Mader. Electronic Text to Accompany Introduction to Biology. (C). 1994. pap. write for info. (0-697-24726-0) Wm C Brown Pubs.

Mader, A., tr. see Booss, B. & Bleecker, D. D.

Mader, Charles L. Numerical Modeling of Water Waves. (Los Alamos Series in Basic & Applied Sciences: No. 8). 1988. 50.00 (0-520-06269-8) U CA Pr.

Mader, Charles L., ed. LASL Phermex Data, Vol. 2. (Los Alamos Scientific Laboratory Series on Dynamic Material Properties: Vol. 2). 768p. 1980. 65.00 (0-520-04010-4) U CA Pr.

— LASL Phermex Data, Vol. 3. (Los Alamos Scientific Laboratory Series on Dynamic Material Properties: Vol. 3). 1980. 65.00 (0-520-04011-2) U CA Pr.

Mader, Charles L., et al, eds. LASL Phermex Data, Vol. 1. (Los Alamos Scientific Laboratory Series on Dynamic Material Properties: Vol. 1). 1980. 65.00 (0-520-04009-0) U CA Pr.

— Los Alamos: Explosives Performance Data. LC 82-40391. (Los Alamos Scientific Laboratory Series on Dynamic Material Properties: Vol. 7). 824p. (C). 1983. 55.00 (0-520-04014-7) U CA Pr.

Mader, D. Hydraulic Proppant Fracturing & Gravel Packing. (Developments in Petroleum Science Ser.: No. 26). 1240p. 1989. 189.75 (0-444-87352-X) Elsevier.

— Palaeoecology of the Flora in Bundsandstein & Keuper in the Triassic of Middle Europe, 2 vols., Set. (Illus.). 1582p. 1990. lib. bdg. 241.00 (0-685-50522-7, Pub. by G Fischer Verlag GW) Lubrecht & Cramer.

***Mader, Detlef.** Aeolian & Adhesion Morphodynamics & Phytoecology in Recent Coastal & Inland Sand & Snow Flats & Dunes from Mainly North Sea & Baltic Sea to Mars & Venus, 2 vols. LC 94-41210. 2348p. 1994. 225.95 (0-8204-2814-0) P Lang Pubs.

— Palaeoecology of the Flora in Buntsandstein & Keuper in the Triassic of Middle Europe, 2 vols. 1600p. 1990. Vol. 1, Buntsandstein. write for info. (0-318-68432-2); Vol. 2, Keuper & Index. write for info. (0-318-68433-0) G F Verlag.

— Palaeoecology of the Flora in Buntsandstein & Keuper in the Triassic of Middle Europe, 2 vols., Set. 1600p. 1990. lib. bdg. 275.00 (1-56081-302-4) G F Verlag.

Mader, Diane C., jt. auth. see Mader, Thomas F.

Mader, Douglas P., et al. Process Control Methods. LC 92-41667. (Six Sigma Research Institute Ser.). 1993. write for info. (0-201-63410-4) Addison-Wesley.

***Mader, Douglas R.** Reptile Medicine & Surgery. LC 95-9672. (Illus.). 624p. 1995. text ed. write for info. (0-7216-5208-5) Saunders.

Mader, Friedrich W. Distant Worlds: The Story of a Voyage to the Planets. Shachtman, Max, tr. LC 75-28859. (Classics of Science Fiction Ser.). (Illus.). vi, 343p. 1976. reprint ed. 15.40 (0-88355-374-0); reprint ed. pap. 10.00 (0-88355-458-5) Hyperion Conn.

Mader, George G., jt. auth. see Lagorio, Henry J.

Mader, Gerald L., ed. Permanent Satellite Tracking Networks for Geodesy & Geodynamics. (International Association of Geodesy Symposia Ser.: Vol. 109). (Illus.). 210p. 1993. pap. write for info. (3-540-55827-6) Spr-Verlag.

— Permanent Satellite Tracking Networks for Geodesy & Geodynamics: Symposium No. 109, Vienna, Austria, August 11-24, 1991. LC 93-2186. (International Association of Geodesy Symposia Ser.: No. 109). 1993. pap. 69.00 (0-387-55827-6) Spr-Verlag.

Mader, Josef. Chip Carving & Relief Carving. (Illus.). 88p. 1987. pap. 14.95 (0-02-000720-5) Macmillan.

Mader, Katherine, jt. auth. see Wolf, Marvin J.

Mader, Robert D., jt. auth. see Adams, James R.

***Mader, Sylvia.** Biology. (C). 1995. student ed write for info. (0-697-28182-5) Wm C Brown Pubs.

— Biology. 3rd ed. 880p. (C). 1990. student ed write for info. (0-697-11247-0) Wm C Brown Pubs.

— Biology. 3rd ed. 880p. (C). 1990. text ed. write for info. (0-697-05638-4) Wm C Brown Pubs.

— Biology. 3rd ed. 880p. (C). 1990. student ed write for info. (0-697-05640-6) Wm C Brown Pubs.

— Biology, 6 pts. 4th ed. 896p. (C). 1992. pap. write for info. (0-697-15096-8) Wm C Brown Pubs.

— Biology, 6 pts. 4th ed. 896p. (C). 1992. student ed write for info. (0-697-12384-7); student ed, disk write for info. (0-697-12386-3) Wm C Brown Pubs.

— Biology. 5th ed. 896p. (C). 1995. pap. write for info. (0-697-21819-8) Wm C Brown Pubs.

— Biology, 6 pts., Pt. I: The Cell. 4th ed. 896p. (C). 1992. text ed. write for info. (0-697-15098-4) Wm C Brown Pubs.

— Biology, 6 pts., Pt. II: Genetic Basics of Life. 4th ed. 896p. (C). 1992. text ed. write for info. (0-697-15099-2) Wm C Brown Pubs.

— Biology, 6 pts., Pt. III: Evolution & Diversity. 4th ed. 896p. (C). 1992. text ed. write for info. (0-697-15100-X) Wm C Brown Pubs.

— Biology, 6 pts., Pt. IV: Plant Structure & Function. 4th ed. 896p. (C). 1992. text ed. write for info. (0-697-15101-8) Wm C Brown Pubs.

— Biology, 6 pts., Pt. V: Biology of Animal Structure & Function. 4th ed. 896p. (C). 1992. text ed. write for info. (0-697-15102-6) Wm C Brown Pubs.

— Biology, 6 pts., Pt. VI: Biology of Behavior & Ecology. 4th ed. 896p. (C). 1992. text ed. write for info. (0-697-15103-4) Wm C Brown Pubs.

— Human Biology. 544p. (C). 1988. pap. write for info. (0-697-05340-7); student ed write for info. (0-697-06384-4); student ed write for info. (0-697-05341-5) Wm C Brown Pubs.

— Human Biology. 2nd ed. 576p. (C). 1989. pap. write for info. (0-697-05635-X); student ed write for info. (0-697-10194-0) Wm C Brown Pubs.

— Human Biology. 2nd ed. 576p. 1990. student ed write for info. (0-697-10195-9) Wm C Brown Pubs.

— Human Biology. 4th ed. 528p. 1994. student ed write for info. (0-697-24182-3) Wm C Brown Pubs.

— Human Biology. 4th ed. 528p. (C). 1994. pap. text ed. write for info. (0-697-15956-6) Wm C Brown Pubs.

— Human Biology. 4th ed. 224p. (C). 1994. student ed write for info. (0-697-15961-2); text ed. write for info. (0-697-15957-4); student ed write for info. (0-697-16236-2) Wm C Brown Pubs.

— Human Reproductive Biology. 2nd ed. 224p. (C). 1991. pap. write for info. (0-697-11805-3) Wm C Brown Pubs.

— Inquiry into Life. 6th ed. 848p. (C). 1990. pap. write for info. (0-697-13280-3); pap. write for info. (0-697-13748-1) Wm C Brown Pubs.

— Inquiry into Life. 6th ed. 848p. (C). 1991. text ed. write for info. (0-697-13747-3) Wm C Brown Pubs.

— Inquiry into Life, 2 vols. 6th ed. 864p. (C). 1991. student ed write for info. (0-697-13752-X) Wm C Brown Pubs.

— Inquiry into Life, 2 vols., I. 6th ed. 864p. 1991. boxed write for info. (0-697-10200-9) Wm C Brown Pubs.

— Inquiry into Life, 2 vols., I. 6th ed. 864p. (C). 1991. write for info. (0-697-13281-1) Wm C Brown Pubs.

— Inquiry into Life, 2 vols., II. 6th ed. 864p. 1991. student ed write for info. (0-697-13169-6) Wm C Brown Pubs.

— Inquiry into Life, 2 vols., II. 6th ed. 864p. (C). 1991. write for info. (0-697-13282-X) Wm C Brown Pubs.

— Inquiry into Life, 2 vols., Set. 6th ed. 864p. (C). 1991. write for info. (0-697-13574-8) Wm C Brown Pubs.

— Inquiry into Life with Student Study Art Notebook. 7th ed. (Illus.). 784p. (C). 1993. pap. text ed. write for info. (0-697-13680-9) Wm C Brown Pubs.

— Inquiry into Life with Student Study Art Notebook. 7th ed. (Illus.). 784p. (C). 1993. text ed. write for info. (0-697-13679-5) Wm C Brown Pubs.

— Inquiry into Life with Student Study Art Notebook. 7th ed. (Illus.). 784p. (C). 1993. Lab manual. student ed write for info. (0-697-13686-8); Study guide. student ed write for info. (0-697-13702-3); Case study wkbk., Critical Thinking. student ed write for info. (0-697-13699-X) Wm C Brown Pubs.

— Inquiry into Life with Student Study Art Notebook. 7th ed. (Illus.). 784p. 1994. Art study notebook. student ed write for info. (0-697-23117-8) Wm C Brown Pubs.

— Introduction to Biology & Student Study Art Notebook. 416p. (C). 1993. pap. text ed. write for info. (0-697-16626-0) Wm C Brown Pubs.

— Introduction to Biology & Student Study Art Notebook. 416p. (C). 1993. text ed. write for info. (0-697-21002-2) Wm C Brown Pubs.

— Introduction to Biology & Student Study Art Notebook. 416p. 1994. student ed write for info. (0-697-23170-4); write for info. (0-318-71645-3) Wm C Brown Pubs.

— Introduction to Biology & Student Study Art Notebook. 416p. (C). 1994. student ed write for info. (0-697-16879-4) Wm C Brown Pubs.

— Understanding Human Anatomy & Physiology. 368p. (C). 1991. student ed write for info. (0-697-12042-2); pap. write for info. (0-697-07856-6) Wm C Brown Pubs.

— Understanding Human Anatomy & Physiology. 2nd ed. 464p. (C). 1993. pap. text ed. write for info. (0-697-13671-X) Wm C Brown Pubs.

— Understanding Human Anatomy & Physiology. 2nd ed. 464p. (C). 1994. text ed. write for info. (0-697-22191-1); Study wkbk. student ed write for info. (0-697-13673-6) Wm C Brown Pubs.

Mader, Sylvia S. Human Biology. 3rd ed. 528p. (C). 1991. pap. text ed. write for info. (0-697-12333-2) Wm C Brown Pubs.

— Human Biology. 3rd ed. 528p. (C). 1991. text ed. write for info. (0-697-13837-2); student ed write for info. (0-697-12335-9) Wm C Brown Pubs.

— Human Biology. 3rd ed. 528p. (C). 1991. student ed write for info. (0-697-12336-7) Wm C Brown Pubs.

— Martha's Vineyard Nature Guide. (Illus.). 96p. (Orig.). 1985. pap. 7.99 (0-317-40346-X) Mader Enter.

Mader, T. R. Unnatural Wolf Transplant in Yellowstone National Park. (C). 1990. pap. text ed. 3.50 (0-944402-04-6) Cmmn Man Inst.

Mader, Thomas F. & Mader, Diane C. Understanding One Another: Communicating Interpersonally. 416p. (C). 1990. pap. write for info. (0-697-06779-3) Brown & Benchmark.

Mader, Troy R. The Death Sentence of AIDS: A Comprehensive Source Book of Quotes by the World's Leading Physicians, Scientists & Researchers. LC 87-72211. (Orig.). 1987. pap. 9.94 (0-944402-00-3) Cmmn Man Inst.

— Wolves & Humans in Conflict: A Pictorial History of Wolves in North America. (Illus.). (C). Date not set. text ed. 24.95 (0-944402-05-4) Cmmn Man Inst.

Madero, Francisco I. The Presidential Succession of 1910. Davis, Thomas, tr. (American University Studies: Ser. IX, Vol. 89). 307p. (C). 1990. text ed. 51.50 (0-8204-1250-3) P Lang Pubs.

Mades, Leonard, tr. see Donoso, Jose.

Madewell, Bruce R., jt. ed. see Theilen, Gordon H.

Madewell, Terry. Glory Holes: An Expert's Guide to Tennessee's Best Fishing. Reeser, Jacki, ed. (Illus.). 120p. (Orig.). 1985. pap. 9.95 (0-9615455-1-8) J T Pub Co.

— Terry Madewell's Catfishing from A to Z: A Manual of Modern Catfishing Techniques. Reeser, Jacki, ed. 52p. 1993. 8.00 (0-9615455-4-2) J T Pub Co.

Madey, jt. ed. see Newman.

Madey, Doren L., jt. auth. see Hill, Paul T.

Madey, J. M., et al, eds. Free Electron Generation of Extreme Ultraviolet Coherent Radiation (Brookhaven-OSA, 1983) AIP Conference Proceedings No. 118. LC 84-71539. (Optical Science & Engineering Ser.: No. 4). 319p. 1984. lib. bdg. 40.50 (0-88318-317-X) Am Inst Physics.

Madey, R., jt. auth. see Jaroniec, M.

Madey, T. E., jt. ed. see Yates, J. T.

Madge, John H. Origins of Scientific Sociology. LC 62-11855. 1967. pap. text ed. 16.95 (0-02-919710-4) Free Pr.

Madge, Nicola, et al. The National Childhood Encephalopathy Study: A 10-Year Follow-Up. (Illus.). 121p. (C). 1993. pap. 19.95 (0-521-45883-8) Cambridge U Pr.

Madge, P. Concise Guide to the JCT Insurance Clauses, 1986. (C). 1987. 110.00 (0-685-33723-5, Pub. by Witherby & Co UK) St Mut.

— Liability Policy Wording & Cover. 2nd ed. (C). 1973. 85.00 (0-685-32744-2, Pub. by Witherby & Co UK) St Mut.

Madge, P., jt. auth. see Eaglestone, F.

Madge, Peter. Civil Engineering Insurance & Bonding. (C). 1987. 175.00 (0-685-33733-2, Pub. by Witherby & Co UK) St Mut.

— Guide to the Indemnity & Insurance Aspects of Building Contracts. (C). 1989. 135.00 (0-685-32807-4, Pub. by Witherby & Co UK) St Mut.

— Liability Policy Wordings & Cover. 150p. 1973. 75.00 (0-948691-04-2, Pub. by Witherby & Co UK) St Mut.

Madge, Peter, ed. Civil Engineering Insurance & Bonding. 144p. 1987. 34.00 (0-7277-0371-4, Pub. by T Telford UK) Am Soc Civil Eng.

Madge, S. J. Domesday of Crown Lands. (Illus.). 499p. 1968. 39.50 (0-7146-1341-X, Pub. by F Cass Pubs UK) Intl Spec Bk.

Madge, Sidney J. Domesday of Crown Lands. LC 67-31560. (Illus.). xvii, 499p. 1968. reprint ed. 49.50 (0-678-05071-6) Kelley.

Madge, Sidney J., ed. Abstracts of Inquisitiones Post Mortem for Gloucestershire Returned into the Court of Chancery During the Plantagenet Period, Pt. IV: 20 Henry III to 29 Edward I, 1236-1300. (British Record Society Index Library Ser.: Vol. 30). 1972. reprint ed. pap. 19.00 (0-8115-1475-7) Periodicals Srv.

An Asterisk (*) at the beginning of an entry indicates that the title is appearing in BIP for the first time.

— Abstracts of Inquisitiones Post Mortem for the City of London Returned into the Court of Chancery During the Tudor Period, Pt. II: 4-9, Elizabeth, 1561-1577. (British Record Society Index Library Ser.: Vol. 26). 1972. reprint ed. pap. 19.00 (*0-8115-1471-4*) Periodicals Srv.

Madge, Steve. Waterfowl: An Identification Guide to the Ducks, Geese & Swans of the World. (Illus.). 288p. 1992. pap. 24.95 (*0-395-46726-8*) HM.

Madge, Steven. Crows & Jays: A Guide to the Crows, Jays, & Magpies of the World. (Illus.). 256p. 1994. 40.00 (*0-395-67171-X*) HM.

Madge, Tim, jt. auth. see Ramwell, Dave.

Madges, William. The Core of Christian Faith: D. F. Strauss & His Catholic Critics. (American University Studies: Theology & Religion: Ser. VII, Vol. 38). 224p. (C). 1988. text ed. 33.00 (*0-8204-0521-3*) P Lang Pubs.

Madges, William, jt. auth. see Hill, Brennan.

Madgett, Mary Ann. Poetic Feelings. (Illus.). 60p. 1995. pap. 12.95x (*0-9645227-9-9*) Madgett Pub. POETIC FEELINGS is a collection of poems about nature, love, death & caring. Includes the poem "A Tree" which can be found in an anthology, "Edge of Twilight." Also includes two poems: "Spoken Words" & "My Prayer" which will be in two anthologies coming out in the spring of '95. From the poem: "The Child Within," Mary Ann Madgett writes: "Look at me/ What do you see/ All the things/ that cannot be/ The hidden lines/ of dreams that's lost/ The tears that flow/ Which time has forgot" To Order: Madgett Publishing, 650 Castro Lane, Springdale, OH 45246, 513-671-0980. Special discount for 5 or more books.** ***Publisher Provided Annotation.

Madgett, Naomi L. Exits & Entrances. LC 77-91712. (Illus.). 69p. (YA). (gr. 9-12). 1978. per. 5.00 (*0-916418-13-8*) Lotus.

— Octavia & Other Poems. LC 87-51637. (Illus.). 117p. (Orig.). (YA). (gr. 9-12). 1988. pap. 8.00 (*0-88378-121-2*) Third World.

— Pink Ladies in the Afternoon. 2nd ed. LC 90-60605. 75p. (YA). (gr. 7-10). 1990. pap. 7.00 (*0-916418-78-2*) Lotus.

— Remembrances of Spring: Collected Early Poems. LC 93-34603. (Lotus Poetry Ser.: Vol. 1). 170p. 1993. 24.95 (*0-87013-345-4*) Mich St U Pr.

— Star by Star. 2nd ed. LC 77-143900. 61p. (YA). (gr. 7-12). 1970. reprint ed. per. 5.00 (*0-916418-00-6*) Lotus.

— A Student's Guide to Creative Writing. LC 79-93055. 134p. (C). 1980. pap. 11.00 (*0-916418-24-3*, Penway Bks) Lotus.

Madgett, Naomi L., ed. A Milestone Sampler: Fifteenth Anniversary Anthology. (Illus.). 130p. (Orig.). (YA). (gr. 9-12). 1988. per., pap. 9.00 (*0-916418-74-X*) Lotus.

Madgett, Naomi L., intro. Adam of Ife: Black Women in Praise of Black Men. LC 91-61410. (Illus.). 235p. (Orig.). 1992. pap. 15.00 (*0-916418-80-4*) Lotus.

Madgulkar, Vyankatesh. The Winds of Fire. Kale, Pramod, tr. 113p. 1975. pap. 2.50 (*0-88253-693-1*) Ind-US Inc.

Madgwick, P. J. Introduction to British Politics. 3rd ed. (C). 1989. pap. 29.00 (*0-09-153561-1*, Pub. by S Thornes UK) Dufour.

— A New Introduction to British Politics. 448p. (Orig.). 1994. pap. 37.50 (*0-7487-1592-4*, Pub. by Stanley Thornes UK) Trans-Atl Phila.

Madgwick, Wendy. Animaze! A Collection of Amazing Nature Mazes. LC 91-46892. (Illus.). 40p. (J). (ps-3). 1992. 13.00 (*0-679-82665-3*) Knopf Bks Yng Read.

— Behold! Spot-the-Difference Bible Stories. LC 93-5506. (Illus.). 48p. (J). (gr. k-3). 1994. 12.00 (*0-679-85333-2*) Random Bks Yng Read.

— Cacti & Other Succulents. LC 91-14934. (Green World Ser.). (Illus.). 48p. (J). (gr. 5-9). 1992. lib. bdg. 22.13 (*0-8114-2737-4*) Raintree Steck-V.

— Citymaze! A Collection of Amazing City Mazes. (Illus.). 40p. (J). (gr. 3 up). 1995. pap. 7.95 (*1-56294-846-6*) Millbrook Pr.

— Flowering Plants. LC 90-9572. (Green World Ser.). (Illus.). 48p. (J). (gr. 5-9). 1990. lib. bdg. 22.13 (*0-8114-2730-7*) Raintree Steck-V.

— Fungi & Lichens. LC 90-9571. (Green World Ser.). (Illus.). 48p. (J). (gr. 5-9). 1990. lib. bdg. 22.13 (*0-8114-2728-5*) Raintree Steck-V.

***Madgwick, Wendy & Courtney, Don.** Citymaze! A Collection of Amazing City Mazes. LC 94-26291. (Illus.). 40p. (YA). (gr. 8 up). 1995. lib. bdg. 12.90 (*1-56294-561-0*) Millbrook Pr.

Madgwick, Wendy, jt. auth. see Huddleston, Ruth.

Madhava, K. G. Western Karnataka: Its Agrarian Relations A.D. 1500-1800. (C). 1991. 29.50 (*81-7013-073-5*, Pub. by Navarang II) S Asia.

Madhava-Vidyaranya. Sankara-Dig-Vijaya: The Traditional Life of Sri Sankaracharya. Tapasyananda, Swami, tr. 1979. pap. 3.95 (*0-87481-484-7*, Pub. by Ramakrishna Math II) Vedanta Pr.

Madhavan, A. More Poems. (Redbird Ser.). 1976. 8.00 (*0-89253-698-5*); pap. text ed. 4.80 (*0-89253-083-9*) Ind-US Inc.

— Poems. 8.00 (*0-89253-772-8*); 4.00 (*0-89253-773-6*) Ind-US Inc.

Madhavan, C. E., jt. ed. see Nori, K. V.

Madhavananda, tr. Uddhava Gita or Last Message of Sri Krishna. 425p. pap. 5.95 (*0-87481-211-9*, Pub. by Advaita Ashrama II) Vedanta Pr.

Madhavananda & Majumdar, Ramesh, eds. Great Women of India. 551p. 1987. 15.95 (*0-87481-111-2*, Pub. by Advaita Ashrama II) Vedanta Pr.

Madhavananda, Swami, tr. Brhadaranyaka Upanishad. 1965. Bilingual ed. pap. 7.95 (*0-87481-063-9*, Pub. by Advaita Ashrama II) Vedanta Pr.

— Minor Upanishads. 1970. pap. 2.00 (*0-87481-061-2*, Pub. by Advaita Ashrama II) Vedanta Pr.

Madhavananda, Swami, tr. see Adhvarindra, Dharmaraja.

Madhavananda, Swami, tr. see Shankara.

Madhaven, C. E., ed. Foundations of Software Technology & Theoretical Computer Science. (Lecture Notes in Computer Science Ser.: Vol. 405). xiii, 339p. 1989. pap. 40.00 (*0-387-52048-1*) Spr-Verlag.

***Madhavi, et al.** Food Antioxidants. (Food Science & Technology Ser.). 708p. 1995. write for info. (*0-8247-9351-X*) Dekker.

Madhavji, N., et al, eds. SDE & F1: Proceedings of the First International Conference on System Development Environments & Factories, Berlin, May 1989. 240p. (C). 1990. pap. text ed. 300.00 (*0-273-08829-7*, Pub. by Pitman Pubng UK) St Mut.

Madhere, Serge. Piti Piti Plen Kay. 90p. 1987. pap. text ed. write for info. (*1-881686-00-0*) Madhere.

— Silo Sajes: Prensip Filozofi Lavi. 103p. 1992. pap. text ed. write for info. (*1-881686-02-7*) Madhere.

— Tezen. 72p. 1989. pap. text ed. write for info. (*1-881686-01-9*) Madhere.

Madhihassan, S. Indian Alchemy or Rasayana. (C). 1991. 12.50 (*81-208-0788-X*, Pub. by Motilal Banarsidass II) S Asia.

Madhok, Bal R. Kashmir: The Storm Center of the World. 280p. 1992. 25.95 (*0-9611614-8-5*); pap. 17.95 (*0-9611614-9-3*) A Ghosh.

Madhok, Balraj. Bungling in Kashmir. 178p. 1975. pap. 2.85 (*0-88253-695-8*) Ind-US Inc.

Madhok, R., et al. Blood, Blood Products, & HIV. 2nd ed. 256p. 1993. 69.00 (*0-412-40400-1*) Chapman & Hall.

Madhok, R., et al, eds. Blood, Blood Products, & AIDS. LC 87-21530. (Contemporary Medicine & Public Health Ser.). 244p. 1988. text ed. 55.00x (*0-8018-3608-5*) Johns Hopkins.

Madhu Bazaz Wangu. Hinduism. (World Religions Ser.). (Illus.). 128p. (YA). (gr. 7-12). 1991. 17.95 (*0-8160-2447-2*) Facts on File.

Madhu, Swaminathan. Linear Circuits Analysis. (Illus.). 850p. 1988. text ed. write for info. (*0-318-62359-5*) P-H.

Madhubuti, Haki R. Black Men, Obsolete, Single, Dangerous? Essays in Discovery, Solution & Hope. LC 89-51325. 1990. 29.95 (*0-88378-134-4*); pap. 14.95 (*0-88378-135-2*) Third World.

— Book of Life. 1992. pap. 7.95 (*0-88378-132-8*) Third World.

— Claiming Earth: Race, Rape, Ritual, Richness in America & the Search for Enlightened Empowerment. 175p. 1994. 19.95 (*0-88378-095-X*) Third World.

— Don't Cry, Scream. 1992. pap. 8.00 (*0-88378-016-X*) Third World.

— Earthquake & Sunrise Missions. 1987. pap. 8.95 (*0-88378-109-3*) Third World.

— Enemies: The Clash of Races. LC 77-12275. (Orig.). 1978. pap. 12.95 (*0-88378-073-9*) Third World.

Madhubuti, Haki R., pseud. From Plan to Planet: Life Studies: The Need for Afrikan Minds & Institutions. LC 72-94350. (Orig.). 1992. pap. 7.95 (*0-88378-066-6*) Third World.

Madhubuti, Haki R. Killing Memory, Seeking Ancestors. LC 85-82523. 58p. (Orig.). (YA). (gr. 9-12). 1987. per. 8.00 (*0-916418-63-4*) Lotus.

— Killing Memory, Seeking Ancestors. (Orig.). 1992. pap. 8.00 (*0-88378-093-3*) Third World.

— Kwanzaa: A Progressive & Uplifting African-American Holiday. 4th ed. (Orig.). 1987. reprint ed. pap. 2.50 (*0-88378-012-7*) Third World.

Madhubuti, Haki R., ed. Black Books Bulletin - Words Work: Black Intellectual Mercenaries. 80p. 1993. pap. 4.95 (*0-685-69762-2*) Third World.

— Confusion by Any Other Name: Essays Exploring the Negative Impact of the Blackman's Guide to Understanding the Blackwoman. 1992. 3.95 (*0-88378-148-4*) Third World.

— Say That the River Turns: The Impact of Gwendolyn Brooks. (Orig.). 1987. pap. 8.95 (*0-88378-118-2*) Third World.

Madhubuti, Haki R., intro. Why L. A. Happened: Implications of the '92 Los Angeles Rebellion. LC 92-63015. 287p. (Orig.). 1993. pap. 14.95 (*0-88378-094-1*) Third World.

Madhubuti, Safisha. Story of Kwanzaa. (J). (gr. 1). 1989. reprint ed. pap. 5.95 (*0-88378-001-1*) Third World.

Madhukar, ed. Growth of Compound Semiconductor Structures. 1988. 45.00 (*0-89252-979-2*, 944) SPIE.

Madhukar, A., ed. Growth of Semiconductor Structures & High Tc Thin Films on Semiconductors. 1990. 53.00 (*0-8194-0336-9*, VOL. 1285) SPIE.

Madhuri, Desai, ed. see Gordon, Douglas H.

Madhvacarya. Srila Madhvacarya's Sri Tattva-Muktavali or Mayavada-Sata-Dusani: The Pearl Necklace of Truths, or 100 Refutations of the Mayavada Fallacy. Kusakrathadasa, tr. (Krsna Library: Vol. 13). 110p. (Orig.). (C). 1988. pap. 8.00 (*0-944833-12-8*) Krsna Inst.

Madianou, Gefou, ed. Alcohol, Gender & Culture. 208p. 1992. 69.95 (*0-415-08667-1*, A9642) Routledge.

Madiebo, Alexander. Memoirs of a Biafran General. LC 75-18600. 350p. 1976. 20.00 (*0-89388-206-2*) Okpaku Communications.

***Madigan.** Dorothy Canfield Fisher. 1995. 24.95 (*0-8057-7645-1*, Twayne) Macmillan.

— Prehospital Emergency Drugs & Pocket Reference. 200p. 1990. 12.95 (*0-8016-3375-3*) Mosby Yr Bk.

Madigan, Arthur, tr. see Alexander of Aphrodisias.

Madigan, Brian C. & Cooper, Frederick A. The Temple of Apollo Bassitas, Vol. 2: The Sculpture. LC 92-23979. (Illus.). 144p. 1992. 50.00 (*0-87661-947-2*) Am Sch Athens.

Madigan, Carol & Ellwood, Ann, eds. Life's Big Instruction Book: The Almanac of Indispensable Information. 912p. 1995. 29.95 (*0-446-51757-7*) Warner Bks.

***Madigan, Carol O. & Elmwood, Ann.** Life's Big Instruction Book: The Almanac of Indispensable Information. 1995. pap. write for info. (*0-446-67157-6*) Warner Bks.

Madigan, Carol O. & Elwood, Ann. Test Your Nineteen Eighties Literacy. 288p. 1990. pap. 8.95 (*0-685-32623-3*) P-H.

Madigan, Carol O., jt. auth. see Elwood, Ann.

Madigan, John E. Manual of Equine Neonatal Medicine. 2nd rev. ed. (Illus.). 363p. 1994. pap. text ed. 29.95 (*0-9629517-0-6*) Live Oak CA.

Madigan, Lee & Gamble, Nancy. The Second Rape: Society's Continued Betrayal of the Victim. 160p. 1991. text ed. 19.95 (*0-669-27189-6*) Free Pr.

Madigan, Margaret. Philosophers: Exploring Ideas Through the Study of Six Great Lives. rev. ed. Patton, Sally J., ed. 120p. (gr. 5-12). 1989. reprint ed. pap. text ed. 14.95 (*0-913705-34-9*) Zephyr Pr AZ.

Madigan, Mark J., ed. Keeping Fires Night & Day: Selected Letters of Dorothy Canfield Fisher. (Illus.). 384p. (C). 1993. 34.95 (*0-8262-0884-3*) U of Mo Pr.

Madigan, Michael T., jt. auth. see Brock, Thomas D.

Madigan, Mike, jt. auth. see Wright, George.

Madigan, Patrick. Aristotle & His Modern Critics: The Uses of Tragedy in the Nontragic Vision. LC 90-72044. 120p. 1992. 22.50 (*0-940866-13-7*) U Scranton Pr.

— Christian Revelation & the Completion of the Aristotelian Revolution. 136p. (Orig.). (C). 1988. lib. bdg. 34.00 (*0-8191-7090-9*); pap. text ed. 19.50 (*0-8191-7091-7*) U Pr of Amer.

— The Modern Project to Rigor: Descartes to Nietzsche. LC 85-22564. (Illus.). 224p. (Orig.). (C). 1986. lib. bdg. 49.50 (*0-8191-5080-0*) U Pr of Amer.

— Penance, Contemplation, & Service: Pivotal Experiences of Christian Spirituality. 232p. (Orig.). 1994. pap. text ed. 14.95 (*0-8146-5911-X*, M Glazier) Liturgical Pr.

Madigan, Patrick, tr. see Baumert, Norbert.

Madigan, Patrick, tr. see Larere, Philippe.

Madigan, Richard E. Taxation of the Shipping Industry. 2nd ed. LC 82-7470. 108p. 1982. text ed. 20.00 (*0-87033-292-9*) Cornell Maritime.

Madigan, Shawn. Spirituality: Rooted in Liturgy. 1989. pap. 13.95 (*0-912405-56-2*) Pastoral Pr.

Madigan, Tim. See No Evil: Blind Devotion & Bloodshed in David Koresh's Holy War. (Illus.). 300p. (Orig.). 1993. pap. 11.95 (*1-56530-063-7*) Summit TX.

Madigan, Timothy J., ed. see Kurtz, Paul.

Madigan, Tom. Boss: The Bill Stroppe Story. (Illus.). 204p. 1984. pap. 13.95 (*0-933506-13-9*) Darwin Pubns.

Madigan, Tom, ed. The Dick Cepek Off-Road Handbook. (Illus.). 224p. 1984. pap. 9.95 (*0-933506-11-2*) Darwin Pubns.

Madill Record Staff. Marshall County, Oklahoma. (Illus.). 348p. 1988. 60.00 (*0-88107-109-9*) Curtis Media.

Madill, W., jt. auth. see Bartlett, R. E.

Madin, Douglas L., ed. The Psychology of Learning & Motivation, Vol. 30. (Illus.). 328p. 1993. text ed. 69.95 (*0-12-543330-1*) Acad Pr.

***Madina, Nuri.** Renaissance: 2000 & Beyond. 44p. (Orig.). 1994. pap. 3.00 (*0-9643333-3-3*) BAPP.

Madinaveitia, Horacio. La Gran Aventura de Don Roberto. (Illus.). 32p. (SPA.). (J). (gr. k-4). 1992. lib. bdg. 13.95 (*1-879567-02-4*, Valeria Bks) Wonder Well.

— Sir Robert's Little Outing. (Illus.). 32p. (J). (gr. k-4). 1991. lib. bdg. 13.95 (*1-879567-01-6*, Valeria Bks); pap. text ed. 7.95 (*1-879567-00-8*, Valeria Bks) Wonder Well.

Madine, Margaret W. Fondue Cooking. LC 77-95289. 1970. 5.95 (*0-88351-010-3*) Test Recipe.

Madis, George. The Winchester Book. 3rd ed. LC 79-8991. (Illus.). 1979. 45.00 (*0-910156-03-4*) Art & Ref.

— Winchester Dates of Manufacture. (Illus.). 1984. 4.95 (*0-910156-05-0*) Art & Ref.

— The Winchester Era. (Illus.). 1985. 14.95 (*0-910156-08-5*) Art & Ref.

— The Winchester Handbook. (Illus.). 320p. (YA). 1981. 19.50 (*0-910156-04-2*) Art & Ref.

— The Winchester Model 12. (Illus.). 1982. 19.95 (*0-910156-06-9*) Art & Ref.

***Madisetti, Vijay.** VLSI Digital Signal Processors: An Introduction to Rapid Prototyping & Design Synthesis. 412p. 1994. 64.95 (*0-7506-9406-8*) Buttrwrth-Heinemann.

Madisetti, Vijay, ed. Modeling & Simulation on Microcomputers, 1990. 138p. 1990. pap. 40.00 (*0-911801-64-2*, MSM90) Soc Computer Sim.

Madisetti, Vijay, et al, eds. Advances in Parallel & Distributed Simulation. (Simulation Ser.: Vol. 23, No. 1). 250p. 1991. 60.00 (*0-911801-78-2*, SS23-1) Soc Computer Sim.

— MASCOTS '94: Second International Workshop on Modeling, Analysis, & Simulation. LC 93-80981. 440p. 1994. text ed. 80.00 (*0-8186-5292-6*, 5292) IEEE Comp Soc.

Madison. Real Estate Finance. 1991. 54.00 (*0-316-54363-2*) Little.

— San Francisco on a Shoestring: The Intelligent Traveler's & Native's Guide to Budget Living. 1995. pap. text ed. 7.95 (*0-912125-07-1*) L E Madison.

Madison, Anna, jt. ed. see Smith, Nick L.

Madison, Arnold. Drugs & You. rev. ed. LC 82-3450. (Illus.). 80p. (J). (gr. 4 up). 1982. lib. bdg. 9.79 (*0-671-43986-3*, Julian Messner); pap. 4.95 (*0-671-49477-5*, Julian Messner) Silver Burdett Pr.

— Drugs & You. rev. ed. Steltenpohl, Jane, ed. (Illus.). 128p. (J). (gr. 4-6). 1990. lib. bdg. 13.98 (*0-671-69147-3*, Julian Messner); pap. 5.95 (*0-671-69148-1*, Julian Messner) Silver Burdett Pr.

— How the Colonists Lived. (YA). (gr. 7 up). 1980. 8.95 (*0-679-20685-X*) McKay.

Madison, Arnold, jt. auth. see Wyndham, Lee.

Madison, Bernice Q. Social Welfare in the Soviet Union. xxvi, 298p. 1968. 39.50 (*0-8047-0654-9*) Stanford U Pr.

Madison, Brian. Alleged Imagery Errors. (C). 1992. pap. text ed. 10.95 (*0-913412-56-2*) Brandon Hse.

— Rectification of Memory-Errors. (C). 1991. pap. text ed. 9.99 (*0-913412-57-0*) Brandon Hse.

Madison Center for Education Staff. Common Sense Guide to American Colleges, 1993-1994. 666p. (Orig.). Date not set. pap. 14.95 (*0-8191-8734-8*) Madison Bks UPA.

Madison, Charles L., jt. auth. see Clark, John B.

Madison, Charles L., jt. auth. see Gauthier, Sharon V.

***Madison County Farm Bureau Women's Committee.** Cookbook 25 Years: Women of the Farm Bureau. 490p. 1995. text ed. 18.95 (*0-9644914-1-9*); pap. text ed. 16.95 (*0-9644914-0-0*) Madison Cty Farm Bur.

***Madison, D. Soyini.** The Woman That I Am: The Literature & Culture of Contemporary Women of Color. 752p. 1993. pap. text ed. 28.00 (*0-312-07956-7*) St Martin.

Madison, D. Soyini, ed. The Woman That I Am: The Literature & Culture of Women of Color. 720p. 1993. 35.00 (*0-312-10012-4*) St Martin.

Madison, Dahlia L. Guaranteed Home Based Business Opportunities. LC 89-90653. 100p. (Orig.). 1989. pap. 12.95 (*0-927043-00-9*) M W Pub.

Madison, Deborah. Savory Way. 1990. 27.50 (*0-553-05780-4*) Bantam.

Madison, Deborah, jt. auth. see Brown, Edward E.

Madison, G. B. The Hermeneutics of Postmodernity: Figures & Themes. LC 87-46089. (Studies in Phenomenology & Existential Philosophy). 224p. 1989. 35.00 (*0-253-32190-5*); pap. text ed. 12.95 (*0-253-20617-0*, MB-617) Ind U Pr.

— The Logic of Liberty. LC 85-27278. (Contributions in Philosophy Ser.: No. 30). 307p. 1986. text ed. 49.95 (*0-313-25018-9*, MLG/, Greenwood Pr) Greenwood.

— The Phenomenology of Merleau-Ponty: A Search for the Limits of Consciousness, Vol. 3. LC 84-5080. (Series in Continental Thought: Vol. 3). xxxvi, 345p. 1981. pap. text ed. 16.95x (*0-8214-0644-2*) Ohio U Pr.

Madison, Gary B., intro. Working Through Derrida. (Studies in Phenomenology & Existential Philosophy). 294p. (Orig.). 1993. 49.95 (*0-8101-1054-7*); pap. 19.95 (*0-8101-1079-2*) Northwestern U Pr.

***Madison, James.** CNC Machining Handbook. (Illus.). 280p. (C). 1995. text ed. 38.95 (*0-8311-3064-4*) Indus Pr.

— The Debates in the Federal Convention of 1787, 2 vols., Set. LC 86-63352. 677p. 1987. 72.95 (*0-87975-388-9*) Prometheus Bks.

— Federalist, No. 10. (Reprint Series in Social Sciences). (C). 1993. reprint ed. pap. text ed. 1.00 (*0-8290-3200-2*, PS-397) Irvington.

— Federalist, No. 51. (Reprint Series in Social Sciences). (C). 1993. reprint ed. pap. text ed. 1.00 (*0-8290-3708-X*, PS-396) Irvington.

— Journal of the Federal Convention. Scott, E. H., ed. LC 78-119938. (Select Bibliographies Reprint Ser.). 1977. reprint ed. 36.95 (*0-8369-5381-9*) Ayer.

— The Mind of the Founder: Sources of the Political Thought of James Madison. rev. ed. Meyers, Marvin, ed. LC 80-54466. 506p. 1981. pap. 20.00 (*0-87451-201-8*) U Pr of New Eng.

— Notes of Debates in the Federal Convention of 1787. rev. ed. LC 84-5080. xxiii, 695p. 1985. 50.00 (*0-8214-0777-5*) Ohio U Pr.

— Notes of Debates in the Federal Convention of 1787. 720p. 1987. reprint ed. pap. 16.95 (*0-393-30405-1*) Norton.

— The Papers of James Madison, 10 vols. Hutchinson, William T. & Rachal, William M., eds. Incl. Vol. 5. 1 August-31 December 1782. LC 62-9114. 1967. lib. bdg. 25.00x (*0-226-36297-3*); 1 January 1783-30 April, 1783. LC 62-9114. 548p. 1969. lib. bdg. 25.00x (*0-226-36298-1*); May 3, 1783-February 20, 1784. LC 62-9114. 1971. lib. bdg. 25.00x (*0-226-36300-7*); LC 62-9114. (Illus.). write for info. (*0-318-56067-4*) U Ch Pr.

— The Papers of James Madison: August 1, 1801-February 28, 1802. Hackett, Mary A. et al, eds. (Secretary of State Ser.: Vol. 2). 576p. (C). 1993. text ed. 60.00 (*0-8139-1403-5*) U Pr of Va.

— The Papers of James Madison: March 1789 to January 1790. with a supplement 24 October 1775-24 January 1789. Rutland, Robert A. & Hobson, Charles F., eds. LC 62-9114. (Vol. 12). 498p. 1979. 37.50 (*0-8139-0803-5*) U Pr of Va.

— The Papers of James Madison: Vol. 11, 7 March 1788 to 1 March 1789. Rutland, Robert A. & Hobson, Charles F., eds. LC 62-9114. 471p. 1977. 37.50 (*0-8139-0739-X*) U Pr of Va.

— The Papers of James Madison: 1 March-30 September 1809. Rutland, Robert A. & Mason, Thomas A., eds. LC 83-6953. (Presidential Ser.: Vol. 1). 414p. 1984. 37.50 (*0-8139-0991-0*) U Pr of Va.

— The Papers of James Madison: 1 October 1809 - 2 November 1810. Stagg, J. C. et al, eds. (Presidential Ser.: Vol. 2). 681p. (C). 1992. text ed. 50.00 (*0-8139-1345-4*) U Pr of Va.

— The Papers of James Madison, Vol. 13: Twenty January Seventeen Ninety to Thirty-One March Seventeen Ninety-One. Rutland, Robert A. & Hobson, Charles F., eds. LC 62-9144. 423p. 1981. 37.50 (*0-8139-0861-2*) U Pr of Va.

— The Papers of James Madison, Vol. 14: April 6, 1791 to March 16, 1793. Rutland, Robert A. & Mason, Thomas A., eds. LC 62-9144. 495p. 1983. 37.50 (*0-8139-0955-4*) U Pr of Va.

— The Papers of James Madison, Vol. 16: Twenty-Seven April 1795-27 March 1797. Stagg, John C. et al, eds. LC 62-9114. (Papers of James Madison). 576p. 1989. text ed. 45.00 (*0-8139-1212-1*) U Pr of Va.

— The Papers of James Madison, Vol. 17: 31 March 1797-3 March 1801, with a Supplement. Mattern, David B. et al, eds. (Papers of James Madison). 656p. 1991. 47.50 (*0-8139-1288-1*) U Pr of Va.

— The Virginia Report of 1799-1800, Touching the Alien & Sedition Laws. Bd. with Virginia Resolutions of December 21, 1789. LC 75-107626. LC 75-107626. (Civil Liberties in American History Ser.). 1970. reprint ed. Set lib. bdg. 35.00 (*0-306-71860-X*) Da Capo.

M

Madison, James, et al. The Federalist Papers. Kramnick, Isaac, ed. 528p. 1987. pap. 10.95 (*0-14-044495-5*, Penguin Classics) Viking Penguin.

— The Papers of James Madison. Brugger, Robert J. et al, eds. LC 85-29516. (Secretary of State Series, 4 March-31 July 1801: Vol. 1). xxx, 526p. 1987. 37.50 (*0-8139-1093-5*) U Pr of Va.

— The Papers of James Madison Volume 15: March 24, 1793-April 20, 1795. Rutland, Robert A. et al, eds. LC 62-9114. xxii, 561p. 1985. 47.50 (*0-8139-1059-5*) U Pr of Va.

Madison, James H. Eli Lilly: A Life, 1885-1977. (Illus.). 342p. 1989. 29.95 (*0-87195-047-2*) Ind Hist Soc.

— Indiana Through Tradition & Change: A History of the Hoosier State & Its People, 1920-1945. (History of Indiana Ser.). 454p. 1982. pap. 9.95 (*0-87195-042-1*) Ind Hist Soc.

— Indiana Through Tradition & Change: A History of the Hoosier State & Its People, 1920-1945. (History of Indiana Ser.). 454p. 1982. 27.50 (*0-87195-043-X*) Ind Hist Soc.

— Indiana to Eighteen Sixteen: The Colonial Period. (History of Indiana Ser.). (Illus.). 520p. 1994. reprint ed. pap. 17.95 (*0-87195-109-6*) Ind Hist Soc.

— The Indiana Way: A State History. LC 85-45071. (Illus.). 364p. 1986. 25.00 (*0-253-32999-X*); pap. 14.95 (*0-253-20609-X*) Ind Hist Soc.

Madison, James H., ed. Heartland: Comparative Histories of the Midwestern States. LC 87-45835. (Midwestern History & Culture Ser.). 318p. 1988. 29.95 (*0-253-31423-2*); pap. 12.95 (*0-253-20576-X*) Ind U Pr.

— Wendell Willkie: Hoosier Internationalist. LC 91-12758. (Illus.). 214p. 1992. text ed. 19.95 (*0-253-33619-8*) Ind U Pr.

Madison, James T., ed. see Venkstern, Tat'kilana.

Madison, Joyce. Great Hoaxes, Swindles, Scandals, Cons, Stings, & Scams. 240p. 1992. 4.99 (*0-451-17361-9*, Sig) NAL-Dutton.

Madison, Kathy. Fun Guide to Anchorage. Lauzen, Elizabeth, ed. (Illus.). 32p. (Orig.). (J). (gr. 1-6). 1987. pap. 3.50 (*0-942553-00-4*) Madison Aves.

Madison, Lloyd. Bad Medicine. large type ed. (Linford Western Library). 304p. 1986. pap. 11.95 (*0-7089-6282-3*, Linford) Ulverscroft.

— Boomer Sawbones. large type ed. (Linford Western Library). 304p. 1986. pap. 11.95 (*0-7089-6279-3*, Linford) Ulverscroft.

— Bullet Breed. large type ed. (Linford Western Library). 304p. 1986. pap. 11.95 (*0-7089-6291-2*, Linford) Ulverscroft.

— The Man from Rio Grande. large type ed. (Linford Western Library). 272p. 1987. pap. 11.95 (*0-7089-6346-3*, Linford) Ulverscroft.

— The Rainmaker of Deadman. large type ed. (Linford Western Library). 304p. 1987. pap. 11.95 (*0-7089-6353-6*, Linford) Ulverscroft.

Madison, Louis. San Francisco on a Shoestring. 7th ed. 176p. 1991. pap. 6.95 (*0-912125-05-5*) L E Madison.

Madison, Louis E. San Francisco on a Shoestring. 8th ed. 1993. pap. 7.95 (*0-912125-06-3*) L E Madison.

— San Francisco on a Shoestring: The Intelligent Traveler's & Native's Guide to Budget Living... 6th ed. 176p. 1990. pap. 6.95 (*0-912125-04-7*) L E Madison.

***Madison, Lucy F.** Joan of Arc. LC 94-23684. (Illus.). (J). 1995. 12.99 (*0-517-12203-0*, Child Classics) Random Hse Value.

Madison, Malcolm. Numerology. 23p. 1985. reprint ed. spiral bd. 3.85 (*0-7873-1243-6*) Mokelumne.

Madison, Maria. The Encounter. 176p. 1990. pap. 4.95 (*0-929654-48-X*, 78) Blue Moon Bks.

— The Reckoning. 1993. pap. 5.95 (*1-56201-042-5*) Blue Moon Bks.

— What Love? 1992. pap. 5.95 (*0-929654-86-2*, 117) Blue Moon Bks.

Madison, Michael, jt. ed. see Chapman, Michael W.

Madison, Michael T. & Dwyer, Jeffrey R. Law of Real Estate Financing. LC 80-53430. 916p. 1981. Supplement, 1991-2. write for info. (*0-685-05307-5*) Warren Gorham & Lamont.

— Law of Real Estate Financing. suppl. ed. LC 80-53430. 916p. 1981. Cumulative supplementation, semi-annually. 120.00 (*0-88262-516-0*) Warren Gorham & Lamont.

— Law of Real Estate Financing. suppl. ed. LC 80-53430. 916p. 1991. Supplement, 1991-1. 70.00 (*0-685-55628-X*) Warren Gorham & Lamont.

Madison, R. Allan, ed. see Denys, Peter.

Madison, Richard. The L. A. Loop: Exploring Los Angeles by Car. LC 92-43867. (Illus.). 64p. (Orig.). 1993. pap. 12.95 (*0-9635143-6-9*) Fun Pubns.

— Signs of Jesus' Return. Eldredge, A., ed. 70p. (Orig.). 1994. pap. 8.95 (*1-885857-00-4*) Four Wnds Pubng.

***Madison, Ron.** Ned & Fred. 12p. (J). (ps-1). 1994. pap. 1.95 (*1-887206-02-7*) Dr R Madison.

— Ned & Fred & Ned, Fred & Friend, 2 bks., Set. (J). (ps-1). 1995. audio, pap. 9.95 (*1-887206-08-6*) Dr R Madison.

— Ned & Fred Set. (J). (ps-1). 1995. audio, pap. 24.95 (*1-887206-06-X*) Dr R Madison.

— Ned, Fred & Friend. 12p. (J). (ps-1). 1995. pap. 1.95 (*1-887206-03-5*) Dr R Madison.

— Ned's Friend. 12p. (J). (ps-1). 1994. pap. 1.95 (*1-887206-01-9*) Dr R Madison.

— Ned's Friend Set. (J). (ps-1). 1995. audio, pap. 19.95 (*1-887206-05-1*) Dr R Madison.

— Ned's Head. 12p. (J). (ps-1). 1993. pap. 1.95 (*1-887206-00-0*) Dr R Madison.

— Ned's Head & Ned's Friend, 2 bks., Set. (J). (ps-1). 1995. audio, pap. 9.95 (*1-887206-07-8*) Dr R Madison.

— Ned's Head Set. (J). (ps-1). 1993. audio, pap. 24.95 (*1-887206-04-3*) Dr R Madison.

Madison-Shaw, Tamara. Sistuh's Sermon on the Mount: The Blood Still Boils. LC XLittlebook. 42p. (Orig.). 1993. 6.00 (*0-940880-43-1*) Open Hand.

Madison Square Pr. Staff. Corporate & Communications Design Annual, No. 2. 1990. pap. 19.95 (*0-8230-5847-6*) Madison Square.

Madison Square Press Staff. International Logos & Trademarks of the 1908s I. 1991. 45.00 (*0-8230-6093-4*) Madison Square.

Madix, Robert J., ed. Surface Reactions. LC 93-49867. (Surface Sciences Ser.: Vol. 34). 1994. 69.00 (*0-387-57605-3*) Spr-Verlag.

Madjar, H., et al, eds. Breast Ultrasound Update. (Illus.). x, 376p. 1995. 100.00 (*3-8055-5860-0*) S Karger.

Madjenovic, Paul J., ed. How to Achieve Credit Card Merchant Status. 64p. 1994. pap. 30.00 (*0-915344-50-5*) Todd Pubns.

***Madkins, Jerry.** Corporate Social Responsibility. 106p. (C). 1994. 18.20 (*1-56870-140-3*) RonJon Pub.

***Madl, F., ed.** The Law of the European Economic Community: Enterprises, Economic Competition & the Economic Function of the State in the Process of Economic Integration. 329p. (C). 1978. 60.00x (*963-05-1330-7*, Pub. by Akad Kiado HU) St Mut.

Madl, Linda. A Tender Magic. Tolley, Carolyn, ed. 288p. (Orig.). 1993. mass mkt. 4.99 (*0-671-73391-5*) PB.

Madland, Helga S., jt. ed. see Leidner, Alan C.

Madlansacay, Len T., jt. auth. see Lewis, Loida N.

Madlem, Peter. Real Estate Securities: The REIT Investment Handbook. 96p. (Orig.). 1995. pap. 12.95 (*0-942641-60-4*) Intl Pub IL.

Madlem, Peter, jt. auth. see Cappiello, Frank.

***Madlener, Josef.** The Philosophy of Love. 1995. 16.95 (*0-533-11369-5*) Vantage.

Madler, Trudy. Why Did Grandma Die? LC 79-23892. (Life & Living from a Child's Point of View Ser.). (Illus.). 32p. (J). (gr. k-6). 1980. lib. bdg. 19.97 (*0-8172-1354-6*) Raintree Steck-V.

— Why Did Grandma Die? (J). (ps-3). 1993. pap. 3.95 (*0-8114-7156-X*) Raintree Steck-V.

Madnick, Stuart E., ed. The Strategic Use of Information Technology. (Executive Bookshelf-Sloan Management Review Ser.). (Illus.). 220p. 1987. 25.00 (*0-19-505048-7*) OUP.

Madnick, Stuart E. & Donovan, John J. Operating Systems. (Illus.). 640p. (C). 1974. text ed. write for info. (*0-07-039455-5*) McGraw.

Mado, Michio. The Animals: Selected Poems. HRM the Empress of Japan, tr. LC 92-10356. (Illus.). 48p. (ENG & JPN.). (J). (ps up). 1992. text ed. 16.95 (*0-689-50574-4*, McElderry) S&S Childrens.

Madoc-Jones, Beryl, jt. ed. see Coates, Jennifer.

Madocks, Susan, tr. see Pedrocco, Filippo.

Madoff. Bacterial L-Forms. (Microbiology Ser.: Vol. 17). 344p. 1986. 150.00 (*0-8247-7480-9*) Dekker.

Madoff, Sarabelle. Mycoplasma & the L Forms of Bacteria. (Illus.). 116p. 1971. text ed. 109.00 (*0-677-14790-2*) Gordon & Breach.

Madoff, Steven H. Michael Gitlin: Sculptures Drawings 1982-1985. (Illus.). 23p. (Orig.). 1985. pap. 10.00 (*0-913263-11-7*) Exit Art.

Madokoro, Hisako. The Adventures of Buster the Puppy, 6 vols., Set. (Illus.). 96p. (J). (gr. k-2). 1991. lib. bdg. 103.60 (*0-8368-0488-0*) Gareth Stevens Inc.

— Buster & the Dandelions. LC 90-47926. (Adventures of Buster the Puppy Ser.). (Illus.). 24p. (J). (gr. k-2). 1991. lib. bdg. 17.27 (*0-8368-0491-0*) Gareth Stevens Inc.

— Buster & the Little Kitten. LC 90-47947. (Adventures of Buster the Puppy Ser.). (Illus.). 24p. (J). (gr. k-2). 1991. lib. bdg. 17.27 (*0-8368-0490-2*) Gareth Stevens Inc.

— Buster Catches a Cold. LC 90-47948. (Adventures of Buster the Puppy Ser.). (Illus.). 24p. (J). (gr. k-2). 1991. lib. bdg. 17.27 (*0-8368-0489-9*) Gareth Stevens Inc.

— Buster in the Field. (Further Adventures of Buster the Puppy Ser.). (Illus.). 24p. (J). 1995. lib. bdg. 12.95 (*0-8368-1301-4*) Gareth Stevens Inc.

— Buster in the Night. (Futher Adventures of Buster the Puppy Ser.). (Illus.). 24p. (J). 1995. lib. bdg. 12.95 (*0-8368-1302-2*) Gareth Stevens Inc.

— Buster in the Night, 2 vols., Set. (Illus.). 48p. (J). 1995. lib. bdg. 25.50 (*0-8368-1300-6*) Gareth Stevens Inc.

— Buster's Blustery Day. LC 90-47927. (Adventures of Buster the Puppy Ser.). (Illus.). 24p. (J). (gr. k-2). 1991. lib. bdg. 17.27 (*0-8368-0494-5*) Gareth Stevens Inc.

— Buster's First Snow. LC 90-47946. (Adventures of Buster the Puppy Ser.). (Illus.). 24p. (J). (gr. k-2). 1991. lib. bdg. 17.27 (*0-8368-0492-9*) Gareth Stevens Inc.

— Buster's First Thunderstorm. LC 90-47869. (Adventures of Buster the Puppy Ser.). (Illus.). 24p. (J). (gr. k-2). 1991. lib. bdg. 17.27 (*0-8368-0493-7*) Gareth Stevens Inc.

Madole, Juanita M. & American Bar Association, Tort & Insurance Practice Staff. The Government Contractor Defense: A Fair Defense or the Contractor's Shield? LC 86-71631. 80p. 1986. 29.95 (*0-89707-252-9*, 519-0055) Amer Bar Assn.

***Madon, Shirin.** Designing Information Systems for Development Planning. 171p. Date not set. 50.00 (*1-872474-11-X*, Pub. by Alfred Waller UK) Paul & Co Pubs.

***Madoni, Don & Wolf, Rich.** Visual Guide to Microsoft Access for Windows 95. 650p. 1995. disk 34.95 (*1-56604-286-0*) Ventana Pr.

Madonna. The Madonna Girlie Show Book. (Illus.). 1994. Incl. CD. cd-rom write for info. (*0-318-72817-6*) Callaway Edns.

Madonna, G. Terry. The Revolutionary Leadership. Walker, Joseph E., ed. LC 76-8955. (Lancaster County During the American Revolution Ser.). (Illus.). 56p. 1976. pap. 5.00 (*0-915010-07-0*) Sutter House.

Madonna Madrigana, Rosa. Whiplash Injuries: Medical Subject Analysis & Research Guide with Bibliography. LC 83-45539. 140p. 1985. 44.50 (*0-88164-094-8*); pap. 39.50 (*0-88164-095-6*) ABBE Pubs Assn.

Madonna, Richard. Orbital Mechanics. LC 88-29051. (C). 1996. write for info. (*0-89464-010-0*) Krieger.

Madore, Barry F. Cepheids: Theory & Observation, Proceedings of the IAU Colloquium 82. 300p. 1985. 59.95 (*0-521-30091-6*) Cambridge U Pr.

Madore, Barry F., ed. New Ideas in Astronomy: A Symposium Celebrating the Sixtieth Birthday of Halton C. Arp. 400p. 1988. 69.95 (*0-521-34562-6*) Cambridge U Pr.

Madore, Barry F. & Tully, Brent R., eds. Galaxy Distances & Deviations from Universal Expansion. 1986. lib. bdg. 112.00 (*90-277-2277-3*) Kluwer Ac.

Madore, Barry F, jt. auth. see Arp, Halton C.

Madore, Barry F.

Madore, Barry F., jt. ed. see Halton, C. Arp.

***Madore, J.** An Introduction to Noncommutative Differential Geometry & Its Applications. (London Mathematical Society Lecture Note Ser.: No. 206). (Illus.). 250p. (C). 1994. pap. write for info. (*0-521-46791-8*) Cambridge U Pr.

Madorma, James. The Complete Guide to Understanding & Caring for Your Home: A Practical Handbook for Knowledgeable Homeowners. (Illus.). 272p. (Orig.). 1991. pap. 18.95 (*1-55870-210-5*) Betterway Bks.

— The Home Buyer's Inspection Guide: Making Investments in Your Home That Pay for Themselves. (Illus.). 176p. (Orig.). 1990. pap. 12.95 (*1-55870-146-X*) Betterway Bks.

***Madosa.** German Dictionary. 148p. 1991. 18.00 (*0-614-00600-7*) Valor Pub.

***Madou, Marc.** Fundamentals of Microfabrication. 512p. 1995. 79.95 (*0-8493-9451-1*, 9451) CRC Pr.

Madou, Marc J. & Morrison, S. Roy. Chemical Sensing with Solid State Devices. 556p. 1989. text ed. 142.00 (*0-12-464965-3*) Acad Pr.

Madous, H. Michael & Newman, Eric P. The First Official U. S. Coins: The Flag Connection. 3rd ed. Alberts, Robert C. et al, eds. (Flag Plaza Standard Ser.: Third Special Edition). 6p. 1989. reprint ed. pap. 1.50 (*0-934021-33-3*) Nat! Flag Foun.

Madow, Leo. Anger. LC 75-162773. 144p. 1974. pap. 6.95 (*0-684-13688-0*, Scribners) S&S Trade.

Madow, Stuart & Sobul, Jeff. The Colour of Your Dreams: The Beatles' Psychedelic Music. 116p. 1992. 13.00 (*0-8059-3261-5*) Dorrance.

Madox, Ford B. The Diary of Madox Brown. Surtees, Virginia, ed. LC 81-51344. (Paul Mellon Centre for Studies in British Art). (Illus.). 320p. (C). 1981. 42.50 (*0-300-02743-5*) Yale U Pr.

Madox, Thomas. Baronia Anglica. LC 79-8369. reprint ed. 78.50 (*0-404-18358-1*) AMS Pr.

— History & Antiquities of the Exchequer, 2 Vols, Set. 2nd ed. 1969. reprint ed. 60.00 (*0-8377-2426-0*) Rothman.

— History & Antiquities of the Exchequer of the Kings of England, in Two Periods, 2 vols., Set. 2nd ed. LC 68-57386. (Illus.). 1969. reprint ed. 95.00 (*0-678-04500-3*) Kelley.

Madras, Neal & Slade, Gordon. The Self-Avoiding Walk. LC 92-28276. (Probability & Its Applications Ser.). xiv, 425p. 1992. 64.50 (*0-8176-3589-0*) Birkhauser.

Madras, Ronald. The Catholic Church & Antisemitism: Poland, 1933-1939. LC 94-4488. (Studies in Antisemitism). 1994. text ed. 48.00 (*3-7186-5568-3*) Gordon & Breach.

Madrazo, Beatrice, jt. auth. see Shirkhoda, Ali.

Madrazo, Gerry M., Jr., ed. Sourcebook for Science Supervisors. 4th ed. 134p. 1993. pap. text ed. 17.95 (*0-87355-114-1*) Natl Sci Tchrs.

Madrid Conference on Optimun Currency Areas Staff. The Economics of Common Currencies: Proceedings. Johnson, Harry G. & Swoboda, Alexander K., eds. LC 73-76382. (Illus.). 302p. reprint ed. pap. 86.10 (*0-8357-8109-7*, 2033935) Bks Demand.

Madrid, Luis, ed. see Mandela, Nelson.

Madrid, Luis, ed. see Marx, Karl & Engels, Frederick.

Madrid, Patrick, ed. & intro. Surprised by Truth: 11 Converts Give the Biblical & Historical Reasons for Becoming Catholic. 280p. (Orig.). 1994. pap. 11.99 (*0-9642610-8-1*) Basilica Pr. Foreword by Scott Hahn, introduction by Patrick Madrid. These intimate personal conversion accounts are packed with compelling biblical & historical proofs for Catholicism. Each year many Evangelicals & Fundamentalists are being surprised by Catholic truth - these converts tell you why. "Conversion involves many strands of theological & personal struggles. SURPRISED BY TRUTH weaves those strands into a tapestry of great beauty." (Kimberly Hahn, co-author of ROME SWEET HOME). "A masterpiece of Catholic apologetics!" (Most Rev. Charles Chaput, Bishop of Rapid City, South Dakota). "A sustained argument for the truth of the Catholic faith...anxieties, doubts, reasons, & affirmations are reported candidly - nothing is held back." (Karl Keating, author of CATHOLICISM & FUNDAMENTALISM). "The converts bring apologetics to life in an exciting way." (Rev. Peter Stravinskas, author of THE BIBLE & THE MASS). "These converts relentlessly sought Christ & were amazed at where they found him." (Rev. Mitchel Pacwa, S.J., author of CATHOLICS & THE NEW AGE). To order: Basilica Press, P.O. Box 85152-134, Dept. B, San Diego, CA 92186, FAX (619) 698-3469.** ***Publisher Provided Annotation.

Madrid, Philip E. & Sun, Shih W. Device Design & Process Window Analysis of a Deep-Submicron CMOS VLSI Technology. LC 92-23863. (Six Sigma Research Institute Ser.). 1992. pap. write for info. (*0-201-63424-4*) Addison-Wesley.

Madrid, Raul M. Overexposed: U. S. Banks Confront the Third World Debt Crisis. 260p. 1990. pap. 40.00 (*0-931035-50-3*) IRRC Inc DC.

Madrid, Renato E. Southern Harvest: A Collection of Stories. viii, 187p. (Orig.). 1987. pap. 10.75 (*971-10-0297-3*, Pub. by New Day Pub PH) Cellar.

***Madrigal.** Open Door to Spanish: A Conversation Course for Beginners, Level 2. 2nd ed. (Illus.). 272p. (C). 1994. pap. text ed. write for info. (*0-13-181538-5*) P-H.

Madrigal, Jose A., jt. auth. see McCrary, William C.

Madrigal, Jose A., ed. see Valerio, Juan F.

Madrigal, Margarita. Madrigals Magic Key to Spanish. 1989. mass mkt. 10.95 (*0-385-41095-6*) Doubleday.

— Open Door to Spanish, Bk. 1. (Illus.). 223p. (C). (gr. 7-12). 1980. pap. text ed. 5.25 (*0-88345-420-3*, 18469); audio 45.00 (*0-686-77563-5*, 58471) Prentice ESL.

— Open Door to Spanish, Bk. 1. 1987. BK. 1. pap. text ed. 16.50 (*0-13-637695-9*) Prentice ESL.

— Open Door to Spanish, Bk. 2. (Open Door to Spanish Ser.). 222p. (J). (gr. 7-12). 1981. teacher ed 1.50 (*0-88345-487-4*, 18474); pap. text ed. 5.25 (*0-88345-427-0*, 18470); audio 45.00 (*0-686-77684-4*, 58472) Prentice ESL.

— Open Door to Spanish, Bk. 2. 1987. pap. text ed. 16.50 (*0-13-637703-3*) Prentice ESL.

— Open Door to Spanish: A Conversation Course for Beginners, Level 1. 2nd ed. LC 94-22581. 256p. 1994. pap. text ed. 28.00 (*0-13-181520-2*) P-H.

— See It & Say It in Spanish. (Orig.). 1961. pap. 5.99 (*0-451-16837-2*, Sig) NAL-Dutton.

Madrigal, Margarita & Dulac, Colette. First Steps in French. (Illus.). (gr. 4-7). 1964. pap. text ed. 3.25 (*0-88345-176-X*, 17473) Prentice ESL.

— See It & Say It in French. 1963. pap. 5.99 (*0-451-16347-8*) NAL-Dutton.

Madrigal, Margarita & Halpert, Inge. See It & Say It in German. (Orig.). 1962. pap. 4.50 (*0-451-15698-6*, AE2929, Sig) NAL-Dutton.

Madrigal, Margarita & Salvadori, Giuseppina. See It & Say It in Italian. (Orig.). 1961. pap. 3.95 (*0-451-15532-7*, AJ1327, Sig) NAL-Dutton.

Madrigal, Sylvia. Farms. (Wonders! Ser.). (Illus.). 24p. (Orig.). (J). (gr. 1-3). 1992. pap. text ed. 29.95 (*1-56334-063-1*); pap. text ed. 6.00 (*1-56334-069-0*) Hampton-Brown.

— Farms: Level 2. (Wonders! Ser.). (Illus.). 24p. (Orig.). 1992. pap. write for info. (*1-56334-228-6*) Hampton-Brown.

— Granjas. (Que Maravilla! Ser.). (Illus.). 24p. (Orig.). (SPA.). (J). (gr. 1-3). 1992. pap. 29.95 (*1-56334-024-0*); pap. 6.00 (*1-56334-038-0*) Hampton-Brown.

— Granjas: Level 2. (Que Maravilla! Ser.). 24p. (Orig.). (SPA.). 1992. pap. write for info. (*1-56334-217-0*) Hampton-Brown.

Madron, Frantisek. Process Plant Performance: Measurement & Data Processing for Optimization & Retrofits. 300p. 1993. text ed. write for info. (*0-13-723875-4*) P-H.

Madron, Thomas W. Local Area Networks: New Technologies, Emerging Standards. 3rd ed. LC 94-11323. 1994. pap. text ed. 29.95 (*0-471-00959-8*) Wiley.

— Local Area Networks: The Second Generation. 2nd ed. 306p. 1990. pap. text ed. 24.95 (*0-471-52250-3*) Wiley.

— Low-Cost E-Mail with UUCP: Integrating UNIX, DOS, Windows & Mac: UNIX to UNIX Copy Program. (Computer Science Ser.). 1994. pap. 39.95 (*0-442-01849-5*) Van Nos Reinhold.

An Asterisk (*) at the beginning of an entry indicates that the title is appearing in BIP for the first time.

— Network Security in the Nineties: Issues & Solutions for Managers. 304p. 1992. pap. text ed. 32.95 (*0-471-54777-8*) Wiley.
— Peer-to-Peer LANS: Networking Two to Ten PCs. 304p. 1993. pap. text ed. 26.95 (*0-471-59091-6*) Wiley.
— Redes de Area Local. 1992. pap. text ed. 27.95 (*968-18-4144-1*, Pub. by Limusa MX) Computer & Tech.

Madron, Thomas W., et al. Using Microcomputers in Research. (Quantitative Applications in the Social Sciences Ser.: Vol. 52). 1985. 9.95 (*0-8039-2457-7*) Sage.

Madry. Lesson Plans for Professional Estheticians. 1979. 54. 95 (*0-87350-084-9*); teacher ed 23.95 (*0-87350-132-2*); student ed 17.95 (*0-87350-357-0*) Milady Pub.

Madry, B. R. Job Seekers Guide. 1987. 13.50 (*0-87350-900-5*); teacher ed 8.00 (*0-87350-902-1*); student ed 6.95 (*0-87350-901-3*) Milady Pub.

Madry, Bobbi R. Milady Illustrated Cosmetology Dictionary. (Illus.). 1985. 27.95 (*0-87350-412-7*) Milady Pub.

Madsen. Mexican-Americans of South Texas, 1974. 2nd ed. 124p. (C). 1973. pap. text ed. 13.50 (*0-03-008431-8*) HB Coll Pubs.
— Print Reading for Engineering & Manufacturing Technology. 96p. 1995. teacher ed, pap. text ed. 14.00 (*0-8273-5236-0*) Delmar.

Madsen, jt. auth. see Covey.

Madsen, tr. see Jackins, Harvey & Meyer.

Madsen, jt. auth. see Shumaker.

Madsen, et al. American Politics in the Heartland. 304p. (C). 1990. pap. text ed. 23.95 (*0-8403-5890-3*) Kendall-Hunt.

Madsen, Albert A., jt. auth. see Curtis, Edward L.

Madsen, Axel. Chanel: A Woman of Her Own. (Illus.). 400p. 1991. pap. 15.95 (*0-8050-1639-2*, Owl) H Holt & Co.
— The Sewing Circle: Hollywood's Greatest Secret--Female Stars Who Loved Other Women. (Illus.). 368p. 1995. 22. 50 (*1-55972-275-4*, Birch Ln Pr) Carol Pub Group.
— Sonia: Artist of the Lost Generation. 1989. 24.95 (*0-318-42506-8*) McGraw.

Madsen, Betty M. & Madsen, Brigham D. North to Montana: Jehus, Bullwackers, & Mule Skinners on the Montana Trail. LC 78-60240. (University of Utah Publications in the American West: No. 13). (Illus.). 318p. reprint ed. pap. 90.70 (*0-8357-4376-4*, 2037207) Bks Demand.

Madsen, Brigham, ed. see Roberts, B. H.

Madsen, Brigham D. Chief Pocatello: The "White Plume" LC 86-6719. (Bonneville Bks.). 154p. reprint ed. pap. 43. 90 (*0-7837-3963-X*, 2043792) Bks Demand.
— Corinne, the Gentile Capital of Utah. LC 80-50202. (Illus.). xii, 331p. 1980. 17.50 (*0-913738-30-1*) Utah St Hist Soc.
— Exploring the Great Salt Lake: The Stansbury Expedition of 1849-50. LC 88-28041. (Publications in the American West: Vol. 22). (Illus.). 960p. 1989. 29.95 (*0-87480-325-X*) U of Utah Pr.
— Glory Hunter: A Biography of Patrick Edward Connor. LC 90-52744. (Publications in the American West: No. 24). (Illus.). 336p. 1990. 27.50 (*0-87480-336-5*) U of Utah Pr.
— Gold Rush Sojourners in Great Salt Lake City, 1849 & 1850. LC 83-12460. (Publications in the American West: Vol. 18). (Illus.). 200p. 1983. 16.95 (*0-87480-227-X*) U of Utah Pr.
— The Lemhi: Sacajawea's People. LC 78-53137. (Illus.). (Orig.). 1980. pap. 7.95 (*0-87004-267-X*) Caxton.
— The Lemhi: Sacajawea's People. LC 78-53137. (Illus.). 214p. (Orig.). reprint ed. pap. 61.00 (*0-8357-4120-6*, 2036951) Bks Demand.
— The Shoshoni Frontier & the Bear River Massacre. LC 85-13389. (Utah Centennial Ser.: Vol.1). (Illus.). 336p. 1985. 19.95 (*0-87480-099-4*) U of Utah Pr.

Madsen, Brigham D., ed. A Forty-Niner in Utah with the Stansbury Exploration of Great Salt Lake: Letters & Journal of John Hudson, 1848-50. LC 81-69864. 227p. 1981. 19.95 (*0-941214-39-7*) Signature Bks.
— The Shoshoni Frontier & the Bear River Massacre. (Illus.). 304p. Date not set. reprint ed. pap. 17.95 (*0-87480-494-9*) U of Utah Pr.

Madsen, Brigham D., jt. auth. see Madsen, Betty M.

Madsen, Carol C. In Their Own Words: The Women & the Story of Nauvoo. LC 93-41762. 250p. 1994. 8.99 (*0-87579-770-9*) Deseret Bk.

Madsen, Charles H., Jr. & Madsen, Clifford K. Teaching Discipline: A Positive Approach for Educational Development. 3rd ed. 318p. (C). 1981. pap. text ed. 27. 95x (*0-89892-053-1*) Contemp Pub Co of Raleigh.

Madsen, Charles H., Jr., jt. auth. see Madsen, Clifford K.

Madsen, Christine. Drinking & Driving. LC 89-31584. (Understanding Drugs Ser.). (Illus.). 62p. (J). (gr. 6-10). 1989. lib. bdg. 13.23 (*0-531-10799-X*) Watts.

Madsen, Claudia, jt. auth. see Madsen, William.

Madsen, Clifford, jt. ed. see Merrion, Margaret.

Madsen, Clifford K. & Kuhn, Terry L. Contemporary Music Education. 2nd rev. ed. LC 77-90672. 186p. (C). 1994. pap. text ed. 17.95x (*0-89892-119-8*) Contemp Pub Co of Raleigh.

Madsen, Clifford K. & Madsen, Charles H., Jr. Experimental Research in Music. (Illus.). 1978. reprint ed. pap. text ed. 23.95 (*0-89892-018-3*) Contemp Pub Co of Raleigh.

Madsen, Clifford K. & Moore, Randall S. Experimental Research in Music - Workbook in Design & Statistical Tests. rev. ed. 1978. 29.95 (*0-89892-017-5*) Contemp Pub Co of Raleigh.

Madsen, Clifford K. & Yarbrough, Cornelia. Competency Based Music Education. 184p. (C). 1985. reprint ed. pap. text ed. 19.95 (*0-89892-061-2*) Contemp Pub Co of Raleigh.

Madsen, Clifford K., jt. auth. see Madsen, Charles H., Jr.

Madsen, Clifford K., jt. auth. see Yarbrough, Cornelia.

Madsen, Clifford K., et al. Research in Music Behavior: Modifying Music Behavior in the Classroom. LC 74-16362. (Illus.). 285p. reprint ed. pap. 81.30 (*0-317-09961-2*, 2020325) Bks Demand.

Madsen, David. The National University: Enduring Dream of the U. S. A. LC 66-22036. 179p. reprint ed. pap. 51. 10 (*0-685-15829-2*, 2027683) Bks Demand.
— Successful Dissertations & Theses: A Guide to Graduate Student Research from Proposal to Completion. 2nd ed. LC 91-21687. (Higher & Adult Education - Social & Behavioral Science Ser.). 238p. 1991. reprint ed. pap. 20. 00 (*1-55542-389-2*) Jossey-Bass.
— Successful Dissertations & Theses: A Guide to Graduate Student Research from Proposal to Completion. LC 82-49039. (Joint Publication in the Jossey-Bass Higher Education Series & the Jossey-Bass Social & Behavioral Science Ser.). 192p. reprint ed. pap. 54.80 (*0-7837-2550-7*, 2042709) Bks Demand.
— Ussa. 1991. mass mkt. 4.99 (*1-55817-475-3*, Pinnacle NY) Windsor NY.
— Vodoun. LC 94-6615. 1994. 23.00 (*0-688-10563-7*) Morrow.

Madsen, David & Jefferis, Alan. Print Reading for Architecture & Construction Technology. 415p. 1994. pap. text ed. 28.95 (*0-8273-5429-0*) Delmar.
— Print Reading for Architecture & Construction Technology. 59p. 1994. teacher ed 14.00 (*0-8273-5430-4*) Delmar.

Madsen, David & Rhode, David, eds. Across the West: Human Population Movement & the Expansion of the Numa. 256p. (C). 1994. text ed. 50.00 (*0-87480-465-5*) U of Utah Pr.

Madsen, David & Shumaker, Terrance. Civil Drafting Technology. 2nd ed. 294p. 1994. pap. text ed. 26.00 (*0-13-100785-8*) P-H.

Madsen, David A. Drafting: Syllabus. 1974. pap. text ed. 8.95 (*0-89420-070-4*, 107015); audio 104.35 (*0-89420-140-9*, 107000) Natl Book.
— Geometric Dimensioning & Tolerancing: Basic Fundamentals. rev. ed. LC 94-17779. (Illus.). 351p. 1995. pap. text ed. 25.00 (*1-56637-064-7*) Goodheart.
— Print Reading for Engineering & Manufacturing Technology. 407p. 1994. pap. text ed. 29.95 (*0-8273-5235-2*) Delmar.

Madsen, David A., jt. auth. see Jefferis, Alan.

Madsen, David A., jt. auth. see Shumaker, Terence M.

Madsen, David A., et al. Engineering Drawing & Design. 1024p. 1991. text ed. 63.95 (*0-8273-2602-5*); trans. 79. 95 (*0-8273-4749-9*); disk 40.00 (*0-8273-4748-0*); 16.75 (*0-8273-4747-2*); 13.95 (*0-685-56321-9*) Delmar.
— Engineering Drawing & Design, Vol. 1. 1024p. 1991. teacher ed 25.00 (*0-8273-2603-3*) Delmar.
— Engineering Drawing & Design, Vol. II. 1024p. 1991. teacher ed write for info. (*0-8273-4765-0*) Delmar.
— Fundamentals of Drafting Technology. rev. ed. LC 93-10536. Orig. Title: Engineering Drawing & Design. 604p. 1994. pap. text ed. 45.95 (*0-8273-5238-7*) Delmar.

Madsen, David B. & O'Connell, James F., eds. Man & Environment in the Great Basin. (SAA Papers: No. 2). 248p. 1982. 25.00 (*0-932839-02-9*) Soc Am Arch.

Madsen, Deborah L. The Postmodernist Allegories of Thomas Pynchon. LC 91-9841. 192p. 1991. text ed. 49. 95 (*0-312-06512-4*) St Martin.
— Rereading Allegory: A Narrative Approach to Genre. LC 94-25350. 1994. write for info. (*0-312-12298-5*) Martin Pr.

Madsen, Deborah L., ed. Visions of America since 1492. LC 94-12856. 1994. text ed. 39.95 (*0-312-12281-0*) St Martin.

Madsen, Donna L. & Nelson, Lynda B. Micro-Typewriter: Tutorial Guide. 56p. 1986. pap. text ed. 5.95 (*1-57094-041-X*) S E Warner Sftware.
— Micro-Typewriter: Tutorial Guide. 2nd ed. 58p. 1987. pap. text ed. 5.95 (*1-57094-042-8*) S E Warner Sftware.
— Micro-Typewriter: Tutorial Guide. 3rd ed. 60p. 1988. pap. text ed. 5.95 (*1-57094-043-6*) S E Warner Sftware.
— Micro-Typewriter: Tutorial Guide. 4th ed. 62p. 1989. pap. text ed. 5.95 (*1-57094-044-4*) S E Warner Sftware.
— Micro-Typewriter: Tutorial Guide. 5th ed. 64p. 1992. pap. text ed. 5.95 (*1-57094-045-2*) S E Warner Sftware.

Madsen, Douglas, jt. auth. see Snow, Peter G.

Madsen, Eric, ed. see Napoleon, Harold.

Madsen, Greg, jt. auth. see McGarry, Richard M.

Madsen, Harold S. Techniques in Testing. (Techniques in Teaching English As a Second Language Ser.). (Illus.). (C). 1983. pap. text ed. 10.50 (*0-19-434132-1*) OUP.

Madsen, Hunter, jt. auth. see Kirk, Marshall.

Madsen, Ib & Milgram, R. James. The Classifying Spaces for Surgery & Cobordism of Manifolds. LC 78-70311. (Annals of Mathematics Studies: No. 92). 1979. 49.50 (*0-691-08225-1*); pap. 24.95 (*0-691-08226-X*) Princeton U Pr.

Madsen, J. B. & Cold, G. E. The Effects of Anaesthetics upon Cerebral Circulation & Metabolism. (Illus.). 150p. 1991. 58.00 (*0-387-82198-8*) Spr-Verlag.

Madsen, Jean. Educational Reform at the State Level: The Politics & Problems of Implementation. LC 93-9072. 1993. write for info. (*0-7507-0280-X*, Falmer Pr) Taylor & Francis.
— Educational Reform at the State Level: The Politics & Problems of Implementation. (Education Policy Perspectives Ser.). 192p. 1994. 65.00 (*0-7507-0206-0*, Falmer Pr) Taylor & Francis.

Madsen, K. B. Theories of Motivation: A Comparative Study of Modern Theories of Motivation. 4th ed. LC 68-22338. 366p. reprint ed. pap. 104.40 (*0-317-10321-0*, 2050861) Bks Demand.

Madsen, K. B., ed. A History of Psychology in Metascientific Perspective. (Advances in Psychology Ser.: 53). 606p. 1988. 138.50 (*0-444-70433-7*, North Holland) Elsevier.

Madsen, K. B. & Mos, Leendert P., eds. Annals of Theoretical Psychology, Vol. 3. LC 84-644088. 368p. 1985. 85.00 (*0-306-41972-6*, Plenum Pr) Plenum.

Madsen, Lyman. There Is No Death: Inspirational Helps for Those Who Serve in Time of Sorrow. LC 89-85212. 125p. 1990. 9.98 (*0-88290-352-7*) Horizon Utah.

Madsen, Lynn. Healing the Wounded Wounds of Childbirth. LC 93-40162. 192p. 1994. pap. text ed. 14.95 (*0-89789-348-4*, Bergin & Garvey) Greenwood.

Madsen, Mark. Confessions of a Country Doctor. Jones, M. L., ed. 117p. (Orig.). 1994. pap. 8.95 (*0-9636072-3-5*) J Honea Pubs.

Madsen, Mark T. Medical Physics Handbook of Nuclear Medicine, Vol. 2. (Illus.). 110p. (Orig.). (C). 1992. pap. text ed. 14.00 (*0-944838-14-6*) Med Physics Pub.

Madsen, Norman P. Ask & You Will Receive: Prayer & the Letter to the Hebrews. 136p. 1989. pap. 9.99 (*0-8272-0018-8*) Chalice Pr.
— Basic Bible Commentary, Vol. 20: John. Deming, Lynne M., ed. LC 94-10965. 160p. (Orig.). 1994. pap. 4.95 (*0-687-02639-3*) Abingdon.
— Basic Bible Commentary, Vol. 23: First & Second Corinthians. Deming, Lynne M., ed. LC 94-10965. 160p. (Orig.). 1994. pap. 4.95 (*0-687-02643-1*) Abingdon.

Madsen, O. Lehrmann, et al, eds. Proceedings: ECOOP 'Ninety-Two, European Conference on Object-Oriented Programming, Utrecht, The Netherlands, June 29-July 3, 1992. LC 92-19991. (Lecture Notes in Computer Science Ser.: Vol. 615). x, 426p. 1992. pap. 63.00 (*0-387-55668-0*) Spr-Verlag.

Madsen, Ole L., et al. Object-Oriented Programming in the BETA Programming Language. LC 93-1150. (C). 1993. pap. text ed. 37.75 (*0-201-62430-3*) Addison-Wesley.

Madsen, Peter & Shafritz, Jay M., eds. Essentials of Government Ethics. 512p. (Orig.). 1992. pap. 15.00 (*0-452-01091-8*, Mer) NAL-Dutton.

Madsen, Peter, jt. ed. see Shafritz, Jay M.

Madsen, R. Scott. The Bomber Mountain Crash: A Wyoming Mystery. rev. ed. LC 90-62431. (Illus.). 104p. 1990. 16.95 (*0-9624665-1-4*); pap. text ed. 7.95 (*0-9624665-0-6*) Mtn Man Pub.

Madsen, Richard. China & the American Dream: A Moral Inquiry. LC 93-45003. (C). 1995. 27.50 (*0-520-08613-9*) U CA Pr.
— Morality & Power in a Chinese Village. LC 83-4887. 200p. 1984. pap. 15.00 (*0-520-05925-5*) U CA Pr.

Madsen, Richard W. & Moeschberger, Melvin L. Introductory Statistics for Business & Economics. (Illus.). 752p. 1983. text ed. write for info. (*0-13-501577-4*) P-H.
— Statistical Concepts with Applications to Business & Economics. 2nd ed. (Illus.). 672p. (C). 1986. text ed. 33. 95 (*0-317-38353-1*) P-H.

Madsen, Richard W., jt. auth. see Isaacson, Dean L.

Madsen, Ross M. Stewart Stork. LC 92-30730. (Illus.). 40p. (J). (ps-3). 1993. 11.99 (*0-8037-1325-8*); lib. bdg. 11.89 (*0-8037-1326-6*) Dial Bks Young.

Madsen, Roy P. Animated Film: Concepts, Methods, Uses. 1976. 24.95 (*0-8488-0830-4*) Amereon Ltd.
— Working Cinema: Learning from the Masters. 392p. (C). 1990. text ed. 44.95 (*0-534-11881-X*); pap. 37.95 (*0-534-11880-1*) Intl Thomson.

Madsen, Sharon, jt. ed. see McCulloch, Myrna.

Madsen, Sheila & Gould, Bette. The Teacher's Book of Lists. 2nd ed. (Illus.). 336p. (J). (gr. k-6). 1994. pap. 19. 95 (*0-673-36074-1*) GdYrBks.

Madsen, Stephan T. Sources of Art Nouveau. LC 75-26819. (Quality Paperbacks Ser.). (Illus.). 1976. pap. 10.95 (*0-306-80024-1*) Da Capo.
— Sources of Art Noveau. Christopherson, Ragnar, tr. LC 74-34464. (Architecture & Decorative Art Ser.). (Illus.). 488p. 1975. reprint ed. lib. bdg. 59.50 (*0-306-70733-0*) Da Capo.

Madsen, Steven K., jt. auth. see Crampton, C. Gregory.

Madsen, Susan A. Christmas: A Joyful Heritage. LC 84-72519. (Illus.). xvi, 93p. 1984. reprint ed. pap. 3.95 (*0-87579-367-3*) Deseret Bk.
— I Walked to Zion: True Stories of Young Pioneers on the Mormon Trail. LC 94-404. ix, 182p. (YA). (gr. 6-12). 1994. 12.95 (*0-87579-848-9*) Deseret Bk.
— The Lord Needed a Prophet. LC 90-81829. (Illus.). 234p. (J). (gr. 3-6). 1990. 10.95 (*0-87579-276-6*) Deseret Bk.

***Madsen, Svend A.** Days with Diam: Or Life at Night. Jones, W. Glyn, tr. 246p. 1995. pap. 24.00 (*1-870041-26-7*) Dufour.
— Virtue & Vice in the Middle Time. Ogier, James M., tr. LC 92-10596. (Library of World Literature in Translation: Vol. 29). 584p. (DAN & ENG.). 1992. 78. 00 (*0-8153-0606-7*) Garland.

Madsen, Truman G. Christ & the Inner Life. 6.95 (*0-88494-345-3*) Bookcraft Inc.
— Defender of the Faith: The B. H. Roberts Story. deluxe ed. 1994. 11.95 (*0-614-03069-2*) Bookcraft Inc.
— Joseph Smith the Prophet. 10.95 (*0-88494-704-1*) Bookcraft Inc.
— The Radiant Life. 1994. 10.95 (*0-88494-938-9*) Bookcraft Inc.

Madsen, W. Handbook of Personal Data Protection. 1026p. 1992. 170.00 (*1-56159-046-0*, Stockton Pr) Groves Dictionaries.

Madsen, Willard J. Conversational Sign Language II: An Intermediate-Advanced Manual. 220p. 1972. pap. 10.95 (*0-913580-00-7*, Clerc Bks) Gallaudet Univ Pr.
— Intermediate Conversational Sign Language. LC 82-81440. (Illus.). 400p. 1982. pap. text ed. 17.95 (*0-913580-79-1*, Clerc Bks) Gallaudet Univ Pr.

Madsen, William. Virgin's Children: Life in an Aztec Village Today. LC 74-88900. 248p. 1970. reprint ed. text ed. 65. 00 (*0-8371-2098-5*, MAVC, Greenwood Pr) Greenwood.

Madsen, William & Madsen, Claudia. A Guide to Mexican Witchcraft. (Illus.). 96p. 1977. pap. 4.50 (*0-912434-10-4*) Ocelot Pr.

Madsen, William G., ed. see Milton, John.

Madson, Arthur. Blue-Eyed Boy. Spelius, Carol, ed. (Orig.). pap. 6.95 (*0-941363-13-9*) Lake Shore Pub.
— Coming up Sequined. 46p. (Orig.). 1991. pap. 7.50 (*1-878660-11-X*) Fireweed WI.

Madson, Chris. When Nature Heals: The Greening of Rocky Mountain Arsenal. 80p. 1990. pap. 14.95 (*0-911797-71-8*) R Rinehart.

Madson, J. Outdoor Life Deer Hunter's Encyclopedia. 1985. 49.95 (*0-943822-53-X*) Times Mir Mag Bk Div.

Madson, John. Stories from Under the Sky. LC 87-34486. (Iowa Heritage Collection Ser.). (Illus.). 206p. 1988. reprint ed. pap. 7.95 (*0-8138-0077-3*) Iowa St U Pr.
— Tallgrass Prairie. (Illus.). 128p. 1993. 29.50 (*1-56044-223-9*) Falcon Pr MT.
— Where the Sky Began: Land of the Tallgrass Prairie. rev. ed. LC 94-31126. (Illus.). 336p. 1994. 24.95 (*0-8138-2513-X*) Iowa St U Pr.

Madtes, Richard E. The Ithaca Chapter of Joyce's Ulysses. LC 83-9248. (Studies in Modern Literature: No. 27). 172p. reprint ed. pap. 49.10 (*0-8357-1460-8*, 2070505) Bks Demand.

Madu, Christian N. Strategic Planning in Technology Transfer to Less Developed Countries. LC 91-22020. 224p. 1992. text ed. 52.95 (*0-89930-629-2*, MTY, Quorum Bks) Greenwood.

Madu, Christian N., ed. Management of New Technologies for Global Competitiveness. LC 92-31712. 400p. 1993. text ed. 59.95 (*0-89930-713-2*, MNH, Quorum Bks) Greenwood.

Madu, Christian N. & Kuei, Chu-Hua. Experimental Statistical Designs & Analysis in Simulation Modeling. LC 92-37467. 224p. 1993. text ed. 65.00 (*0-89930-695-0*, MXS/, Quorum Bks) Greenwood.
— Strategic Total Quality Mangement: Corporate Performance & Product Quality. LC 94-32082. 224p. 1995. text ed. 55.00 (*0-89930-817-1*, Quorum Bks) Greenwood.

Madu, Raphael O. African Symbols, Proverbs & Myths: The Hermeneutics of Destiny. LC 91-42866. (Studies in African & African-American Culture: Vol. 3). 327p. (C). 1993. text ed. 59.80 (*0-8204-1863-3*) P Lang Pubs.

Madubuike, Ihechukwa. Handbook of African Names. 2nd rev. ed. LC 86-50744. 157p. 1994. pap. 12.00 (*0-89410-438-1*) Three Continents.

Madueno, Amalio. Computers for Neighborhoods. 2nd ed. 53p. (C). 1987. pap. 7.50 (*0-317-93050-8*) CIE Inc.

Madugula, I. S. The Acarya: Sankara of Kaladi, a Story. 143p. (C). 1991. reprint ed. text ed. 16.00 (*81-208-0009-5*, Pub. by Motilal Banarsidass II) S Asia.

Madugula, Marty K. & Kennedy, J. B. Single & Compound Angle Members: Structural Analysis & Design. (Illus.). 372p. 1985. 101.00 (*0-85334-364-0*, Pub. by Elsevier Applied Sci UK) Elsevier.

Madugula, Marty K., jt. auth. see Kennedy, John B.

— White Magic: The Origins & Ideas of Black Mental & Cultural Colonialism. 279p. (Orig.). 1994. pap. 12.00 (*1-56411-085-0*) Untd Bros & Sis.

Madupu, Gangadhur, jt. auth. see Hanrahan, Edward J.

Madura, Jeff. Financial Markets & Institutions. 2nd ed. Fenton & Craig, eds. 717p. (C). 1992. text ed. 61.00 (*0-314-87735-5*) West Pub.
— Financial Markets & Institutions. 3rd ed. LC 94-17238. 670p. 1994. text ed. 63.00 (*0-314-04160-5*) West Pub.

M

— International Finance Perspectives. LC 92-75277. 220p. 1993. pap. write for info. (*1-878975-22-6*) Kolb Pub.
— International Financial Management. 3rd ed. Fenton & Craig, eds. LC 85-29501. 728p. (C). 1992. text ed. 60.50 (*0-314-86272-2*) West Pub.
— International Financial Management. 4th ed. LC 94-17237. 650p. 1994. text ed. 65.75 (*0-314-04161-3*) West Pub.
Madura, Jeff & Veit, E. Theodore. Introduction to Financial Management. 750p. (C). 1988. text ed. 65.25 (*0-314-65664-2*) West Pub.
Madura, Jeffrey M. Basic Accounting, (Illus.). 200p. (C). 1981. pap. text ed. 14.95 (*0-916780-16-3*) CES.
— Interpreting Financial Reports for Decision Making. (Illus.). 170p. 1984. 37.95 (*0-916780-22-8*) CES.
Madurga, G. & Lozano, M. Heavy-Ion Collision, La Rabida, Spain, 1982: Proceedings. (Lecture Notes in Physics Ser.: Vol. 168). 429p. 1982. pap. 39.00 (*0-387-11945-0*) Spr-Verlag.
Madurga, G., jt. auth. see Garcia-Leon, M.
Maduro, Otto. Religion & Social Conflicts. Barr, Robert R., tr. LC 82-3439. Orig. Title: Religion y Lucha de Clase. 189p. (Orig.). reprint ed. pap. 53.90 (*0-7837-5512-0*, 2045282) Bks Demand.
Maduro, Otto, jt. ed. see Ellis, Marc H.
Maduro, Roger & Schauerhammer, Ralf. The Holes in the Ozone Scare: The Scientific Evidence That the Sky Isn't Falling. (Illus.). 357p. (Orig.). 1992. pap. 15.00 (*0-9628134-0-0*) Twenty Fst Sci.
Madvig, Donald, tr. see Schweizer, Eduard.
Madvig, Johan N. Adversaria Critica Ad Scriptores Graecos et Latinos, 3 vols., Set. viii, 1703p. 1967. reprint ed. write for info. (*0-318-70779-9*, Pub. by Georg Olms GW) Lubrecht & Cramer.
— Kleine Philologische Schriften. vii, 560p. 1966. reprint ed. write for info. (*0-318-70780-2*, Pub. by Georg Olms GW) Lubrecht & Cramer.
— Opuscula Academica. xi, 779p. 1977. reprint ed. write for info. (*3-487-06456-1*, Pub. by Georg Olms GW) Lubrecht & Cramer.
Madwed, Sidney. How to Use Poetry to Get Better Results in Your Life. 117p. 1991. pap. 11.95 (*0-685-51147-2*) S Madwed.
— How to Use Poetry to Get Better Results in Your Life. 1991. pap. 11.95 (*0-9629490-0-0*) S Madwed.
Madyastha, K. M. Biological Oxidation Systems, Vol. 1. Reddy, C. Channa et al, eds. (Illus.). 534p. 1990. text ed. 105.00 (*0-12-584551-0*) Acad Pr.
***Mae, Linda.** One Too Many Candles of Repentance: Poetry & Prose by Linda Mae. (Illus.). 48p. (Orig.). 1994. pap. 4.95 (*0-9642130-0-1*) Fountain Pen.
Mae-Wan Ho. The Rainbow & the Worm: The Physics of Organisms. 220p. 1993. text ed. 40.00 (*981-02-1486-3*) World Scientific Pub.
Maecha, Alberto, ed. see Bourgeois, Jean-Francois.
Maeda, ed. see NHK Overseas Broadcasting Department Staff & Mizutani, Nobuko.
Maeda, Anthony C. Angels of Twilight: Selected Poems & Songs by Tony Maeda. 20p. (Orig.). 1992. pap. 5.00 (*0-9633301-0-1*) Mustang Pr.
Maeda, Daisaku, jt. auth. see Palmore, Erdman.
Maeda, F. Y. Dirichlet Integrals on Harmonic Spaces. (Lecture Notes in Mathematics Ser.: Vol. 803). 180p. 1980. pap. 25.00 (*0-387-09995-6*) Spr-Verlag.
Maeda, H., jt. ed. see Koprowski, H.
Maeda, Hisayo G. & Craft, Lucille. Japanese Secrets of Beautiful Skin & Weight Control. LC 89-50660. (Illus.). 204p. 1989. pap. 15.95 (*0-8048-1543-7*) C E Tuttle.
Maeda, Jun. Let's Study Japanese. LC 64-24949. (Illus.). 130p. (YA). (gr. 9 up). 1965. pap. 6.95 (*0-8048-0362-5*) C E Tuttle.
Maeda, K., ed. The Fetus As a Patient '87: Proceedings of the 3rd International Symposium, Matsue, Japan, 20-23 July, 1987. (International Congress Ser.: No. 752). 460p. 1987. 136.75 (*0-444-80941-4*, Excerpta Medica) Elsevier.
***Maeda, K. & Shinzato, T., eds.** Dialysis-Related Amyloidosis. (Contributions to Nephrology Ser.: Vol. 112). (Illus.). viii, 192p. 1994. 152.00 (*3-8055-6046-X*) S Karger.
— Effective Hemodiafiltration: New Methods. (Contributions to Nephrology Ser.: Vol. 108). (Illus.). viii, 136p. 1994. 118.50 (*3-8055-5886-4*) S Karger.
Maeda, K., et al, eds. Recent Advances in Perinatology: Proceedings, 4th Asia-Oceania Congress of Perinatology, Tokyo, Japan, April 8-11, 1986. (International Congress Ser.: No. 712). 444p. 1987. 147.25 (*0-444-80842-6*, Excerpta Medica) Elsevier.
— Recent Advances in Renal Research: Contributions from Japan. (Contributions to Nephrology Ser.: Vol. 9). (Illus.). 1978. 39.25 (*3-8055-2826-4*) S Karger.
Maeda, Mitsuo. Laser Dyes: Properties of Organic Compounds for Dye Lasers (Monograph) LC 83-15069. 1984. text ed. 87.00 (*0-12-464980-7*) Acad Pr.
Maeda, Shintaro. Thomas Raccoon's Fantastic Airshow. Thatch, Nancy R., ed. (Books for Students by Students Ser.). (Illus.). 29p. (J). (gr. k-3). 1994. lib. bdg. 14.95 (*0-933849-51-6*) Landmark Edns.
***Maeda, Tetsuo.** The Hidden Army: The Untold Story of Japan's Militray Forces. Kenney, David J., ed. Karpa, Steven, tr. (Illus.). 1995. 24.95 (*1-883695-01-5*) Edition Q.
***Maeda, Yoshiaki, et al, eds.** Symplectic Geometry & Quantization: A Symposium on Symplectic Geometry & Quantization Problems, July 1993, Japan. LC 94-25115. (Contemporary Mathematics Ser.: Vol. 179). 1994. write for info. (*0-8218-0302-6*) Am Math.
Maedel, Lynn & Sommer, Sandra. Blood Cell Morphology, 6 vols. 1993. sl. 100.00 (*0-89189-329-6*) Am Soc Clinical.
— Blood Cell Morphology, 6 vols., Set. 1993. sl. 540.00 (*0-685-74782-4*) Am Soc Clinical.
Maeder, Andre & Renzini, Alvio, eds. Observational Tests of the Stellar Evolution Theory. 1984. lib. bdg. 148.00 (*90-277-1774-5*); pap. text ed. 67.50 (*90-277-1775-3*) Kluwer Ac.
Maeder, Andre, jt. ed. see De Jong, T.
Maeder, Clara F. Autobiography of Clara Fisher Maeder. (American Biography Ser.). 138p. 1991. reprint ed. lib. bdg. 59.00 (*0-7812-8260-8*) Rprt Serv.
Maeder, Edward, jt. auth. see Ricci, Stefania.
Maeder, Gary. God's Will For Your Life. 1991. 8.99 (*0-8423-1097-5*) Tyndale.
Maeder, Roman E. Computer Science with Mathematica: Theory & Practice for Science, Mathematics & Engineering. (Illus.). 384p. (C). 1995. text ed. write for info. (*0-201-56940-X*) Addison-Wesley.
— The Mathematica Programmer. (Illus.). 199p. 1994. disk, pap. 44.95 (*0-12-464990-4*, AP Prof) Acad Pr.
— Programming in Mathematica. 1989. 35.50 (*0-685-31411-1*) Addison-Wesley.
— Programming in Mathematica. 2nd ed. 1991. 31.25 (*0-201-54578-0*) Addison-Wesley.
— Programming in Mathematica. 2nd ed. (Advanced Book Program Ser.). (Illus.). 300p. (C). 1991. text ed. 44.25 (*0-201-54877-1*, Adv Bk Prog) Addison-Wesley.
— Programming in Mathematics. 1989. 35.50 (*0-201-51002-2*) Addison-Wesley.
— Programming in Mathematics. 2nd ed. 200p. (C). 1991. pap. text ed. 34.50 (*0-201-54878-X*, Adv Bk Prog) Addison-Wesley.
Maeder, Thomas. Adverse Reactions. LC 93-31896. 1994. 27.95 (*0-688-11682-5*) Morrow.
Maedke. Information & Records Management. 1987. pap. 26.65 (*0-02-820590-1*) Macmillan.
Maedke, Wilmer O., et al. Consumer Education. LC 77-73301. 528p. (gr. 11-12). 1984. teacher ed 10.67 (*0-02-475740-3*); text ed. 27.96 (*0-02-475720-9*); student ed 7.72 (*0-02-475730-6*) Glencoe.
Maegraith, jt. auth. see Adams.
Maehl, William H. August Bebel, Shadow Emperor of the German Workers. LC 79-51544. (Memoirs of the American Philosophical Society Ser.: Vol. 138). 576p. reprint ed. pap. 164.20 (*0-7837-0542-5*, 2040870) Bks Demand.
— The German Socialist Party: Champion of the First Republic 1918-1933. LC 84-5903. (Memoirs Ser.: Vol. 169). 400p. 1986. 40.00 (*0-87169-169-8*, M169-MAW) Am Philos.
Maehling, Rita F., jt. auth. see Hale, Roger L.
Maehlis, Sally, jt. auth. see Field, Nancy.
Maehly, A. & Williams, R., eds. Forensic Science Progress, Vol. 5. (Illus.). ix, 182p. 1991. 118.00 (*0-387-53203-X*) Spr-Verlag.
Maehly, A. & Williams, R. L. Forensic Science Progress, Vol. 2. (Illus.). 180p. 1988. 129.00 (*0-387-12937-5*) Spr-Verlag.
Maehly, A. & Williams, R. L., eds. Forensic Science Progress, Vol. 3. (Illus.). 140p. 1988. 109.00 (*0-387-18447-3*) Spr-Verlag.
Maehly, A., ed. see Seller, K.
Maehr, David S., jt. auth. see Kale, Herbert W., II.
Maehr, J. M. K-3 Language & Literacy. LC 90-22885. (K-Three Curriculum Ser.). 256p. 1991. Field Test Ed. pap. 22.95 (*0-929816-23-4*) High-Scope.
Maehr, Martin. The Development of Achievement Motivation. (Advances in Motivation & Achievement Ser.: Vol. 3). 347p. 1984. 73.25 (*0-89232-289-6*) Jai Pr.
Maehr, Martin L. Enhancing Motivation. (Advances in Motivation & Achievement Ser.: Vol. 5). 1987. 73.25 (*0-89232-621-2*) Jai Pr.
Maehr, Martin L., ed. Advances in Motivation & Achievement, Vol. 6. 1989. 73.25 (*0-89232-889-4*) Jai Pr.
— Advances in Motivation & Achievement: Motivation & Adulthood, Vol. 4. 1986. 73.25 (*0-89232-544-5*) Jai Pr.
— Advances in Motivation & Achievement: The Effects of School Desegregation on Motivation & Achievement, Vol. 1. 1984. 73.25 (*0-89232-290-X*) Jai Pr.
— Advances in Motivation & Achievement: Women in Science, Vol. 2. 1984. 73.25 (*0-89232-288-8*) Jai Pr.
Maeijer, J. M. & Geens, K., eds. Defensive Measures Against Hostile Takeovers in the Common Market. 232p. 1991. lib. bdg. 99.50 (*0-7923-0834-4*) Kluwer Ac.
Maeir, Clifford L. The Role of Spectroscopy in the Acceptance of the Internally Structured Atom. Cohen, I. Bernard, ed. LC 80-2093. (Development of Science Ser.). (Illus.). 1981. lib. bdg. 55.95 (*0-405-13858-X*) Ayer.
Maekawa, M. & Belady, L. A., eds. Operating Systems Engineering, Amagi, Japan 1980: Proceedings. (Lecture Notes in Computer Science Ser.: Vol. 143). 465p. 1982. pap. 40.00 (*0-387-11604-4*) Spr-Verlag.
Maekawa, M. & Oldekoeft. Operating Systems: Advanced Concepts. (C). 1987. text ed. 59.25 (*0-8053-7121-4*) Benjamin-Cummings.
Maekawa, Z. & Lord, P. Environmental & Architectural Acoustics. LC 92-47247. 1993. write for info. (*1-85861-012-5*) Elsevier.
Maeland, A., jt. ed. see Andresen, A. F.
Maelicke, A., ed. Molecular Biology of Neuroreceptors & Ion Channels. (NATO ASI Series H: Vol. 32). (Illus.). 670p. 1989. 203.00 (*0-387-50380-3*) Spr-Verlag.
— Nicotinic Acetylcholine Receptor. (NATO ASI Series H: Vol. 3). xvi, 489p. 1986. 148.00 (*0-387-17168-1*) Spr-Verlag.
Maelzer, G., ed. Bibliographie zur Geschichte des Pietismus, Vol. 1, Die Werke der Wuerttembergischen Pietisten. 415p. (C). 1972. 104.60 (*3-11-002219-2*) De Gruyter.
Maenchen-Helfen, Otto J. The World of the Huns: Studies in Their History & Culture. Knight, Max, ed. LC 79-94985. (Illus.). 634p. reprint ed. pap. 180.00 (*0-7837-4764-0*, 2044511) Bks Demand.
Maene, Ayako, tr. see Ogaki, Tetsuya.
Maennchen, Julis & Waschke, Ernst-Joachim, eds. Altes Testament - Literatursammlung und Heilige Schrift: Gesammelte Aufsaetze zur Entstehung, Geschichte und Auslegung des Alten Testaments. (Beihefte zur Zeitschrift fuer die Alttestamentliche Wissenschaft Ser.: Bd. 212). viii, 306p. (GER.). (C). 1993. lib. bdg. 106.15 (*3-11-013982-0*) De Gruyter.
Maenza, David. Chicago by Maenza. Fynn, Jay, ed. GCI International Staff, tr. (Illus.). 54p. (ENG, FRE, GER, ITA, JPN, POL & SPA.). 1988. 8.95 (*0-317-90968-1*) D J Maenza Assocs.
Maerd, Dorushka. Sipapu Odyssey. (Phoenix Journals). (Illus.). (Orig.). 1990. pap. 10.00 (*0-922356-11-4*) Amer West Pubs.
Maerk, T. D. & Dunn, G. H., eds. Electron Impact Ionization. (Illus.). 400p. 1985. 113.00 (*0-387-81778-6*) Spr-Verlag.
Maeroff, Gene I. The Empowerment of Teachers: Overcoming the Crisis of Confidence. 152p. (Orig.). (C). 1988. pap. text ed. 16.95 (*0-8077-2908-6*) Tchrs Coll.
— School & College: Partnerships in Education. LC 83-70359. 83p. 1983. pap. text ed. 4.50 (*0-931050-22-7*) Carnegie Fnd Advan Teach.
— The School Smart Parent: A Guide for Knowing What Your Child Should Know - From Infancy Through the End of Elementary School. 1989. 19.95 (*0-8129-1631-X*, Times Bks) Random.
— Team Building for School Change: Equipping Teachers for New Roles. LC 93-19983. (Series on School Reform). 192p. (C). 1993. text ed. 36.00 (*0-8077-3268-0*); pap. text ed. 16.95 (*0-8077-3267-2*) Tchrs Coll.
Maeroff, Gene I., ed. Sources of Inspiration: Fifteen Modern Religious Leaders. LC 92-27494. 308p. (Orig.). 1992. 29.95 (*1-55612-602-6*); pap. 19.95 (*1-55612-556-9*, LL1556) Sheed & Ward MO.
Maerowitz. Fundamental Litigation of Paralegals. 1991. pap. 16.00 (*0-316-54367-5*) Little.
Maerz, George C., jt. ed. see Harlow, Giles D.
Maes, A. A., jt. ed. see Van Rossum, J. H.
Maes, H. E., et al, eds. Solid State Device Research '92: Proceedings of the 22nd European Conference, ESSDERC '92, 14-17 September 1992, Leuven, Belgium. LC 92-23521. 1992. write for info. (*0-444-89478-0*) Elsevier.
Maes, John L. Suffering: A Care Giver's Guide. LC 89-27485. 224p. 1990. pap. 12.95 (*0-687-40570-X*) Abingdon.
Maes, P. & Nardi, D., eds. Meta-Level Architectures & Reflection. 356p. 1988. 87.25 (*0-444-70343-8*, North Holland) Elsevier.
Maes, Pattie, ed. Computational Reflection. (C). 1990. pap. text ed. 180.00 (*0-273-08823-8*, Pub. by Pitman Pubng UK) St Mut.
— Designing Autonomous Agents: Theory & Practice from Biology to Engineering & Back. (Illus.). 200p. 1991. pap. 24.95x (*0-262-63135-0*) MIT Pr.
Maes, Pattie, jt. ed. see Brooks, Rodney A.
Maes, R. A., ed. Topics in Forensic & Analytical Toxicology: Proceedings of the Annual European Meet. of the Internat. Assoc. of FornsicToxicologists, Munich, Aug. 21-25, 1983. (Analytical Chemistry Symposia Ser.: No. 20). 214p. 1984. 89.75 (*0-444-42313-3*, I-139-84) Elsevier.
Maes, R. A., jt. ed. see Brandenberger, H.
Maes, Stan, et al, eds. International Review of Health Psychology, Vol. 1. 237p. 1992. text ed. 86.50 (*0-471-92754-6*) Wiley.
— International Review of Health Psychology, Vol. 2. 230p. 1993. text ed. 99.95 (*0-471-93826-2*) Wiley.
— International Review of Health Psychology, 3, Vol. 3. 1994. text ed. 52.95 (*0-471-94456-4*) Wiley.
— Topics in Health Psychology. LC 88-5646. 314p. 1988. text ed. 166.50 (*0-471-91975-6*) Wiley.
Maest, Ann S., jt. ed. see Kharaka, Yousif K.
Maestas, jt. auth. see Griego, Jose.
Maestas, Bobby. Kawai K-One Sound Making Book. Alexander, Peter L., ed. (Kawai K-One Support Ser.). (Illus.). 138p. (C). 1988. pap. text ed. 19.95 (*0-939067-08-0*) Alexander Pub.
— Korg M-One Sound Making Book: Level 1. Alexander, Peter L., ed. (Korg M-One Support Ser.). (Illus.). 167p. (C). 1989. pap. 21.95 (*0-939067-39-0*) Alexander Pub.
Maestas, Bobby & Goldfield, Paul. Sampling Basics. Alexander, Peter L., ed. 125p. (C). 1989. pap. text ed. 14.95 (*0-939067-82-X*) Alexander Pub.
Maestas, Roberto, jt. auth. see Johansen, Bruce.
Maestas, Ronald W., jt. auth. see Ross, Steven C.
Maestri, William F. Choose Life & Not Death: A Primer on Abortion, Euthanasia, & Suicide. LC 85-28687. 1986. pap. 9.95 (*0-8189-0490-9*) Alba.
— My Advent Journal. 110p. 1990. pap. 5.95 (*0-8189-0599-9*) Alba.
— My Lenten Journal. 128p. 1990. pap. 5.95 (*0-8189-0576-X*) Alba.
— My Rosary Journal: The Great Mysteries. (Illus.). 112p. (Orig.). 1993. pap. 7.95 (*0-8189-0673-1*) Alba.
— My Way of the Cross Journal: A Lenten Journey with Jesus. 105p. (Orig.). 1993. pap. 5.95 (*0-8189-0663-4*) Alba.
— Paul's Pastoral Vision: Pastoral Letters for a Pastoral Church Today. LC 89-203. 240p. (Orig.). 1989. pap. 12.95 (*0-8189-0556-5*) Alba.
— A Priest to Turn To: Biblical & Pastoral Reflections on the Priesthood. LC 88-31418. 256p. (Orig.). 1989. pap. 12.95 (*0-8189-0546-8*) Alba.
— A Time for Peace: Biblical Meditations for Advent. LC 83-22399. 94p. 1983. pap. 4.95 (*0-8189-0463-1*) Alba.
— A Time to Be Re-Born. LC 82-24336. 147p. (Orig.). 1983. pap. 5.95 (*0-8189-0447-X*) Alba.
— What the Church Teaches: A Guide for the Study of Veritatis Splendor. 87p. 1994. pap. 1.50 (*0-8198-3072-0*) Pauline Bks.
— A Word in Season. LC 84-11026. 153p. (Orig.). 1983. pap. 6.95 (*0-8189-0459-3*) Alba.
Maestri, William F., ed. Mary: Model of Justice: Reflections on the Magnificat. LC 86-22304. 87p. (Orig.). 1987. pap. 4.95 (*0-8189-0511-5*) Alba.
***Maestro, Betsy.** Coming to America: The Story of Immigration. LC 94-31110. (Illus.). (J). 1995. 14.95 (*0-590-44151-5*) Scholastic Inc.
Maestro, Betsy. All Aboard Overnight: A Book of Compound Words. (Illus.). 32p. (J). (ps-2). 1992. 14.95 (*0-395-51120-8*, Clarion Bks) HM.
— Bats. LC 93-26153. (Illus.). (J). (gr. 3 up). 1994. 14.95 (*0-590-46150-8*) Scholastic Inc.
— Delivery Van: Words for Town & Country. (Illus.). 32p. (J). (ps-2). 1990. 14.95 (*0-395-51119-4*, Clarion Bks) HM.
— Discovery of the Americas. (J). (ps-3). 1991. lib. bdg. 15.93 (*0-688-06838-3*) Lothrop.
— The Discovery of the Americas Activities Book. (Illus.). 92p. (J). (gr. 1-6). 1992. pap. 7.95 (*0-688-08590-3*) Lothrop.
— Ferryboat. LC 85-47887. (Illus.). 32p. (J). (ps-3). 1986. lib. bdg. 14.89 (*0-690-04520-4*, Crowell Jr Bks) HarpC Child Bks.
— How Do Apples Grow? LC 91-9468. (Let's-Read-&-Find-Out Science Bk.). (Illus.). 32p. (J). (gr. k-4). 1992. 15.00 (*0-06-020055-3*); lib. bdg. 14.89 (*0-06-020056-1*) HarpC Child Bks.
— How Do Apples Grow? LC 91-9468. (Trophy Let's-Read-&-Find-Out Science Bk.: Stage 2). (Illus.). 32p. (J). (gr. k-3). 1993. pap. 4.95 (*0-06-445117-8*, Trophy) HarpC Child Bks.
— A More Perfect Union: The Story of Our Constitution. LC 87-4083. (Illus.). 48p. (J). (gr. 1-5). 1987. 15.95 (*0-688-06839-1*); lib. bdg. 15.88 (*0-688-06840-5*) Lothrop.
— The Story of Money. (Illus.). 48p. (J). (gr. 1 up). 1993. 15.95 (*0-395-56242-2*, Clarion Bks) HM.
— The Story of Money. Cohn, Amy, ed. (Illus.). (J). (gr. 1 up). 1995. reprint ed. pap. 4.95 (*0-688-13304-5*, Mulberry) Morrow.
— The Story of Religion. LC 92-38980. (Illus.). (J). 1994. write for info. (*0-395-62364-2*, Clarion Bks) HM.
— The Story of the Statue of Liberty. LC 85-11324. (Illus.). 40p. (J). (ps-3). 1986. lib. bdg. 12.88 (*0-688-05774-8*) Lothrop.
— The Story of the Statue of Liberty. LC 85-11324. (Illus.). 48p. (J). (gr. k up). 1989. pap. 5.95 (*0-688-08746-9*, Mulberry) Morrow.
— Take a Look at Snakes. (Illus.). (J). 1992. 14.95 (*0-590-44935-4*, Scholastic Hardcover) Scholastic Inc.
— Taxi: A Book of City Words. LC 88-22867. (Illus.). (J). (ps-2). 1989. 14.95 (*0-89919-528-8*, Clarion Bks) HM.
— Taxi: A Book of City Words. LC 88-22867. (Illus.). (J). (ps-3). 1990. reprint ed. pap. 5.95 (*0-395-54811-X*, Clarion Bks) HM.
— Why Do Leaves Change Color? LC 93-9611. (Let's-Read-&-Find-Out Science Bk.). (Illus.). 32p. (J). (gr. k-3). 1994. pap. 4.95 (*0-06-445126-7*, Trophy) HarpC Child Bks.
— Why Do Leaves Change Color? LC 93-9611. (Let's-Read-&-Find-Out Science Bk.). (Illus.). 32p. (J). (gr. k-4). 1994. 15.00 (*0-06-022873-3*); lib. bdg. 14.89 (*0-06-022874-1*) HarpC Child Bks.
Maestro, Betsy & DelVecchio, Ellen. Big City Port. 32p. (J). (gr. k-3). 1984. pap. 4.95 (*0-590-41577-8*) Scholastic Inc.
— Big City Port. LC 85-4339. (Illus.). 32p. (J). (gr. k-3). 1984. text ed. 14.95 (*0-02-762110-3*, Four Winds Pr) S&S Childrens.
Maestro, Betsy & Maestro, Giulio. El Descubrimiento de las Americas. Arturo, Juan G., tr. (Illus.). 48p. (J). (gr. 5-8). 1992. 13.95 (*0-9625162-9-5*) Lectorum Pubns.
— Discovery of the Americas. (J). (gr. 4-7). 1991. 16.00 (*0-688-06837-5*) Lothrop.
— Discovery of the Americas. LC 89-32375. (Illus.). 48p. (J). (gr. k up). 1992. pap. 5.95 (*0-688-11512-8*, Mulberry) Morrow.
— Exploration & Conquest: The Americas After Columbus, 1500-1620. LC 93-48618. (J). 1994. 16.00 (*0-688-09267-5*); lib. bdg. 15.93 (*0-688-09268-3*) Lothrop.
— A More Perfect Union: The Story of Our Constitution. LC 87-4083. (Illus.). 48p. (J). (gr. k up). 1990. pap. 5.95 (*0-688-10192-5*, Mulberry) Morrow.
— Traffic: A Book of Opposites. LC 80-29641. (Illus.). 32p. (J). (ps-1). 1991. 16.00 (*0-517-54427-X*) Crown Bks Yng Read.
— Una Union Mas Perfecta: La Historia de Nuestra Constitucion. Marcuse, Aida, tr. (Illus.). 48p. (J). (gr. 5). 1992. 13.95 (*0-9625162-8-7*) Lectorum Pubns.
Maestro, Giulio. Halloween Howls: Riddles That Are a Scream. LC 83-1419. (Illus.). 64p. (J). (gr. 3-7). 1983. 10.95 (*0-525-44059-3*, DCB) Dutton Child Bks.
— Halloween Howls: Riddles That Are a Scream. LC 83-1419. (Illus.). 64p. (J). (gr. 2-7). 1992. pap. 4.99 (*0-14-036115-4*, Puff Unicorn) Puffin Bks.
— Macho Nacho & Other Rhyming Riddles. LC 93-47137. (Illus.). 48p. (J). (gr. 2-7). 1994. 12.99 (*0-525-45261-3*) Dutton Child Bks.
— More Halloween Howls: Riddles That Come Back to Haunt You. LC 91-23505. (Illus.). 64p. (J). (gr. 2-7). 1992. 12.00 (*0-525-44899-3*, DCB) Dutton Child Bks.

An Asterisk (*) at the beginning of an entry indicates that the title is appearing in BIP for the first time.

— Razzle-Dazzle Riddles. LC 85-3785. (Illus.). 64p. (Orig.). (J). (gr. 2-5). 1985. pap. 5.95 (*0-89919-405-2*, Clarion Bks) HM.
— Riddle Roundup: A Wild Bunch to Beef up Your Word Power. LC 86-33404. (Illus.). 64p. (J). (gr. 2-5). 1989. pap. 6.95 (*0-89919-537-7*, Clarion Bks) HM.
— What's a Frank Frank? Tasty Homograph Riddles. LC 84-5021. (Illus.). 64p. (J). (gr. 2-5). 1984. pap. 6.95 (*0-89919-317-X*, Clarion Bks) HM.
— What's Mite Might? Homophone Riddles to Boost Your Word Power! LC 86-2665. (Illus.). 64p. (J). (gr. 2-5). 1986. pap. 5.95 (*0-89919-435-4*, Clarion Bks) HM.
Maestro, Giulio, jt. auth. see Maestro, Betsy.
Maestro, Giulio, jt. auth. see Maestro, Marco.
Maestro, Marco & Maestro, Giulio. Riddle City USA: A Book of Geography Riddles. LC 93-16665. (Illus.). 64p. (J). (gr. 2-5). 1994. 15.00 (*0-06-023368-0*) HarpC Child Bks.
— Riddle City USA: A Book of Geography Riddles. LC 93-16665. (Illus.). 64p. (J). (gr. 2-5). 1994. lib. bdg. 14.89 (*0-06-023369-9*) HarpC Child Bks.
— Ride the Riddle Express. LC 94-18686. (J). (gr. 2-5). 1996. 12.00 (*0-06-024948-X*); lib. bdg. 11.89 (*0-06-024949-8*) HarpC Child Bks.
Maestro, Vittorio, ed. see Dingus, Lowell, et al.
Maeterlinck, Maurice. Before the Great Silence. Kastenbaum, Robert, ed. LC 76-19580. (Death & Dying Ser.). 1977. reprint ed. lib. bdg. 21.95 (*0-405-09593-7*) Ayer.
— Le Bourgmestre de Stilmonde. 216p. (FRE.). 1967. reprint ed. pap. 11.95 (*0-7859-0931-1*) Fr & Eur.
— Bulles Bleues. 236p. (FRE.). 1948. 14.95 (*0-7859-0014-4*, F66680) Fr & Eur.
— Death. Kastenbaum, Robert, ed. LC 76-19581. (Death & Dying Ser.). 1977. reprint ed. lib. bdg. 19.95 (*0-405-09577-5*) Ayer.
— Devant Dieu. 224p. (FRE.). 1967. reprint ed. pap. 11.95 (*0-7859-4684-5*) Fr & Eur.
— The Great Secret. (Citadel Library of the Mystic Arts). 1989. pap. 7.95 (*0-8065-1155-9*, Citadel Pr) Carol Pub Group.
— L' Hote Inconnu. 196p. (FRE.). 1967. reprint ed. pap. 11.95 (*0-7859-4685-3*) Fr & Eur.
— L' Intelligence des Fleurs. 316p. (FRE.). 1951. 9.95 (*0-7859-0025-X*, F67720) Fr & Eur.
— Light Beyond. De Mattos, Alexander T., tr. LC 70-37844. (Essay Index Reprint Ser.). 1977. reprint ed. 20.95 (*0-8369-2607-2*) Ayer.
— Monna Vanna. 186p. (FRE.). 1967. reprint ed. pap. write for info. (*0-7859-4686-1*) Fr & Eur.
— Monna Vanna: A Play in Three Acts. Coleman, Alexis I., tr. LC 93-10174. 102p. 1993. reprint ed. pap. 11.95 (*1-56114-166-6*) Second Renaissance.
— L' Oiseau Bleu: Feerie en Cinq Actes et Douze Tableaux. 186p. (FRE.). 1976. 34.95 (*0-8288-9898-7*, F118590) Fr & Eur.
— On Emerson & Other Essays. Moses, Montrose J., tr. LC 78-58262. (Essay Index in Reprint Ser.). 1978. reprint ed. 20.50 (*0-8486-3024-6*) Roth Pub Inc.
— Pelleas et Melisande. 70p. (FRE.). 1968. 14.95 (*0-7859-0018-7*, F66750) Fr & Eur.
— La Princesse Isabelle. 196p. (FRE.). 1967. reprint ed. pap. 11.95 (*0-7859-4687-X*) Fr & Eur.
— Le Sablier. 224p. (FRE.). 1967. reprint ed. pap. 11.95 (*0-7859-4633-0*) Fr & Eur.
— Serres Chaudes, Quinze Chansond: La Princesse Maleine. 320p. (FRE.). 1983. pap. 16.95 (*0-7859-4688-8*) Fr & Eur.
— Serres Chaudes. Quinze Chansons. La Princesse Maleine. (Poesie Ser.). 320p. (FRE.). 1983. pap. 13.95 (*2-07-032245-9*) Schoenhof.
— Theatre Inedit. (FRE.). 1967. reprint ed. pap. 11.95 (*0-7859-4703-5*) Fr & Eur.
— The Treasure of the Humble. Sutro, Alfred, tr. LC 77-10276. reprint ed. 20.00 (*0-404-16328-9*) AMS Pr.
— Le Tresor des Humbles. 180p. (FRE.). 1986. pap. 13.95 (*0-7859-4662-4*) Fr & Eur.
— The Unknown Guest. 1975. 7.95 (*0-8216-0220-9*, Univ Bks) Carol Pub Group.
— La Vie des Abeilles. 9.95 (*0-686-56293-3*) Fr & Eur.
— La Vie des Fourmis. 260p. (FRE.). 1969. 39.95 (*0-7859-0021-7*, F66832) Fr & Eur.
— La Vie des Termites. 210p. (FRE.). 1969. 39.95 (*0-8288-9743-3*, 2246009294) Fr & Eur.
— Women, & Four Other Essays. 1991. lib. bdg. 75.00 (*0-8490-4190-2*) Gordon Pr.
Maeterlinck, Maurice, et al. What Is Civilization. LC 68-57342. (Essay Index Reprint Ser.). 1977. 19.95 (*0-8369-0986-0*) Ayer.
***Maevis, Alfred c.** Unknown in the Underground. Date not set. 5.00 (*0-614-05243-2*, UNK10791M) ASFE.
Maevis, Alfred C., ed. see Rapid Excavation & Tunneling Conference Staff.
Maeyama, Y., ed. see Hartner, Willy.
Maezumi, Hakuyu T. & Glassman, Bernard T. The Hazy Moon of Enlightenment: On Zen Practice III. LC 77-81974. (Zen Writings Ser.: Vol. Four). (Illus.). 1978. pap. 8.95 (*0-916820-05-X*) Center Pubns.
Maezumi, Hakuyu T. & Glassman, Bernard T., eds. On Zen Practice: Foundations of Practice. LC 76-9463. (Zen Writings Ser.: Vol. 1). (Illus.). 1976. pap. 5.00 (*0-916820-02-5*) Center Pubns.
Maezumi, Hakuyu T. & Loori, John D. The Way of Everyday Life. LC 78-8309. (Illus.). 1978. pap. 9.95 (*0-916820-06-8*) Center Pubns.
Maezumi, Hakuyu T., jt. auth. see Merzel, Dennis G.
MaFarlane, Gavin. ABC of VAT: And Customs & Excise Terms. 250p. (C). 1991. 34.00 (*1-85431-163-8*, Pub. by Blackstone Pr UK) W W Gaunt.
Mafeje, Archie & Radwan, Samir, eds. Economic & Demographic Change in Africa. (International Studies in Demography). (Illus.). 176p. 1995. 39.95 (*0-19-828892-1*) OUP.
Mafera, G., jt. auth. see Anderson, K.
Maffei, A. English-Konkani. 545p. 1990. reprint ed. 28.00 (*81-206-0626-4*) IBD Ltd.
— Konkani-English. 156p. 1990. reprint ed. 21.00 (*81-206-0627-2*) IBD Ltd.
Maffei, Anthony C. Classroom Computers: A Practical Guide for Effective Teaching. (Illus.). 266p. 1986. 38.95 (*0-89885-251-X*); pap. 20.95 (*0-89885-255-2*) Human Sci Pr.
Maffei, Anthony C. & Buckley, Patricia. Teaching Preschool Math: Foundations & Activities. LC 79-27448. 176p. 1980. 26.95 (*0-87705-492-4*) Human Sci Pr.
Maffei, Anthony C. & Hauck, Teresa M. Purposeful Play with Your Preschooler: A Learning-Based Activity Book. LC 92-20896. 325p. 1992. 24.95 (*0-306-44325-2*, Plenum Insight) Plenum.
Maffei, L., ed. Pathophysiology of the Visual System. (Documenta Ophthalmologica Proceedings Ser.: No. 30). 304p. 1981. lib. bdg. 112.50 (*90-6193-726-4*) Kluwer Ac.
Maffei, Lieta, jt. auth. see Thurer, Robert L.
Maffei, Lieta M., jt. auth. see Hines, Deanna M.
Maffei, N. Money Management Worksheets - IBM. 1991. 24.95 (*0-8306-6621-4*) TAB Bks.
— Money Management Worksheets - IBM PC. 1991. 24.95 (*0-8306-6622-2*) TAB Bks.
Maffei, Paolo. Monsters in the Sky. (Illus.). 1980. 32.50 (*0-262-13153-6*) MIT Pr.
Maffei, Xavier. English - Konkani Dictionary. 566p. 1990. 49.95 (*0-8288-8459-5*) Fr & Eur.
— Konkani English Dictionary. 160p. 1990. 29.95 (*0-8288-8460-9*) Fr & Eur.
— Konkani Grammar. 456p. 1986. 39.95 (*0-8288-8461-7*) Fr & Eur.
Maffesoli, Michel. The Shadow of Dionysus: A Contribution to the Sociology of the Orgy. Palmquist, M. K. & Linse, C., trs. LC 91-41828. 167p. 1992. 59.50 (*0-7914-1239-3*); pap. 19.95 (*0-7914-1240-7*) State U NY Pr.
Maffetone, Philip. High Performance Heart: Effective Training for Health, Fitness & Competition With... 2nd ed. 1994. pap. 10.95 (*0-933201-64-8*) Bicycle Books.
Maffetone, Philip & Mantell, Matthew E. High Performance Heart: Effective Training with the Heart Rate Monitor. LC 91-73663. (Illus.). 128p. (Orig.). 1991. pap. 9.95 (*0-933201-37-0*) Bicycle Books.
Maffetone, Philip B. In Fitness & in Health: Everyone Is an Athlete. 2nd rev. ed. 230p. 1994. pap. 14.95 (*0-9642062-0-X*) D Barmore Prods.
Maffett, Andrew L. Topics for a Statistical Description of Radar Cross Section. (Remote Sensing & Image Processing Ser.). 373p. 1989. text ed. 115.00 (*0-471-61357-6*) Wiley.
***Maffett, Michael.** Neptune's Account. 448p. 1995. 23.95 (*0-9644618-0-3*) Woodvale Pr.
Maffezzoni, C., ed. Modeling & Control of Electric Power Plants: Proceedings of the IFAC Workshop, Como, Italy, 22-23 September 1983. (IFAC Publication). 176p. 1984. 72.00 (*0-08-031163-6*, Pub. by Pergamon Repr UK) Franklin.
Maffi, Mario. Gateways to the Promised Land: Ethnicity & Culture in New York's Lower East Side. (Illus.). 350p. 1994. 45.00 (*0-8147-5509-7*); pap. 17.50 (*0-8147-5508-9*) NYU Pr.
***Maffit, Rocky.** Rhythm & Beauty: The Art of Drumming. (Illus.). 136p. 1995. audio 49.00 (*1-886154-12-0*); 39.00 (*1-886154-13-9*) Phoenix IL.
Maffly-Kipp, Laurie R. Religion & Society in Frontier California. LC 93-24808. (Yale Historical Publications). 256p. Date not set. 25.00 (*0-300-05377-0*) Yale U Pr.
Mafi, Maryam, tr. see Daneshvar, Simin.
Mafi, Perry. The Now That Never Was. 119p. (Orig.). 1992. pap. text ed. 7.95 (*0-9631372-1-2*) P Mafi Writs.
— Wake up from Your Dream. 83p. 1990. pap. text ed. 7.95 (*0-9631372-0-4*) P Mafi Writs.
Mafico, Christopher J. Urban Low Income Housing in Zambabwe. 176p. 1991. 68.95 (*1-85628-226-0*, Pub. by Avebury Pub UK) Ashgate Pub Co.
***Maflin, Andrea.** Decorative Paper: Projects, Techniques, Pull-out Designs. (Illus.). 108p. 1995. pap. 22.95 (*1-57076-027-6*, Trafalgar Sq Pub) Trafalgar.
Mafrou, Edisyon, ed. see Large, Josaphat.
Maga & Tu, eds. Food Additive Toxicology. 552p. 1995. 175.00 (*0-8247-9245-9*) Dekker.
Maga, Joseph A. Smoke in Food Processing. 176p. 1988. 156.00 (*0-8493-5155-3*, TP371) CRC Pr.
Maga, Timothy P. Defending Paradise: The United States & Guam, 1898-1950. 1988. 15.00 (*0-8240-4336-7*) Garland.
— John F. Kennedy & New Frontier Diplomacy, 1961-1963. LC 92-43248. 170p. (C). 1994. lib. bdg. 18.50 (*0-89464-829-2*) Krieger.
— John F. Kennedy & the New Pacific Community, 1961-63. LC 89-36450. 200p. 1990. text ed. 35.00 (*0-312-03639-6*) St Martin.
— The World of Jimmy Carter: U. S. Foreign Policy, 1977-1981. Katsaros, Thomas, ed. 200p. (Orig.). 1994. pap. text ed. 20.00 (*0-936285-23-0*) U New Haven Pr.
***Magad, Eugene L. & Amos, John M.** Total Materials Management: Achieving Maximum Profits Through Materials-Logistics Operations. LC 94-47941. (Materials Management-Logistics Ser.). 1995. write for info. (*0-615-00452-0*, Chap & Hall NY) Chapman & Hall.
Magadatz, Joe. One Thousand One Ways Not to Be Romantic. 1993. pap. 6.95 (*1-883518-27-X*) Casablanca Pr.
— One Thousand One Ways NOT to be Romantic-the Parody! (Illus.). 192p. 1993. pap. 6.95 (*0-88351-827-9*) Casablanca Pr.
Magagna, Jeanne, ed. see Rey, Henri.
Magagna, Victor V. Communities of Grain: Rural Rebellion in Comparative Perspective. LC 90-55720. (Wilder House Series in Politics, History, & Culture). 312p. 1991. 45.00 (*0-8014-2361-9*) Cornell U Pr.
***Magai, Carol & McFadden, Susan H.** The Role of Emotions in Social & Personality Development: History, Theory, & Research. (Emotions, Personality, & Psychotherapy Ser.: 1). 360p. 1995. 45.00 (*0-306-44866-1*, Plenum Pr) Plenum.
Magaia, Lina. Dumba Nengue: Run for Your Life: Peasant Tales of Tragedy in Mozambique. Wolfers, Michael, tr. LC 87-72780. (Illus.). 115p. (C). 1988. 14.95 (*0-86543-073-X*); pap. 6.95 (*0-86543-074-8*) Africa World.
Magal, Lily, pseud. & Arber, Rachel. In the Land of the Golden Fleece. (Illus.). 1993. Album size. 39.50 (*0-317-05873-8*, Pub. by Israel Ministry Def IS) Gefen Bks.
Magalaner, Marvin. Time of Apprenticeship: The Fiction of Young James Joyce. LC 70-140366. (Select Bibliographies Reprint Ser.). 1977. reprint ed. 18.95 (*0-8369-5609-5*) Ayer.
Magalas, L. B. & Gorczyca, S., eds. Internal Friction & Ultrasonic in Solids, Including High-Temperature Superconductors. 876p. (C). 1993. text ed. 225.00 (*0-87849-623-8*, Pub. by Trans Tech SZ) LPS Dist Ctr.
Magalashivili, Lily, see Lily Magal, pseud..
Magalhaes, Hulda, ed. see American Association of Laboratory Animal Science Staff.
Magalini. Dictionary of Medical Syndromes. 3rd ed. (Illus.). 900p. 1990. text ed. 99.00 (*0-397-50882-4*) Lippincott.
Magalit, Isabelo F. Can a Christian Be a Nationalist? 35p. (Orig.). 1993. pap. 3.75 (*971-10-0517-4*, Pub. by New Day Pub PH) Cellar.
***Magallanes, Eduardo.** Querido Alberto: Biografia Autorizado de Juan Gabriel. 1995. pap. 12.00 (*0-684-81548-6*, Scribners) S&S Trade.
Magallon, Ana & Betran, J. Antonio, eds. Isidorus Hispaliensis - Concordantia in Isidori Hispaliensis Etymologias, 2 vols. Bd. CXX. 1200p. Date not set. write for info. (*0-318-71154-0*, Pub. by Georg Olms GW) Lubrecht & Cramer.
Magallon, Ana, ed. see Hispaliensis, Isidorus.
Magallon Martinez, M., ed. Inside Hemophilia: Milestones in Hemophilia & Von Willebrand's Disease in the Last 25 Years, Dedicated to Dr. J. Martin Villar in His Retirement. (Journal: Haemostasis: Vol. 22, No. 5, 1992). (Illus.). 84p. 1992. pap. 42.50 (*3-8055-5717-5*) S Karger.
Magalnick, B. English Reader. 1979. pap. text ed. 6.84 (*0-07-039470-9*) McGraw.
Magalula, Cisco. Implementing Educational Policies in Swaziland. (Discussion Paper Ser.: No. 88). 84p. 1990. 7.95 (*0-8213-1585-4*, 11585) World Bank.
Magan, Geralyn G., ed. Aging, Race & Culture: Issues in Long Term Care. LC 82-72776. 77p. 1982. 6.50 (*0-685-06337-2*) Am Assn Homes.
Magana. Guia Rapida Impresoras Laser: Spanish Guide to Laser Printers. (SPA.). 1990. 12.95 (*0-7859-3700-5*, 8428317801) Fr & Eur.
Magana, Gilardo. Emiliano Zapata y el Agrarismo en Mexico, 5 vols., Set. (Mexico Ser.). 1979. lib. bdg. 1,500.00 (*0-8490-2908-2*) Gordon Pr.
***Magana, Lisa, ed.** Mexican Americans: Are They An Ambivalent Minority? 138p. (C). (gr. 12 up). 1994. pap. text ed. 15.00 (*1-57240-000-5*) T Rivera Ctr.
Magana, Raoul D., jt. auth. see Gelfand, Leo.
Magann, Julia H. Municipal Financial Disclosure: An Empirical Investigation. Farmer, Richard N., ed. LC 83-1106. (Research for Business Decisions Ser.: No. 58). 110p. reprint ed. 31.40 (*0-8357-1394-6*, 2070402) Bks Demand.
Maganza, Dennis, ed. see Fielding, Henry.
Magar, jt. ed. see Conrad.
Magara, K. Compaction & Fluid Migration: Practical Petroleum Geology. (Developments in Petroleum Science Ser.: Vol. 9). 320p. 1978. 113.00 (*0-444-41654-4*) Elsevier.
— Geological Models of Petroleum Entrapment. 340p. 1986. 106.25 (*0-85334-439-6*, Pub. by Elsevier Applied Sci UK) Elsevier.
Magarello, Anthony. Good Reading-Good Writing, A. (Effective Language Arts Program Ser.). (Illus.). 59p. 1981. 4.75 (*0-9602800-7-3*) Comp Pr.
— Good Reading-Good Writing, C. (Effective Language Arts Program Ser.). 61p. 1983. 4.75 (*0-9602800-8-1*) Comp Pr.
Magaret, Pat & Slusser, Donna. Round Robin Quilts: Friendship Quilts of the 90s & Beyond. Weiland, Barbara, ed. LC 94-21147. (Illus.). 112p. (Orig.). 1994. pap. 22.95 (*1-56477-065-6*) That Patchwork.
Magaret, Pat S. & Slusser, Donna I. Watercolor Quilts. Weiland, Barbara, ed. LC 93-8551. (Illus.). 118p. (Orig.). 1993. pap. 24.95 (*1-56477-031-1*, B161) That Patchwork.
***Magarey, D. R.** Buying & Selling Businesses & Companies. 316p. 1989. boxed 69.00 (*0-409-49535-2*, Austral) Butterworth Legal Pubs.
Magarey, Susan, et al, eds. Debutante Nation: Feminism Rewrites History of the 1890's. 224p. 1993. pap. 19.95 (*1-86373-296-9*, Pub. by Allen Unwin AT) Paul & Co Pubs.
Magarian-Gold, Judi, jt. auth. see Mogensen, Sandra.
Magarian-Gold, Judy, jt. auth. see Mogensen, Sandra.
Magarian, Karen, et al. Chiropractic College Admissions & Curriculum Directory: 1988-89. 250p. 1988. pap. write for info. (*0-945947-00-3*) KM Enterprises.
— The Chiropractic College Admissions & Curriculum Directory: 1996-97. 5th ed. 250p. Date not set. lib. bdg. 17.95 (*0-945947-04-6*); pap. 11.95 (*0-614-05274-2*) KM Enterprises.
Magarick, Pat. Casualty Insurance Claims: Coverage-Investigation-Law, 2 vols. 3rd ed. LC 87-16624. 1988. ring bd. 215.00 (*0-87632-559-2*) Clark Boardman Callaghan.
— Casualty Investigation Checklists. 3rd ed. LC 84-23135. 1985. spiral bd. 62.50 (*0-87632-457-X*) Clark Boardman Callaghan.
— Excess Liability: The Law of Extracontractual Liability of Insurers. 3rd ed. LC 88-17495. 1989. ring bd. 135.00 (*0-87632-604-1*) Clark Boardman Callaghan.
— Insurance Law Review. 1990. 125.00 (*0-87632-847-8*) Clark Boardman Callaghan.
Magarick, Pat & Brownlee, Ken. Casualty Investigation Checklists. 4th ed. LC 94-17154. 1994. spiral bd. 80.00 (*0-87632-073-6*) Clark Boardman Callaghan.
Magarick, Ronald H. & Burkman, Ronald T., eds. Reproductive Health Education & Technology: Issues & Future Directions. (Illus.). 144p. (Orig.). (C). 1988. pap. write for info. (*0-318-63707-3*) JHPIEGO.
Magaro, Peter A. Cognition in Schizophrenia & Paranoia: The Integration of Cognitive Processes. LC 80-13870. 351p. 1980. text ed. 69.95 (*0-89859-028-0*) L Erlbaum Assocs.
— Construction of Madness: Emerging Conceptions & Interventions into Psychotic Process. 240p. 1976. 101.00 (*0-08-019904-6*, Pub. by Pergamon Repr UK) Franklin.
Magaro, Peter A., ed. Cognitive Bases of Mental Disorders. (Annual Review of Psychopathology Ser.: Vol. 1). 352p. (C). 1990. text ed. 49.95 (*0-8039-4009-2*); pap. text ed. 24.00 (*0-8039-4010-6*) Sage.
Magaro, Peter A., et al. The Mental Health Industry: A Cultural Phenomenon. LC 77-14434. (Wiley Series on Personality Processes). 288p. reprint ed. pap. 82.10 (*0-317-27956-4*, 2055761) Bks Demand.
Magarrell, Elaine. Blameless Lives. LC 91-66080. 72p. (Orig.). 1991. pap. 10.00 (*0-915380-28-5*) Word Works.
— On Hogback Mountain. LC 84-52606. (Series Nine). 54p. 1985. pap. 7.00 (*0-931846-27-7*) Wash Writers Pub.
Magarshac, David, tr. see Tolstoy, Leo.
Magarshack, David. Chekhov, a Life. LC 69-13983. 431p. 1970. reprint ed. text ed. 79.50 (*0-8371-4095-1*, MACH, Greenwood Pr) Greenwood.
— Stanislavsky: A Life. 432p. 1986. pap. 13.95 (*0-571-13791-1*) Faber & Faber.
Magarshack, David, tr. see Avilov, Lydia.
Magarshack, David, tr. see Chekhov, Anton P.
Magarshack, David, tr. see Chekhov, Anton.
Magarshack, David, ed. see Chekhov, Anton.
Magarshack, David, tr. see Dostoyevsky, Fyodor.
Magarshack, David, tr. see Gogol, Nikolai V.
Magarshack, David, tr. see Leskov, Nikolai S.
Magarshack, David, tr. see Ostrovskii, Aleksandr N.
Magarshack, David, tr. see Ostrovsky, Alexander.
Magarshack, David, tr. see Pasternak, Boris.
Magarshack, David, tr. see Saltykov-Shchedrin, Mikhail.
Magarshack, David, tr. see Schneider, Ilya I.
Magarshak, David, tr. see Chekhov, Anton.
Magas, Branca. The Destruction of Yugoslavia. LC 92-30825. 384p. 1993. 64.95 (*0-86091-376-7*, A3750, Pub. by Verso UK); pap. 19.95 (*0-86091-593-X*, A3754, Pub. by Verso UK) Routledge Chapman & Hall.
— The Widening Gyre: Class & Nation in Yugoslavia. 256p. 1990. 50.00 (*0-86091-262-0*, A3750); pap. 17.95 (*0-86091-975-7*, A3754) Routledge Chapman & Hall.
Magasi, P. Surgery of the Neurogenic Bladder. 150p. 1982. 115.00 (*0-569-08733-3*, Pub. by Collets UK) Pro-Am Music.
— Surgery of the Neurogenic Bladder. 148p. (C). 1982. 54.00x (*963-05-2892-4*) St Mut.
Magat, M., jt. auth. see Haissinsky, M.
Magat, Richard, ed. An Agile Servant: Community Leadership by Community Foundations. LC 89-38377. 1989. 24.95 (*0-87954-330-2*); pap. 15.95 (*0-87954-332-9*) Foundation Ctr.
— Philanthropic Giving: Studies in Varieties & Goals. (Yale Studies on Nonprofit Organizations). (Illus.). 382p. 1989. 55.00 (*0-19-505050-9*) OUP.
Magat, Wesley A. & Viscusi, W. Kip. Informational Approaches to Regulation. (REA Ser.). (Illus.). 371p. 1991. 35.00 (*0-262-13277-X*) MIT Pr.
Magat, Wesley A., jt. auth. see Viscusi, W. Kip.
Magat, Wesley A., et al. Rules in the Making: A Statistical Analysis. LC 85-43555. 182p. 1986. text ed. 22.50 (*0-915707-24-1*) Resources Future.
Magay, M. I. Hungarian-English & English-Hungarian Dictionary for Tourists. 8th ed. 629p. (ENG & HUN.). 1986. 14.95 (*0-8288-1655-7*, M10680) Fr & Eur.
***Magay, T.** English-Hungarian Concise Dictionary. 17th ed. 703p. (HUN.). 1991. 30.50 (*0-7859-8935-8*, 3426266253) Fr & Eur.
— Hungarian-English Concise Dictionary. 3rd ed. (ENG & HUN.). 1991. 30.50 (*0-7859-8942-0*) Fr & Eur.
***Magay, T. & Kiss, L., eds.** Hungarian English & English Hungarian Paperback Dictionary, 2 vols. 1186p. (C). 1991. pap. 60.00x (*963-05-6056-9*, Pub. by Akad Kiado HU) St Mut.
Magay, T. & Lang, I. L. Anglicisms, Americanisms. 320p. (ENG & HUN.). 1991. 14.95 (*0-8288-7190-6*, F88860) Fr & Eur.
— Anglicisms, Americanisms. 320p. (C). 1993. 24.00x (*963-05-6043-7*, Pub. by Akad Kiado HU) St Mut.
***Magay, T. & Orszagh, L.** A Concise Hungarian-English Dictionary. 3rd rev. ed. 1152p. (C). 1993. 54.00x (*963-05-6547-1*, Pub. by Akad Kiado HU) St Mut.
— English-Hungarian Concise Dictionary. 17th ed. 1045p. 1991. 30.50 (*963-05-6025-9*) IBD Ltd.

An Asterisk (*) at the beginning of an entry indicates that the title is appearing in BIP for the first time.

— Hungarian-English Concise Dictionary. 3rd rev. ed. 1152p. 1991. 30.50 (963-05-6047-X) IBD Ltd.

*Magay, T. & Zigany, J., eds. Budalex 88 Proceedings. 580p. (C). 1990. pap. 180.00x (963-05-5863-7, Pub. by Akad Kiado HU) St Mut.

Magay, T., jt. auth. see Kiss, L.

Magay, T., jt. auth. see Orszagh, L.

*Magay, Tomas & Kiss, Laszlo. English Hungarian Standard Dictionary. 541p. 1995. 40.00 (0-7818-0391-8) Hippocrene Bks.

Magazine, Alan H. Environmental Management in Local Government: A Study of Local Response to Federal Mandate. LC 77-12818. (Special Studies). 160p. 1977. text ed. 45.00 (0-275-90269-2, C0269, Praeger Pubs) Greenwood.

Magazine Marketing Service Staff. M. M. S. County Buying Power Index. LC 75-22826. (America in Two Centuries Ser.). 1976. reprint ed. 20.95 (0-405-07698-3) Ayer.

Magazine of Wall Street Staff. Fourteen Methods of Operating in the Stock Market. LC 68-29698. 1968. reprint ed. 12.00 (0-87034-027-1) Fraser Pub Co.

Magaziner, Fred T. & Johnson, Earl, Jr. Pennsylvania Civil Trial Guide, 5 vols., Set. LC 92-20444. 1992. write for info. (0-8205-1825-5) Bender.

Magaziner, Ira & Patinkin, Mark. Silent War. LC 89-40489. 1990. pap. 15.00 (0-679-72827-9, Vin) Random.

Magaziner, Ira C. & Hout, Thomas M. Japanese Industrial Policy. LC 81-80791. (Policy Papers in International Affairs Ser.: No. 15). (Illus.). 120p. 1981. pap. 9.50 (0-87725-515-6) U of Cal IAS.

Magazis, G. A. Greek-English - English-Greek. 863p. 1989. 30.00 (960-226-017-3) IBD Ltd.

*Magda, Kovacs. Microelectronics Dictionary in Three Languages. 1990. pap. 28.50 (0-7859-8964-1) Fr & Eur.

— Microelectronics Dictionary in Three Languages. 381p. (ENG, GER & HUN.). 1990. pap. 28.50 (963-7935-04-5) IBD Ltd.

Magda, Matthew S., ed. Monessen: Industrial Boomtown & Steel Community, 1898-1980. (American Places Ser.). (Illus.). 152p. 1985. pap. text ed. 6.95 (0-89271-029-2) Pa Hist & Mus.

Magdalany, Philip. Criss-Crossing & Watercolor: Manuscript Edition. 1970. pap. 13.00 (0-8222-0251-4) Dramatists Play.

Magdalen. Children in the Church Today: An Orthodox Perspective. (Illus.). 104p. (Orig.). 1990. pap. 7.95 (0-88141-104-3) St Vladimirs.

Magdalen, I. I. Ana P. LC 84-60403. 320p. 1985. 16.95 (0-87951-980-0) Overlook Pr.

Magdalena. The Real Preacher. 1986. 20.00 (0-946270-23-6, Pub. by Pentland Pr UK) St Mut.

Magdaleno, Mauricio. Jose Marti. 1976. lib. bdg. 250.00 (0-8490-2108-1) Gordon Pr.

— Sunburst. Brenner, Anita, tr. LC 74-25390. reprint ed. 17.50 (0-404-58449-7) AMS Pr.

Magdalino, Paul. The Empire of Manuel I Komnenos, 1142-1180. LC 92-13501. (Illus.). 584p. (C). 1993. 89.95 (0-521-30571-3) Cambridge U Pr.

— Tradition & Transformation in Medieval Byzantium. (Collected Studies: No. CS 343). 350p. 1991. text ed. 95.00 (0-86078-295-6, Pub. by Variorum UK) Ashgate Pub Co.

Magdalino, Paul, ed. New Constantines: The Rhythm of Imperial Renewal in Byzantium, 4th-13th Centuries. LC 94-5125. (Publications - Society for the Promotion of Byzantine Studies: Vol. 2). 324p. 1994. text ed. 69.50 (0-86078-409-6, Pub. by Variorum UK) Ashgate Pub Co.

— The Perception of the Past in Twelfth-Century Europe. 256p. 1992. boxed 55.00 (1-85285-066-3) Hambledon Press.

Magdanz, Lee. Color the Inside of Your Brain. (Illus.). 22p. 1989. pap. 9.95 (0-9613949-2-7) R S Pr.

Magdaong-Manginsay, Edna G., jt. auth. see Alonto, Zafrullah M.

Magdelen, Margaret. Transformed by Love: The Way of Mary Magdalen. LC 90-61562. 96p. (Orig.). 1990. pap. 5.95 (0-9623410-5-3) Resurrection.

Magden, Ronald E. A History of Seattle Waterfront Workers 1884-1934. (Illus.). 280p. (Orig.). 1991. pap. 10.00 (0-9629578-0-1) Tacoma Lngshore Comm.

— The Working Longshoreman. (Illus.). 208p. (Orig.). 1991. 10.00 (0-9629616-1-2) Tacoma Lngshore Comm.

Magden, Ronald E. & Martinson, A. D. The Working Waterfront: The Story of Tacoma's Ships & Men. (Illus.). 181p. (Orig.). 1982. pap. 10.00 (0-9629578-2-8) Intl Long WA.

Magder, Ted. Canada's Hollywood: The Canadian State & Feature Films. (State & Economic Life Ser.). 368p. 1993. 50.00 (0-8020-2970-1); pap. 22.95 (0-8020-7433-2) U of Toronto Pr.

Magdi Wahba. English-Arabic Dictionary: Al-Mukhtar. 1989. 39.95 (0-86685-535-1) Intl Bk Ctr.

Magdich, L. N. & Molchanov, V. Y. Acousto-optical Devices & Their Applications. 176p. 1989. text ed. 135.00 (2-88124-677-X) Gordon & Breach.

Magdics, Klara. Studies in the Acoustic Characteristics of Hungarian Speech Sounds. LC 68-65314. (Uralic & Altaic Ser.: Vol. 97). (Illus.). 141p. 1969. pap. text ed. 12.00 (0-87750-041-X) Res Inst Inner Asian Studies.

Magdoff, Fred. Building Soils for Better Crops: Organic Matter Management. LC 92-2362. (Our Sustainable Future Ser.: Vol. 2). xii, 176p. 1993. 22.95 (0-8032-3160-1) U of Nebr Pr.

Magdoff, Harry. Age of Imperialism. LC 69-19788. 1969. 6.00 (0-85345-082-X); pap. 9.00 (0-85345-101-X) Monthly Rev.

— Imperialism: From the Colonial Age to the Present. LC 77-76167. 1979. pap. 10.00 (0-85345-498-1) Monthly Rev.

Magdoff, Harry & Sweezy, Paul. The End of Prosperity: The American Economy in the 1970's. LC 77-76168. 136p. 1977. 7.95 (0-85345-422-1); pap. 2.95 (0-85345-458-2) Monthly Rev.

Magdoff, Harry & Sweezy, Paul M. The Irreversible Crisis. 96p. (Orig.). (C). 1989. pap. 4.50 (0-85345-776-X) Monthly Rev.

— Stagnation & the Financial Explosion. 224p. 1987. 24.00 (0-85345-716-6); pap. 8.00 (0-85345-715-8) Monthly Rev.

Magdoff, Harry, jt. auth. see Sweezy, Paul M.

Magdoff, Harry, jt. ed. see Sweezy, Paul M.

Magdol, Edward. The Antislavery Rank & File: A Social Profile of the Abolitionists' Constituency. LC 85-30191. (Contributions in American History Ser.: No. 117). 188p. 1986. text ed. 49.95 (0-313-24723-4, MRK/, Greenwood Pr) Greenwood.

— A Right to the Land: Essays on the Freedmen's Community. LC 76-39707. (Contributions in American History Ser.: No. 61). (Illus.). 290p. 1977. text ed. 59.95 (0-8371-9409-1, MFC/, Greenwood Pr) Greenwood.

Magdol, Edward & Wakelyn, Jon L. The Southern Common People: Studies in Nineteenth-Century Social History. LC 79-7724. (Contributions in American History Ser.: No. 86). (Illus.). xii, 386p. (C). 1980. text ed. 65.00 (0-313-21403-4, MLL/, Greenwood Pr) Greenwood.

Magee, Alan. Stones & Other Works. (Illus.). 64p. 1987. pap. 16.95 (0-8109-2341-6) Abrams.

Magee, Anthony I., ed. Protein Targeting: A Practical Approach. (Practical Approach Ser.). (Illus.). 276p. 1992. 79.00 (0-19-963206-5); pap. 44.00 (0-19-963210-3) OUP.

Magee, Babette. Screen Printing Primer. LC 85-71229. (Illus.). 92p. 1985. 40.00 (0-88362-077-4, 1331) Graphic Arts Tech Found.

Magee, Babette, jt. auth. see Hohman, Jennifer.

Magee, Benjamin F. History of the Seventy-Second Indiana Volunteer Infantry: Wilder's Lightning Brigade. (Illus.). 800p. 1995. reprint ed. 40.00 (0-9628866-3-7) Blue Acorn Pr.

Magee, Bettie, jt. auth. see Howells, John.

Magee, Brian. In the Light of Christ: The Old Testament Readings at the Easter Vigil. 1994. pap. 21.00 (1-85390-296-9, Pub. by Veritas IE) St Mut.

— Reading for the Funeral Mass. 72p. 1989. pap. 22.00 (0-86217-222-5, Pub. by Veritas IE) St Mut.

— Readings for Your Wedding. 88p. 1989. pap. 22.00 (0-86217-211-X, Pub. by Veritas IE) St Mut.

Magee, Brian, ed. Bless This House: Ritual for the Blessing of a Home. 30p. 1990. 3.95 (1-85390-199-7) Ignatius Pr.

— A Book of Prayers & Blessings. 214p. 1992. reprint ed. 8.99 (0-89283-761-6) Servant.

Magee, Brian, intro. Psalm Prayers for Morning & Evening. 65p. (Orig.). 1991. pap. 5.95 (1-85390-121-0, Pub. by Veritas Publns IE) Ignatius Pr.

Magee, Bryan. Aspects of Wagner. 2nd ed. 112p. 1988. pap. 10.95 (0-19-284012-6) OUP.

— Democratic Revolution. LC 64-25509. 1964. 16.95 (0-8023-1075-3) Dufour.

— The Great Philosophers. (Illus.). 352p. 1988. pap. 11.95 (0-19-282201-2) OUP.

— Philosophy & the Real World: An Introduction to Karl Popper. 120p. (C). 1985. reprint ed. pap. 12.95 (0-87548-436-0) Open Court.

Magee, D. F. & Dalley, A. F. Digestion & the Structure & Function of the Gut. (Continuing Education Ser.: Vol. 8). (Illus.). viii, 360p. 1986. 118.50 (3-8055-4204-6) S Karger.

Magee, David. Bibliography of the Grabhorn Press, Nineteen Fifteen to Nineteen Fifty-Six. LC 75-14603. 1975. 150.00 (0-915346-04-4) A Wofsy Fine Arts.

— The Lifeforce Maximizer. LC 86-81432. (Illus.). 164p. (Orig.). 1986. pap. 39.50 (0-938811-00-2) Life Survival Digest.

Magee, David J. Orthopedic Physical Assessment. 2nd ed. (Illus.). 720p. 1992. text ed. 46.50 (0-7216-4344-2) Saunders.

*Magee, David S. Everything Your Heirs Need to Know: Your Assets, Family History & Final Wishes. 2nd ed. 176p. (Orig.). 1995. pap. 19.95 (0-7931-1308-3, 5608-4502) Dearborn Finan.

Magee, Dennis W. Freshwater Wetlands: A Guide to Common Indicator Plants of the Northeast. LC 80-26876. (Illus.). 240p. 1981. pap. text ed. 16.95x (0-87023-317-3) U of Mass Pr.

Magee, Doug & Newman, Robert. All Aboard ABC. LC 89-29852. (Illus.). (J). (ps). 1990. 14.99 (0-525-65036-9, Cobblehill Bks) Dutton Child Bks.

— All Aboard ABC. (Illus.). 48p. (J). (ps-3). 1994. pap. 4.99 (0-14-055351-7, Puff Unicorn) Puffin Bks.

— Let's Fly from A to Z. LC 91-39774. (Illus.). 48p. (J). (ps-3). 1992. 14.00 (0-525-65105-5, Cobblehill Bks) Dutton Child Bks.

Magee, Elizabeth. Richard Wagner & the Nibelungs. 242p. 1991. 55.00 (0-19-816190-5) OUP.

Magee, Frances T., jt. auth. see Magee, Stephen P.

Magee, Gregory H. Facilities Maintenance Management. (Illus.). 280p. (C). 1988. 79.95 (0-87629-100-0, 67249) R S Means.

Magee, Heno. Hatchet. 1978. pap. 2.95 (0-912262-48-6) Proscenium.

— Hatchet. deluxe ed. 1978. 7.50 (0-912262-47-8) Proscenium.

MaGee, Herman J. Unit Costs of Salaries in Teachers College & Normal Schools. LC 73-177046. (Columbia University. Teachers College. Contributions to Education Ser.: No. 489). reprint ed. 37.50 (0-404-55489-X) AMS Pr.

Magee, J. H. Night of Affliction & Morning of Recovery. LC 77-89397. (Black Heritage Library Collection). 1977. 15.95 (0-8369-8622-9) Ayer.

Magee, J. O. Company Accounts. 445p. (C). 1982. 85.00 (0-685-39820-X, Inst Pur & Supply) St Mut.

Magee, J. Robert. Japan Cheap & Easy: A Practical Guide to Daily Life in Japan. 168p. (Orig.). 1993. pap. 11.95 (4-89684-231-6, Pub. by Yohan Pubns JA) Weatherhill.

Magee, J. S. & Mitchell, M. M., Jr., eds. Fluid Catalytic Cracking: Science & Technology. LC 93-20742. (Studies in Surface Science & Catalysis: Vol. 76). 605p. 1993. 248.50 (0-444-89037-8) Elsevier.

Magee, James E. Your Place in the Cosmos, Vol. I: A Layman's Book of Astronomy & the Mythology of the Eighty-Eight Celestial Constellations & Registry. (Illus.). 530p. (YA). 1985. text ed. 34.45 (0-9614354-0-2) Mosele & Assocs.

— Your Place in the Cosmos, Vol. II: A Layman's Book of Astronomy & the Mythology of the Eighty-Eight Celestial Constellations & Registry. (Illus.). 508p. (YA). 1988. text ed. 34.45 (0-9614354-1-0) Mosele & Assocs.

— Your Place in the Cosmos, Vol. III: A Layman's Book of Astronomy & the Mythology of the Eighty-Eight Celestial Constellations & Registry. (Illus.). 388p. (YA). 1992. text ed. 49.45 (0-9614354-2-9) Mosele & Assocs.

Magee, James J. Mr. Justice Black, Absolutist on the Court. LC 79-11555. (Virginia Legal Studies). 232p. reprint ed. pap. 66.20 (0-685-20396-4, 2030188) Bks Demand.

— A Professional's Guide to Older Adult's Life Review: Releasing the Peace Within. 112p. 1988. text ed. 27.95 (0-669-19413-1) Free Pr.

Magee, Jarlon. Sanctuary of Illusion. LC 91-60468. 1991. pap. 12.95 (0-87212-248-4) Libra.

Magee, Jeff. Bounceback. 1992. pap. 12.95 (0-932845-50-9) Lowell Pr.

Magee, Jeffrey, jt. auth. see Crawford, Richard.

Magee, Jeffrey L. The P Factor: The Personality Jumpstart Advantage. Spaith, Nancey, ed. 250p. 1993. pap. 19.95 (0-9641240-0-9) J Magee Intl.

— Power Charged for Life! Designing A Championship Attitude. Drissel, Nancy, ed. 80p. (Orig.). (C). 1994. pap. 12.95 (0-9641240-1-7) J Magee Intl.

Magee, John. Analyzing Bar Charts for Profits. McDermott, Richard J., ed. (Illus.). 69p. (Orig.). 1993. write for info. (0-910944-03-2) Magee.

— Boethius on Signification & Mind. LC 89-37962. (Philosophia Antiqua Ser.: Vol. LII). xiv, 165p. (Orig.). 1989. pap. text ed. 51.50 (90-04-09096-7) E J Brill.

— Microbe Base - Apple. 1986. text ed., disk 927.00 (0-12-465014-7) Acad Pr.

Magee, John, jt. auth. see Edwards, Robert D.

Magee, Joseph H., jt. auth. see Horwitz, Orville.

Magee, Kathleen, jt. auth. see Brewer, John D.

Magee, Kenneth R. & Saper, Joel R. Clinical & Basic Neurology for Health Professionals. LC 80-27146. 311p. reprint ed. pap. 88.70 (0-318-34979-5, 2030792) Bks Demand.

Magee, Kenneth R., jt. auth. see Simpson, John F.

Magee, Linda. Two Hundred One Group Games. (Game & Party Bks.). 64p. 1984. pap. 4.99 (0-8010-6154-7) Baker Bk.

Magee, Malachy. One Thousand Years of Irish Whiskey. 1991. pap. 12.95 (0-86278-228-7) Dufour.

Magee, Michael C. Basic Science for the Practicing Urologist. LC 82-4561. (Illus.). 250p. 1983. 64.95 (0-521-24567-2) Cambridge U Pr.

Magee, Peter N., ed. Nitrosamines & Human Cancer. LC 82-12952. (Banbury Report Ser.: Vol. 12). 599p. 1982. 67.00 (0-87969-211-1) Cold Spring Harbor.

Magee, Philip S., et al, eds. Pesticide Synthesis Through Rational Approaches: Based on a Symposium Sponsored by the Division of Pesticide Chemistry at the 186th Meeting of the American Chemical Society, Washington, DC, August 28-September 2, 1983. LC 84-11062. (ACS Symposium Ser.: No. 255). (Illus.). 368p. reprint ed. pap. 104.90 (0-7837-1965-5, 2052443) Bks Demand.

Magee-Powell, Marilyn, ed. The Journal of Applied Manufacturing Systems, Vol. 4, Nos. 1 & 2. 80p. 1991. 20.00 (0-9624229-2-4) St Thomas Tech.

Magee, R. Dale, ed. see Boucher, David.

Magee, Richard S., et al. Innovative Site Remediation Technology, Vol. 7: Thermal Destruction. Anderson, William C., ed. LC 93-20786. 140p. 1994. 49.95 (1-883767-07-5) Am Acad Environ.

Magee, Robert. Reading Japanese Around You. 160p. (Orig.). 1994. pap. 11.95 (4-89684-240-5, Pub. by Yohan Pubns JA) Weatherhill.

Magee, Rosemary M. Conversations with Flannery O'Connor. LC 86-22381. (Literary Conversations Ser.). 146p. 1987. 37.50 (0-87805-264-X); pap. 15.95 (0-87805-265-8) U Pr of Miss.

Magee, Rosemary M., ed. Friendship & Sympathy: Communities of Southern Women Writers. LC 91-25615. 1992. 38.50 (0-87805-523-1); pap. 16.95 (0-87805-545-2) U Pr of Miss.

Magee, S. & Tripp, L. Software Engineering Standards: An Annotated Index & Directory. 250p. 1994. 79.50 (0-912702-82-6) Global Eng Doc.

Magee, Sean, ed. see Oaksley, John.

Magee, Stephen P. International Trade & Distortions in Factor Markets. LC 75-25163. (Business Economics & Finance Ser.: No. 6). 158p. reprint ed. pap. 45.10 (0-7837-0701-0, 2041033) Bks Demand.

Magee, Stephen P. & Magee, Frances T. A Plague of Lawyers: Greed & the American Legal System. 1994. write for info. (0-446-51811-5) Warner Bks.

Magee, Stephen P., et al, eds. Black Hole Tariffs & Endogenous Policy Theory: Political Economy in General Equilibrium. (Illus.). (C). 1989. 74.95 (0-521-36247-4); pap. 24.95 (0-521-37700-5) Cambridge U Pr.

Magee, Thomas. Baja California: Business Opportunities & Retirement Guide. 1992. write for info. (1-56559-900-4) HGI Mrktng.

Magee, Tim, et al. A Solar Greenhouse Guide for the Pacific Northwest. 2nd ed. Stewart, Annie & Sassaman, Richard, eds. (Illus.). 91p. 1979. pap. 6.00 (0-934478-26-0) Ecotope.

*Magee, Veda. To Emma. 250p. 1995. text ed. write for info. (1-882194-14-4) TN Valley Pub.

Magee, Wes. Dark Age. 56p. 1982. pap. 11.95 (0-85640-256-7, Pub. by Blackstaff Pr IE) Dufour.

— Legend of the Ragged Boy. (Illus.). 32p. (J). (ps-3). 1993. 14.95 (1-55970-228-1) Arcade Pub Inc.

Magee, William A. & Napper, Elizabeth S. Fluent Tibetan: A Proficiency Oriented Learning System, Novice & Intermediate Levels, 18 tapes, Set of 3. Hopkins, Jeffrey, ed. LC 93-4076. 1025p. 1993. audio, pap. 250.00 (1-55939-021-2) Snow Lion Pubns.

*Magee, William H. Convention & the Art of Jane Austen's Heroines. 320p. (Orig.). 1995. text ed. 69.95x (1-883255-85-6); pap. text ed. 49.95x (1-883255-84-8) Intl Scholars.

Magee, William K. Anglo-Irish Essays. LC 67-26738. (Essay Index Reprint Ser.). 1977. reprint ed. 17.95 (0-8369-0664-0) Ayer.

— Irish Literary Portraits. LC 67-23243. (Essay Index Reprint Ser.). 1977. 17.95 (0-8369-0665-9) Ayer.

Magel, Charles R. A Bibliography on Animal Rights & Related Matters. LC 80-5636. 622p. (C). 1981. lib. bdg. 75.00 (0-8191-1488-X) U Pr of Amer.

— Keyguide to Information Sources on Animal Rights. LC 88-21574. 281p. 1989. pap. 42.50x (0-89950-405-1) McFarland & Co.

Magel, Emil. Folktales from the Gambia: Wolof Fictional Narratives. LC 81-51649. 204p. 1984. 18.00 (0-89410-220-6) Three Continents.

*Mageli, Paul D. The Immigrant Experience. (Magill Bibliographies Ser.). 183p. 1991. 40.00 (0-8108-2793-X) Scarecrow.

Magellan, Mauro. Cambio Chameleon. LC 89-19995. (Illus.). 32p. (J). 1990. 10.95 (0-89334-118-5) Humanics Ltd.

— Home at Last. LC 89-19994. (Illus.). 32p. (J). 1990. 10.95 (0-89334-119-3) Humanics Ltd.

— Max, the Apartment Cat. LC 88-32067. (Illus.). 32p. (J). 1989. 10.95 (0-89334-117-7) Humanics Ltd.

Magenau, John M., III, jt. auth. see Hunt, Raymond G.

Magenda, Burhan. East Kalimantan: The Decline of a Commercial Aristocracy. (Monograph Ser.: No. 70). 120p. 1991. 11.00 (0-87763-036-4) Cornell Mod Indo.

Magendie, Francois.

Magenes, E., jt. auth. see Lions, J. L.

Magenheimer, Kay. First Light to Dawn: A Collection of Poems in Three Parts. LC 92-85139. (Illus.). 496p. 1992. 29.95 (0-9634972-0-0) Runnymede Pr.

Magennis, Hugh, jt. auth. see Clayton, Mary.

*Mager. Complete Letter Writer. 1991. mass mkt. 5.99 (0-671-74419-4) PB.

Mager, Alison, ed. Children of the Past in Photographic Portraits: An Album with 165 Prints. (Illus.). 1978. pap. 7.95 (0-486-23697-8) Dover.

Mager, Gerald M. & Myers, Betty. Developing a Career in the Academy. (SPE Monograph Ser.). 1983. 3.00 (0-933669-22-4) Soc Profs Ed.

Mager, Gus. Sherlocko the Monk: An Original Compilation. Blackbeard, Bill, ed. LC 76-53050. (Classic American Comic Strips Ser.). (Illus.). 1977. 19.75 (0-88355-655-3); pap. 10.00 (0-88355-654-5) Hyperion Conn.

Mager, J. F., ed. Evolution of Artificial Organs: A Festschrift to Dr. George E. Schriner. 30.00 (0-936022-27-2) ICAOT Pr.

*Mager, N. H. Prentice Hall Encyclopedic Dictionary of English Usage. 2nd ed. 1994. pap. 14.95 (0-13-157165-6) P-H.

Mager, N. H. & Mager, S. K. The Great Book of Cost Cutting. LC 84-28565. 565p. 1985. 50.00 (0-932648-59-2) Boardroom.

Mager, Nathan H. The Kondratieff Waves. LC 86-9319. 256p. 1986. text ed. 65.00 (0-275-92149-2, C2149, Praeger Pubs) Greenwood.

Mager, Nathan H. & Mager, S. K. Prentice Hall Encyclopedic Dictionary of English Usage. 2nd ed. LC 92-22944. 1993. text ed. 27.95 (0-13-276858-5) P-H.

Mager, Nathan H. & Mager, Sylvia K. Encyclopedic Dictionary of English Usage. 1973. 24.95 (0-13-275792-3, Reward) P-H.

Mager, Peter P. Design Statistics in Pharmacochemistry. (Chemometrics Research Studies). 661p. 1991. text ed. 356.00 (0-471-92953-0) Wiley.

— Multidimensional Pharmacochemistry: Design of Safer Drugs. LC 82-24362. (Medicinal Chemistry Ser.). 1985. text ed. 189.00 (0-12-465020-1) Acad Pr.

— Multivariate Chemometrics in QSAR: A Dialogue. LC 87-4890. (Chemometrics Research Studies). 345p. 1988. text ed. 258.00 (0-471-91570-X) Wiley.

Mager, Robert F. Developing Attitudes Toward Learning. 2nd ed. LC 83-60499. 1984. pap. 15.95 (1-56103-337-5) Lake Pub Co.

— Goal Analysis. 2nd ed. LC 83-60501. 1984. pap. 15.95 (1-56103-339-1) Lake Pub Co.

— The How to Write a Book Book. (Illus.). 137p. (C). 1991. reprint ed. pap. text ed. 15.95 (1-56103-761-3) Lake Pub Co.

— Making Instruction Work. 1988. pap. 15.95 (1-56103-467-3) Lake Pub Co.

— Measuring Instructional Results. 2nd ed. LC 83-60502. 1984. pap. 15.95 (1-56103-340-5) Lake Pub Co.

— The New Mager Six-Pack. 1984. 84.95 (1-56103-344-8) Lake Pub Co.

— Preparing Instructional Objectives. 2nd rev. ed. LC 83-60503. 1984. pap. 15.95 (1-56103-341-3) Lake Pub Co.

— Troubleshooting: The Troubleshooting Course or Debug d'Bugs. LC 82-81980. 1983. 32p. pap. 15.95 (1-56103-370-7) Lake Pub Co.

An Asterisk (*) at the beginning of an entry indicates that the title is appearing in BIP for the first time.

— What Every Manager Should Know about Training: Or I've Got a Training Problem & Other Odd Ideas. LC 91-78265. 160p. 1992. pap. 15.95 (1-56103-345-6) Lake Pub Co.

Mager, Robert F. & Pipe, Peter. Analyzing Performance Problems or You Really Oughta Wanna. 2nd ed. LC 84-60498. 1984. pap. 15.95 (1-56103-336-7) Lake Pub Co.

— Performance Analysis Job Aid. 1984. 15.95 (1-56103-343-X) Lake Pub Co.

— Quick-Reference Checklist. 1984. 15.95 (1-56103-328-6) Lake Pub Co.

Mager, S. K., jt. auth. see Mager, N. H.

Mager, S. K., jt. auth. see Mager, Nathan H.

Mager, Sylvia K., jt. auth. see Mager, Nathan H.

***Magere, Philippe.** Dictionnaire de l'Allemand dD'Aujourd'hui: German-French, French-German. 743p. (FRE & GER.). 1987. pap. 19.95 (0-7859-8009-1, 2737002699) Fr & Eur.

Magerovskii, Lev. Bibliografiia Gazetnykh Sobranii Russkogo Istoricheskogo Arkhiva za Gody, 1917-1921. LC 91-67666. 136p. (RUS.). 1994. reprint ed. lib. bdg. 100.00 (0-88354-352-4) N Ross.

Magers, Bernard. Seventy-Five Years of Western Electric Tube Manufacturing: A Log Book History of over 750 W.E. Tubes Including Dates of Manufacture. 148p. 1992. pap. 16.95 (0-9632440-1-9) Antique Elect.

Magers, Mary A. Bible Moments with Motions. Zapel, Arthur L., ed. Zapel, Michelle, tr. (Illus.). 53p. (Orig.). (gr. 1-5). 1984. pap. 4.95 (0-916260-27-5, B-183) Meriwether Pub.

— Holy Horoscopes...for Those under the Sign of the Cross. LC 85-50451. 112p. 1985. 8.95 (0-938232-74-6) Winston-Derek.

Magers, Pat, illus. Sing with Me Animal Songs. (Sing with Me Songbooks Ser.). (J). (ps-1). 1987. audio 5.95 (0-394-88809-X) Random Bks Yng Read.

Magers-Rankin, Deborah, ed. see Grover, Margaret J. & Carson, Joseph J.

Magers-Rankin, Deborah, ed. see Tidus, Jeffrey A., et al.

Magers-Rankin, Deborah, ed. see Tidus, Jeffrey A.

Magerstadt, Michael. Antibody Conjugates & Malignant Disease. (Illus.). 248p. 1991. 179.00 (0-8493-6089-7, RC270) CRC Pr.

***Mages, Michael J.** Innate Depravity in American Literature. 286p. (Orig.). (C). 1995. text ed. 64.95 (1-57292-027-0); pap. text ed. 44.95 (1-57292-026-2) Austin & Winfield.

Maget, E., jt. auth. see Le Lionnais, Francois.

Maget, M. Le Pain Anniversaire a Villard D'Arene en Oisans. 246p. 1989. pap. text ed. 46.00 (2-88124-263-4) Gordon & Breach.

Maggal, Moshe M. The Secret of Israel's Victories-Past, Present, & Future. (Illus.). 74p. 7.95 (0-533-04986-5) Vantage.

Maggard, Bill N. TPM That Works: The Theory & Design of Total Productive Maintenance. LC 92-41792. (Illus.). 202p. (C). 1992. text ed. 39.95 (1-882258-01-0, TPMTW) TPM Pr.

Maggard, Margaret, ed. Guide to Private Fortunes, 1993. 3rd ed. 727p. 1992. pap. 225.00 (1-879784-29-7, 600356) Taft Group.

Maggard, Michael J., jt. auth. see Harris, Roy D.

Maggart, Zelda R. & Zintz, Miles V. Corrective Reading. 6th ed. 568p. (C). 1990. pap. write for info. (0-697-10426-5) Brown & Benchmark.

Maggay, Melba P., ed. Communicating Cross-Culturally: Towards a New Context for Missions in the Philippines. 61p. (Orig.). (C). 1989. pap. 6.00 (971-10-0350-3, Pub. by New Day Pub PH) Cellar.

Magge, Kenneth R., jt. auth. see Saper, Joel R.

Maggenti, A. R. General Nematology. (Microbiology Ser.). (Illus.). 372p. 1981. 76.00 (0-387-90588-X) Spr-Verlag.

Maggi, C. A., ed. Nervous Control of the Urogenital System. Vol. 3. 1992. write for info. (0-318-69520-0) Gordon & Breach.

Maggi, Tolstoy M. Fables & Folk Tales. (Illus.). 30p. (J). (ps-1). 1986. 3.95 (0-8120-5727-9) Barron.

Maggi, W., ed. Cost 202 Bis Wideband Digital Telecommunications Networks. 429p. 1991. pap. 50.00 (92-826-1997-4, CD-NA-13195-EN-C) UNIPUB.

Maggied, Hal S. Transportation for the Poor: Research in Rural Mobility. (Studies in Applied Regional Science). 1982. lib. bdg. 49.50 (0-89838-081-2) Kluwer Ac.

Maggin, Elliot S. Batman: The Blue, the Grey & the Bat. O'Neil, Dennis, ed. 64p. 1992. pap. 5.95 (0-930289-75-7) DC Comics.

— Superman: Last Son of Krypton. 20.95 (0-8488-0118-0, Amereon Hse) Amereon Ltd.

Magginetti, R. T., et al. Early Permian Fusulinids from the Owens Valley Group, East-Central California. Stevens, C. E. & Stone, P., eds. (Special Paper Ser.: No. 217). 1988. pap. 4.00 (0-8137-2217-9) Geol Soc.

Maggio, C. A. & Scriabine, A., eds. Alpha-Glucosidease Inhibition: Potential Use in Diabetes: Proceedings of the First Preclinical Workshop on Acarbose. (Drugs in Development Ser.). (Illus.). 285p. (Orig.). 1994. pap. text ed. 75.00 (0-9637603-0-0) Neva Pr.

***Maggio, Carole.** Facerise. 96p. (Orig.). 1995. pap. 12.00 (0-399-51960-2, Perigree Bks) Berkley Pub.

***Maggio, Chris, ed.** The Pet Ferret Owners' Manual. 72p. (Orig.). 1995. lib. bdg. write for info. (0-9646477-1-0); pap. write for info. (0-9646477-2-9) C Maggio.

Maggio, Edward T. Enzyme-Immunoassay. 304p. 1980. 163.00 (0-8493-5617-2, QP519, CRC Reprint) Franklin.

Maggio, Joseph A., jt. auth. see Dahlgren, Emily.

Maggio, Margk & Maze, T. H., eds. Transportation Policy. (Orig.). 1993. pap. 12.00 (0-944285-33-3) Pol Studies.

Maggio, Rosalie. The Beacon Book of Quotations by Women. LC 92-4697. 416p. 1993. 25.00 (0-8070-6764-4) Beacon Pr.

— Beacon Book of Quotations by Women. LC 92-4697. 400p. 1994. pap. 15.00 (0-8070-6765-2) Beacon Pr.

— The Bias-Free Word Finder: A Dictionary of Non-Discriminatory Language. 294p. 1992. pap. 16.00 (0-8070-6003-8) Beacon Pr.

— The Dictionary of Bias-Free Usage: A Guide to Nondiscriminatory Language. 304p. 1991. pap. 25.00 (0-89774-653-8) Oryx Pr.

— How to Say It: Choice Words, Phrases, Sentences & Paragraphs for Every Situation. 428p. 1990. pap. text ed. 15.95 (0-13-424375-7) P-H.

— The Music Box Christmas. LC 90-38529. 128p. (J). (gr. 5 up). 1990. 12.95 (0-688-08851-1) Morrow Jr Bks.

***Maggiolini, M., et al.** Endocrine Disorders in Thalassemia: Physiological Therapeutic Aspects. LC 94-23058. 1994. 86.00 (0-387-58390-4) Spr-Verlag.

— Endocrine Disorders in Thalassemia: Physiological Therapeutic Aspects. LC 94-23058. 1994. write for info. (3-540-58390-4) Spr-Verlag.

Maggioni, M. Julie. Pensees of Pascal: A Study in Baroque Style. LC 79-94181. (Catholic University of America. Studies in Romance Languages & Literatures: No. 39). reprint ed. 37.50 (0-404-50339-X) AMS Pr.

Maggiora, Gerald M., jt. ed. see Johnson, Mark A.

Maggiore, Dolores, ed. Lesbians & Child Custody: A Casebook, Vol. 8. LC 92-5398. (Gay & Lesbian Studies). 280p. 1992. 30.00 (0-8153-0229-0) Garland.

Maggiore, Dolores J. Lesbianism: An Annotated Bibliography & Guide to the Literature, 1976-1986. 2nd ed. LC 92-34699. 268p. 1992. 32.50 (0-8108-2617-8) Scarecrow.

Maggiore, MaryAnn. Salt: A Book of Poems by MaryAnn Maggiore. (Orig.). 1989. pap. 6.95 (0-9623396-0-1) Express PA.

***Maggiori, Herman.** Safe & Secure: How to Travel Safely in a Dangerous World. 144p. (Orig.). 1994. pap. 9.95 (1-878179-13-6) Burning Gate Pr.

Maggiori, Herman J. How to Make the World Your Market: The International Sales & Marketing Handbook. LC 91-73712. (Illus.). 480p. (Orig.). 1992. pap. 24.95 (1-878179-06-3) Burning Gate Pr.

Maggitti, P. Guide to a Well-Behaved Cat. 1993. pap. 9.95 (0-8120-1476-6) Barron.

***Maggitti, Phil.** Before You Buy That Kitten. 1995. pap. 5.95 (0-8120-1336-0) Barron.

— Owning the Right Cat. 1993. 29.95 (1-56465-111-8, 16003) Tetra Pr.

— Owning the Right Dog. 1993. 29.95 (1-56465-110-X, 16001) Tetra Pr.

— Scottish Fold Cats: Everything about Acquisition, Care, Nutrition, Behavior, Health Care, & Breeding. LC 92-36729. (Complete Pet Owner's Manuals Ser.). 88p. 1993. pap. 5.95 (0-8120-4999-3) Barron.

Maggitti, Phil, jt. auth. see Benson, Gary J.

Maggs, Bruce, jt. auth. see Leighton, Thomson F.

***Maggs, C. & Hommersand, M.** Seaweeds of the British Isles Pt. 2B: Corallinales, Hildenbrandiales. Vol. 1. 464p. 1994. pap. 59.95 (0-11-310016-7, HM00167, Pub. by HMSO UK) UNIPUB.

— Seaweeds of the British Isles, Pt. 3A: Rhodophyta - Ceramiales. 464p. 1993. pap. 69.95 (0-11-310045-0, HM00450, Pub. by HMSO UK) UNIPUB.

Maggs, Christopher, ed. Nursing History: The State of the Art. LC 86-32802. 208p. pap. 25.00 (0-7099-4637-6, Pub. by Croom Helm UK) Routledge Chapman & Hall.

Maggs, Colin. Railways of the Cotswolds. (Illus.). 96p. (C). 1987. 45.00 (0-317-90462-0, Pub. by Picton UK) St Mut.

Maggs, Colin G. Branch Lines of Berkshire. (Illus.). 160p. 1993. 26.00 (0-7509-0316-3) A Sutton Pub.

— Branch Lines of Gloucestershire. (Illus.). 160p. 1992. 26.00 (0-86299-959-6) A Sutton Pub.

— Branch Lines of Somerset. LC 92-34655. (Illus.). 160p. 1993. 26.00 (0-7509-0226-4) A Sutton Pub.

— Branch Lines of Warwickshire. (Illus.). 160p. 1993. text ed. 26.00 (0-7509-0317-1) A Sutton Pub.

— Branch Lines of Wiltshire. LC 92-39934. 1992. 26.00 (0-7509-0076-8) A Sutton Pub.

— The Last Days of Steam in Bristol & Somerset. (Last Days of Steam Ser.). (Illus.). 1992. 26.00 (0-7509-0001-6) A Sutton Pub.

— The Swindon to Gloucester Line. (Illus.). 128p. 1991. 29.00 (0-7509-0000-8) A Sutton Pub.

Maggs, Colin G., ed. The Best of the Last Days of Steam. (Illus.). 142p. 1995. 39.95 (0-7509-0353-8) A Sutton Pub.

— Highbridge in Its Heyday: Home of the Somerset & Dorset Railway. 88p. (C). 1985. 39.00 (0-85361-324-9, Pub. by Oakwood UK) St Mut.

Maggs, John, jt. auth. see Thyer, Dennis.

Maggs, Peter B. The Mandelstam & "Der Nister" Files: An Introduction to Stalin-era Prison & Labor Camp Records. (Illus.). 128p. 1995. 29.95 (1-56324-175-7) M E Sharpe.

Maggs, Peter B., jt. auth. see Ioffe, Olimpiad S.

Maggs, Peter B., et al. Computer Law - Cases, Comments, & Questions, Teacher's Manual to Accompany. (American Casebook Ser.). 108p. (C). 1992. pap. text ed. write for info. (0-314-01065-3) West Pub.

— Computer Law, Cases - Comments - Questions. (American Casebook Ser.). 731p. (C). 1991. text ed. 46.00 (0-314-92197-4) West Pub.

Maggs, R. J., jt. ed. see Knapman, C. E.

***Maggs, Sue.** Fifty Fantastic Chicken Dishes. (Step by Step Ser.). 96p. 1994. 9.98 (0-8317-8055-X) Smithmark.

— Step by Step Children's Party Cakes. 96p. 1994. 9.98 (0-8317-7845-8) Smithmark.

Maghan, Jess, jt. ed. see Kelly, Robert J.

Maghimbi, S., jt. auth. see Forster, P. G.

Maghroori, Ray, jt. auth. see Gurtov, Melvin.

***Maghsoud, Moulana S.** A Meditation: Payam-e-del. Angha, Nahid, tr. (Illus.). 65p. (Orig.). 1994. pap. 10.00 (0-918437-05-9) Intl Sufism.

— Psalms of Gods: Avaz-e-Khodayan. Angha, Nahid, tr. (Illus.). 32p. (Orig.). 1991. pap. 8.00 (0-918437-09-1) Intl Sufism.

Maghsoud Sadegh-ibn-Mohammad Angha, jt. auth. see Molana-al-Moazam Hazrat Shah.

Magi, Aldo P. & Walser, Richard, eds. Thomas Wolfe Interviewed, 1929-1938. LC 84-25083. (Southern Literary Studies). (Illus.). viii, 135p. 1985. text ed. 25.00 (0-8071-1229-1) La State U Pr.

Magi, Aldo P., ed. see Hoagland, Clayton & Hoagland, Kathleen.

***Magi Society Staff.** Astrology Really Works! Kramer, Jill, ed. (Illus.). 300p. (Orig.). 1995. pap. 12.95 (1-56170-134-3, 170) Hay House.

Magic Valley Rehabilitation Services, Inc. Staff. An Activities of Daily Living Curriculum for Handicapped Adults. Crumrime, Jeffery C. & Tiller, Chuck, eds. 800p. 1981. reprint ed. pap. 35.00 (0-916671-06-2) Material Dev.

Magid, A., jt. auth. see Goldman, W.

Magid, Alvin. Private Lives - Public Surfaces: Grassroots Perspectives & the Legitimacy Question in Yugoslav Socialism. 500p. 1992. text ed. 60.00 (0-88033-211-5) Col U Pr.

— Urban Nationalism: A Study of Political Development in Trinidad. LC 86-33978. 314p. 1988. 32.95 (0-8130-0853-0) U Press Fla.

Magid, Alvin, jt. ed. see Schoolman, Morton.

Magid, Andy R. Lectures on Differential Galois Theory. LC 94-10431. (University Lecture Ser.: Vol. 5). 1994. pap. 35.00 (0-8218-7004-1) Am Math.

— Rings, Extensions & Cohomology: Proceedings of the Conference on the Occasion of the Retirement of Daniel Zelinsky. LC 94-11105. (Lecture Notes in Pure & Aplied Mathematics: Vol. 159). 241p. 1994. pap. 110.00 (0-8247-9241-6) Col U Pr.

— The Separable Galois Theory of Commutative Rings. LC 74-80286. (Pure & Applied Mathematics Ser.: No. 27). 156p. reprint ed. pap. 44.50 (0-7837-0872-6, 2041180) Bks Demand.

Magid, Andy R., jt. auth. see Lubotsky, Alexander.

Magid, Barry. Freud's Case Studies: Self-Psychological Perspectives. 216p. 1993. 29.95 (0-88163-132-9) Analytic Pr.

Magid, Dubner. Alle Mesholim Fun, 2 vols., Set. 19.50 (0-88482-720-8) Hebrew Pub.

Magid, Henry M. English Political Pluralism: The Problem of Freedom & Organization. LC 41-15264. reprint ed. 20.00 (0-404-04149-3) AMS Pr.

***Magid, Jonathon, et al.** The Web Server Book: Tools & Techniques for Building on Internet Information Sites. 500p. 1995. cd-rom 49.95 (1-56604-234-8) Ventana Pr.

Magid, Ken. The Advice Book: A Question-Answer Book for Those Who Love. 247p. (Orig.). 1993. pap. 19.95 (1-883590-50-7) K M Prods.

Magid, Ken & McKelvey, Carole A. High Risk: Children Without a Conscience. 1989. pap. 11.95 (0-553-34667-9) Bantam.

***Magid, Larry.** The Little Quicken Book, Windows Edition. 375p. 1995. pap. 17.95 (1-56609-185-3) Peachpit Pr.

Magid, Lawrence J. Cruising Online: Larry Magid's Guide to the New Digital Highway. 1994. pap. 25.00 (0-679-75155-6) Random.

— The Little PC Book: A Gentle Introduction to Personal Computers. Orig. Title: Letter to a Computer Novice. (Illus.). 384p. (Orig.). 1993. pap. 17.95 (0-938151-54-1) Peachpit Pr.

Magid, Lynn H. Guide to Dallas Private Schools. Watson, Cristine L., ed. 466p. (Orig.). 1990. pap. 19.95 (0-9627445-0-6) Private-in-Print.

— Guide to Dallas Private Schools. 2nd ed. 550p. (Orig.). 1993. reprint ed. pap. text ed. 24.95 (0-9627445-2-2) Private-in-Print.

Magid, Lynn H. & Kahn, Beth F. A Guide to Dallas Learning Specialists. Lively, Ken, ed. 250p. (Orig.). 1993. pap. text ed. 19.95 (0-9627445-3-0) Private-in-Print.

***Magid, Peter.** OS-2 Warp Uncensored. 1995. pap. 34.99 (1-56884-474-3) IDG Bks.

Magid, Renee & Codkind, Melissa. Work & Personal Life: A Manager's Perspective. Gerould, Philip, ed. LC 93-73207. (Fifty-Minute Ser.). (Illus.). 100p. (Orig.). 1995. pap. 9.95 (1-56052-269-0) Crisp Pubns.

Magid, Renee Y. & Fleming, Nancy E. When Mothers & Fathers Work: Creative Strategies for Balancing Career & Family. LC 86-47817. 208p. reprint ed. pap. 59.30 (0-7837-4240-1, 2043929) Bks Demand.

— When Mothers & Fathers Work: Creative Ways to Succeed with Both Family & Career. 224p. 1989. reprint ed. pap. 3.95 (0-380-70753-5) Avon.

Magid, Zalman, jt. auth. see Sackman, Deena.

***Magida, Arthur J.** Prophet of Rage: The Radical World of Louis Farrakhan & the Nation of Islam. (Illus.). 300p. 1996. 23.95 (1-882605-26-8) Natl Pr Bks.

Magida, Daniel L. The Rules of Seduction. 432p. 1994. pap. 10.00 (0-449-90852-6, Columbine) Fawcett.

Magida, Phylis. Eating, Drinking, & Thinking: A Gourmet Perspective. LC 73-86024. 184p. 1973. 29.95 (0-911012-91-5) Nelson-Hall.

Magida, Phyllis & Grunes, Barbara. Gourmet Fish on the Grill: More than Ninety Easy Recipes for Elegant Entertaining. 160p. (Orig.). 1989. pap. 9.95 (0-8092-4596-5) Contemp Bks.

— Skinny Chocolate: Over One Hundred Sinfully Delicious, Yet Low-Fat Recipes for Cakes, Cookies, Savories & Chocoholic Treats. (Skinny Cookbook Ser.). 210p. 1994. pap. 12.95 (0-940625-80-6) Surrey Bks.

Magida, Phyllis, jt. auth. see Grunes, Barbara.

Magidoff, Robert, jt. auth. see Pinza, Ezio.

Magidson, Jane & Harney, Susan. Shopwalks Paris: Shopping Maps & Guide. (Illus.). 1994. pap. 5.95 (0-9638326-0-3) Shopwalks.

Magie, Allan. Pets, People, Plagues. LC 79-19321. (Better Living Ser.). 1979. pap. 1.25 (0-8127-0233-6) Review & Herald.

Magie, David. Roman Rule in Asia Minor to the End of the Third Century After Christ, 2 vols., 1. LC 75-7328. (Roman History Ser.). 1975. reprint ed. 60.95 (0-405-07099-3) Ayer.

— Roman Rule in Asia Minor to the End of the Third Century After Christ, 2 vols., 2. LC 75-7328. (Roman History Ser.). 1975. reprint ed. 60.95 (0-405-07100-0) Ayer.

— Roman Rule in Asia Minor to the End of the Third Century After Christ, 2 vols., Set. LC 75-7328. (Roman History Ser.). 1975. reprint ed. 121.95 (0-405-07098-5) Ayer.

Magie, David, tr. see Warmington, E. H., ed.

Magie, Dian, jt. auth. see Korza, Pam.

Magie, William F. A Source Book in Physics. LC 63-21307. (Source Books in the History of the Sciences). (Illus.). 634p. reprint ed. pap. 180.00 (0-7837-4118-9, 2057941) Bks Demand.

Magiera, Lana, jt. auth. see Holmes, Janice.

Magill & Will, eds. Schiller: Die Raube. (Bristol German Texts Ser.). (GER.). 1991. 13.95 (0-685-50002-0, Pub. by Brstl Class Pr UK) Focus Info Gr.

Magill, Anne. Designing & Gardening with the Plant Materials & Conditions of North Central Florida (New USDA Zone 9) A Companion Volume to Landscape Design & Gardening Procedures for the Not So Rich. 118p. (Orig.). 1990. pap. 10.95 (0-9627632-1-7) Melrose Garden Pr.

— Landscape Design & Gardening Procedures for the Not So Rich. (Illus.). 104p. (Orig.). 1989. pap. 8.95 (0-9627632-0-9) Melrose Garden Pr.

Magill, Arthur W. Assessing Public Concern for Landscape Quality: A Potential Model to Identify Visual Thresholds. (Illus.). 50p. (Orig.). (C). 1993. pap. text ed. 30.00 (0-7881-0017-3) Diane Pub.

Magill, C. W., jt. auth. see McNiel, N. A.

Magill, Dan. Dan Magill's Bull-Doggerel: Fifty Years of Anecdotes from the Greatest Bulldog Ever. LC 93-79659. (Illus.). 192p. 1993. 16.95 (1-56352-089-3) Longstreet Pr Inc.

— Match Pointers: Courtside with the Winningest Coach in Tennis History. 192p. 1995. 19.95 (1-56352-194-6) Longstreet Pr Inc.

Magill, Frank N. Great Events from History II: Arts & Culture Series, 5 vols., 1. LC 93-28381. 2678p. 1993. write for info. (0-89356-808-2, Magill Bks) Salem Pr.

— Great Events from History II: Arts & Culture Series, 5 vols., Set. LC 93-28381. 2678p. 1993. lib. bdg. 375.00 (0-89356-807-4, Magill Bks) Salem Pr.

— Great Women Writers. 1994. 40.00 (0-8050-2932-X) H Holt & Co.

— Magill's Literary Annual 1984, 2 Vols. LC 77-99209. 996p. 1984. lib. bdg. 55.00 (0-89356-284-X) Salem Pr.

— Masterplots. (Non-fiction, Poetry, Drama Ser.). 1995. cd-rom 500.00 (0-89356-262-9) Salem Pr.

— Masterplots II, 4 vols. LC 86-1910. (American Fiction Ser.). 1863p. (C). 1986. lib. bdg. 365.00 (0-89356-456-7) Salem Pr.

— Masterplots II, 6 vols. (Short Story Ser.). 2763p. 1986. lib. bdg. 425.00 (0-89356-461-3) Salem Pr.

— Masterplots II. 1992. cd-rom 1,295.00 (0-89356-260-2) Salem Pr.

— Masterplots II, 4 vols., Set. LC 87-4639. (British & Commonwealth Fiction Ser.). 1959p. 1987. 365.00 (0-89356-468-0) Salem Pr.

— Masterplots II, 4 vols., Set. (World Fiction Ser.). 1819p. 1988. lib. bdg. 365.00 (0-89356-473-7) Salem Pr.

— The Nobel Prize Winners, 3 vols., Set. (Literature Ser.). 1027p. 1988. lib. bdg. 210.00 (0-89356-541-5) Salem Pr.

— Survey of Social Science, 5 vols. (Government & Politics Ser.). 2500p. 1995. lib. bdg. 375.00 (0-89356-745-0) Salem Pr.

Magill, Frank N., ed. The American Presidents: The Office & the Men, 3 vols. rev. ed. LC 85-30338. (Illus.). 1989. Set: Vol. 1, 284p.; Vol. 2, 290p.; Vol. 3, 303p. 150.00 (0-7172-7166-8) Grolier Inc.

— Critical Survey Index: Cumulative Indexes, 1981-1994. rev. ed. LC 93-18632. 379p. 1994. pap. text ed. 12.95 (0-89356-698-5) Salem Pr.

— Critical Survey of Drama, 7 vols., Set. rev. ed. (English Language Ser.). 3107p. (YA). (gr. 9-12). 1994. lib. bdg. 425.00 (0-89356-851-1, Magill Bks) Salem Pr.

— Critical Survey of Drama: Foreign Language Series, 6 vols., Set. 2509p. (C). 1986. lib. bdg. 350.00 (0-89356-382-X) Salem Pr.

— Critical Survey of Literary Theory, 4 vols., Set. 1900p. 1988. lib. bdg. 300.00 (0-317-67452-8) Pan-Am Publishing Co.

— Critical Survey of Long Fiction, 5 vols., Set. (Foreign Language Ser.). 2396p. 1984. lib. bdg. 275.00 (0-89356-369-2) Salem Pr.

— Critical Survey of Long Fiction, 8 vols., Set. rev. ed. (English Language Ser.). 3352p. 1991. lib. bdg. 475.00 (0-89356-825-2, Magill Bks) Salem Pr.

— Critical Survey of Mystery & Detective Fiction, 4 vols. 1748p. 1989. lib. bdg. 300.00 (0-89356-486-9) Salem Pr.

— Critical Survey of Poetry, 5 vols., Set. LC 84-5365. (Foreign Language Ser.). 2274p. 1984. lib. bdg. 275.00 (0-89356-350-1) Salem Pr.

— Critical Survey of Poetry, 8 vols., Set. rev. ed. (English Language Ser.). 3662p. 1992. lib. bdg. 475.00 (0-89356-834-1, Magill Bks) Salem Pr.

— Critical Survey of Short Fiction, 7 vols., 1. rev. ed. 2819p. 1993. write for info. (0-89356-844-9) Salem Pr.

— Critical Survey of Short Fiction, 7 vols., Set. rev. ed. 2819p. 1993. 425.00 (*0-89356-843-0*) Salem Pr.
— Cyclopedia of Literary Characters II, 4 vols. 1775p. 1990. lib. bdg. 300.00 (*0-89356-517-2*) Salem Pr.
— Cyclopedia of World Authors II. 1640p. 1989. lib. bdg. 300.00 (*0-89356-512-1*) Salem Pr.
— Great Events from History, 3 vols., Set. LC 72-86347. (Ancient & Medieval Ser.). 1854p. 1972. 115.00 (*0-89356-104-5*) Salem Pr.
— Great Events from History, 3 vols., Set. LC 72-86347. (American Fiction Ser.). 2047p. 1975. 115.00 (*0-89356-112-6*) Salem Pr.
— Great Events from History II. LC 94-27299. (Business & Commerce Ser.). 2000p. 1994. lib. bdg. 375.00 (*0-89356-813-9*, Magill Bks) Salem Pr.
— Great Events from History II, 5 vols. LC 95-5035. (Ecology & the Environment Ser.). 2500p. (J). 1995. lib. bdg. 375.00 (*0-89356-751-5*) Salem Pr.
— Great Events from History II, 5 vols., Set. (Science & Technology Ser.). 2386p. 1991. lib. bdg. 375.00 (*0-89356-637-3*, Magill Bks) Salem Pr.
— Great Events from History II, 5 vols., Set. (Human Rights Ser.). 2624p. 1992. lib. bdg. 375.00 (*0-89356-643-8*, Magill Bks) Salem Pr.
— Great Lives from History, 5 vols. (Ancient & Medieval Ser.). 2420p. 1988. lib. bdg. 365.00 (*0-89356-545-8*) Salem Pr.
— Great Lives from History, 5 vols. (American Women Ser.). 2000p. 1995. lib. bdg. 365.00 (*0-89356-892-9*) Salem Pr.
— Great Lives from History, 5 vols., Set. (American Fiction Ser.). 2592p. 1987. 365.00 (*0-89356-529-6*) Salem Pr.
— Great Lives from History, 5 vols., Set. (British & Commonwealth Fiction Ser.). 2683p. 1987. 365.00 (*0-89356-535-0*) Salem Pr.
— Great Lives from History, 5 vols., Set. (Renaissance to 1900 Ser.). 2549p. 1989. lib. bdg. 365.00 (*0-89356-551-2*) Salem Pr.
— Great Lives from History, 5 vols., Set. (Twentieth Century Ser.). 2527p. 1990. lib. bdg. 365.00 (*0-89356-565-2*) Salem Pr.
— Great Lives from History Index. rev. ed. 250p. 1995. pap. text ed. 12.95 (*0-89356-891-0*) Salem Pr.
— Magill Index to Masterplots, 1963-1994: Cumulative Indexes. rev. ed. LC 93-18633. 309p. 1993. pap. text ed. 12.95 (*0-89356-599-7*) Salem Pr.
— Magill's Cinema Annual, 1987. 600p. 1987. 50.00 (*0-89356-406-0*) Salem Pr.
— Magill's Cinema Annual, 1988. 1988. lib. bdg. 50.00 (*0-89356-407-9*) Salem Pr.
— Magill's Cinema Annual, 1989. 556p. 1989. lib. bdg. 50.00 (*0-89356-408-7*, Magill Bks) Salem Pr.
— Magill's Cinema Annual, 1990. 600p. 1990. lib. bdg. 50.00 (*0-89356-409-5*) Salem Pr.
— Magill's Cinema Annual, 1991. 531p. 1991. lib. bdg. 50.00 (*0-89356-410-9*, Magill Bks) Salem Pr.
— Magill's Cinema Annual, 1992. 600p. 1992. lib. bdg. 50.00 (*0-89356-411-7*, Magill Bks) Salem Pr.
— Magill's Cinema Annual, 1993. 600p. 1993. lib. bdg. 50.00 (*0-89356-412-5*, Magill Bks) Salem Pr.
— Magill's Cinema Annual, 1994. 600p. 1994. lib. bdg. 50.00 (*0-89356-413-3*, Magill Bks) Salem Pr.
— Magill's Cinema Annual, 1995. 600p. 1995. lib. bdg. 50.00 (*0-89356-414-1*, Magill Bks) Salem Pr.
— Magill's History of Europe. LC 92-54832. 1992. 219.00 (*0-7172-7173-0*) Grolier Inc.
— Magill's Literary Annual: 1978, 2 vols., Set. LC 77-99209. 1978. lib. bdg. 55.00 (*0-89356-278-5*) Salem Pr.
— Magill's Literary Annual: 1979, 2 vols., Set. LC 77-99209. 1979. 55.00 (*0-89356-279-3*) Salem Pr.
— Magill's Literary Annual: 1989, 2 vols., Set. 937p. 1989. lib. bdg. 65.00 (*0-89356-289-0*, Magill Bks) Salem Pr.
— Magill's Literary Annual 1981, 2 vols., Set. LC 77-99209. 950p. 1981. 55.00 (*0-89356-281-5*) Salem Pr.
— Magill's Literary Annual, 1982, 2 vols., Set. LC 77-99209. 1007p. 1982. 55.00 (*0-89356-282-3*) Salem Pr.
— Magill's Literary Annual, 1983, 2 vols., Set. 938p. 1983. 55.00 (*0-89356-283-1*) Salem Pr.
— Magill's Literary Annual 1985. 1045p. 1985. lib. bdg. 60.00 (*0-89356-285-8*) Salem Pr.
— Magill's Literary Annual, 1986, 2 vols., Set. 988p. 1986. 60.00 (*0-89356-286-6*) Salem Pr.
— Magill's Literary Annual, 1987, 2 vols., Set. 1026p. 1987. 65.00 (*0-89356-287-4*) Salem Pr.
— Magill's Literary Annual, 1988, 2 vols., Set. 950p. 1988. lib. bdg. 65.00 (*0-89356-288-2*) Salem Pr.
— Magill's Literary Annual, 1990. 950p. 1990. lib. bdg. 70.00 (*0-89356-290-4*) Salem Pr.
— Magill's Literary Annual, 1991, 2 vols., Set. 924p. 1991. lib. bdg. 70.00 (*0-89356-291-2*, Magill Bks) Salem Pr.
— Magill's Literary Annual, 1992, 2 vols., Set. 950p. 1992. lib. bdg. 70.00 (*0-89356-292-0*, Magill Bks) Salem Pr.
— Magill's Literary Annual, 1993, 2 vols., Set. 1000p. 1993. lib. bdg. 70.00 (*0-89356-293-9*) Salem Pr.
— Magill's Literary Annual 1994, 2 vols., Set. 1000p. 1994. lib. bdg. 70.00 (*0-89356-294-7*) Salem Pr.
— Magill's Literary Annual, 1995, 2 vols., Set. 1995. lib. bdg. 70.00 (*0-89356-295-5*, Magill Bks) Salem Pr.
— Magill's Medical Guide, Health & Illness, 3 vols. (Illus.). 1000p. 1995. lib. bdg. 270.00 (*0-89356-712-4*) Salem Pr.
— Magill's Quotations in Context: Second Series, 2 vols., Set. LC 65-21011. 1350p. 1969. 75.00 (*0-89356-136-3*) Salem Pr.
— Magill's Survey of American Literature, 2 vols. Incl. Magill's Survey of American Literature Vol. 1. LC 94-25192. 1994. (*1-85435-732-8*); Vol. 2. Magill's Survey of American Literature Vol. 2. LC 94-25192. 1994. (*1-85435-733-6*); LC 94-25192. 1993. Set lib. bdg. 129.95 (*1-85435-734-4*) Marshall Cavendish.
— Magill's Survey of American Literature, 6 vols., Set. LC 91-28113. (Illus.). 2160p. 1991. lib. bdg. 389.95 (*1-85435-437-X*) Marshall Cavendish.
— Magill's Survey of American Literature Vol. 2, Vol. 2. LC 94-25192. (Magill's Survey of American Literature). 1994. write for info. (*1-85435-733-6*) Marshall Cavendish.
— Magill's Survey of Cinema: Foreign Language Films, 8 vols. 3504p. 1985. lib. bdg. 350.00 (*0-89356-243-2*) Salem Pr.
— Magill's Survey of Science, 5 vols. (Earth Science Ser.). 2328p. 1990. lib. bdg. 425.00 (*0-89356-606-3*) Salem Pr.
— Magill's Survey of Science. (Applied Science Ser.). 1993. cd-rom 1,150.00 (*0-89356-270-X*) Salem Pr.
— Magill's Survey of Science, 6 vols., Set. (Life Science Ser.). 2763p. 1991. lib. bdg. 475.00 (*0-89356-612-8*) Salem Pr.
— Magill's Survey of Science, 6 vols., Set. (Physical Science Ser.). 2796p. 1992. lib. bdg. 475.00 (*0-89356-618-7*) Salem Pr.
— Magill's Survey of Science, 6 vols., Set. (Applied Science Ser.). 2918p. 1993. lib. bdg. 475.00 (*0-89356-705-1*) Salem Pr.
— Magill's Survey of World Literature, 6 vols. LC 92-11198. 1992. 389.95 (*1-85435-482-5*) Marshall Cavendish.
— Magill's Survey of World Literature, 6 vols., 1. LC 92-11198. 1992. lib. bdg. write for info. (*1-85435-483-3*) Marshall Cavendish.
— Magill's Survey of World Literature, 6 vols., 2. LC 92-11198. 1992. lib. bdg. write for info. (*1-85435-484-1*) Marshall Cavendish.
— Magill's Survey of World Literature, 6 vols., 3. LC 92-11198. 1992. lib. bdg. write for info. (*1-85435-485-X*) Marshall Cavendish.
— Magill's Survey of World Literature, 6 vols., 4. LC 92-11198. 1992. lib. bdg. write for info. (*1-85435-486-8*) Marshall Cavendish.
— Magill's Survey of World Literature, 6 vols., 5. LC 92-11198. 1992. lib. bdg. write for info. (*1-85435-487-6*) Marshall Cavendish.
— Magill's Survey of World Literature, 6 vols., 6. LC 92-11198. 1992. lib. bdg. write for info. (*1-85435-488-4*) Marshall Cavendish.
— Masterpieces of African-American Literature: Descriptions, Analyses, Characters, Plots, Themes, Critical Evaluations, & Significance of Major Works of Fiction, Non-Fiction, Drama & Poetry. LC 92-52542. 608p. 1992. 45.00 (*0-06-270066-9*, Harper Ref) HarpC.
— Masterpieces of American Literature. LC 93-15940. 736p. 1993. 40.00 (*0-06-270072-3*, Harper Ref) HarpC.
— Masterpieces of Latino Literature. LC 94-8803. 1994. 45.00 (*0-06-270106-1*) HarpC.
— Masterpieces of World Literature. LC 89-45052. 957p. 1991. 45.00 (*0-06-270050-2*, HarpT) HarpC.
— Masterplots. LC 76-5606. 1976. cd-rom write for info. (*0-614-03132-X*) Salem Pr.
— Masterplots. (Fiction Ser.). 1994. cd-rom 500.00 (*0-89356-261-0*) Salem Pr.
— Masterplots, 3 vols. rev. ed. (European Fiction Ser.). 1437p. 1986. lib. bdg. 120.00 (*0-89356-508-3*) Salem Pr.
— Masterplots, 12 vols., Set. rev. ed. LC 76-5606. 7358p. 1976. 450.00 (*0-89356-025-1*) Salem Pr.
— Masterplots, 3 vols., Set. rev. ed. (American Fiction Ser.). 1485p. 1985. lib. bdg. 120.00 (*0-89356-500-8*) Salem Pr.
— Masterplots, 3 vols, Set. rev. ed. (British & Commonwealth Fiction Ser.). 1790p. 1985. lib. bdg. 120.00 (*0-89356-504-0*) Salem Pr.
— Masterplots II, 4 vols. LC 89-10989. (Drama Ser.). 1804p. 1990. pap. 365.00 (*0-89356-491-5*) Salem Pr.
— Masterplots II, 6 vols. (Women's Literature Ser.). 3000p. 1995. lib. bdg. 500.00 (*0-89356-898-8*) Salem Pr.
— Masterplots II, 4 vols., Set. (Nonfiction Ser.). 1745p. 1989. lib. bdg. 365.00 (*0-89356-478-8*) Salem Pr.
— Masterplots II, 4 vols., Set. LC 92-44708. (Juvenile & Young Adult Fiction Ser.). 1695p. (YA). (gr. 6 up). 1991. lib. bdg. 365.00 (*0-89356-579-2*) Salem Pr.
— Masterplots II, 6 vols., Set. (Poetry Ser.). 2980p. 1992. lib. bdg. 425.00 (*0-89356-584-9*) Salem Pr.
— Masterplots II, 3 vols., Set. (African-American Literature Ser.). 1530p. (YA). (gr. 9-12). 1994. lib. bdg. 275.00 (*0-89356-594-6*, Magill Bks) Salem Pr.
— Masterplots II: American Fiction Supplement, 2 vols., Set. 960p. (YA). (gr. 9-12). 1994. lib. bdg. 185.00 (*0-89356-719-1*) Salem Pr.
— The Nobel Prize Winners. (Illus.). 1246p. 1990. lib. bdg. 210.00 (*0-89356-561-X*) Salem Pr.
— The Nobel Prize Winners. (Physiology or Medicine Ser.). (Illus.). 1597p. 1991. lib. bdg. 210.00 (*0-89356-571-7*) Salem Pr.
— The Nobel Prize Winners, 3 vols., Set. (Physics Ser.). 1364p. 1989. lib. bdg. 210.00 (*0-89356-557-1*, Magill Bks) Salem Pr.
— Survey of Contemporary Literature, 12 vols., Set. LC 77-79874. 8531p. 1977. 350.00 (*0-89356-050-2*) Salem Pr.
— Survey of Modern Fantasy Literature, 5 vols., Set. LC 83-15189. 2589p. 1983. 275.00 (*0-89356-450-8*) Salem Pr.
— Survey of Social Science, 5 vols., Set. (Economics Ser.). 2494p. 1991. lib. bdg. 375.00 (*0-89356-725-6*) Salem Pr.
— Survey of Social Science, 6 vols., Set. (Psychology Ser.). 2698p. 1993. lib. bdg. 425.00 (*0-89356-732-9*) Salem Pr.
— Survey of Social Science: Sociology Series, 5 vols., Set. 2244p. 1994. lib. bdg. 375.00 (*0-89356-739-6*) Salem Pr.
Magill, Frank N., intro. Critical Survey of Literary Theory, 4 vols., Set. 1833p. 1988. lib. bdg. 300.00 (*0-89356-390-0*) Salem Pr.
Magill, Frank N. & McNelly, Willis E., eds. Survey of Science Fiction Literature, 5 vols., Set. LC 79-64639. 2549p. 1979. 250.00 (*0-89356-194-0*) Salem Pr.
Magill, Frank N. & Roth, John, eds. Masterpieces of World Philosophy: More Than 100 Classics of the World's Greatest Philosophers Analyzed & Explained. LC 15-8176. 684p. 1991. 40.00 (*0-06-270051-0*, Harper Ref) HarpC.
Magill, Frank N., et al, eds. Magill's Literary Annual: 1977, 2 vols., Set. LC 77-99209. 1977. lib. bdg. 55.00 (*0-89356-077-4*) Salem Pr.
Magill, Gerard, ed. Discourse & Context: An Interdisciplinary Study of John Henry Newman. LC 92-17309. 232p. (C). 1993. 34.95 (*0-8093-1836-9*) S Ill U Pr.
— Personality & Belief: Interdisciplinary Essays on John Henry Newman. 228p. (C). 1994. lib. bdg. 39.50 (*0-8191-9757-2*) U Pr of Amer.
Magill, H. B. The Biography of Francis Schlatter, the Healer: Life, Works & Wanderings - 5000 Healings a Day. 1991. lib. bdg. 75.95 (*0-8490-4130-9*) Gordon Pr.
Magill, Harry B. Biography of Francis Schlatter, the Healer. 198p. 1968. reprint ed. spiral bd. 4.95 (*0-7873-0580-4*) Mokelumne.
Magill, Harry T. & Previtts, Gary J. CPA Professional Responsibilities: An Introduction. 214p. (C). 1991. text ed. 23.95 (*0-538-80121-2*, AT64AA) S-W Pub.
Magill, Jane. Problem Solving in Biochemistry: A Practical Approach. 2nd ed. 323p. (C). 1988. pap. write for info. (*0-02-432100-1*) Macmillan.
Magill, Jane M. & Moore, John B., Jr. Experiments in Biochemistry. (Illus.). 100p. (Orig.). 1978. spiral bd. 6.95x (*0-89641-007-2*) American Pr.
— Experiments in Metabolism. (Illus.). 118p. (Orig.). 1979. spiral bd. 6.95x (*0-89641-013-7*) American Pr.
Magill, John, jt. text see Adams, Lynn.
Magill, John, ed. see Fitzgerald, Gregory & Dillon, John.
Magill, Michele M. Repertoire des References aux Arts et a la Litterature dans "A la Recherche du Temps Perdu" de Marcel Proust. LC 91-65734. (Marcel Proust Studies: Vol. 2). 272p. (FRE.). 1991. lib. bdg. 38.95 (*0-917786-85-8*) Summa Pubns.
Magill, Richard A. Motor Learning: Concepts & Applications. 4th ed. 480p. (C). 1993. boxed write for info. (*0-697-12643-9*) Brown & Benchmark.
Magill, Richard A., et al, eds. Children in Sport. LC 82-82668. 327p. reprint ed. pap. 93.20 (*0-318-34932-9*, 2031470) Bks Demand.
Magill, Robert. Michael's Cut. abr. ed. 260p. 1995. pap. 8.95 (*1-56901-517-1*) NW Pub.
Magill, Robert E., jt. ed. see Coosey, Marshall R.
Magill, Robert E., jt. auth. see Crosby, Marshall R.
Magill, Robert S. Social Policy in American Society. 250p. (C). 1984. pap. 20.95 (*0-89885-278-1*) Human Sci Pr.
Magilligan & Quinn. Endocarditis: Medical & Surgical Management. (Cardiothoracic Surgery Ser.: Vol. 1). 288p. 1986. 110.00 (*0-8247-7580-5*) Dekker.
Magin, M., jt. ed. see Chadwick, C.
Magini, Mauro, ed. X-Ray Diffraction of Ions in Aqueous Solutions: Hydration & Complex Formation. 288p. 1988. 158.00 (*0-8493-6945-2*, QD561, CRC Reprint) Franklin.
Maginn, John L. & Tuttle, Donald L., eds. Managing Investment Portfolios: A Dynamic Process. 2nd ed. LC 89-50465. 775p. (C). 1991. text ed. 125.00 (*0-7913-0322-5*) Warren Gorham & Lamont.
***Maginn, Michael D.** Effective Teamwork. (AMI How-to Ser.). 100p. 1995. 9.95 (*1-884926-42-8*) Amer Media.
— Team Player: A Practical Guide to Team Membership. LC 93-5. 112p. 1993. pap. 10.00 (*1-55623-880-0*) Irwin Prof Pubng.
Maginnes, Al. Outside a Tattoo Booth. Zarucchi, Roy & Page, Carolyn, eds. (Chapbook Ser.). (Illus.). 28p. (Orig.). 1991. pap. 5.00 (*1-879205-16-5*) Nightshade Pr.
Maginnis, John. Cross to Bear: Louisiana Politics 1991 from David Duke to Edwin Edwards. (Illus.). 320p. 1992. 19.95 (*0-9614138-2-4*) Darkhorse Pr.
— The Last Hayride. Phillips, Barbara, ed. LC 84-80875. (Illus.). 354p. (C). 1985. 15.95 (*0-9614138-0-8*); pap. 7.95 (*0-9614138-1-6*) Darkhorse Pr.
Maginnis, Matthew, jt. auth. see Carpenter, Allan.
Magisa, Lenore, ed. see Beil, Drake.
Magison, E. C. Electrical Instruments in Hazardous Locations. 3rd enl. rev. ed. LC 70-184225. 394p. 1978. text ed. 55.00 (*0-87664-376-4*, 1376-4) Instru Soc.
— Intrinsic Safety. LC 84-10852. (Independent Learning Module Ser.). 192p. 1984. text ed. 50.00 (*0-87664-635-6*, 1635-6) Instru Soc.
— Temperature Measurement in Industry. 176p. 1990. text ed. 55.00 (*1-55617-208-7*, A208-7) Instru Soc.
Magison, E. C. & Calder, W. Electrical Safety in Hazardous Locations. rev. ed. LC 83-169373. (Instructional Resource Package Ser.). 185p. 1983. Student Text: 185p. student ed, pap. text ed. 35.00 (*0-87664-704-2*, 1704-2) Instru Soc.
***Magison, Ernest C.** Intrinsic Safety. LC 84-10852. (Independent Learning Module from the Instrument Society of America Ser.). (Illus.). reprint ed. pap. 54.50 (*0-7837-9045-7*, 2049796) Bks Demand.
Magison, Ernest C., jt. auth. see Calder, William.
Magisos, Joel H., et al. Excellence in Vocational Education: Four Levels, Four Perspectives. 39p. 1984. 4.75 (*0-318-22101-2*, IN287) Ctr Educ Trng Employ.
Magister, Thomas. Ecloga Vocum Atticarum. cxlvi, 504p. 1970. reprint ed. write for info. (*0-318-71053-6*, Pub. by Georg Olms GW) Lubrecht & Cramer.
Magistrale, Anthony. The Moral Voyages of Stephen King. LC 88-1076. (Starmont Studies in Literary Criticism: No. 25). iv, vi, 157p. 1989. lib. bdg. 29.00x (*1-55742-071-8*); pap. 19.00x (*1-55742-070-X*) Borgo Pr.
— Obsessions. 48p. (C). 1990. reprint ed. lib. bdg. 23.00x (*0-8095-6853-5*) Borgo Pr.
Magistrale, Anthony, ed. The Shining Reader. LC 89-29631. (Starmont Studies in Literary Criticism: No. 30). xii, 220p. 1990. 33.00x (*1-55742-107-2*) Borgo Pr.
Magistrale, Anthony S. Salvation on the Installment Plan. (Lamont Hall Chapbook Series for Poetry). 20p. 1982. 1.75 (*0-9603840-3-0*) Andrew Mtn Pr.
— Stephen King: The Second Decade: Danse Macabre to the Dark Half. (United States Authors Ser.). 208p. 1992. text ed. 20.95 (*0-8057-3957-2*, 599, Pub. by Royal Botanic Garden UK) Macmillan.
Magistrale, Anthony S., ed. The Dark Descent: Essays Defining Stephen King's Horrorscape. LC 91-36705. (Contributions to the Study of Science Fiction & Fantasy Ser.: No. 48). 248p. 1992. text ed. 47.95 (*0-313-27297-2*, MDU/, Greenwood Pr) Greenwood.
Magistrale, Tony. Landscape of Fear: Stephen King's American Gothic. LC 87-72642. 139p. (C). 1988. 26.95 (*0-87972-404-8*); pap. 13.95 (*0-87972-405-6*) Bowling Green Univ.
Magistrale, Tony, ed. Casebook on "The Stand" LC 93-214779. (Starmont Studies in Literary Criticism: No. 38). xii, 210p. 1992. lib. bdg. 31.00x (*1-55742-251-6*) Borgo Pr.
Magitskii, Efim. Galereiia Vymysla - Stikhi. LC 87-82249. 112p. (RUS.). 1987. 10.00 (*0-911971-27-0*) Effect Pub.
Maglacas, A. Mangay & Simons, J., eds. The Potential of the Traditional Birth Attendant. (WHO Offset Publication Ser.: No. 95). 105p. 1986. pap. 9.60 (*92-4-170095-5*) World Health.
Maglalang, Demetrio M. Agricultural Approach to Family Planning. 159p. 1976. pap. text ed. 9.00 (*0-942717-01-5*) Intl Inst Rural.
Magleby, David B. Direct Legislation: Voting on Ballot Propositions in the United States. LC 83-22265. 284p. reprint ed. pap. 81.00 (*0-7837-4275-4*, 2043967) Bks Demand.
Magleby, David B. & Nelson, Candice J. The Money Chase: Congressional Campaign Finance Reform. 250p. 1990. 31.95 (*0-8157-5434-5*); pap. 12.95 (*0-8157-5433-7*) Brookings.
Magley, Beverly. Arizona Wildflowers. (Interpreting the Great Outdoors Ser.). (Illus.). 32p. (J). (gr. 1-8). 1991. pap. 5.95 (*1-56044-096-1*) Falcon Pr MT.
— California Wildflowers. LC 88-83883. (Interpreting the Great Outdoors Ser.). (Illus.). 32p. (Orig.). (J). (gr. 3-6). 1989. pap. 5.95 (*0-937959-58-8*) Falcon Pr MT.
— The Fire Mountains: The Story of the Cascade Volcanos. LC 88-83884. (Interpreting the Great Outdoors Ser.). (Illus.). 32p. (Orig.). (J). (gr. 3-6). 1989. pap. 5.95 (*0-937959-57-X*) Falcon Pr MT.
— Minnesota Wildflowers: Children's Field Guide. (Illus.). 32p. (Orig.). (J). (gr. 4-7). 1992. pap. 5.95 (*1-56044-117-8*) Falcon Pr MT.
— Montana Wildflowers. (Illus.). 32p. (Orig.). (J). (gr. 4-7). 1992. pap. 5.95 (*1-56044-118-6*) Falcon Pr MT.
— North Carolina Wildflowers: A Children's Field Guide to the State's Most Common Flowers. (Interpreting the Great Outdoors Ser.). (Illus.). 32p. (Orig.). (J). 1993. pap. 5.95 (*1-56044-184-4*) Falcon Pr MT.
— Oregon Wildflowers: Children's Field Guide. (Interpreting the Great Outdoors Ser.). (Illus.). 32p. (Orig.). (J). (gr. 4-7). 1992. pap. 5.95 (*1-56044-035-X*) Falcon Pr MT.
— Scenic Byways. LC 90-80040. (Falcon Guide Ser.). (Illus.). 256p. (Orig.). 1990. pap. 11.95 (*0-937959-94-4*) Falcon Pr MT.
— Scenic Byways II. Bates, Malcolm, ed. (Falcon Guide Ser.). (Illus.). 232p. (Orig.). 1992. pap. 11.95 (*1-56044-112-7*) Falcon Pr MT.
— Texas Wildflowers: A Children's Field Guide to the State's Most Common Flowers. (Interpreting the Great Outdoors Ser.). (Illus.). 32p. (Orig.). (J). 1993. pap. 5.95 (*1-56044-183-6*) Falcon Pr MT.
Magley, Beverly R. Montana Backroads. LC 93-16144. (Montana Geographic Ser.: No. 19). (Illus.). 104p. 1993. 14.95 (*1-56037-033-5*) Am Wrld Geog.
Maglic, Kosta D., ed. Compendium of Thermophysical Property Measurement Methods, Vol. 1: Survey of Measurement Techniques. 806p. 1984. 165.00 (*0-306-41424-4*, Plenum Pr) Plenum.
Maglic, Kosta D., et al, eds. Compendium of Thermophysical Property Measurement Methods, Vol. 2. (Illus.). 666p. 1991. 165.00 (*0-306-43854-2*, Plenum Pr) Plenum.
Maglin, Nan B. & Schniedewind, Nancy, eds. Women & Stepfamilies. (Illus.). 448p. 1990. pap. 18.95 (*0-87722-782-9*) Temple U Pr.
— Women & Stepfamilies: Voices of Anger & Love. LC 88-11719. (Women in the Political Economy Ser.). 448p. (C). 1989. 39.95 (*0-87722-586-9*) Temple U Pr.
Maglin, Nan B., jt. ed. see Perry, Donna.
Maglinte, jt. auth. see Herlinger.
Maglio, Rodolfo, jt. auth. see Jaffe, Philip M.
Maglio, Vincent J. & Cooke, H. B., eds. Evolution of African Mammals. LC 77-19318. (Illus.). 656p. 1979. 88.00 (*0-674-27075-4*) HUP.
Magliocchetti, Bruno & Verna, Anthony, eds. The Motif of the Journey in Nineteenth-Century Italian Literature. LC 94-8388. 1994. 29.95 (*0-8130-1291-0*) U Press Fla.
Magliocco, Maurine, jt. ed. see Hargrove, Anne C.
Magliocco, Sabina. The Two Madonnas: The Politics of Festival in a Sardinian Community. LC 92-16538. (American University Studies: Anthropology & Science: Ser. XI, Vol. 61). 158p. (Orig.). (C). 1993. pap. text ed. 22.95 (*0-8204-1896-X*) P Lang Pubs.
Maglione, Connie A. & Fiore, Carmen A. Voices of the Daughters. LC 89-5031. (Illus.). 335p. 1989. 18.95 (*0-939219-05-0*) Townhouse Pub.
Maglione, Harry, jt. ed. see Emmens, Carol A.
Maglione, Robin S. Alyndoria: Tales of Inner Magic. (Illus.). 71p. (Orig.). (J). (gr. k-12). 1986. pap. 12.00 (*0-910609-11-X*) Gifted Educ Pr.

An Asterisk (*) at the beginning of an entry indicates that the title is appearing in BIP for the first time.

Magliozzi, Ronald S. Treasures from the Film Archives: A Catalog of Short Silent Fiction Films Held by FIAF Archives. LC 88-13500. 856p. 1988. 62.50 (*0-8108-2180-X*) Scarecrow.

Magliozzi, Tom. Car Talk. 1991. mass mkt. 10.00 (*0-440-50364-7*) Dell.

Maglischo, Cheryl W. Biomachanics Workbook to Accompnay Software. 137p. (C). 1991. pap. write for info. (*0-697-14842-4*) Brown & Benchmark.

Maglischo, Ernest W. Swimming Even Faster: A Comprehensive Guide to the Science of Swimming. 2nd ed. LC 92-10769. 755p. (C). 1993. text ed. 39.95 (*1-55934-036-3*) Mayfield Pub.

Maglischo, Ernest W. & Brennan, Cathy F. Swim for the Health of It. 144p. (Orig.). (C). 1985. pap. text ed. 13.95 (*0-87484-588-2*) Mayfield Pub.

Magliveras, S., jt. auth. see Kramer, E.

Maglott, D. R. & Nierman, W. C., eds. American Type Culture Collection Catalogue of Recombinant DNA Materials. 3rd ed. 150p. 1993. pap. text ed. write for info. (*0-930009-51-7*) ATCC.

Maglott, D. R., jt. ed. see Nierman, W. C.

Magnaflux Corporation Staff. Principles of Magnetic Particle Testing. LC 66-29699. (Illus.). 1966. 34.00 (*0-686-21417-X*) Magnaflux.

Magnaghi, Russell M. Miners, Merchants & Midwives: Michigan's Upper Peninsula Italians. LC 87-70604. 113p. (Orig.). 1987. pap. 7.95 (*0-942879-00-7*) Belle Fontaine Pr.

Magnaint-Lopez, Bernard, jt. auth. see Pelletier, Sophie.

Magnan, Bob, ed. One Hundred Forty-Seven Practical Tips for Teaching Professors. LC 92-9593. 48p. 1990. pap. 12.50 (*0-912150-09-2*) Magna Pubns.

Magnan, Bob, ed. see Johnson, Glenn R.

Magnan, Pierre. L' Amant du Poivre d'Ane. 416p. (FRE.). 1991. pap. 13.95 (*0-7859-4379-X*, 2070384292) Fr & Eur.

— La Maison Assassinee. (FRE.). 1985. pap. 13.95 (*0-7859-4224-6*) Fr & Eur.

Magnan, Richard A. Software User Interface Compatibility after Lotus Development Corporation vs Paperback Software International, No. P-93-4. (Illus.). 49p. (Orig.). 1993. pap. text ed. write for info. (*1-879716-04-6*) Ctr Info Policy.

Magnan, Robert, jt. auth. see Schoenfeld, A. Clay.

***Magnan, Rudy A., ed.** Reinventing American Education. (Orig.). Date not set. pap. write for info. (*0-943025-47-8*) Cummngs & Hath.

Magnan, Sally S., ed. Shifting the Instructional Focus to the Learner. LC 55-34379. (Reports of the Northeast Conference on the Teaching of Foreign Languages). 177p. 1990. pap. 10.95 (*0-915432-90-0*) NE Conf Teach Foreign.

***Magnan, William B.** Streets of St. Louis. 260p. (Orig.). 1994. pap. 14.95 (*0-9638816-1-2*) Right Press.

— Streets of St. Louis: An Entertaining History of St. Louis Street Names. 1994. pap. write for info. (*1-881183-02-5*) AIM Pr.

Magnani, David & McMurtry, Newell. Breaking the Boardom: An Annotated Bibliography on Boards & Councils. (Illus.). (Orig.). 1983. pap. 10.00 (*0-934210-08-X*) Devlp Commy.

Magnani, Denise. The Winterthur Garden: Henry Francis du Pont's Romance with the Land. LC 94-14976. 1995. write for info. (*0-8109-3779-4*) Abrams.

Magnani, Duane. Another Jesus, 2 vols., I. 1990. 12.95 (*1-883858-01-1*) Witness CA.

— Another Jesus, 2 vols., II. 1990. 12.95 (*1-883858-02-X*) Witness CA.

— Another Jesus, 2 vols., Set. 1990. pap. 19.95 (*1-883858-00-3*) Witness CA.

— Bible Students? 1983. 11.95 (*1-883858-03-8*) Witness CA.

— Charles Taze Russell - Child Molester. 1986. 4.95 (*1-883858-04-6*) Witness CA.

— Cruel & Unusual Punishment. 1986. 13.95 (*1-883858-05-4*) Witness CA.

— Danger at Your Door. 1987. 13.95 (*1-883858-06-2*, 687) Witness CA.

— Dialogue with Jehovah's Witnesses, 2 vols., I. 1983. 13.95 (*1-883858-08-9*) Witness CA.

— Dialogue with Jehovah's Witnesses, 2 vols., II. 1983. 13.95 (*1-883858-09-7*) Witness CA.

— Dialogue with Jehovah's Witnesses, 2 vols., Set. 1983. 22.95 (*1-883858-07-0*) Witness CA.

— The Heavenly Weatherman. 1987. 11.95 (*1-883858-12-7*) Witness CA.

— The Moneymakers. 1986. 7.95 (*1-883858-14-3*) Witness CA.

— Point-Counterpoint, Vol. 1: False Prophets. 1986. 7.95 (*1-883858-16-X*) Witness CA.

— A Problem of Communication. 1989. 6.95 (*1-883858-17-8*) Witness CA.

— Refutation of Preparing for Child Custody Cases. 1988. 11.95 (*1-883858-18-6*) Witness CA.

— Saleskids. 1986. 14.95 (*1-883858-19-4*) Witness CA.

— The Secret Doctrine of Jehovah's Witnesses. 1983. 4.95 (*1-883858-20-8*) Witness CA.

— Super Index. 1993. pap. 8.95 (*1-883858-21-6*) Witness CA.

— What Makes a Minister? 1986. 4.95 (*1-883858-23-2*) Witness CA.

— Where Is Michael? 1984. 6.95 (*1-883858-24-0*) Witness CA.

— Who Is the Faithful & Wise Servant? rev. ed. 1992. 11.95 (*1-883858-25-9*) Witness CA.

Magnani, Duane & Barrett, Arthur. Eyes of Understanding. 1977. 7.95 (*1-883858-10-0*) Witness CA.

— From Kingdom Hall to Kingdom Come. rev. ed. 1987. 11.95 (*1-883858-11-9*) Witness CA.

— The Watchtower Files. LC 84-28318. 340p. (Orig.). 1985. pap. 10.99 (*0-87123-816-0*) Bethany Hse.

Magnani, Gregorio, jt. ed. see Buchholz, Daniel.

Magnani, M. & De Flora, A., eds. Red Blood Cell Aging. (Advances in Experimental Medicine & Biology Ser.). (Illus.). 380p. 1991. 110.00 (*0-306-44021-0*, Plenum Pr) Plenum.

Magnani, M. & DeLoach, J. R., eds. The Use of Resealed Erythrocytes As Carriers & Bioreactors. (Advances in Experimental Medicine & Biology Ser.: Vol. 326). (Illus.). 357p. (C). 1993. 89.50 (*0-306-44345-7*, Plenum Pr) Plenum.

Magnarella, Paul J. Human Materialism: A Model of Sociocultural Systems & a Strategy for Analysis. LC 93-11146. (Illus.). 192p. 1993. lib. bdg. 29.95 (*0-8130-1233-3*); pap. text ed. 16.95 (*0-8130-1245-7*) U Press Fla.

— The Peasant Venture: Tradition, Migration & Change among Georgian Peasants in Turkey. (Illus.). 175p. 1979. pap. 11.95 (*0-87073-821-6*) Schenkman Bks Inc.

— Tradition & Change in a Turkish Town. 2nd ed. (Illus.). 210p. 1982. 18.95 (*0-87073-153-X*); pap. 13.95 (*0-87073-152-1*) Schenkman Bks Inc.

Magnarelli, Sharon. The Lost Rib. LC 83-46157. 232p. 1985. 38.50 (*0-8387-5074-5*) Bucknell U Pr.

— Reflections - Refractions: Reading Luisa Valenzuela. (American University Studies: Romance Languages & Literature: Ser. II, Vol. 80). 243p. (C). 1988. text ed. 34.50 (*0-8204-0638-4*) P Lang Pubs.

Magne, Emile, ed. see La Fayette, Marie-Madeleine de.

Magne, Jean. From Christianity to Gnosis & from Gnosis to Christianity: An Itinerary Through the Texts to & from the Tree of Paradise. LC 93-7328. (Brown Judaic Studies: No. 286). 251p. 1993. 49.95 (*1-55540-855-9*, 140286) Scholars Pr GA.

***Magne, Lawrence.** Passport to World Band Radio: 1995 Edition. (Radio Database International Ser.). (Illus.). 536p. (Orig.). 1994. pap. 19.95 (*0-914941-35-6*, PAW95P) IBS PA.

— RDI Evaluates the Sony ICF-2010 Receiver. (Radio Database International White Paper Ser.). (Illus.). 22p. (Orig.). 1988. pap. 5.95 (*0-914941-06-2*) IBS PA.

Magne, Lawrence, ed. RDI Evaluates the ICOM IC-R71 Receiver. (Radio Database International White Paper Ser.). (Illus.). 20p. (Orig.). 1988. pap. 5.95 (*0-914941-08-9*) IBS PA.

Magne, Lawrence, et al. Passport Evaluation of the ICOM IC-R9000 Receiver. (Radio Database International White Paper Ser.). (Illus.). 28p. (Orig.). 1990. pap. 5.95 (*0-914941-21-6*, WP14) IBS PA.

— Passport Evaluation of the Japan Radio NRD-93 Receiver. (Radio Database International White Paper Ser.). (Illus.). 17p. (Orig.). 1990. pap. 5.95 (*0-914941-19-4*, WP3) IBS PA.

— Passport Evaluation of the Kenwood R-5000 Receiver. (Radio Database International White Paper Ser.). (Illus.). 31p. (Orig.). 1990. pap. 5.95 (*0-914941-25-9*, WP5) IBS PA.

— Passport Evaluation of the Lowe HF-225 Receiver. (Radio Database International White Paper Ser.). (Illus.). 27p. (Orig.). 1990. pap. 5.95 (*0-914941-22-4*, WP15) IBS PA.

— Passport to World Band Radio: 1996 Edition. (Radio Database International Ser.). (Illus.). 536p. (Orig.). 1995. pap. 19.95 (*0-914941-37-2*, PAW96P) IBS PA.

Magne, P., jt. auth. see Fagot, J.

Magnenat-Thalmann, N. & Thalmann, Daniel. Image Synthesis Theory & Practice. (Computer Science Workbench Ser.). (Illus.). 400p. 1987. 59.00 (*0-387-70023-4*) Spr-Verlag.

— Synthetic Actors in Computer-Generated 3D Films. Kunii, Toshiyasu L., ed. (Computer Science Workbench Ser.). (Illus.). 144p. 1990. 59.00 (*0-387-52214-X*) Spr-Verlag.

Magnenat-Thalmann, N. & Thalmann, Daniel, eds. Computer Animation '90. (Illus.). viii, 242p. 1990. 98.00 (*0-387-70061-7*) Spr-Verlag.

— Computer Animation '91. (Illus.). viii, 256p. 1991. 124.00 (*0-387-70077-3*) Spr-Verlag.

— Computer-Generated Images. (Illus.). x, 497p. 1986. 79.00 (*0-387-70010-2*) Spr-Verlag.

— State-of-the-Art in Computer Animation. (Illus.). viii, 227p. 1989. 109.00 (*0-387-70046-3*) Spr-Verlag.

Magner, Candace A. Phonetic Readings of Brahms Lieder. LC 87-17620. (Illus.). 424p. 1987. 29.50 (*0-8108-2059-5*) Scarecrow.

***Magner, Carolyn.** Life Moses: My Bible Sticker Storybook. (J). (ps-3). 1994. pap. 2.99 (*0-7814-0141-0*) Cook.

— Wonders of Jesus: My Bible Sticker Storybook. (J). (ps-3). 1994. pap. 2.99 (*0-7814-0140-2*) Cook.

Magner, D. Classic Encyclopedia. 1988. pap. 6.99 (*0-517-32168-8*) Random Hse Value.

***Magner, Eilis.** Joske's Law & Procedure at Meetings in Australia. 8th ed. 220p. 1994. 60.00 (*0-455-21276-7*, Pub. by Law Bk Co) W W Gaunt.

— Joske's Law & Procedure at Meetings in Australia. 8th ed. 220p. 1994. pap. 36.00 (*0-455-21277-5*, Pub. by Law Bk Co) W W Gaunt.

***Magner, George.** Chiropractic: The Victim's Perspective. Barrett, Stephen, ed. (Illus.). 220p. 1995. 24.95 (*1-57392-041-X*) Prometheus Bks.

Magner, James A. Men of Mexico. LC 68-55849. (Essay Index Reprint Ser.). 1977. 44.95 (*0-8369-0666-7*) Ayer.

Magner, Jeanadele, jt. auth. see Magner, Ken.

Magner, Ken & Magner, Jeanadele. The Lady's Men. (Illus.). 275p. 1986. 19.95 (*0-9616979-0-3*) Hailstone.

Magner, Lee. Banished. (Silhouette Intimate Moments Ser.). 1994. mass mkt. 3.50 (*0-373-07556-1*, 5-07556-9) Silhouette.

— Standoff. (Silhouette Intimate Moments Ser.). 1993. mass mkt. 3.50 (*0-373-07507-3*, 5-07507-2) Silhouette.

Magner, Lois N. A History of the Life Sciences. 2nd ed. LC 93-34946. 512p. 1994. 39.95 (*0-8247-8942-3*) Dekker.

Magner, Lois N., ed. A History of Medicine. 400p. 1992. 59.75 (*0-8247-8673-4*) Dekker.

Magner, Thomas F. Introduction to the Croatian & Serbian Language. rev. ed. LC 89-37132. 448p. 1990. lib. bdg. 49.50 (*0-271-00685-4*) Pa St U Pr.

— Introduction to the Croatian & Serbian Language. rev. ed. LC 89-37132. 400p. 1995. pap. 25.00 (*0-271-01467-9*) Pa St U Pr.

Magnes, Beatrice. Episodes: A Memoir. 124p. 1977. 10.00 (*0-943376-07-6*) Magnes Mus.

Magnes, Judah L. & Buber, Martin. Arab-Jewish Unity: Testimony Before the Anglo-American Inquiry for the Ihud (Union) LC 75-7678. (Rise of Jewish Nationalism & the Middle East Ser.). 96p. 1975. reprint ed. 15.00 (*0-88355-348-1*) Hyperion Conn.

Magnes, Judah L., et al. Palestine-Divided or United? The Case for a Bi-National Palestine Before the United Nations. LC 80-39531. 104p. 1983. reprint ed. text ed. 59.75 (*0-8371-2617-7*, MAPA, Greenwood Pr) Greenwood.

Magnes, M. & Hafellener, J. Ascomyceten auf Gefaesspflanzen an Ufern von Gebirgsseen in den Ostalpen. (Bibliotheca Mycologica Ser.: Vol. 139). (Illus.). 185p. 1991. pap. 56.00 (*3-443-59040-3*, Pub. by Cramer-Borntraeger GW) Lubrecht & Cramer.

Magness, Lee. Sense & Absence. (Semeia Studies). (C). 1986. text ed. 16.95 (*1-55540-006-X*, 06-06-15); pap. 15.95 (*1-55540-007-8*) Scholars Pr GA.

***Magness, Perre M.** Past Times: Stories of Early Memphis. (Illus.). 288p. 1994. 25.00 (*0-9642929-0-4*) Parkway Press.

Magnet, Charles E. Puppet Dialogues. LC 78-53323. 1978. spiral bd. 4.95 (*0-916406-99-7*) Accent CO.

Magnet, Myron. The Dream & the Nightmare: The Sixties' Legacy to the Underclass. LC 92-23260. 256p. 1993. 20.00 (*0-688-11951-4*) Morrow.

— Dream & the Nightmare: The Sixties' Legacy to the Underclass. 1994. pap. 12.00 (*0-688-13512-9*, Quill) Morrow.

***Magnetic Resonance Annual Staff.** Magnetic Resonance Annual, 1988. fac. ed. Kressel, Herbert Y., ed. LC 85-646023. (Illus.). 357p. Date not set. pap. 101.80 (*0-7837-7223-8*, 2047075) Bks Demand.

Magney, jt. auth. see Erlandsen, Stanley L.

Magni, Laura. Come to the Park. (Look-Behind-The-Picture Bks.). (Illus.). 16p. (J). (ps up). 1989. 8.95 (*0-8120-5994-8*) Barron.

— Goodnight Stories from the Big Tree. (Illus.). 192p. (J). (ps-6). 1990. 9.99 (*0-517-69687-8*) Random Hse Value.

— Two Little Monkeys. (Illus.). 18p. (J). (ps-00). 1992. bds. 3.95 (*1-56397-154-2*) Boyds Mills Pr.

Magnien, E., ed. Biomolecular Engineering in the European Community. 1986. lib. bdg. 294.50 (*90-247-3400-2*) Kluwer Ac.

Magnien, Victor & Lacroix, M. Dictionnaire Grec-Francais: Greek - French Dictionary. 2168p. (FRE & GRE.). 1969. 79.95 (*0-8288-6592-2*, M-6382) Fr & Eur.

***Magnin, Andre & Soulillou, Jacques, eds.** Contemporary Art of Africa. LC 94-42674. 1995. write for info. (*0-8109-4032-9*) Abrams.

Magnin, John D. San Diego County Practical Guide to Divorce. 237p. (Orig.). 1994. 34.95 (*1-885558-00-7*) CA Pract Law.

— San Diego County Practical Guide to Divorce. Rose, Donna L., ed. 237p. (Orig.). 1994. pap. text ed. 29.95 (*1-885558-14-7*) CA Pract Law.

Magno, Cettina T. & Erdman, David V., eds. The Four Zoas by William Blake: A Photographic Facsimile of the Manuscript. LC 84-45891. (Illus.). 1987. 85.00 (*0-8387-5083-4*) Bucknell U Pr.

Magno, Joseph A. & LaMotte, Victor S. The Christian, the Atheist, & Freedom. LC 74-165170. 99p. 1975. 16.95x (*0-913750-08-5*) Transaction Pubs.

Magno, Paul D., jt. auth. see Ginnis, Sol.

Magno, Rosa M. Always There's a Thud: Poems. 115p. (Orig.). 1987. pap. 8.75 (*971-10-0328-7*, Pub. by New Day Pub PH) Cellar.

Magnotta, George, jt. auth. see Price, Robert S.

Magnotti, Shirley. Library Science Research, 1974-1979. 179p. 1983. 15.00 (*0-87875-235-8*) Whitston Pub.

— Masters Theses in Library Science 1960-1969. LC 75-8232. 306p. 1975. 18.00 (*0-87875-074-6*) Whitston Pub.

— Master's Theses in Library Science 1970-1974: Supplement. LC 75-8232. 1976. 10.50 (*0-87875-100-9*) Whitston Pub.

***Magnum, Abbas.** Allah O Akbar: A Journey Through Militant Islam. (Illus.). 320p. (C). 1994. 60.00 (*0-7148-3162-X*, Pub. by Phaidon Press UK) Chronicle Bks.

Magnum Incorporated Staff. Heroes & Anti-Heroes. LC 91-4309. 1992. 65.00 (*0-679-41178-X*) Random.

Magnum Photographers Staff, photos. In Our Time: The Last Five Decades as Seen by the Photographers of Magnum. 1989. 65.00 (*0-393-02767-8*) Norton.

Magnum School, Inc. Staff. Curso Completo de Tiro de Defensa. (Illus.). (SPA.). 1987. 24.95 (*0-945406-01-0*) Magnum Schl.

Magnum School Inc., Staff. Firearms: A Complete Guide for Their Proper Use & Care. 2nd ed. (Illus.). 103p. (YA). 1994. student ed 24.95 (*0-945406-02-9*) Magnum Schl.

Magnus, pseud. Necron. Leighton, Tom, tr. (Illus.). 56p. (Orig.). 1989. pap. 9.95 (*0-87416-072-3*) Catalan Communs.

Magnus. Necron, No. 2. Metz, Bernd, ed. Leighton, Tom, tr. (Illus.). 56p. (Orig.). 1990. pap. 9.95 (*0-87416-118-5*) Catalan Communs.

— Necron Three. Metz, Bernd, ed. Haworth, Philip, tr. (Illus.). 56p. (Orig.). 1991. pap. 10.95 (*0-87416-107-X*) Catalan Communs.

Magnus, Albertus. Albertus Magnus: Egyptian Secrets. 9.95 (*0-685-72555-3*) Wehman.

— Egyptian Secrets or White & Black Art for Man & Beast. 210p. 1993. pap. 16.95 (*1-56459-356-8*) Kessinger Pub.

Magnus, Alfred. Non-Spherical Principal Series Representations of a Semisimple Lie Group. LC 79-10157. (Memoirs Ser.: No. 19/216). 52p. 1979. pap. 17.00 (*0-8218-2216-0*, MEMO 19/216) Am Math.

Magnus, Anne, jt. auth. see Scorgie, Michael.

Magnus, Bernd. Contemporary Continental Philosophy. (Dimensions of Philosophy Ser.). 256p. 1997. 34.50 (*0-8133-0627-2*); pap. 16.95 (*0-8133-0628-0*) Westview.

Magnus, Bernd, et al. Nietzsche's Case: Philosophy As - And Literature. 320p. 1992. 52.50 (*0-415-90094-8*, A2724, Routledge NY); pap. 16.95 (*0-415-90095-6*, A2728, Routledge NY) Routledge.

Magnus, Bernd. Nietzsche's Existential Imperitive. LC 77-9864. (Studies in Phenomenology & Existential Philosophy). 254p. reprint ed. pap. 72.40 (*0-8357-6686-1*, 2056865) Bks Demand.

***Magnus, Bernd & Cullenberg, Stephen, eds.** Whither Marxism? Global Crises in International Perspective. 288p. 1994. 55.00 (*0-415-91042-0*, B4459) Routledge.

— Whither Marxism? Global Crises in International Perspective. 288p. 1994. pap. 17.95 (*0-415-91043-9*, B4463) Routledge.

Magnus, Erica. Around Me. LC 90-26459. (Illus.). 32p. (J). (ps-3). 1992. 13.00 (*0-688-09756-1*); lib. bdg. 12.93 (*0-688-09753-7*) Lothrop.

— The Crossing. LC 94-42372. (J). 1996. write for info. (*0-688-13927-2*); lib. bdg. write for info. (*0-688-13928-0*) Lothrop.

— My Secret Place. LC 93-8701. (Illus.). (J). 1994. write for info. (*0-688-11859-3*); lib. bdg. write for info. (*0-688-11860-7*) Lothrop.

Magnus, Hugo, jt. ed. see Connor, W. R.

***Magnus, I. B. & Kjellstorn, B.** Musical Motifs in Swedish Church Art: The Pictorial Representations of Music & Music-Making in Sweden's Medieval Churches up to 1630. Stevens, Michael, tr. (Illus.). 408p. (ENG & SWE.). 1993. 97.50x (*91-972117-0-2*, Pub. by Almqv & Wiksell SW) Coronet Bks.

Magnus, Jan R. Linear Structures. (Charles Griffin Book Ser.). 224p. 1988. 49.95 (*0-19-520655-X*) OUP.

Magnus, Jan R. & Neudecker, Heinz. Matrix & Differential Calculus with Applications in Statistics & Econometrics. (Series in Probability & Mathematics). 393p. 1988. text ed. 140.00 (*0-471-91516-5*) Wiley.

Magnus, Joann & Bogot, Howard I. An Artist You Don't Have to Be! A Jewish Arts & Crafts Book. 1990. pap. 10.95 (*0-8074-0422-5*, 168504) UAHC.

Magnus, Katie. Jewish Portraits. LC 72-3396. (Essay Index Reprint Ser.). 1977. reprint ed. 20.95 (*0-8369-2912-8*) Ayer.

Magnus, Knut. Trends in Cancer Incidences: Causes & Practical Implications. 1982. text ed. 79.50 (*0-07-039501-2*) McGraw.

Magnus, Knut, ed. Trends in Cancer Incidence: Causes & Practical Implications. LC 81-13205. (Illus.). 446p. 1982. 79.00 (*0-89116-235-6*) Hemisp Pub.

Magnus, Laurie. English Literature in Its Foreign Relations, 1300-1800. LC 68-20238. 1972. reprint ed. 23.95 (*0-405-08775-6*) Ayer.

— A General Sketch of European Literature in the Centuries of Romance. 1977. lib. bdg. 59.95 (*0-8490-1878-1*) Gordon Pr.

— A Primer of Wordsworth. LC 72-3170. (Studies in Wordsworth: No. 29). 1972. reprint ed. lib. bdg. 75.00 (*0-8383-1519-4*) M S G Haskell Hse.

Magnus, Laury. The Track of the Repetend: Syntactic & Lexical Repetition in Modern Poetry. LC 86-47850. (Ars Poetica Ser.: No. 4). 1989. 37.50 (*0-404-62504-5*) AMS Pr.

Magnus, Laury, jt. auth. see Epstein, Jane.

Magnus, Laury, tr. see Goncharov, Ivan.

Magnus, Leonard A., ed. The Tale of the Armament of Igor, A.D. 1185, A Russian Historical Epic. 1977. lib. bdg. 59.95 (*0-8490-2727-6*) Gordon Pr.

Magnus, Magus. Little Puddles. (Poetry I Ser.). (Illus.). 96p. (Orig.). 1994. pap. 10.00 (*0-9638061-0-6*) M DeLeon Bksmith.

Magnus, Mayotte, jt. auth. see Lewinski, Jorge.

Magnus, P. & Sorensen, T. I. Workshop on Genetic Epidemiology. (EUR Ser.: No. 14848). 76p. 1993. pap. 10.00 (*92-826-5469-9*, CD-NA-14848-EN-, Pub. by Europ Com) UNIPUB.

Magnus, R. Body Posture. (C). 1988. 47.50 (*81-205-0061-X*, Pub. by Oxford IBH II) S Asia.

Magnus, Ralph. Afghan Alternatives: Issues, Options & Policies. 229p. (C). 1985. 39.95 (*0-88738-050-6*) Transaction Pubs.

Magnus, Ralph H., ed. Documents on the Middle East. LC 75-93191. 239p. reprint ed. pap. 68.20 (*0-8357-4465-5*, 2037309) Bks Demand.

Magnus, Ralph H. & Naby, Eden. Afghanistan: Marx, Mullah, & Mujahid. 1994. 26.50 (*0-86531-513-2*) Westview.

Magnus, S. W., ed. Butterworths Company Forms Manual. 1988. U.K. pap. 110.00 (*0-406-01630-5*) Butterworth Legal Pubs.

Magnus, W., jt. auth. see Grossman, I.

Magnus, Wilhelm. Collected Papers. Chandler, B. & Baumslag, Gilbert, eds. (Illus.). 735p. 1983. 73.00 (*0-387-90879-X*) Spr-Verlag.

Magnus, Wilhelm, jt. auth. see Chandler, B.

Magnus, Wilhelm, et al. Combinational Group Theory: Presentations of Groups in Terms of Generators & Relations. 1976. reprint ed. pap. text ed. 12.95 (*0-486-63281-4*) Dover.

Magnuson, Carl R., jt. auth. see Chinn, Jennie A.

M

An Asterisk (*) at the beginning of an entry indicates that the title is appearing in BIP for the first time.

*Magnuson, Diana, illus. Animal Lore & Legend - Rabbit: American Indian Legends. LC 94-46600. (J). 1996. write for info. (0-590-22490-5) Scholastic Inc.
— Animal Lore & Legend--Bear: American Indian Legends. LC 94-47935. (J). 1996. write for info. (0-590-22491-3) Scholastic Inc.
— Animal Lore & Legend--Buffalo: American Indian Legends. LC 94-44267. (J). 1995. 4.95 (0-590-22489-1) Scholastic Inc.
— Animal Lore & Legend--Owl. LC 94-43935. (J). 1995. pap. 4.95 (0-590-22488-3) Scholastic Inc.
*Magnuson, Landis K. Circle Stock Theater: Touring American Small Towns, 1900-1950. 192p. 1995. lib. bdg. 32.50 (0-7864-0101-X) McFarland & Co.
Magnuson, Norris. Salvation in the Slums: Evangelical Social Welfare Work, 1865-1920. LC 76-54890. (American Theological Library Association Monograph: No. 10). 315p. 1977. 29.50 (0-8108-1001-8) Scarecrow.
— Salvation in the Slums: Evangelical Social Work, 1865-1920. LC 89-28714. 315p. 1990. reprint ed. pap. text ed. 10.99 (0-8010-6261-6) Baker Bk.
Magnuson, Norris A. & Travis, William G. American Evangelicalism: An Annotated Bibliography. LC 90-33989. 495p. (C). 1990. lib. bdg. 45.00 (0-933951-27-2) Locust Hill Pr.
Magnuson, Paul. Coleridge & Wordsworth: A Lyrical Dialogue. 352p. 1988. text ed. 47.50 (0-691-06732-5) Princeton U Pr.
— Coleridge's Nightmare Poetry. LC 74-4422. 151p. reprint ed. pap. 43.10 (0-685-20582-7, 2030680) Bks Demand.
Magnuson, Roger. Are Gay Rights Right? Making Sense of the Controversy. 149p. 1990. pap. 8.99 (0-88070-336-9, Multnomah Bks) Questar Pubs.
— Education in New France. 240p. 1992. 42.95 (0-7735-0907-0, Pub. by McGill CN) U of Toronto Pr.
— Informed Answers to Gay Rights Questions. 200p. 1994. pap. 9.99 (0-88070-659-7, Multnomah Bks) Questar Pubs.
— Shareholder Litigation, 1984-1990, 3 vols. LC 81-6078. 350.00 (0-685-09306-9) Clark Boardman Callaghan.
Magnuson, Roger J. White-Collar Crime Explosion: How to Protect Yourself & Your Company from Prosecution. 1992. text ed. 24.95 (0-07-039520-9) McGraw.
Magnussen, F., ed. see International Congress of Psychotherapy Staff.
Magnussen, S. Iceland: Country & People. (Illus.). 66p. (Orig.). 1987. pap. 10.00 (0-89918-113-9) Vanous.
Magnusson & Alexa. Transmission Lines & Wave Propagation. 3rd ed. 1991. 59.95 (0-8493-4279-1, TK3221) CRC Pr.
*Magnusson, et al. Tools 13: Technology of Object-Oriented Languages & Systems. (Illus.). 448p. (C). 1994. pap. text ed. 60.00 (0-13-350539-1) P-H.
Magnusson, Boris & Perrot, Jean. Tools 10: Technology of Object-Oriented Languages. 300p. 1993. pap. text ed. 72.00 (0-13-097114-6) P-H.
Magnusson, D., jt. ed. see Gustafson, S. B.
Magnusson, David, ed. Individual Development from an Interactional Perspective: A Longitudinal Study. (Paths Through Life Ser.). 248p. 1987. text ed. 39.95 (0-89859-707-2) L Erlbaum Assocs.
— Toward a Psychology of Situations: An Interactional Perspective. 480p. 1981. text ed. 69.95 (0-89859-061-2) L Erlbaum Assocs.
Magnusson, David & Allen, Vernon L., eds. Human Development: An Interactional Perspective. LC 83-7077. (Developmental Psychology Ser.). 1983. text ed. 65.00 (0-12-465480-0) Acad Pr.
Magnusson, David & Bergman, Lars R., eds. Data Quality in Longitudinal Research. (Illus.). 288p. (C). 1990. 64.95 (0-521-38091-X) Cambridge U Pr.
Magnusson, David & Casaer, Paul, eds. Longitudinal Research on Individual Development: Present Status & Future Prospectives. LC 93-18120. (European Network on Longitudinal Studies on Individual Development: Vol. 7). (Illus.). 350p. (C). 1993. 84.95 (0-521-43478-5) Cambridge U Pr.
Magnusson, David & Endler, Norman S. Personality at the Crossroads. LC 77-4190. 464p. (C). 1977. text ed. 69.95 (0-89859-293-3) L Erlbaum Assocs.
Magnusson, David & Ohman, Arne, eds. Psychopathology: An Interactional Perspective. (Personality, Psychopathology & Psychotherapy Ser.). 394p. 1987. text ed. 92.00 (0-12-465485-1) Acad Pr.
Magnusson, David, jt. ed. see Stattin, Haken.
Magnusson, David, et al, eds. Problems & Methods in Longitudinal Research: Stability & Change. (European Network on Longitudinal Studies on Individual Development). 355p. (C). 1992. 105.00 (0-521-40195-X) Cambridge U Pr.
— Problems & Methods in Longitudinal Research: Stability & Change. (European Network on Longitudinal Studies on Individual Development). (Illus.). 367p. (C). 1994. pap. 34.95 (0-521-46732-2) Cambridge U Pr.
Magnusson, Eirikr & Morris, William, trs. The Story of the Volsungs & Niblungs: With Certain Songs from the Elder Edda. 275p. 1980. reprint ed. 45.00 (0-8154-0518-9) Cooper Sq.
Magnusson, Finnur. The Hidden Class: Culture & Class in a Maritime Setting - Iceland 1880-1942. (Aarhus University North Atlantic Monographs: Vol. 1). (Illus.). 160p. 1990. 48.50 (87-7288-279-4, Pub. by Aarhus Univ Pr DK) Coronet Bks.
Magnusson, L., jt. auth. see Emmi, P. C.
*Magnusson, Lars. The Contest for Control: Metal Industries in Sheffield, Solingen, Remscheid, & Eskilstuna During Industrialization. (Illus.). 224p. 1994. 44.95 (0-85496-952-7) Berg Pubs.
— Mercantilism: The Shaping of an Economic Language. LC 93-43157. 240p. 1994. 65.00x (0-415-07258-1, B3925, Routledge NY) Routledge.
Magnusson, Lars, ed. Evolutionary & Neo-Schumpeterian Approaches to Economics. LC 93-5059. (Recent Economic Thought Ser.). 344p. (C). 1994. lib. bdg. 99.95 (0-7923-9385-6) Kluwer Ac.
— Mercantilism. LC 94-33823. 1995. write for info. (0-415-11600-7) Routledge.
— Mercantilist Economics. LC 93-1423. (Recent Economic Thought Ser.). 288p. (C). 1993. lib. bdg. 84.95 (0-7923-9359-7) Kluwer Ac.
Magnusson, lars, jt. auth. see Isacson, Naths.
Magnusson, M. Eirikr. Thomas Saga Erkibyskups: A Life of Archbishop Thomas Becket, in Icelandic, with English Translation, Notes & Glossary, 2 vols., Set. (Rolls Ser.: No. 65). 1974. reprint ed. 160.00 (0-8115-1133-2) Periodicals Srv.
*Magnusson, Magnus. Tutankhamun & the Discovery of the Tomb. (Jackdaws Ser.). 1992. 24.95 (1-56696-002-9); 32.00 (0-614-07317-0) Golden Owl NY.
Magnusson, Magnus, ed. Larousse Biographical Dictionary. rev. ed. Orig. Title: Cambridge Biographical Dictionary. 1616p. 1994. reprint ed. 50.00 (0-7523-5002-1, Chambers LKC); reprint ed. pap. 29.95 (0-7523-5003-X, Chambers LKC) LKC.
Magnusson, Magnus & Palsson, Hermann, trs. King Harald's Saga: Harald Hardradi of Norway. (Classics Ser.). 1976. pap. 8.95 (0-14-044183-2, Penguin Classics) Viking Penguin.
— Laxdaela Saga. (Classics Ser.). (Orig.). 1969. pap. 9.95 (0-14-044218-9, Penguin Classics) Viking Penguin.
— Njal's Saga. (Classics Ser.). (Orig.). 1960. mass mkt. 9.95 (0-14-044103-4, Penguin Classics) Viking Penguin.
*Magnusson, Michael. Latin Glory: Airline Color Schemes of South America. (Illus.). 112p. 1995. pap. 19.95 (0-7603-0024-0) Motorbooks Intl.
Magnusson, S. & Ottesen, M. Regulatory Proteolytic Enzymes & Their Inhibitors. LC 77-30606. (Proceedings 11th FEBS Meeting, Copenhagen 1977 Ser.: Vol. 47: A6). 1978. 107.00 (0-08-022628-0, Pub. by Pergamon Repr UK) Franklin.
Magnusson, Sally. The Flying Scotsman. (Illus.). 191p. 1982. pap. 5.95 (0-7043-3379-1, Pub. by Quartet UK) Charles River Bks.
— A Shout in the Street: The Story of Church House in Bridgeton. (C). 1992. pap. 35.00 (0-86153-150-7, Pub. by St Andrew UK) St Mut.
Magnusson, Sigurdur A., tr. The Postwar Poetry of Iceland. LC 82-8606. (Iowa Translations Ser.). 228p. (Orig.). 1982. pap. text ed. 17.95x (0-87745-115-X) U of Iowa Pr.
Magnusson, Ulf & Persson, Gunnar. Facets, Phases & Foci: Studies in Lexical Relations in English. (Umea Studies in the Humanities: No. 75). 308p. (Orig.). 1986. pap. text ed. 40.00x (91-7174-253-0) Coronet Bks.
Magnusson, Ulla, jt. ed. see Roderick, Hilliard.
Magnusson, Warren & Sancton, Andrew, eds. City Politics in Canada. LC 83-196724. 346p. reprint ed. pap. 98.70 (0-8357-3782-9, 2036512) Bks Demand.
Magny, jt. auth. see Hurtaut.
Magny, Claude. L' Age du Roman Americain. (BCL1-PS American Literature Ser.). 252p. 1993. reprint ed. lib. bdg. 79.00 (0-7812-6592-4) Rprt Serv.
Magnyickij, A. V., jt. auth. see Pume, N. D.
Magocsi, Paul R. Carpatho-Rusyn Americans. (Peoples of North America Ser.). (Illus.). 112p. (YA). (gr. 5 up). 1990. 17.95 (0-87754-866-8) Chelsea Hse.
— Historical Atlas of East Central Europe, Vol. 1. LC 93-13783. (History of East Central Europe Ser.). (Illus.). 232p. 1995. pap. 39.95 (0-295-97445-1) U of Wash Pr.
— The Russian Americans. Stotsky, Sandra, ed. LC 95-12599. (J). 1995. (0-7910-3367-8) Chelsea Hse.
— The Rusyns of Slovakia: An Historical Survey. LC 93-71875. (East European Monographs: No. CCCLXXXI). 185p. 1994. 28.00 (0-88033-278-6) East Eur Quarterly.
— Ukraine: A Historical Atlas. 64p. 1985. 50.00 (0-8020-3428-4); pap. 27.50 (0-8020-3429-2) U of Toronto Pr.
Magocsi, Paul R., ed. The Persistence of Regional Cultures: Rusyns & Ukrainians in Their Carpathian Homeland & Abroad. 300p. 1993. 42.00 (0-88033-262-X, 365) East Eur Quarterly.
— Texts of the Ukraine "Peace" with Maps. (Revolution & Nationalism in the Modern World Ser.: No. 3). 184p. 1981. reprint ed. pap. 12.00 (0-939738-02-3) Zubal Inc.
— The Ukrainian Experience in the United States: A Symposium. LC 78-59968. (Sources & Documents Ser.). (Orig.). 1979. pap. 7.50 (0-916458-04-0) Harvard Ukrainian.
Magocsi, Paul R., jt. auth. see Hrushevsky, Michaelo.
Magoffin, Jim. Triumph Over Turbulence: Alaska's Luckiest Bush Pilot. (Illus.). 308p. 1993. 29.95 (0-9637806-0-3) J Magoffin.
Magoffin, Susan S. Down the Santa Fe Trail & into Mexico: The Diary of Susan Shelby Magoffin, 1846-1847. Drumm, Stella M., ed. LC 82-2722. (Illus.). xxxvi, 304p. 1982. reprint ed. pap. 9.95 (0-8032-8116-1, Bison Books) U of Nebr Pr.
Magolda, Marcia B. Knowing & Reasoning in College: Gender Related Patterns in Students' Intellectual Development. LC 92-9889. (Higher & Adult Education Ser.). 472p. (C). 1992. 34.95 (1-55542-467-8) Jossey-Bass.
Magoldi, Mary. Daily Close-Ups for Spring. Russell, Bruce, ed. 96p. (J). (gr. k-6). 1984. student ed 9.95 (0-86653-255-2, GA 563) Good Apple.
— Daily Close-Ups for Winter. Russell, Bruce, ed. 96p. (J). (gr. k-6). 1984. student ed 9.95 (0-86653-256-0, GA 562) Good Apple.
Magoldi, Mary & Russell, Bruce. Daily Close-Ups for Fall. 96p. (J). (gr. k-6). 1984. student ed 9.95 (0-86653-254-4, GA 561) Good Apple.
Magolin, Arnold. The Ontology of Bioethics. 57p. (Orig.). 1991. pap. 6.44 (0-685-48279-0) Dayspring Pr.
Magomedov, D. M. The Art of Daghestan: Decorative Applied Art, Paintings, Scultpture & Graphics. 200p. 1981. 125.00 (0-317-14220-8, Pub. by Collets UK) St Mut.
Magon, Ricardo F. Land & Liberty: Anarchist Influences in the Mexican Revolution. Poole, Dave, ed. (Orig.). 1979. pap. 5.50 (0-932366-04-X) Black Thorn Bks.
Magona, Sindiwe. Living, Loving & Lying Awake at Night. (Emerging Voices: New International Fiction Ser.). 208p. 1994. 24.95 (1-56656-147-7); pap. 11.95 (1-56656-141-8) Interlink Pub.
— To My Children's Children. LC 94-4358. (Orig.). 1994. 24.95 (1-56656-163-9); pap. 11.95 (1-56656-152-3) Interlink Pub.
*Magonet, Jonathan, ed. Jewish Explorations of Sexuality. (European Judaism Ser.: Vol. 1). 288p. (C). 1995. pap. text ed. 25.00 (1-57181-029-3) Berghahn Bks.
— Jewish Explorations of Sexuality. (European Judaism Ser.: Vol. 1). 288p. (C). 1995. text ed. 45.00 (1-57181-868-5) Berghahn Bks.
— Returning. LC 78-68143. 1978. pap. 3.95 (0-8197-0468-7) Bloch.
Magonet, Jonathan, jt. auth. see Blue, Lionel.
Magonet, Philip. Practical Hypnotism. 1976. pap. 3.00 (0-87980-123-9) Wilshire.
Magoon, Charles E. Photos at the Archives. 274p. (Orig.). 1981. pap. write for info. (0-318-54244-7) Macmillan.
— Reports of the Law of Civil Government in Territory Subject to Military Occupation by the Military Forces of the United States. 3rd ed. Kavass, Igor I. & Sprudzs, Adolf, eds. LC 72-75029. (International Military Law & History Ser.: Vol. 2). 808p. 1972. reprint ed. lib. bdg. 55.00 (0-930342-39-9, 300920) W S Hein.
Magoon, E. L. Orators of the American Revolution. 456p. 1992. reprint ed. 42.50 (0-8377-2442-2) Rothman.
*Magoon, Eaton B., Jr., et al. Numbah One Day of Christmas: The Hawaii Version of the Twelve Days of Christmas. LC 94-77955. (Illus.). 20p. 1994. 9.95 (1-880188-91-0) Bess Pr.
*Magoon, Leslie B. & Claypool, George E., eds. Alaska North Slope Oil-Rock Correlation Study. (AAPG Studies in Geology: No. 20). (Illus.). xiv, 682p. 1985. pap. 42.00 (0-89181-026-9) AAPG.
*Magoon, Leslie B. & Dow, Wallace G., eds. The Petroleum System: From Source to Trap. (Memoir Ser.: No. 60). (Illus.). xiii, 655p. 1994. 114.00 (0-89181-338-1) AAPG.
Magoon, Orville T. & Baird, W. F., eds. Durability of Stone for Rubble Mound Breakwaters. LC 91-39609. 277p. 1992. pap. text ed. 29.00 (0-87262-863-9) Am Soc Civil Eng.
Magoon, Orville T. & Converse, Hugh, eds. Coastal Zone '83, 3 Vols., Set. 2990p. 1983. pap. 198.00 (0-87262-359-9) Am Soc Civil Eng.
Magoon, Orville T. & Fabbri, Paulo, eds. Coastlines of Italy. 192p. 1989. pap. text ed. 24.00 (0-87262-706-3, 706) Am Soc Civil Eng.
Magoon, Orville T. & Hemsley, J. Michael, eds. Ocean Wave Measurement & Analysis: Proceedings of the Second International Symposium, Honoring Robert L. Wiegel, New Orleans, Louisiana, July 25-28, 1993. LC 94-7190. 1994. write for info. (0-87262-922-8) Am Soc Civil Eng.
Magoon, Orville T. & Neves, Claudio, eds. Coastlines of Brazil. 304p. 1989. pap. text ed. 31.00 (0-87262-707-1, 707) Am Soc Civil Eng.
Magoon, Orville T., jt. ed. see Bolton, H. Suzanne.
Magoon, Orville T., jt. ed. see Cambers, Gillian.
Magoon, Orville T., jt. ed. see Cofer-Shabica, Stephen V.
Magoon, Orville T., jt. ed. see Davidson, D. D.
Magoon, Orville T., jt. ed. see Nagao, Yoshimi.
Magoon, Orville T., et al, eds. Coastal Zone '89, 5 vols. 5240p. 1989. pap. text ed. 480.00 (0-87262-705-5, 705) Am Soc Civil Eng.
— Coastal Zone '91, 4 vols., Set. LC 91-19398. 3800p. 1991. pap. text ed. 325.00 (0-87262-809-4) Am Soc Civil Eng.
— Coastal Zone '93: Proceedings of the Eighth Symposium & Ocean Management, July 19-23, 1993. New Orleans Louisiana. LC 93-2242. 3624p. 1993. 254.00 (0-87262-918-X) Am Soc Civil Eng.
Magoon, Robert A., jt. auth. see Cofer, Richard S., Jr.
Magoon, T. M., et al. Mental Health Counsellors at Work. (C). 1969. 88.00 (0-08-006422-1, Pub. by Pergamon Repr UK) Franklin.
Magor, John. Aliens above Always. A UFO Report. (Illus.). 160p. (Orig.). 1983. pap. 9.95 (0-88839-969-3) Hancock House.
— Pagans in My Blood. 120p. 1992. pap. 14.95 (0-88839-291-5) Hancock House.
Magor, Thomasin. African Warriors: The Samburu. LC 93-47465. Date not set. write for info. (0-8109-1943-5) Abrams.
Magorian, James. America First. LC 92-70840. 156p. (Orig.). 1992. pap. 6.00 (0-930674-37-5) Black Oak.
— At the City Limits. LC 86-72766. (Illus.). 34p. (J). (gr. 3-5). 1987. pap. 3.00 (0-930674-22-7) Black Oak.
— The Beautiful Music. LC 88-71142. (Illus.). 12p. (J). (gr. 2-5). 1988. pap. 3.00 (0-930674-25-1) Black Oak.
— The Bonkly Dribblefink Fables. LC 87-70706. (Illus.). 16p. (J). (gr. 1-4). 1987. pap. 3.00 (0-930674-24-3) Black Oak.
— Borderlands. LC 91-75480. 36p. (Orig.). 1992. pap. 6.00 (0-930674-36-7) Black Oak.
— Catalpa Blossoms. 42p. 1994. 15.00 (0-930674-39-1) Black Oak.
— The Emily Dickinson Jogging Book. LC 84-71315. 60p. 1984. pap. 5.00 (0-930674-13-8) Black Oak.
— Fimperings & Torples. LC 81-69872. (Illus.). 44p. (J). (gr. 4-6). 1981. pap. 3.00 (0-930674-06-5) Black Oak.
— The Great Injun Carnival. LC 81-69873. 48p. 1982. pap. 5.00 (0-930674-07-3) Black Oak.
— Griddlemort & the Beanstalk. LC 83-73615. (Illus.). 64p. 1986. pap. 5.00 (0-930674-21-9) Black Oak.
— Griddlemort Loses His Birthday. LC 88-71604. (Illus.). 32p. (J). (gr. 1-4). 1988. pap. 3.00 (0-930674-29-4) Black Oak.
— Ground-Hog Day. LC 87-70705. (Illus.). 22p. (J). (gr. 3-5). 1987. pap. 3.00 (0-930674-23-5) Black Oak.
— The Hideout of the Sigmund Freud Gang. LC 84-71316. 974p. 1987. pap. 10.00 (0-930674-16-2) Black Oak.
— Ideas for a Bridal Shower. LC 79-53858. 196p. 1980. pap. 5.00 (0-930674-02-2) Black Oak.
— Imaginary Radishes. LC 79-53857. (Illus.). 32p. (J). (gr. 3-5). 1980. 5.00 (0-930674-03-0) Black Oak.
— The Invention of the Afternoon Nap. LC 89-62222. (Illus.). 20p. (J). (gr. 2-5). 1989. pap. 3.00 (0-930674-32-4) Black Oak.
— Karl Marx & the Development of International Communism. LC 85-72861. 44p. 1986. pap. 5.00 (0-930674-18-9) Black Oak.
— Keeper of Fire. (Indian Culture Ser.). (Illus.). 78p. (Orig.). (J). (gr. 4-12). 1984. pap. 6.95 (0-89992-088-8) Coun India Ed.
— The Kingdom of Junk Bonds. LC 88-71143. (Illus.). 24p. (J). (gr. 5-9). 1988. pap. 3.00 (0-930674-27-8) Black Oak.
— The Magic Pretzel. LC 88-71603. (Illus.). 32p. (J). (gr. 2-5). 1988. pap. 3.00 (0-930674-28-6) Black Oak.
— The Man Who Wore Layers of Clothing in the Winter. LC 94-71880. 121p. (Orig.). 1994. pap. 6.00 (0-930674-40-5) Black Oak.
— Mountain Man. LC 88-71606. 40p. 1989. pap. 6.00 (0-930674-31-6) Black Oak.
— Mud Pies. LC 91-70218. (Illus.). 24p. (Orig.). (J). (gr. 4-6). 1991. pap. 3.00 (0-930674-35-9) Black Oak.
— The Palace of Water. LC 90-81003. (Illus.). 16p. (J). (gr. 2-5). 1990. pap. 3.00 (0-930674-33-2) Black Oak.
— Phases of the Moon. LC 77-82560. (Illus.). 40p. 1978. 6.00 (0-930674-01-4) Black Oak.
— Plucked Chickens. LC 80-68263. (Illus.). 32p. (J). (gr. 4-6). 1981. 5.00 (0-930674-04-9) Black Oak.
— Safe Passage. LC 77-87243. (Stone Country Poetry Ser.: No. 4). (Illus.). 1977. pap. text ed. 3.00 (0-930020-03-0) Stone Country.
— Spiritual Rodeo. LC 80-18372. 17p. (Orig.). 1980. pap. 3.00 (0-915124-37-8, Toothpaste) Coffee Hse.
— Spoonproof Jello & Other Poems. LC 90-81004. (Illus.). 16p. (J). (gr. 2-5). 1990. pap. 3.00 (0-930674-34-0) Black Oak.
— Squall Line. LC 85-73614. 52p. 1986. pap. 3.00 (0-930674-19-7) Black Oak.
— The Three Diminutive Pigs. LC 88-71605. (Illus.). 20p. (J). (gr. 1-4). 1988. pap. 3.00 (0-930674-30-8) Black Oak.
— The Tooth Fairy. LC 93-73338. (Illus.). 22p. (Orig.). (J). (gr. 1-3). 1993. pap. 3.00 (0-930674-38-3) Black Oak.
— Training at Home to be a Locksmith. LC 80-68264. 112p. 1981. pap. 6.00 (0-930674-05-7) Black Oak.
— The Walden Pond Caper. LC 83-71263. 148p. 1983. pap. 6.00 (0-930674-11-1) Black Oak.
— The Witches' Olympics. LC 83-71262. 44p. (J). (gr. 4-7). 1983. pap. 5.00 (0-930674-10-3) Black Oak.
Magorian, Michelle. Back Home. LC 84-47629. (Charlotte Zolotow Bk.). 384p. (YA). (gr. 7 up). 1992. pap. 4.95 (0-06-440411-0, Trophy) HarpC Child Bks.
— Good Night, Mr. Tom. LC 80-8444. 336p. (YA). (gr. 7 up). 1982. lib. bdg. 15.89 (0-06-024079-2) HarpC Child Bks.
— Good Night, Mr. Tom. LC 80-8444. (Trophy Bk.). 336p. (J). (gr. 5-9). 1986. pap. 3.95 (0-06-440174-X, Trophy) HarpC Child Bks.
Magos, Adam L., jt. ed. see Lewis, B. Victor.
Magos, Alicia P. The Enduring Ma-Aram Tradition: An Ethnography of a Knaray-a Village in Antique. (Illus.). 147p. 1993. pap. 12.50 (971-10-0506-9, Pub. by New Day Pub PH) Cellar.
Magosci, Paul R. The Russian Americans. (Peoples of North America Ser.). (Illus.). 112p. (YA). (gr. 5 up). 1989. 17.95 (0-87754-899-4) Chelsea Hse.
Magosi, Paul R., ed. see Pekar, Athanasius.
Magoteaux, Cheryl. IPRA Media Guide. (Illus.). 256p. 1984. pap. 9.95 (0-318-03395-X) Intl Rodeo.
Magoulias, Harry J., tr. O City of Byzantium: Annals of Niketas Choniates. LC 81-130890. 476p. (GRE.). 1984. 50.00 (0-8143-1764-2) Wayne St U Pr.
Magoulias, Harry J., tr. see Ducas.
*Magoulias, Michael, ed. Shakespearean Criticism Vol. 26. 422p. 1995. 128.00 (0-8103-8946-0) Gale.
Magoun, Christine, jt. auth. see Danielson, Jan.
Magoun, F. A. & Hodgins, Eric. History of Aircraft. LC 70-169431. (Literature & History of Aviation Ser.). 1972. reprint ed. 40.95 (0-405-03774-0) Ayer.
Magoun, F. Alexander. The Frigate Constitution & Other Historic Ships. (Illus.). 256p. 1987. reprint ed. pap. 10.95 (0-486-25524-7) Dover.
Magoun, Francis P. A Chaucer Gazetteer. LC 61-11293. 173p. reprint ed. pap. 49.40 (0-685-10700-0, 2024058) Bks Demand.
Magoun, Francis P. & Lhonnrot, Elias. The Old Kalevala, & Certain Antecedents. LC 74-78520. 331p. reprint ed. pap. 94.40 (0-7837-4119-7, 2057942) Bks Demand.
Magoun, Francis P., Jr., tr. see Lonnrot, Elias, ed.
Magowan, Robin. Burning the Knife: New & Selected Poems. LC 84-23671. (Poets Now Ser.: No. 8). 134p. 1985. 13.50 (0-8108-1777-2) Scarecrow.
— Looking for Binoculars. 50p. 1976. pap. 8.00 (0-87711-062-X) Story Line.
— Tour de France: The 75th Anniversary Bicycle Race. 175p. 1995. pap. 16.95 (1-884737-13-7) VeloPress.

An Asterisk (*) at the beginning of an entry indicates that the title is appearing in BIP for the first time.

Magowan, Robin & Watson, Graham. Kings of the Road: A Portrait of Racers & Racing. (Illus.). 208p. 1988. 25.95 (*0-88011-297-2*, PMAG0297) Human Kinetics.

Magrab, E. B. Computer Integrated Experimentation. (Environmental & Energetics Ser.). (Illus.). 272p. 1991. 65.00 (*0-387-53291-9*) Spr-Verlag.

— Vibrations of Elastic Structural Members, No. 3. (Mechanics of Structural Systems Ser.). 404p. 1980. lib. bdg. 129.50 (*90-286-0207-0*) Kluwer Ac.

Magrab, Edward B., ed. see ASME, DED Vibrations Conference Staff.

Magrab, Phyllis R. Learning to Learn: Ways to Nurture Your Child's Intelligence. LC 93-50219. 1994. 23.95 (*0-306-44647-2*, Plenum Insight) Plenum.

Magrab, Phyllis R., ed. Improving Psychological Services for Children & Adolescents with Severe Mental Disorders: Clinical Training in Psychology. LC 89-82575. 231p. (Orig.). 1990. pap. text ed. 30.00 (*1-55798-080-2*) Am Psychol.

— Psychological & Behavioral Assessment: Impact on Pediatric Care. 384p. 1984. 65.00 (*0-306-41697-2*, Plenum Pr) Plenum.

Magrabi, Frances M., et al. The Economics of Household Consumption. LC 91-20302. 208p. 1991. text ed. 69.95 (*0-275-93406-3*, C3406, Praeger Pubs); pap. text ed. 17.95 (*0-275-94113-2*, B4113, Praeger Pubs) Greenwood.

Magrass, Yale. Thus Spake the Moguls. 274p. 1981. text ed. 19.95 (*0-87073-578-0*); pap. text ed. 13.95 (*0-87073-579-9*) Schenkman Bks Inc.

Magrassi, P., jt. ed. see Bounhoure, J. P.

Magrath, Allan, jt. auth. see Hardy, Kenneth.

Magrath, Allan J. How to Achieve Zero-Defect Marketing. 192p. 1993. 22.95 (*0-8144-5123-3*) AMACOM.

— Marketing Strategies for Growth in Uncertain Times. Knudsen, Anne, ed. LC 94-20721. 1995. 29.95 (*0-8442-3323-4*, NTC Busn Bks) NTC Pub Grp.

— The Six Imperatives of Marketing: Lessons from the World's Best Companies. 208p. 1992. 22.95 (*0-8144-5042-3*) AMACOM.

Magrath, C. Peter. Yazoo: Law & Politics in the New Republic: The Case of Fletcher v. Peck. LC 66-19584. 259p. reprint ed. pap. 73.90 (*0-685-44067-2*, 2030026) Bks Demand.

Magrath, C. Peter, et al. Strengthening Teacher Education: The Challenges to College & University Leaders. LC 86-46336. (Jossey-Bass Higher Education Ser.). 206p. reprint ed. pap. 58.80 (*0-7837-2524-8*, 2042683) Bks Demand.

Magrath, Derek. Norton Crowood Motoclas: The Complete Story. (Illus.). 160p. 1991. 29.95 (*1-85223-545-4*, Pub. by Crowood UK) Motorbooks Intl.

Magrath, I. T., ed. New Directions in Cancer Treatment. (Illus.). 610p. 1989. pap. 104.00 (*0-387-19063-5*) Spr-Verlag.

Magrath, Ian T. Non-Hodgkins Lymphomas. 1990. 80.00 (*0-683-05895-9*) Williams & Wilkins.

Magrath, Ian T., et al, eds. Pathogenesis of Leukemias & Lymphomas: Environmental Influences. (Progress in Cancer Research & Therapy Ser.: Vol. 27). 430p. 1984. text ed. 148.50 (*0-89004-901-7*) Raven.

Magrath, Myler. Book of Great Irish Lies. 1989. pap. 7.95 (*0-946645-10-8*) Dufour.

Magrath, William B., jt. ed. see Doolette, John B.

Magraw, Daniel B., ed. International Law & Pollution. LC 90-19454. 384p. (C). 1991. text ed. 39.95 (*0-8122-3052-3*) U of Pa Pr.

Magraw, Roger. A History of the French Working Class, 2 vols., 1. 768p. (C). 1992. 54.95 (*0-631-13817-X*) Blackwell Pubs.

— A History of the French Working Class, 2 vols., 2. 768p. (C). 1992. 54.95 (*0-631-18045-1*) Blackwell Pubs.

*__Magraw, Trisha.__ Princess Megan. Bodnar, Judit & Gould, Betsy, eds. (Magic Attic Club Ser.). (Illus.). 64p. (Orig.). (J). (gr. 2-6). 1995. 12.95 (*1-57513-004-1*); pap. 5.95 (*1-57513-005-X*) Magic Attic Club.

— Rodeo Riding Megan. Bodnar, Judit & Gould, Betsy, eds. (Magic Attic Club Ser.). (Illus.). 64p. (Orig.). (J). (gr. 2-6). 1995. 12.95 (*1-57513-012-2*); pap. 5.95 (*1-57513-013-0*) Magic Attic Club.

Magre, Maurice, tr. see Merton, Reginald.

Magrelli, Valerio. Nearsights: Selected Poems. Molino, Anthony, tr. 180p. (C). 1990. 16.95 (*1-55597-133-4*); pap. 10.95 (*1-55597-134-2*) Graywolf.

Magri, Iole F., tr. see Cancogni, Manlio.

Magri, Iole F., tr. see Fargion, Maria L.

Magriel, Paul, ed. Bibliography of Dancing. LC 65-16242. (Illus.). 1972. 20.95 (*0-405-08776-4*) Ayer.

— Chronicles of the American Dance. LC 77-25865. (Series in Dance). (Illus.). 1978. reprint ed. lib. bdg. 35.00 (*0-306-77566-2*) Da Capo.

— Chronicles of the American Dance: From the Shakers to Martha Graham. LC 78-9067. (Quality Paperbacks Ser.). (Illus.). 1978. reprint ed. pap. 7.95 (*0-306-80082-9*) Da Capo.

— Nijinsky, Pavlova, Duncan: Three Lives in Dance. (Series in Dance). 1977. reprint ed. lib. bdg. 35.00 (*0-306-70845-0*); reprint ed. pap. 12.95 (*0-306-80035-7*) Da Capo.

Magriel, Paul, ed. see Mendoza, Daniel.

Magris, Claudio. Danube. Creagh, Patrick, tr. 1990. pap. 11.95 (*0-374-52245-6*, Noonday) FS&G.

Magriso, Yitzchok. Avoth. Barocas, David N., tr. (Torah Anthology - Meam Loez Ser.). 400p. 17.95 (*0-940118-22-X*) Moznaim.

Magritte, Rene, jt. auth. see Robbe-Grillet, Alain.

Magro, A., et al, eds. Central & Peripheral Mechanisms of Cardiovascular Regulation. LC 86-15101. (NATO ASI Series A, Life Sciences: Vol. 109). 554p. 1986. 125.00 (*0-306-42360-X*, Plenum Pr) Plenum.

Magro, Michael V., ed. see New York State Bar Association Staff.

Magruder, Allan B. John Marshall. Morse, John T., Jr., ed. LC 73-128974. (American Statesmen Ser.: No. 10). reprint ed. 45.00 (*0-404-50860-X*) AMS Pr.

*__Magruder, Carter B.__ Recurring Logistic Problems As I Have Observed Them. 134p. (Orig.). (C). 1994. pap. text ed. 45.00 (*0-7881-1310-0*) Diane Pub.

Magruder, Clark, ed. see Torres, Eliseo, et al.

Magruder, Dudley B., Jr. The Two-Dollar Boat: Boat Stories & Other Lies. LC 91-24247. (Illus.). 208p. 1992. 18.95 (*1-56474-000-5*) Fithian Pr.

Magruder, G. Brock & Gilbert, Walter R., Jr. The Book on Cataracts. Curley & Pynn Public Relations Management, Inc. Staff, ed. (Illus.). (Orig.). (C). 1988. pap. text ed. 4.95 (*0-317-93288-8*) G B Magruder.

*__Magruder, J. Scott.__ CARP: User's Guide & Introduction to Authoring Tutorials. 119p. 1991. pap. text ed. 50.00 (*0-933179-07-3*) Bus Account Pubns.

Magruder, James, tr. see Marivaux.

Magruder, Julia. Miss Ayr of Virginia & Other Stories. LC 77-110207. (Short Story Index Reprint Ser.). 1977. 23.95 (*0-8369-3358-3*) Ayer.

*__Magruder, Scott.__ Using a Computer Simulation to Teach General Equilibrium Concepts. 63p. 1989. pap. text ed. 26.50 (*0-931179-03-3*) Bus Account Pubns.

Magryta, Leslie. Introduction to Paralegal Studies: A Skills Approach. LC 92-28396. 350p. (C). 1992. text ed. 34.50 (*0-256-12390-X*) Irwin.

Magsino, Romula, jt. ed. see Miranda, Evelina O.

Magstadt, Thomas H. & Schotten, Peter M. Understanding Politics: Ideas, Instituions & Issues. 3rd ed. LC 92-50018. (Illus.). 603p. (C). 1992. pap. text ed. 37.00 (*0-312-05018-6*) St Martin.

Magstadt, Thomas M. Nations & Governments: Comparative Politics in Regional Perspective. LC 89-63917. 608p. (Orig.). (C). 1991. pap. text ed. 0.40 (*0-312-05291-X*) St Martin.

— Nations & Governments: Comparative Politics in Regional Perspective. 2nd ed. 608p. 1994. pap. text ed. 37.00 (*0-312-08644-X*) St Martin.

Magubane, Bernard. Political Economy of Race & Class in South Africa. LC 78-13917. 364p. 1980. pap. 12.00 (*0-85345-506-6*) Monthly Rev.

— South Africa: From Soweto to Uitenhage: The Political Economy of the South African Revolution. LC 86-73223. 225p. (C). 1989. 35.00 (*0-86543-050-0*); pap. 11.95 (*0-86543-051-9*) Africa World.

— The Ties That Bind: African American Consciousness of Africa. 2nd ed. LC 86-70980. 250p. (C). 1990. 35.00 (*0-86543-036-5*); pap. 10.95 (*0-86543-037-3*) Africa World.

Magubane, Bernard, jt. ed. see Mandaza, Ibbo.

Magubane, Peter. Soweto: The Fruit of Fear: A School Children's Revolt That Ignited a Nation. LC 86-71992. 125p. (C). 1987. 29.95 (*0-86543-041-1*); pap. 14.95 (*0-86543-040-3*) Africa World.

Magubane, Peter, photos. Women of South Africa: Their Fight for Freedom. (Illus.). 128p. 1993. 40.00 (*0-8212-1928-6*); pap. 24.95 (*0-8212-1934-0*) Bulfinch Pr.

Maguet, P., tr. see Pauwels, F.

Maguglin, Robert O. Howard Hughes: His Achievements & Legacy. LC 85-50968. (Illus.). 120p. 1988. pap. 10.95 (*0-917859-22-7*) Sunrise SBCA.

— The Queen Mary: The Official Pictorial History. LC 85-50967. (Illus.). 120p. 1988. pap. 10.95 (*0-917859-21-9*) Sunrise SBCA.

Maguin, Jean-Marie, jt. ed. see Klein, Holger.

Maguin, Jean-Marie, jt. ed. see Willems, Michelee M.

Maguiness, David. Macworld Guide to Microsoft Excel 4. (Illus.). 383p. 1992. 22.95 (*1-878058-40-1*) IDG Bks.

Maguiness, David, jt. auth. see Van Buren, Chris.

Maguiness, David, jt. auth. see Walkenach, John.

Maguiness, Nancy. Giving Back the Elements. 80p. (Orig.). 1993. pap. text ed. 10.00 (*1-879260-19-0*) Evanston Pub.

*__Maguire.__ Dry Land Tourist. Date not set. per. 12.95 (*0-920813-67-4*, Pub. by Sister Vision CN) InBook.

— Respiratory Home Care. (Illus.). 320p. 1990. 34.95 (*0-8016-3490-3*) Mosby Yr Bk.

Maguire & Van Nostrand, eds. Diagnosis of Colorectal & Ovarian Carcinoma: Application of Immunoscintigraphic Technology. (Targeted Diagnosis & Therapy Ser.: Vol. 6). 268p. 1992. 110.00 (*0-8247-8646-7*) Dekker.

*__Maguire, Ann, et al.__ Miscarriage of Justice: An Irish Family's Story of Wrongful Conviction As IRA Terrorists. rev. ed. 176p. 1994. pap. 10.95 (*1-57098-006-3*) R Rinehart.

Maguire, Anne. For Brian's Sake: The Story of the Keenan Sisters. 144p. (Orig.). 1991. pap. 12.95 (*0-85640-481-0*, Pub. by Blackstaff Pr IE) Dufour.

Maguire, Arlene. Dinosaur Pop-Up ABC. (J). 1995. 14.95 (*0-671-89076-X*, Litl Simon S&S) S&S Childrens.

— Life's Changes. LC 91-9353. (Illus.). 32p. (Orig.). (J). (ps-5). 1991. 6.95 (*0-941992-26-8*) Los Arboles Pub.

— We're All Special. (Illus.). 32p. (J). (gr. 4-9). 1995. 12.00 (*0-9641330-3-2*) Portunus Pubng.

Maguire, B. The Botany of the Guayana Highland, Pt. XI. LC 78-9099. (Memoirs Ser.: Vol. 32). (Illus.). 391p. 1981. pap. 40.00 (*0-89327-229-9*) NY Botanical.

— Memoirs of the New York Botanical: No. 17(1), 2 bks. Incl. Botany of the Guayana Highland: Part 7. 1967. (*0-318-59975-9*); Botany of the Chimanta Massif Part 2. 1967. (*0-318-59976-7*); 35.00x (*0-89327-059-8*) NY Botanical.

Maguire, B., et al. The Botany of the Guayana Highland, Pt. 1. (Memoirs Ser.: Vol. 8 (2)). 74p. 1953. 10.00 (*0-89327-030-X*) NY Botanical.

— The Botany of the Guayana Highland, Pt. XII. LC 78-9099. (Memoirs Ser.: Vol. 38). (Illus.). 84p. 1984. 21.00 (*0-89327-255-8*) NY Botanical.

— The Botany of the Guayana Highland, Pt.4 (2) LC 78-9099. (Memoirs Ser.: Vol. 10 (4)). 87p. 1961. 10.00 (*0-89327-038-5*) NY Botanical.

Maguire, Barrie, jt. auth. see Kozel, William.

Maguire, Bassett, et al. The Botany of the Guayana Highland, Pt. XIII. LC 78-9099. (Memoirs Ser.: No. 51). (Illus.). 127p. 1989. pap. text ed. 20.75 (*0-89327-331-7*) NY Botanical.

— The Botany of the Guayana Highland: Part X. LC 78-9099. (Memoirs Ser.: Vol. 29). (Illus.). 288p. 1978. pap. 25.00 (*0-89327-207-8*) NY Botanical.

Maguire, Brenda. Boyne Valley Book & Tape of Irish Legends. 48p. 1987. pap. 14.95 (*0-86278-140-X*, Pub. by OBrien Pr IE) Dufour.

Maguire, Byron W. Cabinetmaking: From Design to Finish. (Illus.). 416p. 1986. pap. 15.50 (*0-13-109737-7*) P-H.

— Cabinetmaking: From Design to Finish. 2nd ed. 416p. 1990. reprint ed. pap. 22.00 (*0-934041-62-8*) Craftsman.

— Carpentry: Framing & Finishing. 352p. 1989. boxed 43.00 (*0-13-115494-X*) P-H.

— Carpentry for Residential Construction. 400p. (Orig.). 1987. pap. 19.75 (*0-934041-21-0*) Craftsman.

— Carpentry in Commercial Construction. 272p. 1988. reprint ed. pap. 19.00 (*0-934041-33-4*) Craftsman.

— Deskbook of Building Construction: Charts, Tables, & Forms. (Illus.). 256p. (C). 1985. pap. text ed. 36.00 (*0-13-202037-8*) P-H.

— European Cabinet & Furniture Making. 1990. pap. 19.95 (*0-13-292053-0*) P-H.

— Exterior Renovation & Restoration of Private Dwellings. LC 92-30703. 272p. 1993. text ed. 30.00 (*0-13-296914-9*) P-H.

— Interior Renovation & Restoration of Private Dwellings. LC 93-37227. 319p. 1994. write for info. (*0-13-474537-X*) P-H.

— Outdoor Building Projects. 1991. boxed 32.00 (*0-13-643354-5*) P-H.

— Remodeling Kitchens, Bathrooms, & Utility Rooms. 240p. 1991. text ed. 35.00 (*0-13-770330-9*) P-H.

Maguire, Carmel, et al. Information Services for Innovative Organizations. LC 93-38540. (Library & Information Science Ser.). (Illus.). 319p. 1994. text ed. 55.00 (*0-12-465030-9*) Acad Pr.

Maguire, D. P., ed. Appropriate Development for Basic Needs. 360p. 1991. text ed. 76.00 (*0-7277-1618-2*, Pub. by T Telford UK) Am Soc Civil Eng.

Maguire, Daniel, jt. auth. see Maguire, Majorie R.

Maguire, Daniel C. Moral Core of Judaism & Christianity: Reclaiming the Revolution. LC 92-39136. 256p. 1993. pap. 15.00 (*0-8006-2689-3*, 1-2689) Augsburg Fortress.

— The Moral Revolution: A Christian Humanist Vision. LC 85-51826. 224p. pap. 12.95 (*0-86683-520-2*, RD 572) Harper SF.

— Reflections of a Catholic Theologian on Visiting an Abortion Clinic. 11p. 1985. pap. 3.00 (*0-915365-10-3*) Cath Free Choice.

Maguire, Daniel C. & Fargnoli, A. Nicholas. On Moral Grounds: The Art - Science of Ethics. 192p. 1991. 21.95 (*0-8245-1123-9*) Crossroad NY.

Maguire, Daniel C., jt. auth. see Maguire, Marjorie R.

Maguire, David J. Computers in Geography. 248p. 1989. pap. text ed. 52.95 (*0-470-21194-6*) Halsted Pr.

Maguire, David J., et al, eds. Geographical Information Systems: Principles & Applications, 2 vols., Set. 1096p. 1991. text ed. 350.00 (*0-470-21789-8*) Halsted Pr.

Maguire, Edward J., ed. Reverend John O'Hanlon's The Irish Emmigrant's Guide to the United States. LC 76-6352. (Irish Americans Ser.). 1976. 25.95 (*0-405-09346-2*) Ayer.

Maguire, Eliza D. Kona Legends. (Illus.). 1966. pap. 4.95 (*0-912180-05-6*) Petroglyph.

Maguire, Eunice D., et al. Art & Holy Powers in the Early Christian House. (Illinois Byzantine Studies: No. II). (Illus.). 264p. 1989. pap. 24.95 (*0-252-06095-4*) U of Ill Pr.

Maguire, F. J. Equipment Availability, Downtime & Utilization. (C). 1986. 150.00 (*0-906297-55-9*, Pub. by ICHCA UK) St Mut.

Maguire, Fidelma, jt. auth. see Corrain, Donnchadh O.

Maguire, Francis J., jt. auth. see Hook, Harry H.

*__Maguire, G. E.__ Anglo-American Policy Towards the Free French. LC 95-11453. (St. Antony's-Macmillan Ser.). 1995. write for info. (*0-312-12710-3*) St Martin.

Maguire, Gabrielle. Our Own Language: An Irish Initiative. (Multilingual Matters Ser.: No. 66). 262p. 1991. 99.00 (*1-85359-096-7*, Pub. by Multilingual Matters UK); pap. 34.95 (*1-85359-095-9*, Pub. by Multilingual Matters UK) Taylor & Francis.

Maguire, Gail H. Care of the Elderly. 321p. 1985. 51.00 (*0-316-54380-2*) Little.

Maguire, Gregory. Missing Sisters. LC 93-8300. 160p. (J). (gr. 5-9). 1994. text ed. 14.95 (*0-689-50590-6*, McElderry) S&S Childrens.

— Oasis. LC 94-42891. (J). 1996. write for info. (*0-395-67019-5*, Clarion Bks) HM.

— The Peace & Quiet Diner. LC 87-36865. (Illus.). 48p. (J). (ps-3). 1988. 5.95 (*0-8193-1176-6*) Parents.

— The Peace-&-Quiet Diner. LC 93-7770. (Parents Magazine Read Aloud Original Ser.). (Illus.). (J). 1994. lib. bdg. 14.60 (*0-8368-0971-8*) Gareth Stevens Inc.

— Seven Spiders Spinning. LC 93-30478. (J). (gr. 1 up). 1994. 13.95 (*0-395-68965-1*, Clarion Bks) HM.

Maguire, Gregory, jt. auth. see Harrison, Barbara G.

Maguire, Henry. Art & Eloquence in Byzantium. (C). 1994. pap. 18.95 (*0-691-03693-4*) Princeton U Pr.

— Earth & Ocean: The Terrestrial World in Early Byzantine Art. LC 86-22551. (Illus.). 174p. 1987. 35.00 (*0-271-00477-0*) Pa St U Pr.

*__Maguire, Henry, ed.__ Byzantine Magic. LC 94-33501. (Dumbarton Oaks Ser.). (Illus.). 216p. (C). 1995. text ed. 30.00 (*0-88402-230-7*) HUP.

— Dumbarton Oaks Papers, No. 47. LC 42-6499. 1993. 78.00 (*0-88402-199-8*) Dumbarton Oaks.

— Dumbarton Oaks Papers No. 48, No. 48. LC 42-6499. (Illus.). 448p. 1995. 100.00x (*0-88402-236-6*) Dumbarton Oaks.

Maguire, Henry, jt. ed. see Laiou, Angeliki E.

Maguire, J. Robert, jt. auth. see Wilker, Jenny S.

*__Maguire, Jack.__ The Christmas Book. 192p. (Orig.). 1994. pap. 4.99 (*0-425-14510-7*) Berkley Pub.

— Creative Storytelling: Choosing, Inventing, & Sharing Tales for Children. (Illus.). 192p. 1985. text ed. write for info. (*0-07-039513-6*) McGraw.

— Creative Storytelling: Choosing, Inventing & Sharing Tales for Children. (Illus.). 200p. 1992. reprint ed. pap. 10.95 (*0-938756-35-4*) Yellow Moon.

— Everyday Letters for All Occasions. 288p. 1995. pap. 4.99 (*0-425-15019-4*) Berkley Pub.

— Everyday Letters for All Occasions. 256p. 1994. 10.95 (*1-56865-085-X*, GuildAmerica) Dblday Bk Music.

— Five Hundred Terrific Ideas for Home Maintenance & Repair. (Illus.). 160p. (Orig.). 1992. spiral bd., pap. 10.99 (*0-671-73716-3*, Fireside) S&S Trade.

— The Halloween Book. 160p. (Orig.). 1992. pap. text ed. 4.99 (*0-425-13537-3*) Berkley Pub.

— O Christmas Tree! A Celebration. (Illus.). 112p. (Orig.). 1992. pap. 7.00 (*0-380-77070-9*) Avon.

— Texas: Amazing but True. (Illus.). 200p. 1984. pap. 14.95 (*0-89015-487-2*) Sunbelt Media.

Maguire, Jack, jt. auth. see Cowan, Tom.

Maguire, Jack, ed. see Cowan, Tom.

Maguire, Jack, jt. auth. see Leahy, Linda R.

Maguire, Jack, jt. auth. see Philadelphia Child Guidance Center Staff.

Maguire, Jack, jt. auth. see Philadelphia Child Guidance Clinic Staff.

Maguire, James H. The Literature of Idaho: An Anthology. LC 85-73199. (Hemingway Western Studies). (Illus.). 336p. 1986. pap. 17.95 (*0-932129-02-1*) Heming W Studies.

Maguire, James H., ed. see Long, Haniel.

Maguire, Jennifer, et al. Torn by the Issues: An Unbiased Review of the Watershed Issues in American Life - a Collaboration of Unlike Minds. Hoey, Fred et al, eds. 400p. (Orig.). 1994. pap. 15.95 (*1-56474-093-5*) Fithian Pr.

Maguire, Jesse. Crossing Over. 1990. mass mkt. 3.99 (*0-8041-0446-8*) Ivy Books.

— Cutting Loose. (Nowhere High Ser.: No. 8). (Orig.). 1992. mass mkt. 3.99 (*0-8041-0850-1*) Ivy Books.

— Getting It Right. 192p. (Orig.). 1991. pap. 3.95 (*0-8041-0847-1*) Ivy Books.

Maguire, John. Universe. 106p. 1989. 19.95 (*0-9621826-0-5*) Ash Pr.

Maguire, John F. Irish in America. LC 69-18784. (American Immigration Collection Ser., No. 1: No. 1). 1969. reprint ed. 27.95 (*0-405-00532-6*) Ayer.

Maguire, John M. Evidence: Common Sense & Common Law. (University Textbook Ser.). 251p. (C). 1990. reprint ed. text ed. 15.00 (*0-88277-413-1*) West Pub.

— Evidence of Guilt: Restrictions upon Its Discovery or Compulsory Disclosure. xi, 1295p. 1982. reprint ed. lib. bdg. 32.50 (*0-8377-0843-5*) Rothman.

— The Lance of Justice: A Semi-Centennial History of the Legal Aid Society 1876-1926. xi, 305p. 1982. reprint ed. lib. bdg. 30.00 (*0-8377-0847-8*) Rothman.

Maguire, John T., jt. auth. see Yeck, John D.

*__Maguire, Jon.__ Silver Wings, Pinks & Greens: Uniforms, Wings & Insignia of USAAF Airmen in WWII. (Illus.). 192p. 1994. 45.00 (*0-88740-578-9*) Schiffer.

*__Maguire, Jon & Conway, John.__ American Flight Jackets, Airmen & Aircraft: A History of U. S. Flyers' Jackets from WWI to Desert Storm. (Illus.). 256p. 1994. 59.95 (*0-88740-511-8*) Schiffer.

— Art of the Flight Jacket: Classic Leather Jackets of World War II. (Illus.). 256p. 1995. 59.95 (*0-88740-794-3*) Schiffer.

*__Maguire, Jon A.__ Gear Up! Flight Clothing & Equipment of USAAF Airmen in World War II. LC 94-68963. (Illus.). 184p. 1995. 45.00 (*0-88740-744-7*) Schiffer.

Maguire, Joseph, jt. ed. see Bale, John.

Maguire, Joseph, jt. auth. see Jarvie, Grant.

Maguire, Kathleen, jt. auth. see Flanagan, Timothy J.

Maguire, Keith. Politics in South Africa: From Vorster to de Klerk. (Political Spotlights Ser.). 280p. (Orig.). 1992. pap. 14.95 (*0-550-20752-X*, Chambers LKC) LKC.

Maguire, Lambert. Social Support Systems in Practice: A Generalist Approach. LC 91-28008. 187p. (C). 1991. 21.95 (*0-87101-189-1*) Natl Assn Soc Wkrs.

Maguire, Lisa, tr. see Hamon, Philippe.

Maguire, M. & Lawton, M. Structure of Business. Aslett, J. R., ed. 224p. (C). 1986. 75.00 (*0-7175-1243-6*, Pub. by S Thornes Pubs UK) St Mut.

*__Maguire, Majorie R. & Maguire, Daniel.__ Aborto: Una Guia para Tomar Decisiones Eticas. 2nd ed. Inda, Caridad & Newberry, Sara, eds. Alvarez, Elena & Rivera, Mary, trs. 19p. (Orig.). (SPA.). 1987. pap. 3.00 (*0-915365-25-1*) Cath Free Choice.

*__Maguire, Marie.__ Men, Women, Passion & Power: Gender Issues in Psychotherapy. 256p. 1995. 55.00x (*0-415-07432-0*, C0171); pap. 17.95 (*0-415-07433-9*, C0172) Routledge.

Maguire, Marion. To Sea with a Lyre. 98p. (C). 1990. 38.00 (*0-9598076-8-3*, Pub. by Pascoe Pub AT) St Mut.

Maguire, Marjorie R. & Maguire, Daniel C. Abortion: A Guide to Making Ethical Choices. Jackman, Paul & Mooney, Anne S., eds. 44p. 1983. pap. 5.00 (*0-915365-00-6*) Cath Free Choice.

*__Maguire, Mary H., ed. & prol.__ Dialogue in a Major Key: Women Scholars Speak. LC 95-3985. 200p. (Orig.). 1995. pap. 20.00 (*0-8141-0881-4*) NCTE.

An Asterisk (*) at the beginning of an entry indicates that the title is appearing in BIP for the first time.

Maguire, Matthew. The Tower. 88p. (Orig.). 1991. pap. 8.95 (*1-55713-133-3*) Sun & Moon CA.

***Maguire, Michael.** Essential Commercial Legislation - Queensland. (Essential Legislation Ser.). 300p. 1995. pap. 39.00 (*0-455-21314-3*, Pub. by Law Bk Co) W W Gaunt.

Maguire, Mike & Pointing, John, eds. Victims of Crime: A New Deal? 256p. 1988. 90.00 (*0-335-15567-7*, Open Univ Pr); pap. 32.00 (*0-335-15566-9*, Open Univ Pr) Taylor & Francis.

Maguire, Mike, jt. ed. see King, Roy D.

Maguire, Mike, et al, eds. The Oxford Handbook of Criminology. LC 93-49443. 900p. 1994. pap. 25.00 (*0-19-876241-0*, Clarendon Pr) OUP.

— The Oxford Handbook of Criminology. LC 93-49443. 900p. 1994. 90.00 (*0-19-876242-9*, Clarendon Pr) OUP.

Maguire, Molly, ed. & intro. The Beat Map of America. (Literary Maps Ser.). (Illus.). (Orig.). 1987. pap. 4.95 (*0-937609-10-2*) Aaron Blakc Pubs.

Maguire, Molly, ed. The Raymond Chandler Mystery Map of Los Angeles. (Literary Maps Ser.). (Orig.). 1986. pap. 4.95 (*0-937609-00-5*) Aaron Blake Pubs.

Maguire, Molly, intro. The Literary Map of Latin America. (Literary Maps Ser.). (Illus.). (Orig.). (J). (gr. 6-12). 1988. pap. 4.95 (*0-937609-12-9*) Aaron Blake Pubs.

— The Literary Map of the American South. (Literary Maps Ser.). (Illus.). (Orig.). (J). (gr. 6-12). 1988. pap. 4.95 (*0-937609-11-0*) Aaron Blake Pubs.

Maguire, Molly, jt. ed. see Silverman, Aaron.

Maguire, Nancy K. Regicide & Restoration: English Tragicomedy, 1660-1671. (Illus.). 280p. (C). 1993. 64.95 (*0-521-41622-1*) Cambridge U Pr.

Maguire, Nancy K., ed. Renaissance Tragicomedy: Explorations in Genre & Politics. LC 85-48060. (Studies in the Renaissance: No. 20). 1986. 34.50 (*0-404-62290-9*) AMS Pr.

Maguire, Patricia. Doing Participatory Research: A Feminist Approach. 305p. (Orig.). 1987. pap. 8.00 (*0-932288-79-0*) Ctr Intl Ed U of MA.

— Women in Development: An Alternative Analysis. 68p. (Orig.). 1984. pap. 4.00 (*0-932288-74-X*) Ctr Intl Ed U of MA.

Maguire, Peter, jt. auth. see Faulkner, Ann.

Maguire, Robert A. Exploring Gogol. LC 94-14416. (Studies of the Harriman Institute). 1995. 45.00 (*0-8047-2320-6*) Stanford U Pr.

— Red Virgin Soil: Soviet Literature in the 1920's. LC 86-24391. 504p. (C). 1987. reprint ed. pap. 16.95 (*0-8014-9447-8*) Cornell U Pr.

Maguire, Robert A., ed. Gogol from the Twentieth Century: Eleven Essays. LC 73-16750. 428p. 1974. 65.00 (*0-691-06268-4*); pap. 18.95 (*0-691-01326-8*) Princeton U Pr.

Maguire, Robert A. & Timberlake, Alan, eds. American Contributions to the Eleventh International Congress of Slavists, Literature, Linguistics, Poetics (Bratislava 1993) 459p. 1993. 29.95 (*0-89357-238-1*) Slavica.

Maguire, Robert A., tr. see Bely, Andrei.

Maguire, Robert A., ed. see Gippius, V. V.

Maguire, Robert A., tr. see Gippius, V. V.

Maguire, Robert A., tr. see Rozewicz, Tadeusz.

Maguire, Robert A., tr. see Szymborska, Wislawa.

Maguire, Sarah, ed. Civil & Criminal Procedure. 265p. (C). 1991. 90.00 (*1-85352-864-1*, Pub. by HLT Pubns UK) St Mut.

Maguire, Steve. Debugging the Development Process. 1994. pap. 24.95 (*1-55615-650-2*) Microsoft.

— Writing Clean Code. 1993. pap. 24.95 (*1-55615-551-4*) Microsoft.

Maguire, Tim, jt. auth. see Schwartz, Natalie.

***Maguire, Tom & Smith, Steve.** Talking Yellow Pages Review, 1994. (Illus.). 131p. 1995. write for info. (*0-88709-061-3*) Simba Info Inc.

Maguire, W. A. Kings in Conflict: Revolutionary War in Ireland & Its Aftermath. 224p. 1990. 29.95 (*0-85640-435-7*, Pub. by Blackstaff Pr IE) Dufour.

Maguire, W. B. All You Need to Know about Joint Replacement. (C). 1990. pap. 24.00 (*0-86439-101-3*, Pub. by Boolarong Pubns AT) St Mut.

Maguire, Wilhelmina. AKIA Spa Cookbook. 71p. (Orig.). 1992. pap. 13.50 (*0-9639039-0-X*) AKIA.

***Magun, Carol.** Circling Eden. 200p. 1995. 19.95 (*0-89733-412-4*) Academy Chi Pubs.

***Magura, Stephen & Rosenblum, Andrew, eds.** Experimental Therapeutics in Addiction Medicine. LC 94-43278. (Journal of Addictive Diseases Ser.). (Illus.). 256p. 1994. lib. bdg. 349.95 (*1-56024-699-5*) Haworth Pr.

Magura, Stephen, et al. Assessing Risk & Measuring Change in Families: The Family Risk Scales. 40p. 1987. pap. 16.95 (*0-87868-275-9*) Child Welfare.

Magurn, Bruce A., ed. Reviews in K-Theory, 1940-1984. LC 85-7481. 811p. 1985. pap. 321.00 (*0-8218-0088-4*, REVKC) Am Math.

Magurran, Anne E. Ecological Diversity & Its Measurement. (Illus.). 215p. 1988. text ed. 49.50 (*0-691-08485-8*); pap. text ed. 17.95 (*0-691-08491-2*) Princeton U Pr.

Magurshak, Dan, tr. see Poggeler, Otto.

***Magy, Tamas.** English-Hungarian Dictionary of Technology & Science, 2 Vols. (ENG & HUN.). 1993. 250.00 (*0-7859-8884-X*) Fr & Eur.

Magyar, B. Guidelines to Planning Atomic Spectometric Analysis. (ANC Ser.: Vol. 4). 274p. 1982. 102.75 (*0-444-99699-0*) Elsevier.

***Magyar, I.** Differential Diagnosis of Internal Diseases: In Russian, 2 vols., Set. 1154p. (RUS.). (C). 1987. 300.00x (*963-05-4233-1*) St Mut.

Magyar, K. Symposium on Pharmacological Agents & Biogenic Amines in the Central Nervous System. 274p. 1973. 53.00 (*0-569-08072-X*, Pub. by Collets UK) Pro-Am Music.

— Symposium on Pharmacology of Catecholaminergic Serotonergic Mechanisms. 203p. 1976. 80.00 (*0-569-08374-5*, Pub. by Collets UK) Pro-Am Music.

Magyar, K., ed. Monoamine Oxidases & Their Selective Inhibition: Proceedings of the Third Congress of the Hungarian Pharmacological Society, Budapest, 1979. LC 80-41281. (Advances in Pharmacological Research & Practice Ser.: Vol. IV). 165p. 1980. 76.00 (*0-08-026389-5*, Pub. by Pergamon Repr UK) Franklin.

Magyar, K., jt. ed. see Vereczkey, L.

Magyar, K., jt. ed. see Vizi, E. S.

Magyar, Laszlo. Reisen in Sud-Afrika in den Jahren 1849-1857. (B. E. Ser.: No. 155). (GER.). 1859. 44.00 (*0-8115-3073-6*) Periodicals Srv.

***Magyar Nemzeti Muzeum Curators Staff.** Baroque Splendor: The Art of the Hungarian Goldsmith. (Illus.). 227p. Date not set. pap. 50.00 (*0-614-07360-X*) Bard Grad Ctr.

Magyar, P., ed. see Czaki, F., et al.

Magyari, E., jt. auth. see Constantinescu, F.

Mah, Julie, ed. see McDonald, Marie.

Mah, Richard S. Chemical Process Structures & Information Flows. (Series in Chemical Engineering). (Illus.). 500p. 1990. text ed. 84.95 (*0-7506-9230-8*) Buttrwrth-Heinemann.

Mah, Ronald. Dinosaur Masks & Puppets. (J). (gr. 2 up). pap. 4.50 (*0-8431-1952-7*, Troubador) Price Stern.

— North America Animal Masks & Hats. Werges, Rosanne, ed. (Illus.). 48p. (Orig.). (J). (gr. k-4). 1988. pap. 4.95 (*0-9615903-2-7*) Symbiosis Bks.

— Predator Prey Puppets & Toys: Eight Paper Animal Projects to Make. (Illus.). 32p. (J). (ps-3). 1986. pap. 3.95 (*0-9615903-1-9*) Symbiosis Bks.

Mah Talat Etemad Moghadam. From the Prophet to the Great Sufi Mir Ghotbeddin Mohammad. 231p. (Orig.). 1982. pap. 12.50 (*0-317-01145-6*) MTO Printing & Pubn Ctr.

Mahabir, Cynthia. Crime & Nation Building in the Caribbean: The Legacy of Legal Barriers. LC 84-5304. 280p. (Orig.). 1985. 24.95 (*0-87073-601-9*); pap. 15.95 (*0-87073-602-7*) Schenkman Bks Inc.

Mahadev, K. Gaslights in Calcutta. 8.00 (*0-89253-677-2*); 4.80 (*0-89253-678-0*) Ind-US Inc.

— The Testament of Nizamulmulk. (Writers Workshop Redbird Ser.). 1975. 8.00 (*0-88253-654-0*); pap. text ed. 4.00 (*0-88253-653-2*) Ind-US Inc.

Mahadeva, A. & Rangacharya, K., eds. The Taitiriya Samhita of the Black Yajurveda, 10 vols. (C). 1986. reprint ed. 185.00 (*81-208-0228-4*, Pub. by Motilal Banarsidass II) S Asia.

Mahadevan, jt. ed. see Ramachandran.

Mahadevan, A. Biochemical Aspects of Plant Disease Resistance: Preformed Inhibitory Substance 'Prohibitions', Pt. 1. (International Bioscience Monographs: No. 11). (Illus.). xiv, 400p. 1989. reprint ed. 59.00 (*0-88065-225-X*, Pub. by Today & Tomorrows P & P II) Scholarly Pubns.

— Biochemical Aspects of Plant Diseases Resistance Vol. 2: Post Infectional Defence Mechanisms. (Illus.). 800p. 1991. 95.00 (*1-55528-231-8*, Pub. by Today & Tomorrows P & P II) Scholarly Pubns.

Mahadevan, A., jt. auth. see Gnanamanickam, S. S.

Mahadevan, K. Population Dynamics in Indian States. 1989. 38.50 (*81-7099-178-1*, Pub. by Mittal II) S Asia.

— Sociology of Fertility: Determinants of Fertility Differentials in South India. 1978. 11.00 (*0-8364-0293-6*) S Asia.

Mahadevan, K., ed. Ecology, Development & Population Problem: Perspectives from India, China & Australia. (C). 1992. 48.00 (*81-7018-735-4*, Pub. by BR Pub II) S Asia.

Mahadevan, K., ed. Fertility Policies of Asian Countries. 288p. (C). 1989. text ed. 29.00 (*0-8039-9570-9*) Sage.

Mahadevan, K., ed. Health Education for Quality of Life. (C). 1992. 33.00 (*0-685-66247-0*, Pub. by BR Pub II) S Asia.

— Women & Population Dynamics: Perspectives from Asia. 320p. (C). 1990. text ed. 25.00 (*0-8039-9615-2*) Sage.

Mahadevan, K. & Sumangala, M. Social Development, Cultural Change, & Fertility Decline: A Study of Fertility Change in Kerala. 160p. (C). 1989. text ed. 17.95 (*0-8039-9536-9*) Sage.

Mahadevan, K., jt. auth. see Aiyappan, A.

Mahadevan, Kuttan & Krishnan, Parameswara, eds. Methodology for Population Studies & Development. LC 92-15028. (Illus.). 428p. (C). 1993. text ed. 42.00 (*0-8039-9431-1*, Sage India Pvt) Sage.

***Mahadevan, Kuttan, et al, eds.** Differential Development & Demographic Dilemma: Perspectives from China & India. (C). 1994. 44.00 (*81-7018-816-4*, Pub. by BR Pub II) S Asia.

— Society & Development in China & India. (C). 1994. 48.00 (*81-7018-812-1*, Pub. by BR Pub II) S Asia.

Mahadevan, Meera. Shulamith. 208p. 1980. pap. 3.25 (*0-86578-061-7*) Ind-US Inc.

Mahadevan, Sridhar, jt. ed. see Connell, Jonathan H.

Mahadevan, T. M. The Hymns of Sankara. 188p. 1986. reprint ed. 15.00 (*81-208-0094-X*, Pub. by Motilal Banarsidass II); reprint ed. pap. 11.00 (*81-208-0097-4*, Pub. by Motilal Banarsidass II) S Asia.

— Sankaracharya. 119p. 1968. 3.95 (*0-318-37165-0*) Asia Bk Corp.

— Upanisads: The Selections from 108 Upanisads. 240p. (Orig.). 1975. pap. 3.20 (*0-88253-985-X*) Ind-US Inc.

Mahadevan, T. M., ed. Spiritual Perspectives: Essays in Mysticism & Metaphysics. 303p. 1975. lib. bdg. 12.00 (*0-89253-021-9*) Ind-US Inc.

Mahadevan, T. M. & Saroja, G. V. Contemporary Indian Philosophy. 282p. 1983. 34.95 (*0-940500-51-5*, Pub. by Sterling II) Asia Bk Corp.

Mahadevan, T. M., tr. see Anantendra-Yati.

Mahadevan, T. M., tr. see Sankaracharya.

Mahadovan, T. K. The Year of the Phoenix, Gandhi's Pivotal Year: 1893-94. 196p. 1985. 5.00 (*0-317-60741-3*) World Without War.

Mahaffey, George, jt. auth. see Kolpas, Norman.

Mahaffey, J. A., jt. ed. see Thompson, R. C.

Mahaffey, Joy, jt. auth. see Peel, Kathy.

Mahaffey, Kathryn R., ed. Dietary & Environmental Lead: Human Health Effects. (Topics in Environmental Health Ser.: Vol. 7). 472p. 1985. 189.75 (*0-444-80609-1*) Elsevier.

Mahaffey, Maryann & Hanks, John W., eds. Practical Politics: Social Work & Political Responsibility. LC 82-80273. 260p. (C). 1982. 21.95 (*0-87101-099-2*) Natl Assn Soc Wkrs.

Mahaffey, Michael W. If You Dare: Out of the Problem & into the Solution. 205p. 1988. 14.95 (*0-317-92496-6*) Mahaffey & Assocs.

Mahaffey, Redge. A Higher Education. 250p. 1989. pap. 7.95 (*0-317-93250-0*) Ramsgate MD.

— Me, Myself & I. (Illus.). 54p. (Orig.). 1990. pap. 3.95 (*0-9622546-1-4*) Ramsgate MD.

***Mahaffey, Richard R.** The Cure. 250p. 1995. pap. 8.95 (*1-56901-888-X*) NW Pub.

— LIMS: Applied Information Management for the Library. 1989. text ed. 62.95 (*0-442-31820-0*) Chapman & Hall.

***Mahaffey, Robert, ed.** Safe Schools: A Handbook for Practitioners. (Illus.). 200p. (Orig.). 1995. pap. 125.00 (*0-88210-304-0*) Natl Assn Principals.

Mahaffey, Vicki. Reauthorizing Joyce. 280p. 1988. 49.95 (*0-521-35250-9*) Cambridge U Pr.

— Reauthorizing Joyce. LC 94-34181. (Florida James Joyce Ser.). 248p. (C). 1995. pap. text ed. 19.95 (*0-8130-1344-5*) U Press Fla.

***Mahaffie, Charles D., Jr.** A Land of Discord Always: Acadia from Its Beginning to the Expulsion of Its Inhabitants 1604-1755. (Illus.). 328p. 1995. 24.95 (*0-89272-362-9*) Down East.

Mahaffy, Carcus & Beck, Lewis W. Prolegomena to Any Future Metaphysics: Kant. (C). 1950. pap. text ed. write for info. (*0-02-319330-1*) Macmillan.

Mahaffy, Ellen. Nothing Was Ever Said. (Illus.). 116p. 1993. 25.00 (*0-89822-109-9*) Visual Studies.

Mahaffy, J. A. A History of Classical Greek Literature, 4 vols. 1972. 1,000.00 (*0-8490-0320-2*) Gordon Pr.

Mahaffy, J. P. Alexander's Empire. 323p. 1981. 35.00 (*0-89005-391-X*) Ares.

Mahaffy, John P. Descartes. LC 71-94277. (Select Bibliographies Reprint Ser.). 1977. 21.95 (*0-8369-5051-8*) Ayer.

— Greek Life & Thought from the Age of Alexander to the Roman Conquest. LC 75-13278. (History of Ideas in Ancient Greece Ser.). 1976. reprint ed. 55.95 (*0-405-07318-6*) Ayer.

Mahaffy, Robert. Francis Joseph His Life & Times: An Essay in Politics. 1972. 59.95 (*0-8490-0190-0*) Gordon Pr.

Mahajan, A. Indian Police-Women. 189p. 1982. 27.95 (*0-318-37063-8*) Asia Bk Corp.

— Problems of the Aged in Unorganized Sector. 106p. (C). 1987. 17.50 (*0-8364-2185-X*, Pub. by Mittal II) S Asia.

***Mahajan, Amar J. & Luthra, Nirupama.** Family & Television: A Sociological Study. (C). 1993. 16.00 (*0-614-04151-1*, Pub. by Gian Publng Hse II) S Asia.

***Mahajan, Amar J. & Luthra, Nirupamja.** Family & Television. (C). 1993. 16.00 (*81-212-0435-6*, Pub. by Gian Publng Hse II) S Asia.

Mahajan, Anil & Nath, Surinder, eds. Application Areas of Anthropology. 1992. 30.00 (*81-85047-90-1*, Pub. by Reliance Pub Hse II) Apt Bks.

Mahajan, Anil, jt. ed. see Joshi, P. C.

Mahajan, Anil, jt. ed. see Nayak, P. K.

Mahajan, Anupam. Ragas in Indian Classical Music. 150p. 1989. audio write for info. (*81-212-0269-8*, Pub. by Gian Publng Hse II) S Asia.

Mahajan, Ashok. The Garden of Fand. (Redbird Ser.). 1976. lib. bdg. 6.75 (*0-89253-122-3*); 4.80 (*0-89253-143-6*) Ind-US Inc.

Mahajan, Carlee S. Ghost's New Old Home. LC 91-65247. (Illus.). 44p. (J). (gr. k-3). 1992. 6.95 (*1-55523-430-5*) Winston-Derek.

Mahajan, G. Evaluation & Development of Ground Water. (C). 1989. 50.00 (*81-7024-241-X*, Pub. by Ashish II) S Asia.

Mahajan, J. P., jt. auth. see Vardharajan, B.

***Mahajan, Kanti K.** Design of Process Equipment: Selected Topics. 3rd ed. (Illus.). 1990. 68.00 (*0-615-00652-3*) Pressure.

***Mahajan, Mehr C., ed.** Looking Back: Autobiography of Mehr Chand Mahajan. (C). 1994. 28.00 (*81-241-0194-9*, Pub. by Har-Anand Pubns II) S Asia.

Mahajan, S. Imperialist Strategy & Moderate Politics: Indian Legislature at Work, 1909-1920. 1983. 24.00 (*0-8364-0979-5*, Pub. by Chanakya II) S Asia.

Mahajan, S., ed. Handbook on Semiconductors, Vol. 3: Materials, Properties, & Preparation. 1800p. 1994. 568.50 (*0-444-88835-7*, North Holland) Elsevier.

Mahajan, S. & Kimerling, L. C. Concise Encyclopedia of Semiconducting Materials & Related Technologies. (Advances in Materials Science & Engineering Ser.: No. 8). 600p. 1992. 270.00 (*0-08-034724-X*, Pergamon Pr) Elsevier.

Mahajan, Satinder N. Political Authority: A Comparative Study. 113p. 1986. 12.00 (*1-881338-72-X*) Nataraj Bks.

Mahajan, T. T. Aspects of Agrarian & Urban History of the Marathas. (C). 1991. 21.00 (*81-7169-162-5*, Pub. by Commonwealth II) S Asia.

— Courts & Administration of Justice under Chhatrapati Shivaji. (C). 1992. 18.00 (*81-7169-198-6*, Commonwealth) S Asia.

— Shivaji & His Diplomats. (C). 1991. 16.00 (*81-7169-110-2*, Pub. by Commonwealth II) S Asia.

Mahajan, V. D. Chief Justice Mehr Chand Mahajan. (C). 1989. 22.00 (*0-89771-766-X*, Pub. by Eastern Book II) St Mut.

— Constitutional Law of India. 600p. 1984. 160.00 (*0-317-54584-1*) St Mut.

— Constitutional Law of India. (C). 1991. text ed. 125.00 (*0-89771-486-5*) St Mut.

— General Clauses Acts (Central & States) 1024p. 1980. 375.00 (*0-317-54585-X*) St Mut.

— A History of India, Set. 1100p. 1990. 310.00 (*0-317-52140-3*, Pub. by S Chand II) St Mut.

— History of Modern India, 2 vols., I:1919-74. 1220p. 1987. 117.00 (*0-317-52141-1*, Pub. by S Chand II) St Mut.

— History of Modern India, 2 vols., II:1974-82. 1220p. 1987. write for info. (*0-318-61351-4*, Pub. by S Chand II) St Mut.

— History of Modern India Nineteen Nineteen to Nineteen Eighty-Two, 2 vols., Set. 1983. text ed. 77.50 (*0-685-14075-X*) Coronet Bks.

— Jurisprudence & Legal Theory. 5th ed. (C). 1987. 75.00 (*0-685-25161-6*) St Mut.

Mahajan, V. D., ed. Constitutional Law of India. 7th ed. (C). 1991. 125.00 (*0-685-39772-6*) St Mut.

— General Clauses Acts (Central & States) 1600p. (C). 1990. 175.00 (*0-685-38601-5*); text ed. 350.00 (*0-89771-487-3*) St Mut.

— General Clauses Acts (Central & States) 6th ed. (C). 1990. 350.00 (*0-685-39693-2*) St Mut.

Mahajan, V. S. Growth of Agriculture & Industry in India. 1985. 13.50 (*0-8364-1443-8*, Pub. by Deep) S Asia.

— Manmohan's India & Other Current Writings. (C). 1994. text ed. 29.00 (*81-7100-640-X*, Pub. by Deep) S Asia.

Mahajan, V. S., ed. Agriculture & Rural Economy in India. 1990. 72.50 (*0-685-40055-7*, Pub. by Deep) S Asia.

Mahajan, Vijay & Pegels, C. Carl, eds. Systems Analysis in Health Care. LC 78-19461. 504p. 1979. text ed. 75.00 (*0-275-90384-2*, C0384, Praeger Pubs) Greenwood.

Mahajan, Vijay & Peterson, Robert A. Models for Innovation Diffusion. (Quantitative Applications in the Social Sciences Ser.: Vol. 48). 1985. 9.95 (*0-8039-2136-5*) Sage.

Mahajan, Virendra N., ed. Aberration Theory Made Simple. (Tutorial Texts Ser.: Vol. TT 6). 157p. 1991. 38.00 (*0-8194-0536-1*) SPIE.

— Selected Papers on Effects of Aberrations in Optical Imaging. LC 92-46455. (Milestone Ser.: Vol. MS74). 1993. write for info. (*0-8194-1215-5*); pap. write for info. (*0-8194-1214-7*) SPIE.

***Mahajan, Yogi.** The Ascent. (C). 1993. text ed. 7.00 (*81-208-1182-8*, Pub. by Motilal Banarsidass II) S Asia.

— Geeta Enlightened. xi, 177p. 1986. 14.00 (*81-208-0066-4*, Pub. by Motilal Banarsidass II); pap. 10.95 (*81-208-0156-3*, Pub. by Motilal Banarsidass II) S Asia.

Mahak, Francine, tr. see SATPREM Staff.

Mahak, Francine T., tr. see Martinez, Eliseo R. & Martinez, Irma C.

Mahak, Francine T., tr. see Taraqqi, Goli.

Mahalanabis, A. K., ed. see IFAC Symposium Staff.

Mahalanobis, P. C. Rabindranath Tagore's Visit to Canada. LC 76-52432. (Studies in Asiatic Literature: No. 57). 1977. lib. bdg. 75.00 (*0-8383-2130-5*) M S G Haskell Hse.

Mahalingam, Indira & Carr, Brian, eds. Logical Foundations: Essays in Honour of D. J. O'Connor. LC 90-31926. 208p. 1991. text ed. 55.00 (*0-312-04737-1*) St Martin.

Mahalingam, Indira, jt. ed. see Carr, Brian.

Mahalingam, N., ed. see Sekkizhaar.

Mahalingam, S. Tribal Cooperative System: A Study of North-East India. (C). 1992. text ed. 21.00 (*81-7033-169-2*, Pub. by Rawat II) S Asia.

Mahalingam, T. V., ed. Inscriptions of the Pallavas. 1988. 120.00 (*0-8364-2300-3*, Pub. by Agam II) S Asia.

Mahalinjam, N., ed. see Tirumulav.

Mahall, Karl. Quality Assessment of Textiles: Damage Detection by Microscopy. LC 93-42572. (Illus.). 322p. 1993. 99.00 (*0-387-57390-9*) Spr-Verlag.

Mahan, A. T. The Influence of Sea Power upon History, 1660-1783. (Illus.). 640p. 1987. reprint ed. pap. 11.95 (*0-486-25509-3*) Dover.

Mahan, Alfred T. Admiral Farragut. LC 68-26360. (American Biography Ser.: No. 32). 1969. reprint ed. lib. bdg. 75.00 (*0-8383-0268-8*) M S G Haskell Hse.

— Admiral Farragut. (History - United States Ser.). 333p. 1992. reprint ed. lib. bdg. 89.00 (*0-7812-6177-5*) Rprt Serv.

— Admiral Farragut. LC 74-108509. 1970. reprint ed. 14.00 (*0-403-00217-6*) Scholarly.

— Armaments & Arbitration. Bd. with Great Illusion: A Reply to Rear Admiral A. T. Mahan. LC 77-147583. LC 77-147583. (Library of War & Peace; Int'l. Organization, Arbitration & Law). 1972. Set lib. bdg. 46.00 (*0-8240-0347-0*) Garland.

— From Sail to Steam: Recollections of Naval Life. LC 68-26817. (American Scene Ser.). 1968. reprint ed. lib. bdg. 37.50 (*0-306-71148-6*) Da Capo.

— From Sail to Steam: Recollections of Naval Life. (American Biography Ser.). 458p. 1991. reprint ed. lib. bdg. 89.00 (*0-7812-8261-6*) Rprt Serv.

— The Gulf & Inland Waters: The Navy in the Civil War. LC 74-140367. (Select Bibliographies Reprint Ser.). 1977. reprint ed. 23.95 (*0-8369-5610-9*) Ayer.

— The Gulf & the Inland Waters. (Illus.). 267p. 1990. reprint ed. 25.00 (*0-916107-89-2*) Broadfoot.

— The Influence of Sea Power upon History, 1660-1783. (Illus.). 1970. 24.95 (*0-316-54382-9*) Little.

— Influence of Sea Power upon the French Revolution & Empire, 2 vols. 1898. 33.00 (*0-403-00193-5*) Scholarly.

An Asterisk (*) at the beginning of an entry indicates that the title is appearing in BIP for the first time.

— The Interest of America in Sea Power, Present & Future. LC 75-137382. (Select Bibliographies Reprint Ser.). 1977. reprint ed. 23.95 (0-8369-5583-8) Ayer.
— Lessons of the War with Spain. LC 79-133526. (Select Bibliographies Reprint Ser.). 1977. reprint ed. 23.95 (0-8369-5558-7) Ayer.
— Life of Nelson: The Embodiment of the Sea Power of Great Britain, 2 Vols. LC 68-26361. (English Biography Ser.: No. 31). 1969. reprint ed. lib. bdg. 99.95 (0-8383-0182-7) M S G Haskell Hse.
— Life of Nelson, the Embodiment of the Sea Power of Great Britain, 2 vols. in 1. 1899. 26.00 (0-403-00076-9) Scholarly.
— Mahan on Naval Strategy: Selections from the Writings of Rear Admiral Alfred Thayer Mahan. LC 90-25401. (Classics of Sea Power Ser.). (Illus.). 432p. 1991. 34.95 (1-55750-556-X) Naval Inst Pr.
— Major Operations of the Navies in the War of American Independence. LC 69-10128. (Illus.). 280p. 1969. reprint ed. text ed. 35.00 (0-8371-1002-5, MAWI, Greenwood Pr) Greenwood.
— The Major Operations of the Navies in the War of American Independence. (BCL1 - U. S. History Ser.). 280p. 1991. reprint ed. lib. bdg. 79.00 (0-7812-6119-8) Rprt Serv.
— Naval Strategy. LC 74-14359. (Illus.). 475p. 1975. reprint ed. text ed. 99.75 (0-8371-7802-9, MANS, Greenwood Pr) Greenwood.
— Sea Power in Its Relations to the War of 1812, 2 Vols. LC 68-26362. (World History Ser.: No. 48). 1969. reprint ed. lib. bdg. 150.00 (0-8383-0181-9) M S G Haskell Hse.
— Sea Power in Relation to the War of 1812, 2 vols., Set. 1993. reprint ed. lib. bdg. 150.00 (0-7812-5190-7) Rprt Serv.
— Types of Naval Officers: Drawn from the History of the British Navy. LC 77-84323. (Essay Index Reprint Ser.). 500p. reprint ed. lib. bdg. 21.75 (0-8290-0473-4) Irvington.
— Types of Naval Officers, Drawn from the History of the British Navy. LC 77-84323. (Essay Index Reprint Ser.). 1977. 25.95 (0-8369-1093-1) Ayer.
Mahan, Ann, jt. auth. see Mahan, John.
Mahan, Asa. Autobiography: Intellectual, Moral, & Spiritual. (American Biography Ser.). 458p. 1991. reprint ed. lib. bdg. 89.00 (0-7812-8262-4) Rprt Serv.
— Autobiography - Intellectual, Moral & Spiritual. LC 75-3269. reprint ed. 45.00 (0-404-59257-0) AMS Pr.
— Doctrine of the Will. LC 75-3270. reprint ed. 42.00 (0-404-59258-9) AMS Pr.
— The Science of Natural Theology. LC 75-3273. reprint ed. 27.50 (0-404-59261-9) AMS Pr.
Mahan, Asa, intro. The Science of Logic: or, An Analysis of the Laws of Thought. reprint ed. pap. 14.95 (0-935005-84-6) Lincoln-Rembrandt.
Mahan, Benton, illus. Goldilocks & the Three Bears. LC 80-27631. 32p. (J). (gr. k-2). 1981. lib. bdg. 9.79 (0-89375-470-6); pap. text ed. 2.50 (0-89375-471-4) Troll Assocs.
Mahan, Brian & Richesin, L. Dale, eds. The Challenge of Liberation Theology: A First-World Response. LC 81-9527. 160p. reprint ed. pap. 45.60 (0-8357-2683-5, 2040219) Bks Demand.
Mahan, Bruce H. University Chemistry. 3rd ed. LC 74-19696. (C). 1975. text ed. write for info. (0-201-04405-6) Addison-Wesley.
Mahan, Bruce M. & Myers, Rollie J. University Chemistry. 4th ed. LC 86-14063. (Chemistry Ser.). (Illus.). 1076p. (C). 1987. text ed. 55.95 (0-201-05833-2); student ed 17.25 (0-201-05835-9); 15.00 (0-201-05838-3) Benjamin-Cummings.
Mahan, Charles, jt. auth. see Young, Diony.
Mahan, Dennis H. Complete Treatise on Field Fortification. LC 68-54797. 268p. 1969. reprint ed. text ed. 35.00 (0-8371-0557-9, MAFF, Greenwood Pr) Greenwood.
Mahan, Gerald D. Many-Particle Physics. 2nd ed. (Physics of Solids & Liquids Ser.). 1046p. 1990. 135.00 (0-306-43423-7, Plenum Pr) Plenum.
Mahan, Gerald D. & Subbaswamy, K. R. Local Density Theory of Polarizability. LC 90-42552. (Physics of Solids & Liquids Ser.). (Illus.). 260p. 1990. 65.00 (0-306-43685-X, Plenum Pr) Plenum.
Mahan, Henry T. Bible Class Commentaries, 6 vols. Incl. Romans. 1984. pap. (0-85234-184-9); 1st & 2nd Corinthians. 1984. pap. (0-85234-194-6); Galatians Thru Colossians. 1984. pap. (0-85234-210-1); 1st & 2nd Thessalonians; 1st & 2nd Timothy. 1984. pap. (0-85234-185-7); Hebrews & James. 1984. pap. (0-85234-187-3); Titus, Philemon, & 1st & 2nd Peter Thru Jude. 1984. pap. (0-85234-211-X); 1984. Set pap. 4.95 (0-685-74589-9) Pilgrim Pubns.
— Bible Class Commentaries, 6 vols., Set. Incl. Romans. 1984. pap. (0-85234-184-9); 1st & 2nd Corinthians. 1984. pap. (0-85234-194-6); Galatians Thru Colossians. 1984. pap. (0-85234-210-1); 1st & 2nd Thessalonians; 1st & 2nd Timothy. 1984. pap. (0-85234-185-7); Hebrews & James. 1984. pap. (0-85234-187-3); Titus, Philemon, & 1st & 2nd Peter Thru Jude. 1984. pap. (0-85234-211-X); 1984. Set pap. 29.95 (0-85234-215-2) Pilgrim Pubns.
— Galatians. 1983. pap. 1.95 (1-56186-510-9) Pilgrim Pubns.
— Gospel of John. 1987. pap. 4.99 (0-85234-238-1, Pub. by Evangel Pr UK) Presby & Reformed.
— With New Testament Eyes. 1993. pap. 8.99 (0-85234-304-3, Pub. by Evangel Pr UK) Presby & Reformed.
Mahan, J. Alex. Vienna: Yesterday & Today. 1976. lib. bdg. 59.95 (0-8490-2797-7) Gordon Pr.
Mahan, Jeffrey H. A Long Way from Solving That One: Psycho-Social & Ethical Implications of Ross Macdonald's Lew Archer Tales. 166p. (C). 1990. lib. bdg. 37.50 (0-8191-7710-5) U Pr of Amer.
Mahan, Jeffrey H., jt. auth. see Kaminsky, Stuart M.
Mahan, Jeffrey H., et al. Shared Wisdom: A Guide to Case Study Reflection in Ministry. LC 93-4458. 144p. (Orig.). 1993. pap. 11.95 (0-687-38335-8) Abingdon.
Mahan, John & Mahan, Ann. Wild Lake Michigan. (Illus.). 128p. 1991. 29.95 (0-89658-132-2) Voyageur Pr.
— Wild Lake Michigan. (Illus.). 128p. 1993. pap. 19.95 (0-89658-184-5) Voyageur Pr.
Mahan, Joseph B. Columbus: Georgia's Fall Line "Trading Town" LC 86-5652. (Illus.). 256p. 1986. 24.95 (0-89781-166-6) Preferred Mktg.
— North American Sun Kings: Keepers of the Flame. 300p. 1992. 30.00 (1-880820-03-X) ISAC Pr.
Mahan, Juneau G. Campus Community Confronts Sexual Assault: A Program for Chemically Dependent Women in Recovery. 1994. 21.95 (1-55691-113-0) Learning Pubns.
Mahan, Lois. Willits Scrapbook: The Way it Was 1958-1974. LC 78-108189. 1975. 4.00 (0-932820-00-X) M P Pubs.
Mahan, Nancie, ed. see Mobley, Chuck & Mobley, Andrea.
Mahan, Nancie S., ed. see Taylor, Richard C.
Mahan, Parker E. & Alling, Charles C., III. Facial Pain. 3rd ed. LC 90-13278. (Illus.). 376p. 1991. 69.50 (0-8121-1252-0) Williams & Wilkins.
Mahan, Sue. Unfit Mothers. Reed, R., ed. LC 81-83616. (Illus.). 125p. (C). 1982. pap. 12.95 (0-88247-622-X) R & E Pubs.
Mahan, Vista A., jt. ed. see Hughes, Alice.
Mahan, Walter L. The Unveiling. LC 92-61369. 392p. 1992. pap. 12.95 (1-55523-562-X) Winston-Derek.
Mahan, Wayne W. Tillich's System. LC 73-91170. 145p. 1974. write for info. (0-911536-52-3) Trinity U Pr.
Mahandas, Narla, jt. ed. see Shohet, Stephen B.
Mahaney, C. J., jt. auth. see Boisvert, Robin.
Mahaney, C. J., jt. auth. see Loftness, John.
Mahaney, Michael C., ed. see Rounds, Joseph B.
Mahaney, Teri. Change Your Mind. rev. ed. 1990. pap. 19.95 (0-9624140-1-8) Supertraining Pr.
Mahaney, W. C. Quaternary Dating Methods. (Developments in Palaeontology & Stratigraphy Ser.: Vol. 7). 1984. 110.25 (0-444-42392-3) Elsevier.
Mahaney, W. C., ed. Quaternary & Environmental Research on East African Mountains. 400p. (C). 1989. text ed. 105.00 (90-6191-794-8, Pub. by A A Balkema NE) Ashgate Pub Co.
Mahaney, William C. Ice on the Equator: Quaternary Geology of Mount Kenya, East Africa. LC 90-41212. (Illus.). xii, 386p. 1990. 65.00 (0-940473-19-4) Wm Caxton.
Mahang, Lois, jt. auth. see Burton, Eric.
Mahant, Edelgard. Free Trade in American-Canadian Relations. Snyder, Louis L., ed. (Anvil Ser.). (Illus.). 232p. (Orig.). (C). 1993. pap. 14.95 (0-89464-522-6) Krieger.
Mahanta, Jogeshwar. Sex, Crime & Society. viii, 112p. (C). 1993. 15.00x (81-7024-548-6, Pub. by Ashish Pub Hse II) Nataraj Bks.
Mahanthappa, K. T. & Brittin, Wesley E., eds. Boulder Lecture Notes in Theoretical Physics, 1969: Vol. 12-A, Ferromagnetism & Quantum Optics, Vol. 12. 220p. 1971. text ed. 134.00 (0-677-14550-0) Gordon & Breach.
— Boulder Lecture Notes in Theoretical Physics, 1969: Vol. 12-B High Energy Collisions of Elementary Particles, Vol. 12. 384p. 1971. text ed. 197.00 (0-677-14560-8) Gordon & Breach.
— Boulder Lecture Notes in Theoretical Physics, 1969: Vol. 12-C, Mathematical Methods in Field Theory & Complex Analytic Varieties, Vol. 12. 296p. 1971. text ed. 190.00 (0-677-14570-5) Gordon & Breach.
Mahanthappa, K. T., jt. ed. see Freund, P. G.
***Mahanti, Neeti.** Tribal Issues: A Non-Conventional Approach. (C). 1994. 14.00x (81-210-0332-6, Pub. by Inter-India Pubns) S Asia.
***Mahanti, S. D. & Jena, P., eds.** Local Order in Condensed Matter Physics. (Illus.). 285p. (C). 1995. lib. bdg. 98.00 (1-56072-220-7) Nova Sci Pubs.
Mahanti, S. D., jt. ed. see Kaplan, T. A.
Mahanty, J., jt. auth. see Das, M. P.
Mahanty, Shukla, jt. auth. see Singh, Bhagawan P.
Mahany, Gene. Mahany on Sales Promotion. LC 81-67753. 120p. 1982. pap. 9.95 (0-8442-3066-9, Crain Bks) NTC Pub Grp.
Mahany, Patricia S. Hurry up, Noah. Beegle, Shirley, ed. (Happy Day Bks.). (Illus.). 24p. (J). (ps-3). 1994. reprint ed. pap. 1.89 (0-7847-0257-8) Standard Pub.
Mahapatra, Jayanta. Burden of Waves & Fruit. LC 85-50522. 100p. 1988. 16.00 (0-89410-477-2); pap. 10.00 (0-89410-478-0) Three Continents.
— Selected Poems. 80p. 1989. pap. 5.95 (0-19-562051-8) OUP.
— Svayamvara & Other Poems. (Redbird Ser.). 1976. 6.75 (0-89253-558-X); 4.00 (0-89253-091-X) Ind-US Inc.
Mahapatra, Jayashree, jt. auth. see Padhy, K. S.
***Mahapatra, L. K.** Tribal Development in India: Myth & Reality. (C). 1994. 15.00x (0-7069-7351-8, Pub. by Vikas II) S Asia.
Mahapatra, L. K., jt. auth. see Das, K. B.
Mahapatra, Sitakant. Beyond the Word: The Multiple Gestures of Tradition. (C). 1993. 14.00 (81-208-1108-9, Pub. by Motilal Banarsidass II) S Asia.
— The Empty Distance Carries... Munda & Oraon Folk - Songs. 1976. lib. bdg. 14.00 (0-89253-096-0); 4.80 (0-89253-146-0) Ind-US Inc.
— The Other Silence. (Redbird Ser.). 1975. 6.75 (0-88253-600-1); pap. text ed. 4.80 (0-88253-599-4) Ind-US Inc.
— Quiet Violence. 4.80 (0-89253-605-5) Ind-US Inc.
— Unending Rhythms: Oral Poetry of Indian Tribes. (Tribal Studies of India Ser.: No. T 145). (C). 1992. 32.00 (81-210-0277-X, Pub. by Inter-India Pubns) S Asia.
Mahapatra, Sitakant & Zide, Norman H. Staying Is Nowhere: An Anthology of Kondh & Paraja Poetry. (Saffronbird Ser.). 1976. lib. bdg. 12.00 (0-89253-126-6); 6.75 (0-89253-142-8) Ind-US Inc.
Mahapatra, Sitakanta, ed. The Realm of the Sacred: Verbal Symbolism & Ritual Structures. (Illus.). 248p. 1993. 26.00 (0-19-562610-9) OUP.
Mahapatro, P. C. Economics of Cotton Handloom Industry in India. 1986. 31.00 (81-7024-060-3, Pub. by Ashish II) S Asia.
Mahapatro, Prafullo C. Economic Development of Tribal India. 1987. 30.00 (81-7024-065-4, Pub. by Ashish II) S Asia.
Mahaprajna, Yuvacharya. Mysteries of Mind. 225p. 1982. 11.00 (0-88065-223-3, Pub. by Today & Tomorrows P & P II) Scholarly Pubns.
Mahar, Dennis J. Frontier Development Policy in Brazil: A Study of Amazonia. LC 78-19750. (Praeger Special Studies). 204p. 1979. text ed. 45.00 (0-275-90385-0, C0385, Praeger Pubs) Greenwood.
— Government Policies & Deforestation in Brazil's Amazon Region. 64p. 1989. 6.95 (0-8213-1174-3, 11174) World Bank.
Mahar, J. Michael, ed. The Untouchables in Contemporary India. LC 79-152039. (Illus.). 528p. reprint ed. pap. 150.50 (0-317-58770-6, 2029654) Bks Demand.
Mahar-Keplinger, Lisa. Grain Elevators. LC 92-29683. (Illus.). 88p. (Orig.). 1993. pap. 19.95 (1-878271-35-0) Princeton Arch.
Mahar, Paul, jt. auth. see Escobar, Ernest.
Maharaj, B., jt. auth. see Charran, R.
Maharaj, Clement. The Dispossessed. (Caribbean Writers Ser.). 128p. 1992. pap. 9.95 (0-435-98928-6, 98928) Heinemann.
Maharaj, Nisargadatta. Consciousness & the Absolute: The Final Talks of Sri Nisargadatta Maharaj. Dunn, Jean, ed. (Illus.). vii, 119p. (Orig.). 1994. pap. 11.95 (0-89386-041-7) Acorn NC.
— I Am That: Talks with Sri Nisargadatta Maharaj. Dikshit, Sudhaker S., ed. Frydman, Maurice, tr. LC 81-66800. (Illus.). xx, 550p. 1994. reprint ed. pap. 19.95 (0-89386-022-0) Acorn NC.
— Prior to Consciousness: Talks with Sri Nisargadatta Maharaj. rev. ed. Dunn, Jean, ed. LC 89-81145. xi, 157p. 1990. pap. 12.95 (0-89386-024-7) Acorn NC.
— Seeds of Consciousness: The Wisdom of Sri Nisargadatta Maharaj. rev. ed. Dunn, Jean, ed. LC 89-81146. 215p. 1990. reprint ed. pap. 13.95 (0-89386-025-5) Acorn NC.
Maharaj, Rabindranath R. & Hunt, Dave. Death of a Guru. rev. ed. LC 84-81212. 208p. 1986. reprint ed. pap. 7.99 (0-89081-434-1) Harvest Hse.
Maharaj, Ratnachandraji, jt. auth. see Shri, Shatavadhani J.
Maharaj, Satyeswarananda G. Mahabharata, Vol. I: The Stories of the Great Epic. LC 93-84705. (Illus.). 528p. (Orig.). 1993. pap. text ed. write for info. (1-877854-24-7) Sanskrit Classics.
***Maharaj, Yogeshwaranand S.** Science of Divine Sound: Divya Shabad Vijnana: A Latest Research on Self & God Realization with the Medium of Sound. Ji, Muktanand S., tr. xi, 160p. 1984. 10.00 (0-614-06354-X, Pub. by Yoga Niketan II) Nataraj Bks.
— Science of Soul: A Practical Exposition of Ancient Method of Visualisation of Soul. Atma-Vijnana. xx, 280p. 1987. 15.00 (0-614-06349-3, Pub. by Yoga Niketan II) Nataraj Bks.
— Science of Vital Force: A New Research of Self & God-Realisation by the Medium of Prana. Saraswati, Muktanand, tr. v, 143p. 1980. 10.00 (0-614-06352-3, Pub. by Yoga Niketan II) Nataraj Bks.
Maharaja, Jagadguru S. Vedic Mathematics: Sixteen Simple Mathematical Formulae from the Vedas. Agrawala, V. S., ed. 367p. (C). 1992. pap. 12.00 (81-208-0164-4, Pub. by Motilal Banarsidass II) S Asia.
Maharaja, Krsna Tirthaji, jt. auth. see Bharati, Jahadhuru Swami Sri.
Maharaja Yogiraja, ed. see Maitriya.
Maharajah of Cooch Behar. Big Game Shooting in Cooch Behar, the Duars & Assam. 1993. reprint ed. 118.00 (1-879356-23-6) Wolfe Pub Co.
Maharajan, M. Gandhian Thought: A Study of Tradition & Modernity. 176p. 1993. text ed. 27.50 (81-207-1336-2, Pub. by Sterling Pubs II) Apt Bks.
Maharam, Lewis G. Maharam's Curve: The Exercise High - How to Get It, How to Keep It. (Illus.). 288p. 1992. 19.95 (0-393-03365-1) Norton.
Maharam, Patsy, jt. auth. see Blackwell, Earl.
Maharg, James. Call to Authenticity: The Essays of Ezequiel Martinez Estrada. LC 77-7175. (Romance Monographs: No. 26). 1977. 26.00 (84-399-7352-7) Romance.
Maharg, Lois, jt. auth. see Burton, Eric.
Maharidge, Dale. And Their Children after Them. 1990. pap. 14.95 (0-679-72878-3) Pantheon.
Maharidge, Dale & Williamson, Michael. And Their Children after Them: The Legacy of Let Us Now Praise Famous Men: James Agee, Walker Evans, & the Rise & Fall of the Cotton in the South. 1989. 24.95 (0-394-57766-3) Pantheon.
— The Last Great American Hobo. LC 92-40480. 1993. 24.95 (1-55958-299-5) Prima Pub.
Maharidge, Dale, jt. auth. see Mather, Jay.
Maharishi Mahesh Yogi. Bhagavad - Gita: A New Translation & Commentary, Chapters 1-6. 373p. 1967. 18.95 (0-89186-000-2); 5.00 (0-89186-002-9) Age Enlight Pr.
— Life Supported by Natural Law: Lectures by His Holiness Maharishi Mahesh Yogi to the World Assembly on Vedic Science, July 9-17, 1975, Washington, D.C. LC 86-14204. (Illus.). 210p. 1986. pap. 12.00 (0-89186-051-7) Age Enlight Pr.
— Love & God. 56p. 1973. 9.00 (0-89186-003-7) Age Enlight Pr.
— Science of Being & Art of Living. rev. ed. 335p. 1966. 18.95 (0-89186-001-0) Age Enlight Pr.
— Transcendental Meditation: Science of Being & Art of Living. (New Age Ser.). 320p. 1988. pap. 4.95 (0-317-67301-7, Sig) NAL-Dutton.
Maharishi Mahesh Yogi, tr. Maharishi Mahesh Yogi on the Bhagavad-Gita. (Orig.). 1990. pap. 8.95 (0-14-002913-3, Penguin Bks) Viking Penguin.
Maharriyum, Thaemas A. Love Communings: Soul Embracings with the Spirit of the Unborn Child. (Illus.). 68p. (Orig.). 1985. write for info. (0-912323-02-7); pap. write for info. (0-912323-01-9) Apollo Phonic.
Maharshi, Ramana. Forty Verses on Reality: Ullabu Narpadu. Cohen, S. S., tr. 46p. 1990. 8.95 (0-7224-0161-2) Element MA.
— The Spiritual Teaching of Ramana Maharshi. (Dragon Editions Ser.). 112p. (Orig.). 1988. pap. 12.00 (0-87773-024-5) Shambhala Pubns.
Mahasattva, Swami Devageet, ed. see Rajneesh, Osho.
Mahasattva Swami Geet Govind, ed. see Osho.
Mahasattva, Swami Krishna, ed. see Rajneesh, Osho.
Mahasattva, Swami Satya, ed. see Rajneesh, Osho.
Mahaska County Historical Society Staff, jt. ed. see KEO-MAH Geneaological Society Staff.
Mahathera, A. P. Concise Pali - English Dictionary. (ENG & PLI.). 1992. reprint ed. 39.95 (0-8288-8462-5) Fr & Eur.
— English Pali Dictionary. (ENG & PLI.). 1992. reprint ed. 49.95 (0-8288-8463-3, F46280) Fr & Eur.
Mahathera, Narada. The Buddha & His Teachings. 412p. (Orig.). 1988. pap. 10.50 (955-24-0025-2, Pub. by Buddhist Pubns Soc CE) Wisdom MA.
Mahathera, Narada, tr. A Manual of Abhidhamma: Abhidhammattha Sangaha. rev. ed. (C). 1990. pap. 10.95 (0-685-48810-1, Pub. by Buddhist Pubns Soc CE) Wisdom MA.
Mahathera, Paravahera V. Buddhist Meditation in Theory & Practice: A General Exposition According to the Pali Canon of the Theravada School. 3rd ed. 496p. (C). 1987. text ed. 12.95 (967-9920-41-0, Buddhist Missionary Society) Wisdom MA.
Mahatme, Anand. Concepts & Procedures in Indian Census. (C). 1988. 21.00 (0-8364-2455-7) S Asia.
Mahaut, Antoine. A New Method for Learning to Play the Transverse Flute. Hadidian, Eileen, tr. LC 88-45497. (Publications of the Early Music Institute). 88p. 1989. pap. 17.95 (0-253-20499-2, MB-499) Ind U Pr.
Mahay, A., jt. ed. see Kaliaguine, S.
Mahboubi. Pediatric Bone Imaging: A Practical Approach. 1989. 117.00 (0-316-54381-0) Little.
Mahdavieh, Y. & Gonzalez, R. C., eds. Advances in Image Analysis. LC 92-25969. 1992. 92.00 (0-8194-1046-2); pap. 77.00 (0-8194-1047-0) SPIE.
Mahdev, P. D., ed. Contributions to Indian Geography, Vol. 7: Urban Geography. 1986. 44.00 (0-8364-1600-7, Pub. by Heritage IA) S Asia.
Mahdi, Louise C., et al, eds. Betwixt & Between: Patterns of Masculine & Feminine Initiation. LC 86-31271. (Reality of the Psyche Ser.). 528p. 1987. 39.95 (0-8126-9047-8); pap. 18.95 (0-8126-9048-6) Open Court.
***Mahdi, Muhsin.** The Thousand & One Nights. LC 95-3212. 1995. pap. 28.75 (90-04-10204-3) E J Brill.
***Mahdi, Muhsin, ed.** The Thousand & One Nights (Alf Layla Wa-Layla) From Earliest Known Sources, Vol. 3. 396p. (ARA & ENG.). 1994. 114.50 (90-04-10106-3) E J Brill.
Mahdi, Muhsin, jt. ed. see Lerner, Ralph.
Mahdi, Mushin. Arabian Nights: The Thousand & One Nights. 1992. 17.00 (0-679-41338-3, Everymans Lib) Knopf.
Mahdi Xan. Sanglax A Persian Guide to the Turkish Language. (Gibb Memorial New Ser.: Vol. 20). 1992. 29.85 (0-906094-31-3, Pub. by Aris & Phillips UK) David Brown.
Mahe, Cathy M., ed. see American Trucking Association Staff.
Mahe, John A., II, et al, eds. Encyclopaedia of New Orleans Artists, 1718-1918. LC 87-80477. xxii, 466p. 1987. 39.95 (0-917860-23-3) Historic New Orleans.
Mahecha, Alberto, ed. see Pollock, Algernon J.
Mahedy, William & Bernardi, Janet. A Generation Alone: Xers Making a Place in the World. LC 94-18634. 182p. (Orig.). 1994. pap. 10.99 (0-8308-1696-8, 1696) InterVarsity.
Mahel, M. & Buday, T., eds. Regional Geology of Czechoslovakia, Pt. 2: The West Carpathians. (Illus.). 723p. 1968. 45.50 (3-510-99066-8) Lubrecht & Cramer.
Mahelona, John, jt. auth. see Johnson, Rubellite K.
Mahendra, B. Dementia. 2nd ed. 1987. lib. bdg. 78.00 (0-7462-0044-7) Kluwer Ac.
— Depression. 1987. lib. bdg. 117.00 (0-85200-983-6) Kluwer Ac.
Mahendra Nath Gupta, see M, pseud..
Mahendravarman. The Farce of the Drunk Monk. Lal, P., tr. 30p. 1973. pap. text ed. 6.00 (0-88253-301-0) Ind-US Inc.
***Maher.** Feminist Classroom. 1995. pap. 14.00 (0-465-02354-1) Basic.
Maher, ed. Evolution of Artificial Organs: A Festschrift to Dr. George E. Schreiner. write for info. (0-318-62543-1) ICAOT Pr.
Maher, Alan E. Complete Soccer Handbook. LC 83-2278. 216p. 1983. 19.95 (0-13-163386-4, Parker Publishing Co) P-H.
Maher, Ann B., et al. Orthopaedic Nursing. LC 92-49447. (Illus.). 704p. 1993. text ed. 89.50 (0-7216-2699-8) Saunders.

Maher, Barry. Getting the Most from Your Yellow Pages Advertising. LC 88-47703. 268p. 1988. 14.95 (*0-8144-7695-3*) AMACOM.
Maher, Barry & Garber, Bernard J. Legend: A Novel. LC 83-83169. 304p. (Orig.). 1987. pap. 12.00 (*0-8334-0024-X*, Spir Lit Lib) Garber Comm.
Maher, Betty. Woman Journeying: Two-Minute Reflections on the Ordinary & the Everyday. 104p. (Orig.). 1994. pap. 7.95 (*1-85607-095-6*, Pub. by Columba Pr IE) Twenty-Third.
Maher, Bill. True Story: A Comedy Novel. 1994. pap. 12.00 (*0-679-75337-0*) Random.
Maher, Brendan, tr. see From, Franz.
Maher, Brendan A. Progress in Experimental Personality Research, Vol. 13. (Serial Publication Ser.). 1984. text ed. 134.00 (*0-12-541413-7*) Acad Pr.
Maher, Brendan A. & Maher, Winifred B., eds. Progress in Experimental Personality Research, Vol. 14. (Serial Publication Ser.). 1986. text ed. 96.00 (*0-12-541414-5*) Acad Pr.
Maher, Brendan A., jt. ed. see Oltmanns, Thomas F.
Maher, Brendan A., jt. ed. see Spitzer, M.
Maher, Brendon, ed. Clinical Psychology & Personality: The Selected Papers of George Kelly. LC 78-10716. 372p. 1979. reprint ed. lib. bdg. 29.50 (*0-88275-772-5*) Krieger.
Maher, Carolyn A. Math Two. 1981. 20.00 (*0-07-039595-0*) McGraw.
Maher, Carolyn A., jt. ed. see Davis, Robert B.
Maher, Charles A., ed. Advances in Psychology & Education, Vol. 1. 1988. 73.25 (*0-89232-842-8*) Jai Pr.
Maher, Charles A. & Bennett, Randy E. Planning & Evaluating Special Education Services. (Illus.). 288p. (C). 1984. text ed. 21.75 (*0-13-679481-5*) P-H.
Maher, Charles A. & Forman, Susan G., eds. A Behavioral Approach to Education of Children & Youth. (Kratochwill-Yesseldyke School Psychology Ser.). 344p. 1987. text ed. 69.95 (*0-89859-634-3*) L Erlbaum Assocs.
Maher, Charles A., jt. ed. see Bennett, Randy E.
Maher, Charles A., jt. auth. see Bollettieri, Nick.
Maher, Charles A., jt. ed. see Schwebel, Milton.
Maher, Chi. Sex Education & Health Matters for Girls. (Attic Handbooks Ser.). (Illus.). 64p. (Orig.). (C). 1990. pap. 7.95 (*0-946211-92-2*, Pub. by Attic IE) InBook.
Maher, E. R., jt. auth. see Hodgson, S. V.
Maher, Edward R. Pilot's Avionics Survival Guide. 1993. text ed. 29.00 (*0-07-039621-3*); pap. text ed. 18.95 (*0-07-039622-1*) McGraw.
— Pilot's Avionics Survival Guide. 1993. pap. 18.95 (*0-8306-4204-8*) TAB Bks.
Maher, F. K. & Waller, P. L. Derham, Maher & Waller: An Introduction to Law. 6th ed. xi, 238p. 1991. 45.00 (*0-455-21015-2*, Pub. by Law Bk Co); pap. 29.00 (*0-455-21016-0*, Pub. by Law Bk Co) W W Gaunt.
Maher, Frances A., jt. auth. see Tetreault, Mary K.
Maher, G. & Cusine, D. J. Law & Practice of Diligence. 1990. 105.00 (*0-406-11121-9*, U.K.) Butterworth Legal Pubs.
Maher, Gerry, ed. see Association of Legal & Social Philosophy.
Maher, Gerry, jt. auth. see McLean, Sheila.
Maher, J. Peter. Papers on Language Theory & History I: Creation & Tradition in Language. (Current Issues in Linguistic Theory Ser.: No. 3). xx, 171p. 1979. 48.00x (*90-272-0904-9*) Benjamins North Am.
Maher, J. Peter, et al, eds. Papers from the Third International Conference on Historical Linguistics, Hamburg, August 22-26, 1977. (Current Issues in Linguistic Theory Ser.: No. 13). xvi, 434p. 1982. 81.00x (*90-272-3505-8*) Benjamins North Am.
Maher, Jacqueline, et al. The Small Business Guide to Hazardous Materials Management. 200p. 1988. ring bd. 48.00 (*0-9621718-0-8*) WSOS Cmnt Action Com.
Maher, James, et al. Illinois Circuit Court Automation Requirements Analysis, Vol. 1. 101p. 1989. 6.00 (*0-685-33616-6*, NERO-228) Natl Ctr St Courts.
Maher, James R., et al. Illinois Circuit Court Automation Requirements Analysis, Vol. 2: Appendices. 77p. 1989. 5.00 (*0-685-33617-4*, NERO-229) Natl Ctr St Courts.
Maher, Jim. Do Video Transcripts Affect the Scope of Appellate Review? An Evaluation in the Kentucky Court of Appeals: A Technical Assistance Report. 140p. 1990. 8.50 (*0-685-38109-9*, NERO,T/A-559) Natl Ctr St Courts.
Maher, John. Coast of Malabar. 176p. 1988. pap. 9.95 (*0-86278-166-3*, Pub. by OBrien Pr IE) Dufour.
Maher, John & Bohls, Kirk. Bleeding Orange. (Illus.). 304p. 1992. pap. 10.95 (*0-312-08145-6*) St Martin.
— Long Live the Longhorns! One Hundred Years of Texas Football. (Illus.). 256p. 1993. 29.95 (*0-312-09328-4*) St Martin.
Maher, John & Briggs, Dennie, eds. An Open Life: Joseph Campbell in Conversation with Michael Toms. LC 88-51185. (Illus.). 144p. (Orig.). 1988. pap. 9.95 (*0-943914-47-7*) Larson Pubns.
Maher, John, jt. auth. see Hoy, Mark.
Maher, John C. International Medical Communication. LC 91-36916. 200p. (C). 1992. pap. text ed. 15.95 (*0-472-08174-8*) U of Mich Pr.
***Maher, John C. & Macdonald, Gaynor, eds.** Diversity in Japanese Culture & Language. LC 94-44932. (Japanese Studies). 1995. write for info. (*0-7103-0477-3*, Pub. by Kegan Paul Intl UK) Routledge Chapman & Hall.
***Maher, John C. & Yashiro, Kyoko, eds.** Multilingual Japan. 180p. 1995. 59.00x (*1-85359-287-0*, Pub. by Multilingual Matters UK) Taylor & Francis.

Maher, John E. Thinker, Sailor, Brother, Spy. 330p. (Orig.). 1995. pap. 10.00 (*0-9643121-0-7*) Maher & Maher. Armed with a doctorate from Harvard, the hero of this novel sallies into academe & becomes a professor of economics, Dean of a business school, critic of the desexualization of women, & dilettante lover. But before all this, he serves as First Lieutenant of the destroyer Hobson during World War II &, recalled to active duty, he becomes Chief Engineer of the destroyer HUNT during the Korean War. His experiences aboard ship are reminiscent of the trials & tribulations portrayed in Herman Wouck's THE CANINE MUTINY. Throughout his errant life, he encounters such leading lights as Mark Van Doren, Mae & Walter Reuther, Vernon Jordan (his family's first babysitter), Jimmy Hoffa, & Vladimir Androsov, a professor from Moscow. The literate byplay between John & his brother Donald, a professor of English & comparative literature, yield amazing insights into the publish-or-perish cuckoo land of university imbroglios. The revelations of a professor's life include the hothouse atmosphere of Wesleyan University &, more extensively, the controversies at Southern Connecticut State University where his charges of plagiarism are said to have helped to unseat the president & where charges of sex discrimination & endless litigation have long harassed the scholarly community. Distributed by Baker & Taylor Books, Box 6920, Bridgewater, NJ 08807-0920; 908- 218-0400.** ***Publisher Provided Annotation.

Maher, John F., ed. Replacement of Renal Function by Dialysis: A Textbook of Dialysis. 3rd enl. ed. (C). 1989. lib. bdg. 277.50 (*0-89838-414-1*) Kluwer Ac.
***Maher, John T., et al.** Maritime Litigation. LC 94-34469. 1994. ring bd. 100.00 (*0-250-40734-5*) Buttrwrth NH.
Maher, Karen J., jt. auth. see Lord, Robert G.
***Maher, Larry.** The Mulligan's Complete Golf Etiquette Handbook. Bicknell, Robert, ed. (Illus.). 64p. 1995. pap. 8.95 (*0-9646234-0-4*) Happy Ft Creat.
Maher, Marie B. Flight for Life. Silvestro, Denise, ed. (Illus.). 232p. (Orig.). 1993. mass mkt. 5.99 (*0-671-74464-X*) PB.
Maher, Mary D. To Bind up the Wounds: Catholic Sister Nurses in the U. S. Civil War. LC 89-2217. (Contributions in Women's Studies: No. 107). 188p. 1989. text ed. 45.00 (*0-313-26458-9*, MRM/, Greenwood Pr) Greenwood.
Maher, Mary L., ed. Expert Systems for Civil Engineers: Technology & Application. 143p. 1987. 26.00 (*0-87262-617-2*) Am Soc Civil Eng.
Maher, Mary L., jt. ed. see Gero, John.
Maher, Mary L., jt. ed. see Kostem, Celal N.
***Maher, Mary L., et al.** Case-Based Reasoning in Design. 350p. 1995. text ed. 70.00 (*0-8058-1831-6*); pap. text ed. 35.00 (*0-8058-1832-4*) L Erlbaum Assocs.
Maher, Mary M. The Places We Save: Wisconsin Chapter of the Nature Conservancy. (Illus.). 88p. (Orig.). 1988. pap. text ed. 11.95 (*0-9619854-0-2*) Nat Conserv WI.
Maher, Mary Z. Modern Hamlets & Their Soliloquies. LC 92-12900. (Studies in Theatre History & Culture). (Illus.). 258p. 1992. 32.95 (*0-87745-380-2*) U of Iowa Pr.
— Modern Hamlets & Their Soliloquies. LC 92-12900. (Studies in Theatre History & Culture). (Illus.). 258p. 1995. pap. 12.95 (*0-87745-504-X*) U of Iowa Pr.
Maher, Michael. Lieutenants: The Evolution of Political Style. LC 90-39105. 208p. 1990. text ed. 49.95 (*0-275-93461-6*, C3461, Praeger Pubs) Greenwood.
— Psychology. 9th ed. (Stonyhurst Philosophical Ser.). 608p. 1982. reprint ed. pap. text ed. 10.00 (*0-87343-051-4*) Magi Bks.
— The Targum Pseudo-Jonathan to Genesis. (Aramaic Bible Ser.). 256p. (Orig.). 1992. pap. text ed. 65.00 (*0-8146-5492-4*) Liturgical Pr.
***Maher, Michael & Deakin, Edward.** Cost Accounting. 4th ed. 1016p. (C). 1993. text ed. 69.95 (*0-256-11657-1*) Irwin.
Maher, Michael, jt. auth. see Deakin, Edward.
Maher, Michael, jt. auth. see Deaking, Edward.
Maher, Michael J., ed. Science & Cultivation of Edible Fungi: Proceedings of the Thirteenth International Congress, Dublin, 1-6 September 1991, 2 vols. (Illus.). 880p. 1991. text ed. 140.00 (*90-5410-021-4*, Pub. by A A Balkema NE) Ashgate Pub Co.
Maher, Michael W., jt. auth. see Deakin, Edward B.
Maher, Michael W., et al. Managerial Accounting: An Introduction to Concepts, Methods, & Uses. 4th ed. 935p. (C). 1991. text ed. 59.00 (*0-15-554768-2*) Dryden Pr.
— Managerial Accounting: An Introduction to Concepts, Methods, & Uses. 5th ed. LC 93-73779. 821p. (C). 1994. text ed. 65.25 (*0-03-098202-2*) Dryden Pr.
Maher Mooney, Bernice. Salt of the Earth: The History of the Catholic Church in Utah, 1776- 1987. 2nd rev. ed. (Illus.). 546p. 1992. 20.00 (*0-9619627-1-2*) Catholic Diocese SLC.
Maher, Patrick. Betting on Theories. LC 92-13817. (Studies in Prabability, Induction & Decision Theory). 384p. (C). 1993. 54.95 (*0-521-41850-X*) Cambridge U Pr.
Maher, Patrick T. Assessor Training Manual for Public Sector Assessment Centers. 2nd ed. LC 93-84900. 225p. (C). 1993. text ed. 99.95 (*0-943865-00-X*); pap. text ed. 59.95 (*0-943865-01-8*) Persnl & Org Dev.
— Designing Emergency Scene Simulations for Police & Fire Promotional Examinations. 65p. (C). 1993. pap. text ed. 14.95 (*0-943865-02-6*) Persnl & Org Dev.
Maher, Peter J., jt. auth. see Danielsen, Niels.
Maher, Richard P. Introduction to Construction Operations. LC 82-1884. 402p. 1982. text ed. 64.95 (*0-471-86136-7*) Wiley.
Maher, Robert. Leadership: Self, School, Community. Bruce, C., ed. 96p. (Orig.). (YA). (gr. 9-12). 1988. pap. 10.00 (*0-88210-217-6*) Natl Assn Student.
Maher, Stuart T. There Must Be Something. (Illus.). 512p. (Orig.). 1992. pap. 30.00 (*0-9633576-0-3*, HV854.M01, Cheyenne West) S Maher.
Maher, Susan M. An Overview of Solutions to Breastfeeding & Sucking Problems. 32p. 1988. pap. 6.50 (*0-912500-31-X*) La Leche.
Maher, Vanessa A., ed. The Anthropology of Breast-Feeding. 176p. 1993. 49.95 (*0-85496-721-4*) Berg Pubs.
— Anthropology of Breast-Feeding. 224p. 1993. pap. 15.95 (*0-85496-814-8*) Berg Pubs.
Maher, William J. The Management of College & University Archives. LC 92-11667. (Society of American Archivists Ser.). (Illus.). 430p. 1992. 49.50 (*0-8108-2568-6*) Scarecrow.
Maher, William P. Fated to Survive. Hall, Ed Y., ed. (Illus.). 180p. (Orig.). 1992. pap. 7.50 (*0-9622166-2-3*) Honoribus Pr.
Maher, Winifred B., jt. auth. see Appley, Mortimer.
Maher, Winifred B., jt. ed. see Maher, Brendan A.
Mahes, Chola. Freedom Convoy. (Illus.). 276p. 1993. pap. 14.95 (*0-8059-3305-0*) Dorrance.
Mahesh, V. B., et al, eds. Regulation of Ovarian & Testicular Function. LC 87-22073. (Advances in Experimental Medicine & Biology Ser.: Vol. 219). (Illus.). 774p. 1987. 135.00 (*0-306-42676-5*, Plenum Pr) Plenum.
***Mahesh, V. S.** Thresholds of Motivation: Nurturing Human Growth in the Organization. 1994. 27.95 (*0-07-462232-3*) McGraw.
Mahesh, Virendra B., jt. ed. see Brann, Darrell W.
Maheshwar, ed. see Aurobindo, Sri.
***Maheshwari, Anil.** Crescent over Kashmir: Politics of Mullaism. (C). 1993. 19.50 (*81-7167-157-8*, Pub. by Rupa II) S Asia.
Maheshwari, B. B. India & Sri Lanka: Economic Relations. 1987. 26.00 (*0-8364-2245-7*, Pub. by Agam II) S Asia.
Maheshwari, B. L. Quality Circles. (C). 1987. 16.00 (*81-204-0235-9*, Pub. by Oxford IBH II) S Asia.
Maheshwari, J. K., et al. Journal of Economic & Taxonomic Botany. (C). 1988. 270.00 (*0-317-62275-7*, Scientific) St Mut.
Maheshwari, Naresh K., jt. auth. see Sharma, R. S.
Maheshwari, R. P. Principles of Business Studies, Vol. 1. 452p. 1990. 42.00 (*81-209-0188-6*, Pub. by Pitambar Pub II) St Mut.
— Principles of Business Studies, Vol. 2. 244p. 1990. pap. 24.50 (*81-209-0189-4*, Pub. by Pitambar Pub II) St Mut.
— Principles of Functional Management. 224p. 1992. 25.00 (*81-209-0448-6*, Pub. by Pitambar Pub II) St Mut.
Maheshwari, R. P. & Singh, B. Principles & Practice of Auditing. 624p. 1988. 65.00 (*81-209-0002-2*, Pub. by Pitambar Pub II) St Mut.
Maheshwari, S. N., ed. Foundations of Software Technology & Theoretical Computer Science. (Lecture Notes in Computer Science Ser.: Vol. 206). ix, 522p. 1985. pap. 49.00 (*0-387-16042-6*) Spr-Verlag.
Maheshwari, S. R. Mandal Commision & Mandalisation: A Critique. (C). 1990. text ed. 21.00 (*81-7022-338-5*, Pub. by Concept II) S Asia.
Maheshwari, Shiriram. The Higher Civil Service in France. (C). 1991. 17.50 (*81-7023-289-9*, Pub. by Allied II) S Asia.
Maheshwari, Shriman. President's Rule in India. 1977. 12.50 (*0-88386-985-3*) S Asia.
***Maheshwari, Shriram.** Rural Development in India: A Public Policy Approach. 2nd ed. LC 94-34877. 280p. 1995. text ed. 24.95 (*0-8039-9209-2*) Sage.
Maheshwary, Sharda, jt. auth. see Gupta, V. K.
***Mahesvarananda, Paramhansa Syami.** Meetings with a Yogi. (C). 1994. 16.00x (*81-7018-795-8*, Pub. by BR Pub II) S Asia.
Maheswar, Neg. Early History of the Vaisnava Faith & Movement in Assam: Sankaradeva & His Times. xx, 400p. 1986. 38.00 (*81-208-0007-9*, Pub. by Motilal Banarsidass II) S Asia.
***Maheu, Louis.** Social Movements & Social Classes. 272p. 1995. text ed. 65.00 (*0-8039-7952-5*) Sage.
Maheu, Robert. Next to Hughes: One Man Helped Build Howard Hughes' Empire, the Other Man Watched it Fall. 1993. mass mkt. 5.99 (*0-06-109033-6*, Harp PBks) HarpC.
Maheux, Anne, jt. auth. see Boggs, Jean S.
Maheux, Anne F. Degas Pastels. (Illus.). 88p. 1988. pap. 19.95 (*0-88884-547-2*, Pub. by Natl Gallery CN) U Ch Pr.
Mahfood, Philip E. TeleSelling: High Performance Business-to-Business Phone. 225p. 1993. reprint ed. pap. 16.95 (*1-55738-500-9*) Probus Pub Co.
Mahfood, Phillip E. The Customer Crisis: Turning an Unhappy Customer into a Life-Long Client. 200p. 1993. 24.95 (*1-55738-421-5*) Probus Pub Co.
— Managing the Home-Based Worker: How to Hire, Motivate & Monitor Employees Who Work at Home. 1994. pap. 19.95 (*1-55738-578-5*) Probus Pub Co.
Mahfouz, Afaf M., jt. ed. see Smith, Joseph H.
***Mahfouz, Baguib.** Children of Gebelaawi. rev. ed. LC 94-45586. 1995. pap. 16.00 (*0-89410-818-2*) Three Continents.
Mahfouz, Nagib. The Beggar: Al Shahad. (ARA.). 1985. pap. 8.95 (*0-86685-151-8*) Intl Bk Ctr.
— The Crime: Al Jar'imah. (ARA.). 1985. pap. 8.95 (*0-86685-147-X*) Intl Bk Ctr.
— The Honeymoon: Shahrel Assel. (ARA.). 1985. pap. 8.95 (*0-86685-161-5*) Intl Bk Ctr.
— Khan el Khalili: (Novel in Arabic) 1987. pap. 8.95 (*0-86685-177-1*) Intl Bk Ctr.
— Love in the Rain: Hebeh Tahtal Matar. (ARA.). pap. 8.95 (*0-86685-154-2*) Intl Bk Ctr.
— Madak Alley. 1980. Arabic. pap. 8.95 (*0-86685-163-1*); English. pap. 11.00 (*0-686-67892-3*) Intl Bk Ctr.
— The Road: Al Tareeq. (ARA.). 1982. pap. 8.95 (*0-86685-152-6*) Intl Bk Ctr.
— Tales of New Cairo: Qahira Al Jadida. pap. 8.95 (*0-86685-150-X*) Intl Bk Ctr.
— Tales of the Black Cat: Khamarat Quet Aswad. (ARA.). 1967. pap. 8.95 (*0-86685-157-7*) Intl Bk Ctr.
— The Thief & the Dogs: Les Wil Kelab. (ARA.). 1976. pap. 8.95 (*0-86685-158-5*) Intl Bk Ctr.
Mahfouz, Naguib. Adrift on the Nile. 1994. 9.95 (*0-385-42333-0*, Anchor NY) Doubleday.
— Arabian Nights & Days. Johnson-Davies, Denys, tr. LC 94-6457. 1995. 22.95 (*0-385-46888-1*) Doubleday.
— Autumn Quail. 1986. pap. 8.50 (*977-424-107-X*, Pub. by Am Univ Cairo Pr UA) Col U Pr.
— Autumn Quail. rev. ed. Rodenbeck, John, ed. Allen, Roger, tr. 1990. reprint ed. mass mkt. 7.95 (*0-385-26454-2*) Doubleday.
— Autumn Quail (Siman wa Khareef) Arabic Novel. (ARA.). (J). (gr. 4-7). 1985. 8.95 (*0-86685-162-3*) Intl Bk Ctr.
— The Beggar. Henry, Kristin W., tr. 1987. pap. 10.50 (*977-424-135-5*, Pub. by Am Univ Cairo Pr UA) Col U Pr.
— The Beggar. 1990. mass mkt. 7.95 (*0-385-26456-9*) Doubleday.
— Beginning & the End. (ARA.). 1985. pap. 8.95 (*0-86685-153-4*) Intl Bk Ctr.
— The Beginning & the End. 1989. mass mkt. 10.00 (*0-385-26458-5*) Doubleday.
— Children of Gebelaawi. rev. ed. Stewart, Philip, tr. 368p. 1990. pap. 16.00 (*0-89410-697-X*) Three Continents.
— Children of the Alley. Theroux, Peter, tr. LC 95-15510. 1996. write for info. (*0-385-42094-3*) Doubleday.
— Fountain & Tomb. Kenneson, James et al, trs. LC 86-51004. (Illus.). 120p. (Orig.). (C). 1988. reprint ed. 22.00 (*0-89410-580-9*); reprint ed. pap. 10.00 (*0-89410-581-7*) Three Continents.
— The Harafish. Cobham, Catherine, tr. LC 93-7782. 1994. 22.95 (*0-385-42324-1*) Doubleday.
— The Harafish. Cobham, Catherine, tr. LC 94-38311. Orig. Title: Malhamat al-Harafish. 1995. pap. 11.00 (*0-385-42335-7*, Anchor NY) Doubleday.
— The Journey of Ibn Fattouma. 1993. mass mkt. 9.95 (*0-385-42334-9*, Anchor NY) Doubleday.
— Midaq Alley. 1992. mass mkt. 9.00 (*0-385-26476-3*, Anchor NY) Doubleday.
— Miramar. Rodenbeck, John, ed. Mahmoud, Fatma M., tr. LC 92-25382. 1993. mass mkt. 8.50 (*0-385-26478-X*, Anchor NY) Doubleday.
— Miramar. 2nd enl. ed. Moussa-Mahmoud, Fatma, tr. LC 89-20627. 173p. 1991. reprint ed. pap. 11.00 (*0-89410-693-7*) Three Continents.
— Palace of Desire. 1992. pap. 11.00 (*0-385-26468-2*, Anchor NY) Doubleday.
— Palace of Desire: The Cairo Trilogy II. 1991. 22.95 (*0-385-26467-4*) Doubleday.
— Palace Walk. Hutchins, William M. & Kenny, Olive E., trs. 1990. 22.95 (*0-385-26465-8*) Doubleday.
— Palace Walk. 1991. pap. 11.00 (*0-385-26466-6*, Anchor NY) Doubleday.
— Respected Sir. 1990. mass mkt. 7.95 (*0-385-26480-1*) Doubleday.
— Search. 1991. mass mkt. 8.00 (*0-385-26460-7*) Doubleday.
— The Search: A Novel. 126p. (Orig.). 1987. pap. 10.50 (*977-424-160-6*, Pub. by Am Univ Cairo Pr UA) Col U Pr.
— Stories of the Neighborhood (Hekayat Haretna) (Novel in Arabic) (ARA.). 1982. 8.95 (*0-86685-156-9*) Intl Bk Ctr.
— Story Without Ending (Hekeyah bela Bidayah) (ARA.). 1982. 8.95 (*0-86685-155-0*) Intl Bk Ctr.
— Sugar Street. 1992. 14.99 (*0-385-26937-4*) Doubleday.
— Sugar Street. Hutchins, William M. & Samaan, Angele B., trs. LC 92-25362. 1993. pap. 11.00 (*0-385-26470-4*, Anchor NY) Doubleday.
— Sugar Street: The Cairo Trilogy III. 1992. 22.50 (*0-385-26469-0*) Doubleday.
— The Thief & the Dogs. 1989. mass mkt. 7.95 (*0-385-26462-3*) Doubleday.
— Time & the Place. 1992. mass mkt. 8.95 (*0-385-26472-0*, Anchor NY) Doubleday.
— Wedding Song. Mursi Saad El Din & Rodenbeck, John, eds. Kennedy, Olive E., tr. 99p. 1985. pap. 8.50 (*977-424-018-9*, Pub. by Am Univ Cairo Pr UA) Col U Pr.
— Wedding Song. 1989. mass mkt. 7.95 (*0-385-26464-X*, Anchor NY) Doubleday.
— Whisperings on the Nile (Saraarah Fouk el Nil) Arabic Novel. (ARA.). 1976. 8.95 (*0-86685-160-7*) Intl Bk Ctr.
***Mahfouz, Naquib.** Adrift on the Nile. braille ed. 227p. 1994. text ed. 18.16 (*1-56956-425-6*, BR9307) W A T Braille.
Mahfuz, Naguib. God's World: An Anthology of Short Stories. Abadir, Akef & Allen, Roger, trs. LC 73-79201. (Studies in Middle Eastern Literatures: No. 2). 1973. pap. 12.00 (*0-88297-044-5*) Bibliotheca.

An Asterisk (*) at the beginning of an entry indicates that the title is appearing in BIP for the first time.

— Mirrors. Allen, Roger, tr. LC 76-47306. (Studies in Middle Eastern Literatures: No. 8). 1977. pap. 12.00 (0-88297-016-X) Bibliotheca.

Mahiau, Louis J. The Plumber's Toolbox Manual. (On-the-Job Reference Ser.). 352p. 1989. pap. 10.00 (0-13-683806-5) P-H.

Mahieu, Wauthier de. Qui a Obstrue la Cascade? Analyse Semantique du Rituel de la Circoncision chez les Komo au Zaire. (Atelier d'Anthropologie Sociale). 464p. 1986. 74.95 (0-521-30043-6) Cambridge U Pr.

Mahin, Andrew. Grasshoppers & Bushcrickets. (Shire Natural History Ser.: No. 25). (Illus.). 24p. 1988. pap. text ed. 5.25 (0-85263-946-5) Lubrecht & Cramer.

Mahinda, Deegalle, jt. ed. see Hoffman, Frank.

Mahindra, Indira. The End Play. (Emerging Voices: New International Fiction Ser.). 192p. 1994. 24.95 (1-56656-175-2); pap. 11.95 (1-56656-166-3) Interlink Pub.

Mahini, Amir. Making Decisions in Multinational Corporations: Managing Relations with Sovereign Governments. LC 87-37591. 225p. 1988. text ed. 55.00 (0-471-84092-0) Wiley.

Mahiri, Jabari. The Day They Stole the Letter J. (Illus.). (Orig.). (J). (gr. 3-5). 1981. pap. 3.95 (0-88378-084-4) Third World.

Mahjoub, Azzam, ed. Adjustment or Delinking? The African Experience. Berrett, A. M., tr. LC 89-9027. (UNU Studies in African Political Economy). (Illus.). 272p. (C). 1990. text ed. 55.00 (0-86232-842-X, Pub. by Zed Books UK); pap. 17.50 (0-86232-843-8, Pub. by Zed Books UK) Humanities.

Mahjoub, Jamal. Navigation of a Rainmaker: An Apocalyptic Vision of War-Torn Africa. (African Writers Ser.). 184p. (Orig.). 1989. pap. 7.95 (0-435-90560-0) Heinemann.

— Wings of Dust. 224p. 1994. pap. 9.95 (0-435-90984-3) Heinemann.

Mahl, Alan R., ed. Interpretive Centers for More Effective Education: Proceedings of the Natural Science Center Conference 1971-Saint Paul, Minnesota. (Illus.). (Orig.). 1972. 5.00 (0-916544-01-X) Natural Sci Youth.

— Leadership to Meet Our Environmental Crisis: Proceedings of the Natural Science Center Conference 1970 - Dayton Ohio. (NCS Conference Proceedings Ser.). (Illus.). (Orig.). 1971. 5.00 (0-916544-00-1) Natural Sci Youth.

Mahl, George. Explorations in Nonverbal & Vocal Behavior. 440p. 1987. 79.95 (0-89859-757-9) L Erlbaum Assocs.

Mahl, Mary R. & Koon, Helene, eds. The Female Spectator: English Women Writers Before 1800. 310p. reprint ed. pap. 88.40 (0-317-27836-3, 2056046) Bks Demand.

Mahlck, Lars O., jt. ed. see Chapman, David W.

Mahle, Benj. Power Teaching. 1989. pap. 9.99 (0-8224-5192-1) Fearon Teach Aids.

Mahlendorf, tr. see Bienek, Horst.

Mahlendorf, Ursula R. The Wellsprings of Literary Creation. LC 84-72198. (Studies in German Literature, Linguistics & Culture: Vol. 18). (Illus.). 292p. 1985. 35.00 (0-938100-34-3) Camden Hse.

Mahlendorf, Ursula R., jt. auth. see Lerner, Arthur.

Mahler, jt. auth. see Brahms.

Mahler, Annie, tr. see Antelme, Robert.

Mahler, Donald A., ed. Dyspnea. (Illus.). 288p. 1990. 40.00 (0-87993-361-5) Futura Pub.

— Pulmonary Disease in the Elderly Patient. LC 92-49321. (Lung Biology in Health & Disease Ser.: Vol. 63). 528p. 1992. 170.00 (0-8247-8752-8) Dekker.

***Mahler, Donald A. & American College of Sports Medicine Staff.** Guidelines for Exercise Testing & Prescription: American College of Sports Medicine. 5th ed. 1995. write for info. (0-683-00023-3) Williams & Wilkins.

Mahler, F., et al, eds. Methoden der Klinischen Kapillarmikroskopie. (Illus.). 168p. 1986. pap. 63.25 (3-8055-4409-X) S Karger.

— Techniques in Clinical Capillary Microscopy. (Mikrozirkulation in Forschung und Klinik; Progress in Applied Microcirculation Ser.: Vol. 11). (Illus.). xii, 152p. 1986. pap. 63.25 (3-8055-4327-1) S Karger.

Mahler, Greg, jt. auth. see March, Roman.

Mahler, Gregory, jt. ed. see Karsh, Efraim.

Mahler, Gregory S. Comparative Politics: An Institutional & Cross-National Approach. 380p. 1984. 24.95 (0-87073-682-5); pap. 15.95 (0-87073-683-3) Schenkman Bks Inc.

— Comparative Politics: An Institutional & Cross-National Approach. 2nd ed. LC 94-21377. 464p. 1994. text ed. 25.80 (0-13-176611-2) P-H.

— Israel: Government & Politics in a Maturing State. 293p. (C). 1989. pap. text ed. 16.00 (0-15-547152-X) HB Coll Pubs.

— The Knesset: Parliament in the Israeli Political System. LC 80-67633. 256p. 1982. 35.00 (0-8386-3071-5) Fairleigh Dickinson.

— New Dimensions of Canadian Federalism. LC 85-46013. 192p. 1987. 36.50 (0-8386-3289-0) Fairleigh Dickinson.

Mahler, Gregory S., comp. Contemporary Canadian Politics: An Annotated Bibliography, 1970-1987. LC 88-21357. (Bibliographies & Indexes in Law & Political Science Ser.: No. 10). 414p. 1988. text ed. 59.95 (0-313-25510-5, MCF/, Greenwood Pr) Greenwood.

Mahler, Gregory S., ed. Israel after Begin. LC 89-28079. (SUNY Series in Israeli Studies). 357p. 1990. 64.50 (0-7914-0367-X); pap. 21.95 (0-7914-0368-8) State U NY Pr.

— Readings on the Israeli Political System: Structures & Processes. LC 81-40031. 450p. (Orig.). 1982. pap. text ed. 37.00 (0-8191-2118-5) U Pr of Amer.

Mahler, Gustav. Symphonies Nos. 1 & 2 in Full Score. 1987. pap. 14.95 (0-486-25473-9) Dover.

Mahler, Margaret. The Selected Papers of Margaret S. Mahler Vol. 2: Separation-Individuation, Vol. 2. LC 94-70014. 270p. 1994. reprint ed. pap. 30.00 (1-56821-224-0) Aronson.

***Mahler, Margaret S.** The Selected Papers of Margaret S. Mahler Vol. 1: Infantile Psychosis & Early Contributions. LC 79-51915. 334p. 1995. pap. text ed. 32.50 (1-56821-421-9) Aronson.

Mahler, Margaret S. & Furer, Manuel. On Human Symbiosis & the Vicissitudes of Individuation Vol. 1: Infantile Psychoses. LC 68-24453. 271p. 1968. text ed. 40.00 (0-8236-3780-8) Intl Univs Pr.

Mahler, Margaret S., et al. The Psychological Birth of the Human Infant. LC 74-77255. 320p. 1975. text ed. 35.00 (0-465-06659-3) Basic.

Mahler, Michael. United States Civil War Revenue Stamp Taxes. LC 88-72215. (C. & S. Revenue Ser.). (Illus.). 384p. 49.95 (0-9603498-3-9) Castenholz Sons.

Mahler, Michael D. Ringed in Steel. 256p. 1987. mass mkt. 4.99 (0-515-09074-3) Jove Pubns.

Mahler, Paul. Informix 4-Gl Tutorial. 1990. pap. text ed. 52.00 (0-13-464173-6) P-H.

— Powerbuilder: Building Client Server Applications. 448p. 1994. pap. 34.95 (0-13-179300-4) P-H.

— Relational Databases & SQL. (Illus.). 1993. pap. write for info. (0-13-772310-5) P-H.

Mahler, Philip H., et al. Precalculus with Applications. 608p. (C). 1995. boxed write for info. (0-697-11656-5) Wm C Brown Pubs.

Mahler, Raphael. Hasidism & the Jewish Enlightenment: Their Confrontation in Galicia & Poland in the First Half of the Nineteenth Century. Orenstein, Eugene et al, trs. 412p. 1990. 29.95 (0-8276-0233-2) JPS Phila.

Mahler, Richard. Guatemala: A Natural Destination. (Natural Destination Ser.). (Illus.). 288p. (Orig.). 1993. pap. 16.95 (1-56261-075-9) John Muir.

Mahler, Richard & Wotkyns, Steele. Belize: A Natural Destination. 288p. (Orig.). 1991. pap. 16.95 (1-56261-011-2) John Muir.

— Belize: A Natural Destination. 2nd ed. LC 93-22122. (Natural Destination Ser.). (Illus.). 304p. (Orig.). 1993. pap. 16.95 (1-56261-141-0) John Muir.

Mahler, Richard, jt. auth. see Goldman, Connie.

***Mahler, Sarah J.** American Dreaming: Immigrant Life on the Margins. LC 95-13473. 1995. write for info. (0-691-03783-3); pap. write for info. (0-691-03782-5) Princeton U Pr.

Mahler, Vincent A. Dependency Approaches to International Political Economy: A Cross-National Study. LC 79-26200. 1980. text ed. 40.50 (0-231-04836-X) Col U Pr.

Mahler, Walter R. Diversified Company: An Endangered Species. 1992. 24.95 (0-914431-03-X) Mahler Pub Co.

Mahler, Walter R. & Drotter, Stephen J. Succession Planning Handbook for the Chief Executive. 300p. 1986. 45.00 (0-914431-01-3) Mahler Pub Co.

Mahler, Walter R. & Moss, Robert. The Highly Diversified Company. 360p. 1989. write for info. (0-318-65383-4) Mahler Pub Co.

Mahlmann, Lewis & Jones, David C. Plays for Young Puppeteers. 328p. (Orig.). 1993. pap. text ed. 14.95 (0-8238-0298-1) Plays.

Mahlmeister, Laura R., jt. auth. see May, Katharyn A.

Mahlmeister, Laura R., jt. auth. see May, Kathryn A.

Mahlum, D. D. & Sikov, M. R., eds. Developmental Toxicology of Energy-Related Pollutants: Proceedings. LC 78-606139. (DOE Symposium Ser.). 661p. 1978. pap. 24.50 (0-87079-113-3, CONF-771017); fiche 9.00 (0-87079-178-8, CONF-771017) DOE.

Mahlum, D. Dennis, jt. ed. see Sikov, Melvin R.

Mahlum, Dennis D., et al, eds. Coal Conversion & the Environment: Chemical, Biomedical, & Ecological Considerations. LC 81-607088. (DOE Symposium Ser.: Proceedings). 622p. 1981. pap. 24.75 (0-87079-128-1, CONF-801039); fiche 9.00 (0-87079-401-9, CONF-801039) DOE.

***Mahmood.** Collins Bridge for Beginners Series Declarer Play. 1995. pap. 8.00 (0-00-218471-0) Collins SF.

— Collins Bridge Series for Begginers Defence. 1995. pap. 8.00 (0-00-218469-9) Collins SF.

Mahmood, Cynthia. Frisian & Free: Study of an Ethnic Minority of The Netherlands. (Illus.). 111p. (Orig.). (C). 1989. pap. text ed. 8.50 (0-88133-418-9) Waveland Pr.

***Mahmood, K.** Reservoir Sedimentation: Impact, Extent, & Mitigation. (Technical Paper Ser.: No. 71). 130p. 1987. 10.95 (0-614-02846-9, 10952) World Bank.

Mahmood, K., et al. Alluvial Channel Data on PC. 1989. disk 350.00 (0-318-41785-5) WRP.

Mahmood, K., et al, eds. Mechanics of Alluvial Channels. LC 87-51101. 536p. 1988. 60.00 (0-918334-63-2) WRP.

Mahmood, Rohana, ed. Peace in the Making. 108p. 1992. 56.50 (0-7103-0419-6, A7252, Pub. by Kegan Paul Intl UK) Routledge Chapman & Hall.

Mahmood, Safdar. Pakistan: Political Roots & Development. 320p. 1990. text ed. 35.00 (81-207-1125-4, Pub. by Sterling Pubs II) Apt Bks.

— Pakistan Divided. 35.00 (1-56744-178-5) Kazi Pubns.

Mahmood, Syed, jt. auth. see Ranis, Gustav.

Mahmood, Tahir. Personal Law in Islamic Countries. (C). 1987. 110.00 (0-685-25711-8) St Mut.

***Mahmood, Zia.** Bridge My Way. 1994. pap. 12.95 (0-9634715-2-X) L Cohen NJ.

Mahmoody, Betty. For the Love of a Child. 1993. mass mkt. 5.99 (0-312-95081-0) St Martin.

— Not Without My Daughter. 1988. mass mkt. 4.95 (0-312-91193-9) St Martin.

Mahmoody, Betty & Hoffer, William. Not Without My Daughter. 1991. reprint ed. mass mkt. 5.99 (0-312-92588-3) St Martin.

— Not Without My Daughter: A True Story. (Paperback Ser.). 574p. 1991. pap. 15.95 (0-8161-5199-7) G K Hall.

Mahmoud, et al. Large Scale Control Systems: Theories & Techniques. (Electrical Engineering & Electronics Ser.: Vol. 26). 384p. 1985. 135.00 (0-8247-7289-X) Dekker.

Mahmoud, Adel A., jt. auth. see Warren, K. S.

Mahmoud, Adel A. F., ed. Tropical & Geographical Medicine, 2nd Ed. Companion Handbook. (Companion Handbook Ser.). (Illus.). 464p. 1994. pap. text ed. 27.50 (0-07-039625-6) Hlth Prof Div.

Mahmoud, Adel A. F., jt. auth. see Warren, Kenneth S.

Mahmoud, Fatma M., tr. see Mahfouz, Naguib.

Mahmoud, Hosam M. Evolution of Random Search Trees. (Interscience Series in Discrete Mathematics: No. 1484). 336p. 1991. text ed. 84.95 (0-471-53228-2) Wiley.

***Mahmoud, K. M.** Non-Linear A-D Converters for Integrated Silicon Smart Sensors. 168p. (Orig.). 1994. pap. 52.50x (90-6275-976-9, Pub. by Delft U Pr NE) Coronet Bks.

Mahmoud, M. S., jt. auth. see Bahnasawi, A. A.

Mahmoud, M. S., et al. Discrete Systems: Analysis, Control & Optimization. (Communications & Control Engineering Ser.). (Illus.). 690p. 1984. 109.00 (0-387-13645-2) Spr-Verlag.

Mahmoud, Magdi S. Computer-Operated Systems Control. (Electrical Engineering & Electronics Ser.: Vol. 70). 680p. 1991. 185.00 (0-8247-8092-2) Dekker.

Mahmoud, Parvine, tr. see Khayyam, Omar.

Mahmoud, Shah. Research & Writing: A Complete Guide & Handbook. (Illus.). 272p. (Orig.). 1992. pap. 18.95 (1-55870-243-1) Betterway Bks.

Mahmoudi, Jalil. A Concordance to the Hidden Words of Baha'u'llah. LC 80-21346. (Orig.). 1980. pap. 0.95 (0-87743-148-5, 368-052) Bahai.

Mahmoudi, Said. The Law of Deep Sea-Bed Mining: A Study of the Progressive Development of International Law Concerning the Management of the Polymetallic Nodules of the Deep Sea-Bed. 362p. 1987. text ed. 121.00x (91-22-01156-0, Pub. by Almqv & Wiksell SW) Coronet Bks.

Mahmoudian, Morteza. Modern Theories of Language: The Empirical Challenge. LC 92-13538. (Sound & Meaning: The Roman Jakobson Series in Linguistics & Poetics). (Illus.). 256p. 1993. text ed. 39.95 (0-8223-1278-6) Duke.

Mahmoudov, Alexei. The Soviet Oil & Natural Gas Industries: Problems of Reserve Estimation. Williams, John, ed. 95p. (Orig.). 1986. pap. text ed. 75.00 (1-55831-029-0) Delphic Associates.

Mahmud. New Temple for Hathor at Memphis, Vol. 1: Egyptology Today. 1978. pap. 32.50 (0-85668-089-3, Pub. by Aris & Phillips UK) David Brown.

Mahmud Ahmad Ghazanfar. Talim ul-Hajj. 94p. (Orig.). 1985. pap. 5.99 (1-56744-399-0) Kazi Pubns.

Mahmud, S. F. A Short History of Islam. rev. ed. (Illus.). 442p. 1989. pap. 17.95 (0-19-577384-5) OUP.

Mahmud, Sayed J. Pillars on Modern India, 1757-1947. 140p. 1994. 16.00 (81-7024-586-9, Pub. by Ashish Pub Hse II) Nataraj Bks.

Mahmud, Shabana. Urdu Language & Literature: A Bibliography of Sources in European Languages. 352p. 1992. text ed. 100.00 (0-7201-2143-4, Mansell Pub) Cassell.

Mahn, Patrick, jt. auth. see Valentine, Tom.

Mahncke, Dieter. Nukleare Mitwirkung: Die Bundesrepublik Deutschland in der atlantischen Allianz 1954-1970. (Beitraege zur Auswaertigen und Internationalen Politik Ser.: Vol. 6). xvi, 274p. (C). 1972. 79.25 (3-11-001820-9) De Gruyter.

Mahnke, Dan. Antique Roads of America: Bicycle Guide for Route 66. (Illus.). 102p. (Orig.). 1992. pap. 9.95 (0-9633853-0-5, TX 3 345 672) D Mahnke.

Mahnke, Doug, jt. auth. see Arcudi, John.

Mahnke, R. Color & Light in Man Made Environments. 1993. pap. 39.95 (0-442-01322-1) Van Nos Reinhold.

Mahnken, Jan. Feeding the Birds. LC 94-16742. (Orig.). 1994. pap. 6.99 (0-517-11845-9, Pub. by Wings Bks) Random.

— Feeding the Birds. Griffith, Roger, ed. LC 83-16365. (Illus.). 192p. (Orig.). 1983. pap. 9.95 (0-88266-361-5, Garden Way Pub) Storey Comm Inc.

— Hosting the Birds: How to Attract Birds to Nest in Your Yard. Mason, Jill, ed. LC 88-45487. (Illus.). 216p. 1989. 21.95 (0-88266-534-0, Garden Way Pub); pap. 10.95 (0-88266-525-1, Garden Way Pub) Storey Comm Inc.

Mahoe, Noelani K., jt. ed. see Elbert, Samuel H.

Mahon, Brid. Land of Milk & Honey: The Story of Traditional Irish Food & Drink. (Illus.). 176p. (Orig.). 1992. pap. 17.95 (1-85371-142-X, Pub. by Poolbeg Pr IE) Dufour.

— A Time to Love. 484p. 1993. pap. 13.95 (1-85371-221-3, Pub. by Poolbeg Pr IE) Dufour.

***Mahon, Connie, et al, eds.** Textbook of Diagnostic Microbiology. LC 94-21550. (Illus.). 1152p. 1995. text ed. 63.00 (0-7216-4028-1) Saunders.

Mahon, Denis. Guercino: Master Painter of Baroque. LC 91-44263. (Illus.). 315p. (Orig.). 1992. pap. 39.95 (0-89468-167-2) Natl Gallery Art.

— Studies in Seicento Art & Theory. LC 73-114544. (Illus.). 351p. 1971. reprint ed. text ed. 35.00 (0-8371-4743-3, MAST, Greenwood Pr) Greenwood.

Mahon, Denis & Turner, Nicholas. The Drawings of Guercino in the Collection of Her Majesty the Queen at Windsor Castle. 450p. 1989. 250.00 (0-521-24476-5) Cambridge U Pr.

Mahon, Derek. The Hunt by Night. rev. ed. LC 82-50938. 63p. 1983. pap. 6.95 (0-916390-17-9) Wake Forest.

— Selected Poems. 198p. 1992. 20.00 (0-670-83575-7, Viking) Viking Penguin.

— Selected Poems. LC 93-2221. 198p. 1993. pap. 12.00 (0-14-058704-7, Penguin Bks) Viking Penguin.

Mahon, Derek, jt. ed. see Fallon, Peter.

Mahon, Derek, tr. see Jaccottet, Philippe.

***Mahon, George, comp.** A Policies & Procedures Handbook for Induction & Foundation Training. 1991. pap. 21.00 (0-614-07448-7, Pub. by Natl Inst Soc Work) St Mut.

Mahon, Gigi. The Last Days of the New Yorker. 1989. pap. 9.95 (0-317-02698-4, Plume) NAL-Dutton.

Mahon, Harold P., et al. Efficient Energy Management. (Illus.). 496p. (C). 1983. 29.95 (0-13-791434-2) P-H.

Mahon, Jana. Coupon & Refund Guide. (Illus.). 52p. (Orig.). 1989. pap. 4.00 (0-685-25744-4) J L Mahon.

***Mahon, John.** Kate Tyrrell "Lady Mariner" The Story of the Extraordinary Woman Who Sailed the Denbighshire Lass. 1995. pap. 11.99 (1-85594-140-6) InBook.

Mahon, John & Pendleton, Thomas A., eds. Fanned & Winnowed Opinions: Shakespearean Essays Presented to Harold Jenkins. 320p. 1988. pap. 67.50 (0-416-00422-9) Routledge Chapman & Hall.

Mahon, John K. History of the Second Seminole War, 1835-1842. rev. ed. LC 85-16443. (Illus.). 401p. 1991. pap. 16.95 (0-8130-1097-7) U Press Fla.

— The War of 1812. (Quality Paperbacks Ser.). (Illus.). xii, 476p. 1991. reprint ed. pap. 15.95 (0-306-80429-8) Da Capo.

Mahon, K. L. Just One Tear. LC 93-80198. (YA). (gr. 5 up). 1994. 10.00 (0-688-13519-6) Lothrop.

Mahon, L. L. Diesel Generator Handbook. (Illus.). 416p. 1992. 195.00 (0-7506-1147-2) Buttrwrth-Heinemann.

Mahon, Lord, ed. see Chesterfield, Philip D.

Mahon, Michael. Foucault's Nietzschean Genealogy: Truth, Power, & the Subject. LC 91-35092. (SUNY Series in Contemporary Continental Philosophy). 255p. 1992. 59.50 (0-7914-1149-4); pap. 19.95 (0-7914-1150-8) State U NY Pr.

Mahon, Rianne. The Politics of Industrial Restructuring: Canadian Textiles. (State & Economic Life Ser.: No. 7). xii, 204p. 1984. 30.00 (0-8020-2538-2); pap. 13.95 (0-8020-6546-5) U of Toronto Pr.

Mahon, Rianne, jt. ed. see Jenson, Jane.

Mahon, Thomas. The Fandango Involvement. 224p. 1981. pap. 2.25 (0-449-14427-5, GM) Fawcett.

***Mahon, Thomas E.** Axis Two. 580p. 1995. pap. 12.95 (1-56901-780-8) NW Pub.

Mahon, Thomas J. Say, Kids! Always Say No to That Junky Stuff, Drugs! (J). 1992. 7.95 (0-533-09698-7) Vantage.

Mahon, Tom. The Special People. LC 93-60738. 144p. 1994. 8.95 (1-55523-635-9) Winston-Derek.

Mahon, William, ed. Proceedings of the Harvard Celtic Colloquium, Vols. VIII/IX. (Harvard Celtic Colloquium Ser.). 253p. (Orig.). 1991. lib. bdg. 32.50 (1-879095-01-7); pap. text ed. 22.50 (1-879095-00-9) Pangur Pubns.

Mahon, William J., jt. ed. see Jefferiss, Paul.

Mahon, William J., tr. see Kirwan, Augustine & Hughes, Thomas.

Mahone-Lonesome, Robyn. Charles R. Drew. (Black Americans of Achievement Ser.). (Illus.). (YA). (gr. 5 up). 1990. 17.95 (1-55546-581-1) Chelsea Hse.

Mahone, Sydne, intro. Moon Marked & Touched by Sun: Plays by African-American Women. 448p. 1994. pap. 15.95 (1-55936-065-8) Theatre Comm.

Mahoney, Anne R. Juvenile Justice in Context. 224p. 1987. 40.00 (1-55553-011-7) NE U Pr.

Mahoney, Barry. Toward Excellence in Caseflow Management: The Experience of the Circuit Court in Wayne County, Michigan. 92p. 1991. pap. text ed. 6.95 (0-685-50610-X, R125) Natl Ctr St Courts.

Mahoney, Bateman & Mahoney, Bill. Macho: Is This What I Really Want? (J). 1986. pap. 6.00 (0-87738-024-4) Youth Ed.

Mahoney, Beverly, jt. ed. see Olsen, Larry.

Mahoney, Bill, jt. auth. see Mahoney, Bateman.

Mahoney-Briscoe, Charlotte, jt. auth. see Briscoe, David.

Mahoney, Carole, jt. auth. see Staples, Danny.

Mahoney, Connie, jt. auth. see Pardini, Alan.

Mahoney, Dan. Detective First Grade. 384p. 1993. 21.95 (0-312-09288-1) St Martin.

— Detective First Grade Vol. 1: A Novel. 1994. pap. 5.99 (0-312-95313-5) St Martin.

— Edge of the City. 464p. 1995. 22.95 (0-312-13058-9) St Martin.

Mahoney, Daniel J. The Liberal Political Science of Raymond Aron: A Critical Introduction. 1991. pap. text ed. 14.95 (0-8476-7716-8) Rowman.

— The Liberal Political Science of Raymond Aron: A Critical Introduction. (C). 1991. text ed. 52.00 (0-8476-7715-X) Rowman.

Mahoney, Daniel J., ed. In Defense of Political Reason: Essays by Raymond Aron. 188p. (C). 1994. lib. bdg. 52.50 (0-8476-7877-6); pap. text ed. 19.95 (0-8476-7878-4) Rowman.

Mahoney, Daniela. Outstanding Oregon Recipes. 120p. 1992. spiral bd. 5.50 (0-941016-87-0) Penfield.

***Mahoney, Denis.** Black Pig Bk. 1: In Red Ochre. 1994. pap. 7.00 (0-614-04109-0) Hozomeen Pr.

Mahoney, Dennis C., et al. Tax Strategies in Divorce. (Family Law Library). 746p. 1991. 135.00 (0-471-55303-4) Wiley.

— Tax Strategies in Divorce. (Family Law Library). 168p. 1993. ring bd. 55.00 (0-471-58858-X) Wiley.

— Tax Strategies in Divorce: 1992 Supplement. 1992. ring bd. 45.00 (0-471-57037-0) Wiley.

Mahoney, Dennis F. The Critical Fortunes of a Romantic Novel: Novalis's Heinrich von Ofterdingen. LC 94-11094. (Studies in German Literature, Linguistics, & Culture). 175p. 1994. 54.95 (1-879751-58-5) Camden Hse.

Mahoney, Dennis J., jt. auth. see Levy, Leonard W.

Mahoney, Dennis J., jt. ed. see Levy, Leonard W.

Mahoney, Dennis J., jt. ed. see Schramm, Peter W.

Mahoney, Donna T. Touching the Face of God: Intimacy & Celibacy in the Priesthood. LC 91-76864. 233p. 1991. pap. 12.95 (0-9631517-0-3) Jeremiah Pr.

*Mahoney, E. F. & Dwiggins, B. H. Automotive Electricity & Electronics: Concepts & Applications. LC 95-15895. 1995. pap. write for info. (0-13-359233-2) P-H.

Mahoney, Edward F. Electricity for Air Conditioning & Refrigeration Technician. 3rd ed. 320p. 1991. pap. text ed. 49.00 (0-13-249418-3) P-H.

— Readings & Interpreting Diagrams in Air Conditioning & Refrigeration. (C). 1983. teacher ed write for info. (0-8359-6484-1, Reston) P-H.

Mahoney, Ellen & Wilcox, Leah. Ready, Set, Read: Best Books to Prepare Preschoolers. LC 83-27087. 1985. 27.50 (0-8108-1684-9) Scarecrow.

Mahoney, Ellen V. Animals. (Ringtales Ser.). (Illus.). 8p. (J). (ps). 1994. vinyl bd. 3.95 (0-8431-3545-X) Price Stern.

— Coping with Safer Sex. Rosen, Ruth, ed. (Coping Ser.). (YA). (gr. 7-12). 1989. lib. bdg. 15.95 (0-8239-0999-9) Rosen Group.

— Food. (Ringtales Ser.). (Illus.). 8p. (J). (ps). 1994. vinyl bd. 3.95 (0-8431-3546-8) Price Stern.

— Now You've Got Your Period. rev. ed. Rosen, Roger, ed. (Coping Ser.). (YA). (gr. 7 up). 1993. lib. bdg. 15.95 (0-8239-1662-6) Rosen Group.

— The Sea. (Ringtales Ser.). (Illus.). 8p. (J). (ps). 1994. vinyl bd. 3.95 (0-8431-3547-6) Price Stern.

— Toys. (Ringtales Ser.). (Illus.). 8p. (J). (ps). 1994. vinyl bd. 3.95 (0-8431-3548-4) Price Stern.

Mahoney, Eugene. Fire Suppression Practices & Procedures. 304p. 1991. pap. 28.25 (0-89303-215-8) P-H.

Mahoney, Eugene J. There's a Light in the Gardibee House & Other Stories. 117p. (Orig.). 1985. pap. 2.95 (0-9615994-0-5) E J Mahoney.

Mahoney, Francis X. & Thor, Carl G. The TQM Trilogy: Using ISO 9000, the Deming Prize, & the Baldrige Award to Establish a System for Total Quality Management. 224p. 1994. 29.95 (0-8144-5105-5) AMACOM.

Mahoney, Gene. Effective Supervisory Practices Study Guide. 112p. (Orig.). 1987. pap. 11.95 (0-945250-00-2) Davis Pub Co.

— Fire Department Oral Interviews: Practices & Procedures. 350p. (C). 1988. pap. text ed. 27.00 (0-87814-911-2) Fire Eng.

— Introduction to Fire Apparatus & Equipment. 2nd ed. LC 85-82103. (Illus.). 524p. (C). 1986. text ed. 36.75 (0-912212-12-8); student ed 20.00 (0-87814-901-5) Fire Eng.

Mahoney, Haynes R. Yarmouth's Proud Packets: The Commodore Hull Didn't Sail So Dull. (Illus.). 46p. 1986. pap. 4.00 (0-9625068-1-8) Hist Soc Yarmouth.

Mahoney, Irene, ed. Marie of the Incarnation: Selected Writings. (Sources of American Spirituality Ser.). 1989. 24.95 (0-8091-0428-8) Paulist Pr.

Mahoney, J. J. Inlets for Supersonic Missiles. (Educ Ser.). (Illus.). 237p. 1991. 57.95 (0-930403-79-7) AIAA.

*Mahoney, Jack. The Golf History of New England: Centennial Edition. 256p. 1995. 35.00 (0-9647426-0-8) J Mahoney.

— Teaching Business Ethics in the U. K., U. S. A. & Europe: A Comparative Study. LC 90-635. 224p. (C). 1990. text ed. 49.95 (0-485-11399-6, Pub. by Athlone Pr UK) Humanities.

— Virginia Broderick: Artist Extraordinary. 1983. pap. 1.00 (0-915866-13-7) Am Cath Pr.

Mahoney, Jack & Vallance, Elizabeth, eds. Business Ethics in a New Europe. LC 92-26437. (Issues in Business Ethics Ser.: Vol. 3). 244p. (C). 1992. lib. bdg. 69.00 (0-7923-1931-1) Kluwer Ac.

Mahoney, James R. & Sakamoto, Clyde, eds. International Trade Education: Issues & Programs. LC 85-216111. (AACJC Issues Ser.: No. 2). 97p. reprint ed. pap. 27.70 (0-7837-2483-7, 2042640) Bks Demand.

Mahoney, Jane & Euhardy, Reenie. Coping with Impaired Mobility. LC 93-40443. (Coping with Aging Ser.). 1994. 18.95 (1-879105-65-9) Singular Publishing.

Mahoney, Jean & Rao, Peggy L. At Home with Japanese Design: Accents, Structure & Spirit. (Illus.). 184p. 1990. 24.95 (4-07-975061-7, Pub. by Shufunomoto Co Ltd JA) C E Tuttle.

Mahoney, Jean, jt. auth. see Rao, Peggy L.

Mahoney, Jim & Sallis, Lela, eds. AACJC Statistical Yearbook, 1991. 1991. 38.50 (0-87117-233-X, 1321) Am Assn Comm Coll.

Mahoney, Jim, ed. see Sellis, Lela.

Mahoney, John. The Making of Moral Theology: A Study of the Roman Catholic Tradition (Martin D'Arcy Memorial Lectures 1981-1982) (Illus.). 384p. 1989. pap. text ed. 19.95 (0-19-826730-4) OUP.

— Seeking the Spirit. 1981. pap. 11.95 (0-87193-187-7) Dimension Bks.

Mahoney, John, ed. see Hungness, Carl.

Mahoney, John F., tr. see Benoit, Hubert.

Mahoney, John L. The Logic of Passion: The Literary Criticism of William Hazlitt. rev. ed. LC 81-67501. 135p. reprint ed. pap. 38.50 (0-7837-5879-0, 2045599) Bks Demand.

— The Whole Internal Universe: Imitation & the New Defense of Poetry in British Criticism, 1660-1830. LC 85-80479. 176p. reprint ed. pap. 50.20 (0-7837-5878-2, 2045598) Bks Demand.

Mahoney, John L., ed. & intro. The English Romantics: Major Poetry & Critical Theory with Selected Modern Critical Essays. 828p. 1978. pap. text ed. 31.00 (0-669-05240-X) Heath.

Mahoney, John L., jt. ed. see Barth, J. Robert.

Mahoney, John L., jt. auth. see Dryden, John.

Mahoney, John L., ed. see Dryden, John.

Mahoney, Joseph F. & Wosh, Peter J., eds. The Diocesan Journal of Michael Augustine Corrigan, 1872-1880, Vol. XXII. (Collections of the New Jersey Historical Society). 443p. 1987. 35.00 (0-911020-17-9) NJ Hist Soc.

Mahoney, Judy. Teach Me English. (Illus.). 20p. 1993. teacher ed, pap. 5.95 (0-934633-25-8) Teach Me.

— Teach Me English. (Illus.). 20p. (J). (ps-6). 1993. audio, pap. 13.95 (0-934633-60-6) Teach Me.

— Teach Me Even More French. (Illus.). 24p. (Orig.). (J). (ps-6). 1995. audio, pap. 14.95 (0-934633-72-X) Teach Me.

— Teach Me Even More Spanish. (Illus.). 20p. (J). (ps-6). Date not set. audio 13.95 (0-934633-67-3) Teach Me.

— Teach Me French. (Illus.). 20p. (FRE.). 1989. teacher ed, pap. 5.95 (0-934633-26-6) Teach Me.

— Teach Me French. rev. ed. (Illus.). 20p. (FRE.). (J). (ps-6). 1989. audio, pap. 13.95 (0-934633-02-9) Teach Me.

— Teach Me French Book Pack. (Illus.). 20p. (Orig.). (J). (ps-6). 1994. audio, pap. 14.95 (0-614-03283-0) Teach Me.

— Teach Me German. (Illus.). 20p. (GER.). 1989. teacher ed, pap. 5.95 (0-934633-27-4) Teach Me.

— Teach Me German. rev. ed. (Illus.). 20p. (GER.). (J). (ps-6). 1989. audio, pap. 13.95 (0-934633-07-X) Teach Me.

— Teach Me Hebrew. Horowitz, Shelly, tr. (Illus.). 20p. 1991. teacher ed, pap. 5.95 (0-934633-28-2) Teach Me.

— Teach Me Hebrew. Horowitz, Shelly, tr. (Illus.). 20p. (J). (ps-6). 1991. audio, pap. 11.95 (0-934633-54-1) Teach Me.

— Teach Me Italian. Grifoni, Maria C., tr. (Illus.). 20p. (ITA.). 1992. teacher ed, pap. 5.95 (0-934633-29-0) Teach Me.

— Teach Me Italian. Grifoni, Maria C., tr. (Illus.). 20p. (ITA.). (J). (ps-6). 1992. audio, pap. 13.95 (0-934633-57-6) Teach Me.

— Teach Me Japanese. Satoh, Naomi, tr. (Illus.). 20p. 1990. teacher ed, pap. 5.95 (0-934633-30-4) Teach Me.

— Teach Me Japanese. Satoh, Naomi, tr. (Illus.). 20p. (J). (ps-6). 1990. audio, pap. 13.95 (0-934633-17-7) Teach Me.

— Teach Me More English. (Illus.). 20p. (Orig.). 1994. audio, pap. text ed. 13.95 (0-934633-66-5) Teach Me.

— Teach Me More English. (Illus.). 20p. (Orig.). 1994. teacher ed, text ed. 6.95 (0-934633-38-X) Teach Me.

— Teach Me More English. (Illus.). 20p. (Orig.). (J). (ps-6). 1994. 6.95 (0-934633-65-7) Teach Me.

— Teach Me More French. (Illus.). 20p. (FRE.). 1989. teacher ed, pap. 6.95 (0-934633-33-9) Teach Me.

— Teach Me More French. (Illus.). 20p. (FRE.). (J). (ps-6). 1989. audio, pap. 13.95 (0-934633-11-8) Teach Me.

— Teach Me More French Book. (Illus.). (Orig.). (J). (ps-6). 1995. audio, boxed 14.95 (0-934633-10-X) Teach Me.

— Teach Me More German. (Illus.). 20p. (GER.). 1990. teacher ed, pap. 6.95 (0-934633-34-7) Teach Me.

— Teach Me More German. (Illus.). 20p. (GER.). (J). (ps-6). 1990. audio, pap. 13.95 (0-934633-23-1) Teach Me.

— Teach Me More Italian. Grifoni, Maria, tr. (Illus.). 20p. (Orig.). (J). (ps-6). 1993. audio, pap. 13.95 (0-934633-63-0) Teach Me.

— Teach Me More Italian. Grifoni, Maria C., tr. (Illus.). 20p. (Orig.). 1993. teacher ed 6.95 (0-934633-35-5) Teach Me.

— Teach Me More Italian. Grifoni, Maria C., tr. (Illus.). 20p. (Orig.). 1993. 6.95 (0-934633-62-2) Teach Me.

— Teach Me More Japanese. Satoh, Naomi, tr. (Illus.). 20p. (JPN.). 1991. teacher ed, pap. 6.95 (0-934633-36-3) Teach Me.

— Teach Me More Japanese. Satoh, Naomi, tr. (Illus.). 20p. (JPN.). (J). (ps-6). 1991. audio, pap. 13.95 (0-934633-20-7) Teach Me.

— Teach Me More Russian. (Illus.). 20p. (Orig.). (J). (ps-6). 1996. audio, pap. 13.95 (0-934633-78-9) Teach Me.

— Teach Me More Spanish. (Illus.). 20p. 1989. teacher ed, pap. 6.95 (0-934633-37-1) Teach Me.

— Teach Me More Spanish. (Illus.). 20p. (J). (ps-6). 1989. audio, pap. 13.95 (0-934633-14-2) Teach Me.

— Teach Me More Spanish Book. (Illus.). 20p. (Orig.). (J). (ps-6). 1995. audio, boxed 14.95 (0-934633-13-4) Teach Me.

— Teach Me Russian. Gybin, Sasha, tr. 20p. (Orig.). 1991. teacher ed, pap. 5.95 (0-934633-31-2) Teach Me.

— Teach Me Russian. Gybin, Sasha, tr. 20p. (Orig.). (J). (ps-6). 1991. audio, pap. 13.95 (0-934633-51-7) Teach Me.

— Teach Me Spanish. (Illus.). 20p. (SPA.). 1989. teacher ed, pap. 5.95 (0-934633-32-0) Teach Me.

— Teach Me Spanish. rev. ed. (Illus.). 20p. (SPA.). (J). (ps-6). 1989. audio, pap. 13.95 (0-934633-05-3) Teach Me.

— Teach Me Spanish Book Pack. (Illus.). 20p. (SPA.). (J). (ps-6). Date not set. audio, pap. 14.95 (0-934633-03-7) Teach Me.

Mahoney, Judy, comp. Sing with Me in English: A Teach Me Tapes Songbook. (Illus.). 26p. (Orig.). (J). (ps-6). 1994. pap. 7.95 (0-934633-90-8) Teach Me.

— Sing with Me in French: A Teach Me Tapes Songbook. (Illus.). 26p. (Orig.). (FRE.). (J). (ps-6). 1994. pap. 7.95 (0-934633-91-6) Teach Me.

— Sing with Me in Spanish: A Teach Me Tapes Songbook. (Illus.). 26p. (Orig.). (SPA.). (J). (ps-6). 1994. pap. 7.95 (0-934633-92-4) Teach Me.

Mahoney, Kate, jt. auth. see Burmeister, George.

*Mahoney, Katherine & Murakami, Linda K. Farewell to Arms: Cleaning up Nuclear Weapons Facilities. 70p. 1993. 15.00 (1-55516-497-8, 4639) Natl Conf State Legis.

Mahoney, Katherine A., jt. auth. see Reed, James B.

Mahoney, Kathleen. Gothic: Architecture & Interiors from the Eighteenth Century to the Present. LC 92-50395. 1993. write for info. (0-670-84446-2, Viking Studio) Studio Bks.

— Gothic Style: Architecture & Interiors from the Eighteenth Century to the Present. LC 94-32731. 1995. write for info. (0-8109-3381-0) Abrams.

— Simple Wisdom: Shaker Sayings, Poems, & Songs. LC 92-50729. 1993. 12.95 (0-670-84808-5, Viking Studio) Studio Bks.

Mahoney, Kathleen E. & Mahoney, Paul, eds. Human Rights in the Twenty-First Century: A Global Challenge. LC 92-15848. 1993. lib. bdg. 270.00 (0-7923-1810-2) Kluwer Ac.

Mahoney, Lawrence. Children & Hope: A History of the Children's Home Society of Florida. (Illus.). 112p. (Orig.). 1987. 22.95 (0-940495-02-3) Pickering Pr.

— The Early Birds: A History of Pan Am's Clipper Ships. (Illus.). 128p. (Orig.). 1987. pap. 12.95 (0-940495-07-4) Pickering Pr.

Mahoney, Lawrence, ed. see Graham, Bob.

Mahoney, Lawrence T. Gator! (Illus.). 72p. (Orig.). 1991. pap. 9.95 (0-89815-404-9) Ten Speed Pr.

Mahoney, M. H. Women in Espionage: A Biographical Dictionary. 1993. lib. bdg. 65.00 (0-87436-743-3) ABC-CLIO.

Mahoney, Marci. Strategic Resumes. Gerould, W. Philip, ed. LC 91-76255. (Fifty-Minute Ser.). (Illus.). 90p. (Orig.). 1993. pap. 9.95 (1-56052-129-5) Crisp Pubns.

Mahoney, Margaret M. Stepfamilies & the Law. 350p. 1994. text ed. 47.50 (0-472-10519-1) U of Mich Pr.

Mahoney, Maria. Sara's World. 1994. 8.95 (0-533-10821-7) Vantage.

Mahoney, Maria F. Meaning in Dreams & Dreaming. 1966. reprint ed. pap. 9.95 (0-8065-0095-6, Citadel Pr) Carol Pub Group.

Mahoney, Marie M. Reflections on Mary's Help Hospital & Seton Medical Center, 1893-1985. 180p. 1986. 25.00 (0-9616516-0-1) Seton Med Ctr.

Mahoney, Michael J. Human Change Processes: The Scientific Foundation of Psychotherapy. LC 90-80675. 608p. 1991. text ed. 55.00 (0-465-03118-8) Basic.

Mahoney, Michael J., ed. Cognitive & Constructive Psychotherapies: Theory, Research, & Practice. (Illus.). 232p. 1994. 38.95 (0-8261-8610-6) Springer Pub.

Mahoney, Michael J. & Freeman, Arthur, eds. Cognition & Psychotherapy. LC 85-3370. 370p. 1985. 60.00 (0-306-41858-4, Plenum Pr) Plenum.

Mahoney, Michael J., jt. ed. see Neimeyer, Robert A.

Mahoney, Michael S. Mathematical Career of Pierre De Fermat. 1601-1665. (C). 1994. pap. 18.95 (0-691-03666-7) Princeton U Pr.

— The Mathematical Career of Pierre de Fermat (1601-1665) LC 72-733. 439p. reprint ed. pap. 125.20 (0-317-08307-4, 2016017) Bks Demand.

Mahoney, Michael S., tr. see Descartes, Rene.

Mahoney, Mick & Murray, Melissa. Verity Bargate Award Plays, 1984. Keefe, Barrie, ed. (Methuen New Theatrescripts Ser.). 64p. 1988. pap. 8.95 (0-413-58930-7, A0305, Pub. by Methuen UK) Heinemann.

Mahoney, Olivia. Edward F. Worst: Craftsman & Educator. (Illus.). 72p. (Orig.). 1985. pap. 9.95 (0-913820-12-1) Chicago Hist.

Mahoney, Olivia, jt. auth. see Foner, Eric.

Mahoney, Patrick, jt. auth. see Chanda, Linda J.

Mahoney, Paul. Difficulties with Rosary Meditation. 1990. 0.50 (0-911988-98-X) AMI Pr.

— Narcotics Investigation Techniques. 1992. 49.95 (0-13-612573-5) P-H.

Mahoney, Paul, jt. ed. see Mahoney, Kathleen E.

Mahoney, Paul T. Narcotics Investigation Techniques. (Illus.). 406p. (C). 1992. text ed. 68.95x (0-398-05803-2) C C Thomas.

— Narcotics Investigation Techniques. (Illus.). 406p. (C). 1992. pap. 37.95x (0-398-06263-3) C C Thomas.

Mahoney, Phillip. Supreme. 80p. 1989. pap. 7.95 (1-55643-053-1) North Atlantic.

Mahoney, R. C. Animal Behavior: Index of New Information with Authors, Subjects & Bibliography. rev. ed. 1994. 49.50 (0-7883-0170-5); pap. 45.50 (0-7883-0171-3) ABBE Pubs Assn.

Mahoney, Robert. Bruce Helander: Curious Collage. LC 93-80843. (Illus.). 112p. 1994. 50.00 (0-9628514-6-9) Grassfield Pr.

Mahoney, Rosemary. Whoredom in Kimmage: Irish Women Coming of Age. LC 94-11848. 1994. 12.95 (0-385-47450-4, Anchor NY) Doubleday.

— Whoredom in Kimmage: Irish Women Coming of Age. LC 93-20294. 320p. 1993. 21.95 (0-395-60201-7) HM.

Mahoney, Ruth C. Animal Communications: Index of New Information with Authors, Subjects & Bibliography. 180p. 1993. 49.50 (1-55914-792-X); pap. 39.50 (1-55914-793-8) ABBE Pubs Assn.

— Animal Testing Alternatives in Health Sciences: Index of New Information with Authors, Subjects & Bibliography. rev. ed. 147p. 1994. 49.50 (0-7883-0368-6); pap. 44.50 (0-7883-0369-4) ABBE Pubs Assn.

Mahoney, Sheila, ed. see Goode, Erica T., et al.

Mahoney, Sheila, ed. see Rosenbaum, Ernest H., et al.

Mahoney, Sheila, ed. see Rosenbaum, Ernest H.

Mahoney, Sheila, ed. see Wheat, Mary E. & Rosenbaum, Ernest H.

Mahoney, Thomas. Law Enforcement Career Planning. (Illus.). 92p. 1989. 27.95 (0-398-05589-0) C C Thomas.

— Law Enforcement Career Planning. (Illus.). 92p. 1989. pap. 15.95 (0-614-02285-1) C C Thomas.

Mahoney, Thomas H., ed. see Burke, Edmund E.

Mahoney, Timothy R. River Towns in the Great West: The Structure of Provincial Urbanization in the American Midwest, 1820-1870. (Illus.). (C). 1990. 49.95 (0-521-36130-3) Cambridge U Pr.

Mahoney, Tom. Merchants of Life: An Account of the American Pharmaceutical Industry. LC 77-167381. (Essay Index Reprint Ser.). 1977. reprint ed. 20.95 (0-8369-2608-0) Ayer.

Mahoney Valley Historical Society Staff. Historical Collections of the Mahoney Valley - (Ohio), Vol. I. 524p. 1993. reprint ed. lib. bdg. 55.00 (0-8328-3225-1) Higginson Bk Co.

Mahoney, William D., jt. auth. see Trauner, Theodore H.

Mahoney, William F. The Active Shareholder: Exercising Your Rights, Increasing Your Profits, & Minimizing Your Risks. 289p. 1993. text ed. 21.95 (0-471-57100-8) Wiley.

— Investor Relations: The Professional's Guide to Financial Marketing & Communications. 1990. 34.95 (0-13-691254-0) NY Inst Finance.

*Mahoni, William, illus. Polynesian Cultural Center - English. 50p. 1995. pap. write for info. (0-9644640-0-4) Polynesian Cult.

Mahoning Valley Historical Society Staff. Historical Collections of the Mahoning Valley (Ohio), Vol. 1. (Illus.). 550p. 1990. reprint ed. pap. 30.00 (1-55613-336-7) Heritage Bk.

Mahony, jt. auth. see Tangney.

Mahony, Ann. Handwriting & Personality: How Graphology Reveals What Makes People Tick. 368p. 1990. mass mkt. 4.95 (0-8041-0575-8) Ivy Books.

Mahony, B. K., intro. MECH 'Ninety-One Australia: Engineering for a Competitive World, Conference 6: Maintenance Engineering: Emerging Technologies & a New Professionalism. (Illus.). 105p. (Orig.). 1991. pap. 38.50 (0-85825-530-8, Pub. by Inst Engrs Aust-EA Bks AT) Accents Pubns.

Mahony, Bertha & Whitney, Elinor. Contemporary Illustrators of Children's Books. (Illus.). 1992. reprint ed. 65.00 (1-55888-944-2) Omnigraphics Inc.

Mahony, J. H., jt. ed. see Stokes, G. S.

Mahony, John J., jt. auth. see Fowkes, N. D.

Mahony, John J., jt. ed. see Fowkes, N. D.

Mahony, Judy R., jt. auth. see Cronan, Mary P.

Mahony, Pat, jt. ed. see Frith, Ruth.

Mahony, Patrick. Cries of the Wolf Man. Chicago Institute for Psychoanalysis Staff, ed. LC 83-26525. (History of Psychoanalysis Ser.: No. 1). xiii, 188p. (C). 1984. text ed. 30.00 (0-8236-1090-X) Intl Univs Pr.

— Psychoanalysis & Discourse. Tuckett, David, ed. (New Library of Psychoanalysis). 250p. (C). 1987. lib. bdg. 42.50 (0-422-61030-5, Pub. by Tavistock UK); pap. 12.95 (0-422-61720-2, Pub. by Tavistock UK) Routledge Chapman & Hall.

Mahony, Patrick F. Barbed Wit & Malicious Humor. 1985. 25.00 (0-941694-12-7) Inst Study Man.

— Escape into the Psychic Kingdom. 1985. 25.00 (0-941694-18-6) Inst Study Man.

— It's Better in America. 1985. 25.00 (0-941694-11-9) Inst Study Man.

— Maurice Maeterlinck. 1985. 25.00 (0-941694-22-4) Inst Study Man.

— Out of the Silence. 1985. 25.00 (0-941694-17-8) Inst Study Man.

— You Can Find a Way. 1985. 25.00 (0-941694-10-0) Inst Study Man.

Mahony, Patrick J. Freud As a Writer. LC 81-14306. 227p. 1981. 35.00 (0-8236-2018-2) Intl Univs Pr.

Mahony, Phillip. Catching Bodies. 80p. 1984. text ed. 20.00 (0-938190-56-3); pap. 7.95 (0-938190-55-5) North Atlantic.

*Mahony, Rhona. Kidding Ourselves: Why Women Won't Achieve Equality Until Men Really Share Parenting & How to Make it Happen. LC 95-5761. 288p. 1995. 23.00 (0-465-08593-8) Basic.

Mahony, Robert, jt. ed. see Rizzo, Betty.

Mahood, G. A., ed. see Gans, P. B., et al.

MaHood, James, ed. see Mosher, Clelia D.

Mahood, Linda. The Magdalenes: Prostitution in the Nineteenth Century. 224p. 1990. 39.95 (0-415-00166-8, A3993) Routledge.

Mahood, M. M. Bit Parts in Shakespeare's Plays. 266p. (C). 1993. 64.95 (0-521-41612-4) Cambridge U Pr.

Mahood, M. M., ed. see Shakespeare, William.

Mahood, Wayne. The Plymouth Pilgrims: A History of the Eighty-Fifth New York Infantry in the Civil War. rev. ed. Martin, David, ed. (Illus.). 367p. (C). 1991. 30.00 (0-944413-22-6) Longstreet Hse.

Mahood, Wayne, ed. Charlie Mosher's Civil War: From Fair Oaks to Andersonville with the Plymouth Pilgrims (85th N. Y. Inf.) (Illus.). 378p. 1994. 30.00 (0-944413-20-X) Longstreet Hse.

Mahood, Wayne, et al. Teaching Social Studies in the Middle & Senior High School. 416p. (C). 1990. write for info. (0-675-21253-7, Merrill Pub Co) Macmillan.

Mahowald, Anthony P., ed. Genetics of Pattern Formation & Growth Control. 272p. 1990. text ed. 159.95 (0-471-56821-X) Wiley.

Mahowald, M. & Priddy, S. Algebraic Topology: (Proceedings of the International Conference) LC 89-15023. (CONM Ser.: Vol. 96). 350p. 1989. pap. 49.00 (0-8218-5102-0, CONM96) Am Math.

Mahowald, Mark. The Metastable Homotopy of S-to-the-N. LC 52-42839. (Memoirs Ser.: No. 1/72). 81p. 1967. pap. 16.00 (0-8218-1272-6, MEMO 1/72) Am Math.

Mahowald, Mark E., jt. ed. see Friedlander, Eric M.

Mahowald, Mary B. Women, Children, & Health Care. LC 92-12912. 320p. 1993. 39.95 (0-19-506346-5) OUP.

Mahowald, Mary B., ed. Philosophy of Woman: An Anthology of Classic & Current Concepts. 2nd ed. LC 83-8433. 480p. (C). 1983. lib. bdg. 34.95 (0-915144-49-2); pap. text ed. 14.95 (0-915144-48-4) Hackett Pub.

An Asterisk (*) at the beginning of an entry indicates that the title is appearing in BIP for the first time.

— Philosophy of Women: An Anthology of Classic to Current Concepts. 3rd ed. LC 94-25616. 544p. (C). 1994. lib. bdg. 37.95x (0-87220-262-3); pap. text ed. 16. 95x (0-87220-261-5) Hackett Pub.

Mahowald, Misha. An Analog VLSI System for Stereoscopic Vision. LC 93-49498. (International Series in Engineering & Computer Science, VLSI, Computer Architecture, & Digital Screen Processing). 232p. (C). 1994. lib. bdg. 95.00 (0-7923-9444-5) Kluwer Ac.

Mahowald, Stephen C. Beyond the Bars: A Journey of Faith in the Modern World. 128p. (Orig.). 1989. pap. 6.95 (0-685-25936-6) Goals Unlimited.

Mahr, B., jt. auth. see Ehrig, H.

Mahr, D., jt. auth. see Boyd, T. J.

Mahr, Daniel, jt. ed. see Boyd, Thomas J.

Mahr, Douglas J., jt. auth. see Ramtha.

Mahr, Theodore C. Early's Valley Campaign: The Battle of Cedar Creek: Showdown in the Shenandoah. (Virginia Civil War Battles & Leaders Ser.). (Illus.). 480p. 1992. 25.00 (1-56190-025-7) H E Howard.

***Mahrer, Alvin R.** The Complete Guide to Experiential Psychotherapy. LC 95-7302. 1995. text ed. 59.95 (0-471-12438-9) Wiley.

— Dream Work in Psychotherapy & Self-Change. 1990. 34. 95 (0-393-70089-5) Norton.

— Experiencing: A Humanistic Theory of Psychology & Psychiatry. 896p. 1989. pap. 47.00 (0-7766-0245-4, Pub. by Univ Ottawa Pr CN) Paul & Co Pubs.

— Experiential Psychotherapy: Basic Practices. 420p. 1989. pap. 33.00 (0-7766-0244-6, Pub. by Univ Ottawa Pr CN) Paul & Co Pubs.

— How to Do Experiential Psychotherapy: A Manual for Practitioners. 170p. 1989. pap. 13.00 (0-7766-0242-X, Pub. by Univ Ottawa Pr CN) Paul & Co Pubs.

— Integrations of Psychotherapies: A Guide for Practicing Therapists. LC 87-26091. 208p. 1989. 38.95 (0-89885-412-1) Human Sci Pr.

— Therapeutic Experiencing: The Process of Change. (Professional Bks.). 1986. 34.95 (0-393-70008-9) Norton.

Mahrer, Debi & Levy, Ruth. Being Torah Teacher's Guide. 116p. 1987. pap. 12.95 (0-685-22217-9) Torah Aura.

Mahry, DiAnna. Muttsey, an Unforgettable Mutt. 1991. 7.95 (0-924663-16-2) Alaskan Viewpoint.

Mahsun, Carol A. Pop Art & the Critics. Kuspit, Donald, ed. LC 87-6032. (Studies in the Fine Arts: Criticism: No. 23). (Illus.). 146p. reprint ed. pap. 42.20 (0-8357-1960-X) Bks Demand.

Mahsun, Carol A., ed. Pop Art: The Critical Dialogue. LC 88-39868. (Studies in the Fine Arts: Criticism: No. 29). Orig. Title: Pop Art: The Critical Dialogue. 258p. reprint ed. 73.60 (0-8357-1922-7, 2070735) Bks Demand.

***Mahta, Tarla.** Sanskrit Play Production in Ancient India. (C). 1995. 34.00x (81-208-1057-0, Pub. by Motilal Banarsidass II) S Asia.

Mahtab, M. Ashraf & Grasso, Piergiorgo. Geomechanics Principles in the Design of Tunnels & Caverns in Rocks. LC 92-32794. (Developments in Geotechnical Engineering Ser.: No. 72). 1992. write for info. (0-444-88308-8) Elsevier.

Mahtani, Aruna, jt. auth. see D'Ardennes, Patricia.

Mahuika, A. T., tr. see Smith, Miriam.

Mahunka, S., jt. ed. see Balogh, J.

Mahurin, Cecil. A Public Rebuttal to Rush Limbaugh. 1993. 10.95 (0-533-10766-0) Vantage.

Mahurin, Matt. Matt Mahurin: Japan & America. Ishiwata, Maya & Luisotti, Theresa, eds. (Illus.). 52p. (ENG & JPN.). 1993. 45.00 (4-947671-01-7, Pub. by RAM Pub JA) Res Art Media.

Mahurin, Ronald P., jt. auth. see Sherratt, Timothy R.

***mahurin, tim.** Jeremy Kooloo. LC 94-20462. (J). (gr. 1-4). 1995. 13.99 (0-525-45203-6, DCB) Dutton Child Bks.

Mahut, Helen, ed. see Walesa, Lech.

Mahvenieradze, V. Political Reality & Political Consciousness. 444p. (C). 1985. 50.00 (0-685-31660-2, Pub. by Collets UK) Pro-Am Music.

Mahy, B. W., ed. The Genetics & Pathogenicity of Negative Strand Viruses. 419p. 1989. 192.50 (0-444-81082-X) Elsevier.

— Virology. (Practical Approach Ser.). 280p. 1985. pap. 39. 00 (0-904147-78-9, IRL Pr) OUP.

Mahy, B. W. & Kolakofsky, D., eds. The Biology of Negative Strand Viruses. 436p. 1987. 177.00 (0-444-80833-7) Elsevier.

Mahy, B. W., jt. auth. see Rowson, K. E.

Mahy, Brian W. & Lvov, Dmitri K., eds. Current Concepts in Virology: From Ivanofsky to the Present. LC 93-3449. 438p. 1993. text ed. 90.00 (3-7186-0568-6) Gordon & Breach.

Mahy, Margaret. Aliens in the Family. (J). (gr. 4-7). 1991. pap. 3.25 (0-590-44898-6, Apple Paperbacks) Scholastic Inc.

— The Birthday Burglar & a Very Wicked Headmistress. LC 92-46599. (Illus.). 144p. (J). (gr. 5 up). 1993. pap. 4.95 (0-688-12470-4, Pub. by Beech Tree Bks) Morrow.

— The Blood-&-Thunder Adventure on Hurricane Peak. LC 89-8098. (Illus.). 144p. (J). (gr. 4-7). 1989. text ed. 13.95 (0-689-50488-8, McElderry) S&S Childrens.

— Boy Who Was Followed Home. LC 75-2866. (Pied Piper Bks.). (Illus.). 32p. (J). (ps-3). 1986. 14.99 (0-8037-0286-8) Dial Bks Young.

— Boy Who Was Followed Home. (J). (ps-3). 1993. pap. 5.99 (0-14-054614-6) Dial Bks Young.

— The Boy Who Was Followed Home. (Pied Piper Bks.). (Illus.). 32p. (J). (ps-3). 1983. pap. 4.95 (0-8037-0903-X) Dial Bks Young.

— Bubble Trouble: And Other Poems & Stories. LC 92-3540. (Illus.). 80p. (J). (gr. 3-7). 1992. text ed. 13.95 (0-689-50557-4, McElderry) S&S Childrens.

— A Busy Day for a Good Grandmother. LC 93-77331. (Illus.). 32p. (J). (ps-3). 1993. text ed. 14.95 (0-689-50595-7, McElderry) S&S Childrens.

— The Catalogue of the Universe. 192p. (YA). (gr. 7 up). 1994. pap. 3.99 (0-14-036600-8) Puffin Bks.

— The Catalogue of the Universe. LC 85-72262. 192p. (YA). (gr. 9 up). 1986. text ed. 15.95 (0-689-50391-1, McElderry) S&S Childrens.

— The Changeover. 224p. (YA). (gr. 7 up). 1994. pap. 3.99 (0-14-036599-0) Puffin Bks.

— The Changeover: A Supernatural Romance. LC 83-83446. 224p. (YA). (gr. 7 up). 1984. text ed. 14.95 (0-689-50303-2, McElderry) S&S Childrens.

— The Chewing-Gum Rescue & Other Stories. (Illus.). 142p. (J). (gr. 3-7). 1991. 12.95 (0-87951-424-8) Overlook Pr.

— The Chewing Gum Rescue & Other Stories. LC 93-35963. 192p. (J). (gr. 5 up). 1994. reprint ed. pap. 4.95 (0-688-12798-3, Pub. by Beech Tree Bks) Morrow.

— Clancy's Cabin. LC 94-46278. (Illus.). (J). 1995. 13.95 (0-87951-592-9) Overlook Pr.

— Dangerous Spaces. 160p. (J). (gr. 5 up). 1993. pap. 3.99 (0-14-036362-9, Puffin) Puffin Bks.

— Dangerous Spaces. (YA). 1991. 12.95 (0-670-83734-2) Viking Child Bks.

— Door in the Air. (J). (gr. 4-7). 1993. pap. 3.50 (0-440-40774-5) Dell.

— The Dragon of an Ordinary Family. LC 91-2513. (Illus.). 48p. (J). (ps-3). 1992. 14.00 (0-8037-1062-3) Dial Bks Young.

— A Fortunate Name. LC 93-560. (J). 1993. 13.95 (0-385-31135-4) Delacorte.

— A Fortunate Name Bk. 2: The Cousins Quartet. (Cousins Quartet Ser.: Bk. 2). (Illus.). (J). (gr. 2-7). 1995. mass mkt. 3.50 (0-440-41065-7) Dell.

— A Fortune Branches Out. LC 93-11441. (Cousins Quartet Ser.: Bk. 3). (Illus.). (J). 1994. 13.95 (0-385-32037-X) Delacorte.

— The Girl with the Green Ear: Stories about Magic in Nature. LC 91-14992. (Illus.). 112p. (J). (gr. 3-7). 1992. 15.00 (0-679-82231-3); lib. bdg. 15.99 (0-679-92231-8) Knopf Bks Yng Read.

— The Girl with the Green Ear: Stories about Magic in Nature. LC 91-14992. (Illus.). 112p. (J). (gr. 3-7). 1993. pap. 3.25 (0-679-84000-1, Bullseye Bks) Knopf Bks Yng Read.

— The Good Fortunes Gang. LC 92-38784. (J). (gr. 5 up). 1993. 13.95 (0-385-31015-3) Delacorte.

— Good Fortunes Gang No. 1: The Cousins Quartet. (J). (gr. 4-7). 1995. pap. 3.50 (0-440-41060-6) Dell.

— The Good Fortunes Gang, Bk. 1: Cousins Quartet. large type ed. (Illus.). (J). (gr. 1-8). 1994. 16.95 (0-7451-2222-1, Galaxy Child Lrg Print) Chivers N Amer.

— The Great Piratical Rumbustification & The Librarian & The Robbers. LC 92-43777. (Illus.). 64p. (J). (gr. 5 up). 1993. pap. 3.95 (0-688-12469-0, Pub. by Beech Tree Bks) Morrow.

— Great Piratical Rumbustification the Librarian & the Robbers. LC 85-45966. (Illus.). 64p. (J). 1986. 11.95 (0-87923-629-9) Godine.

— The Great White Man-Eating Shark: A Cautionary Tale. (Illus.). (J). (ps-3). 1990. 13.99 (0-8037-0749-5) Dial Bks Young.

— The Greatest Show off Earth. (Illus.). 160p. (J). (gr. 3-7). 1994. 13.99 (0-670-85736-X) Viking Child Bks.

— The Haunting. LC 82-3983. 144p. (J). (gr. 5-9). 1982. text ed. 13.95 (0-689-50243-5, McElderry) S&S Childrens.

— The Horrendous Hullabaloo. (Illus.). 28p. (J). (ps-3). 1994. pap. 4.99 (0-14-055322-3) Puffin Bks.

— The Horrendous Hullabaloo. (Illus.). 32p. (J). (ps-3). 1992. 13.00 (0-670-84547-7) Viking Child Bks.

— Keeping House. LC 90-37591. (Illus.). 32p. (J). (gr. k-4). 1991. text ed. 13.95 (0-689-50515-9, McElderry) S&S Childrens.

— A Lion in the Meadow. (Illus.). 32p. (J). (ps-3). 1992. 13. 95 (0-87951-446-9) Overlook Pr.

— Making Friends. LC 89-13246. (Illus.). 32p. (J). (gr. k-3). 1990. text ed. 13.95 (0-689-50498-5, McElderry) S&S Childrens.

— Memory. LC 87-21427. 288p. (J). (gr. 9 up). 1988. text ed. 14.95 (0-689-50446-2, McElderry) S&S Childrens.

— My Mysterious World. LC 95-1291. (Meet the Author Collection). (Illus.). 32p. (J). (gr. 2-5). 1995. 13.95x (1-878450-58-1) R Owen Pubs.

— Nonstop Nonsense. LC 88-8401. (Illus.). 128p. (J). (gr. 1-5). 1989. text ed. 13.95 (0-689-50483-7, McElderry) S&S Childrens.

— The Other Side of Silence. LC 95-8615. (J). 1995. write for info. (0-670-86455-2, Viking) Viking Penguin.

— The Pirate Uncle. (Illus.). 128p. (J). (gr. 3-7). 1994. 13.95 (0-87951-555-4) Overlook Pr.

— The Pirates' Mixed-up Voyage. LC 92-3931. (Illus.). 192p. (J). (gr. 4-8). 1993. 13.99 (0-8037-1350-9) Dial Bks Young.

— The Pirates' Mixed-up Voyage. (Illus.). 192p. (J). 1995. pap. 3.99 (0-14-037128-1) Puffin Bks.

— Pumpkin Man & the Crafty Creeper. (J). (ps-3). 1991. 14. 95 (0-688-10347-2); 14.88 (0-688-10348-0) Lothrop.

— Raging Robots & Unruly Uncles. (Illus.). 94p. (J). (gr. 3-7). 1993. 13.95 (0-87951-469-8) Overlook Pr.

— The Rattlebang Picnic. LC 93-36294. (Illus.). (J). (gr. 3 up). 1994. 14.99 (0-8037-1318-5); lib. bdg. 14.89 (0-8037-1319-3) Dial Bks Young.

— Seven Chinese Brothers. (J). (ps-3). 1990. pap. 14.95 (0-590-42055-0) Scholastic Inc.

— Seven Chinese Brothers. (J). 1992. pap. 3.95 (0-590-42057-7) Scholastic Inc.

— Seventeen Kings & Forty-Two Elephants. LC 87-5311. (Illus.). 32p. (J). (ps-3). 1987. 14.99 (0-8037-0458-5) Dial Bks Young.

— Seventeen Kings & Forty-Two Elephants. Fogelman, Phyllis J., ed. LC 87-5311. (Illus.). 32p. (J). (ps-3). 1990. pap. 4.95 (0-8037-0781-9) Dial Bks Young.

— Los Siete Hermanos Chinos - The Seven Chinese Brothers. (J). (ps-3). 1994. pap. 3.95 (0-590-48131-2) Scholastic Inc.

— A Tall Story & Other Tales. LC 91-62222. (Illus.). 96p. (J). (gr. 3-7). 1992. lib. bdg. 15.95 (0-689-50547-7, McElderry) S&S Childrens.

— Tangled Fortunes. LC 93-32202. (Cousins Quartet Ser.: Bk. 4). (J). 1994. 14.95 (0-385-32066-3) Delacorte.

— The Three-Legged Cat. (Illus.). 32p. (J). (ps-3). 1993. 13. 99 (0-670-85015-2) Viking Child Bks.

— The Three-Legged Cat. (Illus.). 32p. (J). (ps-3). 1995. pap. 4.99 (0-14-055331-2) Puffin Bks.

— Tick Tock Tales. (Illus.). 96p. (J). (gr. k-4). 1994. lib. bdg. 16.95 (0-689-50604-X, McElderry) S&S Childrens.

— The Tricksters. LC 86-33761. 272p. (YA). (gr. 9 up). 1987. text ed. 14.95 (0-689-50400-4, McElderry) S&S Childrens.

— Underrunners. 176p. (J). (gr. 5 up). 1994. pap. 3.99 (0-14-036869-8) Puffin Bks.

— Underrunners. 192p. (J). (gr. 5-9). 1992. 14.00 (0-670-84179-X) Viking Child Bks.

— When the King Rides By. (Illus.). 16p. (Orig.). (J). (ps-2). 1995. 21.95 (1-57255-003-1); pap. 4.95 (1-57255-002-3) Mondo Pubng.

Mahy, Margaret & Chamberlain, Margaret. The Man Whose Mother Was a Pirate. (Illus.). (J). (gr. 3-7). 1987. reprint ed. pap. 4.99 (0-14-050624-1, Puffin) Puffin Bks.

***Mahy, Margarte.** Christmas Tree Tangle. (J). 1994. 15.59 (0-689-50616-3, McElderry) S&S Childrens.

Mahyuddin, Jan, jt. ed. see Gunew, Sneja.

Mai-Aru & Anisson du Perron, J. Dictionnaire Francais-Tahitien et Tahitien-Francais: Tahitian - French - Tahitian Dictionary. 380p. (FRE.). 1973. 39.95 (0-8288-6267-2, M-6383) Fr & Eur.

Mai, Charles F. Secrets of Major Gift Fund Raising. LC 87-25568. 170p. 1987. 25.95 (0-914756-39-7) Taft Group.

Mai Chin. New Chinese Cooking Class Cookbook. 1991. 12. 99 (0-517-03077-2) Random Hse Value.

Mai, Ekkehard, et al. Three Centuries of German Painting & Drawing: From the Collections of the Wallraf-Richartz Musuem, Cologne. LC 85-14261. (Illus.). 224p. 1985. pap. 24.95 (0-295-96437-5, Smithsonian Traveling) U of Wash Pr.

***Mai, Hoang D.** Tinh-Yeu Trong Doi Thuong. 104p. Date not set. pap. text ed. 7.50 (1-885550-03-0) Du-Sinh St Joseph.

Mai, Ludwig H. Men & Ideas in Economics: A Dictionary of World Economists Past & Present. (Quality Paperbacks Ser.: No. 284). 270p. (Orig.). 1977. reprint ed. pap. 9.95 (0-8226-0284-9) Rowman.

Mai, Nguyen T. The Rubber Tree: Memoir of a Vietnamese Woman Who Was an Anti-French Guerrilla, a Publisher & a Peace Activist. 272p. 1994. lib. bdg. 29.95 (0-89950-954-1) McFarland & Co.

Mai, Ulrich, jt. ed. see Buchholt, Helmut.

***Mai, William F., et al.** Plant-Parasitic Nematodes: A Pictorial Key to Genera. 5th ed. (Comstock Book Ser.). (Illus.). 288p. 1996. 49.95x (0-8014-3116-6) Cornell U Pr.

Maia, Fred, jt. auth. see West, Gordon.

Maia Neto, Jose R., jt. auth. see Neto, Jose R.

***Maia, Ronaldo.** More Decorating with Flowers. Otis, Denise, ed. LC 95-2340. 1995. write for info. (0-8109-8141-6, Abradale Pr) Abrams.

Maia, Ronaldo & Otis, Denise. More Decorating with Flowers. (Illus.). 208p. 1991. 60.00 (0-8109-3622-4) Abrams.

Maiakovskii, V. V. Chelovek, Sobytiia Vremiia. 184p. 1984. 75.00 (0-685-12134-8, Pub. by Collets UK) St Mut.

Maibach & Boisits. Neonatal Skin: Structure & Function. (Dermatology Ser.: Vol. 1). 296p. 1982. 110.00 (0-8247-1860-7) Dekker.

Maibach, jt. auth. see Bronaugh.

Maibach, jt. auth. see Orkin.

***Maibach, Edward & Parrot, Roxanne L.** Designing Health Messages: Public Health Practice & Communication Theory. 250p. 1995. text ed. 42.00 (0-8039-5397-6); pap. text ed. 21.95 (0-8039-5398-4) Sage.

Maibach, H., jt. ed. see Roenigk, Henry H.

Maibach, H., jt. auth. see Steigleder, G. K.

Maibach, H. I. & Lowe, N. J., eds. Dermatology. (Models in Dermatology Ser.: No. 1). (Illus.). x, 374p. 1984. 166. 75 (3-8055-3945-2) S Karger.

— Dermatopharmacology & Toxicology. (Models in Dermatology Ser.: No. 2). (Illus.). x, 370p. 1984. 200.00 (3-8055-3947-9) S Karger.

— Models in Dermatology, Vol. 4. x, 298p. 1989. 296.00 (3-8055-4761-7) S Karger.

— Models in Dermatology, 1987, Vol. 3. xvi, 204p. 1987. 200.00 (3-8055-4239-9) S Karger.

Maibach, H. I. & Surber, C., eds. Topical Corticosteroids. (Illus.). viii, 518p. 1991. 253.75 (3-8055-5332-3) S Karger.

Maibach, H. I., jt. ed. see Andersen, K. E.

Maibach, H. I., jt. ed. see Elsner, P.

Maibach, H. I., jt. ed. see Kortin, H. C.

Maibach, Howard, jt. auth. see Reeves, John R.

Maibach, Howard, et al. Handbook of Contact Dermatitis. 350p. 1995. 69.95 (0-8493-7351-4) CRC Pr.

***Maibach, Howard I.** Dermatologic Research Techniques. 240p. 1995. 85.00 (0-8493-8373-0, 8373) CRC Pr.

Maibach, Howard I., ed. Animal Models in Dermatology, Relevance to Human Dermatopharmacology & Dermatotoxicology: Proceedings of a Symposium, University of California Medical School, San Francisco. LC 75-16283. 288p. reprint ed. pap. 82.10 (0-8357-5489-8, 2056327) Bks Demand.

Maibach, Howard I., jt. auth. see Bronaugh, Robert L.

Maibach, Howard I., jt. ed. see Marzulli, Francis N.

Maibach, Howard I., jt. ed. see Menne, Torkil.

Maibach, Howard I., jt. ed. see Shah, V. P.

Maibach, Howard I., jt. ed. see Smith, Eric W.

Maiback, ed. Nickel & the Skin. 1989. 144.00 (0-8493-6976-2, RL803) CRC Pr.

Maiben, Dina, jt. auth. see Zlotowitz, Bernard M.

Maibum, Thomas S., jt. auth. see Turski, Wladyslaw M.

Maickel, R. Biochemical Factors in Alcoholism. LC 66-27641. 1967. 115.00 (0-08-012045-8, Pub. by Pergamon Repr UK) Franklin.

Maid, Amy. Communication As a Second Language, 5 pts. Incl. Pt. 1. Language. 1978. pap. 7.95 (0-916250-28-8); Pt. 2. Ideas. 1978. pap. 7.95 (0-916250-29-6); Pt. 3. Mass Communication. 1978. pap. 7.95 (0-916250-30-X); Pt. 4. Print. 1978. pap. 7.95 (0-916250-31-8); Pt. 5. Airwaves & Beyond. 1978. pap. 7.95 (0-916250-32-6); (Mandala Series in Education). (Illus.). write for info. (0-318-53705-2) Irvington.

— Mindscapes. LC 82-9904. 67p. (J). (gr. 3-8). 1983. pap. 11.95 (0-8290-1001-7) Irvington.

— Write from the Beginning. (Illus.). 94p. (Orig.). (J). (gr. k-5). 1987. pap. 19.95x (0-8290-0993-0) Irvington.

Maid, Amy & Timmekmann, Tim. Something for 10:30: Involvement Cards for Social Skills. rev. ed. LC 77-92392. (Illus.). 158p. (YA). (gr. 7-12). 1987. pap. 29.95x (0-8290-0353-3) Irvington.

Maida, Carl A., et al. The Crisis of Competence: Transitional Stress & the Displaced Worker. LC 89-15825. (Psychosocial Stress Ser.: No. 16). 224p. 1990. 29.95 (0-87630-559-1) Brunner-Mazel.

Maida, Pamela. Freedom of Information Case List, Sept. 1990 Edition. 637p. 1990. per. 20.00 (0-16-026645-9, S/N 027-000-01336-8) USGPO.

Maida, Patricia. Mother of Detective Fiction: The Life & Works of Anna Katharine Green. 120p. 1989. lib. bdg. 24.95 (0-87972-445-5); pap. text ed. 12.95 (0-87972-446-3) Bowling Green Univ.

Maida, Patricia D. & Spornick, Nicholas B. Murder She Wrote: A Study of Agatha Christie's Detective Fiction. 199p. 1982. 16.95 (0-87972-215-0) Bowling Green Univ.

Maida, Peter R., jt. ed. see Volpe, Maria R.

Maida, Shuichi. The Evil Person: Essays on Shin Buddhism. Haneda, Nobuo, tr. & intro. by. LC 88-84034. 101p. (Orig.). (C). 1989. pap. 8.00 (0-9622047-0-6) HHNATC.

— Heard by Me: Essays on My Buddhist Teacher. Haneda, Nobuo, ed. & tr. by. LC 90-82529. 242p. (Orig.). 1992. pap. 15.00 (0-9627231-0-X) Frog Pr.

Maidat, Rita. The Twins Visit Israel. (Shayna & Keppi Ser.). (Illus.). (J). (gr. 3-10). 1978. pap. 2.00 (0-914080-72-5) Shulsinger Sales.

***Maiden, Herman.** Real Estate Brokers' Mathematics: Easy Method. 1995. 9.95 (0-8062-5045-3) Carlton.

Maiden, Martin. Interactive Morphonology: Metaphony in Italy. (Romance Linguistics Ser.). (Illus.). 316p. 1991. 85.00 (0-415-02639-3, A5545) Routledge.

— A Linguistic History of Italian. LC 93-46832. (Longman Linguistics Library). 1994. write for info. (0-582-05929-1, Pub. by Longman UK); pap. write for info. (0-582-05928-3, Pub. by Longman UK) Longman.

Maiden, Martin, jt. ed. see Smith, John C.

Maiden, Mike. The Joshua Generation: God's Conquering Manifesto. Walker, Jeff E., ed. 193p. (Orig.). (C). 1990. pap. text ed. 7.95 (0-9626327-1-6) Victory Chris Ctr.

Maiden, Neil, jt. ed. see Walton, Paul.

Maiden, R. Paul, ed. Employee Assistance Programs in South Africa. LC 92-12236. (Employee Assistance Quarterly Ser.: Vol. 7, No. 3). (Illus.). 145p. 1992. text ed. 29.95 (1-56024-302-3) Haworth Pr.

Maiden, Robert J., jt. auth. see Peterson, Steven A.

Maidens, Melinda, ed. American Technology: Are We Falling Behind? LC 82-15603. 191p. reprint ed. pap. 54. 50 (0-8357-3493-5, 2039752) Bks Demand.

— Immigration: New Americans, Old Questions. LC 81-9914. 198p. reprint ed. pap. 56.50 (0-685-15580-3, 2027220) Bks Demand.

— Life, Death & the Government. fac. ed. LC 80-29094. (Illus.). 200p. 1980. reprint ed. pap. 57.00 (0-7837-8143-1, 2047951) Bks Demand.

— Religion, Morality & the "New Right" LC 82-2333. (Illus.). 224p. reprint ed. pap. 63.90 (0-8357-4242-3, 2037030) Bks Demand.

Maidens, Melinda, jt. ed. see Burr, Jeanne.

Maidigue, Modesto A., jt. auth. see Burgelman, Robert A.

Maidique, Modesto A., jt. auth. see Burgelman, Robert A.

Maidman, Frank, ed. Child Welfare: A Source Book of Knowledge & Practice. 454p. 1984. 32.95 (0-87868-236-8) Child Welfare.

Maidman, M. P. Two Hundred Nuzi Texts from the Oriental Institute of the University of Chicago, Pt. I. (Studies on the Civilization & Culture of Nuzi & the Hurrians: Vol. 6). 449p. (C). 1994. 50.00 (1-883053-05-6) CDL Pr.

Maidman, Maynard P., jt. auth. see Lacheman, Ernest R.

Maidment, David R. Handbook of Hydrology. 1424p. 1993. text ed. 115.50 (0-07-039732-5) McGraw.

Maidment, Fred. Annual Editions: Human Resources 95-96. 5th ed. 256p. 1995. pap. text ed. 12.95 (1-56134-338-2) Dushkin Pub.

***Maidment, Fred H., ed.** Annual Editions: International Business, 95-96. 4th rev. ed. (Illus.). 256p. (C). 1995. pap. text ed. 12.95x (1-56134-361-7) Dushkin Pub.

— Annual Editions: Management 94-95. 3rd rev. ed. (Illus.). 256p. 1994. pap. text ed. 12.95x (1-56134-281-5) Dushkin Pub.

Maidment, James. Chronicle of Perth. LC 72-1038. (Maitland Club, Glasgow. Publications: No. 10). reprint ed. 10.00 (0-404-52939-9) AMS Pr.

— Notices Relative to the Bannatyne Club. LC 70-172715. (Bannatyne Club, Edinburgh. Publications). reprint ed. 25.00 (0-404-52887-2) AMS Pr.

— Scottish Ballads & Songs, Historical & Traditionary, 2 Vols, 1. LC 78-144497. reprint ed. write for info. (0-404-08671-3) AMS Pr.

M

— Scottish Ballads & Songs, Historical & Traditionary, 2 Vols, 2. LC 78-144497. reprint ed. write for info. (*0-404-08672-1*) AMS Pr.

— Scottish Ballads & Songs, Historical & Traditionary, 2 Vols, Set. LC 78-144497. reprint ed. 67.50 (*0-404-08670-5*) AMS Pr.

Maidment, James, ed. see Cokain, Aston.

Maidment, James, ed. see Crowne, John.

Maidment, James, ed. see Lacy, John.

Maidment, James, ed. see Marmion, Shakerley.

Maidment, James, ed. see Tatham, John.

Maidment, James, ed. see Wilson, John.

Maidment, K. J., tr. Minor Attic Orators, Vol. 1. Incl. Antiphon & Andocides. (*0-318-53113-5*); (Loeb Classical Library: No. 308). 15.50 (*0-674-99340-3*) HUP.

Maidment, Margaret. A Manual of Hand-Made Bobbin Lace Work. (Illus.). 1983. 22.50 (*0-7134-3855-X*) Robin & Russ.

Maidment, Patricia. How to Build & Furnish a Dollhouse for 100 Dollars or Less. LC 82-17778. 224p. 1983. pap. write for info. (*0-672-52745-6*) Macmillan.

Maidment, Richard. American Politics Today. 4th ed. (Politics Today Ser.). 248p. 1994. text ed. write for info. (*0-7190-3939-8*, Pub. by Manchester Univ Pr UK); text ed. write for info. (*0-7190-3940-1*, Pub. by Manchester Univ Pr UK) St Martin.

***Maidment, Richard, ed.** Democracy. (The U. S. in the Twentieth Century Ser.). 288p. 1994. pap. 14.95 (*0-340-59686-4*, Pub. by E Arnld UK) St Martin.

***Maidment, Richard & Dawson, Michael, eds.** Key Documents. 288p. 1994. pap. 14.95 (*0-340-59689-9*, Pub. by E Arnld UK) St Martin.

Maidment, Richard & Thompson, Grahame. Managing the United Kingdom: An Introduction to Its Political Economy & Public Policy. (Illus.). 288p. (C). 1993. text ed. 59.95 (*0-8039-8850-8*); pap. text ed. 21.95 (*0-8039-8851-6*) Sage.

Maidment, Richard, jt. ed. see Mitchell, Jeremy.

Maidment, Richard A. The Judicial Response to the New Deal. 204p. 1992. text ed. 59.95 (*0-7190-3332-2*, Pub. by Manchester Univ Pr UK) St Martin.

Maidment, Richard A. & McGrew, Anthony G. The American Political Process. 2nd ed. (Illus.). 224p. 1991. text ed. 49.95 (*0-8039-8525-8*); pap. text ed. 19.95 (*0-8039-8434-0*) Sage.

Maidment, Robert. Decisions: Perspectives for the School Administrator. 48p. 1986. pap. 6.00 (*0-88210-192-7*) Natl Assn Student.

— Robert's Rules of Disorder: A Guide to Mismanagement. 112p. 1990. 6.95 (*0-88289-111-1*) Pelican.

— Straight Talk: A Guide to Saying More with Less. LC 82-12211. 112p. (Orig.). 1983. pap. 5.95 (*0-88289-340-8*) Pelican.

— Tuning In. LC 84-5259. 86p. (Orig.). 1984. pap. 5.95 (*0-88289-439-0*) Pelican.

— Write It Right. LC 87-2247. 112p. (Orig.). 1987. pap. 5.95 (*0-88289-647-4*) Pelican.

Maidment, Robert & Bullock, William. Meetings, Meetings, Meetings: Accomplishing More with Better & Fewer. George, Patricia L., ed. 48p. (Orig.). 1984. pap. 6.00 (*0-88210-162-5*) Natl Assn Principals.

Maidment, Robert & Hanny, Robert. The Group: Dealing with Difficult People. (Illus.). 98p. (Orig.). 1988. pap. 4.95 (*0-935005-92-7*) Lincoln-Rembrandt.

Maidment, William. Triple Play. 160p. (Orig.). 1993. pap. 4.95 (*0-9619930-9-X*) Moonfall Pr VA.

Maidoff, Ilka. Let's Explore the Shore. (Illus.). (J). (gr. 5 up). 1962. 9.95 (*0-8392-3017-6*) Astor-Honor.

Maienschein, Jane. One Hundred Years Exploring Life, 1888-1988, the Marine Biological Laboratory at Woods Hole. 208p. 1989. pap. 24.95 (*0-86720-120-7*) Jones & Bartlett.

— Transforming Traditions in American Biology, 1880-1915. LC 90-15623. (Illus.). 288p. 1991. text ed. 48.00 (*0-8018-4126-7*) Johns Hopkins.

Maienschein, Jane, ed. Defining Biology. LC 86-307. (Illus.). 352p. 1986. 35.00 (*0-674-19615-5*) HUP.

Maier, ed. Ion & Cluster Ion Spectroscopy & Structure. 484p. 1989. 169.25 (*0-444-87283-3*) Elsevier.

Maier, A. English in the Cockpit. 400p. (ENG & GER.). 1986. lib. bdg. 85.00 (*0-8288-3400-8*, F41073) Fr & Eur.

***Maier, Albert M.** Friendly Concern. 14p. (Orig.). 1994. pap. write for info. (*1-885206-13-5*, Iliad Pr) Cader Pubng.

Maier, Ann H. The Day Care Directory: Fairfield County, 1991. 368p. (Orig.). 1991. pap. write for info. (*0-9626513-0-3*) Schl Hse Pubns.

Maier, Anne M. Mother Love, Deadly Love: The Texas Cheerleader Murder Plot. (Illus.). 256p. 1992. 18.95 (*1-55972-137-5*, Birch Ln Pr) Carol Pub Group.

Maier, Arlee S., jt. auth. see Guerin, Gilbert R.

Maier, B., jt. auth. see Suck, J. B.

Maier, Beatrice R., tr. see Graf, Max.

***Maier, C.** Integrated Management of Tentiform Leafminers, Phyllonorycter spp. (Lepidoptera: Gracillariidae), in North American Apple Orchards. (Thomas Say Proceedings Ser.). 82p. 1994. 22.00 (*0-938522-48-5*) Entomol Soc.

Maier, Carol & Salper, Roberta L., eds. Ramon Maria del Valle-Inclan: Questions of Gender. LC 93-42561. 1994. write for info. (*0-8387-5261-6*) Bucknell U Pr.

Maier, Carol, tr. see Armand, Octavio.

Maier, Carol, jt. ed. see Dingwaney, Anuradha.

Maier, Carol, tr. see Sarduy, Severo.

Maier, Carol, jt. ed. see Valis, Noel.

Maier, Charles S. Changing Boundaries of the Political: Essays on the Evolving Balance Between the State & Society, Public & Private in Europe. (Cambridge Studies in Modern Political Economies). (Illus.). 432p. 1987. 69.95 (*0-521-34366-6*); pap. 19.95 (*0-521-34847-1*) Cambridge U Pr.

— In Search of Stability: Explorations in Historical Political Economy. (Studies in Modern Political Economies). 288p. 1988. 54.95 (*0-521-23001-2*); pap. 17.95 (*0-521-34698-3*) Cambridge U Pr.

— Recasting Bourgeois Europe: Stabilization in France, Germany, & Italy in the Decade After World War One. LC 73-2488. 700p. 1988. pap. 24.95 (*0-691-10025-X*) Princeton U Pr.

— The Unmasterable Past: History, Holocaust, & German National Identity. LC 88-11690. 240p. 1988. 33.95 (*0-674-92975-6*) HUP.

— The Unmasterable Past: History, Holocaust, & German National Identity. 240p. 1990. pap. text ed. 12.00 (*0-674-92976-4*) HUP.

Maier, Charles S., ed. Cold War in Europe. LC 90-13075. 420p. (Orig.). (C). 1991. 38.95 (*1-55876-029-6*); pap. text ed. 18.95 (*1-55876-034-2*) Wiener Pubs Inc.

Maier, Charles S. & Bischof, Gunter, eds. The Marshall Plan & Germany: West German Development Within the Framework of the European Recovery Program. LC 89-39742. 536p. 1991. 79.95 (*0-85496-306-5*) Berg Pubs.

Maier, Charles S., jt. auth. see Kistiakowsky, George B.

Maier, Charles S., jt. ed. see Lindberg, Leon N.

Maier, Christoph T. Preaching the Crusades: Mendicant Friars & the Cross in the Thirteenth Century. LC 93-32162. (Studies in Medieval Life & Thought: No. 28). 212p. (C). 1994. 44.95 (*0-521-45246-5*) Cambridge U Pr.

Maier, David & Warren, David. Computing with Logic: Logic Programming with PROLOG. 475p. (C). 1988. pap. text ed. 44.25 (*0-8053-6681-4*) Benjamin-Cummings.

Maier, David, jt. ed. see Atkinson, Malcolm.

Maier, David, jt. ed. see Zdonik, Stanley.

Maier, Donna J. Priests & Power: The Case of the Dente Shrine in Nineteenth-Century Ghana. LC 82-48582. (Illus.). 271p. reprint ed. pap. 77.30 (*0-7837-3717-3*, 2057895) Bks Demand.

Maier, Elaine C. How to Prepare a Legal Citation. 192p. 1986. pap. 11.95 (*0-8120-2960-7*) Barron.

***Maier, Ernest.** Cases in Business to Business Relationship Selling. 4th ed. LC 95-5112. 1995. pap. text ed. write for info. (*0-13-340290-8*) P-H.

Maier, Ernest, et al, eds. Business Library & How to Use It. 300p. 1995. lib. bdg. 45.00 (*0-7808-0026-5*) Omnigraphics Inc.

Maier, Eugene, jt. auth. see Arcidiacono, Michael J.

Maier, Frith. Trekking in Russia & Central Asia, a Traveler's Guide: Urals, Pamirs, Caucasus, Siberia, Lake Baikal, Crimean Peninsula, Kamchatka Peninsula. (Illus.). 320p. 1994. pap. 16.95 (*0-89886-355-4*) Mountaineers.

Maier, G., ed. Case Histories in Offshore Engineering. (CISM International Centre for Mechanical Sciences Ser.: Vol. 283). (Illus.). ix, 365p. 1985. pap. 54.00 (*0-387-81817-0*) Spr-Verlag.

Maier, G., jt. ed. see Brebbia, C. A.

Maier, Gerhard. Biblical Hermeneutics. Yarbrough, Robert W., tr. LC 93-42342. 560p. (Orig.). 1994. pap. 22.00 (*0-89107-767-7*) Crossway Bks.

Maier, Harold G., jt. auth. see Buergenthal, Thomas.

Maier, Harry O. The Social Setting of the Ministry As Reflected in the Writing of Hermas, Clement & Ignatius. (Dissertations SR Ser.: Vol. 1). 232p. (C). 1991. pap. 25.00 (*0-88920-995-2*, Pub. by Wilfrid Laurier CN) Humanities.

Maier, Heinrich. Die Syllogistik Des Aristoteles, 2 vols. in 3, Set. xxiv, 1195p. 1969. reprint ed. write for info. (*0-318-70973-2*, Pub. by Georg Olms GW) Lubrecht & Cramer.

***Maier, Hendrik M.** In the Center of Authority: The Malay Hikayat Merong Mahawangsa. LC 89-157454. (Studies on Southeast Asia). 210p. (Orig.). 1988. pap. 59.90 (*0-7837-8497-X*, 2049304) Bks Demand.

Maier, Henry W. The Mayor Who Made Milwaukee Famous: An Autobiography. LC 92-30042. 304p. 1993. 24.95 (*0-8191-8621-X*) Madison Bks UPA.

Maier, Henry W., et al. Developmental Group Care of Children & Youth: Concepts & Practice. LC 87-7421. (Child & Youth Services Ser.: Vol. 9, No. 2). 233p. 1987. text ed. 49.95 (*0-86656-655-4*) Haworth Pr.

Maier, Johann. Geschichte der Juedischen Religion: Von der Zeit Alexanders des Grossen bis zur Aufklaerung. Mit einem Ausblick auf das 19.-20. Jahrhundert. LC 72-77437. xx, 641p. (GER.). (C). 1972. 60.00 (*3-11-002448-9*) De Gruyter.

Maier, John, jt. ed. see Tollers, Vincent L.

Maier, John R., jt. tr. see Gardner, John C.

Maier, John R., jt. auth. see Kramer, Samuel N.

Maier, Josef. On Hegel's Critique of Kant. LC 39-31564. reprint ed. 20.00 (*0-404-04168-X*) AMS Pr.

Maier, Joseph B. & Waxman, Chaim I., eds. Ethnicity, Identity & History: Essays in Memory of Werner J. Cahnman. LC 82-6928. (Illus.). 350p. 1983. 42.95x (*0-87855-461-0*) Transaction Pubs.

Maier, Joseph B., et al, eds. German Jewry: Its History & Sociology: Selected Essays of Werner J. Cahnman. 250p. 1989. 39.95 (*0-88738-253-3*) Transaction Pubs.

Maier, Jul. J., ed. see Oeglin, Erhart.

Maier, Klaus A., et al. Germany & the Second World War, Vol. 2: Germany's Initial Conquests in Europe. McMurry, Dean S. & Osers, Ewald, trs. (Illus.). 464p. 1991. 75.00 (*0-19-822885-6*, 12188) OUP.

Maier, Leo. The Costs & Benefits of U. S. Agricultural Policies with Imperfect Competition in Food Manufacturing. LC 92-36023. (Government & the Economy Ser.). 328p. 1993. 70.00 (*0-8153-1233-4*) Garland.

Maier, Mark H. City Unions: Managing Discontent in New York City. 214p. 1987. pap. text ed. 15.00 (*0-8135-1229-8*) Rutgers U Pr.

— The Data Game: Controversies in Social Science Statistics. 264p. (C). 1991. 49.95 (*0-87332-588-5*); pap. text ed. 20.95 (*0-87332-768-3*) M E Sharpe.

— The Data Game: Controversies in Social Science Statistics. 2nd rev. ed. (Illus.). 300p. 1995. 55.00 (*1-56324-481-0*); pap. text ed. 21.95 (*1-56324-482-9*) M E Sharpe.

Maier, Michael. Atalanta Fugiens: An Edition of the Emblems, Fugues & Epigrams. Godwin, Joscelyn, tr. LC 89-34804. (Magnum Opus Hermetic Sourceworks Ser.: No. 22). (Illus.). 215p. (Orig.). 1989. And cassette. 50.00 (*0-933999-81-X*); And cassette. pap. 26.00 (*0-933999-82-8*) Phanes Pr.

— Laws of the Fraternity of the Rosie Crosse (Themis Aurea) 14.50 (*0-89314-402-9*) Philos Res.

— The Secrets of Alchemy. 1984. reprint ed. pap. 3.95 (*0-916411-17-6*) Holmes Pub.

Maier, Norman R. Frustration: The Study of Behavior Without a Goal. (Ann Arbor Paperbacks Ser.: No. 48). 264p. reprint ed. pap. 75.30 (*0-317-08177-2*, 2055628) Bks Demand.

— Frustration: The Study of Behavior Without a Goal. LC 81-20092. (Illus.). 264p. 1982. reprint ed. text ed. 59.75 (*0-313-23340-3*, MAFRU, Greenwood Pr) Greenwood.

Maier, Norman R. & Verser, Trudy G. Psychology in Industrial Organizations, 5 Vols. 5th ed. LC 81-81702. (Illus.). 672p. (C). 1981. teacher ed, pap. 1.56 (*0-395-31741-X*) HM.

— Psychology in Industrial Organizations, 5 Vols. 5th ed. LC 81-81702. (Illus.). 672p. (C). 1982. text ed. 55.56 (*0-395-31740-1*) HM.

***Maier, Paul L.** Flames of Rome. 456p. 1995. pap. 10.99 (*0-8254-3297-9*) Kregel.

— The Flames of Rome. LC 90-28622. 456p. 1991. reprint ed. 19.99 (*0-8254-3262-6*) Kregel.

— Josefo: Las Obras Esceniales (Full-Color Edition) (Illus.). 416p. (SPA.). 1995. pap. 24.99 (*0-8254-1457-1*) Kregel.

— Pontius Pilate. 384p. 1995. pap. 10.99 (*0-8254-3296-0*) Kregel.

— Pontius Pilate: A Biographical Novel. LC 68-10585. 384p. 1990. 16.99 (*0-8254-3261-8*) Kregel.

Maier, Paul L., ed. Josefo: Los Escritos Esenciales. Orig. Title: Josephus: The Essential Writings. 400p. (SPA.). 1992. 14.99 (*0-8254-1456-3*) Kregel.

Maier, Paul L., ed. see Josephus, Flavius.

Maier, Pauline. From Resistance to Revolution: Colonial Radicals & the Development of American Opposition to Britain, 1765-1776. 360p. 1992. pap. 11.95 (*0-393-30825-1*) Norton.

— Old Revolutionaries: Political Lives in the Age of Samuel Adams. 1990. pap. 10.95 (*0-393-30663-1*) Norton.

Maier, Richard A. Human Sexuality in Perspective. LC 83-11478. (Illus.). 576p. (C). 1984. write for info. (*0-8304-1107-0*) Nelson-Hall.

Maier, Robert. Location Scouting & Management Handbook: Television, Film & Still Photography. (Illus.). 160p. 1994. pap. 19.95 (*0-240-80152-0*, Focal) Buttrwrth-Heinemann.

Maier, Robert, ed. Norms in Argumentation. (Studies of Argumentation in Pragmatic & Discourse Analysis). 218p. (Orig.). (C). 1989. pap. 67.70 (*90-6765-423-X*) Mouton.

Maier, Robert, jt. ed. see De Graaf, Willibrord.

Maier, Sarah, ed. see Hardy, Thomas.

Maier, Thomas. Newhouse: All the Glitter, Power & Glory in America's Richest Media Empire & the Secretive Man Behind It. 480p. 1994. 24.95 (*0-312-11481-8*, Pub. by Thomas Dunne Bks) St Martin.

Maier, Walter A., III. Aserah: Extrabiblical Evidence. LC 86-15596. (Harvard Semitic Monographs). 274p. 1987. 24.95 (*1-55540-046-9*, 04-00-37) Scholars Pr GA.

Maier, Walter A. & Maier, Walter A. Nahum. 1987. 19.95 (*0-570-04238-0*, 15-1728) Concordia.

Maier, Walter A., jt. auth. see Maier, Walter A.

Maiers, Wolfgang, jt. ed. see Tolman, Charles W.

Maifair, Linda. No Girls Allowed. LC 93-40083. (Ready, Set, Read! Beginning Readers Ser.). (J). 1993. 3.99 (*0-8066-2688-7*, 9-2688, Augsburg) Augsburg Fortress.

Maifair, Linda, jt. auth. see Sussman, Ellen.

Maifair, Linda L. The Case of the Angry Actress. (Darcy J. Doyle, Daring Detective Ser.: Bk. 7). 64p. (J). (gr. 2-5). 1994. pap. 3.99 (*0-310-43301-0*) Zondervan.

— The Case of the Bashful Bully. (Darcy J. Doyle, Daring Detective Ser.: Bk. 6). 64p. (J). (gr. 2-5). 1994. pap. 3.99 (*0-310-43281-2*) Zondervan.

— The Case of the Choosey Cheater. (Darcy J. Doyle, Daring Detective Ser.). 64p. (J). (gr. 2-5). 1993. pap. 3.99 (*0-310-57901-5*) Zondervan.

— The Case of the Creepy Campout. (Darcy J. Doyle, Daring Detective Ser.: Bk. 5). 64p. (J). (gr. 2-5). 1994. pap. 3.99 (*0-310-43271-5*) Zondervan.

— The Case of the Giggling Ghost. (Darcy J. Doyle, Daring Detective Ser.). 64p. (J). (gr. 2-5). 1993. pap. 3.99 (*0-310-57911-2*) Zondervan.

— The Case of the Missing Max. (Darcy J. Doyle, Daring Detective Ser.: Bk. 8). 64p. (J). (gr. 2-5). 1994. pap. 3.99 (*0-310-43311-8*) Zondervan.

— The Case of the Mixed-up Monsters. (Darcy J. Doyle, Daring Detective Ser.). 64p. (J). 1993. pap. 3.99 (*0-310-57921-X*) Zondervan.

— The Case of the Pampered Poodler. (Darcy J. Doyle, Daring Detective Ser.). 64p. (J). (gr. 2-5). 1993. pap. 3.99 (*0-310-57891-4*) Zondervan.

— Eighteen-Wheelers. (Cruisin' Ser.). 48p. (J). (gr. 3-4). 1991. lib. bdg. 11.95 (*1-56065-073-7*) Capstone Pr.

Maifair, Linda L., jt. auth. see Roth, David.

Maifair, Linda Lee. Brothers Don't Know Everything. LC 93-4605. (Illus.). (J). 1993. pap. 3.99 (*0-8066-2635-6*, 9-2635, Augsburg) Augsburg Fortress.

***Maigne, Robert.** Diagnosis & Treatment of Common Pain of Vertebral Origin: A New Approach. Nieves, Walter L., ed. & tr. by. LC 94-29321. Orig. Title: Diagnostic et Traitement des Douleurs Commones d'Origine Rachidienne. 1995. write for info. (*0-683-05376-0*) Williams & Wilkins.

Maiguashca, Raffaella, jt. auth. see Karumanchiri, Luisa.

Maiguashca, Raffaella U., et al. Schede di Lavoro 1. 2nd ed. (Italian Studies). 152p. (C). 1994. student ed 24.95 (*0-8020-7213-5*); teacher ed 20.00 (*0-8020-7226-7*) U of Toronto Pr.

Maiguashea, Raffaella, et al. Schede di Lavoro, No. 1. 1985. teacher ed 5.00 (*0-8020-6599-6*) U of Toronto Pr.

— Schede di Lavoro, No. 2. 1985. teacher ed 5.00 (*0-8020-6601-1*) U of Toronto Pr.

— Schede di Lavoro, Pt. 1. 276p. 1985. Part 1. Wkbk. 276p. student ed 23.95 (*0-8020-6598-8*) U of Toronto Pr.

— Schede di Lavoro, Pt. 2. 200p. 1985. Part 2. Wkbk. 200p. student ed 21.95 (*0-8020-6600-3*) U of Toronto Pr.

***Maihafer.** Oblivion: The Disappearance of West Point Cadet Richard Cox. 288p. 1997. 24.95 (*1-57488-043-8*) Brasseys Inc.

Maihafer, Harry J. Brave Decisions: Moral Courage from the Revolutionary War to Desert Storm. (Association of the U. S. Army Book Ser.). 224p. 1995. 23.95 (*0-02-881108-9*) Brasseys Inc.

— From the Hudson to the Yalu: West Point '49 in the Korean War. LC 93-12948. (Military History Ser.: No. 31). (Illus.). 296p. 1993. 29.50 (*0-89096-554-4*) Tex A&M Univ Pr.

Maik, Thomas A. The Masses Magazine (1911-1917) Odyssey of an Era. LC 93-43979. (Modern American History Ser.). 272p. 1994. 62.00 (*0-8153-1642-9*) Garland.

— A Reexamination of Mark Twain's 'Joan of Arc' LC 92-5601. 168p. 1992. lib. bdg. 79.95 (*0-88946-164-3*) E Mellen.

Maika, Patricia. Virginia Woolf's "Between the Acts" & Jane Harrison's Con-spiracy. Litz, A. Walton, ed. LC 87-13897. (Studies in Modern Literature: No. 78). 102p. reprint ed. 29.10 (*0-8357-1818-2*, 2070736) Bks Demand.

Maiken, Peter T. Night Trains: The Pullman System in the Golden Years of American Rail Travel. LC 92-12586. (Illus.). 416p. 1992. pap. 24.95 (*0-8018-4503-3*) Johns Hopkins.

— Night Trains: The Pullman System in the Golden Years of American Rail Travel. (Illus.). 416p. (C). 1989. boxed 49.95 (*0-9621480-0-8*) Lakme Pr.

Maikmeat. How to Build a Doh. 1986. 10.95 (*0-02-579370-5*) Macmillan.

Maikovich, Andrew J. Sports Quotations: Maxims, Quips & Pronouncements for Writers & Fans. LC 83-20005. 174p. 1984. lib. bdg. 27.50x (*0-89950-100-1*) McFarland & Co.

— Sports Trivia Encyclopedia. 308p. (Orig.). 1991. pap. 9.95 (*0-9631633-0-2*) Write Field Prods.

Maikovich, Andrew J. & Brown, Michele D. Employment Discrimination: A Claims Manual for Employees & Managers. LC 89-42733. 220p. 1989. lib. bdg. 32.50x (*0-89950-436-1*) McFarland & Co.

Mail, Patricia D. & McDonald, David R. Tulapai to Tokay: A Bibliography of Alcohol Use & Abuse Among Native Americans of North America. LC 80-81243. (Bibliographies Ser.). 372p. 1981. 25.00 (*0-87536-253-2*) HRAFP.

Mailand, Harold F. Considerations for the Care of Textiles & Costumes: A Handbook for the Non-Specialist. 1980. 4.00 (*0-317-29210-2*) Ind Mus Art.

***Maile.** "Principles to Apply & Remember" 111p. 1994. pap. 11.95 (*0-929385-59-4*) Light Tech Comns Servs.

Maile, jt. auth. see Wren.

Maile, M. Economics. (Core Business Studies Ser.). 1990. pap. 21.00 (*0-7463-0013-1*, Pub. by Northcote UK) St Mut.

Mailer, F. Josef Strauss: Genius Against His Will. Povey, P., tr. (Illus.). 117p. 1985. text ed. 34.00 (*0-08-026765-3*, Pub. by PPL UK) Elsevier.

Mailer, Norman. Advertisements for Myself. 532p. 1992. reprint ed. pap. text ed. 15.95 (*0-674-00590-2*) HUP.

— An American Dream. LC 64-20280. 288p. 1987. pap. 12.95 (*0-8050-0349-5*, Owl) H Holt & Co.

— Ancient Evenings. 864p. 1988. mass mkt. 7.99 (*0-446-35769-3*) Warner Bks.

— Armies of the Night. 1968. pap. 6.99 (*0-451-14070-2*, AE2317, Sig) NAL-Dutton.

— The Armies of the Night: History As a Novel - The Novel As History. 304p. 1995. pap. 11.95 (*0-452-27279-3*, Plume) NAL-Dutton.

— The Executioner's Song. 1993. 20.00 (*0-679-42471-7*, Modern Lib) Random.

— The Executioner's Song. 1986. mass mkt. 7.99 (*0-446-34521-0*) Warner Bks.

— Harlot's Ghost. 1992. mass mkt. 6.99 (*0-345-37755-9*) Ballantine.

— Harlot's Ghost. 1310p. 1992. 30.00 (*0-394-58832-0*) Random.

— Harlot's Ghost. limited ed. 1310p. 1992. 200.00 (*0-394-58915-7*) Random.

— Harlot's Ghost: A Novel. 1200p. 1992. pap. 15.92 (*0-345-37965-9*, Ballantine Trade) Ballantine.

— How the Wimp Won the War. deluxe ed. 36p. 1991. 75.00 (*0-935716-57-2*) Lord John.

— Huckleberry Finn, Alive at One Hundred. limited ed. 13p. 1985. 18.00 (*0-936897-02-3*) Caliban.

— Marilyn: The Classic. 1989. 17.98 (*0-88365-731-7*) Galahad Bks.

— Miami & the Siege of Chicago. LC 85-82495. 223p. 1986. pap. 9.95 (*0-917657-85-3*, Primus Lib Contemp) D I Fine.

— The Naked & the Dead. 1994. lib. bdg. 27.95x (*1-56849-421-1*) Buccaneer Bks.
— The Naked & the Dead. LC 80-25751. 740p. 1980. pap. 14.95 (*0-8050-0521-8*, Owl) H Holt & Co.
— The Naked & the Dead. (Classics Ser.). 736p. 1990. 30.00 (*0-8050-1273-7*) H Holt & Co.
— Oswald's Tale: An American Mystery. 1995. 30.00 (*0-679-42535-7*) Random.
— Portrait of Picasso as a Young Man. LC 95-1877. 1995. 30.00 (*0-87113-608-2*, Atlntc Mnthly) Grove-Atltic.
— The Prisoner of Sex. LC 85-80630. 240p. 1985. pap. 8.95 (*0-917657-59-4*, Primus Lib Contemp) D I Fine.
— Rivage de Barbarie. (FRE.). 1977. pap. 11.95 (*0-7859-4084-7*) Fr & Eur.
— Tough Guys Don't Dance. 384p. 1985. mass mkt. 5.95 (*0-345-32321-1*) Ballantine.
— Tough Guys Don't Dance. LC 84-42514. 240p. 1984. 16.95 (*0-394-53786-6*) Random.
— Why Are We in Vietnam? A Novel. 216p. 1982. pap. 9.95 (*0-8050-1880-8*, Owl) H Holt & Co.
Mailer, Norman, et al. Black Messiah. 1981. 20.00 (*0-912824-25-5*); pap. 9.00 (*0-912824-26-3*) Vagabond Pr.
Mailer, Stan. The Green Bay & Western: From Moguls to Alcos. Hundman, Robert L. & Lee, Cathy H., eds. LC 88-81184. (Illus.). 350p. 1989. 38.50 (*0-685-22196-2*) Hundman Pub.
Mailhol, Philippe D. Dictionnaire Historique et Heraldique De la Noblesse Francaise, 2 vols., Set. vii, 1452p. reprint ed. write for info. (*0-318-71375-6*, Pub. by Georg Olms GW) Lubrecht & Cramer.
Mailhot, Ernie, et al. The Eastern Airlines Strike: Accomplishments of the Rank-&-File Machinists & Gains for the Labor Movement. LC 91-60839. (Illus.). 94p. (Orig.). (C). 1991. lib. bdg. 35.00 (*0-87348-635-8*); pap. 9.95 (*0-87348-626-9*) Pathfinder NY.
Mailick, Mildred & Rehr, Helen, eds. In the Patient's Interest: Access to Hospital Care. LC 81-15781. 171p. 1982. text ed. 17.50 (*0-88202-136-2*) Watson Pub Intl.
Mailick, Mildred, jt. ed. see Caroff, Phyllis.
Mailick, Sidney, jt. auth. see Hoberman, Solomon.
Mailick, Sidney, jt. ed. see Hoberman, Solomon.
Mailick, Sidney, jt. auth. see Reymond, Henri.
Mailick, Sidney, et al, eds. The Practice of Management Development. LC 88-2398. 226p. 1988. text ed. 55.00 (*0-275-92357-6*, C2357, Praeger Pubs) Greenwood.
***Maillard.** Light in the Company of Women. 1994. pap. text ed. 11.00 (*0-00-647533-7*, Harp PBks) HarpC.
Maillard, Antoine S. Grammar of the Mikmaque Language of Nova Scotia. Bellenger, Joseph M., ed. LC 11-29307. (Library of American Linguistics: Vol. 9). reprint ed. 42.75 (*0-404-50989-4*) AMS Pr.
Maillard, Claude, jt. auth. see Gordon, Coco.
Maillard, Keith. The Knife in My Hands. 336p. 1983. pap. 3.95 (*0-7736-7056-4*, Pub. by Stoddart Pubng CN) Genl Dist Srvs.
Maillbaum, T. S., jt. ed. see Abramsky, S.
Maillet, Antonine. Christopher Cartier of Hazelnut, Also Known As Bear. 76p. 1984. 9.95 (*0-458-98110-9*, Pub. by Stoddart Pubng CN) Genl Dist Srvs.
— The Devil Is Loose! 310p. 1987. 16.95 (*0-8027-0958-3*) Walker & Co.
— Pelagie-la-Charrette. (Orig.). 1987. pap. 11.95 (*0-7145-3966-X*) Riverrun NY.
— Tale of Don l'Orginal. 107p. 1978. 3.95 (*0-7720-1216-4*, Pub. by Stoddart Pubng CN) Genl Dist Srvs.
— The Tales of Don L'Orignal. 107p. 1989. pap. 5.95 (*0-7736-7234-6*, Pub. by Stoddart Pubng CN) Genl Dist Srvs.
Maillet, Dominique. Lexique de l'Informatique. 205p. 1993. pap. 32.00 (*0-7859-5575-5*, 2010200519) Fr & Eur.
Maillet, Julie O. Ethical Issues & Decision in Feeding. 30p. 1989. student ed 10.25 (*0-685-51756-X*); audio 27.50 (*0-88091-051-8*, 1219) Am Dietetic Assn.
Maillet, Lucienne. Subject Control of Film & Video: A Comparison of Three Methods. LC 90-45127. (Studies in Librarianship: No. 11). (C). 1991. pap. text ed. 30.00 (*0-8389-0553-6*, 0553-6) ALA.
***Maillet, Lynda L.** Commercial & Investment Law: Uzbekistan. LC 94-30392. 1994. write for info. (*1-56425-045-8*) Transnatl Juris Pubns.
Maillet, Pierre, et al, eds. The Economics of Choice Between Energy Souces: Proceedings of a Conference Held by the International Economic Association in Tokyo, Japan. 350p. 1987. text ed. 45.00 (*0-312-23677-8*) St Martin.
Maillie, J. B., jt. auth. see Park, W. R.
Maillol, Aristide. Maillol Erotic Woodcuts: One Hundred Thirty-Five Illustrations. 48p. (Orig.). 1988. pap. 3.50 (*0-486-25569-7*) Dover.
— Maillol Nudes: Thirty-Five Lithographs by Aristide Maillol. (Dover Art Library). Orig. Title: The Dialogues of the Courtesans. (Illus.). 1980. pap. 3.50 (*0-486-24000-2*) Dover.
Maillot, Antoine L. La Musique au Theatre. LC 80-2288. 1981. reprint ed. 44.00 (*0-404-18856-7*) AMS Pr.
Maillot, J. La Traduction Scientifique et Technique. 2nd ed. 280p. (FRE.). 1981. 49.95 (*0-8288-2105-4*, M14402) Fr & Eur.
Mailloux, Peter. A Hesitation Before Birth: The Life of Franz Kafka. LC 87-40268. (Illus.). 624p. 1988. 50.00 (*0-87413-331-9*) U Delaware Pr.
Mailloux, Robert, jt. auth. see De Vosjoli, Philippe.
Mailloux, Robert J. Phased Array Antenna Handbook. (Antenna Ser.). 625p. 1993. text ed. 119.00 (*0-89006-502-0*) Artech Hse.
Mailloux, Steven. Interpretive Conventions: The Reader in the Study of American Fiction. LC 81-70712. 232p. 1982. 33.95 (*0-8014-1476-8*); pap. 12.95 (*0-8014-9285-8*) Cornell U Pr.
— Rhetorical Power. LC 89-42878. 208p. 1989. 33.95 (*0-8014-2245-0*); pap. 12.95 (*0-8014-9602-0*) Cornell U Pr.
***Mailloux, Steven, ed.** Rhetoric, Sophistry, Pragmatism. (Literature, Culture, Theory Ser.: No. 15). 290p. (C). 1995. 54.95 (*0-521-46225-8*) Cambridge U Pr.
— Rhetoric, Sophistry, Pragmatism. (Literature, Culture, Theory Ser.: No. 15). 290p. (C). 1995. pap. 16.95 (*0-521-46780-2*) Cambridge U Pr.
Mailloux, Steven & Levinson, Sanford, eds. Interpreting Law & Literature: A Hermeneutic Reader. 502p. (C). 1988. 62.95 (*0-8101-0770-8*); pap. 29.95 (*0-8101-0793-7*) Northwestern U Pr.
Mailloux, Zoe. Sensory Integrative Approaches in Occupational Therapy. LC 87-2878. (Occupational Therapy in Health Care Ser.: Vol. 4, No. 2). 179p. 1987. 39.95 (*0-86656-665-1*) Haworth Pr.
Mailman, Leo. The Handyman Poems. LC 82-71399. 56p. (Orig.). 1982. pap. 5.95 (*0-930090-16-0*) Applezaba.
— The Handyman Poems. deluxe limited ed. LC 82-71399. 56p. (Orig.). 1982. 10.00 (*0-930090-17-9*) Applezaba.
— The Kid Comes Home. LC 76-29868. (Illus.). 1976. pap. 2.00 (*0-685-01523-8*) Duck Down.
— The Kid Comes Home. 1976. 3.00 (*0-685-03276-0*) Maelstrom.
Mailman, Stanley, jt. auth. see Gordon, Charles.
Mails, Thomas. Dog Soldiers. 1976. 20.95 (*0-8488-1089-9*) Amereon Ltd.
— Fools Crow. 1976. 19.95 (*0-8488-1090-2*) Amereon Ltd.
— Mystic Warriors of the Plains. 1976. 20.95 (*0-8488-1091-0*) Amereon Ltd.
— Secret Native American Pathways: A Guide to Inner Peace. LC 88-70671. (Illus.). 312p. 1988. pap. 16.95 (*0-933031-15-7*) Coun Oak Bks.
Mails, Thomas E. The Cherokee People. LC 91-73541. (Illus.). 368p. 1992. 49.95 (*0-933031-45-9*) Coun Oak Bks.
— The Cherokee People. deluxe ed. LC 91-73541. (Illus.). 368p. 1992. ring bd. 250.00 (*0-933031-46-7*) Coun Oak Bks.
— Fools Crow. LC 90-33803. (Illus.). vi, 294p. 1990. reprint ed. pap. 10.95 (*0-8032-8174-9*, Bison Books) U of Nebr Pr.
— Fools Crow - Wisdom & Power. LC 90-85350. (Illus.). 204p. 1991. pap. 16.95 (*0-933031-35-1*) Coun Oak Bks.
— Mystic Warriors of the Plains. 672p. 1994. 49.95 (*1-57178-002-5*) Coun Oak Bks.
— The Mystic Warriors of the Plains: The Culture, Arts, Crafts, & Religion on the Plains Indians. (Illus.). 618p. 1995. pap. 25.00 (*1-56924-843-5*) Marlowe & Co.
— Secret Native American Pathways: A Guide to Inner Peace. 1994. 24.95 (*1-57178-003-3*) Abacus MI.
Mailvaganam, N. P. Repair & Protection of Concrete Structures. 1991. 205.00 (*0-8493-4993-1*, TA681) CRC Pr.
Mailvaganam, N. P., jt. auth. see Rixom, M. R.
Maiman, Jaye. Crazy for Loving. (Robin Miller Mystery Ser.: No. 2). 320p. 1992. pap. 10.95 (*1-56280-025-6*) Naiad Pr.
— I Left My Heart. 303p. (Orig.). 1991. pap. 10.95 (*0-941483-72-X*) Naiad Pr.
— Someone to Watch: A Robin Miller Mystery. 1995. pap. 10.95 (*1-56280-095-7*) Naiad Pr.
— Under My Skin. (Robin Miller Mystery Ser.: No. 3). 320p. 1993. pap. 10.95 (*1-56280-049-3*) Naiad Pr.
Maiman, Judith C. Poems of a Manic Depressive. (Illus.). 96p. (Orig.). 1992. pap. 10.95 (*0-9627860-4-7*) Lone Oak MN.
Maiman, Richard J., jt. auth. see Steamer, Robert J.
Maime, Jane H., jt. auth. see Youngman, Joan M.
Maimes, Steven L., ed. see Carlebach, Shlomo.
Maimo, A. O. I Am Vindicated. rev. ed. (B. E. Ser.: No. 67). 1959. 18.00 (*0-8115-3017-5*) Periodicals Srv.
Maimon, Albert S., ed. see Maimon, Sam B.
Maimon, Sam B. The Beauty of Sephardic Life: Scholarly, Humorous & Personal Reflections. Maimon, Albert S. & Normand, Eugene, eds. 254p. (Orig.). 1993. pap. 15.00 (*0-9636764-0-7*) Marmon Ideas.
Maimondies & Hyamson, Moses. Book of Adoration. (Mishneh Torah Ser.). 330p. 1981. 17.95 (*0-87306-086-5*) Feldheim.
Maimondies & Klein, Isaac. The Book of Agriculture. LC 49-9495. (Yale Judaica Ser.: No. 7). 1979. text ed. 70.00 (*0-300-02223-9*) Yale U Pr.
Maimonides. Book of Knowledge. Hyamson, Moses, tr. (Mishneh Torah Ser.). 1981. 19.95 (*0-87306-085-7*) Feldheim.
— Guide for the Perplexed: A Fifteenth Century Spanish Translation by Pedro de Toledo. Lazar, Moshe & Dilligan, Robert, eds. LC 89-85092. (Sephardic Classical Library: No. 2). (Illus.). 370p. (C). 1989. lib. bdg. 75.00 (*0-911437-49-5*) Labyrinthos.
— Pirkie Avot. Touger, Eliyahu, tr. (Mishne Torah Ser.). 184p. 1994. write for info. (*0-940118-98-X*) Moznaim.
Maimonides, Moses. Code of Maimonides, Bk. 3, Treatise 8, Sanctification Of The New Moon. Gandz, Solomon, tr. (Judaica Ser.: No. 11). 1956. 28.00x (*0-300-00476-1*) Yale U Pr.
— Code of Maimonides, Bk. 3: The Book of Seasons. Gandz, Solomon & Klein, Hyman, trs. (Judaica Ser.: No. 14). 1961. 75.00 (*0-300-00475-3*) Yale U Pr.
— Commentary to Mishnah Aboth. David, Arthur, tr. LC 68-27871. 1968. 9.95 (*0-8197-0154-8*) Bloch.
— Ethical Writings of Maimonides. (Philosophy & Religion Ser.). 182p. (Orig.). 1983. pap. 4.50 (*0-486-24522-5*) Dover.
— Guide for the Perplexed. Friedlander, M., tr. 1904. pap. 7.95 (*0-486-20351-4*) Dover.
— Guide for the Perplexed. 2nd ed. 20.00 (*0-8446-2512-4*) Peter Smith.
— Guide for the Perplexed: Morah Nevochim. Alcharizi, Yehuda & Friedlander, M., trs. 42.50 (*0-87559-079-9*) Shalom.
— Guide of the Perplexed, 2 vols., 1. Pines, Shlomo, tr. LC 62-18113. 1963. 25.00 (*0-226-50232-5*) U Ch Pr.
— The Guide of the Perplexed, 1. Pines, Shlomo, tr. & intro. by. LC 62-18113. 1974. reprint ed. pap. 21.00 (*0-226-50230-9*, P609) U Ch Pr.
— The Guide of the Perplexed, 2. Pines, Shlomo, tr. & intro. by. LC 62-18113. 1974. reprint ed. pap. 24.95 (*0-226-50231-7*, P610) U Ch Pr.
— Maimonides Introduction to the Talmud. 296p. (ENG & HEB.). 1975. pap. 8.95 (*0-910818-06-1*) Judaica Pr.
— Mishneh Torah. abr. ed. Birnbaum, Philip, tr. 755p. (ENG & HEB.). 1944. 21.50 (*0-88482-437-3*); pap. 12.95 (*0-88482-436-5*) Hebrew Pub.
— The Reason of the Laws of Moses. Townley, James, ed. LC 78-97294. 451p. 1970. reprint ed. text ed. 35.00 (*0-8371-2618-5*, MARL, Greenwood Pr) Greenwood.
Maimonides, Moses & Judah, trs. Fathers According to Rabbi Nathan Goldin. (Judaica Ser.: No. 10). 1955. 40.00x (*0-300-00497-4*) Yale U Pr.
Maimonides, Moses & Klein, Isaac. The Book of Women: The Code of Maimonides, Bk. 4. LC 49-9495. (Judaica Ser.: No. 19). 592p. 1972. 60.00 (*0-300-01438-4*) Yale U Pr.
Maimonides, Moses & Twersky, Isadore. Introduction to the Code of Maimonides (Mishneh Torah) LC 79-10347. (Yale Judaica Ser.: No. XXII). 1980. 60.00 (*0-300-02319-7*) Yale U Pr.
— Introduction to the Code of Maimonides (Mishneh Torah) LC 79-10347. (Yale Judaica Ser.: No. XXII). 1982. pap. 20.00 (*0-300-02846-6*) Yale U Pr.
Maimonides, Obadyah. The Treatise of the Pool: Al-Mawala al Hawdiyya. Fenton, Paul, tr. 1981. 23.00 (*0-900860-87-1*, Pub. by Octagon Pr UK) ISHK Bk Service.
Maimonidies. Mishne Torah Hilchot Avodat Kochavim (The Laws of Star Worship & Statues) Touger, Eliyahu, tr. & comment by. (Mishneh Torah Ser.: 3). 239p. 1990. 17.95 (*0-940118-67-X*) Moznaim.
— Mishne Torah Hilchot Berachot - Hilchot Milah Laws of Blessings Laws of Circumcision. Touger, Eliyahu, tr. & comment by. (Mishneh Torah Ser.: 8). 256p. 1991. 17.95 (*0-940118-69-6*) Moznaim.
— Mishne Torah Hilchot Eishut: Laws Pertaining to Marriage. Touyer, Eliyahu, ed. & tr. by. (Mishne Torah Ser.). 337p. 1994. 17.95 (*1-885220-00-6*) Moznaim.
— Mishne Torah Hilchot Eruvin, Holchot Sh'vitat Asor Hilchot Sh'vitat Yom Tov: Laws of Eruvin, Laws of Resting on the 10th of Tishrie, Laws of Resting on Yom Tov. (Mishneh Torah Ser.). (Illus.). 316p. 1993. 17.95 (*0-940118-93-9*) Moznaim.
— Mishne Torah Hilchot Shabbat I: Laws of Shabbat, Pt. I. Touger, Eliyahu, tr. & comment by. (Mishneh Torah Ser.: 9). 296p. 1992. 17.95 (*0-940118-71-8*) Moznaim.
— Mishne Torah Hilchot Shabbat, Pt. 2: Laws of Shabbat. (Mishneh Torah Ser.). 358p. 1993. 17.95 (*0-940118-81-5*) Moznaim.
— Mishne Torah Hilchot Ta'aniot Hilchot Megillah & Chanukah: Laws of Fasts, Laws of Reading the Megillah & of Chanukah. Touger, Eliyah, tr. & comment by. (Mishneh Torah Ser.: 15). 189p. 1991. 17.95 (*0-940118-70-X*) Moznaim.
— Mishne Torah Hilchot Tefilah, Pt. 2: Laws of Prayer & Priestly Blessings. Touger, Eli, tr. (Mishne Torah Ser.: 6). 232p. 1989. 17.95 (*0-940118-30-0*) Moznaim.
— Mishne Torah Hilchot Tefillin U'Mezuza Lu'Sefer Torah: Hilchot Tzizit Laws of Tefillin, Mezuza & Torah Scrolls, Laws of Tzitzit. Touger, Eliyahu, tr. & comment by. (Mishneh Torah Ser.: 7). 139p. 1990. 17.95 (*0-940118-68-8*) Moznaim.
— Mishne Torah, Hilchot Yesodei HaTorah: The Laws (Which Are the) Foundations of the Torah. Touger, Eliyahu, tr. & comment by. (Mishneh Torah Ser.: 1). 300p. 1989. 17.95 (*0-940118-41-6*) Moznaim.
— Mishneh Torah Hilchos Chametz U'Matzah: Laws of Chametz & Matzah. Touger, Eliyahu, tr. & comment by. (Mishneh Torah Ser.: 12). 198p. 1988. 17.95 (*0-940118-21-1*) Moznaim.
— Mishneh Torah Hilchos Melachim V'Milchomoteihem: Laws of Kings & Their Wars. Touger, Eliyahu, tr. & comment by. (Mishneh Torah Ser.). 263p. 1987. 17.95 (*0-940118-34-3*) Moznaim.
— Mishneh Torah Hilchot Bais Habechira: Laws of (God's) Chosen House. Touger, Eliyahu, tr. & comment by. (Mishneh Torah Ser.). 223p. 1986. 17.95 (*0-940118-19-X*) Moznaim.
— Mishneh Torah Hilchot De'ot - Hilchot Talmud Torah: Laws of De'ot - Personality Development Laws of Torah Study. Touger, Eliyahu, tr. & comment by. (Mishneh Torah Ser.: 2). 304p. 1989. 17.95 (*0-940118-23-8*) Moznaim.
— Mishneh Torah Hilchot Kriat Shema Hilchot Tefilah, Part 1: Laws of Kriat Shema & Laws of Prayer. Kaplan, Boruch, tr. & comment by. (Mishneh Torah Ser.: 5). 224p. 1989. 17.95 (*0-940118-24-6*) Moznaim.
— Mishneh Torah Hilchot Shofar, Sukkah, VE Lulav: Laws of the Shofar Sukah & Lulav. Touger, Eliyahu, tr. & comment by. (Mishneh Torah Ser.: 13). 231p. 1988. 17.95 (*0-940118-42-4*) Moznaim.
— Mishneh Torah Hilchot Teshuvah: Laws of Repentance. Touger, Eliyahu, tr. & comment by. (Mishneh Torah Ser.: 4). 241p. 1987. 17.95 (*0-940118-20-3*) Moznaim.
— The Mishneh Torah Series, 19 vols., Set. Touger, Eliyahu, tr. 1989. 375.00 (*0-940118-18-1*) Moznaim.
***Main.** Creating the Successful 21st Century Enterprise. 1997. 25.00 (*0-02-874079-3*) Free Pr.
Main, Barbara Y., jt. ed. see Shoate, Alec.
Main, C. F. & Seng, Peter J., eds. Poems. 4th ed. 490p. (C). 1978. pap. 23.95 (*0-534-00541-1*) Intl Thomson.
Main, Chris J., et al, eds. Clinical Psychology & Medicine: A Behavioral Perspective. LC 81-19978. 384p. 1981. 65.00 (*0-306-40900-3*, Plenum Pr) Plenum.
Main, Denise M., jt. auth. see Main, Elliot K.
Main, Elliot K. & Main, Denise M. Obstetrics & Gynecology: A Pocket Reference. 2nd ed. (Illus.). 450p. 1990. 24.95 (*0-8151-5734-7*, Yr Bk Med Pubs) Mosby Yr Bk.
Main, Ernest. Palestine at the Crossroads. LC 71-180359. reprint ed. 42.50 (*0-404-56291-4*) AMS Pr.
Main, Gwen. This Far by Faith. LC 91-33130. 105p. 1992. pap. 8.95 (*0-944350-21-6*) Friends United.
***Main, Hamish & Williams, Stephen Wynn, eds.** Environmental Housing in Third World Cities. 1994. text ed. 54.95 (*0-471-94831-4*) Wiley.
Main, Iain G. Vibrations & Waves in Physics. 3rd ed. LC 92-33323. (Illus.). 379p. (C). 1993. pap. 29.95 (*0-521-44701-1*) Cambridge U Pr.
— Vibrations & Waves in Physics. 3rd ed. LC 92-33323. (Illus.). 379p. (C). 1993. 79.95 (*0-521-44186-2*) Cambridge U Pr.
Main, Jackson T. Political Parties Before the Constitution. LC 71-184228. 501p. reprint ed. pap. 142.80 (*0-7837-0291-4*, 2040612) Bks Demand.
— Political Parties Before the Constitution. (Illus.). 512p. (C). 1974. reprint ed. pap. text ed. 4.95 (*0-393-00718-9*) Norton.
— The Social Structure of Revolutionary America. LC 65-17146. 340p. reprint ed. pap. 96.90 (*0-317-08695-2*, 2011969) Bks Demand.
— Society & Economy in Colonial Connecticut. LC 84-42892. 420p. 1985. text ed. 49.50x (*0-691-04726-X*) Princeton U Pr.
— The Upper House in Revolutionary America, 1763-1788. LC 67-20753. 323p. reprint ed. pap. 92.10 (*0-317-09462-9*, 2004974) Bks Demand.
Main, Jeremy, jt. auth. see Juran Institute Staff.
Main, Jody, jt. auth. see Portugal, Nancy.
Main, John. Letters from the Heart: Christian Monasticism & the Renewal of Community. 1982. 9.95 (*0-8245-0444-5*) Crossroad NY.
— Modern Spirituality Series. Hallward, Clare, ed. (Modern Spirituality Ser.). 96p. 1988. pap. 4.95 (*0-87243-166-5*) Templegate.
— Present Christ. 128p. (Orig.). 1986. pap. 9.95 (*0-8245-0740-1*) Crossroad NY.
— Word into Silence. LC 80-84660. 96p. 1981. pap. 5.95 (*0-8091-2369-X*) Paulist Pr.
Main, John, jt. ed. see Archer, Clive.
Main, Katy. Baby Animals of the North. (Illus.). 36p. (J). (ps-00). 1992. bds. 9.95 (*0-88240-395-8*) Alaska Northwest.
Main, Kevan L., jt. ed. see Fulks, Wendy.
Main, Laurence. A Bristol Countryway. (C). 1988. pap. 40.00 (*0-904110-80-X*, Pub. by Thornhill Pr UK) St Mut.
— King Alfred's Way. (C). 1988. pap. 29.00 (*0-904110-82-6*, Pub. by Thornhill Pr UK) St Mut.
— A South Coast Way. (C). 1988. pap. 29.00 (*0-904110-86-9*, Pub. by Thornhill Pr UK) St Mut.
— A South Wessex Way. (C). 1988. pap. 29.00 (*0-904110-81-8*, Pub. by Thornhill Pr UK) St Mut.
— A Wiltshire Way. (C). 1988. pap. 40.00 (*0-904110-85-0*, Pub. by Thornhill Pr UK) St Mut.
Main, Lawrence. A Somerset Way. (C). 1988. pap. text ed. 29.00 (*0-904110-79-6*, Pub. by Thornhill Pr UK) St Mut.
Main, Linda & Whitaker, Char. Automating Literacy: A Challenge for Libraries. LC 90-47285. (New Directions in Information Management Ser.: No. 24). 144p. 1991. text ed. 45.00 (*0-313-27528-9*, MLX/, Greenwood Pr) Greenwood.
Main, M. G., et al, eds. Mathematical Foundations of Programming Language Semantics. (Lecture Notes in Computer Science Ser.: Vol. 298). viii, 637p. 1988. pap. 65.00 (*0-387-19020-1*) Spr-Verlag.
— Mathematical Foundations of Programming Semantics: 5th International Conference, Tulane University, New Orleans, Louisiana, USA, March 29 - April 1, 1989 Proceedings. (Lecture Notes in Computer Science Ser.: Vol. 442). vi, 439p. 1990. pap. 39.00 (*0-387-97375-3*) Spr-Verlag.
***Main, Mary.** Tower of Evil. (YA). 1994. pap. 2.95 (*0-8167-3533-6*) Troll Assocs.
Main, Michael & Savitch, Walter. Data Structures & Other Objects: A Second Course in Computer Science. 800p. (C). 1995. pap. text ed. 50.50 (*0-8053-7086-2*) Benjamin-Cummings.
Main, Nanci. New Ark Cookbook: Fresh & Simple Cuisine from the Pacific Northwest. LC 90-1482. 1990. pap. 19.95 (*0-87701-698-4*) Chronicle Bks.
***Main, Norman.** Muirfield: Home of the Honourable Company (1744-1994) (Illus.). 160p. 1995. 39.95 (*1-85158-617-2*, Pub. by Mnstream UK) Trafalgar.
Main, Ronald C. & Zervas, Judy. Keep Your Kids Straight: What Parents Need to Know about Drugs & Alcohol. 126p. 1991. pap. 7.95 (*0-8306-7681-3*, 3681) Sulzburger & Graham Pub.
Main Street Designers Staff, et al. Rush Hour Superchef. LC 83-70952. (Illus.). 256p. (Orig.). 1984. 11.95 (*0-685-07460-9*) Deanne Inc.
Main Street Edition Staff. Footprints on Our Hearts. (Illus.). 32p. 1993. 6.95 (*0-8362-4707-8*) Andrews & McMeel.
Main Street Press Staff, comp. Book of Medieval & Renaissance Alphabets. LC 91-14736. 128p. 1991. pap. 7.95 (*0-8069-8278-0*, Sterling-Main St) Sterling.
Main, Tom. The Ailment & Other Psychoanalytic Essays. 256p. 1989. 40.00 (*1-85343-104-4*) Col U Pr.
Main, Wynell F. An Investigation of Angels. 1992. pap. 6.95 (*0-89137-462-0*) Quality Pubns.

M

Mainardi, Patricia. Art & Politics of the Second Empire: The Universal Expositions of 1855 & 1867. LC 87-6262. 248p. 1987. text ed. 50.00 (0-300-03871-2) Yale U Pr.
— Art & Politics of the Second Empire: The Universal Expositions of 1855 & 1867. 248p. (C). 1990. reprint ed. 22.50 (0-300-04747-9) Yale U Pr.
— The End of the Salon: Art & the State in the Early Third Republic. LC 92-15566. (Illus.). 224p. (C). 1994. 54.95 (0-521-43251-0) Cambridge U Pr.
— The End of the Salon: Art & the State in the Early Third Republic. (Cambridge Studies in New Art History & Criticism). (Illus.). 224p. (C). 1994. pap. 18.95 (0-521-46921-X) Cambridge U Pr.
— Quilts: The Great American Art. xix, 57p. 1985. reprint ed. 8.95 (0-936810-06-8); reprint ed. pap. 3.95 (0-936810-24-6) R&E Miles.
***Mainardi, Patricia, et al.** The Persistence of Classicism. (Illus.). 46p. (Orig.). 1995. pap. 4.50 (0-931102-36-7) S & F Clark Art.
Maine A. T. Club. A Guide to Log Lean-to Construction. (Illus.). 1992. pap. 3.95 (0-917953-47-9) Appalachian Trail.
Maine, Barry, ed. Dos Pasos. (Critical Heritage Ser.). 320p. (C). 1988. text ed. 49.50 (0-415-00229-X) Routledge.
Maine, Basil. Elgar: His Life & Works, 2 vols., Set. LC 74-26065. reprint ed. 32.50 (0-404-13005-4) AMS Pr.
Maine Board of Overseers of the Bar Staff. Maine Manual on Professional Responsibility. rev. ed. 300p. 1994. ring bd. 65.00 (0-89442-082-8) Michie Butterworth.
— Maine Manual on Professional Responsibility, Vol. 2. rev. ed. 370p. 1994. ring bd. 65.00 (1-56257-301-2) Michie Butterworth.
***Maine Commissioners Staff.** Maine at Gettysburg: Report of the Maine Monuments Commission. (Illus.). 602p. 1994. 45.00 (1-879664-23-2) Stan Clark Military.
Maine De Biran, Pierre. Influence of Habit on the Faculty of Thinking. Boehm, Margaret D., tr. LC 79-98854. 227p. 1970. reprint ed. text ed. 35.00 (0-8371-3124-3, MBTH, Greenwood Pr) Greenwood.
Maine, Diana, ed. Science. LC 92-54482. (Picturepedia Ser.). (Illus.). (J). 1993. write for info. (1-56458-248-5) Dorling Kindersley.
Maine Genealogical Society Staff, et al, eds. Vital Records of Mount Desert Island, Maine, 1776-1820: And Other Nearby Islands. LC 90-60973. (Illus.). 96p. 1990. text ed. 20.00 (0-929539-68-0, 68) Picton Pr.
Maine, Henry J. Ancient Law: Its Connection with the Early History of Society & Its Relation to Modern Ideas. Reams, Bernard D., Jr., ed. LC 30-21428. (Historical Reprints in Jurisprudence & Classical Legal Literature Ser.). xxiv, 426p. 1984. reprint ed. lib. bdg. 52.50 (0-89941-249-1, 303180) W S Hein.
Maine, Henry S. Ancient Law. LC 86-6929. (Classics of Anthropology Ser.). 400p. 1986. reprint ed. pap. 19.95 (0-8165-1006-7) U of Ariz Pr.
— Ancient Law: The Connection with the Early History of Society & Its Relation to Modern Ideas. 13.25 (0-8446-0784-3) Peter Smith.
Maine, Henry S., Sr. Ancient Law. 344p. 1987. 16.95 (0-88029-101-X) Dorset Pr.
Maine, Henry S. Dissertations on Early Law & Custom Chiefly Selected from Lectures Delivered at Oxford. LC 74-25768. (European Sociology Ser.). 414p. 1975. reprint ed. 30.95 (0-405-06522-1) Ayer.
— Lectures on the Early History of Institutions: A Sequel to Ancient Law. LC 87-81276. viii, 412p. 1987. reprint ed. lib. bdg. 50.00 (0-89941-562-8, 305200) W S Hein.
— Popular Government. LC 76-26329. 1977. reprint ed. 8.50 (0-913966-14-2) Liberty Fund.
— Village-Communities in the East & West. LC 73-14169. (Perspectives in Social Inquiry Ser.). 430p. 1974. reprint ed. 25.95 (0-405-05513-7) Ayer.
Maine Historical Society. Collections of the Maine Historical Society, 10 vols., Set. reprint ed. 345.00 (0-404-11059-2) AMS Pr.
Maine Historical Society & Maine Historical Society Staff. The Maine Bicentennial Atlas: An Historical Survey. (Illus.). 1976. pap. 10.00 (0-685-03278-7); write for info. (0-915592-23-1) Maine Hist.
***Maine Historical Society Staff.** Collections of the Maine Historical Society, Vol. IV. (Illus.). 433p. (Orig.). 1995. pap. text ed. 28.00 (0-7884-0172-6) Heritage Bk.
Maine Historical Society Staff, jt. auth. see Maine Historical Society.
Maine Joint Special Committee. Report of the Joint Special Committee on Investigation of the Affairs of the Maine State Prison: Made to the Fifty-Third Legislature. LC 74-3832. (Criminal Justice in America Ser.). 1974. reprint ed. 15.95 (0-405-06152-8) Ayer.
Maine Literature Project Staff, ed. Maine Speaks: An Anthology of Maine Literature. LC 89-60344. (Illus.). 466p. (gr. 7-12). 1989. 29.95 (0-9618592-1-0); pap. 17.95 (0-9618592-2-9) Maine Writers.
Maine, Margo. Father Hunger: Fathers, Daughters & Food. 272p. 1991. pap. 12.95 (0-936077-09-3) Gurze Bks.
***Maine, Sandy.** The Soap Book: Simple Herbal Recipes. 96p. 1995. pap. 9.95 (1-883010-14-4) Interweave.
Maine State Bar Association Staff. Maine Media Law Guide. (State Law Ser.). 140p. (Orig.). 1993. pap. text ed. 9.95 (0-913507-42-3) New Forums.
Mainelli, Helen K. Numbers. (Bible Commentary - Old Testament Ser.: No. 5). 136p. 1985. pap. 3.95 (0-8146-1373-X) Liturgical Pr.
Mainer, Jose C., ed. see Fernandez Florez, Wenceslao.
Maines. Heme Oxygenase: Clinical Applications & Functions. 1992. 184.00 (0-8493-5408-0, QP603) CRC Pr.
Maines, David R., ed. Social Organization & Social Process: Essays in Honor of Anselm Strauss. (Communication & Social Order Ser.). 408p. 1991. lib. bdg. 65.95 (0-202-30390-X) Aldine de Gruyter.
Maines, David R., ed. see Blumer, Herbert.
Maines, David R., jt. ed. see Lopata, Helena Z.
Maines, Kenneth. Easy Money, Racing Secrets from Las Vegas. 1974. 10.00 (0-685-57205-6) Byzantine Pr.
Mainfort, Robert, ed. Middle Woodland Settlement & Ceremonialism in the Mid-South & Lower Mississippi Valley: Proceedings of the 1984 Mid-South Archaeological Conference. LC 89-60071. (Archaeological Report Ser.: No. 22). (Illus.). (Orig.). 1989. pap. text ed. write for info. (0-938896-55-5) Mississippi Archives.
Maingon, Charles, jt. auth. see Cova, J. L.
***Maingot, Anthony P.** The United States & the Caribbean. LC 94-28673. 1994. text ed. 52.00 (0-8133-2242-1) Westview.
— The United States & the Caribbean: Challenges of an Asymmetrical Relationship. LC 94-28673. (C). 1994. pap. text ed. 18.95 (0-8133-2241-3) Westview.
Maingot, Anthony P., jt. auth. see Preeg, Ernest H.
Mainguet, M. Desertification: Natural Background & Human Mismanagement. (Physical Environment Ser.: Vol. 9). (Illus.). xvi, 306p. 1991. 159.00 (0-387-52519-X) Spr-Verlag.
Mainguet, Monique. Desertification: Natural Background & Human Mismanagement. LC 94-14998. 1994. 69.00 (0-387-57746-7) Spr-Verlag.
Mainhardt, Ricia, jt. auth. see Varley, John.
Maini, Darshan S. Henry James: The Indirect Vision. 2nd enl. rev. ed. Litz, A. Walton, ed. LC 87-24871. (Studies in Modern Literature: No. 83). 246p. reprint ed. 73.60 (0-8357-1838-7, 2070737) Bks Demand.
— The Spirit of American Literature. viii, 222p. 1988. text ed. 27.50 (0-938719-27-0, Envoy Pr) Apt Bks.
Mainiero, Lina, ed. American Women Writers: A Critical Reference Guide, Vol. 2, F-Le. LC 78-20945. 600p. 1981. 75.00 (0-8044-3152-3, F Ungar Bks) Continuum.
— American Women Writers: A Critical Reference Guide, Vol. 3, Li-R. LC 78-20945. 600p. 1981. 95.00 (0-8044-3153-1, F Ungar Bks) Continuum.
— American Women Writers: A Critical Reference Guide, Vol. 1, A-E. LC 78-20945. 600p. 1979. 95.00 (0-8044-3151-5, F Ungar Bks) Continuum.
Mainiero, Lina & Faust, Langdon L., eds. American Women Writers: A Critical Reference Guide, 4 vols., 4. LC 78-20945. 600p. 1982. 95.00 (0-8044-3155-8, F Ungar Bks) Continuum.
— American Women Writers: A Critical Reference Guide, 4 vols., Set. LC 78-20945. 600p. 1982. 380.00 (0-8044-3150-7, F Ungar Bks) Continuum.
Mainiero, Lisa A. & Tromley, Cheryl L. Developing Managerial Skills in Organizational Behavior: Exercises, Cases, & Readings. 2nd ed. LC 93-5071. 1993. pap. text ed. write for info. (0-13-208190-3) P-H.
Mainkar, T. G. The Making of Vedant. 170p. 1980. 15.95 (0-318-37172-3) Asia Bk Corp.
Mainke, Karl & Tucker, John V. Many-Sorted Logic & Its Applications. 397p. 1993. text ed. 74.95 (0-471-93485-2) Wiley.
Mainland, W. F., ed. see Hoffmann, Ernest.
Mainland, William F., tr. see Von Schiller, Friedrich.
Maino, Charles A. Old Times: San Luis Obispo CA Memoirs. Maino, Jeannette G., ed. 50p. (Orig.). 1990. write for info. (0-318-66925-0) Dry Creeks Bks.
***Maino, Dominick M., ed.** Diagnosis & Management of Special Populations. (Mosby's Optometric Problem Solving Ser.). 1994. write for info. (0-8151-5901-3) Mosby Yr Bk.
Maino, Evelyn, jt. auth. see McMinn, Howard E.
Maino, G., jt. ed. see Carmignani, C.
Maino, G., et al. Simulation of Nonlinear Systems in Physics: ENEA Workshop on Nonlinear Dynamics, Vol. 3. 250p. 1991. text ed. 84.00 (981-02-0402-7) World Scientific Pub.
Maino, G., et al, eds. Nonlinear Phenomena in Physics of Fluids & Plasmas - Proceedings of the ENEA Workshops on Nonlinear Dynamics, Bologna, Italy, October 30-31, 1989. (ENEA Workshop on Nonlinear Dynamics Ser.: Vol. 2). 208p. 1991. text ed. 89.00 (981-02-0363-2) World Scientific Pub.
Maino, Jeannette G. Places, Paths & Passes. 80p. (Orig.). 1991. write for info. (0-941885-07-0) Dry Creeks Bks.
— Speeding into Lost Landscapes. (Orig.). 1982. pap. 5.50 (0-941885-00-3) Dry Creeks Bks.
Maino, Jeannette G., ed. see Maino, Charles A.
Maino, Joseph H., jt. auth. see Aston, Sheree J.
Mainous, Frank D., jt. auth. see Ottman, Robert W.
***Mains, A. A.** Field Security Very Ordinary Intelligence. 1990. 44.00 (0-948251-57-3, Pub. by Picton UK) St Mut.
Mains, David. Eight Survival Skills for Changing Times. LC 92-29671. (Illus.). 156p. 1992. pap. 9.99 (1-56476-036-7, Victor Books) SP Pubns.
— Healing the Dysfunctional Church Family. 168p. 1992. pap. 8.99 (0-89693-050-5) SP Pubns.
— Never Too Late to Dream. 156p. (Orig.). 1993. pap. 8.99 (1-56476-203-3, Victor Books) SP Pubns.
Mains, David & Mains, Karen. Abba: How God Parents Us. LC 88-37312. 160p. (Orig.). 1989. pap. 7.99 (0-87788-002-6) Shaw Pubs.
Mains, David, jt. auth. see Mains, Karen B.
Mains, David, jt. auth. see Mains, Karen.
Mains, David R. & Timberlake, Melissa M. Getting Beyond "How Are You?" LC 92-23325. 1993. pap. 4.99 (1-56476-035-9) SP Pubns.
Mains, Geoffrey. Urban Aboriginals: A Celebration of Leathersexuality. (Illus.). 192p. (Orig.). 1991. reprint ed. pap. 14.95 (0-917342-38-0) Gay Sunshine.
Mains, Karen. Key to an Open Heart. LC 79-51746. 1988. student ed, pap. 8.99 (1-55513-198-0, LifeJourney) Chariot Family.
— Lonely No More. 1993. 14.99 (0-8499-0880-9) Word Inc.
— Open Heart, Open Home. LC 76-1550. 1991. student ed, pap. 8.99 (1-55513-165-4, LifeJourney) Chariot Family.
— With My Whole Heart. rev. ed. 1994. pap. 9.99 (0-88070-681-3, Multnomah Bks) Questar Pubs.
Mains, Karen & Mains, David. Tales of the Resistance. (Illus.). 112p. (J). (gr. 4-7). 1986. 16.99 (0-89191-938-4) Cook.
Mains, Karen, jt. auth. see Hancock, Maxine.
Mains, Karen, jt. auth. see Mains, David.
***Mains, Karen B.** Making Sunday Special. 1994. pap. 8.99 (1-56233-253-8, Star Song Contemp) Star Song TN.
— Open Heart - Open Home. 1989. pap. 3.50 (0-451-15255-7) NAL-Dutton.
— Open Heart-Open Home. 1980. pap. 2.95 (0-451-14183-0, AE2641, Sig) NAL-Dutton.
Mains, Karen B. & Mains, David. Tales of the Kingdom. (Illus.). 112p. (J). (gr. 1 up). 1983. 16.99 (0-89191-560-5) Cook.
Mains, Kristine, jt. auth. see Strumpf, Lori.
Mains, Kristine M., jt. auth. see Strumpf, Lori.
Mains, Laura L., comp. Wisdom from Proverbs: Time-Tested Principles for Living. (Pocketpac Bks.). 112p. (Orig.). 1993. pap. 2.99 (0-87788-845-0) Shaw Pubs.
Mains, Randolph P. The Golden Hour. LC 89-80410. 135p. (Orig.). 1990. pap. 6.00 (0-916383-86-5) Aegina Pr.
Mainstone, Madeleine & Mainstone, Rowland. The Seventeenth Century. LC 80-40039. (Cambridge Introduction to Art Ser.). (Illus.). 100p. 1981. 29.95 (0-521-22162-5); pap. 11.95 (0-521-29376-6) Cambridge U Pr.
Mainstone, Rowland. Hagia Sophia. LC 86-50969. (Illus.). 304p. 1988. 50.00 (0-500-34098-6) Thames Hudson.
Mainstone, Rowland, jt. auth. see Mainstone, Madeleine.
Mainuddin, Rolin G., jt. auth. see Ali, Sheikh R.
Mainwaring, G. B. & Grunwedel, A. Dictionary of the Lepcha Language. (C). 1979. 130.00 (0-89771-111-4, Pub. by Ratna Pustak Bhandar) St Mut.
Mainwaring, John. Memoirs of the Life of George Frederick Handel. LC 80-14096. (Music Ser.). 1980. reprint ed. 32.50 (0-306-76042-8) Da Capo.
Mainwaring, Lynn. Dynamics of Uneven Development. 224p. 1990. text ed. 69.95 (1-85278-319-2, Pub. by E Elgar Pub UK) Ashgate Pub Co.
Mainwaring, Lynn, jt. ed. see George, K. D.
Mainwaring, Marion. Murder in Pastiche or, Nine Detectives All at Sea. LC 89-61889. (Periwig Mystery Ser.: No. 3). 230p. 1989. reprint ed. pap. text ed. 8.95 (0-937672-27-0) Rowan Tree.
Mainwaring, Marion, ed. see Wharton, Edith.
Mainwaring, S. Learning Through Sewing & Pattern Design. 35p. (J). (gr. k-3). 1976. pap. 8.95 (0-931114-86-1) High-Scope.
Mainwaring, S. & Shouse, C. Learning Through Construction. 43p. (J). (gr. k-3). 1983. pap. 8.95 (0-685-51017-4) High-Scope.
Mainwaring, Scott. The Catholic Church & Politics in Brazil, 1916-1985. 352p. 1986. 42.50 (0-8047-1320-0) Stanford U Pr.
***Mainwaring, Scott & Scully, Timothy R., eds.** Building Democratic Instutitions: Party Systems in Latin America. 600p. 1995. 65.00x (0-8047-2307-9) Stanford U Pr.
— Building Democratic Instutitions: Party Systems in Latin America. LC 93-46528. 600p. 1995. pap. 19.95 (0-8047-2305-2) Stanford U Pr.
Mainwaring, Scott & Wilde, Alexander, eds. The Progressive Church in Latin America. LC 88-40324. 340p. (C). 1990. text ed. 32.95 (0-268-01573-2) U of Notre Dame Pr.
Mainwaring, Scott, et al, eds. Issues in Democratic Consolidation: The New South American Democracies in Comparative Perspective. LC 91-50566. (From the Helen Kellogg Institute for International Studies). (C). 1992. text ed. 42.95 (0-268-01210-5) U of Notre Dame Pr.
— Issues in Democratic Consolidation: The New South American Democracies in Comparative Perspective. LC 91-50566. (From the Helen Kellogg Institute for International Studies). (C). 1992. pap. text ed. 19.95 (0-268-01211-3) U of Notre Dame Pr.
Mainwaring, William L. Exploring the Mt. Hood Loop. (Illus.). 64p. (Orig.). 1992. pap. 9.95 (0-918832-00-4) Westridge.
— Exploring the Oregon Coast. 5th ed. LC 77-77250. (Illus.). 1994. pap. 7.95 (0-918832-01-2) Westridge.
Mainwarsng, C. B. & Grunwedel, A. Dictionary of the Lepcha Language. 1979. 80.00 (0-7855-0267-X, Pub. by Ratna Pustak Bhandar) St Mut.
Mainwarsng, M. & Grunwedel, G. Dictionary of the Lepcha Language. 1979. 80.00 (0-7855-0310-2, Pub. by Ratna Pustak Bhandar) St Mut.
***Mainzer, Klaus.** Computer - Neue Fluegel des Geistes? Die Evolution Computergestuetzter Techik, Wissenschaft, Kultur & Philosophie. (Philosophie & Wissenschaft - Transdisziplinaere Studien Ser.: Bd. 9). xii, 882p. (Orig.). (GER.). (C). 1995. pap. text ed. 60.00 (3-11-014808-0) De Gruyter.
— Computer - Neue Fluegel des Geistes? Die Evolution Computergestuetzter Technick, Wissenschaft, Kultur & Philosophie. (Illus.). xii, 882p. (GER.). (C). 1994. lib. bdg. 344.65 (3-11-014004-7) De Gruyter.
— Thinking in Complexity. 1994. pap. 30.00 (0-387-57597-9) Spr-Verlag.
Maio, Eugene, tr. see Pearson, D'Orsay W., ed. & tr.
Maio, Kathy. Popcorn & Sexual Politics: Movie Reviews. 200p. 1991. 21.95 (0-89594-469-3); pap. 9.95 (0-89594-468-5) Crossing Pr.
***Maio, Samuel.** Creating Another Self: Voice in Modern American Personal Poetry. LC 95-6311. 1995. write for info. (0-943549-33-7) TJU Pr.
Maio-sin Wu, Samuel, jt. auth. see Johnston, Daniel.
Maiolo, John R., jt. ed. see Vasoli, Robert H.
Maiolo, Joseph & Brantley, Jill, eds. From Three Sides: Reading for Writers. 288p. (C). 1976. pap. text ed. write for info. (0-13-331876-1) P-H.
Maior, Plinius. C. Plinii Secundi Naturalis Historia, 6 vols. in 3. 1784p. (GER.). 1992. reprint ed. Vol. I, Bd. 1: Libri 1-6, 1866; Bd. 2: Libri 7-15, 1867, Zus, 590p. write for info. (0-318-70543-5, Pub. by Georg Olms GW); reprint ed. Vol. II, Bd. 3: Libri 16-22, 1868; Bd. 4: Libri 23-31, 1871, Zus, 637p. write for info. (0-318-70544-3, Pub. by Georg Olms GW); reprint ed. Vol. III, Bd. 5: Libri 32-37, 1873; Bd. 6: Index Deorum et Hominum, Index Locorum, 1882, Zus, 557p. write for info. (0-318-70545-1, Pub. by Georg Olms GW) Lubrecht & Cramer.
— C. Plinii Secundi Naturalis Historia, 6 vols. in 3, Set. 1784p. (GER.). 1992. reprint ed. write for info. (3-487-09678-1, Pub. by Georg Olms GW) Lubrecht & Cramer.
***Maiorana, Sal.** Relentless: The Hard-Hitting History of Buffalo Bills Football. (Illus.). 480p. 1994. 39.50 (1-885758-00-6) Quality Sports.
— Through the Green: The Mind & Art of a Professional Golfer. (Illus.). 272p. 1993. 21.95 (0-312-09363-2) St Martin.
Maiorana, Victor P. The Analytical Student: Whole Learning for the High School & College Student. LC 94-13031. 1994. 16.95 (0-927516-59-4) ERIC-REC.
— The Analytical Teacher: Whole Teaching, Whole Learning for the High School & College Teacher. LC 94-13030. 1994. 16.95 (0-927516-58-6) ERIC-REC.
— Critical Thinking Across the Curriculum: Building the Analytical Classroom. LC 92-20683. 180p. (Orig.). (C). 1992. pap. text ed. 14.95 (0-927516-35-7) ERIC-REC.
Maiorano, Robert & Brooks, Valerie. Balanchine's Mozartiana: The Making of a Masterpiece. (Illus.). 192p. 1985. 17.95 (0-88191-013-9) Freundlich.
Maiori, Rachel, jt. auth. see Martin, Genevieve A.
Maiorino, Giancarlo. Portrait of Eccentricity: Arcimboldo & the Mannerist Grotesque. (Illus.). 160p. 1991. 28.50 (0-271-00727-3) Pa St U Pr.
Maiorino, Giancarlo. Adam, "New Born & Perfect" The Renaissance Promise of Eternity. LC 86-46144. (Illus.). 172p. (C). 1987. 22.50 (0-253-30405-9) Ind U Pr.
— The Cornucopian Mind & the Baroque Unity of the Arts. LC 89-3894. (Illus.). 224p. 1990. lib. bdg. 32.50 (0-271-00679-X) Pa St U Pr.
— Leonardo da Vinci: The Daedalian Myth-Maker. (Illus.). 320p. 1992. text ed. 35.00 (0-271-00817-2) Pa St U Pr.
Maiotti, Ettore. The Drawing Handbook: Learning from the Masters. 1989. 12.95 (0-517-57283-4, C P Pubs) Crown Pub Group.
— Oil Painting Handbook. 1990. 13.95 (0-517-57624-4, C P Pubs) Crown Pub Group.
— Oil Painting Handbook. 1994. pap. 6.99 (0-517-13133-1) Random.
— The Watercolor Handbook: Learning from the Masters. (Illus.). 160p. 1986. 14.00 (0-517-56306-1, C P Pubs) Crown Pub Group.
Maiping, Chen, tr. see Wang, Anyi.
Mair, A. Student Health Services in Great Britain & North Ireland. LC 66-284040. 1967. 115.00 (0-08-011963-8, Pub. by Pergamon Repr UK) Franklin.
Mair, Christian. Infinitival Complement Clauses in English: A Study of Syntax in Discourse. (Studies in English Language). (Illus.). 350p. (C). 1990. 64.95 (0-521-37035-3) Cambridge U Pr.
Mair, Craig. Mercat Cross & Tolbooth: Understanding Scotland's Old Burghs. 242p. (C). 1989. pap. text ed. 26.00 (0-85976-196-7, Pub. by J Donald) St Mut.
Mair, David, jt. auth. see Roundy, Nancy L.
Mair, Denis C., tr. see Chen-hua & Yu, Chun-Fang.
Mair, Denis C., tr. see Pu, Songling.
Mair, Denis C., tr. see Wang, Meng.
Mair, Denis C., tr. see Yan, Jiaqi.
Mair, Douglas. A Modern Guide to Economic Thought: An Introduction to Comparative Schools of Thought in Economics. 296p. 1992. pap. 22.95 (1-85278-640-X, Pub. by E Elgar Pub UK) Ashgate Pub Co.
Mair, Douglas, ed. The Scottish Contribution to Modern Economic Thought. 1990. text ed. 39.00 (0-08-037723-8, Pub. by Aberdeen U Pr) Macmillan.
Mair, Douglas & Miller, Anne. Modern Guide to Economic Thought: An Introduction to Comparative Schools of Thought in Economics. 288p. 1991. text ed. 69.95 (1-85278-323-0, Pub. by E Elgar Pub UK) Ashgate Pub Co.
Mair, G. L., jt. auth. see Prewett, P. D.
Mair, Gary. Directory of Public Companies: Stockbrokers Bible. 400p. 1993. 49.95 (1-884821-00-6) Wall St Finan.
***Mair, George.** Bette: An Intimate Biography of Bette Midler. (Illus.). 368p. 1995. 22.50 (1-55972-272-X, Birch Ln Pr) Carol Pub Group.
— Family Money. 352p. 1994. pap. 4.99 (0-7860-0010-4, Pinnacle NY) Windsor NY.
— Lethal Ladies. 1993. mass mkt. 4.99 (1-55817-735-3, Pinnacle NY) Windsor NY.
— Oprah Winfrey: The Real Story. LC 94-18112. 1994. 21.95 (1-55972-250-9, Birch Ln Pr) Carol Pub Group.
— Oprah Winfrey: The Real Story. large type ed. LC 95-3696. (Large Print Book Ser.). 1995. pap. 21.95 (1-56895-095-0) Wheeler Pub.
— Star Stalkers. 352p. 1995. pap. 4.99 (0-7860-0138-0) Windsor NY.
— Star Stalkers. 352p. 1995. pap. 4.99 (0-8217-0162-2) Zebra.
Mair, George, jt. auth. see Phillips, Patricia.
Mair, J. Pictorial History of Darvel. (C). 1989. pap. 50.00 (0-907526-40-3, Alloway Pub) St Mut.
— Pictorial History of Galston. (C). 1988. pap. 50.00 (0-907526-37-3, Alloway Pub) St Mut.

M

An Asterisk (*) at the beginning of an entry indicates that the title is appearing in BIP for the first time.

— Pictorial History of Newmilns. (C). 1988. pap. 50.00 (*0-907526-34-9*, Alloway Pub) St Mut.

Mair, John. Book-Keeping Moderniz'd: Or, Merchant-Accounts by Double Entry, According to the Italian Form. Brief, Richard P., ed. LC 77-87276. (Development of Contemporary Accounting Thought Ser.). 1978. reprint ed. lib. bdg. 52.95 (*0-405-10904-0*) Ayer.

— Fourth Forger: William Ireland & the Shakespeare Papers. LC 70-146864. (Select Bibliographies Reprint Ser.). 1977. reprint ed. 21.95 (*0-8369-5631-1*) Ayer.

Mair, Lucy. Primitive Government. 12.00 (*0-8446-2513-2*) Peter Smith.

Mair, Lucy P. Anthropology & Social Change. (London School of Economics Monographs on Social Anthropology: No. 38). 206p. (C). 1971. pap. 14.95 (*0-485-19638-7*, Pub. by Athlone Pr UK) Humanities.

— An Introduction to Social Anthropology. 2nd ed. LC 85-19895. 324p. 1985. reprint ed. text ed. 57.75 (*0-313-24977-6*, MISA, Greenwood Pr) Greenwood.

Mair, Miller. Between Psychology & Psychotherapy: A Poetics of Experience. 272p. 1989. 49.95 (*0-415-00021-1*, A3317); pap. 14.95 (*0-415-00022-X*, A3690) Routledge.

Mair, Nancy & Rinzler, Susan, eds. Simply Vegetarian! 240p. (Orig.). 1993. mass mkt. 4.99 (*0-425-13992-1*) Berkley Pub.

Mair, Peter, ed. The Changing Irish Party System: Organisation, Ideology and Electoral Competition. LC 87-12811. 257p. 1987. text ed. 39.95 (*0-312-01218-7*) St Martin.

— The West European Party System. (Oxford Readings in Politics & Government Ser.). 376p. 1990. 59.00 (*0-19-827584-6*); pap. text ed. 17.95 (*0-19-827583-8*) OUP.

Mair, Peter & Smith, Gordon, eds. Understanding Party System Change in Western Europe. 191p. 1990. text ed. 37.50 (*0-7146-3381-X*, Pub. by F Cass Pubs UK) Intl Spec Bk.

Mair, Peter, jt. auth. see Bartolini, Stefano.

Mair, Peter, jt. ed. see Bartolini, Stefano.

Mair, Peter, jt. auth. see Cranston, Maurice W.

Mair, Peter, jt. ed. see Daalder, Hans.

Mair, Peter, jt. auth. see Katz, Richard S.

Mair, R. J., et al. Repository Tunnel Construction in Deep Clay Formations. 132p. 1992. pap. 16.00 (*92-826-3738-7*, CD-NA-13964-EN-C, Pub. by Europ Com) UNIPUB.

***Mair, Ralf.** The Last Cast: Fishing Reminiscences. 1995. 29.95 (*0-88839-346-6*) Hancock House.

Mair, Susan G., jt. auth. see Ducan, James P.

Mair, Thomas A. Batavia Revisited. (Illus.). 227p. (Orig.). 1990. pap. 12.00 (*0-9628268-0-4*) Benson Mair & Gosselin.

Mair, Victor, et al. Four Introspective Poets: A Concordance to Selected Poems. LC 86-71604. (Arizona State University Center for Asian Studies Monograph Ser.: No. 20). xiii, 243p. (Orig.). 1987. pap. 10.00 (*0-317-58260-7*) ASU Ctr Asian.

Mair, Victor H. Painting & Performance: Chinese Picture Recitation & Its Indian Genesis. LC 88-21591. (Illus.). 302p. 1988. text ed. 30.00 (*0-8248-1100-3*) UH Pr.

— T'ang Transformation Texts: A Study of the Buddhist Contribution to the Rise of Vernacular Fiction & Drama in China. LC 88-37983. (Harvard-Yenching Institute Monograph: No. 28). 300p. 1989. 28.00 (*0-674-86815-3*) HUP.

— Tunhuang Popular Narratives. LC 83-1939. (Cambridge Studies in Chinese History, Literature & Institutions). 400p. 1984. 84.95 (*0-521-24761-6*) Cambridge U Pr.

Mair, Victor H., ed. The Columbia Anthology of Traditional Chinese Literature. LC 93-48174. (Translation from the Asian Classics Ser.). 1,350p. 1994. 65.00 (*0-231-07428-X*) Col U Pr.

— Experimental Essays on Chuang-tzu. LC 83-3615. (Asian Studies at Hawaii: No. 29). 196p. 1989. reprint ed. pap. text ed. 10.00 (*0-8248-0836-3*) UH Pr.

Mair, Victor H., tr. & comment. Wandering on the Way: Early Taoist Tales & Parables of Chuang Tzu. LC 93-46775. 1994. pap. 11.95 (*0-553-37406-0*) Bantam.

Mair, Victor H. & Liu, Yongquan, eds. Characters & Computers. 200p. 1991. 65.00 (*90-5199-061-8*, Pub. by IOS Pr NE) IOS Press.

Mair, Victor H., tr. see Mei Cherng & Wang Bor.

Mair, Victor H., tr. see Pu, Songling.

Mair, W. Austyn & Birdsall, David L. Aircraft Performance. (Aerospace Ser.: No. 5). (Illus.). 304p. (C). 1992. 89.95 (*0-521-36264-4*) Cambridge U Pr.

Mair, William C., et al. Computer Control & Audit. (Illus.). 1977. text ed. 35.25 (*0-89413-063-3*) Inst Inter Aud.

Mairants, Ivor. The Flamenco Guitar: A Complete Method for Playing Flamenco. (Illus.). 200p. 1958. 16.95 (*0-686-09074-8*, 60481-910); lp 9.95 (*0-686-09075-6*, 61609-960) Peer-Southrn.

Maire, Albert. Materials Used to Write Upon Before the Invention of Printing. (Shorey Lost Arts Ser.). 30p. reprint ed. pap. 2.95 (*0-8466-6006-7*, U6) Shorey.

Maire, C. D. Learning to Live for God. 1979. pap. 7.50 (*0-85234-132-6*, Pub. by Evangel Pr UK) Presby & Reformed.

Maire, J. & Waegell, B. Structures, Mecanismes et Spectroscopye: 120, 60 Solutions. (Cours & Documents de Chimie Ser.). 312p. (FRE.). 1969. text ed. 241.00 (*0-677-50160-9*) Gordon & Breach.

Maire, J. C. & Waegell, B. Structures, Mechanisms & Spectroscopy: 120 Problems, 60 Solutions. LC 70-146808. (Documents in Chemistry Ser.). (Illus.). 312p. 1971. text ed. 241.00 (*0-677-30160-X*) Gordon & Breach.

Mairesse, Jacques, jt. ed. see Griliches, Zvi.

Mairet, P. A. R. Orage. 1974. 99.35 (*0-87968-572-7*) Gordon Pr.

Mairet, Philip, tr. see Eliade, Mircea.

Mairet, Philip, tr. see Mounier, Emmanuel.

Mairet, Philip, tr. see Wendel, Francois.

Mairet, Philippe. Pioneer of Sociology: The Life & Letters of Patrick Geddes. LC 78-24782. 1980. reprint ed. 23.00 (*0-88355-859-9*) Hyperion Conn.

Mairowitz, David Z. Kafka for Beginners. (Illus.). 176p. 1994. reprint ed. pap. 11.95 (*0-87816-282-8*) Kitchen Sink.

— Reich for Beginners. (Writers & Readers Documentary Comic Bks.). (Illus.). 176p. 1986. pap. 6.95 (*0-86316-031-X*) Writers & Readers.

Mairowitz, M. & Gonzales, G. Reich for Beginners. 1990. pap. 21.00 (*0-04-021032-4*, Pub. by Northcote UK) St Mut.

Mairs & Hoerauf. The Puget Sound Region: A Portfolio of Computer Maps. (Occasional Papers: No. 3). 1986. pap. 2.95 (*0-318-23323-1*) WWU CPNS.

Mairs, Nancy. In All the Rooms of the Yellow House. 1984. 14.95 (*0-933188-26-9*); pap. 7.95 (*0-933188-27-7*) Blue Moon Pr.

— Ordinary Time: Cycles in Marriage, Faith, & Renewal. LC 92-40421. 256p. 1993. 20.00 (*0-8070-7056-4*) Beacon Pr.

— Ordinary Time: Cycles in Marriage, Faith, & Renewal. 256p. 1994. pap. 12.00 (*0-8070-7057-2*) Beacon Pr.

— Plaintext. LC 85-27043. 154p. 1986. 19.95 (*0-8165-0892-5*) U of Ariz Pr.

— Plaintext. LC 85-27043. 154p. 1992. reprint ed. pap. 13.95 (*0-8165-1337-6*) U of Ariz Pr.

— Remembering the Bone House: An Erotics of Place & Space. LC 94-41563. 288p. 1995. pap. 12.95 (*0-8070-7069-6*) Beacon Pr.

— Voice Lessons: On Becoming a (Woman) Writer. LC 93-31513. 176p. 1994. 15.00 (*0-8070-6006-2*) Beacon Pr.

Mairtin Mac an Ghaill. Young, Gifted & Black: Student-Teacher Relations in the Schooling of Black Youth. 160p. 1988. pap. 29.00 (*0-335-09507-0*, Open Univ Pr) Taylor & Francis.

Mais, D. E., jt. ed. see Halushka, P. V.

Mais, Roger. Black Lightning. (Caribbean Writers Ser.). 159p. (Orig.). (C). 1983. reprint ed. pap. 8.95 (*0-435-98584-1*) Heinemann.

— Brother Man. (Caribbean Writers Ser.). 191p. 1974. pap. 8.95 (*0-435-98585-X*) Heinemann.

— The Hills Were Joyful Together. (Caribbean Writers Ser.). 288p. 1981. pap. 9.95 (*0-435-98586-8*) Heinemann.

Mais, Stuart P. Books & Their Writers. LC 68-54359. (Essay Index Reprint Ser.). 1977. 21.95 (*0-8369-0667-5*) Ayer.

— From Shakespeare to O. Henry: Studies in Literature. rev. ed. LC 68-16952. (Essay Index Reprint Ser.). 1977. 20.95 (*0-8369-0668-3*) Ayer.

— Some Modern Authors. LC 73-128276. (Essay Index Reprint Ser.). 1977. 23.95 (*0-8369-1836-3*) Ayer.

— Why We Should Read. LC 67-26760. (Essay Index Reprint Ser.). 1977. 20.95 (*0-8369-0669-1*) Ayer.

Maisch, J. M. A Manual of Organic Materia Medica: Drugs from Natural Sources. (Alternative Medicine Ser.). 1992. lib. bdg. 275.95 (*0-8490-5441-9*) Gordon Pr.

Maisel. Alexander Technique. 1989. pap. 9.95 (*0-8065-1118-4*, Citadel Pr) Carol Pub Group.

— The Ocular Lens: Structure, Function, & Pathology. 496p. 1985. 165.00 (*0-8247-7297-0*) Dekker.

Maisel, Albert Q. Miracles of Military Medicine. LC 70-167382. (Essay Index Reprint Ser.). 1977. reprint ed. 23.95 (*0-8369-2561-0*) Ayer.

Maisel, Carolyn. Witnessing. LC 78-60979. 59p. 1978. per. 3.75 (*0-934332-07-X*) LEpervier Pr.

Maisel, David, tr. see Coquery-Vidrovitch, Catherine.

Maisel, David, tr. see Neher, Andre.

Maisel, David, tr. see Sternhell, Zeev, et al.

Maisel, David, tr. see Ye'or, Bat.

Maisel, Edward, intro. & sel. The Alexander Technique. 1989. pap. 9.95 (*0-8184-0506-6*) Carol Pub Group.

Maisel, Edward M. Charles T. Griffes: The Life of an American Composer. (Music Book Index Ser.). 347p. 1992. reprint ed. lib. bdg. 89.00 (*0-7812-9464-9*) Rprt Serv.

Maisel, Eric. The Blackbirds of Mulhouse. LC 83-60319. 287p. (Orig.). 1984. pap. 7.95 (*0-910997-01-2*) Maya Pr.

— Dismay. LC 82-61850. 211p. (Orig.). 1983. pap. 7.95 (*0-910997-00-4*) Maya Pr.

— Fearless Creating: A Step-by-Step Guide to Starting & Completing Your Work of Art. LC 95-10427. 1995. write for info. (*0-87477-805-0*) J P Tarcher.

— The Fretful Dancer. LC 86-70631. 128p. (Orig.). 1987. pap. 7.95 (*0-916383-12-1*) Aegina Pr.

— A Life in the Arts: Practical Guidance & Inspiration for Creative & Performing Artists. LC 93-21257. (Inner Work Book Ser.). 272p. 1994. pap. 15.95 (*0-87477-766-6*, J P T-Putnam) Putnam Pub Group.

— Staying Sane in the Arts: A Guide for Creative & Performing Artists. 304p. 1992. 22.95 (*0-87477-693-7*) J P Tarcher.

Maisel, Eric, ed. Artists Speak (Journal Edition) Sketchbooks. 224p. 1993. 20.00 (*0-06-250881-4*) Harper SF.

— Artists Speak (Pocket Edition) Sketchbooks. 224p. 1993. 15.00 (*0-06-250880-6*) Harper SF.

***Maisel, John.** Is Jesus God? (Regular Script) Lee, Margaret, tr. 76p. (CHI.). 1993. pap. 1.50 (*1-56582-016-9*) Christ Renew Min.

— Is Jesus God? (Simplified Script) Lee, Margaret, tr. 76p. (CHI.). 1993. pap. 1.50 (*1-56582-017-7*) Christ Renew Min.

Maisel, L. Sandy. Parties & Elections in America: The Electoral Process. 2nd ed. LC 92-37941. 1993. pap. text ed. write for info. (*0-07-039738-4*) McGraw.

— The Parties Respond: Changes in American Parties & Campaigns. 2nd ed. (Transforming American Politics Ser.). 420p. (C). 1994. pap. text ed. 24.50 (*0-8133-1723-1*) Westview.

Maisel, L. Sandy, ed. Political Parties & Elections in the United States: An Encyclopedia, 2 vols., Set. LC 91-6940. (Reference Library of Social Science: Vol. 498). 1367p. 1991. 150.00 (*0-8240-7975-2*, SS498) Garland.

Maisel, Louis & Cooper, Joseph, eds. The Impact of the Electoral Process. LC 76-47088. (Sage Electoral Studies Yearbook: Vol. 3). (Illus.). 304p. reprint ed. pap. 86.70 (*0-317-08927-7*, 2021926) Bks Demand.

Maisel, Louis S. From Obscurity to Oblivion: Running in the Congressional Primary. rev. ed. LC 81-21994. 208p. 1986. text ed. 28.00x (*0-87049-347-7*); pap. text ed. 14.00x (*0-87049-348-5*) U of Tenn Pr.

Maisel, Merry, ed. see Trotsky, Leon.

Maisel, Sally J. Cruising Solo: The Single Person's Guide to Adventure on the High Seas. (Illus.). 300p. (Orig.). 1993. pap. 14.95 (*0-934377-14-6*) Marin Pubns.

Maisel, Sandy L. & Shade, William G., eds. Parties & Politics in American History: A Reader. LC 94-8022. (Reference Library of the Humanities: Vol. 1724). 296p. 1994. 44.00 (*0-8153-1690-9*, H1724); pap. 18.95 (*0-8153-1323-3*) Garland.

Maisel, Sherman J. Managing the Dollar. (Illus.). 1973. 10.95 (*0-393-05494-2*) Norton.

— Real Estate & Finance. 2nd ed. 570p. (C). 1992. text ed. 56.00 (*0-15-575852-7*) Dryden Pr.

— Real Estate Finance. (Illus.). 448p. (C). 1987. text ed. 46.75 (*0-15-575847-0*) HB Coll Pubs.

Maisels, Charles K. Archaeology in the "Cradle of Civilization" LC 92-2777. (Experience of Archaeology Ser.). 224p. 1992. 75.00 (*0-415-04742-0*, A6070) Routledge.

— The Emergence of Civilization: From Hunting & Gathering to Agriculture, Cities & the State in the Near East. (Illus.). 480p. 1990. 82.50 (*0-415-00168-4*, A4108) Routledge.

— The Emergence of Civilization: From Hunting & Gathering to Agriculture, Cities & the State in the Near East. LC 93-7453. 1993. pap. write for info. (*0-415-09659-6*) Routledge.

Maisey, John G. Santana Fossils: An Illustrated Atlas. 1991. 200.00 (*0-86622-549-8*) TFH Pubns.

Maisey, M. N. Clinical Nuclear Medicine. 1983. 97.50 (*0-7020-1243-2*) Saunders.

Maisey, M. N., et al. Clinical Nuclear Medicine. (Illus.). 525p. 1983. text ed. 121.00 (*0-7216-1087-0*) Saunders.

— Clinical Nuclear Medicine. 2nd ed. (Illus.). 650p. 1991. text ed. 149.50 (*0-397-58327-3*) Lippincott.

Maisey, Michael. Nuclear Medicine: A Clinical Introduction. (Illus.). 125p. 1982. 24.50 (*0-686-33362-4*) Kluwer Ac.

Maislin, Sam. New York Criminal Law Designed for Criminal Justice (Paralegal Students) 3rd ed. 240p. 1990. per. 31.95 (*0-8403-6105-X*) Kendall-Hunt.

Maisner, Heather. Find Mouse in the House. LC 93-3638. (Illus.). 20p. (J). (ps up). 1994. 9.95 (*1-56402-351-6*) Candlewick Pr.

— Find Mouse in the Yard. LC 93-12825. (Illus.). 20p. (J). (ps up). 1994. 9.95 (*1-56402-350-8*) Candlewick Pr.

— The Magic Globel. LC 94-15164. (Illus.). (J). 1995. write for info. (*1-56402-445-8*) Candlewick Pr.

— The Magic Hourglass: A Time-Travel Adventure Game. LC 94-10404. (Illus.). (J). 1995. reprint ed. write for info. (*1-56402-446-6*) Candlewick Pr.

Maisner, Larry. Practical Soccer Tactics. LC 78-64382. (Illus.). 144p. 1979. pap. 4.95 (*0-89037-157-1*) Anderson World.

— Practical Soccer Tactics. 1986. pap. 7.95 (*0-02-028790-9*, Collier S&S) S&S Trade.

Maisner, Larry & Mason, Bill. The Rules of Soccer: Simplified. (Illus.). 16p. 1978. pap. 1.95 (*0-9611406-0-7*) Maisner & Mason.

Maison, K. E. Daumier, Honore: Catalogue Raisonne of the Paintings, Watercolours & Drawings, 2 vols., Set, Vols. 1-2. (Illus.). 1995. reprint ed. Set, Vol. 1: Paintings, 446p. Vol. 2: Watercolours & Drawings, 620p. 350.00 (*1-55660-251-0*) A Wofsy Fine Arts.

Maison, Mary B. Easy Quilts...by Jupiter! Reinstatler, Laura, ed. LC 94-17061. (Quilt Shop Ser.). (Illus.). 72p. (Orig.). 1994. pap. 17.95 (*1-56477-068-0*) That Patchwork.

Maisrikrod, Surin. Thailands Two General Elections in 1992. (Research Notes & Discussions Papers: No. 75). 70p. 1993. pap. 11.50 (*981-3016-52-3*, Pub. by Inst SE Asian Studies SI) Ashgate Pub Co.

Maissel. Handbook of Thin Film Technology. 1995. text ed. 99.95 (*0-07-039743-0*) McGraw.

Maissel, Leon I. & Francombre, Maurice H. Introduction to Thin Films. 308p. 1973. text ed. 177.00 (*0-677-02840-7*) Gordon & Breach.

Maissin, Eugene. French in Mexico & Texas, 1838-1839. Sheppherd, J. L., tr. (Illus.). 1961. 65.00 (*0-685-05002-5*) A Jones.

Maister, David. Managing the Professional Service Firm. 448p. 1993. text ed. 39.95 (*0-02-919782-1*) Free Pr.

Maister, Philippa. The Insider's Atlanta. (Illus.). 252p. (Orig.). 1982. pap. 7.95 (*0-9608596-0-8*) Good Hope GA.

***Maister, Robert.** Ipswich: Town on the Orwell. 112p. 1994. pap. 21.00x (*0-614-00312-1*) St Mut.

Maisto, G., ed. Tax Treatment of Cost-Contribution Arrangements. 324p. 1988. lib. bdg. 104.00 (*90-6544-352-5*) Kluwer Ac.

Maisto, Stephen, jt. auth. see Nirenberg, Ted D.

Maisto, Stephen, et al. Drug Use & Misuse. 2nd ed. (Illus.). 515p. (C). 1994. pap. text ed. write for info. (*0-15-501007-7*) HB Coll Pubs.

Maisto, Stephen A., jt. ed. see Galizio, Mark.

Maisto, Stephen A., et al. Drug Use & Misuse. LC 90-5098. (Illus.). 512p. (C). 1991. pap. text ed. 30.00 (*0-03-014973-8*, RM315.M335) HB Coll Pubs.

Maistre, Joseph. Considerations on France. Lebrun, Richard, tr. (Cambridge Texts in the History of Political Thought Ser.). 288p. (C). 1995. 49.95 (*0-521-46076-X*); pap. 16.95 (*0-521-46628-8*) Cambridge U Pr.

Maistre, Joseph M. de. Essay on the Generative Principle of Political Constitutions. LC 77-24972. 1977. reprint ed. 50.00 (*0-8201-1294-1*) Schol Facsimiles.

Maistrellis, Nicholas, jt. ed. see Zeiderman, Howard.

Maital, Sharone, jt. auth. see Maital, Shlomo.

Maital, Shlomo. Executive Economics: Ten Essential Tools for Managers. 1994. text ed. 24.95 (*0-02-919785-6*) Free Pr.

Maital, Shlomo & Maital, Sharone. Economics & Psychology. Blaug, Mark, ed. (International Library of Critical Writings in Business History). 584p. 1993. 159.95 (*1-85278-693-0*, Pub. by E Elgar Pub UK) Ashgate Pub Co.

Maiti & Goswami, G. Clinical Electro-Cardiography. (C). 1989. 40.00 (*0-89771-373-7*, Current Dist) St Mut.

Maiti, Satyabrata, et al. Handbook of Annual Oilseed Crops. (C). 1988. 18.00 (*81-204-0315-0*, Pub. by Oxford IBH II) S Asia.

Maitland, A. & Sibbett, W. QE8 - Eighth National Quantum Electronics Conference: Special Issue - Journal of Modern Optics, Vol. 35 No. 3. 320p. 1988. pap. 66.00 (*0-85066-899-9*) Taylor & Francis.

***Maitland, Antony, illus.** Stories from Shakespeare. (YA). (gr. 5 up). 1995. 19.95 (*0-689-80037-1*, McElderry) S&S Childrens.

Maitland, Arthur & Dunn, M. H. Laser Physics. LC 76-97205. 425p. reprint ed. pap. 121.20 (*0-317-09014-3*, 2051612) Bks Demand.

***Maitland, Brian.** Japanese Baseball: A Fan's Guide. (Illus.). 140p. (Orig.). 1991. pap. 12.95 (*0-8048-1680-8*) C E Tuttle.

Maitland Club Staff. Catalogue of the Works Printed for the Maitland Club. LC 72-1043. (Maitland Club, Glasgow. Publications: No. 38). reprint ed. 10.00 (*0-404-53011-7*) AMS Pr.

— Miscellany of the Maitland Club, 4 Vols, Set. Macdonald, Alexander et al, eds. LC 72-982. (Maitland Club, Glasgow. Publications: No. 25). reprint ed. 165.00 (*0-404-52971-2*) AMS Pr.

— Publications of the Maitland Club, Numbers 1-75. reprint ed. write for info. (*0-404-52920-8*) AMS Pr.

— Registrum Metellanum, I. LC 72-967. (Maitland Club, Glasgow. Publications: No. 11). reprint ed. 10.00 (*0-404-52941-0*) AMS Pr.

Maitland, David J. Aging As Counterculture: A Vocation for the Later Years. LC 90-7837. 192p. (Orig.). 1990. pap. 12.95 (*0-8298-0869-8*) Pilgrim OH.

Maitland, Edward. Anna Kingsford, 2 vols., Set. 1971. 200.00 (*0-87968-639-1*) Gordon Pr.

— By & By: An Historical Romance of the Future. 460p. 1977. reprint ed. 60.00 (*0-8398-2379-7*) Ultramarine Pub.

— The Higher Law: A Romance, 3 vols. in 2, Set. LC 79-8165. reprint ed. 84.50 (*0-404-62184-8*) AMS Pr.

Maitland, Edward, jt. auth. see Kingsford, Anna B.

Maitland, Edward, jt. tr. see Kingsford, Anna B.

Maitland, Edward, jt. auth. see Kingsford, Anna.

Maitland, Edward, tr. see Trismegistus, Hermes M.

Maitland, F. W. The Constitutional History of England: A Course of Lectures Delivered. LC 92-75950. 578p. 1993. reprint ed. 110.00 (*1-56169-026-0*) W W Gaunt.

— Equity, Also the Forms of Action at Common Law: Two Courses of Lectures. Chaytor, A. H. & Whittaker, W. J., eds. xvi, 412p. 1984. reprint ed. lib. bdg. 37.50 (*0-8377-0824-9*) Rothman.

Maitland, Francis. Chile: Its Land & People. 1976. lib. bdg. 59.95 (*0-8490-1604-5*) Gordon Pr.

Maitland, Frederic. Justice & Police. LC 77-38669. reprint ed. 29.50 (*0-404-09179-2*) AMS Pr.

Maitland, Frederic W. Domesday Book & Beyond: Three Essays in the Early History of England. 550p. 1988. pap. 32.95 (*0-521-34918-4*) Cambridge U Pr.

— Forms of Action at Common Law. (C). 1936. pap. 15.95 (*0-521-09185-3*) Cambridge U Pr.

— Selected Essays. Hazeltine, H. D. et al, eds. LC 68-20316. (Essay Index Reprint Ser). 1977. 20.95 (*0-8369-0670-5*) Ayer.

Maitland, Frederic W., pseud. Selected Historical Essays of F. W. Maitland. LC 85-12552. xxx, 278p. 1985. reprint ed. text ed. 65.00 (*0-313-24954-7*, MSHE, Greenwood Pr) Greenwood.

Maitland, Frederic W. A Sketch of English Legal History. LC 75-41185. 1976. reprint ed. 22.50 (*0-404-14684-8*) AMS Pr.

Maitland, Frederic W., ed. Memoranda de Parliamento: Records of the Parliament Holden at Westminster, 28th February, in the 33rd Year of the Reign of Edward I (1305) (Rolls Ser.: No. 98). 1969. reprint ed. 80.00 (*0-8115-1177-4*) Periodicals Srv.

Maitland, Frederic W., tr. see Gierke, Otto.

Maitland, G. D. Peripheral Manipulation. 3rd ed. 1991. pap. text ed. 42.95 (*0-7506-1031-X*) Buttrwrth-Heinemann.

— Vertebral Manipulation. 5th ed. 400p. 1986. pap. text ed. 44.95 (*0-7506-1333-5*) Buttrwrth-Heinemann.

Maitland, G. D., jt. auth. see Corrigan, Brian.

Maitland, Geoff, jt. auth. see Corrigan, Brian.

Maitland, Iain. The Barclays Guide to Managing Staff for the Small Business. 180p. 1991. pap. 24.95 (*0-631-17482-6*) Blackwell Pubs.

— The Business Planner: A Complete Guide to Raising Finance for Your Business. 200p. 1992. pap. 29.95 (*0-7506-0136-1*) Buttrwrth-Heinemann.

— Getting a Result. 98p. (C). 1994. pap. 18.00x (*0-85292-551-4*, Pub. by IPM Hse UK) St Mut.

— How to Organize a Conference. 160p. 1995. 42.95 (0-566-07552-0) Ashgate Pub Co.
— How to Recruit. 200p. 1991. text ed. 39.95 (0-566-02968-5, Pub. by Gower UK) Ashgate Pub Co.
*Maitland, Ian. Budgeting for Non-Financial Managers: Prepare Effective Budgets & Stick to Them. (Institute of Management Ser.). 275p. 1995. pap. 43.50 (0-273-61712-5, Pub. by Pitman Pub Ltd UK) Trans-Atl Phila.
— Maitland's Film Editing Glossary. 144p. (C). 1990. per., pap. text ed. 18.95 (0-8403-6056-8) Kendall-Hunt.
*Maitland, Jeffrey. Spacious Body: Explorations in Somatic Ontology. 200p. (Orig.). (C). 1995. pap. 12.95 (0-614-02577-X) North Atlantic.
— Spacious Body: Explorations in Somatic Ontology. LC 95-8725. 1995. pap. write for info. (1-55643-188-0) North Atlantic.
Maitland, John A. & Squire, W. Barclay. Fitzwilliam Virginal Book. 2 Vols, 1. 1963. pap. 13.95 (0-486-21068-5) Dover.
— Fitzwilliam Virginal Book. 2 Vols, 2. 1963. pap. 13.95 (0-486-21069-3) Dover.
Maitland, Katherine. Ashes for Gold: A Tale from Mexico. LC 94-14349. (Mondo Folktales ser.). (Illus.). 24p. (Orig.). (J). (gr. k-4). 1994. 23.95 (1-879531-14-3); lib. bdg. 9.95 (1-879531-43-7); pap. 4.95 (1-879531-22-4) Mondo Pubng.
Maitland, Leslie & Taylor, Louis. Historical Sketches of Ottawa. 160p. 1990. 29.95 (0-921149-67-0) Broadview Pr.
Maitland, Leslie, et al. A Guide to Canadian Architectural Styles. 320p. 1992. pap. 19.95 (1-55111-002-4) Broadview Pr.
Maitland, Margaret. Love's Golden Circle. 1978. pap. 1.95 (0-8439-0557-3) Dorchester Pub Co.
Maitland, P. S., et al, eds. The Fresh Waters of Scotland: A National Resource of International Significance. LC 93-46720. 1994. text ed. 89.95 (0-471-94462-9) Wiley.
Maitland, Peter S. The Ecology of Scotland's Largest Lochs. (Monographiae Biologicae: No. 44). 304p. 1981. lib. bdg. 126.50 (90-6193-097-9) Kluwer Ac.
— A Key to British Freshwater Fishes. 1972. 35.00 (0-900386-18-5) St Mut.
Maitland, Richard. Dicky Dandies. 1989. pap. 17.95 (0-317-04321-8) Man-Root.
— Dicky Dandies. deluxe ed. 1989. 25.00 (0-317-04320-X) Man-Root.
— History of the House of Seytoun to the Year 1559. LC 74-172716. reprint ed. 20.00 (0-404-52921-6) AMS Pr.
— Poems of Sir Richard Maitland, Knight of Lethingtoun. Bain, Joseph, ed. LC 77-144427. reprint ed. 41.50 (0-404-52927-5) AMS Pr.
Maitland, Sandra M. The Cedar Glen Secret. (Illus.). 24p. (J). (ps-8). 1983. 6.95 (0-920806-44-9, Pub. by Penumbra Pr CN) U of Toronto Pr.
Maitland, Sara. Ancestral Truths. 304p. 1994. 22.50 (0-8050-2536-7) H Holt & Co.
— Ancestral Truths: A Novel. 304p. 1995. pap. 12.00 (0-8050-3779-9, Owl) H Holt & Co.
— Daughter of Jerusalem: A Novel. LC 95-971. 1995. pap. 12.00 (0-8050-3810-8, Owl) H Holt & Co.
— A Map of the New Country: Women & Christianity. LC 82-13142. 280p. 1984. pap. 13.95 (0-7100-9301-2, RKP) Routledge.
— Three Times Table. 224p. 1994. pap. 12.95 (0-8050-2923-0) H Holt & Co.
Maitland, Sara & Appignanesi, Lisa, eds. The Rushdie File. (Contemporary Issues in the Middle East Ser.). (Illus.). 256p. 1990. pap. 15.95x (0-8156-0248-0) Syracuse U Pr.
Maitland, Terrence & McInerney, Peter. A Contagion of War, Vol. 5. Manning, Robert, ed. LC 83-70671. (Vietnam Experience Ser.). (Illus.). 192p. 1983. 16.95 (0-939526-05-0) Boston Pub Co.
Maitland, Terrence & Weiss, Stephen. Raising the Stakes, Vol. III. Manning, Robert, ed. LC 82-71280. (Vietnam Experience Ser.). (Illus.). 192p. 1982. 16.95 (0-939526-02-6) Boston Pub Co.
Maitland, Terrence, jt. auth. see Doyle, Edward.
Maitland, Thomas, ed. see Dalgarno, George.
Maitland, Thomas, ed. see Drummond, William.
Maitland, William F. English Law & the Renaissance: The Rede Lecture for 1901, with Some Notes. 98p. 1985. reprint ed. lib. bdg. 20.00 (0-8377-0822-2) Rothman.
Maitland, William J. Beginning Weight Training for Young Athletes. (Illus.). 84p. (YA). (gr. 7 up). 1987. pap. 9.95 (0-936759-00-3) Maitland Enter.
— Weight Training for Gifted Athletes. LC 89-90833. (Illus.). 147p. (Orig.). (YA). (gr. 8 up). 1990. pap. 17.95 (0-936759-01-1) Maitland Enter.
— Young Ball Player's Guide to Safe Pitching: Ages Eight Thru Adult with Conditioning, Strengthening. (Illus.). 140p. (YA). (gr. 3 up). 1994. pap. 14.95 (0-936759-14-3) Maitland Enter.
Maitlen, Bonnie, jt. auth. see Ludden, LaVerne.
Maitra, Apurba. We Cried Together. 1983. 11.00 (0-8364-0952-3, Pub. by Mukhopadhyaya II) S Asia.
Maitra, H. Hinduism: The World Ideal. 1972. 34.95 (0-8490-0302-4) Gordon Pr.
Maitra, Kiran. Roy, Comintern & Marxism in India. (C). 1991. 22.00 (81-85169-24-1, Pub. by Naya Prokash IA) S Asia.
Maitra, Kiran S. Naga Folk Tales. 1990. 16.00 (0-685-40057-3, Pub. by Mittal II) S Asia.
Maitra, M. K. Groundwater Management: An Application. (C). 1992. 58.00 (81-7024-466-8, Pub. by Ashish II) S Asia.
Maitra, P., jt. ed. see Tisdell, Clement A.
*Maitra, Priyatosh. The Globalization of Capitalism & Its Impact on Third World: India as a Case Study. LC 95-7549. 1995. text ed. write for info. (0-275-95159-6, Praeger Pubs) Greenwood.
— Indian Economic Development. (C). 1991. 28.00 (81-7024-387-4, Pub. by Ashish II) S Asia.
— Population Technology & Development. 200p. 1986. text ed. 56.95 (0-566-05205-9, Pub. by Avebury Pub UK) Ashgate Pub Co.
Maitra-Sinha, Anjana. Women in a Changing Society. xii, 166p. 1993. 15.95 (1-881338-35-5) Nataraj Bks.
Maitre, H. Joachim, jt. ed. see Hahn, Walter.
*Maitreya, Aegia, pseud. The Holy Absolute: Achieving Immortality. (Illus.). 245p. (Orig.). 1995. pap. write for info. (1-57502-025-4) Morris Pubng.
Maitreya, Ananda, tr. see Buddha.
Maitreya, Aryasanga. Uttaratantra, or Ratnagotravibhaga: Sublime Science of the Great Vehicle to Salvation. Obermiller, E., tr. 225p. 1984. reprint ed. lib. bdg. 27.50 (0-88181-001-0) Canon Pubns.
Maitri, Sandra, ed. see Almaas, A. H.
Maitriya. The Buddha Mimansa. Maharaja Yogiraja, ed. LC 78-70098. reprint ed. 23.50 (0-404-17347-0) AMS Pr.
Maitron, Jean. Dictionnaire Biographique du Mouvement Ouvrier Francais, 8 vols., Set. (FRE.). 295.00 (0-7859-0939-7, M-6384) Fr & Eur.
— Dictionnaire Biographique du Movement Ouvrier Francais: De la Revolution Francaise a la Fondation de la Premiere Internationale (1789-1864, 3 tomes. Incl. Tome I. De A a C. 16.95 (0-685-36060-1); Tome II. De D a L. 19.95 (0-685-36061-X); Tome III. De M a Z. 19.95 (0-685-36062-8); write for info. (0-318-51979-8) Fr & Eur.
*Maity, Bimal. Bengali Phrasebook. (Illus.). 200p. 1995. pap. 5.95 (0-86442-312-8) Lonely Planet.
Maity, J. C., ed. see Nag, N. K.
Maity, M. & Ghosh, G. Integral Calculus (Analysis) (C). 1989. 60.00 (0-89771-395-8, Current Dist) St Mut.
— Vector Analysis (Vect. Alg. & Vect. Calculus) (C). 1989. 85.00 (0-89771-392-3, Current Dist) St Mut.
Maity, M., jt. auth. see Ghosh, G.
Maity, P. K. Folk Ritual of Eastern India. 1988. 21.00 (81-7017-235-7, Pub. by Abhinav II) S Asia.
— Human Fertility Cults & Rituals of Bengal. (C). 1989. 37.50 (81-7017-263-2, Pub. by Abhinav II) S Asia.
Maity, S. K. Masterpieces of Haysala Art: Belur, Halebid, Somnathpur. (Illus.). viii, 52p. 1981. text ed. 35.00 (0-686-32481-1, Pub. by Taraporevala II) Apt Bks.
Maity, S. K., ed. Indological Studies. (C). 1987. 49.00 (81-7017-220-9, Pub. by Abhinav II) S Asia.
Maitz, Don. First Maitz: Selected Works of Don Maitz. LC 88-50651. (Illus.). 96p. 1988. 24.95 (0-942681-01-0) Ursus Imprints.
— First Maitz: Selected Works of Don Maitz. deluxe ed. LC 88-50651. (Illus.). 96p. 1988. boxed 45.00 (0-942681-02-9) Ursus Imprints.
Maitz, Don, illus. Dreamquests: The Art of Don Maitz. 112p. 1993. 29.95 (0-88733-175-0); pap. 17.95 (0-88733-176-9) Underwood-Miller.
Maitzen, H. M., jt. ed. see Van Paradijs, Jan.
*Maiwald, Sue. Exposed! How to Become a Model Without Getting Scammed. (Orig.). (YA). (gr. 7-12). 1994. pap. 4.95 (0-9644526-0-X) Maiwald Prod.
Maiwald, Trudy. Missy & Her Nightlight. 16p. (Orig.). (J). 1994. pap. write for info. (1-56167-153-3) Am Literary Pr.
Maiworm, Friedhelm, et al. Learning in Europe: the Erasmus Experience: A Survey of the 1988-89 Erasmus Students. (Higher Education Policy Ser.: No. 14). 160p. 1991. 45.00 (1-85302-527-5, Pub. by J Kingsley Pubs UK) Taylor & Francis.
Maixner, Paul. Robert Louis Stevenson: The Critical Heritage. (Critical Heritage Ser.). 556p. 1981. 53.00 (0-7100-0505-9, RKP) Routledge.
Maiz, Ramon, ed. see Sieyes, Enmanuel J.
Maize, John C., jt. ed. see Ackerman, A. Bernard.
Maizel, Abby L., ed. see Symposium on Fundamental Cancer Research Staff.
Maizel, Bruno. Food & Beverage Cost Controls. LC 77-142501. 1971. write for info. (0-672-96079-6); text ed. write for info. (0-672-96077-X) Macmillan.
— Food & Beverage Purchasing. LC 77-142502. 1971. write for info. (0-672-96073-7); text ed. write for info. (0-672-96071-0) Macmillan.
Maizel, David, tr. see Revel-Neher, Elisabeth.
Maizelis, I., jt. auth. see Averbakh, Y.
Maizell, Robert, et al. Abstracting Scientific & Technical Literature. LC 78-9756. 316p. 1979. reprint ed. 29.50 (0-88275-703-2) Krieger.
Maizell, Robert E. How to Find Chemical Information: A Guide for Practicing Chemists, Teachers & Students. 2nd ed. 432p. 1987. text ed. 79.95 (0-471-86767-5, Wiley-Interscience) Wiley.
Maizels, Alfred. Commodities in Crisis. (WIDER Studies in Development Economics). (Illus.). 320p. 1992. 64.00 (0-19-828387-3) OUP.
Maizels, Judith K. & Caseldine, Chris, eds. Environmental Change in Iceland: Past & Present. (C). 1991. lib. bdg. 118.00 (0-7923-1209-0) Kluwer Ac.
Maizels, R. M., et al. Parasite Antigens, Parasite Genes: A Laboratory Manual for Molecular Parasitology. (Illus.). 230p. (C). 1992. 59.95 (0-521-41927-1) Cambridge U Pr.
Maizlish, Aaron & Tefft, William. The World Map Directory, 1992-1993: A Practical Guide to U. S. & International Maps. (Illus.). 335p. 1992. pap. 29.95 (0-929591-08-9) Map Link.
*Maizlish, Lisa. The Ring. 32p. (J). 1996. write for info. (0-688-14217-6) Greenwillow.
— The Ring. 32p. (J). 1996. lib. bdg. write for info. (0-688-14218-4) Greenwillow.
Maizlish, Stephen E. The Triumph of Sectionalism: The Transformation of Ohio Politics, 1844-1856. LC 83-11255. 325p. reprint ed. pap. 92.70 (0-7837-1353-3, 2041501) Bks Demand.
Maizlish, Stephen E., jt. auth. see Abzug, Robert H.
Maizlish, Stephen E., jt. ed. see Kushma, John J.
Maizlish, Stephen E., jt. ed. see Reinhartz, Dennis.
Maizys, Donald J. Life in the Passionate Lane. LC 89-91457. 1990. 10.95 (0-87212-230-1) Libra.
Maj, M., et al. Mental Disorders in HIV-1 Infection & AIDS. (WHO Expert Series on Biological Psychiatry: Vol. 5). (Illus.). 100p. 1993. text ed. 24.00 (0-88937-096-6) Hogrefe & Huber Pubs.
Maj, S. P. The Use of Computers for Laboratory Automation. 380p. 1993. 59.95 (0-85186-744-8, R6744) CRC Pr.
*Maja, Pearce A. Wole Soyinka: An Appraisal. 160p. 1994. pap. 17.50 (0-435-91151-1) Heinemann.
Maja-Pearce, Adewale. A Mask Dancing: Nigerian Novelists of the Eighties. (New Perspectives on African Literature Ser.: No. 4). 216p. 1992. lib. bdg. 85.00 (0-905450-92-2, Pub. by H Zell Pubs UK) Bowker-Saur.
— Who's Afraid of Wole Soyinka: Essays on Censorship. (Studies in African Literature). 128p. 1991. pap. 17.50 (0-435-90977-0) Heinemann.
Maja-Pearce, Adewale, ed. The Heinemann Book of African Poetry in English. 224p. 1991. pap. 9.95 (0-435-91323-9) Heinemann.
Majam-Majumdar, R. C. Classical Accounts of India: Rome, Greek. reprint ed. 18.50 (0-8364-0704-0, Pub. by Mukhopadhyaya II) S Asia.
Majapuria, M. Yeti: The Abominable Snowman of the Silent Snows of the Himalayas. (C). 1993. 40.00 (0-7855-0223-8, Pub. by Ratna Pustak Bhandar) St Mut.
Majapuria, M. & Roberts, R. Kumari: Her Worship, Fate of Ex-Kumaries & Sceptical Views. (C). 1993. 60.00 (0-7855-0188-6, Pub. by Ratna Pustak Bhandar) St Mut.
Majaro, Simon. The Creative Marketer. (Marketing Practitioner Ser.). 192p. 1993. pap. 19.95 (0-7506-1708-X) Buttrwrth-Heinemann.
— The Creative Marketer: Published in Association with the Chartered Institute of Marketing. 256p. 1991. 39.95 (0-7506-0096-9) Buttrwrth-Heinemann.
— The Essence of Marketing. LC 93-22068. 176p. 1993. pap. 19.95 (0-13-285354-X) P-H.
— International Marketing: A Strategic Approach to World Markets. 2nd ed. 320p. (C). 1982. pap. text ed. 24.95 (0-04-658240-1) Routledge Chapman & Hall.
Majchrowicz, Martin, jt. auth. see Marco, Michael.
Majchrzak, Ann. The Human Side of Factory Automation: Managerial & Human Resource Strategies for Making Automation Succeed. LC 87-45505. (Management Ser.). 408p. 1988. 39.95 (1-55542-050-8) Jossey-Bass.
Majda, A. J. Compressible Fluid Flow & Systems of Conservation Laws in Several Space Variables. (Applied Mathematical Sciences Ser.: Vol. 53). 160p. 1984. pap. 36.00 (0-387-96037-6) Spr-Verlag.
Majda, A. J., jt. ed. see Chorin, A.
Majda, A. J., et al, eds. Multidimensional Hyperbolic Problems & Computations. (IMA Volumes in Mathematics & Its Applications Ser.: Vol. 29). (Illus.). xiv, 386p. 1990. 44.00 (0-387-97485-7) Spr-Verlag.
Majda, Andrew. The Existence of Multi-Dimensional Shock Fronts. LC 83-3725. (Memoirs of the American Mathematical Society Ser.: No. 43/281). 92p. 1983. pap. 18.00 (0-8218-2281-0, MEMO 43/281) Am Math.
— The Stability of Multi-Dimensional Shock Fronts. LC 82-20636. (Memoirs Ser.: No. 41/275). 95p. 1982. pap. 16.00 (0-8218-2275-6, MEMO 41/275) Am Math.
Majdalany, Jeanne & Wicks, Edith M. The Early Settlements of Stamford, Connecticut, 1641-1700: Including Genealogies of the Stamford Families of the Seventeenth Century. (Illus.). xiv, 211p. (Orig.). 1991. pap. 17.50 (1-55613-394-4) Heritage Bk.
Majeed, Javed. Ungoverned Imaginings: James Mill's the History of British India & Orientalism. (Oxford English Monographs). 270p. 1992. 55.00 (0-19-811786-8) OUP.
*Majeed, Kardar. What Is Behind the IQ? 1995. 12.95 (0-8062-5378-9) Carlton.
*Majer, Diemut. Non-Germans in the Third Reich. (C). 1901. text ed. 130.00 (0-8133-2359-2) Westview.
Majer, J. D., ed. Animals in Primary Succession: The Role of Fauna in Reclaimed Land. (Illus.). 512p. (C). 1989. 110.00 (0-521-33400-4) Cambridge U Pr.
Majer, J. R. The Mass Spectrometer. (Wykeham Science Ser.: No. 44). 160p. 1977. pap. 18.00 (0-85109-550-X) Taylor & Francis.
Majer, J. R. & Berry, M. The Mass Spectrometer. LC 77-15307. (Wykeham Science Ser.: No. 44). 159p. (C). 1977. 18.00 (0-8448-1171-8, Crane Russak) Taylor & Francis.
Majer Krich, Rochelle. Fair Game. 384p. 1993. 17.95 (0-89296-507-X) Mysterious Pr.
Majer, M. & Plotkin, S. A., eds. Strains of Human Viruses. 160p. 1972. 78.50 (3-8055-1401-8) S Karger.
Majer, V., et al. Heats of Vaporization of Fluids. (Studies in Modern Thermodynamics: No. 9). 370p. 1989. 151.50 (0-444-98920-X) Elsevier.
Majeska, George P. Russian Travelers to Constantinople in the Fourteenth & Fifteenth Centuries. LC 82-24255. (Dumbarton Oaks Studies: Vol. 19). (Illus.). 464p. 1984. 35.00 (0-88402-101-7) Dumbarton Oaks.
Majeski, Bill. Doubletalk: Fifty Comedy Duets for Actors. Zapel, Arthur L., ed. LC 90-52981. 208p. (Orig.). 1990. pap. 9.95 (0-916260-66-6, B186) Meriwether Pub.
— Fifty Great Monologs for Student Actors. Zapel, Arthur L., ed. LC 87-14103. 144p. (Orig.). (J). (gr. 10 up). 1987. pap. 9.95 (0-916260-43-7, B-197) Meriwether Pub.
— Gross Encounters of the Worst Kind. 1978. pap. 2.50 (0-87129-076-6, G30) Dramatic Pub.
— Oh, Mr. President. (Orig.). 1985. pap. 6.00 (0-88734-206-X) Players Pr.
Majetschak, Stefan, jt. ed. see Hoffmann, Thomas S.
Majette, Baji, ed. see Allums, Charles.
*Majette, Susan L. When Reality Shines. LC 94-61158. 205p. 1995. pap. 10.95 (1-55523-723-1) Winston-Derek.
Majewski, Arthur. Moneta Polska. (Illus.). 216p. 1991. 19.50 (0-9617557-1-7) Maryt Pub.
Majewski, Arthur J. When Hamtramck & I Were Friends. LC 86-62351. 120p. 1987. 10.00 (0-9617557-0-9) Maryt Pub.
Majewski, Henry F. Paradigm & Parody: Images of Creativity in French Romanticism - Vigny, Hugo, Balzac, Gautier, Musset. LC 88-15419. 192p. 1989. 29.95 (0-8139-1177-X) U Pr of Va.
Majewski, Henry F., jt. ed. see Schor, Naomi.
Majewski, Joe. A Friend for Oscar Mouse. LC 87-5365. (Illus.). 32p. (J). (ps-2). 1991. pap. 3.99 (0-8037-0913-7, Puff Pied Piper) Puffin Bks.
Majewski, S. R., ed. Galaxy Evolution: The Milky Way Perspective. (ASP Conference Series Publications: Vol. 49). 256p. 1993. 40.00 (0-937707-68-6) Astron Soc Pacific.
Majewski, T. & O'Brien, M. J. An Analysis of Historical Ceramics from the Central Salt River Valley of Northeast Missouri. (Illus.). viii, 121p. 1984. 15.00 (0-917111-02-8) Mus Anthro MO.
Majid al Najjar, Abdul. Dawr Hurriyat al Ra'y fi al Wahdah al Fikriyah Bayna al Muslimin: (The Role of Freedom of Opinion in the Intellectual Unity Amongst Muslims) LC 91-44549. (Silsilat Abhath 'Ilmiyah: No. 6). 88p. (Orig.). (ARA.). 1992. pap. 5.00 (1-56564-024-1) IIIT VA.
Majid Ali Khan, tr. see Maulana Muhammad Kandhlawi.
Majid, Anouar. Si Youssef. 160p. 1993. 19.95 (0-7043-7032-8, Pub. by Quartet UK) Interlink Pub.
*Majid, Mimi K. Dangerous Drugs Laws in Malaysia. Date not set. write for info. (0-614-05482-6) Butterworth Legal Pubs.
*Majid, Shahn. Foundations of Quantum Group Theory. (Illus.). 600p. (C). Date not set. write for info. (0-521-46032-8) Cambridge U Pr.
Majidimehr, Amir. One Thousand Questions & Answers about Unix Systems. 1994. pap. text ed. 22.50 (0-13-119884-X) P-H.
— Optimizing Unix for Performance. 1994. pap. text ed. 22.50 (0-13-111551-0) P-H.
*Majied, Atiyah, ed. The Teachings of Both Bible & Holy Qur'an As Taught by, The Most Honorable Elijah Muhammad Messenger of Allah (God) Master Fard Muhammad, Bk. I. (Illus.). 359p. 1995. pap. 15.95 (1-56411-078-8) Untd Bros & Sis.
Majiid Ali Khan, tr. see Maulana Muhammad Kandhlawi.
Majima, H. Asymptotic Analysis for Integrable Connections with Irregular Singular Points. (Lecture Notes in Mathematics Ser.: Vol. 1075). ix, 159p. 1984. pap. 31.10 (0-387-13375-5) Spr-Verlag.
Majithia, M., ed. see Kazansky, V. I.
Majka, Theo J., jt. auth. see Mooney, Patrick H.
Majkowski, J. Epilepsy. (Monographs in Neural Sciences: Vol. 5). (Illus.). xvi, 304p. 1981. pap. 75.25 (3-8055-0635-X) S Karger.
Majkowski, Wladyslaw. People's Poland: Patterns of Social Inequality & Conflict, No. 55. LC 84-15689. (Contributions in Sociology Ser.). (Illus.). xvii, 234p. 1985. text ed. 55.00 (0-313-24614-9, MJP/, Greenwood Pr) Greenwood.
Majkrzak, C., ed. Thin Film Neutron Optical Devices: Mirrors, Supermirrors, Multilayer Monochromators, Polarizers & Beam Guides, Vol. 983. 1988. 45.00 (0-8194-0018-1) SPIE.
Majkut, Paul. Asterion, the Minotaur: A Book of Suspicion, Resentment, Confusion, Regret, Poor Memory, Tales, Poetry, & Conversation. LC 93-16136. 1993. write for info. (0-9632702-3-0) Lightning.
Majluf, Nicholas S., jt. auth. see Hax, Arnoldo C.
Majnaric, Niko. Greek-Serbocroatian Dictionary: Grcko-Hrvatski ili Srpski Rjecnik. 468p. (GRE & SER.). 1983. 29.95 (0-8288-1054-0, F79182) Fr & Eur.
Majno, Guido. The Healing Hand: Man & Wound in the Ancient World. (Commonwealth Fund Publications). 528p. (C). 1991. pap. text ed. 19.95 (0-674-38331-1) HUP.
Majno, Guido & Joris, Isabelle. Cells, Tissues, & Disease. (Illus.). 832p. 1994. 75.00 (0-86542-372-5) Blackwell Sci.
Majone, Giandomenico. Evidence, Argument, & Persuasion in the Policy Process. LC 88-21677. 224p. (C). 1989. text ed. 30.00 (0-300-04159-4) Yale U Pr.
— Evidence, Argument, & Persuasion in the Policy Progress. 224p. (C). 1992. reprint ed. pap. text ed. 12.00 (0-300-05259-6) Yale U Pr.
Majone, Giandomenico, ed. Deregulation or Re-Regulation? Regulatory Reform in Europe & the United States. 272p. 1992. pap. text ed. 24.50 (1-85567-067-4, Pub. by Pinter Pubs UK) St Martin.
*Major. Creative Nursery Book: Imaginative Designs to Make at Home. 1995. 9.99 (0-517-12155-7) Random Hse Value.
— Saint-Exupery: L'ecriture et la Pensee. 28.90 (0-685-37091-7) Fr & Eur.
Major, A. Dynamics in Civil Engineering, 4 vols. 320p. 1980. 500.00 (0-569-00234-6, Pub. by Collets UK) Pro-Am Music.
— Dynamics in Civil Engineering: Foundations for Hammers: Reciprocating Engines, & Other Machines, Vibration Isolation & Damping, Vol. 2. 302p. (C). 1983. 81.00x (963-05-3164-X) St Mut.
— Dynamics in Civil Engineering: Fundamentals in Vibration Theory & Practice Including Machine Foundations, Soil Dynamics, Instrumentation, Vibration Tolerances, Vol. 1. 320p. (C). 1983. 81.00x (963-05-3163-1) St Mut.
— Dynamics in Civil Engineering Vol. 3: Foundations for High-Speed Machinery, Steam & Nuclear Power Plants, Structural Details. 292p. (C). 1983. 81.00x (0-614-00732-1, Pub. by Akad Kiado HU) St Mut.

An Asterisk (*) at the beginning of an entry indicates that the title is appearing in BIP for the first time.

— Dynamics in Civil Engineering Vol. 4: Vibrations in Buildings & Industrial Structures, Dynamics in Hydraulic Structures & Bridges, Vol. 4. 306p. (C). 1983. 81.00x (963-05-3166-6, Pub. by Akad Kiado HU) St Mut.

— Dynamics in Civil Engineering Analysis & Design, 4 vols., Set. (C). 1983. 324.00x (963-05-3162-3) St Mut.

Major, A. Jayne. Breakthrough Parenting: Unlock the Secrets to a Great Relationship with Your Children. 192p. 1993. pap. 9.95 (0-925190-69-1) Fairview Press.

Major, Ann. The Accidental Bridegroom. 1994. mass mkt. 2.99 (0-373-05889-6, 1-05889-0) Harlequin Bks.

— A Cowboy Christmas. 1995. pap. 3.25 (0-373-05967-1, 1-05967-4) Silhouette.

— Destiny's Child. (Western Lovers Ser.). 1995. mass mkt. 3.99 (0-373-88548-2, 1-88548-2) Harlequin Bks.

— Dream Come True. (Men Made in American Ser.). 1994. mass mkt. 3.59 (0-373-45159-8, 1-45159-0) Silhouette.

— The Fairy Tale Girl. (Western Lovers Ser.). 1995. mass mkt. 3.99 (0-373-88521-0, 1-88521-9) Harlequin Bks.

— La Sirene et l'Aventurier. (Rouge Passion Ser.). (FRE.). 1994. pap. 3.50 (0-373-37291-4, 1-37291-1) Harlequin Bks.

— Wild Honey: Man of the Month, Something Wild. (Silhouette Desire Ser.). 1993. mass mkt. 2.99 (0-373-05805-5, 5-05805-2) Silhouette.

— Wild Innocence: (Man of the Month, Something Wild) (Silhouette Desire Ser.). 1994. mass mkt. 2.99 (0-373-05835-7, 5-05835-9) Silhouette.

— Wild Midnight: Something Wild. (Silhouette Desire Ser.). 1993. mass mkt. 2.99 (0-373-05819-5, 5-05819-3) Silhouette.

— The Wrong Man. (Men in America Ser.). 1994. mass mkt. 3.99 (0-373-45188-1, 1-45188-9) Harlequin Bks.

Major, Beverly. Playing Sardines. (Illus.). (J). (ps-2). 1989. pap. 3.95 (0-590-41154-3) Scholastic Inc.

Major, C. I., et al. Papers on the Subfossil Primates of Madagascar, Reprinted from Various Sources. LC 78-72722. 1980. 105.00 (0-404-18301-8) AMS Pr.

Major, Charles. The Bears of Blue River. LC 83-49522. (Library of Indiana Classics). (Illus.). 288p. 1984. 20.00 (0-253-10590-0); pap. 8.95 (0-253-20330-9, MB-330) Ind U Pr.

— Bears of Blue River. reprint ed. lib. bdg. 21.95 (0-88411-094-X, Aeonian Pr) Amereon Ltd.

— Uncle Tom Andy Bill. 350p. 1992. reprint ed. lib. bdg. 26.95 (0-89966-914-X) Buccaneer Bks.

— Uncle Tom Andy Bill: A Story of Bears & Indian Treasure. LC 93-22086. (Library of Indiana Classics). (C). 1993. 17.95 (0-253-33653-8); pap. 10.95 (0-253-33654-6) Ind U Pr.

— When Knighthood Was in Flower. LC 70-126656. reprint ed. 45.00 (0-404-04169-8) AMS Pr.

— When Knighthood Was in Flower. reprint ed. lib. bdg. 21.95 (0-88411-095-8, Aeonian Pr) Amereon Ltd.

— When Knighthood Was in Flower. (BCL1-PS American Literature Ser.). 295p. 1992. reprint ed. lib. bdg. 79.00 (0-7812-6792-7) Rprt Serv.

Major, Clarence. All-Night Visitors. 203p. 1973. pap. 7.50 (0-685-32466-4) Univ Place.

— The Dark & Feeling. LC 73-83162. 196p. 1974. 19.95 (0-89388-118-X) Okpaku Communications.

— The Dark & the Feeling. LC 73-83162. 12.95 (0-89388-119-8) Okpaku Communications.

— Emergency Exit. LC 79-52031. (Illus.). 1979. 15.95 (0-914590-58-8); pap. 6.95 (0-914590-59-6) Fiction Coll.

— Fun & Games. LC 88-45370. 144p. 1990. 15.95 (0-930100-34-4) Holy Cow.

— My Amputations. 205p. 1986. 15.95 (0-914590-96-0) Fiction Coll.

— Reflex & Bone Structure. LC 75-10746. 145p. 1975. pap. 6.95 (0-914590-17-0) Fiction Coll.

— Some Observations of a Stranger at Zuni in the Latter Part of the Century. (New American Poetry Ser.: No. 2). 1990. pap. 9.95 (1-55713-020-5) Sun & Moon CA.

— Surfaces & Masks. LC 88-23673. 91p. (Orig.). 1988. pap. 8.95 (0-918273-43-9) Coffee Hse.

— Swallow the Lake. LC 79-120258. (Wesleyan Poetry Program Ser.: Vol. 54). 64p. 1970. 12.95 (0-8195-2054-3, Wesleyan Univ Pr) U Pr of New Eng.

Major, Clarence, ed. Calling the Wind: Twentieth Century African-American Short Stories. LC 92-52620. 1993. pap. 13.00 (0-06-098201-2, PL) HarpC.

Major, Clarence, intro. Juba to Jive: The Dictionary of African-American Slang. 432p. (Orig.). 1994. pap. 14.95 (0-14-051306-X, Penguin Bks) Viking Penguin.

Major, D. C. Multiobjective Water Resource Planning. (Water Resources Monograph Ser.: Vol. 4). (Illus.). 81p. 1977. 10.00 (0-87590-305-3) Am Geophysical.

Major, David C. & Schwarz, Harry E. Large-Scale Regional Water Resources Planning: The North Atlantic Regional Study. (C). 1990. lib. bdg. 82.00 (0-7923-0711-9) Kluwer Ac.

***Major, Devorah.** An Open Weave. 170p. (Orig.). 1995. pap. 10.95 (1-878067-66-4) Seal Pr Feminist.

Major, Diana. The Acquisition of Modal Auxiliaries in the Language of Children. (Janua Linguarum, Series Minor: No. 195). 1974. pap. text ed. 49.25 (90-279-2664-6) Mouton.

Major, Edward, jt. ed. see Taylor, T. H.

***Major, Eugene O., et al, eds.** Technical Advances in AIDS Research in the Human Nervous System: Proceedings of a NIH Workshop Held in Washington, D. C., October 4-5, 1993. 360p. 1995. 95.00 (0-306-45000-3) Plenum.

Major, Geri. Black Society. 1977. 25.00 (0-87485-075-4) Johnson Chi.

Major, Grace. Take Charge! How to Manage Your Customer Relationships. LC 92-60371. (Executive Edition Ser.). 266p. (Orig.). 1992. 149.00 (0-9632406-2-5); text ed. 27.95 (0-9632406-1-7); pap. text ed. 27.95 (0-9632406-0-9) Sigma Bks.

Major, H. D., ed. see Rashdall, Hastings.

Major, Henry D. Civilization & Religious Values. LC 77-27137. (Hibbert Lectures: 1946). reprint ed. 30.00 (0-404-60431-5) AMS Pr.

Major, Howard. Domestic Architecture of the Early American Republic. 236p. 1993. reprint ed. lib. bdg. 79.00 (0-7812-5299-7) Rprt Serv.

Major, Ivan. Privatization in Eastern Europe: A Critical Approach. (Illus.). 192p. 1993. 49.95 (1-85278-887-9, Pub. by E Elgar Pub UK) Ashgate Pub Co.

***Major, J. Kenneth.** Animal Powered Machines. (C). 1989. pap. 25.00x (0-85263-710-1, Pub. by Shire UK) St Mut.

Major, J. Russell. From Renaissance Monarchy to Absolute Monarchy: French Kings, Nobles, & Estates. LC 93-47260. 1994. text ed. 49.95x (0-8018-4776-1) Johns Hopkins.

— The Monarchy, the Estates & the Aristocracy in Renaissance France. (Collected Studies: No. CS279). 298p. (C). 1988. reprint ed. text ed. 87.50 (0-86078-227-1, Pub. by Variorum UK) Ashgate Pub Co.

— Representative Government in Early Modern France. LC 79-14711. 752p. 1980. text ed. 67.00 (0-300-02300-6) Yale U Pr.

Major, Jack, jt. ed. see Barbour, Michael G.

Major, James. Dulcimer Chord Encyclopedia. 1993. 9.95 (0-87166-613-8, 93858) Mel Bay.

— Mandolin Chord Book. 1984. pap. 4.95 (0-8256-2296-4) Music Sales.

Major, James & Smith, Doug. World Cup Ski Technique 2. (World Cup Ski Technique Ser.). (Illus.). 384p. (Orig.). 1990. 33.00 (0-935240-08-X) Poudre Pr.

Major, James, tr. see Joubert, Georges.

Major, James, jt. auth. see Larsson, Olle.

Major, James R. Representative Institutions in Renaissance France, 1421-1559. LC 82-25305. ix, 182p. (C). 1983. reprint ed. text ed. 59.75 (0-313-23569-4, MAJR, Greenwood Pr) Greenwood.

Major, Jill C., jt. auth. see Chapman, Eugenia.

Major, Jill C., et al. Encircled by Love. LC 89-51133. 97p. 1989. 8.95 (0-87579-247-2) Deseret Bk.

Major, John. Prize Possession: The United States & the Panama Canal, 1903-1979. LC 92-32406. (Illus.). 400p. (C). 1993. 49.95 (0-521-43306-1) Cambridge U Pr.

Major, John, jt. ed. see Love, Robert W., Jr.

Major, John M. Sir Thomas Elyot & Renaissance Humanism. LC 64-11351. 292p. reprint ed. pap. 83.30 (0-7837-6020-5, 2045832) Bks Demand.

Major, John S. Heaven & Earth in Early Han Thought: Chapters Three, Four, & Five of the Huainanzi. (Chinese Philosophy & Culture Ser.). 388p. (C). 1993. 74.50 (0-7914-1585-6); pap. 24.95 (0-7914-1586-4) State U NY Pr.

— The Silk Route. LC 92-38169. (Illus.). (J). 1995. 14.95 (0-06-022924-1); lib. bdg. 14.89 (0-06-022926-8) HarpC.

Major League Baseball Properties, Inc. Staff & Baseball Encyclopedia Editors. The Official Major League Baseball Stat Book, 1991. 416p. 1991. pap. 13.95 (0-02-063381-5, Collier S&S) S&S Trade.

— The Official Major League Baseball Stat Book, 1992. (Illus.). 480p. 1992. pap. 14.95 (0-02-079646-3, Collier S&S) S&S Trade.

Major League Baseball Properties, Inc. Staff & Cader Company, Inc. Staff. The Official Major League Scorebook 1990. 128p. 1990. spiral bd. 9.95 (0-02-029435-2, Collier S&S) S&S Trade.

***Major League Baseball Staff.** Official Rules of Major League Baseball, 1995. (Official Rules Ser.). 201p. (YA). 1995. pap. 8.95 (1-880141-96-5) Triumph Bks.

— Official Rules of Major League Baseball 1996. (Official Rules Ser.). (Illus.). 201p. 1995. pap. 8.95 (1-57243-038-9) Triumph Bks.

— One Hundred Twenty-Five Years of Major League Baseball. (Illus.). 64p. 1994. 14.95 (1-880141-84-1) Triumph Bks.

Major League Baseball Training Staff & Lowenfish, Lee. The Professional Baseball Trainers' Fitness Book. (Orig.). 1988. pap. 12.95 (0-446-38751-7) Warner Bks.

Major, Mabel. Southwest Heritage: Literary History with Bibliography. (BCL1-PS American Literature Ser.). 199p. 1993. reprint ed. lib. bdg. 69.00 (0-7812-6581-9) Rprt Serv.

Major, Mabel, ed. see Duval, John C.

Major, Mark. American-Hungarian Relations, Nineteen Eighteen-Nineteen Forty-Four. LC 74-80001. 288p. 1974. 10.00 (0-87934-036-3) Danubian.

Major, Norma. Joan Sutherland: The Authorized Biography. 1994. 24.95 (0-316-54555-4) Little.

Major-Poetzl, Pamela. Michel Foucault's Archaeology of Western Culture: Toward a New Science of History. LC 81-19689. 295p. reprint ed. pap. 84.10 (0-7837-0308-2, 2040630) Bks Demand.

Major, R. H. India in the Fifteenth Century Being a Collection of Narratives & Voyages to India in the Century Preceeding the Portuguese Discovery of Good Hope from Latin, Persian, Russian & Italian Sources. (C). 1992. reprint ed. 19.00 (81-206-0768-6, Pub. by Asian Educ Servs II) S Asia.

Major, R. H., ed. & tr. Christopher Columbus: Four Voyages to the New World. (Illus.). 240p. 1992. pap. 9.95 (0-8065-1337-3, Citadel Pr) Carol Pub Group.

Major, R. H., ed. see Columbus, Christopher.

Major, Ralph H. Classic Descriptions of Disease: With Biographical Sketches of the Authors. 3rd ed. (Illus.). 712p. 1978. Photocopy ed. 104.95 (0-398-01202-4) C C Thomas.

— Classic Descriptions of Disease: With Biographical Sketches of the Authors. 3rd ed. (Illus.). 712p. 1978. pap. 51.50 (0-398-06265-X) C C Thomas.

Major, Reginald. Justice in the Round: The Trial of Angela Davis. LC 72-84108. 256p. 1973. 35.00 (0-89388-052-3) Okpaku Communications.

Major, Richard H. Life of Prince Henry of Portugal. 487p. 1967. reprint ed. 35.00 (0-7146-1045-3, Pub. by F Cass Pubs UK) Intl Spec Bk.

Major, Robert L. Discipline: The Most Important Subject We Teach. 142p. (Orig.). (C). 1990. pap. text ed. 17.50 (0-8191-7745-8) U Pr of Amer.

Major, S. Architectural Woodwork. 1995. pap. 49.95 (0-442-01402-3) Van Nos Reinhold.

Major, Ted, jt. auth. see Williams, Terence T.

Major, Walter & Hoagland, David. The Complete Guide to Starting a Local Church Counseling Ministry, 3 cass., Set. deluxe ed. Spear, Cindy G. & Johnson, Tamara, eds. 92p. (Orig.). 1993. audio, ring bd. 79.95 (0-941005-92-5) Chrch Grwth VA.

— Counseling: Offering a Needed Touch in Times of Trouble, a Guide for Personal Care-Giving. Spear, Cindy G. & Johnson, Tamara, eds. 144p. (Orig.). 1993. pap. 8.95 (0-941005-91-7) Chrch Grwth VA.

Major, Wilfred, jt. auth. see O'Brien, Joan.

Majorano, Sabatino, sel. Florilegium of Texts from Mother Maria Celeste Crostarosa. 159p. (Orig.). 1993. pap. text ed. 9.95 (0-89243-574-7) Liguori Pubns.

Majors, Alexander. Seventy Years on the Frontier. LC 88-31597. (Illus.). 449p. 1989. reprint ed. pap. 8.95 (0-8032-8158-7, Bison Books) U of Nebr Pr.

— Seventy Years on the Frontier: Alexander Majors' Memoirs of a Lifetime on the Border. (American Biography Ser.). 325p. 1991. reprint ed. lib. bdg. 79.00 (0-7812-8263-2) Rprt Serv.

Majors, Jack H. Communicating the Joy, Pain & Everything. 2nd ed. 176p. (C). 1976. pap. 6.00 (0-937104-00-0) Programs Comm.

Majors, Judith S. Meatless Wonder. LC 82-70644. 1982. pap. 6.95 (0-9602238-5-1) Apple Pr.

— Sugar Free: Goodies. LC 87-70318. pap. 6.95 (0-941905-00-4) Apple Pr.

— Sugar Free: Hawaiian Cookery. LC 87-70229. pap. 6.95 (0-9602238-9-4) Apple Pr.

— Sugar Free: Kids Cookery. LC 79-66220. 1979. pap. 6.95 (0-9602238-1-9) Apple Pr.

— Sugar Free . . . . Family Favorites. LC 84-72670. 1985. pap. 5.95 (0-9602238-7-8) Apple Pr.

— Sugar Free . . . . Good & Easy. LC 85-72597. 1985. pap. 5.95 (0-9602238-8-6) Apple Pr.

— Sugar Free. . . . Sweets & Treats. LC 82-73049. 1982. pap. 6.95 (0-9602238-6-X) Apple Pr.

— Sugar Free . . . That's Me! 1980. mass mkt. 6.95 (0-345-28708-8, Ballantine Trade) Ballantine.

— Sugar Free... Microwavery. LC 80-67167. pap. 6.95 (0-9602238-3-5) Apple Pr.

— Sugar Free-That's Me. LC 78-74029. (Illus.). 1978. pap. 6.95 (0-9602238-0-0) Apple Pr.

Majors, Monroe A. Noted Negro Women. LC 73-138341. (Black Heritage Library Collection). 1977. 29.95 (0-8369-8733-0) Ayer.

— Noted Negro Women. 1972. 99.95 (0-8490-0737-2) Gordon Pr.

Majors, Randall E. Business Communications: Writing, Interviewing, & Speaking at Work. 352p. (C). 1990. pap. text ed. 46.50 (0-06-044183-6) HarpCollege.

— Is This Going to Be on the Test? And Ten Other Questions That Can Save Your College Career. 2nd ed. 260p. 1994. pap. write for info. (0-89787-820-5) Gorsuch Scarisbrick.

Majors, Randall E., jt. auth. see Busby, Rudolph E.

Majors, Richard & Billson, Janet M. Cool Pose: The Dilemma of Black Manhood in America. 176p. 1993. pap. 10.00 (0-671-86572-2, Touchstone Bks) S&S Trade.

— CoolPose: The Dilemmas of Black Manhood in America. 132p. 1992. text ed. 19.95 (0-669-24523-2) Free Pr.

Majors, Richard G. & Gordon, Jacob U. The American Black Male. 1993. pap. text ed. 21.95 (0-8304-1236-0) Nelson-Hall.

Majors, Susan. Child at Work, Vol. 1: Numbers. (Illus.). (Orig.). 1988. pap. 5.95 (0-685-45830-X) Programs Comm.

— Child at Work, Vol. 2: Colors. (Illus.). (Orig.). 1988. pap. 5.95 (0-937104-06-X) Programs Comm.

— Quackers, an Idea Book for Preschool Teachers. rev. ed. 288p. 1986. pap. text ed. 20.00 (0-317-57809-X) Programs Comm.

Majors, William R. Change & Continuity: Tennessee Politics since the Civil War. LC 86-12523. 144p. (Orig.). (C). 1986. pap. 12.95 (0-86554-209-0, P25) Mercer Univ Pr.

— Editorial Wild Oats: Edward Ward Carmack & Tennessee Politics. LC 84-10870. xx, 194p. 1984. 17.50 (0-86554-133-7, MUP/H124) Mercer Univ Pr.

— Volunteer Trails: A Program of Visual Aids for the Study of Tennessee. (Illus.). 80p. 1980. 20.00 (0-939710-06-4) Meridional Pubns.

Majoy, Peter. Doorways to Learning: A Model for Developing the Brain's Full Potential. LC 93-8573. 256p. 1993. 25.00 (0-913705-86-1) Zephyr Pr AZ.

Majozo, Estella C. Jiva Telling Rites: An Initiation. (Orig.). 1991. pap. text ed. 8.00 (0-88378-138-7) Third World.

— Libation. 176p. (Orig.). 1992. 22.00 (0-86316-303-3); pap. 9.95 (0-86316-024-7) Writers & Readers.

Majrani, Marco. Himalayas. 144p. 1994. 19.98 (0-8317-8682-5) Smithmark.

Majul, Cesar A. The Contemporary Muslim Movement in the Philippines. LC 85-21519. 158p. (Orig.). (C). 1985. 15.95 (0-933782-16-0); pap. 8.95 (0-933782-17-9) Mizan Pr.

Majumader, Robin & McLaurin, Allen, eds. Virginia Woolf: The Critical Heritage. (Critical Heritage Ser.). 1975. 69.50 (0-7100-8138-3, RKP) Routledge.

Majumdar, A. K. N-Benzoylphenylhydroxylamine & Its Analogues. 224p. 1972. 89.00 (0-08-016754-3, Pub. by Pergamon Repr UK) Franklin.

Majumdar, Arun. Poverty, Development & Exchange Relations. 175p. 1987. text ed. 15.95 (81-7027-108-8, Pub. by Radiant Pubs II) S Asia.

Majumdar, Asis K. South-East Asia in Indian Foreign Policy. 1983. 22.50 (0-8364-0932-9, Pub. by Naya Prokash IA) S Asia.

Majumdar, Asoke K. Concise History of Ancient India, 3 vols., Set. 1931p. 1983. text ed. 100.00 (0-685-13637-X) Coronet Bks.

Majumdar, B. S., et al, eds. Constitutive Behavior of High-Temperature Composites. (MD Ser.: Vol. 40). 184p. 1992. 50.00 (0-7918-1117-4, G00761) ASME.

Majumdar, D. N. Social Contours of an Industrial City. LC 73-13863. (Illus.). 247p. 1975. reprint ed. text ed. 59.75 (0-8371-6762-0, MASD, Greenwood Pr) Greenwood.

Majumdar, Dipika. Ramendrasundar Trivedi: A Study of His Social & Political Ideas. (C). 1988. 40.00 (81-85195-13-7, Pub. by Minerva II) S Asia.

Majumdar, Gopa. In the Sam Boat: Golden Tales from Bengal. (C). 1994. text ed. 8.50 (81-86112-09-X, Pub. by UBS Pubs Dist II) S Asia.

Majumdar, Ila, jt. auth. see Majumdar, P. S.

Majumdar, J. The Economics of Railway Traction. 528p. 1985. text ed. 85.00 (0-566-00670-7) Ashgate Pub Co.

Majumdar, J. K. Raja Rammohun Roy & Progressive Movement in India. 1988. reprint ed. 72.50 (81-7041-071-1, Pub. by Anmol II) S Asia.

Majumdar, J. K., ed. Indian Speeches & Documents on British Rule, 1821-1918. 1987. 34.95 (0-318-37217-7) Asia Bk Corp.

Majumdar, Jatindra K., jt. auth. see Chanda, Ram P.

Majumdar, K. A Comprehensive Handbook for the Practitioner. (C). 1984. 30.00 (0-89771-354-0, Current Dist) St Mut.

— Handbook of Practical Medicine & Treatment. (C). 1989. 75.00 (0-89771-353-2, Current Dist) St Mut.

— A Medical Handbook for Medical. (C). 1989. 50.00 (0-89771-355-9, Current Dist) St Mut.

Majumdar, Lila. Jorasanko House. (Nehru Library for Children). (Illus.). (J). (gr. 1-9). 1979. pap. 2.50 (0-89744-176-1) Auromere.

Majumdar, M. A Comprehensive Medical Handbook. (C). 1984. 45.00 (0-685-36199-3, Current Dist) St Mut.

Majumdar, M. C., et al, eds. Artificial Intelligence & Other Innovative Computer Applications in the Nuclear Industry. LC 88-9396. (Illus.). 928p. 1988. 150.00 (0-306-42902-0, Plenum Pr) Plenum.

***Majumdar, Margaret A.** Althusser & the End of Leninism? LC 95-3741. 6p. (C). 1995. text ed. 69.95 (0-7453-0888-0, Pub. by Pluto Pr UK); pap. text ed. 22.95 (0-7453-0887-2, Pub. by Pluto Pr UK) Westview.

Majumdar, Mukul, ed. Decentralization in Infinite Horizon Economies. 193p. (C). 1992. text ed. 54.50 (0-8133-8090-1) Westview.

— Equilibrium & Dynamics: Essays in Honour of David Gale. LC 91-25354. 380p. 1992. text ed. 75.00 (0-312-06810-7) St Martin.

Majumdar, P. S. & Majumdar, Ila. Rural Migrants in An Urban Setting. 176p. (C). 1978. text ed. 29.95 (0-87855-330-4) Transaction Pubs.

Majumdar, R. C. Champa: History & Culture of an Indian Colonial Kingdom in the Far East 2nd Century A.D. (C). 1985. 36.00 (0-8364-2802-1, Pub. by Gian Publng Hse II) S Asia.

— Hindu Colonies in the Far East. (C). 1991. reprint ed. 32.00 (0-8364-2740-8, Pub. by Firma KLM) S Asia.

— History of the Freedom Movement in India, Vol. I. (C). 1988. reprint ed. 17.00 (0-8364-2374-7, Pub. by Firma KLM) S Asia.

— History of the Freedom Movement in India, Vol. II. (C). 1988. reprint ed. 17.00 (0-8364-2375-5, Pub. by Firma KLM) S Asia.

— History of the Freedom Movement in India, Vol. III. (C). 1988. reprint ed. 32.50 (0-8364-2376-3, Pub. by Firma KLM) S Asia.

— Suvarnadvipa Ancient Indian Colonies in the Far East, 2 vols., Set. (C). 1986. 110.00 (81-212-0040-7) S Asia.

Majumdar, R. C. & Altekar, A. S. The Vakataka - Gupta Age Circa 200-550 A.D. 515p. 1986. reprint ed. 17.50 (81-208-0026-5, Pub. by Motilal Banarsidass II); reprint ed. pap. 12.50 (81-208-0043-5, Pub. by Motilal Banarsidass II) S Asia.

Majumdar, R. C. & Chopra, P. N. Main Currents of Indian History. 2nd rev. ed. 430p. (C). 1988. text ed. 22.50 (81-207-0770-2, Pub. by Sterling Pubs II) Apt Bks.

Majumdar, Ramesh, jt. ed. see Madhavananda.

Majumdar, Rupendra G. Blunderbuss. (Writers Workshop Redbird Ser.). 1975. 8.00 (0-88253-510-2); pap. text ed. 4.80 (0-88253-509-9) Ind-US Inc.

Majumdar, S. K., ed. Energy, Environment & the Economy. LC 81-82465. xxi, 228p. 1981. 20.00 (0-9606670-0-8) Penn Science.

***Majumdar, S. K., et al, eds.** Biological Diversity: Problems & Challenges. LC 93-87463. (Illus.). x, 461p. (C). 1994. 45.00 (0-945809-09-3) Penn Science.

— Conservation & Resource Management. LC 93-71958. (Illus.). x, 444p. (C). 1993. 45.00 (0-945809-08-5) Penn Science.

— Medicine & Health Care into the Twenty-First Century. LC 95-67144. (Illus.). xii, 613p. 1995. 55.00 (0-945809-11-5) Penn Science.

— Natural & Technological Disasters: Causes, Effects & Preventive Measures. (Illus.). x, 561p. (C). 1992. 45.00 (0-945809-06-9) Penn Science.

— The Oceans: Physical-Chemical Dynamics & Human Impact. LC 94-67523. (Illus.). x, 498p. (C). 1994. 45.00 (0-945809-10-7) Penn Science.

Majumdar, Sachin K., tr. & intro. The Bhagavad Gita: A Scripture for the Future. LC 91-21423. 272p. (Orig.). 1992. 45.00 (0-89581-885-X, Asian Human Pr); pap. 15.00 (0-89581-896-5, Asian Human Pr) Jain Pub Co.

M

Majumdar, Shyamal K. & Miller, E. Willard, eds. Hazardous & Toxic Wastes: Technology Management & Health Effects. LC 83-8317. (Illus.). xxii, 442p. 1984. 35.00 (*0-9606670-2-4*) Penn Science.

— Management of Radioactive Materials & Wastes: Issues & Progress. LC 85-61443. (Illus.). 405p. 1985. 35.00 (*0-9606670-4-0*) Penn Science.

— Pennsylvania Coal: Resources, Technology & Utilization. LC 82-62857. (Illus.). xxvi, 594p. 1983. 30.00 (*0-9606670-1-6*) Penn Science.

— Solid & Liquid Wastes: Management, Methods & Socioeconomic Considerations. LC 84-61472. (Illus.). xxii, 412p. 1984. 35.00 (*0-9606670-3-2*) Penn Science.

Majumdar, Shyamal K., jt. auth. see Riley, Herbert P.

Majumdar, Shyamal K., et al, eds. Air Pollution: Environmental Issues & Health Effects. LC 91-61996. (Illus.). x, 496p. (C). 1991. text ed. 45.00 (*0-945809-05-0*) Penn Science.

— Contaminant Problems & Management of Living Chesapeake Bay Resources. LC 87-62940. xii, 573p. (C). 1987. 40.00 (*0-9606670-7-5*) Penn Science.

— Ecology & Restoration of the Delaware River Basin. LC 88-60133. (Illus.). xiv, 431p. (C). 1988. text ed. 40.00 (*0-9606670-8-3*) Penn Science.

— Endangered & Threatened Species Programs in Pennsylvania & Other States: Causes, Issues & Management. LC 86-61186. (Illus.). xix, 519p. 1986. 40.00 (*0-9606670-5-9*) Penn Science.

— Environmental Consequences of Energy Production: Problems & Prospects. LC 87-61248. (Illus.). 531p. 1987. 40.00 (*0-9606670-6-7*) Penn Science.

— Environmental Radon: Occurrence, Control, & Health Hazards. LC 90-61965. (Illus.). xi, 436p. 1990. text ed. 45.00 (*0-945809-03-4*) Penn Science.

— Global Climate Change: Implications, Challenges & Mitigation Measures. LC 92-85374. (Illus.). xiv, 566p. (C). 1992. text ed. 45.00 (*0-945809-07-7*) Penn Science.

— Management of Hazardous Materials & Wastes: Treatment, Minimization & Environmental Impacts. LC 89-60201. (Illus.). xviii, 474p. (C). 1989. text ed. 45.00 (*0-9606670-9-1*) Penn Science.

— Science Education in the United States: Issues, Crises, Priorities. LC 91-60096. (Illus.). 550p. 1991. text ed. 45.00 (*0-945809-04-2*) Penn Science.

— Water Resources in Pennsylvania: Availability, Quality & Management. LC 89-63978. (Illus.). xiii, 580p. (C). 1990. text ed. 45.00 (*0-945809-02-6*) Penn Science.

— Wetlands Conservation: Emphasis in Pennsylvania. LC 89-61084. (Illus.). xiv, 395p. (C). 1989. text ed. 45.00 (*0-945809-01-8*) Penn Science.

Majumdar, Somendu. Regulation Requirements for Hazardous Materials. LC 92-32345. 688p. 1993. text ed. 70.00i (*0-07-039761-9*) McGraw.

Majumdar, Surendra N. Ao Nagas. LC 77-87507. reprint ed. 12.00 (*0-404-16841-8*) AMS Pr.

Majumdar, Tapas. The Measurement of Utility. LC 74-14113. (Illus.). 149p. 1975. reprint ed. text ed. 35.00 (*0-8371-7785-5*, MAMUT, Greenwood Pr) Greenwood.

Majumdar, Tapas, ed. Nature, Man & the Indian Economy. (Illus.). 432p. 1994. 37.00 (*0-19-562915-9*) OUP.

Majumder, D. Datta, jt. auth. see Chaudhuri, B. B.

Majumder, M. Medical Handbook for the Medical Representative. 7th ed. (C). 1989. 40.00 (*0-685-36201-9*, Current Dist) St Mut.

Majumder, Partha P., ed. Human Population Genetics: A Centennial Tribute to J.B.S. Haldane. LC 93-32262. (Illus.). 348p. (C). 1994. 89.50 (*0-306-44572-7*, Plenum Pr) Plenum.

Majundar, M. K. Microbiology & Immunology - an Encyclopedic Approach. (C). 1989. 90.00 (*0-89771-367-2*, Current Dist) St Mut.

Majundar, Sachindra K. Introduction to Yoga. 1977. pap. 4.95 (*0-8065-0542-7*, Citadel Pr) Carol Pub Group.

Majupuria, Trilok C. Glimpses of Nepal. (Illus.). 327p. 1980. pap. 19.95 (*0-686-92276-X*); pap. text ed. 21.95 (*0-686-98496-X*) Asia Bk Corp.

Majupuria, Trilok C. & Gupta, S. P. Nepal: The Land of Festivals (Religious, Cultural, Social & Historical Festivals) (Illus.). 152p. 1981. 14.95 (*0-940500-83-3*) Asia Bk Corp.

***Majure, Dave.** Direct Hit: Real-World Insights & Common Sense Advice from a Direct Marketing Pro. 1994. 22.95 (*1-55738-821-0*) Probus Pub Co.

Majus, J. & Spaniol, Otto, eds. Data Networks with Satellites. (Informatik-Fachberichte Ser.: Vol. 67). 251p. 1983. pap. 32.00 (*0-387-12311-3*) Spr-Verlag.

***Majzlik.** Party Food for Vegetarians. Date not set. pap. 14.95 (*1-897766-04-1*, Pub. by Jon Pubng UK) InBook.

Mak, Dayton & Kennedy, Charles S. American Ambassadors in a Troubled World: Interviews with Senior Diplomats. LC 92-7398. (Contributions in Political Science Ser.: No. 303). 248p. 1992. text ed. 55.00 (*0-313-28558-6*, MKR, Greenwood Pr) Greenwood.

Mak, Ronald. Writing Compilers & Interpreters: An Applied Approach. 516p. 1991. text ed. 49.95 (*0-471-54712-3*); text ed. 59.95 (*0-471-55580-0*); pap. text ed. 34.95 (*0-471-50968-X*) Wiley.

Mak, T. C., et al. Problems in Inorganic & Structural Chemistry. 284p. 1982. pap. text ed. 32.50x (*962-201-253-1*, Pub. by Chinese Univ HK) Coronet Bks.

Mak, Tak W., ed. The T-Cell Receptors. LC 87-38495. (Illus.). 254p. 1988. 65.00 (*0-306-42708-7*, Plenum Pr) Plenum.

Mak, Tak W., jt. ed. see Bergsagel, Daniel E.

Mak, Thomas C. & Gongdu, Zhou. Crystallography in Modern Chemistry: A Resource Book of Crystal Structures. 1344p. 1992. text ed. 195.00 (*0-471-54702-6*) Wiley.

Makaira, Robert. The Institute. LC 82-16393. 1989. pap. 14.95 (*0-87949-231-7*) Ashley Bks.

***Makana, Carol.** Music Is a Gift of Love Bilingual Masters Series. Montiero & Associates Staff, tr. (Music Is a Gift of Love Self-Esteem Character Development - Self-Esteem Ser.). (Illus.). 238p. (SPA.). (J). (gr. k-3). 1994. ring bd. write for info. (*1-879544-06-7*, H2-H005) Heart to Heart.

— Music Is a Gift of Love Self-Esteem Character Development Complete Program. rev. ed. Montiero & Associates Staff, tr. (Illus.). (J). (gr. k-3). Date not set. 489.00 (*1-879544-11-3*, H2-H 005(CE)) Heart to Heart.

— Music Is a Gift of Love Songbook. (Music Is a Gift of Love Self-Esteem Character Development - Self-Esteem Ser.). (Illus.). 40p. (Orig.). (J). (gr. k-3). 1990. student ed, pap. write for info. (*1-879544-02-4*) Heart to Heart.

— Music Is a Gift of Love Workbook. (Music Is a Gift of Love Self-Esteem Character Development - Self-Esteem Ser.). (Illus.). 71p. (Orig.). (J). (gr. k-3). 1990. student ed, spiral bd. write for info. (*1-879544-01-6*) Heart to Heart.

Makanin, Vladimir. Escape Hatch: Two Novellas. Szporluk, Mary A., tr. LC 94-7869. 1995. 24.00 (*0-87501-110-1*) Ardis Pubs.

Makankov, V., et al. Nonlinear Evolution Equations. 504p. 1993. text ed. 121.00 (*981-02-1448-0*) World Scientific Pub.

***Makanna, Philip.** Ghosts of the Skies: Aviation in the Second World War. 1995. 40.00 (*0-8118-0742-8*) Chronicle Bks.

Makanowitzky, Barbara, tr. see Turgenev, Ivan S.

Makansi, Jason, ed. Managing Steam: An Engineering Guide to Industrial, Commercial, & Utility Systems. 224p. 1986. 52.00 (*0-89116-462-6*) Hemisp Pub.

Makar-Limanov, S., tr. see Sadovskii, L. E. & Sadovskii, A. L.

Makara, jt. auth. see Koike.

Makarczyk, Jerzy. Principles of a New International Economic Order: A Study of International Law in the Making. (C). 1988. lib. bdg. 140.00 (*90-247-3746-X*) Kluwer Ac.

Makarczyk, Jerzy, ed. Essays in International Law in Honour of Judge Manfred Lachs. 1984. lib. bdg. 251.50 (*90-247-3071-6*) Kluwer Ac.

Makarenko, A. S. Collective Family: A Handbook for Russian Parents. Orig. Title: Book for Parents. 11.50 (*0-8446-2515-9*) Peter Smith.

Makari, Victor E. Ibn Taymiyyah's Ethics: The Social Factor. LC 81-1019. (American Academy of Religion Academy Ser.). 246p. (C). 1983. 27.95 (*0-89130-476-2*, 01 01 34) Scholars Pr GA.

Makarim, Sami N. Druze Faith. LC 73-19819. 1974. 25.00 (*0-88206-003-1*) Caravan Bks.

Makarim, Sami N., tr. see Ya'qub, Abu A.

Makario, Michel. Chagall. (Masterworks Ser.). (Illus.). 144p. 1991. 19.99 (*0-517-64646-3*) Random Hse Value.

Makarius, Theodore F. Operation of the Offset Press. (Illus.). (C). 1993. 24.50 (*0-685-66944-0*) Perfect Graphic.

Makaroff, Dmitri, jt. auth. see Duff, Charles.

Makarov. Engineering Artificial Intelligence. 1990. 88.00 (*0-89116-963-6*) Hemisp Pub.

— Modelling Robotic & Flexible Manufacturing Systems. 1990. 93.00 (*0-89116-964-4*) Hemisp Pub.

Makarov, B. M., et al. Selected Problems in Real Analysis. LC 92-15594. (Translations of Mathematical Monographs, 0065-9282: Vol. 107). 392p. 1992. 112.00 (*0-8218-4559-4*) Am Math.

Makarov, Evgeniis S. Crystal Chemistry of Simple Compounds of Uranium, Thorium, Plutonium, Neptunium. Uvarov, E. B., tr. LC 59-14486. 153p. reprint ed. pap. 43.70 (*0-317-08925-0*, 2003366) Bks Demand.

Makarov, I. & Vinogradskaia, T. Theory of Choice & Decision Making. 328p. (C). 1987. 80.00 (*0-685-46646-9*, Pub. by Collets) St Mut.

Makarov, Igor, illus. Romeo & Juliet. LC 92-14523. (Shakespeare: The Animated Tales Ser.). 48p. (J). (gr. 5 up). 1993. pap. 6.99 (*0-679-83874-0*) Knopf Bks Yng Read.

Makarov, S. O. Discussions of Questions in Naval Tactics. Hattendorf, John B. & Huges, Wayne P., eds. Bernadou, J. B., tr. LC 90-6279. (Classics of Sea Power Ser.). 320p. 1990. 34.95 (*0-87021-779-8*) Naval Inst Pr.

Makarov, V. & Matveeva, N., eds. Dictionary of Lexical Difficulties Encountered in Literary Texts. 368p. (C). 1989. 60.00 (*0-685-54119-3*, Pub. by Collets) St Mut.

Makarov, V. M. Reprocessing of Tires & Rubber Wastes. (Applied Science & Industrial Technology Ser.). 1991. text ed. 64.00 (*0-13-932948-X*, 520702) P-H.

***Makarov, Valery L., et al.** Mathematical Economic Theory: Pure & Mixed Types of Economic Mechanisms. (Advanced Textbooks in Economics Ser.: Vol. 33). 1994. write for info. (*0-444-89443-8*) Elsevier.

Makarova, Lena, ed. see Chapin, Melissa C.

Makarova, Marina. For Yesterday. 1985. pap. 5.95 (*0-8248-1000-7*) UH Pr.

Makarovskaia, G. Museum of History & Art in Zagorsk. (Illus.). 200p. (C). 1986. text ed. 100.00 (*0-685-40293-2*, Pub. by Collets) St Mut.

Makarovskaia, G. A. Russian Printed Shawls. 182p. 1986. 88.00 (*0-317-61387-1*, Pub. by Collets UK) Pro-Am Music.

Makarovskaia, Galina. Museum of History & Art: Zagorsk. 200p. (C). 1986. 88.00 (*0-685-21940-2*, Pub. by Collets UK) Pro-Am Music.

Makarowski, William S. Living with Pain. 144p. (Orig.). 1991. pap. 8.95 (*0-929162-24-2*) PIA Pr.

Makaryk, Irena R., ed. Encyclopedia of Contemporary Literary Theory: Approaches, Scholars, Terms. 576p. 1993. 150.00 (*0-8020-5914-7*); pap. 39.95 (*0-8020-6860-X*) U of Toronto Pr.

— Living Record: Essays in Memory of Constantine Bida. 421p. 1991. pap. 40.00 (*0-7766-0306-X*, Pub. by Univ Ottawa Pr CN) Paul & Co Pubs.

Makasheva, R. K. The Pea. Sharma, B. R., tr. 275p. (C). 1984. text ed. 60.00 (*90-6191-431-0*, Pub. by A A Balkema NE) Ashgate Pub Co.

Makato, Ooka, tr. see Fitzsimmons, Thomas, ed. & tr.

Makau, Josina M. Reasoning & Communication: Thinking Critically about Arguments. 251p. (C). 1990. pap. 29.95 (*0-534-12390-2*) Intl Thomson.

Makay, D. Bruce, comp. A Comprehensive Index to Biblical Archaeologist, Vol. 36-45. 225p. 1986. pap. 11.95 (*0-89757-008-1*, Eisenbrauns) Am Sch Orient Res.

***Makay, Ian.** Food for Thought: Being a Compendium of Culinary Quips, Quotes, Anecdotes, Facts, & Recipes by the Great & Not-So-Great. (Illus.). 320p. 1995. 14.95 (*0-89594-762-5*) Crossing Pr.

Makay, John J. Public Speaking: Theory into Practice. (Illus.). 448p. (Orig.). (C). 1992. pap. text ed. 21.50 (*0-03-030823-2*) HB Coll Pubs.

Makay, John J., jt. auth. see Bulsys, Joseph A.

Makay, Leigh. Practicing the Art of Public Speaking. 288p. (C). 1994. per. 18.36 (*0-8403-9368-7*) Kendall-Hunt.

Makay, Stanley P. A Gypsy's Ominous Prophecy. 1995. 24.95 (*0-8062-4984-6*) Carlton.

Makdisi, ed. see Qudamas, Ibn.

Makdisi, George. History & Politics in Eleventh-Century Baghdad. (Collected Studies: No. CS 336). 320p. (ENG & FRE.). 1991. text ed. 89.95 (*0-86078-289-1*, Pub. by Variorum UK) Ashgate Pub Co.

— Religion, Law & Learning in Classical Islam. (Collected Studies: No. CS 347). 336p. 1991. text ed. 89.95 (*0-86078-301-4*, Pub. by Variorum UK) Ashgate Pub Co.

— The Rise of Colleges: Institutions of Learning in Islam & the West. 377p. 1982. 42.00 (*0-85224-375-8*, Pub. by Edinburgh U Pr UK) Col U Pr.

— The Rise of Humanism in Classical Islam & the Christian West. 448p. 1989. 59.00 (*0-85224-630-7*, Pub. by Edinburgh U Pr UK) Col U Pr.

Makdisi, Jean S. Beirut Fragments: A War Memoir. LC 89-26533. 256p. 1990. 19.95 (*0-89255-150-X*) Persea Bks.

— Beirut Fragments: A War Memoir. LC 89-26533. 256p. 1991. reprint ed. pap. 9.95 (*0-89255-164-X*) Persea Bks.

Makdisi, John. Introduction to the Study of Law: Cases & Materials. 325p. 1990. pap. 21.00 (*0-87084-551-9*) Anderson Pub Co.

Makeba, Miriam & Hall, James A. Makeba: My Story. 1989. pap. 11.00 (*0-452-26234-8*, Plume) NAL-Dutton.

Makechnie, George K. Seventy Stories about Boston University, 1923-1993: A Memoir. LC 93-4005. 1993. write for info. (*0-87270-104-2*, Boston University) U Pr of Amer.

Makedon, F., et al, eds. VLSI Algorithms & Architecture. (Lecture Notes in Computer Science Ser.: Vol. 227). viii, 328p. 1986. pap. 39.00 (*0-387-16766-8*) Spr-Verlag.

Makedon, Fillia, jt. ed. see Gloor, Peter A.

Makeham, J. P. & Malcolm, L. R. The Farming Game Now. 2nd ed. (Illus.). 448p. (C). 1993. 79.95 (*0-521-40452-5*); pap. 29.95 (*0-521-42679-0*) Cambridge U Pr.

Makeham, John. Name & Actuality in Early Chinese Thought. LC 93-31922. (SUNY Series in Chinese Philosophy & Culture). 286p. 1994. text ed. 59.50x (*0-7914-1983-5*); pap. 17.95 (*0-7914-1984-3*) State U NY Pr.

Makek, M. Clinical Pathology of Fibro-Osteo-Cemental Lesions in the Cranio-Facial & Jaw Bones. (Illus.). x, 230p. 1983. 127.25 (*3-8055-3704-2*) S Karger.

Makela, Benjamin R., jt. ed. see Vancil, Richard F.

Makela, Chuck. After You've Tried Everything Else: A "More Excellent Way" to Freedom from Addictions. 32p. (Orig.). 1987. pap. 1.00 (*0-9618532-0-4*) Just Pub Hse.

Makela, Constance E. Iron Mining Fun Book for Children: Featuring Orville Ore. (Illus.). 44p. (Orig.). (J). (gr. k-6). 1982. pap. 2.00 (*0-9608686-0-7*) Happy Thoughts & Rainbow.

Makela, M. M. & Neittaanmaki, P. Nonsmooth Optimization: Analysis & Algorithms with Applications to Optimal Control. 300p. (C). 1992. text ed. 48.00 (*981-02-0773-5*) World Scientific Pub.

Makela, Maria. The Munich Secession: Art & Artists in Turn-of-the-Century Munich. (Illus.). 224p. 1992. text ed. 49.50 (*0-691-03982-8*); pap. text ed. 19.95 (*0-691-00287-8*) Princeton U Pr.

Makela, Taisto & Miller, Wallis, eds. Wars of Classification: Architecture & Modernity. (Illus.). 95p. (Orig.). 1991. pap. 8.95 (*0-910413-82-7*) Princeton Arch.

Makela, Virpi, jt. auth. see Lehtipuu, Markus.

Makelainen, P., jt. ed. see Niemi, E.

Maken, Neil. Hand-Cranked Phonographs: It All Started with Edison. (Illus.). 87p. 1993. lib. bdg. 25.95 (*0-9640687-0-2*); pap. 15.95 (*0-9640687-1-0*) Promar Pubng.

Makens, James C. The Marketing Plan Workbook. LC 85-9422. 204p. 1985. pap. text ed. 59.95 (*0-13-558065-X*, Busn) P-H.

— The Marketing Plan Workbook. 240p. 1988. pap. 18.95 (*0-13-558537-6*) P-H.

Makepeace, Chris. Ephemera. 1985. text ed. 59.95 (*0-566-03439-5*) Ashgate Pub Co.

***Makepeace, Joanna.** Corinna's Cause. large type ed. (Historical Romance Ser.). 1994. 18.95 (*0-263-14008-3*, Pub. by Mills & Boon Ltd UK) Chivers N Amer.

— Love's Raging Fires. large type ed. LC 94-19598. 597p. 1995. pap. 18.95 (*0-7862-0300-5*) Thorndike Pr.

Makepeace, Margaret, ed. Trade on the Guinea Coast, 1657-1666: The Correspondence of the English East India Company. LC 91-34443. (African Primary Texts Ser.: No. 5). 158p. (Orig.). 1991. pap. 26.00 (*0-942615-11-5*) U Wis African Stud.

Maker, C. June. Curriculum Development for the Gifted. LC 81-14985. (Illus.). 392p. 1982. 38.00 (*0-89079-130-9*, 2061) PRO-ED.

— Teaching Models in Education of the Gifted. LC 82-1692. (Illus.). 475p. 1982. 39.00 (*0-89079-186-4*, 2066) PRO-ED.

Maker, C. June, ed. Critical Issues in Gifted Education, Vol. I: Defensible Programs for the Gifted. LC 86-17345. 357p. 1986. 37.00 (*0-89079-194-5*, 2069) PRO-ED.

— Critical Issues in Gifted Education, Vol. II: Defensible Programs for Cultural & Ethnic Minorities. LC 88-992. (Critical Issues in Gifted Education Ser.). 347p. 1989. text ed. 35.00 (*0-89079-184-8*, 2072) PRO-ED.

Maker, C. June & Nielson, Aleene B. Teaching Models in Education of the Gifted. 2nd ed. (C). 1994. text ed. 39.00 (*0-89079-609-2*, 6802) PRO-ED.

Maker-Inmon, Janet & Lenier, Minnette. College Reading, Bk. 2. 4th ed. 471p. (C). 1992. pap. 25.95 (*0-534-17082-X*) Intl Thomson.

— College Reading, Bk. 3. 2nd ed. (C). 1997. pap. 25.95 (*0-534-17976-2*) Intl Thomson.

Maker, Janet & Lenier, Minnette. Academic Reading with Active Critical Thinking. (C). 1996. pap. 24.95 (*0-534-22020-7*) Intl Thomson.

— College Reading, Bk. 3. 357p. (C). 1985. pap. 25.95 (*0-534-04269-4*) Intl Thomson.

— Keys to a Powerful Vocabulary: Level I. 2nd ed. (Illus.). 256p. (C). 1988. pap. text ed. write for info. (*0-13-514951-7*) P-H.

— Keys to a Powerful Vocabulary: Level 1. 3rd ed. LC 93-10922. 1993. pap. text ed. 27.20 (*0-13-668948-5*) P-H Gen Ref & Trav.

Maker, Janet, jt. auth. see Lenier, Minnette.

Maker, June C., ed. Critical Issues in Gifted Education, Vol. 3, Vol. III. LC 92-39. 480p. (C). 1992. text ed. 39.00 (*0-89079-549-5*, 2071) PRO-ED.

Maker, William. Philosophy Without Foundations: Rethinking Hegel. (SUNY Series in Hegelian Studies in Philosophy). 308p. (C). 1994. 59.50 (*0-7914-2099-X*); pap. 19.95 (*0-7914-2100-7*) State U NY Pr.

Makerenko, Anton. A Book for Parents. 1977. lib. bdg. 59.95 (*0-8490-1525-1*) Gordon Pr.

***Makey, Miller S., et al.** How to Fly a Kite: A Kiteflier's Manual. (Illus.). 66p. (Orig.). 1992. pap. 3.00 (*0-9631175-9-9*) Am Kite MD.

Makgill, Jacques & Bellenden, Jean. Discours Particulier D'Escosse. Thomson, Thomas, ed. LC 72-172710. (Bannatyne Club, Edinburgh. Publications: No. 5). reprint ed. 17.50 (*0-404-52706-X*) AMS Pr.

Makhan, Rosemary. Biblical Blocks. LC 93-32921. 1993. 7.95 (*1-56477-044-3*) That Patchwork.

— Samplings from the Sea. LC 93-32534. 1993. 7.95 (*1-56477-043-5*) That Patchwork.

Makhankov, V. G. & Pashaev, O. K., eds. Nonlinear Evolution Equations & Dynamical Systems: NEEDS '90. (Research Reports in Physics). (Illus.). 240p. 1991. pap. 69.00 (*0-387-53294-3*) Spr-Verlag.

Makhankov, V. G., et al. The Skyrme Model: Fundamentals, Methods, Applications. LC 92-28266. (Series in Nuclear & Particle Physics). 1993. 98.00 (*0-387-54905-6*) Spr-Verlag.

Makhankov, Vladimir G. Soliton Phenomenology. (Mathematics & Its Applications, Soviet Ser.). 464p. (C). 1990. lib. bdg. 177.50 (*90-277-2830-5*) Kluwer Ac.

Makharita, R. M., jt. ed. see El-Baz, Farouk.

Makheeja, R. D., jt. auth. see Bhandari, M. C.

***Makhigani, Arjun & Gurney, Kevin R.** Mending the Ozone Hole: Science, Technology & Policy. (Illus.). 360p. 1995. 35.00 (*0-262-13308-3*) MIT Pr.

Makhijani, Arjun. From Global Capitalism to Economic Justice: An Inquiry into the Elimination of Systemic Poverty, Violence & Environmental Destruction in the World Economy. LC 91-36571. 192p. (Orig.). 1992. pap. 14.95 (*0-945257-41-4*) Apex Pr.

Makhijani, Arjun & Saleska, Scott. High-Level Dollars, Low-Level Sense: A Critique of Present Policy for the Management of Long-Lived Radioactive Wastes & Discussion of an Alternative Approach. 144p. (Orig.). 1992. pap. 12.95 (*0-945257-42-2*) Apex Pr.

Makhijani, Arjun, ed. see International Physicians for the Prevention of Nuclear War Staff & Institute for Energy & Environmental Research Staff.

Makhlis, F. A. Radiation Physics & Chemistry of Polymers. 300p. 1974. text ed. 74.00x (*0-7065-1431-9*, Pub. by Keter Pub IS) Coronet Bks.

Makhlouf, Gabriel M. & Schultz, Stanley G., eds. Handbook of Physiology, Section 6: The Gastrointestinal System, Vol. II: Neural & Endocrine Biology. (American Physiological Society Book). (Illus.). 736p. 1989. 195.00 (*0-19-520795-5*) OUP.

Makhlouf, Georgia. The Rise of Major Religions. Moeller, Walter O., tr. (Human Story Ser.). Orig. Title: Les Grandes Religions. (Illus.). 77p. (YA). (gr. 7 up). 1988. 12.95 (*0-382-09482-4*) Silver Burdett Pr.

Makhon'ko, K. P. & Malakhov, S. G., eds. Nuclear Meteorology. 388p. 1974. text ed. 96.75 (*0-7065-1445-9*, Pub. by Keter Pub IS) Coronet Bks.

Makhoul, John, jt. auth. see Kazimi, Mujid.

Makhubu, Lydia, et al, eds. Endod II: Phytolacca Dodecandra--Towards the Use of Endod As a Plant-Derived Molluscicide for Control of Schistosomiasis on a Community Self-Help Basis; Report of the Second International Meeting on Endod. (Illus.). 168p. (Orig.). 1987. pap. 13.50 (*0-936876-48-4*) LRIS.

Makhult, Mihaly. Machine Support Design Based on Vibration Calculus. 26.00 (*963-05-1150-9*, Pub. by Akad Kiado HU) St Mut.

Makhviladze, T. M., ed. Lithography in Microelectronics. (Proceedings of the Institute of General Physics of the Academy of Sciences of the U. S. S. R. Ser.: Vol. 8). 207p. 1989. text ed. 115.00 (*0-941743-30-6*) Nova Sci Pubs.

Maki, A., jt. auth. see Dickson, K.

Maki, Alan, jt. auth. see Smith, Gary.

Maki, Arthur G. & Wells, Joseph S. New Wavenumber Calibration Tables from Heterodyne Frequency Measurements. (Illus.). 62p. (Orig.). (C). 1992. pap. text ed. 40.00 (*1-56806-136-6*) Diane Pub.

Maki, Chu. Snowflakes, Sugar, & Salt: Crystals up Close. LC 92-18538. (Illus.). (J). (gr. 1-3). 1993. 18.95 (*0-8225-2903-3*, Lerner Publctns) Lerner Group.

Maki, Daniel P. & Thompson, Maynard. Finite Mathematics. 3rd ed. 1989. text ed. write for info. (*0-07-039751-1*) McGraw.

— Finite Mathematics. 4th ed. LC 94-48013. 1995. 51.50 (*0-07-039763-5*) McGraw.

— Mathematical Models & Applications: With Emphasis on the Social, Life, & Management Sciences. (Illus.). 464p. 1973. text ed. write for info. (*0-13-561670-0*) P-H.

Maki, Dennis R. & Berven, Norman L., eds. Directory of Doctoral Study in Rehabilitation. 2nd ed. 62p. 1992. 10.00 (*1-55620-116-8*, 72253) Am Coun Assn.

Maki, John M. Conflict & Tension in the Far East: Key Documents, 1894-1960. LC 61-17709. 254p. 1961. 20.00 (*0-295-73751-4*) U of Wash Pr.

Maki, John M., ed. Japan's Commission on the Constitution: The Final Report. LC 80-50869. (Asian Law Ser.: No. 7). 424p. 1980. 40.00 (*0-295-95767-0*) U of Wash Pr.

***Maki, Kathleen E., ed.** Small Business Sourcebook, 2 vols. 8th ed. 2971p. 1994. 235.00 (*0-8103-5668-6*) Gale.

Maki, Ken. Big Mac Secrets. 1992. pap. 39.95 (*0-88022-992-6*) Que.

— The EO Travel Guide. LC 93-30018. 1993. pap. text ed. 22.95 (*0-471-00783-8*) Wiley.

— Integrating Macs with Your PC Network. LC 93-49414. 1994. pap. text ed. 27.95 (*0-471-30505-7*) Wiley.

— Macintosh Revelations. LC 94-25117. 1995. text ed. 32.95 (*0-471-05255-8*) Wiley.

Maki, P. & Schilling, C. Writing in Organizations: Purposes, Strategies & Processes. 416p. 1987. pap. text ed. write for info. (*0-07-030361-4*) McGraw.

Maki, Uskali, et al, eds. Rationality, Institutions, & Economic Methodology. LC 93-6926. (Economics As Social Theory Ser.). 272p. 1993. 74.50 (*0-415-07571-8*, B0141); pap. 19.95 (*0-415-09208-6*, B0145) Routledge.

Maki, William S., jt. ed. see Zentall, Thomas R.

Makielski, Kathleen H., jt. auth. see Larrabee, Wayne F., Jr.

***Makiko, Nakano, tr.** Makiko's Diary: A Merchant Wife in 1910 Kyoto. LC 94-39864. (Illus.). 304p. (ENG & JPN.). 1995. 45.00x (*0-8047-2440-7*); pap. 14.95 (*0-8047-2441-5*) Stanford U Pr.

Makil, Perla Q., jt. ed. see Yengoyan, Aram A.

Makin, A. J. International Capital Mobility & External Account Determination. LC 93-44094. 1994. text ed. 55.00 (*0-312-12100-8*) St Martin.

Makin, Ena, ed. see Puccini, Giacomo.

Makin, Jock. The Big Run. 193p. 1992. 59.95 (*1-86302-228-7*, Pub. by Natl Bk Dist AT) St Mut.

Makin, John H. U. S. Fiscal Policy: Its Effects at Home & Abroad. 54p. (Orig.). 1986. pap. text ed. 9.50 (*0-8447-3608-2*) Am Enterprise.

Makin, John H., et al. Balancing Act: Debt, Deficits, & Taxes. 133p. (C). 1990. lib. bdg. 22.25 (*0-685-40157-X*) Am Enterprise.

Makin, Michael. Marina Tsvetaeva: Poetics of Appropriation. LC 93-12218. (Oxford Modern Languages & Literature Monographs). 1994. 60.00 (*0-19-815164-0*, Clarendon Pr) OUP.

Makin, Michael & Toman, Jindrich, eds. On Karel Capek: A Michigan Slavic Colloquium. LC 92-20812. (Materials Ser.: No. 34). 1992. pap. 15.00 (*0-930042-71-9*) Mich Slavic Pubns.

Makin, Peter. Bunting: The Shaping of His Verse. (Illus.). 304p. 1992. 92.00 (*0-19-811254-8*) OUP.

— Pound's Cantos. Rawson, Claude, ed. (Unwin Critical Library). 368p. 1985. pap. text ed. 18.95 (*0-04-811002-7*) Routledge Chapman & Hall.

— Pound's Cantos. 352p. 1992. reprint ed. pap. text ed. 13.95x (*0-8018-4371-5*) Johns Hopkins.

— Provence & Pound. LC 77-76186. 442p. reprint ed. pap. 126.00 (*0-7837-4694-6*, 2044441) Bks Demand.

Makin, Peter J., et al. Managing People at Work. LC 89-8475. 221p. 1989. text ed. 55.00 (*0-89930-505-9*, MKW/, Quorum Bks) Greenwood.

Makin, Royce E. You Are the Christ? Nine One-Act Plays. LC 93-12109. 152p. (Orig.). 1993. pap. 10.99 (*0-8272-4404-5*) Chalice Pr.

Makin, Stephen. Indifference Arguments. LC 93-9799. (Issues in Ancient Philosophy Ser.). (Illus.). 248p. 1994. 54.95 (*0-631-17838-4*) Blackwell Pubs.

Makin, Susan R. A Consumer's Guide to Art Therapy: For Prospective Employers, Clients & Students. 112p. (C). 1994. 29.95 (*0-398-05917-9*) C C Thomas.

— A Consumer's Guide to Art Therapy: For Prospective Employers, Clients & Students. 112p. (C). 1994. pap. 15.95 (*0-398-06511-X*) C C Thomas.

Makinda, Samuel M. Seeking Peace from Chaos: Humanitarian Intervention in Somalia. LC 93-20731. (International Peace Academy Occasional Paper Ser.). 96p. 1993. pap. text ed. 8.95 (*1-55587-477-0*) Lynne Rienner.

— Superpower Diplomacy in the Horn of Africa. LC 86-31379. 272p. 1987. text ed. 49.95 (*0-312-00548-2*) St Martin.

Makinde, M. Akin. African Philosophy, Culture & Traditional Medicine. LC 88-15680. (Monographs in International Studies, Africa Ser.: No. 53). 175p. 1988. pap. text ed. 16.00 (*0-89680-152-7*, Ohio U Ctr Intl) Ohio U Pr.

Makinen, K. K. Biochemical Principles of the Use of Xylitol in Medicine & Nutrition with Special Consideration of Dental Aspects. (Experientia Supplementa Ser.: No. 30). (Illus.). 160p. 1980. 40.95 (*0-8176-0961-X*) Birkhauser.

Makinen, M. Joyce Cary: A Descriptive Bibliography. 264p. 1989. text ed. 100.00 (*0-7201-1985-5*, Mansell Pub) Cassell.

Makinen, Merja, jt. auth. see Gamman, Lorraine.

Makinen, Merja, jt. auth. see Gamman, Lorriane.

Makinen, Paul, tr. see Barenblatt, G. I.

Makinen, Paul, tr. see Kuz'min, A. D., ed.

Makinen, Paul, tr. see Plotnikov, A. F., ed.

Makino, Erika B. Six of Cups: A Circle of Stories. LC 92-70849. (Illus.). 160p. (Orig.). 1992. pap. 8.50 (*0-929151-05-4*) Earth Bks.

Makino, H. Assembly Automation: Proceedings of the 4th International Conference, Tokyo, Japan, 11-13 Oct., 1983. 408p. 1984. 95.00 (*0-444-86768-6*) Elsevier.

Makino, Noboru. Total Forecast Japan: The Nineteen Nineties. 352p. 1993. text ed. 79.95 (*0-304-32717-4*) Cassell.

Makino, S., jt. ed. see Ishikawa, T.

Makino, Sohei & Fukuda, Takeshi, eds. Eosinophils: Biological & Clinical Aspects. 1992. 219.00 (*0-8493-6822-7*, RB145) CRC Pr.

Makino, Yasuko. Japan Through Children's Literature: An Annotated Bibliography. 2nd ed. LC 85-21941. x, 144p. 1985. text ed. 45.00 (*0-313-24611-4*, MJA/, Greenwood Pr) Greenwood.

Makino, Yasuko & Saito, Masaei. A Student Guide to Japanese Sources in the Humanities. LC 93-34031. (Michigan Papers in Japanese Studies: No. 24). ix, 155p. (C). 1994. pap. 17.95 (*0-939512-64-5*) U MI Japan.

Makinodan, T., et al. Aging & the Immune Function. 227p. 1974. text ed. 28.50 (*0-8422-7228-3*) Irvington.

Makinodan, Takashi & Kay, Marguerite M., eds. Handbook of Immunology of Aging. (Series in Aging). 328p. 1981. 113.95 (*0-8493-3144-7*, QP86, CRC Reprint) Franklin.

Makinouchi, Akifumi, ed. Database Systems for Advanced Applications '91: Proceedings of the Second International Symposium on Database Systems for Advanced Applications, April 2-4, 1991, Tokyo, Japan. LC 92-19671. (Advanced Database Research & Development Ser.: Vol. 2). 568p. 1992. text ed. 121.00 (*981-02-1055-8*) World Scientific Pub.

Makins, Geoffrey E. Waymarks: An Artist's Attempt at a Natural Religion. (C). 1988. 51.00 (*1-85072-026-6*, Pub. by W Sessions UK) St Mut.

Makinson. Shrinkproofing of Wool. (Fiber Science Ser.: Vol. 8). 392p. 1979. 125.00 (*0-8247-6776-4*) Dekker.

Makinson, Larry. The Cash Constituents of Congress. 300p. 1992. pap. 32.95 (*0-87187-690-6*) Congr Quarterly.

— Open Secrets: Congressional Money & Politics. 2nd ed. LC 92-5802. 1400p. 1992. 169.95 (*0-87187-689-2*) Congr Quarterly.

— Open Secrets: The Dollar Power of PACs in Congress. 1188p. 1990. 159.95 (*0-87187-579-9*) Congr Quarterly.

— The Price of Admission: Campaign Spending in the 1990 Elections. (Illus.). 160p. 1992. pap. text ed. 19.95 (*0-939715-16-3*) Ctr Politics.

Makinson, Larry & Goldstein, Joshua F. The Cash Constituents of Congress, 1992 Elections. 362p. 1994. pap. 33.95 (*1-56802-010-4*) Congr Quarterly.

— Open Secrets: The Encyclopedia of Congressional Money & Politics. 3rd ed. 1362p. 1994. 169.95 (*1-56802-026-0*) Congr Quarterly.

Makinson, Randell L. Greene & Greene: Architecture As a Fine Art, Vol. 1. LC 76-57792. (Illus.). 288p. 1977. pap. 24.95 (*0-87905-126-4*, Peregrine Smith) Gibbs Smith Pub.

— Greene & Greene: Furniture & Related Designs, Vol. 2. LC 76-57792. (Illus.). 190p. 1983. pap. 24.95 (*0-87905-125-6*, Peregrine Smith) Gibbs Smith Pub.

Makinson, Randell L., jt. auth. see McCoy, Esther.

Makinster, Genie. Ravensloch: Gothic Mystery. LC 83-26303. (Illus.). 141p. (Orig.). 1982. pap. 1.95 (*0-9608742-0-8*) Gemak Pub.

Makintosh, Allan, jt. auth. see Jensen, Jens.

Makita, Akira, et al, eds. Membrane Alterations in Cancer. (GANN Monographs on Cancer Research: No. 29). 312p. 1983. 85.00 (*0-306-41565-8*, Plenum Pr) Plenum.

Makiuchi, Reiko, jt. auth. see Shelley, Rex.

Makiya, Hind & Rogers, Margaret. Design & Technology in the Primary School: Case Studies for Teachers. LC 91-48095. 160p. 1992. 59.95 (*0-415-08089-4*, A7629) Routledge.

Makiya, Kanan. Cruelty & Silence: War, Tyranny, Uprising, & the Arab World. 1994. pap. 10.95 (*0-393-31141-4*) Norton.

— Cruelty & Silence: War, Tyranny, Uprising in the Arab World. (Illus.). 256p. 1993. 22.95 (*0-393-03108-X*) Norton.

— Post-Islamic Classicism: A Visual Essay on the Architecture of Mohamed Makiya. 1993. 69.95 (*0-86356-295-7*, Pub. by Saqi Bks UK) Interlink Pub.

Makiyama, Thomas. Keijutsukai Aikido: Japanese Art of Self Defense. LC 83-61559. (Japanese Arts Ser.). (Illus.). (Orig.). 1983. pap. 11.95 (*0-89750-092-X*, 428) Ohara Pubns.

Makkai & Pare. Accessible Categories: The Foundations of Categorical Model Theory. LC 89-18125. (CONM Ser.: Vol. 104). 176p. 1991. reprint ed. pap. 34.00 (*0-8218-5111-X*, CONM-104) Am Math.

***Makkai, Adam.** Dictionary of American Idioms. 3rd ed. 1995. pap. 12.95 (*0-8120-1248-8*) Barron.

— A Dictionary of Space English. viii, 72p. (Orig.). 1973. pap. 10.00 (*0-933104-23-5*) Jupiter Pr.

— Ecolinguistics: Toward a New Paradigm for the Science of Language. (Open Linguistics Ser.). 600p. 1993. text ed. 89.00 (*1-85567-018-6*, Pub. by Pinter Pubs UK) St Martin.

— Idiom Structure in English. LC 76-144014. (Janua Linguarum, Ser. Major: No. 48). (Illus.). 371p. 1972. text ed. 78.50 (*90-279-2105-9*) Mouton.

— K-Square Equals Thirteen. (Hungarian Poems Ser.). 112p. 1970. 12.00 (*0-933104-18-9*) Jupiter Pr.

— Languages for Peace: A Tribute to Kenneth L. Pike. (Languages for Peace Ser.: No. 1). (Illus.). 32p. (Orig.). 1983. pap. 4.00 (*0-933104-14-6*) Jupiter Pr.

Makkai, Adam, ed. Toward a Theory of Context in Linguistics & Literature: Proceedings of a Conference of the Kelemen Mikes Hungarian Cultural Society, Maastricht, September 21-25, 1971. (De Proprietatibus Litterarum, Ser. Minor: No. 18). pap. 40.00 (*90-279-3273-5*) Mouton.

Makkai, Adam & Lockwood, David G. Readings in Stratificational Linguistics. viii, 331p. 1973. 20.00 (*0-933104-24-3*) Jupiter Pr.

Makkai, Adam & Melby, Alan K. Linguistics & Philosophy: Essays in Honor of Rulon S. Wells. LC 85-20099. (Current Issues in Linguistic Theory Ser.: No. 42). xviii, 472p. 1985. 94.00x (*90-272-3536-8*) Benjamins North Am.

Makkai, Adam, tr. see Alexander, Michael.

Makkai, Adam, et al. A Dictionary of American Idioms. 2nd rev. ed. 480p. 1987. pap. 11.95 (*0-8120-3899-1*) Barron.

— Handbook of Commonly Used Idioms. 2nd ed. 1991. vinyl bd. 6.95 (*0-8120-4614-5*) Barron.

Makkai, Adam, et al, eds. Linguistics at the Crossroads. LC 79-312499. viii, 502p. (C). 1977. pap. 27.00 (*0-933104-02-2*) Jupiter Pr.

Makkai, Michael. Duality & Definability in First Order Logic. LC 93-4868. (Memoirs Ser.: No. 503). 106p. 1993. pap. 30.00 (*0-8218-2565-8*) Am Math.

Makkai, Valerie B., ed. Phonological Theory: Evolution & Current Practice. LC 76-138654. xi, 711p. (C). 1978. reprint ed. pap. 20.00 (*0-933104-05-7*) Jupiter Pr.

Makkar, G. C. Three Number Author Tables. 200p. 1974. 6.00 (*0-88065-153-9*, Messers Today & Tomorrow) Scholarly Pubns.

Makkar, S. P., ed. Law of Culpable Homicide, Murder & Punishment in India. (C). 1990. 125.00 (*0-89771-180-7*) St Mut.

Makkar, S. P. & Hamid, Abdul, eds. Constitutional Law, a Miscellany. (C). 1990. 150.00 (*0-89771-203-X*) St Mut.

Makkay, Janos. Tarantella: Avagy Utazasok a Pokhalon (Egy Pszichoanalizis Tortenete) 63p. (Orig.). 1985. pap. 8.00 (*0-317-99612-6*) Jupiter Pr.

Makkay, Jans. Early Stamp Seals in South-East Europe. 124p. 1984. 62.50 (*0-685-16985-5*, Pub. by Collets UK) Pro-Am Music.

Makker, Sudesh P., jt. auth. see Kher, Kanwal K.

Makkink, Henri J. Philip Massinger & John Fletcher: A Comparison. LC 68-1145. (Studies in Drama: No. 39). 1969. reprint ed. lib. bdg. 49.95 (*0-8383-0669-1*) M S G Haskell Hse.

Makkreel, Rudolf, ed. see Dilthey.

Makkreel, Rudolf A. Imagination & Interpretation in Kant: The Hermeneutical Import of the Critique of Judgment. LC 89-39715. 200p. 1990. 24.95 (*0-226-50276-7*) U Ch Pr.

— Imagination & Interpretation in Kant: The Hermeneutical Import of the Critique of Judgment. xii, 188p. 1994. pap. text ed. 12.95 (*0-226-50277-5*) U Ch Pr.

Makkreel, Rudolf A., ed. Wilhelm Dilthey: Introduction to the Human Sciences. (Selected Works of Wilhelm Dilthey: Vol. I). 539p. 1991. text ed. 65.00 (*0-691-07307-4*); pap. text ed. 19.95 (*0-691-02074-4*) Princeton U Pr.

Makkreel, Rudolf A. & Scanlon, John, eds. Dilthey & Phenomenology. LC 87-8102. (Current Continental Research Ser.: No. 006). 182p. (Orig.). (C). 1987. lib. bdg. 46.00 (*0-8191-6305-8*, Ctr Adv Res) U Pr of Amer.

Makkreel, Rudolf A., ed. see Dilthey, Wilhelm.

Makky, Wagih H., ed. Aviation Security Problem & Related Technologies: Proceedings of a Conference Held 19-20 July 1992, San Diego, California. LC 92-17417. (Critical Reviews of Optical Science & Technology Ser.: Vol. CR42). 1992. 68.00 (*0-8194-0954-5*); pap. 50.00 (*0-8194-0955-3*) SPIE.

Maklad, Nabil F., ed. Ultrasound in Perinatology. (Clinics in Diagnostic Ultrasound Ser.: Vol. 19). (Illus.). 222p. 1986. text ed. 35.95 (*0-443-08365-7*) Churchill.

— Ultrasound in Perinatology. fac. ed. LC 85-29139. (Clinics in Diagnostic Ultrasound Ser.: No. 19). (Illus.). 238p. 1986. reprint ed. pap. 67.90 (*0-7837-7892-9*, 2047648) Bks Demand.

Maklan, David M. The Four-Day Work Week: Blue Collar Adjustment to a Nonconventional Arrangement of Work & Leisure Time. LC 77-14308. (Special Studies). 222p. 1977. text ed. 49.95 (*0-275-90270-6*, C0270, Praeger Pubs) Greenwood.

Makler, Harry M., jt. ed. see Graham, Lawrence S.

Makley, Michael J. The Apprentice Twain. LC 93-91080. 172p. (Orig.). 1994. pap. 6.25 (*0-9636608-1-0*) Estrn Sierra.

— The Hanging of Lucky Bill. 145p. 1993. pap. 9.95 (*0-9636608-0-2*) Estrn Sierra.

Makman, Maynard H. & Stefano, George B., eds. Neuroregulatory Mechanisms in Aging. LC 93-21169. (Studies in Neuroscience). 1993. 127.00 (*0-08-041989-5*, Pergamon Pr) Elsevier.

***Mako, Inc. Staff.** Pediatric Emergency Pocketbook. 96p. 1995. pap. text ed. 8.95 (*1-882742-03-6*) Tarascon Pub.

Mako, William P. U. S. Ground Forces & the Defense of Central Europe. LC 83-2817. (Studies in Defense Policy). 137p. 1983. 26.95 (*0-8157-5444-2*); pap. 9.95 (*0-8157-5443-4*) Brookings.

Makofske, Mary. Disappearance of Gargoyles. 64p. (Orig.). 1988. pap. 5.95 (*0-939395-10-X*) Thorntree Pr.

Makofske, William J. & Edelstein, Michael R., eds. Radon & the Environment. LC 87-35242. (Illus.). 465p. 1988. 39.00 (*0-8155-1161-2*) Noyes.

Makofske, William J. & Karlin, Eric F., eds. Technology, Development & Global Environmental Issues. LC 94-12437. 352p. (C). 1994. 12.00 (*0-673-99181-4*) HarpCollege.

Makolkin, Anna. Name, Hero, Icon: Semiotics of Nationalism Through Heroic Biography. LC 91-48252. (Approaches to Semiotics Ser.: No. 105). xvi, 264p. (C). 1992. lib. bdg. 113.85 (*3-11-013012-2*) Mouton.

— Semiotics of Misogyny Through the Humor of Chekhov & Maugham. LC 92-18419. 260p. 1992. text ed. 89.95 (*0-7734-9570-3*) E Mellen.

Makoondekwa, Joao, jt. auth. see Carter, Hazel.

Makos, Marc. Interviewing & the Smart Job Search. LC 93-28985. 1994. pap. 10.95 (*0-9630394-5-8*) HD Pub.

Makos, Marc L. Resumes for the Smart Job Search: The Ultimate Guide to Writing Resumes in the 90s. LC 92-47008. 160p. 1993. pap. 14.95 (*0-9630394-9-0*) HD Pub.

— The Smart Job Search: A Guide to Proven Methods for Finding a Great Job. LC 91-31232. 308p. 1991. pap. 18.95 (*0-9630394-8-2*) HD Pub.

— The Smart Job Search Series, 3 bks., Set. 580p. 1994. pap. 44.85 (*0-9630394-0-7*) HD Pub.

Makoshi, K., jt. auth. see Ilisca, E.

Makoski, Ellen H. Scenic Parks & Landscape Value. LC 90-39467. (Environment: Problems & Solutions Ser.: Vol. 15). 283p. 1990. 75.00 (*0-8240-0470-1*) Garland.

Makosky, Veronica. Susan Glaspell's Century of American Women: A Critical Interpretation of Her Work. LC 92-23329. 1993. 32.00 (*0-19-507866-7*) OUP.

Makosky, Vivian P., et al, eds. Activities Handbook for the Teaching of Psychology, Vol. 3. (Illus.). 384p. (C). 1990. 25.00 (*1-55798-081-0*) Am Psychol.

Makoto, Ooka. The Colors of Poetry: Essays on Classic Japanese Verse. Fitzsimmons, Thomas, ed. Lento, Takako & Lento, Thomas, trs. (Reflections Ser.: No. 1). 152p. (C). 1991. 19.95 (*0-942668-28-6*); pap. 12.95 (*0-942668-27-8*) Katydid Bks.

— Elegy & Benediction: Selected Poems, 1947-1989. Elliott, William I. & Kazuo, Kawamura, trs. 112p. 1991. text ed. 17.95 (*0-942668-31-6*); pap. 10.95 (*0-942668-32-4*) Katydid Bks.

Makoto, Ooka, ed. A Poet's Anthology: The Range of Japanese Poetry. Beichman, Janine, tr. (Reflections Ser.: No. 3). 224p. (C). 1993. text ed. 29.95 (*0-942668-37-5*); pap. text ed. 19.95 (*0-942668-38-3*) Katydid Bks.

Makoto, Ooka, jt. ed. see Fitzsimmons, Thomas.

Makov, Susan, jt. auth. see Eddington, Patrick.

Makovsky, Andre, ed. see Cisco, Bob.

***Makovsky, David.** Making Peace with the PLO. (C). 1995. text ed. 40.00 (*0-8133-2425-4*); pap. text ed. 15.95 (*0-8133-2426-2*) Westview.

Makower, Joel. The Air & Space Catalog. LC 89-40133. 336p. 1990. pap. 16.95 (*0-679-72038-3*, Vin) Random.

— The E-Factor: The Bottom-Line Approach to Environmentally Responsible Business. LC 93-47227. 304p. 1994. pap. 11.95 (*0-452-27190-8*, Plume) NAL-Dutton.

— The E-Factor: Turning Environmental Responsibility into Good, Green Profits. LC 92-50504. 1993. 23.00 (*0-8129-2057-0*, Times Bks) Random.

— The Green Commuter: Cars, Bikes & Feet: Driving & Vacationing for a Cleaner World. 160p. 1991. pap. 9.95 (*0-915765-95-0*) Krantz Co.

— The Map Catalog. LC 89-43158. 352p. 1990. 27.50 (*0-394-58326-4*) Random.

— The Map Catalog. rev. ed. LC 89-40434. 368p. 1990. pap. 21.00 (*0-679-72767-1*, Vin) Random.

— Map Catalog: Every Kind of Map & Chart on Earth & Even Some above It. LC 92-5358. 1992. pap. 20.00 (*0-679-74257-3*, Vin) Random.

— The Nature Catalog. LC 91-50216. (Vintage Original Ser.). (Illus.). 336p. 1991. pap. 18.00 (*0-679-73300-0*, Vin) Random.

— Spreading the Wealth. 1994. 22.00 (*0-671-88325-9*) S&S Trade.

Makower, Joel, et al. The Green Consumer. rev. ed. (Tilden Press Bks.). 320p. 1993. pap. 11.00 (*0-14-017711-6*, Penguin Bks) Viking Penguin.

Makower, Stanley V. & Blackwell, Basil H., eds. Book of English Essays: Sixteen Hundred to Nineteen Hundred. LC 73-37845. (Essay Index Reprint Ser.). 1977. reprint ed. 29.95 (*0-8369-2609-9*) Ayer.

Makowka. Handbook of Animal Models in Transplantation Research. 1994. 179.95 (*0-8493-3629-5*, RD120) CRC Pr.

***Makowka, Leonard & Sher, Linda S., eds.** Ortho Biotech Handbook of Organ Transplantation. LC 95-1070. 1995. write for info. (*1-57059-188-1*) R G Landes.

Makowka, Leonard, jt. ed. see Sher, Linda S.

Makowski, Colleen L. Quilting, Nineteen Fifteen to Nineteen Eighty-Three: An Annotated Bibliography. LC 85-2497. (Illus.). 165p. 1985. pap. text ed. 20.00 (*0-8108-1813-2*) Scarecrow.

Makowski, Elizabeth M., jt. auth. see Wilson, Katharina M.

Makowski, John F., tr. see Roberts, J. L., III, et al, eds.

Makowski, Sandi, jt. auth. see Kalashian, Susan.

Makowski, William. The Polish People in Canada: A Visual History. LC 86-51039. (Illus.). 300p. 1987. pap. 12.50 (*0-88776-189-5*, U of Toronto Pr) Tundra Bks.

Makowski, Z. S., ed. Analysis Design & Construction of Braced Barrel Vaults. 416p. 1986. 162.00 (0-85334-377-2, Pub. by Elsevier Applied Sci UK) Elsevier.

Makowsky, Michael. Minstrel of Love: A Biography of Satguru Sant Keshavadas. (Illus.). 334p. (Orig.). 1980. pap. 12.00 (0-942508-20-3) Vishwa.

Makowsky, Michael, jt. auth. see Collins, Randall.

Makowsky, Veronica A. Caroline Gordon: A Biography. (Illus.). 276p. 1989. 25.00 (0-19-505718-X) OUP.

Makowsky, Veronica A., ed. see Blackmur, R. P.

Makrakis, Apostolos. The Bible & the World & Triluminal Science. Orthodox Christian Educational Society Staff, ed. Cummings, Denver, tr. 531p. 1950. 24.95 (0-938366-18-1) Orthodox Chr.

— Catechesis of the Orthodox Church. rev. ed. Orthodox Christian Educational Society Staff, ed. 239p. 1969. reprint ed. pap. text ed. 9.95 (0-938366-14-9) Orthodox Chr.

— The City of Zion-The Human Society in Christ, i.e., the Church Built upon a Rock. Orthodox Christian Educational Society Staff, ed. Cummings, Denver, tr. 109p. (C). 1958. pap. 6.95 (0-938366-16-5) Orthodox Chr.

— Commentary on the Psalms of David. Orthodox Christian Educational Society Staff, ed. Cummings, Denver, tr. 990p. 1950. 24.95 (0-938366-19-X) Orthodox Chr.

— Concerning Our Duties to God. Orthodox Christian Educational Society Staff, ed. 170p. 1958. pap. text ed. 5.95 (0-938366-13-0) Orthodox Chr.

— Divine & Sacred Catechism. Orthodox Christian Educational Society Staff, ed. 224p. (C). 1946. 9.95 (0-938366-15-7) Orthodox Chr.

— The Foundation of Philosophy-a Refutation of Skepticism, the True Jesus Christ, the Science of God & Man; the God of the Christians. Orthodox Christian Educational Society Staff, ed. Lekatsos, Anthony & Cummings, Denver, trs. 395p. 1955. 14.96 (0-938366-07-6) Orthodox Chr.

— Freemasonry Known by the Masonic Diploma. Cummings, Denver, tr. 135p. (Orig.). 1956. reprint ed. pap. 5.95 (0-938366-42-4) Orthodox Chr.

— Hellenism & the Unfinished Revolution. Orthodox Christian Educational Society Staff, ed. 191p. (Orig.). 1968. pap. 8.95 (0-938366-26-2) Orthodox Chr.

— The Holy Orthodox Church. Orthodox Christian Educational Society Staff, ed. Lisney, M. I. & Krick, L., trs. 290p. (Orig.). 1980. pap. 12.95 (0-938366-34-3) Orthodox Chr.

— The Human Nature of Christ: Growth & Perfection. Orthodox Christian Educational Society Staff, ed. Cummings, D., tr. 52p. (Orig.). 1965. pap. 3.95 (0-938366-28-9) Orthodox Chr.

— The Innovations of the Roman Church. 82p. (Orig.). 1966. reprint ed. pap. 4.95 (0-938366-39-4) Orthodox Chr.

— Interpretation of the Book of Revelation. Orthodox Christian Educational Society Staff, ed. Alexander, A. G., tr. 564p. 1972. 21.95 (0-938366-12-2) Orthodox Chr.

— Interpretation of the Entire New Testament (Revelation Not Incl),, 2 vols., Set. Orthodox Christian Educational Society Staff, ed. Alexander, Albert G., tr. 2052p. (C). 1949. 44.95 (0-938366-08-4) Orthodox Chr.

— The Interpretation of the Gospel Law. Orthodox Christian Educational Society Staff, ed. Cummings, Denver, tr. 453p. 1955. 15.95 (0-938366-10-6) Orthodox Chr.

— Kyriakodromion (Sunday Sermonary) Orthodox Christian Educational Society Staff, ed. Cummings, D., tr. 637p. 1951. 19.95 (0-938366-20-3) Orthodox Chr.

— Logic: An Orthodox Christian Approach. Orthodox Christian Educational Society Staff, ed. Cummings, Denver, tr. (Logos & Holy Spirit in the Unity of Christian Thought Ser.: Vol. 3). 200p. 1977. reprint ed. pap. 5.95 (0-938366-04-1) Orthodox Chr.

— Memoir of the Nature of the Church of Christ. Orthodox Christian Educational Society Staff, ed. Cummings, Denver, tr. 175p. 1947. 6.95 (0-938366-21-1) Orthodox Chr.

— The Orthodox Approach to Philosophy. Orthodox Christian Educational Society Staff, ed. Cummings, Denver, tr. (Logos & Holy Spirit in the Unity of Christian Thought Ser.: Vol. 1). 82p. 1977. reprint ed. pap. 5.00 (0-938366-06-8) Orthodox Chr.

— Orthodox Christian Meditations (Spiritual Discourses for the Orthodox Christians) Orthodox Christian Educational Society Staff, ed. Cummings, Denver, tr. 143p. (Orig.). 1965. pap. 3.95 (0-938366-22-X) Orthodox Chr.

— The Orthodox Definition of Political Science. Orthodox Christian Educational Society Staff, ed. Cummings, Denver, tr. 163p. 1968. reprint ed. pap. 4.95 (0-938366-31-9) Orthodox Chr.

— An Orthodox-Protestant Debate. Cummings, Denver, tr. 101p. 1949. reprint ed. pap. 4.95 (0-938366-37-8) Orthodox Chr.

— The Paramount Doctrines of Orthodoxy-the Tricompositeness of Man, Apology of A. Makrakis & the Trial of A. Makrakis. Orthodox Christian Educational Society Staff, ed. Cummings, Denver, tr. 904p. 1954. 19.95 (0-938366-17-3) Orthodox Chr.

— Philosophy: An Orthodox Christian Understanding. Orthodox Christian Educational Society Staff, ed. Cummings, Denver, tr. (Logos & Holy Spirit in the Unity of Christian Thought Ser.: Vol. 5). 279p. 1977. reprint ed. pap. 5.00 (0-938366-02-5) Orthodox Chr.

— The Political Philosophy of the Orthodox Church. Orthodox Christian Educational Society Staff, ed. Cummings, Denver, tr. Orig. Title: The Orthodox Definition of Political Science. 163p. (Orig.). (C). 1965. pap. 4.95 (0-938366-11-4) Orthodox Chr.

— Psychology: An Orthodox Christian Perspective. Orthodox Christian Educational Society Staff, ed. Cummings, Denver, tr. (Logos & Holy Spirit in the Unity of Christian Thought Ser.: Vol. 2). 151p. 1977. reprint ed. pap. 5.00 (0-938366-05-X) Orthodox Chr.

— A Revelation of Treasure Hid--Concerning Freedom, Concerning the Motherland, Concerning Justice, Apostolical Canons Respecting Baptism. Orthodox Christian Educational Society Staff, ed. Cummings, Denver, tr. 80p. (Orig.). 1952. pap. 2.95 (0-938366-23-8) Orthodox Chr.

— A Scriptural Refutation of the Pope's Primacy. Cummings, Denver, tr. 171p. (Orig.). 1952. reprint ed. pap. 4.95 (0-938366-40-8) Orthodox Chr.

— Theology: An Orthodox Standpoint. Orthodox Christian Educational Society Staff, ed. Cummings, Denver, tr. (Logos & Holy Spirit in the Unity of Christian Thought Ser.: Vol. 4). 216p. 1977. reprint ed. pap. 5.00 (0-938366-03-3) Orthodox Chr.

— Three Great Friday Sermons & Other Theological Discourses. Orthodox Christian Educational Society Staff, ed. Cummings, Denver, tr. 107p. (Orig.). 1952. pap. 5.95 (0-938366-48-3) Orthodox Chr.

— The Two Contrariant Schools, Concerning the Establishment of a Christian University. Orthodox Christian Educational Society Staff, ed. Cummings, Denver, tr. 87p. (Orig.). 1949. pap. 2.95 (0-938366-27-0) Orthodox Chr.

Makrakis, Apostolos, ed. see Agapius, et al.

Makrakis, Apostolos, jt. auth. see Stratman, Chrysostomos H.

Makram-Ebeid, S. & Tuck, B., eds. Semi-Insulating Three-Four Materials: Evian 1982. 420p. 1980. text ed. 62.95 (0-906812-22-4) Birkhauser.

Makridakis, Spyros. Forecasting, Planning, & Strategy for the 21st Century. 1990. text ed. 35.00 (0-02-919781-3) Free Pr.

Makridakis, Spyros & Wheelwright, Steven. Interactive Forcasting: Univariate & Multivariate Methods. 2nd ed. LC 76-27396. 1978. teacher ed 6.95 (0-8162-5426-5); text ed. 42.00 (0-8162-5416-8) Holden-Day.

Makridakis, Spyros & Wheelwright, Steven C. Forecasting Methods for Management. 5th ed. LC 88-26178. 470p. 1989. text ed. 80.00 (0-471-60063-6) Wiley.

Makridakis, Spyros & Wheelwright, Steven C., eds. Handbook of Forecasting: A Manager's Guide. 2nd ed. 638p. 1987. text ed. 139.95 (0-471-83903-5) Wiley.

Makridakis, Spyros, et al, eds. Forecasting: Methods & Application. 2nd ed. LC 82-23858. (Management Ser.). 923p. 1983. Net. text ed. write for info. (0-471-08610-X) Wiley.

Makrinenko, Leonid I. Acoustics of Auditoriums in Public Buildings. Bradley, J. S., ed. Rattner, R. S., tr. LC 94-16573. 1994. write for info. (1-56396-360-4) Am Inst Physics.

Makris, Barbara L. & Davis-Debeuneure, Linda. Parenting: A Curriculum for the Single Working Mother. 22p. 1983. pap. text ed. 15.00 (0-934966-10-9) Wider Oppor Women.

Makris, Barbara L., jt. auth. see Thomas, Melissa L.

Makris, Kallistos. The God-Inspired Orthodox Julian Calendar vs. the False Gregorian Papal Calendar. Vlesmas, Jerry, tr. 118p. (Orig.). 1971. reprint ed. pap. 4.95 (0-938366-36-X) Orthodox Chr.

Makris, Kathryn. Almost Sisters: The Sisters Scheme. 144p. (Orig.). (YA). 1991. pap. 2.99 (0-380-76035-5, Camelot) Avon.

— Almost Sisters: The Sisters Team. 176p. (Orig.). (J). (gr. 5 up). 1992. pap. 3.50 (0-380-76056-8, Camelot) Avon.

— Almost Sisters, No. 2: The Sisters War. 160p. (Orig.). (YA). 1991. pap. 3.50 (0-380-76055-X, Camelot) Avon.

— The Clean-up Crew. (Eco-Kids Ser.: No. 2). 160p. (Orig.). (J). (gr. 5 up). 1994. pap. 3.50 (0-380-77050-4, Camelot Young) Avon.

— Crosstown. 176p. (Orig.). (YA). 1993. pap. 3.50 (0-380-76226-9, Flare) Avon.

— A Different Way. 192p. (J). 1989. pap. 2.95 (0-380-75728-1, Flare) Avon.

— The Five Cat Club. (Eco-Kids Ser.: No. 1). 176p. (Orig.). (J). (gr. 5 up). 1994. pap. 3.50 (0-380-77049-0, Camelot Young) Avon.

— The Green Team. (Eco-Kids Ser.: No. 3). 160p. (Orig.). (J). (gr. 5 up). 1994. pap. 3.50 (0-380-77051-2, Camelot Young) Avon.

Maksic, Z. B., ed. The Concept of the Chemical Bond, Pt. 2. (Theoretical Models of Chemical Bonding Ser.). (Illus.). 664p. 1990. 301.00 (0-387-51553-4) Spr-Verlag.

— Molecular Spectroscopy, Electronic Structure & Intramolecular Interactions, Pt. 3. (Illus.). x, 638p. 1991. 244.00 (0-387-52252-2) Spr-Verlag.

— Theoretical Treatment of Large Molecules & Their Interactions, Pt. 4. (Illus.). x, 458p. 1991. 244.00 (0-387-52253-0) Spr-Verlag.

Maksimov, M. V. & Gorgonov, G. I. Electronic Homing Systems. Barton, William F., tr. (Radar Library). 300p. 1988. text ed. 49.00 (0-89006-278-1) Artech Hse.

Maksimov, Vladimir. A Man Survives. Hollo, Anselm, tr. LC 75-15657. 106p. 1975. reprint ed. text ed. 45.00 (0-8371-8217-4, MAMSU, Greenwood Pr) Greenwood.

Maksimova, E., jt. auth. see Andrews, E.

Maksimovic-Ambodik, N. M. Emvlevy i Simvoly Seventeen Eighty-Eight, the First Russian Emblem Book. Hippisley, Anthony, ed. LC 89-850. (Symbola et Emblemata Ser.: Vol. 1). 368p. 1989. reprint ed. text ed. 143.00 (90-04-08992-6) E J Brill.

Maksimovic, C. Urban Drainage Modelling--Urban Drainage Catchments. 1986. 150.00 (0-08-034333-3, Pergamon Pr) Elsevier.

Maksimovic, C. & Radojkovic, M., eds. Comparison of Urban Drainage Models with Real Catchment Data: Proceedings of the International Symposium, Dubrovnik, Yogoslavia, 9-11 April 1986. 1986. 228.00 (0-08-032558-0, Pub. by PPL UK) Franklin.

— Computational Modelling & Experimental Methods in Hydraulics - Hydrocomp '89: Proceedings of the International Conference on Interaction of Computational Methods & Measurements in Hydraulics & Hydrology, Dubrovnik, Yugoslavia, 13-16 June 1989. 526p. 1989. 113.50 (1-85166-374-6) Elsevier.

— Urban Drainage Catchments: Selected Worldwide Rainfall-Runoff Data. (Illus.). 382p. 1986. 162.00 (0-08-034086-5, Pub. by PPL UK) Franklin.

Maksimovic, Ljubomir. The Byzantine Provincal Administration under the Palaiologoi. viii, 308p. 1988. pap. 61.00 (90-256-0968-6, Pub. by A M Hakkert NE) Benjamins North Am.

Maksimowicz, Michelle. Focus on Authentic Learning & Assessment in the Middle School. Romano, Louis G., ed. 20p. 1993. pap. text ed. write for info. (0-318-72648-3) MI Middle Educ.

Maksoudian, Krikor. History of Armenia. LC 86-6688. (Center for Armenian Studies). 355p. 1987. 45.95 (0-89130-952-7, 00-19-03); pap. 35.95 (0-89130-953-5) Scholars Pr GA.

Maksoudian, Krikor, ed. see Draskhanakertetsi, Hovhannes.

Maksoudian, Krikor, ed. see Koriun.

Maksoudian, Krikor, tr. see Petrosian, Levon T.

Maksoudian, Krikor H., tr. see Ayvazian, Argam.

Maksy, Mostafa M., jt. auth. see Bernstein, Leopold A.

Maktari, A. M. Water Rights & Irrigation Practices in Lahj: A Study of the Application of Customary & Shri'ah Law in South-West Arabia. LC 76-145606. (Oriental Publications: No. 21). (Illus.). 1972. 59.95 (0-521-07930-6) Cambridge U Pr.

Makuck, Peter. Pilgrims. 1987. pap. 3.50 (0-935331-03-4) Ampersand RI.

— Sunken Lightship. (American Poets Continuum Ser.: No. 19). 1990. 18.00 (0-918526-74-4); pap. 10.00 (0-918526-75-2) BOA Edns.

— Where We Live. (New Poets of America Ser.). 80p. (C). 1982. 14.00 (0-918526-40-X); pap. 7.00 (0-918526-41-8) BOA Edns.

Makuck, Peter, ed. see England, Eugene.

Makuuchi, Masatoshi. Intraoperative Abdominal Ultrasonography. LC 87-21355. (Illus.). 220p. 1987. 110. 00 (0-89640-132-4) Igaku-Shoin.

Makuuchi, Masatoshi, jt. auth. see Kawasaki, Seiji.

***Makward, Christiane P. & Miller, Judith G., eds.** Plays by French & Francophone Women: A Critical Anthology. (Illus.). 320p. (C). 1994. pap. text ed. 17.95x (0-472-08258-2) U of Mich Pr.

— Plays by French & Francophone Women: A Critical Anthology. (Illus.). 320p. (C). 1994. text ed. 47.50x (0-472-10263-X) U of Mich Pr.

Maky, illus. Kung Fu Meditations & Chinese Proverbial Wisdom. LC 73-7731. 1973. pap. 5.00 (0-87407-200-X, FPI) Thor.

Mal, Ajit K. & Singh, Sarva J. Deformation of Elastic Solids. 352p. 1990. text ed. 81.00 (0-13-200700-2) P-H.

Malabre, Alfred L., Jr. Beyond Our Means: How Reckless Borrowing Now Threatens to Overwhelm Us. LC 87-45931. 192p. 1988. pap. 6.95 (0-394-75816-1, Vin) Random.

— Investing for Profit in the 80's. 1983. pap. 3.95 (0-8217-1301-9) Zebra.

— Lost Prophets: An Insider's History of the Modern Economist. 1993. text ed. 27.95 (0-07-103453-6) McGraw.

— Lost Prophets: Insider's View of the Modern Economists. LC 93-4616. 272p. 1993. 27.95 (0-87584-441-3) Harvard Busn.

— Understanding the New Economy. 200p. 1988. text ed. 30.00 (1-55623-117-2) Irwin Prof Pubng.

Malacara, D., ed. Selected Papers on Optical Shop Metrology. 720p. 1990. 114.00 (0-8194-0478-0, VOL. MS18/HC); pap. 99.00 (0-8194-0479-9, VOL. MS18) SPIE.

Malacara, Daniel. Optical Shop Testing. 2nd ed. (Series In Pure & Applied Optics: No. 1349). 792p. 1992. text ed. 115.00 (0-471-52232-5) Wiley.

Malacara, Daniel & Malacara, Zacarias. Handbook of Lens Design. LC 94-18940. (Optical Engineering Ser.: Vol. 44). 600p. 1994. 125.00 (0-8247-9225-4) Dekker.

Malacara, Daniel, jt. ed. see Hariharan, P.

Malacara, Zacarias, jt. auth. see Malacara, Daniel.

Malach, Mary J. Walking Minnesota. (Illus.). 368p. (Orig.). 1991. pap. 14.95 (0-89658-147-0) Voyageur Pr.

Malachosky, Tim & Greene, James. Mae West. deluxe limited ed. (Illus.). 350p. 1993. 85.00 (0-9637169-4-8) Empire Pub CA.

Malachow, et al. Noise & Diffusion in Bistable Nonequilibrium Systems. 168p. (C). 1985. 65.00 (0-685-46638-8, Pub. by Collets) St Mut.

Malachowski, Alan, ed. Reading Rorty: Critical Response to Philosophy & the Mirror of Nature. 288p. 1990. pap. 21. 95 (0-631-16149-X) Blackwell Pubs.

Malachowski, Cindy, jt. auth. see Quinn, Dawn.

Malacinski, George M. Cytoplasmic Organization Systems. (Primers in Developmental Biology Ser.). 448p. 1990. text ed. 65.00 (0-07-039749-X) McGraw.

Malacinski, George M., jt. ed. see Armstrong, John.

Malacinski, George M., et al. Molecular Genetics of Mammalian Cells. 1986. text ed. 58.50 (0-07-039755-4) McGraw.

Malaclypse. Pricipia Discordia. 2nd ed. (Illus.). 100p. (Orig.). 1980. pap. text ed. 6.95 (1-55950-040-9) Loompanics.

Malaclypse the Younger. Principia Discordia. (Illus.). 120p. 1991. reprint ed. pap. 9.95 (0-9626534-2-X) IllumiNet Pr.

Malaga, S., jt. ed. see Santos, F.

Malagalada, J. R., jt. ed. see Holtermuller, K. H.

Malagardis, N. E. & Williams, T. J., eds. Standards in Information Technology & Industrial Control: Contributions from IFIP Working Group 5.4 1988. 294p. 1988. 69.25 (0-444-70403-5, North Holland) Elsevier.

Malagon, Joseph. Cinderella Suicide. LC 83-62348. (Illus.). 70p. (Orig.). 1984. pap. 6.00 (0-318-00451-8) Metropol Press.

Malaise, Joseph, ed. see Groote, Gerard.

Malaisse, F. & Brooks, R. R. The Heavy Metal Tolerant Flora of Southcentral Africa: A Multidisciplinary Approach. 206p. (C). 1985. text ed. 105.00 (90-6191-543-0, Pub. by A A Balkema NE) Ashgate Pub Co.

Malaiya, Y. K. & Rajsuman, R. Bridging Faults & IDDQ Testing. LC 92-30950. 136p. 1992. pap. 35.00 (0-8186-3215-1, 3215) IEEE Comp Soc.

Malaiya, Y. K. & Srimani, P. K. Software Reliability Models: Developments, Evaluation & Applications. LC 90-56332. 136p. 1991. pap. 7.95 (0-8186-2110-9, 2110) IEEE Comp Soc.

Malaiyandi, M., jt. ed. see Suffet, I. H.

Malaka, Tan. From Jail to Jail, 3 vols. Jarvis, Helen, tr. LC 90-47586. (Monographs in International Studies, Southeast Asia Ser.: No. 83). 1209p. (Orig.). 1991. pap. text ed. 55.00 (0-89680-150-0) Ohio U Pr.

Malakhov, A. Mystery of the Earth's Mantle. (Illus.). 204p. 1975. 32.95 (0-8464-0664-0) Beekman Pubs.

Malakhov, N. Fedoskino. (Illus.). 168p. (C). 1984. text ed. 225.00 (0-685-40325-4, Pub. by Collets) St Mut.

Malakhov, S. G., jt. ed. see Makhon'ko, K. P.

Malakhov, V. V. Nematodes: Structure, Development, Classification, & Phylogeny. Bentz, George V., tr. LC 92-38962. (Illus.). 320p. (C). 1993. pap. text ed. 25.00 (1-56098-255-1) Smithsonian.

Malakoff, Edward & Malakoff, Sheila. Pairpoint Lamps. LC 90-63190. (Illus.). 160p. 1990. 95.00 (0-88740-281-X) Schiffer.

Malakoff, Laura Z. Housing Options for the Elderly: The Innovation Process in Community Settings. rev. ed. LC 91-30753. (Studies on Elderly in America). 152p. 1991. 44.00 (0-8153-0525-7) Garland.

Malakoff, Sheila, jt. auth. see Malakoff, Edward.

Malalasekera. Dictionary of Pali Proper Names, 2 vols. (PLI.). 1983. 250.00 (0-8288-1721-9, F 27380) Fr & Eur.

Malalasekera, George P. & Jayatilleke, K. N. Buddhism & the Race Question. LC 77-18853. (Race Question in Modern Thought). 73p. 1978. reprint ed. text ed. 49.50 (0-313-20208-7, MABU, Greenwood Pr) Greenwood.

Malalasekera, W., jt. auth. see Versteeg, H.

***Malam, John.** Goldilocks & the Three Bears. (Story Stickers Ser.). 16p. (J). (ps-2). 1995. pap. write for info. (1-56293-564-X) McClanahan Bk.

— In the Town. (Illus.). 16p. (J). (ps-2). 1995. pap. 1.95 (1-56293-816-9) McClanahan Bk.

— Indiana Jones Explores Egypt. (Illus.). 48p. (J). (gr. 3-7). 1992. 13.95 (1-55970-183-8) Arcade Pub Inc.

— Indiana Jones Explores the Incas. (Indiana Jones Explores Ser.). (Illus.). 48p. (J). (gr. 3-7). 1993. 14.95 (1-55970-199-4) Arcade Pub Inc.

— Jack & the Beanstalk. (Story Stickers Ser.). 16p. (J). (ps-2). 1995. pap. write for info. (1-56293-561-5) McClanahan Bk.

— Little Red Riding Hood. (Story Stickers Ser.). 16p. (J). (ps-2). 1995. pap. write for info. (1-56293-562-3) McClanahan Bk.

— On the Farm. (Illus.). 16p. (J). (ps-2). 1995. pap. write for info. (0-614-02527-3) McClanahan Bk.

— Three Little Pigs. (Story Stickers Ser.). 16p. (J). (ps-2). 1995. pap. write for info. (1-56293-563-1) McClanahan Bk.

Malamat, Abraham. Mari & the Early Israelite Experience. (Schweich Lectures on Biblical Archaeology, British Academy Ser.). 184p. 1992. reprint ed. pap. 21.95 (0-19-726117-5) OUP.

Malamed. Handbook of Local Anesthesia. 3rd ed. (Illus.). 320p. 1991. pap. 42.95 (0-8016-3076-2) Mosby Yr Bk.

— Sedation: A Guide to Patient Management. (Illus.). 624p. 1988. pap. text ed. 45.95 (0-8016-3210-2) Mosby Yr Bk.

Malamed, Stanley F. Medical Emergencies in the Dental Office. 4th rev. ed. LC 92-49542. 466p. 1993. pap. 41.95 (0-8016-6386-5) Mosby Yr Bk.

— Sedation: A Guide to Patient Management. 3rd ed. LC 94-32507. 1994. write for info. (0-8151-5736-3) Mosby Yr Bk.

Malami, Alhaji S. Sir Siddiq Abubakar the Third: Seventeenth Sultan of Sokoto. (Kenya People Ser.). (Illus.). 240p. 1991. 22.95 (0-237-51196-7, Pub. by Evans Bros Ltd UK) Trafalgar.

***Malami, Chris.** The Purple Palace. LC 95-5817. 1995. write for info. (1-883911-05-2) Brandylane.

Malamud. Ingres: Tools for Building an Information Architecture. 1989. text ed. 49.95 (0-442-31800-6) Van Nos Reinhold.

Malamud, Bernard. The Assistant. 304p. 1980. mass mkt. 4.95 (0-380-51474-5, Bard) Avon.

— The Assistant. 304p. 1993. pap. 10.00 (0-380-72085-X) Avon.

— Assistant. 1980. mass mkt. 4.95 (0-380-68338-5) Avon.

— Dubin's Lives. 400p. 1994. 10.95 (0-14-018760-X, Penguin Classics) Viking Penguin.

— The Fixer. 1989. pap. 3.95 (0-685-53965-2, WSP) PB.

— The Fixer. 304p. 1994. pap. 9.95 (0-14-018515-1, Penguin Classics) Viking Penguin.

— The Fixer, the Natural, the Assistant. 1994. 12.98 (1-56731-001-X, MJF Bks) Fine Comms.

An Asterisk (*) at the beginning of an entry indicates that the title is appearing in BIP for the first time.

— God's Grace. 223p. 1982. 13.50 (0-374-16465-7) FS&G.
— God's Grace. (Twentieth Century Classics Ser.). 1995. pap. 9.95 (0-14-018491-0, Penguin Bks) Viking Penguin.
— Idiots First. 212p. 1986. pap. 8.95 (0-374-52010-0) FS&G.
— Long Work, Short Life. (Chapbooks in Literature Ser.). (Illus.). 1985. 5.00 (0-9614940-1-8) Bennington Coll.
— The Natural. 217p. 1980. mass mkt. 4.99 (0-380-50609-2) Avon.
— The Natural. 224p. 1993. pap. 10.00 (0-380-72084-1) Avon.
— The Natural. LC 52-9853. 237p. 1984. pap. 10.00 (0-374-50200-5) FS&G.
— A New Life. 368p. 1988. pap. 8.95 (0-374-52103-4) FS&G.
— A New Life. 208p. 1995. 9.95 (0-14-018681-6, Penguin Classics) Viking Penguin.
— The People: And Other Uncollected Fiction. 1989. 18.95 (0-374-23067-6) FS&G.
— Rembrandt's Hat. 224p. 1973. 11.95 (0-374-24909-1) FS&G.
— The Stories of Bernard Malamud. LC 83-14100. 357p. 1983. 17.95 (0-374-27037-6) FS&G.
— The Stories of Bernard Malamud. 370p. 1984. pap. 8.95 (0-452-25911-8, Plume) NAL-Dutton.
— Stories of Bernard Malamud. 1984. pap. 12.95 (0-452-26354-9, Plume) NAL-Dutton.
— The Stories of Bernard Malamud. limited ed. LC 83-14100. 357p. 1983. 75.00 (0-374-27038-4) FS&G.
— The Tenants. 230p. 1988. pap. 8.95 (0-374-52102-6) FS&G.
— The Tenants. 176p. 1994. 9.95 (0-14-018516-X, Penguin Classics) Viking Penguin.

Malamud, C. Analyzing Novell Networks. 1992. pap. 39.95 (0-442-01302-7) Van Nos Reinhold.

Malamud, Carl. Analyzing Decnet-Osi Phase V. 1991. text ed. 44.95 (0-442-00375-7) Van Nos Reinhold.
— The Book of DEC Systems & Architectures. (Illus.). 256p. 1989. text ed. 50.00 (0-07-039822-4) McGraw.
— Exploring the Internet: A Technical Travelogue. LC 92-16450. 400p. 1992. 26.95 (0-13-296898-3) P-H.
— Stacks: Interoperability in Today's Computer Networks. 320p. 1991. text ed. 48.00 (0-13-484080-1) P-H.

Malamud, Daniel & Tabak, Lawrence, eds. Saliva As a Diagnostic Fluid. LC 93-9077. (Annals Ser.: Vol. 694). 348p. 1993. write for info. (0-89766-787-5); pap. 95.00 (0-89766-788-3) NY Acad Sci.

Malamud-Goti, Jaime. Smoke & Mirrors: The Paradox of the Drug Wars. 117p. 1992. text ed. 27.50 (0-8133-1360-0) Westview.

Malamud, Martha A. A Poetics of Transformation: Prudentius & Classical Mythology. LC 88-43290. (Cornell Studies in Classical Philology). 224p. 1989. 29.95 (0-8014-2249-3) Cornell U Pr.

Malamud, Nathan & Hirano, Asao. Atlas of Neuropathology. 2nd rev. ed. (Illus.). 1974. 120.00 (0-520-02221-1) U CA Pr.

Malamud, Randy. The Language of Modernism. Litz, A. Walton, ed. LC 89-20134. (Studies in Modern Literature: No. 108). 208p. reprint ed. 59.30 (0-8357-2030-6, 2070738) Bks Demand.
— T. S. Eliot's Drama: A Research & Production Sourcebook. LC 91-46960. (Modern Dramatists Research & Production Sourcebooks Ser.: No. 2). 328p. 1992. text ed. 49.95 (0-313-27813-X, MTK, Greenwood Pr) Greenwood.
— Where the Words Are Valid: T.S. Eliot's Communities of Drama. LC 94-22018. (Contributions in Drama & Theatre Studies: Vol. 58). 224p. 1994. text ed. 49.95 (0-313-27818-0, Greenwood Pr) Greenwood.

Malamud Rikles, Carlos D., et al. Historia de Espana: 31. La Epoca de la Ilustracion, Vol. II: Las Indias y la Politica Exterior. 904p. 1992. 189.50x (84-239-4979-6) Elliots Bks.

Malamuth, Charles, tr. see Tarasov-Rodionov, Aleksandr I.

Malamuth, Neil, jt. ed. see Buss, David M.

Malamuth, Neil, jt. auth. see Linz, Daniel.

Malamuth, Neil M. & Donnerstein, Edward. Pornography & Sexual Aggression. 1984. text ed. 69.00 (0-12-466280-3) Acad Pr.
— Pornography & Sexual Aggression. 1986. pap. text ed. 47.00 (0-12-466281-1) Acad Pr.

***Malan.** Individual Psychotherapy. 2nd ed. 288p. 1995. write for info. (0-7506-2387-X, Focal) Buttrwrth-Heinemann.

***Malan, Cesar.** The Cross - Where All Roads Meet. 1994. pap. 6.99 (0-85234-316-7, Pub. by Evangel Pr UK) Presby & Reformed.

Malan, D. H. The Frontier of Brief Psychotherapy: An Example of the Convergence of Research & Clinical Practice. LC 76-9646. (Topics in General Psychiatry Ser.). (Illus.). 388p. 1976. 42.50 (0-306-30895-9, Plenum Pr) Plenum.
— A Study of Brief Psychotherapy. LC 75-30916. 326p. 1976. pap. 24.50 (0-306-20019-8, Plenum Pr) Plenum.
— Toward the Validation of Dynamic Psychotherapy: A Replication. LC 76-10182. 308p. 1976. 59.50 (0-306-30896-7, Plenum Pr) Plenum.

Malan, Dan. The Complete Guide to Classics Illustrated. (U. S. Ser.: Vol. 1). (Illus.). 112p. 1994. reprint ed. 34.95 (0-9631135-6-9); reprint ed. pap. 24.95 (0-9631135-0-X) Malan Class.
— The Complete Guide to Classics Illustrated. (Foreign Ser.: Vol. 2). (Illus.). 116p. 1994. reprint ed. 34.95 (0-9631135-7-7); reprint ed. pap. 24.95 (0-9631135-1-8) Malan Class.
— Gustave Dore: Adrift on Dreams of Splendor. (Illus.). 352p. (C). 1995. 39.95 (0-9631135-8-5) Malan Class.

Malan, David H. Individual Psychotherapy & the Science of Psychodynamics. LC 78-40691. (Postgraduate Psychiatic Ser.). 1979. 34.95 (0-7506-0755-6) Buttrwrth-Heinemann.
— Psychodynamics: Training & Outcome in Brief Psychotherapy. (Illus.). 336p. 1992. 65.00 (0-7506-1545-1) Buttrwrth-Heinemann.

***Malan, F. R.** Bills of Exchange, Cheques & Promissory Notes in South African Law. 441p. 1983. pap. 100.00 (0-409-04074-6, SA) Butterworth Legal Pubs.
— Butterworths Selection of Statutes: Persons & Family Law. 192p. 1990. pap. 41.00 (0-409-01504-0, SA) Butterworth Legal Pubs.
— Provisional Sentence on Bills of Exchange, Cheques & Promissory Notes. 269p. 1986. pap. 92.00 (0-409-04086-X, SA) Butterworth Legal Pubs.

Malan, F. R. & Oelofse, A. N. South African Banking Legislation. 400p. 1991. ring bd. write for info. (0-7021-2572-5, Pub. by Juta SA) W W Gaunt.

Malan, Rian. My Traitor's Heart. LC 90-50145. (Vintage International Ser.). 432p. 1991. pap. 12.00 (0-679-73215-2, Vin) Random.

Malan, S. C., tr. see Saint Ephraem Syrus.

Malana, D., ed. Critical Technologies & Economic Competitiveness. 227p. (C). 1994. lib. bdg. 69.00 (1-56072-091-3) Nova Sci Pubs.

***Maland, Charles.** Frank Capra. (Twayne's Filmmaker Ser.). 1995. pap. 14.95 (0-8057-4501-7, Twayne) Macmillan.

Maland, Charles J. American Visions, the Films of Chaplin, Ford, Capra & Welles, 1936-1941. 1977. 36.95 (0-405-09892-8, 11487) Ayer.
— Chaplin & American Culture: The Evolution of a Star Image. (Illus.). 464p. 1991. text ed. 55.00 (0-691-09440-3); pap. text ed. 17.95 (0-691-02860-5) Princeton U Pr.

Malandain & Verdol. Methode Orange, Bk 1. (Methode Orange Ser.). (Illus.). (gr. 7-12). 1979. text ed. 6.25 (0-88345-407-6) Prentice ESL.

Malandra, Geri H. Unfolding a Mandala: The Buddhist Cave Temples at Ellora. LC 92-8142. (SUNY Series in Buddhist Studies). (Illus.). 348p. (C). 1993. 89.50 (0-7914-1355-1); pap. 29.95 (0-7914-1356-X) State U NY Pr.

Malandro, Loretta A., jt. auth. see Smith, Lawrence J.

Malandro, Loretta A., et al. Nonverbal Communication. 2nd ed. 352p. (C). 1989. pap. text ed. write for info. (0-07-555059-8) McGraw.

Malanga, Gerard. Chic Death. 131p. 1971. 6.50 (0-913219-14-2) Pym-Rand Pr.
— Chic Death. deluxe ed. 131p. 1971. 12.50 (0-913219-16-9) Pym-Rand Pr.
— Equal Time. deluxe ed. 1979. 7.50 (0-317-42210-3) Bellevue Pr.
— Mythologies of the Heart. 180p. (C). 1995. 25.00 (0-87685-994-5); pap. 13.50 (0-87685-993-7) Black Sparrow.
— Mythologies of the Heart. deluxe ed. 180p. (C). 1995. 35.00 (0-87685-995-3) Black Sparrow.
— Rosebud. deluxe ed. (Illus.). 40p. 1975. 25.00 (0-915778-15-7) Penmaen Pr.
— Three Diamonds. LC 91-23551. (Illus.). 220p. (Orig.). 1991. 20.00 (0-87685-838-8); pap. 12.50 (0-87685-837-X) Black Sparrow.
— Three Diamonds. deluxe ed. LC 91-23551. (Illus.). 220p. (Orig.). 1991. 30.00 (0-87685-839-6) Black Sparrow.

Malani, I., jt. auth. see Phadnis, U.

Malanotte-Rizzoli, Paola & Robinson, Allan R., eds. Ocean Processes in Climate Dynamics: Global & Mediterranean Examples: Proceedings of the NATO Advanced Study Institute, Erice, Italy, January 20-February 2, 1993. LC 93-38824. (NATO Advanced Study Institutes Series C, Mathematical & Physical Sciences). 460p. (C). 1993. lib. bdg. 176.00 (0-7923-2624-5) Kluwer Ac.

Malanowski, Jamie. Mr. Stupid Goes to Washington: A Political Satire. LC 92-15474. 224p. 1992. 16.95 (1-55972-132-4, Birch Ln Pr) Carol Pub Group.

Malanowski, K. Stability of Solutions to Convex Problems of Optimization. (Lecture Notes in Control & Information Sciences Ser.: Vol. 93). ix, 137p. 1987. pap. 29.00 (0-387-17589-X) Spr-Verlag.

Malanowski, K. & Mizukami, K., eds. Analysis & Algorithms of Optimization Problems. (Lecture Notes in Control & Information Sciences Ser.: Vol. 82). viii, 240p. 1986. pap. 32.00 (0-387-16660-2) Spr-Verlag.

Malanowski, Stanislaw & Anderko, Andrzej. Modelling Phase Equilibria: Thermodynamic Background & Practical Tools. (Series in Chemical Engineering: No. 1793). 328p. 1992. text ed. 79.95 (0-471-57103-2) Wiley.

Malanowski, Stanislaw & Stephenson, R. Handbooks of Thermodynamics of Organic Compounds for Chemical Engineers. 550p. 1987. 79.00 (0-444-01240-0) Elsevier.

Malanson, G. P., ed. Natural Areas Facing Climate Change. (Illus.). viii, 92p. 1989. pap. 30.00 (90-5103-030-4, Pub. by SPB Acad Pub NE) Koeltz Sci Bks.

Malanson, George P. Riparian Landscapes. LC 92-30617. (Studies in Ecology). (Illus.). 296p. (C). 1993. 59.95 (0-521-38431-1) Cambridge U Pr.

Malantschuk, Gregor. Kierkegaard's Thought. Hong, Howard V. & Hong, Edna H., eds. Hong, Edna H., tr. LC 77-155000. 398p. reprint ed. pap. 113.50 (0-8357-3236-3, 2057130) Bks Demand.

Malaparte, Curzio. Kaputt. Foligno, Cesare, tr. LC 82-61436. 407p. 1982. reprint ed. pap. 12.95 (0-910395-01-2) Marlboro Pr.
— La Peau. (FRE.). 1982. pap. 13.95 (0-7859-4021-9) Fr & Eur.

Malaret, Augusto. Diccionario de Americanismos. 1977. lib. bdg. 250.00 (0-8490-1717-3) Gordon Pr.

Malaria Research Symposium Staff. Malaria Research: Proceedings of the Symposium, Rabat, Morocco, April 1-5, 1974. (WHO Bulletin Reprint Ser.: Vol. 50, No. 3-4). 1974. pap. 7.20 (0-686-16793-7) World Health.

***Malarkey, John.** The Global Adventurer's Handbook: How to Plan, Pay For, & Enjoy Your Extended Vacation. 1995. pap. 9.95 (1-881199-40-1, Perpetual Pr) Progress Media.

Malarkey, John J., III, ed. Term Papers & Reports: The Wilmington College Style Guide. 120p. (Orig.). (C). 1993. pap. text ed. 4.95 (0-9636944-0-5) Wilmington Coll.

Malaro, Marie C. A Legal Primer on Managing Museum Collections. LC 84-23497. 366p. 1985. pap. 19.95 (0-87474-697-3, MALPP) Smithsonian.
— Museum Governance: Mission, Ethics, Policy. 208p. (Orig.). 1994. pap. 16.95 (1-56098-363-9) Smithsonian.

Malas, J. C., jt. ed. see Gunasekera, J. S.

Malasanos, et al. Health Assessment. 4th ed. (Illus.). 848p. 1989. 49.95 (0-8016-3226-9) Mosby Yr Bk.

Malasekera, G. P. Dictionary of Pali Proper Names, 2 vols. (C). 1938. 72.50 (0-86013-269-2, Pub. by Pali Text) Wisdom MA.

Malashenko, Alexei. The Last Red August: A Russian Mystery. Olcott, Anthony, tr. LC 92-35181. 250p. (RUS.). 1993. text ed. 21.00 (0-684-19571-2, Scribners) S&S Trade.

Malashenko, Alexei, jt. auth. see Polonskaya, Ludmila.

Malaspina, Mark, et al. What Works Report No. 1: Air Pollution Solutions. (What Works Ser.). (Illus.). 113p. (Orig.). (C). 1992. pap. text ed. 17.00 (0-9638613-0-1) Environ Exchange.

Malatesha, Rattihalli N. Neuropsychology & Cognition. 1987. lib. bdg. 299.00 (90-247-2752-9) Kluwer Ac.

Malatesha, Rattihalli N. & Aaron, P. G., eds. Reading Disorders: Varieties & Treatment. LC 82-4039. (Perspectives in Neurolinguistics, Neuropsychology & Psycholinguistics Ser.). 1982. text ed. 72.00 (0-12-466320-6) Acad Pr.

Malatesha, Rattihalli N. & Whitaker, Harry A., eds. Dyslexia: A Global Issue. (NATO Advanced Study Institutes Series D: Behavioural & Social Sciences). 1983. lib. bdg. 202.00 (90-247-2909-2) Kluwer Ac.

Malatesta, Carol Z., et al. The Development of Emotion Expression during the First Two Years of Life. (Child Development Monographs: No. 219 54: 1-2). 178p. 1989. pap. text ed. 14.50 (0-226-50285-6) U Ch Pr.

Malatesta, Carol Z. & Izard, Carroll E., eds. Emotion in Adult Development. LC 84-1937. (Illus.). 343p. reprint ed. pap. 97.80 (0-8357-8494-0, 2034769) Bks Demand.

Malatesta, Edward J., ed. see Ricci, Matteo.

Malatesta, Errico. Fra Contadini: A Dialogue on Anarchy. Weir, Jean, tr. (Anarchist Pamphlets Ser.: No. 6). 43p. (Orig.). 1981. pap. 3.00 (0-317-67947-3) Left Bank.
— Malatesta: Life & Ideas. Richards, Vernon, ed. 309p. 1965. pap. 11.00 (0-900384-15-8) Left Bank.

Malatesta, Linda & Kostere, Kim. Maps, Models, & the Structure of Reality. Stephens, Lori, ed. 144p. 1992. pap. 11.95 (1-55552-007-3) Metamorphous Pr.

***Malatesta, Maria, ed.** Society & the Professions in Italy, 1860-1914. (Studies in Italian History & Culture). 275p. (C). 1995. write for info. (0-521-46536-2) Cambridge U Pr.

***Malatich, John M. & Tucker, Wayne C.** Tricks of the Trade for Divers. LC 85-47839. (Illus.). (Orig.). reprint ed. pap. 72.70 (0-7837-9072-4, 2049821) Bks Demand.

Malatinsky, Joseph P. Slovak: Hippocrene Handy Dictionary. (ENG & SLO.). 1994. pap. 8.95 (0-7818-0101-X) Hippocrene Bks.

Malave, Lilliam & Duquette, George, eds. Language, Culture, & Cognition: A Collection of Studies in First & Second Language Acquisition. (Multilingual Matters Ser.: No. 69). 300p. 1991. 99.00 (1-85359-103-3, Pub. by Multilingual Matters UK); pap. 39.95 (1-85359-102-5, Pub. by Multilingual Matters UK) Taylor & Francis.

Malawar, Martin, jt. auth. see Sugarbaker, Paul.

Malawer, Stewart. Federal Regulation of International Business, Vol. 4. LC 80-69834. 1982. text ed. write for info. (0-89834-046-2) Natl Chamber Foun.

Malay, Paula C., tr. see Alvarez, Santiago V.

***Malayan Law Journal Staff, ed.** Mallal's Digest 1993. 1994. write for info. (0-409-99694-7) Butterworth Legal Pubs.

M'albahad, Migl. The Lopez Murders. 103p. (Orig.). 1991. pap. 11.81 (0-685-48263-4) Dayspring Pr.

Malbin, Michael, jt. auth. see Benjamin, Gerald.

Malbin, Michael J., ed. Money & Politics in the United States: Financing Elections in the 1980s. LC 84-2900. 336p. reprint ed. pap. 95.80 (0-8357-4828-6, 2037765) Bks Demand.

Malbois, R. & Sweet, D., eds. Healthy Schools: Proceedings of the 1st European Conference on Health Promotion & the Prevention of Cancer in School, No. EUR 13017. 302p. 1990. pap. 35.00 (92-826-1884-6, CD-NA-13017-EN-C) UNIPUB.

Malbon, Elizabeth S. Iconography of the Sarcophagus of Junius Bassus: Neofitus Iit Ad Deum. (Illus.). 254p. 1990. text ed. 52.50 (0-691-07355-4) Princeton U Pr.
— Narrative Space & Mythic Meaning in Mark. (Biblical Seminar Ser.). (Illus.). 212p. (Orig.). (C). 1991. 15.00 (1-85075-711-9, Pub. by Sheffield Acad UK) CUP Services.

Malbon, Elizabeth S., jt. ed. see Berlin, Adele.

Malbon, Elizabeth S., jt. auth. see McKnight, Edgar V.

Malbrough, Ray T. Charms, Spells & Formulas for the Making & Use of Gris-Gris Bags, Herb Candles, Doll Magick, Incenses, Oils & Powders...to Gain Love, Protection, Prosperity, Luck & Prophetic Dreams. LC 85-45286. (Practical Magick Ser.). (Illus.). 192p. (Orig.). 1986. pap. 6.95 (0-87542-501-1) Llewellyn Pubns.

Malburg, Chris. How to Fire Your Boss. 1991. pap. 4.50 (0-425-12734-6) Berkley Pub.

Malburg, Chris, jt. auth. see Tylczak, Lynn.

Malburg, Christopher R. Accounting for the New Business: How to Do Your Own Accounting Simply, Easily & Accurately. LC 94-8710. (Business Advisors Ser.). 1994. 29.95 (1-55850-350-1); pap. 10.95 (1-55850-349-8) Adams Pubng.
— All in One Business Planning Guide: How to Create Cohesive Plans for Marketing, Sales, Operations, Finance & Cash Flow. LC 94-8709. (Business Advisors Ser.). 1994. 29.95 (1-55850-348-X); pap. 10.95 (1-55850-347-1) Adams Pubng.
— Business Plans to Manage Day to Day Operations: Real-Life Results for Small Business Owners & Operators. LC 92-34809. 288p. 1993. disk 85.00 (0-471-57296-9); pap. 39.95 (0-471-57299-3) Wiley.
— Cash Management Handbook. 1992. disk 89.95 (0-13-116989-0, Busn) P-H.
— Controller's & Treasurer's Desk Reference. 1994. text ed. 69.95 (0-07-911604-3) McGraw.
— How to Write a Knock-Em-Dead Book Proposal: Structuring, Packaging & Presenting Book Ideas That Sell. 200p. (Orig.). 1994. pap. 29.95 (0-9640035-0-3) Writers Res Grp.

Malburg, Christopher R. & Cohen, Marilyn M. The Professional Investor's Tax Guide. LC 92-24043. 1992. write for info. (0-13-726977-3) P-H.

Mal'Cev, A. A., jt. ed. see Fadeev, L. D.

Mal'cev, A. I. Algebraic Systems. Seckler, B. D. & Doohovskoy, A. P., trs. (Grundlehren der Mathematischen Wissenschaften Ser.: Vol. 192). 320p. 1973. 79.00 (0-387-05792-7) Spr-Verlag.

Malchaire, Jacques. Heat Stress Evaluation, Version 2.0. 1993. 120.00 (0-87371-847-X, TK) Lewis Pubs.

Malchiodi, Cathy. Breaking the Silence: Art Therapy with Children from Violent Homes. LC 90-1466. (Illus.). 230p. 1990. 29.95 (0-87630-578-8) Brunner-Mazel.

Malchiodi, Cathy, ed. Art Therapy, Vol. 10, No. 1: Journal of the American Art Therapy Association. (Illus.). 64p. (Orig.). (C). 1993. 16.00 (1-882147-17-0) Am Art Therapy.

Malchiodi, Cathy A., ed. Art Therapy. (Journal of the American Art Therapy Association Ser.: Vol. 10, No. 4). (Illus.). (C). Date not set. pap. 18.00 (1-882147-45-6) Am Art Therapy.
— Art Therapy. (Journal of the American Art Therapy Association Ser.: Vol. 9, No. 1). (Illus.). 60p. (C). 1992. 16.00 (1-882147-00-6) Am Art Therapy.
— Art Therapy. (Journal of the American Art Therapy Association Ser.: Vol. 9, No. 2). 51p. (C). 1992. 16.00 (1-882147-01-4) Am Art Therapy.
— Art Therapy. (Journal of the American Art Therapy Association Ser.: Vol. 9, No. 3). (Illus.). 52p. (C). 1992. 16.00 (1-882147-02-2) Am Art Therapy.
— Art Therapy. (Journal of the American Art Therapy Association Ser.: Vol. 10, No. 3). 66p. (C). 1993. pap. 18.00 (1-882147-19-7) Am Art Therapy.
— Art Therapy: Journal of the American Art Therapy Association, Vol. 10, No. 2. (Illus.). 55p. (Orig.). (C). 1993. 16.00 (1-882147-18-9) Am Art Therapy.
— Art Therapy, Vol. 9, No. 4: Journal of the American Art Therapy Association. (Illus.). 56p. (Orig.). (C). 1992. pap. 18.00 (1-882147-15-4) Am Art Therapy.

Malchiodi, Cathy A., jt. auth. see Riley, Shirley.

Malchow, H. L. Gentlemen Capitalists: The Social & Political World of the Victorian Businessman. LC 89-64241. (Illus.). 450p. 1991. 49.50 (0-8047-1807-5) Stanford U Pr.

Malchow, Howard L. Population Pressures: Emigration & Government in Late Nineteenth-Century Britain. LC 79-64166. (Illus.). 323p. 1979. 18.00 (0-930664-02-7) SPOSS.

Malcles. Les Sources du Travail Bibliographique, 3 tomes. Incl. Tome I. Bibliographies Generales. 22.50 (0-685-35977-8); Set. Bibliographies Specialisees; Sciences Humaines, 2 pts. 46.50 (0-685-35976-X); Tome III. Bibligraphies Specialisees; Sciences Exactes et Techniques. 22.50 (0-685-35979-4); write for info. (0-318-52266-7) Fr & Eur.

***Malcolm.** Honky-Tonk Addict. 200p. Date not set. 8.95 (1-56901-857-X) NW Pub.
— Jean Rhys. 1995. text ed. 24.95 (0-8057-0855-3) Macmillan.
— Scared to Death. 1995. pap. (0-590-55217-1) Scholastic Inc.
— Tolley's Health & Safety at Work Handbook 1995. 900p. (C). 1994. 175.00 (0-85459-945-2, Pub. by Tolley Pubng UK) St Mut.

Malcolm, A. Treatise of Musick, Speculative, Practical & Historical. LC 69-16676. (Music Ser.). 1970. reprint ed. lib. bdg. 75.00 (0-306-71099-4) Da Capo.

Malcolm, Alan D., ed. Molecular Medicine, Vol. 1. 216p. 1985. pap. 34.00 (0-904147-93-2, IRL Pr) OUP.
— Molecular Medicine, Vol. 2. 132p. 1987. pap. 45.00 (0-947946-58-6, IRL Pr) OUP.

Malcolm, Alan D., ed. see GP-Info Symposium Staff.

Malcolm, Aleen. Devlyn Tremayne. 1990. 20.00 (0-7278-4030-4) Severn Hse.
— Kenlaren. 1991. 18.95 (0-7278-4100-9) Severn Hse.

Malcolm, Alix. Falcon's Lure. large type ed. 1991. 21.95 (0-7089-2371-2) Ulverscroft.

Malcolm, Andrew. The Tyranny of the Group. (Quality Paperback Ser.: No. 294). 190p. (Orig.). 1975. reprint ed. pap. 8.00 (0-8226-0294-6) Littlefield.

Malcolm, Andrew H. The Canadians. (Illus.). 416p. 1991. pap. 13.95 (0-312-06921-9) St Martin.
— Final Harvest. 1987. pap. 4.50 (0-451-14852-5, Sig) NAL-Dutton.

M

An Asterisk (*) at the beginning of an entry indicates that the title is appearing in BIP for the first time.

— The Land & People of Canada. LC 90-47560. (Portraits of the Nations Ser.). (Illus.). 240p. (J). (gr. 6 up). 1991. 19.00 (*0-06-022494-0*); lib. bdg. 18.89 (*0-06-022495-9*) HarpC Child Bks.

Malcolm, Andrew H. & Straus, Roger, III. U. S. One: America's Original Main Street. LC 92-43706. 1993. pap. 14.95 (*0-312-09024-2*) St Martin.

Malcolm, Anthea. Counterfeit Heart. 400p. 1991. pap. 3.95 (*0-8217-3425-3*) Zebra.

— Courting of Philippa. 1989. pap. 3.95 (*0-8217-2714-1*) Zebra.

— Frivolous Pretence. 1990. pap. 3.95 (*0-8217-2902-0*) Zebra.

— An Improper Proposal. 400p. 1992. mass mkt. 4.50 (*0-8217-3858-5*) Zebra.

— A Sensible Match. 384p. 1993. mass mkt. 3.99 (*0-8217-4169-1*) Zebra.

— Touch of Scandal. 1991. mass mkt. 4.50 (*0-8217-3603-5*) Zebra.

— Widow's Gambit. 352p. 1993. mass mkt. 3.99 (*0-8217-4075-X*) Zebra.

Malcolm, Clark & Houseman, William, eds. Everybody's Business: A Fund of Retrievable Ideas for Humanizing Life in the Office. LC 85-5872. (Illus.). 112p. 1985. text ed. 30.00 (*0-936658-19-3*) H Miller Res.

Malcolm, Clark, ed. see Grant, Christin N. & Meima, Karla L.

Malcolm, Davis W., tr. see Vernadskii, Georgii.

Malcolm, Dorothea C. Design: Elements & Principles. LC 71-148087. (Illus.). 128p. (J). (gr. 5-12). 1972. 15.95 (*0-87192-039-5*) Davis Mass.

Malcolm, Douglas R., Jr. How to Build Electronic Projects. Goldberg, Joel, ed. LC 79-17829. (Electro-Skills Ser.). (Illus.). 1980. pap. text ed. 11.10 (*0-07-039760-0*) McGraw.

Malcolm, Elizabeth. Ireland Sober, Ireland Free: Drink & Temperance in Nineteenth-Century Ireland. (Irish Studies). 370p. 1986. text ed. 39.95x (*0-8156-2366-6*) Syracuse U Pr.

Malcolm, George A. The Commonwealth of the Philippines. Philippines Commonwealth Constitution 1972 Staff, ed. 1977. 40.95 (*0-8369-6982-0*, 7860) Ayer.

— First Malayan Republic: Story of the Philippines. LC 75-161776. reprint ed. 41.50 (*0-404-09032-X*) AMS Pr.

Malcolm, H. Historical Documents Relating to the Bahama Islands. 1976. lib. bdg. 59.95 (*0-8490-1958-3*) Gordon Pr.

Malcolm, Ian Z. Pursuits of Leisure & Other Essays. LC 68-20317. (Essay Index Reprint Ser.). 1977. reprint ed. 17.95 (*0-8369-0671-3*) Ayer.

— Vacant Thrones: A Volume of Political Portraits. LC 67-28760. (Essay Index Reprint Ser.). 1977. 20.95 (*0-8369-0672-1*) Ayer.

Malcolm, J. Cooper. The Tau: Its Origin & Symbolic Use in Royal Arch Masonry. 1990. pap. 5.95 (*1-55818-173-3*, Sure Fire) Holmes Pub.

Malcolm, J. L. Caesar's Due: Loyalty & King Charles, 1642-1646. (Royal Historical Society Ser.: No. 38). 256p. 1983. 63.00 (*0-901050-90-3*) Boydell & Brewer.

Malcolm, Jahnna N. Freak Show. (J). (gr. 4-7). 1993. pap. 3.25 (*0-590-45853-1*) Scholastic Inc.

— Scared Stiff. 128p. (J). 1991. pap. 2.75 (*0-590-44996-6*, Apple Paperbacks) Scholastic Inc.

— Scared to Death. 144p. (J). 1992. pap. 2.95 (*0-590-44995-8*, Apple Paperbacks) Scholastic Inc.

Malcolm, James A. Origins of the Balfour Declaration. 1983. pap. 3.00 (*0-939484-13-7*) Inst Hist Rev.

Malcolm, Jan. Fortunes. Orig. Title: Roulette. 304p. 1989. reprint ed. pap. 3.95 (*0-380-75492-4*) Avon.

Malcolm, Janet. Collected Essays. 1992. write for info. (*0-679-74046-5*) McKay.

— In the Freud Archives. 1985. pap. 9.00 (*0-394-72922-6*, Vin) Random.

— Journalist & the Murderer. LC 90-50156. 192p. 1990. pap. 10.95 (*0-679-73183-0*, Vin) Random.

— Psychoanalysis: The Impossible Profession. LC 82-40036. 192p. 1982. pap. 10.00 (*0-394-71034-7*, Vin) Random.

— Psychoanalysis: The Impossible Profession. LC 94-72518. 184p. 1994. 20.00 (*1-56821-342-5*) Aronson.

— The Purloined Clinic. LC 92-4498. 1992. 22.50 (*0-679-41232-8*) Knopf.

— The Purloined Clinic: Selected Writings. LC 93-7859. 1993. reprint ed. write for info. (*0-679-74810-5*, Vin) Random.

— The Silent Woman: Sylvia Plath & Ted Hughes. LC 93-33848. 1994. 23.00 (*0-685-70236-7*) Knopf.

— Silent Woman: Sylvia Plath & Ted Hughes. 1994. 23.00 (*0-679-43158-6*) Knopf.

— Silent Woman: Sylvia Plath & Ted Hughes. 1995. pap. 12.00 (*0-679-75140-8*, Vin) Random.

Malcolm, Jean. Table de la Bibliographie de Voltaire par Bengesco: Geneva, 1953, Vol. 1. 1974. 30.00 (*0-8115-0898-6*) Periodicals Srv.

Malcolm, John. A Deceptive Appearance. (Tim Simpson Mystery Ser.). 224p. 1992. text ed. 20.00 (*0-684-19508-9*, Scribners) S&S Trade.

— A Deceptive Appearance. large type ed. LC 93-9001. (Nightingale Ser.). 1993. pap. 14.95 (*0-8161-5780-4*) Hall.

— Plato on the Self-Predication of Forms: Early & Middle Dialogues. 240p. 1991. 59.00 (*0-19-823906-8*) OUP.

— Sheep, Goats & Soap. large type ed. 275p. 1992. pap. 14.95 (*0-8161-5475-9*, Nightingale) Hall.

— Sheep, Goats & Soap: A Tim Simpson Mystery. 224p. 1992. text ed. 19.95 (*0-684-19384-1*, Scribners) S&S Trade.

Malcolm, Joyce L. To Keep & Bear Arms: The Origins of an Anglo-American Right. LC 93-26710. 246p. 1994. 32.50 (*0-674-89306-9*) HUP.

Malcolm, Kari T. We Signed Away Our Lives: How One Family Gave Everything for the Gospel. LC 90-38692. 184p. (Orig.). 1990. pap. 8.99 (*0-8308-1718-2*, 1718) InterVarsity.

— Women at the Crossroads: A Path Beyond Feminism & Traditionalism. LC 82-7228. 215p. (Orig.). 1982. pap. 11.99 (*0-87784-379-1*, 379) InterVarsity.

Malcolm, L. Diccionario Tecnico Frances-Espanol: French - Spanish Technical Dictionary. 544p. (FRE & SPA.). 1973. 39.95 (*0-8288-6242-7*, S-31563) Fr & Eur.

Malcolm, L. R., jt. auth. see Makeham, J. P.

Malcolm, Neil. Soviet Policy Perspectives on Western Europe. LC 89-9846. (Chatham House Papers). 128p. (Orig.). 1989. pap. 14.95 (*0-87609-066-8*) Coun Foreign.

— Soviet Political Scientists & American Politics. LC 83-16122. 256p. 1984. text ed. 39.95 (*0-312-74855-8*) St Martin.

Malcolm, Neil, ed. Russia & Europe: An End to Confrontation? LC 93-27883. 1994. 49.00 (*1-85567-161-1*, Pub. by Pinter Pubs UK) St Martin.

Malcolm, Noel. Bosnia: A Short History. (Illus.). 340p. 1994. 26.95 (*0-8147-5520-8*) NYU Pr.

Malcolm, Noel, ed. see Hobbes, Thomas.

Malcolm, Norman. Wittgenstein: A Religious Point of View? Winch, Peter, ed. LC 93-25808. 152p. 1994. 32.50 (*0-8014-2978-1*) Cornell U Pr.

— Wittgenstein: A Religious Point of View? Winch, Peter, ed. 152p. 1995. pap. 10.95x (*0-8014-8266-6*) Cornell U Pr.

— Wittgensteinian Themes: Essays 1978-1989. Von Wright, Georg H., ed. 256p. 1995. 34.50x (*0-8014-3042-9*) Cornell U Pr.

Malcolm, Paula. Cost Containment Learning Module, No. 7. (Orig.). 1985. pap. text ed. 47.50 (*0-931369-09-6*) Southern IL Univ Sch.

Malcolm, Peter. Libya. LC 92-38756. (Cultures of the World Ser.). (J). 1993. 21.95 (*1-85435-573-2*) Marshall Cavendish.

— Libya, Set. LC 92-38756. (Cultures of the World Ser.). (J). 1993. write for info. (*1-85435-571-6*) Marshall Cavendish.

Malcolm, S., jt. auth. see Emery, A. E.

Malcolm, S., jt. ed. see Humphries, S. E.

Malcolm, W. K., ed. A Blasphemer & Reformer: A Study of James Leslie Mitchell-Lewis Grassic Gibbon. 224p. 1984. text ed. 27.90 (*0-08-030373-0*, Pergamon Pr) Elsevier.

Malcolm X. The Autobiography of Malcolm X. 1987. mass mkt. 5.99 (*0-345-90233-5*) Ballantine.

— The Autobiography of Malcolm X: With the Assistance of Alex Haley. LC 92-52659. 464p. 1992. 20.00 (*0-345-37975-6*, One World) Ballantine.

— By Any Means Necessary. rev. ed. LC 92-64456. (Illus.). 195p. 1993. reprint ed. lib. bdg. 45.00 (*0-87348-759-1*); reprint ed. pap. 15.95 (*0-87348-754-0*) Pathfinder NY.

— The End of White World Supremacy. 160p. 1994. audio 12.95 (*1-55970-271-0*) Arcade Pub Inc.

— February, 1965: The Final Speeches. Clark, Steve, ed. LC 92-62259. (Illus.). 250p. (Orig.). 1992. 50.00 (*0-87348-753-2*); pap. 17.95 (*0-87348-749-4*) Pathfinder NY.

— Habla Malcolm X - Malcolm X Speaks. Koppel, Martin, ed. LC 92-83753. (Illus.). 240p. (SPA.). 1993. lib. bdg. 50.00 (*0-87348-764-8*); pap. 17.95 (*0-87348-733-8*) Pathfinder NY.

— Malcolm X: The Last Speeches. LC 89-61591. 170p. (Orig.). (C). 1992. reprint ed. lib. bdg. 45.00 (*0-87348-544-0*); reprint ed. pap. 16.95 (*0-87348-543-2*) Pathfinder NY.

— Malcolm X on Afro-American History. 3rd ed. LC 72-103696. (Illus.). 93p. 1990. pap. 8.95 (*0-87348-592-0*) Pathfinder NY.

— Malcolm X Speaks. 2nd ed. LC 65-27410. (Illus.). 233p. 1993. reprint ed. lib. bdg. 17.95 (*0-87348-546-7*) Pathfinder NY.

— Malcolm X Speaks Out. 1992. 17.95 (*0-8362-8011-3*); pap. 9.95 (*0-8362-8010-5*) Andrews & McMeel.

— Malcolm X Speeches: January 1965. 1994. 50.00 (*0-87348-780-X*); pap. 16.95 (*0-87348-779-6*) Pathfinder NY.

— Malcolm X Talks to Young People. 29p. (Orig.). 1993. reprint ed. 3.00 (*0-87348-086-4*); reprint ed. lib. bdg. 35.00 (*0-87348-631-5*); reprint ed. pap. 10.95 (*0-87348-628-5*) Pathfinder NY.

— Two Speeches by Malcolm X. 3rd ed. (Orig.). 1993. reprint ed. pap. 3.50 (*0-87348-591-2*) Pathfinder NY.

Malcolm X: Make It Plain Production Team Staff., jt. text see Strickland, William.

Malcolme, David. An Essay on the Antiquities of Great Britain & Ireland. LC 79-103250. 256p. 1983. reprint ed. lib. bdg. 43.00x (*0-89370-783-X*) Borgo Pr.

Malcolme-Lawes, David J. Microcomputers & Laboratory Instrumentation. 2nd ed. LC 88-5794. (Illus.). 284p. 1988. 42.50 (*0-306-42903-9*, Plenum Pr) Plenum.

Malcolmson, Patricia E. English Laundresses: A Social History, 1850-1930. LC 85-24599. (Working Class in European History Ser.). (Illus.). 236p. 1986. 26.95 (*0-252-01293-3*) U of Ill Pr.

Malcolmson, Robert, jt. ed. see Rule, John.

Malcolmson, Robert W. Beyond Nuclear Thinking. 168p. (C). 1990. text ed. 37.95 (*0-7735-0784-1*, Pub. by McGill CN); pap. text ed. 17.95 (*0-7735-0802-3*, Pub. by McGill CN) U of Toronto Pr.

— Nuclear Fallacies: How We Have Been Misguided since Hiroshima. 1985. 39.95 (*0-7735-0585-7*, Pub. by McGill CN); pap. 17.95 (*0-7735-0586-5*, Pub. by McGill CN) U of Toronto Pr.

***Malcom, Ben S. & Martz, Ron.** White Tigers: My Secret War in North Korea. (Illus.). 288p. 1995. 23.95 (*1-57488-016-0*) Brasseys Inc.

Malcom, H. Rooney. Elements of Urban Stormwater Design. LC 89-82034. (Illus.). 134p. (Orig.). (C). 1990. pap. text ed. 30.00 (*1-56049-016-0*) NCSU CE IES.

Malcom, Paul J., jt. auth. see Fitch, Margaret E.

Malcom, Shirley, jt. ed. see Kulm, Gerald.

Malcom, Shirley M., jt. ed. see Kulm, Gerald.

Malcom, Shirley M., jt. auth. see Matyas, Marsha L.

Malcom, Shirley M., jt. ed. see Sosa, Maria.

Malcom, Shirley M., et al, eds. This Year in School Science 1991: Technology for Teaching & Learning. 212p. 1991. 15.95 (*0-87168-428-4*, 91-37S) AAAS.

Malcome, D. J. Programming ALGOL. 1969. 56.00 (*0-08-006385-3*, Pub. by Pergamon Repr UK) Franklin.

Malcomson, Robert & Malcomson, Thomas. HMS Detroit: The Battle for Lake Erie. LC 90-63199. (Illus.). 150p. 1991. 25.95 (*1-55750-053-3*) Naval Inst Pr.

Malcomson, Scott L. Borderlands: Nation & Empire. 250p. 1994. 22.95 (*0-571-19815-5*) Faber & Faber.

Malcomson, Thomas, jt. auth. see Malcomson, Robert.

Malcor, Linda A., jt. auth. see Littleton, C. Scott.

Malczewski, Jacek. The Spatial Planning of Health Services, Vol. 33: Case Studies in Warsaw, Poland. (Progress in Planning Ser.: No. 2). (Illus.). 63p. 1990. pap. 45.00 (*0-08-040171-6*, Pergamon Pr) Elsevier.

Maldague, X. P., ed. Advances in Signal Processing for Nondestructive Evaluation of Materials: Proceedings of the NATO Advanced Research Workshop, Quebec City, Quebec, Canada, August 17-20, 1993. LC 94-6394. (NATO Advanced Study Institutes Series E, Applied Sciences: Vol. 262). 504p. (C). 1994. lib. bdg. 199.50 (*0-7923-2765-9*) Kluwer Ac.

Maldague, Xavier. Non Destructive Evaluation of Materials by Infrared Thermography. LC 92-33616. 1993. 198.00 (*0-387-19769-9*) Spr-Verlag.

Maldague, Xavier P., ed. Infrared Methodology & Technology. LC 92-43489. (Nondestructive Testing Monographs & Tracts: Vol. 7). 1993. pap. text ed. 115.00 (*2-88124-590-0*) Gordon & Breach.

Malde, Harold E. Guidelines for Reviewers of Geological Manuscripts. 28p. 1986. pap. 5.95 (*0-913312-82-7*) Am Geol.

Maldifassi, Jose O. & Abetti, Pier A. Defense Industries in Latin American Countries: Argentina, Brazil, & Chile. LC 93-43070. 280p. 1994. text ed. 59.95 (*0-275-94729-7*, Praeger Pubs) Greenwood.

Maldon. Battle of Maldon & Short Poems from the Saxon Chronicle. Sedgefield, Walter, ed. LC 70-144444. (Belles Lettres Ser., Section I: No. 9). reprint ed. 27.50 (*0-404-53610-7*) AMS Pr.

Maldonado-Bear, Rita & Bear, Larry A. Free Markets, Finance, Ethics, & Law. LC 93-18901. 1993. pap. text ed. write for info. (*0-13-457896-1*) P-H.

Maldonado, C., ed. see International Labour Office Staff.

Maldonado-Capriles, Jenaro & Medina-Gaud, Silverio. Insectos Daninos y Beneficiosos de Puerto Rico: Manual de Laboratorio. 200p. (C). 1987. pap. text ed. 19.95 (*1-881375-16-1*) Libreria Univ.

***Maldonado, Carlos & Garcia, Gilbert.** Chicano Experience - NW. 208p. (C). 1994. per., pap. text ed. 25.95 (*0-7872-0437-4*) Kendall-Hunt.

Maldonado de Ortiz, Candida. Antonio S. Pedreira: Vida y Obra. 192p. (C). 1974. 5.00 (*0-8477-0512-9*); pap. 4.00 (*0-8477-0513-7*) U of PR Pr.

Maldonado-Denis, Manuel. The Emigration Dialectic: Puerto Rico & the U. S. A. LC 80-16640. (Illus.). 168p. (C). 1980. pap. 3.25 (*0-7178-0563-8*) Intl Pubs Co.

Maldonado, Donald, jt. auth. see Chan, Paul D.

Maldonado, J. R., jt. ed. see Celler, G. K.

Maldonado, Jesus M. Esta Era una Vez: Once upon a Time. LC 94-71028. (Illus.). 48p. (ENG & SPA.). (J). (gr. 2-6). 1994. lib. bdg. 14.95 (*0-9636912-1-X*) J M Maldonado.

— In the Still of My Heart. 112p. (Orig.). (C). 1993. pap. text ed. 9.98 (*0-9636912-0-1*) J M Maldonado.

Maldonado, Jorge. Aprenda a Tocar la Guitarra: Learn How to Play the Guitar. (SPA.). 3.95 (*84-7228-612-6*, 220043, Pub. by Edit Clie SP) TSELF.

***Maldonado, Jorge E., ed.** Fundamentos Biblico-Teologicos del Matrimonio y la Familia. LC 94-46256. (SPA.). 1995. pap. write for info. (*0-8028-0929-4*) Eerdmans.

Maldonado, Jose. The Clay Pigeon. 1993. 17.95 (*0-533-10300-2*) Vantage.

Maldonado, Jose, jt. auth. see Lippman, Richard.

Maldonado, Luis A. Cuando Llora un Guerrillero. 89p. 1985. reprint ed. pap. 3.25 (*0-311-37014-4*) Casa Bautista.

***Maldre, Mati & Kruty, Paul.** Walter Burley Griffin in America. LC 95-11632. (Illus.). 1996. write for info. (*0-252-02193-2*) U of Ill Pr.

Male. L' Art Religieux en France, 3 tomes. Incl. Tome III. De la Fin du Moyen Age. 75.00 (*0-8288-9914-2*, F22172); (FRE.). write for info. (*0-318-51926-7*) Fr & Eur.

Male, Belkis C. Woman on the Front Lines. Carmell, Pamella, tr. & intro. by. 88p. 1987. 17.50 (*0-87775-202-8*); pap. 9.95 (*0-87775-203-6*) Unicorn Pr.

Male, Belkis C., ed. see Diaz-Rodriguez, Ernesto.

Male, D. K., et al. Advanced Immunology. 2nd ed. (Illus.). 304p. 1991. 69.95 (*0-397-44771-X*); pap. 45.00 (*0-397-44586-5*, GM0051) Mosby Yr Bk.

Male, Emile. The Gothic Image: Religious Art in France of the Thirteenth Century. Nussey, Dora, tr. (Icon Editions Ser.). (Illus.). 440p. 1973. reprint ed. pap. text ed. 19.00 (*0-06-430032-3*, IN-32, Icon Edns) HarpC.

— Religious Art from the Twelfth to the Eighteenth Century. LC 82-47903. (Illus.). 256p. 1982. pap. 15.95x (*0-691-00347-5*) Princeton U Pr.

— Religious Art in France: The Late Middle Ages: A Study of Medieval Iconography & Its Sources. Bober, Harry, ed. Mathews, Marthiel, tr. (Bollingen Ser.: Vol. XC, No. 3). 600p. 1987. text ed. 97.50 (*0-691-09914-6*) Princeton U Pr.

— Religious Art in France: The Thirteenth Century-A Study of the Origins of Medieval Iconography. Bober, Harry, ed. Mathews, Marthiel, tr. LC 82-11210. (Bollingen Ser.: Vol. XC). (Illus.). 576p. 1984. 110.00 (*0-691-09913-8*) Princeton U Pr.

— Religious Art in France: The Twelfth Century. LC 72-14029. (Bollingen Ser.: No. 90). 1978. 145.00 (*0-691-09912-X*) Princeton U Pr.

Male, George A. Issues in the Education of Minorities: England & the United States. LC 88-38808. 110p. 1989. 22.50 (*0-89341-552-9*, Longwood Academic); pap. 15.00 (*0-89341-553-7*, Longwood Academic) Hollowbrook.

Male, Herbert G. Being in All Respects Ready for Sea. 1993. 19.95 (*1-85756-030-2*, Pub. by Janus Pub UK) Intl Spec Bk.

Male, J. Teach Yourself Modern Persian. (Teach Yourself Ser.). 1979. pap. 8.95 (*0-679-10220-5*) McKay.

Male, James W. & Walski, Thomas M. Water Distribution Systems: A Troubleshooting Manual. (Illus.). 119p. 1990. 74.95 (*0-87371-232-3*, TD485) Lewis Pubs.

Male, James W., et al. Identifying & Reducing Losses in Water Distribution Systems. LC 85-16842. (Illus.). 156p. 1986. 32.00 (*0-8155-1050-0*) Noyes.

Male, Mary C. Creating Exceptional Classrooms: Technology Options for All. LC 93-16215. 1993. pap. text ed. write for info. (*0-205-14695-3*) Allyn.

Male, Roy R. Enter, Mysterious Stranger: American Cloistral Fiction. LC 79-4736. 1979. 22.95 (*0-8061-1544-0*) U of Okla Pr.

Male, S. P. & Stocks, R. K. Competitive Advantage in Construction. 480p. 1992. 115.00 (*0-7506-1075-1*) Buttrwrth-Heinemann.

Male, Stephen, jt. auth. see Kelly, John.

Male, Steven, jt. auth. see Kelly, John.

Male, Steven, jt. auth. see Langford, David.

Malebranch, Nicolas. Philosophical Selections: From the Search after Truth, Dialogue on Metaphysics, Treatise on Nature & Grace. Lennon, Thomas M. et al, trs. LC 92-19801. 288p. (C). 1992. 34.95 (*0-87220-153-8*); pap. text ed. 12.95 (*0-87220-152-X*) Hackett Pub.

Malebranche. Oeuvres: De la Recherche de la Verite, Conversations Chretiennes, Vol. 1. write for info. (*0-318-52179-2*) Fr & Eur.

— Oeuvres Completes. (FRE.). 1978. lib. bdg. 105.00 (*0-8288-3550-0*, M5422) Fr & Eur.

Malebranche, Nicholas. Entretiens sur la Metaphysique et sur la Religion. Doney, Willis, tr. LC 77-86229. (Janus Ser.). 359p. 1980. 20.00 (*0-913870-57-9*) Abaris Bks.

Malebranche, Nicolas. The Search after Truth & Elucidations of the Search after Truth. Lennon, Thomas M. & Olscamp, Paul J., trs. LC 79-23881. Orig. Title: De la Recherche de la Verite & Eclaircissements. 893p. 1980. 89.50 (*0-8142-0246-2*) Ohio St U Pr.

— Treatise on Ethics (Sixteen Eighty-Four) Walton, Craig, tr. & intro. by. LC 92-13823. (International Archives of the History of Ideas Ser.: Vol. 133). 1992. lib. bdg. 106.50 (*0-7923-1763-7*) Kluwer Ac.

— Treatise on Nature & Grace. Riley, Patrick, tr. & intro. by. 224p. 1992. 55.00 (*0-19-824832-6*) OUP.

Malec, Glenn. The Azure Scroll. 257p. (Orig.). 1991. pap. write for info. (*0-9630657-1-8*) Godolphin Hse.

— International Horoscopes, 2 vols., Vol. 1. LC 82-72573. 176p. 16.00 (*0-86690-043-8*, M2643-014) Am Fed Astrologers.

— International Horoscopes, 2 vols., Vol. 2. LC 82-72573. 130p. 16.00 (*0-86690-271-6*, 2530-01) Am Fed Astrologers.

***Malec, Henry A.** Benchmarking Purchasing in the Semiconductor Industry with Sigma Barometers. Ketchum, Carol, ed. 22p. (Orig.). (C). 1991. pap. text ed. 20.00 (*0-945968-09-4*) Ctr Advanced Purchasing.

Malec, Michael A. Essential Statistics for Social Research. 2nd ed. LC 93-5060. 289p. (C). 1993. pap. text ed. 26.50 (*0-8133-1556-5*) Westview.

— Essential Statistics for Social Research. 2nd ed. LC 93-5060. 289p. (C). 1993. text ed. 63.00 (*0-8133-1555-7*) Westview.

Malecha, Scarlet, jt. auth. see Hoyt, Doris.

Malecki, Donald S. Agent's Automobile Guide. 24.00 (*0-942326-01-6*, 26060) Rough Notes.

— Agent's Casualty Guide. 24.00 (*0-942326-03-2*, 26100) Rough Notes.

Malecki, Donald S. & Flitner, Arthur L. Commercial General Liability. 3rd ed. LC 90-62771. 210p. 1990. pap. 30.00 (*0-87218-340-8*) Natl Underwriter.

***Malecki, Donald S. & Gibson, Jack P.** The Additional Insured Book. 2nd ed. 286p. 1994. pap. 49.98 (*1-886813-02-7*) Intl Risk Mgt.

Malecki, Donald S., jt. auth. see Hamilton, Karen L.

Malecki, Donald S., jt. auth. see Wiening, Eric A.

Malecki, Donald S., et al. Commercial Liability Risk Management & Insurance, 2 Vols. 2nd ed. LC 86-72708. 978p. 1986. text ed. 26.00 (*0-89463-049-0*) Am Inst FCPCU.

Malecki, Edward J. Technology & Economic Development: The Dynamics of Local, Regional, & National Change. 495p. 1991. pap. text ed. 49.95 (*0-470-21723-5*) Halsted Pr.

Malecki, I. & Bellert, I. Physical Foundations of Technical Acoustics. LC 64-17267. 1969. 308.00 (*0-08-011097-5*, Pub. by Pergamon Repr UK) Franklin.

Malecki, J., jt. auth. see Hilczer, B.

Malecki, Joseph. Achieving Customer Satisfaction. Hankinson, Mari-Lynn, ed. (AT&T Quality Library). 126p. (Orig.). 1990. pap. 29.95 (*0-932764-21-5*, 500-443) AT&T Customer Info.

Malecki, Joseph & Lee, Janet. Great Performances: The Best in Customer Satisfaction & Customer Service. Hankinson, Mari-Lynn, ed. (AT&T Quality Library). (Illus.). 176p. (Orig.). 1991. pap. 29.95 (*0-932764-28-2*, 500-450) AT&T Customer Info.

Malecki, Maryann. Mom & Dad & I Are Having a Baby! LC 82-81707. (Illus.). 70p. (Orig.). (J). (ps-3). 1982. reprint ed. pap. 6.95 (*0-937604-03-8*) Pennypress.
Malecot, A. Contribution a L'etude De la Force D'articulation En Francais. 1977. 21.15 (*90-279-3176-3*) Mouton.
***Malecot, Andre.** Eye on the Western Stars: A Novel. 176p. (Orig.). 1995. pap. 10.95 (*1-56474-113-3*) Fithian Pr.
— Fundamental French: Language & Culture. LC 63-10567. (Illus.). 1963. 27.50 (*0-89197-184-X*); pap. text ed. 16.95 (*0-89197-766-X*) Irvington.
— Introduction a la Phonetique Francaise. (Janua Linguarum, Ser.: No. 15). 1977. pap. 21.55 (*90-279-3395-2*) Mouton.
Maleev, Vladimir L. Diesel Engine Operation & Maintenance. 1954. text ed. 43.95 (*0-07-039770-8*) McGraw.
Maleev, Vladomir L. Diesel Engine Operation & Maintenance. 1954. text ed. write for info. (*0-07-039772-4*) McGraw.
Malehorn, Hal. Elementary Teacher's Classroom Management Handbook. LC 84-1925. 274p. 1984. pap. text ed. 24.95 (*0-13-260605-4*, Busn) P-H.
Malehorn, Merlin K. & Davenport, Tim. United States Sales Tax Tokens & Stamps: A History & Catalog. LC 93-79632. (Illus.). 403p. 1993. text ed. 49.95 (*0-942596-05-6*) Jade Hse Pubns.
Malek, D. Another Life. 1994. mass mkt. 4.50 (*0-06-108040-3*, Harp PBks) HarpC.
Malek, Doreen O. Above the Law. (Desire Ser.). 1994. mass mkt. 2.99 (*0-373-05869-1*, 1-05869-2) Silhouette.
— The Harder They Fall. (Silhouette Desire Ser.). 1993. pap. 2.89 (*0-373-05778-4*, 5-05778-1) Silhouette.
— Highwayman. 1993. mass mkt. 4.50 (*0-06-108017-9*, Harp PBks) HarpC.
— Marriage in Name Only. (Intimate Moments Ser.). 1995. pap. 3.75 (*0-373-07620-7*, 1-07620-7) Silhouette.
— The Panther & the Pearl. 448p. (Orig.). 1994. pap. 4.99 (*0-8439-3569-3*) Dorchester Pub Co.
— The Raven & the Rose. 432p. 1994. mass mkt. 4.50 (*0-8217-4775-4*) Zebra.
Malek, Doreen O., see Faye Morgan, pseud..
Malek, Emile A. Snail Transmitted Parasitic Diseases, 2 vols., Vol. 1. 352p. 1980. 123.95 (*0-8493-5269-X*, RC119, CRC Reprint) Franklin.
— Snail Transmitted Parasitic Diseases, 2 vols., Vol. 2. 344p. 1980. 123.95 (*0-8493-5270-3*, CRC Reprint) Franklin.
Malek, James S. The Arts Compared: An Aspect of Eighteenth-Century British Aesthetics. LC 74-11088. 176p. reprint ed. pap. 50.20 (*0-7837-3602-9*, 2043467) Bks Demand.
***Malek, Jaromir.** The ABC of Hieroglyphs - Ancient Egyptian Writing. (Illus.). 48p. 1995. pap. 8.95 (*1-85444-052-7*, 0527, Pub. by Ashmolean Mus UK) A Schwartz & Co.
— The Cat in Ancient Egypt. (Illus.). 144p. (C). 1993. 29.95 (*0-7141-0969-X*) U of Pa Pr.
— Egypt. LC 92-50718. (Cradles of Civilization Ser.: Vol. 1). (Illus.). 186p. (C). 1993. 39.95 (*0-8061-2526-8*) U of Okla Pr.
— In the Shadow of the Pyramids: Egypt During the Old Kingdom. LC 86-40188. (Illus.). 128p. 1992. pap. 19.95 (*0-8061-2027-4*) U of Okla Pr.
Malek, Jaromir, jt. auth. see Baines, John.
Malek, M. International Mediation & the Gulf War. 250p. (C). 1991. 175.00 (*0-685-60263-X*, Pub. by Royston Ltd) St Mut.
Malek, M., ed. see Rasquinha, J.
Malek, M. H. Contemporary Issues in European Development Aid. 152p. 1991. text ed. 59.95 (*1-85628-146-9*, Pub. by Avebury Pub UK) Ashgate Pub Co.
Malek, M. M. The Political Economy of Iran under the Shah. 288p. 1987. 42.00 (*0-7099-3519-6*, Pub. by Croom Helm UK) Routledge Chapman & Hall.
Malek, Miroslav, jt. auth. see Lipovski, Jack.
Malek, Miroslaw. High-Performance Computing in Europe. 46p. (Orig.). (C). 1993. pap. text ed. 50.00 (*1-56806-305-9*) Diane Pub.
— Responsive Computing. LC 94-31249. 120p. (C). 1994. lib. bdg. 69.95 (*0-7923-9511-5*) Kluwer Ac.
***Malek, Mo, ed.** Setting Priorities in Health Care. 1994. text ed. 54.95 (*0-471-94394-0*) Wiley.
Malek, Mo, et al, eds. Strategic Issues in Health Care Management. LC 93-18502. 279p. 1993. text ed. 72.00 (*0-471-93964-1*) Wiley.
Malek-Zavarei, M. & Jamshidi, Mohammad. Time-Delay Systems. (North Holland Systems & Control Ser.: Vol. 9). 1987. 105.25 (*0-317-66030-6*) Elsevier.
— Time-Delay Systems: Analysis, Optimization & Applications. (Systems & Control Ser.: No. 8). 500p. 1987. 102.75 (*0-444-70204-0*, North Holland) Elsevier.
Malek-Zavarei, M., jt. auth. see Jamshidi, Mohammad.
Maleki, Reza. Flexible Manufacturing Systems: The Technology & Management. 336p. 1990. text ed. 66.00 (*0-13-321761-2*) P-H.
***Malekian, Farhad.** The Concept of Islamic International Criminal Law: A Comparative Study. 232p. 1994. lib. bdg. 92.00 (*1-85966-085-1*, Pub. by Graham & Trotman UK) Kluwer Ac.
— Condemning the Use of Force in the Gulf Crisis. 116p. (Orig.). 1992. pap. 78.00x (*91-630-1251-0*, Pub. by Almqv & Wiksell SW) Coronet Bks.
— International Criminal Law: The Legal & Critical Analysis of International Crimes, 2 vols., Set. 1121p. 1991. 1,250.00x (*91-630-0244-2*, Pub. by Almqv & Wiksell SW) Coronet Bks.
— The Monopolization of International Criminal Law in the United Nations: A Jurisprudential Approach. 2nd ed. 240p. (Orig.). 1995. pap. 127.50x (*91-630-3196-5*, Pub. by Almqv & Wiksell SW) Coronet Bks.
Malekoff, Andrew, ed. Group Work with Suburbia's Children: Difference, Acceptance & Belonging. (Social Work with Groups Ser.). 127p. 1991. text ed. 29.95 (*1-56024-100-4*) Haworth Pr.
Malekoff, Robert, jt. auth. see Lapchick, Richard E.
Malekzadeh, Ali R., jt. auth. see Nahavandi, Afsaneh.
Malen, Betty, jt. ed. see Fuhrman, Susan H.
Malen, Lenore. Images from Dante. LC 91-62103. (Books by Artists - Poetry Ser.). (Illus.). 32p. (Orig.). 1991. pap. text ed. 14.00 (*1-877675-08-3*) Midmarch Arts-WAN.
***Malenda, John W.** Being. 35p. (Orig.). 1995. pap. 3.50 (*1-886482-01-2*) Guiding Lght.
— Destinations. 180p. 1995. pap. 10.95 (*1-886482-00-4*) Guiding Lght.
Maler, Anne M. Mother Love, Deadly Love: The Texas Cheerleader Murder Plot. 1994. mass mkt. 4.99 (*0-312-95126-4*) St Martin.
Maler, Karl-Goran. Economic Sciences, 1981-1990: The Sveriges Riksbank (Bank of Sweden) Prize in Economic Sciences in Memory of Alfred Nobel. LC 92-37996. (Nobel Lectures, Including Presentation Speeches & Laureates' Biographies Ser.). 400p. 1992. text ed. 86.00 (*981-02-0835-9*); pap. text ed. 46.00 (*981-02-0836-7*) World Scientific Pub.
— Environmental Economics: A Theoretical Inquiry. LC 73-19347. (Illus.). 286p. reprint ed. pap. 81.60 (*0-8357-4678-X*, 2037625) Bks Demand.
Maler, Karl-Goran, jt. auth. see Dasgupta, Partha.
Maler, Karl-Goran, jt. ed. see Dasgupta, Partha.
Maler, T. Explorations in the Department of Peten, Guatemala, Vol. 5, Nos. 1 & 2. Bd. with Prehistoric Ruins of Tikal, Guatemala. 1911. 80.00 (*0-527-01166-5*, MU.PMM) Periodicals Srv.
— Explorations in the Department of Peten, Guatemala, & Adjacent Region, 2 vols., Vol. 4, No. 2. (HU PMM Ser.). 1972. reprint ed. 50.00 (*0-527-01163-0*) Periodicals Srv.
— Explorations in the Department of Peten, Guatemala, & Adjacent Region, 2 vols., Vol. 4, No. 3. (HU PMM Ser.). 1972. reprint ed. pap. 40.00 (*0-527-01164-9*) Periodicals Srv.
— Explorations of the Upper Usumatsintla & Adjacent Region. (HU PMM Ser.: Vol. 4, No. 1). 1972. reprint ed. 30.00 (*0-527-01162-2*) Periodicals Srv.
— Researches in the Central Portion of the Usumatsintla Valley. (HU PMM Ser.). 1974. reprint ed. 50.00 (*0-527-01156-8*) Periodicals Srv.
— Researches in the Usumatsintla Valley, Pt. 2. (HU PMM Ser.). 1974. reprint ed. 80.00 (*0-527-01157-6*) Periodicals Srv.
Malerba-Foran, Joan. When You Look in the Mirror, What Do You See? 20p. (Orig.). (YA). (gr. 7 up). 1985. pap. 2.50 (*0-89486-262-6*) Hazelden.
Malerba, Franco. The Semiconductor Business: The Economics of Rapid Growth & Decline. LC 85-40372. (Economics of Technological Change Ser.). 272p. 1985. text ed. 27.50 (*0-299-10460-5*) U of Wis Pr.
Malerba, L., ed. Italian Cinema, 1945-51. 1976. lib. bdg. 69.95 (*0-8490-2084-0*) Gordon Pr.
Malerich, Charles, jt. auth. see Scharf, Walter.
***Malerstein, A. J.** The Conscious Mind: A Developmental Theory. 163p. (C). 1993. text ed. 22.50 (*0-9644089-1-0*) Cole Valley Pr.
***Malerstein, A. J. & Ahern, Mary.** A Piagetian Model of Character Structure. 252p. (C). 1993. text ed. 22.50 (*0-9644089-0-2*) Cole Valley Pr.
Malerstein, A. J., jt. auth. see Ahern, Mary.
Males, R., jt. ed. see Barrett, Peter.
Males, Richard M., et al. Use of Expert Systems in a Water Utility. (Illus.). 120p. (Orig.). (C). 1994. pap. text ed. 60.00 (*0-7881-0277-X*) Diane Pub.
Malesani, M. G., jt. auth. see Valenti, R.
Malesis, C. H. Where the Trilliums Bloom. 192p. 1991. pap. 11.95 (*0-9631266-0-1*) Poon Crick Pub.
— With Tongue in Cheek. Stablein, Marilyn, ed. (Illus.). 233p. 1990. pap. 11.95 (*0-939116-25-1*) Frontier OR.
Maleska, Eugene. S&S Crossword No. 178. 1994. pap. 7.50 (*0-671-87197-8*, Fireside) S&S Trade.
— S&S Crossword Number 179. 1994. pap. 7.50 (*0-671-87198-6*, Fireside) S&S Trade.
— S&S Large Type Crossword No. 17. 1994. pap. 8.00 (*0-671-87219-2*, Fireside) S&S Trade.
Maleska, Eugene, ed. New York Times Crossword Puzzles, Vol. 34. Date not set. write for info. (*0-8129-2264-6*) Random.
— New York Times Crossword Puzzles, Vol. 37. Date not set. 8.00 (*0-8129-2358-8*) Random.
— S&S Crossword, No. 180. 1994. pap. 7.50 (*0-671-89268-1*, Fireside) S&S Trade.
— Simon & Schuster Crossword, No. 181. 1994. 7.50 (*0-671-89708-X*, Fireside) S&S Trade.
— Simon & Schuster Crossword, No. 182. 1994. 7.50 (*0-671-89710-1*, Fireside) S&S Trade.
— Simon & Schuster Super Crossword, No. 8. 1994. pap. 9.00 (*0-671-89709-8*, Fireside) S&S Trade.
Maleska, Eugene T. Children's Word Games & Crossword Puzzles, Vol. 2. (J). (gr. 2-4). 1988. pap. 7.50 (*0-8129-1692-1*) Random.
— Children's Word Games & Crossword Puzzles, Vol. 3. (J). (gr. 2-4). 1992. pap. 7.00 (*0-8129-1980-7*, Times Bks) Random.
— Crosstalk: Letters to America's Foremost Crossword Puzzle Authority. LC 93-15814. 1993. pap. 12.00 (*0-671-70875-9*, Fireside) S&S Trade.
— Crossword Series, Vol. 161. 1991. pap. 6.95 (*0-671-74047-4*, Fireside) S&S Trade.
— New York Times Daily Crossword Puzzles, Vol. 28. 1991. pap. 7.00 (*0-8129-1899-1*, Times Bks) Random.
— New York Times Daily Crossword Puzzles, Vol. 31. 1992. pap. 8.00 (*0-8129-2043-0*, Times Bks) Random.
— New York Times Daily Crossword Puzzles, Vol. 32. 1992. pap. 7.50 (*0-8129-2082-1*, Times Bks) Random.
— New York Times Daily Crossword Puzzles, Vol. 33. 1993. pap. 7.50 (*0-8129-2183-6*, Times Bks) Random.
— New York Times Daily Crossword Puzzles, Vol. 34. 1993. pap. 8.00 (*0-8129-2209-3*, Times Bks) Random.
— The New York Times Daily Crossword Puzzles: Puns & Anagrams. 1993. pap. 7.50 (*0-8129-2271-9*, Times Bks) Random.
— The New York Times Daily Crossword Puzzles, Vol. 35. 1993. pap. 8.00 (*0-8129-2270-0*, Times Bks) Random.
— The New York Times Daily Crossword Puzzles, Vol. 35, Vol. 24. 1989. 5.95 (*0-8129-1782-0*) Random.
— The New York Times Daily Crossword Puzzles, Vol. 35, Vol. 25. 1989. 6.95 (*0-8129-1837-1*) Random.
— The New York Times Daily Crossword Puzzles, Vol. 35, Vol. 26. 1990. 6.95 (*0-8129-1860-6*) Random.
— The New York Times Daily Crosswords, Vol. 27. 1990. 7.00 (*0-8129-1879-7*, Times Bks) Random.
— The New York Times Large Type Crossword Puzzles, Vol. 4. large type ed. 96p. 1990. pap. 6.95 (*0-8129-1892-4*, Times Bks) Random.
— The New York Times Large Type Crossword Puzzles, Vol. 5. large type ed. 1990. pap. 6.95 (*0-8129-1893-2*, Times Bks) Random.
— The New York Times Sunday Crossword Puzzles, Vol. 15. (Orig.). 1989. 8.00 (*0-8129-1781-2*, Times Bks) Random.
— The New York Times Sunday Crossword Puzzles, Vol. 16. (Orig.). 1990. 7.50 (*0-8129-1839-8*, Times Bks) Random.
— The New York Times Sunday Crossword Puzzles, Vol. 17. (Orig.). 1990. spiral bd. 8.00 (*0-8129-1878-9*, Times Bks) Random.
— The New York Times Sunday Crossword Puzzles, Vol. 18. (Orig.). 1994. pap. 8.00 (*0-8129-2268-9*, Times Bks) Random.
— New York Times Sunday Crossword Puzzles, Vol. 19. 1992. pap. 7.50 (*0-8129-2083-X*, Times Bks) Random.
— The New York Times Toughest Crossword Puzzles, Vol. 1. 1988. 9.00 (*0-8129-1694-8*, Times Bks) Random.
— The New York Times Toughest Crossword Puzzles, Vol. 2. 1989. 9.00 (*0-8129-1828-2*, Times Bks) Random.
— New York Times Toughest Crossword Puzzles, Vol. 3. 1991. pap. 9.00 (*0-8129-1912-2*, Times Bks) Random.
— New York Times Toughest Crossword Puzzles, Vol. 4. 1993. pap. 9.00 (*0-8129-2178-X*, Times Bks) Random.
— A Pleasure in Words. 448p. 1982. pap. 10.95 (*0-671-44775-0*, Fireside) S&S Trade.
— S&S Crossword Puzzle Book. 1991. pap. 6.95 (*0-671-73162-9*, Fireside) S&S Trade.
— Simon & Schuster Crossword Puzzle Book, No. 154. 1990. pap. 5.95 (*0-671-69520-7*) S&S Trade.
— Simon & Schuster Crossword Puzzle Book, No. 155. 1990. pap. 5.95 (*0-671-70638-1*) S&S Trade.
— Simon & Schuster Crossword Puzzle Book, No. 156. 1990. pap. 5.95 (*0-671-70639-X*) S&S Trade.
— Simon & Schuster Crossword Puzzle Book, No. 157. 1990. pap. 6.95 (*0-671-72351-0*) S&S Trade.
— Simon & Schuster Crossword Puzzle Book, No. 158. 1990. pap. 6.95 (*0-671-72352-9*) S&S Trade.
— Simon & Schuster Crossword Puzzle Book, No. 169. 1992. pap. 6.99 (*0-671-79178-8*, Fireside) S&S Trade.
— Simon & Schuster Crossword Puzzle Book, No. 170. 1992. pap. 6.99 (*0-671-79179-6*, Fireside) S&S Trade.
— Simon & Schuster Crossword Puzzle Book Series, No. 162. 1991. pap. 6.95 (*0-671-74048-2*, Fireside) S&S Trade.
— Simon & Schuster Super Crossword Puzzle Book, No. 6. 1990. pap. 8.95 (*0-671-72355-3*) S&S Trade.
— Simon & Schuster's Crossword Puzzle Book, No. 167. 1992. pap. 6.99 (*0-671-77849-8*, Fireside) S&S Trade.
— Simon & Schuster's Crossword Puzzle Book, No. 173. 1993. pap. 7.50 (*0-671-86408-4*, Fireside) S&S Trade.
— Simon & Schuster's Crossword Puzzle Book, No. 1174. 1993. pap. 7.50 (*0-671-86409-2*, Fireside) S&S Trade.
— Simon & Schuster's Crossword Puzzle Book Series, No. 168. 1992. pap. 6.99 (*0-671-77850-1*) S&S Trade.
— Simon & Schuster's Cryptic Crossword Treasury Series, No. 3. 1993. pap. 9.00 (*0-671-73512-8*, Fireside) S&S Trade.
— Simon & Schuster's Super Crossword Book, No. 7. 1992. pap. 9.00 (*0-671-79232-6*, Fireside) S&S Trade.
Maleska, Eugene T., ed. Children's Word Games & Crossword Puzzles, Vol. 1. LC 86-888. 80p. 1986. pap. 7.00 (*0-8129-1243-8*, Times Bks) Random.
— Children's Word Games & Puzzles. 2nd ed. LC 86-886. 80p. (J). (gr. 3 up). 1986. pap. 7.00 (*0-8129-1308-6*) Random.
— New York Times Daily Crossword Puzzles, Vol. 38. 1994. pap. 8.00 (*0-8129-2450-9*, Times Bks) Random.
— The New York Times Daily Crossword Puzzles, Vol. 35, Vol. 30. 1992. 7.50 (*0-8129-1997-1*) Random.
— The New York Times Daily Crossword Puzzles, Vol. 35, Vol. 36. 1994. pap. 8.00 (*0-8129-2340-5*) Random.
— The New York Times Daily Crosswords, Vol. 29. 64p. 1991. pap. 7.00 (*0-8129-1937-8*, Times Bks) Random.
— The New York Times Large Print Crossword Puzzle Omnibus, Vol. 1. large type ed. 1994. pap. 12.00 (*0-679-75144-0*) Random.
— The New York Times Sunday Crossword Puzzles, Vol. II. (Orig.). 1985. pap. 8.00 (*0-8129-1115-6*, Times Bks) Random.
— The New York Times Sunday Crossword Puzzles, Vol. 10. 64p. (Orig.). 1984. spiral bd., pap. 8.00 (*0-8129-1083-4*, Times Bks) Random.
— The New York Times Sunday Crossword Puzzles, Vol. 12. 64p. (Orig.). 1985. pap. 7.50 (*0-8129-1166-0*, Times Bks) Random.
— The New York Times Sunday Crossword Puzzles, Vol. 13. 64p. (Orig.). 1986. pap. 8.00 (*0-8129-1191-1*, Times Bks) Random.
— The New York Times Sunday Crossword Puzzles, Vol. 14. 64p. (Orig.). 1988. pap. 8.00 (*0-8129-1681-6*, Times Bks) Random.
— New York Times Sunday Crossword Puzzles, Vol. 20. 1994. pap. 8.00 (*0-8129-2451-7*, Times Bks) Random.
— The New York Times Sunday Omnibus, Vol. 3. 240p. 1991. pap. 10.00 (*0-8129-1936-X*, Times Bks) Random.
— Simon & Schuster Crossword, No. 175. 1993. pap. 7.50 (*0-671-87194-3*, Fireside) S&S Trade.
— Simon & Schuster Crossword, No. 176. 1993. pap. 7.50 (*0-671-87195-1*, Fireside) S&S Trade.
— Simon & Schuster Crossword Treasury, No. 37. 1993. pap. 8.00 (*0-671-87199-4*, Fireside) S&S Trade.
— Simon & Schuster Large Type Crossword, No. 16. large type ed. 1993. pap. 8.00 (*0-671-87218-4*, Fireside) S&S Trade.
— Simon & Schuster's Crossword Book Of Quotations, No. 13. 1981. pap. 4.95 (*0-686-73805-5*, Fireside) S&S Trade.
— Simon & Schuster's Cryptic Crossword Treasury, No. 2. 1992. pap. 8.99 (*0-671-73511-X*, Fireside) S&S Trade.
— Simon & Schuster's Large Type Crosswords, No. 15. large type ed. 96p. 1993. spiral bd. 8.00 (*0-671-79780-8*, Fireside) S&S Trade.
Maleska, Eugene T. & Samson, John M. Simon & Schuster Crossword Puzzle Book, No. 152. 1989. pap. 6.95 (*0-671-67988-0*, Fireside) S&S Trade.
— Simon & Schuster Crossword Puzzle Book Series, No. 159. 1991. pap. 6.95 (*0-671-73161-0*, Fireside) S&S Trade.
— Simon & Schuster Crossword Puzzle Book Series, No. 177. 1994. 7.50 (*0-671-87196-X*, Fireside) S&S Trade.
— Simon & Schuster Crossword Treasury, No. 35. 1989. pap. 7.95 (*0-671-68732-8*, Fireside) S&S Trade.
Maleska, Eugene T. & Samson, John M., eds. Simon & Schuster Crossword Book Series, No. 165: New Challenges in the Series, Containing 50 Never-Before-Published Puzzles. 64p. 1992. pap. 6.95 (*0-671-75848-9*, Fireside) S&S Trade.
— Simon & Schuster Crossword Puzzle, No. 148. 1989. pap. 6.95 (*0-671-67594-X*, Fireside) S&S Trade.
— Simon & Schuster Crossword Puzzle Book, No. 144. 1988. pap. 5.95 (*0-671-62762-7*, Fireside) S&S Trade.
— Simon & Schuster Crossword Puzzle Book, No. 146. 64p. 1988. spiral bd. 5.95 (*0-671-62764-3*, Fireside) S&S Trade.
— Simon & Schuster Crossword Puzzle Book, No. 149. 1989. pap. 5.95 (*0-671-67983-X*, Fireside) S&S Trade.
— Simon & Schuster Crossword Puzzle Book, No. 150. 1989. pap. 5.95 (*0-671-67985-6*, Fireside) S&S Trade.
— Simon & Schuster Crossword Puzzle Book Series, No. 163. 64p. 1991. pap. 6.95 (*0-671-74915-3*, Fireside) S&S Trade.
— Simon & Schuster Crossword Puzzle Book Series, No. 164. 64p. 1991. pap. 6.95 (*0-671-74916-1*, Fireside) S&S Trade.
— Simon & Schuster Crossword Puzzle Book Series, No. 166: New Challenges in the Series, Containing 50 Never-Before-Published Puzzles. 64p. 1992. pap. 6.95 (*0-671-75849-7*, Fireside) S&S Trade.
— Simon & Schuster's Crossword Puzzle Book No. 183. 64p. 1995. pap. 7.50 (*0-671-51056-8*, Fireside) S&S Trade.
— Simon & Schuster's Crossword Puzzle Book No. 184. 64p. 1995. pap. 7.50 (*0-671-51131-9*, Fireside) S&S Trade.
— Simon & Schuster's Crossword Puzzle Book Series, No. 171. 64p. 1993. spiral bd. 7.00 (*0-671-79787-5*, Fireside) S&S Trade.
— Simon & Schuster's Crossword Puzzle Book Series, No. 172. 64p. 1993. spiral bd. 7.00 (*0-671-79798-0*, Fireside) S&S Trade.
— Simon & Schuster's Large Type Crosswords No. 18. 96p. 1995. pap. 8.00 (*0-671-51134-3*, Fireside) S&S Trade.
Maleska, Eugene T., jt. auth. see Farrar, Margaret P.
Maleska, Eugene T., jt. ed. see Farrar, Margaret P.
Maleska, Eugene T., jt. ed. see Weng, Will.
Maleske, Robert T. Foundations for Gathering & Interpreting Behavioral Data. LC 94-15947. (Illus.). 528p. 1995. text ed. 52.95 (*0-534-23742-8*) Brooks-Cole.
***Maleskey, Gale, et al, eds.** Home Remedies: What Works: Thousands of Americans Reveal Their Favorite, Home-Tested Cures for Everyday Health Problems. LC 94-30876. 1995. write for info. (*0-87596-233-5*) Rodale Pr Inc.
Maleski, Mary A., ed. Fine Tuning: Studies of the Religious Poetry of Herbert & Milton. (Medieval & Renaissance Texts & Studies: Vol. 64). 334p. 1989. 30.00 (*0-86698-048-2*) MRTS.
Malesky, Gale. Take This Book to the Gynecologist with You. 1991. pap. 9.57 (*0-201-52379-5*) Addison-Wesley.
Maleson, Sandra, jt. auth. see Spencer, Janet.
Malet, Hugh. Voyage in a Bowler Hat. 272p. (C). 1989. 50.00 (*0-947712-02-X*, Pub. by S A Baldwin UK) St Mut.
Malet, Lucas, pseud. The History of Sir Richard Calmady: A Romance, 2 vols. in 1. LC 79-8424. reprint ed. 44.50 (*0-404-62015-9*) AMS Pr.
Malet, Marianne D. Violet; or the Danseuse: A Portraiture of the Human Passions & Character, 2 vols. in 1. LC 79-8167. reprint ed. 44.50 (*0-404-62018-3*) AMS Pr.
Malet, Oriel. Daphne Du Maurier: Letters from Menabilly, Portrait of a Friendship. 1994. 25.00 (*0-87131-759-1*) M Evans.
***Malet, R. Maria, et al.** Surrealismo en Cataluna. (Illus.). 208p. (SPA.). 1993. 150.00 (*84-343-0546-1*) Elliots Bks.
Malet, Rosa M. Joan Miro. LC 83-62002. (Illus.). 128p. 1984. 24.95 (*0-8478-0524-7*) Rizzoli Intl.
***Malet-Veale, Decima.** Putting on the Polish: A Guide to Image Enhancement for Men & Women. (Illus.). 488p. 1993. pap. 21.95 (*1-55059-074-X*) Temeron Bks.

M

An Asterisk (*) at the beginning of an entry indicates that the title is appearing in BIP for the first time.

Maletic, Vera. Body Space Expressions: The Development of Rudolf Laban's Movement & Dance Concepts. (Approaches to Semiotics Ser.: No. 75). (Illus.). xvi, 268p. 1987. lib. bdg. 90.80 (*0-89925-141-2*) Mouton.
Maletis, Margaret, jt. auth. see Patton, Sally J.
Maletsky, Evan, ed. Teaching with "Student Math Notes" (Illus.). 124p. 1987. pap. 14.50 (*0-87353-244-9*) NCTM.
Maletsky, Evan & Hirsch, Christian, eds. Activities from the "Mathematics Teacher" LC 81-4028. (Illus.). 140p. (J). (gr. 7 up). 1981. pap. 10.00 (*0-87353-173-6*) NCTM.
***Maletsky, Evan M., ed.** Teaching with "Student Math Notes" Vol. 2. (Illus.). (Orig.). 1994. pap. text ed. write for info. (*0-87353-369-0*) NCTM.
Maletsky, Evan M., jt. auth. see Sobel, Max A.
Maletta, Gabe J. & Pirozzolo, Francis J., eds. Assessment & Treatment of the Elderly Neuropsychiatric Patient. LC 86-9507. (Advances in Neurogerontology Ser.: Vol. 4). 291p. 1986. text ed. 65.00 (*0-275-92112-3*, C2112, Praeger Pubs) Greenwood.
Maletta, Gerry. The Pandora Principle. 500p. 1994. pap. 12.95 (*1-56901-362-4*) NW Pub.
Malette, jt. ed. see Chalouh.
Maletzky, Barry M. Treating the Sexual Offender. 320p. (C). 1990. text ed. 46.00 (*0-8039-3662-1*); pap. text ed. 22.95 (*0-8039-3663-X*) Sage.
Maletzky, Barry M., ed. Multiple-Monitored Electroconvulsive Therapy. 256p. 1981. 119.95 (*0-8493-5940-6*, RC485, CRC Reprint) Franklin.
Malewicki, Douglas J. How to Build the One Hundred Fifty-Five MPG at 55 MPH California Commuter. 2nd ed. (Illus.). 50p. 1982. reprint ed. pap. 15.00 (*0-941730-00-X*); reprint ed. pap. text ed. 15.00 (*0-941730-01-8*) Aero Vis.
— New Unified Performance Graphs & Comparisons for Streamlined Human Powered Vehicles. 20p. 1983. 3.50 (*0-912468-29-7*) CA Rocketry.
— One Hundred Fifty-Five Mile per Gallon California Commuter. 8p. 3.00 (*0-912468-30-0*) CA Rocketry.
Malewicki, Douglas J. & Schwenn, Donald C. Model Rockets from Design to Launch. 1976. teacher ed 9.95 (*0-912468-15-7*, MRDTL-T); student ed 9.95 (*0-912468-16-5*, MRDTL-S) CA Rocketry.
Maley, Alan & Duff, Alan. Drama Techniques in Language Learning: A Resource Book of Communication Activities for Language Teachers. (Cambridge Handbooks for Language Teachers Ser.). (Illus.). 234p. 1983. pap. 16.95 (*0-521-28868-1*) Cambridge U Pr.
— The Inward Ear: Poetry in the Language Classroom. (Cambridge Handbooks for Language Teachers Ser.). (Illus.). 192p. (C). 1989. 42.95 (*0-521-32048-8*); pap. 15.95 (*0-521-31240-X*) Cambridge U Pr.
— Sounds Intriguing: Resource Material for Teachers. 73p. 1979. pap. 10.95 (*0-521-22138-2*); pap. 15.95 (*0-521-22135-8*) Cambridge U Pr.
Maley, Alan, et al. The Mind's Eye: Using Pictures Creatively in Language Learning. 96p. 1981. student ed, pap. 11.95 (*0-521-23332-1*); teacher ed, pap. 11.95 (*0-521-23333-X*) Cambridge U Pr.
Maley, Anne, jt. auth. see Simons, Sandra M.
Maley, Catherine A. Dans le Vent. 3rd ed. 224p. (FRE.). (C). 1990. pap. text ed. 25.50 (*0-03-012663-0*) HB Coll Pubs.
— The Pronouns of Address in Modern Standard French. LC 74-17218. (Romance Monographs: No. 10). 1974. 22.00 (*84-399-2792-4*); pap. 17.00 (*0-686-31732-7*) Romance.
Maley, Catherine A., jt. ed. see King, Larry D.
Maley, F. Miller. Single-Layer Wire Routing & Compaction: Foundations of Computing. 424p. 1990. 45.00 (*0-262-13250-8*) MIT Pr.
Maley, Nancy, jt. auth. see Ellison, Sheila.
Maley, Robin A. & Epstein, Alice L., eds. High Technology in Health Care: Risk Management. LC 93-14154. 296p. 1993. 62.00 (*1-55648-107-1*, 178158) AHPI.
Maley, Terry. Field Geology Illustrated. LC 94-75576. (Illus.). 316p. (Orig.). (C). 1994. pap. text ed. 15.95 (*0-940949-03-2*) Mineral Pubns.
Maley, Terry, jt. ed. see Horowitz, Asher.
Maley, Terry S. Exploring Idaho Geology. LC 86-90540. (Illus.). 232p. (Orig.). 1987. pap. 16.95 (*0-940949-00-8*) Mineral Pubns.
Maley, V. Carlton, Jr. The Theory of Beats & Combination Tones, 1700-1863. LC 90-3350. (Harvard Dissertations in the History of Science Ser.). 184p. 1990. 44.00 (*0-8240-0040-4*) Garland.
Maley, William & Saikal, Fazel H. Political Order in Post-Communist Afghanistan. LC 92-32723. (International Peace Academy Occasional Paper Ser.). 80p. 1992. pap. text ed. 7.95 (*1-55587-361-8*) Lynne Rienner.
Maley, William, jt. ed. see Saikal, Amin.
Maley, Willy. A Spenser Chronology. LC 93-2455. 164p. (C). 1994. lib. bdg. 44.00 (*0-389-21010-2*) B&N Imports.
Malezieux, E., jt. auth. see Malezieux, J.
Malezieux, J. & Malezieux, E. Travaux Publics des Etats-Unis Amerique en 1870 Souvenirs d'Une Mission. (Industrial Antiquities Ser.). (Illus.). 256p. (FRE.). (C). 1989. reprint ed. 150.00 (*1-85297-014-6*, Pub. by Archival Facs UK) St Mut.
Malfatti, Patrizia. Look Inside the Ocean. (Poke & Look Learning Ser.). (Illus.). 16p. (J). (ps-3). 1993. bds. 11.95 (*0-448-40488-5*, G&D) Putnam Pub Group.
Malfatti, Patrizia, tr. Look Around the City. (Poke & Look Learning Bks.). (Illus.). 16p. (J). (ps-3). 1993. bds. 11.95 (*0-448-40187-8*, G&D) Putnam Pub Group.
— Look Inside an Airplane. (Poke & Look Learning Bks.). (Illus.). 16p. (J). (ps-3). 1994. bds. 11.95 (*0-448-40543-1*, G&D) Putnam Pub Group.
Malfetti, James L. & Eidlitz, Elizabeth, eds. Perspectives on Sexuality: A Literary Collection. LC 78-144052. (Illus.). 611p. 1972. pap. text ed. 9.95 (*0-03-082826-0*) Irvington.
Malfetti, James L., jt. auth. see Stewart, Ernest.
Malfliet, W., jt. auth. see Callebaut, D. K.
Malgady, Robert G. & Rodriguez, Orlando, eds. Theoretical & Conceptual Issues in Hispanic Mental Health. LC 93-38655. 274p. 1994. 37.50 (*0-89464-839-X*) Krieger.
Malgavkar, P. D. Biotechnology: Business Possibilities & Prospects. (C). 1988. 12.00 (*81-204-0287-1*, Pub. by Oxford IBH II) S Asia.
— High Technology: Managerial Considerations. (C). 1989. 19.00 (*81-204-0415-7*, Pub. by Oxford IBH II) S Asia.
— Industrial Policy & Prospects 2001 A.D. (C). 1988. 15.00 (*81-204-0282-0*, Pub. by Oxford IBH II) S Asia.
— Technologies for Economic Development. (C). 1987. 18.00 (*81-204-0158-1*, Pub. by Oxford IBH II) S Asia.
Malgavkar, P. D. & Panandiker, V. A. Population & Development. 1982. 18.50 (*0-8364-0923-X*, Pub. by Somaiya) S Asia.
Malgieri, Nick. Great Italian Desserts. 1990. 22.95 (*0-316-54519-8*) Little.
— How to Bake. (Illus.). 1995. 29.95 (*0-06-016819-6*, HarpT) HarpC.
— Nick Malgieri's Perfect Pastry. 320p. 1989. text ed. 27.00 (*0-02-579251-2*) Macmillan.
Malgo, Wim. Begin with Sadat. 2.95 (*0-937422-17-7*) Midnight Call.
— Biblical Counseling. 4.95 (*0-937422-18-5*) Midnight Call.
— Called to Pray. 3.95 (*0-937422-19-3*) Midnight Call.
— Depression & Its Remedy. 1980. 2.95 (*0-937422-03-7*) Midnight Call.
— Fifty Questions Most Frequently Asked about the Second Coming. 3.95 (*0-937422-04-5*) Midnight Call.
— How to Walk with God. 1980. 1.95 (*0-937422-02-9*) Midnight Call.
— In the Beginning Was the End. pap. 4.95 (*0-937422-33-9*) Midnight Call.
— Israel Shall Do Valiantly. 3.95 (*0-937422-05-3*) Midnight Call.
— Israel's God Does Not Lie. 4.95 (*0-937422-06-1*) Midnight Call.
— Jerusalem: Focal Point of the World. 3.95 (*0-937422-08-8*) Midnight Call.
— A New Heaven & a New Earth. 9.95 (*0-937422-32-0*); pap. 6.95 (*0-937422-31-2*) Midnight Call.
— Nuclear Catastrophe in the Mideast. 3.95 (*0-937422-22-3*) Midnight Call.
— On the Border of Two Worlds. 1.95 (*0-937422-10-X*) Midnight Call.
— One Thousand Years Peace...A Utopia? 3.95 (*0-937422-11-8*) Midnight Call.
— Prayer & Revival. 4.95 (*0-937422-12-6*) Midnight Call.
— The Rapture & Its Mystery. pap. 1.95 (*0-937422-13-4*) Midnight Call.
— The Rulership of Heaven. 9.95 (*0-937422-28-2*); pap. 6.95 (*0-937422-27-4*) Midnight Call.
— Russia's Last Invasion. 1980. 3.95 (*0-937422-01-0*) Midnight Call.
— Seven Letters from Heaven. 9.95 (*0-937422-26-6*); pap. 6.95 (*0-937422-25-8*) Midnight Call.
— Seven Signs of a Born Again Person. 1.45 (*0-937422-14-2*) Midnight Call.
— The Sword of the Lord. pap. 2.95 (*0-937422-24-X*) Midnight Call.
— There Shall Be Signs from 1948 to 1982. 1980. 2.95 (*0-937422-00-2*) Midnight Call.
— Twentieth Century Handwriting on the Wall. 4.95 (*0-686-12823-0*) Midnight Call.
— The Wrath of Heaven on Earth. 9.95 (*0-937422-30-4*); pap. 6.95 (*0-937422-29-0*) Midnight Call.
Malgonkar, Mahohar. Distant Drum. 270p. 1974. reprint ed. pap. write for info. (*0-88253-286-3*) Ind-US Inc.
Malgonkar, Manohar. Bandicoot Run. 337p. 1982. 15.00 (*0-86578-134-6*); pap. 6.00 (*0-86578-192-3*) Ind-US Inc.
— Combat of Shadows. 292p. 1968. pap. 2.50 (*0-88253-056-9*) Ind-US Inc.
— The Men Who Killed Gandhi. 192p. 1981. pap. 4.50 (*0-86578-194-X*) Ind-US Inc.
— The Sea Hawk. (Orient Paperbacks Ser.). 293p. 1980. 9.95 (*0-86578-136-2*); pap. 4.95 (*0-86578-069-2*) Ind-US Inc.
Malgonkar, Manohar, jt. auth. see Scindia, Vijaya R.
Malgonkar, Monohar. A Bend in the Ganges. 382p. (C). 1981. reprint ed. pap. 4.00 (*0-88253-772-5*) Ind-US Inc.
Malgorn, G. Dictionnaire Technique Francais-Anglais (French-English Technical Dictionary) 475p. 1972. 105.00 (*0-7859-4831-7*) Fr & Eur.
— English-French Technical Dictionary. 490p. 1976. 91.00 (*2-04-002959-1*) IBD Ltd.
— English-Spanish Technical Dictionary. Rodriguez, M. R. & Armisen, P., trs. 606p. (ENG & SPA.). 1991. 39.00 (*84-283-0923-X*) IBD Ltd.
— French-English Technical Dictionary. 471p. 1975. 91.00 (*2-04-002947-8*) IBD Ltd.
— Spanish-English Dictionary. 4th ed. Rodriguez, M. R. & Armisen, P., trs. 570p. (ENG & SPA.). 1990. 39.00 (*84-283-1354-7*) IBD Ltd.
— Spanish-English Technical Dictionary. 4th ed. (ENG & SPA.). 1990. 39.00 (*0-7859-8966-8*) Fr & Eur.
Malgorn, Guy. Diccionario Tecnico Espanol-Frances: Spanish-French Technical Dictionary. deluxe ed. (FRE & SPA.). 1979. write for info. (*0-8288-4782-7*, S50241) Fr & Eur.
— Diccionario Tecnico Espanol-Ingles. 5th ed. 576p. (ENG & SPA.). 1990. pap. write for info. (*0-7859-4906-2*) Fr & Eur.
— Diccionario Tecnico Ingles-Espanol. 7th ed. 632p. (ENG & SPA.). 1991. pap. 34.95 (*0-7859-3715-3*, 842830923X) Fr & Eur.
— Dictionaire Technique Francais-Espagnol. 2nd ed. 544p. (FRE & SPA.). 1974. 69.95 (*0-8288-6000-9*, M6387) Fr & Eur.
— Dictionnaire Technique Anglais-Francais. 495p. (ENG & FRE.). 1976. 89.95 (*0-8288-5657-5*, M6385) Fr & Eur.
Malgrange, B. Equations Differentielles a Coefficients Polynomiaux. (Progress in Mathematics Ser.: Vol. 96). viii, 232p. 1991. 49.50 (*0-8176-3556-4*) Spr-Verlag.
Malhan, S. Indian Cookery. 143p. 1977. 7.95 (*0-318-36292-9*) Asia Bk Corp.
Malherbe. Oeuvres. 1128p. 35.95 (*0-686-56536-3*) Fr & Eur.
— Oeuvres: Poesies - Lettres. (FRE.). 1971. lib. bdg. 89.95 (*0-8288-3551-9*, F39530) Fr & Eur.
Malherbe, Abraham. Paul & the Thessalonians: The Philosophic Tradition of Pastoral Care. LC 86-45918. 144p. 1987. 12.00 (*0-8006-1963-3*, 1-1963) Augsburg Fortress.
Malherbe, Abraham, tr. Gregory of Nyssa: The Life of Moses. LC 78-56352. (Classics of Western Spirituality Ser.). (Illus.). 1988. pap. 19.95 (*0-8091-2112-3*) Paulist Pr.
Malherbe, Abraham J. Ancient Epistolary Theorists. LC 87-9565. (Society of Biblical Literature Ser.). 98p. 1988. pap. 18.95 (*1-55540-247-X*, 06 03 19) Scholars Pr GA.
— The Cynic Epistles: A Study Edition. LC 77-21619. (Society for Biblical Literature. Sources for Biblical Study Ser.: No. 12). 342p. reprint ed. pap. 97.50 (*0-7837-5447-7*, 2045212) Bks Demand.
— Moral Exhortation, a Greco-Roman Sourcebook. LC 86-5499. (Library of Early Christianity: Vol. 4). 178p. (C). 1986. pap. 12.99 (*0-664-25016-5*, Westminster) Westminster John Knox.
— Paul & the Popular Philosophers. LC 89-36042. 208p. 1989. 25.00 (*0-8006-2410-6*, 1-2410) Augsburg Fortress.
— Social Aspects of Early Christianity. 2nd rev. ed. LC 83-5602. 144p. 1983. reprint ed. pap. 10.00 (*0-8006-1748-7*, 1-1748, Fortress Pr) Augsburg Fortress.
— The World of the New Testament. LC 68-5578. 1984. 12.95 (*0-915547-16-3*) Abilene Christ U.
Malherbe, Abraham J. & Meeks, Wayne A., eds. The Future of Christology: Essays in Honor of Leander E. Keck. LC 92-40265. 288p. 1993. 37.00 (*0-8006-2728-8*, 1-2728, Fortress Pr) Augsburg Fortress.
Malherbe, Ernest G. The Bilingual School. Cordasco, Francesco, ed. LC 77-90547. (Bilingual-Bicultural Education in the U. S. Ser.). 1978. reprint ed. lib. bdg. 19.95 (*0-405-11086-3*) Ayer.
Malherbe, H. H. Viral Cytopathology. 112p. 1980. 98.95 (*0-8493-5567-2*, RC114) CRC Pr.
Malherbe, J. A. Microwave Transmission Line Couplers. LC 88-19338. (Artech House Microwave Library). 231p. reprint ed. pap. 65.90 (*0-7837-3018-7*, 2042922) Bks Demand.
Malherbe, J. A. G. Microwave Transmission Line Filters. LC 78-31243. (Illus.). 352p. reprint ed. pap. 100.40 (*0-8357-5589-4*, 2035220) Bks Demand.
Malhos, Georges, ed. see Voltaire, Francois-Marie de.
Malhotra, Anil K. A Survey of Asia's Energy Prices. LC 94-16612. (Technical Papers: Vol. 248). 1994. write for info. (*0-8213-2860-3*) World Bank.
***Malhotra, Anil K., et al.** The Performance of Asia's Energy Sector, 257. LC 94-30388. (Technical Paper Ser.). 1994. write for info. (*0-8213-3016-0*) World Bank.
Malhotra, Ashok, jt. auth. see Shrader, Douglas W.
Malhotra, D. & Hancock, B. A., eds. Reagents for Better Metallurgy. LC 93-86997. (Illus.). 365p. (Orig.). 1994. pap. 60.00 (*0-87335-128-2*) SMM&E Inc.
Malhotra, D., et al, eds. Evaluation & Optimization of Metallurgical Performance. LC 90-63802. (Illus.). 365p. (Orig.). 1991. pap. 53.50 (*0-87335-097-9*, 979) SMM&E Inc.
***Malhotra, Deepak.** Flotation Plants: Are They Optimized? fac. ed. LC 92-62902. (Illus.). 185p. 1993. reprint ed. pap. 52.80 (*0-7837-7870-8*, 2047627) Bks Demand.
Malhotra, Deepak & Riggs, William F., eds. Chemical Reagents in the Mineral Processing Industry. LC 86-63354. 320p. reprint ed. pap. 91.20 (*0-8357-3484-6*, 2039743) Bks Demand.
Malhotra, I. J. Hindu Vivah Adhiniyam. 303p. (HIN.). 1984. 90.00 (*0-317-54876-X*) St Mut.
— Hindu Vivah Adhiniyam: (Hindu Marriage Act in Hindi) 2nd ed. (HIN.). (C). 1991. 95.00 (*0-685-39628-2*) St Mut.
— Madhyastham Adhiniyam Arbitration Act. (HIN.). (C). 1990. text ed. 60.00 (*0-89771-488-1*) St Mut.
Malhotra, I. J., ed. Hindu Vivah Adhiniyam (Hindu Marriage Act in Hindi) (C). 1991. 85.00 (*0-89771-784-8*, Pub. by Eastern Book II) St Mut.
Malhotra, Inder. Indira Gandhi: A Personal & Political Biography. 363p. 1991. text ed. 35.00 (*1-55553-095-8*) NE U Pr.
Malhotra, Kamal, jt. auth. see Clark, Janice.
Malhotra, M., jt. auth. see Arora, A.
Malhotra, M. L. Redress of Public Grievances. 1993. 30.00 (*81-207-1337-0*, Pub. by Sterling Pubs II) Apt Bks.
Malhotra, Naresh K. Marketing Research: An Applied Orientation. LC 92-13858. 1056p. 1992. text ed. 70.00 (*0-13-555350-4*) P-H.
Malhotra, Naresh K., ed. see Conference of the Academy of Marketing Science (10th, 1986, Anaheim, CA).
Malhotra, Naresh K., ed. see Conference of the Academy of Marketing Science (9th, 1985, Miami Beach, Fl).
Malhotra, O. P. The Law of Industrial Disputes. (C). 1985. 650.00 (*0-685-25683-9*) St Mut.
Malhotra, R. The Indian Islanders: An Anthropological Perspective. (C). 1989. 17.50 (*81-7099-148-X*, Pub. by Mittal II) S Asia.
Malhotra, R., ed. Anthropology of Development: Commemoration Volume in Honour of Professor I. P. Singh. (C). 1992. text ed. 37.50 (*81-7099-328-8*, Pub. by Mittal II) S Asia.
Malhotra, S. L., jt. auth. see Sharma, S. K.
***Malhotra, Sharan.** Divine Darshan. (C). 1994. 20.00 (*81-224-0677-7*, Pub. by Wiley Eastern II) S Asia.
Malhotra, Subhash C. Bibliography on Copper Smelting Nineteen-Forty to Nineteen Seventy-Three. LC 73-87447. 300p. 1973. 31.45 (*0-686-05581-0*) Malhotra.
Malhotra, Sudarshan, ed. Advances in Neural Science, Vol. 1. 1992. 90.25 (*1-55938-356-9*) Jai Pr.
— Advances in Structural Biology, Vol. 1. 1991. 90.25 (*1-55938-292-9*) Jai Pr.
Malhotra, V. M., et al. Condensed Silica Fume in Concrete. 256p. 1987. 217.00 (*0-8493-5657-1*, TP884) CRC Pr.
Malhotra, V. M. & Carino, Nicholas J. Handbook of Nondestructive Testing of Concrete. (Illus.). 336p. 1990. 174.95 (*0-8493-2984-1*, TA440) CRC Pr.
Malhotra, Veena. Kenya under Kenyatta. 1990. 16.00 (*81-85163-16-2*, Pub. by Kalinga) S Asia.
Malhotra, Vinay K. Contemporary Socialist Thought: A Critical Study. 1990. 54.00 (*81-7041-235-8*, Pub. by Anmol II) S Asia.
***Malhotra, Vinay K., ed.** Indo-U. S. Relations in Nineties. (C). 1995. 16.00x (*81-7488-043-7*, Pub. by Anmol II) S Asia.
Malhotra, Vinod. Anesthesia for Renal & Genito-Urologic Surgery. (Illus.). 320p. 1995. 55.00 (*0-07-039877-1*) Hlth Prof Div.
Mali, J. W., ed. Current Problems in Dermatology, Vol. 3. 1970. 66.50 (*3-8055-0484-5*) S Karger.
— Current Problems in Dermatology, Vol. 4. 1972. 77.00 (*3-8055-1248-1*) S Karger.
— Current Problems in Dermatology, Vol. 5. 1973. 71.25 (*3-8055-1380-1*) S Karger.
— Keratinization & Growth Regulation. (Current Problems in Dermatology Ser.: Vol. 6). (Illus.). 250p. 1976. 78.50 (*3-8055-2294-0*) S Karger.
— Some Fundamental Approaches in Skin Research. (Current Problems in Dermatology Ser.: Vol. 9). (Illus.). viii, 152p. 1981. pap. 78.50 (*3-8055-3080-3*) S Karger.
Mali, J. W., ed. see Oholo Biological Conference Staff.
Mali, Jane L., jt. auth. see Herzig, Alison C.
Mali, Jane L., jt. auth. see Herzig, Alison.
Mali, Joseph. The Rehabilitation of Myth: Vico's New Science. 296p. (C). 1992. 64.95 (*0-521-41952-2*) Cambridge U Pr.
Mali, Millicent S. French Faience: Fantaisie et Populaire of the Nineteenth & Twentieth Centuries. (Illus.). 136p. (Orig.). 1986. pap. 25.00 (*0-9603824-2-9*) M S Mali.
— Madame Campan: Educator of Women, Confidante of Queens. LC 78-65428. 1978. pap. text ed. 23.00 (*0-8191-0662-3*) U Pr of Amer.
Malia, Kathleen & Warycka, Sharon. Read, Write, Relate. 220p. (C). 1990. pap. text ed. 18.75 (*0-15-575483-1*) HB Coll Pubs.
Malia, Martin E. The Soviet Tragedy: A History of Socialism in Russia. 500p. 1994. 24.95 (*0-02-919795-3*) Free Pr.
Malia, S. P. Astrological Guidance to Occupations. 83p. 1983. pap. text ed. 5.95 (*0-86590-232-1*, Pub. by Taraporevala II) Apt Bks.
Malian, Ida, jt. auth. see Fox, C. Lynn.
Malibran, Maria & Grernspan, Charlotte. Album Lyrique & Dernieres Pensees. LC 83-7841. (Women Composers Ser.: No. 14). 62p. 1983. reprint ed. lib. bdg. 26.50 (*0-306-76194-7*) Da Capo.
Malick & Bell. Endorphins: Chemistry, Physiology & Clinical Relevance. (Modern Pharmacology-Toxicology Ser.: Vol. 20). 288p. 1982. pap. 140.00 (*0-8247-7201-6*) Dekker.
Malick, J., jt. ed. see Williams, M.
Malick, Jeffrey B., et al, eds. Anxiolytics: Neurochemical, Behavioral, & Clinical Perspectives. (Central Nervous System Pharmacology Set Ser.). 232p. 1983. text ed. 92.50 (*0-89004-731-6*) Raven.
Malicky, Hans, ed. Verhandlungen des Sechsten Internationalen Symposiums uber Entonomofaunistik in Mitteleuropa. 1977. pap. text ed. 103.00 (*90-6193-559-8*) Kluwer Ac.
Malicoat, Galen. Small, Honest Hollows. 32p. (Orig.). 1992. pap. 10.00 (*0-911623-11-6*) I Klang.
Malier, Y., ed. High Performance Concrete: From Material to Structure. 504p. 1992. 89.95 (*0-442-31618-6*) Chapman & Hall.
Malies, Harold. A Short History of the English Microscope, Vol. 11. LC 80-83457. (Illus.). 1981. 20.00 (*0-904962-09-1*) Microscope Pubns.
Malifa, Fata S. Alms for Oblivion. 1993. 17.95 (*0-533-10466-1*) Vantage.
***Maliga, Pal, et al.** Methods in Plant Molecular Biology: A Laboratory Course Manual. LC 94-36570. 1995. write for info. (*0-87969-450-5*) Cold Spring Harbor.
Maliga, Pat, et al, eds. Methods in Plant Molecular Biology: A Laboratory Course Manual. (Illus.). 250p. (C). 1994. pap. text ed. 75.00 (*0-87969-386-X*) Cold Spring Harbor.
Malignon, Jean. Dictionnaire des Ecrivains Francais: Dictionary of French Writers. 576p. (FRE.). 1971. 39.95 (*0-8288-6445-4*, M-6388) Fr & Eur.
— Petit Dictionnaire Rameau. 280p. (FRE.). 1983. pap. 26.95 (*0-7859-7912-3*, 2700703146) Fr & Eur.
Malik, A. India Watching: The Media Game. 149p. 1977. 14.95 (*0-318-37277-0*) Asia Bk Corp.
Malik, B. Survey Search & Seizure. (C). 1988. 375.00 (*0-685-25678-2*) St Mut.
Malik, C. P., ed. Pollen Physiology & Biotechnology. (Advances in Pollen-Spore Research Ser.: Vol. XIX). (Illus.). 196p. 1992. 65.00 (*1-55528-267-9*, Pub. by Today & Tomorrows P & P II) Scholarly Pubns.
— Recent Researches in Palynology: Hensferdinand Linskens Commemoration Volume. (Illus.). 295p. 1984. 50.00 (*1-55528-071-4*, Pub. by Today & Tomorrows P & P II) Scholarly Pubns.
Malik, Charles. A Christian Critique of the University. 118p. (C). 1987. reprint ed. lib. bdg. 16.00 (*0-921075-06-5*) N Waterloo Acad Pr.

An Asterisk (*) at the beginning of an entry indicates that the title is appearing in BIP for the first time.

Malik, Charles, ed. God & Man in Contemporary Islamic Thought. (C). 1972. 24.95 (*0-8156-6035-9*, Am U Beirut) Syracuse U Pr.
Malik, Dipak. Indian Trade Unionism in Developmental Perspective. 1989. 42.00 (*81-7169-002-5*, Pub. by Commonwealth II) S Asia.
Malik, F. B., ed. Condensed Matter Theories, Vol. 1. LC 86-9400. 354p. 1986. 125.00 (*0-306-42284-0*, Plenum Pr) Plenum.
Malik, F. B., jt. ed. see Blum, L.
***Malik, Gaafar M.** Manual of Basic Skills & Clinical Procedures in Medicine. 1994. pap. 18.95 (*0-533-10517-X*) Vantage.
Malik, Hafeez. Sir Sayyid Ahmad Khan & Muslim Modernization in India & Pakistan. LC 80-13905. (Illus.). 288p. 1980. text ed. 51.50 (*0-231-04970-6*) Col U Pr.
— Soviet-American Relations with Pakistan, Iran & Afghanistan. 480p. 1987. text ed. 45.00 (*0-312-00240-8*) St Martin.
Malik, Hafeez, ed. Central Asia: Its Strategic Importance & Future Prospects. LC 93-9083. 1994. text ed. 59.95 (*0-312-10370-0*) St Martin.
— Domestic Determinants of Soviet Foreign Policy Towards South Asia & the Middle East. LC 89-24078. 234p. 1990. text ed. 49.95 (*0-312-04022-9*) St Martin.
— International Security in Southwest Asia. LC 83-24637. 240p. 1984. text ed. 45.00 (*0-275-91222-1*, C1222, Praeger Pubs) Greenwood.
— Iqbal: Poet-Philosopher of Pakistan. LC 75-135475. (Studies in Oriental Culture: No. 7). 460p. reprint ed. pap. 131.10 (*0-317-29701-5*, 2022058) Bks Demand.
Malik, Iftikhar H. Pakistanis in Michigan: A Study of Third Culture & Acculturation. LC 88-84006. (Immigrant Communities & Ethnic Minorities in the U. S. & Canada Ser.: No. 59). 1989. 42.50 (*0-404-19469-9*) AMS Pr.
— U. S. - South Asian Relations. LC 90-34611. 290p. 1991. text ed. 65.00 (*0-312-04892-0*) St Martin.
Malik, Imam & Din, M. R. Muwata. 25.50 (*1-56744-162-9*) Kazi Pubns.
***Malik, J. Mohan, ed.** Great Powers & Regional Powers Bk. One. 173p. (C). 1992. pap. 108.00x (*0-7300-1576-9*, SSS842, Pub. by Deakin Univ AT) St Mut.
— Peace & Security Bk. Three. 96p. (C). 1993. 45.00x (*0-7300-1811-3*, Pub. by Deakin Univ AT) St Mut.
— Regional Conflicts & Security Issues Bk. Two. 263p. (C). 1993. 59.00x (*0-7300-1720-6*, Pub. by Deakin Univ AT) St Mut.
Malik, Justice. Land Acquisition Act. (C). 1990. 65.00 (*0-89771-301-X*) St Mut.
Malik, K. K. Supreme Court Rules Nineteen Sixty-Six. 119p. 1984. 90.00 (*0-317-54869-7*) St Mut.
Malik, Keshav. Between Nobodies & Stars: Stories Portraits. 1985. 11.50 (*0-8364-1490-X*, Pub. by Abhinav II) S Asia.
Malik, M. Limitation Act. (C). 1990. 50.00 (*0-89771-250-1*) St Mut.
Malik, M. A., ed. American Drug Reference. 550p. 1992. 85.00 (*0-9633782-0-1*) Am Drug Ref.
Malik, M. A., et al. Solar Distillation. 1982. 82.00 (*0-08-028679-8*, Pub. by Pergamon Repr UK) Franklin.
Malik, Miroslav, jt. auth. see Bresky, Dushan.
Malik Mueen Azhar. Bibliography of Articles on Iqbal. 64p. (Orig.). 1985. pap. 7.95 (*1-56744-233-1*) Kazi Pubns.
Malik, P. L. Arms Act, Nineteen Fifty-Nine with Rules, 1962. annot. ed. 160p. 1984. 60.00 (*0-317-54868-9*) St Mut.
— Arms Act, 1959: With Rules, 1962. 6th ed. (C). 1990. 45.00 (*0-685-39798-X*) St Mut.
— Arms Act, 1959, with Rules, 1962 (Annotated) (C). 1992. 75.00 (*0-89771-775-9*, Pub. by Eastern Book II) St Mut.
— Central Acts & Ordinances, Nineteen Seventy-Five. 518p. 1976. 180.00 (*0-317-54867-0*) St Mut.
— Commentaries on the Opium Act, 1878. 175p. 1984. 90.00 (*0-317-54866-2*) St Mut.
— Criminal Court Handbook: (Three Major Acts) 15th ed. (C). 1991. 95.00 (*0-685-39748-3*) St Mut.
— Criminal Court Handbook: Three Major Acts. 808p. 1982. 270.00 (*0-317-54865-4*) St Mut.
— Criminal Court Handbook (Minor Acts), 4 vols., Set. (C). 1991. 150.00 (*0-685-39749-1*) St Mut.
— Criminal Court Handbook (Three Major Acts) 18th ed. (C). 1992. 150.00 (*81-7012-489-1*, Pub. by Eastern Book II) St Mut.
— The Customs Act Nineteen Sixty-Two. 649p. 1982. 255.00 (*0-317-54862-X*) St Mut.
— Customs Act, Nineteen Sixty-Two. (C). 1990. 60.00 (*0-685-39355-0*) St Mut.
— Employees Provident Funds & Miscellaneous Provisions Act, 1952. (C). 1992. 60.00 (*0-89771-786-4*, Pub. by Eastern Book II) St Mut.
— Employees Provident Funds & Miscellaneous Provisions Act, 1990. (C). 1990. reprint ed. 50.00 (*0-685-39722-X*) St Mut.
— Employees Provident Funds & Miscellaneous Provisions Act, 1990: With Supplement. (C). 1990. reprint ed. 50.00 (*0-685-47804-1*) St Mut.
— Guide to Foreign Exchange Regulations. 336p. 1981. 135.00 (*0-317-54861-1*) St Mut.
— Handbook of Electricity Laws. (C). 1992. 100.00 (*0-89771-781-3*, Pub. by Eastern Book II) St Mut.
— Handbook of Labour & Industrial Law. 1985. 65.00 (*0-317-56713-6*) St Mut.
— Handbook of Labour & Industrial Law. 4th ed. (C). 1990. 120.00 (*0-685-39653-3*) St Mut.
— Handbook of Labour & Industrial Laws. (C). 1993. 200.00 (*0-7855-0171-1*, Pub. by Eastern Book II) St Mut.
— Handbook of Labour & Industrial Laws. 5th ed. (C). 1993. 100.00 (*81-7012-502-2*, Pub. by Eastern Book II) St Mut.
— Indian Stamp Act (As Applicable in the State of Uttar Pradesh) Alongwith Registration Act (As Applicable in the State of Uttar Pradesh) 3rd ed. (C). 1993. 50.00 (*81-7012-521-9*, Pub. by Eastern Book II) St Mut.
— Indian Stamp Act, 1899 & Indian Registration Act, 1908: (As Applicable in Uttar Pradesh) (C). 1988. 150.00 (*0-685-44304-3*) St Mut.
— Indian Stamp Act, 1899 (As Applicable to U. P.) With Supplement, 1990. (C). 1990. 55.00 (*0-685-39549-9*) St Mut.
— Indian Stamp Act, 1899 (As Applicable to U. P.), 1988. (C). 1990. 55.00 (*0-685-39548-0*) St Mut.
— Industrial Law. 1774p. 1985. 675.00 (*0-317-54859-X*) St Mut.
— Industrial Law. (C). 1990. 400.00 (*0-685-37432-7*); 200.00 (*0-89771-325-7*); text ed. 400.00 (*0-89771-489-X*) St Mut.
— Industrial Law. (C). 1992. 480.00 (*0-7855-0168-1*, Pub. by Eastern Book II) St Mut.
— Industrial Law. 15th ed. (C). 1990. reprint ed. 400.00 (*0-685-39652-5*) St Mut.
— Industrial Law, 1989. 15th ed. (C). 1990. 400.00 (*0-685-39674-6*) St Mut.
— Industries Development & Regulation Act, 1951. 1985. 65.00 (*0-317-56715-2*) St Mut.
— Industries Development & Regulation Act, 1951. (C). 1991. 95.00 (*0-685-39673-8*) St Mut.
— Intermediate Education Act, Nineteen Twenty-One: Together with Amending Acts Regulations & Notifications. 173p. 1982. 75.00 (*0-317-54858-1*) St Mut.
— Labour Laws in U. P. 3rd ed. (C). 1985. 330.00 (*0-685-39658-4*) St Mut.
— Law of Motor Vehicles in U. P. 820p. 1984. 300.00 (*0-685-17750-5*) St Mut.
— The Law Relating to Forests in Uttar Pradesh. 206p. 1984. 110.00 (*0-317-54855-7*) St Mut.
— Law Relating to Weights & Measures. (C). 1991. 125.00 (*0-89771-794-5*, Pub. by Eastern Book II) St Mut.
— Minimum Wages Act. 1985. 120.00 (*0-317-54853-0*) St Mut.
— U. P. Excise Act, 1910: Together with Rules & Notifications. 4th ed. (C). 1991. 95.00 (*0-685-39707-6*) St Mut.
— U. P. Police Regulations. 4th ed. (C). 1991. 95.00 (*0-685-39586-3*) St Mut.
— U. P. Sales Tax Act, Nineteen Forty-Eight: Together with Rules & Notifications. 220p. 1985. 108.00 (*0-317-54852-2*) St Mut.
— U. P. Sales Tax Act, 1948: Together with Rules & Notifications with Supplement. 8th ed. (C). 1990. 65.00 (*0-685-39565-0*) St Mut.
— U.P. Sales Tax Act, 1948, Together with Rules & Notifications. 8th ed. (C). 1989. 33.00 (*0-685-38630-9*) St Mut.
Malik, P. L., ed. Commentaries on Opium Act, 1878: With U. P. Opium Rules, 1961, U. P. Poppy-Head Rules, 1961 & U. P. Opium Smoking Act & Rules. (C). 1984. 40.00 (*0-685-39600-2*) St Mut.
— Customs Act, 1962. 3rd ed. (C). 1990. 105.00 (*0-685-39741-6*) St Mut.
— Employees Provident Funds & Miscellaneous Provisions Act, 1952. (C). 1989. 40.00 (*0-685-38622-8*) St Mut.
— Guide to Foreign Exchange Regulations. 2nd ed. (C). 1991. 95.00 (*0-685-39701-7*) St Mut.
— Industrial Law. 15th ed. (C). 1989. 400.00 (*0-685-36442-9*) St Mut.
— Intermediate Education Act, 1921: Together with Amending Acts, Regulation & Notifications, 1982 with Supplement. (C). 1988. 30.00 (*0-685-39725-4*) St Mut.
— Law of Electricity in U. P. 3rd ed. (C). 1991. 110.00 (*0-685-39723-8*) St Mut.
— Minimum Wages Act with Central & U. P. Rules & Notification Fixing Minimum Wages in Various Industries & Establishments. 7th ed. (C). 1991. 95.00 (*0-685-39622-3*) St Mut.
— Minimum Wages Act with Central & U.P. Rules & Notifications Fixing Minimum Wages in Various Industries & Establishments. (C). 1987. 40.00 (*0-685-38623-6*) St Mut.
— U. P. Industrial Disputes Act, 1947: With Rules & Notifications. (C). 1991. 95.00 (*0-685-39651-7*) St Mut.
Malik, P. L., jt. auth. see Nath, B.
Malik, P. L., jt. auth. see Nath, Bholeshwar.
Malik, P. L., jt. auth. see Saxena, R. P.
Malik, R. J. III-V Semiconductors Materials Devices Materials Processing: Theory & Practices, Vol. 7. 1990. 223.00 (*0-444-87074-1*, HPT V.7) Elsevier.
Malik, S. Comparative Tables of Supreme Court Cases, 1950-1985. 1986. 65.00 (*0-317-56721-7*) St Mut.
— The Complete Digest of Supreme Court Cases (1950 to Date), 16 vols. (C). 1989. Vol I to XIV published. 2,100.00 (*0-685-27878-6*) St Mut.
Malik, S., ed. The Complete Supreme Court Criminal Digest, 1950 to June 1987, 7 vols. (C). 1989. 660.00 (*0-685-27879-4*) St Mut.
— Supreme Court Labour & Service Digest (1950-1986), 4 vols. (C). 1989. 400.00 (*0-685-27880-8*) St Mut.
Malik, S. B. & Mehra, R. K. Principles & Digest of the Arbitration Law. (C). 1990. 120.00 (*0-89771-249-8*) St Mut.
Malik, S. C. Indian Civilization: The Formative Period: A Study of Archaeology & the Anthropology. 204p. (C). 1987. reprint ed. 14.00 (*81-208-0328-0*) S Asia.
— Indian Movements: Some Aspects of Dissent Protest & Reform. 296p. 1978. 14.95 (*0-940500-67-1*, Pub. by Indian Inst Comm II) Asia Bk Corp.
— Modern Civilization: A Crisis of Fragmentation. (C). 1989. 22.50 (*81-7017-255-1*, Pub. by Abhinav II) S Asia.
Malik, S. C., ed. Determinants of Social Status in India. xi, 192p. 1986. 22.00 (*81-208-0073-7*, Pub. by Motilal Banarsidass II) S Asia.
Malik, S. C. & Arora, Savita. Mathematical Analysis. 2nd ed. 1992. text ed. 68.95 (*0-470-21858-4*) Halsted Pr.
Malik, S. C., ed. see Freidman, Maurice.
Malik, S. K. The Quranic Concept of War. 195p. (C). 1986. 95.00 (*81-7002-020-4*, Pub. by Himalayan Bks II) St Mut.
Malik, S. K. & Shah, S. S., eds. Physical & Material Properties of High Temperature Superconductors. (Illus.). 711p. (C). 1994. lib. bdg. 145.00 (*1-56072-114-6*) Nova Sci Pubs.
Malik, S. K., jt. auth. see Graham, G. A.
Malik, S. K., jt. ed. see Gupta, L. C.
Malik, S. Surendra. Supreme Court on Preventive Detention from 1950 to Present. 478p. 1985. 270.00 (*0-317-54842-5*) St Mut.
Malik, Sharad, jt. ed. see Meng, Teresa H.
Malik, Shashi. CSP: A Developer's Guide. 1992. text ed. write for info. (*0-07-039780-5*) McGraw.
Malik, Shashi & Yamauchi, Henry. CSP: A Developer's Guide. LC 92-11092. 1992. text ed. 45.00 (*0-07-039825-9*) McGraw.
Malik, Surendra. Commentaries of U. P. Nagar Mahapalika Act, 1959. 818p. 1985. 345.00 (*0-317-54839-5*) St Mut.
— Commentaries on U. P. Municipalities Act, 1916. 866p. 1984. 360.00 (*0-317-54838-7*) St Mut.
— Commentaries on U. P. Municipalities Act, 1916. (C). 1989. 205.00 (*0-685-39616-9*) St Mut.
— Commentaries on U. P. Municipalities Act, 1984: With Supplement. (C). 1989. reprint ed. 200.00 (*0-685-39621-5*) St Mut.
— Commentaries on U. P. Nagar Mahapalika Adhiniyam, 1959. 5th ed. (C). 1989. 135.00 (*0-685-39611-8*) St Mut.
— Commentaries on U. P. Panchayar Raj Act, 1948. 2nd ed. (C). 1991. 100.00 (*0-685-39599-5*) St Mut.
— Complete Digest of Supreme Court Cases, 16 vols. (C). 1991. Vols. 1-14. 135.00 (*0-318-69177-9*) St Mut.
— Complete Digest of Supreme Court Cases, 16 vols., 15. (C). 1991. 150.00 (*0-685-54753-1*) St Mut.
— Complete Digest of Supreme Court Cases, 16 vols., 16. (C). 1991. 175.00 (*0-89771-692-2*) St Mut.
— The Complete Digest of Supreme Court Cases, 13 vols., Set. 9100p. (C). 1987. 1,235.00 (*0-685-25173-X*) St Mut.
— The Complete Digest of Supreme Court Cases, Vol. XVI. (C). 1991. text ed. 175.00 (*0-685-52020-X*) St Mut.
— The Complete Digest of Supreme Court Cases (Since 1950), Vol. XV. (C). 1991. 150.00 (*0-685-39737-8*) St Mut.
— The Complete Digest of Supreme Court Cases, 1950 to Present, Vol. XIV. 700p. 1987. 125.00 (*0-317-54851-4*) St Mut.
— The Complete Supreme Court Criminal Digest - Second Cumulative Supplement (July 1987 to Dec. 1990) (C). 1991. text ed. 125.00 (*0-89771-494-6*) St Mut.
— The Complete Supreme Court Criminal Digest, 1950 to Present, 8 vols., Set. 800p. 1991. 595.00 (*0-317-54849-2*) St Mut.
— The Complete Supreme Court Criminal Digest, 1950 up to Date, Set, Vols. I, II, III-A, III-B, IV & V. (C). 1987. Set. 660.00 (*0-685-37420-3*) St Mut.
— The Complete Supreme Court Criminal Digest, 1950 up to 1990 with 1st & 2nd Supplements, Set. (C). 1991. text ed. 950.00 (*0-89771-493-8*) St Mut.
— The Complete Supreme Court Labour & Services Digest, 4 vols., Set. (C). 1987. 360.00 (*0-685-25174-8*) St Mut.
— Fundamental Rights Case, 1951-1973. 1078p. 1973. 145.00 (*0-317-54848-4*) St Mut.
— Laws of Preventive Detention - Past & Present. (C). 1988. 59.00 (*0-685-22634-4*) St Mut.
— Supreme Court Decennial Digest 1981-1990, Vol. I. (C). 1993. 180.00 (*81-7012-505-7*, Pub. by Eastern Book II) St Mut.
— Supreme Court Decennial Digest 1981-1990, Vol. II. (C). 1993. 180.00 (*81-7012-515-4*, Pub. by Eastern Book II) St Mut.
— Supreme Court Decennial Digest 1981-1990, Vol. III. (C). 1993. 180.00 (*81-7012-519-7*, Pub. by Eastern Book II) St Mut.
— Supreme Court Judgement on Prime Minister's Election Case. 283p. 1975. 75.00 (*0-317-54841-7*) St Mut.
— Supreme Court Labour & Services Digest, Vol. V. (C). 1991. 95.00 (*0-685-39657-6*) St Mut.
— Supreme Court Labour & Services Digest: 1987-1990. (C). 1991. 200.00 (*0-89771-700-7*) St Mut.
— Supreme Court Labour & Services Digest, 1950-1982, 3 vols. 1532p. 1983. 750.00 (*0-317-54846-8*) St Mut.
— Supreme Court Labour & Services Digest, 1950-1989, 5 vols., Set, Vols. I-IV. (C). 1991. Set. 400.00 (*0-685-39644-4*) St Mut.
— Supreme Court Mandal Commission Case 1992. (C). 1993. 62.50 (*81-7012-498-0*, Pub. by Eastern Book II) St Mut.
— Supreme Court on Essential Commodities Act, 1955. 161p. 1984. 120.00 (*0-317-54843-3*) St Mut.
— Supreme Court on Hindu Law. 247p. 1977. 110.00 (*0-317-54845-X*) St Mut.
— Supreme Court on Interpretation of Statutes. (C). 1977. 35.00 (*0-685-39669-X*) St Mut.
— Supreme Court on Law of Limitation, 1950-1979. 226p. 1981. 75.00 (*0-317-54844-1*) St Mut.
— Supreme Court on Law of Limitation, 1950-1979. (C). 1981. 40.00 (*0-685-39630-4*) St Mut.
— Supreme Court on Preventive Detention, 1950- (C). 1991. 95.00 (*0-685-39581-2*) St Mut.
— Supreme Court on Preventive Detention (1950 up to Date) (C). 1991. 95.00 (*0-685-39730-0*) St Mut.
— Supreme Court on Rent Control & Eviction. (C). 1992. 200.00 (*0-89771-792-9*, Pub. by Eastern Book II); 100.00 (*81-7012-471-9*, Pub. by Eastern Book II) St Mut.
— Supreme Court on Words & Phrases. (C). 1993. 140.00 (*81-7012-510-3*, Pub. by Eastern Book II) St Mut.
— Supreme Court Yearly Digest for 1982. (C). 1983. 55.00 (*0-685-39735-1*) St Mut.
— Supreme Court Yearly Digest for 1985. (C). 1986. 100.00 (*0-685-39734-3*) St Mut.
— Supreme Court Yearly Digest for 1986. (C). 1987. 100.00 (*0-685-39732-7*) St Mut.
— Supreme Court Yearly Digest for 1991. (C). 1992. 320.00 (*0-89771-780-5*, Pub. by Eastern Book II) St Mut.
— Supreme Court Yearly Digest for 1992. (C). 1993. 180.00 (*81-7012-500-6*, Pub. by Eastern Book II) St Mut.
— Supreme Court Yearly Digest, 1989. (C). 1990. 175.00 (*0-685-36438-0*) St Mut.
— Supreme Court Yearly Digest, 1990. (C). 1990. 110.00 (*0-89771-329-X*) St Mut.
— Supreme Court Yearly Digest, 1990. (C). 1991. text ed. 220.00 (*0-89771-491-1*) St Mut.
— U. P. Consolidation of Holdings Act. 250p. 1980. 82.50 (*0-317-54837-9*) St Mut.
— U. P. Consolidation of Holdings Act, 1953: Together with Exhaustive Commentaries, Notifications & Rules. (C). 1991. 95.00 (*0-685-39776-9*) St Mut.
— Yearly Digest of Supreme Court Criminal Cases. 1988. 80.00 (*0-317-54840-9*) St Mut.
Malik, Surendra, ed. The Complete Digest of Supreme Court Cases (Since 1950), Vol. XVI. (C). 1991. 110.00 (*0-685-39736-X*) St Mut.
— The Complete Digest of Supreme Court Cases (Since 1950), Vols. I-XIV. (C). 1991. 135.00 (*0-685-74318-7*) St Mut.
— The Complete Supreme Court Criminal Digest, 1950 up to Date: With Supplement, 1987 Vol., 6 vols., Set, Vols. I, II, III-A, III-B, IV & V. (C). 1990. Set. 660.00 (*0-685-39731-9*) St Mut.
— Supreme Court Labour & Services Digest, 1950-1989, 5 vols., Set. (C). 1989. 200.00 (*0-685-38609-0*) St Mut.
— Supreme Court Labour & Services Digest, 1950-1989, 5 vols., V. (C). 1989. write for info. (*0-318-68183-8*) St Mut.
— Supreme Court Labour & Services Digest, 1950-1989, 5 vols., Vol. III, 1979-1982. (C). 1989. 40.00 (*0-685-38607-4*) St Mut.
— Supreme Court Labour & Services Digest, 1950-1989, 5 vols., Vol. IV, 1983-1986. (C). 1989. 40.00 (*0-685-38608-2*) St Mut.
— Supreme Court Labour & Services Digest, 1950-1989, 5 vols., Vols. I & II, 1950-1978. (C). 1989. 130.00 (*0-685-38606-6*) St Mut.
— Supreme Court Labour & Services Digest (1987-1990), Vol. V. (C). 1991. text ed. 160.00 (*0-89771-490-3*) St Mut.
— Supreme Court on Essential Commodities Act, 1984: With Supplement. (C). 1987. reprint ed. 45.00 (*0-685-39714-9*) St Mut.
— Supreme Court on Tenancy & Land Laws: 1950-1990. (C). 1991. 135.00 (*0-89771-682-5*) St Mut.
— Supreme Court Yearly Digest for 1988. (C). 1989. 140.00 (*0-685-39733-5*) St Mut.
Malik, Syed A. Tale of a Nomadic Soul. (C). 1990. text ed. 19.50 (*81-7018-584-X*, Pub. by BR Pub II) S Asia.
Malik, Uzir A., jt. auth. see Choudhury, Masudul A.
Malik, V. S. & Sridhar, P. Industrial Biotechnology. 633p. 1992. 88.00 (*1-881570-04-5*) Intl Sci Pub.
Malik, Vedpal S. & Lillehoj, Erik P., eds. Antibody Techniques: A Guide for Nonimmunologists. (Illus.). 353p. 1994. pap. 44.95 (*0-12-466460-1*) Acad Pr.
Malik, Vijay. The Banking Regulation Act Nineteen Forty-Nine. 163p. 1984. 90.00 (*0-317-54836-0*) St Mut.
— Criminal Manual. 550p. 1983. 125.00 (*0-317-54611-2*) St Mut.
— Dand Vidhi Nirdeshika. 561p. 1985. 90.00 (*0-317-54607-4*) St Mut.
— Dand Vidhi Nirdeshika: (Three Major Acts in Hindi) Pocket Edition. (HIN.). (C). 1990. 42.00 (*0-685-39745-9*) St Mut.
— Dand Vidhi Nirdeshika (Three Major Acts in Hindi) (C). 1992. 55.00 (*0-89771-777-5*, Pub. by Eastern Book II) St Mut.
— Dandniya Manual: (Three Major Acts, Cr.P.C., I.PC. & Evidence in Hindi) (HIN.). (C). 1990. 90.00 (*0-685-39746-7*) St Mut.
— Dandniya Manual: Three Major Acts in Hindi. 550p. 1983. 135.00 (*0-317-54608-2*) St Mut.
— Drugs & Cosmetics Act, Nineteen Forty. 447p. 1984. 195.00 (*0-317-54604-X*) St Mut.
— Drugs & Cosmetics Act, 1940 Together with Drugs & Cosmetics Rules, 1945, Drugs (Price Control) Order, 1987. (C). 1993. 100.00 (*81-7012-514-6*, Pub. by Eastern Book II) St Mut.
— Drugs & Cosmetics Act, 1940 with Drugs & Cosmetics Rules, 1945, Drugs, Prices Control Order, 1987 & Notifications & Short Notes. (C). 1990. 63.00 (*0-89771-321-4*) St Mut.
— Handbook on Environment & Pollution Control Law. 2nd ed. (C). 1991. 95.00 (*0-685-39583-9*) St Mut.
— Handbook on Environment & Pollution Control Laws. 2nd ed. (C). 1991. 95.00 (*0-685-39718-1*) St Mut.
— The Indian Explosives Act, Eighteen Eighty-Four & Explosive Rules, 1983 Together with Explosive Substances Act, 1908, Gas Cylinders Rules, 1981 & Static & Mobile Pressure Vessels (Unfired) Rules, 1981. 5th ed. (C). 1989. 60.00 (*0-685-37419-X*) St Mut.
— The Indian Explosives Act, 1884 & Explosive Rules, 1983. 255p. 1984. 120.00 (*0-317-54599-X*) St Mut.
— Law for Cinemas & Videos. (C). 1990. 45.00 (*0-685-38602-3*); text ed. 95.00 (*0-89771-495-4*) St Mut.
— Law Relating to Banking & Financial Institutions. (C). 1989. 135.00 (*0-685-39795-5*) St Mut.
— Muslim Law of Marriage, Divorce & Maintenance. 2nd ed. (C). 1988. 60.00 (*0-685-39612-6*) St Mut.

M

An Asterisk (*) at the beginning of an entry indicates that the title is appearing in BIP for the first time.

— National Security Act, 1980. (C). 1991. 110.00 (*0-89771-688-4*) St Mut.
— National Security Act, 1980 along with Other Laws on Preventive Detention - Past & Present. (C). 1991. text ed. 110.00 (*0-89771-496-2*) St Mut.
— Tax on Luxuries in Hotels in U. P. 40p. 1975. 60.00 (*0-317-54595-7*) St Mut.
— Tax on Luxuries in Hotels in U. P. 2nd ed. (C). 1991. 95. 00 (*0-685-39629-0*) St Mut.
— U. P. Land Records Manual. 138p. 1975. 50.00 (*0-317-54592-2*) St Mut.
— Water (Prevention & Control of Pollution) Act, 1974. 2nd ed. (C). 1991. 95.00 (*0-685-39522-7*) St Mut.
Malik, Vijay, ed. Criminal Manual: (Three Major Acts, CRP.C., I.P.C. & Evidence in English) (C). 1990. 90.00 (*0-685-39747-5*) St Mut.
— Indian Explosives Act, 1884 & Explosives Rules, 1983: Together with Explosive Substances Act, 1908, Gas Cylinders Rules, 1981 & Static & Mobile Pressure Vessels (Unfired) Rules, 1981. 5th ed. (C). 1990. 60.00 (*0-685-39706-8*) St Mut.
— Indian Explosives Act, 1984. 1993. 60.00 (*81-7012-520-0*) St Mut.
— Railway Property, Unlawful Possession Act, 1966: Together with R. P. F. Act & Rules. 2nd ed. (C). 1991. 90.00 (*0-89771-687-6*) St Mut.
Malik, Vijay, tr. see Shukla, V. M.
Malik, Vijay, tr. see Shukla, V. M., ed.
Malik, Yogendra. South Asian Intellectuals & Social Change. 1982. 24.00 (*0-8364-0825-X*); 15.00 (*0-686-81181-X*) S Asia.
Malik, Yogendra, ed. Boeings & Bullock Carts: Studies in Change & Continuity in Indian Civilization: Essays in Honour of K. Ishwaran Vol. 1: India Culture & Society. 1990. 42.00 (*81-7001-063-2*, Pub. by Chanakya II) S Asia.
Malik, Yogendra & Marquette, Jesse. Political Mercenaries & Citizen Soldiers: A Profile of North Indian Party Activists. 1990. 24.50 (*81-7001-081-0*, Pub. by Chanakya II) S Asia.
Malik, Yogendra & Vajpeyi, Dhirendra, eds. Boeings & Bullock-Carts Vol. 3: Law Politics & Society in India. (C). 1990. text ed. 34.00 (*81-7001-065-9*, Pub. by Chanakya II) S Asia.
***Malik, Yogendra K. & Singh, V. B.** Hindu Nationalists in India: The Rise of the Bharatiya Janata Party. LC 94-23352. (C). 1994. pap. text ed. 39.95 (*0-8133-8810-4*) Westview.
Malik, Yogendra K. & Vajpeyi, Dhirendra K., eds. India: The Years of Indira Gandhi. (International Studies in Sociology & Social Anthropology: Vol. 47). vi, 148p. (Orig.). 1988. pap. 31.00 (*90-04-08681-1*) E J Brill.
Malik, Yogendra K., jt. ed. see Vajpeyi, Dhirendra.
Malikin, G., jt. ed. see Lam, S.
Malik's Chief Justice. The Art of Lawyer. (C). 1988. 65.00 (*0-685-25710-X*) St Mut.
Malim, Julia, jt. auth. see Jenkin-Pearce, Susie.
Malin, David. A View of the Universe. LC 92-46469. (Illus.). 288p. (C). 1993. 39.95 (*0-521-44477-2*) Cambridge U Pr.
— A View of the Universe. (Illus.). 292p. 1993. 39.95 (*0-933346-66-2*) Sky Pub.
Malin, Edward. Totem Poles of the Pacific Northwest Coast. (Illus.). 195p. 1994. pap. 19.95 (*0-88192-295-1*) Timber.
— A World of Faces: Masks of the Northwest Coast Indians. LC 77-26786. (Illus.). 160p. 1994. pap. 17.95 (*0-917304-05-5*) Timber.
***Malin, Edyth L. & Tunick, Michael H., eds.** Chemistry of Structure-Function Relationships in Cheese: Proceedings of ACS Symposium Held in Chicago, Illinois, August 23-25, 1993. (Advances in Experimental Medicine & Biology Ser.: Vol. 367). 385p. 1995. 95.00 (*0-306-44982-X*) Plenum.
Malin, Fran & Sranzi, Richard, eds. Information America: Sources of Print & Non-Print Materials from Organizations, Industry & Government Agencies & Specialized Publishers. 2nd ed. 900p. 1993. text ed. 150. 00 (*1-55570-078-0*) Neal-Schuman.
Malin, Irving. Nathanael West's Novels. LC 75-188697. (Crosscurrents-Modern Critiques Ser.). 152p. 1972. 7.95 (*0-8093-0577-1*) S Ill U Pr.
— William Faulkner: An Interpretation. LC 76-165664. 109p. 1972. reprint ed. 35.00 (*0-87752-154-9*) Gordian.
Malin, James. John Brown & the Legend of Fifty-Six, 2 vols., Set. LC 70-117588. (Studies in History & Culture: No. 54). 1970. reprint ed. lib. bdg. 150.00 (*0-8383-1021-4*) M S G Haskell Hse.
Malin, James C. Doctors, Devils & the Woman: Fort Scott, Kansas 1870-1890. 122p. 1975. 8.50 (*0-87291-074-1*) Coronado Pr.
— The Grassland of North America: Prolegomena to Its History. 1967. 13.25 (*0-8446-1296-0*) Peter Smith.
— History & Ecology: Studies of the Grassland. Swierenga, Robert P., ed. LC 83-16951. xxx, 376p. 1984. pap. 14.95 (*0-8032-8125-0*) U of Nebr Pr.
— Ironquil-Paint Creek Essays. 183p. 1972. 7.50 (*0-87291-025-3*) Coronado Pr.
— The United States after the World War. LC 77-37897. (Select Bibliographies Reprint Ser.). 1977. reprint ed. 31. 95 (*0-8369-6735-6*) Ayer.
Malin, Karl S. & Valentich, John D., eds. Functional Epithelial Cells in Culture. (Modern Cell Biology Ser.: Vol. 8). 300p. 1989. text ed. 149.95 (*0-471-50810-1*) Wiley.
Malin, Margot E., jt. auth. see Northrup, Herbert R.
Malin, Martin H. Individual Rights Within the Union. 740p. 1987. text ed. 88.00 (*0-87179-537-X*, 0537) BNA.
Malin, Nigel. Services for People with Learning Disabilities. LC 94-5049. 256p. 1994. 65.00x (*0-415-09937-4*, B4665); pap. 22.95 (*0-415-09938-2*, B4669) Routledge.
Malin, Nigel, ed. Reassessing Community Care. (C). 1987. 57.50 (*0-7099-1738-4*, Pub. by Croom Helm UK) Routledge Chapman & Hall.
Malin, Nigel A., ed. Implementing Community Care. LC 93-42337. (C). 1994. write for info. (*0-335-15739-4*, Open Univ Pr); pap. write for info. (*0-335-15738-6*, Open Univ Pr) Taylor & Francis.
Malin, S., jt. auth. see Carmeli, Moshe.
Malin, Stuart. The Greenwich Guide to Stars, Galaxies & Nebulae. (Greenwich Guides to Astronomy Ser.). (Illus.). 96p. (C). 1990. pap. 10.95 (*0-521-37777-3*) Cambridge U Pr.
— The Greenwich Guide to the Planets. (Greenwich Guides to Astronomy Ser.). (Illus.). 96p. (C). 1990. pap. 10.95 (*0-521-37776-5*) Cambridge U Pr.
— Story of the Earth. LC 90-11019. (Exploring the Universe Ser.). (Illus.). 32p. (J). (gr. 4-6). 1991. lib. bdg. 11.89 (*0-8167-2134-3*); pap. text ed. 3.95 (*0-8167-2135-1*) Troll Assocs.
Malina, Bruce J. The New Testament World: Insights from Cultural Anthropology. rev. ed. 224p. 1993. pap. 14.99 (*0-664-25456-X*) Westminster John Knox.
— On the Genre & Message of Revelation: Star Visions & Sky Journeys. 350p. 1995. 19.95 (*1-56563-040-8*) Hendrickson MA.
— Windows on the World of Jesus: Time Travel to Ancient Judea. LC 93-10360. 208p. (Orig.). 1993. pap. 12.99 (*0-664-25457-8*) Westminster John Knox.
Malina, Bruce J. & Neyrey, Jerome H. Calling Jesus Names: The Social Value of Labels in Matthew. LC 88-5821. (Foundations & Facets: Social Facets Ser.). 192p. 1988. pap. 15.95 (*0-944344-05-4*) Polebridge Pr.
Malina, Bruce J. & Rohrbaugh, Richard L. Social-Science Commentary on the Synoptic Gospels. LC 92-359. 432p. 1992. pap. 22.00 (*0-8006-2562-5*, 1-2562, Fortress Pr) Augsburg Fortress.
Malina, Bruce J., jt. auth. see Pilch, John J.
Malina, Frank J. Applied Sciences Research & Utilization of Lunar Resources. 1970. 89.00 (*0-08-015565-0*, Pub. by Pergamon Repr UK) Franklin.
— Life Sciences Research & Lunar Medicine: Proceedings of the 2nd Lunar International Laboratory Symposium Madrid 10-66. LC 66-24187. 1967. 61.00 (*0-08-012526-3*, Pub. by Pergamon Repr UK) Franklin.
— Research in Physics & Chemistry. 1969. 70.00 (*0-08-013400-9*, Pub. by Pergamon Repr UK) Franklin.
Malina, Frank J., ed. Visual Art, Mathematics & Computers: Selections from the Journal Leonardo. 1979. 140.00 (*0-08-021854-7*, Pub. by Pergamon Repr UK) Franklin.
Malina, Joseph F., Jr., ed. Environmental Engineering. 936p. 1989. pap. text ed. 80.00 (*0-87262-711-X*, 711) Am Soc Civil Eng.
Malina, Joseph F., Jr. & Pohland, Frederick G., eds. Design of Anaerobic Processes for the Treatment of Industrial & Municipal Wastes. LC 92-53523. (Water Quality Management Library: Vol. 7). 200p. 1992. text ed. 75.00 (*0-87762-942-0*) Technomic.
Malina, Joshua. Nutshell Classics: The Haunted House. 1988. pap. text ed. 80.00 (*0-938735-99-3*) Classic Theatre Schl.
— Nutshell Classics: The Importance of Being Earnest. 1988. pap. text ed. 55.00 (*0-938735-51-9*) Classic Theatre Schl.
Malina, Judith, tr. see Brecht, Bertolt.
Malina, Robert M., ed. Young Athletes: Biological, Psychological, & Educational Perspectives. (Illus.). 312p. 1988. text ed. 40.00x (*0-87322-173-7*, BMAL0173) Human Kinetics.
Malina, Robert M. & Bouchard, Claude. Growth, Maturation, & Physical Activity. LC 90-25553. (Illus.). 520p. (Orig.). (C). 1991. text ed. 54.00x (*0-87322-321-7*, BMAL0321) Human Kinetics.
Malina, Robert M. & Bouchard, Claude, eds. Sport & Human Genetics. LC 85-18116. 200p. (C). 1986. text ed. 36.00x (*0-87322-011-0*, BMAL0011) Human Kinetics.
Malina, Robert M., jt. ed. see Roche, Alex F.
Malina, Roger F., ed. Proceedings of the Extreme Ultraviolet Astronomy Colloquium. (Illus.). 208p. 1991. 80.00 (*0-08-037303-8*, Pergamon Pr) Elsevier.
Malinconico, L. L., Jr. & Lillie, R. J., eds. Tectonics of the Western Himalayas. (Special Paper Ser.: No. 232). (Illus.). 300p. 1989. pap. 40.00 (*0-8137-2232-2*) Geol Soc.
***Maling, Anne E.** Princess Anne Co., VA: Wills 1783-1871. 255p. (Orig.). 1994. pap. 22.50 (*1-55613-966-7*) Heritage Bk.
— Princess Anne County, Virginia; Land & Probate Records Abstracted from Deed Books Eight to Eighteen, 1755-1783. iv, 117p. (Orig.). 1993. pap. write for info. (*1-55613-731-1*) Heritage Bk.
— Princess Anne County, Virginia, Land & Probate Records Abstracted from Deed Books One to Eighteen 1691-1783. 243p. (Orig.). 1995. pap. text ed. 19.00 (*0-7884-0175-0*) Heritage Bk.
— Princess Anne County, Virginia, Land & Probate Records Abstracted from Deed Books 1-7: 1691-1755. 118p. (Orig.). 1992. pap. 14.50 (*1-55613-620-X*) Heritage Bk.
Maling, Arthur. The Koberg Link. large type ed. 406p. 1981. 12.00 (*0-7089-0674-5*) Ulverscroft.
— A Taste of Treason. large type ed. 416p. 1985. 21.95 (*0-7089-1338-5*) Ulverscroft.
Maling, D. H. Coordinate Systems & Map Projections. rev. ed. (Illus.). 480p. 1993. pap. text ed. 45.00 (*0-08-037233-3*, Pergamon Pr) Elsevier.
— Coordinate Systems & Map Projections. 2nd rev. ed. (Illus.). 480p. 1992. text ed. 120.00 (*0-08-037234-1*, Ed Skills Dallas) Elsevier.
Maling, George C., Jr., ed. see International Conference on Noise Control Engineering Staff.
Malingrey, A. M., ed. see Chrysostomus.
Malingue, Maurice, ed. see Gauguin, Paul.
Malino, Frances & Albert, Phyllis C., eds. Essays in Modern Jewish History: A Tribute to Ben Halpern. LC 80-70585. 500p. 1982. 36.50 (*0-8386-3095-2*) Fairleigh Dickinson.
Malino, Frances & Sorkin, David, eds. From East & West: Jews in a Changing Europe 1750-1870. (Illus.). 256p. 1991. pap. text ed. 21.95 (*0-631-17768-X*) Blackwell Pubs.
Malino, Frances & Wasserstein, Bernard, eds. The Jews in Modern France. LC 84-40591. (Tauber Institute Ser.: No. 4). (Illus.). 368p. 1985. text ed. 40.00 (*0-87451-324-3*) U Pr of New Eng.
Malinoski, Robert R. A Golden Decade of Trains: The 1950's In Color. LC 91-62001. (Illus.). 128p. 1991. 45.00 (*1-878887-06-8*) Morning NJ.
Malinova. Czech-English Technical Dictionary: Cesko-Anglicky Technicky Slovnik. 4th ed. 945p. (CZE & ENG.). 1986. 95.00 (*0-8288-0679-9*, F42070) Fr & Eur.
— English-Czech, Czech-English, Electrotechnic & Electronic Dictionary. (CZE & ENG.). 1985. 49.95 (*0-8288-7202-3*, M1362) Fr & Eur.
Malinova, L. Czech-English - English-Czech Dictionary of Electrical Engineering & Electronics. 924p. 1982. 44.00 (*0-88431-256-9*) IBD Ltd.
Malinove, L. English-Czech & Czech-English Electrotechnical Dictionary. 924p. (C). 1985. 125.00 (*0-89771-909-3*, Pub. by Collets) St Mut.
Malinovski, Alexsandr A., see A. Bogdanoff, pseud..
Malinow, Ana. Manual for (Relatively) Painless Medical Spanish: A Self-Teaching Course. LC 91-47543. (Illus.). 263p. (Orig.). (C). 1992. pap. 14.95 (*0-292-75146-X*) U of Tex Pr.
***Malinowitz, Harriet.** Textual Orientations: Lesbian & Gay Students & the Making of Discourse Communities. Stillman, Peter R., ed. LC 94-36734. 294p. 1995. pap. text ed. 22.00 (*0-86709-353-6*) Boynton Cook Pubs.
Malinowski, Bronislaw. Argonauts of the Western Pacific. (Illus.). 527p. (C). 1984. reprint ed. pap. text ed. 13.95 (*0-88133-084-1*) Waveland Pr.
— Crime & Custom in Savage Society. LC 84-19807. (Illus.). xii, 132p. 1984. reprint ed. text ed. 45.00 (*0-313-24686-6*, MCRC, Greenwood Pr) Greenwood.
— Crime & Custom in Savage Society. (Quality Paperback Ser.: No. 210). 1976. reprint ed. pap. 19.00 (*0-8226-0210-5*) Littlefield.
— A Diary in the Strict Sense of the Term. 360p. 1989. 45. 00 (*0-8047-1706-0*); pap. 16.95 (*0-8047-1707-9*) Stanford U Pr.
— The Dynamics of Culture Change. Kaberry, Phyllis M., ed. LC 75-14599. 171p. 1976. reprint ed. text ed. 35.00 (*0-8371-8216-6*, MADCC, Greenwood Pr) Greenwood.
— Freedom & Civilization. LC 76-40226. 338p. 1977. reprint ed. text ed. 35.00 (*0-8371-9277-3*, MAFA, Greenwood Pr) Greenwood.
— Magic, Science & Religion & Other Essays. LC 84-19290. 274p. 1984. reprint ed. text ed. 55.00 (*0-313-24687-4*, MMSR, Greenwood Pr) Greenwood.
— Magic, Science & Religion & Other Essays. (Illus.). 274p. (C). 1992. reprint ed. pap. text ed. 9.95 (*0-88133-657-2*) Waveland Pr.
— Malinowski among the Magi: The Natives of Mailu. Young, Michael, ed. 250p. (C). 1988. lib. bdg. 57.50 (*0-415-00249-4*) Routledge.
— A Scientific Theory of Culture. LC 44-8385. x, 228p. (C). 1990. reprint ed. pap. 14.95 (*0-8078-4283-4*) U of NC Pr.
— Sex & Repression in Savage Society. LC 85-971. xii, 285p. 1985. pap. text ed. 12.95 (*0-226-50287-2*) U Ch Pr.
— The Sexual Life of Savages. LC 86-47760. (Illus.). 650p. 1987. reprint ed. pap. 19.00 (*0-8070-4607-8*, BP 740) Beacon Pr.
— The Sexual Life of Savages in North-Western Melanesia. 700p. 1982. pap. text ed. 22.50 (*0-7100-6659-7*, RKP) Routledge.
Malinowski, Bronislaw & De La Fuente, Julio. Malinowski in Mexico: The Economics of a Mexican Market System. Drucker-Brown, Susan, ed. (International Library of Anthropology). 246p. 1985. pap. 13.95 (*0-7102-0584-8*, RKP) Routledge.
Malinowski, Bronislaw, jt. auth. see Briffault, Robert.
Malinowski, Edmund R. Factor Analysis in Chemistry. 2nd ed. 368p. 1991. text ed. 75.95 (*0-471-53009-3*) Wiley.
Malinowski, Edmund R. & Howery, Darryl G. Factor Analysis in Chemistry. LC 88-13742. 264p. (C). 1989. reprint ed. lib. bdg. 47.50 (*0-89464-343-6*) Krieger.
Malinowski, Gregory P. & Jahani, Mohammad. An Information Systems Guide for Community Action Agencies. (Illus.). 250p. 1981. 15.00 (*0-936130-04-0*) Intl Sci Tech.
Malinowski, Gregory P., jt. auth. see Cones, Vanessa C.
Malinowski, Grzegorz. Many-Valued Logics. LC 93-36413. (Oxford Logic Guides Ser.: No. 25). 144p. (C). 1994. 39. 95 (*0-19-853787-5*, Clarendon Pr) OUP.
Malinowski, Janet. Nursing Care During the Labor Process. 3rd ed. LC 88-30981. (Illus.). 433p. (C). 1989. pap. text ed. 26.95 (*0-8036-5803-6*) Davis Co.
Malinowski, K., jt. auth. see Brdys, M. A.
Malinowski, Sharon, ed. Black Writers 2: Sketches from Contemporary Authors. 2nd ed. 1993. 89.00 (*0-8103-7788-8*) Gale.
— Gay & Lesbian Literature. 475p. 1993. 85.00 (*1-55862-174-1*) St James Pr.
***Malinowski, Sharon & Abrams, George H. J., eds.** Notable Native Americans. 2nd ed. LC 94-36202. 492p. 1994. 75.00 (*0-8103-9638-6*) Gale.
***Malinowski, Sharon & Brelin, Christa.** The Gay & Lesbian Literary Companion. 1994. pap. 18.95 (*0-7876-0033-4*) Visible Ink Pr.
Malinowski, Stanley B. & Melodia, Thomas V. The Easter Bunny Comes to Forgottenville. 48p. (J). (ps-3). 1988. 11.95 (*0-941316-02-5*) TSM Books.
***Malinowski, Walt.** More Decisive Than Bastogne, Hitler's "Bulge" Dream for Dunkirk II Exploded Green GI's & Vets on Elsenborn Ridge & N. Shoulder Did It! Green GI's & Vets on Elsenborn Ridge & N. Shoulder Did It! (Illus.). 42p. (Orig.). (C). Date not set. pap. write for info. (*0-935648-47-X*) Halldin Pub.
Malinowsky, H. Robert. Science & Technology Annual Reference Review, 1990. 360p. 1990. 55.00 (*0-89774-527-2*) Oryx Pr.
— Science & Technology Annual Reference Review, 1991. 376p. 1991. 74.50 (*0-89774-608-2*) Oryx Pr.
Malinowsky, H. Robert, ed. Best Science & Technology Reference Books for Young People. 232p. 1991. pap. 24. 95 (*0-89774-580-9*) Oryx Pr.
— Reference Sources in Science, Engineering, Medicine, & Agriculture. 328p. 1994. pap. 39.95 (*0-89774-745-3*) Oryx Pr.
— Reference Sources in Science, Engineering, Medicine, & Agriculture. 360p. 1994. 49.95 (*0-89774-742-9*) Oryx Pr.
— Science & Technology Annual Reference Review, 1989. 248p. 1989. 45.00 (*0-89774-487-X*) Oryx Pr.
Malinowsky, H. Robert & Perry, Gerald J. The AIDS Information Sourcebook, 1991-92. 3rd ed. 312p. 1991. pap. 39.95 (*0-89774-598-1*) Oryx Pr.
Malins, D. C. & Sargent, J. R., eds. Biochemical & Biophysical Perspectives in Marine Biology, Vol. 4. 1979. text ed. 178.00 (*0-12-466604-3*) Acad Pr.
Malins, D. C., jt. auth. see Holman, R. J.
Malins, Dana H. How to Write Twice As Fast with the New Word-Shortening System. 53p. 1990. pap. 19.95 (*0-9628032-0-0*) Peninsu MA.
Malins, Donald C. & Ostrander, Gary K., eds. Aquatic Toxicology: Molecular, Biochemical, & Cellular Perspectives. LC 93-6117. 512p. 1993. 60.00 (*0-87371-545-4*, QH90) Lewis Pubs.
Malins, Edward. A Preface to Yeats. 2nd rev. ed. LC 93-39017. (Preface Bks.). 280p. (C). 1994. pap. text ed. 25. 50 (*0-582-09093-8*, Pub. by Longman UK) Longman.
Malins, Geoffrey H. How I Filmed the War. (Great War Ser.: No. 25). (Illus.). 347p. reprint ed. 34.95 (*0-89839-183-0*) Battery Pr.
Malins, Jed. Start Ballroom & Latin Dancing. 56p. 1991. pap. 12.95 (*1-85273-029-3*) Princeton Bk Co.
Malinski, Violet M. & Barrett, Elizabeth A., eds. Martha E. Rogers: Her Life & Her Work. LC 94-6137. 380p. 1994. 50.00 (*0-8036-5807-9*) Davis Co.
Malinski, Y., jt. auth. see Barrett, E. A.
Malinvaud, A. Statistical Methods in Econometrics. 3rd rev. ed. (Studies in Mathematical & Managerial Economics: Vol. 6). 770p. 1980. 121.25 (*0-444-85473-8*, North Holland) Elsevier.
Malinvaud, Edmond. Diagnosing Unemployment. (Caffe Lectures Ser.: No. 1). 180p. (C). 1994. 34.95 (*0-521-44533-7*) Cambridge U Pr.
— Lectures on Microeconomic Theory. rev. ed. Silvey, A., tr. (Advanced Textbooks in Economics Ser.: Vol. 2). 384p. 1985. 39.50 (*0-444-87650-2*, North Holland) Elsevier.
— Mass Unemployment. 160p. 1986. pap. text ed. 14.95 (*0-631-14992-9*) Blackwell Pubs.
— Profitability & Unemployment. LC 79-21472. 1980. 18.95 (*0-521-22999-5*) Cambridge U Pr.
Malis, Carolyn. Juicing. 224p. (Orig.). 1993. mass mkt. 4.99 (*0-380-77185-3*) Avon.
Malis, G. IU. Research on the Etiology of Schizophrenia. LC 61-11828. (International Behavioral Sciences Ser.). (Illus.). 207p. reprint ed. pap. 59.00 (*0-317-10350-4*, 2020657) Bks Demand.
Malisani, Eduardo A. Diccionario de Fisica. 320p. (SPA.). 1987. pap. 55.00 (*0-7859-6402-9*, 8486592402) Fr & Eur.
Malischewsky, P. Surface Waves & Discontinuities. (Developments in Solid Earth Geophysics Ser.: Vol. 16). 1988. 89.75 (*0-444-98959-5*) Elsevier.
Malison, Andrew F. Semiconductors: Industry & Trade Summary. (Illus.). 53p. (Orig.). (C). 1994. pap. text ed. 50.00 (*0-7881-0320-2*) Diane Pub.
Malisow, Betty. Recipes from Minnesota: With Love. (Illus.). 199p. 1981. spiral bd. 9.95 (*0-913703-00-1*, MN29) Branches.
Maliszewski, Michael. Great Traditions of the Martial Arts. (Frontiers of Consciousness Ser.). (Illus.). 300p. 1994. write for info. (*0-8290-2632-0*) Irvington.
Maliszewski, Michael, jt. ed. see Diamond, Seymour.
Malitz, J. Introduction to Mathematical Logic: Set Theory-Computable Functions-Model Theory. (Undergraduate Texts in Mathematics Ser.). (Illus.). 1987. 33.00 (*0-387-90346-1*) Spr-Verlag.
Malitz, Jerome. The Personal Landscapes. LC 89-30114. (Illus.). 272p. 1989. 39.95 (*0-88192-131-9*) Timber.
— Rocky Mountain National Park Dayhiker's Guide: A Scenic Guide to 33 Favorite Hikes Including Longs Peak. LC 92-42538. (Illus.). 144p. (Orig.). 1993. pap. 15. 95 (*1-55566-110-6*) Johnson Bks.
***Malitz, Sidney.** L-DOPA & Behavior. fac. ed. LC 75-181306. (Illus.). 144p. Date not set. pap. 41.10 (*0-7837-7194-0*, 2047105) Bks Demand.
Malitz, Sidney & Sackeim, Harold A., eds. Electroconvulsive Therapy: Clinical & Basic Research Issues. (Annals Ser.: Vol. 462). 424p. 1986. text ed. 98. 00 (*0-89766-319-5*); pap. text ed. 98.00 (*0-89766-320-9*) NY Acad Sci.
Malitza, M., jt. auth. see Guiasu, S.
Maliushitskii, Iurii N. The Centrifugal Model Testing of Waste-Heap Embankments. Schofield, A. N., ed. LC 78-67431. 218p. reprint ed. pap. 62.20 (*0-318-34819-5*, 2031686) Bks Demand.

An Asterisk (*) at the beginning of an entry indicates that the title is appearing in BIP for the first time.

Maliwal, G. L. Salt Tolerance of Crops & Plant Metabolism in Saline Substrate: An Annotated Bibliography, 1940-1980. 1981. 75.00 (*0-685-21852-X*, Pub. by Intl Bk Distr II) St Mut.
— Salt Tolerance of Crops & Plants Metabolism in Saline Substrate: An Annotated Bibliography. (C). 1989. text ed. 135.00 (*0-89771-581-0*, Pub. by Intl Bk Distr II) St Mut.
Maliyamkono, T. L. & Bagachwa, Mboya S. The Second Economy in Tanzania. LC 89-27398. 224p. 1990. lib. bdg. 29.95 (*0-8214-0949-2*) Ohio U Pr.
Maliyamkono, T. L., et al. Training & Productivity in Eastern Africa. (Eastern African Universities Research Project Ser.). 400p. 1982. text ed. 60.00 (*0-435-89582-6*) Heinemann.
Maljkovic-Petkovic, Djero, ed. see Mraovitch, Sima.
Maljkovic-Petkovic, Djuro, ed. see Rajacic, Roy.
Malka, Drucker. Jacob's Rescue: A Holocaust Story. (J). (gr. 4-7). 1994. mass mkt. 3.99 (*0-440-40965-9*) Dell.
***Malkani, Sheila V. & Walsh, Michael F.** The Insider's Guide to Law Firms. 734p. (Orig.). 1994. 79.95 (*0-9637970-3-4*); pap. 28.95 (*0-614-02753-5*) Mobius Pr CO.
Malkasian, C. A. The Big Cry Quandary. 1991. text ed. write for info. (*0-9631541-0-9*) W Dewey.
Malkemes, Fred & Pires, Deborah S. Looking at English, Bk. 3. (Illus.). 288p. (C). 1983. pap. text ed. 14.00 (*0-13-540435-5*) P-H.
— Looking at English: An ESL Text-Workbook for Beginners, Bk. 1. (English As a Second Language Ser.). (Illus.). 256p. (C). 1981. pap. text ed. write for info. (*0-13-540401-0*) P-H.
Malkevich, M. S., jt. auth. see Feigelson, E. M.
Malkevich, V. East-West Economic Co-operation & Technological Exchange. (Problems of the Contemporary World Ser.: No. 100). 161p. 1981. 14.00 (*0-317-46616-X*, Pub. by Collets UK) Pro-Am Music.
***Malkevitch, J. & Froelich, G.** Loads of Codes. (Hi Map: No. 22). Date not set. pap. text ed. 11.99 (*0-614-05307-2*, HM 5622) COMAP Inc.
Malkevitch, Joe, ed. Geometry's Future. (Illus.). 122p. 1991. pap. 5.99 (*0-912843-21-7*) COMAP Inc.
Malkevitch, Joseph. Properties of Planar Graphs with Uniform Vertex & Face Structure. LC 52-42839. (Memoirs Ser.: No. 1/99). 116p. 1970. pap. 16.00 (*0-8218-1299-8*, MEMO 1/99) Am Math.
Malkevitch, Joseph, jt. auth. see Froelich, Gary.
Malkevitch, Joseph, ed. see Guy, Richard K.
Malkevitch, Joseph, ed. see Meyer, Rochelle W. & Meyer, Walter.
***Malkiel, Burton G.** A Random Walk down Wall Street: Including a Life-Cycle Guide to Personal Investing. 6th ed. LC 95-8148. 1995. 25.00 (*0-393-03888-2*) Norton.
— Random Walk down Wall Street: Updated for the 1990s Investor. rev. ed. 1990. 22.95 (*0-393-02793-7*) Norton.
— A Random Walk down Wall Street: Updated for the 1990s Investor. 5th ed. 409p. (C). 1991. pap. 14.95 (*0-393-95961-9*) Norton.
— The Term Structure of Interest Rates: Expectations & Behavior Patterns. LC 66-21836. (Illus.). 293p. reprint ed. pap. 83.60 (*0-317-08743-6*, 2051944) Bks Demand.
Malkiel, Burton G., jt. auth. see Cragg, John G.
Malkiel, Theresa S. Diary of a Shirtwaist Striker. (Literature of American Labor Ser.). 224p. 1990. pap. 12.95 (*0-87546-168-9*) ILR Pr.
Malkiel, Yakov. Diachronic Problems in Phonosymbolism: Edita & Inedita, 1979-1988, Vol. 1. LC 89-17827. vii, 258p. 1990. 89.00x (*979-272-2066-2*) Benjamins North Am.
— Diachronic Studies in Lexicology, Affixation, & Phonology, Vol. II: Edita & Inedita, 1979-1988. LC 91-48116. 250p. 1992. 83.00 (*90-272-2072-7*) Benjamins North Am.
— Etymology. LC 92-20773. 250p. (C). 1993. pap. 27.95 (*0-521-31166-7*) Cambridge U Pr.
— Etymology. LC 92-20773. 250p. (C). 1994. 69.95 (*0-521-32338-X*) Cambridge U Pr.
— From Particular to General Linguistics: Selected Essays 1965-1978. (Studies in Language Companion: No. 3). xxii, 659p. 1983. 127.00x (*90-272-3002-1*) Benjamins North Am.
— Linguistics & Philology in Spanish America: A Survey (1925-1970) (Janua Linguarum, Ser. Minor: No. 97). 179p. (Orig.). 1972. pap. text ed. 36.95 (*90-279-2313-2*) Mouton.
— Patterns of Derivational Affixation in the Cabraniego Dialect of East-Central Asturian. LC 70-627777. (U. C. Publ. in Linguistics Ser.: Vol. 64). 203p. reprint ed. 57.90 (*0-8357-9637-X*, 2015103) Bks Demand.
— Theory & Practice of Romance Etymology: Studies in Language, Culture & History. (Collected Studies: No. CS288). 348p. (C). 1989. lib. bdg. 95.00 (*0-86078-236-0*, Pub. by Variorum UK) Ashgate Pub Co.
Malkiel, Yakov, jt. auth. see Lehmann, Winfred P.
Malkin. Photophysical & Photochemical Properties: Aromatic Compounds. 1992. 225.00 (*0-8493-6802-2*) CRC Pr.
Malkin, Carole. The Journeys of David Toback: As Retold by His Granddaughter. large type ed. 256p. 1992. pap. 15.95 (*0-8027-2665-8*) Walker & Co.
***Malkin, Gary.** Comprehensive Networking Glossary & Acronym Guide. 200p. 1994. pap. text ed. 19.93 (*0-13-319955-X*) P-H.
Malkin, Gary S. The Comprehensive Networking Glossary & Acronym Guide. (Illus.). 200p. 1994. pap. 19.95 (*1-884777-02-3*) Manning Pubns.
Malkin, Harold M. Out of the Mist: The Foundation of Modern Pathology & Medicine During the Nineteenth Century. (Illus.). 422p. 1993. 80.00 (*0-9637689-0-5*); pap. text ed. 35.00 (*0-9637689-1-3*) Vesalius Bks.
Malkin, Irad. Myth & Territory in the Spartan Mediterranean. LC 93-30357. (Illus.). 320p. (C). 1994. 59.95 (*0-521-41183-1*) Cambridge U Pr.
Malkin, Irad, ed. La France et la Mediterranee: Vingt-Sept Siecles d'Interdependance. LC 89-7177. x, 423p. (FRE.). 1990. 103.00 (*90-04-08930-6*) E J Brill.
Malkin, J. Pictorial History of Kilmarnock. (C). 1988. pap. 90.00 (*0-907526-42-X*, Alloway Pub) St Mut.
Malkin, Jain. Hospital Interior Architecture. (Illus.). 448p. 1992. text ed. 149.95 (*0-442-31897-9*) Van Nos Reinhold.
— Medical & Dental Space Planning for the 1990's. 2nd ed. (Illus.). 482p. 1990. text ed. 79.95 (*0-442-26485-2*) Van Nos Reinhold.
Malkin, Jeanette. Verbal Violence in Contemporary Drama: From Handke to Shepard. 256p. (C). 1992. 59.95 (*0-521-38335-8*) Cambridge U Pr.
Malkin, John. Sir Alexander Fleming: Man of Penicillin. 92p. 1985. 30.00 (*0-907526-06-3*, Alloway Pub) St Mut.
Malkin, Marjorie & Howe, Christine Z., eds. Research in Therapeutic Recreation: Concepts & Methods. LC 92-63340. 354p. (C). 1993. boxed 31.95 (*0-910251-53-3*) Venture Pub PA.
Malkin, Marsha, jt. auth. see Anschell, Helen.
Malkin, Martin, ed. see Anschell, Helen & Malkin, Marsha.
Malkin, Mort. Walk It Off! Complete Walking Program to Reduce Weight, Stress, & Hypertension. 1995. pap. text ed. 14.95 (*0-471-55672-6*) Wiley.
— Walking-the Pleasure Exercise: A 60-Day Walking Program for Fitness & Health. LC 85-28263. (Illus.). 208p. 1986. pap. 9.95 (*0-87857-608-8*, 12-212-1) Rodale Pr Inc.
Malkin, Peter & Stein, Harry. Eichmann in My Hands. large type ed. LC 90-41189. 402p. 1990. reprint ed. lib. bdg. 22.95 (*1-56054-055-9*) Thorndike Pr.
Malkin, Peter Z. & Stein, Harry. Eichmann in My Hands. 1990. 22.95 (*0-446-51418-7*) Warner Bks.
Malkin, R., jt. ed. see Barber, J.
Malkind, Samuel N. Commodities for Kids of All Ages. 1993. 10.95 (*0-533-10334-7*) Vantage.
***Malkki, Liisa H.** Purity & Exile: Violence, Memory, & National Cosmology Among Hutu Refugees in Tanzania. LC 94-37099. 1993. lib. bdg. 60.00 (*0-226-50271-6*); pap. text ed. 21.50 (*0-226-50272-4*) U Ch Pr.
Malkmus, George H. Why Christians Get Sick. 144p. (Orig.). 1988. pap. 6.95 (*0-929619-01-3*) Hallelujah Acres.
Malkmus, Lizbeth & Armes, Roy. Arab & African Film Making. 256p. (C). 1991. text ed. 69.95 (*0-86232-916-7*, Pub. by Zed Books UK); pap. 25.00 (*0-86232-917-5*, Pub. by Zed Books UK) Humanities.
Malko, J. Robert, jt. ed. see Enholm, Gregory B.
Malkoc, Anna M. Easy Plays in English. rev. ed. LC 93-16407. 1993. pap. text ed. 8.50 (*0-13-061698-2*) P-H.
Malkoff, Karl. Escape from the Self. 1977. text ed. 37.50 (*0-231-03720-1*) Col U Pr.
— Muriel Spark. LC 68-54456. (Columbia Essays on Modern Writers Ser.: No. 36). 48p. (Orig.). 1968. pap. text ed. 7.50 (*0-231-03063-0*) Col U Pr.
***Malks, Josh.** How to Maintain & Use Your Collector Car. (Illus.). 192p. 1995. pap. 19.95 (*0-7603-0056-9*) Motorbooks Intl.
— Illustrated Duesenberg Buyer's Guide. (Illustrated Buyer's Guide Ser.). (Illus.). 128p. 1993. pap. 16.95 (*0-87938-741-6*) Motorbooks Intl.
Mall, David. In Good Conscience: Abortion & Moral Necessity. LC 82-9918. xii, 212p. 1982. 20.00 (*0-9608410-1-6*); pap. 10.00 (*0-9608410-0-8*) Kairos Bks.
Mall, David, ed. When Life & Choice Collide: Essays on Rhetoric & Abortion, Vol. 1 To Set the Dawn Free. LC 93-20573. (Words in Conflict Ser.). (Illus.). 368p. 1994. 30.00 (*0-9608410-3-2*); pap. 15.00 (*0-9608410-2-4*) Kairos Bks.
Mall, David & Watts, Walter F., eds. Psychological Aspects of Abortion. LC 79-88679. 168p. 1979. pap. text ed. 17.95 (*0-313-27053-8*, P7053, Greenwood Pr) Greenwood.
Mall, David, jt. ed. see Horan, Dennis J.
Mall, E. Jane. How to Become Wealthy Publishing a Newsletter. 4th ed. 110p. 1990. pap. 17.50 (*0-934311-65-X*) Intl Wealth.
— How to Become Wealthy Publishing a Newsletter. 5th ed. 110p. 1992. pap. 17.50 (*1-56150-016-X*) Intl Wealth.
— Kitty, My Rib. LC 59-10977. 1971. reprint ed. pap. 7.99 (*0-570-03113-3*, 12-2347) Concordia.
Mall, E. Jane, jt. auth. see Powers, Betty.
Mall, Elyse, jt. auth. see Waters, Margaret.
Mall-Haefeli, Marianne, ed. Hormonale Kontrazeption: Eine Standortbestimmung. (Illus.). viii, 148p. 1983. 47.25 (*3-8055-3767-0*) S Karger.
— Moderne Kontrazeption: Fortbildungskurs der Schweizerischen Gesellschaft fuer Familien Planung. (Gynaekologische Rundschau Journal: Vol. 18, No. 3-4). (Illus.). 1978. pap. 19.25 (*3-8055-2939-2*) S Karger.
Mall, Jill C. & Kaufman, Barry. Esteem Architecture: The Esteem Building Card Game. 55p. 1993. 14.95 (*1-884780-05-9*) Phoenix Pubng.
Mall, K. Jane. How to Become Wealthy Publishing a Newsletter. 6th ed. 110p. 1993. pap. 17.50 (*1-56150-066-6*) Intl Wealth.
Mall, Loren. Public Land & Mining Law. 3rd ed. LC 81-68524. 464p. 1982. student ed. pap. 29.50 (*0-409-23018-9*) Butterworth Legal Pubs.
Mall, Victor. Pathway in the Sky. 132p. (Orig.). (RUS.). 1993. pap. 10.00 (*0-922792-57-7*) Gnosis Pr.
Malla, Bansilal. Sculptures of Kashmir. 1990. 73.00 (*0-8364-2521-9*, Pub. by Agam Kala Prakashan) S Asia.
Malla, Kamal P. English in Nepalese Education. 1977. 35.00 (*0-7855-0272-6*, Pub. by Ratna Pustak Bhandar) St Mut.
— English in Nepalese Education. (C). 1977. 35.00 (*0-89771-074-6*, Pub. by Ratna Pustak Bhandar) St Mut.
Malla, Maria. El Reinado de la Paz: The Coming Kingdom of Peace. (SPA.). 2.25 (*84-7228-462-X*, 220758, Pub. by Edit Clie SP) TSELF.
Malla, Ramesh B., ed. Dynamic Response & Progressive Failure of Special Structures: Proceedings of the Technical Sessions on Response of Truss & Truss-Type Structures During Progressive Failure & Dynamic Loading & Analysis of Structures. LC 93-40323. 1993. write for info. (*0-87262-946-5*) Am Soc Civil Eng.
Malla, Samal B., jt. ed. see Ohba, Hideaki.
Malla, Sarah B., jt. auth. see Ohba, Hideaki.
Mallabarman, Adwaita. A River Called Titash. Bardhan, Kalpana, tr. & aft. by. LC 92-46698. 1993. 45.00 (*0-520-38040-1*); pap. 15.00 (*0-520-08050-5*) U CA Pr.
Mallaby, Sebastian. After Apartheid: The Future of South Africa. LC 91-50190. (Illus.). 275p. 1992. 21.50 (*0-8129-1938-6*, Times Bks) Random.
— After Apartheid: The Future of South Africa. 1993. pap. 14.00 (*0-8129-2204-2*, Times Bks) Random.
Mallach, Alan. Inclusionary Housing Programs: Policies & Practices. LC 84-7055. 288p. 1984. text ed. 22.95 (*0-88285-100-4*) Transaction Pubs.
Mallach, Efrem, ed. see Sondak, Norman E.
Mallach, Stanley, jt. auth. see Curtis, Verna P.
Mallada, Victor F., tr. see Pineda y Ramirez, Antonio de.
***Mallakh, Dorothea E., ed.** Energy Watchers Five: Energy & Development Revisited: Twenty Years & Beyond & the United States & North America: International Implications for Supply & Demand. (Illus.). 189p. 1994. pap. 24.00 (*0-918714-40-0*) Intl Res Ctr Energy.
— Energy Watchers Two: Phoenix Like OPEC: Changing Structures, Markets, & Future Stability & the Oil-Gas Relationship. LC 90-81130. (Illus.). 189p. 1991. 24.00 (*0-918714-26-5*) Intl Res Ctr Energy.
Mallakh, Dorothea H., ed. Energy Watchers, No. 1: Shadow OPEC: New Element for Stability? & A "Reintegrated" Oil Industry: Implications for Supply, Marketing, Pricing, & Investment. 150p. 1990. pap. 24.00 (*0-918714-19-2*) Intl Res Ctr Energy.
***Mallakh, Ragaei E.** The Economic Development of the United Arab Emirates. 215p. 1981. 20.00 (*0-7099-0209-3*) Intl Res Ctr Energy.
— The Middle East, Pacific Basin, & the United States: Refining & Petrochemicals. LC 86-81024. (Illus.). 180p. 1986. pap. 36.00 (*0-918714-10-9*) Intl Res Ctr Energy.
— Qatar: Development of an Oil Economy. (Illus.). 183p. 1979. 10.95 (*0-85664-848-5*) Intl Res Ctr Energy.
— Qatar: Energy & Development. LC 84-29317. (Illus.). 184p. 1985. 21.00 (*0-7099-0955-1*, Pub. by Croom Helm UK) Routledge Chapman & Hall.
— Saudi Arabia: Rush to Development. (Illus.). 472p. 1982. 26.00 (*0-7099-0905-5*) Intl Res Ctr Energy.
***Mallakh, Ragaei E., ed.** OPEC: Twenty Years & Beyond. LC 81-7531. (Illus.). 270p. 1982. 21.00 (*0-86531-163-3*) Intl Res Ctr Energy.
***Mallakh, Ragaei E. & Atta, Jacob K.** The Absorptive Capacity of Kuwait. LC 81-2020. (Illus.). 204p. 1981. 20.00 (*0-669-04541-1*) Intl Res Ctr Energy.
Mallakh, Ragaei El, jt. ed. see El Mallakh, Dorothea H.
Mallakh, Ragaei El, et al. Implications of Regional Development in the Middle East for U. S. Trade, Capital Flows, & Balance of Payments. LC 77-73035. 1977. pap. 5.00 (*0-918714-01-X*) Intl Res Ctr Energy.
Mallalieu, H. L. The Dictionary of British Watercolour Artists Up to 1920: Vol. 2, The Plates. (Illus.). 284p. 1979. 69.50 (*0-902028-63-4*) Antique Collect.
— The Dictionary of British Watercolour Artists up to 1920: Vol. 3. (Illus.). 288p. 1991. 69.50 (*1-85149-111-2*) Antique Collect.
— Understanding Watercolours. (Understanding Ser.). (Illus.). 1985. 49.50 (*0-907462-39-1*) Antique Collect.
Mallalieu, Huon, ed. The Illustrated History of Antiques: Essential Reference for All Antiques Lovers & Collectors. LC 93-71301. (Illus.). 640p. 1993. reprint ed. 29.98 (*1-56138-332-5*) Courage Bks.
Mallalieu, J. P. W. Very Ordinary Seaman. 253p. pap. 7.00 (*0-583-12808-4*, Pub. by Granada UK) Academy Chi Pubs.
Mallalieu, Jonathan. The Prince of Wales & Stories. 272p. 1993. pap. 17.95 (*1-897580-11-8*, Pub. by Phoenix Hse UK) Trafalgar.
Mallalieu, M. L. The Dictionary of British Watercolour Artists up to 1920: Vol. 1, The Text. 2nd ed. 304p. 1986. 79.50 (*1-85149-025-6*) Antique Collect.
Mallam, R. Clark. Indian Creek Memories: A Sense of Place. LC 87-60995. (Illus.). 200p. (Orig.). 1987. 13.00 (*0-9618412-1-4*); pap. 6.00 (*0-9618412-0-6*) Prairie Song Pr.
Mallam, R. Clark, jt. auth. see Alex, Lynn M.
Mallamace, F., jt. ed. see Corti, M.
Mallampally, Padma, jt. ed. see Sauvant, Karl P.
Mallan, Chicki. Belize Handbook. 2nd ed. LC 92-21235. 263p. (Orig.). 1993. pap. 13.95 (*0-918373-95-6*) Moon Pubns CA.
— Belize Handbook. 3rd ed. (Moon Travel Handbooks Ser.). (Illus.). 268p. (Orig.). 1995. pap. 14.95 (*1-56691-030-7*) Moon Pubns CA.
— Cancun Handbook & Mexico's Caribbean Coast. 4th ed. LC 94-4896. 260p. 1994. pap. 13.95 (*1-56691-050-1*) Moon Pubns CA.
— Catalina Island Handbook: A Guide to California's Channel Islands. 4th ed. (Illus.). 250p. (Orig.). 1992. pap. 10.95 (*0-918373-75-1*) Moon Pubns CA.
— Central Mexico Handbook: Mexico City & Other Colonial Cities within the Highland States. LC 94-9364. 350p. 1994. pap. 15.95 (*1-56691-023-4*) Moon Pubns CA.
— Yucatan Penninsula Handbook: The Gulf of Mexico to the Caribbean Sea. 5th ed. LC 94-4898. 400p. 1994. pap. 15.95 (*1-56691-024-2*) Moon Pubns CA.
Mallan, Chicki, jt. auth. see Cummings, Joe.
Mallan, John T., jt. auth. see Welton, David A.
Mallan, Kerry. Children As Storytellers. LC 92-20527. 87p. 1992. pap. text ed. 14.00 (*0-435-08779-7*, 08779) Heinemann.
Mallan, Lloyd, ed. see Neruda, Pablo, et al.
Mallan, Sandra. Caring in Emergencies. (Skills for Caring Ser.). (Illus.). 48p. (Orig.). 1993. pap. text ed. 12.00 (*0-443-04622-0*) Churchill.
Mallander, J. O., jt. auth. see Sangharakshita.
Mallard, Catherine O., jt. auth. see Barnum, Barbara S.
***Mallard, Colin D.** Mr. President: A Spiritual Journey. LC 95-90227. (Orig.). 1995. pap. text ed. 15.95 (*0-9646040-4-3*) Wild Duck Pubng.
Mallard, G. E. & Aronson, D. E., eds. U. S. Geological Survey Toxic Substances Hydrology Program: Proceedings of the Technical Meeting, 1991. (Illus.). 730p. (Orig.). (C). 1994. pap. text ed. 195.00 (*0-7881-0438-1*) Diane Pub.
Mallard, Robert Q. Montevideo-Maybank: Some Memoirs of a Southern Christian. 1977. text ed. 21.95 (*0-8369-9230-X*, 9084) Ayer.
Mallard, William. Language & Love: Introduction to Augustine's Religious Thought Through the Confessions Story. LC 93-9070. 1994. 35.00 (*0-271-01037-1*); pap. 16.95 (*0-271-01038-X*) Pa St U Pr.
— The Reflection of Theology in Literature: A Case Study in Theology & Culture. LC 76-14036. 271p. 1977. write for info. (*0-911536-64-7*) Trinity U Pr.
***Mallarme, Stephane.** Collected Poems. Weinfield, Henry, tr. & comment by. LC 94-26794. 1994. 25.00 (*0-520-08188-9*) U CA Pr.
— Correspondance, 3 tomes. Mondor, ed. Incl. Tome I. 1862-1871. 15.95 (*0-7859-0022-5*, F67220); Tome II. 1871-1885. 15.95 (*0-7859-0023-3*, F67221); Tome III. 1886-1889. 19.95 (*0-7859-0024-1*, F67222); (FRE.). write for info. (*0-318-51969-0*) Fr & Eur.
— Correspondence, 1890-1891, Vol. 4. (FRE.). 1973. pap. 65.00 (*0-7859-3969-5*) Fr & Eur.
— Correspondence, 1893-1894, Vol. 6. (FRE.). 1981. pap. 55.00 (*0-7859-3959-8*) Fr & Eur.
— Correspondence, 1894-1895, Vol. 7. (FRE.). 1982. pap. 75.00 (*0-7859-3965-2*) Fr & Eur.
— Correspondence, 1896, Vol. 8. (FRE.). 1983. pap. 65.00 (*0-685-68103-3*) Fr & Eur.
— Correspondence, 1897, Vol. 9. (FRE.). 1983. pap. 75.00 (*0-7859-3966-0*) Fr & Eur.
— Herodias. Mills, Clark, tr. LC 77-10277. reprint ed. 27.50 (*0-404-16329-7*) AMS Pr.
— Igitur; Divagations; Un Coup de Des. (Poesie Ser.). 443p. (Orig.). (FRE.). 1976. pap. 13.95 (*2-07-032157-6*) Schoenhof.
— Igitur, Divagations, un Coup de Des. (FRE.). 1976. pap. 10.95 (*0-8288-3864-X*, M2440) Fr & Eur.
— Oeuvres Completes. deluxe ed. Mondor & Jean-Aubry, eds. (Pleiade Ser.). (FRE.). 1945. 77.95 (*2-07-010326-9*) Schoenhof.
— Poems. Fry, Roger, tr. LC 77-10279. 320p. reprint ed. 32.00 (*0-404-16330-0*) AMS Pr.
— Poesies: (Poesies Choix de vers de Circonstance; Poemes d'Enfance et de Jeunesse) (Poesie Ser.). (FRE.). Date not set. pap. 11.95 (*2-07-032716-7*) Schoenhof.
— Poesies: Poesies Choix de Vers de Circonstance. (FRE.). 1966. pap. 10.95 (*0-8288-3865-8*, F67270) Fr & Eur.
— Selected Letters of Stephane Mallarme. Lloyd, Rosemary, ed. & tr. by. 272p. 1988. 27.50 (*0-226-48841-1*) U Ch Pr.
— Selected Poems. MacIntyre, C. F., tr. (C). 1957. pap. 10.00 (*0-520-00801-4*) U CA Pr.
— Selected Poetry & Prose. Caws, Mary A., ed. & intro. by. LC 81-18899. 128p. 1982. pap. 9.95 (*0-8112-0823-0*, NDP529) New Directions.
Mallarme, Stephane, tr. The Raven. (Illustrated Book Reprints Ser.: Raven Bks.). (Illus.). reprint ed. boxed 75.00 (*0-932256-00-7*) Pilgrim Pr Corp NY.
Mallarme, Stephane, tr. see Poe, Edgar Allan.
Mallarme, Stephane, et al. Le Tombeau de Charles Baudelaire. LC 77-11490. reprint ed. 54.00 (*0-404-16350-5*) AMS Pr.
Mallary, Peter T. Houses of New England. 1988. 14.99 (*0-517-65750-3*) Random Hse Value.
***Mallary, R. DeWitt.** Lenox (Mass.) & the Berkshire Highlands. (Illus.). 363p. 1995. reprint ed. lib. bdg. 42.50 (*0-8328-4465-9*) Higginson Bk Co.
Mallas, John H. & Kreimer, Evered. The Messier Album. LC 78-63243. (Illus.). 256p. 1978. 19.95 (*0-933346-04-2*) Sky Pub.
Mallasch, Marion. Passion's Harvest. 1981. pap. 2.75 (*0-89083-724-4*) Zebra.
Mallasz, Gitta, tr. Talking with Angels. 445p. 1995. pap. 15.95 (*3-85630-505-X*, Pub. by Daimon Verlag SZ) Atrium Pubs.
Mallat, Chibli. The Renewal of Islamic Law: Muhammad Bager As-Sadr, Najaf, & the Shi'i International. LC 92-23821. (Cambridge Middle East Library: No. 29). 280p. (C). 1993. 54.95 (*0-521-43319-3*) Cambridge U Pr.
Mallat, Chibli, ed. Islam & Public Law. (Arab & Islamic Laws Ser.). (C). 1993. lib. bdg. 100.00 (*1-85333-768-4*) Kluwer Ac.
Mallat, Chibli, jt. ed. see Allan, J. A.
Mallay, Jack D. & Vaughn, Warren. Elvis: The Messiah? 172p. 1993. pap. 9.95 (*1-883795-00-1*) TCB Pub.
Malle, Louis. Au Revoir les Enfants. Hollo, Anselm, tr. (Illus.). 224p. 1988. pap. 8.95 (*0-8021-3114-X*) Grove-Atltic.
— Au Revoir les Enfants. (Gallimard Ser.). 132p. (FRE.). 1987. pap. 27.95 (*2-07-071187-0*) Schoenhof.

— Malle on Malle. French, Philip, ed. (Directors on Directors Ser.). (Illus.). 224p. 1992. 19.95 (*0-571-16237-1*) Faber & Faber.

Malle, Louis & Carriere, Jean-Claude. Milou in May: or May Fools. Pilling, Jayne, tr. (Illus.). 79p. (Orig.). 1990. pap. 9.95 (*0-571-14497-7*) Faber & Faber.

Malle, Silvana. The Economic Organisation of War Communism, 1918-1921. (Cambridge Russian, Soviet & Post-Soviet Studies: No. 47). 480p. 1985. 84.95 (*0-521-30292-7*) Cambridge U Pr.

— Employment Planning in the Soviet Union: Continuity & Change. LC 90-8898. 350p. 1991. text ed. 55.00 (*0-312-05326-6*) St Martin.

Mallea, Eduardo. History of an Argentine Passion. Miller, Yvette E., ed. Lichtblau, Myron I., tr. LC 82-20816. 222p. 1983. pap. 13.95 (*0-935480-10-2*) Lat Am Lit Rev Pr.

Mallea, John R. Schooling in a Plural Canada. 120p. 1989. 69.00 (*1-85359-030-4*, Pub. by Multilingual Matters UK); pap. 24.95 (*1-85359-029-0*, Pub. by Multilingual Matters UK) Taylor & Francis.

Mallea, John R. & Shea, Edward C. Multiculturalism & Education: A Select Bibliography. LC 80-481969. (Ontario Institute for Studies in Education, Symposium Ser.: No. 9). 300p. reprint ed. pap. 85.50 (*0-685-20792-7*, 2030103) Bks Demand.

Mallek, Henry. Women's Advantage Diet. 1990. mass mkt. 4.95 (*0-671-67676-8*) PB.

Mallen, Ronald E. & Allen, Richard B., eds. Defense Counsel Practice Management Manual: Achieving Excellence in a Defense Practice. 200p. 1991. 65.00 (*0-9621989-2-7*) IADC IL.

***Mallen, Ronald E. & Smith, Jeffrey M.** Legal Malpractice, Vol. 1. 4th ed. LC 95-5502. 700p. (C). 1995. text ed. write for info. (*0-314-05492-8*) West Pub.

— Legal Malpractice, Vol. 2. 4th ed. LC 95-5502. 700p. (C). 1995. text ed. write for info. (*0-314-05493-6*) West Pub.

— Legal Malpractice, Vol. 3. 4th ed. LC 95-5502. 700p. (C). 1995. text ed. write for info. (*0-314-05494-4*) West Pub.

— Legal Malpractice: Volumes 1 & 2. 3rd ed. 2000p. 1988. text ed. write for info. (*0-314-06927-5*) West Pub.

***Mallen, Terry.** Taking Charge of Your Child's Education: Nine Steps to Becoming a Learning Ally. LC 94-72481. (Illus.). 200p. (Orig.). 1995. pap. 14.95 (*0-9642369-9-0*) Acumen Pr.

Mallender, Paul & Rayson, Jane. How to Make Applications in the Family Proceedings Court. (C). 1992. pap. 38.00 (*1-85431-201-4*, Pub. by Blackstone Pr UK) W W Gaunt.

Maller, Dick & Feinman, Jeffrey. Twenty-One Days to a Trained Dog. 1979. pap. 8.00 (*0-671-25193-7*, Fireside) S&S Trade.

Maller, J. The Therapeutic Community with Chronic Mental Patients. (Bibliotheca Psychiatrica Ser.: No. 146). 1971. pap. 35.25 (*3-8055-1157-4*) S Karger.

Maller, Julius B. Cooperation & Competition: An Experimental Study in Motivation. LC 74-177049. (Columbia University. Teachers College. Contributions to Education Ser.: No. 384). reprint ed. 37.50 (*0-404-55384-2*) AMS Pr.

Maller, R. A., jt. auth. see Pakes, Anthony G.

Malleret, Thierry. Conversion of the Defense Industry in the Former Soviet Union. LC 92-11692. (Occasional Papers: Vol. 23). 1992. 12.85 (*0-913449-30-X*) Inst EW Stud.

Mallerich, Dallas. Greenberg's Guide to Toy Trains. LC 90-70539. (Illus.). 288p. 1990. pap. 17.95 (*0-87069-579-7*, Wallace-Hmestead) Chilton.

Mallery, G., et al. The Sioux Indians: A Socio-Ethnological History. (Illus.). 1897. 22.50 (*0-914074-06-7*, J M C & Co) Amereon Ltd.

Mallery, Garrick. Picture-Writing of the American Indians. 1972. 79.95 (*0-8490-0836-0*) Gordon Pr.

— Picture-Writing of the American Indians, 2 vols., 1. (Illus.). 822p. 1972. reprint ed. pap. 11.95 (*0-486-22842-8*) Dover.

— Picture-Writing of the American Indians, 2 vols., 2. (Illus.). 822p. 1972. reprint ed. pap. 11.95 (*0-486-22843-6*) Dover.

Mallery, Otto T. Economic Union & Durable Peace. LC 76-142663. (Essay Index Reprint Ser.). 1977. reprint ed. 18. 95 (*0-8369-2778-8*) Ayer.

Mallery, Paul. Bridge & Trestle Handbook. (Illus.). 160p. 1992. pap. 18.95 (*0-911868-79-8*, C79) Carstens Pubns.

— Design Handbook for Model Railroads. (Illus.). 68p. 1990. pap. 8.95 (*0-911868-71-2*, C71) Carstens Pubns.

— Electrical Handbook for Model Railroads, Vol. 1. (Carstens Hobby Bks.). (Illus.). 68p. 1987. pap. 7.95 (*0-911868-21-6*, C21) Carstens Pubns.

— Electrical Handbook for Model Railroads, Vol. 2. rev. ed. (Carstens Hobby Bks.). 1982. pap. 8.95 (*0-911868-43-7*) Carstens Pubns.

— Operation Handbook for Model Railroads. (Illus.). 200p. 1991. pap. 12.95 (*0-911868-74-7*, C74) Carstens Pubns.

— Trackwork Handbook for Model Railroads. 3rd ed. (Hobby Bks.: No. C86). (Illus.). 112p. 1994. pap. 13.95 (*0-911868-86-0*) Carstens Pubns.

Mallery, Paul, jt. auth. see George, Darren.

Mallery, Richard D., ed. Masterworks of Autobiography. LC 70-111848. (Essay Index Reprint Ser.). 1977. 40.95 (*0-8369-1760-X*) Ayer.

— Masterworks of Travel & Exploration. LC 73-111849. (Essay Index Reprint Ser.). 1977. 34.95 (*0-8369-1761-8*) Ayer.

***Mallery, Susan.** The Best Bride. (Special Edition Ser.). 1995. pap. 3.50 (*0-373-09933-9*, 1-09933-2) Silhouette.

— Cowboy Daddy. 1994. mass mkt. 3.50 (*0-373-09898-7*, 1-09898-7) Harlequin Bks.

— A Dad for Billie. (Silhouette Special Edition Ser.). 1993. mass mkt. 3.50 (*0-373-09834-0*, 5-09834-8) Silhouette.

— Father in Training. (Special Edition Ser.). 1995. mass mkt. 3.75 (*0-373-09969-X*, 1-09969-6) Silhouette.

— Justin's Bride. (Historical Ser.). 1995. pap. 4.50 (*0-373-28870-0*, 1-28870-3) Harlequin Bks.

— Marriage on Demand. (Special Edition Ser.). 1995. pap. 3.75 (*0-373-09939-8*, 1-09939-9) Silhouette.

— More Than Friends. 1993. mass mkt. 3.39 (*0-373-09802-2*, 5-09802-5) Silhouette.

— The Only Way Out. (Intimate Moments Ser.). 1995. mass mkt. 3.75 (*0-373-07646-0*, 1-07646-2) Silhouette.

— Tempting Faith. (Silhouette Intimate Moments Ser.). 1994. mass mkt. 3.50 (*0-373-07554-5*, 5-07554-4) Silhouette.

Malleson, George B. Battlefields of Germany, from the Outbreak of the Thirty-Years' War. LC 68-54798. 360p. 1971. reprint ed. text ed. 38.50 (*0-8371-5017-5*, MABG, Greenwood Pr) Greenwood.

Malleson, George B., ed. see Kaye, John W.

Malless, Stan & McQain, Jeff. The Elements of English: A Glossary of Basic Terms for Literature, Composition, & Grammar. 86p. 1988. pap. 6.95 (*0-8191-6803-3*) U Pr of Amer.

Malless, Stan & McQuain, Jeff. A Handlist to English: Basic Terms for Literature, Composition, & Grammar. LC 86-9176. 48p. (Orig.). (C). 1986. pap. text ed. 10.50 (*0-8191-5408-3*) U Pr of Amer.

Mallet, D., ed. Viscount Henry St. John Bolingbroke: The Works, 5 vols., Set. (Anglistica & Americana Ser.: No. 13). 1968. reprint ed. 637.00 (*0-685-66435-X*, 05102021, Pub. by Georg Olms GW) Lubrecht & Cramer.

Mallet, David. Works of David Mallet, 3 Vols, Set. LC 74-144567. reprint ed. 165.00 (*0-404-08580-6*) AMS Pr.

Mallet Du Pan, Jacques. Considerations on the Nature of the French Revolution & on the Causes Which Prolong Its Duration. LC 74-13491. xxii, 114p. 1975. reprint ed. 30.00 (*0-86527-032-5*) Fertig.

Mallet, Francoise. The Illusionist. Briffault, Herma, tr. LC 75-12335. (Homosexuality Ser.). (ENG.). 1975. reprint ed. 15.95 (*0-405-07383-6*) Ayer.

Mallet, Jerry J., jt. auth. see Bartch, Marian R.

Mallet-Joris, Francoise. Adriana Sposa. (FRE.). 1991. pap. 12.95 (*0-7859-3284-4*, 2277230626) Fr & Eur.

— Allegra. 416p. 1976. 25.00 (*0-686-56296-8*) Fr & Eur.

— Un Chagrin d'Amour et d'Ailleurs. (FRE.). 1983. pap. 6.95 (*0-7859-3111-2*) Fr & Eur.

— La Chambre Rouge. 284p. (FRE.). 1955. 9.95 (*0-8288-9836-7*, F110720) Fr & Eur.

— Le Clin d'Oeil de l'Ange. (FRE.). 1985. pap. 12.95 (*0-7859-2909-6*) Fr & Eur.

— Cordelia. 300p. (FRE.). 1956. 8.95 (*0-8288-9837-5*, F110730) Fr & Eur.

— Dickie-Roi. (FRE.). 1982. pap. 12.95 (*0-7859-3106-6*) Fr & Eur.

— Divine. (FRE.). 1992. pap. 12.95 (*0-7859-3438-3*) Fr & Eur.

— L' Empire Celeste. 400p. (FRE.). 1973. 13.95 (*0-8288-9838-3*, F110740) Fr & Eur.

— J'Aurais Voulu Jouer de L'Accordeon. 128p. 1976. 9.95 (*0-686-56302-6*) Fr & Eur.

— Le Jeu du Souterrain. 288p. (FRE.). 1973. pap. 10.95 (*0-7859-1467-6*, 2253011592); pap. 3.95 (*0-685-73293-2*) Fr & Eur.

— Lettre a Moi-Meme. 304p. (FRE.). 1970. 6.95 (*0-8288-9839-1*, F110761) Fr & Eur.

— La Maison de Papier. 272p. (FRE.). 1970. 10.95 (*0-8288-9910-X*, F140728); pap. 3.95 (*0-686-56308-5*) Fr & Eur.

— Les Mensonges. (FRE.). 1956. 6.95 (*0-8288-9840-5*, F110780) Fr & Eur.

— Les Personnages. 462p. (FRE.). 1973. 13.95 (*0-8288-9841-3*, F110790); pap. 3.95 (*0-686-56311-5*) Fr & Eur.

— Le Rempart des Beguines. 1951. 8.95 (*0-686-56312-3*); 10.95 (*0-8288-9842-1*, F110801) Fr & Eur.

— Le Rire de Laura. (FRE.). 1987. pap. 12.95 (*0-7859-3392-1*) Fr & Eur.

— Les Signes et les Prodiges. 416p. (FRE.). 1966. pap. 10.95 (*0-8288-9843-X*, F110821); pap. 3.95 (*0-686-56316-6*) Fr & Eur.

— Trilingual Psychological Dictionary, Vol. 3: German-English-French. 592p. 1978. pap. 55.00 (*0-7859-0061-6*, M12024) Fr & Eur.

— La Tristesse de la Cerf-Volant. (FRE.). 1989. pap. 12.95 (*0-7859-3279-8*, 2277225967) Fr & Eur.

— Trois Ages de la Nuit. (FRE.). 1992. pap. 13.95 (*0-7859-4774-4*) Fr & Eur.

Mallet, M. Dominique. Les Rapports des Grecs avec l'Egypte. 218p. 1980. 30.00 (*0-89005-299-9*) Ares.

Mallet, Paul H. Northern Antiquities. LC 68-57868. (Bohn's Antiquarian Library). reprint ed. 56.00 (*0-404-50020-X*) AMS Pr.

— Northern Antiquities; or, a Description of the Manners, Customs, Religion & Laws of the Ancient Danes, & Other Northern Nations, 2 vols. Feldman, Burton & Richardson, Robert, eds. LC 78-60889. (Myth & Romanticism Ser.: Vol. 16). 840p. 1979. lib. bdg. 15.00 (*0-8240-3565-8*) Garland.

Mallet, Robert, ed. see Gide, Andre.

Mallet, Serge. Essays on the New Working Class. Howard, Dick & Savage, Dean, eds. LC 75-34904. 240p. (Orig.). (C). 1975. 25.00 (*0-914386-13-1*); pap. 15.00 (*0-914386-14-X*) Telos Pr.

Mallet, Serge, ed. The New Working Class. Shepherd, Andree, tr. 210p. 1975. 32.50 (*0-85124-131-X*, Pub. by Spokesman Bks UK) Coronet Bks.

Mallett. Frozen Food Production. 1994. text ed. 179.95 (*0-442-30867-1*) Van Nos Reinhold.

Mallett, jt. auth. see Grundy, Ken.

Mallett, A. S. Mallet: John Mallet, the Huguenot, & His Descendants, 1694-1894. 342p. 1992. reprint ed. lib. bdg. 53.00 (*0-8328-2207-8*); reprint ed. pap. 43.00 (*0-8328-2208-6*) Higginson Bk Co.

— The Union-Castle Line. 1990. 59.00 (*0-9516038-1-7*, Pub. by Ship Pictorial Pubng UK) St Mut.

Mallett, A. S. & Bell, A. M. The Pirrie Kylsant Motorships 1915-1932. 1990. 39.00 (*0-9509453-0-7*, Pub. by Ship Pictorial Pubng UK) St Mut.

Mallett, Annette Y., jt. auth. see Mallett, Daryl F.

Mallett, Ashley. Clarrie Grimmett: The Bradman of Spin. pap. 16.95 (*0-7022-2531-2*, Pub. by Univ Queensland Pr AT) Intl Spec Bk.

Mallett, D. T. Index of Artists, International: Biographical. 28.50 (*0-8446-1297-9*) Peter Smith.

— Supplement to Index of Artists. 28.50 (*0-8446-1298-7*) Peter Smith.

Mallett, Daryl, jt. ed. see Hewett, Jerry.

Mallett, Daryl F. & Mallett, Annette Y. The Work of Elizabeth Chater: An Annotated Bibliography & Guide. Clarke, Boden, ed. LC 93-333. (Bibliographies of Modern Authors Ser.: No. 27). 80p. Date not set. pap. 11.00x (*0-89370-490-3*) Borgo Pr.

— The Work of Elizabeth Chater: An Annotated Bibliography & Guide. Clarke, Boden, ed. LC 93-333. (Bibliographies of Modern Authors Ser.: No. 27). 80p. 1994. lib. bdg. 21.00x (*0-89370-390-7*) Borgo Pr.

Mallett, Daryl F. & Reginald, Robert. Reginald's Science Fiction & Fantasy Awards: A Comprehensive Guide to the Awards & Their Winners. enl. rev. ed. LC 92-24445. (Borgo Literary Guides Ser.: No. 1). 248p. 1993. pap. 21.00x (*0-8095-1200-9*) Borgo Pr.

— Reginald's Science Fiction & Fantasy Awards: A Comprehensive Guide to the Awards & Their Winners. 3rd enl. rev. ed. LC 92-24445. (Borgo Literary Guides Ser.: No. 1). 248p. 1993. 31.00x (*0-8095-0200-3*) Borgo Pr.

Mallett, Daryl F., ed. see Bamberger, W. C.

Mallett, Daryl F., ed. see Burgess, Brio.

Mallett, Daryl F., ed. see Cox, Greg.

Mallett, Daryl F., jt. auth. see Hall, Hal W.

Mallett, Daryl F., jt. ed. see Hall, Hal W.

Mallett, Daryl F., ed. see Harbottle, Philip & Holland, Stephen.

Mallett, Daryl F., jt. auth. see Hewett, Jerry.

Mallett, Daryl F., ed. see Indick, Ben P.

Mallett, Daryl F., ed. see Science Fiction Research Association Staff.

Mallett, Daryl F., ed. see Wood, Martine.

Mallett, David. Inch by Inch: The Garden Song. LC 93-38352. (Illus.). 32p. (J). (ps-3). 1995. 13.95 (*0-06-024303-1*) HarpC Child Bks.

— Inch by Inch: The Garden Song. LC 93-38352. (Illus.). 32p. (J). (ps-3). 1995. lib. bdg. 13.89 (*0-06-024304-X*) HarpC Child Bks.

Mallett, Gavin, ed. see Conference on Applications of X-Ray Analysis (14th: 1965, Denver).

Mallett, James K., ed. Ministry of Governance. 255p. (Orig.). 1987. pap. 12.00 (*0-934616-31-0*) Canon Law Soc.

Mallett, Jane, jt. auth. see Pritchard, A. P.

Mallett, Jerry & Bartch, Marian. Booker's Bunch, Bk. 1. 80p. (J). (gr. 3-4). 1988. lib. bdg. 9.74 (*0-8000-4735-4*, 036417) Perma-Bound.

— Booker's Bunch, Bk. 2. 88p. (J). (gr. 3-4). 1988. lib. bdg. 9.74 (*0-8000-4736-2*, 036418) Perma-Bound.

— Clearly Old Ernie. 151p. (J). (gr. 4-7). 1989. lib. bdg. 8.45 (*0-8000-3303-5*, 055786) Perma-Bound.

— Good Old Ernie. 127p. (J). (gr. 4-7). 1978. lib. bdg. 7.65 (*0-8479-1992-7*, 120716) Perma-Bound.

— Poor Old Ernie. 96p. (J). (gr. 4-7). 1988. reprint ed. lib. bdg. 8.45 (*0-8479-9036-2*, 239600) Perma-Bound.

Mallett, Jerry & Ervin, Timothy. Fold & Cut Stories. 56p. (Orig.). (J). (ps-5). 1992. pap. text ed. 9.95 (*0-913853-26-7*, 32538, Alleyside) Highsmith Pr.

— Sound & Action Stories. 48p. (Orig.). (J). (ps-3). 1992. pap. text ed. 6.95 (*0-913853-23-2*, 32534, Alleyside) Highsmith Pr.

***Mallett, Jerry & Polette, Keith.** World Folktales: A Multicultural Approach to Whole Language, Vol. 1. LC 94-21691. 66p. (J). (gr. k-2). 1994. pap. 10.95 (*0-917846-43-5*, Alleyside) Highsmith Pr.

— World Folktales: A Multicultural Approach to Whole Language, Vol. 2. LC 94-21691. 60p. 1994. pap. 10.95 (*0-917846-44-3*, Alleyside) Highsmith Pr.

— World Folktales: A Multicultural Approach to Whole Language, Vol. 3. LC 94-21691. 89p. (J). (gr. 6-8). 1994. pap. 10.95 (*0-917846-45-1*, Alleyside) Highsmith Pr.

***Mallett, Jerry, et al.** Selling Adventure Travel: Marketing Today's Travel. Adventure Travel Society Staff, ed. (Illus.). (Orig.). Date not set. pap. 29.95 (*1-885789-04-1*) Advent Trvl Soc.

Mallett, Jerry J. Library Skills Activities Kit: Puzzles, Games, Bulletin Boards & Other Interest-Rousers for the Elementary School Library. 1980. spiral bd. 24.95 (*0-87628-535-3*) Ctr Appl Res.

— Reading Bulletin Boards & Displays Kit. 288p. 1987. pap. 19.95 (*0-318-32867-4*, Busn) P-H.

Mallett, Jerry J. & Ervin, Timothy S. Elevator. (Illus.). 23p. (J). (ps-2). 1992. 9.40 (*0-7804-3989-9*, 088542) Perma-Bound.

— Elevator: Paper Big Book. (Illus.). 23p. (Orig.). (J). (ps-2). 1992. pap. 22.00 (*0-7804-3988-0*, 088544) Perma-Bound.

— Elevator: Perma Big Book. (Illus.). 23p. (J). (ps-2). 1992. 47.50 (*0-7804-3987-2*, 088543) Perma-Bound.

— Good Day, Blue Goose. (Illus.). 28p. (J). (ps-2). 1992. 9.40 (*0-7804-3992-9*, 120051) Perma-Bound.

— Good Day, Blue Goose: Paper Big Book. (Illus.). 28p. (Orig.). (J). (ps-2). 1992. pap. 22.00 (*0-7804-3990-2*, 120052) Perma-Bound.

— Good Day, Blue Goose: Perma Big Book. (Illus.). 28p. (J). (ps-2). 1992. 47.50 (*0-7804-3991-0*, 120053) Perma-Bound.

Mallett, Jerry J., jt. auth. see Bartch, Marian R.

Mallett, Margaret. Making Facts Matter: Reading Non-Fiction 5-11. 160p. 1992. pap. 27.00 (*1-85396-165-5*, Pub. by Paul Chapman UK) Taylor & Francis.

Mallett, Marshall. Handbook of Anatomy & Physiology for Students of Medical Radiation Technology. (Illus.). 280p. (C). 1984. text ed. 30.00 (*0-916973-00-X*) Burnell Co.

Mallett, Michael. The Borgias: The Rise & Fall of a Renaissance Dynasty. (Illus.). 368p. 1987. reprint ed. pap. 10.00 (*0-89733-238-5*) Academy Chi Pubs.

Mallett, Philip, ed. Kipling Considered. 192p. 1989. text ed. 39.95 (*0-312-26157-8*) St Martin.

Mallett, R. H., et al, eds. Effects of Piping Restraints on Piping Integrity: Pressure Vessels & Piping Conference, 1980, San Francisco, CA. LC 80-66028. (PVP Ser.: No. 40). 323p. pap. 92.10 (*0-317-58256-9*, 2056394) Bks Demand.

***Mallett, Reginald.** God's Coming in Christ: An Advent Study for Adults. LC 95-11871. 1995. write for info. (*0-687-00574-4*) Abingdon.

Mallette, Bruce I. & Howard, Richard P., eds. Monitoring & Assessing Intercollegiate Athletics. LC 85-645339. (New Directions for Institutional Research Ser.: No. IR 74). 100p. 1992. 16.95 (*1-55542-756-1*) Jossey-Bass.

***Mallette, Gloria.** When We Practice to Deceive. 224p. 1995. 4.95 (*0-87067-865-5*) Holloway.

Mallette, Kathleen & Tomlinson, Joann. Benchmarking: Focus on World-Class Practices. Serritella, Susan, ed. (AT&T Quality Library). 126p. (Orig.). 1992. pap. 29.95 (*0-932764-24-X*, 500-454) AT&T Customer Info.

Mallette, Richard. Spenser, Milton, & Renaissance Pastoral. LC 78-73154. 224p. 1980. 32.50 (*0-8387-2412-4*) Bucknell U Pr.

Mallette, Vincent P., jt. auth. see Watkins, Christopher D.

Mallevialle & Suf. Influence & Removal - Organics in Drinking Water Treatment. 1992. 89.95 (*0-87371-386-9*, TD449) Lewis Pubs.

Malley. Clinical Blood Gases: Invasive & Noninvasive Techniques & Applications. (Illus.). 400p. 1990. text ed. 44.00 (*0-7216-5861-X*) Saunders.

Malley, B., tr. see Pradera, Victor.

Malley, Barbara & Allen, Frances. Poetry with a Purpose. 128p. (J). (gr. 4-7). 1987. pap. 11.95 (*0-86653-415-6*, GA 1018) Good Apple.

Malley, Barbara B. Rhyme Time. 1992. pap. 11.99 (*0-86653-968-9*) Fearon Teach Aids.

***Malley, E. Louise.** Treasury of Animal Stories. 1994. 10.98 (*0-7858-0213-4*) Bk Sales Inc.

Malley, Elaine, tr. see Seara Vazquez, M.

Malley, J. D. Optimal Unbiased Estimation of Variance Components. (Lecture Notes in Statistics Ser.: Vol. 39). ix, 146p. 1986. pap. 32.00 (*0-387-96449-5*) Spr-Verlag.

***Malley, James D.** Statistical Applications of Jordan Algebras. LC 94-28225. (Lecture Notes in Statistics Ser.: Vol. 91). 1994. 29.00 (*0-387-94341-2*) Spr-Verlag.

Malley, Richard C. Graven by the Fishermen Themselves: Scrimshaw in Mystic Seaport Museum. (Illus.). 156p. 1983. pap. 19.95 (*0-913372-27-7*) Mystic Seaport.

— In Their Hours of Ocean Leisure: Scrimshaw in the Cold Spring Harbor Whaling Museum. 96p. 1993. 19.50 (*0-9636361-0-3*) Whaling Mus.

Malley, Sarah H., jt. auth. see Lightbody, Nancy K.

Malley, Stephen. The Kids' Guide to the Nineteen Ninety-Two Summer Olympics. (Illus.). 80p. (J). (gr. 3-7). 1992. pap. 12.95 (*0-316-54534-1*, Spts Illus Kids) Little.

Mallgrave, Harry F., ed. Otto Wagner: Reflections on the Raiment of Modernity. (Issues & Debates Ser.). (Illus.). 436p. 1993. 55.00 (*0-89236-258-8*); pap. 29.95 (*0-89236-257-X*) J P Getty Trust.

Mallgrave, Harry F., ed. see Semper, Gottfried.

Mallgrave, Harry F., tr. see Vischer, Robert, et al.

Mallgrave, Harry F., tr. see Wagner, Otto.

Malli, G. L., ed. Relativistic & Electron Correlation Effects in Molecules. (NATO ASI Series B, Physics: Vol. 318). (Illus.). 482p. 1994. 129.50 (*0-306-44625-1*, Plenum Pr) Plenum.

Mallia, Marianne, ed. Twenty-Five Years of Excellence: A History of the Texas Heart Institute. (Illus.). 300p. (C). 1989. 35.00 (*0-317-91336-0*) TX Heart Inst Found.

Malliani, A., et al, eds. Neural Mechanisms & Cardiovascular Disease: Proceedings of the International Symposium Held in S. Margherita Ligure, Italy, in May 1985. (FIDIA Research Ser.). 650p. 1987. 146.00 (*0-387-96454-1*) Spr-Verlag.

Malliaris, T. G. Stochastic Methods in Economics & Finance. (Advanced Textbooks in Economics Ser.: Vol. 17). 304p. 1982. 40.00 (*0-444-86201-3*, North Holland) Elsevier.

Malliavin, M. P. Seminaire d'Algebre Paul Dubreil et Marie-Paule Malliavin. (Lecture Notes in Mathematics Ser.: Vol. 1146). iv, 420p. (ENG & FRE.). 1985. pap. 49.60 (*0-387-15686-0*) Spr-Verlag.

Malliavin, M. P., ed. Seminaire d'Algebre Paul Dubreil et Marie-Paule Malliavin. (Lecture Notes in Mathematics Ser.: Vol. 1029). 339p. 1983. pap. 38.70 (*0-387-12699-6*) Spr-Verlag.

— Seminaire d'Algebre Paule Dubreil et Marie-Paul Malliavin. (Lecture Notes in Mathematics Ser.: Vol. 1404). ix, 410p. 1989. pap. 51.30 (*0-387-51812-6*) Spr-Verlag.

***Malliavin, Paul, et al.** Integration & Probability. (Graduate Texts in Mathematics Ser.: Vol. 157). 1995. write for info. (*0-387-94409-5*) Spr-Verlag.

Mallick. Fiber-Reinforced Composites: Materials, Manufacturing & Designs. (Mechanical Engineering Ser.: Vol. 83). 576p. 1993. 165.00 (*0-8247-9031-6*) Dekker.

An Asterisk (*) at the beginning of an entry indicates that the title is appearing in BIP for the first time.

Mallick, B. S. Money, Banking & Trade in Mughal India. (C). 1991. 22.50 (*0-685-59783-0*, Pub. by Rawat II) S Asia.

Mallick, Joan. Anorexia. Head, J. J., ed. LC 86-72198. (Carolina Biology Readers Ser.: No. 173). (Illus.). 16p. (Orig.). (YA). (gr. 10 up). 1987. pap. text ed. 2.75 (*0-89278-373-7*, 45-9773) Carolina Biological.

Mallick, M. R. Bail-Law & Practice. (C). 1990. 110.00 (*0-89771-175-0*) St Mut.

Mallick, P. K. Fibre-Reinforced Composites. 450p. 1988. 70.00 (*0-318-37729-2*) T-C Pubns CA.

Mallick, P. K. & Newman, S. Composite Materials Technology: Processes & Properties. 400p. (C). 1991. text ed. 89.95 (*1-56990-056-6*) Hanser-Gardner.

Mallick, Ross. Development Policy of a Communist Government: West Bengal Since 1977. LC 92-20010. (Cambridge South Asian Studies: No. 54). (Illus.). 240p. (C). 1994. 59.95 (*0-521-43292-8*) Cambridge U Pr.

Mallick, S., jt. auth. see Francon, Maurice.

Mallick, S. K. & Gupta, A. P. Reinforced Concrete. 4th ed. (C). 1987. pap. 14.00 (*81-204-0047-X*, Pub. by Oxford IBH II) S Asia.

Mallier, A. T. & Rosser, M. J. Women & the Economy: A Comparative Study of Britain & the United States. LC 86-4011. 1986. text ed. 35.00 (*0-312-88732-9*) St Martin.

Mallier, A. T. & Shafto, T. A. The Economics of Flexible Retirement. (Illus.). 180p. 1992. text ed. 75.00 (*0-12-466610-8*) Acad Pr.

Mallier, T. & Shafto, T., eds. Economics of Labour Markets & Management. (C). 1989. 130.00 (*0-09-173166-6*, Pub. by S Thornes Pubs UK) St Mut.

Mallik, Asok K., et al. Kinematic Analysis & Synthesis of Mechanisms. LC 93-37108. 1994. 79.95 (*0-8493-9121-0*, TJ175) CRC Pr.

Mallik, C. C. A Short Textbook of Medical Jurisprudence. 1985. 100.00 (*0-317-38795-2*, Current Dist) St Mut.

Mallik, G. N. Philosophy of Vaisnava Religion. 1972. 59.95 (*0-8490-0829-8*) Gordon Pr.

Mallin, Chris A., jt. auth. see Davidson, Ian R.

***Mallin, Eric S.** Inscribing the Time: Shakespeare & the End of Elizabethan England. LC 94-28943. (New Historicism: 33). 1995. 40.00 (*0-520-08623-6*) U CA Pr.

***Mallin, Gail.** Debt of Honour. large type ed. (Historical Romance Ser.). 1994. 18.95 (*0-263-14006-7*, Pub. by Mills & Boon Ltd UK) Chivers N Amer.

Mallin, Gail, jt. auth. see Andrew, Sylvia.

Mallin, Jay. Covering Castro: The Rise & Fall of Cuba's Communist Dictator. 250p. 1992. 21.95 (*0-944273-09-2*) U S Cuba Inst.

Mallin, Jay, Sr. Covering Castro. 200p. (C). 1994. 32.95 (*1-56000-156-9*) Transaction Pubs.

— Covering Castro: Rise & Decline of Cuba's Communist Dictator. LC 93-46178. 1994. 25.00 (*1-884750-00-1*) U S Cuba Inst.

Mallin, Jay. Ernesto 'Che' Guevara: Modern Revolutionary, Guerilla Theorist. Rahmas, D. Steve, ed. (Outstanding Personalities Ser.: No. 53). 32p. (Orig.). (gr. 7-12). 1973. lib. bdg. 4.95 (*0-87157-556-6*) SamHar Pr.

— The Great Managua Earthquake. Rahmas, D. Steve, ed. (Events of Our Times Ser.: No. 14). 32p. (Orig.). (gr. 7-12). 1974. student ed, lib. bdg. 4.95 (*0-87157-715-1*) SamHar Pr.

Mallin, Jay, ed. Strategy for Conquest: Communist Documents on Guerrilla Warfare. LC 71-102688. 1970. 19.95 (*0-87024-144-3*) U of Miami Pr.

— Terror & Urban Guerillas: A Study of Tactics & Documents. LC 79-163842. 1983. 13.95 (*0-87024-223-7*) U of Miami Pr.

Mallin, Robert E. Rx for Lean Living. 156p. 1979. pap. 4.95 (*0-933914-00-8*) Lone Raven.

Mallinckrodt, Anita . A Dream Left High & Dry: Town of Dortmund. (Illus.). 20p. (Orig.). 1992. pap. text ed. 4.00 (*0-931227-05-4*) Mallinckrodt Comm.

Mallinckrodt, Anita M. From Knights to Pioneers: One German Family in Westphalia & Missouri. LC 93-16891. (Illus.). 560p. (C). 1994. 45.00x (*0-8093-1917-9*) S Ill U Pr.

— Historic Augusta: Its Buildings & People, 1820-1900. (Illus.). 100p. (Orig.). 1994. pap. text ed. 8.50 (*0-931227-06-2*) Mallinckrodt Comm.

— Historical Highlights - Augusta, Missouri: From Town Board Records, 1855-1903. (Illus.). 28p. (Orig.). 1990. pap. text ed. 5.00 (*0-931227-04-6*) Mallinckrodt Comm.

— How They Came: German Immigration from Prussia to Missouri. (Illus.). 50p. (Orig.). 1989. pap. 6.25 (*0-931227-02-X*) Mallinckrodt Comm.

— What They Did: Public Activities of German Immigrants in Missouri. 20p. 1995. 4.00 (*0-931227-09-7*) Mallinckrodt Comm.

— What They Thought Vol. II: Missouri's German Immigrants Assess Their World 1860s. 32p. 1995. 5.00 (*0-931227-08-9*) Mallinckrodt Comm.

— Why They Left: German Immigration from Prussia to Missouri. rev. ed. (Illus.). 34p. 1989. reprint ed. pap. 5.25 (*0-931227-03-8*) Mallinckrodt Comm.

***Mallinckrodt, Anita M., abr.** What They Thought Vol. I: Missouri's German Immigrants Assess Their World, 1850s. 44p. 1995. 6.00 (*0-931227-07-0*) Mallinckrodt Comm.

Mallinckrodt, Robert G. Nobody's Imperfect: New Thinking from the Perfection-Now Position. LC 91-68407. (Perfection-Now Story Ser.: Vol. 1). 257p. (Orig.). 1992. pap. 12.95 (*0-9631888-0-1*) Silver Crest.

Mallinger, Allan & Dewyze, Jeannette. Too Perfect. 224p. 1993. pap. 8.00 (*0-449-90800-3*, Columbine) Fawcett.

Mallinof, Estell, ed. see Shosteck, Robert.

Mallinoff, Estelle, ed. see Burmeister, Walter F.

Mallinoff, Estelle, ed. see Garvey, Edward B.

Mallinson, Graham. Rumanian. (Descriptive Grammars Ser.). 384p. 1986. 72.50 (*0-7099-3537-4*, Pub. by Croom Helm UK) Routledge Chapman & Hall.

***Mallinson, Ian.** Keyworking in Social Care: A Structured Approach to Provision. 1995. 70.00 (*1-871177-06-5*, Pub. by Whiting & Birch UK); pap. 32.95 (*1-871177-12-X*, Pub. by Whiting & Birch UK) Paul & Co Pubs.

Mallinson, Jane, et al. H'mong Batik: A Textile Technique from Laos. LC 88-90587. (Illus.). 87p. (Orig.). 1988. pap. 12.50 (*0-9620278-0-4*) Mallinson Info Servs.

Mallinson, Jean. Margaret Atwood & Her Works (Poetry) (Canadian Author Studies). 65p. (C). 1985. pap. text ed. 9.95 (*0-920802-96-6*, Pub. by ECW Press CN) Genl Dist Srvs.

Mallinson, John. The Foundations of Magnetic Recording. 2nd ed. (Illus.). 217p. 1993. text ed. 39.95 (*0-12-466626-4*) Acad Pr.

— Magneto-Resistive Heads: Fundamentals & Applications. (Electromagnetism Ser.). (Illus.). 250p. 1995. boxed write for info. (*0-12-466630-2*) Acad Pr.

Mallinson, Linda. Contemporary Personnel: A Word Processing Simulation. 278p. (C). 1991. pap. text ed. write for info. (*0-13-173444-X*) P-H.

Mallinson, Vernon. None Can Be Called Deformed. Phillips, William R. & Rosenberg, Janet, eds. LC 79-6917. (Physically Handicapped in Society Ser.). 1980. reprint ed. lib. bdg. 24.95 (*0-405-13124-0*) Ayer.

Mallion, ed. see Sand, George.

Mallios, A. Topological Algebras: Selected Topics. (North Holland Mathematics Studies: Vol. 124). 536p. 1986. 95.00 (*0-444-87966-8*, North Holland) Elsevier.

Mallios, William S. Statistical Modeling: Applications in Contemporary Issues. LC 89-31303. 248p. (C). 1989. text ed. 41.95 (*0-8138-0307-1*) Iowa St U Pr.

Mallis, A. George, jt. auth. see Van Allan, Leroy.

Mallis, Arnold, et al. Handbook of Pest Control. 7th ed. (Illus.). 1990. 89.00 (*0-317-99622-3*) Franzak & Foster.

Mallis, Jackie. Diamonds in the Dust: Discover & Develop Your Child's Gifts. 448p. (Orig.). 1982. pap. 14.95 (*0-86617-020-0*) Multi Media TX.

— Diamonds in the Dust: Discover & Develop Your Child's Gifts. 2nd ed. 448p. (Orig.). 1992. pap. 19.95 (*0-86617-056-1*) Multi Media TX.

— Effective Composition: A Problem-Solving Process. 100p. 1988. pap. 15.95 (*0-86617-040-5*) Multi Media TX.

— Mosaics. (Pathways to Poetry Ser.). 95p. 1984. pap. 15.95 (*0-86617-030-8*) Multi Media TX.

Mallis, Jackie, ed. Ideas for Teaching Gifted Students, 8 bks., Set. Incl. English. 192p. pap. 29.95 (*0-86617-022-7*); Language Arts. 203p. 1980. pap. 29.95 (*0-86617-021-9*); Mathematics. 240p. 1980. pap. 29.95 (*0-86617-027-X*); Music. 206p. pap. 29.95 (*0-86617-028-6*); Science. 245p. 1980. pap. 29.95 (*0-86617-026-X*); Social Studies-Elementary. 200p. 1980. pap. 29.95 (*0-86617-023-5*); Social Studies-Secondary. 154p. 1980. pap. 29.95 (*0-86617-024-3*); Visual Arts. 162p. 1980. pap. 29.95 (*0-86617-025-1*); 1980. Set pap. text ed. 199.95 (*0-86617-029-4*) Multi Media TX.

Mallis, Jacqueline. Earn Cash Creating Word Puzzles. (Illus.). 160p. (Orig.). 1993. 19.95 (*0-86617-055-3*) Multi Media TX.

Mallison, Constance, text. Variations: Seven Los Angeles Painters, Vol. II. LC 83-80463. (Illus.). 51p. (Orig.). 1983. pap. 10.00 (*0-911291-08-3*) Fellows Cont Art.

Mallison, Francoise, jt. ed. see Eck, Diana L.

Mallison, Francoise, jt. ed. see Entwistle, Alan W.

Mallison, George. Color at Home & Abroad. LC 72-132388. reprint ed. 39.50 (*0-404-00198-X*) AMS Pr.

Mallison, Sally V. & Mallison, Thomas W. Settlements & the Law: A Juridicial Analysis of the Israeli Settlements in the Occupied Territories. (Illus.). 1982. pap. 1.00 (*0-318-01027-5*) Am Educ Trust.

Mallison, Sally V. & Mallison, W. Thomas. Armed Conflict in Lebanon, 1982: Humanitarian Law in a Real World Setting. (Illus.). 86p. 1985. pap. 8.95 (*0-318-01034-8*) Am Educ Trust.

Mallison, Thomas W., jt. auth. see Mallison, Sally V.

Mallison, W. T., Jr. The Balfour Declaration: An Appral in International Law. (Information Papers: No. 4). 52p. 1971. pap. text ed. 1.00 (*0-937694-20-7*) Assn Arab-Amer U Grads.

Mallison, W. Thomas, jt. auth. see Mallison, Sally V.

Mallmann, Jacob E. Shelter Island & Presbyterian Church. 1976. 23.95 (*0-8488-0874-6*) Amereon Ltd.

Mallmann, Joanne, jt. auth. see Dittl, Barbara.

Mallmann, Wolfgang, ed. & intro. Armament & Disarmament in the 1980s. LC 92-21182. (Library of Contemporary History, Stuttgart). 288p. 1995. 52.95 (*0-85496-383-9*) Berg Pubs.

Malloch, Christian A., tr. see Wieser, Friedrich von.

Malloch, D. Macleod, jt. auth. see Morton, George A.

Malloch, David. Moulds: Their Isolation, Cultivation & Identification. LC 81-195429. (Illus.). 107p. reprint ed. pap. 30.50 (*0-8357-3996-1*, 2036696) Bks Demand.

Malloch, David, jt. auth. see Ker, John.

Malloch, Theodore R. Beyond Reductionism. 290p. 1983. text ed. 29.50 (*0-8290-1292-3*) Irvington.

— Issues in International Trade & Development Policy. LC 87-2469. 192p. 1987. text ed. 55.00 (*0-275-92356-8*, C2356, Praeger Pubs) Greenwood.

Mallock, William H. The New Republic: Or, Culture, Faith & Philosophy in an English Country House. LC 75-30033. 376p. reprint ed. 34.50 (*0-404-14036-X*) AMS Pr.

— Studies of Contemporary Superstition. LC 72-333. (Essay Index Reprint Ser.). 1977. reprint ed. 23.95 (*0-8369-2804-0*) Ayer.

***Mallon, A.** The Religion of Egypt. (African Heritage Classical Research Studies Ser.). Date not set. 10.00 (*0-938818-37-6*) ECA Assoc.

— Religion of Egypt. (African Studies). reprint ed. 10.00 (*0-685-56712-5*) ECA Assoc.

Mallon, Bill, et al. Quest for Gold: The Encyclopedia of American Olympians. LC 84-966. (Illus.). 496p. 1984. pap. 26.00 (*0-88011-217-4*, PMAL0217) Human Kinetics.

Mallon, Elias D., ed. Neighbors: Islam in North America. 112p. (Orig.). 1989. pap. 5.95 (*0-377-00198-8*) Friendship Pr.

Mallon, Florencia E. Peasant & Nation: The Making of Postcolonial Mexico & Peru. LC 93-34677. 1994. 55.00 (*0-520-08504-3*); pap. 19.00 (*0-520-08505-1*) U CA Pr.

Mallon, Florenica E. The Defense of Community in Peru's Central Highlands: Peasant Struggle & Capitalist Transition, 1860-1940. LC 83-42565. 400p. 1983. 59.50x (*0-691-07647-2*); pap. 17.95x (*0-691-10140-X*) Princeton U Pr.

Mallon, G. W. Bankers Versus Consumers. 1972. 59.95 (*0-87968-703-7*) Gordon Pr.

Mallon, Maurus E. Ex Novo Mundo: Ten Tales of the Americas. LC 91-60949. 126p. (Orig.). 1991. pap. write for info. (*0-88100-074-4*) Natl Writ Pr.

— A Matter of Conscience. LC 89-64249. 112p. (Orig.). (C). 1990. pap. 6.95 (*0-88100-067-1*) Natl Writ Pr.

Mallon, Richard D. & Sourrouille, Juan V. Economic Policymaking in a Conflict Society: The Argentine Case. LC 74-21227. (Center for International Affairs Ser.). 288p. 1975. 32.00 (*0-674-22930-4*) HUP.

Mallon, Sarah R., ed. see Handy, Isaac W.

Mallon, Thomas. Aurora, No. 7. 246p. 1992. pap. 8.95 (*0-393-30848-0*) Norton.

— Book of One's Own. 318p. 1995. reprint ed. pap. 14.00 (*1-886913-02-1*) Hungry Mind.

— Henry & Clara. 1994. 22.95 (*0-395-59071-X*) Ticknor & Fields.

— Henry & Clara. large type ed. LC 95-721. 1995. write for info. (*0-7862-0420-6*) Thorndike Pr.

— Rockets & Rodeos & Other American Spectacles. LC 92-33189. 256p. 1993. 19.95 (*0-89919-939-9*) Ticknor & Fields.

— Stolen Words: Forays into the Origins & Ravages of Plagiarism. 320p. 1991. pap. 9.95 (*0-14-014440-4*) Viking Penguin.

Mallon, William J., et al. Orthopaedics for the House Officer. (Illus.). 200p. 1990. 20.00 (*0-683-05420-1*) Williams & Wilkins.

Mallone, George. Arming for Spiritual Warfare: How Christians Can Prepare to Fight the Enemy. LC 90-46663. 200p. (Orig.). 1991. pap. 9.99 (*0-8308-1734-4*, 1734) InterVarsity.

Mallonee, Barbara C., et al. Minute by Minute: A History of the Baltimore Monthly Meetings of Friends, Homewood & Stony Run. (Illus.). 308p. (Orig.). 1992. pap. 17.00 (*0-9635053-1-9*) Baltimore Monthly.

Mallonee, Dennis. The Coming of Aphrodite. (Illus.). 32p. (Orig.). 1992. pap. 3.95 (*0-929729-00-5*) Heroic Pub CA.

— Eternity Smith, Bk. 1. (Illus.). 64p. (Orig.). 1988. pap. 7.95 (*0-317-91226-7*) Heroic Pub CA.

— Flare, Bk. 1. (Illus.). 64p. (Orig.). 1988. pap. 7.95 (*0-317-91227-5*) Heroic Pub CA.

— League of Champions, Bk. 1. (Illus.). 160p. (Orig.). 1990. pap. 9.95 (*0-929729-01-3*) Heroic Pub CA.

Malloney, George A., et al. Three Sacred Byzantine Poets. Vaporis, Nomikos V., ed. 74p. 1979. pap. 3.25 (*0-685-02339-7*) Holy Cross Orthodox.

Mallorca, Jacqueline & Verdon, Renee. Convection Cuisine: Great Taste & Maximum Results from Your Convection Oven, Including 250 Newly Created Recipes. LC 88-16359. (Illus.). 320p. 1988. 22.95 (*0-688-08100-2*) Hearst Bks.

Mallord, Lauri A. No More Black Days: Complete Freedom from Depression, Eating Disorders & Other Compulsive Behaviors. 128p. (Orig.). 1992. pap. 5.95 (*0-9630069-0-8*) Whi Stone.

Mallory. Profitable No Load Mutual Fund. 1988. 37.95 (*0-930233-11-5*) Windsor.

Mallory, A. W. Guidelines for Centrifugal Blast Cleaning. (Illus.). 1984. pap. text ed. 15.00 (*0-938477-09-9*) SSPC.

Mallory, Bob F., jt. auth. see Cargo, David N.

Mallory, Bruce & New, Rebecca. Diversity & Developmentally Appropriate Practice in Early Childhood Education: Challenges for Early Childhood Education. (Early Childhood Education Ser.). (C). 1993. text ed. 41.00 (*0-8077-3300-8*); pap. text ed. 17.95 (*0-8077-3299-0*) Tchrs Coll.

Mallory, Bruce L., jt. auth. see Mulick, James.

Mallory, Charles. Direct Mail Magic. Brett, Elaine, ed. LC 90-83478. (Fifty-Minute Ser.). (Illus.). 73p. (Orig.). 1991. pap. 9.95 (*1-56052-075-2*) Crisp Pubns.

— Publicity Power: A Practical Guide to Effective Promotion. Crisp, Michael G., ed. LC 88-92737. (Fifty-Minute Ser.). (Illus.). 96p. (Orig.). 1989. pap. 9.95 (*0-931961-82-3*) Crisp Pubns.

— Workhealing: The Healing Process for You & Your Job. 128p. (Orig.). 1993. pap. 8.95 (*0-87516-664-4*) DeVorss.

Mallory, Daniel, jt. auth. see Clay, Henry.

Mallory, Doug. Football Drill Book. LC 93-34346. (Illus.). 192p. (Orig.). 1993. pap. 12.95 (*0-940279-72-X*) Masters Pr IN.

Mallory, Eva L. Riding the Right Roads. (Illus.). 640p. 1989. ring bd. 25.00 (*0-685-28999-0*) Right Roads Pubns.

Mallory, Franklin B. Serial Numbers of U. S. Martial Arms. LC 82-63083. 112p. 1983. pap. 15.00 (*0-9603306-1-5*) Springfield Res Serv.

— Serial Numbers of U. S. Martial Arms. 208p. 1990. pap. 20.00 (*0-9603306-4-X*) Springfield Res Serv.

— Serial Numbers of U. S. Martial Arms. 320p. 1995. pap. 30.00 (*0-9603306-5-8*) Springfield Res Serv.

— Serial Numbers of U. S. Martial Arms, Vol. 2. 209p. 1986. pap. 20.00 (*0-9603306-3-1*) Springfield Res Serv.

Mallory, George. Boswell the Biographer. 1972. 59.95 (*0-87968-778-9*) Gordon Pr.

Mallory, George L., jt. auth. see Bury, Charles H.

Mallory, H. S. Backgrounds of Book Reviewing. 1972. 59.95 (*0-87968-693-6*) Gordon Pr.

Mallory, J. P. In Search of the Indo-Europeans: Language, Archaeology & Myth. 1991. pap. 19.95 (*0-500-27616-1*) Thames Hudson.

Mallory, J. P., jt. auth. see Telegin, D. Ya.

Mallory, James, Jr., jt. auth. see Cosgrove, Mark.

Mallory, James D., Jr., jt. auth. see Kubetin, Cynthia A.

Mallory, Ken, jt. auth. see Kraus, Scott.

***Mallory, Kenneth.** Families of the Deep Blue Sea. LC 95-7039. (Saltwater Secrets Ser.). (Illus.). 32p. (J). 1995. 14.95 (*0-88106-886-1*); lib. bdg. 15.88 (*0-88106-887-X*); pap. 6.95 (*0-88106-885-3*) Charlesbridge Pub.

Mallory, Kenneth, Jr. Practice Soccer by Yourself. (Illus.). 272p. 1985. pap. 10.95 (*0-89651-606-7*) B L Pub.

Mallory, Kenneth. The Red Sea. (New England Aquarium Book Ser.). (Illus.). 48p. (J). (gr. 5-7). 1991. 14.95 (*0-531-15213-8*); lib. bdg. 15.82 (*0-531-10993-3*) Watts.

— Water Hole: And the Rebirth of a Tropical Forest. LC 92-14360. (Illus.). 56p. (J). (gr. 5-8). 1992. 15.95 (*0-531-15250-2*); lib. bdg. 16.87 (*0-531-11154-7*) Watts.

Mallory, Kenneth & Conley, Andrea. Rescue of the Stranded Whales. 48p. (J). (gr. 3 up). 1989. pap. 14.95 (*0-671-67122-7*, S&S Bks Young Read) S&S Childrens.

Mallory, Kenneth, jt. ed. see Kaufman, Les.

Mallory, Lee. I Write Your Name. Odom, Robert, Jr., ed. (Poetry Ser.). 1990. write for info. (*0-9626168-0-X*) Prometh Pr CA.

Mallory, Lee, ed. see Edelman, Bart.

Mallory, Lee, ed. see Haim.

Mallory, Lee, ed. see Odom, Robert, Jr.

Mallory, Maria, ed. see Williams, Terry.

Mallory, Nina A., jt. auth. see Sullivan, Edward J.

Mallory, Perry M., ed. see Tetsola, John.

Mallory, Roosevelt. Radcliff, No. Four: New Jersey Showdown. (Orig.). 1976. pap. 2.25 (*0-87067-085-9*, BH085) Holloway.

Mallory, Steven R. Software Development & Quality Assurance for the Healthcare Manufacturing Industries. 316p. 1994. 169.00 (*0-935184-58-9*) Interpharm.

Mallory, Susan B. & Leal-Khouri, Susana. An Illustrated Dictionary of Dermatologic Syndromes. LC 94-15125. (Illus.). 250p. 1994. 54.95 (*1-85070-458-9*) Prthnon Pub.

Mallory, Tess. Jewels of Time. 400p. (Orig.). 1994. mass mkt., pap. text ed. 4.99 (*0-505-51976-3*) Dorchester Pub Co.

Mallory, Thomas. King Arthur & His Knights of the Round Table. Lanier, Sidney & Pyle, Howard, eds. (Illus.). 288p. (J). (gr. 4-6). 1950. 13.95 (*0-448-06016-7*, G&D) Putnam Pub Group.

Mallory, Virgil S. Lower Tertiary Biostratigraphy of the California Coast Ranges. LC 59-1390. 460p. reprint ed. pap. 131.10 (*0-317-29061-4*, 2023745) Bks Demand.

Mallory, Walter H. China: Land of Famine. LC 76-39655. (Select Bibliographies Reprint Ser.). 1977. reprint ed. 23.95 (*0-8369-9940-1*) Ayer.

Mallory, William & Simpson-Housley, Paul, eds. Geography & Literature: A Meeting of the Disciplines. LC 86-22968. (Illus.). 192p. 1989. pap. text ed. 16.95x (*0-8156-2464-6*) Syracuse U Pr.

Mallos, Tess. Barbecue Cookbook. 1994. 9.99 (*0-517-10251-X*) Random Hse Value.

— The Complete Middle East Cookbook. (Illus.). 384p. 1993. 34.95 (*0-8048-1982-3*) C E Tuttle.

Mallotte, Stan. Painless Path to Proper Punctuation. 1990. pap. 8.95 (*0-312-04399-6*) St Martin.

Mallouk, Brenda M. Accounting: The Basis for Business Decisions: Problem Supplement II Solutions Manual. (C). 1990. pap. text ed. write for info. (*0-07-551001-4*, Pub. by McGraw-H Ryerson CN) McGraw.

— Adders 'N Keyes: One Month in the Life of a Sole Proprietorship. 2nd ed. (C). 1991. pap. text ed. write for info. (*0-07-551221-1*, Pub. by McGraw-H Ryerson CN) McGraw.

— Problems Plus Solutions in Financial Accounting. Smythe, Kelly, ed. 124p. (C). 1991. pap. text ed. write for info. (*0-07-551340-4*, Pub. by McGraw-H Ryerson CN) McGraw.

— Problems, Problems & More Problems in Accounting. Smythe, Kelly, ed. (C). 1991. reprint ed. pap. text ed. write for info. (*0-07-551331-5*, Pub. by McGraw-H Ryerson CN) McGraw.

Mallouk, Thomas E., ed. Advances in the Synthesis & Reactivity of Solids, Vol. 2. 1991. 90.25 (*1-55938-330-5*) Jai Pr.

Mallouk, Thomas E. & Harrison, D. Jed, eds. Interfacial Design & Chemical Sensing. LC 94-19957. (Symposium Ser.: Vol. 561). 338p. 1994. 94.95 (*0-8412-2931-7*) Am Chemical.

Mallove, Eugene F. Fire from Ice: Searching for the Truth Behind the Cold Fusion Furor. 352p. 1991. text ed. 22.95 (*0-471-53139-1*) Wiley.

Mallove, Eugene F. & Matloff, Gregory L. The Starflight Handbook: A Pioneer's Guide to Interstellar Travel. 274p. 1989. text ed. 27.95 (*0-471-61912-4*) Wiley.

***Mallow.** Vipers. 1996. write for info. (*0-89464-877-2*) Krieger.

Mallow, Jeffry V. Science Anxiety. Hackworth, Robert & Howland, Joseph, eds. (Illus.). 200p. (Orig.). 1986. 12.95 (*0-943202-18-3*) H & H Pub.

Mallowe, Mike. Meatman. 1989. pap. 3.95 (*1-55817-201-7*, Pinnacle NY) Windsor NY.

Mallowe, Mike, jt. auth. see McCarthy, Bill.

Mallowe, Mike, jt. auth. see McCarthy, William.

Mallows, D. F. & Pickering, W. J. Stress Analysis Problems in SI Units. LC 71-171465. 1972. 117.00 (*0-08-016293-2*, Pub. by Pergamon Repr UK) Franklin.

M

An Asterisk (*) at the beginning of an entry indicates that the title is appearing in BIP for the first time.

Malloy. Common-Sense Geriatrics. 1991. pap. 38.95 (*0-86542-107-2*) Blackwell Sci.
— Economic Sanctions & U. S. Trade. 1990. 175.00 (*0-316-54515-5*) Little.

Malloy & Hartshorn. Acute Care Nursing in the Home: A Holistic Approach. (Illus.). 606p. 1988. text ed. 36.50 (*0-397-54661-0*) Lippincott.

Malloy, jt. ed. see Conway.

Malloy, tr. see Gallegos, Romula.

Malloy, Alex G. Comic Book Artists. 352p. 1993. pap. 14.95 (*0-87069-707-2*, Wallace-Hmestead) Chilton.
— Comics Values Annual: The Comic Book Price Guide. 448p. 1992. pap. 15.95 (*0-87069-654-8*) Chilton.
— Comics Values Annual, 1993-94: The Comic Books Price Guide. 608p. 1993. pap. 15.95 (*0-87069-683-1*) Chilton.
— Comics Values Annual, 1994-95. 624p. 1994. pap. 12.95 (*0-87069-725-0*) Chilton.
— Price Guide to Medieval Coins in the Christian J. Thomsen Collection, Vol. 1. 1993. 9.50 (*0-915018-46-2*) Attic Bks.

***Malloy, Alex G., ed.** Comics Values Annual, 1996: The Comic Book Price Guide. 4th ed. (Illus.). 592p. 1995. pap. 14.95 (*0-930625-35-8*, Antque Trdr Bks) Antique Trader.

***Malloy, Alex G. & Wells, Stuart W.** Comic Collectibles & Their Values. 352p. 1995. pap. 15.95 (*0-87069-724-2*) Chilton.

Malloy, Alex G., jt. auth. see Sydenham, Edward A.

Malloy, Cathy, ed. see Souza, Fernando R.

Malloy, Charles. The Poems of Emerson: Selected Criticism from the Coming Age & the Arena, 1899-1905. LC 80-2539. 1981. 32.50 (*0-404-19265-3*) AMS Pr.

Malloy, Dick, jt. auth. see Ott, John S.

Malloy, Ione. Southie Won't Go: A Teacher's Diary of the Desegregation of South Boston High School. LC 86-16563. (Illus.). 304p. 1986. 29.95 (*0-252-01276-3*) U of Ill Pr.

Malloy, James M. Bolivia: The Uncompleted Revolution. LC 77-101486. (Pitt Latin American Ser.). 406p. reprint ed. 115.80 (*0-8357-9751-1*, 2015449) Bks Demand.
— The Politics of Social Security in Brazil. LC 78-53994. (Latin American Ser.). (Illus.). 232p. 1979. 49.95 (*0-8229-3385-3*) U of Pittsburgh Pr.

Malloy, James M., ed. Authoritarianism & Corporatism in Latin America. LC 76-6669. (Latin American Ser.). 552p. (C). 1977. pap. 19.95 (*0-8229-5275-0*) U of Pittsburgh Pr.

Malloy, James M. & Gamarra, Eduardo. Revolution & Reaction: Bolivia, 1964-1985. 256p. 1987. 29.95 (*0-88738-159-6*) Transaction Pubs.
— Revolution & Reaction: Bolivia, 1964-1992. 2nd ed. 1992. 32.95 (*1-56000-032-5*) Transaction Pubs.

Malloy, James M. & Gamarra, Eduardo, eds. Latin America & Caribbean Contemporary Record, 1988-1989, Vol. VIII. x, 1100p. 1993. 380.00 (*0-8419-1290-4*) Holmes & Meier.

Malloy, James M. & Seligson, Mitchell A., eds. Authoritarians & Democrats: Regime Transition in Latin America. LC 86-25035. (Latin American Ser.). (Illus.). 288p. (C). 1987. 49.95 (*0-8229-3551-1*); pap. 15.95 (*0-8229-5387-0*) U of Pittsburgh Pr.

Malloy, James M., jt. auth. see Conaghan, Catherine M.

Malloy, Jerry, comp. Sol White's History of Colored Base Ball, with Other Documents on the Early Black Game, 1886-1936. rev. ed. LC 94-20992. Orig. Title: Sol White's Official Base Ball Guide. 1995. reprint ed. text ed. 25.00 (*0-8032-4771-0*) U of Nebr Pr.

Malloy, John. Winning Investment Strategies. 1991. 49.95 (*0-8306-6741-5*) TAB Bks.

Malloy, John B. Winning Investment Strategies: Using Security Analysis to Build Wealth. 1990. text ed. 22.95 (*0-07-155094-1*) McGraw.
— Winning Investment Strategies: Using Security Analysis to Build Wealth. 1990. 22.95 (*0-8306-3509-2*) TAB Bks.

Malloy, John F., jt. auth. see Turner, William C.

Malloy, Joseph L., ed. Catechism for Inquirers. 4th ed. 1984. pap. 4.95 (*0-8091-5012-3*) Paulist Pr.

Malloy, Joseph T., tr. see Diez, Klemens, pseud.

Malloy, Linda Jo, jt. auth. see Malloy, Ruth L.

Malloy, Mary. African Americans in the Maritime Trades: A Guide to Resources in New England. (Museum Monograph Ser.). (Illus.). 1990. pap. text ed. 6.50 (*0-937854-30-1*) Kendall Whaling.

Malloy, Mary G. & Jacobs, Marion. Genealogical Abstracts Montgomery County Sentinel, 1855-1899. 1987. 24.00 (*0-317-68194-X*) Montgomery Co Hist.

Malloy, Merrit. Irish-American Funny Quotes. LC 94-26206. 128p. 1994. pap. 5.95 (*0-8069-0753-3*) Sterling.
— The People Who Didn't Say Goodbye. LC 82-45932. 1985. mass mkt. 10.00 (*0-385-18784-X*, Dolp) Doubleday.

Malloy, Merrit, comp. I Purr, Therefore I Am: Never Before Collected Observations on All Things Cat. LC 94-7563. 1994. 19.95 (*0-8431-3583-2*); 10.95 (*0-8431-3782-7*) Putnam Pub Group.

Malloy, Merrit & Rose, Marsha. The Comedians' Quote Book: Quick Takes from the Great Comics. LC 92-41346. 128p. 1993. pap. 5.95 (*0-8069-0324-4*) Sterling.

Malloy, Merrit, jt. auth. see Engel, Peter.

Malloy, Michael. Am I My Brother's Keeper? The AIDs Crisis & the Church. 149p. (Orig.). 1990. pap. 7.95 (*0-8341-1329-5*) Beacon Hill.

Malloy, Michael P. The Corporate Law of Banks: Regulation of Corporate & Securities Activities of Depository Institutions, 2 vols., Set. 1800p. 1987. 160.00 (*0-316-54462-0*) Little.
— Economic Sanctions in U. S. International Trade. 1989. write for info. (*0-318-63269-1*) Little.

Malloy, Patrick, et al. Oraciones del los Fieles, 1993. Wilde, James A. & Castillo Demezas, Ana V., eds. (Annual Book Ser.). 96p. 1992. pap. 5.95 (*0-915531-01-1*) OR Catholic.
— Prayers of the Faithful 1993. 2nd ed. (Annual Book Ser.). 96p. 1992. pap. 5.95 (*0-915531-00-3*) OR Catholic.

Malloy, Robin P. Law & Economics: A Comparative Approach to Theory & Practice. 166p. 1990. pap. text ed. 16.50 (*0-314-72586-5*) West Pub.
— Planning for Serfdom: Legal Economic Discourse & Downtown Development. LC 90-29188. 208p. (C). 1991. text ed. 29.95 (*0-8122-3055-8*) U of Pa Pr.

***Malloy, Robin P. & Braun, Christopher K., eds.** Law & Economics: New & Critical Perspectives. (Critic of Institutions Ser.: Vol. 4). 472p. (C). 1995. pap. text ed. 29.95 (*0-8204-2627-X*) P Lang Pubs.

Malloy, Robin P. & Evensky, Jerry, eds. Adam Smith & the Philosophy of Law & Economics. LC 94-9710. (Law & Philosophy Library: Vol. 20). 240p. (C). 1994. lib. bdg. 88.50 (*0-7923-2796-9*) Kluwer Ac.

***Malloy, Roderick A.** Malloy's Guide to Sports Cards Values. 400p. 1995. pap. 15.95 (*0-87069-726-9*) Chilton.
— Malloy's Sports Collectibles Value Guide. LC 92-50673. 448p. 1993. pap. 17.95 (*0-87069-689-0*) Chilton.

Malloy, Ruth L. China Guide. 8th rev. ed. Stein & Cardoza, eds. (Passport Press Travel Guides Ser.). (Illus.). 704p. 1994. pap. 17.95 (*1-883323-06-1*, Passpt Pr) Open Rd Pub.
— Fielding's People's Republic of China 1993. (Illus.). 784p. 1992. pap. 17.00 (*0-688-11148-3*) Morrow.

***Malloy, Ruth L. & Malloy, Linda Jo.** Hong Kong & Macao Guide. Stein, J., ed. LC 94-66043. 304p. 1994. pap. 13.95 (*1-883323-13-4*) Open Rd Pub.

Malloy, Tom. Profiles of the Past: A Illustrated History of Ashburnham, Gardner, Hubbardston, Templeton, Westminster & Winchendon, Massachusetts. LC 83-63344. (Illus.). 192p. (Orig.). 1984. pap. 8.95 (*0-912395-02-8*) Millers River Pub Co.

Malloy, William. The Mystery Book of Days. 224p. 1990. 15.95 (*0-89296-422-7*) Mysterious Pr.

Malloy, William M. Senate Documents, Treaties, Conventions, International Acts, Protocols, & Agreements Between the United States of America & Other Powers, 4 vols., Set. reprint ed. lib. bdg. 395.00 (*0-403-00246-X*) Scholarly.

Mallozzi, John S. & DeLillo, Nicholas J. Computability with Pascal. LC 83-24450. (Illus.). 193p. (C). 1984. text ed. 26.95 (*0-685-07560-5*) P-H.

Malluche, H. H., ed. Bone Disease in Renal Failure. (Mineral & Electrolyte Metabolism Journal: Vol. 17, No. 4). (Illus.). 92p. 1992. pap. 54.50 (*3-8055-5506-7*) S Karger.

Malluche, H. H. & Faugere, Marie-Claude. Atlas of Mineralized Bone Histology. (Illus.). xiii, 136p. 1986. 191.25 (*3-8055-4201-1*) S Karger.

Mallwitz, Alfred, jt. auth. see Heyder, Wolfgang.

Mally, E. Logische Schriften: Grosses Logikfragment, Grundgesetze des Sollens. LC 73-135106. (Synthese Historical Library: No. 3). 347p. (GER.). 1971. lib. bdg. 94.00 (*90-277-0174-1*) Kluwer Ac.

Mally, E. Louise. A Treasury of Animal Stories. 1976. 23.95 (*0-8488-0764-2*) Amereon Ltd.

Mally, Lynn. Culture of the Future: The Proletkult Movement in Revolutionary Russia. 1989. 40.00 (*0-520-06577-8*) U CA Pr.

Malm, Karen. Behavior Management in K-6 Classrooms. 128p. 1992. 11.95 (*0-8106-0365-9*) NEA.

Malm, Krister & Wallis, Roger. Media Policy & Music Activity. LC 92-13299. 288p. 1993. 59.95 (*0-415-05019-7*, A9861, Routledge NY); pap. 17.95 (*0-415-05020-0*, B0411, Routledge NY) Routledge.

Malm, Richard. Perfected Praise. 96p. (Orig.). 1988. pap. 6.99 (*0-914903-62-4*) Destiny Image.

Malm, William P. Japanese Music & Musical Instruments. LC 59-10411. (Illus.). 300p. 1959. pap. 27.95 (*0-8048-1648-4*) C E Tuttle.
— Music Cultures of the Pacific, the Near East & Asia. 2nd ed. (Illus.). 1977. pap. text ed. 34.00 (*0-13-607994-6*) P-H.
— Music Cultures of the Pacific, the Near East, & Asia. 3rd ed. LC 94-48578. (History of Music Ser.). 1995. pap. text ed. 50.67 (*0-13-182387-6*) P-H.
— Nagauta: The Heart of Kabuki Music. LC 73-6260. (Illus.). 344p. 1973. reprint ed. text ed. 49.75 (*0-8371-6900-3*, Greenwood Pr) Greenwood.
— Six Hidden Views of Japanese Music. (Ernest Bloch Lectures: No. 6). 1986. 45.00 (*0-520-05045-2*) U CA Pr.

Malman, Laurie. Federal Income Taxation: Problems, Cases & Materials. Solomon, Lewis D. & Hesck, Jerome H., eds. (American Casebook Ser.). 440p. 1994. pap. text ed. write for info. (*0-314-04150-8*) West Pub.

Malman, Laurie L., et al. Federal Income Taxation: Problems, Cases, & Materials. LC 94-4266. (American Casebook Ser.). 979p. 1994. text ed. 47.00 (*0-314-03503-6*) West Pub.

Malmat, Bonnie. Through the Window of the Past Abstracts of the Washington Reporter: August 1, 1814-December 30, 1816. 222p. 1993. pap. text ed. 19.95 (*1-55856-151-X*) Closson Pr.

Malmat, Bonnie, comp. Abstracts of the Washington County Reporter 1808-1814. 323p. 1990. pap. text ed. 19.95 (*1-55856-041-6*) Closson Pr.

Malmaud, Roslyn. Work & Marriage: The Two-Profession Couple. LC 84-104. (Research in Clinical Psychology Ser.: No. 10). 299p. reprint ed. pap. 85.30 (*0-8357-1543-4*, 2070403) Bks Demand.

Malmberg, Bertil. Linguistique Generale et Romane: Etudes en Allemand, Anglais, Espagnol et Francais. (Janua Linguarum, Series Major: No. 66). 1973. 112.35 (*90-279-2429-5*) Mouton.

Malmberg, Bertil, ed. Readings in Modern Linguistics: An Anthology. 384p. (Orig.). 1972. pap. text ed. 70.80 (*0-685-03446-1*) Mouton.

Malmberg, Carl, tr. see Kristensen, Tom.

Malmberg, Carl, tr. see Paludan, Jacob.

Malmberg, Gunnar. Metropolitan Growth & Migration in Peru. (University of Umea Geographical Reports: No. 9). (Illus.). 266p. (Orig.). 1988. pap. 87.50x (*91-7174-329-4*, Pub. by Umea U Bibl SW) Coronet Bks.

Malmberg, Lars, tr. see Bergfeldt, Inga.

Malmberg, Russell, et al, eds. Molecular Biology of Plants: A Laboratory Course Manual. LC 85-11036. 150p. (Orig.). (C). 1985. text ed. 28.00 (*0-87969-184-0*) Cold Spring Harbor.

Malmberg, Sieglinde, jt. auth. see O'Shea-Roche, Annette.

Malmberg, Torsten. Human Territoriality. (New Babylon Studies in the Social Sciences). 352p. 1980. 18.25 (*90-279-3199-2*); 57.70 (*3-10-800346-1*) Mouton.
— Human Territoriality: A Survey on the Behavioral Territories of Man with Preliminary Analysis & Discussion of Meaning. 1979. pap. 23.10 (*3-10-800384-4*) Mouton.

Malmendier, C. L. & Alaupovic, P., eds. Eicosanoids, Apolipoproteins, Lipoprotein Particles, & Atherosclerosis. LC 88-28929. (Advances in Experimental Medicine & Biology Ser.: Vol. 243). (Illus.). 372p. 1988. 89.50 (*0-306-43037-1*, Plenum Pr) Plenum.
— Lipoproteins & Atherosclerosis. LC 87-2345. (Advances in Experimental Medicine & Biology Ser.: Vol. 210). 266p. 1987. 69.50 (*0-306-42487-8*, Plenum Pr) Plenum.

Malmendier, C. L., et al, eds. Hypercholesterolemia, Hypocholesterolemia, Hypertriglyceridemia in Vivo Kinetics. LC 91-2557. (Advances in Experimental Medicine & Biology Ser.: Vol. 285). (Illus.). 434p. 1991. 105.00 (*0-306-43814-3*, Plenum Pr) Plenum.

Malmesbury, James H. Diaries & Correspondence of the Earl of Malmesbury, 4 Vols, 1. 2nd ed. LC 73-121023. reprint ed. write for info. (*0-404-04171-X*) AMS Pr.
— Diaries & Correspondence of the Earl of Malmesbury, 4 Vols, 2. 2nd ed. LC 73-121023. reprint ed. write for info. (*0-404-04172-8*) AMS Pr.
— Diaries & Correspondence of the Earl of Malmesbury, 4 Vols, 3. 2nd ed. LC 73-121023. reprint ed. write for info. (*0-404-04173-6*) AMS Pr.
— Diaries & Correspondence of the Earl of Malmesbury, 4 Vols, 4. 2nd ed. LC 73-121023. reprint ed. write for info. (*0-404-04174-4*) AMS Pr.
— Diaries & Correspondence of the Earl of Malmesbury, 4 Vols, Set. 2nd ed. LC 73-121023. reprint ed. 265.00 (*0-404-04170-1*) AMS Pr.

Malmgreen, Gail, ed. Religion in the Lives of English Women, 1760-1930. LC 86-45172. (Illus.). 224p. (C). 1986. 29.95 (*0-253-34973-7*) Ind U Pr.

Malmgreen, Gail, jt. ed. see Lebowitz, Arieh.

Malmgren, Carl D. Fictional Space in the Modernist & Postmodernist American Novel. 240p. 1985. 36.50 (*0-8387-5067-2*) Bucknell U Pr.
— Worlds Apart: Narratology of Science Fiction. LC 90-25045. 222p. 1991. 22.50 (*0-253-33645-7*) Ind U Pr.

Malmgren, Dallin. Is This for a Grade? A Survival Guide for Teaching in the 90s. LC 94-70041. 200p. (Orig.). 1994. pap. 9.95 (*0-931722-98-5*) Corona Pub.

Malmgren, Harold B., jt. auth. see Turner, William C.

Malmin, Jack. El Otro Lado (The Other Side) The True Story of Marcus Hooks--Smuggler. LC 90-70919. (Illus.). 1991. 19.95 (*0-9627198-0-3*) Trailblazer Pub.

Malmin, Ken. Bible Research - Revised. (Illus.). 202p. 1976. pap. 13.95 (*0-914936-71-9*) Bible Temple.

Malmin, Ken & Conner, Kevin. New Testament Survey. 1975. 4.95 (*0-914936-22-0*) Bible Temple.
— Old Testament Survey. 1974. 4.95 (*0-914936-21-2*) Bible Temple.

Malmin, Ken P., jt. auth. see Conner, Kevin J.

Malmivuo, Jaakko & Plonsey, Robert. Bioelectromagnetism: Principles & Applications of Bioelectric & Biomagnetic Fields. (Illus.). 480p. 1995. 98.00 (*0-19-505823-2*) OUP.

***Malmkjaer, Kirsten.** The Linguistics Encyclopedia. (Illus.). 592p. 1995. pap. 24.95 (*0-415-12566-9*, C0435) Routledge.

Malmkjaer, Kirsten, ed. The Linguistics Encyclopedia. (Illus.). 640p. 1991. 120.00 (*0-415-02942-2*, A6266) Routledge.

Malmkjar, Kirsten, jt. auth. see Knowles, Murray.

Malmlow, Eric G. How to Do Your Prudent Entrepreneurial Planning: From Ideas to Your First Billion-Dollar Sale. 1993. pap. 21.95 (*0-533-10367-3*) Vantage.

Malmn, Y. & Rouhiainen, Veikko, eds. Reliability & Safety of Processes & Manufacturing Systems: Proc. of the Twelfth Annual Symp. of the Society of Reliability Engineers, Scandinavian Chapter, 1-3 October 1991, Tampere, Finland. 380p. 1991. 102.00 (*1-85166-710-5*) Elsevier.

Malmont, Valerie S. Death Pays the Rose Rent: A Tori Miracle Mystery. LC 93-42075. 1994. 20.00 (*0-671-86967-1*) S&S Trade.

Malmouth, Charles, tr. see Ilf, Ilya & Petrov, Eugene.

***Malmquist, Carl P.** Homicide: A Psychiatric Perspective. 1995. boxed 45.00 (*0-88048-690-2*, 8690) Am Psychiatric.

Malmquist, O. N. The First Hundred Years: A History of the Salt Lake Tribune, 1871-1971. LC 74-158989. (Illus.). 496p. 1971. 8.00 (*0-913738-21-2*) Utah St Hist Soc.

Malmsheimer, Richard. Doctors Only: The Evolving Image of the American Physician. LC 88-5685. (Contributions in Medical Studies: No. 25). 185p. 1988. text ed. 55.00 (*0-313-23465-5*, MAD/, Greenwood Pr) Greenwood.

Malmstad, John, ed. see Khodasevich, Vladislav.

Malmstad, John E. Andrey Bely: Spirit of Symbolism. (Illus.). 352p. 1987. 52.50 (*0-8014-1984-0*); pap. 22.95 (*0-8014-9445-1*) Cornell U Pr.

Malmstad, John E., tr. see Bely, Andrei.

Malmstad, John E., ed. see Bely, Andrey.

Malmstadt, Howard V., et al. Microcomputers & Electronic Instrumentation: Making the Right Connections. LC 94-1407. 1994. 75.00 (*0-8412-2861-2*) Am Chemical.
— Addbook One: Experiments in Digital & Analog Electronics. (Addbook Ser.: Bk. 1). 1977. pap. text ed. 17.00 (*0-89704-019-8*) E&L Instru.

Malmstadt, Susan & Freier, Marilynn. Exercise SeniorStyle Guide for Instructors. rev. ed. 56p. 1993. 7.95 (*1-877673-10-2*, EXG) Cottonwood Pr.

Malmstrom, B. Nobel Lectures in Chemistry 1981-1990. 800p. 1993. text ed. 122.00 (*981-02-0788-3*); pap. text ed. 61.00 (*981-02-0789-1*) World Scientific Pub.

Malmstrom, B., jt. auth. see Ehrenberg, A.

Malmstrom, Jean.

Malmstrom, Karin & Nash, Nancy. The Man with the Key Is Not Here: A Key to What They Really Mean in China. Davies, Shann, ed. (Illus.). (Orig.). 1990. pap. text ed. 5.95 (*0-9626164-0-0*) Pacific Venture.

Malmstrom, Margit. Modeling the Figure in Clay. (Illus.). 144p. 1980. 24.95 (*0-8230-3097-0*, Watsn-Guptill) Watsn-Guptill.

Malmstrom, Margit, jt. auth. see Etter, Howard.

Malmstrom, Marilyn. My Tongue Is the Pen: How Audiocassettes Can Serve the Nonreading World. LC 91-66074. 224p. (Orig.). 1991. pap. 16.00 (*0-88312-812-8*); fiche 16.00 (*0-88312-732-6*) Summer Instit Ling.

Malmstrom, Richard, jt. ed. see Pierce, Dianne.

Malmstrom, S. Bonnier's Swedish Dictionary: Bonniers Svenska Ordbok. 744p. (SWE.). 1986. 150.00 (*0-8288-2072-4*, F60694) Fr & Eur.

Malmuth, Mason. Blackjack Essays. Loomis, Lynne, ed. 224p. 1991. pap. 19.95 (*1-880685-05-1*) Two Plus NV.
— Gambling Theory & Other Topics. 4th ed. Loomis, Lynne, ed. 315p. 1994. pap. text ed. 29.95 (*1-880685-03-5*) Two Plus NV.
— Poker Essays. Loomis, Lynne, ed. 262p. (Orig.). 1991. pap. text ed. 24.95 (*1-880685-09-4*) Two Plus NV.
— Winning Concepts in Draw & Lowball. 2nd ed. Levis, Bob, ed. 378p. 1993. pap. text ed. 24.95 (*1-880685-07-8*) Two Plus NV.

Malmuth, Mason & Loomis, Lynne. Fundamentals of Craps. (Illus.). 70p. 1993. pap. 3.95 (*1-880685-14-0*) Two Plus NV.
— Fundamentals of Poker. 2nd ed. (Illus.). 70p. 1992. pap. 3.95 (*1-880685-11-6*) Two Plus NV.
— Fundamentals of "Twenty-One" (Illus.). 70p. 1993. pap. 3.95 (*1-880685-13-2*) Two Plus NV.
— Fundamentals of Video Poker. (Illus.). 70p. (Orig.). 1993. pap. 3.95 (*1-880685-12-4*) Two Plus NV.

Malmuth, Mason, jt. auth. see Sklansky, David.

Malnar, Joy M. & Vodvarka, Frank. The Interior Dimension: A Theoretical Approach to Enclosed Space. LC 91-6291. (Illus.). 464p. 1992. text ed. 54.95 (*0-442-23739-1*) Van Nos Reinhold.

Malnassy, Phillip G. Laboratory Investigations into the World of Plants. 104p. 1991. spiral bd. 13.95 (*0-8403-7085-7*) Kendall-Hunt.

Malnati, Peggy, ed. see Trantina, Gerry & Nimmer, Ron.

Malnati, Richard, jt. auth. see Donigian, Jeremiah.

Malnic, Jutta, jt. auth. see Mowaljarlai, David.

Malnig, Anita. Where the Waves Break: Life at the Edge of the Sea. LC 84-9614. (Nature Watch Bks.). (Illus.). 48p. (J). (gr. 2-5). 1985. lib. bdg. 19.95 (*0-87614-226-9*, Carolrhoda) Lerner Group.
— Where the Waves Break: Life at the Edge of the Sea. (Nature Watch Bks.). (Illus.). 48p. (J). (gr. 2-5). 1987. reprint ed. pap. 6.95 (*0-87614-477-6*, Lerner Publctns) Lerner Group.

Malnig, Anita, jt. auth. see Malnig, Lawrence R.

Malnig, Julie. Dancing till Dawn: A Century of Exhibition Ballroom Dance. LC 91-33482. (Contributions to the Study of Music & Dance Ser.: No. 25). 192p. 1992. text ed. 45.00 (*0-313-27647-1*, MND, Greenwood Pr) Greenwood.
— Dancing Till Dawn: A Century of Exhibition Ballroom Dance. (Illus.). 174p. 1995. pap. 15.95 (*0-8147-5528-3*) NYU Pr.

Malnig, Lawrence R. & Malnig, Anita. What Can I Do with a Major In...? How to Choose & Use Your College Major. LC 83-73269. 250p. 1984. 26.95 (*0-9612678-1-X*) Abbott Pr.

Malo, David. Hawaiian Antiquities. 4th ed. (Special Publication Ser.: No. 2). (Illus.). 278p. (C). 1987. reprint ed. pap. 19.95 (*0-910240-15-9*) Bishop Mus.
— Ka Mo'olelo Hawaii (Hawaiian Antiquities) Chun, Malcolm N., ed. (Illus.). 178p. (Orig.). (HAW.). 1987. pap. 12.95 (*0-938603-01-9*) Folk Press.

Malo, G. Panamanian Problem. 1993. 22.95 (*0-935047-17-4*) Americas Group.

Malo, Jean-Jacques & Williams, Tony, eds. Vietnam War Films: Over Six Hundred Feature, Made-for-TV, Pilot & Short Movies, 1939-1992, from the United States, Vietnam, France, Belgium, Australia, Hong Kong, South Africa, Great Britain & Other Countries. LC 92-56662. (Illus.). 592p. 1994. lib. bdg. 55.00 (*0-89950-781-6*) McFarland & Co.

Malo, John. Basic Canoeing for Pathfinders: A Youth Enrichment Skill. rev. ed. Gattis, L. S., ed. (Illus.). (Orig.). 1987. pap. 5.00 (*0-936241-17-9*) Cheetah Pub.

Maloba, Wunyabari O. Mau Mau & Kenya: An Analysis of a Peasant Revolt. LC 92-31421. (Blacks in the Diaspora Ser.). 240p. 1993. 35.00 (*0-253-33664-3*) Ind U Pr.

Maloch, David T. Marketing Guide for Small Business. 62p. (Orig.). 1989. pap. 7.95 (*0-9623457-0-9*) Perfidia Pr.

An Asterisk (*) at the beginning of an entry indicates that the title is appearing in BIP for the first time.

Malocsay, Zoltan. Opening Forbidden Lakes: Fishing Colorado's Watersheds - Without Getting Arrested. (Illus.). 144p. 1992. pap. write for info. (*0-9629250-1-2*) Squeezy Pr.
— Trails Guide to Pikes Peak Country. 4th ed. (Illus.). 1991. pap. write for info. (*0-9629250-0-4*) Squeezy Pr.
Malody, Chuck, ed. see Zagat, Eugene H., Jr. & Zagat, Nina S.
Malody, Peggy, ed. see Ferrell, Valli Smith.
Malody, Raymond L. The Chinese Call Me Teacher. LC 92-61876. 192p. (Orig.). 1992. pap. 10.95 (*0-939644-89-4*) Media Pub.
Malof, Joseph. A Manual of English Meters. LC 78-823. 236p. 1978. reprint ed. text ed. 55.00 (*0-313-20293-1*, MAMEM, Greenwood Pr) Greenwood.
***Maloff, Chalda & Wood, Susan M.** Business & Social Etiquette with Disabled People: A Guide to Getting along with Persons Who Have Impairments of Mobility, Vision, Hearing or Speech. 162p. 1988. pap. 24.95 (*0-398-06266-8*) C C Thomas.
— Business & Social Etiquette with Disabled People: A Guide to Getting along with Persons Who Have Impairments of Mobility, Vision, Hearing or Speech. 162p. (C). 1988. 39.95 (*0-398-05463-0*) C C Thomas.
Maloff, Chalda & Zears, Russell W. Computers in Nutrition. LC 79-4339. (Illus.). 368p. reprint ed. pap. 104.90 (*0-8357-5587-8*, 2035218) Bks Demand.
***Maloff, Joel.** 1994-1995 Internet Access Providers Marketplace Analysis. (Illus.). 159p. 1995. pap. text ed. 200.00 (*1-57074-258-8*) Greyden Pr.
Maloine Staff. Dictionnaire Medical Illustre De Semiologie Patronymique. (FRE.). 1979. 49.95 (*0-8288-4798-3*, M6149) Fr & Eur.
— Nouvelle Encyclopedie du Cheval. 784p. (FRE.). 1992. 225.00 (*0-8288-9443-4*) Fr & Eur.
Maloiy, G. M., jt. ed. see Jewell, P. A.
Malok, jt. auth. see Porter, Bern.
Malon, P., jt. ed. see Blaha, K.
Malone. Physical & Occupational Therapy: Drug Implications for Practice. (Illus.). 299p. 1989. text ed. 31.50 (*0-397-50757-7*) Lippincott.
Malone, jt. auth. see Moore, Wesley S.
Malone, Andrew E. Irish Drama. LC 65-16243. 1972. 30.95 (*0-405-08777-2*, Pub. by Blom Pubns UK) Ayer.
Malone, Ann P. Sweet Chariot: Slave Family & Household Structure in Nineteenth-Century Louisiana. LC 91-50787. (Fred W. Morrison Series in Southern Studies). (Illus.). xvi, 369p. (C). 1992. 39.95 (*0-8078-2026-1*) U of NC Pr.
Malone, Anne-Frisbie. Santa's Workshop: A Punch-Out Village & Characters. (Illus.). (J). (gr. 4-7). 1993. pap. 2.95 (*0-486-27622-8*) Dover.
Malone, Barbara. Florida Seafood. 36p. (Orig.). 1982. pap. 2.75 (*0-940844-09-5*) Wellspring.
Malone, Bartlett Y. Whipt 'Em Everytime: The Diary of Bartlett Yancey Malone Co H 6th North Carolina Regiment. Pierson, William W., Jr. & Wiley, Bell I., eds. (Illus.). 131p. 1992. reprint ed. 20.00 (*0-916107-37-X*) Broadfoot.
Malone, Bill C. Country Music, U. S. A. rev. ed. LC 84-21896. (Illus.). 576p. 1985. 27.95 (*0-292-71095-X*); pap. 17.95 (*0-292-71096-8*) U of Tex Pr.
— Singing Cowboys & Musical Mountaineers: Southern Culture & the Roots of Country Music. LC 92-12430. (Mercer University Lamar Memorial Lecture Ser.: No. 34). 160p. 1993. 24.95 (*0-8203-1483-8*) U of Ga Pr.
— Singing Cowboys, Musical Mountaineers: Southern Culture & the Roots of Country Music. LC 92-12430. (Brown Thrasher Bks.). 168p. 1994. pap. 12.95 (*0-8203-1679-2*) U of Ga Pr.
— Southern Music - American Music. LC 79-4005. (New Perspectives on the South Ser.). (Illus.). 224p. 1979. 24.00 (*0-8131-0300-2*) U Pr of Ky.
Malone, Bill C. & McCulloh, Judith, eds. Stars of Country Music. (Quality Paperbacks Ser.). (Illus.). 476p. 1991. reprint ed. pap. 14.95 (*0-306-80444-1*) Da Capo.
— Stars of Country Music: Uncle Dave Macon to Johnny Rodriguez. LC 75-15848. (Music in American Life Ser.). 488p. 1975. 29.95 (*0-252-00527-9*) U of Ill Pr.
Malone, C. B., jt. auth. see Bowler, N. P.
Malone, Caroline. English Heritage Book of Avebury. (Illus.). 154p. 1989. pap. 34.95 (*0-7134-5960-3*, Pub. by Batsford UK) Trafalgar.
Malone, Caroline, jt. ed. see Stoddart, Simon.
Malone, Carolyn. Availability to Ticketing. (Illus.). 135p. (C). 1985. pap. text ed. 21.95 (*0-917063-07-4*) Travel Text.
Malone, Dandridge M. Small Unit Leadership: A Commonsense Approach. (Illus.). 180p. (Orig.). 1983. pap. 12.95 (*0-89141-173-9*) Presidio Pr.
Malone, David. Hattie & Huey: An Arkansas Tour. LC 89-4837. 208p. 1989. pap. 11.95 (*1-55728-107-6*) U of Ark Pr.
Malone, Dumas. Jefferson & His Time. (History - United States Ser.). 1993. reprint ed. lib. bdg. write for info. (*0-7812-4885-X*) Rprt Serv.
— Jefferson & His Time: The Sage of Monticello, Vol. 6. (Illus.). 512p. 1981. 29.95 (*0-316-54463-9*) Little.
— Jefferson & His Time: The Sage of Monticello, Vol. 6. (Illus.). 512p. 1982. pap. 15.95 (*0-316-54478-7*) Little.
— Jefferson & the Ordeal of Liberty, Vol. 3. (Jefferson & His Time Ser.). 1962. 29.95 (*0-316-54475-2*) Little.
— Jefferson & the Ordeal of Liberty, Vol. 3. (Jefferson & His Time Ser.). 1969. pap. 15.95 (*0-316-54469-8*) Little.
— Jefferson & the Rights of Man, Vol. 2. (Jefferson & His Time Ser.). (Illus.). 1951. 29.95 (*0-316-54473-6*) Little.
— Jefferson & the Rights of Man, Vol. 2. (Jefferson & His Time Ser.). (Illus.). 1968. pap. 15.95 (*0-316-54470-1*) Little.
— Jefferson the President: First Term, 1801-1805, Vol. 4. LC 48-5972. (Jefferson & His Time Ser.). (Illus.). 1970. 29.95 (*0-316-54467-1*) Little.
— Jefferson the President: First Term, 1801-1805, Vol. 4. LC 48-5972. (Jefferson & His Time Ser.). (Illus.). 1971. pap. 15.95 (*0-316-54466-3*) Little.
— Jefferson the President: Second Term, 1805-1809, Vol. 5. (Jefferson & His Time Ser.). 1974. 29.95 (*0-316-54465-5*) Little.
— Jefferson the President: Second Term, 1805-1809, Vol. 5. (Jefferson & His Time Ser.). 1975. pap. 15.95 (*0-316-54464-7*) Little.
— Jefferson the Virginian, Vol. 1. (Jefferson & His Time Ser.). (Illus.). 1948. 29.95 (*0-316-54474-4*) Little.
— Jefferson the Virginian, Vol. 1. (Jefferson & His Time Ser.). (Illus.). 1967. pap. 15.95 (*0-316-54472-8*, LB78) Little.
— The Public Life of Thomas Cooper, 1783-1839. LC 75-3122. reprint ed. 46.00 (*0-404-59117-5*) AMS Pr.
— Saints in Action. LC 70-142664. (Essay Index Reprint Ser.). 1977. 18.95 (*0-8369-2062-7*) Ayer.
— Thomas Jefferson: A Brief Biography. (Monticello Monograph Ser.). (Illus.). 48p. (Orig.). Date not set. reprint ed. pap. 4.95 (*1-882886-00-3*) T J Mem Fnd.
— Thomas Jefferson As Political Leader. LC 78-21568. 75p. 1979. reprint ed. text ed. 35.00 (*0-313-20730-5*, MATJ, Greenwood Pr) Greenwood.
Malone, Dumas, ed. see Jefferson, Thomas.
Malone, E. E. Malone: Jeremiah Dumas Malone, a Genealogical Outline. (Illus.). 159p. 1993. reprint ed. lib. bdg. 35.00 (*0-8328-3713-X*); reprint ed. pap. 25.00 (*0-8328-3714-8*) Higginson Bk Co.
Malone, E. T., Jr. The View from Wrightsville Beach. (Illus.). (Orig.). 1988. pap. 8.95 (*0-9621668-0-4*) Lit Lantern.
Malone, E. T., Jr., jt. auth. see Walser, Richard.
Malone, Edgar W., jt. auth. see Hart, William C.
Malone, Edmond. Cursory Observations on the Poems Attributed to Thomas Rowley: The Second Edition, Revised & Augmented. 2nd rev. ed. LC 92-2372. (Augustan Reprints Ser.: No. 123 (1966)). reprint ed. 12.00 (*0-404-70123-X*, PR3344) AMS Pr.
— Inquiry into the Authenticity of Certain Miscellaneous Papers & Legal Instruments Published 1795 & Attributed to Shakespeare, Queen Elizabeth & Henry, Earl of Southampton. 440p. 1970. reprint ed. 32.50 (*0-7146-2514-0*, Pub. by F Cass Pubs UK) Intl Spec Bk.
Malone, Edmond, jt. auth. see Reynolds, Joshua.
Malone, Edmond, jt. auth. see Ritson, Joseph.
Malone, Edmond, ed. see Shakespeare, William.
Malone, Edmund. Inquiry into the Authenticity of Certain Miscellaneous Papers & Legal Instruments. LC 73-96356. (Eighteenth Century Shakespeare Ser.: No. 22). vii, 424p. 1970. reprint ed. lib. bdg. 45.00 (*0-678-05123-2*) Kelley.
***Malone, Eileen.** The Complete Guide to Writers' Groups & Workshops: Where to Find Them & How to Get the Most Out of Them. 304p. 1995. pap. 12.95 (*0-8065-1642-9*, Citadel Pr) Carol Pub Group.
Malone, Eloise F., jt. auth. see Cochran, Charles L.
Malone, Fred. Bees Don't Get Arthritis. (Illus.). 179p. 1992. pap. 13.95 (*0-914960-60-1*) Academy Bks.
Malone, Gifford D. Political Advocacy & Cultural Communication: Organizing the Nation's Public Diplomacy. (Exxon Education Foundation Series on Rhetoric & Political Discourse: Vol. 11). 178p. (Orig.). (C). 1988. lib. bdg. 41.00 (*0-8191-6619-7*, Pub. by White Miller Center); pap. text ed. 20.00 (*0-8191-6620-0*) U Pr of Amer.
Malone, H. E. The Determination of Hydrazine-Hydrazide Groups. (C). 1970. 172.00 (*0-08-015871-4*, Pub. by Pergamon Repr UK) Franklin.
Malone, Hank. Survival Evasion & Escape. Iddings, Kathleen, ed. LC 84-82407. 92p. (Orig.). 1985. per. 5.95 (*0-931721-00-8*) La Jolla Poets.
Malone, J. B. The Complete Wicklow Way: A Step-by-Step Guide. rev. ed. 127p. 1994. pap. 8.95 (*0-86278-158-2*, Pub. by OBrien Pr IE) Dufour.
Malone, James H. No-Job Dad. LC 92-15873. (Illus.). 30p. (J). (gr. 1-2). 1992. 13.95 (*1-878217-06-2*) Victory Press.
Malone, Joanne. Stencilling: A Practical & Inspirational Guide to Decorative Ideas for Interiors, Furnishings, Clothing, Stationery & More. LC 92-38336. (Illus.). 132p. 1993. pap. 14.95 (*0-8069-0360-0*) Sterling.
Malone, John. The Civil War Quiz Book. (Quill Quiz Bk.). (Illus.). 224p. 1992. pap. 9.00 (*0-688-11269-2*, Quill) Morrow.
— The Native American Quiz Book. LC 93-8539. 1994. 9.00 (*0-688-11021-5*, Quill) Morrow.
— One Hundred Twenty-Five Most Asked Questions about Cats, & the Answers. 1992. 13.00 (*0-688-10552-1*) Morrow.
— The One Hundred Twenty-Five Most Asked Questions about Dogs. LC 92-38538. 1993. 14.00 (*0-688-11311-7*) Morrow.
— The One Hundred Twenty-Five Most Asked Questions about Horses: And the Answers. LC 93-40777. 1994. 15.00 (*0-688-11312-5*) Morrow.
— The World War Two Quiz Book. (Illus.). 224p. 1991. pap. 9.00 (*0-688-10872-5*, Quill) Morrow.
Malone, John & Baldwin, Paul. One Hundred One Ways to Say Merry Christmas for Less Than Twenty-Five Dollars. LC 92-7447. 1992. 8.00 (*0-688-11361-3*) Morrow.
Malone, John C. Theories of Learning: A Historical Approach. 342p. (C). 1991. text ed. 48.95 (*0-534-05760-8*) Brooks-Cole.
Malone, Joseph J. Pine Trees & Politics. Bruchey, Stuart, ed. LC 78-53552. (Development of Public Land Law in the U. S. Ser.). 1979. reprint ed. lib. bdg. 19.95 (*0-405-11380-3*) Ayer.
Malone, Joseph L. The Science of Linguistics in the Art of Translation: Some Tools from Linguistics for the Analysis & Practice of Translation. LC 87-13888. (Linguistics Ser.). 241p. 1988. 89.50 (*0-88706-653-4*); pap. 29.95 (*0-88706-654-2*) State U NY Pr.
— Tiberian Hebrew Phonology. LC 92-43400. x, 204p. 1993. 45.00 (*0-931464-75-7*) Eisenbrauns.
Malone, Katherine & Schneider, Jane. Cat Dissection Laboratory Manual. Pullins, ed. 450p. (C). 1992. pap. text ed. 41.50 (*0-314-93925-3*) West Pub.
Malone, Kathryn E. Biology of Human Sexuality Workbook: A Student Study Guide. 192p. 1992. spiral bd. 17.95 (*0-8403-7981-1*) Kendall-Hunt.
Malone, Kelly & Lagoria, Georgianna. A Little Hawaiian Cookbook. (Illus.). 60p. 1994. 6.95 (*0-8118-0642-1*) Chronicle Bks.
Malone, Kemp. Chapters on Chaucer. LC 79-4628. 240p. 1979. reprint ed. text ed. 38.50 (*0-313-21260-0*, MACHC, Greenwood Pr) Greenwood.
— Literary History of Hamlet. LC 65-15886. (Studies in Shakespeare: No. 24). 1969. reprint ed. lib. bdg. 75.00 (*0-8383-0593-8*) M S G Haskell Hse.
Malone, Kemp, ed. Deor. (Old English Ser.). 1966. pap. text ed. 9.95 (*0-89197-566-7*) Irvington.
Malone, Larry, jt. auth. see McGlathery, Glenn.
Malone, Lawrence. Coordinated Urban Economic Development: A Case Study Analysis. Linger, Juyne, ed. 269p. (Orig.). 1978. pap. 17.50 (*0-317-04920-8*) Natl Coun Econ Dev.
Malone, Lawrence J., ed. see Smith, Adam.
Malone, Lee, jt. auth. see Malone, Paul.
Malone, Leo J. Basic Concepts in Chemistry. 4th ed. LC 93-38490. 1994. text ed. write for info. (*0-471-53590-7*) Wiley.
MaLone, Leo J. Basic Concepts of Chemistry. 3rd ed. LC 88-5909. 276p. 1989. teacher ed 17.50 (*0-471-85120-5*); trans. 140.00 (*0-471-85118-3*) Wiley.
Malone, Linda A. Environmental Regulation of Land Use. LC 90-267. (Environmental Ser.). 1990. ring bd. 145.00 (*0-87632-739-0*) Clark Boardman Callaghan.
Malone, Linda A., et al. Stanford Environmental Law Journal, Vol. 12. 220p. (C). 1993. pap. 15.00 (*0-942007-36-0*) Stanford Enviro.
Malone, Linda C., jt. auth. see Ostle, Bernard.
Malone, Maggie. Christmas Scrapcrafts. LC 91-23273. (Illus.). 144p. 1991. 24.95 (*0-8069-6804-4*) Sterling.
— Christmas Scrapcrafts. (Illus.). 136p. (J). (gr. 5-10). 1992. pap. 12.95 (*0-8069-6805-2*) Sterling.
— Five Hundred Full-Size Patchwork Patterns. LC 85-9906. (Illus.). 168p. (Orig.). 1985. pap. 10.95 (*0-8069-6230-5*) Sterling.
— One Hundred Twenty Patterns for Traditional Patchwork Quilts. LC 82-19671. (Illus.). 256p. 1983. pap. 12.95 (*0-8069-7716-7*) Sterling.
— One Thousand One Patchwork Designs. LC 81-85037. (Illus.). 224p. (Orig.). 1990. pap. 14.95 (*0-8069-7604-7*) Sterling.
— Patchwork Quilt Patterns: More Than One Hundred Designs for Making Your Own Heirloom Quilt. 1989. 10.99 (*0-517-68790-9*) Random Hse Value.
— Quilting Shortcuts. LC 86-14440. (Illus.). 168p. (Orig.). 1986. 10.95 (*0-8069-4786-1*); pap. 9.95 (*0-8069-4788-8*) Sterling.
— Quilting Shortcuts. (Illus.). 168p. (Orig.). (C). 1989. reprint ed. lib. bdg. 29.00x (*0-8095-7518-3*) Borgo Pr.
Malone, Martin J., jt. auth. see Levinson, David.
Malone, Marvin. Wormwood Regulars. 40p. (Orig.). 1986. pap. 4.00 (*0-935390-11-1*) Wormwood Bks & Mag.
Malone, Mary. Connie Chung: Broadcast Journalist. LC 91-25396. (Contemporary Women Ser.). (Illus.). 128p. (J). (gr. 6 up). 1992. lib. bdg. 17.95 (*0-89490-332-2*) Enslow Pubs.
— Dorothea L. Dix: Hospital Founder. (Discovery Biographies Ser.). (Illus.). 80p. (J). (gr. 2-6). 1991. reprint ed. lib. bdg. 12.95 (*0-7910-1436-3*) Chelsea Hse.
— Liliuokalani: Queen of Hawaii. (Discovery Biographies Ser.). (Illus.). 80p. (J). (gr. 2-6). 1993. reprint ed. lib. bdg. 12.95 (*0-7910-1413-4*) Chelsea Hse.
— Maya Lin: Architect & Artist. LC 94-5333. (People to Know Ser.). (Illus.). 112p. (YA). (gr. 6 up). 1995. lib. bdg. 17.95 (*0-89490-499-X*) Enslow Pubs.
Malone, Melinda. Reflections. 40p. 1993. pap. text ed. 13.00 (*1-885156-06-5*) Animas Quilts.
***Malone, Michael.** Apostolic Digest. abr. ed. 190p. Date not set. pap. 9.95 (*1-885692-00-5*) Cath Treas.
— Dingley Falls. 1989. mass mkt. 4.95 (*0-671-67180-4*) PB.
— Dingley Falls. LC 93-5836. 1994. pap. 10.00 (*0-671-87529-9*, WSP) PB.
— Foolscap. 1991. 19.95 (*0-316-54527-9*) Little.
— Foolscap. Rosenman, Jane, ed. LC 92-42591. 400p. 1993. reprint ed. pap. 10.00 (*0-671-78857-4*, WSP) PB.
— Handling Sin. Rosenman, Jane, ed. 672p. 1993. pap. 10.00 (*0-671-87526-4*, WSP) PB.
— Microprocessor: A Biography with CD-ROM for Mac. 1994. pap. 39.95 (*0-387-94145-2*) Spr-Verlag.
— Time's Witness. Rosenman, Jane, ed. 562p. 1994. pap. 10.00 (*0-671-87527-2*, WSP) PB.
— Times Witness. Peters, Sally, ed. 592p. 1991. reprint ed. mass mkt. 5.95 (*0-671-70318-8*) PB.
— Uncivil Seasons. Rosenman, Jane, ed. 320p. 1993. pap. 12.00 (*0-671-87528-0*, WSP) PB.
***Malone, Michael P.** The Battle for Butte: Mining & Politics on the Northern Frontier, 1864-1906. LC 95-14591. (Illus.). 281p. (C). 1995. reprint ed. pap. write for info. (*0-917298-34-9*) MT Hist Soc.
— C. Ben Ross & the New Deal in Idaho. LC 69-14207. (Illus.). 217p. 1970. 20.00 (*0-295-95060-9*) U of Wash Pr.
Malone, Michael P., ed. Historians & the American West. LC 82-17550. xii, 449p. 1983. 30.00 (*0-8032-3071-0*) U of Nebr Pr.
Malone, Michael P. & Etulain, Richard W. The American West: A Twentieth-Century History. LC 88-26840. (Illus.). xii, 347p. 1989. pap. 14.95 (*0-8032-8167-6*) U of Nebr Pr.
Malone, Michael P., et al. Montana: A History of Two Centuries. rev. ed. LC 91-21742. (Illus.). 480p. 1991. text ed. 40.00 (*0-295-97120-7*); pap. 19.95 (*0-295-97129-0*) U of Wash Pr.
***Malone, Michael S.** Microprocessor a Biography. 1994. cd-rom 29.95 (*0-387-94342-0*) Spr-Verlag.
Malone, Michael S., jt. auth. see Davidow, William H.
Malone, Myrtle D., ed. MGM Grand Hotel, Inc. Hotel-Casino-Theme Park: Grand Opening Commemorative. (Illus.). 135p. 1993. 20.00 (*1-881547-17-5*) Pioneer Pubns.
Malone, Myrtle D., ed. see Black, Geoff & Colson, Brett.
Malone, Myrtle D., ed. see Sheehan, Jack.
Malone, Nancy, ed. Where Love & People Are: Creative Ministry Program 1990 Fellows Yearbook. LC 90-50105. (Illus.). 125p. (Orig.). 1990. pap. text ed. 14.95 (*1-55605-149-2*) Wyndhall Pr.
Malone, Nancy A., ed. As Tentative As Flight. LC 89-40279. 84p. (C). 1989. pap. text ed. 14.95 (*1-55605-065-8*) Wyndhall Pr.
Malone, P. M. Into the High Branches. (Deep Woods Trilogy Ser.: Bk. II). (Illus.). 196p. (Orig.). (J). (gr. 1-8). 1992. pap. text ed. 11.95 (*0-9631957-1-9*) Raspberry Hill.
— Out of the Nest. (Deep Woods Trilogy Ser.: Bk. I). (Illus.). 198p. (Orig.). (J). (gr. 1-8). 1991. pap. text ed. 11.95 (*0-9631957-0-0*) Raspberry Hill.
— To Find a Way Home. (Deep Woods Trilogy Ser.: Bk. III). (Illus.). 200p. (Orig.). (J). (gr. 1-8). 1993. pap. text ed. 11.95 (*0-9631957-2-7*) Raspberry Hill.
Malone, Patrick. Skulking Way of War. 1991. 29.95 (*0-8191-8067-X*) Madison Bks UPA.
Malone, Patrick M. Canals & Industry: Engineering in Lowell, 1821-1880. (Illus.). 27p. (Orig.). 1983. pap. 2.50 (*0-942472-07-1*) Lowell Museum.
— The Skulking Way of War: Technology & Tactics among the New England Indians. LC 92-22740. (Illus.). 160p. 1993. reprint ed. pap. 13.95 (*0-8018-4554-8*) Johns Hopkins.
Malone, Patrick M., jt. auth. see Gordon, Robert B.
Malone, Paul. Louisiana Plantation Homes: A Return to Splendor. LC 84-25369. (Illus.). 160p. 1986. 36.95 (*0-88289-403-X*) Pelican.
— The Majesty of the Garden District. LC 93-41390. (Illus.). 160p. 1994. 21.95 (*1-56554-014-X*) Pelican.
Malone, Paul & Malone, Lee. The Majesty of New Orleans. LC 91-29043. (Illus.). 112p. 1992. 19.95 (*0-88289-863-9*) Pelican.
— The Majesty of the Felicianas. LC 88-29072. (Illus.). 96p. 1989. 15.95 (*0-88289-712-8*) Pelican.
— Majesty of the River Road. LC 87-31160. (Illus.). 128p. 1988. 15.95 (*0-88289-674-1*) Pelican.
Malone, Paul B., III. Abuse 'Em & Lose 'Em: Eighteen Leadership Styles That Were Made in Hell. LC 90-70734. (Illus.). 240p. (Orig.). 1990. pap. 11.95 (*0-9616548-2-1*) Synergy Pr.
— Love 'Em & Lead 'Em. LC 86-60237. (Illus.). 192p. (Orig.). 1986. 18.95 (*0-9616548-1-3*); pap. 10.95 (*0-9616548-0-5*) Synergy Pr.
***Malone, Paul S.** In an Arid Land: Thirteen Stories of Texas. LC 94-16972. 232p. 1995. 21.50 (*0-87565-140-2*) Tex Christian.
Malone, Peter. Movie Christs: And Antichrists. (Illus.). 172p. (Orig.). 1990. 10.95 (*0-8245-1003-8*) Crossroad NY.
— Traces of God: Understanding God's Presence in the World Today. 64p. (Orig.). 1991. pap. text ed. 6.95 (*0-8146-2074-4*) Liturgical Pr.
Malone, Robert L. Songs of the Shore. (Illus.). 72p. 1981. 8.95 (*0-9606234-0-X*) Ark & Arbor.
Malone, Romeo. Salona Travis in the Virgin Islands. LC 90-61069. 256p. 1990. 14.95 (*0-944957-05-6*) Rivercross Pub.
Malone, Russell. Irish America. (U. S. A. Guides Ser.). 300p. (Orig.). 1994. pap. 14.95 (*0-7818-0173-7*) Hippocrene Bks.
Malone, Shelley B. & Strunk, Phyllis B. Postcards of Old Key West. (Illus.). 64p. (Orig.). 1989. pap. write for info. (*0-318-65765-1*) S B Malone & P B Strunk.
Malone, Susan, jt. auth. see Waldrep, Kent.
Malone, Susan, jt. auth. see Weisbeck, Chuck.
Malone, Susan M. By the Book. LC 92-74829. 256p. 1993. 18.00 (*1-880909-00-6*) Baskerville.
Malone, Sylvester L. Dr. Edward McGlynn. 1978. 19.95 (*0-405-10841-9*, 11847) Ayer.
Malone, Thomas E., jt. ed. see Porter, Roger J.
Malone, Thomas F. International Networks for Addressing Issues of Global Change. (Illus.). 244p. 1994. pap. 2.00 (*0-914446-06-1*) Sigma Xi.
Malone, Vernon, jt. auth. see Dodge, Steve.
Malone, Wex S. Essays on Torts. LC 85-82407. 400p. 1986. lib. bdg. 49.00 (*0-940448-13-0*) LSU Law Pubns.
Malone, William F. & Koth, David L. Tylman's Theory & Practice of Fixed Prosthodontics. 8th ed. 461p. 1989. 59.50 (*0-912791-48-9*) Ishiyaku Euro.
Malone, Willie. Your New Beginning: Step Two. 64p. (Orig.). 1983. pap. 2.50 (*0-88144-008-6*) Christian Pub.
Malone, Willie J. Buck Van Huss: The Legend. 160p. 1989. 15.00 (*0-317-93444-9*); pap. 6.95 (*0-317-93445-7*) Willane Pub.
Maloney & Grindle. Textbook of Phacoemulsification. LC 87-28607. (Illus.). 1988. 68.00 (*0-918916-06-2*) Lasenda.
Maloney, jt. auth. see Phagan-Schostok.
Maloney, tr. see Ryokan.
Maloney, et al. Consumer Guide to Modern Cataract Surgery. LC 85-80392. (Illus.). 1986. pap. 12.95 (*0-918916-05-4*) Lasenda.

M

Maloney, Betty, jt. auth. see Blombery, Alec M.
Maloney, Betty, jt. auth. see Blombery, Alec.
Maloney, Betty, jt. auth. see Thompson, Patricia.
Maloney, Betty, jt. auth. see Thomson, Patricia.
Maloney, Clarence. Dimensions of Morning Sky. 1964. pap. 10.00 (0-685-62611-3) Atlantis Edns.
— People of the Maldive Islands. (Illus.). 432p. 1980. text ed. 27.95 (0-86131-158-2, Pub. by Orient Longman Ltd II) Apt Bks.
Maloney, Clarence, ed. The Evil Eye. LC 76-16861. (Illus.). 334p. 1983. pap. text ed. 17.50 (0-231-05825-X) Col U Pr.
Maloney, Clarence & Raju, K. V. Managing Irrigation Together: Practice & Policy in India. LC 94-7771. 340p. 1994. 36.00 (0-8039-9175-4) Sage.
***Maloney, David J., Jr.** Maloney's Antiques & Collectibles Resource Directory. 3rd ed. 560p. 1995. pap. 24.95 (0-930625-40-4, Antique Trdr Bks) Antique Trader.
— Maloney's Antiques & Collectibles Resource Directory, 1994-1995. (Illus.). 512p. 1993. pap. 22.95 (0-87069-706-4, Wallace-Hmestead) Chilton.
Maloney, Dennis. Lost in Language: Translations from the Japanese & Spanish. 24p. (Orig.). 1989. pap. text ed. 2.00 (1-877800-00-7) Springhse Editions.
— The Pine Hut Poems. 1983. pap. 4.00 (0-934834-41-5) White Pine.
— Selected Poems. 100p. 1990. 17.50 (0-87775-232-X); pap. 7.95 (0-87775-231-1) Unicorn Pr.
— Sitting in Circles. Keida, Yusuke, tr. 112p. (ENG & JPN.). 1987. pap. 8.00 (0-934834-87-3) White Pine.
Maloney, Dennis, ed. On Turtle's Back: A Biogeographic Anthology of New York State Poetry. 1978. 10.00 (0-685-05388-1); pap. 4.50 (0-685-05389-X) White Pine.
Maloney, Dennis, tr. see Akiko, Yosano.
Maloney, Dennis, tr. see Jiminez, Juan R.
Maloney, Dennis, tr. see Machado, Antonio.
Maloney, Dennis, tr. see Neruda, Pablo.
Maloney, Dennis, ed. see Oppenheimer, Joel.
Maloney, Dennis, jt. ed. see Seaton, J. P.
Maloney, Dennis M. Protection of Human Research Subjects: A Practical Guide to Federal Laws & Regulations. LC 84-4873. 442p. 1984. 69.50 (0-306-41522-4, Plenum Pr) Plenum.
Maloney, E. S., jt. auth. see Miller, Conrad.
***Maloney, Eddie & Hoffman, William.** Tough Guy. 384p. 1995. pap. 4.99 (0-7860-0168-2) Windsor NY.
***Maloney, Edward & Thorpe, Donald.** Tora Tora, Pearl Harbor: The Aircraft & Airmen, Dec. 7, 1941. (Illus.). 1991. pap. 24.95 (0-614-03027-7, WW II Pubns) Aviation.
Maloney, Edward T. Northrop Flying Wings. 1975. pap. 14.95 (0-915464-00-4, WW II Pubns) Aviation.
Maloney, Elberrt S. & Powers, Judith. Waterway Guide Chartbook: Norfolk to Jacksonville. 72p. (C). 1990. student ed 54.95 (0-915962-52-7) Argus GA.
Maloney, Elbert S. Chapman Piloting: Seamanship & Small Boat Handling. deluxe ed. 1993. 50.00 (0-688-11684-1) Morrow.
— Chapman Piloting, Seamanship & Small Boat Handling. 61th ed. 1993. 35.00 (0-688-11683-3) Morrow.
— Chapman Piloting, Seamanship & Small Boat Handling. 60th ed. (Illus.). 652p. 1991. 32.50 (0-688-10425-8, Hearst Marine Bks); boxed 50.00 (0-688-11092-4, Hearst Marine Bks) Morrow.
— Chapman's Nautical Guide: Communications Afloat. (Illus.). 144p. 1991. pap. 14.95 (0-688-09823-1, Hearst Marine Bks) Morrow.
— Dutton's Navigation & Piloting. 14th ed. (Illus.). 664p. 1985. 59.95 (0-87021-157-9) Naval Inst Pr.
— Problems & Answers in Navigation & Piloting. 2nd ed. 83p. 1985. pap. 6.95 (0-87021-150-1) Naval Inst Pr.
Maloney, Elliott C. Semitic Interference in Marcan Syntax. LC 80-13016. (Society of Biblical Literature Dissertation Ser.: No. 51). 1981. pap. 22.95 (0-89130-406-1, 06-01-51) Scholars Pr GA.
***Maloney, Eugene.** The Blue Myth: Corruption & Mismanagement in America's Police Force. 336p. 1994. pap. 5.99 (1-56171-334-1, S P I Bks) Sure Sellers.
Maloney, G. & Rogers-Gardner, Barbara J. Loving the Christ in You: A Spiritual Path to Self-Esteem. LC 87-18431. 128p. (Orig.). 1987. 7.95 (0-940989-15-8) Meyer Stone Bks.
Maloney, Gary, ed. see American Political Network, Inc. Staff & LTV Corporation Staff.
Maloney, Gene. Fire Department Lieutenant Captain Battalion Chief: Score High on Firefighter Promotion Exams. 1990. pap. 14.00 (0-13-318361-0, Arco Test) P-H Gen Ref & Trav.
Maloney, George. Death Where Is Your Sting? LC 84-9216. 155p. (Orig.). 1984. pap. 6.95 (0-8189-0470-4) Alba.
— Inward Stillness. 1974. pap. 14.95 (0-87193-062-5) Dimension Bks.
— Jesus, Set Me Free! Inner Freedom Through Contemplation. 1979. pap. 14.95 (0-87193-096-X) Dimension Bks.
— Listen, Prophets! 192p. 1974. pap. 14.95 (0-87193-059-5) Dimension Bks.
— Mary, the Womb of God. 1983. pap. 14.95 (0-87193-057-9) Dimension Bks.
— Nesting in the Rock. 1981. pap. 14.95 (0-87193-002-1) Dimension Bks.
— On the Road to Perfection: How Humility Fits in Today's Society. 144p. 1995. pap. 8.95 (1-56548-035-X) New City.
— That Your Joy May Be Complete: The Secret of Becoming a Joyful Person. LC 93-47943. 1994. 8.95 (1-56548-062-7) New City.
Maloney, George, ed. God's Exploding Love. LC 86-28802. 164p. (Orig.). 1987. pap. 7.95 (0-8189-0514-X) Alba.
Maloney, George A. Be Filled with the Fullness of God: Living with the Indwelling Trinity. 144p. (Orig.). 1993. pap. 8.95 (1-56548-024-4) New City.
— Called to Intimacy. LC 83-3782. 164p. 1983. pap. 6.95 (0-8189-0452-6) Alba.
— Communion of Saints. 200p. (Orig.). 1988. pap. 6.95 (0-914544-73-X) Living Flame Pr.
— Deep Calls to Deep: A Christian Spirituality of the Heart. 160p. 1993. pap. 11.95 (0-87193-286-5) Dimension Bks.
— Entering into the Heart of Jesus: Meditations on the Indwelling Trinity in St. John's Gospel. LC 87-30659. 170p. 1988. pap. 8.95 (0-8189-0527-1) Alba.
— God's Community of Love: Living with the Indwelling Trinity. 144p. (Orig.). 1993. pap. 8.95 (1-56548-042-2) New City.
— God's Incredible Mercy. LC 88-30108. 183p. (Orig.). 1989. pap. 9.95 (0-8189-0544-1) Alba.
— Indwelling Presence. 114p. (Orig.). 1985. pap. 6.95 (0-914544-62-4) Living Flame Pr.
— Journey into Contemplation. 144p. (Orig.). 1983. pap. 5.95 (0-914544-51-9) Living Flame Pr.
— Manna in the Desert. 120p. (Orig.). 1984. pap. 6.95 (0-914544-54-3) Living Flame Pr.
— Second Dawn of Life. 102p. (Orig.). 1990. pap. 6.95 (0-914544-78-0) Living Flame Pr.
— The Silence of Surrendering Love: Body, Soul, Spirit Integration. LC 85-28636. 189p. 1986. pap. 7.95 (0-8189-0494-1) Alba.
— The Spirit Broods over the World. LC 92-40239. 192p. 1993. pap. 9.95 (0-8189-0633-2) Alba.
— Who Do You Say You Are? Christ's Love for Us. 119p. (Orig.). 1986. pap. 6.95 (0-914544-64-0) Living Flame Pr.
— Why Not Become Totally Fire? The Power of Fiery Prayer. LC 89-39315. 144p. 1990. pap. 7.95 (0-8091-3122-6) Paulist Pr.
— Your Sins Are Forgiven You: Rediscovering the Sacrament of Reconciliation. LC 93-43836. 1994. pap. 7.95 (0-8189-0691-X) Alba.
Maloney, George A., tr. & intro. Pseudo-Macarius: The Fifty Spiritual Homilies & the Great Letter. LC 92-4736. (Classics of Western Spirituality Ser.). 320p. 1992. 24.95 (0-8091-0455-5); pap. 17.95 (0-8091-3312-1) Paulist Pr.
Maloney, George S. A Theology of Uncreated Energies of God. LC 78-55049. (Pere Marquette Lectures). 1978. 10.00 (0-87462-516-5) Marquette.
Maloney, Gilles & Frohn, Winnie, eds. Hippocrates - Concordantia in Corpus Hippocraticum, 6 vols., Set. (Alpha Omega, Reihe A Ser.: No. LXXV). xxiii, 4869p. (GER.). 1986. lib. bdg. 1,025.70 (3-487-07740-X, Pub. by Georg Olms GW) Lubrecht & Cramer.
— Hippocrates - Concordantia in Corpus Hippocraticum, 6 vols., Vol. 6. (Alpha Omega, Reihe A Ser.: No. LXXV). vi, 487p. (GER.). 1986. lib. bdg. write for info. (3-487-09130-5, Pub. by Georg Olms GW) Lubrecht & Cramer.
Maloney, J. Christopher. The Mundane Matter of the Mental Language. (Cambridge Studies in Philosophy). (Illus.). (C). 1989. 64.95 (0-521-37031-0) Cambridge U Pr.
Maloney, J. J. Beyond the Wall. 1973. per. 3.00 (0-912678-05-4, Greenfld Rev Pr) Greenfld Rev Lit.
— The Pariah's Handbook. LC 92-32968. 1992. write for info. (0-9617499-3-8) Woods Colt Pr.
Maloney, James C. A Critical Edition of Mira De Amescua's "La Fe De Hungria" & "El Monte De la Piedad", Vol. 7. 149p. 1975. pap. 7.00 (0-912788-06-2) Tulane Romance Lang.
Maloney, James H. Studebaker Cars. (Illus.). 320p. 1994. 39.95 (0-87938-884-6) Motorbooks Intl.
Maloney, John. The Professionalization of Economics: Alfred Marshall & the Dominance of Orthodoxy. 248p. (C). 1990. pap. 19.95 (0-88738-345-9) Transaction Pubs.
Maloney, John C., ed. see Attitude Research Conference Staff.
Maloney, Karen B. Infant Food & Nutrition of Newborn: Medical Subject Analysis with Reference Bibliography. LC 85-48104. 150p. 1987. 39.50 (0-88164-480-3); pap. 34.50 (0-88164-481-1) ABBE Pubs Assn.
Maloney, Kerry, jt. ed. see Barry, William.
Maloney, L., tr. see Buhler, Walther.
Maloney, Linda, tr. see Aristide, Jean-Bertrand.
Maloney, Linda, tr. see Drewermann, Eugen.
Maloney, Linda, ed. see Rezende, Ricardo F.
Maloney, Linda M. All That God Hath Done with Them: The Narration of the Works of God in the Early Christian Community as Described in the Acts of the Apostles. LC 90-40424. (American University Studies: Theology & Religion: Ser. VII, Vol. 91). 238p. (C). 1991. text ed. 42.95 (0-8204-1410-7) P Lang Pubs.
— The Captain from Connecticut: The Life & Naval Times of Isaac Hull. (Illus.). 540p. 1986. text ed. 47.50 (0-930350-90-1) NE U Pr.
— Proclamation Five: Pentecost 3: Interpreting the Lessons of the Church Year, Ser. C. LC 92-22973. 1994. pap. 4.50 (0-8006-4200-7, Fortress Pr) Augsburg Fortress.
Maloney, Linda M., tr. see Haussling, Angelus A., et al, eds.
Maloney, Linda M., tr. see Richter, Klemens.
Maloney, Linda M., tr. see Schnelle, Udo.
Maloney, Linda M., tr. see Soelle, Dorothee.
Maloney, Linda M., tr. see Theissen, Gerd.
Maloney, Linda M., tr. see Vorgrimler, H.
Maloney, M. J. Book-Keeping - A Guide for Beginners, Vol. 1: Worked Solutions. (C). 1986. 40.00 (0-85950-654-1, Pub. by S Thornes Pubs UK) St Mut.
Maloney, Mack. Freedmon Express. (Wingman Ser.: No. 7). 1990. mass mkt. 3.99 (0-8217-4022-9) Zebra.
— The Ghost War. 448p. 1993. mass mkt. 4.50 (0-8217-4223-X) Zebra.
— The Lucifer Crusade. (Wingman Ser.: No. 3). 432p. 1987. pap. 3.95 (0-8217-2232-8) Zebra.
— Return from the Inferno. (Wingman Ser.: No. 9). 1991. pap. 3.95 (0-8217-3510-1) Zebra.
— Skyfire. (Wingman Ser.: No. 8). 1990. pap. 3.95 (0-8217-3121-1) Zebra.
— Thunder Alley. 432p. 1988. pap. 3.95 (0-8217-2405-3) Zebra.
— Thunder in the East. (Wingman Ser.: No. 4). 432p. 1988. pap. 3.95 (0-8217-2453-3) Zebra.
— Twisted Cross. (Wingman Ser.: No. 5). 400p. 1991. pap. 3.95 (0-8217-2553-X) Zebra.
— War Heaven. 432p. 1991. mass mkt. 4.95 (0-8217-3414-8) Zebra.
— War of the Sun. (Wingman Ser.: No. 10). 1992. mass mkt. 3.99 (0-8217-3773-2) Zebra.
Maloney, Marina. The Knight of the Sand Castle. LC 92-85410. (Illus.). 44p. (J). (gr. k-4). 1993. pap. 5.95 (1-55523-553-0) Winston-Derek.
Maloney, Mark. Wingman. 464p. 1987. pap. 3.95 (0-8217-2015-5) Zebra.
Maloney, Martin J. & Rubenstein, Paul M. Writing for the Media. 1980. text ed. write for info. (0-13-970558-9) P-H.
Maloney, Martin J., jt. auth. see Rubenstein, Paul M.
Maloney, Mary E. Dermatologic Surgical Suite: Design & Materials. (Practical Manuals in Dermatologic Surgery Ser.). (Illus.). 105p. 1991. pap. text ed. 32.00 (0-443-08688-5) Churchill.
Maloney, Michael & Kranz, Rachel. Straight Talk about Anxiety & Depression. (Straight Talk Ser.). 128p. (YA). (gr. 5-12). 1991. lib. bdg. 16.95 (0-8160-2434-0) Facts on File.
— Straight Talk about Eating Disorders. (Straight Talk Ser.). 128p. (YA). (gr. 7-12). 1991. 16.95 (0-8160-2414-6) Facts on File.
***Maloney, Michael, et al.** Pocket Guide to Fly Casting. (Illus.). 28p. 1995. spiral bd. 12.95 (1-886127-10-7) Greycliff Pub.
Maloney, Michael P. A Clinician's Guide to Forensic Psychological Assessment. 288p. (C). 1985. text ed. 35.00 (0-02-919850-X) Free Pr.
Maloney, Michael P. & Ward, Michael P. Psychological Assessment: A Conceptual Approach. 1976. text ed. 29.95 (0-19-502027-8) OUP.
Maloney, P. Dennis, ed. see Lehner, Devony.
Maloney, Pat, Sr. & Pasqual, Jack. Winning the Million Dollar Lawsuit. LC 82-21175. 258p. 1982. text ed. 99.50 (0-87624-848-2, Inst Busn Plan) P-H.
Maloney, Pat, jt. auth. see Singer, Amy.
Maloney, Patricia L. Practical Guidance for Parents of the Visually Handicapped Preschooler. (Illus.). 88p. 1981. spiral bd. 21.95x (0-398-04583-6) C C Thomas.
Maloney, R. Kay, ed. Personnel Development in Libraries. (Issues in Library & Information Sciences Ser.: No. 3). 1977. pap. text ed. 15.00 (0-8135-0843-6) Rutgers U SICLS.
Maloney, Ralph. Twenty-Four Hour Drink Book. (Illus.). 1962. 10.95 (0-8392-1121-X) Astor-Honor.
Maloney, Robert C. The Way of Vincent de Paul: A Contemporary Spirituality in the Service of the Poor. 3rd ed. 176p. 1992. 9.95 (1-56548-001-5) New City.
***Maloney, Robert P.** He Hears the Cry of the Poor: On the Spirituality of Vincent de Paul. LC 95-9621. 1995. 9.95 (1-56548-034-1) New City.
Maloney, Roy T. A Magnet Called Earth: The Universe Quick & Easy. (Illus.). 400p. (Orig.). (C). 1989. pap. 16.95 (0-913257-06-0) Dropzone Pr.
— Real Estate Quick & Easy. 10th ed. 400p. 1990. 16.95 (0-913257-03-6, Publishers Group) Dropzone Pr.
— Roy's Rot: Rules of Thumb to Wit & Wisdom. LC 85-7015. (Illus.). 1985. pap. 12.95 (0-913257-01-X) Dropzone Pr.
Maloney, Roy T., ed. see Kramer, Mark H.
Maloney, Sean M. Securing Command of the Sea: NATO Naval Planning, 1948-1954. (Illus.). 256p. 1994. 38.95 (1-55750-562-4) Naval Inst Pr.
Maloney, Stephen R. Speaker's Portable Answer Book. LC 93-8251. 1993. 29.95 (0-13-501016-0) P-H.
— Talk Your Way to the Top: Communication Secrets of the Ceos. 1992. 19.95 (0-13-882788-5, Busn) P-H.
Maloney, Thomas M. Modern Particleboard & Dry-Process Fiberboard Manufacturing. LC 76-47094. (Forest Industries Book Ser.). (Illus.). 1993. 59.00 (0-87930-288-7) Miller Freeman.
Maloney, Thomas S., tr. Roger Bacon: Three Treatments of Universals. (Medieval & Renaissance Texts & Studies: Vol. 66). 176p. 1989. 20.00 (0-86698-075-X) MRTS.
Maloney, Timothy. Electricity: Fundamental Concepts & Applications. 1992. teacher ed 26.00 (0-8273-4677-8) Delmar.
Maloney, Timothy J. Electric Circuits: Principles & Applications. (Illus.). 896p. (C). 1984. 32.15 (0-685-07187-1) P-H.
— Electric Circuits: Principles & Applications. 2nd ed. 864p. 1988. boxed 41.00 (0-13-247735-1) P-H.
— Electricity: Fundamental Concepts & Applications. 448p. 1992. 46.95 (0-8273-4675-1) Delmar.
— Industrial Solid State Electronics. 2nd ed. (Illus.). 624p. (C). 1985. text ed. 75.00 (0-13-463423-3) P-H.
— Solid-State Electronics: Principles & Applications. 535p. (C). 1994. pap. text ed. 33.50 (0-9639857-4-4) Dirk Pubng.
Maloney, Walter C. A Sketch of the History of Key West, Florida. Peters, Thelma B., ed. & intro. by. LC 68-21658. (Floridiana Facsimile & Reprint Ser.). xxi, 85p. 1968. reprint ed. 16.95 (0-8130-0157-9) U Press Fla.
Maloni, Ruby. European Merchant Capital & the Indian Economy: A Historical Reconstruction Based on Surat Factory Records 1630-1668. (C). 1992. 30.00 (81-85425-50-7, Pub. by Manohar II) S Asia.
Malony, H. Newton. Church Organization Development: Perspectives & Resources. LC 86-81285. (Orig.). 1986. pap. 16.95 (0-9609928-2-0) Integ Pr.
— Integration Musings: Thoughts on Being A Christian Professional. LC 86-81512. (Orig.). 1986. pap. 16.33 (0-9609928-3-9) Integ Pr.
— Psychology of Religion: Personalities, Problems, & Possibilities. LC 90-38821. (Psychology & Christianity Ser.). 560p. (Orig.). 1990. pap. text ed. 29.99 (0-8010-6268-3) Baker Bk.
— The Psychology of Religion for Ministry. LC 94-41661. (Integration Bks.). 144p. 1994. pap. 12.95 (0-8091-3483-7) Paulist Pr.
— Relaxation for Christians. (Orig.). 1992. mass mkt. 4.99 (0-345-36649-2) Ballantine.
— Settling Conflict Without Waging War: Nine Strategies for Win-Win Relationships. LC 94-34802. 1995. 15.99 (0-8054-1095-3) Broadman.
Malony, H. Newton, ed. Is There a Shrink in the Lord's House? How Psychologists Can Help the Church. LC 86-81513. (Orig.). 1986. pap. 12.95 (0-9609928-4-7) Integ Pr.
— Spirit-Centered Wholeness: Beyond the Psychology of Self. LC 87-23028. (Studies in the Psychology of Religion: Vol. 2). 256p. 1987. lib. bdg. 89.95 (0-88946-246-1) E Mellen.
Malony, H. Newton & Southard, Samuel, eds. Handbook of Religious Conversion. 314p. (Orig.). 1992. 25.95 (0-89135-086-1) Religious Educ.
Malony, H. Newton & Spilka, Bernard, eds. Religion in Psychodynamic Perspective: The Contributions of Paul W. Pruyser. 254p. 1991. 37.50 (0-19-506234-5) OUP.
Malony, H. Newton, jt. ed. see Rosik, Christopher H.
Malony, H. Newton, jt. auth. see Sanders, Randolph K.
Maloof, Judy. Over Her Dead Body: The Construction of Male Subjectivity in Onetti. LC 93-44115. (American University Studies, Series XXII: Vol. 24). 200p. (C). 1995. text ed. 41.95 (0-8204-2450-1) P Lang Pubs.
Maloof, Karen. For My Child: An Album of Family Memories from Parent to Child. (Illus.). 48p. (J). 1994. 17.95 (0-8249-8659-8, Ideals Child) Hambleton-Hill.
Maloof, Karen, illus. For My Grandchild: An Album of Memories from Grandparent to Grandchild. 56p. 1992. 17.95 (0-8249-8545-1, Ideals Child) Hambleton-Hill.
***Maloof, Rich.** Joe Satriani Riff by Riff. 91p. Date not set. pap. 17.95 (0-89524-851-4, 02506314) Cherry Lane.
Maloof, Sam. Sam Maloof: Woodworker. (Illus.). 1989. pap. 45.00 (0-87011-910-9) Kodansha.
Malor, J., et al, eds. Annotations to the Acts & Regulations of the Australian Parliament. 227.00 (0-409-49007-5) Butterworth Legal Pubs.
Malory, Sir Thomas. Le Morte d'Arthur. 1994. 20.00 (0-679-60099-X, Modern Lib) Random.
***Malory, Thomas.** Arthur & the Sword. LC 95-9968. (J). 1995. write for info. (0-689-31987-8, Atheneum S&S) S&S Trade.
— King Arthur & His Knights. Vinaver, Eugene, ed. (Illus.). 1975. pap. 9.95 (0-19-501905-9) OUP.
— Malory Works. 2nd ed. Vinaver, Eugene, ed. (Oxford Standard Authors Ser.). 1977. pap. 16.95 (0-19-281217-3) OUP.
— Morte D'Arthur. Brewer, D. S., ed. LC 68-22420. (York Medieval Texts Ser.). 166p. (C). 1968. pap. 9.95 (0-8101-0031-2) Northwestern U Pr.
— Le Morte D'Arthur. Field, P. J., ed. LC 77-22498. (London Medieval & Renaissance Ser.). 284p. 1978. 34.50 (0-8419-0333-6) Holmes & Meier.
— Le Morte D'Arthur. Lumiansky, Robert M., ed. 768p. 1986. pap. 19.95 (0-02-022560-1, Collier S&S) S&S Trade.
— Le Morte d'Arthur. (Learning Channel's Great Books Ser.). 1993. pap. 9.00 (0-679-74956-X) Random.
— Morte D'Arthur. abr. ed. Sanders, C. R. & Ward, C. E., eds. 1979. reprint ed. pap. text ed. 10.95 (0-89197-308-7) Irvington.
— Le Morte d'Arthur. (BCL1-PR English Literature Ser.). 148p. 1992. reprint ed. lib. bdg. 69.00 (0-7812-7189-4) Rprt Serv.
— Le Morte D'Arthur, 2 vols., 1. Cowen, Janet, ed. (English Library). 1970. mass mkt. 9.95 (0-14-043043-1, Penguin Classics) Viking Penguin.
— Le Morte D'Arthur, 2 vols., 2. Cowen, Janet, ed. (English Library). 1970. mass mkt. 6.95 (0-14-043044-X, Penguin Classics) Viking Penguin.
— Morte D'Arthur, 3 Vols. in 2, Set. Sommer, H. Oskar, ed. LC 78-172839. reprint ed. 185.00 (0-404-04175-2) AMS Pr.
— Sir Thomas Malory: Views & Re-Views. Hanks, D., Jr., ed. LC 91-11928. (Studies in the Middle Ages: No. 19). 1991. 39.50 (0-404-61449-3) AMS Pr.
— Tales of King Arthur. 1989. pap. 20.00 (0-8052-0891-7) Schocken.
— The Works of Sir Thomas Malory, Vol. I. 3rd rev. ed. Vinaver, Eugene, ed. (Oxford English Texts Ser.). 611p. 1990. 135.00 (0-19-812344-2) OUP.
— The Works of Sir Thomas Malory, Vol. II. 3rd rev. ed. Vinaver, Eugene, ed. (Oxford English Texts Ser.). 654p. 1990. 135.00 (0-19-812345-0) OUP.
— The Works of Sir Thomas Malory, Vol. III. 3rd rev. ed. Vinaver, Eugene, ed. (Oxford English Texts Ser.). 680p. 1990. 145.00 (0-19-812346-9) OUP.
***Malos, Ellen, ed. & comp.** The Politics of Housework. 256p. 1995. 45.00 (1-873797-19-2); pap. 19.95 (1-873797-18-4) Paul & Co Pubs.
Malos, Ellen, jt. auth. see Hague, Gill.
Malot, Hector. En Famille, Tome 1. (Folio - Junior Ser.: No. 131). (Illus.). 220p. (FRE.). (J). (gr. 5-10). 1980. pap. 9.95 (2-07-033131-8) Schoenhof.
— En Famille, Tome 2. (Folio - Junior Ser.: No. 132). (Illus.). 221p. (FRE.). (J). (gr. 5-10). 1980. pap. 9.95 (2-07-033132-6) Schoenhof.

An Asterisk (*) at the beginning of an entry indicates that the title is appearing in BIP for the first time.

— Sans Famille, Tome 1. (Folio - Junior Ser.: No. 612). (Illus.). 351p. (FRE.). (J). (gr. 5-10). 1990. pap. 10.95 (2-07-033612-3) Schoenhof.

— Sans Famille, Tome 2. (Folio - Junior Ser.: No. 617). (Illus.). 417p. (FRE.). (J). (gr. 5-10). 1991. pap. 10.95 (2-07-033617-4) Schoenhof.

Malot, Hector H. Nobody's Boy. 301p. 1991. reprint ed. lib. bdg. 29.95x (0-89966-760-0) Buccaneer Bks.

— Nobody's Girl. 301p. 1991. reprint ed. lib. bdg. 29.95x (0-89966-759-7) Buccaneer Bks.

Malotki, Ekkehart. Hopi Time: A Linguistic Analysis of the Temporal Concepts in the Hopi Language. (Trends in Linguistics, Studies & Monographs: No. 20). xxii, 677p. 1983. 141.95 (90-279-3349-9) Mouton.

— The Magic Hummingbird. (Illus.). 32p. (J). (gr. 1-5). 1995. 14.95 (1-885772-03-3) Kiva Pubng.

***Malotki, Ekkehart, ed. & tr.** The Bedbugs' Night Dance & Other Hopi Sexual Tales: Mumuspi'yyungqa Tuutuwutsi. 224p. (C). 1995. text ed. 35.00 (0-8032-3190-3) U of Nebr Pr.

Malotki, Ekkehart, photos. Tapamveni: The Rock Art Galleries of Petrified Forest & Beyond. LC 94-17796. (Illus.). 1994. 24.95 (0-945695-05-5) Petrified Forest Mus Assn.

Malotki, Ekkehart & Lomatuway'ma, Michael. Hopi Coyote Tales: Istutuwutsi. LC 83-23412. (American Tribal Religions Ser.: Vol. 9). (Illus.). viii, 343p. 1984. pap. 13. 95 (0-8032-8123-4) U of Nebr Pr.

— Maasaw: Profile of a Hopi God. LC 87-163. (American Tribal Religions Ser.: Vol. 11). (Illus.). x, 273p. 1987. 35. 00 (0-8032-3118-0) U of Nebr Pr.

— Stories of Maasaw: A Hopi God. LC 87-164. (American Tribal Religions Ser.: Vol. 10). (Illus.). 357p. 1987. reprint ed. pap. 101.80 (0-7837-8895-9, 2049606) Bks Demand.

Malotki, Ekkehart, ed. see Lomatuway'ma, Michael, et al.

Malotki, Ekkehart, et al. Gullible Coyote Una'ihi: A Bilingual Collection of Hopi Coyote Stories. LC 85-14101. (Illus.). 193p. reprint ed. pap. 55.10 (0-7837-5050-1, 2044728) Bks Demand.

Malott, Adele, jt. auth. see Malott, Gene.

Malott, Gene & Malott, Adele. Get up & Go: A Guide for the Mature Traveler. LC 89-11715. 336p. 1989. pap. 10. 95 (0-933469-06-3) Gateway Bks.

***Malott, Gene E.** 1995 Senior Media Directory. rev. ed. 1995. lib. bdg. 95.00 (0-9629034-4-2) GEM Pub Group.

Malott, Jack C. & Fodor, Joseph, III. The Art & Science of Medical Radiography. 7th ed. LC 92-49306. 297p. 1993. pap. 35.95 (0-8016-6321-0) Mosby Yr Bk.

Malott, Richard, et al. Behavior Analysis & Behavior Modification: An Introduction. LC 78-380. (Illus.). 442p. (Orig.). 1978. reprint ed. pap. 11.00 (0-917472-06-3); reprint ed. write for info. (0-318-51872-4) F Fournies.

Malott, Richard. Contingency Management in Education & Other Equally Exciting Places. 2nd ed. (Illus.). 260p. 1972. reprint ed. teacher ed write for info. (0-318-51874-0); reprint ed. pap. text ed. 10.00 (0-917472-07-1) F Fournies.

Malott, Richard W., et al. Elementary Principles of Behavior. 2nd ed. 512p. 1992. pap. text ed. 43.33 (0-13-260241-5) P-H.

Malou, Job. The Dinka Vowel System. LC 88-60939. (Publications in Linguistics: No. 82). (Illus.). 100p. 1988. pap. 20.00 (0-88312-008-9); fiche 8.00 (0-88312-451-3) Summer Instit Ling.

Malouf, David. Child's Play: The Bread of Time To Come. 282p. 1994. pap. 7.95 (0-8076-1351-7) Braziller.

— David Malouf: Selected Poems. 120p. (Orig.). 1992. pap. 10.00 (0-207-17280-3, Pub. by Angus & Robertson AT) HarpC.

— First Things Last. 58p. 1981. text ed. 16.95 (0-7022-1564-3, Pub. by Univ Queensland Pr AT) Intl Spec Bk.

— The Great World: A Novel. LC 93-15510. 1993. pap. 12. 00 (0-679-74836-9, Vin) Random.

— An Imaginary Life. LC 77-18601. 154p. 1985. reprint ed. pap. 7.95 (0-8076-1114-X) Braziller.

— Neighbours in a Thicket. 2nd ed. 1980. pap. 12.95 (0-7022-1547-3, Pub. by Univ Queensland Pr AT) Intl Spec Bk.

— Remembering Babylon. LC 93-7888. 1993. 20.00 (0-679-42724-4) Pantheon.

— Remembering Babylon. 1994. pap. 10.00 (0-679-74951-9, Vin) Random.

Malouf, Dian L. Cattle Kings of Texas. LC 91-73402. (Illus.). 176p. 1991. 39.95 (0-941831-69-8) Beyond Words Pub.

Malouf, Doug & Pivar, William H. The Real Estate Sales Survival Kit: Success Strategies for the 1990's. (Illus.). 248p. 1990. pap. 24.95 (0-7931-0084-4, 1913-13) Dearborn Finan.

Malouf, George H. Maloof: The Ghassani Legacy. (Illus.). 608p. 1992. text ed. 150.00 (0-9632681-0-4) Malouf Prods.

Malouf, John L., jt. auth. see Haas, Leonard J.

Malouf, Marcellene & DeLeon, David. From Daddy with Love. (Illus.). 34p. (J). 1993. 16.95 (0-9639680-0-9) Malouf-Christopherson.

***Malouf, Waldy & Finn, Molly.** The Hudson River Valley Cook Book: A Leading American Chef Savors the Region's Bounty. 409p. 1995. write for info. (0-201-62253-X) Addison-Wesley.

***Maloux, Maurice.** Dictionnaire de l'Humour et du Libertinage. 360p. (FRE.). 1983. 34.95 (0-7859-7835-6, 2226017674) Fr & Eur.

— Dictionnaire des Proverbes, Sentences, et Maximes. (FRE.). 1994. pap. 32.40 (0-7859-8887-4) Fr & Eur.

— Dictionnaire des Proverbs, Sentences, et Maximes: Larousse Dictionary of Proverbs, Sayings & Maxims. 2nd ed. 628p. (FRE.). 1990. pap. write for info. (0-7859-4738-8) Fr & Eur.

— Larousse Dictionnaire des Proverbes, Sentences et Maximes. (FRE.). 1992. 59.95 (0-7859-7648-5, 2033409066) Fr & Eur.

Malov, V. & Immirzi, F. Telemechanics. LC 63-10018. (International Series of Monographs on Automation & Automatic Control: Vol. 1). 1964. 52.00 (0-08-013841-1, Pub. by Pergamon Repr UK) Franklin.

Malovitzki, Sinai. Parshas Lech. (Bible in Yiddish Ser.). (Illus.). 160p. (YID.). (YA). 1987. teacher ed 10.00 (0-944704-03-4) Sinai Heritage.

— Parshas Nitzuvim. (Bible in Yiddish Ser.). (Illus.). 150p. (YID.). (J). 1988. pap. 5.00 (0-944704-61-1) Sinai Heritage.

— Parshas Yisroy. (Bible in Yiddish Ser.). (Illus.). 400p. (YID.). (J). 1988. lib. bdg. 25.00 (0-944704-19-0) Sinai Heritage.

— Parshaw Va'Yeilech. (Bible in Yiddish Ser.). (Illus.). 95p. (YID.). (YA). 1988. pap. 5.00 (0-944704-62-X) Sinai Heritage.

— Zochor Veshomor. (Bible in Yiddish Ser.). (Illus.). 200p. (YID.). (C). 1987. reprint ed. pap. text ed. 7.00 (0-944704-67-0) Sinai Heritage.

Malowicki, Sinai. An Illustrated Guide to the Korbanos & Menachos. Fruchter, Yaakov, ed. (Illus.). 136p. (Orig.). 1991. pap. text ed. 7.50 (0-914131-99-0) Torah Umesorah.

Malowicky, Sinai, ed. see Teitelbaum, Eli.

Maloy, B. Patrick. Law in Sports: Liability Cases in Management & Administration. 202p. 1988. pap. text ed. write for info. (0-697-14819-X) Brown & Benchmark.

Maloy, Jacqueline. Teeth. (Real Readers Ser.: Level Blue). (Illus.). 32p. (J). (gr. 1-4). 1989. lib. bdg. 19.97 (0-8172-3520-5); pap. 3.95 (0-8114-6722-8) Raintree Steck-V.

Maloy, K. & Patterson, M. Birth or Abortion: Private Struggles in a Political World. (Illus.). 420p. (C). 1992. 26.95 (0-306-44327-9, Plenum Pr) Plenum.

Maloy, Kate. Toward a New Science of Instruction. 73p. (Orig.). (C). 1994. pap. text ed. 25.00 (0-7881-0595-7) Diane Pub.

Maloy, N. G. Local Government Finance & Accounts. xiii, 470p. 1982. pap. 65.00 (0-455-20366-0, Pub. by Law Bk Co) W W Gaunt.

Maloy, Otis C. Plant Disease Control: Principles & Practice. LC 92-39600. 360p. 1993. text ed. 64.95 (0-471-57317-5) Wiley.

Maloy, Richard H. Your Questions Answered about Florida Divorce Law. 2nd ed. LC 77-81168. (Your Questions Answered on Florida Law Ser.). 1984. pap. 3.50 (0-89317-023-2) Windward Pub.

— Your Questions Answered about Florida Law & Family Relationships in Life & Death. LC 77-93147. (Your Questions Answered on Florida Law Ser.). 1978. pap. 1.95 (0-89317-026-7) Windward Pub.

— Your Questions Answered about Florida Law & Your Continuing Obligations after Divorce. LC 77-93148. (Your Questions Answered on Florida Law Ser.). 1978. pap. 1.95 (0-89317-025-9) Windward Pub.

Maloy, Richard H. & Bird, David D. Bankruptcy Practice Deskbook, 3 vols. suppl. ed. 2400p. 1992. Latest supp. 10/92. 47.00 (1-56257-155-9) Butterworth Legal Pubs.

— Bankruptcy Practice Deskbook, 3 vols., 3. 2400p. 1991. 100.00 (0-88063-730-7) Butterworth Legal Pubs.

— Bankruptcy Practice Deskbook, 3 vols., Set. 2400p. 1994. ring bd. 285.00 (0-88063-779-X) Michie Butterworth.

— Bankruptcy Practice Deskbook, 3 vols., Vols. 1 & 2. 2400p. 1991. 205.00 (0-88063-729-3) Butterworth Legal Pubs.

Maloy, Richard H. & McDuff, Wilbur S. Bender's Florida Forms: Pleadings, 14 vols. 1968. write for info. (0-8205-1101-3) Bender.

Maloy, Robert W., jt. auth. see Edwards, Sharon A.

Maloy, Robert W., jt. auth. see Jones, Byrd L.

Maloy, Stanley. Experimental Techniques in Bacterial Genetics. 196p. (Orig.). 1989. spiral bd. 37.50 (0-86720-118-5) Jones & Bartlett.

Maloy, Stanley R., et al. Microbial Genetics. 2nd ed. 1994. boxed 5.50 (0-86720-248-3) Jones & Bartlett.

Malpa, Alfred P., jt. auth. see Fenn, Patricia.

Malpas, J. E. The Mirror of Meaning: Donald Davidson & the Theory of Interpretation. 296p. (C). 1992. 54.95 (0-521-41721-X) Cambridge U Pr.

Malpas, J. E., ed. see Donagan, Alan.

***Malpas, James S., et al, eds.** Myeloma: Biology & Management. (Illus.). 592p. 1995. 98.00 (0-19-262480-6) OUP.

Malpas, Phillip A. True Messiah. 160p. 1989. 7.95 (0-913004-67-7, 352) Point Loma Pub.

Malpass, Eric. The Long Long Dances. large type ed. 354p. 1982. 15.95 (0-7089-0825-X) Ulverscroft.

— Oh, My Darling Daughter. large type ed. 384p. 1982. 15. 95 (0-7089-0881-0) Ulverscroft.

— Summer Awakening. large type ed. 336p. 1983. 15.95 (0-7089-0961-2) Ulverscroft.

Malpass, Michael A., ed. Provincial Inca: Archaeological & Ethnohistorical Assessment of the Impact of the Inca State. LC 93-30296. (Illus.). 290p. 1993. pap. text ed. 25.95 (0-87745-426-4) U of Iowa Pr.

Malpass, Peter & Means, Robin, eds. Implementing Housing Policy. LC 92-23835. 1993. 90.00 (0-335-15751-3, Open Univ Pr); pap. 32.00 (0-335-15750-5, Open Univ Pr) Taylor & Francis.

Malpass, Roy S., jt. ed. see Lonner, Walter J.

Malpazzi, Frances, jt. ed. see Frontain, Raymone-Jean.

Malpede, Karen. A Monster Has Stolen the Sun. LC 87-60431. 224p. (Orig.). 1987. pap. 11.50 (0-910395-24-1) Marlboro Pr.

— Women in Theatre: Compassion & Hope. LC 84-26138. 304p. 1985. 14.95 (0-87910-035-4) Limelight Edns.

Malpezzi, Frances M. & Clements, William M. Italian-American Folklore: Proverbs, Songs, Games, Folktales, Foodways, Superstitions, Folk Remedies & More. (American Folklore Ser.). (Illus.). 272p. 1992. 24. 95 (0-87483-279-9); pap. 14.95 (0-87483-278-0) August Hse.

Malpezzi, Stephen & Ball, Gwendolyn. Rent Control in Developing Countries. (Discussion Paper Ser.: No. 129). 100p. 1991. 7.95 (0-8213-1910-8, 11910) World Bank.

Malphrus, Benjamin K. The History of Radio Astronomy & the National Radio Astronomy Observatory: Evolution Toward Big Science. (C). 1995. write for info. (0-89464-841-1) Krieger.

Malphurs, Aubrey. Developing a Vision for Ministry in the Twenty-First Century. LC 91-42503. 192p. (Orig.). 1992. pap. 11.99 (0-8010-6286-1) Baker Bk.

— Maximizing Your Effectiveness: How to Discover & Develop Your Divine Design. (Illus.). 256p. (Orig.). 1995. pap. 13.99 (0-8010-6317-5) Baker Bk.

— Planting Growing Churches for the Twenty-First Century: A Comprehensive Guide for New Churches & Those Desiring Renewal. LC 92-20932. 1992. 19.99 (0-8010-6295-0) Baker Bk.

— Pouring New Wine into Old Wineskins: How to Change a Church Without Destroying It. LC 93-10368. 224p. (Orig.). 1993. pap. 12.99 (0-8010-6301-9) Baker Bk.

— Vision America: A Strategy for Reaching a Nation. LC 94-11200. (Illus.). 256p. (Orig.). 1994. pap. 11.99 (0-8010-6313-2) Baker Bk.

Malphurs, J. G. Amusement for Your Bible Hour. 1961. pap. 0.60 (0-88027-100-0) Firm Foun Pub.

— Let's Do Something. 1958. pap. 0.60 (0-88027-099-3) Firm Foun Pub.

— My Hand in His. 1961. 5.00 (0-88027-012-8) Firm Foun Pub.

Malpighi, Stefania, tr. see Eggenberger, David, ed.

Malpine, D. Botanical Atlas. 1989. 14.99 (0-517-68132-3) Random Hse Value.

Malraux, Andre. Antimemoires: Miroir des Limbes. (Folio Ser.: No. 23). 1972. 14.95 (2-07-036023-7) Schoenhof.

— Les Chenes Qu'on Abat. (FRE.). 1970. pap. 10.95 (0-8288-3709-0, M3706) Fr & Eur.

— Condition Humaine. (Folio Ser.: No. 1). (FRE.). 1933. 9.95 (2-07-036001-6) Schoenhof.

— La Condition Humaine. (FRE.). 1972. pap. 11.95 (0-8288-3710-4, F110891) Fr & Eur.

— Les Conquerants. 256p. (FRE.). 1954. 10.95 (0-8288-9844-8, F110901); 3.95 (0-686-56321-2) Fr & Eur.

— The Conquerors. Becker, Stephen, tr. LC 72-91594. 210p. 1991. pap. 10.95 (0-226-50290-2) U Ch Pr.

— La Corde et les Souris: Avec Les Hotes de Passage, Les Chenes Qu'On Abat (Version Difinitive), La Tete d'Obsidienne (Version Definitive), Lazare. 1976. 4.95 (0-686-56322-0) Fr & Eur.

— Espoir. (Folio Ser.: No. 20). (FRE.). 1937. 12.95 (2-07-036020-2) Schoenhof.

— L' Espoir. (FRE.). 1972. pap. 15.95 (0-8288-3711-2, F110911) Fr & Eur.

— L' Homme Precaire et la Litterature. 330p. (FRE.). 1977. pap. 19.95 (0-7859-1349-1, 2070295559) Fr & Eur.

— Les Hotes de Passage: Comprend les 3 Premiers Chapitres du Tome 2 de Le Memoir des Limbes. 240p. (FRE.). 1975. 17.95 (0-7859-0106-X, M3708) Fr & Eur.

— Man's Fate. 1965. pap. text ed. write for info. (0-07-553654-4) McGraw.

— Man's Fate. Chevalier, Haakon M., tr. 1965. pap. 4.50 (0-685-06615-0, Modern Lib) Random.

— Man's Fate. 1969. pap. 5.95 (0-394-70479-7) Random.

— Man's Fate. 1990. pap. 11.00 (0-679-72574-1, Vin) Random.

— Man's Hope. Gilbert, Stuart & Macdonald, Alastair, trs. LC 83-42699. 511p. 1984. 10.95 (0-394-60478-4, Modern Lib) Random.

— Metamorphose des Dieux: L'Intemporel. (Illus.). 424p. (FRE.). 1976. 125.00 (0-7859-1282-7, 2070108619) Fr & Eur.

— La Metaorphose des Dieux: Le Surnatel, Vol. 1. (Illus.). 386p. (FRE.). 1977. 125.00 (0-7859-1283-5, 2070109070) Fr & Eur.

— Miroir des Limbes. Tome 2: Corde et les Souris. (Folio Ser.: No. 731). (FRE.). 1986. pap. 13.95 (2-07-036731-2) Schoenhof.

— Le Miroir des Limbes, Vol. 1: Antimemoires. (FRE.). 1972. pap. 17.95 (0-8288-3712-0, F110871) Fr & Eur.

— Le Miroir des Limbes, Vol. 2: La Corde et les Souris. (FRE.). 1986. pap. 16.95 (0-8288-3713-9, M11056) Fr & Eur.

— Oraisons funebres: Discours Prononces par l'Auteur 1958-1965. (Coll. Soleil). 13.50 (0-685-34270-0) Fr & Eur.

— Picasso's Mask. annot. ed. Guicharnaud, June, tr. & anno. by. LC 94-34604. (Illus.). 285p. 1995. pap. 13.95 (0-306-80629-0) Da Capo.

— Romans. Incl. Conquerants. 1947. (0-318-63593-3); Condition Humaine. 1947. (0-318-63594-1); Espoir. 1947. (0-318-63595-X); 1947. write for info. (0-318-63592-5) Fr & Eur.

— Romans. deluxe ed. 864p. (FRE.). 1978. 110.00 (0-7859-1621-0, 2070103293) Fr & Eur.

— Scenes Choisies. 8.50 (0-685-34268-9) Fr & Eur.

— The Temptation of the West. Hollander, Robert, tr. 136p. 1991. pap. 10.95 (0-226-50291-0) U Ch Pr.

— Tentation de l'Occident. pap. 6.95 (0-685-34271-9) Fr & Eur.

— La Tentation de l'Occident. (FRE.). 1972. pap. 10.95 (0-7859-3096-5) Fr & Eur.

— Le Triangle Noir: Laclos, Goysa, Saint-Just. 13.15 (0-685-34272-7) Fr & Eur.

— The Voices of Silence. Gilbert, Stuart, tr. LC 77-92101. (Bollingen Ser.: Vol. XXIV: A). (Illus.). 661p. 1978. reprint ed. 95.00x (0-691-09941-3); reprint ed. pap. 24. 95 (0-691-01821-9) Princeton U Pr.

— Voie Royale. (Coll. Soleil). 1954. 12.50 (0-7859-0612-6) Fr & Eur.

— The Walnut Trees of Altenburg. Fielding, A. W., tr. LC 88-37363. 224p. 1989. lib. bdg. 40.00 (0-86527-392-8) Fertig.

— The Walnut Trees of Altenburg. Fielding, A. W., tr. LC 88-37363. 234p. 1992. pap. 11.95 (0-226-50289-9) U Ch Pr.

Malsam, Margaret. Camping Circus. (Illus.). 120p. 1986. pap. 7.95 (0-9616108-0-8) Beaumont Bks.

Malsam, Margaret, ed. see Sadow, Sue.

Malsam, Margaret, ed. see Weyer, Ruth C.

Malsam, Margaret A. Meditations for Today's Married Christians: Profiles of Married Saints for Troubled Times. LC 94-70558. 64p. (Orig.). 1994. pap. 5.99 (0-9616108-8-3) Beaumont Bks.

Malsch, Brownson. Indianola: The Mother of Western Texas. limited ed. LC 88-8557. (Illus.). 363p. (C). 1988. 60.00 (0-938349-27-9) State House Pr.

Malseed. Pharmacology: Drug Therapy & Nursing Considerations. 944p. 1995. write for info. (0-397-55061-8) Lippincott.

Malseed, Roger T. & Girton, Sandra E. Pharmacology: Drug Therapy & Nursing Considerations. 3rd ed. (Illus.). 893p. 1990. text ed. 35.95 (0-397-54677-7) Lippincott.

Malseed, Roger T. & Harrigan. Textbook of Pharmacology & Nursing Care: Using the Nursing Process. LC 64-3737. (Illus.). 1749p. 1988. text ed. 52.50 (0-397-54432-4) Lippincott.

Malseva, F. Alexei Savrasov. 407p. 1977. 60.00 (0-317-14216-X, Pub. by Collets UK) St Mut.

Malshe, Milind S. Literary Classification. 200p. 1993. text ed. 35.00 (81-85218-35-8, Pub. by Prestige II) Advent Bks Div.

Malson, Micheline R., et al, eds. Black Women in America: Social Science Perspectives. 348p. 1990. pap. 15.95 (0-226-50296-1) U Ch Pr.

— Feminist Theory in Practice & Process. 320p. 1989. lib. bdg. 30.00 (0-226-50293-7); pap. 16.95 (0-226-50294-5) U Ch Pr.

Malster, Robert. Ipswich: Town on the Orwell. 112p. (C). 1988. 45.00 (0-900963-92-1, Pub. by T Dalton UK) St Mut.

— Lowestoft: East Coast Port. 128p. 1994. pap. 21.00 (0-86138-013-4, Pub. by T Dalton UK) St Mut.

— Saved from the Sea: The Story of Life-Saving Services on the East Anglian Coast. 296p. 1994. 42.00 (0-900963-32-8, Pub. by T Dalton UK) St Mut.

— Wherries & Waterways. 176p. 1994. 36.00 (0-86138-042-8, Pub. by T Dalton UK) St Mut.

Malstrom. Manufacturing Cost Engineering Handbook. (Cost Engineering Ser.: Vol. 5). 472p. 1984. 140.00 (0-8247-7126-5) Dekker.

— WEESKA Manufacturing Cost Estimating. (What Every Engineer Should Know Ser.: Vol. 6). 208p. 1981. 49.75 (0-8247-1511-X) Dekker.

Malstrom, Stan. Be Your Own Doctor by Using Natural Methods. (Tree of Knowledge Ser.: No. 4). 34p. pap. 3.95 (0-913923-37-0) Woodland UT.

— Herbal Remedies, No. II. 40p. pap. 2.95 (0-913923-13-3) Woodland UT.

— Herbal Remedies for Common Diseases. (Tree of Knowledge Ser.: No. 2). 30p. pap. 3.95 (0-913923-35-4) Woodland UT.

— Natural Approach to Female Problems. (Tree of Knowledge Ser.: No. 7). 31p. pap. 3.95 (0-913923-41-9) Woodland UT.

— Natural First Aid. (Tree of Knowledge Ser.: No. 5). 19p. pap. 3.95 (0-913923-38-9) Woodland UT.

— Natural Treatment for Childhood Diseases. (Tree of Knowledge Ser.: No. 6). 29p. pap. 3.95 (0-913923-40-0) Woodland UT.

— Own Your Own Body. 400p. 12.95 (0-913923-23-0) Woodland UT.

— Own Your Own Body. LC 76-58968. 414p. 1980. reprint ed. pap. 5.95 (0-87983-215-0) Keats.

— Roots of Disease. (Tree of Knowledge Ser.: No. 1). 26p. pap. 3.95 (0-913923-34-6) Woodland UT.

— Your Colon, Its Character, Care & Therapy. (Tree of Knowledge Ser.: No. 3). 34p. pap. 3.95 (0-913923-36-2) Woodland UT.

Malt, Ronald A. The Practice of Surgery. LC 92-22929. (Illus.). 512p. 1993. text ed. 210.00 (0-7216-1811-1) Saunders.

Malt, Ronald A., jt. ed. see Morris, Peter J.

Malt, Ronald A., et al. Complex Operations at Massachusetts General Hospital. (Illus.). 272p. 1983. text ed. 115.00 (0-7216-6008-8) Saunders.

Malta, Robert G., jt. auth. see Hall, Robert G.

Malta, Victor G. Espejos Negros y los Caminos del Silencio. 90p. (Orig.). (SPA.). 1992. pap. 8.00 (0-9623552-4-0) Ed Arcas.

Maltagliati, Raoul. How to Dream Your Lucky Lotto Numbers: Manual & Dictionary for Forecasting the Future & Lotto Numbers Through the Interpretation of Dreams. 2nd ed. LC 90-35093. (How-to Ser.). (Illus.). 128p. (Orig.). 1994. pap. 3.95 (0-87542-483-X) Llewellyn Pubns.

Maltbie, Cynthis, jt. auth. see Mays, Bruce.

Maltbie, Milo R. English Local Government of To-Day: A Study of the Relations of Central & Local Government. LC 74-76664. (Columbia University. Studies in the Social Sciences: No. 23). reprint ed. 27.50 (0-404-51023-X) AMS Pr.

Maltby, ed. Latin Love Elegy. vi, 143p. 1991. reprint ed. 11. 00 (0-685-48558-7) Bolchazy-Carducci.

M

Maltby, Arthur & Maltby, Jean. Ireland in the Nineteenth Century: A Breviate of Official Publications. (Guides to Official Publications: Vol. 4). (Illus.). 1979. 120.00 (*0-08-023688-X*, Pub. by Pergamon Repr UK) Franklin.

Maltby, Arthur & McKenna, Brian. Irish Official Publications: A Guide to Republic of Ireland Papers, with a Breviate of Reports 1922-1972. LC 80-40873. (Guides to Official Publications: Vol. 7). 388p. 1980. 158.00 (*0-08-023703-7*, Pub. by Pergamon Repr UK) Franklin.

Maltby, E. & Wollersen, T., eds. Soils & Their Management: A Sino-European Perspective: Proc. of a Workshop Jointly Organized by the People's Republic of China & the EEC, held in China, April 1988. 396p. 1990. 86.50 (*1-85166-427-0*) Elsevier.

Maltby, Gordon. Porsche 356. (Illus.). 160p. 1991. 29.95 (*0-87938-551-0*) Motorbooks Intl.

Maltby, Gregory M., jt. auth. see Obiakor, Festus E.

Maltby, Gregory P., jt. ed. see Cooper, Lloyd G.

Maltby, Jean, jt. auth. see Maltby, Arthur.

Maltby, L. & Calow, P. Methods in Ecotoxicology. 224p. 1994. pap. 34.00 (*0-632-03549-8*, Pub. by Blckwell Sci Pubns UK) Blackwell Sci.

***Maltby, Lewis L.** A State of Emergency in the American Workplace. 23p. (Orig.). 1990. pap. 3.50 (*0-914031-15-5*) Amer Civil Lib.

Maltby, Paul. Dissident Postmodernists: Barthelme, Coover, Pynchon. LC 91-25115. (Pennsylvania Studies in Contemporary American Fiction). 232p. (C). 1992. text ed. 29.95 (*0-8122-3064-7*) U of Pa Pr.

Maltby, Ralph. The Complete Golf Club Fitting Plan. (Illus.). 400p. 1986. pap. 38.50 (*0-9606792-7-8*) R Maltby.

— Golf Club Assembly Manual: Basic & Advanced Techniques. (Illus.). 36p. 1981. pap. 4.95 (*0-9606792-3-5*) R Maltby.

Maltby, Ralph & Wilson, Mark. Golf Club Repair in Pictures. 4th ed. (Illus.). 340p. 1989. pap. 4.95 (*0-9606792-8-6*) R Maltby.

***Maltby, Ralph D.** Golf Club Design, Fitting, Alteration & Repair. rev. ed. (Illus.). 890p. 1995. 39.95 (*0-927956-05-5*) R Maltby.

— Golf Club Design, Fitting, Alteration & Repair. 2nd ed. (Illus.). 720p. 1984. 44.95 (*0-9606792-4-3*) R Maltby.

Maltby, Richard. Harmless Entertainment: Hollywood & the Ideology of Consensus. LC 82-10244. 425p. 1983. 35.00 (*0-8108-1548-6*) Scarecrow.

***Maltby, Richard & Craven, Ian.** Hollywood Cinema: An Introduction. LC 94-3794. 1995. 64.95 (*0-631-15706-9*); pap. 24.95 (*0-631-15732-8*) Blackwell Pubs.

Maltby, Richard, Jr., jt. auth. see Galli, E. R.

Maltby, T. J. Practical Handbook of the Oriya Language. 214p. (ENG & ORI.). 1986. 39.95 (*0-8288-8464-1*) Fr & Eur.

Maltby, Tony. Women & Pensions in Britain & Hungary: A Cross-National & Comparative Case Study of Social Dependency. 260p. 1994. 59.95 (*1-85628-630-4*, Pub. by Avebury Pub UK) Ashgate Pub Co.

Maltby, William S. The Black Legend in England: The Development of Anti-Spanish Sentiment, 1558-1660. LC 78-161356. (Duke Historical Publications). 188p. reprint ed. pap. 53.60 (*0-8357-7291-8*, 2023764) Bks Demand.

Maltenfort, George G. Corrugated Shipping Containers: An Engineering Approach. LC 87-83603. (Illus.). 291p. 1988. 94.50 (*0-9616302-1-3*) Jelmar Pub.

— Performance & Evaluation of Shipping Containers. LC 89-63845. (Illus.). 488p. 1990. 97.50 (*0-9616302-3-X*) Jelmar Pub.

— Understanding Statistics. LC 92-28704. 128p. 1993. 62.00 (*0-9616302-8-0*) Jelmar Pub.

Malter, Alan J., jt. auth. see Jensen, Merle H.

Malter, Heinrich, ed. see Steinschneider, Moritz.

Malterre, Elona. The Last Wolf of Ireland. (J). (gr. 4-9). 1990. 13.95 (*0-395-54381-9*, Clarion Bks) HM.

***Maltese, John A.** The Selling of Supreme Court Nominees. LC 95-3536. (Interpreting American Politics Ser.). 232p. 1995. 26.95 (*0-8018-5102-5*) Johns Hopkins.

— The Selling of Supreme Court Nominees. LC 95-3536. (Interpreting American Politics Ser.). 1995. pap. write for info. (*0-8018-5103-3*) Johns Hopkins.

— Spin Control: The White House Office of Communications & the Management of Presidential News. 2nd rev. ed. LC 93-29368. (Illus.). xii, 323p. (C). 1994. pap. 15.95 (*0-8078-4452-7*) U of NC Pr.

Maltezou, S., et al. Hazardous Waste Management. 364p. 1989. text ed. 105.00 (*1-85148-027-7*, Tycooly Pub) Weidner & Sons.

Malthus, Thomas R. Definitions in Political Economy: Preceded by an Inquiry into the Rules Which Ought to Guide Political Economists in the Definition & Use of Their Terms. LC 86-7468. (Reprints of Economic Classics Ser.). 1986. reprint ed. 35.00 (*0-678-00018-2*) Kelley.

— An Essay on Principle of Population. (English Library). 1983. mass mkt. 8.95 (*0-14-043206-X*, Penguin Classics) Viking Penguin.

— An Essay on the Principle of Population, 2 vols. James, Patricia, ed. 640p. 1990. 150.00 (*0-521-32361-4*) Cambridge U Pr.

— An Essay on the Principle of Population. Winch, Donald, ed. (Cambridge Texts in the History of Political Thought Ser.). 448p. (C). 1992. 39.95 (*0-521-41954-9*); pap. 11.95 (*0-521-42972-2*) Cambridge U Pr.

— An Essay on the Principle of Population. Gilbert, Geoffrey, ed. (World's Classics Ser.). 208p. 1994. pap. 7.95 (*0-19-283096-1*) OUP.

— An Essay on the Principle of Population. Appleman, Philip, ed. (Critical Editions in the History of Ideas Ser.). 256p. (C). 1976. pap. text ed. 9.95 (*0-393-09202-X*) Norton.

— Essay on the Principle of Population or a View of Its Past & Present Effects on Human Happiness. 7th ed. LC 86-7453. (Reprints of Economic Classics Ser.). xv, 551p. 1986. reprint ed. lib. bdg. 49.50 (*0-678-00838-8*) Kelley.

— The Measure of Value Stated & Illuminated. LC 87-17246. (Reprints of Economic Classics Ser.). 1989. reprint ed. 22.50 (*0-678-00603-2*) Kelley.

— Pamphlets of Thomas Robert Malthus 1800-1817. LC 77-117389. (Reprints of Economic Classics Ser.). 1970. reprint ed. lib. bdg. 39.50 (*0-678-00646-6*) Kelley.

— Population: The First Essay. 1959. pap. 12.95 (*0-472-06031-7*, 31, Ann Arbor Bks) U of Mich Pr.

— Principles of Political Economy: Considered with a View to Their Practical Application. 2nd ed. LC 86-10606. (Reprints of Economic Classics Ser.). 1986. reprint ed. 45.00 (*0-678-00038-7*) Kelley.

— Principles of Political Economy: Variorum Edition, 2 vols., Set. Pullen, John, ed. 1990. 135.00 (*0-521-24775-6*) Cambridge U Pr.

Malthus, Thomas R., et al. The Malthus Library Catalogue: The Personal Collection of Thomas Robert Malthus at Jesus College, Cambridge University. 150p. 1983. 46.00 (*0-08-029386-7*, Pergamon Pr) Elsevier.

Malti-Douglas, Fedwa. Blindness & Autobiography: Al-Ayyam of Taha Husayn. 248p. 1988. text ed. 37.50 (*0-691-06733-3*) Princeton U Pr.

— Men, Women, & God(s) Nawal El Saadawi & Arab Feminist Poetics. LC 94-44255. 277p. 1995. 45.00 (*0-520-20071-3*); pap. 17.00 (*0-520-20072-1*) U CA Pr.

— Woman's Body, Woman's Word: Gender & Discourse in Arabo-Islamic Writing. 213p. 1992. text ed. 39.50 (*0-691-06856-9*); pap. text ed. 12.95 (*0-691-01488-4*) Princeton U Pr.

Malti-Douglas, Fedwa, jt. auth. see Douglas, Allen.

Maltin, Leonard. The Art of the Cinematographer: A Survey & Interviews with Five Masters. 1978. reprint ed. pap. 7.95 (*0-486-23686-2*) Dover.

— The Disney Films. rev. ed. LC 95-14024. 1995. write for info. (*0-7868-6163-0*) Hyperion.

— The Disney Films. 3rd ed. (Illus.). 352p. 1995. pap. 15.95 (*0-7868-8137-2*) Hyperion.

— Leonard Maltin's Movie & Video Guide, 1993. 1520p. 1992. pap. 17.00 (*0-452-26857-5*, Plume) NAL-Dutton.

— Leonard Maltin's Movie & Video Guide, 1994. 1584p. 1993. pap. 18.00 (*0-452-27085-5*, Plume) NAL-Dutton.

— Leonard Maltin's Movie & Video Guide, 1994. 1552p. 1993. pap. 7.99 (*0-451-17766-5*, Sig) NAL-Dutton.

— Leonard Maltin's Movie & Video Guide, 1995. 1584p. 1994. pap. 17.95 (*0-452-27327-7*, Plume) NAL-Dutton.

— Leonard Maltin's Movie & Video Guide, 1995. 1994. disk, pap. 29.99 (*0-451-18339-8*, Sig) NAL-Dutton.

— Leonard Maltin's Movie & Video Guide, 1995: The 25th Anniversary Edition. 1600p. (Orig.). 1994. pap. 7.99 (*0-451-18172-7*, Sig) NAL-Dutton.

— Leonard Maltin's Movie & Video Guide 1996. 1600p. 1995. pap. 7.99 (*0-451-18505-6*, Sig) NAL-Dutton.

— Leonard Maltin's Movie & Video Guide 1996. rev. ed. 1584p. 1995. pap. 19.95 (*0-452-27467-2*, Plume) NAL-Dutton.

— Leonard Maltin's Movie Encyclopedia: Career Profiles of More Than 2,000 Actors & Filmmakers, Past & Present. 1088p. 1994. 34.95 (*0-525-93635-1*, Dutton) NAL-Dutton.

— Leonard Maltin's Movie Encyclopedia: Career Profiles of More Than 2,000 Actors & Filmmakers, Past & Present. 992p. 1995. 19.95 (*0-452-27058-8*, Plume) NAL-Dutton.

— Leonard Maltin's TV Movies & Video Guide, 1993. 1536p. (Orig.). 1992. pap. 7.99 (*0-451-17381-3*, Sig) NAL-Dutton.

— Of Mice & Magic: A History of American Animated Cartoons. LC 87-20234. 1987. pap. 22.95 (*0-452-25993-2*, Plume) NAL-Dutton.

— Selected Short Subjects: From Spanky to the Three Stooges. LC 83-7580. (Quality Paperbacks Ser.). (Illus.). 236p. 1983. reprint ed. pap. 12.95 (*0-306-80204-X*) Da Capo.

Maltin, Leonard, ed. Leonard Maltin's TV Movies, 1985-86. 1000p. 1984. pap. 12.95 (*0-452-25787-5*, Plume) NAL-Dutton.

Maltin, Leonard & Bann, Richard W. The Little Rascals: The Life & Times of Our Gang. enl. ed. LC 92-16724. 1992. pap. 18.00 (*0-517-58325-9*, Crown) Crown Pub Group.

Maltin, Rick. Sales Magic. 1988. 109.00 (*0-87280-526-3*, 560, Asher-Gallant) Caddylak Systs.

Maltman. Geological Maps: An Introduction. 1990. text ed. 51.95 (*0-442-30307-6*) Chapman & Hall.

Malton, James. Georgian Dublin. 1984. pap. 6.95 (*0-85105-425-0*, Pub. by Colin Smythe Ltd UK) Dufour.

Maltoni, Cesare, et al. Experimental Research on Acrylonitrile Carcinogenesis. LC 86-62753. (Illus.). 225p. 1987. 160.00 (*0-911131-41-8*) Princeton Sci Pubs.

— Experimental Research on Methylene Chloride Carcinogenesis. LC 86-61069. (Illus.). 225p. 1987. 160.00 (*0-911131-39-6*) Princeton Sci Pubs.

Maltoni, Cesare, et al, eds. Experimental Research on Trichloroethylene Carcinogenesis. LC 85-63664. (Illus.). 393p. 1986. 220.00 (*0-911131-40-X*) Princeton Sci Pubs.

— Experimental Research on Vinylidene Chloride Carcinogenesis. LC 85-61066. (Archives of Industrial Carcinogenesis Ser.). (Illus.). 250p. 160.00 (*0-911131-36-1*) Princeton Sci Pubs.

Maltsberger, John T. Suicide Risk: The Formulation of Clinical Judgement. LC 86-2415. 176p. 1986. 45.00x (*0-8147-5398-1*); pap. 16.50x (*0-8147-5399-X*) NYU Pr.

Maltsev, Yuri N., intro. Requiem for Marx. 301p. (Orig.). 1993. pap. text ed. 18.00 (*0-945466-13-7*) Ludwig von Mises.

Malty, Martin E. Pushing the Faith: Proselytism & Civility in a Pluralistic World. 256p. 1988. 19.95 (*0-8245-0871-8*) Crossroad NY.

Maltz, Alan S. Celebrities of Nature: Endangered & Selected Species of Florida. (Post Card Pictorial Ser.). 50p. 1991. pap. 12.95 (*0-9626677-1-4*) Light Key West.

— Key West Color. (Illus.). 192p. 1995. 50.00 (*0-9626677-2-2*) Light Key West.

— Key West Sunsets: A Postcard Pictorial. 2nd ed. (Illus.). 1990. pap. 12.95 (*0-9626677-0-6*) Light Key West.

Maltz, Albert. Afternoon in the Jungle: The Selected Short Stories of Albert Maltz. 1971. pap. 2.75 (*0-87140-256-4*) Liveright.

Maltz, Albert, jt. auth. see Wald, Malvin.

Maltz, Betty. El Cielo: Heaven: A Bright & Glorious. (SPA.). 5.00 (*84-7645-493-7*, 223584, Pub. by Edit Clie SP) TSELF.

— Una Visita a la Eternidad: My Glimpse of Eternity. (SPA.). 4.25 (*84-7228-513-8*, 220923, Pub. by Edit Clie SP) TSELF.

Maltz, Earl M. Civil Rights, the Constitution & Congress, 1863-1869. LC 90-32818. xii, 196p. 1990. 25.00 (*0-7006-0467-7*) U Pr of KS.

— Rethinking Constitutional Law: Originalism, Interventionism, & the Politics of Judicial Review. LC 93-30266. 158p. 1994. 27.50 (*0-7006-0653-X*) U Pr of KS.

Maltz, M. D., et al. Mapping Crime in Its Community Setting: Event Geography Analysis. (Illus.). 152p. 1990. 68.00 (*0-387-97381-8*) Spr-Verlag.

Maltz, Maxwell. Five Minutes to Happiness. 1962. 10.95 (*0-8392-1033-7*) Astor-Honor.

— Magic Power of Self-Image. 1989. mass mkt. 5.99 (*0-671-70461-3*) PB.

— Magic Power of Self-Image Psychology. 1989. pap. 7.95 (*0-13-545096-9*) P-H.

— Magic Power of Self-Image Psychology: The New Way to a Bright Full Life. 1986. 5.95 (*0-13-545319-4*, Reward) P-H.

— Psycho-Cybernetics. 1973. pap. 7.00 (*0-87980-127-1*) Wilshire.

Maltz, Michael D. Recidivism. LC 83-15911. (Quantitative Studies in Social Relations). 1984. text ed. 47.00 (*0-12-468980-9*) Acad Pr.

Maltz, Wendy. The Sexual Healing Journey: A Guide for Survivors of Sexual Abuse. LC 90-55934. (Illus.). 368p. 1992. reprint ed. pap. 13.00 (*0-06-092155-2*, PL) HarpC.

Maltz, Wendy & Holman, Beverly. Incest & Sexuality: A Guide to Understanding & Healing. 192p. 1986. pap. 13.95 (*0-669-14085-6*) Free Pr.

Maltzahn, Wendelin V. Deutscher Bucherschatz des 16, 17 und 18, Bis um die Mitte des 19 Jahrhunderts. x, 627p. 1966. reprint ed. write for info. (*0-318-71842-1*, Pub. by Georg Olms GW) Lubrecht & Cramer.

Maltzan, Heinrich F. Reise Nach Sudarabien. (Illus.). 422p. reprint ed. write for info. (*0-318-71530-9*, Pub. by Georg Olms GW) Lubrecht & Cramer.

Maltzman, Jeffrey. Jobs in Paradise. LC 92-53297. 448p. 1993. pap. 13.00 (*0-06-273186-6*, Harper Ref) HarpC.

Maltzoff, Nicholas. Basic Structure Practice in Russian. 80p. 1991. pap. 12.95 (*0-8442-4260-8*, Passport Bks) NTC Pub Grp.

— Essentials of Russian Grammar. 352p. 1984. pap. 17.95 (*0-8442-4244-6*, Natl Textbk) NTC Pub Grp.

— Everyday Conversations in Russian. 64p. 1983. pap. 4.95 (*0-8442-4241-1*, Natl Textbk) NTC Pub Grp.

Maluccio, Anthony, et al. Permanency Planning for Children: Concepts & Methods. 350p. 1986. text ed. 32.50 (*0-422-78840-6*, 4074, Pub. by Tavistock UK); pap. text ed. 14.95 (*0-422-78850-3*, 4075, Pub. by Tavistock UK) Routledge Chapman & Hall.

Maluccio, Anthony N., ed. Promoting Competence in Clients: A New-Old Approach to Social Work Intervention. LC 80-1056. (Illus.). 1981. 27.95 (*0-02-919830-5*) Free Pr.

— Promoting Competence in Clients: A New-Old Approach to Social Work Practice. 370p. 1985. pap. 17.95 (*0-02-919860-7*) Free Pr.

Maluccio, Anthony N., jt. ed. see Sinanoglu, Paula A.

Maluccio, John, jt. auth. see Thomas, Duncan.

Maludzinska, G. Dictionary of Analyical Chemistry in English, German, French, Polish & Russian. 392p. (ENG, FRE, GER, POL & RUS.). 1990. 225.00 (*0-8288-9226-1*) Fr & Eur.

Maludzinska, G., ed. Dictionary of Analytical Chemistry: English, German, French, Polish & Russian. 400p. (ENG, FRE, GER, POL & RUS.). 1991. 143.00 (*0-444-98729-0*) Elsevier.

Maluf, Leonard, tr. see Feuillet, Andre.

Maluf, Leonard, tr. see Lafont, Ghislain.

***Malus, Michael.** Before the End of the Day. 1995. pap. 15.95 (*1-55065-055-6*) InBook.

Maluso, Diane, jt. ed. see Lott, Bernice.

Maluszynski, Jan, jt. auth. see Deransert, Pierre.

Maluszynski, Jan, jt. auth. see Nilsson, Ulf.

Maluszynski, Jan, et al, eds. Programming Language Implementation & Logic Programming: 3rd International Symposium, PLILP '91, Passau, Germany, August 26-28, 1991 Proceedings. (Lecture Notes in Computer Science Ser.: Vol. 528). xi, 433p. 1991. pap. 41.00 (*0-387-54444-5*) Spr-Verlag.

Maluszynski, M., ed. Current Options for Cereal Improvement: Doubled Haploids, Mutants & Heterosis. (Advances in Agricultural Biotechnology Ser.). (C). 1988. lib. bdg. 71.50 (*0-7923-0064-5*) Kluwer Ac.

Malvadkar, C. B., tr. see Gyachev, L. V., ed.

Malval, Fritz J. Dictionary Catalog of the George Foster Peabody Collection of Negro Literature & History, 2 vols., Set. 1972. text ed. 315.00 (*0-8371-6065-0*, HIL/, Greenwood Pr) Greenwood.

— A Guide to the Archives of Hampton Institute. LC 85-5599. (Bibliographies & Indexes in Afro-American & African Studies: No. 5). vi, 599p. 1985. text ed. 125.00 (*0-313-24968-7*, MGH/, Greenwood Pr) Greenwood.

Malvaney, Sam. At the Beach. LC 85-62693. (Illus.). 104p. 1985. 12.95 (*0-935180-17-6*) Mutual Pub HI.

Malvar, Henrique S. Digital Signal Compression. 1994. 55.00 (*0-13-605882-5*) P-H.

— Signal Processing with Lapped Transforms. (Telecommunications Library). 375p. 1992. text ed. 69.00 (*0-89006-467-9*) Artech Hse.

Malvasia, Carlo C. The Life of Guido Reni. Enggass, Catherine & Enggass, Robert, trs. LC 80-11650. (Illus.). 150p. 1981. 28.50 (*0-271-00264-6*) Pa St U Pr.

Malvavkar, C. B., tr. see Zelenin, A. N., et al, eds.

Malve, Eduardo, jt. auth. see Ureta, Floreal.

Malveaux, Julianne. Sex, Lies & Stereotypes: Perspectives of a Mad Economist. 350p. (Orig.). 1994. pap. 14.95 (*0-9636952-5-8*) Pines One.

Malveaux, Julianne M., jt. ed. see Simms, Margaret C.

Malveaux, Roy L. Signs of the Times. 1992. 10.00 (*0-533-10023-2*) Vantage.

Malven, Paul V. Mammalian Neuroendocrinology. 1993. 55.00 (*0-8493-8757-4*, QP356) CRC Pr.

Malvern, L. E., ed. see Midwestern Mechanics Conference Staff.

Malvern, Lawrence E. Introduction to the Mechanics of a Continuous Medium. 1977. text ed. 93.00 (*0-13-487603-2*) P-H.

Malvezzi, Virgilio. Historia de los Primeros Anos del Reinado de Felipe IV. Shaw, D. L., ed. (Serie B: Textos, VII). (Illus.). 206p. (Orig.). (SPA.). (C). 1968. pap. 45.00 (*0-900411-01-5*, Pub. by Tamesis Bks Ltd UK) Boydell & Brewer.

Malville, J. McKim & Putnam, Claudia. Prehistoric Astronomy in the Southwest. rev. ed. LC 93-17712. (Illus.). 112p. 1993. pap. 9.95 (*1-55566-116-5*) Johnson Bks.

Malville, John M. Time & Eternal Change. 128p. 1991. text ed. 25.00 (*81-207-1288-9*, Pub. by Sterling Pubs II) Apt Bks.

Malvino, Albert P. AC Circuits: A Whole-Brain Learning System. (APPLE II Ser.: No. 2). (Illus.). 224p. (Orig.). (C). 1987. disk, pap. text ed. 19.95 (*1-56048-102-1*, 102) Malvino Inc.

— Basic Semiconductors: A Whole-Brain Learning System. (APPLE II Ser.: No. 3). (Illus.). 288p. (Orig.). (C). 1987. disk, pap. text ed. 19.95 (*1-56048-103-X*, 103) Malvino Inc.

— DC Circuits: A Whole-Brain Learning System. (APPLE II Ser.: No. 1). (Illus.). 224p. (Orig.). (C). 1986. text ed., disk 19.95 (*1-56048-101-3*, 101E) Malvino Inc.

— Digital Computer Electronics: An Introduction to Microcomputers. 2nd ed. LC 83-8952. (Illus.). 384p. 1983. text ed. 39.95 (*0-07-039901-8*); text ed. write for info. (*0-07-040023-7*) McGraw.

— Electronic Instrumentation Fundamentals. (Illus.). 1967. text ed. 39.95 (*0-07-039847-X*) McGraw.

— Electronic Principles. LC 92-36587. 1992. write for info. (*0-02-808845-X*) Glencoe.

— Electronic Principles. 1989. Experiments. write for info. (*0-07-040022-9*) McGraw.

— Electronic Principles. 2nd ed. (Illus.). 1979. text ed. 42.95 (*0-07-039867-4*) McGraw.

— Electronic Principles. 3rd ed. 1984. text ed. 42.95 (*0-07-039912-3*) McGraw.

— Electronic Principles. 4th ed. 992p. 1989. text ed. 39.95 (*0-07-039957-3*) McGraw.

— Electronic Principles. 4th ed. 1989. text ed. write for info. (*0-07-040021-0*) McGraw.

— Electronic Principles. 5th ed. 1992. 44.95 (*0-02-800845-6*) Macmillan.

— Principios de Electronica. 2nd ed. 1984. text ed. 5.95 (*0-07-039914-X*) McGraw.

— Quik-Lab for AC Circuits - Conventional-Flow Version: A Whole-Brain Learning System. (IBM (MS-DOS) Ser.: No. 2). (Illus.). 224p. (C). 1989. student ed, disk 16.45 (*1-56048-812-3*, 802C) Malvino Inc.

— Quik-Lab for Basic Electronics - Electron-Flow Version: A Whole-Brain Learning System. (IBM (MS-DOS) Ser.: No. 3). (Illus.). 240p. (C). 1988. student ed, disk 16.45 (*1-56048-803-4*, 803E) Malvino Inc.

— Quik-Lab II for Advanced Electronics. (IBM PC Series, CGA, Hercules, EGA - VGA Graphics). (Illus.). 164p. (C). 1991. student ed 18.45 (*1-56048-984-7*, 984); disk write for info. (*0-318-68964-2*) Malvino Inc.

— Quik-Lab II for Basic Electronics: Electron-Flow Edition. (IBM PC Series, CGA, Hercules, EGA - VGA Graphics). (Illus.). 192p. (Orig.). (C). 1991. student ed 18.45 (*1-56048-983-9*, 983) Malvino Inc.

— Quik-Lab Two for AC Circuits: Electron-Flow Edition. (EGA - VGA - Hercules Graphics Ser.). (Illus.). 188p. (Orig.). (C). 1991. student ed 18.45 (*1-56048-982-0*, 982) Malvino Inc.

— Quik-Lab Two for DC Circuits: Electron-Flow Edition. (EGA - VGA - Hercules Graphics Ser.). (Illus.). 176p. (Orig.). (C). 1990. student ed 18.45 (*1-56048-981-2*, 981) Malvino Inc.

— Quik-Lab(II) for AC Circuits: Conventional-Flow Edition. (CGA, Hercules, EGA - VGA Graphics Ser.). (Illus.). 188p. (Orig.). (C). 1991. student ed, pap. 18.45 (*1-56048-986-3*, 982C) Malvino Inc.

— Quik-Lab(II) for DC Circuits: Conventional-Flow Edition. (CGA, Hercules, EGA - VGA Graphics Ser.). (Illus.). 176p. (C). 1990. student ed 18.45 (*1-56048-985-5*, 981C) Malvino Inc.

— Resistive & Reactive Circuits. (Illus.). 640p. (C). 1974. text ed. 38.95 (*0-07-039856-9*) McGraw.

— Semiconductor Circuit Approximations: An Introduction to Transistors & Integrated Circuits; Experiments for Semiconductor Circuit Approximations. 4th ed. 128p. 1985. text ed. 42.95 (*0-07-039898-4*); 17.95 (*0-07-039899-2*) McGraw.

— Theory of AC Circuits. (Illus.). 304p. (Orig.). (C). 1989. pap. text ed. 16.95 (*1-56048-302-4*, 302) Malvino Inc.

An Asterisk (*) at the beginning of an entry indicates that the title is appearing in BIP for the first time.

— Theory of AC Circuits - Quik-Lab for AC Circuits: Conventional-Flow Version, 2 bks., Bks. 1 & 2. (IBM Package Ser.: No. 2). (Illus.). (Orig.). (C). 1989. Bk. 1: 304 pp., Feb., 1989; Bk. 2: 224 pp., March, 1989. disk 24.95 (*1-56048-383-0*, 3802C) Malvino Inc.

— Theory of AC Circuits - Quik-Lab for AC Circuits: Electron-Flow Version, 2 bks., Bks. 1 & 2. (IBM Package Ser.: No. 2). (Illus.). (Orig.). (C). 1989. Bk. 1: 304 pp., Feb. 1989; Bk. 2: 224 pp., March, 1989. disk 24.95 (*1-56048-382-2*, 3802E) Malvino Inc.

— Theory of AC Circuits - Quik-Lab Two for AC Circuits: Electron-Flow Edition Package, 2 vols. (EGA - VGA - Hercules Graphics Ser.). (Illus.). 480p. (Orig.). (C). pap. text ed. 26.95 (*1-56048-399-7*, 3982); Bk. 1: 03/1989, 304p. write for info. (*0-318-68173-0*); Bk. 2: 1991, 176p. write for info. (*0-318-68174-9*) Malvino Inc.

— Theory of AC Circuits - Quik-Lab(II) for AC Circuits Package: Conventional-Flow Edition, 2 bks., Set. (CGA, Hercules, EGA - VGA Graphics Ser.). (Illus.). 492p. (Orig.). (C). 1991. pap. text ed. 26.95 (*1-56048-397-0*, 3982C) Malvino Inc.

— Theory of DC Circuits: Conventional-Flow Edition. (Illus.). 272p. (Orig.). (C). 1989. pap. text ed. 16.95 (*1-56048-301-6*, 301C) Malvino Inc.

— Theory of DC Circuits - Quik-Lab Two for DC Circuits: Electron-Flow Edition Package, 2 vols. (EGA - VGA - Hercules Graphics Ser.). (Illus.). 448p. (Orig.). (C). pap. text ed. 26.95 (*1-56048-398-9*, 3981); Bk. 1: 01/1989, 272p. write for info. (*0-318-68171-4*); Bk. 2: 1990, 176p. write for info. (*0-318-68172-2*) Malvino Inc.

— Theory of DC Circuits - Quik-Lab(II) for DC Circuits Package: Conventional Flow Edition, 2 bks., Set. (CGA, Hercules, EGA - VGA Graphics Ser.). (Illus.). 448p. (Orig.). (C). 1990. pap. text ed. 26.95 (*1-56048-396-2*, 3981C) Malvino Inc.

— Transistor Circuit Approximations. 3rd ed. LC 79-18580. (Illus.). 1980. text ed. 42.95 (*0-07-039878-X*) McGraw.

— Troubleshooting for Electronics. (IBM PC Ser.). (Illus.). 82p. (C). 1990. student ed 12.50 (*1-56048-901-4*, 904) Malvino Inc.

Malvino, Albert P. & Leach, Donald P. Digital Principles & Applications. 3rd ed. LC 80-19631. (Illus.). 496p. (C). 1981. text ed. 43.95 (*0-07-039875-5*) McGraw.

— Digital Principles & Applications. 4th ed. 544p. 1985. text ed. 42.95 (*0-07-039883-6*) McGraw.

Malvino, Albert P. & Malvino, Joanna. Quik-Lab(II) for Basic Electronics: Conventional-Flow Edition. (CGA, Hercules, EGA - VGA Graphics Ser.). (Illus.). 192p. (Orig.). (C). 1991. student ed, pap. 18.45 (*1-56048-987-1*, 983C) Malvino Inc.

Malvino, Albert P. & Malvino, Joanna M. Quik-Lab for AC Circuits - Electron-Flow Version: A Whole-Brain Learning System. (IBM (MS-DOS) Ser.: No. 2). (Illus.). 224p. (C). 1989. student ed, disk 16.45 (*1-56048-802-6*, 802E) Malvino Inc.

— Quik-Lab for Basic Electronics - Conventional-Flow Version: A Whole-Brain Learning System. (IBM (MS-DOS) Ser.: No. 3). (Illus.). 240p. (C). 1988. Incl. software. student ed, disk 16.45 (*1-56048-813-1*, 803C) Malvino Inc.

— Theory of DC Circuits: Electron-Flow Edition. (Illus.). 272p. (Orig.). (C). 1989. pap. text ed. 16.95 (*1-56048-300-8*, 301E) Malvino Inc.

Malvino, Albert P., jt. auth. see Leach, Donald P.

Malvino, Albert P., jt. auth. see Zbar, Paul B.

Malvino, Joanna, jt. auth. see Malvino, Albert P.

Malvino, Joanna M., jt. auth. see Malvino, Albert P.

Malviya, A. K. Management of Exports Marketing in India. (C). 1990. 94.00 (*0-8364-2641-X*, Pub. by Chugh Pubns II) S Asia.

Malviya, Achla, jt. auth. see Rani, Seema.

Malwal, Bona. People & Power in Sudan: The Struggle for National Stability. (Sudan Studies: No. 6). 273p. 1981. 25.00 (*0-903729-78-4*, Pub. by Ithaca UK) Evergreen Dist.

— The Sudan: A Second Challenge to Nationhood. LC 85-4761. (Illus.). 48p. (Orig.). 1985. pap. text ed. 4.95 (*0-936508-13-2*) Barber Pr.

Malwal, Bona & Kok, Peter N. Crisis in the Sudan: Re-Thinking the Future. 1994. pap. 15.95 (*0-936508-35-3*) Barber Pr.

— Crisis in the Sudan: Re-Thinking the Future. 1995. 29.95 (*0-936508-34-5*) Barber Pr.

Maly. Design of Testable VSLI Circuits. 1994. write for info. (*0-8493-7281-X*) CRC Pr.

Maly, Eugene H. Romans. LC 79-55806. (New Testament Message Ser.: Vol. 9). 144p. 1980. pap. 10.95 (*0-8146-5132-1*) Liturgical Pr.

Maly, Kenneth. The Path of Archaic Thinking: Unfolding the Work of John Sallis. (Contemporary Continental Philosophy Ser.). 352p. 1995. text ed. 64.50 (*0-7914-2355-7*); pap. text ed. 21.95 (*0-7914-2356-5*) State U NY Pr.

Maly, Kenneth, tr. see Heidegger, Martin.

Maly, Kenneth, tr. see Petzet, Heinrich W.

Maly, Kurt & Hanson, Allen R. Fundamentals of the Computing Sciences. (Illus.). 1978. Reference ed. pap. text ed. write for info. (*0-13-335240-4*) P-H.

Maly, M. Romans. 1989. pap. 21.00 (*0-86217-009-5*, Pub. by Veritas IE) St Mut.

Maly, W., jt. ed. see Director, S. W.

Maly, Wojciech. Atlas of IC Technologies: An Introduction to VLSI Processes. (Illus.). 330p. (C). 1987. pap. text ed. 36.75 (*0-8053-6850-7*) Benjamin-Cummings.

Malyala, Panduranga R. Aum: (Amen) rev. ed. Malyala, Raghu, ed. (Illus.). 44p. 1993. pap. text ed. 5.00 (*0-938924-38-9*) Sri Shirdi Sai.

— Basil Plant (Tulasi Plant) Worship among the World. (Illus.). 1982. 2.00 (*0-938924-06-0*) Sri Shirdi Sai.

— Bhagavadgeeta-Bible-Khuran (Krishna-Jesus Mohammad) Date not set. 3.99 (*0-938924-04-4*) Sri Shirdi Sai.

— Himalayas Tibet & McMohan Line. Date not set. 2.99 (*0-938924-09-5*) Sri Shirdi Sai.

— History of Indians in South & North America. Date not set. 2.99 (*0-938924-07-9*) Sri Shirdi Sai.

— Interrelationship Between Atom-Body-Universe (Anda-Pinda-Brah Manda) Date not set. 1.99 (*0-938924-08-7*) Sri Shirdi Sai.

— Mantras-Meaning (from Physics & Chemistry Stand Point of View) Date not set. 3.99 (*0-938924-05-2*) Sri Shirdi Sai.

— New Clear Energy: Rudra Abhisekam. (Illus.). 120p. 1983. 5.00 (*0-938924-11-7*) Sri Shirdi Sai.

— Sri Ganesh Puja (Worship of God of Obstacles) (Illus.). 56p. 1982. 5.00 (*0-938924-03-6*) Sri Shirdi Sai.

— Sri Sarasvati Puja: Goddess of Knowledge & Education. (Illus.). 28p. 1982. 2.00 (*0-938924-10-9*) Sri Shirdi Sai.

— Temples & Idol Worship. Date not set. 4.99 (*0-938924-02-8*) Sri Shirdi Sai.

— Upanayanam (Thread Marriage) (Illus.). 20p. 1983. pap. text ed. 2.00 (*0-938924-15-X*) Sri Shirdi Sai.

— Vishnu Sahasranamam. (Illus.). 18p. (Orig.). 1986. pap. text ed. 5.00 (*0-938924-28-1*) Sri Shirdi Sai.

— Why Cow Protection? Date not set. 1.99 (*0-938924-01-X*) Sri Shirdi Sai.

Malyala, Panduranga R., frwd. Yagna (The Eternal Energy) (Illus.). 36p. (Orig.). 1984. pap. text ed. 5.00x (*0-938924-23-0*) Sri Shirdi Sai.

Malyala, Pandurangarao. Daily Prayers. (Illus.). (Orig.). 1984. pap. 2.00 (*0-938924-24-9*) Sri Shirdi Sai.

Malyala, Raghu, ed. see Malyala, Panduranga R.

Malyaskaya, Great R., tr. see Idelchik, I. E.

Malygin, E. G., et al. Physicochemical Biology: Restriction-Modification Enzymes; Cell-Model Membrane Interactions, Vol. 9. Skulachev, V. P., ed. (Soviet Scientific Reviews Ser.: Vol. 9, Pt. 2). ii, 98p. 1989. text ed. 65.00 (*3-7186-4917-9*) Gordon & Breach.

Malynes, Gerard De. A Treatise of the Canker of Englands Common Wealth. LC 77-7412. (English Experience Ser.: No. 880). 1977. reprint ed. lib. bdg. 10.50 (*90-221-0880-5*) Walter J Johnson.

Malyshev, D. V., tr. see Sharkovsky, A. N., et al.

Malyshev, V. A. & Minlos, R. A. Gibbs Random Fields: Cluster Expansions. (C). 1991. lib. bdg. 122.50 (*0-7923-0232-X*) Kluwer Ac.

— Linear Infinite Particle Operators. LC 94-42578. (Translations of Mathematical Monographs: Vol. 143). 298p. (ENG & RUS.). 1995. 125.00 (*0-8218-0283-6*) Am Math.

Malyshev, V. V., et al. Optimization of Observation & Control Processes. (Educ Ser.). (Illus.). 400p. 1992. 65.95 (*1-56347-040-3*) AIAA.

Malz, Betty. Angels Watching over Me. LC 85-26322. 128p. 1986. 11.99 (*0-8007-9056-1*) Chosen Bks.

— Heaven: A Bright & Glorious Place. LC 89-9879. 1989. 11.99 (*0-8007-9145-2*) Chosen Bks.

— Making Your Husband Feel Loved. LC 90-55273. 228p. (Orig.). 1991. pap. 9.99 (*0-88419-276-8*, Creation Hse) Strang Comms Co.

— Morning Jam Sessions: Devotions to Get Your Day off to a Flying Start! LC 92-27969. 384p. 1992. 12.99 (*0-8007-9204-1*) Chosen Bks.

— My Glimpse of Eternity. LC 77-22671. 126p. 1983. pap. 7.99 (*0-8007-9066-9*) Chosen Bks.

— My Glimpse of Eternity. LC 77-22671. 1985. pap. 3.99 (*0-8007-8363-8*) Revell.

— Prayers That Are Answered. LC 79-24532. 168p. 1980. pap. 7.99 (*0-8007-9095-2*) Chosen Bks.

— Prayers That Are Answered. 1981. pap. 3.50 (*0-451-14948-3*, Sig) NAL-Dutton.

— Super Natural Living: Letting God Invade Every Day of Your Life. pap. 3.99 (*0-8007-8611-4*) Revell.

— Touching the Unseen World. LC 91-10142. 1991. 11.99 (*0-8007-9180-0*) Chosen Bks.

— Women in Tune: Five Secrets for Survival in Today's Hectic World. LC 87-23384. 192p. 1995. pap. 7.99 (*0-8007-9220-3*) Chosen Bks.

Malzac, R. P. Dictionnaire Francais-Malgache. 861p. (FRE.). 1953. pap. 59.95 (*0-8288-6876-X*, M-6390) Fr & Eur.

Malzahn, Judith C. The How to of Pineneedle Art & Basketry. (Illus.). 30p. (Orig.). 1985. pap. write for info. (*0-9614565-0-7*) Judith Malzahn.

Malzahn, Manfred. Germany 1945-1949: A Sourcebook. (Illus.). 288p. (C). 1991. text ed. 49.95 (*0-415-00840-9*, A5510) Routledge.

Malzan, Jerry G., jt. auth. see Djokovic, D. Z.

Malzberg, Barry. Beyond Apollo. 1989. pap. 3.50 (*0-88184-551-5*) Carroll & Graf.

— Galaxies. 128p. 1989. pap. 2.95 (*0-88184-491-8*) Carroll & Graf.

Malzberg, Barry & Greenberg, Martin H., eds. Classic Tales of Horror & the Supernatural. 608p. 1991. pap. 15.00 (*0-688-10963-2*, Quill) Morrow.

Malzberg, Barry, jt. auth. see Pronzini, Bill.

Malzberg, Barry N. The Passage of the Light: The Recursive Science Fiction of Barry N. Malzberg. LC 94-65656. x, 281p. 1994. pap. 14.00 (*0-915368-59-5*) New Eng SF Assoc.

— Underlay. 256p. 1986. pap. 4.95 (*0-930330-41-2*) Intl Polygonics.

Malzberg, Barry N. & Greenberg, Martin H., eds. The Science Fiction of Mark Clifton. LC 80-20977. (Alternatives Ser.). 318p. 1980. 17.95 (*0-8093-0985-8*) S Ill U Pr.

Malzberg, Barry N., ed. see Neville, Kris.

Malzberg, Barry N., jt. auth. see Pronzini, Bill.

Malzberg, Benjamin. Social & Biological Aspects of Mental Disease. Grob, Gerald N., ed. LC 78-22573. (Historical Issues in Mental Health Ser.). (Illus.). 1980. reprint ed. lib. bdg. 28.95 (*0-405-11926-7*) Ayer.

***Mama, Amina.** Beyond the Masks: Race, Gender & Subjectivity. LC 95-8479. (Critical Psychology Ser.). 1995. write for info. (*0-415-03543-0*); pap. write for info. (*0-415-03544-9*) Routledge.

Mamaev, B. M. & Krivosheina, N. P. The Larvae of the Gall Midges (Diptera & Cecidomyiidae) Roskam, J. C., ed. Wieffering, J. H., tr. (Illus.). 302p. (C). 1992. text ed. 95.00 (*90-6191-787-5*, Pub. by A A Balkema NE) Ashgate Pub Co.

Mamak, Alexander F. Colour, Culture & Conflict: A Study of Pluralism in Fiji. (Illus.). 1979. pap. text ed. 21.00 (*0-08-023353-8*, Pergamon Pr) Elsevier.

Mamak, Alexander F., ed. see Young Nations Conference, Sidney, 1976 Staff.

Mamalakis, Markos J. The Growth & Structure of the Chilean Economy: From Independence to Allende. LC 74-29729. (Economic Growth Center, Yale University Publication Ser.). 412p. 1976. reprint ed. pap. 117.50 (*0-8357-8158-5*, 2033811) Bks Demand.

— Historical Statistics of Chile: Banking, & Financial Services, Vol. 5. LC 78-66721. (Illus.). xcii, 532p. 1985. text ed. 195.00 (*0-313-25136-3*, MHC/5, Greenwood Pr) Greenwood.

— Historical Statistics of Chile: Forestry & Related Activities, Vol. 3. LC 78-66721. (Illus.). lxxxvii, 443p. 1982. text ed. 175.00 (*0-313-20855-7*, MHC/3, Greenwood Pr) Greenwood.

Mamalakis, Markos J., comp. Historical Statistics of Chile: Demography & Labor Force, Vol. 2. LC 79-54051. (Illus.). 420p. 1980. text ed. 175.00 (*0-313-20854-9*, MHC/2, Greenwood Pr) Greenwood.

— Historical Statistics of Chile: Government Services & Public Sector & a Theory of Services, Vol. 6. LC 78-66721. 976p. 1989. text ed. 215.00 (*0-313-26563-1*, MHC/6, Greenwood Pr) Greenwood.

— Historical Statistics of Chile: Money, Prices, & Credit Services, Vol. 4. LC 78-66721. (Illus.). lxxviii, 510p. 1983. text ed. 175.00 (*0-313-20856-5*, MHC/4, Greenwood Pr) Greenwood.

— Historical Statistics of Chile: National Accounts. LC 78-66721. 262p. 1978. text ed. 175.00 (*0-313-20619-8*, MHC/1, Greenwood Pr) Greenwood.

Mamaliga, Emil, jt. auth. see Dowell, Linus J.

Mamantov, C. B., jt. ed. see Mamantov, Gleb.

Mamantov, Gleb, ed. Molten Salts: Characterization & Analysis. LC 75-88481. (Illus.). 627p. reprint ed. pap. 178.70 (*0-317-07980-8*, 2055007) Bks Demand.

Mamantov, Gleb & Mamantov, C. B., eds. Advances in Molten Salt Chemistry, Vol. 5. 290p. 1983. 115.50 (*0-444-42238-2*) Elsevier.

Mamantov, Gleb & Marassi, Roberto, eds. Molten Salt Chemistry: An Introduction & Selected Applications. (C). 1987. lib. bdg. 154.50 (*90-277-2483-0*) Kluwer Ac.

Mamantov, Gleb & Popov, Alexander. Chemistry of Nonaqueous Solutions. LC 93-40038. 1994. write for info. (*1-56081-546-9*) VCH Pubs.

Mamantov, Gleb, ed. see International Symposium on Molten Salts Staff.

Mamantov, Gleb, et al, eds. Advances in Molten Salt Chemistry, Vol. 6. 362p. 1987. 159.00 (*0-444-42822-4*) Elsevier.

Mamantov, I. A., ed. see Altman, Moses S.

Mamatas, Emanuel. The No Hair-Loss Hair Care Book: With Hair Replacement Solutions & Treatments. 1988. pap. 14.95 (*0-13-623018-0*) P-H.

***Mamatey.** Rise of the Habsburg Empire. 1994. pap. 9.50 (*0-89464-920-5*) Krieger.

Mamatey, Victor S. Rise of the Habsburg Empire: 1526-1815. LC 77-15525. (Berkshire Studies). 192p. 1978. reprint ed. pap. text ed. 10.50 (*0-88275-639-7*) Krieger.

Mamay, Carl O., photos. Opinions Six: Philatelic Expertizing - An Inside View. (Opinions Ser.). (Illus.). ii, 226p. 1992. text ed. 32.50 (*0-911989-25-0*) Philatelic Found.

Mamayev, O. I. Temperature-Salinity Analysis of World Ocean Waters. (Oceanography Ser.: Vol. 11). 374p. 1975. 133.50 (*0-444-41251-4*) Elsevier.

Mambert, W. A. Elements of Effective Communication: Idea Power Tactics. LC 71-141366. 1971. pap. 6.95 (*0-87491-141-9*) Acropolis.

— On Becoming an Educated Person: A Practical Handbook for Developing Your Basic Thinking, Problem Solving & Communicating Skills. LC 80-81014. 1982. pap. text ed. 14.95 (*0-941822-00-1*) C E R I Pr.

— Presenting Technical Ideas: A Guide to Audience Communication. LC 67-28335. (Wiley Series on Human Communication). (Illus.). 229p. reprint ed. pap. 65.30 (*0-317-10710-0*, 2055175) Bks Demand.

Mambuca, Annette, ed. Free at Last: Daily Meditations by & for Inmates. LC 93-84893. 375p. (Orig.). 1993. pap. 9.95 (*0-942421-54-X*) Hazelden.

— Free at Last: Daily Meditations by & for Inmates. LC 93-84893. 375p. (Orig.). 1993. pap. 9.95 (*1-56838-070-4*) Hazelden.

Mamchak, P. Susan & Mamchak, Steven R. Complete Communications Manual for Coaches & Athletic Directors. 328p. 1989. pap. text ed. 34.95 (*0-13-159229-7*, Busn) P-H.

— Complete School Communications Manual: With Sample Letters, Forms, Bulletins, Policies & Memos. LC 83-21298. 486p. 1984. text ed. 39.95 (*0-13-162850-X*, Busn) P-H.

— Educator's Treasury of Stories for All Occasions. LC 92-17483. 1992. write for info. (*0-13-240805-8*, Parker Publishing Co) P-H.

— School Administrator's Encyclopedia. LC 81-22492. 414p. 1982. text ed. 27.95 (*0-13-792390-2*, Parker Publishing Co) P-H.

— School Administrator's Public Speaking Portfolio: With Model Speeches & Anecdotes. 360p. 1983. 34.95 (*0-13-792556-5*, Parker Publishing Co) P-H.

— Teacher's Communication Resource Book. LC 85-16730. 233p. 1986. pap. text ed. 22.95 (*0-13-888355-6*, Busn) P-H.

— Two Thousand Two Gems of Educational Wit & Humor. LC 93-47894. 1994. write for info. (*0-13-489683-1*, Parker Publishing Co) P-H.

Mamchak, Steven R., ed. see Frailey, Lester E.

Mamchak, Steven R., jt. auth. see Mamchak, P. Susan.

Mamchak, Steven R., jt. auth. see Mamchak, Susan.

Mamchak, Steven R., jt. auth. see Susan, P.

Mamchak, Susan & Mamchak, Steven R. The New Encyclopedia of School Letters. 416p. 1990. 39.95 (*0-13-612656-1*) P-H.

— Teacher's Time Management Survival Kit: Ready-To-Use Techniques & Materials. LC 93-3737. 1993. write for info. (*0-13-014374-X*) P-H.

Mamdani, Mahmood. Imperialism & Fascism in Uganda. ix, 125p. (Orig.). 1984. 15.95 (*0-86543-028-4*); pap. 6.95 (*0-86543-029-2*) Africa World.

— The Myth of Population Control: Family, Caste & Class in an Indian Village. LC 72-81761. (Illus.). 176p. 1973. pap. 11.00 (*0-85345-284-9*) Monthly Rev.

— Politics & Class Formation in Uganda. LC 75-15348. 337p. 1976. 16.50 (*0-85345-378-0*) Monthly Rev.

Mame & Plon. Catechisme de l'Eglise Catholique. (FRE.). 1992. pap. 59.95 (*0-7859-1006-9*, 2728905495) Fr & Eur.

Mamedov, Seville. Azerbaijany-English, English-Azerbaijany Concise Dictionary. (Concise Dictionaries Ser.). 400p. (Orig.). (AZE & ENG.). 1994. pap. 11.95 (*0-7818-0244-X*) Hippocrene Bks.

Mamen, Moojan. Studies in the Babi & Baha'i Religions, Vol. 5: Essays in Honor of the late H. M. Balyuzi. 1989. 32.50 (*0-933770-72-3*); pap. 24.95 (*0-933770-44-8*) Kalimat.

Mamertinus, Claudius. Die Neujahrsrede Des Konsuls Claudius Mamertinus Vor Dem Kaiser Julian. (Basler Beitrage Zur Geschichtswissenschaft Ser.: No. 10). 254p. 1980. write for info. (*3-487-07045-6*, Pub. by Georg Olms GW) Lubrecht & Cramer.

Mamet, D., et al. The Ensemble Studio Theatre Marathon '84. 94p. (Orig.). 1985. pap. 4.95 (*0-88145-030-8*) Broadway Play.

Mamet, David. American Buffalo. LC 77-78079. 128p. 1988. pap. 7.95 (*0-8021-5057-8*) Grove-Atltic.

— American Buffalo. limited ed. (Illus.). 118p. 1992. 350.00 (*0-685-70226-X*) Arion Pr.

— The Cabin: Reminiscence & Diversions. 1992. 20.00 (*0-679-41558-0*) Random.

— The Cabin: Reminiscence & Diversions. LC 93-10493. 1993. pap. 10.00 (*0-679-74720-6*, Vin) Random.

— Cryptogram & Other Plays. 1995. pap. 9.00 (*0-679-74653-6*) Random.

— Five Television Plays: A Waitress in Yellowstone; Bradford; The Museum of Science & Industry Story; A Wasted Weekend; We Will Take You There. 224p. 1990. pap. 12.95 (*0-8021-3171-9*) Grove-Atltic.

— Glengarry Glenn Ross. LC 83-49380. 112p. 1988. pap. 7.95 (*0-8021-3091-7*) Grove-Atltic.

— Goldberg Street: Short Plays & Monologues. LC 84-7310. 156p. 1989. pap. 10.95 (*0-8021-5104-3*) Grove-Atltic.

— Homicide: A Screenplay. 1992. pap. 9.95 (*0-8021-3308-8*) Grove-Atltic.

— House of Games. LC 86-32013. (Illus.). 160p. 1987. pap. 7.95 (*0-8021-3028-3*) Grove-Atltic.

— A Life in the Theatre. LC 77-91884. 120p. 10.95 (*0-8021-5067-5*) Grove-Atltic.

— A Life with No Joy in It: And Other Plays & Pieces. 1994. pap. 4.75 (*0-8222-1321-4*) Dramatists Play.

— Oleanna. 1993. 4.75 (*0-8222-1343-5*) Dramatists Play.

— Oleanna. LC 92-637. 128p. 1993. 20.00 (*0-679-42411-3*) Pantheon.

— Oleanna. LC 92-50638. 1993. pap. 10.00 (*0-679-74536-X*, Vin) Random.

— On Directing. LC 89-40695. 128p. 1991. 18.95 (*0-670-83033-X*, Viking) Viking Penguin.

— On Directing Film. 128p. 1992. pap. 10.95 (*0-14-012722-4*, Penguin Bks) Viking Penguin.

— Passover. (Illus.). 64p. 1995. 14.95 (*0-312-13141-0*) St Martin.

— Reunion & Dark Pony. 64p. 1990. pap. 8.95 (*0-8021-5171-X*) Grove-Atltic.

— The Revenge of the Space Pandas. 1978. 5.00 (*0-87129-532-6*, R26) Dramatic Pub.

— Sexual Perversity in Chicago & the Duck Variations. LC 77-91885. 128p. 1988. 8.95 (*0-8021-5011-X*) Grove-Atltic.

— The Shawl & Prairie du Chien. LC 85-14884. 120p. 1985. pap. 6.95 (*0-8021-5172-8*) Grove-Atltic.

— Short Plays & Monologues. 1981. pap. 4.75 (*0-8222-0720-6*) Dramatists Play.

— Speed-the-Plow. 128p. 1988. pap. 8.95 (*0-8021-3046-1*) Grove-Atltic.

— Three Children's Plays: The Poet & the Rent; The Frog Prince; The Revenge of the Space Pandas or Binky Rudich & the Two-Speed Clock. 144p. (J). (gr. 3-7). pap. 8.95 (*0-8021-5173-6*) Grove-Atltic.

— The Village: A Novel. LC 94-4342. 1994. 21.95 (*0-316-54572-4*) Little.

— We're No Angels. 144p. 1990. pap. 7.95 (*0-8021-3202-2*) Grove-Atltic.

— The Woods, Lakeboat, Edmond. 288p. 1987. 10.95 (*0-8021-5109-4*) Grove-Atltic.

— Writing in Restaurants. 176p. 1987. pap. 8.95 (*0-14-008981-0*, Penguin Bks) Viking Penguin.

Mamet, David & Silverstein, Shel. Things Change. (Illus.). 64p. 1988. pap. 7.95 (*0-8021-3047-X*) Grove-Atltic.

Mamin-Sibiryak, D. N. Grey Neck. LC 88-2100. (Illus.). 32p. (J). (gr. k-3). 1988. 13.95 (*0-88045-068-1*) Stemmer Hse.

M

Mamis, Justin. The Nature of Risk: Stock Market Survival & the Meaning of Life. (Illus.). 256p. 1993. pap. 12.45 (*0-201-62235-1*) Addison-Wesley.

— When to Sell for the 90's: Inside Strategies for Stock-Market Profits. LC 94-22970. (Illus.). 350p. (C). 1994. pap. text ed. 20.00 (*0-87034-116-2*) Fraser Pub Co.

Mamiya, Christin J. Pop Art & Consumer Culture: American Super Market. LC 91-18892. (American Studies Ser.). (Illus.). 227p. 1991. text ed. 35.00 (*0-292-77653-5*); pap. 17.95 (*0-292-76540-1*) U of Tex Pr.

Mamiya, Lawrence, jt. auth. see Lincoln, C. Eric.

Mamleev, Jurii. Vzglid 12 Nichto: Rasskazy. LC 88-83825. (Illus.). 328p. (RUS.). 1989. 32.00 (*0-911971-42-4*); pap. 25.00 (*0-911971-43-2*) Effect Pub.

Mammana, Dennis. Start Exploring Space: A Fact-Filled Coloring Book. (Start Exploring Ser.). (Illus.). 128p. (Orig.). (J). (gr. 3 up). 1991. pap. 8.95 (*0-89471-864-9*) Running Pr.

Mammem, Lori. TAAS Master Social Studies Grade Four. (TAAS Master Ser.). (Illus.). 144p. 1993. pap. text ed. 19.95 (*0-944459-92-7*) ECS Lrn Systs.

Mammen, E. F., et al, eds. Treatment of Bleeding Disorders with Blood Components. (Reviews of Hematology: Vol. I). 1980. 49.95 (*0-915340-01-1*) PJD Pubns.

Mammen, Lori. Passageways: Vocabulary Activities to Build Writing Skills. 96p. 1992. pap. text ed. 12.95 (*0-944459-62-5*) ECS Lrn Systs.

— Springboards for Reading, Grades 3-6: 48 Strategic Reading Lessons. (ECS Activity Book for Language Arts Ser.). 96p. 1993. pap. text ed. 11.95 (*0-944459-69-2*) ECS Lrn Systs.

— Springboards for Reading, Grades 7-12: 38 Strategic Reading Lessons. (ECS Activity Book for Language Arts Ser.). 80p. 1993. pap. text ed. 10.95 (*0-944459-70-6*) ECS Lrn Systs.

— TAAS Master Reading Teacher Training Manual - Elementary. (Illus.). 64p. 1992. pap. text ed. 7.95 (*0-944459-41-2*) ECS Lrn Systs.

— TAAS Master Reading Teacher Training Manual - Secondary. 64p. 1992. pap. text ed. 7.95 (*0-944459-42-0*) ECS Lrn Systs.

— TAAS Master Social Studies Grade Eight. (TAAS Master Ser.). (Illus.). 144p. (Orig.). 1993. pap. 19.95 (*0-944459-91-9*) ECS Lrn Systs.

— TAAS Master Writing, Exit Level: Teacher's Handbook for Texas Assessment of Academic Skills. 112p. (Orig.). 1990. pap. text ed. 14.95 (*0-944459-13-7*) ECS Lrn Systs.

— TAAS Master Writing, Gr. Eight-Gr. Nine: Teacher's Handbook for Texas Assessment of Academic Skills. (Illus.). 128p. 1990. pap. text ed. 15.95 (*0-944459-12-9*) ECS Lrn Systs.

— TAAS Master Writing, Gr. 2-12: Teacher Training Manual. 64p. (Orig.). (C). 1990. pap. text ed. 7.95 (*0-944459-24-2*) ECS Lrn Systs.

— TAAS Master Writing, Grade 2 - Grade 3: Teacher's Handbook for Texas Assessment of Academic Skills. (Illus.). 128p. (Orig.). 1990. pap. text ed. 15.95 (*0-944459-09-9*) ECS Lrn Systs.

— TAAS Master Writing, Grades Four & Five: Teacher's Handbook for Texas Assessment of Academic Skills. (Illus.). 128p. (Orig.). 1990. pap. text ed. 15.95 (*0-944459-10-2*) ECS Lrn Systs.

— TAAS Master Writing, Grades Six & Seven: Teacher's Handbook for Texas Assessment of Academic Skills. (Illus.). 128p. 1990. pap. text ed. 15.95 (*0-944459-11-0*) ECS Lrn Systs.

— TAAS Master Writing Teacher Training Manual. rev. ed. 64p. 1991. pap. 9.95 (*0-944459-25-0*) ECS Lrn Systs.

— TAAS Quick Review Reading: Exit Level. (Illus.). 96p. 1992. pap. text ed. 12.95 (*0-944459-39-0*) ECS Lrn Systs.

— TAAS Quick Review Reading, Grade 8. (Illus.). 96p. 1992. pap. 12.95 (*0-944459-38-2*) ECS Lrn Systs.

— TAAS Quick Review Writing: Exit Level. 64p. 1991. pap. text ed. 9.95 (*0-944459-30-7*) ECS Lrn Systs.

— TAAS Quick Review Writing: Grade 3. (Illus.). 64p. 1991. pap. text ed. 9.95 (*0-944459-26-9*) ECS Lrn Systs.

— TAAS Quick Review Writing: Grade 5. (Illus.). 64p. 1991. pap. text ed. 9.95 (*0-944459-27-7*) ECS Lrn Systs.

— TAAS Quick Review Writing: Grade 7. 64p. 1991. pap. text ed. 9.95 (*0-944459-28-5*) ECS Lrn Systs.

— TAAS Quick Review Writing: Grade 9. 64p. 1991. pap. text ed. 9.95 (*0-944459-29-3*) ECS Lrn Systs.

— TEAMS Vocabulary Plus: Learning & Using TEAMS Vocabulary Words, 3 vols. (Illus.). 120p. (J). 1988. Grade 3. pap. text ed. 7.95 (*0-944459-00-5*); Grade 5. pap. text ed. 7.95 (*0-944459-01-3*); Grade 7. pap. text ed. 7.95 (*0-944459-02-1*) ECS Lrn Systs.

— Writing Prompts Plus: Preparing Students for the TEAMS Composition Test, 4 vols. (Illus.). 160p. (J). 1988. Grade 3. pap. text ed. 7.95 (*0-944459-03-X*); Grade 5. pap. text ed. 7.95 (*0-944459-04-8*); Grade 7. pap. text ed. 7.95 (*0-944459-05-6*); Grade 9. pap. text ed. 7.95 (*0-944459-06-4*) ECS Lrn Systs.

— Writing Warm-Ups. 80p. (gr. k-6). 1989. pap. text ed. 9.95 (*0-944459-07-2*) ECS Lrn Systs.

— Writing Warm-Ups. 80p. (YA). (gr. 7-12). 1989. pap. text ed. 9.95 (*0-944459-08-0*) ECS Lrn Systs.

— Writing Warm-ups Two K-6: Quick, Creative, & Challenging Writing Exercises. 80p. 1992. pap. text ed. 9.95 (*0-944459-45-5*) ECS Lrn Systs.

— Writing Warm-ups Two 7-12: Quick, Creative, & Challenging Writing Exercises. 80p. 1992. pap. text ed. 9.95 (*0-944459-46-3*) ECS Lrn Systs.

Mammen, Lori, ed. see Graft, Janine & McNamee, Dan.

Mammen, Lori, ed. see McNamee, Dan & Graft, Janine.

Mammen, Lori, jt. auth. see Parker, Violette.

Mammen, Lori, et al. TAAS Master Reading, Exit Level: Teacher's Handbook for Texas Assessment of Academic Skills. (Illus.). 112p. (Orig.). 1990. pap. text ed. 14.95 (*0-944459-23-4*) ECS Lrn Systs.

— TAAS Master Reading, Grades 6-7: Teacher's Handbook for Texas Assessment of Academic Skills. (Illus.). 112p. (Orig.). 1990. pap. text ed. 14.95 (*0-944459-21-8*) ECS Lrn Systs.

— TAAS Master Reading, Grades 8-9: Teacher's Handbook for Texas Assessment of Academic Skills. (Illus.). 112p. (Orig.). 1990. pap. text ed. 14.95 (*0-944459-22-6*) ECS Lrn Systs.

Mammen, P. M. Communalism vs. Communism: A Study of the Socio-Religious Communities & Political Parties in Kerala, 1892-1970. 1981. 18.50 (*0-8364-0041-0*) S Asia.

— Gandhian Utopia: Its Relevance & Justification. 1988. 12. 50 (*81-85195-09-9*, Pub. by Minerva II) S Asia.

Mammerickx, Jacqueline, jt. auth. see Langseth, Marcus G.

Mammerickx, M., jt. ed. see Burny, A.

Mammitzsch, Ulrich. Evolution of the Garbhadhatu Mandala. (C). 1991. 64.00 (*81-85179-70-0*, Pub. by Aditya Prakashan II) S Asia.

Mammitzsch, Ulrich, tr. see Huizinga, Johan.

Mammitzsch, Ulrich H., tr. see Seckel, Dietrich.

Mammone, Richard J. Computational Methods of Signal Recovery & Recognition. (Series in Telecommunications: No. 1794). 448p. 1992. text ed. 86.95 (*0-471-85384-4*) Wiley.

Mammone, Richard J., ed. Artificial Neural Networks for Speech & Vision. LC 93-32966. 1993. write for info. (*0-412-54850-X*, Chap & Hall NY) Chapman & Hall.

Mammone, Richard J. & Zeevi, Yehoshua, eds. Neural Networks: Theory & Applications. (Illus.). 355p. 1991. text ed. 49.95 (*0-12-467050-4*) Acad Pr.

Mamola, Claire. Japanese Women Writers in English Translation, Vol. 2: An Annotated Bibliography. LC 89-1319. 480p. 1992. 72.00 (*0-8240-7077-1*, H1317) Garland.

Mamola, Claire Z. Japanese Women Writers in English Translation: An Annotated Bibliography. 500p. 1989. 60. 00 (*0-8240-3048-6*) Garland.

Mamone, Robert A., jt. auth. see Lee, William W.

Mamonova, Tatyana. Russian Women's Studies: Essays on Sexism in Soviet Culture. (Athene Ser.). (Illus.). 198p. 1988. text ed. 45.00 (*0-08-036482-9*, Pergamon Pr); pap. text ed. 17.95 (*0-08-036481-0*, Pergamon Pr) Elsevier.

— Russian Women's Studies: Essays on Sexism in the Soviet Culture. (Athene Ser.). 198p. (C). text ed. 45.00 (*0-8077-6211-3*); pap. text ed. 17.95 (*0-8077-6210-5*) Tchrs Coll.

Mamonova, Tatyana, ed. Women & Russia: Feminist Writings from the Soviet Union. Park, Rebecca & Fitzpatrick, Catherine A., trs. LC 82-73963. 297p. reprint ed. pap. 84.70 (*0-7837-1386-X*, 2041562) Bks Demand.

Mamonova, Tatyana & Folsom, Chandra N., contribs. Women's Glasnost Vs. Naglost: Stopping Russian Backlash. LC 93-15181. 208p. 1993. text ed. 49.95 (*0-89789-339-5*, H339, Bergin & Garvey); pap. text ed. 18.95 (*0-89789-340-9*, G340, Bergin & Garvey) Greenwood.

Mamorsky, Jeffrey D. Employee Benefits Handbook. 3rd ed. 1992. Supplemented annually, write for info. 129.00 (*0-7913-1069-8*) Warren Gorham & Lamont.

— Employee Benefits Law: Erisa & Beyond, 2 vols. 1100p. 1986. reprint ed. ring bd. 135.00 (*0-318-21430-X*, 00557) NY Law Pub.

Mamorsky, Jeffrey D., ed. Employee Benefits Handbook. 3rd ed. 1991. text ed. 115.00 (*0-685-69669-3*, EBH) Warren Gorham & Lamont.

— Journal of Compensation & Benefits. 129.00 (*0-685-69672-3*, JCB) Warren Gorham & Lamont.

Mamorsky, Jeffrey D., jt. ed. see Duva, Joseph W.

Mamot, Patricio R. People Power: Profile of Filipino Heroism. (Illus.). 227p. (Orig.). 1986. pap. 13.75 (*971-10-0295-7*, Pub. by New Day Pub PH) Cellar.

Mamourian, Arsene, tr. see Khrakhouni, Zareh.

Mamourian, Arsene, tr. see Mavian, Vahram.

Mampaso, A., et al, eds. Infrared Astronomy. (Illus.). 432p. (C). 1994. 64.95 (*0-521-46462-5*) Cambridge U Pr.

Mamrak, Sandra, et al. The Integrated Chameleon Architecture: Translating Electronic Documents with St. 208p. 1994. pap. text ed. 40.00 (*0-13-056418-4*) P-H.

*__Mamulyan, A.__ English-Russian Comprehensive Law Dictionary. 389p. (ENG & RUS.). 1993. 95.00 (*0-614-00407-1*, 5874650016) Fr & Eur.

Mamyrin, B. A. & Tolstikhin, I. N. Helium Isotopes in Nature. (Developments in Geochemistry Ser.: No. 3). 274p. 1984. 79.50 (*0-444-42180-7*, I-0073-84) Elsevier.

Mamzic, Charles L., ed. Statistical Process Control. LC 94-9020. (Practical Guides for Measurement & Control Ser.). 1994. write for info. (*1-55617-511-6*) Instru Soc.

Man, Bruce, jt. auth. see Koolhaas, Rem.

Man-ch'ing, Cheng. Cheng Man-ch'ings Advanced T'ai-chi Form Instructions. 3rd ed. Wile, Douglas, tr. (Illus.). 162p. (Orig.). 1985. pap. 10.95 (*0-912059-03-6*) Sweet Ch I Pr.

— Lao Tzu: My Words Are Very Easy to Understand. 2nd ed. Gibbs, Tam & Huang, Juh-Hua, trs. 256p. (CHI & ENG.). 1981. pap. 12.95 (*0-913028-91-6*) North Atlantic.

— A Simplified Explanation of Man & His Culture. Hennessy, Mark, tr. 200p. (Orig.). (C). 1995. pap. 12.95 (*1-883319-26-9*) Frog CA.

— Tai Chi Ch'uan: A Simplified Method of Calisthenics for Health & Self Defense. Tseng, Beauson, tr. (Illus.). 160p. (Orig.). 1981. pap. 8.95 (*0-913028-85-1*) North Atlantic.

Man-Ching, Cheng, et al. Cheng-Tzu's Thirteen Treatises on T'ai Chi Ch'uan. Jeng, Benjamin P. & Jeng Lo, Benjamin P., trs. (Illus.). 226p. 1985. 18.95 (*0-938190-45-8*) North Atlantic.

Man Chong Fung, tr. Be Perfect. 2nd ed. 160p. (CHI.). 1982. pap. write for info. (*0-941598-03-9*) Living Spring Pubns.

Man, Eagle, jt. auth. see McGaa, Ed.

Man, Edward H. The Nicobar Islands & Their People. LC 77-86996. (Royal Anthropological Institute of Great Britain & Ireland. Publication Ser.). reprint ed. 29.50 (*0-404-16767-5*) AMS Pr.

Man, Felix H. Graham Sutherland: The Graphic Work, 1922-1970. 234p. 1970. 125.00 (*1-55660-107-7*) A Wofsy Fine Arts.

Man, Glenn. Radical Visions: American Film Renaissance, 1967-1976. LC 94-3049. (Contributions in the Study of Popular Culture Ser.: No. 41). 232p. 1994. text ed. 55.00 (*0-313-29306-6*, Greenwood Pr) Greenwood.

Man Ho, Kwok & O'Brien, Joanne, eds. The Eight Immortals of Taoism: Legends & Fables of Popular Taoism. O'Brien, Joanne, tr. (Illus.). 160p. 1991. pap. 8.95 (*0-452-01070-5*, Mer) NAL-Dutton.

Man, John. D-Day Atlas. 1994. 24.95 (*0-8160-3137-1*) Facts on File.

— Dinosaurs. 1988. 4.98 (*0-671-06145-3*) S&S Trade.

— The Survival of Jan Little. large type ed. (General Ser.). (Illus.). 768p. 1993. 21.95 (*0-7089-2809-9*) Ulverscroft.

Man, John, jt. auth. see Smith, Frank S.

Man, John, jt. auth. see Yathy, Pin.

Man, K. W. Contact Mechanics Using Boundary Elements. LC 94-72216. (Topics in Engineering Ser.: Vol. 22). 200p. 1994. 86.00 (*1-56252-258-2*) Computational Mech MA.

Man-Kit, Dominic, jt. ed. see Shapley, Robert.

*__Man, Michael.__ Poetry in the Raw with Narrations Describing the Acts: A Perspicacity Towards Life. (Illus.). 160p. (C). Date not set. text ed. write for info. (*0-9633226-0-5*) BMN Intl.

Man, N. K., et al, eds. Blood Purification in Perspective: New Insights & Future Trends. 65.00 (*0-936022-28-0*) ICAOT Pr.

*__Man, Nguyen-Khoa, et al.__ Long-Term Hemodialysis. LC 95-14248. 1995. write for info. (*0-7923-3477-9*) Kluwer Ac.

*__Man, Rosamond.__ Mezze: Greek, Turkish & Middle Eastern Dishes. (Illus.). 160p. 1995. 35.00 (*1-85964-049-4*) Paul & Co Pubs.

Man Si-wai, jt. ed. see McMillen, Donald H.

Man-Sik, Chae. Peace under Heaven: A Modern Korean Novel. Kyung-Ja, Chun & Eckert, Carter J., trs. LC 92-31807. 272p. 1993. 44.95 (*1-56324-112-9*); pap. text ed. 18.95 (*1-56324-172-2*) M E Sharpe.

Man, W. K. Muslim Separatism: The Moros of Southern Philippines & the Malays of Southern Thailand. (South-East Asian Social Science Monographs). (Illus.). 260p. 1990. pap. 29.95 (*0-19-588924-X*) OUP.

Man-yong, Han, et al. Korean Dance, Theater, & Cinema. Korean National Commission for UNESCO, ed. (Korean Art, Folklore, Language, & Thought Ser.: No. 4). (Illus.). viii, 204p. 1983. 20.00 (*0-89209-017-0*) Pace Intl Res.

Mana, Tawa & Youyouseyah. When Hopi Children Were Bad: A Monster Story. (Illus.). 41p. (Orig.). (J). (gr. k-5). 1989. pap. 6.95 (*0-940113-20-1*) Sierra Oaks Pub.

*__Manabe, Johji.__ Appleseed Data Book, Bk. 1. (Illus.). 128p. 1995. pap. 12.95 (*1-56971-103-8*) Dark Horse Comics.

— Outlanders, Bk. 4. (Illus.). 168p. 1995. pap. 12.95 (*1-56971-069-4*) Dark Horse Comics.

— Outlanders Collection, Vol. 1. Warner, Chris, ed. Lewis, David & Smith, Toren, trs. (Outlanders Ser.). (Illus.). 148p. 1989. pap. 9.95 (*1-878574-05-1*) Dark Horse Comics.

— Outlanders Collection, Vol. 2. Warner, Chris, ed. Lewis, Dana & Smith, Toren, trs. (Outlanders Ser.). (Illus.). 148p. 1990. pap. 10.95 (*1-878574-14-0*) Dark Horse Comics.

Manach, Jorge. La Crisis de la Alta Cultura en Cuba; Indagacion del Choteo. (Coleccion Cuba y Sus Jueces Ser.). 96p. (SPA.). 1991. reprint ed. pap. 9.95 (*0-89729-606-0*) Ediciones.

— Marti: Apostle of Freedom. (Illus.). 9.50 (*0-8159-6201-0*) Devin.

— Teoria de la Frontera. 171p. 1970. 3.00 (*0-8477-2412-3*) U of PR Pr.

Manachino, Albert J. Dark Bible. (Willie Button Stories Ser.). 12p. (Orig.). 1985. pap. 2.25 (*0-9634181-1-4*) Argo Pr.

Manachino, Albert J., jt. auth. see Ambrose, Michael.

Management Accounting Practices Committee. Accounting for Software Used Internally. (Issues Paper). 24p. 5.00 (*0-86641-122-4*, 85178) Inst Mgmt Account.

Management Advisory Publications Staff. Computer Auditing & Security Manual: Operations & Systems Audits. 1976. 75.00 (*0-940706-03-2*, MAP-5) Management Advisory Pubns.

Management Development Research Ctr. Staff, ed. Vision Management: Translating Strategy into Action. LC 91-20051. 194p. 1992. 30.00 (*0-915299-80-1*) Prod Press.

Management Graphics Limited Staff. Successful Business Presentations with Harvard Graphics 3.0. (Illus.). 256p. (C). 1992. pap. text ed. 25.95 (*0-201-56890-X*) Addison-Wesley.

Management Information Systems Staff. Management Information Systems in Higher Education: The State of the Art. Johnson, Charles B. & Katzenmeyer, William G., eds. LC 74-109171. 215p. reprint ed. pap. 61.30 (*0-317-42171-9*, 2026206) Bks Demand.

Management of an Accounting Practice Committee, American Institute of Certified Public Accountants. Human Resources. LC 94-17000. (Management Ser.). 1994. write for info. (*0-87051-151-3*) Am Inst CPA.

Management Resources Project Staff. Governing the Empire State: An Insider's Guide. (Illus.). 256p. (Orig.). 1988. pap. 9.95 (*0-9621102-0-5*) Mgt Resc Proj.

Management Roundtable, Inc. Staff. CAD-CAM Manager's Complete Anthology. (Illus.). 176p. (Orig.). 1987. per. 75.00 (*0-932007-11-2*, B54) Mgmt Roundtable.

Management Roundtable, Inc. Staff, ed. CAD-CAM Databases: Implementation & Planning Strategies. (Illus.). 350p. 1986. spiral bd. 295.00 (*0-932007-08-2*, B00045) Mgmt Roundtable.

*__Management Services Staff.__ Working with Insurance & Managed Care Plans: Guide for Getting Paid. (Orig.). 1995. pap. write for info. (*0-07-600744-8*) Hlthcare Mgmt Grp.

Management Techniques Research Committee Staff, prod. Control Points in School Business Management. 24p. 1979. 6.00 (*0-910170-10-X*, 2805) Assn Sch Busn.

Manahan. Fundamentals of Environmental Chemistry. 1992. 49.95 (*0-87371-587-X*, TD193) Lewis Pubs.

— Hazardous Waste Chemistry: Toxicology & Treatment. 1990. 69.95 (*0-87371-209-9*, TD1030) Lewis Pubs.

Manahan, Nancy, jt. auth. see Curb, Rosemary.

Manahan, Nancy, jt. ed. see Curb, Rosemary.

Manahan, Stanley E. Environmental Chemistry. 5th ed. 565p. 1991. 59.95 (*0-87371-425-3*, QD31) Lewis Pubs.

— Environmental Chemistry. 6th ed. 650p. 1994. 59.95 (*1-56670-088-4*, L1088) Lewis Pubs.

— Toxicological Chemistry: A Guide to Toxic Substances in Chemistry. 2nd ed. (Illus.). 310p. 1992. 74.95 (*0-87371-621-3*, RA1219) Lewis Pubs.

Manahan, William. Eat for Health: Fast & Simple Ways of Eliminating Diseases Without Medical Assistance. Lipsett, Suzanne, ed. LC 88-81722. 252p. 1988. pap. 10. 95 (*0-915811-11-1*) H J Kramer Inc.

Manak, Dave, et al. Bullwinkle & Rocky. (Illus.). 96p. 1992. 4.95 (*0-87135-876-X*) Marvel Entmnt.

*__Manak, Frank.__ American Freedom: Why the Colonists Risked Their Lives, Their Fortunes & Their Sacred Honor. LC 95-60858. (Illus.). 250p. (Orig.). 1995. pap. 12.95 (*0-9634940-7-4*) York Pub.

Manak, Mark M., jt. ed. see Keller, George H.

Manaka, Y. Chinese Massage: Quick & Easy. 7.95 (*0-685-70676-1*) Wehman.

Manaka, Yoshio, et al. The Layman's Guide to Acupuncture. LC 72-78590. (Illus.). 144p. 1972. 12.50 (*0-8348-0072-1*); pap. 10.95 (*0-8348-0107-8*) Weatherhill.

— Chasing the Dragon's Tail. 300p. 1994. pap. 40.00 (*0-912111-32-1*) Paradigm Publns.

Manaker, George H. Interior Plantscapes. 2nd ed. (Illus.). 320p. 1987. text ed. 79.00 (*0-13-469321-3*) P-H.

Manalo, Kathleen H., jt. auth. see Stowasser, Barbara F.

Manamon, James Mc., jt. ed. see Kiemen, Mathias C.

Manamura, Robert. Asian Roots, Western Soil: Japanese Influences in American Culture. Schildgen, Robert, ed. (Illus.). 32p. (Orig.). 1993. pap. 5.99 (*0-942744-02-0*) Berkeley Art.

Manandhar, N. P., ed. Medicinal Plants of Nepal Himalaya. 87p. (C). 1980. 75.00 (*0-89771-096-7*, Pub. by Ratna Pustak Bhandar) St Mut.

Manara, Milo. The Art of Manara. LeClerc, Jacinthe, tr. 80p. 1994. 29.95 (*1-56163-100-0*, Eurotica) NBM.

— Art of Spanking. Bell, Elisabeth, tr. 96p. 1993. pap. 17.95 (*1-56163-090-X*, Eurotica) NBM.

— An Author in Search of Six Characters: The African Adventures of Giuseppe Bergman, Pt. 1. Surbeck, Jean-Jacques, tr. (Illus.). 80p. (Orig.). 1989. pap. 11.95 (*0-87416-071-5*) Catalan Communs.

— Butterscotch. 64p. 1994. pap. 12.95 (*1-56163-109-4*, Eurotica) NBM.

— Butterscotch: The Flavor of the Invisible. Metz, Bernd, ed. Leighton, Tom, tr. (Illus.). 72p. 1988. pap. 10.95 (*0-87416-047-2*) Catalan Communs.

— Click! A Woman under the Influence. 2nd ed. Leighton, Tom, tr. (Illus.). 64p. 1987. pap. 9.95 (*0-87416-055-3*) Catalan Communs.

— Click One. Leighton, Tom, tr. 48p. 1993. pap. 9.95 (*1-56163-084-5*, Eurotica) NBM.

— Click Two. Huntley, Michael, tr. 72p. 1993. 45.00 (*1-56163-061-6*, Eurotica); pap. 12.95 (*1-56163-062-4*, Eurotica) NBM.

— Dies Irae, Pt. 2: The African Adventures of Giuseppe Bergman. Metz, Bernd, ed. Bell, Elizabeth, tr. (Illus.). 88p. (Orig.). 1990. pap. 11.95 (*0-87416-077-4*) Catalan Communs.

— Great Adventure. Metz, Bernd, ed. (Adventures of Giuseppe Bergman Ser.). (Illus.). 120p. (Orig.). 1988. pap. 12.95 (*0-87416-063-4*) Catalan Communs.

— Hidden Camera. Metz, Bernd, ed. Gaudiano, Stefano, tr. (Illus.). 49p. (Orig.). 1990. pap. 9.95 (*0-87416-098-7*) Catalan Communs.

— Hidden Camera. 48p. (Orig.). 1994. pap. 10.95 (*1-56163-114-0*, Eurotica) NBM.

— Perchance to Dream: The Indian Adventures of Giuseppe Bergman. Metz, Bernd, ed. Bell, Elizabeth, tr. (Illus.). 120p. (Orig.). 1990. pap. 12.95 (*0-87416-086-3*) Catalan Communs.

— Shorts. Leighton, Tom, tr. (Illus.). 49p. (Orig.). 1989. pap. 9.95 (*0-87416-060-X*) Catalan Communs.

— Shorts. 48p. (Orig.). 1995. pap. 9.95x (*1-56163-128-0*, Eurotica) NBM.

*__Manara, Milo & Pratt, Hugo.__ El Gaucho. 144p. 1995. 28. 95x (*1-56163-129-9*, Comics Lit) NBM.

— Indian Summer. 152p. 1994. pap. 19.95 (*1-56163-107-8*, Comics Lit) NBM.

*__Manard, Barbara & Perone, Christopher.__ Hospice Care: An Introduction & Review of the Evidence. 40p. 1994. 10.50 (*0-931207-23-1*) Natl Hospice.

Manarin, Louis, ed. Confederate Veteran Index, 3 vols, Set. 1990. 300.00 (*0-916107-15-9*) Broadfoot.

An Asterisk (*) at the beginning of an entry indicates that the title is appearing in BIP for the first time.

Manarin, Louis H. Fifteenth Virginia Infantry. (Virginia Regimental Histories Ser.). (Illus.). 125p. 1990. 19.95 (*0-930919-95-5*) H E Howard.

Manarin, Louis H. & Dowdey, Clifford. The History of Henrico County. LC 84-7323. (Illus.). 581p. reprint ed. pap. 165.60 (*0-7837-1924-8*, 2042139) Bks Demand.

Manarin, Louis H. & Wallace, Lee A., Jr. Richmond Volunteers: The Volunteer Companies of the City of Richmond & Henrico County, Virginia, 1861-1865. LC 72-100103. 312p. reprint ed. pap. 89.00 (*0-8357-9815-1*, 2014632) Bks Demand.

Manarin, Louis H., jt. ed. see Dowdey, Clifford.

Manas, Vincent T., ed. National Plumbing Code Handbook. (Illus.). 1957. text ed. 74.50 (*0-07-039850-X*) McGraw.

Manas-Zloczower, Ica & Tadmor, Zehev, eds. Mixing & Compounding of Polymers: Theory & Practice. LC 93-33468. (Progress in Polymer Processing Ser.). (C). 1993. text ed. write for info. (*1-56990-156-2*) Hanser-Gardner.

***Manasek, F. J.** Uncommon Values: A Rare Book Dealer's World. 148p. 1995. 20.00 (*1-883817-02-1*) Anglers & Scholars.

Manasi, Mark. Inside OS - 2 2.1. 3rd ed. 900p. 1993. pap. 34.95 (*1-56205-206-3*) New Riders Pub.

***Manasi, Mark, et al.** Inside MS-DOS 6.22. 3rd ed. LC 94-35118. (Illus.). 1632p. (Orig.). 1995. pap. 39.99 (*1-56205-414-7*) New Riders Pub.

Manasian, N. English-Russian Frequency Glossary of Quantum Generators. 272p. (C). 1983. 90.00 (*0-685-46842-9*, Pub. by Collets) St Mut.

Manasreh, M. O. Semiconductor Quantum Wells & Superlattices for Long-Wavelength Infrared Detectors. LC 92-32246. (Materials Ser.). 265p. (C). 1992. text ed. 85.00 (*0-89006-603-5*) Artech Hse.

Manasreh, M. O., et al, eds. Physics & Applications of Defects in Advanced Semiconductors. (Materials Research Society Symposium Proceedings Ser.: Vol. 325). 1994. text ed. 71.00 (*1-55899-224-3*) Materials Res.

Manassah, Sallie. Lansing: Capital, Campus, & Cars. (Illus.). 240p. (C). 1986. 24.95 (*0-8143-2123-2*) Wayne St U Pr.

Manassah, Sallie M., et al. Lansing: Capital, Campus, & Cars. Moffett, Joyce, ed. (Contemporary Image Ser.). 240p. (C). 1986. 24.95 (*0-9616743-1-8*) Wayne St U Pr.

Manasse, A. Lorri & Schoeppler, Claire. A Banker's Guide to Better Service, Bigger Profits. 1989. pap. 49.95 (*1-55840-053-2*) Exec Ent Pubns.

***Manasse, Geoff & Swallow, Jean.** Making Love Visible: In Celebration of Gay & Lesbian Families. LC 95-6467. (Illus.). 176p. 1995. pap. 18.95 (*0-89594-778-1*) Crossing Pr.

***Manassen-Mori, Charlotte.** Sayonara My Friend Love Annie. (Illus.). 247p. 1994. 19.95 (*0-85572-239-8*) Seven Hills Bk.

Manassewitsch, Vadim. Frequency Synthesizers: Theory & Design. 3rd ed. LC 86-18968. 624p. 1987. text ed. 115.00 (*0-471-01116-9*) Wiley.

Manaster. Handbook in Radiology, Vol. 9: Neuroradiology: The Spine & Spinal Cord. 1990. 21.95 (*0-8151-7859-X*, Yr Bk Med Pubs) Mosby Yr Bk.

— Handbooks in Radiology, Vol. 2: Skeletal Radiology. 464p. 1989. pap. 31.95 (*0-8151-5754-1*, Yr Bk Med Pubs) Mosby Yr Bk.

Manaster, jt. auth. see Selmi.

***Manaster, Benjamin.** Skyla. Caso, Adolfo, ed. LC 94-43023. 246p. 1995. 21.95 (*0-8283-2002-0*) Branden Pub Co.

Manaster, Guy J. & Corsini, Raymond J. Individual Psychology: Theory & Practice. LC 81-82887. 322p. 1982. pap. 19.95 (*0-87581-274-0*) Adler Sch Prof Psy.

Manaster, Jane. The Pecan Tree. LC 93-49563. (Corrie Herring Hooks Ser.: No. 27). (Illus.). 112p. 1994. 17.95 (*0-292-75153-2*) U of Tex Pr.

***Manaster, Kenneth A.** Environmental Protection & Justice: Readings & Commentary on Environmental Law & Practice. LC 95-7757. 1995. write for info. (*0-87084-253-6*) Anderson Pub Co.

Manaster, Kenneth A., jt. auth. see Selmi, Daniel P.

Manaster-Ramer, Alexis, ed. Mathematics of Language: Proceedings of a Conference Held at the University of Michigan, Ann Arbor, October, 1984. LC 87-9183. ix, 401p. (C). 1987. 83.00x (*1-55619-032-8*) Benjamins North Am.

Manaster, Robert A., ed. see Daldorph, Brian.

Manat, G. P., ed. Guide to Books on Black Americans. (Illus.). 454p. 1994. lib. bdg. 98.00 (*1-56072-174-X*) Nova Sci Pubs.

— Politics & Economics of the Soviet Union: An Annotated Bibliography. 82p. (C). 1992. pap. text ed. 59.00 (*1-56072-048-4*) Nova Sci Pubs.

Manatt, Katherine K. Not the Marrying Kind: A Story of Love, Life, & Travel. 1992. 18.95 (*0-533-09570-0*) Vantage.

***Manatt, Richard.** When Right Is Wrong: Fundamentalists & the Public Schools. LC 94-61497. 150p. 1994. pap. text ed. 24.50 (*1-56676-222-7*) Technomic.

Manaugh, Geoffrey M. Fifteen Year Eternity. LC 92-80378. 88p. (Orig.). 1992. pap. 8.95 (*0-9632397-0-8*) Plenilunium.

Manay, N. Shakuntala & Shadaksharaswamy, M. Foods Facts & Principles. (C). 1987. pap. 17.50 (*0-85226-731-2*, Pub. by Wiley Eastern II) S Asia.

Manber, Beverly, ed. see Lickson, Charles P.

Manber, David. Zachary of the Wings. 88p. (YA). (gr. 9-12). 1993. lib. bdg. 10.95 (*1-879567-27-X*) Wonder Well.

Manber, U., jt. ed. see Baeza-Yates, Ricardo A.

Manber, Udi. Introduction to Algorithms: A Creative Approach. (Illus.). (C). 1989. text ed. 55.95 (*0-201-12037-2*) Addison-Wesley.

Manby, Thomas. Journal of the Voyages of the H. M. S. Discovery & Chatham. 230p. Date not set. write for info. (*0-87770-459-7*) Ye Galleon.

Manca, Alessandra, jt. ed. see Manca, Luigi.

Manca, John & Cosgrove, Vincent. Tin for Sale. 320p. 1993. reprint ed. mass mkt. 4.99 (*0-380-71034-X*) Avon.

— Tin for Sale: My Career in Organized Crime & the NYPD. 288p. 1991. 20.00 (*0-688-09466-X*) Morrow.

Manca, Joseph. The Art of Ercole de' Roberti. (C). 1992. 150.00 (*0-521-39462-7*) Cambridge U Pr.

— Titian Five Hundred. 1993. 0.70 (*0-89468-194-X*) Natl Gallery Art.

***Manca, Luigi & Manca, Alessandra, eds.** Gender & Utopia in Advertising: A Critical Reader. 1995. 14.95 (*0-8156-8119-4*) Syracuse U Pr.

Manca, Marie A. Harmony & the Poet: The Creative Ordering of Reality. (De Proprietatibus Litterarum, Series Major: No. 4). 1978. 34.00 (*90-279-3086-4*) Mouton.

Mancall, Mark. Russia & China: Their Diplomatic Relations to 1728. LC 74-85077. (Harvard East Asian Ser.: No. 61). 412p. reprint ed. pap. 117.50 (*0-685-20531-2*, 2029993) Bks Demand.

***Mancall, Peter C.** Deadly Medicine: Indians & Alcohol in Early America. (Illus.). 296p. 1995. 29.95 (*0-8014-2762-2*) Cornell U Pr.

— Envisioning America: English Plans for Colonies in North America 1580-1640. 208p. 1995. pap. text ed. 8.65 (*0-312-09670-4*) St Martin.

— Valley of Opportunity: Economic Culture along the Upper Susquehanna, 1700-1800. LC 90-55719. (Illus.). 240p. 1991. 31.95 (*0-8014-2503-4*) Cornell U Pr.

***Mancall, Peter C., ed.** Envisioning America: English Plans for the Colonization of North America, 1580-1640. (Illus.). 208p. 1995. 35.00 (*0-312-12252-7*) St Martin.

— Roll on, River: Rivers in the Lives of the American People. large type ed. (Discovery Through the Humanities Ser.). (Illus.). 185p. (Orig.). 1990. write for info. (*0-910883-58-0*) Natl Coun Aging.

Mance, A. E. Thoughts of a Country Doctor, an Immigrant's Son: In Poetry, 2 vols., Vol. II. 1990. pap. 9.95 (*0-685-61021-7*) McClain.

Mance, Azell. How to Buy a Car Without Getting Cheated. LC 92-60561. (Illus.). 208p. (Orig.). 1993. pap. 29.95 (*0-9633258-0-9*) Share The Know.

Mance, G. Pollution Threat of Heavy Metals in Aquatic Environments. 372p. 1987. 101.00 (*1-85166-039-9*, Pub. by Elsevier Applied Sci UK) Elsevier.

Mancebo, pseud. Villa Sara. LC 90-62235. 240p. (Orig.). 1990. 16.95 (*0-9626993-1-4*) Armadillo Niche.

Mancebo, Manuel R. El Domino Azul. LC 80-66398. (Coleccion Caniqui Ser.). 146p. (Orig.). (SPA.). 1982. pap. 7.95 (*0-89729-259-6*) Ediciones.

***Mancer, Cliff.** Guide to New Zealand Estate Planning & Tax. 297p. 1994. pap. 30.00 (*0-455-21263-5*, Pub. by Law Bk Co) W W Gaunt.

Mancer, Clifford J. Taxation Questions. vii, 122p. 1990. pap. 21.00 (*0-455-21005-5*, Pub. by Law Bk Co) W W Gaunt.

***Manceron, Anne.** Revolution Francais Dictionnaire General. 385p. (FRE.). 1989. 75.00 (*0-7859-8189-6*, 2877420329) Fr & Eur.

Manceron, Claude. The Age of the French Revolution, Vol. 1: Twilight of the Old Order (1774-1778) 1989. 14.95 (*0-318-41868-1*, Touchstone Bks) S&S Trade.

— Revolution Francaise, Dictionnaire Biographique. 571p. (FRE.). 1989. 95.00 (*0-7859-8188-8*, 2877420086) Fr & Eur.

— Toward the Brink. (French Revolution Ser.: Vol. 4). (Illus.). 1983. 22.95 (*0-394-51533-1*) Knopf.

Manchanda, S. C., jt. auth. see Shabbir, Mahammod.

Manchel, Frank. Film Study: A Resource Guide. LC 72-3262. 422p. 1973. 27.50 (*0-8386-1225-3*) Fairleigh Dickinson.

— Film Study, Vol. 1: An Analytical Bibliography, 4 vols. enl. rev. ed. LC 85-45026. (Illus.). 976p. 1991. 65.00 (*0-8386-3186-X*) Fairleigh Dickinson.

— Film Study, Vol. 1: An Analytical Bibliography, 4 vols., 2. enl. rev. ed. LC 85-45026. (Illus.). 976p. 1991. 65.00 (*0-8386-3412-5*) Fairleigh Dickinson.

— Film Study, Vol. 1: An Analytical Bibliography, 4 vols., 3. enl. rev. ed. LC 85-45026. (Illus.). 976p. 1991. 65.00 (*0-8386-3413-3*) Fairleigh Dickinson.

— Film Study, Vol. 1: An Analytical Bibliography, 4 vols., 4. enl. rev. ed. LC 85-45026. (Illus.). 976p. 1991. 65.00 (*0-8386-3414-1*) Fairleigh Dickinson.

Manchen-Helfen, Otto J. Journey to Tuva. Leighton, Alan, tr. 1992. pap. 15.00 (*1-878986-04-X*) Ethnogphics Pr.

Manchester. Computer Weekly's Guide to Three Hundred Key It Companies. 1991. pap. 160.00 (*0-85384-026-1*) Buttrwrth-Heinemann.

Manchester & Bradford. Review of Textile Progress. 538p. 1972. 75.00 (*0-686-63796-8*) St Mut.

Manchester, A. H. A Modern Legal History of England & Wales, 1750-1950. 1980. pap. 63.00 (*0-406-62264-7*); boxed 76.00 (*0-406-62263-9*) Butterworth Legal Pubs.

— Sources of English Legal History, 1750-1950. 1984. 102.00 (*0-406-51659-6*, U.K.) Butterworth Legal Pubs.

Manchester, A. H., jt. ed. see Ives, E. W.

Manchester Business School Staff. European Business Rankings Annual. 450p. 1992. 160.00 (*1-873477-00-7*, 055560-M94609) Gale.

Manchester, Carol. French Tea. LC 92-45129. 1993. 17.00 (*0-688-11355-9*) Hearst Bks.

Manchester, Colin. Sex Shops & the Law. 200p. 1986. text ed. 55.95 (*0-566-05232-6*, Pub. by Dartmth Pub UK) Ashgate Pub Co.

Manchester, Colin, jt. auth. see Leng, Roger.

Manchester, Diana, ed. Germany Philatelic Society Fortieth Anniversary Anthology. (Illus.). (Orig.). 1989. pap. write for info. (*0-318-65953-0*) D Manchester.

Manchester, Frederick, ed. see Babbitt, Irving.

Manchester, Frederick, jt. tr. see Prabhavananda, Swami.

Manchester, Herbert. Four Centuries of Sport in America. 2nd ed. (Fifty Greatest Bks.). (Illus.). 245p. 1992. reprint ed. 49.00 (*1-56416-031-9*) Derrydale Pr.

— Four Centuries of Sport in America 1490-1890. LC 68-21221. (Illus.). 1972. reprint ed. 55.95 (*0-405-08778-0*, Pub. by Blom Pubns UK) Ayer.

Manchester Historic Association Staff. Manchester Historic Association Collections, Vol. V: 1908. 416p. (Orig.). 1992. pap. text ed. 27.00 (*1-55613-682-X*) Heritage Bk.

— Manchester Historic Association Collections, Vol. VI: 1911. (Illus.). xxxvi, 384p. (Orig.). 1992. pap. text ed. 26.00 (*1-55613-683-8*) Heritage Bk.

— Manchester Historic Association Collections, Vol. IV: 1908-1910. (Illus.). 339p. (Orig.). 1992. reprint ed. pap. 23.50 (*1-55613-625-0*) Heritage Bk.

— Manchester Historic Association Collections, Vol. III: 1902-1903. (Illus.). 235p. (Orig.). reprint ed. pap. 23.50 (*1-55613-624-2*) Heritage Bk.

— Manchester Historic Association Collections, Vol. 1: 1896-1899. (Illus.). 329p. 1992. reprint ed. pap. 22.50 (*1-55613-574-2*) Heritage Bk.

— Manchester Historic Association Collections, Vol. 2: 1900-1901. (Illus.). 138p. 1992. reprint ed. pap. 22.50 (*1-55613-575-0*) Heritage Bk.

Manchester, Jason H., jt. auth. see Ouellette, Robert J.

Manchester, Joe. Balloon Shot. 1968. pap. 2.75 (*0-8222-0093-7*) Dramatists Play.

— Run, Thief Run! 1964. pap. 3.00 (*0-8222-0977-2*) Dramatists Play.

Manchester, Keith, jt. auth. see Roberts, Charlotte.

Manchester, Lydia & Bogart, Geoffrey S. Contracting & Volunteerism in Local Government. (Special Report Ser.). 224p. (Orig.). 1988. pap. text ed. 30.00 (*0-87326-933-0*) Intl City-Cnty Mgt.

Manchester, Lydia & Valente, Carl. Service Delivery in the Nineties: Alternative Approaches for Local Governments. Farr, Cheryl, ed. 189p. (Orig.). 1989. pap. text ed. 38.00 (*0-87326-926-8*) Intl City-Cnty Mgt.

Manchester, Martin L. The Philosophical Foundations of Humboldt's Linguistic Doctrines. LC 85-9209. (Studies in the History of the Language Sciences: No. 32). xii, 216p. 1985. 48.00x (*90-272-4514-2*) Benjamins North Am.

Manchester Open Learning Staff. Achieving Goals Through Teamwork. 216p. (Orig.). 1993. pap. text ed. 22.95 (*0-7494-1142-2*, Pub. by Kogan Page UK) Nichols Pub.

— Creating Customer Loyalty. 216p. (Orig.). 1993. pap. text ed. 22.95 (*0-7494-1139-2*, Pub. by Kogan Page UK) Nichols Pub.

— Handling Conflict & Negotiation. 216p. (Orig.). 1993. pap. text ed. 22.95 (*0-7494-1140-6*, Pub. by Kogan Page UK) Nichols Pub.

— Making Effective Presentations. 216p. (Orig.). 1993. pap. text ed. 22.95 (*0-7494-1138-4*, Pub. by Kogan Page UK) Nichols Pub.

— Managing People & Employee Relations. 216p. (Orig.). 1993. pap. text ed. 22.95 (*0-7494-1141-4*, Pub. by Kogan Page UK) Nichols Pub.

— Planning & Managing Change. 216p. (Orig.). 1993. pap. text ed. 22.95 (*0-7494-1143-0*, Pub. by Kogan Page UK) Nichols Pub.

Manchester, Richard B. Amazing Facts: The Indispensable Collection of True Life Facts & Feats. 1991. pap. 7.95 (*0-88486-043-4*) Arrowood Pr.

— Incredible Facts. 1990. pap. 8.95 (*0-88486-036-1*) Arrowood Pr.

— Incredible Facts: The Indispensable Collection of True Life Facts & Oddities. 1994. 7.98 (*0-88365-708-2*) Galahad Bks.

— Mammoth Book of Crossword Puzzles. 1989. pap. 8.95 (*0-88486-030-2*) Arrowood Pr.

— Mammoth Book of Crossword Puzzles. 412p. 1988. reprint ed. pap. 8.95 (*0-912608-74-9*) Mid Atlantic.

— Mammoth Book of Fun & Games. 1991. pap. 8.95 (*0-88486-044-2*) Arrowood Pr.

Manchester, Richard B. Mammoth Book of Word Games. 1990. pap. 8.95 (*0-88486-031-0*) Arrowood Pr.

***Manchester, Richard B.** Pencil Pastimes Book of Fun & Games. 1994. pap. 8.95 (*0-88486-098-1*, Bristol Park Bks) Arrowood Pr.

— The Pencil Pastimes Book of Seek-a-Word. (Pencil Pastimes Ser.). 1992. pap. 6.95 (*0-88486-055-8*) Arrowood Pr.

— Pencil Pastimes Book of Word Games. (Pencil Pastimes Ser.). 1992. pap. 7.95 (*0-88486-056-6*) Arrowood Pr.

Manchester, William. American Caesar: Douglas MacArthur, 1880-1964. 1058p. (gr. 7 up). 1983. mass mkt. 6.95 (*0-440-30424-5*, LE) Dell.

— American Caesar: Douglas MacArthur 1880-1964. LC 78-8004. (Illus.). 1978. 35.00 (*0-316-54498-1*) Little.

— Arms of Krupp: 1587-1968. 1983. mass mkt. 7.99 (*0-553-25992-X*) Bantam.

— The Death of a President: November 1963. LC 88-45174. 752p. 1988. pap. 16.00 (*0-06-091531-5*, HarpT) HarpC.

— Disturber of the Peace: The Life of H. L. Mencken. 2nd ed. LC 86-6999. (Illus.). 376p. 1986. pap. 18.95 (*0-87023-544-3*) U of Mass Pr.

— The Glory & the Dream: A Narrative History of America, 1932-1972. 1408p. 1984. pap. 23.50 (*0-553-34589-3*) Bantam.

— Goodbye, Darkness. 1987. mass mkt. 6.99 (*0-440-32907-8*, LE) Dell.

— In Our Time: The World As Seen by Magnum Photographers. 456p. 1994. pap. 39.95 (*0-393-31129-5*) Norton.

— The Last Lion: Biography of Winston Churchill, 1932-40. (Illus.). 800p. 1988. 40.00 (*0-316-54512-0*) Little.

— The Last Lion: Winston Spencer Churchill Visions of Glory, 1874-1932. LC 82-24972. (Illus.). 1983. 35.00 (*0-316-54503-1*) Little.

— The Last Lion - Winston Spencer Churchill: Alone, 1932-1940. 1989. pap. 16.95 (*0-385-31331-4*, Delta) Dell.

— One Brief Shining Moment: Remembering Kennedy. (Illus.). 280p. 1988. pap. 16.95 (*0-316-54511-2*) Little.

— A World Lit Only by Fire: The Medieval Mind & the Renaissance - Portrait of an Age. 1993. pap. 12.95 (*0-316-54556-2*) Little.

Manchette, Jean-Patrick. L' Affaire N'Gustro. 224p. (FRE.). 1987. pap. 10.95 (*0-7859-4270-X*, 2070378543) Fr & Eur.

— Fatale. (FRE.). 1983. pap. 8.95 (*0-7859-4192-4*) Fr & Eur.

Manchise, Louis J., jt. auth. see Lobel, Ira B.

Mancho Duque, Maria J., ed. see Jesus, Teresa de.

Mancho, Maria J. The Text & Concordance of the Tratado de la Generacion de la Criatura: I-51 Biblioteca Nacional, Madrid. (Spanish Medical Texts Ser.: No. 11). 10p. 1987. 10.00 (*0-940639-07-6*) Hispanic Seminary.

Manchot, C. The Cutaneous Arteries of the Human Body. (Illus.). 149p. 1983. 145.00 (*0-387-90792-0*) Spr-Verlag.

Manci, William E. Farming & the Environment. LC 93-13046. (Environment Alert! Ser.). (J). 1993. 17.27 (*0-8368-0731-6*) Gareth Stevens Inc.

Mancia, Mauro. In the Gaze of Narcissus: Memory, Affects, & Creativity. 220p. (C). 1994. pap. 31.95 (*1-85575-042-2*, Pub. by Karnac Bks UK) Brunner-Mazel.

Mancia, Mauro & Marini, Gabriella. The Diencephalon & Sleep. 432p. 1990. 67.00 (*0-88167-682-9*) Raven.

Manciaux, M., ed. Handicaps in Childhood. (Child Health & Development Ser.: Vol. 1). (Illus.). x, 182p. 1982. 66.50 (*3-8055-2935-X*) S Karger.

Manciaux, M., et al. Sante de la Mere et de l'Enfant: Nouveaux Concepts en Pediatrie Sociale. 2nd ed. (Illus.). 504p. 1984. lib. bdg. 35.00 (*0-318-04482-X*) S M P F Inc.

Mancing, Howard. The Chivalric World of Don Quijote: Style, Structure, & Narrative Technique. LC 81-10475. (Illus.). 252p. 1982. text ed. 28.00 (*0-8262-0350-7*) U of Mo Pr.

— The Golden Age Comedia: Text, Theory, & Performance. Ganelin, Charles, ed. LC 93-1959. 432p. 1994. 44.00 (*1-55753-042-4*) Purdue U Pr.

Mancini. Decision Making in Emergency Nursing. (Illus.). 218p. (C). 1987. 32.95 (*1-55664-003-X*) Mosby Yr Bk.

— Sounds & Scores. 1995. audio, pap. text ed. 29.95 (*0-89898-666-4*, XW1705) CPP Belwin.

— Sounds & Scores. 1995. cd-rom, pap. text ed. 32.95 (*0-89898-667-2*, XW1705) CPP Belwin.

Mancini, ed. Upper Cretaceous & Paleogene Biostratigraphy & Lithostratigraphy of the Eastern Gulf Coastal Plain, No. T372. (IGC Field Trip Guidebooks Ser.). 128p. 1989. 28.00 (*0-87590-561-7*) Am Geophysical.

Mancini, Anthony. Godmother. LC 93-70895. 288p. 1993. 21.95 (*1-55611-376-5*) D I Fine.

— Menage. LC 88-45470. 1989. 16.95 (*1-55611-117-7*) D I Fine.

— Talons. 1991. 19.95 (*1-55611-234-3*) D I Fine.

— The Yellow Gardenia. 1990. 18.95 (*1-55611-209-2*) D I Fine.

Mancini, Elaine. Struggles of the Italian Film Industry During Fascism, 1930-1935. LC 85-1069. (Studies in Cinema: No. 34). (Illus.). 310p. reprint ed. pap. 88.40 (*0-8357-1655-4*, 2070506) Bks Demand.

Mancini, F., ed. Quantum Field Theory: Proceedings of the International Symposium in Honour of Hiroomi Umezawa, Positano, Salerno, Italy, 5-7 June, 1985. 696p. 1986. 84.75 (*0-444-87001-6*) Elsevier.

Mancini, G. B., ed. Clinical Applications of Cardiac Digital Angiography. (Illus.). 336p. 1988. text ed. 108.50 (*0-88167-361-7*) Raven.

Mancini, Genevieve. Uncaring Eyes Can Never See. 1979. 2.95 (*0-686-26182-8*) G Mancini.

Mancini, George. Instant Keyboard: Starter Pack. (Illus.). 48p. pap. 14.95 (*0-7119-1514-8*, AM71424) Music Sales.

Mancini, Gloria. The Falling Away. 1993. pap. text ed. 5.95 (*0-9637646-0-8*) A & O Christ Minist.

Mancini, Henry & Matthais, Johnny. The Hollywood Musicals. 1981. pap. 12.95 (*0-89898-506-4*) CPP Belwin.

Mancini, Henry, jt. auth. see Galway, James.

Mancini, Janet K. Strategic Styles: Coping in the Inner City. LC 79-56773. 349p. reprint ed. pap. 99.50 (*0-8357-6519-9*, 2035890) Bks Demand.

Mancini, M., et al. Treatment of Severe Hypercholesterolemia in the Prevention of Coronary Heart Disease - 2. Gotto, A. M., Jr. et al, eds. viii, 274p. 1990. 63.25 (*3-8055-5085-5*) S Karger.

***Mancini, Marc.** Conducting Tours. 2nd ed. LC 95-10906. 1995. write for info. (*0-8273-7471-2*) Delmar.

— Selling Destinations: Geography for the Travel Professional. 2nd ed. LC 94-13909. 1995. pap. 35.95 (*0-538-63450-2*) S-W Pub.

Mancini, Mario, jt. ed. see Stokes, Joseph, III.

Mancini, Mark. Time Management. LC 93-3443. (Business Skills Express Ser.). 176p. 1993. pap. 10.00 (*1-55623-888-6*) Irwin Prof Pubng.

Mancini, Mary E. Decision Making in Trauma Management: A Multidisciplinary Approach. (Illus.). 464p. (C). 1990. 44.00 (*1-55664-227-X*) Mosby Yr Bk.

Mancini, Matthew. Alexis de Tocqueville. (Twayne's World Authors Ser.). 184p. 1993. text ed. 22.95 (*0-8057-4305-7*, Twayne) Macmillan.

Mancini, Pat M., ed. Contemporary Latin American Short Stories. 480p. 1979. pap. 1.95 (*0-449-30844-8*, Prem) Fawcett.

Mancini, Richard. American Legends of the Wild West. LC 91-58653. (Illus.). 128p. 1992. 12.98 (*1-56138-119-5*) Courage Bks.

— Everything You Need to Know about Living with a Single Parent. rev. ed. (Need to Know Library). (YA). (gr. 7-12). 1995. lib. bdg. 15.95 (*0-8239-2118-2*) Rosen Group.

Mancini, Richard E. Indians of the Southeast. (First Americans Ser.). (Illus.). 96p. (YA). (gr. 5-8). 1991. lib. bdg. 18.95 (*0-8160-2390-5*) Facts on File.

Mancini, Robert E. Pharmacy: Pretest Self-Assessment & Review. (Pretest Specialty Level Ser.). 256p. Date not set. pap. text ed. 29.95 (*0-07-052010-0*) Hlth Prof Div.

Mancini, Stephen C. & Rich, Shellie. Criminal Law & Procedure. (Lex Paralegal Ser.). 249p. (C). 1992. pap. 39.95 (*1-881643-08-5*) Carleston Pub.

Mancke, Richard B. Mexican Oil & Natural Gas: Political, Strategic & Economic Implications. LC 78-27095. 175p. 1979. text ed. 49.95 (*0-275-90386-9*, C0386, Praeger Pubs) Greenwood.

Manclark, C. R. & Hennessen, W., eds. Pertussis. (Developments in Biological Standardization Ser.: Vol. 61). (Illus.). xii, 600p. 1986. pap. 240.00 (*3-8055-4210-0*) S Karger.

Manco-Johnson, Michael L., et al. Diagnostic Ultrasound Test & Syllabus, Vol. 23. (Professional Self-Evaluation & Continuing Education Program Ser.). (Illus.). 700p. 1988. 150.00 (*1-55903-023-2*) Am Coll Radiology.

***Mancoff, Debra N.** The Return of King Arthur: The Legend Through Victorian Eyes. LC 95-6473. 1995. write for info. (*0-8109-3782-4*) Abrams.

Mancoff, Debra N., ed. The Arthurian Revival: Essays on Form, Tradition, & Transformation. LC 92-8108. (Illus.). 360p. 1992. 49.00 (*0-8153-0060-3*, H1419) Garland.

Mancoff, Neal A. & Weiner, David M. Nonqualified Deferred Compensation Arrangements. 1990. 145.00 (*0-685-24500-4*) Clark Boardman Callaghan.

Mancoff, Neil & Steinberg, Allen. Qualified Deferred Compensation Plans: Forms, 1 vol. LC 83-23222. 798p. 1990. 135.00 (*0-317-11358-5*) Clark Boardman Callaghan.

***Mancosu, Paolo.** Philosophy of Mathematics & Mathematical Practices in the Seventeenth Century. (Illus.). 336p. 1995. 65.00 (*0-19-508463-2*) OUP.

Mancour, T. L. Spartacus. Stern, Dave, ed. (Star Trek: The Next Generation Ser.: No. 20). 288p. (Orig.). 1992. mass mkt. 5.50 (*0-671-76051-3*) PB.

Mancusi-Ungaro, Donna. Dante & the Empire. (American University Studies: Romance Languages & Literature: Ser. II, Vol. 49). 201p. 1987. text ed. 73.95 (*0-8204-0337-7*) P Lang Pubs.

Mancusi-Ungaro, Harold R., Jr. Michelangelo: The Bruges Madonna & the Piccolomini Altar. LC 70-151582. (College Ser.: No. 11). (Illus.). 240p. reprint ed. 68.40 (*0-8357-9387-7*, 2013192) Bks Demand.

Mancuso. Couplings & Joints: Design, Selection & Application. (Mechanical Engineering Ser.: Vol. 45). 488p. 1986. 140.00 (*0-8247-7400-0*) Dekker.

Mancuso, Anthony. California Incorporator: 1.0. 336p. 1990. disk 129.00 (*0-87337-027-9*) Nolo Pr.

— The California NonProfit Corporation Handbook. 6th ed. 1991. pap. 29.95 (*0-87337-139-9*) Nolo Pr.

— The California Professional Corporation Handbook. 5th ed. LC 93-40930. 1993. pap. 34.95 (*0-87337-234-4*) Nolo Pr.

— Form Your Own Limited Liability Company: National. 300p. 1996. 29.95 (*0-87337-307-3*) Nolo Pr.

— How to Form a California Nonprofit Corporation with Corporate Records. 3rd ed. LC 94-36211. (Illus.). 400p. 1995. disk, ring bd. 49.95 (*0-87337-278-6*) Nolo Pr.

— How to Form a Nonprofit Corporation: 2nd National Edition, Set, incl. disk. 2nd ed. (Illus.). 368p. 1994. pap. 39.95 (*0-87337-259-X*) Nolo Pr.

— How to Form Your Own California Corporation: With Corporate Records Binder & Disk. 288p. 1994. pap. 39.95 (*0-87337-248-4*) Nolo Pr.

— How to Form Your Own Florida Corporation. 3rd ed. 225p. (Orig.). 1990. disk, pap. 39.95 (*0-87337-145-3*) Nolo Pr.

— How to Form Your Own New York Corporation. 3rd ed. LC 94-24780. 272p. 1994. disk, pap. 39.95 (*0-87337-277-8*) Nolo Pr.

— How to Form Your Own Texas Corporation, Set, incl. disk. 4th ed. 1988. disk, pap. 39.95 (*0-87337-255-7*) Nolo Pr.

— Taking Care of Your Corporation Vol. 2: Key Corporate Decisions Made Easy. 1995. disk, pap. 39.95 (*0-87337-276-X*) Nolo Pr.

— Taking Care of Your Corporation Vol. 2: Key Corporate Decisions Made Easy. 320p. 1995. 3.5 hd, pap. 39.95 (*0-614-04421-9*) Nolo Pr.

Mancuso, Anthony, et al. Computed Tomography & Magnetic Resonance Imaging of the Head & Neck. 2nd ed. (Illus.). 504p. 1985. 99.95 (*0-683-05476-7*) Williams & Wilkins.

Mancuso, Anthony A. Workbook for MRI & CT of the Head & Neck. 2nd ed. (Illus.). 236p. 1989. 60.00 (*0-683-05478-3*) Williams & Wilkins.

Mancuso, George A., jt. auth. see Lane, Caren B.

Mancuso, James C. & Shaw, Mildred L., eds. Cognition & Personal Structure: Computer Access & Analysis. LC 87-13770. 352p. 1988. text ed. 65.00 (*0-275-92606-0*, C2606, Praeger Pubs) Greenwood.

Mancuso, James C., ed. see Adams-Webber, Jack R.

Mancuso, James C., jt. auth. see Adams-Weber, James.

Mancuso, Jon R., jt. ed. see South, David W.

Mancuso, Joseph. The Entrepreneur's Handbook, 2 vols., 1. LC 74-82601. reprint ed. pap. 63.30 (*0-317-27677-8*, 2025055) Bks Demand.

— The Entrepreneur's Handbook, 2 vols., 2. LC 74-82601. reprint ed. pap. 61.80 (*0-317-27678-6*) Bks Demand.

— Four Hundred & Two Things You Must Know Before Starting a New Business. 1980. pap. 9.95 (*0-13-329128-6*, Busn) P-H.

— How to Buy & Manage a Franchise. 1993. pap. 11.00 (*0-671-76775-5*, Fireside) S&S Trade.

— How to Get a Business Loan: Featuring Andrew Tobias' MANAGING YOUR MONEY Software. 1993. Includes diskette. disk 45.00 (*0-679-74465-7*) Random.

— How to Start, Finance, & Manage Your Own Small Business. 1990. pap. 17.00 (*0-671-76356-3*) P-H.

— Managing Technology Products, Vol. 1. LC 74-82598. (Modern Frontiers in Applied Science Ser.). 184p. reprint ed. pap. 52.50 (*0-685-15314-2*, 2027161) Bks Demand.

— Winning with the Power of Persuasion: Mancuso's Secrets for Small Business Success. LC 93-9176. 304p. 1993. 19.95 (*0-7931-0517-X*, 561559) Dearborn Finan.

Mancuso, Joseph, ed. Marketing Technology Products. LC 77-352039. (Technology Products Ser.: No. 2). (Illus.). 205p. reprint ed. pap. 58.50 (*0-8357-4182-6*, 2036960) Bks Demand.

Mancuso, Joseph C. Mastering Technical Writing. 1990. pap. 29.95 (*0-201-52350-7*) Addison-Wesley.

— Technical Editing. 208p. 1991. text ed. 44.00 (*0-13-898503-0*, 640704) P-H.

— Technical Editing. 191p. 1994. 44.00 (*0-9643750-0-1*) Training Edge.

***Mancuso, Joseph R.** Mancuso's Small Business Basics: Start, Buy or Franchise Your Way to a Successful Business. (Small Business Sourcebooks Ser.). 188p. 1996. 17.95 (*1-57071-077-5*); pap. 9.95 (*1-57071-076-7*) Sourcebks.

— Mancuso's Small Business Resource Guide. (Small Business Sourcebooks Ser.). 1995. pap. 9.95 (*1-57071-066-X*) Sourcebks.

— Mancuso's Small Business Resource Guide. rev. ed. (Small Business Sourcebooks Ser.). 160p. 1995. 17.95 (*1-57071-067-8*) Sourcebks.

— Mid-Career Entrepreneur: How to Start a Business & Be Your Own Boss. 235p. 1993. pap. 17.95 (*0-7931-0719-9*, 561410) Dearborn Finan.

Mancuso, Joseph R., jt. auth. see Baumback, Clifford M.

Mancuso, Laurence. Liturgical Music: Dogmatica & Other Selections, Vol. II. (Monastic Offices at New Skete Ser.). 107p. 1978. pap. 15.00 (*0-9607924-2-2*) Monks of New Skete.

— Liturgical Music: Selection for Vespers, Matins, & Liturgy, Vol. I. (Monastic Offices at New Skete Ser.). 172p. 1975. 18.00 (*0-9607924-0-6*); pap. 15.00 (*0-9607924-1-4*) Monks of New Skete.

Mancuso, Laurence, tr. The Prayerbook: Book of Hours. (Illus.). 752p. 1976. 35.00 (*0-9607924-3-0*) Monks of New Skete.

— Troparia & Kondakia. 452p. 1984. 49.50 (*0-9607924-7-3*) Monks of New Skete.

Mancuso, Laurence, tr. see Monks of New Skete Staff.

Mancuso, Laurence, ed. see Monks of New Skete Staff.

Mancuso, Laurence, tr. see Monks of New Skete Staff.

Mancuso, Laurence, ed. see Monks of New Skete Staff.

Mancuso, Laurence, tr. see Monks of New Skete Staff.

Mancuso, Laurence, tr. see Monks of New Skete.

Mancuso, Laurence, tr. see onks of New Skete, M.

Mancuso, Laurence, tr. see The, Monks of New Skete Staff.

***Mancuso, Maureen.** The Ethical World of British MPs. 248p. 1995. 44.95 (*0-7735-1261-6*) U of Toronto Pr.

Mancuso, Maureen, et al, eds. Leaders & Leadership in Canada. 448p. 1994. pap. 29.95 (*0-19-540922-1*) OUP.

Mancuso, Robert A. Question the Direction: A Program for Teaching Careful Listening & the Questioning of Unclear Directions. (J). (gr. 1-7). 1988. student ed 29.95 (*1-55999-065-1*) LinguiSystems.

Mancuso, S., ed. Achievements in Gynecology. (Contributions to Gynecology & Obstetrics Ser.: Vol. 17). (Illus.). vi, 130p. 1989. 78.50 (*3-8055-4825-7*) S Karger.

— Achievements in Gynecology 1989-90. (Contributions to Gynecology & Obstetrics Ser.: Vol. 18). (Illus.). x, 186p. (C). 1991. 144.00 (*3-8055-5122-3*) S Karger.

— Current Status of Fetal Medicine & Its Future, 1989: Journal: Fetal Therapy, Vol. 4, Suppl. 1. (Illus.). vi, 134p. 1990. pap. 39.25 (*3-8055-5284-X*) S Karger.

Mancuso, Ted & Hill, Frank. Kung Fu for Young People. LC 82-80287. (Specialties Ser.). 96p. (Orig.). (J). (ps-7). 1982. pap. 9.95 (*0-89750-079-2*, 416) Ohara Pubns.

Mancuso, Ted, jt. auth. see Lam, Kwon W.

Mancuso, Tony. Taking Care of Your Corporation Vol. 1: Director & Shareholder Meetings Made Easy. 300p. 1994. 26.95 (*0-87337-223-9*) Nolo Pr.

Mancy. Environmental Health Sciences. 1995. write for info. (*0-87371-028-2*) Lewis Pubs.

Manda, Swami Jyotir. Yoga Stories & Parables. (Illus.). 1976. pap. 6.99 (*0-934664-41-2*) Yoga Res Foun.

Mandabach, Frederick A., jt. auth. see Adams, Stephen.

Mandahar, C. L., ed. Plant Viruses: Structure & Replication. (Illus.). 368p. 1989. 270.00 (*0-8493-6947-9*, QR351) CRC Pr.

— Plant Viruses, Vol. II: Pathology. (Illus.). 368p. 1990. 271.00 (*0-8493-6948-7*, QR351) CRC Pr.

Mandahl-Barth, G. Intermediate Hosts of Schistosoma: African Biomphalaria & Bulinus. (Monograph Ser.: No. 37). 132p. (ENG, FRE & SPA.). 1958. 5.60 (*92-4-140037-4*) World Health.

Mandal, Anil K. Assessment of Urinary Sediment by Electron Microscopy: Applications in Renal Disease. LC 87-14153. 284p. 1987. 69.50 (*0-306-42521-1*, Plenum Pr) Plenum.

Mandal, Anil K. & Jennette, J. Charles, eds. Diagnosis & Management of Renal Disease & Hypertension. 2nd ed. LC 93-73562. (Illus.). 548p. (C). 1994. boxed 98.50 (*0-89089-557-0*) Carolina Acad Pr.

— Diagnosis & Management of Renal Disease & Hypertension. LC 87-29884. 556p. reprint ed. pap. 158.50 (*0-7837-2850-6*, 2057622) Bks Demand.

Mandal, Ashis K., jt. auth. see Thadepalli, Haragopal.

***Mandal, B. N., ed.** Mathematical Techniques for Water Wave Problems. (Advances in Fluid Mechanics Ser.). 300p. 1996. text ed. 118.00 (*1-85312-413-3*) Computational Mech MA.

Mandal, Bankim C. Srikanthacarita: A Mahakavya of Mankhaka. (C). 1992. 24.00 (*0-8364-2798-X*, Pub. by Sanskrit Pustake) S Asia.

***Mandal, Bibhat K., et al.** Lecture Notes on Infectious Diseases. LC 95-8411. 1995. write for info. (*0-632-03351-7*) Blackwell Sci.

Mandal, Gobinda C. Rural Development: Retrospect & Prospect. (C). 1992. text ed. 16.00 (*81-7022-396-2*, Pub. by Concept II) S Asia.

Mandal, J. N., ed. First Indian Geotextiles Conference on Reinforced Soil & Teotextiles: Proceedings. (C). 1988. 44.00 (*81-204-0377-0*, Pub. by Oxford IBH II) S Asia.

***Mandal, J. N. & Divshikar, D. G.** Soil Testing in Civil Engineering. (Illus.). 256p. 1995. 85.00 (*90-5410-233-0*) Balkema RSA.

Mandal, N. C., jt. auth. see Dasgupta, M. K.

***Mandal, R.** Privatisation in the Third World. (C). 1994. 22.50x (*0-7069-7318-6*, Pub. by Vikas II) S Asia.

Mandal, Tirtha. Women Revolutionaries of Bengal, 1905-1939. (C). 1991. text ed. 14.00 (*81-85195-41-2*, Pub. by Minerva II) S Asia.

Mandala, Elias C. Work & Control in a Peasant Economy: A History of the Lower Tchiri Valley in Malawi, 1859-1960. LC 90-50093. 480p. (Orig.). (C). 1990. text ed. 49.50 (*0-299-12490-8*); pap. text ed. 22.50 (*0-299-12494-0*) U of Wis Pr.

Mandali, Monique. Everyone's Mandala Coloring Book, Vol. 2. (Illus.). 48p. (Orig.). 1994. pap. 8.95 (*1-56044-295-6*) Falcon Pr MT.

Mandali, Monique, illus. Everyone's Mandala Coloring Book. 48p. (Orig.). 1991. pap. 8.95 (*1-56044-014-7*) Falcon Pr MT.

Mandarino, Joseph A. & Anderson, Violet. Monteregian Treasures: The Minerals of Mont Saint-Hilaire, Quebec. (Illus.). 350p. 1989. 94.95 (*0-521-32632-X*) Cambridge U Pr.

Mandat-Grancey, Edmond. Cow-boys & Colonels: Narrative of a Journey Across the Prairie & over the Black Hills of Dakota. LC 83-23583. (Illus.). 378p. reprint ed. pap. 107.80 (*0-7837-1840-3*, 2042036) Bks Demand.

Mandava & Ito. Countercurrent Chromatography: Theory & Practice. (Chromatographic Science Ser.: Vol. 44). 752p. 1988. 199.00 (*0-8247-7815-4*) Dekker.

Mandava, N. Bhushan, ed. Handbook of Natural Pesticides: Methods, 2 vols., Vol. I: Theory, Practice, & Detection. 552p. 1985. 214.95 (*0-8493-3651-1*, SB951, CRC Reprint) Franklin.

— Handbook of Natural Pesticides: Methods, 2 vols., Vol. II: Isolation & Identification. 576p. 1985. 214.95 (*0-8493-3652-X*, SB957, CRC Reprint) Franklin.

— Plant Growth Substances. LC 79-18933. (ACS Symposium Ser.: No. 111). 1979. 43.95 (*0-8412-0518-3*) Am Chemical.

Mandava, N. Bhushan & Morgan, E. David, eds. Handbook of Natural Pesticides: Pheromones, 2 pts., Pt. A: Insect Olfaction & Molecular Structure. 224p. 1988. Pt. A, Insect Olfaction & Molecular Structure, 224 pgs. 195.95 (*0-8493-3657-0*, SB951) CRC Pr.

— Handbook of Natural Pesticides: Pheromones, 2 pts., Pt. B: Pheromones of Diptera. 368p. 1988. Pt. B, Pheromones of Diptera, 368 pgs. 216.95 (*0-8493-3658-9*, SB951) CRC Pr.

Mandavdhare, S. M. Caste & Land Relations in India. 1989. 46.00 (*81-85024-50-2*, Pub. by Uppal Pub Hse II) S Asia.

Mandaville, James P. The Flora of Eastern Saudi Arabia. (Illus.). 600p. 1990. 125.00 (*0-7103-0371-8*, A4186, Pub. by Kegan Paul Intl UK) Routledge Chapman & Hall.

Mandaza, Ibbo & Magubane, Bernard, eds. Whither South Africa? LC 86-73224. 250p. (C). 1988. 29.95 (*0-86543-048-9*); pap. 9.95 (*0-86543-049-7*) Africa World.

Mande, C., jt. ed. see Bonnelle, C.

Mande, Pierre. The Broken E String: A Collection of Short Stories. (Illus.). 67p. 1988. 7.95 (*0-935087-17-6*) Wright Pub Co.

Mandekic, Anthony V. Your Heavenly Children-Alleluia! LC 82-90171. 170p. (Orig.). 1983. pap. text ed. 6.00 (*0-9608312-0-7*) Mandekic.

***Mandel.** Analysis of Two-Way Layouts. 1994. (*0-412-98611-6*) Chapman & Hall.

— Cardiac Arrhythmias. 3rd ed. 860p. 1995. write for info. (*0-397-51185-X*) Lippincott.

— Trotsky As an Alternative. 256p. (Orig.). 1995. 64.95x (*1-85984-995-4*, C0500, Pub. by Verso UK); pap. 18.95 (*1-85984-085-X*, C051, Pub. by Verso UK) Routledge Chapman & Hall.

Mandel & Wagoner. Atlas of Corneal Disease. 160p. 1989. text ed. 164.00 (*0-7216-2160-0*) Saunders.

Mandel, Adrienne, ed. see De Marivaux, Pierre C.

Mandel, Adrienne S., tr. see De Marivaux, Pierre C.

Mandel, Alan. The S. E. X. Blackjack System. LC 86-70882. (Illus.). 224p. (Orig.). 1987. pap. 12.95 (*0-9616765-0-7*) Bronx Bks.

Mandel, Allan, et al, contribs. Community Indicators: Improving Community Management. (Policy Research Project Report Ser.: No. 6). 149p. 1974. 3.00 (*0-318-00177-2*) LBJ Sch Pub Aff.

Mandel, B. J. Statistics for Management: A Practical Introduction to Statistics. 5th ed. LC 83-73694. 528p. 1984. 25.00 (*0-685-81631-1*, 0-910486) Dangary Pub.

Mandel, Bob. Heart over Heels: Fifty Ways Not to Lose Your Lover. LC 88-31159. 272p. (Orig.). 1988. pap. 9.95 (*0-89087-541-3*) Celestial Arts.

— Open Heart Therapy. LC 84-45360. 160p. (Orig.). 1984. pap. 8.95 (*0-89087-408-5*) Celestial Arts.

— Two Hearts Are Better Than One. LC 85-29922. 220p. (Orig.). 1986. pap. 9.95 (*0-89087-454-9*) Celestial Arts.

— Wake up to Wealth. LC 93-38528. 1994. 9.95 (*0-89087-709-2*) Celestial Arts.

Mandel, Bob, jt. auth. see Ray, Sondra.

Mandel, C. Applied Network Optimization. LC 79-40808. 1980. text ed. 101.00 (*0-12-468350-9*) Acad Pr.

Mandel, C. E., Jr. Tutorial: Environmental Stress Screening. rev. ed. 125p. 1991. pap. 100.00 (*1-877862-09-6*) Inst Environ Sci.

Mandel, C. E., Jr. & Livesay, Billy R. Defect Induced Failure Mechanisms: Accelerated by Environmental Stress Screening. rev. ed. LC 62-38584. 200p. (Orig.). 1990. pap. text ed. 100.00 (*1-877862-04-5*) Inst Environ Sci.

Mandel, Charlotte. A Disc of Clear Water. LC 80-25317. (Illus.). 66p. (Orig.). 1981. pap. 5.00 (*0-938158-00-7*) Saturday Pr.

— Doll. (Illus.). 24p. 1986. pap. 4.00 (*0-938535-74-9*) Salt-Works Pr.

— Keeping Him Alive. Little, Geraldine C., ed. 32p. (Orig.). 1990. pap. 4.50 (*0-943710-04-9*); pap. text ed. 4.50 (*0-685-46214-5*) Silver App Pr.

— The Life of Mary, a Poem-Novella. LC 87-28677. (Illus.). 72p. (Orig.). 1988. pap. 7.00 (*0-938158-10-4*) Saturday Pr.

— The Life of Mary, a Poem-Novella. LC 87-28677. (Orig.). 1993. digital audio 9.00 (*0-938158-14-7*) Saturday Pr.

— The Marriages of Jacob: A Poem Novella. LC 91-10855. 110p. (Orig.). 1991. pap. 10.00 (*0-916288-32-3*) Micah Pubns.

Mandel, Charlotte, et al, eds. Saturday's Women. LC 82-10278. (Eileen W. Barnes Award Ser.). 102p. (Orig.). 1982. pap. 6.50 (*0-938158-02-3*) Saturday Pr.

Mandel, David. Rabotiagi: Perestroika & after Viewed from Below. 288p. (C). 1993. text ed. 34.00 (*0-85345-879-0*); pap. text ed. 16.00 (*0-85345-878-2*) Monthly Rev.

Mandel, Dorothy. Uncommon Eloquence: A Biography of Angna Enters. LC 86-17386. (Illus.). 368p. (Orig.). 1986. 24.50 (*0-912869-07-0*) Arden Pr.

Mandel, Edmund. The Right Path: The Autobiography of a Survivor. LC 94-6632. 1994. 29.50 (*0-88125-498-3*) Ktav.

Mandel, Elias, jt. auth. see Meilach, Dona Z.

Mandel, Ellen, jt. auth. see Lydon, Michael.

Mandel, Ernest. Beyond Perestroika. 300p. 1988. 60.00 (*0-86091-223-X*, Pub. by Verso UK); pap. 18.95 (*0-86091-935-8*, Pub. by Verso UK) Routledge Chapman & Hall.

— Beyond Perestroika: The Future of Gorbachev's U. S. S. R. rev. ed. Fagan, Gus, tr. 300p. 1991. 64.95 (*0-86091-339-2*, A6355, Pub. by Verso UK); pap. 18.95 (*0-86091-549-2*, A6359, Pub. by Verso UK) Routledge Chapman & Hall.

— Bureaucracy: A Marxist Theory. 320p. 1991. 59.95 (*0-86091-321-X*, A5359, Pub. by Verso UK); pap. 18.95 (*0-86091-548-4*, A5761, Pub. by Verso UK) Routledge Chapman & Hall.

— Delightful Murder: A Social History of the Crime Story. LC 85-8679. vii, 152p. 1985. text ed. 24.95 (*0-8166-1463-6*); pap. text ed. 9.95 (*0-8166-1464-4*) U of Minn Pr.

— Introduction to Marxism. (C). 1982. pap. text ed. 14.95 (*0-86104-389-8*) Westview.

— Introduction to Marxist Economic Theory. 2nd ed. Pathfinder Press Staff, ed. LC 73-82169. 80p. 1992. reprint ed. lib. bdg. 30.00 (*0-87348-314-6*); reprint ed. pap. 9.95 (*0-87348-315-4*) Pathfinder NY.

— Late Capitalism. 624p. 1987. pap. 19.95 (*0-86091-703-7*, Pub. by Verso UK) Routledge Chapman & Hall.

— Long Waves of Capitalist Development: A Marxist Interpretation. rev. ed. 360p. 1995. pap. 22.95 (*1-85984-037-X*, C0480, Pub. by Verso UK) Routledge Chapman & Hall.

— Marxist Economic Theory, 2 vols., 2. Pearce, Brian, tr. LC 68-13658. 417p. reprint ed. pap. 118.90 (*0-8357-6204-1*, 2034336) Bks Demand.

— Marxist Economic Theory, 2 vols., Vol. 1. Pearce, Brian, tr. LC 68-13658. 383p. reprint ed. pap. 109.20 (*0-8357-6203-3*, 2034336) Bks Demand.

— The Meaning of the Second World War. 210p. 1986. 50.00 (*0-86091-130-6*, Pub. by Verso UK); pap. 15.95 (*0-86091-842-4*, Pub. by Verso UK) Routledge Chapman & Hall.

— The Place of Marxism in History. LC 93-12067. (Revolutionary Studies). 112p. (C). 1994. pap. 9.95 (*0-391-03814-1*) Humanities.

— The Second Slump: A Marxist Analysis of Recession in the Seventies. 226p. 1985. pap. 15.95 (*0-86091-728-2*) Routledge Chapman & Hall.

Mandel, Ernest & Novack, George. The Marxist Theory of Alienation. 2nd rev. ed. LC 72-96599. (Illus.). 94p. 1995. reprint ed. lib. bdg. 30.00 (*0-87348-229-8*); reprint ed. pap. 10.95 (*0-87348-230-1*) Pathfinder NY.

Mandel, Evelyn. The Art of Aging. Frost, Miriam, ed. Orig. Title: The Gray Matter. (Illus.). 176p. (Orig.). 1982. 14.95 (*0-86683-754-X*) Harper SF.

Mandel, Geoffrey, ed. see Chijiiwa, Hideaki.

Mandel, Gregory. Word 6 for Windows Essentials. (Illus.). 400p. 1994. 29.95 (*1-56609-106-3*) Peachpit Pr.

Mandel, Hal W., jt. auth. see Bleich, Ronald L.

Mandel, Harvey P. Short-Term Psychotherapy & Brief Treatment Techniques: An Annotated Bibliography, 1920-1980. LC 81-221. 704p. 1981. 95.00 (*0-306-40658-6*, Plenum Pr) Plenum.

Mandel, Harvey P. & Marcus, Sander I. The Psychology of Underachievement: Differential Diagnosis & Differential Treatment. LC 87-37127. (Personality Processes Ser.). 397p. 1988. text ed. 60.00 (*0-471-84855-7*) Wiley.

Mandel, Heidi, jt. auth. see Mandel, Linda.

An Asterisk (*) at the beginning of an entry indicates that the title is appearing in BIP for the first time.

Mandel, J., et al. Proceedings of the Fourth Mountain Copper Mountain Conference on Multigrid Methods. (Proceedings in Applied Mathematics Ser.: No. 41). xii, 438p. 1989. pap. 44.50 (*0-89871-248-3*) Soc Indus-Appl Math.

Mandel, Jerome. Geoffrey Chaucer: Building the Fragments of the Canterbury Tales. LC 91-55041. 256p. (C). 1992. 39.50 (*0-8386-3454-0*) Fairleigh Dickinson.

Mandel, Jerome, jt. ed. see Stevens, Martin.

Mandel, John. Analysis of Two-Way Layouts. LC 93-48326. 1994. 69.95 (*0-442-01212-8*) Chapman & Hall.
— Evaluation & Control of Measurements. (Quality & Reliability Ser.: Vol. 26). 272p. 1991. 99.75 (*0-8247-8531-2*) Dekker.
— The Statistical Analysis of Experimental Data. LC 83-20599. (Mathematics Ser.). 448p. 1984. reprint ed. pap. 9.95 (*0-486-64666-1*) Dover.

Mandel, L. American Cars. 1984. 24.95 (*0-517-44767-3*) Random Hse Value.

Mandel, L. & Wolf, E., eds. Coherence & Quantum Optics Five. LC 83-23067. 1280p. 1984. 160.00 (*0-306-41517-8*, Plenum Pr) Plenum.
— Selected Papers on Coherence & Fluctuations of Light (1850-1966), MS19. 976p. 1990. pap. 115.00 (*0-8194-0440-3*) SPIE.
— Selected Papers on Coherence & Fluctuations of Light (1850-1966), MS19/HC. 976p. 1990. 130.00 (*0-8194-0439-X*) SPIE.

Mandel, Lazaro, jt. ed. see Eaton, Douglas C.

Mandel, Lazaro J. & Benos, Dale J., eds. Current Topics in Membranes & Transport, Vol. 27. (Serial Publication Ser.). 320p. 1986. text ed. 143.00 (*0-12-153327-1*) Acad Pr.

***Mandel, Leonard & Wolf, Emil.** Optical Coherence & Quantum Optics. (Illus.). 1000p. (C). 1995. write for info. (*0-521-41711-2*) Cambridge U Pr.

Mandel, Linda & Mandel, Heidi. The Treasure of Trash: A Recycling Story. LC 92-41222. (Illus.). 48p. (J). (gr. 4 up). 1993. pap. 12.95 (*0-89529-575-X*) Avery Pub.

Mandel, Margaret. Teddy Bears & Steiff Animals, Second Series. (Illus.). 200p. 1987. 19.95 (*0-89145-356-3*, 1817) Collector Bks.
— Teddy Bears, Annalee Animals. 1990. 19.95 (*0-89145-419-5*) Collector Bks.

Mandel, Margaret F. Teddy Bears & Steiff Animals. (Illus.). 288p. 1991. pap. 9.95 (*0-89145-267-2*) Collector Bks.

Mandel, Mike. Mike Mandel: Making Good Time. (Illus.). 72p. 1989. 27.50 (*0-918290-00-7*) Clatworthy.

Mandel, Miriam. Reading Hemingway: The Facts in the Fictions. LC 94-14481. 609p. 1995. 72.50 (*0-8108-2870-7*) Scarecrow.

Mandel, Morris, jt. auth. see Mandelbaum, Sylvia.

Mandel, Neville. The Arabs & Zionism Before World War One. LC 73-78545. 1977. pap. 11.00 (*0-520-03940-8*) U CA Pr.

Mandel, Oscar. August von Kotzebue: The Comedy, the Man. LC 88-43438. (Illus.). 44p. 1990. lib. bdg. 25.00 (*0-271-00668-4*) Pa St U Pr.
— The Book of Elaborations. LC 85-114320. 320p. 1985. 17.95 (*0-8112-0962-8*); pap. 12.95 (*0-8112-1023-5*, NDP643) New Directions.
— Collected Lyrics & Epigrams. LC 81-410. 104p. 1982. 9.50 (*0-89807-025-2*) Spectrum Prods.
— Collected Plays, 2 vols, 1. LC 70-134738. 1971. write for info. (*0-87775-000-9*) Spectrum Prods.
— Collected Plays, 2 vols, 2. LC 70-134738. 1971. write for info. (*0-87775-001-7*) Spectrum Prods.
— Collected Plays, 2 vols, Set. LC 70-134738. 1971. 24.00 (*0-914502-04-2*); pap. 16.00 (*0-914502-05-0*) Spectrum Prods.
— The Kukkurrik Fables: 43 Mini-Plays for All Media. LC 86-63083. (Illus.). 116p. (Orig.). 1987. pap. 4.25 (*0-914502-06-9*) Spectrum Prods.
— The Patriots of Nantucket: A Romantic Comedy of the American Revolution. LC 75-37367. 84p. 1976. pap. 4.90 (*0-914502-02-6*) Spectrum Prods.
— Philoctetes & the Fall of Troy: Plays, Documents, Iconography, Interpretations. LC 80-28524. (Illus.). 287p. reprint ed. pap. 81.80 (*0-7837-6021-3*, 2045833) Bks Demand.
— Sigismund, Prince of Poland: A Baroque Entertainment. LC 88-204. (Illus.). 72p. (Orig.). (C). 1988. lib. bdg. 25.50 (*0-8191-6930-7*); pap. text ed. 13.50 (*0-8191-6931-5*) U Pr of Amer.
— Simplicities: Poems. LC 74-79131. 64p. 1974. pap. 4.00 (*0-914502-01-8*) Spectrum Prods.
— The Virgin & the Unicorn: Four Plays by Oscar Mandel. LC 93-83430. (Orig.). 1993. pap. 15.95 (*0-914502-10-7*) Spectrum Prods.

Mandel, Oscar, ed. The Theatre of Don Juan: A Collection of Plays & Views, 1630-1963. LC 86-1491. (Illus.). x, 731p. 1986. pap. 30.00 (*0-8032-8137-4*) U of Nebr Pr.

Mandel, Oscar, tr. Five Comedies of Medieval France. LC 82-13499. 158p. (C). 1982. reprint ed. pap. text ed. 18.50 (*0-8191-2668-3*) U Pr of Amer.

Mandel, Oscar, tr. see Corneille, Thomas.

Mandel, Oscar, ed. see De Marivaux, Pierre C.

Mandel, Oscar, tr. see Moliere.

Mandel, Oscar, jt. auth. see Sutherland, John.

Mandel, Oscar, tr. see Tieck, Ludwig.

Mandel, P., et al, eds. From Optical Bistability Towards Optical Computing: The European Joint Optical Bistability Project. 362p. 1987. 107.75 (*0-444-70159-1*, North Holland) Elsevier.

Mandel, Patricia. Selection VII: American Paintings from the Museum's Collection 1800-1930. LC 77-70393. (Illus.). 243p. 1977. 22.00 (*0-911517-37-5*) Mus of Art RI.

Mandel, Patricia C., jt. auth. see O'Brien, Maureen C.

Mandel, Patricia C. F. Fair Wilderness: American Paintings in the Collection of the Adirondack Museum. Gilborn, Alice W. et al, eds. (Illus.). 176p. 1990. pap. 39.95 (*0-910020-40-X*) Adirondack Mus.

***Mandel, Paul & DeFeudis, Francis V., eds.** CNS Receptors: From Molecular Pharmacology to Behavior. LC 83-11175. (Advances in Biochemical Psychopharmacology Ser.: No. 37). (Illus.). reprint ed. pap. 150.20 (*0-7837-9571-8*, 2060320) Bks Demand.

***Mandel, Peter.** Acu-Impulsor Therapy: Treatment with Piezoelectric Impulses. Baker, Christopher & Harrison, Judith, trs. (Illus.). 190p. 1988. text ed. 59.00 (*3-925806-11-3*) Medicina Bio.
— Energy Emission Analysis: New Application of Kirlian Photography for Holistic Health. Greenberg, John, tr. (Illus.). 197p. 1987. text ed. 59.00 (*3-922026-39-7*) Medicina Bio.
— Esogetics: The Sense & Nonsense of Sickness & Pain. Kristen, S. & Allanach, J., trs. (Illus.). 182p. (Orig.). 1993. pap. text ed. 25.00 (*3-925806-71-7*) Medicina Bio.
— If One Lived on the Equator. Page, Carolyn, ed. & illus. by. (Chapbook Ser.). 36p. (Orig.). 1993. pap. 6.95 (*1-879205-42-4*) Nightshade Pr.
— The Official Cat I. Q. Test: Find out How Smart Your Cat Really Is. LC 90-55581. (Illus.). 64p. (Orig.). 1991. pap. 8.00 (*0-06-096592-4*, PL) HarpC.
— The Official Dog I.Q. Test. 60p. 1995. pap. 6.95 (*1-56625-015-3*) Bonus Books.
— Practical Compendium of Colorpuncture. Baker, Christopher, tr. (Illus.). 269p. 1986. text ed. 112.00 (*3-925806-08-3*) Medicina Bio.
— Red Cat, White Cat. (J). 1994. 14.95 (*0-8050-2929-X*) H Holt & Co.

Mandel, Richard D. Weavings from Nahuala: A Mayan Tradition. Cilella, Salvatore G., ed. McRae, Patricia B., tr. (Illus.). 28p. (SPA.). (C). 1992. write for info. (*0-9627858-1-4*) Columbia Mus Art.

Mandel, Robert. The Changing Face of National Security. LC 94-17982. (Contributions in Military Studies Ser.: No. 156). 176p. 1994. text ed. 49.95 (*0-313-28519-5*, Greenwood Pr) Greenwood.
— Conflict over the World's Resources: Background, Trends, Case Studies, & Considerations for the Future. LC 88-15489. (Contributions in Political Science Ser.: No. 225). 156p. 1988. text ed. 42.95 (*0-313-26129-6*, MCQ/) Greenwood.
— Irrationality in International Confrontation. LC 87-7588. (Contributions in Political Science Ser.: No. 185). 162p. 1987. text ed. 49.95 (*0-313-25950-X*, MIY/, Greenwood Pr) Greenwood.

Mandel, Sally. Time to Sing. 1990. mass mkt. 4.95 (*0-06-100066-3*, Harp PBks) HarpC.

Mandel, Siegfried, tr. see Kerenyi, Karl.

Mandel, Siegfried, tr. see Salome, Lou A.

Mandel, Siegfried, ed. see Salome, Lou A.

Mandel, Siegfried, tr. see Salome, Lou.

Mandel, Steve. Effective Presentation Skills. 2nd rev. ed. Gerould, Philip, ed. (Fifty-Minute Ser.). 100p. 1993. pap. 9.95 (*1-56052-202-X*) Crisp Pubns.
— Technical Presentation Skills. rev. ed. Gerould, W. Philip, ed. LC 93-74052. (Illus.). 100p. (Orig.). 1994. pap. 9.95 (*1-56052-263-1*) Crisp Pubns.

Mandel, Steven, et al, eds. Minor Head Trauma. LC 92-49619. 1993. 98.00 (*0-387-97943-3*) Spr-Verlag.

Mandel, Suzy, jt. auth. see Ziefert, Harriet.

Mandel, Theo S. Windows vs. OS 2: The GUI-OOUI War: An Up-Close Look at Computer User Interfaces. (Illus.). 352p. 1994. text ed. 29.95 (*0-442-01750-2*) Van Nos Reinhold.

***Mandel, Thomas & Van Der Leun, Gerard.** Rules of the Net: How to Live & Thrive in Cyberspace Once You've Finally Arrived. 224p. 1996. pap. 12.00 (*0-7868-8135-6*) Hyperion.

Mandel, Thomas E., jt. ed. see Green, Marjorie K.

Mandel, Tom. Erat. deluxe ed. (Burning Deck Poetry Ser.). 24p. (Orig.). 1981. pap. 10.00 (*0-930900-99-5*) Burning Deck.
— Four Strange Books. 128p. (Orig.). (C). 1990. pap. 12.00 (*0-9623399-1-1*) Gaz NJ.
— Letters of the Law. (New American Poetry Ser.: No. 15). 121p. (Orig.). 1994. pap. 10.95 (*1-55713-164-3*) Sun & Moon CA.
— Ready to Go. LC 81-4904. 69p. (Orig.). 1981. pap. 4.00 (*0-87886-113-0*, Greenfld Rev Pr) Greenfld Rev Lit.
— Realism. (Burning Deck Poetry Ser.). 80p. (Orig.). 1991. pap. 8.00 (*0-930901-70-3*) Burning Deck.
— Realism. deluxe ed. (Burning Deck Poetry Ser.). 80p. (Orig.). 1991. Signed. pap. 15.00 (*0-930901-71-1*) Burning Deck.

Mandel, William. The Soviet Far East & Central Asia. LC 75-30111. (Institute of Pacific Relations Ser.). reprint ed. 16.50 (*0-404-59545-6*) AMS Pr.

Mandel, William J., jt. ed. see Griffin, Jerry C.

***Mandel, William M.** Chernobyl Victims at Polesskoe. (Illus.). 60p. (Orig.). 1994. pap. 19.95 (*1-57205-747-5*) Rector Pr.
— A Part of Mine Own Country. 300p. (Orig.). 1995. pap. 20.00 (*0-7605-2332-0*) Rector Pr.
— Russia Re-Examined: The Land, the People & How They Live. (Illus.). 250p. (Orig.). 1994. pap. 29.95 (*1-57205-729-7*) Rector Pr.
— Russian Street-Corner Democracy. (Illus.). 60p. (Orig.). 1994. pap. 19.95 (*1-57205-749-1*) Rector Pr.
— Soviet but Not Russian. rev. ed. (Illus.). 280p. (C). 1994. 24.95 (*1-57205-730-0*) Rector Pr.
— Soviet People Speak: Interviews by & Letters to William Mandel, 1989-1992. (Illus.). 100p. (Orig.). 1994. pap. 19.95 (*1-57205-731-9*) Rector Pr.
— Soviet Women. (Illus.). 250p. (Orig.). 1994. pap. 29.95 (*1-57205-728-9*) Rector Pr.
— U. S. S. R. Life: Fifty Letters to William Mandel Written Before & after the August 1991 Coup. (Illus.). 60p. (Orig.). 1994. pap. 19.95 (*1-57205-750-5*) Rector Pr.

Mandela, Nelson. Long Walk to Freedom: The Autobiography of Nelson Mandela. 1994. 24.95 (*0-316-54585-6*) Little.
— Nelson Mandela: The Struggle Is My Life. 2nd ed. LC 90-63060. 281p. 1990. lib. bdg. 50.00 (*0-87348-594-7*); pap. 15.95 (*0-87348-593-9*) Pathfinder NY.
— Nelson Mandela: Intensifiquemos la Lucha: Discursos en Africa, Europa y Norteamerica. Madrid, Luis, ed. & intro. by. LC 90-63059. (Illus.). 112p. (Orig.). (SPA.). 1990. lib. bdg. 35.00 (*0-87348-598-X*); pap. 13.95 (*0-87348-597-1*) Pathfinder NY.
— Nelson Mandela Speaks: Forging a Democratic, Nonracial South Africa. Clark, Steve, ed. LC 93-85689. (Illus.). 296p. (Orig.). 1993. lib. bdg. 50.00 (*0-87348-775-3*); pap. 18.95 (*0-87348-774-5*) Pathfinder NY.
— Nelson Mandela Speeches 1990: 'Intensify the Struggle to Abolish Apartheid' (Illus.). (Orig.). (C). 1990. pap. 6.00 (*0-87348-595-5*) Pathfinder NY.
— No Easy Walk to Freedom. (African Writers Ser.). (Illus.). 189p. 1990. pap. 8.95 (*0-435-90782-4*, 90782) Heinemann.

Mandela, Nelson & Castro, Fidel. How Far We Slaves Have Come! LC 91-66760. (Illus.). 72p. (Orig.). (C). 1991. lib. bdg. 30.00 (*0-87348-497-5*); pap. 8.95 (*0-87348-729-X*) Pathfinder NY.
— Que Lejos Hemos Llegado los Esclavos! Sudafrica y Cuba En el Mundo De Hoy. LC 91-66761. (Illus.). 83p. (Orig.). (SPA.). 1991. pap. 10.95 (*0-87348-732-X*) Pathfinder NY.

Mandela, Winnie. A Part of My Soul Went with Him. Benjamin, Anne & Benson, Mary, eds. LC 85-21632. (Illus.). 164p. 1985. 14.95 (*0-393-02215-3*); pap. 6.95 (*0-393-30290-3*) Norton.

***Mandelbaum, Allen.** Metamorphoses of Ovid. 1995. pap. 15.00 (*0-15-600126-8*) HarBrace.
— Odyssey of Homer: A New Verse Translation. (Illus.). 1990. 38.00 (*0-520-07021-6*) U CA Pr.
— The Savantasse of Montparnasse. (Illus.). 203p. 1987. 19.95 (*0-935296-70-0*); pap. 12.95 (*0-935296-71-9*) Sheep Meadow.

Mandelbaum, Allen, tr. The Metamorphoses of Ovid. LC 93-8118. 1993. 40.00 (*0-15-170529-1*) HarBrace.

Mandelbaum, Allen, tr. see Alighieri, Dante.

Mandelbaum, Allen, tr. see Dante Alighieri.

Mandelbaum, Allen, tr. see Ovid.

Mandelbaum, Allen, tr. see Virgil.

Mandelbaum, Bernard. Choose Life. 1972. pap. 8.95 (*0-8197-0006-1*) Bloch.
— Tales of the Fathers of the Conservative Movement. LC 89-63758. (Illus.). 80p. 1990. pap. 6.95 (*0-88400-140-7*) Shengold.
— Wisdom of Solomon Schechter. 1963. pap. 2.50 (*0-8381-3103-4*) United Syn Bk.
— You Are Not Alone. LC 88-43148. 96p. 1989. 8.95 (*0-88400-132-6*); pap. 6.95 (*0-88400-133-4*) Shengold.

Mandelbaum, David G. The Plains Cree, Vol 37, Pt. 2. LC 76-43772. reprint ed. 21.00 (*0-404-15626-6*) AMS Pr.
— Society in India, Vol. I: Continuity & Change. 392p. 1970. pap. 16.00 (*0-520-01893-1*) U CA Pr.
— Society in India, Vol. II: Change & Continuity. 408p. 1970. pap. 16.00 (*0-520-01895-8*) U CA Pr.
— Women's Seclusion & Men's Honor: Sex Roles in North India, Bangladesh, & Pakistan. LC 87-36547. 153p. 1988. 24.95 (*0-8165-1043-1*) U of Ariz Pr.
— Women's Seclusion & Men's Honor: Sex Roles in North India, Bangladesh, & Pakistan. LC 87-36547. (Illus.). 153p. 1993. reprint ed. pap. text ed. 12.95 (*0-8165-1400-3*) U of Ariz Pr.

Mandelbaum, David G., ed. see Sapir, Edward.

Mandelbaum, Dorothy R. Making Life Choices: Current Research Findings on Work, Family & Children. 256p. write for info. (*0-275-90005-3*, C0005, Praeger Pubs) Greenwood.

Mandelbaum, Howard & Myers, Eric. Screen Deco. (Illus.). 224p. 1987. pap. 15.95 (*0-312-01087-7*) St Martin.

Mandelbaum, Hugo. Jewish Life in Village Communities of Southern Germany. (Illus.). 96p. 1986. 6.95 (*0-87306-382-1*) Feldheim.

Mandelbaum, Irving J. A History of the Mishnaic Law of Agriculture: Kilayim. Neusner, Jacob, ed. LC 81-1462. (Brown Judaic Studies: No. 26). (C). 1982. pap. text ed. 19.00 (*0-89130-465-7*, 14 00 26) Scholars Pr GA.

Mandelbaum, Irving J., ed. & tr. The Talmud of the Land of Israel, a Preliminary Translation & Explanation, Vol. 4: Kilayim. LC 90-10979. (Chicago Studies in the History of Judaism). (Illus.). 480p. 1991. lib. bdg. 75.00 (*0-226-57661-2*) U Ch Pr.

Mandelbaum, Jonathan, tr. see Bouloiseau, Marc.

Mandelbaum, Jonathan, tr. see Furet, Francois.

Mandelbaum, Jonathan, tr. see Pera, Marcello.

Mandelbaum, Jonathan, tr. see Plessis, Alain.

Mandelbaum, Ken. Not since Carrie: Forty Years of Broadway Musical Flops. (Illus.). 368p. 1991. 24.95 (*0-312-06428-4*) St Martin.
— Not since Carrie: Forty Years of Broadway Musical Flops. (Illus.). 384p. 1992. pap. 14.95 (*0-312-08273-8*) St Martin.

Mandelbaum, Lyn. Consider Yourself Lucky. LC 79-91629. (Illus.). 52p. (Orig.). 1979. pap. 6.00 (*0-935694-00-5*) St Edns.
— Consider Yourself Lucky. deluxe ed. LC 79-91629. (Illus.). 52p. (Orig.). 1979. pap. 12.00 (*0-686-31786-6*) St Edns.
— SAY! deluxe limited ed. (Illus.). 1982. pap. 10.00 (*0-935694-02-1*) St Edns.

Mandelbaum, Maurice. The Phenomenology of Moral Experience. LC 72-13895. (Johns Hopkins Paperbacks Ser.: No. 65). 336p. reprint ed. pap. 95.80 (*0-8357-6745-0*, 2035400) Bks Demand.
— Philosophy, Science, & Sense Perception: Historical and Critical Studies. 288p. 1964. 49.50x (*0-8018-0450-7*); pap. 14.95x (*0-8018-0451-5*) Johns Hopkins.
— Purpose & Necessity in Social Theory. LC 86-46283. 224p. 1987. text ed. 30.00x (*0-8018-3470-8*) Johns Hopkins.

Mandelbaum, Maurice H. The Anatomy of Historical Knowledge. LC 76-46945. 240p. reprint ed. pap. 68.40 (*0-8357-5463-4*, 2024133) Bks Demand.
— History, Man & Reason: A Study in Nineteenth-Century Thought. LC 75-150042. 565p. reprint ed. pap. 161.10 (*0-317-08083-0*, 2019946) Bks Demand.
— The Problem of Historical Knowledge: An Answer to Relativism. LC 74-152993. (Select Bibliographies Reprint Ser.). 1977. reprint ed. 24.95 (*0-8369-5745-8*) Ayer.

Mandelbaum, Michael. The Fate of Nations: The Search for National Security in the Nineteenth & Twentieth Centuries. (Illus.). 384p. 1988. 17.95 (*0-521-35527-3*); pap. 17.95 (*0-521-35790-X*) Cambridge U Pr.
— Making Markets. Islam, Shafiqul, ed. 208p. 1992. pap. 14.95 (*0-87609-129-X*) Coun Foreign.
— The Nuclear Future. LC 82-74068. (Cornell Studies in Security Affairs). 131p. 1983. pap. 9.95 (*0-8014-9254-8*) Cornell U Pr.
— The Nuclear Question. LC 79-388. 1980. pap. 19.95 (*0-521-29614-5*) Cambridge U Pr.
— The Rise of Nations in the Soviet Union: American Foreign Policy & the Disintegration of the U. S. S. R. 104p. 1991. pap. 14.95 (*0-87609-100-1*) Coun Foreign.

Mandelbaum, Michael, ed. America's Defense. LC 87-35705. 360p. 1989. 45.00 (*0-8419-1156-8*); pap. 24.95 (*0-8419-1157-6*) Holmes & Meier.
— Central Asia & the World: Kazakhstan, Krygyzstan, Tajikistan, Turkmenistan, & Uzbekistan. LC 94-7846. 150p. 1994. 16.95 (*0-87609-167-2*) Coun Foreign.
— The Other Side of the Table: The Soviet Approach to Arms Control. 192p. 1990. pap. 16.95 (*0-87609-071-4*) Coun Foreign.
— Western Approaches to the Soviet Union. 128p. 1988. pap. 10.95 (*0-87609-048-X*) Coun Foreign.

Mandelbaum, Michael, jt. auth. see Bialer, Seweryn.

Mandelbaum, Michael, ed. see Mochizuki, Mike M., et al.

Mandelbaum, Paul, ed. First Words. LC 93-4809. 1993. 20.00 (*0-945575-71-8*) Algonquin Bks.

Mandelbaum, Paulette, ed. Acid Rain: Economic Assessment. LC 85-17021. (Environmental Science Research Ser.: Vol. 33). 302p. 1985. 75.00 (*0-306-42102-X*, Plenum Pr) Plenum.

Mandelbaum, Pili. You Be Me, I'll Be You. (Illus.). 40p. (J). (ps-3). 1990. 13.95 (*0-916291-27-8*) Kane-Miller Bk.
— You Be Me, I'll Be You. (Illus.). 40p. (J). (ps-3). reprint ed. pap. 6.95 (*0-916291-47-2*) Kane-Miller Bk.

Mandelbaum, R., jt. ed. see Harper, J.

Mandelbaum, Seymour J. Boss Tweed's New York. 216p. 1990. pap. 8.95 (*0-929587-20-0*, Elephant Paperbacks) I R Dee.
— Boss Tweed's New York. Cantor, Norman F., ed. LC 81-13368. (New Dimensions in History Ser.: Historical Cities). (Illus.). ix, 196p. 1982. reprint ed. text ed. 49.75 (*0-313-23259-8*, MATY, Greenwood Pr) Greenwood.

***Mandelbaum, Seymour J., et al, eds.** Explorations in Planning Theory. 450p. (C). 1995. text ed. 44.95x (*0-88285-153-5*); pap. text ed. 21.95x (*0-88285-154-3*) Ctr Urban Pol Res.

***Mandelbaum, Sylvia & Mandel, Morris.** Marriage: Duet or Duel. 270p. 1992. 14.95 (*965-229-027-0*, Pub. by Gefen Pub Hse IS) Gefen Bks.

Mandelblatt, Abe & Mandelblatt, Malka. Abe & Malka's One Hundred Guitar Accompaniment Patterns. (Illus.). 200p. 1974. pap. 17.95 (*0-8256-2812-1*, AM41369) Music Sales.

Mandelblatt, Malka, jt. auth. see Mandelblatt, Abe.

Mandelbrojt, S. Principles & Methods. LC 75-170339. (Dirichlet Ser.). 166p. 1971. lib. bdg. 71.50 (*90-277-0214-4*) Kluwer Ac.

Mandelbrojt-Sweeney, Mireille. Anglais Medical: Medical English. 168p. (ENG & FRE.). 1992. 49.95 (*0-7859-6918-9*, 2225827028) Fr & Eur.

Mandelbrot, Benoit & Scholz, Christopher H. Fractals in Geophysics. 350p. 1990. 34.50 (*0-8176-2206-3*) Birkhauser.

Mandelbrot, Benoit, jt. auth. see Hirst, Bill.

Mandelbrot, Benoit B. The Fractal Geometry of Nature. LC 81-15085. (Illus.). 460p. (C). 1995. text ed. write for info. (*0-7167-1186-9*) W H Freeman.

Mandeles, Stanley. Nucleic Acid Sequence Analysis. LC 79-186389. (Molecular Biology Ser.). 282p. 1972. text ed. 53.00 (*0-231-03130-0*) Col U Pr.

Mandelis, Andreas. Non-Destructive Evaluation. 1993. text ed. 80.00 (*0-13-147430-8*) P-H.

Mandelis, Andreas, ed. Photoacoustic & Thermal Wave Phenomena in Semiconductors. 480p. 1987. 91.00 (*0-444-01226-5*) P-H.
— Principles & Perspectives of Photothermal & Photoacoustic Phenomena. 1991. 110.00 (*0-444-01641-4*) P-H.

Mandelis, Andreas & Christofides, Constantinos. Physics, Chemistry, & Technology of Solid State Gas Sensor Devices. LC 93-6565. (Chemical Analysis Ser.: Vol. 125). 352p. 1993. Alk. paper. text ed. 69.95 (*0-471-55885-0*) Wiley.

Mandelker, Amy. Framing Anna Karenina: Tolstoy, the Woman Question, & the Victorian Novel. LC 93-5570. (Theory & Interpretation of Narrative Ser.). 241p. 1993. 39.50 (*0-8142-0613-1*) Ohio St U Pr.

Mandelker, Daniel, jt. auth. see Ewald, William.

M

*__Mandelker, Daniel R.__ Land Use Law. 3rd ed. 632p. 1993. 85.00 (1-55834-126-9) Michie Butterworth.
— Land Use Law with 1992 Cumulative Supplement. 2nd ed. 572p. 1988. 43.00 (0-87473-388-X) Michie Butterworth.
— NEPA Law & Litigation. LC 92-24290. 1992. ring bd. 145.00 (0-87632-904-0) Clark Boardman Callaghan.
Mandelker, Daniel R. & Cunningham, Roger A. Planning & Control of Land Development. 3rd ed. (Contemporary Legal Education Ser.). 893p. 1990. text ed. 46.00 (0-87473-669-2) Michie Butterworth.
Mandelker, Daniel R. & Ewald, William R., Jr. Street Graphics & the Law. 3rd ed. LC 87-71118. (Illus.). 207p. 1988. lib. bdg. 52.95 (0-685-18628-8); pap. 35.95 (0-918286-50-6) Planners Pr.
Mandelker, Daniel R. & Montgomery. Housing in America: Problems & Perspectives. LC 73-7689. 1973. pap. 19.95 (0-672-61346-8, Bobbs) Macmillan.
Mandelker, Daniel R. & Netsch, Dawn Clark. State & Local Government in a Federal System. 3rd ed. (Contemporary Legal Education Ser.). 828p. 1990. 40.00 (0-87473-584-X) Michie Butterworth.
— State & Local Government in a Federal System. 3rd suppl. ed. (Contemporary Legal Education Ser.). 828p. 1992. Supplement 1992. 6.00 (0-685-57756-2) Michie Butterworth.
Mandelker, Daniel R., et al. Federal Land Use Law: Limitations, Procedures, Remedies. LC 86-17099. (Real Property-Zoning Ser.). 1986. ring bd. 145.00 (0-87632-516-9) Clark Boardman Callaghan.
— Intergovernmental Decisionmaking for Environmental Protection & Public Works. (Illus.). 85p. (Orig.). (C). 1994. pap. text ed. 35.00x (0-7881-1516-2) Diane Pub.
Mandelker, Ira L. Religion, Society, & Utopia in Nineteenth-Century America. LC 84-47. 200p. 1984. lib. bdg. 25.00 (0-87023-436-6) U of Mass Pr.
Mandelker, Lester, jt. ed. see Glasofer, Seymour.
Mandelkern, L. An Introduction to Macromolecules. 2nd ed. 180p. 1983. pap. 36.00 (0-387-90796-3) Spr-Verlag.
Mandelkern, Leo, ed. see Flory, Paul J.
Mandelkern, Mark. Constructive Continuity. LC 82-24358. (Memoirs of the American Mathematical Society Ser.: No. 42/277). 117p. 1983. pap. 17.00 (0-8218-2277-2, MEMO 42/277) Am Math.
Mandelkern, Nicholas, ed. see Bamberger, David.
*__Mandelkern, Nicholas D. & Weber, Vicki L.__ The Jewish Holiday Home Companion: A Parent's Guide to Family Celebration. (Illus.). 96p. Date not set. pap. 4.50 (0-87441-566-7) Behrman.
Mandelkern, S. Heichal Hakodesh Concordance to the Old Testament, 1 vol. 95.00 (0-87559-163-9) Shalom.
Mandelkorn, Philip, ed. To Know Your Self: The Essential Teachings of Swami Satchidananda. LC 77-80901. 250p. 1988. pap. 9.95 (0-932040-34-9) Integral Yoga Pubns.
Mandell. Acute Rheumatic & Immunological Disease: Management of the Critically Ill Patient. 640p. 1994. 195.00 (0-8247-9125-8) Dekker.
— Imaging Strategies in Pediatric Orthopedics. Date not set. 500.00 (0-685-65361-7) Mosby Yr Bk.
*__Mandell, Arnold J., ed.__ Neurobiological Mechanismms of Adaptation & Behavior. fac. ed. LC 74-14475. (Advances in Biochemical Psychopharmacology Ser.: No. 13). (Illus.). 314p. Date not set. pap. 89.50 (0-7837-7189-4, 2047110) Bks Demand.
Mandell, Arnold J., jt. ed. see Usdin, Earl.
Mandell, Barbara & Penn, Roger. Off the Beaten Track: Spain. LC 93-10704. (Illus.). 315p. (Orig.). 1993. pap. 14.95 (1-56440-296-7) Globe Pequot.
Mandell, Betty R., jt. auth. see Schram, Barbara A.
Mandell, Charlotte, tr. see Blanchot, Maurice.
Mandell, Colleen J. & Fiscus, Edward D. Understanding Exceptional People. (Illus.). 517p. (C). 1981. text ed. 54. 25 (0-8299-0394-1) West Pub.
Mandell, Colleen J., jt. auth. see Fiscus, Edward D.
Mandell, G. L., et al, eds. Pentoxifylline & Analogues: Effects on Leukocyte Function. (Illus.). x, 232p. 1990. 157.00 (3-8055-5302-1) S Karger.
Mandell, Gail P. Life into Art: Conversations with Seven Contemporary Biographers. 229p. 1991. 27.50 (1-55728-180-7) U of Ark Pr.
— Madeleva, 1994: One Woman's Life. LC 94-5932. (Madeleva Lectures). 64p. (Orig.). 1994. pap. 4.95 (0-8091-3499-3) Paulist Pr.
— The Phoenix Paradox: A Study of Renewal Through Change in the "Collected Poems" & "Last Poems" of D. H. Lawrence. LC 83-10563. 288p. 1984. 24.50 (0-8093-1121-6) S Ill U Pr.
Mandell, Gerald L. Principles & Practice of Infectious Disease. 4th ed. 1994. 249.95 (0-443-08935-3) Churchill.
*__Mandell, Gerald L. & Bleck, Thomas P., eds.__ Central Nervous System & Eye Infections. LC 94-41262. (Atlas of Infectious Diseases Ser.: Vol. 3). 1995. write for info. (0-443-07700-2) Current Med.
*__Mandell, Gerald L. & Brook, Itzhak, eds.__ Upper Respiratory & Head & Neck Infections. LC 95-1977. (Atlas of Infectious Diseases Ser.: Vol. 4). 1995. write for info. (0-443-07710-X) Current Med.
Mandell, Gerald L., et al. Principles & Practice of Infectious Diseases: Antimicrobial Therapy, 1992. LC 91-36236. 184p. reprint ed. pap. 52.50 (0-7837-6255-0, 2045967) Bks Demand.
— Principles & Practice of Infectious Diseases: Antimicrobial Therapy, 1993-1994. 200p. 1993. 14.95 (0-443-08938-8) Churchill.
— Principles & Practice of Infectious Diseases: Antimicrobial Therapy, 1993-1994. LC 93-194225. reprint ed. pap. 54.50 (0-7837-9616-1, 2060373) Bks Demand.
— Principles & Practice of Infectious Diseases: Handbook of Antimicrobial Therapy. 166p. (Orig.). 1992. 19.95 (0-443-08818-7) Churchill.
Mandell, Gerald L., et al, eds. Anti-Infective Therapy. LC 85-3135. 536p. reprint ed. pap. 152.80 (0-7837-1615-X, 2041907) Bks Demand.
— Principles & Practice of Infectious Diseases. 2nd ed. LC 84-13076. (Illus.). 1800p. 1988. pap. 180.00 (0-8357-6554-7, 2035919) Bks Demand.
— Principles & Practice of Infectious Diseases. 3rd ed. (Illus.). 2340p. 1990. text ed. 225.00 (0-443-08686-9) Churchill.
Mandell, Harvey & Spiro, Howard, eds. When Doctors Get Sick. LC 87-14104. (Illus.). 484p. 1987. 27.50 (0-306-42653-6, Plenum Med Bk) Plenum.
Mandell, Jack. Workers' Compensation. (Illus.). 93p. 1992. pap. 35.00 (0-317-57854-5) NJ Inst CLE.
Mandell, James, ed. see Mandell, Terri.
*__Mandell, Jim.__ The Studio Business Book. Jewett, Andy, ed. (Illus.). 274p. (Orig.). 1994. pap. 34.95 (0-918371-04-X, MixBooks) Cardinal Busn Media.
Mandell, Jim, ed. see Mandell, Terri.
Mandell, Joan G. & Damon, Linda. Group Treatment for Sexually Abused Children. LC 89-7462. 170p. 1989. pap. text ed. 25.00 (0-89862-516-5) Guilford Pr.
Mandell, Jonathan & Rubin, Sy. Trump Tower. 200p. 1984. 30.00 (0-8184-0354-3, Citadel Pr) Carol Pub Group.
*__Mandell, Judy.__ Book Editors Talk to Writers. LC 94-41641. 1995. pap. text ed. 12.95 (0-471-00391-3) Wiley.
Mandell, Judy, ed. Fiction Writers Guidelines: Over 260 Periodical Editors' Instructions Reproduced & Indexed. 2nd ed. LC 92-53504. 400p. 1992. pap. 31.50x (0-89950-673-9) McFarland & Co.
Mandell, Judy, jt. auth. see Rochester, Lois.
Mandell, L., jt. auth. see Menger, F. M.
Mandell, Lewis. The Credit Card Industry: A History. (Twayne's Evolution of American Business Ser.: No. 4). 200p. (C). 1990. text ed. 26.95 (0-8057-9810-2, Twayne); pap. 14.95 (0-8057-9816-1, Twayne) Macmillan.
— Credit Card Use in the United States. LC 72-86124. 120p. 1972. pap. 8.00 (0-87944-129-1) Inst Soc Res.
— Credit Card Use in the United States. LC 72-86124. (Illus.). 121p. reprint ed. pap. 34.50 (0-7837-5275-X, 2045013) Bks Demand.
— The Demand for Money in Israel, 1955-1967. LC 75-192. (Business Economics & Finance Ser.: No. 3). 132p. reprint ed. pap. 37.70 (0-7837-0785-1, 2041099) Bks Demand.
Mandell, Lewis & O'Brien, Thomas J. Investments. (Illus.). 576p. (C). 1991. Addtl. materials avail. text ed. write for info. (0-02-375340-4) Macmillan.
Mandell, Margery. Self-Made Americans: Interviews with Dreamers, Visionaries & Entrepreneurs. Dorszynski, Alexia, ed. 288p. 1995. 24.00 (0-9634249-9-8) Gift Future Two Thous.
Mandell, Margery, jt. auth. see Godin, Seth.
Mandell, Marshall. Dr. Mandell's Lifetime Arthritis Relief System. 336p. 1986. mass mkt. 4.99 (0-425-09355-7) Berkley Pub.
Mandell, Muriel. Fantastic Book of Logic Puzzles. LC 86-5980. (Illus.). 128p. 1987. pap. 4.95 (0-8069-4756-X) Sterling.
— Physics Experiments for Children. LC 68-9308. Orig. Title: Science for Children. (Illus.). (J). (gr. 3-10). 1968. reprint ed. pap. 2.95 (0-486-22033-8) Dover.
— Simple Kitchen Experiments: Learning Science with Everyday Foods. LC 92-41479. (Illus.). 128p. 1993. pap. 13.95 (0-8069-8414-7) Sterling.
— Simple Kitchen Experiments: Learning Science with Everyday Foods. (Illus.). 128p. 1994. pap. 4.95 (0-8069-8415-5) Sterling.
— Simple Science Experiments with Everyday Materials. LC 88-31201. (Illus.). 128p. (J). (gr. 4-10). 1989. 13.95 (0-8069-6794-3) Sterling.
— Simple Science Experiments with Everyday Materials. LC 88-31201. (Illus.). 128p. (YA). (gr. 4-10). 1990. pap. 4.95 (0-8069-5764-6) Sterling.
— Simple Weather Experiments with Everyday Materials. LC 90-37915. (Illus.). 128p. (J). (gr. 4-10). 1990. 13.95 (0-8069-7296-3) Sterling.
— Simple Weather Experiments with Everyday Materials. LC 90-37915. (Illus.). 128p. (J). (gr. 4 up). 1991. pap. 4.95 (0-8069-7295-5) Sterling.
— Two Hundred & Twenty Easy-to-Do Science Experiments for Young People: Three Complete Books. (Juveniles Ser.). 287p. (J). (gr. 3 up). 1985. pap. 10.50 (0-486-24874-7) Dover.
Mandell, Myrna P., jt. ed. see Gage, Robert W.
Mandell, Patricia. Massachusetts: Off the Beaten Path. LC 91-25494. (Illus.). 160p. 1992. pap. 9.95 (0-87106-242-9) Globe Pequot.
Mandell, Patricia, jt. auth. see Vollmer, Ryan.
Mandell, Peter, et al. Low Back Pain: An Historical & Contemporary Overview of the Occupational Medical & Psychosocial Issues of Chronic Back Pain. LC 89-42576. 219p. 1989. 39.00 (1-55642-082-X) SLACK Inc.
Mandell, Richard. The Bats. LC 80-83027. 170p. (Orig.). 1981. pap. 4.50 (0-9605008-0-4) Hermes Hse.
Mandell, Richard, ed. see Jean, Raymond.
Mandell, Richard D. The Nazi Olympics. LC 86-19347. (Sport & Society Ser.). (Illus.). 344p. 1987. pap. 12.95 (0-252-01325-5) U of Ill Pr.
— The Olympics of 1972: A Munich Diary. LC 90-23544. 223p. reprint ed. pap. 63.60 (0-7837-5239-3, 2044973) Bks Demand.
— Sport: A Cultural History. LC 83-20017. (Illus.). 384p. 1986. text ed. 47.50 (0-231-05470-X); pap. text ed. 17. 50 (0-231-05471-8) Col U Pr.
Mandell, Robert B. Contact Lens Practice. 4th ed. (Illus.). 1040p. (C). 1988. text ed. 86.95x (0-398-05509-2) C C Thomas.
Mandell, Sara & Freedman, David N. The Relationship Between Herodotus' History & Primary History. LC 93-16100. (USF Studies in the History of Judaism: No. 60). 207p. 1992. 44.95 (1-55540-838-9, 240060) Scholars Pr GA.
Mandell, Stephen, jt. auth. see Kirszner, Laurie.
Mandell, Stephen R., jt. auth. see Kirszner, Laurie G.
Mandell, Steve L., jt. auth. see Hopper, Grace M.
*__Mandell, Steven.__ Dr. Mandell's Ultimate PC Desk Reference. 2nd ed. 628p. 1995. 26.99 (1-56761-533-3) Alpha Bks IN.
Mandell, Steven L. Basic Program Instructor Manual. 2nd ed. 349p. 1989. pap. text ed. 13.95 (0-314-57501-4) West Pub.
— BASIC Programming Today: A Structured Approach. (Illus.). 325p. (Orig.). (C). 1986. teacher ed 12.95 (0-314-96642-0); pap. text ed. 33.75 (0-314-93199-6) West Pub.
— BASIC Programming Today: A Structured Approach. 2nd ed. Perlee, Clyde, ed. 560p. (Orig.). (C). 1990. pap. text ed. 47.25 (0-314-47602-4) West Pub.
— Beginning BASIC for the Commodore 64. (Illus.). 160p. (Orig.). 1985. pap. text ed. 33.75 (0-314-85264-6) West Pub.
— Building LOGO Skills: Terrapin Book B. 376p. (gr. 4-6). 1986. pap. text ed. 28.75 (0-314-89685-6); teacher ed, pap. text ed. 35.00 (0-314-88708-3) West Pub.
— The Commodore 64 Guidebook. (Illus.). 170p. (Orig.). 1985. pap. text ed. 31.00 (0-314-85261-1) West Pub.
— Complete BASIC Programming. (Illus.). 349p. 1984. pap. text ed. 28.50 (0-314-77921-3) West Pub.
— Computer Fundamentals with BASIC. 304p. 1985. text ed. 35.50 (0-314-89689-9) West Pub.
— Computers & Data Processing: Concepts & Applications. 3rd ed. (Illus.). 512p. (C). 1984. text ed. 33.00 (0-314-85262-X) West Pub.
— Computers & Data Processing: Concepts & Applications with BASIC. 3rd ed. (Illus.). 292p. (C). 1984. text ed. 35.00 (0-314-87560-3) West Pub.
— Computers & Data Processing Today. (Illus.). 161p. (C). 1983. student ed 10.75 (0-314-71106-6); pap. text ed. 28.50 (0-314-69663-6) West Pub.
— Computers & Data Processing Today with BASIC. (Illus.). 510p. (C). pap. text ed. 29.50 (0-314-70646-1) West Pub.
— Computers & Data Processing Today with BASIC. 2nd ed. (Illus.). 472p. (C). 1985. pap. text ed. 35.50 (0-314-96079-1) West Pub.
— Computers & Data Processing Today with Pascal. (Illus.). 332p. (C). 1983. pap. text ed. 29.50 (0-314-70647-X) West Pub.
— Computers & Data Processing Today with Pascal. 2nd ed. (Illus.). 472p. (C). 1986. pap. text ed. 50.75 (0-314-96080-5) West Pub.
— Computers & Information Processing: Concepts & Applications. 6th ed. Perlee, Clyde, ed. 512p. (C). 1992. text ed. 50.75 (0-314-92964-9) West Pub.
— Computers & Information Processing: Concepts & Applications with BASIC. Perlee, Clyde, ed. (Illus.). 174p. (C). 1987. pap. text ed. 15.00 (0-314-35299-6) West Pub.
— Computers & Information Processing: Concepts & Applications with BASIC. 6th ed. Perlee, Clyde, ed. 512p. (C). 1992. text ed. 54.75 (0-314-89569-8) West Pub.
— Computers, Data Processing & the Law: Text & Cases. (Illus.). 1083p. 1984. text ed. 69.25 (0-314-70624-0); pap. text ed. 40.50 (0-314-69664-4) West Pub.
— Exploring Software Today: Apple II Version. (Illus.). 253p. (C). 1986. text ed. 37.00 (0-314-87127-6) West Pub.
— Instructor Manual to Computer Basics. 499p. 1991. pap. text ed. write for info. (0-314-82969-5) West Pub.
— Introduction to BASIC Programming. 2nd ed. LC 84-17393. (Illus.). 175p. 1984. pap. text ed. 16.00 (0-314-85263-8) West Pub.
— Introduction to BASIC Programming. 3rd ed. 248p. (C). 1987. pap. text ed. 31.25 (0-314-34731-3) West Pub.
— Introduction to Computers Using the Apple II. Perlee, Clyde, ed. (Illus.). 539p. (C). 1985. pap. text ed. 52.75 (0-314-85265-4) West Pub.
— Introduction to Computers Using the IBM & MS DOS PCs: Popular Commercial Software Version. 3rd ed. Perlee, Clyde, ed. 674p. (C). 1991. pap. text ed. 54.50 (0-314-79211-2) West Pub.
— Introduction to Computers Using the IBM & MS DOS PCs: West 2.5 Version. 439p. 1987. pap. text ed. 51.25 (0-314-32170-5); teacher ed, pap. text ed. write for info. (0-314-35263-5) West Pub.
— Introduction to Computers Using the IBM & MS DOS PC's (Commercial Software Version) 499p. 1987. pap. text ed. 41.75 (0-314-32171-3) West Pub.
— Introduction to Computers Using the IBM PC. Perlee, Clyde, ed. 547p. (C). pap. text ed. 38.00 (0-314-85267-0) West Pub.
— Introduction to Computers Using the Macintosh. Perlee, Clyde, ed. 724p. (C). 1992. pap. text ed. 54.25 (0-314-88729-6) West Pub.
— Introduction to Computers Using the TRS 80 Model III. (Illus.). 535p. (C). 1986. pap. text ed. 52.75 (0-314-85266-2) West Pub.
— Microcomputing Today. 150p. 1995. pap. write for info. (0-314-04624-0) West Pub.
— Pascal Programming Today. LC 86-24610. (Illus.). 550p. (Orig.). (C). 1987. pap. text ed. 54.25 (0-314-33935-3); teacher ed, pap. text ed. 19.95 (0-314-97186-6) West Pub.
— A Pascal Supplement for Computers & Data Processing Today. 143p. (C). 1983. pap. text ed. write for info. (0-314-77494-7) West Pub.
— Personal Computer Desk Reference. 608p. 1993. 32.95 (0-9637426-0-4); pap. 23.95 (0-9637426-1-2) Rawhide Pr.
— Principles of Data Processing. 3rd ed. (Illus.). 164p. 1984. teacher ed write for info. (0-314-77924-8) West Pub.
— Principles of Information Processing. 4th ed. 225p. (C). 1988. pap. text ed. 32.50 (0-314-68950-8) West Pub.
— Turbo Pascal Programming Today. (Illus.). 561p. (Orig.). (C). 1987. pap. text ed. 51.50 (0-314-34628-7); teacher ed, pap. text ed. 19.95 (0-314-35260-0) West Pub.
— Working with Application Software - IBM-PC. (Illus.). 253p. (C). 1986. text ed. 41.00 (0-314-96495-9) West Pub.
— Working with Application Software - TRS-80. (Illus.). 242p. (C). 1986. text ed. 41.00 (0-314-96493-2) West Pub.
Mandell, Steven L., jt. auth. see Baumann, Susan K.
Mandell, Steven L., jt. auth. see Brenan, Kathleen M.
Mandell, Steven L., jt. auth. see Clark, Ann L.
Mandell, Steven L., jt. auth. see Flyn, Meredith.
Mandell, Steven L., jt. auth. see Hopper, Grace M.
Mandell, Steven L., et al. Introduction to Business: Concepts & Applications. (Illus.). 594p. (C). 1981. text ed. 54.75 (0-8299-0393-3) West Pub.
— Introduction to Business Concepts & Applications: Test Bank. 93p. (C). 1980. pap. text ed. write for info. (0-8299-0527-8) West Pub.
— Word Processing for Legal Professionals Using WordPerfect 5.1. LC 95-2009. 1995. spiral bd. 31.50 (0-314-05250-X) West Pub.
Mandell, Terri. Power Shmoozing: The New Etiquette for Social & Business Success. Mandell, Jim, ed. 200p. (Orig.). 1993. pap. 11.95 (0-9623062-9-0) First Hse Pr.
— When Good People Throw Bad Parties. Mandell, James, ed. 100p. (Orig.). 1994. pap. 6.95 (0-9623062-7-4) First Hse Pr.
Mandell, Walt. The Rabbi Who Couldn't Die. Green, Nate, ed. LC 90-83818. 376p. (Orig.). 1992. pap. 8.95 (0-9627343-4-9) Drawbridge Pr.
Mandelsberg, Rose G. Bizarre Murderers. 1991. mass mkt. 4.95 (1-55817-486-9, Pinnacle NY) Windsor NY.
— Cult Killers. 1991. mass mkt. 4.95 (1-55817-528-8, Pinnacle NY) Windsor NY.
— From the Files of True Detective: Crimes of Passion. (Illus.). 448p. 1993. mass mkt. 4.99 (1-55817-684-5, Pinnacle NY) Windsor NY.
— Medical Murderers: From the Files of True Detective. 1992. mass mkt. 4.99 (1-55817-582-2, Pinnacle NY) Windsor NY.
— Torture Killers. 1991. mass mkt. 4.95 (1-55817-506-7, Pinnacle NY) Windsor NY.
Mandelsberg, Rose G., ed. From the Files of True Detective: Bizarre Murders II. (Illus.). 448p. 1993. mass mkt. 4.99 (1-55817-760-4, Pinnacle NY) Windsor NY.
— From the Files of True Detective: Family Slaughters. (Illus.). 448p. 1993. mass mkt. 4.99 (1-55817-711-6, Pinnacle NY) Windsor NY.
— From the Files of True Detective: Greed Killers. (Illus.). 448p. 1994. mass mkt. 4.99 (1-55817-888-0, Pinnacle NY) Windsor NY.
— From the Files of True Detective: Mass Murderers. (Illus.). 448p. 1993. mass mkt. 4.99 (1-55817-777-9, Pinnacle NY) Windsor NY.
— From the Files of True Detective: Spouse Killers. (Illus.). 448p. 1994. mass mkt. 4.99 (1-55817-785-X, Pinnacle NY) Windsor NY.
— From the Files of True Detective: The Crimes of the Rich & Famous. (Illus.). 448p. 1992. mass mkt. 4.99 (1-55817-630-6, Pinnacle NY) Windsor NY.
— From the Files of True Detective: The Mutilators. (Illus.). 448p. 1993. mass mkt. 4.99 (1-55817-768-X, Pinnacle NY) Windsor NY.
— From the Files of True Detective: Torture Killers II. (Illus.). 448p. 1994. mass mkt. 4.99 (1-55817-793-0, Pinnacle NY) Windsor NY.
— From the Files of True Detective: Unsolved Mysteries. (Illus.). 448p. 1992. mass mkt. 4.99 (1-55817-654-3, Pinnacle NY) Windsor NY.
— From the Files of True Detective Magazine: Cop Killers. (Illus.). 448p. 1992. mass mkt. 4.99 (1-55817-603-9, Pinnacle NY) Windsor NY.
— Hitmen. (True Detective Ser.). 448p. 1994. mass mkt. 4.99 (0-7860-0048-1) Windsor NY.
— Hooker Killers. 448p. 1994. pap. 4.99 (0-7860-0006-6, Pinnacle NY) Windsor NY.
— Killer Teens. 448p. 1994. mass mkt. 4.99 (1-55817-895-3, Pinnacle NY) Windsor NY.
— Murders in Paradise. (True Detective Ser.). 448p. 1994. mass mkt. 4.99 (0-7860-0037-6) Windsor NY.
— Predators. (True Detective Ser.). 448p. 1994. mass mkt. 4.99 (0-7860-0028-7) Windsor NY.
— Stranglers. 448p. 1994. pap. 4.99 (0-7860-0015-5, Pinnacle NY) Windsor NY.
Mandelshtam, Osip. The Eyesight of Wasps. Greene, James, tr. 160p. 1989. 29.50 (0-8142-0478-3) Ohio St U Pr.
Mandel'shtam, Osip. Osip Mandelstam's Stone. LC 80-7545. (Lockert Library of Poetry in Translation). 268p. reprint ed. pap. 76.40 (0-8357-6930-5, 2037989) Bks Demand.
Mandelshtam, Osip. Selected Poems. Greene, James, tr. & sel. by. 144p. 1992. 9.95 (0-14-018474-0, Penguin Classics) Viking Penguin.
Mandelstam, et al. Quarterly Review of Literature: The 1970s, Prose, Vol. XVIII, Nos. 3-4. 1970. pap. 15.00 (0-317-05323-X) Quarterly Rev.
Mandelstam, Dorothy, ed. Incontinence & Its Management. 2nd ed. LC 85-27001. 288p. 1986. pap. 25.00 (0-7099-3580-3, Pub. by Croom Helm UK) Routledge Chapman & Hall.

M

An Asterisk (*) at the beginning of an entry indicates that the title is appearing in BIP for the first time.

Mandelstam, Michael. How to Get Equipment for Disability. 3rd ed. 528p. 1993. pap. 55.00 (*1-85302-190-3*, Pub. by J Kingsley Pubs UK) Taylor & Francis.

Mandelstam, Michael, comp. How to Get Equipment for Disability. 374p. 1990. pap. 33.00 (*1-85302-095-8*, Pub. by J Kingsley Pubs UK) Taylor & Francis.

— How to Get Equipment for Disability 1992. 2nd ed. 528p. 1992. pap. 49.00 (*1-85302-128-8*, Pub. by J Kingsley Pubs UK) Taylor & Francis.

***Mandelstam, Michael & Schwehr, Belinda.** Community Care Practice & the Law. LC 95-5881. 450p. 1995. pap. 32.00 (*1-85302-273-X*, Pub. by J Kingsley Pubs UK) Taylor & Francis.

Mandelstam, Nadezhda. Hope Against Hope. LC 77-124984. 448p. (C). 1976. pap. 13.95 (*0-689-70530-1*, 218, Pub. by Ctrl Bur voor Schimmel NE) Macmillan.

— Mozart & Salieri. 1994. pap. 11.00 (*0-679-75619-1*, Vin) Random.

Mandelstam, Osip. Critical Prose & Letters. 2nd ed. Harris, Jane G. & Anthony, C., eds. (Illus.). 725p. (C). 1990. pap. 19.95 (*0-88233-164-7*) Ardis Pubs.

— Fifty Poems. Meares, Bernard, tr. LC 76-52274. 120p. (Orig.). 1977. pap. 8.95 (*0-89255-006-6*) Persea Bks.

— Moscow Notebooks. McKane, Richard & McKane, Elizabeth, trs. 80p. (Orig.). 1991. pap. 14.95 (*1-85224-126-8*, Pub. by Bloodaxe Bks UK) Dufour.

— Stone. Tracy, Robert, tr. & intro. by. 250p. 1993. pap. 14.00 (*0-00-272145-7*, Pub. by HarpC UK) HarpC.

— Tristia. 1988. pap. 9.95 (*0-88268-069-2*) Station Hill Pr.

Mandelstam, S. L., ed. Spectrochemical Analysis in the U. S. S. R. 112p. 1982. pap. 19.25 (*0-08-028747-6*, Pergamon Pr) Elsevier.

Mandelstam, Stanley, jt. auth. see Yourgrau, Wolfgang.

Mandelstein, Cornelia, ed. see Losee, Michael.

Mandelstein, Paul. Nightingale & the Wind. LC 93-31056. 32p. (J). (gr. 4 up). 1994. 17.95 (*0-8478-1787-3*) Rizzoli Intl.

Mandelstein, Paul, ed. see Losee, Michael.

Mandelstein, Paul, ed. see Utz, Peter.

Mander, Clive, jt. auth. see Barnes, Maurice.

Mander, Jerry. Four Arguments for the Elimination of Television. LC 77-12558. 1978. pap. 8.95 (*0-688-08274-2*, Quill) Morrow.

— In the Absence of the Sacred: The Failure of Technology & the Survival of the Indian Nations. LC 91-13869. 400p. 1991. 25.00 (*0-87156-739-3*) Sierra.

— In the Absence of the Sacred: The Failure of Technology & the Survival of the Indian Nations. LC 91-13869. 464p. 1992. reprint ed. pap. 14.00 (*0-87156-509-9*) Sierra.

Mander, John. Berlin: Hostage for the West. LC 79-9953. (Illus.). 124p. 1979. reprint ed. text ed. 49.75 (*0-313-20996-0*, MABE, Greenwood Pr) Greenwood.

— The Writer & Commitment. LC 75-18402. 215p. 1975. reprint ed. text ed. 59.75 (*0-8371-8332-4*, MAWCO, Greenwood Pr) Greenwood.

Mander-Jones, Phyllis. Catalogue of the Manuscripts in the Library of the Royal Geographical Society of Australasia (South Australian Branch) Inc. (C). 1981. 75.00 (*0-7855-0333-1*, Pub. by Royal Geograp Soc AT) St Mut.

Mander, Linden. Some Dependent Peoples of the South Pacific. LC 75-30071. (Institute of Pacific Relations Ser.). reprint ed. 84.50 (*0-404-59544-8*) AMS Pr.

Mander, Mary S., ed. Communications in Transition: Issues & Debates in Current Research. LC 83-13985. 352p. 1983. text ed. 42.95 (*0-275-91040-7*, C1040, Praeger Pubs) Greenwood.

Mander, Matthias. The Cassowary. Mitchell, Michael, tr. (Studies in Austrian Literature, Culture, & Thought. Translation Ser.). 340p. 1994. pap. 23.95 (*0-929497-73-2*) Ariadne CA.

Mander, R. & Mitchinson, J. Hamlet Through the Ages: A Pictorial Record from 1709. Marshall, H., ed. 1977. lib. bdg. 150.00 (*0-8490-1929-X*) Gordon Pr.

Mander, Raymond & Mitchenson, Joe. The Theatres of London. LC 78-11808. 292p. 1979. reprint ed. text ed. 59.75 (*0-313-21227-9*, MATL, Greenwood Pr) Greenwood.

Mander, Rosemary. Bereavement in Childbearing. LC 94-13658. (Illus.). 240p. 1994. pap. 19.95 (*0-632-03826-8*, Pub. by Blckwell Sci Pubns UK) Blackwell Sci.

— Care of the Mother Grieving a Baby Relinquished for Adoption. 228p. 1995. 59.95 (*1-85628-597-9*, Pub. by Avebury Pub UK) Ashgate Pub Co.

Mander, W. J. An Introduction to Bradley's Metaphysics. 192p. 1994. 39.95 (*0-19-824090-2*) OUP.

Mandera, Franklin R. An Inquiry into the Effects of Bilingualism on Native & Non-Native Americans: Viewed in Sociopsychologic & Cultural Terms. Cordasco, Francesco, ed. LC 77-90548. (Bilingual-Bicultural Education in the U. S. Ser.). 1978. lib. bdg. 24.95 (*0-405-11087-1*) Ayer.

Manderick, Bernard, jt. ed. see Manner, Reinhard.

Manderino, John. Sam & His Brother Len. LC 94-9992. 248p. 1994. 19.95 (*0-89733-407-8*) Academy Chi Pubs.

Manderino, Ned. Actor As Artist. 176p. (Orig.). 1991. pap. 10.95 (*0-9601194-7-7*) Manderino Bks.

— All about Method Acting. 192p. (Orig.). 1985. pap. 10.95 (*0-9601194-3-4*) Manderino Bks.

— The Transpersonal Actor: Reinterpreting Stanislavski. rev. ed. 240p. (Orig.). 1989. pap. 14.95 (*0-9601194-5-0*) Manderino Bks.

Manderscheid, Ronald W. & Sonnenschein, Mary A. Mental Health, United States, 1990. (Illus.). 278p. 1990. per., pap. 14.00 (*0-16-026885-0*, S/N 017-024-014) USGPO.

Manderson, Desmond. From Mr. Sin to Mr. Big: A History of Australian Drug Laws. (Illus.). 278p. 1994. pap. 24.95 (*0-19-553531-6*) OUP.

Manderson, Lenore, jt. auth. see Crouch, Mira.

Mandes, Ric, jt. auth. see Russell, Erskine.

Mandesson, A. Greek-English, English-Greek Dictionary, with a Complete & Accurate System for the Pronunciation of the Words, 2 vols. 1380p. 1961. Greek-English, 1380p. 34.00 (*0-88431-922-9*, Pub. by U Politecnica); English-Greek, 1102p. 34.00 (*0-88431-125-2*, Pub. by U Politecnica) IBD Ltd.

Mandetta, Anne & Gustaveson, Patricia. Abortion to Zoophilia: A Sourcebook of Sexual Facts. LC 75-31909. (Illus.). 1975. pap. text ed. 3.00 (*0-89055-114-6*) Carolina Pop Ctr.

Mandeville, A. Glenn. Contemporary Doll Stars: Forty Years of the Best. (Illus.). 192p. 1992. pap. 14.95 (*0-87588-385-0*) Hobby Hse.

— The Golden Age of Collectible Dolls, 1946. 144p. 1990. 25.00 (*0-87588-350-8*) Hobby Hse.

Mandeville, Bernard. Aesop Dress'd: or A Collection of Fables Writ in Familiar Verse. LC 92-23720. (Augustan Reprints Ser.: No. 120 (1966)). reprint ed. 12.00 (*0-404-70120-5*, PR3545) AMS Pr.

— Collected Works Vol. II: A Treatise of the Hypochondriack & Hysterick Passions, Vulgarly Call'd the Hypo in Men an Vapours in Women. xxiv, 288p. 1981. reprint ed. write for info. (*3-487-07037-5*, Pub. by Georg Olms GW) Lubrecht & Cramer.

— Collected Works Vol. III: The Fable of the Bees: or, Private Vices Publick Benefits. 404p. 1983. reprint ed. write for info. (*3-487-07177-0*, Pub. by Georg Olms GW) Lubrecht & Cramer.

— Collected Works Vol. IV: The Fable of the Bees, Pt. II. 456p. 1980. reprint ed. write for info. (*3-487-07038-3*, Pub. by Georg Olms GW) Lubrecht & Cramer.

— Collected Works Vol. V: Free Thoughts on Religion, the Church, & National Happiness. xxii, 364p. 1987. reprint ed. write for info. (*3-487-07782-5*, Pub. by Georg Olms GW) Lubrecht & Cramer.

— Collected Works Vol. VI: An Enquiry into the Origin of Honour, & the Usefulness of Christianity in War. xi, 240p. 1990. reprint ed. write for info. (*3-487-09315-4*, Pub. by Georg Olms GW) Lubrecht & Cramer.

— The Fable of the Bees. 416p. 1989. pap. 10.95 (*0-14-044541-2*, Penguin Classics) Viking Penguin.

— The Fable of the Bees. LC 02-15833. 13p. (C). 1987. reprint ed. pap. 2.00 (*0-942153-19-7*) Entropy Conserv.

— The Fable of the Bees (F. B. Kaye Edition), 2 vols., Set. LC 88-646. 1988. 30.00 (*0-86597-072-6*); pap. 15.00 (*0-86597-075-0*) Liberty Fund.

— Free Thoughts on Religion, the Church, & National Happiness. LC 77-17171. 1981. reprint ed. lib. bdg. 60.00 (*0-8201-1300-X*) Schol Facsimiles.

— The Mischiefs That Ought Justly to Be Apprehended from a Whig-Government. LC 92-544. (Augustan Reprints Ser.: No. 174 (1975)). reprint ed. 12.00 (*0-404-70174-4*, DA503) AMS Pr.

— A Modest Defence of Publick Stews: or An Essay upon Whoring, As It Is Now Practis'd in These Kingdoms. LC 92-23890. (Augustan Reprints Ser.: No. 162 (1973)). reprint ed. 12.00 (*0-404-70162-0*, HQ185) AMS Pr.

— A Modest Defense of Publick Stews. 1972. 95.95 (*0-8490-0656-2*) Gordon Pr.

— A Treatise of the Hypochondriack & Hysterick Diseases. LC 76-45623. 1976. reprint ed. 60.00 (*0-8201-1277-1*) Schol Facsimiles.

— The Virgin Unmask'd. LC 75-14288. 256p. 1975. reprint ed. lib. bdg. 50.00 (*0-8201-1155-4*) Schol Facsimiles.

Mandeville, D. C., jt. ed. see Holmyard, E. J.

Mandeville, Francine. Midnight in Paris. (Lucky in Love Ser.: No. 9). 320p. 1992. mass mkt. 3.99 (*0-8217-3865-8*) Zebra.

***Mandeville, Glenn.** Alexander Dolls Collection Price Guide, Vol. 2. 128p. 1995. pap. 11.95 (*0-87588-435-0*) Hobby Hse.

— Glenn Mandeville's Madame Alexander Dolls Value Guide. 128p. 1993. pap. 9.95 (*0-87588-406-7*, 4532) Hobby Hse.

***Mandeville, Glenn A.** Doll Fashion Anthology & PG. 4th ed. 200p. 1994. pap. 12.95 (*0-87588-413-X*) Hobby Hse.

— Ginny: An American Toddler Doll. rev. ed. 152p. 1994. 12.95 (*0-87588-415-6*, 4688) Hobby Hse.

Mandeville, Jerry, tr. see Dolson, Gina, ed.

Mandeville, John. Mandeville's Travels from the French, Pt. 1. Hamelius, P., ed. (EETS, OS Ser.: No. 153). 1916. 36.00 (*0-527-00150-3*) Periodicals Srv.

— The Travels of Sir John Mandeville. Moseley, Charles W., tr. (Classics Ser.). 208p. 1984. pap. 9.95 (*0-14-044435-1*, Penguin Classics) Viking Penguin.

Mandeville, Joyce, jt. auth. see Foster, Susan.

Mandeville, Joyce C. & Foster, Susen. Historic Inns of California's Gold Country Cookbook & Guide. (Illus.). 112p. (Orig.). 1993. pap. 12.95 (*0-9637112-0-2*) Hist Inns CA.

Mandeville, Lisa K. & Troiano, Nan H. High Risk Intrapartum Care. (Illus.). 352p. 1992. pap. 39.95 (*0-397-54811-7*) Lippincott.

Mandeville, M., et al. Solar Alcohol: The Fuel Revolution. rev. ed. (Illus.). 128p. 1980. pap. 8.95 (*0-940828-00-6*) Olympic Pub.

Mandeville, Mildred S., ed. The Used Book Price Guide: Five Year Edition, 2 vols., Set. Incl. A-K May 1967 to May 1972. 376p. 1977. (*0-318-55347-3*); L-Z May 1968 to May 1973. 368p. 1977. reprint ed. (*0-911182-72-1*); 1977. 59.00 (*0-911182-73-X*) Price Guide.

— Used Book Price Guide: Five Year Edition, 1977 Supplement. 479p. 1977. 49.00 (*0-911182-76-4*) Price Guide.

— Used Book Price Guide: Five Year, 1983 Edition. 536p. 1983. 79.00 (*0-685-05650-3*) Price Guide.

Mandeville, Sylvia. Amigos de Dios. Gutierrez, Edna L., tr. (Serie Apunta Con Tu Dedo). 24p. 1980. pap. 7.50 (*0-311-38532-X*, Edit Mundo) Casa Bautista.

Mandeville, Sylvia & Pierson, Lance. Conoce a Jesus. Gutierrez, Edna L., tr. (Pointing Out Bks.). 24p. 1980. pap. 7.50 (*0-311-38531-1*, Edit Mundo) Casa Bautista.

Mandeville, Thomas. Understanding Novelty: Information, Technological Change, & the Patent System. Dervin, Brenda, ed. (Communication & Information Science Ser.). 144p. (C). 1995. text ed. write for info. (*0-89391-632-3*); pap. text ed. write for info. (*1-56750-004-8*) Ablex Pub.

Mandi, Peter. Education & Economic Growth in the Developing Countries. 226p. 1981. 67.50 (*0-569-08693-0*, Pub. by Collets UK) St Mut.

— Education & Economic Growth in the Developing Countries. 224p. (C). 1981. 60.00x (*963-05-2781-2*, Pub. by Akad Kiado HU) St Mut.

Mandia, M. Structures of the Level One Standard Modules for the Affine Lie Algebra. LC 86-28797. (Memoirs of the American Mathematical Society Ser.: Vol. 66/362). 146p. 1987. pap. text ed. 25.00 (*0-8218-2423-6*, MEMO 66/362) Am Math.

Mandia, Patricia M. Comedic Pathos: Black Humor in Mark Twain's Fiction. LC 91-52757. 176p. 1991. lib. bdg. 27.50x (*0-89950-642-9*) McFarland & Co.

***Mandiberg, James M., ed.** Innovations in Japanese Mental Health Services. LC 85-644749. (New Directions for Mental Health Services Ser.: No. 60). 91p. (Orig.). 1993. pap. 17.95 (*1-55542-697-2*) Jossey-Bass.

Mandich, D. R. & Placek, J. A. Russian Heraldry & Nobility. (Illus.). 700p. 1992. 135.00 (*0-9633063-9-1*) Dramco Pubs.

***Mandiela.** Guyana Betrayal. Date not set. per. 9.95 (*0-920813-80-1*, Pub. by Sister Vision CN) InBook.

Mandil, S. H., et al, eds. Health Informatics in Africa: HELINA 93. (International Congress Ser.: Vol. 1055). 240p. 1993. 168.50 (*0-444-81752-2*, Excerpta Medica) Elsevier.

Mandilaras, Basil G. The Verb in the Greek Non-literary Papyri. 493p. 1973. 47.00 (*0-685-47544-1*, Pub. by A M Hakkert NE) Benjamins North Am.

***Mandile.** Outdoor Photographer's Bible. 1995. pap. (*0-385-47271-4*) Doubleday.

Mandinach, Ellen B. & Cline, Hugh F. Classroom Dynamics: Implementing a Technology-Based Learning Environment. 224p. 1993. text ed. 49.95 (*0-8058-0555-9*) L Erlbaum Assocs.

***Mandino, Og.** El Angel Numero Doce - The Twelfth Angel. De La Luz Broissin F., Maria, tr. 192p. (SPA.). 1995. pap. 10.00 (*0-449-91016-4*) Fawcett.

— A Better Way to Live. large type ed. 176p. 1992. pap. 14.95 (*0-8161-5234-9*) G K Hall.

— Better Way to Live: For the First Time, Og Mandino Shares His Personal Success Story. 1991. mass mkt. 5.50 (*0-553-28674-9*) Bantam.

— Choice. 1986. mass mkt. 5.50 (*0-553-24576-7*) Bantam.

— Christ Commission. 1983. mass mkt. 5.50 (*0-553-27742-1*) Bantam.

— The God Memorandum. rev. ed. (Illus.). 1991. 8.95 (*0-8119-0657-4*) LIFETIME.

— The Greatest Gift in the World. LC 76-43508. (Illus.). 128p. 1989. reprint ed. 12.95 (*0-8119-0274-9*) LIFETIME.

— The Greatest Miracle in the World. 1983. mass mkt. 5.50 (*0-553-27972-6*) Bantam.

— Greatest Miracle in the World. large type ed. 1988. pap. 9.95 (*0-8027-2605-4*) Walker & Co.

— The Greatest Miracle in the World. 1993. reprint ed. lib. bdg. 16.95 (*1-56849-089-5*) Buccaneer Bks.

— The Greatest Miracle in the World. LC 75-12823. 128p. 1991. reprint ed. 14.95 (*0-8119-0255-2*) LIFETIME.

— Greatest Salesman in the World. LC 68-10798. (J). (gr. 9 up). 1987. 12.95 (*0-8119-0067-3*) LIFETIME.

— The Greatest Salesman in the World. 1983. mass mkt. 5.50 (*0-553-27757-X*) Bantam.

— Greatest Salesman in the World. large type ed. (Large Print Inspirational Ser.). 60p. 1986. pap. 8.95 (*0-8027-2557-0*) Walker & Co.

— The Greatest Salesman in the World. 1993. reprint ed. lib. bdg. 16.95 (*1-56849-090-9*) Buccaneer Bks.

— The Greatest Salesman in the World, Part Two: The End of the Story. 1989. mass mkt. 5.50 (*0-553-27699-9*) Bantam.

— The Greatest Secret in the World. LC 79-175423. 200p. 1972. 10.95 (*0-8119-0212-9*) LIFETIME.

— Greatest Secret in the World. 1983. mass mkt. 5.50 (*0-553-28038-4*) Bantam.

— The Greatest Success in the World. 1984. mass mkt. 5.50 (*0-553-27825-8*) Bantam.

— Mission Success! 176p. (Orig.). 1987. mass mkt. 4.99 (*0-553-26500-8*) Bantam.

— Og Mandino. deluxe ed. 1991. 12.99 (*0-517-05587-2*) Random Hse Value.

— Og Mandino's Great Trilogy: Includes: The Greatest Salesman in the World, The Greatest Secret in the World, & The Greatest Miracle in the World. deluxe ed. 336p. 1991. ring bd. 49.95 (*0-8119-0750-3*) LIFETIME.

— Og Mandino's Great Trilogy - Greatest Salesman, Secret & Miracle in the World. 420p. (J). 1995. 12.98 (*0-8119-0428-8*) LIFETIME.

— The Return of the Rag Picker. large type ed. 1993. 20.95 (*1-56895-017-9*) Wheeler Pub.

— Return of the Ragpicker. 1993. pap. 4.99 (*0-553-29993-X*) Bantam.

— Secrets for Success & Happiness. LC 95-12226. 1995. 22.00 (*0-449-90691-4*, Columbine) Fawcett.

— The Spellbinder's Gift. LC 94-26383. 1994. 18.50 (*0-449-90690-6*, Columbine) Fawcett.

— The Twelfth Angel. 1994. mass mkt. 4.99 (*0-449-22303-5*) Fawcett.

— University Success. 1983. pap. 14.95 (*0-553-34535-4*) Bantam.

Mandino, Og & Kaye, Buddy. Gift of Acabar. 1983. mass mkt. 5.50 (*0-553-26084-7*) Bantam.

Mandino, Og, jt. auth. see Dewey, Edward R.

Mandl, F. Quantum Mechanics. (Manchester Physics Ser.: No. 1173). 301p. 1992. text ed. 91.95 (*0-471-92971-9*); pap. text ed. 54.95 (*0-471-93155-1*) Wiley.

— Quantum Mechanics. x, 267p. 1994. reprint ed. pap. text ed. 8.95 (*0-486-67864-4*) Dover.

— Statistical Physics. 2nd ed. (Manchester Physics Ser.). 386p. 1988. pap. text ed. 47.95 (*0-471-91533-5*) Wiley.

Mandl, F. & Shaw, G. Quantum Field Theory. LC 84-5229. 354p. 1985. pap. text ed. 69.95 (*0-471-90650-6*) Wiley.

— Quantum Field Theory. 358p. 1993. pap. text ed. 67.95 (*0-471-94186-7*) Wiley.

***Mandl, Franz.** Quantum Mechanics. fac. ed. LC 91-24255. (The Manchester Physics Ser.). 314p. 1992. reprint ed. pap. 89.50 (*0-7837-8284-5*, 2049066) Bks Demand.

— Statistical Physics. 2nd ed. LC 87-8283. (Manchester Physics Ser.). (Illus.). 406p. reprint ed. pap. 115.80 (*0-8357-3091-3*, 2039348) Bks Demand.

Mandl, G. Mechanics of Tectonic Faulting: Models & Basic Concepts. (Developments in Structural Geology Ser.: No. 1). 407p. 1988. 77.00 (*0-444-42946-8*) Elsevier.

Mandl, Heinz & Lesgold, Alan M., eds. Learning Issues for Intelligent Tutoring Systems. (Cognitive Science Ser.). (Illus.). 225p. 1988. pap. 39.00 (*0-387-96616-1*) Spr-Verlag.

Mandl, Heinz, jt. ed. see Jonassen, David H.

Mandl, Heinz, jt. ed. see Tiberghien, Andree.

Mandl, Heinz, et al, eds. Learning & Comprehension of Text. LC 83-14050. (Illus.). 470p. reprint ed. pap. 134.00 (*0-8357-4211-3*, 2036988) Bks Demand.

Mandl, Ines, ed. Collagenase. LC 73-173997. (Illus.). 222p. 1972. text ed. 169.00 (*0-677-15190-X*) Gordon & Breach.

Mandl, Matthew. Basics of Electricity & Electronics. (Illus.). 448p. 1975. 42.00 (*0-13-060228-0*) P-H.

— Fundamentals of Electronics. 3rd ed. 1973. pap. text ed. 43.00 (*0-13-338160-9*) P-H.

— Introduction to Digital Logic Techniques & Systems. LC 82-13337. (Illus.). 201p. (C). 1983. 43.00 (*0-8359-3175-7*, Reston) P-H.

— Maintenance & Repair of Video Cassette Recorders. (Illus.). 304p. (C). 1986. text ed. 44.80 (*0-13-545526-X*) P-H.

— Repairing & Maintaining Your Own Stereo System. (Illus.). 176p. 1983. text ed. 45.00 (*0-13-773515-4*) P-H.

— Unusual Mathematical Puzzles, Tricks, & Oddities. (Illus.). 128p. 1984. 19.95 (*0-13-938150-3*); pap. 15.95 (*0-13-938101-5*) P-H.

Mandl, P. Analytical Treatment of One-Dimensional Markov Processes. LC 68-59694. (Grundlehren der Mathematischen Wissenschaften Ser.: Vol. 151). 1969. 64.00 (*0-387-04142-7*) Spr-Verlag.

Mandl, P. & Huskova, M., eds. Asymptotic Statistics: Proceedings of the Fifth Prague Symposium, Held from September 4-9, 1993. (Contributions to Statistics Ser.). x, 474p. 1994. pap. 98.00 (*0-387-91488-9*) Spr-Verlag.

— Asymptotic Statistics 2: Proceedings of the Prague Symposium on Asymptotic Physics, 3rd, Aug. 29-Sept. 2, 1983. 462p. 1984. 82.00 (*0-444-87525-5*) Elsevier.

Mandl, P., ed. see Prague Symposium on Asymptatic Statistics Staff.

Mandle, jt. auth. see Edelman.

Mandle, Jay R. Not Slave, Not Free: The African American Economic Experience since the Civil War. LC 91-27995. (Illus.). 152p. 1992. pap. text ed. 14.95 (*0-8223-1220-4*) Duke.

— Patterns of Caribbean Development: An Interpretive Essay on Economic Change. (Caribbean Studies: Vol. 2). 168p. 1982. text ed. 24.00 (*0-677-06000-9*) Gordon & Breach.

Mandle, Jay R. & Mandle, Joan D. Caribbean Hoops: The Development of West Indian Basketball. LC 94-4491. (Caribbean Studies: Vol. 8). 1994. text ed. 31.00 (*2-88449-106-6*); pap. text ed. 16.00 (*2-88449-107-4*) Gordon & Breach.

Mandle, Jay R., jt. auth. see Ferleger, Louis A.

Mandle, Joan D., jt. auth. see Mandle, Jay R.

Mandle, Julia B. & Rothschild, Deborah M. Sites of Recollection: Four Altars & a Rap Opera. LC 92-50560. (Illus.). 112p. (Orig.). 1992. pap. 22.95 (*0-913697-15-X*) U of Pa Pr.

Mandlebaum, Bernard. Live with Meaning. 1980. pap. 7.95 (*0-87677-182-7*) Hartmore.

Mandler, George. Cognitive Psychology: An Essay in Cognitive Science. 144p. (C). 1985. text ed. 29.95 (*0-89859-537-1*); pap. 6.95 (*0-89859-659-9*) L Erlbaum Assocs.

— Mind & Body: Psychology of Emotion & Stress. (C). 1984. pap. text ed. 12.95 (*0-393-95346-7*) Norton.

— Mind & Emotion. LC 81-14291. 296p. 1982. reprint ed. 25.50 (*0-89874-350-8*) Krieger.

Mandler, George, jt. auth. see Mandler, Jean M.

Mandler, Jean M. Stories, Scripts, & Scenes: Aspects of Schema Theory. 144p. (C). 1984. text ed. 29.95 (*0-89859-446-4*) L Erlbaum Assocs.

Mandler, Jean M. & Mandler, George. Thinking: From Association to Gestalt. LC 81-13347. (Perspectives in Psychology Ser.). x, 300p. 1982. reprint ed. text ed. 59.75 (*0-313-23261-X*, MATK, Greenwood Pr) Greenwood.

Mandler, Peter, ed. The Uses of Charity: The Poor on Relief in the Nineteenth-Century Metropolis. LC 90-30496. (Shelby Cullom Davis Center Ser.). (Illus.). 264p. (C). 1990. text ed. 34.95x (*0-8122-8214-0*) U of Pa Pr.

Mandler, Peter & Pedersen, Susan, eds. After the Victorians: Private Conscience & Public Duty in Modern Britain. LC 93-17693. 1994. write for info. (*0-415-07056-2*) Routledge.

M

Mandlowitz, Lynda. Como Conseguir el Empleo Que Usted Desea. (Careers in Depth Ser.). (Illus.). 128p. 1980. lib. bdg. 7.97 (*0-8239-0517-9*) Rosen Group.

Mandoe, Bonnie. Vegetarian Nights: Fresh from Hawaii. LC 93-49055. 1994. 17.95 (*0-89087-712-2*) Celestial Arts.

Mandolesi, N. & Vittorio, N., eds. The Cosmic Microwave Background: Twenty-Five Years Later. (C). 1990. lib. bdg. 115.50 (*0-7923-0849-2*) Kluwer Ac.

Mandorilli, Lavanya, jt. auth. see Tymes, Elna R.

Mandouvalos, N. Scattering Operator, Eisenstein Series, Inner Product Formula & "Maass-Selberg" Relations for Kleinian Groups. LC 89-180. (MEMO Ser.: Vol. 78/400). 87p. 1989. pap. 16.00 (*0-8218-2463-5*, MEMO 78/400) Am Math.

Mandover, Joan. Because I Care. large type ed. (Linford Romance Library). 1990. pap. 12.95 (*0-7089-6823-6*) Ulverscroft.

— My Love Has Wings. large type ed. (Linford Romance Library). 224p. 1989. pap. 11.95 (*0-7089-6688-8*, Linford) Ulverscroft.

Mandowsky, E., ed. see Ripa, Cesare, pseud.

Mandrak, Nicholas E. & Crossman, E. J. A Checklist of Ontario Freshwater Fishes: Annotated with Distribution Maps. (Illus.). 1994. pap. 15.95 (*0-88854-402-2*, Pub. by Royal Ont Mus CN) U of Toronto Pr.

Mandrekar, V. & Salehi, H., eds. Prediction Theory & Harmonic Analysis. 446p. 1983. 105.25 (*0-444-86597-7*, I-121-83, North Holland) Elsevier.

Mandrell, Barbara. Get to the Heart: My Story. 1991. mass mkt. 5.99 (*0-553-29243-9*) Bantam.

Mandrell, James. Don Juan & the Point of Honor: Seduction, Patriarchal Society, & Literary Tradition. (Illus.). 336p. 1992. text ed. 32.50 (*0-271-00781-8*) Pa St U Pr.

Mandrell, Louise. All American Hero: A Story about the Meaning of Veterans Day. (Louise Mandrell's Holiday Adventure Ser.). (J). (gr. 4-7). 1993. 12.95 (*1-56530-010-6*) Summit TX.

— Candy's Frog Prince: A Story about the Meaning of Valentines Day. (J). (gr. 4-7). 1993. 12.95 (*1-56530-046-7*) Summit TX.

— End of the Rainbow: A Story about the Meaning of St. Patrick's Day. (J). (gr. 4-7). 1993. 12.95 (*1-56530-047-5*) Summit TX.

— Eye of an Eagle: A Story about the Meaning of Columbus Day. (Louise Mandrell's Holiday Adventure Ser.). (J). (gr. 4-7). 1993. 12.95 (*1-56530-009-2*) Summit TX.

— Kimi's American Dream: A Story about the Meaning of Martin Luther King Day. (J). (gr. 4-7). 1993. 12.95 (*1-56530-045-9*) Summit TX.

— Peril in Evans Woods: A Story about the Meaning of Easter. (J). (ps-3). 1993. 12.95 (*1-56530-053-X*) Summit TX.

— Sunrise over the Harbor: A Story about the Meaning. (J). (ps-3). 1993. 12.95 (*1-56530-048-3*) Summit TX.

— Twin Disasters: A Story about the Meaning of Labor Day. (J). (gr. 4-7). 1993. 12.95 (*1-56530-041-6*) Summit TX.

Mandrell, Louise & Collins, Ace. All in a Day's Work: A Story about the Meaning of Mother's Day. (Illus.). 32p. (J). (gr. 1-4). 1993. 12.95 (*1-56530-036-X*) Summit TX.

— Best Man for the Job: A Story about the Meaning of Father's Day. (Illus.). 32p. (J). (gr. 1-4). 1993. 12.95 (*1-56530-039-4*) Summit TX.

— Eddie Finds a Hero: A Story about the Meaning of Memorial Day. (Illus.). 32p. (J). (gr. 1-4). 1993. 12.95 (*1-56530-037-8*) Summit TX.

— Jonathan's Gift: A Story about the Meaning of Christmas. 32p. 1992. 12.95 (*1-56530-014-9*) Summit TX.

— Jonathan's Gifts: A Story about the Meaning of Christmas. (Illus.). 32p. (J). (gr. 1-4). 1992. 12.95 (*1-56530-012-2*) Summit TX.

— A Mission for Jenny: A Story about the Meaning of Flag Day. (Illus.). 32p. (J). (gr. 1-4). 1993. 12.95 (*1-56530-038-6*) Summit TX.

— Peril in Evans Woods: A Story about the Meaning of Easter. (Illus.). 32p. (J). (gr. 1-4). 1993. 12.95 (*1-56530-035-1*) Summit TX.

— Runaway Thanksgiving: A Story about the Meaning of Thanksgiving. (Illus.). 32p. (J). (gr. 1-4). 1992. 12.95 (*1-56530-011-4*) Summit TX.

— Sunrise over the Harbor: A Story about the Meaning of Independence Day. LC 93-310. (Children's Holiday Adventure Ser.: Vol. 16). (Illus.). 32p. (J). 1993. 12.95 (*1-56530-040-8*) Summit TX.

Mandrell, Regina M. Our Family: Facts & Fancies: The Crary & Related Families. Coker, William S. et al, eds. (Southern History & Genealogy Ser.). (Illus.). 276p. 1993. pap. text ed. 27.50 (*1-882695-05-4*) Patagonia Pr.

***Mandri, Flora G.** Jose Donoso's House of Fiction: A Dramatic Construction of Time & Place. (Latin American Literature & Culture Ser.). 200p. 1995. text ed. 32.95x (*0-8143-2526-2*) Wayne St U Pr.

Mandrioli, Dino. Advances in Object Oriented Software Engineering. 1992. text ed. 64.00 (*0-13-006578-1*) P-H.

Mandrioli, Dino & Ghezzi, Carlo. Theoretical Foundations of Computer Sciences. 504p. (C). 1993. reprint ed. lib. bdg. 59.95 (*0-89464-798-9*) Krieger.

Mandrou, Robert. From Humanism to Science, 1480-1700. LC 92-29506. (Classics in the History & Philosophy of Science Ser.: Vol. 11). 1992. pap. write for info. (*2-88124-568-4*) Gordon & Breach.

— Introduction to Modern France, 1500-1640: An Essay in Historical Psychology. Hallmark, R. E., tr. LC 75-28239. (Illus.). 285p. 1976. 35.00 (*0-8419-0245-3*) Holmes & Meier.

Mandruzzato, G. P., ed. The Risk at Delivery. (Contributions to Gynecology & Obstetrics Ser.: Vol. 3). (Illus.). 1977. 39.25 (*3-8055-2421-8*) S Karger.

Mandry, Allene. Effective Teaching: There's Only One Way. LC 86-62494. 86p. (Orig.). 1987. pap. 6.95 (*0-88247-762-5*) R & E Pubs.

Mandt, Jinger, jt. ed. see Lange, Marie A.

Mandus, Brother, ed. For Women Only. (C). 1990. pap. 35.00 (*0-85305-246-8*, Pub. by J Arthur Ltd UK) St Mut.

Mandy, W. J., jt. ed. see Inman, F. P.

Mandyczewski, Eusebius, ed. see Brahms, Johannes.

Mandyczewski, Eusebius, ed. see Schubert, Franz.

Mandyczewski, Eusibius, ed. see Schubert, Franz.

Mane, R. Ergodic Theory & Differentiable Dynamics. (Ergebnisse der Mathematik und Ihrer Grenzgebiete Ser.: Vol. 8). (Illus.). 330p. 1987. 89.00 (*0-387-15278-4*) Spr-Verlag.

Mane, Robert. Henry Adams on the Road to Chartres. LC 74-154502. 296p. reprint ed. pap. 84.40 (*0-7837-2295-8*, 2057383) Bks Demand.

***Manea, Norman.** The Black Envelope. Camiller, Patrick, tr. LC 94-39253. 336p. (ENG & RUM.). 1995. 25.00 (*0-374-11397-1*) FS&G.

— Compulsory Happiness. Coverdale, Linda, tr. LC 92-38608. (FRE & ROM.). 1993. 22.00 (*0-374-12785-9*) FS&G.

— Compulsory Happiness. Coverdale, Linda, tr. LC 94-17021. (Writings from an Unbound Europe Ser.). 264p. 1994. pap. 13.95 (*0-8101-1190-X*) Northwestern U Pr.

— October, Eight O'Clock: Stories. LC 91-36377. 216p. 1993. pap. 12.00 (*0-8021-3371-1*) Grove-Atltic.

— On Clowns: The Dictator & the Arts; Essays. LC 91-23866. 178p. 1993. pap. 12.00 (*0-8021-3375-4*) Grove-Atltic.

Manedov, Russell. Soviet Military Medicine: Research Subject Index with Bibliography. LC 88-47621. 150p. 1988. 44.50 (*0-88164-722-5*); pap. 39.50 (*0-88164-723-3*) ABBE Pubs Assn.

Maneesha, Ma P., ed. see Osho.

Maneesha, Ma Prem, ed. see Rajneesh, Osho.

Maneesha, Sambodhi M., ed. see Rajneesh, Osho.

Manekeller, Wolfgang. Hundert Briefe Deutsch fuer Export & Import. 176p. 1983. pap. 10.50 (*3-468-41111-1*) Langenscheidt.

— So Bewirbt Man Sich. 160p. (GER.). 1980. pap. 8.95 (*3-581-66255-8*) Langenscheidt.

— So schreibt man Geschaeftsbriefe. 160p. (GER.). 1982. pap. 8.95 (*3-581-66229-9*) Langenscheidt.

***Maneker, Jerry S.** Applied Sociology: Sociological Understanding & Its Application. 70p. (Orig.). (C). 1994. pap. text ed. 14.50 (*0-8191-9777-7*) U Pr of Amer.

Manekin, Charles H. The Logic of Gersonides: A Translation of Sefer ha-Heqqesh ha-Yashar (the Book of the Correct Syllogism) of Rabbi Levi ben Gershom with Introduction, Commentary, & Analytical Glossary. (New Synthese Historical Library). 364p. (C). 1991. lib. bdg. 115.50 (*0-7923-1513-8*) Kluwer Ac.

Manela, Roger, jt. auth. see Ferman, Louis A.

Manelfe, Claude, ed. Imaging of the Spine & Spinal Cord. 928p. 1992. 189.00 (*0-88167-863-5*) Raven.

Maneli, Mieczyslaw. Perelman's New Rhetoric As Philosophy & Methodology for the Next Century. LC 93-18161. (Library of Rhetorics: Vol. 1). 151p. (C). 1994. lib. bdg. 80.50 (*0-7923-2166-9*) Kluwer Ac.

Manelis, G. B., et al. Chemistry Reviews: Pulsed NMR Study of Molecular Motion in Solids, Vol. 14. Vol'pin, M. E., ed. (Soviet Scientific Reviews Ser.: Vol. 14, Pt. 2). ii, 92p. 1989. pap. text ed. 46.00 (*3-7186-4959-4*) Gordon & Breach.

Manelis, Judith, et al. The Seventeenth Epilepsy International Symposium. (Advances in Epileptology Ser.: Vol. 17). 526p. 1989. 155.00 (*0-88167-520-2*) Raven.

Manell, P. & Johansson, S. G., eds. The Impact of Computer Technology on Drug Information: Proceedings of the IFIP-IMIA Working Conference, Uppsala, Sweden, October 26-28, 1981. 262p. 1982. 48.75 (*0-444-86451-2*, North Holland) Elsevier.

Manen, Lucie. Bel Canto: The Teaching of the Classical Italian Song-Schools, Its Decline & Restoration. (Illus.). 88p. 1987. pap. 22.95 (*0-19-317109-0*) OUP.

Manenc, J. Structural Thermodynamics of Alloys. Corcoran, N., tr. LC 73-83564. Orig. Title: Thermodynamique Structurale Des Alliages. (Illus.). 1973. lib. bdg. 64.00 (*90-277-0346-9*) Kluwer Ac.

Manenkov, A. A. A New Class of Modified Polymers. 246p. (C). 1992. text ed. 77.00 (*1-56072-032-8*) Nova Sci Pubs.

Manenkov, A. A., ed. Laser Techniques for Investigation of Defects in Semiconductors & Dielectrics. (Proceedings of the Institute of General Physics of the Academy of Sciences of the U. S. S. R. Ser.: Vol. 4). 204p. (C). 1988. text ed. 105.00 (*0-941743-15-2*) Nova Sci Pubs.

Manent, Pierre. An Intellectual History of Liberalism. Balinski, Rebecca, tr. LC 94-3110. (New French Thought Ser.). 1994. 19.95 (*0-691-03437-0*) Princeton U Pr.

Maner, Jerome H., jt. auth. see Pond, Wilson G.

Maner, Robert E. Making the Small Church Grow. 101p. 1982. pap. 5.95 (*0-8341-0741-4*) Beacon Hill.

***Manera, Elizabeth, ed.** Substitute Teaching Handbook. 160p. 1995. pap. 20.00 (*0-912099-06-2*) Kappa Delta Pi.

Manera, Elizabeth S., et al. Annotated Writer's Guide to Professional Educational Journals. 188p. 1982. pap. 9.95 (*0-9609782-0-8*) Bobets.

***Manera, Nancy & Donoghue, Simon J.** Mixed Nuts. 1983. 5.00 (*0-87129-576-8*, M59) Dramatic Pub.

Maners, Wendelin, jt. auth. see Gimbel, Cheryl.

Manes & Cheng. The Marginal Approach to Joint Cost Allocation: Theory & Application. (Studies in Accounting Research: No. 29). 219p. 1988. 20.00 (*0-86539-068-1*) Am Accounting.

Manes, Christopher. Green Rage: Radical Environmentalism & the Unmaking of Civilization. 1991. pap. 12.95 (*0-316-54532-5*) Little.

Manes, Ernest G. Predicate Transformer Semantics. (Cambridge Tracts in Theoretical Computer Science Ser.: No. 33). 233p. (C). 1992. 44.95 (*0-521-42036-9*) Cambridge U Pr.

Manes, Ernest G. & Arbib, Michael A. Algebraic Approaches to Program Semantics. (Texts & Monographs in Computer Science). (Illus.). 355p. 1986. 85.00 (*0-387-96324-3*) Spr-Verlag.

Manes, Ernest G., jt. ed. see Arbib, Michael A.

Manes, Joan, jt. ed. see Wolfson, Nessa.

Manes, L., ed. Actinides: Chemistry & Physical Properties. (Structure & Bonding Ser.: Vol. 59-60). (Illus.). 250p. 1985. 106.00 (*0-387-13752-1*) Spr-Verlag.

Manes, Rene P. The Effects of United States Oil Import Policy on the Petroleum Industry. Bruchey, Stuart, ed. LC 78-22696. (Energy in the American Economy Ser.). (Illus.). 1979. lib. bdg. 35.95 (*0-405-11999-2*) Ayer.

Manes, Ronald D. & Silver, Michael. Solicitor - Client Privilege in Canadian Law. 256p. 1993. text ed. 77.50 (*0-409-80654-4*) Butterworth Legal Pubs.

Manes, Rose T. Prima Vera: Springtime. Costa, Gwen, ed. LC 90-21706. 1991. pap. 13.95 (*0-87949-330-5*) Ashley Bks.

***Manes, Stephen.** An Almost Perfect Game. LC 94-18192. 1995. 14.95 (*0-590-44432-8*) Scholastic Inc.

— Be a Perfect Person. (J). 1983. pap. 3.50 (*0-553-15580-6*) Bantam.

— Be a Perfect Person in Just Three Days! (Illus.). 64p. (J). (gr. 3-6). 1982. 14.95 (*0-89919-064-2*, Clarion Bks) HM.

— The Boy Who Turned into a TV Set. (Illus.). 32p. (Orig.). (J). (gr. 2-5). 1983. pap. 2.50 (*0-380-62000-6*, Camelot) Avon.

— Chocolate-Covered Ants. (J). (gr. 4-7). 1993. pap. 2.95 (*0-590-40961-1*) Scholastic Inc.

— Comedy High. 176p. (YA). (gr. 7 up). 1992. 13.95 (*0-590-44436-0*, Scholastic Hardcover) Scholastic Inc.

— Comedy High. (YA). 1994. pap. 3.50 (*0-590-44437-9*) Scholastic Inc.

— The Great Gerbil Roundup. (Illus.). 105p. (J). (gr. 3-7). 1988. 13.95 (*0-15-232490-9*, HB Juv Bks) HarBrace.

— The Great Gerbil Roundup. LC 88-2266. (Trophy Bk.). (Illus.). 112p. (J). (gr. 3-7). 1991. reprint ed. pap. 3.95 (*0-06-440375-0*, Trophy) HarpC Child Bks.

— The Hooples' Horrible Holiday. 128p. (Orig.). (J). (gr. 3-7). 1986. pap. 2.50 (*0-380-89740-7*, Camelot) Avon.

— Hooples on the Highway. 96p. 1985. pap. 2.50 (*0-380-69989-3*, Camelot) Avon.

— It's New!, It's Improved!, It's Terrible! (J). (gr. 2-6). 1989. pap. 3.50 (*0-553-15682-9*, Skylark) Bantam.

— Make Four Million Dollars by Next Thursday! (J). (gr. 3-7). 1992. 3.50 (*0-553-15908-9*, Skylark) Bantam.

— Some of the Adventures of Rhode Island Red. LC 89-35397. (Illus.). 128p. (J). (gr. 3-7). 1990. lib. bdg. 11.89 (*0-397-32348-4*, Lipp Jr Bks) HarpC Child Bks.

Manes, Stephen & Andrews, Paul. Gates. 1994. 14.00 (*0-671-88074-8*, Touchstone Bks) S&S Trade.

— Gates: How Microsoft's Mogul Reinvented an Industry - & Made Himself the Richest Man in America. LC 92-15994. 1993. 25.00 (*0-385-42075-7*) Doubleday.

Manes, Stephen & Somerson, Paul. StarFixer: The Ultimate WordStar Enhancement. (Business Productivity Library). 1994. disk 29.95 (*0-553-34462-5*) Bantam.

Manese, Wilfredo R. Employment Testing, Validation & the Law: A Primer. 213p. 1979. 25.00 (*0-9604586-0-3*) EGM Ent.

— Fair & Effective Employment Testing: Administrative, Psychometric, & Legal Issues for the Human Resources Professional. LC 85-27151. (Illus.). 157p. 1986. text ed. 49.95 (*0-89930-171-1*, MFE/, Quorum Bks) Greenwood.

— Occupational Job Evalution: A Research-Based Approach to Job Classification. LC 87-32280. 177p. 1988. text ed. 49.95 (*0-89930-261-0*, MOL/, Quorum Bks) Greenwood.

***Maness, Larry.** Nantucket Revenge: A Jake Eaton Mystery. 208p. 1995. 19.95 (*0-89141-566-1*, Lyford Bks) Presidio Pr.

Maness, Malia. Curious Kimo. LC 93-86143. (Illus.). 32p. (J). (ps-3). 1993. 9.95 (*0-9633493-0-9*) Pacific Greetings.

— The Toad That Taught Flying. LC 93-86144. (Illus.). 32p. (J). (ps-3). 1993. 9.95 (*0-9633493-1-7*) Pacific Greetings.

Maness, Terry S. & Zietlow, John T. Short-Term Financial Management: Text, Cases, & Readings. Burvikovs, ed. LC 92-32830. 550p. (C). 1993. text ed. 67.00 (*0-314-01268-0*) West Pub.

Manetho. Aegyptiaca, Etc. Warmington, E. H., ed. Bd. with Tetrabiblios (Loeb Classical Library: No. 350). (ENG & GRE.). 15.50 (*0-674-99385-3*) HUP.

Manette, Jan. The Working Girl in a Man's World. LC 66-22896. 223p. 1966. 5.00 (*0-915988-01-1*) Reading Gems.

Manetti, Antonio. The Fat Woodworker. Martone, Valerie, tr. LC 90-55850. (Illus.). 88p. (Orig.). 1991. pap. 10.00 (*0-934977-23-2*) Italica Pr.

Manetti, Giovanni. Theories of the Sign in Classical Antiquity. Richardson, Christine, tr. LC 92-28924. (Advances in Semiotics Ser.). 224p. (ENG & ITA.). 1993. 35.00 (*0-253-33684-8*) Ind U Pr.

Manevich, Eleanor D. Such Were the Times: A Personal View of the Lysenko Era in the U. S. S. R. LC 89-64119. 100p. 1990. pap. 9.95 (*0-938875-22-1*) Pittenbruach Pr.

Manevitz, Alan Z., jt. ed. see Talbott, John A.

Maney, A. S. Faith for Living. (C). 1989. pap. 21.00 (*1-85072-112-2*, Pub. by W Sessions UK) St Mut.

Maney, Ann & Wells, Susan, eds. Professional Responsibilities in Protecting Children: A Public Health Approach to Child Sexual Abuse. LC 87-32798. 237p. 1988. text ed. 55.00 (*0-275-92966-3*, C2966, Praeger Pubs) Greenwood.

Maney, Ardith & Bykerk, Loree. Consumer Politics: Protecting Public Interests on Capitol Hill. LC 93-30980. (Contributions in Political Science Ser.: No. 343). 200p. 1994. text ed. 49.95 (*0-313-26428-7*, Greenwood Pr) Greenwood.

Maney, Ardith, jt. auth. see Bykerk, Loree.

Maney, Ardith L. Still Hungry after All These Years: Food Assistance Policy from Kennedy to Reagan. LC 88-7711. (Studies in Social Welfare Policies & Programs). 203p. 1989. text ed. 49.95 (*0-313-26327-2*, MSY, Greenwood Pr) Greenwood.

Maney, Carla. The Maze. (J). 1993. 7.95 (*0-533-10152-2*) Vantage.

Maney, Jill M. Emily Dickinson in Amherst: A Guide. (Famous Footsteps Ser.). (Illus.). (Orig.). 1989. pap. 4.95 (*0-929709-05-5*) Computer Lab.

***Maney, Kevin.** Megamedia Shakeout: The Inside story of the Leaders & the Losers in the Exploding Communications Industry. LC 94-43311. 1995. text ed. 24.95 (*0-471-10719-0*) Wiley.

Maney, Mabel. The Case of the Good-for-Nothing Girlfriend: A Nancy Clue Mystery. LC 94-29820. (Illus.). 180p. (Orig.). 1994. lib. bdg. 24.95 (*0-939416-90-5*); pap. 10.95 (*0-939416-91-3*) Cleis Pr.

— The Case of the Not-So-Nice Nurse. 160p. (Orig.). 1993. 24.95 (*0-939416-75-1*); pap. 9.95 (*0-939416-76-X*) Cleis Pr.

— A Ghost in the Closet. (Nancy Clue & the Hardly Boys Ser.). 180p. 1995. 24.95 (*1-57344-013-2*); pap. 10.95 (*1-57344-012-4*) Cleis Pr.

Maney, Patrick. Franklin D. Roosevelt. (Twentieth Century American Biography Ser.). 272p. 1992. pap. 14.95 (*0-8057-7786-5*) Macmillan.

Maney, Patrick J. The Roosevelt Presence: A Biography of F. D. R. (Twayne's Twentieth-Century American Biography Ser.). 250p. (C). 1992. pap. 14.95 (*0-8057-9825-0*, Twayne) Macmillan.

— The Roosevelt Presence: A Biography of F. D. R. (Twayne's Twentieth-Century American Biography Ser.). 250p. (C). 1993. text ed. 26.95 (*0-8057-7758-X*, Twayne) Macmillan.

Maney, R. Wayne. Marching to Cold Harbor: Victory & Failure, 1864. LC 94-27111. (Illus.). 280p. (C). 1994. 29.95 (*0-942597-65-6*) White Mane Pub.

Manferto, Valeria. Florida. 1992. 14.98 (*0-8317-3392-6*) Smithmark.

Manfield, Elizabeth. The Fifth Kiss. 224p. 1992. pap. 3.99 (*0-515-08910-9*) Jove Pubns.

Manfield, Philip. Split Self-Split Object: Understanding & Treating Borderline, Narcissistic, & Schizoid Disorders. LC 91-44052. 384p. 1992. 47.50 (*0-87668-460-6*) Aronson.

Manford, Alan, ed. see Hardy, Thomas.

Manford, Florence. Chips Around the World. 1992. 10.95 (*0-533-10057-7*) Vantage.

Manford, Toby, jt. auth. see Appleyard, R. T.

Manfred, F. R., jt. auth. see De Vries, Kets.

Manfred, F. R., jt. auth. see Kets de Vries.

Manfred, Frederick. Conquering Horse. 352p. 1959. pap. 4.50 (*0-451-08739-9*, W8739, Sig) NAL-Dutton.

— Conquering Horse. LC 83-5826. xvi, 355p. 1983. reprint ed. pap. 11.95 (*0-8032-8119-6*, Bison Books) U of Nebr Pr.

— Duke's Mixture. (Prairie Plains Ser.). 260p. (YA). (gr. 8). 1994. pap. 15.95 (*0-931170-55-9*) Ctr Western Studies.

— Flowers of Desire. LC 89-23569. 248p. 1989. 19.95 (*0-9624298-0-5*); pap. 10.95 (*0-9624298-1-3*) Dancing Badger.

— The Frederick Manfred Reader. Rezmerski, John C., ed. & intro. by. (Illus.). 458p. (Orig.). (YA). (gr. 10 up). 1995. pap. 18.95 (*0-930100-67-0*) Holy Cow.

— The Golden Bowl: Golden Anniversary Edition. LC 92-5627. 250p. 1992. pap. 9.95 (*0-9632157-0-1*) SD Human Fnd.

— King of Spades. 352p. 1995. mass mkt. 4.50 (*0-451-18424-6*, Sig) NAL-Dutton.

— Lord Grizzly. 1994. pap. 4.50 (*0-451-18413-0*, Sig) NAL-Dutton.

— Lord Grizzly. LC 82-24739. (Illus.). xviii, 285p. 1983. reprint ed. pap. 9.95 (*0-8032-8118-8*, Bison Books) U of Nebr Pr.

— The Manly-Hearted Woman. LC 84-25716. xvi, 185p. 1985. 20.00 (*0-8032-3092-3*); pap. 6.50 (*0-8032-8127-7*) U of Nebr Pr.

— No Fun on Sunday. LC 89-40738. 296p. 1990. 19.95 (*0-8061-2273-0*) U of Okla Pr.

— Of Lizards & Angels: A Saga of Siouxland. LC 91-50865. 624p. 1992. 22.95 (*0-8061-2417-2*) U of Okla Pr.

— Of Lizards & Angels: A Saga of Siouxland. LC 91-50865. 626p. (C). 1993. pap. 15.95 (*0-8061-2514-4*) U of Okla Pr.

— Prime Fathers. LC 86-27847. 190p. 1988. 15.95 (*0-935704-36-1*); pap. 9.95 (*0-935704-37-X*) Howe Brothers.

— Riders of Judgment. 352p. 1995. pap. 4.99 (*0-451-18425-4*, Sig) NAL-Dutton.

— Scarlet Plume. (The/Buckskin Man Tales Ser.: Bk. 3). 368p. 1995. 4.50 (*0-451-18423-8*, Sig) NAL-Dutton.

— Scarlet Plume. LC 83-5788. xviii, 365p. 1983. reprint ed. pap. 12.95 (*0-8032-8120-X*, Bison Books) U of Nebr Pr.

— The Selected Letters of Frederick Manfred, 1932-1954. Huseboe, Arthur R. & Nelson, Nancy O., eds. LC 88-4798. (Illus.). viii, 421p. 1989. 40.00 (*0-8032-2344-7*) U of Nebr Pr.

— Winter Count. deluxe limited ed. 1966. 75.00 (*0-911506-05-5*) Thueson.

— Winter Count: Poems. 1978. pap. 3.50 (*0-914476-78-5*) Thorp Springs.

— Winter Count II Bk. I. 1987. 40.00 (*0-911506-20-9*) Thueson.

An Asterisk (*) at the beginning of an entry indicates that the title is appearing in BIP for the first time.

Manfred, Frederick F. Lord Grizzly. 352p. (YA). 1964. pap. 4.50 (*0-451-08311-3*, E8311, Sig) NAL-Dutton.

Manfred, Freya. American Roads. LC 79-51029. 96p. 1984. pap. 8.95 (*0-87951-958-4*) Overlook Pr.

— American Roads: A Book of Poems. LC 79-51029. 96p. 1980. 14.95 (*0-87951-100-1*); 50.00 (*0-87951-103-6*) Overlook Pr.

— A Goldenrod Will Grow. 1971. pap. 2.75 (*0-911506-10-1*) Thueson.

Manfred, Hofer, jt. auth. see Eckel, Denis.

Manfred, Madge, jt. auth. see Strenski, Ellen.

Manfred, Riedel, jt. ed. see Mittelstrass, Juergen.

Manfred, Victor & Glutchison, John. Current Approaches to African Linguistics, Vol. 7. (Publications in African Languages & Linguistics: No. 11). 235p. 1990. pap. 77.15 (*90-6765-498-1*) Mouton.

Manfredi, Christopher P. The Paradox of Liberal Constitutionalism: Judicial Power & the Charter of Rights & Freedoms. LC 92-50725. 1993. pap. 19.95 (*0-8061-2527-6*) U of Okla Pr.

Manfredi, John. The Social Limits of Art. LC 82-8661. (Illus.). 208p. 1982. lib. bdg. 25.00 (*0-87023-372-6*) U of Mass Pr.

Manfredi, Renee. Where Love Leaves Us. LC 93-28456. (Iowa Short Fiction Award Ser.). 158p. 1994. 22.95 (*0-87745-444-2*) U of Iowa Pr.

Manfredi-Romanini, Maria G. & Bolognani-Fantin, Anna M. Polysaccharides & Glycoconjugates in Invertebrates & Polysaccharides & Glycoconjugates in Non-Mammalian Vertebrates. (Handbook of Histochemistry, Poly-saccharides Ser.: Vol. 11, Pt. 5). (Illus.). 450p. 1991. text ed. 255.00 (*1-56081-324-5*, Pub. by Gustav Fischer Verlag) VCH Pubs.

Manfredi, Ron. Sex Love & the Sad Soul. LC 91-67437. 60p. (Orig.). 1992. pap. 7.00 (*1-56002-127-6*) Aegina Pr.

Manfredi, Stephen J. AIDS: Answers for Everyone. 96p. (Orig.). (YA). (gr. 6-12). 1989. pap. text ed. 9.95 (*0-929496-01-9*) Treehaus Comns.

Manfredo, Michael J. Influencing Human Behavior: Theory & Applications in Recreation & Tourism & Natural Resources Management. LC 91-67445. 400p. (C). 1992. text ed. 37.95 (*0-915611-35-X*) Sagamore Pub.

Manfredo, Ralph P. Electronic Transformers & Inductors - U.S. Markets & Opportunities: 1993-1998 Analysis & Forecasts. 370p. 1994. pap. text ed. 1,900.00 (*1-878218-48-4*) World Info Tech.

Manfredonia, S. J. Twenty Eight Styles for Student Practice. (SPA.). 1984. 10.95 (*0-87350-149-7*) Milady Pub.

Manfull. The Stage in Action. 672p. 1992. per. 30.95 (*0-8403-7624-3*) Kendall-Hunt.

***Mang, Christa.** Senegal. (Bradt Country Guides Ser.). 96p. (Orig.). 1994. pap. 15.95 (*1-56440-555-9*, Pub. by Bradt Pubns UK) Globe Pequot.

— Zaire. (Bradt Country Guides Ser.). (Illus.). 224p. (Orig.). 1994. pap. 15.95 (*1-56440-557-5*, Pub. by Bradt Pubns UK) Globe Pequot.

Mang, H., jt. auth. see Kuhn, G.

Mang, Herbert & Meschke, Gunther. Computational Mechanics of Reinforced Concrete Structures. (Fundamentals & Advances in the Engineering Sciences Ser.). 350p. 1993. 108.00 (*3-528-06390-4*, Pub. by Vieweg & Sohn GW) Ballen Bkslr.

Mang, Herbert J., Jr., jt. auth. see Palmisano, Donald J.

Mang, Karl. History of Modern Furniture. (Illus.). 295p. 1979. 35.00 (*0-8109-1066-7*) Abrams.

Mang, T. S., ed. Physiological Monitoring & Early Detection Diagnostic Methods. 1992. 53.00 (*0-8194-0787-9*, 1641) SPIE.

***Mangajin Magazine Editors.** Mangajin's Basic Japanese Grammar Through Comics, Pt. 2. (Illus.). 160p. (Orig.). (JPN.). 1995. pap. 14.95 (*0-9634335-4-7*) Mangajin.

Mangal, S. K. General Psychology. 320p. (C). 1988. text ed. 30.00 (*81-207-0723-0*, Pub. by Sterling Pubs II) Apt Bks.

— Psychology: An Introduction to Human Behavior. 231p. 1990. text ed. 27.95 (*81-207-1242-0*, Pub. by Sterling Pubs II) Apt Bks.

Mangalam, S. J. Historical Geography & Toponomy of Andhra Pradesh. 260p. (C). 1987. 38.50 (*81-85055-99-8*, Pub. by Sundeep II) S Asia.

Mangaliso, Nomazengele A. The South African Mosaic: A Sociological Analysis of Post-Apartheid Conflict. 144p. (Orig.). 1994. lib. bdg. 42.50 (*0-8191-9505-7*); pap. text ed. 29.50 (*0-8191-9506-5*) U Pr of Amer.

Mangalwadi, Vishal. When the New Age Gets Old: Looking for a Greater Spirituality. LC 92-36926. 287p. (Orig.). 1993. pap. 12.99 (*0-8308-1770-0*, 1770) InterVarsity.

— The World of Gurus. 1987. 12.00 (*0-8364-2046-2*, Pub. by Usha II) S Asia.

— The World of Gurus. rev. ed. Hoeksema, Kurt, ed. LC 92-19113. 1992. pap. 11.95 (*0-940895-03-X*) Cornerstone IL.

Mangan, Celine, et al. The Targums of Job, Proverbs, & Qohelet. (Aramaic Bible Ser.). 256p. 1991. text ed. 65.00 (*0-8146-5490-8*) Liturgical Pr.

***Mangan, Charles, ed.** Walking with the Pilgrim Pope: Pope John Paul II Speaks Through Words & Pictures. 56p. Date not set. pap. 4.95 (*1-882972-43-0*) Queenship Pub.

Mangan, Charles M. Woman of Many Titles. LC 91-61498. (Illus.). 64p. (Orig.). 1991. pap. 4.00 (*1-877678-16-3*) Riehle Found.

Mangan, Dave, jt. auth. see Wilson, Ken.

Mangan, Frank. El Paso in Pictures. LC 70-184833. (Illus.). 174p. 1971. 30.00 (*0-930208-02-1*) Mangan Books TX.

Mangan, Frank & Mangan, Judy. Ruidoso Country. (Illus.). 192p. 1994. 39.95 (*0-930208-33-1*) Mangan Books TX.

Mangan, Frank, ed. see Metz, Leon C.

Mangan, G. The Biology of Human Personality. (International Series in Experimental Social Psychology: Vol. 25). 470p. 1982. 240.00 (*0-08-026781-5*, Pub. by Pergamon Repr UK) Franklin.

Mangan, Gerald. Waiting for the Storm. 64p. (Orig.). 1990. pap. 15.95 (*1-85224-110-1*, Pub. by Bloodaxe Bks UK) Dufour.

Mangan, Gordon L. Review of Published Research on the Relationship of Some Personality Variables to ESP Scoring Level. (Parapsychological Monograph Ser.: No. 1). 1958. pap. 5.00 (*0-912328-03-7*) Parapsych Foun.

Mangan, I., jt. auth. see Keogh, S.

Mangan, J. A., ed. Pleasure, Profit, Proselytism: British Culture & Sport at Home & Abroad, 1700-1914. 250p. 1986. 35.00 (*0-7146-3289-9*, Pub. by F Cass Pubs UK); pap. 16.50 (*0-7146-4050-6*, Pub. by F Cass Pubs UK) Intl Spec Bk.

— A Significant Social Revolution: Cross-Cultural Aspects of the Evolution of Compulsory Education. 232p. 1994. 37.50 (*0-7130-0189-5*, Pub. by Woburn Pr) Intl Spec Bk.

Mangan, J. A. & Park, Roberta J., eds. From "Fair Sex" to Feminism: Sport & the Socialization of Women in the Industrial & Post-Industrial Eras. LC 86-17529. 224p. 1986. 35.00 (*0-7146-3288-0*, Pub. by F Cass Pubs UK); pap. 14.95 (*0-7146-4049-2*, Pub. by F Cass Pubs UK) Intl Spec Bk.

Mangan, J. A., jt. ed. see Baker, William J.

Mangan, James A., ed. The Imperial Curriculum: Racial Images & Education in the British Colonial Experience. LC 92-19350. 272p. 1993. 59.95 (*0-415-06883-5*, B0172) Routledge.

— Making Imperial Mentalities: Socialisation & British Imperialism. (Studies in Imperialism). 1990. text ed. 59.95 (*0-7190-2864-7*, Pub. by Manchester Univ Pr UK) St Martin.

Mangan, James A. & Walvin, James, eds. Manliness & Morality: Middle-Class Masculinity in Britain & America, 1800-1940. LC 86-33923. 288p. 1991. reprint ed. text ed. 24.95 (*0-7190-2367-X*, Pub. by Manchester Univ Pr UK) St Martin.

Mangan, James A., jt. ed. see Staudohar, Paul D.

Mangan, James C. The Prose Writings of James Clarence Mangan. O'Donoghue, D. J., ed. LC 75-28826. reprint ed. 49.50 (*0-404-13818-7*) AMS Pr.

Mangan, James C., tr. Poets & Poetry of Munster: A Selection of Irish Songs by the Poets of the Last Century. 5th ed. LC 75-28824. reprint ed. 34.50 (*0-404-13816-0*) AMS Pr.

***Mangan, James J., ed.** Robert Whyte's Famine Ship Diary: The Journey of an Irish Immigrant Vessel. 128p. 1995. pap. 14.95 (*1-85635-091-6*) Dufour.

Mangan, John J. Life, Character & Influence of Desiderius Erasmus of Rotterdam, 2 Vols. LC 73-147113. reprint ed. 78.50 (*0-404-04178-7*) AMS Pr.

Mangan, Judy, jt. auth. see Mangan, Frank.

Mangan, Judy, ed. see Metz, Leon C.

***Mangan, Kathy.** Above the Tree Line. LC 94-70462. (Poetry Ser.). 64p. 1995. pap. 11.95 (*0-88748-191-4*) Carnegie-Mellon.

Mangan, Michael. Preface to Shakespeare's Tragedies. (Preface Bks.). (Illus.). 243p. (C). 1991. pap. text ed. 28.50 (*0-582-35503-6*, 79012) Longman.

Mangan, Sherry. Blackness of a White Night: Stories & Poems. Brooks, Marshall, ed. LC 86-20666. 64p. 1987. 13.50 (*0-933292-16-3*); pap. 6.50 (*0-933292-17-1*) Arts End.

Mangan, Velda B., ed. see Bair, Elmer O.

Manganaro, Marc. Myth, Rhetoric, & the Voice of Authority: A Critique of Frazer, Eliot, Frye, & Campbell. 240p. (C). 1992. text ed. 32.50 (*0-300-05194-8*) Yale U Pr.

Manganaro, Marc, ed. Modernist Anthropology: From Fieldwork to Text. 340p. (C). 1990. text ed. 52.50 (*0-691-06846-1*); pap. text ed. 15.95 (*0-691-01480-9*) Princeton U Pr.

Manganelli, Giorgio. All the Errors. Martin, Henry, tr. LC 90-5489. 158p. 1990. 20.00 (*0-929701-07-0*); pap. 10.00 (*0-929701-06-2*) McPherson & Co.

***Manganelli, Raymond L. & Klein, Mark M.** The Reengineering Handbook: A Step-by-Step Guide to Business Transformation. LC 94-26609. 288p. 1994. 29.95 (*0-8144-0236-4*) AMACOM.

Manganese Bronze, Ltd. Staff. Complex Aluminum Bronze Alloys with Improved Mechanical Corrosion-Resistance Properties. 79p. 1970. 11.85 (*0-317-34500-1*, 56) Intl Copper.

Manganiello, Dominic. T. S. Eliot & Dante. LC 88-15871. 192p. 1989. text ed. 39.95 (*0-312-02104-6*) St Martin.

Mangano. Preoperative Cardiac Assessment: A Society of Cardiovascular Anesthesiologists Mono. (Illus.). 200p. 1990. text ed. 38.00 (*0-397-51089-6*) Lippincott.

Mangano, Antonio. Sons of Italy: A Social & Religious Study of the Italians in America. LC 75-145488. (American Immigration Library). xii, 264p. 1971. reprint ed. lib. bdg. 33.95 (*0-89198-020-2*) Ozer.

Mangano, Joseph. Health Information Management. Karaffa, Melanie, ed. 260p. 1993. 49.95 (*1-878487-54-X*, ME051) Practice Mgmt Info.

Mangano, Joseph J. Living Legacy: How Nineteen Sixty-Four Changed America. LC 93-26725. 228p. (Orig.). (C). 1993. pap. text ed. 24.50 (*0-8191-9270-8*) U Pr of Amer.

Manganyi, N. Chabani. Treachery & Innocence: Psychology & Racial Difference in South Africa. 164p. 1992. 50.00 (*1-873836-05-8*, Pub. by H Zell Pubs UK) Bowker-Saur.

Manganyi, N. Chabani & Du Toit, Andre, eds. Political Violence & the Struggle in South Africa. LC 90-30359. 304p. 1990. text ed. 55.00 (*0-312-04662-6*) St Martin.

Manganyi, Noel C. Alienation & the Body in Racist Society: A Study of the Society That Invented Sow. LC 74-81854. 1977. text ed. 13.95 (*0-88357-053-X*) NOK Pubs.

Mangarella, Gina I., ed. see Mangarella, Michael A.

Mangarella, Michael A. The Art of Dealing Poker, Vol. II. Mangarella, Gina I., ed. (Illus.). 208p. (Orig.). (C). 1991. pap. 9.95 (*1-877725-12-9*) Video One Prodns.

Mangas, Brian. Carrot Delight. (J). 1990. pap. 5.95 (*0-671-67886-8*, S&S Bks Young Read) S&S Childrens.

— Carrot Delight. (Illus.). 32p. (J). (ps-1). 1991. pap. 2.25 (*0-671-73278-1*, Litl Simon S&S) S&S Childrens.

— Follow that Puppy. (J). (ps-6). 1993. pap. 4.95 (*0-671-87171-4*, S&S Bks Young Read) S&S Childrens.

— A Nice Surprise for Father Rabbit. (Illus.). 32p. (J). (ps-1). 1991. pap. 2.25 (*0-671-73277-3*, Litl Simon S&S) S&S Childrens.

— Sshaboom! LC 91-24764. (Illus.). 40p. (J). (ps-1). 1993. pap. 14.00 (*0-671-75538-2*, S&S Bks Young Read) S&S Childrens.

— You Don't Get a Carrot Unless You're a Bunny. (J). 1989. pap. 5.95 (*0-671-67201-0*, Litl Simon S&S) S&S Childrens.

— You Don't Get a Carrot Unless You're a Bunny. LC 88-19763. (Illus.). 32p. (J). (ps-00). 1991. pap. 2.25 (*0-671-74200-0*, Litl Simon S&S) S&S Childrens.

Mangas Manjarres, Julio, et al. Historia de Espana: 2. Espana Romana, Vol. II: La Sociedad, el Derecho y la Cultura. 764p. 1992. 189.50x (*84-239-4984-2*) Elliots Bks.

Mangasarian, Leon, ed. see Jafarian, Boghos.

***Mangasarian, Olvi L.** Nonlinear Programming. LC 94-36844. (Classics in Applied Mathematics Ser.: Vol. 10). 1994. 28.50 (*0-89871-341-2*) Soc Indus-Appl Math.

Mangat, Gurbachan S. Indian National Army: Role in India's Struggle for Freedom. (C). 1991. text ed. 26.00 (*0-685-50085-3*, Pub. by Classical Pub II) S Asia.

Mangat, S. S. Policeman's Guide to Crime & Criminal Investigation. (C). 1979. 160.00x (*0-685-39588-X*) St Mut.

Mange, Alyce E. The Near Eastern Policy of the Emperor Napoleon III. LC 74-12762. (Illinois Studies in the Social Sciences). 150p. 1975. reprint ed. text ed. 49.75 (*0-8371-7742-1*, MAEN, Greenwood Pr) Greenwood.

Mange, Arthur P. & Mange, Elaine J. Genetics: Human Aspects. 2nd rev. ed. LC 89-19662. (Illus.). 591p. (C). 1990. text ed. 51.95x (*0-87893-501-0*) Sinauer Assocs.

Mange, Arthur P., jt. auth. see Mange, Elaine J.

Mange, D. Microprogrammed Systems: An Introduction to Firmware Theory. 400p. 1992. pap. 49.95 (*0-442-31551-1*) Chapman & Hall.

Mange, Daniel. Analysis & Synthesis of Logic Systems. 700p. (C). 1986. text ed. 29.00 (*0-89006-188-2*) Artech Hse.

Mange, Elaine J. & Mange, Arthur P. Basic Human Genetics. LC 93-17808. (Illus.). 491p. 1993. text ed. 47.95 (*0-87893-495-2*) Sinauer Assocs.

Mange, Elaine J., jt. auth. see Mange, Arthur P.

Mange, Maria A. & Maurer, Heinz F. Heavy Minerals in Colour. (Illus.). 128p. (C). 1992. text ed. 79.95 (*0-412-43910-7*, A7197) Chapman & Hall.

— Heavy Minerals in Colour. (Illus.). 128p. 1989. 90.00 (*0-04-445564-X*) Routledge Chapman & Hall.

Mangel, Charles, jt. auth. see Gifford, Frank.

***Mangel, Gary D.** Corporate's Struggle with Ethics (The Lures & the Lies) A Guide to Climbing the Corporate Ladder. LC 95-75256. 152p. (Orig.). 1995. pap. 12.95 (*1-887057-13-7*) A M Publ IA.

Mangel, M., ed. Sex Allocation & Sex Change: Experiments & Models. LC 90-45411. (LLSCI Ser.: Vol. 22). 205p. 1990. pap. text ed. 43.00 (*0-8218-1172-X*, LLSCI-22) Am Math.

Mangel, M., et al, eds. Pest Control: Operations & Systems Analysis in Fruit Fly Management. (NATO ASI Series G Ecological Sciences: No. 11). xii, 465p. 1986. 128.00 (*0-387-16088-4*) Spr-Verlag.

Mangel, Marc. Decision & Control in Uncertain Resource Systems. (Mathematics in Science & Engineering Ser.). 1984. text ed. 75.00 (*0-12-468720-2*) Acad Pr.

Mangel, Marc & Clark, Colin W. Dynamic Modeling in Behavioral Ecology. (Monographs in Behavior & Ecology). (Illus.). 380p. 1988. 55.00 (*0-691-08505-6*); pap. 19.95 (*0-691-08506-4*) Princeton U Pr.

***Mangels.** Essential Star Wars. Date not set. pap. 18.00 (*0-345-39535-2*) Ballantine.

***Mangels, George.** Frank's World: The Odyssey of a Fleshy Lump. LC 94-44487. 1995. 22.95 (*0-312-11791-4*) St Martin.

Mangels, Reed, jt. auth. see Wasserman, Debra.

***Mangelsdorf, Guenter.** Die Ortswuestungen des Havellandes: Historisch-Archaeologische Beitraege Zur Wuestungkunde der Mark Brandenburg. (Veroeffentlichungen der Historischen Kommission Zu Berlin Ser.: Bd. 86). 338p. (GER.). (C). 1994. lib. bdg. 110.80 (*3-11-014086-1*) De Gruyter.

Mangelsdorf, J., et al. River Morphology. (Physical Environment Ser.: Vol. 7). (Illus.). 264p. 1990. 110.00 (*0-387-51108-3*) Spr-Verlag.

Mangelsdorf, Paul C. Corn: Its Origin, Evolution, & Development. LC 72-95454. 288p. 1974. 30.00 (*0-674-17175-6*) HUP.

Mangelsdorf, Tom. History of Steinbeck's Cannery Row. LC 86-50500. (Illus.). 216p. 1991. pap. 14.95 (*0-934136-35-1*) Western Tanager.

Mangelsdorff, David, jt. ed. see Gal, Reuven.

Mangelsdorff, Rich. Selected Essays. (American Dust Ser.: No. 8). 1977. pap. 2.95 (*0-913218-50-2*) Dustbooks.

Mangelsen, Mary A., ed. see Schwartz, George & Cayten, C. Gene.

Mangelsen, Thomas D. A Time for Singing. LC 93-36772. (Illus.). 32p. (J). (ps-3). 1994. 13.99 (*0-525-65096-2*, Cobblehill Bks) Dutton Child Bks.

Mangelsen, Tom. Images of Nature. (Illus.). 224p. 1989. 60.00 (*0-88363-789-8*) H L Levin.

Mangen, David & Peterson, Warren A. Research Instruments in Social Gerontology: Clinical & Social Psychology, Vol. 1. LC 81-16449. 666p. (C). 1982. text ed. 44.95 (*0-8166-0991-8*) U of Minn Pr.

Mangen, David J. & Peterson, Warren A., eds. Research Instruments in Social Gerontology: Social Roles & Social Participation, Vol. 2. LC 81-16449. 538p. (C). 1982. text ed. 44.95 (*0-8166-1096-7*) U of Minn Pr.

— Research Instruments in Social Gerontology, Vol. 3: Health, Program Evaluation, & Demography. LC 81-16449. 469p. 1984. text ed. 44.95 (*0-8166-1112-2*) U of Minn Pr.

Mangen, David J., et al, eds. Measurement of Intergenerational Relations. LC 87-28466. (Sage Focus Editions Ser.: No. 92). 253p. reprint ed. pap. 72.20 (*0-7837-6579-7*, 2046144) Bks Demand.

Manger, Jason. Database Graphics Programming: A Guide for Xbase Developers Using dGE. 324p. (Orig.). 1993. pap. 48.50 (*1-85058-504-0*, Pub. by Sigma Press UK) Coronet Bks.

— The Essential Internet Information Guide. 515p. 1994. pap. text ed. 27.95 (*0-07-707905-1*) McGraw.

— UNIX - the Complete Book: A Guide for the Professional User. 468p. (Orig.). 1991. pap. 67.50 (*1-85058-219-X*, Pub. by Sigma Press UK) Coronet Bks.

***Manger, Jason J.** The World-Wide Web, Mosaic & More. 1995. pap. text ed. 34.95 (*0-07-709132-9*) McGraw.

Manger, Leif, ed. Communal Labour in the Sudan. (Bergen Studies in Social Anthropology: No. 41). 150p. 1988. pap. 13.95 (*0-936508-71-X*) Barber Pr.

***Manger, Leif O.** From the Mountains to the Plains: The Integration of the Lafofa Nuba into Sudanese Society. (Scandinavian Institute of African Studies). 173p. (Orig.). 1994. pap. 37.50x (*91-7106-336-6*, Pub. by Almqv & Wiksell SW) Coronet Bks.

— The Sand Swallows Our Land. (Bergen Studies in Social Anthropology: No. 24). 137p. (Orig.). 1985. pap. text ed. 11.95 (*0-936508-60-4*, Pub. by Bergen Univ Dept Social Anthro NO) Barber Pr.

Manger, Leif O., ed. Trade & Traders in the Sudan. (Bergen Studies in Social Anthropology: No. 32). 284p. 1985. pap. text ed. 13.95 (*0-936508-64-7*, Pub. by Bergen Univ Dept Social Anthro NO) Barber Pr.

Manger, W. M. Catecholamines in Normal & Abnormal Cardiac Function. (Advances in Cardiology Ser.: Vol. 30). (Illus.). xxiv, 152p. 1982. 78.50 (*3-8055-3516-3*) S Karger.

***Manger, William M., ed.** Pheochromocytoma: A Clinical & Experimental Overview. 2nd ed. 700p. (C). 1995. write for info. (*0-393-71028-9*) Norton.

Manget, Ansley. My Secrets of Living: A French Woman Tells about Her Love Affair with Life & Its Joys. (Illus.). 96p. (Orig.). 1989. pap. 12.50 (*0-9622760-0-6*) A Manget.

Manget, J. Jacob. Bibliotheca Chemica Curiosa, 2 vols., Set. Date not set. write for info. (*0-318-71843-X*, Pub. by Georg Olms GW) Lubrecht & Cramer.

Mangham, I. L. Interactions & Interventions in Organizations. LC 78-2602. (Wiley Series on Individuals, Groups & Organizations). (Illus.). 166p. reprint ed. pap. 47.40 (*0-685-23759-1*, 2032833) Bks Demand.

Mangham, Iain, jt. auth. see Bate, Paul.

Mangham, Iain L. The Politics of Organizational Change. LC 79-23. (Contributions in Economics & Economic History Ser.: No. 26). 221p. 1979. text ed. 49.95 (*0-313-20981-2*, MPC/, Greenwood Pr) Greenwood.

Mangham, Iain L., ed. Organization Analysis & Development: A Social Construction of Organizational Behaviour. LC 86-26713. (Industrial Psychology & Organization Behaviour Ser.). 283p. reprint ed. pap. 80.70 (*0-7837-6162-7*, 2045884) Bks Demand.

Mangham, Iain L. & Overington, Michael A. Organizations As Theatre: A Social Psychology of Dramatic Appearances. LC 86-19199. 224p. reprint ed. pap. 63.90 (*0-7837-6163-5*, 2045885) Bks Demand.

Manghnani, M. H., jt. auth. see Akimoto, S.

Manghnani, Murli H. & Syono, Yasuhiko, eds. High Pressure Research in Mineral Physics. (Mineral Physics Ser.: Vol. 2). (Illus.). 498p. 1987. 60.00 (*0-87590-066-6*) Am Geophysical.

Manghnani, Murli H., jt. auth. see Syono, Yasuhiko.

Mangiafico, Luciano. Contemporary American Immigrants: Patterns of Filipino, Korean, & Chinese Settlement in the United States. LC 87-17752. 229p. 1988. text ed. 49.95 (*0-275-92726-1*, C2726, Praeger Pubs) Greenwood.

***Mangiaracina, Michael F.** Courtroom Testimony Concepts. Garrison, Kathleen M., ed. 98p. 1994. pap. text ed. 14.95 (*0-9644837-0-X*) Garrison Desktop.

— So You Want to Buy a Handgun! Read This Before Going Any Further. Garrison, Kathleen M., ed. (Illus.). 91p. (Orig.). 1995. pap. text ed. 11.95 (*0-9644837-1-8*) Garrison Desktop.

Mangiarotti, L. & Sardanashvily, G. New Lagrangian & Hamiltonian Methods in Field Theory. 300p. 1995. text ed. 71.00 (*981-02-1587-8*) World Scientific Pub.

Mangieri, John, jt. ed. see Collins, Cathy.

Mangieri, John N., ed. Excellence in Education. LC 85-50539. 248p. 1985. 25.00 (*0-87565-020-1*) Tex Christian.

Mangieri, John N., jt. auth. see Block, Cathy C.

Mangieri, Rose M. My Companion to Know, Love, & Serve. LC 73-158919. (Know, Love, & Serve Catechisms Ser.). (Illus.). 85p. (Orig.). (J). (ps-1). 1977. pap. 5.50 (*0-913382-45-0*, 103-7) Prow Bks-Franciscan.

Mangili, Lauren, jt. auth. see Mazzeo, Karen.

***Mangin, P. & Ludes, B.** Acta Medicinae Legalis 1994: Proceedings of the XVIIth Congress of the International Academy of Legal Medicine. 560p. 1995. pap. 143.00 (*3-540-58847-7*) Spr-Verlag.

Mangin, Patrice J., ed. see Technical Association of the Pulp & Paper Industry Staff.

***Mangine, Robert E., ed.** Physical Therapy of the Knee. 2nd ed. LC 95-12053. (Clinics in Physical Therapy Ser.). 1995. write for info. (*0-443-08916-7*) Churchill.

— Physical Therapy of the Knee. LC 87-24284. (Clinics in Physical Therapy Ser.: Vol. 19). (Illus.). 264p. reprint ed. pap. 75.30 (0-7837-1611-7, 2041903) Bks Demand.

Manginello, Frank P. & DiGeronimo, Theresa F. Your Premature Baby: Everything You Need to Know about the Childbirth Treatment & Parenting of Premature Infants. 296p. 1991. pap. text ed. 14.95 (0-471-53587-7) Wiley.

Mangini, A., jt. auth. see Bernardi, F.

Mangini, A., et al. Summary of Some of My Research on Organosulphur Compounds; Rotational Isomerism of Vinyl Ethers & Sulfides; The Effect of Organic Sulfur Compounds on Oxidation Processes of Hydrocarbon Fuels. Senning, A., ed. (Sulfer Report Ser.: Vol. 7, No. 5). 83p. 1987. pap. text ed. 78.00 (3-7186-4804-0) Gordon & Breach.

***Mangini-Gonzalez, Shirley.** Memories of Resistance: Women's Voices from the Spanish Civil War. LC 94-29752. 1995. 25.00 (0-300-05816-0) Yale U Pr.

Mangiola, Leslie, jt. auth. see Heath, Shirley B.

Mangione, Jerre. Mount Allegro: A Memoir of Italian-American Life. LC 88-45636. 320p. 1989. reprint ed. pap. 12.00 (0-06-097215-7, PL 7215, PL) HarpC.

— A Passion for Sicillians: The World Around Danilo Dolici. 320p. (C). 1985. pap. 18.95 (0-88738-606-7) Transaction Pubs.

— Reunion in Sicily. LC 84-1855. (Morningside Bk.). 285p. 1984. reprint ed. text ed. 43.00 (0-231-05840-3); reprint ed. pap. text ed. 16.00 (0-231-05841-1) Col U Pr.

Mangione, Jerre & Morreale, Ben. La Storia: Five Centuries of the Italian American Experience. LC 92-52553. (Illus.). 528p. 1993. reprint ed. pap. 15.00 (0-06-092441-1, PL) HarpC.

Mangione, S., jt. auth. see Gerace, P.

Mangione, Thomas W., jt. auth. see Fowler, Floyd J., Jr.

Manglapus, Raul S. Japan in Southeast Asia: Collision Course. LC 76-14709. 1976. text ed. 3.75 (0-87003-004-3) Carnegie Endow.

— Philippines, the Silenced Democracy. LC 75-3342. 221p. reprint ed. pap. 63.00 (0-8357-8982-9, 2033523) Bks Demand.

— Will of the People: Original Democracy in Non-Western Societies. LC 86-29594. (Studies in Freedom: No. 4). 200p. 1987. text ed. 49.95 (0-313-25837-6, MWG/, Greenwood Pr) Greenwood.

Mangles, J., jt. auth. see Irby, C.

Mango, Andrew. Turkey: The Challenge of a New Role. LC 94-10581. (Washington Papers). 140p. 1994. text ed. 45.00 (0-275-94985-0, Praeger Pubs); pap. text ed. 12.95 (0-275-94986-9, Praeger Pubs) Greenwood.

Mango, Cyril. Byzantine Architecture. LC 85-62749. (History of World Architecture Ser.). (Illus.). 224p. 1985. pap. 29.95 (0-8478-0615-4) Rizzoli Intl.

— Byzantium & Its Image: History & Culture of the Byzantine Empire & Its Heritage. (Collected Studies: CS191). (Illus.). 360p. (C). 1984. reprint ed. lib. bdg. 101.95 (0-86078-139-9, Pub. by Variorum UK) Ashgate Pub Co.

— Studies on Constantinople. (Collected Studies: Vol. 394). 288p. 1993. 89.95 (0-86078-372-3, Pub. by Variorum UK) Ashgate Pub Co.

Mango, Cyril, ed. The Art of the Byzantine Empire 312-1453: Sources & Documents. (Medieval Academy Reprints for Teaching Ser.). 272p. 1986. reprint ed. pap. text ed. 12.95 (0-8020-6627-5) U of Toronto Pr.

Mango, Cyril, tr. & comment. Nikephoros, Patriarch of Constantinople, Short History. LC 89-17058. (Dumbarton Oaks Texts Ser.: Vol. 10). (Illus.). 264p. 1990. 30.00 (0-88402-184-X, MANI, Dumbarton Rsch Lib) Dumbarton Oaks.

Mango, Karin N. Hearing Loss. Perrotta, Mary, ed. LC 90-19746. (Venture Bks.). (Illus.). 144p. (YA). (gr. 7-12). 1991. lib. bdg. 14.77 (0-531-12519-X) Watts.

— Mapmaking. LC 83-25084. (Illus.). 112p. (J). (gr. 4 up). 1984. lib. bdg. 9.29 (0-671-45518-4, Julian Messner) Silver Burdett Pr.

Mango, Marlia M., jt. ed. see Boyd, Susan A.

Mango, Wanda P. Grandma's Home Kitchen: Where Lessons & Life Were Mixed with Love: Family Recipes & Traditions of Grandma's Swedish Bakery, Door County. 128p. (Orig.). 1994. pap. write for info. (0-942495-38-1) Amherst Pr.

***Mangold.** Duden Woerterbuch Vol. 6: Aussptache. 794p. (GER.). 1990. 49.95 (0-614-00369-5, 341120916X) Fr & Eur.

Mangold, George B. Labor Argument in the American Protective Tariff Discussion. LC 73-156433. (American Labor Ser., No. 2). 1971. reprint ed. 15.95 (0-405-02931-4) Ayer.

Mangold, Helmut K., ed. Handbook of Chromatography: Lipids, 2 vols., Vol. I. 624p. 1984. 180.95 (0-8493-3037-8, QD305, CRC Reprint) Franklin.

— Handbook of Chromatography: Lipids, 2 vols., Vol. II. 368p. 1984. 141.95 (0-8493-3038-6, QD305, CRC Reprint) Franklin.

Mangold, Lori & Mangold, Scott. The Professional Pet Sitter: Your Guide to Starting & Operating a Successful Service. 100p. 1994. pap. 29.95 (0-9635442-1-7) Paws for Awhile.

Mangold, M. A. How to Buy a Small Business. rev. ed. LC 86-91533. 31p. 1987. pap. 3.50 (0-87576-126-7) Pilot Bks.

Mangold, Margaret M., ed. La Causa Chicana: The Movement for Justice. LC 72-92083. 236p. reprint ed. pap. 67.30 (0-685-24010-X, 2031597) Bks Demand.

Mangold, Nancy R. Changing Auditors & the Effect on Earnings, Auditors' Opinions & Stock Prices. Farmer, Richard, ed. LC 87-19128. (Research for Business Decisions Ser.: No. 93). 147p. reprint ed. pap. 49.90 (0-8357-1786-0, 2070404) Bks Demand.

Mangold, Paul, jt. auth. see Gipson, Morrell.

Mangold, Peter. National Security & Internatinal Politics: The Search for Security. 144p. 1990. 59.95 (0-415-02295-9, A4665) Routledge.

Mangold, Sally, ed. A Teacher's Guide to the Special Educational Needs of Blind & Visually Handicapped Children. LC 82-4025. 164p. 1982. pap. 18.95 (0-89128-108-8) Am Foun Blind.

Mangold, Sally S., jt. auth. see Olson, Myrna R.

Mangold, Scott, jt. auth. see Mangold, Lori.

Mangold, Tom & Penycate, John. The Tunnels of Cu Chi. 320p. 1986. mass mkt. 5.99 (0-425-08951-7) Berkley Pub.

Mangone, Gerard J. Concise Marine Almanac. 1990. 58.00 (0-8448-1674-4) Taylor & Francis.

— The Idea & Practice of World Government. LC 74-3620. 278p. 1975. reprint ed. text ed. 59.75 (0-8371-7453-8, MAPW, Greenwood Pr) Greenwood.

— Marine Policy for America. 2nd enl. rev. ed. LC 88-4890. (Illus.). 400p. (C). 1988. text ed. 55.00 (0-8448-1537-3) Taylor & Francis.

Mangone, Gerard J., ed. International Straits. (Special Issue of Ocean Development & International Law Ser.: Vol. 18, No. 4). 106p. 1987. pap. 22.00 (0-8448-1534-9) Taylor & Francis.

Mangonon, P. L., Jr., ed. see Metallurgical Society of AIME Staff.

Mangonon, P. L.

Mangraviti, James, jt. auth. see Babitsky, Steven J.

Mangraviti, James, jt. auth. see Babitsky, Steven.

Mangrum, Charles T., II. Learning to Study, Bk. D. 2nd ed. 80p. (J). (gr. 4). 1994. teacher ed 3.95 (0-89061-733-3); pap. 8.00 (0-89061-726-0) Jamestown Pubs.

— Learning to Study, Bk. E. 2nd ed. 96p. (J). (gr. 5). 1994. teacher ed 3.95 (0-89061-734-1); pap. 8.00 (0-89061-727-9) Jamestown Pubs.

— Learning to Study, Bk. F. 2nd ed. 96p. (J). (gr. 6). 1994. teacher ed 3.95 (0-89061-735-X); pap. 8.00 (0-89061-728-7) Jamestown Pubs.

— Learning to Study, Bk. G. 2nd ed. 96p. (J). (gr. 7). 1994. teacher ed 3.95 (0-89061-736-8); pap. 8.00 (0-89061-729-5) Jamestown Pubs.

— Learning to Study, Bk. H. 2nd ed. 96p. (J). (gr. 8). 1994. teacher ed 3.95 (0-89061-737-6); pap. 8.00 (0-89061-730-9) Jamestown Pubs.

— Learning to Study, Bks. B-C. 2nd ed. 80p. (J). (gr. 2-3). 1994. teacher ed 3.95 (0-89061-732-5); pap. 8.00 (0-89061-725-2) Jamestown Pubs.

— Learning to Study, 6 bks., Bks.B-H. 2nd ed. (J). (gr. 2-8). 1994. teacher ed 23.70 (0-89061-731-7) Jamestown Pubs.

— Learning to Study, 6 bks., Set, Bks. B-H. 2nd ed. (J). (gr. 2-8). 1994. Set. pap. 48.00 (0-89061-724-4) Jamestown Pubs.

Mangrum, Charles T. & Strichart, Stephen S. Peterson's Guide to Colleges with Programs for Students with Learning Disabilities. 4th ed. LC 94-4760. 684p. (C). 1994. 31.95 (1-56079-400-3) Petersons Guides.

Mangrum, Charles T., II, jt. auth. see Strichart, Stephen S.

Mangrum, Grace S. From Mourning into Morning. LC 89-92263. (Illus.). (Orig.). 1989. pap. 8.50 (0-9624524-0-8) G S Mangrum.

Mangrum, R. Collin, jt. auth. see Firmage, Edwin B.

Mangrum, Robert G. Route Step March: Edwin M Stanton's Special Military Units & the Prosecution of the War, 1862-1865. 237p. 1980. 28.95 (0-89126-091-9) MA-AH Pub.

Manguel. Dictionary of Imaginery Places. 1980. 24.95 (0-02-579310-1) Macmillan.

Manguel, Alberto. Black Water Two: More Tales of the Fantastic. 1990. pap. 17.50 (0-517-57559-0, C P Pubs) Crown Pub Group.

— The Gates of Paradise: An Anthology of Erotic Short Fiction. 1993. 18.00 (0-517-88050-4, C P Pubs) Crown Pub Group.

— News from a Foreign Country Came. 1991. 19.00 (0-517-58343-7, C P Pubs) Crown Pub Group.

Manguel, Alberto, ed. Black Water: The Book of Fantastic Literature. 992p. 1984. pap. 16.00 (0-517-55269-8, C P Pubs) Crown Pub Group.

Manguel, Alberto, ed. & intro. Other Fires: Short Fiction by Latin American Women. 224p. 1985. 12.00 (0-517-55870-X, C P Pubs) Crown Pub Group.

Manguel, Alberto, ed. Soho Square, No. 3. 286p. 1993. 19.95 (0-7475-0716-3, Pub. by Bloomsbury Pub Ltd UK) Trafalgar.

Manguel, Alberto & Guadalupi, Gianni. The Dictionary of Imaginary Places. (Illus.). 1987. pap. 18.95 (0-15-626054-9, Harvest Bks) HarBrace.

Manguel, Alberto & Stephenson, Craig. In another Part of the Forest: An Anthology of Gay Short Fiction. LC 93-38181. 1994. 20.00 (0-517-88156-X, C P Pubs) Crown Pub Group.

Manguel, Alberto, tr. see Yourcenar, Marguerite.

Manguin, Pierre-Yves, jt. ed. see Bouchon, Genevieve.

Mangum, Bryant. A Fortune Yet: Money in the Art of F. Scott Fitzgerald's Short Stories. LC 91-9442. 254p. 1991. 30.00 (0-8153-0083-2, H1421) Garland.

***Mangum, Cary R. & Garvis, Ralph W.** Being: The Metamorphosis of Consciousness. (Illus.). 162p. (Orig.). 1992. pap. 12.95 (1-879337-00-2) Garrett Pub.

Mangum, Charles T., II, jt. auth. see Forgan, Harry W.

Mangum, Diane L. Carry on, Caroline. 1993. pap. 6.95 (0-88494-883-8) Bookcraft Inc.

***Mangum, Eric & Stubbs, Dean.** 87 Superstar Guitar Sounds on a Stompbox Budget. (Illus.). 112p. (Orig.). 1995. pap. text ed. 14.95 (0-89524-883-2, HL02503100) Cherry Lane.

— FX - 87 Superstar Sounds on a Stompbox Budget. 90p. 1995. pap. write for info. (0-614-03544-9) Cherry Lane.

Mangum, Garth & Blumell, Bruce. The Mormons' War on Poverty: A History of LDS Welfare, 1830-1990. LC 92-35616. (Publications in Mormon Studies: Vol. 8). 320p. 1993. 29.95 (0-87480-414-0) U of Utah Pr.

Mangum, Garth, jt. auth. see Walsh, John.

Mangum, Garth L. The Operating Engineers: The Economic History of a Trade Union. LC 63-19144. (Publications in Industrial Relations). 366p. reprint ed. pap. 104.40 (0-317-55365-8, 2029171) Bks Demand.

Mangum, Garth L. & Glenn, Lowell M. Employing the Disadvantaged in the Federal Civil Service. LC 79-626166. (Policy Papers in Human Resources & Industrial Relations Ser.: No. 13). (Orig.). 1969. pap. 5.00 (0-87736-113-4) U of Mich Inst Labor.

Mangum, Garth L. & Philips, Peter, eds. Three Worlds of Labor Economics. LC 87-26423. 392p. (C). 1988. 51.95 (0-87332-455-2); pap. 25.95 (0-87332-456-0) M E Sharpe.

Mangum, Garth L. & Seninger, Stephen F. Coming of Age in the Ghetto, a Dilemma of Youth Unemployment: A Report to the Ford Foundation. (PSEW Ser.: No. 33). 1978. text ed. 16.00 (0-8018-2125-8) Johns Hopkins.

Mangum, Garth L. & Walsh, John. Union Resilience in Troubled Times: The Story of the Operating Engineers, AFL-CIO, 1960-1993. (Labor & Human Resources Ser.). (Illus.). 294p. 1994. text ed. 49.95 (1-56324-452-7); pap. text ed. 21.95 (1-56324-453-5) M E Sharpe.

Mangum, Garth L., jt. auth. see Hildebrand, George H.

Mangum, Garth L., jt. auth. see Levitan, Sar A.

Mangum, Garth L., jt. ed. see Levitan, Sar A.

Mangum, Garth L., jt. auth. see Nemore, Arnold L.

Mangum, Karen. Life's Simple Pleasure Cookbook. 160p. 1990. 24.95 (0-8163-0927-2) Pacific Pr Pub Assn.

— Life's Simple Pleasures: Fine Vegetarian Cooking for Sharing & Celebration. 1990. 24.95 (0-8163-1114-5) Pacific Pr Pub Assn.

Mangum, Kim, et al. Voter Purging: The Perils & the Promise. 50p. 1990. 15.00 (0-685-56594-7) CPA Washington.

Mangum, Neil C. Battle of the Rosebud: Prelude to the Little Bighorn. LC 87-50694. (Montana & the West Ser.: Vol. 5). (Illus.). 200p. (C). 1987. 35.00 (0-912783-11-7) Upton Sons.

Mangum, Richard K. & Mangum, Sherry G. Flagstaff Album: Flagstaff's First Fifty Years in Photographs, 1876-1926. (Illus.). 64p. (Orig.). 1993. pap. 9.95 (0-9632265-4-1) Hexagon Pr.

— Flagstaff Hikes: One-Hundred-Thirty-Four Day Hikes Around Flagstaff, Arizona. 3rd rev. ed. (Illus.). 264p. 1995. pap. 14.95 (0-9632265-7-6) Hexagon Pr.

— Flagstaff Historic Walk: A Stroll Through Old Downtown. (Illus.). 64p. (Orig.). 1993. pap. 6.95 (0-9632265-3-3) Hexagon Pr.

— Sedona Hikes: One Hundred Twenty-One Hikes, Five Vortex Sites Around Sedona, Arizona. 2nd rev. ed. (Illus.). 256p. 1994. reprint ed. pap. 14.95 (0-9632265-6-8) Hexagon Pr.

Mangum, Sherry G., jt. auth. see Mangum, Richard K.

Mangum, Stephen L., jt. auth. see Hsieh, Ching-Yao.

***Mangum, William.** Job Search Workbook: A Companion to the Book...99 Minutes to Your Ideal Job. Weckbaugh, Ernest, ed. 116p. (Orig.). 1995. student ed, pap. 12.95 (1-881474-04-6) TMI Pubng.

***Mangum, William T.** 99 Minutes to Your Ideal Job. LC 94-34132. 1995. text ed. 29.95 (0-471-11125-2); pap. text ed. 12.95 (0-471-11126-0) Wiley.

Mangun, Vesta. The Best of Vesta Mangun. (Illus.). 180p. (Orig.). 1987. pap. write for info. (0-9619753-0-X) Pentecostals Alexandria.

— Vesta Mangun Continues. 87p. (Orig.). 1990. pap. 6.00 (0-9619753-1-8) Pentecostals Alexandria.

Mangun, William, ed. Wildlife Conservation & Public Policy. (Orig.). 1991. pap. 12.00 (0-944285-22-8) Pol Studies.

Mangun, William R., ed. American Fish & Wildlife Policy: The Human Dimension. LC 91-47741. (Illus.). 288p. (C). 1992. 27.50 (0-8093-1821-0) S Ill U Pr.

— Public Policy Issues in Wildlife Management. LC 91-20774. (Contributions in Political Science Ser.: No. 286). 208p. 1991. text ed. 47.95 (0-313-28010-X, MIW, Greenwood Pr) Greenwood.

Mangun, William R., jt. auth. see Henning, Daniel H.

Mangus, A. L. Changing Aspects of Rural Relief. LC 74-165685. (Research Monograph Ser.: Vol. 14). 1971. reprint ed. lib. bdg. 29.50 (0-306-70346-7) Da Capo.

Mangus, A. R., jt. auth. see Asch, Berta.

Mangus, Brent, jt. auth. see Pfeiffer, Ron.

***Mangus, Brent C. & Pfeiffer, Ronald P.** Concepts of Athletic Training. LC 95-1456. 1995. write for info. (0-87620-839-1) Jones & Bartlett.

Mangus, Jim. Shawnee Pottery: An Identification & Value Guide. 1993. 24.95 (0-89145-574-4) Collector Bks.

***Mangusso, Mary C. & Haycox, Stephen W., eds.** Interpreting Alaska's History: An Anthology. LC 94-24909. 480p. 1995. pap. 24.95 (0-295-97432-X) U of Wash Pr.

Mangusso, Mary C., jt. auth. see Haycox, Stephen W.

Manhard, Stephen J. The Goof-Proofer: The Sure-Fire Way to Improve Your Speaking & Writing. 96p. 1987. pap. 4.95 (0-02-040610-X, Pub. by Gebrueder Borntraeger GW) Macmillan.

Manhart, Marcia Y. Objects & Drawings from the Sanford M. & Diane Besser Collection. 94p. 1992. pap. 25.00 (1-884240-01-1) Arkansas Art Ctr.

Manhas, J. S., jt. auth. see Singh, R. K.

Manhas, Maghar S. & Bose, Ajay K. Synthesis of Penicillin, Cephalosporin C, & Analogs. LC 69-13151. (New Directions in Organic Chemistry Ser.). 132p. reprint ed. pap. 37.70 (0-685-16176-5, 2027101) Bks Demand.

Manhattan, Avro. Catholic Imperialism & World Freedom. LC 73-161336. (Atheist Viewpoint Ser.). 528p. 1972. reprint ed. 31.95 (0-405-03810-0) Ayer.

— The Vatican Billions. LC 83-72654. 304p. 1983. pap. 11.50 (0-937958-16-6) Chick Pubns.

— The Vatican Moscow Washington Alliance. LC 82-73082. 352p. (Orig.). pap. 11.50 (0-937958-12-3) Chick Pubns.

Manheim, Carol J. The Myofascial Release Manual. 2nd ed. LC 94-13677. 214p. 1994. 38.00 (1-55642-241-5) SLACK Inc.

Manheim, Carol J. & Lavett, Diane K. The Myofascial Release Manual. LC 89-42574. (Illus.). 135p. (Orig.). (C). 1989. pap. text ed. 35.00 (1-55642-108-7, 40559) SLACK Inc.

— The Self-Healing Body: Craniosacral Therapy & Sonato-Emotional Release. LC 89-42578. 250p. (Orig.). 1989. pap. text ed. 30.00 (1-55642-250-4) SLACK Inc.

Manheim, Jarol. Public Diplomacy & American Foreign Policy. (Illus.). 240p. (C). 1994. 39.95 (0-19-508737-2); pap. text ed. 14.95 (0-19-508738-0) OUP.

Manheim, Jarol B. All of the People, All the Time: Strategic Communication & American Politics. LC 90-39657. 272p. 1991. text ed. 36.95 (0-87332-796-9) M E Sharpe.

Manheim, Jarol B. & Rich, Richard C. Empirical Political Analysis: Research Methods in Political Science. 3rd ed. 399p. (C). 1991. text ed. 48.95 (0-8013-0407-5, 78216) Longman.

— Empirical Political Analysis: Research Methods in Political Science. 4th ed. LC 94-9003. 480p. (C). 1995. text ed. 47.95 (0-8013-1307-4) Longman.

Manheim, Karl, tr. see Jaspers, Karl.

Manheim, Marvin. Fundamentals of Transportation Systems Analysis: Basic Concepts, Vol. 1. 1979. 55.00x (0-262-13129-3) MIT Pr.

Manheim, Marvin, jt. auth. see Coleman, David.

Manheim, Michael. Eugene O'Neill's New Language of Kinship. LC 82-3190. 256p. 1982. pap. 16.95 (0-8156-2277-5) Syracuse U Pr.

Manheim, R., tr. see Corbin, Henry.

Manheim, R., tr. see Jacobi, Jolande.

Manheim, Ralph, tr. Hesse, Hermann: Hesse As Painter (with 20 Full-Page Watercolors) (Illus.). 46p. 1980. 10.00 (3-518-03176-7, Pub. by Suhr Verlag GW) Intl Bk Import.

Manheim, Ralph, tr. see Andersch, Alfred.

Manheim, Ralph, tr. see Auerbach, Erich.

Manheim, Ralph, tr. see Babinger, Franz.

Manheim, Ralph, tr. see Bachofen, J. J.

Manheim, Ralph, ed. see Brecht, Bertolt.

Manheim, Ralph, tr. see Brecht, Bertolt.

Manheim, Ralph, ed. see Brecht, Bertolt.

Manheim, Ralph, tr. see Brecht, Bertolt.

Manheim, Ralph, tr. see Broch, Hermann.

Manheim, Ralph, tr. see Buber-Neumann, Margarete.

Manheim, Ralph, tr. see Buch, Hans C.

Manheim, Ralph, tr. see Cassirer, Ernst.

Manheim, Ralph, tr. see Celine, Louis-Ferdinand D.

Manheim, Ralph, tr. see Ende, Michael.

Manheim, Ralph, tr. see Freud, Sigmund.

Manheim, Ralph, tr. see Gary, Romain.

Manheim, Ralph, tr. see Grass, Gunter.

Manheim, Ralph, tr. see Grimm, Jacob & Grimm, Wilhelm K.

Manheim, Ralph, tr. see Grimm, Wilhelm K.

Manheim, Ralph, tr. see Handke, Peter.

Manheim, Ralph, tr. see Heidegger, Martin.

Manheim, Ralph, tr. see Heine, Helme.

Manheim, Ralph, tr. see Hitler, Adolf.

Manheim, Ralph, tr. see Hoffmann, E. T.

Manheim, Ralph, tr. see Jacobi, Jolande.

Manheim, Ralph, tr. see Jaspers, Karl.

Manheim, Ralph, tr. see Jung, Carl G.

Manheim, Ralph, tr. see Kerenyi, C.

Manheim, Ralph, tr. see Kis, Danilo.

Manheim, Ralph, tr. see Mrozek, Slawomir.

Manheim, Ralph, tr. see Neumann, Erich.

Manheim, Ralph, tr. see Proust, Marcel.

Manheim, Ralph, tr. see Raddatz, Fritz.

Manheim, Ralph, tr. see Reich, Wilhelm.

Manheim, Ralph, tr. see Rouaud, Jean.

Manheim, Ralph, tr. see Serge, Victor.

Manheim, Ralph, jt. ed. see Willett, John.

Manheim, Theodore, et al. Sources in Educational Research: A Selected & Annotated Bibliography, Vol. 1. LC 68-64690. 319p. reprint ed. pap. 91.00 (0-685-16227-3, 2027601) Bks Demand.

***Manheimer, Aron H., ed.** The Jewish Condition: Essays on Contemporary Judaism Honoring Rabbi Alexander M. Schindler. (Orig.). 1995. pap. 12.00 (0-8074-0540-X, 160006) UAHC.

***Manheimer, Eric.** Islam: Evolution & Development. 144p. 1994. per., pap. text ed. 18.95 (0-8403-9570-1) Kendall-Hunt.

Manheimer, Ronald, ed. Older Americans Almanac. 800p. 1994. 99.50 (0-8103-8348-9, 065000) Gale.

Manheimer, Ronald J. Developing Arts & Humanities Programming with the Elderly. LC 83-25864. (RASD Adult Services in Action Ser.: No. 2). 13p. 1984. pap. 2.00 (0-8389-5656-4) ALA.

***Manheimer, Ronald J., ed.** The Second Middle Age: Looking Differently at Life Beyond Fifty. LC 95-7303. 1995. 17.95 (0-7876-0481-X) Visible Ink Pr.

Manheimer, Ronald J., jt. ed. see Grant, H. Roger.

***Manheimer, Ronald J., et al.** Older Adult Education: A Guide to Research, Programs, & Policies. LC 95-10277. 1995. text ed. write for info. (0-313-28878-X, Greenwood Pr) Greenwood.

Manheimer, W. M. & Lashmore-Davies, C. N. MHD & Microinstabilities in Confined Plasma. (Plasma Physics Ser.). (Illus.). 300p. 1989. 166.00 (0-85274-282-7) IOP Pub.

An Asterisk (*) at the beginning of an entry indicates that the title is appearing in BIP for the first time.

Manheimer, Wallace M. An Introduction to Trapped-Particle Instability in Tokamaks. LC 77-8530. (ERDA Critical Review Ser.: Advances in Fusion Science & Engineering). 104p. 1977. pap. 10.50 (*0-87079-105-2*, TID-27157); fiche 9.00 (*0-87079-251-2*, TID-27157) DOE.

Manhire, Bill. The New Land: A Picture Book. 1990. pap. 9.95 (*0-7900-0107-1*, A0437) Heinemann.

Manhire, Bill, jt. ed. see McLeod, Marion.

Manhire, Wilson. The Examination Candidate's Guide to Scale & Arpeggio Piano Playing. 66p. 1991. reprint ed. text ed. 59.00 (*0-7812-9320-0*) Rprt Serv.

Manhoff, jt. auth. see Vogel.

Manhoff, David, jt. auth. see Vogel, Stephen.

Manhoff, David H., jt. auth. see Vogel, Stephen N.

Manhold, John H. & Black, Cecelia. Practical Dental Management: Patients & Practice. 300p. (Orig.). 1984. pap. 9.50 (*0-912791-04-7*) Ishiyaku Euro.

Mani, A., jt. ed. see Sandhu, K. S.

Mani, Anna. Wind Energy Resource Survey for India. (C). 1990. text ed. 34.00 (*81-7023-297-X*, Pub. by Allied II) S Asia.

Mani, B. N. Laws of Dharmasastra. (C). 1989. 58.00 (*81-7013-025-5*) S Asia.

Mani, Dinesh, jt. auth. see Misra, S. G.

Mani, Dinesh, jt. ed. see Misra, S. G.

Mani, G. S., ed. Evolutionary Dynamics of Genetic Diversity: Proceedings of a Symposium Held in Manchester, England, March 29-30, 1983. (Lecture Notes in Biomathematics Ser.: Vol. 53). vii, 312p. 1984. pap. 40.70 (*0-387-12903-0*) Spr-Verlag.

Mani, Gomathi. Education in the International Context. 1990. text ed. 30.00 (*81-207-1220-X*, Pub. by Sterling Pubs II) Apt Bks.

Mani, J. C. & Dornand, J., eds. Lymphocyte Activation & Differentiation: Fundamental & Clinical Aspects. 960p. (C). 1988. lib. bdg. 276.95 (*0-89925-446-2*) De Gruyter.

— Lymphocyte Activation & Differentiation: Fundamental & Clinical Aspects. 960p. (C). 1988. lib. bdg. 276.95 (*3-11-010760-0*) De Gruyter.

Mani, J. C., jt. auth. see Mousseron-Canet, M.

Mani, M. N. Techniques of Teaching Blind Children. 1993. text ed. 27.50 (*81-207-1393-1*, Pub. by Sterling Pubs II) Apt Bks.

Mani, M. S. Butterflies of the Himalaya. 1986. lib. bdg. 124.50 (*90-6193-545-8*) Kluwer Ac.

— Fundamentals of High Altitude Biology. rev. ed. 1990. 28.00 (*81-204-0493-9*, Pub. by Oxford IBH II) S Asia.

Mani, M. S. & Giddings, L. E. Ecology of Highlands. (Monographiae Biologicae: No. 40). (Illus.). 236p. 1980. lib. bdg. 112.50 (*90-6193-093-6*) Kluwer Ac.

Mani, Salah A. & Al-Shaikly, Salah. The Euro-Arab Dialogue: A Study in Associative Diplomacy. LC 83-9763. 230p. 1983. text ed. 29.95 (*0-312-26690-1*) St Martin.

Mani, Vettam. Puranic Encyclopaedia. (C). 1989. 75.00 (*81-208-0597-6*) S Asia.

Maniaci, Matthew, jt. auth. see Comollo, Richard.

Maniak, Angela J. Audit Report Writing Manual. 196p. 1990. pap. 49.00 (*1-55520-132-6*) Probus Pub Co.

— Maximizing the Value of Your Audit Reports: Managing Quality & Timeliness. 100p. 1991. text ed. 95.00 (*0-9629337-0-8*) A J Maniak.

***Maniam.** In a Far Country, Vol. 1. (Skoob Pacifica Ser.). 1995. pap. 11.95 (*1-871438-14-4*) Atrium Pubs.

— Return, Vol. 1. (Skoob Pacifica Ser.). 1995. pap. 11.95 (*1-871438-04-7*) Atrium Pubs.

***Maniam, K. S.** Sensous Horizons, Vol. 1. (Skoob Pacifica Ser.). 1995. pap. 11.95 (*1-871438-69-1*) Atrium Pubs.

Manias, Paul & May, Fiona. The Americas. (Family Library of World Travel). (Illus.). 64p. 1985. pap. 4.95 (*0-933521-14-6*) AGT Pub.

Maniates, Chris, ed. Chicago Prop Finders Handbook: 1991. 3rd ed. 600p. 1991. write for info. (*0-9625639-1-9*) Print Grp.

Maniates, Christian, ed. Chicago Prop Finders Handbook. 596p. 1990. write for info. (*0-9625639-0-0*) Print Grp.

Maniates, Maria R. Mannerism in Italian Music & Culture, 1530-1630. LC 78-11236. (Illus.). xx, 678p. 1979. 55.00 (*0-8078-1319-2*) U of NC Pr.

Maniates, Maria R., ed. Music Discourse from Classical to Early Modern Times: Editing & Translating Texts: Papers Given at the Twenty-Sixth Annual Conference on Editorial Problems, University of Toronto, 19-20 October 1990. LC 92-45274. 1993. 37.50 (*0-685-66356-6*) AMS Pr.

Maniatis, K. Assessment of Incineration of Industrial Wastes, EUR 14136. 114p. 1992. pap. 17.00 (*92-826-3855-3*, CD-NA-14136-EN-C, Pub. by Europ Com) UNIPUB.

Maniatis, T., et al. Molecular Cloning: A Laboratory Manual. LC 81-68891. 555p. reprint ed. pap. 158.20 (*0-7837-1892-6*, 2042096) Bks Demand.

Maniatis, Y., ed. Archaeometry: Proceedings of the 25th International Symposium. 720p. 1989. 143.75 (*0-444-87333-3*) Elsevier.

***Maniatty, Taramesha.** Glory Trail. Thatch, Nancy R., ed. LC 95-8701. (Books for Students by Students Ser.). (Illus.). 29p. (J). (gr. 5-8). 1995. lib. bdg. 14.95 (*0-933849-59-1*) Landmark Edns.

Manibhai, ed. see Aurobindo, Sri.

Manicas, Peter T. History & Philosophy of the Social Sciences. 352p. 1988. pap. text ed. 16.95 (*0-631-16583-5*) Blackwell Pubs.

— War & Democracy. 384p. 1989. text ed. 49.95 (*0-631-15836-7*) Blackwell Pubs.

Manichuk, Jurii V. A Problem of Comparative Legal Method: Comparison of Buyers's Remedies for Breach of Delivery of Sale of Goods in Canadian Common Law & Ukrainian. 150p. 1994. 64.95 (*1-880921-45-6*); pap. 44.95 (*1-880921-44-8*) Austin & Winfield.

Manickam, Sudararaj. Social Setting of Christian Conversion in South India: The Impact of the Wesleyan Methodists Missionaries. 306p. (Orig.). 1977. pap. 57.50 (*3-515-02639-8*) Coronet Bks.

Manickam, V. S. Ecological Studies on the Fern Flora of the Palni Hills (S. India) (International Bioscience Ser.: No. 5). 76p. 1984. 19.00 (*1-55528-103-6*, Messers Today & Tomorrow) Scholarly Pubns.

— Fern Flora of the Palni Hills (S. India) (International Bioscience Ser.: No. 11). 200p. 1986. 27.00 (*1-55528-072-2*, Messers Today & Tomorrow) Scholarly Pubns.

Manickam, V. S. & Irudayaraj, V. Cytology of Ferns of the Western Ghats South India. (Illus.). 109p. 1988. 35.00 (*1-55528-099-4*, Pub. by Today & Tomorrows P & P II) Scholarly Pubns.

Manicom, Ann, jt. ed. see Campbell, Marie.

Manicom, Linzi, jt. ed. see Walters, Shirley.

Manier, Edward. The Young Darwin & His Cultural Circle. (Studies in the History of Modern Science: No. 2). 1978. lib. bdg. 70.00 (*90-277-0856-8*) Kluwer Ac.

— The Young Darwin & His Cultural Circle. (Studies in the History of Modern Science: No. 2). 1978. pap. text ed. 36.50 (*90-277-0857-6*) Kluwer Ac.

Manier, Edward, et al, eds. Abortion: New Directions for Policy Studies. LC 76-51617. 198p. reprint ed. pap. 56.50 (*0-8357-5017-5*, 2024363) Bks Demand.

***Maniere, Jacques.** Cuisine a la Valeur: The Art of Steam Cooking. Lyness, Stephanie, tr. & adapt. by. LC 94-32732. 1995. write for info. (*0-688-10507-6*) Morrow.

Maniet, Albert, ed. Plautus: Plaute, Lexique Inverse, Listes Grammaticales, Releves Divers. Vol. XVIII. viii, 201p. 1969. write for info. (*0-318-71975-4*, Pub. by Georg Olms GW) Lubrecht & Cramer.

— Plautus - Plaute, Asinaria: Index Verborum, Lexiques Inverses, Releves Lexicaux et Grammaticaux. Vol. XXVI. Date not set. write for info. (*0-318-71978-9*, Pub. by Georg Olms GW) Lubrecht & Cramer.

— Plautus - Plaute, Asinaria. Index Verboru, Lexiques Inverses, Releves Lexicaux et Grammaticaux. (Alpha-Omega, Reihe A Ser.: Bd. XXVI). x, 211p. (GER.). 1992. write for info. (*3-487-09465-7*, Pub. by Georg Olms GW) Lubrecht & Cramer.

— Plautus - Plaute, Lexique Inverse. Listes Grammaticales. Releves Divers. Bd. XVIII. viii, 201p. 1969. write for info. (*0-318-70660-1*, Pub. by Georg Olms GW) Lubrecht & Cramer.

Maniet, Albert & Paquot, Annette, eds. Plautus - Plaute, Amphitryon: Index Verborum, Lexiques Inverses, Releves Lexicaux et Grammaticaux. Vol. XIX. vii, 217p. 1970. write for info. (*0-318-71976-2*, Pub. by Georg Olms GW) Lubrecht & Cramer.

— Plautus - Plaute, Amphitryon. Index Verborum, Lexiques Inverses, Releves Lexicaux et Grammaticaux. Bd. XIX. vii, 217p. 1970. write for info. (*0-318-70661-X*, Pub. by Georg Olms GW) Lubrecht & Cramer.

Maniet, Albert, ed. see Plautus.

Maniet, Monique. CatMinder. 100p. 1991. 19.95 (*0-914783-52-1*) Charles.

— DogMinder. 98p. 1991. 19.95 (*0-914783-53-X*) Charles.

Manifold, Deirdre. Karl Marx: True or False Prophet? LC 87-82937. (Illus.). 150p. (Orig.). 1987. pap. 8.95 (*0-945001-00-2*) GSG & Assocs.

Manifold, Gay. George Sand's Gabriel. LC 92-15368. (Contributions in Drama & Theatre Studies: No. 49). 184p. 1992. text ed. 45.00 (*0-313-28390-7*, MOX, Greenwood Pr) Greenwood.

— George Sand's Theatre Career. LC 84-28098. (Theater & Dramatic Studies: No. 28). (Illus.). 206p. reprint ed. pap. 58.80 (*0-8357-1653-8*, 2070596) Bks Demand.

Manifold, J. S. The Music in English Drama. 1988. reprint ed. lib. bdg. 75.00 (*0-7812-0242-6*) Rprt Serv.

Manifold, John S. The Music in English Drama from Shakespeare to Purcell. LC 70-181207. 208p. 1956. reprint ed. 49.00 (*0-403-01617-7*) Scholarly.

Manigat, Leslie F., jt. ed. see Heine, Jorge.

Maniguet, Xavier. The Jaws of Death: Shark As Predator Man As Prey. Christie, David A., tr. LC 93-31533. (Illus.). 352p. (Orig.). 1994. pap. 19.95 (*0-924486-64-3*) Sheridan.

— Survival: How to Prevail in Hostile Environments. Roberts, Ivanka, tr. LC 93-16118. 454p. (ENG & FRE.). 1994. 35.00 (*0-8160-2518-5*) Facts on File.

Manikyamba, P. Women in Panchayti Raj Structures. 180p. 1989. 22.50 (*81-212-0286-8*, Pub. by Gian Publng Hse II) S Asia.

Manikyanandi. Pariksamukham (with Prameya-ratna-mala, by Anantavirya) Ghoshal, Sarat C., ed. & comment by. LC 73-3845. reprint ed. 57.50 (*0-404-57711-3*) AMS Pr.

Manilius. Astronomica. (Loeb Classical Library: No. 469). 510p. (C). 1978. text ed. 18.95 (*0-674-99516-3*) HUP.

— Five Books of Manilius. 190p. 1953. 7.00 (*0-86690-128-0*, E1096-014) Am Fed Astrologers.

Manilius, Marcus. Astronomica, 5 vols. in 2, Set. cxcvii, 627p. 1972. reprint ed. write for info. (*3-487-04271-1*, Pub. by Georg Olms GW) Lubrecht & Cramer.

Maniloff, Jack, et al, eds. Mycoplasmas: Molecular Biology & Pathogenesis. LC 92-49746. 609p. 1992. 109.00 (*1-55581-050-0*) Am Soc Microbio.

Manin, Ju. I., et al. Seven Papers on Algebra, Algebraic Geometry & Algebraic Topology. LC 51-5559. (Translations Ser.: No. 2, Vol. 63). 279p. 1967. 50.00 (*0-8218-1763-9*, TRANS 2-63) Am Math.

Manin, Philippe, jt. auth. see Groux, Jean.

Manin, Yu I. A Course in Mathematical Logic. Ewing, J. H. et al, eds. Koblitz, Neal, tr. (Graduate Tests in Mathematics Ser.: Vol. 53). xiii, 286p. 1991. reprint ed. 49.00 (*0-387-90243-0*) Spr-Verlag.

— Cubic Forms: Algebra, Geometry, Arithmetic. rev. ed. (North Holland Mathematical Library: Vol. 4). 340p. 1986. 95.00 (*0-444-87823-8*, North Holland) Elsevier.

— Gauge Field Theory & Complex Geometry. (Grundlehren Ser.: Vol. 289). x, 297p. 1988. 98.00 (*0-387-18275-6*) Spr-Verlag.

— K-Theory, Arithmetic & Geometry. (Lecture Notes in Mathematics Ser.: Vol. 1289). v, 399p. 1987. pap. 54.40 (*0-387-18571-2*) Spr-Verlag.

— Mathematics & Physics. (Progress in Physics Ser.: No. 3). 112p. (C). 1981. 29.50 (*0-8176-3027-9*) Birkhauser.

Manin, Yu. I., jt. auth. see Kobzarev, I. Yu.

Manin, Yu. I., jt. auth. see Kostrikin, A. I.

Manin, Yu I., tr. see Kostrikin, A. I. & Shararevich, I. R., eds.

Manin, Yuri I. Topics in Noncommutative Geometry. 163p. 1991. text ed. 37.50 (*0-691-08588-9*) Princeton U Pr.

Maning, Kyle. Blood Storm. 288p. (Orig.). 1990. pap. 3.50 (*0-8439-2815-8*) Dorchester Pub Co.

— Killpoint. (Z-Comm Ser.). 288p. (Orig.). 1989. pap. 3.50 (*0-8439-2679-1*) Dorchester Pub Co.

— Z Comm. (Swastika Ser.). 288p. (Orig.). 1988. pap. 3.50 (*0-8439-2652-X*) Dorchester Pub Co.

— Z-Comm: Mia. 288p. pap. 3.50 (*0-8439-2691-0*) Dorchester Pub Co.

Maning, Maryann, et al. Theme Immersion: Inquiry-Based Curriculum in Elementary & Middle Schools. LC 93-43027. (Illus.). 192p. (YA). 1994. pap. text ed. 19.50 (*0-435-08806-8*) Heinemann.

Manion, C. L., jt. ed. see Taylor, J. G.

Manion, Christopher, jt. auth. see Stone, Deborah J.

Manion, Jo. Change from Within: Nurse Intrapreneurs As Health Care Innovators. 171p. (Orig.). (C). 1990. pap. 26.75 (*0-685-39092-6*, G-178) Am Nurses Pub.

Manion, John S. General Terry's Last Statement to Custer: New Evidence on the Mary Adam's Affidavit. (Custer Monograph: No. 8). (Illus.). 60p. 1983. 12.00 (*0-940696-09-6*) Monroe County Lib.

Manion, Judith, et al. Research Guide to Congress: How to Make Congress Work for You. 2nd ed. 204p. 1991. text ed. 75.00 (*1-880955-00-8*) Legi-Slate.

Manion, Lawrence, jt. auth. see Cohen, Louis.

Manion, Margaret M. & Muir, Bernard J., eds. Medieval Texts & Images; Studies of Manuscripts from the Middle Ages. LC 91-8868. 224p. 1991. text ed. 50.00 (*3-7186-5133-5*, Z6) Gordon & Breach.

Manion, Margaret M., et al. Medieval & Renaissance Manuscripts in New Zealand. LC 88-51139. (Illus.). 1989. 45.00 (*0-500-23544-9*) Thames Hudson.

Manion, Martha L. Writings about Henry Cowell: An Annotated Bibliography. LC 82-81925. (I.S.A.M. Monographs: No. 16). (Illus.). 368p. (Orig.). 1982. pap. 15.00 (*0-914678-17-5*) Inst Am Music.

Manion, Melanie. Retirement of Revolutionaries in China: Public Policies, Social Norms, Private Interests. LC 92-32031. (Illus.). 224p. (C). 1993. text ed. 35.00 (*0-691-08653-2*) Princeton U Pr.

Manion, Paul D. Scleroderris Canker in Conifers. (Forestry Sciences Ser.). 1984. lib. bdg. 98.00 (*90-247-2912-2*) Kluwer Ac.

— Tree Disease Concepts. 2nd rev. ed. 1990. text ed. 80.00 (*0-13-929423-6*, 510101) P-H.

Manion, Paul D. & Lachance, Denis, eds. Forest Decline Concepts. LC 92-73742. (Illus.). vi, 250p. (Orig.). 1992. pap. 36.00 (*0-89054-143-4*) Am Phytopathol Soc.

Manion, Timothy E. American Hunting & Fishing Guide. 292p. (Orig.). pap. 9.95 (*0-9612936-1-6*) Manion Outdoors Co.

— Wild Game & Country Cooking. 200p. 1983. spiral bd. 9.95 (*0-9612936-0-8*) Manion Outdoors Co.

***Manions International Auction Staff.** American Military Collectibles Price Guide. 1995. pap. 16.95 (*0-930625-47-1*) Antique Trader.

— Foreign Military Collectibles Price Guide. 1995. pap. 16.95 (*0-930625-44-7*) Antique Trader.

Maniotes, jt. auth. see Quasney.

Maniotes, John, jt. auth. see Quansey, James S.

Maniotes, John, jt. auth. see Quasney, James S.

Maniquis, Robert M. & Donato, Clorinda, eds. The Encyclopedie & the Age of Revolution. (Illus.). 232p. (C). 1992. text ed. 65.00 (*0-8161-0527-8*) G K Hall.

Manire, James, jt. auth. see Goeldner, C. R.

Maniruzzaman, Talukder. Group Interests & Political Changes. 271p. 1982. 29.95 (*0-318-37236-3*) Asia Bk Corp.

— Group Interests & Political Changes: Studies of Pakistan & Bangladesh. 1982. 24.00 (*0-8364-0892-6*) S Asia.

Manis, Andrew M. Southern Civil Religions in Conflict: Black & White Baptists & Civil Rights, 1947-1957. LC 86-25028. 170p. 1987. 22.00 (*0-8203-0931-1*) U of Ga Pr.

Manis, Jerome G. Serious Social Problems. (C). 1983. teacher ed write for info. (*0-318-57567-1*, H80450); text ed. 44.00 (*0-205-08044-8*, H80443); write for info. (*0-318-57568-X*, H80468) Allyn.

Manis, Laura G. Assertion Training Workshop: Leader Guide. LC 83-83316. 240p. 1984. pap. 19.95 (*0-918452-63-5*); pap. write for info. (*0-918452-64-3*) Learning Pubns.

— Womanpower: A Manual for Workshops in Personal Effectiveness. LC 76-54156. 1977. pap. text ed. 6.75 (*0-910328-10-2*) Sulzburger & Graham Pub.

Manis, Rod. UNIX Relational Database Management: Application Development in the UNIX Environment. 1988. pap. text ed. 70.00 (*0-13-938622-X*) P-H.

Manis, Rod, et al. Relational Database Management in the Unix Environment. (Illus.). 576p. (C). 1988. pap. text ed. 28.00 (*0-13-771833-0*) P-H.

Manis, Vincent C. & Little, James J. The Schematics of Computation. LC 94-21432. 1995. text ed. 50.67 (*0-13-834284-9*) P-H.

Maniscalco, Joe. Old Barn: Springtime. Wheeler, Penny E., ed. 32p. (J). (gr. 2-4). 1988. pap. 3.95 (*0-8280-0423-4*) Review & Herald.

Manitonquat, see Medicine Story, pseud..

***Manix, E. F. & Mannix, J. E.** Leading Cases on Australian Income Tax. 7th ed. 800p. 1993. pap. 90.00 (*0-409-30653-3*, Austral) Butterworth Legal Pubs.

Manjarres, J. M., ed. see Menendez Pidal, Ramon.

Manjikian, Hagon, et al. Houshamatian of Arf-Dashnaktsutium Album - Atlas, Vol. I: Diutsaznamart. 1992. 45.00 (*0-9635278-0-0*) ARF Central.

Manjon, Maite, jt. auth. see Read, Jan.

Manju, jt. auth. see Pandeya, Ram C.

Manjusri, jt. auth. see Sadhvi, Jaina.

Mank, Gregory W. Abbott & Costello Meet Frankenstein: The Original Shooting Script. Riley, Philip J., ed. LC 89-63447. (Universal Filmscript Series: Classic Comedy Films: Vol. 1). (Illus.). 168p. (Orig.). 1990. pap. 19.95 (*1-882127-10-2*) Magicimage Filmbooks.

— Frankenstein Meets the Wolf Man: The Original Shooting Script. Riley, Philip J., ed. LC 90-61037. (Universal Filmscript Series: Classic Horror Films). (Illus.). (Orig.). 1990. pap. 19.95 (*1-882127-13-7*) Magicimage Filmbooks.

— The Ghost of Frankenstein: The Original Shooting Script. Riley, Philip J., ed. LC 90-61038. (Universal Filmscript Series: Classic Horror Films). (Illus.). (Orig.). 1990. pap. 19.95 (*1-882127-15-3*) Magicimage Filmbooks.

— Hollywood Cauldron: Thirteen Horror Films from the Genre's Golden Age. LC 92-56663. (Illus.). 428p. 1993. lib. bdg. 37.50 (*0-89950-865-0*) McFarland & Co.

— The Hollywood Hissables. LC 88-28163. (Illus.). 530p. 1989. 49.50 (*0-8108-2134-6*) Scarecrow.

— The House of Frankenstein: The Original Shooting Script. Riley, Philip J., ed. LC 90-61039. (Universal Filmscript Series: Classic Horror Films). (Illus.). (Orig.). 1991. pap. 19.95 (*1-882127-17-X*) Magicimage Filmbooks.

— Karloff & Lugosi: The Story of a Haunting Collaboration, with a Complete Filmography of Their Films Together. LC 90-42734. 384p. 1990. lib. bdg. 38.50x (*0-89950-437-X*) McFarland & Co.

— Son of Frankenstein: The Original Shooting Script. Riley, Philip J., ed. LC 89-92188. (Universal Filmscript Series: Classic Horror Films: Vol. 3). (Illus.). 256p. (Orig.). 1990. pap. 19.95 (*1-882127-11-0*) Magicimage Filmbooks.

M

Mank, Mary S. Steps to Learning: A Handbook of Developmental Activities. LC 83-62303. 125p. (Orig.). (C). 1985. pap. text ed. 8.50 (*0-88247-723-4*) R & E Pubs.

Manka, R., jt. ed. see Zralek, M.

Mankabady, S. The Law of Collision at Sea. 608p. 1987. 128.25 (*0-444-70307-1*) Elsevier.

Mankad, Vipul N. & Moore, Blaine R., eds. Sickle Cell Disease: Pathophysiology, Diagnosis, & Management. LC 91-32168. 432p. 1992. text ed. 85.00 (*0-275-92503-X*, C2503, Praeger Pubs) Greenwood.

Mankbadi, R. R., et al, eds. Computational Aero- & Hydro-Acoustics 1993. LC 93-71634. (FED Ser.: Vol. 147). 131p. 1993. pap. 35.00 (*0-7918-0955-2*, H00787) ASME.

***Mankbadi, Reda R.** Transition, Turbulence & Noise, 287. LC 94-21221. (International Engineering & Computer Science, VLSI, Computer Architecture, & Digital Screen Processing Ser.). 400p. (C). 1994. lib. bdg. 125.00 (*0-7923-9481-X*) Kluwer Ac.

Mankekar, D. R. Indira Era. 200p. 1986. 22.00 (*0-317-61127-5*, Pub. by Navrang) S Asia.

— One Way Free Flow. 171p. 1978. 11.95 (*0-318-37286-X*) Asia Bk Corp.

— The Press Versus the Government. 187p. 1978. 14.95 (*0-318-37288-6*) Asia Bk Corp.

— Sheer Anecdotages Leaves from a Reporter's Diary. 1984. 12.50 (*0-8364-1167-6*, Pub. by Allied II) S Asia.

Manker, Dayton A. Invasion from Heaven. pap. 5.99 (*0-88019-073-6*) Schmul Pub Co.

Mankey, Bob, jt. auth. see Shafer, Jack.

Mankiewicz, Rene H. The Liability Regime of the International Air Carrier. 288p. 1981. 104.00 (*90-268-1170-5*) Kluwer Law Tax Pubs.

Mankiller, Wilma & Wallis, Michael. Mankiller: A Chief & Her People. (Illus.). 304p. 1993. 22.95 (*0-312-09868-5*) St Martin.

— Mankiller: A Chief & Her People. 320p. 1994. pap. 13.95 (*0-312-11393-5*) St Martin.

Mankin, David, ed. see Horace.

Mankin, Donald A. Toward a Post-Industrial Psychology: Emerging Perspectives on Technology, Work, Education, & Leisure. LC 78-5302. 227p. reprint ed. pap. 64.70 (*0-317-28058-9*, 2055773) Bks Demand.

Mankin, Paul A. Precious Irony: The Theatre of Jean Giraudoux. LC 78-165146. (Studies in French Literature: No. 19). 195p. (Orig.). 1971. pap. text ed. 34.70 (*90-279-1918-6*) Mouton.

Mankivell, Edmund, jt. auth. see Clark, Paul.

Mankiw. Macroeconomics. 2nd ed. 514p. 1994. 57.95x (*0-87901-722-8*); student ed, pap. 12.95x (*0-87901-723-6*) Worth.

Mankiw, Dorothy. Lesson Plans for the Van Dean Manual. Rubenstein, Israel, ed. 1977. ring bd., vinyl bd 51.95 (*0-87350-074-1*) Milady Pub.

Mankiw, N. Gregory. Macroeconomics. 514p. (C). 1992. text ed. 54.95 (*0-87901-502-0*); student ed, pap. 10.95 (*0-87901-503-9*); boxed 7.95x (*0-87901-597-7*) Worth.

Mankiw, N. Gregory, ed. Monetary Policy. (Illus.). 360p. 1994. lib. bdg. 50.00 (*0-226-50308-9*) U Ch Pr.

Mankiw, N. Gregory & Romer, David, eds. New Keynesian Economics, Vol. 1: Imperfect Competition & Sticky Prices. (Illus.). 340p. 1991. pap. 21.00 (*0-262-63133-4*) MIT Pr.

— New Keynesian Economics, Vol. 2: Coordination Failures & Real Rigidities. (Illus.). 340p. 1991. pap. 21.00 (*0-262-63134-2*) MIT Pr.

An Asterisk (*) at the beginning of an entry indicates that the title is appearing in BIP for the first time.

Manko, David J. A General Model of Legged Locomotion on Natural Terrain. LC 92-13547. (International Series in Engineering & Computer Science, VLSI, Computer Architecture, & Digital Screen Processing). 128p. (C). 1992. lib. bdg. 73.00 (0-7923-9247-7) Kluwer Ac.

Manko, Howard H. Soldering Handbook for Printed Circuits & Surface Mounting. 2nd ed. 1991. text ed. 74.95 (0-442-01206-3) Van Nos Reinhold.

Manko, Howard M. Soldering Handbook for Printed Circuits & Surface Mounting. 1986. text ed. 74.95 (0-442-26423-2) Van Nos Reinhold.

— Solders & Soldering: Materials, Design, Production, & Analysis for Reliable Bonding. 3rd ed. 1992. text ed. 59.00 (0-07-039970-0) McGraw.

***Man'ko, V. I. & Markov, M. A., eds.** Research in Quantum Field Theory: Proceedings of the Lebedev Physics Institute, Vol. 214. 217p. (C). 1995. lib. bdg. 96.00 (1-56072-221-5) Nova Sci Pubs.

Man'ko, V. I., jt. ed. see Dodonov, V. V.

Manko, V. I.

Mankodi, K. Queen's Stepwell at Patan. (C). 1992. 120.00 (81-900184-0-X, Pub. by Franco-Indian II) S Asia.

Man'Kovskaia, L. Khiva: A Reserve of Khorezm Architiecture. 264p. 1982. 358.00 (0-317-61312-X, Pub. by Collets UK) Pro-Am Music.

***Mankowitz.** Change of Life. 1995. pap. 15.00 (0-919123-15-5) Atrium Pubs.

— Samson Riddle. 8.95 (0-87677-102-9) Hartmore.

Mankowitz, Wolf. Make Me an Offer & a Kid for Two Farthings. (Illus.). 208p. 1991. pap. 13.95 (0-233-98548-4, Pub. by A Deutsch UK) Trafalgar.

Manktelow, K. I. & Over, D. E. Inference & Understanding: A Philosophical & Psychological Perspective. (International Library of Psychology). 244p. 1990. 55.00 (0-415-00784-4, A4728); pap. 16.50 (0-415-00785-2, A4732) Routledge.

Manktelow, K. I. & Over, D. E., eds. Rationality: Psychological & Philosophical Perspectives. LC 92-47072. (International Library of Psychology). (Illus.). 320p. 1993. 74.50 (0-415-06955-6, A7779, Routledge NY) Routledge.

Manktelow, R. T. Microvascular Reconstruction. (Illus.). 245p. 1986. 313.00 (0-387-15271-7) Spr-Verlag.

Manktelow, Roger. Routes to Hospital: A Sociological Analysis of the Paths to Psychiatric Hospitalization. LC 94-9576. 1994. 51.95 (1-85628-492-1, Pub. by Avebury Pub UK) Ashgate Pub Co.

Manley, jt. ed. see Ho.

***Manley, Albert E.** A Legacy Continues: The Manley Years at Spelman College, 1953-1976. LC 95-1335. (Illus.). 246p. (C). 1995. lib. bdg. 38.00 (0-8191-9880-3, Open Univ Pr) U Pr of Amer.

Manley, Atwood. Rushton & His Times in American Canoeing. (Illus.). 224p. 1968. pap. 16.95 (0-8156-0141-7) Syracuse U Pr.

***Manley, Belinda.** Through Streets Broad & Narrow: A Life Search to Find the Best Way to Live out the Message of Love to All Men As Revealed by Christ in His Life on Earth. Huntington, Gertrude E., ed. (Illus.). 300p. (Orig.). 1995. pap. 17.00 (1-882260-05-8) Carrier Pigeon.

Manley, Brent, jt. auth. see Hamman, Bob.

Manley-Casimir, Michael E. & Luke, Carmen, eds. Children & Television: A Challenge for Education. LC 87-2469. 334p. 1987. text ed. 59.95 (0-275-92355-X, C2355, Praeger Pubs) Greenwood.

Manley-Casimir, Michael E., jt. ed. see Cochrane, Donald B.

Manley, D. Look & Learn about People, Places & Things. (Illus.). (J). (gr. 2-6). 5.98 (0-517-45795-4) Random Hse Value.

Manley, David, ed. see Hyland, Terry L. & Reilly, Hugh J.

Manley, David E. A Root of Jesse. (Illus.). 320p. (Orig.). 1995. pap. 10.95 (0-89407-090-8) Strawberry Hill.

Manley, Dean V., ed. see Asham, Roger & Ford, Horace.

Manley, Deborah. Animals. (It's Fun Finding out about Ser.). 48p. 1990. 4.99 (0-517-69617-7) Random Hse Value.

— Bible Times. (It's Fun Finding out about Ser.). 48p. (J). 1990. 4.99 (0-517-69616-9) Random Hse Value.

— How to Make a Rainbow: Great Things to Make & Do for Seven Year Olds. LC 93-23331. (Illus.). 64p. (Orig.). (J). (gr. 1-4). 1994. pap. 2.95 (1-85697-929-6, Kingfisher LKC) LKC.

— Long Ago. (It's Fun Finding out about Ser.). (Illus.). 48p. (J). (ps-6). 1990. 4.99 (0-517-69615-0) Random Hse Value.

— The Nile: A Traveller's Anthology. (Illus.). 256p. 1991. 29.95 (0-304-34062-6, Pub. by Cassell UK) Sterling.

— People & Places. (It's Fun Finding out about Ser.). (Illus.). 48p. (J). (ps-6). 1990. 4.99 (0-517-69614-2) Random Hse Value.

— Peppermint Mice: Great Things to Make & Do for Six Year Olds. LC 93-23330. (Illus.). 64p. (Orig.). (J). (gr. 1-4). 1994. pap. 2.95 (1-85697-928-8, Kingfisher LKC) LKC.

Manley, Delarivier. The New Atalantis. Ballaster, Rosalind, ed. (Women's Classics Ser.). 600p. 1992. text ed. 55.00x (0-8147-5478-3) NYU Pr.

— The New Atlantis. 336p. 1993. 11.95 (0-14-043370-8, Penguin Classics) Viking Penguin.

Manley, Delariviere. Lucius, the First Christian King of Britain: A Tragedy. LC 92-24018. (Augustan Reprints Ser.: Nos. 253-254 (1989)). reprint ed. 18.50 (0-404-70253-8) AMS Pr.

Manley, Francis, ed. see Pace, Richard.

Manley, Frank. Two Masters: Prior Engagements. LC 87-24619. (Illus.). 176p. (Orig.). 1987. pap. 8.95 (0-932419-14-3) Cherokee.

Manley, Frank & Watkins, Floyd C. Some Poems & Some Talk about Poetry. LC 84-13061. 134p. 1985. 15.95 (0-87805-230-5) U Pr of Miss.

Manley, Frank, ed. see Chapman, George.

Manley, Frank, ed. see More, St. Thomas.

Manley, G. T. Nuevo Auxiliar Biblico: New Bible Handbook. (SPA.). 18.95 (84-7645-211-X, 223257, Pub. by Edit Clie SP) TSELF.

Manley, Inza. Effects of the Germanic Invasions on Gaul, 234-284 A. D. LC 34-2822. (University of California Publications in Social Welfare: Vol. 17, No. 2). 124p. reprint ed. pap. 35.40 (0-317-29059-2, 2021449) Bks Demand.

Manley, J., et al, eds. Proceedings of the Third European Conference on Mathematics in Industry. (C). 1990. lib. bdg. 150.00 (0-7923-0807-7) Kluwer Ac.

***Manley, Joan B.** She Flew No Flags. LC 94-27623. (J). 1995. 15.95 (0-395-71130-4) HM.

Manley, Joan H., et al. Qu'est-ce Qu'on Dit? LC 93-43695. (ENG & FRE.). 1994. text ed. 47.95 (0-8384-4487-3) Heinle & Heinle.

— Qu'est-ce Qu'on Dit? LC 93-43695. (ENG & FRE.). 1994. pap. 15.95 (0-8384-4489-X) Heinle & Heinle.

Manley, Joey. The Death of Donna-May Dean. 256p. 1992. pap. 8.95 (0-312-07702-5) St Martin.

Manley, Johanna. The Lament of Eve. 160p. (Orig.). (C). 1993. pap. 6.68 (0-9622536-2-6) Monastery Bks.

Manley, Johanna, comp. The Bible & the Holy Fathers for Orthodox: Daily Scripture Readings & Commentary. LC 89-90759. (Illus.). 1136p. 1990. 45.00 (0-9622536-0-X) Monastery Bks.

— Grace for Grace: The Psalter & the Holy Fathers. LC 92-80344. (Illus.). 768p. 1992. 32.00 (0-9622536-1-8) Monastery Bks.

***Manley, Johanna, ed. & comp.** Isaiah Through the Ages. LC 95-3251. 1094p. 1995. 40.00 (0-9622536-3-4) Monastery Bks.

Manley, John. Atlas of Prehistoric Britain. (Illus.). 160p. 1989. 39.95 (0-19-520807-2) OUP.

Manley, John F. & Dolbeare, Kenneth M., eds. The Case Against the Constitution: From the Antifederalists to the Present. LC 87-4640. 200p. 1987. pap. text ed. 22.95 (0-87332-433-1) M E Sharpe.

Manley, Joyce A. Arapahoe City to Fairmount: From a Ghost Town to a Community. 128p. (Orig.). 1989. pap. write for info. (0-318-65759-7) J A Manley.

Manley, Lawrence. Convention, Fifteen Hundred to Seventeen Fifty. LC 79-27773. 365p. 1980. 37.50 (0-674-17015-6) HUP.

— Literature & Culture in Early Modern London. LC 93-51069. (Illus.). 538p. (C). 1995. 59.95 (0-521-46161-8) Cambridge U Pr.

— London in the Age of Shakespeare. LC 86-20476. 384p. 1987. 35.00 (0-271-00445-2) Pa St U Pr.

Manley, Marc W., jt. auth. see Glynn, Thomas J.

Manley, Mark. Devils Coin. 1990. pap. 3.95 (0-8217-3094-0) Zebra.

Manley, Mary. Memoirs of the Life of Mrs. Manley, Author of the Atalantis. 3rd ed. LC 71-37701. reprint ed. 29.00 (0-404-56765-7) AMS Pr.

Manley, Mary D. Novels, Seventeen Hundred Five to Seventeen Fourteen, 7 Vols. in Two, Set. LC 75-161934. 1971. 200.00 (0-8201-1094-9) Schol Facsimiles.

Manley, Michael. Jamaica: Struggle in the Periphery. (Illus.). 259p. 1982. 15.95 (0-906495-97-0); pap. 7.95 (0-906495-98-9) Writers & Readers.

— The Politics of Change: A Jamaican Testament. rev. ed. 1990. pap. 15.95 (0-88258-029-9) Howard U Pr.

— The Poverty of Nations. 122p. (C). 1991. text ed. 42.00 (0-7453-0314-5, Pub. by Pluto Pr UK); pap. text ed. 12.95 (0-7453-0449-4, Pub. by Pluto Pr UK) Westview.

— Up the down Escalator: Development & the Economy, a Jamaican Case Study. (Illus.). 320p. 1987. 24.50 (0-88258-112-0) Howard U Pr.

Manley, Michael T., jt. auth. see Geesink, Rudolph G.

Manley, Micheal. A Voice At the Workplace: Reflections on Colonialism and the Jamaican Worker. 1991. 29.95 (0-88258-067-1); pap. 15.95 (0-88258-068-X) Howard U Pr.

Manley, Molly. Talkaty Talker. (Illus.). 24p. (J). (ps-1). 1994. 9.95 (1-56397-195-X) Boyds Mills Pr.

Manley, Norris C. First Love. 149p. (Orig.). 1993. pap. 10.00 (1-880365-44-8) Prof Pr NC.

Manley, Robert H. Guyana Emergent: The Post Independence Struggle for Nondependent Development. 180p. 1982. 18.95 (0-87073-375-3); pap. text ed. 11.95 (0-87073-349-4) Schenkman Bks Inc.

Manley, Robert N. Nebraska: Our Pioneer Heritage. 199p. 1993. 14.95 (0-685-72261-9) J & L Lee.

Manley, Roger. Signs & Wonders: Outsider Art Inside North Carolina. LC 89-60598. (Illus.). 152p. 1989. pap. 19.95 (0-88259-957-7, U of NC Pr) NCMA.

Manley, Roger & Van Parys, Michelle, eds. Dear Mr. Ripley: A Compendium of Curioddities from the Believe It or Not! Archives. LC 92-23246. 1993. 19.95 (0-8212-1968-5) Little.

Manley, Rosie, jt. auth. see Brackett, Karen.

Manley, Stephen. Feast at Your Fingertips: The Ultimate Catalog of Fabulous Foods by Mail. (Illus.). 192p. 1992. pap. 9.95 (0-8065-1379-9, Citadel Pr) Carol Pub Group.

— Meditations in Matthew: A Daily Devotional. 128p. 1992. pap. 7.50 (0-8341-1427-5) Beacon Hill.

— More Than Words. 32p. (YA). 1988. pap. 1.95 (0-8341-1236-1) Beacon Hill.

Manley, Stephen L. Journey into Wholeness. 96p. (Orig.). 1983. pap. 5.95 (0-8341-0832-1) Beacon Hill.

Manley, Walter, II. Executive's Handbook of Model Business Conduct Codes. 1991. 34.95 (0-13-296757-X) P-H.

— Handbook of Good Business Practice: Corporate Codes of Conduct. 288p. 1992. pap. 39.00 (0-415-06232-2, B0183) Routledge.

Manley, Walter, II & Shrode, William A. Critical Issues in Business Conduct: Legal, Ethical, & Social Challenges for the 1990s. LC 90-30009. 336p. 1990. text ed. 55.00 (0-89930-570-9, MCZ/, Quorum Bks) Greenwood.

Manley, Will. For Library Directors Only: Talking about Trustees. Bd. with For Library Trustees Only: Living with Your Director. LC 92-50942. 122p. (0-89950-827-8) LC 92-50942. (Illus.). 114p. 1993. Set pap. 23.50 (0-89950-826-X) McFarland & Co.

— The Manley Art of Librarianship. LC 92-56664. (Illus.). 248p. 1993. lib. bdg. 23.95x (0-89950-866-9) McFarland & Co.

— The Truth about Catalogers. (Illus.). 128p. 1995. pap. 22.50 (0-7864-0103-6) McFarland & Co.

— Uncensored Thoughts: Pot Shots from a Public Librarian. (Illus.). 173p. 1994. lib. bdg. 23.95 (0-89950-992-4) McFarland & Co.

— Unintellectual Freedoms: Opinions of a Public Librarian. LC 90-53505. (Illus.). 174p. 1991. lib. bdg. 23.95x (0-89950-575-9) McFarland & Co.

— Unprofessional Behavior: Confessions of a Public Librarian. LC 91-40350. (Illus.). 208p. 1992. lib. bdg. 23.95 (0-89950-690-9) McFarland & Co.

— Unsolicited Advice: Observations of a Public Librarian. LC 92-50311. (Illus.). 208p. 1992. lib. bdg. 23.95x (0-89950-745-X) McFarland & Co.

Manlove, C. N. C. S. Lewis: His Literary Achievement. LC 87-4775. 224p. 1987. text ed. 39.95 (0-312-00899-6) St Martin.

— Science Fiction: Ten Explorations. LC 85-14738. 224p. 1986. 22.50 (0-87338-326-5) Kent St U Pr.

Manlove, Colin. Christian Fantasy: From Twelve Hundred to the Present. LC 91-47494. (C). 1992. text ed. 32.95 (0-268-00790-X) U of Notre Dame Pr.

— Chronicles of Narnia: The Patterning of a Fantastic World. (Masterwork Studies). 160p. 1993. text ed. 22.95 (0-8057-8800-X, Twayne); pap. 12.95 (0-8057-8801-8, Twayne) Macmillan.

— Critical Thinking: A Guide to Interpreting Literary Texts. LC 89-30824. 180p. 1989. text ed. 35.00 (0-312-03166-1) St Martin.

Manlove, Colin N. The Impulse of Fantasy Literature. LC 82-15335. 188p. reprint ed. pap. 53.60 (0-7837-0570-0, 2040914) Bks Demand.

— Modern Fantasy: Five Studies. LC 74-31798. 316p. reprint ed. pap. 90.10 (0-685-15589-7, 2026346) Bks Demand.

Manlove, Donald C., ed. see Riley, James W.

***Manlowe, Jennifer L.** Faith Born of Seduction: Sexual Trauma, Body Image, & Religion. 230p. 1995. 40.00 (0-8147-5517-8); pap. 16.95 (0-8147-5529-1) NYU Pr.

Manly, Bryan F. The Design & Analysis of Research Studies. (Illus.). 352p. (C). 1992. 94.95 (0-521-41453-9); pap. 37.95 (0-521-42580-8) Cambridge U Pr.

***Manly, Bryan F., Jr.** Multivariate Statistical Methods: A Primer. 2nd ed. 1994. pap. 26.95 (0-412-60300-4, Blackie & Son-Chapman NY) Routledge Chapman & Hall.

Manly, Bryan F. Randomization & Monte Carlo Methods in Biology. 256p. 1990. 65.00 (0-412-36710-6, A5017) Chapman & Hall.

— Stage-Structured Populations: Sampling, Analysis & Simulation. (Population & Community Biology Ser.). (Illus.). 160p. 1990. 49.95 (0-412-35060-2, A4128) Chapman & Hall.

— The Statistics of Natural Selection. 500p. 1987. pap. text ed. 37.50 (0-412-30700-6) Chapman & Hall.

Manly, Bryan F., et al. Resource Selection by Animals: Statistical Design & Analysis for Field Studies. LC 92-36062. 1992. write for info. (0-412-40140-1) Chapman & Hall.

Manly, Howard, jt. auth. see Turnbull, Walter.

Manly Inc. Staff. Value of a Dollar: 1901-1920. 400p. 1993. 75.00 (0-8103-6841-2, 101638) Gale.

Manly, John M. Manly Anniversary Studies in Language & Literature. LC 68-22110. (Essay Index Reprint Ser.). 1977. reprint ed. 24.95 (0-8369-0673-X) Ayer.

— Specimens of Pre-Shakespearean Drama. (BCL1-PR English Literature Ser.). 1992. reprint ed. lib. bdg. 75.00 (0-7812-7152-5) Rprt Serv.

— Specimens of the Pre-Shakespearean Drama, 2 Vols, Set. LC 67-18432. 1897. 40.00 (0-8196-0200-0) Biblo.

Manly, John M. & Rickert, E. Contemporary American Literature. LC 74-4436. (American Literature Ser.: No. 49). 1974. lib. bdg. 75.00 (0-8383-2048-1) M S G Haskell Hse.

Manly, John M. & Rickert, Edith. Contemporary American Literature, Bibliographies & Study Outlines. (BCL1-PS American Literature Ser.). 378p. 1992. reprint ed. lib. bdg. 89.00 (0-7812-6620-3) Rprt Serv.

— Contemporary British Literature. LC 73-21795. (English Literature Ser.: No. 33). 1974. lib. bdg. 49.95 (0-8383-1827-4) M S G Haskell Hse.

Manly, Louise. Manly Family: Account of the Descendants of Captain Basil Manly of the Revolution, & Related Families. (Illus.). 351p. 1994. reprint ed. lib. bdg. 64.50 (0-8328-4029-7); reprint ed. pap. 54.50 (0-8328-4030-0) Higginson Bk Co.

Manly, Myrna. The Math Problem Solver: Reasoning Skills for Application. LC 92-38293. 1993. pap. 10.60 (0-8092-3764-4) Contemp Bks.

Manly, Peter L. The Twenty-cm Schmidt-Cassegrain Telescope. LC 93-42045. (Illus.). 256p. (C). 1994. 29.95 (0-521-43360-6) Cambridge U Pr.

— Unusual Telescopes. (Illus.). 200p. (C). 1992. 39.95 (0-521-38200-9) Cambridge U Pr.

— Unusual Telescopes. (Illus.). 238p. (C). 1995. pap. 19.95 (0-521-48393-X) Cambridge U Pr.

Manly, William L. Death Valley in '49. LC 77-2273. 1977. reprint ed. pap. 30.95 (0-912494-23-9) Chalfant Pr.

— Death Valley in '49. 1992. reprint ed. lib. bdg. 75.00 (0-7812-5063-3) Rprt Serv.

Manmohan, Mehra. Harley Granville Barker: A Critical Study of the Major Plays. 1982. 16.00 (0-686-38375-3) S Asia.

***Mann.** Atlas of Acupuncture. Date not set. (0-7506-1678-4) Buttrwrth-Heinemann.

— A Bird in the Hand. 1994. 22.00 (0-671-88995-8); pap. 12.00 (0-671-88994-X) P-H Gen Ref & Trav.

— A Bird in the Hand. 1994. pap. 12.00 (0-671-89779-9) P-H Gen Ref & Trav.

— Chest Radiology. (SPA.). 1992. 24.70 (0-8016-7031-4) Mosby Yr Bk.

— Handbooks in Radiology, Vol. 3: Chest Radiology. 256p. 1988. pap. 26.95 (0-8151-5758-4, Yr Bk Med Pubs) Mosby Yr Bk.

— Meridians of Acupuncture. 174p. 1964. text ed. 39.95 (0-433-20303-X) Buttrwrth-Heinemann.

— Millennium Prophecies. 1995. pap. text ed. 7.95 (1-85230-685-8) Element MA.

— Study Guide to Smith Essentials. 452p. 1991. pap. text ed. 21.25 (0-314-54025-3) West Pub.

— Textbook of Acupuncture. (Illus.). 640p. 1987. text ed. 95.00 (0-433-20312-9) Buttrwrth-Heinemann.

Mann & Lazier. Dynamics of Marine Ecosystems. 1991. pap. 49.95 (0-86542-082-3) Blackwell Sci.

Mann, et al. Handbook in Diagnostic-Prescriptive Teaching in the Elementary Schools. (C). 1987. text ed. 79.95 (0-205-10491-6, H04914) Allyn.

Mann, A. T. The Divine Plot: Astrology, Reincarnation, Cosmology & History. (Illus.). 288p. 1991. pap. 15.95 (1-85230-232-1) Element MA.

— Elements of Reincarnation. 1995. pap. 9.95 (1-85230-698-X) Element MA.

— The Elements of the Tarot. (Elements of...Ser.). (Illus.). 144p. 1993. pap. 9.95 (1-85230-422-7) Element MA.

— Life Time Astrology. 288p. 1990. pap. 15.95 (1-85230-234-8) Element MA.

— Sacred Architecture. 1993. pap. 19.95 (1-85230-391-3) Element MA.

— Sacred Sexuality. 1995. pap. 19.95 (1-85230-658-0) Element MA.

Mann, Abby. A Child Is Waiting. 16.95 (0-89190-629-0, Am Repr) Amereon Ltd.

— Massacre at Wounded Knee. (Orig.). 1979. pap. 2.50 (0-89083-542-X) Zebra.

— Shocking True Story of the McMartin Child Abuse Trial. 1993. 25.00 (0-394-56472-3, Villard Bks) Random.

Mann, Alan E., jt. auth. see Weiss, Mark L.

Mann, Albert. Report on the Diatoms of the Albatross Voyage in the Pacific Ocean, 1888-1904. 1978. reprint ed. pap. text ed. 59.00 (3-87429-132-4) Koeltz Sci Bks.

***Mann, Albert W.** Civil War Militia, History of the 45th Regiment, M. V. M., "The Cadet Regiment" (Illus.). 562p. 1995. reprint ed. lib. bdg. 62.00 (0-8328-4626-0) Higginson Bk Co.

***Mann, Alfred.** The Great Composer As Teacher & Student: Theory & Practice of Composition. unabridged ed. LC 94-28795. (Illus.). 176p. 1994. pap. text ed. 10.95 (0-486-28316-X) Dover.

— Handel's Orchestral Music: Orchestral Concertos, Organ Concertos, Water Music, & Music for the Royal Fireworks. (Monuments of Western Music Ser.). (Illus.). 1995. text ed. 35.00 (0-02-871382-6) Schirmer Bks.

— Randall Thompson: A Choral Legacy. 1983. pap. 10.00 (0-911318-12-7) E C Schirmer.

— The Study of Fugue. 352p. 1987. reprint ed. pap. 9.95 (0-486-25439-9) Dover.

— The Study of Fugue. LC 81-4183. (Illus.). x, 341p. 1981. reprint ed. text ed. 65.00 (0-313-22623-7, MASF, Greenwood Pr) Greenwood.

Mann, Alfred, pref. Modern Music Librarianship: Essays in Honor of Ruth Watanabe. LC 89-30559. (Festschrift Ser.: No. 8). (Illus.). 200p. 1989. lib. bdg. 48.00 (0-918728-93-2) Pendragon NY.

Mann, Alfred K. Neutrino Interactions with Electrons & Protons. LC 93-23103. (Key Papers in Physics). 160p. 1993. text ed. 45.00 (1-56396-228-4, AIP Pr) Am Inst Physics.

***Mann, Alfred K. & Cline, David B., eds.** Discovery of Weak Neutral Currents: The Weak Interaction Before & After. LC 94-70515. (AIP Conference Proceeding Ser.: Vol. 300). 676p. 1994. 145.00 (1-56396-306-X) Am Inst Physics.

Mann, Alfred N., jt. auth. see Murthy, Belur N.

Mann, Allen, ed. Selected Papers on Zoom Lenses. LC 93-32573. (Milestone Ser.: Vol. MS 85). 1993. write for info. (0-8194-1389-5); pap. write for info. (0-8194-1388-7) SPIE.

***Mann, Anthony T.** Real World Programming with Visual Basic. (Illus.). 1100p. (Orig.). 1995. pap. text ed. 45.00 (0-672-30619-0) Sams.

Mann, Arthur. LaGuardia Comes to Power: 1933. LC 81-4124. (Illus.). 199p. 1981. reprint ed. text ed. 49.75 (0-313-22787-X, MALC, Greenwood Pr) Greenwood.

Mann, Arthur, ed. see Kantowicz, Edward.

Mann, Arthur R., jt. intro. see Hamilton, William H.

Mann, Barry. Sigmund Freud. LC 92-42548. (Biographies Ser.). (J). 1993. 19.93 (0-86625-491-9); 14.95 (0-685-66534-8) Rourke Pubns.

Mann, Betty M. The Devore - DeVore Families, 1500-1992. 800p. 1992. 60.00 (0-917231-13-9) Ferguson Comns Pubs.

Mann, Bob. Bob Mann's Automatic Golf Complete. (Illus.). 128p. (Orig.). 1992. pap. 9.99 (0-671-74049-0, Fireside) S&S Trade.

— Bob Manns Proven Golf Method. 64p. 1990. pap. 6.99 (0-517-01998-1) Random Hse Value.

Mann, Brenda J., jt. auth. see Spradley, James P.

An Asterisk (*) at the beginning of an entry indicates that the title is appearing in BIP for the first time.

Mann, Brian. The Secular Madrigals of Filippo Di Monte, 1521- 1603. LC 83-1061. (Studies in Musicology: No. 64). 497p. reprint ed. pap. 141.70 (*0-8357-1402-0*, 2070483) Bks Demand.

Mann, Brian, ed. Paolo Quagliati: Recercate, et Canzone, Libro Primo a Quattro Voci, Rome, 1601. LC 94-1961. (Italian Instrumental Music of the Sixteenth & Early Seventeenth Centuries Ser.: Vol. 15). 168p. 1994. 62.00 (*0-8240-4514-9*) Garland.

***Mann, Bruce.** Jimi Hendrix. (CD Bks.). (Illus.). 120p. 1994. pap. 7.99 (*1-886894-09-4*, MBS Paperbk) Mus Bk Servs.

Mann, Bruce H. Neighbors & Strangers: Law & Community in Early Connecticut. LC 87-6001. (Studies in Legal History). 216p. reprint ed. pap. 61.60 (*0-7837-6858-3*, 2046687) Bks Demand.

Mann, C. David & Kelley, Martin N., eds. RETC Proceedings, 1985. LC 85-70960. (Rapid Excavation & Tunneling Conference Ser.). (Illus.). 1278p. 1985. 75.00 (*0-89520-441-X*, 441-X) SMM&E Inc.

Mann, C. John, jt. ed. see Hunter, Regina L.

Mann, C. S. Mark: A New Translation with Introduction & Commentary, Vol. 27. LC 85-4433. (Illus.). 744p. 1986. 42.00 (*0-385-03253-6*, Anchor NY) Doubleday.

Mann, C. S., jt. ed. see Albright, William F.

Mann, C. V. & Glass, R. E. Surgical Treatment of Anal Incontinence. (Illus.). xiii, 160p. 1991. 198.00 (*0-387-19640-4*) Spr-Verlag.

Mann, Cameron. Concordance to the English Poems of George Herbert. 277p. reprint ed. lib. bdg. 79.00 (*0-7812-0251-5*) Rprt Serv.

— Concordance to the English Poems of George Herbert. 1971. reprint ed. 49.00 (*0-403-01089-6*) Scholarly.

Mann, Carleton H. How Schools Use Their Time: Time Allotment Practice in 444 Cities. LC 72-177051. (Columbia University. Teachers College. Contributions to Education Ser.: No. 333). reprint ed. 37.50 (*0-404-55333-8*) AMS Pr.

Mann, Carol. Modigliani. LC 90-72012. (World of Art Ser.). (Illus.). 216p. 1991. pap. 14.95 (*0-500-20176-5*) Thames Hudson.

— The Nineteenth Hole: Favorite Golf Stories. LC 92-10801. (Illus.). 256p. 1992. 19.95 (*0-681-41455-3*) Longmeadow Pr.

Mann, Catherine L., jt. auth. see Hooper, Peter.

Mann, Charles C. & Plummer, Mark L. The Aspirin Wars: Money, Medicine, & One Hundred Years of Rampant Competition. LC 90-28735. (Illus.). 416p. 1991. 24.50 (*0-394-57894-5*) Knopf.

— The Aspirin Wars: Money, Medicine, & 100 Years of Rampant Competition. 432p. 1993. pap. 16.95 (*0-87584-401-4*) Harvard Busn.

— The Aspirin Wars: Money, Medicine & 100 Yeas of Rampant Competition. 1993. pap. text ed. 16.95 (*0-07-103398-X*) McGraw.

— Noah's Choice: The Future of Endangered Species. LC 94-25807. 1995. 24.00 (*0-679-42002-9*) Knopf.

Mann, Charles C., jt. auth. see Crease, Robert P.

Mann, Charles E., ed. see Hutchinson, John Wallace.

***Mann, Charles F.** Madeleine Delbrel: A Life Beyond Boundaries. LC 95-67111. 192p. 1995. pap. 14.95 (*0-9645600-9-7*) New Wrld Pr.

Mann, Charles K. & Huddleston, Barbara, eds. Food Policy: Frameworks for Analysis & Action. LC 85-42526. (Illus.). 256p. 1986. 29.95 (*0-253-34342-9*) Ind U Pr.

Mann, Charles K. & Ruth, Stephen R., eds. Expert Systems in Developing Countries: Practice & Promise. 288p. (C). 1992. pap. text ed. 49.00 (*0-8133-8397-8*) Westview.

Mann, Charles K., et al. Seeking Solutions: Framework & Cases for Small Enterprise Development Programs. LC 89-2568. (Library of Management for Development, Case Study Ser.). (Illus.). xv, 434p. (C). 1989. pap. text ed. 29.95 (*0-931816-77-7*) Kumarian Pr.

***Mann, Charles K., et al, eds.** Seeking Solutions: Case Leader's Guide. fac. ed. LC 90-35169. (Kumarian Press Library of Management for Development). 199p. 1994. pap. 56.80 (*0-7837-7583-0*, 2047336) Bks Demand.

Mann, Chris. Chris Mann on Grammar. LC 90-61818. 90p. 1990. pap. 10.95 (*0-939044-30-7*) Lingua Pr.

***Mann, Clarence E.** Bring on the Clowns: An Assessment of the Origin of the Shih Tzu. 1995. 18.95 (*0-533-11461-6*) Vantage.

Mann, Coramae R. Female Crime & Delinquency. LC 82-16052. (Illus.). xv, 352p. 1984. 34.50 (*0-8173-0144-5*) U of Ala Pr.

— Unequal Justice: A Question of Color. LC 92-25110. (Blacks in the Diaspora Ser.). 320p. (C). 1993. 35.00 (*0-253-33676-7*); pap. 14.95 (*0-253-20783-5*) Ind U Pr.

— When Women Kill. LC 95-15374. (Series in Violence). 1996. write for info. (*0-7914-2811-7*); pap. write for info. (*0-7914-2812-5*) State U NY Pr.

Mann, D. G., ed. International Diatom Symposium, 7th, Philadelphia, Aug. 1982: Proceedings. (Illus.). 541p. 1984. lib. bdg. 135.00 (*3-87429-217-7*) Koeltz Sci Bks.

***Mann, Dale, ed.** Making Change Happen? fac. ed. LC 78-21849. (Policy Analysis & Education Ser.). 363p. 1978. reprint ed. pap. 103.50 (*0-7837-8645-X*, 2047943) Bks Demand.

Mann, Dale, et al. Chasing the American Dream: Jobs, Schools, & Employment Training Programs in New York State: Technical Report. LC 85-106191. 47p. (Orig.). 1980. pap. 3.00 (*0-88156-005-7*) Comm Serv Soc NY.

— Chasing the American Dream: Jobs, Schools, & Employment Training Programs in New York State: Technical Report. LC 85-106191. 228p. (Orig.). 1981. 12.00 (*0-88156-006-5*) Comm Serv Soc NY.

Mann, Daniel. Programming the 29K RISC Family. LC 93-10610. (Innovative Technology Ser.). 1993. pap. text ed. 37.00 (*0-13-091893-8*) P-H.

Mann, Dave. Harley-Davidson Performance Parts Directory. 1993. pap. 19.95 (*0-87938-774-2*) Motorbooks Intl.

Mann, David. The Elizabethan Player: Contemporary Stage Presentations. (Illus.). 272p. (C). 1991. text ed. 75.00 (*0-415-04896-6*, A5091) Routledge.

— Races, Chases & Crashes. (Illus.). 144p. 1994. pap. text ed. 14.95 (*0-87938-859-5*) Motorbooks Intl.

Mann, David D., comp. A Concordance to the Plays & Poems of Sir George Etherege. LC 84-27917. xi, 445p. 1985. text ed. 125.00 (*0-313-20976-6*, MPO/, Greenwood Pr) Greenwood.

Mann, David D., ed. see Congreve, William.

Mann, David K. The Nineteen Seventy-Two Invasion of Military Region 1: Fall of Quang Tri & Defense of Hue. 93p. 1993. reprint ed. pap. 11.50x (*0-923135-62-6*) Dalley Bk Service.

***Mann, David M., et al.** A Color Atlas & Text of Adult Dementias. LC 94-43604. 1994. 99.95 (*0-7234-1784-9*) Wolfe Pub.

Mann, David S., ed. Government in the Palmetto State: Toward the 21st Century. (Government in South Carolina Ser.). (Illus.). 176p. (Orig.). 1993. pap. 18.00 (*0-917069-07-2*) Univ SC Inst Pub Affairs.

Mann, David W. A Simple Theory of the Self. 160p. (C). 1994. 25.00 (*0-393-70172-7*) Norton.

Mann, David W., jt. auth. see Gold, Martin.

Mann, Dean, ed. Environmental Policy. (Orig.). 1980. pap. 12.00 (*0-918592-43-7*) Pol Studies.

Mann, Dean, jt. ed. see Feldman, David.

Mann, Dean E., jt. ed. see Ingram, Helen M.

Mann, Dean E., jt. auth. see Wyner, Alan J.

Mann, Denise, jt. ed. see Spigel, Lynn.

Mann, Derek. Mann at Sea. 1994. 16.95 (*0-533-10952-3*) Vantage.

Mann, Don, jt. auth. see Carter, W. Horace.

Mann, Donald C., jt. ed. see Holtman, Arthur F.

Mann, E. A. Boundaries & Identities: Muslims, Work & Status in Aligarh. (Illus.). 188p. (C). 1992. text ed. 28.50 (*0-8039-9422-2*) Sage.

Mann, E. B. Brett Randall, Gambler. large type ed. (Linford Western Library). 352p. 1988. pap. 11.95 (*0-7089-6527-X*, Linford) Ulverscroft.

Mann, Edwin J. The Deaf & Dumb. 1972. 59.95 (*0-8490-0002-5*) Gordon Pr.

Mann, Eleanor, ed. see Thomsen, Thomas C.

Mann, Eleanor, jt. auth. see Thomsen, Thomas C.

Mann, Eleanor, ed. see Thomsen, Thomas C.

Mann, Emily. Still Life. 1981. pap. 4.75 (*0-8222-1081-9*) Dramatists Play.

Mann, Eric. Taking on General Motors: A Case Study of the UAW Campaign to Keep GM Van Nuys Open. (Illus.). 408p. (Orig.). (C). 1987. pap. 20.00 (*0-89215-141-2*) U Cal LA Indus Rel.

Mann, Erika. Last Year of Thomas Mann. Graves, Richard, tr. LC 72-126323. (Biography Index Reprint Ser.). 1977. 17.95 (*0-8369-8029-8*) Ayer.

Mann, Ernest. Free I Got. 3269p. (Orig.). (C). 1993. pap. 8.95 (*0-9620301-1-2*) Little Free.

— I Was Robot: (Utopia Now Possible) 320p. (C). 1990. pap. 7.95 (*0-9620301-0-4*) Little Free.

Mann, F. A. The Legal Aspect of Money. 5th ed. 600p. 1992. 165.00 (*0-19-825650-7*) OUP.

— Notes & Comments on Cases in International Law, Commercial Law, & Arbitration. LC 92-15318. 304p. (C). 1993. 62.00 (*0-19-825798-8*, Clarendon Pr) OUP.

Mann, Felilx. Reinventing Acupuncture: A New Concept of Ancient Medicine. LC 92-27735. 1993. 36.95 (*0-7506-0844-7*) Buttrwrth-Heinemann.

Mann, Felix. Acupuncture. rev. ed. (Illus.). 192p. 1973. pap. 8.00 (*0-394-71727-9*, Vin) Random.

— Acupuncture. 2nd ed. LC 92-20085. 1992. pap. 22.50 (*0-7506-0700-9*) Buttrwrth-Heinemann.

— Acupuncture, the Ancient Chinese Art of Healing. (Illus.). 19.50 (*0-8446-4583-4*) Peter Smith.

— Atlas of Acupuncture: Points & Meridians in Relation to Surface Anatomy. 656p. 1966. text ed. 55.00 (*0-433-20301-3*) Buttrwrth-Heinemann.

Mann, Floyd C. & Hoffman, L. Richard. Automation & the Worker: A Study of Social Change in Power Plants. LC 83-12978. (Illus.). xiv, 272p. 1983. reprint ed. text ed. 59.75 (*0-313-24222-4*, MAUW, Greenwood Pr) Greenwood.

Mann, Frederick G. & Saunders, Bernard C. Introduction to Practical Organic Chemistry. 2nd ed. LC 66-84573. 219p. reprint ed. pap. 62.50 (*0-317-08940-4*, 2003647) Bks Demand.

Mann, Friedhelm, et al, eds. Gregorii Nysseni Sermones, Pars II. LC 64-42055. (Gregorius Nyssenus Opera Ser.: Vol. X, Tomus 1). (Illus.). cclxiii, 176p. (LAT.). 1990. 105.25 (*90-04-08123-2*) E J Brill.

Mann, Fritz A. Foreign Affairs in English Courts. 300p. 1986. 59.00 (*0-19-825564-0*) OUP.

Mann, G., ed. Internationale Bibliographie Zur Geschichte der Medzin, 1875-1901. 589p. 1971. write for info. (*0-318-71806-5*, Pub. by Georg Olms GW) Lubrecht & Cramer.

Mann, G., jt. auth. see Haufe, G.

Mann, G. C., et al, eds. Applied Radionuclide Metrology: Proceedings of the International Committee for Radionuclide Metrology Seminar, Geel, Belgium, 16-17 May 1983. (International Journal of Applied Radiation & Isotopes Ser.: Vol. 34, No. 8). 286p. 1984. pap. 28.00 (*0-08-030271-8*, Pergamon Pr) Elsevier.

***Mann, George.** Theatre Lethbridge: A History of Theatrical Production in Lethbridge, Alberta (1885-1988) (Illus.). 440p. (Orig.). 1993. pap. 29.95 (*1-55059-055-3*) Temeron Bks.

Mann, George V., ed. Coronary Heart Disease: The Dietary Sense & Nonsense. (Illus.). 150p. (Orig.). 1993. pap. 17.95 (*1-85756-072-8*, Pub. by Janus Pubng UK) Paul & Co Pubs.

***Mann, Gerald.** Common Sense Religion: A Guide for Renewing Your Christian Faith. LC 94-27348. 1994. pap. 8.95 (*1-56977-566-4*) McCracken Pr.

— Commonsense Christianity. 1989. 13.95 (*0-318-41360-4*) Harper SF.

— When One Day at a Time Is Too Long: Practical Answers to 42 of Life's Questions. LC 94-1589. 256p. 1994. 17.95 (*1-56977-563-X*) McCracken Pr.

— When the Bad Times Are Over for Good: Transforming Trouble into Triumph. LC 93-78997. 225p. 1993. 17.95 (*1-56977-560-5*) McCracken Pr.

Mann, Gerhard. Holstein Horses. (Breed Ser.). 1977. pap. 4.95 (*0-88376-017-7*) Dreenan Pr.

Mann, Gertrude, jt. auth. see Rabinsky, Leatrice.

Mann, Glennis A., jt. auth. see Pray, Bobbie A.

***Mann, Golo, et al, eds.** Historia Universal. (Illus.). (SPA.). 1989. pap. 1,595.00x (*84-239-4409-3*) Elliots Bks.

Mann, Gurinder S., jt. ed. see Hawley, John S.

Mann, H., jt. ed. see Sieberth, H. G.

Mann, H. H. Fodder Crops of Western India. (C). 1991. 125.00 (*81-7136-028-9*, Pub. by Periodical Expert India) St Mut.

Mann, H. K. Radiation Sterilization of Plastic Medical Devices: Seminar under the Auspices of the University of Lowell, Mass., March 1979. 128p. 1980. pap. 25.00 (*0-08-025067-X*, Pergamon Pr) Elsevier.

Mann, H. S. Arid Zone Research & Development. 531p. 1980. 300.00 (*0-317-62029-0*, Scientific) St Mut.

Mann, H. S., jt. auth. see Spooner, B.

Mann, Hal. Color Conexion Bilingual Dictionary. 1993. pap. 7.95 (*0-9635301-0-0*) Color Cognate.

Mann, Harold H. Social Framework of Agriculture. LC 67-29802. 1967. 49.50 (*0-678-08007-0*) Kelley.

— Social Framework of Agriculture. Thorner, Daniel, ed. (Illus.). 501p. 1968. 37.50 (*0-7146-2333-4*, Pub. by F Cass Pubs UK) Intl Spec Bk.

Mann, Heinrich. Henry King of France. LC 84-22682. 800p. 1987. 25.00 (*0-87951-999-1*); pap. 15.95 (*0-87951-224-5*) Overlook Pr.

— In the Land of Cockaigne. Clark, A. D., tr. 388p. 1995. reprint ed. lib. bdg. 45.00 (*0-86527-419-3*) Fertig.

— Man of Straw. LC 92-34082. 286p. 1995. 35.00 (*0-86527-412-6*) Fertig.

— Man of Straw. 304p. 1992. 9.95 (*0-14-018137-7*, Penguin Classics) Viking Penguin.

— Young Henry of Navarre. Sutton, Eric, tr. LC 84-42673. 585p. 1986. reprint ed. Tusk. 25.00 (*0-87951-981-9*); reprint ed. Tusk. pap. 14.95 (*0-87951-206-7*) Overlook Pr.

Mann, Helen S. Charles Ezra Sprague. Brief, Richard P., ed. LC 77-87277. (Development of Contemporary Accounting Thought Ser.). 1978. reprint ed. lib. bdg. 19.95 (*0-405-10905-9*) Ayer.

Mann, Henry B. Addition Theorems: The Addition Theorems of Group Theory & Number Theory. LC 76-16766. 124p. 1976. reprint ed. text ed. 15.50 (*0-88275-418-1*) Krieger.

Mann, Herman. The Female Review: Life of Deborah Sampson, the Female Soldier in the War of the Revolution. LC 72-2603. (American Women Ser.: Images & Realities). 276p. 1978. reprint ed. 21.95 (*0-405-04476-3*) Ayer.

— The Female Review; or, Memoirs of an American Young Lady. LC 78-64079. reprint ed. 37.50 (*0-404-17069-2*) AMS Pr.

— Historical Annals of Dedham, from Its Settlement in 1635 to 1847. 136p. 1995. reprint ed. pap. 22.50 (*0-8328-4663-5*) Higginson Bk Co.

Mann, Horace. Lectures on Education. LC 70-89197. (American Education: Its Men, Imstitutions & Ideas, Ser. 1). 1978. reprint ed. 19.95 (*0-405-01437-6*) Ayer.

— On the Art of Teaching. 32p. 1990. 8.95 (*1-55709-129-3*) Applewood.

— Slavery: Letters & Speeches. LC 79-81126. (Black Heritage Library Collection). 1977. 32.95 (*0-8369-8623-7*) Ayer.

— Slavery, Letters & Speeches. LC 70-82205. (Anti-Slavery Crusade in America Ser.). 1970. reprint ed. 32.95 (*0-405-00643-8*) Ayer.

Mann, Hugh. Hugh Mann Writes. 106p. (Orig.). 1993. pap. 15.00 (*0-9623892-0-X*) Hugh Mann.

Mann, J. Bibliography of Fatigue Materials Component & Structure 1838-1950. LC 71-102401. 1970. 136.00 (*0-08-006754-9*, Pub. by Pergamon Repr UK) Franklin.

Mann, J., et al. Natural Products: Their Chemistry & Biological Significance. LC 93-28148. 1994. pap. text ed. 44.95 (*0-470-20002-2*) Halsted Pr.

Mann, J. A. Cotton Trade of Great Britain: Its Rise, Progress & Present Extent. (Illus.). 134p. 1968. reprint ed. 29.50 (*0-7146-1405-X*, Pub. by F Cass Pubs UK) Intl Spec Bk.

Mann, J. C. Staindrop Quaker Meeting House. (C). 1988. 25.00 (*1-85072-118-1*, Pub. by W Sessions UK) St Mut.

Mann, J. J., ed. Models of Depressive Disorders: Psychological, Biological, & Genetic Perspectives. (Depressive Illness Ser.: Vol. 2). (Illus.). 195p. 1989. 39.50 (*0-306-43277-3*, Plenum Pr) Plenum.

Mann, J. J. & Kuper, David J., eds. Biology of Depressive Disorders, Set. (Depressive Illness Ser.: Vols. 3 & 4). (Illus.). 1993. 69.50 (*0-685-67873-3*, Plenum Pr) Plenum.

Mann, J. J. & Kupfer, David J., eds. Biology of Depressive Disorders Pt. A: A Systems Perspective. (Depressive Illness Ser.: Vol. 3). (Illus.). 270p. (C). 1993. 45.00 (*0-306-44295-7*, Plenum Pr) Plenum.

— Biology of Depressive Disorders Pt. B: Subtypes of Depression & Comorbid Disorders. (Depressive Illness Ser.: Vol. 4). (Illus.). 175p. (C). 1993. 37.50 (*0-306-44296-5*, Plenum Pr) Plenum.

Mann, J. John, ed. The Phenomenology of Depressive Illness. (Depressive Illness Ser.: Vol. 1). 263p. 1988. 42.95 (*0-89885-369-9*) Human Sci Pr.

Mann, J. Johnston. The Art of Dapping. 1989. 25.00 (*0-7223-2094-9*, Pub. by A H S Ltd UK) St Mut.

— Fishing for Fun. 90p. (C). 1989. 34.00 (*0-7223-2181-3*, Pub. by A H S Ltd UK) St Mut.

Mann, J. Y. Bibliography on the Fatigue of Materials, Components & Structures, Vol. 3: 1961-1965. 510p. 1983. 205.00 (*0-08-025449-7*, Pub. by Pergamon Repr UK) Franklin.

— Bibliography on the Fatigue of Materials, Components & Structures, Vol. 4: 1966-1969. 509p. 1990. 216.00 (*0-08-040507-X*, Pub. by PPL UK) Franklin.

Mann, Jack. Gees' First Case. 1970. 6.50 (*0-685-33435-X*) Bookfinger.

— Glass Too Many. 1973. 6.50 (*0-685-33436-8*) Bookfinger.

— Grey Shapes. 1970. 6.50 (*0-685-26775-X*) Bookfinger.

— Her Ways Are Death. 287p. 1981. 6.50 (*0-686-73102-6*) Bookfinger.

— Maker of Shadows. 1977. 6.50 (*0-685-88837-1*) Bookfinger.

— Nightmare Farm. 1975. 6.50 (*0-685-54480-X*) Bookfinger.

— The Ninth Life. 1970. 6.50 (*0-685-26776-8*) Bookfinger.

Mann, Jackie & Mann, Sunnie. Yours Till the End. large type ed. (Charnwood Library). 1992. 23.95 (*0-7089-8680-3*) Ulverscroft.

— Yours Till the End: Two Survivors of the Hostage Crisis - Their Amazing Story. (Illus.). 272p. 1993. pap. 9.95 (*0-7493-1336-6*, Pub. by W Heinemann Ltd) Trafalgar.

Mann, Jacob. The Bible As Read & Preached in the Old Synagogue, Vol. 1. rev. ed. (Library of Biblical Studies). 1970. 69.50 (*0-87068-083-8*) Ktav.

— The Responsa of the Babylonian Geonim As a Source of Jewish History. LC 73-2215. (Jewish People; History, Religion, Literature Ser.). 1973. reprint ed. 25.95 (*0-405-05279-0*) Ayer.

Mann, James. Rediscovery of Man: The Complete Short Science Fiction of Cordwainer Smith. Smith, Cordwainer, ed. LC 93-84365. xvi, 671p. 1993. 24.95 (*0-915368-56-0*) New Eng SF Assoc.

— Time-Limited Psychotherapy. LC 72-96631. (Commonwealth Fund Publications). 212p. 1980. pap. 16.95 (*0-674-89191-0*) HUP.

Mann, James & Goldman, Robert. A Casebook in Time-Limited Psychotherapy. LC 93-74812. 192p. 1995. pap. 25.00 (*1-56821-210-0*) Aronson.

— A Casebook in Time-Limited Psychotherapy. LC 86-32209. 192p. reprint ed. pap. 54.80 (*0-8357-4756-5*, 2037682) Bks Demand.

Mann, James, jt. auth. see Buckley, Martin.

Mann, James A., ed. see Smith, Cordwainer.

Mann, James E., Jr., jt. auth. see Simmonds, James G.

Mann, Jeff, jt. ed. see Cranston, Meg.

***Mann, Jessica.** Mrs. Knox's Profession. 160p. 1994. 16.95 (*0-7451-8646-7*, Black Dagger) Chivers N Amer.

Mann, Jill. Apologies to Women. (C). 1991. pap. 9.95 (*0-521-42376-7*) Cambridge U Pr.

— Langland & Allegory. (Morton W. Bloomfield Lectures on Medieval English Literature Ser.: Vol. II). (C). 1992. 5.00 (*1-879288-15-X*) Medieval Inst.

Mann, Jill, jt. ed. see Boitani, Piero.

Mann, Jim. Ad Sales: Interviews with Twenty-Three Top Magazine Executives. Carroll, Theodus, ed. 1987. 59.95 (*0-918110-15-7*) Hanson Pub Grp.

— Magazine Editing: Its Art & Practice. 1985. 59.95 (*0-918110-12-2*) Hanson Pub Grp.

Mann, Jim, ed. NESFA Index to Short Science Fiction for 1988. 136p. 1990. 12.00 (*0-915368-43-9*) New Eng SF Assoc.

— NESFA Index to Short Science Fiction for 1989. 164p. 1992. 12.00 (*0-915368-48-X*) New Eng SF Assoc.

— NESFA Index to Short SF: 1987. (Index Ser.). 139p. 1989. pap. 12.00 (*0-915368-41-2*) New Eng SF Assoc.

— NESFA Index to the Science Fiction Magazines & Original Anthologies, 1986. (Index Ser.). 82p. 1988. pap. 8.00 (*0-915368-32-3*) New Eng SF Assoc.

Mann, Jim, jt. auth. see Ball, Madaleine.

Mann, Jim, jt. auth. see Longstaff, Roberta.

***Mann, John.** Bacteria & Anti-Bacterial Agents. LC 95-7004. (Biochemical & Medicinal Chemistry Ser.). 1995. write for info. (*0-7167-4508-9*) W H Freeman.

— Chemical Aspects of Biosynthesis. (Chemistry Primers Ser.: No. 20). (Illus.). 96p. (C). 1995. text ed. 29.95 (*0-19-855677-2*); pap. text ed. 9.95 (*0-19-855676-4*) OUP.

— Murder, Magic, & Medicine. (Illus.). 240p. 1992. 29.95 (*0-19-855561-X*) OUP.

— Murder, Magic, & Medicine. (Illus.). 240p. 1994. reprint ed. pap. 14.95 (*0-19-855854-6*) OUP.

— Rudi: Fourteen Years with My Teacher. Asay, Diane, ed. 343p. (Orig.). 1987. pap. 14.95 (*0-915801-04-3*) Rudra Pr.

Mann, John & Short, Lar. The Body of Light: History & Practical Techniques for Awakening Your Subtle Body. (Illus.). 192p. (Orig.). 1993. reprint ed. 12.95 (*0-8048-1992-0*) C E Tuttle.

Mann, John, jt. auth. see Richard, Michel P.

Mann, John A. & Everone, Chadd. Fountains of Youth: Secrets of Life Extension. 1995. pap. 14.95 (*0-914171-76-3*) Ronin Pub.

Mann, John C., jt. auth. see Pomeroy, John N.

Mann, John E. Southampton Past & Present. 96p. 1987. 30.00 (*0-905392-53-1*) St Mut.

— Southampton People Eminent Sotonians & Assorted Characters. (C). 1989. 39.00 (*1-85455-021-7*, Pub. by Ensign Pubns & Print UK) St Mut.

Mann, John E. & Whatley, Derek. Brannon's Southampton. (C). 1989. 39.00 (*1-85455-042-X*, Pub. by Ensign Pubns & Print UK) St Mut.

Mann, Jonathan, et al, eds. AIDS in the World, 1992. 1037p. 1992. text ed. 50.00 (*0-674-01265-8*); pap. text ed. 24.95 (*0-674-01266-6*) HUP.

M

An Asterisk (*) at the beginning of an entry indicates that the title is appearing in BIP for the first time.

Mann, Josiah S. Before the Wedding Bell Rings: A Marriage Preparation Manual. 96p. 1986. pap. 5.95 (*0-937673-02-1*) Peacock Ent LA.

Mann, Judy. The Difference: Growing up Female in America. 336p. 1994. 22.95 (*0-446-51707-0*) Warner Bks.

— The Difference: Growing up Female in America. 1995. pap. write for info. (*0-446-67118-5*) Warner Bks.

— Mann for All Seasons. 1990. 19.95 (*0-942361-22-9*) MasterMedia Ltd.

— Mann for All Seasons: Wit & Wisdom from the Washington Post's Judy Mann. LC 90-39907. 320p. 1991. pap. 9.95 (*0-942361-38-5*) MasterMedia Ltd.

Mann, Jules. Get Naked And. . . Mycue, Edward, ed. (Took Modern Poetry in English Ser.: No. 5). (Illus.). 28p. (Orig.). 1991. pap. 4.00 (*0-9625855-8-0*) Norton Coker Pr.

Mann, Julia, jt. auth. see Wadsworth, Alfred P.

Mann, K. Tribal Women in Changing Society. 178p. 1987. 21.00 (*0-8364-2034-9*, Pub. by Mittal II) S Asia.

Mann, K. & Jones, E. Leeches Hirudinea: Their Structure Physiology Ecology & Embryology. LC 61-17953. (International Series of Monographs on Pure & Applied Mathematics: Vol. 11). 1962. 89.00 (*0-08-009585-2*, Pub. by Pergamon Repr UK) Franklin.

Mann, K. H. Ecology of Coastal Waters: A Systems Approach. LC 81-40321. (Studies in Ecology: Vol. 8). (Illus.). 300p. 1981. pap. 20.00 (*0-520-04734-6*) U CA Pr.

Mann, K. H., jt. ed. see Barnes, R. S.

Mann, K. H., jt. auth. see Elliott, J. M.

Mann, Karen B. The Language that Makes George Eliot's Fiction. LC 83-257. 240p. reprint ed. pap. 68.40 (*0-8357-6621-7*, 2035266) Bks Demand.

Mann, Ken & Jones, Gary. Downsizing Computer Systems. (Illus.). 350p. 1995. pap. 29.95 (*0-7506-0907-9*) Buttrwrth-Heinemann.

Mann, Kenneth. Defending White-Collar Crime: A Portrait of Attorneys at Work. LC 84-17357. (Yale Studies on White-Collar Crime). 282p. 1985. text ed. 42.00 (*0-300-03254-4*) Yale U Pr.

***Mann, Kenny.** The Guinea Coast: Oyo, Benin, Ashanti. LC 95-16060. (African Kingdoms of the Past Ser.). 1995. write for info. (*0-87518-657-2*, Dillon Silver Burdett) Silver Burdett Pr.

— The Guinea Coast: Oyo, Benin, Ashanti. LC 95-16060. (African Kingdoms of the Past Ser.). (J). 1995. pap. write for info. (*0-382-39177-2*, Dillon Silver Burdett) Silver Burdett Pr.

— I Am Not Afraid! Based on a Masai Tale. LC 92-13811. (Illus.). (J). 1993. pap. 3.50 (*0-553-37108-8*, Little Rooster); mass mkt. 9.99 (*0-553-09119-0*, Little Rooster) Bantam.

Mann, Kenton, jt. auth. see Farrell, Isabel.

Mann, Kirk. The Making of an English 'Underclass'? The Social Divisions of Welfare & Labour. 192p. 1991. 90.00 (*0-335-09719-7*, Open Univ Pr); pap. 32.00 (*0-335-09718-9*, Open Univ Pr) Taylor & Francis.

***Mann, Klaus.** Mephisto. Smyth, Robin, tr. 272p. 1995. 11.95 (*0-14-018918-1*, Penguin Classics) Viking Penguin.

— Pathetic Symphony: A Biographical Novel about Tchaikovsky. LC 85-50532. (Illus.). 380p. 1985. reprint ed. pap. 9.95 (*0-910129-24-X*) Wiener Pubs Inc.

— Siblings & the Children's Story. Alexander, Tanya & Eyre, Peter, trs. 160p. 1991. 19.95 (*0-7145-2939-7*) M Boyars Pubs.

— The Turning Point: The Autobiography of Klaus Mann. LC 83-27414. 420p. 1984. reprint ed. 18.95 (*0-910129-13-4*); reprint ed. pap. 9.95 (*0-910129-14-2*) Wiener Pubs Inc.

Mann, Kristin. Marrying Well: Marriage, Status & Social Change among the Educated Elite in Colonial Lagos. (African Studies: No. 47). (Illus.). 204p. 1985. 64.95 (*0-521-30701-5*) Cambridge U Pr.

Mann, Kristin & Roberts, Richard. Law in Colonial Africa. (Social History of Africa Ser.). 264p. 1991. text ed. 45.00 (*0-435-08053-9*) Heinemann.

— Law in Colonial Africa. LC 90-25784. (Social History of Africa Ser.). 264p. (C). 1991. pap. 22.95 (*0-435-08055-5*) Heinemann.

Mann, Laurie, ed. The Noreascon 3 Memory Book. (Illus.). 64p. 1991. 7.00 (*0-9603146-7-9*) MA Convent Fandom.

Mann, Lawrence, Jr. Maintenance Management. rev. ed. LC 81-47628. 512p. 1983. text ed. 49.95 (*0-669-04715-5*) Free Pr.

Mann, Leon, jt. auth. see Janis, Irving L.

Mann, Leonard. Life-Size Living. Sherer, Michael L., ed. (Orig.). 1986. pap. 6.55 (*0-89536-820-X*, 6829) CSS OH.

Mann, Lester, jt. ed. see Reynolds, Cecil R.

Mann, Lloyd & Mann, Wilma. Dialogos Evangelisticos (Dialogues That Witness) Para Alcanzar a Mas Jovenes para Cristo (Reaching Youth for Christ) 96p. (SPA.). 1991. pap. 3.50 (*0-311-12334-1*) Casa Bautista.

Mann, M. A. & Jackson, K. C. Fashion: An Interdisciplinary Review. (C). 1987. pap. text ed. 90.00 (*0-900739-97-5*, Pub. by Textile Institue UK) St Mut.

Mann, Marek. Annie's City Adventures. Max, Jill, ed. Verlag, Mangold, tr. LC 91-21302. (Magic Mountain Fables Ser.). (Illus.). 24p. (J). (gr. k-3). 1991. lib. bdg. 14.60 (*1-56074-031-0*) Garrett Ed Corp.

— Annie's High Sea Adventure. Max, Jill & Bradford, Elizabeth, eds. Verlag, Mangold, tr. LC 91-21305. (Magic Mountain Fables Ser.). (Illus.). 24p. (J). (gr. k-3). 1991. lib. bdg. 14.60 (*1-56074-027-2*) Garrett Ed Corp.

— Dino, the Star Keeper. Max, Jill, ed. Verlag, Mangold, tr. LC 91-21304. (Magic Mountain Fables Ser.). (Illus.). 24p. (J). (gr. k-3). 1991. lib. bdg. 14.60 (*1-56074-028-0*) Garrett Ed Corp.

Mann, Marek, jt. auth. see Gipson, Morrell.

Mann, Maria, jt. auth. see Roberts, John.

Mann, Maria A. La Mere dans la Litterature Francaise, 1678-1831. (American University Studies: Romance Languages & Literature: Ser. II, Vol. 92). 299p. (C). 1989. text ed. 40.10 (*0-8204-0878-6*) P Lang Pubs.

Mann, Martan. Jazz Improvisation for the Classical Pianist. (Illus.). 221p. (Orig.). 1989. pap. 29.95 (*0-8256-1229-2*, AM10000) Music Sales.

— New Age Improvisation for the Classical Pianist. (Illus.). 48p. 1992. pap. 14.95 (*0-8256-1286-1*, AM80169) Music Sales.

Mann, Marty. Marty Mann Answers Your Questions about Drinking & Alcoholism. 112p. 1970. 3.95 (*0-318-15340-8*) Natl Coun Alcoholism.

Mann, Mary T. Life of Horace Mann. LC 73-89396. (Black Heritage Library Collection). 1977. 28.95 (*0-8369-8624-5*) Ayer.

Mann, Mary T., tr. see Sarmiento, Domingo F.

Mann, Maybelle. The American Art Union. rev. ed. LC 87-70145. (Illus.). 128p. (C). 1987. pap. 14.95 (*0-9618779-0-1*) ALM Assocs.

— Walter Launt Palmer. LC 84-50506. (Illus.). 192p. 1989. 35.00 (*0-88740-001-9*) Schiffer.

Mann, Michael. The Sources of Social Power, Vol. 1: A History of Power from the Beginning to AD 1760. (Illus.). 608p. 1986. 89.95 (*0-521-30851-8*); pap. 29.95 (*0-521-31349-X*) Cambridge U Pr.

— The Sources of Social Power, Vol. 2: The Rise of Classes & Nation States, 1760-1914. (Illus.). 816p. (C). 1993. 79.95 (*0-521-44015-7*); pap. 24.95 (*0-521-44585-X*) Cambridge U Pr.

— States, War & Capitalism: Studies in Political Sociology. pap. 18.95 (*0-631-18509-7*) Blackwell Pubs.

Mann, Michael, jt. auth. see Crompton, Rosemary.

Mann, Michael J., et al. Innovative Site Remediation Technology, Vol. 3: Soil Washing - Soil Flushing. Anderson, William C., ed. LC 93-20786. 160p. 1994. 49.95 (*1-883767-03-2*) Am Acad Environ.

***Mann, Moke.** Hawaiian Fishing Traditions. 2nd ed. Kawaharada, Dennis, ed. & intro. by. LC 91-60467. 96p. 1994. pap. 7.95 (*0-9623102-3-9*) Kalamaku Pr.

Mann, N. H. & Carr, N. G., eds. Photosynthetic Prokaryotes. (Biotechnology Handbooks Ser.: Vol. 6). (Illus.). 286p. 1991. 69.50 (*0-306-43879-8*, Plenum Pr) Plenum.

Mann, Nancy R. The Keys to Excellence: The Story of the Deming Philosophy. 138p. 1987. text ed. 16.95 (*0-9614986-0-9*) Prestwick Bks.

Mann, Nancy R., et al. Methods for the Statistical Analysis of Reliability & Life Data. LC 73-20461. (Probability & Mathematical Statistics Ser.). 564p. 1974. text ed. 145.00 (*0-471-56737-X*, Wiley-Interscience) Wiley.

***Mann, Nicholas R.** His Story: Masculinity in the Post-Patriarchal World. LC 95-12264. (Male Mysteries Ser.). 336p. 1995. pap. text ed. 14.95 (*1-56718-458-8*) Llewellyn Pubns.

— Sedona-Sacred Earth: Ancient Lore, Modern Myths - A Guide to the Red Rock Country. rev. ed. Thompson, Margaret & Dye, Nancy, eds. (Illus.). 108p. 1990. pap. 10.95 (*0-9622707-3-3*) Zivah Pubs.

Mann, Nicholas R. & Sutton, Marcia. Giants of Gaia. (Illus.). 204p. (Orig.). 1995. pap. 15.95 (*0-914732-32-3*) Bro Life Inc.

Mann, Nome. Come Dance with Me. 1985. 5.09 (*0-935513-00-0*) Samara Pubns.

Mann, P., et al, eds. Geologic & Tectonic Development of the North American-Caribbean Plate Boundary in Hispaniola. (Special Paper Ser.: No. 262). (Illus.). 1992. pap. 98.75 (*0-8137-2262-4*) Geol Soc.

Mann, Pamela. Children in Care Revisited. LC 84-9915. 192p. 1984. text ed. 29.95 (*0-312-13234-6*) St Martin.

— The Frog Princess? LC 95-7907. (Illus.). (J). 1995. write for info. (*0-8368-1352-9*) Gareth Stevens Inc.

Mann, Patricia S. Micro-Politics: Agency in a Postfeminist Era. LC 93-28965. 264p. 1994. pap. 17.95 (*0-8166-2049-0*) U of Minn Pr.

— Micro-Politics: Agency in a Postfeminist Era. LC 93-28965. 264p. 1994. text ed. 44.95 (*0-8166-2048-2*) U of Minn Pr.

Mann, Patrick C., ed. see Michigan State University, Institute of Public Utilities Conference Staff.

Mann, Patrick C., et al. An Economic Analysis of the Electric Utility Sector in the Ohio River Basin Region. 77p. 1979. write for info. (*0-318-59910-4*) Assn U Busn & Econ Res.

Mann, Paul. The Britannia Contract. 448p. 1993. 21.00 (*0-88184-933-2*) Carroll & Graf.

— The Ganja Coast. LC 93-46505. 336p. 1995. 22.50 (*0-449-90769-4*, Columbine) Fawcett.

— Season of the Monsoon. LC 92-54998. 352p. 1993. 20.00 (*0-449-90768-6*, Columbine) Fawcett.

— Season of the Monsoon. 1995. mass mkt. 5.99 (*0-8041-1259-2*) Ivy Books.

— The Theory-Death of the Avant-Garde. LC 90-49768. 160p. 1991. 29.95 (*0-253-33672-4*) Ind U Pr.

***Mann, Paul, ed.** Geologic & Tectonic Development of the Caribbean Plate Boundary in Southern Central America. LC 94-41170. (Special Papers: Vol. 295). 1995. pap. 100.00 (*0-8137-2295-0*) Geol Soc.

Mann, Pauline. Wedding Flowers. (Illus.). 64p. 1985. 19.95 (*0-7134-4636-6*, Pub. by Batsford UK) Trafalgar.

Mann, Peggy. La Historia de Maria Wanna: O Como te Dana la Marihuana. Ramirez, Gloria & Gatti, Maria N., trs. (Illus.). 44p. (Orig.). (SPA.). (J). (gr. 1-6). 1990. pap. text ed. 3.95 (*0-942493-15-X*) Woodmere Press.

— The Mary Wanna Teacher's Guide. 20p. (gr. 3-6). 1989. pap. 4.50 (*0-318-50074-4*) Woodmere Press.

— Pot Safari: A Visit to the Top Marijuana Researchers. rev. ed. LC 82-91050. 133p. (Orig.). (YA). (gr. 9-12). 1987. pap. 6.95 (*0-942493-01-X*) Woodmere Press.

— The Sad Story of Mary Wanna or How Marijuana Harms You. rev. ed. 40p. (J). (gr. 1-6). 1990. pap. 3.95 (*0-318-50073-6*) Woodmere Press.

— Twelve Is Too Old. 140p. (YA). (gr. 6-9). 1987. pap. 6.95 (*0-942493-00-1*) Woodmere Press.

Mann, Peggy & Houlton, Betsy. Ms. Cramm on Pot: The Real Story about Marijuana. (Illus.). 21p. (YA). (gr. 6-12). 1991. pap. 1.75 (*0-89486-738-5*, 5512B) Hazelden.

Mann, Peggy, jt. auth. see Moran, Bill.

Mann, Penny J. Best Friends. (Miss Penny's Adventures Ser.: No. 1). 48p. 1993. pap. 5.00 (*0-9638742-0-9*) Good News Express.

— Center Lane... Turn Only. No. 2. 64p. Date not set. pap. write for info. (*0-318-72210-0*) Good News Express.

— Don't Die, Marvin. No. 3. 80p. Date not set. pap. write for info. (*0-318-72211-9*) Good News Express.

Mann, Pete, jt. ed. see Jones, Merrick.

Mann, Pete M., jt. auth. see Mann, Rebecca C.

Mann, Peter. Tesnic. 216p. 1994. pap. 16.00 (*0-8059-3556-8*) Dorrance.

***Mann, Peter & Lewis, Candace.** Annotated Insurance Contracts Act. 300p. 1994. pap. 65.00 (*0-455-21255-4*, Pub. by Law Bk Co) W W Gaunt.

Mann, Peter, jt. auth. see Dan, Uri.

Mann, Peter A. Blueprint Reading for the Construction Trades. (C). 1984. text ed. write for info. (*0-318-57574-4*, Reston) P-H.

— Illustrated Residential & Commercial Construction. 448p. 1988. pap. text ed. 50.00 (*0-13-453250-3*) P-H.

Mann, Peter H. Methods of Social Investigation. 256p. 1985. pap. 21.95 (*0-631-14019-0*) Blackwell Pubs.

Mann, Philip H. Guide for Educating Mainstreamed Students. 1991. pap. 34.95 (*0-205-13225-1*, Longwood Div) Allyn.

Mann, Philip H., et al. Basic Phonic Analysis Skills: Teacher's Guide & Student Worksheets. 297p. 1982. 33.95 (*0-205-07804-4*, H78041) Allyn.

Mann, Phillip. Wulfsyarn. 368p. 1993. mass mkt. 4.99 (*0-380-71717-4*, AvoNova) Avon.

— Wulfsyarn: A Mosaic. LC 92-15039. 1992. 22.00 (*0-688-11881-X*) Morrow.

Mann, Prem S. Introductory Statistics. 800p. (C). 1991. Net. text ed. write for info. (*0-471-52733-5*) Wiley.

— Introductory Statistics. 2nd ed. LC 94-42931. (C). 1995. text ed. write for info. (*0-471-31009-3*) Wiley.

— Introductory Statistics: With Supplemental Chapter on Design of Experiments. 1994. text ed. write for info. (*0-471-31057-3*) Wiley.

— Statistics for Business & Economics. LC 94-26247. 879p. 1994. text ed. 67.95 (*0-471-58969-1*) Wiley.

Mann, R., et al, eds. Gravitation: A BANFF Summer Institute: BANFF Center, Alberta, Canada, 12-25 August 1990. 650p. (C). 1991. text ed. 130.00 (*981-02-0751-4*) World Scientific Pub.

***Mann, R. B. & Mclenaghan, R. G.** General Relativity & Relativistic Astrophysics-Proceedings of the 5th Canadian Conference. 500p. 1994. text ed. 118.00 (*981-02-1916-4*) World Scientific Pub.

Mann, R. D., ed. Adverse Drug Reactions. (Illus.). 240p. 1987. 65.00 (*1-85070-137-7*) Prthnon Pub.

— The History of the Management of Pain: From Early Principles to Present Practice. (History of Medicine Ser.). (Illus.). 200p. 1988. 58.00 (*1-85070-183-0*) Prthnon Pub.

— Oral Contraceptives & Breast Cancer: The Implications of the Present Findings for Informed Consent & Informed Choice. (Illus.). 406p. 1990. 65.00 (*1-85070-282-9*) Prthnon Pub.

— Risk & Consent to Risk in Medicine. (Illus.). 234p. 1989. 65.00 (*1-85070-263-2*) Prthnon Pub.

Mann, R. D., jt. ed. see Costello, J. F.

Mann, R. D., et al. William Withering & the Foxglove. 1986. lib. bdg. 218.50 (*0-85200-950-X*) Kluwer Ac.

Mann, R. E., et al, eds. A Textbook of Pharmaceutical Medicine. (Illus.). 500p. 1993. text ed. 135.00 (*1-85070-341-8*) Prthnon Pub.

Mann, R. J. Our Miss Brooks - Str. rev. ed. 1978. 4.95 (*0-87129-253-X*, O25) Dramatic Pub.

— Our Miss Brooks & the Christmas Carol. 1954. pap. 2.50 (*0-87129-209-2*, O26) Dramatic Pub.

Mann, R. S. Culture & Integration of Indian Tribes. 193p. (C). 1993. 60.00x (*81-85880-03-4*, Pub. by Print Hse II) St Mut.

— Social Change & Social Research: An Indian Perspective. (C). 1988. 38.00 (*81-7022-200-1*, Pub. by Concept II) S Asia.

Mann, Ralph. After the Gold Rush: Society in Grass Valley & Nevada City, California, 1849-1870. LC 81-52825. (Illus.). 320p. 1982. 37.50 (*0-8047-1136-4*) Stanford U Pr.

— Glasnost: Gateway to World Revival. rev. ed. 304p. 1989. 2.99 (*0-88368-212-5*) Whitaker Hse.

Mann, Randy, jt. auth. see Loffman, Tom.

Mann, Randy, ed. see Loffman, Tom.

Mann, Rebecca B. Behavior Mismatch: How to Manage Problem Employees Whose Actions Don't Match Your Expectations. LC 93-24873. 176p. 1993. 19.95 (*0-8144-5121-7*) AMACOM.

Mann, Rebecca C. & Mann, Pete M. Essay Writing: Methods & Models. 416p. (C). 1990. pap. 23.95 (*0-534-12168-3*) Intl Thomson.

Mann, Richard. Elvis Presley. (SPA.). 4.95 (*84-7228-491-3*, 220347, Pub. by Edit Clie SP) TSELF.

Mann, Richard, jt. auth. see Brown, Jonathan.

***Mann, Richard A. & Roberts, Barry S.** Essentials of Business Law & the Legal Environment. 5th ed. LC 94-28022. 1000p. 1994. text ed. 61.50 (*0-314-04529-5*) West Pub.

— Smith & Roberson's Business Law. 9th ed. Bruckner, ed. LC 93-21510. 1250p. (C). 1993. text ed. 68.50 (*0-314-02712-2*) West Pub.

Mann, Richard D. The Light of Consciousness: Explorations in Transpersonal Psychology. LC 83-18088. 177p. 1984. 39.50 (*0-87395-905-1*); pap. 12.95 (*0-87395-906-X*) State U NY Pr.

Mann, Richard G. El Greco & His Patrons: Three Major Projects. (Cambridge Studies in the History of Art). (Illus.). 178p. 1989. pap. 27.95 (*0-521-38943-7*) Cambridge U Pr.

Mann, Richard G., jt. auth. see Brown, Jonathan.

Mann, Richard I. Travel Guide Indonesia. (Holiday Sports of Tomorrow Ser.). (Illus.). 200p. 1991. pap. 14.95 (*981-00-2393-6*, Pub. by Singapore Natl Print Ltd SI) Intl Spec Bk.

Mann, Richard O., jt. auth. see Mann, Steven W.

Mann, Rink. Backyard Sugarin' 3rd rev. ed. (Illus.). 96p. 1991. pap. 8.00 (*0-88150-216-2*) Countryman.

***Mann, Rip & Mann, Tammi.** Hewing Contemporary Bowls. LC 94-24311. (Schiffer Book for Woodcarvers Ser.). (Illus.). 64p. (Orig.). 1995. pap. 12.95 (*0-88740-710-2*) Schiffer.

— Sculpting Traditional Bowls. LC 94-66374. (Illus.). 48p. (Orig.). 1994. pap. 12.95 (*0-88740-698-X*) Schiffer.

Mann, Robert. Andrei Bely's Petersburg & the Cult of Dionysus. (Illus.). 124p. (C). 1987. 12.50 (*0-87291-170-5*) Coronado Pr.

— The Dionysian Art of Isaac Babel. (Illus.). 134p. (Orig.). (C). 1994. pap. 12.50 (*0-936041-08-0*) Barbary Coast Bks.

— Lances Sing: A Study of the Igor Tale. 231p. (Orig.). 1990. pap. 16.95 (*0-89357-208-X*) Slavica.

— Rails 'Neath the Palms. (Illus.). 220p. 1984. 29.95 (*0-933506-08-2*) Darwin Pubns.

— Russian Apocalypse: Songs & Tales about the Coming of Christianity to Russia. 151p. (C). 1987. 12.95 (*0-87291-172-1*) Coronado Pr.

Mann, Robert E., jt. ed. see Wilson, R. Jean.

***Mann, Robert W. & Murphy, Sean P.** Regional Atlas of Bone Disease: A Guide to Pathologic & Normal Variation in the Human Skeleton. (Illus.). 224p. 1990. pap. 29.95 (*0-398-06267-6*) C C Thomas.

— Regional Atlas of Bone Disease: A Guide to Pathologic & Normal Variation in the Human Skeleton. (Illus.). 224p. (C). 1990. text ed. 44.95 (*0-398-05675-7*) C C Thomas.

Mann, Robert W., ed. see McCullough, Christopher J.

Mann, Robert W., jt. auth. see McCullough, Christopher J.

Mann, Roger, jt. ed. see Rosenfield, Aaron.

Mann, Roger A. & Coughlin, Michael J., eds. Surgery of the Foot & Ankle. 6th rev. ed. LC 92-19174. Orig. Title: Surgery of the Foot & Ankle. 1703p. 1992. 245.00 (*0-8016-6683-X*) Mosby Yr Bk.

Mann, Roland. Cat & Mouse: Wearin' 'N Tearin' (Illus.). 110p. 1991. pap. 9.95 (*1-56398-000-2*) Malibu Graphics.

— Cat & Mouse Collection. Ulm, Chris, ed. (Illus.). 139p. (J). 1990. pap. 9.95 (*0-944735-70-3*) Malibu Graphics.

Mann, Ronald D. Hormone Replacement Therapy & Breast Cancer Risk. (Illus.). 320p. 1992. 78.00 (*1-85070-399-X*) Prthnon Pub.

— Modern Drug Use. 1984. lib. bdg. 160.50 (*0-85200-717-5*) Kluwer Ac.

Mann, Ronald D., ed. Patient Information in Medicine. (Illus.). 200p. 1991. text ed. 35.00 (*1-85070-367-1*) Prthnon Pub.

Mann, Ronald J. Infections of the Hand. LC 87-21434. 204p. reprint ed. pap. 58.20 (*0-7837-2726-7*, 2043106) Bks Demand.

Mann, Ronald L. Personal Relationship Inventory (PRI) Manual for Scoring & Interpretation. 91p. (Orig.). 1994. pap. 18.00 (*1-879858-03-7*) Behaviordyne.

Mann, Rs. K. Tribal Cultures & Change. (C). 1989. 42.00 (*0-685-32674-8*, Pub. by Mittal II) S Asia.

Mann, Russell A. USL Journalism Manual of Style & Format. LC 86-90665. 115p. (Orig.). 1986. pap. 9.95 (*0-940205-00-9*) Journalism Style.

Mann, Ruth, jt. auth. see Horowitz, Estelle.

Mann, S., et al, eds. Biomineralization: Chemical & Biochemical Perspectives. LC 89-14840. 541p. 1989. lib. bdg. 220.00 (*0-89573-672-1*) VCH Pubs.

Mann, Sally. At Twelve: Portraits of Young Women. (Illus.). 56p. 1988. pap. 19.95 (*0-89381-330-3*) Aperture.

— At Twelve: Portraits of Young Women. (Illus.). 56p. 1988. 35.00 (*0-89381-296-X*) Aperture.

— Immediate Family. (Illus.). 88p. 1992. 40.00 (*0-89381-518-7*) Aperture.

— Immediate Family. 1994. pap. 24.95 (*0-89381-523-3*) Aperture.

— Still Time. (Illus.). 80p. 1994. pap. 29.95 (*0-89381-593-4*) Aperture.

***Mann, Sita.** Secrets in the Attic. (Rainbow Romances Ser.). 160p. 1994. 14.95 (*0-7090-4997-8*, 909, Hale-Parkwest) Parkwest Pubns.

Mann, Stanley. Triggers: A New Approach to Self-Motivation. 216p. 1986. text ed. 25.95 (*0-13-930793-1*) P-H.

Mann, Stanley C. One Against the Storm. LC 80-54238. (Illus.). 221p. (Orig.). pap. 6.95 (*0-938662-00-7*) Quest Utah.

Mann, Stephanie & Blakeman, M. C. Safe Homes, Safe Neighborhoods. 256p. 1993. pap. 14.95 (*0-87337-195-X*) Nolo Pr.

***Mann, Steve.** The Mann Fantasy Baseball Guide 1995. 192p. 1995. pap. 11.00 (*0-06-273331-1*, Harper Ref) HarpC.

— The Small Talk Resource Guide. 2nd ed. 225p. (Orig.). 1994. pap. 40.00 (*0-9642181-0-0*) Creat Digital.

— The Smalltalk Resource Guide. 3rd ed. 300p. 1995. pap. write for info. (*0-9642181-1-9*) Creat Digital.

Mann, Steven. Being Ill: Personal & Social Meanings. 204p. 1982. text ed. 26.50 (*0-8290-0720-2*) Irvington.

— Being Ill: Personal & Social Meanings. 204p. 1985. reprint ed. pap. text ed. 12.95 (*0-8290-1661-9*) Irvington.

An Asterisk (*) at the beginning of an entry indicates that the title is appearing in BIP for the first time.

Mann, Steven W. & Mann, Richard O. Windows 3.1 Demystified: Tips, Tricks & Techniques. (Illus.). 512p. 1991. pap. 24.95 (*0-8306-3800-8*, 3800, Windcrest) TAB Bks.

Mann, Stuart H., jt. auth. see Johnson, Edward R.

Mann, Sunnie. Holding On. 192p. 1991. 34.95 (*0-7475-0665-5*, Pub. by Bloomsbury Pub Ltd UK) Trafalgar.

Mann, Sunnie, jt. auth. see Mann, Jackie.

Mann, Susan. Local Merchants & the Chinese Bureaucracy, 1750-1950. LC 86-14403. (Illus.). 296p. 1987. 39.50 (*0-8047-1341-3*) Stanford U Pr.

Mann, Susan A. Agrarian Capitalism in Theory & Practice. LC 89-22656. (Illus.). xvi, 212p. (C). 1990. 34.95 (*0-8078-1885-2*) U of NC Pr.

Mann, Susan G. The Short Story Cycle: A Genre Companion & Reference Guide. 243p. 1988. lib. bdg. 49.95 (*0-318-39872-9*, MSS/, Greenwood Pr) Greenwood.

Mann, T. Spermatophores: Development, Structure, Biochemical Attributes & Role in the Transfer of Spermatozoa. (Zoophysiology Ser.: Vol. 15). (Illus.). 240p. 1984. 105.00 (*0-387-13583-9*) Spr-Verlag.

Mann, T. & Lutwak-Mann, C. Male Reproductive Function & Semen. (Illus.). 498p. 1981. 142.00 (*0-387-10383-X*) Spr-Verlag.

Mann, Tammi, jt. auth. see Mann, Rip.

Mann, Thomas. The Black Swan. Trask, Willard R., tr. 155p. 1990. 22.00 (*0-520-07008-9*); pap. 12.00 (*0-520-07009-7*) U CA Pr.

— Buddenbrooks. LC 92-52929. 1994. 20.00 (*0-679-41737-0*) Knopf.

— Buddenbrooks. 1984. pap. 15.00 (*0-394-72637-5*) Random.

— Buddenbrooks. 1994. pap. 15.00 (*0-679-75260-9*) Random.

— Buddenbrooks. Lowe-Porter, H. T., tr. 644p. 1988. reprint ed. lib. bdg. 45.95 (*0-89966-599-3*) Buccaneer Bks.

— Buddenbrooks: The Decline of a Family. Woods, John E., tr. LC 92-18990. 1993. 35.00 (*0-679-41994-2*) Knopf.

— Children & Fools. Scheffauer, Herman G., tr. LC 71-142268. (Short Story Index Reprint Ser.). 1977. 18.95 (*0-8369-3752-X*) Ayer.

— Confessions of Felix Krull. 1993. 21.00 (*0-8446-6715-3*) Peter Smith.

— Confessions of Felix Krull Con. 1992. pap. 11.00 (*0-679-73904-1*, Vin) Random.

— Confessions of Felix Krull, Confidence Man. 382p. 1969. pap. 9.00 (*0-394-70496-7*, Vin) Random.

— Death in Venice. 1976. 11.95 (*0-8488-0574-7*) Amereon Ltd.

— Death in Venice. Heller, Erich, tr. (Modern Library College Editions). (C). 1970. pap. text ed. write for info. (*0-07-553669-2*, T99) McGraw.

— Death in Venice. Kolb, Clayton, ed. & tr. by. (Critical Editions Ser.). (C). 1994. pap. text ed. 6.95 (*0-393-96013-7*) Norton.

— Death in Venice. Appelbaum, Stanley, tr. & comment by. LC 95-2967. (Thrift Editions Ser.). 1995. pap. 1.00 (*0-486-28714-9*) Dover.

— Death in Venice. 451p. 1983. reprint ed. lib. bdg. 12.95 (*0-89966-455-5*) Buccaneer Bks.

— Death in Venice & Other Stories. 400p. (Orig.). 1991. 17.00 (*0-679-40666-2*, Everymans Lib) Knopf.

— Death in Venice & Other Stories. Luke, David, tr. & intro. by. 320p. (Orig.). 1988. mass mkt. 5.95 (*0-553-21333-4*) Bantam.

— Death in Venice & Seven Other Stories. 1954. pap. 4.95 (*0-394-70003-1*) Random.

— Death in Venice & Seven Other Stories. Lowe-Porter, Helen T., tr. (International Ser.). 1989. pap. 10.00 (*0-679-72206-8*, Vin) Random.

— Death in Venice & Seven Other Stories. Lowe-Porter, Helen T., tr. LC 92-25325. 1992. 15.50 (*0-679-60040-X*, Modern Lib) Random.

— Doctor Faustus. 1992. 20.00 (*0-679-41328-6*, Everymans Lib) Knopf.

— Doctor Faustus. 1992. 20.00 (*0-679-40996-3*, Everymans Lib) Knopf.

— Dr. Faustus. 1992. pap. 14.00 (*0-679-73905-X*, Vin) Random.

— Doctor Faustus: The Life of the German Composer Adrian Leverk Uhn As Told by a Friend. Lowe-Porter, Helen T., tr. LC 92-24703. 1992. 18.50 (*0-679-60042-6*, Modern Lib) Random.

— Doctor Faustus: The Life of the German Composer, Adrian Leverkuhn As Told by a Friend. LC 48-8940. 1971. pap. 11.00 (*0-394-71297-8*, Vin) Random.

— A Guide to Library Research Methods. LC 87-1565. 224p. 1987. 23.00 (*0-19-504943-8*) OUP.

— A Guide to Library Research Methods. LC 87-1565. 224p. 1990. pap. 9.95 (*0-19-504944-6*) OUP.

— The Holy Sinner. Lowe-Porter, Helen T., tr. 1992. 30.00 (*0-520-07672-9*); pap. 14.00 (*0-520-07671-0*) U CA Pr.

— Joseph & His Brothers. 1948. 60.00 (*0-394-43132-4*) Knopf.

— The Letters of Thomas Mann, 1889-1955. Winston, Richard & Winston, Clara, eds. Winston, Clara, tr. 1990. 47.50 (*0-520-07004-6*); pap. 13.00 (*0-520-06968-4*) U CA Pr.

— Letters to Paul Amann, Nineteen Fifteen to Nineteen Fifty-Two. Wegener, Herbert, ed. Winston, Richard & Winston, Clara, trs. LC 60-7258. 196p. reprint ed. pap. 55.90 (*0-317-08259-0*, 2001955) Bks Demand.

— Library Research Models: A Guide to Classification, Cataloging, & Computers. (Illus.). 264p. (C). 1994. reprint ed. pap. 12.95 (*0-19-509395-X*) OUP.

— Library Research Models: A Guide to Classifications, Catalogs, & Computers. LC 92-34311. (Illus.). 264p. 1993. 25.00 (*0-19-508190-0*) OUP.

— Lotte in Weimar: The Beloved Returns. Lowe-Porter, Helen T., tr. 475p. 1990. 30.00 (*0-520-07006-2*); pap. 14.00 (*0-520-07007-0*) U CA Pr.

— Magic Mountain. 1956. 30.00 (*0-394-43458-7*) Knopf.

— Magic Mountain. 1976. 31.95 (*0-8488-0576-3*) Amereon Ltd.

— Magic Mountain. Lowe-Porter, Helen T., tr. (C). 1967. pap. text ed. write for info. (*0-07-553665-X*, 30993) McGraw.

— Magic Mountain. 740p. 1969. pap. 10.95 (*0-394-70497-5*) Random.

— The Magic Mountain. 1992. 15.00 (*0-679-73645-X*, Vin) Random.

— The Magic Mountain. Lowe-Porter, Helen T., tr. LC 92-25324. 1992. 19.00 (*0-679-60041-8*, Modern Lib) Random.

— The Magic Mountain. 1995. 35.00 (*0-679-44183-2*) Knopf.

— The Magic Mountain. 340p. 1983. reprint ed. lib. bdg. 28.95 (*0-89966-454-7*) Buccaneer Bks.

— Mario the Magician. 1991. reprint ed. lib. bdg. 19.95 (*1-56849-035-6*) Buccaneer Bks.

— Nocturnes. LC 79-140336. (Short Story Index Reprint Ser.). 1977. 11.95 (*0-8369-3728-7*) Ayer.

— Order of the Day. LC 79-80389. (Essay Index Reprint Ser.). 1977. 21.95 (*0-8369-1060-5*) Ayer.

— Past Masters, & Other Papers. Lowe-Porter, Helen T., tr. LC 68-25605. (Essay Index Reprint Ser.). 1977. 17.95 (*0-8369-0674-8*) Ayer.

— Reflections of a Nonpolitical Man. Morris, Walter D., tr. 452p. 1987. reprint ed. pap. 14.95 (*0-8044-6482-0*, F Ungar Bks) Continuum.

— Royal Highness. Curtis, A. Cecil, tr. 360p. 1992. 30.00 (*0-520-07674-5*); pap. 4.00 (*0-520-07673-7*) U CA Pr.

— Stories of Three Decades. Lowe-Porter, Helen T., tr. LC 61-66696. 1979. 9.95 (*0-394-60483-0*, Modern Lib) Random.

— The Tables of the Law. Lowe-Porter, H. T., tr. (Austrian-German Culture Ser.). 64p. 1995. 25.00 (*0-933806-63-9*) Black Swan CT.

— Thomas Mann's "Goethe & Tolstoy" otes & Sources. Koelb, Clayton, ed. & tr. by. Scott, Alcyone, tr. LC 82-13497. 267p. 1984. pap. 76.10 (*0-7837-8388-4*, 2059199) Bks Demand.

— Tonio Kroger. Wilkinson, ed. (Bristol German Texts Ser.). 228p. (GER.). 1968. 14.95 (*1-85399-345-X*, Pub. by Brstl Class Pr UK) Focus Info Gr.

— Tonio Kroger. 126p. (GER.). (C). 1992. reprint ed. pap. text ed. 6.95 (*0-88133-655-6*) Waveland Pr.

— Transposed Heads. 1959. pap. 8.00 (*0-394-70086-4*, Vin) Random.

Mann, Thomas E., ed. A Question of Balance: The President, the Congress, & Foreign Policy. 265p. 1990. 34.95 (*0-8157-5454-X*); pap. 14.95 (*0-8157-5453-1*) Brookings.

Mann, Thomas E. & Ornstein, Norman J. Congress, the Press, & the Public. 212p. (C). 1994. 36.95 (*0-8157-5462-0*); pap. 16.95 (*0-8157-5461-2*) Brookings.

— Renewing Congress: A Second Report. 86p. (C). 1993. pap. 9.95 (*0-8157-5459-0*) Brookings.

Mann, Thomas E. & Ornstein, Norman J., eds. The American Elections of Nineteen Eighty-Two. LC 83-11843. (AEI Studies: No. 389). (Illus.). 223p. reprint ed. pap. 63.60 (*0-7837-1079-8*, 2041609) Bks Demand.

Mann, Thomas E. & Orren, Gary R., eds. Media Polls in American Politics. 172p. (C). 1992. 28.95 (*0-8157-5456-6*); pap. 10.95 (*0-8157-5455-8*) Brookings.

Mann, Thomas E. & Orstein, Norman J. Renewing Congress: A First Report. 76p. (C). 1992. pap. 9.95 (*0-8157-5457-4*) Brookings.

Mann, Thomas E., jt. ed. see Jennings, M. Kent.

Mann, Thomas W. The Book of the Torah. LC 87-25079. 1988. pap. 15.99 (*0-8042-0085-8*, John Knox) Westminster John Knox.

Mann, Thomas W., Jr. Financing Information Services: Problems Changing Approaches & New Opportunities for Academic & Research Libraries. Spyers-Duran, Peter, ed. LC 84-15729. (New Directions in Librarianship Ser.: No. 6). (Illus.). vi, 197p. 1985. text ed. 49.95 (*0-313-24644-0*, SPY/) Greenwood.

Mann, Thomas W. To Taste & See: Exploring the Incarnation & the Ambiquities of Faith. LC 91-48103. 160p. (Orig.). 1992. pap. 12.95 (*0-8298-0933-3*) Pilgrim OH.

Mann, Thomas W., Jr., jt. ed. see Spyers-Duran, Peter.

Mann, Thorbjoern. Building Economics for Architects. (Illus.). 224p. 1992. text ed. 39.95 (*0-442-00389-7*) Van Nos Reinhold.

Mann, V. Seeds That Grew to Be a Hundred. LC 59-1209. 32p. 1975. pap. 1.89 (*0-570-06091-5*) Concordia.

Mann, Valerie K., jt. auth. see Kelly, Thomas J., Jr.

Mann, Victor. He Remembered to Say "Thank You" (Arch Bks.). (Illus.). 32p. (J). (ps-4). 1976. pap. 1.99 (*0-570-06103-2*, 59-1221) Concordia.

Mann, Vivian, et al, eds. Convivencia: Jews, Muslims, & Christians in Medieval Spain. (Illus.). 272p. (Orig.). 1992. 50.00 (*0-8076-1283-9*); pap. 25.00 (*0-8076-1286-3*) Braziller.

Mann, Vivian B., ed. Gardens & Ghettos: The Art of Jewish Life in Italy. (Illus.). 250p. 1989. 65.00 (*0-520-06824-6*); pap. 32.50 (*0-520-06825-4*) U CA Pr.

Mann, Vivian B. & Tucker, Gordon, eds. The Seminar on Jewish Art: Proceedings. 37p. (Orig.). 1985. pap. 6.00 (*0-87334-029-9*) Jewish Sem.

Mann, Vivian B., et al. The Jewish Museum. (Illus.). 128p. 1993. 29.95 (*1-85759-015-5*) Scala Books.

— The Jewish Museum. (Illus.). 128p. 1993. 29.95 (*0-685-74831-6*, Pub. by P Wilson Pubs) Sothebys Pubns.

Mann, W. B., et al, eds. Radioactivity & Its Measurement. 2nd ed. LC 79-40881. (Illus.). 1980. text ed. 100.00 (*0-08-025028-9*, Pub. by Aberdeen U Pr) Macmillan.

Mann, W. B., jt. auth. see Debertin, K.

Mann, W. B., jt. ed. see Hutchinson, J. M.

Mann, W. B., et al, eds. Radioactivity Measurements: Principles & Practice. (International Journal of Applied Radiation & Isotopes Ser.: No. ARI 228 JARI 39). Orig. Title: Applied Radiation & Isotopes, Vol 39, No. 8. 220p. 1991. pap. 44.00 (*0-08-037037-3*, Pergamon Pr); pap. text ed. 30.00 (*0-08-037239-2*, Pergamon Pr) Elsevier.

Mann, W. Robert, jt. auth. see Taylor, Angus E.

Mann, Warner. The Healing Power of Inversion Thinking from Soul to Body. LC 85-91344. (Metaphysics for Everyone Ser.: No. 1). (Illus.). 250p. (Orig.). 1986. 14.95 (*0-9615973-0-5*); pap. 9.95 (*0-9615973-1-3*) Cos Sci Orange.

Mann, Wayne M. Obliquely Wild. Hammack, Susan M. & Hammack, Edie, eds. (Illus.). 476p. 1982. pap. 9.95 (*0-9608904-0-8*) Mann Found.

***Mann, William.** Ant Hill Odyssey. (American Autobiography Ser.). 338p. 1995. reprint ed. lib. bdg. 89.00 (*0-7812-8585-2*) Rprt Serv.

— James Galway's Music in Time. 384p. (C). 1983. pap. text ed. 42.95 (*0-13-509240-X*) P-H.

— Politics on the Net. (Illus.). 416p. (Orig.). 1995. pap. 24.99 (*0-7897-0286-X*) Que.

— Space & Time In Landscape Architectural History. 290p. 1981. 15.00 (*0-318-17832-X*, Landscape Architecture) Am Landscape Arch.

Mann, William, ed. see Baptist De La Salle, John.

Mann, William, tr. see Schwinger, Wolfram.

Mann, William A. Landscape Architecture: An Illustrated History in Timelines, Site Plans, & Biography. 480p. (Orig.). 1993. pap. text ed. 42.95 (*0-471-59465-2*) Wiley.

Mann, William C. & Lane, Joseph P. Assistive Technology for Persons with Disabilities: The Role of Occupational Therapy. 300p. (C). 1991. pap. text ed. 38.00 (*0-910317-71-2*) Am Occup Therapy.

Mann, William C. & Thompson, Sandra A., eds. Discourse Description: Diverse Linguistic Analysis of a Fund-Raising Text. LC 91-46957. (Pragmatics & Beyond New Ser.: No. 16). x, 409p. 1992. 118.00x (*1-55619-282-7*); pap. 29.95 (*1-55619-287-8*) Benjamins North Am.

Mann, William D. Fads & Fancies of Representative Americans at the Beginning of the Twentieth Century... LC 75-1857. (Leisure Class in America Ser.). (Illus.). 1978. reprint ed. 150.95 (*0-405-06923-5*) Ayer.

Mann, William P. Wasting Time with Windows. 320p. 1993. 19.95 (*0-672-30345-0*) Sams.

Mann, William P. & Prestwood, Brian. Edutainment Comes Alive! (Illus.). 500p. (Orig.). 1994. pap. 34.95 (*0-672-30450-3*) Sams.

Mann, Wilma, jt. auth. see Mann, Lloyd.

Mann, Woody. Anthology of Blues Guitar. (Illus.). 160p. 1993. pap. 19.95 (*0-8256-0315-3*, Oak) Music Sales.

— The Complete Robert Johnson. (Illus.). 96p. 1991. pap. 12.95 (*0-8256-0314-5*, OK64965, Oak) Music Sales.

— Six Early Blues Guitarists. (Illus.). 112p. 1973. pap. 14.95 (*0-8256-0135-5*, OK62703, Oak) Music Sales.

Manna & Waldinger, Richard. The Logical Basis for Computer Programming: Informal Reasoning, Vol. 1. (C). 1985. text ed. 40.95 (*0-201-18260-2*) Addison-Wesley.

Manna, Anthony L. & Symons, Cynthia W. Children's Literature for Health Awareness. LC 92-29737. (Illus.). 629p. 1992. 49.50 (*0-8108-2582-1*) Scarecrow.

Manna, Anthony L., ed. see Virginia Hamilton Conference Staff.

***Manna, Dawn D.** Lesbian Stew: Cartoon Creations. (Illus.). 72p. 1995. 7.50 (*0-9636909-6-5*) Lavender Crystal.

— Lesbian Stew: Cartoon Creations by Dawn D. Manna. (Illus.). 72p. (Orig.). 1995. pap. 7.50 (*0-9636909-5-7*) Lavender Crystal.

Manna, Gunomoy. The Shal Forest. (C). 1990. text ed. 18.00 (*81-7017-268-3*, Pub. by Abhinav II) S Asia.

Manna, John S. & Katzenstein, Herbert. The Global Legal Environment of Direct Marketing in the 21st Century. LC 92-30636. 56p. (Orig.). (C). 1992. pap. 8.00 (*1-881901-00-9*) LEGAS.

Manna, M., jt. auth. see Ghosh, G.

Manna, Sibendu. Mother Goddess Candi: (Its Socio Ritual Impact on the Folk Life) 1993. 36.00 (*81-85094-60-8*, Pub. by Punthi Pus II) S Asia.

Manna, Z. Lectures on the Logic of Computer Programming. LC 79-93153. (CBMS-NSF Regional Conference Ser.: No. 31). iv, 49p. 1980. pap. text ed. 14.50 (*0-89871-164-9*) Soc Indus-Appl Math.

Manna, Z. & Pnueli, A. The Temporal Logic of Reactive Systems Vol. 1: Specification. (Illus.). 392p. 1991. 49.95 (*0-387-97664-7*) Spr-Verlag.

Manna, Zohar. Introduction to Mathematical Theory of Computation. (Computer Science Ser.). (Illus.). 360p. (C). 1974. text ed. write for info. (*0-07-039910-7*) McGraw.

***Manna, Zohar & Pnueli, Amir.** Temporal Verification of Reactive Systems: Safety. LC 95-5442. 1995. write for info. (*0-387-94459-1*) Spr-Verlag.

Manna, Zohar & Waldinger, Richard. The Logical Basis for Computer Programming: Combined Volume. (Computer Science Ser.). (Illus.). 736p. (C). 1993. text ed. 46.25 (*0-201-54886-0*) Addison-Wesley.

— The Logical Basis for Computer Programming, Vol. II: Deductive Systems. (Computer Science Ser.). (Illus.). 608p. (C). 1990. text ed. 40.95 (*0-201-18261-0*) Addison-Wesley.

Mannaioni & Clendenin. Clinical Pharmacology of Drug Dependence. (Illus.). 282p. 1984. 25.00 (*88-299-0213-6*, Pub. by Piccin Nueva Libraria) Ishiyaku Euro.

Mannaioni, P. F. Clinical Pharmacology of Drug Dependence. 282p. 1984. pap. text ed. 32.00 (*1-57235-060-1*) Piccin NY.

Mannan, M. A. Issues of Small Enterprise Development: The Case of a Developing Economy. 120p. 1993. 59.95 (*1-85628-544-8*, Pub. by Avebury Pub UK) Ashgate Pub Co.

Mannan, M. M. Islamic Economics in Theory & Practice. 16.95 (*1-56744-092-4*) Kazi Pubns.

Mannari, Hiroshi, jt. auth. see Marsh, Robert M.

Manne, A. S., ed. Economic Equilibrium: Model Formulation & Solution. (Mathematical Programming Studies: Vol. 23). 252p. 1986. pap. 51.50 (*0-444-87883-1*, North Holland) Elsevier.

Manne, Alan & Richels, Richard. Buying Greenhouse Insurance: The Economic Costs of CO2 Emission Limits. (Illus.). 192p. 1992. 29.95x (*0-262-13280-X*) MIT Pr.

Manne, Henry G. & Miller, Roger L., eds. Auto Safety Regulation: The Cure or the Problem? LC 76-1676. 1976. 15.95 (*0-913878-09-X*) T Horton & Dghts.

Manne, Henry G. & Wallich, Henry C. The Modern Corporation & Social Responsibility. LC 72-91865. (Rational Debate Ser.: No. 6). 120p. reprint ed. pap. 34.20 (*0-8357-4511-2*, 2037368) Bks Demand.

Manne, Henry G., ed. see Dorn, James A.

Manne, S., ed. Scanning Probe Microscopies. 1992. 53.00 (*0-8194-0785-2*) SPIE.

Manned Lunar Flight Symposium Staff. Manned Lunar Flight: Proceedings of the Symposium, Denver, 1961. Morgenthaler, G. W. & Jacobs, H., eds. (Advances in the Astronautical Sciences Ser.: Vol. 10). 1963. 35.00 (*0-87703-011-1*, Pub. by Am Astro Soc) Univelt Inc.

***Mannello, Timothy.** A CQI System for Healthcare: How the Williamsport Hospital Brings Quality to Life. LC 94-46508. 1995. write for info. (*0-527-76290-3*) Qual Resc.

Manner, A. English - Tulu Dictionary. 660p. 1987. 79.95 (*0-8288-8465-X*) Fr & Eur.

— English-Tulu. 651p. 1987. 33.00 (*0-88431-264-X*) IBD Ltd.

— English-Tulu Dictionary. (C). 1987. reprint ed. 35.00 (*0-8364-2404-2*, Pub. by Asian Educ Servs II) S Asia.

— Tulu-English. 687p. 1983. 27.00 (*0-88431-263-1*) IBD Ltd.

— Tulu English Dictionary. 696p. 1983. 79.95 (*0-8288-8466-8*) Fr & Eur.

Manner, Eeva L. Fog Horses. Barkan, Stanley H., ed. Poom, Rilva, tr. (Review Chapbook Ser.: No. 19: Finnish Poetry). 48p. 1988. 15.00 (*0-89304-820-8*, CCC185); pap. 5.00 (*0-89304-821-6*) Cross-Cultrl NY.

Manner, Reinhard & Manderick, Bernard, eds. Parallel Problem Solving from Nature, 2: Proceedings of the Second Conference on Parallel Problem Solving from Nature, Brussels, Belgium, 28-30 September, 1992. LC 92-23499. 1992. write for info. (*0-444-89730-5*, North Holland) Elsevier.

Manner, Reinhard, jt. ed. see Schwefel, H. P.

Mannering, Dennis E. Attitudes Are Contagious ... Are Yours Worth Catching? Mason, Virgina & Samson, Christopher, eds. 68p. reprint ed. pap. text ed. 3.50 (*0-945890-00-1*) Options Unltd.

— Everyday Heroes. Mannering, Wendy K. & Mason, Virginia, eds. 91p. 1992. write for info. (*0-945890-02-8*) Options Unltd.

Mannering, Dennis E. & Wilde, Kevin. How Good Managers Become Great Leaders. Mason, Virginia, ed. 163p. 1989. 35.00 (*0-945890-01-X*) Options Unltd.

Mannering, Fred L. & Kilareski, Walter P. Principles of Highway Engineering & Traffic Analysis. LC 08-938364. 251p. 1990. Net. text ed. write for info. (*0-471-63532-4*); teacher ed 13.50 (*0-471-51959-6*) Wiley.

Mannering, Wendy K., ed. see Mannering, Dennis E.

Manners. Hitchhiker's Guide to Electronics in the 90's. 1990. pap. 32.95 (*0-85384-020-2*) Buttrwrth-Heinemann.

— Living with the Chip. 1995. pap. (*0-412-61690-4*) Chapman & Hall.

Manners, G. South Wales in the Sixties: Studies in Industrial Geography. LC 64-21689. 1964. 120.00 (*0-08-010759-1*, Pub. by Pergamon Repr UK) Franklin.

Manners, George E., Jr., jt. auth. see Jewell, Donald O.

Manners, Gerald. The Changing World Market for Iron Ore, 1950-1980: An Economic Geography. LC 70-146734. 400p. reprint ed. pap. 114.00 (*0-317-26471-0*, 2023806) Bks Demand.

Manners, Gerald, jt. auth. see McDivitt, James M.

Manners, Gerald, et al. Regional Development in Britain. 2nd ed. LC 79-42901. (Illus.). 440p. reprint ed. pap. 125.40 (*0-685-20595-9*, 2030529) Bks Demand.

Manners, H. & Carroll, M. E. Movement Education Leading to Gymnastics 4-7: A Session by Session Approach to Key Stage 1. 168p. 1991. pap. 29.00 (*0-7507-0007-6*, Falmer Pr) Taylor & Francis.

Manners, H., jt. ed. see Carroll, M. E.

***Manners, Hazel K.** A Framework for Physical Education in the Early Years. LC 94-45068. 1995. pap. 24.95 (*0-7507-0417-9*, Falmer Pr) Taylor & Francis.

Manners, Ian R. North Sea Oil & Environmental Planning: The United Kingdom Experience. LC 81-16170. 344p. (C). 1982. text ed. 37.50 (*0-292-76475-8*) U of Tex Pr.

Manners, J. G. Principles of Plant Pathology. 2nd ed. LC 92-29558. (Illus.). 288p. (C). 1993. 89.95 (*0-521-43402-5*); pap. 32.95 (*0-521-43564-1*) Cambridge U Pr.

Manners, L. J. An Acre of England. 160p. 1980. pap. 35.00 (*0-905418-06-9*, Pub. by Gresham Bks UK) St Mut.

Manners, R., jt. auth. see Vivian, A.

Manners, Robert, jt. auth. see Kaplan, David.

Manners, Robert A., jt. auth. see Kaplan, David.

Manners, Ruth A. Quick & Easy Vegetarian Cookbook. 1994. pap. 10.95 (*0-87131-738-9*) M Evans.

M

Manners, Ruth A. & Mannners, William. The Quick & Easy Vegetarian Cookbook. LC 78-2259. 288p. 1978. 12.50 (0-87131-260-3); pap. 7.95 (0-87131-303-0) M Evans.

Mannes, David. Music Is My Faith: An Autobiography. LC 78-9601. (Music Reprint Ser.: 1978). (Illus.). 1978. reprint ed. lib. bdg. 37.50 (0-306-77595-6) Da Capo.

Mannes, Philip. Tables of Bullet Performance. Wolfe, Dave, ed. 407p. (Orig.). 1980. text ed. 17.50 (0-935632-06-9); pap. text ed. 17.50 (0-935632-05-0) Wolfe Pub Co.

Mannes, Willibald. Techniques of Staircase Construction. (Illus.). 112p. 1986. text ed. 49.95 (0-442-26086-5) Chapman & Hall.

Mannetje, L. T. & Jones, R. M. P.R.O.S.E.A., Vol. IV: (Forages) PUDOC Staff, ed. 250p. (C). 1991. text ed. 500.00 (0-89771-636-1, Pub. by Intl Bk Distr II) St Mut.

Mannetje, L't., ed. Measurement of Grassland Vegetation. 260p. (Orig.). 1978. pap. text ed. 33.00 (0-85198-404-5) CAB Intl.

Mannett, Luana, ed. see Morrall, June.

Mannetter, Terrence A., ed. Text & Concordance of the Leyes de Estilo, MS5764: Biblioteca Nacional, Madrid. (Spanish Legal Texts Ser.: No. 6). 8p. (SPA.). 1989. 10.00 (0-940639-43-2) Hispanic Seminary.

Mannetter, Terrence A., et al, eds. Text & Concordance of the Leyes del Estilo, MS. Z.III.11, Escorial. (Spanish Legal Texts Ser.: No. 8). 6p. 1990. 10.00 (0-940639-47-5) Hispanic Seminary.

Mannetti, William. Dinosaurs in Your Backyard. LC 81-7998. (Illus.). 160p. (J). (gr. 4-7). 1982. text ed. 13.95 (0-689-30906-6, Atheneum Bks Young) S&S Childrens.

Manneville, P., et al, eds. Cellular Automata & Modeling of Complex Physical Systems. (Proceedings in Physics Ser.: Vol. 46). (Illus.). 350p. 1990. 72.00 (0-387-51933-5, 3776) Spr-Verlag.

Manneville, Paul, ed. Dissipative Structures & Weak Turbulence. 485p. 1990. text ed. 69.95 (0-12-469260-5) Acad Pr.

Manney, Gerald, jt. auth. see De Santis, Richard.

Mannhardt, Karl-Heinz. Dictionary of Energy Science: Nuclear & Non-Nuclear Energy. 166p. (ENG & GER.). 1981. 110.00 (0-8288-0700-0, M 15045); 75.00 (0-8288-2292-1, M15046); 110.00 (0-8288-2293-X, M 15047) Fr & Eur.

Mannhardt, Werner G., tr. see Muller, Herbert W.

Mannhardt, Wilhelm. Mythologische Forschungen Aus Dem Nachlasse, 2 vols. in 1. Bolle, Kees W., ed. LC 77-79142. (Mythology Ser.). (GER.). 1978. reprint ed. lib. bdg. 42.95 (0-405-10551-7) Ayer.

Mannheim. Regeln und Sprache Des Sports, 2 vols., Set. (GER.). 55.00 (3-411-01362-1, M-7601) Fr & Eur.

Mannheim, Bruce. The Language of the Inka since the European Invasion. (Illus.). 346p. 1991. text ed. 25.00 (0-292-74663-6) U of Tex Pr.

Mannheim, Bruce, jt. ed. see Huizer, Gerrit.

Mannheim, Bruce, jt. ed. see Tedlock, Dennis.

Mannheim, Hermann. Group Problems in Crime & Punishment. 2nd enl. ed. LC 73-108234. (Criminology, Law Enforcement, & Social Problems Ser.: No. 117). 1972. 25.00 (0-87585-117-7) Patterson Smith.

— Juvenile Delinquency in an English Middletown: With New Intro. by Author Added. LC 73-108226. (Criminology, Law Enforcement, & Social Problems Ser.: No. 109). (Illus.). 144p. 1970. reprint ed. 22.00 (0-87585-109-6) Patterson Smith.

— Pioneers of Criminology. enl. ed. LC 78-108238. (Criminology, Law Enforcement, & Social Problems Ser.: No. 121). (C). 1972. pap. 17.00 (0-87585-902-X) Patterson Smith.

— Pioneers of Criminology. 2nd enl. ed. LC 78-108238. (Criminology, Law Enforcement, & Social Problems Ser.: No. 121). (C). 1972. 30.00 (0-87585-121-5) Patterson Smith.

Mannheim, Karl. Conservatism: A Contribution to the Sociology of Knowledge. Kettler, David et al, eds. King, Elizabeth, tr. (International Library of Sociology). 256p. (C). 1986. text ed. 49.95 (0-7102-0338-1, RKP) Routledge.

— Diagnosis of Our Time: Wartime Essays of a Sociologist. LC 86-22787. (International Library of Sociology & Social Reconstruction). 190p. 1987. reprint ed. text ed. 52.50 (0-313-25165-7, MDIA) Greenwood.

— Essays in the Sociology of Culture. (Classics in Sociology Ser.). 1992. 49.95 (0-415-07553-X, A6974) Routledge.

— Ideology & Utopia: An Introduction to the Sociology of Knowledge. LC 68-77694. 354p. 1955. pap. 12.95 (0-15-643955-7, Harvest Bks) HarBrace.

— Structures of Thinking. Kettler, David et al, eds. (International Library of Sociology). 240p. 1985. pap. 15.95 (0-7102-0730-1, RKP) Routledge.

— Systematic Sociology: An Introduction to the Study of Society. Eros, J. S. & Stewart, W. A., eds. LC 83-22743. (International Library of Sociology & Social Reconstruction). xxx, 169p. 1984. reprint ed. text ed. 49.75 (0-313-24378-6, MASY) Greenwood.

Mannheimer, Marc, jt. auth. see Ehrlich, Jefferey.

Mannheimer, Monica. The Generations in Meredith's Novels. (Gothenburg Studies in English: No. 23). 199p. (Orig.). 1972. pap. 40.00x (0-317-65793-3) Coronet Bks.

***Mannheimer, Steve.** Pacer Power. 210p. 1994. pap. 16.95 (1-878208-48-9) Guild Pr IN.

Mannhold, Raimund, jt. auth. see Rekker, Roelof F.

Manni, Alessandra & Sollins, Susan. Eternal Metaphors: New Art from Italy. LC 89-85331. 72p. 1989. 20.00 (0-916365-28-X) Ind Curators.

Manni, Andrea, jt. auth. see Santen, Richard J.

Manniche. Musical Instruments from the Tomb of Tutankhamun. (Tutankhamuns Tomb Ser.: Vol. 6). 1976. 34.00 (0-900416-05-X, Pub. by Aris & Phillips UK) David Brown.

Manniche, Lisa. City of the Dead: Thebes in Egypt. LC 87-5022. (British Museum Publications). (Illus.). x, 160p. (C). 1987. 27.50 (0-226-50339-9) U Ch Pr.

Manniche, Lise. An Ancient Egyptian Herbal. (Illus.). 176p. (Orig.). 1989. pap. 19.95 (0-292-70415-1) U of Tex Pr.

— The Ancient Egyptians. (British Museum Activity Bks.). (Illus.). 16p. (J). 1995. pap. 5.95 (0-500-27787-7) Thames Hudson.

— Music & Musicians in Ancient Egypt. 1992. pap. 10.95 (0-486-27171-4) Dover.

— Sexual Life in Ancient Egypt. (Illus.). 127p. 1987. 35.00 (0-7103-0202-9, Pub. by Kegan Paul Intl UK) Routledge Chapman & Hall.

— The Wall Decoration of Three Theban Tombs. (Illus.). 31p. (Orig.). 1988. pap. 87.50x (87-7289-036-3, Pub. by Almqv & Wiksell SW) Coronet Bks.

Manniche, Peter. Living Democracy in Denmark. LC 73-98779. 237p. 1970. reprint ed. text ed. 59.75 (0-8371-3985-6, MADD, Greenwood Pr) Greenwood.

Mannick. Advances in Surgery, Vol. 20. 1986. 59.95 (0-8151-5751-7, Yr Bk Med Pubs) Mosby Yr Bk.

Mannick, jt. auth. see Greenhalgh.

Mannick, A. R. Mauritius: The Development of a Plural Society. 174p. 1979. 34.50 (0-85124-249-9, Pub. by Spokesman Bks UK) Coronet Bks.

Mannikka, Eleanor. Selected Topics in Cataloging Asian Art. 1989. 20.00 (0-685-46055-X) Visual Resources Assn.

Mannin, Ethel. The Saga of Sammy-Cat. (J). (gr. 1-3). 1969. reprint ed. 2.59 (0-08-013397-5, Pergamon Pr) Elsevier.

— Women & the Revolution. 1976. lib. bdg. 59.95 (0-8490-2834-5) Gordon Pr.

Manninen, V., ed. see Paavo Nurmi Symposium Staff.

Manninezhath, Thomas. Harmony of Religions: Vedanta Siddhanta Samaramam of Tayumanavar. (C). 1993. text ed. 22.50 (81-208-1001-5, Pub. by Motilal Banarsidass II) S Asia.

***Manning.** Building Community: The Human Side of Work. (GC-Principles of Management Ser.). 1996. text ed. 44.95 (0-538-83586-9) S-W Pub.

— Human Biology. (Illus.). 576p. 1991. 32.95 (0-8016-5850-0) Mosby Yr Bk.

— Total Quality Management: A Systems Approach. (C). 1994. text ed. 8.95 (0-87709-053-X, BF053X) S-W Pub.

Manning, jt. auth. see Mewett.

Manning, jt. auth. see Rugh.

Manning, Al G. Eye of Newt in My Martini: A Certified Public Accountant Turned Occultist Tells Why & How. LC 81-84169. (Illus.). 1981. 12.95 (0-941698-00-9); pap. 6.95 (0-941698-01-7) Pan Ishtar.

— Helping Yourself with E.S.P. 1989. pap. text ed. 8.95 (0-13-386384-0) P-H.

— Helping Yourself with Psycho-Cosmic Power. LC 68-12433. 1983. pap. 6.95 (0-941698-06-8) Pan Ishtar.

— Helping Yourself with Real Spirit Contact. LC 89-92375. 180p. (Orig.). 1990. pap. 7.95 (0-941698-18-1) Pan Ishtar.

— Helping Yourself with the Power of Gnostic Magic. LC 79-13447. 1984. reprint ed. pap. 7.95 (0-941698-11-4) Pan Ishtar.

— Helping Yourself with White Witchcraft. 1986. 9.95 (0-13-386565-7, Reward); 6.95 (0-13-386573-8, Reward) P-H.

— How to Get the Most Out of Life. LC 88-90687. 180p. (Orig.). 1988. pap. 7.95 (0-941698-17-3) Pan Ishtar.

— Life after Death? Sex? Dinner? The Lighter Side of the Occult. LC 83-60386. 144p. (Orig.). 1983. pap. 6.95 (0-941698-07-6) Pan Ishtar.

— The Magic of New Ishtar Power. LC 77-4502. 229p. 1986. reprint ed. pap. 7.95 (0-941698-13-0) Pan Ishtar.

— Mighty Maverick Magick: The Essence of Victorious Living. 180p. 1983. 12.95 (0-941698-08-4); pap. 6.95 (0-941698-09-2) Pan Ishtar.

— The Miracle of Universal Psychic Power. LC 73-13512. 1974. 14.95 (0-13-585729-5) Pan Ishtar.

— Miracle of Universal Psychic Power: How to Build Your Way to Prosperity. 1986. 5.95 (0-13-585794-5, Parker Publishing Co) P-H.

— Miracle Spiritology. LC 75-19350. 1975. 13.95 (0-13-585745-7) Pan Ishtar.

— The Miraculous Laws of Universal Dynamics. 1964. pap. 6.95 (0-317-46046-3) Pan Ishtar.

— Moon Lore & Moon Magic. 1980. 14.95 (0-13-600668-X) Pan Ishtar.

— Rainbows Falling on My Head: The Magic of the Great God Pan. LC 82-90133. (Illus.). 1982. 12.95 (0-941698-02-5); pap. 6.95 (0-941698-03-3) Pan Ishtar.

— Real Ritual Magick: For People Ready to Enjoy Life Now. LC 86-63701. 180p. (Orig.). 1987. pap. 7.95 (0-941698-15-7) Pan Ishtar.

— Your Golden Key to Success: A Self Help Odyssey. LC 82-60767. (Illus.). 1982. 12.95 (0-941698-04-1); pap. 6.95 (0-941698-05-X) Pan Ishtar.

Manning, Al G. & Manning, Rachel L. Faerie Tales Are True-Get Your Share. LC 85-80465. 180p. (Orig.). 1986. pap. 7.95 (0-941698-12-2) Pan Ishtar.

— You're Beautiful: Quick Reference Self Help Program for All Situations. LC 87-62127. 1987. pap. 7.95 (0-941698-16-5) Pan Ishtar.

Manning, Al G., jt. auth. see Manning, Rachel L.

Manning, Alice H. Meadow City Milestones: A Collection of Historical Sketches. (Illus.). 94p. (Orig.). 1987. pap. 4.95 (0-9618052-1-8) Daily Hampshire.

Manning, Anita S. PB: Shattered Dreams. 62p. 1991. pap. 3.00 (0-9630309-0-6) Way Out Ministr.

Manning, Anne. The Maiden & Married Life of Mary Powell, Afterwards Mistress Milton, 2 vols. in 1. Bd. with Household of Sir Thomas Moore. LC 79-8166. LC 79-8166. reprint ed. 44.50 (0-404-62021-3) AMS Pr.

— Valentine Duval: An Autobiography. (Art, History & the Connoisseur Ser.). (Illus.). 142p. (C). 1990. reprint ed. 19.95 (1-879080-00-1) Clios Cabinet.

Manning, Aubrey & Dawkins, Marian S. An Introduction to Animal Behaviour. 4th ed. (Illus.). 350p. (C). 1992. 69.95 (0-521-41759-7); pap. 24.95 (0-521-42792-4) Cambridge U Pr.

Manning, Audrey & Serpell, James, eds. Animals & Society: Changing Perspectives. LC 93-10557. 1994. write for info. (0-415-09155-1) Routledge.

Manning, Barbara. Genealogical Abstracts from Newspapers of the German Reformed Church, 1830-1839. viii, 328p. (Orig.). 1992. pap. 25.00 (1-55613-626-9) Heritage Bk.

— Genealogical Abstracts from Newspapers of the German Reformed Church, 1840-1843. 344p. (Orig.). 1995. pap. text ed. 25.00 (0-7884-0177-7) Heritage Bk.

Manning, Barbralu. Kids Mean Business: How to Turn Your Love of Children into a Profitable & Wonderfully Satisfying Business. LC 84-21830. 199p. (Orig.). 1985. pap. 9.95 (0-911781-03-X) Live Oak Pubns.

Manning, Bayless & Hanks, James J., Jr. Legal Capital. 3rd ed. (University Textbook Ser.). 213p. 1990. pap. text ed. 17.00 (0-88277-799-8) Foundation Pr.

Manning, Bernard L. The Hymns of Wesley & Watts. 1987. pap. 5.99 (0-88019-220-8) Schmul Pub Co.

— The Hymns of Wesley & Watts. 144p. (C). 1988. pap. text ed. 9.95 (0-7162-0455-X, Epworth Pr) TPI PA.

Manning, Bertina S. Chrysler Art Museum of Provincetown, Inaugural Exhibition. (Illus.). 115p. 1958. pap. 7.50 (0-940744-00-7) Chrysler Museum.

Manning, Beverley. Index to American Women Speakers, Eighteen Twenty-Eight to Nineteen Seventy-Eight. LC 79-26928. viii, 672p. 1980. lib. bdg. 42.50 (0-8108-1282-7) Scarecrow.

— We Shall Be Heard: An Index to Speeches by American Women, 1978-1985. LC 88-6644. 626p. 1988. 62.50 (0-8108-2122-2) Scarecrow.

Manning, Bill. Beacon Small Group Bible Studies, Joel-Jonah. 76p. (Orig.). 1987. pap. 3.95 (0-8341-1207-8) Beacon Hill.

Manning, Brenda, jt. auth. see Richlin, Laurie.

Manning, Brenda H. Cognitive Self-Instruction (CSI) for Classroom Processes. LC 90-32701. 370p. (C). 1991. 89.50 (0-7914-0479-X); pap. 29.95 (0-7914-0480-3) State U NY Pr.

Manning, Brennan. ABBA's Child. LC 94-14008. 192p. (Orig.). 1994. pap. 10.00 (0-89109-826-7) NavPress.

— The Gentle Revolutionaries. 1979. pap. 8.95 (0-87193-012-9) Dimension Bks.

— Lion & Lamb: The Relentless Tenderness of Jesus. LC 86-15409. (Quality Paper Ser.). 224p. 1986. pap. 8.99 (0-8007-9083-9) Chosen Bks.

— Prophets & Lovers: In Search of the Holy Spirit. 1985. pap. 8.95 (0-87193-013-7) Dimension Bks.

— The Ragamuffin Gospel: Embracing the Unconditional Love of God. 238p. (Orig.). 1993. pap. 8.99 (0-88070-631-7, Multnomah Bks) Questar Pubs.

— The Signature of Jesus: On the Pages of Our Lives. Heaney, Liz, ed. 210p. 1992. reprint ed. pap. 8.99 (0-88070-479-9, Multnomah Bks) Questar Pubs.

— Stranger to Self-Hatred. 1981. pap. 8.95 (0-87193-156-7) Dimension Bks.

— The Wisdom of Accepted Tenderness. 1979. pap. 8.95 (0-87193-110-9) Dimension Bks.

***Manning, Carol S.** Female Tradition in Southern Literature: Essays on Southern Women. 1994. pap. 13.95 (0-252-06444-5) U of Ill Pr.

— With Ears Opening Like Morning Glories: Eudora Welty & the Love of Storytelling. LC 85-921. (Contributions in Women's Studies: No. 58). xv, 221p. 1985. text ed. 55.00 (0-313-24776-5, MWE/, Greenwood Pr) Greenwood.

Manning, Carol S., ed. The Female Tradition in Southern Literature. LC 92-9375. 272p. (C). 1993. text ed. 34.95 (0-252-01951-2) U of Ill Pr.

Manning, Caroline. Immigrant Woman & Her Job. LC 73-129407. (American Immigration Collection Ser. 2). (Illus.). 1975. reprint ed. 14.95 (0-405-00560-1) Ayer.

Manning, Charles A. Learn to Earn: How to Choose the Best Private Career School for Yourself. 200p. 1991. pap. 11.95 (1-880153-91-2) AmericaWORKS.

— The Return of Gold Fever. 322p. 1992. pap. 19.95 (1-880153-99-8) AmericaWORKS.

— Toward a New (Work) World Order. 193p. 1992. pap. 14.95 (1-880153-96-3) AmericaWORKS.

— The Truth about School Accreditation. 232p. 1992. pap. 12.95 (1-880153-88-2) AmericaWORKS.

— Two Thousand Ninety-Five: An Interactive Futures Novel. 300p. (Orig.). 1995. pap. 14.95 (1-880153-95-5) AmericaWORKS.

Manning, Clarence A. Forgotten Republics. LC 79-136891. (Illus.). 264p. 1971. reprint ed. text ed. 49.75 (0-8371-5334-4, MAFO, Greenwood Pr) Greenwood.

— Ukrainian Literature: Studies of the Leading Authors. LC 70-86771. (Essay Index Reprint Ser.). 1977. reprint ed. 20.95 (0-8369-2244-1) Ayer.

Manning, Clarence A., tr. see Korolenko, Vladimir G.

Manning, Clark, jt. auth. see Vanrenen, Louis J.

Manning, Conrad. Sandbox: A Study in the Optimal Lifestyle. 175p. (Orig.). pap. 14.95 (0-9618479-0-5) Sandbox Inc.

Manning, Constance. Measurement of Image Accuracy. (C). 1991. pap. text ed. 11.11 (0-913412-58-9) Brandon Hse.

Manning, D. Disaster Technology: An Annotated Bibliography. 300p. 1976. 125.00 (0-08-019984-4, Pub. by Pergamon Repr UK) Franklin.

***Manning, D. A.** Introduction to Industrial Minerals. LC 94-72021. 276p. 1995. pap. 34.50 (0-412-55550-6) Chapman & Hall.

Manning, D. A., et al, eds. Geochemistry of Clay-Pore Fluid Interactions. LC 92-39558. (Mineralogical Society Ser.: Vol. 4). 1993. write for info. (0-412-48980-5) Chapman & Hall.

Manning, Daniel F. Traveling Light. (Illus.). (Orig.). 1979. pap. 5.00 (0-933192-00-2) Dancin Bee.

Manning, David J. The Mind of Jeremy Bentham. LC 84-6551. ix, 118p. 1984. reprint ed. text ed. 39.75 (0-313-22579-6, MAMJ, Greenwood Pr) Greenwood.

Manning, Diane & Ritchie, Donald A. Hill Country Schoolteacher: Memories from the One-Room School & Beyond. (Twayne's Oral History Ser.: No. 3). 224p. (C). 1990. text ed. 22.95 (0-8057-9102-7, Pub. by Royal Botanic Garden UK) Macmillan.

Manning, Donna & Frances, Allen J., eds. Combination Pharmacotherapy & Psychotherapy for Depression. LC 90-103. (Progress in Psychiatry Ser.: No. 26). 125p. 1990. text ed. 26.50 (0-88048-194-3) Am Psychiatric.

Manning, Doug. Comforting Those Who Grieve. LC 84-48226. 80p. 1987. pap. 9.00 (0-06-065424-4) Harper SF.

— Don't Take My Grief Away: What to Do When You Lose a Loved One. LC 84-47730. 144p. 1984. pap. 11.00 (0-06-065417-1, RD 522) Harper SF.

— When Love Gets Tough. 1990. pap. 9.00 (0-06-250561-0, Hazelden SF) Harper SF.

***Manning, Edward.** Tin Can Tales & Vagabonds. 1995. 16.95 (0-8062-5272-3) Carlton.

Manning, Ellis L., jt. ed. see Reynolds, Neil B.

***Manning, Eugenia, illus.** DeSoto Parish History. 1994. 50.00 (0-9644415-0-0) DeSoto Hist & Geneal.

Manning, Francis S. & Thompson, Richard. Oilfield Processing, Vol. 1: Natural Gas. 420p. 1991. 79.95 (0-87814-343-2, P4475) PennWell Bks.

Manning, Francis S., jt. auth. see Canjar, Lawrence N.

Manning, Francis V., tr. see Bernard, Pierre R.

Manning, Frank. Creative Chip Carving. rev. ed. (Illus.). 48p. 1984. pap. 2.95 (0-486-23735-4) Dover.

Manning, Frank & Philibert, J. M., eds. Customs in Conflict: The Anthropology of a Changing World. 320p. 1990. pap. text ed. 19.95 (0-921149-34-4) Broadview Pr.

***Manning, Frank A.** Fetal Medicine: Principles & Practice. LC 94-44480. (C). 1995. text ed. 115.00 (0-8385-2572-5) Appleton & Lange.

Manning, Frank E., ed. The World of Play. LC 82-83395. (Association for the Anthropological Study of Play: Vol. 7). 232p. (Orig.). (C). 1983. pap. text ed. 24.00 (0-88011-059-7, PMAN0059) Human Kinetics.

Manning, Frank E., jt. ed. see Flaherty, David H.

Manning, Frederic. The Vigil of Brunhild: A Narrative Poem. LC 90-26796. 76p. 1990. reprint ed. lib. bdg. 49.95 (0-7734-9986-5) E Mellen.

Manning, G., jt. auth. see Reece, B.

Manning, Gary & Manning, Maryann, eds. Whole Language: Beliefs & Practices, K-8. 240p. 1989. 16.95 (0-8106-1482-0) NEA.

Manning, Gary, et al. Reading & Writing in the Middle Grades: A Whole-Language View. 64p. 1990. 8.95 (0-8106-3071-0) NEA.

Manning, Gary L., jt. auth. see Murphy Manning, Maryann.

Manning, George & Curtis, Kent. Communication: The Miracle of Dialogue. (Human Side of Work Ser.). 303p. (C). 1988. pap. 22.95 (0-538-21252-7, U252) S-W Pub.

— Ethics at Work: Fire in a Dark World. (Human Side of Work Ser.). 265p. (C). 1988. pap. 22.95 (0-538-21254-3, U254) S-W Pub.

— Groupstrength: Quality Circles at Work. (Human Side of Work Ser.). 292p. (C). 1988. pap. 22.95 (0-538-21258-6, U258) S-W Pub.

— Human Behavior: Why People Do What They Do. (Human Side of Work Ser.). 317p. (C). 1988. pap. 22.95 (0-538-21253-5, U253) S-W Pub.

— Leadership: Nine Keys to Success. (Human Side of Work Ser.). 292p. (C). 1988. pap. 22.95 (0-538-21256-X, U256) S-W Pub.

— Morale: Quality of Work Life. (Human Side of Work Ser.). 340p. (C). 1988. pap. 22.95 (0-538-21255-1, U255) S-W Pub.

— Performance: Managing for Excellence. (Human Side of Work Ser.). 337p. (C). 1988. pap. 22.95 (0-538-21257-8, U257) S-W Pub.

— Stress Without Distress: Rx for Burnout. (Human Side of Work Ser.). 273p. (C). 1988. pap. text ed. 147.95 (0-538-21250-0, U251) S-W Pub.

***Manning, Gerald L. & Reece, Barry L.** Selling Today. 6th ed. LC 94-35214. 1995. text ed. write for info. (0-205-16446-3) P-H.

— Selling Today: A Personal Approach. 4th ed. 570p. 1989. teacher ed write for info. (0-318-66325-2, H27253); text ed. 48.00 (0-205-12102-0, H21025); vhs write for info. (0-318-66327-9, H21066); write for info. (0-318-66326-0, H21041) Allyn.

— Selling Today: An Extension of the Marketing Concept. 5th ed. 570p. (C). 1991. text ed. 54.00 (0-205-13250-2) Allyn.

Manning, Gerry. COBOL Basics. 2nd ed. 400p. 1984. pap. text ed. write for info. (0-394-33572-4) Random.

Manning, Gordon P. Life in the Colchester Reef Lighthouse. (Illus.). 1958. pap. 2.00 (0-939384-01-9) Shelburne.

Manning, Harvey. Backpacking, One Step At a Time. 1986. pap. 13.00 (0-394-72939-0, Vin) Random.

— Hiking the I-90 Greenway: From Puget Sound to the Cascades. LC 93-6011. (Illus.). 224p. 1993. pap. 12.95 (0-89886-369-4) Mountaineers.

— Walking the Beach to Bellingham. LC 86-21516. 272p. 1986. 18.95 (0-88089-018-5) Madrona Pubs.

***Manning, Harvey & Manning, Penny.** Walks & Hikes in the Foothills & Lowlands Around Puget Sound. (Illus.). 224p. 1995. pap. 12.95 (0-89886-431-3) Mountaineers.

An Asterisk (*) at the beginning of an entry indicates that the title is appearing in BIP for the first time.

— Walks & Hikes on the Beaches. (Illus.). 224p. 1995. pap. 12.95 (*0-89886-411-9*) Mountaineers.

Manning, Harvey, jt. auth. see Spring, Ira.

Manning, Henry. The Fourth Dimension Simply Explained. 12.00 (*0-8446-2522-1*) Peter Smith.

Manning, Hiram. Manning on Decoupage. (Illus.). 256p. 1980. reprint ed. pap. 7.95 (*0-486-24028-2*) Dover.

Manning, J. & Robinson, R. Introduction to Chemical Industry. LC 65-22671. (Commonwealth & International Library). 1965. 121.00 (*0-08-010836-9*, Pub. by Pergamon Repr UK) Franklin.

Manning, Jane. New Vocal Repertory: An Introduction. LC 93-30975. (Illus.). 292p. 1994. pap. 22.95 (*0-19-816413-0*) OUP.

Manning, Jason. Battle of the Teton Basin. (High Country Ser.: No. 3). 352p. (Orig.). 1994. pap. 4.50 (*0-451-17829-7*, Sig) NAL-Dutton.

— The Border Captains. (Flintlock Ser.: Vol. 2). 352p. (Orig.). 1995. pap. 4.50 (*0-451-18287-1*, Sig) NAL-Dutton.

— Flintlock. 352p. (Orig.). 1994. pap. 4.50 (*0-451-18133-6*, Sig) NAL-Dutton.

— Gone to Texas. (Flintlock Ser.: Vol. 3). 352p. (Orig.). 1995. mass mkt. 4.50 (*0-451-18500-5*, Sig) NAL-Dutton.

— Green River Rendezvous. (High Country Ser.: No. 2). 352p. 1993. pap. 4.50 (*0-451-17714-2*, Sig) NAL-Dutton.

— Gunsmoke on the Sierra Line. 1989. pap. 2.95 (*0-8217-2632-3*) Zebra.

— High Country. 352p. (Orig.). 1993. pap. 4.50 (*0-451-17680-4*, Sig) NAL-Dutton.

— Revenge in Little Texas. 1990. pap. 2.95 (*0-8217-2898-9*) Zebra.

— Showdown at Seven Springs. 224p. 1992. pap. 3.50 (*0-8217-3999-9*) Zebra.

— Texas Blood Kill. 1991. pap. 3.50 (*0-8217-3577-2*) Zebra.

— Texas Gundown. 1990. pap. 2.95 (*0-8217-2970-5*) Zebra.

— Texas Helltown. 1990. pap. 2.95 (*0-8217-3218-8*) Zebra.

Manning, Jerome A. Estate Planning. 4th ed. 746p. 1991. text ed. 110.00 (*0-685-54556-3*, D1-0160) PLI.

— Estate Planning - with Supplement. 3rd ed. 661p. 1982. 125.00 (*0-685-69426-7*) PLI.

— Estate Planning & 1989 Supplement. 3rd ed. LC 87-63222. 735p. 1988. 95.00 (*0-685-69427-5*) PLI.

Manning, John, ed. Abraham Fraunce, Symbolicae Philosophiae Liber. Haan, Estelle, tr. LC 89-45845. (Studies in the Emblem: No. 7). 1991. 63.00 (*0-404-63707-8*) AMS Pr.

— The Emblems of Thomas Palmer: Two Hundred Poosees. LC 87-45812. (Studies in the Emblem: No. 2). 1988. 72.45 (*0-404-63702-7*) AMS Pr.

***Manning, John & Waterston, Elizabeth.** The Collected Poems of Robert Louis Stevenson, Vol. 1. (Collected Works of Robert Louis Stevenson: Vol. 1). (Illus.). 300p. 1994. 35.00 (*0-7486-0503-7*, Pub. by Edinburgh U Pr UK) Col U Pr.

Manning, John, jt. auth. see Thornton, Mark.

Manning, John C. Applied Principles of Hydrology. 2nd ed. (Illus.). 320p. (C). 1991. pap. write for info. (*0-02-375710-8*) Macmillan.

Manning, John J., intro. The First & Second Parts of Sir John Hayward's "Life & Raigne of King Henrie IIII" (Royal Historical Society: Camden Fourth Ser.: No. 42). 462p. (C). 1991. text ed. 39.00 (*0-86193-129-7*) Boydell & Brewer.

Manning, John J., ed. see Hayward, John.

Manning, John R. Diffusion Kinetics for Atoms in Crystals. LC 68-20921. 274p. reprint ed. pap. 78.10 (*0-317-09190-5*, 2005790) Bks Demand.

Manning, Joseph F. The Miracle of Agape Love. 160p. 1977. pap. 2.99 (*0-88368-079-3*) Whitaker Hse.

Manning, Kathleen, jt. auth. see Stage, Frances K.

Manning, Ken. Renegade Blue. abr. ed. 370p. 1995. pap. 9.95 (*1-56901-441-8*) NW Pub.

Manning, Kenneth R. Black Apollo of Science: The Life of Ernest Everett Just. (Illus.). 416p. 1983. 35.00 (*0-19-503299-3*) OUP.

— Black Apollo of Science: The Life of Ernest Everett Just. (Illus.). 416p. 1985. pap. 12.95 (*0-19-503498-8*) OUP.

Manning, Kenneth R., ed. MIT: Shaping the Future. (Illus.). 210p. 1992. pap. 9.95 (*0-262-63141-5*) MIT Pr.

Manning, Kitty. The Between People. 256p. (Orig.). (C). 1990. pap. 11.99 (*1-85594-012-4*, Pub. by Attic IE) InBook.

Manning, Laura L. The Dispute Processing Model of Public Policy Evolution: The Case of Endangered Species Policy Changes from 1973 to 1983. LC 90-39465. (Environment: Problems & Solutions Ser.: Vol. 14). 504p. 1990. 95.00 (*0-8240-2520-2*) Garland.

Manning, Laurence A. Bibliography of the Ionosphere: An Annotated Survey Through 1960. xvi, 613p. 1962. 69.50 (*0-8047-0125-3*) Stanford U Pr.

Manning, Linda. Dinosaur Days. LC 93-28443. (Illus.). 32p. (J). (ps-2). 1993. lib. bdg. 12.95 (*0-8167-3315-5*); pap. 3.95 (*0-8167-3316-3*) BrdgeWater.

Manning, Loretta, jt. auth. see Rayfield, Sylvia.

Manning, M. C., jt. ed. see Ahern, T. J.

Manning, M. I., jt. ed. see Meadowcroft, D. B.

Manning, M. J. Phylogeny of Immunological Memory. (Developments in Immunology Ser.: Vol. 10). 1980. 73.50 (*0-444-80255-X*) Elsevier.

***Manning, M. Lee.** Celebrating Diversity: Multicultural Education in Middle Level Schools. 142p. (C). 1994. pap. text ed. 22.00 (*1-56090-089-X*) Natl Middle Schl.

— Developmentally Appropriate Middle Level Schools. LC 93-34185. 1993. write for info. (*0-87173-132-0*) ACEI.

Manning, M. Lee & Baruth, Leroy G. Students at Risk. LC 93-50125. 1994. pap. text ed. 32.00 (*0-205-15464-6*) Allyn.

Manning, M. Lee, jt. auth. see Baruth, Leroy G.

Manning, Mari C. For Women Only: A Guide to Healthy Living. 68p. 1992. pap. text ed. 5.95 (*0-9617800-5-3*) Zebra Run Pr.

Manning, Marilyn. Leadership Skills for Women. Crisp, Mike, ed. LC 88-72261. (Fifty-Minute Ser.). (Orig.). 1989. pap. 9.95 (*0-931961-62-9*) Crisp Pubns.

Manning, Marilyn & Barnes, Carolyn. Professional Excellence for Secretaries. Crisp, Michael, ed. LC 87-73561. (Fifty-Minute Ser.). (Illus.). 80p. 1988. pap. 9.95 (*0-931961-52-1*) Crisp Pubns.

***Manning, Marilyn & Haddock, Patricia.** The NAFE Guide to Starting Your Own Business: A Handbook for Entrepreneurial Women. 156p. 1995. pap. 15.00 (*0-7863-0408-1*) Irwin Prof Pubng.

Manning, Marilyn, jt. auth. see Haddock, Patricia.

Manning, Marilyn, jt. auth. see Rietz, Helen L.

***Manning, Martha.** Undercurrents: A Therapist's Reckoning with Depression. LC 94-33043. 1995. 20.00 (*0-06-251183-1*) Harper SF.

— Undercurrents: A Therapist's Reckoning with Depression. LC 94-33043. 1995. pap. 12.00 (*0-06-251184-X*) Harper SF.

Manning, Maryann, jt. ed. see Manning, Gary.

Manning, Maryann M., et al. Reading & Writing in the Primary Grades. 80p. 1987. 9.95 (*0-8106-1697-1*) NEA.

Manning, Matthew. Link: Extraordinary Gifts of a Teenage Psychic. (Illus.). 176p. 1987. pap. 10.95 (*0-86140-283-9*, Pub. by Colin Smythe Ltd UK) Dufour.

Manning, Maurice. The Blueshirts. 2nd ed. (Illus.). 276p. 1987. reprint ed. pap. 21.95 (*0-7171-1515-1*, Pub. by Gill & MacMill IE) Irish Bks Media.

Manning, Maxine & Locke, Mattie. Inservice Manual Continuing Education Programs for Long Term Care. (Illus.). 137p. (C). 1986. ring bd. 33.95 (*1-877735-12-4*, 115) M&H Pub Co TX.

***Manning, Michael.** The Spider Garden. 96p. 1995. pap. 11.95x (*1-56163-117-5*, Amerotica) NBM.

Manning, Michael R., jt. ed. see Jackson, Conrad N.

Manning, Mick. A Ruined House. LC 93-21295. (Read & Wonder Ser.). 32p. (J). (ps up). 1994. 14.95 (*1-56402-453-9*) Candlewick Pr.

Manning-Miller, Linda, ed. Recovery: A Directory to Texas Substance Abuse Treatment Facilities. LC 92-13107. 448p. 1992. pap. 16.95 (*1-55622-144-4*) Wordware Pub.

Manning, Morris, jt. auth. see Mewett, Alan.

Manning, Nichola. All Down to a River. 64p. (Orig.). 1984. pap. 5.95 (*0-89807-112-7*) Illuminati.

— Frenchwoman Poems. 1978. pap. 3.95 (*0-930090-03-9*) Applezaba.

— Historical Document. 32p. 1982. pap. 4.95 (*0-930090-14-4*) Applezaba.

— Save Save Save Save. 1986. 14.95 (*0-930090-27-6*); pap. 7.95 (*0-930090-26-8*) Applezaba.

— Save Save Save Save. deluxe limited ed. 1986. Signed & Lettered. 20.00 (*0-930090-25-X*) Applezaba.

Manning, Nick. The Therapeutic Community Movement: Charisma & Routinisation. (Therapeutic Communities Ser.). 256p. 1989. 49.50 (*0-415-02913-9*) Routledge.

Manning, Olivia. The Balkan Trilogy. 1982. pap. 9.95 (*0-14-005936-9*, Penguin Bks) Viking Penguin.

— The Levant Trilogy. 576p. 1983. pap. 8.95 (*0-14-005962-8*, Penguin Bks) Viking Penguin.

— Summer Companions. (Inflation Fighter Ser.). 192p. 1982. pap. write for info. (*0-8439-1120-4*) Dorchester Pub Co.

Manning, P., jt. ed. see Wagner, J.

Manning, P. R. & DeBakey, L., eds. Medicine: Preserving the Passion. (Illus.). 315p. 1988. 50.00 (*0-387-96361-8*) Spr-Verlag.

Manning, Patrick. Slavery & African Life: Occidental, Oriental & African Slave Trades. (African Studies: No. 67). (Illus.). 264p. (C). 1990. pap. 18.95 (*0-521-34867-6*) Cambridge U Pr.

Manning, Patrick J., jt. ed. see Wagner, Joseph E.

Manning, Patrick J., et al, eds. The Biology of the Laboratory Rabbit. 2nd ed. (American College of Laboratory Animal Medicine Ser.). (Illus.). 483p. 1994. text ed. 120.00 (*0-12-469235-4*) Acad Pr.

***Manning, Patrick L.** In Search of the Senior Tour. 1994. 16.95 (*0-533-11133-1*) Vantage.

Manning, Paul. Martin Bormann: Nazi in Exile. (Illus.). 320p. (C). 1981. 14.95 (*0-8184-0309-8*) Carol Pub Group.

Manning, Pauline, ed. see Potter, Neal & Christy, Francis T.

Manning, Penny, jt. auth. see Manning, Harvey.

***Manning, Peter.** Electronic & Computer Music. 2nd ed. (Illus.). 408p. 1994. pap. text ed. 22.00 (*0-19-816329-0*) OUP.

Manning, Peter B., jt. auth. see Thorner, Marvin E.

Manning, Peter J. Byron & His Fictions. LC 78-7943. 297p. reprint ed. pap. 84.70 (*0-7837-3667-3*, 2043540) Bks Demand.

— Reading Romantics: Texts & Contexts. 336p. 1990. 45.00 (*0-19-505787-2*) OUP.

Manning, Peter K. Organizational Communication. (Communication & Social Order Ser.). 260p. 1992. lib. bdg. 44.95 (*0-202-30401-9*); pap. text ed. 22.95 (*0-202-30402-7*) Aldine de Gruyter.

— Semiotics & Fieldwork. (Qualitative Research Methods Ser.: Vol. 7). 96p. (C). 1987. text ed. 21.50 (*0-8039-2761-4*); pap. text ed. 9.50 (*0-8039-2640-5*) Sage.

— Symbolic Communication: Signifying Calls & Police Response. (Organization Studies: No. 9). 290p. 1989. 40.00 (*0-262-13234-6*) MIT Pr.

Manning, Peter K. & Zucker, Martine. The Sociology of Mental Health & Illness. LC 76-16067. (Studies in Sociology). (C). 1976. pap. text ed. write for info. (*0-672-61265-8*, Bobbs) Macmillan.

Manning, Phil. Afoot in the South: Walks in the Natural Areas of North Carolina. LC 92-46868. (Orig.). 1993. pap. 12.95 (*0-89587-099-1*) Blair.

***Manning, Phillip.** Palmetto Journal: Walks in the Natural Areas of South Carolina. LC 94-49584. (Illus.). (Orig.). 1995. pap. 13.95 (*0-89587-124-6*) Blair.

Manning, Rachel L. Your Spirit Guides Are Thoroughbreds: A Self Help Manual for Mule Headed People. LC 86-62341. 160p. (Orig.). 1988. pap. 7.95 (*0-941698-14-9*) Pan Ishtar.

Manning, Rachel L. & Manning, Al G. Puck'em All: We've Got the Magick. 150p. (Orig.). 1985. pap. 7.95 (*0-941698-10-6*) Pan Ishtar.

Manning, Rachel L., jt. auth. see Manning, Al G.

Manning, Raymond B. & Chace, Fenner A. Decapod & Stomatopod Crustacea from Ascension Island, South Atlantic Ocean. LC 90-10365. (Smithsonian Contributions to Zoology Ser.: No. 503). 97p. reprint ed. pap. 27.70 (*0-8357-2752-1*, 2039868) Bks Demand.

***Manning, Renfro C.** Schools for All Learners: Beyond the Bell Curve. LC 94-34139. 1994. 29.95 (*1-883001-06-4*) Eye On Educ.

— The Teacher Evaluation Handbook. 224p. 1988. 27.95 (*0-13-888389-0*) P-H.

***Manning, Richard.** Earth's Foundation: A Grassland Manifesto. LC 95-10073. 1995. 23.95 (*0-670-85342-9*, Viking) Viking Penguin.

— A Good House: Building a Life on the Land. (Illus.). 256p. 1994. pap. 11.95 (*0-14-023407-1*, Penguin Bks) Viking Penguin.

— Last Stand: A Riveting Expose of Environmental Pillage & a Lone Journalist's Struggle to Keep Faith. 192p. 1992. reprint ed. pap. 10.95 (*0-14-017293-9*, Penguin Bks) Viking Penguin.

Manning, Richard B. Impotence: How to Overcome It; the Authoritative Layman's Guide to Sexual Potency. rev. ed. 252p. 1989. pap. 14.95 (*0-685-12382-0*) HealthProInk.

— Impotence - How to Overcome It. 1989. pap. 14.95 (*0-933803-12-5*) HealthProInk.

Manning, Richard W., jt. auth. see Jones, J. Knox, Jr.

Manning, Rita C. Speaking from the Heart: A Feminist Perspective on Ethics. 224p. (C). 1992. text ed. 49.00 (*0-8476-7733-8*); pap. text ed. 14.95 (*0-8476-7734-6*) Rowman.

Manning, Robert, ed. The Aftermath: The Legacy of War, 1975-1985. (Vietnam Experience Ser.). (Illus.). 192p. 1986. 16.30 (*0-201-11273-6*) Addison-Wesley.

— Combat Photographer: Vietnam Through G.I. Lenses. (Vietnam Experience Ser.). (Illus.). 192p. 1984. 16.30 (*0-201-11266-3*) Addison-Wesley.

— The False Peace: The Beginning of the End, 1972-1974. (Vietnam Experience Ser.). (Illus.). 192p. 1986. 16.30 (*0-201-11272-8*) Addison-Wesley.

— Fighting for Time: The War Changes Time, 1969-1970. (Vietnam Experience Ser.). (Illus.). 192p. 1984. 16.30 (*0-201-11267-1*) Addison-Wesley.

— A Nation Divided: The War at Home, 1945-1972. (Vietnam Experience Ser.). (Illus.). 192p. 1984. 16.30 (*0-201-11263-9*) Addison-Wesley.

— South Vietnam on Trial: The Test of Vietnamization, 1970-1973. (Vietnam Experience Ser.). (Illus.). 192p. 1984. 16.30 (*0-201-11264-7*) Addison-Wesley.

— Thunder from Above: The War in the Air Through 1968. (Vietnam Experience Ser.). (Illus.). 192p. 1984. 16.30 (*0-201-11265-5*) Addison-Wesley.

— The Vietnam Experience: The Fall of the South, The False Peace 1972-74, The Aftermath 1975-85. write for info. (*0-318-60206-7*) Addison-Wesley.

— Words of War. (Vietnam Experience Ser.). (Illus.). 192p. 1988. 16.30 (*0-201-11943-9*) Addison-Wesley.

Manning, Robert, ed. see Boston Publishing Co. Editors.

Manning, Robert, ed. see Boston Publishing Co. Staff.

Manning, Robert, ed. see Dougan, Clark & Fulghum, David.

Manning, Robert, ed. see Dougan, Clark & Lipsman, Samuel L.

Manning, Robert, ed. see Dougan, Clark & Weiss, Stephen.

Manning, Robert, ed. see Doyle, Edward G. & Lipsman, Samuel L.

Manning, Robert, ed. see Doyle, Edward G., et al.

Manning, Robert, ed. see Doyle, Edward G. & Lipsman, Samuel L.

Manning, Robert, ed. see Doyle, Edward & Maitland, Terrence.

Manning, Robert, ed. see Doyle, Edward & Weiss, Stephen.

Manning, Robert, ed. see Lipsman, Samuel L. & Weiss, Stephen.

Manning, Robert, ed. see Maitland, Terrence & McInerney, Peter.

Manning, Robert, ed. see Maitland, Terrence & Weiss, Stephen.

Manning, Robert, ed. see Morrocco, John.

Manning, Robert A. Asian Policy: The New Soviet Challenge in the Pacific - A Twentieth Century Fund Paper. 150p. 1988. 18.95 (*0-87078-245-2*); pap. 8.95 (*0-87078-244-4*) TCFP-PPP.

Manning, Robert E. Studies in Outdoor Recreation. LC 85-15447. (Illus.). 184p. 1986. pap. text ed. 19.95x (*0-87071-345-0*) Oreg St U Pr.

Manning, Robert J. Interpreting Otherwise Than Heidegger: Emmanuel Levinas's Ethics As First Philosophy. LC 92-45191. 270p. 1993. text ed. 38.95 (*0-8207-0246-3*); pap. text ed. 19.95 (*0-8207-0253-6*) Duquesne.

Manning, Roberta T. The Crisis of the Old Order in Russia: Gentry & Government. LC 81-47933. (Studies of the Russian Institute, Columbia University & Harvard Series in Ukrainian Studies). (Illus.). 576p. 1982. text ed. 75.00x (*0-691-05349-9*); lib. bdg. 24.95x (*0-691-10189-2*) Princeton U Pr.

— The Crisis of the Old Order in Russia: Gentry & Government. LC 81-47933. (Studies of the Russian Institute). Date not set. reprint ed. pap. 162.80 (*0-7837-9378-2*, 2060122) Bks Demand.

Manning, Roberta T., jt. ed. see Getty, J. Arch.

Manning, Roger B. Hunters & Poachers: A Cultural & Social History of Unlawful Hunting in England 1485-1640. (Illus.). 280p. 1993. 49.95 (*0-19-820324-1*) OUP.

— Village Revolts: Social Protest & Popular Disturbances in England, 1509-1640. (Illus.). 368p. 1988. 82.00 (*0-19-820116-8*) OUP.

Manning, Rosemary. Green Smoke. large type ed. 224p. (J). (gr. 3-7). 1991. 16.95 (*0-7451-1318-4*, Galaxy Child Lrg Print) Chivers N Amer.

— Heraldry. (Junior Reference Ser.). (Illus.). (J). (gr. 7 up). 1975. 14.95 (*0-7136-0108-6*) Dufour.

***Manning, Russ.** Exploring the Big South Fork: A Handbook to the National River & Recreation Area. (Illus.). 252p. (Orig.). 1994. pap. 15.95 (*0-9625122-6-5*) Mtn Laurel Pl.

— The Historic Cumberland Plateau: An Explorer's Guide. LC 92-15007. (Outdoor Tennessee Ser.). (Illus.). 360p. (Orig.). (C). 1992. 29.95 (*0-87049-765-0*); pap. 14.95 (*0-87049-766-9*) U of Tenn Pr.

Manning, Russ & Jamieson, Sondra. The Best of the Big South Fork National River & Recreation Area: A Hiker's Guide to Trails & Attractions. (Tag-Along Bks.). (Illus.). 92p. (Orig.). 1989. pap. 4.95 (*0-9625122-0-6*) Mtn Laurel Pl.

— The Best of the Big South Fork National River & Recreation Area: A Hiker's Guide to Trails & Attractions. 2nd ed. (Tag-Along Bks.). (Illus.). 112p. (Orig.). 1990. pap. 6.95 (*0-9625122-4-9*) Mtn Laurel Pl.

— The Best of the Great Smoky Mountains National Park: A Hikers Guide to Trails & Attractions. (Tag-Along Bks.). (Illus.). 256p. (Orig.). 1991. pap. 10.95 (*0-9625122-2-2*) Mtn Laurel Pl.

— Historic Knoxville & Knox County Bicentennial Edition: A Walking & Touring Guide. (Tag-Along Bks.). (Illus.). 256p. (Orig.). 1990. pap. 8.95 (*0-9625122-3-0*) Mtn Laurel Pl.

— The South Cumberland & Fall Creek Falls Recreation Area & State Park: A Hiker's Guide to Trails & Attractions. (Tag-Along Bks.). (Illus.). 112p. (Orig.). 1990. pap. text ed. 6.95 (*0-9625122-1-4*) Mtn Laurel Pl.

— Tennessee's South Cumberland: A Hiker's Guide to Trails & Attractions. 2nd ed. (Tag-along Bks.). Orig. Title: The South Cumberland & Fall Creek Falls. (Illus.). 144p. 1994. pap. 8.95 (*0-9625122-7-3*) Mtn Laurel Pl.

— Trails of the Big South Fork National River & Recreation Area: Hiking, Horse, & Biking Trails. 3rd ed. (Tag-Along Bks.). (Illus.). 256p. 1995. pap. 10.95 (*0-9625122-5-7*) Mtn Laurel Pl.

Manning, S. W. The Absolute Chronology of the Aegean Early Bronze Age: Archaeology, Radiocarbon & History. (Monographs in Mediterranean Archaeology). (Illus.). 235p. 1992. 30.00 (*1-85075-336-9*, Pub. by Sheffield Acad UK) CUP Services.

Manning, Sam, jt. auth. see Greenhill, Basil.

Manning, Samuel F., jt. auth. see McIntosh, David C.

Manning, Shirley, ed. see Young, Ronald D. & Fennell, Robert A.

Manning, Shirley, ed. see Young, Ronald D.

Manning, Susan A. Ecstasy & the Demon: Feminism & Nationalism in the Dances of Mary Wigman. LC 92-32232. (C). 1993. 30.00 (*0-520-08193-5*) U CA Pr.

— The Puritan-Provincial Vision: Scottish & American Literature in the Nineteenth Century. (Cambridge Studies in American Literature & Culture: No. 41). 270p. (C). 1990. 59.95 (*0-521-37237-2*) Cambridge U Pr.

Manning, Susan A., ed. see Scott, Walter.

Manning, Thomas G. U. S. Coast Survey vs. Naval Hydrographic Office: A 19th-Century Rivalry in Science & Politics. LC 87-25524. (History of American Science & Technology Ser.). 216p. 1988. 24.50 (*0-8173-0390-1*) U of Ala Pr.

Manning, W. H. The Genealogical & Biographical History of the Manning Family of New England & Descendants from Settlement in America to Present Time. (Illus.). 865p. 1989. reprint ed. lib. bdg. 140.00 (*0-8328-0850-4*); reprint ed. pap. 130.00 (*0-8328-0851-2*) Higginson Bk Co.

— Report on the Excavations at USK, 1965-196, Vol. IV: The Fortress Excavations, 1972-74 & Minor Excavations on the Fortress & Favian Fort. xviii, 194p. 1989. 60.00 (*0-7083-1050-8*, Pub. by U of Wales UK) Bks Intl VA.

Manning, W. H., ed. The Roman Pottery, Vol. 5: Report on the Excavations at Usk, 1965-1976. (Illus.). xviii, 461p. 1993. 60.00 (*0-7083-1173-3*, Pub. by U of Wales UK) Bks Intl VA.

Manning, W. J. & Feder, W. A. Biomonitoring Air Pollutants with Plants. (Pollution Monitoring Ser.: No. 2). (Illus.). 142p. 1980. 41.50 (*0-85334-916-9*, Pub. by Elsevier Applied Sci UK) Elsevier.

Manning, Willard G., Jr., jt. ed. see Frank, Richard G.

Manning, Willard G., et al. The Costs of Poor Health Habits. 223p. (C). 1991. 34.50 (*0-674-17485-2*) HUP.

Manning, William, jt. auth. see Fuller, Floyd.

Manning, William R. Early Diplomatic Relations Between the United States & Mexico. LC 77-158857. reprint ed. 37.50 (*0-404-04181-7*) AMS Pr.

— Early Diplomatic Relations Between the United States & Mexico. (BCL1 - U. S. History Ser.). 406p. 1991. reprint ed. lib. bdg. 99.00 (*0-7812-6075-2*) Rprt Serv.

— The Nootka Sound Controversy. LC 65-27195. 1969. reprint ed. 22.95 (*0-405-03678-7*) Ayer.

***Manningham.** Airmanship Technique & Safety: The Best of Dan Manningham. 1995. pap. text ed. 18.95 (*0-07-009426-8*) TAB Bks.

M

An Asterisk (*) at the beginning of an entry indicates that the title is appearing in BIP for the first time.

Manningham, John. Diary of John Manningham. Bruce, John, ed. LC 17-1264. (Camden Society, London. Publications, First Ser.: No. 99). reprint ed. 49.50 (*0-404-50199-0*) AMS Pr.

— The Diary of John Manningham of the Middle Temple, 1602-1603: Newly Edited in Complete & Unexpurgated Form from the Original Manuscript in the British Museum. LC 74-22553. 485p. reprint ed. pap. 138.30 (*0-8357-6520-2*, 2035891) Bks Demand.

Mannino, Angelica L., jt. auth. see Mannino, Marc P.

Mannino, Edward F. Lender Liability & Banking Litigation. 700p. 1989. ring bd. 98.00 (*0-317-05405-8*, 00611) NY Law Pub.

Mannino, Fortune. Practice of Mental Health Consultation. 1975. 24.95 (*0-89876-082-8*) Gardner Pr.

Mannino, Fortune V., ed. Mental Health & Social Change: Fifty Years of Orthopsychiatry, No. 7. LC 74-26634. (Studies in Modern Society: Political & Social Issues). 34.50 (*0-404-11277-3*) AMS Pr.

***Mannino, J. Davis.** The Moon Ups & the Sun Downs. (Illus.). 150p. (C). 1995. 20.00 (*0-9647388-0-5*) Teddy-Bear Pub.

Mannino, Marc P. & Mannino, Angelica L. La Cola Magica de Marjorie. Norman-Grumbley, Patricia, tr. LC 93-86116. (Illus.). 32p. (Orig.). (SPA.). (J). (gr. k-3). 1993. pap. 7.95 (*0-9638340-1-0*) Sugar Sand.

— Marjorie's Magical Tail. LC 93-86041. (Illus.). 32p. (Orig.). (J). (ps-5). 1993. pap. 7.95 (*0-9638340-0-2*) Sugar Sand.

Mannino, Philip. ABCs of Audio-Visual Equipment & the School Projectionist Manual. 2nd ed. pap. 4.00 (*0-911328-01-7*) Sch Proj Club.

— Organizing a School Projectionist Club. pap. 0.75 (*0-685-48118-2*) Sch Proj Club.

Mannion, A. M. & Bowlby, S. R. Environmental Issues in the Nineteen Hundred Nineties. 349p. 1992. pap. text ed. 44.95 (*0-471-93326-0*) Wiley.

Mannion, Antoinette M. Global Environmental Change. 1991. pap. text ed. 57.95 (*0-470-21678-6*) Halsted Pr.

Mannion, C. L., jt. ed. see Taylor, J. G.

Mannion, John B., jt. auth. see Evans, John P.

Mannion, John J. Irish Settlements in Eastern Canada: A Study of Cultural Transfer & Adaptation. LC 73-84354. (University of Toronto, Department of Geography Research Publications: No. 12). (Illus.). 231p. reprint ed. pap. 65.90 (*0-8357-6387-0*, 2035742) Bks Demand.

Mannion, Michael T. Abortion & Healing: A Cry to Be Whole. 2nd ed. LC 86-60382. (Illus.). 96p. (Orig.). 1986. pap. 5.95 (*0-934134-35-9*) Sheed & Ward MO.

— Post-Abortion Aftermath: A Comprehensive Consideration. LC 94-21556. 192p. (Orig.). 1994. pap. 12.95 (*1-55612-708-1*) Sheed & Ward MO.

— Spiritual Reflections of a Pro-Life Pilgrim. LC 86-63590. (Illus.). 60p. (Orig.). 1987. pap. 3.50 (*1-55612-060-5*) Sheed & Ward MO.

Mannion, Michael T., jt. auth. see Crawford, Douglas R.

Mannion, Sean. Ireland's Friendly Dolphin. (Illus.). 128p. (Orig.). (YA). (gr. 7-11). 1991. pap. 9.95 (*0-86322-122-X*, Pub. by Brandon Bk Pubs IE) Irish Bks Media.

Mannis, Mark J. & Smith, Morton E. Case Studies in Ophthalmology for Medical Students. 1989. student ed 10.00 (*0-317-94085-6*); teacher ed 15.00 (*0-317-94086-4*) Am Acad Ophthal.

***Mannis, Mark J., et al, eds.** Eye & Skin Disease. LC 95-14343. 1995. write for info. (*0-7817-0269-0*) Raven.

Mannison, D. S., et al, eds. Ovironmental Philosophy. (Monograph Ser.: No. 2). vi, 386p. (C). 1980. pap. text ed. 21.00 (*0-909596-39-5*) Ridgeview.

Mannix, Daniel P. Freaks: We Who Are Not As Others. (Illus.). 124p. 1990. 50.00 (*0-940642-26-3*) Re Search Pubns.

— Freaks: We Who Are Not As Others. rev. ed. Juno, Andrea & Vale, V., eds. (Illus.). 128p. 1990. pap. 13.99 (*0-940642-20-4*) Re Search Pubns.

Mannix, Darlene. Be a Better Student: Lessons & Worksheets for Teaching Behavior Management in Grades 4-9. 280p. 1989. spiral bd. 29.95 (*0-87628-009-2*) Ctr Appl Res.

— Life Skills Activities for Secondary Students with Special Needs. LC 95-12270. (Illus.). 1995. write for info. (*0-87628-541-8*) Ctr Appl Res.

— Life Skills Activities for Special Children. 352p. 1991. spiral bd. 27.95 (*0-87628-547-7*) Ctr Appl Res.

— Oral Language Activities for Special Children. 238p. 1986. pap. 24.95 (*0-87628-637-6*) P-H.

— Social Skills Activities for Special Children. LC 93-12222. (Illus.). 1993. spiral bd. 27.95 (*0-87628-868-9*) Ctr Appl Res.

Mannix, J. E., jt. auth. see Manix, E. F.

Mannix, Patrick. The Rhetoric of Antinuclear Fiction: Persuasive Strategies in Novels & Films. LC 91-55466. 192p. 1992. 36.50 (*0-8387-5218-7*) Bucknell U Pr.

Mannle, Henry W. & Hirschel, David. Fundamental of Criminology. (Illus.). 512p. 1988. text ed. 28.00 (*0-317-62576-4*) P-H.

Mannners, William, jt. auth. see Manners, Ruth A.

Manno, Christopher E. & Gartner, Steven J. Doing Business in Europe: Before & After 1992. Merritt, Raymond W. & Ennico, Clifford M., eds. (Corporate Counseling Monograph Ser.). 125p. (Orig.). 1991. pap. 35.00 (*0-942954-46-7*) NYS Bar.

Manno, Karen, jt. auth. see Patton, Tim.

Manno, Rosemary, tr. Camourade: Selected Poems of Paul Laraque. LC 87-71704. 116p. 1988. pap. 9.95 (*0-915306-71-9*) Curbstone.

Manno, V. & Ring, J., eds. Infrared Detection Techniques for Space Research: Proceedings-E S L A B-E S R I N Symposium, 5th, Noordwijk, The Netherlands, 1971. LC 70-179894. (Astrophysics & Space Science Library: No. 30). 344p. 1972. lib. bdg. 103.00 (*90-277-0226-8*) Kluwer Ac.

Manno, V., ed. see ESLAB-ESRIN Symposium Staff.

Manno, Vittorio, jt. auth. see Bonnet, Roger M.

Mannocci, Lino. The Etchings of Claude Lorrain. 256p. (C). 1989. text ed. 85.00 (*0-300-04222-1*) Yale U Pr.

Mannoia, V. James, Jr. What Is Science? An Introduction to the Structure & Methodology of Science. LC 79-47988. (Illus.). 149p. 1980. pap. text ed. 15.00 (*0-8191-0989-4*) U Pr of Amer.

Mannon. Emergency Encounters. 1992. pap. 25.00 (*0-86720-189-4*) Jones & Bartlett.

Mannon, James M. American Gridmark: Why You've Always Suspected That Measuring Up Doesn't Count. LC 90-39598. 208p. (Orig.). 1990. pap. 9.95 (*0-943173-55-8*) Harbinger AZ.

— Caring for the Burned: Life & Death in a Hospital Burn Center. 274p. (C). 1985. 44.95x (*0-398-05089-9*) C C Thomas.

— Caring for the Burned: Life & Death in a Hospital Burn Center. 1985. 42.50 (*0-318-23303-7*) Phoenix Soc.

Mannone, F., ed. Safety in Tritium Handling Technology: Based on the Lectures Given During the Eurocourse on 'Safety in Tritium Handling Technology' Held at the Joint Research Centre Ispra, Italy, April 28-30, 1993. LC 93-30126. (Eurocourses: Nuclear Science & Technology Ser.). 248p. (C). 1993. lib. bdg. 85.00 (*0-7923-2511-7*) Kluwer Ac.

Mannoni, Edith. Classic French Paperweights. Jokelson, Paul & Selman, Lawrence H., eds. LC 84-61013. (Illus.). 60p. 1984. 35.00 (*0-933756-06-2*) Paperwght Pr.

Mannoni, Luciana & Mannoni, Tiziano. Marble: The History of Culture. LC 86-160034. (Illus.). 284p. reprint ed. pap. 81.00 (*0-8357-4254-7*, 2037043) Bks Demand.

Mannoni, Maud. The Child, His "Illness," & the Others. 292p. 1970. reprint ed. pap. 32.95 (*0-946439-39-7*, Pub. by Karnac Bks UK) Brunner-Mazel.

Mannoni, Octave. Freud: The Theory of the Unconscious. Bruce, Renaud, tr. 215p. 1986. pap. text ed. 15.95 (*0-86091-834-3*, Pub. by Verso UK) Routledge Chapman & Hall.

— Prospero & Caliban: The Psychology of Colonization. 230p. 1990. 44.50 (*0-472-09430-0*); pap. 15.95 (*0-472-06430-4*) U of Mich Pr.

Mannoni, Tiziano, jt. auth. see Mannoni, Luciana.

***Mannors, Ruth A. & Mannors, William.** The Quick & Easy Vegetarian Cookbook. 240p. 1995. 11.95 (*1-56865-133-3*, GuildAmerica) Dblday Bk Music.

Mannors, William, jt. auth. see Mannors, Ruth A.

Manns, Charles G., jt. auth. see Temperley, Nicholas.

Manns, James W. Reid & His French Disciples: Aesthetics & Metaphysics. (Brill's Studies in Intellectual History: Vol. 45). 250p. 1994. 65.75 (*90-04-09942-5*, NLG110) E J Brill.

Manns, Timothy. A Guide to Grand Canyon Village Historic District. (Illus.). 24p. 1978. pap. 4.95 (*0-938216-05-8*) GCNHA.

Manns, Tom & Coleman, Michael. Software Quality Assurance. (Computer Science Ser.). (Illus.). 140p. (C). 1988. pap. text ed. 30.00 (*0-333-45991-1*, Pub. by Macmill Press UK) Scholium Intl.

Manns, William, et al. Painted Ponies: American Carousel Art. Riley, Dru, ed. LC 86-51050. (Illus.). 256p. 1986. 40.00 (*0-939549-01-8*) Zon Intl Pub.

***Mannucci, P. M., ed.** Current Therapy of Von Willebrand's Disease. (Journal: Haemostasis: Vol. 24, No. 5, 1994). (Illus.). 64p. 1994. pap. 42.50 (*3-8055-6078-8*) S Karger.

Mannucci, P. M. & D'Angelo, A., eds. Urokinase: Basic & Clinical Aspects. LC 81-68958. (Serono Symposia Ser.: Vol. 48). 276p. 1982. text ed. 97.00 (*0-12-469280-X*) Acad Pr.

***Mannucci, P. M., et al, eds.** Viral Safety of Plasma-Derived Replacement Factors for Hemophilia: How Safe is Safe? (Journal: Vox Sanguinis Ser.: Vol. 67, Supplement 4, 1994). (Illus.). iv, 28p. 1994. pap. 13.00 (*3-8055-6066-4*) S Karger.

Mannuzzu, Salvatore. Procedura. 1993. 20.00 (*0-679-40082-6*) Random.

Mannweiler, Ulrich, ed. Light Metals, 1994. LC 94-75197. 1249p. 1994. 164.00 (*0-87339-264-7*) Minerals Metals.

Mannyng, Robert. Robert of Brunne's Handlyng Synne, Pts. 1-2. Furnivall, Frederic J., ed. (EETS, OS Ser.: No. 119, 123). 1974. reprint ed. 52.00 (*0-527-00117-1*) Periodicals Srv.

Mano, jt. auth. see Rico.

Mano, D. Keith. Topless. 1991. 17.50 (*0-679-40275-6*) Random.

Mano, M. Morris. Computer Engineering. (Illus.). 576p. 1988. text ed. 74.00 (*0-13-162926-3*) P-H.

— Computer System Architecture. 3rd ed. LC 92-12094. 528p. 1992. text ed. 74.00 (*0-13-175563-3*) P-H.

— Digital Design. 2nd ed. 592p. 1990. text ed. 74.00 (*0-13-212937-X*) P-H.

— Digital Logic & Computer Design. 1979. text ed. 48.00 (*0-13-214510-3*) P-H.

Mano, Noriichi, ed. see Tokyo Metropolitan Institute for Neuroscience.

Mano, Sadako. Little Furry Friends. (How to Draw & Paint Ser.). (Illus.). 32p. (Orig.). 1989. pap. 5.95 (*0-929261-86-0*, HT189) W Foster Pub.

Mano-Zissi, Djordje, jt. ed. see Wiseman, James.

Manoa. Manoa: Summer 1994: A Pacific Journal of International Writing. Shepard, Robert & Stewart, Frank, eds. 1994. pap. 15.00 (*1-55597-223-3*) Graywolf.

Manocchio, Anthony J. & Dunn, Jimmy. Time Game: Two Views of a Prison. 1970. pap. 19.95 (*0-8039-0920-9*) Sage.

Manocha & Srivastava. Algebra & Its Applications. (Lecture Notes in Pure & Applied Mathematics Ser.: Vol. 91). 416p. 1984. 140.00 (*0-8247-7165-6*) Dekker.

Manoff, Richard K. Have We Become Surrogates for Failure? Proposing a New Nutrition Education. LC 93-27281. (Martin J. Forman Memorial Lecture Ser.: Vol. 6). (Illus.). 32p. (Orig.). 1993. pap. 7.00 (*0-915173-25-5*) Helen Keller Intl.

Manoff, Robert K., ed. The Buck Starts Here: Enterprise & the Arts. 165p. 1984. 11.95 (*0-917103-00-9*) Vol Lawyers Arts.

Manoff, Robert K. & Schudson, Michael, eds. Reading the News. LC 86-72639. 256p. 1986. pap. 11.16 (*0-394-74649-X*) Pantheon.

Manoff, Tom. Music: A Living Language. (Illus.). 350p. (C). 1982. pap. text ed. 29.95 (*0-393-95194-4*); lp 22.95 (*0-393-95228-2*) Norton.

— Music: A Living Language. (Illus.). 350p. (C). 1982. Instr's. manual. teacher ed, pap. text ed. write for info. (*0-393-95220-7*) Norton.

— The Music Kit. (C). 1984. Instr's. recordings. write for info. (*0-393-99134-2*) Norton.

— The Music Kit. (C). 1984. Instr's. manual. teacher ed, pap. text ed. write for info. (*0-393-95301-7*) Norton.

— The Music Kit. 2nd ed. (C). 1984. pap. text ed. 39.95 (*0-393-95298-3*) Norton.

— The Music Kit. 3rd ed. (C). 1994. teacher ed, pap. text ed. write for info. (*0-393-96326-8*) Norton.

— The Music Kit, Wkbk., rhythm reader, scorebook. 3rd ed. 391p. (C). 1994. text ed., digital audio 41.95x (*0-393-96325-X*) Norton.

Manoff, Tom & Miller, John. The Music Kit: CAI (Computered Assisted Instruction) Version for the Apple II. 2nd ed. (Orig.). (C). 1988. pap. text ed. 44.95 (*0-393-95686-5*) Norton.

— The Music Kit: Computer - Assisted Instruction. (C). 1994. mac hd, pap. text ed. 46.95x (*0-393-96330-6*); pap. text ed. 46.95x (*0-393-96327-6*) Norton.

Manogaran, Chelvadurai. Ethnic Conflict & Reconciliation in Sri Lanka. LC 87-16247. 248p. 1987. text ed. 22.00 (*0-8248-1116-X*) UH Pr.

***Manogaran, Chelvadurai & Pfaffenberger, Brian, eds.** The Sri Lankan Tamils: Ethnicity & Identity. LC 94-3552. (C). 1994. pap. text ed. 42.95 (*0-8133-8845-7*) Westview.

Manohar, Murli. The Art of Conveyancing & Pleading. 290p. 1974. 45.00 (*0-317-54573-6*) St Mut.

— Art of Conveyancing & Pleading. (C). 1990. 35.00 (*0-685-39760-2*) St Mut.

— Dand Prakriya Vyakhyan (Code of Criminal Procedure in Hindi) 212p. 1981. 45.00 (*0-317-54574-4*) St Mut.

Manohar, Murli, ed. The Art of Conveyancing & Pleadings. (C). 1989. reprint ed. 65.00 (*0-685-37458-0*) St Mut.

— Pralekhan aur Abhivechan: (The Art of Conveyancing & Pleading in Hindi) 2nd ed. (HIN.). (C). 1991. 95.00 (*0-685-39756-4*) St Mut.

Manohar Rao, M. J. Filtering & Control of Macroeconomic Systems: A Control System Incorporating the Kalman Filter for the Indian Economy. (Contributions to Economic Analysis Ser.: No. 160). 280p. 1987. 69.25 (*0-444-70188-5*, North Holland) Elsevier.

Manoharan, S., jt. auth. see Singh, K. S.

Manoj Kumar Srivastava. Succession to Rule under Dehli Sultan. 1990. 24.00 (*81-7169-053-X*, Commonwealth) S Asia.

Manolagas, Stavros & Olefsky, Jerrold M., eds. Metabolic Bone & Mineral Disorders. (Contemporary Issues in Endocrinology & Metabolism Ser.: Vol. 5). (Illus.). 254p. 1988. text ed. 63.00 (*0-443-08586-2*) Churchill.

***Manolagas, Stavros C. & Olefsky, Jerrold M., eds.** Metabolic Bone & Mineral Disorders. fac. ed. LC 88-22864. (Contemporary Issues in Endocrinology & Metabolism Ser.: No. 5). (Illus.). 266p. 1988. reprint ed. pap. 75.90 (*0-7837-7877-5*, 2047634) Bks Demand.

Manolakis, Dimitris G., jt. auth. see Proakis, John G.

***Manoleas, Peter, ed.** The Cross-Cultural Practice of Clinical Case Management in Mental Health. LC 94-47011. 1995. text ed. 24.95 (*1-56024-874-2*) Haworth Pr.

***Manolis, Argie, ed.** Teddy Bear Sourcebook for Collectors & Artists. (Illus.). 356p. (Orig.). 1995. pap. 18.99 (*1-55870-386-1*) Betterway Bks.

Manolis, Charlie, jt. auth. see Webb, Grahame.

Manolis, G. & Davies, T., eds. Boundary Element Techniques in Geomechanics. LC 93-72574. (Computational Engineering Ser.). 548p. 1993. 224.00 (*1-56252-183-7*) Computational Mech MA.

Manolis, G. D. Boundary Element Techniques in Geomechanics. 1993. 224.00 (*1-85861-024-9*, Pub. by Elsevier Applied Sci UK) Elsevier.

Manolis, G. D. & Beskos, D. E. Boundary Element Methods in Elastodynamics. 288p. 1988. text ed. 75.00 (*0-04-620019-3*) Routledge Chapman & Hall.

***Manoliu-Manea, Maria.** Discourse & Pragmatic Constraints on Grammatical Choices: A Grammar of Surprises. Price, Glanville, ed. LC 94-39160. (Linguistic Ser.: Vol. 57). 1994. write for info. (*0-444-82043-4*, North Holland) Elsevier.

Manolopoulos, D. E., jt. auth. see Fowler, P. W.

Manon, Melvin & H, Jose I. Operacion Estrella: Con Caamano, la Resistencia y la Inteligencia Cubana. (Illus.). iii, 178p. (Orig.). (SPA.). 1989. pap. 15.00 (*0-89729-524-2*) Ediciones.

Manooch, Charles S., III. Fisherman's Guide: Fishes of the Southeastern United States. LC 84-60641. (Illus.). 376p. 1984. 29.95 (*0-917134-07-9*) NC Natl Sci.

***Manooja, D. C.** Adoption Law & Practice. (C). 1993. 32.00x (*81-7100-581-0*, Pub. by Deep) S Asia.

Manor, Giora, ed. Israel Dance Annual: 1982. (Illus.). 1982. pap. 6.50 (*0-934682-08-9*) Emmett.

— Israel Dance Annual 1980. (Illus.). 1980. pap. 6.50 (*0-934682-06-2*) Emmett.

— Israel Dance Annual 1981. (Illus.). 1981. pap. 6.50 (*0-934682-07-0*) Emmett.

— Israel Dance Annual 1983. (Illus.). 1983. pap. 6.50 (*0-934682-09-7*) Emmett.

— Israel Dance Annual 1984. (Illus.). 1984. pap. 6.50 (*0-934682-10-0*) Emmett.

— Israel Dance Annual 1985. 1985. pap. 7.95 (*0-934682-12-7*) Emmett.

— Israel Dance Annual 1986. (Illus.). 1986. pap. 9.95 (*0-934682-15-1*) Emmett.

Manor Healthcare Corporation Staff & Switkes, Betty. Armchair Fitness. (Illus.). 64p. 1984. write for info. (*0-917025-00-8*) Manor Health.

Manor, J. Curtis. Adventures from the Pentateuch. 1994. 17.95 (*1-56794-068-4*) Star Bible.

Manor, James. The Expedient Utopian: Bandaranaike & Ceylon. (Illus.). (C). 1990. 64.95 (*0-521-37191-0*) Cambridge U Pr.

— Political Change in an Indian State, Mysore, 1917-1955. 1978. 12.50 (*0-8364-0069-0*) S Asia.

— Power, Poverty, & Poison: Disaster & Response in an Indian City. LC 92-40655. (Illus.). 200p. 1993. 28.50 (*0-8039-9466-4*) Sage.

Manor, James, ed. Rethinking Third World Politics. 352p. (C). 1991. pap. text ed. 23.95 (*0-582-07458-4*, 78937) Longman.

— Rethinking Third World Politics. 352p. (C). 1992. text ed. 60.95 (*0-582-07459-2*, 78936) Longman.

Manor, James, jt. ed. see Colclough, Christopher.

***Manos, Constantine, photos.** American Color. (Illus.). 96p. 1995. 29.95 (*0-393-03912-9*) Norton.

Manos, Dennis M. & Flamm, Daniel L., eds. Plasma Etching: An Introduction. (Plasma Materials Interactions Ser.). 476p. 1989. text ed. 84.95 (*0-12-469370-9*) Acad Pr.

Manos, Nikki L. & Rochelson, Meri-Jane, eds. Transforming Genres: New Approaches to British Fiction of the 1890s. LC 94-9855. 1994. text ed. 39.95 (*0-312-12154-7*) St Martin.

Manos, Paris & Manos, Susan. Collectible Male Action Figures: G.I. Joe, Captain Action, & Ken. 1990. pap. 14.95 (*0-89145-411-X*) Collector Bks.

— The Wonder of Barbie. (Illus.). 136p. 1990. pap. 9.95 (*0-89145-336-9*, 1808) Collector Bks.

— The World of Barbie Dolls. (Illus.). 144p. 1990. pap. 9.95 (*0-89145-229-X*) Collector Bks.

Manos, Susan, jt. auth. see Manos, Paris.

Manougian, M. N. All You Need to Know about the Lottery: Play to Win. LC 91-3240. (Illus.). 114p. 1991. 12.95 (*0-931541-23-9*); pap. 5.95 (*0-931541-24-7*) Mancorp Pub.

— Basic Algebra. 2nd ed. (Illus.). 480p. (C). 1994. text ed. 29.50 (*0-931541-32-8*) Mancorp Pub.

— Precalculus Algebra & Trigonometry. 2nd ed. LC 86-34332. 1987. 29.50 (*0-931541-07-7*) Mancorp Pub.

Manoukian, E. B. Modern Concepts & Theorems of Mathematical Statistics. (Series in Statistics). 175p. 1985. 42.00 (*0-387-96186-0*) Spr-Verlag.

Manoukian, Edward B. Mathematical Nonparametric Statistics. 340p. 1986. text ed. 156.00 (*2-88124-093-3*) Gordon & Breach.

— Remoralization. (Pure & Applied Mathematics Ser.). 1983. text ed. 75.00 (*0-12-469450-0*) Acad Pr.

Manousos, Anthony. Spiritual Linkage with Russians. LC 91-68220. 32p. (Orig.). 1992. pap. 3.00 (*0-87574-301-3*, PHP 301) Pendle Hill.

Manousos, Stephen E. & Tilden, Scott W. The Professional Look: The Complete Guide to Desktop Publishing. Benhari, Ted, ed. (Illus.). 275p. (Orig.). 1990. pap. 19.95 (*0-932309-40-2*) Venture Persp Pr.

Manovich, Lev, jt. ed. see Efimova, Alla.

Manovich, Lev, tr. see Efimova, Alla & Manovich, Lev, eds.

Manovrier, Lynne. Animal Farm: A Study Guide. (Novel-Ties Ser.). (J). (gr. 6-10). 1983. student ed, teacher ed 15.95 (*0-88122-021-3*) Lrn Links.

Manraj, A. Shakoor & Haines, Paul D. The Law on Speeding & Radar. 2nd ed. 168p. 1991. 45.00 (*0-409-90376-0*) Butterworth Legal Pubs.

Manring, Rob, ed. see Panamarioff, Rob & Pikok, Bob.

Manrique, Beatriz. Hola Bebe. (Illus.). (Orig.). (SPA.). 1987. pap. 5.00 (*980-6017-09-9*); pap. 5.00 (*0-944499-23-6*) Editorial Amer.

***Manrique, Jaime.** Federico Garcia Lorca. Duberman, Martin, ed. (Lives of Notable Gay Men & Lesbians Ser.). (Illus.). 168p. (YA). (gr. 9 up). 1995. lib. bdg. 19.95 (*0-7910-2320-6*) Chelsea Hse.

— Federico Garcia Lorca. Duberman, Martin, ed. (Lives of Notable Gay Men & Lesbians Ser.). (Illus.). 168p. (YA). (gr. 9 up). 1995. pap. 9.95 (*0-7910-2888-7*) Chelsea Hse.

— Latin Moon in Manhattan. LC 92-40802. 1993. pap. 9.95 (*0-312-08835-3*) St Martin.

Manrique, Jorge. Poesias Completas. Perez Priego, Miguel A., ed. (Nueva Austral Ser.: Vol. 152). (SPA.). 1991. pap. text ed. 24.95x (*84-239-1952-8*) Elliots Bks.

***Manroe, C.** Designing with Collectibles. 1994. pap. 10.99 (*0-517-13296-6*) Random.

Manroe, Candace O. Designing with Collectibles. LC 92-30120. (Illus.). 144p. 1993. 25.00 (*0-671-76103-X*) S&S Trade.

— For Your Home: Family Rooms. 1994. pap. 11.95 (*0-316-65210-5*) Little.

— For Your Home: Fireplaces & Hearths. 1994. pap. 11.95 (*0-316-54756-5*) Little.

— For Your Home: Flood Treatments. 1994. pap. 11.95 (*0-316-65211-3*) Little.

— For Your Home: Lighting Ideas. 1994. pap. 11.95 (*0-316-54757-3*) Little.

An Asterisk (*) at the beginning of an entry indicates that the title is appearing in BIP for the first time.

— Storage Made Easy. LC 95-13633. 1995. write for info. (*1-56799-216-1*, Friedman-Fairfax); pap. write for info. (*1-56799-211-0*, Friedman-Fairfax) M Friedman Pub Grp Inc.

— Storage Made Easy: Great Ideas for Organizing Everything in Your Home. (Illus.). 128p. 1995. 14.95 (*1-56865-128-7*, GuildAmerica) Dblday Bk Music.

Manroe, Candance O. Decorative Eggs. 1992. 14.99 (*0-517-06032-9*) Random Hse Value.

Manross, William W. Episcopal Church in the United States, 1800-1840: A Study in Church Life. LC 38-38020. (Columbia University. Studies in the Social Sciences: No. 441). reprint ed. 21.00 (*0-404-51441-3*) AMS Pr.

Manry, Douglas. The Land the Cleves Built. Sloan, Stephen, ed. (Illus.). 32p. (J). (gr. 2-5). 1989. write for info. (*0-9622316-0-6*) Sloan Manry Pubs.

***Mans, Lorenzo.** The Mango Grove. 41p. 1993. pap. text ed. 3.95 (*1-885901-11-9*) Presbyters Peartree.

Mansaray, Alasan. A Haunting Heritage: An African Saga in America. LC 93-87204. 320p. 1994. 21.95 (*0-9639497-5-6*) Sahara Pubng.

Mansbach, Richard W. & Vasquez, John A. In Search of Theory: A New Paradigm for Global Politics. LC 80-19365. 544p. 1983. text ed. 56.00 (*0-231-05060-7*); pap. text ed. 21.50 (*0-231-05061-5*) Col U Pr.

Mansbach, Richard W., jt. auth. see Ferguson, Yale H.

Mansbach, Richard W., jt. auth. see Lee, Manwoo.

Mansbach, Steven A., ed. Standing in the Tempest: Painters of the Hungarian Avante-Garde, 1908-1930. (Illus.). 240p. 1991. 47.50 (*0-262-13274-5*) MIT Pr.

Mansberg, Ruth, jt. auth. see Carlin, Vivian F.

Mansbridge, Albert. Fellow Men. LC 73-117329. (Biography Index Reprint Ser.). 1977. 23.95 (*0-8369-8021-2*) Ayer.

Mansbridge, Jane, jt. ed. see Okin, Susan M.

Mansbridge, Jane J. Beyond Adversary Democracy. xiv, 412p. 1983. pap. text ed. 16.95 (*0-226-50355-0*) U Ch Pr.

— Why We Lost the E. R. A. LC 86-6954. (Illus.). xii, 328p. 1986. lib. bdg. 35.00 (*0-226-50357-7*); pap. text ed. 13. 95 (*0-226-50358-5*) U Ch Pr.

Mansbridge, Jane J., ed. Beyond Self-Interest. LC 89-38629. 332p. 1990. pap. text ed. 16.95 (*0-226-50360-7*) U Ch Pr.

Mansbridge, Michael. John Nash: A Complete Catalogue. LC 90-52872. (Illus.). 1991. 75.00 (*0-8478-1308-8*) Rizzoli Intl.

Manschreck, Clyde L. A History of Christianity in the World: From Persecution to Uncertainty. 2nd ed. (Illus.). 352p. (C). 1984. text ed. 61.00 (*0-13-389354-5*) P-H.

— Melanchthon: The Quiet Reformer. LC 73-21263. (Illus.). 350p. 1975. reprint ed. text ed. 38.50 (*0-8371-6131-2*, MAMQ, Greenwood Pr) Greenwood.

Mansdoerfer, Caroline B. I Plead the Fifth: The Story of Alpha One Trek America. LC 93-93634. (Illus.). 125p. (Orig.). 1993. pap. 12.95 (*0-9638663-0-3*) Alpha One Crusades.

Mansdorf, jt. auth. see Roseman.

Mansdorf, S. Z. Complete Guide to Industrial Safety in Manufacturing. LC 93-4986. 1993. 69.95 (*0-13-159633-0*) P-H.

Mansdorf, S. Z., jt. auth. see Frosberg, Krister.

Mansel. A Color Atlas of Breast Diseases. 128p. 1993. 49.50 (*0-8151-5756-8*, Yr Bk Med Pubs) Mosby Yr Bk.

Mansel, Henry L. The Gnostic Heresies of the First & Second Centuries. Lightfoot, J. B., ed. LC 78-63170. (Heresies of the Early Christian & Medieval Era Ser.: Second Ser.). reprint ed. 47.50 (*0-404-16185-5*) AMS Pr.

— Limits of Religious Thought Examined. LC 72-172840. reprint ed. 45.00 (*0-404-04182-5*) AMS Pr.

Mansel, Philip. The Court of France, 1789-1830. (Illus.). 236p. (C). 1991. pap. 22.95 (*0-521-42398-8*) Cambridge U Pr.

Mansel, R. E. Recent Developments in the Study of Benign Breast Disease. 4th ed. (Illus.). 200p. 1992. 68.00 (*1-85070-386-8*) Prthnon Pub.

Mansel, R. E., ed. Recent Developments in the Study of Benign Breast Disease: The Proceedings of the 5th International Symposium on Benign Breast Disease. 5th ed. LC 93-41022. (Illus.). 280p. (C). 1993. pap. text ed. 45.00 (*1-85070-532-1*) Prthnon Pub.

***Mansel, Robert E. & Bundred, Nigel J.** Color Atlas of Breast Diseases. LC 94-44123. (Illus.). (J). 1994. 45.00 (*0-7234-1721-0*, Yr Bk Med Pubs) Mosby Yr Bk.

Mansell, Chris. Redshift - Blueshift. 64p. (C). 1990. 27.00 (*0-9587972-1-8*, Pub. by Pascoe Pub AT) St Mut.

— Shining Like a Jinx. (Amelia Chapbooks Ser.). 48p. (Orig.). 1989. pap. 8.95 (*0-936545-11-9*) Amelia.

***Mansell, Colette.** A Collector's Guide to British Dolls since 1920. (Illus.). 390p. Date not set. 45.00 (*0-7091-9380-7*, Pub. by R Hale Ltd UK) Antique Collect.

Mansell, Dom. Dinosaurs Came to Town. (J). (ps-3). 1991. 13.95 (*0-316-54584-8*) Little.

— My Old Teddy. LC 91-71830. (Illus.). 32p. (J). (ps). 1992. 12.95 (*1-56402-035-5*) Candlewick Pr.

— My Old Teddy. LC 91-71830. (Illus.). 32p. (J). (ps). 1994. pap. 3.99 (*1-56402-282-X*) Candlewick Pr.

Mansell, Donald E. & Mansell, Vesta W. Sure As the Dawn. LC 93-3782. 1993. 9.95 (*0-8280-0723-3*) Review & Herald.

Mansell, Gilbert. Working with the Computer. 156p. 1971. pap. 64.00 (*0-08-016014-X*, Pub. by Pergamon Repr UK) Franklin.

Mansell, Joanna. Illusion of Paradise. large type ed. 1992. 18.95 (*0-263-12944-6*, MB029, Pub. by Mills & Boon Ltd UK) Chivers N Amer.

— Istanbul Affair. 1994. mass mkt. 2.99 (*0-373-11662-4*, 1-11662-3) Harlequin Bks.

— The Touch of Aphrodite. (Presents Ser.). 1994. mass mkt. 2.99 (*0-373-11684-5*, 1-11684-7) Harlequin Bks.

Mansell, Lilene, ed. see Skinner, Edith.

Mansell, Mary, ed. see Birnholz, Mary B., et al.

Mansell, Maureen E. By the Power of Their Dreams: Songs, Prayers, & Sacred Shields of the Plains Indians. LC 93-8148. (Illus.). 96p. 1994. 16.95 (*0-8118-0460-7*) Chronicle Bks.

Mansell, Nigel & Sheu, Jeremy. Nigel Mansell's Indy Car Racing. LC 93-11913. (Illus.). 160p. 1993. 24.95 (*0-87938-836-6*) Motorbooks Intl.

Mansell, Robin E. The New Telecommunications: A Political Economy of Network Evolution. (C). 1994. text ed. 65.00 (*0-8039-8535-5*); pap. text ed. 24.95 (*0-8039-8536-3*) Sage.

Mansell, Vesta W., jt. auth. see Mansell, Donald E.

Mansell, Wade, jt. auth. see Conaghan, Joanne.

Manselli, Raoul. St. Francis of Assisi. Duggan, Paul, tr. 365p. 1988. 24.95 (*0-8199-0880-0*, Frncscn Herld) Franciscan Pr.

Mansen, Cynthia, et al, eds. Women of Mystery. 336p. (Orig.). 1993. mass mkt. 5.99 (*0-425-13747-3*) Berkley Pub.

Manser, Anthony R. Sartre: A Philosophic Study. LC 81-765. 280p. 1981. reprint ed. text ed. 38.50 (*0-313-22827-2*, MASPS, Greenwood Pr) Greenwood.

Manser, Anthony R. & Stock, Guy, eds. The Philosophy of F. H. Bradley. 336p. 1987. pap. 26.00 (*0-19-824972-1*) OUP.

***Manser, J.E.** Economics: A Foundation Course for the Built Environment. 290p. 1994. 24.50 (*0-419-18260-8*) Wiley.

Manser, Jose. The Joseph Shops, London, 1979-1988. (Architecture in Detail Ser.). (Illus.). 60p. 1991. pap. 42. 95 (*0-442-30827-2*) Van Nos Reinhold.

— Rodney Kinsman: The Logical Art of Furniture. (Illus.). 112p. 1992. 29.95 (*1-85702-010-3*, Pub. by Fourth Estate UK) Trafalgar.

Manser, Martin. Get to the Roots: A Dictionary of Word & Phrase Origins. 272p. (Orig.). 1992. pap. 10.00 (*0-380-71473-6*) Avon.

— Melba Toast, Bowie's Knife & Caesar's Wife: A Dictionary of Eponyms. 256p. 1990. pap. 7.95 (*0-380-70877-9*) Avon.

Manser, Martin & McQuain, Jeffrey, eds. The World Almanac Guide to Good Word Usage. 288p. 1991. reprint ed. pap. 8.95 (*0-380-71449-3*) Avon.

Manser, Roger. Failed Transitions: The Eastern European Economy Since the Fall of Communism. LC 93-26990. 1994. 22.95 (*1-56584-119-0*) New Press NY.

Manser, William. Control from Brussels. (C). 1993. text ed. 26.95 (*0-201-62421-4*) Addison-Wesley.

Manser, William, jt. auth. see Bannock, Graham.

Mansergh, Ian & Broom, Linda. The Mountain Pygmy Possum. (Natural History Ser.). 1992. pap. 19.95 (*0-86840-085-8*, Pub. by New South Wales Univ Pr AT) Intl Spec Bk.

Mansergh, N. The Commonwealth & the Nations: Studies in British Commonwealth Relations. 229p. 1968. reprint ed. 20.00 (*0-8464-0261-0*) Beekman Pubs.

Mansergh, Nicholas. The Commonwealth Experience, 2 vols. rev. ed. Incl. Vol. 1. Durham Report to the Anglo-Irish Treaty. 1982. pap. 12.95 (*0-8020-6515-5*); Vol. 2. From British to Multiracial Commonwealth. 1982. 27.50 (*0-8020-2492-0*); Vol. 2. From British to Multiracial Commonwealth. 1982. pap. 12.95 (*0-8020-6516-3*); 1982. Set. Set pap. 25.00 (*0-8020-6497-3*) U of Toronto Pr.

— The Commonwealth Experience, 2 vols., Set. rev. ed. Incl. Vol. 1. Durham Report to the Anglo-Irish Treaty. 1982. pap. 12.95 (*0-8020-6515-5*); Vol. 2. From British to Multiracial Commonwealth. 1982. 27.50 (*0-8020-2492-0*); Vol. 2. From British to Multiracial Commonwealth. 1982. pap. 12.95 (*0-8020-6516-3*); 1982. 50.00 (*0-8020-2477-7*) U of Toronto Pr.

— The Irish Question, 1840-1921: A Commentary on Anglo-Irish Relations & on Social & Political Forces in Ireland in the Age of Reform & Revolution. 3rd ed. 341p. reprint ed. pap. 97.20 (*0-317-55700-9*, 2029338) Bks Demand.

— Survey of British Commonwealth Affairs: Problems of Wartime Cooperation & Post-War Change, 1939-1952. 470p. 1968. reprint ed. 37.50 (*0-7146-1496-3*, Pub. by F Cass Pubs UK) Intl Spec Bk.

— The Unresolved Question: The Anglo-Irish Settlement & Its Undoing 1912-72. 384p. (C). 1991. text ed. 40.00 (*0-300-05069-0*) Yale U Pr.

Mansergh, Nicholas, ed. Commonwealth Perspectives. LC 58-11381. (Duke University Commonwealth Studies Center: No. 8). 224p. reprint ed. 63.90 (*0-8357-9100-9*, 2017911) Bks Demand.

***Mansfeld, F., et al.** H. H. Uhlig Memorial Symposium. 330p. 1995. pap. 58.00 (*1-56677-085-8*, PV 94-26) Electrochem Soc.

Mansfeld, Florian, ed. see Electrochemical Society Staff.

Mansfeld, Guenter. Die Fibeln der Heuneburg 1950-1970: Ein Beitrag zur Geschichte der Spaethallstattfibel Heuneburgstudien II. LC 72-75868. (Roemisch Germanische Forschungen Ser.: Vol. 33). (Illus.). xii, 299p. (C). 1973. 200.00 (*3-11-003769-6*) De Gruyter.

Mansfeld, Jaap. Heresiography in Context: Hippolytus' Elenchos As a Source for Greek Philosophy. LC 92-6285. (Philosophia Antiqua Ser.: Vol. 56). xvii, 391p. 1992. 97.25 (*90-04-09616-7*) E J Brill.

— Prolegomena: Questions to Be Settled before the Study of an Author or a Text. LC 94-16216. (Philosophia Antiqua Ser.: Vol. 61). 1994. 57.25 (*90-04-10084-9*) E J Brill.

— Studies in Later Greek Philosophy & Gnosticism. (Collected Studies: No. CS292). 334p. (C). 1989. lib. bdg. 89.95 (*0-86078-240-9*, Pub. by Variorum UK) Ashgate Pub Co.

Mansfield. Corrosion Mechanisms. (Mansfield Chemical Industries Ser.: Vol. 28). 472p. 1987. 175.00 (*0-8247-7627-5*) Dekker.

— Parasitic Diseases: The Chemotherapy, Vol. 2. 248p. 1984. 140.00 (*0-8247-7050-1*) Dekker.

Mansfield, Arlene F. Descendants of Conrad Bower, Martin Easterday Sr., John Hoover Sr., & Gabriel Swinehart Sr. Families: From Colonial Maryland to Ohio in the Early 1800's. 490p. 1993. 32.50 (*0-9635981-0-4*) Coyote Tales.

Mansfield, Bruce. Interpretations of Erasmus c1750-1920: Man on His Own. (Erasmus Studies: No. 11). 480p. 1992. 75.00 (*0-8020-5950-3*) U of Toronto Pr.

Mansfield, C. M. Early Breast Cancer: Its History & Results of Treatment. Wolsky, A., ed. (Experimental Biology & Medicine Ser.: Vol. 5). (Illus.). 120p. 1976. 39.25 (*3-8055-2300-9*) S Karger.

— Therapeutic Radiology. 650p. 1988. write for info. (*0-444-01249-4*, Excerpta Medica) Elsevier.

Mansfield, Carmella E. Writing Business Letters & Reports. 1986. pap. write for info. (*0-02-682970-3*) Macmillan.

Mansfield, Carmella E. & Bahniuk, Margaret H. Writing Business Letters & Reports. 1981. teacher ed write for info. (*0-672-97375-8*); pap. write for info. (*0-672-97374-X*) Macmillan.

Mansfield, Carmella E., jt. auth. see Kratochwil, Friedrich V.

Mansfield, Charles B. Paraguay, Brazil, & the Plate. LC 79-128414. reprint ed. 55.00 (*0-404-04183-3*) AMS Pr.

Mansfield, Clay B. & Cunningham, Timothy W. Pension Funds: A Commonsense Guide to a Common Goal. LC 92-12182. 190p. 1992. 37.50 (*1-55623-810-X*) Irwin Prof Pubng.

***Mansfield, D. L.** History of Dummerston - from Vermont Historical Gazetteer, Vol. V. (Illus.). 216p. 1995. reprint ed. lib. bdg. 32.50 (*0-8328-4656-2*) Higginson Bk Co.

Mansfield, Danielle F. Good-Bye, Baby Venus. LC 92-44490. 1993. 39.50 (*0-8191-9028-4*) U Pr of Amer.

Mansfield, Dick. Central New York Mountain Biking: The 30 Best Back Road & Trail Rides in Upstate New York. LC 94-2715. 176p. 1994. pap. 12.95 (*0-937921-50-5*) Acorn Pub.

— Runners Guide to Cross Country-Skiing. 2nd ed. (Illus.). 160p. 1990. pap. 10.95 (*0-937921-49-1*) Acorn Pub.

— Skating on Skis. (Illus.). 144p. 1988. pap. 9.95 (*0-937921-37-8*) Acorn Pub.

— Vermont Mountain Biking: The Best Back Road & Trail Rides in Southern Vermont. LC 88-355596. (Illus.). 176p. 1989. pap. 10.95 (*0-937921-48-3*) Acorn Pub.

Mansfield, Dick, jt. auth. see Heed, Peter.

Mansfield, Don L., jt. ed. see Bochkarev, Andrei G.

Mansfield, E. D., jt. auth. see Abbott, Evelyn.

Mansfield, E. H. The Bending & Stretching of Plates. 2nd ed. (Illus.). (C). 1989. 79.95 (*0-521-33304-0*) Cambridge U Pr.

Mansfield, Edward D. The Legal Rights, Liabilities & Duties of Women. LC 78-72352. (Free Love in America Ser.). reprint ed. 28.50 (*0-404-60951-1*) AMS Pr.

— Memoirs of the Life & Services of Daniel Drake, M.D. 1993. reprint ed. lib. bdg. 89.00 (*0-7812-5386-1*) Rprt Serv.

— Memoirs of the Life & Services of Daniel Drake, M.D., Physician, Professor, & Author. LC 75-108. (Mid-American Frontier Ser.). 1975. reprint ed. 34.95 (*0-405-06875-1*) Ayer.

— Personal Memories: Social, Political, & Literary. LC 72-133527. (Select Bibliographies Reprint Ser.). 1977. reprint ed. 23.95 (*0-8369-5559-5*) Ayer.

— Personal Memories, Social, Political & Literary. LC 74-125707. (American Journalists Ser.). 1971. reprint ed. 35.95 (*0-405-01688-3*) Ayer.

— Personal Memories, Social, Political, & Literary, with Sketches of Many Noted People. (American Biography Ser.). 348p. 1991. reprint ed. lib. bdg. 79.00 (*0-7812-8264-0*) Rprt Serv.

— Power, Trade, & War. LC 93-13700. 1994. 35.00 (*0-691-03288-2*) Princeton U Pr.

Mansfield, Edwin. Applied Microeconomics. LC 92-47402. (C). 1993. text ed. 59.95 (*0-393-96431-0*) Norton.

— Basic Statistics: With Applications. (C). 1986. text ed. 44. 95 (*0-393-95393-9*); Instr's. manual & test item file. teacher ed, pap. text ed. write for info. (*0-393-95402-1*); Incl. problems, exercises & case studies. student ed, pap. text ed. 12.95 (*0-393-95396-3*) Norton.

— Economics: Principles, Problems, Decisions. (C). 1992. pap. text ed. 49.95 (*0-393-96230-X*) Norton.

— Economics: Principles, Problems, Decisions. (C). 1992. pap. text ed. 16.95 (*0-393-96172-9*) Norton.

— Economics: Principles, Problems, Decisions. 5th ed. (C). 1986. student ed 11.95 (*0-685-43273-4*) Norton.

— Economics: Principles, Problems, Decisions. 7th ed. (C). 1992. text ed. 54.95 (*0-393-96138-9*) Norton.

— Innovation, Technology & the Economy: The Selected Essays of Edwin Mansfield. LC 95-5533. (Economists of the Twentieth Century Ser.). 1995. write for info. (*1-85898-035-6*, Pub. by E Elgar Pub UK) Ashgate Pub Co.

— Intellectual Property Protection, Foreign Direct Investment, & Technology Transfer. LC 93-49386. (IFC Discussion Paper Ser.: No. 19). 54p. 1994. write for info. (*0-8213-2759-3*) World Bank.

— Leading Economic Controversies of 1995. 150p. (C). 1995. pap. text ed. 9.95 (*0-393-96711-5*) Norton.

— Managerial Economics. (Illus.). (C). 1990. disk write for info. (*0-318-65466-0*) Norton.

— Managerial Economics. (C). 1992. pap. text ed. 14.95 (*0-393-96286-5*) Norton.

— Managerial Economics. (C). 1993. pap. text ed. write for info. (*0-393-96285-7*) Norton.

— Managerial Economics. LC 95-1115. (C). 1996. text ed. write for info. (*0-393-96775-1*) Norton.

— Managerial Economics. 2nd ed. (C). 1992. text ed. 59.95 (*0-393-96284-9*) Norton.

— Microeconomics: Theory - Applications. 8th ed. LC 92-43629. (C). 1993. text ed. 59.95 (*0-393-96417-5*) Norton.

— Microeconomics: Theory & Applications. (C). 1985. pap. text ed. 13.95 (*0-393-95403-X*); Case studies & review exercises. write for info. (*0-318-58339-9*) Norton.

— Microeconomics: Theory & Applications. 6th ed. (C). 1988. Shorter ed. text ed. 44.45 (*0-393-95637-7*) Norton.

— Microeconomics: Theory & Applications. 7th ed. (Illus.). (C). 1990. text ed. 52.95 (*0-393-96036-6*) Norton.

— Microeconomics: Theory & Applications. 7th ed. (Illus.). (C). 1991. disk write for info. (*0-318-68251-6*) Norton.

— MYSTAT Software to Accompany Managerial Economics. (Illus.). (C). 1991. write for info. (*0-318-68574-4*) Norton.

— Principles of Macroeconomics. (C). 1989. disk write for info. (*0-318-63403-1*) Norton.

— Principles of Macroeconomics. (Illus.). (C). 1992. pap. text ed. 12.95 (*0-393-96174-5*) Norton.

— Principles of Macroeconomics. 7th ed. (Illus.). (C). 1992. pap. text ed. 39.95 (*0-393-96173-7*) Norton.

— Principles of Macroeconomics: Reading Issues & Cases. 4th ed. (C). 1983. pap. text ed. 5.95 (*0-393-95340-8*) Norton.

— Principles of Microeconomics. 1980. trans. write for info. (*0-318-54693-0*); write for info. (*0-318-54692-2*) Norton.

— Principles of Microeconomics. (C). 1986. teacher ed write for info. (*0-318-59752-7*); teacher ed write for info. (*0-318-59753-5*) Norton.

— Principles of Microeconomics. (Illus.). (C). 1992. student ed, pap. text ed. 12.95 (*0-393-96176-1*) Norton.

— Principles of Microeconomics. (Illus.). (C). 1992. Computer test item file avail. student ed write for info. (*0-393-96179-6*) Norton.

— Principles of Microeconomics. (Illus.). (C). 1992. student ed, pap. text ed. write for info. (*0-393-96178-8*) Norton.

— Principles of Microeconomics. 6th ed. (C). 1989. teacher ed write for info. (*0-318-63396-5*); trans. write for info. (*0-318-63399-X*); disk write for info. (*0-318-63398-1*); write for info. (*0-318-63397-3*) Norton.

— Principles of Microeconomics. 7th ed. (Illus.). (C). 1992. pap. text ed. 39.95 (*0-393-96175-3*) Norton.

— Principles of Microeconomics: Readings, Issues & Cases. 4th ed. (C). 1983. teacher ed write for info. (*0-318-56814-4*); pap. text ed. 5.95 (*0-393-95331-9*) Norton.

— Statistics for Business & Economics. (C). 1987. Test item file. pap. text ed. write for info. (*0-393-95575-3*) Norton.

— Statistics for Business & Economics: Methods & Applications. 900p. (C). 1991. pap. text ed. write for info. (*0-393-96082-X*) Norton.

— Statistics for Business & Economics: Methods & Applications. 5th ed. LC 93-7702. (C). 1994. pap. text ed. 57.95 (*0-393-96460-4*) Norton.

— Statistics for Business & Economics: Problems, Exercises, & Case Studies. 5th ed. LC 93-22745. (C). 1994. pap. text ed. 18.95 (*0-393-96488-4*) Norton.

Mansfield, Edwin, ed. Managerial Economics & Operations Research: Techniques, Applications, Cases. 5th ed. 500p. (C). 1987. pap. text ed. 14.95 (*0-393-95590-7*) Norton.

Mansfield, Edwin & Behravesh, Nariman. Economics U. S. A. (C). 1989. disk write for info. (*0-318-63778-2*) Norton.

— Economics U. S. A. (Illus.). (C). 1992. student ed, pap. text ed. 18.95 (*0-393-96160-5*); student ed, pap. text ed. 16.95 (*0-393-96159-1*); student ed write for info. (*0-393-96163-X*) Norton.

— Economics U. S. A. (Illus.). (C). 1992. pap. text ed. write for info. (*0-393-96161-3*); student ed, pap. text ed. write for info. (*0-393-96162-1*) Norton.

— Economics U. S. A. 2nd ed. (C). 1989. trans. write for info. (*0-318-63779-0*) Norton.

— Economics U. S. A. 3rd ed. (Illus.). (C). 1992. pap. text ed. 42.95 (*0-393-96146-X*) Norton.

— Economics U. S. A. 4th ed. (C). 1995. pap. text ed. 39. 95x (*0-393-96641-0*) Norton.

— Economics U.S.A, Telecourse review guide. 4th ed. (C). 1995. pap. text ed. 19.95 (*0-393-96670-4*) Norton.

— Economics U.S.A, Test item file. (C). 1995. pap. text ed. write for info. (*0-393-96672-0*) Norton.

— Economics U.S.A, Text review guide. 4th ed. (C). 1995. pap. text ed. 17.95 (*0-393-96648-8*) Norton.

Mansfield, Edwin & Mansfield, Elizabeth, eds. The Economics of Technical Change. (International Library of Critical Writings in Business History: Vol. 31). (Illus.). 500p. 1993. 159.95 (*1-85278-783-X*, Pub. by E Elgar Pub UK) Ashgate Pub Co.

Mansfield, Edwin, jt. auth. see Kelley, Elizabeth S.

Mansfield, Edwin, ed. see Teubal, Morris.

Mansfield, Elisabeth. Lady Lu. large type ed. LC 90-44228. 302p. 1990. reprint ed. bds. 18.95 (*1-56054-050-8*) Thorndike Pr.

Mansfield, Elizabeth. The Accidental Romance. 208p. 1994. pap. text ed. 3.99 (*0-515-11481-2*) Jove Pubns.

— The Bartered Bride. 224p. 1994. pap. text ed. 4.50 (*0-515-11521-5*) Jove Pubns.

— Bartered Bride. 5p. 1994. pap. 3.99 (*0-515-81152-1*) Jove Pubns.

— A Brilliant Mismatch. 224p. 1991. pap. text ed. 4.50 (*0-515-10545-7*) Jove Pubns.

— Christmas Kiss. 1991. pap. 4.50 (*0-515-10520-1*) Jove Pubns.

— The Counterfeit Husband. 224p. 1993. pap. 3.99 (*0-515-09010-7*) Jove Pubns.

— The Fifth Kiss. large type ed. LC 94-28138. 341p. 1994. pap. 17.95 (*0-8161-7471-7*) Hall.

— The Frost Fair. 224p. 1987. pap. 3.99 (*0-515-08961-3*) Jove Pubns.

— Her Heart's Captain. 192p. 1993. pap. 3.99 (*0-515-09060-3*) Jove Pubns.

M

— Her Man of Affairs. 224p. 1986. pap. 3.99 (*0-515-08799-8*) Jove Pubns.
— The Lady Disguised. large type ed. LC 90-10775. 358p. 1990. bds. 18.95 (*0-89621-972-0*) Thorndike Pr.
— The Magnificent Masquerade. 224p. 1994. pap. 3.99 (*0-515-11460-X*) Jove Pubns.
— The Magnificent Masquerade. large type ed. LC 90-35643. 393p. 1990. reprint ed. bds. 18.95 (*1-56054-009-5*) Thorndike Pr.
— Mother's Choice. 208p. (Orig.). 1994. pap. 3.99 (*0-515-11386-7*) Jove Pubns.
— My Lord Murderer. 256p. 1992. pap. text ed. 4.50 (*0-515-08743-2*) Jove Pubns.
— Passing Fancies. 224p. (Orig.). 1993. pap. 3.99 (*0-515-09175-8*) Jove Pubns.
— Poor Caroline. 224p. (Orig.). Date not set. pap. text ed. 5.99 (*0-515-11659-9*) Jove Pubns.
— A Prior Engagement. 240p. 1990. pap. text ed. 4.50 (*0-515-10398-5*) Jove Pubns.
— A Regency Charade. 224p. 1987. pap. 3.99 (*0-515-08916-8*) Jove Pubns.
— The Reluctant Flirt. 208p. 1987. pap. 3.99 (*0-515-08937-0*) Jove Pubns.
— Winter Wonderland. 1993. pap. 3.99 (*0-515-11234-8*) Jove Pubns.
*__Mansfield, Elizabeth, ed.__ The Trespasser. 288p. 1995. 9.95 (*0-14-018800-2*, Penguin Classics) Viking Penguin.
Mansfield, Elizabeth, ed. see Lawrence, D. H.
Mansfield, Elizabeth, jt. ed. see Mansfield, Edwin.
Mansfield, F. & Bertocci, U., eds. Electrochemical Corrosion Testing - STP 727. 411p. 1981. 36.00 (*0-8031-0704-8*, 04-727000-27) ASTM.
Mansfield, F., jt. auth. see Wilson, F.
Mansfield, H. O. Norfolk Churches: Their Foundations, Architecture & Furnishings. 208p. 1994. 30.00 (*0-900963-57-3*, Pub. by T Dalton UK) St Mut.
Mansfield, H. P. Key to Understanding the Scriptures. 1989. pap. 4.95 (*0-317-02705-0*, Pub. by Logos Pubns AT) Majco.
Mansfield, Harold. Billion Dollar Battle: The Story Behind the "Impossible" 727 Project. Gilbert, James B., ed. LC 79-7283. (Flight: Its First Seventy-Five Years Ser.). (Illus.). 1980. reprint ed. lib. bdg. 19.95 (*0-405-12192-X*) Ayer.
— Vision: A Saga of the Sky. Gilbert, James B., ed. LC 79-7284. (Flight: Its First Seventy-Five Years Ser.). (Illus.). 1980. reprint ed. lib. bdg. 37.95 (*0-405-12193-8*) Ayer.
Mansfield, Harvey C. America's Constitutional Soul. LC 90-19210. (Series in Constitutional Thought). 224p. 1991. 35.00 (*0-8018-4114-3*) Johns Hopkins.
Mansfield, Harvey C., Jr. America's Constitutional Soul. (Series in Constitutional Thought). 224p. 1993. reprint ed. pap. 13.95 (*0-8018-4634-X*) Johns Hopkins.
Mansfield, Harvey C. Illustrations of Presidential Management: Johnson's Cost Reduction & Tax Increase Campaigns. (Administrative History of the Johnson Presidency Ser.). 75p. 1988. 6.00 (*0-89940-307-7*) LBJ Sch Pub Aff.
— Lake Cargo Coal Rate Controversy. LC 73-76629. (Columbia University. Studies in the Social Sciences: No. 373). reprint ed. 22.50 (*0-404-51373-5*) AMS Pr.
— Responsible Citizenship: Ancient & Modern. LC 94-41697. (Kritikos Professorship in the Humanities Ser.). 1994. 5.00 (*0-87114-228-7*) U of Oreg Bks.
— The Spirit of Liberalism. LC 78-7809. 144p. reprint ed. pap. 41.10 (*0-7837-5936-3*, 2045735) Bks Demand.
Mansfield, Harvey C., Jr. Taming the Prince: The Ambivalence of Modern Executive Power. 310p. 1989. text ed. 29.95 (*0-02-919980-8*) Free Pr.
— Taming the Prince: The Ambivalence of Modern Executive Power. LC 92-31982. 384p. 1993. reprint ed. pap. 16.95 (*0-8018-4589-0*) Johns Hopkins.
Mansfield, Harvey C., Jr., ed. see Burke, Edmund E.
Mansfield, Harvey C., Jr., ed. see Jefferson, Thomas.
Mansfield, Harvey C., Jr., tr. see Machiavelli, Niccolo.
Mansfield, Helene. Contessa. 1984. pap. 3.95 (*0-8217-1336-1*) Zebra.
Mansfield, Howard. Cosmopolis: Yesterday's Cities of the Future. LC 89-25159. 172p. (C). 1990. 10.00 (*0-88285-131-4*) Ctr Urban Pol Res.
— In the Memory House. 288p. 1993. 19.95 (*1-55591-162-5*) Fulcrum Pub.
— In the Memory House. 288p. 1995. pap. 12.95 (*1-55591-247-8*) Fulcrum Pub.
Mansfield, J. A Collector's Guide to Modern Australian Ceramics. (Illus.). 128p. 1989. text ed. 60.00 (*0-947131-09-4*) Gordon & Breach.
*__Mansfield, Janet.__ Contemporary Ceramic Art in Australia & New Zealand. 1995. 60.00 (*976-8097-32-9*) IPG Chicago.
— Salt-Glaze Ceramics. 144p. 1992. 39.95 (*0-8019-8344-4*) Chilton.
Mansfield, John M. Parasitic Diseases: Immunology, Vol. 1. 336p. 1981. 140.00 (*0-8247-1409-1*) Dekker.
Mansfield, K., jt. ed. see Murry, J. M.
Mansfield, Katherine. Bliss, & Other Short Stories. 1977. 23.95 (*0-8369-4240-X*, 6051) Ayer.
— The Collected Letters of Katherine Mansfield, Vol. III: 1919-1920. O'Sullivan, Vincent & Scott, Margaret, eds. 328p. 1993. 55.00 (*0-19-812615-8*) OUP.
— The Doll's House. (Creative's Collection of Classic Short Stories Ser.). 32p. (J). (gr. 4 up). 1986. lib. bdg. 13.95 (*0-88682-056-1*) Creative Ed.
— The Garden Party. (Creative Short Stories Ser.). (YA). (gr. 4-12). 1989. 13.95 (*0-88682-342-0*, 97216-098) Creative Ed.
— The Garden Party: Katherine Mansfield's New Zealand Stories. (Illus.). 188p. (C). 1988. 40.00 (*0-941533-38-7*) New Amsterdam Bks.
— The Garden Party & Other Stories. 304p. 1991. 15.00 (*0-679-40539-9*, Everymans Lib) Knopf.
— In a German Pension. 128p. 1990. mass mkt. 9.95 (*0-14-018149-0*, Penguin Classics) Viking Penguin.
— In a German Pension: Thirteen Stories. LC 95-1144. (Thrifty Editions). 1995. 1.00 (*0-486-28719-X*) Dover.
— Journal. (FRE.). 1983. pap. 19.95 (*0-7859-4193-2*) Fr & Eur.
— Memories of LM. (Illus.). 240p. 1990. pap. 13.95 (*0-86068-745-7*, Pub. by Virago Pr UK) Trafalgar.
— Novels & Novelists. reprint ed. 49.00 (*0-403-02290-8*) Somerset Pub.
— Stories by Katherine Mansfield. LC 90-50474. 368p. 1991. pap. 12.00 (*0-679-73374-4*, Vin) Random.
Mansfield, Kenneth. Coarse Fishing for Beginners. (Illus.). 160p. (Orig.). 1974. pap. 14.95 (*0-572-01176-8*) Trans-Atl Phila.
Mansfield, Luther, ed. see Melville, Herman.
Mansfield, Lynda & Waldmann, Christopher H. Don't Touch My Heart: Helping Parents Deal with the Pain of an Unattached Child. LC 94-5508. (Illus.). 128p. (Orig.). 1994. pap. 10.00 (*0-89109-820-8*) Pinon Press.
Mansfield, Lyndon E. Primer of Immunology. 1991. 25.00 (*0-07-039919-0*) McGraw.
Mansfield, M., tr. see Di Coppo, Giovanni.
*__Mansfield-Marcoux, Michael J.__ A New Life for Mark Benson. 290p. 1995. pap. 8.95 (*0-7610-0023-2*) NW Pub.
Mansfield, Margaret. Black Like Me Notes. 1971. pap. 4.50 (*0-8220-0245-0*) Cliffs.
Mansfield, Mary C. The Humiliation of Sinners: Public Penance in Thirteenth-Century France. (Illus.). 336p. 1994. 37.95 (*0-8014-2939-0*) Cornell U Pr.
Mansfield, Maynard J. Intermediate Real Analysis. LC 78-15379. 222p. 1979. reprint ed. lib. bdg. 20.50 (*0-88275-712-1*) Krieger.
— Introduction to Topology. LC 63-2175. 126p. 1972. reprint ed. 15.50 (*0-88275-042-9*) Krieger.
Mansfield, Maynard J., jt. ed. see Barrett, Robert A.
*__Mansfield, Michael.__ Presumed Guilty: The British Legal System Exposed. 304p. 1995. pap. 13.95 (*0-7493-1253-X*, Pub. by Mandarin Bks UK) Trafalgar.
Mansfield, Michael W., jt. ed. see Nimmo, Dan.
Mansfield, Niall. Window System: A User's Guide. 2nd ed. (C). 1995. pap. text ed. 10.00 (*0-201-54438-5*) Addison-Wesley.
— X Window System: An Overview. (C). 1993. pap. text ed. 26.95 (*0-201-56512-9*) Addison-Wesley.
Mansfield, P. & Hahn, E. L., eds. NMR Imaging: Recent Developments & Future Prospects. (Royal Society Discussion Volumes Ser.). (Illus.). 150p. (C). 1991. 64.95 (*0-521-40460-6*) Cambridge U Pr.
Mansfield, Patti G. As by a New Pentecost. 179p. 1992. pap. 9.95 (*0-940535-44-0*, UP 144) Franciscan U Pr.
— More of God. 220p. 1990. pap. 7.50 (*0-940535-32-7*, UP132) Franciscan U Pr.
— Proclaim His Marvelous Deeds: How to Give a Personal Testimony. 96p. (Orig.). 1987. pap. 3.75 (*0-940535-06-8*, UP107) Franciscan U Pr.
Mansfield, Peter. The Arabs. 1990. pap. 9.95 (*0-14-013574-X*, Penguin Bks) Viking Penguin.
— The Arabs. rev. ed. (Pelican Ser.). 528p. 1985. pap. 8.95 (*0-14-022561-7*, Penguin Bks) Viking Penguin.
— The Arabs. rev. ed. 560p. 1992. reprint ed. pap. 12.00 (*0-14-014768-3*, Penguin Bks) Viking Penguin.
— The Bates Method. (Alternative Health Ser.). (Illus.). 166p. (Orig.). 1994. pap. 12.95 (*0-8048-3003-7*) C E Tuttle.
— Flower Remedies. (Tuttle Alternative Health Ser.). (Illus.). 120p. (Orig.). 1995. pap. 14.95 (*0-8048-3005-3*) C E Tuttle.
— A History of the Middle East. 368p. 1992. pap. 13.95 (*0-14-016989-X*, Penguin Bks) Viking Penguin.
Mansfield, Phyllis K. Pregnancy for Older Women: Assessing the Medical Risks. LC 86-9440. 240p. 1986. text ed. 55.00 (*0-275-92184-0*, C2184, Praeger Pubs) Greenwood.
Mansfield, Richard. Desktop Publishing with WordPerfect 6. 1993. pap. 24.95 (*1-56604-049-3*) Ventana Pr.
— Desktop Publishing with WordPerfect 6 for Windows. (Illus.). 350p. 1994. pap. 24.95 (*1-56604-086-8*) Ventana Pr.
— Visual Guide to Visual Basic for Windows: The Illustrated, Plain-English Encyclopedia to the Windows Programming Language. 3rd ed. (Illus.). 1405p. 1995. pap. 29.95 (*0-318-72824-9*) Ventana Pr.
— The Visual Guide to Visual Basic for Windows: The Illustrated Plain-English Encyclopedia to the Windows Programming Language - for Version 3. 2nd ed. (Illus.). 1300p. 1993. 29.95 (*1-56604-063-9*) Ventana Pr.
— Visual Guide to Visual Basic 4.0 for Windows. 3rd ed. (Illus.). 1405p. 1995. disk, pap. 34.95 (*1-56604-192-9*) Ventana Pr.
— WordPerfect 5 Solutions. 126p. (Orig.). 1989. pap. 14.95 (*0-929307-04-6*) GP Pubns.
Mansfield, Richard & Brannon, Charles. The Windows 95 Book. (Illus.). 700p. 1995. disk 29.95 (*1-56604-154-6*) Ventana Pr.
*__Mansfield, Richard & Petroutsos, Evangelos.__ Visual BASIC Power Toolkit: Cutting-Edge Tools & Techniques for Programmers. LC 94-41205. 918p. 1994. audio, pap. 39.95 (*1-56604-190-2*) Ventana Pr.
— Visual Basic 4.0 Power Toolkit: Cutting-Edge Tools & Techniques for Power Programmers. 2nd ed. 950p. 1995. cd-rom 49.95 (*1-56604-263-1*) Ventana Pr.
— Windows 95 Power Toolkit. 600p. 1995. cd-rom 49.95 (*1-56604-319-0*) Ventana Pr.
Mansfield, Richard & Weitkamp, Galen. Recursive Aspects of Descriptive Set Theory. (Oxford Logic Guides Ser.). 1985. 22.50 (*0-19-503602-6*) OUP.
Mansfield, Richard H. Progress of the Breed: A History of U. S. Holsteins. Hastings, Robert H., ed. LC 85-60730. 350p. 1985. 34.95 (*0-9614711-0-7*) Holstein-Friesian.
Mansfield, Richard S. & Busse, Thomas V. The Psychology of Creativity & Discovery: Scientists & Their Work. LC 80-29219. 164p. 1981. 32.95 (*0-88229-653-1*) Nelson-Hall.
Mansfield, Roger. Company Strategy & Organizational Design. LC 85-25062. 192p. 1986. text ed. 32.50 (*0-312-15328-7*) St Martin.
Mansfield, Roger, ed. Frontiers of Management: Research & Practice. 240p. 1990. 67.50 (*0-415-04455-3*, A4013) Routledge.
Mansfield, Roger & Poole, Michael. International Perspectives on Management & Organization. 164p. 1981. text ed. 50.95 (*0-566-00469-0*) Ashgate Pub Co.
*__Mansfield, Ron.__ Compact Guide to Microsoft Office Professional. LC 94-68438. 1191p. 1994. pap. 29.99 (*0-7821-1604-3*) Sybex.
— Compact Guide to the Microsoft Office. LC 93-87701. 779p. 1994. pap. 29.99 (*0-7821-1483-0*) Sybex.
— DOS Quick & Easy Reference. LC 93-85945. 149p. 1993. 6.99 (*0-7821-1379-6*) Sybex.
— DOS 6.2 Quick & Easy. LC 94-66292. 205p. 1994. pap. 19.99 (*0-7821-1582-9*) Sybex.
— Mastering Word 6 for Windows. 2nd ed. LC 94-69306. 1994. pap. 29.99 (*0-7821-1639-6*) Sybex.
— Mastering Word 6 for Windows: Special Edition. LC 93-86591. 971p. 1993. 29.99 (*0-7821-1399-0*) Sybex.
— Microsoft Office for the Mac Compact Guide. 1994. pap. 29.99 (*0-7821-1394-X*) Sybex.
— Word for Windows Quick & Easy Reference. LC 93-87028. 150p. 1993. 6.99 (*0-7821-1380-X*) Sybex.
Mansfield, S., jt. auth. see Schlecter, R.
Mansfield, Scott. Engineering Design for Process Facilities. 300p. 1993. text ed. 48.00i (*0-07-040010-5*) McGraw.
Mansfield, Stephanie. The Richest Girl in the World. 480p. 1994. mass mkt. 4.99 (*1-55817-792-2*, Pinnacle NY) Windsor NY.
Mansfield, Stephen S. Princess Anne County & Virginia Beach: A Pictorial History. LC 88-30917. (Illus.). 224p. 1992. 24.95 (*0-89865-743-1*) Donning Co.
Mansfield, Steve. Photographing Airplanes. 1991. pap. 24.95 (*0-943231-43-4*) Howell Pr VA.
Mansfield, Sue, ed. see Mill, John Stuart.
*__Mansfield, Victor.__ Synchronicity, Science, & Soulmaking. 328p. 1995. pap. 17.95 (*0-8126-9304-3*) Open Court.
Mansfield, William L. California Real Estate Practice. 480p. 1994. text ed. 34.80 (*0-13-121187-0*) P-H.
Manshard, W. Die Staedte des Tropischen Afrika. (Urbanisierung der Erde Ser.: Vol. 1). (Illus.). 258p. (GER.). 1977. lib. bdg. 68.60 (*3-443-39070-6*, Pub. by Gebrueder Borntraeger GW) Lubrecht & Cramer.
Manshard, W. & Fischnich, O. E. Man & Environment. 108p. (C). 1975. pap. 23.00 (*0-08-019673-X*, Pergamon Pr) Elsevier.
Manshard, W., jt. auth. see Ruddle, K.
Mansheim, Gerald, jt. auth. see Gebhard, David.
Manshel, Lisa. Nap Time: The True Story of Sexual Abuse at a Suburban Day Care Center. 1991. mass mkt. 4.95 (*0-8217-3262-5*) Zebra.
*__Manship, Henry.__ History of Great Yarmouth, 2 vols., Set. Palmer, Charles J., ed. (Illus.). 823p. 1995. reprint ed. lib. bdg. 92.50 (*0-8328-4650-3*) Higginson Bk Co.
Mansingh, Surjit. India's Search for Power: Indira Gandhi's Foreign Policy, 1966-82. 1984. 29.95 (*0-8039-9475-3*) Sage.
Mansinha, L., ed. see NATO Advanced Study Institute Staff.
Mansion, Jean E. French Reference Grammar for Schools & Colleges. LC 72-98855. 247p. 1971. reprint ed. text ed. 59.75 (*0-8371-3125-1*, MAFG, Greenwood Pr) Greenwood.
— Harrap's New College French & English Dictionary. (ENG & FRE.). 39.95 (*0-317-45640-7*) Fr & Eur.
— Harrap's New Standard French & English Dictionary. (ENG & FRE.). 1980. 125.00 (*0-8288-0061-8*, M6310) Fr & Eur.
— Harrap's New Standard French & English Dictionary, Pt. 1: French to English, 2 vols. (ENG & FRE.). 125.00 (*0-317-45641-5*) Fr & Eur.
— Harrap's New Standard French & English Dictionary, Pt. 2: English to French, 2 vols. (ENG & FRE.). 125.00 (*0-317-45642-3*) Fr & Eur.
Mansir, A. Richard. How to Build Ship Models: A Beginner's Guide. (Moonraker Bks.). (Illus.). 64p. (Orig.). 1984. reprint ed. pap. 7.95 (*0-8168-0004-9*, 20004, TAB-Aero) TAB Bks.
— Quest for the Northeast Passage. (Sea Adventure Ser.). (Illus.). 112p. (Orig.). 1989. pap. 15.95 (*0-929834-01-1*) Kittiwake Pubns.
Manske, Fred A., Jr. Secrets of Effective Leadership: A Practical Guide to Success. LC 87-16870. (Illus.). 167p. 1988. 17.95 (*0-943703-00-X*); pap. 9.95 (*0-943703-01-8*) Leader Educ Dev.
— Secrets of Effective Leadership - A Practical Guide to Success. 2nd rev. ed. (Illus.). 210p. 1990. 19.95 (*0-943703-03-4*) Leader Educ Dev.
Manske, R. & Rodrigo, R. G., eds. The Alkaloids: Chemistry & Pharmacology, Vol. 20. (Serial Publication Ser.). 1982. text ed. 148.00 (*0-12-469520-5*) Acad Pr.
Manske, R. F. & Holmes, H. L., eds. The Alkaloids: Chemistry & Pharmacology, Vol. 21. (Serial Publication Ser.). 1983. text ed. 148.00 (*0-12-469521-3*) Acad Pr.
Manske, R. G., ed. The Alkaloids, Vol. 19: Chemistry & Physiology. 1981. text ed. 148.00 (*0-12-469519-1*) Acad Pr.
Manske, R. H., ed. The Alkaloids: Chemistry & Pharmacology, Vol 22. (Serial Publication Ser.). 1983. text ed. 148.00 (*0-12-469522-1*) Acad Pr.
Manske, R. H. & Rodrigo, R. G., eds. The Alkaloids: Chemistry & Physiology, Vol. 18. LC 50-5522. 1981. text ed. 170.00 (*0-12-469518-3*) Acad Pr.
Manske, R. H., ed. see Brossi, Arnold.
Manske, R. H., et al, eds. The Alkaloids: Chemistry & Physiology. write for info. (*0-318-50224-0*) Acad Pr.
Manske, Ron. A Polish Love Story. LC 79-84322. (Illus.). 144p. 1979. pap. 2.50 (*0-89221-060-5*) New Leaf.
Manski, Charles F. Analog Estimation Methods in Econometrics. (Monographs in Statistics & Applied Probability). 250p. 1988. text ed. 45.00 (*0-412-01141-7*, 9961, Chap & Hall NY) Chapman & Hall.
— Identification Problems in the Social Sciences. LC 94-29313. (Illus.). 184p. (C). 1995. text ed. 29.95 (*0-674-44283-0*, MANIDE) HUP.
Manski, Charles F. & Garfinkel, Irwin, eds. Evaluating Welfare & Training Programs. (Illus.). 364p. (C). 1992. 45.00 (*0-674-27017-7*) HUP.
Manski, Charles F. & Wise, David A. College Choice in America. (Illus.). 240p. 1983. 32.00 (*0-674-14125-3*) HUP.
Mansmann, Patricia A. & Neuhausel, Patricia A. Life after Survival: A Therapeutic Approach for Adult Children of Alcoholics. (Illus.). 56p. (YA). (gr. 9 up). 1986. pap. text ed. 6.95 (*0-940967-00-6*) Genesis Pub PA.
— Life after Survival: A Therapeutic Approach for Adult Children of Alcoholics. 2nd rev. ed. (Illus.). 88p. 1989. pap. text ed. 6.95 (*0-940967-01-4*) Genesis Pub PA.
Manso, Gilbert, jt. auth. see Whalen, Freda.
Manso, Peter. Brando: The Biography. (Illus.). 1172p. 1994. 29.95 (*0-7868-6063-4*) Hyperion.
— Brando: The Biography. (Illus.). 1172p. 1995. pap. 15.95 (*0-7868-8128-3*) Hyperion.
Manson, Ainslie. A Dog Came, Too: A True Story. LC 91-44891. (Illus.). 32p. (J). (gr. 1-5). 1993. text ed. 13.95 (*0-689-50567-1*, McElderry) S&S Childrens.
Manson-Bahr & Bell. Manson's Tropical Diseases. 19th ed. 960p. 1988. text ed. 155.00 (*0-7020-1187-8*) Saunders.
*__Manson, C. J., ed.__ Directory of Geoscience Libraries, U. S. & Canada. 4th ed. 1992. 35.00 (*0-934485-20-8*) Geosci Info.
Manson, Christopher. A Farmyard Song. LC 91-46238. (Illus.). 32p. (J). (gr. k). 1992. 14.95 (*1-55858-169-3*); lib. bdg. 14.88 (*1-55858-170-7*) North-South Bks NYC.
— Maze: A Riddle in Words & Pictures. (Illus.). 96p. 1985. pap. 8.95 (*0-8050-1088-2*, Owl) H Holt & Co.
— The Tree in the Wood. LC 92-23524. (Illus.). 32p. (J). (gr. k-3). 1994. pap. 5.95 (*1-55858-320-3*) North-South Bks NYC.
Manson, Christopher, illus. Good King Wenceslas. LC 94-17443. (J). 1994. 14.95 (*1-55858-321-1*); lib. bdg. 14.88 (*1-55858-322-X*) North-South Bks NYC.
Manson, Christopher, illus. & adapt. The Tree in the Wood: An Old Nursery Song. LC 92-23524. 32p. (J). (gr. k-3). 1993. 14.95 (*1-55858-192-8*); lib. bdg. 14.88 (*1-55858-193-6*) North-South Bks NYC.
Manson, Cynthia, ed. Crime a La Carte. 256p. (Orig.). 1994. pap. 4.99 (*0-451-18052-6*, Sig) NAL-Dutton.
— Death on the Verandah. 304p. 1995. pap. text ed. 4.99 (*0-425-14836-X*, Prime Crime) Berkley Pub.
— Death on the Verandah: Mystery Stories of the South. 288p. 1994. 19.95 (*0-7867-0055-6*) Carroll & Graf.
— Grifters & Swindlers. 240p. 1993. 18.95 (*0-88184-931-6*) Carroll & Graf.
— Mystery Cats Three: More Feline Felonies by Lilian Jackson Braun, Patricia Highsmith, Edward D. Hoch, & 14 Others. 256p. (Orig.). 1995. pap. 4.99 (*0-451-18293-6*, Sig) NAL-Dutton.
— Women of Mystery: Stories from Ellery Queen's Mystery Magazine & Alfred Hitchcock's Mystery Magazine, Vol. II. 352p. 1994. 21.95 (*0-7867-0140-4*) Carroll & Graf.
Manson, Cynthia & Ardai, Charles, eds. FutureCrime: An Anthology of the Shape of Crime to Come. LC 91-55185. 336p. 1992. 21.95 (*1-55611-312-9*) D I Fine.
— New England Crime Chowder. LC 92-52741. 250p. 1992. pap. 11.95 (*1-55882-127-9*, Lib Crime Classics) Intl Polygonics.
*__Manson, Cynthia & Scarborough, Constance, eds.__ The Haunted Hour. 256p. (Orig.). 1995. pap. 4.99 (*0-425-15010-0*, Prime Crime) Berkley Pub.
Manson, Cynthia & Stern, Adam, eds. Silver Screams: Murder Goes Hollywood. LC 94-19561. 1994. 8.95 (*0-681-00753-2*) Longmeadow Pr.
Manson, Cynthia, jt. ed. see Jordan, Cathleen.
Manson, Dan W., ed. Alkaline Papermaking: A TAPPI Press Anthology of Published Papers, 1982-1992. LC 92-28279. 1992. 148.00 (*0-89852-271-4*, 0101R204) TAPPI.
Manson, Dan W., ed. see Technical Associaton of the Pulp & Paper Industry Staff.
Manson, Frank A. The Adventures of Prince Albert & the Royal Dinosaurs. (Prince Albert Ser.: No. 1). (Illus.). 144p. (J). (gr. 2-7). 1990. 11.95 (*0-918339-17-0*) Vandamere.
Manson, Frank A., jt. auth. see Cagle, Malcolm W.
Manson, G., jt. auth. see Cherryholmes, C.
Manson, Gary A. & Ridd, Merrill K. New Perspectives on Geographic Education: Putting Theory into Practice. 224p. 1977. per. 16.95 (*0-8403-1782-4*) Kendall-Hunt.
Manson, Grant. Frank Lloyd Wright to 1910: The First Golden Age. 1958. pap. 29.95 (*0-442-26130-6*) Van Nos Reinhold.
Manson-Hing, Lincoln R. Fundamentals of Dental Radiography. 3rd ed. LC 89-7971. (Illus.). 269p. 1989. pap. text ed. 39.50 (*0-8121-1253-9*) Williams & Wilkins.
Manson, J. D. Outline of Periodontics. 2nd ed. (Dental Practitioners' Handbook Ser.: No. 33). (Illus.). 207p. 1989. pap. text ed. 55.00 (*0-7236-1763-5*, Pub. by John Wright UK) Buttrwrth-Heinemann.
*__Manson, J. D. & Eley, B. M.__ Outline of Periodontics. 3rd ed. LC 95-7449. 1995. write for info. (*0-7236-1018-5*) Wright UK.
*__Manson, Jane.__ Tales from the Cryptkeeper. (Illus.). (J). (gr. 1-4). 1995. pap. 3.50 (*0-590-25088-4*) Scholastic Inc.

M

An Asterisk (*) at the beginning of an entry indicates that the title is appearing in BIP for the first time.

Manson, Janet M. Diplomatic Ramifications of Unrestricted Submarine Warfare, 1939-1941. LC 90-34130. (Contributions in Military Studies: No. 104). 326p. 1990. text ed. 55.00 (*0-313-26894-0*, MGC, Greenwood Pr) Greenwood.

***Manson, JoAnn E., et al, eds.** Prevention of Myocardial Infarction. (Illus.). 416p. 1995. 65.00 (*0-19-508582-5*) OUP.

Manson, John A., jt. auth. see Hertzberg, Richard W.

Manson, Lionel A., jt. ed. see Kates, Morris.

Manson, Margaret M., ed. Immunochemical Protocols. LC 91-41416. (Methods in Molecular Biology Ser.: Vol. 10). (Illus.). 496p. 1992. 89.50 (*0-89603-204-3*); spiral bd. 69. 50 (*0-89603-270-1*) Humana.

Manson, Marsden. The Yellow Peril in Action: A Possible Chapter in History. (Imaginary Wars & Battles Ser.: No. 2). 58p. Date not set. lib. bdg. write for info. (*0-89370-356-7*); pap. write for info. (*0-89370-456-3*) Borgo Pr.

Manson, Morse P., jt. auth. see Geist, Harold.

Manson, S., jt. auth. see Gray, I. H.

Manson, Spero M., et al, eds. Psychosocial Research on American Indian & Alaska Native Youth: An Indexed Guide to Recent Dissertations. LC 84-6583. (Bibliographies & Indexes in Psychology Ser.: No. 1). (Illus.). viii, 228p. 1984. text ed. 59.95 (*0-313-23991-6*, MPY/) Greenwood.

Manson, T. W. A Companion to the Bible. 2nd ed. Rowley, H. H., ed. 592p. 1963. pap. 31.95 (*0-567-02197-1*, Pub. by T & T Clark UK) Bks Intl VA.

Manson, Veronica. International Employee Stock Ownership Plans (ESOPS) for Multinational Corporations. (Illus.). 59p. (Orig.). 1993. pap. 25.00 (*0-926902-24-5*) NCEO.

Manson, William. RIDDLES OF EROS: Exploring, Sex, Psyche & Culture. LC 93-38164. 128p. (Orig.). (C). 1994. lib. bdg. 39.50 (*0-8191-9369-0*); pap. text ed. 19. 50 (*0-8191-9370-4*) U Pr of Amer.

Manson, William C. The Psychodynamics of Culture: Abram Kardiner & Neo-Freudian Anthropology. LC 88-17778. (Contributions to the Study of Anthropology Ser.: No. 3). 162p. 1988. text ed. 49.95 (*0-313-26267-5*, MDY/, Greenwood Pr) Greenwood.

Manson, William R. Will You Murder Your African American Children? A Challenge to Parental Caregivers. (Illus.). 672p. 1994. pap. 8.95 (*0-8059-3560-6*) Dorrance.

Mansoor, Ali M., jt. auth. see Hemming, Richard.

Mansoor, Christine. The Scandal of the Century: The Mansoor Amarna Expose. 1995. 19.95 (*0-8062-4976-5*) Carlton.

Mansoor, Menahem. Biblical Hebrew Step by Step: A Significant Breakthrough for Learning Biblical Hebrew. 1978. pap. 13.99 (*0-8010-6041-9*); audio 7.99 (*0-8010-6074-5*) Baker Bk.

— Biblical Hebrew Step by Step II: Readings from the Book of Genesis. 230p. (Orig.). (C). 1984. pap. 13.99 (*0-8010-6151-2*); audio 7.99 (*0-8010-6198-9*) Baker Bk.

— Contemporary Hebrew. LC 75-1813. 1976. pap. text ed. 12.95x (*0-87441-251-X*) Behrman.

— Easy Hebrew Phrase Book: Over 770 Basic Phrases for Every Day Use. LC 94-43467. 1995. pap. text ed. write for info. (*0-486-28556-1*) Dover.

— Jewish History & Thought: An Introduction. 591p. 1992. 39.50 (*0-88125-403-7*, 91-34985); pap. 19.95 (*0-88125-404-5*) Ktav.

— Key to Biblical Hebrew Step by Step, No. 1. 1978. pap. 9.99 (*0-8010-6100-8*) Baker Bk.

— Modern Hebrew Literature Reader for Advanced Students, 2 vols, 1. 1971. 16.95 (*0-87068-579-1*) Ktav.

— Modern Hebrew Literature Reader for Advanced Students, 2 vols, 2. 1971. 16.95 (*0-685-02918-2*) Ktav.

Mansoor, Menahem, ed. see Pakuda, Bahya I.

Mansoor, Menham. Key to the Biblical Hebrew, No. 2. 1985. 7.99 (*0-8010-6182-2*) Baker Bk.

Mansoori, G. A., jt. ed. see Haile, J. M.

Mansoori, G. Ali. Thermodynamics: The Application of Classical & Statistical Thermodynamics to the Prediction of Equilibrium Properties. (Advances in Thermodynamics Ser.: Vol. 8). 300p. 1991. 41.00 (*0-8448-1681-7*, Crane Russak) Taylor & Francis.

Mansoori, G. Ali & Chorn, Larry, eds. C Seven Plus Fraction Characterization. (Advances in Thermodynamics Ser.). (Illus.). 240p. (C). 1989. text ed. 83.00 (*0-8448-1565-9*) Taylor & Francis.

Mansoori, G. Ali & Matteoli, Enrico, eds. Fluctuation Theory of Mixtures, Vol. 2. (Advances in Thermodynamics Ser.: Vol. 2). 350p. 1990. 83.00 (*0-8448-1630-2*, Crane Russak) Taylor & Francis.

Mansour. Pesticide Prediction in Soils, Plants, & Aquatic Systems. 1993. 79.95 (*0-87371-616-7*, TD879) Lewis Pubs.

***Mansour, Awad & Rumman, Ali.** A Journey to the World of Computers: A Computer Reader for Kids. Dabbour, Mohammed M., tr. LC 94-71602. (Illus.). 48p. (J). (gr. 1-3). 1995. 14.95 (*1-884187-06-4*) AMICA Pub Hse.

Mansour, Camille. Beyond Alliance: Israel in U. S. Foreign Policy. LC 93-28046. 1994. 37.50 (*0-231-08492-7*) Col U Pr.

— Beyond Alliance: Israel in U. S. Foreign Policy. 340p. 1994. 37.50 (*0-614-02727-6*) Inst Palestine.

Mansour, Camille, jt. ed. see Khalidi, Rashid.

Mansour, Fawzy. The Arab World: Nation, State & Democracy. Wolfers, Michael, tr. LC 90-47485. (Studies in African Political Economy). 176p. (C). 1992. text ed. 17.50 (*0-86232-884-5*, Pub. by Zed Books UK); pap. 17. 50 (*0-86232-885-3*, Pub. by Zed Books UK) Humanities.

Mansour, Gerda. Multilingualism & Nation Building. LC 92-31458. (Multilingual Matters Ser.: No. 91). 1993. 74.00 (*1-85359-175-0*, Pub. by Multilingual Matters UK); pap. 24.95 (*1-85359-174-2*, Pub. by Multilingual Matters UK) Taylor & Francis.

Mansour, Joyce. Cries & Claws: Poetry by Joyce Mansour. Pallister, Jan, tr. 31p. 1987. 5.00 (*0-934477-00-0*) Edits Autrui.

— Flash Card. Beach, Mary, tr. LC 77-19313. (FRE.). 1978. pap. 5.00x (*0-916156-33-8*) Cherry Valley.

— Screams. Gavronsky, Serge, tr. 100p. (Orig.). 1995. pap. 10.00 (*0-942996-25-9*) Post Apollo Pr.

Mansour, M., jt. ed. see Schweitzer, G. E.

Mansour, M., et al, eds. Robustness of Dynamic Systems with Parameter Uncertainties. LC 92-27728. (Monte Verita Ser.). ix, 315p. 1992. 73.50 (*0-8176-2791-X*) Birkhauser.

Mansour, Mansour H. The Maliki School of Law, Spread & Domination in North & West Africa, 8th-14th Centuries. 350p. 1995. 64.95 (*1-880921-81-2*); pap. 44.95 (*1-880921-80-4*) Austin & Winfield.

Mansour, Muneer. I Escaped From Them. 312p. (ARA.). 1992. pap. 15.00 (*0-9631952-0-4*) Katchi Pub.

Mansouri, F. & Scanio, J. J. Quantum Gravity & Beyond: Essays in Honor of Louis Witten on His Retirement. 392p. 1993. text ed. 116.00 (*981-02-1290-9*) World Scientific Pub.

Mansourian, B., jt. ed. see Davies, M.

Manspeaker, Nancy. Jonathan Edwards: Bibliographical Synopses. LC 81-9491. (Studies in American Religion: Vol. 3). (Illus.). xviii, 278p. 1981. lib. bdg. 89.95 (*0-88946-907-5*) E Mellen.

Manspeizer, W., ed. Triassic-Jurassic Rifting: Continental Breakup & the Origin of the Atlantic Passive Margins, 2 vols. (Developments in Geotectonics Ser.: No. 22). 1038p. 1989. 287.25 (*0-444-42903-4*) Elsevier.

Mansson, Margret, jt. ed. see Sunner, Stig.

Mansson, Sven-Axel. Cultural Conflict & the Swedish Sexual Myth: The Male Immigrant's Encounter with Swedish Sexual & Cohabitation Culture. 246p. (C). 1993. pap. text ed. 19.95 (*0-935016-52-X*, Hanover Hse) Excelsior Music Pub Co.

— Cultural Conflict & the Swedish Sexual Myth: The Male Immigrant's Encounter with Swedish Sexual & Cohabitation Culture. LC 93-10324. (Contributions in Sociology Ser.: No. 107). 248p. 1993. text ed. 55.00 (*0-313-28920-4*, GM8920, Greenwood Pr) Greenwood.

Manstavicius, E. & Schweiger, F., eds. Analytic & Probabilistic Methods in Number Theory. (New Trends in Probability & Statistics Ser.: No. 2). 400p. 1992. 225. 00 (*90-6764-094-8*) Coronet Bks.

Manstead, Antony, jt. ed. see Wagner, Hugh.

Manstead, Antony S. Emotion in Social Life: A Special Issue on Cognition & Emotion, Vol. 5, Issues 5 & 6. 128p. 1991. text ed. 37.50 (*0-86377-174-2*) L Erlbaum Assocs.

Manstead, Antony S. & Hewstone, MIles, eds. The Blackwell Encyclopedia of Social Psychology. (Illus.). (C). 1994. text ed. 125.00 (*0-631-18146-6*) Blackwell Pubs.

Manstead, S. R., jt. ed. see Semin, Gun R.

Manston, Peter B. Manston's Flea Markets, Antique Fairs & Auctions of Britain. LC 87-16221. (Illus.). 286p. (Orig.). 1987. pap. 9.95 (*0-931367-10-7*) Travel Keys.

— Manston's Flea Markets, Antique Fairs & Auctions of France. LC 86-30909. (Manston's Travel Key Guide Ser.). (Illus.). 196p. 1987. 9.95 (*0-931367-06-9*) Travel Keys.

— Manston's Flea Markets, Antique Fairs & Auctions of Germany. LC 86-30908. (Illus.). 224p. 1987. pap. 9.95 (*0-931367-08-5*) Travel Keys.

— Manston's Italy. (Illus.). 352p. 1990. pap. 10.95 (*0-931367-12-3*) Travel Keys.

— Manston's Travel Key Britain. LC 89-4488. (Illus.). 384p. (Orig.). 1989. pap. 9.95 (*0-931367-11-5*) Travel Keys.

Mansukhana, Gobind Sigh. Maharaja Ranjit Singh. (Illus.). 1982. 7.25 (*0-89744-247-4*) Auromere.

Mansukhani, G. S. Indian Classical Music & Sikh Kirtan. 1983. 17.50 (*0-8364-0993-0*, Pub. by Oxford IBH II) S Asia.

Mansukhani, Gobin S., ed. & tr. Hymns from the Holy Granth. 1976. pap. 2.75 (*0-89253-063-4*) Ind-US Inc.

Mansukhani, Gobind S., jt. auth. see Dogra, Ramesh C.

Mansum, C. J. Elsevier's Dictionary of Building Construction. 472p. (DUT, ENG, FRE & GER.). 1985. reprint ed. 250.00 (*0-8288-9297-0*, M7920) Fr & Eur.

Mansur, Salim, jt. auth. see Choudhry, Nanda K.

***Mansur, Yusuf M.** Fuzzy Sets & Economics: Applications of Fuzzy Mathematics to Non-Cooperative Oligopoly. LC 94-34104. 208p. 1995. 63.95 (*1-85898-206-5*, Pub. by E Elgar Pub UK) Ashgate Pub Co.

Mansure, Irene. The Scar. abr. ed. 210p. 1995. pap. 8.95 (*1-56901-437-X*) NW Pub.

Mansuripur, Masud. The Physical Principles of Magneto-Optical Recording. LC 93-48553. (Illus.). 720p. (C). 1994. 99.95 (*0-521-46124-3*) Cambridge U Pr.

Mansvelt-Beck, B. J. The Treatises of Later Han: Their Author, Sources, Contents & Place in Chinese Historiography. LC 90-2156. (Sinica Leidensia Ser.: Vol. 21). xii, 296p. 1990. pap. 60.75 (*90-04-08895-4*) E J Brill.

Mant, Gilbert, ed. Soldier Boy: The Letters & Memoirs of Gunner W. J. Duffell 1915-1918. 192p. 1993. 24.95 (*0-86417-429-2*, Pub. by Kangaroo Pr AT); pap. 14.95 (*0-86417-418-7*, Pub. by Kangaroo Pr AT) Seven Hills Bk.

Mant, Gilbert, intro. Soldier Boy: The Letters & Memoirs of Gunner W. J. Duffell 1915-1918. 168p. (C). 1992. text ed. 75.00 (*0-907590-39-X*, Pub. by SPA Bks Ltd UK) St Mut.

***Mant, Janice M.** The Next Margaret. 144p. 1995. lib. bdg. 33.00 (*0-8095-4858-5*) Borgo Pr.

Mant, Richard. The Simpliciad. LC 91-3947. 62p. 1991. reprint ed. 35.00 (*1-85477-076-4*, Pub. by Woodstock Bks UK) Cassell.

Mantai, Kenneth E. A Field Guide to the Aquatic Life of Chautauqua County. (Marginal Media Bioguide Ser.: No. 5). (Illus.). 48p. 1983. pap. 3.00 (*0-942788-10-9*) Iris Visual.

Manteau-Bonamy, H. M. Immaculate Conception & the Holy Spirit: The Marian Teachings of Father Kolbe. 2nd ed. Geiger, Bernard M., ed. Arnandez, Richard, tr. LC 77-93104. (Illus.). 172p. 1992. reprint ed. pap. 6.00 (*0-913382-00-0*, 101-20) Prow Bks-Franciscan.

Mantee, Paul. Bruno of Hollywood. LC 93-90462. 240p. 1994. 18.00 (*0-345-38379-6*) Ballantine.

— In Search of the Perfect Ravioli. 208p. (Orig.). 1991. pap. 9.00 (*0-345-37261-1*, Available Pr) Ballantine.

Mantegazza, Giovanna. The Cat. LC 91-73872. (Illus.). 12p. (J). (ps-1). 1992. 6.95 (*1-56397-032-5*) Boyds Mills Pr.

— Dog. (J). (ps). 1993. 6.95 (*1-56397-200-X*) Boyds Mills Pr.

— The Hippopotamus. LC 91-73871. (Illus.). 12p. (J). (ps-1). 1992. 6.95 (*1-56397-033-3*) Boyds Mills Pr.

Mantegazza, Giovanni. Our Little Boat. (Tubby Books ser.). (Illus.). 20p. (J). (gr. 3 up). 1994. 3.95 (*1-55550-994-0*) Universe.

— Our Little Helicopter. (Tubby Bks.). (Illus.). 20p. (J). (ps). 1994. bds. 3.95 (*1-55550-997-5*) Universe.

— Our Little Jeep. (Tubby Books ser.). (Illus.). 20p. (J). (gr. 3 up). 1994. 3.95 (*1-55550-999-1*) Universe.

— Our Little Rocket Ship. (Tubby Bks.). (Illus.). 20p. (J). (ps). 1994. bds. 3.95 (*1-55550-995-9*) Universe.

— Our Little Submarine. (Illus.). 20p. (J). (gr. 3 up). 1994. 3.95 (*1-55550-998-3*) Universe.

— Our Little Train. (Tubby Books ser.). (Illus.). 20p. (J). (gr. 3 up). 1994. 3.95 (*1-55550-996-7*) Universe.

Mantegazzini. The Environmental Risks from Biotechnology. 1992. text ed. 47.50 (*0-86187-658-X*, Pub. by Pinter Pubs UK) St Martin.

Mantegna, Gian F. & High, Steven. Oneiric Threshold: An Installation by Alastair Noble. 1993. 5.00 (*0-935519-16-5*) Anderson Gal.

***Mantegna, Gianfranco.** Graphis Designer Products 94. (Illus.). 240p. 1994. 69.00 (*0-8230-6375-5*) Watsn-Guptill.

Manteiga, Robert C. The Poetry of Rafael Alberti: A Visual Approach. (Serie A: Monagrafias, LXXV). 130p. (C). 1978. 45.00 (*0-7293-0069-2*, Pub. by Tamesis Bks Ltd UK) Boydell & Brewer.

Manteiga, Roberto C., et al, eds. Critical Approaches to the Writings of Juan Benet. LC 83-40010. 183p. (C). 1984. 25.00 (*0-87451-270-0*) U Pr of New Eng.

— Feminine Concerns in Contemporary Spanish Fiction by Women. 186p. 35.00 (*0-916379-49-3*) Scripta.

Mantel, Herman & Mantel, Hugo. Mantel's Folks Redner: Mantel's Sermons & Address in Yiddish Language for All Jewish Holidays & Many Other Occasions. 320p. 27. 50 (*0-87559-148-5*) Shalom.

Mantel, Hilary. A Change of Climate. 354p. 1994. text ed. 22.00 (*0-689-12201-2*, Atheneum S&S) S&S Trade.

— A Place of Greater Safety. 864p. 1993. 25.00 (*0-689-12168-7*, Atheneum S&S) S&S Trade.

Mantel, Hugo. Studies in the History of the Sanhedrin. LC 61-7391. (Harvard Semitic Studies: No. 17). 389p. reprint ed. pap. 110.90 (*0-7837-4121-9*, 2057944) Bks Demand.

Mantel, Hugo, jt. auth. see Mantel, Herman.

Mantel, Linda H. & Bliss, Dorothy E., eds. The Biology of Crustacea Vol. 5: Physiological Regulation. 400p. 1983. text ed. 125.00 (*0-12-106405-0*) Acad Pr.

Mantel, Linda H., jt. ed. see Bliss, Dorothy E.

Mantel, Samuel J., jt. auth. see Meredith, Jack R.

***Mantell.** Kidnapped in Catacombs. (J). 1995. 3.50 (*0-679-87071-7*) Random.

Mantell, Charles L. Solid Wastes: Origin, Collection, Processing, & Disposal. LC 74-26930. (Illus.). 1143p. reprint ed. pap. 180.00 (*0-685-23821-0*, 2056602) Bks Demand.

— Tin: Its Mining, Production, Technology, & Applications. 2nd ed. LC 29-22211. (ACS Monograph: No. 51). 1949. 47.95 (*0-8412-0257-5*) Am Chemical.

Mantell, Charles L., jt. auth. see Galanti, Anthony V.

***Mantell, David M.** True Americanism: Green Berets & War Resisters; a Study of Commitment. LC 74-2230. (Foresight Books in Psychology). (Illus.). 293p. 1974. reprint ed. pap. 83.60 (*0-7837-8947-5*, 2049658) Bks Demand.

Mantell, Gideon A. The Medals of Creation: Or, First Lessons in Geology & the Study of Organic Remains, 2 vols., 1. 2nd rev. ed. Gould, Stephen J., ed. LC 79-8334. (History of Paleontology Ser.). (Illus.). 1980. reprint ed. lib. bdg. 44.95 (*0-405-12717-0*) Ayer.

— The Medals of Creation: Or, First Lessons in Geology & the Study of Organic Remains, 2 vols., 2. 2nd rev. ed. Gould, Stephen J., ed. LC 79-8334. (History of Paleontology Ser.). (Illus.). 1980. reprint ed. lib. bdg. 44. 95 (*0-405-12718-9*) Ayer.

— The Medals of Creation: Or, First Lessons in Geology & the Study of Organic Remains, 2 vols., Set. 2nd rev. ed. Gould, Stephen J., ed. LC 79-8334. (History of Paleontology Ser.). (Illus.). 1980. reprint ed. lib. bdg. 88. 95 (*0-405-12716-2*) Ayer.

Mantell, Laurie. Murder & Chips. large type ed. 368p. 1989. 17.95 (*0-7089-2028-4*) Ulverscroft.

— Murder in Vain. large type ed. 357p. 1989. 17.95 (*0-7089-1978-2*) Ulverscroft.

— Murder to Burn. large type ed. (Linford Romance Library). 368p. 1987. pap. 11.95 (*0-7089-6391-9*, Linford) Ulverscroft.

Mantell, Martin E. Johnson, Grant, & the Politics of Reconstruction. LC 72-13452. 209p. 1973. text ed. 42.00 (*0-231-03507-1*) Col U Pr.

Mantell, Matthew E., jt. auth. see Maffetone, Philip.

Mantell, Michael. Ticking Bombs: Defusing Violence in the Workplace. LC 93-44770. 300p. 1994. text ed. 25.00 (*0-7863-0189-9*) Irwin Prof Pubng.

Mantell, Michael & Harper, Stephen. Creating Successful Communities: A Guidebook to Growth Management Strategies. LC 89-15473. (Illus.). 230p. (Orig.). 1989. 39. 95 (*1-55963-030-2*) Island Pr.

Mantell, Michael A., ed. Managing National Park System Resources: A Handbook on Legal Duties, Opportunities, & Tools. LC 89-20993. 288p. 1990. pap. 23.50 (*0-89164-114-9*) World Wildlife Fund.

Mantell, Michael R. Don't Sweat the Small Stuff: P.S. It's All Small Stuff! LC 88-1596. 240p. (Orig.). 1988. pap. 9.95 (*0-915166-56-9*) Impact Pubs CA.

Mantell, Murray I. Handbook for Living: A Reference for Personal & Public Issues. LC 92-80647. (Illus.). 200p. (Orig.). 1992. lib. bdg. 19.95 (*1-56675-040-7*); pap. 12.95 (*1-56675-041-5*) Mnemosyne.

Mantell, Paul & Hart, Avery. Beauty & the Beast. (X-Men Picturebacks Ser.). (Illus.). 24p. (Orig.). (J). (ps-3). 1995. pap. 2.50 (*0-679-86931-X*) Random Bks Yng Read.

— The Brood. (X-Men Digest Novels Ser.). (Illus.). 112p. (Orig.). (J). (gr. 2 up). 1994. pap. 3.50 (*0-679-86568-3*, Bullseye Bks) Random Bks Yng Read.

— The Wedding of Cyclops. (X-Men Picturebacks Ser.). (Illus.). 24p. (Orig.). (J). (ps-3). 1995. pap. 2.50 (*0-679-86932-8*) Random Bks Yng Read.

— X-Men in the Savage Land. (X-Men Digest Novels Ser.). (Illus.). 112p. (Orig.). (J). (gr. 2 up). 1994. pap. 3.50 (*0-679-86700-7*, Bullseye Bks) Random Bks Yng Read.

Mantell, Paul, jt. auth. see Hart, Avery.

Mantellini, Rafael, tr. see D'Annunzio, Gabriele.

Mantello, Frank, tr. see Thuroczy, Janos.

Manten, A., jt. auth. see Hulshof, O.

Manten, A. A. Symposia & Symposium Publications: A Guide for Organisers, Lecturers, & Editors of Scientific Meetings. LC 76-837. (Illus.). 176p. reprint ed. pap. 50. 20 (*0-317-09783-0*, 2051677) Bks Demand.

Manten, A. A. & Timman, T., eds. Information Policy & Scientific Research. 170p. 1983. 56.50 (*0-444-86611-6*, I-170-83) Elsevier.

Manternach, Janaan & Pfeifer, Carl. Creative Catechist. rev. ed. LC 91-90951. 160p. (Orig.). 1991. pap. 9.95 (*0-89622-490-2*) Twenty-Third.

Manternach, Janaan & Pfeifer, Carl J. And the Children Pray: A Practical Book for Prayerful Catechists. LC 89-85064. 192p. (Orig.). 1989. spiral bd. 9.95 (*0-87793-412-6*) Ave Maria.

— How to Be a Better Catechist: Answers to Questions Catechists Ask Most. LC 89-61927. 112p. (Orig.). 1989. pap. 5.95 (*1-55612-268-3*) Sheed & Ward MO.

Manternach, Janaan, jt. auth. see Pfeifer, Carl J.

Mantero, F., et al. Endocrinology of Hypertension-Symposium. 1983. text ed. 156.00 (*0-12-469980-4*) Acad Pr.

Mantero, Manuel & Craige, Betty J. Manuel Mantero: New Songs for the Ruins of Spain. LC 84-46101. 120p. 1986. 29.50 (*0-8387-5094-X*) Bucknell U Pr.

Manteuffel, Tadeusz. The Formation of the Polish State: The Period of Ducal Rule. LC 81-11583. 173p. reprint ed. pap. 49.40 (*0-318-39776-5*, 2033178) Bks Demand.

Mantey, J. R., jt. auth. see Dana, H. E.

Manthe, George L. Inside Dope. (Illus.). 177p. 1984. 15.95 (*0-911603-00-X*); pap. 9.95 (*0-911603-01-8*) Cube Pubns.

Manthei & Assoc. Staff. How to Operate the Macintosh with System 7. Reid, Christine, ed. (Illus.). 80p. (Orig.). 1991. pap. text ed. 125.00 (*0-917792-86-6*) OneOnOne Comp Trng.

Manthei, George. A Gourmet's Fables & Fare. Taylor, Vernon, ed. (Illus.). 140p. 1994. pap. 9.95 (*1-878816-00-4*) Schildge Pub.

— Wild & Famous Fish & Game Cookbook. Taylor, Vernon, ed. (Illus.). 140p. 1992. spiral bd. 9.95 (*1-878816-01-2*) Schildge Pub.

***Manthey, Cynthia.** Pre-K Math: Concepts from Global Sources. (Illus.). 160p. (Orig.). 1995. lib. bdg. 25.95 (*0-89334-246-7*, 2477054); pap. 15.95 (*0-89334-240-8*, 2408054) Humanics Ltd.

— With Respect for Others: Activities for a Global Neighborhood. (Illus.). 160p. (Orig.). 1995. lib. bdg. 27. 95 (*0-89334-247-5*, 2475054); pap. 17.95 (*0-89334-241-6*, 2416054) Humanics Ltd.

Manthey, Cynthia M. With Respect, Vol. 1P: Successful Primary Theme Activities. 100p. (J). (ps-1). 1992. pap. text ed. 11.95 (*0-9634651-0-4*); audio 9.95 (*0-9634651-1-2*) Qual Instruct.

Manthey, F. Die Sprachphilosophie des Hl, Thomas Von Aquin. (Philosophy Reprints Ser.). (GER.). reprint ed. lib. bdg. 45.00 (*0-697-00042-7*) Irvington.

Manthey, Gerda. Fuchsias. Christie, David, tr. (Illus.). 204p. 1991. 41.95 (*0-88192-187-4*) Timber.

Manthey, John. Chemistry & Biochemistry of Plant Nutrition. 1994. 99.95 (*0-87371-942-5*, S592) Lewis Pubs.

Manthey, Marie. The Practice of Primary Nursing. 96p. 1980. 19.95 (*0-86542-000-9*) Creative Nursing.

Manthey-Zorn, Otto, tr. see Kant, Immanuel.

Manthorne. Fascination & Other Bar Stories. (NFS Canada Ser.). Date not set. pap. 9.95 (*0-921881-16-9*, Pub. by Gynergy-Ragweed CN) InBook.

— Ghost Motel. (NFS Canada Ser.). 1994. pap. 9.95 (*0-921881-31-2*, Pub. by Gynergy-Ragweed CN) InBook.

***Manthorne, Jackie.** Deadly Reunion. 1995. pap. 10.95 (*0-921881-32-0*) InBook.

— Last Resort: A Harriet Hubbley Mystery. 192p. 1995. pap. 10.95 (*0-921881-34-7*, Pub. by Gynergy-Ragweed CN) InBook.

— Without Wings. 192p. (Orig.). 1993. pap. 9.95 (*0-921881-29-0*, Pub. by Gynergy-Ragweed CN) InBook.

An Asterisk (*) at the beginning of an entry indicates that the title is appearing in BIP for the first time.

Manthorne, Jane, et al, eds. Idea Sourcebook for Young Adult Programs. 1973. 2.00 (0-89073-015-6) Boston Public Lib.

Manthorne, Katherine E. Tropical Renaissance: North American Artists Exploring Latin America, 1839-1879. (Illus.). 235p. 1989. 55.00 (0-87474-714-7); pap. 24.95 (0-87474-715-5) Smithsonian.

Manthorp, Beryl. Towards Ballet: Dance Training for the Very Young. LC 87-62262. (Illus.). 88p. 1987. 10.95 (0-916622-60-6, Dance Horizons) Princeton Bk Co.

Manthorpe, Jill & Atherton, Celia. Grandparent's Rights. (C). 1989. 35.00 (0-86242-079-2, Pub. by Age Concern Eng UK) St Mut.

Manthorpe, Victoria, ed. see Smith, Richard G.

Manthuruthil, Jose, jt. ed. see Hamilton, Joseph H.

Manthy, Robert S. Natural Resource Commodities: A Century of Statistics, Prices, Output, Consumption, Foreign Trade & Employment in the U. S., 1870-1973. LC 78-8429. (Resources for the Future Ser.). 1978. text ed. 25.00 (0-8018-2142-8) Johns Hopkins.

— Natural Resource Commodities: A Century of Statistics: Prices, Output, Consumption, Foreign Trade, & Employment in the United States, 1870-1973. Tron, Joan R., ed. LC 78-8429. 254p. reprint ed. pap. 72.40 (0-8357-4682-8, 2037629) Bks Demand.

Mantice, James. Slash Your Advertising Costs Now! An Easy-Access Guide to Spending Less & Getting More for Your. 210p. 1991. pap. 32.95 (0-85013-172-3) Dartnell Corp.

Mantice, Jim. Bug Off! Fifty Simple Ways to Protect Yourself from Burglars, Thieves, Muggers, Con-Artists, & Other Lowlifes. (Illus.). 96p. (Orig.). 1992. pap. 5.95 (0-9631380-0-6) Walnut Grove Pubs.

Mantin, Peter. Questions of Evidence: The Twentieth Century World. (Illus.). 128p. 1987. pap. 15.95 (0-09-170221-6, Pub. by S Thornes UK) Dufour.

Mantin, Peter & Lankester, Colin. From Romanov to Gorbachev: Russia in the 20th Century. 96p. (Orig.). 1989. pap. 14.95x (0-09-182378-1, Pub. by Stanley Thornes UK) Trans-Atl Phila.

Mantin, Peter & Mantin, Ruth. The Islamic World: Beliefs & Civilisation 600-1600. (Cambridge History Programme Ser.). (Illus.). 64p. (C). 1993. pap. 9.25 (0-521-40609-9) Cambridge U Pr.

Mantin, Peter & Pulley, R. Investigation Sources. (Hutchinson History Ser.). (C). 1989. 50.00 (0-09-182339-0, Pub. by S Thornes UK) Dufour.

Mantin, Peter & Pulley, Richard. Medicine Through the Ages: A Study in Development. 128p. (Orig.). 1988. pap. 19.95 (0-7487-0268-7, Pub. by Stanley Thornes UK) Trans-Atl Phila.

— The Roman World: From Republic to Empire. (Cambridge History Programme Ser.). (Illus.). 80p. (J). (gr. 6 up). 1993. pap. 10.25 (0-521-40608-0) Cambridge U Pr.

Mantin, Peter, jt. auth. see Lankester, Colin.

Mantin, Ruth, jt. auth. see Mantin, Peter.

Mantinband. Dizzy Dervish. (J). Date not set. 13.95 (0-06-020226-2, HarpT); lib. bdg. 13.89 (0-06-020227-0, HarpT) HarpC.

Mantinband, Gerda B. Blabbermouths. LC 91-3006. (J). (ps-3). 1992. 14.00 (0-688-10602-1); lib. bdg. 13.93 (0-688-10604-8) Greenwillow.

Mantinband, Gerda B., adapt. & ret. Three Clever Mice. LC 91-48171. (Illus.). 32p. (J). (gr. k up). 1993. 14.00 (0-688-11369-9); lib. bdg. 13.93 (0-688-11370-2) Greenwillow.

Mantinband, James H. Dictionary of Greek Literature. (Quality Paperback Ser.: No. 145). 409p. 1966. reprint ed. pap. 12.95 (0-8226-0145-1) Littlefield.

— Dictionary of Latin Literature. (Quality Paperback Ser.: No. 152). 303p. 1964. reprint ed. pap. 9.95 (0-8226-0152-4) Littlefield.

Mantinband, James H., tr. see Vergil.

***Manting, Dorien.** Dynamics in Marriage & Cohabitation: An Intertemporal, Life Course Analysis of First Union Formation & Dissolution. 210p. 1994. pap. 25.00 (90-5170-295-7, Pub. by Thesis Pubs NE) IBD Ltd.

Mantione, Anthony J., jt. auth. see Munoz, Rafael A.

Mantione, Denise. Chatty Hats & Other Props. (Illus.). 148p. 1990. teacher ed 22.95 (0-937857-17-3, 1581) Speech Bin.

Mantione, Denise A. Speech-Language In-Services for Colleagues in Education (SLICE) 112p. (J). (ps-12). 1992. 24.95 (0-937857-33-5, 1510) Speech Bin.

Mantis, Elizabeth M. Woman, Root of Love. Renolds, Sallie, ed. (Poetry Ser.). 52p. 1989. pap. text ed. 6.95 (0-317-93533-X) Maya NY.

***Mantius, Peter.** Shell Game. LC 95-8564. 1995. write for info. (0-312-13169-0) St Martin.

***Mantle.** All My Octobers. 1995. mass mkt. 5.99 (0-06-109212-6, Harp PBks) HarpC.

Mantle, Burns, ed. The Best Plays of 1919-1920. LC 75-19860. (Best Plays Series). 1978. 30.95 (0-405-09168-0) Ayer.

— The Best Plays of 1928-1929. LC 75-19860. (Best Plays Series). 1976. 30.95 (0-405-09169-9) Ayer.

— The Best Plays of 1929-1930. LC 75-19860. (Best Plays Series). 1975. 30.95 (0-405-09170-2) Ayer.

— The Best Plays of 1930-1931. LC 75-19860. (Best Plays Series). 1977. 30.95 (0-405-09171-0) Ayer.

— The Best Plays of 1938-1939. LC 75-19860. (Best Plays Series). 1977. 30.95 (0-405-09174-5) Ayer.

Mantle, Greg, jt. auth. see Wedge, Peter.

Mantle, Jill, jt. auth. see Powden, Margaret.

Mantle, Jonathan. Archbishop: The Life & Times of Robert Runcie. (Illus.). 360p. 1992. 29.95 (1-85619-058-7, Sinclair-Stevenson) Trafalgar.

Mantle, Margaret. Some Just Clap Their Hands: Raising a Handicapped Child. LC 85-15026. 264p. 1985. 16.95 (0-915361-24-8, 097331); pap. 12.95 (0-685-10635-7) Modan-Adama Bks.

Mantle, Mickey. All My Octobers: My Memories of 12 World Series When the Yankees Ruled Baseball. 272p. 1994. 23.00 (0-06-017747-0, HarpT) HarpC.

— Mickey Mantle: My Favorite Summer, 1956. 1992. mass mkt. 5.99 (0-440-21203-0) Dell.

Mantle, Mickey & Gluck, Herb. The Mick. 288p. 1987. mass mkt. 4.99 (0-515-08599-5) Jove Pubns.

Mantle, Mickey & Rothgeb, Lew. Mickey Mantle: The American Dream Comes to Life. (Illus.). 120p. 1994. 24.95 (0-915611-89-9) Sagamore Pub.

Mantle, T. J., et al, eds. Glutathione S-Transferases & Carcinogenesis. 268p. 1987. 115.00 (0-85066-394-6) Taylor & Francis.

Mantlo, et al. Cloak & Dagger: Predator & Prey. 64p. 1988. 5.95 (0-87135-125-0) Marvel Entmnt.

— Power Pack - Cloak & Dagger. 64p. 1989. 7.95 (0-87135-601-5) Marvel Entmnt.

Mantlo, Bill & Guice, Jackson. Swords of the Swashbucklers. 64p. 1984. 5.95 (0-87135-002-5) Marvel Entmnt.

Manto, Mike & Dawson, Mike. Sorting Out OPNQRYF: The Desktop Guide to Open Query File. (Illus.). 154p. (Orig.). 1994. pap. 69.95 (1-884322-20-4) Comp Applicatns.

Manto, Saadat H. Kingdom's End & Other Stories. Hasan, Khalid, tr. 272p. 1988. 18.95 (0-86091-183-7, Pub. by Verso UK) Routledge Chapman & Hall.

***Mantoani, Tim.** Photographic Global Notes: Global Notes, 2 vols., Vol. I & II. (Illus.). 317p. 1994. pap. 29.95 (1-883403-23-5, H 707, Silver Pixel Pr) Saunders Photo.

Mantock, Jim, jt. auth. see Phillips, W. Scott.

Manton, Denis. Tigers in the Park. (Illus.). 32p. (J). (ps-2). 1992. 15.95 (0-09-174525-X, Pub. by Hutchinson UK) Trafalgar.

— Wolf Comes to Town. LC 93-37918. (J). 1994. 13.99 (0-525-45281-8, DCB) Dutton Child Bks.

Manton, E. Lennox. Roman North Africa. (Illus.). 144p. 1988. 39.95 (1-85264-007-3, Pub. by Seaby UK) Trafalgar.

Manton, Jo. Gods, Beasts & Men. 212p. (C). 1974. 40.00 (0-685-33820-7, Pub. by S Thornes Pubs UK) St Mut.

Manton, Jo, jt. auth. see Gittings, Robert.

Manton, Kenneth G. & Stallard, Eric. Chronic Disease Modelling: Measurement & Evaluation of the Risks of Chronic Disease Processes. (Charles Griffin Series--Mathematics in Medicine: No. 2). (Illus.). 288p. 1988. 69.00 (0-19-520617-7) OUP.

— Recent Trends in Mortality Analysis. LC 83-11736. (Studies in Population). 1984. text ed. 72.00 (0-12-470020-9) Acad Pr.

Manton, Kenneth G., et al. Statistical Applications Using Fuzzy Sets. (Probability & Mathematical Statistics Ser.). 320p. 1994. text ed. 59.95 (0-471-54561-9) Wiley.

Manton, Kenneth G., et al, eds. Forecasting the Health of Elderly Populations. LC 92-48819. (Series in Statistics in the Health Sciences). 1993. 59.00 (0-387-97953-0) Spr-Verlag.

Manton, Richard. The Blue Train. 1993. pap. 5.95 (1-56201-043-3) Blue Moon Bks.

— Bombay Bound: Voluptuous Years As the Viceroy's Emissary in the Indian Rajah's Court. 1989. pap. 4.50 (0-8216-5042-4, Univ Books) Carol Pub Group.

— Deep South. (Orig.). 1993. pap. text ed. 5.95 (1-56201-061-1) Blue Moon Bks.

— Elaine Cox. 1993. pap. 5.95 (1-56201-041-7) Blue Moon Bks.

— Noreen. 1992. pap. 5.95 (0-929654-89-7, 110) Blue Moon Bks.

— Pleasure Beach. 1993. pap. 5.95 (1-56201-034-4) Blue Moon Bks.

— Tropic of Venus. (Victorian Era Ser.). (Orig.). 1990. pap. text ed. 5.95 (0-929654-69-2, 86) Blue Moon Bks.

— La Vie Parisienne. 1988. pap. 4.95 (0-929654-66-8, 09) Blue Moon Bks.

— Villa Rosa. (Orig.). 1989. pap. 4.50 (0-929654-13-7, 47) Blue Moon Bks.

Manton, Richard, ed. A Victorian Sampler. 1992. pap. 5.95 (1-56201-019-0, 118) Blue Moon Bks.

Manton, Thomas. Commentary on Jude. LC 88-12127. 384p. reprint ed. lib. bdg. 20.99 (0-8254-3240-5); reprint ed. pap. 14.99 (0-8254-3239-1) Kregel.

— A Commentary on Jude. 376p. (C). 1989. reprint ed. 17.95 (0-85151-553-3) Banner of Truth.

— James. (Geneva Commentaries Ser.). 1983. 21.95 (0-85151-074-4) Banner of Truth.

— James. LC 94-47149. (Classic Commentaries Ser.). 224p. (Orig.). 1995. pap. 17.99 (0-89107-832-0) Crossway Bks.

— Psalm 119, 3 vols. 580p. 1990. 79.95 (0-85151-576-2) Banner of Truth.

— Works of Thomas Manton, 22 Vols, Set. LC 76-172841. reprint ed. 465.00 (0-404-04200-7) AMS Pr.

— The Works of Thomas Manton, 3 vols., Vol. 1. 500p. (YA). 1993. 25.95 (0-85151-648-3) Banner of Truth.

— The Works of Thomas Manton, 3 vols., Vol. 2. 500p. (YA). 1993. 25.95 (0-85151-649-1) Banner of Truth.

— The Works of Thomas Manton, 3 vols., Vol. 3. 500p. (YA). 1993. 25.95 (0-85151-650-5) Banner of Truth.

Mantooth, C., et al. Family Preservation: A Treatment Manual for Reducing Couple Violence. 188p. 1987. 18.95 (1-882948-00-9) Family Violence.

Mantooth, Frank. Best Chord Changes for the Most Requested Standards. (Keyboards-Guitar Ser.). 216p. (C). 1990. pap. text ed. 19.95 (0-88188-853-2, 00359125) H Leonard.

— Best Chord Changes for the World's Greatest Standards. 1990. pap. 19.95 (0-88188-852-4, HL 00359124) H Leonard.

***Mantooth, H. Alan.** Modeling with an Analog Hardware Description Language. (International Series in Engineering & Computer Science, Natural Language Processing & Machine Translation). 296p. (C). 1994. lib. bdg. 95.00 (0-7923-9516-6) Kluwer Ac.

Mantooth, Tonya, jt. auth. see Kayser, Thomas A.

Mantoura, R. F. & Martin, J. M., eds. Ocean Margin Processes in Global Change. 301p. 1991. teacher ed write for info. (0-318-68474-8); text ed. 149.95 (0-471-92979-4); trans. write for info. (0-318-68476-4); write for info. (0-318-68475-6); write for info. (0-318-68477-2) Wiley.

Mantoura, R. F., et al. Ocean Margin Processes in Global Change. (Dahlem Workshop Reports - Physical, Chemical, Earth Sciences). 469p. 1991. text ed. 214.95 (0-471-92673-6) Wiley.

Mantoux. Alexis de Tocqueville Livre du Centenaire (1859-1959) 8.95 (0-8288-6094-7, F74630) Fr & Eur.

Mantoux, Etienne. The Carthaginian Peace or the Economic Consequences of Mr. Keynes. Wilkins, Mira, ed. LC 78-3936. (International Finance Ser.). 1979. reprint ed. lib. bdg. 23.95 (0-405-11237-8) Ayer.

Mantovani, Alberto. Tumor-Associated Leukocytes: Pathophysiology & Therapeutic Applications. LC 93-50704. (Molecular Biology Intelligence Unit Ser.). 1994. 89.95 (1-57059-013-3) R G Landes.

***Mantran, Robert, ed.** Great Dates in Islamic History. LC 95-12883. (Great Dates Ser.). 1996. write for info. (0-8160-2935-0) Facts on File.

Mantreswara. Phala Deepika. Kapoor, G. S., tr. (C). 1991. 17.00 (0-8364-2769-6, Pub. by Ranjan Pubs II) S Asia.

Mantsch, H. H., jt. ed. see Birge, R. R.

Mantsch, Pat & Whitney, Jane, eds. Gifts from the Earth: A Basketmakers Field Guide to Midwest Botanicals. LC 88-50438. (Illus.). 50p. (Orig.). 1988. pap. 14.95 (0-9614795-1-5) Wild Willow.

Mantsch, Pat S., ed. see TerBeest, Char.

Mantuanus, Baptista. Adulescentia: The Ecologues of Mantuan. Wilhelm, James J., ed. Piepho, Lee, tr. LC 89-16967. (World Literature in Translation Ser.: Vol. 14). 206p. 1989. 52.00 (0-8240-3309-4) Garland.

Mantus, Roberta. Design Guidelines for Desktop Publishing. 128p. 1992. text ed. 16.95 (0-8273-5075-9) Delmar.

— Design Guidelines for Desktop Publishing: Instructor's Guide. 1992. 8.00 (0-8273-5076-7) Delmar.

***Mantyla, Karen.** Consultative Sales Power: Achieving Sales Excellence. Gerould, Philip, ed. (Fifty-Minute Ser.). (Illus.). 110p. (Orig.). 1994. pap. 9.95 (1-56052-304-2) Crisp Pubns.

Mantyla, Martti. Introduction to Solid Modeling. 144p. (C). 1995. text ed. write for info. (0-7167-8015-1, Computer Sci Pr) W H Freeman.

Mantyla, Martti, jt. auth. see Shah, Jami J.

Mantz, R. & Murry, John Middleton. Life of Katherine Mansfield. LC 75-42109. (English Literature Ser.: No. 33). 1974. lib. bdg. 75.00 (0-8383-1882-7) M S G Haskell Hse.

Mantzarides, Giorgios I. Orthodox Spiritual Life. LC 94-13034. 1994. write for info. (0-917651-35-9) Holy Cross Orthodox.

Mantzaridis, Georgios I. The Deification of Man: St. Gregory Palamas & the Orthodox Tradition. Sherrard, Liadain, tr. (Contemporary Greek Theologians Ser.: No. 2). 137p. (Orig.). 1984. pap. 9.95 (0-88141-027-6) St Vladimirs.

Mantzius, Karl. History of Theatrical Art in Ancient & Modern Times, 6 Vols, Set. (Illus.). 72.00 (0-8446-0786-X) Peter Smith.

Manucci, Niccolao. Storia Do Mogor, or Mogul India 1653-1708, 4 vols., Set. Irvine, William, tr. reprint ed. text ed. 125.00 (0-685-13412-1) Coronet Bks.

***Manucy, Albert.** Artillery Through the Ages: A Short Illustrated History of Cannon, Emphasizing Types Used in America. (Illus.). 92p. (Orig.). (C). 1994. pap. text ed. 45.00x (0-7881-0745-3) Diane Pub.

— Artillery Through the Ages: A Short Illustrated History of Cannon, Emphasizing Types Used in America. (Illus.). 96p. (Orig.). 1985. reprint ed. pap. 2.75 (0-16-003405-1, S/N 024-005-00159-0) USGPO.

— Florida's Menendez, Captain General of the Ocean Sea. LC 66-5157. (Illus.). 104p. (Orig.). 1965. pap. 4.95 (0-917553-04-7) St Augustine Hist.

— The Houses of St. Augustine, Fifteen Sixty-Five to Eighteen Twenty-One. rev. ed. LC 65-67871. (Illus.). 179p. (Orig.). 1978. 25.00 (0-917553-03-9); pap. 8.95 (0-917553-02-0) St Augustine Hist.

— The Houses of St. Augustine, 1565-1821. (Florida Sand Dollar Book Ser.). (Illus.). 184p. (C). 1992. reprint ed. pap. 11.95 (0-8130-1103-5) U Press Fla.

— Menendez: Pedro Menendez de Aviles: Captain General of the Ocean Sea. LC 92-5128. (Illus.). 112p. 1992. 14.95 (1-56164-015-8); pap. 7.95 (1-56164-016-6) Pineapple Pr.

Manucy, Albert & Torres-Reyes, Ricardo. The Forts of Old San Juan. LC 73-83358. (Illus.). 96p. 1989. pap. 16.95 (0-85699-085-X) Chatham Pr.

Manuel, David. Like a Mighty River. LC 77-90948. (Illus.). 220p. 1977. 5.95 (0-932260-02-0) Rock Harbor.

— Medjugorje under Siege. LC 92-80352. 180p. (Orig.). 1992. 8.95 (1-55725-052-9) Paraclete MA.

Manuel, David, ed. see Ford, Camie & Hale, Sunny.

Manuel, David, jt. auth. see Marshall, Peter.

Manuel Di Bella, Jose. Nailed to the Wound. Polkinhorn, Harry, tr. (Baja California Literature in Translation Ser.). 162p. 1993. pap. 12.50 (1-879691-14-0) SDSU Press.

Manuel, Don J. El Conde Lucanor. (SPA.). 9.95 (84-241-5615-3) E Torres & Sons.

***Manuel, Elisabeth.** Cette Ombre Familiere - Dark Companion. Suther, Judith, tr. 230p. (Orig.). (FRE.). 1995. pap. 18.00 (0-9645677-0-9) Starbks.

Manuel, Frank E. The Broken Staff: Judaism Through Christian Eyes. (Illus.). 363p. (C). 1992. 39.95 (0-674-08370-9) HUP.

— The Changing of the Gods. LC 82-40475. 216p. 1983. text ed. 30.00 (0-87451-254-9) U Pr of New Eng.

— A Portrait of Isaac Newton. (Quality Paperbacks Ser.). (Illus.). 512p. 1990. reprint ed. pap. 13.95 (0-306-80400-X) Da Capo.

— The Realities of American-Palestine Relations. LC 72-596. 378p. 1975. reprint ed. text ed. 69.50 (0-8371-5999-7, MARA, Greenwood Pr) Greenwood.

— A Requiem for Karl Marx. LC 94-48452. (Illus.). 272p. (C). 1995. 24.95 (0-674-76326-2) HUP.

— Shapes of Philosophical History. (Modern Revivals in Philosophy Ser.). 176p. 1994. 54.95 (0-7512-0210-X, Pub. by Gregg Revivals UK) Ashgate Pub Co.

— Shapes of Philosophical History. 166p. 1965. 22.50 (0-8047-0248-9) Stanford U Pr.

— Shapes of Philosophical History. LC 65-13111. (Harry Camp Lectures at Stanford University). 111p. reprint ed. pap. 30.00 (0-7837-4069-7, 2044025) Bks Demand.

Manuel, Frank E., ed. The Age of Reason. (Paperbook Series in History). (Illus.). 64p. (C). 1993. reprint ed. pap. text ed. 2.00 (1-877891-11-8) Paperbook Pr Inc.

Manuel, Frank E. & Manuel, Fritzie P. Utopian Thought in the Western World. LC 79-12382. 902p. 1979. 50.00 (0-674-93185-8) Belknap Pr.

— Utopian Thought in the Western World. LC 79-12382. 902p. 1982. pap. 23.50 (0-674-93186-6) Belknap Pr.

Manuel, Fritzie P., jt. auth. see Manuel, Frank E.

Manuel, Juan. Cinco Tractados. Ayerbe-Chaux, Reinaldo, ed. (Spanish Ser.: No. 51). 1989. 25.00 (0-940639-36-X) Hispanic Seminary.

— Count Lucanor: A Collection of Medieval Spanish Stories. England, ed. (Hispanic Classics Ser.). 1987. 55.00 (0-85668-325-6, Pub. by Aris & Phillips UK); pap. 25.00 (0-85668-326-4, Pub. by Aris & Phillips UK) David Brown.

Manuel, Juan, et al. The Book of Count Lucanor & Patronio: A Translation of Don Juan Manuel's El Conde Lucanor. LC 76-24342. (Studies in Romance Languages: No. 16). 207p. reprint ed. pap. 59.00 (0-7837-5812-X, 2045479) Bks Demand.

Manuel, Madelynne. The Epiphany: Sequel to The Interlopers I. 401p. (Orig.). 1993. pap. 6.99 (0-9635714-1-9) M Manuel Prods.

— The Interlopers I. Henson, Mari, ed. (Illus.). 290p. (Orig.). 1992. pap. 6.99 (0-9635714-0-0) M Manuel Prods.

Manuel, Mark. A Geography of South Australia. LC 93-33370. 1991. pap. 19.95 (0-521-42330-9) Cambridge U Pr.

Manuel, Mark, et al. Our Coast. (J). 1994. pap. write for info. (0-318-72422-7) Cambridge U Pr.

***Manuel, Paul Christopher.** Uncertain Outcome: The Politics of the Portuguese Transition to Democracy. 214p. (C). 1994. lib. bdg. 36.50 (0-8191-9651-7) U Pr of Amer.

Manuel, Peggy C. Jose & Cardo. (Illus.). 32p. (gr. k-3). 1983. pap. 3.50 (971-10-0104-7, Pub. by New Day Pub PH) Cellar.

Manuel, Peter. Cassette Culture: Popular Music & Technology in North India. LC 92-27626. (Chicago Studies in Ethnomusicology). 365p. (C). 1993. pap. text ed. 22.00 (0-226-50401-8) U Ch Pr.

— Cassette Culture: Popular Music & Technology in North India. LC 92-27626. (Chicago Studies in Ethnomusicology). 365p. (C). 1993. lib. bdg. 52.00 (0-226-50399-2) U Ch Pr.

— Essays on Cuban Music: North American & Cuban Perspectives. 348p. (C). 1992. lib. bdg. 42.00 (0-8191-8430-6) U Pr of Amer.

— Popular Musics of the Non-Western World: An Introductory Survey. (Illus.). 314p. 1990. reprint ed. pap. 18.95 (0-19-506334-1) OUP.

— Thumri in Historical & Stylistic Perspectives. 1989. 47.50 (81-208-0673-5, Pub. by Motilal Banarsidass II) S Asia.

***Manuel, Peter, et al.** Caribbean Currents: Caribbean Music from Rumba to Reggae. LC 95-3152. (Illus.). 288p. (C). 1995. lib. bdg. 39.95 (1-56639-338-8); pap. 18.95 (1-56639-339-6) Temple U Pr.

Manuel, Roland. Maurice Ravel: Music Book Index. 152p. 1993. reprint ed. lib. bdg. 69.00 (0-7812-9616-1) Rprt Serv.

Manuel, Ron C., ed. Minority Aging: Sociological & Social Psychological Issues. LC 82-930. (Contributions in Ethnic Studies: No. 8). xvii, 285p. 1982. text ed. 55.00 (0-313-22541-9, MAG/, Greenwood Pr) Greenwood.

Manuel, Seco. Diccionario de Dudas y Dificultades de la Lengua Espanola. 9th ed. 568p. (SPA.). 1991. write for info. (0-7859-5013-3) Fr & Eur.

Manuel, Susan, jt. auth. see Hopkins, Jerry.

***Manuel, Ted.** Five-Hundred-One Types of People Who Can Cause You to Have a Bad Hair Day. Ramirez, Doreen, ed. 100p. (Orig.). 1995. write for info. (0-9628011-5-1) Desert Palm Pub.

— Jerks Who Are They? And from Where Do They Come? Ramirez, Doreen, ed. (Illus.). 100p. (Orig.). 1995. write for info. (0-9628011-3-5) Desert Palm Pub.

— The PMS-Prudent Mans Survival Cookbook. Ramirez, Doreen, ed. 100p. (Orig.). 1995. write for info. (0-9628011-4-3) Desert Palm Pub.

***Manuel, Ted & Ramirez, Doreen.** The PMS Handbook for Men. rev. ed. (Illus.). 56p. (Orig.). 1994. write for info. (0-9628011-1-9) Desert Palm Pub.

***Manuel, Ted, et al.** Five-Hundred-One Things to Do When Your Computer Crashes!! 100p. (Orig.). 1995. write for info. (0-9628011-2-7) Desert Palm Pub.

Manuele, Fred A. Essays on the Practice of Safety. LC 92-32859. 1993. pap. 39.95 (0-442-01401-5) Van Nos Reinhold.

An Asterisk (*) at the beginning of an entry indicates that the title is appearing in BIP for the first time.

Manuelian, Jack. World War III According to Nostradamus: A Book of Prophecy. 148p. (ENG & FRE.). 1995. pap. 12.00 (*1-885591-00-4*) Morris Pubng.

Manuelian, P. M., tr. Proverbs from the Armenian. LC 80-13387. (Illus.). 150p. 1980. 8.95 (*0-933706-20-0*) Ararat Pr.

Manuelian, P. M., ed. see Papazian, K. S.

Manuell, Guy. Floating Down Under: Foreign Exchange in Australia. xxi, 366p. 1986. pap. 56.50 (*0-455-20698-8*, Pub. by Law Bk Co) W W Gaunt.

Manuelli, Rodolfo E. & Sargent, Thomas J. Exercises in Dynamic Macroeconomic Theory. LC 86-25767. (Illus.). 224p. (C). 1987. pap. 25.95 (*0-674-27476-8*) HUP.

Manufacturers Group Staff. OnRamp: The Traveler's Radio & Entertainment Guide. (Western Edition Ser.). 169p. (Orig.). 1991. pap. 4.95 (*1-880126-00-1*); pap. 4.95 (*1-880126-02-8*); pap. 4.95 (*1-880126-01-X*) Pacif Pr.

Manuila, A., ed. Progress in Medical Terminology. (Illus.). xii, 116p. 1981. pap. 63.25 (*3-8055-2112-X*) S Karger.

Manuila, A., et al. Dictionnaire Francais de Medicine et de Biologie, Vol. 4. 580p. (FRE.). 1975. 1,195.00 (*0-8288-5856-X*, M15420) Fr & Eur.

— Dictionnaire Francais de Medicine et de Biologie, Vol. 4: Annexes. 580p. (FRE.). 1975. 325.00 (*0-7859-4432-X*, 2225287767) Fr & Eur.

Manuila, Alexandre. French Dictionary of Medicine & Biology: Dictionnaire Francais de Medicine et de Biologie, 20 vols. (FRE.). 1981. 450.00 (*0-8288-1817-7*, M15579) Fr & Eur.

— Petit Dictionnaire Medical. 4th ed. 566p. (FRE.). 1985. pap. 49.95 (*0-7859-4942-9*) Fr & Eur.

***Manuila, Ludmila.** Dictionnaire Medical. 5th ed. 504p. (FRE.). 1991. pap. 39.95 (*0-7859-7833-X*, 2225827958) Fr & Eur.

***Manuila, Ludmila, et al.** Dictionnaire Medical de Poche. 1994. write for info. (*0-7859-7862-3*, 2-253-08521-9) Fr & Eur.

Manuilov, V., ed. Encyclopaedia of Lermontov. 784p. (RUS.). (C). 1981. 150.00 (*0-685-46862-3*, Pub. by Collets) St Mut.

Manunder, W. F., ed. see Munby, Denys.

Manus, Morton. Guitar Chord Dictionary. 40p. 1975. 4.95 (*0-88284-153-X*, 377) Alfred Pub.

— How to Play Guitar Chords & Strums. (Alfred Handy Guide Ser.). 48p. (Orig.). 1992. pap. text ed. 4.50 (*0-88284-231-5*, 1890) Alfred Pub.

— How to Play the Guitar. (Alfred Handy Guide Ser.). 48p. 1980. 4.50 (*0-88284-152-1*, 1888) Alfred Pub.

— How to Play the Recorder. (Alfred Handy Guide Ser.). (Orig.). 1984. pap. 4.95 (*0-88284-200-5*, 298) Alfred Pub.

— Organ Chord Dictionary. (Alfred Handy Guide Ser.). 48p. 1978. 3.95 (*0-88284-156-4*, 283) Alfred Pub.

— Piano Chord Dictionary. (Alfred Handy Guide Ser.). 48p. 1978. 4.95 (*0-88284-154-8*, 285) Alfred Pub.

Manus, Ron, jt. auth. see Hall, Steve.

Manus, Rosanne. Making Words Work Quick & Easy. 369p. 1993. ring bd. 79.95 (*0-913956-70-8*) EBSCO.

Manus, Rosanne M. The Skillful Teacher's Handbook: Effectively Teaching Regular & Special Education Students. (Illus.). 416p. (C). 1990. spiral bd. 56.95 (*0-398-05702-8*) C C Thomas.

Manus, Steven. How to Play the Harmonica. (Alfred Handy Guide Ser.). 48p. 1978. 4.95 (*0-88284-157-2*, 284) Alfred Pub.

Manus, Willard. Connubial Bliss. 1989. pap. 9.95 (*0-915572-82-6*) Panjandrum.

— The Fighting Men. 192p. 1982. 14.95 (*0-915572-55-9*); pap. 6.95 (*0-915572-54-0*) Panjandrum.

— Other Women, Other Men. 1988. pap. 9.95 (*0-915572-38-9*) Panjandrum.

Manuscriptors Guild Members. Around the Corner: Tenth Anniversary Anthology. Fowler, Dot & Price, Pat, eds. (Illus.). 150p. (Orig.). Date not set. pap. text ed. 12.50 (*0-9637150-1-1*) Talent By Lb.

Manuscripts International Staff, ed. see Mounts, Willard.

Manushina, T., ed. Early Russian Embroidery in the Zagorsk Museum Collection. 294p. (ENG & RUS.). 1983. 56.00 (*0-317-57331-4*, Pub. by Collets UK) St Mut.

Manushkin. Joys of the Sabbath. (J). 1995. 14.00 (*0-671-88333-X*, S&S Bks Young Read) S&S Childrens.

Manushkin, Fran. Hello World. LC 91-71337. (Mickey's World Tour Ser.). (Illus.). 32p. (J). (ps-1). 1991. 8.95 (*1-56282-059-1*) Disney Pr.

— Latkes & Applesauce: A Hannukah Story. (Illus.). (J). (ps-2). 1992. 4.95 (*0-590-42265-0*, Blue Ribbon Bks) Scholastic Inc.

— Latkes & Applesauce: A Hanukkah Story. (J). (ps-2). 1990. 12.95 (*0-590-42261-8*, Scholastic Hardcover) Scholastic Inc.

— Let's Go Riding in Our Strollers. LC 92-72935. (Illus.). 32p. (J). (ps-00). 1993. 13.95 (*1-56282-390-6*); lib. bdg. 13.89 (*1-56282-391-4*) Hyprn Child.

— Let's Go Riding in Our Strollers. LC 92-72935. (Illus.). 32p. (J). (ps-k). Date not set. pap. 4.95 (*0-7868-1038-6*) Hyprn Ppbks.

— Lulu's Mixed-Up Movie. LC 94-49734. (Angel Corners Ser.: No. 3). 1995. 3.99 (*0-14-037200-8*) Puffin Bks.

— My Christmas Safari. LC 92-28643. (Illus.). 32p. (J). (ps-1). 1993. 13.99 (*0-8037-1294-4*); lib. bdg. 13.89 (*0-8037-1295-2*) Dial Bks Young.

— One Hundred One Dalmatians Counting Book & Puppy, Set. (Illus.). 32p. (J). (ps-1). 1993. Boxed set incl. plush puppy. boxed 16.95 (*1-56282-572-0*) Disney Pr.

— Peeping & Sleeping. LC 93-26297. (Illus.). (J). (ps-3). 1994. 14.95 (*0-395-64339-2*, Clarion Bks) HM.

— Puppies & Kittens. (Golden Little Look-Look Book Ser.). (Illus.). 24p. (J). (ps-00). 1989. pap. write for info. (*0-307-11806-1*, Golden Bks) Western Pub.

— Rachel, Meet Your Angel! 96p. (J). 1995. pap. 3.99 (*0-14-037198-2*) Puffin Bks.

— This Is the Matzoh that Papa Brought Home. LC 94-9952. (J). (ps-2). 1995. 14.95 (*0-590-47146-5*) Scholastic Inc.

— Toby Takes the Cake. 96p. (J). 1995. pap. 3.99 (*0-14-037199-0*) Puffin Bks.

— Walt Disney-One Hundred One Dalmatas: Un Libro para Contar. Santacruz, Daniel, tr. LC 93-70677. (Libros Buena Vista Ser.). (Illus.). 32p. (SPA.). (J). 1994. lib. bdg. 13.89 (*1-56282-697-2*); pap. 5.95 (*1-56282-568-2*) Disney Pr.

— Walt Disney's One Hundred One Dalmatians: A Counting Book. LC 90-85426. (Illus.). 32p. (J). (ps-00). 1991. 9.95 (*1-56282-012-5*); lib. bdg. 9.89 (*1-56282-032-X*) Disney Pr.

— Walt Disney's One Hundred One Dalmatians: A Counting Book. LC 92-53493. (Illus.). 32p. (J). (ps-00). 1993. reprint ed. pap. 4.95 (*1-56282-324-8*) Disney Pr.

Manuso, James S. Occupational Clinical Psychology. LC 82-19065. 350p. 1983. text ed. 59.95 (*0-275-91041-5*, C1041, Praeger Pubs) Greenwood.

Manusov, Eugene & Wald, Mike. Character Steins: A Collector's Guide. LC 84-45009. (Illus.). 272p. 1987. 45.00 (*0-8453-4784-5*, Cornwall Bks) Assoc Univ Prs.

Manusov, Eugene V., jt. auth. see Manusov, Patricia L.

Manusov, Patricia L. & Manusov, Eugene V. A Collectors Guide to Diesinger Steins. (Illus.). 96p. (Orig.). 1991. pap. 24.95 (*0-9629458-0-3*) Bristol Pr.

Manuz, Roger, ed. Contemporary Literary Criticism: Yearbook 1989, Vol. 59: The Year in Fiction, Poetry, Drama & World Literature & the Year's New Authors, Prizewinners, Obituaries, & Outstanding Literary Events, Vol. 59. (Illus.). 525p. 1990. text ed. 122.00 (*0-8103-4433-5*) Gale.

Manvel, B., jt. auth. see Bose, R. C.

Manvell, Roger. Elizabeth Inchbald: England's Principal Woman Dramatist & Independent Woman of Letters in 18th Century London. LC 87-21247. (Biography Study Ser.). (Illus.). 232p. (Orig.). (C). 1988. lib. bdg. 50.00 (*0-8191-6633-2*) U Pr of Amer.

— Ingmar Bergman: An Appreciation. LC 79-6697. (Dissertations on Film, 1980 Ser.). 1980. lib. bdg. 20.95 (*0-405-12936-X*) Ayer.

Manvell, Roger, ed. Experiment in the Film. LC 73-124017. (Literature of Cinema Ser.). 1975. reprint ed. 20.95 (*0-405-01623-9*) Ayer.

Manvell, Roger, intro. Selected Comedies: Elizabeth Inchbald. (Illus.). 372p. (Orig.). (C). 1988. lib. bdg. 49.00 (*0-8191-6635-9*) U Pr of Amer.

Manvell, Roger & Jowett, Garth S., eds. The Cinema, 1950. LC 77-11380. (Aspects of Film Ser.). (Illus.). 1978. reprint ed. lib. bdg. 18.95 (*0-405-11139-8*) Ayer.

— The Cinema, 1951. LC 77-18644. (Aspects of Film Ser.). (Illus.). 1978. reprint ed. lib. bdg. 18.95 (*0-405-11145-2*) Ayer.

— The Cinema, 1952. LC 77-18645. (Aspects of Film Ser.). (Illus.). 1978. reprint ed. lib. bdg. 18.95 (*0-405-11146-0*) Ayer.

Manvell, Roger, ed. see Dickinson, Thorold & De La Roche, Catherine.

Manvell, Roger, jt. auth. see Fleming, Michael.

Manvell, Roger, ed. see Hardy, Forsyth.

Manvell, Roger, ed. see Jarratt, Vernon.

Manvell, Roger, ed. see Sadoul, Georges.

Manvell, Roger, ed. see Wollenberg, H. H.

Manville, Daniel E. Prisoners Self-Help Litigation Manual. 2nd rev. ed. LC 83-15406. 684p. (Orig.). 1983. pap. 17.50 (*0-379-20831-8*) Oceana.

— Prisoners Self-Help Litigation Manual. 2nd suppl. ed. LC 83-15406. 684p. (Orig.). 1983. lib. bdg. 30.00 (*0-379-20830-X*) Oceana.

Manville, Daniel E. & Brezna, George N. Post-Conviction Remedies: A Self-Help Manual. LC 88-1464. 571p. 1988. lib. bdg. 35.00 (*0-379-20778-8*); pap. 17.50 (*0-379-20779-6*) Oceana.

Manville, Daniel E., jt. auth. see Boston, John.

Manville, Douglas, ed. see Oliver, George.

Manville, Phillip B. The Origins of Citizenship in Ancient Athens. 309p. 1990. text ed. 39.50 (*0-691-09442-X*) Princeton U Pr.

Manwani, S. N. Evolution of Art & Architecture in Central India: With Special Reference to the Kalachuris of Ratanpur. (C). 1988. 70.00 (*0-8364-2338-0*, Pub. by Agam Kala Prakashan) S Asia.

Manwaring, A., ed. Marathi Proverbs. (C). 1991. reprint ed. 15.00 (*81-206-0704-X*, Pub. by Asian Educ Servs II) S Asia.

***Manwaring, Charles W.** A Digest of the Early Connecticut Probate Records, 3 Vols., Set. 2224p. 1995. reprint ed. 150.00 (*0-8063-1472-9*) Genealog Pub.

Manwaring, G. E. & Dobree, Bonamy. Floating Republic: The Mutinies at Spithead & the Nore, 1797. (Illus.). 299p. 1966. reprint ed. 30.00 (*0-7146-1197-2*, BHA-01497, Pub. by F Cass Pubs UK) Intl Spec Bk.

***Manwaring, Kim H. & Crone, Kerry R.** Neuroendoscopy. 121p. 1991. 40.00 (*0-913113-57-3*) M Liebert.

Manwaring, Max G. Gray Area Phenomena: Confronting the New World Disorder. (Studies in Global Security). (C). 1993. pap. text ed. 39.50 (*0-8133-8748-5*) Westview.

Manwaring, Max G. & Prisk, Court, eds. El Salvador at War: An Oral History of Conflict from the 1979 Insurrection to the Present. LC 88-18741. (Illus.). 555p. 1989. per. 16.00 (*0-16-001693-2*, S/N 008-020-01145-2) USGPO.

Manwaring, Max G. & Sabrosky, Alan N. Defending Europe: The Iberian Connection. 144p. (C). 1929. pap. text ed. 17.00 (*0-8133-7183-X*) Westview.

Manwaring, Randle. A Study of Hymn-Writing & Hymn-Singing in the Christian Church. LC 90-47020. (Texts & Studies in Religion: Vol. 50). 188p. 1990. lib. bdg. 79.95 (*0-88946-798-6*) E Mellen.

Manwood, John. A Treatise of the Lawes of the Forest. LC 76-57398. (English Experience Ser.: No. 814). 1977. reprint ed. lib. bdg. 51.00 (*90-221-0814-7*) Walter J Johnson.

Manx Gaelic Society. Manx, a Course in the Spoken Language. pap. 8.95 (*0-89979-025-9*) British Am Bks.

Many, Joyce & Cox, Carole, eds. Reader Stance & Literary Understanding: Exploring the Theories, Research, & Practice. LC 92-17318. 288p. 1992. text ed. 55.00 (*0-89391-874-1*); pap. text ed. 22.50 (*0-89391-916-0*) Ablex Pub.

Many, Wesley A. & Friker, Walter. Building Computer Literacy: Levels A thru I. (Illus.). 1985. teacher ed 9.50 (*0-932957-01-3*); pap. 6.75 (*0-932957-00-5*) Natl School.

Manyak, Anne, jt. ed. see Almquist, Alan J.

Manyan, Gladys. The Country Seasons Cookbook. LC 74-80292. (Illus.). 184p. 1985. reprint ed. pap. 8.95 (*0-941216-25-X*) Cay-Bel.

— Recipes & Escapades from a Countrywoman's Journal. LC 87-71572. (Illus.). 248p. 1987. 17.50 (*0-941216-45-4*); pap. 9.95 (*0-941216-38-1*) Cay-Bel.

***Manyarrows, Victoria L.** Songs from the Native Lands. LC 95-67634. 96p. 1995. pap. 9.95 (*0-9645234-1-8*) Nopal Pr.

***Manyika & Durrant-Whyte.** Data Fusion & Sensor Management. (Illus.). 289p. 1994. write for info. (*0-13-303132-2*) P-H.

Manyon, L. A., tr. see Bloch, Marc.

Manyoni, Angelika. Consistence of Phenotype: A Study of Gottfried Benn's Views on Lyrical Poetry. LC 83-5462. (American University Studies: Germanic Languages & Literature: Ser. I, Vol. 698). 346p. (Orig.). (C). 1983. pap. text ed. 36.30 (*0-8204-0011-4*) P Lang Pubs.

***Man'yoshu, English.** The Ten Thousand Leaves: A Translation of the Man'yoshu, Japan's Premier Anthology of Classical Poetry, Vol. 1. LC 80-8561. (Princeton Library of Asian Translations). (Illus.). 418p. 1987. reprint ed. pap. 119.20 (*0-7837-8176-8*, 2047881) Bks Demand.

Manypenny, George W. Our Indian Wards. LC 68-54844. (American Scene Ser.). 1972. reprint ed. lib. bdg. 35.00 (*0-306-71140-0*) Da Capo.

Manz, A. F. The Welding Power Handbook (WPH) 208p. 1973. 13.00 (*0-914096-04-4*, WPH) Am Welding.

Manz, Beatrice F. The Rise & Rule of Tamerlane. (Studies in Islamic Civilization). (Illus.). 250p. (C). 1989. 64.95 (*0-521-34595-2*) Cambridge U Pr.

— The Rise & Rule of Tamerlane. (Studies in Islamic Civilization). (Illus.). 238p. (C). 1991. pap. 19.95 (*0-521-40614-5*) Cambridge U Pr.

***Manz, Beatrice F., ed.** Central Asia in Historical Perspective. (John M. Olin Critical Issues Ser.). (C). 1994. text ed. 54.95 (*0-8133-8801-5*) Westview.

Manz, Beatrice F., ed. see Fletcher, Joseph F., Jr.

Manz, Beatriz. Refugees of a Hidden War: The Aftermath of Counterinsurgency in Guatemala. LC 87-10169. (Anthropological Studies of Contemporary Issues). (Illus.). 283p. 1987. 74.50 (*0-88706-675-5*); pap. 24.95 (*0-88706-676-3*) State U NY Pr.

— Repatriation & Reintegration: An Arduous Process in Guatemala. 72p. (Orig.). 1988. pap. 7.50 (*0-924046-02-3*) Ctr EPRA.

Manz, Charles C. Mastering Self-Leadership: Empowering Yourself for Personal Excellence. 168p. 1991. pap. 15.95 (*0-13-560863-5*) P-H.

— Super Leadership. 1990. pap. 10.00 (*0-425-12356-1*, Berkley Trade) Berkley Pub.

Manz, Charles C. & Sims, Henry P., Jr. Business Without Bosses: How Self-Managing Teams are Building High Performance Companies. LC 93-7864. 256p. 1993. text ed. 24.95 (*0-471-57700-6*) Wiley.

***Manz, Kenneth W.** The Challenge of Recycling Refrigerants. Turpin, Joanna & Checket-Hanks, B. A., eds. LC 94-34530. (Illus.). 200p. 1995. 37.95 (*1-885863-00-4*) Busn News.

Manz, Olaf & Wolf, Thomas R. Representations of Solvable Groups. (London Mathematical Society Lecture Note Ser.: No. 185). 320p. (C). 1993. pap. 42.95 (*0-521-39739-1*) Cambridge U Pr.

Manzaloui, Mahmoud, ed. Arabic Short Stories Nineteen Forty-Five to Nineteen Sixty-Five. 1986. pap. 20.00 (*977-424-121-5*, Pub. by Am Univ Cairo Pr UA) Col U Pr.

— Arabic Writing Today: Drama. (American Research Center in Egypt, Publications Ser.: Vol. 2). 643p. (Orig.). 1977. pap. 12.50 (*0-936770-00-7*, Pub. by Amer Res Ctr Egypt UA) Eisenbrauns.

Manzanares, C. Lo Que Usted Necesita Saber-Nueva Era (What You Need to Know about-New Age) (SPA.). Date not set. 2.49 (*1-56063-165-5*, 489071) Editorial Unilit.

Manzanares, Cesar. Ovnis: Cual Es la Verdad? (SPA.). 1992. 3.99 (*1-56063-178-3*, 490264) Editorial Unilit.

***Manzano, Juan F.** The Autobiography of a Slave: A Bilingual Edition. Schulman, Ivan A., ed. Garfield, Evelyn P., tr. (Latin American Literature & Culture Ser.). 160p. (C). 1996. 34.95 (*0-8143-2537-8*); pap. 16.95 (*0-8143-2538-6*) Wayne St U Pr.

Manzano, Juan F. & De La Concepcion Valdes, Gabriel. Two Cuban Poets, 2 vols. in 1. (B. E. Ser.: No. 54). 1937. Two works in one unit. 39.00 (*0-8115-3005-1*) Periodicals Srv.

Manzano, M. Extensions of First-Order Logic. (Cambridge Tracts in Theoretical Computer Science Ser.). 350p. (C). 1992. write for info. (*0-521-35435-8*) Cambridge U Pr.

Manzano, Mariano O. Dictionary of Synonyms & Antonyms: Diccionario de Sinonimos y Antonimos. 3rd ed. 368p. (SPA.). 1990. write for info. (*0-7859-4956-9*) Fr & Eur.

Manzano, R. Whitney, jt. auth. see Cho, David Y.

Manzano, R. Whitney, jt. auth. see Cho, Paul Y.

Manzano, Roy R. Pelly's Exciting Adventures. (Illus.). (J). 1993. 9.95 (*0-533-10526-9*) Vantage.

Manzardo, Lori, illus. Current Techniques in Neurosurgery. 240p. 1993. text ed. 175.00 (*1-878132-01-6*) Current Med.

Manzella. Infectious Disease, No. 2: Outpatient IBM 5. 1991. write for info. (*0-933755-26-0*) Mosby Yr Bk.

Manzella, John L. The Businessman's Guide to Free Trade. (Illus.). 90p. (C). 1989. pap. 9.95 (*0-926566-00-8*) Free Trade Consults.

— Mexico & NAFTA: The Real Impact. 1994. write for info. (*0-614-04810-9*); write for info. (*0-614-06601-8*) Free Trade Consults.

— Opportunity in Mexico: A Small Business Guide. 1992. write for info. (*0-614-06600-X*) Free Trade Consults.

***Manzella, John L. & Walker, Tony.** Opportunity in Mexico: A Small Business Guide. (Illus.). 1992. write for info. (*0-614-04809-5*) Free Trade Consults.

Manzer, Alison. The Bank Act Annotated. 624p. 1993. boxed 80.00 (*0-409-89901-1*, CN) Butterworth Legal Pubs.

Manzer, Ronald. Public Policies & Political Development in Canada. 256p. 1985. pap. 19.95 (*0-8020-6559-7*) U of Toronto Pr.

— State Education in Canada: Public Policy & Public Philosophy. 367p. 1994. 50.00 (*0-8020-0604-3*); pap. 19.95 (*0-8020-7209-7*) U of Toronto Pr.

Manzer, Ronald A. Public Policies & Political Development in Canada. LC 86-110537. (Illus.). 250p. reprint ed. pap. 71.30 (*0-7837-0527-1*, 2040853) Bks Demand.

Manzetti, Luigi. Institutions, Parties, & Coalitions in Argentine Politics. LC 93-12872. (Latin American Ser.). 408p. (C). 1994. text ed. 75.00 (*0-8229-3755-7*) U of Pittsburgh Pr.

— The International Monetary Fund & Economic Stabilization: The Argentine Case. LC 90-24565. 256p. 1991. text ed. 59.95 (*0-275-93397-0*, C3397, Praeger Pubs) Greenwood.

Manzetti, Luigi, jt. auth. see Snow, Peter G.

Manzi, Deborah B. & Weaver, Patricia. Head Injury: The Acute Care Phase. LC 86-42910. 150p. 1987. pap. 18.00 (*1-55642-001-3*) SLACK Inc.

Manzi, J. J. & Castagna, M., eds. Clam Mariculture in North America. (Developments in Aquaculture & Fisheries Science Ser.: No. 19). 461p. 1989. 115.50 (*0-444-87300-7*) Elsevier.

M

***Manzi, Raffaele. Christian Multi-Media Catalogue for Multi-Lingual Ministries. Ulrich, Sharon S., ed. 384p. (Orig.). 1994. pap. 100.00 (*0-9644029-1-2*) Means NJ.**

If you are in an everyday process of attempting to disseminate Biblical truths to people of culture & language different from yourself, this soon-to-be-published book, CHRISTIAN MULTI-MEDIA CATALOGUE FOR MULTI-LINGUAL MINISTRIES, by Raffaele Manzi from MEANS' INC., is for you. This book will be available in two formats; computer diskettes 3 1/2 & 5 inches & hard page notebook. As this is a resource that will be revised & updated yearly, update information will be made available to original purchasers at a reduced price. THE CHRISTIAN MULTI-MEDIA CATALOGUE FOR MULTI-LINGUAL MINISTRIES, cites over 1,000 distributors & lists over 350 different languages. It indexes by languages, countries of origin, & countries by which these distributors are located, & also has an alphabetical index of all producers, publishers & distributors. The cost paid prior to publication is $75 to missionaries, & $100 to all other organizations & agencies. After publication, the price will be $100 for missionaries & $120 to organizations & agencies. For further information or order forms write MEANS' INC., 488 Parker Ave., Hackensack, NJ 07601; 201-488-6727.

Publisher Provided Annotation.

— Italian-American Experience in Georgia. (Illus.). 135p. (Orig.). Date not set. pap. 25.00 (*0-9644029-0-4*) Means NJ.

Manzini, Ezio. The Material of Invention: Materials & Design. (Illus.). 256p. 1989. 50.00 (*0-262-13242-7*) MIT Pr.

— The Material of Invention: Materials & Design. 250p. (C). 1989. text ed. 135.00 (*0-85072-247-0*) St Mut.

Manzini, Maria R. Locality: A Theory & Some of Its Empirical Consequences. (Linguistic Inquiry Monographs: No. 19). (Illus.). 255p. 1992. 37.50 (*0-262-13279-6*); pap. 17.95 (*0-262-63140-7*) MIT Pr.

Manzione, Carol K. Christ's Hospital of London, 1552-1598: Passing Deed of Pity. LC 94-16865. 232p. 1995. 37.50 (*0-945636-71-7*) Susquehanna U Pr.

Manzione, Joseph. I Am Looking to the North for My Life: Sitting Bull, 1876-1881. (Publications in the American West: Vol. 25). (Illus.). 300p. 1994. reprint ed. pap. 14.95 (*0-87480-461-2*) U of Utah Pr.

An Asterisk (*) at the beginning of an entry indicates that the title is appearing in BIP for the first time.

Manzione, Louis T. Applications of Computer-Aided Engineering in Injection Molding. 1988. 83.00 (0-685-22187-3) T-C Pubns CA.

— Applications of Computer Aided Engineering in Injection Molding. 302p. (C). 1987. text ed. 94.50 (1-56990-057-4) Hanser-Gardner.

Manzo. Content Area Reading: A Heuristic Approach. 528p. (C). 1990. text ed. write for info. (0-675-20652-9, Merrill Pub Co) Macmillan.

Manzo, jt. auth. see Blum.

Manzo, Anthony & Manzo, Ula C. Literary Disorders: Holistic Diagnosis & Remediation. (Illus.). 515p. (C). 1992. text ed. 48.00 (0-03-072633-6) HB Coll Pubs.

Manzo, Anthony V. & Manzo, Ula C. Literacy Disorders: Holistic Diagnosis & Remediation. 512p. (C). 1993. lib. bdg. write for info. (0-03-072566-6); Test bank. pap. text ed. 2.00 (0-03-097349-X) HB Coll Pubs.

— Teaching Children to Be Literate: A Reflective Approach. (Illus.). 640p. (C). 1994. write for info. (0-15-300560-2) HB Coll Pubs.

Manzo, Anthony V., et al. Informal Reading-Thinking Inventory (IR-TI) An Informal Reading Inventory (IRI) with Options for Assessing Additional Elements of Higher-Order Literacy. 224p. (C). 1994. pap. text ed. write for info. (0-15-500956-7) HB Coll Pubs.

***Manzo, Bettina.** The Animal Rights Movement in the U. S., 1975-1990: An Annotated Bibliography. LC 94-19622. 306p. 1994. text ed. 39.50 (0-8108-2732-8) Scarecrow.

Manzo, David P. Hollywood Blues. LC 88-70449. 97p. (Orig.). 1989. pap. 6.00 (0-916383-57-1) Aegina Pr.

Manzo, Kathryn A. Domination, Resistance, & Social Change in South Africa: The Local Effects of Global Power. LC 92-9116. 304p. 1992. text ed. 59.95 (0-275-94364-X, C4364, Praeger Pubs) Greenwood.

Manzo, Luigi. Advances in Neurotoxicology: Proceedings of the International Congress on Neurotoxicology, Varese, 27-30 September 1979. LC 80-40319. (Illus.). 404p. 1980. 174.00 (0-08-024953-1, Pub. by Pergamon Repr UK) Franklin.

Manzo, Ula C., jt. auth. see Manzo, Anthony V.

Manzo, Ula C., jt. auth. see Manzo, Anthony.

***Manzo, Vicki.** Ralph's Favorite Christmas Present. LC 93-95025. (Illus.). 64p. (Orig.). (J). 1995. pap. 8.00 (1-56002-409-7, Univ Edtns) Aegina Pr.

Manzoni, Alessandro. The Betrothed. Penman, Bruce, tr. (Classics Ser.). 720p. 1984. pap. 11.95 (0-14-044274-X, Penguin Classics) Viking Penguin.

— On the Historical Novel. Bermann, Sandra, tr. LC 83-10583. x, 134p. 1984. 20.00 (0-8032-3084-2) U of Nebr Pr.

Manzoor, M. Heat Flow Through Extended Surface Heat Exchangers. (Lecture Notes in Engineering Ser.: Vol. 5). 277p. 1983. pap. 37.00 (0-387-13047-0) Spr-Verlag.

Manzur, Ibn. Lisan al Arab, 15 vols., Set. 600p. (ARA & ENG.). 1979. 295.00 (0-86685-541-6) Intl Bk Ctr.

Manzur, Meher. Exchange Rates, Prices & World Trade: New Methods, Evidence & Implications. 224p. 1992. 77.50 (0-415-08589-6, A9688) Routledge.

Mao. Exponential Stability of Stochastic Differential Equations. LC 94-6019. (Pure & Applied Mathematics Ser.: Vol. 182). 328p. 1994. 125.00 (0-8247-9080-4) Dekker.

Mao, Ashikho D. Nagas: Problems & Politics. x, 206p. 1992. 19.95 (1-881338-30-4) Nataraj Bks.

— Nagas: Problems & Politics. (C). 1992. 24.00 (81-7024-486-2, Pub. by Ashish II) S Asia.

Mao Dun. Rainbow. Zelin, Madeleine, tr. LC 91-31273. (Voices from Asia Ser.: No. 4). 255p. 1992. 38.00 (0-520-07327-4); pap. 13.00 (0-520-07328-2) U CA Pr.

— Spring Silkworms & Other Stories. 2nd ed. 1980. 9.95 (0-8351-0615-2) China Bks.

Mao, James C. Corporate Financial Decisions. LC 75-18149. (Illus.). 600p. (C). 1976. text ed. 19.95 (0-915944-00-6) Pavan Pubs.

Mao, Li, ed. Ancient Way to Keep Fit. Luzeng, Song et al, trs. LC 92-81013. 1992. 20.00 (0-679-74371-5) Random.

— Ancient Way to Keep Fit. Luzeng, Song et al, trs. LC 92-81013. 224p. 1992. 20.00 (0-936070-14-5) Shelter Pubns.

Mao, Lina, tr. see Wittet, Scott & Wong, Debbie.

Mao, Nathan K., tr. see Ch'ien, Chung-Shu.

***Mao Tse-Tung.** A Critique of Soviet Economics. Roberts, Moss, tr. LC 77-70971. reprint ed. pap. 44.80 (0-7837-9611-0, 2060368) Bks Demand.

— Five Essays on Philosophy. 1977. 5.95 (0-8351-0451-6) China Bks.

— Mao's China: Party Reform Documents, 1942-44. Compton, Boyd, tr. LC 82-6102. lii, 278p. 1982. reprint ed. text ed. 59.75 (0-313-23593-7, MAMAC, Greenwood Pr) Greenwood.

Mao, Tse-tung. Quotations from Chairman Mao. 312p. (C). 1990. 7.95 (0-8351-2388-X) China Bks.

Mao Tse-tung. Snow Glistens on the Great Wall: The Complete Poetical Works of Mao Tse-Tung. Wen-yee, Ma, ed. Wen-Yee, Ma, tr. (Illus.). 208p. (Orig.). 1985. 17.95 (0-915520-78-8); pap. 9.95 (0-915520-79-6) Santa Barb Pr.

— Ten Poems & Lyrics by Mao Tse-tung. Wang Hui-Ming, tr. & illus. by. LC 74-21248. 72p. 1975. 15.00 (0-87023-178-2); pap. 8.95 (0-87023-182-0) U of Mass Pr.

Mao Tse-Tung, et al. China: The March Toward Unity. LC 75-36225. reprint ed. 37.50 (0-404-14475-6) AMS Pr.

Mao Tun, Dun. Spring Silkworms & Other Stories. 2nd ed. Shapiro, Sidney, tr. 237p. (C). 1979. 9.95 (0-917056-90-6, Pub. by Foreign Lang Pr CH) Cheng & Tsui.

Mao Wall, Lina, teller. Judge Rabbit & the Tree Spirit: A Folktale from Cambodia. LC 90-26240. (Illus.). 32p. (J). (gr. k-5). 1991. 13.95 (0-89239-071-9) Childrens Book Pr.

Mao Zedong. Report from Xunwu. Thompson, Roger R., tr. LC 89-21776. (Illus.). 304p. 1990. 32.50 (0-8047-1678-1) Stanford U Pr.

Maolain, Ciaran O. The Radical Right: An International Dictionary. 500p. 1980. lib. bdg. 131.25 (0-87436-514-7) ABC-CLIO.

***Maomao, Deng.** Deng Xiaoping: My Father. 512p. 1995. 27.50 (0-465-01625-1) Basic.

Maor, Eli. E: The Story of a Number. (Illus.). 232p. 1993. text ed. 24.95 (0-691-03390-0) Princeton U Pr.

— To Infinity & Beyond: A Cultural History of the Infinite. (Illus.). 1991. 49.50 (0-8176-3325-1) Birkhauser.

— To Infinity & Beyond: A Cultural History of the Institute. (Illus.). 294p. 1991. pap. text ed. 16.95 (0-691-02511-8) Princeton U Pr.

Maoshing Ni. Chinese Herbology Made Easy. (Illus.). 150p. 1986. pap. text ed. 14.50 (0-937064-12-2) SevenStar Comm.

Maoshing Ni & Daoshing Ni. Golden Message: A Guide to Spiritual Life with Self-Study Program for Learning the Integral Way. LC 90-61067. 1993. pap. 11.95 (0-937064-36-X) SevenStar Comm.

Maoz, Benjamin, et al. Doctors & Their Feelings: A Pharmacology of Medical Caring. LC 91-29032. 168p. 1992. text ed. 55.00 (0-275-93990-1, C3990, Praeger Pubs) Greenwood.

Ma'oz, M., ed. Studies on Palestine During the Ottoman Period. 224p. 1979. text ed. 35.00 (965-223-589-X, Pub. by Magnes Press IS) Eisenbrauns.

Ma'oz, Moshe. Palestinian Leadership on the West Bank: The Changing Role of the Arab Mayors under Jordan & Israel. (Illus.). 232p. 1984. 40.00 (0-7146-3234-1, Pub. by F Cass Pubs UK); pap. 19.50 (0-7146-4046-8, Pub. by F Cass Pubs UK) Intl Spec Bk.

— Syria & Israel: From War to Peacemaking. 320p. 1995. 45.00 (0-19-828018-1) OUP.

Maoz, Zeev. National Choices & International Processes. (Cambridge Studies in International Relations: No. 8). (Illus.). 624p. (C). 1990. 84.95 (0-521-36595-3) Cambridge U Pr.

— Paradoxes of War: On the Art of National Self-Entrapment. (Studies in International Conflict: Vol. 3). 384p. 1989. 70.00 (0-04-445113-X) Routledge Chapman & Hall.

Map & Geography Round Table of the American Library Staff, jt. ed. see Koepp, Donna P.

***Map International, Inc. Staff.** Use It...or Lose It. 176p. 1994. boxed 19.95 (0-7872-0127-8) Kendall-Hunt.

MAP Staff. EDI Management, Security, Audit & Internal Controls Manual (Map-29) (Security, Audit & Control Ser.). 200p. 1993. student ed. ring bd. 390.00 (0-940706-50-4) Management Advisory Pubns.

Map, Walter. De Nugis Curialium. James, Montagu R., ed. (Anecdota Oxoniensia Ser.: No. 14). 1988. reprint ed. 71.50 (0-404-63964-X) AMS Pr.

— Gualteri Mapes De Nugis Curialium Distinctiones Quinque. Wright, Thomas, ed. (Camden Society, London. Publications, First Ser.: No. 50). reprint ed. 60.00 (0-404-50150-8) AMS Pr.

— Latin Poems Commonly Attributed to Walter Mapes. Wright, Thomas, ed. (Camden Society, London. Publications, First Ser.: No. 16). reprint ed. 95.00 (0-404-50116-8) AMS Pr.

Mapa, Joseph, jt. ed. see Turner, Gerald P.

Mapanje, Jack. The Chattering Wagtails of Mikuyu Prison. (African Writers Ser.). 1993. pap. 9.95 (0-435-91198-8) Heinemann.

— Of Chameleons & Gods. (African Writers Ser.). (Orig.). (C). 1991. pap. 8.95 (0-435-91194-5) Heinemann.

Mapel, David. Social Justice Reconsidered: The Problem of Appropriate Precision in a Theory of Justice. LC 88-30131. 184p. 1989. 24.95 (0-252-01598-3) U of Ill Pr.

Mapel, David R., jt. ed. see Nardin, Terry.

Mapes. Name Games. 1985. pap. 5.95 (0-86530-077-1) Incentive Pubns.

***Mapes, Bruce E.** Child Eyewitness Testimony: Ecological Sexual Abuse Investigations. LC 94-41029. 1995. write for info. (0-88422-154-7) Clinical Psych.

***Mapes, Carrie & Gold, Judith.** Goldilocks & the Three Bears. (Folktale Theme Ser.: Vol. 2). (Illus.). 64p. (J). (gr. k-2). 1995. teacher ed, pap. text ed. 6.95 (1-55799-373-4, EMC 525) Evan-Moor Corp.

— Jack & the Beanstalk. (Folktale Theme Ser.: Vol. 1). (Illus.). 64p. (J). (gr. k-2). 1995. teacher ed, pap. text ed. 6.95 (1-55799-372-6, EMC 524) Evan-Moor Corp.

— The Little Red Hen. (Folktale Theme Ser.: Vol. 5). (Illus.). 64p. (J). (gr. k-2). 1995. teacher ed, pap. text ed. 6.95 (1-55799-376-9, EMC 528) Evan-Moor Corp.

— Little Red Riding Hood. (Folktale Theme Ser.: Vol. 4). (Illus.). 64p. (J). (gr. k-2). 1995. teacher ed, pap. text ed. 6.95 (1-55799-375-0, EMC 527) Evan-Moor Corp.

— The Three Little Pigs. (Folktale Theme Ser.: Vol. 3). (Illus.). 64p. (J). (gr. k-2). 1995. teacher ed, pap. text ed. 6.95 (1-55799-374-2, EMC 526) Evan-Moor Corp.

— The Ugly Duckling. (Folktale Theme Ser.: Vol. 6). (Illus.). 64p. (J). (gr. k-2). 1995. teacher ed, pap. text ed. 6.95 (1-55799-377-7, EMC 529) Evan-Moor Corp.

Mapes, E. K. Escritos Ineditos de R. Dario. 224p. 3.80 (0-318-22345-7) Hispanic Inst.

Mapes Monde Staff, ed. see Woods, Edith D.

Mapes, Olin V. Westmoreland Nee Neville. (Orig.). 1992. pap. 28.50 (1-55613-615-3) Heritage Bk.

Mapes, Victor. Duse & the French. LC 68-56485. 1972. reprint ed. 19.95 (0-405-08779-9) Ayer.

Maple. Superstition, Are You Superstitious? 1979. pap. 2.00 (0-87980-245-6) Wilshire.

Maple, Frank F. Dynamic Interviewing: An Introduction to Counseling. (Human Services Guides Ser.: Vol. 41). 160p. (C). 1985. pap. text ed. 17.95 (0-8039-2513-1) Sage.

Maple, M. B. & Fischer, O., eds. Superconductivity in Ternary Compounds II: Superconductivity & Magnetism. (Topics in Current Physics Ser.: Vol. 34). (Illus.). 335p. 1982. 63.00 (0-387-11814-4) Spr-Verlag.

Maple, M. B., jt. ed. see Fischer, O.

Maple, Marilyn. On the Wings of a Butterfly: A Story about Life & Death. LC 91-50854. (Illus.). 32p. (Orig.). (J). (gr. 1-6). 1992. 18.95 (0-943990-69-6); pap. 9.95 (0-943990-68-8) Parenting Pr.

Maple Summer Workshop & Symposium. Mathematical Computation with Maple V - Ideas & Applications: Proceedings of the Maple Summer Workshop & Symposium, University of Michigan, Ann Arbor, June 28-30, 1993. Lee, Thomas, ed. LC 93-21604. viii, 199p. 1993. pap. 34.50 (0-8176-3724-9) Birkhauser.

Maple, Terry & Archibald, Erika. Zoo Man: Inside the Zoo Revolution. LC 91-61926. (Illus.). 224p. 1992. 19.95 (1-56352-016-8) Longstreet Pr Inc.

Maples, Ann W. The Day the Music Stopped. LC 89-52187. 189p. 1990. 9.95 (1-55523-316-3) Winston-Derek.

Maples, Deirdre M., jt. auth. see Graw, LeRoy H.

Maples, Edna H., jt. auth. see Stewart, Patricia A.

Maples, J. D. & Maplesden, Doug. Deadly Design. 256p. 1994. pap. 8.95 (1-56901-267-9) NW Pub.

Maples, Robert E. Petroleum Refinery Process Economics. LC 92-37931. 384p. 1993. 74.95 (0-87814-384-X, P4488) PennWell Bks.

Maples, Ruth M., ed. see Bollinger, Orenia.

***Maples, W. C.** NSUCO Oculomotor Test. Bleything, Willard, ed. (Illus.). 60p. (Orig.). (C). 1994. lib. bdg. 18.00 (0-943599-74-1) OEPF.

Maples, Wallace R. Opportunities in Aerospace Careers. (Illus.). 160p. 1991. 13.95 (0-8442-8650-8, VGM Career Bks); pap. 10.95 (0-8442-8651-6, VGM Career Bks) NTC Pub Grp.

Maples, William R. & Browning, Michael. Dead Men do Tell Tales. LC 94-12290. 1994. 22.95 (0-385-47490-3) Doubleday.

Maplesden, Doug, jt. auth. see Maples, J. D.

Maplet, John. A Greene Forest, or a Naturall Historie. LC 79-84122. (English Experience Ser.: No. 941). 244p. 1979. reprint ed. lib. bdg. 18.00 (90-221-0941-0) Walter J Johnson.

***Maplin Staff.** Audio IC Projects. (Maplin Ser.). 208p. 1995. pap. 19.95 (0-7506-2121-4, Focal) Buttrwrth-Heinemann.

— Auto Electronics Projects. (Maplin Ser.). 208p. 1995. pap. 19.95 (0-7506-2296-2, Focal) Buttrwrth-Heinemann.

— TV & Video Projects. (Maplin Ser.). 208p. 1995. pap. 19.95 (0-7506-2297-0, Focal) Buttrwrth-Heinemann.

Mapother, William R. Kentucky Collections: Practice Systems Library Manual. LC 79-91144. ring bd. 120.00 (0-317-03196-1) Lawyers Cooperative.

— Kentucky Collections: Practice Systems Library Manual. suppl. ed. LC 79-91144. 1993. Suppl. 1993. 65.00 (0-317-04715-9) Lawyers Cooperative.

***Mapou, Robert L. & Spector, Jack, eds.** Clinical Neuropsychological Assessment: A Cognitive Approach. (Critical Issues in Neuropsychology Ser.: Vol. 1). 360p. 1995. 65.00 (0-306-44869-6, Plenum Pr) Plenum.

Mapp. Frock Coats & Epaulets. 1985. pap. 9.95 (0-915463-24-5) Green Hill.

***Mapp, Alf J., Jr.** Bed of Honor. 480p. 1995. pap. 12.95 (1-56901-717-4) NW Pub.

— The Golden Dragon: Alfred the Great & His Times. (Illus.). 254p. 1991. reprint ed. pap. 12.95 (0-8191-7826-8) Madison Bks UPA.

— Thomas Jefferson: A Strange Case of Mistaken Identity. 512p. 1989. 24.95 (0-8191-5782-1); pap. 14.95 (0-8191-7454-8) Madison Bks UPA.

— Thomas Jefferson: Passionate Pilgrim - the Presidency, the Founding of the University, & the Private Battle. (Illus.). 472p. 1991. 24.95 (0-8191-8053-X) Madison Bks UPA.

Mapp, Alf J. Thomas Jefferson: Passionate Pilgrim: The Presidency & the Founding of the University. 1993. pap. 16.95 (1-56833-020-0) Madison Bks UPA.

Mapp, Barbara A. Just Like Grandma Used to Make. (Illus.). 308p. (Orig.). 1992. pap. 14.95 (0-9627087-9-8) Mt Olive Coll Pr.

Mapp, Edward. Directory of Blacks in the Performing Arts. 2nd ed. LC 89-30477. 612p. 1990. 57.50 (0-8108-2222-9) Scarecrow.

Mapp, Edward, ed. Puerto Rican Perspectives. LC 73-20175. 179p. 1974. 20.00 (0-8108-0691-6) Scarecrow.

Mapp, Edward, jt. auth. see Kisch, John.

Mapp, Larry G. The Harbrace College Workbook, Form 11B. 11th ed. 360p. (C). 1990. pap. text ed. 18.75 (0-15-531881-0); pap. text ed. 5.50 (0-15-531882-9) HB Coll Pubs.

Mapp, Nigel, jt. ed. see Norris, Christopher.

Mapp, Wayne D. The Iran-United States Claims Tribunal: The First Ten Years: an Assessment of the Tribunal's Jurisprudence & Its Contribution to International Arbitration. LC 92-40259. (Melland Schill Monographs in International Law). 1993. text ed. 79.95 (0-7190-3790-5, Pub. by Manchester Univ Pr UK) St Martin.

Mappen, Marc. Jerseyana: The Underside of New Jersey History. LC 91-41139. (Illus.). 235p. (C). 1992. text ed. 40.00 (0-8135-1818-0); pap. 14.95 (0-8135-1819-9) Rutgers U Pr.

— Witches & Historians: Interpretations of Salem. LC 78-2579. (American Problem Studies). 126p. 1980. pap. 9.50 (0-88275-653-2) Krieger.

Mappes, Thomas A. & Zembaty, Jane S. Biomedical Ethics. 3rd ed. 672p. (C). 1991. text ed. write for info. (0-07-040126-8) McGraw.

— Social Ethics: Morality & Social Policy. 4th ed. 544p. (C). 1992. pap. text ed. write for info. (0-07-040133-0) McGraw.

***Mappin, Don.** Mortal Enemies: Sentinels. 150p. (YA). (gr. 10). 1995. pap. text ed. 15.00 (0-9641722-2-4) Black Gate.

Mapplethorpe Estates Staff. Mapplethorpe. 1992. 500.00 (0-679-41842-3) Random.

Mapplethorpe, Robert. The Black Book. 128p. 1986. 50.00 (0-312-08302-5) St Martin.

— Black Book. (Illus.). 112p. 1988. pap. 24.95 (0-312-02166-6) St Martin.

— Flowers. (Illus.). 108p. 1990. 60.00 (0-8212-1781-X) Bulfinch Pr.

— Flowers. (Illus.). 108p. 1993. pap. 29.95 (0-8212-2019-5) Bulfinch Pr.

— Flowers Vol. 1, Mini ed. (Illus.). 108p. 1994. 9.95 (0-8212-2151-5) Bulfinch Pr.

— Lady: Lisa Lyon. 1991. 40.00 (0-312-05289-8); pap. 24.95 (0-312-05290-1) St Martin.

— Some Women. (Illus.). 120p. 1992. pap. 29.95 (0-8212-1937-5) Bulfinch Pr.

— Some Women, Mini ed. (Illus.). 120p. 1995. 10.95 (0-8212-2197-3) Bulfinch Pr.

Mapplethorpe, Robert, photos. Robert Mapplethorpe: Certain People. (Illus.). 132p. 1985. 55.00 (0-942642-14-7) Twelvetrees Pr.

Mapplethorpe, Robert, jt. auth. see Marshall, Richard.

Maprayil, Cyriac. The Soviets & Afghanistan. 129p. 1986. 19.95 (81-85047-07-3) Asia Bk Corp.

Maps International AB Staff & GLA Kartor AB Staff. Earth MAPBOOK - Environmental Atlas. (Mapbook Ser.). 187p. 1993. 18.95 (1-879856-25-5) Interarts.

Maps International AB Staff, jt. auth. see Liber Kartor AB Staff.

Maps International Staff, et al. Earth Factbook - Facts & Maps. (Mapbook Ser.). (Illus.). 183p. 1993. 15.95 (1-879856-28-X) Interarts.

Mapson, J. Wendell, Jr. The Ministry of Music in the Black Church. 1984. pap. 9.00 (0-8170-1057-2) Judson.

***Mapson, Jo-Ann.** Blue Rodeo. 1995. pap. 12.00 (0-06-092635-X, PL) HarpC.

— Blue Rodeo: A Novel. LC 93-46453. 352p. 1994. 22.00 (0-06-016944-3, HarpT) HarpC.

— Blue Rodeo: A Novel. large type ed. LC 94-12999. 536p. 1994. 21.95 (0-7862-0280-7) Thorndike Pr.

— Fault Line. LC 89-62971. 240p. 1989. pap. 11.95 (0-944870-02-3) Pacific Writers Pr.

— Hank & Chloe. large type ed. LC 93-13683. 1993. 24.95 (0-7927-1718-X, Curley Lrg Print); pap. 22.95 (0-7927-1699-X, Curley Lrg Print) Chivers N Amer.

— Hank & Chloe. 320p. 1994. reprint ed. pap. 12.00 (0-06-092464-0, PL) HarpC.

Mapstone, Bryan. Making Wooden Toys for All Ages. (Illus.). 172p. 1990. 19.95 (0-7153-9382-0, Pub. by D & C Pub UK) Sterling.

— Making Wooden Toys for All Ages. LC 92-44019. (Illus.). 172p. (YA). (gr. 10-12). 1993. pap. 17.95 (0-7153-9809-1, Pub. by D & C Pub UK) Sterling.

Mapstone, Edna. Footsteps of Faith. (Illus.). 32p. (Orig.). (J). (gr. 1-5). 1993. student ed 3.99 (0-87509-528-3) Chr Pubns.

Mapstone, Richard. Policing in a Divided Society: A Study of Part-Time Policing in Northern Ireland. 139p. 1994. 51.95 (1-85628-598-7, Pub. by Avebury Pub UK) Ashgate Pub Co.

Maqay, T. & Orszagh, Laszlo, eds. A Concise English-Hungarian Dictionary. 1056p. 1990. 39.95 (0-19-864170-2) OUP.

Maqsood, Rosalyn. Petra: A Travellers' Guide. (Illus.). 192p. 1994. 29.95 (1-873938-12-8, Pub. by Garnet Pubng Ltd UK) Paul & Co Pubs.

Maqsood, Ruqaiyyah W. The Separated Ones: Jesus, the Pharisees, & Islam. 192p. 1992. pap. 17.50 (0-334-02498-6, SCM Pr) TPI PA.

***Maquet, Charles.** Larousse Dictionnaire Analogique. 11th ed. 600p. (FRE.). 1971. 55.00 (0-7859-7645-0, 2033402185) Fr & Eur.

Maquet, J. Introduction to Aesthetic Anthropology. (Other Realities Ser.: No. 1). 110p. (C). 1971. pap. text ed. 11.50 (0-89003-041-3) Undena Pubns.

Maquet, Jacques P. Africanity: The Cultural Unity of Black Africa. Rayfield, Joan R., tr. (Illus.). 1972. pap. 9.95 (0-19-519700-3) OUP.

— Civilizations of Black Africa. Rayfield, Joan R., tr. 1972. pap. 15.95 (0-19-501464-2) OUP.

— The Sociology of Knowledge. Locke, John F., tr. LC 70-168963. 318p. 1973. reprint ed. text ed. 59.75 (0-8371-6236-X, MASK, Greenwood Pr) Greenwood.

Maquet, Jacques P., ed. see Fernandez, James, et al.

Maquet, Jacques P., ed. see Greenberg, J., et al.

Maquet, Jaques P. The Aesthetic Experience: An Anthropologist Looks at the Visual Arts. LC 85-8232. (Illus.). 277p. 1986. text ed. 50.00 (0-300-03342-7) Yale U Pr.

— The Aesthetic Experience: An Anthropologist Looks at the Visual Arts. LC 85-8232. (Illus.). 277p. 1988. pap. 22.00 (0-300-04134-9) Yale U Pr.

Maquet, Jaques P., ed. see Mintz, S., et al.

Maquet, P. G. Biomechanics of the Hip. (Illus.). 320p. 1984. 199.00 (0-387-13257-0) Spr-Verlag.

— Biomechanics of the Knee. 2nd ed. (Illus.). 330p. 1983. 184.00 (0-387-12489-6) Spr-Verlag.

Maquet, P. G., tr. see Braune, W. & Fischer.

Maquiavelo, Nicolas. El Principe. (Biblioteca De Cultura Basica Ser.). 621p. 1986. 11.50 (0-8477-0727-X) U of PR Pr.

An Asterisk (*) at the beginning of an entry indicates that the title is appearing in BIP for the first time.

M

— El Principe (Comentado Por Napoleon Bonaparte) Jungl, Eli L., tr. (Nueva Austral Ser.: Vol. 215). (SPA.). 1991. pap. text ed. 24.95x (*84-239-7215-1*) Elliots Bks.

Maquiso, Mechizedek. Institutional Planning & Development: A Primer. x, 172p. 1983. pap. 12.50 (*971-10-0054-7*, Pub. by New Day Pub PH) Cellar.

***Maqutu, W. C.** Contemporary Family Law of Lesotho: A Historical & Critical Commentary. 389p. 1992. 75.00 (*99911-30-04-7*, Pub. by Nat Univ Lesotho LO) W W Gaunt.

Mar, Alexander D. Collected Works. 1972. 500.00 (*0-87968-887-4*) Gordon Pr.

Mar, B. W., et al, eds. Managing High Technology: An Interdisciplinary Perspective: Based on Papers from the 3rd International Conference on Interdisciplinary Research Seattle, Wash. 1-3 Aug., 1984. 420p. 1985. 100.00 (*0-444-87762-2*, North Holland) Elsevier.

Mar Gregorios, Paulos. Science for Sane Societies. LC 86-25282. (Patterns of World Spirituality Ser.). 247p. 1987. pap. 8.95 (*0-913757-70-5*, New Era Bks) Paragon Hse.

Mar-Lena. The Enchantress. 73p. 1992. pap. 10.50 (*0-9634497-0-2*) Leja Pubns.

***Mara.** Breeding & Keeping Frogs. 1995. (*0-7938-0130-3*) TFH Pubns.

— Garter & Ribbon Snakes. 1995. pap. text ed. (*0-7938-0269-5*) TFH Pubns.

— Milk Snakes. 1995. pap. text ed. 7.95 (*0-7938-0250-4*) TFH Pubns.

— Pinesnakes. 1995. pap. text ed. (*0-7938-0262-8*) TFH Pubns.

Mara, D. Duncan & Do Monte, Marecos. Waste Stabilization Ponds: Proceedings of an IAWPRC Specialized Conference Held in Lisbon, Portugal, 29 June - 2 July 1987. (Water Science & Technology Ser.: 19). (Illus.). 402p. 1988. pap. 54.00 (*0-08-035598-6*, Pergamon Pr) Elsevier.

Mara, David D. Sewage Treatment in Hot Climates. LC 75-23421. 437p. reprint ed. pap. 124.60 (*0-8357-3399-8*, 2039656) Bks Demand.

Mara, Joseph, jt. auth. see Newman, Betsy.

Mara, Mary J., jt. auth. see Daniels, Jerry.

Mara, P. El Arca (The Ark) (SPA.). Date not set. 4.99 (*1-56063-310-7*, 490448) Editorial Unilit.

— El Pesebre (The Manger) (SPA.). Date not set. bds. 4.99 (*1-56063-311-5*, 490449) Editorial Unilit.

Mara, Pam. The Greeks Pop-up. (Tarquin Pop-up Ser.). (Illus.). 32p. (Orig.). (J). (gr. 3 up). 1985. pap. 7.95 (*0-906212-33-2*, Pub. by Tarquin UK) Parkwest Pubns.

Mara, Rachna. Of Customs & Excise: Short Fiction. 1991. pap. 14.95 (*0-929005-25-2*, Pub. by Second Story Pr CN) InBook.

Mara, Thalia. First Steps in Ballet: Basic Exercises at the Barre. LC 75-37100. (Illus.). 64p. (Orig.). (J). (gr. 2-5). 1987. reprint ed. pap. 6.95 (*0-916622-53-3*) Princeton Bk Co.

— Fourth Steps in Ballet: On Your Toes! Basic Pointe Work. LC 74-181476. (Illus.). 64p. (YA). (gr. 9-12). 1987. reprint ed. pap. 6.95 (*0-916622-56-8*) Princeton Bk Co.

— The Language of Ballet: A Dictionary. LC 78-181477. (Illus.). 120p. 1987. reprint ed. pap. 9.95 (*0-87127-037-4*) Princeton Bk Co.

— Second Steps in Ballet: Basic Center Exercises. LC 75-37101. (Illus.). 64p. (Orig.). (J). (gr. 4-6). 1987. reprint ed. pap. 6.95 (*0-916622-54-1*) Princeton Bk Co.

— Third Steps in Ballet: Basic Allegro Steps. LC 70-181475. (Illus.). 64p. (Orig.). (YA). (gr. 6-9). 1987. reprint ed. pap. 6.95 (*0-916622-55-X*) Princeton Bk Co.

Mara, Tim. The Thames & Hudson Manual of Screen Printing. (Illus.). 1979. 18.95 (*0-500-67019-6*) Thames Hudson.

Mara, W. P. Venomous Snakes of the World. (TS Ser.). (Illus.). 224p. 1993. text ed. 29.95 (*0-86622-522-6*, TS-189) TFH Pubns.

Mara, Will P. Amphibians: Look & Learn. (Illus.). 64p. 7.95 (*0-7938-0067-6*, KD006) TFH Pubns.

— Snakes: Look & Learn. (Illus.). 64p. 1993. 7.95 (*0-7938-0074-9*, KD003) TFH Pubns.

— Turtles As a Hobby. (Illus.). 96p. 1993. 7.95 (*0-86622-324-X*, TT013) TFH Pubns.

***Mara, William P.** The Fragile Frog. LC 95-1409. (Illus.). (J). 1995. write for info. (*0-8075-2580-4*) A Whitman.

Marabell, George P. Frederick Libby & the American Peace Movement, 1921-1941. 1981. 30.95 (*0-405-14094-0*) Ayer.

Marabin, Jean. L' U. R. S. S. un Portrait en Couleurs. (Illus.). 276p. (FRE.). 1960. lib. bdg. 19.95 (*0-8288-3980-8*) Fr & Eur.

Marable, Manning. Black American Politics: From the Washington Marches to Jesse Jackson. rev. ed. (Haymarket Ser.). 384p. 1985. text ed. 32.95 (*0-86091-108-X*, Pub. by Verso UK); pap. text ed. 12.95 (*0-86091-816-5*, Pub. by Verso UK) Routledge Chapman & Hall.

— Black American Politics: From the Washington Marches to Jesse Jackson. 2nd ed. 416p. 1993. 64.95 (*0-86091-205-1*, A1915, Pub. by Verso UK) Routledge Chapman & Hall.

— Black American Politics: From the Washington Marches to Jesse Jackson, Vol. 1. 2nd ed. 416p. 1992. pap. 18.95 (*0-86091-923-4*, A1919, Pub. by Verso UK) Routledge Chapman & Hall.

— Blackwater: Historical Studies in Race, Class Consciousness & Revolution. 1992. pap. 14.95 (*0-87081-274-2*) Univ Pr Colo.

— The Crisis of Color & Democracy: Essays on Race, Class & Power. (Orig.). 1992. 29.95 (*0-9628838-3-2*); pap. 14.95 (*0-9628838-2-4*) Common Courage.

— How Capitalism Underdeveloped Black America. LC 82-61153. 300p. 1983. 30.00 (*0-89608-166-4*); pap. 15.00 (*0-89608-165-6*) South End Pr.

— Race, Reform, & Rebellion: The Second Reconstruction in Black America, 1945-1990. rev. ed. LC 90-19215. 1991. pap. 15.95 (*0-87805-493-6*) U Pr of Miss.

— Race, Reform, & Rebellion: The Second Reconstruction in Black America, 1945-1990. 2nd rev. ed. LC 90-19215. 1991. 37.50 (*0-87805-505-3*) U Pr of Miss.

— W. E. B. Du Bois: Black Radical Democrat. (Twentieth Century American Biography Ser.: No. 3). 304p. 1986. text ed. 26.95 (*0-8057-7750-4*, Pub. by Royal Botanic Garden UK) Macmillan.

— W. E. B. Du Bois: Black Radical Democrat, No. 3. (Twentieth Century American Biography Ser.: No. 3). (Illus.). 261p. 1987. pap. 14.95 (*0-8057-7771-7*, Pub. by Royal Botanic Garden UK) Macmillan.

Marabotto, Don C. & St. Catherine of Genoa. The Spiritual Doctrine of St. Catherine of Genoa. LC 88-50267. 328p. 1989. reprint ed. pap. 9.00 (*0-89555-335-X*) TAN Bks Pubs.

Maracchi, G., jt. ed. see Fantechi, R.

Maracle. Ravensong. (NFS Canada Ser.). 1993. pap. 12.95 (*0-88974-044-5*, Pub. by Press Gang CN) InBook.

— Sojourner's Truth & Other Stories. (NFS Canada Ser.). 1999. pap. 10.95 (*0-88974-023-2*, Pub. by Press Gang CN) InBook.

***Maracle & Freire.** Onkwehonwe-Neha. 1994. per. 6.95 (*0-920813-93-3*, Pub. by Sister Vision CN) InBook.

Maracle, Brian. Crazywater: Native Voices on Addiction & Recovery. 224p. 1994. pap. 10.95 (*0-14-017287-4*, Penguin Bks) Viking Penguin.

Maracle, David K. Mohawk, Let's Speak. 102p. 1990. 7.95 (*0-88432-723-X*, AFMH99) Audio-Forum.

— Mohawk, Let's Speak. 100p. 1993. 7.95 (*0-88432-707-8*, AFMH10); audio 44.95 (*0-88432-706-X*, AFMH10) Audio-Forum.

— Mohawk, One Thousand Useful Words. 158p. 1992. 10.95 (*0-88432-710-8*, AFMH94) Audio-Forum.

***Maracle, Lee.** Sundogs. 214p. (Orig.). 1992. pap. 10.95 (*0-919441-41-6*, Pub. by Theytus Bks Ltd CN) Orca Bk Pubs.

Maracotta, Lindsay. Everything We Wanted. 432p. 1988. pap. 3.95 (*1-55817-115-0*, Pinnacle NY) Windsor NY.

Maracz, Laszlo K. & Muysken, Pieter, eds. Configurationality: The Typology of Asymmetries. (Studies in Generative Grammar). vi, 236p. (Orig.). (C). 1989. pap. 64.30 (*90-6765-405-1*) Mouton.

Maradudin, A. A. & Nardelli, G. F., eds. Elementary Excitations in Solids: The Cortina Lectures, July 1966, & Selected Lectures from the Conference on Localized Excitations, Milan, July 25-26, 1966. LC 68-26772. 536p. reprint ed. pap. 152.80 (*0-317-30349-X*, 2024719) Bks Demand.

Maradudin, A. A., jt. auth. see Horton, G. K.

Maradudin, A. A., jt. ed. see Horton, G. K.

Marafiote, Richard A. The Custody of Children: A Behavioral Assessment Model. LC 85-12217. 290p. 1985. 54.50 (*0-306-41874-6*, Plenum Pr) Plenum.

Marafioti, P. Mario. Caruso's Method of Voice Production: The Scientific Culture of the Voice. (Illus.). 336p. 1981. reprint ed. pap. 7.95 (*0-486-24180-7*) Dover.

Maragos, G. D. The First Five Years of Life Pediatrics for Parents. 240p. (C). 1990. 50.00 (*81-85017-49-2*, Pub. by Interprint II) St Mut.

Maragos, George D., ed. Seminar on Ambulatory Pediatrics: Journal: Paediatrician, Vol. 5, No. 3. (Illus.). 1977. 24.00 (*3-8055-2433-1*) S Karger.

— Seminar on Geographical Pediatrics. (Journal: Paediatrician: Vol. 6, No. 2). (Illus.). 1977. 25.00 (*3-8055-2795-0*) S Karger.

— Seminar on Human Genetics. (Journal: Paediatrician: Vol. 6, No. 6). (Illus.). 1978. 25.00 (*3-8055-2909-0*) S Karger.

— Seminar on Immunological Aspects of Kidney Diseases in Children. (Journal: Paediatrician: Vol. 10, No. 5-6). (Illus.). 164p. 1981. pap. 56.00 (*3-8055-3488-4*) S Karger.

— Seminar on Infectious Diseases in Childhood. (Journal: Paediatrician: Vol. 8, No. 1-2). (Illus.). 1979. pap. 53.00 (*3-8055-3027-7*) S Karger.

— Seminar on Neonatology. (Journal: Paediatrician: Vol. 5, No. 5). (Illus.). 1977. 24.00 (*3-8055-2702-0*) S Karger.

— Seminar on Office Pediatrics, Part II. (Journal: Paediatrician: Vol. 8, No. 3). (Illus.). 1979. pap. 26.50 (*3-8055-3074-9*) S Karger.

— Seminar on Pediatric Allergy. (Journal: Paediatrician: Vol. 5, No. 4). (Illus.). 80p. 1977. 24.00 (*3-8055-2648-2*) S Karger.

— Seminar on Pediatric Cardiology. (Journal: Paediatrician: Vol. 7, No. 1-3). (Illus.). 1978. pap. 74.50 (*3-8055-2912-0*) S Karger.

— Seminar on Public Health, Pt. I. (Journal: Paediatrician: Vol. II, No. 1-2, 1982). (Illus.). iv, 120p. 1982. pap. 56.50 (*3-8055-3533-3*) S Karger.

— Seminar on Public Health, Pt. 2. (Journal: Paediatrician: Vol. II, No. 3-4). (Illus.). 126p. 1982. pap. 61.75 (*3-8055-3532-5*) S Karger.

Maragos, Nicolas E. Holy Cross Liturgical Hymnal. 159p. (Orig.). (ENG & GRE.). 1988. text ed. 8.95 (*0-917651-49-9*); ring bd. 5.95 (*0-917651-29-4*) Holy Cross Orthodox.

Maragoudakis, M. E., et al, eds. Angiogenesis: Molecular Biology, Clinical Aspects. (NATO ASI, Series A, Life Sciences: Vol. 263). (Illus.). 366p. (C). 1994. text ed. 105.00 (*0-306-44713-4*, Plenum Pr) Plenum.

— Angiogenesis in Health & Diseases. (NATO ASI Series A, Life Sciences: Vol. 227). (Illus.). 394p. (C). 1992. 110.00 (*0-306-44196-9*, Plenum Pr) Plenum.

Marah, John K. Pan-African Education: The Last Stage of Educational Developments. LC 88-1696. (Studies in African Education: Vol. 2). 336p. 1989. lib. bdg. 99.95 (*0-88946-186-4*) E Mellen.

— The Son of a Chief. 1995. 15.95 (*0-533-11324-5*) Vantage.

***Marah, Meredith.** What It's Like to Live Now. LC 94-22688. 1995. 21.95 (*0-553-09600-1*) Bantam.

Marahimin, Ismail. And the War Is Over. Novel. McGlynn, John H., tr. LC 86-10625. 173p. 1987. 16.95 (*0-8071-1340-9*) La State U Pr.

***Maraia, Richard.** The Impact of Short Interspersed Elements (SINEs) on the Host Genome. (Molecular Biology Intelligence Unit Ser.). 272p. 1995. write for info. (*1-57059-277-2*) R G Landes.

***Maraini.** The Silent Duchess. 1993. 23.95 (*1-55082-053-2*, Pub. by Quarry Pr CN) InBook.

Maraini, Daca. Only Prostitutes Marry in May. 378p. 1994. pap. 18.00 (*0-920717-81-0*) Guernica Editions.

***Maraini, Dacia.** Bagheria. Kitto, Dick & Spottiswood, Elspeth, trs. 119p. 1995. 30.00 (*0-7206-0926-7*, Pub. by P Owen Ltd UK) Dufour.

— Isolina. Williams, Sian, tr. 152p. 1994. 30.00 (*0-7206-0897-X*, Pub. by P Owen Ltd UK) Dufour.

— The Silent Duchess. Kitto, Dick & Spottiswoode, Elspeth, trs. 235p. 1992. 30.00 (*0-7206-0859-7*, Pub. by P Owen Ltd UK) Dufour.

— Woman at War. Benetti, Mara & Spottiswood, Elspeth, trs. LC 88-81204. Orig. Title: Donna in Guerra. 282p. (Orig.). 1989. pap. 14.50 (*0-934977-12-7*) Italica Pr.

Marais, Gill. Right over the Mountain: Travels with a Tibetan Medicine Man. (Illus.). 160p. 1990. pap. 13.95 (*1-85230-150-3*) Element MA.

Marais, Johan. A Complete Guide to Snakes of South Africa. 284p. 1992. 37.50 (*1-86812-439-8*, Pub. by Southern Bk Pubs) Krieger.

Marais, Johannes S. Cape Coloured People, Sixteen Fifty-Two to Nineteen Thirty-Seven. LC 74-15065. reprint ed. 44.00 (*0-404-12106-3*) AMS Pr.

— Colonization of New Zealand. LC 77-137258. reprint ed. 24.75 (*0-404-04184-1*) AMS Pr.

Marais, Marin. Pieces a Une et a Deux Violes. Hsu, John & McDowell, Bonney, eds. (Instrumental Works: Vol. 1). (Illus.). 1980. lib. bdg. 150.00 (*0-8450-7201-3*) Broude.

Maraist, Frank L. Admiralty in a Nutshell. 2nd ed. (Nutshell Ser.). 379p. (C). 1992. reprint ed. pap. text ed. 17.50 (*0-314-64765-1*) West Pub.

***Maraj, Pandit Bhopaul.** On Hinduism: From Darkness to Light. (Illus.). 250p. (Orig.). 1994. pap. write for info. (*0-615-00040-1*) K Maraj.

Marak, Julius L. Garo Customary Laws & Practices: A Sociological Study. 1986. 27.50 (*0-8364-1568-X*, KL Mukhopadhyay) S Asia.

***Maral, G.** VSAT Networks. (Series in Communication & Distribution). 1995. text ed. 49.95 (*0-471-95302-4*) Wiley.

Maral, G. & Bousquet, M. Satellite Communication System: Systems, Techniques & Technology. 2nd ed. David, S., tr. (Communication & Distributed Systems Ser.). 688p. 1993. text ed. 89.95 (*0-471-93032-6*, Wiley-Interscience) Wiley.

Maraldo, John C., tr. see Dumoulin, Heinrich.

Maraldo, John C., jt. ed. see Heisig, James W.

Maraldo, Pamela J., et al. Talking Points: A Public Policy Guide to Key Issues in Nursing & Health Care. 2nd ed. 132p. 1991. 19.95 (*0-88737-449-2*) Natl League Nurse.

Maram, Sheldon L., jt. auth. see Greenfield, Gerald M.

Maram, Sheldon L., et al. Hispanic Workers in the Garment & Restaurant Industries in Los Angeles County. (Research Report Ser.: No. 12). 123p. (Orig.). (C). 1980. ring bd. 5.00 (*0-935391-11-8*, RR-12) UCSD Ctr US-Mex.

Marambaud, Pierre. William Byrd of Westover, 1674-1744. LC 70-151251. 307p. reprint ed. pap. 87.50 (*0-685-15935-3*, 2027069) Bks Demand.

Marambaud, Pierre, jt. auth. see Fontenilles, Alfred.

Maramonosch, Karl, ed. see Maramorosch, Karl, et al.

Maramorosch, Karl. Advances in Cell Culture, Vol. 3. (Serial Publication Ser.). 1984. text ed. 126.00 (*0-12-007903-8*) Acad Pr.

— Viroids & Satellites: Molecular Parasites at the Frontier of Life. 176p. 1991. 115.00 (*0-8493-6783-2*, QP552) CRC Pr.

Maramorosch, Karl, ed. Advances in Cell Culture, Vol. 4. (Serial Publication Ser.). 1985. text ed. 126.00 (*0-12-007904-6*) Acad Pr.

— Advances in Cell Culture, Vol. 5. (Serial Publication Ser.). 1987. text ed. 126.00 (*0-12-007905-4*) Acad Pr.

— Biotechnology Advances in Invertebrate Pathology & Cell Culture. 511p. 1987. text ed. 154.00 (*0-12-470255-4*) Acad Pr.

— Methods in Virology, Vol. 7. 1984. text ed. 118.00 (*0-12-470207-4*) Acad Pr.

— Plant Diseases of Viral, Viroid, Mycoplasma, & Uncertain Etiology. LC 92-21544. 190p. (C). 1993. text ed. 71.50 (*0-8133-1616-2*) Westview.

Maramorosch, Karl & Harris, Kerry F. Plant Diseases & Vectors: Ecology & Epidemiology. 1981. text ed. 95.00 (*0-12-470240-6*) Acad Pr.

Maramorosch, Karl & Koprowski, Hilary, eds. Methods in Virology, Vol. 8. 1984. text ed. 138.00 (*0-12-470208-2*) Acad Pr.

Maramorosch, Karl & McIntosh, Arthur H., eds. Insect Cell Biotechnology. LC 93-33795. 1994. 137.00 (*0-8493-4597-9*, CRC Reprint) Franklin.

Maramorosch, Karl & McKelvey, John J., Jr., eds. Subviral Pathogens of Plants & Animals: Viroids & Prions. 1985. text ed. 72.00 (*0-12-470230-9*) Acad Pr.

Maramorosch, Karl & Raychaudhuri, S. P., eds. Mycoplasma Diseases of Crops. (Illus.). 450p. 1987. 142.00 (*0-387-96646-3*) Spr-Verlag.

Maramorosch, Karl & Sato, Gordon H., eds. Advances in Cell Culture, Vol. 6. (Serial Publication Ser.). 339p. 1988. text ed. 126.00 (*0-12-007906-2*) Acad Pr.

Maramorosch, Karl & Sato, Gordon H, eds. Advances in Cell Culture, Vol. 7. (Serial Publication Ser.). 289p. 1989. 130.00 (*0-685-31296-8*) Acad Pr.

Maramorosch, Karl & Sherman, K. E., eds. Viral Insecticides for Biological Control. 1985. text ed. 148.00 (*0-12-470295-3*) Acad Pr.

Maramorosch, Karl, jt. ed. see Harris, Kerry F.

Maramorosch, Karl, jt. ed. see Lauffer, Max A.

Maramorosch, Karl, jt. ed. see McIntosh, Arthur H.

Maramorosch, Karl, et al. Advances in Virus Research, Vol. 38. (Serial Publication Ser.). 457p. 1990. text ed. 110.00 (*0-12-039838-9*) Acad Pr.

— Advances in Virus Research, Vols. 1-18 & 21-24. Lauffer, Max A. & Maramorosch, Karl, eds. Incl. Vol. 1. 1953. 66.00 (*0-12-039801-X*); Vol. 5. 1958. 70.00 (*0-12-039805-2*); (Serial Publication Ser.). write for info. (*0-318-50222-4*) Acad Pr.

Maramorosch, Karl, et al, eds. Advances in Virus Research, Vol. 30. (Serial Publication Ser.). 368p. 1986. text ed. 128.00 (*0-12-039830-3*) Acad Pr.

— Advances in Virus Research, Vol. 31. (Serial Publication Ser.). 464p. 1986. text ed. 128.00 (*0-12-039831-1*) Acad Pr.

— Advances in Virus Research, Vol. 32. (Serial Publication Ser.). 300p. 1987. text ed. 109.00 (*0-12-039832-X*) OneOnOne Comp Trng.

— Advances in Virus Research, Vol. 33. (Serial Publication Ser.). 300p. 1987. text ed. 109.00 (*0-12-039833-8*) Acad Pr.

— Advances in Virus Research, Vol. 34. (Serial Publication Ser.). 327p. 1988. text ed. 109.00 (*0-12-039834-6*) Acad Pr.

— Advances in Virus Research, Vol. 35. (Serial Publication Ser.). 501p. 1988. text ed. 109.00 (*0-12-039835-4*) Acad Pr.

— Advances in Virus Research, Vol. 36. (Serial Publication Ser.). 356p. 1989. text ed. 109.00 (*0-12-039836-2*) Acad Pr.

— Advances in Virus Research, Vol. 37. (Serial Publication Ser.). 349p. 1989. text ed. 99.00 (*0-12-039837-0*) Acad Pr.

— Advances in Virus Research, Vol. 39. (Illus.). 355p. 1991. text ed. 94.00 (*0-12-039839-7*) Acad Pr.

— Advances in Virus Research, Vol. 40. (Illus.). 291p. 1991. text ed. 72.00 (*0-12-039840-0*) Acad Pr.

— Advances in Virus Research, Vol. 41. (Illus.). 472p. 1992. text ed. 95.00 (*0-12-039841-9*) Acad Pr.

— Advances in Virus Research, Vol. 42. (Illus.). 421p. 1992. text ed. 90.00 (*0-12-039842-7*) Acad Pr.

— Advances in Virus Research, Vol. 43. (Illus.). 398p. 1994. text ed. 90.00 (*0-12-039843-5*) Acad Pr.

— Advances in Virus Research, Vol. 44. (Illus.). 473p. 1994. text ed. 99.00 (*0-12-039844-3*) Acad Pr.

— Advances in Virus Research, Vol. 45. (Illus.). 327p. 1995. boxed 75.00 (*0-614-05260-2*) Acad Pr.

— Advances in Virus Research Vol. 45, Vol. 45. (Illus.). 347p. 1995. boxed 75.00 (*0-12-039845-1*) Acad Pr.

Maramorsch, Karl, ed. Biotechnology for Biological Control of Pests & Vectors. 248p. 1991. 179.00 (*0-8493-4836-6*, RA639) CRC Pr.

Maran, A. G. & Birrell. Logan Turner's Diseases of the Nose, Throat & Ear. 10th ed. (Illus.). 456p. 1987. pap. 40.00 (*0-7236-0945-4*, Pub. by John Wright UK) Buttrwrth-Heinemann.

Maran, A. G., jt. auth. see Stell, P. M.

Maran, Arnold & Lund, Valarie. Clinical Rhinology. (Illus.). 240p. 1990. text ed. 105.00 (*0-86577-358-0*) Thieme Med Pubs.

Maran, Graphics. Marangraphics' Poster. 1993. pap. write for info. (*0-13-036989-6*) P-H.

***Maran Graphics Staff.** Computers Simplified. 2nd ed. 1995. pap. 19.99 (*1-56884-676-2*) IDG Bks.

— Computers Visual Pocket Guide. 1995. pap. 14.99 (*1-56884-675-4*) IDG Bks.

— Internet Simplified. 1995. pap. 19.99 (*1-56884-658-4*) IDG Bks.

— Macintosh Simplified. 1995. pap. 19.99 (*1-56884-679-7*) IDG Bks.

— Microsoft Office 4.2 for Windows Simplified. 1995. pap. 27.99 (*1-56884-673-8*) IDG Bks.

— Microsoft Works 95 Simplified. 1995. pap. 19.99 (*1-56884-677-0*) IDG Bks.

— MS DOS 6.22 Visual Pocket Guide. 1995. pap. 14.99 (*1-56884-674-6*) IDG Bks.

— Multimedia Simplified. 1995. pap. 19.99 (*1-56884-680-0*) IDG Bks.

— 3-D Visual Dictionary of Computing. 1995. pap. 19.99 (*1-56884-678-9*) IDG Bks.

— Windows 95 Simplified. 1995. pap. 19.99 (*1-56884-662-2*) IDG Bks.

— Windows 95 Visual Pocket Guide. 1995. pap. 14.99 (*1-56884-661-4*) IDG Bks.

***Maran Graphics Staff & Maran, Ruth.** Excel 5 Visual Pocket Guide. 1994. pap. 14.99 (*1-56884-667-3*) IDG Bks.

— Lotus 1-2-3 R5 for Windows Visual Pack Guide: Visual Pocket Guide. 1995. pap. 14.99 (*1-56884-671-1*) IDG Bks.

— Lotus 1-2-3 R5 Simplified. expanded ed. 1994. pap. 19.99 (*1-56884-670-3*) IDG Bks.

— MS-DOS 6.2 Simplified Education Edition. 1995. pap. 14.99 (*1-56884-653-3*) IDG Bks.

— Windows 3.1 Simplified. 1995. pap. 14.99 (*1-56884-652-5*) IDG Bks.

— Word 6 for Windows Simplified. 1994. pap. 14.99 (*1-56884-659-2*) IDG Bks.

— WordPerfect 6 for Windows Simplified. expanded ed. 1995. pap. 19.99 (*1-56884-665-7*) IDG Bks.

— WP 5.1 for DOS Simplified Educ Ed. 1995. pap. 14.99 (*1-56884-663-0*) IDG Bks.

— WP 6.1 for Windows Visual Pocket Guide. 1995. pap. 14.99 (*1-56884-668-1*) IDG Bks.

***Maran Graphics Staff, Richard.** Computers Simplified. 1994. pap. 14.99 (*1-56884-651-7*) IDG Bks.

Maran, Meredith, jt. auth. see Heron, Ann.

Maran, Michael. Make Your Own Will: A Guide to Making a Michigan Statutory Will Without a Lawyer. (Illus.). 96p. (Orig.). 1990. pap. 4.95 (*0-936343-04-4*) Grand River.

— The Michigan Divorce Book: A Guide to Doing an Uncontested Divorce Without an Attorney (without Minor Children) 2nd ed. (Illus.). 192p. 1989. pap. 18.95 (*0-685-29559-1*); pap. 24.95 (*0-685-29560-5*) Grand River.

— The Michigan Divorce Book: A Guide to Doing an Uncontested Divorce Without an Attorney (without Minor Children) 3rd ed. (Illus.). 272p. 1993. pap. 27.95 (*0-936343-08-7*); pap. 21.95 (*0-936343-07-9*) Grand River.

— The Michigan Power of Attorney Book: A Guide to Making Financial, Health Care & Custodial Powers of Attorney Without a Lawyer. (Illus.). 140p. (Orig.). 1991. pap. 5.95 (*0-936343-05-2*) Grand River.

Maran, Rene. Batouala. LC 87-23642. (African Writers Ser.). (Orig.). 1987. pap. 8.95 (*0-435-90135-4*) Heinemann.

— Batouala. (Orig.). 1989. reprint ed. lib. bdg. 25.95 (*0-89966-640-X*) Buccaneer Bks.

Maran, Richard. In Full Color Windows 3.1 Expanded. (J). 1993. pap. 12.95 (*0-13-458241-1*) P-H.

— Lotus One-Two-Three for Windows. 1992. pap. 12.95 (*0-13-000779-X*) P-H.

— MaranGraphics Learn At First Sight MS-DOS 6.2. LC 93-41751. 1993. pap. 12.95 (*0-13-301672-2*) P-H.

— Microsoft Excel 5.0 for Windows. 1994. pap. 12.95 (*0-13-291261-9*) P-H.

— Microsoft Word 6.0 for Windows. 1993. pap. 19.95 (*0-13-104431-1*) P-H.

— Windows 3.1 Al Instante, Windows 3.1 Simplified. 1994. pap. 12.95 (*0-13-123316-5*) P-H.

— WordPerfect 6.0 for Windows. 1994. pap. 14.95 (*0-13-104449-4*) P-H.

Maran, Richard & Feistmantl, Eric. Computers Simplified: MaranGraphics Simplified Computer Guide. LC 93-12260. 160p. (J). 1993. Academic edition. pap. text ed. 16.80 (*0-13-095324-5*) P-H Gen Ref & Trav.

— MaranGraphics Simplified Computer Guide: Computers Simplified. LC 92-45349. 1993. write for info. (*0-13-001687-X*) P-H.

Maran, Richard, jt. auth. see Maran, Ruth.

Maran, Rita. Torture: The Role of Ideology in the French-Algerian War. LC 88-37478. 230p. 1989. text ed. 55.00 (*0-275-93248-6*, C3248, Praeger Pubs) Greenwood.

***Maran, Ruth.** Excel 5 Simplified. expanded ed. 1994. pap. 19.99 (*1-56884-664-9*) IDG Bks.

— Lotus 1-2-3 Release 2.3 Simplified. 160p. (C). 1993. pap. text ed. 17.40 (*0-13-064619-9*) P-H.

— Windows 3.1 Simplified. expanded ed. 1994. pap. 19.99 (*1-56884-654-1*) IDG Bks.

— Windows 3.1 Visual Pocket Guide. 1994. pap. 14.99 (*1-56884-650-9*) IDG Bks.

— Word 2.0 for Windows Simplified. 144p. (C). 1994. pap. text ed. 16.40 (*0-13-064635-0*) P-H.

— Word 6 for Windows Simplified. expanded ed. 1994. pap. 19.99 (*1-56884-660-6*) IDG Bks.

— Word 6 for Windows Visual Pocket Guide. 1994. pap. 14. 99 (*1-56884-666-5*) IDG Bks.

— WordPerfect 6 for DOS Simplified. 1994. pap. 14.99 (*1-56884-657-6*) IDG Bks.

— WordPerfect 6 for Windows Simplified. 1994. pap. 14.99 (*1-56884-656-8*) IDG Bks.

— WordPerfect 6.0 for DOS. 112p. pap. 12.95 (*0-13-002197-0*) P-H.

— WordPerfect 6.0 for DOS Simplified. 144p. (C). 1993. pap. text ed. 10.00 (*0-13-064676-8*) P-H.

Maran, Ruth & Maran, Richard. Excel 4.0 for Windows Simplified. 144p. (C). 1993. pap. text ed. 10.00 (*0-13-106303-0*) P-H.

— MaranGraphics' Simplified Computer Guide for Microsoft MS-DOS 6.0. LC 93-7169. 128p. 1993. pap. 12.95 (*0-13-064650-4*) P-H.

— MaranGraphics' Simplified Computer Guide for WordPerfect 5.1 for DOS. 2nd ed. LC 93-3098. 96p. 1993. pap. 12.95 (*0-13-106295-6*) P-H.

— MS-DOS Simplified. 160p. (C). 1994. pap. text ed. 17.40 (*0-13-064643-1*) P-H.

— Windows 3.1 Simplified. 144p. (C). 1993. pap. text ed. 17. 40 (*0-13-064627-X*) P-H.

— WordPerfect 5.1 for DOS Simplified: MaranGraphics Simplified Computer Guide. LC 93-20144. 96p. (C). 1993. pap. text ed. 16.80 (*0-13-106253-0*) Prentice ESL.

Maran, Ruth, jt. auth. see Maran Graphics Staff.

Maran, Stephen, ed. The Encyclopedia of Astronomy & Astrophysics. (Illus.). 1000p. 1992. text ed. 129.95 (*0-442-26364-3*) Van Nos Reinhold.

Maran, Stephen P., jt. ed. see French, Bevan M.

Maranatha Church Staff, ed. see Barr, Joan & Barr, Jack.

Maranda, D. & Daigle, A. Lexique des Ascenceurs et Monte-Charge: Francais-Anglais, Anglais-Francais. 32p. (ENG & FRE.). 1978. pap. 7.95 (*0-8288-5249-9*, M9224) Fr & Eur.

Maranda, Pierre. French Kinship Structure & History. (Janua Linguarum, Series Practica: No. 169). 1974. pap. text ed. 44.65 (*3-10-800096-9*) Mouton.

Maranda, Pierre, ed. Soviet Structural Folkloristics: Texts by Meletinsky, Nekludov, Novik, & Segal, with Tests of the Approach by Jilek & Jilek-Aall, Reid, & Layton, Vol. 1. LC 73-79892. (Approaches to Semiotics Ser.: No. 42). 194p. 1974. 41.35 (*90-279-2683-2*) Mouton.

Maranda, Pierre, jt. ed. see Pouillon, Jean.

Maranda, William. Stories of String. LC 93-93977. (Illus.). 184p. 1994. pap. 12.00 (*1-56002-359-7*, Univ Edtns) Aegina Pr.

Marandel, J. Patrice. Francois de Nome: Mysteries of a Seventeenth-Century Neapolitan Painter. (Illus.). 64p. (Orig.). 1992. pap. 14.95 (*0-939594-27-7*) Menil Found.

— The French Painting Tradition. LC 87-71234. (Illus.). 32p. (Orig.). 1987. pap. 3.50 (*0-918881-18-8*) Columbus Mus Art.

— Manfred Schwartz: The Last Ten Years. LC 73-93335. (Illus.). 1974. 3.00 (*0-911517-27-8*) Mus of Art RI.

Marandel, J. Patrice, intro. Gray Is the Color: An Exhibition of Grisaille Painting, 13th-20th Centuries. LC 73-92776. (Illus.). 1974. pap. 9.95 (*0-914412-08-6*) Inst for the Arts.

Marando, jt. auth. see Florestano.

Marangolo, M. & Fiorentini, G., eds. Small Cell Lung Cancer: Proceedings of the International Conference on Small Cell Lung Cancer, Ravenna, Italy, 27-28 March, 1987. (Advances in the Biosciences Ser.: Vol. 72). (Illus.). 175p. 1988. 92.00 (*0-08-036631-7*, Pergamon Pr) Elsevier.

Marangoly, George. Dollarinte Nattil (Short Stories in Malayalam) 120p. (Orig.). (MAL.). 1989. write for info. (*0-318-65118-1*) Printindia.

Marangoni, Roy D., jt. auth. see Beckwith, Thomas G.

Marangos, P. J. & Lal, H., eds. Emerging Strategies in Neuroprotection. (Advances in Neuroprotection Ser.). (Illus.). xviii, 359p. 1992. 99.00 (*0-8176-3544-0*) Birkhauser.

MaranGraphics' Development Group. MaranGraphics Learn at First Sight Excel 5 for Windows Expanded. LC 94-17894. 1994. 19.95 (*0-13-310723-X*) P-H.

MaranGraphics' Development Group Staff. MaranGraphics' Development Group Learn at First Sight Windows 3.1. 1994. write for info. (*0-318-72421-9*) P-H.

MaranGraphics Development Group Staff. MaranGraphics Learn at First Sight Lotus 1-2-3 for Windows Release 4. LC 93-34098. (J). 1994. write for info. (*0-13-458233-0*) P-H.

— MaranGraphics Learn at First Sight Word 6 for Windows. LC 94-10475. 1994. write for info. (*0-13-149246-2*) P-H.

MaranGraphics Staff. Computers Simplified-Expanded Edition. 1994. pap. 19.95 (*0-13-304080-1*) P-H.

— Lotus for Windows (Rel. 4.0) Academic Edition. 1994. pap. text ed. 10.00 (*0-13-126954-2*) P-H.

— Ms-Dos 6.2. 1993. pap. 12.95 (*0-685-70706-7*) P-H.

— MS-Dos 6.2 Academic Edition. 1994. pap. text ed. 10.00 (*0-13-111436-0*) P-H.

MaranGraphics Staff & Development. WP 6.0 for Windows Academic Edition. 1994. pap. text ed. 10.00 (*0-13-124744-1*) P-H.

Maranhao, Tullio. Therapeutic Discourse & Socratic Dialogue: A Cultural Critique. LC 86-40056. (Rhetoric of the Human Sciences Ser.). 256p. 1986. text ed. 22.50 (*0-299-10920-8*) U of Wis Pr.

Maranhao, Tullio, ed. The Interpretation of Dialogue. LC 89-5074. (Illus.). 368p. 1990. pap. text ed. 17.95 (*0-226-50434-4*) U Ch Pr.

— The Interpretation of Dialogue. LC 89-5074. (Illus.). 368p. 1990. lib. bdg. 42.00 (*0-226-50433-6*) U Ch Pr.

Marani, A., ed. Advances in Environmental Modelling: Proceedings of a Symposium Held 22-26 June 1987, Venice, Italy, Sponsored by the International Society for Ecological Modelling (ISEM) (Developments in Environmental Modelling Ser.: No. 13). 690p. 1989. 141.00 (*0-444-98894-7*) Elsevier.

Marani, E., ed. Outgrowth in the Nervous System During Development & Maturity: Proceedings of the First Erasmus Winterschool, 5-10 February 1990. 348p. 1990. 45.00 (*90-265-1143-4*, Pub. by Swets Pub Serv NE) Taylor & Francis.

Marani, Enrico. Topographic Histochemistry of the Cerebellum. LC 86-12132. (Progress in Histochemistry & Cytochemistry Ser.: Vol. 16, No. 4). (Illus.). 169p. 1986. pap. 105.00 (*0-89574-221-7*, Pub. by Gustav Fischer Verlag) VCH Pubs.

***Maraniss, David.** First in His Class: The Biography of Bill Clinton. 1995. 25.00 (*0-671-87109-9*) S&S Trade.

Maraniss, James, tr. see Benitez-Rojo, Antonio.

Maraniss, James E., tr. see Benitez-Rojo, Antonio.

Maraniss, Linda, ed. see Center for Environmental Education Staff.

***Marano, Americo.** Italian I. (C). Date not set. pap. text ed. write for info. (*1-884155-03-0*) Day & Nite Pub.

— Italian II. (C). Date not set. pap. text ed. write for info. (*1-884155-02-2*) Day & Nite Pub.

Marano, Christopher, ed. see Master, Chan & Chang, Sheng-yen.

Marano, Philomena. Word Sandwiches. (J). (gr. 1 up). 1994. pap. 1.95 (*0-590-47588-6*) Scholastic Inc.

Marano, Russell. Pockets of Love. 58p. 1984. 5.00 (*0-318-03893-5*) Back Fork Bks.

— Poems from a Mountain Ghetto. (Illus.). 76p. (Orig.). 1979. pap. 5.00 (*0-686-37048-1*) Back Fork Bks.

Maranon, Gregorio. Amiel. (Nueva Austral Ser.: Vol. 23). (SPA.). 1991. pap. text ed. 24.95x (*84-239-1823-8*) Elliots Bks.

Maranon, Rafael. Evidencias Olvidadas - Forgotten Truths. 80p. (SPA.). 1992. pap. 3.95 (*84-7645-576-3*) TSELF.

Marans, David, jt. auth. see Pospesel, Howard.

Marans, J. Eugene. Manual of Foreign Investment in the United States. LC 83-27189. (International Practice Ser.). 1984. text ed. 95.00 (*0-07-081899-1*) Shepards-McGraw.

Marans, J. Eugene, et al, eds. Manual of Foreign Investment in the United States. 2nd ed. LC 93-25765. 1993. text ed. 175.00 (*0-07-172469-9*) Shepards-McGraw.

Marans, Nelly, tr. see Arminjon, Blaise.

Marans, Nelly, tr. see Auboyer, Jeannine.

Marans, Nelly, tr. see Cochini, Christian.

Marans, Nelly, tr. see De Foucauld, Charles.

Marans, Nelly, ed. see Varillon, Francois.

Marans, R. W. & Stokols, Daniel, eds. Environmental Simulation: Research & Policy Issues. (Illus.). 310p. (C). 1993. 49.50 (*0-306-44388-0*, Plenum Pr) Plenum.

Marans, Robert W. & Fly, J. Mark. Recreation & the Quality of Urban Life: Recreational Resources, Behaviors, & Evaluations of People in the Detroit Region. 240p. (Orig.). 1981. pap. 16.00 (*0-87944-273-5*) Inst Soc Res.

— Recreation & the Quality of Urban Life: Recreational Resources, Behaviors, & Evaluations of People in the Detroit Region. LC 81-623446. (Institute for Social Research, Research Report Ser.). (Illus.). 240p. (Orig.). reprint ed. pap. 68.40 (*0-7837-5255-5*, 2044992) Bks Demand.

Marans, Robert W. & Spreckelmeyer, Kent F. Evaluating Built Environments: A Behavioral Approach. (Illus.). 249p. (C). 1981. 20.00 (*0-87944-272-7*) Inst Soc Res.

— Evaluating Built Environments: A Behavioral Approach. LC 81-6709. (Illus.). 250p. reprint ed. pap. 71.30 (*0-7837-5266-0*, 2045004) Bks Demand.

Marans, Robert W. & Wellman, John D. The Quality of Nonmetropolitan Living: Evaluations, Behaviors, & Expectations of Northern Michigan Residents. LC 78-69913. (Illus.). 352p. 1978. 20.00 (*0-87944-227-1*); pap. 12.00 (*0-87944-226-3*) Inst Soc Res.

— The Quality of Nonmetropolitan Living: Evaluations, Behaviors, & Expectations of Northern Michigan Residents. LC 78-69913. 279p. reprint ed. pap. 79.60 (*0-7837-5692-5*, 2044983) Bks Demand.

Marans, Robert W., et al. Perceptions of Life Quality in Rural America: An Analysis of Survey Data from Four Studies. LC 80-50377. (University of Michigan Institute for Social Research Report Ser.). 118p. reprint ed. pap. 33.70 (*0-317-42021-6*, 2025967) Bks Demand.

— Waterfront Living: A Report on Permanent & Seasonal Residents in Northern Michigan. LC 76-620083. 301p. 1976. pap. 12.00 (*0-87944-218-2*) Inst Soc Res.

— Waterfront Living: A Report on Permanent & Seasonal Residents in Northern Michigan. LC 76-620083. (Illus.). 301p. reprint ed. pap. 85.80 (*0-7837-5252-0*, 2044989) Bks Demand.

Maranto, Cheryl D. & Bruscia, Kenneth E. Methods of Teaching & Training the Music Therapist. (Studies on Music Therapy Education: Vol. 2). 71p. (Orig.). (C). 1988. pap. text ed. 20.00 (*1-878216-02-3*) Temple U Esther Boyer.

— Perspectives on Music Therapy Education & Training, Vol. 1. (Studies on Music Therapy Education). 212p. (Orig.). (C). 1987. pap. text ed. 25.00 (*1-878216-01-5*) Temple U Esther Boyer.

Maranto, Cheryl D. & Bruscia, Kenneth E., eds. Master's Theses in Music Therapy: Index & Abstracts. (Studies on Music Therapy Education). 149p. (Orig.). (C). 1988. pap. text ed. 25.00 (*1-878216-03-1*) Temple U Esther Boyer.

Maranto, Robert. Politics & Bureaucracy in the Modern Presidency: Careerists & Appointees in the Reagan Administration. LC 92-30014. (Contributions in Political Science Ser.: No. 311). 200p. 1993. text ed. 52.95 (*0-313-28332-X*, MTR/, Greenwood Pr) Greenwood.

Maranto, Robert & Schultz, David. A Short History of the United States Civil Service. 228p. (Orig.). (C). 1991. lib. bdg. 49.00 (*0-8191-8213-5*); pap. text ed. 30.00 (*0-8191-8214-1*) U Pr of Amer.

Marantz, Alec P. On the Nature of Grammatical Relations. 300p. (Orig.). 1983. 37.50 (*0-262-13193-5*); pap. 17.50 (*0-262-63090-7*) MIT Pr.

Marantz, Kenneth & Marantz, Sylvia. Artists of the Page: Interviews with Children's Book Illustrators. LC 91-50951. 240p. 1992. lib. bdg. 32.50x (*0-89950-701-8*) McFarland & Co.

Marantz, Kenneth, jt. auth. see Marantz, Sylvia.

Marantz, Kenneth, et al. The Picturebook: Source & Resource for Art Education. 92p. (Orig.). 1994. pap. 15. 00 (*0-937652-68-7*) Natl Art Ed.

Marantz, Kenneth A., jt. auth. see Marantz, Sylvia S.

Marantz, Sylvia & Marantz, Kenneth. Multicultural Picture Books: Art for Understanding Others. (Professional Growth Ser.). 200p. 1994. pap. text ed. 28.95 (*0-938865-22-6*) Linworth Pub.

Marantz, Sylvia, jt. auth. see Marantz, Kenneth.

Marantz, Sylvia S. Picture Books for Looking & Learning: Awakening Visual Perceptions through the Art of Children's Books. 216p. 1992. pap. 24.50 (*0-89774-716-X*) Oryx Pr.

***Marantz, Sylvia S. & Marantz, Kenneth A.** The Art of Children's Picture Books: A Selective Reference Guide. 2nd ed. LC 94-16308. (Garland Reference Library of the Humanities Ser.). 320p. 1994. 38.00 (*0-8153-0937-6*, H1636) Garland.

Maranville, Rabbit. Run, Rabbit, Run. 120p. (Orig.). 1991. pap. 9.95 (*1-55643-081-7*) North Atlantic.

Maranville, Walter R. Run, Rabbit, Run: The Hilarious & Mostly True Tales of Rabbit Maranville. 1991. pap. 9.95 (*0-910137-44-7*) Soc Am Baseball Res.

Maranz, David E. Peace Is Everything: World View of Muslims in the Senegambia. LC 92-83905. (International Museum of Cultures Publications: No. 28). xiv, 314p. 1993. pap. 32.00 (*0-88312-816-0*); fiche 24.00 (*0-88312-581-1*) Summer Instit Ling.

Maraqten, Mohammed. Die Semitischen Personennamen in Den Alt- und Reichsamaischen Inschriften Aus Vorderasien. (Texte und Studien Zur Orientalistik Ser.: Vol. 5). vi, 250p. 1988. write for info. (*3-487-09042-2*, Pub. by Georg Olms GW) Lubrecht & Cramer.

Marar, Eve. More Haunted House Stories. (Illus.). 96p. (Orig.). (J). 1988. pap. 1.95 (*0-942025-64-4*) Kidsbks.

Marar, K. Narayana, tr. see Siddheswarananda, Swami.

Maras, Raymond J. Innocent XI, Pope of Christian Unity. (Church & the World Ser.). xiv, 356p. 1984. 42.85 (*0-940121-02-6*) Cross Cultural Pubns.

Marasa, Paul, jt. ed. see Rind, Bruce.

Marasanov, V. English-Russian Dictionary of Civil Aviation. 534p. (C). 1989. 135.00 (*0-685-37113-1*, Pub. by Collets) St Mut.

Marasas, W. F., et al. Toxigenic Fusarium Species: Identity & Mycotoxicology. LC 82-42779. 350p. 1984. 45.00 (*0-271-00348-0*) Pa St U Pr.

Maraschi, L., et al, eds. BL Lac Objects. (Lecture Notes in Physics Ser.: Vol. 334). xii, 500p. 1989. 73.00 (*0-387-51389-2*, 3453) Spr-Verlag.

Maraschiello, Christopher A. Wallace P. Roudebush: Spirit of the Institution. 100p. (Orig.). 1993. pap. text ed. write for info. (*0-918761-04-2*) Miami U Pubns.

Marasco, M. C., ed. Complete Commodity Futures Directory. rev. ed. 550p. Date not set. ring bd. 175.00 (*0-685-45274-3*) Christopher Res.

Marasco, Robert. Burnt Offerings. 1993. reprint ed. lib. bdg. 18.95x (*0-89968-437-8*, Lghtyr Pr) Buccaneer Bks.

Marascuilo, Leonard A., jt. auth. see Serlin, Ronald C.

Marashi, Medhi, ed. & pref. Persian Studies in North America, Studies in Honor of Mohammad Ali Jazayery. LC 93-12142. (Illus.). 560p. (ENG & PER.). 1994. boxed, lib. bdg. 60.00x (*0-936347-35-X*) Iran Bks.

Marashi, Mehdi. Persian Contemporary Spoken. 136p. (C). 1986. 14.95 (*0-88432-557-1*, AFPE91); digital audio 185.00 (*0-88432-132-0*, AFPE01) Audio-Forum.

Marashio, Nancy. Writing: A Window to Our Minds. (Writing Teachers at Work Ser.). 172p. 1982. pap. text ed. 6.50 (*1-883920-03-5*) Nat Writing Proj.

***Marasinghe, E. W., ed.** Bimbamana of Gautamiyasastra: As Hexard by Sariputra. (C). 1994. 14.00 (*81-7030-417-2*, Pub. by Sri Satguru Pubns II) S Asia.

Marasinghe, Lakshman. Contract of Sale in International Trade Law. 300p. 1992. boxed 85.00 (*0-409-99628-9*) Michie Butterworth.

Marasinghe, M. L. & Conklin, William E., eds. Essays on Third World Perspectives in Jurisprudence. xvii, 442p. 1984. pap. 50.00 (*9971-70-035-2*) Butterworth Legal Pubs.

Maraspini, A. L. Study of an Italian Village. 1968. pap. text ed. 36.00 (*90-279-6039-9*) Mouton.

Marassi, Roberto, jt. ed. see Mamantov, Gleb.

Marat, Jean-Paul. Polish Letters, 2 vols. 1972. 200.00 (*0-8490-0871-9*) Gordon Pr.

Marateck, Samuel L. BASIC. 3rd ed. 533p. (C). 1986. pap. text ed. 37.25 (*0-15-504505-9*) Dryden Pr.

— FORTRAN 77. 584p. 1983. 26.00 (*0-685-30163-X*) HarBrace.

— Pascal. 823p. 1991. Net. text ed. write for info. (*0-471-60546-8*); teacher ed. disk write for info. (*0-318-63966-1*); disk write for info. (*0-318-63967-X*); disk write for info. (*0-318-63968-8*); disk write for info. (*0-471-55016-7*); disk write for info. (*0-318-63970-X*); disk write for info. (*0-318-63971-8*); disk write for info. (*0-471-55017-5*); write for info. (*0-318-63969-6*) Wiley.

— Pascal Genie 3.5 Mac Disk & Booklet Supplement & Pascal Set. text ed. write for info. (*0-471-11047-7*) Wiley.

— Turbo Mac 3.5. suppl. ed. Date not set. text ed., disk write for info. (*0-471-11050-7*) Wiley.

— Turbo Pascal. 102p. 1991. teacher ed 28.00 (*0-471-53551-6*); Net. text ed. write for info. (*0-471-60547-6*); teacher ed 24.50 (*0-471-53556-7*); disk 25.00 (*0-471-55574-6*); disk 25.00 (*0-471-55576-2*); write for info. (*0-471-53549-4*); 1.00 (*0-471-55170-8*); 1.00 (*0-471-55030-2*) Wiley.

Marateck, Samuel L. & Pattis, Richard E. Pascal & Karel the Robot: A Gentle Introduction to the Art of Programming - Dynamic Set. (C). 1991. Net. pap. text ed. write for info. (*0-471-55029-9*) Wiley.

— Turbo Pascal & Karel the Robot. (C). 1991. Net. pap. text ed. write for info. (*0-471-55107-4*) Wiley.

Marathe, K. B., jt. ed. see Fraser, J. Nelson.

Marathe, K. B., tr. see Fraser, J. Nelson & Marathe, K. B., eds.

Marathe, Kishore B. & Martucci, G. The Mathematical Foundations of Gauge Theories. LC 92-18717. (Studies in Mathematical Physics: Vol. 5). 1992. write for info. (*0-444-89708-9*, North Holland) Elsevier.

Marathe, M. P., et al, eds. Studies in Jainism. 267p. 1986. pap. 9.50 (*0-8364-1665-1*, Pub. by Abhinav II) S Asia.

Marathe, Sharad S. Regulation & Development: India's Policy Experience of Controls over India. 2nd ed. 340p. (C). 1990. text ed. 16.95 (*0-8039-9628-4*) Sage.

Marathe, Sudhakar. T. S. Elliot's Shakespeare Criticism. 1989. 20.00 (*81-7018-534-3*, Pub. by BR Pub II) S Asia.

Marathi, Ashish R., tr. see Alkunchwar, Mehesh.

Maratka, Z. Illustrated Terminology, Definitions & Diagnostic Criteria in Digestive Endoscopy: Atlas. rev. ed. (Illus.). 1992. 46.00 (*0-926592-09-2*) Normed Verlag.

Maratka, Zdenek. Terminology, Definitions & Diagnostic Criteria in Digestive Endoscopy: OMED Database of Digestive Endoscopy. enl. rev. ed. (Illus.). 130p. (C). 1989. disk 64.00 (*0-926592-02-5*) Normed Verlag.

— Terminology, Definitions & Diagnostic Criteria in Digestive Endoscopy: OMED Database of Digestive Endoscopy. 2nd enl. rev. ed. (Illus.). 130p. (C). 1989. text ed. 35.00 (*0-926592-01-7*) Normed Verlag.

Maratka, Zdenek & Ottenjann, R., eds. Inflammation in Gut: Esophagitis, Duodenitis, Segmental Colitis. (Bibliotheca Gastroenterologica Ser.: No. 9). (Illus.). 1970. pap. 47.25 (*3-8055-0043-2*) S Karger.

Maratos, Daniel C. & Hill, Marnesba D. Escritores de la Diaspora Cubano-Cuban Exile Writers: Manual Bibliografico-A Bibliographic Handbook. LC 85-31756. vvi, 391p. 1986. 42.50 (*0-8108-1878-7*) Scarecrow.

Maratsos, Michael P. The Use of Definite & Indefinite Reference in Young Children: An Experimental Study of Semantic Acquisition. 158p. reprint ed. pap. 45.10 (*0-317-27554-2*, 2024500) Bks Demand.

Maratsos, Michael P., jt. ed. see Gunnar, Megan R.

An Asterisk (*) at the beginning of an entry indicates that the title is appearing in BIP for the first time.

Maratta, Katie. Silent Pictures. 128p. 1992. pap. 9.95 (*0-943728-49-5*) Lone Eagle Pub.

Maravall Casesnoves, Dario. Diccionario de Matematica Moderna. 332p. (SPA.). 1975. pap. 19.95 (*0-8288-5814-4*, S50009) Fr & Eur.

Maravall, Jose A. Culture of the Baroque: Analysis of a Historical Structure. Cochran, Terry, tr. (Theory & History of Literature Ser.: Vol. 25). 330p. (Orig.). 1986. text ed. 16.95x (*0-8166-1443-1*); pap. text ed. 16.95 (*0-8166-1445-8*) U of Minn Pr.

— Utopia & Counterutopia in the "Quixote" Felkel, Robert W., tr. LC 90-20768. 254p. 1991. text ed. 29.95 (*0-8143-2294-8*) Wayne St U Pr.

Maravanyika, O. E. Implementing Educational Policies in Zimbabwe. No. 91. 44p. 1990. write for info. (*0-318-70278-9*, 11588) World Bank.

Maravel, Alexandra, jt. auth. see Rossides, Eugene T.

Maravel, William. Southwest Virginia in the Civil War: The Battles for Saltville. (Virginia Civil War Battles & Leaders Ser.). (Illus.). 192p. 1992. 19.95 (*1-56190-026-5*) H E Howard.

Maravelas, Paul, ed. & tr. Texts Pertaining to the Invention of the Balloon in 1782. Carpenter, Scott, tr. (Illus.). 28p. 1985. text ed. 95.00x (*0-318-19997-1*) P Maravelas.

Maravell, Nicholas P. Alex Katz: The Complete Prints, 1947-1983. (Illus.). 252p. 1983. 125.00 (*1-55660-063-1*) A Wofsy Fine Arts.

Maraviglia, B. Physics of NMR Spectroscopy in Biology & Medicine: Proceedings of the International School of Physics Enrico Fermi, Course C, Varenna, Italy, 8-18 July 1986. (Enrico Fermi International Summer School of Physics Ser.: Vol. 100). 456p. 1988. 141.00 (*0-444-87108-X*, North Holland) Elsevier.

Maraviglia, B., ed. Nuclear Magnetic Double Resonance: Varenna on Lake Como, Villa Monastero, 13-12 October 1992. LC 93-48564. 1994. write for info. (*0-444-81823-5*, North Holland) Elsevier.

Maravilla, Kenneth R. & Cohen, Wendy A. MRI Atlas of the Spine. 456p. 1991. 163.50 (*0-88167-755-8*) Raven.

Maravillas, Matilde. Innocents on the Road. 450p. (Orig.). 1993. pap. 10.00 (*0-915214-23-7*, Wrds Worth Pr) Current.

— Summers in Star Valley. 435p. (Orig.). 1991. pap. 14.95 (*0-915214-21-0*) Current.

— Summers in Star Valley. 2nd rev. ed. 454p. (Orig.). 1992. pap. 14.95 (*0-915214-25-3*) Current.

Marazon, Renee A. The Marazon Planning System: Developmental Planning for Early Childhood. rev. ed. Keller, Debra S., ed. (Understanding Developmental Objectives Ser.: Vol. A). (Illus.). 234p. (C). 1994. pap. text ed. 49.50 (*1-885673-00-0*) Lrning Gear.

— The Marazon Planning System: Developmental Planning for Early Childhood. rev. ed. Keller, Debra S., ed. (System in Practice Ser.: Vol. B). (Illus.). 172p. (C). 1994. pap. text ed. 49.50 (*1-885673-08-6*) Lrning Gear.

Marazzi, Richard & Fiorito, Len. Aaron to Zuverink: Baseball Players of the Fifties. 552p. 1984. mass mkt. 4.50 (*0-380-68445-4*, 68445) Avon.

***Marbach, Carl.** Carmina Scripturarum: Antiphonas et Responsoria ex Sacro Scripturae Fonte in Libros Liturgicos Sanctae Ecclesiae Romanae: Derivata, Collegit et Editit. 595p. (LAT.). 1994. lib. bdg. 163.50x (*3-487-00348-1*, Pub. by Georg Olms GW) Lubrecht & Cramer.

Marbach, Eduard. Mental Representation & Consciousness: Towards a Phenomenological Theory of Representation & Reference. LC 92-42687. (Contributions to Phenomenology Ser.: Vol. 14). 208p. (C). 1993. lib. bdg. 97.00 (*0-7923-2101-4*) Kluwer Ac.

Marbach, Ellen S., et al. Nutrition in a Changing World: A Curriculum for Primary Level. LC 79-11776. (Illus.). (Orig.). (J). (gr. 1-3). 1979. pap. 8.95 (*0-8425-1660-3*) BYU Scholarly.

Marbach, Ethel. The Cabbage Moth & the Shamrock. LC 91-575. (Illus.). 32p. (J). (ps-2). 1991. 9.00 (*0-671-74864-5*, Green Tiger S&S) S&S Childrens.

Marbaker, Thomas D. History of the Eleventh New Jersey Volunteers. Martin, David G., ed. (Illus.). 490p. (C). 1990. reprint ed. 32.00 (*0-944413-13-7*, 203) Longstreet Hse.

Marban, Edilberto. El Mundo Iberoamericano: Hombres en Su Historia. 390p. (C). (gr. 10-12). 1974. pap. text ed. 6.95 (*0-88345-066-6*, 18084) Prentice ESL.

— Puerto Rico: Cuna y Forja (Historia de la Isla Desde su Descubriiento en 1493 Hasta el Ultimo Periedo de Munoz en 1965) LC 86-81158. (Coleccion Textos Ser.). (Illus.). 298p. (Orig.). (SPA.). 1987. pap. 19.00 (*0-89729-405-X*) Ediciones.

Marban, Jorge A. La Florida: Cinco Siglos de Historia Hispanica. LC 78-70500. (Coleccion de Estudios Hispanicos - Hispanic Studies Collection). (Illus.). 1979. pap. 6.00 (*0-89729-214-6*) Ediciones.

Marbe, Karl, jt. auth. see Thumb, Albert.

Marberger, M., ed. Thermal Tissue Ablation. (Journal: European Urology: Vol. 23, Suppl. 1, 1993). (Illus.). iv, 72p. 1993. pap. 37.00 (*3-8055-5799-X*) S Karger.

Marberger, Michael, et al. Stone Surgery. (Practice of Surgery Ser.). (Illus.). 320p. 1991. text ed. 195.00 (*0-443-03522-9*) Churchill.

Marberry. Innovations in Healthcare Design. 1995. text ed. 59.95 (*0-442-01867-3*) Van Nos Reinhold.

Marberry, Sara. Color in the Office: Design Trends from 1950 to 1990 & Beyond. LC 93-1363. 1994. text ed. 49.95 (*0-442-00944-5*) Van Nos Reinhold.

***Marberry, Sara O. & Zagon, Laurie.** The Power of Color: Creating Healthy Interior Spaces. LC 94-23831. (Construction Business & Management Library). 1995. text ed. 49.95 (*0-471-07685-6*) Wiley.

Marberry, Thomas. The Randall House Bible Commentary: Galatians, Ephesians, Philippians, & Colossians. Picirilli, Robert E. et al, eds. (Bible Commentary Ser.). 400p. 1988. 24.95 (*0-89265-134-2*) Randall Hse.

Marbet, U., jt. ed. see Beglinger, C.

Marble, Alexander, ed. see Christlieb, A. Richard & Soeldner, J. Stuart.

Marble, Alice. Courting Danger. 1992. mass mkt. 5.99 (*0-312-92813-0*) St Martin.

Marble, Allan E. Surgeons, Smallpox, & the Poor: A History of Medicine & Social Conditions in Nova Scotia, 1749-1799. (Illus.). 352p. 1993. 39.95 (*0-7735-0988-7*, Pub. by McGill CN) U of Toronto Pr.

Marble, Annie R. Heralds of American Literature. LC 67-26761. (Essay Index Reprint Ser.). 1977. 22.95 (*0-8369-0675-6*) Ayer.

— Nobel Prize Winners in Literature, 1901-1931. LC 70-84324. (Essay Index Reprint Ser.). 1977. 30.95 (*0-8369-1185-7*) Ayer.

— Thoreau: His Home, Friends & Books. 1972. 59.95 (*0-8490-1204-X*) Gordon Pr.

— Thoreau: His Home, Friends & Books. LC 73-85906. reprint ed. 34.50 (*0-404-04185-X*) AMS Pr.

— Thoreau: His Home, Friends & Books. (BCL1-PS American Literature Ser.). 343p. 1992. reprint ed. lib. bdg. 89.00 (*0-7812-6884-2*) Rprt Serv.

Marble, Duane F. Two Computer Programs for the Analysis of Simple Markov Chains. (Discussion Paper Ser.: No. 6). 1964. pap. 10.00 (*1-55869-128-6*) Regional Sci Res Inst.

Marble, Effie M. Beautiful Bristol. (Illus.). 150p. 1988. pap. 7.95 (*0-933704-73-9*) Dawn Pr.

Marble, Melinda, jt. ed. see Chao Gunther, Herb.

Marbrook, John, jt. ed. see Watson, James D.

Marburg, Lahn, jt. ed. see Deutsche Blindenstudienstalt Staff.

Marburg, Theodore, ed. see Levasseur, Emile.

Marburger, Carl L., jt. auth. see Hansen, Barbara J.

Marburger, Carl L., jt. auth. see Henderson, Anne T.

Marburger, Carl L., jt. auth. see NCCE Staff.

Marburger, Heinz, jt. ed. see Luck, Kai von.

Marbury, jt. auth. see Piper.

Marbury, Mary O. Favorite Flies & Their History. 1989. 17.98 (*1-55521-241-7*) Bk Sales Inc.

Marbut, Curtis F., jt. auth. see Shantz, Homer L.

Marbut, F. B. News from the Capital: The Story of Washington Reporting. LC 76-132484. (New Horizons in Journalism Ser.). (Illus.). 328p. 1971. 12.50 (*0-8093-0495-3*) S Ill U Pr.

Marc, Alexandre, jt. auth. see Gopal, Gita.

***Marc, Alexandre, et al.** Social Action Progress & Social Funds: A Review of Design & Implementation in Sub-Saharan Africa. LC 94-48191. (Discussion Paper Ser.: No. 274). 174p. 1995. 10.95 (*0-8213-3167-1*, 13167) World Bank.

***Marc, David.** Bonfire of the Humanities: Television, Subliteracy, & Long-Term Memory Loss. (Television Ser.). (Illus.). 224p. 1995. 24.95 (*0-8156-0321-5*) Syracuse U Pr.

— Comic Visions: Television Comedy & American Culture. (Media Studies). 224p. 1989. text ed. 39.95 (*0-04-445284-5*); pap. text ed. 14.95 (*0-04-445285-3*) Routledge Chapman & Hall.

— Demographic Vistas: Television in American Culture. LC 83-12329. 224p. 1984. pap. text ed. 17.95 (*0-8122-1164-2*) U of Pa Pr.

***Marc, David & Thompson, Robert J.** Prime Time, Prime Movers: From I Love Lucy to L. A. Law--America's Greatest TV Shows & the People Who Created Them. (Television Ser.). (Illus.). 350p. 1995. pap. 14.95 (*0-8156-0311-8*) Syracuse U Pr.

— Prime Time, Prime Movers: The Inside Story of the Inside People Who Made American Television. (Illus.). 350p. 1992. 22.95 (*0-316-54589-9*) Little.

Marc, Franz. Franz Marc: Letters from the War. Lankheit, Klaus & Steffen, Uwe, eds. Dieckmann, Liselotte, tr. LC 91-23987. (American University Studies: Fine Arts: Ser. XX, Vol. 16). (Illus.). 113p. (C). 1992. text ed. 29.95 (*0-8204-1588-X*) P Lang Pubs.

Marc, Franz, jt. tr. see Kandinsky, Wassily.

Marc Love Productions Staff. Thinking about Nutrition. 92p. 1992. per. 13.95 (*0-8403-8011-9*) Kendall-Hunt.

Marc, Michel, ed. see Labiche, Eugene.

MARC Standards Office Staff, prod. US-MARC Code List for Countries. 1993. LC 93-38625. 1993. write for info. (*0-8444-0825-5*) Lib Congress.

MARC Standards Office Staff, jt. auth. see Network Development Staff.

MARC Standards Office Staff, jt. ed. see Network Development Staff.

Marc, Stephen. Urban Notions. LC 84-180996. (Illus.). 70p. 1983. 15.00 (*0-915109-01-8*); pap. 8.00 (*0-915109-02-6*) Ataraxia.

Marca, David & Bock, Geoffrey. Groupware: Software for Computer-Supported Cooperative Work. LC 91-37373. (Illus.). 592p. (C). 1992. text ed. 75.00 (*0-8186-2637-2*, 2637) IEEE Comp Soc.

Marca, David A. & McGowan, Clement L. IDEFO - SADT Business Process & Enterprise Modelling. 392p. 1993. pap. 65.00 (*0-9638750-0-0*) Eclectic Solns.

Marcaccio, Kathleen Y., jt. auth. see Young.

Marcaccio, Michael D. The Hapgoods Three Earnest Brothers. LC 77-5102. (Illus.). 271p. reprint ed. pap. 77.30 (*0-8357-3136-7*, 2039399) Bks Demand.

Marcais, Georges, jt. auth. see Diehl, Charles.

Marcangelo, Jo. Italian Vegetarian Cooking. 160p. 1989. pap. 9.95 (*0-89281-343-1*) Inner Tradit.

Marcano-Garcia, Pablo. La Criminelidad y la Crisis de las Prisiones en Puerto Rico. 144p. (Orig.). (SPA.). 1985. pap. 9.00 (*0-685-24434-2*) Editorial El Coqui.

Marcante, Duilio. This Is Diving. 2nd ed. Busuttili, Mike, tr. (This Is...Ser.). (Illus.). 160p. 1989. 24.95 (*0-911378-96-0*) Sheridan.

Marcantel, David E., jt. auth. see Gelhay, Patrick.

Marceau, Felicien. Les Anneese Courtes. (FRE.). 1973. pap. 10.95 (*0-7859-4016-2*) Fr & Eur.

— Bergere Legere. 288p. (FRE.). 1973. pap. 8.95 (*0-7859-4012-X*, 2070364437) Fr & Eur.

— Chair et Cuir. (FRE.). 1974. pap. 10.95 (*0-7859-4028-6*) Fr & Eur.

— Le Corps de Mon Enemi. (FRE.). 1978. pap. 10.95 (*0-7859-4096-0*) Fr & Eur.

— Creezy. (FRE.). 1972. pap. 10.95 (*0-7859-3995-4*) Fr & Eur.

— Les Elans du Coeur. (FRE.). 1973. pap. 8.95 (*0-7859-4002-2*) Fr & Eur.

— L' Homme du Roi. (FRE.). 1972. pap. 8.95 (*0-7859-3996-2*) Fr & Eur.

— L' Oeuf. 160p. (FRE.). 1980. pap. 8.95 (*0-7859-4138-X*, 2070372383) Fr & Eur.

Marceau, Gabrielle Z. Anti-Dumping & Anti-Trust Issues in Free Trade Areas. 320p. 1995. 89.00 (*0-19-825920-4*) OUP.

Marceau, Jane. A Family Business: The Making of an International Business Elite. (Illus.). 240p. (C). 1989. 64.95 (*0-521-26731-5*) Cambridge U Pr.

Marceau, Jane, ed. Reworking the World: Organisations, Technologies, & Cultures in Comparative Perspective. LC 92-32150. (Studies in Organization: No. 42). x, 514p. 1992. lib. bdg. 79.95 (*3-11-013158-7*) De Gruyter.

Marceau, Marcel. Pimporello: A Fable for All Ages. 1991. 28.00 (*0-7206-0813-9*, Pub. by Peter Owen Ltd UK) Dufour.

Marceau, William C. The Eucharist in Theodore de Beze & St. Francis de Sales. LC 93-15464. (Toronto Studies in Theology: Vol. 59). (Illus.). 136p. 1993. text ed. 69.95 (*0-7734-9693-9*) E Mellen.

— Henri Bergson et Joseph Malegue: La convergence de Deux Pensees. (Stanford French & Italian Studies: No. 50). 144p. (Orig.). (FRE.). 1988. pap. 46.50 (*0-915838-66-4*) Anma Libri.

— Optimism in the Works of St. Francis De Sales. LC 89-29359. (Toronto Studies in Theology: Vol. 41). 336p. 1989. lib. bdg. 99.95 (*0-88946-990-3*) E Mellen.

Marcel, A. J. & Bisiach, E., eds. Consciousness in Contemporary Science. (Illus.). 416p. 1992. reprint ed. pap. 35.00 (*0-19-852237-1*) OUP.

***Marcel Dekker, Inc. Staff.** Chemically Resistant Masonry. (Illus.). 1982. 125.00 (*0-8247-1586-1*) NACE Intl.

— Corrosion-Resistant Plastic Composites in Chemical Plant Design. (Plastics Engineering Ser.: Vol. 18). (Illus.). 572p. 1988. 145.00 (*0-8247-7687-9*) NACE Intl.

Marcel, Gabriel. The Existential Background of Human Dignity. LC 62-13814. (William James Lectures: 1961-1962). 188p. reprint ed. pap. 53.60 (*0-317-09026-7*, 2011022) Bks Demand.

— Homo Viator: Introduction to a Metaphysic of Hope. Crauford, Emma, tr. 27.25 (*0-8446-2529-9*) Peter Smith.

— The Mystery of Being, 2 vols. in 1. Hague, Rene, tr. LC 77-27179. (Gifford Lectures: 1949-50). 432p. reprint ed. 61.50 (*0-404-60504-4*) AMS Pr.

— Mystery of Being, Vol. II: Faith & Reality. 198p. (C). 1984. reprint ed. pap. text ed. 16.00 (*0-8191-3311-6*) U Pr of Amer.

— Philosophy of Existence. Harai, Manya, tr. LC 73-80390. (Essay Index Reprint Ser.). 1977. 18.95 (*0-8369-1094-X*) Ayer.

— The Philosophy of Existentialism. 132p. 1995. pap. 7.95 (*0-8065-0901-5*, 84, Citadel Pr) Carol Pub Group.

— Royce's Metaphysics. LC 56-11854. 200p. reprint ed. pap. 57.00 (*0-317-08060-1*, 2055292) Bks Demand.

— Royce's Metaphysics. Ringer, Virginia & Ringer, Gordon, trs. LC 74-33746. 180p. 1975. reprint ed. text ed. 49.75 (*0-8371-7978-5*, MARO, Greenwood Pr) Greenwood.

— Tragic Wisdom & Beyond. Jolin, Stephen & McCormick, Peter, trs. LC 72-96700. (Studies in Phenomenology & Existential Philosophy). 256p. (C). 1973. pap. 16.95 (*0-8101-0614-0*) Northwestern U Pr.

Marcel, George, ed. see Moorman, John R.

Marcel, Glenn P. Juggling the Truth. LC 89-61781. 200p. 1989. 14.95 (*0-935773-21-5*) Charleston Pr.

Marcel, Mario & Arenas, Alberto. Social Security Reform in Chile. 47p. 1992. pap. text ed. write for info. (*0-940602-46-6*) IADB.

Marcel, Mario & Arenas, Alberto, eds. Reformas a la Seguridad Social En Chile. 1991. write for info. (*0-940602-41-5*) IADB.

Marcel, Pierre C. El Bautismo: Sacramento del Pacto de Gracia. Padilla, C. Rene, tr. 288p. (Orig.). (SPA.). 1991. pap. text ed. 10.99 (*0-8028-0912-5*) Eerdmans.

Marcel Socias Studio Staff, ed. see Julivert, Maria A.

Marcelin, Pierre, jt. auth. see Thoby-Marcelin, Philippe.

Marcell, David W. Progress & Pragmatism: James, Dewey, Beard & the American Idea of Progress. LC 72-818. (Contributions in American Studies: No. 9). 402p. 1974. text ed. 75.00 (*0-8371-6387-0*, MPR/, Greenwood Pr) Greenwood.

Marcell, Raleigh, Jr. The Infamous Soothing System of Professor Maillard. (Illus.). 23p. (Orig.). 1981. pap. 3.00 (*0-88680-093-5*) I E Clark.

— The Middle of Nowhere. (Illus.). 28p. (Orig.). 1982. pap. 3.00 (*0-88680-130-3*) I E Clark.

Marcell, Rita & Newton, Robert. A New Manual of Classification. LC 94-172. 1994. 69.95 (*0-566-07547-4*, Pub. by Gower UK) Ashgate Pub Co.

Marcella, A. J., Jr., et al. Automated System for Contingency Planning & Disaster Recovery. Campbell, Lee A., ed. (Took Kit Ser.). 88p. 1992. 200.00 (*0-89413-276-8*) Inst Inter Aud.

Marcella, Albert. Auditing IBM's Customer Information Control System. 178p. 1991. pap. 20.00 (*0-89413-240-7*) Inst Inter Aud.

Marcella, Albert J., Jr. & Chan, Sally. EDI Security, Control, & Audit. (Telecommunications Library). 185p. 1993. text ed. 69.00 (*0-89006-610-8*) Artech Hse.

Marcella, Gabriel, ed. Warriors in Peacetime: The Military & Democracy in Latin America, New Directions for U.S. Policy. LC 94-1380. 190p. (C). 1994. 35.00 (*0-7146-4585-0*, Pub. by F Cass Pubs UK); pap. 19.50 (*0-7146-4115-4*) Intl Spec Bk.

Marcelle, R., et al, eds. Biological Control of Photosynthesis. (Advances in Agricultural Biotechnology Ser.). 1986. lib. bdg. 95.50 (*90-247-3287-5*) Kluwer Ac.

— Photosynthesis & Plant Development. 1979. lib. bdg. 136.50 (*90-6193-595-4*) Kluwer Ac.

Marcelli, A., jt. ed. see Bianconi, A.

Marcelli, M. Pinto. Ecologia Liquenica nos Manguezais do Sul-Sudeste Brasileiro. (Bibliorheca Lichenologica Ser.: Vol. 47). (Illus.). (POR.). 1992. pap. text ed. 108.00 (*3-443-58026-2*, Pub. by Cramer-Borntraeger GW) Lubrecht & Cramer.

Marcellino. Picture Book 2. (Illus.). (J). Date not set. 15.00 (*0-06-205064-8*); lib. bdg. 14.89 (*0-06-205065-6*) HarpC Child Bks.

— Picture Book 3. (Illus.). (J). Date not set. 15.00 (*0-06-205066-4*); lib. bdg. 14.89 (*0-06-205067-2*) HarpC Child Bks.

Marcellinus, Ammianus. The Later Roman Empire (A.D. 353-378) Hamilton, Walter, ed. 640p. 1986. pap. 12.95 (*0-14-044406-8*, Penguin Classics) Viking Penguin.

— Rerum Gestarum Libri Qui Supersunt, Vols. I & II. (GER.). 1963. write for info. (*0-318-70575-3*, Pub. by Georg Olms GW); Vol. I: Libri 14-25, pages xii, 1-387. write for info. (*3-296-10401-1*, Pub. by Georg Olms GW); Vol. II: Libri 26-31, pages iv, 389-604. write for info. (*0-318-70576-1*, Pub. by Georg Olms GW) Lubrecht & Cramer.

Marcello, jt. auth. see Nedaud.

Marcello, Beth & Bohn, Earl. Passport to Pittsburgh: The New Airport & the International City. Turner, James E. & Hughs, Mary, eds. LC 93-31594. 320p. 1993. text ed. 45.00 (*0-9630029-6-1*) Community Comm.

Marcello, John A., jt. auth. see Desmond, Glenn M.

***Marcello, Leo L.** Blackrobe's Love Letters. (Occasional Publications Ser.: No. 4). 39p. (Orig.). 1994. pap. 5.95 (*1-883275-02-4*) Xavier Rev.

— The Secret Proximity of Everywhere. 32p. (C). 1994. 8.00 (*1-884725-01-5*) Blue Heron LA.

Marcello, Leo L., ed. see Scantelbury, Joy, et al.

Marcello, Ronald E., ed. Building the Death Railway: The Ordeal of American POWs in Burma, 1942-1945. LC 92-97641. 368p. 1993. 24.95 (*0-8420-2428-X*) Scholarly Res Inc.

Marcello, Ronald E., jt. ed. see La Forte, Robert S.

Marcellus, Daniel H. Programming Expert Systems in Turbo Prolog. (Illus.). 256p. (C). 1989. text ed. 34.00 (*0-13-295841-4*) P-H.

— Systems Programming for Small Computers. (C). 1984. pap. 23.95 (*0-13-881656-5*) P-H.

Marcellus, Nonius. De Compendiosa Doctrina Libri XX, 3 vols., Set. Lindsay, W. M., ed. xlii, 997p. 1971. reprint ed. write for info. (*0-318-71187-7*, Pub. by Georg Olms GW) Lubrecht & Cramer.

Marcellus Nonius. Dictionary of Republican Latin. Lindsay, W. M., ed. 120p. reprint ed. lib. bdg. 25.87 (*0-685-13739-2*, Pub. by Georg Olms GW) Lubrecht & Cramer.

Marcelo, Dascal, jt. ed. see Cohen, Avner.

Marcelo, J. J. Ships Afire. Arvio, Sarah, tr. 336p. (Orig.). 1988. pap. 7.95 (*0-380-89741-5*) Avon.

Marcenac, L. N. Encyclopedia of Horses: Encyclopedie du Cheval. 4th ed. 2224p. (FRE.). 1981. 150.00 (*0-8288-2342-1*, M6397) Fr & Eur.

Marcey, Sally. Choice Adventures, No. 11: The Silverlake Stranger. LC 92-36889. (J). 1993. 4.99 (*0-8423-5048-9*) Tyndale.

— Choice Adventures, No. 3: The Underground Railroad. (J). (gr. 3-7). 1991. lib. bdg. 4.99 (*0-8423-5027-6*) Tyndale.

March, ed. see Ionesco, Eugene.

March, ed. see Sophocles.

March, A. C. A Glossary of Buddhist Terms. 3rd ed. (Bibliotheca Indo-Buddhica Ser.: No. 25). 99p. (C). 1986. reprint ed. text ed. 6.00 (*81-7030-025-8*) S Asia.

March, Alden. History & Conquest of the Philippines & Our Other Island Possessions. LC 04-111744. (American Imperialism: Viewpoints of United States Foreign Policy, 1898-1941 Ser.). 1970. reprint ed. 25.95 (*0-405-02038-4*) Ayer.

March, Andrew L., ed. Recommended Reference Books in Paperback. 2nd ed. LC 92-15875. 350p. 1992. lib. bdg. 47.50 (*1-56308-067-2*) Libs Unl.

March, Andrew L. & March, Kathryn G. The Mushroom Basket: A Gourmet Introduction to the Best Common Mushrooms of the Southern Rocky Mountains, with Applications Throughout the Northern Hemisphere, & Tidbits of Mushroom Lore from Europe Russia & China. LC 82-90153. (Illus.). 162p. (Orig.). 1982. pap. 11.95 (*0-940206-02-1*) Meridian Hill.

March, Andrew L., jt. auth. see March, Kathryn G.

March, Ausias. Ausias March: Selected Poems. Terry, Arthur, ed. LC 76-29514. (Edinburgh Bilingual Library). 1977. 20.00 (*0-292-70323-6*) Lib Soc Sci.

March, Candida, jt. ed. see Wallace, Tina.

March, Carol. Choosing an Airline Career: In-Depth Descriptions of Entry-Level Positions, Travel Benefits, How to Apply & Interview. LC 91-77885. (Illus.). 160p. 1992. pap. 16.95 (*0-9631614-0-7*) Capri Pub.

M

An Asterisk (*) at the beginning of an entry indicates that the title is appearing in BIP for the first time.

March, Connie S. The Complete Care Plan Manual for Long-Term Care. LC 91-44365. 143p. (Orig.). 1992. 37.95 (*1-55648-085-7*, 130105) AHPI.

March, David. D'Albert S'Expose: Aubrey Beardsley's Drawings for Mademoiselle de Maupin. LC 85-90379. (Illus.). 48p. 1985. pap. 20.00 (*0-9615493-0-0*) D March.

— Priapusa, Manicure & Fardeuse; or the Reine des ribauds in the Land of the Queen of Love. (Illus.). 32p. (Orig.). 1988. pap. 100.00 (*0-9615493-1-9*) D March.

March, Francis A. A Comparative Grammar of the Anglo-Saxon Language. 1977. 59.95 (*0-8490-1651-7*) Gordon Pr.

— Thesaurus Dictionary of the English Language. (Illus.). 1994. reprint ed. lib. bdg. 48.00 (*0-7808-0011-7*) Omnigraphics Inc.

March, George P. Cossacks of the Brotherhood: The Zaporog Kosh of the Dniepr River. LC 89-27980. (American University Studies: History: Ser. IX, Vol. 86). 264p. 1990. text ed. 51.00 (*0-8204-1191-4*) P Lang Pubs.

March, Ivan, et al. The Complete Penguin Guide to Compact Discs & Cassettes. rev. ed. 1400p. 1993. pap. 23.50 (*0-14-046918-4*, Penguin Bks) Viking Penguin.

— The Penguin Guide to Bargain Compact Discs & Cassettes: Bargain Buys in Classical Music. 720p. (Orig.). 1992. pap. 17.50 (*0-14-046919-2*, Penguin Bks) Viking Penguin.

— The Penguin Guide to Compact Discs & Cassettes. rev. ed. 1376p. 1995. pap. 23.50 (*0-14-046958-3*, Penguin Bks) Viking Penguin.

— The Penguin Guide to Opera on Compact Disc. 688p. 1993. pap. 17.50 (*0-14-046957-5*, Penguin Bks) Viking Penguin.

March, J. Problems in Advanced Organic Chemistry. LC 70-176119. 431p. reprint ed. pap. 122.90 (*0-8357-9093-2*, 2055049) Bks Demand.

March, J., et al. Open Plan Office Acoustical Privacy. (Illus.). 1884. pap. text ed. 39.95 (*0-931673-00-3*) J March Pub Grp.

March, James & Simon, Herbert. Organizations. 2nd ed. LC 92-42143. 1993. 24.95 (*0-631-18631-X*) Blackwell Pubs.

March, James G. Autonomy As a Factor in Group Organization. Zuckerman, Harriet & Merton, Robert K., eds. LC 79-9012. (Dissertations on Sociology Ser.). 1980. lib. bdg. 34.95 (*0-405-12980-7*) Ayer.

— Decisions & Organizations. 300p. 1988. pap. text ed. 32.95 (*0-631-16856-7*) Blackwell Pubs.

— A Primer on Decision Making: How Decisions Happen. LC 94-4414. 1994. text ed. 29.95 (*0-02-920035-0*) Free Pr.

***March, James G. & Olsen, Johan P.** Democratic Governance. 1995. 30.00 (*0-02-874054-8*) Free Pr.

March, James G., jt. auth. see Cohen, Michael D.

March, James G., jt. auth. see Lave, Charles A.

***March, Jared A.** The New Jersey Book of Golf: Golf Directory & Travel Guide. rev. ed. LC 94-96807. (Illus.). 1995. pap. write for info. (*0-931673-01-1*) J March Pub Grp.

March, Jerry. Advanced Organic Chemistry: Reactions, Mechanisms, & Structures. 4th ed. 1495p. 1992. text ed. 59.95 (*0-471-60180-2*) Wiley.

March, Jerry, jt. auth. see Bettelheim, Frederick.

March, Jessica. Illusions. 1988. mass mkt. 5.95 (*0-446-35943-2*) Warner Bks.

— Obsessions. 1990. mass mkt. 5.95 (*0-446-35227-6*) Warner Bks.

— Obsessions. 1991. reprint ed. 22.95 (*0-7278-4178-5*) Severn Hse.

— Sensations. 432p. (Orig.). 1993. pap. 5.99 (*0-451-40356-8*, Onyx) NAL-Dutton.

— Temptations. 1989. mass mkt. 4.95 (*0-446-35226-8*) Warner Bks.

— Temptations. 528p. 1991. reprint ed. 22.95 (*0-7278-4125-4*) Severn Hse.

***March, John S.** Anxiety Disorders in Children & Adolescents. 448p. 1995. lib. bdg. 40.00 (*0-89862-834-2*) Guilford Pr.

March, Joseph M. The Wild Party: The Lost Classic. LC 94-11682. (Illus.). 1994. 22.00 (*0-679-42450-4*) Pantheon.

***March, Karen.** The Stranger Who Bore Me: Adoptee-Birth Mother Interactions. 192p. 1995. 45.00 (*0-8020-0447-4*); pap. 17.95 (*0-8020-7235-6*) U of Toronto Pr.

March, Kathleen, ed. An Anthology of Galician Short Stories: Asi Vai o Conto. LC 91-25884. (Hispanic Literature Ser.: Vol. 13). 248p. 1991. lib. bdg. 89.95 (*0-7734-9749-8*) E Mellen.

March, Kathleen, tr. see Belli, Gioconda.

March, Kathleen N. Festa da Palabra: An Anthology of Contemporary Galician Women Poets. (American University Studies: Romance Languages & Literature: Ser. II, Vol. 51). 254p. (C). 1989. text ed. 41.50 (*0-8204-1022-5*) P Lang Pubs.

March, Kathleen N., ed. First Galician Studies Conference, 1985. 375p. (Orig.). 1987. pap. text ed. 20.00 (*0-89101-067-X*) U Maine Pr.

March, Kathryn G. & March, Andrew L. The Wild Plant Companion: A Fresh Understanding of Herbal Food & Medicine. (Illus.). 200p. (Orig.). 1986. pap. 11.95 (*0-940206-03-X*) Meridian Hill.

— The Wild Taste: Plant & Mushroom Recipes for the Knowledgeable Cook. LC 88-90947. (Illus.). 320p. (Orig.). 1989. pap. 19.95 (*0-940206-04-8*) Meridian Hill.

March, Kathryn G., jt. auth. see March, Andrew L.

March, L., ed. The Architecture of Form. LC 74-80354. (Cambridge Urban & Architectural Studies: No. 4). (Illus.). 552p. 1976. 125.00 (*0-521-20528-X*) Cambridge U Pr.

March, L. G., jt. auth. see Forde, L. A.

March, Lionel. Frank Lloyd Wright: The Phoenix Papers, 2 vols., Set. Zygas, K. Paul & Johnson, Linda N., eds. (Illus.). 320p. 1995. 79.95 (*1-884320-08-2*) ASU Herberger Ctr.

March, Louise. Gold Dust. 1980. 20.00 (*0-686-33124-9*) Rochester Folk Art.

March, Lourdes, jt. auth. see Rios, Alicia.

March, Marion. Creative Typography. (Illus.). 144p. 1988. 27.95 (*0-89134-258-3*, 30079) North Light Bks.

March, Marion D. & McEvers, Joan. The Only Way to... Learn about Horary & Electional Astrology. (Only Way to Learn Ser.: Vol. VI). 256p. (Orig.). 1994. pap. 12.95 (*0-935127-29-1*) ACS Pubns.

— The Only Way to...Learn About Relationships, Vol. 5. (Only Way to Learn Ser.: Vol. V). (Orig.). 1992. pap. 12.95 (*0-935127-21-6*) ACS Pubns.

— The Only Way to...Learn about Tomorrow, Vol. 4. (Only Way to Learn Ser.: Vol. IV). 290p. (Orig.). 1988. pap. 12.95 (*0-917086-65-1*) ACS Pubns.

— The Only Way to...Learn Astrology: Basic Principles, Vol. 1. (Only Way to Learn Ser.: Vol. I). (Illus.). 320p. (Orig.). 1981. pap. 12.95 (*0-917086-00-7*) ACS Pubns.

— The Only Way To...Learn Astrology: Horoscope Analysis, Vol. 3. (Only Way to Learn Ser.: Vol. III). 272p. 1982. pap. 12.95 (*0-917086-43-0*) ACS Pubns.

— The Only Way To...Learn Astrology: Math & Interpretation Techniques, Vol. 2. 2nd rev. ed. (Only Way to Learn Ser.: Vol. II). (Illus.). 264p. 1981. reprint ed. pap. 12.95 (*0-917086-26-0*) ACS Pubns.

March, Melisand. The Site. 320p. 1989. pap. 3.95 (*0-8439-2812-3*) Dorchester Pub Co.

March, Michael. Description of a Struggle: The Vintage Book of Contemporary Eastern European Writing. 1994. pap. 14.00 (*0-679-74514-9*, Vin) Random.

March, N. H. Atomic Dynamics in Liquids. 1991. pap. 8.95 (*0-486-66598-4*) Dover.

— Chemical Physics of Liquids. 336p. 1990. text ed. 190.00 (*2-88124-722-9*) Gordon & Breach.

— Electron Correlation in Molecules & Condensed Phases. LC 95-4195. (Physics of Solids & Liquids Ser.). 440p. 1995. 115.00 (*0-306-44844-0*, Plenum Pr) Plenum.

March, N. H., jt. auth. see Srivastava, S. K.

March, Norman H. Chemical Bonds Outside Metal Surfaces. LC 86-5022. (Physics of Solids & Liquids Ser.). 294p. 1986. 75.00 (*0-306-42059-7*, Plenum Pr) Plenum.

— Electron Density Theory of Atoms & Molecules. (Theoretical Chemistry Ser.). (Illus.). 339p. 1991. text ed. 116.00 (*0-12-470525-1*) Acad Pr.

— Liquid Metals. 1968. 57.00 (*0-08-012331-7*, Pub. by Pergamon Repr UK) Franklin.

— Liquid Metals: Concepts & Theory. (Cambridge Monographs on Mathematical Physics). 250p. (C). 1990. 130.00 (*0-521-30279-X*) Cambridge U Pr.

— Self-Consistent Fields in Atoms. 1975. text ed. 106.00 (*0-08-017819-7*, Pub. by Pergamon Repr UK) Franklin.

March, Norman H. & Deb, B. M., eds. Single-Particle Density in Physics & Chemistry. (Techniques of Physics Ser.). 385p. 1988. text ed. 115.00 (*0-12-470518-9*) Acad Pr.

March, Norman H. & Mucci, J. F. Chemical Physics of Free Molecules. (Illus.). 360p. (C). 1992. 49.50 (*0-306-44270-1*, Plenum Pr) Plenum.

March, Norman H. & Pings, C. J. Physics & Chemistry of Liquids: Special Topics - Proceedings of the XV Solvay Conference on Chemistry: Electrostatic Interaction & the Structure of Water, 2 pts., Set. 388p. 1978. pap. text ed. 345.00 (*0-677-40285-6*) Gordon & Breach.

March, Norman H. & Tosi, Mario P. Coulomb Liquids: Monograph. 1984. text ed. 129.00 (*0-12-470520-0*) Acad Pr.

March, Norman H. & Tosi, Mario P., eds. Polymers, Liquid Crystals & Low-Dimensional Solids. (Physics of Solids & Liquids Ser.). 622p. 1984. 135.00 (*0-306-41641-7*, Plenum Pr) Plenum.

March, Norman H., jt. auth. see Alonso, Julio A.

March, Norman H., jt. auth. see Jones, William.

March, Norman H., jt. ed. see Lundqvist, S. O.

March, Norman H., et al, eds. Amorphous Solids & the Liquid State. LC 85-12031. (Physics of Solids & Liquids Ser.). 560p. 1985. 135.00 (*0-306-41947-5*, Plenum Pr) Plenum.

March of the Living Operations Office Staff, et al. Study Guide for the March of the Living. (Illus.). (Orig.). 1992. pap. 24.95 (*0-930029-06-2*) Central Agency.

March, Peter R. Desert Warpaint. (Osprey Colour Library). (Illus.). 128p. 1992. pap. 15.95 (*1-85532-193-9*, Pub. by Osprey Pubng Ltd UK) Motorbooks Intl.

March, Peyton C. Nation at War. LC 72-109779. 407p. 1970. reprint ed. text ed. 45.00 (*0-8371-4269-5*, MANW, Greenwood Pr) Greenwood.

March, Randolph B. Thirty Years of Army Life on the Border. Comprising Descriptions of the Indian Nomads of the Plains, Explorations... (American Biography Ser.). 442p. 1991. reprint ed. lib. bdg. 89.00 (*0-7812-8265-9*) Rprt Serv.

March, Ray. A Paradise Called Pebble Beach. Peters, Sally, ed. 1992. pap. 40.00 (*0-671-77722-X*) PB.

March, Ray, ed. California Golf: The Complete Guide. 3rd ed. (Illus.). 608p. 1991. 16.95 (*0-935701-16-8*) Foghorn Pr.

March, Raymond & Hughes, Richard. Quadrupole Storage Mass Spectrometry. (Chemical Analysis Ser.). 471p. 1989. text ed. 120.00 (*0-471-85794-7*) Wiley.

March, Raymond E. & Todd, John F., eds. Practical Applications of Ion Trap Mass Spectrometry. (Modern Mass Spectrometry Ser.). 464p. 1995. 89.95 (*0-8493-8251-3*, 8251) CRC Pr.

— Practical Applications of Ion Trap Mass Spectrometry. (Modern Mass Spectrometry Ser.). 432p. 1995. 125.00 (*0-8493-4452-2*, 4452) CRC Pr.

— Practical Aspects of Ion Trap Mass Spectrometry Vol. II: Ion Trap Instrumentation. LC 95-14146. (Modern Mass Spectrometry Ser.). 352p. 1995. 89.95 (*0-8493-8253-X*, 8253) CRC Pr.

March, Richard & Tambimuttu, M. J., comps. T. S. Eliot. LC 68-55850. (Essay Index Reprint Ser.). 1977. 21.95 (*0-8369-0676-4*) Ayer.

March, Rita N., jt. auth. see Shires, H. Bess.

March, Robert H. Physics for Poets. 3rd ed. 1992. pap. text ed. write for info. (*0-07-040245-0*) McGraw.

March, Robert M. Honoring the Customer: Marketing & Selling to the Japanese. 224p. 1991. text ed. 24.95 (*0-471-55073-6*) Wiley.

— The Japanese Negotiator: Subtlety & Strategy Beyond Western Logic. LC 88-80129. 240p. 1988. 18.95 (*0-87011-887-0*) Kodansha.

— The Japanese Negotiator: Subtlety & Strategy Beyond Western Logic. 197p. 1991. pap. 9.00 (*4-7700-1462-7*) Kodansha.

— Working for a Japanese Company: Managing Relationships in a Multicultural Organization. 176p. 1992. 19.00 (*4-7700-1533-X*) Kodansha.

March, Robert T. The Investment Side of Corporate Cash Management. LC 88-3100. 246p. 1988. text ed. 55.00 (*0-89930-333-1*, MHI/, Quorum Bks) Greenwood.

March, Robert W. Taste of Steel. 224p. pap. 2.50 (*0-8439-2022-X*) Dorchester Pub Co.

March, Roman & Mahler, Greg. Annual Editions: Canadian Politics 93-94. 3rd ed. 256p. 1993. pap. text ed. 12.95 (*1-56134-191-6*) Dushkin Pub.

March, S. T., ed. Entity-Relationship Approach: Proceedings of the 6th International Conference, New York, NY, 9-11 Nov., 1987. 522p. 1988. 107.75 (*0-444-70440-X*, North Holland) Elsevier.

***March, Sam.** A Marxist Defense of the L.A. Rebellion. 1992. pap. 2.50 (*0-89567-106-9*) World View Forum.

March, Sam, jt. auth. see Gutierrez, Teresa.

March, Stephen, jt. ed. see Brinkmeyer, Robert.

March, W. Eugene. Israel & the Politics of Land: A Theological Case Study. LC 93-40125. 112p. (Orig.). 1994. pap. 12.99 (*0-664-25121-8*) Westminster John Knox.

March, W. Eugene, ed. Texts & Testaments: Critical Essays on the Bible & Early Church Fathers. LC 79-92585. 321p. 1980. write for info. (*0-911536-80-9*) Trinity U Pr.

March, Wayne F. Practical Ophthalmic Problems for Allied Health Professionals. (Allied Health Professions Monograph). 148p. 1984. 12.50 (*0-87527-329-7*) Green.

March, William. Bad Seed. adapted ed. 1956. pap. 4.75 (*0-8222-0088-0*) Dramatists Play.

— The Bad Seed. 1993. reprint ed. lib. bdg. 21.95 (*1-56849-107-7*) Buccaneer Bks.

— Company K. LC 89-38395. (Library of Alabama Classics). 260p. 1989. pap. 14.50 (*0-8173-0480-0*) U of Ala Pr.

— Company K. 18.95 (*0-89190-097-7*, Am Repr) Amereon Ltd.

— Trial Balance: The Collected Short Stories of William March. LC 87-5900. (Library of Alabama Classics). 536p. 1987. reprint ed. pap. 16.95 (*0-8173-0372-3*) U of Ala Pr.

Marchac, D. Surgery of Basal Cell Carcinoma. (Illus.). 130p. 1987. 114.00 (*0-387-18034-6*) Spr-Verlag.

Marchac, D., ed. Craniofacial Surgery. (Illus.). 540p. 1987. 266.00 (*0-387-16924-5*) Spr-Verlag.

Marc'hadour, Germain. The Bible in the Works of Thomas More, 2 vols., Set. 1098p. 1969. text ed. 167.50 (*90-6004-107-0*, Pub. by B De Graaf NE) Coronet Bks.

Marchais, Pierre. Glossaire de Psychiatrie: Glossary of Psychiatry. 238p. (FRE.). 1970. 79.95 (*0-8288-6537-X*, M-6398) Fr & Eur.

Marchaj, C. A. Aero-Hydrodynamics of Sailing. exp. rev. ed. (Illus.). 746p. 1988. text ed. 59.95 (*0-87742-993-6*) Intl Marine.

Marchaj, Zeslaw A. Aero-Hydrodynamics of Sailing. 1980. 40.00 (*0-396-07739-0*, Putnam) Putnam Pub Group.

Marchak, M. Patricia. The Integrated Circus: The New Right & the Restructuring of Global Markets. 1991. 44.95 (*0-7735-0845-7*, Pub. by McGill CN); pap. 17.95 (*0-7735-1149-0*, Pub. by McGill CN) U of Toronto Pr.

Marchal, Alain, jt. auth. see Hardcastel, William J.

Marchal, C. The Three-Body Problem. (Studies in Astronautics: No. 4). 576p. 1990. 166.75 (*0-444-87440-2*) Elsevier.

***Marchal, Gaston-Louis.** Arras et l'Art Au XIX Siecle Dictionnaire des Peintres, Sculpteurs, Graveurs, Architectes: 1800-1919. 310p. (FRE.). 1987. pap. 115.00 (*0-7859-8205-1*, 2900643066) Fr & Eur.

Marchal, Jean-Yves. La Petite Region Dambohimanambola (Sous-Prefecture de Betafo) La Colonisation Agricole au Moyan-Quest Malgache. (Atlas des Structures Agraires au Sud de Sahara Ser.: No. 2). (Illus.). 122p. (FRE.). 1974. pap. text ed. 55.40 (*90-279-7935-9*) Mouton.

Marchal, Michael. Adapting the Liturgy. LC 89-10241. 312p. (Orig.). (C). 1989. pap. 11.95 (*0-89390-139-3*) Resource Pubns.

— Parish Funerals: A Guide to the Order of Christian Funerals. 74p. 1987. pap. 3.25 (*0-930467-65-5*) Liturgy Tr Pubns.

Marchall, C. Alan. What Ever Happened to the Black Panthers. 250p. (Orig.). 1993. pap. 17.95 (*0-9633029-2-2*) Marshall MD.

Marchalonis, John J. Antigen Specific T Cell Receptors & Factors, 2 vols., Set. 336p. 1987. 305.00 (*0-8493-6169-9*, QR185) CRC Pr.

— The Lymphocyte: Structure & Function. 2nd ed. (Immunology Ser.: Vol. 37). 440p. 1988. 165.00 (*0-8247-7797-2*) Dekker.

Marchalonis, John J., ed. Contemporary Topics in Immunobiology, Vol. 12: Immunobiology of Parasites & Parasitic Infections. LC 79-179761. 518p. 1984. 95.00 (*0-306-41418-X*, Plenum Pr) Plenum.

Marchalonis, John J., et al, eds. Cancer Biology Reviews, Vol. 1. LC 80-644712. (Illus.). 368p. 1980. reprint ed. pap. 99.40 (*0-7837-0741-X*, 2041063) Bks Demand.

— Cancer Biology Reviews, Vol. 2. LC 80-644712. (Illus.). 294p. 1981. reprint ed. pap. 83.80 (*0-7837-0742-8*) Bks Demand.

— Cancer Biology Reviews, Vol. 3. LC 80-644712. (Illus.). 223p. 1982. reprint ed. pap. 63.60 (*0-7837-0743-6*) Bks Demand.

Marchalonis, Shirley. Critical Essays on Mary Wilkins Freeman. (Critical Essays on American Literature Ser.). 200p. 1991. text ed. 45.00 (*0-8161-7306-0*, Hall Reference) Macmillan.

— Girls in the Groves of Academe: College Fiction, 1865-1940. LC 94-41573. (Illus.). 225p. 1995. text ed. 45.00 (*0-8135-2175-0*); pap. text ed. 16.00 (*0-8135-2176-9*) Rutgers U Pr.

— The Worlds of Lucy Larcom, 1824-1893. LC 88-28660. (Illus.). 336p. 1989. 40.00 (*0-8203-1113-8*) U of Ga Pr.

Marchalonis, Shirley, ed. Patrons & Protegees: Gender, Friendship, & Writing in Nineteenth-Century America. LC 87-42735. 250p. 1988. 40.00 (*0-8135-1270-0*) Rutgers U Pr.

— Patrons & Protegees: Gender, Friendship, & Writing in Nineteenth-Century America. 243p. (C). 1991. pap. text ed. 16.00 (*0-8135-1690-0*) Rutgers U Pr.

Marcham, F. G., jt. auth. see Stephenson, Carl.

Marcham, Frederick G., jt. ed. see Stephenson, Carl.

Marcham, William, jt. ed. see Lovell, Percy.

Marchand, C. Roland. The American Peace Movement & Social Reform, 1898-1918. LC 70-166382. 360p. 1972. 67.50x (*0-691-04609-3*) Princeton U Pr.

— The American Peace Movement & Social Reform, 1898-1918. LC 70-166382. Date not set. reprint ed. pap. 131.40 (*0-7837-9379-0*, 2060123) Bks Demand.

Marchand, Clement. Vanishing Villages. (Prose Ser.: No. 19). 234p. 1993. pap. 13.00 (*0-920717-73-X*) Guernica Editions.

Marchand, Donald A. The Politics of Privacy, Computers, & Criminal Justice Records: Controlling the Social Costs of Technological Change. LC 80-80675. xvi, 433p. 1980. text ed. 34.95 (*0-87815-030-7*) Info Resources.

Marchand, Donald A., jt. ed. see Horton, Forest W., Jr.

***Marchand-Ennery, Rabbin.** Dictionnaire de la Bible Hebraique. 3rd ed. 304p. (FRE & HEB.). 1986. pap. 19.95 (*0-7859-8086-5*, 2853320456) Fr & Eur.

— French-Hebrew Dictionary: Dictionnaire Francais-Hebreu. 302p. (FRE & HEB.). 1981. 13.95 (*0-8288-0460-5*, F19230) Fr & Eur.

Marchand, Erich W. Gradient Index Optics. 1978. text ed. 71.00 (*0-12-470750-5*) Acad Pr.

Marchand, J. P., ed. see NATO Advanced Study Institute Staff.

Marchand, James W. The Sounds & Phonemes of Wulfila's Gothic. (Janua Linguarum, Series Practica: No. 25). 1973. pap. text ed. 49.25 (*90-279-2432-5*) Mouton.

***Marchand, Leslie A.** What Comes Uppermost: Byron's Letters & Journals, Supplementary Volume. 128p. 1994. 29.50 (*0-87413-576-1*) U Delaware Pr.

Marchand, Leslie A., ed. Lord Byron: Selected Letters & Journals. LC 82-9720. 408p. 1984. pap. 10.95 (*0-674-53912-5*) Belknap Pr.

Marchand, Leslie A., ed. see Byron, George G.

***Marchand, Marianne H. & Parpart, Jane L., eds.** Feminism - Postmodernism - Development. LC 94-23866. (International Studies of Women & Place). 272p. (Orig.). 1995. 59.95 (*0-415-10523-4*, B4140) Routledge.

— Feminism - Postmodernism - Development. LC 94-23866. (International Studies of Women & Place). 272p. (Orig.). 1995. pap. 17.95 (*0-415-10524-2*, B4144) Routledge.

Marchand, Maurice G., et al. The Performance of Public Enterprises: Concepts & Measurement. LC 84-10124. (Studies in Mathematical & Managerial Economics: Vol. 33). 296p. 1984. 77.00 (*0-444-87551-4*) Elsevier.

Marchand, Peter. North Woods: An Inside Look at the Nature of Forests in the Northeast. (Illus.). 160p. 1987. pap. 9.95 (*0-910146-64-0*) AMC Books.

— What Good Is a Cactus? LC 94-65088. (Illus.). 32p. (Orig.). (J). (gr. 3-6). 1994. pap. 9.95 (*1-879373-83-1*) R Rinehart.

Marchand, Peter J. Life in the Cold: An Introduction to Winter Ecology. 2nd ed. LC 91-5037. (Illus.). 256p. 1991. pap. 16.95 (*0-87451-556-4*) U Pr of New Eng.

***Marchand, Phillip.** Deadly Spirits. 224p. 1995. 15.95 (*0-7737-5641-8*, Pub. by Stoddart Publng CN) Pubs Dist MI.

Marchand, Roger. Meeting Jesus in Holy Communion. 32p. (J). (gr. 1-3). 1984. pap. 2.95 (*0-89243-202-0*) Liguori Pubns.

Marchand, Roland. Advertising the American Dream: Making Way for Modernity, 1920-1940. LC 84-28082. 1985. 50.00 (*0-520-05253-6*); pap. 19.00 (*0-520-05885-2*) U CA Pr.

Marchand, Sidney A. Attempt to Re-Assemble the Old Settlers in Family Groups. 1965. 12.50 (*0-87511-079-7*) Claitors.

Marchant. Design for Fire Safety. 120p. 1999. text ed. write for info. (*0-7506-1081-6*) Buttrwrth-Heinemann.

Marchant, jt. auth. see Cook.

Marchant, Alan B. Optical Recording: A Technical Overview. (Illus.). 364p. (C). 1990. text ed. 58.25 (*0-201-76247-1*) Addison-Wesley.

Marchant, Brian & Marchant, Heather. A Boy Named Chong. 40p. (J). (gr. k-9). 1993. pap. 11.95 (*1-885298-00-5*); vhs 14.95 (*1-885298-01-3*) Project Chong.

Marchant, David. Understanding Shmittah. 1987. 12.95 (*0-317-57129-X*) Feldheim.

Marchant, E. C. Thucydides, Bk. 1. 334p. 1982. reprint ed. 23.75 (*0-86292-027-2*, Pub. by Brstl Class Pr UK) Focus Info Gr.

An Asterisk (*) at the beginning of an entry indicates that the title is appearing in BIP for the first time.

Marchant, E. C. & Wiedemann, T., eds. Thucydides, Bk. II. 239p. reprint ed. 16.00 (*0-86516-041-4*) Bolchazy-Carducci.

Marchant, E. C., ed. see Xenophon.

Marchant, Fred. Tipping Point. LC 93-61079. 80p. (Orig.). 1994. per. 10.00 (*0-915380-30-7*) Word Works.

Marchant, Heather, jt. auth. see Marchant, Brian.

Marchant, James. Alfred Russel Wallace: Letters & Reminiscences. LC 74-26273. (History, Philosophy & Sociology of Science Ser.). 1975. reprint ed. 38.95 (*0-405-06601-5*) Ayer.

Marchant, James & Jowett, Garth S., eds. The Cinema in Education. LC 77-11381. (Aspects of Film Ser.). (Illus.). 1978. reprint ed. lib. bdg. 13.95 (*0-405-11140-1*) Ayer.

Marchant, James, ed. see Inge, William R.

Marchant, John & Prater, Tony. Shorebirds: An Identification Guide. (Illus.). 416p. 1991. pap. 29.95 (*0-395-60237-8*) HM.

Marchant, Kerena. Sounds Like Skipper. large type ed. 1989. 17.95 (*0-7089-2059-4*) Ulverscroft.

Marchant, Mary & Williamson, Handy, Jr., eds. Achieving Diversity: The Status & Progress of Women & African Americans in the Agricultural Economics Profession. LC 93-39458. (Studies on Industrial Productivity). 248p. 1994. 40.00 (*0-8153-1537-6*) Garland.

Marchant, Mary A. Political Economic Analysis of U. S. Dairy Policies & European Community Dairy Policy Comparisons. LC 92-40968. (Government & the Economy Ser.). 280p. 1993. 62.00 (*0-8153-1231-8*) Garland.

Marchant, Maurice P. Participative Management in Academic Libraries. LC 76-8740. (Contributions in Librarianship & Information Science Ser.: No. 16). 320p. 1977. text ed. 45.00 (*0-8371-8935-7*, MPM/, Greenwood Pr) Greenwood.

— Why Adults Use the Public Library: A Research Perspective. LC 93-31053. 125p. 1994. pap. text ed. 24.00 (*1-56308-193-8*) Libs Unl.

Marchant, Robert. Principles of Wordsworth's Poetry. (C). 1986. 110.00 (*0-9502723-3-7*, Pub. by Brynmill Pr Ltd UK) St Mut.

Marchant-Smith, D. J. & Haslem, P. R. Small Arms & Cannons. (Brassey's Battlefield Weapons Systems & Technology Ser.: Vol. 5). 160p. 1982. text ed. 30.00 (*0-08-028330-6*, Pergamon Pr); pap. text ed. 18.95 (*0-08-028331-4*, Pergamon Pr) Elsevier.

Marchant, Stephen & Higgins, P. J., eds. The Handbook of Australian, New Zealand & Antarctic Birds, Vol. 2: Raptors to Lapwings. (Illus.). 1048p. 1994. 295.00 (*0-19-553069-1*) OUP.

Marchant, Stephen & Higgins, Peter, eds. The Handbook of Australian, New Zealand & Antarctic Birds, 2 vols., Set. 1994. 590.00 (*0-19-521066-2*) OUP.

Marchant, Stephen & Higgins, Peter M., eds. The Handbook of Australian, New Zealand & Antarctic Birds, Vol. 1, Pts. A & B: Ratites to Ducks. (Illus.). 1406p. 1991. 295.00 (*0-19-553068-3*) OUP.

Marchant, Tim, jt. auth. see Grootaert, Christiaan.

Marchant, Tim J., jt. auth. see Murphy, Josette.

Marchant, Timothy, jt. auth. see Grootaert, Christiaan.

Marchant, Tony. Thick As Thieves. Incl. Dealt With. 1988. (*0-318-57268-0*); London Calling. 1988. (*0-318-57269-9*); 1988. Set pap. 7.95 (*0-413-51070-0*, A0292) Heinemann.

— Welcome Home, Raspberry & The Lucky Ones. (Methuen Theatrescripts Ser.). 1988. pap. 7.95 (*0-413-53820-6*, A0313) Heinemann.

Marchant, W. In Praise of Ale. 1972. 59.95 (*0-8490-0391-1*) Gordon Pr.

Marchant, William. To Be Continued. 1952. pap. 2.75 (*0-8222-1156-4*) Dramatists Play.

Marchant, William, tr. see Bourget, Paul C.

Marchbank, Brenda. Durham Quilting. (Illus.). 1988. 27.50 (*0-85219-737-3*) Branford.

Marchbank, Pearce, ed. Elvis: In His Own Words. (Illus.). 128p. 1977. pap. 15.95 (*0-86001-487-8*, OP40310) Omnibus NY.

— With the Beatles: The Historic Photographs of Dezo Hoffman. (Illus.). 128p. Date not set. pap. 19.95 (*0-685-69181-0*) Omnibus NY.

— With the Beatles: The Historic Photographs of Dezo Hoffmann. (Illus.). 128p. (Orig.). 1982. pap. 17.95 (*0-7119-0111-2*, OP41961) Omnibus NY.

Marche, Pierre, jt. auth. see Meyer, Philippe.

Marchegiani, Irene, tr. see Spaziani, Maria L.

Marchel, Ernst. Florida. (Windsor Destination Guides Ser.). (Illus.). 56p. 1992. pap. 12.95 (*1-874111-02-2*, Pub. by Windsor Bks UK) Seven Hills Bk.

Marchello, Joseph M. Control of Air Pollution Sources. LC 74-79923. (Chemical Processing & Engineering Ser.: No. 7). (Illus.). 640p. reprint ed. pap. 180.00 (*0-685-23500-9*, 2029003) Bks Demand.

Marchello, Joseph M. & Gomezplata, Albert, eds. Gas-Solids Handling in the Process Industries. LC 76-151314. (Chemical Processing & Engineering Ser.: No. 8). (Illus.). 336p. reprint ed. pap. 95.80 (*0-7837-0677-4*, 2041011) Bks Demand.

Marchello, Joseph M. & Kelly, John J., eds. Gas Cleaning for Air Quality Control: Industrial & Environmental Health & Safety Requirements. LC 73-78559. (Chemical Processing & Engineering Ser.: No. 2). (Illus.). 432p. reprint ed. pap. 123.20 (*0-7837-4306-8*, 2043997) Bks Demand.

Marchello, Martin, jt. auth. see Gaida, Urban.

Marchenko, E. Masters of World Painting in the Museums of the Soviet Union. (Illus.). 160p. 1975. 55.00 (*0-8464-0617-9*) Beekman Pubs.

Marchenko, G. N., jt. auth. see Petrov.

Marchenko, G. N., jt. auth. see Tarchevsky, I. A.

Marchenko, Gennady P. Detection of Enzymes on Electrophoretic Gels: A Handbook. 352p. 1994. 95.00 (*0-8493-8935-6*, 8935) CRC Pr.

Marchenko, V. A., jt. auth. see Agranovich, Z. S.

Marchenko, Vladimir A. Nonlinear Equations & Operator Algebras. (C). 1987. lib. bdg. 95.00 (*90-277-2654-X*) Kluwer Ac.

— Sturm-Liouville Operators & Applications. (Operator Theory Ser.: Vol. 22). 392p. 1986. 127.00 (*0-8176-1794-9*) Birkhauser.

Marchesani, Robert A., jt. ed. see Anson, Jack L.

Marchesani, Robert F., Jr., jt. ed. see Anson, Jack L.

Marcheschi, Graziano. Wheat & Weeds & the Wolf of Gubbio: Stories & Prayers for People Who Pray & for People Who Don't. (Illus.). 136p. (Orig.). 1993. pap. 9.95 (*1-55612-661-1*) Sheed & Ward MO.

Marcheschi, Graziano & Marcheschi, Nancy S. Scripture at Weddings: Choosing & Proclaiming the Word of God. 128p. (Orig.). 1992. pap. 4.00 (*0-929650-62-X*, READ/W) Liturgy Tr Pubns.

Marcheschi, Nancy S., jt. auth. see Marcheschi, Graziano.

Marchese, Angelo. Diccionario de Retorica, Critica y Terminologia Literaria. 3rd ed. 448p. (SPA.). 1991. pap. 45.00 (*0-7859-5927-0*, 8434483866) Fr & Eur.

Marchese, Francis T., ed. Understanding Images: Finding Meaning in Digital Imagery. LC 93-42645. (TELOS - The Electronic Library of Science). 1995. 49.95 (*0-387-94148-7*) Spr-Verlag.

Marchese, Lynell. Tense-Aspect & the Development of Auxiliaries in Kru Languages. LC 86-60586. (Publications in Lingustics: No. 78). (Illus.). 200p. (Orig.). (C). 1986. fiche 24.00 (*0-88312-407-6*) Summer Instit Ling.

Marchese, Raymond. Our Turn, Whitey. Costa, Gwen, ed. LC 91-22351. (Orig.). 1992. pap. 13.95 (*0-87949-316-X*) Ashley Bks.

Marchese, Ronald. Family Holdings: Turkish Nomadic Flatweaves. 32p. (Orig.). 1991. pap. 15.00 (*0-914489-09-7*) Univ Miss-KS Art.

Marchese, Theodore J. The Search Committee Handbook. 56p. 1988. 12.00 (*0-685-45302-2*) Coll & U Personnel.

Marchesi, Blanche. Singer's Pilgrimage. Farkas, Andrew, ed. LC 76-29951. (Opera Biographies Ser.). (Illus.). 1977. reprint ed. lib. bdg. 29.95 (*0-405-09692-5*) Ayer.

— Singer's Pilgrimage. LC 77-1941. (Music Reprint Ser.: 1978). (Illus.). 1978. reprint ed. lib. bdg. 37.50 (*0-306-70878-7*) Da Capo.

Marchesi, Carlo, ed. Ambulatory Monitoring: Cardiovascular System & Applied Applications. (Developments in Cardiovascular Medicine Ser.). 1984. lib. bdg. 145.00 (*0-89838-642-X*) Kluwer Ac.

Marchesi, Mathilde. Bel Canto: Theoretical & Practical Vocal Method. 1970. reprint ed. pap. text ed. 8.95 (*0-486-22315-9*) Dover.

— Marchesi & Music: Passages from the Life of a Famous Singing-Teacher. LC 77-27354. (Music Reprint Ser.: 1978). 1978. reprint ed. lib. bdg. 39.50 (*0-306-77577-8*) Da Capo.

Marchesi, Michele. Object Oriented Programming & Smalltalk V. 352p. 1994. pap. text ed. 35.80 (*0-13-630294-7*) P-H.

Marchesi, Stephen, illus. Don Quixote & Sancho Panza. LC 90-24098. 80p. (YA). (gr. 6 up). 1992. text ed. 16.95 (*0-684-19235-7*, C Scribner Sons Young) S&S Childrens.

Marchessault, R. H. & Skaar, Christen, eds. Surfaces & Coatings Related to Paper & Wood. LC 66-27617. (C). 1967. 39.95x (*0-8156-5017-5*) Syracuse U Pr.

Marchesseau, Daniel. Marie Laurencin: Catalogue Raisonne of the Graphic Work. (Illus.). 184p. (FRE.). 1981. pap. 135.00 (*1-55660-064-X*) A Wofsy Fine Arts.

— Marie Laurencin: Catalogue Raisonne of the Paintings. (Illus.). 554p. (FRE.). 1986. 575.00 (*1-55660-065-8*) A Wofsy Fine Arts.

Marcheteau, M., et al. French-English - English-French Economic, Commercial & Financial Pocket Dictionary. 2nd ed. 620p. (ENG & FRE.). 1990. pap. 27.00 (*2-266-02239-3*, Presses Pocket) IBD Ltd.

Marcheteau, Michel. Dictionary of Commercial & Economic English: Dictionnaire de L'Anglais Economique et Commercial. 2nd ed. 620p. (ENG & FRE.). 1990. pap. 24.95 (*0-8288-0075-8*, M513) Fr & Eur.

Marchetta, C., jt. ed. see Martuscelli, E.

Marchetta, Camille. Lovers & Friends. 480p. 1991. mass mkt. 4.95 (*0-380-70812-4*) Avon.

— Lovers & Friends. Grose, William, ed. 480p. 1995. mass mkt. 5.99 (*0-671-86926-4*) PB.

Marchette, Nyven J. Ecological Relationships & Evolution of the Rickettsiae, Vol. I. 176p. 1982. 110.00 (*0-8493-6125-7*, QR353, CRC Reprint) Franklin.

Marchette, Nyven J., ed. Ecological Relationships & Evolution of the Rickettsiae, Vol. II. 192p. 1982. 110.00 (*0-8493-6126-5*, QR353, CRC Reprint) Franklin.

Marchetti, Albert. Beating the Odds; Alternative Treatments That Have Worked Miracles Against Cancer. 1990. mass mkt. 4.95 (*0-312-92236-1*) St Martin.

— Common Cures for Common Ailments: A Doctor's Guide to Nonprescription, Over-the-Counter Medicines & His Recommendations for Their Use. LC 77-16114. 368p. 1981. pap. 8.95 (*0-8128-6107-8*, Scrbrough Hse) Madison Bks UPA.

Marchetti, Gina. Romance & the "Yellow Peril" Race, Sex, & Discursive Strategies in Hollywood Fiction. LC 92-10878. 1993. 40.00 (*0-520-07974-4*); pap. 14.00 (*0-520-08495-0*) U CA Pr.

Marchetti, N., jt. auth. see Rodriguez, F.

Marchetti-Spaccamela, A., et al. Theoretical Computer Science: Proceedings of the 4th Italian Conference. 372p. 1992. text ed. 121.00 (*981-02-1258-5*) World Scientific Pub.

Marchetti, Tony. Automotive Engine Overhaul. Gorham, Kelly, ed. (Automotive Ser.). 23p. (Orig.). Date not set. student ed. 7.00 (*0-8064-0009-9*, A35); audio 299.00 (*0-8064-0008-0*, A35) Bergwall.

Marchetto, Ezio. The Catholic Church & the Phenomenon of Migration: On Overview. 26p. 1989. 5.00 (*0-934733-45-7*) Ctr Migration.

Marchetto, Ezio, comp. A Directory of Italian American Associations in the Tri-State Area: Connecticut, Eastern New Jersey & New York. 200p. 1989. 14.95 (*0-934733-44-9*) Ctr Migration.

Marchevsky, Alberto & Bartels, Peter. Image Analysis: A Primer for Pathologists. 368p. 1995. 105.00 (*0-7817-0170-8*) Raven.

Marchevsky, Alberto M. Surgical Pathology. (Lung Biology in Health & Disease Ser.: Vol. 44). 704p. 1990. 190.00 (*0-8247-8106-6*) Dekker.

Marchevsky, Alberto M. & Kaneko, Mamoru. Surgical Pathology of the Mediastinum. 2nd ed. 352p. 1992. 104.00 (*0-88167-818-X*) Raven.

Marchi, Dudley M. Montaigne among the Moderns: Receptions of the Essais. LC 94-29461. 350p. (C). 1994. text ed. 49.95 (*1-57181-007-2*) Berghahn Bks.

Marchi, Ena, jt. auth. see Galdo, Giovanna.

Marchi, Francesco. I Cinquecentisti: The Cinquecontisti Five-Accounts Theorists. Brief, Richard P., ed. LC 80-1510. (Dimensions of Accounting Theory & Practice Ser.). (ITA.). 1980. reprint ed. lib. bdg. 23.95 (*0-405-13535-1*) Ayer.

Marchi, Jane G., ed. The Foreign Policies of Caribbean & Central American Countries. 282p. (C). 1991. 21.95 (*0-935501-22-3*, LA218) U Miami N-S Ctr.

Marchiafava, Louis J. The Houston Police, Eighteen Seventy-Eight to Nineteen Forty-Eight. LC 77-81468. (Rice University Studies: Vol. 63, No. 2). (Illus.). 119p. (Orig.). (C). 1977. pap. 10.00 (*0-89263-232-1*) Rice Univ.

Marchiano, Michele. Ferrari by Zagato. (Illus.). 156p. 39.95 (*88-7911-003-9*, Pub. by Giorgio Nada Editore IT) Howell Pr VA.

— Zagato: Fiat 8VZ, Alfa Romeo 1900 SSZ. (Illus.). 110p. 19.95 (*88-7672-008-1*, Pub. by Giorgio Nada Editore IT) Howell Pr VA.

— Zagato: Seventy Years in the Fast Lane. (Illus.). 184p. 55.00 (*88-7911-021-7*, Pub. by Giorgio Nada Editore IT) Howell Pr VA.

Marchildon, Gregory P. Mergers & Acquisitions. (International Library of Critical Writings in Business History: No. 3). 500p. 1991. text ed. 169.95 (*1-85278-430-X*, Pub. by E Elgar Pub UK) Ashgate Pub Co.

Marchildon, Gregory P. & McDowall, Duncan, eds. Canadian Multinationals & International Finance. LC 92-12975. 185p. 1992. text ed. 37.50 (*0-7146-3481-6*, Pub. by F Cass Pubs UK) Intl Spec Bk.

Marchington, Mick. Managing the Team: A Guide to Total Employee Involvement. LC 92-15428. (Human Resource Management in Action Ser.). 1992. pap. 39.95 (*0-631-18677-8*) Blackwell Pubs.

Marchini, Ron & Fong, Leo. Power Training in Kung-Fu & Karate. Cocoran, John & Scurra, John, eds. LC 74-14128. (Specialties Ser.). (Illus.). 1974. pap. text ed. 17.95 (*0-89750-047-4*, 400) Ohara Pubns.

Marchini, Ronald L. The Ultimate Martial Art: Renbukai, Vol. II. 144p. 1982. pap. 7.95 (*0-940522-01-2*) ROMARC Inc.

— The Ultimate Martial Art: Renbukai, Vol. III. 152p. 1982. pap. 7.95 (*0-940522-02-0*) ROMARC Inc.

— The Ultimate Martial Art: Renbukai, Vol. 1. 128p. (Orig.). (C). 1981. pap. 6.95 (*0-940522-00-4*) ROMARC Inc.

Marchinko, Richard. Rogue Warrior 2 Red Cell. 1994. 22.00 (*0-671-79956-8*) PB.

Marchinton, R. Larry, jt. ed. see Miller, Karl V.

Marchione, Joanne. Margaret Newman: Health As Expanding Consciousness. (Notes on Nursing Theories Ser.: Vol. 6). (Illus.). 60p. 1992. 18.95 (*0-8039-4796-8*); pap. 8.95 (*0-8039-4797-6*) Sage.

***Marchione, Margherita.** The Adventurous Life of Philip Mazzei. LC 95-6188. (ENG & ITA.). 1995. pap. write for info. (*0-8191-9927-3*) U Pr of Amer.

— Americans of Italian Heritage. (Illus.). 246p. (Orig.). (C). 1995. lib. bdg. 47.00 (*0-8191-9825-0*); pap. text ed. 28.50 (*0-8191-9826-9*) U Pr of Amer.

— Peter & Sally Sammartino: Biographical Notes. (Illus.). 320p. 1994. 24.95 (*0-8453-4855-8*, Cornwall Bks) Assoc Univ Prs.

— Philip Mazzei: World Citizen (Jefferson's "Zealous Whig") 158p. (C). 1994. lib. bdg. 36.50 (*0-8191-9698-3*) U Pr of Amer.

Marchione, Margherita, ed. Lettere di Clemente Rebora 1897-1930, Vol. 1. 680p. 1976. 20.00 (*0-916322-17-3*) Am Inst Ital Stud.

— Lettere di Clemente Rebora 1930-1957, Vol. 2. 410p. 1982. 20.00 (*0-916322-13-0*) Am Inst Ital Stud.

— Philip Mazzei: My Life & Wanderings. unabridged ed. Scalia, S. Eugene, tr. LC 80-69637. (Illus.). 472p. (Orig.). (C). 1980. 40.00 (*0-916322-03-3*); pap. 20.00 (*0-916322-04-1*) Am Inst Ital Stud.

— Philip Mazzei: Selected Writings & Correspondence, 1730-1816, 3 vols., Set. (ENG & ITA.). 1983. 150.00 (*0-685-06725-4*) Am Inst Ital Stud.

— Philip Mazzei: The Comprehensive Microform Edition of His Papers, 1730-1816. LC 81-12382. 171p. 1982. 450.00 (*0-527-62471-3*) Kraus Intl.

Marchione, Margherita, ed. & tr. Philip Mazzei: Jefferson's "Zealous Whig" LC 75-29945. 350p. 1975. 9.95 (*0-916322-01-7*); pap. 17.50 (*0-916322-02-5*) Am Inst Ital Stud.

Marchione, Margherita, et al, eds. Phillip Mazzei: Selected Writings & Correspondence, 3 vols., Set. (Illus.). 200.00 (*0-685-43295-5*) Mazzei.

Marchione, Margherita, tr. Twentieth Century Italian Poetry: A Bilingual Anthology. LC 72-6634. 302p. 1974. 10.00 (*0-8386-1245-8*) Am Inst Ital Stud.

Marchione, Margherita & Mussini, Gianni, eds. Carteggio Angelini-Prezzolini. 330p. 1983. 20.00 (*0-916322-15-7*) Am Inst Ital Stud.

Marchione, Margherita & Prezzolini, Giuseppe. L' Imagine Tesa: The Life & Works of Clemente Rebora. enl. ed. 410p. 1974. reprint ed. 10.00 (*0-916322-16-5*) Am Inst Ital Stud.

Marchioness of Londonberry & Hyde, H. M., eds. Russian Journals of Martha & Catherine Wilmot. LC 71-115597. (Russia Observed Ser.). (Illus.). 1971. reprint ed. 29.95 (*0-405-03139-4*) Ayer.

Marchioness of Tavistock & Levin, Angela. A Chance to Live. (Illus.). 288p. 1993. pap. 11.95 (*0-7472-3790-5*, Pub. by Headline UK) Trafalgar.

***Marchionini, Gary, abr.** Information Seeking in Electronic Environments. (Series in Human-Computer Interaction: No. 9). (Illus.). 200p. (C). 1995. 49.95 (*0-521-44372-5*) Cambridge U Pr.

Marchiony, William. The New House Buyer Guide. LC 86-70558. (Illus.). 120p. (Orig.). 1986. student ed, pap. text ed. 18.95 (*0-938411-00-4*) Carefree Living.

Marchiori, Roberto, jt. illus. see Mariotti, Mario.

Marchioro, Carlo & Pulvirenti, Mario. Mathematical Theory of Incompressible Non-Viscous Fluids. LC 93-4683. (Applied Mathematical Sciences Ser.: Vol. 96). 1993. 49.00 (*0-387-94044-8*) Spr-Verlag.

Marchioro, Carlo, et al. Vortex Methods in Two-Dimensional Fluid Dynamics. (Lecture Notes in Physics Ser.: Vol. 203). iii, 137p. 1984. pap. 17.00 (*0-387-13352-6*) Spr-Verlag.

Marchisio, Linda. With a Little of Both. (Illus.). 19p. (J). (gr. k-5). 1987. teacher ed 15.95 (*0-9624224-1-X*); audio 8.95 (*0-9624224-0-1*) Rainbow Bend.

Marchisio, Sergio & DiBlase, Antonietta. The Food & Agriculture Organization (FAO) (International Organization & the Evolution of World Society Ser.). 268p. 1990. lib. bdg. 120.00 (*0-7923-1012-8*) Kluwer Ac.

Marchlewski, J. B. Antysemityzm a Robotnicy. 94p. reprint ed. 20.00 (*0-318-23360-6*) Szwede Slavic.

***Marchlowitz, Birgit.** Freikirchlicher Gemeindeaufbau: Geschichtliche und Empirische Untersuchung Baptistischen Gemeindeverstaendnisses. (Arbeiten zur Praktischen Theologie Ser.: Bd. 7). 362p. (GER.). (C). 1994. lib. bdg. 167.70 (*3-11-014371-2*) De Gruyter.

Marchmont, Arthur W. By Right of Sword. 1976. lib. bdg. 15.30 (*0-89968-064-X*, Lghtyr Pr) Buccaneer Bks.

— In the Name of a Woman. 1976. lib. bdg. 16.30 (*0-89968-065-8*, Lghtyr Pr) Buccaneer Bks.

— Marlwych Mystery; or, Parson Thring's Secret. 1976. lib. bdg. 15.80 (*0-89968-066-6*, Lghtyr Pr) Buccaneer Bks.

— Miser Hoadley's Secret: A Detective Story. 1976. lib. bdg. 14.85 (*0-89968-067-4*, Lghtyr Pr) Buccaneer Bks.

— The Mystery of Mortimore Strange. 1976. lib. bdg. 16.70 (*0-89968-068-2*, Lghtyr Pr) Buccaneer Bks.

Marchok, Janice M. Oh No! Not My Electric Blanket, Too? A Guide to a Healthier Home. DeSimone, Patricia & Conway, Katherine, eds. LC 91-72193. (Illus.). 183p. (Orig.). 1991. pap. 14.95 (*0-9629215-0-5*) Jetmarc Grp.

Marchon-Arnaud, Catherine. A Gallery of Games. LC 93-25053. (Young Artisan Ser.). (Illus.). 60p. (J). (gr. 3 up). 1994. 12.95 (*0-395-68379-3*) Ticknor & Flds Bks Yng Read.

Marchuk. Computational Processes & Systems. 1994. 59.95 (*0-8493-8947-X*, QA297) CRC Pr.

Marchuk, jt. auth. see Programming Staff.

Marchuk, G. I., ed. see IFIP Technical Conference Staff.

***Marchuk, Guri I.** Adjoint Equations & Analysis of Complex Systems. LC 94-22318. (Mathematics & Its Applications Ser.: 295). 480p. (C). 1995. lib. bdg. 218.00 (*0-7923-3013-7*) Kluwer Ac.

Marchuk, Gurii I. Mathematical Models in Environmental Problems. (Studies in Mathematics & Its Applications: Vol. 16). 218p. 1986. 72.00 (*0-444-87965-X*, North Holland) Elsevier.

— Mathematical Models in Immunology. Balakrishnan, A. V., ed. LC 83-8269. (Translations Series in Mathematics & Engineering). (Illus.). 378p. 1983. pap. text ed. 72.00 (*0-911575-01-4*) Optimization Soft.

— Methods of Numerical Mathematics. 2nd ed. (Applications of Mathematics Ser.: Vol. 2). (Illus.). 510p. 1982. 55.00 (*0-387-90614-2*) Spr-Verlag.

— Numerical Methods for Nuclear Reactor Calculations. LC 59-9229. (Soviet Journal of Atomic Energy: Supplement Ser.: Nos. 3-4, 1958). 300p. reprint ed. pap. 85.50 (*0-317-08317-1*, 2020653) Bks Demand.

Marchuk, Gurii I. & Belykh, L. N., eds. Mathematical Modeling in Immunology & Medicine. 396p. 1983. 61.75 (*0-444-86588-8*, I-36-83, North Holland) Elsevier.

Marchuk, Gurii I. & Kagan, B. A. Dynamics of Ocean Tides. (C). 1989. lib. bdg. 165.50 (*90-277-2552-7*) Kluwer Ac.

Marchuk, Gurii I. & Lebedev, V. I. Numerical Methods in the Theory of Neutron Transport. 620p. 1986. text ed. 260.00 (*3-7186-0182-6*); pap. text ed. 46.00 (*3-7186-0210-5*) Gordon & Breach.

Marchuk, Gurii I. & Shaidurov, V. V. Difference Methods & their Extrapolations. (Applications of Mathematics Ser.: Vol. 19). (Illus.). 334p. 1983. 39.00 (*0-387-90794-7*) Spr-Verlag.

Marchuk, Gurii I., et al. Monte Carlo Methods in Atmospheric Optics. (Optical Sciences Ser.: Vol. 12). (Illus.). 1980. 40.00 (*0-387-09402-4*) Spr-Verlag.

M

An Asterisk (*) at the beginning of an entry indicates that the title is appearing in BIP for the first time.

Marchuk, Guril I. Differential Equations & Numerical Mathematics: Proceedings of a U. S. S. R. Council of Ministers for Science & Technology, Moscow. LC 81-81912. (Illus.). 176p. 1982. 68.00 (*0-08-026491-3*, D120, Pub. by Pergamon Repr UK) Franklin.

Marchuk, Guril I. & Kagan, B. A. Ocean Tides: Mathematical Models & Numerical Experiments. Cartwright, D. E., tr. LC 82-18898. (Illus.). 240p. 1984. 122.00 (*0-08-026236-8*, Pub. by Pergamon Repr UK) Franklin.

Marchuk, Guril I. & Nisevich, N. I., eds. Mathematical Methods in Clinical Practice. (Illus.). 150p. 1980. 46.00 (*0-08-025493-4*, Pub. by Pergamon Repr UK) Franklin.

Marchuk, William N. A Life Science Lexicon. 224p. (C). 1991. pap. write for info. (*0-697-12133-X*) Wm C Brown Pubs.

Marci, Randolph B. The Prairie Traveler: The Classic Handbook for American Pioneers. (Illus.). 240p. 1994. pap. 10.00 (*0-399-51865-7*, Perigree Bks) Berkley Pub.

Marcia, James E., et al. Ego Identity: A Handbook for Psychosocial Research. LC 93-2919. 1993. 98.00 (*0-387-94033-2*) Spr-Verlag.

— Ego Identity: A Handbook for Psychosocial Research. (Illus.). 400p. 1993. write for info. (*3-540-94033-2*) Spr-Verlag.

***Marcial, Gene.** Secrets of the Street: The Dark Side of Making Money. 1995. text ed. 20.00 (*0-07-040255-8*) McGraw.

Marciano, Teresa & Sussman, Marvin B., eds. Families & the Prospect of Nuclear Attack Holocaust. LC 86-18320. (Marriage & Family Review Ser.: Vol. 10, No. 2). 139p. 1986. text ed. 32.95 (*0-86656-374-1*) Haworth Pr.

Marciano, Theresa D. & Sussman, Marvin B., eds. Wider Families: New Traditional Family Forms. LC 91-19686. (Marriage & Family Review Ser.). (Illus.). 182p. 1993. lib. bdg. 39.95 (*1-56024-167-5*); pap. 14.95 (*1-56024-271-X*) Haworth Pr.

***Marcic, Dorothy.** Organizational Behavior: Experiences & Cases. 4th ed. 400p. 1995. pap. text ed. 31.50 (*0-314-04596-1*) West Pub.

Marcic, Dorothy & Puffer, Sheila. International Management: Cases & Exercises. Szilagyi, ed. 200p. (C). Date not set. pap. text ed. 29.00 (*0-314-02828-5*) West Pub.

Marciel, Scot, jt. ed. see Czinkota, Michael R.

Marcil-Lacoste, Louise. Claude Buffier & Thomas Reid: Two Common-Sense Philosophers. (McGill-Queen's Studies in the History of Religion). 224p. 1982. 44.95 (*0-7735-1003-6*, Pub. by McGill CN) U of Toronto Pr.

Marcil, William M. & Tigges, Kent N., eds. The Person with AIDS: A Personal & Professional Perspective. LC 88-43550. (Illus.). 292p. 1991. pap. 28.00 (*1-55642-098-6*) SLACK Inc.

Marcil, William M., jt. auth. see Tigges, Kent N.

Marcilhac, Felix. Jean Dunand: His Life & Works. (Illus.). 352p. 1991. 95.00 (*0-8109-3202-4*) Abrams.

— Orloff (Chana) Catalogue Raisonne of the Sculptures. (Illus.). 256p. (FRE.). 1991. 150.00 (*1-55660-191-3*) A Wofsy Fine Arts.

— Rene Lalique: The Complete Work in Glass. 1100p. (FRE.). 1989. 350.00 (*1-55660-113-1*) A Wofsy Fine Arts.

Marcin, Marietta M. The Herbal Tea Garden: Planning, Planting, Harvesting & Brewing. Webb, Sandra, ed. LC 92-54653. (Illus.). 224p. (Orig.). 1993. pap. 12.95 (*0-88266-827-7*, Garden Way Pub) Storey Comm Inc.

Marcinello, Angela, ed. see Peterson, David & Denney, Dick.

***Marciniak.** English-Polish Dictionary of Computer-Science. 671p. (ENG & POL.). 1991. 45.00 (*0-7859-7515-2*, 8301090200) Fr & Eur.

Marciniak, A. & Jankowski, M. English-Polish Dictionary of Computer Science. 671p. 1991. 40.00 (*83-01-09020-0*) IBD Ltd.

Marciniak, Andrzej. Numerical Solutions of the N-Body Problem. 1985. lib. bdg. 103.00 (*90-277-2058-4*) Kluwer Ac.

Marciniak, Barbara. Bringers of the Dawn: Teachings from the Pleiadians. Thomas, Tera L., ed. LC 92-12393. 260p. (Orig.). 1992. pap. 10.95 (*0-939680-98-X*) Bear & Co.

— Earth: Pleiadian Keys to the Living Library. Thomas, Tera, ed. 240p. (Orig.). 1994. pap. 12.95 (*1-879181-21-5*) Bear & Co.

Marciniak, Bonita S. Seatwork Relief: Board Activities for Primary Teachers. 122p. 1991. pap. 15.95 (*0-9630787-0-4*) Scal-Mar.

Marciniak, James & Marciniak, Steven. Beyond the Silvered Pane. (Illus.). 1978. 5.95 (*0-940244-08-X*) Flying Buffalo.

Marciniak, John J., ed. Encyclopedia of Software Engineering, 2 vols., 1. 624p. 1994. text ed. write for info. (*0-471-54001-3*) Wiley.

— Encyclopedia of Software Engineering, 2 vols., 2. 624p. 1994. text ed. write for info. (*0-471-54002-1*) Wiley.

— Encyclopedia of Software Engineering, 2 vols., Vol. 2. 1453p. 1994. Set. text ed. 295.00 (*0-471-54004-8*) Wiley.

Marciniak, John J. & Reifer, Donald J. Software Acquisition Management: Managing the Acquisition of Custom Software Systems. 290p. 1990. text ed. 59.95 (*0-471-50643-5*) Wiley.

Marciniak, John J., jt. auth. see Evans, Michael W.

Marciniak, Steven, jt. auth. see Marciniak, James.

Marciniszyn, A., ed. see Carella, C. J. & Siembieda, Kevin.

Marciniszyn, A., ed. see Carella, C. J. & Siembieda, K.

Marciniszyn, A., ed. see Cartier, Randi & Siembieda, Kevin.

Marciniszyn, A., ed. see Nowak, Pat & Siembieda, Kevin.

Marciniszyn, Alex, ed. see Balent, Matthew.

Marciniszyn, Alex, ed. see Carella, C. J., et al.

Marciniszyn, Alex, ed. see Christian, D., et al.

Marciniszyn, Alex, ed. see Greenberg, Daniel & Siembieda, Kevin.

Marciniszyn, Alex, ed. see McCall, Randy & Siembieda, Kevin.

Marciniszyn, Alex, ed. see Reed, Gary.

Marciniszyn, Alex, ed. see Siembieba, Kevin.

Marciniszyn, Alex, ed. see Siembieda, Kevin, et al.

Marciniszyn, Alex, ed. see Siembieda, Kevin.

Marciniszyn, Alex, ed. see Siembieda, Kevin & Long, Kevin.

Marciniszyn, Alex, ed. see Siembieda, Kevin & Siembieda, Maryann.

Marciniszyn, Alex, ed. see Siembieda, Kevin.

Marciniszyn, Alex, ed. see Siembieda, Kevin & Bartold, Thomas.

Marciniszyn, Alex, ed. see Siembieda, Kevin.

Marciniszyn, Alex, ed. see Siembieda, Kevin & Long, Kevin.

Marciniszyn, Alex, ed. see Siembieda, Kevin.

Marciniszyn, Alex, ed. see Siembieda, Kevin & Long, Kevin.

Marciniszyn, Alex, ed. see Siembieda, Kevin & Henry, Truman.

Marciniszyn, Alex, ed. see Siembieda, Kevin.

Marciniszyn, Alex, ed. see Trostle, Jape & Siembieda, Kevin.

Marciniszyn, Alex, ed. see Wallis, James & Siembieda, Kevin.

Marciniszyn, Alex, ed. see Wallis, James & Sienbieda, Kevin.

Marciniszyn, Alex, ed. see Wujcik, Erick & Balent, Matthew.

Marciniszyn, Alex, ed. see Wujcik, Erick.

Marciniszyn, Alex, ed. see Wujcik, Erick & Siembieda, Kevin.

Marciniszyn, Alex, ed. see Wujcik, Erick.

Marcinizyn, A., ed. see Breaux, Wayne & Siembieda, Kevin.

Marcinizyn, A., ed. see Nowak, Patrick & Siembieda, Kevin.

Marcinizyn, A., ed. see Siembieda, K. & Carella, C. J.

Marcinizyn, A., ed. see Siembieda, Kevin & Zeleznik, John.

Marcinizyn, Alex, ed. see Carella, C. J. & Siembieda, Kevin.

***Marcinko.** Leadership Secrets of the Rogue Warrior. Date not set. mass mkt. 6.00 (*0-671-54514-0*) PB.

— Leadership Secrets of the Rogue Warrior. 1996. 20.00 (*0-671-54515-9*) PB.

Marcinko, David. Infections of the Foot: Diagnosis, Management. 325p. 1994. 69.95 (*0-8016-7018-7*) Mosby Yr Bk.

Marcinko, David & Weisman, John. Rogue Warrior. Regan, Judith & McCarthy, Paul, eds. 352p. 1992. 23.00 (*0-671-70390-0*) PB.

Marcinko, David E. Comprehensive Textbook of Hallux Valgus Reconstruction. 304p. 1992. 91.00 (*0-8016-3171-8*) Mosby Yr Bk.

— Medical & Surgical Therapeutics of the Foot & Ankle. (Illus.). 968p. 1992. 125.00 (*0-683-05549-6*) Williams & Wilkins.

Marcinko, Richard & Weisman, John. Red Cell. Regan, Judith & McCarthy, Paul, eds. (Rogue Warrior Ser.: No. 2). 416p. 1994. reprint ed. mass mkt. 5.99 (*0-671-79957-6*) PB.

— Rogue Warrior. Regan, Judith & McCarthy, Paul, eds. 480p. 1993. pap. 6.50 (*0-671-79593-7*, Pocket Star Bks) PB.

— Rogue Warrior: Green Team. 1995. 23.00 (*0-615-00609-4*) PB.

— Rogue Warrior III: Green Team. McCarthy, Paul, ed. 352p. 1995. 23.00 (*0-671-89671-7*) PB.

Marcinkowski, M. J. Unified Theory of the Mechanical Behavior of Matter. LC 78-27799. 275p. reprint ed. pap. 78.40 (*0-317-28028-7*, 2055722) Bks Demand.

Marcinsizyn, Alex, ed. see Siembieda, Kevin.

Marcion Of Sinope. The Gospel of the Lord. Hill, James H., tr. LC 78-63171. (Heresies of the Early Christian & Medieval Era Ser.: Second Ser.). reprint ed. 27.50 (*0-404-16186-3*) AMS Pr.

Marciszewski, Witold. Logic from a Rhetorical Point of View. LC 93-45843. (Grundlagen der Kommunikation & Kognition (Foundations of Communication & Cognition) Ser.). xv, 312p. (C). 1993. lib. bdg. 118.50 (*3-11-013683-X*) De Gruyter.

Marciszewski, Witold, ed. Dictionary of Logic As Applied in the Study of Language: Concepts - Methods - Theories. 464p. 1981. lib. bdg. 145.50 (*90-247-2123-7*) Kluwer Ac.

Marck, Jan V. D. Arman Selected Works. LC 74-18537. (Illus.). 48p. 1974. 8.00 (*0-686-99820-0*) Mus Contemp Art.

Marck, Jeffrey C., jt. auth. see Jackson, Frederick H.

Marck, John T. The First Ladies of the United States. (Illus.). 45p. (Orig.). 1993. pap. text ed. 19.95 (*1-884604-01-3*) Creative Impress.

— Maryland, the Seventh State: A History. 2nd ed. (Illus.). 230p. (YA). (gr. 9-12). 1994. pap. 19.95 (*1-884604-02-1*) Creative Impress.

—Maryland, the Seventh State: A History. 3rd ed. 432p. (J). (gr. 4 up). 1995. 29.95 (*1-884604-03-X*) Creative Impress. MARYLAND THE SEVENTH STATE A HISTORY, 3RD EDITION. Now in Hardback, this is a comprehensive book covering many aspects of the State of Maryland. The front cover displays a color Maryland State Flag, & the back cover displays a color picture of the Great Seal of Maryland. The book starts with a complete chronology, covering major events in Maryland's history from 10, 000 B.C. to present day. The first section deals with the founding of the State of Maryland, as well as the American Revolutionary War, the War of 1812 & the Civil War, & how these relate to Maryland. Also included are pictures & descriptions of all State Symbols & the Great Seal as well as all former Great Seals. This Third Edition includes In-Depth information on all counties of Maryland & Baltimore City. Included in this section is information on their founding, as well as historical places of interest. Provided for each county & Baltimore City is a map & a picture of its seal, as well as Maryland Counties & their County Seat, Order of Establishment, Population, Regions, & State Parks & Forests. Also included is a chronology of Maryland's Barons of Baltimore, Lords of Proprietary & Governors from 1625 to present day. Additionally, this Third Edition contains United States stamps commemorating Maryland, & Obsolete Bank Notes & miscellaneous documents from Maryland's past. Other general information on Maryland & trivia & interesting facts questions & answers are provided. Suitable for all ages, this is the only book of its kind to include all aspects in one volume. This new Third Edition also contains many illustrations & photographs. 432 pages, $29.95 Other books by the author are THE PRESIDENTS OF THE UNITED STATES, IBSN 1-884604-00-5 & THE FIRST LADIES OF THE UNITED STATES, ISBN 1-0884604-01-3. These books include a picture & signature of each president, & a picture of each First Lady. Both include biographical information. Order directly from: Creative Impressions, Ltd., P.O. Box 188, Glen Arm, MD. 21057. (410) 592-7068. ***Publisher Provided Annotation.***

— The Presidents of the United States. (Illus.). 45p. (Orig.). 1993. pap. text ed. 19.95 (*1-884604-00-5*) Creative Impress.

Marck, Patricia, jt. ed. see Field, Peggy A.

Marckwardt, Albert H. Principal & Subsidiary Dialect Areas in the North-Central States. Bd. with English Loan Words in the Low German Dialect of Westphalia, Missouri. (Publications of the American Dialect Society: No. 27). 32p. 1957. Set pap. 2.35 (*0-8173-0627-7*) U of Ala Pr.

Marckwardt, Albert H. & Moore, Samuel. Historical Outlines of English Sounds & Inflections. 1957. pap. 15.00x (*0-911586-22-9*) Wahr.

Marckwardt, Wilhelm, ed. International Guide to MARC Databases & Services: National Magnetic Tape, CD-ROM, & Online Services & Databases. 3rd rev. ed. (UBCIM Publications). 250p. 1993. reprint ed. lib. bdg. 100.00 (*3-598-10987-3*) K G Saur.

Marco, Carolyn, jt. auth. see Gach, Michael.

Marco, Gayle J. & Lucas, Anthony J. Media Instructor's Manual to Accompany Boone-Kurtz, Contemporary Business, 7-E. 7th ed. 267p. (C). 1993. pap. text ed. 22.75 (*0-03-097989-7*) Dryden Pr.

— Video Instructor's Manual to Accompany Boone-Kurtz, Contemporary Business. 7th ed. 186p. (C). 1993. pap. text ed. 4.50 (*0-03-076343-6*) Dryden Pr.

Marco, Gino J., et al, eds. Regulation of Agrochemicals: A Driving Force in Their Evolution. LC 91-19736. (Illus.). 188p. 1991. 44.95 (*0-8412-2089-1*); pap. 34.95 (*0-8412-2085-9*) Am Chemical.

— Silent Spring Revisited. 1987. 32.95 (*0-8412-0980-4*); pap. 19.95 (*0-317-59798-1*) Am Chemical.

Marco, Guy A. & Andrews, Frank, eds. Encyclopedia of Recorded Sound in the United States. LC 93-18166. (Reference Library of the Humanities: Vol. 936). (Illus.). 968p. 1993. Acid-free paper. 125.00 (*0-8240-4782-6*, H936) Garland.

Marco, Guy A., jt. auth. see Bryant, E. T.

Marco, Guy A., tr. see Zarlino, Gioseffo.

Marco, Joaquin. Literatura Hispanoamericana: Del Modernismo a Nuestros Dias. (Nueva Austral Ser.: Vol. 17). (SPA.). 1991. pap. text ed. 34.95x (*84-239-1817-3*) Elliots Bks.

Marco, Juan B., et al, eds. Stochastic Hydrology & its Use in Water Resources Systems Simulation & Optimization. LC 93-19300. (NATO Advanced Study Institutes Series E, Applied Sciences: Vol. 237). 1993. lib. bdg. 181.00 (*0-7923-2288-6*) Kluwer Ac.

***Marco, Lou.** ISPF - REXX Development for Experienced Programmers. (Illus.). 400p. (C). 1995. 3.5 hd, pap. text ed. 35.00 (*1-878956-50-7*) CBM Bks.

***Marco, Michael & Majchrowicz, Martin.** Current Issues in Research & Treatment of Kaposi's Sarcoma: The KS Project Report. 85p. (Orig.). (C). 1994. pap. text ed. 30.00 (*0-7881-1386-0*) Diane Pub.

Marco, T., tr. see Honegger, Marc.

Marco, Tomas. Spanish Music in the Twentieth Century. Franzen, Cola, tr. LC 92-14270. 269p. (C). 1993. 42.50 (*0-674-83102-0*) HUP.

Marco, Tomas, tr. see Honegger, Marc.

***Marcoci, Roxana.** Gardens in Bloom. LC 94-32480. (Celebrations in Art Ser.). 1995. write for info. (*1-56799-163-7*, MetroBooks) M Friedman Pub Grp Inc.

— Mothers & Children. LC 94-32474. (Celebrations in Art Ser.). 1995. write for info. (*1-56799-162-9*, MetroBooks) M Friedman Pub Grp Inc.

Marcombe, David. English Small Town Life: Retford 1520-1642. (Illus.). 320p. 1994. 35.00 (*1-85041-067-4*); pap. 17.95 (*1-85041-068-2*) Paul & Co Pubs.

— Nottingham & the Great War. (C). 1984. text ed. 40.00 (*0-685-22174-1*, Pub. by Univ Nottingham UK) St Mut.

— Sounding Boards: Oral Testimony & the Local Historian. 90p. 1994. pap. 10.00 (*1-85041-075-5*, Pub. by U Nottingham UK) Paul & Co Pubs.

Marcombe, David, jt. auth. see Bourne, Terry.

Marcondes de Souza Filho, Danilo. Language & Action: A Reassessment of Speech Act Theory. LC 84-4055. (P & B Ser.: Vol. V, No. 6). x, 165p. (Orig.). 1985. pap. 50.00x (*0-915027-01-1*) Benjamins North Am.

Marconi, Catherine L., ed. Handspan of Red Earth: An Anthology of American Farm Poems. LC 90-21163. (Illus.). 197p. 1991. pap. 12.95 (*0-87745-326-8*) U of Iowa Pr.

Marconi, Gilberto, jt. ed. see O'Collins, Gerald.

Marconi, Joe. Beyond Branding: How Savvy Marketers Use Brand Extension to Create Products & Open New Markets. 225p. 1993. 24.95 (*1-55738-428-2*) Probus Pub Co.

— Crisis Marketing: When Bad Things Happen to Good Companies. 225p. 1992. 22.95 (*1-55738-246-8*) Probus Pub Co.

— Getting the Best from Your Ad Agency: Everything Marketers Need to Know about Working with Agencies - from Creative, Media Planning, Budgeting & Market Strategy to Campaign Execution & Evaluation. 200p. 1991. 24.95 (*1-55738-179-8*) Probus Pub Co.

Marconi, Joseph, ed. Indexed Periodicals. LC 76-12242. 1976. 90.00 (*0-87650-005-X*) Pierian.

Marconi, Paolo. Atlas of Rome. (Illus.). 600p. 1992. 250.00 (*0-941419-70-3*) Marsilio Pubs.

Marconis, E. J. The Sanctuary of Memphis; or Hermes - Masonic Rituals. 230p. 1993. pap. 19.95 (*1-56459-311-8*) Kessinger Pub.

Marconnet, P. & Komi, P., eds. Muscular Function in Exercise & Training. (Medicine & Sport Science Ser.: Vol. 26). (Illus.). viii, 272p. 1987. 158.50 (*3-8055-4598-3*) S Karger.

Marconnet, P. & Poortmans, J., eds. Physiological Chemistry of Training & Detraining. (Medicine & Sport Science Ser.: Vol. 17). (Illus.). xii, 264p. 1984. 158.50 (*3-8055-3764-6*) S Karger.

Marconnet, P., et al, eds. Muscle Fatigue Mechanisms in Exercise & Training. (Medicine & Sport Science Ser.: Vol. 34). (Illus.). viii, 244p. 1992. 198.50 (*3-8055-5483-4*) S Karger.

Marcontell, Paul. The Down-the-Aisle Directory: The Wedding Resource Book for the N.Y.-Tri-State Area. (Illus.). 448p. 1991. 35.00 (*0-9627895-0-X*) MRS Pubns.

***Marcoon, Bruce.** Second Glances. (Illus.). 128p. 1994. pap. 8.50 (*0-8059-3705-6*) Dorrance.

Marcorich, Miroslav. Studies in Graeco-Roman Religions & Gnosticism. 194p. (C). 1988. text ed. 40.00 (*90-04-08624-2*) E J Brill.

Marcos, Anastasios C., jt. ed. see Draper, Thomas W.

Marcos, Natalio F. Scribes & Translators: Septuagint & Old Latin in the Books. LC 94-9717. (Supplements to Vetus Testamentum Ser.). 1994. 57.25 (*90-04-10043-1*) E J Brill.

Marcos, Plinio, et al. Three Contemporary Brazilian Plays in Bilingual Edition. Szoka, Elzbieta & Bratcher, Joe, eds. Marques, Lydia & Pinto, Lelina, trs. (Illus.). 525p. (Orig.). (C). 1988. pap. 20.00 (*0-685-24272-2*) Host Pubns.

Marcos, Rafael, tr. see Gatje, Charles T. & Gatje, John F.

Marcos Sanchez, Maria D., ed. see Casona, Alejandro.

Marcosson, Isaac F. Adventures in Interviewing. LC 80-130996. reprint ed. 21.50 (*0-404-04186-8*) AMS Pr.

— Anaconda. LC 75-41771. (Companies & Men: Business Enterprises in America Ser.). (Illus.). 1976. reprint ed. 40.95 (*0-405-08085-9*) Ayer.

— Marse Henry: A Biography of Henry Watterson. LC 74-156200. (Illus.). 269p. 1971. reprint ed. text ed. 59.75 (*0-8371-6150-9*, MAMH) Greenwood.

— Turbulent Years. LC 71-90661. (Essay Index Reprint Ser.). 1977. 30.95 (*0-8369-1305-1*) Ayer.

— Wherever Men Trade: The Romance of the Cash Register. LC 72-5062. (Technology & Society Ser.). (Illus.). 310p. 1972. reprint ed. 21.95 (*0-405-04713-4*) Ayer.

Marcot, Roy M. Civil War Chief of Sharpshooters, Hiram Berdan, Military Commander & Firearms Inventor. LC 89-92286. (Illus.). 342p. 1992. 59.95 (*0-9611494-1-8*) Northwood Heritage Pr.

— Spencer Repeating Firearms. (Illus.). 316p. 1990. 60.00x (*1-884849-14-8*) R & R Bks.

— Spencer Repeating Firearms. 2nd rev. ed. LC 89-92524. (Illus.). 316p. 1989. reprint ed. 59.95 (*0-9611494-3-4*) Northwood Heritage Pr.

Marcotorchino, J. F., et al, eds. Data Analysis in Real Life Environment. (Advanced Series in Management: Vol. 8). 1985. 82.00 (*0-444-87692-8*) Elsevier.

Marcotte. Biomechanics in Orthodontics. 200p. 1990. 52.00 (*1-55664-168-0*) Mosby Yr Bk.

— Management of Asymmetrics in Orthodontics. 200p. Date not set. 49.50 (*1-55664-304-7*) Mosby Yr Bk.

Marcotte, Armand & Druffel, Ann. Past Lives, Future Growth. 200p. (Orig.). 1993. pap. 8.95 (*1-878901-79-6*) Hampton Roads Pub Co.

— The Psychic & the Detective. 160p. (Orig.). 1995. pap. 10.95 (*1-57174-029-5*) Hampton Roads Pub Co.

Marcotte, David B., jt. ed. see Nadelson, Carol C.

An Asterisk (*) at the beginning of an entry indicates that the title is appearing in BIP for the first time.

Marcotte, J., jt. auth. see Detienne, M. G.

Marcotty, M. W. & Ledgard, Henry. The World of Programming Languages. (Books on Professional Computing). (Illus.). 385p. 1986. pap. 46.00 (*0-387-96440-1*) Spr-Verlag.

Marcotty, Michael. Software Implementation. 2nd ed. 300p. 1991. pap. 49.20 (*0-13-823493-0*) P-H.

Marcou, Diane, ed. see Haimes, Allen N.

Marcou, Jules, Jr. Jules Marcou on the Taconic System in North America: An Original Anthology. Albritton, Claude C., ed. LC 77-6527. (History of Geology Ser.). (Illus.). 1978. lib. bdg. 65.95 (*0-405-10448-0*) Ayer.

Marcou, Richard. How to Cook...Roadkill: "Goremet Cooking" (Illus.). 96p. (Orig.). 1993. reprint ed. 9.95 (*0-9637062-0-9*) MCB Pubns.

***Marcouiller, David W.** Tourism Planning. LC 95-8753. (Bibliography Ser.: No. 316). 1995. write for info. (*0-86602-316-X*) Coun Plan Librarians.

Marcouiller, David W., jt. auth. see Jepson, Edward J.

***Marcoulides, George A. & Schumacker, Randall E., eds.** Advanced Structural Equation Modeling Techniques. 300p. 1996. text ed. 45.00 (*0-8058-1819-7*) L Erlbaum Assocs.

Marcoux, J. Paul. Guilbert de Pixerecourt: French Melodrama in the Early Nineteenth Century. LC 92-7271. (Studies in French Theatre: Vol. 1). 154p. 1993. 43.95 (*0-8204-1905-2*) P Lang Pubs.

Marcoux, J. Paul, tr. see Feydeau, Georges.

Marcoux, Marcene. Cursillo: Anatomy of a Movement. LC 81-20704. 290p. 1995. 50.00 (*0-931186-00-5*) Lambeth Pr.

Marcoux, Phil. ISO Nine Thousand Compatible Electronic Assembly Workmanship Guidelines. 102p. (C). 1993. student ed 295.00 (*1-884817-01-7*) PPM Assocs.

— Printed Circuit Assembly Design Guidelines. 258p. (C). 1992. student ed 395.00 (*1-884817-00-9*) PPM Assocs.

— Printed Circuit Assembly Inspection, Rework, & Repair Techniques. 115p. (C). 1993. student ed 65.00 (*1-884817-02-5*) PPM Assocs.

Marcoux, Phil P. Fine Pitch Surface Mount Technology: Quality, Design, & Manufacturing Techniques. (Illus.). 300p. 1992. text ed. 59.95 (*0-442-00862-7*) Van Nos Reinhold.

Marcov, Diane, jt. auth. see Steiner, Dieter.

Marcove, Ralph C. & Arlen. Atlas of Bone Pathology: With Clinical & Radiographic Correlations. (Illus.). 688p. 1992. text ed. 150.00 (*0-397-51077-2*) Lippincott.

Marcove, Ralph C., jt. auth. see Arlen, Myron.

***Marcovich, Miroslav.** Patristic Textual Criticism. LC 94-24542. (Illinois Classical Studies, Supplement: Vol. 6). 1994. pap. write for info. (*0-7885-0046-5*) Scholars Pr GA.

— Prosper of Aquitaine - De Providentia Dei: Text, Translation & Commentary. LC 89-36313. (Supplements to Vigiliae Christianae Ser.: No. X). xii, 137p. 1989. text ed. 41.25 (*90-04-09090-8*) E J Brill.

— Studies in Greek Poetry. 249p. 1991. pap. 39.95 (*1-55540-603-3*) Scholars Pr GA.

Marcovich, Miroslav, ed. Alcestis Barcinonensis: Text & Commentary. LC 87-37212. (Mnemosyne, Bibliotheca Classica Batava Ser.: No. 103). 117p. (Orig.). 1988. pap. 25.25 (*90-04-08600-5*) E J Brill.

— Athenagoras: Legatio Pro Christianis. (Patristische Texte und Studien Ser.: Vol. 31). xii, 158p. (C). 1990. lib. bdg. 90.80 (*0-89925-689-9*) De Gruyter.

— Athenagoras: Legatio Pro Christianis. (Patristische Texte Und Studien Ser.: Vol. 31). xii, 158p. (C). 1990. lib. bdg. 90.80 (*3-11-011881-5*) De Gruyter.

— Hippolytus Refutatio Omnium Haeresium. (Patristische Texte und Studien Ser.: Vol. 25). xvi, 541p. 1986. lib. bdg. 242.35 (*0-89925-211-7*) De Gruyter.

— Hoppolytus Refutatio Omnium Haeresium. (Patristische Texte Und Studien Ser.: Vol. 25). xvi, 541p. 1986. lib. bdg. 242.35 (*3-11-008751-0*) De Gruyter.

— Iustini Martyris Apologiae Pro Christianis. (Patristische Texte und Studies: Bd. 38). 223p. (GRE.). (C). 1994. lib. bdg. 90.80 (*3-11-014180-9*) De Gruyter.

— Pseudo-Iustinus: Cohortatio ad Graecos - De Monarchia - Oratio ad Graecos. (Patristische Texte und Studien Ser.: Vol. 32). x, 161p. (C). 1990. lib. bdg. 90.80 (*0-89925-708-9*) De Gruyter.

— Pseudo-Iustinus: Cohortatio ad Graecos - De Monarchia - Oratio ad Graecos. (Patristische Texte Und Studien Ser.: Vol. 32). x, 161p. (C). 1990. lib. bdg. 90.80 (*3-11-012135-2*) De Gruyter.

***Marcozzi, Beth A. & Shapiro, Lawrence E.** My Best Friend Is Me. (Illus.). 45p. (Orig.). (J). (ps-3). 1995. pap. 9.95 (*1-882732-25-1*) Ctr Applied Psy.

Marcrander, Meg, jt. auth. see Luetje, Carolyn.

Marcroft, Karen. Fulbert Firefly. LC 85-90463. (Illus.). 48p. (J). (gr. 3-8). 1986. 14.95 (*0-935849-00-9*) Marcroft Prods.

Marcu, E. D. Nationalism in the Sixteenth Century. LC 75-39172. 1975. 8.50 (*0-913870-08-0*) Abaris Bks.

Marcu, Valeriu. Men & Forces of Our Time. LC 68-29231. (Essay Index Reprint Ser.). 1977. reprint ed. 19.95 (*0-8369-0678-0*) Ayer.

Marcucci, Domenico. Rezando el Rosario Con Fray Angelic. (Illus.). 1991. pap. 2.50 (*0-8189-0620-0*) Alba.

— Through the Rosary with Fra Angelico. Lane, Edmund C., tr. (Illus.). 48p. (Orig.). 1989. pap. 2.50 (*0-8189-0557-3*) Alba.

Marcucci, Robert G. & Schoen, Harold L. Beginning Algebra. (C). 1990. 90.36 (*0-395-52954-9*) HM.

Marcucci, Robert G., jt. auth. see Schoen, Harold L.

Marcuccio, Phyllis & Marshall, Sheila, eds. A Strategy for Change. (Illus.). 176p. 1993. pap. text ed. 17.50 (*0-87355-118-4*) Natl Sci Tchrs.

***Marcum, Betty.** The New Cairn Terrier. LC 95-13520. 1995. write for info. (*0-87605-073-9*) Howell Bk.

***Marcum, Deanna.** Preservation Education Institute Final Report. 13p. 1990. pap. 10.00 (*1-887334-02-5*) Comm Preserv & Access.

Marcum, Deanna B. Good Books in a Country Home: The Public Library as Cultural Force in Hagerstown, Maryland. LC 93-14463. 208p. 1994. text ed. 49.95 (*0-313-28626-4*, Greenwood Pr) Greenwood.

Marcum, John A. Angolan Revolution: The Anatomy of an Explosion, 1950-1962, Vol. 1. (Studies in Communism, Revisionism & Revolution). 1969. 45.00 (*0-262-13048-3*) MIT Pr.

— Education in South Africa: Reform or Transform? (Significant Issues Ser.). (C). 1994. pap. text ed. 9.95 (*0-89206-190-1*) CSI Studies.

Marcum, John A., ed. Education, Race, & Social Change in South Africa. LC 82-60256. (Perspectives on Southern Africa Ser.: No. 34). 180p. 1982. pap. 11.00 (*0-520-04899-7*) U CA Pr.

Marcum, Richard & Myers, Reyburn W. Message of the Locust. 200p. 1988. 17.95 (*0-940375-06-0*) WindRiver Pub.

Marcum, Robert. Angel of Armageddon. 1992. pap. 9.95 (*0-88494-854-4*) Bookcraft Inc.

— Death of a Tsar. LC 94-22709. 383p. 1994. 15.95 (*0-87579-914-0*) Deseret Bk.

— Dominions of the Gadiantons. 1991. pap. 9.95 (*0-88494-813-7*) Bookcraft Inc.

— Sting of the Scorpion. 1993. pap. 9.95 (*0-88494-889-7*) Bookcraft Inc.

Marcum, Walt. Living in the Light: Leading Youth to Deeper Spirituality. LC 94-12860. 112p. (Orig.). 1993. pap. 11.95 (*0-687-39235-7*) Abingdon.

— Sharing Groups in Youth Ministry. 1991. pap. 10.95 (*0-687-38344-7*) Abingdon.

Marcus. Celestial Raise. 230p. (Orig.). 1987. 24.95 (*0-9618316-0-X*); pap. 21.95 (*0-941131-01-7*) ASSK Pub.

— Letters Ursula Nordstrom. (J). Date not set. 17.00 (*0-06-023625-6*); lib. bdg. 17.00 (*0-06-023624-8*) HarpC Child Bks.

***Marcus & Oudar, eds.** Corrosion Mechanisms in Theory & Practice. (Corrosion Technology Ser.: vol. 8). 574p. 1995. write for info. (*0-8247-9592-X*) Dekker.

Marcus, jt. auth. see Cook.

Marcus, jt. auth. see Marinsky.

Marcus, Aaron. Graphic Design for Electronic Documents & User Interfaces. (ACM Press Tutorial Ser.). (Illus.). 288p. (C). 1991. pap. text ed. 34.50 (*0-201-54364-8*) Addison-Wesley.

— Multimedia Interface Design Studio. 1995. 40.00 (*0-679-75999-9*) Random.

Marcus, Aaron, jt. auth. see Baecker, Ronald M.

Marcus, Abraham. The Middle East on the Eve of Modernity: Aleppo in the Eighteenth Century. (Study of the Middle East Institute Ser.). 418p. (C). 1992. pap. 14. 50 (*0-231-06595-7*) Col U Pr.

— The Middle East on the Eve of Modernity: Culture & Society in Eighteenth-Century Aleppo. (Study of the Middle East Institute Ser.). (Illus.). 1989. text ed. 45.00 (*0-231-06594-9*) Col U Pr.

Marcus, Abraham & Lenk, John D. Computers for Technicians. (Illus.). 400p. 1973. text ed. 40.00 (*0-13-166181-7*) P-H.

Marcus, Abraham & Marcus, W. Basic Electricity. 4th ed. 1973. 34.48 (*0-13-060152-7*) P-H.

Marcus, Abraham & Thomson, Charles M. Electricity for Technicians. 3rd ed. (Illus.). 512p. (C). 1982. text ed. 52. 00 (*0-13-248666-0*) P-H.

Marcus, Abraham, jt. auth. see Gritter, W. V.

Marcus, Abraham, et al, eds. The Biochemistry of Plants Vol. 15: A Comprehensive Treatise. (Molecular Biology Ser.). 1100p. 1989. text ed. 213.00 (*0-12-675415-2*) Acad Pr.

Marcus, Adrianne. Divided Weather. 64p. (Orig.). 1985. 25. 00 (*0-931757-24-X*); pap. 15.00 (*0-931757-25-8*) Pterodactyl Pr.

— Faced with Love. (Orig.). 1978. pap. 4.50 (*0-914278-13-4*) Copper Beech.

Marcus, Alan. Acute Abdominal Syndromes: Their Diagnosis & Treatment According to Combined Chinese-Western Medicine. LC 91-77707. 161p. (Orig.). 1991. pap. text ed. 16.95 (*0-936185-31-7*) Blue Poppy.

Marcus, Alan I. Cancer from Beef: The DES Controversy, Federal Food Regulation, & Consumer Confidence in Modern America. LC 93-21505. 1994. text ed. 38.50 (*0-8018-4700-1*) Johns Hopkins.

— Plague of Strangers: Social Groups & the Origins of City Services in Cincinnati 1819-1870. (Urban Life & Urban Landscape Ser.). 256p. 1991. 42.50 (*0-8142-0550-X*) Ohio St U Pr.

Marcus, Alan I. & Segal, Howard P. Technology in America: A Brief History. 380p. (C). 1989. pap. text ed. 16.00 (*0-15-589762-4*) HB Coll Pubs.

***Marcus, Alan R.** Relocating Eden: The Image & Politics of Inuit Exile in the Canadian Arctic. (Illus.). 304p. 1995. pap. 19.95 (*0-87451-659-5*) U Pr of New Eng.

Marcus, Alfred A. The Adversary Economy: Business Responses to Changing Government Requirements. LC 83-17674. (Illus.). xvi, 260p. 1984. text ed. 65.00 (*0-89930-055-3*, MAV/, Quorum Bks) Greenwood.

— Business & Society: Ethics, Government, & the World Economy. LC 92-23081. 704p. (C). 1992. text ed. 60.95 (*0-256-08866-7*) Irwin.

— Controversial Issues in Energy Policy. (Controversial Issues In Public Policy Ser.: Vol. 2). (Illus.). 200p. (C). 1992. 38.00 (*0-8039-3969-8*); pap. 17.50 (*0-8039-3970-1*) Sage.

— Promise & Performance: Choosing & Implementing an Environmental Policy. LC 79-8290. (Contributions in Political Science Ser.: No. 39). 204p. 1980. text ed. 55. 00 (*0-313-20707-0*, MPT/, Greenwood Pr) Greenwood.

Marcus, Alfred A., et al, eds. Business Strategy & Public Policy: Perspectives from Industry & Academia. LC 86-30388. 334p. 1987. text ed. 75.00 (*0-89930-172-X*, MBS/, Quorum Bks) Greenwood.

Marcus, Arbeiter. Say No to Chronic Pain. 1994. 20.00 (*0-671-79892-8*) S&S Trade.

Marcus, Audrey F. & Zwerin, Raymond A. Like a Maccabee. (Illus.). (J). (gr. k-3). 1991. 11.95 (*0-8074-0445-4*, 102564) UAHC.

— Shabbat Can Be. Syme, Daniel B., ed. (Illus.). (J). (gr. k-3). 1979. 10.95 (*0-8074-0023-8*) UAHC.

Marcus, Audrey F. & Zwerin, Raymond A., eds. The Jewish Principals Handbook. LC 83-70198. 525p. (C). 1983. pap. text ed. 45.00 (*0-86705-035-7*) A R E Pub.

— The New Jewish Teachers Handbook. LC 94-70560. 480p. (Orig.). 1994. teacher ed, pap. text ed. write for info. (*0-86705-033-0*) A R E Pub.

Marcus, Audrey F., jt. auth. see Zwerin, Raymond A.

Marcus, Audrey F., jt. auth. see Zwerm, Raymond A.

Marcus Aurelius. The Commentaries of the Emperor Marcus Antoninus: Containing His Maxims of Science & Rules of Life, Wrote for His Own Use & Address'd to Himself. LC 77-158297. (Augustan Translators Ser.). reprint ed. 49.50 (*0-404-54103-8*) AMS Pr.

— Meditations. (Loeb Classical Library: No. 58). 448p. 1930. 18.95 (*0-674-99064-1*) HUP.

— Meditations. Staniforth, Maxwell, tr. (Classics Ser.). (YA). (gr. 9 up). 1964. mass mkt. 8.95 (*0-14-044140-9*, Penguin Classics) Viking Penguin.

— Meditations. Grube, G. M. A., ed. & tr. by. LC 83-22722. (HPC Classics Ser.). 170p. (C). 1984. reprint ed. lib. bdg. 21.50 (*0-915145-78-2*); reprint ed. pap. text ed. 5.75 (*0-915145-79-0*) Hackett Pub.

— The Meditations of Marcus Aurelius Antoninus & a Selection from the Letters of Marcus & Fronto. Rutherford, R. B. & Farquharson, A. S., trs. 224p. 1990. 49.95 (*0-19-814761-9*) OUP.

Marcus, B., jt. auth. see Adler, R. L.

***Marcus, Ben.** The Age of Wire & String: Stories. LC 95-4131. 1995. write for info. (*0-679-42660-4*) Knopf.

Marcus, Brian, jt. auth. see Lind, Douglas.

Marcus, Bruce. Muck Arbour. Ashbery, John, ed. LC 74-5984. 64p. 1975. 7.95 (*0-87955-500-9*) O'Hara.

***Marcus, Clare C.** House As a Mirror of Self: Exploring the Deeper Meaning of Home. (Illus.). 350p. 1995. 24.95 (*0-943233-92-5*) Conari Press.

— People Places. 1990. text ed. 49.95 (*0-442-31929-0*) Van Nos Reinhold.

Marcus, Daniel, ed. see Paper Tiger Television Collective Staff.

Marcus, Daniel A. Differential Equations: An Introduction. 656p. (C). 1991. write for info. (*0-697-11681-6*) Wm C Brown Pubs.

— Number Fields (Universitext) LC 77-21467. 1995. text ed. 39.00 (*0-387-90279-1*) Spr-Verlag.

***Marcus, David.** From Balaam to Jonah: Anti-Prophetic Satire in the Hebrew Bible. LC 95-6409. (Brown Judaic Studies: No. 301). 1995. write for info. (*0-7885-0101-1*) Scholars Pr GA.

— Jephthah & His Vow. 80p. 1986. 25.00 (*0-89672-136-1*); pap. 15.00 (*0-89672-135-3*) Tex Tech Univ Pr.

— A Manual of Akkadian. LC 78-63068. 1978. pap. text ed. 19.50 (*0-8191-0608-9*) U Pr of Amer.

— A Manual of Babylonian Jewish Aramaic. LC 80-6073. 104p. (Orig.). (C). 1981. pap. text ed. 16.00 (*0-8191-1363-8*) U Pr of Amer.

Marcus, David, ed. New Irish Writing. 3.95 (*0-7043-3101-2*, Pub. by Quartet UK) Charles River Bks.

Marcus, Dora, jt. auth. see Dressel, Paul L.

Marcus, Edward, ed. A New Canaan Private in the Civil War: Letters of Justus M. Silliman, Seventeenth Connecticut Volunteers. (Illus.). 117p. 1984. 7.50 (*0-939958-01-5*) New Canaan.

Marcus, Edward & Marcus, Mildred R. Investment & Development Possibilities in Tropical Africa. Wilkins, Mira, ed. LC 76-29767. (European Business Ser.). 1977. reprint ed. lib. bdg. 25.95 (*0-405-09781-6*) Ayer.

Marcus, Edward, jt. auth. see Marcus, Gerald.

Marcus, Edward, jt. ed. see Schmukler, Nathan.

Marcus, Elizabeth. All about Mountains & Volcanoes. LC 83-4834. (Question & Answer Bks.). (Illus.). 32p. (J). (gr. 3-6). 1984. lib. bdg. 10.59 (*0-89375-969-4*); pap. text ed. 2.95 (*0-89375-970-8*) Troll Assocs.

— Amazing World of Plants. LC 83-4836. (Question & Answer Bks.). (Illus.). 32p. (J). (gr. 3-6). 1984. lib. bdg. 10.59 (*0-89375-967-8*); pap. text ed. 2.95 (*0-89375-968-6*) Troll Assocs.

— Our Wonderful Seasons. LC 82-17372. (Question & Answer Bks.). (Illus.). 32p. (J). (gr. 3-6). 1983. lib. bdg. 10.59 (*0-89375-896-5*); pap. text ed. 2.95 (*0-89375-897-3*) Troll Assocs.

— Rocks & Minerals. LC 82-17424. (Question & Answer Bks.). (Illus.). 32p. (J). (gr. 3-6). 1983. lib. bdg. 10.59 (*0-89375-876-0*); pap. text ed. 2.95 (*0-89375-877-9*) Troll Assocs.

Marcus, Elliott, et al. An Introduction to the Neurosciences. 2nd ed. (Illus.). 750p. Date not set. student ed, text ed. 69.50 (*0-683-05542-9*) Williams & Wilkins.

Marcus, Eric. Is It a Choice? Answers to Three Hundred of the Most Frequently Asked Questions about Gays & Lesbians. LC 92-56425. 240p. 1993. pap. 10.00 (*0-06-250664-1*) Harper SF.

— Making History: The Struggle for Gay & Lesbian Equal Rights. LC 90-56389. (Illus.). 544p. 1993. pap. 14.00 (*0-06-092222-2*, PL) HarpC.

— The Male Couple's Guide: Finding a Man, Making a Home, Building a Life. enl. ed. LC 91-58673. 320p. 1992. reprint ed. pap. 15.00 (*0-06-096936-9*, PL) HarpC.

— Why Suicide? Answers to 200 of the Most Frequently Asked Questions about Suicide, & Assisted Suicide. 240p. 1995. pap. 10.00 (*0-06-251166-1*) Harper SF.

***Marcus, Eric & Louganis, Greg.** Breaking the Surface: A Life. 1995. 23.00 (*0-679-43703-7*) Random.

Marcus, G. J. The Conquest of the North Atlantic. (Illus.). 1981. 29.95 (*0-19-520252-X*) OUP.

Marcus, Gary F., et al. Overregularization in Language Acquisition. 100p. 1992. pap. text ed. 9.75 (*0-226-50456-5*) U Ch Pr.

Marcus, Geoffrey. The Maiden Voyage. (Illus.). 340p. 1991. reprint ed. lib. bdg. 32.95x (*0-89966-792-9*) Buccaneer Bks.

Marcus, George, jt. auth. see Hiesinger, Kathryn.

Marcus, George E., ed. Perilous States: Conversations on Culture, Politics, & Nation. (Late Editions: Cultural Studies for the End of the Century). (Illus.). 360p. 1993. lib. bdg. 54.95 (*0-226-50446-8*); pap. 18.95 (*0-226-50447-6*) U Ch Pr.

— Rereading Cultural Anthropology. LC 92-21908. 416p. 1992. lib. bdg. 44.95 (*0-8223-1279-4*); pap. text ed. 14. 95 (*0-8223-1297-2*) Duke.

— Technoscientific Imaginaries: Conversations, Profiles, & Memoirs. 576p. 1995. lib. bdg. 65.00 (*0-226-50443-3*); pap. text ed. 22.50 (*0-226-50444-1*) U Ch Pr.

Marcus, George E. & Fischer, Michael M. Anthropology As Cultural Critique: An Experimental Moment in the Human Sciences. LC 85-20686. xiv, 206p. (Orig.). 1986. pap. 11.95 (*0-226-50449-2*) U Ch Pr.

Marcus, George E. & Hall, Peter D. Lives in Trust: The Fortunes of Dynastic Families in Late Twentieth-Century America. 380p. 1992. text ed. 56.00 (*0-8133-0464-4*) Westview.

— Lives in Trust: The Fortunes of Dynastic Families in Late Twentieth-Century America. 380p. (C). 1992. pap. text ed. 21.50 (*0-8133-0467-9*) Westview.

Marcus, George E. & Hanson, Russell L., eds. Reconsidering the Democratic Public. LC 92-33653. 464p. 1993. 55.00 (*0-271-00917-9*); pap. 15.95 (*0-271-00927-6*) Pa St U Pr.

***Marcus, George E. & Myers, Fred R., eds.** The Traffic in Culture: Refiguring Anthropology & Art. LC 94-39487. 1995. 48.00 (*0-520-08846-8*); pap. 17.95 (*0-520-08847-6*) U CA Pr.

Marcus, George E., jt. ed. see Clifford, James.

***Marcus, George E., et al.** With Malice Toward Some: How People Make Civil Liberties Judgments. (Cambridge Studies in Political Psychology & Public Opinion). (Illus.). 304p. (C). 1995. write for info. (*0-521-43396-7*); pap. write for info. (*0-521-43997-3*) Cambridge U Pr.

***Marcus, George H.** Functionalist Design: An Ongoing History. (Illus.). 176p. (Orig.). 1995. pap. 29.95 (*3-7913-1423-8*, Pub. by Prestel) TeNeues.

Marcus, George H., jt. auth. see Hiesinger, Kathryn B.

Marcus, Gerald & Marcus, Edward. Optimizing Ocean Current Crossings. 16p. Date not set. pap. text ed. 15.00 (*1-882502-18-3*) US Sail Assn.

***Marcus, Gregory, et al.** Credit Survival Guide Instructor's Manual. Johnson, Robert W., ed. 162p. (Orig.). 1995. teacher ed, pap. 14.95 (*0-9635779-8-0*) Am Bureau Info.

Marcus, Greil. Dead Elvis: A Chronicle of a Cultural Obsession. LC 92-17939. 1992. pap. 14.00 (*0-385-41719-5*, Anchor NY) Doubleday.

— The Dustbin of History. LC 95-8876. (Illus.). 240p. (C). 1995. 22.95 (*0-674-21857-4*) HUP.

— Lipstick Traces: A Secret History of the Twentieth Century. LC 88-24678. (Illus.). 512p. 1989. 37.00 (*0-674-53580-4*) HUP.

— Lipstick Traces: A Secret History of the Twentieth Century. (Illus.). 512p. 1990. pap. text ed. 16.95 (*0-674-53581-2*) HUP.

— Mystery Train. 3rd ed. 1990. pap. 13.95 (*0-452-26712-9*, Plume) NAL-Dutton.

Marcus, Greil, ed. see Bangs, Lester.

Marcus, Hans, jt. auth. see Beaumont, Ben.

Marcus, Harold, ed. see Sellassie, Haile.

***Marcus, Harold G.** Haile Sellassie I: The Formative Years, 1892-1936. LC 94-48486. 1995. 49.95 (*1-56902-007-8*); pap. 16.95 (*1-56902-008-6*) Red Sea Pr.

— A History of Ethiopia. LC 93-17987. 280p. 1993. 35.00 (*0-520-08121-8*) U CA Pr.

— A History of Ethiopia. 1995. pap. 13.95 (*0-520-20247-3*) U CA Pr.

— The Life & Times of Menelik II: Ethiopia 1844-1913. LC 94-48485. 1995. 49.95 (*1-56902-009-4*); pap. 16.95 (*1-56902-010-8*) Red Sea Pr.

— The Politics of Empire: Ethiopia, Great Britain & the United States, 1941-1974. LC 94-48479. 1995. 49.95 (*1-56902-005-1*); pap. 16.95 (*1-56902-006-X*) Red Sea Pr.

Marcus, Henry S. Intermodal Movement of Marine Containers. Date not set. 15.00 (*1-56172-007-0*) MIT Sea Grant.

— Marine Transportation Management. LC 86-22188. 352p. 1986. text ed. 59.95 (*0-86569-158-4*, Auburn Hse) Greenwood.

Marcus, Howard. Basketball Basics: Drills, Techniques & Strategies for Coaches. 160p. 1991. pap. 10.95 (*0-8092-3958-2*) Contemp Bks.

Marcus, I. Moshe's Adventures in Brachaland. (YA). 1990. 7.95 (*0-89906-990-8*) Mesorah Pubns.

Marcus, I. M., et al. An Interdisciplinary Approach to Accident Patterns in Children. (SRCD M: Vol. 25, No. 2). 1960. pap. 15.00 (*0-527-01584-9*) Periodicals Srv.

Marcus, Irene W. & Marcus, Paul. Into the Great Forest: A Story for Children Away from Parents for the First Time. LC 92-56871. (Books to Help Children Ser.). (Illus.). (J). 1993. lib. bdg. 17.27 (*0-8368-0932-7*) Gareth Stevens Inc.

M

— Into the Great Forest: A Story for Children Away from Parents for the First Time. LC 91-37636. (Illus.). 32p. (J). (ps-3). 1992. pap. 8.95 (*0-945354-40-1*) Magination Pr.

— Scary Night Visitors: A Story for Children with Bedtime Fears. LC 92-56874. (Books to Help Children Ser.). (J). 1993. lib. bdg. 17.27 (*0-8368-0935-1*) Gareth Stevens Inc.

— Scary Night Visitors: A Story for Children with Bedtime Fears. LC 90-41919. (Illus.). 32p. (J). (ps-2). 1990. 16.95 (*0-945354-26-6*); pap. 8.95 (*0-945354-25-8*) Magination Pr.

Marcus, Irving. The Portable Dictionary of Real Estate Terminology. 120p. 1983. pap. 11.95 (*0-8283-1739-9*) Branden Pub Co.

Marcus, Irving H. How to Test & Improve Your Wine Judging Ability. 2nd ed. (Illus.). 96p. (C). 1974. pap. 5.00 (*0-913840-28-9*) Wine Pubns.

Marcus, Irwin M. & Francis, John J., eds. Masturbation: From Infancy to Senescence. LC 73-16855. 634p. 1975. text ed. 55.00 (*0-8236-3150-8*) Intl Univs Pr.

Marcus, J. & Stauff, E. Radio Remote Control & Telemetry & Application to Missiles. LC 65-14225. 1966. 110.00 (*0-08-010136-4*, Pub. by Pergamon Repr UK) Franklin.

M

Marcus, Jacob R. The American Jewish Woman: A Documentary History. 1981. 45.00 (*0-87068-752-2*) Ktav.

— The Colonial American Jew, 1492-1776, Vols. I, II, & III. 1650p. 1994. reprint ed. text ed. 75.00 (*0-8143-1403-1*) Wayne St U Pr.

— Communal Sick-Care in the German Ghetto. 335p. 1978. reprint ed. pap. 11.95 (*0-87820-202-1*) Hebrew Union Coll Pr.

— An Introduction to Early American Jewish History. (Texts & Studies). (HEB.). 1971. 10.00 (*0-911934-09-X*) Am Jewish Hist Soc.

— Israel Jacobson: The Founder of the Reform Movement in Judaism. 167p. 1972. 10.00 (*0-87820-000-2*) Hebrew Union Coll Pr.

— The Jew in the Medieval World: A Source Book, 315-1791. LC 71-97295. 504p. 1975. reprint ed. text ed. 35.00 (*0-8371-2619-3*, MAJM, Greenwood Pr) Greenwood.

— The Jew in the Medieval World: A Source Book: 315-1791. 504p. 1990. reprint ed. pap. text ed. 12.95 (*0-87820-209-9*) Hebrew Union Coll Pr.

— Studies in American Jewish History. 225p. 1969. 15.00 (*0-87820-003-7*) Hebrew Union Coll Pr.

— This I Believe: Documents of American Jewish Life. LC 90-33814. 304p. 1990. 30.00 (*0-87668-782-6*) Aronson.

— To Count a People: American Jewish Population Data, 1585-1984. LC 89-22458. (Illus.). 274p. (C). 1990. lib. bdg. 52.50 (*0-8191-7583-8*) U Pr of Amer.

— United States Jewry, 1776-1985, Vol. I: The Sephardic Period. LC 89-5723. (Illus.). 852p. 1989. 49.95 (*0-8143-2186-0*) Wayne St U Pr.

— United States Jewry, 1776-1985, Vol. II: The Germanic Period, Pt. 1. LC 89-5723. (Illus.). 451p. 1990. text ed. 39.95 (*0-8143-2187-9*) Wayne St U Pr.

— United States Jewry 1776-1985, Vol. III: The Germanic Period, Pt. 2. LC 89-5723. (Illus.). 957p. 1993. text ed. 59.95 (*0-8143-2188-7*) Wayne St U Pr.

— United States Jewry, 1776-1985, Vol. IV: The East European Period, the Emergence of the American Jew, Epilogue. (Illus.). 952p. 1993. 64.95 (*0-8143-2189-5*) Wayne St U Pr.

Marcus, Jacob R., ed. The American Jewish Woman: 1654-1980. 1981. 19.95 (*0-87068-751-4*) Ktav.

— An Index to the Picture Collection of the American Jewish Archives. (Publications of the American Jewish Archives: No. 9). 90p. 1977. pap. 7.50 (*0-87820-005-3*) Hebrew Union Coll Pr.

— The Jew in the American World: A Source Book. 800p. 1995. text ed. 59.95x (*0-8143-2547-5*) Wayne St U Pr.

— The Jew in the American World: A Source Book. 800p. 1995. pap. text ed. 24.95x (*0-8143-2548-3*) Wayne St U Pr.

Marcus, Jacob R. & Daniels, Judith M., eds. The Concise Dictionary of American Jewish Biography. LC 94-20231. 750p. 1994. 200.00 (*0-926019-74-0*) Carlson Pub.

Marcus, Jacob R. & Peck, Abraham J. The American Rabbinate: A Century of Continuity & Change 1883-1983. 300p. 1985. text ed. 25.00 (*0-88125-076-7*) Ktav.

Marcus, Jacob R. & Peck, Abraham J., eds. Among the Survivors of the Holocaust - 1945: The Landsberg DP Camp Letters of Major Irving Heymount, United States Army. (Monographs of the American Jewish Archives: No. 10). 111p. 1982. pap. 7.95 (*0-87820-012-6*) Hebrew Union Coll Pr.

— Studies in the American Jewish Experience, Vol. I. 128p. 1981. pap. 10.00 (*0-87820-010-X*) Hebrew Union Coll Pr.

Marcus, Jacob R., jt. auth. see Katz, Irving I.

Marcus, James, tr. see Parise, Goffredo.

Marcus, James, tr. see Sciascia, Leonardo.

Marcus, Jane. Art & Anger: Reading Like a Woman. 320p. (C). 1988. pap. 21.50 (*0-8142-0460-0*) Ohio St U Pr.

— Virginia Woolf & the Languages of Patriarchy. LC 86-45470. 240p. 1987. pap. 10.95 (*0-253-20410-0*, MB-410) Ind U Pr.

Marcus, Jane, ed. New Feminist Essays on Virginia Woolf. LC 80-51823. xx, 272p. 1981. 30.00 (*0-8032-3070-2*) U of Nebr Pr.

— Virginia Woolf: A Feminist Slant. LC 82-24787. 296p. reprint ed. pap. 84.40 (*0-8357-4129-X*, 2057064) Bks Demand.

Marcus, Jane, intro. The Young Rebecca: Writings of Rebecca West, 1911-17. LC 89-31300. 416p. 1989. pap. 12.95 (*0-253-23101-9*) Ind U Pr.

Marcus, Jay B. Success from Within: Discovering the Inner State That Creates Personal Fulfillment & Business Success. LC 90-62354. (Illus.). 200p. 1990. pap. 11.95 (*0-923569-04-9*) Maharishi Intl U Pr.

Marcus, Jerry. Abraham, Isaac, Jacob & Zev. LC 81-70363. 225p. 1982. 13.95 (*0-941394-00-X*) Brittany Pubns.

— The Salvation Peddler. LC 87-71614. 235p. 1988. 15.95 (*0-941394-01-8*) Brittany Pubns.

Marcus, Joanna. A Few Days in Endel. large type ed. 317p. 1980. 12.00 (*0-7089-0468-8*) Ulverscroft.

Marcus, Joel. The Mystery of the Kingdom of God. (Society of Biblical Literature Dissertation Ser.). 270p. (C). 1986. pap. 14.95 (*0-89130-984-5*) Scholars Pr GA.

— The Way of the Lord: Christological Exegesis of the Old Testament in the Gospel of Mark. 256p. 1992. text ed. 25.00 (*0-664-21949-7*) Westminster John Knox.

Marcus, John. The Complete Job Interview Handbook. 163p. 7.95 (*0-318-41634-4*, 216) Am Bartenders.

Marcus, John J. The Complete Job Interview Handbook. 3rd ed. 192p. 1994. pap. 10.00 (*0-06-273266-8*, Harper Ref) HarpC.

Marcus, John T. Sub Specie Historiae: Essays in the Manifestations of Historical & Moral Consciousness. LC 76-50285. 328p. 1980. 40.00 (*0-8386-2057-4*) Fairleigh Dickinson.

***Marcus, Jonathan.** The National Front & French Politics: The Resistible Rise of Jean-Marie Le Pen. LC 95-12259. 1995. pap. write for info. (*0-8147-5535-6*) NYU Pr.

— The National Front & French Politics: The Resistible Rise of Jean-Marie Le Pen. LC 95-12259. 256p. 1995. 45.00 (*0-8147-5534-8*) NYU Pr.

Marcus, Joseph. The Newly Discovered Original Hebrew of Ben Sira (Ecclesiasticus xxxii, 16-xxxiv, 1) The Fifth Manuscript & a Prosodic Version of Ben Sira (Ecclesiasticus xxii, 22-xxiii, 9) 28p. 1931. 10.00 (*0-685-70562-5*, Ctr Judaic Studies) Eisenbrauns.

— Social & Political History of the Jews in Poland, 1919-1939. LC 82-22420. (New Babylon Studies in the Social Sciences: No. 37). xviii, 569p. 1983. 115.40 (*90-279-3239-5*) Mouton.

Marcus, Joseph, ed. Growing up in Groups: The Russian Day Care Center & the Israeli Kibbutz. (Illus.). 318p. 1972. text ed. 87.00 (*0-677-04800-9*) Gordon & Breach.

Marcus, Joyce. Emblem & State in the Classic Maya Lowlands: An Epigraphic Approach to Territorial Organization. LC 76-5213. (Illus.). 203p. 1976. 20.00 (*0-88402-066-5*) Dumbarton Oaks.

— The Inscriptions at Calakmul. (Technical Reports: No. 21). (Orig.). 1987. pap. 8.00 (*0-915703-15-7*) U Mich Mus Anthro.

— Late Intermediate Occupation at Cerro Azul, Peru. (Technical Reports: No. 20). xvi, 112p. (Orig.). 1987. pap. 8.00 (*0-915703-12-2*) U Mich Mus Anthro.

— Mesoamerican Writing Systems: Propaganda, Myth, & History in Four Ancient Civilizations. LC 92-9091. (Illus.). 550p. 1992. text ed. 55.00 (*0-691-09474-8*) Princeton U Pr.

Marcus, Joyce, ed. Debating Oaxaca Archaeology. LC 90-42333. (Anthropological Papers: No. 84). (Illus.). x, 270p. (Orig.). 1990. pap. 18.00 (*0-915703-22-X*) U Mich Mus Anthro.

***Marcus, Joyce & Zeitlin, Judith F., eds.** Caciques & Their People: A Volume in Honor of Ronald Spores. LC 94-34805. (Anthropological Papers:Museum of Anthropology: No. 89). 1995. write for info. (*0-915703-37-8*) U Mich Mus Anthro.

Marcus, Joyce, ed. see De Diez Canseco, Maria R.

Marcus, Joyce, jt. auth. see Flannery, Kent V.

Marcus, Joyce, jt. ed. see Flannery, Kent V.

Marcus, Joyce, ed. see Hodge, Mary G.

Marcus, Joyce, ed. see Hopkins, Joseph W., III.

Marcus, Judith. Georg Lukacs & Thomas Mann: A Study in Sociology of Literature. LC 92-27069. (C). 1994. reprint ed. pap. 15.00 (*0-391-03787-0*) Humanities.

— Georg Lukacs & Thomas Mann: A Study in the Sociology of Literature. LC 86-1261. 208p. 1988. lib. bdg. 27.50 (*0-87023-486-2*) U of Mass Pr.

Marcus, Judith & Tar, Zoltan, eds. Foundations of the Frankfurt School of Social Research. 384p. 1984. pap. 21.95x (*0-87855-963-9*) Transaction Pubs.

Marcus, Judith & Tarr, Zoltan, eds. Georg Lukacs: Theory, Culture, & Politics. 224p. 1989. 39.95 (*0-88738-244-4*) Transaction Pubs.

Marcus, Judith, ed. see Lukacs, Georg.

Marcus, Julie. A World of Difference: Islam & Gender Hierarchy in Turkey. LC 92-29104. 208p. (C). 1992. text ed. 49.95 (*1-85649-185-4*, Pub. by Zed Books UK); pap. 17.50 (*1-85649-186-2*, Pub. by Zed Books UK) Humanities.

Marcus, Julie, ed. Women in Anthropology. 1992. pap. 24.95 (*0-522-84466-9*) Intl Spec Bk.

Marcus, Kenneth K. The National Government & the Natural Gas Industry, 1946-56: A Study in the Making of a National Policy. Bruchey, Stuart, ed. LC 78-22697. (Energy in the American Economy Ser.). (Illus.). 1979. lib. bdg. 91.95 (*0-405-12000-1*) Ayer.

Marcus, Laura. Auto-Biographical Discourses: Theory, Criticism, Practice. LC 93-47153. 1994. text ed. 79.95 (*0-7190-3642-9*, Pub. by Manchester Univ Pr UK) St Martin.

— Virginia Woolf. 1990. 40.00 (*0-7463-0721-7*, Pub. by Northcote House UK) St Mut.

— Virginia Woolfe. (Writers & Their Work Ser.). 96p. (Orig.). 1994. pap. text ed. 11.50 (*0-7463-0726-8*, Pub. by Northcote House UK) Trans-Atl Phila.

Marcus, Laura & Nead, Linda, eds. The Actuality of Walter Benjamin. (New Formations Ser.: No. 20). 176p. (C). 1993. pap. 19.95 (*0-85315-761-8*, Pub. by Lawrence & Wishart UK) Humanities.

Marcus, Laura, ed. see Lowndes, Marie B.

Marcus, Laurence R., jt. auth. see Johnson, Janet R.

Marcus, Laurence R., jt. auth. see Stickney, Benjamin D.

Marcus, Laurence R., et al. The Path to Excellence: Quality Assurance in Higher Education. Fife, Jonathan D., ed. LC 83-146405. (ASHE-ERIC Higher Education Report Ser.: No. 1, 1983). 68p. (Orig.). 1983. pap. 7.50 (*0-913317-00-4*) GWU Schl E&HD.

Marcus, Laurie R., ed. see Scott, Carlton T.

Marcus, Leah S. The Politics of Mirth: Jonson, Herrick, Milton, Marvell, & the Defense of Old Holiday Pastimes. LC 86-7133. (Illus.). 328p. (C). 1987. 29.00 (*0-226-50451-4*) U Ch Pr.

— The Politics of Mirth: Jonson, Herrick, Milton, Marvell, & the Defense of Old Holiday Pastimes. LC 86-7133. (Illus.). 328p. (C). 1989. pap. text ed. 15.95 (*0-226-50452-2*) U Ch Pr.

— Puzzling Shakespeare: Local Reading & Its Discontents. (New Historicism Ser.: No. 6). (Illus.). 280p. 1989. 45.00 (*0-685-30558-9*); pap. 13.00 (*0-520-07191-3*) U CA Pr.

***Marcus, Leonard, et al.** Renegotiating Health Care: Resolving Conflicts to Build Collaboration. (Health Ser.). 1995. 32.95 (*0-7879-0151-2*) Jossey-Bass.

Marcus, Leonard C. Veterinary Biology & Medicine of Captive Amphibians & Reptiles. LC 80-24859. 251p. reprint ed. pap. 71.60 (*0-685-20937-7*, 2056518) Bks Demand.

Marcus, Leonard S. Margaret Wise Brown: Awakened by the Moon. LC 91-17305. (Illus.). 352p. 1992. 25.00 (*0-8070-7048-3*) Beacon Pr.

— Margaret Wise Brown: Awakened by the Moon. (Illus.). 364p. 1994. pap. 15.00 (*0-8070-7049-1*) Beacon Pr.

— Petrouchka: A Ballet Cut-Out Book. (Illus.). 16p. (J). (gr. 3-6). 1983. pap. 12.95 (*0-87923-469-5*) Godine.

Marcus, Leonard S., intro. Seventy-Five Years of Children Book Week Posters. (Illus.). (J). (ps up). 1994. 30.00 (*0-679-85106-2*) Knopf Bks Yng Read.

Marcus, Leonard S., sel. Lifelines: A Poetry Anthology Patterned on the Stages of Life. LC 93-26413. 112p. (YA). (gr. 6 up). 1994. 15.99 (*0-525-45164-1*, DCB) Dutton Child Bks.

Marcus, Linda. Our Days in the Garden. (Illus.). 72p. (Orig.). (C). 1989. pap. 9.95 (*0-317-93848-7*) L Marcus Unlimited.

Marcus, Lloyd E. Agape: A Solution for World Peace. 48p. 1993. pap. 5.95 (*0-8059-3408-1*) Dorrance.

Marcus, Lois, jt. auth. see Dorman, Ruth.

Marcus, M. E-Radial Processes & Random Fourier Series. LC 87-12569. (MEMO Ser.: No. 68/368). 181p. 1987. pap. text ed. 25.00 (*0-8218-2432-5*, MEMO 68/368) Am Math.

Marcus, M., ed. see Eberlein, Ernst, et al.

Marcus, M. B. Geometrical & Statistical Aspects of Probability in Banach Spaces. Fernique, X. et al, eds. (Lecture Notes in Mathematics Ser.: Vol. 1193). iv, 128p. 1986. pap. 20.00 (*0-387-16487-1*) Spr-Verlag.

Marcus, Maeva. The Documentary History of the Supreme Court of the United States, 1789-1800, Vol. 3: The Justices on Circuit, 1795-1800. 1990. text ed. 79.00 (*0-231-08870-1*) Col U Pr.

— Truman & the Steel Seizure Case: The Limits of Presidential Power. LC 93-43419. (Constitutional Conflicts Ser.). 424p. 1994. pap. text ed. 17.95 (*0-8223-1417-7*) Duke.

Marcus, Maeva, ed. The Documentary History of the Supreme Court of the United States, 1789-1800, Vol. IV: Organizing the Federal Judiciary Legislation & Commentaries. 832p. 1992. text ed. 75.00 (*0-231-08871-X*) Col U Pr.

— Origins of the Federal Judiciary: Essays on the Judiciary Act of 1789. (Illus.). 288p. 1992. 39.95 (*0-19-506721-5*, 1528) OUP.

***Marcus, Maeva, et al, eds.** The Documentary History of the Supreme Court of the United States, 1789-1800 Vol. 5: Suits Against the States. LC 85-3794. 686p. 1995. 125.00 (*0-231-08872-8*) Col U Pr.

— The Documentary History of the Supreme Court of the United States, 1789-1800, Vol. 2: The Justices on Circuit, 1790-1794. 550p. 1989. text ed. 99.50 (*0-231-08869-8*) Col U Pr.

Marcus, Marvin. Matrices & Matlab: A Tutorial. 736p. 1992. text ed. 61.00 (*0-13-562901-2*) P-H.

— Paragons of the Ordinary: The Biographical Literature of Mori Ogai. LC 92-26583. (SHAPS Library of Asian Studies). 1993. text ed. 45.00 (*0-8248-1450-9*) UH Pr.

— A Survey of Finite Mathematics. LC 92-43550. (Illus.). 496p. 1993. reprint ed. pap. 12.95 (*0-486-67553-X*) Dover.

Marcus, Marvin, ed. Introduction to Modern Algebra. (Pure & Applied Mathematics Ser.: Vol. 47). 504p. 1978. 130.00 (*0-8247-6479-X*) Dekker.

Marcus, Marvin & Minc, Henryk. Introduction to Linear Algebra. 288p. 1988. reprint ed. pap. text ed. 7.95 (*0-486-65695-0*) Dover.

— A Survey of Matrix Theory & Matrix Inequalities. 192p. 1992. reprint ed. pap. 6.95 (*0-486-67102-X*) Dover.

Marcus, Melvin L., et al. Cardiac Imaging: A Companion to Braunwald's Heart Disease. (Illus.). 1344p. 1990. text ed. 138.00 (*0-7216-5862-8*) Saunders.

Marcus, Michael. Landlord-Tenant Rights in Oregon. 4th ed. (Legal Ser.). 304p. 1992. 12.95 (*0-88908-833-0*) Self-Counsel Pr.

— Trial Preparation for Prosecutors. (Trial Practice Library). 1989. text ed. 125.00 (*0-471-84895-6*) Wiley.

Marcus, Michael B. & Pisier, Gilles. Random Fourier Series with Application to Harmonic Analysis. LC 81-47145. (Annals of Mathematics Studies: No.101). 192p. 1981. 35.00x (*0-691-08289-8*); pap. 14.95 (*0-691-08292-8*) Princeton U Pr.

Marcus, Michelle I. Emblems of Identity & Prestige: The Seals & Sealings from Hasanlu, Iran : Commentary & Catalog. LC 94-15048. (Hansanlu Special Studies: Vol. 3). 1995. write for info. (*0-924171-26-X*) U PA Mus Pubns.

Marcus, Mildred R., jt. auth. see Marcus, Edward.

Marcus, Millicent. An Allegory of Form: Literary Self-Consciousness in the "Decameron" (Stanford French & Italian Studies: No. 18). viii, 136p. 1979. pap. 46.50 (*0-915838-21-4*) Anma Libri.

— Filmmaking by the Book: Italian Cinema & Literary Adaptation. (Illus.). 384p. 1993. text ed. 48.50 (*0-8018-4454-1*); pap. text ed. 15.95 (*0-8018-4455-X*) Johns Hopkins.

— Italian Film in the Light of Neorealism. 480p. 1987. pap. text ed. 22.95 (*0-691-10208-2*) Princeton U Pr.

Marcus, Mordecai. Assistant Notes. 1972. pap. 4.50 (*0-8220-0214-0*) Cliffs.

— Emily Dickinson: Selected Poem Notes. 102p. (Orig.). (C). 1982. pap. text ed. 3.95 (*0-8220-0432-1*) Cliffs.

— Poems of Robert Frost: An Explication. 288p. (C). 1991. text ed. 35.00 (*0-8161-7267-6*, Hall Reference) Macmillan.

Marcus, Morton. The Armies Encamped in the Fields Beyond the Unfinished Avenues: Prose Poems. enl. ed. (Illus.). 80p. (C). 1988. reprint ed. pap. 5.95 (*0-9621321-0-1*) Brown Bear.

— Big Winds, Glass Mornings, Shadows Cast by Stars: Poems: 1972-1980. 3rd ed. 80p. 1988. reprint ed. pap. 5.95 (*0-9621321-1-X*) Brown Bear.

— Origins. (Illus.). (Orig.). 1973. pap. 8.00 (*0-87711-045-X*) Story Line.

— Origins. 3rd ed. (Illus.). 80p. (Orig.). 1988. reprint ed. pap. 2.95 (*0-9621321-2-8*) Brown Bear.

— Pages from a Scrapbook of Immigrants. LC 88-30234. 130p. (Orig.). 1988. pap. 8.95 (*0-918273-47-1*) Coffee Hse.

— The Santa Cruz Mountain Poems. 2nd ed. (Illus.). 72p. reprint ed. pap. 12.95 (*0-932319-03-3*) Capitola Bk.

Marcus, Moshe & Mizel, Victor. Limiting Equations for Problems Involving Long Range Memory. LC 83-3752. (Memoirs of the American Mathematical Society Ser.: No. 43/278). 64p. 1983. pap. 17.00 (*0-8218-2278-0*, MEMO 43/278) Am Math.

Marcus, Naomi, tr. see Tamarov, Vladislav.

Marcus, Neiman. Pure & Simple: An Incircle Cookbook. 1993. 19.95 (*0-15-175122-6*) HarBrace.

Marcus, Norman. Broadcast & Cable Management. 368p. (C). 1986. text ed. 44.00 (*0-13-083577-3*) P-H.

Marcus, P., et al, eds. Modifications of Passive Films: Papers Presented at the European Symposium on Modifications of Passive Films. (European Federation of Corrosion Publications Ser.: No. 12). 345p. 1993. pap. 140.00 (*0-901716-52-9*, Pub. by Inst Materials UK) Ashgate Pub Co.

Marcus, Paul. The Entrapment Defense: With 1992 Cumulative Supplement. 762p. 1989. 85.00 (*0-87473-432-0*) Michie Butterworth.

— Prosecution & Defense of Criminal Conspiracy Cases. 1978. Updates. ring bd. write for info. (*0-8205-1365-2*) Bender.

— Thorsons Introductory Guide to Acupuncture: A Patient's Guide. (Illus.). 1992. pap. 6.95 (*0-7225-2531-1*) Thorsons SF.

Marcus, Paul & Rosenberg, Alan, eds. Healing Their Wounds: Psychotherapy with Holocaust Survivors & Their Families. LC 89-8638. 320p. 1989. text ed. 55.00 (*0-275-92948-5*, C2948, Praeger Pubs) Greenwood.

Marcus, Paul, jt. auth. see Luel, Steven.

Marcus, Paul, jt. auth. see Marcus, Irene W.

Marcus, Philip L., jt. ed. see Balbert, Peter.

Marcus, Phillip L. Standish O'Grady. LC 74-124647. (Irish Writers Ser.). 92p. 1975. 8.50 (*0-8387-7751-1*); pap. 1.95 (*0-8387-7660-4*) Bucknell U Pr.

— Yeats & Artistic Power. 320p. (C). 1992. text ed. 45.00 (*0-8147-5471-6*) NYU Pr.

— Yeats & the Beginning of the Irish Renaissance. 2nd ed. LC 86-22969. (Irish Studies). 336p. 1987. reprint ed. pap. text ed. 14.95 (*0-8156-2398-4*) Syracuse U Pr.

Marcus, Phillip L., ed. see Yeats, William Butler.

Marcus, R. Psychosis & Near Psychosis: Ego Function, Symbol Structure & Treatment. 328p. 1993. 69.00 (*0-387-97765-1*) Spr-Verlag.

Marcus, R. D., et al. Pneumatic Conveying of Solids. 528p. 1990. 99.95 (*0-412-21490-3*, 6647) Chapman & Hall.

Marcus, R. Kenneth, ed. Glow Discharge Spectroscopies. LC 93-10300. (Modern Analytical Chemistry Ser.). 514p. 1993. 95.00 (*0-306-44396-1*, Plenum Pr) Plenum.

Marcus, Ralph. Law in the Apocrypha. LC 29-9822. (Columbia University. Oriental Studies: No. 26). reprint ed. 15.00 (*0-404-50516-3*) AMS Pr.

Marcus, Randall E. Orthopaedics: Problems in Primary Care. Karaffa, Melanie C., ed. (Illus.). 400p. (C). 1991. text ed. 49.95 (*1-878487-33-7*) Practice Mgmt Info.

Marcus, Richard, ed. Digital Video 3. rev. ed. (Illus.). 230p. (Orig.). 1982. reprint ed. pap. text ed. 25.00 (*0-940690-04-7*) Soc Motion Pic & TV Engrs.

***Marcus, Richard L., et al.** Civil Procedure: A Modern Approach. 2nd ed. (American Casebook Ser.). 1177p. (C). 1995. text ed. 51.00 (*0-314-06105-3*) West Pub.

— Civil Procedure, a Modern Approach, Teacher's Manual For. 2nd ed. (American Casebook Ser.). 450p. (C). 1995. pap. text ed. write for info. (*0-314-06902-X*) West Pub.

Marcus, Richard L. Civil Procedure, a Modern Approach, 1994. suppl. ed. 200p. 1994. pap. text ed. 12.00 (*0-314-04320-9*) West Pub.

— Family & Medical Leave: Policies & Procedures. LC 94-13466. (Employee Benefits Library). 1994. text ed. 75.00 (*0-471-04195-5*) Wiley.

An Asterisk (*) at the beginning of an entry indicates that the title is appearing in BIP for the first time.

Marcus, Richard L. & Sherman, Edward F. Complex Litigation, Cases & Materials on Advanced Civil Procedure: Teacher's Manual. 2nd ed. (American Casebook Ser.). 1026p. (C). 1993. reprint ed. text ed. 51.50 (*0-314-00769-5*); reprint ed. pap. text ed. write for info. (*0-314-01192-7*) West Pub.

Marcus, Richard L., et al. Civil Procedure: A Modern Approach, 1991 Supplement. (American Casebook Ser.). 151p. (C). 1993. reprint ed. pap. text ed. 11.00 (*0-314-88748-2*) West Pub.

— Civil Procedure, Cases & Materials. (American Casebook Ser.). 1027p. 1992. reprint ed. text ed. 46.00 (*0-314-49349-2*) West Pub.

— A Modern Approach, Teacher's Manual to Accompany Civil Procedure. (American Casebook Ser.). 342p. 1989. pap. text ed. write for info. (*0-314-54545-X*) West Pub.

Marcus, Robert. Encyclopedia of Florida. (Encyclopedia of the United States Ser.). 600p. 1985. reprint ed. lib. bdg. 79.00 (*0-403-09979-X*) Somerset Pub.

— Osteoporosis. (Illus.). 352p. 1994. 8.00 (*0-86542-266-4*) Blackwell Sci.

Marcus, Robert, ed. American Voices: Readings in History & Literature, 2 vols., Set. (Illus.). (C). 1992. reprint ed. Net. pap. text ed. 10.36 (*0-685-61616-9*) Brandywine Press.

— American Voices: Readings in History & Literature, Vol. I. (Illus.). (C). 1992. reprint ed. Vol. 1, 385p. pap. write for info. (*1-881089-04-5*) Brandywine Press.

— American Voices: Readings in History & Literature, Vol. 2. (Illus.). (C). 1992. reprint ed. pap. write for info. (*1-881089-05-3*) Brandywine Press.

*__Marcus, Robert D. & Burner, David.__ America Firsthand: From Settlement to Reconstruction. 3rd ed. 292p. (C). 1994. pap. text ed. 24.66 (*0-312-10162-7*); pap. text ed. 19.95 (*0-312-10163-5*) St Martin.

Marcus, Robert D. & Burner, David, eds. American Scene: Varieties of American History, 2 vols. LC 73-136426. (Orig.). (C). 1971. teacher ed write for info. (*0-89197-020-7*); Vol. 1 Colonial Period To 1877. pap. text ed. 11.95 (*0-89197-018-5*); Vol. 2 Since 1865. pap. text ed. 11.95 (*0-8290-1409-8*); pap. text ed. 9.95 (*0-89197-019-3*) Irvington.

Marcus, Robert H., ed. see Stine, Robert J.

*__Marcus, Ronald.__ Stamford Connecticut - a Bibliography: An Annotated, xxii, 284p. (Orig.). 1995. pap. 49.95 (*1-886054-13-4*) Stamford Hist Soc.

Marcus, Rudolphy A. Theories of Chemical Reactions Rates. (Twentieth Century Chemistry Ser.). 400p. 1997. text ed. 109.00 (*981-02-1505-3*); pap. text ed. 53.00 (*981-02-1506-1*) World Scientific Pub.

Marcus, Rudy. Intersection: Journal of the Guild for Psychological Studies, Vol. I. 110p. (Orig.). (C). 1993. pap. text ed. 9.95 (*0-917479-16-5*) Guild Psy.

Marcus, Russell. English-Lao, Lao-English Dictionary. rev. ed. LC 77-116487. 416p. (ENG & LAO.). 1970. pap. 16.95 (*0-8048-0909-7*) C E Tuttle.

— Forms of Man: The Buddhist Vision of Thawan Duchanee. (Illus.). 76p. 1975. pap. 12.00 (*0-916020-01-0*) Books Marcus.

Marcus, Russell, ed. Lao Proverbs. Phengsy, Novanta, tr. (Illus.). 56p. 1969. pap. 6.00 (*0-916020-00-2*) Books Marcus.

Marcus, Ruth B. Modalities: Philosophical Essays. 288p. 1993. 45.00 (*0-19-507698-2*) OUP.

— Modalities: Philosophical Essays. 288p. 1995. pap. 19.95 (*0-19-509657-6*) OUP.

Marcus, Ruth E., ed. see Bauer, Lawrence M., III.

Marcus, Ruth E., ed. see Bodian, Nat G. & Luedtke, Robert.

Marcus, S. T., et al. Experimental General Chemistry. 448p. (C). 1988. pap. text ed. write for info. (*0-07-054420-4*) McGraw.

Marcus, Samuel H. Basics of Structural Steel Design. 2nd ed. 480p. 1981. write for info. (*0-8359-0420-2*, Reston) P-H.

Marcus, Sander I., jt. auth. see Mandel, Harvey P.

Marcus, Sandra, ed. Knowledge Acquisition: Selected Research & Commentary. (C). 1990. lib. bdg. 55.50 (*0-7923-9062-8*) Kluwer Ac.

Marcus, Sherman J. The Bilingual Puzzle Book: Rompecabezas Para Personas Bilingues. 143p. (Orig.). 1986. pap. 4.95 (*0-9610444-2-X*) Cambita Bks.

— The Veterinarian's Puzzle Book: Continuing Education the Fun Way. 140p. (Orig.). 1983. pap. 4.95 (*0-9610444-0-3*) Cambita Bks.

Marcus, Stanley. David Smith: The Sculptor & His Work. LC 83-45148. (Illus.). 208p. 1983. 39.95 (*0-8014-1510-1*) Cornell U Pr.

— The Viewpoints of Stanley Marcus: A Ten-Year Perspective. 400p. 1995. 24.95 (*0-929398-86-6*) UNTX Pr.

Marcus, Steve, jt. auth. see Dornbusch, Rudiger.

Marcus, Steven. Engels, Manchester, & the Working Class. 288p. 1985. reprint ed. pap. 8.95 (*0-393-30237-7*) Norton.

— Freud & the Culture of Psychoanalysis: Studies in the Transition from Victorian Humanism to Modernity. 280p. 1987. reprint ed. pap. 7.95 (*0-393-30410-8*) Norton.

— Representations: Essays on Literature & Society. 384p. 1990. text ed. 42.00 (*0-231-07400-X*); pap. text ed. 16.50 (*0-231-07401-8*) Col U Pr.

Marcus, Steven, ed. see Esman, Aaron H.

Marcus, Steven E., jt. auth. see Seiderman, Arthur S.

Marcus, Susan A. & McDonald, Penny. Tools for the Cooperative Classroom. (Illus.). 128p. (Orig.). 1990. pap. text ed. 19.95 (*0-932935-27-3*) IRI-Skylght.

*__Marcus, Sybil.__ A World of Fiction: Twenty Timeless Short Stories. LC 94-31206. 1995. pap. write for info. (*0-201-82520-1*) Addison-Wesley.

Marcus, Tessa. Modernizing Super-Exploitation: Restructuring South African Agriculture. LC 89-5835. 256p. (C). 1989. text ed. 55.00 (*0-86232-844-6*, Pub. by Zed Books UK); pap. 19.95 (*0-86232-845-4*, Pub. by Zed Books UK) Humanities.

Marcus, W., jt. auth. see Marcus, Abraham.

Marcus, Walz. Molekulare Analysen zur Expression von Beta-Lactam-Genen bei Acremonium Chrysogenum. (Bibliotheca Mycologica Ser.: Vol. 147). (Illus.). 101p. (GER.). 1992. pap. text ed. 47.00 (*3-443-59048-9*, Pub. by Cramer-Borntraeger GW) Lubrecht & Cramer.

Marcus, Y. & Ben-Dor, L., eds. International Congress of Pure & Applied Chemistry, 25th, Jerusalem, 1975: Proceedings. 1977. 41.00 (*0-08-020952-1*, Pub. by Pergamon Repr UK) Franklin.

Marcus, Y., jt. ed. see Kertes, A. S.

Marcus, Yizhak. Introduction to Liquid State Chemistry. LC 76-40230. 375p. reprint ed. pap. 106.90 (*0-685-20596-7*, 2030530) Bks Demand.

— Ion Solvation. LC 85-6436. (Illus.). 314p. reprint ed. pap. 89.50 (*0-7837-4392-0*, 2044132) Bks Demand.

Marcus, Yizhak, jt. ed. see Marinsky, Jacob A.

Marcuse, Aida, tr. Lizard's Song. (Books in Spanish). (Illus.). 32p. (SPA.). (J). (ps up). 1994. reprint ed. pap. 4.95 (*0-688-13201-4*, Mulberry) Morrow.

Marcuse, Aida, tr. see Cowcher, Helen.

Marcuse, Aida, tr. see Dr. Seuss.

Marcuse, Aida, tr. see Hutchins, Pat.

Marcuse, Aida, tr. see Joyce, Susan.

Marcuse, Aida, tr. see Kalan, Robert.

Marcuse, Aida, tr. see Kellogg, Steven.

Marcuse, Aida, tr. see Maestro, Betsy & Maestro, Giulio.

Marcuse, Aida, tr. see Perrault, Charles.

Marcuse, Aida, tr. see Potter, Beatrix.

Marcuse, Aida, tr. see Singer, Isaac Bashevis.

Marcuse, Aida, tr. see Singer, Marilyn.

Marcuse, Aida, tr. see William, Vera B.

Marcuse, Aida, tr. see Williams, Vera B.

Marcuse, Aida, tr. see Williams, Vera.

Marcuse, Aida, tr. see Zemach, Margot.

Marcuse, Aida D., tr. see Conlon, Laura.

Marcuse, Aida E. Caperucita Roja y la Luna de Papel. (Illus.). 24p. (Orig.). (SPA.). (J). (gr. k-6). 1993. lib. bdg. 7.50 (*1-56492-103-4*) Laredo.

Marcuse, Aida E., tr. see Brown, Margaret W.

Marcuse, Aida E., tr. see Castaneda, Omar S.

Marcuse, Aida E., tr. see Coerr, Eleanor.

Marcuse, Aida E., tr. see Conlon, Laura.

Marcuse, Aida E., tr. see Dr. Seuss.

Marcuse, Aida E., tr. see Hallinan, P. K.

Marcuse, Aida E., tr. see McCall, Barbara A.

Marcuse, Dietrich. Principles of Optical Fiber Measurements. LC 80-2339. 1981. text ed. 79.00 (*0-12-470980-X*) Acad Pr.

— Principles of Quantum Electronics. LC 79-8857. 1980. text ed. 85.00 (*0-12-471050-6*) Acad Pr.

— Theory of Dielectric Optical Waveguides. 2nd ed. (Quantum Electronics Ser.). (Illus.). 380p. 1991. text ed. 69.95 (*0-12-470951-6*) Acad Pr.

Marcuse, Gary, jt. auth. see Whitaker, Reg.

Marcuse, Herbert. The Aesthetic Dimension: Toward a Critique of Marxist Aesthetics. LC 76-9001. 1978. reprint ed. pap. 12.00 (*0-8070-1519-9*, BPA17) Beacon Pr.

— Counterrevolution & Revolt. LC 79-179150. 140p. 1972. reprint ed. pap. 12.00 (*0-8070-1533-4*, BPA23) Beacon Pr.

— Eros & Civilization: A Philosophical Inquiry into Freud. LC 66-3219. 320p. 1974. reprint ed. pap. 15.00 (*0-8070-1555-5*, BP496) Beacon Pr.

— Essay on Liberation. LC 69-15591. 1969. reprint ed. pap. 12.00x (*0-8070-0595-9*) Beacon Pr.

— From Luther to Popper. De Pres, Joris, tr. 227p. 1983. pap. text ed. 15.95 (*0-86091-781-9*, Pub. by Verso UK) Routledge Chapman & Hall.

— Hegel's Ontology & the Theory of Historicity. 350p. 1987. 37.50 (*0-262-13221-4*) MIT Pr.

— One-Dimensional Man: Studies in the Ideology of Advanced Industrial Society. LC 91-18246. 320p. 1992. pap. 15.00 (*0-8070-1417-6*) Beacon Pr.

— Reason & Revolution: Hegel & the Rise of Social Theory. 2nd ed. LC 89-35982. (Humanities Paperback Library). 456p. (C). 1991. reprint ed. pap. 18.50 (*0-391-02999-1*) Humanities.

— Soviet Marxism: A Critical Analysis. LC 57-10943. 271p. 1985. pap. text ed. 17.00 (*0-231-08379-3*) Col U Pr.

Marcuse, Herbert & Popper, Karl. Revolution or Reform: A Confrontation. LC 75-12192. (Studies in Ethics & Society Ser.: Vol. 2). Orig. Title: Revolution oder Reform. 120p. 1976. 16.95 (*0-89044-020-4*) Transaction Pubs.

Marcuse, Joel. Domestic Enemies. abr. ed. 298p. 1994. pap. 9.95 (*1-56901-303-9*) NW Pub.

Marcuse, Maxwell F. Tin Pan Alley in Gaslight. LC 58-59691. (Illus.). 1959. pap. 7.00 (*0-87282-084-X*) Am Life Foun.

Marcuse, Michael. Reference Guide for English Studies. 1990. 120.00 (*0-520-05161-0*); pap. 40.00 (*0-520-07992-2*) U CA Pr.

Marcussen, A. Jan. National Sunday Law. 94p. (Orig.). 1989. pap. 1.50 (*0-912145-03-X*) MMI Pr.

— National Sunday Law. rev. ed. (Illus.). 97p. (Orig.). 1986. reprint ed. pap. 1.50 (*0-912145-08-0*, 9600-1001) MMI Pr.

Marcussen, Henrik S. & Torp, Jens E. The Internationalization of Capital. 192p. (C). 1982. pap. 17.50 (*0-905762-77-0*, Pub. by Zed Books UK) Humanities.

Marcussen, Henrik S., jt. ed. see Van Dijk, Meine P.

Marcussen, Lars. Third World Housing in Social & Spatial Development: The Case of Jakarta Housing in Social & Spatial Development. 205p. 1990. text ed. 68.95 (*1-85628-085-3*, Pub. by Avebury Pub UK) Ashgate Pub Co.

Marcusson, Pat. The Beartooth Fishing Guide. LC 85-80382. (Falcon Guide Ser.). (Illus.). 144p. (Orig.). 1985. pap. 7.95 (*0-934318-33-6*) Falcon Pr MT.

Marcuvitz, N., et al, eds. Waveguide Handbook. (Electromagnetic Waves Ser.). 446p. 1986. boxed 82.00 (*0-86341-058-8*, EW021) Inst Elect Eng.

Marcuvitz, Nathan, jt. auth. see Felsen, Leopold B.

Marcuzzi, G. European Ecosystems. (Biogeographica Ser.: Vol. 15). 1979. lib. bdg. 307.50 (*90-6193-216-5*) Kluwer Ac.

Marcuzzo, Maria C. & Rosselli, Annalisa. Ricardo & the Gold Standard: The Foundations of the International Money Order. 180p. 1991. text ed. 65.00 (*0-312-05327-4*) St Martin.

Marcy, Carl. Presidential Commissions. LC 72-8109. (Studies in American History & Government). 156p. 1973. reprint ed. lib. bdg. 25.00 (*0-306-70532-X*) Da Capo.

Marcy, Carl, et al, eds. Common Sense in U. S. - Soviet Trade. 1983. pap. 5.00 (*0-318-00157-8*) Am Comm US Soviet.

Marcy, Joseph H., jt. ed. see Cook, D. Ryan.

Marcy, Michel, jt. auth. see Nutting, Teresa.

Marcy, Randolph B. Prairie Traveler. (Illus.). 356p. 1968. reprint ed. 25.00 (*0-87928-001-8*) Corner Hse.

— The Prairie Traveler. 256p. 1988. reprint ed. pap. 10.95 (*0-918222-89-3*) Applewood.

Marcy, Sam. Anatomy of the Economic Crisis. 120p. 1982. pap. 3.25 (*0-89567-077-1*) World View Forum.

— The Bolsheviks & War. 165p. 1985. 4.95 (*0-89567-080-1*) World View Forum.

— Czechoslovakia Nineteen Sixty-Eight: The Class Character of the Events. 62p. 3.00 (*0-89567-002-X*) World View Forum.

— Eurocommunism, New Form of Reformism. 52p. 1978. pap. 3.00 (*0-89567-026-7*) World View Forum.

— Generals over the White House: The Impact of the Military-Industrial Complex. 59p. 3.00 (*0-89567-042-9*) World View Forum.

— High-Tech, Low Pay. 217p. 1986. 5.95 (*0-89567-083-6*) World View Forum.

— Imperialism & the Crisis in the Socialist Camp. 57p. 1979. pap. 3.50 (*0-89567-030-5*) World View Forum.

— The Klan & the Government: Foes or Allies. 80p. 1983. pap. 2.95 (*0-89567-079-8*) World View Forum.

— Perestroika: A Marxist Critique. 409p. 1990. 12.95 (*0-89567-102-6*) World View Forum.

— Poland: Behind the Crisis. 168p. 1982. pap. 3.95 (*0-89567-076-3*) World View Forum.

— Problems of the Soviet Economic Reforms. 1992. pap. 2.50 (*0-89567-091-7*) World View Forum.

— Reindustrialization: The Menace Behind the Promise. 56p. 1981. pap. 3.50 (*0-89567-045-3*) World View Forum.

— Selected Articles: 1981-82. 89p. 1982. pap. 2.50 (*0-89567-078-X*) World View Forum.

— Soviet Socialism: Utopian or Scientific? 1992. pap. 2.50 (*0-89567-107-7*) World View Forum.

Marcy, Sam, et al. China, the Struggle Within. 2nd ed. 116p. 1972. pap. 4.00 (*0-89567-008-9*) World View Forum.

Marcy, Samuel J. Equal & Distinct Genders: Representation of Women by Women & Men by Men. LC 92-74961. 160p. (Orig.). 1993. pap. 15.00 (*0-9634728-0-1*) EJUT Bks.

Marcy, William, ed. Patent Policy: Government, Academic, & Industry Concepts. LC 78-9955. (ACS Symposium Ser.: No. 81). 1978. 27.95 (*0-8412-0454-3*) Am Chemical.

Marcyzinski-Music, Karen K. Health Care Solutions: Designing Community-Based Systems That Work. LC 94-9469. (Health Ser.). 256p. 1994. boxed 29.95 (*0-7879-0010-9*) Jossey-Bass.

Marczali, Henry. Hungary in the Eighteenth Century. LC 75-135818. (Eastern Europe Collection Ser.). 1971. reprint ed. 24.95 (*0-405-02760-5*) Ayer.

Marczenko, Z., et al, eds. Dictionary of Analytical Reagents. 2000p. 1993. 975.00 (*0-412-35150-1*, A9622) Chapman & Hall.

Marczewski, J. Histoire Quantitative: Buts et Methodes. Bd. with Produit de l'Agriculture Francaise de 1700 a 1958: Estimation du Produit au XVIII Siecle. (Economies et Societes Series AF: No. 1). 1961. Set pap. (*0-8115-0625-8*) Periodicals Srv.

— Le Produit Physique de l'Economie Francaise de 1789 a 1913: (Comparaison avec la Grande-Bretagne) Bd. with Industrie Francaise de 1789 a 1964: Sources at Methodes. (Economies et Societes Series AF: No. 4). 1965. Set pap. (*0-8115-0628-2*) Periodicals Srv.

Marczewski, Jan. Inflation & Unemployment in France: A Quantitative Analysis. LC 77-25490. (Praeger Special Studies). 222p. 1978. text ed. 55.00 (*0-275-90305-2*, C0305, Praeger Pubs) Greenwood.

Mardam-Bey, Farouk, jt. auth. see Kassir, Samir.

Marden. Minorities in American Society. (C). 1991. text ed. 51.00 (*0-06-044215-8*) HarpCollege.

Marden, Brice. Brice Marden: New Paintings, Drawings, Etchings. (Illus.). 48p. 1993. 25.00 (*1-880146-07-X*) M Marks Inc.

— A Brice Marden Sketchbook. (Illus.). 108p. Date not set. pap. 29.95 (*1-881616-49-5*) Dist Art Pubs.

Marden, Brice, tr. see Bann, Stephen, et al.

Marden, Hal. Payofski's Dyscovery. LC 85-45701. 110p. 1986. 12.95 (*0-253-34301-1*) Ind U Pr.

*__Marden, John I.__ Analyzing & Modeling Rank Data. LC 94-49214. 1998. write for info. (*0-412-99521-2*) Chapman & Hall.

Marden, Morris. Geometry of Polynomials. rev. ed. LC 66-20882. (Mathematical Surveys Ser.: Vol. 3). 260p. 1989. 49.00 (*0-8218-1503-2*, SURV-3) Am Math.

*__Marden, Orison S.__ Character: The Grandest Thing in the World. (Illus.). 55p. 1995. pap. 5.00 (*0-89540-297-1*) Sun Pub.

— An Iron Will. 52p. 1995. pap. 4.50 (*0-89540-283-1*) Sun Pub.

— The Miracle of Right Thought. 339p. 1995. pap. 28.00 (*0-89540-311-0*) Sun Pub.

Marden, Parker G., et al. Population in the Global Arena: Actors, Values, Policies, & Futures. LC 81-7211. (Duke Press Global Issues Ser.). xvii, 146p. 1982. pap. 14.95 (*0-8223-0584-4*) Duke.

Marden, Patricia C. & Barchers, Suzanne I. Cooking up World History: Multicultural Recipes & Resources. (Illus.). 225p. 1994. pap. text ed. 22.50 (*1-56308-116-4*) Teacher Ideas Pr.

Marden, Patricia C., jt. auth. see Barchers, Suzanne I.

Marden, Philip S. Detours (Passable but Unsafe) LC 68-54360. (Essay Index Reprint Ser.). 1977. 19.95 (*0-8369-0677-2*) Ayer.

Marden, Robert. Fifteen Selected Sonatas for Piano. 1950. pap. 9.95 (*0-8256-2073-2*) Music Sales.

M

Marden, William. Marden's Guide to Manhattan Booksellers. 412p. (Orig.). 1994. pap. 12.95 (*0-9636646-0-3*) Marden Bks.

— Marden's Guide to Manhattan Booksellers, 1996. 400p. 1995. pap. 12.95 (*0-9636646-1-1*) Marden Bks.

Marder, A. R., ed. The Physical Metallurgy of Zinc Coated Steel: Proceedings. LC 93-80903. 333p. 1994. 50.00 (*0-87339-260-4*) Minerals Metals.

Marder, A. R., ed. see International Conference on Phase Transformations in Ferrous Alloys Staff.

Marder, A. R., ed. see Metallurgical Society of AIME Staff.

Marder, Amy. Your Healthy Pet: A Practical Guide to Raising Happier, Healthier Dogs & Cats. LC 93-27730. 1994. pap. 14.95 (*0-87596-185-1*) Rodale Pr Inc.

Marder, Arthur J., et al. Old Friends, New Enemies: The Royal Navy & the Imperial Japanese Navy, 1936-1945, Vol. 2: The Pacific War. (Illus.). 664p. 1990. 69.00 (*0-19-820150-8*) OUP.

Marder, Danie, jt. auth. see Guinn, Dorothy.

Marder, Daniel. Arnold Andre Transcripts: A Reconstruction. LC 92-46364. (Illus.). 224p. 1993. 21.00 (*0-912526-59-9*) Lib Res.

— Exiles at Home: A Story of Literature in Nineteenth Century America. LC 84-17303. 382p. (Orig.). 1985. pap. text ed. 30.00 (*0-8191-4285-9*) U Pr of Amer.

— Hugh Henry Brackenridge. (Twayne's United States Authors Ser.). 1967. pap. 13.95 (*0-8084-0162-9*, T114) NCUP.

— Mrs. Arnold & Her General. 395p. 1995. pap. 9.95 (*1-56901-619-4*) NW Pub.

Marder, Daniel, ed. see Brackenbridge, Hugh H.

Marder, Estelle, jt. auth. see Marder, William.

Marder, Joyce S. Surviving the Start-up Years in Your Own Business. (Illus.). 172p. (Orig.). 1991. pap. 7.95 (*1-55870-200-8*) Betterway Bks.

Marder, Larry. Larry Marder's Beanworld, Bk. 1. 1990. 32.95 (*0-913035-88-2*); pap. 9.95 (*0-913035-89-0*) Eclipse Bks.

— Larry Marder's Beanworld, Bk. 2. (Illus.). 1991. 32.95 (*1-56060-091-8*); pap. 9.95 (*1-56060-094-2*) Eclipse Bks.

Marder, Leslie. Calculus of Several Variables. LC 75-318221. (Problem Solvers Ser.: No. 2). 90p. reprint ed. pap. 25.70 (*0-8357-7970-X*, 2023263) Bks Demand.

Marder, Louis, ed. Speak the Speech: The Shakespeare Quotation Book. LC 93-4842. 400p. 1994. 25.00 (*0-06-270070-7*, Harper Ref) HarpC.

— Speak the Speech: The Shakespeare Quotation Book. 496p. 1995. pap. 15.00 (*0-06-272063-5*) HarpC.

Marder, Norma. An Eye for Dark Places. LC 92-38577. 1993. 19.95 (*0-316-54606-2*) Little.

Marder, Seth R., et al, eds. Materials for Nonlinear Optics: Chemical Perspectives. LC 90-25768. (ACS Symposium Ser.: No. 455). (Illus.). 750p. 1991. 129.95 (*0-8412-1939-7*) Am Chemical.

Marder, Stephen. A Supplementary Russian-English Dictionary. xv, 522p. (Orig.). (ENG & RUS.). 1992. pap. 27.95 (*0-89357-228-4*) Slavica.

Marder, Stephen R., et al, eds. Clinical Use of Neuroleptic Plasma Levels. LC 93-16126. 144p. 1993. text ed. 26.00 (*0-88048-524-8*) Am Psychiatric.

Marder, Sue E. Legal Forms, Contracts & Advice for Horse Owners. 110p. 1991. pap. 19.95 (*0-914327-37-2*) Breakthrgh NY.

Marder, Sue E., jt. auth. see Winter, Tony.

Marder, William. The History & Technique of a New Diffusion Process. 1980. pap. 25.00 (*0-9607480-5-9*) Marder.

Marder, William & Marder, Estelle. Anthony, the Man, the Company, the Cameras. Duncan, Robert G., ed. LC 81-90597. 384p. 1982. 135.00 (*0-9607480-0-8*) Marder.

— Anthony, the Man, the Company, the Cameras. limited ed. Duncan, Robert G., ed. LC 81-90597. 384p. 1982. 200.00 (*0-685-05986-3*) Marder.

— Pioneers of Photography. 91p. 1991. pap. 28.00 (*0-9607480-3-2*) Marder.

Marder, William D., jt. auth. see American Medical Association Staff.

Marder, William D., jt. auth. see Wolinsky, Fredric D.

Mardesic, S., ed. see Segal, J.

Mardh, P. A. & Schleifer, K. H., eds. Coagulase-Negative Staphylococci. (Illus.). 222p. (Orig.). 1986. 71.00x (*91-22-00783-0*, Pub. by Almqv & Wiksell SW) Coronet Bks.

Mardh, Peter-Anders, et al. Chlamydia. (Illus.). 358p. 1989. 72.00 (*0-306-42965-9*, Plenum Med Bk) Plenum.

Mardh, Peter-Anders, et al, eds. Chlamydial Infections: Proceedings, 5th International Symposium, Lund, Sweden, June 15-19, 1982. (Fernstrom Foundation Ser.: Vol. 2). 454p. 1982. 104.75 (*0-444-80431-5*, I-293-82) Elsevier.

Mardia, K. V. The Scientific Foundations of Jainism. 1990. 23.00 (*81-208-0658-1*, Pub. by Motilal Banarsidass II) S Asia.

Mardia, K. V., ed. The Art of Statistical Science: A Tribute to G. S. Watson. (Probability & Mathematical Statistics: Applied Probability & Statistics Section Ser.: No. 1345). 317p. 1992. text ed. 190.00 (*0-471-93110-1*) Wiley.

Mardia, K. V., et al. Multivariate Analysis. LC 79-40922. (Probability & Mathematical Statistics Ser.). 1980. pap. text ed. 65.00 (*0-12-471252-5*) Acad Pr.

Mardiguian, Michael. Grounding & Bonding. LC 88-80528. (Electromagnetic Interference & Compatibility Ser.: Vol. 2). (Illus.). 408p. 1988. 130.00 (*0-944916-02-3*) D White Consult.

— How to Control Electrical Noise. 2nd ed. Price, Edward R., ed. LC 81-70305. (Illus.). 87p. 1983. text ed. 29.00 (*0-932263-22-4*) D White Consult.

Mardiguian, Michael, jt. auth. see White, Donald R.

Mardiguian, Michel. Interference Control in Computers & Microprocessor-Based Equipment. (Illus.). 110p. 1984. text ed. 69.00 (*0-932263-23-2*) D White Consult.

Mardin, Serif. Religion & Social Change in Modern Turkey: The Case of Bediuzzaman Said Nursi. LC 89-4280. (SUNY Series in Near Eastern Studies). 267p. (C). 1989. 64.50 (*0-88706-996-7*); pap. 21.95 (*0-88706-997-5*) State U NY Pr.

Mardin, Yusuf. Colloquial Turkish. (Trubner's Colloquial Manuals Ser.). 1976. pap. 14.95 (*0-7100-8415-3*, RKP) Routledge.

Mardiquian, Michael. Electromagnetic Control in Components & Devices. LC 88-80524. (Electromagnetic Interference & Compatibility Ser.: Vol. 5). (Illus.). 492p. 1988. 85.00 (*0-944916-05-8*) D White Consult.

— Electrostatic Discharge Understand, Simulate & Fix ESD. Problems. LC 85-80686. (Illus.). 205p. 1985. 89.00 (*0-932263-27-5*) D White Consult.

— EMI Control Methodology & Procedures. LC 88-81458. (Electromagnetic Interference & Compatibility Ser.: Vol. 8). (Illus.). 347p. 1988. 275.00 (*0-944916-08-2*) D White Consult.

Mardirosian, Tom. Saved from Obscurity. 1989. pap. 4.75 (*0-8222-0991-8*) Dramatists Play.

— Subfertile. 1991. pap. 4.75 (*0-8222-1092-4*) Dramatists Play.

Mardirossian, F., et al, eds. Clusters & Groups of Galaxies. 704p. 1984. lib. bdg. 204.50 (*90-277-1772-9*) Kluwer Ac.

Mardock, Robert W., jt. ed. see Richmond, Robert W.

Mardon, D. K. An Illustrated Catalogue of the Rothschild Collection of Fleas (Siphonaptera) in the British Museum (Natural History) Pygiopsyllidae, Vol. VI. (Illus.). 306p. 1987. 135.00 (*0-318-36425-5*) OUP.

Mardon, Thomas W. Lans: Applications of IEEE-Ansi 802 Standards. 1989. text ed. 39.95 (*0-471-62049-1*) Wiley.

***Mardorf, Judy.** When a Drunk Driver Kills: A Widow's Survival. Krumm, LaRue, ed. LC 94-96787. (Illus.). 128p. (Orig.). 1994. pap. 7.95 (*0-9643936-3-8*) Taleteller.

***Mardrus.** Thousand Nights & One Night Vol. 2. 1993. pap. 14.95 (*0-415-04540-1*) Routledge Chapman & Hall.

— Thousand Nights & One Night Vol. 3. 1993. pap. 13.75 (*0-415-04541-X*) Routledge Chapman & Hall.

— Thousand Nights & One Night Vol. 4. 1993. pap. 13.75 (*0-415-04542-8*) Routledge Chapman & Hall.

***Mardus, Craig B.** How to Make Worry Work For You: Simple & Practical Lessons on How to Be Happy. 114p. 1995. 14.95 (*0-446-51967-7*) Warner Bks.

— How to Make Worry Work for You: Simple & Practical Lessons on How to Be Happy. 1996. mass mkt. write for info. (*0-446-60315-5*) Warner Bks.

***Mardyks, Raymond.** Sedona Starseed: A Galactic Initiation. (Illus.). 145p. (Orig.). 1995. pap. 14.95 (*0-9644180-0-2*) Star Heart.

Mardzhanishvili, K. K., jt. auth. see Bogolyubov, N. N.

Mardzhanishvili, M. A. Analysis of the Spatial Behavior & Size of Modern Buildings for Earthquake-Proof Design. Dhillion, K. S., tr. 145p. (C). 1985. text ed. 90.00 (*90-6191-595-3*, Pub. by A A Balkema NE) Ashgate Pub Co.

— Seismic Design of Frame-Panel Buildings & Their Structural Members. Dhillon, K. S., tr. 131p. (C). 1984. text ed. 90.00 (*90-6191-424-8*, Pub. by A A Balkema NE) Ashgate Pub Co.

— Theoretical & Experimental Analysis of Members of Earthquake Proof Frame Panel Buildings. (C). 1987. 28. 50 (*0-8364-2121-3*, Pub. by Oxford IBH II) S Asia.

Mardzhanishvilli, L., jt. auth. see Mardzhanishvilli, M. A.

Mardzhanishvilli, M. A. & Mardzhanishvilli, L. Theoretical & Experimental Analysis of Members of Earthquake-Proof Frame Panel Buildings. Dhillon, K., tr. 180p. (C). 1986. text ed. 90.00 (*90-6191-472-8*, Pub. by A A Balkema NE) Ashgate Pub Co.

Mare, jt. auth. see Smith.

Mare, Gerhard. Ethnicity & Politics in South Africa. LC 92-33428. 144p. (C). 1993. reprint ed. text ed. 49.95 (*1-85649-207-9*, Pub. by Zed Books UK); reprint ed. pap. 17.50 (*1-85649-208-7*, Pub. by Zed Books UK) Humanities.

Mare, Gerhard & Hamilton, Georgina. An Appetite for Power: Buthelezi's Inkatha & South Africa. LC 87-21527. (Illus.). 270p. 1988. 35.00 (*0-253-30812-7*) Ind U Pr.

Mare, Margaret L. Eduard Morike: The Man & the Poet. LC 72-7860. (Illus.). 275p. 1973. reprint ed. lib. bdg. 19. 75 (*0-8371-6538-5*, MEMO, Greenwood Pr) Greenwood.

Mare, Margaret L., ed. see Lichtenberg, G. C.

Mare, Nancy N., jt. auth. see Smith, Lorraine C.

Mare, Vladimir. What Is Our Future, America? (Illus.). 1985. 24.95 (*0-933517-00-9*) V & M World Wide.

Mare, W. Harold. Archaeology of the Jerusalem Area. LC 85-73719. 1986. 19.99 (*0-8010-6126-1*) Baker Bk.

Marea, Cameron G., jt. auth. see Werner, Lynne A.

Marecek, Mary. Breaking Free from Partner Abuse: Voices of Battered Women Caught in the Cycle of Domestic Violence. enl. rev. ed. Orig. Title: Say "No!" to Violence. (Illus.). 96p. 1993. pap. 7.95 (*0-930934-74-1*) Morning Glory.

Marechal, A., ed. Space Optics. 398p. 1974. text ed. 252.00 (*0-677-50680-5*) Gordon & Breach.

Marechal, A., ed. see CNRS Staff.

Marechal, Chantal A., ed. In Quest of Marie de France, a Twelfth-Century Poet. LC 92-24244. (Illus.). 308p. 1992. text ed. 99.95 (*0-7734-9586-X*) E Mellen.

Marechal, Ernest, jt. auth. see Kennedy, Joseph P.

Marechal, G., ed. Eurographics '87: Proceedings of the European Computer Graphics Conference & Exhibition, Amsterdam, The Netherlands, August 24-28, 1987. 584p. 1987. 105.25 (*0-444-70291-1*, North Holland) Elsevier.

Marechal, Pierre S. Dictionnaire Des Athees Anciens et Modernes. 438p. reprint ed. write for info. (*0-318-71376-4*, Pub. by Georg Olms GW) Lubrecht & Cramer.

Marechal-Ross, Patricia, jt. auth. see Steele, Ross.

***Marechera.** House of Hunger. (African Writers Ser.). 154p. (C). 1995. pap. 10.95 (*0-435-90986-X*) Heinemann.

***Marechera, Dambudzo.** The Black Insider. Date not set. pap. 7.99 (*0-85315-739-1*, Pub. by Lawrence & Wishart UK) Humanities.

— Black Sunlight. (African Writers Ser.). (Orig.). (C). 1981. pap. 9.95 (*0-435-90237-7*) Heinemann.

***Maredia, Karen & Bedford, Bruce.** Proceedings of the USAID Latin America Caribbean Region Biosafety Workshop (1993) (Illus.). 51p. (Orig.). (C). 1994. pap. text ed. 35.00x (*0-7881-1504-9*) Diane Pub.

Maree, Aaron. Brownies, Shortbreads & Toll House Cookies: One Hundred Fifty Delights for Teas & Desserts. 1992. 30.00 (*0-207-17741-4*, Pub. by Angus & Robertson AT) HarpC.

— Chocolate Delights. (Illus.). 64p. 1993. 10.00 (*0-207-18036-9*, Pub. by Angus & Robertson AT) HarpC.

— Encyclopedia of Patisserie. 368p. 1994. 35.00 (*0-207-18478-X*, Pub. by Angus & Robertson AT) HarpC.

— Festive Treats. (Illus.). 64p. 1993. 10.00 (*0-207-18038-5*, Pub. by Angus & Robertson AT) HarpC.

— Petits Fours. (Illus.). 64p. 1993. 10.00 (*0-207-18035-0*, Pub. by Angus & Robertson AT) HarpC.

— Sweet Treats. (Illus.). 64p. 1993. 10.00 (*0-207-18037-7*, Pub. by Angus & Robertson AT) HarpC.

Maree, Johann, ed. The Independent Trade Unions, 1974-1984: Ten Years of the South African Labour Bulletin. 500p. 1987. pap. text ed. 17.95 (*0-86975-307-X*, Pub. by Ravan Pr ZA) Ohio U Pr.

Mareel, Marc M., et al. Mechanisms of Invasion & Metastasis. (Illus.). 608p. 1991. 237.00 (*0-8493-6254-7*, RC269) CRC Pr.

Marei, H. Basic Technical Dictionary: French-English-German-Arabic. 363p. (ARA, ENG, FRE & GER.). 1973. lib. bdg. 125.00 (*0-7859-0804-8*, M-9752) Fr & Eur.

Marei, Sayed A. The World Food Crisis. 2nd ed. LC 77-14527. (Illus.). 144p. reprint ed. pap. 41.10 (*0-685-20308-5*, 2030346) Bks Demand.

Marek, Charles R., ed. Low-Temperature Properties of Bithuminous Materials & Compacted Bithuminous Paving Mixtures - STP 628. 1977. 11.00 (*0-8031-0194-5*, 04 628000 08) ASTM.

Marek, Charles R., jt. ed. see Schreuders, Hans G.

Marek, Donna. Creme De Carmel: The Story of the Lively Personalities Who Shaped California's Fabled Castal Kingdom. LC 94-65083. (Illus.). 160p. 1994. 29.95 (*1-879373-88-2*) R Rinehart.

Marek, Edmund A & Lewis, Melanie. Laboratory Investigations for General Science, Part II. (Illus.). 101p. (C). 1982. pap. text ed. 6.95x (*0-89641-078-1*) American Pr.

Marek, Edmund A., et al. Laboratory Investigations for General Science Part I. (Illus.). 89p. 1982. pap. text ed. 6.95x (*0-89641-111-7*) American Pr.

Marek, George R., ed. World Treasury of Grand Opera: Its Triumphs, Trials & Great Personalities. LC 74-167383. (Essay Index Reprint Ser.). 1977. reprint ed. 35.95 (*0-8369-2463-0*) Ayer.

***Marek, Jayne.** Women Editing Modernism: "Little" Magazines & Literary History. (Illus.). 248p. (Orig.). (C). 1995. text ed. 34.95 (*0-8131-1937-5*); pap. 14.95 (*0-8131-0854-3*) U Pr of Ky.

***Marek, Karen.** Manual to Develop Guidelines. Date not set. write for info. (*0-614-02742-X*, NP-97) Am Nurses Pub.

Marek, Milos & Schreiber, Igor. Chaotic Behaviour of Deterministic Dissipative Systems. (Illus.). 378p. (C). 1992. pap. 39.95 (*0-521-43830-6*) Cambridge U Pr.

Marek, Milos, jt. auth. see Kubicek, M.

***Marek, Pavel, et al.** Simulation-Based Reliability Assessment for Structural Engineers. 320p. 1995. write for info. (*0-8493-8286-6*, 8286) CRC Pr.

Marek, V. W. & Trusczynski, M. Nonmonotonic Logic: Context-Dependent Reasoning. Loveland, D. W., ed. (Artificial Intelligence Ser.). x, 396p. 1993. 79.00 (*0-387-56448-9*) Spr-Verlag.

Marek, Wiktor. Elements of Logic & Foundations of Mathematics in Problems. 1983. lib. bdg. 90.00 (*90-277-1084-8*) Kluwer Ac.

Marek, Wiktor & Onyszkiewicz, Janusz. Elements of Logic & Foundations of Mathematics in Problems. 1985. pap. text ed. 44.50 (*90-277-2131-9*) Kluwer Ac.

Marek, Wiktor, jt. ed. see Nerode, Anil.

MarElia, Beatrice. The Great Mirage. LC 85-15117. 1986. pap. 13.95 (*0-87949-249-X*) Ashley Bks.

Marelli, Maria E., tr. see Feldman, Cathy, ed.

Marello, Carla, jt. ed. see Fordyce, Rachel.

Maremaa, T. Oops! Macintosh: What to Do When Things Go Wrong. (Illus.). 320p. (Orig.). 1993. pap. 16.95 (*1-56529-291-X*) Que.

***Mareman, Tom.** Filemaker Pro for Dummies. 1995. pap. 19.99 (*1-56884-906-0*) IDG Bks.

Maremmani, Icro, jt. ed. see Tagliamonte, Alessandro.

Maren, Alianna, et al. Handbook of Neural Computing Applications. 448p. 1990. text ed. 79.00 (*0-12-471260-6*) Acad Pr.

Maren, Michael. The Land & People of Kenya. LC 88-22959. (Portraits of the Nations Ser.). (Illus.). 208p. (J). (gr. 6 up). 1989. 19.00 (*0-397-32334-4*, Lipp Jr Bks); lib. bdg. 18.89 (*0-397-32335-2*, Lipp Jr Bks) HarpC Child Bks.

Marenbon, John. Early Medieval Philosophy, 480-1150. 224p. 1988. pap. text ed. 13.95 (*0-415-00070-X*) Routledge.

— Later Medieval Philosophy Eleven Fifty to Thirteen Fifty. 248p. (C). 1987. lib. bdg. 35.00 (*0-685-19266-0*, Routledge NY) Routledge Chapman & Hall.

— Later Medieval Philosophy (1150-1350) An Introduction. 248p. 1991. pap. 15.95 (*0-415-06807-X*, A6265) Routledge.

Marenco, E. K. The Transformation of Sikh Society. 342p. 1976. 24.95 (*0-318-36785-8*) Asia Bk Corp.

Marenco, Ethne K. Transformation of Sikh Society. (Illus.). 342p. 1972. pap. 16.95 (*0-913244-08-2*) Hapi Pr.

Marengo, Franco D. Rules of the Italian Political Game. 144p. 1981. text ed. 53.95 (*0-566-00301-5*) Ashgate Pub Co.

Marenka, Stephen R., jt. auth. see Watkins, Christopher D.

Marenkov, O. S., ed. Handbook of Partial Attenuation Coefficients of Characteristic X-Ray Radiation. 207p. 1994. lib. bdg. 97.00 (*1-56072-102-2*) Nova Sci Pubs.

Marenkov, O. S. & Komyak, N. I., eds. Handbook of Photon-Interaction Coefficients in Radio Isotope-Excited X-Ray Fluorescence Analysis. 225p. (C). 1990. text ed. 115.00 (*0-941743-79-9*) Nova Sci Pubs.

Marenn, Lea. Salvador's Children: A Song for Survival. (Helen Hooven Santmyer Prize in Women's Studies). 240p. 1993. 24.95 (*0-8142-0593-3*) Ohio St U Pr.

Marennyi, Ya. I. Tunnels with In-Situ Pressed Concrete Lining. Zeidler, R. B., ed. (Illus.). 256p. 1993. text ed. 80.00 (*90-5410-141-5*, Pub. by A A Balkema NE) Ashgate Pub Co.

Marentette, Lawrence, jt. auth. see Kellman, Robert.

Marenzio, Luca. Madrigali a Quatto Cinque E Sei Voci, Libro Primo 1588: Luca Marenzio, the Secular Works, No. 7. Ledbetter, Steven, ed. xxvi, 167p. 1977. pap. 50. 00 (*0-8450-7107-6*) Broude.

— Il Sesto libro de' madrigali a sei voci (1595) Myers, Patricia, ed. (Luca Marenzio: the Secular Works: Vol. 6). xxxv, 220p. (ITA.). 1983. pap. 50.00 (*0-8450-7106-8*) Broude.

— Ten Madrigals for Mixed Voices. Arnold, Denis, ed. 1985. 18.95 (*0-19-343675-2*) OUP.

***Marer, et al.** Transforming State Industrial Enterprises. (C). 1995. text ed. 59.95 (*0-8133-2704-0*); pap. text ed. 19.95 (*0-8133-2705-9*) Westview.

Marer, Patrick J. The Safe & Effective Use of Pesticides: Pesticide Application Compendium 1. LC 87-73550. 400p. 1988. 30.00 (*0-931876-83-4*, 3324) ANR Pubns CA.

Marer, Patrick J., ed. Residential, Industrial & Institutional Pest Control: Pesticide Application Compendium 2. (Illus.). 232p. (Orig.). 1991. pap. 25.00 (*0-931876-93-1*, 3334) ANR Pubns CA.

***Marer, Patrick J. & Grimes, Mark, eds.** Forest & Right-of-Way Pesticide Application: Pesticide Application Compendium 4. Date not set. pap. 25.00 (*1-879906-19-8*, 3336) ANR Pubns CA.

Marer, Patrick J., et al. Wood Preservation: Pesticide Application Compendium 3. LC 92-63207. (Illus.). 92p. 1992. pap. 15.00 (*1-879906-05-8*, 3335) ANR Pubns CA.

Marer, Paul. Dollar GNPs of the U.S.S.R. & Eastern Europe. LC 85-45101. 256p. reprint ed. pap. 73.00 (*0-7837-4273-8*, 2043965) Bks Demand.

— U. S. Financing of East-West Trade: The Political Economy of Government Credits & the National Interest. (Studies in East European & Soviet Planning, Development, & Trade: No. 22). (Illus.). 1975. pap. text ed. 5.00 (*0-89249-030-6*) Intl Development.

Marer, Paul & Montias, John M., eds. East European Integration & East-West Trade. LC 79-3181. (Studies in East European & Soviet Planning, Development, & Trade: No. 28). (Illus.). 448p. reprint ed. pap. 128.90 (*0-685-44450-3*, 2056710) Bks Demand.

Marer, Paul & Siwinski, Wlodzimierz, eds. Creditworthiness & Reform in Poland: Western & Polish Perspectives. LC 87-26962. 372p. 1988. 40.00 (*0-253-31472-0*); pap. 25.00 (*0-253-20477-1*, MB-477) Ind U Pr.

Marer, Paul & Tabaczynski, Eugeniusz, eds. Polish-U. S. Industrial Cooperation in the 1980's: Findings of a Joint Research Project. LC 81-47884. (Illus.). 448p. 1982. 25. 00 (*0-253-34529-4*) Ind U Pr.

Marer, Paul & Van Veen, Pieter, eds. Advances in International Comparative Management: East European Economic Trends & East-West Trade, Pt. II: Foreign Trade Policies & Controversies. 1987. write for info. (*0-318-62529-6*) Jai Pr.

— Advances in International Comparative Management: East European Economic Trends & East-West Trade, Set. 1987. 73.25 (*0-89232-822-3*) Jai Pr.

— Advances in International Comparative Management: East European Economic Trends & East-West Trade, Suppl. 2, 3 pts. 1987. Pt. I: Region-Wide Economic Trends. write for info. (*0-318-62528-8*); Pt. III: Country Perspectives. write for info. (*0-318-62530-X*) Jai Pr.

Marer, Paul, jt. ed. see Koves, Andras.

Marer, Paul, et al. Historically Planned Economies: A Guide to the Data. LC 92-17667. 260p. 1992. 24.95 (*0-8213-2147-1*, 12147) World Bank.

***Marer, Sharon & Piwonski, Shirley.** Sedona, Responding to the Call. (Illus.). 200p. (Orig.). 1994. pap. 12.95 (*1-885782-89-6*) Sources of Light.

***Mares, Benny.** Executive Protection: A Professional's Guide to Bodyguarding. 112p. 1994. pap. 12.00 (*0-87364-798-X*) Paladin Pr.

Mares, Bill & Bryan, Frank. Out of Order: The Very Unofficial Vermont State House Archives. LC 91-66745. (Illus.). 128p. 1991. pap. 9.95 (*0-933050-88-7*) New Eng Pr VT.

Mares, Bill, jt. auth. see Bryan, Frank.

Mares, David R. The Evolution of U. S. - Mexican Agricultural Relations: The Changing Roles of the Mexican State & Mexican Agricultural Producers. (Research Report Ser.: No. 16). 44p. (Orig.). (C). 1981. pap. 5.00 (*0-935391-15-0*, RR-16) UCSD Ctr US-Mex.

— Penetrating International Markets: Theoretical Considerations & Mexican Agriculture. (Political Economy of International Change Ser.). 296p. 1987. text ed. 46.00 (*0-231-06346-6*) Col U Pr.

Mares, E. A. The Unicorn Poem & Flowers & Songs of Sorrow. 74p. (Orig.). 1992. pap. 8.95 (*0-931122-65-1*) West End.

Mares, E. A., tr. see Lamadrid, Enrique R., ed.

Mares, E. A., et al. Padre Martinez: New Perspectives from Taos. (Illus.). 151p. (Orig.). 1988. pap. 9.95 (*0-9609818-3-7*) M Rogers Mus.

Mares, F. H., ed. see Shakespeare, William.

Mares, George C. The History of the Typewriter Successor to the Pen. LC 85-90315. (Illus.). 320p. 1985. 24.95 (*0-911160-87-6*) Post Group.

Mares, Michael, jt. auth. see Jones, L. R.

Mares, Michael A. Heritage at Risk: Oklahoma's Hidden Treasure. (Illus.). 73p. (Orig.). 1988. pap. 20.00 (*1-883090-02-4*) OK Museum.

Mares, Michael A. & Schmidly, David J. Latin American Mammalogy: History, Biodiversity, & Conservation. LC 91-10264. (Oklahoma Museum of Natural History Publication Ser.). (Illus.). 480p. 1991. 55.00 (*0-8061-2343-5*) U of Okla Pr.

Mares, Michael A., et al. Guide to the Mammals of Salta Province, Argentina: Guia De los Mamiferos de la Provincia De Salta, Argentina. LC 89-40219. (Oklahoma Museum of Natural History Publication Ser.). (Illus.). 320p. 1990. 35.00 (*0-8061-2187-4*) U of Okla Pr.

***Mares, Milan.** Computation Over Fuzzy Quantities. 176p. 1994. 69.95 (*0-8493-7635-1*) CRC Pr.

Mares, Penny. In Control: Hel with Incontinence. (C). 1989. 35.00 (*0-86242-088-1*, Pub. by Age Concern Eng UK) St Mut.

Mares, Stanislav. Introduction to Applied Geophysics. 556p. 1984. lib. bdg. 182.00 (*90-277-1424-X*) Kluwer Ac.

Mares, Stanislav, ed. see Karous, Milos, et al.

Mares, William. Making Beer. rev. ed. LC 93-43381. (Illus.). 1994. 16.00 (*0-679-43237-X*) Knopf.

Mares, William J. Making Beer. 1994. pap. 16.00 (*0-679-75502-0*) Knopf.

Maresca, B. & Lindquist, S., eds. Heat Shock. (Illus.). 344p. 1991. 98.00 (*0-387-54111-X*) Spr-Verlag.

***Maresca, Bruno & Kobayashi, George S.** Molecular Biology of Pathogenic Fungi: A Laboratory Manual. 577p. 1994. spiral bd. 95.00 (*0-914386-27-1*) Telos Pr.

Maresca, Bruno, et al, eds. Molecular Biology & Its Application to Medical Mycology. LC 92-49124. (NATO ASI Ser.: Vol. 69). 1993. write for info. (*3-540-54609-X*); 179.00 (*0-387-54609-X*) Spr-Verlag.

Maresca, Frank, et al. American Self-Taught. LC 93-267. 1993. 75.00 (*0-394-58212-8*) Knopf.

Maresca, John J. To Helsinki: The Conference on Security & Cooperation in Europe, 1973-75. 2nd ed. LC 87-22261. xv, 315p. (C). 1987. pap. text ed. 20.95 (*0-8223-0791-X*) Duke.

Maresca, Joseph W., Jr. & Hillger, Robert W. Chemicals Stored in USTs: Characteristics & Leak Detection. (Illus.). 61p. (Orig.). (C). 1992. pap. text ed. 40.00 (*1-56806-114-5*) Diane Pub.

Maresca, Joseph W., Jr., et al. Volumetric Leak Detection Methods for Underground Fuel Storage Tanks. LC 89-71008. (Pollution Technology Review Ser.: No. 180). (Illus.). 356p. 1990. 57.00 (*0-8155-1230-9*) Noyes.

Maresca, Thomas E. Three English Epics: Studies of Troilus & Criseyde, The Faerie Queen, & Paradise Lost. LC 79-1080. 238p. reprint ed. pap. 67.90 (*0-7837-6022-1*, 2045834) Bks Demand.

Maresca, Tom. Mastering Wine: A Learner's Manual. 1992. pap. 12.95 (*0-8021-3298-7*) Grove-Atltic.

— Right Wine. 1992. pap. 12.95 (*0-8021-3297-9*) Grove-Atltic.

Maresca, Tom, jt. auth. see Darrow, Diane.

Marescaux, C., et al, eds. Generalized Non-Convulsive Epilepsy: Focus on GABA-B Receptors. LC 92-2422. (Journal of Neural Transmission Ser.: Suppl. 35). (Illus.). 160p. 1992. pap. 73.00 (*0-387-82340-9*) Spr-Verlag.

An Asterisk (*) at the beginning of an entry indicates that the title is appearing in BIP for the first time.

Maresceau, Marc, ed. The European Community's Commercial Policy after 1992: The Legal Dimension. LC 92-44287. 488p. (ENG & FRE.). (C). 1993. lib. bdg. 117.50 (*0-7923-2131-6*) Kluwer Ac.

Mareschal, M., ed. Microscopic Simulations of Complex Flows. LC 90-46797. (NATO ASI Series B, Physics: Vol. 229). (Illus.). 380p. 1990. 105.00 (*0-306-43687-6*, Plenum Pr) Plenum.

Mareschal, M. & Holian, B. L., eds. Microscopic Simulations of Complex Hydrodynamic Phenomena. (NATO ASI Series B, Physics: Vol. 292). (Illus.). 436p. (C). 1992. 115.00 (*0-306-44226-4*, Plenum Pr) Plenum.

Maresh, M. Audit in Obstetrics & Gynaecology. (Illus.). 224p. 1994. write for info. (*0-632-03352-5*) Blackwell Sci.

Maresic, Josip. Phraseological Dictionary of the Serbian & Croatian Languages: Frazeoloski Rjecnik Hrvatskog Ili Srpskog Jezika. 808p. 1982. 49.95 (*0-8288-1998-X*, F78630) Fr & Eur.

Marestier, Jean-Baptiste. Memoir on Steamboats of the United States of America, Printed by the Royal Press, Paris, 1824. Withington, Sidney, tr. LC 57-59433. (Marine Historical Association, Publication Ser.: No. 31). 100p. reprint ed. pap. 28.50 (*0-8357-2794-7*, 2039920) Bks Demand.

Maret, Elizabeth. Women of the Range: Women's Roles in the Texas Beef Cattle Industry. LC 92-45787. (Illus.). 176p. 1993. 32.00 (*0-89096-532-3*); pap. 12.95 (*0-89096-541-2*) Tex A&M Univ Pr.

Mareth, E. & Kelly, R. Number Skills. 1980. text ed. 8.85 (*0-07-040341-4*) McGraw.

Maretis, D. K., jt. auth. see Hoffmann, G. R.

Maretski, Thomas, jt. auth. see Chrisman, Noel.

Marett, Allan, ed. Musica Asiatica, No. 6. (Illus.). 200p. (C). 1991. 69.95 (*0-521-39050-8*) Cambridge U Pr.

Marett, Cora B. & Leggon, Cheryl B., eds. Research in Race & Ethnic Relations, Vol. 1. 199p. 1979. 73.25 (*0-89232-064-8*) Jai Pr.

Marett, Paul. Information Law & Practice. 250p. 1991. text ed. 69.95 (*0-566-05402-7*, Pub. by Gower UK) Ashgate Pub Co.

Marett, Robert R. Faith, Hope & Charity in Primitive Religion. LC 77-27193. (Gifford Lectures: 1931-32). reprint ed. 15.00 (*0-404-60487-0*) AMS Pr.

— Faith, Hope & Charity in Primitive Religion. LC 72-80150. 1972. reprint ed. 24.95 (*0-405-08780-2*, Pub. by Blom Pubns UK) Ayer.

— Sacraments of Simple Folk. LC 77-27192. (Gifford Lectures: 1932-33). reprint ed. 36.50 (*0-404-60488-9*) AMS Pr.

— The Threshold of Religion. LC 76-44755. reprint ed. 34.50 (*0-404-15950-8*) AMS Pr.

Marett, Robert R., ed. see Spencer, Baldwin.

Marett, Valerie. Immigrants Settling in the City: Ugandan Asians in Leicester. 256p. 1992. 52.00 (*0-7185-1283-9*, Pub. by Pinter Pubs UK) St Martin.

Maretti, Valerio, ed. see Colombo, Gioachino.

Maretzek, Max. Crochets & Quavers: Or Revelations of an Opera Manager in America. 2nd ed. LC 65-23397. (Music Ser.). 1966. reprint ed. lib. bdg. 39.50 (*0-306-70915-5*) Da Capo.

— Crotchets & Quavers: On Revelations of an Opera Manager in America. (American Biography Ser.). 346p. 1991. reprint ed. lib. bdg. 79.00 (*0-7812-8266-7*) Rprt Serv.

Maretzki, Thomas W., ed. see Kennedy, Raymond.

Mareus, Leonard J., jt. auth. see Dubler, Nancy N.

Marey, Etienne J. Movement. LC 70-169333. (Literature of Cinema, Ser. 2). (Illus.). 344p. 1979. reprint ed. 23.95 (*0-405-03900-X*) Ayer.

Marfault, Jean, jt. auth. see Mermet, Charles.

Marfia, Jim. U. S. Open: Ft. Worth 1984. (Illus.). 98p. (Orig.). 1985. pap. 5.00 (*0-931462-40-1*) Chess Ent Inc.

— U. S. Open: 1983. (U. S. Tournament Ser.). (Illus.). 100p. (Orig.). 1984. pap. 6.00 (*0-931462-29-0*) Chess Ent Inc.

Marfia, Jim, ed. Queen's Gambit with Bf4. 36p. (Orig.). 1985. pap. 2.50 (*0-931462-42-8*) Chess Ent Inc.

Marfia, Jim & Watson, John. U. S. Open: St. Paul 1982. (Illus.). 83p. (Orig.). 1982. pap. 5.00 (*0-931462-21-5*) Chess Ent Inc.

Marfia, Jim, tr. see Botvinnik, Mikhail M.

Marfia, Jim, tr. see Botvinnik, Mikhail.

Marfia, Jim, tr. see Bronstein, David.

Marfia, Jim, tr. see Cvetkov, Alexander.

Marfia, Jim, tr. see Estrin, Yakov B.

Marfia, Jim, tr. see Kortchnoi, Viktor & Cavallaro, Lenny.

Marfo, K., jt. ed. see Thornburn, M. J.

Marfo, Kofi, ed. Early Intervention in Transition: Current Perspectives on Programs for Handicapped Children. LC 91-15312. 368p. 1991. text ed. 65.00 (*0-275-93470-5*, C3470, Praeger Pubs) Greenwood.

— Parent-Child Interaction & Developmental Disabilities: Theory, Research, & Intervention. LC 87-25908. 395p. 1988. text ed. 65.00 (*0-275-92835-7*, C2835, Praeger Pubs) Greenwood.

Marfo, Kofi, et al, eds. Child Disabilities in Developing Countries. LC 85-20871. 1985. text ed. 49.95 (*0-275-90217-X*, C0217, Praeger Pubs) Greenwood.

Marfori, Mark D. Feng Shui: Discover Money, Health & Love. (Illus.). 192p. (Orig.). 1994. pap. 13.95 (*0-9637748-4-0*) Dragon Pub.

Marfunin, A. S. Composition, Structure, & Properties of Mineral Matter: Concepts, Results, & Problems. (Advanced Mineralogy Ser.: Vol. 1). (Illus.). 562p. 1994. 133.00 (*0-387-57254-6*) Spr-Verlag.

Marfunin, Arnold S., ed. Advanced Mineralogy, Vol. 2. LC 94-13315. 1995. 133.00 (*0-387-57255-4*) Spr-Verlag.

Marfurt, K. J. Numerical Modeling of Seismic Wave Propagation. Kelly, K. R., ed. (Geophysics Reprint Ser.: No. 13). 525p. 1990. text ed. 75.00 (*1-56080-011-9*, 473) Soc Expl Geophys.

Marg, Elwyn. Computer-Assisted Eye Examination. (Illus.). 1980. 15.00 (*0-911302-40-9*) San Francisco Pr.

Marg, Walter, jt. auth. see Hirzel, Rudolf.

Margadant, Jo B. Madame le Professeur: Women Educators in the Third Republic. (Illus.). 349p. (C). 1990. text ed. 57.50 (*0-691-05593-9*); pap. text ed. 17.95 (*0-691-00864-7*) Princeton U Pr.

Margadant, Ted W. Urban Rivalries in the French Revolution. LC 92-9563. (Illus.). 504p. (C). 1992. text ed. 69.50 (*0-691-05687-0*); pap. text ed. 24.95 (*0-691-00891-4*) Princeton U Pr.

Margah, Irish, jt. auth. see Monroe, Elvira.

Margairaz, A. & Merkli, R. The Taxation of Corporations in Switzerland. (Orig.). 1983. pap. text ed. 59.00 (*90-6544-132-8*) Kluwer Law Tax Pubs.

— Taxation of Holding Companies in Switzerland. 160p. 1983. 31.00 (*0-686-41002-5*) Kluwer Ac.

***Margalef, Ramon, ed.** Limnology Now: Paradigm of Planetary Problems. LC 94-3431. 1994. 194.50 (*0-444-89826-3*) Elsevier.

Margalef-Roig, J. & Dominguez, E. Outerelo. Differential Topology. LC 92-10918. (North-Holland Mathematics Studies: Vol. 173). 1992. write for info. (*0-444-88434-3*, North Holland) Elsevier.

Margalit, Avishai, jt. auth. see Halbertal, Moshe.

Margalit, Avishai, jt. ed. see Ullman-Margalit, Edna.

Margalit, Baruch. The Ugaritic Poem of AQHT: Text - Transaltion - Commentary. xviii, 534p. (C). 1989. lib. bdg. 161.55x (*0-89925-472-1*) De Gruyter.

— The Ugaritic Poem of AQHT: Text - Translation - Commentary. xviii, 534p. (C). 1989. lib. bdg. 161.55x (*3-11-011632-4*) De Gruyter.

Margalit, M. Effective Technology: Integration for Disabled Children: The Family Perspective. xxii, 226p. 1990. 49.00 (*0-387-97256-0*) Spr-Verlag.

Margalit, Malka. Loneliness among Children with Special Needs: Theory, Research, Coping, & Intervention. LC 93-32707. 1993. 69.00 (*0-387-94158-4*) Spr-Verlag.

Margalit, Nehemiah, ed. see Symposium on Power Sources for Biomedical Implantable Applications Staff.

Margalith, Aaron M., jt. auth. see Adler, Cyrus.

Margalith, P. Z. Pigment Microbiology. LC 92-38097. 1992. write for info. (*0-412-41050-8*) Chapman & Hall.

Marganne, Marie-Helene. L' Ophtalmologie dans l'Egypte d'apres les Papyrus Litteraires Grecs. (Studies in Ancient Medicine: No. 8). 272p. (FRE.). 1994. 80.00 (*90-04-09907-7*, NLG140) E J Brill.

***Margaret Gates & Associates Staff, et al.** Care & Community in Modern Society: Passing on the Tradition of Service to Future Generations. LC 95-13733. (Nonprofit Sector Ser.). 1995. 39.95 (*0-7879-0109-1*) Jossey-Bass.

Margaret Louise Margaret Cloret de la Touche. The Love & Service of God, Infinite Love. O'Connell, Patrick, tr. LC 86-51580. 230p. 1987. reprint ed. pap. 10.00 (*0-89555-310-4*) TAN Bks Pubs.

Margaret Therese of Jesus. The Way Back to Wisdom. (Illus.). 147p. (Orig.). 1988. pap. 10.38 (*0-9625008-0-1*) Wisdoms Pub Hse.

Margaretten, Selma, jt. ed. see Barcia, Jose R.

Margaretten, Selma, tr. see Castro, Americo.

Margaris, N. S. & Mooney, Harold A., eds. Components of Productivity of Mediterranean-Climate Regions: Basic & Applied Aspects. (Tasks for Vegetation Science Ser.: No. 4). viii, 280p. 1981. lib. bdg. 107.50 (*90-6193-944-5*) Kluwer Ac.

Margaris, N. S., jt. ed. see Fantechi, R.

Margaris, N. S., et al, eds. Being Alive on Land: Proceedings of the International Symposium on Adaptations to Terrestrial Environment, Held in Halkidiki, Greece, 1982. (Tasks for Vegetation Science Ser.). 334p. 1984. 72.00 (*0-318-01972-8*) Kluwer Ac.

Margaritondo, Giorgio. Introduction to Synchrotron Radiation. (Illus.). 296p. 1988. 45.00 (*0-19-504524-6*) OUP.

Margaritondo, Giorgio, ed. Electronic Structure of Semiconductor Heterojunctions. (C). 1988. lib. bdg. 144.00 (*90-277-2823-2*); pap. text ed. 68.00 (*90-277-2824-0*) Kluwer Ac.

Margaritondo, Giorgio & Weaver, J. H., eds. Synchrotron Radiation. (Reprint Bks.). 128p. 1986. pap. text ed. 18.00 (*0-917853-19-9*, RB46) Am Assn Physics.

Margaritondo, Giorgio, jt. ed. see Capasso, F.

Margaritondo, Giorgio, et al, eds. High-Tc Superconducting Thin Films, Devices & Applications: Proceedings of the Topical Conference of the AVS, Atlanta, GA, October 1988. (AIP Conference Proceedings Ser., American Vacuum Society Ser.: No. 182, 6). (Illus.). 450p. 1989. 70.00 (*0-88318-382-X*) Am Inst Physics.

Margarshack, David, tr. & intro. The Amazon & Other Stories. LC 76-23884. 282p. 1987. reprint ed. 21.00 (*0-88355-495-X*) Hyperion Conn.

Margaryan, Alfred, jt. auth. see Piliavin, Michael A.

Margasahayam, Ravi N., jt. auth. see Drago, Raymond J.

Margate, Rosaline N., ed. see Thomas, William.

Margen, Sheldon, jt. auth. see Univ. of California at Berkeley Wellness Letter Editors.

Margenat, Assumpta. Wild Card. McIntosh, Sheila, tr. 165p. (Orig.). 1992. pap. 8.95 (*1-879679-04-3*) Women Translation.

Margenat, Hugo. Complete Works of Hugo Margenat. (Puerto Rico Ser.). 1979. lib. bdg. 600.00 (*0-8490-2892-2*) Gordon Pr.

Margenau, Eric. Sports Without Pressure: A Guide for Parents & Coaches of Young Athletes. LC 89-16998. 156p. 1990. pap. 9.95 (*0-89876-165-4*) Brunner-Mazel.

Margenau, Eric, ed. The Encyclopedic Handbook of Private Practice. LC 87-19624. 1050p. 1990. text ed. 120.00 (*0-89876-151-4*) Gardner Pr.

Margenau, H. & Kestner, N. Theory of Intermolecular Forces. 2nd ed. LC 79-142172. 1969. text ed. 172.00 (*0-08-016502-8*, Pub. by Pergamon Repr UK) Franklin.

Margenau, Henry. The Miracle of Existence. LC 83-4972. xii, 143p. 1984. 22.50 (*0-918024-26-9*); pap. 15.00 (*1-881987-03-5*) Ox Bow.

— The Nature of Physical Reality: A Philosophy of Modern Physics. LC 77-86356. 1977. reprint ed. 35.00 (*0-918024-02-1*); reprint ed. pap. 17.00 (*0-918024-03-X*) Ox Bow.

— Open Vistas. LC 83-60547. x, 256p. 1983. reprint ed. 26.00 (*0-918024-27-7*); reprint ed. pap. 14.00 (*0-918024-28-5*) Ox Bow.

— Physics & Philosophy: Selected Essays. (Episteme Ser.: No. 6). 1978. lib. bdg. 84.00 (*90-277-0901-7*) Kluwer Ac.

— Thomas & the Physics of Nineteen Fifty-Eight: A Confrontation. LC 58-9679. (Aquinas Lectures). 1958. 10.00 (*0-87462-123-2*) Marquette.

Margenau, Henry & Varghese, Roy A., eds. Cosmos, Bios, Theos: Scientists Reflect on Science, Religion, & the Origins of the Universe, Life, & Homo Sapiens. LC 92-7685. 299p. (C). 1992. pap. 17.95 (*0-8126-9186-5*) Open Court.

Margenau, Henry, jt. auth. see LeShan, Lawrence.

Margenau, Henry, jt. auth. see Lindsay, R. Bruce.

Margenau, James R. & Sentlowitz, Michael. How to Study Mathematics. LC 77-5560. (Illus.). 32p. 1977. pap. 5.00 (*0-87353-115-9*) NCTM.

Margeneau, H., ed. Integrative Principles of Modern Thought. (Current Topics of Contemporary Thought Ser.: Vol. 3). 532p. (C). 1972. text ed. 141.00 (*0-677-14150-5*) Gordon & Breach.

Marger, Martin N. Elites & Masses: An Introduction to Political Sociology. 2nd ed. 344p. (C). 1987. text ed. 42.95 (*0-534-07434-0*) Intl Thomson.

— Race & Ethnic Relations: American & Global Perspectives. 2nd ed. 591p. (C). 1991. text ed. 43.95 (*0-534-13950-7*) Intl Thomson.

— Race & Ethnic Relations: American & Global Perspectives. 3rd ed. 607p. 1994. text ed. 48.95 (*0-534-20809-6*) Intl Thomson.

Marger, Martin N., jt. ed. see Olsen, Marvin E.

Margeret, Jacques. The Russian Empire & Grand Duchy of Muscovy: A Seventeenth-Century French Account. Dunning, Chester S., ed. & tr. by. LC 82-20126. (Illus.). 235p. 1983. 49.95 (*0-8229-3805-7*) U of Pittsburgh Pr.

Margerison, Charles. Making Management Development Work: Achieving Success in the Nineties. 1991. pap. text ed. 24.95 (*0-07-707382-7*) McGraw.

— Managerial Consulting Skills: A Practical Guide. 256p. 1988. text ed. 41.95 (*0-566-02793-3*, Pub. by Gower UK) Ashgate Pub Co.

Margerison, D., jt. auth. see Green, J. R.

Margerit, Robert. Mont-Dragon. (FRE.). 1973. pap. 10.95 (*0-7859-4018-9*) Fr & Eur.

Margeson, Hank, photos. Quail Plantations of South Georgia & North Florida. LC 91-3054. (Illus.). 120p. 1991. 34.95 (*0-8203-1386-6*) U of Ga Pr.

Margeson, John, ed. see Shakespeare, William.

Margeson, Sue. Viking. LC 93-32593. (Eyewitness Bks.). (Illus.). 64p. (J). (gr. 5 up). 1994. 16.00 (*0-679-86002-9*); lib. bdg. 16.99 (*0-679-96002-3*) Knopf Bks Yng Read.

Margeton, Stephen G. & Meredith, Willis C. Law Library Preservation Issues: Books, Microforms & Electronic Media. (Law Library Information Reports: Vol. 16). 85p. 1994. pap. text ed. 100.00 (*0-87802-095-0*) Glanville.

Margetson, George R. England in the West Indies. 1977. lib. bdg. 59.95 (*0-8490-1769-6*) Gordon Pr.

— Songs of Life. LC 76-39095. (Black Heritage Library Collection). 1977. reprint ed. 15.95 (*0-8369-9033-1*) Ayer.

Margetts, Barrie M., ed. Design Concepts in Nutritional Epidemiology. (Illus.). 432p. 1991. 69.95 (*0-19-261873-3*) OUP.

Margetts, Helen & Smyth, Gareth, eds. Turning Japanese? Britain with a Permanent Party of Government. 224p. (C). 1994. pap. 29.95 (*0-85315-785-5*, Pub. by Lawrence & Wishart UK) Humanities.

Margetts, Juliet, ed. Who's Who in Business & Industry in the U. K. 1000p. 1991. lib. bdg. 250.00 (*1-55862-155-5*) St James Pr.

Margetts, Martina, jt. contrib. see Britton, Alison.

Marggraff, Jim, jt. auth. see Schweidler, Rob.

Margham, J. P., jt. auth. see Hale, W. G.

Margherita, Gayle. The Romance of Origins: Language & Sexual Difference in Middle English Literature. LC 94-12610. 256p. (Orig.). (C). 1994. text ed. 34.95 (*0-8122-3217-8*); pap. text ed. 14.95 (*0-8122-1502-8*) U of Pa Pr.

Margherita, Marchione. Clemente Rebora: A Man's Quest for the Absolute. LC 78-7632. (Twayne's World Authors Ser.). 180p. 1979. 12.50 (*0-8057-6362-7*) Am Inst Ital Stud.

Marghon, Blandine. The Bible: The Greatest Stories. (Illus.). 160p. 1992. 16.95 (*0-687-03115-X*) Abingdon.

Margic, Joyce D., jt. auth. see Palumbo, P. J.

Margin, Alex r., Jr., jt. auth. see Benhart, John E.

Margineanu, D., jt. auth. see Schoffeniels, E.

Marginson, Simon. Education & Public Policy in Australia. LC 92-44907. (Illus.). 288p. (C). 1992. pap. write for info. (*0-521-43963-9*) Cambridge U Pr.

— Education & Public Policy in Australia. LC 92-44907. (Illus.). 288p. (C). 1993. 59.95 (*0-521-43345-2*) Cambridge U Pr.

Marginter, Peter. The Baron & the Fish. Bangerter, Lowell A., tr. & aft. by. (Studies in Austrian Literature, Culture, & Thought. Translation Ser.). 311p. (Orig.). 1992. pap. 22.00 (*0-929497-46-5*) Ariadne CA.

Margiotta, Franklin D., ed. Brassey's Encyclopedia of Military History & Biography. (Illus.). 1232p. 1994. 44.95 (*0-02-881096-1*) Brasseys Inc.

Margison, G. P., jt. ed. see Canonico, A.

Margitic, Milorad R. Essai sur la Mythologie du Cid. LC 76-22508. (Romance Monographs: No. 22). 1976. 30.00 (*84-399-5848-X*) Romance.

Margitic, Milorad R., ed. Le Cid: Tragi-Comedie. LC 89-6655. (Purdue University Monographs in Romance Languages: Vol. 28). lxxxv, 302p. (FRE.). 1989. 106.00x (*1-55619-067-0*); pap. 27.95 (*1-55619-068-9*) Benjamins North Am.

Margitondo, Giorgio, et al, eds. HIGH Tc Superconducting Thin Films, Devices, & Applications. LC 88-83947. (Conference Proceeding Ser.: No. 182). 450p. 1989. lib. bdg. 60.50 (*0-88318-383-8*) Am Inst Physics.

Marglin, Frederique A. & Marglin, Stephen A., eds. Dominating Knowledge: Development, Culture, & Resistance. (WIDER Studies in Development Economics). 312p. 1990. 49.95 (*0-19-828694-5*) OUP.

— Dominating Knowledge: Development, Culture, & Resistance. (WIDER Studies in Development Economics). 312p. 1994. reprint ed. pap. 24.95 (*0-19-828838-7*) OUP.

Marglin, Frederique A., jt. ed. see Banuri, Tariq.

Marglin, Stephen, jt. ed. see Apffel-Marglin, Frederique.

Marglin, Stephen A. Growth, Distribution, & Prices. LC 83-18569. 584p. 1987. pap. 12.95 (*0-674-36416-3*) HUP.

— Value & Price in the Labor-Surplus Economy. (Illus.). 1976. 45.00 (*0-19-828194-3*) OUP.

Marglin, Stephen A. & Schor, Juliet B., eds. The Golden Age of Capitalism: Reinterpreting the Postwar Experience. (WIDER Studies in Development Economics). 344p. 1992. pap. 24.95 (*0-19-828741-0*) OUP.

Marglin, Stephen A., jt. ed. see Marglin, Frederique A.

Margo, Curtis & Grossniklaus. Ocular Histopathology: A Guide to Differential Diagnosis. (Illus.). 352p. 1990. text ed. 115.00 (*0-7216-3291-2*) Saunders.

Margo, Curtis, et al, eds. Diagnostic Problems in Clinical Ophthalmology. LC 92-49132. (Illus.). 896p. 1993. text ed. 89.50 (*0-7216-3659-4*) Saunders.

Margo, Glen, jt. ed. see Krieger, Nancy.

Margo, Robert A. Race & Schooling in the South, Eighteen Eighty to Nineteen Fifty: An Economic History. LC 90-11249. (National Bureau of Economic Research Long Term Factors in Economic Development Ser.). (Illus.). 176p. 1990. 24.95 (*0-226-50510-3*) U Ch Pr.

— Race & Schooling in the South, 1880-1950: An Economic History. (National Bureau of Economic Research Long Term Factors in Economic Development Ser.). (Illus.). x, 164p. 1994. pap. text ed. 12.95 (*0-226-50511-1*) U Ch Pr.

Margo, Rod D. Aviation Insurance. 2nd ed. 1989. 199.00 (*0-406-28811-9*, U.K.) Butterworth Legal Pubs.

Margoilin, Philip. Gone But Not Forgotten. 1994. mass mkt. 6.50 (*0-553-56903-1*) Bantam.

Margolese, Richard G., ed. Breast Cancer. LC 83-10059. (Contemporary Issues in Oncology Ser.: Vol. 1). (Illus.). 318p. reprint ed. pap. 90.70 (*0-7837-6240-2*, 2045954) Bks Demand.

Margolf, Charles W. Federal Coal Lease Readjustments: Will Reason Prevail? 120p. (Orig.). (C). 1988. pap. text ed. 15.00 (*0-317-91386-7*) C W Margolf.

***Margolick, David.** At the Bar. 1995. pap. 13.00 (*0-671-88787-4*, Touchstone Bks) S&S Trade.

— Undue Influence: The Battle for the Johnson & Johnson Fortune. LC 92-27521. 1993. 23.00 (*0-688-06425-6*) Morrow.

— Undue Influence: The Epic Battle for the Johnson & Johnson Fortune. 1994. pap. 15.00 (*0-688-13787-3*, Quill) Morrow.

***Margolies.** Pump & Circumstance, Vol. 1. 1995. pap. text ed. 8.95 (*0-8212-2192-2*) Bulfinch Pr.

Margolies, Alan, ed. see Fitzgerald, F. Scott.

Margolies, Barbara A. Kanu of Kathmandu: A Journey to Nepal. LC 92-12482. (Illus.). 40p. (J). (gr. 1-4). 1992. text ed. 14.95 (*0-02-762282-7*, Four Winds Pr) S&S Childrens.

— Olbalbal: A Day in Maasailand. LC 93-19744. (Illus.). 32p. (J). (gr. 1-4). 1994. text ed. 15.95 (*0-02-762284-3*, Four Winds Pr) S&S Childrens.

— Warriors, Wigmen, & Crocodile People: Journeys in Papua New Guinea. LC 92-27475. (Illus.). 40p. (J). (gr. 1-5). 1993. text ed. 14.95 (*0-02-762283-5*, Four Winds Pr) S&S Childrens.

Margolies, David. Monsters of the Deep: Social Dissolution in Shakespeare's Tragedies. 176p. 1994. text ed. 19.95 (*0-7190-3441-8*, Pub. by Manchester Univ Pr UK) St Martin.

— Novel & Society in Elizabethan England. LC 84-20369. 204p. 1985. 38.50 (*0-389-20538-9*, BNB-08100) B&N Imports.

***Margolies, David & Joannou, Maroula, eds.** Heart of the Heartless World: Essays in Cultural Resistance. LC 95-2979. (C). 1995. text ed. 79.95 (*0-7453-0981-X*, Pub. by Pluto Pr UK) Westview.

Margolies, Edward. Which Way Did He Go? The Private Eye in Dashiell Hammett, Raymond Chandler, Chester Himes, & Ross MacDonald. LC 81-1061. 130p. 1982. 25.00 (*0-8419-0436-7*); pap. 15.00 (*0-8419-0790-0*) Holmes & Meier.

Margolies, Eva. The Best of Friends, the Worst of Enemies. 1987. 4.50 (*0-317-61573-4*) PB.

— Undressing the American Male: Men with Sexual Problems & What You Can Do to Help Them. LC 93-30970. 1994. 22.95 (*0-525-93832-X*, Dutton) NAL-Dutton.

— Undressing the American Male: Men with Sexual Problems & What You Can Do to Help Them. 288p. 1995. 12.95 (*0-452-27444-3*, Plume) NAL-Dutton.

Margolies, Jacob. Hank Aaron: Home Run King. Mathews, V., ed. LC 91-29776. (First Bks.). (Illus.). 64p. (J). (gr. 3-6). 1992. lib. bdg. 13.23 (*0-531-20075-2*) Watts.

— Kareem Abdul-Jabbar: Basketball Great. LC 91-31662. (First Bks.). (Illus.). 64p. (J). (gr. 3-6). 1992. lib. bdg. 13.93 (*0-531-20076-0*) Watts.

— The Negro Leagues: The Story of Black Baseball. (African-American Experience Ser.). (Illus.). 144p. (YA). (gr. 7-12). 1993. lib. bdg. 14.98 (*0-531-11130-X*) Watts.

— The Negro Leagues: The Story of Black Baseball. (African-American Experience Ser.). (Illus.). (YA). (gr. 7-12). 1994. pap. 6.95 (*0-531-15694-X*) Watts.

*__Margolies, John.__ Home Away from Home: Motels in America. 128p. 1995. 29.95 (*0-8212-2162-0*) Bulfinch Pr.

— Palaces of Dreams: Movie Theater Postcards. 1993. 8.95 (*0-8212-2017-9*) Bulfinch Pr.

— Pump & Circumstance: The Glory Days of the Gas Station. LC 93-12966. (Illus.). 125p. 1993. 29.95 (*0-8212-1995-2*) Bulfinch Pr.

Margolies, John & Gwathmey, Emily. Signs of Our Times. LC 92-37283. 96p. 1993. 21.95 (*1-55859-209-1*) Abbeville Pr.

Margolies, John & Gwathmey, Emily M. Ticket to Paradise: American Movie Theatres & How We Had Fun. (Illus.). 144p. 1991. 29.95 (*0-8212-1829-8*) Bulfinch Pr.

Margolies, Luise, jt. auth. see Gasparini, Graziano.

Margolies, Morris B. A Gathering of Angels: Angels in Jewish Life & Literature. 288p. (Orig.). 1994. pap. 12.00 (*0-345-38104-1*, Ballantine Trade) Ballantine.

Margolin, David I., ed. Cognitive Neuropsychology in Clinical Practice. (Illus.). 560p. 1992. 60.00 (*0-19-506422-4*) OUP.

Margolin, Gayla, jt. auth. see Jacobson, Neil S.

Margolin, Jean-Claude. Erasme: Le Prix des Mots et de L'Homme. (Collected Studies: No. CS241). 318p. (FRE.). (C). 1986. reprint ed. text ed. 95.00 (*0-86078-189-5*, Pub. by Variorum UK) Ashgate Pub Co.

— Erasme dans son Miroir et dans son Sillage. (Collected Studies: No. CS257). 320p. (ENG & FRE.). (C). 1987. reprint ed. text ed. 95.00 (*0-86078-205-0*, Pub. by Variorum UK) Ashgate Pub Co.

— Humanism in Europe at the Time of the Renaissance. Farthing, John L., tr. LC 89-8093. 88p. 1989. pap. 7.95 (*0-939464-49-7*) Labyrinth Pr.

*__Margolin, Jeannine & Margolin, Malcolm.__ Another Way of Living. 1995. 37.00 (*0-8095-4988-3*) Borgo Pr.

Margolin, Judith, ed. Foundation Fundamentals: A Guide for Grantseekers. 5th ed. 1994. pap. 24.95 (*0-87954-543-7*) Foundation Ctr.

Margolin, Judith B. The Individual's Guide to Grants. LC 83-2252. 314p. 1983. 19.95 (*0-306-41309-4*, Plenum Pr) Plenum.

Margolin, Judith B., ed. Financing a College Education: The Essential Guide for the 90s. (Illus.). 320p. 1989. 24.95 (*0-306-43071-1*, Plenum Pr) Plenum.

— Financing a College Education: The Essential Guide for the 90's. LC 88-37657. (Illus.). 320p. 1989. pap. 14.95 (*0-306-43281-1*, Plenum Pr) Plenum.

— Foundation Center's User-Friendly Guide: Grantseeker's Guide to Resources. 3rd ed. 1994. pap. text ed. 14.95 (*0-87954-541-0*) Foundation Ctr.

Margolin, Laura I., jt. ed. see Burns, Michael E.

Margolin, Leslie. Goodness Personified: The Emergence of Gifted Children. LC 93-47411. (Social Problems & Social Issues Ser.). 208p. 1994. lib. bdg. 37.95 (*0-202-30526-0*); pap. 18.95 (*0-202-30527-9*) Aldine de Gruyter.

Margolin, Malcolm. The Earth Manual: How to Work on Wild Land Without Taming It. rev. ed. (Illus.). 240p. 1985. reprint ed. pap. 16.00 (*0-930588-18-5*) Heyday Bks.

— The Earth Manual: How to Work on Wild Land Without Taming It. (Illus.). 239p. 1991. reprint ed. lib. bdg. 39.00x (*0-8095-4962-X*) Borgo Pr.

— The East Bay Out: A Personal Guide to the East Bay Regional Parks. rev. ed. (Illus.). 256p. 1988. pap. 12.50 (*0-930588-15-0*) Heyday Bks.

— The East Bay Out: A Personal Guide to the East Bay Regional Parks. (Illus.). 227p. 1991. reprint ed. lib. bdg. 31.00x (*0-8095-4965-4*) Borgo Pr.

— The Ohlone Way: Indian Life in the San Francisco-Monterey Bay Area. LC 78-56826. (Illus.). 182p. (Orig.). 1978. pap. 12.95 (*0-930588-01-0*) Heyday Bks.

— The Ohlone Way: Indian Life in the San Francisco-Monterey Bay Area. 182p. (Orig.). 1991. reprint ed. lib. bdg. 33.00x (*0-8095-4958-1*) Borgo Pr.

Margolin, Malcolm, comment. The Way We Lived: California Indian Reminiscences, Stories, & Songs. rev. ed. (Illus.). 320p. 1993. pap. 14.95 (*0-930588-55-X*) Heyday Bks.

Margolin, Malcolm, ed. Native Ways: California Indian Stories & Memories. (Illus.). 160p. (J). (gr. 4-6). 1994. pap. 7.95 (*0-930588-73-8*) Heyday Bks.

— The Way We Lived: California Indian Reminiscences, Stories, & Songs. rev. ed. (Illus.). 260p. (C). 1993. lib. bdg. 37.00x (*0-8095-4983-2*) Borgo Pr.

Margolin, Malcolm, tr. Mourning Dove: A Yurok-English Tale. (Bilingual Chapbook Ser.: No. 1). 12p. (C). 1993. reprint ed. lib. bdg. 20.00x (*0-8095-4982-4*) Borgo Pr.

*__Margolin, Malcolm & Montijo, Yolanda.__ Native Ways: California Indian Stories & Memories. (Illus.). 128p. 1995. lib. bdg. 23.00x (*0-8095-4985-9*) Borgo Pr.

Margolin, Malcolm, jt. ed. see Gendar, Jeannine.

Margolin, Malcolm, jt. auth. see Margolin, Jeannine.

Margolin, Malcolm, ed. see Martin, Carol O.

Margolin, Malcolm, jt. auth. see Pitcher, Don.

*__Margolin, Phillip.__ After Dark. LC 94-41997. 384p. 1995. 23.95 (*0-385-47548-9*) Doubleday.

— Heartstone. 1995. mass mkt. 6.50 (*0-553-56978-3*) Bantam.

Margolin, Phillip M. Gone, but Not Forgotten. LC 93-21859. 1993. 22.00 (*0-385-47002-9*) Doubleday.

Margolin, Victor, intro. Design Discourse: History, Theory, Criticism. LC 89-33920. (Illus.). 304p. 1989. lib. bdg. 55.00 (*0-226-50513-8*); pap. text ed. 17.95 (*0-226-50514-6*) U Ch Pr.

*__Margolin, Victor & Buchanan, Richard, eds.__ The Idea of Design. (Design Issues Reader Ser.). (Illus.). 315p. (C). 1995. pap. 17.00x (*0-262-63166-0*) MIT Pr.

Margolin, Victor, jt. ed. see Buchanan, Richard.

Margoliouth, B. Liturgy of the Nile. 1979. pap. 4.95 (*0-89981-052-7*) Eastern Orthodox.

Margoliouth, D. S. The Relations Between Arabs & Israelis Prior to the Rise of Islam. (British Academy, London, Schweich Lectures on Biblical Archaeology Series, 1930). 1974. reprint ed. pap. 20.00 (*0-8115-1263-0*) Periodicals Srv.

Margoliouth, D. S., tr. see Miskawayh, et al.

Margoliouth, David S. Analecta Orientalia Ad Poeticam Aristoteleam. vi, 243p. reprint ed. write for info. (*0-318-71531-7*, Pub. by Georg Olms GW) Lubrecht & Cramer.

— Cairo, Jerusalem, & Damascus, Three Chief Cities of the Egyptian Sultans. LC 80-1918. (Illus.). reprint ed. 54.50 (*0-404-18980-6*) AMS Pr.

— The Early Development of Mohammedanism. LC 77-27156. (Hibbert Lectures: 1913). reprint ed. 34.50 (*0-404-60415-3*) AMS Pr.

— Mohammed & the Rise of Islam. LC 73-14455. reprint ed. 45.00 (*0-404-58273-7*) AMS Pr.

— Mohammed & the Rise of Islam. LC 73-38361. (Select Bibliographies Reprint Ser.). 1977. reprint ed. 37.95 (*0-8369-6778-X*) Ayer.

Margoliovth, D. S., tr. see Mez, Adam.

*__Margolis.__ Woof! 1995. write for info. (*0-517-88451-8*) Random Hse Value.

Margolis, Alan M. & Monahan, Thomas J. United Kingdom: Medical Laboratory Science, Occupational Therapy, Physiotherapy. LC 79-49614. (World Education Ser.). 192p. reprint ed. pap. 54.80 (*0-8357-7534-8*, 2036247) Bks Demand.

*__Margolis, Andrew.__ The Fax Modem Source Book. pap. text ed. 39.95 (*0-471-95072-6*) Wiley.

Margolis, Anne, ed. see Honeywell, Jerry L.

Margolis, Anne T. Henry James & the Problem of Audience: An International Act. LC 84-24073. (Studies in Modern Literature: No. 49). 267p. reprint ed. pap. 76.10 (*0-8357-1624-4*, 2070507) Bks Demand.

Margolis, Art. Computer Technician' Handbook. 3rd ed. 1989. pap. text ed. 26.95 (*0-07-157547-2*) McGraw.

— Computer Technician's Handbook. 2nd ed. (Illus.). 490p. pap. 19.95 (*0-8306-1939-9*) TAB Bks.

— Computer Technician's Handbook. 3rd ed. (Illus.). 512p. 1989. 32.95 (*0-8306-9279-7*); pap. 24.95 (*0-8306-3279-4*) TAB Bks.

— Troubleshooting & Repairing Personal Computers. 2nd ed. 1992. text ed. 34.95 (*0-07-157667-3*); pap. text ed. 23.95 (*0-07-157666-5*) McGraw.

— Troubleshooting & Repairing Personal Computers. 2nd ed. 544p. 1991. 34.95 (*0-8306-2187-3*, 3504, Windcrest); pap. 23.95 (*0-8306-2186-5*, Windcrest) TAB Bks.

— Troubleshooting & Repairing Personal Computers. 3rd ed. LC 93-39124. (Glencoe Tech Ser.). 1993. write for info. (*0-02-802003-0*) Macmillan.

— Troubleshooting & Repairing the New Personal Computer. (Illus.). 416p. (Orig.). 1987. 26.95 (*0-8306-0209-7*) TAB Bks.

— Troubleshooting & Repairing Your Commodore 128. (Illus.). 400p. 1988. 27.95 (*0-8306-9099-9*, 3099) TAB Bks.

— Troubleshooting & Repairing Your Commodore 64. (Illus.). 288p. (Orig.). 1985. 22.95 (*0-8306-0889-3*, 1889) TAB Bks.

Margolis, Barbara A. & Moller, Jonathan R., eds. The National Protocol Directory, 1987. (Illus.). 83p. (Orig.). 1987. pap. 6.00 (*0-9619228-0-X*) NYC Mayors Comm Protocol.

Margolis, Bernard P., jt. auth. see Bixler, James P.

Margolis, Bob, ed. see Dvorak, Thomas L., et al.

Margolis, Bob, jt. auth. see Weber, Rhoda B.

Margolis, Carolyn, jt. auth. see Viola, Herman J.

Margolis, Carolyn J. & Danis, Jan S. Magnificent Voyagers: The U. S. Exploring Expedition, 1838-1842. Viola, Herman J., ed. LC 85-40192. 304p. (Orig.). 1985. pap. 27.50 (*0-87474-945-X*, VIMVP) Smithsonian.

Margolis, Carolyn J., jt. ed. see Viola, Herman J.

Margolis, Daniel J. & Schoenberg, Elliot S., eds. Curriculum, Community, Commitment: Views on the American Jewish Day School in Memory of Bennett I. Solomon. LC 93-2812. 1993. 24.95 (*0-87441-545-4*) Behrman.

*__Margolis, Deborah P.__ Freud & His Mother: Preoedipal Aspects of Freud's Personality. LC 94-44328. Date not set. 30.00 (*1-56821-448-0*) Aronson.

Margolis, Edwin & Moses, Stanley. The Elusive Quest: The Struggle for Equality of Educational Opportunity. LC 87-27076. (Illus.). 170p. (Orig.). 1992. pap. 16.50 (*0-945257-46-5*) Apex Pr.

Margolis, F. G. & Unanyants, T. P. Production of Complex Fertilizers. 146p. 1971. text ed. 73.50 (*0-7065-1024-0*, Pub. by Keter Pub IS) Coronet Bks.

Margolis, F. L. & Getchell, T. V., eds. Molecular Neurobiology of the Olfactory System: Molecular, Membranous, & Cytological Studies. LC 88-14821. (Illus.). 398p. 1988. 95.00 (*0-306-42858-X*, Plenum Pr) Plenum.

Margolis, Fredric, jt. auth. see Stockard, Oliva.

Margolis, Fredric H. & Bell, Chip R. Instructing for Results. rev. ed. LC 86-50409. Orig. Title: Managing the Learning Process. 128p. 1986. pap. text ed. 24.95 (*0-88390-196-X*) Pfeiffer & Co.

Margolis, Gary. The Day We Still Stand Here. LC 82-4773. (Contemporary Poetry Ser.). 96p. 1983. pap. 7.95 (*0-8203-0635-5*) U of Ga Pr.

— Falling Awake. LC 85-16509. (Contemporary Poetry Ser.). 128p. 1986. 15.00 (*0-8203-0825-0*); pap. 6.95 (*0-8203-0826-9*) U of Ga Pr.

Margolis, H. A. Spectra & the Steenrod Algebra. (Mathematical Library: Vol. 29). 500p. 1984. 105.25 (*0-444-86516-0*, North Holland) Elsevier.

Margolis, Harold J. Inhibitory Control Theory: A Mind-Body Theory of Sensory Signaling & Stressor Accommodation. 681p. (C). 1991. lib. bdg. 57.00 (*1-879646-04-8*) Silogram.

— Stress: A Mind-Body Approach to Understanding & Overcoming Stress. (Frontiers of Consciousness Ser.). 750p. 1990. text ed. 69.50 (*0-685-26542-0*) Irvington.

Margolis, Harry A. Title Fifty-Nine; Tort Claims Against Public Entities, Amendments to May 1, 1984: Comments & Annotations. LC 84-208513. (Illus.). vii, 352p. 1984. pap. 28.00 (*0-933902-10-7*) Gann Law Bks.

Margolis, Harry S. Elderlaw Forms Manual: Essential Documents for Representing the Older Client. 500p. 1992. ring bd. 99.00 (*0-316-54629-1*) Little.

Margolis, Howard. Paradigms & Barriers: How Habits of Mind Govern Scientific Beliefs. LC 92-44650. (Illus.). 288p. (C). 1993. lib. bdg. 40.00 (*0-226-50522-7*); pap. text ed. 15.95 (*0-226-50523-5*) U Ch Pr.

— Patterns, Thinking, & Cognition: A Theory of Judgement. (Illus.). xii, 332p. 1988. pap. text ed. 16.95 (*0-226-50528-6*) U Ch Pr.

— Selfishness, Altruism & Rationality: A Theory of Social Choice. LC 84-2620. xii, 194p. 1984. pap. text ed. 12.95 (*0-226-50524-3*) U Ch Pr.

Margolis, Isidor & Markowitz, Sidney L. Jewish Holidays & Festivals. (Illus.). 132p. (Orig.). 1995. pap. 6.95 (*0-8065-0285-1*, Citadel Pr) Carol Pub Group.

Margolis, James M. Decorating Plastics. 135p. (C). 1986. text ed. 39.95 (*1-56990-058-2*) Hanser-Gardner.

— Engineering Thermoplastics: Properties & Applications. (Plastics Engineering Ser.: Vol. 8). 408p. 1985. 140.00 (*0-8247-8051-5*) Dekker.

— Instrumentation for Thermoplastic Processing. 1988. 35.00 (*0-685-22189-X*) T-C Pubns CA.

— Instrumentation for Thermoplastics Processing. 99p. (C). 1988. text ed. 39.95 (*1-56990-059-0*) Hanser-Gardner.

— Medical & Hospital Plastic Products: A Special Report on New Applications & Research. LC 83-15199. (Series of Special Reports: No. 10). 180p. reprint ed. pap. 51.30 (*0-7837-0695-2*, 2041028) Bks Demand.

Margolis, James M., ed. Conductive Polymers & Plastics. (Illus.). 224p. 1989. 42.50 (*0-412-01431-9*, Chap & Hall NY) Chapman & Hall.

Margolis, James M., et al. Rationality, Relativism & the Human Sciences. 1986. lib. bdg. 95.00 (*90-247-3271-9*) Kluwer Ac.

Margolis, John D. Joseph Wood Krutch: A Writer's Life. LC 80-182. (Illus.). 272p. reprint ed. pap. 77.60 (*0-685-20456-1*, 2029849) Bks Demand.

Margolis, Jonathan. Cleese Encounters: The Unauthorized Biography of Monty Python Veteran John Cleese. (Illus.). 304p. 1993. pap. 12.95 (*0-312-09769-7*) St Martin.

*__Margolis, Jonathan & Morris, Gabrielle.__ The Commuter's Tale. (Illus.). 224p. 1993. pap. 8.95 (*1-85592-631-8*) Trafalgar.

Margolis, Joseph. Culture & Cultural Entities. LC 83-4635. 170p. 1983. lib. bdg. 74.50 (*90-277-1574-2*) Kluwer Ac.

— The Flux of History & the Flux of Science. LC 93-4134. 1993. 40.00 (*0-520-08319-9*) U CA Pr.

— Historied Thought, Constructed World: A Conceptual Primer for the Turn of the Millennium. 382p. 1995. 48.00 (*0-520-20113-2*) U CA Pr.

— Interpretation Radical but Not Unruly: The New Puzzle of the Arts & History. LC 94-15598. 1995. 42.00 (*0-520-08769-0*) U CA Pr.

— Persons & Minds: The Prospects of Nonreductive Materialism. (Synthese Library: No. 121). 1977. lib. bdg. 70.00 (*90-277-0854-1*); pap. text ed. 36.50 (*90-277-0863-0*) Kluwer Ac.

— Philosophy Looks at the Arts: Contemporary Readings in Aesthetics. 3rd ed. LC 88-12303. 592p. (C). 1987. 39.95 (*0-87722-439-0*); pap. 27.95 (*0-87722-440-4*) Temple U Pr.

— Science Without Unity: Reconciling the Human & Natural Sciences. 368p. (C). 1987. text ed. 45.00 (*0-631-15173-7*) Blackwell Pubs.

— Texts without Referents: Reconciling Science & Narrative. (Persistance of Reality Ser.). 400p. 1988. text ed. 54.95 (*0-631-16319-0*) Blackwell Pubs.

— The Truth about Relativism. 240p. (C). 1991. pap. text ed. 21.95 (*0-631-18178-4*) Blackwell Pubs.

Margolis, Joseph, ed. see Farias, Victor.

Margolis, Joseph, jt. ed. see Rockmore, Tom.

Margolis, Judy, jt. auth. see English, Sandal.

Margolis, Julius, ed. Analysis of Public Output. (Universities-National Bureau Conference Ser.: No. 23). 425p. 1970. text ed. 111.10 (*0-87014-220-8*) Natl Bur Econ Res.

— The Analysis of Public Output: A Conference of the Universities - National Bureau Committee for Economic Research. LC 78-119997. (Universities-National Bureau Conference Ser.: No. 23). (Illus.). 427p. reprint ed. pap. 121.70 (*0-8357-7565-8*, 2056886) Bks Demand.

— The Public Economy of Urban Communities: Papers Presented at the 2nd Conference on Urban Public Expenditures, Feb. 21-22, 1964. LC 77-86404. (Resources for the Future, Inc. Publications). 288p. reprint ed. 55.00 (*0-404-60339-4*) AMS Pr.

Margolis, Julius, jt. auth. see Hanson, Royce.

Margolis, Karen, ed. see Klaniczay, Gabor.

*__Margolis, L. & Guoot, C.__ Pacific Salmon Life Histories. 608p. 1991. 65.00 (*0-7748-0359-2*) U of Wash Pr.

Margolis, Lawrence. Executive Agreements & Presidential Power in Foreign Policy. LC 85-12484. 172p. 1985. text ed. 49.95 (*0-275-90023-1*, C0023, Praeger Pubs) Greenwood.

Margolis, Marianne F., ed. see Stieglitz, Alfred.

Margolis, Matthew & Siegal, Mordecai. Woof! My Twenty-Five Years of Training Dogs. LC 93-40002. 1994. reprint ed. 20.00 (*0-517-59148-0*, Crown) Crown Pub Group.

Margolis, Matthew & Swan, Catherine. The Dog In Your Life. LC 82-40037. (Illus.). 368p. 1982. pap. 14.00 (*0-394-71174-2*, Vin) Random.

Margolis, Matthew, jt. auth. see Sendak, Maurice.

Margolis, Matthew, jt. auth. see Siegal, Mordecai.

Margolis, Max L. The Book of Joshua in Greek According to the Critically Restored Text with an Apparatus Containing the Variants of the Principal Recensions & of the Individual Witnesses, Pt. 5: Joshua 19: 39 - 24: 33. LC 91-21422. xxvi, 457p. 1992. pap. 35.00 (*0-900268-66-2*) Eisenbrauns.

Margolis, Maxine E. Mothers & Such: Views of American Women & Why They Changed. LC 83-12369. (Illus.). 360p. (C). 1984. pap. 14.00 (*0-520-05596-9*) U CA Pr.

Margolis, Maxine L. Little Brazil: An Ethnography of Brazilian Immigrants in New York City. LC 93-13699. (Illus.). 328p. 1994. text ed. 49.50 (*0-691-03348-X*); pap. text ed. 14.95 (*0-691-00056-5*) Princeton U Pr.

— The Moving Frontier: Social & Economic Change in a Southern Brazilian Community. LC 73-7730. (Latin American Monographs: Ser. 2, No. 11). (Illus.). 292p. reprint ed. pap. 83.30 (*0-7837-5074-9*, 2044772) Bks Demand.

Margolis, Maxine L. & Carter, William E., eds. Brazil: Anthropological Perspectives. LC 79-11843. (Illus.). 448p. 1979. text ed. 53.00 (*0-231-04714-2*) Col U Pr.

Margolis, Maxine L., jt. ed. see Murphy, Martin F.

Margolis, Michael. Viable Democracy. LC 79-5053. 1979. text ed. 29.95 (*0-312-83886-7*) St Martin.

Margolis, Michael, ed. Free Expression, Public Support, & Censorship: Examining Government's Role in the Arts in Canada & the United States. LC 93-30572. 160p. (Orig.). Date not set. lib. bdg. 46.50 (*0-8191-9289-9*); pap. text ed. 18.50 (*0-8191-9290-2*) U Pr of Amer.

Margolis, Michael & Green, John C., eds. Machine Politics, Sound Bites, & Nostalgia: On Studying Political Parties. LC 92-32648. 78p. (Orig.). (C). 1992. lib. bdg. 34.00 (*0-8191-8855-7*); pap. text ed. 10.50 (*0-8191-8856-5*) U Pr of Amer.

Margolis, Michael & Mauser, Gary A. Manipulating Public Opinion. 423p. (C). 1989. pap. 24.95 (*0-534-11121-1*) Intl Thomson.

Margolis, Nadia. Joan of Arc in History, Literature, & Film: A Select, Annotated Bibliography. LC 90-39611. 432p. 1990. 50.00 (*0-8240-4638-2*, H1224) Garland.

Margolis, Nadia, tr. see De Pizan, Christine.

Margolis, Nancy, ed. see Griffin, Farah J. & Rony, Fatimah T.

Margolis, Nancy H., ed. see Adcock, Craig, et al.

Margolis, Nancy H., ed. see Bloemink, Barbara J., et al.

Margolis, Nancy H., ed. see Fleming, Jeff.

Margolis, Nancy H., ed. see Kuspit, Donald, et al.

Margolis, Nancy H., ed. see Larson, John C. & Fleming, Jeff.

Margolis, Nancy H., ed. see Lineker, Bruce, et al.

Margolis, Neal & Harmon, N. Paul. Accounting Essentials. 2nd ed. LC 85-12332. 319p. 1985. pap. text ed. 14.95 (*0-471-82721-5*) Wiley.

Margolis, Otto S. Acute Grief: Loss of an Adult Child. LC 87-18315. 208p. 1988. text ed. 55.00 (*0-275-91304-X*, C1304, Praeger Pubs) Greenwood.

— Grief & the Meaning of the Funeral. 1979. 17.95 (*0-405-12501-1*) Ayer.

Margolis, Otto S., ed. Acute Grief: Counseling the Bereaved. LC 80-21020. (Foundation of Thanatology Ser.). 320p. 1981. text ed. 52.00 (*0-231-04586-7*) Col U Pr.

Margolis, Otto S. & Cherico, Daniel J. Thanatology Abstracts, 1977. 1980. 19.95 (*0-405-12503-8*) Ayer.

— Thanatology Abstracts 1979. 1981. 18.95 (*0-405-14222-6*, 19702) Ayer.

Margolis, Otto S., jt. auth. see Cherico, Daniel J.

Margolis, Otto S., et al, eds. Loss, Grief, & Bereavement: A Guide for Counseling. LC 85-12260. 176p. 1985. text ed. 49.95 (*0-275-90144-0*, C0144, Praeger Pubs) Greenwood.

Margolis, P. E. & Darnell, P. A. Software Engineering in C. (Books on Professional Computing). (Illus.). 500p. 1989. pap. 32.00 (*0-387-96574-2*) Spr-Verlag.

Margolis, P. E., jt. auth. see Darnell, P. A.

Margolis, Philip. Random House Personal Computer Dictionary. 1991. pap. 10.00 (*0-679-73480-5*) Random.

Margolis, R. K., jt. auth. see Margolis, R. U.

Margolis, R. U. & Margolis, R. K., eds. Neurobiology of Glycoconjugates. (Illus.). 472p. 1989. 105.00 (*0-306-43128-9*, Plenum Pr) Plenum.

Margolis, Richard J. Secrets of a Small Brother. LC 84-3478. (Illus.). 40p. (J). (gr. 1-4). 1984. text ed. 12.95 (*0-02-762280-0*, Mac Bks Young Read) S&S Childrens.

Margolis, Robin, jt. auth. see Goodman-Malmuth, Leslie.

Margolis, S., jt. auth. see Mayne, R.

Margolis, Seth, ed. see Hijuelos, Oscar.

Margolis, Seth, ed. see McMurtry, Larry.

Margolis, Seth J. Losing Isaiah. LC 92-38301. 384p. 1993. 22.95 (*1-56282-807-X*) Hyperion.

— Losing Isaiah. 400p. 1994. reprint ed. pap. text ed. 5.99 (*0-515-11539-8*) Jove Pubns.

Margolis, Simeon. The Practice of Medicine: A Self-Assessment Guide. 4th ed. 315p. 1989. pap. text ed. 36.50 (*0-8385-7891-8*, A7891-3) Appleton & Lange.

An Asterisk (*) at the beginning of an entry indicates that the title is appearing in BIP for the first time.

Margolis, Simeon, ed. The Johns Hopkins Handbook of Drugs: Specially Edited & Organized by Disease for People over 50. LC 93-7465. 1200p. 1993. 39.95 (*0-929661-07-9*, Random) Rebus.

Margolis, Stephen & Wasserberger, Jonathan. Pharmacology & Therapeutics in Emergency Care. LC 82-122. (Illus.). 410p. (Orig.). 1985. pap. 16.95 (*0-940122-03-0*) Mosby Multi-Media.

Margolis, Susanna. Adventuring in the Pacific: The Sierra Club Travel Guide to the Islands of Polynesia, Melanesia, & Micronesia. LC 87-23558. (Adventure Travel Guide Ser.). (Illus.). 400p. 1988. pap. 12.95 (*0-87156-780-6*) Sierra.

Margolis, Susanna & Harmon, Ginger. Walking Europe from Top to Bottom. LC 85-18469. (Adventure Travel Guide Ser.). (Illus.). 320p. (Orig.). 1986. pap. 10.95 (*0-87156-752-0*) Sierra.

***Margolis, Victor.** The Platespinner: Playing with Time. 300p. (Orig.). 1995. pap. 14.95 (*0-9642973-8-8*) Marik Pubg.

Margolis, Vivienne, et al. Fanfare for a Feather: Seventy-Seven Ways to Celebrate Practically Anything. LC 91-16134. (Illus.). 176p. (Orig.). (C). 1991. pap. 9.95 (*0-89390-202-0*) Resource Pubns.

Margolius, Harry S., jt. ed. see Greenbaum, Lowell M.

***Margolius, Ivan.** Church of the Sacred Heart: Prague 1922-33: Joze Plecnik. (Architecture in Detail Ser.). (Illus.). 60p. (Orig.). (C). 1995. pap. 29.95 (*0-7148-3351-7*, Pub. by Phaidon Press UK) Chronicle Bks.

Margoliuth, David S. Mohammed. LC 79-2875. 151p. 1981. reprint ed. 23.00 (*0-8305-0044-8*) Hyperion Conn.

Margoliuth, David S., tr. see Zaydan, Jirji.

Margolus, Norman, jt. auth. see Toffoli, Tommaso.

Margon, Lester. Construction of American Furniture Treasures. (Illus.). 168p. 1975. reprint ed. pap. 7.95 (*0-486-23056-2*) Dover.

Margoninski, Y., ed. see Israeli Vacuum Congress Staff.

Margopoulos, Richard. Tales of the Black Diamond. (Illus.). 80p. (Orig.). 1993. pap. 8.95 (*0-9623841-9-4*) Fantagor Pr.

Margoschis, Richard. Recording Natural History Sounds. (Illus.). 1979. 8.95 (*0-913714-24-0*); pap. 5.95 (*0-913714-25-9*) Legacy Books.

Margoshes, David. Saskatchewan. (Discover Canada Ser.). (Illus.). 144p. (J). (gr. 4 up). 1992. lib. bdg. 20.55 (*0-516-06618-8*) Childrens.

Margossian, Marzbed, jt. ed. see Der Hovanessian, Diana.

Margot, Alain G. The Chinese Community in Vietnam under the French. LC 93-24943. 196p. 1993. pap. 39.95 (*0-7734-1941-1*) E Mellen.

Margraf, Wolfgang. Untersuchungen zur Production und Reingung eines gelben Farbstoffes des Basidiomyceten: Pleurotus ostreatus (Jacq. ex Fr.) Kummer. (Bibliotheca Mycologica Ser.: No. 93). (Illus.). 95p. (GER.). 1984. 26.00 (*3-7682-1412-5*) Lubrecht & Cramer.

Margrave, John L., ed. Modern High Temperature Science. 480p. 1984. 115.00 (*0-89603-072-5*) Humana.

***Margrave-Jones, Clive V.** Mellows: The Law of Succession. 5th ed. 680p. 1993. pap. text ed. 66.00 (*0-406-02438-3*, UK) Butterworth Legal Pubs.

Margrave-Jones, Clive V., jt. auth. see Rodgers, Christopher P.

Margrave-Jones, Clive V., et al, eds. Butterworths Wills, Probate & Administration Service, 2 vols. 1990. Set, U.K. ring bd. 460.00 (*0-406-12500-7*, U.K.) Butterworth Legal Pubs.

Margroff, Robert E., jt. auth. see Anthony, Piers.

Margry, Pierre, ed. Decouvertes et Establissements des francais dans l'ouest et dans le sud de l'Amerique septentrionale: 1614-1754, 6 vols., Set. Incl. Vol. 1. Voyages des francais sur les Grands Lacs et Decouverte de l'Ohio et du Mississippi (1614-1684) reprint ed. (*0-318-50550-9*); Vol. 2. Lettres de Cavelier de la Salle et Correspondance Relative a ses Entreprises (1678-1685) reprint ed. (*0-318-50551-7*); Vol. 3. Recherche des Bouches du Mississippi et Voyage a Travers le Continent Depuis les Cotes du Texas jusqu'a Quebec (1669-1698) reprint ed. (*0-318-50552-5*); Vol. 4. Decouverte par mer des bouches du Mississippi et etablissement de Lemoyne d'Iberville sur le golfe du Mexique (1694-1703) reprint ed. (*0-318-50553-3*); Vol. 5. Premiere Formation d'une Chaine de Postes entre le Fleuve Saint-Laurent et le Golfe du Mexique (1683-1724) reprint ed. (*0-318-50554-1*); Vol. 6. Exploration des Affluents du Mississippi et Decouverte des Montagnes Rocheuses (1679-1754) reprint ed. (*0-318-50555-X*); 750.00 (*0-404-04230-9*) AMS Pr.

Marguardt, Michael & Reynolds, Angus. The Global Learning Organization. LC 93-2391. 336p. 1993. text ed. 25.00 (*1-55623-839-8*) Irwin Prof Pubng.

Marguerite d'Angouleme. Correspondance: Annees 1521-1522, Vol. 1. Briconnet, Guillaume et al, eds. 238p. (FRE.). 1975. pap. 49.95 (*0-7859-5530-5*) Fr & Eur.

Marguerite D'Angouleme. The Heptameron. Machen, Arthur, tr. LC 76-48439. (Library of World Literature Ser.). 1985. reprint ed. lib. bdg. 30.00 (*0-88355-574-3*) Hyperion Conn.

— L' Heptameron des Nouvelles, 4 vols. 1500p. (FRE.). 1969. 350.00 (*0-7859-5531-3*) Fr & Eur.

— La Navire Ou Consolation du Roi Francois 1er a Sasoeur Marguerite: Edition Critique. Marichal, Robert, ed. 347p. (FRE.). 1956. pap. 115.00 (*0-7859-5533-X*) Fr & Eur.

— Poesies du Roi Francois 1er, de Louise de Savoie, Duchesse D'Angouleme, de Marguerite, Reine de Navarre. 243p. (FRE.). 1970. reprint ed. 75.00 (*0-7859-5529-1*) Fr & Eur.

Marguerite De Navarre. L' Heptameron. Francois, ed. (Coll. Prestige). 27.95 (*0-685-34187-9*); pap. 14.95 (*0-685-34186-0*) Fr & Eur.

***Marguerite of Angouleme.** Theatre Profane. Reynolds-Cornell, Regine, tr. 238p. 1992. pap. 8.00 (*1-895537-06-1*, DH90, Pub. by Dovehouse CN) MRTS.

***Marguerite, Yves.** Dictionnaires des Reves. 385p. (FRE.). 1990. pap. 38.95 (*0-7859-8639-1*, 226801004x) Fr & Eur.

Margueron, C. Modern Saturn Italian-French, French-Italian Dictionary: Dictionnaire Moderne Saturne Italien-Francais-Italien. 1600p. (FRE & ITA.). 1983. 85.00 (*0-8288-0370-6*, M6833) Fr & Eur.

Margueron, C. & Folena, G. Larousse Apollo French-Italian, Italian-French Dictionary: Dictionnaire Larousse Apollo Francais-Italien-Francais. 992p. (FRE & ITA.). 1980. 22.95 (*0-8288-0369-2*, M14295) Fr & Eur.

***Margueron, Claude & Eolena, Gianfranco.** Dictionnaire General Francais-Italien, Italien-Francais. 1994. write for info. (*0-7859-7661-2*, 2034513347) Fr & Eur.

Marguerre, K. Mechanics of Vibrations. Wolfel, H., ed. (Mechanics of Structural Systems Ser.: No. 2). 282p. 1979. lib. bdg. 65.00 (*90-286-0086-8*) Kluwer Ac.

Marguez, Gustavo. El Seguro Social En Venezuela. 56p. 1992. write for info. (*0-940602-54-7*) IADB.

***Marguez, Joseph A.** East & West of the Sangre De Cristos No. 1: La Familia De Cordoba. Simms, Charlene G., ed. (Illus.). 162p. (Orig.). 1991. pap. text ed. write for info. (*0-9628974-1-8*) El Escrito.

Marguglio. Environmental Management Systems. 208p. 1991. 59.75 (*0-8247-8523-1*) Dekker.

Marguglio, B. W., ed. Quality Systems in the Nuclear Industry - STP 616. 700p. 1977. 37.75 (*0-8031-0197-X*, 04-616000-34) ASTM.

Margules, C. R. & Austin, M. P., eds. Nature Conservation. (C). 1991. 60.00 (*0-643-05089-2*, Pub. by CSIRO AT) Intl Spec Bk.

Margulias, Ivan & Meish, Charles. Skoda. (Illus.). 192p. 1992. 49.95 (*1-85532-237-4*, Pub. by Osprey Pubng Ltd UK) Motorbooks Intl.

***Margulies.** Say Please: Shari Lewis' Baby Lamb Chop. (J). 1995. 4.25 (*0-307-12874-1*, Golden Pr) Western Pub.

Margulies, Alfred. The Empathic Imagination. (C). 1989. 22.95 (*0-393-70076-3*) Norton.

Margulies, Alice. Compassion. (Illus.). 64p. (YA). (gr. 7-12). 1990. lib. bdg. 14.95 (*0-8239-1108-X*) Rosen Group.

Margulies, Dan, jt. auth. see Masie, Elliott.

Margulies, Donald. Found a Peanut. 1984. pap. 4.75 (*0-8222-0417-7*) Dramatists Play.

— The Loman Family Picnic. (Illus.). 120p. 1994. 8.99 (*1-56865-097-3*, GuildAmerica) Dblday Bk Music.

— The Loman Family Picnic. rev. ed. 1994. pap. 4.75 (*0-8222-0684-6*) Dramatists Play.

— The Model Apartment. 1990. pap. 4.75 (*0-8222-0767-2*) Dramatists Play.

— Pitching to the Star & Other Short Plays. 1993. 4.75 (*0-8222-1358-3*) Dramatists Play.

— Sight Unseen. 1992. pap. 4.75 (*0-8222-1317-6*) Dramatists Play.

— Sight Unseen: And Other Plays. 304p. (Orig.). 1995. pap. 14.95 (*1-55936-103-4*) Theatre Comm.

— What's Wrong with This Picture. 75p. (Orig.). 1988. pap. 4.95 (*0-88145-059-6*) Broadway Play.

Margulies, Edward & Rebello, Stephen. Bad Movies We Love. (Illus.). 352p. (Orig.). 1993. pap. 12.00 (*0-452-27005-7*, Plume) NAL-Dutton.

Margulies, Harold & Bloch, Lucille S. Foreign Medical Graduates in the United States. LC 69-18040. (Commonwealth Fund Publications). (Illus.). 1990. 23.50 (*0-674-30875-1*) HUP.

Margulies, Herbert F. The Decline of the Progressive Movement in Wisconsin 1890-1920. LC 68-63073. 310p. 1968. 7.50 (*0-87020-060-7*) State Hist Soc Wis.

— The Mild Reservationists & the League of Nations Controversy in the Senate. LC 89-4702. 264p. 1989. text ed. 39.00 (*0-8262-0693-X*) U of Mo Pr.

Margulies, Julia, jt. auth. see Weintraub, Dov.

Margulies, Nancy. Mapping Inner Space: Learning & Teaching Mind Mapping. (Illus.). 128p. 1991. 24.95 (*0-913705-56-X*) Zephyr Pr AZ.

— Yes, You Can...Draw! Rose, Diana, ed. (Illus.). 75p. (Orig.). 1991. pap. text ed. 29.95 (*0-905553-35-7*, Pub. by Accel Lrn Sys UK) Acclrtd Learn.

Margulies, Sam. Getting Divorced Without Ruining Your Life. 304p. (Orig.). 1992. pap. 12.00 (*0-671-72826-1*, Fireside) S&S Trade.

Margulies, Sheldon. Everyday Doctoring: A New Approach to the Logic & Reasoning of Neurology & Medicine. (Illus.). 575p. (Orig.). 1986. pap. text ed. 14.95 (*0-9617669-0-5*) Panda Pub Co.

Margulies, Sheldon & Lasson, Kenneth. Learning Law: The Mastery of Legal Logic. LC 92-71953. 150p. (C). 1992. pap. text ed. 9.95 (*0-89089-494-9*) Carolina Acad Pr.

Margulies, Sylvia R. Pilgrimage to Russia: The Soviet Union & the Treatment of Foreigners, 1924-1937. 302p. 1968. 30.00 (*0-299-04720-2*) U of Wis Pr.

Margulies, Teddy S. Walt Disney's Snow White & the Seven Dwarfs. (Look-Look Bks.). (Illus.). 24p. (J). (ps-3). 1993. pap. 1.95 (*0-307-12686-2*, 12686, Golden Pr) Western Pub.

Margulis. Alimentary Tract Radiology, No. 4. (Illus.). 2216p. 1989. 299.00 (*0-8016-3191-2*) Mosby Yr Bk.

Margulis, et al. The Five Kingdom Coloring Book. (Illus.). (C). 1993. 21.50 (*0-06-500843-X*) HarpCollege.

Margulis, Alexander, jt. ed. see Eisenberg, Ronald L.

Margulis, Alexander R. & Burhenne, H. Joachim, eds. Practical Alimentary Tract Radiology. LC 92-18766. 512p. 1992. 95.00 (*0-8016-3133-5*) Mosby Yr Bk.

***Margulis, Daniel.** Professional Photoshop: Color Correction, Retouching, & Image Manipulation with Adobe Photoshop. LC 94-33545. (Illus.). 1995. pap. text ed. 49.95 (*0-471-01873-2*) Wiley.

Margulis, Daniel & Schroeder, John. The Literate Typographer. (Illus.). 240p. 1984. pap. 20.00 (*0-938304-03-8*) Cornell Daily.

Margulis, Daniel & Schroeder, John, eds. A Century at Cornell. (Illus.). 232p. 1980. 19.95 (*0-938304-00-3*) Cornell Daily.

Margulis, G. A. Discrete Subgroups of Semisimple Lie Groups. (Ergebnisse der Mathematik und Ihrer Grenzgebiete Ser.: Vol. 17). ix, 338p. 1991. 85.00 (*0-387-12179-X*) Spr-Verlag.

***Margulis, L. & Schwartz, K.** Five Kingdoms: Life on Earth. 1995. cd-rom 79.00 (*3-540-14500-1*); cd-rom 79.00 (*3-540-14501-X*) Spr-Verlag.

***Margulis, L., et al.** Protoctist Glossary. 1995. cd-rom 79.00 (*3-540-14510-9*); cd-rom 79.00 (*3-540-14199-5*) Spr-Verlag.

Margulis, Lynn. Early Life. (Biology Ser.). (Illus.). 160p. (C). 1982. pap. text ed. 25.00 (*0-86720-005-7*) Jones & Bartlett.

— Origins of Life, 2 vols., Vol. 1. 2nd ed. 392p. 1970. text ed. 205.00 (*0-677-13320-0*) Gordon & Breach.

— Origins of Life, 2 vols., Vol. 2. 2nd ed. 246p. 1971. text ed. 135.00 (*0-677-13630-7*) Gordon & Breach.

— Protoctista Glossary. 288p. (Orig.). (C). 1993. boxed 50.00 (*0-86720-081-2*) Jones & Bartlett.

— Sharing with Children: New Ideas on the Evolution of Life. (Illus.). 23p. (Orig.). (C). 1985. pap. 3.00 (*0-918374-21-9*) City Coll Wk.

— Symbiosis in Cell Evolution: Microbial Evolution in the Archean & Proterozoic Eons. 2nd ed. LC 92-14565. (C). 1995. text ed. write for info. (*0-7167-7028-8*); pap. text ed. write for info. (*0-7167-7029-6*) W H Freeman.

Margulis, Lynn, ed. International Society for Evolutionary Protistology. 1984. lib. bdg. 94.00 (*90-277-1765-6*) Kluwer Ac.

Margulis, Lynn & Fester, Rene, eds. Symbiosis As a Source of Evolutionary Innovation: Speciation & Morphogensis. 408p. 1991. 45.00 (*0-262-13269-9*) MIT Pr.

Margulis, Lynn & Olendzenski, Lorraine, eds. Environmental Evolution: Effects of the Origin & Evolution of Life on Planet Earth. (Illus.). 400p. 1992. 37.50 (*0-262-13273-7*) MIT Pr.

Margulis, Lynn & Sagan, Dorion. Microcosmos: Four Billion Years of Microbial Evolution. 304p. 1991. pap. 10.00 (*0-671-74798-3*, Touchstone Bks) S&S Trade.

— Mystery Dance: On the Evolution of Human Sexuality. 224p. 1992. pap. 12.00 (*0-671-79226-1*, Touchstone Bks) S&S Trade.

— Origins of Sex: Three Billion Years of Genetic Recombination. 259p. (Orig.). (C). 1990. pap. 17.00 (*0-300-04619-7*) Yale U Pr.

Margulis, Lynn & Schwartz, Karlene V. Five Kingdoms. 2nd ed. (Biology Ser.). 376p. (C). 1995. pap. text ed. write for info. (*0-7167-1912-6*) W H Freeman.

Margulis, Lynn, ed. see Khakhina, Liya N.

Margulis, Lynn, jt. ed. see Ponnamperuma, Cyril.

Margulis, Lynn, jt. auth. see Sagan, Dorion.

Margulis, Lynn, et al. Handbook of Protoctista. (C). 1989. boxed 225.00 (*0-86720-052-9*) Jones & Bartlett.

Margulis, Rena K. The Complete Guide to Whitewater Rafting Tours: California Edition, 1986. (Complete Guide to Whitewater Rafting Tours Ser.). (Illus.). 304p. (Orig.). 1986. pap. 11.95 (*0-9616150-0-1*) Aquatic Adv Pubns.

— The Complete Guide to Whitewater Rafting Tours: Western States Edition. 2nd rev. ed. (Complete Guide to Whitewater Rafting Tours Ser.). (Illus.). 448p. (Orig.). 1988. pap. 12.95 (*0-9616150-2-8*) Aquatic Adv Pubns.

Marguth, F., et al, eds. Neurovascular Surgery: Specialized Neurosurgical Techniques. (Advances in Neurosurgery Ser.: Vol. 7). (Illus.). 420p. 1979. pap. 63.00 (*0-387-09675-2*) Spr-Verlag.

Marharishi Mahesh Yogi. Transcendental Meditation. 320p. 1973. pap. 4.95 (*0-451-14081-8*, Sig) NAL-Dutton.

Marheine, Allen H. You Belong. LC 79-21954. (Orig.). 1980. pap. 3.95 (*0-8298-0380-7*) Pilgrim OH.

— You Belong: A Handbook for Church Members. rev. ed. 96p. 1995. pap. 4.95 (*0-8298-1104-4*) Pilgrim OH.

Marhoefer, Patricia E. Caring for the Developing Child Workbook. 2nd ed. 1992. 13.95 (*0-8273-4902-5*) Delmar.

Marhoefer, Patricia E. & Vadnais, Lisa A. Caring for the Developing Child. 2nd ed. 1992. teacher ed 13.00 (*0-8273-4682-4*); text ed. 29.95 (*0-8273-4681-6*) Delmar.

Mari, Jean-Luc & Coppens, Francoise. Seismic Well Surveying. 128p. (C). 1991. 140.00 (*2-7108-0605-3*, Pub. by Edits Technip FR) St Mut.

Mari, Jean-Luc, jt. auth. see Glangeaud, Franois.

***Mari, Jean-Luc, et al.** Full Waveform Acoustic Data Processing. (Illus.). 136p. 1994. pap. text ed. 54.00 (*2-7108-0664-9*) Technip.

Mari-Mutt, Jose & Bellinger, Peter F. Catalog of the Neotropical Collembola. LC 89-70038. (Flora & Fauna Handbook Ser.: No. 5). 256p. (Orig.). 1990. pap. text ed. 39.95 (*1-877743-00-3*) Sandhill Crane.

Mar'I, Sami K. Arab Education in Israel. 1978. 39.95x (*0-8156-0145-X*) Syracuse U Pr.

Maria, Gerarda & Middendorp, Kooiman-van. The Hero in the Feminine Novel. 174p. (C). 1966. text ed. 75.00 (*0-8383-0576-8*) M S G Haskell Hse.

***Maria, Jack S.** Indian Vegetarian Cookery. 176p. 1995. pap. 11.95 (*0-7126-2409-0*, Pub. by Rider UK) Trafalgar.

Maria, Katherine. Reading Comprehension Instruction: Issues & Strategies. LC 90-70057. 306p. (C). 1990. pap. text ed. 29.50 (*0-912752-20-3*) York Pr.

Maria, Lucia, et al. Alexej Jawlensky, 1890-1914, Vol. 1: Catalogue Raisonne of the Oil Paintings. (Illus.). 560p. 1991. 395.00 (*0-85667-398-6*) Sothebys Pubns.

***Mariabelem, pseud.** Furtively I Come: A Poetic Journey into Mysticism. 68p. (Orig.). (C). 1994. pap. 6.00 (*0-9626221-4-1*) Vista Pubns FL.

— A Hurtadillas Vengo. 154p. (Orig.). (SPA.). (C). Date not set. pap. 6.00 (*0-9626221-5-X*) Vista Pubns FL.

Mariah, Nelson. Are We Winning Yet? 1991. 19.50 (*0-394-57576-8*) Random.

Mariah, Paul. Apparitions of a Black Pauper's Suit. 1988. 2.00 (*0-318-41323-X*) Man-Root.

— Apparitions of a Black Pauper's Suit. deluxe ed. 1988. write for info. (*0-318-64675-7*) Man-Root.

— Apparitions of a Black Pauper's Suit: Thirteen Eulogies. 1975. pap. 2.00 (*0-686-18839-X*) Man-Root.

— Dances with Dali. Date not set. 6.00 (*0-317-05628-X*) Man-Root.

— The Electric Holding Company. 1988. 2.00 (*0-318-41324-8*) Man-Root.

— The Electric Holding Company. deluxe ed. 1988. 3.00 (*0-318-41325-6*) Man-Root.

— Letter to Robert Duncan While Bending the Bow. 1988. pap. 2.50 (*0-686-18848-9*) Man-Root.

— Personae Non Gratae. 32p. 1977. pap. 1.95 (*0-686-19032-7*) Man-Root.

— Selected Poems Nineteen Sixty to Nineteen Seventy-Five. 1978. 8.95 (*0-686-18930-2*) Man-Root.

— Six Imaginary Letters of Young Caesar, 81 BC. 1988. 1.50 (*0-318-41328-0*) Man-Root.

— This Light Will Spread: Selected Poems Nineteen Sixty to Nineteen Seventy-Five. deluxe ed. 15.00 (*0-686-25740-5*) Man-Root.

— This Light Will Spread: Selected Poems Nineteen Sixty to Nineteen Seventy-Five. limited ed. pap. 8.95 (*0-686-25741-3*) Man-Root.

Mariama Ba. So Long a Letter. Modupe' Bode'-Thomas, tr. (African Writers Ser.). 96p. (Orig.). (YA). 1989. pap. 8.95 (*0-435-90555-4*, 90555) Heinemann.

***Marian.** Cruising Guide to the Tennessee River, Tenn-Tom Waterway, & Lower Tombrigbee River. 1995. pap. text ed. 29.95 (*0-07-064415-2*) Intl Marine.

Marian Goodman Gallery Staff, ed. see Buch, Benjamin H.

Marian, Jim. Growing up Christian. 156p. 1992. pap. 1.60 (*0-89693-802-6*) SP Pubns.

— Leading Your Students in Worship. 156p. (Orig.). 1993. pap. 8.99 (*1-56476-086-3*, Victor Books) SP Pubns.

Marian, Stanton, ed. see Jones, Ernest, et al.

***Marian, Thomas W.** Cruising Guide to the Northeast's Inland Waterways: Hudson River, New York State Canals... LC 94-27926. 1995. text ed. 39.95 (*0-07-158011-5*) McGraw.

Marian, Thomas W. & Rumsey, W. J. A Cruising Guide to the Tennessee River, Tenn-Tom Waterway & Lower Tombigee River. 1991. text ed. 39.95 (*0-07-054291-0*) McGraw.

Mariana. Miss Flora McFlimsey & the Baby New Year. rev. ed. LC 86-15339. (Illus.). 40p. (J). (ps-2). 1988. 11.95 (*0-688-04533-2*); lib. bdg. 11.88 (*0-688-04534-0*) Lothrop.

— Miss Flora McFlimsey's Birthday. rev. ed. LC 86-15269. (Illus.). 40p. (J). (ps-2). 1987. 11.95 (*0-688-04537-5*) Lothrop.

— Miss Flora McFlimsey's Christmas Eve. rev. ed. LC 86-15259. (Illus.). 40p. (J). (ps-2). 1988. 11.95 (*0-688-04282-1*); lib. bdg. 11.88 (*0-688-04283-X*) Lothrop.

— Miss Flora McFlimsey's Easter Bonnet. rev. ed. LC 86-15268. (Illus.). 40p. (J). (gr. k-3). 1987. 9.95 (*0-688-04535-9*); lib. bdg. 8.88 (*0-688-04536-7*) Lothrop.

— Miss Flora McFlimsey's Halloween. rev. ed. LC 86-15270. (Illus.). 40p. (J). (ps-2). 1987. 11.95 (*0-688-04549-9*) Lothrop.

— Miss Flora McFlimsey's May Day. rev. ed. LC 86-15252. (Illus.). 40p. (J). (ps-3). 1987. 9.95 (*0-688-04545-6*) Lothrop.

Marianacci, Dante, jt. ed. see Talbot, George.

Marianccio, Dave. All I Really Need to Know I Learned from Watching Star Trek. 1994. 14.00 (*0-517-59798-5*, Crown) Crown Pub Group.

Mariane, Emma. Our Yesterdays in Brandywine Hundred. 1992. 15.95 (*0-533-10088-7*) Vantage.

— Through Open Doors. 1990. 13.95 (*0-533-08832-1*) Vantage.

Marianetti, M. C. Religion & Politics in Aristophanes' Clouds. Bd. 24. Date not set. write for info. (*0-318-70702-0*, Pub. by Georg Olms GW) Lubrecht & Cramer.

Marianetti, Marie C. Religion & Politics in Aristophanes' Clouds. (Altertumswissenschaftliche Texte und Studien Ser.: Vol. 24). x, 140p. (GER.). 1992. pap. 22.35 (*3-487-09633-1*, Pub. by Georg Olms GW) Lubrecht & Cramer.

***Mariani, Cliff.** Police Supervisor's Test Manual. 290p. Date not set. ring bd. 19.95 (*0-930137-84-1*) Looseleaf Law.

Mariani, G., ed. Activated Prothrombin Complex Concentrates: Managing Hemophilia With Factor VIII Inhibitor. LC 81-23358. 256p. 1982. text ed. 65.00 (*0-275-91373-2*, C1373, Praeger Pubs) Greenwood.

Mariani, G., et al, eds. Desmopressin in Bleeding Disorders. (NATO ASI Series A, Life Sciences: Vol. 242). (Illus.). 386p. (C). 1993. 105.00 (*0-306-44414-3*, Plenum Pr) Plenum.

Mariani, Giorgio. Spectacular Narratives: Representations of Class & War in Stephen Crane & the American 1890s. LC 91-47738. (American University Studies: American Literature: Ser. XXIV, Vol. 37). 184p. 1993. 36.95 (*0-8204-1875-7*) P Lang Pubs.

Mariani, J. A., ed. see Nishinuma, Y. & Espesser, R.

Mariani, John. America Eats Out: An Illustrated History of Restaurants, Taverns, Coffee Shops, Speakeasies, & Other Establishments That Have Fed Us for 350 Years. (Illus.). 288p. 1991. 25.00 (*0-688-09996-3*) Morrow.

Mariani, John & Von Bidder, Alex. The Four Seasons: A History of America's Premier Restaurant. LC 94-8642. 1994. 35.00 (*0-517-59147-2*) Crown Pub Group.

M

Mariani, John F. Dictionary of American Food & Drink. 1994. pap. 19.95 (*0-688-10139-9*) Morrow.
— Mariani's Coast-To-Coast Dining Guide. LC 84-41003. 704p. (Orig.). 1986. pap. 12.95 (*0-8129-1309-4*, Times Bks) Random.
***Mariani, John F. & Meltzer, Peter D.** Passport to New York Restaurants 1995. 182p. 1994. 9.95 (*0-937413-09-7*) Passport NYC.
— Passport to New York Restaurants. 1996. rev. ed. 182p. 1995. pap. 9.95 (*0-937413-10-0*) Passport NYC.
Mariani, L., jt. ed. see Cobelli, C.
Mariani, Michael M., jt. auth. see Schlesinger, Edward S.
Mariani, Paul. Lost Puritan: A Life of Robert Lowell. LC 93-48018. (Illus.). 1994. 27.50 (*0-393-03661-8*) Norton.
— Lost Puritan: A Life of Robert Lowell. (Illus.). 560p. 1996. pap. 15.00 (*0-393-31374-3*, Norton Paperbks) Norton.
Mariani, Paul J. Salvage Operations: New & Selected Poems. 1990. 17.95 (*0-393-02863-1*) Norton.
— Salvage Operations: New & Selected Poems. 1991. pap. 9.95 (*0-393-30759-X*) Norton.
— A Usable Past: Essays on Modern & Contemporary Poetry. LC 84-2613. 280p. 1984. lib. bdg. 30.00 (*0-87023-445-5*) U of Mass Pr.
— William Carlos Williams: A New World Naked. 1990. pap. 14.95 (*0-393-30672-0*) Norton.
Mariani, Paul L. Dream Song. 1994. pap. 16.95 (*1-56924-947-4*) Marlowe & Co.
— William Carlos Williams: The Poet & His Critics. LC 75-8645. 285p. reprint ed. pap. 81.30 (*0-317-27974-2*, 2025611) Bks Demand.
Mariani, Phil, jt. ed. see Kruger, Barbara.
Mariani, Philomena, ed. Critical Fictions: The Politics of Imaginative Writing. LC 89-650815. (Discussions in Contemporary Culture Ser.: No. 7). 304p. (Orig.). 1991. pap. 15.95 (*0-941920-24-0*) Bay Pr.
Mariani, U., tr. see Zangrilli, Franco, ed.
Mariani, Umberto, tr. see Bonaviri, Giuseppe.
Mariani, V. Michelangelo, the Painter. (Illus.). 1987. 39.99 (*0-517-10208-0*) Random Hse Value.
Marianna, Mayer. Baba Yaga & Vasilisa the Brave. LC 90-38514. (Illus.). 40p. (J). (ps-3). 1994. 16.00 (*0-688-08500-8*); 15.93 (*0-688-08501-6*) Morrow Jr Bks.
***Mariano, Bernard J. & West, Jill.** Espresso Encyclopedia. (Illus.). 208p. (Orig.). 1994. pap. 12.95 (*0-9643222-1-8*) Trendex Intl.
Mariano, John H. The Italian Contribution to American Democracy. LC 74-17938. (Italian American Experience Ser.). (Illus.). 336p. 1975. reprint ed. 23.95 (*0-405-06409-8*) Ayer.
— The Italian Immigrant & Our Courts. LC 74-17939. (Italian American Experience Ser.). (Illus.). 88p. 1975. reprint ed. pap. 14.95 (*0-405-06410-1*) Ayer.
Mariano, Joseph N., jt. auth. see Brossi, Mario.
Mariano, Nicky. Berenson Archive: An Inventory of Correspondence Compiled on the Centenary of the Birth of Bernard Berenson, 1865-1959. Berenson, Bernard, ed. LC 65-28597. (Illus.). 134p. 1965. 19.00 (*0-674-06750-9*) HUP.
Mariano, Patrick S., ed. Advances in Electron Transfer Chemistry, Vol. 1. 1991. 90.25 (*1-55938-167-1*) Jai Pr.
— Advances in Electron Transfer Chemistry, Vol. 2. 1992. 90.25 (*1-55938-168-X*) Jai Pr.
— Advances in Electron Transfer Chemistry, Vol. 3. 1993. 90.25 (*1-55938-320-8*) Jai Pr.
Mariano, Roberto. Advances in Statistical Analysis & Statistical Computing, Vol. 1. 1986. 73.25 (*0-89232-467-8*) Jai Pr.
Mariano, Roberto S., ed. Advances in Statistical Analysis & Statistical Computing, Vol. 2. 1987. 73.25 (*0-89232-826-6*) Jai Pr.
— Advances in Statistical Analysis & Statistical Computing, Vol. 3. 1991. 73.25 (*1-55938-069-1*) Jai Pr.
Mariano, Roberto S., jt. ed. see Clemente, Lilia C.
Mariano, Thomas. America in Chaos: America's Second Civil War. Huhn, Patricia, ed. 105p. (Orig.). 1994. pap. 5.00 (*1-877637-10-6*) Mariano Pub.
— Essays of an American Peasant. Tate, Laura O., ed. (Illus.). 96p. (Orig.). 1989. pap. text ed. write for info. (*1-877637-00-9*) Mariano Pub.
— Opinions of an American Peasant. Allison, Carrie C., ed. (Illus.). 256p. (Orig.). 1989. pap. write for info. (*1-877637-01-7*) Mariano Pub.
— Potshot Reviews: Of Southern Colorado Ghostowns. Tate, Laura, ed. (Illus.). 282p. (Orig.). 1991. pap. 10.00 (*1-877637-04-1*) Mariano Pub.
— Rhymes from the Books of Ham: Mormon Deceptions. Huhn, Patricia, ed. 105p. (Orig.). 1993. pap. 5.00 (*1-877637-09-2*) Mariano Pub.
— Western Tales of Southern Colorado: To Know the West. 2nd ed. (Illus.). 312p. 1991. pap. 13.95 (*1-877637-03-3*) Mariano Pub.
Marians of the Immaculate Conception Staff, ed. Divine Mercy: Re-Translation & Outline of Pope John Paul II's Encyclical Rich in Mercy. LC 87-62983. 76p. 1988. pap. text ed. write for info. (*0-944203-07-8*) Marian Pr.
— Now Is the Time for Mercy: The Message & Devotion to the Divine Mercy. LC 87-62981. 114p. 1988. pap. text ed. write for info. (*0-944203-05-1*) Marian Pr.
— Tell My Priests: Words of Our Lord to Priests about His Mercy As Revealed to Sister Faustina Kowalska. LC 87-62982. 112p. 1988. pap. text ed. write for info. (*0-944203-08-6*) Marian Pr.
Marians of the Immaculate Conception Staff, ed. see Kosicki, George W.
Marianska, Anna, tr. see Koscialkowska, Janina.
Marianska-Peleg, Miriam & Peleg, Mordecai. Witnesses: Life in Occupied Krakow. 208p. 1991. 25.00 (*0-415-06523-2*, A6636) Routledge.
Mariant, Giulian, ed. Pathophysiology of Plasma Protein Metabolism. 416p. 1985. 105.00 (*0-306-41771-5*, Plenum Pr) Plenum.
Marias Aguilera, Julian. Reason & Life: The Introduction to Philosophy. Reid, Kenneth S. & Sarmiento, Edward, trs. LC 74-25891. 413p. 1975. reprint ed. text ed. 75.00 (*0-8371-7866-5*, MARLI, Greenwood Pr) Greenwood.
Marias, Javier. All Souls. Costa, Marguaret J., tr. 210p. (Orig.). 1993. pap. 12.00 (*0-00-271283-0*, Pub. by HarperCollins UK) Harper SF.
Marias, Julian. Acerca de Ortega. (Nueva Austral Ser.: Vol. 214). (SPA.). 1991. pap. text ed. 24.95 (*84-239-7214-3*) Elliots Bks.
— A Biography of Philosophy. Raley, Harold C., tr. LC 83-6939. 269p. 1984. pap. 76.70 (*0-7837-8393-0*, 2059204) Bks Demand.
— History of Philosophy. 22th ed. (YA). (gr. 7-12). 1966. pap. 9.95 (*0-486-21739-6*) Dover.
— Jose Ortega y Gasset: Circumstances & Vocation. Lopez-Morillas, Frances M., tr. LC 71-88141. 490p. reprint ed. pap. 139.70 (*0-8357-9729-5*, 2016239) Bks Demand.
— Miguel de Unamuno. Lopez-Morillas, Frances M., tr. LC 66-18251. 236p. reprint ed. pap. 67.90 (*0-7837-2296-6*, 2057384) Bks Demand.
— Philosophy As Dramatic Theory. Parsons, James, tr. LC 72-84669. 1970. 32.50 (*0-271-00100-3*) Pa St U Pr.
— The Structure of Society. Raley, Harold C., tr. LC 84-185. 248p. 1986. 26.50 (*0-8173-0181-X*) U of Ala Pr.
— Understanding Spain. Lopez-Morillas, Frances M., tr. 464p. (C). 1992. pap. text ed. 18.95 (*0-472-08188-8*) U of Mich Pr.
Marias, Julian & Michigan University Press Staff. Understanding Spain. LC 89-77991. 462p. 1990. 32.50 (*0-8477-0888-8*) U of PR Pr.
Mariategui, Jose C. Seven Interpretive Essays on Peruvian Reality. Urquidi, Marjory, tr. 335p. 1988. reprint ed. pap. 12.95 (*0-292-77611-X*) U of Tex Pr.
Maric, D. Adapting Working Hours to Modern Needs: The Time Factor in the New Approach to Working Conditions. viii, 50p. 1980. 20.00 (*92-2-101659-5*) Intl Labour Office.
Maricella, tr. see Collins, D'Andre.
***Maricevic, Vivienne, photos.** Male to Female: La Cage aux Folles. (Illus.). 140p. Date not set. 39.95 (*3-905514-86-9*) Dist Art Pubs.
Marich, Stephen, jt. intro. see O'Rourke, Mike D.
Marichal, Carlos. A Century of Debt Crises in Latin America: From Independence to the Great Depression, 1820-1930. 352p. 1989. text ed. 55.00 (*0-691-07792-4*); pap. text ed. 19.95 (*0-691-02299-2*) Princeton U Pr.
— Luis Munoz Rivera. (Puerto Rico Ser.). 1979. lib. bdg. 59.95 (*0-8490-2965-1*) Gordon Pr.
Marichal, Robert, ed. see D'Angouleme, Marguerite.
Marichal, Robert, ed. see Marguerite D'Angouleme.
Marick, Brian. Craft of Software Testing. 553p. 1994. text ed. 50.00 (*0-13-177411-5*) P-H.
Marie - Queen of Roumania. Story of My Life, 2 Vols, Set. LC 73-135820. (Eastern Europe Collection Ser.). 1971. reprint ed. 70.95 (*0-405-02793-1*) Ayer.
Marie, Anna & Hager, Everett G. Baja California Travels Series: General Index, Vols. 1-49. (Baja California Travels Ser.: No. 50). 124p. 1991. 50.00 (*0-87093-250-0*) Dawsons.
Marie, Anna & Hager, Everett G., eds. Index to California Historical Society Quarterly, Vols. 41-54. 1977. pap. 12.95 (*0-910312-40-0*) Calif Hist.
Marie, Christy. The Case of the Broken Heart. 1992. 8.95 (*0-533-09325-2*) Vantage.
Marie, D. Tears for Ashan. LC 88-63766. (Illus.). 32p. (J). (ps-3). 1989. 11.95 (*0-9621681-0-6*) Creative Pr Works.
Marie-Daly, Bernice. Ecofeminism: Sacred Matter - Sacred Mother. (Teilhard Studies). 1991. 3.50 (*0-89012-064-1*) Anima Pubns.
Marie-Daly, Bernice & Rae, Eleanor. Created in Her Image: Models of the Feminine Divine. 160p. 1990. 18.95 (*0-8245-1013-5*) Crossroad NY.
Marie, Danielle. Straight from the Heart: Authors, Celebrities & Others Share Their Philosophies on Making a Difference in the World. LC 92-70221. (Illus.). 160p. 1992. pap. 10.95 (*1-880741-09-1*) Dickens Pr.
Marie, De France. Fables. Spiegel, Harriet, ed. LC 88-148665. (Toronto Medieval Texts & Translations Ser.: No. 5). (Illus.). 291p. (ENG & FRE.). reprint ed. pap. 83.00 (*0-7837-4287-8*, 2043979) Bks Demand.
Marie De France. French Mediaeval Romances from the Lays of Marie De France. Mason, Eugene, tr. LC 75-41188. reprint ed. 24.50 (*0-404-14571-X*) AMS Pr.
Marie, Evelyn. My Tree. (Illus.). 24p. (J). (gr. k-2). 1987. pap. 3.95 (*0-9614746-5-3*) Berry Bks.
Marie, J. B. Glossary of Human Rights. 339p. (ENG & FRE.). 1981. pap. 59.95 (*0-8288-1519-4*, M12410) Fr & Eur.
Marie, Jean, jt. auth. see Edwards, Jean.
Marie, Jeanne. Moving Through Your ABC's. LC 92-9944. (Everyday Concept Ser.). (Illus.). 32p. (J). (ps-2). Date not set. 11.95 (*1-56065-166-0*) Capstone Pr.
Marie, Joseph. Medical Vocabulary. 1972. 59.95 (*0-8490-0597-3*) Gordon Pr.
Marie, Lois. Does Your Marriage Suffer from TMS? (Traveling Mate Syndrome) LC 92-93583. 105p. 1993. pap. 9.00 (*0-9635410-0-5*) Beginnings.
***Marie, Lyn.** The Lion's Lair. 400p. (Orig.). Date not set. pap. 12.95 (*0-7610-0308-8*) NW Pub.
Marie, Nancy. Country Christmas. (Jimmy & Sweet Sue's Bks.). (Illus.). 36p. (J). (gr. k-5). 1979. 5.95 (*0-941595-00-5*) Heldreth Pub.
***Marie, Rosena.** Gospel Way of Life. LC 94-16405. 144p. (Orig.). 1994. pap. 5.00 (*1-880033-17-8*) Faith Pub OH.
Marie, S. Handbook of Sweeteners. 1991. text ed. 110.00 (*0-442-31433-7*) Chapman & Hall.
Marie, Sharon. Granny's Crooked Teeth. (J). 1993. 7.95 (*0-533-10602-8*) Vantage.
Marieb, Elaine N. A&P Coloring Workbook. 4th ed. (C). 1994. pap. text ed. 20.50 (*0-8053-4171-4*) Benjamin-Cummings.
— The A&P Coloring Workbook: A Complete Study Guide. 3rd ed. 350p. (C). 1991. write for info. (*0-318-69059-4*) Addison-Wesley.
— Essentials of Human Anatomy & Physiology. 3rd ed. (Illus.). 464p. (C). 1991. teacher ed 11.95 (*0-8053-4805-0*); pap. text ed. 31.25 (*0-8053-4804-2*); pap. text ed. 17.25 (*0-685-54329-3*) Addison-Wesley.
— Essentials of Human Anatomy & Physiology. 4th ed. LC 93-24550. (C). 1994. pap. text ed. 34.50 (*0-8053-4170-6*) Benjamin-Cummings.
— Human Anatomy. (C). 1992. text ed. 63.50 (*0-8053-4060-2*) Benjamin-Cummings.
— Human Anatomy & Physiology. (Illus.). 1050p. (C). 1989. teacher ed 13.95 (*0-8053-0120-8*); text ed. 56.95 (*0-8053-0122-4*); student ed, teacher ed 430.25 (*0-8053-0119-4*); student ed 25.75 (*0-8053-0106-2*); trans. 322.75 (*0-8053-0109-7*); 13.95 (*0-8053-0108-9*) Benjamin-Cummings.
— Human Anatomy & Physiology. 2nd ed. Adams, Melinda, ed. 1104p. (C). 1992. teacher ed write for info. (*0-8053-4128-5*); text ed. 66.75 (*0-8053-4120-X*); trans. write for info. (*0-8053-4124-2*); disk 268.95 (*0-8053-4125-0*); 11.95 (*0-8053-4123-4*) Addison-Wesley.
— Human Anatomy & Physiology. 2nd ed. 1985. Cat Edition. spiral bd. 34.50 (*0-8053-6726-8*); Fetal Pig Edition. spiral bd. 29.25 (*0-8053-6727-6*) Benjamin-Cummings.
— Human Anatomy & Physiology. 3rd ed. LC 94-27422. (Life Sciences Ser.). (C). 1995. text ed. 69.95 (*0-8053-4281-8*) Benjamin-Cummings.
— Human Anatomy & Physiology: The Pig Version. 3rd ed. (Illus.). 700p. (C). 1989. teacher ed write for info. (*0-318-64657-9*); pap. text ed. 37.75 (*0-8053-0111-9*); trans. write for info. (*0-318-64658-7*) Benjamin-Cummings.
— Human Anatomy & Physiology Brief Lab Manual. 3rd ed. Adams, Melinda, ed. 552p. (C). 1993. pap. text ed. 36.75 (*0-8053-4807-7*); disk 68.50 (*0-8053-4808-5*); 12.95 (*0-8053-4811-5*) Benjamin-Cummings.
— Human Anatomy & Physiology Laboratory Manual, Brief Version. 500p. 1987. student ed 13.95 (*0-8053-6734-9*) Benjamin-Cummings.
— Human Anatomy & Physiology Laboratory Manual, Brief Version. 2nd ed. 500p. (C). 1987. pap. text ed. 33.50 (*0-8053-6733-0*) Benjamin-Cummings.
— Human Anatomy Laboratory Manual: With Cat Dissections. 480p. 1992. teacher ed 13.95 (*0-8053-4051-3*) Benjamin-Cummings.
— Human Anatomy Laboratory Manual: With Cat Dissections. 4th ed. 480p. (C). 1992. spiral bd. 35.50 (*0-8053-4050-5*) Benjamin-Cummings.
Mariechild, Diane. The Inner Dance: A Guide to Psychological & Spiritual Unfolding. LC 87-19849. 180p. (Orig.). 1987. pap. 10.95 (*0-89594-245-3*) Crossing Pr.
— Lesbian Sacred Sexuality. LC 94-4125. (Illus.). 144p. (Orig.). 1995. pap. 24.95 (*0-914728-81-4*) Wingbow Pr.
— Mother Wit: A Guide to Healing & Psychic Development. rev. ed. 200p. 1989. pap. 12.95 (*0-89594-358-1*) Crossing Pr.
— Open Mind: Women's Daily Inspirations for Becoming Mindful. LC 94-26377. 1995. pap. 11.00 (*0-06-251093-2*) Harper SF.
Mariejol, Jean H. Philip II, the First Modern King. 1977. 22.95 (*0-8369-6948-0*, 7829) Ayer.
Mariel, Pierre. Dictionnaire des Societes Secretes en Occident. (FRE.). 1971. pap. 29.95 (*0-8288-6450-0*, M-6642) Fr & Eur.
Mariella, Cinzia. Passport to Italy. rev. ed. LC 93-21189. (Illus.). 48p. (J). (gr. 5-8). 1994. lib. bdg. 14.77 (*0-531-14295-7*) Watts.
Marien, Bert. Bibliografica Critica Degli Studi Plotiniani: Con rassegna della loro recensioni. Cilento, V., ed. (Classical Studies Ser.). (ITA.). reprint ed. lib. bdg. 47.00 (*0-697-00043-5*) Irvington.
Marien, Matthaeus. Iconum Biblicarum. (Illus.). 320p. 1981. reprint ed. 34.95 (*0-939688-06-9*) Directed Media.
Marien, Michael. Future Survey Annual 1992. 1992. 35.00 (*0-930292-43-X*) World Future.
— World Futures & the United Nations: An Annotated Guide to 250 Recent Books & Reports. LC 95-13952. (Future Survey Guidebooks Ser.: Vol. 1). 1995. pap. 25.00 (*0-930242-49-1*) World Future.
Marien, Michael, ed. Future Survey Annual, 1979: A Guide to Recent Books & Articles Concerning Trends, Forecasts, & Policy Proposals. 280p. 1980. pap. 35.00 (*0-930242-10-6*) World Future.
— Future Survey Annual, 1981-82. 1983. 35.00 (*0-930242-17-3*) World Future.
— Future Survey Annual, 1983: A Guide to the Recent Literature of Trends, Forecasts, & Policy Proposals, Vol. 4. 250p. 1984. pap. 35.00 (*0-930242-23-8*) World Future.
— Future Survey Annual, 1984: A Guide to the Recent Literature of Trends, Forecasts & Policy Proposals. 240p. 1985. pap. 25.00 (*0-930242-26-2*) Transaction Pubs.
— Future Survey Annual, 1985. 208p. 1986. pap. 25.00 (*0-930242-29-7*) Transaction Pubs.
— Future Survey Annual, 1986. 220p. 1987. pap. 25.00 (*0-930242-32-7*) Transaction Pubs.
— Future Survey Annual, 1987. 210p. 1988. pap. 25.00 (*0-930242-34-3*) Transaction Pubs.
— Future Survey Annual, 1988-89: A Guide to the Recent Literature of Trends, Forecasts & Policy Proposals. 212p. 1989. 35.00 (*0-930242-35-1*) World Future.
— Future Survey Annual, 1990. 196p. 1990. 35.00 (*0-930242-38-6*) World Future.
— Future Survey Annual, 1991. 1991. pap. 35.00 (*0-930242-42-4*) World Future.
— Future Survey Annual, 1992: A Guide to the Recent Literature of Trends, Forecasts, & Policy Proposals. 192p. (C). 1993. pap. text ed. 35.00 (*0-930242-43-2*) Transaction Pubs.
— Future Survey Annual 1993. 1993. 35.00 (*0-930242-44-0*) World Future.
— Future Survey Annual, 1995. 1995. pap. 35.00 (*0-930242-50-5*) World Future.
Marien, Michael & Jennings, Lane, eds. What I Have Learned: Thinking about the Future Then & Now. LC 86-14958. 219p. 1987. text ed. 45.00 (*0-313-25071-5*, MWL/, Greenwood Pr) Greenwood.
Marien, Michael, et al, eds. Future Survey Annual, 1980-81: A Guide to the Recent Literature of Trends, Forecasts, & Policy Proposals. 280p. (Orig.). 1981. pap. 35.00 (*0-930242-13-0*) World Future.
Marier, Donald & Stoiaken, Larry, eds. Alternative Sources of Energy. (Orig.). 1988. pap. 5.95 (*0-917328-92-2*) ASEI.
— Alternative Sources of Energy: Cogeneration Wind. (Orig.). 1988. pap. 5.95 (*0-917328-91-4*) ASEI.
— Alternative Sources of Energy: Hydropower. (Orig.). 1988. pap. 5.95 (*0-917328-90-6*) ASEI.
Marier, Donald, ed. see Kessler, et al.
Marier, Donald, jt. ed. see Stoiaken, Larry.
Marier, Donald, ed. see Wilson & Frumerman.
Marier, Robert L., jt. auth. see D'Ambrosia, Robert.
Marier, Robert L., jt. ed. see Edwards, Janine C.
Marier, Thomas, tr. see Graf, Fritz.
Marier, Thomas, tr. see Zimmermann, Bernhard.
***Marietta, Don, Jr. & Embree, Lester, eds.** Environmental Philosophy & Environmental Activism. 224p. (C). 1995. lib. bdg. 52.50 (*0-8476-8055-X*) Rowman.
— Environmental Philosophy & Environmental Activism. 224p. (C). 1995. pap. text ed. 21.95 (*0-8476-8056-8*) Rowman.
Marietta, Don E., Jr. For People & the Planet: Holism & Humanism in Environmental Ethics. (Environmental Ethics, Values, & Policy Ser.). 256p. (C). 1994. text ed. 44.95 (*1-56639-246-2*); pap. text ed. 19.95 (*1-56639-247-0*) Temple U Pr.
Mariette, Auguste E. Abydos (Egyptienne), 3 vols. in 1. vii, 749p. reprint ed. write for info. (*3-487-06719-6*, Pub. by Georg Olms GW) Lubrecht & Cramer.
— Catalogue General Des Monuments D'Abydos Decouverts Pendant les Fouilles De Cette Ville. viii, 596p. reprint ed. write for info. (*0-318-71377-2*, Pub. by Georg Olms GW) Lubrecht & Cramer.
— Denderah, 6 vols. in 2, Set. vi, 363p. 1980. reprint ed. write for info. (*3-487-07002-2*, Pub. by Georg Olms GW) Lubrecht & Cramer.
— Karnak. 208p. reprint ed. write for info. (*0-318-71378-0*, Pub. by Georg Olms GW) Lubrecht & Cramer.
— Les Mastabas De l'Ancien Empire. 592p. 1976. reprint ed. write for info. (*3-487-05987-8*, Pub. by Georg Olms GW) Lubrecht & Cramer.
Mariger, Randall P. Consumption Behavior & the Effects of Government Fiscal Policies. (Economic Studies: No. 158). (Illus.). 312p. 1986. 32.00 (*0-674-16635-3*) HUP.
Marigny, Jean. Vampires: Restless Creatures of the Night. (Discoveries Ser.). 1994. pap. 12.95 (*0-8109-2869-8*) Abrams.
Marigold, Lys, jt. auth. see Popcorn, Faith.
Marija, Landa. English & Serbocroatian Economics Dictionary: Privredno-Poslovni Recnik Englesko-Srpskohrvatski. 358p. (ENG & SER.). 1986. 49.95 (*0-8288-0122-3*, F126828) Fr & Eur.
— Serbocroatian-English Business Dictionary: Privredno-Poslovni Recnik Srpskohrvatsko-Engleski. 260p. (ENG & SER.). 1984. 29.95 (*0-8288-4414-3*, F110100); 24.95 (*0-8288-0121-5*, F18170) Fr & Eur.
Marijnissen, Roger H. Bosch (Hieronymus) the Complete Works. (Illus.). 516p. 1987. boxed 250.00 (*1-55660-229-4*) A Wofsy Fine Arts.
Marik, Ray. Special Education Students Write. (Writing Teachers at Work Ser.). 145p. (C). 1982. pap. text ed. 7.00 (*1-883920-04-3*) Nat Writing Proj.
Marik, V., et al, eds. Advanced Topics in Artificial Intelligence: Proceedings of the International Summer School, Prague, Czechoslavakia, July 6-17, 1992. LC 92-17999. (Lecture Notes in Artificial Intelligence Ser.: Vol. 617). ix, 484p. 1992. pap. 67.00 (*0-387-55681-8*) Spr-Verlag.
— Artificial Intelligence in Higher Education: CEPES-UNESCO International Symposium, Prague, CSFR, October 23-25, 1989 Proceedings. (Lecture Notes in Computer Science, Lecture Notes in Artificial Intelligence Ser.: Vol. 451). ix, 247p. 1990. pap. 33.00 (*0-387-52952-7*) Spr-Verlag.
— Database & Expert Systems Applications: Fourth International Conference, DEXA '93 Prague, Czech Republic, September 6-8, 1993 Proceedings. (Lecture Notes in Computer Science Ser.: Vol. 720). 768p. 1994. pap. 96.00 (*0-387-57234-1*) Spr-Verlag.
Marikhin, V. A., jt. ed. see Myasnikova, L.
Maril, Nadja. American Lighting: 1840-1940. LC 89-84163. (Illus.). 160p. 1989. 29.95 (*0-88740-177-5*) Schiffer.
— American Lighting 1840-1940. (Illus.). 160p. 1995. 39.95 (*0-88740-879-6*) Schiffer.
— Me, Molly Midnight, the Artist's Cat. LC 77-22708. (Illus.). 40p. (J). (gr. k up). 1977. 12.95 (*0-916144-15-1*); pap. 5.95 (*0-916144-16-X*) Stemmer Hse.
— Runaway Molly Midnight, the Artist's Cat. LC 80-17097. (Illus.). 40p. (J). (gr. k up). 1980. 12.95 (*0-916144-62-3*) Stemmer Hse.

An Asterisk (*) at the beginning of an entry indicates that the title is appearing in BIP for the first time.

*__Maril, Robert L.__ The Bay Shrimpers of Texas: Rural Fishermen in a Global Economy. (Rural America Ser.). (Illus.). 320p. 1995. 35.00x (*0-7006-0703-X*); pap. 17.95 (*0-7006-0704-8*) U Pr of KS.

— Cannibals & Condos: Texans & Texas along the Gulf Coast. LC 86-5759. (Tarleton State University Southwestern Studies in the Humanities: No. 3). 136p. 1986. 13.95 (*0-89096-276-6*) Tex A&M Univ Pr.

— Living on the Edge of America: At Home on the Texas-Mexico Border. LC 91-46457. 200p. 1992. 24.50 (*0-89096-505-6*) Tex A&M Univ Pr.

— Poorest of Americans: The Mexican Americans of the Lower Rio Grande Valley of Texas. LC 89-40015. 228p. (C). 1990. pap. 11.95 (*0-268-01581-3*) U of Notre Dame Pr.

— Texas Shrimpers: Community, Capitalism, & the Sea. LC 82-45897. (Illus.). 256p. 1983. 18.00 (*0-89096-147-6*) Tex A&M Univ Pr.

Marill, Alvin H. The Complete Films of Edward G. Robinson. 1990. pap. 15.95 (*0-8065-1181-8*, Citadel Pr) Carol Pub Group.

— The Films of Robert Mitchum. (Citadel Film Series Library). (Illus.). 256p. 1995. pap. 17.95 (*0-8065-1594-5*, Citadel Pr) Carol Pub Group.

— The Films of Sidney Poitier. (Illus.). 1978. text ed. 14.95 (*0-8065-0612-1*, Citadel Pr) Carol Pub Group.

— More Theatre: Stage to Screen to Television, 2 vols. 1648p. 1993. Vol. I: A-L. write for info. (*0-318-70222-3*); Vol. II: M-Z. write for info. (*0-318-70223-1*) Scarecrow.

— More Theatre: Stage to Screen to Television, 2 vols., Set. LC 93-4687. 1648p. 1993. 149.50 (*0-8108-2717-4*) Scarecrow.

Marill, Alvin H. & Kennedy, Arthur. The Films of Anthony Quinn. (Illus.). 256p. 1975. 12.00 (*0-8065-0470-6*, Citadel Pr); pap. 7.95 (*0-8065-0570-2*, Citadel Pr) Carol Pub Group.

Marilla, A. Bibliography of Henry Vaughan. LC 72-6142. (English Literature Ser.: No. 33). 1972. reprint ed. lib. bdg. 39.95 (*0-8383-1598-4*) M S G Haskell Hse.

Marilla, E. L. The Central Problem of Paradise Lost: The Fall of Man. (Essays & Studies on English Language & Literature: Vol. 15). 1972. reprint ed. pap. 15.00 (*0-8115-0213-9*) Periodicals Srv.

— Three Odes of Keats. (Essays & Studies on English Language & Literature: Vol. 24). (Orig.). 1962. pap. 15.00 (*0-8115-0222-8*) Periodicals Srv.

Marilla, E. L., ed. The Secular Poems of Henry Vaughan. (Essays & Studies on English Language & Literature: Vol. 21). 1974. reprint ed. pap. 35.00 (*0-8115-0219-8*) Periodicals Srv.

Marilue. Bobby Bear & the Friendly Ghost. LC 85-61830. (Bobby Bear Ser.). (Illus.). 32p. (J). (ps-1). 1985. 6.95 (*0-87783-204-8*) Oddo.

— Bobby Bear at the Circus. LC 89-62708. (Bobby Bear Ser.). (Illus.). 32p. (J). (ps-2). 1990. lib. bdg. 12.95 (*0-87783-252-8*) Oddo.

— Bobby Bear Meets Cousin Boo. LC 80-82952. (Bobby Bear Ser.). (Illus.). 32p. (J). (ps-1). 1981. lib. bdg. 9.95 (*0-87783-155-6*) Oddo.

— Bobby Bear's Christmas. LC 77-83628. (Illus.). 32p. (J). (ps-1). 1978. lib. bdg. 9.95 (*0-87783-142-4*) Oddo.

— Bobby Bear's Kite Contest. LC 87-62507. (Bobby Bear Ser.). (Illus.). 32p. (J). (ps-1). 1988. lib. bdg. 11.45 (*0-87783-219-6*) Oddo.

— Bobby Bear's Magic Show. LC 89-62707. (Bobby Bear Ser.). (Illus.). 32p. (J). (ps-2). 1990. lib. bdg. 12.95 (*0-87783-253-6*) Oddo.

— Bobby Bear's New Home. LC 78-190265. (Bobby Bear Ser.). (Illus.). 32p. (J). (ps-1). 1973. lib. bdg. 9.95 (*0-87783-054-1*); audio 7.94 (*0-87783-184-X*) Oddo.

— Bobby Bear's Red Raft. LC 71-190266. (Bobby Bear Ser.). (Illus.). 32p. (J). (ps-1). 1973. lib. bdg. 9.95 (*0-87783-055-X*); audio 7.94 (*0-87783-185-8*) Oddo.

— Bobby Bear's Thanksgiving. LC 77-83623. (Bobby Bear Ser.). (Illus.). 32p. (J). (ps-1). 1978. lib. bdg. 9.95 (*0-87783-143-2*) Oddo.

Marimuthu, K. M. & Gopinath, P. M., eds. Recent Trends in Medical Genetics: Proceedings of the Conference on Recent Trends in Medical Genetics, Madras, India, 8-10 December, 1983. (Illus.). 350p. 1986. 125.00 (*0-08-031993-9*, Pergamon Pr) Elsevier.

Marin, A. Royo, jt. auth. see De Montfort, Louis M.

Marin, Alan. Macroeconomic Policy. 224p. 1992. 77.50 (*0-415-08379-6*, A9691) Routledge.

Marin, Alan, jt. ed. see Estrin, Saul.

Marin, Albert. Unconditional Surrender: U. S. Grant & the Civil War. LC 93-20041. (Illus.). 208p. (J). (gr. 5-9). 1994. lib. bdg. 20.00 (*0-689-31837-5*, Atheneum Bks Young) S&S Childrens.

Marin, Alexis, jt. auth. see Guillou, Lucien.

*__Marin, Antonio R.__ Elevation to the Most Blessed Trinity. Parrot, J. Edward, ed. Bolivar Plaza Staff, tr. (Illus.). 125p. (C). Date not set. pap. write for info. (*1-877905-29-1*) Am Soc Defense TFP.

— The Great Unknown: The Holy Ghost & His Gifts. 179p. (Orig.). 1991. pap. 13.50 (*1-881008-00-2*) Am Soc Defense TFP.

Marin, B. P., ed. Plant Vacuoles: Their Importance in Solute Compartmentation in Cells & Their Applications in Plant Biotechnology. LC 87-14121. (NATO ASI Series A, Life Sciences: Vol. 134). (Illus.). 578p. 1987. 135.00 (*0-306-42613-7*, Plenum Pr) Plenum.

Marin, Barbara V., jt. auth. see Marin, Gerardo.

Marin, Bayard. Inside Justice: A Comparative Analysis Practices & Procedures for the Determination of Offenses Against Discipline in Prisons of Great Brtain & the United States. LC 81-65465. 416p. 1983. 60.00 (*0-8386-3086-3*) Fairleigh Dickinson.

Marin, Bernd, ed. Generalized Political Exchange: Antagonistic Cooperation & Integrated Policy Circuits. 284p. (C). 1991. pap. text ed. 50.00 (*0-8133-8291-2*) Westview.

— Governance & Generalized Exchange: Self-Organizing Policy Networks in Action. 386p. (C). 1991. pap. text ed. 61.00 (*0-8133-8292-0*) Westview.

Marin, Bloc. Votre Livre du Bord, 2 vols., Vol. 1. (C). 1989. 105.00x (*0-685-74324-1*, Pub. by Imray Laurie Norie & Wilson UK) St Mut.

— Votre Livre du Bord, 2 vols., Vol. 2. (C). 1989. 105.00x (*0-685-74325-X*, Pub. by Imray Laurie Norie & Wilson UK) St Mut.

Marin, Cheech. Me Llamo Cheech, el Chofer dle Autobus de la Escuela. 16p. (Orig.). (SPA.). (J). 1992. cd-rom, pap. 13.98 (*1-56668-202-9*) BMG Kidz.

— My Name Is Cheech the School Bus Driver. 16p. (J). 1992. cd-rom, pap. 13.98 (*1-56668-178-2*, 70508-2); audio, pap. 9.98 (*1-56668-177-4*, 70508-4) Rincon Rodanthe.

Marin, Diego. La Civilizacion Espanola. rev. ed. (Illus.). (C). 1969. text ed. 35.25 (*0-03-080033-1*) HB Coll Pubs.

— Poesia Paisajistica Espanola, 1940-1970: Estudio Y Antologia. (Serie A: Monagrafias, LVII). 296p. (SPA.). (C). 1976. 40.00 (*0-7293-0026-9*, Pub. by Tamesis Bks Ltd UK) Boydell & Brewer.

Marin, Diego & Tayler, Neale H. La Vida Espanola. rev. ed. LC 55-7036. (Illus.). (SPA.). 1955. reprint ed. pap. text ed. 7.95 (*0-89197-973-5*) Irvington.

Marin, Estela, ed. see Becker, Greg.

Marin, Gerardo & Marin, Barbara V. Research with Hispanic Populations. (Applied Social Research Methods Ser.: Vol. 23). (Illus.). 160p. 1991. 37.00 (*0-8039-3720-2*); pap. 16.95 (*0-8039-3721-0*) Sage.

Marin, Gerardo, et al. Latin American Psychology: A Guide to Research & Training. LC 87-17409. 220p. (Orig.). 1987. pap. 30.00 (*0-912704-84-5*) Am Psychol.

Marin-Guzman, Roberto. Popular Dimensions of the 'Abbasid Revolution: A Case Study of Medieval Islamic Social History. 160p. (Orig.). 1990. reprint ed. pap. 12.00 (*9977-88-004-2*) Three Continents.

Marin, Javier J., tr. see Barclay, William.

Marin, John. Letters of John Marin. Seligmann, Herbert J., ed. LC 77-109780. 1971. reprint ed. text ed. 45.00 (*0-8371-4270-9*, MALE, Greenwood Pr) Greenwood.

— The Selected Writings of John Marin. (American Biography Ser.). 241p. 1991. reprint ed. lib. bdg. 69.00 (*0-7812-8267-5*) Rprt Serv.

Marin, John A., jt. auth. see Calabria, Antonio.

Marin, Louis. Food for Thought. Hjort, Mette, tr. LC 88-29342. (Parallax: Re-Visions of Culture & Society Ser.). 304p. 1989. text ed. 42.50x (*0-8018-3476-7*) Johns Hopkins.

— Portrait of the King. LC 87-19093. (Theory & History of Literature Ser.: Vol. 57). 305p. 1988. text ed. 39.95 (*0-8166-1603-5*); pap. text ed. 15.95 (*0-8166-1604-3*) U of Minn Pr.

— The Semiotics of the Passion Narratives. Johnson, Alfred M., Jr., tr. LC 80-18199. (Pittsburgh Theological Monographs: No. 25). 1980. 12.95 (*0-915138-23-9*) Pickwick.

— To Destroy Painting. Hjort, Mette, tr. (Illus.). 224p. 1994. lib. bdg. 39.95 (*0-226-50534-0*); pap. text ed. 15.95 (*0-226-50535-9*) U Ch Pr.

— Utopics: The Semiological Play of Textual Spaces. Vollrath, Robert, tr. LC 90-31499. (Contemporary Studies in Philosophy & the Human Sciences). 312p. (C). 1984. text ed. 55.00 (*0-391-02859-6*) Humanities.

Marin, M. A., et al. El Teatro Cervantes De Alcala De Henares: 1602-1866: Estudio y Documentos. (Series C: Fuentes Para La Historia Del Teatro En Espana: No. 18). (Illus.). 390p. (Orig.). (C). 1990. pap. 53.00 (*0-7293-0310-1*, Pub. by Tamesis Bks Ltd UK) Boydell & Brewer.

Marin, Marguerite V. Social Protest in an Urban Barrio: A Study of the Chicano Movement, 1966-1974. Fisher, Sethard, ed. (Class, Ethnicity, Gender, & the Democratic Nation Ser.). 320p. (C). 1990. lib. bdg. 53.00 (*0-8191-7962-0*) U Pr of Amer.

MARIN, Maritime Research Institute Netherlands Staff. Marine Jubilee, Nineteen Ninety-Two: Special Jubilee Volume. LC 92-13876. (Developments in Marine Technology Ser.: Vol. 9). 1992. write for info. (*0-444-89469-1*) Elsevier.

Marin, Mark. The Island Epicurean. 118p. 1986. 13.95 (*0-317-67969-4*) Antilles Schl.

Marin Martinez, Juan M., ed. see De Vega, Lope.

*__Marin, Michael.__ Endovascular Stented Grafts for the Treatment of Vascular Diseases. Veith, Frank J., ed. (Medical Intelligence Unit Ser.). 168p. 1995. write for info. (*1-57059-273-X*) R G Landes.

Marin, Michael L. Endoluminal Stent-Grafts for the Treatment of Vascular Diseases. (Medical Intelligence Unit Ser.). 115p. 1994. 89.95 (*1-57059-090-7*, LN9090) R G Landes.

Marin, Peter. Freedom & Its Discontents: Reflections on Four Decades of American Moral Experience. 265p. 1995. 22.00 (*1-883642-24-8*) Steerforth Pr.

Marin, Ramon. Fiestas Populares de Ponce y la Villa de Ponce. 1994. 12.95 (*0-8477-0189-1*) U of PR Pr.

Marin, Reymundo, jt. auth. see De Marin, Maria V.

Marin, Reymundo, jt. auth. see Marin, Viramontes.

Marin, Reymundo, jt. auth. see Viramontes de Marin, Maria.

Marin, Roselyn. Helping Obese Children: Weight Control Groups That Really Work. 1990. pap. 19.95 (*1-55691-049-5*, 495) Learning Pubns.

— I'm a Winner! 1991. write for info. (*1-55691-075-4*) Learning Pubns.

Marin, S. E. Basic Japanese-English-Japanese Conversation Dictionary. 50th ed. (ENG & JPN.). 1982. pap. 6.95 (*0-8288-1610-7*, M14399) Fr & Eur.

Marin Staff. Diccionario Marin de al Lengua Espanola, Vol. 2. 1668p. (SPA.). 1982. 250.00 (*0-8288-2017-1*, S2556) Fr & Eur.

— Gran Diccionario Infantil Marin, 4 vols., Set. 840p. (SPA.). 1979. 250.00 (*0-8288-4807-6*, S50032) Fr & Eur.

— Gran Mundo Infantil, 3 vols., Set. 1792p. (SPA.). 1979. 375.00 (*0-8288-4808-4*, S50489) Fr & Eur.

— El Mundo de la Cultura: Enciclopedia Formativa Marin, 12 vols., Set. 2400p. (SPA.). 1978. 395.00 (*0-8288-5255-3*, S50488) Fr & Eur.

Marin, Viramontes & Marin, Reymundo. La Historia de los Estados Unidos: La Diversidad de sus Pueblos. (Illus.). 425p. (Orig.). (SPA.). 1991. 26.50 (*0-685-34820-2*); pap. 20.00 (*0-927065-02-9*) Marin Chula Vista.

Marina, R. Fernandez, et al. The Sober Generation: A Topology of Competent Adolescent Coping in Modern Puerto Rico. 798p. 1969. 7.50 (*0-8477-2475-1*); pap. 6.00 (*0-8477-2476-X*) U of PR Pr.

Marinacci, Alberto A. Applied Electromyography. LC 68-25208. 308p. reprint ed. pap. 87.80 (*0-8357-5676-9*, 2003766) Bks Demand.

Marinacci, Barbara & Marinacci, Rudy. California's Spanish Place-Names: What They Mean & How They Got There. LC 88-20114. (Illus.). 267p. 1988. pap. 9.95 (*0-935382-68-2*) Tioga Pub Co.

Marinacci, Barbara, jt. auth. see Ray, Eleanor.

Marinacci, Rudy, jt. auth. see Marinacci, Barbara.

*__Marinaccio, Dave.__ All I Really Need to Know I Learned from Watching Star Trek. 1995. pap. 10.00 (*0-517-88386-4*, Crown) Crown Pub Group.

*__Marinaro, M. & Morasso, P. G., eds.__ ICANN '94. 1488p. 1994. pap. text ed. 109.00 (*0-387-19887-3*) Spr-Verlag.

Marinaro, M. & Scarpetta, G. Structure: From Physics to General Systems - Festschrift Volume in Honor of Caianiello's 70th Birthday. 832p. 1993. text ed. 162.00 (*981-02-1291-7*) World Scientific Pub.

Marinaro, Vincent C. In the Ring of the Rise. (Illus.). 184p. 1987. reprint ed. 29.95 (*0-941130-59-2*) Lyons & Burford.

Marinas, Amante P., Sr. Pananandata Yantok at Daga: Filipino Stick & Dagger. (Illus.). 88p. 1988. pap. 16.00 (*0-87364-447-6*) Paladin Pr.

Marinatos, Nanno. Minoan Religion: Ritual Process, Image, & Symbol. Denny, Frederick M., ed. LC 92-11628. (Studies in Comparative Religion). (Illus.). 316p. (C). 1993. text ed. 49.95 (*0-87249-744-5*) U of SC Pr.

Marinatos, Nanno & Agg, Robin H., eds. Greek Sanctuaries: New Approaches. LC 92-30812. (Illus.). 336p. 1993. 49.95 (*0-415-05384-6*, A7941) Routledge.

Marinbach, Bernard. Galveston: Ellis Island of the West. LC 82-10609. (Modern Jewish History Ser.). 288p. (C). 1984. 74.50 (*0-87395-700-8*); pap. 24.95 (*0-87395-701-6*) State U NY Pr.

Marinberg, Simon. Four-Dimensional Realism: Method Depiction of Four-Dimensional Space in Painting. 70p. 1992. pap. 29.95 (*0-9634628-0-6*) White Grp.

Marincola, Paula. ICA Street Sights. LC 80-84550. (Illus.). 1980. pap. 7.00 (*0-88454-056-1*) U of Pa Contemp Art.

— ICA Street Sights 2. (Illus.). 24p. 1982. pap. 7.00 (*0-88454-028-6*) U of Pa Contemp Art.

Marincola, Paula & Crimp, Douglas. Image Scavengers: Photography. 1982. pap. 10.00 (*0-88454-031-6*) U of Pa Contemp Art.

Marincola, Paula, ed. see Stroud, Marion B., et al.

Marindin, Hope, ed. Handbook for Single Adoptive Parents. 88p. 1992. pap. 15.00 (*0-9634045-0-4*) Comm Single Adopt.

*__Marine.__ Prentice Hall Teachers Resource Guide to the Internet. 1995. pap. text ed. 22.95 (*0-13-337395-9*) P-H.

Marine, April. Internet: Getting Started. rev. ed. 1993. pap. 28.00 (*0-13-289596-X*) P-H.

Marine, April, jt. auth. see International SRI Staff.

Marine Biological Laboratory Staff. Serial Publications. 1983. 10.00 (*0-685-52862-6*) Marine Bio.

Marine Biological Laboratory Staff & Woods Hole Oceanographic Institution, Woods Hole, Massachusetts Staff. Catalog of the Library of the Institute for World Economics, 7 pts. Incl. Title Catalog, 12 vols. 1971. lib. bdg. 1,215.00 (*0-8161-0937-0*, Hall Library); write for info. (*0-318-52339-6*, Hall Library) G K Hall.

Marine Corps Association Staff. Guidebook for Marines. 15th ed. 560p. 1986. pap. 5.00 (*0-940328-07-0*) Marine Corps.

— Leatherneck Laffs. 96p. 1980. reprint ed. 1.50 (*0-686-32444-7*) Marine Corps.

Marine Law Institute, Staff. North Atlantic Water Dependent Use Study, Vol. 3: An Executive Summary. 32p. (Orig.). 1989. pap. 2.00 (*0-685-31980-6*) Univ S ME Marine Law Inst.

Marine Law Institute, Staff, ed. North Atlantic Water Dependent Use Study, 3 vols., Vols. I-III. (Orig.). 1989. Set: Vol.I, 320p.; Vol. II, 296p.; Vol. III, 32p. pap. 20.00 (*0-9618224-0-6*) Univ S ME Marine Law Inst.

Marine Law Institute, Staff & Boston University Institute for Employment Policy, Staff. North Atlantic Water Dependent Use Study, Vol. 2: Guidebook to the Economics of Waterfront Planning & Water Dependent Uses. 296p. (Orig.). 1989. pap. 10.00 (*0-9618224-3-0*) Univ S ME Marine Law Inst.

Marine Law Institute, Staff & Robinson & Cole Land Use, Staff. North Atlantic Water Dependent Use Study, Vol. 1: Managing the Shoreline for Water Dependent Uses. (Handbook of Legal Tools). (Orig.). 1989. pap. 10.00 (*0-9618224-2-2*) Univ S ME Marine Law Inst.

Marine Libraries Assocoation. Marine Transport: A Guide to Libraries. 76p. 1983. pap. 65.00 (*0-946347-00-X*, Pub. by Witherby & Co UK) St Mut.

Marine, Michael. One Hundred One Ways to Get Rid of a Lettuce Head Doll. 96p. (Orig.). 1984. pap. 4.95 (*0-8439-2200-1*) Dorchester Pub Co.

Marine Research Society Staff. The Pirates Own Book: Authentic Narratives of the Most Celebrated Sea Robbers. LC 93-12468. Orig. Title: The Pirates Own Book: or Authentic Narratives of the Lives, Exploits, & Executions of the Most Celebrated Sea Robbers. (Illus.). 496p. 1993. reprint ed. pap. 8.95 (*0-486-27607-4*) Dover.

*__Marineau, Michele.__ The Road to China. Ouriou, Susan, tr. 144p. (YA). 1995. pap. 8.95 (*0-88995-129-2*, Pub. by Red Deer CN) BookWorld Dist.

Marineau, Rene F. Jacob Levy Moreno, 1889-1974: Father of Psychodrama, Sociometry, & Group Psychotherapy. (International Library of Group Psychotherapy & Group Process). 224p. 1990. 57.50 (*0-415-04383-2*, A3968); pap. 16.95 (*0-415-04110-4*, A3972) Routledge.

Marinelli, Anthony. Conscience & Catholic Faith: Love & Fidelity. 1991. pap. 4.95 (*0-8091-3263-X*) Paulist Pr.

— The Word Made Flesh: An Overview of the Catholic Faith. LC 92-45629. 320p. 1993. pap. 9.95 (*0-8091-3391-1*) Paulist Pr.

Marinelli, David, tr. see Blaukopf, Kurt.

Marinelli, David, tr. see Gozzano, Guido.

Marinelli, David N., tr. see Maron, Monika.

Marinelli, David N., tr. see Ripellino, Angelo M.

*__Marinelli, Donald, ed.__ Arthur Giron's Edith Stein: A Dramaturgical Sourcebook. (Dramaturgical Sourcebook Ser.). (Illus.). 210p. 1994. pap. 15.95 (*0-88748-178-7*) Carnegie-Mellon.

Marinelli, Giovanni. Commentaria in Libros Hippocratis. 280p. reprint ed. write for info. (*0-318-72047-7*, Pub. by Georg Olms GW) Lubrecht & Cramer.

Marinelli, Irene. Family Spirituality for Busy People. 104p. (Orig.). 1991. pap. 4.95 (*0-87973-149-4*) Our Sunday Visitor.

Marinelli, Janet, ed. The Environmental Gardner. (Plants & Gardens Ser.). (Illus.). 1992. per., pap. 6.95 (*0-945352-70-0*, Sterling) Bklyn Botanic.

— Going Native: Biodiversity in Our Own Backyards. (21st-Century Gardening Ser.). (Illus.). 1994. per., pap. 6.95 (*0-945352-85-9*) Bklyn Botanic.

*__Marinelli, Janet & Bierman-Lytle, Paul.__ Your Natural Home: A Complete Sourcebook & Design Manual for Creating a Healthy, Beautiful, & Environmentally Sensitive House. LC 94-46327. 1995. 40.00 (*0-316-09302-5*); pap. 19.95 (*0-316-09303-3*) Little.

Marinelli, Janet & Kourik, Robert. The Naturally Elegant Home: Environmental Style. LC 92-13887. 1992. 45.00 (*0-316-54612-7*) Little.

Marinelli, Patti J. & Laughlin, Lizette M. Puentes: Spanish for Intensive & High-Beginner Courses. LC 93-38316. 1994. pap. 25.95 (*0-8384-4298-6*) Heinle & Heinle.

— Puentes: Spanish for Intensive & High-Beginner Courses. LC 93-38316. 1994. pap. 45.95 (*0-8384-2163-6*) Heinle & Heinle.

Marinelli, Peter V. Ariosto & Boiardo: The Origins of "Orlando Furioso" LC 87-4993. 256p. 1987. text ed. 31.00 (*0-8262-0636-0*) U of Mo Pr.

Marinelli, Robert P. & Dell Orto, Arthur E., eds. The Psychological & Social Impact of Disability. 3rd ed. LC 91-4809. 384p. (C). 1991. 36.95 (*0-8261-2212-4*) Springer Pub.

Marinello, Grace. Me, Myself, & I: A Program on Alcoholism & Its Effect on Family for Older Students. 16p. 1993. 3.95 (*1-884063-06-3*) Mar Co Prods.

Mariner, Elwyn, jt. auth. see Levitan, Donald.

*__Mariner, Jo.__ Dreaming a Sacred Place. 24p. 1993. 5.00 (*1-885796-00-5*) Kali Momma.

Mariner, Steven A., jt. auth. see Nara, Robert O.

Mariner, Tom. Continents. LC 89-17285. (Earth in Action Ser.). (Illus.). 32p. (J). (gr. 3-8). 1990. lib. bdg. 9.95 (*1-85435-195-8*) Marshall Cavendish.

— Deserts. LC 89-17278. (Earth in Action Ser.). (Illus.). 32p. (J). (gr. 3-8). 1990. lib. bdg. 9.95 (*1-85435-192-3*) Marshall Cavendish.

— Earth in Action Series, 6 vols. (Illus.). (J). (gr. 3-8). 1990. lib. bdg. 59.70 (*1-85435-189-3*) Marshall Cavendish.

— Mountains. LC 89-17280. (Earth in Action Ser.). (Illus.). 32p. (J). (gr. 3-8). 1990. lib. bdg. 9.95 (*1-85435-193-1*) Marshall Cavendish.

— Oceans. LC 89-9823. (Earth in Action Ser.). (Illus.). 32p. (J). (gr. 3-8). 1990. lib. bdg. 9.95 (*1-85435-190-7*) Marshall Cavendish.

— Rivers. LC 89-9824. (Earth in Action Ser.). (Illus.). 32p. (J). (gr. 3-8). 1990. lib. bdg. 9.95 (*1-85435-191-5*) Marshall Cavendish.

— Rocks. LC 89-17321. (Earth in Action Ser.). (Illus.). 32p. (J). (gr. 3-8). 1990. lib. bdg. 9.95 (*1-85435-194-X*) Marshall Cavendish.

Mariner, Tom & Ellis, Anyon. The Dillon Press Book of the Earth. LC 94-16855. (J). (gr. 3 up). 1994. text ed. 16.95 (*0-87518-640-8*, Mac Bks Young Read) S&S Childrens.

Mariner, William. An Account of the Natives of the Tonga Islands in the South Pacific Ocean, 2 vols., Set. LC 75-35204. reprint ed. 124.50 (*0-404-14290-7*) AMS Pr.

Mariners Museum Library - Newport News - Virginia Staff. Catalog of Maps, Ships' Papers & Logbooks. 1970. lib. bdg. 110.00 (*0-8161-0686-X*, Hall Library) G K Hall.

— Catalog of Marine Photographs, 5 Vols, Set. 1970. lib. bdg. 545.00 (*0-8161-0685-1*, Hall Library) G K Hall.

— Catalog of Marine Prints & Paintings, 3 Vols, Set. 1970. lib. bdg. 330.00 (*0-8161-0684-3*, Hall Library) G K Hall.

— Dictionary Catalog of the Library of the Mariners Museum, 9 Vols, Set. 1970. lib. bdg. 980.00 (*0-8161-0674-6*, Hall Library) G K Hall.

Marinescu, Gheorgha, jt. auth. see Cristescu, Romulus.

Marinescu, Ioana. Gene Networks in Cancer Genesis & Reversion. 1995. write for info. (*0-8493-4831-5*) CRC Pr.

Marinetti, F. T. Let's Murder the Moonshine. Flint, R. W. & Coppotelli, Arthur A., trs. (Sun & Moon Classics Ser.: No. 12). 1990. pap. 12.95 (*1-55713-101-5*) Sun & Moon CA.
— Mots En Liberte Futuristes. pap. 20.00 (*0-87556-216-7*) Saifer.
— The Untameables. Coppotelli, Arthur A., tr. (Sun & Moon Classics Ser.: No. 28). 1994. pap. 10.95 (*1-55713-064-7*) Sun & Moon CA.
Marinetti, G. V. Disorders of Lipid Metabolism. LC 89-72205. (Illus.). 240p. 1990. 50.00 (*0-306-43431-8*, Plenum Pr) Plenum.
Marinetti, Guido, ed. Lipid Chromatographic Analysis, Vol. 3. LC 75-42515. 300p. reprint ed. pap. 85.50 (*0-8357-9085-1*, 2017689) Bks Demand.
Marinetti, Guido V., ed. Lipid Chromatographic Analysis, Vol. 1. 2nd ed. LC 75-42515. 351p. reprint ed. pap. 100.10 (*0-7837-0008-3*, 2017689) Bks Demand.
— Lipid Chromatographic Analysis, Vol. 2. 2nd ed. LC 75-42515. 383p. reprint ed. pap. 109.20 (*0-7837-0009-1*) Bks Demand.
Marinez de Irizarry, Marina & Alcaraz Vda De Vivoni, Yuyu. Cooking in San German, Puerto Rico. 1991. pap. 9.95 (*0-533-09278-7*) Vantage.
Maring, K. W. & Van Dijk, A. Brikkenaar, eds. Education of the Engineer for Innovative & Entrepreneurial Activity. 470p. (Orig.). 1982. pap. text ed. 42.50 (*90-6275-088-5*, Pub. by Delft U Pr NE) Coronet Bks.
Maring, Margaret. Louisiana Creole & Cajun. 64p. 1984. pap. 3.49 (*0-942320-14-X*) Am Cooking.
Maring, Norman H. & Hudson, Winthrop S. Baptist Manual of Polity & Practice. rev. ed. 1991. 24.00 (*0-8170-1171-4*) Judson.
Maring, R. H., jt. auth. see Kaler, S. P.
Maringer, Robert E., jt. auth. see Marschall, Charles W.
Marini. Physiologic Basis of Mechanical Ventilation. 1991. 45.00 (*0-8151-5793-2*, Yr Bk Med Pubs) Mosby Yr Bk.
Marini, A. Diccionario Enciclopedico Electronica. 376p. 1989. 39.95 (*0-7859-6503-3*) Fr & Eur.
Marini, Anthony, jt. ed. see Violato, Claudio.
Marini-Bettolo, G. B., ed. Chemical Events in the Atmosphere & Their Impact on the Environment: Proceedings of a Study at the Pontifical Academy of Sciences, Nov., 7-11, 1983. 702p. 1986. 248.75 (*0-444-99513-7*) Elsevier.
— A Modern Approach to the Protection of the Environment: Proceedings of a Study Week Held in the Vatican, 2-7 November 1987. (Pontifical Academiae Scientiarum Scripta Ser.). (Illus.). 602p. 1990. 94.00 (*0-08-040816-8*, Pergamon Pr) Elsevier.
— Towards a Second Green Revolution: From Chemical to New Biological Tehcnologies in Agriculture in the Tropics. (Developments in Agricultural & Managed-Forest Ecology Ser.: Vol. 19). 532p. 1988. 166.75 (*0-444-98927-7*) Elsevier.
Marini, C. P. Spinal Cord Protection During Surgery on the Thoracic & Thoraco-Abdominal Aorta. (Medical Intelligence Unit Ser.). write for info. (*1-57059-084-2*) R G Landes.
Marini, Gabriella, jt. auth. see Mancia, Mauro.
Marini, John. The Politics of Budget Control: Congress, the Presidency & Growth of the Administrative State. 300p. 1992. 45.00 (*0-8448-1716-3*, Crane Russak); pap. 21.00 (*0-8448-1717-1*, Crane Russak) Taylor & Francis.
Marini, John A., jt. ed. see Jones, Gordon S.
Marini, John J. & Ravenscraft, Sue A. Principles: Practice of Mechanical Ventilation. (Illus.). 544p. 1994. write for info. (*0-683-05556-9*) Williams & Wilkins.
Marini, John J. & Wheeler, Arthur. Critical Care Medicine. 344p. (Orig.). 1989. pap. text ed. 34.00 (*0-683-05554-2*) Williams & Wilkins.
Marini, Luis A., ed. Manual de Odontologia Infantil. 463p. (Orig.). (SPA.). (C). 1982. 12.00 (*0-8477-2330-5*) U of PR Pr.
Marini, Marcelle. Jacques Lacan: The French Context. Tomiche, Anne, tr. LC 92-9652. 310p. (ENG & FRE.). (C). 1993. 45.00 (*0-8135-1851-2*); pap. 18.00 (*0-8135-1852-0*) Rutgers U Pr.
Marini, Maurizio, jt. auth. see Hoopes, Donelson.
Marini, Paola, ed. see Rearick, W. R., et al.
Marini, Stephen A. Radical Sects of Revolutionary New England. LC 81-6913. 220p. 1982. 32.00 (*0-674-74625-2*) HUP.
Marinjnissen, R. H. Paintings-Genuine, Fraud, Fake: Modern Methods of Examining Paintings. (Illus.). 413p. 1987. text ed. 65.00 (*0-313-25874-0*, MPF/, Greenwood Pr) Greenwood.
***Marinkas, Paul L., ed.** Organic Energetic Compounds. (Illus.). 298p. (C). 1994. lib. bdg. 89.00 (*1-56072-201-0*) Nova Sci Pubs.
Marinker, Simon. Informed Consent to Surgery: Everything You Always Wanted to Know about Your Operaton but Were Afraid to Ask. 114p. (Orig.). 1991. pap. 11.95 (*0-9694811-0-1*) Gordon Soules Bk.
Marinkov, Dusica, tr. see Cardu, Petru.
***Marino.** English-Italian Phraseological Medical Dictionaries. 526p. (ENG & ITA.). 1985. 115.00 (*0-7859-7516-0*, 8828902795) Fr & Eur.
— Modern Bioelectricity. 737p. 1988. 250.00 (*0-8247-7788-3*) Dekker.
Marino, Andrew & Ray, Joel. The Electric Wilderness. 1986. pap. 12.50 (*0-911302-55-7*) San Francisco Pr.
Marino, Bernard D. Handbook of Capital Expenditure Management. 256p. 1986. text ed. 59.95 (*0-13-372541-3*) P-H.
Marino, Bradley, jt. ed. see Fernandopulle, Rushika.
Marino, C., ed. SuperComputer Applications in Automotive Research & Engineering Development. 452p. 1986. 115.00 (*0-931215-29-3*) Computational Mech MA.
Marino, Carlos & Diaz-Guerrero, Rogelio. Diccionario de Terminos Mineralogicos y Cristalograficos. 608p. (SPA.). 1991. 75.00 (*0-7859-5731-6*, 8420652377) Fr & Eur.
Marino, Daniel A. A Whirl Around the World. 180p. Date not set. pap. 9.95 (*0-9633159-0-0*) Jemet Bks.
Marino, Emiliano. The Sailmaker's Apprentice: A Guide for the Self-Reliant Sailor. 512p. 1994. 39.95 (*0-07-157980-X*) McGraw.
***Marino, G., et al, eds.** Biochemistry of Vitamin B6 & PQQ. (Advances in Life Science Ser.). 384p. 1994. 85.00 (*0-8176-5067-9*) Birkhauser.
— Biochemistry of Vitamin B6 & PQQ. (Advances in Life Sciences Ser.). 1994. write for info. (*3-7643-5067-9*) Birkhauser.
Marino, Giovan B. La Lira - Archivio Tematico Della Lirica Italiana. (Archivio Tematico Della Lirica Italiana - Atli Ser.: Vol. 1). vii, 488p. 1992. write for info. (*3-487-09526-2*, Pub. by Georg Olms GW) Lubrecht & Cramer.
Marino, Gordon. Kierkegaard's Anthropology. (Orig.). 1995. pap. write for info. (*0-87462-604-8*) Marquette.
Marino, Jan. The Day That Elvis Came to Town. 208p. (J). (gr. 5). 1993. reprint ed. pap. 3.50 (*0-380-71672-0*, Camelot) Avon.
— Day That Elvis Came to Town, Vol. 1. (YA). (gr. 9-12). 1991. 15.95 (*0-316-54618-6*) Little.
— Eighty-Eight Steps to September. 160p. (J). (gr. 3-7). 1991. pap. 2.95 (*0-380-71001-3*, Camelot) Avon.
— For the Love of Pete. 208p. (J). (gr. 4 up). 1994. pap. 3.50 (*0-380-72281-X*, Camelot) Avon.
— For the Love of Pete: A Novel. LC 92-36465. (J). 1993. 14.95 (*0-316-54627-5*) Little.
— Like Some Kind of Hero. 224p. (YA). 1993. pap. 3.50 (*0-380-72010-8*, Flare) Avon.
— Like Some Kind of Hero. (J). (gr. 7 up). 1992. 14.95 (*0-316-54626-7*) Little.
— The Mona Lisa of Salem Street: A Novel. LC 94-34666. (J). 1995. 14.95 (*0-316-54614-3*) Little.
Marino, Jane. Sing Us a Story: Using Music in Preschool & Family Story Times. LC 93-6389. 215p. 1994. 40.00 (*0-8242-0847-1*) Wilson.
Marino, Jane & Houlihan, Dorothy F. Mother Goose Time: Library Programs for Babies & Their Caregivers. 172p. 1992. 30.00 (*0-8242-0850-1*) Wilson.
Marino, John, et al. The Raam Book (The Race Across America Book) The Official Guide & History of the Race Across America & the Ultra-Marathon Cycling Association. (Illus.). 250p. (Orig.). 1988. 9.95 (*0-924272-01-5*) Info Net Pub.
Marino, John A. Pastoral Economics in The Kingdom of Naples. LC 87-9196. (Studies in Historical & Political Science: 106th Series, No. 1). 400p. 1988. text ed. 52.50x (*0-8018-3437-6*) Johns Hopkins.
Marino, Joseph L. Matrimonial & Family Law, MFL: Covering Domestic Relations, General Obligations, Family Court, with Practice Commentaries. Vol. 9A: 10. write for info. (*0-318-58376-3*) West Pub.
Marino, Joseph S., ed. Biblical Themes in Religious Education. LC 83-16124. 294p. (Orig.). 1983. pap. 16.95 (*0-89135-038-1*) Religious Educ.
Marino, Juan P. Tratado de Evangelismo Personal: Treatise on Personal Evangelism. (SPA.). 4.95 (*84-399-7102-8*, 220901, Pub. by Edit Clie SP) TSELF.
Marino, Kenneth E. Forcasting Your Company's Sales & Profits: Quickly, Easily & Realistically. (Entrepreneur's Guide Ser.). 1990. pap. 22.95 (*1-55738-143-7*) Probus Pub Co.
Marino, Kim. Best Resumes for Accountants & Financial Professionals. 208p. 1994. text ed. 37.50 (*0-471-59542-X*); pap. text ed. 14.95 (*0-471-59543-8*) Wiley.
— The College Student's Resume Guide. LC 92-12689. 132p. 1992. pap. 9.95 (*0-89815-505-3*) Ten Speed Pr.
— The College Students Resume Guide: How to Write Your Own Professional Resume. (Illus.). 80p. (Orig.). (C). 1989. pap. write for info. (*0-318-65774-0*) Tangerine Pr.
— The College Students Resume Guide: How to Write Your Own Professional Resume. LC 89-27364. (Illus.). 80p. (Orig.). (C). 1990. pap. 8.95 (*0-9624284-9-3*) Tangerine Pr.
— The College Student's Resume Guide: How to Write Your Own Professional Resume. (Illus.). 96p. (C). 1991. pap. 9.95 (*0-9624284-7-7*) Tangerine Pr.
— Just Resumes: Two Hundred Powerful & Proven Successful Resumes to Get That Job. 256p. 1991. pap. text ed. 12.95 (*0-471-54856-1*) Wiley.
— The Resume Guide for Women of the Nineties. (Illus.). 128p. (Orig.). 1990. pap. 11.95 (*0-9624284-8-5*) Tangerine Pr.
— The Resume Guide for Women of the Nineties. LC 92-13552. 132p. (Orig.). 1992. pap. 11.95 (*0-89815-504-5*) Ten Speed Pr.
— Resumes for Educational Professionals. LC 93-47212. 1994. pap. text ed. 14.95 (*0-471-31144-8*) Wiley.
— Resumes for the Health Care Professional. 208p. 1993. pap. text ed. 12.95 (*0-471-55862-1*) Wiley.
Marino, M. A. & Luthin. Seepage & Groundwater. (Developments in Water Science Ser.: Vol. 13). 490p. 1982. 146.25 (*0-444-41975-6*) Elsevier.
Marino, Maria B., jt. ed. see Rodriguez-Monino, Antonio.
Marino, Michael F., 3rd. Labor & Employment in Pennsylvania: Guide to Employment Laws, Regulations & Practices. 430p. 1993. ring bd. 89.50 (*0-409-25674-9*) Michie Butterworth.
***Marino, Michael F., III & Richeson, J. David.** Employment in Florida: A Guide to Employment Laws, Regulations, & Practices. suppl. ed. 1994. ring bd. 38.50 (*0-614-03179-6*) Butterworth Legal Pubs.
Marino, Michael F., 3rd & Richeson, J. David. Employment in Florida: A Guide to Employment Laws, Regulations, & Practices. LC 92-26520. 450p. 1994. ring bd. 89.50 (*0-409-25666-8*) Michie Butterworth.
Marino, Michael F., III, jt. auth. see Liddle, Jeffrey L.
Marino, Michael F., et al. The Virginia Employer's Guide to Labor Law. LC 83-171872. (Illus.). 1982. 45.00 (*0-685-08125-7*) VA Chamber Com.
Marino, Miguel A., ed. Subsurface Flow & Contamination: Methods of Analysis & Parameter Uncertainty. (AWRA Monograph Ser.: No. 8). (Illus.). 118p. reprint ed. pap. 33.70 (*0-8357-3170-7*, 2039433) Bks Demand.
Marino, Nancy. La Serranilla Espanola. 153p. 1990. 29.50 (*0-916379-45-0*) Scripta.
Marino, Paul L. The ICU Book. LC 90-5622. (Illus.). 713p. 1991. text ed. 49.50 (*0-8121-1306-3*) Williams & Wilkins.
***Marino, Ragi.** Flying High: The Airplane in Quilt. (Illus.). 72p. (Orig.). Date not set. pap. 17.95 (*0-929950-18-6*) ME Pubns.
Marino, Raul, Jr., jt. ed. see Rasmussen, Theodore.
***Marino, Riccardo & Tomei, Patrizio.** Nonlinear Control Design: Geometric, Adaptive, & Robust. LC 94-47038. (Information & System Sciences Ser.). 1995. write for info. (*0-13-342635-1*) P-H.
***Marino, Rod.** Quincy Invasion. (Illus.). 56p. (J). 1995. pap. 8.00 (*0-8059-3733-1*) Dorrance.
Marino, T. J. & Sheff, Donald A. Freelance Photographer's Handbook. LC 79-6821. (Illus.). 140p. 1980. pap. write for info. (*0-672-52634-4*) Macmillan.
Marino, Tony. Intergalatic Grudge Match. LC 92-12845. (Widgets Ser.). (J). (gr. 2). 1992. lib. bdg. 13.99 (*1-56239-154-2*) Abdo & Dghtrs.
— Ratchet Hood. LC 92-12841. (Widgets Ser.). (YA). 1992. lib. bdg. 13.99 (*1-56239-152-6*) Abdo & Dghtrs.
— Scraboolee Jubilee. LC 92-12840. (Widgets Ser.). (YA). 1992. lib. bdg. 13.99 (*1-56239-153-4*) Abdo & Dghtrs.
Marino, V. English-Italian Dictionary of Medical Phraseology. 526p. 1985. 114.00 (*88-289-0279-5*) IBD Ltd.
Marino, Vito, jt. auth. see Lonstein, Albert I.
Marino, Vito R. & Furfero, Anthony C. The Official Price Guide to Frank Sinatra Collectibles - Records & CDs. (Illus.). 304p. 1993. pap. 12.00 (*0-87637-903-X*, House of Collect) Ballantine.
Marinoff, Irene. The Heresy of National Socialism. 1976. lib. bdg. 59.95 (*0-8490-1945-1*) Gordon Pr.
Marinone, N., ed. All the Greek Verbs. 352p. 1990. pap. text ed. 17.50 (*0-89341-629-0*, Longwood Academic) Hollowbrook.
Marinone, N. & Guala, F. Complete Handbook of Greek Verbs. 353p. 1972. 9.95 (*0-87774-001-1*) Schoenhof.
Marinone, Nino, ed. Xenophanes - Lessico Di Senofane. (Alpha-Omega, Reihe A Ser.: Bd. XX). 117p. 1972. reprint ed. write for info. (*3-487-04216-9*, Pub. by Georg Olms GW) Lubrecht & Cramer.
Marinone, Nino, jt. ed. see Lomanto, Valeria.
Marinos, Alex, jt. auth. see Louis, Diana F.
Marinos Of Neapolis. Life of Proclus & Commentary on the "Dedomena" of Euclid Extant Works. (Ancient Greek & Roman Writers Ser.). xvi, 107p. 1977. 20.00 (*0-89005-218-2*) Ares.
Marinos, Paul G., ed. Engineering Geology of Ancient Works, Monuments & Historical Sites: Proceedings of an International Symposium, Athens, 19-23 September 1988, 3 vols., Set. 2000p. (C). 1988. text ed. 340.00 (*90-6191-793-X*, Pub. by A A Balkema NE) Ashgate Pub Co.
Marinov, C. A. & Neittaanmaki, P. Mathematical Models in Electrical Circuits: Theory & Applications. (C). 1991. lib. bdg. 77.50 (*0-7923-1155-8*) Kluwer Ac.
Marinovic, N., ed. Electrotechnology in Mining. (Advances in Mining Science & Technology Ser.: No. 6). 638p. 1990. 184.75 (*0-444-88272-3*) Elsevier.
Marinozzi, V., ed. Ultrastructural Kidney Pathology. (Journal: Applied Pathology: Vol. 2, No. 4, 1984). (Illus.). 52p. 1985. pap. 38.50 (*3-8055-4251-8*) S Karger.
Marinsky & Marcus. Ion Exchange & Solvent Extraction, Vol. 5. 298p. 1973. 170.00 (*0-8247-6061-1*) Dekker.
— Ion Exchange & Solvent Extraction, Vol. 7. 312p. 1977. 185.00 (*0-8247-6571-0*) Dekker.
— Ion Exchange & Solvent Extraction, Vol. 8. 448p. 1981. 185.00 (*0-8247-1333-8*) Dekker.
— Ion Exchange & Solvent Extraction, Vol. 11. 400p. 1993. 215.00 (*0-8247-8472-3*) Dekker.
— Ion Exchange & Solvent Extraction: A Series of Advances, Vol. 12. 456p. 1995. 195.00 (*0-8247-9382-X*) Dekker.
— Ion Exchange & Solvent Extraction, Vol. 10: A Series of Advances. 296p. 1988. 185.00 (*0-8247-7688-7*) Dekker.
— Ion Exchange & Solvent Extraction, Vol. 9: A Series of Advances. 504p. 1985. 185.00 (*0-8247-7120-6*) Dekker.
Marinsky, Jacob A., ed. Ion Exchange, Vol. 1. LC 66-29027. 436p. reprint ed. pap. 124.30 (*0-685-15961-2*, 2027832) Bks Demand.
— Ion Exchange, Vol 2. LC 66-29027. 256p. reprint ed. pap. 73.00 (*0-317-08361-9*, 2055055) Bks Demand.
Marinsky, Jacob A. & Marcus, Yizhak, eds. Ion Exchange & Solvent Extraction, 3. LC 66-29027. 168p. reprint ed. pap. 47.90 (*0-685-15832-2*, 2027813) Bks Demand.
— Ion Exchange & Solvent Extraction, 4. LC 66-29027. reprint ed. pap. 70.30 (*0-685-15833-0*) Bks Demand.
— Ion Exchange & Solvent Extraction, Vol. 6: A Series of Advances. LC 73-645531. (Illus.). 315p. reprint ed. pap. 89.80 (*0-7837-4207-X*, 2027813) Bks Demand.
Mario, L. Profugo De la Sal. LC 78-56759. 1978. pap. 5.00 (*0-89729-206-5*) Ediciones.
Mario, Luis. Ciencia y Arte del Verso Castellano. LC 91-72151. (Coleccion Polymita Ser.). 506p. (Orig.). (SPA.). 1991. pap. 24.95 (*0-89729-607-9*) Ediciones.
— Cuba en Mis Versos. LC 92-74962. (Coleccion Espejo de Paciencia Ser.). 140p. (Orig.). (SPA.). 1993. pap. 12.00 (*0-89729-662-1*) Ediciones.
— Esta Mujer. LC 83-81719. (Coleccion Espejo de Paciencia Ser.). 77p. (Orig.). (SPA.). 1984. pap. 6.00 (*0-89729-338-X*) Ediciones.
— La Misma. LC 88-81864. (Coleccion Espejo de Paciencia Ser.). 131p. (Orig.). (SPA.). 1990. pap. 9.95 (*0-89729-498-X*) Ediciones.
— Poesia y Poetas. LC 83-81718. (Coleccion Polymita Ser.). 126p. (Orig.). (SPA.). 1984. pap. 8.95 (*0-89729-337-1*) Ediciones.
Mario, Thomas. Playboy's New Bar Guide. LC 70-136582. 1984. pap. 3.95 (*0-515-07937-5*) Playboy Pbks.
Mariolle, Elaine & Shermer, Michael B. The Woman Cyclist: Training & Racing Techniques. (Illus.). 224p. (Orig.). 1988. pap. 12.95 (*0-8092-4941-3*) Contemp Bks.
Mariological Society of America, Burlingame, Calif. Convention, 1989. Marian Studies: Proceedings, Vol. 40, Vol. 40. 279p. 12.00 (*0-318-50039-6*) Mariological Soc.
Mariological Society of America, East Aurora Convention, 1988. Marian Studies: Proceedings, Vol. 39, Vol. 39. 224p. 12.00 (*0-318-50038-8*) Mariological Soc.
Mariological Society of America. New York City Convention, 1980. Marian Studies: Proceedings, Vol. 31. 238p. 12.00 (*0-318-14800-5*) Mariological Soc.
Mariological Society of America, Providence, R. I., Convention, 1990. Marian Studies: Proceedings, Vol. 41, Vol. 41. 203p. 12.00 (*0-317-04171-1*) Mariological Soc.
Mariological Society of America Staff. Marian Studies: Proceedings, Chicago Convention, 1991, Vol. 42. 1991. 12.00 (*0-317-04172-X*) Mariological Soc.
Mariological Society of America. Tampa, Fla. Convention, 1986. Marian Studies: Proceedings, Vol. 37. 279p. 12.00 (*0-317-01324-6*) Mariological Soc.
Mariolopoulos, E. Compendium in Astronomy. 1982. lib. bdg. 112.50 (*90-277-1373-1*) Kluwer Ac.
Marion, A. Introduction to Image Processing. 1991. 54.95 (*0-442-31202-4*) Chapman & Hall.
Marion, Bruce W. Organization & Performance of the U. S. Food System. LC 85-45106. 576p. 1985. text ed. 60.00 (*0-669-11220-8*) Free Pr.
Marion, Craig A., ed. see Renfro, Nancy & Sullivan, Debbie.
***Marion, D.** Josephine's Catastrophes: Three Great Cat Tales. LC 94-30493. (J). 1995. 15.95 (*0-382-24909-7*); pap. 5.95 (*0-382-24910-0*) Silver Burdett Pr.
— Josephine's Catastrophes: Three Great Cat Tales. LC 94-30493. (J). 1995. lib. bdg. 17.95 (*0-382-24908-9*) Silver Burdett Pr.
***Marion, Dawn D.** The Wizard & the Golden Acorns. Lingard, Tim, ed. (Continuing Adventures of Timothy Glean). (Illus.). 36p. (Orig.). (J). (gr. k-3). 1994. pap. write for info. (*1-885986-00-9*) Glean Pubns.
Marion, Frances. Valley People. LC 70-144161. (Short Story Index Reprint Ser.). 1977. reprint ed. 20.95 (*0-8369-3776-7*) Ayer.
Marion, Frieda. China Half-Figures Called Pincushion Dolls. LC 74-178257. (Illus.). 1977. reprint ed. 7.95 (*0-89145-058-0*) J Palmer.
***Marion, Gina.** Creative Hardanger. (Illus.). 80p. 1995. pap. 12.95 (*1-86351-136-9*, Pub. by S Milner AT) Sterling.
Marion, James B. & Heald, Mark A. Classical Electromagnetic Radiation. 2nd ed. Vondeling, John & Pachuta, Kate, eds. (Illus.). 488p. (C). 1980. text ed. 57.25 (*0-15-507638-8*); teacher ed, pap. text ed. 28.50 (*0-15-507639-6*) SCP.
Marion, Jean-Luc. God Without Being: Hors-Texte. Carlson, Thomas A., tr. (Religion & Postmodernism Ser.). 264p. 1991. 32.00 (*0-226-50540-5*) U Ch Pr.
— God Without Being: Hors-Texte. Carlson, Thomas A., tr. 258p. 1995. pap. text ed. 13.95 (*0-226-50541-3*) U Ch Pr.
***Marion, Jeff D.** Lost & Found. 64p. 1994. pap. 9.95 (*1-885912-02-1*) Sows Ear Pr.
— Lost & Found. (Illus.). 64p. 1994. 19.95 (*1-885912-03-X*) Sows Ear Pr.
— Vigils, Selected Poems. LC 89-17896. 1989. pap. 9.95 (*0-913239-62-3*) Appalach Consortium.
Marion, Jerry B. Physics in the Modern World. 2nd ed. 648p. (C). 1980. text ed. 53.25 (*0-15-570602-0*) SCP.
Marion, Jerry B. & Hornyak, William F. General Physics with Bioscience Essays. 606p. (C). 1985. lib. bdg. 58.95 (*0-471-89878-3*) Krieger.
— Physics for Scientists & Engineers, Vols. 1 & 2. (C). 1982. student ed 22.75 (*0-685-07039-5*) SCP.
Marion, Jerry B. & Thornton, Stephen T. Classical Dynamics of Particles & Systems. 3rd ed. 725p. (C). 1988. teacher ed 20.00 (*0-15-507641-8*); text ed. 58.75 (*0-15-507640-X*); teacher ed, pap. text ed. 17.00 (*0-15-507642-6*) SCP.
Marion, Jerry B., ed. see International Conference on Fast Neutron Physics Staff.
***Marion, Kathryn A.** Success in the 'Real World' The Graduate's Complete Guide to Making the Most of Your Career (& Your Life)! LC 95-90069. 64p. (Orig.). 1995. pap. 5.95 (*0-9645391-5-2*) Educ Reality.
Marion, Kenneth P. Volunteer Firefighter. (Illus.). 32p. (J). (ps-2). 1990. pap. 4.00 (*0-945878-00-1*) JK Pub.
Marion, Marian. Guidance of Young Children. 4th ed. (Illus.). 336p. (C). 1995. pap. write for info. (*0-02-376061-3*) Macmillan.
Marion, Merrick J. College Undercover: What Every Student Needs to Know. LC 93-60309. 117p. (Orig.). 1994. pap. 12.95 (*1-56912-098-6*) Wharton Pub.
Marion, Nancy E. A History of Federal Crime Control Initiatives, 1960-1993. LC 93-48214. (Criminology & Crime Control Policy Ser.). 288p. 1994. text ed. 55.00 (*0-275-94649-5*, Praeger Pubs) Greenwood.
Marion, Paul. Apples & Oranges. LC 86-81721. 28p. (Orig.). 1986. pap. 4.00 (*0-931507-02-2*) Loom Pr.

An Asterisk (*) at the beginning of an entry indicates that the title is appearing in BIP for the first time.

— Middle Distance. 64p. (Orig.). 1988. pap. 4.95 (*0-931507-04-9*) Loom Pr.

— Strong Place: Poems Seventy-Four to Eighty-Four. LC 84-82241. 64p. (Orig.). 1984. pap. 4.95 (*0-931507-00-6*) Loom Pr.

Marion, Paul, ed. The Loom Reader. 16p. (Orig.). 1986. pap. 2.50 (*0-931507-01-4*) Loom Pr.

Marion, Paul, ed. see Berstein, Stanley, et al.

Marion, Peller. Crisis-Proof Your Career: Finding Job Security in an Insecure Time. LC 92-39825. 1993. 17.95 (*1-55972-181-2*, Birch Ln Pr) Carol Pub Group.

Marion, Robert. Intern Blues: The Private Ordeals of Three Young Doctors. 384p. 1990. mass mkt. 5.99 (*0-449-21898-8*, Crest) Fawcett.

— Learning to Play God. 1993. mass mkt. 4.99 (*0-449-22192-X*) Fawcett.

— Was George Washington Really the Father of Our Country? A Clinical Geneticist Looks at World History. LC 93-26588. (Illus.). 206p. 1993. 22.07 (*0-201-62255-6*) Addison-Wesley.

Marion, Sheila. Tap Dance (A Dictionary in Labanotation) Cook et al, eds. (Illus.). 60p. (Orig.). 1986. pap. text ed. 20.00 (*0-9602002-5-8*) Ray Cook.

Marion-Wild, E. C. The Prologue of the Gospel of St. John: Esoteric Studies. Roboz, Helga & Roboz, Steven, trs. 19p. 1984. pap. 3.75 (*0-919924-22-0*) Anthroposophic.

Marion, William. Client-Server Strategies: Implementations in the IBM Environment. 1994. text ed. 40.00 (*0-07-040539-5*) McGraw.

Mariott, Bernadette M., ed. Nutritional Needs in Hot Environments: Applications for Military Personnel in Field Operations. 392p. (Orig.). (C). 1993. pap. text ed. 39.00 (*0-309-04840-0*) Natl Acad Pr.

Mariotte, Edme. The Motion of Water & Other Fluids: Being a Treatise of Hydrostaticks. Albritton, Claude C. & Albritton, Claude C., eds. Desaguliers, J. T., tr. (History of Geology Ser.). (Illus.). 1978. reprint ed. lib. bdg. 30.95 (*0-405-10449-9*) Ayer.

Mariotte, F., tr. see Little, Ruth.

Mariotti, Federico A., tr. see Hunter, Wayne & Hunter, Emily.

Mariotti, Frederico A., tr. see Hunter, Emily.

Mariotti, J. M., jt. ed. see Alloin, D. M.

Mariotti, Jean-Marie, jt. ed. see Alloin, Danielle M.

***Mariotti, John L.** The Power of Partnerships: The Next Step Beyond TQM, Reengineering & Lean Production : A Competitive Cornerstone for the 21st Century. LC 95-1579. 1995. write for info. (*1-55786-717-8*) Blackwell Pubs.

Mariotti, Mario. Hand Games. (Illus.). 32p. (J). (ps-4). 1992. 11.95 (*0-916291-43-X*) Kane-Miller Bk.

— Hands Off! (Illus.). 40p. (J). (ps-4). 1990. 10.95 (*0-916291-29-4*) Kane-Miller Bk.

— Hanimations. Orig. Title: Rimani. (Illus.). 40p. (J). (ps-4). 1989. 10.95 (*0-916291-22-7*) Kane-Miller Bk.

— Humages. (Illus.). (Orig.). (J). 1991. pap. 8.95 (*0-671-75233-2*, Green Tiger S&S) S&S Childrens.

— Humands. (Illus.). (J). 1991. pap. 8.95 (*0-671-75235-9*, Green Tiger S&S) S&S Childrens.

Mariotti, Mario & Marchiori, Roberto, illus. Hanimals. Orig. Title: Animani. 40p. (Orig.). (J). (gr. 4 up). 1991. pap. 8.95 (*0-671-75232-4*, Green Tiger S&S) S&S Childrens.

Mariotti, Richard & Fife, Bruce. How to Be a Literary Agent: An Introductory Guide to Literary Representation. LC 94-15179. 190p. (Orig.). 1995. pap. 16.00 (*0-941599-26-4*) Piccadilly Bks.

***Mariotti, Steve & Towle, Tony.** How to Start & Run a Business Entrepreneur: The Guide for the Young. 1995. pap. 15.00 (*0-8129-2627-7*, Times Bks) Random.

Maris, Edward. Coins of New Jersey. (Illus.). 1987. reprint ed. pap. 15.00 (*0-685-05536-1*) S J Durst.

Maris, Mariann, ed. see Narada Media Staff.

***Maris, Michael & Monton, Dennis.** Looking Forever Young. (YA). 1995. write for info. (*1-879234-30-0*) Leisure TX.

Maris, Nicolae. Social Progressive Credit System. (Illus.). 36p. 1994. 4.95 (*0-8059-3438-3*) Dorrance.

Maris, Ron. Are You There, Bear? LC 84-4180. (Illus.). 32p. (J). (ps-1). 1985. 15.00 (*0-688-03997-9*); lib. bdg. 14.93 (*0-688-03998-7*) Greenwillow.

— Ducks Quack. LC 91-58726. (Illus.). 14p. (J). (ps). 1992. 4.95 (*1-56402-080-0*) Candlewick Pr.

— Frogs Jump. LC 91-58730. (Illus.). 14p. (J). (ps). 1992. 4.95 (*1-56402-081-9*) Candlewick Pr.

— Hello, Baby Badger. (Illus.). 32p. (J). (ps-1). Date not set. 16.95 (*1-85681-261-8*, Pub. by J MacRae UK) Trafalgar.

— I Wish I Could Fly. LC 86-9797. (Illus.). 32p. (J). (ps-1). 1987. 13.95 (*0-688-06654-2*); lib. bdg. 13.88 (*0-688-06655-0*) Greenwillow.

— I Wish I Could Fly. (J). 1989. pap. 19.95 (*0-590-72461-4*) Scholastic Inc.

— In My Garden. LC 87-8773. (Illus.). 32p. (J). (ps-1). 1988. reprint ed. 13.00 (*0-688-07631-9*) Greenwillow.

— Is Anyone Home? LC 85-5436. (Illus.). 32p. (J). (ps-2). 1986. 16.00 (*0-688-05899-X*) Greenwillow.

— My Book. (Picture Puffins Ser.). (Illus.). 32p. (J). (ps-1). 1986. pap. 3.95 (*0-14-050523-7*, Puffin) Puffin Bks.

— Rescuing Robot. (Illus.). 32p. (J). (ps-00). 1992. 16.95 (*1-85681-260-X*, Pub. by J MacRae UK) Trafalgar.

Maris, Ronald, ed. Understanding & Preventing Suicide: Plenary Papers of the First Combined Meeting of the AAS & IASP. LC 88-175957. (Illus.). 142p. reprint ed. pap. 40.50 (*0-7837-1204-9*, 2041736) Bks Demand.

Maris, Ronald W. Pathways to Suicide: A Survey of Self-Destructive Behaviors. LC 80-24520. (Illus.). 399p. 1981. reprint ed. pap. 113.80 (*0-7837-1111-5*, 2041641) Bks Demand.

Maris, Ronald W., ed. Biology of Suicide: Journal of Suicide & Life-Treatening Behaviors, Vol. 16, No. 2. LC 86-14207. 216p. 1986. lib. bdg. 35.00 (*0-89862-578-5*) Guilford Pr.

— Understanding & Preventing Suicide, Vol. 18, No. 1. 118p. 1988. lib. bdg. 17.50 (*0-89862-583-1*) Guilford Pr.

Maris, Ronald W., et al, eds. Assessment & Prediction of Suicide. LC 91-35408. 697p. 1992. lib. bdg. 55.00 (*0-89862-791-5*) Guilford Pr.

Mariscal, George. Contradictory Subjects: Quevedo, Cervantes & Seventeenth-Century Spanish Culture. LC 91-13369. 248p. 1991. 27.95 (*0-8014-2604-9*) Cornell U Pr.

Marisch, Gerald. The W. D. Gann Method of Trading. 1990. 50.00 (*0-930233-42-5*) Windsor.

Mariska, John T. The Solar Transition Region. (Cambridge Astrophysics Ser.: No. 23). (Illus.). 275p. (C). 1993. 59.95 (*0-521-38261-0*) Cambridge U Pr.

Marison, Fiscar, tr. The Passion of Our Lord. 302p. 1980. pap. 5.95 (*0-911988-38-6*) AMI Pr.

Marison, Fiscar, tr. see Agreda, Mary.

***Marissen, Michael.** The Social & Religious Designs of J. S. Bach's Brandenburg Concertos. LC 94-28688. 1995. 24.95 (*0-691-03739-6*) Princeton U Pr.

Marist Parents' Club Staff, ed. A Touch of Atlanta. (Illus.). 256p. 1990. 16.95 (*0-9626204-0-8*) Marist Parents.

Maristed, Kai. Out after Dark. LC 92-34341. 1993. 22.00 (*1-877946-30-3*) Permanent Pr.

Maritain, Jacques. Approaches to God. O'Reilly, Peter, tr. LC 78-16555. 128p. 1978. reprint ed. text ed. 55.00 (*0-313-20606-6*, MATG, Greenwood Pr) Greenwood.

— Approches Sans Entraves. 595p. (FRE.). 1973. 39.95 (*0-7859-5534-8*) Fr & Eur.

— Art & Scholasticism: With Other Essays. Scanlan, J. F., tr. LC 70-152196. (Essay Index Reprint Ser.). 1977. reprint ed. 16.95 (*0-8369-2241-7*) Ayer.

— Art et Scolastique. 4th ed. 280p. (FRE.). 1965. 19.95 (*0-8288-9854-5*, F111960) Fr & Eur.

— Bergsonian Philosophy & Thomism. LC 68-8068. (Illus.). 383p. 1968. reprint ed. text ed. 65.00 (*0-8371-0559-5*, MABP, Greenwood Pr) Greenwood.

— Carnet de Notes. 2nd ed. (Illus.). 424p. (FRE.). 1965. 34.95 (*0-8288-9887-1*, F11670) Fr & Eur.

— A Christian Looks at the Jewish Question. LC 73-2216. (Jewish People; History, Religion, Literature Ser.). 1980. reprint ed. 19.95 (*0-405-05280-4*) Ayer.

— Christianity & Democracy. Bd. with Rights of Man & Natural Law. LC 83-80191. LC 83-80191. 250p. 1986. Set pap. 12.95 (*0-89870-030-2*) Ignatius Pr.

— Christianity & Democracy. Anson, Doris C., tr. LC 72-6765. (Essay Index Reprint Ser.). 1980. reprint ed. 18.95 (*0-8369-7243-0*) Ayer.

— Court Traite de l'Existence et de l'Existant. 238p. (FRE.). 1964. 11.95 (*0-8288-9846-4*, F111680) Fr & Eur.

— Creative Intuition in Art & Poetry. LC 55-5537. (Bollingen Ser.: No. 35). 517p. 1981. reprint ed. pap. 147.40 (*0-7837-8592-5*, 2049407) Bks Demand.

— De Bergson a Thomas d'Aquin. 336p. (FRE.). 1944. pap. write for info. (*0-7859-4608-X*) Fr & Eur.

— De la Grace et de l'Humanite de Jesus. 2nd ed. 156p. (FRE.). 1967. 15.95 (*0-8288-9848-0*, F111690) Fr & Eur.

— De l'Eglise du Christ. 430p. (FRE.). 1970. 15.95 (*0-8288-9847-2*, F111685) Fr & Eur.

— The Degrees of Knowledge. McInerny, Ralph, ed. Phelan, Gerald B., tr. LC 94-45159. (Collected Works of Jacques Maritain: Vol. 7). (ENG & FRE.). (C). 1995. text ed. 34.95x (*0-268-00876-0*) U of Notre Dame Pr.

— Dieu et la Permission du Mal. 3rd ed. 116p. (FRE.). 1963. 13.95 (*0-8288-9849-9*, F111710) Fr & Eur.

— Distinguer Pour Unir: Les Degres du Savoir. 8th ed. 946p. (FRE.). 1959. 59.95 (*0-8288-9850-2*, F111720) Fr & Eur.

— Education at the Crossroads. (Terry Lecture Ser.). 132p. (C). 1943. pap. 12.00 (*0-300-00163-0*, Y15) Yale U Pr.

— Elements de Philosophie: Introduction Generale a la Philosophie. 33th ed. 240p. 1963. pap. 29.95 (*0-7859-5126-1*, F111730) Fr & Eur.

— Freedom & the Modern World. O'Sullivan, Richard, tr. LC 77-150414. 231p. (C). 1971. reprint ed. 35.00 (*0-87752-147-6*) Gordian.

— L' Homme et l'Etat. 2nd ed. 212p. (FRE.). 1965. 15.95 (*0-8288-9851-0*, F111740) Fr & Eur.

— Humanisme Integral. 320p. 1968. 9.95 (*0-7859-0698-3*) Fr & Eur.

— An Introduction to Philosophy. LC 89-61354. 1989. pap. 12.95 (*0-87061-164-X*) Chr Classics.

— An Introduction to the Basic Problems of Moral Philosophy. Borgerhoff, Cornelia N., tr. LC 90-32535. (Illus.). 224p. 1990. 14.95 (*0-87343-052-2*) Magi Bks.

— L' Intuition Creatrice dans l'Art et dans la Poesie. (Illus.). 424p. (FRE.). 1966. 69.95 (*0-8288-9911-8*, F16910) Fr & Eur.

— Maritain-Mounier: Correspondance, 1929-1939. Mounier, Emmanuel, ed. 272p. (FRE.). 1973. 34.95 (*0-7859-0107-8*, M3734) Fr & Eur.

— Le Mystere d'Israel. 302p. (FRE.). 1990. pap. 29.95 (*0-7859-1601-6*, 222003173X) Fr & Eur.

— Notebooks. Evans, Joseph W., tr. LC 83-26743. (Illus.). 320p. 1984. 12.95 (*0-87343-050-6*) Magi Bks.

— On the Philosophy of History. LC 73-128059. 1973. reprint ed. 27.50 (*0-678-02760-9*) Kelley.

— On the Use of Philosophy: Three Essays. LC 81-13338. 71p. 1982. reprint ed. text ed. 42.50 (*0-313-23199-0*, MAUP, Greenwood Pr) Greenwood.

— Paysanne de la Garonne. 405p. 1966. 29.95 (*0-8288-7445-X*) Fr & Eur.

— Le Payson de Garonne: Un Vieux Laic s'Interroge a propos du Temps Present. 19.95 (*0-685-34274-3*) Fr & Eur.

— Le Peche de l'Ange. De La Trinite & Journet, eds. 248p. (FRE.). 1961. pap. 39.95 (*0-686-56360-3*) Fr & Eur.

— Person & the Common Good. 1966. pap. 5.95 (*0-268-00204-5*) U of Notre Dame Pr.

— La Philosophie Morale: Examen Historique et Critique des Grandes Systemes. 592p. (FRE.). 1960. 39.95 (*0-8288-9852-9*, F111820) Fr & Eur.

— Pour une Philosophie de l'Education. 254p. (FRE.). 1960. 18.95 (*0-8288-9853-7*, F111830) Fr & Eur.

— A Preface to Metaphysics: Seven Lectures on Being. LC 74-157346. (Select Bibliographies Reprint Ser.). 1979. reprint ed. 20.95 (*0-8369-5807-1*) Ayer.

— Ransoming the Time. Binsse, Harry L., tr. LC 70-165665. 322p. 1972. reprint ed. 50.00 (*0-87752-153-0*) Gordian.

— Reflections on America. LC 74-26882. 205p. 1975. reprint ed. 35.00 (*0-87752-166-2*) Gordian.

— Reflexions sur l'Amerique. 224p. (FRE.). 1958. pap. 9.95 (*0-7859-5536-4*) Fr & Eur.

— Religion et Culture. 174p. (FRE.). 1991. pap. 12.95 (*0-7859-1447-1*, 2220031578) Fr & Eur.

— Responsabilite de l'Artiste. 128p. 1961. 9.95 (*0-686-56367-0*) Fr & Eur.

— Responsibility of the Artist. LC 70-150415. 120p. 1972. reprint ed. 30.00 (*0-87752-145-X*) Gordian.

— Rights of Man & Natural Law. LC 74-150416. 120p. 1971. reprint ed. 25.00 (*0-87752-146-8*) Gordian.

— Scholasticism & Politics. LC 72-353. (Essay Index Reprint Ser.). 1977. reprint ed. 18.95 (*0-8369-2805-9*) Ayer.

— Situation de la Poesie. 2nd ed. 144p. (FRE.). 1964. 10.95 (*0-8288-9912-6*, F16911) Fr & Eur.

— St. Thomas & the Problem of Evil. (Aquinas Lectures). 1942. 10.00 (*0-87462-106-2*) Marquette.

— Theonas. LC 74-84325. (Essay Index Reprint Ser.). 1977. 19.95 (*0-8369-1095-8*) Ayer.

— Three Reformers: Luther-Descartes-Rousseau. LC 78-98780. 234p. 1970. reprint ed. text ed. 35.00 (*0-8371-2825-0*, MATR, Greenwood Pr) Greenwood.

— True Humanism. Adamson, M. R., tr. LC 71-114888. (Select Bibliographies Reprint Ser.). 1977. 30.95 (*0-8369-5292-8*) Ayer.

— True Humanism. 3rd ed. Adamson, Margot, tr. LC 71-98781. 304p. 1970. reprint ed. text ed. 41.50 (*0-8371-2902-8*, MAHU, Greenwood Pr) Greenwood.

Maritain, Jacques & Maritain, Raissa. Oeuvres Completes: Vol. 1: 1906-1920, 15 vols. 1175p. 1986. 79.00 (*2-8271-0338-9*) I B C A.

— Oeuvres Completes, Vol. III: 1924-1929, 15 vols., Set. 1472p. (FRE.). 1985. 79.99 (*2-8271-0287-0*) I B C A.

— Oeuvres Completes, Vol. IV: 1929-1932, 15 vols. 1259p. (FRE.). 1983. 72.99 (*2-8271-0259-5*, Pub. by Editions Univ SZ) I B C A.

— Oeuvres Completes, Vol. V: 1932-1935, 15 vols. 1153p. (FRE.). 1982. 72.99 (*2-8271-0224-2*, Pub. by Editions Univ SZ) I B C A.

— Oeuvres Completes, Vol. VI: 1935-1938, 15 vols. 1317p. (FRE.). 1984. 72.99 (*2-8271-0275-7*, Pub. by Editions Univ SZ) I B C A.

— Oeuvres Completes, Vol. X: 1952-1959, 15 vols. 1234p. (FRE.). 1985. 79.99 (*2-8271-0302-8*) I B C A.

— Oeuvres Completes, Vol. 7: Nineteen Thirty-Nine to Nineteen Forty-Three. Allion, J. et al, eds. 1402p. (FRE.). (C). 1988. 87.49 (*2-8271-0388-5*, Pub. by Editions Univ SZ) I B C A.

Maritain, Raissa. Raissa's Journal. LC 72-95648. 425p. 1974. 12.95 (*0-87343-041-7*) Magi Bks.

— St. Thomas Aquinas, the Angel of the Schools: A Book for Children & the Child-Like. (Illus.). 127p. (Orig.). (J). (gr. 3-7). 1993. pap. 5.50 (*0-935952-95-0*) Angelus Pr.

Maritain, Raissa, jt. auth. see Maritain, Jacques.

Maritain, Raissa, jt. auth. see Maritan, Jacques.

Maritan, Jacques & Maritain, Raissa. Oeurves Completes, Vol. 2: Nineteen Twenty to Nineteen Twenty-Three, 15 vols. Allion, J. et al, eds. 1331p. 1987. 79.99 (*2-8271-0350-8*) I B C A.

Maritime Books Staff. A-Z of Ships Badges, 1919-1989, Vol. 1. (C). 1986. text ed. 100.00 (*0-685-38766-6*, Pub. by Maritime Bks UK) St Mut.

— A-Z of Ships Badges, 1919-1989, Vol. 2. (C). 1986. text ed. 100.00 (*1-870842-02-2*, Pub. by Maritime Bks UK) St Mut.

— Aircraft of the Royal Navy since Nineteen Forty-Five. (C). 1986. 59.00 (*0-907771-06-8*, Pub. by Maritime Bks UK) St Mut.

— Badges & Battle Honours of HM Ships. (C). 1986. text ed. 290.00 (*0-907771-26-2*, Pub. by Maritime Bks UK) St Mut.

— British Warships & Auxiliaries, 1990-91. (C). 1986. text ed. 59.00 (*0-907771-44-0*, Pub. by Maritime Bks UK) St Mut.

— British Warships since Nineteen Forty-Five, Pt. 1. (C). 1986. text ed. 40.00 (*0-9506323-4-1*, Pub. by Maritime Bks UK) St Mut.

— British Warships since Nineteen Forty-Five, Pt. 2. (C). 1986. text ed. 40.00 (*0-685-38788-7*, Pub. by Maritime Bks UK) St Mut.

— British Warships since Nineteen Forty-Five, Pt. 4. (C). 1986. text ed. 40.00 (*0-907771-12-2*, Pub. by Maritime Bks UK) St Mut.

— British Warships since Nineteen Forty-Five, Pt. 5. (C). 1986. text ed. 50.00 (*0-907771-13-0*, Pub. by Maritime Bks UK) St Mut.

— Channel Sweep. (C). 1986. text ed. 60.00 (*0-907771-40-8*, Pub. by Maritime Bks UK) St Mut.

— Chatham Dockyard Story. (C). 1986. text ed. 70.00 (*0-948193-30-1*, Pub. by Maritime Bks UK) St Mut.

— Cruisers of the Royal & Commonwealth Navies. (C). 1986. text ed. 100.00 (*0-907771-35-1*, Pub. by Maritime Bks UK) St Mut.

— Encyclopaedia of Fleet Air Arm. (C). 1986. text ed. 130.00 (*0-85059-760-9*, Pub. by Maritime Bks UK) St Mut.

— Encyclopedia of HM Submarines, 1901-55. (C). 1986. text ed. 600.00 (*0-907771-42-4*, Pub. by Maritime Bks UK) St Mut.

— Falklands Task Force Portfolio, Pt. 1. (C). 1986. text ed. 90.00 (*0-907771-02-5*, Pub. by Maritime Bks UK) St Mut.

— Falklands Task Force Portfolio, Pt. 2. (C). 1986. text ed. 90.00 (*0-907771-03-3*, Pub. by Maritime Bks UK) St Mut.

— Fifty Years of Naval Tugs. (C). 1986. text ed. 50.00 (*0-907771-25-4*, Pub. by Maritime Bks UK) St Mut.

— Grand Scuttle - The Sinking of the German Fleet at Scapa Flow. (C). 1986. text ed. 40.00 (*0-86228-099-0*, Pub. by Maritime Bks UK) St Mut.

— Heritage of Ships. (C). 1986. text ed. 80.00 (*0-285-62855-0*, Pub. by Maritime Bks UK) St Mut.

— HMS Ark Royal - The Ship & Her Men. (C). 1986. text ed. 35.00 (*0-907771-39-4*, Pub. by Maritime Bks UK) St Mut.

— HMS Bulwark, 1948-84. (C). 1986. text ed. 50.00 (*0-907771-27-0*, Pub. by Maritime Bks UK) St Mut.

— HMS Ganges - Roll on My Dozen. (C). 1986. text ed. 130.00 (*0-685-38769-0*, Pub. by Maritime Bks UK) St Mut.

— HMS Hermes, 1959-84. (C). 1986. text ed. 100.00 (*0-907771-16-5*, Pub. by Maritime Bks UK); pap. text ed. 50.00 (*0-907771-17-3*, Pub. by Maritime Bks UK) St Mut.

— HMS Plymouth - Her Story. (C). 1986. pap. text ed. 35.00 (*0-685-38787-9*, Pub. by Maritime Bks UK) St Mut.

— Jackspeak RN Slanguage. (C). 1986. text ed. 90.00 (*0-685-38775-5*, Pub. by Maritime Bks UK) St Mut.

— Laugh with the Navy Too. (C). 1986. text ed. 50.00 (*0-907771-01-7*, Pub. by Maritime Bks UK) St Mut.

— Modern Military Techniques Carriers. (C). 1986. pap. text ed. 30.00 (*0-583-31003-6*, Pub. by Maritime Bks UK) St Mut.

— Modern Military Techniques Combined: OPS. (C). 1986. pap. text ed. 40.00 (*0-583-31004-4*, Pub. by Maritime Bks UK) St Mut.

— Modern Military Techniques Submarines. (C). 1986. pap. text ed. 40.00 (*0-583-31009-5*, Pub. by Maritime Bks UK) St Mut.

— Naval Wrecks of Scapa Flow. (C). 1986. text ed. 80.00 (*0-685-38772-0*, Pub. by Maritime Bks UK) St Mut.

— Our Falklands War. (C). 1986. text ed. 60.00 (*0-907771-08-4*, Pub. by Maritime Bks UK) St Mut.

— Portsmouth Built Warships, 1497-1967. (C). 1986. text ed. 50.00 (*0-685-38768-2*, Pub. by Maritime Bks UK) St Mut.

— The Royal Navy at Malta, Vol. 1: The Victorian Era. (C). 1986. text ed. 190.00 (*0-907771-43-2*, Pub. by Maritime Bks UK) St Mut.

— The Royal Navy at Portland since Eighteen Forty-Five. (C). 1986. text ed. 100.00 (*0-907771-29-7*, Pub. by Maritime Bks UK) St Mut.

— The Royal Navy in Focus, 1930-39. (C). 1986. text ed. 60.00 (*0-907771-04-1*, Pub. by Maritime Bks UK) St Mut.

— The Royal Navy in Focus, 1940-49. (C). 1986. text ed. 60.00 (*0-907771-11-4*, Pub. by Maritime Bks UK) St Mut.

— The Royal Navy in Focus, 1950-59. (C). 1986. text ed. 50.00 (*0-907771-22-X*, Pub. by Maritime Bks UK) St Mut.

— The Royal Navy in Focus, 1960-69. (C). 1986. text ed. 50.00 (*0-907771-33-5*, Pub. by Maritime Bks UK) St Mut.

— Sea Power in the Falklands. (C). 1986. text ed. 100.00 (*0-03-069534-1*, Pub. by Maritime Bks UK) St Mut.

— Ships & Aircraft of the Royal Navy. (C). 1986. pap. text ed. 50.00 (*0-907771-23-8*, Pub. by Maritime Bks UK) St Mut.

— Submarine Versus U Boat. (C). 1986. text ed. 130.00 (*0-685-38782-8*, Pub. by Maritime Bks UK) St Mut.

— Warrior - The First & Last. (C). 1986. text ed. 75.00 (*0-907771-34-3*, Pub. by Maritime Bks UK) St Mut.

— We Joined the Navy (Winton) (C). 1986. text ed. 60.00 (*0-907771-38-6*, Pub. by Maritime Bks UK) St Mut.

— Wrecks of Scapa Flow. (C). 1986. text ed. 65.00 (*0-685-38773-9*, Pub. by Maritime Bks UK) St Mut.

Maritime Books Staff, ed. Chatham Built Warships since Eighteen Eighty. (C). 1986. text ed. 60.00 (*0-907771-07-6*, Pub. by Maritime Bks UK) St Mut.

— Devonport Dockyard Story. (C). 1986. text ed. 49.00 (*0-907771-14-9*, Pub. by Maritime Bks UK) St Mut.

— The Ship That Torpedoed Herself. (C). 1986. text ed. 45.00 (*0-685-38770-4*, Pub. by Maritime Bks UK) St Mut.

— This Great Harbour Scapa Flow. (C). 1986. text ed. 200.00 (*0-685-38771-2*, Pub. by Maritime Bks UK) St Mut.

Maritz, J. S. & Lwin, T. Empirical Bayes Methods. 250p. 1989. 55.00 (*0-412-27760-3*, A2933) Chapman & Hall.

***Maritz, Linette.** Soft Furnishings with Your Overlocker: A Step-by-Step Creative Guide to over Fifty Projects. (Illus.). 80p. 1995. pap. 12.95 (*1-85368-473-2*, Pub. by New Holland Pubs UK) Sterling.

Mariuaux. The Triumph of Love. Magruder, James, tr. 1994. pap. 4.75 (*0-8222-1415-6*) Dramatists Play.

Marius. Dutch Painters of the Nineteenth Century. Norman, Geraldine, ed. (Illus.). 328p. 1975. 69.50 (*0-902028-21-9*) Antique Collect.

Marius, Richard. After the War. LC 94-2927. 640p. (J). 1994. reprint ed. pap. 14.95 (*1-55853-273-0*) Rutledge Hill Pr.

— Bound for the Promised Land. LC 93-18163. (C). 1993. reprint ed. pap. 12.95 (*1-55853-226-9*) Rutledge Hill Pr.

— The Coming of Rain. LC 91-23076. 448p. 1991. reprint ed. pap. 12.95 (*1-55853-142-4*) Rutledge Hill Pr.

— A Short Guide to Writing about History. 2nd ed. LC 94-8774. (C). 1994. 10.50 (*0-673-52348-9*) HarpCollege.

M

— A Short Guide to Writing about History. 2nd ed. 192p. 1995. reprint ed. pap. 13.95 (*1-886746-07-9*) Talman Pub.

— A Writer's Companion. 3rd ed. 1994. pap. text ed. write for info. (*0-07-040526-3*) McGraw.

Marius, Richard & Frome, Keith W., eds. The Columbia Book on Civil War Poetry. LC 94-6481. 350p. 1994. 24.95 (*0-231-10002-7*) Col U Pr.

Marius, Richard & Wiener, Harvey S. The McGraw-Hill College Handbook. 3rd ed. 1991. text ed. write for info. (*0-07-040416-X*) McGraw.

— The McGraw-Hill College Handbook. 3rd ed. 1992. Wkbk. student ed, pap. text ed. write for info. (*0-07-040437-2*) McGraw.

— The McGraw-Hill College Handbook. 4th ed. LC 93-29714. 1994. text ed. write for info. (*0-07-040481-X*) McGraw.

Marius, Richard C. After the War: A Novel. 1992. 24.50 (*0-394-58322-1*) Knopf.

— A Short Guide to Writing about History. (C). 1987. pap. text ed. 7.50 (*0-316-54621-6*) Little.

— Writer's Companion. 2nd ed. 1991. pap. text ed. 14.95 (*0-07-040441-0*) McGraw.

Marius, Richard C., et al. A Short Guide to Writing about History. (C). 1989. pap. text ed. 16.00 (*0-673-39998-2*) HarpCollege.

Mariuzzi, G., jt. ed. see Tosi, Piero.

M

Marivaux. La Dispute. Wertenbaker, Timberlake, tr. 1989. pap. 2.75 (*0-87129-126-6*, L71) Dramatic Pub.

— False Admissions. Wertenbaker, Timberlake, tr. 1992. pap. 5.45 (*0-87129-124-X*, F51) Dramatic Pub.

— Successful Strategies. Wertenbaker, Timberlake, tr. 1992. pap. 5.45 (*0-87129-125-8*, S82) Dramatic Pub.

Marivaux, A. Oeuvres de Jeunesse. (FRE.). 1972. lib. bdg. 95.00 (*0-8288-3552-7*, F48070) Fr & Eur.

— Romans - Recits, Contes et Nouvelles. (FRE.). 1949. lib. bdg. 85.00 (*0-8288-3553-5*, F48100) Fr & Eur.

— Theatre Complet. (FRE.). 1950. lib. bdg. 110.00 (*0-8288-3554-3*, F48010) Fr & Eur.

— Theatre Complete. deluxe ed. Coulet, Henri & Gilot, Michel, eds. 11376p. (FRE.). 1993. 150.00 (*0-7859-0967-2*, 2070112594) Fr & Eur.

Marivaux, Pierre C. Theatre Complet. rev. ed. Arland, Marcel, ed. (Bibliotheque de la Pleiade Ser.). 1125p. (FRE.). 1989. pap. 49.95 (*0-685-11591-7*, 2040173455) Fr & Eur.

— Vie de Marianne. (FRE.). 1966. pap. 17.95 (*0-7859-0053-5*, M11000) Fr & Eur.

Marivaux, Pierre de. L' Ecole des Meres: La Mere Confidente. (FRE.). pap. write for info. (*0-7859-3178-3*, 2253063266) Fr & Eur.

— La Surprise de l'Amour; La Second Surprise de l'Amour. (FRE.). 1991. pap. 12.95 (*0-7859-3165-1*, 2253057290) Fr & Eur.

Marix-Evans, Martin. The Twelve Days of Christmas. (Petites Ser.). (Illus.). 80p. 1993. 5.95 (*0-88088-780-X*) Peter Pauper.

Marix, Janne, ed. Les Musiciens de la Cour de Bourgogne au XVe Siecle, 1420-1467. LC 76-4478. (Illus.). reprint ed. 42.50 (*0-404-56627-8*) AMS Pr.

Mariz, Cecilia L. Coping with Poverty: Pentecostals & Christian Base Communities in Brazil. LC 93-12511. 224p. (C). 1993. 39.95 (*1-56639-112-1*); pap. 16.95 (*1-56639-113-X*) Temple U Pr.

Marj. Into the Silence: Healing the Wounds of Abuse. Hanlon, Judy, ed. 112p. (Orig.). 1992. pap. 9.95 (*0-96303388-1-8*) White Oak NY.

Marjani, Fathollah, tr. see Shariati, Ali.

Marjara, Harinder S. Contemplations of Created Things: Science in Paradise Lost. 408p. 1992. 50.00 (*0-8020-2750-4*) U of Toronto Pr.

Marjil de Jesus, Antonio, et al. A Spanish Manuscript Letter on the Lacandones, in the Archives of the Indies at Seville. Tozzer, Alfred M., ed. & tr. by. LC 83-83343. (Illus.). 1984. pap. 10.00 (*0-911437-03-7*) Labyrinthos.

Marjolis, J. Engineering Thermoplastics. 390p. 1987. 80.00 (*0-318-37721-7*) T-C Pubns CA.

Marjoram, D. T. Further Exercises in Modern Mathematics. 1966. 6.95 (*0-08-011969-7*, Pergamon Pr) Elsevier.

— Modern Mathematics in Secondary Schools. 1964. text ed. 6.95 (*0-08-010719-2*, Pergamon Pr); pap. text ed. 5.40 (*0-08-010718-4*, Pergamon Pr) Elsevier.

Marjoribanks, Kevin, ed. The Foundations of Students' Learning. 294p. 1991. text ed. 70.00 (*0-08-037259-7*, Pergamon Pr); pap. text ed. 25.00 (*0-08-037260-0*, Pergamon Pr) Elsevier.

***Marjorie, Benson.** Yellowstone. LC 94-34461. (Wonders of the World Ser.). (J). 1995. lib. bdg. write for info. (*0-8114-6365-6*) Raintree Steck-V.

Marjorowicz & Christiansen. Cardiovascular Nursing. 443p. 1989. 26.95 (*0-87434-167-1*) Springhouse Pub.

***Mark.** But Ossifer, It's Not My Fault. 1994. pap. 4.99 (*0-918259-62-2*) CCC Pubns.

— Handbook of Physical & Mechanical Testing of Paper & Paperboard, Vol. 1. 672p. 1983. 190.00 (*0-8247-1871-2*) Dekker.

— The Inclusive Gospel: Mark. Hays-Lohrey, Steven, tr. & intro. by. 89p. (Orig.). Date not set. pap. 8.95 (*0-915117-70-3*) New Earth Pubns.

Mark & Junior. Survival Licks & Bar Room Tricks. (Illus.). 76p. 1991. pap. text ed. 8.95 (*0-931759-51-X*) Centerstream Pub.

Mark & Mattson. Water Quality Measurement: The Modern Analytical Techniques. (Pollution Engineering & Technology Ser.: Vol. 18). 496p. 1981. 165.00 (*0-8247-1334-6*) Dekker.

Mark, A. J., jt. auth. see Heimlich, E. P.

Mark-Age Staff. One Thousand Keys to the Truth: Spiritual Guidelines for Latter Days & Second Coming. LC 75-40976. 156p. 1976. pap. 7.00 (*0-912322-51-9*) Mark-Age.

Mark, Alexandra. Marriage Made in Heaven. LC 89-50407. 256p. 1989. pap. 14.95 (*0-914918-90-7*, Whitford Pr) Schiffer.

Mark, Alexandra, jt. auth. see Horowitz, Israel A.

***Mark, Arlene M.** Words for Worship. LC 95-12504. 240p. (Orig.). 1995. pap. 15.95 (*0-8361-9037-8*) Herald Pr.

Mark, Barbara A. & Smith, Howard L. Essentials of Finance in Nursing. 304p. 1987. 60.00 (*0-87189-614-1*) Aspen Pub.

***Mark, Bonnie S. & Incorvaia, James, eds.** The Handbook of Infant, Child & Adolescent Psychotherapy Vol. I: A Guide to Diagnosis & Treatment. LC 94-44248. 1995. 50.00 (*1-56821-444-8*) Aronson.

Mark, Charles C. Reluctant Bureaucrats: The Struggle to Establish the National Endowment for the Arts. 256p. 1991. per. 19.95 (*0-8403-6547-0*) Kendall-Hunt.

Mark, Christensen. Aloha. 1994. 21.00 (*0-671-87023-8*) S&S Trade.

***Mark, Christopher.** Early Benjamin Britten: A Study of Stylistic & Technical Evolution. rev. ed. LC 94-49172. (Outstanding Dissertations in Music from British Universities). (Illus.). 368p. 1995. 83.00 (*0-8153-1870-7*) Garland.

Mark, Dave. Learn C on the Macintosh. 1991. pap. 36.95 (*0-201-56785-7*) Addison-Wesley.

— Learn C Plus Plus on the PC. 1993. disk 39.95 (*0-201-62622-5*) Addison-Wesley.

— Learning C Plus Plus on the Macintosh: Includes a Special Version of Symantec's C Plus Plus Compiler. LC 93-61. 1993. pap. 36.95 (*0-201-62204-1*) Addison-Wesley.

— Macintosh C Programming Primer, Vol. 1: Inside the Toolbox Using Think C. 2nd ed. 1992. pap. 29.95 (*0-201-60838-3*) Addison-Wesley.

— Macintosh Pascal Programming Primer, Vol. I: Inside the Toolbox Using Think Pascal. 1990. pap. 26.95 (*0-201-57084-X*) Addison-Wesley.

— Macintosh Programming Primer, Vol. II: Mastering the Toolbox Using Think C. 1990. pap. 28.95 (*0-201-57016-5*) Addison-Wesley.

— MW Ultimate Mac Program: Methods of Th. 1994. Incl. diskette. pap. 39.95 (*1-56884-195-7*) IDG Bks.

Mark, Dave & Reed, Cartwright. Macintosh Programming Primer: Inside the Toolbox Using THINK's LightspeedC. 400p. 1989. pap. 24.95 (*0-201-15662-8*) Addison-Wesley.

Mark, G., jt. auth. see Williams, J.

***Mark, Gareth L.** Estates Without Wills. (Basics Ser.). (Illus.). 56p. (Orig.). Date not set. pap. write for info. (*0-9617478-1-1*) Lineages Inc.

Mark, Grigorii. Graver (Engraver) Stikhotvoreniia (poems) LC 91-71433. 132p. (Orig.). (RUS.). (C). 1991. pap. 12.00 (*0-911971-65-3*) Effect Pub.

***Mark, Groucho & Thurber, James.** Groucho & Me. (Illus.). 390p. 1995. reprint ed. pap. 14.95 (*0-306-80666-5*) Da Capo.

Mark, Hans. The Space Station: A Personal Journey. LC 86-32892. (Illus.). viii, 264p. 1987. 26.95 (*0-8223-0727-8*) Duke.

Mark, Hans, et al. Traditional Moral Values in the Age of Technology. (Andrew R. Cecil Lectures on Moral Values in a Free Society: Vol. VIII). 210p. 1987. text ed. 16.50 (*0-292-78098-2*) U of Tex Pr.

Mark, Harry B., Jr., jt. auth. see Mattson, James S.

Mark, Harry H. Optokinetics: A Treatise on the Motions of Lights. LC 81-71626. (Illus.). 150p. 1982. 9.95 (*0-9608152-0-1*) H Mark-Corbett.

Mark, Herman F. Concise Encyclopedia of Polymer Science & Engineering. 1341p. 1990. text ed. 199.00 (*0-471-51253-2*) Wiley.

— Encyclopedia of Polymer Science & Engineering Database, 1985-1990. 1990. pap. text ed. 209.67 (*0-471-52226-0*) Wiley.

— From Small Organic Molecules to Large: A Century of Progress. Seeman, Jeffrey I., ed. LC 92-30099. (Profiles, Pathways, & Dreams Ser.). (Illus.). 148p. 1993. 24.95 (*0-8412-1776-9*) Am Chemical.

Mark, Herman F., ed. see Alfrey, Turner.

Mark, Herman F., jt. ed. see Seymour, R.

Mark, Herman F., jt. ed. see Seymour, Raymond B.

Mark, Howard. Principles & Practice of Spectroscopic Calibration. (Chemical Analysis: a Series of Monographs on Analytical Chemistry & Its Applications: No. 1075). 192p. 1991. text ed. 84.95 (*0-471-54614-3*) Wiley.

Mark, Howard & Workman, Jerry. Statistics in Spectroscopy. (Illus.). 313p. 1991. text ed. 64.95 (*0-12-472530-9*) Acad Pr.

Mark, Ira S. The Sanctuary of Athena Nike in Athens: Architectural Stages & Chronology. LC 93-37431. (Hesperia Ser.: Suppl. 26). (Illus.). xv, 160p. 1993. pap. 50.00 (*0-87661-526-4*) Am Sch Athens.

***Mark, J. & Williams, G.** The Psychological Treatment of Depression: A Guide to Theory & Practice of Cognitive Behavior. 2nd ed. LC 94-44552. 312p. 1995. pap. 19.95 (*0-415-12874-9*, A7433) Routledge.

Mark, J., et al. Food Industries. Maunder, W. F. & Fleming, M. C., eds. (Reviews of U. K. Statistical Sources Ser.: Vol. XXVIII). 480p. (C). 1991. text ed. 155.00 (*0-412-35660-0*, A5607) Chapman & Hall.

Mark, J. E., jt. ed. see Schaefer, D. W.

Mark, J. E., et al, eds. Computational Methods in Materials Science. (Materials Research Society Symposium Proceedings Ser.: Vol. 278). 1992. text ed. 62.00 (*1-55899-173-5*) Materials Res.

— Hybrid Organic-Inorganic Composites. LC 95-7108. (Symposium Ser.: Vol. 585). 1995. write for info. (*0-8412-3148-6*) Am Chemical.

Mark, James, jt. auth. see Lomben, David O.

Mark, James E. & Erman, Burak. Elastomeric Polymer Networks. 433p. 1991. text ed. 94.00 (*0-13-249483-3*) P-H.

— Rubberlike Elasticity: A Molecular Primer. LC 88-5518. 196p. 1988. text ed. 75.95 (*0-471-61499-8*) Wiley.

Mark, James E. & Lal, Joginder, eds. Elastomers & Rubber Elasticity. LC 82-11320. (ACS Symposium Ser.: No. 193). 578p. 1982. lib. bdg. 65.95 (*0-8412-0729-1*) Am Chemical.

Mark, James E., jt. ed. see Lal, Joginder.

Mark, James E., et al. Inorganic Polymers. 304p. 1991. text ed. 73.00 (*0-13-465881-7*, 520804) P-H.

— Physical Properties of Polymers. 2nd ed. LC 92-35330. (Illus.). 409p. 1993. 59.95 (*0-8412-2505-2*); pap. 44.95 (*0-8412-2506-0*) Am Chemical.

Mark, James E., et al, eds. Science & Technology of Rubber. 2nd ed. (Illus.). 751p. 1994. text ed. 85.00 (*0-12-472525-2*) Acad Pr.

Mark, Jan. Fun with Mrs. Thumb. LC 92-54955. (Illus.). 32p. (J). (ps up). 1993. 9.95 (*1-56402-247-1*) Candlewick Pr.

— Handles. large type ed. (J). (gr. 1-8). 1991. 16.95 (*0-7451-0760-5*, Galaxy Child Lrg Print) Chivers N Amer.

— In Black & White & Other Stories. large type ed. 216p. (J). (gr. 3-7). 1992. 16.95 (*0-7451-1584-5*, Galaxy Child Lrg Print) Chivers N Amer.

— Silly Tails. LC 92-38679. (Illus.). 32p. (J). (gr. k-3). 1993. text ed. 13.95 (*0-689-31843-X*, Atheneum Bks Young) S&S Childrens.

Mark, Jan, ed. The Oxford Book of Children's Stories. 478p. (J). 1993. 25.00 (*0-19-214228-3*) OUP.

— The Oxford Book of Children's Stories. 480p. (J). 1995. pap. 14.95 (*0-19-282397-3*) OUP.

Mark, Jeffrey P. An Analysis of Usury. 1980. lib. bdg. 250.00 (*0-8490-3085-4*) Gordon Pr.

— The Modern Idolatry: Being an Analysis of Usury & the Pathology of Debt. 1980. lib. bdg. 250.00 (*0-8490-3078-1*) Gordon Pr.

— Saving & Spending. 1980. lib. bdg. 59.95 (*0-8490-3083-8*) Gordon Pr.

Mark, Jeffrey P., jt. auth. see Mark, Vernon H.

Mark, Joan. The King of the World in the Land of the Pygmies. LC 94-16285. 1995. text ed. 30.00 (*0-8032-3182-2*) U of Nebr Pr.

— A Stranger in Her Native Land: Alice Fletcher & the American Indians. LC 87-30201. (Women in the West Ser.). (Illus.). xx, 428p. 1988. 40.00 (*0-8032-3128-8*); pap. 16.95 (*0-8032-8156-0*) U of Nebr Pr.

Mark, Joan, jt. auth. see Camden, Thomas.

Mark, Joan T. Four Anthropologists. LC 80-25414. 1980. 20.00 (*0-88202-190-7*) Watson Pub Intl.

Mark, Joan T., ed. see Gay, E. Jane.

Mark, Jonathan, jt. auth. see Westheimer, Ruth.

Mark, Joseph. Life: You Are the Dreamer. 20p. 1994. pap. text ed. write for info. (*1-885206-08-9*, Iliad Pr) Cader Pubng.

Mark, Kathleen. Meteorite Craters. LC 86-19244. (Illus.). 288p. 1987. 9.95 (*0-8165-0902-6*) U of Ariz Pr.

Mark, L. S., et al, eds. Ergonomics & Human Factors. (Recent Research in Psychology Ser.). (Illus.). 291p. 1987. pap. 47.00 (*0-387-96511-4*) Spr-Verlag.

***Mark, Libby & Lefrak, Babs.** Snow. LC 95-14811. 1995. pap. write for info. (*0-399-52166-6*, Perigree Bks) Berkley Pub.

Mark, Linda, ed. Reference Sources 1977. LC 77-79318. 1977. 75.00 (*0-87650-084-X*) Pierian.

— Reference Sources 1978. LC 77-79318. 1978. 75.00 (*0-87650-096-3*) Pierian.

— Reference Sources 1979. LC 77-79318. 1980. 75.00 (*0-87650-117-X*) Pierian.

Mark, Lisbeth, jt. auth. see Binswanger, Barbara.

Mark, M., ed. see Daitch, Susan, et al.

Mark Map Co. Staff. Captain's Atlas: Jet Route Two Edition. (Illus.). 80p. 1994. pap. 15.95 (*0-916413-24-1*) Aviation.

Mark, Mary E. Indian Circus. LC 93-5089. 1993. 40.00 (*0-8118-0531-X*) Chronicle Bks.

— Passport. LC 74-13170. 58p. 1976. pap. 9.95 (*0-912810-14-9*) Lustrum Pr.

— Streetwise. (Illus.). 78p. (Orig.). 1991. pap. 24.95 (*0-89381-487-3*) Aperture.

Mark, Melvin M. & Shotland, R. Lance, eds. Multiple Methods in Program Evaluation. LC 85-644749. (New Directions for Program Evaluation Ser.: No. PE 35). 1987. 17.95 (*1-55542-943-2*) Jossey-Bass.

Mark, Michael, ed. The Music Educator & Community Music. (Best of MEJ Ser.). (Illus.). 104p. 1992. teacher ed 13.50 (*1-56545-006-X*) Music Ed Natl.

Mark, Michael L. Contemporary Music Education. 2nd ed. 368p. (C). 1985. text ed. 29.00 (*0-02-871220-X*) Schirmer Bks.

— Source Readings in Music Education History. rev. ed. 270p. Date not set. pap. 19.95x (*1-57171-002-7*) Lincoln-Rembrandt.

Mark, Michael L. & Gary, Charles. A History of American Music Education. 404p. 1991. text ed. 40.00 (*0-02-871365-6*) Schirmer Bks.

Mark Mon-Chang Hsieh. The U. S. - Republic of China (Taiwan) Fisheries Negotiations, 1989, No. 4. 84p. 1991. 6.00 (*0-925153-16-8*, 105) Occasional Papers.

Mark, Neil, ed. see Kleinfeld, Vincent A., et al.

Mark, Norm, jt. auth. see Morris, Marie.

Mark, Norman. Norman Mark's Chicago: Walking, Bicycling & Driving Tours of the City. 4th ed. LC 93-25222. (Illus.). 392p. (Orig.). 1993. pap. 12.95 (*1-55652-197-9*) Chicago Review.

Mark Of Ephesus. Encyclical Letter of St. Mark of Ephesus. pap. 0.50 (*0-89981-021-7*) Eastern Orthodox.

Mark, Olshaker. Edge. Date not set. 21.00 (*0-517-58044-6*, Crown) Crown Pub Group.

Mark, P., jt. auth. see Lampert, M. A.

Mark, Patricia, jt. auth. see Hanson, Jeanne.

Mark, Peter A. Africans in European Eyes: the Portrayal of Black Africans in Fourteenth & Fifteenth Century Europe. LC 74-25878. (Foreign & Comparative Studies Program, Eastern Africa Ser.: No. 16). 98p. 1975. pap. 3.00 (*0-915984-13-X*) Syracuse U Foreign Comp.

— The Wild Bull & the Sacred Forest: Form, Meaning & Change in Senegambian Initiation Masks of the Diola. (RES Monographs on Anthropology & Aesthetics). (Illus.). 208p. (C). 1992. 74.95 (*0-521-41346-X*) Cambridge U Pr.

Mark Publishing Staff. Beautiful Things to Make for Baby. 1991. pap. 8.95 (*0-937769-21-5*) Mark Inc CA.

— Beautiful Things to Make for Brides: Clever Ideas for a Perfect Wedding. 1991. pap. 8.95 (*0-937769-18-5*) Mark Inc CA.

— Bouquet of Memories from the Heart. 1991. 9.95 (*0-937769-15-0*) Mark Inc CA.

— Country Fair. 1991. pap. 8.95 (*0-937769-19-3*) Mark Inc CA.

— More Reflections from the Heart Journals: Friendship. 1991. 11.95 (*0-937769-23-1*) Mark Inc CA.

— Reflections from the Heart: Children & Grandchildren. 1991. 11.95 (*0-937769-22-3*) Mark Inc CA.

— Soft Toys to Sew. 1991. pap. 8.95 (*0-937769-20-7*) Mark Inc CA.

Mark, Rebecca. The Dragon's Blood: Feminist Intertextuality in Eudora Welty's 'The Golden Apples' LC 93-29518. 320p. 1994. text ed. 35.00 (*0-87805-661-0*) U Pr of Miss.

Mark, Rebecca, ed. see Stein, Gertrude.

Mark, Richard E. Cell Wall Mechanics of Tracheids. 1967. 100.00 (*0-685-45682-X*) Elliots Bks.

Mark, Robert. Becoming a Professional Pilot. LC 93-32866. 1993. text ed. 27.95 (*0-07-040485-2*) TAB Bks.

— Becoming a Professional Pilot. 1994. pap. 17.95 (*0-8306-4146-7*); pap. text ed. 17.95 (*0-07-040486-0*) TAB Bks.

— Experiments in Gothic Structure. (Illus.). 176p. 1982. pap. 12.95 (*0-262-63095-8*) MIT Pr.

— Joy of Flying. 3rd ed. 1994. pap. 15.95 (*0-8306-4432-6*) TAB Bks.

— The Joy of Flying. 3rd ed. LC 93-33783. 1994. pap. text ed. 15.95 (*0-07-040487-9*) McGraw.

— Light, Wind & Structure: The Mystery of the Master Builders. LC 89-334736. (Sloan New Liberal Arts Ser.). (Illus.). 209p. 1990. 37.50 (*0-262-13246-X*) MIT Pr.

— Light, Wind & Structure: The Mystery of the Master Builders. (New Liberal Art Ser.). (Illus.). 234p. 1994. pap. 19.95x (*0-262-63158-X*) MIT Pr.

— Light, Wind & Structure: The Mystery of the Master Builders. 1990. text ed. write for info. (*0-07-040403-8*) McGraw.

Mark, Robert, ed. Architectural Technology up to the Scientific Revolution: The Art & Structure of Large-Scale Buildings. (New Liberal Arts Ser.). 272p. 1994. pap. 19.95x (*0-262-63157-1*) MIT Pr.

Mark, Robert & Cakmak, Ahmet S., eds. The Hagia Sophia: From the Age of Justinian to the Present. (C). 1992. 95.00 (*0-521-41677-9*) Cambridge U Pr.

Mark, Ron. Jugger's Rain. 60p. 1992. pap. 5.95 (*1-56850-009-2*) Chicago Plays.

— Satan in Wonderland. 65p. 1994. pap. 5.95 (*1-56850-042-4*) Chicago Plays.

Mark, Sam, tr. see KCRR Staff & Fay, Jennifer.

Mark, Samuel, ed. Latino Volunteer & Non-Profit Organizations: A Directory. 135p. 1989. pap. text ed. 20.00 (*1-883638-11-9*) Rose Inst.

Mark, Sara, ed. Mystery Mansion: House Math. LC 93-25398. (I Love Math Ser.). (Illus.). 64p. (J). (gr. k-2). 1993. write for info. (*0-8094-9986-X*) Time-Life.

— The Mystery of the Sunken Treasure: Sea Math. (I Love Math Ser.). (Illus.). 64p. (J). 1993. write for info. (*0-8094-9994-0*) Time-Life.

Mark, Sara, ed. see Time-Life Bks. Editors.

Mark, Sara, ed. see Time Life Editors.

Mark, Sara, ed. see Time-Life for Children Staff.

Mark, Sara, ed. see Time-Life Inc. Editors.

Mark, Ted. The Man from O.R.G.Y. Thy Neighbor's Orgy. 272p. (Orig.). 1981. pap. 2.25 (*0-89083-701-5*) Zebra.

— The Man from O.R.G.Y. No. 2: The Tight End. 1981. pap. 2.50 (*0-89083-823-2*) Zebra.

— A Stroke of Genius. (Orig.). 1982. pap. 2.50 (*0-89083-976-X*) Zebra.

Mark, Teresa. She Changes: A Goddess Myth for Modern Women. 226p. (Orig.). 1991. pap. 12.95 (*1-878980-03-3*) Delphi IL.

Mark The Deacon. Life of Porphyry, Bishop of Gaza. 1973. pap. 2.95 (*0-89981-041-1*) Eastern Orthodox.

Mark, Thomas C. Spinoza's Theory of Truth. LC 72-3721. 151p. reprint ed. pap. 43.10 (*0-317-09237-5*, 2006117) Bks Demand.

Mark, V. H., et al, eds. Colloquium on the Use of Embryonic Cell Transplantation for Correction of CNS Disorders. (Journal: Applied Neurophysiology: Vol 47, No. 1-2). (Illus.). 96p. 1984. pap. 28.00 (*3-8055-3952-5*) S Karger.

Mark, Vernon H. Reversing Memory Loss: Medically Proven Methods for Regaining, Strengthening, & Preserving... 256p. 1993. pap. 12.95 (*0-395-65371-1*) HM.

Mark, Vernon H. & Mark, Jeffrey P. Brain Power: A Neurosurgeon's Complete Program to Maintain & Enhance Brain Fitness Throughout Your Life. 256p. 1991. pap. 11.95 (*0-395-55001-7*) HM.

Mark, William. The Chinese Gourmet: Authentic Ingredients & Traditional Recipes from the Kitchens of China. LC 94-14138. 1994. 39.95 (*1-57145-006-8*) Thunder Bay CA.

Mark Williams Company Staff. ANSI C: A Lexical Guide. 522p. 1988. pap. text ed. 57.00 (*0-13-037814-3*) P-H.

An Asterisk (*) at the beginning of an entry indicates that the title is appearing in BIP for the first time.

Mark Wilson & Staff. The Golf Club Identification & Price Guide. 2nd ed. (Illus.). 1989. write for info. (*0-927956-00-4*) R Maltby.

Mark, Yudel, jt. auth. see Efron, S.

***Mark Zweig & Associates, Inc. Staff.** Principal's Survey of A-E-P & Environmental Consulting Firms, 1994. 254p. (Orig.). 1994. pap. text ed. 195.00 (*1-885002-02-5*) M Zweig Assocs.

Mark Zweig & Associates Staff. Management Ideas That Work! White, Frederick D., ed. 236p. (Orig.). 1993. pap. text ed. 39.00 (*0-9630705-8-4*) M Zweig Assocs.

— Mark Zweig & Associates Financial Performance Survey of Environmental Consulting Firms, 1993. 244p. (Orig.). 1992. pap. text ed. 225.00 (*0-9630705-3-3*) M Zweig Assocs.

— Satellite Office Survey of A-E-P & Environmental Consulting Firms, 1994. 200p. (Orig.). 1994. pap. text ed. 195.00 (*1-885002-03-3*) M Zweig Assocs.

Mark Zweig & Associates Staff & Getz, Lowell V. Mark Zweig & Associates Valuation Survey of A-E-P & Environmental Service Firms, 1994. 3rd ed. 243p. 1993. pap. 225.00 (*0-9630705-4-1*) M Zweig Assocs.

Mark Zweig & Associates Staff & Usrey, Nancy J. Insider's Guide to SF254-255 Preparation, 1993. 138p. (Orig.). 1993. pap. 79.00 (*0-9630705-6-8*) M Zweig Assocs.

Markakis, John. Military Marxist Regimes in Africa. 250p. 1986. 34.50 (*0-7146-3295-3*, Pub. by F Cass Pubs UK) Intl Spec Bk.

— National & Class Conflict in the Horn of Africa. (African Studies: No. 55). (Illus.). 344p. 1987. 74.95 (*0-521-33362-8*) Cambridge U Pr.

— National & Class Conflict in the Horn of Africa. (Illus.). 336p. (C). 1990. pap. 19.95 (*0-86232-961-2*, Pub. by Zed Books UK) Humanities.

Markakis, John & Ayela, Nega. Class & Revolution in Ethiopia. LC 85-62178. 160p. 1986. 19.95 (*0-932415-04-0*); pap. 7.95 (*0-932415-05-9*) Red Sea Pr.

Markakis, John, jt. ed. see Fukui, Katsuyoshi.

Markakis, Pericles, ed. Anthocyanins As Food Colors. LC 81-22902. (Food Science & Technology Ser.). 1982. text ed. 85.00 (*0-12-472550-3*) Acad Pr.

Markale, Jean. The Celts: Uncovering the Mythic & Historic Origins of Western Culture. LC 92-47488. (Illus.). 320p. (ENG & FRE.). 1993. pap. 14.95 (*0-89281-413-6*) Inner Tradit.

— King of the Celts: Arthurian Legends & Celtic Tradition. 320p. (Orig.). 1993. pap. 14.95 (*0-89281-452-7*) Inner Tradit.

— Merlin: Priest of Nature. 1995. pap. 12.95 (*0-89281-517-5*) Inner Tradit.

— Petit Dictionnaire de Mythologie Celtique. 224p. (FRE.). 1986. pap. 36.95 (*0-7859-7970-0*, 2726600778) Fr & Eur.

— Women of the Celts. 315p. 1986. pap. 14.95 (*0-89281-150-1*) Inner Tradit.

Markan, Kristina & Fischer, Uwe. Untersuchungen zur Immissionsbelastung der Berliner Forsten: Deposition & Bioindikation. (Dissertationes Botanicae Ser.: Vol. 170). (Illus.). 258p. (GER.). 1991. pap. 63.00 (*3-443-64082-6*, Pub. by Cramer-Borntraeger GW) Lubrecht & Cramer.

Markandaya, Kamala. Nectar in a Sieve. 192p. 1956. pap. 5.99 (*0-451-16836-4*, AE2291, Sig) NAL-Dutton.

Markandya, Anil & Richardson, Julie, eds. Environmental Economics: A Reader. LC 92-36048. 288p. 1993. text ed. 49.95 (*0-312-09476-0*); pap. text ed. 19.95 (*0-312-09477-9*) St Martin.

Markarian, Margie & Hauss, Deborah, eds. The Incentive Travel Case Study Book. (Illus.). 160p. 1990. text ed. 125.00 (*0-9626880-0-2*) SITE.

Markatos, N. C., ed. Computer Simulation for Fluid Flow, Heat & Mass Transfer, & Combustion in Reciprocating Engines: Proceedings of the International Center for Heat & Mass Transfer. 500p. 1989. 184.00 (*0-89116-392-1*) Hemisp Pub.

Markatos, N. C., et al, eds. Numerical Simulation of Fluid Flow & Heat Mass Transfer Processes. (Lecture Notes in Engineering Ser.: Vol. 18). 505p. 1986. pap. 49.00 (*0-387-16377-8*) Spr-Verlag.

Markby, William. Elements of Law: Considered with Reference to Principles of General Jurisprudence. 4th ed. LC 94-75656. 456p. 1994. reprint ed. 92.00 (*1-56169-087-2*) W W Gaunt.

Marke, Julius J. Vignettes of Legal History: Second Series. (Illus.). xiv, 274p. 1977. lib. bdg. 15.00 (*0-8377-0833-8*) Rothman.

Marke, Julius J. & Henke, Dan F. Planning the Law Library As a Legal Information Center. (Law Library Information Reports: Vol. 6). 146p. 1985. pap. 100.00 (*0-87802-081-0*) Glanville.

Marke, Julius J. & Sloane, Richard. Legal Research & Law Library Management. 750p. 1986. reprint ed. ring bd. 90.00 (*0-318-21438-5*, 00572) NY Law Pub.

Marke, Kay, comp. Neal-Schuman Index to Card Games. 200p. (Orig.). 1990. 29.95 (*1-55570-052-7*) Neal-Schuman.

Markel, et al, eds. The Portable Pediatrician. (Illus.). 396p. 1992. pap. text ed. 38.95 (*1-56053-007-3*) Hanley & Belfus.

Markel, Geraldine & Greenbaum, Judith. Not Lazy, Crazy, or Dumb: Performance Breakthroughs for Adolescents & Young Adults with Learning Difficulties. 250p. (Orig.). 1995. pap. text ed. write for info. (*0-87822-349-5*) Res Press.

Markel, Howard & Oski, Frank A. The H. L. Mencken Baby Book. (Illus.). 224p. 1989. 18.95 (*0-932883-22-2*) Hanley & Belfus.

Markel, Lester. Public Opinion & Foreign Policy. (History - United States Ser.). 227p. 1993. reprint ed. lib. bdg. 79.00 (*0-7812-4814-0*) Rprt Serv.

Markel, Lester, ed. Global Challenge to the United States: A Study of the Problems, the Perils, & the Proposed Solutions Involved in Washington's Search for a New Role. LC 75-18807. 241p. (C). 1975. 20.00 (*0-8386-1822-7*) Fairleigh Dickinson.

Markel, Lester, et al. Public Opinion & Foreign Policy. LC 78-167404. (Essay Index Reprint Ser.). 1977. reprint ed. 21.95 (*0-8369-7242-2*) Ayer.

Markel, Michael H. Business Writing Essentials. LC 87-60507. 224p. (C). 1987. pap. text ed. 13.00 (*0-312-00737-X*); Instr's. manual. teacher ed write for info. (*0-318-62508-3*); Instr's. ed. teacher ed write for info. (*0-318-62509-1*) St Martin.

— Technical Writing: Situations & Strategies. 3rd ed. LC 90-71634. 650p. (C). 1992. pap. text ed. 0.56 (*0-312-06757-7*) St Martin.

— Technical Writing Essentials. LC 87-60508. 224p. (C). 1987. pap. text ed. 13.00 (*0-312-00736-1*) St Martin.

— Technical Writing Essentials. LC 87-60508. 224p. (C). 1988. teacher ed, pap. text ed. 0.16 (*0-312-01288-8*) St Martin.

***Markel, Michelle.** Gracias, Rosa. LC 94-25979. (Illus.). (J). 1995. write for info. (*0-8075-3024-7*) A Whitman.

Markel, Mike. Writing in the Technical Fields: A Step-by-Step Guide for Engineers, Scientists, & Technicians. LC 93-26817. (Illus.). 1994. 29.95 (*0-7803-1059-4*, PC03855); text ed. 32.95 (*0-7803-1036-5*, PP03855); pap. 19.95 (*0-685-71166-8*, PP003855) Inst Electrical.

Markel, Robert, jt. auth. see Rangel-Ribeiro, Victor.

Markel, Roberta. Music Through the Recorder. pap. 5.95 (*0-89524-056-4*) Cherry Lane.

— Pop Goes the Recorder. pap. 7.95 (*0-89524-497-7*) Cherry Lane.

***Markel, Ronald G.** Barron's Complete Pet Owner's Manual: Kingsnakes & Milksnakes. 1995. pap. 5.95 (*0-8120-4240-9*) Barron.

— Kingsnakes & Milk Snakes. (Illus.). 144p. 1989. 29.95 (*0-86622-664-8*, TS-125) TFH Pubns.

Markel, Stephen. Origins of the Indian Planetary Deities. LC 93-41911. (Studies in Asian Thought & Religion: Vol. 16). (Illus.). 284p. 1994. text ed. 89.95 (*0-7734-9401-4*) E Mellen.

Markel, Stephen, ed. World of Jade. 1992. 64.00 (*81-85026-20-3*, Pub. by Marg) S Asia.

Markell, David. Expanded Ministry to Youth: Program Guidelines. (Christian Education Ministries Ser.). 1977. pap. 3.95 (*0-89367-021-9*) Light & Life.

Markell, Jan. Angeles en Campos Concentracion: Angels in the Camp. (SPA.). 4.95 (*84-7228-785-8*, 220038, Pub. by Edit Clie SP) TSELF.

— Waiting for a Miracle: Devotions for Those Who Are Physically Weak. 1993. pap. 8.99 (*0-8010-6297-7*) Baker Bk.

Markell, Jeff. Electrical Wiring for the Home. 288p. 1991. text ed. 48.00 (*0-13-248006-9*) P-H.

— The Sailor's Weather Guide. (Illus.). 285p. 1995. pap. 19.95 (*0-924486-91-0*) Sheridan.

Markels, Bobby. Being Here. (Mendocino Malady Ser.). (Illus.). 80p. 1984. reprint ed. pap. 5.00 (*1-880991-04-7*) Stone Pub.

— How to Be a Human Bean. (Illus.). 24p. (J). (gr. 3 up). 1989. reprint ed. pap. 3.50 (*1-880991-01-2*) Stone Pub.

— Lately I've Been Thinking. (Mendocino Malady Ser.). (Illus.). 64p. (Orig.). 1990. pap. 6.95 (*1-880991-05-5*) Stone Pub.

— Popper. (Nonny Ser.). 80p. (Orig.). 1986. pap. 5.95 (*1-880991-07-1*) Stone Pub.

Markels, Julian. Melville & the Politics of Identity: From King Lear to Moby Dick. LC 92-21497. 176p. 1993. 29.95 (*0-252-01995-4*); pap. 13.95 (*0-252-06302-3*) U of Ill Pr.

Markels, Robin B. A New Perspective in Cohesion on Expository Paragraphs. LC 83-14561. (Studies in Writing & Rhetoric). 120p. (Orig.). 1984. pap. text ed. 12.95 (*0-8093-1152-6*) S Ill U Pr.

Marken, Jack W. American Indian: Language & Literature. LC 76-4624. (Goldentree Bibliographies Series in Language & Literature). (C). 1978. pap. text ed. write for info. (*0-88295-553-5*) Harlan Davidson.

Marken, Jack W. & Hoover, Herbert T. Bibliography of the Sioux. LC 80-20106. (Native American Bibliography Ser.: No. 1). 388p. 1980. 27.50 (*0-8108-1356-4*) Scarecrow.

Marken, Mitchell W. Pottery from Spanish Shipwrecks, 1500-1800. LC 93-34787. (Illus.). 280p. (C). 1994. lib. bdg. 39.95 (*0-8130-1268-6*) U Press Fla.

Marken, Richard S. Mind Readings: Experimental Studies of Purpose. (Illus.). 212p. 1992. pap. text ed. 18.00 (*0-9624154-3-X*) Control Systs Group.

Markens, Isaac. The Hebrews in America: A Series of Historical & Biographical Sketches. LC 74-29504. (Modern Jewish Experiences Ser.). 1975. reprint ed. 33.95 (*0-405-06731-3*) Ayer.

Marker, jt. auth. see Smith.

Marker, A. J. Properties & Characteristics of Optical Glass II, Vol. 1327. 1990. 53.00 (*0-8194-0388-1*) SPIE.

Marker, A. J., ed. Properties & Characteristics of Optical Glass. 1988. 45.00 (*0-8194-0005-X*, 970) SPIE.

Marker, B. R., jt. ed. see McCall, G. J.

Marker, Chris. La Jetee: Cine-Roman. LC 92-14634. (Illus.). 256p. (ENG & FRE.). 1992. 34.95 (*0-942299-66-3*) Zone Bks.

Marker, Frederick & Marker, Lise-Lone. Ibsen's Lively Art: A Performance Study of the Major Plays. (Illus.). 280p. (C). 1989. 59.95 (*0-521-26643-2*) Cambridge U Pr.

Marker, Frederick J. Hans Christian Andersen & the Romantic Theatre: A Study of Stage Practices in the Prenaturalistic Scandinavian Theatre. LC 74-151377. (Illus.). 256p. reprint ed. pap. 73.00 (*0-317-09116-6*, 2014356) Bks Demand.

Marker, Frederick J. & Marker, Lise-Lone. Edward Gordon Craig & "The Pretenders" A Production Revisited. LC 80-27481. (Special Issues Ser.). (Illus.). 148p. 1981. 19.95 (*0-8093-0966-1*) S Ill U Pr.

— Ingmar Bergman: A Life in the Theatre. 2nd ed. (Directors in Perspective Ser.). (Illus.). 280p. (C). 1992. 69.95 (*0-521-42082-2*); pap. 21.95 (*0-521-42121-7*) Cambridge U Pr.

Marker, Frederick J., ed. see Bergman, Ingmar.

Marker, Gary. Publishing, Printing, & the Origins of Intellectual Life in Russia, 1700-1800. LC 84-42893. 312p. 1985. text ed. 47.50x (*0-691-05441-X*) Princeton U Pr.

Marker, Gary, ed. Reinterpreting Russian History: Readings, 860-1860's. LC 92-46294. 1994. 48.00 (*0-19-507857-8*); pap. 17.95 (*0-19-507858-6*) OUP.

Marker, Gordon A. Internal Migration & Economic Opportunity: France, 1872-1911. Bruchey, Stuart, ed. LC 80-2815. (Dissertations in European Economic History Ser.). (Illus.). 1981. lib. bdg. 30.95 (*0-405-13999-3*) Ayer.

***Marker, Kenneth H.** Sometime This Summer. 480p. 1995. pap. 9.95 (*1-56901-613-5*) NW Pub.

Marker, Lise-Lone. David Belasco: Naturalism in the American Theatre. LC 74-2970. 271p. reprint ed. pap. 77.30 (*0-8357-3421-8*, 2039678) Bks Demand.

Marker, Lise-Lone, ed. see Bergman, Ingmar.

Marker, Lise-Lone, jt. auth. see Marker, Frederick J.

Marker, Lise-Lone, jt. auth. see Marker, Frederick.

***Marker, Rita.** Deadly Compassion. 328p. 1995. mass mkt. 5.99 (*0-380-72332-8*) Avon.

— Deadly Compassion: The Death of Ann Humphry & the Truth about Euthanasia. LC 92-39736. 1993. 18.00 (*0-688-12221-3*) Morrow.

Marker, Rita L. Euthanasia: Killing or Caring? (Orig.). (C). 1992. pap. 2.00 (*0-919225-36-5*) Life Cycle Bks.

Marker, Sherry. London. (Great Cities Library). (Illus.). 64p. (J). (gr. 3-7). 1990. lib. bdg. 14.95 (*1-56711-023-1*) Blackbirch.

Marker, W. & Helmut, H. Battles of World History. 438p. 1978. 175.00 (*0-317-57279-2*, Pub. by Collets UK) St Mut.

Markert, Bernd, ed. Plants As Biomonitors: Indicators for Heavy Metals in the Terrestrial Environment. LC 92-34620. 500p. 1993. 200.00 (*1-56081-272-9*) VCH Pubs.

Markert, Bernd, jt. ed. see Lieth, Helmut.

Markert, Christopher. Seeing Well Again Without Your Glasses. (Illus.). 128p. Date not set. 17.95 (*0-8464-4288-4*) Beekman Pubs.

Markert, Clement L., ed. Isozymes, 4 vols. 1975. write for info. (*0-318-50288-7*) Acad Pr.

Markert, Clement L., et al. Isozymes: Proceedings of the Seventh International Congress. 328p. 1994. text ed. 105.00 (*981-02-1449-9*) World Scientific Pub.

Markert, Jenny. Arctic Foxes. (Nature Books Ser.). 32p. (J). (gr. 2-6). 1991. lib. bdg. 22.79 (*0-89565-710-4*) Childs World.

— Camels. (Nature Books Ser.). 32p. (J). (gr. 2-6). 1991. lib. bdg. 22.79 (*0-89565-719-8*) Childs World.

— Cheetahs. (Nature Books Ser.). 32p. (J). (gr. 2-6). 1991. lib. bdg. 22.79 (*0-89565-716-3*) Childs World.

— Clouds. (J). (gr. 4-7). 1993. 15.95 (*1-56846-060-0*) Creative Ed.

— Elephants. (Nature Books Ser.). 32p. (J). 1991. lib. bdg. 22.79 (*0-89565-724-4*) Childs World.

— Giraffes. (Nature Books Ser.). 32p. (J). (gr. 2-6). 1991. lib. bdg. 22.79 (*0-89565-723-6*) Childs World.

— Glacier National Park. (Nature Books Ser.). (ENG & SPA.). (J). (gr. 2-6). 1992. lib. bdg. 22.79 (*0-89565-858-5*) Childs World.

— Glaciers & Icebergs. LC 92-32498. (Vision Bks.). (ENG & SPA.). (J). (gr. 2-6). 1993. lib. bdg. 22.79 (*1-56766-004-5*) Childs World.

— Glaciers & Icebergs. LC 92-32498. (Vision Bks.). (ENG & SPA.). (J). (gr. 2-6). 1993. lib. bdg. 15.95 (*1-56766-034-7*) Childs World.

— Grand Canyon. (Nature Book Ser.). (ENG & SPA.). (J). (gr. 2-6). 1992. lib. bdg. 22.79 (*0-89565-856-9*) Childs World.

— Grand Canyon. (Nature Bks.). (ENG & SPA.). (J). (gr. 2-6). 1992. pap. 22.79 (*1-56766-032-0*) Childs World.

— Kangaroos. (Nature Books Ser.). 32p. (J). 1991. lib. bdg. 22.79 (*0-89565-715-5*) Childs World.

— Moose. (Nature Books Ser.). 32p. (J). 1991. lib. bdg. 22.79 (*0-89565-713-9*) Childs World.

— Ocean Resources. LC 93-12204. (J). (gr. 5 up). 1994. lib. bdg. 18.95 (*0-88682-599-7*) Creative Ed.

— Octopuses. (Nature Books Ser.). (J). (gr. 2-6). 1992. lib. bdg. 22.79 (*0-89565-836-4*) Childs World.

— Penguins. (Nature Books Ser.). 32p. (J). 1991. lib. bdg. 22.79 (*0-89565-709-0*) Childs World.

— Polar Bears. (Nature Books Ser.). 32p. (J). (gr. 2-6). 1991. lib. bdg. 22.79 (*0-89565-708-2*) Childs World.

— Reptiles. (Nature Books Ser.). (J). (gr. 1-8). 1992. lib. bdg. 22.79 (*0-89565-850-X*) Childs World.

— Tigers. (Nature Books Ser.). 32p. (J). (gr. 2-6). 1991. lib. bdg. 22.79 (*0-89565-722-8*) Childs World.

— Water. (Images Ser.). (J). (gr. 5 up). 1992. lib. bdg. 16.95 (*0-88682-431-1*) Creative Ed.

— Wildcats. (Nature Books Ser.). 32p. (J). (gr. 2-6). 1991. lib. bdg. 22.79 (*0-89565-704-X*) Childs World.

— Wolves. (Nature Books Ser.). 32p. (J). (gr. 2-6). 1991. lib. bdg. 22.79 (*0-89565-711-2*) Childs World.

— Yellowstone. (Vision Bks.). (ENG & SPA.). (J). (gr. 2-6). 1992. lib. bdg. 22.79 (*0-89565-859-3*) Childs World.

— Yosemite. (Nature Books Ser.). (ENG & SPA.). (J). (gr. 2-6). 1992. lib. bdg. 22.79 (*0-89565-857-7*) Childs World.

— Yosemite. (Nature Bks.). (ENG & SPA.). (J). (gr. 2-6). 1992. lib. bdg. 22.79 (*1-56766-033-9*) Childs World.

— Zebras. (Nature Books Ser.). (J). (gr. 2-6). 1992. lib. bdg. 22.79 (*0-89565-839-9*) Childs World.

Markert, Jenny M. Hippos. LC 92-29743. (Naturebooks Ser.). (J). (gr. 2-6). 1993. lib. bdg. 22.79 (*1-56766-003-7*) Childs World.

Markert, Lawrence W. Arthur Symons: Critic of the Seven Arts. Kuspit, Donald, ed. LC 87-22802. (Studies in the Fine Arts: Criticism: No. 25). 190p. reprint ed. 54.20 (*0-8357-1845-X*, 2070739) Bks Demand.

— The Bloomsbury Group: A Reference Guide. 400p. (C). 1989. text ed. 45.00 (*0-8161-8936-6*, Hall Reference) Macmillan.

— Riddle & Incest. (New Poets Ser.: Vol. 3). 1974. pap. 1.95 (*0-932616-03-8*) New Poets Chestnut Hills.

Markert, Linda R. Contemporary Technology: Innovations, Issues, & Perspectives. LC 92-25952. 473p. 1993. 33.00 (*0-87006-990-X*) Goodheart.

Markert, Ludwig. Struktur und Bezeichnung des Scheltworts. (Beiheft 40 zur Zeitschrift fuer die Alttestamentliche Wissenschaft Ser.). (C). 1977. text ed. 134.60 (*3-11-005813-8*) De Gruyter.

Markesinis, B. S. & Munday, R. J. Outline of the Law of Agency. 3rd ed. 1992. U. K. pap. 30.00 (*0-406-00145-6*) Butterworth Legal Pubs.

Markesinis, Basil S. The German Law of Torts. 3rd ed. (Illus.). 840p. 1994. 110.00 (*0-19-876356-5*) OUP.

Markesinis, Basil S., ed. The Gradual Convergence: Foreign Influences & English Law on the Eve of the 21st Century. 320p. 1994. pap. 52.00 (*0-19-825828-3*) OUP.

Markesinis, Basil S. & Deakin, Simon F. Tort Law. rev. ed. LC 93-43258. 900p. 1994. write for info. (*0-19-876293-3*, Clarendon Pr) OUP.

— Tort Law. 3rd rev. ed. LC 93-43258. 816p. 1994. 75.00 (*0-19-876292-5*, Old Oregon Bk Store) OUP.

Markesinis, Basil S., jt. auth. see Lawson, Frederick H.

***Market House Books Staff, comp.** A Dictionary of Accounting. (Oxford Paperback Reference Ser.). 350p. 1995. pap. 12.95 (*0-19-280029-9*) OUP.

— The Oxford Dictionary for the Business World. 1022p. 1994. 24.00 (*0-19-863125-1*) OUP.

— The Oxford Dictionary of Abbreviations. 416p. 1993. pap. 9.95 (*0-19-280003-5*) OUP.

***Market Intellience Staff.** Profiles of U. S. Polymer & Fine Chemical Manufacturers. 1995. 995.00 (*0-7889-0242-3*) Frost & Sullivan.

Market Intelligence Staf. European Silicon Sensor Markets. 250p. 1993. 2,400.00 (*1-56753-536-4*) Frost & Sullivan.

Market Intelligence Staff. Abbott Labs: What's Not in the Annual Report. 321p. (Orig.). 1992. 995.00 (*1-56753-378-7*) Frost & Sullivan.

— Acoustic & Vibration Sensors & Test Equipment: Opening of Under-Penetrated Global Markets. 276p. (Orig.). 1992. 1,695.00 (*1-56753-054-0*) Frost & Sullivan.

— Agricultural Biotechnology: Staggering Opportunities in World's Largest Market. 323p. (Orig.). 1992. 1,895.00 (*1-56753-037-0*) Frost & Sullivan.

— Agricultural Biotechnology Markets. 263p. 1994. 1,995.00 (*0-7889-0071-4*) Frost & Sullivan.

— AIDS: Diagnostic, Monitoring & Therapeutic Markets: Technology Assessment & Financial Impact. 211p. 1993. 2,495.00 (*1-56753-519-4*) Frost & Sullivan.

— Air Emission Monitor & Analyzer Markets: Clean Air Act Opens Windows of Opportunity. 189p. (Orig.). 1992. 1,695.00 (*1-56753-040-0*) Frost & Sullivan.

— Air Pollution Control Equipment Markets. 202p. 1993. 2,900.00 (*1-56753-543-7*) Frost & Sullivan.

— Alternate Cite Acute Care Equipment & Supply Markets: Quest for Cost Reductions Foster Ambulatory Center Group. 260p. 1993. 1,695.00 (*1-56753-495-3*) Frost & Sullivan.

— Alternate Cite Respiratory Therapy Markets. 250p. 1994. 2,195.00 (*0-7889-0072-2*) Frost & Sullivan.

— Analytical Instrumentation Markets: Product Sophistication Meets Tough Environmental Regulations & Biotech Research Demands. 255p. (Orig.). 1992. 2,295.00 (*1-56753-059-1*) Frost & Sullivan.

— Anesthesia & Gas Monitoring Equipment Markets: Rapid Transition to Multi Parameter Integration & Open Systems. 224p. 1992. 1,895.00 (*1-56753-389-2*) Frost & Sullivan.

— Anesthesia Drug Markets: Patent Expirations Have Players Scrambling to Develop Short Duration Drugs. 233p. 1992. 1,995.00 (*1-56753-419-8*) Frost & Sullivan.

— Animal Health Products: Who's Hogging the Market? 312p. 1993. 1,895.00 (*1-56753-434-1*) Frost & Sullivan.

— Anti-Infective Markets: Manufacturers Build Resistance Against Generic Competition & Evolving Microbials. 229p. 1993. 1,995.00 (*1-56753-494-5*) Frost & Sullivan.

— Antisubmarine Warfare Markets. 227p. 1993. 2,900.00 (*1-56753-540-2*) Frost & Sullivan.

— Autoimmune Disease Therapeutic Markets: New Therapies Target Causes, Not Symptoms. 320p. 1992. 1,895.00 (*1-56753-077-X*) Frost & Sullivan.

— Baxter International: A Strategic Analysis of Success in World Markets. 249p. 1992. 995.00 (*1-56753-285-3*) Frost & Sullivan.

— Biotechnology Food & Nutrition Products Markets: Genetic Engineering Leads Industry into New Era. 196p. (Orig.). 1992. 1,895.00 (*1-56753-072-9*) Frost & Sullivan.

— Biotechnology Instrumentation & Software: Pharmaceutical Growth Expands Supplier Markets. 293p. 1993. 1,895.00 (*1-56753-468-6*) Frost & Sullivan.

— Bristol-Myers Squibb: World's Largest Pharmaceutical Sales Force in Action. 210p. (Orig.). 1992. 995.00 (*1-56753-047-8*) Frost & Sullivan.

— The Business of Macintosh: Beyond Apple, Achieving Success in the World Market. 1994. 1,895.00 (*1-56753-973-4*) Frost & Sullivan.

M

— Cable & Wire Network Markets. 250p. 1993. 3,900.00 (*1-56753-535-6*) Frost & Sullivan.
— Canadian Telecommunication Equipment & Service Markets: Digital Wireless Communications Take Off. 340p. 1994. 2,295.00 (*1-56753-989-0*) Frost & Sullivan.
— Cancer Diagnostic Imaging Markets. 410p. 1994. 2,295.00 (*0-7889-0139-7*) Frost & Sullivan.
— Cardiac Catheters: Forecasts for 22 Products in an Evolving Market. 413p. 1993. 1,995.00 (*1-56753-426-0*) Frost & Sullivan.
— Cellular & PCS Telephone Pager & Accessory Markets: Time to Focus on Applications. 600p. (Orig.). 1994. 2,295.00 (*0-685-70940-X*) Frost & Sullivan.
— Client-Server in the Nineteen Nineties: A Strategic Assessment of Market Potential. 342p. 1993. 1,495.00 (*1-56753-503-8*) Frost & Sullivan.
— Clinical Laboratory Disposable Markets: Chemistry Tests & Reagents, Toxicology & Pathology Supplies. 416p. 1993. 1,895.00 (*1-56753-520-8*) Frost & Sullivan.
— Clinical Laboratory Disposable Markets: Microbiology, Hematology & Immunology. 413p. 1993. 1,695.00 (*1-56753-521-6*) Frost & Sullivan.
— Color in the Mainstream Office: Six Complementary Desktop Technologies Paint the Color Market. 249p. (Orig.). 1992. 1,495.00 (*1-56753-070-2*) Frost & Sullivan.
— Companion Animal Therapeutic Markets: Profiting from Human Pharmaceutical Research. 276p. (Orig.). 1992. 1,895.00 (*1-56753-381-7*) Frost & Sullivan.
— Contraceptive & Fertility Product Markets: Manufacturers Respond to Changing Demographics. 373p. 1993. 2,195.00 (*1-56753-529-1*) Frost & Sullivan.
— Contract Manufacturing Services Market: Revenues Quadruple by the Year 2000. 322p. 1993. 1,495.00 (*1-56753-441-4*) Frost & Sullivan.
— Corrective & Protective Eyewear Markets: New Technologies Alter Marketing Strategies. 297p. 1993. 1,695.00 (*1-56753-481-3*) Frost & Sullivan.
— The Crisis in Healthcare Financing: The Move Toward Universal Access. 246p. (Orig.). 1992. 395.00 (*1-56753-045-1*) Frost & Sullivan.
— Customer Engineering: A Measurement-Based Sales System Designed to Increase Marketing Profitability. 336p. 1993. 95.00 (*1-56753-492-9*) Frost & Sullivan.
— Dental Electronics & Equipment Markets: Dentists Look to Esthetics for New Revenues. 314p. (Orig.). 1992. 1,695.00 (*1-56753-031-1*) Frost & Sullivan.
— Desktop Manufacturing Systems: Rapid Prototyping Techniques Take the World by Storm. 231p. (Orig.). 1992. 1,895.00 (*1-56753-046-X*) Frost & Sullivan.
— Diabetes Product Markets: Product Penetration Increases with Patient Awareness. 300p. 1992. 1,995.00 (*1-56753-404-X*) Frost & Sullivan.
— Diagnostic Electronics & Imaging Equipment Markets: A Detailed Database on a 13 Billion Dollar Market. 370p. 1992. 995.00 (*1-56753-086-9*) Frost & Sullivan.
— Digital Signal Processor, DSP, Markets: Cost Barriers Broken, Hypergrowth Expected Within 18 months. 265p. (Orig.). 1992. 1,695.00 (*1-56753-073-7*) Frost & Sullivan.
— Disposable Medical Product Markets: PPE Demand Creates Specialty Products. 299p. 1992. 1,495.00 (*1-56753-417-1*) Frost & Sullivan.
— Disposable Medical Product Markets, Vol. Two: Respiratory Disease & Infection Control Dominiate Trends for Growth. 297p. 1993. 1,495.00 (*1-56753-474-0*) Frost & Sullivan.
— Distributed Control Systems in Process Industries: End-Users Focus on Smaller, More Modular & Hybrid DCS's. 361p. (Orig.). 1993. 1,495.00 (*1-56753-657-3*) Frost & Sullivan.
— Distribution Channel Analysis of Desktops, Portables & Commercial Workstations: Understanding Distribution Patterns Is the Key to Survival. 234p. 1993. 1,295.00 (*1-56753-428-7*) Frost & Sullivan.
— Dynamic Growth in World Display Markets: Competition Between Flat Panel Technology & CRT Technology Heats Up. 210p. (Orig.). 1992. 1,495.00 (*1-56753-030-3*) Frost & Sullivan.
— EC Market for Fish, Farmed Fish & Products (Europe) 240p. (Orig.). 1992. 3,200.00 (*1-56753-651-4*, E1574) Frost & Sullivan.
— Eight Hundred Service Markets: Portability Unleashes Competition. 302p. 1993. 1,695.00 (*1-56753-514-3*) Frost & Sullivan.
— Electronic Warfare Outside the U. S. 1993. 3,200.00 (*1-56753-479-1*) Frost & Sullivan.
— Electronics Design Automation Software Tools Market: Hot Segments: ASIC, Mixed Signal, MCM. 246p. (Orig.). 1992. 1,295.00 (*1-56753-401-5*) Frost & Sullivan.
— Electrostatic Discharge (ESD) Control Product Markets: Industrial Shakeout: Price Wars, Emerging Applications & New Products. 318p. 1993. 1,895.00 (*1-56753-467-8*) Frost & Sullivan.
— Eli Lilly: Innovation, Diversification & Globalization. 250p. 1993. 995.00 (*1-56753-432-5*) Frost & Sullivan.
— Emerging & Niche Oriented Auto ID Product Markets: Enormous Growth Potential. 268p. 1993. 1,895.00 (*1-56753-523-2*) Frost & Sullivan.
— Endoscope & Peripheral Equipment Markets. 310p. 1994. 1,995.00 (*0-7889-0044-7*) Frost & Sullivan.
— Endoscopes & Peripheral Equipment Markets: Technology Pays off - Less Invasive Procedures Benefit Physicians & Patients. 319p. 1992. 1,895.00 (*1-56753-175-X*) Frost & Sullivan.
— Endoscopic Accessory Markets: A Fresh Look: New Instruments for New Procedures. 268p. 1993. 1,895.00 (*1-56753-449-X*) Frost & Sullivan.
— Entrepreneurial Opportunities in Telecommunications: Shifting Technologies, Regulation, End-User Requirements Drive Opportunities. 209p. (Orig.). 1992. 995.00 (*1-56753-060-5*) Frost & Sullivan.
— Environmental Technology Market Sourcebook. 410p. 1994. 945.00 (*0-7889-0170-2*) Frost & Sullivan.
— Environmental Test Equipment Markets. 360p. 1994. 1,695.00 (*0-7889-0045-5*) Frost & Sullivan.
— European Adhesive Label Markets. 334p. (Orig.). 1994. 3,800.00 (*0-7889-0115-X*) Frost & Sullivan.
— European Adhesive Tape Markets. 280p. 1994. 3,800.00 (*0-7889-0111-7*) Frost & Sullivan.
— European Advanced Building Control System Markets. 279p. 1994. 3,950.00 (*0-7889-0040-4*) Frost & Sullivan.
— European Advanced Control Markets. 250p. 1994. 3,950.00 (*0-7889-0024-2*) Frost & Sullivan.
— European Advanced Motion Control Markets. 212p. 1994. 3,950.00 (*0-7889-0096-X*) Frost & Sullivan.
— European Air Pollution Control Equipment. 1995. write for info. (*0-7889-0233-4*) Frost & Sullivan.
— European Air Pollution Monitoring Equipment Markets. 268p. 1995. 3,950.00 (*0-7889-0187-7*, 3119-15) Frost & Sullivan.
— European Airway Management Device Markets. 320p. 1995. 3,900.00 (*0-7889-0205-9*, 3164-56) Frost & Sullivan.
— European All Culture Reagent Markets. 373p. 1995. 3,500.00 (*0-7889-0263-6*) Frost & Sullivan.
— European Anaesthetic Product Markets. (Orig.). 1994. 3,800.00 (*0-7889-0120-6*) Frost & Sullivan.
— European Animal Feed Markets. 245p. 1994. 3,800.00 (*0-7889-0059-5*) Frost & Sullivan.
— European Antihypertensive Drug Markets. 1995. 3,800.00 (*0-7889-0254-7*) Frost & Sullivan.
— European Antiviral Drug & Vaccine Markets. 400p. 1994. 3,800.00 (*0-7889-0016-1*) Frost & Sullivan.
— European Arthritis Markets. 230p. 1994. 3,800.00 (*0-7889-0153-2*) Frost & Sullivan.
— European Asthma Treatment Product Markets: Shift in Use of Single-Agent Bronchodialation. 250p. 1994. 3,800.00 (*1-56753-941-6*) Frost & Sullivan.
— European Automated Material Handling Markets. 475p. 1994. 3,950.00 (*1-56753-980-7*) Frost & Sullivan.
— European Biopesticides & Related Agricultural Biotechnology Markets: New Market Growth Accompanied by Intense Competition. 385p. 1993. 4,200.00 (*1-56753-582-8*) Frost & Sullivan.
— European Biotechnology Pharmaceutical Markets: The Lucrative Business of Genetic Engineering. 450p. (Orig.). 1993. 3,500.00 (*1-56753-623-9*) Frost & Sullivan.
— European Cardiac Catheter Markets: Healthcare System Differences Require Regional Specific Strategies. 400p. 1994. 3,800.00 (*1-56753-940-8*) Frost & Sullivan.
— European Chemical Industry. 514p. 1994. 3,800.00 (*0-7889-0152-4*) Frost & Sullivan.
— European Clinical Diagnostics Industry Manufacturers & Suppliers: Detailed Profiles of 148 Industry Leaders. (Orig.). 1993. 1,500.00 (*1-56259-621-7*) Frost & Sullivan.
— European Commercial & Industrial Composite Markets. 225p. 1993. 4,300.00 (*1-56753-531-3*) Frost & Sullivan.
— European Commercial-Industrial Security Markets. 273p. 1994. 3,300.00 (*1-56753-928-9*) Frost & Sullivan.
— European Commercial Workstation Markets. 307p. 1994. 3,800.00 (*0-7889-0173-7*) Frost & Sullivan.
— European Confectionery Equipment Markets: Chocolate Confectionery Production Machinery. 150p. 1993. 1,750.00 (*1-56753-560-7*) Frost & Sullivan.
— European Confectionery Equipment Markets: Confectionery Packaging Machinery. 150p. 1993. 1,750.00 (*1-56753-562-3*) Frost & Sullivan.
— European Consumer Telephony Markets. 438p. 1993. 3,950.00 (*1-56753-541-0*) Frost & Sullivan.
— European Cosmetic & Toiletries Industry Company Profiles. (Orig.). 1992. 495.00 (*1-56753-630-1*, E1582) Frost & Sullivan.
— European Cosmetics & Toiletries Packaging Markets. 299p. 1993. 2,900.00 (*1-56753-518-6*) Frost & Sullivan.
— European Datacommunication Services Market. 200p. 1994. 3,900.00 (*0-7889-0077-3*) Frost & Sullivan.
— European Dietary Supplement Markets. 350p. 1995. 3,800.00 (*0-7889-0188-5*, 3005-88) Frost & Sullivan.
— European Disposable Non-Woven Markets. 275p. 1994. 2,100.00 (*0-7889-0069-2*) Frost & Sullivan.
— European Drug Delivery System Markets. 400p. 1994. 3,800.00 (*0-7889-0005-6*) Frost & Sullivan.
— European Durable Non-Woven Markets. 207p. 1994. 2,100.00 (*0-7889-0070-6*) Frost & Sullivan.
— European EFT-POS Terminal Markets. 115p. 1993. 1,800.00 (*1-56753-883-5*) Frost & Sullivan.
— European Electromagnetic Compatibility Markets: EMC Materials Components. 250p. (Orig.). 1994. 1,750.00 (*1-56753-888-6*) Frost & Sullivan.
— European Electromagnetic Compatibility Markets: EMC Test Facilities & Equipment. 250p. (Orig.). 1994. 1,750.00 (*1-56753-889-4*) Frost & Sullivan.
— European Electromagnetic Compatibility Markets: EMC Testing & Consultancy Services. 300p. (Orig.). 1994. 1,750.00 (*1-56753-890-8*) Frost & Sullivan.
— European Electronic Access Markets. 236p. (Orig.). 1992. 2,450.00 (*1-56753-648-4*) Frost & Sullivan.
— European Electronic Data Interchange Markets. 425p. 1994. 3,450.00 (*0-7889-0174-5*, 1924-73) Frost & Sullivan.
— European Electronic Image Management System Markets. 265p. 1994. 3,900.00 (*1-56753-939-4*) Frost & Sullivan.
— European Electronic Navigation Equipment Markets. 350p. (Orig.). 1993. 3,900.00 (*1-56753-884-3*) Frost & Sullivan.
— European Electronic Navigation Equipment Markets: New Opportunities Emerging in Consumer Applications. (Orig.). 1993. 3,900.00 (*1-56753-621-2*) Frost & Sullivan.
— European Electronic Switch Markets. 146p. 1993. 1,750.00 (*1-56753-537-2*) Frost & Sullivan.
— European EMC Product & Services Supply Markets. 212p. 1994. 975.00 (*0-7889-0060-9*) Frost & Sullivan.
— European Environmental Consultancy Industry. 195p. 1994. 1,500.00 (*0-7889-0009-9*) Frost & Sullivan.
— European Environmental Laboratory Testing Markets. 309p. 1994. 3,950.00 (*0-7889-0054-4*) Frost & Sullivan.
— European EPOS-EFT POS Terminal Markets: Electronic Funds Transfer at Point of Sale, EFT-POS Markets. 148p. 1993. 1,800.00 (*1-56753-567-4*) Frost & Sullivan.
— European EPOS-EFT POS Terminal Markets: Electroonic Point of Sale Markets. 148p. 1993. 1,800.00 (*1-56753-566-6*) Frost & Sullivan.
— European EPOS Terminal Markets. 116p. 1993. 1,800.00 (*1-56753-882-7*) Frost & Sullivan.
— European Ethical Skin Care Product Markets: Recent Surge in Scientific Interest in Dermatology Promotes Growth. 300p. 1993. 3,800.00 (*1-56753-555-0*) Frost & Sullivan.
— European Fabric Washing & Household Care Markets. 234p. 1993. 2,400.00 (*1-56753-922-X*) Frost & Sullivan.
— European Fabric Washing & Household Products. 211p. 1993. 2,400.00 (*1-56753-921-1*) Frost & Sullivan.
— European Facilities Management Markets. 287p. (Orig.). 1992. 3,700.00 (*1-56753-645-X*, E1600) Frost & Sullivan.
— European Facsimilie Scanning & OCR Markets. 475p. 1994. 3,700.00 (*0-7889-0039-0*) Frost & Sullivan.
— European Fibre Optic Communications Markets. 164p. 1994. 2,400.00 (*1-56753-993-9*) Frost & Sullivan.
— European Fibre Optic Sensor Markets: Growing User Acceptance Generates Competition & Sustains Industry Growth. 416p. 1994. 3,800.00 (*1-56753-929-7*) Frost & Sullivan.
— European Flexible Manufacturing System Markets. 206p. (Orig.). 1994. 3,800.00 (*0-7889-0114-1*) Frost & Sullivan.
— European Fluid & Drug Delivery Systems Market: Extensive Forecasts Document Country Differences & Usage Trends. 344p. 1992. 1,895.00 (*1-56753-078-8*) Frost & Sullivan.
— European Food Acid Markets. 194p. 1994. 3,800.00 (*0-7889-0066-8*) Frost & Sullivan.
— European Food & Drink Strategies. (Orig.). 1994. 3,800.00 (*0-7889-0117-6*) Frost & Sullivan.
— European Food Processing Equipment Markets. 437p. (Orig.). 1994. 3,950.00 (*0-7889-0105-2*) Frost & Sullivan.
— European Fractional Horsepower Motor Markets. 533p. (Orig.). 1994. 3,950.00 (*0-7889-0104-4*) Frost & Sullivan.
— European Fragrance & Flavour Markets. 193p. 1994. 1,900.00 (*0-7889-0047-1*); 1,900.00 (*0-7889-0046-3*) Frost & Sullivan.
— The European Functional Fluids Market. 240p. 1993. 4,200.00 (*1-56753-510-0*) Frost & Sullivan.
— European Gas Sensor Markets. 386p. 1994. 3,950.00 (*1-56753-983-1*) Frost & Sullivan.
— European General System for Mobile Communications (GSM) A Strategic Report. 233p. (Orig.). 1994. 3,900.00 (*1-56753-896-7*) Frost & Sullivan.
— The European Generic Drugs Market. 207p. 1993. 3,900.00 (*1-56753-509-7*) Frost & Sullivan.
— European Heat Exchanger Markets. 370p. 1994. 3,950.00 (*0-7889-0172-9*) Frost & Sullivan.
— European Hospital Infection Control Equipment & Supply Market: Governmental Responses to AIDS Stimulate Product Demand. 350p. 1992. 1,895.00 (*1-56753-080-X*) Frost & Sullivan.
— European Hospital Information System Markets. 200p. 1994. 3,500.00 (*1-56753-977-7*) Frost & Sullivan.
— European Hybrid Circuit Markets. 293p. 1993. 3,700.00 (*1-56753-595-X*) Frost & Sullivan.
— European Hydraulic Equipment Markets. 1995. 3,950.00 (*0-7889-0253-9*) Frost & Sullivan.
— European Immunohaematology Reagents & Instruments. (Orig.). 1993. 1,500.00 (*0-685-70179-4*) Frost & Sullivan.
— European Immunotherapeutics Markets. 334p. 1994. 3,800.00 (*0-7889-0017-X*) Frost & Sullivan.
— European Impact & Non-Impact Printer Markets. 336p. 1995. 3,800.00 (*0-7889-0219-9*, 3049-73) Frost & Sullivan.
— European Industrial Battery & Fuel Cell Markets. 257p. 1994. 3,900.00 (*0-7889-0010-2*) Frost & Sullivan.
— European Industrial Switch Markets. 87p. 1993. 1,750.00 (*1-56753-539-9*) Frost & Sullivan.
— European Industrial Vision System Markets. 1995. 3,950.00 (*0-7889-0251-2*) Frost & Sullivan.
— European Industrial Weighing Machinery Markets. 196p. (Orig.). 1994. 3,950.00 (*0-7889-0124-9*) Frost & Sullivan.
— European Infectious & Sexually Transmitted Disease Diagnostic Product Markets. 276p. 1994. 3,800.00 (*0-685-71264-8*) Frost & Sullivan.
— European Information System Outsourcing Markets. 357p. 1994. 3,900.00 (*0-7889-0029-3*) Frost & Sullivan.
— European Integral Horsepower Motor Markets. 470p. 1994. 3,950.00 (*0-7889-0042-0*) Frost & Sullivan.
— European Intelligent LAN Hub Markets. 240p. 1994. 2,750.00 (*1-56753-978-5*) Frost & Sullivan.
— European Intra-Ocular Lens Markets. 104p. 1994. 1,750.00 (*0-7889-0004-8*) Frost & Sullivan.
— European Keyboard - Keyswitches Market. 119p. 1993. 1,750.00 (*1-56753-538-0*) Frost & Sullivan.
— European Laboratory Analytical Instrument Markets: Chromatography & LIMS. 209p. 1994. 1,950.00 (*1-56753-951-3*) Frost & Sullivan.
— European Laboratory Analytical Instrument Markets: Magnetic Field, Thermal & Other Analysis. 242p. 1994. 1,950.00 (*1-56753-953-X*) Frost & Sullivan.
— European Laboratory Analytical Instrument Markets: Spectroscopy & Spectrography. 228p. 1994. 1,950.00 (*1-56753-952-1*) Frost & Sullivan.
— European Laminated & Extrusion Material & Machinery Markets. 283p. 1995. 3,800.00 (*0-7889-0182-6*, 3098-10) Frost & Sullivan.
— European LAN Support & Maintenance Markets. 227p. 1994. 3,300.00 (*0-7889-0035-8*) Frost & Sullivan.
— European Liquid - Solid & Liquid - Liquid Separations Equipment Markets. 1994. 3,800.00 (*1-56753-949-1*) Frost & Sullivan.
— European Lithium Battery Markets. 280p. 1994. 3,900.00 (*1-56753-994-7*) Frost & Sullivan.
— European Low Voltage Switch & Fusegear Markets. 395p. (Orig.). 1994. 3,950.00 (*0-7889-0118-4*) Frost & Sullivan.
— European Lubricant Addictive Markets. 176p. 1994. 4,200.00 (*1-56753-970-X*) Frost & Sullivan.
— European Market for Access Control Lock & Identification Products. 1993. 3,450.00 (*1-56753-493-7*) Frost & Sullivan.
— European Market for Automatic Identification Equipment: Need to Improve Productivity & Manufacturing Efficiencies Fuels Increased Implementation. 216p. (Orig.). 1992. 1,495.00 (*1-56753-058-3*) Frost & Sullivan.
— The European Market for Computer Maintenance. 1993. 3,900.00 (*1-56753-482-1*) Frost & Sullivan.
— The European Market for Digital Telecommunications. 277p. 1993. 3,800.00 (*1-56753-526-7*) Frost & Sullivan.
— The European Market for Distributed Control Systems. 295p. 1993. 4,200.00 (*1-56753-485-6*) Frost & Sullivan.
— European Market for Fillers & Fibers. 250p. 1993. 4,400.00 (*1-56753-585-2*) Frost & Sullivan.
— European Market for Hydrocolloids & Emulsifiers Used in the Food Industry. 238p. 1994. 3,800.00 (*1-56753-965-3*) Frost & Sullivan.
— European Market for Industrial Nondestructive Test Equipment & Consumables: Acoustic, Ultrasonic, Eddy Current, Liquid Penetrant & Magnetic Testing & Thermography. 196p. 1993. 2,950.00 (*1-56753-583-6*) Frost & Sullivan.
— European Market for Industrial Nondestructive Test Equipment & Consumables: Radiography & Optical Inspection. 240p. 1993. 2,950.00 (*1-56753-584-4*) Frost & Sullivan.
— The European Market for Industrial Power Transmissions: Chains, Belts & Mechanical Couplings. 156p. 1993. 1,500.00 (*1-56753-513-5*) Frost & Sullivan.
— The European Market for Industrial Power Transmissions: Clutches, Brakes & Hydraulic Couplings. 134p. 1993. 1,500.00 (*1-56753-512-7*) Frost & Sullivan.
— The European Market for Industrial Power Transmissions: Gears, Industrial Gearboxes , Geared Motors & Mechanical Variators. 164p. 1993. 1,500.00 (*1-56753-511-9*) Frost & Sullivan.
— European Market for Mobile Data Communications. 260p. 1993. 3,900.00 (*1-56753-452-X*) Frost & Sullivan.
— European Market for Personal Data Recorders with Radio Frequency Communications Market. 150p. 1993. 1,750.00 (*1-56753-469-4*) Frost & Sullivan.
— European Market for Personal Data-Recorders with Integral Bar Code Scanners Market. 150p. 1993. 1,750.00 (*1-56753-470-8*) Frost & Sullivan.
— European Market for Personal Data Recorders with Programmable Portable Data Recorders Market. 150p. 1993. 1,750.00 (*1-56753-471-6*) Frost & Sullivan.
— European Market for Uninterruptible Power Supplies. 277p. 1993. 3,900.00 (*1-56753-893-2*) Frost & Sullivan.
— The European Market for Variable Speed Drives. 216p. 1993. 3,900.00 (*1-56753-522-4*) Frost & Sullivan.
— The European Market for X-Ray Diagnostic Images. 1993. 3,900.00 (*1-56753-501-1*) Frost & Sullivan.
— European Medical Diagnostic Ultrasound Equipment Markets. 430p. 1995. 3,800.00 (*0-7889-0189-3*, 1968-50) Frost & Sullivan.
— European Medical Ventilator Markets. 250p. 1994. 3,800.00 (*0-7889-0085-4*) Frost & Sullivan.
— European Membrane Separation System Markets. 581p. 1994. 3,950.00 (*0-7889-0176-1*, 1996-10) Frost & Sullivan.
— European Metallic Welding Equipment & Consumables Markets. (Orig.). 1994. 3,950.00 (*0-7889-0133-8*) Frost & Sullivan.
— European Minimally Invasive Surgical Equipment Markets. 324p. 1994. 3,800.00 (*1-56753-974-2*) Frost & Sullivan.
— European Mobility Aid & Associated Paramedical Product Markets. 385p. 1994. 3,800.00 (*1-56753-971-8*) Frost & Sullivan.
— European Multilayer & Flexible Printed Circuit Board Markets. 212p. 1993. 1,895.00 (*1-56753-592-5*) Frost & Sullivan.
— European Multilayer & Flexible Printed Circuit Board Markets: Declining Prices Force Shakeout. 230p. 1993. 1,895.00 (*1-56753-508-9*) Frost & Sullivan.
— European Multimedia Markets. 439p. 1995. 3,700.00 (*0-7889-0179-6*, 3133-73) Frost & Sullivan.
— European Network Systems Integration & Outsourcing: A Strategic Report. 255p. 1993. 3,900.00 (*1-56753-596-8*) Frost & Sullivan.
— European Neuroleptic Drug Markets. 1995. 3,800.00 (*0-7889-0259-8*) Frost & Sullivan.

An Asterisk (*) at the beginning of an entry indicates that the title is appearing in BIP for the first time.

— European Non Isotopic Immunoassay Product Markets. 374p. (Orig.). 1994. 3,800.00 (*1-56753-891-6*) Frost & Sullivan.
— European Oleochemical Markets. 236p. 1995. 3,800.00 (*0-7889-0203-2*, 1911-48) Frost & Sullivan.
— European Ophthalmic Diagnostic Markets. 94p. 1994. 1,750.00 (*0-7889-0003-X*) Frost & Sullivan.
— European Ophthalmic Laser Markets. 113p. 1994. 1,750.00 (*0-7889-0002-1*) Frost & Sullivan.
— European Original Equipment Market for Automotive Chasis Components. 445p. 1994. 3,950.00 (*0-7889-0025-0*) Frost & Sullivan.
— European Orthopaedic Soft Goods & Cast Room Markets. (Orig.). 1994. 3,800.00 (*0-7889-0125-7*) Frost & Sullivan.
— European Osteoporosis Treatment Product Markets. 1995. 4,000.00 (*0-7889-0258-X*) Frost & Sullivan.
— European OTC Analgesic Markets. 304p. 1995. 3,800.00 (*0-7889-0221-0*, 3063-52) Frost & Sullivan.
— European over the Counter Cough & Cold Medicine Markets. 392p. 1994. 3,800.00 (*0-7889-0141-9*) Frost & Sullivan.
— European Packaging Machinery Markets. 347p. 1994. 3,950.00 (*1-56753-999-8*) Frost & Sullivan.
— European Payphone Markets. 265p. 1994. 3,800.00 (*0-7889-0108-7*) Frost & Sullivan.
— European Payphone Markets: Radical Shifts in Purchasing Patterns & Technology. 850p. 1992. 1,895.00 (*1-56753-335-3*) Frost & Sullivan.
— European PC LAN Market: Highest Growth Rates Found in Germany & Spain. 365p. (Orig.). 1992. 1,695.00 (*1-56753-042-7*) Frost & Sullivan.
— European Personal Communications Network Markets. 356p. 1995. 3,800.00 (*0-7889-0248-2*) Frost & Sullivan.
— European Portable Electric Power Tool Markets. 363p. 1994. 3,950.00 (*0-7889-0028-5*) Frost & Sullivan.
— European Position Sensor Markets: New Opportunities Spring from an Ever-Increasing Range of Applications. 219p. 1993. 3,950.00 (*1-56753-704-9*) Frost & Sullivan.
— European Positive Displacement (PD) Pump Market. 147p. 1993. 1,700.00 (*1-56753-587-9*) Frost & Sullivan.
— European Positive Displacement (PD) Pump Markets. 152p. 1993. 1,700.00 (*1-56753-589-5*) Frost & Sullivan.
— European Powder Coating Markets. 360p. 1994. 3,800.00 (*0-7889-0101-X*) Frost & Sullivan.
— European Power Supply Manufacturer Profiles. 240p. 1993. 795.00 (*1-56753-586-0*) Frost & Sullivan.
— European Prescription Psychotropic Rheumaceutical Markets. 420p. 1995. 3,800.00 (*0-7889-0215-6*, 3066-52) Frost & Sullivan.
— European Printing Ink Markets. 241p. 1995. 3,900.00 (*0-7889-0220-2*, 1906-48) Frost & Sullivan.
— European Private Mobile Radio Markets. 1995. 3,800.00 (*0-7889-0255-5*) Frost & Sullivan.
— European Process Analytical Instruments Markets: Complex Process Analysers. 190p. 1993. 1,900.00 (*1-56753-571-2*) Frost & Sullivan.
— European Process Analytical Instruments Markets: Process Gas Analysers. 190p. 1993. 1,900.00 (*1-56753-569-0*) Frost & Sullivan.
— European Process Control Valve & Actuator Markets. 320p. 1994. 3,950.00 (*0-7889-0011-0*) Frost & Sullivan.
— European Professional Lighting Equipment Markets. 327p. 1994. 3,950.00 (*0-7889-0056-0*) Frost & Sullivan.
— European Radio Paging Hardware & Service Markets. 257p. 1993. 3,895.00 (*1-56753-506-2*) Frost & Sullivan.
— European Rapid Microbiology Markets. 559p. 1994. 3,800.00 (*1-56753-979-3*) Frost & Sullivan.
— European Refraction Correction Markets. 103p. 1994. 1,750.00 (*0-7889-0001-3*) Frost & Sullivan.
— European Rehabilitation Support Markets. 344p. 1995. 3,800.00 (*0-7889-0181-8*, 1977-54) Frost & Sullivan.
— European Relay Markets. 408p. (Orig.). 1994. 3,400.00 (*0-7889-0086-2*) Frost & Sullivan.
— European Research Biochemical Markets. 280p. 1993. 3,800.00 (*1-56753-604-2*) Frost & Sullivan.
— European Research Biochemical Markets: Molecular Biology Stimulates & Rejuvenates the Marketplace. 290p. 1993. 3,800.00 (*1-56753-559-3*) Frost & Sullivan.
— European Residential Security Markets. 244p. 1994. 3,000.00 (*1-56753-968-8*) Frost & Sullivan.
— European RX to OTC Switching Markets. 154p. 1994. 3,800.00 (*0-7889-0102-8*) Frost & Sullivan.
— European Sensor Markets: Old-Line Sensors at Risk, Silicon Micro-Machined Technologies in the Forefront. 414p. (Orig.). 1992. 1,495.00 (*1-56753-035-4*) Frost & Sullivan.
— European Septicaemia & Septic Shock Therapy Markets: Increasing Numbers of Patients Paralleled by Decreasing Treatment Costs. 285p. 1993. 3,800.00 (*1-56753-558-5*) Frost & Sullivan.
— European Single Layer Printed Circuit Board Markets. 240p. 1993. 1,895.00 (*1-56753-591-7*) Frost & Sullivan.
— European Single-Layer Printed Circuit Board Markets: Declining Prices Force Shakeout. 230p. 1993. 1,895.00 (*1-56753-507-0*) Frost & Sullivan.
— European Smart Card Markets. 368p. 1994. 3,800.00 (*1-56753-990-4*) Frost & Sullivan.
— European Special & Diabetic Food Markets. 260p. 1994. 3,800.00 (*0-7889-0058-7*) Frost & Sullivan.
— European Specialty Paper Markets. 1994. 3,800.00 (*0-7889-0180-X*, 3091-48) Frost & Sullivan.
— European Stand Alone Bridge & Router Markets: Expanding Communications Needs Prompt Dynamic Changes in Applications & Technology. 237p. 1994. 2,750.00 (*1-56753-950-5*) Frost & Sullivan.
— European Stroke Therapy Markets. 240p. 1994. 3,800.00 (*0-7889-0051-X*) Frost & Sullivan.
— European Switched Mode Power Supply Markets. 260p. 1994. 3,800.00 (*0-7889-0055-2*) Frost & Sullivan.
— European Synthetic Lubricant Markets. 184p. 1994. 3,800.00 (*0-7889-0154-0*) Frost & Sullivan.
— European Technical Workstation Markets. 264p. 1994. 3,800.00 (*0-7889-0167-2*) Frost & Sullivan.
— European Thrombotic-Thrombolytic Markets. 1995. 3,800.00 (*0-7889-0216-4*, 3067-52) Frost & Sullivan.
— European Uninterruptible Power Supply & Power Conditioning Markets. 250p. (Orig.). 1993. 3,900.00 (*1-56753-885-1*) Frost & Sullivan.
— European Union Chemical Industry & the GATT Agreement. 360p. 1995. 2,995.00 (*0-7889-0222-9*, 3090-48) Frost & Sullivan.
— European Value-Added Service Markets. 240p. 1994. 3,800.00 (*0-7889-0084-6*) Frost & Sullivan.
— European Videoconferencing Markets. 360p. 1994. 3,900.00 (*0-7889-0166-4*) Frost & Sullivan.
— European Waste to Energy Markets. 250p. 1994. 3,950.00 (*0-7889-0100-1*) Frost & Sullivan.
— European Water Pollution Monitoring Instrument Markets. 1995. 3,950.00 (*0-7889-0249-0*) Frost & Sullivan.
— European Water Treatment Chemical Markets. 209p. 1993. 4,400.00 (*1-56753-530-5*) Frost & Sullivan.
— Far East Variable Speed Drive Market. 250p. 1994. 2,295.00 (*0-7889-0023-4*) Frost & Sullivan.
— Fetal, Neonatal & Infant Monitoring Markets. 364p. (Orig.). 1994. 2,195.00 (*0-7889-0074-9*) Frost & Sullivan.
— Fiber Optic Communication Application Markets: Fiber in the Loop & Lans Light the Way. 340p. (Orig.). 1992. 1,895.00 (*1-56753-402-3*) Frost & Sullivan.
— Field - on Site Wastewater Analytical Instrumentation Markets: Era of Portability Dawns, Regulation Tightens. 231p. 1993. 1,495.00 (*1-56753-423-6*) Frost & Sullivan.
— Financial & Marketing Analysis of the World Sensor Industry. 370p. 1993. 1,295.00 (*1-56753-445-7*) Frost & Sullivan.
— Fine Chem Source 1994. 292p. 1994. 545.00 (*0-318-72951-2*) Frost & Sullivan.
— Fluid & Drug Delivery System Markets: Patients on the Move: Patches, Ambulatory Packs & Implants. 305p. 1993. 2,295.00 (*1-56753-502-X*) Frost & Sullivan.
— Fractional Horsepower Electric Motor Markets: Who's Winning, Who's Losing & Why? 323p. 1993. 2,395.00 (*1-56753-505-4*) Frost & Sullivan.
— Generic Prescription Pharmaceutical Markets: Patent Expirations Breathe New Life into Generic Competitors. 314p. 1993. 1,995.00 (*1-56753-480-5*) Frost & Sullivan.
— Global Personal Communication System Markets. 460p. 1994. 2,995.00 (*0-7889-0146-X*) Frost & Sullivan.
— Global Strategic Assessment of Personal Communications: It's All Here. 609p. 1993. 1,695.00 (*1-56753-424-4*) Frost & Sullivan.
— Haematology Reagents & Instruments. (Orig.). 1993. 1,500.00 (*0-685-70180-8*) Frost & Sullivan.
— Hazardous Waste Management Equipment & Service Markets: Bright Spot for Defense Contractors to Go Commercial. 185p. (Orig.). 1992. 1,895.00 (*1-56753-399-X*) Frost & Sullivan.
— Hazardous Waste Management Markets. 310p. 1995. 2,295.00 (*0-7889-0195-8*, S117-15) Frost & Sullivan.
— The Healthcare Compendium: A Demographic & Statistical Analysis Beyond Government Sources. 240p. (Orig.). 1992. 695.00 (*1-56753-052-4*) Frost & Sullivan.
— Healthcare Market Engineering. (Orig.). 1994. 95.00 (*0-7889-0053-6*) Frost & Sullivan.
— Healthcare Scenarios in the Year 2000: A Common Sense Look at Four Alternatives to Get Us There. 279p. 1993. 95.00 (*1-56753-421-X*) Frost & Sullivan.
— Home Diagnostic & Monitoring Markets: FDA & Distribution Issues Characterize a Changing Marketplace. 230p. 1992. 1,895.00 (*1-56753-405-8*) Frost & Sullivan.
— Hospital Infection Control Equipment & Supply Markets: Human & Monetary Costs Shape Sterilization & Disinfection Industries. 213p. 1993. 1,995.00 (*1-56753-443-0*) Frost & Sullivan.
— Hospital Procedures & Diagnoses Data Vol. II: Healthcare Compendium. 1995. 1,495.00 (*0-7889-0243-1*) Frost & Sullivan.
— Imitating Human Reasoning: The Viability & Commercialization of Neural Networks & Fuzzy Logic. 227p. (Orig.). 1992. 1,895.00 (*1-56753-061-3*) Frost & Sullivan.
— Immunodiagnostic Markets: Long-Term R & D Pays Off. 213p. 1992. 1,995.00 (*1-56753-408-2*) Frost & Sullivan.
— Impact & Non-Impact Printer Markets: Marketing Strategies Focus on Applications, Not Technology. 423p. (Orig.). 1992. 1,495.00 (*1-56753-034-6*) Frost & Sullivan.
— Incontinence & Ostomy Product Markets: Aggressive Marketers Target Alternate Sites. 340p. 1993. 1,695.00 (*1-56753-457-0*) Frost & Sullivan.
— Industrial Automation Market Sourcebook. 310p. 1994. 545.00 (*0-7889-0083-8*) Frost & Sullivan.
— Industrial Bus Interface Board Markets: Higher Performance & Open Systems Stimulate World Growth. 305p. (Orig.). 1992. 1,695.00 (*1-56753-029-X*) Frost & Sullivan.
— Industrial Market Engineering. 476p. 1994. 95.00 (*0-7889-0052-8*) Frost & Sullivan.
— Industrial Personal & Occupational Safety Monitor, Device & Accessory Markets: Business Steps up Compliance Efforts. 454p. 1992. 1,495.00 (*1-56753-409-0*) Frost & Sullivan.
— Industrial Temperature Measurement & Control in Western Europe: Market for Controllers. 200p. 1993. 1,950.00 (*1-56753-581-X*) Frost & Sullivan.
— Industrial Temperature Measurement & Control in Western Europe: Market for Temperature Sensors, Converters & Transmitters. 200p. 1992. 1,950.00 (*1-56753-579-8*) Frost & Sullivan.
— Industrial Temperature Measurement & Control in Western Europe: Market for Thermometers, Indicators & Recorders. 200p. 1993. 1,950.00 (*1-56753-580-1*) Frost & Sullivan.
— Intelligent Vehicle Highway System Markets. 394p. 1993. 1,850.00 (*1-56753-550-X*) Frost & Sullivan.
— International Telecommunications Standards. 307p. 1993. 795.00 (*1-56753-701-4*) Frost & Sullivan.
— The International Telecommunications Standards Service. 225p. Date not set. 795.00 (*1-56753-597-6*) Frost & Sullivan.
— Johnson & Johnson: Global Expansion in the Face of Intense Competition. 250p. (Orig.). 1993. 1,295.00 (*1-56753-624-7*) Frost & Sullivan.
— Laboratory Equipment Markets: A Detailed Database on a 25 Billion Dollar Market. 270p. 1992. 995.00 (*1-56753-082-6*) Frost & Sullivan.
— LAN & WAN Connectivity Markets: Routes, Bridges & Gateways: Are They Obsolete? 287p. 1993. 1,695.00 (*1-56753-430-9*) Frost & Sullivan.
— LAN Support Services. 1993. 3,200.00 (*1-56753-478-3*) Frost & Sullivan.
— LAN-WAN Network Management Software Service & System Markets: Your First Source about Outsourcing. 198p. 1992. 1,695.00 (*1-56753-663-8*) Frost & Sullivan.
— Latin American Telecommunications Service & Equipment Markets: Emphasis on Service Offers Investment Opportunities to Equipment Manufacturers. 375p. 1994. 2,695.00 (*1-56753-937-8*) Frost & Sullivan.
— Legal Information System Markets (U. S.) 262p. 1992. 2,250.00 (*1-56753-666-2*, A2502) Frost & Sullivan.
— Long Distance & Reseller Markets: Small Players Rise Again. 295p. 1992. 1,695.00 (*1-56753-385-X*) Frost & Sullivan.
— Man Made Fibres in the European Community: Proportion of Imports Expected too Exceed 10 Percent of Market by 1997. 248p. 1993. 4,500.00 (*1-56753-556-9*) Frost & Sullivan.
— Market for Antifungals. 310p. 1992. 3,700.00 (*1-56753-674-3*, A2500) Frost & Sullivan.
— Market for Bathroom Products & Deodorants (Europe) 305p. 1992. 1,250.00 (*1-56753-736-7*, E1580) Frost & Sullivan.
— Market for Celllular Communications (Europe) 272p. 1992. 3,850.00 (*1-56753-746-4*, E1586) Frost & Sullivan.
— Market for Dairy Products (Europe) Butter Cheese & Fermented Products. 400p. 1992. 1,200.00 (*1-56753-726-X*, E1616) Frost & Sullivan.
— Market for Dairy Products (Europe) Milk, Cream & Dairy Drinks. 290p. 1992. 1,200.00 (*1-56753-725-1*, E1617) Frost & Sullivan.
— Market for Dairy Products (Europe) Yogurt, Dairy Desserts & Ice Cream. 325p. 1992. 1,200.00 (*1-56753-724-3*, E1618) Frost & Sullivan.
— Market for Facsimile Equipment (Europe) 259p. 1992. 3,800.00 (*1-56753-711-1*, E1562) Frost & Sullivan.
— Market for Fragrances (Europe) 383p. 1992. 1,250.00 (*1-56753-710-3*, E1576) Frost & Sullivan.
— Market for Hair Care (Europe) 397p. 1992. 1,250.00 (*1-56753-708-1*, E1579) Frost & Sullivan.
— Market for Hazardous Waste Management (Europe) 412p. 1992. 3,900.00 (*1-56753-707-3*, E1590) Frost & Sullivan.
— Market for Heat Exchangers (U. S.) 253p. 1992. 2,450.00 (*1-56753-706-5*, A2547) Frost & Sullivan.
— Market for High Power Semi-Conductors (Europe) 386p. 1992. 2,300.00 (*0-685-70257-X*) Frost & Sullivan.
— Market for Information Technology (IT) Security Products & Services (Europe) 415p. 1992. 3,400.00 (*1-56753-787-1*, E1513) Frost & Sullivan.
— Market for Intravenous Therapy & Interal Nutrition (Europe) 405p. 1992. 3,800.00 (*1-56753-784-7*, E1584) Frost & Sullivan.
— Market for LAN Value Added Resellers (U. S.) 300p. 1992. 2,400.00 (*1-56753-781-2*, A2456) Frost & Sullivan.
— Market for Liquid - Solid Separation Equipment (U. S.) 301p. 1992. 2,800.00 (*1-56753-780-4*, A2568) Frost & Sullivan.
— Market for Local Area Network (LAN) Maintenance (Europe) 272p. 1992. 3,200.00 (*1-56753-779-0*, E1556) Frost & Sullivan.
— Market for Low Power Semiconductors - Smart Power ICs (Europe) 387p. 1992. 2,300.00 (*1-56753-778-2*, E1614) Frost & Sullivan.
— Market for Make-up (Europe) 394p. 1992. 1,250.00 (*1-56753-777-4*, E1577) Frost & Sullivan.
— Market for Manufacturing Systems Integration (U. S.) 250p. 1992. 2,400.00 (*1-56753-775-8*, A2551) Frost & Sullivan.
— Market for Meat & Meat Products (Europe) Carcass Meats. 382p. 1992. 1,200.00 (*1-56753-774-X*, E1619) Frost & Sullivan.
— Market for Meat & Meat Products (Europe) Comminuted Meat Products. 389p. 1992. 1,200.00 (*1-56753-773-1*, E1621) Frost & Sullivan.
— Market for Meat & Meat Products (Europe) Prepared Meat & Associated Products. 411p. 1992. 1,200.00 (*1-56753-772-3*, E1620) Frost & Sullivan.
— Market for Metropolitan Area Networks (U. S.) 233p. 1992. 3,300.00 (*1-56753-770-7*, A2540) Frost & Sullivan.
— Market for Military Automated Mission Planning (U. S.) 300p. 1992. 2,700.00 (*1-56753-769-3*, A2516) Frost & Sullivan.
— Market for Military C3I (Europe) 302p. 1992. 2,900.00 (*1-56753-768-5*, E1632) Frost & Sullivan.
— Market for Military Passive Night Vision (U. S.) 250p. 1992. 2,450.00 (*1-56753-755-3*, A2495) Frost & Sullivan.
— Market for Military Power Supplies (U. S.) 250p. 1992. 2,700.00 (*1-56753-756-1*, A2541) Frost & Sullivan.
— Market for Multichip Modules (MCMs) (U. S.) 215p. 1992. 2,200.00 (*1-56753-760-X*, A2530) Frost & Sullivan.
— Market for Multimedia (Europe) 340p. 1992. 3,700.00 (*1-56753-762-6*, E1646) Frost & Sullivan.
— Market for North American Video & Audio Post-Production Equipment (U. S.) 200p. 1992. 1,450.00 (*1-56753-765-0*) Frost & Sullivan.
— Market for Oral Hygiene Products (Europe) 384p. 1992. 1,250.00 (*1-56753-800-2*, E1581) Frost & Sullivan.
— Market for Outsourcing Services (U. S.) 246p. 1992. 2,450.00 (*1-56753-802-9*, A2497) Frost & Sullivan.
— Market for Pet Healthcare Products (Europe) 405p. 1992. 3,800.00 (*1-56753-823-1*, E1608) Frost & Sullivan.
— Market for Process Control: Flow & Level Instrumentation. 176p. 1993. 1,900.00 (*1-56753-490-2*) Frost & Sullivan.
— Market for Process Control: Temperature Instrumentation. 180p. 1993. 1,900.00 (*1-56753-489-9*) Frost & Sullivan.
— Market for Process Control Pressure - Differentiation Pressure Instrumentation. 180p. 1993. 1,900.00 (*1-56753-491-0*) Frost & Sullivan.
— Market for Professional Studio & Portable Video Equipment in North America (U. S.) 200p. 1992. 1,450.00 (*1-56753-805-3*, A2462) Frost & Sullivan.
— Market for Skin Care (Europe) 394p. 1992. 1,250.00 (*1-56753-809-6*, E1578) Frost & Sullivan.
— Market for Trunked Radio Equipment for SMRs & Users (U. S.) 225p. 1992. 2,900.00 (*1-56753-819-3*, A2510) Frost & Sullivan.
— Market for TV Transmission Systems Technology in North America (U. S.) 397p. 1992. 1,850.00 (*1-56753-820-7*, A2461) Frost & Sullivan.
— Market for UNIX (Europe) 350p. 1992. 3,900.00 (*1-56753-821-5*, E1593) Frost & Sullivan.
— Market for VANs (Europe) 291p. 1992. 3,900.00 (*1-56753-855-X*, E1601) Frost & Sullivan.
— Mechanical Springs Markets. 360p. 1994. 1,895.00 (*0-7889-0090-0*) Frost & Sullivan.
— Medical - Surgical Market '94. 346p. 1994. 595.00 (*1-56753-934-3*) Frost & Sullivan.
— Medical & Dental Suction & Irrigation Equipment Markets: Environment & Infection Control Issues Encourage Innovations. 279p. 1993. 1,695.00 (*1-56753-451-1*) Frost & Sullivan.
— Medical Catheter Markets: New Applications, Technologies, & Safety Issues Overcome Cost Containment. 245p. (Orig.). 1992. 1,895.00 (*1-56753-057-5*) Frost & Sullivan.
— Medical Device Markets: A Detailed Database on a 41 Billion Dollar Market. 240p. 1992. 995.00 (*1-56753-085-0*) Frost & Sullivan.
— Medical Diagnostic Electronics Products: Market Share Analysis, 1991. 246p. (Orig.). 1992. 1,495.00 (*1-56753-064-8*) Frost & Sullivan.
— Medical Disposables Markets: A Detailed Database on a 45 Billion Dollar Market. 340p. 1992. 995.00 (*1-56753-084-2*) Frost & Sullivan.
— Medical Image Management Markets: Telemedicine Is Here: PACS & Teleradiology Lead the Way. 215p. (Orig.). 1992. 1,895.00 (*1-56753-079-6*) Frost & Sullivan.
— Medical Monitoring Markets: A Detailed Database on a 6 Billion Dollar Market. 480p. 1992. 995.00 (*1-56753-087-7*) Frost & Sullivan.
— Medical Services Market: Increasing Cost Constraints Put 20 Billion Dollar Business Up for Grabs. 379p. (Orig.). 1992. 1,295.00 (*1-56753-036-2*) Frost & Sullivan.
— Medical Waste Management & Disposable Markets: Regulations, Regulations & More Regulations Promote Rapid Technological Innovations. 315p. 1992. 1,895.00 (*1-56753-382-5*) Frost & Sullivan.
— Membrane Separation Systems Market (Europe) 387p. 1992. 3,600.00 (*1-56753-860-6*, E1594) Frost & Sullivan.
— Microdisk Drives vs Flash Memory Cards: World Technology Battle over Form, Function, Power, Capacity, Price & Access. 259p. (Orig.). 1992. 1,695.00 (*1-56753-056-7*) Frost & Sullivan.
— MIL-SPEC, Ruggedized, & Commercially Rugged Computer Market: Purchasing Shifts Toward Commercial Products Offering Portability. 322p. (Orig.). 1992. 1,495.00 (*1-56753-071-0*) Frost & Sullivan.
— Military Electro-Optics Equipment Markets: Despite Peace Dividend, Numerous Segments Still Hot. 174p. (Orig.). 1992. 1,695.00 (*1-56753-065-6*) Frost & Sullivan.
— Military Reconnaissance Market (U. S.) 350p. 1992. 2,600.00 (*1-56753-865-7*, A2521) Frost & Sullivan.
— Military Simulation & Training Systems Market: Increased Networking Propels Mission Simulation. 251p. 1993. 1,695.00 (*1-56753-447-3*) Frost & Sullivan.
— MobilCom 'Ninety-Four. 248p. 1994. 595.00 (*1-56753-933-5*) Frost & Sullivan.
— Mobile Communication Service Markets: Enhanced Offerings Expand User-Base. 396p. 1993. 1,695.00 (*1-56753-465-1*) Frost & Sullivan.
— Modem Markets: Survival of the Fastest. 265p. 1992. 1,495.00 (*1-56753-388-4*) Frost & Sullivan.
— Molecular Probe Markets: Hoffman-La Roche Bids for Dominance. 230p. (Orig.). 1992. 1,895.00 (*1-56753-379-5*) Frost & Sullivan.
— Monoclonal Antibody Markets. 320p. 1994. 2,295.00 (*0-7889-0057-9*) Frost & Sullivan.

M

— Monoclonal Antibody Markets: Enormous Potential in Diagnostic & Therapeutic Products, Cancer Leads the Way. 267p. (Orig.). 1992. 1,995.00 (*1-56753-048-6*) Frost & Sullivan.
— Motor Control & Accessories Market (U. S.) 284p. 1992. 2,400.00 (*1-56753-868-1*, A2494) Frost & Sullivan.
— Motor Control, Feedback Elements & Variable Speed Drive Markets: Technology Advancements & Production Methods Transform Industry. 306p. 1993. 2,400.00 (*1-56753-483-X*) Frost & Sullivan.
— Non PCB Mounted Thermal Management Component Markets. 1993. 1,750.00 (*1-56753-477-5*) Frost & Sullivan.
— North American Air Pollution Control Equipment: Deadline 1995 - Compliance with CAAA Phase I. 325p. (Orig.). 1992. 1,695.00 (*1-56753-336-1*) Frost & Sullivan.
— North American Automotive Sensor Markets: Legislation Guarantees Growth, New Technologies Guarantee Battle Royale. 342p. 1992. 1,895.00 (*1-56753-394-9*) Frost & Sullivan.
— North American Industrial Operator Interface Device & Software Markets. 298p. 1994. 2,195.00 (*0-7889-0142-7*) Frost & Sullivan.
— North American Power Semiconductor Markets: Who's Got the Power? Vendors Target Portability & Energy Efficiency. 300p. 1994. 1,995.00 (*0-7889-0026-9*) Frost & Sullivan.
— North American T1 Equipment Markets: LAN Interconnectivity, Hybrid Networks Accurate Growth. 520p. (Orig.). 1992. 1,695.00 (*1-56753-375-2*) Frost & Sullivan.
— Obstetrics & Gynecological Pharmaceutical Markets: New Delivery Systems for Changing Lifestyles. 288p. 1993. 1,995.00 (*1-56753-453-8*) Frost & Sullivan.
— Ophthalmic Diagnostic Equipment Markets: Industry Focuses on Automated Equipment & Corneal Topography. 343p. 1992. 1,695.00 (*1-56753-414-7*) Frost & Sullivan.
— Ophthalmic Pharmaceuticals: Successful Laboratory Results Equal Market Success. 180p. (Orig.). 1992. 1,895.00 (*1-56753-337-X*) Frost & Sullivan.
— Ophthalmic Surgical Device Markets: New IDL Technology Improves Reimbursement Outlook. 204p. 1992. 1,695.00 (*1-56753-418-X*) Frost & Sullivan.
— Opportunities & Directions in Antisense & Other Oligonucleotide-Based Technologies. 218p. 1993. 1,495.00 (*1-56753-603-4*) Frost & Sullivan.
— Opthalmic Product Markets: Manufacturers Seek Ways to Penetrate Untapped Markets. 400p. 1993. 1,995.00 (*1-56753-572-0*) Frost & Sullivan.
— OptoSource '94. 396p. 1994. 595.00 (*1-56753-959-9*) Frost & Sullivan.
— Pain Management: Expiring Patents Open OTC Markets. 332p. 1993. 1,995.00 (*1-56753-488-0*) Frost & Sullivan.
— Patient Monitoring Markets: Integrated Non-Invasive Products Enhance Manufacturer Opportunities. 317p. (Orig.). 1992. 1,995.00 (*1-56753-396-5*) Frost & Sullivan.
— PC LAN Markets: Downsizing, Peer to Peer & FDDI-Copper Stir the Pot. 380p. (Orig.). 1992. 1,495.00 (*1-56753-380-9*) Frost & Sullivan.
— PCB Mounted Thermal Management Component Markets. 1993. 1,750.00 (*1-56753-476-7*) Frost & Sullivan.
— Pen, Palmtop, & Notebook Computer & Peripheral Markets: Applications, Applications, Applications. 364p. (Orig.). 1992. 1,495.00 (*1-56753-069-9*) Frost & Sullivan.
— Perfumery, Cosmetic & Toiletry Chemical Markets in the European Community: Perfumery & Cosmetic Chemicals. 189p. 1994. 2,750.00 (*1-56753-606-9*) Frost & Sullivan.
— Perfumery, Cosmetic & Toiletry Chemical Markets in the European Community: Toiletry Chemicals. 186p. 1994. 2,750.00 (*1-56753-605-0*) Frost & Sullivan.
— Personal Protection Safety Product Markets. 170p. 1994. 1,650.00 (*0-7889-0031-5*); 1,650.00 (*0-7889-0032-3*) Frost & Sullivan.
— Pharmaceutical Market Outlook. 53p. 1994. 695.00 (*0-7889-0065-X*) Frost & Sullivan.
— Pharmaceutical Markets: A Detailed Database on a 94 Billion Dollar Market. 270p. 1992. 995.00 (*1-56753-083-4*) Frost & Sullivan.
— Pharmasource '94. 311p. 1994. 595.00 (*1-56753-985-8*) Frost & Sullivan.
— Pickles & Chutney Markets. 263p. 1993. 1,200.00 (*1-56753-553-4*) Frost & Sullivan.
— Polymers-Plastics Market 1994. 239p. 1994. 545.00 (*0-7889-0033-1*) Frost & Sullivan.
— Positive Displacement Pumps: European Positive Displacement (PD) Pump Markets. 160p. 1993. 1,700.00 (*1-56753-588-7*) Frost & Sullivan.
— Power Transmission Sourcebook. 309p. 1994. 545.00 (*0-7889-0008-0*) Frost & Sullivan.
— Premises Wiring Systems (U. S.) 350p. 1992. 3,300.00 (*1-56753-906-8*, A2479) Frost & Sullivan.
— Private-Line Service Markets: High-Capacity T-Services, CAPS to Grow Vigorously. 287p. 1993. 1,695.00 (*1-56753-908-4*) Frost & Sullivan.
— Process Control Markets Instrumentation. Hammersley, Milmoth, ed. 230p. 1992. pap. text ed. 995.00 (*1-56753-910-6*) Frost & Sullivan.
— Process Control Source 1994. 250p. 1994. 545.00 (*0-7889-0041-2*) Frost & Sullivan.
— Profiles of European Clinical Diagnostic Industry. 313p. 1993. 1,500.00 (*0-685-71265-6*) Frost & Sullivan.
— Profiles of European Computer Equipment & Service Suppliers. 253p. 1994. 975.00 (*0-7889-0007-2*) Frost & Sullivan.
— Profiles of European Datacommunications Equipment & Service Suppliers. 364p. 1994. 950.00 (*1-56753-995-5*) Frost & Sullivan.
— Profiles of European Electro-Mechanical Component Suppliers. 350p. 1994. 895.00 (*0-685-71483-7*) Frost & Sullivan.
— Profiles of European Electronic Chemical Companies. 305p. 1995. 1,500.00 (*0-7889-0246-6*) Frost & Sullivan.
— Profiles of European Electronic Test & Measurement Suppliers. 366p. 1994. 950.00 (*1-56753-984-X*) Frost & Sullivan.
— Profiles of European OTC Pharmaceutical Manufacturers & Suppliers: Continued Growth in a 45 Billion Dollar Industry. 300p. 1993. 1,495.00 (*1-56753-557-7*) Frost & Sullivan.
— Profiles of European Pneumatic & Hydraulic Equipment Suppliers. (Orig.). 1994. 950.00 (*0-7889-0116-8*) Frost & Sullivan.
— Profiles of European Printed Circuit Board Manufacturers: A Market Assessment. 225p. 1993. 695.00 (*1-56753-564-X*) Frost & Sullivan.
— Profiles of European Suppliers of Process Control Instrumentation. 364p. 1994. 995.00 (*1-56753-955-6*) Frost & Sullivan.
— Profiles of PCB Manufacturers. 298p. 1994. 995.00 (*0-7889-0140-0*) Frost & Sullivan.
— Profiles of U. S. Test & Measurement Equipment Manufacturers. 308p. 1994. 995.00 (*1-56753-969-6*) Frost & Sullivan.
— RBOC Strategies in Data Communications. 180p. 1993. 2,400.00 (*1-56753-547-X*) Frost & Sullivan.
— RBOC Strategies in Information Services. 180p. 1993. 2,400.00 (*1-56753-548-8*) Frost & Sullivan.
— Regional Holding Companies Refocus Channel Efforts: Returning to Home Regions & Telecon Products. 341p. (Orig.). 1992. 1,295.00 (*1-56753-049-4*) Frost & Sullivan.
— Robot Markets: Increased Plant Automation Translates to 10 Percent Annual Growth. 277p. 1993. 1,895.00 (*1-56753-472-4*) Frost & Sullivan.
— Satellite Communications in North American Commercial Systems (U. S.) 200p. 1992. 2,900.00 (*1-56753-916-5*, A2473) Frost & Sullivan.
— Sauces & Dressing Markets. 295p. 1993. 1,200.00 (*1-56753-551-8*) Frost & Sullivan.
— Scanning & OCR Devices (U. S.) 385p. 1992. 2,900.00 (*1-56753-917-3*, A2524) Frost & Sullivan.
— Scanning & OCR Market (Europe) 270p. 1992. 3,700.00 (*1-56753-918-1*, E1595) Frost & Sullivan.
— Seasoning & Condiment Markets. 319p. 1993. 1,200.00 (*1-56753-552-6*) Frost & Sullivan.
— Sensor Market 'Ninety-Four. 244p. 1994. 545.00 (*1-56753-932-7*) Frost & Sullivan.
— Site Cleanup under Superfund, DOD & DOE Markets: High Growth Potential. 268p. 1993. 1,495.00 (*1-56753-458-9*) Frost & Sullivan.
— Soft Tissue Implant Markets: Manufacturers Address Regulations & Defend Against Litigation. 221p. 1993. 1,895.00 (*1-56753-454-6*) Frost & Sullivan.
— Speech, Image, & Video Data Compression Markets: Chips, Board, & Software Transcend Data Cram Barriers. 208p. (Orig.). 1992. 1,895.00 (*1-56753-075-3*) Frost & Sullivan.
— Standalone Facsimile Equipment Market (U. S.) 200p. 1992. 2,900.00 (*1-56753-827-4*, A2515) Frost & Sullivan.
— Strategic Analysis of System Integration & Outstanding Markets. 420p. 1993. 1,495.00 (*1-56753-464-3*) Frost & Sullivan.
— Strategies for Marketing Cosmetics & Toiletries in Europe: Competitive Positioning in a 33 Billion Dollar Marketplace. 469p. 1993. 3,800.00 (*1-56753-565-8*) Frost & Sullivan.
— Survey of Rapid Prototyping End-Users: First Generation a Smashing Success, End-Users Waiting for Next Generation Systems. 425p. (Orig.). 1992. 1,695.00 (*1-56753-398-1*) Frost & Sullivan.
— Telecom Distribution Channel Analysis: Complex Issues, Trends & Channel Definitions Clarified. 377p. 1992. 995.00 (*1-56753-415-5*) Frost & Sullivan.
— Telecom Sourcebook, 1993. 1993. 545.00 (*1-56753-594-1*) Frost & Sullivan.
— Telecommunications Market Sourcebook '95. 298p. 1995. 595.00 (*0-7889-0217-2*, 2827-63) Frost & Sullivan.
— Telemanagement Systems, Software, & Services Market: Who's Winning, Who's Losing, & Why. 303p. (Orig.). 1992. 1,495.00 (*1-56753-044-3*) Frost & Sullivan.
— Test & Measurement Equipment '94. 298p. 1994. 545.00 (*1-56753-960-2*) Frost & Sullivan.
— Therapeutic & Surgical Equipment Markets: New Technologies Flourish Despite Slow FDA Approval & Reimbursement Issues. 251p. 1993. 1,895.00 (*1-56753-427-9*) Frost & Sullivan.
— Therapeutic Surgical & Electronic Device Markets: A Detailed Database on a 13 Billion Dollar Market. 280p. 1992. 995.00 (*1-56753-081-8*) Frost & Sullivan.
— U. S. Absorbable & Erodible Biomaterial Product Markets: Emerging Technologies Create Multi-Billion Dollar Industry. 333p. 1995. 1,995.00 (*0-7889-0206-7*, S239S4) Frost & Sullivan.
— U. S. Air Emissions Monitor & Analyzer Markets: Multiple Environmental Regulations Continue to Drive Growth. 400p. (Orig.). 1994. 1,895.00 (*1-56753-892-4*) Frost & Sullivan.
— U. S. Air Pollution Control Markets. 410p. 1994. 2,395.00 (*0-7889-0149-4*) Frost & Sullivan.
— U. S. Allergy & Asthma Markets. 300p. 1994. 3,295.00 (*0-7889-0158-3*) Frost & Sullivan.
— U. S. Allergy & Asthma Treatment Markets: New Approaches in Therapy Promise Major Breakthroughs. 240p. 1993. 2,295.00 (*1-56753-544-5*) Frost & Sullivan.
— U. S. Analytical Instruments in Process Control. 1994. 1,995.00 (*0-7889-0147-8*) Frost & Sullivan.
— U. S. & International Production Market for T. V. & New Video Technologies (U. S.), 2 vols., Set. 1992. 2,450.00 (*1-56753-840-1*, A2258) Frost & Sullivan.
— U. S. Anesthesia & Gas Monitoring Equipment Markets Continuing Development of Integrated & Compact Products. 210p. 1994. 1,995.00 (*0-7889-0027-7*) Frost & Sullivan.
— U. S. Antifungal Markets: High Growth Era for Systemic & OTC Products. 340p. (Orig.). 1994. 2,495.00 (*1-56753-899-1*) Frost & Sullivan.
— U. S. Autoimmune Disease Markets. 370p. 1994. 2,395.00 (*0-7889-0138-9*) Frost & Sullivan.
— U. S. Autoimmune Disease Therapeutic Markets: Betaseron & Other New Compounds Advance Through Clinical Trials. 450p. 1993. 1,995.00 (*1-56753-545-3*) Frost & Sullivan.
— U. S. Automotive Hard Parts Markets. 460p. 1994. 2,395.00 (*0-7889-0063-3*) Frost & Sullivan.
— U. S. Biopharmaceutical Markets: Wall Street Dries Up: Growth Through Alliances. 345p. 1994. 1,995.00 (*0-7889-0088-9*) Frost & Sullivan.
— U. S. Biotech Company Profiles: An In-Depth Look at 100 Leading Industry Innovators. 1995. 1,695.00 (*0-7889-0169-9*, 5085-80) Frost & Sullivan.
— U. S. Cable Television & Associated Technology Product Markets. (Orig.). 1994. 2,295.00 (*0-614-00722-4*) Frost & Sullivan.
— U. S. Call Processing Equipment Markets: Popularity of Call Centers & Computer Integration Creates a Dramatic Revolution. 401p. 1993. 2,895.00 (*1-56753-703-0*) Frost & Sullivan.
— U. S. Cellular & PCS Telephone, Pager & Accessory Markets: Time to Focus on Applications. 546p. 1993. 2,295.00 (*1-56753-705-7*) Frost & Sullivan.
— U. S. Communications Test Equipment Markets. 260p. 1994. 1,895.00 (*0-614-00344-X*) Frost & Sullivan.
— U. S. Complex Carbohydrate Therapeutics Markets. 1994. 2,195.00 (*0-7889-0135-4*) Frost & Sullivan.
— U. S. Computer Outlet to Laser Disk (Cold) Markets. 256p. 1994. 2,495.00 (*0-7889-0095-1*) Frost & Sullivan.
— U. S. Computers in the Banking Industry Markets. (Orig.). 1994. 1,995.00 (*0-7889-0137-0*) Frost & Sullivan.
— U. S. Customer Receptions of Diagnostic Imaging Equipment: Users Evaluate Manufacturers. 250p. 1993. 1,195.00 (*1-56753-573-9*) Frost & Sullivan.
— U. S. Data Compression Markets: Established Standards Set Stage for Rhenomenal Growth Quarterly. 1995. 2,995.00 (*0-7889-0214-8*) Frost & Sullivan.
— U. S. Data Compression Product Markets: Video Compression Leads Growth Through the 1990s. 207p. (Orig.). 1994. 1,895.00 (*1-56753-926-2*) Frost & Sullivan.
— U. S. Desktop Video Markets: The First Definitive Business & Technology Assessment. 450p. 1993. 1,895.00 (*1-56753-841-X*) Frost & Sullivan.
— U. S. E-Mail & Voice Mail Markets. 266p. (Orig.). 1992. 2,900.00 (*1-56753-656-5*) Frost & Sullivan.
— U. S. Earth Moving Equipment Markets. 313p. 1994. 1,995.00 (*0-7889-0143-5*) Frost & Sullivan.
— The U. S. EFT - POS Debit Terminal Market. 279p. 1993. 2,900.00 (*1-56753-527-5*) Frost & Sullivan.
— U. S. Electro-Optical Instrument & Inspection System Markets. 336p. 1994. 2,195.00 (*0-7889-0144-3*) Frost & Sullivan.
— U. S. Electronic Access Control System Markets Requirements: High Security Promote Biometric Identification. 250p. 1994. 1,895.00 (*1-56753-998-X*) Frost & Sullivan.
— U. S. Electronic-Electrical Adhesive, Sealant & Coating Markets: Growth Applications Swing Toward Polyimide. 250p. 1993. 2,895.00 (*1-56753-574-7*) Frost & Sullivan.
— U. S. Emergency & Trauma Care Device Markets: New Technologies Focus on Safety & Ease of Use. 410p. (Orig.). 1994. 1,895.00 (*0-7889-0119-2*) Frost & Sullivan.
— U. S. Enclosed Geardrive & Gearmotor Markets: Another Traditional Domestic Market under International Pressure. 298p. 1993. 2,395.00 (*1-56753-546-1*) Frost & Sullivan.
— U. S. Ethical Nutrition Markets: Manufacturers Target Home Healthcare for Growth. 1994. 1,895.00 (*0-7889-0061-7*) Frost & Sullivan.
— U. S. Federal Non-DOD Physical Security Equipment Markets: Government Market Still Provides Lucrative Growth. 325p. (Orig.). 1994. 1,995.00 (*0-7889-0113-3*) Frost & Sullivan.
— U. S. Field & On-Site Waste Water Analytical Instrument Markets. 360p. 1995. 1,995.00 (*0-7889-0150-8*) Frost & Sullivan.
— U. S. Filtration Product Markets: A Comprehensive Overview of Four Filtration Types: Macro, Micro, Ultra, & Reverse Osmosis. 1994. 1,995.00 (*1-56753-996-3*) Frost & Sullivan.
— U. S. Fine & Ultrafine Filtration Product Markets: Capturing Smaller Particles Generates Larger Dollars. 470p. 1994. 1,995.00 (*1-56753-966-1*) Frost & Sullivan.
— U. S. Fitness & Exercise Equipment Markets: How Is the Industry Shaping Up? 520p. (Orig.). 1994. 1,895.00 (*0-685-71179-X*) Frost & Sullivan.
— U. S. Fluid & Drug Delivery System Markets. (Orig.). 1994. 2,295.00 (*0-7889-0097-8*) Frost & Sullivan.
— U. S. Gasket Packaging & Mechanical Sealing Device Markets. 246p. 1993. 2,895.00 (*1-56753-577-1*) Frost & Sullivan.
— U. S. Genitourological Pharmaceutical & Diagnostic Markets: Competitors Focus on Quality of Life for an Aging Population. 1995. 2,495.00 (*0-7889-0202-4*, 5080-52) Frost & Sullivan.
— U. S. Ground Based & Ship Based Electronic Warfare Markets. 400p. 1992. 2,700.00 (*1-56753-692-1*, A2377) Frost & Sullivan.
— U. S. Healthcare Compendium Vol. I: A Demographic & Statistical Analysis. 221p. (Orig.). 1994. 795.00 (*0-7889-0127-3*) Frost & Sullivan.
— U. S. Home Diagnostic & Monitoring Product Markets: Cost Containment Pressures Motivate Self-Testing. 289p. 1994. 1,995.00 (*0-7889-0018-8*) Frost & Sullivan.
— U. S. Home Improvement Product Markets: DIY: A Bright Spot in a Mature Construction Industry. 290p. (Orig.). 1993. 2,595.00 (*1-56753-629-8*) Frost & Sullivan.
— U. S. Hospital Infection Control Equipment & Supply Markets: New Product Development Substantially Alters Market Share. 360p. 1994. 2,295.00 (*1-56753-961-0*) Frost & Sullivan.
— U. S. Hospital Information Systems Market. 388p. 1992. 2,600.00 (*1-56753-683-2*, A2546) Frost & Sullivan.
— U. S. Hospital Kit & Tray Markets: Manufacturers Meet User Demands with Customization & Safety Features. 358p. 1994. 1,895.00 (*0-7889-0107-9*) Frost & Sullivan.
— U. S. Hospital Respiratory Therapy Markets: Vendors Strategize in the Face of Economic Pressures. 290p. 1994. 1,995.00 (*1-56753-945-9*) Frost & Sullivan.
— U. S. Hot Melt Markets: Technology Is Geared for Fast Packaging Applications. 271p. (Orig.). 1994. 2,995.00 (*1-56753-895-9*) Frost & Sullivan.
— U. S. Hydraulic Power Component Markets: Applications Open Opportunities As Industry Experiences Resurgance. 1995. 2,495.00 (*0-7889-0250-4*) Frost & Sullivan.
— U. S. Immunodiagnostic Markets: Industry Leader Aggressively Pursues Market Share Through New Instrumentation. 350p. 1994. 2,295.00 (*0-7889-0087-0*) Frost & Sullivan.
— U. S. Implantable & Interventional Cardiovascular Device Markets. (Orig.). 1994. 2,295.00 (*0-7889-0130-3*) Frost & Sullivan.
— U. S. Industrial Air Filtration Markets. (Orig.). 1994. 1,995.00 (*0-7889-0129-X*) Frost & Sullivan.
— U. S. Industrial & Scientific Laser System Markets Expanding Industrial Sales Lead Resurgence. (Orig.). 1994. 1,895.00 (*0-7889-0132-X*) Frost & Sullivan.
— U. S. Industrial Battery Markets. 289p. 1995. 2,495.00 (*0-7889-0163-X*) Frost & Sullivan.
— U. S. Industrial Gas Sensor Markets: Migration from Traditional to More Innovative Technologies. 237p. 1994. 1,895.00 (*0-7889-0037-4*) Frost & Sullivan.
— U. S. Industrial Scale & Weighing Equipment Markets: Systems Approach Tilts the Balance. 350p. 1993. 2,395.00 (*1-56753-515-1*) Frost & Sullivan.
— U. S. Industrial Solvent Markets: New Environmental Legislation Changes Market Dynamics. 260p. 1994. 2,295.00 (*0-7889-0078-1*) Frost & Sullivan.
— U. S. Intravenous Equipment & Supply Markets, Vol. Three: Infusion Devices. 155p. 1993. 1,295.00 (*1-56753-534-8*) Frost & Sullivan.
— U. S. Intravenous Equipment & Supply Markets, Vol. One: Intravenous Solutions. 101p. 1993. 1,295.00 (*1-56753-532-1*) Frost & Sullivan.
— U. S. Intravenous Equipment & Supply Markets, Vol. Two: Vascular Access Devices. 182p. 1993. 1,295.00 (*1-56753-533-X*) Frost & Sullivan.
— U. S. ISDN Customer Premise Equipment (CPE) Markets. 294p. 1994. 3,300.00 (*1-56753-927-0*) Frost & Sullivan.
— U. S. LAN Systems Integration Markets. 240p. 1994. 1,995.00 (*0-7889-0014-5*) Frost & Sullivan.
— U. S. Large Cogeneration Equipment Markets: Competition Intensifies As Industry Matures. 1995. 2,395.00 (*0-7889-0213-X*, 5008-10) Frost & Sullivan.
— U. S. Liquid & Solid Separation Equipment Markets. (Orig.). 1994. 1,895.00 (*0-7889-0128-1*) Frost & Sullivan.
— U. S. Long Distance & Reseller Service Markets. 755p. 1994. 1,995.00 (*0-7889-0157-5*) Frost & Sullivan.
— U. S. Low End Workstations for the Commercial Marketplace. 261p. 1994. 1,995.00 (*0-7889-0177-X*, 2610-70) Frost & Sullivan.
— U. S. Lubricant Additive Markets. 215p. 1993. 2,900.00 (*1-56753-599-2*) Frost & Sullivan.
— U. S. Mail Service Pharmacy Markets: Distribution Channel Comes of Age in the Face of Economic Pressures. 450p. 1994. 2,995.00 (*1-56753-936-X*) Frost & Sullivan.
— U. S. Manufacturing Systems Integration. 283p. 1994. 2,495.00 (*0-7889-0062-5*) Frost & Sullivan.
— The U. S. Market for Centrifugal & Turbine Pumps. 210p. 1993. 2,200.00 (*1-56753-487-2*) Frost & Sullivan.
— The U. S. Market for Flat Panel Display: Readout Types. 1993. 1,650.00 (*1-56753-497-X*) Frost & Sullivan.
— The U. S. Market for Flat Panel Displays: Display Systems. 1993. 1,650.00 (*1-56753-498-8*) Frost & Sullivan.
— The U. S. Market for Flat Panel Displays: Panel Types. 1993. 1,650.00 (*1-56753-499-6*) Frost & Sullivan.
— The U. S. Market for Integral Horsepower Adjustable Speed Drives. 147p. 1993. 2,800.00 (*1-56753-486-4*) Frost & Sullivan.
— The U. S. Market for Private Satellige Networks. 212p. 1993. 2,900.00 (*1-56753-549-6*) Frost & Sullivan.
— U. S. Medical & Pharmaceutical Packaging Markets: Manufacturers Focus on Cost Containment & Waste Reduction. 300p. (Orig.). 1993. 1,695.00 (*1-56753-628-X*) Frost & Sullivan.
— U. S. Medical Disposable Product Markets: Specialized Products Show Greatest Growth. 316p. 1995. 1,895.00 (*0-7889-0191-5*) Frost & Sullivan.

— U. S. Medical Disposable Product Markets, Vol. 3: Needles, Syringes & Related Products. 370p. (Orig.). 1994. 1,895.00 (*1-56753-924-6*) Frost & Sullivan.

— U. S. Medical Waste Management & Disposal Markets: Huge Impact on Alternate Cites Due to Stringent Regulation Enforcement. 560p. 1994. 1,995.00 (*0-7889-0012-9*) Frost & Sullivan.

— U. S. Men's Personal Care Product Markets: Manufacturers Shift Focus in Response to Changing Attitudes. 371p. 1994. 1,895.00 (*0-7889-0019-6*) Frost & Sullivan.

— U. S. Military & Commercial Infrared System Markets: Emerging Materials, Price Reduction Offer Excellent Opportunities. 1995. 2,495.00 (*0-7889-0204-0*) Frost & Sullivan.

— U. S. Military Command Control, Communications, & Intelligence, C3I: Service Markets. 510p. 1993. 2,495.00 (*1-56753-590-9*) Frost & Sullivan.

— U. S. Military Display Markets. 343p. 1995. 2,195.00 (*0-7889-0156-7*, S207-16) Frost & Sullivan.

— U. S. Military Electronic Warfare Markets. 600p. 1994. 2, 950.00 (*0-7889-0022-6*) Frost & Sullivan.

— U. S. Military Non-Mission Avionics Equipment Markets: Aircraft Upgrades, New Technologies Offset Declining Defense Budget. 600p. 1994. 2,195.00 (*1-56753-976-9*) Frost & Sullivan.

— U. S. Military Satellite Communications Equipment Markets: Budget Constraints Bring Spending Down to Earth. 364p. 1993. 2,295.00 (*1-56753-601-8*) Frost & Sullivan.

— U. S. Military Trainer Markets. (Orig.). 1994. 2,900.00 (*0-7889-0126-5*) Frost & Sullivan.

— U. S. Military Trainers & Simulator Markets, Vols. I & II. 806p. 1993. 2,900.00 (*1-56753-622-0*) Frost & Sullivan.

— U. S. Military Unmanned Vehicle & Robotics Markets. 200p. 1994. 1,995.00 (*0-7889-0000-5*) Frost & Sullivan.

— U. S Modem Markets: Wireless Saves the Day. 350p. 1994. 1,995.00 (*1-56753-986-6*) Frost & Sullivan.

— U. S. Network Management System & Service Markets. 272p. 1994. 2,800.00 (*1-56753-988-2*) Frost & Sullivan.

— U. S. Network Systems Integration Markets: New Revenue Growth Offers Great Potential to New Entrants. 180p. 1993. 3,150.00 (*1-56753-610-7*) Frost & Sullivan.

— U. S. Neurodiagnostic & Neurosurgical Equipment Markets. 1995. 1,995.00 (*0-7889-0198-2*, 5197-57) Frost & Sullivan.

— U. S. Neurodiagnostic & Neurosurgical Product Markets. 414p. 1995. 1,995.00 (*0-7889-0151-6*) Frost & Sullivan.

— U. S. OEM Coating Markets. 256p. 1994. 2,395.00 (*0-7889-0145-1*) Frost & Sullivan.

— U. S. On-Premises Telecommunications Equipment Markets. 217p. 1994. 2,595.00 (*1-56753-946-7*) Frost & Sullivan.

— U. S. Operator Services & Card Calling Markets. 334p. (Orig.). 1994. 1,895.00 (*0-7889-0030-7*) Frost & Sullivan.

— U. S. Ophthalmic Diagnostic Equipment Markets: Manufacturers Visualize High Growth from Emerging Technologies. 320p. 1994. 1,895.00 (*0-7889-0050-1*) Frost & Sullivan.

— U. S. Ophthalmic Surgical Device Markets. 288p. (Orig.). 1994. 1,895.00 (*0-7889-0103-6*) Frost & Sullivan.

— U. S. Oral OTC Markets: Line Extensions & Rx to OTC Switches Support Self Medication Trends. 360p. 1994. 1, 995.00 (*1-56753-930-0*) Frost & Sullivan.

— U. S. Organ Transplantation Products & Artificial Organs. 310p. 1994. 1,995.00 (*0-7889-0165-6*) Frost & Sullivan.

— U. S. Orthopedic Prosthetic Device & Ins. 367p. 1994. 2, 295.00 (*0-7889-0081-1*) Frost & Sullivan.

— U. S. Orthopedic Soft Goods & Cast Room Product Markets. 453p. 1994. 1,995.00 (*0-7889-0079-X*) Frost & Sullivan.

— U. S. Osteoporosis Markets. 412p. 1994. 2,295.00 (*0-7889-0122-2*) Frost & Sullivan.

— U. S. Patient & Mobility Aid Markets. 345p. 1994. 1,895. 00 (*0-7889-0155-9*) Frost & Sullivan.

— U. S. Patient & Mobility Aid Markets: Niche Markets on the Move. (Orig.). 1994. 1,895.00 (*0-7889-0123-0*) Frost & Sullivan.

— U. S. Patient Monitoring Markets. 368p. 1995. 2,195.00 (*0-7889-0161-3*) Frost & Sullivan.

— U. S. PC - Workstation Storage Strategies: Technology Tradeoffs: How Big? How Much? 320p. 1994. 1,695.00 (*1-56753-991-2*) Frost & Sullivan.

— U. S. Plastic Compounding Industry: Sophisticated Blends & Alloys Replace Engineered Resins. 270p. 1993. 3,295. 00 (*1-56753-615-8*) Frost & Sullivan.

— U. S. Portable Power Tool Consumable Markets. 380p. 1994. 2,295.00 (*0-7889-0159-1*) Frost & Sullivan.

— U. S. Power Supply Manufactures Profiles. 310p. 1994. 975.00 (*0-7889-0112-5*) Frost & Sullivan.

— U. S. Prescription Gastrointestinal Pharmaceutical Markets in a Period of Transition. 1994. 2,495.00 (*0-7889-0064-1*) Frost & Sullivan.

— U. S. Prescription Generic Pharmaceutical Markets. (Quarterly Planning Ser.). 260p. 1993. 3,295.00 (*0-7889-0099-4*) Frost & Sullivan.

— U. S. Prescription Neurological - Psychotherapeutic Pharmaceuticals: R & D Efforts Paying Off. 300p. 1993. 2,295.00 (*1-56753-617-4*) Frost & Sullivan.

— U. S. Prescription Respiratory Pharmaceutical Markets: New Asthma Treatment Guidelines Breathe Life into Industry. 300p. 1994. 2,295.00 (*1-56753-962-9*) Frost & Sullivan.

— U. S. Pressure Sensitive Adhesive Markets: Recycling Technology & Label Applications Lead the Way. 233p. 1993. 3,295.00 (*1-56753-614-X*) Frost & Sullivan.

— U. S. Programmable Logic Controller Markets. 370p. 1994. 2,995.00 (*0-7889-0148-6*) Frost & Sullivan.

— U. S. Protein Ingredients Markets. 281p. 1993. 2,900.00 (*1-56753-516-X*) Frost & Sullivan.

— U. S. Public Data Service Markets: LAN Interconnection, High Bandwidth Applications Fuel Fast-Packet Surge. 340p. 1994. 2,495.00 (*1-56753-964-5*) Frost & Sullivan.

— U. S. Radio Frequency Identification Equipment Markets Demand Fueled by Transportation Industry. 1995. 2, 195.00 (*0-7889-0241-5*) Frost & Sullivan.

— U. S. Radio Paging Equipment & Service Markets: An Economical & Efficient Option for Everyone. 425p. 1994. 2,395.00 (*0-7889-0186-9*, 2748-62) Frost & Sullivan.

— U. S. Rehabilitation Product Markets. 300p. 1994. 1,895. 00 (*0-7889-0048-X*) Frost & Sullivan.

— U. S. Relay Markets: Shift from Conventional to Solid State Technology. 363p. 1994. 1,895.00 (*1-56753-967-X*) Frost & Sullivan.

— U. S. Research Biochemical Markets: Cross-Discipline Applications Multiply Commercial Value of Products. 350p. (Orig.). 1994. 2,995.00 (*1-56753-898-3*) Frost & Sullivan.

— U. S. Residential Security Markets. 214p. 1994. 2,495.00 (*1-56753-938-6*) Frost & Sullivan.

— U. S. Residential Security Product & Service Markets: Increase in Homeowner Investment Promotes Industry Growth. (Orig.). 1993. 2,450.00 (*1-56753-640-9*) Frost & Sullivan.

— U. S. Sales Automation Software Markets: Customizing, Implementation, Training & Services Explode. 300p. 1994. 1,795.00 (*1-56753-992-0*) Frost & Sullivan.

— U. S. Septecemia & Septic Shock Markets: The Search for Therapy Continues: New Agents & Their Potential. 250p. 1994. 2,895.00 (*1-56753-935-1*) Frost & Sullivan.

— U. S. Sexually Transmitted Disease, Diagnostic & Therapeutic Markets. (Orig.). 1994. 2,295.00 (*0-7889-0136-2*) Frost & Sullivan.

— U. S. Small Compressor & Vacuum Pump Markets. 342p. 1995. 2,295.00 (*0-7889-0160-5*) Frost & Sullivan.

— U. S. Specialty Biocide Markets: EPA Regulations Redefine Industry Focus. 510p. 1994. 1,995.00 (*1-56753-997-1*) Frost & Sullivan.

— U. S. Telecommunications Multimedia Markets. 189p. 1994. 2,295.00 (*0-7889-0073-0*) Frost & Sullivan.

— U. S. Telecommunications Network Security & Reliability Equipment & Service Markets. 221p. 1995. 2,495.00 (*0-7889-0178-8*, 2821-60) Frost & Sullivan.

— U. S. Thrombosis Markets: Anticoagulants, Antithrombotics & Thrombolytics: New Drugs, New Indications Expand Market. 290p. 1994. 2,495.00 (*1-56753-957-2*) Frost & Sullivan.

— U. S. Two Way Land Mobile Radio Markets: Traditional Markets Being Affected by Evolving Technologies & Regulatory Conditions. 276p. 1993. 2,900.00 (*1-56753-568-2*) Frost & Sullivan.

— U. S. Uninterruptible Power Supply Markets. 217p. 1993. 2,900.00 (*1-56753-575-5*) Frost & Sullivan.

— U. S. Urology Product Markets: Infection Control in an Aging Population Stimulates Growth. 250p. 1993. 1,995. 00 (*1-56753-619-0*) Frost & Sullivan.

— U. S. Virtual Reality Hardware, Software, System & Service Markets: Current Applications Show Great Promise. 320p. 1993. 2,795.00 (*1-56753-563-1*) Frost & Sullivan.

— U. S. Voc Recovery & Destruction Equipment Markets: Regulations Spark New Acquisition Activity. 210p. 1993. 1,895.00 (*1-56753-600-X*) Frost & Sullivan.

— U. S. Voice Messaging Service Markets. 349p. 1994. 1, 995.00 (*0-7889-0168-0*) Frost & Sullivan.

— U. S. Vxlbus Instrumentation Markets. 207p. 1993. 2,900. 00 (*1-56753-576-3*) Frost & Sullivan.

— U. S. Water Soluble Polymers: Green Thinking Means Growth Despite Overcapacity. 300p. 1993. 2,950.00 (*1-56753-616-6*) Frost & Sullivan.

— U. S. Wire & Cable Markets: Ten Applications & Eight Industries Led by Telecommunications & Consumer Electronics. 488p. 1993. 3,900.00 (*1-56753-611-5*) Frost & Sullivan.

— U. S. Wireless Office Equipment Markets: Anytime, Anywhere Communications. 360p. 1994. 2,295.00 (*0-7889-0094-3*) Frost & Sullivan.

— U. S. Wound Management Markets: The Quest for Less Damaging, More Active Products. 300p. (Orig.). 1994. 2,295.00 (*1-56753-887-8*) Frost & Sullivan.

— Virtual Reality Markets: Hardware, Software, Systems & Services. 320p. Date not set. 2,795.00 (*1-56753-593-3*) Frost & Sullivan.

— Voice Messaging Service Markets. 220p. 1993. 1,695.00 (*1-56753-431-7*) Frost & Sullivan.

— Voice Recognition, Response & Synthesis Markets: Explosive Growth Across All Segments. 284p. 1992. 1, 695.00 (*1-56753-410-4*) Frost & Sullivan.

— West European Industrial Enzyme Markets: New Applications Emerge Out of Changing Technology. 248p. (Orig.). 1993. 3,800.00 (*1-56753-897-5*) Frost & Sullivan.

— West European Market for Fluorochemicals. 443p. 1993. 4,450.00 (*1-56753-554-2*) Frost & Sullivan.

— West European Pulp & Paper Chemical Markets. 322p. 1994. 3,800.00 (*1-56753-598-4*) Frost & Sullivan.

— Western European Market for Chiral Reagents & Instrumentation Markets. 196p. 1993. 4,200.00 (*1-56753-578-X*) Frost & Sullivan.

— Western European Synthetic Adhesive Markets. 342p. 1994. 3,800.00 (*1-56753-975-0*) Frost & Sullivan.

— Western European Thermoplastic Elastomer Markets. 191p. 1993. 4,300.00 (*1-56753-517-8*) Frost & Sullivan.

— Western European Water-Soluble Polymer Markets. 237p. 1994. 3,800.00 (*1-56753-942-4*) Frost & Sullivan.

— Word Diagnostic Imaging Equipment Markets: A Comprehensive Snapshot on Medical Imaging Modalities & Related Products. 570p. 1994. 2,895.00 (*1-56753-987-4*) Frost & Sullivan.

— World Analog & Mix Signal IC Markets. 377p. 1993. 1, 895.00 (*1-56753-473-2*) Frost & Sullivan.

— World Arthritis Treatment Products: Rx, OTC & Prosthetics: OTC Changes Dynamics of Rx Markets. 280p. 1993. 2,295.00 (*1-56753-496-1*) Frost & Sullivan.

— World Audiology Product Markets: Competitors Keep Their Ears to the Ground for Hints of Improving Sales. 310p. 1994. 1,695.00 (*0-7889-0106-0*) Frost & Sullivan.

— World Audiology Product Markets: Consumer Advertising Overcoming the Stigma. 349p. 1992. 1,495. 00 (*1-56753-390-6*) Frost & Sullivan.

— World Barcode Equipment Markets. 410p. 1995. 1,995.00 (*0-7889-0162-1*) Frost & Sullivan.

— World Barcode Equipment Markets: Fast Paybacks, Customer Awareness Creates Recession Proof Growth. 262p. 1993. 1,895.00 (*1-56753-462-7*) Frost & Sullivan.

— World Biomedical Sensor Markets. 250p. 1994. 1,895.00 (*0-7889-0036-6*) Frost & Sullivan.

— World Biomedical Sensor Markets: Cross Contamination & Ease of Use Reshape the Industry. 1992. 1,695.00 (*1-56753-416-3*) Frost & Sullivan.

— World Biomedical Sensor Markets: Cross Contamination & Ease of Use Reshape the Industry. 341p. 1992. 1,695. 00 (*1-56753-422-8*) Frost & Sullivan.

— World Blood Banking; & Plasma Product Markets: Patient & Healthcare Professionals Shape Product Development. 340p. 1994. 1,695.00 (*1-56753-931-9*) Frost & Sullivan.

— World Cancer Therapeutic Markets: Strategic Alliances Globalize the Marketplace. 295p. 1993. 2,495.00 (*1-56753-524-0*) Frost & Sullivan.

— World Cancer Therapeutic Markets by Disease Cite: Accelerated R & D Intensifies Race for Cure. 400p. (Orig.). 1994. 2,895.00 (*1-56753-886-X*) Frost & Sullivan.

— World Cancer Therapeutic Pharmaceuticals Market: Biotech Becomes Big Business. 258p. (Orig.). 1992. 2, 295.00 (*1-56753-063-X*) Frost & Sullivan.

— World Cardiovascular Diagnostic & Therapeutic Equipment Markets: Multi-Billion Dollar Battle, Technology Advances vs Cost Constraints. 313p. (Orig.). 1992. 1,995.00 (*1-56753-043-5*) Frost & Sullivan.

— World Cardiovascular Drug Markets: Primary Prevention Creates Opportunities. 430p. (Orig.). 1994. 2,695.00 (*1-56753-925-4*) Frost & Sullivan.

— World Cell Therapy Markets: Harnessing the Power of the Cell. 1995. 2,895.00 (*0-7889-0193-1*, 5033-52) Frost & Sullivan.

— World Cellular & PCN Telephone, Pager & Accessories Markets: Changes ... Changes ... Changes. 630p. 1992. 1, 695.00 (*1-56753-334-5*) Frost & Sullivan.

— World Clinical Laboratory Instrument Markets: Cost Containment...Consolidation...Point of Care; Report #909-56. 306p. 1994. 2,195.00 (*1-56753-702-2*) Frost & Sullivan.

— World Computer Numerical Controller Market: Waking up to Japanese Manufacturing Expertise. 219p. (Orig.). 1992. 1,495.00 (*1-56753-039-7*) Frost & Sullivan.

— World Computer Numerical Controller Markets: User Interest Sparked by 32-Bit Architecture & Graphics Capabilities. 221p. 1993. 1,695.00 (*1-56753-612-3*) Frost & Sullivan.

— World Contrast Media Markets: New Dynamics in an Evolving Market. (Orig.). 1994. 2,295.00 (*0-7889-0121-4*) Frost & Sullivan.

— World Data Acquisition Boards, Systems & Software: New Entrants Flood the Market. 231p. 1993. 1,895.00 (*1-56753-466-X*) Frost & Sullivan.

— World Dental Product Markets: Esthetics Expand Globally. 313p. 1993. 1,995.00 (*1-56753-528-3*) Frost & Sullivan.

— World Diagnostic Imaging Company Profiles. 478p. (Orig.). 1994. 1,595.00 (*0-7889-0131-1*) Frost & Sullivan.

— World Diagnostic Imaging Contrast Media: Manufacturers Vie for Japanese Market. 216p. 1993. 1, 995.00 (*1-56753-439-2*) Frost & Sullivan.

— World Digital Signal Processor (DSP) Markets: Increasing Price - Performance Ratio Generates New Applications. 250p. (Orig.). 1994. 1,995.00 (*1-56753-894-0*) Frost & Sullivan.

— World Discrete Electronic Active Device Markets: New Opportunities Arise in Telecommunications & Medical Applications. 245p. 1993. 1,495.00 (*1-56753-436-8*) Frost & Sullivan.

— World Discrete Electronic Passive Device Markets: Century-Old Technology Thrives on Leading-Edge Telecommunication Products. 273p. 1992. 1,495.00 (*1-56753-406-6*) Frost & Sullivan.

— World Discrete Manufacturing Software Markets: Shop Floor Goes High Tech - 3 Million Dollar Market Doubles. 248p. 1993. 1,495.00 (*1-56753-420-1*) Frost & Sullivan.

— World Electronic Cleaning Equipment Markets: Spurred by Regulations, North America Leads "Clean" Revolution. 231p. (Orig.). 1992. 1,495.00 (*1-56753-397-3*) Frost & Sullivan.

— World Electronic Data Interchange Market: Countries Trading Partners Press for Cooperation & Standards. 561p. (Orig.). 1992. 1,895.00 (*1-56753-848-7*) Frost & Sullivan.

— World Electronic Switch Markets. 289p. (Orig.). 1994. 1, 995.00 (*0-7889-0093-5*) Frost & Sullivan.

— World Embedded Controller Markets: Industry Goes Mainstream with 386 & Power PC. 370p. 1994. 1,995.00 (*0-7889-0038-2*) Frost & Sullivan.

— World Emerging Sensor Technologies: High Growth Markets Uncovered. 317p. 1993. 1,495.00 (*1-56753-456-2*) Frost & Sullivan.

— World Fetal, Neonatal & Infant Monitor Markets: Manufacturers Push Hi-Tech Products Through One-Stop Shopping. 433p. (Orig.). 1992. 1,995.00 (*1-56753-033-8*) Frost & Sullivan.

— World Fiber Optic Communication Markets: Cable, Transmitters, Connectors, Couplers, Receivers. 244p. 1993. 1,695.00 (*1-56753-463-5*) Frost & Sullivan.

— World Fiber Optic Sensor Markets: Phenomenal Growth Across All Segments by Medical Applications. 335p. 1993. 1,495.00 (*1-56753-435-X*) Frost & Sullivan.

— World Flow Sensor Markets: Moderate Overall Growth Belies High Growth Opportunities. 466p. 1993. 1,695.00 (*1-56753-475-9*) Frost & Sullivan.

— World Frame Relay Markets: Preparing for ATM. 305p. 1993. 1,995.00 (*1-56753-542-9*) Frost & Sullivan.

— World Gastrointestinal Drug Markets: Generic Competition Intensified As Block Buster Drugs Lose Patent Protection. 537p. (Orig.). 1992. 2,295.00 (*1-56753-400-7*) Frost & Sullivan.

— World Gene Therapy Markets: Gene-Based Services & Products to Provide Numerous Commercial Opportunities. (Illus.). 475p. 1994. 2,995.00 (*0-7889-0076-5*) Frost & Sullivan.

— World Geographic Information Systems Software & Service Markets. (Orig.). 1994. 1,995.00 (*0-7889-0134-6*) Frost & Sullivan.

— World Growth Factor Markets: Tissue Applications Poised for Commercialization. 300p. (Orig.). 1993. 2, 495.00 (*1-56753-620-4*) Frost & Sullivan.

— World Human Vaccine Markets: Over 60 Productions: Which Competitors Are Attacking Viruses? 478p. 1993. 2,295.00 (*1-56753-460-0*) Frost & Sullivan.

— World Image Processing & Enhancement Equipment: Clinical Applications Open Market to New Entrants. 287p. 1993. 1,695.00 (*1-56753-849-5*) Frost & Sullivan.

— World Indoor Air Quality Monitoring & Building Control System Markets: Opportunities for Non-Traditional Suppliers. 326p. 1994. 1,895.00 (*0-7889-0034-X*) Frost & Sullivan.

— World Industrial - Broadcast Solid State Camera & System Markets: Picture This...Revenues Double. 322p. 1993. 1,695.00 (*1-56753-438-4*) Frost & Sullivan.

— World Industrial & Scientific Laser Systems Markets: Rebounding Global Economy Eases Price Wars. 538p. 1993. 1,695.00 (*1-56753-446-5*) Frost & Sullivan.

— World Intelligent Materials Handling Markets: Installation of Modular Designs & Integrated Systems on the Rise. 576p. 1993. 1,695.00 (*1-56753-459-7*) Frost & Sullivan.

— World Machine Tool Cutting Tool Markets: Expansion Driven by Innovation: New Materials, New Coatings, New Geometries. 283p. 1992. 1,495.00 (*1-56753-384-1*) Frost & Sullivan.

— World Machine Vision System, Component & Software Markets: Innovative, Affordable & Reliable Solutions Lead Way to Billion Dollar Industry. 389p. (Orig.). 1992. 1,495.00 (*1-56753-376-0*) Frost & Sullivan.

— World Market for Electronic Ceramics: Developments Enable Next Generation Products. 345p. (Orig.). 1992. 1,695.00 (*1-56753-066-4*) Frost & Sullivan.

— World Medical Diagnostic Ultrasound Imaging Equipment Markets at the Forefront of Diagnostic. 1995. 2,495.00 (*0-7889-0247-4*) Frost & Sullivan.

— World Medical Image Management Markets: Minipacs & Facility-to-Facility Teleradiology Offer Cost Effective Solutions. 310p. 1994. 2,495.00 (*0-7889-0082-X*) Frost & Sullivan.

— World Medical Imaging & Therapeutic Immunoconjugate Markets: Competitors Refocusing R&D & Marketing Strategies. 351p. 1994. 2,695.00 (*1-56753-954-8*) Frost & Sullivan.

— World Medical Laser Markets: Manufacturers Focus on Alternate Cites & New Applications. 332p. 1993. 1,995. 00 (*1-56753-440-6*) Frost & Sullivan.

— World Medical Resonance Imaging Markets: Dedicated Imaging Coils Lead Shift to Lower Field Systems. 250p. (Orig.). 1994. 2,495.00 (*0-685-71178-1*) Frost & Sullivan.

— World Memory IC Markets. 386p. 1995. 2,195.00 (*0-7889-0164-8*) Frost & Sullivan.

— World Microdisk Drive & PCMCIA Flash Memory Card Markets: Flash Encroaches on Hard Drives Even as Capacities Increase. 250p. 1994. 1,995.00 (*1-56753-958-0*) Frost & Sullivan.

— World Micromachine & Microstructure Markets: Technology Qualified: After Sensors, the Real Search for Applications Begins. 1992. 1,695.00 (*1-56753-395-7*) Frost & Sullivan.

— World Microscope & Spectrometer Markets: Hyphenate Technologies & Software Enhancements Spawn New Breed of Inspection & Testing Equipment. 427p. 1992. 1,895.00 (*1-56753-393-0*) Frost & Sullivan.

— World Military Microwave Component & Assembly Markets. 213p. (Orig.). 1994. 1,895.00 (*0-7889-0110-9*) Frost & Sullivan.

— World Mobile Data Communications Markets: Market Emerges, Alliances Follow Quickly. 400p. 1994. 1,995. 00 (*0-7889-0013-7*) Frost & Sullivan.

— World Multi-chip Module Markets: From Concept Through Testing Applications Drive the Technology. 288p. (Orig.). 1992. 1,695.00 (*1-56753-053-2*) Frost & Sullivan.

— World Multimedia Application Markets. 370p. 1994. 1, 995.00 (*0-7889-0049-8*) Frost & Sullivan.

— World Multimedia Application Markets: The Complete Market & Sales Targeting Tool. 338p. 1993. 2,495.00 (*1-56753-425-2*) Frost & Sullivan.

— World Multimedia Hardware & Software Markets. (Quarterly Business Planning Ser.). 425p. 1994. 2,995.00 (*0-7889-0020-X*) Frost & Sullivan.

— World Multimedia Hardware & Software Markets: Finally a Definition. 430p. (Orig.). 1992. 1,495.00 (*1-56753-403-1*) Frost & Sullivan.

— World Niche & Specialized Sensor Markets: Growth Potential Lies in Exploring New Applications. 219p. 1993. 1,295.00 (*1-56753-411-2*) Frost & Sullivan.

— World Non-Destructive Test Equipment Markets: Increasing Automation & Integration Represent Wave of the Future. 383p. 1992. 1,495.00 (*1-56753-407-4*) Frost & Sullivan.

— World Nuclear Medical Imaging, NMI, Market: Radiopharmaceutical Applications Drive Double-Digit Growth Despite Cost-Benefit Concerns. 323p. (Orig.). 1992. 2,295.00 (*1-56753-074-5*) Frost & Sullivan.

— World On-Line Transaction Terminal Markets: Communicaiton & Information Technologies Go Retail. 550p. 1993. 1,695.00 (*1-56753-876-2*) Frost & Sullivan.

— World Ophthalmic Pharmaceutical Markets: Technology Driven Products for Shifting Global Economies. 470p. (Orig.). 1994. 2,395.00 (*1-56753-923-8*) Frost & Sullivan.

— World Optical Disk Drive & Media Markets. 1995. 2,995.00 (*0-7889-0190-7*, S177-73) Frost & Sullivan.

— World Orthopedic & Prosthetic Product Markets: Impact of Lifestyles, Demographics & Biomaterials. 627p. 1992. 1,995.00 (*1-56753-386-8*) Frost & Sullivan.

— World OTC Dermatology Pharmaceutical Markets. 1995. 2,295.00 (*0-7889-0196-6*, 960-52) Frost & Sullivan.

— World PBX & Key System Markets. 553p. 1994. 2,295.00 (*0-7889-0021-8*) Frost & Sullivan.

— World PC-Based Instrumentation & Software Markets: Invading the Laboratory & Industrial Environments. 447p. 1992. 1,895.00 (*1-56753-076-1*) Frost & Sullivan.

— World PC Card Markets: PCMCIA Standard Opens the Flood Gates. 250p. 1993. 1,495.00 (*1-56753-448-1*) Frost & Sullivan.

— World PC Card Markets: Peripheral & Flash Cards Byte into Ram Share. 320p. 1994. 1,995.00 (*0-7889-0089-7*) Frost & Sullivan.

— World Pen, Palmtop & Notebook Computer & Peripheral Markets: Solid Profits in Accessories, but Will PDA's Follow? 370p. 1993. 1,995.00 (*1-56753-608-5*) Frost & Sullivan.

— World Prescription Dermatology Markets. 380p. 1994. 2,695.00 (*0-7889-0043-9*) Frost & Sullivan.

— World Pressure Sensor Markets: Fiber Optic & Silicon Micromachine Technologies Usher in New Era of Growth. 340p. 1994. 1,695.00 (*1-56753-982-3*) Frost & Sullivan.

— World Pressure Sensor Markets: Micromachined Applications Rejuvenate Growth. 219p. (Orig.). 1992. 1,495.00 (*1-56753-051-6*) Frost & Sullivan.

— World Process Controller Markets: PC-Based Technology Offers New Opportunity in a Highly Competitive Environment. 320p. 1994. 1,995.00 (*0-7889-0098-6*) Frost & Sullivan.

— World Process Flow Control Markets: Electronics Revolutionizes Values & Accessories, Pumps & Controllers. 168p. (Orig.). 1992. 1,495.00 (*1-56753-050-8*) Frost & Sullivan.

— World Programmable Logic Controller & Software Markets: Downsizing, Eroding Brand Loyalty & New Entrants Challenge Leader. 300p. 1992. 1,495.00 (*1-56753-391-4*) Frost & Sullivan.

— World Programmable Logic Controller & Software Markets: Software & Service Become Key Industry Issues. 298p. 1993. 1,695.00 (*1-56753-613-1*) Frost & Sullivan.

— World Proximity & Displacement Sensor Markets: Applications Boom with the Advent of Smaller, Smarter & Faster Sensors. 340p. 1993. 1,495.00 (*1-56753-433-3*) Frost & Sullivan.

— World Recorder, Datalogger & Indicator Markets: Niche Recorder Segments Counter PC-Based Data Acquisition. 297p. (Orig.). 1992. 1,495.00 (*1-56753-038-9*) Frost & Sullivan.

— World Renal & Hemodialysis Equipment & Supplies Market: U. S. Struggles with Cost Constraints While Europe & Japan Expand. 309p. 1992. 1,895.00 (*1-56753-383-3*) Frost & Sullivan.

— World Renal & Hemodialysis Equipment & Supply Markets: Cost Containment Pressures Influence World Markets. 347p. 1994. 1,995.00 (*0-7889-0015-3*) Frost & Sullivan.

— World Satellite Communications Equipment Markets: VSAT 7 Mobile Applications Unleash SatCom. 394p. 1993. 1,695.00 (*1-56753-437-6*) Frost & Sullivan.

— World Satellite Communications in Developing Countries (Wordlwide) 397p. 1992. 3,700.00 (*1-56753-877-0*, W1597) Frost & Sullivan.

— World Semiconductor Production Equipment Markets: Increased Productivity Justifies Higher Prices, Industry Profits. 300p. 1994. 1,995.00 (*1-56753-948-3*) Frost & Sullivan.

— World SMT Manufacturing Equipment Markets: End-User Demands Prompt Explosive Growth - Test & Inspection Revenues Double. 315p. 1993. 1,695.00 (*0-685-66576-3*) Frost & Sullivan.

— World Standard & Special Machine Tool Markets: Competitors Move into New Segments. 444p. 1993. 2,395.00 (*1-56753-504-6*) Frost & Sullivan.

— World Switching Power Supply Markets: European Standards, New Technologies & Increased Defense Cuts Redirect the Markets. 349p. 1993. 1,895.00 (*1-56753-484-8*) Frost & Sullivan.

— World Telecom & Datacom Test Equipment Markets: Fiber, TIMS, & PC-Based Instrumentation Stimulate Growth. 432p. (Orig.). 1992. 1,895.00 (*1-56753-067-2*) Frost & Sullivan.

— World Telecommunications Services Database 1994. 1994. 595.00 (*1-56753-981-5*) Frost & Sullivan.

— World Teleconferencing System & Service Markets: Look Who's Talking. 410p. 1993. 1,695.00 (*1-56753-450-3*) Frost & Sullivan.

— World Test & Measurement Equipment Markets: Multiple Trends Converge to Promote Impressive ATE & Time Growth. 288p. (Orig.). 1992. 1,895.00 (*1-56753-032-X*) Frost & Sullivan.

— World Test & Measurement Equipment Markets: The Industry Makes a Comeback As Technology Advances & New Markets Emerge. 630p. 1994. 1,695.00 (*1-56753-947-5*) Frost & Sullivan.

— World Transducer-Sensor Technology Assessment: A Qualitative Analysis of the State of the Art Based on More Than 500 Interviews with Industry Experts. 342p. 1992. 1,495.00 (*1-56753-392-2*) Frost & Sullivan.

— World Ultrasound Imaging Markets: Manufacturers Focus on Developing Niche Applications. 365p. 1993. 2,295.00 (*1-56753-618-2*) Frost & Sullivan.

— World Uninterruptible Power Supply Markets: Increased Awareness of Data & Equipment Protection Sustains Growth. 336p. 1994. 2,195.00 (*1-56753-972-6*) Frost & Sullivan.

— World Uninterruptible Power Supply Markets: Mission Critical Applications & Fierce Competition Characterize Markets. 271p. (Orig.). 1992. 1,895.00 (*1-56753-028-1*) Frost & Sullivan.

— World Voice Processing Application & End-User Markets: Technologies Merge, Obstacles Recede. 460p. 1994. 1,895.00 (*1-56753-963-7*) Frost & Sullivan.

— World Welding Equipment Markets: Automation: the Future Direction. 320p. 1993. 1,495.00 (*1-56753-442-2*) Frost & Sullivan.

— World Workstation Markets: Proven Applications, with New Pentium-Power PC Chips, Attract New Users. 306p. 1993. 1,995.00 (*1-56753-609-3*) Frost & Sullivan.

— World Wound Closure Products: Staplers Invade Suture Markets. 345p. 1992. 1,695.00 (*1-56753-387-6*) Frost & Sullivan.

— World X-Ray & Computed Tomography Equipment Markets: Manufacturers Exploit Niche Opportunities & Polarized Markets. 293p. (Orig.). 1992. 1,895.00 (*1-56753-041-9*) Frost & Sullivan.

— World 3-D Diagnostic Medical Imaging Equipment & Software Markets: Dramatic Global Expansion Led by Clinical Applications & Ultrasound Technology. 250p. 1992. 1,995.00 (*1-56753-413-9*) Frost & Sullivan.

— Worldwide Telecom Services Markets: Comprehensive Forecast of Basic, Mobile, Private Line, & Value-Added Services by Five Geographic Regions. 305p. (Orig.). 1992. 1,495.00 (*1-56753-068-0*) Frost & Sullivan.

— Wound Management Products in Europe. 300p. 1993. 3,900.00 (*1-56753-500-3*) Frost & Sullivan.

*__Market Intelligence Staff, contrib.__ European Laser System Markets. 360p. 1994. 3,950.00 (*0-7889-0109-5*) Frost & Sullivan.

Market Knowledge, Inc. Staff, ed. U. S. S. R. Business Guide & Directory, 1991. 800p. 1991. lib. bdg. 395.00 (*0-9624436-5-4*) Triumph Bks.

Market, M. Frances, tr. see Gruen, Anselm.

Market Research Staff. Sports-Fitness-Leisure Market. (Fact File Ser.). 50p. 1990. pap. 37.50 (*0-87005-723-5*) Fairchild.

Marketdata Enterprises, Inc. Staff. Dieter Beware! The Complete Consumer Guide to Weight Loss Programs. 88p. 1991. pap. 19.95 (*0-9632529-0-9*) Mktdata Ent.

Marketing Consultants International Inc. Staff. Who, What & Where in Communications Security. Nye, J. Michael, ed. (Illus.). 124p. 1986. pap. 75.00 (*0-937195-25-1*) Mktg Consult Intl.

Marketing Graphics Corporation Staff & Lewis, Jan. Using IBM PC Storyboard: The Guide to Applications. 320p. (C). 1988. pap. 24.95 (*0-685-19365-9*) P-H.

Marketing, V. G. The Corval Formula. (Illus.). 56p. 1994. 14.95 (*0-9641184-0-8*) V G Mktg.

Markevich, A. P. Russian-Ukrainian-Latin Zoological Dictionary. 410p. 1983. 39.95 (*0-8288-2393-6*, M 15541) Fr & Eur.

Markevitch, Dimitry. Cello Story. Seder, Florence, tr. (Illus.). 192p. (Orig.). 1984. pap. 13.95 (*0-87487-406-8*) Summy-Birchard.

— The Solo Cello: A Bibliography of the Unaccompanied Violoncello Literature. LC 89-23355. (Reference Books in Music: No. 12). x, 113p. 1989. pap. 14.95 (*0-914913-11-5*) Fallen Leaf.

Markewich, Reese. Definitive Bibliography of Harmonically Sophisticated Tonal Music. LC 77-104898. 1970. pap. 4.95 (*0-9600160-2-3*) Markewich.

— Inside Outside: Substitute Harmony in Modern Jazz & Pop Music. LC 67-7697. 102p. 1967. pap. 4.95 (*0-9600160-0-7*) Markewich.

— The New Expanded Bibliography of Jazz Compositions Based on the Chord Progressions of Standard Tunes. LC 74-84745. 1974. pap. 4.95 (*0-9600160-5-8*) Markewich.

*__Markey.__ Italo Calvino. 1998. text ed. 22.95 (*0-8057-4510-6*) Macmillan.

Markey, Barb & Hunt, Tad. Airways: Rising to the Challenge of Managing COPD. Allen, Susan D. & Holloran, Colleen A., eds. (Illus.). 56p. Date not set. pap. text ed. 3.50 (*0-916999-13-0*) HERC Inc.

Markey, Christian E. California Family Law: Practice & Procedure, 7 vols. 1978. Updates. ring bd. write for info. (*0-8205-1179-X*) Bender.

Markey, Daniel J., Jr. & Donnelly, Mary Q. Criminal Law for Paralegals. LC 93-17337. 1994. text ed. 28.95 (*0-538-70861-1*) S-W Pub.

Markey, Frances V. Imaginative Behavior of Preschool Children. LC 75-35075. (Studies in Play & Games). 1976. reprint ed. 15.95 (*0-405-07925-7*) Ayer.

*__Markey, Janice.__ Journey into the Red Eye: The Poetry of Sylvia Plath - a Critique. 1994. pap. 14.99 (*0-7043-4316-9*) Interlink Pub.

Markey, Karen. Subject Access to Visual Resources Collections: A Model for the Computer Construction of Thematic Catalogs. LC 86-7658. (New Directions in Information Management Ser.: No. 11). 209p. 1986. text ed. 49.95 (*0-313-24031-0*, MSI/) Greenwood.

— Subject Searching in Library Catalogs: Before & After the Introduction of Online Catalogs. LC 84-7226. (Library, Information, & Computer Science Ser.: No. 4). (Illus.). 192p. (Orig.). 1984. pap. 21.00 (*0-933418-54-X*) OCLC Online Comp.

Markey, Kevin & Sutton, Caroline. More How Do They Do That? LC 92-22201. 1993. 18.00 (*0-688-10129-1*) Morrow.

Markey, Penny, ed. see Wilmshurst, Ann.

Markey, Ronald, jt. auth. see Teglovic, Eugene.

Markey, T. L. & Greppin, John A., eds. When Worlds Collide: The Bellagio Papers. xii, 478p. 1989. pap. 65.00 (*0-89720-090-X*) Karoma.

Markey, T. L., jt. ed. see Shevoroshkin, Vitalij V.

Markey, T. L., et al. Germanic & Its Dialects: A Grammar of Protogermanic, Vol. 3. 525p. 1977. 100.00x (*90-272-0981-2*) Benjamins North Am.

Markey, Thomas L. Frisian. (Contributions to the Sociology of Language Ser.: No. 30). 1979. text ed. 70.80 (*90-279-3128-3*) Mouton.

Markfield, Wallace. Multiple Orgasms. limited ed. 1977. 35.00 (*0-89723-006-X*) Bruccoli.

— To an Early Grave. 1994. lib. bdg. 24.95x (*1-56849-402-5*) Buccaneer Bks.

Markgraf, Carl. J. M. Barrie: An Annotated Secondary Bibliography. LC 89-84405. (British Authors, 1880-1920 Ser.). 440p. (C). 1989. 35.00 (*0-944318-03-7*) ELT Pr.

Markgraf, J. F., ed. Collimators for Thermal Neutron Radiography: An Overview. (C). 1987. lib. bdg. 69.50 (*90-277-2568-3*) Kluwer Ac.

*__Markgraf, Richard.__ Diversions: Fifty Comic Short Stories. LC 95-90221. 128p. (Orig.). 1995. pap. 8.95 (*0-9646025-0-4*) WMKB Ent.

Markgraf, Vera, jt. ed. see Diaz, Henry R.

Markgraf, Vera, et al. Pollen Flora of Argentina: Modern Spore & Pollen Types of Pteridophyta, Gymnospermae, & Angiospermae with a Spore Morphologic Key & Photomicrographs of the Genera of the Fuego-Patagonian Pteridophyta by Marta A. Morbelli. LC 78-3770. (Illus.). 220p. reprint ed. pap. 62.70 (*0-7837-5051-X*, 2044729) Bks Demand.

*__Markham.__ Managing Stress. 1995. pap. text ed. 11.95 (*1-85230-631-9*) Element MA.

*__Markham, Adam.__ A Brief History of Pollution. LC 94-22231. 1994. text ed. 39.95 (*0-312-12368-X*) St Martin.

— A Brief History of Pollution. LC 94-22231. 1995. pap. write for info. (*0-312-12369-8*) St Martin.

— Brief History Pollution. 1993. 16.95 (*1-85383-213-8*, Pub. by Erthscan Pubns UK) Island Pr.

— The Environment. (World Issues Ser.). (Illus.). 48p. (J). (gr. 5 up). 1988. 13.95 (*0-685-58320-1*); lib. bdg. 18.60 (*0-86592-286-1*) Rourke Corp.

Markham, Andrew. What Happened in History? 144p. 1989. per. 14.95 (*0-8403-5645-5*) Kendall-Hunt.

*__Markham, Ann.__ The Cat with a Black Ring. 1995. 7.95 (*0-533-11337-7*) Vantage.

Markham, Beryl. The Illustrated West with the Night. Sunshine, Linda, ed. LC 94-11150. 1994. 29.95 (*1-55670-385-6*) Stewart Tabori & Chang.

Markham, Bonnie J. The Nitty-Gritty for Ministers' Wives. LC 88-11750. (Illus.). 208p. (Orig.). 1988. pap. 6.99 (*0-932581-34-X*) Word Aflame.

Markham, C. B., jt. auth. see Winsor, Justin.

Markham, Clements. Antarctic Obsession. Holland, Clive, ed. & intro. by. (Antarctic Classics Ser.). (Illus.). 208p. (C). 1989. pap. 51.00 (*0-948285-09-5*, Pub. by Archival Facs UK) St Mut.

— Markham in Peru: The Travels of Clements R. Markham, 1852-1853. Blanchard, Peter, ed. (Illus.). 168p. (Orig.). 1991. text ed. 25.00 (*0-292-71132-8*); pap. 10.95 (*0-292-75127-3*) U of Tex Pr.

Markham, Clements R. History of Peru. 1976. lib. bdg. 69.95 (*0-8490-1983-4*) Gordon Pr.

— Incas of Peru. LC 79-84877. (Illus.). reprint ed. 47.50 (*0-404-04188-4*) AMS Pr.

— The War Between Peru & Chile 1879-1882. 1976. lib. bdg. 59.95 (*0-8490-2805-1*) Gordon Pr.

Markham, Clements R., ed. Book of the Knowledge of All the Kingdoms, Lands & Lordships That Are in the World. (Hakluyt Society Works Ser.: No. 2, Vol. 29). (Illus.). 1972. reprint ed. 26.00 (*0-8115-0346-1*) Periodicals Srv.

— Early Spanish Voyages to the Strait of Magellan. (Hakluyt Society Works Ser.: No. 2, Vol. 28). (Illus.). 1972. reprint ed. 45.00 (*0-8115-0345-3*) Periodicals Srv.

— The Guanches of Tenerife, the Holy Image of Our Lady of Candelaria, with the Spanish Conquest & Settlement, by the Friar Alonso de Espinosa. (Hakluyt Society Ser.: No. 2, Vol. 21). (Illus.). 1969. reprint ed. 40.00 (*0-8115-0341-0*) Periodicals Srv.

— The Voyages of Pedro Fernandez de Quiros, 1595-1606, 2 vols. in 1. (Hakluyt Society Works Ser.: No. 2, Vols. 14 & 15). (Illus.). 1974. reprint ed. 99.00 (*0-8115-0336-4*) Periodicals Srv.

— The War of Quito, by Pedro de Cieza de Leon, & Other Inca Documents. (Hakluyt Society Works Ser.: No. 2, Vol. 31). 1974. reprint ed. 35.00 (*0-8115-0347-X*) Periodicals Srv.

Markham, Clements R., ed. see De Gamboa, Pedro S.

Markham-David, Sally. Hands & Feet. LC 93-28978. (Voyages Ser.). (Illus.). (J). 1994. 4.25 (*0-383-03746-8*) SRA Schl Grp.

— It Takes All Kinds. LC 93-21246. (Voyages Ser.). (Illus.). (J). 1994. 4.25 (*0-383-03753-0*) SRA Schl Grp.

— Mouths & Noses. LC 93-29008. (Illus.). (J). 1994. 4.25 (*0-383-03764-6*) SRA Schl Grp.

— The Secrets of a Garden. LC 93-29003. (Voyages Ser.). (Illus.). (J). 1994. 4.25 (*0-383-03773-5*) SRA Schl Grp.

— Tail Tales. LC 93-6631. (J). 1994. pap. write for info. (*0-383-03718-2*) SRA Schl Grp.

Markham, Dewey, Jr. Wine Basics: A Quick & Easy Guide. LC 92-27315. 208p. 1993. pap. text ed. 12.95 (*0-471-58258-1*) Wiley.

Markham, Doyle. Llamas Are the Ultimate: Training, Feeding, Packing, Hunting, Fishing & Care. LC 90-92191. (Illus.). 292p. (Orig.). 1990. pap. 14.95 (*0-9628326-0-X*) Snake Riv Llamas.

Markham, E. A., ed. Hinterland: Caribbean Poetry from the West Indies & Britain. LC 89-82062. 336p. (Orig.). 1990. 40.00 (*1-85224-086-5*, Pub. by Bloodaxe Bks UK); pap. 21.00 (*1-85224-087-3*, Pub. by Bloodaxe Bks UK) Dufour.

Markham, Edwin. Songs & Stories, Selected & Annotated. 1977. 31.95 (*0-8369-4268-X*, 6066) Ayer.

Markham, Edwin, et al. Children in Bondage. LC 76-89753. (American Labor, from Conspiracy to Collective Bargaining Ser., No. 1). 411p. 1974. reprint ed. 25.95 (*0-405-02140-2*) Ayer.

Markham, Felix M. Napoleon. (Illus.). 1989. pap. 4.50 (*0-451-62653-2*, ME2273, Ment) NAL-Dutton.

Markham, George. Guns of the Elite: Special Forces Firearms, 1940 to the Present. 2nd ed. (Illus.). 176p. 1995. 29.95 (*1-85409-198-0*, Pub. by Arms & Armour UK) Sterling.

— Guns of the Wild West: Firearms of the American Frontier 1849-1917. (Illus.). 160p. 1993. pap. 19.95 (*1-85409-197-2*) Sterling.

— The Markham Method: Twenty Thousand Dollars in 20 Days. (Illus.). 74p. 1988. pap. 19.95 (*1-56610-003-8*) Data Comms Grp.

Markham, Gervase. The English Housewife. Best, Michael R., ed. (C). 1986. text ed. 49.95 (*0-7735-0582-2*, Pub. by McGill CN) U of Toronto Pr.

— English Housewife. 1994. pap. 19.95 (*0-7735-1103-2*, Pub. by McGill CN) U of Toronto Pr.

*__Markham, Gretchen.__ Dempsey's Hot Summer: The July Adventure of a Cape Cod Dog. LC 95-76153. (Illus.). 30p. (Orig.). (J). (gr. 1-3). 1995. pap. 9.95 (*1-887146-01-6*) Art Works.

— A Gift for Dempsey: The Christmas Adventure of a Cape Cod Dog. LC 95-94230. (Illus.). 30p. (Orig.). (J). (gr. 1-3). 1995. pap. 9.95 (*1-887146-00-8*) Art Works.

— I Never Promised to Tell You Everything. 1994. 14.95 (*0-533-10752-0*) Vantage.

— Suddenly a Widow. 1990. 10.95 (*0-533-08850-X*) Vantage.

Markham, Hugh. Scale Model Aircraft from Vac-Form Kits. 1980. 45.00 (*0-905418-34-4*, Pub. by Gresham Bks UK) St Mut.

Markham, Ian S. Plurality & Christian Ethics. (New Studies in Christian Ethics: No. 4). 229p. (C). 1994. 54.95 (*0-521-45328-3*) Cambridge U Pr.

*__Markham, Ian S., ed. & intro.__ A World Religions Reader. (Illus.). 416p. (C). 1996. write for info. (*0-631-18239-X*); pap. write for info. (*0-631-18242-X*) Blackwell Pubs.

Markham, James J., ed. Medical Aspects of Claims. LC 90-86334. 314p. (C). 1991. pap. 26.00 (*0-89462-060-6*) IIA.

— Principles of Workers Compensation Claims. LC 90-86333. 229p. (C). 1992. pap. text ed. 26.00 (*0-89462-059-2*) IIA.

— Property Loss Adjusting, 2 vols., Set. LC 90-80137. (C). 1990. pap. 24.00 (*0-89462-050-9*) IIA.

Markham, James J., et al. The Claims Environment. LC 93-71086. 423p. (C). 1993. pap. text ed. 35.00 (*0-89462-078-9*) IIA.

Markham, Jerald H. The Botetourt Artillery. (Virginia Regimental Histories Ser.). (Illus.). 95p. 1987. 19.95 (*0-318-32502-0*) H E Howard.

Markham, Jerry W. Commodities Regulation: Fraud, Manipulation & Other Claims, 2 vols., Set. LC 87-12979. (Securities Law Ser.). 1987. ring bd. 250.00 (*0-87632-552-5*) Clark Boardman Callaghan.

— The History of Commodity Futures Trading & Its Regulation. 320p. 1986. text ed. 75.00 (*0-275-92313-4*, C2313, Praeger Pubs) Greenwood.

*__Markham, Jerry W. & Hazen, Thomas L.__ Broker-Dealer Operations under Securities & Commodities Law: Financial Responsibility, Credit Regulation, Customer Protection, 2 vols., Set. (Securities Ser.). 1995. ring bd. write for info. (*0-614-06263-2*) Clark Boardman Callaghan.

Markham, John. The Beverley Arms: The Story of a Hotel. (C). 1989. text ed. 35.00 (*0-948929-00-6*) St Mut.

— Final Class. (C). 1989. text ed. 35.00 (*0-948929-38-3*) St Mut.

— Friary Families. (C). 1989. text ed. 35.00 (*0-948929-03-0*) St Mut.

— Hunting Scenes. (C). 1989. text ed. 35.00 (*0-948929-20-0*) St Mut.

— Keep the Home Fires Burning. (C). 1989. text ed. 40.00 (*0-948929-14-6*) St Mut.

— The Old Tiger Inn, Beverley. (C). 1989. text ed. 35.00 (*0-948929-15-4*) St Mut.

— Streets of Hedon. (C). 1989. text ed. 35.00 (*0-948929-24-3*) St Mut.

— Streets of Hull. (C). 1989. text ed. 35.00 (*0-948929-43-X*) St Mut.

— Streets of Hull: A History of Their Names. (C). 1989. text ed. 35.00 (*0-948929-07-3*) St Mut.

An Asterisk (*) at the beginning of an entry indicates that the title is appearing in BIP for the first time.

— Successful Business Communication. 201p. 1978. pap. 55.00 (*0-900886-21-8*, Pub. by Witherby & Co UK) St Mut.

Markham, John J. E., II, jt. auth. see Krietzberg, Ellen.

Markham, K. R. Techniques of Flavonoid Identification. (Biological Techniques Ser.). 1982. text ed. 66.00 (*0-12-472680-1*) Acad Pr.

Markham, Lois. Discoveries That Changed Science. (Twenty Events Ser.). (Illus.). 48p. (J). (gr. 4-8). 1994. lib. bdg. 22.80 (*0-8114-4936-X*) Raintree Steck-V.

— Helen Keller. LC 92-24942. (First Bks.). (Illus.). 64p. (J). (gr. 5-8). 1993. lib. bdg. 13.93 (*0-531-20104-X*) Watts.

— Inventions That Changed Modern Life. LC 93-17022. (Twenty Events Ser.). (Illus.). 48p. (J). (gr. 5-7). 1993. lib. bdg. 22.80 (*0-8114-4930-0*) Raintree Steck-V.

— Theodore Roosevelt. (World Leaders - Past & Present Ser.). (Illus.). 112p. (YA). (gr. 5 up). 1985. lib. bdg. 17.95 (*0-87754-553-7*) Chelsea Hse.

— Theodore Roosevelt. LC 90-48981. (American Cavalcade Ser.). (Illus.). 96p. (J). (gr. 6-10). 1991. lib. bdg. 9.95 (*1-55905-098-5*) Marshall Cavendish.

Markham, M. Roland. Alcar, the Captive Creole. LC 77-170701. (Black Heritage Library Collection). 1977. reprint ed. 21.95 (*0-8369-8891-4*) Ayer.

Markham, Marion M. The April Fool's Day Mystery. 64p. (J). 1993. pap. 3.50 (*0-380-71716-6*, Camelot Young) Avon.

— The April Fool's Day Mystery. LC 90-41318. (Illus.). 48p. (J). (gr. 2-6). 1991. 13.95 (*0-395-56235-X*) HM.

— The Birthday Party Mystery. 64p. (J). (gr. 1-4). 1990. reprint ed. pap. 2.95 (*0-380-70968-6*, Camelot Young) Avon.

— The Christmas Present Mystery. (Illus.). 64p. (J). 1990. pap. 2.95 (*0-380-70966-X*, Camelot) Avon.

— The Halloween Candy Mystery. 64p. (J). (gr. 1-4). 1990. reprint ed. pap. 2.95 (*0-380-70965-1*, Camelot Young) Avon.

— The St. Patrick's Day Shamrock Mystery. LC 94-36716. (J). 1995. 12.95 (*0-395-72137-7*) HM.

— The Thanksgiving Day Parade Mystery. (Illus.). 64p. (J). 1990. pap. 2.95 (*0-380-70967-8*, Camelot) Avon.

— The Valentine's Day Mystery. LC 92-8391. (Illus.). 48p. (J). (gr. 2-5). 1992. 13.95 (*0-395-61589-5*) HM.

Markham, R., et al, eds. Modification of Cells. LC 74-81326. 350p. 1975. 96.50 (*0-444-10699-5*, North Holland) Elsevier.

Markham, Robert. Colonel Sun. 1993. mass mkt. 4.99 (*0-06-100568-1*, Harp PBks) HarpC.

Markham, Sara. Workers, Women, & Afro-Americans: Images of the United States in German Travel Literature, from 1923 to 1933. (American University Studies: Germanic Languages & Literature: Ser. I, Vol. 45). 317p. 1986. text ed. 49.90 (*0-8204-0266-4*) P Lang Pubs.

Markham, Sydney F. Climate & the Energy of Nations. LC 77-10234. 248p. reprint ed. 42.50 (*0-404-16214-2*) AMS Pr.

*__Markham, Ursula.__ Creating a Positive Self-Image: Simple Techniques to Transform Your Life. 1995. pap. text ed. 10.95 (*1-85230-622-X*) Element MA.

— Elements of Visualization. 1989. pap. 9.95 (*1-85230-076-0*) Element MA.

— Hypnosis. (Alternative Health Ser.). (Illus.). 128p. 1993. pap. 12.95 (*0-8048-1835-5*) C E Tuttle.

— Life Scripts: How to 'Talk' to Yourself for Positive Results. LC 93-44410. 1994. pap. 12.95 (*1-85230-432-4*) Element MA.

— Living with Change: Positive Techniques for Transforming Your Life. 1993. pap. 11.95 (*1-85230-380-8*) Element MA.

— Memory Power: How to Improve Your Ability to Learn & Remember. 160p. 1994. pap. 15.95 (*0-09-177578-7*, Vermilion) Trafalgar.

— Women under Pressure: A Practical Guide for Today's Woman. LC 93-16174. (Orig.). 1990. pap. 11.95 (*1-85230-138-4*) Element MA.

— Your Four Point Plan for Life: How to Achieve a Balance Between the Physical, Emotional, Mental & Spiritual Aspects of Ourselves. (Illus.). 144p. 1991. pap. 12.95 (*1-85230-212-7*) Element MA.

*__Markham, William.__ Autobiography of William Colfax Markham. (American Autobiography Ser.). 241p. 1995. reprint ed. lib. bdg. 79.00 (*0-7812-8586-0*) Rprt Serv.

Markham, William T. A Consumer's Guide to Social Research. 128p. 1994. per., pap. text ed. 17.45 (*0-8403-6500-4*) Kendall-Hunt.

Markham, William T., jt. auth. see Simerson, Byron K.

Markholt, Ottilie, ed. To Live in Dignity: Pierce County Labor, 1883-1989. (Illus.). (Orig.). 1989. pap. 10.00 (*0-9624071-0-0*) Pierce Cty Labor.

Marki, Ivan. The Trial of the Poet: An Interpretation of the First Edition of "Leaves of Grass" LC 76-18792. 1976. text ed. 46.50 (*0-231-03984-0*) Col U Pr.

Marki, L. & Weigandt, R., eds. Radical Theory. 754p. 1986. 107.75 (*0-444-86765-1*) Elsevier.

Marki, L. & Wiegandt, R., eds. Theory of Radicals. (Colloquia Mathematica Societatis Janos Bolyai Ser.: Vol. 61). 310p. 1993. 165.75 (*0-444-81528-7*, North Holland) Elsevier.

Marki, Susan R. Derivative Financial Products. 224p. 1991. 45.00 (*0-88730-455-9*) Harper Busn.

Markides, Kyriacos C. Fire in the Heart: Healers, Sages & Mystics. 320p. 1992. pap. 12.95 (*0-14-019285-9*, Arkana) Viking Penguin.

— Homage to the Sun. 1988. pap. 10.95 (*0-14-019024-4*, Penguin Bks) Viking Penguin.

— Magus of Strovolos. 1989. pap. 11.00 (*0-14-019034-1*, Penguin Bks) Viking Penguin.

— Riding with the Lion: In Search of Mystical Christianity. 384p. 1995. 24.95 (*0-670-85780-7*, Arkana) Viking Penguin.

Markides, Kyriacos C., ed. Aging & Health: Perspectives on Gender, Race, Ethnicity, & Class. (Focus Editions Ser.: Vol. 104). 288p. (C). 1989. text ed. 49.95 (*0-8039-3206-5*); pap. text ed. 24.95 (*0-8039-3207-3*) Sage.

Markides, Kyriacos C. & Cooper, Cary L. Retirement in Industrialized Societies: Social, Psychological & Health Factors. 331p. 1987. text ed. 170.00 (*0-471-91040-6*) Wiley.

Markides, Kyriacos C. & Mindel, Charles S. Aging & Ethnicity. LC 86-13910. (Library of Social Research: Vol. 163). 256p. (Orig.). (C). 1987. text ed. 49.95 (*0-8039-2728-2*); pap. text ed. 24.95 (*0-8039-2729-0*) Sage.

Markides, Kyriacos C., et al. Aging Stress & Health. 290p. 1989. text ed. 101.50 (*0-471-92157-2*) Wiley.

Markides, Kyriakos S. & Cooper, Cary L., eds. Retirement in Industrialized Societies: Social, Psychological, & Health Factors. LC 86-19016. 343p. reprint ed. pap. 97.80 (*0-7837-4766-7*, 2044520) Bks Demand.

Markie, Peter J. A Professor's Duties: Ethical Issues in College Teaching. (Issues in Academic Ethics Ser.). 224p. (C). 1994. lib. bdg. 54.50 (*0-8476-7951-9*); pap. text ed. 21.95 (*0-8476-7952-7*) Rowman.

Markiewicz, Dana. The Mexican Revolution & the Limits of Agrarian Reform, 1915-1946. LC 93-12003. 216p. 1993. lib. bdg. 40.00 (*1-55587-321-9*) Lynne Rienner.

Markiewicz, David. Fortune in the Desert. (Illus.). 28p. 1984. pap. 8.95 (*0-913814-22-9*) Nevada Pubns.

Markin, Carole. Bad Dates: Celebrities & Other Talented Types Reveal Their Worst Nights Out. 256p. 1990. pap. 9.95 (*0-8065-1158-3*, Citadel Pr) Carol Pub Group.

Markin, Dennis L. Through the Fire: A Collection of Poems. 1993. 8.95 (*0-533-10148-4*) Vantage.

Markin, Ed & Beloit, Christian. Skidmarks in the Sky: An Irreverent Look at Aviation History. Sload, Pamela, ed. LC 85-807. (Illus.). 152p. (Orig.). 1986. pap. 4.95 (*0-9615223-0-5*) Flaming Hooker Pr.

Markin, R. E. The Alzheimer's Cope Book: The Complete Care Manual for Patients & Their Families. 1992. pap. 7.95 (*0-8065-1370-5*, Citadel Pr) Carol Pub Group.

Marking, L. L. & Kimerke, R. A., eds. Aquatic Toxicology: 2nd Conference- STP 667. 403p. 1979. 37.75 (*0-8031-0279-8*, 667, 04-667000-16) ASTM.

Markish, Ester. Stol Dolgoe Vozvrashchenie. LC 84-60572. (Illus.). 320p. (Orig.). (RUS.). 1989. pap. 22.00 (*0-89830-084-3*) Russica Pubs.

Markish, Shimon. Erasmus & the Jews. Olcott, Anthony, tr. LC 85-16454. 1986. lib. bdg. 25.00 (*0-226-50590-1*) U Ch Pr.

Markison, Robert & Kilgore, Eugene, eds. The Injured Hand. (Illus.). 256p. 1990. 55.00 (*0-8151-5746-0*, QMJ-1, Yr Bk Med Pubs) Mosby Yr Bk.

Markisz, John A. Musculoskeletal Imaging. 1991. 156.00 (*0-316-54613-5*) Little.

Markisz, John A. & Levine, Martin P. Applied Contemporary Chemistry. 3rd ed. (Illus.). 152p. 1989. 13.95 (*0-89529-406-0*) Avery Pub.

Markisz, John A., jt. auth. see Aquilia, Michael G.

Markisz, John A., jt. auth. see Knowles, James R.

Markisz, John A., jt. auth. see Zirinsky, Kenneth.

Markisz, John A., et al. MRI Atlas of the Pelvis: Normal Anatomy & Pathology. LC 92-14015. (Illus.). 248p. 1993. 135.00 (*0-683-05557-7*) Williams & Wilkins.

Markko, K., et al, eds. Columbia Poetry Review, No. 4. (Orig.). (C). 1991. pap. text ed. 8.00 (*0-932026-25-7*) Columbia College Chi.

Markland, jt. auth. see Pirkle.

Markland, Cecily, ed. see Deaton, Dennis R.

Markland, Robert D. Topics in Management Science. 3rd ed. 847p. 1989. teacher ed write for info. (*0-471-50100-X*); Net. text ed. write for info. (*0-471-61786-5*) Wiley.

Markland, Robert E. & Sweigart, James R. Quantitative Methods: Applications to Managerial Decision Making. LC 87-2025. 560p. 1987. Net. text ed. write for info. (*0-471-87885-5*) Wiley.

— Quantitative Methods: Applications to Managerial Decision Making. LC 87-2025. 560p. 1990. teacher ed 58.00 (*0-471-62445-4*) Wiley.

*__Markland, Robert E., et al.__ Operations Management: Concepts in Manufacturing & Services. LC 94-30524. 800p. 1994. text ed. 65.25 (*0-314-04398-5*) West Pub.

*__Markle.__ Outside & Inside You. (Illus.). (J). 1996. pap. 4.95 (*0-689-71896-9*, Aladdin Paperbacks) S&S Childrens.

— Science in a Bottle. 1995. pap. (*0-590-47595-9*) Scholastic Inc.

Markle, Allan, jt. auth. see Rinn, Roger C.

Markle, Donald E. Spies & Spymasters of the Civil War. LC 93-36068. 235p. 1994. write for info. (*0-7818-0227-X*) Hippocrene Bks.

*__Markle, Gerald E.__ Gray Zone: Meditations on the Holocaust. 128p. (C). 1995. text ed. 39.50x (*0-7914-2643-2*); pap. text ed. 12.95x (*0-7914-2644-0*) State U NY Pr.

Markle, Helen M. Criminal Psychology: A Medical Subject Analysis & Research Index with Bibliography. LC 83-71651. 138p. 1985. 37.50 (*0-88164-024-7*); pap. 29.50 (*0-88164-025-5*) ABBE Pubs Assn.

— History of Prisons - Index of Modern Authors & Subjects with Guide for Rapid Research. LC 90-56266. 200p. 1991. 44.50 (*1-55914-306-1*); pap. 39.50 (*1-55914-307-X*) ABBE Pubs Assn.

— Prisons: Index of Modern Information. LC 88-47617. 150p. 1988. 44.50 (*0-88164-862-0*); pap. 39.50 (*0-88164-863-9*) ABBE Pubs Assn.

— Sex & Orgasm Research: Index of Modern Information. rev. ed. LC 88-48009. 150p. 1991. 44.50 (*1-55914-478-5*); pap. 39.50 (*1-55914-479-3*) ABBE Pubs Assn.

— Sex & the Biology of Coitus: Index of Modern Authors & Subjects with Guide for Rapid Research. LC 88-47980. 153p. 1991. 44.50 (*1-55914-220-0*); pap. 39.50 (*1-55914-221-9*) ABBE Pubs Assn.

— Sexually Transmitted Diseases & Appearance of Warts & Papillomas: Index of Modern Authors & Subjects with Guide for Rapid Research. LC 90-56248. 190p. 1991. 44.50 (*1-55914-264-2*); pap. 39.50 (*1-55914-265-0*) ABBE Pubs Assn.

Markle, Sandra. Digging Deeper: Investigations into Rocks, Shocks, Quakes, & Other Earthy Matters. LC 86-27412. (Illus.). 128p. (J). (gr. 4-9). 1987. 15.00 (*0-688-05986-4*) Lothrop.

— Discovering More Science Secrets. (J). (ps-3). 1993. pap. 2.50 (*0-590-44879-X*) Scholastic Inc.

— Earth Alive! (Illus.). 48p. (J). (gr. 4-7). 1991. 14.95 (*0-688-09360-4*) Lothrop.

— Earth Alive! (J). (ps). 1991. lib. bdg. 14.88 (*0-688-09361-2*) Lothrop.

— Exploring Autumn. (Exploring Seasons Ser.: Bk. 4). 160p. (YA). 1993. pap. 3.50 (*0-380-71910-X*, Camelot) Avon.

— Exploring Autumn: A Season of Science Activities, Puzzlers, & Games. LC 90-24209. (Illus.). 160p. (J). (gr. 3-7). 1991. text ed. 14.95 (*0-689-31620-8*, Atheneum Bks Young) S&S Childrens.

— Exploring Spring. 128p. (J). (gr. 4-7). 1992. pap. 2.99 (*0-380-71319-5*, Camelot) Avon.

— Exploring Spring: A Season of Science Activities, Puzzlers & Games. LC 89-394. (Illus.). 128p. (J). (gr. 3-7). 1990. text ed. 14.95 (*0-689-31341-1*, Atheneum Bks Young) S&S Childrens.

— Exploring Summer. 176p. (J). (gr. 7-8). 1991. reprint ed. pap. 2.95 (*0-380-71320-9*, Camelot) Avon.

— Exploring Summer: A Season of Science Activities, Puzzlers, & Games. LC 86-17322. 160p. (J). (gr. 3-7). 1987. text ed. 14.95 (*0-689-31212-1*, Atheneum Bks Young) S&S Childrens.

— Exploring Winter. LC 84-3049. (Illus.). 160p. (J). (gr. 3-7). 1984. text ed. 14.95 (*0-689-31065-X*, Atheneum Bks Young) S&S Childrens.

— Exploring Winter. 160p. (J). (gr. 7 up). 1992. reprint ed. pap. 2.99 (*0-380-71321-7*, Camelot) Avon.

— The Kids' Earth Handbook. LC 90-27478. (Illus.). 64p. (J). (gr. 3-7). 1991. text ed. 13.95 (*0-689-31707-7*, Atheneum Bks Young) S&S Childrens.

— Math Mini-Mysteries. LC 92-11217. (Illus.). 64p. (J). (gr. 3-7). 1993. text ed. 14.95 (*0-689-31700-X*, Atheneum Bks Young) S&S Childrens.

— Measuring Up: Experiments, Puzzles & Games Exploring Measurement. LC 94-19240. (J). 1995. text ed. 15.95 (*0-689-31904-5*, Atheneum S&S) S&S Trade.

— Outside & Inside Birds. LC 93-38910. (Illus.). 40p. (J). (ps-3). 1994. text ed. 15.95 (*0-02-762312-2*, Bradbury S&S) S&S Childrens.

— Outside & Inside Snakes. (Illus.). (J). (ps-3). 1995. 16.00 (*0-02-762315-7*, Mac Bks Young Read) S&S Childrens.

— Outside & Inside Spiders. LC 93-22643. (Illus.). 40p. (J). (ps-3). 1994. text ed. 15.95 (*0-02-762314-9*, Bradbury S&S) S&S Childrens.

— Outside & Inside Trees. LC 92-5145. (Illus.). 40p. (J). (ps-3). 1993. text ed. 15.95 (*0-02-762313-0*, Bradbury S&S) S&S Childrens.

— Outside & Inside You. LC 90-37791. (Illus.). 40p. (J). (ps-3). 1991. text ed. 15.95 (*0-02-762311-4*, Bradbury S&S) S&S Childrens.

— Pioneering Frozen Worlds. LC 95-15971. (J). 1996. write for info. (*0-689-31824-3*, Aladdin Paperbacks) S&S Childrens.

— Pioneering Ocean Depths. LC 93-33555. (J). 1994. text ed. 15.95 (*0-689-31823-5*, Atheneum S&S) S&S Trade.

— Pioneering Space. LC 91-24936. (Illus.). 40p. (J). (gr. 3-7). 1992. text ed. 14.95 (*0-689-31748-4*, Atheneum Bks Young) S&S Childrens.

— Power Up: Experiments, Puzzles & Games Exploring Electricity. LC 88-7772. (Illus.). 48p. (J). (gr. 3-7). 1989. text ed. 14.95 (*0-689-31442-6*, Atheneum Bks Young) S&S Childrens.

— Primary Science Sampler. (Computers & Science Ser.). 112p. (J). (gr. 1-3). 1980. 9.95 (*0-88160-008-3*, LW 110) Learning Wks.

— A Rainy Day. LC 91-17059. (Illus.). 32p. (J). (ps-2). 1993. 14.95 (*0-531-05976-6*); lib. bdg. 14.99 (*0-531-08576-7*) Orchard Bks Watts.

— Science Mini-Mysteries. LC 87-17420. (Illus.). 72p. (J). (gr. 3-7). 1988. text ed. 14.95 (*0-689-31291-1*, Atheneum Bks Young) S&S Childrens.

— Science Sampler. (Computers & Science Ser.). 112p. (J). (gr. 4-8). 1980. 9.95 (*0-88160-031-8*, LW 216) Learning Wks.

— Science to the Rescue. LC 92-41096. (Illus.). 48p. (J). (gr. 3-7). 1994. text ed. 15.95 (*0-689-31783-2*, Atheneum Bks Young) S&S Childrens.

— Weather, Electricity, Environmental Investigations. (Enrichment & Gifted Ser.). 112p. (J). (gr. 4-6). 1982. 9.95 (*0-88160-082-2*, LW 902) Learning Wks.

— What Happens Next? (Illus.). 48p. (J). (gr. k-4). 1995. 14.95 (*1-56352-232-2*) Longstreet Pr Inc.

— The Young Scientist's Guide to Successful Science Projects. LC 89-45290. (Illus.). 128p. (J). (gr. 3-7). lib. bdg. 12.88 (*0-688-07217-8*) Lothrop.

— The Young Scientist's Guide to Successful Science Projects. LC 89-45290. (Illus.). 128p. (J). (gr. 3 up). 1990. pap. 6.95 (*0-688-09137-7*, Pub. by Beech Tree Bks) Morrow.

Markle, Sandras. Science: Just Add Salt. (J). (gr. 4-7). 1994. pap. 2.95 (*0-590-46537-6*) Scholastic Inc.

Markle, Susan M. Designs for Instructional Designers. 1990. spiral bd. 17.80 (*0-87563-366-8*) Stipes.

— Good Frames & Bad: A Grammar of Frame Writing. 2nd ed. LC 71-91153. 324p. reprint ed. pap. 92.40 (*0-317-09852-7*, 2017002) Bks Demand.

Marklew, Gilly, illus. The Little Book of Poems. LC 92-29126. (J). 1993. 7.95 (*1-85697-887-7*, Kingfisher LKC) LKC.

*__Marklew, Victoria.__ Cash, Crisis & Corporate Governance: The Role of National Finance Systems in Industrial Restructuring. LC 95-8273. 1995. write for info. (*0-472-10504-3*) U of Mich Pr.

Markley, Deborah. Availability of Capital in Rural America: Problems & Options. (New Alliances for Rural America Ser.). 60p. (Orig.). 1988. pap. text ed. 6.00 (*1-55877-018-6*) Natl Governor.

Markley, J. Gerald. The Life of Lazarillo De Tormes. LC 55-34585. 80p. (C). 1954. pap. write for info. (*0-02-376160-1*, LLA37) Macmillan.

Markley, J. Gerald, tr. Epic of the Cid. LC 61-14564. 1961. pap. 3.95 (*0-672-60259-8*, LLA77, Bobbs) Macmillan.

Markley, Klare S. Fatty Acids: Their Chemistry, Properties, Production & Uses, 5 pts., Pt. I. 2nd ed. LC 82-8934. 3888p. (C). 1982. lib. bdg. 84.75 (*0-685-73475-7*) Krieger.

— Fatty Acids: Their Chemistry, Properties, Production & Uses, 5 pts., Pt. II. 2nd ed. LC 82-8934. 3888p. (C). 1982. lib. bdg. 90.50 (*0-685-73476-5*) Krieger.

— Fatty Acids: Their Chemistry, Properties, Production & Uses, 5 pts., Set. 2nd ed. LC 82-8934. 3888p. (C). 1982. lib. bdg. 450.00 (*0-89874-576-4*) Krieger.

Markley, Merle, jt. ed. see Berryman, Jack H.

Markley, Nelson G. Introduction to Probability. rev. ed. 1991. 18.00 (*0-536-04960-2*) Ginn Pr.

Markley, O. W., jt. ed. see Center for the Study of Social Policy-SRI International Staff.

Markley, O. W., jt. auth. see Wygant, Alice C.

*__Markley, Oliver W. & McCuan, Walter R., eds.__ America Beyond 2001: Opposing Viewpoints. LC 94-46738. (Opposing Viewpoints Ser.). 1995. lib. bdg. 19.95 (*1-56510-293-2*); pap. 11.55 (*1-56510-292-4*) Greenhaven.

Markley, R. W., jt. auth. see Sheeler, W. D.

Markley, Rayner W. Handwriting Workbook. Evans, A. R., ed. (Welcome to English Ser.). 1977. student ed 3.45 (*0-89285-043-4*) ELS Educ Servs.

— Spot Drills, Bk. 1. (Illus.). 142p. 1983. pap. text ed. 8.95 (*0-19-434125-9*) OUP.

— Spot Drills, Bk. 2. (Illus.). 142p. 1987. pap. text ed. 8.95 (*0-19-434126-7*) OUP.

— Spot Drills, Bk. 3. (Illus.). 142p. 1987. pap. text ed. 8.95 (*0-19-434127-5*) OUP.

Markley, Robert. Fallen Languages: Crises of Representation in Newtonian England, 1660-1740. (Illus.). 288p. 1993. 37.50 (*0-8014-2588-3*) Cornell U Pr.

*__Markley, Robert, ed.__ Virtual Realities & Their Discontents. 197p. 1995. text ed. 38.50x (*0-8018-5225-0*); pap. text ed. 14.95x (*0-8018-5226-9*) Johns Hopkins.

Markley, Robert & Finke, Laurie, eds. From Renaissance to Restoration: Metamorphoses of the Drama. 206p. 1984. 16.00 (*0-934958-03-3*) Bellflower.

Marklin, Megan. The Summoned. Zion, Claire, ed. 320p. (Orig.). 1993. mass mkt. 4.99 (*0-671-76098-X*) PB.

Markline, Judy, et al. Thinking on Paper: A Writing Process Workbook. 256p. (C). 1991. pap. text ed. 22.00 (*0-03-052204-8*) HB Coll Pubs.

Markmam, Charles W. Prehispanic Settlement Dynamics in Central Oaxaca, Mexico: A View from the Miahuatlan Valley. (Publications in Anthropology: No. 26). (Illus.). 185p. 1981. pap. 11.85 (*0-935462-17-1*) Vanderbilt Pubns.

Markman, Charles W. & Kreisa, Paul P. Investigations at the Deere Creek Site: Early Woodland Camping Locality in Rock Island County, Illinois. (Northern Illinois University Archaelogical Research Ser.: No. 1). (Illus.). 70p. 1984. pap. 4.95 (*0-917039-00-9*) N Ill Anthro.

Markman, Ellen M. Categorization & Naming in Children: Problems of Induction. (Learning, Development & Conceptual Change Ser.). (Illus.). 264p. 1991. reprint ed. pap. 13.95 (*0-262-63136-9*, Bradford Bks) MIT Pr.

Markman, Howard, jt. auth. see Notarius, Clifford.

Markman, Howard, ed. see Notarius, Clifford.

Markman, Howard, et al. Fighting for Your Marriage: Preventing Divorce & Preserving a Lasting Love. LC 94-9277. (Social Behavioral Sciences Ser.). 328p. 1994. boxed 23.00 (*1-55542-700-6*) Jossey-Bass.

Markman, Maurie. Regional Antineoplastic Drug Delivery in the Management of Malignant Disease. LC 90-15596. (Series in Contemporary Medicine & Public Health). 220p. 1991. text ed. 65.00x (*0-8018-4166-6*) Johns Hopkins.

Markman, Maurie & Hoskins, William, eds. Cancer of the Ovary. LC 92-49712. 464p. 1993. 131.50 (*0-88167-970-4*) Raven.

Markman, Peter T., jt. auth. see Markman, Roberta H.

Markman, R. & Brecque, L. Obsession: The Stalking of Theresa Saldana. 1994. 22.00 (*0-688-10970-5*) Morrow.

Markman, Roberta H. & Markman, Peter T. The Flayed God: The Mythology of Mesoamerica. LC 91-58158. 496p. 1994. pap. 20.00 (*0-06-250749-4*) Harper SF.

— Masks of the Spirit: Image & Metaphor in Mesoamerica. (Illus.). 375p. 1989. 65.00 (*0-520-06418-6*) U CA Pr.

— Masks of the Spirit: Image & Metaphor in Mesoamerica. (Illus.). 276p. (C). 1994. pap. 27.50 (*0-520-08654-6*) U CA Pr.

Markman, Roberta H. & Waddell, Marie L. Ten Steps in Writing the Research Paper. 5th ed. 160p. (C). 1994. pap. 8.95 (*0-8120-1868-0*) Barron.

Markman, Roberta H., et al. Ten Steps in Writing the Research Paper. 4th ed. 160p. 1989. pap. 7.95 (*0-8120-4151-8*) Barron.

Markman, Roger. Classic Aircraft in Aviation Art. (Illus.). 96p. 1994. 49.95 (*0-943231-64-7*) Howell Pr VA.

***Markman, Ronald & LaBrecque, Ron.** Obsessed: The Anatomy of a Stalker. (Illus.). 304p. 1995. reprint ed. mass mkt. 5.99 (0-380-76650-7) Avon.

Markman, Sidney D. Architecture & Urbanization in Colonial Chiapas, Mexico. LC 81-68194. (Memoirs Ser.: Vol. 153). 443p. 1984. 50.00 (0-87169-153-1, M153-MAS) Am Philos.

— Architecture & Urbanization of Colonial Central America Vol. II: A Geographical Gazetteer of Primary Documentary, Literary & Visual Sources. (Monographs). (Illus.). 350p. (C). 1995. text ed. 40.00 (0-87918-080-3) ASU Lat Am St.

— Architecture & Urbanization of Colonial Central America, Vol. I Vols. I & II: Primary Documentary & Literary Sources. (Illus.). 285p. 1994. text ed. 35.00 (0-87918-078-1) ASU Lat Am St.

— Colonial Architecture of Antigua, Guatemala. LC 66-13634. (American Philosophical Society, Memoirs Ser.: No. 64). 355p. reprint ed. pap. 101.20 (0-7837-2681-3, 2043058) Bks Demand.

— Colonial Central America: A Bibliography. LC 76-23299. 360p. 1977. 5.00 (0-87918-023-4) ASU Lat Am St.

— The Horse in Greek Art. LC 72-88057. (Illus.). 1969. reprint ed. 25.00 (0-8196-0247-7) Biblo.

Markmann, Charles, tr. see Fanon, Frantz.

Markmann, Charles L., tr. see Lemaitre, Solange.

Markmann, Erika. Grow It! An Indoor - Outdoor Gardening Guide for Kids. LC 90-45043. (Illus.). 48p. (J). (gr. 2-7). 1991. lib. bdg. 11.99 (0-679-91528-1); pap. 6.95 (0-679-81528-7) Random Bks Yng Read.

Marko-Geenen, Suzette & Caillat, Carleen. Preparer & Reussir le TOEFL. 158p. (FRE.). 1993. pap. 49.95 (0-7859-1003-4, 2708115367) Fr & Eur.

Marko, H., et al, eds. Processing Structures for Perception & Action. LC 87-34522. 278p. 1988. lib. bdg. 100.00 (0-89573-682-9, Pub. by Deutsche Forschungsgemeinschaft) VCH Pubs.

Marko, Istavan E. Oxidations. (Oxford Chemistry Primers Ser.: No. 6). (Illus.). 96p. (C). 1995. text ed. 29.95 (0-19-855665-9); pap. text ed. 9.95 (0-19-855664-0) OUP.

Marko, Katherine M. Away to Fundy Bay. LC 84-25680. (Walker's American History Series for Young People). (Illus.). 128p. (J). (gr. 4 up). 1985. 11.95 (0-8027-6576-9); lib. bdg. 12.85 (0-8027-6594-7) Walker & Co.

— Hang Out the Flag. LC 92-349. 160p. (J). (gr. 3-7). 1992. text ed. 13.95 (0-02-762320-3, Mac Bks Young Read) S&S Childrens.

— Pocket Babies. (First Bks.). (Illus.). 64p. (J). (gr. 4-6). 1995. lib. bdg. 13.93 (0-531-20211-9) Watts.

Marko, V., ed. Determination of Beta-Blockers in Biological Material. (Techniques & Instrumentation in Analytical Chemistry Ser.: Vol. 4C). 334p. 1989. 148.75 (0-444-87305-8) Elsevier.

Markoe, Glenn. Phoenician Bronze & Silver Bowls from Cyprus & the Mediterranean. LC 83-18305. (UC Publications in Classical Studies: Vol. 26). 1985. pap. 60.00 (0-520-09663-0) U CA Pr.

— Phoenician Bronze & Silver Bowls from Cyprus & the Mediterranean. fac. ed. LC 83-18305. (University of California Publication, Classical Studies: No. 26). (Illus.). 392p. 1985. pap. 111.80 (0-7837-8612-3, 2059167) Bks Demand.

Markoe, Merrill. How to Be Hap-Hap-Happy Like Me. LC 94-10344. 224p. 1994. 18.95 (0-670-85332-1, Viking) Viking Penguin.

— How to Be Hap-Hap-Happy Like Me. 224p. 1995. pap. 8.95 (0-14-023369-5, Penguin Bks) Viking Penguin.

— What the Dogs Have Taught Me: And Other Amazing Things I've Learned. 256p. 1993. pap. 10.00 (0-14-016682-3, Penguin Bks) Viking Penguin.

Markoe, Merrill, ed. Late Night with David Letterman: The Book. LC 85-40390. 206p. 1985. pap. 8.95 (0-394-74191-9, Villard Bks) Random.

***Markoff, Annabelle.** Receptive Oral Language Inventory. Martin, Nancy, ed. 64p. 1995. 40.00 (0-87879-996-6, 996-6); pap. 17.00 (0-87879-997-4, 996-6) Acad Therapy.

Markoff, Annabelle M. Quick Cognitive Inventory (QCI) 39p. (Orig.). 1990. student ed. pap. text ed. 12.00 (0-87879-643-6); 30.00 (0-685-31303-4); 15.00 (0-87879-644-4) Acad Therapy.

— Within Reach: Academic Achievement Through Parent-Teacher Communication. LC 92-17388. 1992. 16.50 (0-87879-955-9) Acad Therapy.

Markoff, John, jt. auth. see Hafner, Katie.

Markoff, Mortimer & Platt, Frederic W. The Art of Playing the Piano: Conversations with Mortimer Markoff. Holmes, Merlyn, ed. LC 93-38483. (Illus.). 144p. (Orig.). 1993. pap. 14.95 (0-9639221-7-3) London Rd Bks.

Markolin, Caroline. Thomas Bernhard & His Grandfather Johannes Freumbichler: Our Grandfathers Are Our Teachers. Hartweg, Petra, tr. LC 92-38175. 1993. 27.50 (0-929497-51-1) Ariadne CA.

***Markolo, Peter G.** Separating & Identifying Food Dyes by Paper Chromatography. Neidig, H. A., ed. (Modular Laboratory Program in Chemistry Ser.). 12p. (C). 1989. pap. text ed. 1.25x (0-87540-372-7) Chem Educ Res.

Markoosie. Harpoon of the Hunter: Markoosie. (Illus.). 84p. 1974. pap. 10.95 (0-7735-0232-7, Pub. by McGill CN) U of Toronto Pr.

Markos, Carol, jt. auth. see Awtrey, Amy.

Markos, Prudence D., jt. auth. see Sullivan, Patricia E.

Markosian, Becky T. & Thayne, Emma L. Hope & Recovery: A Mother-Daughter Story about Anorexia Nervosa, Bulimia, & Manic Depression. Rosoff, Iris, ed. LC 91-36619. (Illus.). 176p. (YA). (gr. 9-12). 1992. lib. bdg. 15.33 (0-531-11140-7) Watts.

Markotic. Ancient Europe & the Mediterranean. 1977. 65.00 (0-85668-083-4, Pub. by Aris & Phillips UK) David Brown.

***Markotic, Nicole.** Yellow Pages. 192p. 1995. pap. 10.95 (0-88995-132-2, Pub. by Red Deer CN) BookWorld Dist.

Markoutsas, Elaine. Showcase of Interior Design: Midwest Edition. 2nd ed. 235p. 1993. 37.50 (0-9624596-7-4) Vitae Pub.

Markov, A. A. & Nagorny, N. M. The Theory of Algorithms. (C). 1988. lib. bdg. 201.50 (90-277-2773-2) Kluwer Ac.

***Markov, A. S.** Dictionary of Scientific & Technical Terminology: English-French-German-Dutch-Russian. 496p. (DUT, FRE & GER.). 1984. 155.00 (0-7859-7151-3) Fr & Eur.

Markov, A. S., et al. Dictionary of Scientific & Technical Terminology. 1984. lib. bdg. 34.50 (0-318-01661-3) Kluwer Ac.

Markov, I. V. Crystal Growth for Beginners - Fundamentals of Nucleation, Crystal Growth & Epitaxy. 436p. 1995. text ed. 67.00 (981-02-1531-2) World Scientific Pub.

Markov, K. Z. Advances in Mathematical Modeling of Composite Materials. (Series on Advances in Mathematics). 304p. 1994. text ed. 81.00 (981-02-1644-0) World Scientific Pub.

Markov, M. A. Electromagnetic Fields & Biomembranes. Blank, Martin, ed. LC 87-29276. 326p. 1988. 85.00 (0-306-42778-8, Plenum Pr) Plenum.

— Invariants & the Evolution of Nonstationary. 370p. 1989. 145.00 (0-941743-49-7) Nova Sci Pubs.

Markov, M. A., ed. The Physical Effects in the Gravitational Field of Black Holes. (Proceedings of the Lebedev Physics Institute Ser.: Vol. 169). 262p. (C). 1987. text ed. 125.00 (0-941743-04-7) Nova Sci Pubs.

— Squeezed & Correlated States of Quantum Systems. (Proceedings of the Lebedev Physics Institute Ser.). 242p. (C). 1993. lib. bdg. 89.00 (1-57072-117-3) Nova Sci Pubs.

— Squeezed & Correlated States of Quantum Systems. Dodonov, V. V. et al, trs. LC 93-20853. 1993. 89.00 (1-56072-117-0) Nova Sci Pubs.

— Theory of Nonstationary Quantum Oscillators: Proceedings of the Lebedev Physics Institute, Vol. 198. 181p. (C). 1992. lib. bdg. 114.00 (1-56072-076-X) Nova Sci Pubs.

Markov, M. A., jt. ed. see Man'ko, V. I.

Markov, M. A., et al. Quantum Gravity: Proceedings of the Fifth Seminar. 176p. 1991. text ed. 130.00 (981-02-0440-X) World Scientific Pub.

Markov, M. A., et al, eds. Group Theoretical Methods in Physics: Proceedings of the Second Zvenigorod Seminar on Group Theoretical Methods in Physics, Zvenigorod, USSR, 24-26th November 1982, 3 vols., Vol. 1. 1615p. 1985. text ed. 580.00 (3-7186-0245-8) Gordon & Breach.

— Group Theoretical Methods in Physics: Proceedings of the Second Zvenigorod Seminar on Group Theoretical Methods in Physics, Zvenigorod, USSR, 24-26th November 1982, 3 vols., Vol. 2. 1615p. 1987. text ed. 304.00 (3-7186-0246-6) Gordon & Breach.

— Group Theoretical Methods in Physics: Proceedings of the Second Zvenigorod Seminar on Group Theoretical Methods in Physics, Zvenigorod, USSR, 24-26th November 1982, 3 vols., Vol. 3. 1615p. 1987. Set. text ed. 778.00 (3-7186-0247-4); text ed. 270.00 (3-7186-0301-2) Gordon & Breach.

— Group Theoretical Methods in Physics: Proceedings of the Third Yurmala Seminar, U. S. S. R., May, 1956, 2 vols., Set. 1388p. 1986. lib. bdg. 328.00 (90-6764-072-7, Pub. by VSP NE) Coronet Bks.

— Quantum Gravity: Proceedings of the Third Seminar, Moscow, 1984. 716p. 1985. 130.00 (9971-978-90-3) World Scientific Pub.

Markov, Sergei, jt. auth. see McFaul, Michael.

Markov, V. & Jeong, T. H., eds. Three-Dimensional Holography '89. 1990. 77.00 (0-8194-0282-6, VOL. 1238) SPIE.

***Markov, Vladimir.** Russian Futurism: A History. 600p. (Orig.). 1994. pap. 79.95 (0-7605-0379-6) Rector Pr.

— Russian Futurism: A History. rev. ed. (Illus.). 690p. (Orig.). 1994. pap. 79.95 (0-7605-0521-7) Rector Pr.

Markov, Vladimir & Worth, Dean S., eds. From Los Angeles to Kiev: Papers on the Occasion of the Ninth International Congress of Slavists (Kiev 1983) (UCLA Slavic Studies: Vol. 7). 250p. 1983. 24.95 (0-89357-119-9) Slavica.

Markov, Vladimir, ed. see Kuzmin, Mikhail A.

Markov, Yuri. Winning with the Slav. (Batsford Chess Library). 1994. pap. 19.95 (0-8050-3283-5) H Holt & Co.

Markova, Aelita K. The Teaching & Mastery of Language. Szekely, Beatrice B., ed. Vale, Michel, tr. LC 78-65595. 293p. reprint ed. pap. 83.60 (0-317-41987-0, 2026124) Bks Demand.

Markova, Dawna. The Art of the Possible: A Compassionate Approach to Understanding the Way People Think, Learn & Communicate. 260p. (Orig.). 1991. pap. 12.95 (0-943233-12-7) Conari Press.

— The Art of the Possible: A Compassionate Approach to Understanding the Way People Think, Learn & Communicate. 250p. (Orig.). 1991. reprint ed. lib. bdg. 33.00x (0-8095-5856-4) Borgo Pr.

— No Enemies Within: A Creative Process for Discovering What's Right about What's Wrong. 300p. (Orig.). 1994. pap. 12.95 (0-943233-64-X) Conari Press.

— No Enemies Within: An Intuitive Process for Discovering What's Right About What's Wrong. 300p. 1994. lib. bdg. 33.00x (0-8095-5880-7) Borgo Pr.

Markova, Dawna & Powell, Anne. How Your Child Is Smart: A Life-Changing Approach to Learning. 200p. (Orig.). 1992. pap. 9.95 (0-943233-38-0) Conari Press.

— How Your Child Is Smart: A Life-Changing Approach to Learning. (Illus.). 200p. (Orig.). (C). 1993. reprint ed. lib. bdg. 27.00x (0-8095-5869-6) Borgo Pr.

Markova, G. A. The Grand Palace of the Dremlin (Bol'shoi Kremlevskii Dvorets) 1981p. 1981. 100.00 (0-317-14237-2, Pub. by Collets UK) Pro-Am Music.

Markova, I. & Foppa, K., eds. The Dynamics of Dialogue. 200p. 1990. 54.00 (0-387-91388-2) Spr-Verlag.

Markova, Ivana. Paradigms, Thought, & Language. LC 81-22022. (Illus.). 241p. reprint ed. pap. 68.70 (0-8357-3098-0, 2039355) Bks Demand.

Markova, Ivana & Foppa, Klaus, eds. Asymmetries in Dialogue. 300p. (C). 1991. text ed. 69.50 (0-389-20980-5) B&N Imports.

***Markova, Ivana, et al, eds.** Mutualities in Dialogue. (Illus.). 270p. (C). 1995. write for info. (0-521-49595-4); pap. write for info. (0-521-49941-0) Cambridge U Pr.

Markova, Ivena, ed. The Social Context of Language. LC 77-3861. 251p. reprint ed. pap. 71.60 (0-685-20650-5, 2030436) Bks Demand.

Markova, N., jt. ed. see Kadieva, D.

Markovchick, Vincent J., et al, eds. Emergency Medicine Secrets. (Illus.). 350p. (Orig.). 1993. pap. text ed. 35.95 (1-56053-051-0) Hanley & Belfus.

Markovic, Debra, ed. see Albert, Eleanor.

Markovic, Mihailo. The Contemporary Marx. 224p. 1986. 40.00 (0-685-12447-9, Bertrand Russell Soc) St Mut.

— Dialectical Theory of Meaning. 1984. lib. bdg. 167.00 (90-277-1596-3) Kluwer Ac.

— From Affluence to Praxis: Philosophy & Social Criticism. (Ann Arbor Paperbacks Ser.: No. 191). 1974. pap. 17.95 (0-472-06191-7, Ann Arbor Bks) U of Mich Pr.

Markovic, Mihailo & Petrovic, Gajo, eds. Praxis. (Boston Studies in the Philosophy of Science: No. XXXVI; Synthese Library, No. 134). 1979. lib. bdg. 112.50 (90-277-0727-8); pap. text ed. 51.50 (90-277-0968-8) Kluwer Ac.

Markovic, V., ed. Radiation Processing: Fourth International Meeting on Radiation Processing, Dubrovnik, Yugoslavia, October 1982, 2 vols., Set. 980p. 1984. pap. 155.00 (0-08-029162-7, Pergamon Pr) Elsevier.

Markovich. Pueblo Style & Regional Architecture. 1992. pap. 34.95 (0-442-01173-3) Van Nos Reinhold.

Markovich, Alex. The Home Owner's Survival Manual. 1992. 17.99 (0-517-06522-3) Random Hse Value.

Markovich, Denise. Effective Asset-Liability Management for the Community Bank. 1989. 49.00 (1-55520-047-8) Probus Pub Co.

Markovich, Efimov I. Bremia Dobra: Russkii Pisatel' Kak Vlastitel' Dum. LC 93-15793. 204p. (Orig.). (RUS.). 1993. pap. 14.00 (1-55779-064-7) Hermitage.

Markovits, Andrei S., ed. The Political Economy of West Germany: Modell Deutschland. LC 81-20996. 240p. 1982. text ed. 55.00 (0-275-90854-2, C0854, Praeger Pubs) Greenwood.

Markovits, Andrei S. & Gorski, Philip S. The German Left: Red, Green, & Beyond. (Europe & the International Order Ser.). 416p. (C). 1993. 55.00 (0-19-521051-4); pap. text ed. 16.95 (0-19-521053-0) OUP.

Markovits, Andrei S. & Sysyn, Frank E., eds. Nationbuilding & the Politics of Nationalism: Essays on Austrian Galicia. LC 80-53800. (Harvard Ukrainian Research Institute Monograph). 345p. 1990. pap. 17.00 (0-674-60312-5) Harvard Ukrainian.

***Markovits, Inge.** Imperfect Justice: A German Diary. 250p. 1995. 42.00 (0-19-825814-3); pap. 18.95 (0-19-825961-1) OUP.

Markovitz, Andrei S. & Silverstein, Mark, eds. The Politics of Scandal: Power & Process in Liberal Democracies. LC 88-11045. 288p. (C). 1989. 39.50 (0-8419-1097-9); pap. 19.95 (0-8419-1098-7) Holmes & Meier.

Markovitz, Irving L., ed. Studies in Power & Class in Africa. (Illus.). 415p. (C). 1987. 45.00 (0-19-504129-1); pap. text ed. 18.95 (0-19-504130-5) OUP.

Markovitz, Paul, et al. Guidelines for the Evaluation of File Transfer, Access & Management Implementations. (Illus.). 99p. (Orig.). (C). 1994. pap. text ed. 45.00 (0-7881-0624-4) Diane Pub.

Markovski, B. L. & Vinitsky, S. I. Adiabatic Representation in Quantum Theory: Rigorous Results & Applications. 400p. 1995. text ed. 86.00 (981-02-0847-2) World Scientific Pub.

Markovski, Venko. Goli Otok-Island of Death: A Diary in Letters. 229p. 1984. text ed. 54.00 (0-88033-055-4) East Eur Quarterly.

Markovsky, Barry. Advances in Group Processes, Vol. 4. Lawler, Edward J. et al, eds. 1987. 73.25 (0-89232-733-2) Jai Pr.

Markovsky, Barry, jt. ed. see Lawler, Edward J.

Markow, Herbert L. Small Boat Law. LC 77-154289. (Illus.). 435p. (Orig.). (C). 1977. pap. 40.00 (0-934108-00-5) H L Markow.

— Small Boat Law: Nineteen Seventy-Eight Supplement. LC 79-88475. 144p. (C). 1979. pap. 20.00 (0-934108-01-3) H L Markow.

— Small Boat Law: Nineteen Seventy-Nine to Nineteen Eighty Supplement. LC 77-154289. 174p. 1981. pap. 24.00 (0-934108-02-1) H L Markow.

— Small Boat Law: 1981-1983 Supplement. LC 77-154289. 274p. (C). 1984. pap. text ed. 36.00 (0-934108-03-X) H L Markow.

Markow, Jack. The Art of Cartooning. (Illus.). 80p. 1990. pap. 9.00 (0-399-51626-3, Perigree Bks) Berkley Pub.

Markow, Peter G. Biochemistry of the Human Body. 80p. (C). 1994. 11.54 (1-56870-030-X) RonJon Pub.

— Estimating the Calorie Content of Nuts. Neidig, H. A., ed. (Modular Laboratory Program in Chemistry Ser.). 12p. (C). 1993. pap. text ed. 1.25x (0-87540-428-6) Chem Educ Res.

***Markow, Radiance.** Going Around the Bend. (Orig.). (J). (gr. 3-6). 1995. lib. bdg. 15.00 (0-88092-167-6); pap. 5.00 (0-88092-166-8) Royal Fireworks.

Markow, Theresa A., ed. Developmental Instability: Its Origins & Evolutionary Implications: Proceedings of the International Conference, Tempe, Arizona, U. S. A., 14-15 June 1993. LC 94-1934. (Contemporary Issues in Genetics & Evolution Ser.: Vol. 2). 436p. (C). 1994. lib. bdg. 199.00 (0-7923-2678-4) Kluwer Ac.

Markow-Totevy, G., jt. auth. see Bree, Germaine.

Markow-Totevy, Georges. Henry James. Griffiths, John, tr. (C). 1969. text ed. 16.00 (0-8464-1164-4) Beekman Pubs.

***Markowiak, Linda.** Courting Valerie. (Superromance Ser.). 1995. 3.50 (0-373-70629-4, 1-70629-0) Harlequin Bks.

Markowich, P. A. Semiconductor Equations. (Illus.). 250p. 1990. 64.00 (0-387-82157-0) Spr-Verlag.

— The Stationary Semiconductor Device Equations. (Computational Microelectronics Ser.). (Illus.). 210p. 1986. 73.00 (0-387-81892-8) Spr-Verlag.

Markowicz. Learning to Use WordPerfect 5.1. (Shelly Cashman Ser.). (Illus.). 260p. (C). 1992. teacher ed, per. 19.00 (0-87835-767-X) Boyd & Fraser.

Markowicz, jt. ed. see Van Grieken.

Markowitsch, H. J., ed. Information Processing by the Brain: Views & Hypotheses from a Physiological-Cognitive Perspective. LC 87-22542. 272p. 1988. 69.00 (0-920887-15-5) Hogrefe & Huber Pubs.

— Transient Global Amnesia & Related Disorders. LC 90-4811. (Illus.). 260p. 1990. text ed. 58.00 (0-920887-70-8) Hogrefe & Huber Pubs.

Markowitsch, Hans J. Intellectual Functions & the Brain: A Historical Perspective. LC 92-1482. (Illus.). 240p. 1992. text ed. 78.00 (0-88937-081-8) Hogrefe & Huber Pubs.

***Markowitz, Darryl.** What Is in a Word. 410p. Date not set. pap. 9.95 (1-56901-653-4) NW Pub.

Markowitz, Endel. Abracadabra. (Illus.). write for info. (0-318-56833-0) Haymark.

— Below the Belt. 78p. T.V. Shooting Script. write for info. (0-318-56910-8) Haymark.

— The Cross & the Star. 360p. write for info. (0-318-60925-8) Haymark.

— The Encyclopedia Yiddishanica. LC 79-89973. (Illus.). 450p. 1980. 19.95 (0-933910-02-9); pap. write for info. (0-933910-04-5) Haymark.

— Kid-Ish Yiddish. (Illus.). 44p. (J). 1993. lib. bdg. 16.95 (0-933910-05-3) Haymark.

— Manhattan Moxie. write for info. (0-318-60926-6) Haymark.

— Vagrancy: Book of Poetry. write for info. (0-318-60927-4) Haymark.

Markowitz, Fran. A Community in Spite of Itself: Soviet Jewish Emigres in New York. LC 92-31989. (Ethnographic Inquiry Ser.). 320p. (C). 1993. 49.00 (1-56098-200-4); pap. 19.95 (1-56098-225-X) Smithsonian.

Markowitz, Gerald, jt. auth. see Rosner, David.

Markowitz, Gerald, jt. ed. see Rosner, David.

Markowitz, Gerald E. & Rosner, David, eds. Slaves of the Depression: Workers' Letters about Life on the Job. LC 87-6671. 272p. 1987. 41.50 (0-8014-1956-5); pap. 15.95 (0-8014-9464-8) Cornell U Pr.

Markowitz, Gerald E., jt. auth. see Park, Marlene.

Markowitz, Hal & Stevens, Victor, eds. Behavior of Captive Wild Animals. LC 77-18156. (Illus.). 320p. 1978. text ed. 35.95 (0-88229-385-0) Nelson-Hall.

Markowitz, Harold, Jr. Distance Education: Staff Handbook. Kozoll, Charles E., ed. 59p. (Orig.). 1990. pap. 13.95 (1-877847-06-2) Univ IL UCOCE&PS.

Markowitz, Harry M. Mean-Variance Analysis in Portfolio Choice & Capital Markets. 1990. pap. 21.95 (0-631-17854-6) Blackwell Pubs.

— Portfolio Selection: Efficient Diversification of Investments. 1991. 37.95 (1-55786-108-0) Blackwell Pubs.

Markowitz, Harvey, jt. auth. see Hoxie, Frederick E.

Markowitz, Jerome. Triumphs & Trials of an Organ Builder. (Illus.). 195p. 1989. 20.00 (0-9624896-0-3) Vox Humana.

Markowitz, Milton, jt. auth. see Taranta, Angelo.

Markowitz, Morris J. & Lam, Michael. How to Beat the Street with Plan Z: The New Strategy for Safe & Lucrative Investing in the Money Markets. LC 93-16552. 272p. 1993. text ed. 24.95 (0-471-58286-7) Wiley.

Markowitz, Ruth J. My Daughter, the Teacher: Jewish Teachers in the New York City Schools. LC 92-37565. 288p. (C). 1993. text ed. 40.00 (0-8135-1974-8); pap. text ed. 15.00 (0-8135-1975-6) Rutgers U Pr.

Markowitz, Sidney L. What You Should Know about Jewish Religion, History, Ethics & Culture. 240p. 1992. pap. 8.95 (0-8065-0811-6, Citadel Pr) Carol Pub Group.

Markowitz, Sidney L., jt. auth. see Margolis, Isidor.

Markowitz, William, ed. see International Astronomical Union Staff.

Markowski, Benedict. Carissima: A Lyric Drama. rev. ed. LC 81-479565. (Illus.). 140p. 1980. ring bd. 25.00 (0-9614820-0-1) Poets Mark.

— Kopernik the Great Humanist. (Illus.). 1973. 1.00 (0-685-37750-4) Endurance.

Markowski, Carol. Tomart's Price Guide to Character & Promotional Glasses Including Pepsi, Coke, Fast-Food, Peanut Butter & Jelly Glasses; Plus Dairy & Milk Bottles. 2nd rev. ed. LC 89-51636. (Illus.). 160p. 1993. pap. 24.95 (0-914293-18-4) Tomart Pubns.

***Markowski, George.** The DOS Windows Book. 240p. (C). 1994. per., pap. text ed. 24.95 (0-8403-9968-5) Kendall-Hunt.

An Asterisk (*) at the beginning of an entry indicates that the title is appearing in BIP for the first time.

Markowski, Hieronymus. De Libanio Socratis Defensore. No. 40. viii, 196p. 1970. reprint ed. write for info. (*0-318-70974-0*, Pub. by Georg Olms GW) Lubrecht & Cramer.

Markowski, Michael A. ARV: The Encyclopedia of Aircraft Recreational Vehicles. LC 83-51822. (Sport Aviation Ser.: Bk. 7). (Illus.). (Orig.). 1984. pap. 19.95 (*0-938716-10-7*) Markowski Intl.

— Ultralight Flight: The Pilot's Handbook of Ultralight Knowledge. LC 81-71889. (Ultralight Aviation Ser.: No. 3). (Illus.). 206p. (Orig.). 1984. 20.95 (*0-938716-07-7*); pap. 14.95 (*0-938716-06-9*) Markowski Intl.

— Ultralight Technique: How to Fly & Navigate Ultralight Air Vehicles. LC 83-50057. (Ultralight Aviation Ser.: No. 5). (Illus.). (Orig.). 1983. pap. 15.95 (*0-938716-12-3*) Markowski Intl.

Markowski, Michael A., ed. see Lambie, Jack.

Marks. Behavioral Psychotherapy. 133p. 1986. 23.95 (*0-7236-0875-X*, Pub. by John Wright UK) Buttrwrth-Heinemann.

— Biochemistry. 2nd ed. (Board Review Ser.). 1994. 19.95 (*0-685-75161-9*) Williams & Wilkins.

— Biochemistry. 3rd ed. (National Medical Ser.). 1993. 25.00 (*0-685-75166-X*) Williams & Wilkins.

— Prostate & Cancer: A Family Guide to Diagnosis, Treatment & Survival. 1995. 24.95 (*1-55561-072-2*) Fisher Bks.

— Prostate & Cancer: A Family Guide to Diagnosis, Treatment & Survival. 1995. pap. text ed. 14.95 (*1-55561-078-1*) Fisher Bks.

— Retinoids in Cutaneous Malignancy. 205p. 1991. 135.00 (*0-632-02646-4*) Blackwell Sci.

Marks, jt. auth. see Willis.

Marks, A., jt. auth. see Tingay, G.

***Marks, Abby.** Study Skills: Tools for Active Learning. 1994. pap. text ed. 22.95 (*0-8273-5437-1*) Delmar.

Marks, Alan. Commando Attack. 256p. (Orig.). 1986. reprint ed. pap. 2.95 (*0-8439-2419-5*) Dorchester Pub Co.

— Nowhere to be Found. LC 87-32729. (Illus.). 28p. (J). (ps up). 1991. pap. 14.95 (*0-88708-062-6*, Picture Book Studio) S&S Childrens.

— Social Psychology. 194p. 1995. student ed. pap. text ed. 13.95x (*0-87901-749-X*) Worth.

— Thief's Daughter. (J). (ps-3). 1994. 11.00 (*0-374-37481-3*) FS&G.

Marks, Alan, ed. Over the Hills & Far Away: A Book of Nursery Rhymes. LC 94-10263. (Illus.). 1994. 19.95 (*1-55858-285-1*) North-South Bks NYC.

Marks, Alan, ed. & illus. Ring-a-Ring o' Roses & a Ding, Dong Bell: A Collection of Nursery Rhymes. LC 91-15222. 96p. (J). (gr. k up). 1991. pap. 19.95 (*0-88708-187-8*, Picture Book Studio) S&S Childrens.

Marks, Alfred. I've Taken a Page in the Bible. 208p. 1987. 14.95 (*0-86051-348-3*, Pub. by Robson UK) Parkwest Pubns.

Marks, Alfred H., tr. see Ihara, Saikaku.

Marks, Alfred H., tr. see Mishima, Yukio.

Marks, Aminta. A Pieta for the Dispossessed: The Grace of Palestinians. LC 93-80534. (Illus.). 170p. (Orig.). 1994. pap. 12.00 (*0-9626898-2-3*) Grindstone Pr.

— So It Is: In the Image of God He Created Them (Poems) LC 90-82231. (Illus.). 179p. (Orig.). 1990. pap. 12.00 (*0-9626898-0-7*) Grindstone Pr.

— Sweet Water & Polar: Poems from the Length of a Marriage. LC 92-81196. 177p. (Orig.). 1992. pap. 12.00 (*0-9626898-1-5*) Grindstone Pr.

***Marks, Andrew R.** The Rabbi & the Poet: Victor Reichert & Robert Frost. LC 93-72556. (Illus.). 64p. (Orig.). 1994. pap. 12.00 (*1-885934-01-7*) Andover Green.

Marks, Anne W., ed. N P T: Paradoxes & Problems. LC 75-826. 1975. pap. 1.50 (*0-87003-022-1*) Carnegie Endow.

***Marks, Anthony & Rye, Howard.** Learn to Play Blues. (Learn to Play Ser.). (Illus.). 64p. (J). (gr. 1 up). 1995. lib. bdg. 15.96 (*0-88110-765-4*, Usborne); pap. 9.95 (*0-7460-1677-8*, Usborne) EDC.

Marks, Anthony E., ed. Prehistory & Paleoenvironments in the Central Negev, Israel Vol. I, Pt. 1: The Avdat-Aqev Area. LC 75-40116. (Institute for the Study of Earth & Man: Reports of Investigations Ser.: No. 2). (Illus.). 392p. 1976. pap. 27.50 (*0-87074-153-5*) SMU Press.

— Prehistory & Paleoenvironments in the Central Negev, Israel Vol. II, Pt. 2: The Avdat-Aqev Area & the Harif. LC 75-40116. (Institute for the Study of Earth & Man: Reports of Investigations Ser.: No. 2). (Illus.). x, 368p. 1977. pap. 25.00 (*0-89643-000-6*) SMU Press.

— Prehistory & Paleoenvironments in the Central Negev, Israel, Vol. III: The Advat-Aqev Area, Pt.3. LC 75-40116. (Institute for the Study of Earth & Man: Reports of Investigations Ser.: No. 2). (Illus.). xvi, 368p. 1983. pap. 35.00 (*0-89643-113-4*) SMU Press.

Marks, Anthony E. & Mohammed-Ali, Abbas, eds. Late Prehistory of the Eastern Sahel: The Mesolithic & Neolithic of Shaqadud, Sudan. LC 90-52656. (Illus.). 304p. 1991. pap. text ed. 29.95 (*0-87074-310-4*) SMU Press.

Marks, Anthony E., jt. ed. see Wendorf, Fred.

Marks, Barbara, jt. auth. see Knipe, Judy.

Marks, Barry A. E. E. Cummings. (United States Authors Ser.: No. 46). 1965. text ed. 19.95 (*0-8057-0176-1*, Twayne) Macmillan.

Marks, Bayly E., ed. see Glenn, William W.

***Marks-Beale, Abby.** Study Skills Instructor's Guide: The Tools for Active Learning. 84p. 1994. teacher ed 16.00 (*0-8273-5439-8*) Delmar.

Marks, Ben. Forbidden Entry: Installations by George Geyer, Lilla Locurto, Carol Newborg, Karen Frimkiss Wolff. (Illus.). 24p. (Orig.). 1990. pap. 8.00 (*0-945192-05-3*) USC Fisher Gallery.

Marks, Betty. Light & Easy Diabetes Cuisine. 256p. 1990. pap. 12.95 (*0-89586-640-4*, HP Books) Berkley Pub.

— The Microwave Diabetes Cookbook. (Illus.). 256p. (Orig.). 1991. pap. 10.95 (*0-940625-26-1*, Publishers Group) Surrey Bks.

Marks, Brian & Hannah, Ian. Heat & Light. 80p. 1993. pap. 22.00 (*0-86153-169-8*, Pub. by St Andrew UK) St Mut.

Marks, Burton. Animals. LC 91-3656. (Read-a-Picture Ser.). (Illus.). 24p. (J). (gr. k-2). 1992. lib. bdg. 9.89 (*0-8167-2415-6*); pap. text ed. 2.95 (*0-8167-2416-4*) Troll Assocs.

— Bear's Boat. (Go-Along Book Ser.). (Illus.). 10p. (J). (ps-3). 1993. 4.99 (*0-89577-516-6*, Random) RD Assn.

— Colors & Numbers. LC 91-17493. (Read-a-Picture Ser.). (Illus.). 24p. (J). (gr. k-2). 1992. lib. bdg. 9.89 (*0-8167-2411-3*); pap. text ed. 2.95 (*0-8167-2412-1*) Troll Assocs.

— Let's Go. LC 91-9986. (Read-a-Picture Ser.). (Illus.). 24p. (J). (gr. k-2). 1992. lib. bdg. 9.89 (*0-8167-2413-X*); pap. text ed. 2.95 (*0-8167-2414-8*) Troll Assocs.

— Penguin's Plane. (Go-Along Book Ser.). (Illus.). 10p. (J). (ps). 1993. 4.99 (*0-89577-517-4*, Random) RD Assn.

— Pig's Car. LC 92-62552. (Go-Along Bks.). (Illus.). 10p. (J). (ps-1). 1993. 4.99 (*0-89577-476-3*) RD Assn.

— Rhymes & Stories. LC 91-3663. (Read-a-Picture Ser.). (Illus.). 24p. (J). (gr. k-2). 1992. lib. bdg. 9.89 (*0-8167-2409-1*); pap. 2.95 (*0-8167-2410-5*) Troll Assocs.

Marks, Cara. God Bless You. (Illus.). 1993. 6.50 (*0-8378-5446-6*) Gibson.

Marks, Cara G. The Handbook of Hebrew Calligraphy. LC 90-728. 208p. 1990. 30.00 (*0-87668-798-2*) Aronson.

Marks, Carole. Farewell--We're Good & Gone: The Great Black Migration. LC 88-45454. (Blacks in the Diaspora Ser.). (Illus.). 222p. 1989. 37.95 (*0-253-33642-2*); pap. 12.95 (*0-253-20520-4*, MB-520) Ind U Pr.

Marks, Cathy & Marks, Steve. Swing, Dawn of a New Era: The Alternative Lifestyle. LC 94-75819. 320p. 1994. 24.95 (*0-9640903-0-9*) M S W Pubng.

Marks, Celia. Come into My Kitchen. 1969. spiral bd. 12.95 (*0-9606574-0-1*) Plum Nelly.

Marks, Charles & Marks, Peter H. Fundamentals of Cardiac Surgery. LC 93-12008. 1993. write for info. (*0-412-54310-9*, Chap & Hall NY) Chapman & Hall.

Marks, Claude. World Artists, 1950-1980. LC 84-13152. (Illus.). 928p. 1984. 83.00 (*0-8242-0707-6*) Wilson.

Marks, Claude, ed. World Artists, 1980-1990. 432p. 1991. 58.00 (*0-8242-0827-7*) Wilson.

Marks, Coleen, jt. ed. see Groth, Patricia C.

Marks, Copeland. The Burmese Kitchen. 1994. pap. 12.95 (*0-87131-768-0*) M Evans.

— The Exotic Kitchens of Indonesia: Recipes from the Outer Islands. LC 89-23322. (Illus.). 322p. 1989. 19.95 (*0-87131-576-9*) M Evans.

— Exotic Kitchens of Indonesia: Recipes from the Outer Islands. 1993. pap. 10.95 (*0-87131-737-0*) M Evans.

— False Tongues & Sunday Bread: A Guatemalan & Mayan Cookbook. LC 93-70896. (Illus.). 416p. 1993. pap. 14.95 (*1-55611-379-X*) D I Fine.

— The Great Book of Couscous: Classic Cuisines of Morocco, Algeria & Tunisia. LC 94-71117. 384p. 1994. 24.95 (*1-55611-420-6*) D I Fine.

— Sephardic Cooking: Six Hundred Recipes Created in Exotic Sephardic Kitchens from Morocco to India. LC 91-55191. 560p. 1992. 24.95 (*1-55611-318-8*) D I Fine.

— Sephardic Cooking: Six Hundred Recipes Created in Exotic Sephardic Kitchens from Morocco to India. LC 94-71112. 560p. 1994. pap. 14.95 (*1-55611-419-2*, Primus) D I Fine.

Marks, Copeland & Kim, Manjo. The Korean Kitchens of Korea: Classic Recipes from the Land of the Morning Calm. LeBlond, Bill, ed. LC 92-38968. (Illus.). 224p. 1993. pap. 11.95 (*0-8118-0321-X*) Chronicle Bks.

Marks, Copeland & Soeharjo, Mintari. The Indonesian Kitchen. LC 80-23103. 288p. 1984. pap. 12.00 (*0-689-70667-7*, 309, Pub. by Ctrl Bur voor Schimmel NE) Macmillan.

Marks, Copeland & Thein, Aung. The Burmese Kitchen. LC 87-22242. (Illus.). 288p. 1987. 19.95 (*0-87131-524-6*) M Evans.

Marks, D. J. & Donnelly, J. Introduction to Physical Inorganic Chemistry. 283p. reprint ed. pap. 80.70 (*0-317-27828-2*, 2025248) Bks Demand.

Marks, Daniel, ed. Foundations of Empire: Archaeology & Art of the Eurasian Steppes. Zirin, Mary F., tr. LC 91-70732. (Illus.). 250p. (Orig.). (C). 1991. pap. 12.00 (*1-878986-02-3*) Ethnographics Pr.

— Rulers from the Steppe: State Formation on the Inner Eurasian Periphery. Zirin, Mary F., tr. LC 90-84794. (Ethnographics Monographs). (Illus.). 328p. (Orig.). (C). 1991. pap. 12.00 (*1-878986-01-5*) Ethnographics Pr.

Marks, David & Kammann, Richard. The Psychology of the Psychic. LC 80-7458. (Science & the Paranormal Ser.). 232p. (C). 1980. 26.95x (*0-87975-121-5*) Prometheus Bks.

Marks, David F. Theories of Image Formation. 1986. lib. bdg. 45.00 (*0-913412-18-X*) Brandon Hse.

Marks, David M. Testing Very Big Systems. 1992. text ed. 35.00 (*0-07-040433-X*) McGraw.

— Testing Very Big Systems. 240p. 1991. 39.95 (*0-8306-2555-0*) TAB Bks.

Marks, Dawn B. Basic Medical Biochemistry. (Illus.). 550p. 1995. write for info. (*0-683-05595-X*) Williams & Wilkins.

— Biochemistry. 2nd ed. (Board Review Ser.). (Illus.). 330p. 1994. 19.95 (*0-683-05597-6*) Williams & Wilkins.

Marks, Diana, ed. see Marks, Joseph.

Marks, Dorrit K., ed. Women & Grass Roots Democracy in the Americas. (University of Miami North-South Center Ser.). 100p. (C). 1993. pap. text ed. 14.95 (*1-56000-685-4*) Transaction Pubs.

Marks, Dustin D. Cheating at Blackjack: (And Advantage Play) LC 94-76753. (Illus.). 232p. (Orig.). 1994. pap. 19.95 (*1-56866-071-5*) Index Pub Grp.

— Cheating at Blackjack: The Dark Side of Gambling. (Illus.). 320p. (Orig.). 1995. pap. 19.95 (*1-56866-073-1*) Index Pub Grp.

— Mothers Maiden Name. (Illus.). 100p. (Orig.). 1995. pap. 39.95 (*1-56866-098-7*) Index Pub Grp.

Marks, E. S. & Elsdon, K. T. Adults in the Colleges of Further Education. (C). 1991. 45.00 (*1-85041-042-9*, Pub. by Univ Nottingham UK) St Mut.

***Marks, Edward & Lewis, William.** Triage for Failing States. 52p. (Orig.). (C). 1994. pap. text ed. 40.00x (*0-7881-1192-2*) Diane Pub.

Marks, Edward S. Entry Strategies in School Consultation. (School Practitioner Ser.). 1995. lib. bdg. 27.95 (*0-89862-368-5*, 2368) Guilford Pr.

Marks, Elaine. Critical Essays on Simone de Beauvoir. (Critical Essays Ser.). 280p. 1987. text ed. 45.00 (*0-8161-8836-X*) G K Hall.

Marks, Elaine, ed. Homosexualities & French Literature: Cultural Contexts Critical Texts. LC 78-25659. 392p. 1990. reprint ed. pap. 16.95 (*0-8014-9766-3*) Cornell U Pr.

Marks, Elaine & De Courtivron, Isabelle, eds. New French Feminisms, An Anthology. LC 81-40413. (Women's Studies Ser.). 304p. (C). 1987. reprint ed. pap. 14.00 (*0-8052-0681-7*) Schocken.

Marks, Elaine, ed. see Gide, Andre.

***Marks, Ellen L.** Case Management in Service Integration: A Concept Paper. 32p. 1994. pap. text ed. 8.00 (*0-926582-13-5*) NCCP.

Marks, Emerson R. Coleridge on the Language of Verse. LC 80-8562. (Essays in Literature Ser.). 116p. 1981. 21.95 (*0-691-06458-X*) Princeton U Pr.

— Coleridge on the Language of Verse. LC 80-8562. (Princeton Essays in Literature Ser.). Date not set. reprint ed. pap. 36.80 (*0-7837-9380-4*, 2060124) Bks Demand.

— Relativist & Absolutist: The Early Neoclassical Debate in England. LC 75-23348. 171p. 1975. reprint ed. text ed. 49.75 (*0-8371-8348-0*, MARAB, Greenwood Pr) Greenwood.

Marks, Esther S., et al, eds. Primary Eyecare in Systematic Disease. LC 94-10704. (C). 1994. text ed. 90.00 (*0-8385-7997-3*) Appleton & Lange.

Marks, Ethel, jt. auth. see Marks, Stanley.

Marks, Ethel M., jt. auth. see Marks, Stanley J.

***Marks, Eugene.** Lemonade Gravy. 1994. pap. 4.95 (*0-9644648-0-2*) Band Hope Pub.

Marks, F. Helena. The Sonata. 1977. text ed. 16.95 (*0-8369-8188-X*) Ayer.

— The Sonata, Its Form & Meaning as Exemplified in the Piano Sonatas by Mozart: A Descriptive Analysis. 167p. 1990. reprint ed. lib. bdg. 59.00 (*0-7812-9170-4*) Rprt Serv.

— The Sonata, Its Form & Meaning As Exemplified in the Piano Sonatas by Mozart: A Descriptive Analysis with Musical Examples. LC 78-66911. (Encore Music Editions Ser.). (Illus.). 1980. reprint ed. 21.50 (*0-88355-751-7*) Hyperion Conn.

Marks, Frederick. Power & Peace: The Diplomacy of John Foster Dulles. LC 92-42442. 296p. 1993. text ed. 49.95 (*0-275-94497-2*, C4497, Praeger Pubs) Greenwood.

***Marks, Frederick W.** A Catholic Handbook for Engaged & Newly Married Couples. LC 94-72069. 126p. (Orig.). 1994. pap. 5.00 (*1-880033-14-3*) Faith Pub OH.

Marks, Frederick W., III. Independence on Trial: Foreign Affairs & the Making of the Constitution. 2nd ed. LC 86-11876. 256p. (Orig.). (C). 1986. 35.00 (*0-8420-2272-4*); pap. text ed. 14.95 (*0-8420-2273-2*) Scholarly Res Inc.

***Marks, Frederick W.** Power & Peace: The Diplomacy of John Foster Dulles. LC 92-42442. 296p. 1995. pap. text ed. 19.95 (*0-275-95232-0*, Praeger Pubs) Greenwood.

Marks, Frederick W., III. Wind over Sand: The Diplomacy of Franklin Roosevelt. LC 86-24976. (Illus.). 472p. 1990. pap. 18.00 (*0-8203-1270-3*) U of Ga Pr.

Marks, G. Harrap's Dictionnaire d'Argot: French to English, English to French Slang Dictionary. rev. ed. 879p. 1986. pap. 45.00 (*0-7859-4824-4*, M6308) Fr & Eur.

Marks, G. Warren, ed. The Planning & Engineering Interface with a Modernized Land Data System. LC 80-66123. 269p. 1980. pap. 28.00 (*0-87262-243-6*) Am Soc Civil Eng.

Marks, Gary. Unions in Politics: Britain, Germany, & the United States in the Nineteenth & Early Twentieth Centuries. 256p. 1989. text ed. 45.00 (*0-691-07801-7*); pap. text ed. 15.95 (*0-691-02304-2*) Princeton U Pr.

Marks, Gary & Diamond, Larry. Reexamining Democracy. 352p. (C). 1992. text ed. 32.00 (*0-8039-4641-4*) Sage.

Marks, Gary, jt. ed. see Lemke, Christiane.

Marks, Genee. Integration of Children into Regular Schools Each an Individual (ECT 324) 168p. (C). 1989. 66.00 (*0-7300-0706-5*, Pub. by Deakin Univ AT) St Mut.

Marks, Genee, jt. auth. see Mousley, Judith.

Marks, Geoffry W., comp. Call to Remembrance: Connecting the Heart to Baha'u'llah. 308p. 1992. 30.00 (*0-87743-237-6*) Bahai.

Marks, George P. The Black Press Views American Imperialism (1898-1900) 1973. 24.95 (*0-405-01985-8*, 19466) Ayer.

Marks, George V. & Lall, Bhagirath, eds. Organization & Management of Public Transport Projects: Proceedings of a Conference Sponsored by the Public Transport Committee of the Urban Transportation Division. 320p. 1985. 34.00 (*0-87262-458-7*) Am Soc Civil Eng.

Marks, Gerald & Caesar, Irving. Sing a Song of Safety. 80p. Date not set. pap. write for info. (*0-318-72238-0*) Music Sales.

Marks, Graham. Webster & the Witch. (Illus.). 40p. (J). (gr. k-3). 1987. 15.95 (*0-340-35564-6*, Pub. by H & S UK) Trafalgar.

Marks, H. Law & Administration: Leading Articles Law & Administration Relating to Nuclear Energy. LC 59-8165. (Progress in Nuclear Energy Ser.: Vol. 1). 1959. 410.00 (*0-08-009184-9*, Pub. by Pergamon Repr UK) Franklin.

Marks, Hilary. Food & Farming in the Fifteen Republics of the Former U. S. S. R. A Market Survey. (Illus.). 200p. 1992. 650.00 (*1-85573-096-0*, Pub. by Woodhead Pubng UK) St Mut.

Marks, Hilary F. A Hundred Years of British Food & Farming: A Statistical Survey. Britton, Denis K., ed. 300p. 1989. 130.00 (*0-85066-452-7*, Pub. by Tay Francis Ltd UK) Taylor & Francis.

Marks, Howard & Marks, Kristin. Networking Windows, NetWare Edition. (Illus.). (Orig.). 1992. disk, pap. 24.95 (*0-672-30206-3*) Sams.

Marks, Isaac M. Behavioural Psychotherapy: Maudsley Pocket Book of Clinical Management. (Illus.). 150p. 1986. pap. 22.50 (*0-317-56190-1*, Yr Bk Med Pubs) Mosby Yr Bk.

— Cure & Care of Neuroses. LC 87-33350. 329p. 1981. reprint ed. 21.00 (*0-88048-162-5*) Am Psychiatric.

— Fears, Phobias & Rituals: Panic, Anxiety, & Their Disorders. (Illus.). 704p. 1987. 55.00 (*0-19-503927-0*) OUP.

— Living with Fear. 320p. 1980. pap. text ed. 9.95 (*0-07-040396-1*) McGraw.

Marks, Isaac M. & Scott, Robert A., eds. Mental Health Care Delivery: Innovations, Impediments & Implementation. (Illus.). 250p. (C). 1990. 69.95 (*0-521-38494-X*) Cambridge U Pr.

Marks, J. Benzodiazepines, Use, Overuse, Misuse, & Abuse. 2nd ed. 1985. lib. bdg. 42.50 (*0-85200-870-8*) Kluwer Ac.

Marks, J. & Pare, C. Scientific Basis of Drug Therapy in Psychiatry: Symposium St. Bertholomews Hospital, London, Sept. 1964. LC 65-16261. 1965. 99.00 (*0-08-011195-5*, Pub. by Pergamon Repr UK) Franklin.

Marks, J., jt. ed. see Glatt, M. M.

Marks, James G. & Deleo. Contact & Occupational Dermatology. 346p. 1992. 69.00 (*0-8016-3123-8*) Mosby Yr Bk.

Marks, James G., Jr., jt. auth. see Lookingbill, Donald P.

Marks, James R. & Craigie, John D. Sharing the Risk: How the Nation's Businesses, Homes, & Autos Are Insured. 2nd rev. ed. LC 81-65769. 191p. reprint ed. pap. 54.50 (*0-685-23719-2*, 2032707) Bks Demand.

Marks, James R., et al. Handbook of Educational Supervision: A Guide for the Practitioner. 3rd ed. 529p. 1985. 44.95 (*0-685-10755-8*, H82993) Allyn.

***Marks, Jane.** The Hidden Children: The Secret Survivors of the Holocaust. 336p. 1995. pap. 12.00 (*0-449-90686-8*) Fawcett.

— We Have a Problem: A Parent's Sourcebook. LC 92-7391. 320p. 1992. 23.95 (*0-88048-504-3*) Am Psychiatric.

— We Have a Problem: A Parent's Sourcebook. 1993. mass mkt. 5.99 (*0-06-104298-6*, Harp PBks) HarpC.

Marks, Jason. Around the World in Seventy-Two Days: The Race Between Pulitzer's Nellie Bly & Cosmopolitan's Elizabeth Bisland. LC 92-73586. (Illus.). 261p. (Orig.). 1993. pap. 12.95 (*0-9633696-1-X*) Gemittarius.

they traversed. To order: Publishers Distribution Service (PDS), (800) 507-BOOK, Baker & Taylor, Ingram, Pacific Pipeline. Special library hardcover discount. ***Publisher Provided Annotation.***

— Twelve Who Made It Big. LC 81-68767. (Illus.). 112p. (Orig.). 1981. pap. write for info. (*0-9606858-0-4*) Alumni Assn.

Marks, Jeannette A. English Pastoral Drama. LC 76-173175. 1972. reprint ed. 20.95 (*0-405-08781-0*, Pub. by Blom Pubns UK) Ayer.

— Through Welsh Doorways. LC 78-167463. (Short Story Index Reprint Ser.). 1977. reprint ed. 20.95 (*0-8369-3989-1*) Ayer.

Marks, Jeffrey S. Lasting Images Price Guide to Adult Entertainment & Fantasy Art Pinup Cards. (Illus.). 60p. (Orig.). 1994. 14.95 (*0-9641536-0-2*) Lasting Images.

Marks, Joan H., ed. Advocacy in Health Care. LC 86-283. (Contemporary Issues in Biomedicine, Ethics, & Society Ser.). 160p. 1986. 39.50 (*0-89603-092-X*) Humana.

Marks, Joel & Ames, Roger T., eds. Emotions in Asian Thought: A Dialogue in Comparative Philosophy. LC 94-2723. 1994. pap. 19.95 (*0-7914-2224-0*) State U NY Pr.

— Emotions in Asian Thought: A Dialogue in Comparative Philosophy. LC 94-2723. 1995. 59.50 (*0-7914-2223-2*) State U NY Pr.

***Marks, John.** Lost Quotes. LC 94-60808. 81p. (Orig.). 1994. pap. 5.95 (*0-9642648-0-3*) Toranaga Pr.

— Science & the Making of the Modern World. xiv, 507p. 1984. pap. text ed. 29.50 (*0-435-54781-X*) Heinemann.

Marks, John D. Search - Manchurian Candidate. 1980. write for info. (*0-394-59583-1*) Random.

— The Search for the "Manchurian Candidate" The CIA & Mind Control. 228p. 1991. pap. 10.95 (*0-393-30794-8*) Norton.

Marks, John H. & Rogers, Virgil M. A Beginner's Handbook to Biblical Hebrew. LC 58-7434. xiv, 174p. 1958. text ed. 15.95x (*0-687-02616-4*) Abingdon.

Marks, John L., et al. Teaching Elementary School Mathematics for Understanding. 5th ed. 416p. 1985. text ed. write for info. (*0-07-040423-2*) McGraw.

Marks, Jonathan. Human Biodiversity: Genes, Race, & History. (Foundations of Human Behavior Ser.). 336p. 1995. lib. bdg. 46.95 (*0-202-02032-0*); pap. 23.95 (*0-202-02033-9*) Aldine de Gruyter.

Marks, Jonathan, jt. auth. see Staski, Edward.

***Marks, Joseph.** Wall Street in Your Pocket. Marks, Diana, ed. 170p. (Orig.). 1995. pap. write for info. (*1-885591-77-2*) Morris Pubng.

Marks, Joseph J. Instant Writing Course. (Illus.). 32p. 1980. Discounts 10-49 copies $2.63., 50-99 copies $2.10 ea., 100 or more copies $1.75 ea. pap. text ed. 3.50 (*0-8134-2086-5*) Interstate.

Marks, Kate. Circle of Song - Songs, Chants & Dances for Ritual & Celebration. LC 93-73300. (Illus.). 304p. (Orig.). 1994. pap. 17.95 (*0-9637489-0-4*) Full Circle MA.

Marks-Kaufman, Robin, jt. auth. see Kanarek, Robin B.

Marks, Kenneth E., et al. Electronic Collection Maintenance & Video Archiving. (Supplement to Computers in Libraries Ser.: No. 54). 175p. 1994. pap. 42.50 (*0-88736-830-1*) Learned Info.

Marks, Kristin, jt. auth. see Marks, Howard.

Marks, Lara V. Model Mothers: Jewish Mothers & Maternity Provision in East London 1870-1939. (Oxford Historical Monographs). (Illus.). 360p. 1994. 53.00 (*0-19-820454-X*) OUP.

Marks, Larry. Unemployment: A State of Mind. (Illus.). 80p. 1994. 29.00 (*1-56216-223-3*); pap. 14.00x (*1-56216-224-1*) Systems Co.

Marks, Laurie J. Dancing Jack. 256p. 1993. mass mkt. 4.99 (*0-88677-578-7*) DAW Bks.

— The Watcher's Mask. 288p. (Orig.). 1992. mass mkt. 4.99 (*0-88677-510-8*) DAW Bks.

Marks, Lawrence E. Sensory Processes: The New Psychophysics. 1974. text ed. 59.00 (*0-12-472950-9*) Acad Pr.

— The Unity of the Senses. (Cognition & Perception Ser.). 1978. text ed. 85.00 (*0-12-472960-6*) Acad Pr.

Marks, Lawrence E., ed. see Hammeal, Robin J. & Bornstein, Marc H.

Marks, Leonard, jt. auth. see Walsh, Charles V.

Marks, Leonard M., ed. see Chitrabhanu, Gurudev S.

Marks, Lillian B. Reister's Desire: The Origin of Reisterstown... with a Genealogical History of the Reister Family. LC 75-18893. (Illus.). 1976. 15.00 (*0-938420-16-X*) MD Hist.

Marks, Lillian S. On Printing in the Tradition. 24p. 1989. 8.00 (*0-929722-31-0*) CA State Library Fndtn.

— Touch Typing Made Simple. LC 85-4431. (Made Simple Ser.). (Illus.). 192p. 1985. pap. 12.95 (*0-385-19426-9*) Doubleday.

Marks, Linda. Living with Vision: Reclaiming the Power of the Heart. (Orig.). 1991. pap. 12.95 (*0-904575-53-5*, Coventure Ltd) Sigo Pr.

Marks, Linda, jt. auth. see Feiden, Karyn.

Marks, Lindy L., et al. Chinoperl Papers,1983, No. 12. Shadick, Harold et al, eds. (Chinoperl Papers). 171p. (Orig.). 1984. pap. 10.00 (*0-318-23301-0*) Chinoperl.

Marks, Londa. Londa Tarot. 24p. 1993. 15.00 (*0-88079-664-2*) US Games Syst.

Marks, M. I. Broadribb's Introductory Pediatric Nursing. (Illus.). 592p. (C). 1994. pap. text ed. 25.95 (*0-397-54946-6*, Lippincott Nursing) Lippincott.

— Pediatric Infectious Diseases for the Practitioner. (Comprehensive Manuals in Pediatrics Ser.: Vol. 3). (Illus.). 890p. 1984. 138.00 (*0-387-96010-4*) Spr-Verlag.

Marks, M. L. Jews among the Indians: Tales of Adventure & Conflict in the Old West. LC 92-81618. 200p. 1992. 21.95 (*0-9632965-0-7*) Benison Bks.

— Jews among the Indians: Tales of Adventure & Conflict in the Old West. LC 92-81618. 190p. 1995. pap. 14.95 (*0-9632965-1-5*) Benison Bks.

Marks, Manuel H. & Corn, Herman, eds. Atlas of Adult Orthodontics: Functional & Esthetic Enhancement. LC 86-21469. (Illus.). 645p. 1989. text ed. 149.50 (*0-8121-1023-4*) Williams & Wilkins.

Marks-Maran, Diane, jt. auth. see Hunt, Jennifer M.

Marks, Martha & Blake, Robert. Al Corriente: Curso Intermedio de Espanol. 1993. Realia kit. write for info. (*0-07-040472-0*) McGraw.

— Al Corriente: Curso Intermedio de Espanol. 2nd ed. 1993. pap. text ed. write for info. (*0-07-040467-4*) McGraw.

— Al Corriente: Curso Intermedio de Espanol. 2nd ed. 1993. Tapescript. write for info. (*0-07-040471-2*) McGraw.

— Al Corriente: Curso Intermedio de Espanol. 2nd ed. 1993. Wkbk. & lab bk. student ed, pap. text ed. write for info. (*0-07-040469-0*) McGraw.

Marks, Martin M. Music & the Silent Film: Contexts & Case Studies, 1895-1924. (Illus.). 352p. Date not set. 40.00 (*0-19-506891-2*) OUP.

Marks, Mary E. Cooking with Southern Accents: A Collection of Old & New Recipes. (Illus.). (Orig.). 1988. pap. 10.00 (*0-9621561-0-8*) M E Marks.

Marks, Matthew, intro. American Prints, 1860-1960: From the Collection of Matthew Marks. LC 85-71125. (Illus.). 32p. 1985. pap. 5.90 (*0-9614940-0-X*) Bennington Coll.

Marks, Mitchell L. From Turmoil to Triumph: New Life After Mergers, Acquisitions, & Downsizing. LC 94-4758. 1994. text ed. 24.95 (*0-02-920055-5*) Free Pr.

Marks, Morton, jt. auth. see Polnauer, Frederick.

Marks, Neville & Rodnight, Richard, eds. Research Methods In Neurochemistry, Vol. 5. LC 72-222263. 334p. 1981. 79.50 (*0-306-40583-0*, Plenum Pr) Plenum.

— Research Methods in Neurochemistry, Vol. 6. 392p. 1985. 89.50 (*0-306-41751-0*, Plenum Pr) Plenum.

Marks, Norton E., jt. ed. see Durlabhji, Subhash.

Marks, P. L., et al. Late Eighteenth Century Vegetation of Central & Western New York State on the Basis of Original Land Surveys. (New York State Museum Bulletin Ser.: No. 484). (Illus.). 55p. (Orig.). 1992. pap. 7.50 (*1-55557-225-1*) NYS Museum.

Marks, Patricia. Bicycles, Bangs & Boomers: The New Woman in the Popular Press. LC 89-25110. (Illus.). 232p. 1990. text ed. 25.00 (*0-8131-1704-6*) U Pr of Ky.

Marks, Patricia, jt. auth. see Savory, Jerold J.

Marks, Paula M. Precious Dust: The North American Gold Rush Era, 1848-1900. LC 93-28196. 1994. 25.00 (*0-688-10566-1*) Morrow.

— Precious Dust: The Saga of the Western Gold Rush. LC 94-22488. 1995. pap. 14.00 (*0-06-258588-6*) HarpC.

— Turn Your Eyes Toward Texas: Pioneers Sam & Mary Maverick. LC 88-27573. (Centennial Series of the Association of Former Students: No. 30). 344p. 1989. 29.50 (*0-89096-380-0*) Tex A&M Univ Pr.

Marks, Paula M., jt. auth. see Hall, Sarah H.

Marks, Percy. The Plastic Age: A Novel. LC 80-17959. (Lost American Fiction Ser.). 352p. 1980. reprint ed. 12.95 (*0-8093-0984-X*) S Ill U Pr.

Marks, Peter, jt. auth. see Marks, Walter.

Marks, Peter H., jt. auth. see Marks, Charles.

Marks, R. & Robinson, A. T. Principles of Weaving. 249p. (C). 1986. pap. text ed. 85.00 (*0-900739-79-7*, Pub. by Textile Institue UK) St Mut.

Marks, R. J. & Jackson, R. Aspects of Civil Engineering Contract Procedure. 3rd ed. LC 84-25569. (International Library of Science, Technology, Engineering, & Social Studies Ser.). 1985. text ed. 121.00 (*0-08-031637-9*, Pub. by Pergamon Repr UK) Franklin.

***Marks, R. L.** Studying Electrochemical Cells & Reduction Potentials. Neidig, H. A., ed. (Modular Laboratory Program in Chemistry Ser.). 12p. (C). 1992. pap. text ed. 1.25x (*0-87540-418-9*) Chem Educ Res.

Marks, R. M., et al. Atlas of Skin Pathology. (Current Histopathology Ser.). 1986. lib. bdg. 177.50 (*0-85200-324-2*) Kluwer Ac.

Marks, R. M. Roxburgh's Common Skin Diseases. 16th ed. (Illus.). 296p. 1994. pap. 49.50 (*0-412-41130-X*) Chapman & Hall.

Marks, R. M., ed. Topics in Topicals. 1985. lib. bdg. 82.50 (*0-85200-891-0*) Kluwer Ac.

Marks, R. M., et al, eds. The Physical Nature of the Skin. (C). 1988. lib. bdg. 95.00 (*0-85200-977-1*) Kluwer Ac.

Marks, R. M. & Payne, P. A. Bioengineering & the Skin. (Illus.). 320p. 1982. lib. bdg. 109.50 (*0-85200-314-5*) Kluwer Ac.

Marks, R. M. & Plewig, Gerd, eds. Stratum Corneum. (Illus.). 300p. 1983. pap. 60.00 (*0-387-11704-0*) Spr-Verlag.

Marks, Randy. Guide to Nations Best Outlets: Outlet Bound. 1993. pap. 6.95 (*0-9631319-1-5*) Outlet Mktg.

— Outletbound: Guide to the Nation's Best Outlets. 150p. 1992. pap. 6.95 (*0-9631319-2-3*) Outlet Mktg.

— Outletbound: Guide to the Nation's Best Outlets, 1992 Edition. 124p. 1991. pap. 6.95 (*0-9631319-0-7*) Outlet Mktg.

Marks, Randy, ed. Outletbound, 1994: Guide to the Nation's Best Outlets. (Illus.). 175p. (Orig.). 1993. pap. 6.95 (*0-9631319-3-1*) Outlet Mktg.

***Marks, Richard.** Remembering Things of the Good Old Days. LC 93-73607. 48p. 1993. pap. text ed. 8.00 (*1-885935-01-3*) Appalchn Log.

— Stained Glass in England During the Middle Ages. (Illus.). 376p. 1993. 85.00 (*0-8020-0592-6*) U of Toronto Pr.

Marks, Richard & Morgan, Nigel. The Golden Age of English Manuscript Painting: 1200-1500. LC 80-12985. (Illus.). 120p. 1981. 25.00 (*0-8076-0971-4*) Braziller.

Marks, Richard G. The Image of Bar Kokhba in Traditional Jewish Literature: False Messiah & National Hero. LC 92-34744. (Hermeneutics: Studies in the History of Religions). 224p. 1993. 35.00 (*0-271-00939-X*); pap. 15.95 (*0-271-00940-3*) Pa St U Pr.

Marks, Richard L. Cortes: The Great Adventurer & the Fate of Aztec Mexico. LC 92-37170. 1993. 27.50 (*0-679-40609-3*) Knopf.

— Three Men of the Beagle. 272p. 1992. pap. 11.00 (*0-380-71838-3*) Avon.

Marks, Robert. Hamlet: Another Interpretation. LC 80-50694. 1980. 16.00 (*0-9605486-0-2*) Leda Pr.

Marks, Robert A. Effective Collection System for Delinquent Consumer Accounts. LC 79-13231. 39p. 1979. pap. 3.95 (*0-87576-082-1*) Pilot Bks.

Marks, Robert B. Rural Revolution in South China: Peasants & the Making of History in Haifeng County, 1570-1930. LC 83-16980. (Illus.). 368p. 1984. 32.50 (*0-299-09530-4*) U of Wis Pr.

Marks, Robert J., II. Fuzzy Logic Technology & Applications I. LC 94-14291. (IEEE Technology Update Ser.). 1994. write for info. (*0-7803-1383-6*) Inst Electrical.

Marks, Robert J., II & Thomas, J. B., eds. Advanced Topics in Shannon Sampling & Interpolation Theory. LC 92-25590. (Texts in Electrical Engineering Ser.). (Illus.). 376p. 1992. 69.00 (*0-387-97906-9*) Spr-Verlag.

***Marks, Ronald.** Sun-Damaged Skin. 1992. 19.95 (*0-614-06225-X*); 19.95 (*0-614-07393-6*, M Dunitz) Scovill Paterson.

***Marks, Ronald, ed.** Eczema. 1992. 95.00 (*0-614-06223-3*); 95.00 (*0-614-07391-X*, M Dunitz) Scovill Paterson.

— The Environmental Threat to the Skin. 1992. 115.00 (*0-614-06224-1*); 115.00 (*0-614-07392-8*, M Dunitz) Scovill Paterson.

***Marks, Ronald & Cunliffe, W. J., eds.** Skin Therapy. 1994. 29.95 (*1-85317-137-9*) Scovill Paterson.

Marks, Ronald, jt. auth. see Lowe, Nicholas.

***Marks, Ronald, et al.** Clinical Signs & Procedures in Dermatology. 1994. 65.00 (*0-948269-44-8*) Scovill Paterson.

Marks, Ruth A. Through It All. LC 87-73017. 1990. 11.95 (*0-8158-0448-2*) Chris Mass.

***Marks, S. J.** Something Grazes Our Hair: Poems. fac. rev. ed. LC 90-44637. 84p. 1991. pap. 25.00 (*0-7837-8078-8*, 2047831) Bks Demand.

Marks, S. N., ed. see Meares, L. G. & Hymowitz, C. E.

Marks, Sally. The Illusion of Peace: International Relations, 1918-1933. (Making of the Twentieth Century Ser.). (Illus.). (C). 1976. pap. text ed. 14.50 (*0-312-40635-5*) St Martin.

— Innocent Abroad: Belgium at the Paris Peace Conference of 1919. LC 80-13698. 461p. reprint ed. pap. 131.40 (*0-7837-2458-6*, 2042611) Bks Demand.

Marks, Sandy & Bell, Richard. The Best of the Sports Fan: Sports Trivia Games & More for All Sports Fans. 40p. write for info. (*0-9633505-0-1*) Strike Two Pr.

***Marks, Sharon F.** It Pays to Praise. (Self-Guided Workshop Ser.). 64p. (Orig.). 1995. pap. 8.95 (*0-917917-07-3*) Miles River.

Marks, Shelly, jt. auth. see Allen, Marie.

Marks, Sheryl, jt. ed. see VanGelder, Naneene.

Marks, Shirley F. Please Don't Call My Dog a Dog. LC 92-73384. (Illus.). 96p. 1993. pap. 9.95 (*0-942963-29-6*) Distinctive Pub.

Marks, Shula. The Ambiguities of Dependence in South Africa: Class, Nationalism, & the State in Twentieth-Century Natal. LC 85-7609. (Johns Hopkins Studies in Atlantic History & Culture Ser.). (Illus.). 188p. reprint ed. pap. 53.60 (*0-7837-6189-9*, 2045911) Bks Demand.

— Class, Race & Gender in South Africa: The Nursing Profession & The Making of Apartheid. LC 93-29470. 1994. 65.00 (*0-312-10643-2*) St Martin.

Marks, Shula, ed. Not Either an Experimental Doll: The Separate World of Three South African Women. LC 88-12867. (Illus.). 234p. (Orig.). 1988. 29.95 (*0-253-34843-9*); pap. 10.95 (*0-253-28640-9*) Ind U Pr.

Marks, Shula & Engels, Dagmar, eds. Contesting Colonial Hegemony: Gramsci & Imperialism. 240p. 1994. text ed. 59.50 (*1-85043-733-5*, Pub. by I B Tauris UK) St Martin.

Marks, Shula & Trapido, Stanley. The Politics of Race, Class & Nationalism in Twentieth Century South Africa. LC 86-27554. (Illus.). (C). 1987. pap. text ed. 30.50 (*0-582-64490-9*, 74623) Longman.

Marks, Shula, ed. see MacMillan, Hugh.

Marks, Siegfried, ed. Political Constraints on Brazil's Economic Development: (North-South Center, University of Miami, in Cooperation with the Getulio Vargas Foundation & University of Sao Paulo) LC 92-42842. 160p. (C). 1993. pap. text ed. 18.95 (*1-56000-683-8*) Transaction Pubs.

Marks, Stanley & Marks, Ethel. The U. S. Consumer Market, 1991. 65p. 1991. pap. 25.00 (*0-685-60575-2*) Bur Intl Aff.

Marks, Stanley J. The Defeat, Disgrace, & Dishonor! The Reagan-Bush Regimes: 1981-1993. 300p. (Orig.). 1993. write for info. (*0-938780-28-X*); pap. write for info. (*0-938780-27-1*) Bur Intl Aff.

— If This Be Treason...! The Reagan-Casey-Bush Conspiracy That Defeated President Jimmy Carter in the 1980 Presidential Election. 160p. (Orig.). 1995. pap. 15.95 (*0-938780-29-8*) Bur Intl Aff.

— If This Be Treason...! The Reagan-Casey-Bush Conspiracy That Defeated President Jimmy Carter in the 1980 Presidential Election. 160p. (Orig.). 1995. 22.95 (*0-938780-30-1*) Bur Intl Aff.

— A Year in the Lives of the Damned: Reagan-Reaganism 1986. 1988. pap. 14.95 (*0-685-17796-3*) Bur Intl Aff.

— A Year in the Lives of the Damned! Reagan-Reaganism, 1986. 292p. (Orig.). 1988. pap. 14.95 (*0-685-60574-4*) Bur Intl Aff.

Marks, Stanley J. & Marks, Ethel M. Jews, Judaism & the United States: The Impact of Judaism Upon the American People. LC 90-80500. 210p. (Orig.). 1991. 21.95 (*0-938780-20-4*); pap. 19.95 (*0-938780-21-2*) Bur Intl Aff.

— Judaism Looks at Christianity: 7 BC-1985 C. E. 295p. 1986. pap. 13.95 (*0-938780-10-7*) Bur Intl Aff.

— U. S. Consumer Market 1987. 1987. pap. 14.95 (*0-938780-11-5*) Bur Intl Aff.

— Yes, Americans, a Conspiracy Murdered JFK! (Illus.). 216p. (Orig.). Date not set. pap. 16.95 (*0-938780-25-5*) Bur Intl Aff.

— Yes, Americans, a Conspiracy Murdered JFK! LC 92-71289. (Illus.). 220p. (Orig.). 1992. text ed. 22.50 (*0-685-59494-7*); pap. 14.50 (*0-685-59495-5*); pap. text ed. 14.50 (*0-685-59496-3*) Bur Intl Aff.

Marks, Stephanie, ed. see Lewis, Ann E.

Marks, Stephen G., jt. auth. see Samuelson, William F.

Marks, Stephen V. & Maskus, Keith E., eds. The Economics & Politics of World Sugar Policies. LC 92-42179. (Studies In International Trade Policy). 190p. (C). 1993. text ed. 42.50 (*0-472-10428-4*) U of Mich Pr.

Marks, Steve, jt. auth. see Marks, Cathy.

Marks, Steven. Gallows Lane. LC 92-14289. 59p. (Orig.). 1993. pap. 6.00 (*0-88734-250-7*) Players Pr.

— Gallows Lane. LC 89-51875. (Illus.). 80p. (Orig.). (C). 1989. pap. 8.95 (*0-9624685-0-9*) Tyger Pr.

Marks, Steven G. Road to Power: The Trans-Siberian Railroad & the Colonization of Asian Russia, 1850-1917. LC 90-55734. (Illus.). 272p. 1991. 32.95 (*0-8014-2533-6*) Cornell U Pr.

Marks, Stuart A. Southern Hunting in Black & White: Nature, History & Ritual in a Carolina Community. (Illus.). 345p. 1993. text ed. 39.50 (*0-691-09452-7*); pap. text ed. 16.95 (*0-691-02851-6*) Princeton U Pr.

Marks, Sylvia K. Sir Charles Grandison: The Compleat Conduct Book. LC 85-47800. 176p. 1986. 36.50 (*0-8387-5090-7*) Bucknell U Pr.

Marks, T. & Robinson, L. Principles of Weaving. 256p. 1976. 90.00 (*0-686-63793-3*) St Mut.

Marks, T., ed. see Corneille, Pierre.

Marks, T., jt. auth. see Robinson, S.

***Marks, T. A.** Maoist Insurgency Since Vietnam. LC 95-5364. 270p. 1995. 39.50 (*0-7146-4606-7*, Pub. by F Cass Pubs UK); pap. 19.50 (*0-7146-4123-5*, Pub. by F Cass Pubs UK) Intl Spec Bk.

***Marks-Tarlow, Terry.** Creativity Inside Out: Learning Through Multiple Intelligences. Apple, Mali, ed. 400p. (Orig.). (YA). 1995. teacher ed, pap. 31.20 (*0-201-49044-7*) Altrntv Pub Grp.

Marks, Ted, jt. auth. see Mryglot, Gerard.

Marks, Thomas C., Jr. & Cooper, John F., Jr. Florida Constitutional Law. LC 92-71955. 600p. (C). 1992. lib. bdg. 60.00 (*0-89089-492-2*) Carolina Acad Pr.

Marks, Thomas C., Jr. & Cooper, John F. State Constitutional Law in a Nutshell. (Nutshell Ser.). 329p. 1988. pap. text ed. 18.50 (*0-314-41748-6*) West Pub.

Marks, Tobin J., ed. Bonding Energetics in Organometallic Compounds. LC 90-36268. (ACS Symposium Ser.: No. 428). (Illus.). 292p. 1990. 64.95 (*0-8412-1791-2*) Am Chemical.

Marks, Tobin J. & Fischer, Dieter, eds. Organometallics of the F-Elements. (NATO Advanced Study Institutes Ser.: C-44). 1979. lib. bdg. 117.00 (*90-277-0990-4*) Kluwer Ac.

Marks, Tobin J. & Fragala, Ignzio L., eds. Fundamental & Technological Aspects of Organo-f-Element Chemistry. 1985. lib. bdg. 129.50 (*90-277-2053-3*) Kluwer Ac.

Marks, Tracy. The Art of Chart Interpretation: A Step-by-Step Method of Analyzing, Synthesizing & Understanding the Birth Chart. LC 86-9683. 180p. (Orig.). 1986. pap. 9.95 (*0-916360-29-6*) CRCS Pubns CA.

— The Art of Chart Synthesis. LC 78-68664. 1979. pap. 6.00 (*0-933620-03-9*) Sag Rising.

— The Astrology of Self-Discovery: An In-Depth Exploration of the Potentials Revealed in the Birth Chart. LC 85-7844. 288p. (Orig.). 1986. pap. 13.95 (*0-916360-20-2*) CRCS Pubns CA.

— Planetary Aspects: From Conflict to Cooperation. rev. ed. LC 86-26445. 220p. (Orig.). 1987. pap. 12.95 (*0-916360-32-6*) CRCS Pubns CA.

— Your Secret Self: Illuminating the Mysteries of the Twelfth House. 288p. (Orig.). 1989. pap. 12.95 (*0-916360-43-1*) CRCS Pubns CA.

Marks, Trevor, ed. see Steward, W. E. & Stubbs, T. A.

Marks, V., jt. ed. see Hubbard, R.

Marks, Vernon J., et al. The Effects of Crushed Particles in Asphalt Mixtures. (Illus.). 52p. (Orig.). (C). 1992. pap. text ed. 29.95 (*1-56806-093-9*) Diane Pub.

Marks, Vic, jt. ed. see Holmes, Bob.

Marks, Vincent, jt. ed. see Williams, David L.

Marks, Vincent, jt. auth. see Williams, David.

Marks, Walter & Marks, Peter. The Butler Did It. 1981. pap. 4.75 (*0-8222-0167-4*) Dramatists Play.

Marks, William C. No More Mac & Cheese: A Bachelor's Guide to Cooking with Ease. (Illus.). 56p. 1990. ring bd. write for info. (*0-9628453-0-2*) Marks Pub CA.

Marks, Winifred. How to Give a Speech. 136p. (C). 1980. 40.00 (*0-85292-255-8*, Pub. by IPM Hse UK) St Mut.

— Politics & Personnel Management: An Outline History, 1960-1976. 240p. (C). 1978. 50.00 (*0-85292-189-6*) St Mut.

Marks, Wizard. Letters from Palenque. (U. S. A. Poetry Chapbook Ser.: No. 5). (Illus.). 16p. (Orig.). 1985. pap. 3.00 (*0-937724-06-8*) Shadow Pr.

An Asterisk (*) at the beginning of an entry indicates that the title is appearing in BIP for the first time.

Marksbury, Richard A., ed. The Business of Marriage: Transformations in Oceanic Matrimony. LC 93-1008. (Association for Social Anthropology in Oceania Monographs: No. 14). 280p. (C). 1994. text ed. 49.95 (*0-8229-3762-X*); pap. text ed. 19.95 (*0-8229-5511-3*) U of Pittsburgh Pr.

Marksbury, Tina, illus. Nighty-Night, Teddy Beddy Bear. (Cuddle Cloth Bks.). 12p. (J). (ps). 1986. 4.99 (*0-394-88244-X*) Random Bks Yng Read.

Markschies, Christoph, jt. auth. see Boehlig, Alexander.

Markson, David. Collected Poems. LC 92-18999. 96p. (Orig.). 1993. pap. 9.95 (*1-56478-033-3*) Dalkey Arch.

— Springer's Progress. LC 90-2731. 240p. 1990. reprint ed. pap. 9.95 (*0-916583-57-0*) Dalkey Arch.

— Wittgenstein's Mistress. LC 87-73068. 240p. 1988. 20.00 (*0-916583-25-2*) Dalkey Arch.

— Wittgenstein's Mistress. 1990. pap. 11.95 (*0-916583-50-3*) Dalkey Arch.

Markson, Elizabeth W., ed. Older Women: Issues & Prospects. LC 81-48025. (Boston University Gerontology Ser.). 352p. 1984. text ed. 19.95 (*0-669-09777-2*) Free Pr.

Markson, Elizabeth W., jt. ed. see Hess, Beth B.

Markstein, G. Nonsteady Flame Propagation. LC 64-14805. (Agardograph Ser.: Vol. 75). 1964. 140.00 (*0-08-010736-2*, Pub. by Pergamon Repr UK) Franklin.

Markstein, George. Chance Awakening. large type ed. 1978. 15.95 (*0-7089-0239-1*) Ulverscroft.

— The Man from Yesterday. 1984. pap. 2.95 (*0-345-25851-7*) Ballantine.

— Soul Hunters. 416p. 1988. pap. 3.95 (*1-55817-062-6*, Pinnacle NY) Windsor NY.

— Traitor for a Cause. large type ed. 368p. 1983. 15.95 (*0-7089-0948-5*) Ulverscroft.

— The Ultimate Issue. 336p. (Orig.). 1981. pap. 2.75 (*0-345-29031-3*) Ballantine.

Markstein, Linda. Developing Reading Skills: Beginning. 160p. 1987. pap. 15.95 (*0-8384-2824-X*, Newbury) Heinle & Heinle.

— Developing Reading Skills: Beginning. 2nd ed. LC 93-45815. 1994. pap. 17.95 (*0-8384-4987-5*) Heinle & Heinle.

— Write Now, Bk. 2. 1987. pap. text ed. write for info. (*0-13-969726-8*) Prentice ESL.

Markstein, Linda & Grunbaum, Dorien. What's the Story? Photographs for Language Practice, 4 bks. (English As a Second Language Bk.). 1981. pap. text ed. 9.50 (*0-685-73375-0*, 75037); Teacher's manual. teacher ed 10.95 (*0-582-79787-X*, 75042); Bk. 1: Beginning. write for info. (*0-582-79783-7*, 75038); Bk. 2: Low-Intermediate. write for info. (*0-582-79784-5*, 75039); Bk. 3: High-Intermediate. write for info. (*0-582-79785-3*, 75040); Bk. 4: Advanced. write for info. (*0-582-79786-1*, 75041); 95.00 (*0-582-79788-8*) Longman.

Markstein, Linda & Hirasawa, Louise. Developing Reading Skills: Advanced. 2nd ed. 232p. 1983. pap. 7.95 (*0-8384-2989-0*, Newbury); pap. 17.95 (*0-8384-2988-2*, Newbury) Heinle & Heinle.

— Developing Reading Skills: Intermediate. 1981. pap. 15.95 (*0-8384-2826-6*, Newbury) Heinle & Heinle.

— Developing Reading Skills: Intermediate. 1982. pap. 7.95 (*0-8384-3055-4*, Newbury) Heinle & Heinle.

— Developing Reading Skills: Intermediate. 2nd ed. LC 93-46179. 1994. pap. 17.95 (*0-8384-5774-6*) Heinle & Heinle.

— Expanding Reading Skills, Intermediate 2. 2nd rev. ed. LC 92-27000. 1993. pap. 17.95 (*0-8384-2644-1*) Heinle & Heinle.

Markstein, Linda, jt. auth. see O'Neill, Robert.

Markstein, Linda R. & Hirasawa, Louise. Expanding Reading Skills: Advanced. 2nd ed. 1990. pap. 17.95 (*0-8384-3098-8*, Newbury) Heinle & Heinle.

Markstein, Rudolf, jt. ed. see Winlow, William.

Markum, J. A. & Silva, M. P. Beginning Electronic Fabrication. 2nd ed. (Illus.). 160p. 1986. pap. text ed. 8.50 (*0-911908-07-2*) Tech Ed Pr.

Markum, J. A. & Silva, P. Intermediate Electronic Fabrication. 2nd ed. 192p. 1984. pap. 8.50 (*0-911908-09-9*) Tech Ed Pr.

Markum, Patricia M. The Congressman's Daughter. 144p. (J). (gr. 5-8). 1994. pap. 2.99 (*0-87406-674-3*) Willowisp Pr.

Markun, Leo. Mrs. Grundy: A History of Four Centuries of Morals Intended to Illuminate Present Problems in Great Britain & the United States. 1930. 69.00 (*0-403-00130-7*) Scholarly.

***Markun, Patricia.** Mystery on Taboga Island. 160p. (J). (gr. 5-8). 1995. pap. 2.99 (*0-87406-727-8*) Willowisp Pr.

Markun, Patricia M. The Little Painter of Sabana Grande. LC 91-35230. (Illus.). 32p. (J). (ps-2). 1993. text ed. 14.95 (*0-02-762205-3*, Bradbury S&S) S&S Childrens.

Markunas, Joe & Apelt, Lisa. Tax Guide for the Intimidated, 1995 Edition. 2nd ed. 240p. 1994. pap. 10.95 (*1-56414-144-6*) Career Pr Inc.

Markus. Introduction to the Spectral Theory of Polynomial Operator Pencils. LC 88-23499. (MMONO Ser.: No. 71). 250p. 1988. 110.00 (*0-8218-4523-3*, MMONO-71) Am Math.

Markus, A. F. A Look at Socialism. (Illus.). 169p. (Orig.). (C). 1986. pap. 5.95 (*0-317-00935-4*) A F Markus.

Markus, A. F., et al. Psychological Problems in General Practice. (Oxford General Practice Ser.: No. 15). (Illus.). 424p. 1989. pap. 37.50 (*0-19-261529-7*) OUP.

***Markus, Andrew.** Australian Race Relations. 266p. 1995. pap. 19.95 (*1-86373-554-2*, Pub. by Allen Unwin AT) Paul & Co Pubs.

Markus, Andrew L. The Willow in Autumn: Ryutei Tanehiko, 1783-1842. (Harvard-Yenching Institute Monograph: No. 35). 290p. (C). 1993. 28.00 (*0-674-95351-7*) HUP.

Markus, Georg. Crime at Mayerling: The Life & Death of Mary Vetsera. De Bussy, Carvel, tr. LC 94-6491. 150p. 1995. pap. 14.95 (*0-929497-94-5*) Ariadne CA.

Markus, Gilbert. Bartolome de las Casas: The Gospel of Liberation. 1989. pap. 22.00 (*1-85390-082-6*, Pub. by Veritas IE) St Mut.

Markus, Gregory B. Analyzing Panel Data. LC 79-91899. (Quantitative Applications in the Social Sciences Ser.: Vol. 18). (Illus.). 72p. 1979. pap. 9.95 (*0-8039-1372-9*) Sage.

Markus, Gyorgy. Language & Production. 1986. lib. bdg. 90.00 (*90-277-2169-6*) Kluwer Ac.

Markus, Hazel R. & Kitayama, Shinobu, eds. Emotion & Culture: Empirical Studies of Mutual Influence. 398p. 1994. 40.00 (*1-55798-224-4*) Am Psychol.

Markus, Hella. Budapest Prestel Guide. Kluge-Fabenyi, Julia, ed. (Prestel Travel Guide Ser.). (Illus.). 192p. 1994. pap. 19.95 (*3-7913-1329-0*, Pub. by Prestel) TeNeues.

Markus, John. Communications Circuits Ready-Reference. (Illus.). 160p. 1982. pap. text ed. 22.95 (*0-07-040460-7*) McGraw.

— Diccionario de Electronica y Tecnica Nuclear. 1052p. (ENG & SPA.). 125.00 (*84-267-0003-9*, S-14264) Fr & Eur.

— Electronics Projects Ready-Reference. (Illus.). 180p. 1982. pap. text ed. 22.95 (*0-07-040459-3*) McGraw.

— Enciclopedia de Circuitos Electronicos. 888p. (SPA.). 1977. 125.00 (*0-8288-5403-3*, S14349) Fr & Eur.

— English & Spanish Dictionary of Electronics & Nuclear Technology. 1052p. (ENG & SPA.). 1985. 195.00 (*0-8288-0705-1*, S14264) Fr & Eur.

— Manual de Circuitos Electronicos. 984p. 1974. 125.00 (*0-7859-0873-0*, S-30723) Fr & Eur.

— Modern Electronic Circuits Reference Manual. (Illus.). 1980. text ed. 97.00 (*0-07-040446-1*) McGraw.

— Special Circuits Ready-Reference. (Illus.). 230p. 1982. pap. text ed. 22.95 (*0-07-040461-5*) McGraw.

— Vocabulario Ingles-Espanol de Electronica y Tecnica Nuclear. 2nd ed. 196p. (ENG & SPA.). pap. 39.95 (*84-267-0247-3*, S-30684) Fr & Eur.

Markus, John & Sclater, Neil. McGraw-Hill Electronics Dictionary. 5th ed. LC 93-39212. 1994. text ed. 49.50 (*0-07-040434-8*) McGraw.

Markus, Julia. Dared & Done: The Marriage of Elizabeth Barrett & Robert Browning. LC 94-11573. 1995. 30.00 (*0-679-41602-1*) Knopf.

Markus, Julia, ed. Elizabeth Barrett Browning's Casa Guidi Windows. LC 77-24944. 1977. 12.00 (*0-930252-00-4*) Browning Inst.

***Markus, Kurt.** Boxers. 112p. 1995. 50.00 (*0-944092-36-5*) Twin Palms Pub.

— Boxers. limited ed. 112p. 1995. 150.00 (*0-944092-37-3*) Twin Palms Pub.

Markus, L. Lectures in Differentiable Dynamics. rev. ed. LC 80-16847. (CBMS Regional Conference Series in Mathematics: No. 3). 77p. 1980. pap. 16.00 (*0-8218-1695-0*, CBMS-3) Am Math.

Markus, L. & Meyer, K. R. Generic Hamiltonian Dynamical Systems Are Neither Integrable Nor Ergodic. LC 74-8095. (Memoirs Ser.: No. 1/144). 52p. 1974. pap. 17.00 (*0-8218-1844-9*, MEMO 1/144) Am Math.

Markus, Lawrence, jt. auth. see Auslander, Louis.

Markus, R. A. The End of Ancient Christianity. 272p. (C). 1991. 59.95 (*0-521-32716-4*) Cambridge U Pr.

— The End of Ancient Christianity. 272p. (C). 1991. pap. 16.95 (*0-521-33949-9*) Cambridge U Pr.

— Sacred & Secular: Studies on Augustine & Latin Christianity. (Collected Studies: CS 465). 350p. 1994. 89.95 (*0-86078-450-9*, Pub. by Variorum UK) Ashgate Pub Co.

Markus, Richard M. & Palmer, George H. Trial Handbook for Ohio Lawyers. 3rd ed. LC 72-97628. 354p. 105.00 (*0-317-00553-7*) Lawyers Cooperative.

— Trial Handbook for Ohio Lawyers. 3rd suppl. ed. LC 72-97628. 354p. 1993. Suppl. 1993. 52.50 (*0-317-05566-6*) Lawyers Cooperative.

Markus, Robert A. Saeculum: History & Society in the Theology of St. Augustine. LC 71-87136. 264p. reprint ed. pap. 75.30 (*0-318-34820-9*, 2031687) Bks Demand.

Markus, S. The Mechanicals of Vibrations of Cylindrical Shells. (Studies in Applied Mechanics: No. 17). 180p. 1988. 92.00 (*0-685-23112-7*) Elsevier.

Markus, Thomas A. Buildings & Power: Freedom & Control in the Origin of Modern Building Types. LC 92-33282. (Illus.). 352p. 1993. 75.00 (*0-415-07664-1*, B2360, Routledge NY); pap. 29.95 (*0-415-07665-X*, B2364, Routledge NY) Routledge.

— Visions of Perfection: Architecture & Utopian Thought. 24p. 1985. 29.00 (*0-906474-45-0*, Pub. by Third Eye Centre UK) St Mut.

Markus, Tom. Actor Behaves: From Audition to Performance. 237p. (Orig.). 1992. pap. 14.95 (*0-573-69901-1*) French.

***Markus, Vasyl.** Religion & Nationalism in Soviet Ukraine after 1945. 46p. 1994. write for info. (*0-9609822-6-4*) Ukrainian Studies Fund.

Markusen, Ann R. The Politics of Regions: The Economics & Politics of Territory. LC 87-4359. 320p. (C). 1987. 55.50 (*0-8476-7394-4*, R7394) Rowman.

— Profit Cycles, Oligopoly & Regional Development. 336p. 1985. 40.00 (*0-262-13201-X*) MIT Pr.

Markusen, Ann R. & Yudken, Joel. Dismantling the Cold War Economy. LC 91-55463. 320p. 1993. reprint ed. pap. 16.00 (*0-465-01665-0*) Basic.

Markusen, Ann R., jt. auth. see Hall, Peter.

Markusen, Ann R., et al. High Tech America: The What, How, Where & Why of the Sunrise Industries. 256p. 1986. text ed. 39.95 (*0-04-338139-1*) Routledge Chapman & Hall.

— The Rise of the Gunbelt: The Military Remapping of Industrial America. (Illus.). 360p. 1991. 42.00 (*0-19-506648-0*) OUP.

Markusen, Eric & Kopf, David. The Holocaust & Strategic Bombing: Genocide & Total War in the 20th Century. 230p. 1995. text ed. 34.95 (*0-8133-7532-0*) Westview.

***Markusen, James R.** International Trade: Theory & Evidence. LC 94-24782. 1994. text ed. 46.50 (*0-07-040447-X*) McGraw.

Markusen, James R. & Scheffman, D. T. Speculation & Monopoly in Urban Development: Analytical Foundations with Evidence for Toronto. LC 80-490583. (Ontario Economic Council Research Studies: No.10). (Illus.). 173p. reprint ed. pap. 49.40 (*0-685-46307-9*, 2036697) Bks Demand.

Markushevich, A. Introduction to the Classical Theory of Abelian Functions. LC 91-36838. 175p. 1992. 123.00 (*0-8218-4542-X*, MMONO-96) Am Math.

Markushevich, A. I. Theory of Functions of a Complex Variable, 3 vols. in 1. 2nd ed. Silverman, Richard A., tr. LC 77-8515. 1977. text ed. 48.00 (*0-8284-0296-5*) Chelsea Pub.

Markuson, Barbara E. & Woods, Elaine W. Networks for Networkers II: Critical Issues for Libraries in the National Network Environment. 250p. 1993. 45.00 (*1-55570-128-0*) Neal-Schuman.

Markuson, Carolyn, jt. auth. see Tobias, Joyce.

Markuson, Gloria C., jt. auth. see Warren, Oscar L.

***Markussen, Birgitte & Henrik, Hans, eds.** Advocacy & Indigenous Film-Making Number One of Intervention: Nordic Papers in Critical Anthropology. 74p. 1995. pap. 15.00 (*87-89825-09-8*) Smyrna.

Markussen, J. Human Insulin by Tryptic Transpeptidations of Porcine Insulin & Biosynthetic Precursors. 1987. lib. bdg. 95.00 (*0-7462-0058-7*) Kluwer Ac.

Markuszewski, Richard & Blaustein, Bernard D., eds. Fossil Fuels Utilization: Environmental Concerns. LC 86-20673. (ACS Symposium Ser.: No. 319). (Illus.). ix, 385p. 1986. 82.95 (*0-8412-0990-1*) Am Chemical.

Markuszewski, Richard & Wheelock, T. D., eds. Processing & Utilization of High-Sulfur Coals, No. III. (Coal Science & Technology Ser.: No. 16). 830p. 1990. 218.00 (*0-444-88719-9*) Elsevier.

***Markvart, Thomas, ed.** Solar Electricity. 228p. 1994. pap. text ed. 34.95 (*0-471-94161-1*) Wiley.

Markward, Anne. Monument Valley. (Illus.). 64p. 1992. 24.95 (*0-944197-22-1*); pap. 14.95 (*0-944197-20-5*) Companion CA.

Markwardt, Bruno. Geschichte der Deutschen Poetik. Incl. Vol. 1. Barock und Fruehaufklaerung. 3rd enl. ed. xii, 512p. 1977. 107.00 (*3-11-004020-4*); Vol. 2. Aufklaerung, Rokoko, Sturm und Drang. 2nd ed. viii, 692p. 1970. 137.00 (*3-11-002679-1*); Vol. 3. Klassik und Romantik. 2nd ed. viii, 730p. 1971. 148.00 (*3-11-003584-7*); Vol. 4. Neunzehnte Jahrhundert. viii, 750p. 1959. 112.00 (*3-11-005329-2*); Vol. 5. Zwanzigste Jahrhundert. viii, 1032p. 1967. 152.00 (*3-11-000169-1*); (Grundriss der Germanischen Philologie Ser.: Vol. 13, Nos. 1-5). (GER.). (C). write for info. (*0-318-51617-9*) De Gruyter.

Markway, Barbara, et al. Dying of Embarrassment: Help for Social Anxiety & Social Phobia. 204p. (Orig.). (C). 1992. 24.95 (*1-879237-24-5*); pap. 11.95 (*1-879237-23-7*) New Harbinger.

Markwell, Bernard K. The Anglican Left: Radical Social Reformers in the Church of England & the Protestant Episcopal Church, 1846-1954. LC 91-28031. (Chicago Studies in the History of American Religion Ser.: Vol. 13). 325p. 1991. 60.00 (*0-926019-26-0*) Carlson Pub.

Markwell, F. C. Tracing Your Ancestors in Warwickshire. (C). 1987. 50.00 (*0-317-89865-5*, Pub. by Birmingham Midland Soc UK) St Mut.

Markwell, F. C., jt. auth. see Saul, Pauline.

Marlais, Michael. Conservative Echoes in Fin-de-Siecle Parisian Art Criticism. (Illus.). 272p. 1992. text ed. 35.00 (*0-271-00773-7*) Pa St U Pr.

Marlais, Michael & Doezema, Marianne. Americans & Paris. LC 90-1866. (Illus.). 62p. (Orig.). 1991. pap. 12.95 (*0-295-97102-9*) U of Wash Pr.

Marland, Folly, ed. see French Ramblers Association Staff.

Marland, Hilary. Medicine & Society in Wakefield & Huddersfield 1780-1870. (Cambridge History of Medicine Ser.). (Illus.). 250p. 1987. 79.95 (*0-521-32575-7*) Cambridge U Pr.

Marland, Hilary, ed. The Art of Midwifery: Early Modern Midwives in Europe. LC 92-49026. (Wellcome Institute Series in the History of Medicine). (Illus.). 256p. 1993. 74.50 (*0-415-06425-2*, B2344, Routledge NY) Routledge.

***Marlatt, Daphne & Warland, Betsy.** Two Women in a Birth. 170p. 1994. pap. 13.00 (*1-55071-003-6*) Guernica Editions.

Marlatt, G. Alan & Gordon, Judith R., eds. Relapse Prevention: Maintenance Strategies in the Treatment of Addictive Behaviors. LC 84-19319. (Guilford Clinical Psychology & Psychotherapy Ser.). 558p. 1985. lib. bdg. 46.95 (*0-89862-009-0*) Guilford Pr.

Marlatt, G. Alan & Nathan, P. E., eds. Behavioral Approaches to Alcoholism. LC 77-620035. (NIAAA-RUCAS Alcoholism Treatment Ser.: No. 2). 1978. pap. 6.00 (*0-911290-48-6*) Rutgers Ctr Alcohol.

Marlatt, G. Alan, jt. ed. see Donovan, Dennis M.

Marlatt, William P., ed. see Conejo Valley Genealogical Society, Inc. Staff.

Marlborough, John C. Letters & Dispatches of John Churchill, First Duke of Marlborough from 1702-1712, 5 vols., Set. Murray, George, ed. LC 68-54801. 1969. reprint ed. text ed. 295.00 (*0-8371-2663-0*, MUJC) Greenwood.

— Letters & Dispatches of John Churchill, First Duke of Marlborough from 1702-1712, 5 vols., Vol. 2. Murray, George, ed. LC 68-54801. 1969. reprint ed. text ed. 75.00 (*0-8371-0829-2*, MUJE) Greenwood.

— Letters & Dispatches of John Churchill, First Duke of Marlborough from 1702-1712, 5 vols., Vol. 3. Murray, George, ed. LC 68-54801. 1969. reprint ed. text ed. 75.00 (*0-8371-0830-6*, MUJF) Greenwood.

— Letters & Dispatches of John Churchill, First Duke of Marlborough from 1702-1712, 5 vols., Vol. 4. Murray, George, ed. LC 68-54801. 1969. reprint ed. text ed. 75.00 (*0-8371-0831-4*, MUJG) Greenwood.

— Letters & Dispatches of John Churchill, First Duke of Marlborough from 1702-1712, 5 vols., Vol. 5. Murray, George, ed. LC 68-54801. 1969. reprint ed. text ed. 75.00 (*0-8371-0832-2*, MUJH) Greenwood.

Marlborough, Sarah J. Letters of Sarah, Duchess of Marlborough. LC 77-37708. reprint ed. 29.50 (*0-404-56766-5*) AMS Pr.

Marle, Charles. Multiphase Flow in Porous Media. LC 79-56345. 356p. (Orig.). 1981. pap. 49.00 (*0-87201-569-6*) Gulf Pub.

***Marle, Charles M.** Multiphase Flow in Porous Media. (Illus.). 272p. (C). 1981. pap. text ed. 93.00 (*2-7108-0404-2*) Technip.

Marle, Charles-Michel, jt. auth. see Libermann, Paulette.

Marle, Hans van, tr. see Huizinga, Johan.

Marle, Inc. Staff, ed. see Robalto, Matilde A.

***Marler, Don C.** Historic Hineston. 192p. (Orig.). 1991. pap. 12.00 (*0-9646846-7-5*) Dogwood TX.

***Marler, Don C. & McManus, Jane P.** The Cherry Winche Country: History of the Redbones. 70p. (Orig.). 1993. pap. 5.00 (*0-9646846-6-7*) Dogwood TX.

Marler, E. E., comp. Pharmacological & Chemical Synonyms. 9th ed. 500p. 1990. reprint ed. 253.25 (*0-444-90487-5*) Elsevier.

***Marler, E. E., ed.** Pharmacological & Chemical Synonyms: A Collection of Names of Drugs, Pesticides & Other Compounds Drawn from the Medical Literature of the World. 10th ed. 608p. 1994. 257.25 (*0-444-82081-7*) Elsevier.

Marler, Ezra. Golden Nuggets of Thought, 4 vols., 1. pap. 3.50 (*0-88494-007-1*) Bookcraft Inc.

— Golden Nuggets of Thought, 4 vols., 2. pap. 3.50 (*0-88494-053-5*) Bookcraft Inc.

— Golden Nuggets of Thought, 4 vols., 3. pap. 3.50 (*0-88494-068-3*) Bookcraft Inc.

— Golden Nuggets of Thought, 4 vols., 4. pap. write for info. (*0-88494-102-7*) Bookcraft Inc.

Marler, George C. The Admiral Issue of Canada. (Illus.). 566p. 1982. 35.00 (*0-933580-08-8*) Am Philatelic Society.

Marler, Jack C., jt. ed. see Kennedy, Leonard A.

Marler, Joe F., III. His Deadly Wound Was Healed. 1992. 10.95 (*0-533-10027-5*) Vantage.

***Marler, John & Wermuth, Andrew.** Youth of the Apocalypse: And the Last True Rebellion. (Illus.). 194p. (Orig.). (YA). 1995. pap. 7.00 (*0-938635-89-1*) St Herman AK.

Marler, Malcolm. Ideas for Homebound Ministries. Nelson, Becky, ed. 41p. (Orig.). 1993. pap. text ed. 4.95 (*1-56309-072-4*, New Hope) Womans Mission Union.

Marler, Patti, jt. auth. see Mattia, Jan B.

Marler, Regina, ed. The Selected Letters of Vanessa Bell. LC 92-50782. (Illus.). 648p. 1993. 35.00 (*0-679-41939-X*) Pantheon.

***Marler, Tim.** Introduction to Oil & Gas Enviornmental Project Management. LC 94-23716. 1994. write for info. (*0-87814-430-7*) PennWell Bks.

Marles, Fay. The Politics of Nursing in Victorian 1987. (C). 1989. pap. 51.00 (*0-7300-0691-3*, NPR803, Pub. by Deakin Univ AT) St Mut.

Marles, J., jt. auth. see Bowen, T.

Marlette, Doug. Faux Bubba: Bill & Hillary Go to Washington. LC 92-56829. 112p. 1993. pap. 10.00 (*0-8129-2073-2*, Times Bks) Random.

— Gone with the Kudzu. 192p. 1995. pap. 12.95 (*1-55853-336-2*) Rutledge Hill Pr.

Marlette, Jerry. Interstate: A History of Interstate Public Service Rail Operations. Riehle, Ginger, ed. LC 87-35740. (Illus.). 272p. 1991. text ed. 48.00 (*0-933449-07-0*) Transport Trails.

***Marlewski-Probert, Bonnie.** A Parent's Guide to Buying That First Horse: How-to Find the Ideal Horse for Your Family & Avoid Buying a Lemon! Haertel, Kandee, ed. (Illus.). 164p. (Orig.). 1995. pap. 16.95 (*0-9646181-0-9*) K&B Products.

Marley, C. F. Battleships, Sailors & High-Seas Action. 94p. 1991. pap. 9.90 (*0-9631610-0-8*) Audubon Hills.

Marley, Claire, jt. auth. see Julian, Desmond.

Marley, Daniel T., ed. see Heiserman, Russell L. & Barber, Preston.

***Marley, Dave.** Database Marketing: Micromarketing for Your Company, & Your Career. (Illus.). 224p. 1995. pap. 29.95 (*0-945442-15-7*) Silverpoint Pr.

— Employee Incentive Contests: For Improved Marketing, Customer Service, & Morale. (Illus.). 224p. 1995. pap. 19.95 (*0-945442-18-1*) Silverpoint Pr.

— Essential Computer Skills for Lifetime Career Success. (Illus.). 224p. 1995. pap. 29.95 (*0-945442-17-3*) Silverpoint Pr.

— High Interest Hobbies for a High Energy Life. (Illus.). 224p. 1995. pap. 24.95 (*0-945442-16-5*) Silverpoint Pr.

Marley, David. Pirates & Privateers of the Americas: An Illustrated Encyclopedia. 250p. 1994. lib. bdg. 60.00 (*0-87436-751-4*) ABC-CLIO.

An Asterisk (*) at the beginning of an entry indicates that the title is appearing in BIP for the first time.

***Marley, David F.** Trafalgar 1805. 1995. pap. 14.95 (1-85532-479-2, Pub. by Osprey UK) Stackpole.

Marley, E., jt. auth. see Leigh, D.

Marley, John. Handwriting Analysis Made Easy. 1978. pap. 10.00 (0-87980-045-3) Wilshire.

Marley, Judy. Behold the Man: Seven Meditations on the Passion, Death & Resurrection of Jesus. (Illus.). 48p. (Orig.). 1990. pap. 3.50 (0-9623410-2-9) Resurrection.

Marley, Mary L. Organic Brain Pathology & the Bender-Gestalt Test: A Differential Diagnostic. 264p. 1983. text ed. 38.00 (0-8089-1425-1, 792683, Grune) Saunders.

Marley, W. & Morgan, K. Health Physics. (Progress in Nuclear Energy Ser.: Vol. 1). 1959. 250.00 (0-08-009283-7, Pub. by Pergamon Repr UK) Franklin.

Marliani, Marco A. Ildegonda. Gosset, Philip, ed. (Italian Opera Ser., 1810-1840). 1986. 97.00 (0-8240-6559-X) Garland.

Marliave, Joseph De. Beethoven's Quartets. Andrews, Hilda, tr. pap. 9.95 (0-486-20694-7) Dover.

Marlin, A. E., ed. Concepts in Pediatric Neurosurgery. (Concepts in Pediatric Neurosurgery Ser.: Vol. 9). (Illus.). viii, 236p. 1989. 169.75 (3-8055-4835-4) S Karger.

— Concepts in Pediatric Neurosurgery, Vol. 7. (Illus.). viii, 240p. 1987. 168.00 (3-8055-4396-4) S Karger.

— Concepts in Pediatric Neurosurgery, Vol. 8. (Illus.). viii, 224p. 1988. 149.00 (3-8055-4622-X) S Karger.

— Concepts in Pediatric Neurosurgery, Vol. 11. (Illus.). viii, 164p. 1991. 172.00 (3-8055-5328-5) S Karger.

— Concepts in Pediatric Neurosurgery Series, Vol. 10. (Illus.). 262p. 1990. 202.50 (3-8055-5022-7) S Karger.

— Selected Proceedings of the Annual Meeting of the American Society of Pediatric Neurosurgeons, San Juan, Puerto Rico, January 1991. (Journal of Pediatric Neurosurgery: Vol. 18, Nos. 5-6, 1992). (Illus.). iv, 108p. 1992. pap. 89.00 (3-8055-5711-6) S Karger.

Marlin, Alice T., ed. see Cannon, James S.

Marlin, Alice T., ed. see Council on Economic Priorities Staff, et al.

Marlin, Alice T., et al. Students Shopping for a Better World. 262p. 1993. 7.49 (0-685-64983-0) CEP.

Marlin, Arthur E., jt. auth. see Gaskill, Sarah J.

Marlin-Bennett, Renee. Food Fights: International Regimes & the Politics of Agricultural Trade Disputes. LC 93-18535. 1993. text ed. 33.00 (2-88124-588-9) Gordon & Breach.

Marlin, C. D. Coroutines. (Lecture Notes in Computer Science Ser.: Vol. 95). (Illus.). 246p. 1980. pap. 28.00 (0-387-10256-6) Spr-Verlag.

Marlin, Emily. Genograms: The New Tool for Exploring the Personality, Career, & Love Patterns You Inherit. 160p. (Orig.). 1989. pap. 10.95 (0-8092-4494-2) Contemp Bks.

— Relationships in Recovery: Healing Strategies for Couples & Families. LC 89-45687. 288p. 1990. pap. 8.95 (0-00-001645-4, PL) HarpC.

— Relationships in Recovery: Healing Strategies for Couples & Families. LC 89-45687. 288p. 1990. pap. 12.00 (0-06-096436-7, PL) HarpC.

Marlin, George, ed. see Chesterton, G. K.

Marlin, George J., et al, eds. The Quotable Paul Johnson: A Topical Compilation of His Wit, Wisdom & Satire. LC 94-18893. 1994. 30.00 (0-374-24075-2); pap. 14.00 (0-374-52423-8) FS&G.

Marlin, Ira J., jt. auth. see Justus, Adalu.

Marlin, John. Heavens to Betsy! And Other Curious Sayings. 1993. pap. 9.00 (0-06-272011-2) HarpC.

Marlin, John T. Cities of Opportunity: Finding the Best Place to Work, Live & Prosper in the 1990s & Beyond. 400p. 1988. 24.95 (0-942361-07-5); pap. 13.95 (0-942361-06-7) MasterMedia Ltd.

— The Livable Cities Almanac: How over 100 Metropolitan Areas Compare in Economic Health, Air Quality, Water Quality, Crime Rate, Life Expectancy, Health Services, Recreational Opportunities, & More. 384p. 1992. pap. 14.00 (0-685-52542-2, Harper Ref) HarpC.

Marlin, John T., et al. Book of World City Rankings. LC 85-25298. 766p. (C). 1986. text ed. 49.95 (0-02-920230-2) Free Pr.

Marlin, T. E., et al, eds. Advanced Process Control Applications: Warren Centre Industrial Case Studies of Opportunities & Benefits. 380p. 1988. pap. text ed. 40.00 (1-55617-121-8, A121-8) Instru Soc.

***Marlin, Thomas.** Process Control: Designing Processes & Control Systems for Dynamic Performance. LC 94-45967. (Chemical Engineering Ser.). 1995. text ed. write for info. (0-07-040491-7) McGraw.

Marlin, William, ed. see Fuller, R. Buckminster.

Marling, Arthur E., jt. ed. see Checck, William R.

Marling, Clare F., jt. auth. see Marling, William E.

Marling, Karal A. As Seen on TV: The Visual Culture of Everyday Life in the 1950s. LC 94-2814. (Illus.). 336p. 1994. 24.95 (0-674-04882-2, MARSEE) HUP.

— Blue Ribbon: A Social & Pictorial History of the Minnesota State Fair. LC 90-5738. (Illus.). 328p. 1990. 39.95 (0-87351-251-0); pap. 24.95 (0-87351-252-9) Minn Hist.

— The Colossus of Roads: Myth & Symbol along the American Highway. LC 84-5079. (Illus.). 152p. (C). 1984. pap. text ed. 14.95 (0-8166-1303-6) U of Minn Pr.

— Edward Hopper. Broude, Norma, ed. LC 91-33473. (Rizzoli Art Ser.). (Illus.). 24p. (Orig.). 1992. pap. 7.95 (0-8478-1514-5); pap. 47.70 (0-8478-5623-2) Rizzoli Intl.

— George Washington Slept Here: Colonial Revivals & American Culture, 1876-1896. LC 87-33026. (Illus.). 496p. 1988. text ed. 47.50 (0-674-34951-2) HUP.

— In Search of the Corn Queen: Pictures from the Heartland. (American Scene Ser.). 96p. (C). 1994. pap. 27.50 (1-881616-18-5) Dist Art Pubs.

— Tom Benton & His Drawings: A Biographical Essay & Collection of His Sketches, Studies & Mural Cartoons. LC 85-992. (Illus.). 232p. 1985. 35.00 (0-8262-0480-5) U of Mo Pr.

— Wall-to-Wall America: A Cultural History of Post Office Murals in the Great Depression. LC 82-2622. (Illus.). 364p. 1982. pap. text ed. 15.95 (0-8166-1117-3) U of Minn Pr.

Marling, Karal A. & Wetenhall, John. Iwo Jima: Monuments, Memories, & the American Hero. (Illus.). 300p. (C). 1991. text ed. 24.95 (0-674-46980-1) HUP.

Marling, Karal A., jt. ed. see Foy, Jessica H.

Marling, William. The American Roman Noir: Hammett, Cain, & Chandler. LC 94-25550. 256p. 1995. 35.00 (0-8203-1658-X) U of Ga Pr.

Marling, William E. Raymond Chandler. (Twayne's United States Authors Ser.: No. 508). 184p. (C). 1986. text ed. 20.95 (0-8057-7472-6, Twayne) Macmillan.

Marling, William E. & Marling, Clare F. The Marling Menu-Master for France. 112p. (Orig.). 1971. pap. 7.95 (0-912818-03-4) Altarinda Bks.

— Marling Menu-Master for Germany. 88p. (Orig.). 1970. pap. 7.95 (0-912818-01-8) Altarinda Bks.

— The Marling Menu-Master for Italy. 108p. (Orig.). 1971. pap. 7.95 (0-912818-02-6) Altarinda Bks.

— The Marling Menu-Master for Spain. 96p. (Orig.). 1973. pap. 7.95 (0-912818-04-2) Altarinda Bks.

***Marlis, Stefanie.** Sheet of Glass. 40p. (Orig.). 1994. pap. 8.00 (0-912449-47-0) Floating Island.

— Slow Joy. LC 89-40260. (Brittingham Prize in Poetry Ser.). 90p. 1989. pap. 10.95 (0-299-12304-9) U of Wis Pr.

— Slow Joy. LC 89-40260. (Brittingham Prize in Poetry Ser.). 90p. (C). 1990. 17.95 (0-299-12300-6) U of Wis Pr.

Marlitt, Richard. Matters of Proportion: The Portland Residential Architecture of Whidden & Lewis. (Illus.). 96p. (Orig.). 1989. pap. 12.95 (0-87595-177-5) Oregon Hist.

— Nineteenth Street. rev. ed. LC 78-73291. (Illus.). 218p. 1978. 19.95 (0-87595-000-0); pap. 12.95 (0-87595-138-4) Oregon Hist.

Marlock, Dennis & Dowling, John. License to Steal: Traveling Con Artists: Their Games, Their Rules - Your Money. 304p. 1993. text ed. 30.00 (0-87364-751-3) Paladin Pr.

***Marlon, Kim.** The Artful Tax Dodger. 312p. (Orig.). 1995. pap. 22.00 (0-89447-311-5) Cypress.

***Marlor.** Introduction to WordPerfect. (C). 1995. pap. text ed. write for info. (0-8053-6361-0) Benjamin-Cummings.

Marlor, Clark S. The Society of Independent Artists: The Exhibition Record, 1917-1944. LC 84-14867. (Illus.). 600p. 1984. 64.00 (0-8155-5063-4) Sound View Pr.

Marlor Editors. Gardener's Notebook: Makes Gardening More Fun & Helps You Produce Better Results! (Illus.). 96p. (Orig.). 1991. pap. 7.95 (0-943400-60-0) Marlor Pr.

— Kid's Vacation Diary: A Fun Diary & Vacation Book for Use While Traveling! (Illus.). 96p. (Orig.). (J). (gr. 1-7). 1991. pap. 6.95 (0-943400-56-2) Marlor Pr.

Marlor Press Editors. Complete Trip Diary. rev. ed. (Illus.). 96p. 1994. pap. 8.95 (0-943400-78-3) Marlor Pr.

— My Camp Book: A Guide to Journaling Summer Camp Experiences for Kids 8-15. (Illus.). 96p. 1994. pap. 8.95 (0-943400-77-5) Marlor Pr.

***Marlow, A. J.** Technical Documentation. 2nd ed. (Illus.). 248p. (Orig.). (C). Date not set. pap. 29.95 (1-85554-216-1, Pub. by NCC Blackwell UK) Blackwell Pubs.

Marlow, Cecilia A., ed. Directory of Directories 1988: Publishers Volume. (Directory of Directories Ser.). 608p. 1987. 155.00 (0-8103-2509-8) Gale.

Marlow, Christine. Research Methods for Generalist Social Work. (C). 1993. pap. 36.95 (0-534-14838-7) Brooks-Cole.

Marlow, Clare. Beginning to Teach: Primary Teaching Explained. 144p. 1994. pap. 23.00 (1-85346-259-4) Taylor & Francis.

Marlow, David. Yearbook. 1972. pap. 1.95 (0-449-23551-3, Crest) Fawcett.

— Yearbook. 228p. 1982. pap. 2.50 (0-449-70029-1, Juniper) Fawcett.

— Yearbook. 1984. pap. 2.50 (0-449-70000-3) Fawcett.

Marlow, Dorothy R. Textbook of Pediatric Nursing. 6th ed. (Illus.). 1358p. 1988. text ed. 64.95 (0-7216-6100-9) Saunders.

Marlow, Elisabeth & Morrison, Veronique. A la Page: Culture et Litterature. 320p. (C). 1985. pap. text ed. 22.75 (0-03-063244-7) HB Coll Pubs.

— A la Page - Grammaire. 4th ed. 240p. (C). 1985. pap. text ed. 26.75 (0-03-063246-3) HB Coll Pubs.

Marlow, Eugene. Corporate Television Programming. 140p. 1992. 39.95 (0-86729-312-8) Knowledge Indus.

— Managing Corporate Media. 2nd ed. (Illus.). 198p. (C). 1989. 39.95 (0-86729-265-2) Knowledge Indus.

Marlow, Eugene & Secunda, Eugene. Shifting Time & Space: The Story of Videotape. LC 90-7808. 192p. 1991. text ed. 49.95 (0-275-93408-X, C3408, Praeger Pubs) Greenwood.

***Marlow, Eugene & Sileo, Janice.** Winners! Producing Effective Electronic Media. LC 94-30435. 158p. 1995. pap. 26.95 (0-534-24090-9) Intl Thomson.

***Marlow, Gordon R.** Vincent's Revenge - Laissez-Faire-Next Ten Miles: A Flurry of Rage & Crows. 224p. (Orig.). 1996. pap. 7.95 (1-887500-00-6) Baillie Caymar Pubns.

Marlow, H. LeRoy. Carving Carousel Animals: From One-Eighth Scale to Full Size. LC 88-37050. (Illus.). 208p. (Orig.). 1989. pap. 19.95 (0-8069-6802-8) Sterling.

— Classic Carousel Carving: From One-Eighth Scale to Full Size. LC 92-23217. (Illus.). 168p. 1993. pap. 19.95 (0-8069-8252-7) Sterling.

Marlow, H. Leroy. Woodcrafting Heritage Toys: A Treasury of Classic Projects. (Illus.). 192p. 1987. 24.95 (0-8306-7863-8, 2863) TAB Bks.

Marlow, Hugh. Managing Change: A Strategy for Our Time. 174p. (C). 1975. 60.00 (0-85292-122-5) St Mut.

— Managing Change: A Strategy for Our Time-Key Questions & Working Papers. 68p. (C). 1975. 42.00 (0-85292-123-3) St Mut.

— Success: Individual, Corporate & National. 416p. (C). 1984. 125.00 (0-85292-336-8) St Mut.

Marlow, James E. Charles Dickens: The Uses of Time. LC 92-50683. 1993. write for info. (0-945636-48-2) Susquehanna U Pr.

***Marlow, Jean, ed.** Actors' Audition Speeches. 128p. 1995. pap. 11.95 (0-435-08664-2); pap. 11.95 (0-435-08663-4) Heinemann.

Marlow, Jean, ed. see Marlow, Jean, et al.

Marlow, Jean, et al. Focus on Microcomputers in the Middle School. Romano, Louis G. & Marlow, Jean, eds. 30p. (Orig.). 1986. pap. 3.00 (0-918449-06-5) MI Middle Educ.

Marlow, Joyce. Anne. large type ed. 1990. 21.95 (0-7089-2240-6) Ulverscroft.

— A Basket of Lilies. 192p. 1994. 17.95 (0-8034-9051-8, Avalon Bks) Bouregy.

— Maggie's Man. 1994. 17.95 (0-8034-9082-8, 094512) Bouregy.

— Sarah. large type ed. 576p. 1989. 17.95 (0-7089-2029-2) Ulverscroft.

Marlow, L. & Sauber, S. Richard. Handbook of Divorce Mediation. LC 88-18791. (Illus.). 528p. 1990. 80.00 (0-306-43286-2, Plenum Pr) Plenum.

Marlow, Lenard. Divorce & the Myth of Lawyers. 160p. 1992. 19.95 (0-9632741-0-4); pap. 10.95 (0-9632741-1-2) Harlan Pr.

Marlow, Louis. Seven Friends. (Illus.). 176p. 1992. text ed. 45.00 (1-872736-07-6, Pub. by Mandrake Pr UK) Holmes Pub.

— Seven Friends. LC 76-58445. (English Biography Ser.: No. 31). 1977. lib. bdg. 48.95 (0-8383-2132-1) M S G Haskell Hse.

— Welsh Ambassadors: Powys Lives & Letters. LC 73-157126. 273p. 1971. text ed. 27.95 (0-912568-04-6) Colgate U Pr.

Marlow, Mary E. Handbook for the Emerging Woman. 1988. pap. 8.95 (0-89865-672-9) Donning Co.

— Handbook for the Emerging Woman: Awakening the Unlimited Power of the Feminine Spirit. rev. ed. 208p. 1993. reprint ed. pap. 10.95 (1-878901-78-8) Hampton Roads Pub Co.

— Jumping Mouse: A Story about Inner Trust. 104p. (Orig.). 1995. pap. 10.95 (1-57174-014-7) Hampton Roads Pub Co.

Marlow, Max. Growth. 1993. 20.00 (0-7278-4445-8) Severn Hse.

— Meltdown. 320p. 1992. 24.95 (0-450-53785-4, Pub. by H & S UK) Trafalgar.

— Shadow at Evening. 1995. lib. bdg. 22.00 (0-7278-4699-X) Severn Hse.

— Where the River Rises. 1994. 22.00 (0-7278-4583-7) Severn Hse.

Marlow, Michael S., et al, eds. Geology & Offshore Resources of Pacific Island Arcs: New Ireland & Manus Region, Papua New Guinea. (Earth Science Ser.: Vol. 9). (Illus.). 288p. 1988. pap. 24.00 (0-933687-10-9) Circum-Pacific.

Marlow, Sandra K. Radiation Victims Before Chernobyl: A Guide to Repositories of Information. (Bibliographies & Indexes in Science & Technology Ser.: No. 7). 1992. 49.95 (0-313-26105-9, MRV, Greenwood Pr) Greenwood.

Marlow, Steve, ed. Interstate Radio Map. (Illus.). 64p. (Orig.). 1985. pap. text ed. 2.95 (0-910887-00-4) TMS Pub.

Marlow, Terry. Target Blue. 304p. 1993. mass mkt. 4.99 (0-515-11056-6) Jove Pubns.

— Target Blue. 272p. 1991. 21.95 (0-399-13564-2, Putnam) Putnam Pub Group.

Marlow, Tim. Schiele. 112p. 1994. 14.98 (0-8317-6115-6) Smithmark.

Marlow, W. H. Mathematics for Operations Research. LC 93-24974. (Illus.). 483p. 1993. reprint ed. pap. 12.95 (0-486-67723-0) Dover.

Marlowe, Ann. The Winnowing Winds. large type ed. 1981. 12.00 (0-7089-0580-3) Ulverscroft.

Marlowe, Christopher. Complete Plays. Steanie, J. B., ed. Incl. Dido Queen of Carthage. 1969. (0-318-55022-9); Massacre at Paris. 1969. (0-318-55023-7); Tamburlaine, Parts 1 & 2. 1969. (0-318-55024-5); Edward Second. 1969. (0-318-55025-3); Doctor Faustus. 1969. (0-318-55026-1); (English Library). (Orig.). 1969. Set pap. 10.95 (0-14-043037-7, Penguin Classics) Viking Penguin.

— The Complete Works of Christopher Marlowe: Dr. Faustus, Vol. II. Gill, Roma, ed. (Oxford English Texts Ser.). (Illus.). 184p. 1990. 69.00 (0-19-812769-3) OUP.

— The Complete Works of Christopher Marlowe: Edward II, Vol. III. LC 94-9290. (English Texts Ser.). (Illus.). 188p. 1995. 59.00 (0-19-812278-0, Clarendon Pr) OUP.

— The Complete Works of Christopher Marlowe Vol. IV: The Jew of Malta. Gill, Roma, ed. (Oxford English Texts Ser.). (Illus.). 180p. 1995. 55.00 (0-19-812770-7) OUP.

— A Concordance to the Plays, Poems, & Translations of Christopher Marlowe. Fehrenbach, Robert J. et al, eds. LC 81-67175. (Cornell Concordances Ser.). 1710p. 1982. 99.50 (0-8014-1420-2) Cornell U Pr.

— Doctor Faustus. 1976. 3.00 (0-8488-0765-0) Amereon Ltd.

— Doctor Faustus. Jump, John D., ed. LC 62-51712. 144p. 1982. pap. 9.50 (0-8419-0826-5) Holmes & Meier.

— Doctor Faustus. Rudall, Nicholas, ed. (Plays for Performance Ser.). 69p. 1991. text ed. 15.95 (0-929587-60-X); pap. 7.95 (0-929587-56-1) I R Dee.

— Doctor Faustus. (Study Texts Ser.). 1984. pap. text ed. 4.29 (0-582-35390-4, 72213) Longman.

— Doctor Faustus. Barnet, Sylvan, ed. 1969. pap. 3.95 (0-451-52378-4, Sig Classics) NAL-Dutton.

— Doctor Faustus. 1989. pap. 3.50 (0-451-52228-1) NAL-Dutton.

— Doctor Faustus. Jump, John D., ed. (Methuen English Classics Ser.). 1965. pap. 8.95 (0-415-03960-6, NO. 2311) Routledge.

— Dr. Faustus. unabridged ed. LC 94-7856. (Thrift Editions Ser.). 64p. 1994. pap. text ed. 1.00 (0-486-28208-2) Dover.

— Doctor Faustus. 2nd ed. Gill, Roma, ed. (New Mermaid Ser.). (C). 1990. pap. text ed. 6.95 (0-393-90059-2) Norton.

— Doctor Faustus. LC 73-133704. (Tudor Facsimile Texts. Old English Plays Ser.: No. 102). reprint ed. 49.50 (0-404-53402-3) AMS Pr.

— Doctor Faustus: A 1604-Version Edition. Keefer, Michael, ed. 250p. 1991. 29.95 (0-921149-56-5); pap. 11.95 (0-921149-59-X) Broadview Pr.

— Doctor Faustus & Other Plays. Bevington, David & Rasmussen, Eric, eds. (World's Classics Ser.). 528p. 1995. 55.00 (0-19-812159-8); pap. 9.95 (0-19-282737-5) OUP.

— Edward II. Forker, Charles R., ed. LC 93-28184. (Revels Plays Ser.). 1994. text ed. 79.95 (0-7190-1536-7, Pub. by Manchester Univ Pr UK) St Martin.

— Edward Second. Charleton, H. B. & Waller, R. D., eds. LC 66-23027. (Works & Life of Christopher Marlowe Ser.: Vol. 6). 226p. 1966. reprint ed. 35.00 (0-87752-191-3) Gordian.

— Edward the Second. Merchant, W. Moelwyn, ed. (New Mermaid Ser.). (C). 1976. pap. text ed. 4.95 (0-393-90018-5) Norton.

— The Famous Tragedy of the Rich Jew of Malta. LC 70-25427. (English Experience Ser.: No. 334). 76p. 1971. reprint ed. 20.00 (90-221-0334-X) Walter J Johnson.

— The Jew of Malta. Bawcutt, N. W., ed. LC 83-80370. (Revels Plays Ser.). 207p. 1988. text ed. 14.95 (0-7190-1618-5, Pub. by Manchester Univ Pr UK) St Martin.

— The Jew of Malta. Bawcutt, N. W., ed. LC 77-17261. (Revels Plays Ser.). 223p. reprint ed. pap. 63.60 (0-8357-4031-5, 2036723) Bks Demand.

— The Jew of Malta. Van Fossen, Richard W., ed. LC 63-14699. (Regents Renaissance Drama Ser.). xxx, 122p. 1991. reprint ed. 14.95 (0-8032-0270-9); reprint ed. pap. 7.95 (0-8032-5270-6) U of Nebr Pr.

— The Jew of Malta. Bennett, H. S., ed. Bd. with Massacre at Paris. LC 66-23027. (Works & Life of Christopher Marlowe Ser.: Vol. 3). 267p. 1966. reprint ed. 35.00 (0-87752-189-1) Gordian.

— The Life of Marlowe. Tucker Brooke, C. F., ed. Bd. with Tragedy of Dido Queen of Carthage. (Works & Life of Christopher Marlowe Ser.: Vol. 1). 238p. 1966. reprint ed. 35.00 (0-87752-194-8) Gordian.

— Marlowe: Complete Plays & Poems. rev. ed. Pendry, E. D., ed. 582p. 1991. pap. 9.95 (0-460-87043-2, Everyman's Classic Lib) C E Tuttle.

— Marlowe's Poems. Martin, L. C., ed. LC 66-23027. (Works & Life of Christopher Marlowe Ser.: Vol. 4). 304p. 1966. reprint ed. 35.00 (0-87752-193-X) Gordian.

— The Massacre at Paris: With the Death of the Duke of Guise. LC 73-25759. (English Experience Ser.: No. 335). 1971. reprint ed. 8.00 (90-221-0335-8) Walter J Johnson.

— Tamburlaine. Harper, J. W., ed. (New Mermaid Ser.). (C). 1976. pap. text ed. 5.95 (0-393-90021-5) Norton.

— Tamburlaine the Great. Cunningham, J. S., ed. LC 81-47596. (Revels Plays Ser.). 354p. (C). 1981. text ed. 34.50 (0-8018-2669-1) Johns Hopkins.

— Tamburlaine the Great, 2 pts. Ellis-Fermor, V. M., ed. LC 66-23027. (Works & Life of Christopher Marlowe Ser.: Vol. 2). 321p. 1966. reprint ed. 35.00 (0-87752-192-1) Gordian.

— Tamburlaine the Great, Parts I & II. Jump, John D., ed. LC 67-10666. (Regents Renaissance Drama Ser.). xxvi, 205p. (C). 1967. pap. 6.95 (0-8032-5271-4, Bison Books) U of Nebr Pr.

— The Tragical History of Doctor Faustus. Kocher, Paul H., ed. (Crofts Classics Ser.). 96p. 1950. pap. text ed. write for info. (0-88295-054-1) Harlan Davidson.

— The Tragical History of Doctor Faustus. Boas, Frederick S., ed. (Works & Life of Christopher Marlowe Ser.: Vol. 5). 221p. 1966. reprint ed. 35.00 (0-87752-190-5); reprint ed. pap. 12.50 (0-685-01942-X) Gordian.

— Works & Life of Christopher Marlowe, 6 Vols, Set. Case, R. H., ed. 1644p. 1966. reprint ed. 175.00 (0-87752-067-4) Gordian.

Marlowe, Christopher & Chapman, George. Hero & Leander. LC 77-172844. (Renaissance Library: No. 1). reprint ed. 27.50 (0-404-07871-0) AMS Pr.

Marlowe, Christopher & Nash, Thomas. Dido. LC 70-133703. (Tudor Facsimile Texts. Old English Plays Ser.: No. 72). reprint ed. 49.50 (0-404-53372-8) AMS Pr.

Marlowe, Dan J. The Name of the Game is Death. LC 92-50690. (Vintage Crime - Black Lizard Ser.). 1993. pap. 9.00 (0-679-73848-7, Vin) Random.

— The Name of the Game Is Death. LC 87-72064. 144p. 1988. reprint ed. pap. 4.95 (0-88739-042-0, Blk Lizard) Creat Arts Bk.

— Never Live Twice. LC 87-72065. 160p. 1988. reprint ed. pap. 4.95 (0-88739-043-9, Blk Lizard) Creat Arts Bk.

— Strongarm. LC 87-72704. 160p. 1988. reprint ed. pap. 4.95 (0-88739-041-2, Blk Lizard) Creat Arts Bk.

— The Vengeance Man. LC 87-72705. 160p. 1988. reprint ed. pap. 4.95 (0-88739-040-4, Blk Lizard) Creat Arts Bk.

Marlowe, David, jt. auth. see Crowne, Douglas P.

An Asterisk (*) at the beginning of an entry indicates that the title is appearing in BIP for the first time.

***Marlowe, Gertrude W.** Ransom for Many: A Life of Maggie Lena Walker. 225p. 1995. 50.00 (*0-926019-83-X*) Carlson Pub.

***Marlowe, Howard J.** Internetworking Lans & Wans: Coexistence of Dissimilar Protocols Within a Common Media. 247p. 1994. pap. 32.80 (*0-89412-242-8*) Aegean Park Pr.

Marlowe, J. I., jt. auth. see Salomone, L. H.

Marlowe, John, jt. auth. see Ross, Victor J.

Marlowe, Katharine. Heart's Desires. 1991. 19.95 (*1-55611-226-2*) D I Fine.

— Nightfall. 352p. 1993. 21.95 (*0-312-85482-X*) Tor Bks.

— Nightfall. 352p. 1994. mass mkt. 4.99 (*0-8125-2415-2*) Tor Bks.

— Secrets. LC 91-55173. 272p. 1992. 19.95 (*1-55611-273-4*) D I Fine.

— Secrets. 400p. 1993. pap. 4.99 (*0-8439-3415-8*) Dorchester Pub Co.

Marlowe, Katherine. Heart's Desires. 400p. 1992. reprint ed. pap. 4.99 (*0-8439-3315-1*) Dorchester Pub Co.

— Secrets: A Novel. large type ed. LC 92-10729. 459p. 1992. reprint ed. lib. bdg. 20.95 (*1-56054-430-9*) Thorndike Pr.

Marlowe, Lynn G., et al. California State Capitol Restoration: A Pictorial History. 2nd ed. Worsley, John C. & Dwyer, Dale E., eds. (Orig.). 1988. pap. 5.50 (*0-318-41105-9*) Cal State Leg.

Marlowe, Monroe & Reed, Bobbie. Creative Bible Learning for Adults. LC 77-76206. (International Center for Learning Handbooks Ser.). 192p. 1977. pap. 6.99 (*0-8307-0480-9*, 9900152) Regal.

Marlowe, Stephen. Deborah's Legacy. 1983. pap. 3.75 (*0-8217-1153-9*) Zebra.

— The Lighthouse at the End of the World: A Tale of Edgar Allan Poe. LC 95-15477. 1995. write for info. (*0-525-94049-9*, Dutton) NAL-Dutton.

Marm, Ingvald & Sommerfelt, Alf. Teach Yourself Norwegian. (Teach Yourself Ser.). 1992. 19.95 (*0-8288-8376-9*) Fr & Eur.

Marm, Ingvald, jt. auth. see Sommerfelt, A.

Marmaduke. Marmaduke Multiply's Merry Method of Making Minor Mathematicians. Bleiler, E. F., ed. viii, 170p. pap. 3.50 (*0-486-22773-1*) Dover.

Marmain, Jacques, jt. auth. see Belyakov, R. A.

Marmar, Earl S. & Terry, James L., eds. Atomic Processes in Plasma. LC 92-71474. (AIP Conference Proceedings Ser.: No. 257). (Illus.). 200p. (C). 1992. 90.00 (*0-88318-939-9*) Am Inst Physics.

Marmarelis, V. Z., ed. Advanced Methods of Physiological System Modeling, Vol. 2. (Illus.). 310p. 1989. 79.50 (*0-306-43259-5*, Plenum Pr) Plenum.

— Advanced Methods of Physiological System Modeling, Vol. 3. (Illus.). 270p. 1994. 85.00 (*0-306-44819-X*, Plenum Pr) Plenum.

Marmarelis, Vasilis Z., intro. Advanced Methods of Physiological System Modeling, Vol. I. (Illus.). 344p. (C). 1987. reprint ed. text ed. 35.00 (*0-941639-01-0*) USC Biomedical.

Marmasse, Claude. Enzyme Kinetics. 242p. 1977. text ed. 114.00 (*0-677-05420-3*) Gordon & Breach.

— Microscopes & Their Uses. 342p. 1980. text ed. 62.00 (*0-677-05510-2*) Gordon & Breach.

Marme, et al. Plasmalemma & Tonoplast: Their Functions in the Plant Cell. (Developments in Plant Biology Ser.: Vol. 7). 446p. 1982. 127.75 (*0-444-80409-9*) Elsevier.

***Marmel, Elaine.** Building Databases with Approach 3. 1994. text ed. 49.95 (*0-471-05252-3*) Wiley.

— Building Databases with Approach 3. LC 94-31731. 1994. pap. text ed. 24.95 (*0-471-05253-X*) Wiley.

— The Mac User's PC - the PC User's Mac. (Illus.). 784p. (Orig.). 1993. pap. 24.95 (*0-672-48545-1*) Hayden.

— Word for Windows Six Solutions. LC 93-41283. 1994. pap. text ed. 24.95 (*0-471-30413-1*) Wiley.

Marmel, Elaine J. Lotus 1-2-3 Release 4 for Windows Solutions. (Solutions Ser.). 640p. (Orig.). 1993. pap. text ed. 24.95 (*0-471-59839-9*) Wiley.

— Using Quicken 2 for Windows. 1992. pap. 22.95 (*1-56529-070-4*) Que.

— Word for Windows Two Quickstart. (QuickStart Ser.). (Illus.). (Orig.). 1992. pap. 21.95 (*0-88022-920-9*) Que.

— Word 6.0 for the Mac Solutions. 1994. pap. text ed. 24.95 (*0-471-00809-5*) Wiley.

Marmeladov, Yuri. Dostoevsky's Secret Code: The Allegory of Elijah the Prophet. MacPherson, Jay, tr. 125p. (C). 1987. 12.50 (*0-87291-171-3*) Coronado Pr.

Marmelstein, Robert. Great Game Graphics. 1994. pap. 29.95 (*1-55851-380-9*) M&T Bks.

Marmini, Paola, jt. auth. see Totaro, Mariella.

Marmion, Daniel M. Handbook of U. S. Colorants: Foods, Drugs, Cosmetics, & Medical Devices. 3rd ed. 576p. 1991. text ed. 115.00 (*0-471-50074-7*) Wiley.

Marmion, Shakerley. Dramatic Works of Shakerley Marmion. Maidment, James & Logan, W. H., eds. LC 67-18423. 1972. reprint ed. 24.95 (*0-405-08760-8*, Pub. by Blom Pubns UK) Ayer.

Marmo, Costantino, jt. ed. see Eco, Umberto.

Marmo, Michael. More Profile Than Courage: The New York City Transit Strike of 1966. LC 89-36179. (SUNY Series in American Labor History). 333p. 1990. 64.50 (*0-7914-0261-4*); pap. 21.95 (*0-7914-0262-2*) State U NY Pr.

Marmol, Jose. Amalia: A Romance of the Argentine. Serrano, Mary J., tr. 1977. lib. bdg. 250.00 (*0-8490-1410-7*) Gordon Pr.

Marmolya, Gary A. Gems of the Necklace: Images of the Cleveland Metropolitan Parks. (Illus.). 136p. 1993. 50.00 (*1-883538-00-9*) Photographs Elite.

Marmon, Shaun. Eunuchs & Sacred Boundaries in Islamic Society. (Studies in Middle Eastern History). (Illus.). 192p. 1995. 35.00 (*0-19-507101-8*) OUP.

***Marmor.** Medical Care & American Democracy. (Political Pampheleteer Ser.). (C). 1994. text ed. 3.00 (*0-673-99778-2*) HarpCollege.

Marmor, Andrei. Interpretation & Legal Theory. (Clarendon Law Ser.). 208p. 1992. 45.00 (*0-19-825691-4*) OUP.

— Interpretation & Legal Theory. (Clarendon Law Ser.). 208p. 1995. reprint ed. pap. 24.00 (*0-19-825906-9*, Old Oregon Bk Store) OUP.

***Marmor, Andrei, ed.** Law & Interpretation: Essays in Legal Philosophy. 388p. 1995. 55.00 (*0-19-825875-5*) OUP.

Marmor, Judd. Psychiatry in Transition. 2nd ed. 464p. (C). 1994. pap. 24.95 (*1-56000-736-2*) Transaction Pubs.

Marmor, Leonard. Arthritis Surgery. LC 75-45362. 559p. reprint ed. pap. 159.40 (*0-8357-5770-6*, 2056018) Bks Demand.

Marmor, Leonard, jt. auth. see Houts, Marshall.

Marmor, Michael F., jt. ed. see Zinn, Keith M.

Marmor, Solomon. Organic Chemistry: A Brief Course. 520p. (C). 1987. text ed. 48.00 (*0-15-567555-9*); teacher ed. pap. text ed. 8.50 (*0-15-567556-7*) SCP.

Marmor, Theodore R. The Politics of Medicare. 2nd ed. (Social Institutions & Social Change Ser.). 192p. 1995. lib. bdg. 33.95x (*0-202-30399-3*); pap. text ed. 15.95 (*0-202-30425-6*) Aldine de Gruyter.

— Understanding Health Care Reform. 288p. 1994. 35.00 (*0-300-05878-0*); pap. 14.00 (*0-300-05879-9*) Yale U Pr.

Marmor, Theodore R. & Christianson, Jon B. Health Care Policy: A Political Economy Approach. LC 82-822. 232p. reprint ed. pap. 66.20 (*0-8357-4772-7*, 2037709) Bks Demand.

Marmor, Theodore R. & Mashaw, Jerry L., eds. Social Security: Beyond the Rhetoric of Crisis. (Studies from the Project on the Federal Social Role). 272p. 1988. 45.00 (*0-691-07776-2*); pap. 14.95 (*0-691-02285-2*) Princeton U Pr.

Marmor, Theodore R., et al. America's Misunderstood Welfare State: Persistent Myths, Enduring Realities. LC 90-80240. 268p. 1992. reprint ed. pap. 14.00 (*0-465-00123-8*) Basic.

Marmor, Theodore R., et al, eds. Economic Security & Intergenerational Justice: A Look at North America. LC 94-7382. 350p. 1994. 65.00 (*0-87766-619-9*); pap. 29.50 (*0-87766-620-2*) Urban Inst.

Marmora, Lelio. Return in Latin America. 50p. (Orig.). 1989. pap. 7.50 (*0-924046-09-0*) Ctr EPRA.

Marmora, Lelio & Gurrieri, Jorge. Return to Rio de la Plata: Response to the Return of Exiles to Argentina & Uruguay. 52p. (Orig.). 1988. pap. 7.50 (*0-924046-05-8*) Ctr EPRA.

Marmorstein, Armohom, tr. see Reinman, Jacob J.

Marmorstein, Arthur. Studies in Jewish Theology: The Arthur Marmorstein Memorial Volume. Rabbinowitz, Joseph & Lew, Meyer S., eds. LC 76-39174. (Essay Index Reprint Ser.). 1977. reprint ed. 23.95 (*0-8369-2702-8*) Ayer.

Marmorstein, Jerome & Marmorstein, Nanette. Awakening from Depression: A Mind-Body Approach to Emotional Recovery. LC 91-27523. 160p. (Orig.). 1992. pap. 9.95 (*0-88007-190-7*) Woodbridge Pr.

Marmorstein, Malcolm. Will the Real Jesus Christ Please Stand Up? 1965. pap. 2.75 (*0-8222-1259-5*) Dramatists Play.

Marmorstein, Nanette, jt. auth. see Marmorstein, Jerome.

Marmot, Michael & Elliott, Paul, eds. Coronary Heart Disease Epidemiology: From Aetiology to Public Health. (Illus.). 600p. 1992. 49.95 (*0-19-262124-6*) OUP.

Marmur, Dow. The Star of Return: Judaism after the Holocaust. LC 90-19911. (Contributions to the Study of Religion Ser.: No. 29). 176p. 1991. text ed. 49.95 (*0-313-27604-8*, MRJ/, Greenwood Pr) Greenwood.

Marmur, Mildred, tr. see Flaubert, Gustave.

Marmura, Michael E., ed. Islamic Theology & Philosophy: Studies in Honor of George F. Hourani. LC 83-408. 339p. 1984. 64.50 (*0-87395-746-6*); pap. 24.95 (*0-87395-747-4*) State U NY Pr.

Marnau, Alfred, jt. ed. see Kokoschka, Olda.

Marne, Patricia. Reveal the Secrets in Doodles: Learn to Analyse Your Doodles. 128p. 1995. pap. 8.95 (*0-572-01427-9*, Pub. by Foulsham UK) Atrium Pubs.

***Marnef, Guido.** Antwerp in the Age of Reformation: Underground Protestantism in a Commercial Metropolis, 1550-1577. (Studies in Historical & Political Science, 112th Series (1994)). (Illus.). 360p. 1995. text ed. 48.50x (*0-8018-5169-6*) Johns Hopkins.

Marnel, Elaine. Quicken 6 Quick Reference. (Quick Reference Ser.). 1992. pap. 9.95 (*1-56529-116-6*) Que.

Marnelius, R., jt. auth. see Brink, L.

Marnell, Deborah J. Career Warfare: Rising above the Trenches. Howard, Dee J., ed. 290p. (Orig.). 1990. pap. 19.95 (*0-9624316-0-5*) Platinum Career.

***Marnell, Tim.** Drug Identification Bible. 2nd ed. LC 94-93967. (Illus.). 458p. (Orig.). 1995. pap. 29.95 (*0-9635626-0-6*) Drug Identif.

Marneros, A. & Tsuang, Ming T., eds. Affective & Schizoaffective Disorders: Similarities & Differences. 304p. 1990. 96.00 (*0-387-52071-6*) Spr-Verlag.

Marneros, A., et al, eds. Negative vs. Positive Schizophrenia. (Illus.). 464p. 1991. 119.00 (*0-387-54388-0*) Spr-Verlag.

***Marneros, Andreas, et al, eds.** Schizophrenia: Psychotic Continuum or Distinct Entities. LC 94-47536. 1995. write for info. (*3-540-58820-5*); write for info. (*0-387-58820-5*) Spr-Verlag.

Marnett, Lawrence J. Arachidonic Acid Metabolism & Tumor Initiation. (Prostaglandins, Leukotrienes, & Cancer Ser.). 1985. lib. bdg. 75.50 (*0-89838-729-9*) Kluwer Ac.

Marnett, Lawrence J., ed. Frontiers in Molecular Toxicology. LC 92-10062. (Illus.). 294p. 1992. 26.95 (*0-8412-2428-5*); student ed 16.95 (*0-685-59402-5*) Am Chemical.

Marney, Carlyle. The Carpenter's Son: But Who Do You Say That I Am? (Sermons) 96p. 1984. reprint ed. pap. 6.95 (*0-913029-02-5*) Stevens Bk Pr.

— The Crucible of Redemption: The Meaning of the Cross-Resurrection Event (Sermons) 64p. 1984. reprint ed. pap. 6.95 (*0-913029-04-1*) Stevens Bk Pr.

— Faith in Conflict. (Abingdon Classics Ser.). (Orig.). 1992. reprint ed. pap. 4.95 (*0-687-12646-0*) Abingdon.

— Priests to Each Other. (Church Classics Ser.). 130p. 1991. reprint ed. pap. text ed. 8.95 (*0-9628455-2-3*) Smyth & Helwys.

— Priests to Each Other. 125p. 1985. reprint ed. pap. 8.95 (*0-913029-06-8*) Stevens Bk Pr.

Marney, Dean. Dirty Socks Don't Win Games. 128p. (J). (gr. 3-7). 1992. pap. 2.95 (*0-590-44880-3*, Apple Paperbacks) Scholastic Inc.

— Jack-O'-Lantern That Ate My Brother. (J). (gr. 4-7). 1994. pap. 2.95 (*0-590-47731-5*) Scholastic Inc.

— You, Me, & Gracie Makes Three. (J). (gr. 6-8). 1989. pap. 2.50 (*0-590-41637-5*, Apple Paperbacks) Scholastic Inc.

Marney-Petix, V. C. Internetworking: The Complete Solution (Training Edition) (Illus.). 300p. 1993. pap. 29.95 (*1-880548-12-7*) Numidia Pr.

— LANs! LANs! LANs! (Illus.). 200p. (Orig.). 1994. pap. 24.95 (*1-880548-38-0*) Numidia Pr.

— Mastering Advanced Internetworking. (Self-Paced Learning Ser.). 188p. (Orig.). 1993. 24.95 (*1-880548-24-0*) Numidia Pr.

— Mastering Advanced Internetworking. (Self-Paced Learning Ser.). 164p. (Orig.). 1993. pap. 24.95 (*1-880548-25-9*) Numidia Pr.

— Mastering Internetworking. (Illus.). 145p. (Orig.). 1992. pap. 27.95 (*1-880548-04-6*) Numidia Pr.

— Mastering Internetworking. 2nd ed. Parker, Carole, ed. (Self-Paced Learning Ser.). (Illus.). 170p. (Orig.). 1994. pap. 24.95 (*1-880548-05-4*) Numidia Pr.

Marney-Petix, V. C., jt. auth. see Brigham, Ellen.

Marney-Petix, V. C., jt. auth. see Lewis, Sadie.

Marney-Petix, Victoria. Networking & Data Communications for Business. (C). 1985. text ed. 34.00 (*0-8359-4881-1*, Reston) P-H.

Marnham, Patrick. The Man Who Wasn't Maigret. large type ed. (Illus.). 560p. 1993. 23.95 (*0-7089-8712-5*, Charnwood) Ulverscroft.

— The Man Who Wasn't Maigret: A Portrait of Georges Simenon. LC 92-16351. 1993. 25.00 (*0-374-20171-4*) FS&G.

— Man Who Wasn't Maigret: A Portrait of Georges Simenon. 1994. pap. 14.95 (*0-15-600059-8*) HarBrace.

— So Far from God: A Journey to Central America. large type ed. (Mainstream Ser.). 329p. 1987. reprint ed. 8.47 (*1-85089-127-3*, Pub. by ISIS UK) Transaction Pubs.

Marni, Archimede. Allegory in French Heroic Poem of the 17th Century. LC 72-122994. (Studies in French Literature: No. 45). 1970. reprint ed. lib. bdg. 59.95 (*0-8383-1127-X*) M S G Haskell Hse.

Marnie, Eve. LoveStart: Pre-Birth Bonding. 142p. (SPA.). pap. 10.00 (*84-86344-88-3*, 139) Hay House.

Marnik, George F., jt. auth. see Donaldson, Gordon A., Jr.

Marnik, George F., jt. ed. see Donaldson, Gordon A., Jr.

Maro, Richard. Prisoner of Fear: My Long Road to Freedom from Anxiety Disease, Panic Attacks & Agoraphobia. 250p. (Orig.). 1990. pap. 12.95 (*0-9628509-0-X*) Hickory Grove Pr.

Marocco, James D. Hawaii's Great Awakening. 52p. (Orig.). 1991. pap. 5.95 (*1-881227-02-2*) Bartimaeus.

— You Can Be a Winner in the Invisible War: The Power of Binding & Loosing. 96p. (Orig.). 1992. pap. 5.95 (*1-881227-00-6*) Bartimaeus.

Marocco, James D. & Yonggi Cho, Paul. Closing the Forbidden Door: An Expose of the Demonic. 160p. (Orig.). 1992. pap. 9.95 (*1-881227-01-4*) Bartimaeus.

Marochnik, L. S., et al. Astrophysics & Space Physics Reviews: The Distribution of Mass & Angular Momentum in the Solar System, Vol. 8. Syunyaev, R. A., ed. (Soviet Scientific Reviews Ser.: Vol. 8, Pt. 3). ii, 62p. 1989. pap. text ed. 40.00 (*3-7186-4986-1*) Gordon & Breach.

***Maroda, Karen J.** The Power of Countertransference: Innovations in Analytic Technique. LC 94-23505. 200p. 1995. pap. 25.00 (*1-56821-431-6*) Aronson.

— Power of the Countertransference: Innovations in Analytic Technique. (Series on Psychotherapy & Counselling: No. 1420). 183p. 1991. text ed. 44.95 (*0-471-92626-4*) Wiley.

***Marohn, Richard C.** The Last Gunfighter: John Wesley Hardin. LC 95-13255. (Early West Ser.). 1995. write for info. (*0-932702-99-6*) Creative Texas.

***Marohn, Richard C., ed.** Adolescent Psychiatry, Vol. 21. 1996. write for info. (*0-88163-195-7*) Analytic Pr.

— Adolescent Psychiatry, Vol. 22. 1997. write for info. (*0-88163-196-5*) Analytic Pr.

— Adolescent Psychiatry, Vol. 23. 1998. write for info. (*0-88163-197-3*) Analytic Pr.

— Adolescent Psychiatry, Vol. 24. 1999. write for info. (*0-88163-198-1*) Analytic Pr.

— Adolescent Psychiatry Vol. 20: The Annals of the American Society for Adolescent Psychiatry. 552p. 1995. 45.00 (*0-88163-194-9*) Analytic Pr.

Marohn, Richard C., jt. ed. see Feinstein, Sherman C.

Marois, M., ed. From Theoretical Physics to Biology: Proceedings of the International Conference, 3rd, Versailles, 1971. 1973. 94.50 (*3-8055-1578-2*) S Karger.

Marois, M., ed. see International Conference on Man & Computer Staff.

Marois, Maurice. Development of Chemotherapeutic Agents for Parasitic Diseases. 1976. 46.25 (*0-444-10996-X*, North Holland) Elsevier.

— Towards a Plan of Actions for Mankind. 558p. 1975. 82.00 (*0-444-10722-3*, North Holland) Elsevier.

Marois, Roger. Vocabulaire Francais-Anglais, Anglais-Francais D'archeologie Prehistorique: French - English, English - French Vocabulary of Prehistoric Archaeology. 116p. (ENG & FRE.). 1972. pap. 29.95 (*0-8288-6427-6*, M-6399) Fr & Eur.

Marola, Lewis J. Do I Miss My Uterus? (Illus.). 80p. 1994. pap. 9.95 (*0-8059-3465-0*) Dorrance.

Marold, Edith. Kenningkunst. viii, 232p. 1983. 100.80 (*3-11-007621-7*) De Gruyter.

***Marolda, Edward J.** By Sea, Air, & Land: An Illustrated History of the U. S. Navy & the War in Southeast Asia. (Illus.). 410p. (Orig.). 1995. pap. text ed. 43.00 (*0-945274-10-6*) Naval Hist Ctr.

Marolda, Edward J. & Fitzgerald, Oscar P. United States Navy & the Vietnam Conflict, V. 2: From Military Assistance to Combat 1959-1963. LC 76-600006. (Illus.). 607p. 1986. 22.00 (*0-16-002044-1*, S/N 008-046-00114-6) USGPO.

Marolda, Edward J. & Lesher, James, eds. A Bibliography of the U. S. Navy & the Conflict in Southeast Asia, 1950-1975. 2nd ed. 100p. (Orig.). (C). 1994. pap. text ed. 35.00 (*0-7881-0268-0*) Diane Pub.

Marolda, Edward J., ed. see Tensor Industries, Inc. Staff.

Marolda, Maria. Cuisenaire Alphabet Book. 64p. (J). (gr. k-4). 1980. pap. text ed. 8.95 (*0-914040-78-2*) Cuisenaire.

Marole, L. T. & De Goma, F. S. English-Venda Dictionary. 22.50 (*0-87559-185-X*) Shalom.

Marolles, Michel de. Tableaux Du Temple Des Muses, Repr. Of 1655 Ed. Bd. with Iconologia or Moral Problems. LC 75-27876. LC 75-27876. (Renaissance & the Gods Ser.: Vol. 31). (Illus.). 1976. Set lib. bdg. 36.00 (*0-8240-2080-4*) Garland.

Marolli, G. Dizionario Tecnico Italiano-Inglese, Inglese-Italiano. 2048p. (ENG & ITA.). 1978. 250.00 (*0-685-42439-1*, M-9197) Fr & Eur.

— Dizionario Tecnico Tedesco-Italiano e Italiano-Tedesco. 2038p. (ITA.). 1991. lib. bdg. 250.00 (*0-685-54279-3*) Fr & Eur.

— English - Italian, Italian - English Technical Dictionary: Dizonarion Tecnico Inglese-Italiano e Italiano-Inglese. 11th ed. 2216p. (ENG & ITA.). 1989. lib. bdg. 275.00 (*0-8288-3367-2*, M9197) Fr & Eur.

— Italian-English - English-Italian Technical Dictionary. (ENG & ITA.). 1991. 234.00 (*0-7859-8945-5*) Fr & Eur.

— Italian-English - English-Italian Technical Dictionary. 12th ed. (Illus.). 1960p. 1991. 234.00 (*88-203-1852-0*) IBD Ltd.

Marom, E., et al, eds. Applications of Holography & Optical Data Processing: Proceedings of an International Conference, Jerusalem, 1976. 1977. 299.00 (*0-08-021625-0*, Pub. by Pergamon Repr UK) Franklin.

Marom, G. & Wagner, H. D., eds. Microphenomena in Advanced Composites. LC 93-3941. 1993. 280.00 (*1-85861-035-4*, Pub. by Elsevier Applied Sci UK) Elsevier.

Maron, Linda. Rescue 911. LC 93-26636. 192p. 1993. 12.98 (*0-681-45256-0*) Longmeadow Pr.

— Rescue 911: Extraordinary Stories. 320p. (Orig.). 1995. pap. text ed. 4.99 (*0-425-14382-1*) Berkley Pub.

Maron, Margaret. Baby Doll Games. 208p. 1995. mass mkt. 5.50 (*0-446-40418-7*, Mysterious Paperbk) Warner Bks.

— Baby Doll Games. large type ed. (Mystery Ser.). 448p. 1992. 21.95 (*0-7089-2775-0*) Ulverscroft.

— Bloody Kin. 224p. 1995. mass mkt. 5.50 (*0-446-40416-0*, Mysterious Paperbk) Warner Bks.

— Bootlegger's Daughter. 272p. 1992. 18.95 (*0-89296-445-6*) Mysterious Pr.

— Bootlegger's Daughter. 272p. 1993. mass mkt. 5.50 (*0-446-40323-7*, Mysterious Paperbk) Warner Bks.

— Death in Blue Folders. large type ed. (Mystery Ser.). 400p. 1992. 21.95 (*0-7089-2665-7*) Ulverscroft.

— Death of a Butterfly. large type ed. 1991. 21.95 (*0-7089-2465-4*) Ulverscroft.

— Fugitive Colors. 272p. 1995. 18.95 (*0-89296-567-3*) Mysterious Pr.

— Fugitive Colors. 1996. mass mkt. write for info. (*0-446-40393-8*, Mysterious Paperbk) Warner Bks.

— One Coffee With. 192p. 1995. mass mkt. 5.50 (*0-446-40415-2*, Mysterious Paperbk) Warner Bks.

— One Coffee With. large type ed. 1991. 21.95 (*0-7089-2433-6*) Ulverscroft.

— The Right Jack. 272p. (Orig.). 1995. mass mkt. 5.50 (*0-446-40417-9*, Mysterious Paperbk) Warner Bks.

— The Right Jack. large type ed. (Mystery Ser.). 480p. (Orig.). 1992. 21.95 (*0-7089-2730-0*) Ulverscroft.

— Shooting at Loons. 240p. 1994. 18.95 (*0-89296-447-2*) Mysterious Pr.

— Shooting at Loons. 256p. 1995. mass mkt. 5.50 (*0-446-40424-1*, Mysterious Paperbk) Warner Bks.

— Shooting at Loons. large type ed. 1994. pap. 19.95 (*1-56895-083-7*) Wheeler Pub.

— Southern Discomfort. 224p. 1994. mass mkt. 5.50 (*0-446-40080-7*, Mysterious Paperbk) Warner Bks.

— Southern Discomfort, Bk. II. 256p. 1993. 17.95 (*0-89296-446-4*) Mysterious Pr.

Maron, Michael. Michael Maron's Makeover Miracles. LC 93-12100. 1994. 30.00 (*0-517-58430-1*, Crown) Crown Pub Group.

Maron, Monika. The Defector. Marinelli, David N., tr. 250p. (Orig.). 1988. 16.95 (*0-930523-40-7*); pap. 8.95 (*0-930523-41-5*) Readers Intl.

— Flight of Ashes. Marinelli, David N., tr. 188p. 1986. 16.95 (*0-930523-22-9*); pap. 8.95 (*0-930523-23-7*) Readers Intl.

— Silent Close No. 6. Marinelli, David N., tr. 192p. (Orig.). (C). 1993. 19.95 (*0-930523-93-8*); pap. 11.95 (*0-930523-94-6*) Readers Intl.

Marona, Bonnie. Kiss Me, But Not Goodbye. 220p. (Orig.). 1989. pap. 4.59 (*0-9621680-0-9*) Circle M Pubns.

M

Maronde, R. F., ed. Topics in Clinical Pharmacology & Therapeutics. (Illus.). 530p. 1986. 138.00 (0-387-96196-8) Spr-Verlag.

*Marone, C. J. & Blanpied, M. L., eds. Faulting, Friction, & Earthquake Mechanics Pt. II. (PAGEOPH Topical Volumes Ser.). 516p. 1994. 42.50 (0-8176-5099-7) Birkhauser.

*Marone, Chris J. & Blanpied, Michael L., eds. Faulting, Friction, & Earthquake Mechanics. (Pageoph Tropic Volumes Ser.). 404p. 1994. 34.50 (0-8176-5073-3) Birkhauser.

Marone, G., ed. Chemical Mediators & Cellular Interactions in Clinical Immunology. (Journal: International Archives of Allergy & Applied Immunology: Vol. 99 Nos. 2-4). (Illus.). 348p. 1993. 289.00 (3-8055-5723-X) S Karger.

— Chemical Mediators & Cellular Interactions in Clinical Immunology. (International Archives of Allergy & Applied Immunology Ser.: Vol. 99, Nos. 2-4, 1992). (Illus.). 346p. 1993. reprint ed. 196.00 (3-8055-5757-4) S Karger.

— Human Basophils & Mast Cells, Set. (Chemical Immunology Ser.: Vols. 61 & 62). (Illus.). xx, 470p. 1995. 352.00 (3-8055-6129-6) S Karger.

— Human Basophils & Mast Cells: Biological Aspects. (Chemical Immunology Ser.: Vol. 61). (Illus.). x, 230p. 1995. 192.00 (3-8055-6127-X) S Karger.

Marone, G., jt. ed. see Ricci, M.

*Marone, Gianni, ed. Human Basophils & Mast Cells: Clinical Aspects. (Chemical Immunology Ser.: Vol. 62). (Illus.). x, 240p. 1995. 200.00 (3-8055-6128-8) S Karger.

Marone, Nicky. How to Father a Successful Daughter. 336p. 1989. reprint ed. pap. text ed. 4.95 (0-449-21687-X, Crest) Fawcett.

— What's Stopping You? Overcome Learned Helplessness & Do What You Never Dreamed Possible. 272p. 1993. pap. 11.00 (0-671-79647-X, Fireside) S&S Trade.

— Women & Risk: How to Master Your Fears & Do What You Never Thought You Could Do. 288p. 1992. 19.95 (0-685-50328-3) St Martin.

Marone, Phillip J. Shoulder Injuries in Sports. LC 91-44364. 188p. 1992. 93.50 (0-8342-0338-3) Raven.

Maroney, Marion L. A Guide to Metal & Plastic Finishing. (Illus.). 120p. 1990. 18.95 (0-8311-3028-8) Indus Pr.

Maroney, Mary. Executive Wordpower. 1988. 27.97 (0-87280-201-9, 3403, Asher-Gallant) Caddylak Systs.

Marongiu, Pietro & Newman, Graeme. Vengeance: The Fight Against Injustice. 192p. 1987. 41.75 (0-8476-7540-8) Rowman.

Maroni, Gustavo. An Atlas of Drosophila Genes: Sequences & Molecular Features. LC 92-35001. 432p. 1993. 80.00 (0-19-507116-6) OUP.

Maroni, Joe. Fifty Elementary Duets for Snare Drum. (Building Excellence Ser.). 1993. 5.95 (0-685-64626-2, 94628) Mel Bay.

— Fifty Syncopated Solos for Snare Drum. (Building Excellence Ser.). 1993. 5.95 (0-685-64628-9, 94629) Mel Bay.

— Fundamental Principles of Drumming. (Building Excellence Ser.). 1993. 8.95 (1-56222-057-8, 94492) Mel Bay.

— Fundamentals of Rhythm for the Drummer. (Building Excellence Ser.). 1993. 8.95 (1-56222-058-6, 94493) Mel Bay.

— One Hundred Rhythm Etudes for Snare Drum. (Building Excellence Ser.). 1993. 5.95 (0-685-64627-0, 94627) Mel Bay.

Maroni, Lisa, tr. see Croceetti, Enzo & Giordano, Mario.

Maroni, Lisa, tr. see Crocetti, Enzo & Giordano, Mario.

Maroni, V. A., ed. Synthesis-Characterization & Novel Applications of Molecular Sieve Materials: Materials Research Society Symposium Proceedings, Vol. 233. 1991. text ed. 68.00 (1-55899-127-1) Materials Res.

Maronski, J. & Rupinska, M. Computer Networks Terminology. 73p. 1980. pap. 7.50 (83-01-01179-3, M-9061) Fr & Eur.

*Maroon, Fred, photos. The Supreme Court: Of the United States. (Illus.). 176p. 1995. 45.00 (1-56566-093-5) Thomasson-Grant.

— The Supreme Court: Of the United States. (Illus.). 176p. 1995. pap. 24.95 (1-56566-097-8) Thomasson-Grant.

Maroon, Fred J. Century Ended, Century Begun: The Catholic University of America. LC 90-36773. (Illus.). 144p. 1990. 29.95 (0-8132-0735-5) Cath U Pr.

— Maroon on Georgetown. LC 85-80974. (Illus.). 128p. 1985. 34.00 (0-934738-15-7) Thomasson-Grant.

— The United States Capitol. LC 92-35906. (Illus.). 192p. 1993. 45.00 (1-55670-316-3); pap. 24.95 (1-55670-319-8) Stewart Tabori & Chang.

Maroon, Fred J., jt. auth. see Beach, Edward L.

Marosi, E., jt. auth. see Torok, J.

Marot, Helen. American Labor Unions. LC 70-89754. (American Labor, from Conspiracy to Collective Bargaining Ser., No. 1). 1974. reprint ed. 19.95 (0-405-02141-0) Ayer.

— Creative Impulse in Industry: A Proposition for Educators. Stein, Leon, ed. LC 77-70514. (Work Ser.). 1977. reprint ed. lib. bdg. 19.95 (0-405-10183-X) Ayer.

Marot, M., jt. auth. see Rohonyi, K.

Maroto, Angel R., ed. see Ballesteros, Antonio M.

Marotta, Gary, ed. see Miller, Joan V.

*Marotta, Kenny. A House in the Piazza. (Prose Ser.: No. 36). 300p. 1995. 15.00 (1-55071-032-X) Guernica Editions.

*Marotta, Lori. Four Children's Adventures. (J). 1995. 10.95 (0-8062-5205-7) Carlton.

Marotta, M. E. The Code Book: Cryptology. 1986. lib. bdg. 79.95 (0-8490-3567-8) Gordon Pr.

Marotta, Terry. I Thought He Was a Speed Bump: And Other Excuses from Life in the Fast Lane. 176p. 1994. pap. 9.95 (0-9638603-0-5) Ravenscroft.

Marotta, Theodore W. & Herubin, Charles A. Basic Construction Materials: Methods & Testing. 4th ed. LC 92-14288. 480p. (C). 1992. text ed. 36.00 (0-13-059585-3) P-H.

*Marotti, Arthur F. Critical Essays on John Donne. (Critical Essays on British Literature Ser.). 1994. lib. bdg. 42.00x (0-8161-8769-X, Twayne) Macmillan.

— John Donne: Coterie Poet. LC 85-40765. 389p. reprint ed. pap. 110.90 (0-7837-4618-0, 2044339) Bks Demand.

— Manuscript, Print, & the English Renaissance Lyric. 336p. 1995. 45.00 (0-8014-2291-4); pap. 19.95 (0-8014-8238-0) Cornell U Pr.

Marotti, Arthur F., et al, eds. Reading with a Difference: Gender, Race, & Cultural Identity: A Criticism Book. LC 93-28532. 400p. 1993. pap. 16.95 (0-8143-2493-2) Wayne St U Pr.

Marotti, Giorgio. Black Characters in the Brazilian Novel. Marotti, Maria O. & Lawton, Harry, trs. (Afro-American Culture & Society Monograph Ser.: Vol. 6). (Illus.). 448p. 1987. 50.95 (0-934934-24-X); pap. 19.95 (0-934934-25-8) UCLA CAAS.

Marotti, Maria O. The Duplicating Imagination: Twain & the Twain Papers. LC 88-19560. 1990. lib. bdg. 30.00 (0-271-00650-1) Pa St U Pr.

*Marotti, Maria O., ed. & intro. Italian Women Writers from the Renaissance to the Present: Revising the Canon. LC 95-14888. 1996. write for info. (0-271-01505-5); pap. write for info. (0-271-01506-3) Pa St U Pr.

Marotti, Maria O., tr. see Marotti, Giorgio.

Marotz-Baden, Ramona, ed. see Hennon, Charles B. & Brubaker, Timothy H.

Marotz, Lynn & Cross, Marie. Computerized Testmaker & Testbank to Accompany Health, Safety & Nutrition for the Young Child. 3rd ed. 1993. 39.95 (0-8273-6061-4) Delmar.

Marotz, Lynn R., jt. auth. see Allen, K. Eileen.

Marotz, Lynn R., et al. Health, Safety, & Nutrition for the Young Child. 3rd ed. LC 92-18290. 545p. 1993. pap. text ed. 30.95 (0-8273-4932-7) Delmar.

— Instructor's Guide for Health, Safety & Nutrition for the Young Child. 3rd ed. 85p. 1993. teacher ed 14.00 (0-8273-4933-5) Delmar.

— Study Guide for Health, Safety & Nutrition for the Young Child. 3rd ed. 169p. 1993. student ed 13.95 (0-8273-6060-6) Delmar.

Maroudas, A. & Kuettner, K., eds. Methods in Cartilage Research. 370p. 1990. text ed. 165.00 (0-12-473280-1) Acad Pr.

Maroun, F. B. Diastematomyelia. LC 75-17393. (Illus.). 144p. 1976. 10.60 (0-87527-143-X) Green.

Maroun, Jack, ed. Decision Making in Business. 3rd rev. ed. LC 90-19566. 216p. (C). 1991. pap. text ed. write for info. (0-935732-28-4) Roxbury Pub Co.

Marousek, Theresa, et al. Laparoscopy & You. (Illus.). 40p. 1994. pap. 3.60 (0-317-59849-X) Budlong.

*Marousis, Jim, et al. Road School. 1995. pap. 12.95 (0-933025-36-X) Blue Bird Pub.

*Marov, Mikhail Y., et al. Nonequilibrium Aeronomic Processes: A Kinetic Approach to the Mathematical Modeling. LC 95-11944. 1995. write for info. (0-7923-3451-5) Kluwer Ac.

Marovic, D. Play the King's Indian Defense. (Chess Ser.). (Illus.). 242p. 1983. 29.95 (0-08-029727-7, Pergamon Pr); pap. 19.90 (0-08-029726-9, Pergamon Pr) Elsevier.

— Play the Queen's Gambit. (PECH Pergamon Chess Ser.). 200p. 1991. write for info. (0-08-029765-X, 6201, Pub. by CHES UK); pap. 29.95 (0-08-029764-1, 6201, Pub. by CHES UK) Macmillan.

Marovic, Drazen. An Active Repertoire for Black. 184p. 1992. pap. 16.95 (0-8050-2320-8, Pub. by Batsford Chess UK) H Holt & Co.

*Marovitz. Abraham Cahan. 1995. text ed. 26.95 (0-8057-3993-9) Macmillan.

Marovitz, Sanford E., jt. ed. see DeMott, Robert J.

Marovitz, Sanford E., jt. ed. see Gohdes, Clarence.

Marowitz, Charles. Burnt Bridges: A Souvenir of the Singing Sixties & Beyond. (Illus.). 245p. 1992. 34.95 (0-340-49659-2, Pub. by H & S UK) Trafalgar.

— Clever Dick. 1989. pap. 4.75 (0-8222-0216-6) Dramatists Play.

— Directing the Action: Acting & Directing in Contemporary Theatre. (Acting Ser.). 1991. pap. 12.95 (1-55783-072-X) Applause Theatre Bk Pubs.

— Disciples. 71p. 1987. pap. 4.75 (0-8222-0313-8) Dramatists Play.

— The Marowitz Shakespeare: Adaptations & Collages of Hamlet, Macbeth, the Taming of the Shrew, Measure for Measure & The Merchant of Venice. 288p. 1990. pap. 15.00 (0-7145-2651-7) M Boyars Pubs.

— Potboilers: Three Black Comedies. 192p. (Orig.). 1987. pap. 11.95 (0-7145-2862-5) M Boyars Pubs.

— Prospero's Staff: Acting & Directing in the Contemporary Theatre. LC 85-45887. (Illus.). 196p. 1986. 29.95 (0-253-34622-3) Ind U Pr.

— Recycling Shakespeare. (Illus.). 256p. 1991. 32.95 (1-55783-093-2); pap. 14.95 (1-55783-094-0) Applause Theatre Bk Pubs.

— Sex Wars: Free Adaptations of Ibsen & Strinberg. LC 82-1133. 192p. 1983. 16.95 (0-7145-2721-1); pap. 9.95 (0-7145-2722-X) M Boyars Pubs.

— Sherlock's Last Case. 1984. pap. 4.75 (0-8222-1021-5) Dramatists Play.

— Wilde West. 1988. pap. 4.75 (0-8222-1256-0) Dramatists Play.

Marowitz, Charles, tr. see Ionesco, Eugene.

Marowski, Daniel G. & Gunton, Sharon R., eds. Contemporary Literary Criticism, Vol. 35. LC 76-38938. 691p. 1985. 122.00 (0-8103-4409-2) Gale.

— Contemporary Literary Criticism, Vol. 36. LC 76-38938. 700p. 1986. 122.00 (0-8103-4410-6) Gale.

— Contemporary Literary Criticism, Vol. 37. LC 76-38938. 600p. 1986. 122.00 (0-8103-4411-4) Gale.

— Contemporary Literary Criticism, Vol. 38. LC 76-38938. 600p. 1986. 122.00 (0-8103-4412-2) Gale.

— Contemporary Literary Criticism, Vol. 39. LC 76-38938. 700p. 1986. 122.00 (0-8103-4413-0) Gale.

— Contemporary Literary Criticism, Vol. 40. LC 76-38938. 600p. 1986. 122.00 (0-8103-4414-9) Gale.

Marowski, Daniel G. & Matuz, Roger. Contemporary Literary Criticism, Vol. 49, Vol. 49. 1988. 122.00 (0-8103-4423-8) Gale.

Marowski, Daniel G. & Matuz, Roger, eds. Contemporary Literary Criiticism, Vol. 46. LC 76-38938. 650p. 1987. 122.00 (0-8103-4420-3) Gale.

— Contemporary Literary Criticism, Vol. 41. 1986. 122.00 (0-8103-4415-7) Gale.

— Contemporary Literary Criticism, Vol. 42. 779p. 1987. 122.00 (0-8103-4416-5) Gale.

— Contemporary Literary Criticism, Vol. 43. 795p. 1987. 122.00 (0-8103-4417-3) Gale.

— Contemporary Literary Criticism, Vol. 44. 626p. 1987. 122.00 (0-8103-4418-1) Gale.

— Contemporary Literary Criticism, Vol. 47. LC 76-38938. 650p. 1988. 122.00 (0-8103-4421-1) Gale.

— Contemporary Literary Criticism, Vol. 50. 600p. 1988. 122.00 (0-8103-4424-6) Gale.

— Contemporary Literary Criticism, Vol. 51. 600p. 1988. 122.00 (0-8103-4425-4) Gale.

— Contemporary Literary Criticism, Vol. 52. 1989. 122.00 (0-8103-5430-6) Gale.

— Contemporary Literary Criticism, Vol. 53. 1989. 122.00 (0-8103-4427-0) Gale.

— Contemporary Literary Criticism, Vol. 54. 1989. 122.00 (0-8103-4428-9) Gale.

— Contemporary Literary Criticism, Vol. 48, Vol. 48. (Contemporary Literary Criticism Ser.). 600p. 1988. 122.00 (0-8103-4422-X) Gale.

Marowski, Daniel G. & Stine, Jean, eds. Contemporary Literary Criticism, Vol. 33, Vol. 33. 680p. 1985. 122.00 (0-8103-4407-6) Gale.

Marowski, Daniel G., ed. see Matuz, Roger.

Marowsky, G. & Smirnov, V. V., eds. Coherent Raman Spectroscopy: Recent Advances. (Proceedings in Physics Ser.: Vol. 63). (Illus.). 320p. 1992. 79.00 (0-387-54993-5) Spr-Verlag.

Marozas, Donald S. & May, Deborah C. Issues & Practices in Special Education. 290p. (C). 1988. pap. text ed. 25.95 (0-582-28639-5, 71663) Longman.

Marpinard, Alain, jt. auth. see Motet, Gilles.

Marple, Elliot & Olson, Bruce H. National Bank of Commerce of Seattle, 1889-1969: Territorial to Worldwide Banking in Eighty Years, Including the Story of the Marine Bancorporation. LC 72-134228. (Illus.). 1972. 24.95 (0-87015-189-4) Pacific Bks.

Marple, Lawrence S., Jr. Digital Special Analysis with Applications in C & Matlab. 1993. text ed. write for info. (0-13-015140-8) P-H.

— Digital Spectral Analysis with Applications. (Illus.). 480p. 1987. text ed. 79.00 (0-13-214149-3) P-H.

Marples, David R. Chernobyl & Nuclear Power in the U. S. S. R. LC 86-42967. 192p. 1986. pap. 15.95 (0-312-00457-5) St Martin.

— The Social Impact of the Chernobyl Disaster. 316p. 1988. pap. 16.95 (0-312-02513-0) St Martin.

— Ukraine under Perestroika: Ecology, Economics & the Workers' Revolt. LC 91-8110. 255p. 1991. text ed. 49.95 (0-312-06196-X); pap. 16.95 (0-312-06197-8) St Martin.

Marples, Morris. White Horses & Other Hill Figures. (Illus.). 224p. 1991. pap. 16.00 (0-86299-759-3) A Sutton Pub.

*Marples, N. J. & Macrae-Gibson, O. D. Critical Discography of Readings in Old English. 1988. 5.00 (0-614-01293-7) Medieval Inst.

Marples, Theodore. Show Dogs: Their Points & Characteristics. 1991. lib. bdg. 88.95 (0-8490-5238-6) Gordon Pr.

Marquadt, William H., jt. ed. see Crumley, Carole E.

Marquand, C. & Croft, D. Thermofluids: An Integrated Approach to Thermodynamics & Fluid Mechanics Principles. LC 93-8776. 403p. 1994. pap. text ed. 44.95 (0-471-94184-0) Wiley.

Marquand, Christina, jt. auth. see Sedgwick, Sarah C.

Marquand, David, jt. ed. see Crouch, Colin.

Marquand, Ed. Graphic Design Presentations. (Illus.). 160p. 1986. text ed. 36.95 (0-442-26167-5) Van Nos Reinhold.

— Graphic Designs Presentations. 28.95 (0-685-19129-X) Van Nos Reinhold.

— How to Prepare Roughs, Comps & Mockups. LC 84-71518. 96p. 1985. 12.50 (0-88108-014-4); pap. 8.95 (0-88108-019-5) Art Dir.

— How to Prepare Your Portfolio. rev. ed. Weiler, Marie, ed. LC 81-66881. (Illus.). 128p. 1994. text ed. 14.50 (0-88108-144-2) Art Dir.

— How to Prepare Your Portfolio. 3rd ed. Date not set. 14.50 (0-88108-129-9); pap. 10.95 (0-88108-130-2) Art Dir.

— How to Prepare Your Portfolio: A Guide for Students & Professionals. (Illus.). 138p. 1981. 12.50 (0-910158-69-X); pap. 10.95 (0-910158-70-3) Art Dir.

Marquand, Ed, jt. auth. see Kotz, Susanne.

Marquand, H. A. The Dynamics of Industrial Combination. LC 79-38262. (Evolution of Capitalism Ser.). 218p. 1972. reprint ed. 17.95 (0-405-04143-8) Ayer.

Marquand, John P. The Black Cargo. LC 74-26118. (Labor Movement in Fiction & Non-Fiction Ser.). reprint ed. 39.50 (0-404-58453-5) AMS Pr.

— H. M. Pulham, Esq. 432p. 1986. reprint ed. pap. 11.00 (0-89733-231-8) Academy Chi Pubs.

— Haven's End. LC 77-130064. (Short Story Index Reprint Ser.). 1977. 23.95 (0-8369-3663-9) Ayer.

— The Late George Apley. 1994. lib. bdg. 24.95x (1-56849-446-7) Buccaneer Bks.

— The Late George Apley: A Novel in the Form of a Memoir. (YA). (gr. 7 up). 1937. 18.95 (0-685-03075-X) Little.

— Mr. Moto & Mr. Moto Is So Sorry. 1976. 15.95 (0-89387-016-1) Amereon Ltd.

— No Hero. reprint ed. lib. bdg. 21.95 (0-88411-141-5, Aeonian Pr) Amereon Ltd.

— Point of No Return. 559p. 1985. pap. 12.00 (0-89733-174-5) Academy Chi Pubs.

— Thank You Mr. Moto. reprint ed. lib. bdg. 21.95 (0-88411-142-3, Aeonian Pr) Amereon Ltd.

— Wickford Point. 11.25 (0-8446-2666-X) Peter Smith.

Marquand, Josephine. Life: Its Nature, Origins & Distribution. (Contemporary Science Library). (Illus.). (C). 1971. reprint ed. pap. text ed. 1.65 (0-393-00589-5) Norton.

Marquand, E. A. Luftwaffe Methods in the Selection of Offensive Weapons: Karlsruhe Study, Vol. 2. (USAF Historical Studies: No. 187). 182p. 1955. reprint ed. pap. 30.95 (0-89126-150-8) MA-AH Pub.

Marquard, Odo. Farewell to Matters of Principle: Philosophical Studies. Wallace, Robert, tr. (Odeon Ser.). 160p. 1989. 32.00 (0-19-505114-9) OUP.

— In Defense of the Accidental (Apologie des Zufallingen) Philosophical Studies. Wallace, Robert M., tr. 144p. 1991. 39.95 (0-19-505632-9); pap. 15.95 (0-19-507252-9) OUP.

Marquard, Steven. The Distortion Theory of Macro-Economic Forecasting: A Guide for Econimists & Investors. LC 93-42761. 224p. 1994. text ed. 59.95 (0-89930-910-0, Quorum Bks) Greenwood.

Marquardt, jt. auth. see Talbot.

*Marquardt, Arthur H. The New Americans. LC 94-71586. 635p. (Orig.). (YA). (gr. 9-12). 1994. pap. 32.50 (0-940121-19-0, P212, Cross Roads Bks) Cross Cultural Pubns.

Marquardt, Barbara S. How to Paint from Start to Finish: Tips & Techniques for Practicing Painters. 57p. (Orig.). 1991. student ed 11.95 (0-9629638-0-1) Artmarq.

Marquardt, Dorothy A. A Guide to the Supreme Court. LC 76-47338. (Illus.). 1977. 7.95 (0-672-52168-7, Bobbs) Macmillan.

Marquardt, Dorothy. A., jt. ed. see Ward, Martha E.

Marquardt, Frederic S. Before Bataan & After. LC 73-161770. reprint ed. 41.50 (0-404-09033-8) AMS Pr.

Marquardt, H. Michael & Walters, Wesley P. Inventing Mormonism: Tradition & the Historical Record. LC 93-13603. (Illus.). 280p. 1994. text ed. 28.95 (1-56085-039-6) Signature Bks.

Marquardt, Hanne. Reflex Zone Therapy of the Feet. 160p. (Orig.). 1984. pap. 14.95 (0-89281-234-6) Inner Tradit.

Marquardt, James F. & Sullivan, James F. Laboratory Manual for General Physics. 3rd ed. 144p. 1990. spiral bd. 15.95 (0-8403-8202-2) Kendall-Hunt.

Marquardt, James F., Sr., jt. auth. see Gilligan, Lawrence G.

Marquardt, Joachim. Romische Staatsverwaltung, 3 vols., 1. LC 75-7329. (Roman History Ser.). 1972. reprint ed. 32.95 (0-405-08997-X) Ayer.

— Romische Staatsverwaltung, 3 vols., 2. LC 75-7329. (Roman History Ser.). 1975. reprint ed. 40.95 (0-405-07103-5) Ayer.

— Romische Staatsverwaltung, 3 vols., 3. LC 75-7329. (Roman History Ser.). 1975. reprint ed. 40.95 (0-405-07104-3) Ayer.

— Romische Staatsverwaltung, 3 vols., Set. LC 75-7329. (Roman History Ser.). 1975. reprint ed. 121.95 (0-405-07101-9) Ayer.

*Marquardt, Karl H. Captain Cook's Endeavour. (Anatomy of the Ship Ser.). (Illus.). 138p. 1995. 36.95 (1-55750-118-1) Naval Inst Pr.

— Eighteenth-Century Rigs & Rigging. (Illus.). (C). 1992. 56.95 (1-881093-00-X) Phoen Pubns.

Marquardt, Kathleen. Animalscam: The Beastly Abuse of Human Rights. LC 93-24500. 221p. 1993. 24.00 (0-89526-498-6) Regnery Pub.

Marquardt, Linda A., jt. ed. see Heltne, Paul G.

Marquardt, M., jt. auth. see Himmelweit, F.

Marquardt, Manfred. John Wesley's Social Ethics: Praxis & Principles. Gunter, W. Stephen & Steely, John E., trs. 224p. 1992. pap. 19.95 (0-687-20494-1) Abingdon.

Marquardt, Marsha. Colorful Ghost. 16p. (J). (gr. 1). 1989. pap. text ed. 3.00 (1-882225-05-8) Tott Pubns.

— Little Ghost Goes to School. (Illus.). 12p. (Orig.). (J). (gr. 1). 1993. pap. text ed. write for info. (1-882225-12-0) Tott Pubns.

— Little Ghost's Vacation. 8p. (J). (gr. 1). 1990. pap. text ed. 2.50 (1-882225-01-5) Tott Pubns.

— Rotten Reggie. 12p. (J). (gr. 1). 1990. pap. text ed. 3.00 (1-882225-00-7) Tott Pubns.

— Tommy Snake. 8p. (J). (gr. 1). 1989. pap. text ed. 3.00 (1-882225-02-3) Tott Pubns.

Marquardt, Max. Wilbur, Orville & the Flying Machine. (Real Readers Ser.: Level Green). (Illus.). 32p. (J). (gr. 1-4). 1989. lib. bdg. 19.97 (0-8172-3530-2); pap. 4.95 (0-8114-6735-X) Raintree Steck-V.

— Working Dogs. (Real Readers Ser.: Level Red). (Illus.). 32p. (J). (gr. 1-4). 1989. lib. bdg. 19.97 (0-8172-3506-X); pap. 3.95 (0-8114-6711-2) Raintree Steck-V.

Marquardt, Mervin A. The Temptation of Jesus. (Arch Bks.). (Illus.). 24p. (J). (gr. k-4). 1986. pap. 1.99 (0-570-06204-7, 59-1427) Concordia.

Marquardt, Michael & Stump, Robert W. Training: Issues & Answers for the Eighties. 1982. pap. 6.00 (0-87771-030-9) Grad School.

Marquardt, Michael J. & Engel, Dean W. Global Human Resource Development. LC 92-17719. (Human Resource Development Ser.). 288p. 1992. pap. text ed. 31.80 (0-13-357930-1) P-H.

Marquardt, R., jt. ed. see Lemp, M. A.

Marquardt, Ronald G., jt. auth. see Karnes, Frances A.

An Asterisk (*) at the beginning of an entry indicates that the title is appearing in BIP for the first time.

*Marquardt Sr., James F. & Sullivan, James F. Physics for Technology Lab Manual. 4th ed. (Illus.). 150p. (C). 1995. 15.95 (0-9626661-7-3) Gilmar Pub.

Marquardt, Thomas P. Acquired Neurogenic Disorders. (Illus.). 208p. 1982. text ed. write for info. (0-13-003814-8) P-H.

Marquardt, Thomas P., jt. auth. see Peterson, Harold A.

Marquardt, Virginia H., jt. ed. see Roman, Gail H.

Marquardt, William C., jt. ed. see Beaty, Barry J.

Marquardt, William H., ed. Culture & Environment in the Domain of the Calusa. (Institute of Archaeology & Paleoenvironmental Studies, Monograph: No. 1). 448p. (C). 1992. pap. 25.00 (1-881448-00-2) U FL Inst Arch & Paleoenv.

— Regional Centers in Archaeology: Prospects & Problems. LC 77-82743. (Research Ser.: No. 14). (Illus.). 40p. 1977. pap. 4.00 (0-943414-15-6) MO Arch Soc.

*Marquart. Everything's a Verb. 1995. pap. text ed. 7.95 (0-89823-162-0) New Rivers Pr.

*Marquart, Debra, et al. A Circle of Four. 1989. 5.00 (0-941127-07-9) Dacotah Terr Pr.

Marquart, James W., jt. auth. see Crouch, Ben M.

Marquart, James W., et al. The Rope, the Chair, & the Needle: Capital Punishment in Texas, 1923-1990. LC 93-15717. (Illus.). 328p. (C). 1994. 24.95 (0-292-75158-3) U of Tex Pr.

Marquart, Judith L. Fearless Living. 192p. (Orig.). pap. 9.95 (0-935236-48-1) Genl Med Pub.

Marquart, Kurt. The Church & Her Fellowship, Ministry, & Governance. Preus, Robert et al, eds. LC 89-84112. (Confessional Lutheran Dogmatics Ser.: Vol. 9). 280p. 1990. 14.50 (0-9622791-9-6) Luth Confess Res.

Marquart, Kurt E., et al, eds. A Lively Legacy: Essays in Honor of Robert Preus. 224p. (Orig.). 1985. 13.95 (0-9615927-0-2); pap. 11.95 (0-9615927-1-0) Concordia Theo Sem.

Marquart, M. Jesus' Second Family. (Arch Bks.). (J). (gr. k-2). 1977. pap. 1.99 (0-570-06111-3, 59-1229) Concordia.

Marques Cavalcante, J. C. English-Portuguese Dictionary of Economic & Commercial Terms: Dicionario Ingles-Portugues de Termos Economicos e Comercials. 408p. (ENG & POR.). 1982. pap. 49.95 (0-8288-0119-3, M14431) Fr & Eur.

Marques, Lydia, tr. see Marcos, Plinio, et al.

Marques, M. J. B., et al, eds. Public Health & Protection of the Population: Proceedings of the First International Congress on Public Health & Sanitary Protection of the Population, Held in Funchal, Madeira, 3-7 Oct., 1988. (International Congress Ser.: No. 840). 390p. 1989. 113.00 (0-444-81085-4, Excerpta Medica) Elsevier.

Marques, M. M., jt. ed. see Faergemand, O.

Marques, Nina M. Diccionari Escolar Catala-Castella, Castella-Catala. 4th ed. 500p. (SPA.). 1991. pap. 27.95 (0-7859-5842-8, 8427304609) Fr & Eur.

Marques, R. Mariana O el Alba. 243p. (SPA.). 1968. 7.50 (0-8288-7059-4, S5041) Fr & Eur.

Marques, Rene. The Look. LC 82-80438. (Senda Narrativa Ser.). Orig. Title: La Mirada. (Illus.). 91p. (Orig.). 1983. pap. 11.95 (0-918454-29-8) Senda Nueva.

Marques, Sarah. La Lengua Que Heredamos: Curso del Espanol para Bilingues. 2nd ed. 400p. (C). 1991. Net. pap. text ed. write for info. (0-471-53215-0) Wiley.

Marques Villanueva, Francisco. Lopede Vega's: Vida & Valores. LC 87-25561. 369p. 1988. pap. 20.00 (0-8477-3522-2) U of PR Pr.

Marquess, Harlan E., jt. ed. see Galler, Meyer.

Marquess, William H. Lives of the Poet: The First Century of Keats Biography. LC 84-43064. 224p. 1985. 28.50 (0-271-00390-1) Pa St U Pr.

Marquet, Jean F., ed. Surgery & Pathology of the Middle Ear. 1985. lib. bdg. 185.50 (0-89838-707-8) Kluwer Ac.

Marquet, Luis. Diccionari d'Electronica. 208p. (CAT.). 1977. pap. 9.95 (0-8288-5304-5, S50184) Fr & Eur.

Marquet, Luis, jt. auth. see Espunes, I.

Marquette, Catherine M., jt. auth. see Lloyd, Cynthia B.

*Marquette Electronics Staff. Affinity Reference for BioMedical. 256p. 1995. boxed 24.95 (0-7872-0065-4) Kendall-Hunt.

Marquette, Jesse, jt. auth. see Malik, Yogendra.

Marquez, Alberto T., ed. War Memories of the Alcala Veterans. (Illus.). 158p. (Orig.). 1992. pap. 8.00 (971-10-0461-5, Pub. by New Day Pub PH) Cellar.

Marquez, Alex & Marquez, Marta. The New Interpreters Handbook. 116p. (Orig.). (C). 1987. pap. text ed. 20.00 (0-943407-00-1) Iberia Lang.

Marquez, Antonio, jt. ed. see Anaya, Rudolfo A.

Marquez, Barbara, et al. Usted y Su Artritis. 97p. (Orig.). (SPA.). 1986. 10.00 (1-879552-20-5) Stanford CRDP.

Marquez, Benjamin. LULAC: The Evolution of a Mexican American Political Organization. LC 92-28983. (Illus.). 153p. (C). 1993. text ed. 25.00 (0-292-75152-4); pap. 11.95 (0-292-75154-0) U of Tex Pr.

Marquez Bessa, Antonio. Diccionario Politico para Occidente. 288p. (SPA.). 1978. pap. 14.95 (0-8288-5149-2, S50003) Fr & Eur.

Marquez, Edrie J. Amazing AMC Muscle: Complete Development & Racing History of the Cars from American Motors. (Illus.). 224p. 1988. pap. 9.98 (0-87938-300-3) Motorbooks Intl.

Marquez, Enrique. Jose Lezama Lima: Bases y Genesis de un Sistema Poetico. LC 90-41160. (American University Studies: Latin American Literature: Ser. XXII, Vol. 12). 225p. (C). 1991. text ed. 41.95 (0-8204-1377-1) P Lang Pubs.

Marquez, Esther T., jt. auth. see Decker, Robert.

Marquez, Gabriel G. El Amor en los Tiempos de Colera. 9th ed. 360p. (SPA.). 1989. pap. 24.95 (0-7859-4987-9) Fr & Eur.

— The Autumn of the Patriarch. 288p. 1994. lib. bdg. 29.00 (0-8095-9137-5) Borgo Pr.

— El Coronel No Tiene Quien Le Escriba. 6th ed. 151p. (SPA.). 1990. pap. 13.95 (0-7859-4983-6) Fr & Eur.

— Cronica De una Muerte Anunciada. 250p. (SPA.). 1983. pap. 10.95 (0-7859-4985-2) Fr & Eur.

— The Handsomest Drowned Man in the World: A Tale for Children. Rabazza, Gregory, tr. LC 92-44055. (J). Date not set. 13.95 (0-88682-587-3) Creative Ed.

— La Hojarasca. 6th ed. 184p. (SPA.). 1986. pap. 17.95 (0-7859-4982-8) Fr & Eur.

— La Increible y Triste Historia De la Candida Erendira y De Su Abuela Desalmada. 160p. (SPA.). 1987. pap. 18.95 (0-7859-4988-7) Fr & Eur.

— Ojos de Perro Azul. 136p. 1987. pap. 17.95 (0-7859-5176-8) Fr & Eur.

— One Hundred Years of Solitude. 1976. 23.95 (0-8488-1429-0) Amereon Ltd.

— One Hundred Years of Solitude. large type ed. Rabassa, Gregory, tr. LC 92-22859. (General Ser.). 533p. 1993. 21.95 (0-8161-5483-X) G K Hall.

— El Otono Del Patriarca. 263p. (SPA.). 1987. pap. 24.95 (0-7859-4984-4) Fr & Eur.

— Strange Pilgrims. Grossman, Edith, tr. LC 93-12257. 1993. 21.00 (0-679-42566-7) Knopf.

— Strange Pilgrims. 208p. 1994. 10.95 (0-14-023940-5, Penguin Bks) Viking Penguin.

Marquez, Gabriel G., tr. see Cepeda Samudio, Alvaro.

*Marquez, Gustavo, ed. Reforming the Labor Market in a Liberalized Economy. 220p. 1995. 18.50 (0-940602-96-2) IADB.

Marquez-Hardy Design Staff. Graphic Standards & Public Relations Manual. enl. ed. Keller, Shelly G., ed. (Partnerships for Change Ser.: No. 3). 95p. 1991. 25.00 (0-929722-48-5) CA State Library Fndtn.

Marquez, Hector P. La Prefiguracion Como Recurso: Estilistico En Amalia. (Coleccion Polymita Ser.). 14p. (Orig.). (SPA.). 1989. pap. 3.00 (0-89729-552-8) Ediciones.

Marquez, Hudson. Monkey Island... a Fantastic Guide to New Orleans. (Illus.). 100p. (Orig.). 1992. pap. 8.95 (0-917905-04-0) Faust Pub Co.

*Marquez, Ismael P. La Retorica de la Violencia en Tres Novelas Peruanas. LC 92-27681. (University Texas Studies in Contemporary Spanish-American Fiction: Vol. 7). 130p. (C). 1994. text ed. 35.95 (0-614-00676-7) P Lang Pubs.

Marquez, Jaime, jt. ed. see Klein, Lawrence R.

Marquez, Jaime, ed. see Klein, Lawrence.

Marquez, Marta, jt. auth. see Marquez, Alex.

Marquez, Nancy. Aprendiendo con Movimientos: Metodo TPR Espanol (for Beginners) 3rd ed. 50p. 1991. pap. 8.95 (1-56018-471-X) Sky Oaks Prodns.

— L' Enseignement par le Mouvement: Total Physical Response French (for Beginners) 2nd ed. 50p. 1991. pap. 8.95 (1-56018-482-5) Sky Oaks Prodns.

— Learning with Movements: Total Physical Response English (for Beginners) 3rd ed. 50p. 1992. pap. 8.95 (1-56018-483-3) Sky Oaks Prodns.

Marquez, Nancy & Perez, Theresa. Portraits of Mexican Americans. 96p. (J). (gr. 4-8). 1991. 10.95 (0-86653-605-1, GA1324) Good Apple.

Marquez, Robert, ed. Latin American Revolutionary Poetry - Poesia Revolucionaria Latinoamericana: A Bilingual Anthology. LC 73-90079. 503p. reprint ed. pap. 135.90 (0-7837-3907-9, 3043755) Bks Demand.

Marquez, Robert, ed. see Guillen, Nicolas.

Marquez-Ruarte, Jorge, jt. auth. see Aghevli, Bijan B.

Marquez, Sandra, jt. auth. see Wagner, Candy.

Marquez-Sterling, Carlos. A la Ingerencia Extrana la Virtud Domestica: Biografia de Manuel Marquez Sterling. LC 86-81071. (Coleccion Cuba y Sus Jueces Ser.). (Illus.). 267p. (Orig.). (SPA.). 1986. pap. 12.00 (0-89729-425-4) Ediciones.

Marquez-Sterling, Manuel. Fernan Gonzalez, First Count of Castile: The Man & the Legend. LC 80-15095. (Romance Monographs: No. 40). (Illus.). 160p. 1980. 24.00 (84-499-4056-7) Romance.

Marquez-Villanueva, Francisco, ed. Harvard University Conference in Honor of Gabriel Miro (1879-1930) LC 82-83312. (Harvard Studies in Romance Languages: No. 39). (Orig.). (SPA.). 1982. pap. 8.00 (0-940940-39-6) Harvard U Romance Lang & Lit.

Marquina, jt. ed. see Wolfe.

Marquis, Alice G. Hopes & Ashes: The Birth of Modern Times, 1929-1939. 261p. 1986. text ed. 27.95 (0-02-920250-7) Free Pr.

Marquis, Arnold. A Guide to America's Indians: Ceremonials, Reservations, & Museums. LC 74-5315. (Illus.). 280p. 1974. pap. 19.95 (0-8061-1148-8) U of Okla Pr.

Marquis, Bessie L. & Huston. Management Decision-Making for Nurses: One Hundred One Case Studies. (Illus.). 393p. 1987. text ed. 26.95 (0-397-54663-7, Lippincott Nursing) Lippincott.

Marquis, Bessie L. & Huston, Carol J. Leadership Roles & Management Functions. (Illus.). 528p. 1991. pap. 28.50 (0-397-54876-1) Lippincott.

— Management Decision Making for Nurses: 119 Case Studies. 2nd ed. (Illus.). 464p. (C). 1994. pap. text ed. 27.95 (0-397-55056-1, Lippincott Nursing) Lippincott.

Marquis, Bessie L., jt. auth. see Huston.

Marquis, Clarke R. & Sarrett, Daniel P. IL Continuing Education for RE Practitioners. 2nd ed. 1994. pap. 14.95 (0-7931-1124-2, 152001-02, Real Estate Ed) Dearborn Finan.

Marquis, D. R., jt. comp. see Teris, C. V.

Marquis de Sade. Filosofiya V Buduare - Philosophy in the Bedroom. rev. ed. Armalinsky, Mikhail, tr. & intro. by. (Illus.). 196p. (RUS.). 1993. pap. 9.00 (0-916201-14-7) M I P Co.

Marquis, Derek A. Till Debt Due Us Part: The Step-by-Step Guide to Getting Out of Debt & Managing Your Money. 1993. pap. 16.95 (1-883163-23-4) DC Pubs & Mgmt.

— Until Debt Due Us Part: A Step-by-Step Guide to Getting Out of Debt in 1990s. (Illus.). 143p. (Orig.). 1992. pap. text ed. 16.95 (0-685-54730-2); pap. text ed. 29.95 (0-685-54731-0) Pubs Dist Ctr Inc.

Marquis, Doc, ed. see Peterson, Alan H.

Marquis, Don. Archy & Mehitabel. 1976. 26.95 (0-8488-0831-2) Amereon Ltd.

— Archy & Mehitabel. 207p. 1989. reprint ed. lib. bdg. 21.95 (0-89966-596-9) Buccaneer Bks.

— Carter, & Other People. LC 75-142269. (Short Story Index Reprint Ser.). 1977. 20.95 (0-8369-3753-8) Ayer.

— Chapters for the Orthodox. LC 74-130066. (Short Story Index Reprint Ser.). 1977. 21.95 (0-8369-3665-5) Ayer.

— Sun Dial Time. LC 79-132119. (Short Story Index Reprint Ser.). 1977. 20.95 (0-8369-3676-0) Ayer.

— When the Turtles Sing & Other Unusual Tales. LC 70-130065. (Short Story Index Reprint Ser.). 1977. reprint ed. 19.95 (0-8369-3664-7) Ayer.

Marquis, Donald M. In Search of Buddy Bolden: First Man of Jazz. LC 77-10958. (Illus.). xix, 176p. (C). 1993. pap. 9.95 (0-8071-1857-5) La State U Pr.

— In Search of Buddy Bolden: First Man of Jazz. LC 80-18335. (Illus.). xix, 176p. 1980. reprint ed. pap. 7.95 (0-306-80130-2) Da Capo.

Marquis, G. Welton. Twentieth-Century Music Idioms. LC 81-4197. xvi, 269p. 1981. reprint ed. text ed. 38.50 (0-313-22624-5, MATC, Greenwood Pr) Greenwood.

Marquis, Judith K., ed. Contemporary Issues in Pesticide Toxicology & Pharmacology. (Concepts in Toxicology Ser.: Vol. 2). (Illus.). xii, 108p. 1986. 71.25 (3-8055-4215-1) S Karger.

— A Guide to General Toxicology. 2nd rev. ed. (Continuing Education Ser.: Vol. 5). (Illus.). x, 294p. 1989. 54.50 (3-8055-4924-5) S Karger.

Marquis, Judith K., jt. ed. see Homburger, F.

Marquis, June H. Weekends for Two: The Mid-Atlantic Area. 2nd ed. 108p. 1989. pap. 7.95 (0-89709-177-9) Liberty Pub.

Marquis, Kent H., ed. see National Institute of Justice Staff & United States Department of Justice Staff.

Marquis, M. Ann & Addy-Trout, Elaine. CASE Study: Communication & Self-Esteem. LC 92-21826. (YA). (gr. 5-12). 1992. pap. 35.00 (0-930599-75-6) Thinking Pubns.

Marquis, Margaret. Lunchtime in Pittsburgh. 40p. (Orig.). 1988. pap. 4.95 (0-9621737-0-3) Pittsburgh Promo.

Marquis, Max. Undignified Death: A Detective Inspector Harry Timberlake Mystery. 192p. 1994. 18.95 (0-312-11087-1, Pub. by Thomas Dunne Bks) St Martin.

Marquis Of Landsdowne Staff, ed. see Petty, William.

*Marquis of Ruvigny & Raineval. The Blood Royal of Britain: Being a Roll of the Living Descendants of Edward IV & Henry VII, Kings of England, & James III, King of Scotland. (Illus.). 632p. 1994. 45.00 (0-614-03827-8, 5046) Genealog Pub.

— The Blood Royal of Britain & the Plantagenet Roll of the Blood Royal, Set. 1994. 235.00 (0-614-03832-4, 5051) Genealog Pub.

— The Plantagenet Roll of the Blood Royal: The Anne of Exeter Volume, Containing the Descendants of Anne (Plantagenet), Duchess of Exeter. (Illus.). 842p. 1994. 50.00 (0-614-03829-4, 5048) Genealog Pub.

— The Plantagenet Roll of the Blood Royal: The Clarence Volume, Containing the Descendants of George, Duke of Clarence. (Illus.). 730p. 1994. 50.00 (0-614-03828-6, 5047) Genealog Pub.

— The Plantagenet Roll of the Blood Royal: The Isabel of Essex Volume, Containing the Descendants of Isabel (Plantagenet), Countess of Essex & Eu. (Illus.). 698p. 1994. 45.00 (0-614-03830-8, 5049) Genealog Pub.

— The Plantagenet Roll of the Blood Royal: The Mortimer-Percy Volume, Containing the Descendants of Lady Elizabeth Perry, Nee Mortimer. (Illus.). 650p. 1994. 45.00 (0-614-03831-6, 5050) Genealog Pub.

Marquis, Robert E., jt. ed. see Bennett, Peter B.

Marquis, T. G. English-Canadian Literature. 1972. 59.95 (0-8490-0108-0) Gordon Pr.

Marquis, Thomas B. The Cheyennes of Montana. Weist, Thomas D., ed. LC 78-59715. 1978. 19.95 (0-917256-04-2) Ref Pubns.

— Custer, Cavalry & Crows. (Source Custeriana Ser.: No. 6). (Illus.). 1975. 20.00 (0-88342-041-4) Old Army.

— Keep the Last Bullet for Yourself: The True Story of Custer's Last Stand. Irvine, Keith & Faherty, Robert, eds. LC 75-39093. (Illus.). 192p. 1976. pap. 8.95 (0-917256-14-X) Ref Pubns.

Marquis, Thomas B., tr. Wooden Leg: A Warrior Who Fought Custer. LC 31-10067. (Illus.). xii, 389p. 1962. pap. 10.95 (0-8032-5124-6, Bison Books) U of Nebr Pr.

*Marquis Who's Who Staff, ed. Index to Marquis Who's Who Publications 1996. 1996. write for info. (0-8379-1433-7) Marquis.

— Who's Who in America 1995, 3 vols. 49th ed. 5000p. 1994. 450.00 (0-8379-0159-6) Marquis.

—Who's Who in America 1996, 3 vols. 50th ed. 5000p. 1995. 459.95 (0-8379-0167-7) Marquis.
"We make very heavy use of WHO'S WHO IN AMERICA in our library. It's used daily to check biographical facts on people of distinction."--MARIE WATERS, HEAD OF COLLECTION DEVELOPMENT, UNIVERSITY OF CALIFORNIA AT LOS ANGELES. Marquis Who's Who is proud to announce the Golden Anniversary 50th Edition of WHO'S WHO IN AMERICA. This, the world's preeminent biographical resource, keeps pace with a changing America with more than 17,500 new entries each year. AND it speeds research with the Geographic/Professional Indexes. ANNUAL UPDATING enables Marquis Who's Who to bring users more new names & to update more existing entries each year. Every entry is selected & researched to ensure the most current, accurate biographical data for Who's Who users. The Geographical/Professional Indexes makes WHO'S WHO IN AMERICA an even more useful research tool. Now users can identify & locate prospective partners & new clients by profession in any of 38 categories, as well as by country, state, or province, or city. Essential for quickly finding the entries you need. More than 92,000 leaders decision-makers, & innovators from every important field - business, finance, government, education, science & technology, the arts & more - are profiled in this Golden Anniversary 50th Edition. Entries include name, occupation, vital statistics, parents, marriage, children, education, career, civic & political activities, writings & creative works, awards, professional memberships, & office address. When you need authoritative, accurate facts on our nation's leaders, go to the preeminent record of American achievement that offers new information EVERY year: Marquis WHO'S WHO IN AMERICA. *Publisher Provided Annotation.*

— Who's Who in American Law. 9th deluxe ed. 1996. write for info. (0-8379-3512-1) Marquis.

—Who's Who in American Law 1996-1997. 9th ed. 1200p. 1996. 275.00 (0-8379-3511-3) Marquis.
Here's an important collection of some 30,000 biographical sketches of leading attorneys, judges, educators & other top professionals in the legal field. Entries detail principal occupation, fields of practice or interest, education, bar memberships, civic & political activities, military service, awards & honors, professional memberships, & home/office addresses. Contains a Professional Index, which lists non-practicing attorneys, such as judges, academics & non-attorneys who work in the legal field, as well as a Fields of Practice Index. *Publisher Provided Annotation.*

— Who's Who in American Nursing 1996-1997. 900p. 1995. 149.95 (0-8379-1004-8) Marquis.

— Who's Who in Entertainment, 1992-1993. 2nd rev. ed. 702p. 1992. 235.00 (0-8379-1851-0) Marquis.

— Who's Who in Finance & Industry 1996-1997. 29th ed. 920p. 1995. 259.95 (0-8379-0330-0) Marquis.

— Who's Who in Religion, 1992-1993. 4th ed. 580p. 1992. 129.00 (0-8379-1604-6) Marquis.

— Who's Who in Science & Engineering. 3rd deluxe ed. 1996. (0-8379-5755-9) Marquis.

— Who's Who in Science & Engineering. 3rd ed. 1300p. 1996. 259.95 (0-8379-5754-0) Marquis.

— Who's Who in the East Classic ed. 26th ed. 1996. write for info. (0-8379-0628-8) Marquis.

— Who's Who in the East Deluxe ed. 26th ed. 1996. write for info. (0-8379-0629-6) Marquis.

— Who's Who in the Midwest Classic ed. 25th ed. 1996. write for info. (0-8379-0726-8) Marquis.

— Who's Who in the Midwest Deluxe ed. 25th ed. 1996. write for info. (0-8379-0727-6) Marquis.

— Who's Who in the West 1996-1997. 25th ed. 975p. 1995. 259.95 (0-8379-0926-0) Marquis.

— Who's Who in the World. 12th ed. 1567p. 1995. 329.95 (0-8379-1113-3) Marquis.

— Who's Who in the World Classic ed. 14th ed. 1996. write for info. (0-8379-1117-6) Marquis.

—Who's Who in the World 1996. 13th ed. 1300p. 1995. 339.95 (0-8379-1115-X) Marquis.
This single volume affords instant access to more than 35,000 individual biographies of the people whose activities are shaping today's world. Among those profiled are prominent government figures, high-ranking military officers, leaders of the largest

M

corporations in each country, heads of religious organizations, pioneers in science, the arts & many more. ***Publisher Provided Annotation.***

— Who's Who of American Women, 1993-1994. 18th rev. ed. 1083p. 1993. 225.00 (*0-8379-0418-8*) Marquis.

— Who's Who of American Women 1995-1996. 19th ed. 1150p. 1995. 239.00 (*0-8379-0420-X*) Marquis. WHO'S WHO OF AMERICAN WOMEN 1995-1996 is the one essential reference to depend on for accurate & detailed facts on American women of achievement. This new edition includes in-depth biographical profiles of more than 29,000 prominent, accomplished women - more than 17,500 new entries are included & an additional 11,500 are updated with the most current information. ***Publisher Provided Annotation.***

M

— Who's Who of Emerging Leaders in America, 1993-1994. 4th ed. 758p. 1992. 229.00 (*0-8379-7203-5*) Marquis.

Marquis Who's Who Staff, jt. ed. see American Board of Medical Specialties.

Marquist, Collen & Frasl, Jack. Crystalline Communion, Vol. II: Mineral Properties for Healing & Integration. (Illus.). 48p. (Orig.). 1991. pap. 7.95 (*0-9620201-1-7*) Earthlight WA.

Marquit, E., tr. see Goldman, I. I. & Krivchenkov, V. D.

Marquit, Erwin. The Socialist Countries: General Features of Political, Economic, & Cultural Life. 2nd ed. LC 83-9329. (Studies in Marxism: Vol. 3). 226p. 1983. 19.95 (*0-930656-31-8*); pap. 9.95 (*0-930656-32-6*) MEP Pubns.

Marquit, Erwin, et al, eds. Dialectical Contradictions: Contemporary Marxist Discussions. LC 81-8462. (Studies in Marxism: Vol. 10). 222p. (C). 1982. 19.95 (*0-930656-19-9*); pap. 9.95 (*0-930656-20-2*) MEP Pubns.

Marqusee, Mike & Heffernan, Richard. One Member, No Vote: Inside Kinnock's Labour Party. 280p. 1992. 59.95 (*0-86091-351-1*, A9739, Pub. by Verso UK); pap. 19.95 (*0-86091-561-1*, A9743, Pub. by Verso UK) Routledge Chapman & Hall.

Marr, C. D. Ramaria of Western Washington. 1973. 30.00 (*3-7682-0902-4*) Lubrecht & Cramer.

Marr, David. American Worlds since Emerson. LC 87-5989. 248p. (C). 1988. lib. bdg. 30.00x (*0-87023-588-5*) U of Mass Pr.

— Vision. 397p. (C). 1995. pap. text ed. 30.95 (*0-7167-1567-8*) W H Freeman.

Marr, David & White, Christine, eds. Postwar Vietnam: Dilemmas in Socialist Development. (Southeast Asia Program Ser.: No. 3). (Illus.). x, 254p. (Orig.). (C). 1988. pap. text ed. 12.00 (*0-87727-120-8*) Cornell SE Asia.

Marr, David G. Vietnam. (World Bibliographical Ser.). 1993. lib. bdg. 110.00 (*1-85109-092-4*) ABC-CLIO.

— Vietnam 1945: The Quest for Power. (Illus.). 587p. 1995. 50.00 (*0-520-07833-0*) U CA Pr.

— Vietnamese Tradition on Trial, 1920-1945. (Illus.). 450p. 1981. pap. 16.00 (*0-520-05081-9*) U CA Pr.

***Marr, Diane D.** Gender Specific Treatment. 1994. pap. 21. 95 (*1-55691-066-5*) Learning Pubns.

Marr, Dick. Bicycle Gearing: A Practical Guide: Everything You Will Ever Need to Know to Use & Choose the Best Gearing Strategies for Pleasure & Performance Cycling. LC 89-2986. (Illus.). 136p. (Orig.). 1989. pap. 8.95 (*0-89886-184-5*) Mountaineers.

Marr, G. V., ed. Handbook on Synchrotron Radiation, Vol. 2. 840p. 1988. 241.00 (*0-444-87046-6*, North Holland) Elsevier.

Marr, George S. Periodical Essayist of the Eighteenth Century. LC 76-93249. 264p. 1970. reprint ed. 75.00 (*0-87753-026-2*) Phaeton.

— Periodical Essayists of the Eighteenth Century: With Illustrative Extracts from the Rare Periodicals. LC 77-99261. (English Book Trade Ser.). 1971. reprint ed. 37. 50 (*0-678-00726-8*) Kelley.

Marr-Hugunin, Lynn. A History of Wrestling at Iowa State University, 1912-1985. (Illus.). 324p. (Orig.). 1987. pap. 24.95 (*0-9617912-0-9*) Nichols Wrestling.

Marr, Jack J., ed. see Wood, Simeon.

Marr, Jerry, jt. auth. see Bergland, Eric O.

Marr, John C. Fishery & Resource Management in Southeast Asia. LC 75-36946. (Resources for the Future Ser.). 76p. 1976. pap. 7.50 (*0-8018-1826-5*) Johns Hopkins.

— Fishery & Resource Management in Southeast Asia. LC 75-36946. (RFF-PISFA Paper Ser.: No. 7). 75p. reprint ed. pap. 25.00 (*0-685-20404-9*, 2030209) Bks Demand.

Marr, John N. & Roessler, Richard T. Supervision & Management: A Guide to Modifying Work Behavior. LC 93-36797. (Illus.). 240p. (C). 1994. pap. 20.00 (*1-55728-306-0*) U of Ark Pr.

Marr, John S. A Breath of Air & a Breath of Smoke. LC 70-161362. (Illus.). 48p. (J). (gr. 3 up). 1970. 4.95 (*0-87131-038-4*) M Evans.

Marr, Joseph J., jt. auth. see Boyd, Robert F.

Marr, Phebe & Lewis, William, eds. Riding the Tiger: The Middle East Challenge after the Cold War. 253p. (C). 1993. text ed. 58.00 (*0-8133-8479-6*); pap. text ed. 19.95 (*0-8133-8663-2*) Westview.

Marr, Rebecca A. The Everytourist Guide to the Springs. (Illus.). 64p. (Orig.). 1992. pap. 4.95 (*0-9631093-0-8*) Marr & Assocs.

***Marr, Richard, et al.** Insurance Data Quality. 158p. 1995. student ed, pap. 25.00 (*1-877796-14-X*); pap. text ed. 75. 00 (*1-877796-13-1*) IDMA.

— Systems Development & Project Management Study Guide. 3rd ed. 179p. 1994. pap. text ed. 25.00 (*1-877796-12-3*) IDMA.

Marr, Ron. Christianity That Really Works. 320p. 1993. pap. 5.99 (*0-88368-271-0*) Whitaker Hse.

Marr, Thomas G., jt. ed. see Bell, George I.

Marr, Warren & Ward, Mayhelle. Minorities & the American Dream: A Bicentennial Perspective. 1976. 19. 95 (*0-405-09117-6*, 19461) Ayer.

Marra, Alan A. Technology of Wood Bonding: Principles in Practice. (Structural Engineering Ser.). (Illus.). 608p. 1992. text ed. 59.95 (*0-442-00797-3*) Chapman & Hall.

Marra, Dorothy B., jt. auth. see Medina, Francis X.

Marra, James L. Advertising Copywriting: Techniques for Improving Your Writing Skills. 240p. 1993. pap. text ed. write for info. (*0-13-007774-7*) P-H.

— Advertising Creativity. 208p. (C). 1989. pap. text ed. write for info. (*0-13-015009-6*) P-H.

Marra, Michele. The Aesthetics of Discontent: Politics & Reclusion in Medieval Japanese Literature. LC 90-25540. (Illus.). 248p. 1991. text ed. 35.00 (*0-8248-1336-7*); pap. text ed. 14.95 (*0-8248-1364-2*) UH Pr.

— Representations of Power: The Literary Politics of Medieval Japan. LC 93-10236. (Illus.). 256p. (C). 1993. lib. bdg. 36.00 (*0-8248-1535-1*); pap. text ed. 15.95 (*0-8248-1556-4*) UH Pr.

Marra, Reggie. The Quality of Effort: Integrity in Sport & Life for Student-Athletes, Parents, & Coaches. LC 90-84335. 113p. (Orig.). 1991. pap. 11.50 (*0-9627828-0-7*) From Heart Pr.

Marra, William A. Happiness & Christian Hope: Being Joyful in a Fallen World. rev. ed. 202p. 1994. text ed. 13.95 (*0-912141-09-3*) Roman Cath Bks.

Marrable, A. W. The Foal in the Womb. (Illus.). 142p. 1990. pap. 21.00 (*0-85131-345-0*, Pub. by J A Allen & Co UK) St Mut.

Marrack, Eleanor. Cezanne. 1993. 5.98 (*1-55521-823-7*) Bk Sales Inc.

— Van Gogh. 1992. 5.98 (*1-55521-763-X*) Bk Sales Inc.

Marraffino, Elizabeth. Blue Moon Ruby Tuesday. (Illus.). 60p. (Orig.). 1981. pap. 3.00 (*0-936556-02-1*) Contact Two.

Marrakchi. Phototonic Switching & Interconnects. (Optical Engineering Ser.: Vol. 40). 464p. 1994. 165.00 (*0-8247-8931-8*) Dekker.

Marran, David. The Cub Fan's Quiz Book. LC 85-12859. 182p. 1985. pap. 7.95 (*0-912083-12-3*) Diamond Communications.

Marran, Vincent P. The Major Looks over His Shoulder: A Medical Memoir of World War II. 180p. 1989. pap. 11. 95 (*0-942383-08-7*) Manor Hse Pub.

***Marranca, Bonnie.** The Hudson Valley Reader: Writings from the 17th Century to the Present. (Illus.). 404p. 1995. pap. 15.95 (*0-87951-598-8*) Overlook Pr.

— Theatrewritings. 1984. 28.50 (*0-933826-67-2*); pap. 12. 95x (*0-933826-68-0*) PAJ Pubns.

Marranca, Bonnie, ed. American Dreams: The Imagination of Sam Shepard. LC 80-85438. 223p. 1981. pap. 14.95 (*0-933826-13-3*) PAJ Pubns.

— American Garden Writing: Gleanings from Garden Lives Then & Now. LC 87-73280. 325p. 23.95 (*1-55554-029-5*) PAJ Pubns.

— The Theatre of Images. (PAJ Publications). (Illus.). 176p. 1995. reprint ed. pap. text ed. 14.95x (*0-8018-5243-9*) Johns Hopkins.

Marranca, Bonnie, intro. Hudson Valley Lives. (Illus.). 432p. 1991. 23.95 (*0-87951-411-6*) Overlook Pr.

Marranca, Bonnie, ed. see Stein, Gertrude.

Marranda, Bonnie & Dasupta, Gautam, eds. Interculturalism & Performance: Writings from PAJ. 1991. 35.00 (*1-55554-057-0*); pap. 14.95 (*1-55554-058-9*) PAJ Pubns.

Marrandette, David G. Golf Playoffs: Sourcebook of Major Championship Men's & Women's Amateur & Professional Playoffs, 1876-1990. LC 90-53506. 165p. 1991. lib. bdg. 38.50x (*0-89950-552-X*) McFarland & Co.

Marrapodi, Betty. Clock That Went Meow. (Illus.). 31p. (J). (gr. k up). 1970. pap. 7.50 (*0-88680-030-7*); pap. 2.50 (*0-88680-029-3*) I E Clark.

— Doctor Hoo. (Illus.). 22p. (J). (gr. 1-6). 1973. pap. 7.50 (*0-88680-039-0*); pap. 2.00 (*0-88680-038-2*) I E Clark.

Marrapodi, Michele, et al, eds. Shakespeare's Italy: Dramatic Function of Italian Location in Renaissance Drama. LC 93-13596. 1994. text ed. 69.95 (*0-7190-4089-2*, Pub. by Manchester Univ Pr UK) St Martin.

Marraro, Howard R. The New Education in Italy. LC 78-63692. (Studies in Fascism: Ideology & Practice). reprint ed. 47.00 (*0-404-16954-6*) AMS Pr.

Marraro, Howard R., ed. Diplomatic Relations Between the United States & the Kingdom of the Two Sicilies, 2 vols., Set. 1951. 45.00 (*0-913298-56-5*) S F Vanni.

Marras, William S., et al. Dynamic Measures of Low Back Performance. 20p. (C). 1993. pap. 8.00 (*0-932627-52-8*, 174-ER-93) Am Indus Hygiene.

Marras, William S., et al, eds. Ergonomics of Manual Work. 774p. 1993. 175.00 (*0-7484-0060-5*) Taylor & Francis.

Marrase, Yara. Ingles Facil Para Todos. 153p. 1985. pap. 2.95 (*1-884249-03-5*) Pub Especiales.

— Ingles Facil Para Todos en Video Cassette. 153p. 1992. pap. 29.50 (*1-884249-05-1*) Pub Especiales.

— Ingles Para Ciudadania Americana. 48p. 1989. pap. 2.75 (*1-884249-08-6*, TX 2-507-729) Pub Especiales.

— Ingles Para Ciudadania Americana. 48p. 1989. pap. 12.00 (*1-884249-09-4*, TX 2-507-729) Pub Especiales.

— Ingles Para la Mujer. 125p. 1988. pap. 2.95 (*1-884249-06-X*, TX 2-278-579) Pub Especiales.

— Ingles Para los Trabajadores. Date not set. pap. 2.95 (*1-884249-10-8*, TXU 572-393); pap. 12.00 (*1-884249-11-6*, TXU 572-393) Pub Especiales.

— Ingles Primario. 121p. 1981. pap. 2.95 (*1-884249-00-0*, TX 742-377) Pub Especiales.

— Ingles Primario en Ninety Minutos. 121p. 1989. pap. 2.95 (*1-884249-01-9*, TX 2-705-779) Pub Especiales.

— Spanish for Americans. 88p. 1983. pap. 2.95 (*1-884249-02-7*, TX 139-381) Pub Especiales.

Marrast, Robert & Marrast, Sylvie. Theatre Espagnol du XVI Siecle. (FRE.). 1983. lib. bdg. 100.00 (*0-7859-3862-1*) Fr & Eur.

Marrast, Sylvie, jt. auth. see Marrast, Robert.

Marrat, Florence. The Dead Man's Message: An Occult Romance. Reginald, R. & Menville, Douglas, eds. LC 75-46290. (Supernatural & Occult Fiction Ser.). 1976. reprint ed. lib. bdg. 17.95 (*0-405-08150-2*) Ayer.

***Marre.** Contemporary Diesel Spotter's Guide. 2nd ed. 352p. 1995. pap. text ed. 19.95 (*0-89024-257-7*, 01068) Kalmbach.

Marre, J. The Structural Analysis of Granitic Rocks. 128p. 1986. 43.75 (*0-444-01078-5*) Elsevier.

***Marre, Louis A. & Sommers, Gregory J.** Frisco in Color. (Illus.). 1995. 49.95 (*1-878887-50-5*) Morning NJ.

Marrelli. Handbook of Home Health Standards & Documentation. 312p. 1993. spiral bd. 24.95 (*0-8016-7661-4*) Mosby Yr Bk.

— Handbook of Home Health Standards & Documentation Guidelines for Reimbursement. 256p. 1988. spiral bd. 25. 95 (*0-8016-2934-9*) Mosby Yr Bk.

— The Nurse Manager's Survival Guide: Practical Answers. 352p. 1993. pap. 25.95 (*0-8016-6449-7*) Mosby Yr Bk.

Marrelli, Tina M. Nursing Documentation Handbook. 300p. 1991. spiral bd. 19.95 (*0-8016-3120-3*) Mosby Yr Bk.

Marren, Joseph H. Mergers & Acquisitions: A Valuation Handbook. 450p. 1992. 90.00 (*1-55623-676-X*) Irwin Prof Pubng.

— Mergers & Acquisitions: Will You Overpay? LC 84-72811. 1985. 57.00 (*0-87094-581-5*) Irwin Prof Pubng.

Marrero, Domingo. El Centauro: Persona y Pensamiento De Ortega y Gasset. (UPREX, Ensayo Ser.: No. 30). 319p. (C). 1974. pap. 1.50 (*0-8477-0030-5*) U of PR Pr.

Marrero, J. Espada. Madre y Hogar. 50p. (SPA.). 1990. reprint ed. pap. 1.95 (*0-311-07302-6*) Casa Bautista.

Marrero, Levi. Cuba Economia y Sociedad, 15 vols., Vol. I. (Illus.). 1979. Vol. 1. 30.00 (*84-359-0128-5*) Ediciones.

— Cuba Economia y Sociedad, 15 vols., Vol. I. 2nd ed. (Illus.). 1992. 30.00 (*84-399-8831-1*) Ediciones.

— Cuba Economia y Sociedad, Vols. II-VII. (Illus.). 1979. 20.00 (*0-685-73234-7*) Ediciones.

— Cuba Economia y Sociedad, Vols. VIII-XIII. (Illus.). 1979. 30.00 (*0-685-73235-5*) Ediciones.

— Cuba Economia y Sociedad, Vols. XIV-XV. (Illus.). 1979. 35.00 (*0-685-73236-3*) Ediciones.

— Los Esclavos y la Virgen del Cobre: Dos Siglos de Lucha Por la Libertad en Cuba. LC 79-56290. (Coleccion Cuba y Sus Jueces Ser.). (Illus.). 32p. (Orig.). (SPA.). 1982. pap. 3.00 (*0-89729-243-X*) Ediciones.

Marrero, Rafael A., ed. see Ayala, Julio R.

Marrero, Robert. Dracula: The Vampire Legend on Film. (Illus.). 128p. 1992. pap. 12.95 (*0-9634982-0-7*) Fantasma Bks.

— Giant Monster Movies: An Illustrated Survey. (Illus.). 256p. (Orig.). 1994. pap. 17.95 (*0-9634982-2-3*) Fantasma Bks.

— Vampire Movies: An Illustrated Guide to Seventy-Two Years of Vampire Movies. (Illus.). 176p. 1994. pap. 19. 95 (*0-9634982-3-1*) Fantasma Bks.

— Vintage Monster Movies. (Illus.). 160p. 1993. pap. 12.95 (*0-9634982-1-5*) Fantasma Bks.

Marrese, Michael & Richter, Sandor, eds. The Challenge of Simultaneous Economic Relations with East & West. 220p. 1990. 70.00 (*0-8147-5453-8*) NYU Pr.

Marrese, Michael & Vanous, Jan. Soviet Subsidization of Trade with Eastern Europe: A Soviet Perspective. LC 83-192. (Research Ser.: No. 52). (Illus.). xxvi, 250p. 1983. pap. 14.50 (*0-87725-152-5*) U of Cal IAS.

Marrese, Michael A., ed. Advances in Electronic Circuit Packaging: Proceedings of the 4th International Electronic Circuit Packaging Symposium, Vol. 4. LC 72-187719. 502p. reprint ed. pap. 143.10 (*0-8357-5159-7*, 2020718) Bks Demand.

Marrett, Barbara & Neal, John. Mahina Tiare, Pacific Passages. LC 92-91094. (Illus.). 306p. 1993. 27.95 (*0-918074-05-3*); pap. 19.95 (*0-918074-04-5*) Pacific Intl.

Marrett, Cora B. & Leggon, Cheryl B. Research in Race & Ethnic Relations, Vol. 4. 1986. 73.25 (*0-89232-361-2*) Jai Pr.

Marrett, Cora B. & Leggon, Cheryl B., eds. Research in Race & Ethnic Relations, Vol. 2. 250p. 1980. lib. bdg. 73.25 (*0-89232-141-5*) Jai Pr.

— Research in Race & Ethnic Relations, Vol. 5. 1987. 73.25 (*0-89232-614-X*) Jai Pr.

Marrett, Cora B., jt. auth. see Wilkinson, Louise C.

Marrevee, William. The Popular Guide to the Mass. 174p. (Orig.). 1992. pap. 9.95 (*0-912405-93-7*) Pastoral Pr.

Marriage, Margaret S., jt. auth. see Mincoff, Elizabeth.

***Marrian, C. R., et al, eds.** Materials - Fabrication & Patterning at the Nanoscale. (Symposium Proceedings Ser.: Vol. 380). 1995. text ed. 83.00 (*1-55899-283-9*) Materials Res.

Marrian, Christie, ed. Technology of Proximal Probe Lithography. LC 93-8684. (Institutes for Advanced Optical Technologies Ser.: Vol. IS 10). 1993. write for info. (*0-8194-1232-5*); pap. write for info. (*0-8194-1233-3*) SPIE.

Marric, J. J. Gideon's Art. 1990. pap. 3.50 (*0-8217-3149-1*) Zebra.

— Gideon's Day. 1989. pap. 3.95 (*0-8217-2721-4*) Zebra.

— Gideon's Day. large type ed. 1972. 21.95 (*0-85456-138-2*) Ulverscroft.

— Gideon's Drive. 224p. 1991. pap. 3.50 (*0-8217-3322-2*) Zebra.

— Gideon's Drive. large type ed. 1978. 21.95 (*0-7089-0164-6*) Ulverscroft.

— Gideon's Fire. 1989. pap. 3.50 (*0-8217-2845-8*) Zebra.

— Gideon's Fire. large type ed. 1974. 21.95 (*0-85456-264-8*) Ulverscroft.

— Gideon's Fog. 224p. 1991. pap. 3.50 (*0-8217-3276-5*) Zebra.

— Gideon's Force. large type ed. 1980. 12.00 (*0-7089-0422-X*) Ulverscroft.

— Gideon's Lot. 1990. pap. 3.50 (*0-8217-2927-6*) Zebra.

— Gideon's March. 192p. 1994. 16.95 (*0-7451-8640-8*, Black Dagger) Chivers N Amer.

— Gideon's March. 1990. pap. 3.50 (*0-8217-2876-8*) Zebra.

— Gideon's Men. 1990. pap. 3.50 (*0-8217-3219-6*) Zebra.

— Gideon's Men. large type ed. 1975. 21.95 (*0-85456-325-3*) Ulverscroft.

— Gideon's Month. 1989. pap. 3.95 (*0-8217-2766-4*) Zebra.

— Gideon's Month. large type ed. 1975. 21.95 (*0-85456-313-X*) Ulverscroft.

— Gideon's Night. 1989. pap. 3.50 (*0-8217-2734-6*) Zebra.

— Gideon's Power. 1990. pap. 3.50 (*0-8217-3105-X*) Zebra.

— Gideon's Press. 1990. pap. 3.50 (*0-8217-3243-9*) Zebra.

— Gideon's Press. large type ed. 1977. 12.00 (*0-7089-0031-3*) Ulverscroft.

— Gideon's Ride. 1990. pap. 3.50 (*0-8217-2900-4*) Zebra.

— Gideon's Ride. large type ed. 1974. 12.00 (*0-85456-234-6*) Ulverscroft.

— Gideon's Risk. 1989. pap. 3.50 (*0-8217-2823-7*) Zebra.

— Gideon's River. 1990. pap. 3.50 (*0-8217-3079-7*) Zebra.

***Marric, J. J., pseud.** Gideon's River. 224p. 1995. 16.95 (*0-7451-8654-8*, Black Dagger) Chivers N Amer.

Marric, J. J. Gideon's Sport. 1990. pap. 3.50 (*0-8217-3128-9*) Zebra.

— Gideon's Sport. large type ed. 334p. 1980. 12.00 (*0-7089-0462-9*) Ulverscroft.

— Gideon's Staff. 1989. pap. 3.50 (*0-8217-2797-4*) Zebra.

— Gideon's Vote. 1990. pap. 3.50 (*0-8217-2971-3*) Zebra.

— Gideon's Week. 1989. pap. 3.95 (*0-8217-2722-2*) Zebra.

— Gideon's Week. large type ed. 1969. 12.00 (*0-85456-659-7*) Ulverscroft.

— Gideon's Wrath. 1990. pap. 3.50 (*0-8217-3050-9*) Zebra.

— Gideon's Wrath. large type ed. 1975. 21.95 (*0-85456-342-3*) Ulverscroft.

Marrie, Thomas J., ed. Q Fever, Vol. I: The Disease. 545p. 1990. 167.00 (*0-8493-5984-8*, RC182) CRC Pr.

Marriet, Jane & Topaz, Muriel, revs. Study Guide for Intermediate Labanotation. rev. ed. 110p. (C). 1995. pap. 22.95 (*0-932582-58-3*) Dance Notation.

Marriett, Jane, jt. auth. see Miller, Buzz.

Marrin, Albert. America in Vietnam: The Elephant & the Tiger. (Illus.). 256p. (YA). (gr. 7 up). 1992. 16.00 (*0-670-84063-7*) Viking Child Bks.

— Aztecs & Spaniards: Cortes & the Conquest of Mexico. LC 85-28782. (Illus.). 224p. (YA). (gr. 5 up). 1986. text ed. 15.95 (*0-689-31176-1*, Atheneum Bks Young) S&S Childrens.

— Cowboys, Indians, & Gunfighters: The Story of the Cattle Kingdom. LC 92-5727. (Illus.). 196p. (J). (gr. 5 up). 1993. text ed. 22.95 (*0-689-31774-3*, Atheneum Bks Young) S&S Childrens.

— Eighteen Twelve: The War Nobody Won. LC 84-21623. (Illus.). 192p. (YA). (gr. 5 up). 1985. text ed. 15.95 (*0-689-31075-7*, Atheneum Bks Young) S&S Childrens.

— Hitler. LC 93-13057. 256p. (J). (gr. 7 up). 1993. reprint ed. pap. 5.99 (*0-14-036526-5*, Puffin) Puffin Bks.

— Inca & Spaniard: Pizarro & the Conquest of Peru. LC 88-29372. (Illus.). 224p. (YA). (gr. 5 up). 1989. text ed. 15. 95 (*0-689-31481-7*, Atheneum Bks Young) S&S Childrens.

— Mao Tse-Tung & His China. LC 93-3799. 288p. (J). (gr. 7 up). 1993. reprint ed. pap. 5.99 (*0-14-036478-1*, Puffin) Puffin Bks.

— Napoleon & the Napoleonic Wars. LC 93-13067. 288p. (J). (gr. 7 up). 1993. pap. 5.99 (*0-14-036479-X*, Puffin) Puffin Bks.

— Napoleon & the Napoleonic Wars. (YA). 1991. 14.99 (*0-670-83480-7*) Viking Child Bks.

— The Sea King: Sir Francis Drake & His Times. (J). (gr. 5-9). 1995. 18.00 (*0-689-31887-1*, Atheneum Bks Young) S&S Childrens.

— The Sea Rovers: Pirates, Privateers & Buccaneers. LC 83-15886. (Illus.). 224p. (YA). (gr. 6 up). 1984. text ed. 15. 95 (*0-689-31029-3*, Atheneum Bks Young) S&S Childrens.

— The Secret Armies: Spies, Counterspies, & Saboteurs in World War II. LC 85-7944. (Illus.). 192p. (YA). (gr. 5 up). 1985. lib. bdg. 14.95 (*0-689-31165-6*, Atheneum Bks Young) S&S Childrens.

— The Spanish-American War. LC 90-935. (Illus.). 192p. (YA). (gr. 5 up). 1991. text ed. 15.95 (*0-689-31663-1*, Atheneum Bks Young) S&S Childrens.

— Stalin: Russia's Man of Steel. LC 93-3798. 256p. (J). (gr. 7 up). 1993. pap. 5.99 (*0-14-032605-7*, Puffin) Puffin Bks.

— Struggle for a Continent: The French & Indian Wars: 1690-1760. LC 86-26508. (Illus.). 232p. (YA). (gr. 5 up). 1987. lib. bdg. 15.95 (*0-689-31313-6*, Atheneum Bks Young) S&S Childrens.

— Victory in the Pacific. LC 82-6707. (Illus.). 224p. (YA). (gr. 6 up). 1983. text ed. 15.95 (*0-689-30948-1*, Atheneum Bks Young) S&S Childrens.

— Virginia's General: Robert E. Lee & the Civil War. LC 94-13353. (J). 1994. text ed. 19.95 (*0-689-31838-3*, Atheneum S&S) S&S Trade.

— The War for Independence: The Story of the American Revolution. LC 87-13711. (Illus.). 288p. (YA). (gr. 5 up). 1988. text ed. 15.95 (*0-689-31390-X*, Atheneum Bks Young) S&S Childrens.

An Asterisk (*) at the beginning of an entry indicates that the title is appearing in BIP for the first time.

— The Yanks Are Coming: The United States in the First World War. LC 86-3585. (Illus.). 256p. (YA). (gr. 5 up). 1986. text ed. 15.95 (*0-689-31209-1*, Atheneum Bks Young) S&S Childrens.

*__Marin, Richard B.__ A Glance Back in Time: Life in Colonial New Jersey (1704-1770) As Depicted in News Accounts of the Day. 359p. (Orig.). 1994. pap. 25.00 (*0-7884-0089-4*) Heritage Bk.

Marrinan, Michael. Painting Politics for Louis-Philippe: Art & Ideology in Orleanist France. LC 87-24636. 239p. (C). 1988. text ed. 50.00 (*0-300-03853-4*) Yale U Pr.

Marriner & Tomey. Case Studies in Nursing Management. (Illus.). 364p. 1990. pap. 26.95 (*0-8016-5848-9*) Mosby Yr Bk.

— Nursing Theorists & Their Work. 2nd ed. (Illus.). 480p. 1989. pap. text ed. 29.95 (*0-8016-3249-8*) Mosby Yr Bk.

Marriner, Brian. On Death's Bloody Trail. 1994. mass mkt. 4.99 (*0-312-95170-1*) St Martin.

Marriner, Paul. Ausable River, NY. (River Journal Ser.: Vol. 1, No. 4). (Illus.). 48p. 1994. pap. 14.95 (*1-878175-43-2*) F Amato Pubns.

Marriner, Paul C. Atlantic Salmon: A Fly Fishing Primer. LC 92-31271. 192p. 1992. 24.95 (*0-8329-0473-2*) New Win Pub.

Marriner-Tomey, Ann. Guide to Nurse Management. 4th ed. 528p. 1991. pap. 27.95 (*0-8016-6326-1*) Mosby Yr Bk.

Marriner-Tomey, Ann, ed. Nursing Theorists & Their Work. 3rd ed. LC 93-996. 496p. 1993. pap. 29.95 (*0-8016-6764-X*) Mosby Yr Bk.

— Transformational Leadership in Nursing. LC 92-15283. 197p. 1992. pap. 26.95 (*0-8016-6875-1*) Mosby Yr Bk.

Marrion, Alastair R., ed. The Chemistry & Physics of Coatings. 186p. 1994. 39.95 (*0-85186-994-7*, R6994) CRC Pr.

Marrion, Robert & Fosten, Don. The British Army 1914-18. (Men-at-Arms Ser.: No. 81). (Illus.). 48p. pap. 11.95 (*0-85045-287-2*, 9021, Pub. by Osprey UK) Stackpole.

— The German Army 1914-18. (Men-at-Arms Ser.: No. 80). (Illus.). 48p. pap. 11.95 (*0-85045-283-X*, 9020, Pub. by Osprey UK) Stackpole.

Marriot, Alice & Ramlin, Carol. Plains Indian Mythology. 224p. 1977. pap. 10.95 (*0-452-00766-6*, Mer) NAL-Dutton.

Marriott. Bedside Cardiac Diagnosis. (Illus.). 315p. 1992. text ed. 49.95 (*0-397-51085-3*) Lippincott.

Marriott & Conover. Advanced Concepts in Arrhythmias. 2nd ed. (Illus.). 432p. 1989. text ed. 39.95 (*0-8016-3239-0*) Mosby Yr Bk.

Marriott, Alice. Hell on Horses & Women. LC 53-5479. (C). 1993. pap. 14.95 (*0-8061-2482-2*) U of Okla Pr.

— Maria: The Potter of San Ildefonso. LC 48-2101. (Civilization of the American Indian Ser.: Vol. 27). (Illus.). 320p. 1987. pap. 15.95 (*0-8061-2048-7*) U of Okla Pr.

— Maria: The Potter of San Ildefonso. rev. ed. LC 48-2101. (Civilization of the American Indian Ser.: Vol. 27). (Illus.). 1976. reprint ed. 24.95 (*0-8061-0176-8*) U of Okla Pr.

— The Ten Grandmothers. LC 45-1584. (Civilization of the American Indian Ser.: Vol. 26). 306p. 1983. pap. 13.95 (*0-8061-1825-3*) U of Okla Pr.

*__Marriott, Anne.__ The Circular Coast: Poems New & Selected. 80p. 1995. lib. bdg. 27.00 (*0-8095-4532-2*) Borgo Pr.

— Letters from Some Islands: New Poems. 96p. 1995. lib. bdg. 25.00 (*0-8095-4561-6*) Borgo Pr.

— A Long Way to Oregon: Selected Short Stories. 107p. 1995. lib. bdg. 27.00 (*0-8095-4563-2*) Borgo Pr.

Marriott, Bernadette M., ed. see Institute of Medicine, Committee on Military Nutrition Research Staff.

Marriott, Catherina. Impressions. 96p. (C). 1989. 65.00 (*1-85183-032-4*, Silent Bks) St Mut.

Marriott, Charles. Modern Movement in Painting. 1977. lib. bdg. 80.00 (*0-8490-2269-X*) Gordon Pr.

Marriott, D. L., jt. ed. see Garrett, G. G.

Marriott, F. H. Basic Mathematics for the Biological & Social Sciences. LC 73-99863. (C). 1970. 104.00 (*0-08-006663-1*, Pub. by Pergamon Repr UK) Franklin.

Marriott, F. H., ed. Dictionary of Statistical Terms. 5th ed. 1990. pap. text ed. 76.95 (*0-470-21349-3*) Halsted Pr.

Marriott, F. H., jt. auth. see Krzanowski, W J.

Marriott, F. H., jt. auth. see Krzanowski, W. J.

Marriott, G. L., ed. see Macarius The Elder Of Egypt.

Marriott, G. R., tr. see De Laveleye, Emile.

Marriott, Henry. ECG-PDQ. (Illus.). 258p. (Orig.). 1987. pap. 19.00 (*0-683-05572-0*) Williams & Wilkins.

Marriott, Henry J. Pearls & Pitfalls in Electrocardiography: Pithy Practical Points. LC 90-5594. (Illus.). 157p. 1990. pap. text ed. 29.00 (*0-8121-1334-9*) Williams & Wilkins.

— Rhythm Quizlets: Self Assessment. LC 87-2802. (Illus.). 189p. 1987. pap. text ed. 29.00 (*0-8121-1110-9*) Williams & Wilkins.

— Rhythm Quizlets II. (Illus.). 113p. 1992. student ed 16.95 (*0-944132-73-1*) Skidmore Roth Pub.

Marriott, Henry L. ECG Ready Reference. 1991. pap. 14.95 (*0-944132-22-7*) Skidmore Roth Pub.

Marriott, J. A. English History in Shakespeare. LC 75-174685. (Studies in Shakespeare: No. 24). 1971. reprint ed. lib. bdg. 59.95 (*0-8383-1337-X*) M S G Haskell Hse.

Marriott, J. B. & Merz, M., eds. High Temperature Alloys: Their Exploitable Potential. 538p. 1988. 119.00 (*1-85166-174-3*) Elsevier.

Marriott, James W., ed. Modern Essays & Sketches. LC 68-22928. (Essay Index Reprint Ser.). 1977. 18.95 (*0-8369-0679-9*) Ayer.

Marriott, John. The Culture of Labourism. 1991. text ed. 50.00 (*0-7486-0248-8*, Pub. by Edinburgh U Pr UK) Col U Pr.

— The Culture of Labourism: The East End Between the Wars. 244p. 1993. pap. 25.00 (*0-7486-0285-2*, Pub. by Edinburgh U Pr UK) Col U Pr.

— Disaster at Sea. (Illus.). 200p. 1989. pap. 9.95 (*0-87052-764-9*) Hippocrene Bks.

Marriott, John A. English Political Institutions: An Introductory Study. 4th ed. LC 74-9169. 348p. 1975. reprint ed. text ed. 69.50 (*0-8371-7621-2*, MAEP, Greenwood Pr) Greenwood.

— The Makers of Modern Italy: Napoleon to Mussolini. LC 74-30842. (Illus.). 228p. 1975. reprint ed. text ed. 59.75 (*0-8371-7936-X*, MAMA, Greenwood Pr) Greenwood.

— Second Chambers. LC 78-102250. (Select Bibliographies Reprint Ser.). 1977. 29.95 (*0-8369-5135-2*) Ayer.

— This Realm of England. LC 78-140368. (Select Bibliographies Reprint Ser.). 1977. reprint ed. 23.95 (*0-8369-5611-7*) Ayer.

*__Marriott, Leo.__ British Airways. (ABC Ser.). (Illus.). 96p. 1994. pap. 9.95 (*0-7110-1972-X*, Pub. by Ian Allan Pub UK) Howell Pr VA.

Marriott, McKim, ed. India Through Hindu Categories. (Illus.). 228p. (C). 1990. 32.00 (*0-8039-9636-5*) Sage.

Marriott, Michael. The Dordogne. (Crowood Travel Guides Ser.). (Illus.). 320p. 1992. pap. 24.95 (*1-85223-461-X*, Pub. by Crowood Pr UK) Trafalgar.

Marriott, Michelle. Old King Cole & Friends. (Soap Opera Ser.). (J). (gr. 4 up). 1990. 9.95 (*0-85953-446-4*) Childs Play.

Marriott, Neil & Chandler, Roy. Management Accounting: A Spreadsheet Approach. LC 92-40486. 1993. 35.90 (*0-13-555152-8*) P-H.

Marriott, Neil, jt. auth. see Olde, Peter.

Marriott, Norman G. Principles of Food Sanitation. 1989. text ed. 59.95 (*0-442-31807-3*) Chapman & Hall.

— Principles of Food Sanitation. 3rd ed. 1993. text ed. 59.95 (*0-442-01201-2*) Chapman & Hall.

— Principles of Food Sanitation. 3rd ed. LC 93-48000. (Food Science & Technology Ser.). 1994. text ed. 59.95 (*0-412-05501-5*) Chapman & Hall.

Marriott, S. Extramural Empires: Service & Self-Interest in English University Adult Education 1873-1983. (C). 1984. 60.00 (*0-902031-94-5*, Pub. by Univ Nottingham UK) St Mut.

Marriott, Salima S., jt. auth. see Kamara, Michael A.

Marriott, Stuart. Picture Books in the Primary School Classroom. 160p. 1991. pap. 27.00 (*1-85396-144-2*, Pub. by P Chapman Pub UK) Taylor & Francis.

Marriott, Stuart, ed. Extra-Mural Empires: Service & Self-Interest in English University Adult Education 1873-1983. 137p. (C). 1984. 60.00 (*0-317-94042-2*, Pub. by Univ Nottingham UK) St Mut.

Marriott, T. Pagan Land. 1982. pap. 2.95 (*0-449-14446-1*) Fawcett.

Marriott, Thomas. The Pagan Land. large type ed. 688p. 1983. 23.95 (*0-7089-8124-0*, Charnwood) Ulverscroft.

Marriott, Val & Timblick, Terry, eds. Loneliness: How to Overcome It. (C). 1989. 30.00 (*0-86242-077-6*, Pub. by Age Concern Eng UK) St Mut.

Marris, Andrew W. & Stoneking, Charles E. Advanced Dynamics. LC 76-8007. 318p. 1976. reprint ed. 25.50 (*0-88275-403-3*) Krieger.

Marris, Copeland. Varied Kitchens of India. LC 86-2028. 1991. pap. 12.95 (*0-87131-672-2*) M Evans.

Marris, Peter & Rein, Martin. Dilemmas of Social Reform: Poverty & Community Action in the U. S. 2nd ed. LC 81-16361. (C). 1982. pap. text ed. 7.95 (*0-226-50657-6*) U Ch Pr.

Marris, Robin. Reconstructing Keynesian Economics with Imperfect Competition: A Desk-Top Simulation. 300p. 1991. text ed. 69.95 (*1-85278-541-1*, Pub. by E Elgar Pub UK) Ashgate Pub Co.

Marris, Robin & Wood, Adrian, eds. Corporate Economy: Growth, Competition, & Innovative Potential. (Studies in Technology & Society). 479p. 1971. 46.50 (*0-674-17252-3*) HUP.

Marris, Robin, jt. auth. see Edigi, Massimo.

Marris, Robin, jt. ed. see Rosenbloom, Richard S.

*__Marris, Stephan.__ Deficits & the Dollar: The World Economy at Risk. fac. ed. LC 85-17303. (Policy Analyses in International Economics Ser.: Vol. 14). 384p. 1985. reprint ed. pap. write for info. (*0-7837-7774-4*, 2047530) Bks Demand.

— Deficits & the Dollar: The World Economy at Risk. fac. ed. LC 85-17303. (Policy Analyses in International Economics Ser.: Vol. 14). 40p. 1985. reprint ed. pap. 25.00 (*0-7837-7775-2*) Bks Demand.

*__Marris, Stephen.__ Deficits & the Dollar: The World Economy at Risk. LC 87-29887. (Policy Analyses in International Economics Ser.: 14). (Illus.). 416p. 1987. reprint ed. pap. 118.60 (*0-7837-7776-0*, 2047531) Bks Demand.

— Managing the World Economy: Will We Ever Learn? LC 84-19344. (Essays in International Finance Ser.: No. 155). 1984. pap. text ed. 8.00 (*0-88165-062-5*) Princeton U Int Finan Econ.

Marris, T. Information Processing with COBOL. (Illus.). 160p. (Orig.). 1989. pap. text ed. 16.95 (*0-7131-3636-7*, Pub. by E Arnold UK) Routledge Chapman & Hall.

Marritt Company Staff. Strategies for Insurance Coverages. 1995. ring bd. 397.00 (*0-930868-57-9*) Merritt Co.

Marro, Barbara. 8 Ways to a Happy Life. LC 94-985. 128p. (Orig.). 1994. pap. 9.95 (*1-56825-018-5*) Rainbow Books.

Marro, Giovanni, jt. auth. see Basile, Giuseppe.

Marro, J., jt. auth. see Garrido, P. L.

Marro, Joaquin, ed. see Granada Seminar on Computational Physics Staff.

*__Marrocco, Nancy.__ Homemade Christians. Koch, Carl, ed. (Illus.). 64p. (Orig.). (J). 1995. pap. 7.95 (*0-88489-381-2*) St Marys.

Marrocco, W. Thomas. Fourteenth Century Italian Cacce. 2nd rev. ed. LC 60-13484. (Medieval Academy Bks.: No. 39). 1961. 20.00 (*0-910956-16-2*) Medieval Acad.

Marrocha, Jean, jt. auth. see Haasl, Beth.

Marron, Carol. Yellowstone. LC 88-18643. (National Parks Ser.). (Illus.). 48p. (J). (gr. 4-5). 1988. text ed. 13.95 (*0-89686-405-7*, Crstwood Hse) Silver Burdett Pr.

Marron, Carol A. Just One of the Family. (Use Your Imagination Ser.). (J). (ps-3). 1993. pap. 4.95 (*0-8114-8404-1*) Raintree Steck-V.

— Someone Just Like Me. (Use Your Imagination Ser.). (J). (ps-3). 1993. pap. 4.95 (*0-8114-8407-6*) Raintree Steck-V.

Marron, Henri, jt. auth. see Leclercq, Dom H.

Marron, J. Function Estimates. LC 86-14203. (CONM Ser.: Vol. 59). 178p. 1986. pap. text ed. 30.00 (*0-8218-5062-8*, CONM-59) Am Math.

Marron, Jamie. Smart Eyes. write for info. (*0-318-59574-5*) Addison-Wesley.

Marron, Margaret, ed. see Weakland, Steve.

Marrone, Nila G. Situaciones. 314p. (C). 1987. pap. text ed. write for info. (*0-07-553735-4*) McGraw.

Marrone, Robert. Body of Knowledge: An Introduction to Body - Mind Psychology. LC 89-28863. (Transpersonal & Humanistic Psychology Ser.). 160p. 1990. 49.50 (*0-7914-0387-4*); pap. 16.95 (*0-7914-0388-2*) State U NY Pr.

Marrone, Russell. The Wizard's Quest. LC 87-50268. (Illus.). 102p. (J). (gr. 3-5). 1987. 7.95 (*1-55523-078-4*) Winston-Derek.

Marrone, Sandy. St. Louis Blues & Other Song Hits of 1914. 1990. pap. 7.95 (*0-486-26383-5*) Dover.

Marrone, Steven P. Truth & Scientific Knowledge in the Thought of Henry of Ghent. LC 84-62885. (Speculum Anniversary Monographs: No. 11). 164p. 1985. 20.00 (*0-910956-91-X*); pap. 12.00 (*0-910956-92-8*) Medieval Acad.

— William Auvergne & Robert Grosseteste: New Ideas of Truth in the Early Thirteenth Century. LC 82-61375. 328p. 1983. 49.50x (*0-691-05383-9*) Princeton U Pr.

— William of Auvergne & Robert Grosseteste: New Ideas of Truth in the Early Thirteenth Century. LC 82-61375. Date not set. reprint ed. pap. 94.40 (*0-7837-9381-2*, 2060125) Bks Demand.

Marrone, Teresa, et al. Dressing & Cooking Wild Game. LC 87-15445. (Hunting & Fishing Library). (Illus.). 160p. 1987. 19.95 (*0-86573-020-2*) Cy De Cosse.

Marrone, Wenda W., jt. auth. see Muscari, Ann.

Marroquin, Lorenzo. Pax: Peace. Goldberg, Isaac & Schierbrand, W. V., trs. 1977. lib. bdg. 59.95 (*0-8490-2417-X*) Gordon Pr.

Marrosu, M. G., et al, eds. Trends in Neuroimmunology. LC 90-6764. (Illus.). 178p. 1990. 55.00 (*0-306-43510-1*, Plenum Pr) Plenum.

Marrou, Henri I. History of Education in Antiquity. 482p. (C). 1982. pap. text ed. 16.95 (*0-299-08814-6*) U of Wis Pr.

Marrou, Henri-Irenee, ed. see Moreau, Jacques.

Marrow, Alfred J. The Practical Theorist: The Life & Work of Kurt Lewin. LC 77-1400. 319p. reprint ed. pap. 91.00 (*0-317-28352-9*, 2022551) Bks Demand.

Marrow, Deborah. The Art Patronage of Maria de'Medici. LC 82-1951. (Studies in Baroque Art History: No. 4). (Illus.). 191p. reprint ed. pap. 54.50 (*0-8357-1303-2*, 2070026) Bks Demand.

Marrow, James, et al. The Golden Age of Dutch Manuscript Painting. LC 89-85967. (Illus.). 320p. 1990. 65.00 (*0-8076-1227-8*) Braziller.

Marrow, James H. The Hours of Simon de Varie. LC 93-28120. (Getty Museum Monographs on Illuminated Manuscripts). (Illus.). 304p. 1994. 95.00 (*0-89236-284-7*) J P Getty Trust.

Marrow, Linda, ed. see Adams, Faye.

Marrow, Linda, ed. see Andrews, V. C.

Marrow, Linda, ed. see Barnett, Jill.

Marrow, Linda, ed. see Cates, Kimberly.

Marrow, Linda, ed. see Davis, Kathryn L.

Marrow, Linda, ed. see Deveraux, Jude.

Marrow, Linda, ed. see Friday, Nancy.

Marrow, Linda, ed. see Garwood, Julie.

Marrow, Linda, ed. see Haeger, Diane.

Marrow, Linda, ed. see Hall, Paris.

Marrow, Linda, ed. see Hughes, D. T.

Marrow, Linda, ed. see Jensen, Kathryn.

Marrow, Linda, ed. see Lael Miller, Linda.

Marrow, Linda, ed. see Laiman, Leah.

Marrow, Linda, ed. see McNaught, Judith.

Marrow, Linda, ed. see McNaught, Judith, et al.

Marrow, Linda, ed. see McNaught, Judith.

Marrow, Linda, ed. see Miller, Linda L.

Marrow, Linda, ed. see O'Brien, Judith.

Marrow, Linda, ed. see Perry, Michael R.

Marrow, Linda, ed. see Pickard, Nancy.

Marrow, Linda, ed. see Quinn, Elizabeth.

Marrow, Linda, ed. see Rogers, Marylyle.

Marrow, Linda, ed. see Schechter, Harold.

Marrow, Linda, ed. see Stewart, Mariah.

Marrow, Linda, ed. see Thorton, Penny.

Marrow, Linda, ed. see Verge, Lisa A.

*__Marrow, Stanley B.__ The Gospel of John: A Reading. LC 94-44922. 416p. (Orig.). 1995. pap. 19.95 (*0-8091-3550-7*) Paulist Pr.

— Paul, His Letters & Theology: An Introduction to Paul's Epistles. 288p. (Orig.). 1986. pap. 12.95 (*0-8091-2744-X*) Paulist Pr.

Marrs, Carol. The Complete Book of Speech Communication: A Workbook of Ideas & Activities for Students of Speech & Theatre. Zapel, Arthur L., ed. LC 91-47621. (Illus.). 176p. (Orig.). 1992. pap. text ed. 12.95 (*0-916260-87-9*, B142) Meriwether Pub.

Marrs, Carol R. Pet Cobwebs. (Illus.). 112p. (J). (gr. 1 up). 1988. 12.95 (*0-9621234-0-4*) Funny Farm Pr.

Marrs, Donald. Executive in Passage: Career in Crisis - The Door to Uncommon Fulfillment. LC 89-6780. 304p. 1990. 19.95 (*0-925887-89-7*) Barring Sky Pub.

Marrs, Edwin W., Jr. A Descriptive Catalogue of the Letters of Charles & Mary Anne Lamb in the W. Hugh Peal Collection, University of Kentucky Libraries. LC 84-50664. (University of Kentucky Libraries Occasional Papers). 48p. 1984. lib. bdg. 15.00 (*0-917519-02-7*) U of KY Libs.

Marrs, Edwin W., Jr., ed. see Carlyle, Thomas.

Marrs, Edwin W., Jr., ed. see Lamb, Charles & Lamb, Mary A.

Marrs, Elijah P. Life & History of the Rev. Elijah P. Marrs. LC 70-89395. (Black Heritage Library Collection). 1977. 16.95 (*0-8369-8625-3*) Ayer.

— Life & History of the Rev. Elijah P. Marrs. (American Biography Ser.). 146p. 1991. reprint ed. lib. bdg. 59.00 (*0-7812-8268-3*) Rprt Serv.

Marrs, Jere M. ARexx: "Some Issues in Programming" LC 93-186535. 164p. 1993. pap. text ed. 30.00 (*0-9636575-0-X*) Tech Res NW.

— ARexx from the Beginning: A Self-Study Workbook. 200p. (Orig.). 1994. pap. text ed. 20.00 (*0-9636575-1-8*) Tech Res NW.

Marrs, Jim. Crossfire: The Plot That Killed Kennedy. (Illus.). 620p. 1990. pap. 13.95 (*0-88184-648-1*) Carroll & Graf.

— Enigma Files. 1995. 23.00 (*0-517-59755-1*, Harmony) Crown Pub Group.

Marrs, John. Substance & Shadow. Mendel, Kathleen L., ed. LC 94-60397. 64p. (Orig.). (C). 1994. pap. 7.95 (*1-878142-34-8*) Telstar TX.

Marrs, Pauline D. Second Season. 1979. pap. 1.75 (*0-449-50012-8*, Coventry) Fawcett.

Marrs, Richard P., ed. Assisted Reproductive Technologies. LC 93-1410. 1993. 80.00 (*0-86542-203-6*) Blackwell Sci.

*__Marrs, Ronald W. & Kolm, Kenneth E., eds.__ Interpretation of Windflow Characteristics from Eolian Landforms. fac. ed. LC 82-15673. (Geological Society of America, Special Paper Ser.: No. 192). (Illus.). 114p. 1982. reprint ed. pap. 32.50 (*0-7837-7941-0*, 2047697) Bks Demand.

***Marrs, Samuel. The Angels Laughed: The Promotion of a Dunghill Beggar. Mel, Jeanne, ed. (Illus.). 200p. (Orig.). 1995. pap. 12.95 (*0-9645387-0-9*) Yeshurun Pub.**

EARTH: A.D. 2000 - The evil empire has arrived. In one final, calculated power-grab, the secret brotherhood has united the earth in one global government. It is the culmination of a plan set in motion & nurtured for thousands of years. Their purpose for global unification is to repel a long-anticipated invasion of the planet Earth from outer space. This invasion will be led by a former Jewish carpenter from Nazareth, who will be carrying out another plan, which was set in motion from before the beginning of time. The prelude to this final drama has already begun. A modern-day prophet recounts his life before & after his call from God, revelations & dreams he received for the times ahead, & visions he was shown while out-of-body. His revelations include: the identity of "THE ANTICHRIST," "THE 666 BEAST," & "THE FALSE PROPHET," the truth about "THE GREAT APOSTASY" & "THE ABOMINATION OF DESOLATION" - & the proclaiming of "THE DAY OF THE LORD." The Dunghill Beggar's promotion to the office of prophet was so unlikely - so totally unexpected - that when it was announced, THE ANGELS LAUGHED! Order from: Yeshurun Publishing, P.O. Box 720849, Dallas, TX 75372-0849; 214-823-6421. ***Publisher Provided Annotation.***

Marrs, Suzanne. The Welty Collection: A Guide to the Eudora Welty Manuscripts & Documents at the Mississippi Department of Archives & History. LC 88-17537. (Illus.). 244p. 1988. text ed. 35.00 (*0-87805-366-2*) U Pr of Miss.

Marrs, Texe. America Shattered: Unmasking the Plot to Destroy Our Families & Our Country. (Illus.). 160p. (Orig.). 1992. pap. 6.95 (*0-9620086-6-4*) Living Truth Pubs.

— Big Sister Is Watching You. 1993. pap. 9.95 (*0-9620086-9-9*) Living Truth Pubs.

— Dark Majesty: The Secret Brotherhood & the Magic of a Thousand Points of Light. (Illus.). 272p. (Orig.). 1992. pap. 9.95 (*0-9620086-7-2*) Living Truth Pubs.

— Dark Secrets of the New Age: Satan's Plan for a One-World Religion. LC 86-72066. 256p. (Orig.). 1987. pap. 9.99 (*0-89107-421-X*) Crossway Bks.

— Mega Forces: Signs & Wonders of the Coming Chaos. 266p. 1988. pap. 8.95 (*0-9620086-0-5*) Living Truth Pubs.

— Millennium. (Illus.). 272p. (Orig.). 1990. pap. 9.95 (*0-9620086-5-6*) Living Truth Pubs.

— Mystery Mark of the New Age: Satan's Design for World Domination. LC 87-72056. 1988. pap. 9.99 (*0-89107-479-1*) Crossway Bks.

M

— New Age Cults & Religions. 1990. pap. 9.95 (*0-9620086-8-0*) Living Truth Pubs.
— The Personal Robot Book. (Illus.). 181p. 1985. pap. 14.95 (*0-317-39383-9*) Robot Inst Am.
— Ravaged by the New Age: Satan's Plan to Destroy Our Kids. LC 88-83897. (Illus.). 272p. (Orig.). 1989. pap. 8.95 (*0-9620086-1-3*) Living Truth Pubs.
— Texe Marrs Book of New Age Cults & Religions. (Illus.). 336p. 1990. 17.95 (*0-9620086-4-8*) Living Truth Pubs.
Marrs, Texe & Marrs, Wanda. New Age Lies to Women. 256p. 1990. 8.95 (*0-9620086-3-X*) Living Truth Pubs.
Marrs, Texe & Read, Karen. The Woman's Guide to Military Service. 2nd ed. 176p. 1987. pap. 8.95 (*0-89709-152-3*) Liberty Pub.
Marrs, Texe W. Careers with Robots. LC 87-24550. 221p. reprint ed. pap. 63.00 (*0-8357-3487-0*, 2039746) Bks Demand.
— How to Prepare for the Armed Forces Test (ASVAB) write for info. (*0-318-58787-4*) S&S Trade.
Marrs, Timothy C., jt. auth. see Ballantyne, Bryan.
Marrs, Wanda, jt. auth. see Marrs, Texe.
Marrus, Michael R. The Holocaust in History. 288p. 1989. pap. 11.95 (*0-452-00953-7*, Mer) NAL-Dutton.
— Samuel Bronfman: The Life & Times of Seagram's Mr. Sam. LC 91-31775. (Illus.). 551p. 1991. 35.00 (*0-87451-571-8*) U Pr of New Eng.
— The Unwanted: European Refugees in the Twentieth Century. (Illus.). 371p. 1985. 30.00 (*0-19-503615-8*) OUP.
— The Unwanted: European Refugees in the Twentieth Century. (Illus.). 371p. 1987. pap. 10.95 (*0-19-505186-6*) OUP.
***Marrus, Michael R. & Paxton, Robert O.** Vichy France & the Jews. 448p. 1995. pap. 17.95 (*0-8047-2499-7*) Stanford U Pr.
Marrus, R., ed. Physics of Highly-Ionized Atoms. (NATO ASI Series B, Physics). (Illus.). 472p. 1989. 115.00 (*0-306-43321-4*, Plenum Insight) Plenum.
Marrus, Stephanie K. Building the Strategic Plan: Find, Analyze, & Present the Right Information. LC 92-47381. 358p. (C). 1994. reprint ed. lib. bdg. 48.50 (*0-89464-835-7*) Krieger.
Marryat, Captain. The Children of the New Forest. Butts, Dennis, ed. (World's Classics Ser.). 352p. 1992. pap. 7.95 (*0-19-282725-1*) OUP.
— The Children of the New Forest. 1990. reprint ed. lib. bdg. 21.95 (*0-89966-700-7*) Buccaneer Bks.
Marryat, Florence. There Is No Death. 1975. 69.95 (*0-8490-1192-2*) Gordon Pr.
Marryat, Frederick. Japhet in Search of a Father, 3 vols. in 2, 1. LC 79-8425. reprint ed. write for info. (*0-404-62023-X*) AMS Pr.
— Japhet in Search of a Father, 3 vols. in 2, 2. LC 79-8425. reprint ed. write for info. (*0-404-62024-8*) AMS Pr.
— Japhet in Search of a Father, 3 vols. in 2, Set. LC 79-8425. reprint ed. 84.50 (*0-404-62022-1*) AMS Pr.
— Mr. Midshipman Easy. LC 89-13600. (Classics of Naval Literature Ser.). 448p. 1990. reprint ed. 32.95 (*0-87021-590-6*) Naval Inst Pr.
— The Phantom Ship, 3 vols. in 1. LC 79-8168. reprint ed. 44.50 (*0-404-62026-4*) AMS Pr.
***Mars.** Towards Very Large Knowledge Bases. LC 95-75768. 1995. 92.00 (*90-5199-217-3*) IOS Press.
***Mars, Diana.** Mixed-up Matrimony. (Desire Ser.). 1995. mass mkt. 3.25 (*0-373-05942-6*, 1-05942-7) Silhouette.
— Peril in Paradise. (Desire Ser.). 1995. pap. 2.99 (*0-373-05906-X*, 1-05906-2) Silhouette.
Mars, Florence & Eden, Lynn. Witness in Philadelphia. LC 76-50660. (Illus.). 296p. 1989. pap. 11.95 (*0-8071-1566-5*) La State U Pr.
Mars, Gerald. Cheats at Work: An Anthology of Workplace Crime. 260p. 1994. 62.95 (*1-85521-379-6*, Pub. by Dartmth Pub UK); pap. 26.95 (*1-85521-528-4*, Pub. by Dartmth Pub UK) Ashgate Pub Co.
Mars, Gerald & Mars, Valerie, eds. Food, Culture, & History. (London Food Seminar Ser.: Vol. I). 220p. 1993. pap. 20.00 (*0-9521746-0-X*, Pub. by London Food Seminar UK) Bosphorus Bks.
Mars, James. Life of James Mars: A Slave Born & Sold in Connecticut. LC 76-89394. (Black Heritage Library Collection). 1869. 9.00 (*0-8369-8626-1*) Ayer.
Mars, Jon C. Fitness First Training Diary. (Illus.). 126p. 1990. spiral bd. 9.95 (*0-9626519-0-7*) AOJ Pub Corp.
***Mars-Jones.** The Waters of Thirst. pap. 11.00 (*0-679-75960-3*) Random.
***Mars-Jones, Adam.** Monopolies of Loss. Date not set. pap. 3.99 (*0-517-13070-X*) Random.
— Monopolies of Loss. LC 93-42197. 1994. pap. 11.00 (*0-679-74415-0*, Vin) Random.
— Monopolies of Loss: Stories. LC 92-54803. 1993. 21.00 (*0-679-41940-3*, Knopf) Random.
— The Waters of Thirst. LC 93-35938. 1994. 20.00 (*0-679-41941-1*) Knopf.
Mars-Jones, Adam, ed. Mae West Is Dead: Recent Lesbian & Gay Fiction. 2nd ed. 320p. 1987. pap. 9.95 (*0-571-14898-0*) Faber & Faber.
***Mars, Kasey.** The Dream. 416p. 1995. pap. 4.99 (*0-7860-0203-4*) Windsor NY.
— Silent Rose. 512p. 1994. mass mkt. 4.99 (*0-7860-0081-3*) Windsor NY.
Mars, Louis B. Crisis of Possession in Voodoo. Collins, Kathleen, tr. LC 76-51943. 1977. 10.00 (*0-918408-07-5*); pap. 4.95 (*0-918408-00-8*) Reed & Cannon.
Mars, P. & Poppelbaum, W. J. Stochastic & Deterministic Averaging Processors. (Computing Ser.: No. 1). (Illus.). 176p. 1981. boxed 107.00 (*0-906048-44-3*, CM906) Inst Elect Eng.
***Mars, Phil, et al.** Learning Algorithms: Theory & Applications in Signal Processing. 256p. 1995. write for info. (*0-8493-7896-6*, 7896) CRC Pr.
Mars, Valerie, jt. ed. see Mars, Gerald.
Marsa, Francisco. Normative Dictionary & Guide to the Spanish Language: Diccionario Normative y Guia De la Lengua Espanol. 2nd ed. 480p. (SPA.). 1990. write for info. (*0-7859-4954-2*) Fr & Eur.
Marsack, Robyn. Sylvia Plath. (Open Guides to Literature Ser.). 112p. 1992. 75.00 (*0-335-09353-1*, Open Univ Pr); pap. 22.00 (*0-335-09352-3*, Open Univ Pr) Taylor & Francis.
Marsack, Robyn, tr. see Bouvier, Nicolas.
Marsack, Robyn, tr. see Monsaingeon, Bruno, ed.
Marsak, L. M., ed. The Nature of Historical Inquiry. LC 74-16092. 220p. 1986. reprint ed. 18.50 (*0-88275-221-9*) Krieger.
Marsal, D. Logik, Dedeutung & Mathematik: Die Konstruktion Einer Fundamentalsprache der Wissenschaften. 152p. (GER.). 1987. pap. 33.60 (*0-685-33223-3*, Pub. by Schweizerbart'sche GW) Lubrecht & Cramer.
— Statistics for Geoscientists. (Illus.). 220p. 1987. 70.00 (*0-08-026268-6*, Pergamon Pr); pap. 44.00 (*0-08-026260-0*, Pergamon Pr) Elsevier.
***Marsalek & Torno.** Urban Storm Drainage, No. WST29/1-2. (Water Science & Technology Ser.: No. 29/1-2). 1995. pap. 220.00 (*0-08-042498-8*, Pergamon Pr) Elsevier.
Marsalek, J. Head Losses at Selected Sewer Manholes. (Special Report Ser.: No. 52). 87p. (Orig.). 1985. pap. text ed. 35.00 (*0-917084-13-6*) Am Public Works.
***Marsalis, Wynton.** Marsalis on Music. (Illus.). 175p. 1995. 25.00 (*0-393-03881-5*) Norton.
Marsalis, Wynton & Stewart, Frank. Sweet Swing Blues on the Road. LC 93-4740. 1994. 29.95 (*0-393-03514-X*) Norton.
Marsan, C. Ajmone, jt. ed. see Caputto, R.
Marsan, Jean-Claude. Montreal in Evolution: Historical Analysis of the Development of Montreal Architecture & Urban Environment. (Illus.). 488p. 1981. 32.95 (*0-7735-0339-0*, Pub. by McGill CN) U of Toronto Pr.
— Montreal in Evolution: Historical Analysis of the Development of Montreal Architecture & Urban Environment. (Illus.). 456p. (C). 1990. reprint ed. pap. text ed. 22.95 (*0-7735-0798-1*, Pub. by McGill CN) U of Toronto Pr.
Marsan, M. Ajmone, ed. Application & Theory of Petri Nets, 1993: Proceedings of the 14th International Conference, Chicago, Illinois, USA, June 21-25, 1993. (Lecture Notes in Computer Science Ser.: Vol. 691). ix, 591p. 1993. pap. 78.00 (*0-387-56863-8*) Spr-Verlag.
Marsan, M. Ajmone, et al. Modeling with Generalized Stochastic Petri Nets. LC 94-20916. (Series in Parallel Computing). 1994. text ed. 69.95 (*0-471-93059-8*) Wiley.
— Performance Models of Multiprocessor Systems. (Computer Systems Ser.). 300p. 1986. 42.00 (*0-262-01093-3*) MIT Pr.
Marsand, Joseph & Griffith, Francis. Spelling the Easy Way. 2nd ed. (Easy Way Ser.). 320p. 1988. pap. 9.95 (*0-8120-3346-9*) Barron.
Marsano, Daniel T. Sir Day the Knight. (Illus.). 48p. (J). (gr. k-6). 1993. 15.00 (*1-883960-11-8*) Henry Quill.
— Sun Day, the Not-Quite Knight. (Illus.). 48p. (J). (gr. k-6). 1994. lib. bdg. 15.00 (*1-883960-13-4*) Henry Quill.
Marsboom, R. P., jt. ed. see Lewi, Paul J.
Marsch, E. & Schwenn, R., eds. Solar Wind Seven: Proceedings of the Third COSPAR Colloquium Held in Goslar, Germany, 16-20 September 1991. LC 92-20040. (COSPAR Colloquia Ser.: Vol. 3). 1992. 225.00 (*0-08-042049-4*, Pergamon Pr) Elsevier.
Marsch, E., jt. auth. see Tu, C. Y.
Marschak, Jacob. Economic Information, Decision, & Prediction, 3 Vols., Vol. I. (Theory & Decision Library: No. 7). 389p. 1980. pap. text ed. 36.50 (*90-277-1195-X*) Kluwer Ac.
— Economic Information, Decision, & Prediction, 3 Vols., Vol. II. (Theory & Decision Library: No. 7). 362p. 1980. pap. text ed. 36.50 (*90-277-1196-8*) Kluwer Ac.
— Economic Information, Decision, & Prediction, 3 Vols., Vol. III. (Theory & Decision Library: No. 7). 399p. 1981. pap. text ed. 36.50 (*90-277-1197-6*) Kluwer Ac.
Marschak, Jacob & Radner, Roy. Economic Theory of Teams. LC 78-99832. (Cowles Foundation for Research in Economics at Yale University. Monograph Ser.: No. 22). 357p. reprint ed. pap. 101.80 (*0-8357-8107-0*, 2033812) Bks Demand.
Marschak, Thomas, et al. Strategy for R & D: Studies in the Microeconomics of Development. LC 67-28248. (Econometrics & Operations Research Ser.: Vol. 8). (Illus.). 1967. 87.00 (*0-387-03945-7*) Spr-Verlag.
Marschall, B., tr. see Resch, H. & Beck, E.
Marschall, Charles W. & Maringer, Robert E. Dimensional Instability-an Introduction. 1977. 133.00 (*0-08-021305-7*, Pub. by Pergamon Repr UK) Franklin.
Marschall, Ken, illus. Hindenburg an Illustrated History: Reliving the Era of the Great Airships. 228p. 1994. 60.00 (*0-446-51784-4*) Warner Bks.
— Titanic: An Illustrated History. 224p. 1995. pap. 29.95 (*0-7868-8147-X*) Hyperion.
Marschall, Ken, jt. auth. see Sauder, Eric.
Marschall, Laurence A. The Supernova Story. LC 88-17978. (Illus.). 316p. 1988. 22.95 (*0-306-42955-1*, Plenum Pr) Plenum.
— The Supernova Story. LC 93-43454. (Science Library). (C). 1994. pap. 12.95 (*0-691-03633-0*) Princeton U Pr.
Marschall, Mark. Yellowstone Trails, A Hiking Guide. (Illus.). 159p. 1990. 4.95 (*0-89288-197-6*) Yellowstone Assn.
Marschall, R., ed. Aspects of Seismic Reflection Data Processing. (C). 1990. lib. bdg. 129.50 (*0-7923-0846-8*) Kluwer Ac.
Marschall, Richard. America's Great Comic-Strip Artists. (Illus.). 288p. 1989. 55.00 (*0-89659-917-5*) Abbeville Pr.
Marschall, Richard, ed. see Caniff, Milton.
Marschall, Richard, ed. see Gould, Will.
Marschall, Richard, ed. see Herriman, George.
Marschall, Richard, ed. see McCay, Winsor.
Marschall, Richard, ed. see Segar, E. C.
Marschall, Richard, ed. see Sterrett, Cliff.
Marschall, Richard A. Numerical Solution of the Helmholtz Equation. 110p. (C). 1993. text ed. 142.00 (*0-9636418-0-8*) Marschall Acoustics.
***Marschall, Rick.** Golden Age of Television. 192p. 1994. 14.98 (*0-8317-3926-6*) Smithmark.
— New Country Music: Today's Brightest Stars. (Illus.). 96p. 1993. 12.98 (*0-8317-6307-8*) Smithmark.
Marschall, Rick, ed. see McCay, Winsor.
Marschall, Rick, ed. see Sterrett, Cliff.
Marschall von Bieberstein, F. A. Flora Taurico Caucasicia, Exhibens Stirpes Phaenogamas, in Charsoneso Taurica & Regionibus Caucasicis Sponte Cresentes, 3vols. in 2. 1972. reprint ed. 200.00 (*3-7682-0762-5*) Lubrecht & Cramer.
Marscharck, Mark, jt. ed. see De Vega, Manuel.
Marschark, Marc. Psychological Development of Deaf Children. LC 92-16491. 1993. 39.95 (*0-19-506899-8*) OUP.
Marschark, Marc & Clark, M. Diane, eds. Psychological Perspectives on Deafness. 400p. 1992. text ed. 79.95 (*0-8058-1054-4*) L Erlbaum Assocs.
Marschner, Alison, tr. see Destexhe, Alain.
Marschner, Horst. Mineral Nutrition of Higher Plants. 2nd ed. (Illus.). 848p. 1995. pap. text ed. 49.95 (*0-12-473543-6*); boxed 120.00 (*0-12-473542-8*) Acad Pr.
Marsden. Elementary Classical Analysis. 2nd ed. LC 92-41432. (C). 1995. text ed. write for info. (*0-7167-2105-8*) W H Freeman.
— Movement Disorders I & II. 864p. 1995. write for info. (*0-7506-2232-6*, Focal) Buttrwrth-Heinemann.
— Vector Calculus. 3rd ed. (C). 1995. text ed. write for info. (*0-7167-1931-2*) W H Freeman.
Marsden, tr. see Polo, Marco.
Marsden, Alan & Pople, Anthony, eds. Computer Representations & Models in Music. (Illus.). 309p. 1991. text ed. 72.00 (*0-12-473545-2*) Acad Pr.
Marsden, Andrew K., ed. see International Congress of Emergency Surgery, 5th: 1981: Brighton, Sussex.
***Marsden, Bill.** Geography 11-16: Rekindling Good Practice. 224p. 1995. pap. text ed. 24.95x (*1-85346-296-9*, Pub. by D Fulton UK) Taylor & Francis.
***Marsden, Bill & Hughes, Jo, eds.** Primary School Geography. 176p. 1994. pap. 29.00x (*1-85346-281-0*, Pub. by D Fulton UK) Taylor & Francis.
Marsden, C. A. & Heal, D. J. Central Serotonin Receptors & Psychotropic Drugs. (Frontiers in Pharmacology & Therapeutics Ser.). (Illus.). 334p. 1992. 135.00 (*0-632-02883-1*) Blackwell Sci.
Marsden, C. D., ed. The Assessment & Therapy of Parkinsonism. (New Trends in Clinical Neurology Ser.). (Illus.). 105p. 1990. 65.00 (*1-85070-318-3*) Prthnon Pub.
Marsden, C. D. & Fahn, S. Movement Disorders 3. (BIMR Ser.: Vol. 12). (Illus.). 416p. 1994. 75.00 (*0-7506-1412-9*) Buttrwrth-Heinemann.
Marsden, C. David, ed. Treating Spasticity: Pharmacological Advances. LC 89-15214. 72p. 1989. text ed. 16.00 (*0-920887-56-2*) Hogrefe & Huber Pubs.
Marsden, C. David & Fahn, Stanley, eds. Movement Disorders Two (BIMR Neurology Vol. 7) (Butterworths International Medical Reviews; Urology Ser.). 468p. 1987. text ed. 75.00 (*0-407-02299-6*) Buttrwrth-Heinemann.
Marsden, C. David & Fowler, Timothy J., eds. Clinical Neurology. 460p. 1989. 47.00 (*0-88167-527-X*) Raven.
Marsden, C. David, tr. see Benecke, R. & Conrad, B., eds.
Marsden, C. David, et al, eds. Madopar HBS. (Journal: European Neurology: Vol. 27, Suppl. 1). (Illus.). vi, 142p. 1987. pap. 41.75 (*3-8055-4692-0*) S Karger.
Marsden, Carl A., jt. ed. see Andrews, John N.
Marsden, Charles A., jt. ed. see Heal, David J.
Marsden, David. The End of Economic Man? Custom & Competition in the Labor Market. LC 85-26108. 256p. 1986. text ed. 39.95 (*0-312-25069-X*) St Martin.
Marsden, David, ed. Pay & Employment in the New Europe. 256p. 1992. 59.95 (*1-85278-564-0*, Pub. by E Elgar Pub UK) Ashgate Pub Co.
Marsden, David, jt. auth. see Oakley, Peter.
Marsden, Dennis. Workless: An Exploration of the Social Contract Between Society & the Worker. 2nd enl. rev. ed. (Illus.). 275p. 1982. pap. 14.95 (*0-7099-1723-6*, Pub. by Croom Helm UK) Routledge Chapman & Hall.
Marsden, Edward W. The Travels of Marco Polo. 1987. 17.95 (*0-88029-135-4*) Dorset Pr.
Marsden, Eric W. Greek & Roman Artillery: Historical Development. LC 71-440116. 253p. reprint ed. pap. 72.20 (*0-685-20914-8*, 2052244) Bks Demand.
— Greek & Roman Artillery: Technical Treatises. LC 74-595763. 312p. reprint ed. pap. 89.00 (*0-685-20913-X*, 2052243) Bks Demand.
Marsden, Eva, jt. auth. see Stevenson, Tony.
***Marsden, George.** Reforming Fundamentalism: Fuller Seminary & the New Evangelicalism. LC 95-10335. 1995. write for info. (*0-8028-0870-0*) Eerdmans.
— Reforming Fundamentalism: Fuller Seminary & the New Evangelicalism. LC 87-22243. 331p. reprint ed. pap. 94.40 (*0-7837-3185-X*, 2042789) Bks Demand.
Marsden, George M. Fundamentalism & American Culture: The Shaping of Twentieth-Century Evangelicalism, 1870-1925. 1982. pap. 11.95 (*0-19-503083-4*) OUP.
— Religion & American Culture. 288p. (C). 1990. pap. text ed. 17.50 (*0-15-576583-3*) HB Coll Pubs.
— The Soul of the American University: From Protestant Establishment to Established Non-Belief. (Illus.). 448p. 1994. 35.00 (*0-19-507046-1*) OUP.
— Understanding Fundamentalism & Evangelicalism. 216p. (Orig.). 1990. pap. 10.99 (*0-8028-0539-6*) Eerdmans.
Marsden, George M. & Longfield, Bradley J., eds. The Secularization of the Academy. (Religion in America Ser.). 288p. (C). 1992. 42.00 (*0-19-507351-7*); pap. text ed. 17.95 (*0-19-507352-5*) OUP.
Marsden, Gordon, ed. Victorian Values: Personalities & Perspectives in Nineteenth Century Society. (Illus.). 248p. (Orig.). (C). 1990. pap. text ed. 21.95 (*0-582-03685-2*, 78418) Longman.
Marsden, Hilda, ed. see Bronte, Anne.
Marsden, J., et al. Dynamics & Control of Multibody Systems. LC 89-15019. (CONM Ser.: Vol. 97). 468p. 1992. pap. 55.00 (*0-8218-5104-7*, CONM97) Am Math.
— Reduction, Symmetry & Phases in Mechanics. LC 90-1143. (MEMO Ser.: Vol. 88/436). 110p. 1990. pap. text ed. 20.00 (*0-8218-2498-8*, MEMO 88/436) Am Math.
***Marsden, Jean I.** The Re-Imagined Text: Shakespeare, Adaptation, & Eighteenth-Century Literary Theory. LC 94-3399. 208p. 1995. text ed. 30.00 (*0-8131-1901-4*) U Pr of Ky.
Marsden, Jean I., ed. see Cohen, Derek.
Marsden, Jerrold. Multi-Variable Calculus. LC 92-38049. (C). 1995. text ed. write for info. (*0-7167-2443-X*) W H Freeman.
Marsden, Jerrold E. Lectures on Geometric Methods in Mathematical Physics. LC 80-54307. (CBMS-NSF Regional Conference Ser.: No. 37). v, 97p. 1981. pap. text ed. 21.00 (*0-89871-170-3*) Soc Indus-Appl Math.
— Lectures on Mechanics. (London Mathematical Society Lecture Note Ser.: No. 174). (Illus.). 272p. (C). 1992. pap. 37.95 (*0-521-42844-0*) Cambridge U Pr.
Marsden, Jerrold E., ed. Fluids & Plasmas: Geometry & Dynamics. LC 84-3011. (Contemporary Mathematics Ser.: Vol. 28). 448p. 1988. reprint ed. pap. 49.00 (*0-8218-5028-8*, CONM-28) Am Math.
Marsden, Jerrold E. & Hoffman, Michael. Basic Complex Analysis. 2nd ed. (Illus.). 620p. (C). 1987. write for info. (*0-318-61032-9*) W H Freeman.
— Basic Complex Analysis. 2nd ed. LC 86-18413. (Mathematics Ser.). (Illus.). 620p. (C). 1995. text ed. write for info. (*0-7167-1814-6*) W H Freeman.
Marsden, Jerrold E. & Hughes, Thomas J. Mathematical Foundations of Elasticity. (Illus.). 576p. 1994. reprint ed. pap. text ed. 14.95 (*0-486-67865-2*) Dover.
***Marsden, Jerrold E. & Ratiu, Tudor S.** Introduction to Mechanics & Symmetry: A Basic Exposition of Classical Mechanical Systems. LC 94-10793. (Text in Applied Mathematics Ser.: 17). 1994. pap. text ed. 42.50 (*0-387-94347-1*) Spr-Verlag.
— Introduction to Mechanics & Symmetry: A Basic Exposition of Classical Mechanical Systems. LC 94-10793. (Texts in Applied Mathematics Ser.: Vol. 17). 1994. 64.50 (*0-387-97275-7*) Spr-Verlag.
Marsden, Jerrold E. & Tromba, Anthony. Vector Calculus. 3rd ed. LC 87-24595. (Illus.). 704p. (C). 1995. text ed. write for info. (*0-7167-1856-1*) W H Freeman.
Marsden, Jerrold E. & Weinstein, Alan. Calculus I: Undergraduate Texts in Mathematics. 2nd ed. (Illus.). 300p. 1990. pap. 24.00 (*0-387-90974-5*) Spr-Verlag.
— Calculus II. 2nd ed. (Undergraduate Texts in Mathematics Ser.). (Illus.). 300p. 1994. pap. 24.00 (*0-387-90975-3*) Spr-Verlag.
— Calculus III. 2nd ed. Ewing, J. H. et al, eds. (Undergraduate Texts in Mathematics Ser.). (Illus.). xv, 341p. 1991. reprint ed. pap. 28.00 (*0-387-90985-0*) Spr-Verlag.
Marsden, Jerrold E., jt. auth. see Abraham, Ralph H.
Marsden, Jerrold E., jt. auth. see Chorin, Alexandre J.
Marsden, Jerrold E., ed. see Lichtenberg, A. J. & Lieberman, M. A.
Marsden, Jerrold E., et al. Basic Multivariable Calculus. xv, 533p. 1993. write for info. (*3-540-97976-X*) Spr-Verlag.
— Basic Multivariable Calculus. LC 92-38049. 1993. 49.00 (*0-387-97976-X*) Spr-Verlag.
***Marsden, John.** The Fury of the Northmen: Saints, Shrines & Sea-Raiders in the Viking Age. (Illus.). 208p. 1995. 24.95 (*0-312-13080-5*, Pub. by Thomas Dunne Bks) St Martin.
— Letters from the Inside. LC 93-41185. (J). 1994. 13.95 (*0-395-68985-6*) HM.
— Northanhymbre Saga: The History of the Anglo-Saxon Kings of Northumbria. (Illus.). 288p. 1992. 39.95 (*1-85626-055-0*) Trafalgar.
— So Much to Tell You. (YA). (gr. 7 up). 1990. pap. 4.99 (*0-449-70374-6*, Juniper) Fawcett.
— So Much to Tell You. 112p. (YA). (gr. 7 up). 1989. 14.95 (*0-316-54877-4*, Joy St Bks) Little.
— Tomorrow, When the War Began. LC 94-29299. (J). 1995. 13.95 (*0-395-70673-4*) HM.
Marsden, John & Barlow, Nic. The Illustrated Border Ballads: The Anglo-Scottish Frontier. (Illus.). 192p. 1991. 34.95 (*0-292-73863-3*) U of Tex Pr.
Marsden, John & House, Iain. Chemistry of Gold Extraction. 400p. 1992. text ed. 105.00 (*0-13-131517-X*) P-H.
***Marsden, Jonathan.** Cliveden. (Illus.). 96p. 1995. pap. 10.95 (*0-7078-0245-8*, Pub. by Natl Trust UK) Trafalgar.
Marsden, Kathryn. The Food Combining Diet: Lose Weight the Hay Way. 224p. 1993. pap. 8.00 (*0-7225-2790-X*) Thorsons SF.
— Super Skin. (Illus.). 1993. reprint ed. pap. 12.00 (*0-7225-2798-5*) Thorsons SF.
Marsden, Keith. African Entrepreneurs: Pioneers of Development. (IFC Discussion Paper Ser.: No. 9). 76p. 1990. English. pap. 7.95 (*0-8213-1693-1*, 11693); French. pap. 7.95 (*0-8213-1782-2*, 11782) World Bank.
Marsden, Keith & Belot, Therese. Private Enterprise in Africa: Creating a Better Environment. (Discussion Papers Ser.: No. 17). 80p. 1987. 7.95 (*0-8213-0945-5*, 20017) World Bank.

M

An Asterisk (*) at the beginning of an entry indicates that the title is appearing in BIP for the first time.

Marsden, Lorna M. The Descent of the God the Continuing Incarnation. (C). 1988. 59.00 (1-85072-093-2, Pub. by W Sessions UK) St Mut.

Marsden, Michael. Practice of Banking 1. 225p. 1985. lib. bdg. 41.00 (0-86010-580-6); pap. text ed. 29.50 (0-86010-563-6) G & T Inc.

— Practice of Banking 1, Vol. 5. 150p. 1985. student ed 20.50 (0-86010-588-1) G & T Inc.

Marsden, Michael T., jt. ed. see Browne, Ray B.

Marsden, Michael T., et al. Movies As Artifacts. LC 82-6300. 288p. (C). 1982. text ed. 32.95 (0-88229-453-9) Nelson-Hall.

Marsden, Norton. A Beginner's Guide to Canaries. (Beginner's Guide Ser.). (Illus.). 64p. 1986. 3.95 (0-86622-301-0, T-102) TFH Pubns.

Marsden, Pater V. & Lin, Nan, eds. Social Structure & Network Analysis. LC 82-10564. (Sage Focus Editions Ser.: No. 57). 319p. reprint ed. pap. 91.00 (0-7837-1115-8, 2041645) Bks Demand.

***Marsden, Peter.** Sociological Methodology. 432p. Date not set. text ed. 59.95 (1-55786-592-2) Blackwell Pubs.

Marsden, Peter V., ed. Linear Models in Social Research. LC 81-9402. (Illus.). 336p. reprint ed. pap. 95.80 (0-7837-1114-X, 2041644) Bks Demand.

Marsden, Philip. The Crossing Place: A Journey among the Armenians. 272p. (Orig.). 1994. pap. 13.00 (1-56836-052-5) Kodansha.

***Marsden, R. G., ed.** The High Latitude Heliosphere: Proceedings of the 28th ESLAB Symposium, 19-21 April 1994, Friedrichshafen, Germany. LC 94-39754. 498p. 1994. lib. bdg. 125.00 (0-7923-3229-6) Kluwer Ac.

— The Sun & the Heliosphere in Three Dimensions. (Astrophysics & Space Science Library). 1986. lib. bdg. 150.00 (90-277-2198-X) Kluwer Ac.

Marsden, Ralph W., ed. Politics, Minerals, & Survival: Proceedings of a Symposium. LC 74-27310. 103p. reprint ed. pap. 29.40 (0-8357-6792-2, 2035469) Bks Demand.

***Marsden, Richard.** The Text of the Old Testament in Anglo-Saxon England. (Studies in Anglo-Saxon England: No. 15). (Illus.). 400p. (C). 1995. write for info. (0-521-46477-3) Cambridge U Pr.

Marsden, Simon. Journal of a Ghost Hunter: In Search of the Dead from Ireland to Transylvania. 1994. 24.95 (1-55859-872-3) Abbeville Pr.

Marsden, Terry. Constructing the Countryside. (C). 1993. pap. text ed. 21.50 (0-8133-1912-9) Westview.

Marsden, Terry & Little, Jo. Political, Social & Economic Perspectives on the International Food System. 271p. 1990. text ed. 68.95 (1-85628-001-2, Pub. by Avebury Pub UK) Ashgate Pub Co.

Marsden, Terry, jt. auth. see Murdoch, Jonathan.

Marsden, Terry, et al. Rural Restructuring: Global Processes & Their Responses. (Critical Perspectives on Rural Change Ser.: Vol. I). 224p. (C). 1990. text ed. 38.50 (0-389-20947-3) B&N Imports.

Marsden, Terry, et al, eds. Rural Restructuring: Global Processes & Local Responses, Vol. 1. (Critical Perspectives on Rural Change Ser.). 224p. (C). 1990. lib. bdg. 79.00 (0-8464-1517-8) Beekman Pubs.

— Technological Change & the Rural Environment, Vol. 2. (Critical Perspectives on Rural Change Ser.). 224p. (C). 1990. lib. bdg. 79.00 (0-8464-1518-6) Beekman Pubs.

Marsden, Victor E., ed. see Nilus.

Marsden, W. E. Educating the Respectable: A Study of Fleet Road Board School Hampstead, 1879-1903. 296p. 1991. text ed. 37.50 (0-7130-0184-4, Pub. by F Cass Pubs UK) Intl Spec Bk.

— Unequal Education Provision in England & Wales: The Nineteenth-Century Roots. (Illus.). 269p. 1987. text ed. 30.00 (0-7130-0178-X, Pub. by Woburn Pr) Intl Spec Bk.

Marsden, Walter. Resting Places in East Anglia. 1993. pap. 15.00 (0-86025-897-1, Pub. by Ian Henry Pubns UK) Empire Pub Srvs.

Marsden, William. Malay-English Dictionary. (ENG & MAY.). 1977. reprint ed. 101.95 (0-518-19003-X) Ayer.

Marsden, William E., jt. ed. see Goodenow, Ronald K.

Marseille, Claudia. Conflict Management: Negotiating Indian Water Rights. (Western Natural Resources Policy Ser.: No. 102). 38p. reprint ed. pap. 25.00 (0-7837-5766-2, 2045431) Bks Demand.

Marsella, Anne. The Lost & Found, & Other Stories. LC 93-46128. 198p. 1994. 25.00 (0-8147-5502-X); pap. 11.95 (0-8147-5503-8) NYU Pr.

***Marsella, Anthony.** Toys from Occupied Japan. (Illus.). 144p. (Orig.). 1995. pap. 29.95 (0-88740-875-3) Schiffer.

Marsella, Anthony J., jt. ed. see Robillard, Albert B.

Marsella, Anthony J., et al, eds. Amidst Peril & Pain: The Mental Health & Well-Being of the World's Refugees. 410p. 1994. text ed. 45.00 (1-55798-223-6) Am Psychol.

— The Measurement of Depression: Clinical, Biological, Psychological, & Psychosocial Perspectives. LC 86-29552. 411p. 1987. lib. bdg. 65.00 (0-89862-694-3) Guilford Pr.

Marsella, Joy, jt. auth. see Hilgers, Thomas L.

Marsella, Joy A. The Promise of Destiny: Children & Women in the Stories of Louisa May Alcott. LC 82-15573. (Contributions to the Study of Childhood & Youth Ser.: No. 2). xxiv, 166p. 1983. text ed. 45.00 (0-313-23603-8, MLO/, Greenwood Pr) Greenwood.

Marselli, Mark. Classic Harley-Davidson Big Twins. (Enthusiast Color Ser.). (Illus.). 96p. 1994. pap. 12.95 (0-87938-922-2) Motorbooks Intl.

Marsenich, Bob. Ready, Aim, Change: A Toolbook for Managing Personal Change. 218p. (Orig.). 1989. pap. 11.95 (0-9622988-3-2) Seaglass Pubns.

***Marsh.** Death & the Dancing Footman. 1995. mass mkt. (0-425-14655-3) Berkley Pub.

— Killer Dolphin. 1995. mass mkt. 4.99 (0-425-14657-X) Berkley Pub.

— Mornings of Gold. 1995. mass mkt. 4.99 (0-440-21627-3) Dell.

Marsh, ed. Handbook of Lipid Bilayers. 1990. 156.95 (0-8493-3255-9, QP751) CRC Pr.

Marsh & Bernard. New Book of Rock Lists. 1994. pap. 15.00 (0-671-78700-4, Fireside) S&S Trade.

Marsh, jt. auth. see Hunt.

Marsh, A. Collection of Teaching Documents & Case Studies: Industrial Relations in Engineering. LC 66-21142. 1966. 60.00 (0-08-011606-X, Pub. by Pergamon Repr UK) Franklin.

Marsh, A. H. History of the Court of Chancery & of the Rise & Development of the Doctrines of Equity. viii, 140p. 1985. reprint ed. lib. bdg. 22.50 (0-8377-0820-6) Rothman.

Marsh, Agnes. Textbook of Social Dancing. (Ballroom Dance Ser.). 1986. lib. bdg. 79.95 (0-8490-3314-4) Gordon Pr.

— Textbook of Social Dancing. (Ballroom Dance Ser.). 1985. lib. bdg. 75.95 (0-87700-817-5) Revisionist Pr.

Marsh, Alan, jt. auth. see McKay, Stephen.

Marsh, Alton K. Tips on Buying Cessna Singles. rev. ed. (Illus.). 202p. (Orig.). 1989. reprint ed. pap. 19.95 (0-9622781-0-6) Buyers Guides.

Marsh, Alton K. & Graham, Jim. Stealth & Future Military Aircraft, 1988. 252p. 1988. pap. 147.00 (0-935453-25-3) Pasha Pubns.

Marsh, Andrew J. Debates & Proceedings in the Constitutional Convention of the State of Nevada. LC 76-39613. 959p. 1976. reprint ed. lib. bdg. 45.00 (0-930342-32-1, 300990) W S Hein.

Marsh, Arthur. Employee Relations Policy & Decision Making. 248p. 1982. text ed. 79.95 (0-566-00540-9) Ashgate Pub Co.

— Trade Union Handbook. 5th ed. 400p. 1991. text ed. 99.95 (0-566-02975-8, Pub. by Gower UK) Ashgate Pub Co.

Marsh, Arthur & Ryan, Victoria. Historical Directory of Trade Unions: Engineering, Iron & Steel, Coal, Mining, Agriculture, Chemicals, Vol. 2. 379p. 1984. text ed. 90.00 (0-566-02161-7) Ashgate Pub Co.

— Historical Directory of Trade Unions: Vol. 1: Non-Manual Unions. 256p. 1980. text ed. 90.00 (0-566-02160-9) Ashgate Pub Co.

Marsh, Arthur, jt. ed. see Kaye, Seymour P.

Marsh, Arthur, et al. Historical Directory of Trade Unions, Vol. 4: Cotton, Wool & Worsted Linen & Jute & Other Textiles. 574p. 1994. 93.95 (0-85967-900-4, Pub. by Scolar Pr UK) Ashgate Pub Co.

Marsh, Benjamin C. An Introduction to City Planning: Democracy's Challenge to the American City. LC 73-11939. (Metropolitan America Ser.). 1977. reprint ed. 13.95 (0-405-05401-7) Ayer.

***Marsh, Betsa.** The Eccentric Traveler: A World of Curious Adventures. 128p. 1995. pap. 14.95 (0-9646636-0-0) Eccentric Pr.

Marsh, Betty F. Past & Repast. (Illus.). 88p. (Orig.). 1981. pap. 5.95 (0-933992-16-5) Coffee Break.

Marsh, Bill. The Philadelphia Inquirer Map & Guide to Center City Philadelphia & Surrounding Area. Bookman, Ken, ed. (Illus.). 52p. (Orig.). 1993. pap. 7.99 (0-9634709-2-2); (0-9634709-3-0) Phila Newspapers.

Marsh, Blanche. Hitch up the Buggy. (Illus.). 152p. 1977. 4.95 (0-317-03228-3) Sandlapper Pub Co.

Marsh, Brian. The Last Trophy: Africa Is a Woman. 2nd ed. Jordan, Andrea & Jordan, David, eds. 304p. 1990. text ed. 24.95 (0-9624807-1-1); pap. text ed. 12.95 (0-9624807-0-3) PHS Pub Div.

Marsh, Brian T. Overland Models: The First Ten Years. (Illus.). 1987. spiral bd. 39.00 (0-9617955-1-4, OMI 2013) Overland Models.

— Overland Models: The First Ten Years. limited ed. (Illus.). 1987. 57.00 (0-9617955-0-6, OMI 2014) Overland Models.

Marsh, C. Duke. California Workers' Compensation Citator. (Personal Injury Library). 296p. 1993. text ed. 138.00 (0-471-59539-X) Wiley.

Marsh-Caldwell, Anne. Emilia Wyndham, 3 vols. in 2, Set. LC 79-8169. reprint ed. 84.50 (0-404-62030-2) AMS Pr.

Marsh, Carl J. Raleigh & Related Families. LC 88-70909. (Illus.). 1988. 20.00 (0-9619972-0-6) C & L Pubns.

Marsh, Carol. Deserat Enemy. large type ed. 268p. 1989. 17.95 (0-7089-1934-0) Ulverscroft.

— Enchanted Valley. large type ed. 1990. pap. 12.95 (0-7089-6911-9, Trailtree Bookshop) Ulverscroft.

— For the Love of Lucy. large type ed. 304p. 1989. 17.95 (0-7089-1996-0) Ulverscroft.

— Happily Ever After. large type ed. (Linford Romance Library). 1989. pap. 11.95 (0-7089-6785-X, Trailtree Bookshop) Ulverscroft.

— In Her Own Light. 1993. mass mkt. 4.99 (0-440-21362-2) Dell.

— Laird of Imchay. large type ed. (Linford Romance Library). 240p. 1992. pap. 14.95 (0-7089-7206-3, Trailtree Bookshop) Ulverscroft.

— A Match for Melanie. large type ed. 1991. pap. 13.95 (0-7089-6981-X) Ulverscroft.

— Nurse under Suspicion. large type ed. 287p. 1989. 17.95 (0-7089-1962-6) Ulverscroft.

— A Primrose for Sarah. large type ed. 288p. 1989. 17.95 (0-7089-2042-X) Ulverscroft.

— Silver Link. 1994. mass mkt. 4.99 (0-440-21624-9) Dell.

Marsh, Carol G., jt. auth. see Harris-Warrick, Rebecca.

Marsh, Carole. A-Plus Very Good! Secrets of Good Writing for Students. (Quantum Leap Ser.). (Orig.). (J). (gr. 4-12). 1994. 24.95 (1-55609-272-5); pap. text ed. 14.95 (0-935326-63-4) Gallopade Pub Group.

— Abstinence Makes the Heart Grow Fonder. (Smart Sex Stuff Ser.). (J). (gr. 2-12). 1994. 24.95 (1-55609-273-3); pap. 14.95 (1-55609-208-3) Gallopade Pub Group.

— AIDS-Zits: A "Sextionary" for Kids. (Smart Sex Stuff Ser.). (Orig.). (J). (gr. 2-12). 1994. 24.95 (1-55609-263-6); pap. 14.95 (1-55609-210-5) Gallopade Pub Group.

— Alabama & Other State Greats (Biographies) (Carole Marsh Alabama Bks.). (Illus.). (YA). (gr. 3-12). 1994. lib. bdg. 24.95 (1-55609-469-8); pap. 14.95 (1-55609-468-X); disk 29.95 (0-7933-1338-4) Gallopade Pub Group.

— Alabama Bandits, Bushwackers, Outlaws, Crooks, Devils, Ghosts, Desperadoes & Other Assorted & Sundry Characters! (Carole Marsh Alabama Bks.). (Illus.). (YA). (gr. 3-12). 1994. lib. bdg. 24.95 (0-7933-0041-X); pap. 14.95 (0-7933-0040-1); disk 29.95 (0-7933-0042-8) Gallopade Pub Group.

— The Alabama Bookstore Book: A Surprising Guide to Our State's Bookstores & Their Specialties for Students, Teachers, Writers & Publishers. (Carole Marsh Alabama Bks.). (Illus.). 1994. lib. bdg. 24.95 (0-7933-2855-1); pap. 14.95 (0-7933-2856-X); disk 29.95 (0-7933-2857-8) Gallopade Pub Group.

— Alabama Classic Christmas Trivia: Stories, Recipes, Activities, Legends, Lore & More! (Carole Marsh Alabama Bks.). (Illus.). (YA). (gr. 3-12). 1994. lib. bdg. 24.95 (0-7933-0044-4); pap. 14.95 (0-7933-0043-6); disk 29.95 (0-7933-0045-2) Gallopade Pub Group.

— Alabama Coastales! (Carole Marsh Alabama Bks.). (J). 1994. lib. bdg. 24.95 (0-7933-6938-X) Gallopade Pub Group.

— Alabama Coastales! (Carole Marsh Alabama Bks.). (Illus.). (YA). (gr. 3-12). 1994. lib. bdg. 24.95 (1-55609-465-5); pap. 14.95 (1-55609-120-6); disk 29.95 (0-7933-1334-1) Gallopade Pub Group.

— Alabama "Crinkum-Crankum" A Funny Word Book about Our State. (Carole Marsh Alabama Bks.). (Illus.). (J). 1994. lib. bdg. 24.95 (0-7933-4810-2); pap. 14.95 (0-7933-4811-0); disk 29.95 (0-7933-4812-9) Gallopade Pub Group.

— Alabama Dingbats! Bk. 1: A Fun Book of Games, Stories, Activities & More about Our State That's All in Code! for You to Decipher. (Carole Marsh Alabama Bks.). (Illus.). (J). (gr. 3-12). 1994. lib. bdg. 24.95 (0-7933-3773-9); pap. 14.95 (0-7933-3774-7); disk 29.95 (0-7933-3775-5) Gallopade Pub Group.

— Alabama Festival Fun for Kids! (Carole Marsh Alabama Bks.). (Illus.). (YA). (gr. 3-12). 1994. lib. bdg. 24.95 (0-7933-3926-X); pap. 14.95 (0-7933-3927-8); disk 29.95 (0-7933-3928-6) Gallopade Pub Group.

— The Alabama Hot Air Balloon Mystery. (Carole Marsh Alabama Bks.). (Illus.). (J). (gr. 2-9). 1994. 24.95 (0-7933-2318-5); pap. 14.95 (0-7933-2319-3); disk 29.95 (0-7933-2320-7) Gallopade Pub Group.

— Alabama Jeopardy! Answers & Questions about Our State! (Carole Marsh Alabama Bks.). (Illus.). (J). (gr. 3-12). 1994. lib. bdg. 24.95 (0-7933-4079-9); pap. 14.95 (0-7933-4080-2); disk 29.95 (0-7933-4081-0) Gallopade Pub Group.

— Alabama "Jography" A Fun Run Thru Our State! (Carole Marsh Alabama Bks.). (Illus.). (YA). (gr. 3-12). 1994. lib. bdg. 24.95 (1-55609-461-2); pap. 14.95 (1-55609-092-7); disk 29.95 (0-7933-1327-9) Gallopade Pub Group.

— Alabama Kid's Cookbook: Recipes, How-to, History, Lore & More! (Carole Marsh Alabama Bks.). (Illus.). (YA). (gr. 3-12). 1994. lib. bdg. 24.95 (0-7933-0082-7); pap. 14.95 (0-7933-0081-9); disk 29.95 (0-7933-0083-5) Gallopade Pub Group.

— The Alabama Library Book: A Surprising Guide to the Unusual Special Collections in Libraries Across Our State for Students, Teachers, Writers & Publishers - Includes Reproducible Mailing Labels Plus Activities for Young People! (Carole Marsh Alabama Bks.). (Illus.). 1994. lib. bdg. 24.95 (0-7933-3008-4); pap. 14.95 (0-7933-3009-2); disk 29.95 (0-7933-3010-6) Gallopade Pub Group.

— The Alabama Media Book: A Surprising Guide to the Amazing Print, Broadcast & Online Media of Our State for Students, Teachers, Writers & Publishers - Includes Reproducible Mailing Labels Plus Activities for Young People! (Carole Marsh Alabama Bks.). (Illus.). 1994. lib. bdg. 24.95 (0-7933-3161-7); pap. 14.95 (0-7933-3162-5); disk 29.95 (0-7933-3163-3) Gallopade Pub Group.

— The Alabama Mystery Van Takes Off! Book 1: Handicapped Alabama Kids Sneak Off on a Big Adventure. (Carole Marsh Alabama Bks.). (Illus.). (J). (gr. 3-12). 1994. 24.95 (0-7933-4964-8); pap. 14.95 (0-7933-4965-6); disk 29.95 (0-7933-4966-4) Gallopade Pub Group.

— Alabama Quiz Bowl Crash Course! (Carole Marsh Alabama Bks.). (Illus.). (YA). (gr. 3-12). 1994. lib. bdg. 24.95 (1-55609-467-1); pap. 14.95 (1-55609-466-3); disk 29.95 (0-7933-1333-3) Gallopade Pub Group.

— Alabama Rollercoasters! (Carole Marsh Alabama Bks.). (Illus.). (YA). (gr. 3-12). 1994. lib. bdg. 24.95 (0-7933-5224-X); pap. 14.95 (0-7933-5225-8); disk 29.95 (0-7933-5226-6) Gallopade Pub Group.

— Alabama School Trivia: An Amazing & Fascinating Look at Our State's Teachers, Schools & Students! (Carole Marsh Alabama Bks.). (Illus.). (YA). (gr. 3-12). 1994. lib. bdg. 24.95 (0-7933-0079-7); pap. 14.95 (0-7933-0049-5); disk 29.95 (0-7933-0080-0) Gallopade Pub Group.

— Alabama Silly Basketball Sportsmysteries, Vol. I. (Carole Marsh Alabama Bks.). (Illus.). (YA). (gr. 3-12). 1994. lib. bdg. 24.95 (0-7933-0047-9); pap. 14.95 (0-7933-0046-0); disk 29.95 (0-7933-0048-7) Gallopade Pub Group.

— Alabama Silly Basketball Sportsmysteries, Vol. II. (Carole Marsh Alabama Bks.). (Illus.). (YA). (gr. 3-12). 1994. lib. bdg. 24.95 (0-7933-1562-X); pap. 14.95 (0-7933-1563-8); disk 29.95 (0-7933-1564-6) Gallopade Pub Group.

— Alabama Silly Football Sportsmysteries, Vol. I. (Carole Marsh Alabama Bks.). (Illus.). (YA). (gr. 3-12). 1994. lib. bdg. 24.95 (1-55609-464-7); pap. 14.95 (1-55609-463-9); disk 29.95 (0-7933-1329-5) Gallopade Pub Group.

— Alabama Silly Football Sportsmysteries, Vol. II. (Carole Marsh Alabama Bks.). (Illus.). (YA). (gr. 3-12). 1994. lib. bdg. 24.95 (0-7933-1339-2); pap. 14.95 (0-7933-1340-6); disk 29.95 (0-7933-1341-4) Gallopade Pub Group.

— Alabama Silly Trivia! (Carole Marsh Alabama Bks.). (Illus.). (YA). (gr. 3-12). 1994. lib. bdg. 24.95 (1-55609-460-4); pap. 14.95 (1-55609-038-2); disk 29.95 (0-7933-1326-0) Gallopade Pub Group.

— Alabama Timeline: A Chronology of Alabama History, Mystery, Trivia, Legend, Lore & More. (Carole Marsh Alabama Bks.). (Illus.). (J). (gr. 3-12). 1994. lib. bdg. 24.95 (0-7933-5875-2); pap. 14.95 (0-7933-5876-0); disk 29.95 (0-7933-5877-9) Gallopade Pub Group.

— Alabama's (Most Devastating!) Disasters & (Most Calamitous!) Catastrophies! (Carole Marsh Alabama Bks.). (Illus.). (YA). (gr. 3-12). 1994. lib. bdg. 24.95 (0-7933-0038-X); pap. 14.95 (0-7933-0037-1); disk 29.95 (0-7933-0039-8) Gallopade Pub Group.

— Alabama's Unsolved Mysteries (& Their "Solutions") Includes Scientific Information & Other Activities for Students. (Carole Marsh Alabama Bks.). (Illus.). (J). (gr. 3-12). 1994. lib. bdg. 24.95 (0-7933-5722-5); pap. 14.95 (0-7933-5723-3); disk 29.95 (0-7933-5724-1) Gallopade Pub Group.

— Alaska & Other State Greats (Biographies) (Carole Marsh Alaska Bks.). (Illus.). (YA). (gr. 3-12). 1994. lib. bdg. 24.95 (1-55609-483-3); pap. 14.95 (1-55609-482-5); disk 29.95 (0-7933-1354-6) Gallopade Pub Group.

— Alaska Bandits, Bushwackers, Outlaws, Crooks, Devils, Ghosts, Desperadoes & Other Assorted & Sundry Characters! (Carole Marsh Alaska Bks.). (Illus.). (YA). (gr. 3-12). 1994. lib. bdg. 24.95 (0-7933-0094-0); pap. 14.95 (0-7933-0093-2); disk 29.95 (0-7933-0095-9) Gallopade Pub Group.

— The Alaska Bookstore Book: A Surprising Guide to Our State's Bookstores & Their Specialties for Students, Teachers, Writers & Publishers. (Carole Marsh Alaska Bks.). (Illus.). 1994. lib. bdg. 24.95 (0-7933-2858-6); pap. 14.95 (0-7933-2859-4); disk 29.95 (0-7933-2860-8) Gallopade Pub Group.

— Alaska Classic Christmas Trivia: Stories, Recipes, Activities, Legends, Lore & More! (Carole Marsh Alaska Bks.). (Illus.). (YA). (gr. 3-12). 1994. lib. bdg. 24.95 (0-7933-0097-5); pap. 14.95 (0-7933-0096-7); disk 29.95 (0-7933-0098-3) Gallopade Pub Group.

— Alaska Coastales. (Carole Marsh Alaska Bks.). (J). 1994. lib. bdg. 24.95 (0-7933-7266-6) Gallopade Pub Group.

— Alaska Coastales. (Carole Marsh Alaska Bks.). (Illus.). (YA). (gr. 3-12). 1994. lib. bdg. 24.95 (1-55609-479-5); pap. 14.95 (1-55609-478-7); disk 29.95 (0-7933-1353-8) Gallopade Pub Group.

— Alaska "Crinkum-Crankum" A Funny Word Book about Our State. (Carole Marsh Alaska Bks.). (Illus.). (J). 1994. lib. bdg. 24.95 (0-7933-4813-7); pap. 14.95 (0-7933-4814-5); disk 29.95 (0-7933-4815-3) Gallopade Pub Group.

— Alaska Dingbats! Bk. 1: A Fun Book of Games, Stories, Activities & More about Our State That's All in Code! for You to Decipher. (Carole Marsh Alaska Bks.). (Illus.). (J). (gr. 3-12). 1994. lib. bdg. 24.95 (0-7933-3776-3); pap. 14.95 (0-7933-3777-1); disk 29.95 (0-7933-3778-X) Gallopade Pub Group.

— Alaska Festival Fun for Kids! (Carole Marsh Alaska Bks.). (Illus.). (YA). (gr. 3-12). 1994. lib. bdg. 24.95 (0-7933-3929-4); pap. 14.95 (0-7933-3930-8); disk 29.95 (0-7933-3931-6) Gallopade Pub Group.

— The Alaska Hot Air Balloon Mystery. (Carole Marsh Alaska Bks.). (Illus.). (J). (gr. 2-9). 1994. 24.95 (0-7933-2327-4); pap. 14.95 (0-7933-2328-2); disk 29.95 (0-7933-2329-0) Gallopade Pub Group.

— Alaska Jeopardy! Answers & Questions about Our State! (Carole Marsh Alaska Bks.). (Illus.). (J). (gr. 3-12). 1994. lib. bdg. 24.95 (0-7933-4082-9); pap. 14.95 (0-7933-4083-7); disk 29.95 (0-7933-4084-5) Gallopade Pub Group.

— Alaska "Jography" A Fun Run Thru Our State! (Carole Marsh Alaska Bks.). (Illus.). (YA). (gr. 3-12). 1994. lib. bdg. 24.95 (1-55609-473-6); pap. 14.95 (1-55609-472-8); disk 29.95 (0-7933-1343-0) Gallopade Pub Group.

— Alaska Kid's Cookbook: Recipes, How-to, History, Lore & More! (Carole Marsh Alaska Bks.). (Illus.). (YA). (gr. 3-12). 1994. lib. bdg. 24.95 (0-7933-0106-8); pap. 14.95 (0-7933-0105-X); disk 29.95 (0-7933-0107-6) Gallopade Pub Group.

— The Alaska Library Book: A Surprising Guide to the Unusual Special Collections in Libraries Across Our State for Students, Teachers, Writers & Publishers - Includes Reproducible Mailing Labels Plus Activities for Young People! (Carole Marsh Alaska Bks.). (Illus.). 1994. lib. bdg. 24.95 (0-7933-3011-4); pap. 14.95 (0-7933-3012-2); disk 29.95 (0-7933-3013-0) Gallopade Pub Group.

— The Alaska Media Book: A Surprising Guide to the Amazing Print, Broadcast & Online Media of Our State for Students, Teachers, Writers & Publishers - Includes Reproducible Mailing Labels Plus Activities for Young People! (Carole Marsh Alaska Bks.). (Illus.). 1994. lib. bdg. 24.95 (0-7933-3164-1); pap. 14.95 (0-7933-3165-X); disk 29.95 (0-7933-3166-8) Gallopade Pub Group.

— The Alaska Mystery Van Takes Off! Book 1: Handicapped Alaska Kids Sneak Off on a Big Adventure. (Carole Marsh Alaska Bks.). (Illus.). (J). (gr. 3-12). 1994. 24.95 (*0-7933-4967-2*); pap. 14.95 (*0-7933-4968-0*); disk 29.95 (*0-7933-4969-9*) Gallopade Pub Group.

— Alaska Quiz Bowl Crash Course! (Carole Marsh Alaska Bks.). (Illus.). (YA). (gr. 3-12). 1994. lib. bdg. 24.95 (*1-55609-481-7*); pap. 14.95 (*1-55609-480-9*); disk 29.95 (*0-7933-1352-X*) Gallopade Pub Group.

— Alaska Rollercoasters! (Carole Marsh Alaska Bks.). (Illus.). (YA). (gr. 3-12). 1994. lib. bdg. 24.95 (*0-7933-5227-4*); pap. 14.95 (*0-7933-5228-2*); disk 29.95 (*0-7933-5229-0*) Gallopade Pub Group.

— Alaska School Trivia: An Amazing & Fascinating Look at Our State's Teachers, Schools & Students! (Carole Marsh Alaska Bks.). (Illus.). (YA). (gr. 3-12). 1994. lib. bdg. 24.95 (*0-7933-0103-3*); pap. 14.95 (*0-7933-0102-5*); disk 29.95 (*0-7933-0104-1*) Gallopade Pub Group.

— Alaska Silly Basketball Sportsmysteries, Vol. I. (Carole Marsh Alaska Bks.). (Illus.). (YA). (gr. 3-12). 1994. lib. bdg. 24.95 (*0-7933-0100-9*); pap. 14.95 (*0-7933-0099-1*); disk 29.95 (*0-7933-0101-7*) Gallopade Pub Group.

— Alaska Silly Basketball Sportsmysteries, Vol. II. (Carole Marsh Alaska Bks.). (Illus.). (YA). (gr. 3-12). 1994. lib. bdg. 24.95 (*0-7933-1565-4*); pap. 14.95 (*0-7933-1566-2*); disk 29.95 (*0-7933-1567-0*) Gallopade Pub Group.

— Alaska Silly Football Sportsmysteries, Vol. I. (Carole Marsh Alaska Bks.). (Illus.). (YA). (gr. 3-12). 1994. lib. bdg. 24.95 (*1-55609-477-9*); pap. 14.95 (*1-55609-476-0*); disk 29.95 (*0-7933-1345-7*) Gallopade Pub Group.

— Alaska Silly Football Sportsmysteries, Vol. II. (Carole Marsh Alaska Bks.). (Illus.). (YA). (gr. 3-12). 1994. lib. bdg. 24.95 (*0-7933-1346-5*); pap. 14.95 (*0-7933-1347-3*); disk 29.95 (*0-7933-1348-1*) Gallopade Pub Group.

— Alaska Silly Trivia! (Carole Marsh Alaska Bks.). (Illus.). (YA). (gr. 3-12). 1994. lib. bdg. 24.95 (*1-55609-471-X*); pap. 14.95 (*1-55609-470-1*); disk 29.95 (*0-7933-1342-2*) Gallopade Pub Group.

— Alaska Timeline: A Chronology of Alaska History, Mystery, Trivia, Legend, Lore & More. (Carole Marsh Alaska Bks.). (Illus.). (J). (gr. 3-12). 1994. lib. bdg. 24.95 (*0-7933-5878-7*); pap. 14.95 (*0-7933-5879-5*); disk 29.95 (*0-7933-5880-9*) Gallopade Pub Group.

— Alaska's (Most Devastating!) Disasters & (Most Calamitous!) Catastrophies! (Carole Marsh Alaska Bks.). (Illus.). (YA). (gr. 3-12). 1994. lib. bdg. 24.95 (*0-7933-0091-6*); pap. 14.95 (*0-7933-0090-8*); disk 29.95 (*0-7933-0092-4*) Gallopade Pub Group.

— Alaska's Unsolved Mysteries (& Their "Solutions") Includes Scientific Information & Other Activities for Students. (Carole Marsh Alaska Bks.). (Illus.). (J). (gr. 3-12). 1994. lib. bdg. 24.95 (*0-7933-5725-X*); pap. 14.95 (*0-7933-5726-8*); disk 29.95 (*0-7933-5727-6*) Gallopade Pub Group.

— Arizona: A(dama) to Z(oroaster) (Carole Marsh Arizona Bks.). (J). 1994. lib. bdg. 24.95 (*0-7933-7317-4*); pap. text ed. 14.95 (*0-7933-7316-6*); disk 29.95 (*0-7933-7318-2*) Gallopade Pub Group.

— Arizona & Other State Greats (Biographies) (Carole Marsh Arizona Bks.). (Illus.). (YA). (gr. 3-12). 1994. lib. bdg. 24.95 (*1-55609-507-4*); pap. 14.95 (*1-55609-506-6*); disk 29.95 (*0-7933-1373-2*) Gallopade Pub Group.

— Arizona Bandits, Bushwackers, Outlaws, Crooks, Devils, Ghosts, Desperadoes & Other Assorted & Sundry Characters! (Carole Marsh Arizona Bks.). (Illus.). (YA). (gr. 3-12). 1994. lib. bdg. 24.95 (*0-7933-0118-1*); pap. 14.95 (*0-7933-0117-3*); disk 29.95 (*0-7933-0119-X*) Gallopade Pub Group.

— The Arizona Bookstore Book: A Surprising Guide to Our State's Bookstores & Their Specialties for Students, Teachers, Writers & Publishers. (Carole Marsh Arizona Bks.). (Illus.). 1994. lib. bdg. 24.95 (*0-7933-2861-6*); pap. 14.95 (*0-7933-2862-4*); disk 29.95 (*0-7933-2863-2*) Gallopade Pub Group.

— Arizona Classic Christmas Trivia: Stories, Recipes, Activities, Legends, Lore & More! (Carole Marsh Arizona Bks.). (Illus.). (YA). (gr. 3-12). 1994. lib. bdg. 24.95 (*0-7933-0121-1*); pap. 14.95 (*0-7933-0120-3*); disk 29.95 (*0-7933-0122-X*) Gallopade Pub Group.

— Arizona Coastales! (Carole Marsh Arizona Bks.). (J). 1994. lib. bdg. 24.95 (*0-7933-7267-4*) Gallopade Pub Group.

— Arizona Coastales! (Carole Marsh Arizona Bks.). (Illus.). (YA). (gr. 3-12). 1994. lib. bdg. 24.95 (*1-55609-503-1*); pap. 14.95 (*1-55609-502-3*); disk 29.95 (*0-7933-1369-4*) Gallopade Pub Group.

— Arizona "Crinkum-Crankum" A Funny Word Book about Our State. (Carole Marsh Arizona Bks.). (Illus.). (J). 1994. lib. bdg. 24.95 (*0-7933-4816-1*); pap. 14.95 (*0-7933-4817-X*); disk 29.95 (*0-7933-4818-8*) Gallopade Pub Group.

— Arizona Dingbats! Bk. 1: A Fun Book of Games, Stories, Activities & More about Our State That's All in Code! for You to Decipher. (Carole Marsh Arizona Bks.). (Illus.). (J). (gr. 3-12). 1994. lib. bdg. 24.95 (*0-7933-3779-8*); pap. 14.95 (*0-7933-3780-1*); disk 29.95 (*0-7933-3781-X*) Gallopade Pub Group.

— Arizona Festival Fun for Kids! (Carole Marsh Arizona Bks.). (Illus.). (YA). (gr. 3-12). 1994. lib. bdg. 24.95 (*0-7933-3932-4*); pap. 14.95 (*0-7933-3933-2*); disk 29.95 (*0-7933-3934-0*) Gallopade Pub Group.

— The Arizona Hot Air Balloon Mystery. (Carole Marsh Arizona Bks.). (Illus.). (J). (gr. 2-9). 1994. 24.95 (*0-7933-2336-3*); pap. 14.95 (*0-7933-2337-1*); disk 29.95 (*0-7933-2338-X*) Gallopade Pub Group.

— Arizona Jeopardy! Answers & Questions about Our State! (Carole Marsh Arizona Bks.). (Illus.). (J). (gr. 3-12). 1994. lib. bdg. 24.95 (*0-7933-4085-3*); pap. 14.95 (*0-7933-4086-1*); disk 29.95 (*0-7933-4087-X*) Gallopade Pub Group.

— Arizona "Jography" A Fun Run Thru Our State! (Carole Marsh Arizona Bks.). (Illus.). (YA). (gr. 3-12). 1994. lib. bdg. 24.95 (*1-55609-498-1*); pap. 14.95 (*1-55609-497-3*); disk 29.95 (*0-7933-1359-7*) Gallopade Pub Group.

— Arizona Kid's Cookbook: Recipes, How-to, History, Lore & More! (Carole Marsh Arizona Bks.). (Illus.). (YA). (gr. 3-12). 1994. lib. bdg. 24.95 (*0-7933-0130-0*); pap. 14.95 (*0-7933-0129-7*); disk 29.95 (*0-7933-0131-9*) Gallopade Pub Group.

— The Arizona Library Book: A Surprising Guide to the Unusual Special Collections in Libraries Across Our State for Students, Teachers, Writers & Publishers - Includes Reproducible Mailing Labels Plus Activities for Young People! (Carole Marsh Arizona Bks.). (Illus.). 1994. lib. bdg. 24.95 (*0-7933-3014-9*); pap. 14.95 (*0-7933-3015-7*); disk 29.95 (*0-7933-3016-5*) Gallopade Pub Group.

— The Arizona Media Book: A Surprising Guide to the Amazing Print, Broadcast & Online Media of Our State for Students, Teachers, Writers & Publishers - Includes Reproducible Mailing Labels Plus Activities for Young People! (Carole Marsh Arizona Bks.). (Illus.). 1994. lib. bdg. 24.95 (*0-7933-3167-6*); pap. 14.95 (*0-7933-3168-4*); disk 29.95 (*0-7933-3169-2*) Gallopade Pub Group.

— The Arizona Mystery Van Takes Off! Book 1: Handicapped Arizona Kids Sneak Off on a Big Adventure. (Carole Marsh Arizona Bks.). (Illus.). (J). (gr. 3-12). 1994. 24.95 (*0-7933-4970-2*); pap. 14.95 (*0-7933-4971-0*); disk 29.95 (*0-7933-4972-9*) Gallopade Pub Group.

— Arizona Quiz Bowl Crash Course! (Carole Marsh Arizona Bks.). (Illus.). (YA). (gr. 3-12). 1994. lib. bdg. 24.95 (*1-55609-505-8*); pap. 14.95 (*1-55609-504-X*); disk 29.95 (*0-7933-1368-6*) Gallopade Pub Group.

— Arizona Rollercoasters! (Carole Marsh Arizona Bks.). (Illus.). (YA). (gr. 3-12). 1994. lib. bdg. 24.95 (*0-7933-5230-4*); pap. 14.95 (*0-7933-5231-2*); disk 29.95 (*0-7933-5232-0*) Gallopade Pub Group.

— Arizona School Trivia: An Amazing & Fascinating Look at Our State's Teachers, Schools & Students! (Carole Marsh Arizona Bks.). (Illus.). (YA). (gr. 3-12). 1994. lib. bdg. 24.95 (*0-7933-0127-0*); pap. 14.95 (*0-7933-0126-2*); disk 29.95 (*0-685-45932-2*) Gallopade Pub Group.

— Arizona Silly Basketball Sportsmysteries, Vol. I. (Carole Marsh Arizona Bks.). (Illus.). (YA). (gr. 3-12). 1994. lib. bdg. 24.95 (*0-7933-0124-6*); pap. 14.95 (*0-7933-0123-8*); disk 29.95 (*0-7933-0125-4*) Gallopade Pub Group.

— Arizona Silly Basketball Sportsmysteries, Vol. II. (Carole Marsh Arizona Bks.). (Illus.). (YA). (gr. 3-12). 1994. lib. bdg. 24.95 (*0-7933-1568-9*); pap. 14.95 (*0-7933-1569-7*); disk 29.95 (*0-7933-1570-0*) Gallopade Pub Group.

— Arizona Silly Football Sportsmysteries, Vol. I. (Carole Marsh Arizona Bks.). (Illus.). (YA). (gr. 3-12). 1994. lib. bdg. 24.95 (*1-55609-501-5*); pap. 14.95 (*1-55609-500-7*); disk 29.95 (*0-7933-1361-9*) Gallopade Pub Group.

— Arizona Silly Football Sportsmysteries, Vol. II. (Carole Marsh Arizona Bks.). (Illus.). (YA). (gr. 3-12). 1994. lib. bdg. 24.95 (*0-7933-1362-7*); pap. 14.95 (*0-7933-1363-5*); disk 29.95 (*0-7933-1364-3*) Gallopade Pub Group.

— Arizona Silly Trivia! (Carole Marsh Arizona Bks.). (Illus.). (YA). (gr. 3-12). 1994. lib. bdg. 24.95 (*1-55609-496-5*); pap. 14.95 (*1-55609-495-7*); disk 29.95 (*0-7933-1358-9*) Gallopade Pub Group.

— Arizona Timeline: A Chronology of Arizona History, Mystery, Trivia, Legend, Lore & More. (Carole Marsh Arizona Bks.). (Illus.). (J). (gr. 3-12). 1994. lib. bdg. 24.95 (*0-7933-5881-7*); pap. 14.95 (*0-7933-5882-5*); disk 29.95 (*0-7933-5883-3*) Gallopade Pub Group.

— Arizona's (Most Devastating!) Disasters & (Most Calamitous!) Catastrophies! (Carole Marsh Arizona Bks.). (Illus.). (YA). (gr. 3-12). 1994. lib. bdg. 24.95 (*0-7933-0115-7*); pap. 14.95 (*0-7933-0114-9*); disk 29.95 (*0-7933-0116-5*) Gallopade Pub Group.

— Arizona's Unsolved Mysteries (& Their "Solutions") Includes Scientific Information & Other Activities for Students. (Carole Marsh Arizona Bks.). (Illus.). (J). (gr. 3-12). 1994. lib. bdg. 24.95 (*0-7933-5728-4*); pap. 14.95 (*0-7933-5729-2*); disk 29.95 (*0-7933-5730-6*) Gallopade Pub Group.

— Arkansas & Other State Greats (Biographies) (Carole Marsh Arkansas Bks.). (Illus.). (YA). (gr. 3-12). 1994. lib. bdg. 24.95 (*1-55609-494-9*); pap. 14.95 (*1-55609-493-0*); disk 29.95 (*0-7933-1389-9*) Gallopade Pub Group.

— Arkansas Bandits, Bushwackers, Outlaws, Crooks, Devils, Ghosts, Desperadoes & Other Assorted & Sundry Characters! (Carole Marsh Arkansas Bks.). (Illus.). (YA). (gr. 3-12). 1994. lib. bdg. 24.95 (*0-7933-0142-4*); pap. 14.95 (*0-7933-0141-6*); disk 29.95 (*0-7933-0143-2*) Gallopade Pub Group.

— The Arkansas Bookstore Book: A Surprising Guide to Our State's Bookstores & Their Specialties for Students, Teachers, Writers & Publishers. (Carole Marsh Arkansas Bks.). (Illus.). 1994. lib. bdg. 24.95 (*0-7933-2864-0*); pap. 14.95 (*0-7933-2865-9*); disk 29.95 (*0-7933-2866-7*) Gallopade Pub Group.

— Arkansas Classic Christmas Trivia: Stories, Recipes, Activities, Legends, Lore & More! (Carole Marsh Arkansas Bks.). (Illus.). (YA). (gr. 3-12). 1994. lib. bdg. 24.95 (*0-7933-0145-9*); pap. 14.95 (*0-7933-0144-0*); disk 29.95 (*0-7933-0146-7*) Gallopade Pub Group.

— Arkansas Coastales! (Carole Marsh Arkansas Bks.). (J). 1994. lib. bdg. 24.95 (*0-7933-7268-2*) Gallopade Pub Group.

— Arkansas Coastales! (Carole Marsh Arkansas Bks.). (Illus.). (YA). (gr. 3-12). 1994. lib. bdg. 24.95 (*1-55609-490-6*); pap. 14.95 (*1-55609-489-2*); disk 29.95 (*0-7933-1385-6*) Gallopade Pub Group.

— Arkansas "Crinkum-Crankum" A Funny Word Book about Our State. (Carole Marsh Arkansas Bks.). (Illus.). (J). 1994. lib. bdg. 24.95 (*0-7933-4819-6*); pap. 14.95 (*0-7933-4820-X*); disk 29.95 (*0-7933-4821-8*) Gallopade Pub Group.

— Arkansas Dingbats! Bk. 1: A Fun Book of Games, Stories, Activities & More about Our State That's All in Code! for You to Decipher. (Carole Marsh Arkansas Bks.). (Illus.). (J). (gr. 3-12). 1994. lib. bdg. 24.95 (*0-7933-3782-8*); pap. 14.95 (*0-7933-3783-6*); disk 29.95 (*0-7933-3784-4*) Gallopade Pub Group.

— Arkansas Festival for Kids! (Carole Marsh Arkansas Bks.). (Illus.). (YA). (gr. 3-12). 1994. lib. bdg. 24.95 (*0-7933-3935-9*); pap. 14.95 (*0-7933-3936-7*); disk 29.95 (*0-7933-3937-5*) Gallopade Pub Group.

— The Arkansas Hot Air Balloon Mystery. (Carole Marsh Arkansas Bks.). (Illus.). (J). (gr. 2-9). 1994. 24.95 (*0-7933-2345-2*); pap. 14.95 (*0-7933-2346-0*); disk 29.95 (*0-7933-2347-9*) Gallopade Pub Group.

— Arkansas Jeopardy! Answers & Questions about Our State! (Carole Marsh Arkansas Bks.). (Illus.). (J). (gr. 3-12). 1994. lib. bdg. 24.95 (*0-7933-4088-8*); pap. 14.95 (*0-7933-4089-6*); disk 29.95 (*0-7933-4090-X*) Gallopade Pub Group.

— Arkansas "Jography" A Fun Run Thru Our State! (Carole Marsh Arkansas Bks.). (Illus.). (YA). (gr. 3-12). 1994. lib. bdg. 24.95 (*1-55609-485-X*); pap. 14.95 (*1-55609-088-9*); disk 29.95 (*0-7933-1375-9*) Gallopade Pub Group.

— Arkansas Kid's Cookbook: Recipes, How-to, History, Lore & More! (Carole Marsh Arkansas Bks.). (Illus.). (YA). (gr. 3-12). 1994. lib. bdg. 24.95 (*0-7933-0154-8*); pap. 14.95 (*0-7933-0153-X*); disk 29.95 (*0-7933-0155-6*) Gallopade Pub Group.

— The Arkansas Library Book: A Surprising Guide to the Unusual Special Collections in Libraries Across Our State for Students, Teachers, Writers & Publishers - Includes Reproducible Mailing Labels Plus Activities for Young People! (Carole Marsh Arkansas Bks.). (Illus.). 1994. lib. bdg. 24.95 (*0-7933-3017-3*); pap. 14.95 (*0-7933-3018-1*); disk 29.95 (*0-7933-3019-X*) Gallopade Pub Group.

— The Arkansas Media Book: A Surprising Guide to the Amazing Print, Broadcast & Online Media of Our State for Students, Teachers, Writers & Publishers - Includes Reproducible Mailing Labels Plus Activities for Young People! (Carole Marsh Arkansas Bks.). (Illus.). 1994. lib. bdg. 24.95 (*0-7933-3170-6*); pap. 14.95 (*0-7933-3171-4*); disk 29.95 (*0-7933-3172-2*) Gallopade Pub Group.

— The Arkansas Mystery Van Takes Off! Book 1: Handicapped Arkansas Kids Sneak Off on a Big Adventure. (Carole Marsh Arkansas Bks.). (Illus.). (J). (gr. 3-12). 1994. 24.95 (*0-7933-4973-7*); pap. 14.95 (*0-7933-4974-5*); disk 29.95 (*0-7933-4975-3*) Gallopade Pub Group.

— Arkansas Quiz Bowl Crash Course! (Carole Marsh Arkansas Bks.). (Illus.). (YA). (gr. 3-12). 1994. lib. bdg. 24.95 (*1-55609-492-2*); pap. 14.95 (*1-55609-491-4*); disk 29.95 (*0-7933-1384-8*) Gallopade Pub Group.

— Arkansas Rollercoasters! (Carole Marsh Arkansas Bks.). (Illus.). (YA). (gr. 3-12). 1994. lib. bdg. 24.95 (*0-7933-5233-9*); pap. 14.95 (*0-7933-5234-7*); disk 29.95 (*0-7933-5235-5*) Gallopade Pub Group.

— Arkansas School Trivia: An Amazing & Fascinating Look at Our State's Teachers, Schools & Students! (Carole Marsh Arkansas Bks.). (Illus.). (YA). (gr. 3-12). 1994. lib. bdg. 24.95 (*0-7933-0151-3*); pap. 14.95 (*0-7933-0150-5*); disk 29.95 (*0-7933-0152-1*) Gallopade Pub Group.

— Arkansas Silly Basketball Sportsmysteries, Vol. I. (Carole Marsh Arkansas Bks.). (Illus.). (YA). (gr. 3-12). 1994. lib. bdg. 24.95 (*0-7933-0149-1*); pap. 14.95 (*0-7933-0147-5*); disk 29.95 (*0-685-45933-0*) Gallopade Pub Group.

— Arkansas Silly Basketball Sportsmysteries, Vol. II. (Carole Marsh Arkansas Bks.). (Illus.). (YA). (gr. 3-12). 1994. lib. bdg. 24.95 (*0-7933-1571-9*); pap. 14.95 (*0-685-45934-9*); disk 29.95 (*0-7933-1573-5*) Gallopade Pub Group.

— Arkansas Silly Football Sportsmysteries, Vol. I. (Carole Marsh Arkansas Bks.). (Illus.). (YA). (gr. 3-12). 1994. lib. bdg. 24.95 (*1-55609-488-4*); pap. 14.95 (*1-55609-487-6*); disk 29.95 (*0-7933-1377-5*) Gallopade Pub Group.

— Arkansas Silly Football Sportsmysteries, Vol. II. (Carole Marsh Arkansas Bks.). (Illus.). (YA). (gr. 3-12). 1994. lib. bdg. 24.95 (*0-7933-1378-3*); pap. 14.95 (*0-7933-1379-1*); disk 29.95 (*0-7933-1380-5*) Gallopade Pub Group.

— Arkansas Silly Trivia! (Carole Marsh Arkansas Bks.). (Illus.). (YA). (gr. 3-12). 1994. lib. bdg. 24.95 (*1-55609-484-1*); pap. 14.95 (*1-55609-083-8*); disk 29.95 (*0-7933-1374-0*) Gallopade Pub Group.

— Arkansas Timeline: A Chronology of Arkansas History, Mystery, Trivia, Legend, Lore & More. (Carole Marsh Arkansas Bks.). (Illus.). (J). (gr. 3-12). 1994. lib. bdg. 24.95 (*0-7933-5884-1*); pap. 14.95 (*0-7933-5885-X*); disk 29.95 (*0-7933-5886-8*) Gallopade Pub Group.

— Arkansas's (Most Devastating!) Disasters & (Most Calamitous!) Catastrophies! (Carole Marsh Arkansas Bks.). (Illus.). (YA). (gr. 3-12). 1994. lib. bdg. 24.95 (*0-7933-0139-4*); pap. 14.95 (*0-7933-0138-6*); disk 29.95 (*0-7933-0140-8*) Gallopade Pub Group.

— Arkansas's Unsolved Mysteries (& Their "Solutions") Includes Scientific Information & Other Activities for Students. (Carole Marsh Arkansas Bks.). (Illus.). (J). (gr. 3-12). 1994. lib. bdg. 24.95 (*0-7933-5731-4*); pap. 14.95 (*0-7933-5732-2*); disk 29.95 (*0-7933-5733-0*) Gallopade Pub Group.

— Astronomy for Kids: Milky Way & Mars Bars. (Quantum Leap Ser.). (Illus.). (J). 1994. 24.95 (*0-7933-0012-6*); pap. 14.95 (*0-7933-0013-4*); disk 29.95 (*0-7933-0014-2*) Gallopade Pub Group.

— Autumn: Silly Trivia. (Quantum Leap Ser.). (Orig.). (J). (gr. 2-6). 1994. 24.95 (*1-55609-274-1*) Gallopade Pub Group.

— Autumn: Silly Trivia. (Quantum Leap Ser.). (Orig.). (J). (gr. 2-6). 1994. pap. 14.95 (*0-685-14606-5*) Gallopade Pub Group.

— Avast, Ye Slobs! Alabama Pirate Trivia. (Carole Marsh Alabama Bks.). (Illus.). (YA). (gr. 3-12). 1994. lib. bdg. 24.95 (*0-7933-0088-6*); pap. 14.95 (*0-7933-0087-8*); disk 29.95 (*0-7933-0089-4*) Gallopade Pub Group.

— Avast, Ye Slobs! Alaska Pirate Trivia. (Carole Marsh Alaska Bks.). (Illus.). (YA). (gr. 3-12). 1994. lib. bdg. 24.95 (*0-7933-0112-2*); pap. 14.95 (*0-7933-0111-4*); disk 29.95 (*0-7933-0113-0*) Gallopade Pub Group.

— Avast, Ye Slobs! Arizona Pirate Trivia. (Carole Marsh Arizona Bks.). (Illus.). (YA). (gr. 3-12). 1994. lib. bdg. 24.95 (*0-7933-0136-X*); pap. 14.95 (*0-7933-0135-1*); disk 29.95 (*0-7933-0137-8*) Gallopade Pub Group.

— Avast, Ye Slobs! Arkansas Pirate Trivia. (Carole Marsh Arkansas Bks.). (Illus.). (YA). (gr. 3-12). 1994. lib. bdg. 24.95 (*0-7933-0160-2*); pap. 14.95 (*0-7933-0159-9*); disk 29.95 (*0-7933-0161-0*) Gallopade Pub Group.

— Avast, Ye Slobs! California Pirate Trivia. (Carole Marsh California Bks.). (Illus.). (YA). (gr. 3-12). 1994. lib. bdg. 24.95 (*0-7933-0184-X*); pap. 14.95 (*0-7933-0183-1*); disk 29.95 (*0-7933-0185-8*) Gallopade Pub Group.

— Avast, Ye Slobs! Colorado Pirate Trivia. (Carole Marsh Colorado Bks.). (Illus.). (YA). (gr. 3-12). 1994. lib. bdg. 24.95 (*0-7933-0208-0*); pap. 14.95 (*0-7933-0207-2*); disk 29.95 (*0-7933-0209-9*) Gallopade Pub Group.

— Avast, Ye Slobs! Connecticut Pirate Trivia. (Carole Marsh Connecticut Bks.). (Illus.). (YA). (gr. 3-12). 1994. lib. bdg. 24.95 (*0-7933-0232-3*); pap. 14.95 (*0-7933-0231-5*); disk 29.95 (*0-7933-0233-1*) Gallopade Pub Group.

— Avast, Ye Slobs! Delaware Pirate Trivia. (Carole Marsh Delaware Bks.). (Illus.). (YA). (gr. 3-12). 1994. lib. bdg. 24.95 (*0-7933-0256-0*); pap. 14.95 (*0-7933-0255-2*); disk 29.95 (*0-7933-0257-9*) Gallopade Pub Group.

— Avast, Ye Slobs! Florida Pirate Trivia. (Carole Marsh Florida Bks.). (Illus.). (YA). (gr. 3-12). 1994. lib. bdg. 24.95 (*0-7933-0304-4*); pap. 14.95 (*0-7933-0303-6*); disk 29.95 (*0-7933-0305-2*) Gallopade Pub Group.

— Avast, Ye Slobs! Georgia Pirate Trivia. (Carole Marsh Georgia Bks.). (Illus.). (YA). (gr. 3-12). 1994. lib. bdg. 24.95 (*0-7933-0328-1*); pap. 14.95 (*0-7933-0327-3*); disk 29.95 (*0-7933-0329-X*) Gallopade Pub Group.

— Avast, Ye Slobs! Hawaii Pirate Trivia. (Carole Marsh Hawaii Bks.). (Illus.). (YA). (gr. 3-12). 1994. lib. bdg. 24.95 (*0-7933-0352-4*); pap. 14.95 (*0-7933-0351-6*); disk 29.95 (*0-7933-0353-2*) Gallopade Pub Group.

— Avast, Ye Slobs! Idaho Pirate Trivia. (Carole Marsh Idaho Bks.). (Illus.). (YA). (gr. 3-12). 1994. lib. bdg. 24.95 (*0-7933-0376-1*); pap. 14.95 (*0-7933-0375-3*); disk 29.95 (*0-7933-0377-X*) Gallopade Pub Group.

— Avast, Ye Slobs! Illinois Pirate Trivia. (Carole Marsh Illinois Bks.). (Illus.). (YA). (gr. 3-12). 1994. lib. bdg. 24.95 (*0-7933-0400-8*); pap. 14.95 (*0-7933-0399-0*); disk 29.95 (*0-7933-0401-6*) Gallopade Pub Group.

— Avast, Ye Slobs! Indiana Pirate Trivia. (Carole Marsh Indiana Bks.). (Illus.). (YA). (gr. 3-12). 1994. lib. bdg. 24.95 (*0-7933-0424-5*); pap. 14.95 (*0-7933-0423-7*); disk 29.95 (*0-685-45926-8*) Gallopade Pub Group.

— Avast, Ye Slobs! Iowa Private Trivia. (Carole Marsh Iowa Bks.). (Illus.). (YA). (gr. 3-12). 1994. lib. bdg. 24.95 (*0-7933-0448-2*); pap. 14.95 (*0-7933-0447-4*); disk 29.95 (*0-7933-0449-0*) Gallopade Pub Group.

— Avast, Ye Slobs! Kansas Pirate Trivia. (Carole Marsh Kansas Bks.). (Illus.). (YA). (gr. 3-12). 1994. lib. bdg. 24.95 (*0-7933-0472-5*); pap. 14.95 (*0-7933-0471-7*); disk 29.95 (*0-7933-0473-3*) Gallopade Pub Group.

— Avast, Ye Slobs! Kentucky Pirate Trivia. (Carole Marsh Kentucky Bks.). (Illus.). (J). (gr. 3-8). 1994. lib. bdg. 24.95 (*0-7933-0496-2*); pap. 14.95 (*0-7933-0495-4*); disk 29.95 (*0-685-45938-1*) Gallopade Pub Group.

— Avast, Ye Slobs! Louisiana Pirate Trivia. (Carole Marsh Louisiana Bks.). (Illus.). (J). (gr. 3-8). 1994. lib. bdg. 24.95 (*0-7933-0520-9*); pap. 14.95 (*0-7933-0519-5*); disk 29.95 (*0-7933-0521-7*) Gallopade Pub Group.

— Avast, Ye Slobs! Maine Pirate Trivia. (Carole Marsh Maine Bks.). (Illus.). (J). (gr. 3-8). 1994. lib. bdg. 24.95 (*0-7933-0545-4*); pap. 14.95 (*0-7933-0544-6*); disk 29.95 (*0-7933-0546-2*) Gallopade Pub Group.

— Avast, Ye Slobs! Maryland Pirate Trivia. (Carole Marsh Maryland Bks.). (Illus.). (J). (gr. 3-8). 1994. lib. bdg. 24.95 (*0-7933-0569-1*); pap. 14.95 (*0-7933-0568-3*); disk 29.95 (*0-7933-0570-5*) Gallopade Pub Group.

— Avast, Ye Slobs! Massachusetts Pirate Trivia. (Carole Marsh Massachusetts Bks.). (Illus.). (J). (gr. 3-8). 1994. lib. bdg. 24.95 (*0-7933-0593-4*); pap. 14.95 (*0-7933-0592-6*); disk 29.95 (*0-7933-0594-2*) Gallopade Pub Group.

— Avast, Ye Slobs! Nevada Pirate Trivia. (Carole Marsh Nevada Bks.). (Illus.). (J). 1994. lib. bdg. 24.95 (*0-7933-0763-5*); pap. 14.95 (*0-7933-0762-7*); disk 29.95 (*0-7933-0764-3*) Gallopade Pub Group.

— Avast, Ye Slobs! New Hampshire Pirate Trivia. (Carole Marsh New Hampshire Bks.). (Illus.). (J). 1994. lib. bdg. 24.95 (*0-7933-0787-2*); pap. 14.95 (*0-7933-0786-4*); disk 29.95 (*0-7933-0788-0*) Gallopade Pub Group.

— Avast, Ye Slobs! New Jersey Pirate Trivia. (Carole Marsh New Jersey Bks.). (Illus.). (J). 1994. lib. bdg. 24.95 (*0-7933-1809-2*); pap. 14.95 (*0-7933-1810-6*); disk 29.95 (*0-7933-1811-4*) Gallopade Pub Group.

An Asterisk (*) at the beginning of an entry indicates that the title is appearing in BIP for the first time.

— Avast, Ye Slobs! New Mexico Pirate Trivia. (Carole Marsh New Mexico Bks.). (Illus.). (J). 1994. lib. bdg. 24.95 (0-7933-0811-9); pap. 14.95 (0-7933-0810-0); disk 29.95 (0-7933-0812-7) Gallopade Pub Group.
— Avast, Ye Slobs! New York Pirate Trivia. (Carole Marsh New York Bks.). (Illus.). (J). 1994. lib. bdg. 24.95 (0-7933-0835-6); pap. 14.95 (0-7933-0834-8); disk 29.95 (0-7933-0836-4) Gallopade Pub Group.
— Avast, Ye Slobs! North Carolina Pirate Trivia. (Carole Marsh North Carolina Bks.). (Illus.). (J). 1994. lib. bdg. 24.95 (0-7933-0859-3); pap. 14.95 (0-7933-0858-5); disk 29.95 (0-7933-0860-7) Gallopade Pub Group.
— Avast, Ye Slobs! North Dakota Pirate Trivia. (Carole Marsh North Dakota Bks.). (Illus.). (J). 1994. lib. bdg. 24.95 (0-7933-0883-6); pap. 14.95 (0-7933-0882-8); disk 29.95 (0-7933-0884-4) Gallopade Pub Group.
— Avast, Ye Slobs! Ohio Pirate Trivia. (Carole Marsh Ohio Bks.). (Illus.). (J). 1994. lib. bdg. 24.95 (0-7933-0908-5); pap. 14.95 (0-7933-0907-7); disk 29.95 (0-7933-0909-3) Gallopade Pub Group.
— Avast, Ye Slobs! Oklahoma Pirate Trivia. (Carole Marsh Oklahoma Bks.). (Illus.). (J). 1994. lib. bdg. 24.95 (0-7933-0932-8); pap. 14.95 (0-7933-0931-X); disk 29.95 (0-7933-0933-6) Gallopade Pub Group.
— Avast, Ye Slobs! Oregon Pirate Trivia. (Carole Marsh Oregon Bks.). (Illus.). (J). 1994. lib. bdg. 24.95 (0-7933-0956-5); pap. 14.95 (0-7933-0955-7); disk 29.95 (0-685-45979-9) Gallopade Pub Group.
— Avast, Ye Slobs! Pennsylvania Pirate Trivia. (Carole Marsh Pennsylvania Bks.). (Illus.). (J). 1994. lib. bdg. 24.95 (0-7933-0980-8); pap. 14.95 (0-7933-0979-4); disk 29.95 (0-7933-0981-6) Gallopade Pub Group.
— Avast, Ye Slobs! Rhode Island Pirate Trivia. (Carole Marsh Rhode Island Bks.). (Illus.). (J). 1994. lib. bdg. 24.95 (0-7933-1004-0); pap. 14.95 (0-7933-1003-2); disk 29.95 (0-7933-1005-9) Gallopade Pub Group.
— Avast, Ye Slobs! South Carolina Pirate Trivia. (Carole Marsh South Carolina Bks.). (Illus.). (J). 1994. lib. bdg. 24.95 (0-7933-1028-8); pap. 14.95 (0-7933-1027-X); disk 29.95 (0-7933-1029-6) Gallopade Pub Group.
— Avast, Ye Slobs! South Dakota Pirate Trivia. (Carole Marsh South Dakota Bks.). (Illus.). (J). 1994. lib. bdg. 24.95 (0-7933-1052-0); pap. 14.95 (0-7933-1051-2); disk 29.95 (0-7933-1053-9) Gallopade Pub Group.
— Avast, Ye Slobs! Tennessee Pirate Trivia. (Carole Marsh Tennessee Bks.). (Illus.). (J). 1994. lib. bdg. 24.95 (0-7933-1076-8); pap. 14.95 (0-7933-1075-X); disk 29.95 (0-7933-1077-6) Gallopade Pub Group.
— Avast, Ye Slobs! Texas Pirate Trivia. (Texas Bks.). (Illus.). (J). 1990. lib. bdg. 24.95 (0-7933-1100-4); pap. 14.95 (0-7933-1099-7); disk 29.95 (0-685-45953-5) Gallopade Pub Group.
— Avast, Ye Slobs! The Book of Silly Pirate Trivia. (Triviatime Ser.). (Illus.). (Orig.). (J). (gr. 1-12). 1994. lib. bdg. 24.95 (1-55609-281-4); pap. 14.95 (0-935326-82-0) Gallopade Pub Group.
— Avast, Ye Slobs! Utah Pirate Trivia. (Carole Marsh Utah Bks.). (Illus.). (J). 1994. lib. bdg. 24.95 (0-7933-1124-1); pap. 14.95 (0-7933-1123-3); disk 29.95 (0-7933-1125-X) Gallopade Pub Group.
— Avast, Ye Slobs! Vermont Pirate Trivia. (Carole Marsh Vermont Bks.). (Illus.). (J). 1994. lib. bdg. 24.95 (0-7933-1148-9); pap. 14.95 (0-685-45958-6); disk 29.95 (0-7933-1149-7) Gallopade Pub Group.
— Avast, Ye Slobs! Virginia Pirate Trivia. (Carole Marsh Virginia Bks.). (Illus.). (J). 1994. lib. bdg. 24.95 (0-7933-1172-1); pap. 14.95 (0-7933-1171-3); disk 29.95 (0-7933-1173-X) Gallopade Pub Group.
— Avast, Ye Slobs! Washington, D.C. (Carole Marsh Washington, D.C. Bks.). (Illus.). (YA). (gr. 3-12). 1994. lib. bdg. 24.95 (0-7933-0280-3); pap. 14.95 (0-7933-0279-X); disk 29.95 (0-7933-0281-1) Gallopade Pub Group.
— Avast, Ye Slobs! Washington Pirate Trivia. (Carole Marsh Washington Bks.). (Illus.). (J). 1994. lib. bdg. 24.95 (0-7933-1196-9); pap. 14.95 (0-7933-1195-0); disk 29.95 (0-7933-1197-7) Gallopade Pub Group.
— Avast, Ye Slobs! West Virginia Pirate Trivia. (Carole Marsh West Virginia Bks.). (Illus.). (J). 1994. lib. bdg. 24.95 (0-7933-1220-5); pap. 14.95 (0-7933-1219-1); disk 29.95 (0-7933-1221-3) Gallopade Pub Group.
— Avast, Ye Slobs! Wisconsin Pirate Trivia. (Carole Marsh Wisconsin Bks.). (Illus.). (J). 1994. lib. bdg. 24.95 (0-7933-1244-2); pap. 14.95 (0-7933-1243-4); disk 29.95 (0-7933-1245-0) Gallopade Pub Group.
— Avast, Ye Slobs! Wyoming Pirate Trivia. (Carole Marsh Wyoming Bks.). (Illus.). (J). 1994. lib. bdg. 24.95 (0-7933-1268-X); pap. 14.95 (0-7933-1267-1); disk 29.95 (0-7933-1269-8) Gallopade Pub Group.
— Avast, Ye Slobs!: Michigan Pirate Trivia. (Carole Marsh Michigan Bks.). (Illus.). (J). (gr. 3 up). 1994. lib. bdg. 24.95 (0-7933-0617-5); pap. 14.95 (0-7933-0616-7); disk 29.95 (0-7933-0618-3) Gallopade Pub Group.
— Avast, Ye Slobs!: Minnesota Pirate Trivia. (Carole Marsh Minnesota Bks.). (Illus.). (J). (gr. 3 up). 1994. lib. bdg. 24.95 (0-7933-0641-8); pap. 14.95 (0-7933-0640-X); disk 29.95 (0-7933-0642-6) Gallopade Pub Group.
— Avast, Ye Slobs!: Mississippi Pirate Trivia. (Carole Marsh Mississippi Bks.). (Illus.). (J). (gr. 3 up). 1994. lib. bdg. 24.95 (0-7933-0666-3); pap. 14.95 (0-7933-0665-5); disk 29.95 (0-7933-0667-1) Gallopade Pub Group.
— Avast, Ye Slobs!: Missouri Pirate Trivia. (Carole Marsh Missouri Bks.). (Illus.). (J). (gr. 3 up). 1994. lib. bdg. 24.95 (0-7933-0690-6); pap. 14.95 (0-7933-0689-2); disk 29.95 (0-7933-0691-4) Gallopade Pub Group.
— Avast, Ye Slobs!: Montana Pirate Trivia. (Carole Marsh Montana Bks.). (J). (gr. 3 up). 1994. lib. bdg. 24.95 (0-7933-0715-5); pap. 14.95 (0-7933-0714-7); disk 29.95 (0-7933-0716-3) Gallopade Pub Group.
— Avast, Ye Slobs!: Nebraska Pirate Trivia. (Carole Marsh Nebraska Bks.). (Illus.). (J). (gr. 3 up). 1994. lib. bdg. 24.95 (0-7933-0739-2); pap. 14.95 (0-7933-0738-4); disk 29.95 (0-7933-0740-6) Gallopade Pub Group.
— The Backyard Searcher's Extra Terrestrial Log Book. (Quantum Leap Ser.). (Illus.). (J). (gr. 4-9). 1994. lib. bdg. 24.95 (1-55609-282-2); pap. 14.95 (0-935326-27-8) Gallopade Pub Group.
— Bat Cave Mystery. (History Mystery Ser.). (Orig.). (J). (gr. 3-8). 1994. lib. bdg. 24.95 (1-55609-154-0); pap. 14.95 (0-935326-72-3) Gallopade Pub Group.
— Be a Fourth Grader Forever! How to Live, Love, & Learn with the Open-Minded Optimism, Eagerness & Joy of a Nine Year Old. 1994. 24.95 (1-55609-900-2); pap. 14.95 (1-55609-901-0) Gallopade Pub Group.
— The Beast & the Kansas Bed & Breakfast. (Carole Marsh Kansas Bks.). (J). (gr. 3-12). 1994. 24.95 (1-55609-371-3); pap. 14.95 (1-55609-372-1); disk 29.95 (1-55609-373-X) Gallopade Pub Group.
— The Beast of the Alabama Bed & Breakfast. (Carole Marsh Alabama Bks.). (Illus.). (YA). (gr. 3-12). 1994. lib. bdg. 24.95 (0-7933-1332-5); pap. 14.95 (0-7933-1331-7); disk 29.95 (0-7933-1330-9) Gallopade Pub Group.
— The Beast of the Arizona Bed & Breakfast. (Carole Marsh Arizona Bks.). (Illus.). (YA). (gr. 3-12). 1994. lib. bdg. 24.95 (0-7933-1365-1); pap. 14.95 (0-7933-1366-X); disk 29.95 (0-7933-1367-8) Gallopade Pub Group.
— The Beast of the Arkansas Bed & Breakfast. (Carole Marsh Arkansas Bks.). (Illus.). (YA). (gr. 3-12). 1994. lib. bdg. 24.95 (0-7933-1381-3); pap. 14.95 (0-7933-1382-1); disk 29.95 (0-7933-1383-X) Gallopade Pub Group.
— The Beast of the Colorado Bed & Breakfast. (Carole Marsh Colorado Bks.). (Illus.). (YA). (gr. 3-12). 1994. lib. bdg. 24.95 (0-7933-1413-5); pap. 14.95 (0-7933-1414-3); disk 29.95 (0-7933-1415-1) Gallopade Pub Group.
— The Beast of the Connecticut Bed & Breakfast. (Carole Marsh Connecticut Bks.). (Illus.). (YA). (gr. 3-12). 1994. lib. bdg. 24.95 (0-7933-1429-1); pap. 14.95 (0-7933-1430-5); disk 29.95 (0-7933-1431-3) Gallopade Pub Group.
— The Beast of the Delaware Bed & Breakfast. (Carole Marsh Delaware Bks.). (Illus.). (YA). (gr. 3-12). 1994. lib. bdg. 24.95 (0-7933-1447-X); pap. 14.95 (0-7933-1448-8); disk 29.95 (0-7933-1449-6) Gallopade Pub Group.
— The Beast of the Florida Bed & Breakfast. (Carole Marsh Florida Bks.). (Illus.). (YA). (gr. 3-12). 1994. lib. bdg. 24.95 (0-7933-1493-3); pap. 14.95 (0-7933-1494-1); disk 29.95 (0-7933-1495-X) Gallopade Pub Group.
— The Beast of the Georgia Bed & Breakfast. (Carole Marsh Georgia Bks.). (Illus.). (YA). (gr. 3-12). 1994. lib. bdg. 24.95 (0-7933-1512-3); pap. 14.95 (0-7933-1513-1); disk 29.95 (0-7933-1514-X) Gallopade Pub Group.
— The Beast of the Hawaii Bed & Breakfast. (Carole Marsh Hawaii Bks.). (Illus.). (YA). (gr. 3-12). 1994. lib. bdg. 24.95 (0-7933-1531-X); pap. 14.95 (0-7933-1532-8); disk 29.95 (0-7933-1533-6) Gallopade Pub Group.
— The Beast of the Idaho Bed & Breakfast. (Carole Marsh Idaho Bks.). (Illus.). (YA). (gr. 3-12). 1994. lib. bdg. 24.95 (0-7933-1550-6); pap. 14.95 (0-7933-1551-4); disk 29.95 (0-7933-1552-2) Gallopade Pub Group.
— The Beast of the Illinois Bed & Breakfast. (Carole Marsh Illinois Bks.). (Illus.). (YA). (gr. 3-12). 1994. lib. bdg. 24.95 (0-7933-1590-5); pap. 14.95 (0-7933-1591-3); disk 29.95 (0-7933-1592-1) Gallopade Pub Group.
— The Beast of the Indiana Bed & Breakfast. (Carole Marsh Indiana Bks.). (Illus.). (YA). (gr. 3-12). 1994. lib. bdg. 24.95 (0-7933-1609-X); pap. 14.95 (0-7933-1610-3); disk 29.95 (0-7933-1611-1) Gallopade Pub Group.
— The Beast of the Iowa Bed & Breakfast. (Carole Marsh Iowa Bks.). (Illus.). (YA). (gr. 3-12). 1994. lib. bdg. 24.95 (0-7933-1628-6); pap. 14.95 (0-7933-1629-4); disk 29.95 (0-7933-1630-8) Gallopade Pub Group.
— The Beast of the Kentucky Bed & Breakfast. (Carole Marsh Kentucky Bks.). (Illus.). (J). (gr. 3-8). 1994. lib. bdg. 24.95 (0-7933-1650-2); pap. 14.95 (0-7933-1651-0); disk 29.95 (0-7933-1652-9) Gallopade Pub Group.
— The Beast of the Louisiana Bed & Breakfast. (Carole Marsh Louisiana Bks.). (Illus.). (J). (gr. 3-8). 1994. lib. bdg. 24.95 (0-7933-1669-3); pap. 14.95 (0-7933-1670-7); disk 29.95 (0-7933-1671-5) Gallopade Pub Group.
— The Beast of the Maine Bed & Breakfast. (Carole Marsh Maine Bks.). (Illus.). (J). (gr. 3-8). 1994. lib. bdg. 24.95 (0-7933-1681-2); pap. 14.95 (0-7933-1682-0); write for info. (0-7933-1683-9) Gallopade Pub Group.
— The Beast of the Maryland Bed & Breakfast. (Carole Marsh Maryland Bks.). (Illus.). (J). (gr. 3-8). 1994. lib. bdg. 24.95 (0-7933-1690-1); pap. 14.95 (0-7933-1691-X); disk 29.95 (0-7933-1692-8) Gallopade Pub Group.
— The Beast of the Massachusetts Bed & Breakfast. (Carole Marsh Massachusetts Bks.). (Illus.). (J). (gr. 3-8). 1994. lib. bdg. 24.95 (0-7933-1699-5); pap. 14.95 (0-7933-1700-2); disk 29.95 (0-7933-1701-0) Gallopade Pub Group.
— The Beast of the Michigan Bed & Breakfast. (Carole Marsh Michigan Bks.). (Illus.). (J). (gr. 3 up). 1994. lib. bdg. 24.95 (0-7933-1708-8); pap. 14.95 (0-7933-1709-6); disk 29.95 (0-7933-1710-X) Gallopade Pub Group.
— The Beast of the Minnesota Bed & Breakfast. (Minnesota Bks.). (Illus.). (J). (gr. 3 up). 1994. lib. bdg. 24.95 (0-7933-1714-2); pap. 14.95 (0-7933-1715-0); disk 29.95 (0-7933-1716-9) Gallopade Pub Group.
— The Beast of the Mississippi Bed & Breakfast. (Mississippi Bks.). (Illus.). (J). (gr. 3 up). 1994. lib. bdg. 24.95 (0-7933-0644-2); pap. 14.95 (0-7933-1726-6); disk 29.95 (0-7933-1727-4) Gallopade Pub Group.
— The Beast of the Missouri Bed & Breakfast. (Missouri Bks.). (Illus.). (J). (gr. 3 up). 1994. lib. bdg. 24.95 (0-7933-1734-7); pap. 14.95 (0-7933-1735-5); disk 29.95 (0-685-45946-2) Gallopade Pub Group.
— The Beast of the Montana Bed & Breakfast. (Montana Bks.). (Illus.). (J). (gr. 3 up). 1994. lib. bdg. 24.95 (0-7933-1743-6); pap. 14.95 (0-7933-1744-4); disk 29.95 (0-7933-1745-2) Gallopade Pub Group.
— The Beast of the Nebraska Bed & Breakfast. (Carole Marsh Nebraska Bks.). (Illus.). (J). (gr. 3 up). 1994. lib. bdg. 24.95 (0-7933-1752-5); pap. 14.95 (0-7933-1753-3); disk 29.95 (0-7933-1754-1) Gallopade Pub Group.
— The Beast of the Nevada Bed & Breakfast. (Carole Marsh Nevada Bks.). (Illus.). (J). 1994. lib. bdg. 24.95 (0-7933-1761-4); pap. 14.95 (0-7933-1762-2); disk 29.95 (0-7933-1763-0) Gallopade Pub Group.
— The Beast of the New Hampshire Bed & Breakfast. (Carole Marsh New Hampshire Bks.). (Illus.). (J). 1994. lib. bdg. 24.95 (0-7933-1770-3); pap. 14.95 (0-7933-1771-1); disk 29.95 (0-7933-1772-X) Gallopade Pub Group.
— The Beast of the New Jersey Bed & Breakfast. (Carole Marsh New Jersey Bks.). (Illus.). (J). 1994. lib. bdg. 24.95 (0-7933-1779-7); pap. 14.95 (0-7933-1780-0); disk 29.95 (0-7933-1781-9) Gallopade Pub Group.
— The Beast of the New Mexico Bed & Breakfast. (Carole Marsh New Mexico Bks.). (Illus.). (J). 1994. lib. bdg. 24.95 (0-7933-1812-2); pap. 14.95 (0-7933-1813-0); disk 29.95 (0-7933-1814-9) Gallopade Pub Group.
— The Beast of the New York Bed & Breakfast. (Carole Marsh New York Bks.). (Illus.). (J). 1994. lib. bdg. 24.95 (0-7933-1821-1); pap. 14.95 (0-7933-1822-X); disk 29.95 (0-7933-1823-8) Gallopade Pub Group.
— The Beast of the North Dakota Bed & Breakfast. (Carole Marsh North Dakota Bks.). (Illus.). (J). 1994. lib. bdg. 24.95 (0-7933-1839-4); pap. 14.95 (0-7933-1840-8); disk 29.95 (0-7933-1841-6) Gallopade Pub Group.
— The Beast of the Ohio Bed & Breakfast. (Carole Marsh Ohio Bks.). (Illus.). (J). 1994. lib. bdg. 24.95 (0-7933-0905-0); pap. 14.95 (0-7933-1848-3); disk 29.95 (0-7933-1849-1) Gallopade Pub Group.
— The Beast of the Oklahoma Bed & Breakfast. (Carole Marsh Oklahoma Bks.). (Illus.). (J). 1994. lib. bdg. 24.95 (0-7933-1869-6); pap. 14.95 (0-7933-1870-X); disk 29.95 (0-7933-1871-8) Gallopade Pub Group.
— The Beast of the Oregon Bed & Breakfast. (Carole Marsh Oregon Bks.). (Illus.). (J). 1994. lib. bdg. 24.95 (0-7933-1901-3); pap. 14.95 (0-7933-1902-1); disk 29.95 (0-7933-1903-X) Gallopade Pub Group.
— The Beast of the Pennsylvania Bed & Breakfast. (Carole Marsh Pennsylvania Bks.). (Illus.). (J). 1994. lib. bdg. 24.95 (0-7933-1933-1); pap. 14.95 (0-7933-1934-X); disk 29.95 (0-7933-1935-8) Gallopade Pub Group.
— The Beast of the Rhode Island Bed & Breakfast. (Carole Marsh Rhode Island Bks.). (Illus.). (J). 1994. lib. bdg. 24.95 (0-7933-1965-X); pap. 14.95 (0-7933-1966-8); disk 29.95 (0-7933-1967-6) Gallopade Pub Group.
— The Beast of the South Carolina Bed & Breakfast. (Carole Marsh South Carolina Bks.). (Illus.). (J). 1994. lib. bdg. 24.95 (0-7933-1995-1); pap. 14.95 (0-7933-1996-X); disk 29.95 (0-7933-1997-8) Gallopade Pub Group.
— The Beast of the South Dakota Bed & Breakfast. (Carole Marsh South Dakota Bks.). (Illus.). (J). 1994. lib. bdg. 24.95 (0-7933-2026-7); pap. 14.95 (0-7933-2027-5); disk 29.95 (0-7933-2028-3) Gallopade Pub Group.
— The Beast of the Tennessee Bed & Breakfast. (Carole Marsh Tennessee Bks.). (Illus.). (J). 1994. lib. bdg. 24.95 (0-7933-2056-9); pap. 14.95 (0-7933-2057-7); disk 29.95 (0-7933-2058-5) Gallopade Pub Group.
— The Beast of the Texas Bed & Breakfast. (Carole Marsh Texas Bks.). (Illus.). (J). 1994. lib. bdg. 24.95 (0-7933-2086-0); pap. 14.95 (0-7933-2087-9); disk 29.95 (0-7933-2088-7) Gallopade Pub Group.
— The Beast of the Utah Bed & Breakfast. (Carole Marsh Utah Bks.). (Illus.). (J). 1994. lib. bdg. 24.95 (0-7933-2117-4); pap. 14.95 (0-7933-2118-2); disk 29.95 (0-7933-2119-0) Gallopade Pub Group.
— The Beast of the Vermont Bed & Breakfast. (Carole Marsh Vermont Bks.). (Illus.). (J). 1994. lib. bdg. 24.95 (0-7933-2149-2); pap. 14.95 (0-7933-2150-6); disk 29.95 (0-7933-2151-4) Gallopade Pub Group.
— The Beast of the Virginia Bed & Breakfast. (Carole Marsh Virginia Bks.). (Illus.). (J). 1994. lib. bdg. 24.95 (0-7933-2179-4); pap. 14.95 (0-7933-2180-8); disk 29.95 (0-7933-2181-6) Gallopade Pub Group.
— The Beast of the Washington Bed & Breakfast. (Carole Marsh Washington Bks.). (Illus.). (J). 1994. lib. bdg. 24.95 (0-7933-2212-X); pap. 14.95 (0-7933-2213-8); disk 29.95 (0-7933-2214-6) Gallopade Pub Group.
— The Beast of the Washington, D.C. Bed & Breakfast. (Carole Marsh Washington, D.C. Bks.). (Illus.). (YA). (gr. 3-12). 1994. lib. bdg. 24.95 (0-7933-1468-2); pap. 14.95 (0-7933-1469-0); disk 29.95 (0-7933-1470-4) Gallopade Pub Group.
— The Beast of the West Virginia Bed & Breakfast. (Carole Marsh West Virginia Bks.). (Illus.). (J). 1994. lib. bdg. 24.95 (0-7933-2244-8); pap. 14.95 (0-7933-2245-6); disk 29.95 (0-7933-2246-4) Gallopade Pub Group.
— The Beast of the Wisconsin Bed & Breakfast. (Carole Marsh Wisconsin Bks.). (Illus.). (J). 1994. lib. bdg. 24.95 (0-7933-2276-6); pap. 14.95 (0-7933-2277-4); disk 29.95 (0-7933-2278-2) Gallopade Pub Group.
— The Beast of the Wyoming Bed & Breakfast. (Carole Marsh Wyoming Bks.). (Illus.). (J). 1994. lib. bdg. 24.95 (0-7933-2300-2); pap. 14.95 (0-7933-2301-0); disk 29.95 (0-7933-2302-9) Gallopade Pub Group.
— The Best Book of Black Biographies. (Our Black Heritage Ser.). (J). (gr. 3-12). 1994. lib. bdg. 24.95 (1-55609-330-6); pap. 14.95 (1-55609-329-2); disk 29.95 (1-55609-331-4) Gallopade Pub Group.
— The Best of the Alaska Bed & Breakfast. (Carole Marsh Alaska Bks.). (Illus.). (YA). (gr. 3-12). 1994. lib. bdg. 24.95 (0-7933-1349-X); pap. 14.95 (0-7933-1350-3); disk 29.95 (0-7933-1351-1) Gallopade Pub Group.
— The Best of the California Bed & Breakfast. (Carole Marsh California Bks.). (Illus.). (YA). (gr. 3-12). 1994. lib. bdg. 24.95 (0-7933-1397-X); pap. 14.95 (0-7933-1398-8); disk 29.95 (0-7933-1399-6) Gallopade Pub Group.
— The Best of the North Carolina Bed & Breakfast. (Carole Marsh North Carolina Bks.). (Illus.). (J). 1994. lib. bdg. 24.95 (0-7933-1830-0); pap. 14.95 (0-7933-1831-9); disk 29.95 (0-7933-1832-7) Gallopade Pub Group.
— The Big Instruction Book of Small Business: (Alabama Edition) (Carole Marsh Alabama Bks.). (Illus.). 1994. lib. bdg. 39.95 (0-7933-2324-X); pap. 29.95 (0-7933-2779-2) Gallopade Pub Group.
— The Big Instruction Book of Small Business: (Alaska Edition) (Carole Marsh Alaska Bks.). (Illus.). 1994. lib. bdg. 39.95 (0-7933-2325-8); pap. 29.95 (0-7933-2780-6) Gallopade Pub Group.
— The Big Instruction Book of Small Business: (Arizona Edition) (Carole Marsh Arizona Bks.). (Illus.). 1994. lib. bdg. 39.95 (0-7933-2342-8); pap. 29.95 (0-7933-2781-4) Gallopade Pub Group.
— The Big Instruction Book of Small Business: (California Edition) (Carole Marsh California Bks.). (Illus.). 1994. lib. bdg. 39.95 (0-7933-2360-6); pap. 29.95 (0-7933-2782-2) Gallopade Pub Group.
— The Big Instruction Book of Small Business: (Colorado Edition) (Carole Marsh Colorado Bks.). (Illus.). 1994. lib. bdg. 39.95 (0-7933-2369-X); pap. 29.95 (0-7933-2783-0) Gallopade Pub Group.
— The Big Instruction Book of Small Business: (Connecticut Edition) (Carole Marsh Connecticut Bks.). (Illus.). 1994. lib. bdg. 39.95 (0-7933-2378-9); pap. 29.95 (0-7933-2784-9) Gallopade Pub Group.
— The Big Instruction Book of Small Business: (Delaware Edition) (Carole Marsh Delaware Bks.). (Illus.). 1994. lib. bdg. 39.95 (0-7933-2387-8); pap. 29.95 (0-7933-2785-7) Gallopade Pub Group.
— The Big Instruction Book of Small Business: (Florida Edition) (Carole Marsh Florida Bks.). (Illus.). 1994. lib. bdg. 39.95 (0-7933-2405-X); pap. 29.95 (0-7933-2787-3) Gallopade Pub Group.
— The Big Instruction Book of Small Business: (Georgia Edition) (Carole Marsh Georgia Bks.). (Illus.). 1994. lib. bdg. 39.95 (0-7933-2414-9); pap. 29.95 (0-7933-2788-1) Gallopade Pub Group.
— The Big Instruction Book of Small Business: (Hawaii Edition) (Carole Marsh Hawaii Bks.). (Illus.). 1994. lib. bdg. 39.95 (0-7933-2423-8); pap. 29.95 (0-7933-2789-X) Gallopade Pub Group.
— The Big Instruction Book of Small Business: (Idaho Edition) (Carole Marsh Idaho Bks.). (Illus.). 1994. lib. bdg. 39.95 (0-7933-2432-7); pap. 29.95 (0-7933-2790-3) Gallopade Pub Group.
— The Big Instruction Book of Small Business: (Illinois Edition) (Carole Marsh Illinois Bks.). (Illus.). 1994. lib. bdg. 39.95 (0-7933-2441-6); pap. 29.95 (0-7933-2791-1) Gallopade Pub Group.
— The Big Instruction Book of Small Business: (Indiana Edition) (Carole Marsh Indiana Bks.). (Illus.). 1994. lib. bdg. 39.95 (0-7933-2450-5); pap. 29.95 (0-7933-2792-X) Gallopade Pub Group.
— The Big Instruction Book of Small Business: (Iowa Edition) (Carole Marsh Iowa Bks.). (Illus.). 1994. lib. bdg. 39.95 (0-7933-2459-9); pap. 29.95 (0-7933-2793-8) Gallopade Pub Group.
— The Big Instruction Book of Small Business: (Kansas Edition) (Carole Marsh Kansas Bks.). (Illus.). 1994. lib. bdg. 39.95 (0-7933-2468-8); pap. 29.95 (0-7933-2794-6) Gallopade Pub Group.
— The Big Instruction Book of Small Business: (Kentucky Edition) (Carole Marsh Kentucky Bks.). (Illus.). 1994. lib. bdg. 39.95 (0-7933-2477-7); pap. 29.95 (0-7933-2795-4) Gallopade Pub Group.
— The Big Instruction Book of Small Business: (Louisiana Edition) (Carole Marsh Louisiana Bks.). (Illus.). 1994. lib. bdg. 39.95 (0-685-72456-5); pap. 29.95 (0-7933-2796-2) Gallopade Pub Group.
— The Big Instruction Book of Small Business: (Maine Edition) (Carole Marsh Maine Bks.). (Illus.). 1994. lib. bdg. 39.95 (0-7933-2495-5); pap. 29.95 (0-7933-2797-0) Gallopade Pub Group.
— The Big Instruction Book of Small Business: (Maryland Edition) (Carole Marsh Maryland Bks.). (Illus.). 1994. lib. bdg. 39.95 (0-7933-2504-8); pap. 29.95 (0-7933-2798-9) Gallopade Pub Group.
— The Big Instruction Book of Small Business: (Massachusetts Edition) (Carole Marsh Massachusetts Bks.). (Illus.). 1994. lib. bdg. 39.95 (0-7933-2513-7); pap. 29.95 (0-7933-2799-7) Gallopade Pub Group.
— The Big Instruction Book of Small Business: (Michigan Edition) (Carole Marsh Michigan Bks.). (Illus.). 1994. lib. bdg. 39.95 (0-7933-2522-6); pap. 29.95 (0-7933-2800-4) Gallopade Pub Group.
— The Big Instruction Book of Small Business: (Minnesota Edition) (Carole Marsh Minnesota Bks.). (Illus.). 1994. lib. bdg. 39.95 (0-7933-2531-5); pap. 29.95 (0-7933-2801-2) Gallopade Pub Group.
— The Big Instruction Book of Small Business: (Mississippi Edition) (Carole Marsh Mississippi Bks.). (Illus.). 1994. lib. bdg. 39.95 (0-7933-2540-4); pap. 29.95 (0-7933-2802-0) Gallopade Pub Group.
— The Big Instruction Book of Small Business: (Missouri Edition) (Carole Marsh Missouri Bks.). (Illus.). 1994. lib. bdg. 39.95 (0-7933-2549-8); pap. 29.95 (0-7933-2803-9) Gallopade Pub Group.

M

— The Big Instruction Book of Small Business: (Montana Edition) (Carole Marsh Montana Bks.). (Illus.). 1994. lib. bdg. 39.95 (*0-7933-2558-7*); pap. 29.95 (*0-7933-2804-7*) Gallopade Pub Group.
— The Big Instruction Book of Small Business: (Nebraska Edition) (Carole Marsh Nebraska Bks.). (Illus.). 1994. lib. bdg. 39.95 (*0-7933-2567-6*); pap. 29.95 (*0-7933-2805-5*) Gallopade Pub Group.
— The Big Instruction Book of Small Business: (Nevada Edition) (Carole Marsh Nevade Bks.). (Illus.). 1994. lib. bdg. 29.95 (*0-7933-2576-5*); ring bd. 29.95 (*0-7933-2806-3*) Gallopade Pub Group.
— The Big Instruction Book of Small Business: (New Hampshire Edition) (Carole Marsh New Hampshire Bks.). (Illus.). 1994. lib. bdg. 39.95 (*0-7933-2585-4*); pap. 29.95 (*0-7933-2807-1*) Gallopade Pub Group.
— The Big Instruction Book of Small Business: (New Jersey Edition) (Carole Marsh New Jersey Bks.). (Illus.). 1994. lib. bdg. 39.95 (*0-7933-2594-3*); pap. 29.95 (*0-7933-2808-X*) Gallopade Pub Group.
— The Big Instruction Book of Small Business: (New Mexico Edition) (Carole Marsh New Mexico Bks.). (Illus.). 1994. lib. bdg. 39.95 (*0-685-72457-3*); pap. 29.95 (*0-7933-2809-8*) Gallopade Pub Group.
— The Big Instruction Book of Small Business: (New York Edition) (Carole Marsh New York Bks.). (Illus.). 1994. lib. bdg. 39.95 (*0-7933-2612-5*); pap. 29.95 (*0-7933-2810-1*) Gallopade Pub Group.
— The Big Instruction Book of Small Business: (North Carolina Edition) (Carole Marsh North Carolina Bks.). (Illus.). 1994. lib. bdg. 39.95 (*0-7933-2621-4*); pap. 29.95 (*0-7933-2811-X*) Gallopade Pub Group.
— The Big Instruction Book of Small Business: (North Dakota Edition) (Carole Marsh North Dakota Bks.). (Illus.). 1994. lib. bdg. 39.95 (*0-7933-2630-3*); pap. 29.95 (*0-7933-2812-8*) Gallopade Pub Group.
— The Big Instruction Book of Small Business: (Ohio Edition) (Carole Marsh Ohio Bks.). (Illus.). 1994. lib. bdg. 39.95 (*0-7933-2639-7*); pap. 29.95 (*0-7933-2813-6*) Gallopade Pub Group.
— The Big Instruction Book of Small Business: (Oklahoma Edition) (Carole Marsh Oklahoma Bks.). (Illus.). 1994. lib. bdg. 39.95 (*0-7933-2648-6*); pap. 29.95 (*0-7933-2814-4*) Gallopade Pub Group.
— The Big Instruction Book of Small Business: (Oregon Edition) (Carole Marsh Oregon Bks.). (Illus.). 1994. lib. bdg. 39.95 (*0-7933-2657-5*); pap. 29.95 (*0-7933-2815-2*) Gallopade Pub Group.
— The Big Instruction Book of Small Business: (Pennsylvania Edition) (Pennsylvaniza Bks.). (Illus.). 1994. lib. bdg. 39.95 (*0-7933-2666-4*); pap. 29.95 (*0-7933-2816-0*) Gallopade Pub Group.
— The Big Instruction Book of Small Business: (Rhode Island Edition) (Carole Marsh Rhode Island Bks.). (Illus.). 1994. lib. bdg. 39.95 (*0-7933-2675-3*); pap. 29.95 (*0-7933-2817-9*) Gallopade Pub Group.
— The Big Instruction Book of Small Business: (South Carolina Edition) (Carole Marsh South Carolina Bks.). (Illus.). 1994. lib. bdg. 39.95 (*0-7933-2684-2*); pap. 29.95 (*0-7933-2818-7*) Gallopade Pub Group.
— The Big Instruction Book of Small Business: (South Dakota Edition) (Carole Marsh South Dakota Bks.). (Illus.). 1994. lib. bdg. 39.95 (*0-7933-2693-1*); pap. 29.95 (*0-7933-2819-5*) Gallopade Pub Group.
— The Big Instruction Book of Small Business: (Tennessee Edition) (Carole Marsh Tennessee Bks.). (Illus.). 1994. lib. bdg. 39.95 (*0-7933-2702-4*); pap. 29.95 (*0-7933-2820-9*) Gallopade Pub Group.
— The Big Instruction Book of Small Business: (Texas Edition) (Carole Marsh Texas Bks.). (Illus.). 1994. lib. bdg. 39.95 (*0-7933-2711-3*); pap. 29.95 (*0-7933-2821-7*) Gallopade Pub Group.
— The Big Instruction Book of Small Business: (Utah Edition) (Carole Marsh Utah Bks.). (Illus.). 1994. lib. bdg. 39.95 (*0-7933-2720-2*); pap. 29.95 (*0-7933-2822-5*) Gallopade Pub Group.
— The Big Instruction Book of Small Business: (Vermont Edition) (Carole Marsh Vermont Bks.). (Illus.). 1994. lib. bdg. 39.95 (*0-7933-2729-6*); pap. 29.95 (*0-7933-2823-3*) Gallopade Pub Group.
— The Big Instruction Book of Small Business: (Virginia Edition) (Carole Marsh Virginia Bks.). (Illus.). 1994. lib. bdg. 39.95 (*0-7933-2738-5*); pap. 29.95 (*0-7933-2824-1*) Gallopade Pub Group.
— The Big Instruction Book of Small Business: (Washington D. C. Edition) (Washington, D.C. Bks.). (Illus.). 1994. lib. bdg. 39.95 (*0-7933-2396-7*); pap. 29.95 (*0-7933-2786-5*) Gallopade Pub Group.
— The Big Instruction Book of Small Business: (Washington Edition) (Carole Marsh Washington Bks.). (Illus.). 1994. lib. bdg. 39.95 (*0-7933-2747-4*); pap. 29.95 (*0-7933-2825-X*) Gallopade Pub Group.
— The Big Instruction Book of Small Business: (West Virginia Edition) (Carole Marsh West Virginia Bks.). (Illus.). 1994. lib. bdg. 39.95 (*0-7933-2756-3*); pap. 29.95 (*0-7933-2826-8*) Gallopade Pub Group.
— The Big Instruction Book of Small Business: (Wisconsin Edition) (Carole Marsh Wisconsin Bks.). (Illus.). 1994. lib. bdg. 39.95 (*0-7933-2765-2*); pap. 29.95 (*0-7933-2827-6*) Gallopade Pub Group.
— The Big Instruction Book of Small Business: (Wyoming Edition) (Carole Marsh Wyoming Bks.). (Illus.). 1994. lib. bdg. 39.95 (*0-7933-2774-1*); pap. 29.95 (*0-7933-2828-4*) Gallopade Pub Group.
— The Big Rio of Ross Perot! (Carole Marsh Biographies Ser.). (J). 1994. lib. bdg. 24.95 (*0-7933-6942-8*); pap. text ed. 14.95 (*0-7933-6943-6*); disk 29.95 (*0-7933-6941-X*) Gallopade Pub Group.
— Bill S: Shakespeare for Kids. (Quantum Leap Ser.). (Illus.). (J). (gr. 4-12). 1994. lib. bdg. 24.95 (*1-55609-156-7*); pap. 14.95 (*0-935326-10-3*) Gallopade Pub Group.
— The Biltmore House Classroom Gamebook. (Carole Marsh Bks.). (Illus.). (Orig.). (J). (gr. 1-12). 1994. lib. bdg. 24.95 (*0-935326-83-9*) Gallopade Pub Group.
— Black Business. (Our Black Heritage Ser.). (J). (gr. 4-12). 1994. lib. bdg. 24.95 (*1-55609-327-6*); pap. 14.95 (*1-55609-326-8*); disk 29.95 (*1-55609-328-4*) Gallopade Pub Group.
— Black "Jography" The Paths of Our Black Pioneers. (Our Black Heritage Ser.). (J). (gr. 3-12). 1994. lib. bdg. 24.95 (*1-55609-321-7*); pap. 14.95 (*1-55609-320-9*); disk 29.95 (*1-55609-322-5*) Gallopade Pub Group.
— Black Trivia, A-Z. (Our Black Heritage Ser.). (J). (gr. 3-12). 1994. lib. bdg. 24.95 (*1-55609-318-7*); pap. 14.95 (*1-55609-317-9*); disk 29.95 (*1-55609-319-5*) Gallopade Pub Group.
— Blackbeard the Pirate's Missing Head Mystery Spook Kit. (S. P. A. R. K. Ser.). (Illus.). (J). (ps-6). 1994. lib. bdg. 24.95 (*0-935326-19-7*) Gallopade Pub Group.
— The Blood & Guts Dingbats Book. (Carole Marsh Dingbats Book Ser.). (Illus.). (YA). (gr. 3-12). 1994. lib. bdg. 24.95 (*0-7933-5398-X*); pap. 14.95 (*0-7933-5399-8*); disk 29.95 (*0-7933-5400-5*) Gallopade Pub Group.
— Bow Wow! Alabama Dogs in History, Mystery, Legend, Lore, Humor & More! (Carole Marsh Alabama Bks.). (Illus.). (J). (gr. 3-12). 1994. lib. bdg. 24.95 (*0-7933-3467-5*); pap. 14.95 (*0-7933-3468-3*); disk 29.95 (*0-7933-3469-1*) Gallopade Pub Group.
— Bow Wow! Alaska Dogs in History, Mystery, Legend, Lore, Humor & More! (Carole Marsh Alaska Bks.). (Illus.). (J). (gr. 3-12). 1994. lib. bdg. 24.95 (*0-7933-3470-5*); pap. 14.95 (*0-7933-3471-3*); disk 29.95 (*0-7933-3472-1*) Gallopade Pub Group.
— Bow Wow! Arizona Dogs in History, Mystery, Legend, Lore, Humor & More! (Carole Marsh Arizona Bks.). (Illus.). (J). (gr. 3-12). 1994. lib. bdg. 24.95 (*0-7933-3473-X*); pap. 14.95 (*0-7933-3474-8*); disk 29.95 (*0-7933-3475-6*) Gallopade Pub Group.
— Bow Wow! Arkansas Dogs in History, Mystery, Legend, Lore, Humor & More! (Carole Marsh Arkansas Bks.). (Illus.). (J). (gr. 3-12). 1994. lib. bdg. 24.95 (*0-7933-3476-4*); pap. 14.95 (*0-7933-3477-2*); disk 29.95 (*0-7933-3478-0*) Gallopade Pub Group.
— Bow Wow! California Dogs in History, Mystery, Legend, Lore, Humor & More! (Carole Marsh California Bks.). (Illus.). (J). (gr. 3-12). 1994. lib. bdg. 24.95 (*0-7933-3479-9*); pap. 14.95 (*0-7933-3480-2*); disk 29.95 (*0-7933-3481-0*) Gallopade Pub Group.
— Bow Wow! Colorado Dogs in History, Mystery, Legend, Lore, Humor & More! (Carole Marsh Colorado Bks.). (Illus.). (J). (gr. 3-12). 1994. lib. bdg. 24.95 (*0-7933-3482-9*); pap. 14.95 (*0-7933-3483-7*); disk 29.95 (*0-7933-3484-5*) Gallopade Pub Group.
— Bow Wow! Connecticut Dogs in History, Mystery, Legend, Lore, Humor & More! (Carole Marsh Connecticut Bks.). (Illus.). (J). (gr. 3-12). 1994. lib. bdg. 24.95 (*0-7933-3485-3*); pap. 14.95 (*0-7933-3486-1*); disk 29.95 (*0-7933-3487-X*) Gallopade Pub Group.
— Bow Wow! Delaware Dogs in History, Mystery, Legend, Lore, Humor & More! (Carole Marsh Delaware Bks.). (Illus.). (J). (gr. 3-12). 1994. lib. bdg. 24.95 (*0-7933-3488-8*); pap. 14.95 (*0-7933-3489-6*); disk 29.95 (*0-7933-3490-X*) Gallopade Pub Group.
— Bow Wow! Florida Dogs in History, Mystery, Legend, Lore, Humor & More! (Carole Marsh Florida Bks.). (Illus.). (J). (gr. 3-12). 1994. lib. bdg. 24.95 (*0-7933-3494-2*); pap. 14.95 (*0-7933-3495-0*); disk 29.95 (*0-7933-3496-9*) Gallopade Pub Group.
— Bow Wow! Georgia Dogs in History, Mystery, Legend, Lore, Humor & More! (Carole Marsh Georgia Bks.). (Illus.). (J). (gr. 3-12). 1994. lib. bdg. 24.95 (*0-7933-3497-7*); pap. 14.95 (*0-7933-3498-5*); disk 29.95 (*0-7933-3499-3*) Gallopade Pub Group.
— Bow Wow! Hawaii Dogs in History, Mystery, Legend, Lore, Humor & More! (Carole Marsh Hawaii Bks.). (Illus.). (J). (gr. 3-12). 1994. lib. bdg. 24.95 (*0-7933-3500-0*); pap. 14.95 (*0-7933-3501-9*); disk 29.95 (*0-7933-3502-7*) Gallopade Pub Group.
— Bow Wow! Idaho Dogs in History, Mystery, Legend, Lore, Humor & More! (Carole Marsh Idaho Bks.). (Illus.). (J). (gr. 3-12). 1994. lib. bdg. 24.95 (*0-7933-3503-5*); pap. 14.95 (*0-7933-3504-3*); disk 29.95 (*0-7933-3505-1*) Gallopade Pub Group.
— Bow Wow! Illinois Dogs in History, Mystery, Legend, Lore, Humor & More! (Carole Marsh Illinois Bks.). (Illus.). (J). (gr. 3-12). 1994. lib. bdg. 24.95 (*0-7933-3506-X*); pap. 14.95 (*0-7933-3507-8*); disk 29.95 (*0-7933-3508-6*) Gallopade Pub Group.
— Bow Wow! Indiana Dogs in History, Mystery, Legend, Lore, Humor & More! (Carole Marsh Indiana Bks.). (Illus.). (J). (gr. 3-12). 1994. lib. bdg. 24.95 (*0-7933-3509-4*); pap. 14.95 (*0-7933-3510-8*); disk 29.95 (*0-7933-3511-6*) Gallopade Pub Group.
— Bow Wow! Iowa Dogs in History, Mystery, Legend, Lore, Humor & More! (Carole Marsh Iowa Bks.). (Illus.). (J). (gr. 3-12). 1994. lib. bdg. 24.95 (*0-7933-3512-4*); pap. 14.95 (*0-7933-3513-2*); disk 29.95 (*0-7933-3514-0*) Gallopade Pub Group.
— Bow Wow! Kansas Dogs in History, Mystery, Legend, Lore, Humor & More! (Carole Marsh Kansas Bks.). (Illus.). (J). (gr. 3-12). 1994. lib. bdg. 24.95 (*0-7933-3515-9*); pap. 14.95 (*0-7933-3516-7*); disk 29.95 (*0-7933-3517-5*) Gallopade Pub Group.
— Bow Wow! Kentucky Dogs in History, Mystery, Legend, Lore, Humor & More! (Kentucky Bks.). (Illus.). (J). (gr. 3-12). 1994. lib. bdg. 24.95 (*0-7933-3518-3*); pap. 14.95 (*0-7933-3519-1*); disk 29.95 (*0-7933-3520-5*) Gallopade Pub Group.
— Bow Wow! Louisiana Dogs in History, Mystery, Legend, Lore, Humor & More! (Carole Marsh Louisiana Bks.). (Illus.). (J). (gr. 3-12). 1994. lib. bdg. 24.95 (*0-7933-3521-3*); pap. 14.95 (*0-7933-3522-1*); disk 29.95 (*0-7933-3523-X*) Gallopade Pub Group.
— Bow Wow! Maine Dogs in History, Mystery, Legend, Lore, Humor & More! (Carole Marsh Maine Bks.). (Illus.). (J). (gr. 3-12). 1994. lib. bdg. 24.95 (*0-7933-3524-8*); pap. 14.95 (*0-7933-3525-6*); disk 29.95 (*0-7933-3526-4*) Gallopade Pub Group.
— Bow Wow! Maryland Dogs in History, Mystery, Legend, Lore, Humor & More! (Carole Marsh Maryland Bks.). (Illus.). (J). (gr. 3-12). 1994. lib. bdg. 24.95 (*0-7933-3527-2*); pap. 14.95 (*0-7933-3528-0*); disk 29.95 (*0-7933-3529-9*) Gallopade Pub Group.
— Bow Wow! Massachusetts Dogs in History, Mystery, Legend, Lore, Humor & More! (Massachuseets Bks.). (Illus.). (J). (gr. 3-12). 1994. lib. bdg. 24.95 (*0-7933-3530-2*); pap. 14.95 (*0-7933-3531-0*); disk 29.95 (*0-7933-3532-9*) Gallopade Pub Group.
— Bow Wow! Michigan Dogs in History, Mystery, Legend, Lore, Humor & More! (Carole Marsh Michigan Bks.). (Illus.). (J). (gr. 3-12). 1994. lib. bdg. 24.95 (*0-7933-3533-7*); pap. 14.95 (*0-7933-3534-5*); disk 29.95 (*0-7933-3535-3*) Gallopade Pub Group.
— Bow Wow! Minnesota Dogs in History, Mystery, Legend, Lore, Humor & More! (Carole Marsh Minnesota Bks.). (Illus.). (J). (gr. 3-12). 1994. lib. bdg. 24.95 (*0-7933-3536-1*); pap. 14.95 (*0-7933-3537-X*); disk 29.95 (*0-7933-3538-8*) Gallopade Pub Group.
— Bow Wow! Mississippi Dogs in History, Mystery, Legend, Lore, Humor & More! (Carole Marsh Mississippi Bks.). (Illus.). (J). (gr. 3-12). 1994. lib. bdg. 24.95 (*0-7933-3539-6*); pap. 14.95 (*0-7933-3540-X*); disk 29.95 (*0-7933-3541-8*) Gallopade Pub Group.
— Bow Wow! Missouri Dogs in History, Mystery, Legend, Lore, Humor & More! (Carole Marsh Missouri Bks.). (Illus.). (J). (gr. 3-12). 1994. lib. bdg. 24.95 (*0-7933-3542-6*); pap. 14.95 (*0-7933-3543-4*); disk 29.95 (*0-7933-3544-2*) Gallopade Pub Group.
— Bow Wow! Montana Dogs in History, Mystery, Legend, Lore, Humor & More! (Carole Marsh Montana Bks.). (Illus.). (J). (gr. 3-12). 1994. lib. bdg. 24.95 (*0-7933-3545-0*); pap. 14.95 (*0-7933-3546-9*); disk 29.95 (*0-7933-3547-7*) Gallopade Pub Group.
— Bow Wow! Nebraska Dogs in History, Mystery, Legend, Lore, Humor & More! (Carole Marsh Nebraska Bks.). (Illus.). (J). (gr. 3-12). 1994. lib. bdg. 24.95 (*0-7933-3548-5*); pap. 14.95 (*0-7933-3549-3*); disk 29.95 (*0-7933-3550-7*) Gallopade Pub Group.
— Bow Wow! Nevada Dogs in History, Mystery, Legend, Lore, Humor & More! (Carole Marsh Nevada Bks.). (Illus.). (J). (gr. 3-12). 1994. lib. bdg. 24.95 (*0-7933-3551-5*); pap. 14.95 (*0-7933-3552-3*); disk 29.95 (*0-7933-3553-1*) Gallopade Pub Group.
— Bow Wow! New Hampshire Dogs in History, Mystery, Legend, Lore, Humor & More! (Carole Marsh New Hampshire Bks.). (Illus.). (J). (gr. 3-12). 1994. lib. bdg. 24.95 (*0-7933-3554-X*); pap. 14.95 (*0-7933-3555-8*); disk 29.95 (*0-7933-3556-6*) Gallopade Pub Group.
— Bow Wow! New Jersey Dogs in History, Mystery, Legend, Lore, Humor & More! (Carole Marsh New Jersey Bks.). (Illus.). (J). (gr. 3-12). 1994. lib. bdg. 24.95 (*0-7933-3557-4*); pap. 14.95 (*0-7933-3558-2*); disk 29.95 (*0-7933-3559-0*) Gallopade Pub Group.
— Bow Wow! New Mexico Dogs in History, Mystery, Legend, Lore, Humor & More! (Carole Marsh New Mexico Bks.). (Illus.). (J). (gr. 3-12). 1994. lib. bdg. 24.95 (*0-7933-3560-4*); pap. 14.95 (*0-7933-3561-2*); disk 29.95 (*0-7933-3562-0*) Gallopade Pub Group.
— Bow Wow! New York Dogs in History, Mystery, Legend, Lore, Humor & More! (Carole Marsh New York Bks.). (Illus.). (J). (gr. 3-12). 1994. lib. bdg. 24.95 (*0-7933-3563-9*); pap. 14.95 (*0-7933-3564-7*); disk 29.95 (*0-7933-3565-5*) Gallopade Pub Group.
— Bow Wow! North Carolina Dogs in History, Mystery, Legend, Lore, Humor & More! (Carole Marsh North Carolina Bks.). (Illus.). (J). (gr. 3-12). 1994. lib. bdg. 24.95 (*0-7933-3566-3*); pap. 14.95 (*0-7933-3567-1*); disk 29.95 (*0-7933-3568-X*) Gallopade Pub Group.
— Bow Wow! North Dakota Dogs in History, Mystery, Legend, Lore, Humor & More! (Carole Marsh North Dakota Bks.). (Illus.). (J). (gr. 3-12). 1994. lib. bdg. 24.95 (*0-7933-3569-8*); pap. 14.95 (*0-7933-3570-1*); disk 29.95 (*0-7933-3571-X*) Gallopade Pub Group.
— Bow Wow! Ohio Dogs in History, Mystery, Legend, Lore, Humor & More! (Carole Marsh Ohio Bks.). (Illus.). (J). (gr. 3-12). 1994. lib. bdg. 24.95 (*0-7933-3572-8*); pap. 14.95 (*0-7933-3573-6*); disk 29.95 (*0-7933-3574-4*) Gallopade Pub Group.
— Bow Wow! Oklahoma Dogs in History, Mystery, Legend, Lore, Humor & More! (Carole Marsh Oklahoma Bks.). (Illus.). (J). (gr. 3-12). 1994. lib. bdg. 24.95 (*0-7933-3575-2*); pap. 14.95 (*0-7933-3576-0*); disk 29.95 (*0-7933-3577-9*) Gallopade Pub Group.
— Bow Wow! Oregon Dogs in History, Mystery, Legend, Lore, Humor & More! (Oregon Bks.). (Illus.). (J). (gr. 3-12). 1994. lib. bdg. 24.95 (*0-7933-3578-7*); pap. 14.95 (*0-7933-3579-5*); disk 29.95 (*0-7933-3580-9*) Gallopade Pub Group.
— Bow Wow! Pennsylvania Dogs in History, Mystery, Legend, Lore, Humor & More! (Pennsylvania Bks.). (Illus.). (J). (gr. 3-12). 1994. lib. bdg. 24.95 (*0-7933-3581-7*); pap. 14.95 (*0-7933-3582-5*); disk 29.95 (*0-7933-3583-3*) Gallopade Pub Group.
— Bow Wow! Rhode Island Dogs in History, Mystery, Legend, Lore, Humor & More! (Rhode Island Bks.). (Illus.). (J). (gr. 3-12). 1994. lib. bdg. 24.95 (*0-7933-3584-1*); pap. 14.95 (*0-7933-3585-X*); disk 29.95 (*0-7933-3586-8*) Gallopade Pub Group.
— Bow Wow! South Carolina Dogs in History, Mystery, Legend, Lore, Humor & More! (South Carolina Bks.). (Illus.). (J). (gr. 3-12). 1994. lib. bdg. 24.95 (*0-7933-3587-6*); pap. 14.95 (*0-7933-3588-4*); disk 29.95 (*0-7933-3589-2*) Gallopade Pub Group.
— Bow Wow! South Dakota Dogs in History, Mystery, Legend, Lore, Humor & More! (South Dakota Bks.). (Illus.). (J). (gr. 3-12). 1994. lib. bdg. 24.95 (*0-7933-3590-6*); pap. 14.95 (*0-7933-3591-4*); disk 29.95 (*0-7933-3592-2*) Gallopade Pub Group.
— Bow Wow! Tennessee Dogs in History, Mystery, Legend, Lore, Humor & More! (Tennessee Bks.). (Illus.). (J). (gr. 3-12). 1994. lib. bdg. 24.95 (*0-7933-3593-0*); pap. 14.95 (*0-7933-3594-9*); disk 29.95 (*0-7933-3595-7*) Gallopade Pub Group.
— Bow Wow! Texas Dogs in History, Mystery, Legend, Lore, Humor & More! (Texas Bks.). (Illus.). (J). (gr. 3-12). 1994. lib. bdg. 24.95 (*0-7933-3596-5*); pap. 14.95 (*0-7933-3597-3*); disk 29.95 (*0-7933-3598-1*) Gallopade Pub Group.
— Bow Wow! Utah Dogs in History, Mystery, Legend, Lore, Humor & More! (Utah Bks.). (Illus.). (J). (gr. 3-12). 1994. lib. bdg. 24.95 (*0-7933-3599-X*); pap. 14.95 (*0-7933-3600-7*); disk 29.95 (*0-7933-3601-5*) Gallopade Pub Group.
— Bow Wow! Vermont Dogs in History, Mystery, Legend, Lore, Humor & More! (Vermont Bks.). (Illus.). (J). (gr. 3-12). 1994. lib. bdg. 24.95 (*0-7933-3602-3*); pap. 14.95 (*0-7933-3603-1*); disk 29.95 (*0-7933-3604-X*) Gallopade Pub Group.
— Bow Wow! Virginia Dogs in History, Mystery, Legend, Lore, Humor & More! (Virginia Bks.). (Illus.). (J). (gr. 3-12). 1994. lib. bdg. 24.95 (*0-7933-3605-8*); pap. 14.95 (*0-7933-3606-6*); disk 29.95 (*0-7933-3607-4*) Gallopade Pub Group.
— Bow Wow! Washington D. C. Dogs in History, Mystery, Legend, Lore, Humor & More! (Washington, D.C. Bks.). (Illus.). (J). (gr. 3-12). 1994. lib. bdg. 24.95 (*0-7933-3491-8*); pap. 14.95 (*0-7933-3492-6*); disk 29.95 (*0-7933-3493-4*) Gallopade Pub Group.
— Bow Wow! Washington Dogs in History, Mystery, Legend, Lore, Humor & More! (Washington Bks.). (Illus.). (J). (gr. 3-12). 1994. lib. bdg. 24.95 (*0-7933-3608-2*); pap. 14.95 (*0-7933-3609-0*); disk 29.95 (*0-7933-3610-4*) Gallopade Pub Group.
— Bow Wow! West Virginia Dogs in History, Mystery, Legend, Lore, Humor & More! (West Virginia Bks.). (Illus.). (J). (gr. 3-12). 1994. lib. bdg. 24.95 (*0-7933-3611-2*); pap. 14.95 (*0-7933-3612-0*); disk 29.95 (*0-7933-3613-9*) Gallopade Pub Group.
— Bow Wow! Wisconsin Dogs in History, Mystery, Legend, Lore, Humor & More! (Wisconsin Bks.). (Illus.). (J). (gr. 3-12). 1994. lib. bdg. 24.95 (*0-7933-3614-7*); pap. 14.95 (*0-7933-3615-5*); disk 29.95 (*0-7933-3616-3*) Gallopade Pub Group.
— Bow Wow! Wyoming Dogs in History, Mystery, Legend, Lore, Humor & More! (Wyoming Bks.). (Illus.). (J). (gr. 3-12). 1994. lib. bdg. 24.95 (*0-7933-3617-1*); pap. 14.95 (*0-7933-3618-X*); disk 29.95 (*0-7933-3619-8*) Gallopade Pub Group.
— The Boy-Is-This-Place-Big Biltmore House Spark Kit. (S. P. A. R. K. Ser.). (Illus.). (Orig.). (J). (gr. 3-12). 1994. lib. bdg. 24.95 (*0-935326-22-7*) Gallopade Pub Group.
— California & Other State Greats (Biographies) (Carole Marsh California Bks.). (Illus.). (YA). (gr. 3-12). 1994. lib. bdg. 24.95 (*1-55609-521-X*); pap. 14.95 (*1-55609-520-1*); disk 29.95 (*0-7933-1405-4*) Gallopade Pub Group.
— California Bandits, Bushwackers, Outlaws, Crooks, Devils, Ghosts, Desperadoes & Other Assorted & Sundry Characters! (Carole Marsh California Bks.). (Illus.). (YA). (gr. 3-12). 1994. lib. bdg. 24.95 (*0-7933-0166-1*); pap. 14.95 (*0-7933-0165-3*); disk 29.95 (*0-7933-0167-X*) Gallopade Pub Group.
— The California Bookstore Book: A Surprising Guide to Our State's Bookstores & Their Specialties for Students, Teachers, Writers & Publishers. (Carole Marsh California Bks.). (Illus.). 1994. lib. bdg. 24.95 (*0-7933-2867-5*); pap. 14.95 (*0-7933-2868-3*); disk 29.95 (*0-7933-2869-1*) Gallopade Pub Group.
— California Classic Christmas Trivia: Stories, Recipes, Activities, Legends, Lore & More! (Carole Marsh California Bks.). (Illus.). (YA). (gr. 3-12). 1994. lib. bdg. 24.95 (*0-7933-0169-6*); pap. 14.95 (*0-7933-0168-8*); disk 29.95 (*0-7933-0170-X*) Gallopade Pub Group.
— California Coastales! (Carole Marsh California Bks.). (J). 1994. lib. bdg. 24.95 (*0-7933-7269-0*) Gallopade Pub Group.
— California Coastales! (Carole Marsh California Bks.). (Illus.). (YA). (gr. 3-12). 1994. lib. bdg. 24.95 (*1-55609-517-1*); pap. 14.95 (*1-55609-516-3*); disk 29.95 (*0-7933-1401-1*) Gallopade Pub Group.
— California "Crinkum-Crankum" A Funny Word Book about Our State. (Carole Marsh California Bks.). (Illus.). (J). 1994. lib. bdg. 24.95 (*0-7933-4822-6*); pap. 14.95 (*0-7933-4823-4*); disk 29.95 (*0-7933-4824-2*) Gallopade Pub Group.
— California Dingbats! Bk. 1: A Fun Book of Games, Stories, Activities & More about Our State That's All in Code! for You to Decipher. (Carole Marsh California Bks.). (Illus.). (J). (gr. 3-12). 1994. lib. bdg. 24.95 (*0-7933-3785-2*); pap. 14.95 (*0-7933-3786-0*); disk 29.95 (*0-7933-3787-9*) Gallopade Pub Group.
— California Festival Fun for Kids! (Carole Marsh California Bks.). (Illus.). (YA). (gr. 3-12). 1994. lib. bdg. 24.95 (*0-7933-3938-3*); pap. 14.95 (*0-7933-3939-1*); disk 29.95 (*0-7933-3940-5*) Gallopade Pub Group.
— The California Hot Air Balloon Mystery. (Carole Marsh California Bks.). (Illus.). (J). (gr. 2-9). 1994. 24.95 (*0-7933-2354-1*); pap. 14.95 (*0-7933-2355-X*); disk 29.95 (*0-7933-2356-8*) Gallopade Pub Group.

An Asterisk (*) at the beginning of an entry indicates that the title is appearing in BIP for the first time.

— California Jeopardy! Answers & Questions about Our State! (Carole Marsh California Bks.). (Illus.). (J). (gr. 3-12). 1994. lib. bdg. 24.95 (*0-7933-4091-8*); pap. 14.95 (*0-7933-4092-6*); disk 29.95 (*0-7933-4093-4*) Gallopade Pub Group.

— California "Jography" A Fun Run Thru Our State! (Carole Marsh California Bks.). (Illus.). (YA). (gr. 3-12). 1994. lib. bdg. 24.95 (*1-55609-511-2*); pap. 14.95 (*1-55609-510-4*); disk 29.95 (*0-685-45935-7*) Gallopade Pub Group.

— California Kid's Cookbook: Recipes, How-to, History, Lore & More! (Carole Marsh California Bks.). (Illus.). (YA). (gr. 3-12). 1994. lib. bdg. 24.95 (*0-7933-0178-5*); pap. 14.95 (*0-7933-0177-7*); disk 29.95 (*0-7933-0179-3*) Gallopade Pub Group.

— The California Library Book: A Surprising Guide to the Unusual Special Collections in Libraries Across Our State for Students, Teachers, Writers & Publishers - Includes Reproducible Mailing Labels Plus Activities for Young People! (Carole Marsh California Bks.). (Illus.). 1994. lib. bdg. 24.95 (*0-7933-3020-3*); pap. 14.95 (*0-7933-3021-1*); disk 29.95 (*0-7933-3022-X*) Gallopade Pub Group.

— The California Media Book: A Surprising Guide to the Amazing Print, Broadcast & Online Media of Our State for Students, Teachers, Writers & Publishers - Includes Reproducible Mailing Labels Plus Activities for Young People! (Carole Marsh California Bks.). (Illus.). 1994. lib. bdg. 24.95 (*0-7933-3173-0*); pap. 14.95 (*0-7933-3174-9*); disk 29.95 (*0-7933-3175-7*) Gallopade Pub Group.

— The California Mystery Van Takes Off! Bk. 1: Handicapped California Kids Sneak Off on a Big Adventure. (Carole Marsh California Bks.). (Illus.). (J). (gr. 3-12). 1994. 24.95 (*0-7933-4976-1*); pap. 14.95 (*0-7933-4977-X*); disk 29.95 (*0-7933-4978-8*) Gallopade Pub Group.

— California Quiz Bowl Crash Course! (Carole Marsh California Bks.). (Illus.). (YA). (gr. 3-12). 1994. lib. bdg. 24.95 (*1-55609-519-8*); pap. 14.95 (*1-55609-518-X*); disk 29.95 (*0-7933-1400-3*) Gallopade Pub Group.

— California Rollercoasters! (Carole Marsh California Bks.). (Illus.). (YA). (gr. 3-12). 1994. lib. bdg. 24.95 (*0-7933-5236-3*); pap. 14.95 (*0-7933-5237-1*); disk 29.95 (*0-7933-5238-X*) Gallopade Pub Group.

— California School Trivia: An Amazing & Fascinating Look at Our State's Teachers, Schools & Students! (Carole Marsh California Bks.). (Illus.). (YA). (gr. 3-12). 1994. lib. bdg. 24.95 (*0-7933-0175-0*); pap. 14.95 (*0-7933-0174-2*); disk 29.95 (*0-7933-0176-9*) Gallopade Pub Group.

— California Silly Basketball Sportsmysteries, Vol. I. (Carole Marsh California Bks.). (Illus.). (YA). (gr. 3-12). 1994. lib. bdg. 24.95 (*0-7933-0172-6*); pap. 14.95 (*0-7933-0171-8*); disk 29.95 (*0-7933-0173-4*) Gallopade Pub Group.

— California Silly Basketball Sportsmysteries, Vol. II. (Carole Marsh California Bks.). (Illus.). (YA). (gr. 3-12). 1994. lib. bdg. 24.95 (*0-7933-1574-3*); pap. 14.95 (*0-7933-1575-1*); disk 29.95 (*0-7933-1576-X*) Gallopade Pub Group.

— California Silly Football Sportsmysteries, Vol. I. (Carole Marsh California Bks.). (Illus.). (YA). (gr. 3-12). 1994. lib. bdg. 24.95 (*1-55609-515-5*); pap. 14.95 (*1-55609-514-7*); disk 29.95 (*0-7933-1396-1*) Gallopade Pub Group.

— California Silly Football Sportsmysteries, Vol. II. (Carole Marsh California Bks.). (Illus.). (YA). (gr. 3-12). 1994. lib. bdg. 24.95 (*0-7933-1394-5*); pap. 14.95 (*0-7933-1395-3*); disk 29.95 (*0-685-74235-0*) Gallopade Pub Group.

— California Silly Trivia! (Carole Marsh California Bks.). (Illus.). (YA). (gr. 3-12). 1994. lib. bdg. 24.95 (*1-55609-509-0*); pap. 14.95 (*1-55609-508-2*); disk 29.95 (*0-7933-1390-2*) Gallopade Pub Group.

— California Timeline: A Chronology of California History, Mystery, Trivia, Legend, Lore & More. (Carole Marsh California Bks.). (Illus.). (J). (gr. 3-12). 1994. lib. bdg. 24.95 (*0-7933-5887-6*); pap. 14.95 (*0-7933-5888-4*); disk 29.95 (*0-7933-5889-2*) Gallopade Pub Group.

— California's (Most Devastating!) Disasters & (Most Calamitous!) Catastrophies! (Carole Marsh California Bks.). (Illus.). (YA). (gr. 3-12). 1994. lib. bdg. 24.95 (*0-7933-0163-7*); pap. 14.95 (*0-7933-0162-9*); disk 29.95 (*0-7933-0164-5*) Gallopade Pub Group.

— California's Unsolved Mysteries (& Their "Solutions") Includes Scientific Information & Other Activities for Students. (Carole Marsh California Bks.). (Illus.). (J). (gr. 3-12). 1994. lib. bdg. 24.95 (*0-7933-5734-9*); pap. 14.95 (*0-7933-5735-7*); disk 29.95 (*0-7933-5736-5*) Gallopade Pub Group.

— Carole Marsh Kentucky Books, 45 bks. (Fullbook State Ser.). (Illus.). (J). (gr. 3-8). 1994. pap. 602.75 (*0-7933-5156-1*) Gallopade Pub Group.

— Carole Marsh Kentucky Books, 45 bks., Set. (Fullbook State Ser.). (Illus.). (J). (gr. 3-8). 1994. lib. bdg. 1,052.75 (*0-7933-1292-2*) Gallopade Pub Group.

— Carole Marsh Louisiana Books, 44 bks., Set. (Fullbook State Ser.). (Illus.). (J). (gr. 3-8). 1994. lib. bdg. 1,027.80 (*0-7933-1293-0*); pap. 587.80 (*0-7933-5158-8*) Gallopade Pub Group.

— Carole Marsh Maine Books, 44 bks., Set. (Fullbook State Ser.). (Illus.). (J). (gr. 3-8). 1994. lib. bdg. 1,027.80 (*0-7933-1294-9*); pap. 587.80 (*0-7933-5160-X*) Gallopade Pub Group.

— Carole Marsh Massachusetts Books, 44 bks., Set. (Fullbook State Ser.). (Illus.). (J). (gr. 3-8). 1994. lib. bdg. 1,027.80 (*0-7933-1296-5*); pap. 587.80 (*0-7933-5164-2*) Gallopade Pub Group.

— Castle Hayne. (Carole Marsh Short Story Ser.). (Illus.). 60p. (J). (gr. 4-12). 1994. lib. bdg. 19.95 (*1-55609-159-1*); pap. 14.95 (*1-55609-241-5*) Gallopade Pub Group.

— The Charming Ghost of Charleston Set. (Carole Marsh Mysteries Ser.). 1994. teacher ed 125.00 (*0-7933-6958-4*) Gallopade Pub Group.

— Chill Out: Scary Alabama Tales Based on Frightening Alabama Truths. (Carole Marsh Alabama Bks.). (Illus.). (J). 1994. lib. bdg. 24.95 (*0-7933-4657-6*); pap. 14.95 (*0-7933-4658-4*); disk 29.95 (*0-7933-4659-2*) Gallopade Pub Group.

— Chill Out: Scary Alaska Tales Based on Frightening Alaska Truths. (Carole Marsh Alaska Bks.). (Illus.). (J). 1994. lib. bdg. 24.95 (*0-7933-4660-6*); pap. 14.95 (*0-7933-4661-4*); disk 29.95 (*0-7933-4662-2*) Gallopade Pub Group.

— Chill Out: Scary Arizona Tales Based on Frightening Arizona Truths. (Carole Marsh Arizona Bks.). (Illus.). (J). 1994. lib. bdg. 24.95 (*0-7933-4663-0*); pap. 14.95 (*0-7933-4664-9*); disk 29.95 (*0-7933-4665-7*) Gallopade Pub Group.

— Chill Out: Scary Arkansas Tales Based on Frightening Arkansas Truths. (Carole Marsh Arkansas Bks.). (Illus.). (J). 1994. lib. bdg. 24.95 (*0-7933-4666-5*); pap. 14.95 (*0-7933-4667-3*); disk 29.95 (*0-7933-4668-1*) Gallopade Pub Group.

— Chill Out: Scary California Tales Based on Frightening California Truths. (Carole Marsh California Bks.). (Illus.). (J). 1994. lib. bdg. 24.95 (*0-7933-4669-X*); pap. 14.95 (*0-7933-4670-3*); disk 29.95 (*0-7933-4671-1*) Gallopade Pub Group.

— Chill Out: Scary Colorado Tales Based on Frightening Colorado Truths. (Carole Marsh Colorado Bks.). (Illus.). (J). 1994. lib. bdg. 24.95 (*0-7933-4672-X*); pap. 14.95 (*0-7933-4673-8*); disk 29.95 (*0-7933-4674-6*) Gallopade Pub Group.

— Chill Out: Scary Connecticut Tales Based on Frightening Connecticut Truths. (Carole Marsh Connecticut Bks.). (Illus.). (J). 1994. lib. bdg. 24.95 (*0-7933-4675-4*); pap. 14.95 (*0-7933-4676-2*); disk 29.95 (*0-7933-4677-0*) Gallopade Pub Group.

— Chill Out: Scary Delaware Tales Based on Frightening Delaware Truths. (Carole Marsh Delaware Bks.). (Illus.). (J). 1994. lib. bdg. 24.95 (*0-7933-4678-9*); pap. 14.95 (*0-7933-4679-7*); disk 29.95 (*0-7933-4680-0*) Gallopade Pub Group.

— Chill Out: Scary Florida Tales Based on Frightening Florida Truths. (Carole Marsh Florida Bks.). (Illus.). (J). 1994. lib. bdg. 24.95 (*0-7933-4681-9*); pap. 14.95 (*0-7933-4682-7*); disk 29.95 (*0-7933-4683-5*) Gallopade Pub Group.

— Chill Out: Scary Georgia Tales Based on Frightening Georgia Truths. (Carole Marsh Georgia Bks.). (Illus.). (J). 1994. lib. bdg. 24.95 (*0-7933-4684-3*); pap. 14.95 (*0-7933-4685-1*); disk 29.95 (*0-7933-4686-X*) Gallopade Pub Group.

— Chill Out: Scary Hawaii Tales Based on Frightening Hawaii Truths. (Carole Marsh Hawaii Bks.). (Illus.). (J). 1994. lib. bdg. 24.95 (*0-7933-4687-8*); pap. 14.95 (*0-7933-4688-6*); disk 29.95 (*0-7933-4689-4*) Gallopade Pub Group.

— Chill Out: Scary Idaho Tales Based on Frightening Idaho Truths. (Carole Marsh Idaho Bks.). (Illus.). (J). 1994. lib. bdg. 24.95 (*0-7933-4690-8*); pap. 14.95 (*0-7933-4691-6*); disk 29.95 (*0-7933-4692-4*) Gallopade Pub Group.

— Chill Out: Scary Illinois Tales Based on Frightening Illinois Truths. (Carole Marsh Illinois Bks.). (Illus.). (J). 1994. lib. bdg. 24.95 (*0-7933-4693-2*); pap. 14.95 (*0-7933-4694-0*); disk 29.95 (*0-7933-4695-9*) Gallopade Pub Group.

— Chill Out: Scary Indiana Tales Based on Frightening Indiana Truths. (Carole Marsh Indiana Bks.). (Illus.). (J). 1994. lib. bdg. 24.95 (*0-7933-4696-7*); pap. 14.95 (*0-7933-4697-5*); disk 29.95 (*0-7933-4698-3*) Gallopade Pub Group.

— Chill Out: Scary Iowa Tales Based on Frightening Iowa Truths. (Carole Marsh Iowa Bks.). (Illus.). (J). 1994. lib. bdg. 24.95 (*0-7933-4699-1*); pap. 14.95 (*0-7933-4700-9*); disk 29.95 (*0-7933-4701-7*) Gallopade Pub Group.

— Chill Out: Scary Kansas Tales Based on Frightening Kansas Truths. (Carole Marsh Kansas Bks.). (Illus.). (J). 1994. lib. bdg. 24.95 (*0-7933-4702-5*); pap. 14.95 (*0-7933-4703-3*); disk 29.95 (*0-7933-4704-1*) Gallopade Pub Group.

— Chill Out: Scary Kentucky Tales Based on Frightening Kentucky Truths. (Carole Marsh Kentucky Bks.). (Illus.). (J). 1994. lib. bdg. 24.95 (*0-7933-4705-X*); pap. 14.95 (*0-7933-4706-8*); disk 29.95 (*0-7933-4707-6*) Gallopade Pub Group.

— Chill Out: Scary Louisiana Tales Based on Frightening Louisiana Truths. (Carole Marsh Louisiana Bks.). (Illus.). (J). 1994. lib. bdg. 24.95 (*0-7933-4708-4*); pap. 14.95 (*0-7933-4709-2*); disk 29.95 (*0-7933-4710-6*) Gallopade Pub Group.

— Chill Out: Scary Maine Tales Based on Frightening Maine Truths. (Carole Marsh Maine Bks.). (Illus.). (J). 1994. lib. bdg. 24.95 (*0-7933-4711-4*); pap. 14.95 (*0-7933-4712-2*); disk 29.95 (*0-7933-4713-0*) Gallopade Pub Group.

— Chill Out: Scary Maryland Tales Based on Frightening Maryland Truths. (Carole Marsh Maryland Bks.). (Illus.). (J). 1994. lib. bdg. 24.95 (*0-7933-4714-9*); pap. 14.95 (*0-7933-4715-7*); disk 29.95 (*0-7933-4716-5*) Gallopade Pub Group.

— Chill Out: Scary Massachusetts Tales Based on Frightening Massachusetts Truths. (Massachusetts Bks.). (Illus.). (J). 1994. lib. bdg. 24.95 (*0-7933-4717-3*); pap. 14.95 (*0-7933-4718-1*); disk 29.95 (*0-7933-4719-X*) Gallopade Pub Group.

— Chill Out: Scary Michigan Tales Based on Frightening Michigan Truths. (Carole Marsh Michigan Bks.). (Illus.). (J). 1994. lib. bdg. 24.95 (*0-7933-4720-3*); pap. 14.95 (*0-7933-4721-1*); disk 29.95 (*0-7933-4722-X*) Gallopade Pub Group.

— Chill Out: Scary Minnesota Tales Based on Frightening Minnesota Truths. (Carole Marsh Minnesota Bks.). (Illus.). (J). 1994. lib. bdg. 24.95 (*0-7933-4723-8*); pap. 14.95 (*0-7933-4724-6*); disk 29.95 (*0-7933-4725-4*) Gallopade Pub Group.

— Chill Out: Scary Mississippi Tales Based on Frightening Mississippi Truths. (Carole Marsh Mississippi Bks.). (Illus.). (J). 1994. lib. bdg. 24.95 (*0-7933-4726-2*); pap. 14.95 (*0-7933-4727-0*); disk 29.95 (*0-7933-4728-9*) Gallopade Pub Group.

— Chill Out: Scary Missouri Tales Based on Frightening Missouri Truths. (Carole Marsh Missouri Bks.). (Illus.). (J). 1994. lib. bdg. 24.95 (*0-7933-4729-7*); pap. 14.95 (*0-7933-4730-0*); disk 29.95 (*0-7933-4731-9*) Gallopade Pub Group.

— Chill Out: Scary Montana Tales Based on Frightening Montana Truths. (Carole Marsh Montana Bks.). (Illus.). (J). 1994. lib. bdg. 24.95 (*0-7933-4732-7*); pap. 14.95 (*0-7933-4733-5*); disk 29.95 (*0-7933-4734-3*) Gallopade Pub Group.

— Chill Out: Scary Nebraska Tales Based on Frightening Nebraska Truths. (Carole Marsh Nebraska Bks.). (Illus.). (J). 1994. lib. bdg. 24.95 (*0-7933-4735-1*); pap. 14.95 (*0-7933-4736-X*); disk 29.95 (*0-7933-4737-8*) Gallopade Pub Group.

— Chill Out: Scary Nevada Tales Based on Frightening Nevada Truths. (Carole Marsh Nevada Bks.). (Illus.). (J). 1994. lib. bdg. 24.95 (*0-7933-4738-6*); pap. 14.95 (*0-7933-4739-4*); disk 29.95 (*0-7933-4740-8*) Gallopade Pub Group.

— Chill Out: Scary New Hampshire Tales Based on Frightening New Hampshire Truths. (Carole Marsh New Hampshire Bks.). (Illus.). (J). 1994. lib. bdg. 24.95 (*0-7933-4741-6*); pap. 14.95 (*0-7933-4742-4*); disk 29.95 (*0-7933-4743-2*) Gallopade Pub Group.

— Chill Out: Scary New Jersey Tales Based on Frightening New Jersey Truths. (Carole Marsh New Jersey Bks.). (Illus.). (J). 1994. lib. bdg. 24.95 (*0-7933-4744-0*); pap. 14.95 (*0-7933-4745-9*); disk 29.95 (*0-7933-4746-7*) Gallopade Pub Group.

— Chill Out: Scary New Mexico Tales Based on Frightening New Mexico Truths. (Carole Marsh New Mexico Bks.). (Illus.). (J). 1994. lib. bdg. 24.95 (*0-7933-4747-5*); pap. 14.95 (*0-7933-4748-3*); disk 29.95 (*0-7933-4749-1*) Gallopade Pub Group.

— Chill Out: Scary New York Tales Based on Frightening New York Truths. (Carole Marsh New York Bks.). (Illus.). (J). 1994. lib. bdg. 24.95 (*0-7933-4750-5*); pap. 14.95 (*0-7933-4751-3*); disk 29.95 (*0-7933-4752-1*) Gallopade Pub Group.

— Chill Out: Scary North Carolina Tales Based on Frightening North Carolina Truths. (Carole Marsh North Carolina Bks.). (Illus.). (J). 1994. lib. bdg. 24.95 (*0-7933-4753-X*); pap. 14.95 (*0-7933-4754-8*); disk 29.95 (*0-7933-4755-6*) Gallopade Pub Group.

— Chill Out: Scary North Dakota Tales Based on Frightening North Dakota Truths. (Carole Marsh North Dakota Bks.). (Illus.). (J). 1994. lib. bdg. 24.95 (*0-7933-4756-4*); pap. 14.95 (*0-7933-4757-2*); disk 29.95 (*0-7933-4758-0*) Gallopade Pub Group.

— Chill Out: Scary Ohio Tales Based on Frightening Ohio Truths. (Carole Marsh Ohio Bks.). (Illus.). (J). 1994. lib. bdg. 24.95 (*0-7933-4759-9*); pap. 14.95 (*0-7933-4760-2*); disk 29.95 (*0-7933-4761-0*) Gallopade Pub Group.

— Chill Out: Scary Oklahoma Tales Based on Frightening Oklahoma Truths. (Oklahoma Bks.). (Illus.). (J). 1994. lib. bdg. 24.95 (*0-7933-4762-9*); pap. 14.95 (*0-7933-4763-7*); disk 29.95 (*0-7933-4764-5*) Gallopade Pub Group.

— Chill Out: Scary Oregon Tales Based on Frightening Oregon Truths. (Oregon Bks.). (Illus.). (J). 1994. lib. bdg. 24.95 (*0-7933-4765-3*); pap. 14.95 (*0-7933-4766-1*); disk 29.95 (*0-7933-4767-X*) Gallopade Pub Group.

— Chill Out: Scary Pennsylvania Tales Based on Frightening Pennsylvania Truths. (Pennsylvania Bks.). (Illus.). (J). 1994. lib. bdg. 24.95 (*0-7933-4768-8*); pap. 14.95 (*0-7933-4769-6*); disk 29.95 (*0-7933-4770-X*) Gallopade Pub Group.

— Chill Out: Scary Rhode Island Tales Based on Frightening Rhode Island Truths. (Rhode Island Bks.). (Illus.). (J). 1994. lib. bdg. 24.95 (*0-7933-4771-8*); pap. 14.95 (*0-7933-4772-6*); disk 29.95 (*0-7933-4773-4*) Gallopade Pub Group.

— Chill Out: Scary South Carolina Tales Based on Frightening South Carolina Truths. (South Carolina Bks.). (Illus.). (J). 1994. lib. bdg. 24.95 (*0-7933-4774-2*); pap. 14.95 (*0-7933-4775-0*); disk 29.95 (*0-7933-4776-9*) Gallopade Pub Group.

— Chill Out: Scary South Dakota Tales Based on Frightening South Dakota Truths. (South Dakota Bks.). (Illus.). (J). 1994. lib. bdg. 24.95 (*0-7933-4777-7*); pap. 14.95 (*0-7933-4778-5*); disk 29.95 (*0-7933-4779-3*) Gallopade Pub Group.

— Chill Out: Scary Tennessee Tales Based on Frightening Tennessee Truths. (Tennessee Bks.). (Illus.). (J). 1994. lib. bdg. 24.95 (*0-7933-4780-7*); pap. 14.95 (*0-7933-4781-5*); disk 29.95 (*0-7933-4782-3*) Gallopade Pub Group.

— Chill Out: Scary Texas Tales Based on Frightening Texas Truths. (Texas Bks.). (Illus.). (J). 1994. lib. bdg. 24.95 (*0-7933-4783-1*); pap. 14.95 (*0-7933-4784-X*); disk 29.95 (*0-7933-4785-8*) Gallopade Pub Group.

— Chill Out: Scary Utah Tales Based on Frightening Utah Truths. (Utah Bks.). (Illus.). (J). 1994. lib. bdg. 24.95 (*0-7933-4786-6*); pap. 14.95 (*0-7933-4787-4*); disk 29.95 (*0-7933-4788-2*) Gallopade Pub Group.

— Chill Out: Scary Vermont Tales Based on Frightening Vermont Truths. (Vermont Bks.). (Illus.). (J). 1994. lib. bdg. 24.95 (*0-7933-4789-0*); pap. 14.95 (*0-7933-4790-4*); disk 29.95 (*0-7933-4791-2*) Gallopade Pub Group.

— Chill Out: Scary Virginia Tales Based on Frightening Virginia Truths. (Virginia Bks.). (Illus.). (J). 1994. lib. bdg. 24.95 (*0-7933-4792-0*); pap. 14.95 (*0-7933-4793-9*); disk 29.95 (*0-7933-4794-7*) Gallopade Pub Group.

— Chill Out: Scary Washington D. C. Tales Based on Frightening Washington D. C. Truths. (Washington, D.C. Bks.). (Illus.). (J). 1994. lib. bdg. 24.95 (*0-7933-4798-X*); pap. 14.95 (*0-7933-4799-8*); disk 29.95 (*0-7933-4800-5*) Gallopade Pub Group.

— Chill Out: Scary Washington Tales Based on Frightening Washington Truths. (Washington Bks.). (Illus.). (J). 1994. lib. bdg. 24.95 (*0-7933-4795-5*); pap. 14.95 (*0-7933-4796-3*); disk 29.95 (*0-7933-4797-1*) Gallopade Pub Group.

— Chill Out: Scary West Virginia Tales Based on Frightening West Virginia Truths. (West Virginia Bks.). (Illus.). (J). 1994. lib. bdg. 24.95 (*0-7933-4801-3*); pap. 14.95 (*0-7933-4802-1*); disk 29.95 (*0-7933-4803-X*) Gallopade Pub Group.

— Chill Out: Scary Wisconsin Tales Based on Frightening Wisconsin Truths. (Wisconsin Bks.). (Illus.). (J). 1994. lib. bdg. 24.95 (*0-7933-4804-8*); pap. 14.95 (*0-7933-4805-6*); disk 29.95 (*0-7933-4806-4*) Gallopade Pub Group.

— Chill Out: Scary Wyoming Tales Based on Frightening Wyoming Truths. (Wyoming Bks.). (Illus.). (J). 1994. lib. bdg. 24.95 (*0-7933-4807-2*); pap. 14.95 (*0-7933-4808-0*); disk 29.95 (*0-7933-4809-9*) Gallopade Pub Group.

— Choose-Your-Own-Ending Sex Ed Adventures. (Smart Sex Stuff Ser.). 60p. (Orig.). 1994. 24.95 (*1-55609-283-0*); pap. 14.95 (*1-55609-226-1*) Gallopade Pub Group.

— Christopher Columbus Comes to Alabama! Includes Reproducible Activities for Kids! (Carole Marsh Alabama Bks.). (Illus.). (J). (gr. 3-12). 1994. lib. bdg. 24.95 (*0-7933-3620-1*); pap. 14.95 (*0-7933-3621-X*); disk 29.95 (*0-7933-3622-8*) Gallopade Pub Group.

— Christopher Columbus Comes to Alaska! Includes Reproducible Activities for Kids! (Carole Marsh Alaska Bks.). (Illus.). (J). (gr. 3-12). 1994. lib. bdg. 24.95 (*0-7933-3623-6*); pap. 14.95 (*0-7933-3624-4*); disk 29.95 (*0-7933-3625-2*) Gallopade Pub Group.

— Christopher Columbus Comes to Arizona! Includes Reproducible Activities for Kids! (Carole Marsh Arizona Bks.). (Illus.). (J). (gr. 3-12). 1994. lib. bdg. 24.95 (*0-7933-3626-0*); pap. 14.95 (*0-7933-3627-9*); disk 29.95 (*0-7933-3628-7*) Gallopade Pub Group.

— Christopher Columbus Comes to Arkansas! Includes Reproducible Activities for Kids! (Carole Marsh Arkansas Bks.). (Illus.). (J). (gr. 3-12). 1994. lib. bdg. 24.95 (*0-7933-3629-5*); pap. 14.95 (*0-7933-3630-9*); disk 29.95 (*0-7933-3631-7*) Gallopade Pub Group.

— Christopher Columbus Comes to California! Includes Reproducible Activities for Kids! (Carole Marsh California Bks.). (Illus.). (J). (gr. 3-12). 1994. lib. bdg. 24.95 (*0-7933-3632-5*); pap. 14.95 (*0-7933-3633-3*); disk 29.95 (*0-7933-3634-1*) Gallopade Pub Group.

— Christopher Columbus Comes to Colorado! Includes Reproducible Activities for Kids! (Carole Marsh Colorado Bks.). (Illus.). (J). (gr. 3-12). 1994. lib. bdg. 24.95 (*0-7933-3635-X*); pap. 14.95 (*0-7933-3636-8*); disk 29.95 (*0-7933-3637-6*) Gallopade Pub Group.

— Christopher Columbus Comes to Connecticut! Includes Reproducible Activities for Kids! (Carole Marsh Connecticut Bks.). (Illus.). (J). (gr. 3-12). 1994. lib. bdg. 24.95 (*0-7933-3638-4*); pap. 14.95 (*0-7933-3639-2*); disk 29.95 (*0-7933-3640-6*) Gallopade Pub Group.

— Christopher Columbus Comes to Delaware! Includes Reproducible Activities for Kids! (Carole Marsh Delaware Bks.). (Illus.). (J). (gr. 3-12). 1994. lib. bdg. 24.95 (*0-7933-3641-4*); pap. 14.95 (*0-7933-3642-2*); disk 29.95 (*0-7933-3643-0*) Gallopade Pub Group.

— Christopher Columbus Comes to Florida! Includes Reproducible Activities for Kids! (Carole Marsh Florida Bks.). (Illus.). (J). (gr. 3-12). 1994. lib. bdg. 24.95 (*0-7933-3647-3*); pap. 14.95 (*0-7933-3648-1*); disk 29.95 (*0-7933-3649-X*) Gallopade Pub Group.

— Christopher Columbus Comes to Georgia! Includes Reproducible Activities for Kids! (Carole Marsh Georgia Bks.). (Illus.). (J). (gr. 3-12). 1994. lib. bdg. 24.95 (*0-7933-3650-3*); pap. 14.95 (*0-7933-3651-1*); disk 29.95 (*0-7933-3652-X*) Gallopade Pub Group.

— Christopher Columbus Comes to Hawaii! Includes Reproducible Activities for Kids! (Carole Marsh Hawaii Bks.). (Illus.). (J). (gr. 3-12). 1994. lib. bdg. 24.95 (*0-7933-3653-8*); pap. 14.95 (*0-7933-3654-6*); disk 29.95 (*0-7933-3655-4*) Gallopade Pub Group.

— Christopher Columbus Comes to Idaho! Includes Reproducible Activities for Kids! (Carole Marsh Idaho Bks.). (Illus.). (J). (gr. 3-12). 1994. lib. bdg. 24.95 (*0-7933-3656-2*); pap. 14.95 (*0-7933-3657-0*); disk 29.95 (*0-7933-3658-9*) Gallopade Pub Group.

— Christopher Columbus Comes to Illinois! Includes Reproducible Activities for Kids! (Carole Marsh Illinois Bks.). (Illus.). (J). (gr. 3-12). 1994. lib. bdg. 24.95 (*0-7933-3659-7*); pap. 14.95 (*0-7933-3660-0*); disk 29.95 (*0-7933-3661-9*) Gallopade Pub Group.

— Christopher Columbus Comes to Indiana! Includes Reproducible Activities for Kids! (Carole Marsh Indiana Bks.). (Illus.). (J). (gr. 3-12). 1994. lib. bdg. 24.95 (*0-7933-3662-7*); pap. 14.95 (*0-7933-3663-5*); disk 29.95 (*0-7933-3664-3*) Gallopade Pub Group.

— Christopher Columbus Comes to Iowa! Includes Reproducible Activities for Kids! (Carole Marsh Iowa Bks.). (Illus.). (J). (gr. 3-12). 1994. lib. bdg. 24.95 (*0-7933-3665-1*); pap. 14.95 (*0-7933-3666-X*); disk 29.95 (*0-7933-3667-8*) Gallopade Pub Group.

M

— Christopher Columbus Comes to Kansas! Includes Reproducible Activities for Kids! (Carole Marsh Kansas Bks.). (Illus.). (J). (gr. 3-12). 1994. lib. bdg. 24.95 (*0-7933-3668-6*); pap. 14.95 (*0-7933-3669-4*); disk 29.95 (*0-7933-3670-8*) Gallopade Pub Group.

— Christopher Columbus Comes to Kentucky! Includes Reproducible Activities for Kids! (Carole Marsh Kentucky Bks.). (Illus.). (J). (gr. 3-12). 1994. lib. bdg. 24.95 (*0-7933-3671-6*); pap. 14.95 (*0-7933-3672-4*); disk 29.95 (*0-7933-3673-2*) Gallopade Pub Group.

— Christopher Columbus Comes to Louisiana! Includes Reproducible Activities for Kids! (Carole Marsh Louisiana Bks.). (Illus.). (J). (gr. 3-12). 1994. lib. bdg. 24.95 (*0-7933-3674-0*); pap. 14.95 (*0-7933-3675-9*); disk 29.95 (*0-7933-3676-7*) Gallopade Pub Group.

— Christopher Columbus Comes to Maine! Includes Reproducible Activities for Kids! (Carole Marsh Maine Bks.). (Illus.). (J). (gr. 3-12). 1994. lib. bdg. 24.95 (*0-7933-3677-5*); pap. 14.95 (*0-7933-3678-3*); disk 29.95 (*0-7933-3679-1*) Gallopade Pub Group.

— Christopher Columbus Comes to Maryland! Includes Reproducible Activities for Kids! (Carole Marsh Maryland Bks.). (Illus.). (J). (gr. 3-12). 1994. lib. bdg. 24.95 (*0-7933-3680-5*); pap. 14.95 (*0-7933-3681-3*); disk 29.95 (*0-7933-3682-1*) Gallopade Pub Group.

M

— Christopher Columbus Comes to Massachusetts! Includes Reproducible Activities for Kids! (Massachuseets Bks.). (Illus.). (J). (gr. 3-12). 1994. lib. bdg. 24.95 (*0-7933-3683-X*); pap. 14.95 (*0-7933-3684-8*); disk 29.95 (*0-7933-3685-6*) Gallopade Pub Group.

— Christopher Columbus Comes to Michigan! Includes Reproducible Activities for Kids! (Carole Marsh Michigan Bks.). (Illus.). (J). (gr. 3-12). 1994. lib. bdg. 24.95 (*0-7933-3686-4*); pap. 14.95 (*0-7933-3687-2*); disk 29.95 (*0-7933-3688-0*) Gallopade Pub Group.

— Christopher Columbus Comes to Minnesota! Includes Reproducible Activities for Kids! (Carole Marsh Minnesota Bks.). (Illus.). (J). (gr. 3-12). 1994. lib. bdg. 24.95 (*0-7933-3689-9*); pap. 14.95 (*0-7933-3690-2*); disk 29.95 (*0-7933-3691-0*) Gallopade Pub Group.

— Christopher Columbus Comes to Mississippi! Includes Reproducible Activities for Kids! (Carole Marsh Mississippi Bks.). (Illus.). (J). (gr. 3-12). 1994. lib. bdg. 24.95 (*0-7933-3692-9*); pap. 14.95 (*0-7933-3693-7*); disk 29.95 (*0-7933-3694-5*) Gallopade Pub Group.

— Christopher Columbus Comes to Missouri! Includes Reproducible Activities for Kids! (Carole Marsh Missouri Bks.). (Illus.). (J). (gr. 3-12). 1994. lib. bdg. 24.95 (*0-7933-3695-3*); pap. 14.95 (*0-7933-3696-1*); disk 29.95 (*0-7933-3697-X*) Gallopade Pub Group.

— Christopher Columbus Comes to Montana! Includes Reproducible Activities for Kids! (Carole Marsh Montana Bks.). (Illus.). (J). (gr. 3-12). 1994. lib. bdg. 24.95 (*0-7933-3698-8*); pap. 14.95 (*0-7933-3699-6*); disk 29.95 (*0-7933-3700-3*) Gallopade Pub Group.

— Christopher Columbus Comes to Nebraska! Includes Reproducible Activities for Kids! (Carole Marsh Nebraska Bks.). (Illus.). (J). (gr. 3-12). 1994. lib. bdg. 24.95 (*0-7933-3701-1*); pap. 14.95 (*0-7933-3702-X*); disk 29.95 (*0-7933-3703-8*) Gallopade Pub Group.

— Christopher Columbus Comes to Nevada! Includes Reproducible Activities for Kids! (Carole Marsh Nevada Bks.). (Illus.). (J). (gr. 3-12). 1994. lib. bdg. 24.95 (*0-7933-3704-6*); pap. 14.95 (*0-7933-3705-4*); disk 29.95 (*0-7933-3706-2*) Gallopade Pub Group.

— Christopher Columbus Comes to New Hampshire! Includes Reproducible Activities for Kids! (Carole Marsh New Hampshire Bks.). (Illus.). (J). (gr. 3-12). 1994. lib. bdg. 24.95 (*0-7933-3707-0*); pap. 14.95 (*0-7933-3708-9*); disk 29.95 (*0-7933-3709-7*) Gallopade Pub Group.

— Christopher Columbus Comes to New Jersey! Includes Reproducible Activities for Kids! (Carole Marsh New Jersey Bks.). (Illus.). (J). (gr. 3-12). 1994. lib. bdg. 24.95 (*0-7933-3710-0*); pap. 14.95 (*0-7933-3711-9*); disk 29.95 (*0-7933-3712-7*) Gallopade Pub Group.

— Christopher Columbus Comes to New Mexico! Includes Reproducible Activities for Kids! (Carole Marsh New Mexico Bks.). (Illus.). (J). (gr. 3-12). 1994. lib. bdg. 24.95 (*0-7933-3713-5*); pap. 14.95 (*0-7933-3714-3*); disk 29.95 (*0-7933-3715-1*) Gallopade Pub Group.

— Christopher Columbus Comes to New York! Includes Reproducible Activities for Kids! (Carole Marsh New York Bks.). (Illus.). (J). (gr. 3-12). 1994. lib. bdg. 24.95 (*0-7933-3716-X*); pap. 14.95 (*0-7933-3717-8*); disk 29.95 (*0-7933-3718-6*) Gallopade Pub Group.

— Christopher Columbus Comes to North Carolina! Includes Reproducible Activities for Kids! (Carole Marsh North Carolina Bks.). (Illus.). (J). (gr. 3-12). 1994. lib. bdg. 24.95 (*0-7933-3719-4*); pap. 14.95 (*0-7933-3720-8*); disk 29.95 (*0-7933-3721-6*) Gallopade Pub Group.

— Christopher Columbus Comes to North Dakota! Includes Reproducible Activities for Kids! (Carole Marsh North Dakota Bks.). (Illus.). (J). (gr. 3-12). 1994. lib. bdg. 24.95 (*0-7933-3722-4*); pap. 14.95 (*0-7933-3723-2*); disk 29.95 (*0-7933-3724-0*) Gallopade Pub Group.

— Christopher Columbus Comes to Ohio! Includes Reproducible Activities for Kids! (Carole Marsh Ohio Bks.). (Illus.). (J). (gr. 3-12). 1994. lib. bdg. 24.95 (*0-7933-3725-9*); pap. 14.95 (*0-7933-3726-7*); disk 29.95 (*0-7933-3727-5*) Gallopade Pub Group.

— Christopher Columbus Comes to Oklahoma! Includes Reproducible Activities for Kids! (Carole Marsh Oklahoma Bks.). (Illus.). (J). (gr. 3-12). 1994. lib. bdg. 24.95 (*0-7933-3728-3*); pap. 14.95 (*0-7933-3729-1*); disk 29.95 (*0-7933-3730-5*) Gallopade Pub Group.

— Christopher Columbus Comes to Oregon! Includes Reproducible Activities for Kids! (Oregon Bks.). (Illus.). (J). (gr. 3-12). 1994. lib. bdg. 24.95 (*0-7933-3731-3*); pap. 14.95 (*0-7933-3732-1*); disk 29.95 (*0-7933-3733-X*) Gallopade Pub Group.

— Christopher Columbus Comes to Pennsylvania! Includes Reproducible Activities for Kids! (Pennsylvania Bks.). (Illus.). (J). (gr. 3-12). 1994. lib. bdg. 24.95 (*0-7933-3734-8*); pap. 14.95 (*0-7933-3735-6*); disk 29.95 (*0-7933-3736-4*) Gallopade Pub Group.

— Christopher Columbus Comes to Rhode Island! Includes Reproducible Activities for Kids! (Rhode Island Bks.). (Illus.). (J). (gr. 3-12). 1994. lib. bdg. 24.95 (*0-7933-3737-2*); pap. 14.95 (*0-7933-3738-0*); disk 29.95 (*0-7933-3739-9*) Gallopade Pub Group.

— Christopher Columbus Comes to South Carolina! Includes Reproducible Activities for Kids! (South Carolina Bks.). (Illus.). (J). (gr. 3-12). 1994. lib. bdg. 24.95 (*0-7933-3740-2*); pap. 14.95 (*0-7933-3741-0*); disk 29.95 (*0-7933-3742-9*) Gallopade Pub Group.

— Christopher Columbus Comes to South Dakota! Includes Reproducible Activities for Kids! (South Dakota Bks.). (Illus.). (J). (gr. 3-12). 1994. lib. bdg. 24.95 (*0-7933-3743-7*); pap. 14.95 (*0-7933-3744-5*); disk 29.95 (*0-7933-3745-3*) Gallopade Pub Group.

— Christopher Columbus Comes to Tennessee! Includes Reproducible Activities for Kids! (Tennessee Bks.). (Illus.). (J). (gr. 3-12). 1994. lib. bdg. 24.95 (*0-7933-3746-1*); pap. 14.95 (*0-7933-3747-X*); disk 29.95 (*0-7933-3748-8*) Gallopade Pub Group.

— Christopher Columbus Comes to Texas! Includes Reproducible Activities for Kids! (Texas Bks.). (Illus.). (J). (gr. 3-12). 1994. lib. bdg. 24.95 (*0-7933-3749-6*); pap. 14.95 (*0-7933-3750-X*); disk 29.95 (*0-7933-3751-8*) Gallopade Pub Group.

— Christopher Columbus Comes to Utah! Includes Reproducible Activities for Kids! (Utah Bks.). (Illus.). (J). (gr. 3-12). 1994. lib. bdg. 24.95 (*0-7933-3752-6*); pap. 14.95 (*0-7933-3753-4*); disk 29.95 (*0-7933-3754-2*) Gallopade Pub Group.

— Christopher Columbus Comes to Vermont! Includes Reproducible Activities for Kids! (Vermont Bks.). (Illus.). (J). (gr. 3-12). 1994. lib. bdg. 24.95 (*0-7933-3755-0*); pap. 14.95 (*0-7933-3756-9*); disk 29.95 (*0-7933-3757-7*) Gallopade Pub Group.

— Christopher Columbus Comes to Virginia! Includes Reproducible Activities for Kids! (Virginia Bks.). (Illus.). (J). (gr. 3-12). 1994. lib. bdg. 24.95 (*0-7933-3758-5*); pap. 14.95 (*0-7933-3759-3*); disk 29.95 (*0-7933-3760-7*) Gallopade Pub Group.

— Christopher Columbus Comes to Washington! Includes Reproducible Activities for Kids! (Washington Bks.). (Illus.). (J). (gr. 3-12). 1994. lib. bdg. 24.95 (*0-7933-3761-5*); pap. 14.95 (*0-7933-3762-3*); disk 29.95 (*0-7933-3763-1*) Gallopade Pub Group.

— Christopher Columbus Comes to Washington D. C.! Includes Reproducible Activities for Kids! (Washington, D.C. Bks.). (Illus.). (J). (gr. 3-12). 1994. lib. bdg. 24.95 (*0-7933-3644-9*); pap. 14.95 (*0-7933-3645-7*); disk 29.95 (*0-7933-3646-5*) Gallopade Pub Group.

— Christopher Columbus Comes to West Virginia! Includes Reproducible Activities for Kids! (West Virginia Bks.). (Illus.). (J). (gr. 3-12). 1994. lib. bdg. 24.95 (*0-7933-3764-X*); pap. 14.95 (*0-7933-3765-8*); disk 29.95 (*0-7933-3766-6*) Gallopade Pub Group.

— Christopher Columbus Comes to Wisconsin! Includes Reproducible Activities for Kids! (Wisconsin Bks.). (Illus.). (J). (gr. 3-12). 1994. lib. bdg. 24.95 (*0-7933-3767-4*); pap. 14.95 (*0-7933-3768-2*); disk 29.95 (*0-7933-3769-0*) Gallopade Pub Group.

— Christopher Columbus Comes to Wyoming! Includes Reproducible Activities for Kids! (Wyoming Bks.). (Illus.). (J). (gr. 3-12). 1994. lib. bdg. 24.95 (*0-7933-3770-4*); pap. 14.95 (*0-7933-3771-2*); disk 29.95 (*0-7933-3772-0*) Gallopade Pub Group.

— Coastales. 1994. 24.95 (*1-55609-106-0*) Gallopade Pub Group.

— The Color Purple & All That Jazz. (Our Black Heritage Ser.). (J). (gr. 3-12). 1994. lib. bdg. 24.95 (*1-55609-315-2*); pap. 14.95 (*1-55609-314-4*); disk 29.95 (*1-55609-316-0*) Gallopade Pub Group.

— Colorado & Other State Greats (Biographies) (Carole Marsh Colorado Bks.). (Illus.). (YA). (gr. 3-12). 1994. lib. bdg. 24.95 (*1-55609-534-1*); pap. 14.95 (*1-55609-533-3*); disk 29.95 (*0-7933-1421-6*) Gallopade Pub Group.

— Colorado Bandits, Bushwackers, Outlaws, Crooks, Devils, Ghosts, Desperadoes & Other Assorted & Sundry Characters! (Carole Marsh Colorado Bks.). (Illus.). (YA). (gr. 3-12). 1994. lib. bdg. 24.95 (*0-7933-0190-4*); pap. 14.95 (*0-7933-0189-0*); disk 29.95 (*0-7933-0191-2*) Gallopade Pub Group.

— The Colorado Bookstore Book: A Surprising Guide to Our State's Bookstores & Their Specialties for Students, Teachers, Writers & Publishers. (Carole Marsh Colorado Bks.). (Illus.). 1994. lib. bdg. 24.95 (*0-7933-2870-5*); pap. 14.95 (*0-7933-2871-3*); disk 29.95 (*0-7933-2872-1*) Gallopade Pub Group.

— Colorado Classic Christmas Trivia: Stories, Recipes, Activities, Legends, Lore & More! (Carole Marsh Colorado Bks.). (Illus.). (YA). (gr. 3-12). 1994. lib. bdg. 24.95 (*0-7933-0193-9*); pap. 14.95 (*0-7933-0192-0*); disk 29.95 (*0-7933-0194-7*) Gallopade Pub Group.

— Colorado Coastales! (Carole Marsh Colorado Bks.). (J). 1994. lib. bdg. 24.95 (*0-7933-7270-4*) Gallopade Pub Group.

— Colorado Coastales! (Carole Marsh Colorado Bks.). (Illus.). (YA). (gr. 3-12). 1994. lib. bdg. 24.95 (*1-55609-530-9*); pap. 14.95 (*1-55609-529-5*); disk 29.95 (*0-7933-1417-8*) Gallopade Pub Group.

— Colorado "Crinkum-Crankum" A Funny Word Book about Our State. (Carole Marsh Colorado Bks.). (Illus.). (J). 1994. lib. bdg. 24.95 (*0-7933-4825-0*); pap. 14.95 (*0-7933-4826-9*); disk 29.95 (*0-7933-4827-7*) Gallopade Pub Group.

— Colorado Dingbats! Bk. 1: A Fun Book of Games, Stories, Activities & More about Our State That's All in Code! for You to Decipher. (Carole Marsh Colorado Bks.). (Illus.). (J). (gr. 3-12). 1994. lib. bdg. 24.95 (*0-7933-3788-7*); pap. 14.95 (*0-7933-3789-5*); disk 29.95 (*0-7933-3790-9*) Gallopade Pub Group.

— Colorado Festival Fun for Kids! (Carole Marsh Colorado Bks.). (Illus.). (YA). (gr. 3-12). 1994. lib. bdg. 24.95 (*0-7933-3941-3*); pap. 14.95 (*0-7933-3942-1*); disk 29.95 (*0-7933-3943-X*) Gallopade Pub Group.

— The Colorado Hot Air Balloon Mystery. (Carole Marsh Colorado Bks.). (Illus.). (J). (gr. 2-9). 1994. 24.95 (*0-7933-2363-0*); pap. 14.95 (*0-7933-2364-9*); disk 29.95 (*0-7933-2365-7*) Gallopade Pub Group.

— Colorado Jeopardy! Answers & Questions about Our State! (Carole Marsh Colorado Bks.). (Illus.). (J). (gr. 3-12). 1994. lib. bdg. 24.95 (*0-7933-4094-2*); pap. 14.95 (*0-7933-4095-0*); disk 29.95 (*0-7933-4096-9*) Gallopade Pub Group.

— Colorado "Jography" A Fun Run Thru Our State! (Carole Marsh Colorado Bks.). (Illus.). (YA). (gr. 3-12). 1994. lib. bdg. 24.95 (*1-55609-525-2*); pap. 14.95 (*1-55609-524-4*); disk 29.95 (*0-7933-1407-0*) Gallopade Pub Group.

— Colorado Kid's Cookbook: Recipes, How-to, History, Lore & More! (Carole Marsh Colorado Bks.). (Illus.). (YA). (gr. 3-12). 1994. lib. bdg. 24.95 (*0-7933-0202-1*); pap. 14.95 (*0-7933-0201-3*); disk 29.95 (*0-7933-0203-X*) Gallopade Pub Group.

— The Colorado Library Book: A Surprising Guide to the Unusual Special Collections in Libraries Across Our State for Students, Teachers, Writers & Publishers - Includes Reproducible Mailing Labels Plus Activities for Young People! (Carole Marsh Colorado Bks.). (Illus.). 1994. lib. bdg. 24.95 (*0-7933-3023-8*); pap. 14.95 (*0-7933-3024-6*); disk 29.95 (*0-7933-3025-4*) Gallopade Pub Group.

— The Colorado Media Book: A Surprising Guide to the Amazing Print, Broadcast & Online Media of Our State for Students, Teachers, Writers & Publishers - Includes Reproducible Mailing Labels Plus Activities for Young People! (Carole Marsh Colorado Bks.). (Illus.). 1994. lib. bdg. 24.95 (*0-7933-3176-5*); pap. 14.95 (*0-7933-3177-3*); disk 29.95 (*0-7933-3178-1*) Gallopade Pub Group.

— The Colorado Mystery Van Takes Off! Bk. 1: Handicapped Colorado Kids Sneak Off on a Big Adventure. (Carole Marsh Colorado Bks.). (Illus.). (J). (gr. 3-12). 1994. 24.95 (*0-7933-4979-6*); pap. 14.95 (*0-7933-4980-X*); disk 29.95 (*0-7933-4981-8*) Gallopade Pub Group.

— Colorado Quiz Bowl Crash Course! (Carole Marsh Colorado Bks.). (Illus.). (YA). (gr. 3-12). 1994. lib. bdg. 24.95 (*0-685-45927-6*); pap. 14.95 (*1-55609-531-7*); disk 29.95 (*0-7933-1416-X*) Gallopade Pub Group.

— Colorado Rollercoasters! (Carole Marsh Colorado Bks.). (Illus.). (YA). (gr. 3-12). 1994. lib. bdg. 24.95 (*0-7933-5239-8*); pap. 14.95 (*0-7933-5240-1*); disk 29.95 (*0-7933-5241-X*) Gallopade Pub Group.

— Colorado School Trivia: An Amazing & Fascinating Look at Our State's Teachers, Schools & Students! (Carole Marsh Colorado Bks.). (Illus.). (YA). (gr. 3-12). 1994. lib. bdg. 24.95 (*0-7933-0199-8*); pap. 14.95 (*0-7933-0198-X*); disk 29.95 (*0-7933-0200-5*) Gallopade Pub Group.

— Colorado Silly Basketball Sportsmysteries, Vol. I. (Carole Marsh Colorado Bks.). (Illus.). (YA). (gr. 3-12). 1994. lib. bdg. 24.95 (*0-7933-0196-3*); pap. 14.95 (*0-7933-0195-5*); disk 29.95 (*0-7933-0197-1*) Gallopade Pub Group.

— Colorado Silly Basketball Sportsmysteries, Vol. II. (Carole Marsh Colorado Bks.). (Illus.). (YA). (gr. 3-12). 1994. lib. bdg. 24.95 (*0-7933-1577-8*); pap. 14.95 (*0-7933-1578-6*); disk 29.95 (*0-7933-1579-4*) Gallopade Pub Group.

— Colorado Silly Football Sportsmysteries, Vol. I. (Carole Marsh Colorado Bks.). (Illus.). (YA). (gr. 3-12). 1994. lib. bdg. 24.95 (*1-55609-528-7*); pap. 14.95 (*1-55609-527-9*); disk 29.95 (*0-7933-1409-7*) Gallopade Pub Group.

— Colorado Silly Football Sportsmysteries, Vol. II. (Carole Marsh Colorado Bks.). (Illus.). (YA). (gr. 3-12). 1994. lib. bdg. 24.95 (*0-7933-1410-0*); pap. 14.95 (*0-7933-1411-9*); disk 29.95 (*0-7933-1412-7*) Gallopade Pub Group.

— Colorado Silly Trivia! (Carole Marsh Colorado Bks.). (Illus.). (YA). (gr. 3-12). 1994. lib. bdg. 24.95 (*1-55609-523-6*); pap. 14.95 (*1-55609-522-8*); disk 29.95 (*0-7933-1406-2*) Gallopade Pub Group.

— Colorado Timeline: A Chronology of Colorado History, Mystery, Trivia, Legend, Lore & More. (Carole Marsh Colorado Bks.). (Illus.). (J). (gr. 3-12). 1994. lib. bdg. 24.95 (*0-7933-5890-6*); pap. 14.95 (*0-7933-5891-4*); disk 29.95 (*0-7933-5892-2*) Gallopade Pub Group.

— Colorado's (Most Devastating!) Disasters & (Most Calamitous!) Catastrophies! (Carole Marsh Colorado Bks.). (Illus.). (YA). (gr. 3-12). 1994. lib. bdg. 24.95 (*0-7933-0187-4*); pap. 14.95 (*0-7933-0186-6*); disk 29.95 (*0-7933-0188-2*) Gallopade Pub Group.

— Colorado's Unsolved Mysteries (& Their "Solutions") Includes Scientific Information & Other Activities for Students. (Carole Marsh Colorado Bks.). (Illus.). (J). (gr. 3-12). 1994. lib. bdg. 24.95 (*0-7933-5737-3*); pap. 14.95 (*0-7933-5738-1*); disk 29.95 (*0-7933-5739-X*) Gallopade Pub Group.

— Columbia Lastname: The Schwarzchild Radius, Bk. 1. (Columbia Lastname Ser.). (Orig.). (YA). (gr. 4 up). 1994. lib. bdg. 24.95 (*1-55609-284-9*); pap. text ed. 14.95 (*0-935326-62-6*) Gallopade Pub Group.

— Connecticut & Other State Greats (Biographies) (Carole Marsh Connecticut Bks.). (Illus.). (YA). (gr. 3-12). 1994. lib. bdg. 24.95 (*1-55609-547-3*); pap. 14.95 (*1-55609-546-5*); disk 29.95 (*0-7933-1437-2*) Gallopade Pub Group.

— Connecticut Bandits, Bushwackers, Outlaws, Crooks, Devils, Ghosts, Desperadoes & Other Assorted & Sundry Characters! (Carole Marsh Connecticut Bks.). (Illus.). (YA). (gr. 3-12). 1994. lib. bdg. 24.95 (*0-7933-0214-5*); pap. 14.95 (*0-7933-0213-7*); disk 29.95 (*0-7933-0215-3*) Gallopade Pub Group.

— The Connecticut Bookstore Book: A Surprising Guide to Our State's Bookstores & Their Specialties for Students, Teachers, Writers & Publishers. (Carole Marsh Connecticut Bks.). (Illus.). 1994. lib. bdg. 24.95 (*0-7933-2873-X*); pap. 14.95 (*0-7933-2874-8*); disk 29.95 (*0-7933-2875-6*) Gallopade Pub Group.

— Connecticut Classic Christmas Trivia: Stories, Recipes, Activities, Legends, Lore & More! (Carole Marsh Connecticut Bks.). (Illus.). (YA). (gr. 3-12). 1994. lib. bdg. 24.95 (*0-7933-0217-X*); pap. 14.95 (*0-7933-0216-1*); disk 29.95 (*0-7933-0218-8*) Gallopade Pub Group.

— Connecticut Coastales. (Carole Marsh Connecticut Bks.). (Illus.). (YA). (gr. 3-12). 1994. lib. bdg. 24.95 (*1-55609-543-0*); pap. 14.95 (*1-55609-542-2*); disk 29.95 (*0-7933-1433-X*) Gallopade Pub Group.

— Connecticut Coastales! (Carole Marsh Connecticut Bks.). (J). 1994. lib. bdg. 24.95 (*0-7933-7271-2*) Gallopade Pub Group.

— Connecticut "Crinkum-Crankum" A Funny Word Book about Our State. (Carole Marsh Connecticut Bks.). (Illus.). (J). 1994. lib. bdg. 24.95 (*0-7933-4828-5*); pap. 14.95 (*0-7933-4829-3*); disk 29.95 (*0-7933-4830-7*) Gallopade Pub Group.

— Connecticut Dingbats! Bk. 1: A Fun Book of Games, Stories, Activities & More about Our State That's All in Code! for You to Decipher. (Carole Marsh Connecticut Bks.). (Illus.). (J). (gr. 3-12). 1994. lib. bdg. 24.95 (*0-7933-3791-7*); pap. 14.95 (*0-7933-3792-5*); disk 29.95 (*0-7933-3793-3*) Gallopade Pub Group.

— Connecticut Festival Fun for Kids! (Carole Marsh Connecticut Bks.). (Illus.). (YA). (gr. 3-12). 1994. lib. bdg. 24.95 (*0-7933-3944-8*); pap. 14.95 (*0-7933-3945-6*); disk 29.95 (*0-7933-3946-4*) Gallopade Pub Group.

— The Connecticut Hot Air Balloon Mystery. (Carole Marsh Connecticut Bks.). (Illus.). (J). (gr. 2-9). 1994. 24.95 (*0-7933-2372-X*); pap. 14.95 (*0-7933-2373-8*); disk 29.95 (*0-7933-2374-6*) Gallopade Pub Group.

— Connecticut Jeopardy! Answers & Questions about Our State! (Carole Marsh Connecticut Bks.). (Illus.). (J). (gr. 3-12). 1994. lib. bdg. 24.95 (*0-7933-4097-7*); pap. 14.95 (*0-7933-4098-5*); disk 29.95 (*0-7933-4099-3*) Gallopade Pub Group.

— Connecticut "Jography" A Fun Run Thru Our State! (Carole Marsh Connecticut Bks.). (Illus.). (YA). (gr. 3-12). 1994. lib. bdg. 24.95 (*1-55609-538-4*); pap. 14.95 (*1-55609-537-6*); disk 29.95 (*0-7933-1423-2*) Gallopade Pub Group.

— Connecticut Kid's Cookbook: Recipes, How-to, History, Lore & More! (Carole Marsh Connecticut Bks.). (Illus.). (YA). (gr. 3-12). 1994. lib. bdg. 24.95 (*0-7933-0226-9*); pap. 14.95 (*0-7933-0225-0*); disk 29.95 (*0-7933-0227-7*) Gallopade Pub Group.

— The Connecticut Library Book: A Surprising Guide to the Unusual Special Collections in Libraries Across Our State for Students, Teachers, Writers & Publishers - Includes Reproducible Mailing Labels Plus Activities for Young People! (Carole Marsh Connecticut Bks.). (Illus.). 1994. lib. bdg. 24.95 (*0-7933-3158-7*); pap. 14.95 (*0-7933-3159-5*); disk 29.95 (*0-7933-3160-9*) Gallopade Pub Group.

— The Connecticut Media Book: A Surprising Guide to the Amazing Print, Broadcast & Online Media of Our State for Students, Teachers, Writers & Publishers - Includes Reproducible Mailing Labels Plus Activities for Young People! (Carole Marsh Connecticut Bks.). (Illus.). 1994. lib. bdg. 24.95 (*0-7933-3179-X*); pap. 14.95 (*0-7933-3180-3*); disk 29.95 (*0-7933-3181-1*) Gallopade Pub Group.

— The Connecticut Mystery Van Takes Off! Book 1: Handicapped Connecticut Kids Sneak Off on a Big Adventure. (Carole Marsh Connecticut Bks.). (Illus.). (J). (gr. 3-12). 1994. 24.95 (*0-7933-4982-6*); pap. 14.95 (*0-7933-4983-4*); disk 29.95 (*0-7933-4984-2*) Gallopade Pub Group.

— Connecticut Quiz Bowl Crash Course! (Carole Marsh Connecticut Bks.). (Illus.). (YA). (gr. 3-12). 1994. lib. bdg. 24.95 (*1-55609-545-7*); pap. 14.95 (*1-55609-544-9*); disk 29.95 (*0-7933-1432-1*) Gallopade Pub Group.

— Connecticut Rollercoasters! (Carole Marsh Connecticut Bks.). (Illus.). (YA). (gr. 3-12). 1994. lib. bdg. 24.95 (*0-7933-5242-8*); pap. 14.95 (*0-7933-5243-6*); disk 29.95 (*0-7933-5244-4*) Gallopade Pub Group.

— Connecticut School Trivia: An Amazing & Fascinating Look at Our State's Teachers, Schools & Students! (Carole Marsh Connecticut Bks.). (Illus.). (YA). (gr. 3-12). 1994. lib. bdg. 24.95 (*0-7933-0223-4*); pap. 14.95 (*0-7933-0222-6*); disk 29.95 (*0-7933-0224-2*) Gallopade Pub Group.

— Connecticut Silly Basketball Sportsmysteries, Vol. I. (Carole Marsh Connecticut Bks.). (Illus.). (YA). (gr. 3-12). 1994. lib. bdg. 24.95 (*0-7933-0220-X*); pap. 14.95 (*0-7933-0219-6*); disk 29.95 (*0-7933-0221-8*) Gallopade Pub Group.

— Connecticut Silly Basketball Sportsmysteries, Vol. II. (Carole Marsh Connecticut Bks.). (Illus.). (YA). (gr. 3-12). 1994. lib. bdg. 24.95 (*0-7933-1580-8*); pap. 14.95 (*0-7933-1581-6*); disk 29.95 (*0-685-45929-2*) Gallopade Pub Group.

— Connecticut Silly Football Sportsmysteries, Vol. I. (Carole Marsh Connecticut Bks.). (Illus.). (YA). (gr. 3-12). 1994. lib. bdg. 24.95 (*1-55609-541-4*); pap. 14.95 (*1-55609-540-6*); disk 29.95 (*0-7933-1425-9*) Gallopade Pub Group.

— Connecticut Silly Football Sportsmysteries, Vol. II. (Carole Marsh Connecticut Bks.). (Illus.). (YA). (gr. 3-12). 1994. lib. bdg. 24.95 (*0-7933-1426-7*); pap. 14.95 (*0-7933-1427-5*); disk 29.95 (*0-7933-1428-3*) Gallopade Pub Group.

— Connecticut Silly Trivia! (Carole Marsh Connecticut Bks.). (Illus.). (YA). (gr. 3-12). 1994. lib. bdg. 24.95 (*1-55609-536-8*); pap. 14.95 (*1-55609-535-X*); disk 29.95 (*0-7933-1422-4*) Gallopade Pub Group.

— Connecticut Timeline: A Chronology of Connecticut History, Mystery, Trivia, Legend, Lore & More. (Carole Marsh Connecticut Bks.). (Illus.). (J). (gr. 3-12). 1994. lib. bdg. 24.95 (*0-7933-5893-0*); pap. 14.95 (*0-7933-5894-9*); disk 29.95 (*0-7933-5895-7*) Gallopade Pub Group.

— Connecticut's (Most Devastating!) Disasters & (Most Calamitous!) Catastrophies! (Carole Marsh Connecticut Bks.). (Illus.). (YA). (gr. 3-12). 1994. lib. bdg. 24.95 (*0-7933-0211-0*); pap. 14.95 (*0-7933-0210-2*); disk 29.95 (*0-7933-0212-9*) Gallopade Pub Group.

— Connecticut's Unsolved Mysteries (& Their "Solutions") Includes Scientific Information & Other Activities for Students. (Carole Marsh Connecticut Bks.). (Illus.). (J). (gr. 3-12). 1994. lib. bdg. 24.95 (*0-7933-5740-3*); pap. 14.95 (*0-7933-5741-1*); disk 29.95 (*0-7933-5742-X*) Gallopade Pub Group.

— Could Your Kid Die "Laughing"? AIDS & Today's Adolescent. (Smart Sex Stuff Ser.). (Orig.). 1994. 24.95 (*1-55609-262-8*); pap. 14.95 (*1-55609-225-3*) Gallopade Pub Group.

— Crazy Comet Classroom Gamebook. (Carole Marsh Bks.). (Illus.). (Orig.). (J). (gr. 3-12). 1994. pap. 19.95 (*0-935326-87-1*) Gallopade Pub Group.

— The Crazy Comet Silly Trivia Book. (Gallopade Galaxy Ser.). (Illus.). 60p. (Orig.). (J). (gr. 2-12). 1994. pap. 14.95 (*0-935326-64-2*) Gallopade Pub Group.

— Cross Staff: A Fictional Journal of Eleanor Dare. (Lost Colony Collection). (Illus.). 200p. (Orig.). 1994. pap. 14.95 (*0-935326-44-8*) Gallopade Pub Group.

— Crosstaff: Journal Writing Activity Kit. (Carole Marsh Bks.). (Illus.). (Orig.). (J). (gr. 4-12). 1994. pap. 14.95 (*0-935326-23-5*) Gallopade Pub Group.

— Delaware & Other State Greats (Biographies) (Carole Marsh Delaware Bks.). (Illus.). (YA). (gr. 3-12). 1994. lib. bdg. 24.95 (*1-55609-558-9*); pap. 14.95 (*1-55609-557-0*); disk 29.95 (*0-7933-1455-0*) Gallopade Pub Group.

— Delaware Bandits, Bushwackers, Outlaws, Crooks, Devils, Ghosts, Desperadoes & Other Assorted & Sundry Characters! (Carole Marsh Delaware Bks.). (Illus.). (YA). (gr. 3-12). 1994. lib. bdg. 24.95 (*0-7933-0238-2*); pap. 14.95 (*0-7933-0237-4*); disk 29.95 (*0-7933-0239-0*) Gallopade Pub Group.

— The Delaware Bookstore Book: A Surprising Guide to Our State's Bookstores & Their Specialties for Students, Teachers, Writers & Publishers. (Carole Marsh Delaware Bks.). (Illus.). 1994. lib. bdg. 24.95 (*0-7933-2876-4*); pap. 14.95 (*0-7933-2877-2*); disk 29.95 (*0-7933-2878-0*) Gallopade Pub Group.

— Delaware Classic Christmas Trivia: Stories, Recipes, Activities, Legends, Lore & More! (Carole Marsh Delaware Bks.). (Illus.). (YA). (gr. 3-12). 1994. lib. bdg. 24.95 (*0-7933-0241-2*); pap. 14.95 (*0-7933-0240-4*); disk 29.95 (*0-7933-0242-0*) Gallopade Pub Group.

— Delaware Coastales. (Carole Marsh Delaware Bks.). (Illus.). (YA). (gr. 3-12). 1994. lib. bdg. 24.95 (*1-55609-554-6*); pap. 14.95 (*1-55609-553-8*); disk 29.95 (*0-7933-1451-8*) Gallopade Pub Group.

— Delaware Coastales! (Carole Marsh Delaware Bks.). (J). 1994. lib. bdg. 24.95 (*0-7933-7272-0*) Gallopade Pub Group.

— Delaware "Crinkum-Crankum" A Funny Word Book about Our State. (Carole Marsh Delaware Bks.). (Illus.). (J). 1994. lib. bdg. 24.95 (*0-7933-4831-5*); pap. 14.95 (*0-7933-4832-3*); disk 29.95 (*0-7933-4833-1*) Gallopade Pub Group.

— Delaware Dingbats! Bk. 1: A Fun Book of Games, Stories, Activities & More about Our State That's All in Code! for You to Decipher. (Carole Marsh Delaware Bks.). (Illus.). (J). (gr. 3-12). 1994. lib. bdg. 24.95 (*0-7933-3794-1*); pap. 14.95 (*0-7933-3795-X*); disk 29.95 (*0-7933-3796-8*) Gallopade Pub Group.

— Delaware Festival Fun for Kids! (Carole Marsh Delaware Bks.). (Illus.). (YA). (gr. 3-12). 1994. lib. bdg. 24.95 (*0-7933-3947-2*); pap. 14.95 (*0-7933-3948-0*); disk 29.95 (*0-7933-3949-9*) Gallopade Pub Group.

— The Delaware Hot Air Balloon Mystery. (Carole Marsh Delaware Bks.). (Illus.). (J). (gr. 2-9). 1994. 24.95 (*0-685-37849-7*); pap. 14.95 (*0-7933-2382-7*); disk 29.95 (*0-7933-2383-5*) Gallopade Pub Group.

— Delaware Jeopardy! Answers & Questions about Our State! (Carole Marsh Delaware Bks.). (Illus.). (J). (gr. 3-12). 1994. lib. bdg. 24.95 (*0-7933-4100-0*); pap. 14.95 (*0-7933-4101-9*); disk 29.95 (*0-7933-4102-7*) Gallopade Pub Group.

— Delaware "Jography" A Fun Run Thru Our State! (Carole Marsh Delaware Bks.). (Illus.). (YA). (gr. 3-12). 1994. lib. bdg. 24.95 (*1-55609-551-1*); pap. 14.95 (*1-55609-550-3*); disk 29.95 (*0-7933-1439-9*) Gallopade Pub Group.

— Delaware Kid's Cookbook: Recipes, How-to-, History, Lore & More! (Carole Marsh Delaware Bks.). (Illus.). (YA). (gr. 3-12). 1994. lib. bdg. 24.95 (*0-7933-0250-1*); pap. 14.95 (*0-7933-0249-8*); disk 29.95 (*0-7933-0251-X*) Gallopade Pub Group.

— The Delaware Library Book: A Surprising Guide to the Unusual Special Collections in Libraries Across Our State for Students, Teachers, Writers & Publishers - Includes Reproducible Mailing Labels Plus Activities for Young People! (Carole Marsh Delaware Bks.). (Illus.). 1994. lib. bdg. 24.95 (*0-7933-3026-2*); pap. 14.95 (*0-7933-3027-0*); disk 29.95 (*0-7933-3028-9*) Gallopade Pub Group.

— The Delaware Media Book: A Surprising Guide to the Amazing Print, Broadcast & Online Media of Our State for Students, Teachers, Writers & Publishers - Includes Reproducible Mailing Labels Plus Activities for Young People! (Carole Marsh Delaware Bks.). (Illus.). 1994. lib. bdg. 24.95 (*0-7933-3182-X*); pap. 14.95 (*0-7933-3183-8*); disk 29.95 (*0-7933-3184-6*) Gallopade Pub Group.

— The Delaware Mystery Van Takes Off! Book 1: Handicapped Delaware Kids Sneak Off on a Big Adventure. (Carole Marsh Delaware Bks.). (Illus.). (J). (gr. 3-12). 1994. 24.95 (*0-7933-4985-0*); pap. 14.95 (*0-7933-4986-9*); disk 29.95 (*0-7933-4987-7*) Gallopade Pub Group.

— Delaware Quiz Bowl Crash Course! (Carole Marsh Delaware Bks.). (Illus.). (YA). (gr. 3-12). 1994. lib. bdg. 24.95 (*1-55609-556-2*); pap. 14.95 (*1-55609-555-4*); disk 29.95 (*0-7933-1450-X*) Gallopade Pub Group.

— Delaware Rollercoasters! (Carole Marsh Delaware Bks.). (Illus.). (YA). (gr. 3-12). 1994. lib. bdg. 24.95 (*0-7933-5245-2*); pap. 14.95 (*0-7933-5246-0*); disk 29.95 (*0-7933-5247-9*) Gallopade Pub Group.

— Delaware School Trivia: An Amazing & Fascinating Look at Our State's Teachers, Schools & Students! (Carole Marsh Delaware Bks.). (Illus.). (YA). (gr. 3-12). 1994. lib. bdg. 24.95 (*0-7933-0247-1*); pap. 14.95 (*0-7933-0246-3*); disk 29.95 (*0-7933-0248-X*) Gallopade Pub Group.

— Delaware Silly Basketball Sportsmysteries, Vol. I. (Carole Marsh Delaware Bks.). (Illus.). (YA). (gr. 3-12). 1994. lib. bdg. 24.95 (*0-7933-0244-7*); pap. 14.95 (*0-7933-0243-9*); disk 29.95 (*0-7933-0245-5*) Gallopade Pub Group.

— Delaware Silly Basketball Sportsmysteries, Vol. II. (Carole Marsh Delaware Bks.). (Illus.). (YA). (gr. 3-12). 1994. lib. bdg. 24.95 (*0-7933-1456-9*); pap. 14.95 (*0-7933-1457-7*); disk 29.95 (*0-7933-1458-5*) Gallopade Pub Group.

— Delaware Silly Football Sportsmysteries, Vol. I. (Carole Marsh Delaware Bks.). (Illus.). (YA). (gr. 3-12). 1994. lib. bdg. 24.95 (*0-7933-1441-0*); pap. 14.95 (*0-7933-1442-9*); disk 29.95 (*0-7933-1443-7*) Gallopade Pub Group.

— Delaware Silly Football Sportsmysteries, Vol. II. (Carole Marsh Delaware Bks.). (Illus.). (YA). (gr. 3-12). 1994. lib. bdg. 24.95 (*0-7933-1444-5*); pap. 14.95 (*0-7933-1445-3*); disk 29.95 (*0-7933-1446-1*) Gallopade Pub Group.

— Delaware Silly Trivia! (Carole Marsh Delaware Bks.). (Illus.). (YA). (gr. 3-12). 1994. lib. bdg. 24.95 (*1-55609-549-X*); pap. 14.95 (*1-55609-548-1*); disk 29.95 (*0-7933-1438-0*) Gallopade Pub Group.

— Delaware Timeline: A Chronology of Delaware History, Mystery, Trivia, Legend, Lore & More. (Carole Marsh Delaware Bks.). (Illus.). (J). (gr. 3-12). 1994. lib. bdg. 24.95 (*0-7933-5896-5*); pap. 14.95 (*0-7933-5897-3*); disk 29.95 (*0-7933-5898-1*) Gallopade Pub Group.

— Delaware's (Most Devastating!) Disasters & (Most Calamitous!) Catastrophies! (Carole Marsh Delaware Bks.). (Illus.). (YA). (gr. 3-12). 1994. lib. bdg. 24.95 (*0-7933-0235-8*); pap. 14.95 (*0-7933-0234-X*); disk 29.95 (*0-7933-0236-6*) Gallopade Pub Group.

— Delaware's Unsolved Mysteries (& Their "Solutions") Includes Scientific Information & Other Activities for Students. (Carole Marsh Delaware Bks.). (Illus.). (J). (gr. 3-12). 1994. lib. bdg. 24.95 (*0-7933-5743-8*); pap. 14.95 (*0-7933-5744-6*); disk 29.95 (*0-7933-5745-4*) Gallopade Pub Group.

— Dinosaur Trivia for Kids: I'm Saury! (Quantum Leap Ser.). (Illus.). (Orig.). (J). (gr. 2 up). 1994. lib. bdg. 24.95 (*1-55609-162-1*); pap. 14.95 (*0-935326-54-5*) Gallopade Pub Group.

— The Dragons & Dungeons Dingbats Book. (Carole Marsh Dingbats Book Ser.). (Illus.). (YA). (gr. 3-12). 1994. lib. bdg. 24.95 (*0-7933-5395-5*); pap. 14.95 (*0-7933-5396-3*); disk 29.95 (*0-7933-5397-1*) Gallopade Pub Group.

— The Drawers of Ocracoke. (Carole Marsh Short Story Ser.). (Illus.). (Orig.). (J). (ps-7). 1994. 24.95 (*1-55609-163-X*); pap. 14.95 (*1-55609-236-9*) Gallopade Pub Group.

— Everready Editorial: How to Write a New Book Every Day! (Lifewrite Ser.). 1994. 24.95 (*1-55609-956-8*); lib. bdg. 24.95 (*1-55609-954-1*); pap. text ed. 14.95 (*1-55609-955-X*); disk 29.95 (*1-55609-957-6*) Gallopade Pub Group.

— First AIDS: Frank Facts for Kids. (Smart Sex Stuff Ser.). (Orig.). 1994. 24.95 (*1-55609-153-2*); pap. 14.95 (*1-55609-205-9*) Gallopade Pub Group.

— Florida & Other State Greats (Biographies) Florida Bks. (Illus.). (YA). (gr. 3-12). 1994. lib. bdg. 24.95 (*1-55609-426-4*); pap. 14.95 (*1-55609-425-6*); disk 29.95 (*0-7933-1501-8*) Gallopade Pub Group.

— Florida Bandits, Bushwackers, Outlaws, Crooks, Devils, Ghosts, Desperadoes & Other Assorted & Sundry Characters! (Carole Marsh Florida Bks.). (Illus.). (YA). (gr. 3-12). 1994. lib. bdg. 24.95 (*0-7933-0286-2*); pap. 14.95 (*0-7933-0285-4*); disk 29.95 (*0-7933-0287-0*) Gallopade Pub Group.

— The Florida Bookstore Book: A Surprising Guide to Our State's Bookstores & Their Specialties for Students, Teachers, Writers & Publishers. (Carole Marsh Florida Bks.). (Illus.). 1994. lib. bdg. 24.95 (*0-7933-2882-9*); pap. 14.95 (*0-7933-2883-7*); disk 29.95 (*0-7933-2884-5*) Gallopade Pub Group.

— Florida Classic Christmas Trivia: Stories, Recipes, Activities, Legends, Lore & More! (Carole Marsh Florida Bks.). (Illus.). (YA). (gr. 3-12). 1994. lib. bdg. 24.95 (*0-7933-0289-7*); pap. 14.95 (*0-7933-0288-9*); disk 29.95 (*0-7933-0290-0*) Gallopade Pub Group.

— Florida Coastales. (Carole Marsh Florida Bks.). (Illus.). (YA). (gr. 3-12). 1994. lib. bdg. 24.95 (*1-55609-422-1*); pap. 14.95 (*1-55609-118-4*); disk 29.95 (*0-7933-1497-6*) Gallopade Pub Group.

— Florida Coastales! (Carole Marsh Florida Bks.). (J). 1994. lib. bdg. 24.95 (*0-7933-7274-7*) Gallopade Pub Group.

— Florida "Crinkum-Crankum" A Funny Word Book about Our State. (Carole Marsh Florida Bks.). (Illus.). (J). 1994. lib. bdg. 24.95 (*0-7933-4834-X*); pap. 14.95 (*0-7933-4835-8*); disk 29.95 (*0-7933-4836-6*) Gallopade Pub Group.

— Florida Dingbats! Bk. 1: A Fun Book of Games, Stories, Activities & More about Our State That's All in Code! for You to Decipher. (Carole Marsh Florida Bks.). (Illus.). (J). (gr. 3-12). 1994. lib. bdg. 24.95 (*0-7933-3800-X*); pap. 14.95 (*0-7933-3801-8*); disk 29.95 (*0-7933-3802-6*) Gallopade Pub Group.

— Florida Festival Fun for Kids! (Carole Marsh Florida Bks.). (Illus.). (YA). (gr. 3-12). 1994. lib. bdg. 24.95 (*0-7933-3953-7*); pap. 14.95 (*0-7933-3954-5*); disk 29.95 (*0-7933-3955-3*) Gallopade Pub Group.

— The Florida Hot Air Balloon Mystery. (Carole Marsh Florida Bks.). (Illus.). (J). (gr. 2-9). 1994. 24.95 (*0-7933-2399-1*); pap. 14.95 (*0-7933-2400-9*); disk 29.95 (*0-7933-2401-7*) Gallopade Pub Group.

— Florida Jeopardy! Answers & Questions about Our State! (Carole Marsh Florida Bks.). (Illus.). (J). (gr. 3-12). 1994. lib. bdg. 24.95 (*0-7933-4106-X*); pap. 14.95 (*0-7933-4107-8*); disk 29.95 (*0-7933-4108-6*) Gallopade Pub Group.

— Florida "Jography" A Fun Run Thru Our State! (Carole Marsh Florida Bks.). (Illus.). (YA). (gr. 3-12). 1994. lib. bdg. 24.95 (*1-55609-418-3*); pap. 14.95 (*1-55609-048-X*); disk 29.95 (*0-7933-1487-9*) Gallopade Pub Group.

— Florida Kid's Cookbook: Recipes, How-To, History, Lore & More! (Carole Marsh Florida Bks.). (Illus.). (YA). (gr. 3-12). 1994. lib. bdg. 24.95 (*0-7933-0298-6*); pap. 14.95 (*0-7933-0297-8*); disk 29.95 (*0-7933-0299-4*) Gallopade Pub Group.

— The Florida Library Book: A Surprising Guide to the Unusual Special Collections in Libraries Across Our State for Students, Teachers, Writers & Publishers - Includes Reproducible Mailing Labels Plus Activities for Young People! (Carole Marsh Florida Bks.). (Illus.). 1994. lib. bdg. 24.95 (*0-7933-3032-7*); pap. 14.95 (*0-7933-3033-5*); disk 29.95 (*0-7933-3034-3*) Gallopade Pub Group.

— The Florida Media Book: A Surprising Guide to the Amazing Print, Broadcast & Online Media of Our State for Students, Teachers, Writers & Publishers - Includes Reproducible Mailing Labels Plus Activities for Young People! (Carole Marsh Florida Bks.). (Illus.). 1994. lib. bdg. 24.95 (*0-7933-3188-9*); pap. 14.95 (*0-7933-3189-7*); disk 29.95 (*0-7933-3190-0*) Gallopade Pub Group.

— The Florida Mystery Van Takes Off! Book 1: Handicapped Florida Kids Sneak Off on a Big Adventure. (Carole Marsh Florida Bks.). (Illus.). (J). (gr. 3-12). 1994. 24.95 (*0-7933-4988-5*); pap. 14.95 (*0-7933-4989-3*); disk 29.95 (*0-7933-4990-7*) Gallopade Pub Group.

— Florida Quiz Bowl Crash Course! (Carole Marsh Florida Bks.). (Illus.). (YA). (gr. 3-12). 1994. lib. bdg. 24.95 (*1-55609-424-8*); pap. 14.95 (*1-55609-423-X*); disk 29.95 (*0-7933-1496-8*) Gallopade Pub Group.

— Florida Rollercoasters! (Carole Marsh Florida Bks.). (Illus.). (YA). (gr. 3-12). 1994. lib. bdg. 24.95 (*0-7933-5251-7*); pap. 14.95 (*0-7933-5252-5*); disk 29.95 (*0-7933-5253-3*) Gallopade Pub Group.

— Florida School Trivia: An Amazing & Fascinating Look at Our State's Teachers, Schools & Students! (Carole Marsh Florida Bks.). (Illus.). (YA). (gr. 3-12). 1994. lib. bdg. 24.95 (*0-7933-0295-1*); pap. 14.95 (*0-7933-0294-3*); disk 29.95 (*0-7933-0296-X*) Gallopade Pub Group.

— Florida Silly Basketball Sportsmysteries, Vol. I. (Carole Marsh Florida Bks.). (Illus.). (YA). (gr. 3-12). 1994. lib. bdg. 24.95 (*0-7933-0292-7*); pap. 14.95 (*0-7933-0291-9*); disk 29.95 (*0-7933-0293-5*) Gallopade Pub Group.

— Florida Silly Basketball Sportsmysteries, Vol. II. (Carole Marsh Florida Bks.). (Illus.). (YA). (gr. 3-12). 1994. lib. bdg. 24.95 (*0-7933-1502-6*); pap. 14.95 (*0-7933-1503-4*); disk 29.95 (*0-7933-1504-2*) Gallopade Pub Group.

— Florida Silly Football Sportsmysteries, Vol. I. (Carole Marsh Florida Bks.). (Illus.). (YA). (gr. 3-12). 1994. lib. bdg. 24.95 (*1-55609-421-3*); pap. 14.95 (*1-55609-420-5*); disk 29.95 (*0-7933-1489-5*) Gallopade Pub Group.

— Florida Silly Football Sportsmysteries, Vol. II. (Carole Marsh Florida Bks.). (Illus.). (YA). (gr. 3-12). 1994. lib. bdg. 24.95 (*0-7933-1490-9*); pap. 14.95 (*0-7933-1491-7*); disk 29.95 (*0-7933-1492-5*) Gallopade Pub Group.

— Florida Silly Trivia! (Carole Marsh Florida Bks.). (Illus.). (YA). (gr. 3-12). 1994. lib. bdg. 24.95 (*1-55609-417-5*); pap. 14.95 (*1-55609-037-4*); disk 29.95 (*0-7933-1486-0*) Gallopade Pub Group.

— Florida Timeline: A Chronology of Florida History, Mystery, Trivia, Legend, Lore & More. (Carole Marsh Florida Bks.). (Illus.). (J). (gr. 3-12). 1994. lib. bdg. 24.95 (*0-7933-5902-3*); pap. 14.95 (*0-7933-5903-1*); disk 29.95 (*0-7933-5904-X*) Gallopade Pub Group.

— Florida's (Most Devastating!) Disasters & (Most Calamitous!) Catastrophies! (Carole Marsh Florida Bks.). (Illus.). (YA). (gr. 3-12). 1994. lib. bdg. 24.95 (*0-7933-0283-8*); pap. 14.95 (*0-7933-0282-X*); disk 29.95 (*0-7933-0284-6*) Gallopade Pub Group.

— Florida's Unsolved Mysteries (& Their "Solutions") Includes Scientific Information & Other Activities for Students. (Carole Marsh Florida Bks.). (Illus.). (J). (gr. 3-12). 1994. lib. bdg. 24.95 (*0-7933-5749-7*); pap. 14.95 (*0-7933-5750-0*); disk 29.95 (*0-7933-5751-9*) Gallopade Pub Group.

— For Your Eyes Only: Silly, Secret & Scary Code & Spy Trivia for Kids. (Carole Marsh Tennessee Bks.). (Illus.). (YA). (gr. 3-12). 1994. lib. bdg. 24.95 (*0-7933-5413-7*); pap. 14.95 (*0-7933-5414-5*); disk 29.95 (*0-7933-5415-3*) Gallopade Pub Group.

— The Fortune Cookie Christmas. (Illus.). (Orig.). (J). (gr. 3 up). 1994. 24.95 (*1-55609-285-7*); pap. 14.95 (*0-935326-53-7*) Gallopade Pub Group.

— The Four Hundred Year Old Cookbook. (Naked Gourmet Ser.). (Orig.). 1994. 24.95 (*1-55609-167-2*); pap. 14.95 (*1-55609-000-5*) Gallopade Pub Group.

— A Fun Book of Olympic Trivia A-Z: 1886-1996! (J). 1994. lib. bdg. 24.95 (*0-7933-6876-6*); pap. text ed. 14.95 (*0-7933-6875-8*); disk 29.95 (*0-7933-6877-4*) Gallopade Pub Group.

— Gee! Ology: Trivia for Kids. (Scientifically Speaking Ser.). (Illus.). (J). (gr. 3-12). 1994. lib. bdg. 24.95 (*1-55609-305-5*); pap. 14.95 (*1-55609-306-3*); disk 29.95 (*1-55609-307-1*) Gallopade Pub Group.

— Georgia & Other State Greats (Biographies) (Carole Marsh Georgia Bks.). (Illus.). (YA). (gr. 3-12). 1994. lib. bdg. 24.95 (*1-55609-392-6*); pap. 14.95 (*1-55609-391-8*); disk 29.95 (*0-7933-1520-4*) Gallopade Pub Group.

— Georgia Bandits, Bushwackers, Outlaws, Crooks, Devils, Ghosts, Desperadoes & Other Assorted & Sundry Characters! (Carole Marsh Georgia Bks.). (Illus.). (YA). (gr. 3-12). 1994. lib. bdg. 24.95 (*0-7933-0310-9*); pap. 14.95 (*0-7933-0309-5*); disk 29.95 (*0-7933-0311-7*) Gallopade Pub Group.

— The Georgia Bookstore Book: A Surprising Guide to Our State's Bookstores & Their Specialties for Students, Teachers, Writers & Publishers. (Carole Marsh Georgia Bks.). (Illus.). 1994. lib. bdg. 24.95 (*0-7933-2885-3*); pap. 14.95 (*0-7933-2886-1*); disk 29.95 (*0-7933-2887-X*) Gallopade Pub Group.

— Georgia Classic Christmas Trivia: Stories, Recipes, Activities, Legends, Lore & More! (Carole Marsh Georgia Bks.). (Illus.). (YA). (gr. 3-12). 1994. lib. bdg. 24.95 (*0-7933-0313-3*); pap. 14.95 (*0-7933-0312-5*); disk 29.95 (*0-7933-0314-1*) Gallopade Pub Group.

— Georgia Coastales. (Carole Marsh Georgia Bks.). (Illus.). (YA). (gr. 3-12). 1994. lib. bdg. 24.95 (*1-55609-233-4*); pap. 14.95 (*1-55609-117-6*); disk 29.95 (*0-7933-1516-6*) Gallopade Pub Group.

— Georgia Coastales! (Carole Marsh Georgia Bks.). (J). 1994. lib. bdg. 24.95 (*0-7933-7275-5*) Gallopade Pub Group.

— Georgia "Crinkum-Crankum" A Funny Word Book about Our State. (Carole Marsh Georgia Bks.). (Illus.). (J). 1994. lib. bdg. 24.95 (*0-7933-4837-4*); pap. 14.95 (*0-7933-4838-2*); disk 29.95 (*0-7933-4839-0*) Gallopade Pub Group.

— Georgia Dingbats! Bk. 1: A Fun Book of Games, Stories, Activities & More about Our State That's All in Code! for You to Decipher. (Carole Marsh Georgia Bks.). (Illus.). (J). (gr. 3-12). 1994. lib. bdg. 24.95 (*0-7933-3803-4*); pap. 14.95 (*0-7933-3804-2*); disk 29.95 (*0-7933-3805-0*) Gallopade Pub Group.

— Georgia Festival Fun for Kids! (Carole Marsh Georgia Bks.). (Illus.). (YA). (gr. 3-12). 1994. lib. bdg. 24.95 (*0-7933-3956-1*); pap. 14.95 (*0-7933-3957-X*); disk 29.95 (*0-7933-3958-8*) Gallopade Pub Group.

— The Georgia Hot Air Balloon Mystery. (Carole Marsh Georgia Bks.). (Illus.). (J). (gr. 2-9). 1994. 24.95 (*0-7933-2408-4*); pap. 14.95 (*0-7933-2409-2*); disk 29.95 (*0-7933-2410-6*) Gallopade Pub Group.

— Georgia Jeopardy! Answers & Questions about Our State! (Carole Marsh Georgia Bks.). (Illus.). (J). (gr. 3-12). 1994. lib. bdg. 24.95 (*0-7933-4109-4*); pap. 14.95 (*0-7933-4110-8*); disk 29.95 (*0-7933-4111-6*) Gallopade Pub Group.

— Georgia Jography: A Fun Run Through the Peach State. (Statemeant Ser.). (Illus.). 50p. (Orig.). (J). (gr. 4-8). 1994. pap. 14.95 (*0-935326-93-6*) Gallopade Pub Group.

— Georgia Kid's Cookbook: Recipes, How-To, History, Lore & More! (Carole Marsh Georgia Bks.). (Illus.). (YA). (gr. 3-12). 1994. lib. bdg. 24.95 (*0-7933-0322-2*); pap. 14.95 (*0-7933-0321-4*); disk 29.95 (*0-7933-0323-0*) Gallopade Pub Group.

— The Georgia Library Book: A Surprising Guide to the Unusual Special Collections in Libraries Across Our State for Students, Teachers, Writers & Publishers - Includes Reproducible Mailing Labels Plus Activities for Young People! (Carole Marsh Georgia Bks.). (Illus.). 1994. lib. bdg. 24.95 (*0-7933-3035-1*); pap. 14.95 (*0-7933-3036-X*); disk 29.95 (*0-7933-3037-8*) Gallopade Pub Group.

— The Georgia Media Book: A Surprising Guide to the Amazing Print, Broadcast & Online Media of Our State for Students, Teachers, Writers & Publishers - Includes Reproducible Mailing Labels Plus Activities for Young People! (Carole Marsh Georgia Bks.). (Illus.). 1994. lib. bdg. 24.95 (*0-7933-3191-9*); pap. 14.95 (*0-7933-3192-7*); disk 29.95 (*0-7933-3193-5*) Gallopade Pub Group.

— The Georgia Mystery Van Takes Off! Book 1: Handicapped Georgia Kids Sneak Off on a Big Adventure. (Carole Marsh Georgia Bks.). (Illus.). (J). (gr. 3-12). 1994. 24.95 (*0-7933-4991-5*); pap. 14.95 (*0-7933-4992-3*); disk 29.95 (*0-7933-4993-1*) Gallopade Pub Group.

— Georgia Quiz Bowl Crash Course! (Carole Marsh Georgia Bks.). (Illus.). (YA). (gr. 3-12). 1994. lib. bdg. 24.95 (1-55609-384-5); pap. 14.95 (1-55609-383-7); disk 29.95 (0-7933-1515-8) Gallopade Pub Group.

— Georgia Rollercoasters! (Carole Marsh Georgia Bks.). (Illus.). (YA). (gr. 3-12). 1994. lib. bdg. 24.95 (0-7933-5254-1); pap. 14.95 (0-7933-5255-X); disk 29.95 (0-7933-5256-8) Gallopade Pub Group.

— Georgia School Trivia: An Amazing & Fascinating Look at Our State's Teachers, Schools & Students! (Carole Marsh Georgia Bks.). (Illus.). (YA). (gr. 3-12). 1994. lib. bdg. 24.95 (0-7933-0319-2); pap. 14.95 (0-7933-0318-4); disk 29.95 (0-7933-0320-6) Gallopade Pub Group.

— Georgia Silly Basketball Sportsmysteries, Vol. I. (Carole Marsh Georgia Bks.). (Illus.). (YA). (gr. 3-12). 1994. lib. bdg. 24.95 (0-7933-0316-8); pap. 14.95 (0-7933-0315-X); disk 29.95 (0-7933-0317-6) Gallopade Pub Group.

— Georgia Silly Basketball Sportsmysteries, Vol. II. (Carole Marsh Georgia Bks.). (Illus.). (YA). (gr. 3-12). 1994. lib. bdg. 24.95 (0-7933-1521-2); pap. 14.95 (0-7933-1522-0); disk 29.95 (0-7933-1523-9) Gallopade Pub Group.

— Georgia Silly Football Sportsmysteries, Vol. I. (Carole Marsh Georgia Bks.). (Illus.). (YA). (gr. 3-12). 1994. lib. bdg. 24.95 (1-55609-394-2); pap. 14.95 (1-55609-393-4); disk 29.95 (0-7933-1508-5) Gallopade Pub Group.

— Georgia Silly Football Sportsmysteries, Vol. II. (Carole Marsh Georgia Bks.). (Illus.). (YA). (gr. 3-12). 1994. lib. bdg. 24.95 (0-7933-1509-3); pap. 14.95 (0-7933-1510-7); disk 29.95 (0-7933-1511-5) Gallopade Pub Group.

— Georgia Silly Trivia Book. (Statemeant Ser.). (Illus.). 48p. (Orig.). (J). (gr. 2-12). 1994. pap. 14.95 (0-935326-61-8) Gallopade Pub Group.

— Georgia Timeline: A Chronology of Georgia History, Mystery, Trivia, Legend, Lore & More. (Carole Marsh Georgia Bks.). (Illus.). (J). (gr. 3-12). 1994. lib. bdg. 24. 95 (0-7933-5905-8); pap. 14.95 (0-7933-5906-6); disk 29. 95 (0-7933-5907-4) Gallopade Pub Group.

— Georgia's (Most Devastating!) Disasters & (Most Calamitous!) Catastrophies! (Carole Marsh Georgia Bks.). (Illus.). (YA). (gr. 3-12). 1994. lib. bdg. 24.95 (0-7933-0307-9); pap. 14.95 (0-7933-0306-0); disk 29.95 (0-7933-0308-7) Gallopade Pub Group.

— Georgia's Unsolved Mysteries (& Their "Solutions") Includes Scientific Information & Other Activities for Students. (Carole Marsh Georgia Bks.). (Illus.). (J). (gr. 3-12). 1994. lib. bdg. 24.95 (0-7933-5752-7); pap. 14.95 (0-7933-5753-5); disk 29.95 (0-7933-5754-3) Gallopade Pub Group.

— The Ghost & Graveyards Dingbats Book. (Carole Marsh Dingbats Book Ser.). (Illus.). (YA). (gr. 3-12). 1994. lib. bdg. 24.95 (0-7933-5386-6); pap. 14.95 (0-7933-5387-4); disk 29.95 (0-7933-5388-2) Gallopade Pub Group.

— The Ghost of Glencastle Set. (Carole Marsh Mysteries Ser.). 1994. 125.00 (0-7933-6961-4) Gallopade Pub Group.

— Ghost of the Bed & Breakfast. (Ghostest with the Mostest Ser.). (Illus.). 48p. (J). (ps-7). 1994. 24.95 (1-55609-155-9); pap. 14.95 (1-55609-239-3) Gallopade Pub Group.

— Go Queen Go! Chess for Kids. (Quantum Leap Ser.). (Illus.). 48p. (J). (gr. k-12). 1994. 24.95 (1-55609-160-5); pap. 14.95 (0-935326-14-6) Gallopade Pub Group.

— Gold Shines Forever! The Discovery & Recovery of the Spanish Treasure Ship Atocha. (Carole Marsh Florida Bks.). (J). 1994. lib. bdg. 24.95 (0-7933-7586-X); pap. 14.95 (0-7933-7319-0) Gallopade Pub Group.

— Grits R Us Cookbook. (Naked Gourmet Ser.). (Orig.). 1994. 24.95 (1-55609-168-0); pap. 14.95 (1-55609-003-X) Gallopade Pub Group.

— The Hairy Horrors Dingbats Book. (Carole Marsh Dingbats Book Ser.). (Illus.). (YA). (gr. 3-12). 1994. lib. bdg. 24.95 (0-7933-5404-8); pap. 14.95 (0-7933-5405-6); disk 29.95 (0-7933-5406-4) Gallopade Pub Group.

— Halloween: Silly Trivia. (Quantum Leap Ser.). (Orig.). (J). (gr. 2-9). 1994. lib. bdg. 24.95 (1-55609-169-9); pap. 14. 95 (1-55609-017-X) Gallopade Pub Group.

— The Hard-to-Believe-But-True! Book of Alabama History, Mystery, Trivia, Legend, Lore, Humor & More. (Carole Marsh Alabama Bks.). (Illus.). (YA). (gr. 3-12). 1994. lib. bdg. 24.95 (0-7933-0085-1); pap. 14.95 (0-7933-0084-3); disk 29.95 (0-7933-0086-X) Gallopade Pub Group.

— The Hard-to-Believe-But-True! Book of Alaska History, Mystery, Trivia, Legend, Lore, Humor & More. (Carole Marsh Alaska Bks.). (Illus.). (YA). (gr. 3-12). 1994. lib. bdg. 24.95 (0-7933-0109-2); pap. 14.95 (0-7933-0108-4); disk 29.95 (0-7933-0110-6) Gallopade Pub Group.

— The Hard-to-Believe-But-True! Book of Arizona History, Mystery, Trivia, Legend, Lore, Humor & More. (Carole Marsh Arizona Bks.). (Illus.). (YA). (gr. 3-12). 1994. lib. bdg. 24.95 (0-7933-0133-5); pap. 14.95 (0-7933-0132-7); disk 29.95 (0-7933-0134-3) Gallopade Pub Group.

— The Hard-to-Believe-But-True! Book of Arkansas History, Mystery, Trivia, Legend, Lore, Humor & More. (Carole Marsh Arkansas Bks.). (Illus.). (YA). (gr. 3-12). 1994. lib. bdg. 24.95 (0-7933-0157-2); pap. 14.95 (0-7933-0156-4); disk 29.95 (0-7933-0158-0) Gallopade Pub Group.

— The Hard-to-Believe-But-True! Book of California History, Mystery, Trivia, Legend, Lore, Humor & More. (Carole Marsh California Bks.). (Illus.). (YA). (gr. 3-12). 1994. lib. bdg. 24.95 (0-7933-0181-5); pap. 14.95 (0-7933-0180-7); disk 29.95 (0-7933-0182-3) Gallopade Pub Group.

— The Hard-to-Believe-But-True! Book of Colorado History, Mystery, Trivia, Legend, Lore, Humor & More. (Carole Marsh Colorado Bks.). (Illus.). (YA). (gr. 3-12). 1994. lib. bdg. 24.95 (0-7933-0205-6); pap. 14.95 (0-7933-0204-8); disk 29.95 (0-7933-0206-4) Gallopade Pub Group.

— The Hard-to-Believe-But-True! Book of Connecticut History, Mystery, Trivia, Legend, Lore, Humor & More. (Carole Marsh Connecticut Bks.). (Illus.). (YA). (gr. 3-12). 1994. lib. bdg. 24.95 (0-7933-0229-3); pap. 14.95 (0-7933-0228-5); disk 29.95 (0-7933-0230-7) Gallopade Pub Group.

— The Hard-to-Believe-But-True! Book of Delaware History, Mystery, Trivia, Legend, Lore, Humor & More. (Carole Marsh Delaware Bks.). (Illus.). (YA). (gr. 3-12). 1994. lib. bdg. 24.95 (0-7933-0253-6); pap. 14.95 (0-7933-0252-8); disk 29.95 (0-7933-0254-4) Gallopade Pub Group.

— The Hard-to-Believe-But-True! Book of Florida History, Mystery, Trivia, Legend, Lore, Humor & More. (Carole Marsh Florida Bks.). (Illus.). (YA). (gr. 3-12). 1994. lib. bdg. 24.95 (0-7933-0301-X); pap. 14.95 (0-7933-0300-1); disk 29.95 (0-7933-0302-8) Gallopade Pub Group.

— The Hard-to-Believe-But-True! Book of Georgia History, Mystery, Trivia, Legend, Lore, Humor & More. (Carole Marsh Georgia Bks.). (Illus.). (YA). (gr. 3-12). 1994. lib. bdg. 24.95 (0-7933-0325-7); pap. 14.95 (0-7933-0324-9); disk 29.95 (0-7933-0326-5) Gallopade Pub Group.

— The Hard-to-Believe-But-True! Book of Hawaii History, Mystery, Trivia, Legend, Lore, Humor & More. (Carole Marsh Hawaii Bks.). (Illus.). (YA). (gr. 3-12). 1994. lib. bdg. 24.95 (0-7933-0349-4); pap. 14.95 (0-7933-0348-6); disk 29.95 (0-7933-0350-8) Gallopade Pub Group.

— The Hard-to-Believe-But-True! Book of Idaho History, Mystery, Trivia, Legend, Lore, Humor & More. (Carole Marsh Idaho Bks.). (Illus.). (YA). (gr. 3-12). 1994. lib. bdg. 24.95 (0-7933-0373-7); pap. 14.95 (0-7933-0372-9); disk 29.95 (0-7933-0374-5) Gallopade Pub Group.

— The Hard-to-Believe-But-True! Book of Illinois History, Mystery, Trivia, Legend, Lore, Humor & More. (Carole Marsh Illinois Bks.). (Illus.). (YA). (gr. 3-12). 1994. lib. bdg. 24.95 (0-7933-0397-4); pap. 14.95 (0-7933-0396-6); disk 29.95 (0-7933-0398-2) Gallopade Pub Group.

— The Hard-to-Believe-But-True! Book of Indiana History, Mystery, Trivia, Legend, Lore, Humor & More. (Carole Marsh Indiana Bks.). (Illus.). (YA). (gr. 3-12). 1994. lib. bdg. 24.95 (0-7933-0421-0); pap. 14.95 (0-7933-0420-2); disk 29.95 (0-7933-0422-9) Gallopade Pub Group.

— The Hard-to-Believe-But-True! Book of Iowa History, Mystery, Trivia, Legend, Lore, Humor & More. (Carole Marsh Iowa Bks.). (Illus.). (YA). (gr. 3-12). 1994. lib. bdg. 24.95 (0-7933-0445-8); pap. 14.95 (0-7933-0444-X); disk 29.95 (0-7933-0446-6) Gallopade Pub Group.

— The Hard-to-Believe-But-True! Book of Kansas History, Mystery, Trivia, Legend, Lore, Humor & More. (Carole Marsh Kansas Bks.). (Illus.). (YA). (gr. 3-12). 1994. lib. bdg. 24.95 (0-7933-0469-5); pap. 14.95 (0-7933-0468-7); disk 29.95 (0-7933-0470-9) Gallopade Pub Group.

— The Hard-to-Believe-But-True! Book of Kentucky History, Mystery, Trivia, Legend, Lore, Humor & More. (Carole Marsh Kentucky Bks.). (Illus.). (J). (gr. 3-8). 1994. lib. bdg. 24.95 (0-7933-0493-8); pap. 14.95 (0-7933-0492-X); disk 29.95 (0-7933-0494-6) Gallopade Pub Group.

— The Hard-to-Believe-But-True! Book of Louisiana History, Mystery, Trivia, Legend, Lore, Humor & More. (Carole Marsh Louisiana Bks.). (Illus.). (J). (gr. 3-8). 1994. lib. bdg. 24.95 (0-7933-0517-9); pap. 14.95 (0-7933-0516-0); disk 29.95 (0-7933-0518-7) Gallopade Pub Group.

— The Hard-to-Believe-But-True! Book of Maine History, Mystery, Trivia, Legend, Lore, Humor & More. (Carole Marsh Maine Bks.). (Illus.). (J). (gr. 3-8). 1994. lib. bdg. 24.95 (0-7933-0542-X); pap. 14.95 (0-7933-0541-1); disk 29.95 (0-7933-0543-8) Gallopade Pub Group.

— The Hard-to-Believe-But-True! Book of Maryland History, Mystery, Trivia, Legend, Lore, Humor & More. (Carole Marsh Maryland Bks.). (Illus.). (J). (gr. 3-8). 1994. lib. bdg. 24.95 (0-7933-0566-7); pap. 14.95 (0-7933-0565-9); disk 29.95 (0-7933-0567-5) Gallopade Pub Group.

— The Hard-to-Believe-But-True! Book of Massachusetts History, Mystery, Trivia, Legend, Lore, Humor & More. (Carole Marsh Massachusetts Bks.). (Illus.). (J). (gr. 3-8). 1994. lib. bdg. 24.95 (0-7933-0590-X); pap. 14.95 (0-7933-0589-6); disk 29.95 (0-7933-0591-8) Gallopade Pub Group.

— The Hard-to-Believe-But-True! Book of Michigan History, Mystery, Trivia, Legend, Lore, Humor & More. (Carole Marsh Michigan Bks.). (Illus.). (J). (gr. 3 up). 1994. lib. bdg. 24.95 (0-7933-0614-0); pap. 14.95 (0-7933-0613-2); disk 29.95 (0-7933-0615-9) Gallopade Pub Group.

— The Hard-to-Believe-But-True! Book of Minnesota History, Mystery, Trivia, Legend, Lore, Humor & More. (Carole Marsh Minnesota Bks.). (Illus.). (J). (gr. 3 up). 1994. lib. bdg. 24.95 (0-7933-0638-8); pap. 14.95 (0-7933-0637-X); disk 29.95 (0-7933-0639-6) Gallopade Pub Group.

— The Hard-to-Believe-But-True! Book of Mississippi History, Mystery, Trivia, Legend, Lore, Humor & More. (Carole Marsh Mississippi Bks.). (Illus.). (J). (gr. 3 up). 1994. lib. bdg. 24.95 (0-7933-0663-9); pap. 14.95 (0-7933-0662-0); disk 29.95 (0-7933-0664-7) Gallopade Pub Group.

— The Hard-to-Believe-But-True! Book of Missouri History, Mystery, Trivia, Legend, Lore, Humor & More. (Carole Marsh Missouri Bks.). (Illus.). (J). (gr. 3 up). 1994. lib. bdg. 24.95 (0-7933-0687-6); pap. 14.95 (0-7933-0686-8); disk 29.95 (0-7933-0688-4) Gallopade Pub Group.

— The Hard-to-Believe-But-True! Book of Montana History, Mystery, Trivia, Legend, Lore, Humor & More. (Carole Marsh Montana Bks.). (Illus.). (J). (gr. 3 up). 1994. lib. bdg. 24.95 (0-7933-0712-0); pap. 14.95 (0-7933-0711-2); disk 29.95 (0-7933-0713-9) Gallopade Pub Group.

— The Hard-to-Believe-But-True! Book of Nebraska History, Mystery, Trivia, Legend, Lore, Humor & More. (Carole Marsh Nebraska Bks.). (Illus.). (J). (gr. 3 up). 1994. lib. bdg. 24.95 (0-7933-0736-8); pap. 14.95 (0-7933-0735-X); disk 29.95 (0-7933-0737-6) Gallopade Pub Group.

— The Hard-to-Believe-But-True! Book of Nevada History, Mystery, Trivia, Legend, Lore, Humor & More. (Carole Marsh Nevada Bks.). (Illus.). (J). 1994. lib. bdg. 24.95 (0-7933-0760-0); pap. 14.95 (0-7933-0759-7); disk 29.95 (0-7933-0761-9) Gallopade Pub Group.

— The Hard-to-Believe-But-True! Book of New Hampshire History, Mystery, Trivia, Legend, Lore, Humor & More. (Carole Marsh New Hampshire Bks.). (Illus.). (J). 1994. lib. bdg. 24.95 (0-7933-0784-8); pap. 14.95 (0-7933-0783-X); disk 29.95 (0-7933-0785-6) Gallopade Pub Group.

— The Hard-to-Believe-But-True! Book of New Jersey History, Mystery, Trivia, Legend, Lore, Humor & More. (Carole Marsh New Jersey Bks.). (Illus.). (J). 1994. lib. bdg. 24.95 (0-7933-1806-8); pap. 14.95 (0-7933-1807-6); disk 29.95 (0-7933-1808-4) Gallopade Pub Group.

— The Hard-to-Believe-But-True! Book of New Mexico History, Mystery, Trivia, Legend, Lore, Humor & More. (Carole Marsh New Mexico Bks.). (Illus.). (J). 1994. lib. bdg. 24.95 (0-7933-0808-9); pap. 14.95 (0-7933-0807-0); disk 29.95 (0-7933-0809-7) Gallopade Pub Group.

— The Hard-to-Believe-But-True! Book of New York History, Mystery, Trivia, Legend, Lore, Humor & More. (Carole Marsh New York Bks.). (Illus.). (J). 1994. lib. bdg. 24.95 (0-7933-0832-1); pap. 14.95 (0-7933-0831-3); disk 29.95 (0-7933-0833-X) Gallopade Pub Group.

— The Hard-to-Believe-But-True! Book of North Carolina History, Mystery, Trivia, Legend, Lore, Humor & More. (Carole Marsh North Carolina Bks.). (Illus.). (J). 1994. lib. bdg. 24.95 (0-7933-0856-9); pap. 14.95 (0-7933-0855-0); disk 29.95 (0-7933-0857-7) Gallopade Pub Group.

— The Hard-to-Believe-But-True! Book of North Dakota History, Mystery, Trivia, Legend, Lore, Humor & More. (Carole Marsh North Dakota Bks.). (Illus.). (J). 1994. lib. bdg. 24.95 (0-7933-0880-1); pap. 14.95 (0-7933-0879-8); disk 29.95 (0-7933-0881-X) Gallopade Pub Group.

— The Hard-to-Believe-But-True! Book of Ohio History, Mystery, Trivia, Legend, Lore, Humor & More. (Carole Marsh Ohio Bks.). (Illus.). (J). 1994. lib. bdg. 24.95 (0-7933-0904-2); pap. 14.95 (0-7933-0903-4); disk 29.95 (0-7933-0906-9) Gallopade Pub Group.

— The Hard-to-Believe-But-True! Book of Oklahoma History, Mystery, Trivia, Legend, Lore, Humor & More. (Carole Marsh Oklahoma Bks.). (Illus.). (J). 1994. lib. bdg. 24.95 (0-7933-0929-8); pap. 14.95 (0-7933-0928-X); disk 29.95 (0-7933-0930-1) Gallopade Pub Group.

— The Hard-to-Believe-But-True! Book of Oregon History, Mystery, Trivia, Legend, Lore, Humor & More. (Carole Marsh Oregon Bks.). (Illus.). (J). 1994. lib. bdg. 24.95 (0-7933-0953-0); pap. 14.95 (0-7933-0952-2); disk 29.95 (0-7933-0954-9) Gallopade Pub Group.

— The Hard-to-Believe-But-True! Book of Pennsylvania History, Mystery, Trivia, Legend, Lore, Humor & More. (Carole Marsh Pennsylvania Bks.). (Illus.). (J). 1994. lib. bdg. 24.95 (0-7933-0977-8); pap. 14.95 (0-7933-0976-X); disk 29.95 (0-7933-0978-6) Gallopade Pub Group.

— The Hard-to-Believe-But-True! Book of Rhode Island History, Mystery, Trivia, Legend, Lore, Humor & More. (Carole Marsh Rhode Island Bks.). (Illus.). (J). 1994. lib. bdg. 24.95 (0-7933-1001-6); pap. 14.95 (0-7933-1000-8); disk 29.95 (0-7933-1002-4) Gallopade Pub Group.

— The Hard-to-Believe-But-True! Book of South Carolina History, Mystery, Trivia, Legend, Lore, Humor & More. (Carole Marsh South Carolina Bks.). (Illus.). (J). 1994. lib. bdg. 24.95 (0-7933-1025-3); pap. 14.95 (0-7933-1024-5); disk 29.95 (0-7933-1026-1) Gallopade Pub Group.

— The Hard-to-Believe-But True! Book of South Dakota History, Mystery, Trivia, Legend, Lore, Humor & More. (Carole Marsh South Dakota Bks.). (Illus.). (J). 1994. lib. bdg. 24.95 (0-7933-1049-0); pap. 14.95 (0-7933-1048-2); disk 29.95 (0-7933-1050-4) Gallopade Pub Group.

— The Hard-to-Believe-But-True! Book of Tennessee History, Mystery, Trivia, Legend, Lore, Humor & More. (Carole Marsh Tennessee Bks.). (Illus.). (J). 1994. lib. bdg. 24.95 (0-7933-1073-3); pap. 14.95 (0-7933-1072-5); disk 29.95 (0-7933-1074-1) Gallopade Pub Group.

— The Hard-to-Believe-But-True! Book of Texas History, Mystery, Trivia, Legend, Lore, Humor & More. (Carole Marsh Texas Bks.). (Illus.). (J). 1994. lib. bdg. 24.95 (0-7933-1097-0); pap. 14.95 (0-7933-1096-2); disk 29.95 (0-7933-1098-9) Gallopade Pub Group.

— The Hard-to-Believe-But-True! Book of Utah History, Mystery, Trivia, Legend, Lore, Humor & More. (Carole Marsh Utah Bks.). (Illus.). (J). 1994. lib. bdg. 24.95 (0-7933-1121-7); pap. 14.95 (0-7933-1120-9); disk 29.95 (0-7933-1122-5) Gallopade Pub Group.

— The Hard-to-Believe-But-True! Book of Vermont History, Mystery, Trivia, Legend, Lore, Humor & More. (Carole Marsh Vermont Bks.). (Illus.). (J). 1994. lib. bdg. 24.95 (0-7933-1145-4); pap. 14.95 (0-7933-1144-6); write for info. (0-7933-1146-2) Gallopade Pub Group.

— The Hard-to-Believe-But-True! Book of Virginia History, Mystery, Trivia, Legend, Lore, Humor & More. (Carole Marsh Virginia Bks.). (Illus.). (J). 1994. lib. bdg. 24.95 (0-7933-1169-1); pap. 14.95 (0-7933-1168-3); disk 29.95 (0-7933-1170-5) Gallopade Pub Group.

— The Hard-to-Believe-But-True! Book of Washington, D.C. History, Mystery, Trivia, Legend, Lore, Humor & More. (Carole Marsh Washington, D.C. Bks.). (Illus.). (YA). (gr. 3-12). 1994. lib. bdg. 24.95 (0-685-45931-4); pap. 14.95 (0-7933-0276-5); disk 29.95 (0-7933-0278-1) Gallopade Pub Group.

— The Hard-to-Believe-But-True! Book of Washington History, Mystery, Trivia, Legend, Lore, Humor & More. (Carole Marsh Washington Bks.). (Illus.). (J). 1994. lib. bdg. 24.95 (0-7933-1193-4); pap. 14.95 (0-7933-1192-6); disk 29.95 (0-7933-1194-2) Gallopade Pub Group.

— The Hard-to-Believe-But-True! Book of West Virginia History, Mystery, Trivia, Legend, Lore, Humor & More. (Carole Marsh West Virginia Bks.). (Illus.). (J). 1994. lib. bdg. 24.95 (0-7933-1217-5); pap. 14.95 (0-7933-1216-7); disk 29.95 (0-7933-1218-3) Gallopade Pub Group.

— The Hard-to-Believe-But-True! Book of Wisconsin History, Mystery, Trivia, Legend, Lore, Humor & More. (Carole Marsh Wisconsin Bks.). (Illus.). (J). 1994. lib. bdg. 24.95 (0-7933-1241-8); pap. 14.95 (0-7933-1240-X); disk 29.95 (0-7933-1242-6) Gallopade Pub Group.

— The Hard-to-Believe-But-True! Book of Wyoming History, Mystery, Trivia, Legend, Lore, Humor & More. (Carole Marsh Wyoming Bks.). (Illus.). (J). 1994. lib. bdg. 24.95 (0-7933-1265-5); pap. 14.95 (0-7933-1264-7); disk 29.95 (0-7933-1266-3) Gallopade Pub Group.

— The Haunt of Hope Plantation. (History Mystery Ser.). (Illus.). (Orig.). (J). (gr. 3-9). 1994. 24.95 (1-55609-170-2); pap. 14.95 (0-935326-03-0) Gallopade Pub Group.

— The Haunt of Hope Plantation S. P. A. R. K. Kit. (S. P. A. R. K. Ser.). (Illus.). (Orig.). (J). (gr. 3-12). 1994. pap. 24.95 (0-935326-21-9) Gallopade Pub Group.

— The Haunt of Hope Plantation Set. (Carole Marsh Mysteries Ser.). 1994. 125.00 (0-7933-6947-9) Gallopade Pub Group.

— The Haunted Christmas Tree Mystery. (Carole Marsh Mysteries & Novel Ser.). (Illus.). (gr. 2-9). 1994. 24.95 (1-55609-267-9); pap. 14.95 (1-55609-266-0); disk 29.95 (1-55609-270-9) Gallopade Pub Group.

— Hawaii: Silly Basketball Sportsmysteries, Vol. I. (Carole Marsh Hawaii Bks.). (Illus.). (YA). (gr. 3-12). 1994. lib. bdg. 24.95 (0-7933-0340-0); pap. 14.95 (0-7933-0339-7); disk 29.95 (0-7933-0341-9) Gallopade Pub Group.

— Hawaii & Other State Greats (Biographies) (Carole Marsh Hawaii Bks.). (Illus.). (YA). (gr. 3-12). 1994. lib. bdg. 24. 95 (1-55609-577-5); pap. 14.95 (1-55609-576-7); disk 29. 95 (0-7933-1539-5) Gallopade Pub Group.

— Hawaii Bandits, Bushwackers, Outlaws, Crooks, Devils, Ghosts, Desperadoes & Other Assorted & Sundry Characters! (Carole Marsh Hawaii Bks.). (Illus.). (YA). (gr. 3-12). 1994. lib. bdg. 24.95 (0-7933-0334-6); pap. 14.95 (0-7933-0333-8); disk 29.95 (0-7933-0335-4) Gallopade Pub Group.

— The Hawaii Bookstore Book: A Surprising Guide to Our State's Bookstores & Their Specialties for Students, Teachers, Writers & Publishers. (Carole Marsh Hawaii Bks.). (Illus.). 1994. lib. bdg. 24.95 (0-7933-2888-8); pap. 14.95 (0-7933-2889-6); disk 29.95 (0-7933-2890-X) Gallopade Pub Group.

— Hawaii Classic Christmas Trivia: Stories, Recipes, Activities, Legends, Lore & More! (Carole Marsh Hawaii Bks.). (Illus.). (YA). (gr. 3-12). 1994. lib. bdg. 24. 95 (0-7933-0337-0); pap. 14.95 (0-7933-0336-2); disk 29. 95 (0-7933-0338-9) Gallopade Pub Group.

— Hawaii Coastales. (Carole Marsh Hawaii Bks.). (Illus.). (YA). (gr. 3-12). 1994. lib. bdg. 24.95 (1-55609-573-2); pap. 14.95 (1-55609-572-4); disk 29.95 (0-7933-1535-2) Gallopade Pub Group.

— Hawaii Coastales! (Hawaii Bks.). (J). 1994. lib. bdg. 24.95 (0-7933-7276-3) Gallopade Pub Group.

— Hawaii "Crinkum-Crankum" A Funny Word Book about Our State. (Carole Marsh Hawaii Bks.). (Illus.). (J). 1994. lib. bdg. 24.95 (0-7933-4840-4); pap. 14.95 (0-7933-4841-2); disk 29.95 (0-7933-4842-0) Gallopade Pub Group.

— Hawaii Dingbats! Bk. 1: A Fun Book of Games, Stories, Activities & More about Our State That's All in Code! for You to Decipher. (Carole Marsh Hawaii Bks.). (Illus.). (J). (gr. 3-12). 1994. lib. bdg. 24.95 (0-7933-3806-9); pap. 14.95 (0-7933-3807-7); disk 29.95 (0-7933-3808-5) Gallopade Pub Group.

— Hawaii Festival Fun for Kids! (Carole Marsh Hawaii Bks.). (Illus.). (YA). (gr. 3-12). 1994. lib. bdg. 24.95 (0-7933-3959-6); pap. 14.95 (0-7933-3960-X); disk 29.95 (0-7933-3961-8) Gallopade Pub Group.

— The Hawaii Hot Air Balloon Mystery. (Carole Marsh Hawaii Bks.). (Illus.). (J). (gr. 2-9). 1994. 24.95 (0-7933-2417-3); pap. 14.95 (0-7933-2418-1); disk 29.95 (0-7933-2419-X) Gallopade Pub Group.

— Hawaii Jeopardy! Answers & Questions about Our State! (Carole Marsh Hawaii Bks.). (Illus.). (J). (gr. 3-12). 1994. lib. bdg. 24.95 (0-7933-4112-4); pap. 14.95 (0-7933-4113-2); disk 29.95 (0-7933-4114-0) Gallopade Pub Group.

— Hawaii "Jography" A Fun Run Thru Our State! (Carole Marsh Hawaii Bks.). (Illus.). (YA). (gr. 3-12). 1994. lib. bdg. 24.95 (1-55609-568-6); pap. 14.95 (1-55609-567-8); disk 29.95 (0-7933-1525-5) Gallopade Pub Group.

— Hawaii Kid's Cookbook: Recipes, How-to, History, Lore & More! (Carole Marsh Hawaii Bks.). (Illus.). (YA). (gr. 3-12). 1994. lib. bdg. 24.95 (0-7933-0346-X); pap. 14.95 (0-7933-0345-1); disk 29.95 (0-7933-0347-8) Gallopade Pub Group.

— The Hawaii Library Book: A Surprising Guide to the Unusual Special Collections in Libraries Across Our State for Students, Teachers, Writers & Publishers - Includes Reproducible Mailing Labels Plus Activities for Young People! (Carole Marsh Hawaii Bks.). (Illus.). 1994. lib. bdg. 24.95 (0-7933-3038-6); pap. 14.95 (0-7933-3039-4); disk 29.95 (0-7933-3040-8) Gallopade Pub Group.

An Asterisk (*) at the beginning of an entry indicates that the title is appearing in BIP for the first time.

— The Hawaii Media Book: A Surprising Guide to the Amazing Print, Broadcast & Online Media of Our State for Students, Teachers, Writers & Publishers - Includes Reproducible Mailing Labels Plus Activities for Young People! (Carole Marsh Hawaii Bks.). (Illus.). 1994. lib. bdg. 24.95 (*0-7933-3194-3*); pap. 14.95 (*0-7933-3195-1*); disk 29.95 (*0-7933-3196-X*) Gallopade Pub Group.

— The Hawaii Mystery Van Takes Off! Book 1: Handicapped Hawaii Kids Sneak Off on a Big Adventure. (Carole Marsh Hawaii Bks.). (Illus.). (J). (gr. 3-12). 1994. 24.95 (*0-7933-4994-X*); pap. 14.95 (*0-7933-4995-8*); disk 29.95 (*0-7933-4996-6*) Gallopade Pub Group.

— Hawaii Quiz Bowl Crash Course! (Carole Marsh Hawaii Bks.). (Illus.). (YA). (gr. 3-12). 1994. lib. bdg. 24.95 (*1-55609-575-9*); pap. 14.95 (*1-55609-574-0*); disk 29.95 (*0-7933-1534-4*) Gallopade Pub Group.

— Hawaii Rollercoasters! (Carole Marsh Hawaii Bks.). (Illus.). (YA). (gr. 3-12). 1994. lib. bdg. 24.95 (*0-7933-5257-6*); pap. 14.95 (*0-7933-5258-4*); disk 29.95 (*0-7933-5259-2*) Gallopade Pub Group.

— Hawaii School Trivia: An Amazing & Fascinating Look at Our State's Teachers, Schools & Students! (Carole Marsh Hawaii Bks.). (Illus.). (YA). (gr. 3-12). 1994. lib. bdg. 24.95 (*0-7933-0343-5*); pap. 14.95 (*0-7933-0342-7*); disk 29.95 (*0-7933-0344-3*) Gallopade Pub Group.

— Hawaii Silly Basketball Sports Mysteries. (Carole Marsh Hawaii Bks.: Vol. II). (Illus.). (YA). (gr. 3-12). 1994. lib. bdg. 24.95 (*0-7933-1540-9*); pap. 14.95 (*0-7933-1541-7*); disk 29.95 (*0-7933-1542-5*) Gallopade Pub Group.

— Hawaii Silly Football Sportsmysteries, Vol. I. (Carole Marsh Hawaii Bks.). (Illus.). (YA). (gr. 3-12). 1994. lib. bdg. 24.95 (*1-55609-571-6*); pap. 14.95 (*1-55609-570-8*); disk 29.95 (*0-7933-1527-1*) Gallopade Pub Group.

— Hawaii Silly Football Sportsmysteries, Vol. II. (Carole Marsh Hawaii Bks.). (Illus.). (YA). (gr. 3-12). 1994. lib. bdg. 24.95 (*0-7933-1528-X*); pap. 14.95 (*0-7933-1529-8*); disk 29.95 (*0-7933-1530-1*) Gallopade Pub Group.

— Hawaii Silly Trivia! (Carole Marsh Hawaii Bks.). (Illus.). (YA). (gr. 3-12). 1994. lib. bdg. 24.95 (*1-55609-566-X*); pap. 14.95 (*1-55609-565-1*); disk 29.95 (*0-7933-1524-7*) Gallopade Pub Group.

— Hawaii Timeline: A Chronology of Hawaii History, Mystery, Trivia, Legend, Lore & More. (Carole Marsh Hawaii Bks.). (Illus.). (J). (gr. 3-12). 1994. lib. bdg. 24.95 (*0-7933-5908-2*); pap. 14.95 (*0-7933-5909-0*); disk 29.95 (*0-7933-5910-4*) Gallopade Pub Group.

— Hawaii's (Most Devastating!) Disasters & (Most Calamitous!) Catastrophies! (Carole Marsh Hawaii Bks.). (Illus.). (YA). (gr. 3-12). 1994. lib. bdg. 24.95 (*0-7933-0331-1*); pap. 14.95 (*0-7933-0330-3*); disk 29.95 (*0-7933-0332-X*) Gallopade Pub Group.

— Hawaii's Unsolved Mysteries (& Their "Solutions") Includes Scientific Information & Other Activities for Students. (Carole Marsh Hawaii Bks.). (Illus.). (J). (gr. 3-12). 1994. lib. bdg. 24.95 (*0-7933-5755-1*); pap. 14.95 (*0-7933-5756-X*); disk 29.95 (*0-7933-5757-8*) Gallopade Pub Group.

— Hello in There: Poetry to Read to the Unborn Baby. (Unborn Baby Ser.). 1994. 24.95 (*1-55609-250-4*); pap. 14.95 (*1-55609-251-2*) Gallopade Pub Group.

— Helping Kids Write Better - By Writing on a Computer. (Books for Teachers). (Illus.). 1994. teacher ed 24.95 (*0-7933-0033-9*) Gallopade Pub Group.

— Ho Lee Chow! Chinese for Kids. (Of All the Gaul Ser.). (J). (gr. k-6). 1994. 24.95 (*0-7933-7355-7*); 14.95 (*0-7933-7357-3*); pap. 14.95 (*0-7933-7356-5*); audio 14.95 (*0-7933-7360-3*); vhs 14.95 (*0-7933-7359-X*); cd-rom 14.95 (*0-7933-7361-1*); disk 14.95 (*0-7933-7358-1*) Gallopade Pub Group.

— The Hot Air Balloon Mystery. (Carole Marsh Mysteries Ser.). (Illus.). (gr. 2-9). 1994. 24.95 (*1-55609-265-2*); pap. 14.95 (*1-55609-264-4*); disk 29.95 (*1-55609-268-7*) Gallopade Pub Group.

— Hot Shot: Photography for Kids. (Quantum Leap Ser.). (Illus.). (Orig.). (J). (gr. 3-12). 1994. 24.95 (*1-55609-171-0*); pap. 14.95 (*0-935326-79-0*) Gallopade Pub Group.

— How to Find an Extra Terrestrial in Your Own Backyard. (Tomorrow's Books for Today's Children). (Illus.). (J). 1994. 24.95 (*0-935326-09-X*) Gallopade Pub Group.

— How to Get Your Kid Out of School... Without AIDS, a Disease, or a Baby! (Smart Sex Stuff Ser.). (Orig.). 1994. 24.95 (*1-55609-286-5*); pap. 14.95 (*1-55609-224-5*) Gallopade Pub Group.

— How to Make a Million Writing Books for Kids! (Carole Marsh Life Write Bks.). 1994. 24.95 (*0-7933-7371-9*); pap. 14.95 (*0-7933-7372-7*); audio 14.95 (*0-7933-7375-1*); vhs 14.95 (*0-7933-7374-3*); disk 14.95 (*0-7933-7373-5*) Gallopade Pub Group.

— How to Make a Million Writing for the New Interactive Multimedia & CD-ROM Market. (How to Make a Million! Ser.). (Illus.). (Orig.). 1994. lib. bdg. 24.95 (*0-7933-7623-8*); pap. 14.95 (*0-7933-7624-6*) Gallopade Pub Group.

— How to Raise the Children You Wish Your Parents Had Raised. 1994. 24.95 (*1-55609-902-9*); pap. 14.95 (*1-55609-903-7*) Gallopade Pub Group.

— How to Start a California Library: At Home or School - A Book for All Ages. (Carole Marsh California Bks.). (Illus.). (J). (gr. 3 up). 1994. lib. bdg. 24.95 (*0-7933-4247-3*); pap. 14.95 (*0-7933-4248-1*); disk 29.95 (*0-7933-4249-X*) Gallopade Pub Group.

— How to Start a Colorado Library: At Home or School - A Book for All Ages. (Carole Marsh Colorado Bks.). (Illus.). (J). (gr. 3 up). 1994. lib. bdg. 24.95 (*0-7933-4250-3*); pap. 14.95 (*0-7933-4251-1*); disk 29.95 (*0-7933-4252-X*) Gallopade Pub Group.

— How to Start a Connecticut Library: At Home or School - A Book for All Ages. (Carole Marsh Connecticut Bks.). (Illus.). (J). (gr. 3 up). 1994. lib. bdg. 24.95 (*0-7933-4253-8*); pap. 14.95 (*0-7933-4254-6*); disk 29.95 (*0-7933-4255-4*) Gallopade Pub Group.

— How to Start a Delaware Library: At Home or School - A Book for All Ages. (Carole Marsh Delaware Bks.). (Illus.). (J). (gr. 3 up). 1994. lib. bdg. 24.95 (*0-7933-4256-2*); pap. 14.95 (*0-7933-4257-0*); disk 29.95 (*0-7933-4258-9*) Gallopade Pub Group.

— How to Start a Florida Library: At Home or School - A Book for All Ages. (Carole Marsh Florida Bks.). (Illus.). (J). (gr. 3 up). 1994. lib. bdg. 24.95 (*0-7933-4259-7*); pap. 14.95 (*0-7933-4260-0*); disk 29.95 (*0-7933-4261-9*) Gallopade Pub Group.

— How to Start a Georgia Library: At Home or School - A Book for All Ages. (Carole Marsh Georgia Bks.). (Illus.). (J). (gr. 3 up). 1994. lib. bdg. 24.95 (*0-7933-4262-7*); pap. 14.95 (*0-7933-4263-5*); disk 29.95 (*0-7933-4264-3*) Gallopade Pub Group.

— How to Start a Hawaii Library: At Home or School - A Book for All Ages. (Carole Marsh Hawaii Bks.). (Illus.). (J). (gr. 3 up). 1994. lib. bdg. 24.95 (*0-7933-4265-1*); pap. 14.95 (*0-7933-4266-X*); disk 29.95 (*0-7933-4267-8*) Gallopade Pub Group.

— How to Start a Kansas Library: At Home or School - A Book for All Ages. (Carole Marsh Kansas Bks.). (Illus.). (J). (gr. 3 up). 1994. lib. bdg. 24.95 (*0-7933-4280-5*); pap. 14.95 (*0-7933-4281-3*); disk 29.95 (*0-7933-4282-1*) Gallopade Pub Group.

— How to Start a Kentucky Library: At Home or School - A Book for All Ages. (Carole Marsh Kentucky Bks.). (Illus.). (J). (gr. 3 up). 1994. lib. bdg. 24.95 (*0-7933-4283-X*); pap. 14.95 (*0-7933-4284-8*); disk 29.95 (*0-7933-4285-6*) Gallopade Pub Group.

— How to Start a Louisiana Library: At Home or School - A Book for All Ages. (Carole Marsh Louisiana Bks.). (Illus.). (J). (gr. 3 up). 1994. lib. bdg. 24.95 (*0-7933-4286-4*); pap. 14.95 (*0-7933-4287-2*); disk 29.95 (*0-7933-4288-0*) Gallopade Pub Group.

— How to Start a Maine Library: At Home or School - A Book for All Ages. (Carole Marsh Maine Bks.). (Illus.). (J). (gr. 3 up). 1994. lib. bdg. 24.95 (*0-7933-4289-9*); pap. 14.95 (*0-7933-4290-2*); disk 29.95 (*0-7933-4291-0*) Gallopade Pub Group.

— How to Start a Maryland Library: At Home or School - A Book for All Ages. (Carole Marsh Maryland Bks.). (Illus.). (J). (gr. 3 up). 1994. lib. bdg. 24.95 (*0-7933-4292-9*); pap. 14.95 (*0-7933-4293-7*); disk 29.95 (*0-7933-4294-5*) Gallopade Pub Group.

— How to Start a Massachusetts Library: At Home or School - A Book for All Ages. (Massachuseets Bks.). (Illus.). (J). (gr. 3 up). 1994. lib. bdg. 24.95 (*0-7933-4295-3*); pap. 14.95 (*0-7933-4296-1*); disk 29.95 (*0-7933-4297-X*) Gallopade Pub Group.

— How to Start a Michigan Library: At Home or School - A Book for All Ages. (Carole Marsh Michigan Bks.). (Illus.). (J). (gr. 3 up). 1994. lib. bdg. 24.95 (*0-7933-4298-8*); pap. 14.95 (*0-7933-4299-6*); disk 29.95 (*0-7933-4300-3*) Gallopade Pub Group.

— How to Start a Minnesota Library: At Home or School - A Book for All Ages. (Carole Marsh Minnesota Bks.). (Illus.). (J). (gr. 3 up). 1994. lib. bdg. 24.95 (*0-7933-4301-1*); pap. 14.95 (*0-7933-4302-X*); disk 29.95 (*0-7933-4303-8*) Gallopade Pub Group.

— How to Start a Mississippi Library: At Home or School - A Book for All Ages. (Carole Marsh Mississippi Bks.). (Illus.). (J). (gr. 3 up). 1994. lib. bdg. 24.95 (*0-7933-4304-6*); pap. 14.95 (*0-7933-4305-4*); disk 29.95 (*0-7933-4306-2*) Gallopade Pub Group.

— How to Start a Missouri Library: At Home or School - A Book for All Ages. (Carole Marsh Missouri Bks.). (Illus.). (J). (gr. 3 up). 1994. lib. bdg. 24.95 (*0-7933-4307-0*); pap. 14.95 (*0-7933-4308-9*); disk 29.95 (*0-7933-4309-7*) Gallopade Pub Group.

— How to Start a Montana Library: At Home or School - A Book for All Ages. (Carole Marsh Montana Bks.). (Illus.). (J). (gr. 3 up). 1994. lib. bdg. 24.95 (*0-7933-4310-0*); pap. 14.95 (*0-7933-4311-9*); disk 29.95 (*0-7933-4312-7*) Gallopade Pub Group.

— How to Start a Nebraska Library: At Home or School - A Book for All Ages. (Carole Marsh Nebraska Bks.). (Illus.). (J). (gr. 3 up). 1994. lib. bdg. 24.95 (*0-7933-4313-5*); pap. 14.95 (*0-7933-4314-3*); disk 29.95 (*0-7933-4315-1*) Gallopade Pub Group.

— How to Start a Nevada Library: At Home or School - A Book for All Ages. (Carole Marsh Nevada Bks.). (Illus.). (J). (gr. 3 up). 1994. lib. bdg. 24.95 (*0-7933-4316-X*); pap. 14.95 (*0-7933-4317-8*); disk 29.95 (*0-7933-4319-4*) Gallopade Pub Group.

— How to Start a New Hampshire Library: At Home or School - A Book for All Ages. (Carole Marsh New Hampshire Bks.). (Illus.). (J). (gr. 3 up). 1994. lib. bdg. 24.95 (*0-685-49562-0*); pap. 14.95 (*0-7933-4320-8*); disk 29.95 (*0-685-49563-9*) Gallopade Pub Group.

— How to Start a New Jersey Library: At Home or School - A Book for All Ages. (Carole Marsh New Jersey Bks.). (Illus.). (J). (gr. 3 up). 1994. lib. bdg. 24.95 (*0-7933-4322-4*); pap. 14.95 (*0-7933-4323-2*); disk 29.95 (*0-7933-4324-0*) Gallopade Pub Group.

— How to Start a New Mexico Library: At Home or School - A Book for All Ages. (Carole Marsh New Mexico Bks.). (Illus.). (J). (gr. 3 up). 1994. lib. bdg. 24.95 (*0-7933-4325-9*); pap. 14.95 (*0-7933-4326-7*); disk 29.95 (*0-7933-4327-5*) Gallopade Pub Group.

— How to Start a New York Library: At Home or School - A Book for All Ages. (Carole Marsh New York Bks.). (Illus.). (J). (gr. 3 up). 1994. lib. bdg. 24.95 (*0-7933-4328-3*); pap. 14.95 (*0-7933-4329-1*); disk 29.95 (*0-7933-4330-5*) Gallopade Pub Group.

— How to Start a North Carolina Library: At Home or School - A Book for All Ages. (Carole Marsh North Carolina Bks.). (Illus.). (J). (gr. 3 up). 1994. lib. bdg. 24.95 (*0-7933-4331-3*); pap. 14.95 (*0-7933-4332-1*); disk 29.95 (*0-7933-4333-X*) Gallopade Pub Group.

— How to Start a North Dakota Library: At Home or School - A Book for All Ages. (Carole Marsh North Dakota Bks.). (Illus.). (J). (gr. 3 up). 1994. lib. bdg. 24.95 (*0-7933-4334-8*); pap. 14.95 (*0-7933-4335-6*); disk 29.95 (*0-7933-4336-4*) Gallopade Pub Group.

— How to Start a Pennsylvania Library: At Home or School - A Book for All Ages. (Pennsylvania Bks.). (Illus.). (J). (gr. 3 up). 1994. lib. bdg. 24.95 (*0-7933-4346-1*); pap. 14.95 (*0-7933-4347-X*); disk 29.95 (*0-7933-4348-8*) Gallopade Pub Group.

— How to Start a Rhode Island Library: At Home or School - A Book for All Ages. (Rhode Island Bks.). (Illus.). (J). (gr. 3 up). 1994. lib. bdg. 24.95 (*0-7933-4349-6*); pap. 14.95 (*0-7933-4350-X*); disk 29.95 (*0-7933-4351-8*) Gallopade Pub Group.

— How to Start a South Carolina Library: At Home or School - A Book for All Ages. (South Carolina Bks.). (Illus.). (J). (gr. 3 up). 1994. lib. bdg. 24.95 (*0-7933-4352-6*); pap. 14.95 (*0-7933-4353-4*); disk 29.95 (*0-7933-4354-2*) Gallopade Pub Group.

— How to Start a South Dakota Library: At Home or School - A Book for All Ages. (South Dakota Bks.). (Illus.). (J). (gr. 3 up). 1994. lib. bdg. 24.95 (*0-7933-4355-0*); pap. 14.95 (*0-7933-4356-9*); disk 29.95 (*0-7933-4357-7*) Gallopade Pub Group.

— How to Start a Tennessee Library: At Home or School - A Book for All Ages. (Tennessee Bks.). (Illus.). (J). (gr. 3 up). 1994. lib. bdg. 24.95 (*0-7933-4358-5*); pap. 14.95 (*0-7933-4359-3*); disk 29.95 (*0-7933-4360-7*) Gallopade Pub Group.

— How to Start a Texas Library: At Home or School - A Book for All Ages. (Texas Bks.). (Illus.). (J). (gr. 3 up). 1994. lib. bdg. 24.95 (*0-7933-4361-5*); pap. 14.95 (*0-7933-4362-3*); disk 29.95 (*0-7933-4363-1*) Gallopade Pub Group.

— How to Start a Utah Library: At Home or School - A Book for All Ages. (Utah Bks.). (Illus.). (J). (gr. 3 up). 1994. lib. bdg. 24.95 (*0-7933-4364-X*); pap. 14.95 (*0-7933-4365-8*); disk 29.95 (*0-7933-4366-6*) Gallopade Pub Group.

— How to Start a Vermont Library: At Home or School - A Book for All Ages. (Vermont Bks.). (Illus.). (J). (gr. 3 up). 1994. lib. bdg. 24.95 (*0-7933-4367-4*); pap. 14.95 (*0-685-49564-7*); disk 29.95 (*0-7933-4369-0*) Gallopade Pub Group.

— How to Start a Virginia Library: At Home or School - A Book for All Ages. (Virginia Bks.). (Illus.). (J). (gr. 3 up). 1994. lib. bdg. 24.95 (*0-7933-4370-4*); pap. 14.95 (*0-7933-4371-2*); disk 29.95 (*0-7933-4372-0*) Gallopade Pub Group.

— How to Start a Washington DC Library: At Home or School - A Book for All Ages. (Washington, D.C. Bks.). (Illus.). (J). (gr. 3 up). 1994. lib. bdg. 24.95 (*0-7933-4376-3*); pap. 14.95 (*0-7933-4377-1*); disk 29.95 (*0-7933-4378-X*) Gallopade Pub Group.

— How to Start a Washington Library: At Home or School - A Book for All Ages. (Washington Bks.). (Illus.). (J). (gr. 3 up). 1994. lib. bdg. 24.95 (*0-7933-4373-9*); pap. 14.95 (*0-7933-4374-7*); disk 29.95 (*0-7933-4375-5*) Gallopade Pub Group.

— How to Start a West Virginia Library: At Home or School - A Book for All Ages. (West Virginia Bks.). (Illus.). (J). (gr. 3 up). 1994. lib. bdg. 24.95 (*0-7933-4379-8*); pap. 14.95 (*0-7933-4380-1*); disk 29.95 (*0-7933-4381-X*) Gallopade Pub Group.

— How to Start a Wisconsin Library: At Home or School - A Book for All Ages. (Wisconsin Bks.). (Illus.). (J). (gr. 3 up). 1994. lib. bdg. 24.95 (*0-7933-4382-8*); pap. 14.95 (*0-7933-4383-6*); disk 29.95 (*0-7933-4384-4*) Gallopade Pub Group.

— How to Start a Wyoming Library: At Home or School - A Book for All Ages. (Wyoming Bks.). (Illus.). (J). (gr. 3 up). 1994. lib. bdg. 24.95 (*0-7933-4385-2*); pap. 14.95 (*0-7933-4386-0*); disk 29.95 (*0-7933-4387-9*) Gallopade Pub Group.

— How to Start an Alabama Library: At Home or School - A Book for All Ages. (Carole Marsh Alabama Bks.). (Illus.). (J). (gr. 3 up). 1994. lib. bdg. 24.95 (*0-7933-4235-X*); pap. 14.95 (*0-7933-4236-8*); disk 29.95 (*0-7933-4237-6*) Gallopade Pub Group.

— How to Start an Alaska Library: At Home or School - A Book for All Ages. (Carole Marsh Alaska Bks.). (Illus.). (J). (gr. 3 up). 1994. lib. bdg. 24.95 (*0-7933-4238-4*); pap. 14.95 (*0-7933-4239-2*); disk 29.95 (*0-7933-4240-6*) Gallopade Pub Group.

— How to Start an Arizona Library: At Home or School - A Book for All Ages. (Carole Marsh Arizona Bks.). (Illus.). (J). (gr. 3 up). 1994. lib. bdg. 24.95 (*0-7933-4241-4*); pap. 14.95 (*0-7933-4242-2*); disk 29.95 (*0-7933-4243-0*) Gallopade Pub Group.

— How to Start an Arkansas Library: At Home or School - A Book for All Ages. (Carole Marsh Arkansas Bks.). (Illus.). (J). (gr. 3 up). 1994. lib. bdg. 24.95 (*0-7933-4244-9*); pap. 14.95 (*0-7933-4245-7*); disk 29.95 (*0-7933-4246-5*) Gallopade Pub Group.

— How to Start an Idaho Library: At Home or School - A Book for All Ages. (Carole Marsh Idaho Bks.). (Illus.). (J). (gr. 3 up). 1994. lib. bdg. 24.95 (*0-7933-4268-6*); pap. 14.95 (*0-7933-4269-4*); disk 29.95 (*0-7933-4270-8*) Gallopade Pub Group.

— How to Start an Illinois Library: At Home or School - A Book for All Ages. (Carole Marsh Illinois Bks.). (Illus.). (J). (gr. 3 up). 1994. lib. bdg. 24.95 (*0-7933-4271-6*); pap. 14.95 (*0-7933-4272-4*); disk 29.95 (*0-7933-4273-2*) Gallopade Pub Group.

— How to Start an Indiana Library: At Home or School - A Book for All Ages. (Carole Marsh Indiana Bks.). (Illus.). (J). (gr. 3 up). 1994. lib. bdg. 24.95 (*0-7933-4274-0*); pap. 14.95 (*0-7933-4275-9*); disk 29.95 (*0-7933-4276-7*) Gallopade Pub Group.

— How to Start an Iowa Library: At Home or School - A Book for All Ages. (Carole Marsh Iowa Bks.). (Illus.). (J). (gr. 3 up). 1994. lib. bdg. 24.95 (*0-7933-4277-5*); pap. 14.95 (*0-7933-4278-3*); disk 29.95 (*0-7933-4279-1*) Gallopade Pub Group.

— How to Start an Ohio Library: At Home or School - A Book for All Ages. (Carole Marsh Ohio Bks.). (Illus.). (J). (gr. 3 up). 1994. lib. bdg. 24.95 (*0-7933-4337-2*); pap. 14.95 (*0-7933-4338-0*); disk 29.95 (*0-7933-4339-9*) Gallopade Pub Group.

— How to Start an Oklahoma Library: At Home or School - A Book for All Ages. (Carole Marsh Oklahoma Bks.). (Illus.). (J). (gr. 3 up). 1994. lib. bdg. 24.95 (*0-7933-4340-2*); pap. 14.95 (*0-7933-4341-0*); disk 29.95 (*0-7933-4342-9*) Gallopade Pub Group.

— How to Start an Oregon Library: At Home or School - A Book for All Ages. (Oregon Bks.). (Illus.). (J). (gr. 3 up). 1994. lib. bdg. 24.95 (*0-7933-4343-7*); pap. 14.95 (*0-7933-4344-5*); disk 29.95 (*0-7933-4345-3*) Gallopade Pub Group.

— How You Know When Your Ass Is Grass. (Of All the Gaul Ser.). 1994. pap. 14.95 (*1-55609-203-2*) Gallopade Pub Group.

— How You Know When Your Tush Is Turf. (Of All the Gaul Ser.). (YA). 1994. lib. bdg. 24.95 (*0-7933-6924-X*); pap. text ed. 14.95 (*0-7933-6923-1*); disk 29.95 (*0-7933-6925-8*) Gallopade Pub Group.

— I Con..If You Con(dom) The Ins & Outs of Contraception for the Sexually Active Girl or Boy. (Smart Sex Stuff Ser.). (Orig.). 1994. pap. 14.95 (*1-55609-209-1*) Gallopade Pub Group.

— Idaho & Other State Greats (Biographies) (Carole Marsh Idaho Bks.). (Illus.). (YA). (gr. 3-12). 1994. lib. bdg. 24.95 (*1-55609-592-9*); pap. 14.95 (*1-55609-591-0*); disk 29.95 (*0-7933-1558-1*) Gallopade Pub Group.

— Idaho Bandits, Bushwackers, Outlaws, Crooks, Devils, Ghosts, Desperadoes & Other Assorted & Sundry Characters! (Carole Marsh Idaho Bks.). (Illus.). (YA). (gr. 3-12). 1994. lib. bdg. 24.95 (*0-7933-0358-3*); pap. 14.95 (*0-7933-0357-5*); disk 29.95 (*0-7933-0359-1*) Gallopade Pub Group.

— The Idaho Bookstore Book: A Surprising Guide to Our State's Bookstores & Their Specialties for Students, Teachers, Writers & Publishers. (Carole Marsh Idaho Bks.). (Illus.). 1994. lib. bdg. 24.95 (*0-7933-2891-8*); pap. 14.95 (*0-7933-2892-6*); disk 29.95 (*0-7933-2893-4*) Gallopade Pub Group.

— Idaho Classic Christmas Trivia: Stories, Recipes, Activities, Legends, Lore & More! (Carole Marsh Idaho Bks.). (Illus.). (YA). (gr. 3-12). 1994. lib. bdg. 24.95 (*0-7933-0361-3*); pap. 14.95 (*0-7933-0360-5*); disk 29.95 (*0-7933-0362-1*) Gallopade Pub Group.

— Idaho Coastales. (Carole Marsh Idaho Bks.). (Illus.). (YA). (gr. 3-12). 1994. lib. bdg. 24.95 (*1-55609-588-0*); pap. 14.95 (*1-55609-587-2*); disk 29.95 (*0-7933-1554-9*) Gallopade Pub Group.

— Idaho Coastales! (Carole Marsh Idaho Bks.). (J). 1994. lib. bdg. 24.95 (*0-7933-7277-1*) Gallopade Pub Group.

— Idaho "Crinkum-Crankum" A Funny Word Book about Our State. (Carole Marsh Idaho Bks.). (Illus.). (J). 1994. lib. bdg. 24.95 (*0-7933-4843-9*); pap. 14.95 (*0-7933-4844-7*); disk 29.95 (*0-7933-4845-5*) Gallopade Pub Group.

— Idaho Dingbats! Bk. 1: A Fun Book of Games, Stories, Activities & More about Our State That's All in Code! for You to Decipher. (Carole Marsh Idaho Bks.). (Illus.). (J). (gr. 3-12). 1994. lib. bdg. 24.95 (*0-7933-3809-3*); pap. 14.95 (*0-7933-3810-7*); disk 29.95 (*0-7933-3811-5*) Gallopade Pub Group.

— Idaho Festival Fun for Kids! (Carole Marsh Idaho Bks.). (Illus.). (YA). (gr. 3-12). 1994. lib. bdg. 24.95 (*0-7933-3962-6*); pap. 14.95 (*0-7933-3963-4*); disk 29.95 (*0-7933-3964-2*) Gallopade Pub Group.

— The Idaho Hot Air Balloon Mystery. (Idaho Bks.). (Illus.). (J). (gr. 2-9). 1994. 24.95 (*0-7933-2426-2*); pap. 14.95 (*0-7933-2427-0*); disk 29.95 (*0-7933-2428-9*) Gallopade Pub Group.

— Idaho Jeopardy! Answers & Questions about Our State! (Carole Marsh Idaho Bks.). (Illus.). (J). (gr. 3-12). 1994. lib. bdg. 24.95 (*0-7933-4115-9*); pap. 14.95 (*0-7933-4116-7*); disk 29.95 (*0-7933-4117-5*) Gallopade Pub Group.

— Idaho "Jography" A Fun Run Thru Our State! (Carole Marsh Idaho Bks.). (Illus.). (YA). (gr. 3-12). 1994. lib. bdg. 24.95 (*1-55609-583-X*); pap. 14.95 (*1-55609-582-1*); disk 29.95 (*0-7933-1544-1*) Gallopade Pub Group.

— Idaho Kid's Cookbook: Recipes, How-to, History, Lore & More! (Carole Marsh Idaho Bks.). (Illus.). (YA). (gr. 3-12). 1994. lib. bdg. 24.95 (*0-7933-0370-2*); pap. 14.95 (*0-7933-0369-9*); disk 29.95 (*0-7933-0371-0*) Gallopade Pub Group.

— The Idaho Library Book: A Surprising Guide to the Unusual Special Collections in Libraries Across Our State for Students, Teachers, Writers & Publishers - Includes Reproducible Mailing Labels Plus Activities for Young People! (Carole Marsh Idaho Bks.). (Illus.). 1994. lib. bdg. 24.95 (*0-7933-3041-6*); pap. 14.95 (*0-7933-3042-4*); disk 29.95 (*0-7933-3043-2*) Gallopade Pub Group.

— The Idaho Media Book: A Surprising Guide to the Amazing Print, Broadcast & Online Media of Our State for Students, Teachers, Writers & Publishers - Includes Reproducible Mailing Labels Plus Activities for Young People! (Carole Marsh Idaho Bks.). (Illus.). 1994. lib. bdg. 24.95 (*0-7933-3197-8*); pap. 14.95 (*0-7933-3198-6*); disk 29.95 (*0-7933-3199-4*) Gallopade Pub Group.

— The Idaho Mystery Van Takes Off! Book 1: Handicapped Idaho Kids Sneak Off on a Big Adventure. (Carole Marsh Idaho Bks.). (Illus.). (J). (gr. 3-12). 1994. 24.95 (*0-7933-4997-4*); pap. 14.95 (*0-7933-4998-2*); disk 29.95 (*0-7933-4999-0*) Gallopade Pub Group.

— Idaho Quiz Bowl Crash Course! (Carole Marsh Idaho Bks.). (Illus.). (YA). (gr. 3-12). 1994. lib. bdg. 24.95 (*1-55609-590-2*); pap. 14.95 (*1-55609-589-9*); disk 29.95 (*0-685-45925-X*) Gallopade Pub Group.

— Idaho Rollercoasters! (Carole Marsh Idaho Bks.). (Illus.). (YA). (gr. 3-12). 1994. lib. bdg. 24.95 (*0-7933-5260-6*); pap. 14.95 (*0-7933-5261-4*); disk 29.95 (*0-7933-5262-2*) Gallopade Pub Group.

— Idaho School Trivia: An Amazing & Fascinating Look at Our State's Teachers, School & Students! (Carole Marsh Idaho Bks.). (Illus.). (YA). (gr. 3-12). 1994. lib. bdg. 24.95 (*0-7933-0367-2*); pap. 14.95 (*0-7933-0366-4*); disk 29.95 (*0-7933-0368-0*) Gallopade Pub Group.

— Idaho Silly Basketball Sportsmysteries. (Carole Marsh Idaho Bks.: Vol. II). (Illus.). (YA). (gr. 3-12). 1994. lib. bdg. 24.95 (*0-7933-1559-X*); pap. 14.95 (*0-7933-1560-3*); disk 29.95 (*0-7933-1561-1*) Gallopade Pub Group.

— Idaho Silly Basketball Sportsmysteries, Vol. I. (Carole Marsh Idaho Bks.). (Illus.). (YA). (gr. 3-12). 1994. lib. bdg. 24.95 (*0-7933-0364-8*); pap. 14.95 (*0-7933-0363-X*); disk 29.95 (*0-7933-0365-6*) Gallopade Pub Group.

— Idaho Silly Football Sportsmysteries, Vol. I. (Carole Marsh Idaho Bks.). (Illus.). (YA). (gr. 3-12). 1994. lib. bdg. 24.95 (*1-55609-586-4*); pap. 14.95 (*1-55609-585-6*); disk 29.95 (*0-7933-1546-8*) Gallopade Pub Group.

— Idaho Silly Football Sportsmysteries, Vol. II. (Carole Marsh Idaho Bks.). (Illus.). (YA). (gr. 3-12). 1994. lib. bdg. 24.95 (*0-7933-1547-6*); pap. 14.95 (*0-7933-1548-4*); disk 29.95 (*0-7933-1549-2*) Gallopade Pub Group.

— Idaho Silly Trivia! (Carole Marsh Idaho Bks.). (Illus.). (YA). (gr. 3-12). 1994. lib. bdg. 24.95 (*1-55609-581-3*); pap. 14.95 (*1-55609-580-5*); disk 29.95 (*0-7933-1543-3*) Gallopade Pub Group.

— Idaho Timeline: A Chronology of Idaho History, Mystery, Trivia, Legend, Lore & More. (Carole Marsh Idaho Bks.). (Illus.). (J). (gr. 3-12). 1994. lib. bdg. 24.95 (*0-7933-5911-2*); pap. 14.95 (*0-7933-5912-0*); disk 29.95 (*0-7933-5913-9*) Gallopade Pub Group.

— Idaho's (Most Devastating!) Disasters & (Most Calamitous!) Catastrophies! (Carole Marsh Idaho Bks.). (Illus.). (YA). (gr. 3-12). 1994. lib. bdg. 24.95 (*0-7933-0355-9*); pap. 14.95 (*0-7933-0354-0*); disk 29.95 (*0-7933-0356-7*) Gallopade Pub Group.

— Idaho's Unsolved Mysteries (& Their "Solutions") Includes Scientific Information & Other Activities for Students. (Carole Marsh Idaho Bks.). (Illus.). (J). (gr. 3-12). 1994. lib. bdg. 24.95 (*0-7933-5758-6*); pap. 14.95 (*0-7933-5759-4*); disk 29.95 (*0-7933-5760-8*) Gallopade Pub Group.

— If My Alabama Mama Ran the World! (Carole Marsh Alabama Bks.). (Illus.). (YA). (gr. 3-12). 1994. lib. bdg. 24.95 (*0-7933-1335-X*); pap. 14.95 (*0-7933-1336-8*); disk 29.95 (*0-7933-1337-6*) Gallopade Pub Group.

— If My Alaska Mama Ran the World! (Carole Marsh Alaska Bks.). (Illus.). (YA). (gr. 3-12). 1994. lib. bdg. 24.95 (*0-7933-1355-4*); pap. 14.95 (*0-7933-1356-2*); disk 29.95 (*0-7933-1357-0*) Gallopade Pub Group.

— If My Arizona Mama Ran the World! (Carole Marsh Arizona Bks.). (Illus.). (YA). (gr. 3-12). 1994. lib. bdg. 24.95 (*0-7933-1370-8*); pap. 14.95 (*0-7933-1371-6*); disk 29.95 (*0-7933-1372-4*) Gallopade Pub Group.

— If My Arkansas Mama Ran the World! (Carole Marsh Arkansas Bks.). (Illus.). (YA). (gr. 3-12). 1994. lib. bdg. 24.95 (*0-7933-1386-4*); pap. 14.95 (*0-7933-1387-2*); disk 29.95 (*0-7933-1388-0*) Gallopade Pub Group.

— If My California Mama Ran the World! (Carole Marsh California Bks.). (Illus.). (YA). (gr. 3-12). 1994. lib. bdg. 24.95 (*0-7933-1402-X*); pap. 14.95 (*0-7933-1403-8*); disk 29.95 (*0-7933-1404-6*) Gallopade Pub Group.

— If My Colorado Mama Ran the World! (Carole Marsh Colorado Bks.). (Illus.). (YA). (gr. 3-12). 1994. lib. bdg. 24.95 (*0-7933-1418-6*); pap. 14.95 (*0-7933-1419-4*); disk 29.95 (*0-7933-1420-8*) Gallopade Pub Group.

— If My Connecticut Mama Ran the World! (Carole Marsh Connecticut Bks.). (Illus.). (YA). (gr. 3-12). 1994. lib. bdg. 24.95 (*0-7933-1434-8*); pap. 14.95 (*0-7933-1435-6*); disk 29.95 (*0-7933-1436-4*) Gallopade Pub Group.

— If My Delaware Mama Ran the World! (Carole Marsh Delaware Bks.). (Illus.). (YA). (gr. 3-12). 1994. lib. bdg. 24.95 (*0-7933-1452-6*); pap. 14.95 (*0-7933-1453-4*); disk 29.95 (*0-7933-1454-2*) Gallopade Pub Group.

— If My Florida Mama Ran the World! (Carole Marsh Florida Bks.). (Illus.). (YA). (gr. 3-12). 1994. lib. bdg. 24.95 (*0-7933-1498-4*); pap. 14.95 (*0-7933-1499-2*); disk 29.95 (*0-7933-1500-X*) Gallopade Pub Group.

— If My Georgia Mama Ran the World! (Carole Marsh Georgia Bks.). (Illus.). (YA). (gr. 3-12). 1994. lib. bdg. 24.95 (*0-7933-1517-4*); pap. 14.95 (*0-7933-1518-2*); disk 29.95 (*0-7933-1519-0*) Gallopade Pub Group.

— If My Hawaii Mama Ran the World! (Carole Marsh Hawaii Bks.). (Illus.). (YA). (gr. 3-12). 1994. lib. bdg. 24.95 (*0-7933-1536-0*); pap. 14.95 (*0-7933-1537-9*); disk 29.95 (*0-7933-1538-7*) Gallopade Pub Group.

— If My Idaho Mama Ran the World! (Carole Marsh Idaho Bks.). (Illus.). (YA). (gr. 3-12). 1994. lib. bdg. 24.95 (*0-7933-1555-7*); pap. 14.95 (*0-7933-1556-5*); disk 29.95 (*0-7933-1557-3*) Gallopade Pub Group.

— If My Illinois Mama Ran the World! (Carole Marsh Illinois Bks.). (Illus.). (YA). (gr. 3-12). 1994. lib. bdg. 24.95 (*0-7933-1595-6*); pap. 14.95 (*0-7933-1596-4*); disk 29.95 (*0-7933-1597-2*) Gallopade Pub Group.

— If My Indiana Mama Ran the World! (Carole Marsh Indiana Bks.). (Illus.). (YA). (gr. 3-12). 1994. lib. bdg. 24.95 (*0-7933-1613-8*); pap. 14.95 (*0-7933-1614-6*); disk 29.95 (*0-7933-1615-4*) Gallopade Pub Group.

— If My Iowa Mama Ran the World! (Carole Marsh Iowa Bks.). (Illus.). (YA). (gr. 3-12). 1994. lib. bdg. 24.95 (*0-7933-1633-2*); pap. 14.95 (*0-7933-1634-0*); disk 29.95 (*0-7933-1635-9*) Gallopade Pub Group.

— If My Kansas Mama Ran the World. (Statemeant Ser.). (J). (gr. 3-12). 1994. 24.95 (*1-55609-374-8*); pap. 14.95 (*1-55609-375-6*); disk 29.95 (*1-55609-376-4*) Gallopade Pub Group.

— If My Kentucky Mama Ran the World! (Carole Marsh Kentucky Bks.). (Illus.). (J). (gr. 3-8). 1994. lib. bdg. 24.95 (*0-7933-1655-3*); pap. 14.95 (*0-7933-1656-1*); disk 29.95 (*0-7933-1657-X*) Gallopade Pub Group.

— If My Louisiana Mama Ran the World! (Carole Marsh Louisiana Bks.). (Illus.). (J). (gr. 3-8). 1994. lib. bdg. 24.95 (*0-7933-1674-X*); pap. 14.95 (*0-7933-1675-8*); disk 29.95 (*0-7933-1676-6*) Gallopade Pub Group.

— If My Maine Mama Ran the World! (Carole Marsh Maine Bks.). (Illus.). (J). (gr. 3-8). 1994. lib. bdg. 24.95 (*0-7933-1687-1*); pap. 14.95 (*0-7933-1688-X*); disk 29.95 (*0-7933-1689-8*) Gallopade Pub Group.

— If My Mama Ran the World. (J). 1994. 24.95 (*1-55609-287-3*); pap. 14.95 (*0-318-37385-8*) Gallopade Pub Group.

— If My Maryland Mama Ran the World! (Carole Marsh Maryland Bks.). (Illus.). (J). (gr. 3-8). 1994. lib. bdg. 24.95 (*0-7933-1693-6*); pap. 14.95 (*0-7933-1694-4*); disk 29.95 (*0-7933-1695-2*) Gallopade Pub Group.

— If My Massachusetts Mama Ran the World! (Carole Marsh Massachusetts Bks.). (Illus.). (J). (gr. 3-8). 1994. lib. bdg. 24.95 (*0-7933-1702-9*); pap. 14.95 (*0-7933-1703-7*); disk 29.95 (*0-7933-1704-5*) Gallopade Pub Group.

— If My Michigan Mama Ran the World! (Carole Marsh Michigan Bks.). (Illus.). (J). (gr. 3 up). 1994. lib. bdg. 24.95 (*0-7933-1723-1*); pap. 14.95 (*0-7933-1724-X*); disk 29.95 (*0-7933-1725-8*) Gallopade Pub Group.

— If My Minnesota Mama Ran the World! (Carole Marsh Minnesota Bks.). (Illus.). (J). (gr. 3 up). 1994. lib. bdg. 24.95 (*0-7933-1717-7*); pap. 14.95 (*0-7933-1718-5*); disk 29.95 (*0-7933-1719-3*) Gallopade Pub Group.

— If My Mississippi Mama Ran the World! (Carole Marsh Mississippi Bks.). (Illus.). (J). (gr. 3 up). 1994. lib. bdg. 24.95 (*0-7933-1728-2*); pap. 14.95 (*0-7933-1729-0*); disk 29.95 (*0-7933-1730-4*) Gallopade Pub Group.

— If My Missouri Mama Ran the World! (Carole Marsh Missouri Bks.). (Illus.). (J). (gr. 3 up). 1994. lib. bdg. 24.95 (*0-7933-1737-1*); pap. 14.95 (*0-7933-1738-X*); disk 29.95 (*0-7933-1739-8*) Gallopade Pub Group.

— If My Montana Mama Ran the World! (Carole Marsh Montana Bks.). (Illus.). (J). (gr. 3 up). 1994. lib. bdg. 24.95 (*0-7933-1746-0*); pap. 14.95 (*0-7933-1747-9*); disk 29.95 (*0-7933-1748-7*) Gallopade Pub Group.

— If My Nebraska Mama Ran the World! (Carole Marsh Nebraska Bks.). (Illus.). (J). (gr. 3 up). 1994. lib. bdg. 24.95 (*0-7933-1755-X*); pap. 14.95 (*0-7933-1756-8*); disk 29.95 (*0-7933-1757-6*) Gallopade Pub Group.

— If My Nevada Mama Ran the World! (Carole Marsh Nevada Bks.). (Illus.). (J). 1994. lib. bdg. 24.95 (*0-7933-1764-9*); pap. 14.95 (*0-7933-1765-7*); disk 29.95 (*0-7933-1766-5*) Gallopade Pub Group.

— If My New Hampshire Mama Ran the World! (Carole Marsh New Hampshire Bks.). (Illus.). (J). 1994. lib. bdg. 24.95 (*0-7933-1773-8*); pap. 14.95 (*0-7933-1774-6*); disk 29.95 (*0-7933-1775-4*) Gallopade Pub Group.

— If My New Jersey Mama Ran the World! (Carole Marsh New Jersey Bks.). (Illus.). (J). 1994. lib. bdg. 24.95 (*0-7933-1782-7*); pap. 14.95 (*0-7933-1783-5*); disk 29.95 (*0-7933-1784-3*) Gallopade Pub Group.

— If My New Mexico Mama Ran The World! (Carole Marsh New Mexico Bks.). (Illus.). (J). 1994. lib. bdg. 24.95 (*0-7933-1815-7*); pap. 14.95 (*0-7933-1816-5*); disk 29.95 (*0-7933-1817-3*) Gallopade Pub Group.

— If My New York Mama Ran the World! (Carole Marsh New York Bks.). (Illus.). (J). 1994. lib. bdg. 24.95 (*0-7933-1827-0*); pap. 14.95 (*0-7933-1828-9*); disk 29.95 (*0-7933-1829-7*) Gallopade Pub Group.

— If My North Carolina Mama Ran the World! (Carole Marsh North Carolina Bks.). (Illus.). (J). 1994. lib. bdg. 24.95 (*0-7933-1833-5*); pap. 14.95 (*0-7933-1834-3*); disk 29.95 (*0-7933-1835-1*) Gallopade Pub Group.

— If My North Dakota Mama Ran the World! (Carole Marsh North Dakota Bks.). (Illus.). (J). 1994. lib. bdg. 24.95 (*0-7933-1842-4*); pap. 14.95 (*0-7933-1843-2*); disk 29.95 (*0-7933-1844-0*) Gallopade Pub Group.

— If My Ohio Mama Ran the World! (Carole Marsh Ohio Bks.). (Illus.). (J). 1994. lib. bdg. 24.95 (*0-7933-1850-5*); pap. 14.95 (*0-7933-1851-3*); disk 29.95 (*0-7933-1852-1*) Gallopade Pub Group.

— If My Oklahoma Mama Ran the World! (Carole Marsh Oklahoma Bks.). (Illus.). (J). 1994. lib. bdg. 24.95 (*0-7933-1875-0*); pap. 14.95 (*0-7933-1876-9*); disk 29.95 (*0-7933-1877-7*) Gallopade Pub Group.

— If My Oregon Mama Ran the World! (Carole Marsh Oregon Bks.). (Illus.). (J). 1994. lib. bdg. 24.95 (*0-7933-1910-2*); pap. 14.95 (*0-7933-1911-0*); disk 29.95 (*0-7933-1912-9*) Gallopade Pub Group.

— If My Pennsylvania Mama Ran the World! (Carole Marsh Pennsylvania Bks.). (Illus.). (J). 1994. lib. bdg. 24.95 (*0-7933-1939-0*); pap. 14.95 (*0-7933-1940-4*); disk 29.95 (*0-7933-1941-2*) Gallopade Pub Group.

— If My Rhode Island Mama Ran the World! (Carole Marsh Rhode Island Bks.). (Illus.). (J). 1994. lib. bdg. 24.95 (*0-7933-1974-9*); pap. 14.95 (*0-7933-1975-7*); disk 29.95 (*0-7933-1976-5*) Gallopade Pub Group.

— If My South Carolina Mama Ran the World! (Carole Marsh South Carolina Bks.). (Illus.). (J). 1994. lib. bdg. 24.95 (*0-7933-2003-8*); pap. 14.95 (*0-7933-2004-6*); disk 29.95 (*0-7933-2005-4*) Gallopade Pub Group.

— If My South Dakota Mama Ran the World! (Carole Marsh South Dakota Bks.). (Illus.). (J). 1994. lib. bdg. 24.95 (*0-7933-2035-6*); pap. 14.95 (*0-7933-2036-4*); disk 29.95 (*0-7933-2037-2*) Gallopade Pub Group.

— If My Tennessee Mama Ran the World! (Carole Marsh Tennessee Bks.). (Illus.). (J). 1994. lib. bdg. 24.95 (*0-7933-2065-8*); pap. 14.95 (*0-7933-2066-6*); disk 29.95 (*0-7933-2067-4*) Gallopade Pub Group.

— If My Texas Mama Ran the World! (Carole Marsh Texas Bks.). (Illus.). (J). 1994. lib. bdg. 24.95 (*0-7933-2094-1*); pap. 14.95 (*0-7933-2095-X*); disk 29.95 (*0-7933-2096-8*) Gallopade Pub Group.

— If My Utah Mama Ran the World! (Carole Marsh Utah Bks.). (Illus.). (J). 1994. lib. bdg. 24.95 (*0-7933-2126-3*); pap. 14.95 (*0-7933-2127-1*); disk 29.95 (*0-7933-2128-X*) Gallopade Pub Group.

— If My Vermont Mama Ran the World! (Carole Marsh Vermont Bks.). (Illus.). (J). 1994. lib. bdg. 24.95 (*0-7933-2158-1*); pap. 14.95 (*0-7933-2159-X*); disk 29.95 (*0-7933-2160-3*) Gallopade Pub Group.

— If My Virginia Mama Ran the World! (Carole Marsh Virginia Bks.). (Illus.). (J). 1994. lib. bdg. 24.95 (*0-7933-2187-5*); pap. 14.95 (*0-7933-2188-3*); disk 29.95 (*0-7933-2189-1*) Gallopade Pub Group.

— If My Washington, D.C. Mama Ran the World! (Carole Marsh Washington, D.C. Bks.). (Illus.). (YA). (gr. 3-12). 1994. lib. bdg. 24.95 (*0-7933-1477-1*); pap. 14.95 (*0-7933-1478-X*); disk 29.95 (*0-7933-1479-8*) Gallopade Pub Group.

— If My Washington Mama Ran the World! (Carole Marsh Washington Bks.). (Illus.). (J). 1994. lib. bdg. 24.95 (*0-7933-2221-9*); pap. 14.95 (*0-7933-2222-7*); disk 29.95 (*0-7933-2223-5*) Gallopade Pub Group.

— If My West Virginia Mama Ran the World! (Carole Marsh West Virginia Bks.). (Illus.). (J). 1994. lib. bdg. 24.95 (*0-7933-2253-7*); pap. 14.95 (*0-7933-2254-5*); disk 29.95 (*0-7933-2255-3*) Gallopade Pub Group.

— If My Wisconsin Mama Ran the World! (Carole Marsh Wisconsin Bks.). (Illus.). (J). 1994. lib. bdg. 24.95 (*0-7933-2285-5*); pap. 14.95 (*0-7933-2286-3*); disk 29.95 (*0-7933-2287-1*) Gallopade Pub Group.

— If My Wyoming Mama Ran the World. (Carole Marsh Wyoming Bks.). (Illus.). (J). 1994. lib. bdg. 24.95 (*0-7933-2309-6*); pap. 14.95 (*0-7933-2310-X*); disk 29.95 (*0-7933-2311-8*) Gallopade Pub Group.

— Illinois & Other State Greats (Biographies) (Carole Marsh Illinois Bks.). (Illus.). (YA). (gr. 3-12). 1994. lib. bdg. 24.95 (*1-55609-416-7*); pap. 14.95 (*1-55609-415-9*); disk 29.95 (*0-7933-1598-0*) Gallopade Pub Group.

— Illinois Bandits, Bushwackers, Outlaws, Crooks, Devils, Ghosts, Desperadoes & Other Assorted & Sundry Characters! (Carole Marsh Illinois Bks.). (Illus.). (YA). (gr. 3-12). 1994. lib. bdg. 24.95 (*0-7933-0382-6*); pap. 14.95 (*0-7933-0381-8*); disk 29.95 (*0-7933-0383-4*) Gallopade Pub Group.

— The Illinois Bookstore Book: A Surprising Guide to Our State's Bookstores & Their Specialties for Students, Teachers, Writers & Publishers. (Carole Marsh Illinois Bks.). (Illus.). 1994. lib. bdg. 24.95 (*0-7933-2894-2*); pap. 14.95 (*0-7933-2895-0*); disk 29.95 (*0-7933-2896-9*) Gallopade Pub Group.

— Illinois Classic Christmas Trivia: Stories, Recipes, Activities, Legends, Lore & More! (Carole Marsh Illinois Bks.). (Illus.). (YA). (gr. 3-12). 1994. lib. bdg. 24.95 (*0-7933-0385-0*); pap. 14.95 (*0-7933-0384-2*); disk 29.95 (*0-7933-0386-9*) Gallopade Pub Group.

— Illinois Coastales. (Carole Marsh Illinois Bks.). (J). 1994. lib. bdg. 24.95 (*0-7933-7278-X*) Gallopade Pub Group.

— Illinois Coastales. (Carole Marsh Illinois Bks.). (Illus.). (YA). (gr. 3-12). 1994. lib. bdg. 24.95 (*1-55609-412-4*); pap. 14.95 (*1-55609-411-6*); disk 29.95 (*0-7933-1594-8*) Gallopade Pub Group.

— Illinois "Crinkum-Crankum" A Funny Word Book about Our State. (Carole Marsh Illinois Bks.). (Illus.). (J). 1994. lib. bdg. 24.95 (*0-7933-4846-3*); pap. 14.95 (*0-7933-4847-1*); disk 29.95 (*0-7933-4848-X*) Gallopade Pub Group.

— Illinois Dingbats! Bk. 1: A Fun Book of Games, Stories, Activities & More about Our State That's All in Code! for You to Decipher. (Carole Marsh Illinois Bks.). (Illus.). (J). (gr. 3-12). 1994. lib. bdg. 24.95 (*0-7933-3812-3*); pap. 14.95 (*0-7933-3813-1*); disk 29.95 (*0-7933-3814-X*) Gallopade Pub Group.

— Illinois Festival Fun for Kids! (Carole Marsh Illinois Bks.). (Illus.). (YA). (gr. 3-12). 1994. lib. bdg. 24.95 (*0-7933-3965-0*); pap. 14.95 (*0-7933-3966-9*); disk 29.95 (*0-7933-3967-7*) Gallopade Pub Group.

— The Illinois Hot Air Balloon Mystery. (Carole Marsh Illinois Bks.). (Illus.). (J). (gr. 2-9). 1994. 24.95 (*0-7933-2435-1*); pap. 14.95 (*0-7933-2436-X*); disk 29.95 (*0-7933-2437-8*) Gallopade Pub Group.

— Illinois Jeopardy! Answers & Questions about Our State! (Carole Marsh Illinois Bks.). (Illus.). (J). (gr. 3-12). 1994. lib. bdg. 24.95 (*0-7933-4118-3*); pap. 14.95 (*0-7933-4119-1*); disk 29.95 (*0-7933-4120-5*) Gallopade Pub Group.

— Illinois "Jography" A Fun Run Thru Our State! (Carole Marsh Illinois Bks.). (Illus.). (YA). (gr. 3-12). 1994. lib. bdg. 24.95 (*1-55609-407-8*); pap. 14.95 (*1-55609-406-X*); disk 29.95 (*0-7933-1584-0*) Gallopade Pub Group.

— Illinois Kid's Cookbook: Recipes, How-to, History, Lore & More! (Carole Marsh Illinois Bks.). (Illus.). (YA). (gr. 3-12). 1994. lib. bdg. 24.95 (*0-7933-0394-X*); pap. 14.95 (*0-7933-0393-1*); disk 29.95 (*0-7933-0395-8*) Gallopade Pub Group.

— The Illinois Library Book: A Surprising Guide to the Unusual Special Collections in Libraries Across Our State for Students, Teachers, Writers & Publishers - Includes Reproducible Mailing Labels Plus Activities for Young People! (Carole Marsh Illinois Bks.). (Illus.). 1994. lib. bdg. 24.95 (*0-7933-3044-0*); pap. 14.95 (*0-7933-3045-9*); disk 29.95 (*0-685-41937-1*) Gallopade Pub Group.

— The Illinois Media Book: A Surprising Guide to the Amazing Print, Broadcast & Online Media of Our State for Students, Teachers, Writers & Publishers - Includes Reproducible Mailing Labels Plus Activities for Young People! (Carole Marsh Illinois Bks.). (Illus.). 1994. lib. bdg. 24.95 (*0-7933-3200-1*); pap. 14.95 (*0-7933-3201-X*); disk 29.95 (*0-7933-3202-8*) Gallopade Pub Group.

— The Illinois Mystery Van Takes Off! Book 1: Handicapped Illinois Kids Sneak Off on a Big Adventure. (Carole Marsh Illinois Bks.). (Illus.). (J). (gr. 3-12). 1994. 24.95 (*0-7933-5000-X*); pap. 14.95 (*0-7933-5001-8*); disk 29.95 (*0-7933-5002-6*) Gallopade Pub Group.

— Illinois Quiz Bowl Crash Course! (Carole Marsh Illinois Bks.). (Illus.). (YA). (gr. 3-12). 1994. lib. bdg. 24.95 (*1-55609-414-0*); pap. 14.95 (*1-55609-413-2*); disk 29.95 (*0-7933-1593-X*) Gallopade Pub Group.

— Illinois Rollercoasters! (Carole Marsh Illinois Bks.). (Illus.). (YA). (gr. 3-12). 1994. lib. bdg. 24.95 (*0-7933-5263-0*); pap. 14.95 (*0-7933-5264-9*); disk 29.95 (*0-7933-5265-7*) Gallopade Pub Group.

— Illinois School Trivia: An Amazing & Fascinating Look at Our State's Teachers, Schools & Students! (Carole Marsh Illinois Bks.). (Illus.). (YA). (gr. 3-12). 1994. lib. bdg. 24.95 (*0-7933-0391-5*); pap. 14.95 (*0-7933-0390-7*); disk 29.95 (*0-7933-0392-3*) Gallopade Pub Group.

— Illinois Silly Basketball Sportsmysteries, Vol. I. (Carole Marsh Illinois Bks.). (Illus.). (YA). (gr. 3-12). 1994. lib. bdg. 24.95 (*0-7933-0388-5*); pap. 14.95 (*0-7933-0387-7*); disk 29.95 (*0-7933-0389-3*) Gallopade Pub Group.

— Illinois Silly Basketball Sportsmysteries, Vol. II. (Carole Marsh Illinois Bks.). (Illus.). (YA). (gr. 3-12). 1994. lib. bdg. 24.95 (*0-7933-1599-9*); pap. 14.95 (*0-7933-1600-6*); disk 29.95 (*0-7933-1601-4*) Gallopade Pub Group.

— Illinois Silly Football Sportsmysteries. (Carole Marsh Illinois Bks.: Vol. II). (Illus.). (YA). (gr. 3-12). 1994. lib. bdg. 24.95 (*0-7933-1587-5*); pap. 14.95 (*0-7933-1588-3*); disk 29.95 (*0-7933-1589-1*) Gallopade Pub Group.

— Illinois Silly Football Sportsmysteries, Vol. I. (Carole Marsh Illinois Bks.). (Illus.). (YA). (gr. 3-12). 1994. lib. bdg. 24.95 (*1-55609-410-8*); pap. 14.95 (*1-55609-409-4*); disk 29.95 (*0-7933-1586-7*) Gallopade Pub Group.

— Illinois Silly Trivia! (Carole Marsh Illinois Bks.). (Illus.). (YA). (gr. 3-12). 1994. lib. bdg. 24.95 (*1-55609-405-1*); pap. 14.95 (*1-55609-113-3*); disk 29.95 (*0-7933-1583-2*) Gallopade Pub Group.

— Illinois Timeline: A Chronology of Illinois History, Mystery, Trivia, Legend, Lore & More. (Carole Marsh Illinois Bks.). (Illus.). (J). (gr. 3-12). 1994. lib. bdg. 24.95 (*0-7933-5914-7*); pap. 14.95 (*0-7933-5915-5*); disk 29.95 (*0-7933-5916-3*) Gallopade Pub Group.

— Illinois's (Most Devastating!) Disasters & (Most Calamitous!) Catastrophies! (Carole Marsh Illinois Bks.). (Illus.). (YA). (gr. 3-12). 1994. lib. bdg. 24.95 (*0-7933-0379-6*); pap. 14.95 (*0-7933-0378-8*); disk 29.95 (*0-7933-0380-X*) Gallopade Pub Group.

— Illinois's Unsolved Mysteries (& Their "Solutions") Includes Scientific Information & Other Activities for Students. (Carole Marsh Illinois Bks.). (Illus.). (J). (gr. 3-12). 1994. lib. bdg. 24.95 (*0-7933-5761-6*); pap. 14.95 (*0-7933-5762-4*); disk 29.95 (*0-7933-5763-2*) Gallopade Pub Group.

— In Good Taste! Cannibalism - Who Did It, Where, When, How & Why. (Extreme History). 1994. 24.95 (*0-7933-7362-X*); 14.95 (*0-7933-7364-6*); pap. 14.95 (*0-7933-7363-8*); audio 14.95 (*0-7933-7367-0*); vhs 14.95 (*0-7933-7366-2*); cd-rom 14.95 (*0-7933-7368-9*); disk 14.95 (*0-7933-7365-4*) Gallopade Pub Group.

— Indiana & Other State Greats (Biographies) (Carole Marsh Indiana Bks.). (Illus.). (YA). (gr. 3-12). 1994. lib. bdg. 24.95 (*1-55609-437-X*); pap. 14.95 (*1-55609-436-1*); disk 29.95 (*0-7933-1616-2*) Gallopade Pub Group.

— Indiana Bandits, Bushwackers, Outlaws, Crooks, Devils, Ghosts, Desperadoes & Other Assorted & Sundry Characters! (Carole Marsh Indiana Bks.). (Illus.). (YA). (gr. 3-12). 1994. lib. bdg. 24.95 (*0-7933-0406-7*); pap. 14.95 (*0-7933-0405-9*); disk 29.95 (*0-7933-0407-5*) Gallopade Pub Group.

— The Indiana Bookstore Book: A Surprising Guide to Our State's Bookstores & Their Specialties for Students, Teachers, Writers & Publishers. (Carole Marsh Indiana Bks.). (Illus.). 1994. lib. bdg. 24.95 (*0-7933-2897-7*); pap. 14.95 (*0-7933-2898-5*); disk 29.95 (*0-7933-2899-3*) Gallopade Pub Group.

— Indiana Classic Christmas Trivia: Stories, Recipes, Activities, Legends, Lore & More! (Carole Marsh Indiana Bks.). (Illus.). (YA). (gr. 3-12). 1994. lib. bdg. 24.95 (*0-7933-0409-1*); pap. 14.95 (*0-7933-0408-3*); disk 29.95 (*0-7933-0410-5*) Gallopade Pub Group.

— Indiana Coastales. (Carole Marsh Indiana Bks.). (Illus.). (YA). (gr. 3-12). 1994. lib. bdg. 24.95 (*1-55609-433-7*); pap. 14.95 (*1-55609-432-9*); disk 29.95 (*0-7933-1617-0*) Gallopade Pub Group.

— Indiana Coastales! (Carole Marsh Indiana Bks.). (J). 1994. lib. bdg. 24.95 (*0-7933-7279-8*) Gallopade Pub Group.

— Indiana "Crinkum-Crankum" A Funny Word Book about Our State. (Carole Marsh Indiana Bks.). (Illus.). (J). 1994. lib. bdg. 24.95 (*0-7933-4849-8*); pap. 14.95 (*0-7933-4851-X*); disk 29.95 (*0-7933-4852-8*) Gallopade Pub Group.

— Indiana Dingbats! Bk. 1: A Fun Book of Games, Stories, Activities & More about Our State That's All in Code! for You to Decipher. (Carole Marsh Indiana Bks.). (Illus.). (J). (gr. 3-12). 1994. lib. bdg. 24.95 (0-7933-3815-8); pap. 14.95 (0-7933-3816-6); disk 29.95 (0-7933-3817-4) Gallopade Pub Group.

— Indiana Festival Fun for Kids! (Carole Marsh Indiana Bks.). (Illus.). (YA). (gr. 3-12). 1994. lib. bdg. 24.95 (0-7933-3968-5); pap. 14.95 (0-7933-3969-3); disk 29.95 (0-7933-3970-7) Gallopade Pub Group.

— The Indiana Hot Air Balloon Mystery. (Carole Marsh Indiana Bks.). (Illus.). (J). (gr. 2-9). 1994. 24.95 (0-7933-2444-0); pap. 14.95 (0-7933-2445-9); disk 29.95 (0-7933-2446-7) Gallopade Pub Group.

— Indiana Jeopardy! Answers & Questions about Our State! (Carole Marsh Indiana Bks.). (Illus.). (J). (gr. 3-12). 1994. lib. bdg. 24.95 (0-7933-4121-3); pap. 14.95 (0-7933-4122-1); disk 29.95 (0-7933-4123-X) Gallopade Pub Group.

— Indiana "Jography" A Fun Run Thru Our State! (Carole Marsh Indiana Bks.). (Illus.). (YA). (gr. 3-12). 1994. lib. bdg. 24.95 (1-55609-428-0); pap. 14.95 (1-55609-102-8); disk 29.95 (0-7933-1603-0) Gallopade Pub Group.

— Indiana Kid's Cookbook: Recipes, How-to, History, Lore & More! (Carole Marsh Indiana Bks.). (Illus.). (YA). (gr. 3-12). 1994. lib. bdg. 24.95 (0-7933-0418-0); pap. 14.95 (0-7933-0417-2); disk 29.95 (0-7933-0419-9) Gallopade Pub Group.

— The Indiana Library Book: A Surprising Guide to the Unusual Special Collections in Libraries Across Our State for Students, Teachers, Writers & Publishers - Includes Reproducible Mailing Labels Plus Activities for Young People! (Carole Marsh Indiana Bks.). (Illus.). 1994. lib. bdg. 24.95 (0-7933-3047-5); pap. 14.95 (0-7933-3048-3); disk 29.95 (0-7933-3049-1) Gallopade Pub Group.

— The Indiana Media Book: A Surprising Guide to the Amazing Print, Broadcast & Online Media of Our State for Students, Teachers, Writers & Publishers - Includes Reproducible Mailing Labels Plus Activities for Young People! (Carole Marsh Indiana Bks.). (Illus.). 1994. lib. bdg. 24.95 (0-7933-3203-6); pap. 14.95 (0-7933-3204-4); disk 29.95 (0-7933-3205-2) Gallopade Pub Group.

— The Indiana Mystery Van Takes Off! Book 1: Handicapped Indiana Kids Sneak Off on a Big Adventure. (Carole Marsh Indiana Bks.). (Illus.). (J). (gr. 3-12). 1994. 24.95 (0-7933-5003-4); pap. 14.95 (0-7933-5004-2); disk 29.95 (0-7933-5005-0) Gallopade Pub Group.

— Indiana Quiz Bowl Crash Course! (Carole Marsh Indiana Bks.). (Illus.). (YA). (gr. 3-12). 1994. lib. bdg. 24.95 (1-55609-435-3); pap. 14.95 (1-55609-434-5); disk 29.95 (0-7933-1612-X) Gallopade Pub Group.

— Indiana Rollercoasters! (Carole Marsh Indiana Bks.). (Illus.). (YA). (gr. 3-12). 1994. lib. bdg. 24.95 (0-7933-5266-5); pap. 14.95 (0-7933-5267-3); disk 29.95 (0-7933-5268-1) Gallopade Pub Group.

— Indiana School Trivia: An Amazing & Fascinating Look at Our State's Teachers, Schools & Students! (Carole Marsh Indiana Bks.). (Illus.). (YA). (gr. 3-12). 1994. lib. bdg. 24.95 (0-7933-0415-6); pap. 14.95 (0-7933-0414-8); disk 29.95 (0-7933-0416-4) Gallopade Pub Group.

— Indiana Silly Basketball Sportsmysteries, Vol. I. (Carole Marsh Indiana Bks.). (Illus.). (YA). (gr. 3-12). 1994. lib. bdg. 24.95 (0-7933-0412-1); pap. 14.95 (0-7933-0411-3); disk 29.95 (0-7933-0413-X) Gallopade Pub Group.

— Indiana Silly Basketball Sportsmysteries, Vol. II. (Carole Marsh Indiana Bks.). (Illus.). (YA). (gr. 3-12). 1994. lib. bdg. 24.95 (0-7933-1618-9); pap. 14.95 (0-7933-1619-7); disk 29.95 (0-7933-1620-0) Gallopade Pub Group.

— Indiana Silly Football Sportsmysteries, Vol. I. (Carole Marsh Indiana Bks.). (Illus.). (YA). (gr. 3-12). 1994. lib. bdg. 24.95 (1-55609-431-0); pap. 14.95 (1-55609-430-2); disk 29.95 (0-7933-1605-7) Gallopade Pub Group.

— Indiana Silly Football Sportsmysteries, Vol. II. (Carole Marsh Indiana Bks.). (Illus.). (YA). (gr. 3-12). 1994. lib. bdg. 24.95 (0-7933-1606-5); pap. 14.95 (0-7933-1607-3); disk 29.95 (0-7933-1608-1) Gallopade Pub Group.

— Indiana Silly Trivia! (Carole Marsh Indiana Bks.). (Illus.). (YA). (gr. 3-12). 1994. lib. bdg. 24.95 (1-55609-427-2); pap. 14.95 (1-55609-101-X); disk 29.95 (0-7933-1602-2) Gallopade Pub Group.

— Indiana Timeline: A Chronology of Indiana History, Mystery, Trivia, Legend, Lore & More. (Carole Marsh Indiana Bks.). (Illus.). (J). (gr. 3-12). 1994. lib. bdg. 24.95 (0-7933-5917-1); pap. 14.95 (0-7933-5918-X); disk 29.95 (0-7933-5919-8) Gallopade Pub Group.

— Indiana's (Most Devastating!) Disasters & (Most Calamitous!) Catastrophies! (Carole Marsh Indiana Bks.). (Illus.). (YA). (gr. 3-12). 1994. lib. bdg. 24.95 (0-7933-0403-2); pap. 14.95 (0-7933-0402-4); disk 29.95 (0-7933-0404-0) Gallopade Pub Group.

— Indiana's Unsolved Mysteries (& Their "Solutions") Includes Scientific Information & Other Activities for Students. (Carole Marsh Indiana Bks.). (Illus.). (J). (gr. 3-12). 1994. lib. bdg. 24.95 (0-7933-5764-0); pap. 14.95 (0-7933-5765-9); disk 29.95 (0-7933-5766-7) Gallopade Pub Group.

— Iowa & Other State Greats (Biographies) (Carole Marsh Iowa Bks.). (Illus.). (YA). (gr. 3-12). 1994. lib. bdg. 24.95 (1-55609-459-0); pap. 14.95 (1-55609-458-2); disk 29.95 (0-7933-1636-7) Gallopade Pub Group.

— Iowa Bandits, Bushwackers, Outlaws, Crooks, Devils, Ghosts, Desperadoes & Other Assorted & Sundry Characters! (Carole Marsh Iowa Bks.). (Illus.). (YA). (gr. 3-12). 1994. lib. bdg. 24.95 (0-7933-0430-X); pap. 14.95 (0-7933-0429-6); disk 29.95 (0-7933-0431-8) Gallopade Pub Group.

— The Iowa Bookstore Book: A Surprising Guide to Our State's Bookstores & Their Specialties for Students, Teachers, Writers & Publishers. (Carole Marsh Iowa Bks.). (Illus.). 1994. lib. bdg. 24.95 (0-7933-2900-0); pap. 14.95 (0-7933-2901-9); disk 29.95 (0-7933-2902-7) Gallopade Pub Group.

— Iowa Classic Christmas Trivia: Stories, Recipes, Activities, Legends, Lore & More! (Carole Marsh Iowa Bks.). (Illus.). (YA). (gr. 3-12). 1994. lib. bdg. 24.95 (0-7933-0433-4); pap. 14.95 (0-7933-0432-6); disk 29.95 (0-7933-0434-2) Gallopade Pub Group.

— Iowa Coastales. (Carole Marsh Iowa Bks.). (Illus.). (YA). (gr. 3-12). 1994. lib. bdg. 24.95 (1-55609-455-8); pap. 14.95 (1-55609-454-X); disk 29.95 (0-7933-1632-4) Gallopade Pub Group.

— Iowa Coastales! (Carole Marsh Iowa Bks.). (J). 1994. lib. bdg. 24.95 (0-7933-7280-1) Gallopade Pub Group.

— Iowa "Crinkum-Crankum" A Funny Word Book about Our State. (Carole Marsh Iowa Bks.). (Illus.). (J). 1994. lib. bdg. 24.95 (0-7933-4853-6); pap. 14.95 (0-7933-4854-4); disk 29.95 (0-7933-4855-2) Gallopade Pub Group.

— Iowa Dingbats! Bk. 1: A Fun Book of Games, Stories, Activities & More about Our State That's All in Code! for You to Decipher. (Carole Marsh Iowa Bks.). (Illus.). (J). (gr. 3-12). 1994. lib. bdg. 24.95 (0-7933-3818-2); pap. 14.95 (0-7933-3819-0); disk 29.95 (0-7933-3820-4) Gallopade Pub Group.

— Iowa Festival Fun for Kids! (Carole Marsh Iowa Bks.). (Illus.). (YA). (gr. 3-12). 1994. lib. bdg. 24.95 (0-7933-3971-5); pap. 14.95 (0-7933-3972-3); disk 29.95 (0-7933-3973-1) Gallopade Pub Group.

— The Iowa Hot Air Balloon Mystery. (Carole Marsh Iowa Bks.). (Illus.). (J). (gr. 2-9). 1994. 24.95 (0-7933-2453-X); pap. 14.95 (0-7933-2454-8); disk 29.95 (0-7933-2455-6) Gallopade Pub Group.

— Iowa Jeopardy! Answers & Questions about Our State! (Carole Marsh Iowa Bks.). (Illus.). (J). (gr. 3-12). 1994. lib. bdg. 24.95 (0-7933-4124-8); pap. 14.95 (0-7933-4125-6); disk 29.95 (0-7933-4126-4) Gallopade Pub Group.

— Iowa "Jography" A Fun Run Thru Our State! (Carole Marsh Iowa Bks.). (Illus.). (YA). (gr. 3-12). 1994. lib. bdg. 24.95 (1-55609-450-7); pap. 14.95 (1-55609-085-4); disk 29.95 (0-7933-1622-7) Gallopade Pub Group.

— Iowa Kid's Cookbook: Recipes, How-to, History, Lore & More! (Carole Marsh Iowa Bks.). (Illus.). (YA). (gr. 3-12). 1994. lib. bdg. 24.95 (0-7933-0442-3); pap. 14.95 (0-7933-0441-5); disk 29.95 (0-7933-0443-1) Gallopade Pub Group.

— The Iowa Library Book: A Surprising Guide to the Unusual Special Collections in Libraries Across Our State for Students, Teachers, Writers & Publishers - Includes Reproducible Mailing Labels Plus Activities for Young People! (Carole Marsh Iowa Bks.). (Illus.). 1994. lib. bdg. 24.95 (0-7933-3050-5); pap. 14.95 (0-7933-3051-3); disk 29.95 (0-7933-3052-1) Gallopade Pub Group.

— The Iowa Media Book: A Surprising Guide to the Amazing Print, Broadcast & Online Media of Our State for Students, Teachers, Writers & Publishers - Includes Reproducible Mailing Labels Plus Activities for Young People! (Carole Marsh Iowa Bks.). (Illus.). 1994. lib. bdg. 24.95 (0-7933-3206-0); pap. 14.95 (0-7933-3207-9); disk 29.95 (0-7933-3208-7) Gallopade Pub Group.

— The Iowa Mystery Van Takes Off! Book 1: Handicapped Iowa Kids Sneak Off on a Big Adventure. (Carole Marsh Iowa Bks.). (Illus.). (J). (gr. 3-12). 1994. 24.95 (0-7933-5006-9); pap. 14.95 (0-7933-5007-7); disk 29.95 (0-7933-5008-5) Gallopade Pub Group.

— Iowa Quiz Bowl Crash Course! (Carole Marsh Iowa Bks.). (Illus.). (YA). (gr. 3-12). 1994. lib. bdg. 24.95 (1-55609-457-4); pap. 14.95 (1-55609-456-6); disk 29.95 (0-7933-1631-6) Gallopade Pub Group.

— Iowa Rollercoasters! (Carole Marsh Iowa Bks.). (Illus.). (YA). (gr. 3-12). 1994. lib. bdg. 24.95 (0-7933-5269-X); pap. 14.95 (0-7933-5270-3); disk 29.95 (0-7933-5271-1) Gallopade Pub Group.

— Iowa School Trivia: An Amazing & Fascinating Look at Our State's Teachers, Schools & Students! (Carole Marsh Iowa Bks.). (Illus.). (YA). (gr. 3-12). 1994. lib. bdg. 24.95 (0-7933-0439-3); pap. 14.95 (0-7933-0438-5); disk 29.95 (0-7933-0440-7) Gallopade Pub Group.

— Iowa Silly Basketball Sportsmysteries, Vol. I. (Carole Marsh Iowa Bks.). (Illus.). (YA). (gr. 3-12). 1994. lib. bdg. 24.95 (0-7933-0436-9); pap. 14.95 (0-7933-0435-0); disk 29.95 (0-7933-0437-7) Gallopade Pub Group.

— Iowa Silly Basketball Sportsmysteries, Vol. II. (Carole Marsh Iowa Bks.). (Illus.). (YA). (gr. 3-12). 1994. lib. bdg. 24.95 (0-7933-1637-5); pap. 14.95 (0-7933-1638-3); disk 29.95 (0-7933-1639-1) Gallopade Pub Group.

— Iowa Silly Football Sportsmysteries, Vol. I. (Carole Marsh Iowa Bks.). (Illus.). (YA). (gr. 3-12). 1994. lib. bdg. 24.95 (1-55609-453-1); pap. 14.95 (1-55609-452-3); disk 29.95 (0-7933-1624-3) Gallopade Pub Group.

— Iowa Silly Football Sportsmysteries, Vol. II. (Carole Marsh Iowa Bks.). (Illus.). (YA). (gr. 3-12). 1994. lib. bdg. 24.95 (0-7933-1625-1); pap. 14.95 (0-7933-1626-X); disk 29.95 (0-7933-1627-8) Gallopade Pub Group.

— Iowa Silly Trivia! (Carole Marsh Iowa Bks.). (Illus.). (YA). (gr. 3-12). 1994. lib. bdg. 24.95 (1-55609-449-3); pap. 14.95 (1-55609-084-6); disk 29.95 (0-7933-1621-9) Gallopade Pub Group.

— Iowa Timeline: A Chronology of Iowa History, Mystery, Trivia, Legend, Lore & More. (Carole Marsh Iowa Bks.). (Illus.). (J). (gr. 3-12). 1994. lib. bdg. 24.95 (0-7933-5920-1); pap. 14.95 (0-7933-5921-X); disk 29.95 (0-7933-5922-8) Gallopade Pub Group.

— Iowa's (Most Devastating!) Disasters & (Most Calamitous!) Catastrophies! (Carole Marsh Iowa Bks.). (Illus.). (YA). (gr. 3-12). 1994. lib. bdg. 24.95 (0-7933-0426-1); pap. 14.95 (0-7933-0427-X); disk 29.95 (0-7933-0428-8) Gallopade Pub Group.

— Iowa's Unsolved Mysteries (& Their "Solutions") Includes Scientific Information & Other Activities for Students. (Carole Marsh Iowa Bks.). (Illus.). (J). (gr. 3-12). 1994. lib. bdg. 24.95 (0-7933-5767-5); pap. 14.95 (0-7933-5768-3); disk 29.95 (0-7933-5769-1) Gallopade Pub Group.

— Island of the Calamari. (Carole Marsh Short Story Ser.). (Illus.). (Orig.). (J). (ps-7). 1994. 24.95 (1-55609-172-9); pap. 14.95 (0-317-66069-1) Gallopade Pub Group.

— Jason Hewitt! German for Kids. (J). 1994. lib. bdg. 24.95 (0-7933-6879-0); pap. text ed. 14.95 (0-7933-6878-2); disk 29.95 (0-7933-6880-4) Gallopade Pub Group.

— Jungle Gym! A Monkey's Eye View of the World's Jungles Yesterday, Today & Tomorrow? 36p. (J). (gr. 3-5). 1994. lib. bdg. 24.95 (0-7933-7346-8); pap. 14.95 (0-7933-7347-6); disk 29.95 (0-7933-7348-4) Gallopade Pub Group.

— Jurassic Ark! Alabama Dinosaurs & Other Prehistoric Creatures. (Carole Marsh State Bks.). (J). (gr. k-12). 1994. lib. bdg. 24.95 (0-7933-7428-6); pap. 14.95 (0-7933-7429-4); disk 29.95 (0-7933-7430-8) Gallopade Pub Group.

— Jurassic Ark! Alaska Dinosaurs & Other Prehistoric Creatures. (Carole Marsh Alaska Bks.). (J). (gr. k-12). 1994. lib. bdg. 24.95 (0-7933-7431-6); pap. 14.95 (0-7933-7432-4); disk 29.95 (0-7933-7433-2) Gallopade Pub Group.

— Jurassic Ark! Arizona Dinosaurs & Other Prehistoric Creatures. (Carole Marsh State Bks.). (J). (gr. k-12). 1994. lib. bdg. 24.95 (0-7933-7434-0); pap. 14.95 (0-7933-7435-9); disk 29.95 (0-7933-7436-7) Gallopade Pub Group.

— Jurassic Ark! Arkansas Dinosaurs & Other Prehistoric Creatures. (Carole Marsh State Bks.). (J). (gr. k-12). 1994. lib. bdg. 24.95 (0-7933-7437-5); pap. 14.95 (0-7933-7438-3); disk 29.95 (0-7933-7439-1) Gallopade Pub Group.

— Jurassic Ark! California Dinosaurs & Other Prehistoric Creatures. (Carole Marsh State Bks.). (J). (gr. k-12). 1994. lib. bdg. 24.95 (0-7933-7440-5); pap. 14.95 (0-7933-7441-3); disk 29.95 (0-7933-7442-1) Gallopade Pub Group.

— Jurassic Ark! Colorado Dinosaurs & Other Prehistoric Creatures. (Carole Marsh State Bks.). (J). (gr. k-12). 1994. lib. bdg. 24.95 (0-7933-7443-X); pap. 14.95 (0-7933-7444-8); disk 29.95 (0-7933-7445-6) Gallopade Pub Group.

— Jurassic Ark! Connecticut Dinosaurs & Other Prehistoric Creatures. (Carole Marsh State Bks.). (J). (gr. k-12). 1994. lib. bdg. 24.95 (0-7933-7446-4); pap. 14.95 (0-7933-7447-2); disk 29.95 (0-7933-7448-0) Gallopade Pub Group.

— Jurassic Ark! Delaware Dinosaurs & Other Prehistoric Creatures. (Carole Marsh State Bks.). (J). (gr. k-12). 1994. lib. bdg. 24.95 (0-7933-7449-9); pap. 14.95 (0-7933-7450-2); disk 29.95 (0-7933-7451-0) Gallopade Pub Group.

— Jurassic Ark! Florida Dinosaurs & Other Prehistoric Creatures. (Carole Marsh State Bks.). (J). (gr. k-12). 1994. lib. bdg. 24.95 (0-7933-7455-3); pap. 14.95 (0-7933-7456-1); disk 29.95 (0-7933-7457-X) Gallopade Pub Group.

— Jurassic Ark! Georgia Dinosaurs & Other Prehistoric Creatures. (Carole Marsh State Bks.). (J). (gr. k-12). 1994. lib. bdg. 24.95 (0-7933-7458-8); pap. 14.95 (0-7933-7459-6); disk 29.95 (0-7933-7460-X) Gallopade Pub Group.

— Jurassic Ark! Hawaii Dinosaurs & Other Prehistoric Creatures. (Carole Marsh State Bks.). (J). (gr. k-12). 1994. lib. bdg. 24.95 (0-7933-7461-8); pap. 14.95 (0-7933-7462-6); disk 29.95 (0-7933-7463-4) Gallopade Pub Group.

— Jurassic Ark! Idaho Dinosaurs & Other Prehistoric Creatures. (Carole Marsh State Bks.). (J). (gr. k-12). 1994. lib. bdg. 24.95 (0-7933-7464-2); pap. 14.95 (0-7933-7465-0); disk 29.95 (0-7933-7466-9) Gallopade Pub Group.

— Jurassic Ark! Illinois Dinosaurs & Other Prehistoric Creatures. (Carole Marsh State Bks.). (J). (gr. k-12). 1994. lib. bdg. 24.95 (0-7933-7467-7); pap. 14.95 (0-7933-7468-5); disk 29.95 (0-7933-7469-3) Gallopade Pub Group.

— Jurassic Ark! Indiana Dinosaurs & Other Prehistoric Creatures. (Carole Marsh State Bks.). (J). (gr. k-12). 1994. lib. bdg. 24.95 (0-7933-7470-7); pap. 14.95 (0-7933-7471-5); disk 29.95 (0-7933-7472-3) Gallopade Pub Group.

— Jurassic Ark! Iowa Dinosaurs & Other Prehistoric Creatures. (Carole Marsh State Bks.). (J). (gr. k-12). 1994. lib. bdg. 24.95 (0-7933-7473-1); pap. 14.95 (0-7933-7474-X); disk 29.95 (0-7933-7475-8) Gallopade Pub Group.

— Jurassic Ark! Kansas Dinosaurs & Other Prehistoric Creatures. (Carole Marsh State Bks.). (J). (gr. k-12). 1994. lib. bdg. 24.95 (0-7933-7476-6); pap. 14.95 (0-7933-7477-4); disk 29.95 (0-7933-7478-2) Gallopade Pub Group.

— Jurassic Ark! Kentucky Dinosaurs & Other Prehistoric Creatures. (Carole Marsh State Bks.). (J). (gr. k-12). 1994. lib. bdg. 24.95 (0-7933-7479-0); pap. 14.95 (0-7933-7480-4); disk 29.95 (0-7933-7481-2) Gallopade Pub Group.

— Jurassic Ark! Louisiana Dinosaurs & Other Prehistoric Creatures. (Carole Marsh State Bks.). (J). (gr. k-12). 1994. lib. bdg. 24.95 (0-7933-7482-0); pap. 14.95 (0-7933-7483-9); disk 29.95 (0-7933-7484-7) Gallopade Pub Group.

— Jurassic Ark! Maine Dinosaurs & Other Prehistoric Creatures. (Carole Marsh State Bks.). (J). (gr. k-12). 1994. lib. bdg. 24.95 (0-7933-7485-5); pap. 14.95 (0-7933-7486-3); disk 29.95 (0-7933-7487-1) Gallopade Pub Group.

— Jurassic Ark! Maryland Dinosaurs & Other Prehistoric Creatures. (Carole Marsh State Bks.). (J). (gr. k-12). 1994. lib. bdg. 24.95 (0-7933-7488-X); pap. 14.95 (0-7933-7489-8); disk 29.95 (0-7933-7490-1) Gallopade Pub Group.

— Jurassic Ark! Massachusetts Dinosaurs & Other Prehistoric Creatures. (Carole Marsh State Bks.). (J). (gr. k-12). 1994. lib. bdg. 24.95 (0-7933-7491-X); pap. 14.95 (0-7933-7492-8); disk 29.95 (0-7933-7493-6) Gallopade Pub Group.

— Jurassic Ark! Michigan Dinosaurs & Other Prehistoric Creatures. (Carole Marsh State Bks.). (J). (gr. k-12). 1994. lib. bdg. 24.95 (0-7933-7494-4); pap. 14.95 (0-7933-7495-2); disk 29.95 (0-7933-7496-0) Gallopade Pub Group.

— Jurassic Ark! Minnesota Dinosaurs & Other Prehistoric Creatures. (Carole Marsh State Bks.). (J). (gr. k-12). 1994. lib. bdg. 24.95 (0-7933-7497-9); pap. 14.95 (0-7933-7498-7); disk 29.95 (0-7933-7499-5) Gallopade Pub Group.

— Jurassic Ark! Mississippi Dinosaurs & Other Prehistoric Creatures. (Carole Marsh State Bks.). (J). (gr. k-12). 1994. lib. bdg. 24.95 (0-7933-7500-2); pap. 14.95 (0-7933-7501-0); disk 29.95 (0-7933-7502-9) Gallopade Pub Group.

— Jurassic Ark! Missouri Dinosaurs & Other Prehistoric Creatures. (Carole Marsh State Bks.). (J). (gr. k-12). 1994. lib. bdg. 24.95 (0-7933-7503-7); pap. 14.95 (0-7933-7504-5); disk 29.95 (0-7933-7505-3) Gallopade Pub Group.

— Jurassic Ark! Montana Dinosaurs & Other Prehistoric Creatures. (Carole Marsh State Bks.). (J). (gr. k-12). 1994. lib. bdg. 24.95 (0-7933-7506-1); pap. 14.95 (0-7933-7507-X); disk 29.95 (0-7933-7508-8) Gallopade Pub Group.

— Jurassic Ark! Nebraska Dinosaurs & Other Prehistoric Creatures. (Carole Marsh State Bks.). (J). (gr. k-12). 1994. lib. bdg. 24.95 (0-7933-7509-6); pap. 14.95 (0-7933-7510-X); disk 29.95 (0-7933-7511-8) Gallopade Pub Group.

— Jurassic Ark! Nevada Dinosaurs & Other Prehistoric Creatures. (Carole Marsh State Bks.). (J). (gr. k-12). 1994. lib. bdg. 24.95 (0-7933-7512-6); pap. 14.95 (0-7933-7513-4); disk 29.95 (0-7933-7514-2) Gallopade Pub Group.

— Jurassic Ark! New Hampshire Dinosaurs & Other Prehistoric Creatures. (Carole Marsh State Bks.). (J). (gr. k-12). 1994. lib. bdg. 24.95 (0-7933-7515-0); pap. 14.95 (0-7933-7516-9); disk 29.95 (0-7933-7517-7) Gallopade Pub Group.

— Jurassic Ark! New Jersey Dinosaurs & Other Prehistoric Creatures. (Carole Marsh State Bks.). (J). (gr. k-12). 1994. lib. bdg. 24.95 (0-7933-7518-5); pap. 14.95 (0-7933-7519-3); disk 29.95 (0-7933-7520-7) Gallopade Pub Group.

— Jurassic Ark! New Mexico Dinosaurs & Other Prehistoric Creatures. (Carole Marsh State Bks.). (J). (gr. k-12). 1994. lib. bdg. 24.95 (0-7933-7521-5); pap. 14.95 (0-7933-7522-3); disk 29.95 (0-7933-7523-1) Gallopade Pub Group.

— Jurassic Ark! New York Dinosaurs & Other Prehistoric Creatures. (Carole Marsh State Bks.). (J). (gr. k-12). 1994. lib. bdg. 24.95 (0-7933-7524-X); pap. 14.95 (0-7933-7525-8); disk 29.95 (0-7933-7526-6) Gallopade Pub Group.

— Jurassic Ark! North Carolina Dinosaurs & Other Prehistoric Creatures. (Carole Marsh State Bks.). (J). (gr. k-12). 1994. lib. bdg. 24.95 (0-7933-7527-4); pap. 14.95 (0-7933-7528-2); disk 29.95 (0-7933-7529-0) Gallopade Pub Group.

— Jurassic Ark! North Dakota Dinosaurs & Other Prehistoric Creatures. (Carole Marsh State Bks.). (J). (gr. k-12). 1994. lib. bdg. 24.95 (0-7933-7530-4); pap. 14.95 (0-7933-7531-2); disk 29.95 (0-7933-7532-0) Gallopade Pub Group.

— Jurassic Ark! Ohio Dinosaurs & Other Prehistoric Creatures. (Carole Marsh State Bks.). (J). (gr. k-12). 1994. lib. bdg. 24.95 (0-7933-7533-9); pap. 14.95 (0-7933-7534-7); disk 29.95 (0-7933-7535-5) Gallopade Pub Group.

— Jurassic Ark! Oklahoma Dinosaurs & Other Prehistoric Creatures. (Carole Marsh State Bks.). (J). (gr. k-12). 1994. lib. bdg. 24.95 (0-7933-7536-3); pap. 14.95 (0-7933-7537-1); disk 29.95 (0-7933-7538-X) Gallopade Pub Group.

— Jurassic Ark! Oregon Dinosaurs & Other Prehistoric Creatures. (Carole Marsh State Bks.). (J). (gr. k-12). 1994. lib. bdg. 24.95 (0-7933-7539-8); pap. 14.95 (0-7933-7540-1); disk 29.95 (0-7933-7541-X) Gallopade Pub Group.

— Jurassic Ark! Pennsylvania Dinosaurs & Other Prehistoric Creatures. (Carole Marsh State Bks.). (J). (gr. k-12). 1994. lib. bdg. 24.95 (0-7933-7542-8); pap. 14.95 (0-7933-7543-6); disk 29.95 (0-7933-7544-4) Gallopade Pub Group.

— Jurassic Ark! Rhode Island Dinosaurs & Other Prehistoric Creatures. (Carole Marsh State Bks.). (J). (gr. k-12). 1994. lib. bdg. 24.95 (0-7933-7545-2); pap. 14.95 (0-7933-7546-0); disk 29.95 (0-7933-7547-9) Gallopade Pub Group.

— Jurassic Ark! South Carolina Dinosaurs & Other Prehistoric Creatures. (Carole Marsh State Bks.). (J). (gr. k-12). 1994. lib. bdg. 24.95 (0-7933-7548-7); pap. 14.95 (0-7933-7549-5); disk 29.95 (0-7933-7550-9) Gallopade Pub Group.

— Jurassic Ark! South Dakota Dinosaurs & Other Prehistoric Creatures. (Carole Marsh State Bks.). (J). (gr. k-12). 1994. lib. bdg. 24.95 (0-7933-7551-7); pap. 14.95 (0-7933-7552-5); disk 29.95 (0-7933-7553-3) Gallopade Pub Group.

— Jurassic Ark! Tennessee Dinosaurs & Other Prehistoric Creatures. (Carole Marsh State Bks.). (J). (gr. k-12). 1994. lib. bdg. 24.95 (0-7933-7554-1); pap. 14.95 (0-7933-7555-X); disk 29.95 (0-7933-7556-8) Gallopade Pub Group.

— Jurassic Ark! Texas Dinosaurs & Other Prehistoric Creatures. (Carole Marsh State Bks.). (J). (gr. k-12). 1994. lib. bdg. 24.95 (0-7933-7557-6); pap. 14.95 (0-7933-7558-4); disk 29.95 (0-7933-7559-2) Gallopade Pub Group.

— Jurassic Ark! Utah Dinosaurs & Other Prehistoric Creatures. (Carole Marsh State Bks.). (J). (gr. k-12). 1994. lib. bdg. 24.95 (0-7933-7560-6); pap. 14.95 (0-7933-7561-4); disk 29.95 (0-7933-7562-2) Gallopade Pub Group.

— Jurassic Ark! Vermont Dinosaurs & Other Prehistoric Creatures. (Carole Marsh State Bks.). (J). (gr. k-12). 1994. lib. bdg. 24.95 (0-7933-7563-0); pap. 14.95 (0-7933-7564-9); disk 29.95 (0-7933-7565-7) Gallopade Pub Group.

— Jurassic Ark! Virginia Dinosaurs & Other Prehistoric Creatures. (Carole Marsh State Bks.). (J). (gr. k-12). 1994. lib. bdg. 24.95 (0-7933-7566-5); pap. 14.95 (0-7933-7567-3); disk 29.95 (0-7933-7568-1) Gallopade Pub Group.

— Jurassic Ark! Washington, D. C. Dinosaurs & Other Prehistoric Creatures. (Carole Marsh State Bks.). (J). (gr. k-12). 1994. lib. bdg. 24.95 (0-7933-7452-9); pap. 14.95 (0-7933-7453-7); disk 29.95 (0-7933-7454-5) Gallopade Pub Group.

— Jurassic Ark! Washington Dinosaurs & Other Prehistoric Creatures. (Carole Marsh State Bks.). (J). (gr. k-12). 1994. lib. bdg. 24.95 (0-7933-7569-X); pap. 14.95 (0-7933-7570-3); disk 29.95 (0-7933-7571-1) Gallopade Pub Group.

— Jurassic Ark! West Virginia Dinosaurs & Other Prehistoric Creatures. (Carole Marsh State Bks.). (J). (gr. k-12). 1994. lib. bdg. 24.95 (0-7933-7572-X); pap. 14.95 (0-7933-7573-8); disk 29.95 (0-7933-7574-6) Gallopade Pub Group.

— Jurassic Ark! Wisconsin Dinosaurs & Other Prehistoric Creatures. (Carole Marsh State Bks.). (J). (gr. k-12). 1994. lib. bdg. 24.95 (0-7933-7575-4); pap. 14.95 (0-7933-7576-2); disk 29.95 (0-7933-7577-0) Gallopade Pub Group.

— Jurassic Ark! Wyoming Dinosaurs & Other Prehistoric Creatures. (Carole Marsh Wyoming Bks.). (J). (gr. k-12). 1994. lib. bdg. 24.95 (0-7933-7578-9); pap. 14.95 (0-7933-7579-7); disk 29.95 (0-7933-7580-0) Gallopade Pub Group.

— Kansas & Other State Greats (Biographies) (Carole Marsh Kansas Bks.). (J). (gr. 3-12). 1994. 24.95 (1-55609-362-4); pap. 14.95 (1-55609-363-2); disk 29.95 (1-55609-364-0) Gallopade Pub Group.

— Kansas Bandits, Bushwackers, Outlaws, Crooks, Devils, Ghosts, Desperadoes & Other Assorted & Sundry Characters! (Carole Marsh Kansas Bks.). (Illus.). (YA). (gr. 3-12). 1994. lib. bdg. 24.95 (0-7933-0454-7); pap. 14.95 (0-7933-0453-9); disk 29.95 (0-7933-0455-5) Gallopade Pub Group.

— The Kansas Bookstore Book: A Surprising Guide to Our State's Bookstores & Their Specialties for Students, Teachers, Writers & Publishers. (Carole Marsh Kansas Bks.). (Illus.). 1994. lib. bdg. 24.95 (0-7933-2903-5); pap. 14.95 (0-7933-2904-3); disk 29.95 (0-7933-2905-1) Gallopade Pub Group.

— Kansas Classic Christmas Trivia: Stories, Recipes, Activities, Legends, Lore & More! (Carole Marsh Kansas Bks.). (Illus.). (YA). (gr. 3-12). 1994. lib. bdg. 24.95 (0-7933-0457-1); pap. 14.95 (0-7933-0456-3); disk 29.95 (0-7933-0458-X) Gallopade Pub Group.

— Kansas Coastales. (Statemeant Ser.). (J). 1994. lib. bdg. 24.95 (1-55609-365-9); pap. 14.95 (1-55609-366-7); disk 29.95 (1-55609-367-5) Gallopade Pub Group.

— Kansas Coastales! (Carole Marsh Kansas Bks.). (J). 1994. lib. bdg. 24.95 (0-7933-7281-X) Gallopade Pub Group.

— Kansas "Crinkum-Crankum" A Funny Word Book about Our State. (Carole Marsh Kansas Bks.). (Illus.). (J). 1994. lib. bdg. 24.95 (0-7933-4856-0); pap. 14.95 (0-7933-4857-9); disk 29.95 (0-7933-4858-7) Gallopade Pub Group.

— Kansas Dingbats! Bk. 1: A Fun Book of Games, Stories, Activities & More about Our State That's All in Code! for You to Decipher. (Carole Marsh Kansas Bks.). (Illus.). (J). (gr. 3-12). 1994. lib. bdg. 24.95 (0-7933-3821-2); pap. 14.95 (0-7933-3822-0); disk 29.95 (0-7933-3823-9) Gallopade Pub Group.

— Kansas Festival Fun for Kids! (Carole Marsh Kansas Bks.). (Illus.). (YA). (gr. 3-12). 1994. lib. bdg. 24.95 (0-7933-3974-X); pap. 14.95 (0-7933-3975-8); disk 29.95 (0-7933-3976-6) Gallopade Pub Group.

— The Kansas Hot Air Balloon Mystery. (Carole Marsh Kansas Bks.). (Illus.). (J). (gr. 2-9). 1994. 24.95 (0-7933-2462-9); pap. 14.95 (0-7933-2463-7); disk 29.95 (0-7933-2464-5) Gallopade Pub Group.

— Kansas Jeopardy! Answers & Questions about Our State! (Carole Marsh Kansas Bks.). (Illus.). (J). (gr. 3-12). 1994. lib. bdg. 24.95 (0-7933-4127-2); pap. 14.95 (0-7933-4128-0); disk 29.95 (0-7933-4129-9) Gallopade Pub Group.

— Kansas "Jography" A Fun Run Thru Your State. (Statemeant Ser.). (J). (gr. 3-12). 1994. lib. bdg. 24.95 (1-55609-353-5); pap. 14.95 (1-55609-354-3); disk 29.95 (1-55609-355-1) Gallopade Pub Group.

— Kansas Kid's Cookbook: Recipes, How-to, History, Lore & More! (Carole Marsh Kansas Bks.). (Illus.). (YA). (gr. 3-12). 1994. lib. bdg. 24.95 (0-7933-0466-0); pap. 14.95 (0-7933-0465-2); disk 29.95 (0-7933-0467-9) Gallopade Pub Group.

— The Kansas Library Book: A Surprising Guide to the Unusual Special Collections in Libraries Across Our State for Students, Teachers, Writers & Publishers - Includes Reproducible Mailing Labels Plus Activities for Young People! (Carole Marsh Kansas Bks.). (Illus.). 1994. lib. bdg. 24.95 (0-7933-3053-X); pap. 14.95 (0-7933-3054-8); disk 29.95 (0-7933-3055-6) Gallopade Pub Group.

— The Kansas Media Book: A Surprising Guide to the Amazing Print, Broadcast & Online Media of Our State for Students, Teachers, Writers & Publishers - Includes Reproducible Mailing Labels Plus Activities for Young People! (Carole Marsh Kansas Bks.). (Illus.). 1994. lib. bdg. 24.95 (0-7933-3209-5); pap. 14.95 (0-7933-3210-9); disk 29.95 (0-7933-3211-7) Gallopade Pub Group.

— The Kansas Mystery Van Takes Off! Book 1: Handicapped Kansas Kids Sneak Off on a Big Adventure. (Carole Marsh Kansas Bks.). (Illus.). (J). (gr. 3-12). 1994. 24.95 (0-7933-5009-3); pap. 14.95 (0-7933-5010-7); disk 29.95 (0-7933-5011-5) Gallopade Pub Group.

— Kansas Quiz Bowl Crash Course. (Statemeant Ser.). (J). (gr. 3-12). 1994. lib. bdg. 24.95 (1-55609-359-4); pap. 14.95 (1-55609-360-8); disk 29.95 (1-55609-361-6) Gallopade Pub Group.

— Kansas Rollercoasters! (Carole Marsh Kansas Bks.). (Illus.). (YA). (gr. 3-12). 1994. lib. bdg. 24.95 (0-7933-5272-X); pap. 14.95 (0-7933-5273-8); disk 29.95 (0-7933-5274-6) Gallopade Pub Group.

— Kansas School Trivia: An Amazing & Fascinating Look at Our State's Teachers, Schools & Students! (Carole Marsh Kansas Bks.). (Illus.). (YA). (gr. 3-12). 1994. lib. bdg. 24.95 (0-7933-0463-6); pap. 14.95 (0-7933-0462-8); disk 29.95 (0-7933-0464-4) Gallopade Pub Group.

— Kansas Silly Basketball Sportsmysteries, Vol. I. (Carole Marsh Kansas Bks.). (Illus.). (YA). (gr. 3-12). 1994. lib. bdg. 24.95 (0-7933-0460-1); pap. 14.95 (0-7933-0459-8); disk 29.95 (0-7933-0461-X) Gallopade Pub Group.

— Kansas Silly Basketball Sportsmysteries, Vol. II. (Carole Marsh Kansas Bks.). (Illus.). (YA). (gr. 3-12). 1994. lib. bdg. 24.95 (0-7933-1640-5); pap. 14.95 (0-7933-1641-3); disk 29.95 (0-7933-1642-1) Gallopade Pub Group.

— Kansas Silly Football Mystery, Vol. I. (Statemeant Ser.). (J). (gr. 3-12). 1994. lib. bdg. 24.95 (1-55609-368-3); pap. 14.95 (1-55609-369-1); disk 29.95 (1-55609-370-5) Gallopade Pub Group.

— Kansas Silly Football Mystery, Vol. II. (Statemeant Ser.). (J). (gr. 3-12). 1994. lib. bdg. 24.95 (1-55609-377-2); pap. 14.95 (0-318-41972-6); disk 29.95 (1-55609-379-9) Gallopade Pub Group.

— Kansas Silly Trivia. (Statemeant Ser.). (J). (gr. 3-12). 1994. lib. bdg. 24.95 (0-318-41973-4); pap. 14.95 (1-55609-351-9); disk 29.95 (1-55609-352-7) Gallopade Pub Group.

— Kansas Timeline: A Chronology of Kansas History, Mystery, Trivia, Legend, Lore & More. (Carole Marsh Kansas Bks.). (Illus.). (J). (gr. 3-12). 1994. lib. bdg. 24.95 (0-7933-5923-6); pap. 14.95 (0-7933-5924-4); disk 29.95 (0-7933-5925-2) Gallopade Pub Group.

— Kansas's (Most Devastating!) Disasters & (Most Calamitous!) Catastrophies! (Carole Marsh Kansas Bks.). (Illus.). (YA). (gr. 3-12). 1994. lib. bdg. 24.95 (0-7933-0451-2); pap. 14.95 (0-7933-0450-4); disk 29.95 (0-7933-0452-0) Gallopade Pub Group.

— Kansas's Unsolved Mysteries (& Their "Solutions") Includes Scientific Information & Other Activities for Students. (Carole Marsh Kansas Bks.). (Illus.). (J). (gr. 3-12). 1994. lib. bdg. 24.95 (0-7933-5770-5); pap. 14.95 (0-7933-5771-3); disk 29.95 (0-7933-5772-1) Gallopade Pub Group.

— Kentucky & Other State Greats (Biographies) (Carole Marsh Kentucky Bks.). (Illus.). (J). (gr. 3-8). 1994. lib. bdg. 24.95 (1-55609-448-5); pap. 14.95 (1-55609-447-7); disk 29.95 (0-7933-1658-8) Gallopade Pub Group.

— Kentucky Bandits, Bushwackers, Outlaws, Crooks, Devils, Ghosts, Desperadoes & Other Assorted & Sundry Characters! (Carole Marsh Kentucky Bks.). (Illus.). (J). (gr. 3-8). 1994. lib. bdg. 24.95 (0-7933-0478-4); pap. 14.95 (0-7933-0477-6); disk 29.95 (0-7933-0479-2) Gallopade Pub Group.

— The Kentucky Bookstore Book: A Surprising Guide to Our State's Bookstores & Their Specialties for Students, Teachers, Writers & Publishers. (Carole Marsh Kentucky Bks.). (Illus.). 1994. lib. bdg. 24.95 (0-7933-2906-X); pap. 14.95 (0-7933-2907-8); disk 29.95 (0-7933-2908-6) Gallopade Pub Group.

— Kentucky Classic Christmas Trivia: Stories, Recipes, Activities, Legends, Lore & More! (Carole Marsh Kentucky Bks.). (Illus.). (J). (gr. 3-8). 1994. lib. bdg. 24.95 (0-7933-0481-4); pap. 14.95 (0-7933-0480-6); disk 29.95 (0-7933-0482-2) Gallopade Pub Group.

— Kentucky Coastales. (Carole Marsh Kentucky Bks.). (Illus.). (J). (gr. 3-8). 1994. lib. bdg. 24.95 (1-55609-444-2); pap. 14.95 (1-55609-443-4); disk 29.95 (0-7933-1654-5) Gallopade Pub Group.

— Kentucky Coastales! (Carole Marsh Kentucky Bks.). (J). 1994. lib. bdg. 24.95 (0-7933-7282-8) Gallopade Pub Group.

— Kentucky "Crinkum-Crankum" A Funny Word Book about Our State. (Carole Marsh Kentucky Bks.). (Illus.). (J). 1994. lib. bdg. 24.95 (0-7933-4859-5); pap. 14.95 (0-7933-4860-9); disk 29.95 (0-7933-4861-7) Gallopade Pub Group.

— Kentucky Dingbats! Bk. 1: A Fun Book of Games, Stories, Activities & More about Our State That's All in Code! for You to Decipher. (Carole Marsh Kentucky Bks.). (Illus.). (J). (gr. 3-12). 1994. lib. bdg. 24.95 (0-7933-3824-7); pap. 14.95 (0-7933-3825-5); disk 29.95 (0-7933-3826-3) Gallopade Pub Group.

— Kentucky Festival Fun for Kids! (Carole Marsh Kentucky Bks.). (Illus.). (YA). (gr. 3-12). 1994. lib. bdg. 24.95 (0-7933-3977-4); pap. 14.95 (0-7933-3978-2); disk 29.95 (0-7933-3979-0) Gallopade Pub Group.

— The Kentucky Hot Air Balloon Mystery. (Carole Marsh Kentucky Bks.). (Illus.). (J). (gr. 2-9). 1994. 24.95 (0-7933-2471-8); pap. 14.95 (0-7933-2472-6); disk 29.95 (0-7933-2473-4) Gallopade Pub Group.

— Kentucky Jeopardy! Answers & Questions about Our State! (Carole Marsh Kentucky Bks.). (Illus.). (J). (gr. 3-12). 1994. lib. bdg. 24.95 (0-7933-4130-2); pap. 14.95 (0-7933-4131-0); disk 29.95 (0-7933-4132-9) Gallopade Pub Group.

— Kentucky "Jography" A Fun Run Thru Our State! (Carole Marsh Kentucky Bks.). (Illus.). (J). (gr. 3-8). 1994. lib. bdg. 24.95 (1-55609-439-6); pap. 14.95 (1-55609-109-5); disk 29.95 (0-7933-1644-8) Gallopade Pub Group.

— Kentucky Kid's Cookbook: Recipes, How-To, History, Lore & More! (Carole Marsh Kentucky Bks.). (Illus.). (J). (gr. 3-8). 1994. lib. bdg. 24.95 (0-7933-0490-3); pap. 14.95 (0-7933-0489-X); disk 29.95 (0-7933-0491-1) Gallopade Pub Group.

— The Kentucky Library Book: A Surprising Guide to the Unusual Special Collections in Libraries Across Our State for Students, Teachers, Writers & Publishers - Includes Reproducible Mailing Labels Plus Activities for Young People! (Carole Marsh Kentucky Bks.). (Illus.). 1994. lib. bdg. 24.95 (0-7933-3056-4); pap. 14.95 (0-7933-3057-2); disk 29.95 (0-7933-3058-0) Gallopade Pub Group.

— The Kentucky Media Book: A Surprising Guide to the Amazing Print, Broadcast & Online Media of Our State for Students, Teachers, Writers & Publishers - Includes Reproducible Mailing Labels Plus Activities for Young People! (Carole Marsh Kentucky Bks.). (Illus.). 1994. lib. bdg. 24.95 (0-7933-3212-5); pap. 14.95 (0-7933-3213-3); disk 29.95 (0-7933-3214-1) Gallopade Pub Group.

— The Kentucky Mystery Van Takes Off! Book 1: Handicapped Kentucky Kids Sneak Off on a Big Adventure. (Carole Marsh Kentucky Bks.). (Illus.). (J). (gr. 3-12). 1994. 24.95 (0-7933-5012-3); pap. 14.95 (0-7933-5013-1); disk 29.95 (0-7933-5014-X) Gallopade Pub Group.

— Kentucky Quiz Bowl Crash Course! (Carole Marsh Kentucky Bks.). (Illus.). (J). (gr. 3-8). 1994. lib. bdg. 24.95 (1-55609-446-9); pap. 14.95 (1-55609-445-0); disk 29.95 (0-7933-1653-7) Gallopade Pub Group.

— Kentucky Rollercoasters! (Carole Marsh Kentucky Bks.). (Illus.). (YA). (gr. 3-12). 1994. lib. bdg. 24.95 (0-7933-5275-4); pap. 14.95 (0-7933-5276-2); disk 29.95 (0-7933-5277-0) Gallopade Pub Group.

— Kentucky School Trivia: An Amazing & Fascinating Look at Our State's Teachers, Schools & Students! (Carole Marsh Kentucky Bks.). (Illus.). (J). (gr. 3-8). 1994. lib. bdg. 24.95 (0-7933-0487-3); pap. 14.95 (0-7933-0486-5); disk 29.95 (0-7933-0488-1) Gallopade Pub Group.

— Kentucky Silly Basketball Sportsmysteries, Vol. I. (Carole Marsh Kentucky Bks.). (Illus.). (J). (gr. 3-8). 1994. lib. bdg. 24.95 (0-7933-0484-9); pap. 14.95 (0-7933-0483-0); disk 29.95 (0-7933-0485-7) Gallopade Pub Group.

— Kentucky Silly Basketball Sportsmysteries, Vol. II. (Carole Marsh Kentucky Bks.). (Illus.). (J). (gr. 3-8). 1994. lib. bdg. 24.95 (0-7933-1659-6); pap. 14.95 (0-7933-1660-X); disk 29.95 (0-7933-1661-8) Gallopade Pub Group.

— Kentucky Silly Football Sportsmysteries, Vol. I. (Carole Marsh Kentucky Bks.). (Illus.). (J). (gr. 3-8). 1994. lib. bdg. 24.95 (1-55609-442-6); pap. 14.95 (1-55609-441-8); disk 29.95 (0-7933-1646-4) Gallopade Pub Group.

— Kentucky Silly Football Sportsmysteries, Vol. II. (Carole Marsh Kentucky Bks.). (Illus.). (J). (gr. 3-8). 1994. lib. bdg. 24.95 (0-7933-1647-2); pap. 14.95 (0-7933-1648-0); disk 29.95 (0-7933-1649-9) Gallopade Pub Group.

— Kentucky Silly Trivia! (Carole Marsh Kentucky Bks.). (J). (gr. 3-8). 1994. lib. bdg. 24.95 (1-55609-438-8); pap. 14.95 (1-55609-040-4); disk 29.95 (0-7933-1643-X) Gallopade Pub Group.

— Kentucky Timeline: A Chronology of Kentucky History, Mystery, Trivia, Legend, Lore & More. (Carole Marsh Kentucky Bks.). (Illus.). (J). (gr. 3-12). 1994. lib. bdg. 24.95 (0-7933-5926-0); pap. 14.95 (0-7933-5927-9); disk 29.95 (0-7933-5928-7) Gallopade Pub Group.

— Kentucky's (Most Devastating!) Disasters & (Most Calamitous!) Catastrophies! LC 00-7933. (Carole Marsh Kentucky Bks.). (Illus.). (J). (gr. 3-8). 1994. lib. bdg. 24.95 (0-7933-0475-X); pap. 14.95 (0-7933-0474-1); disk 29.95 (0-685-45937-3) Gallopade Pub Group.

— Kentucky's Unsolved Mysteries (& Their "Solutions") Includes Scientific Information & Other Activities for Students. (Carole Marsh Kentucky Bks.). (Illus.). (J). (gr. 3-12). 1994. lib. bdg. 24.95 (0-7933-5773-X); pap. 14.95 (0-7933-5774-8); disk 29.95 (0-7933-5775-6) Gallopade Pub Group.

— Kids & Space: Look Forward, Plan, Prepare, Go! (Quantum Leap Ser.). (Illus.). (J). (gr. 3-8). 1994. lib. bdg. 24.95 (0-7933-0003-7); pap. 14.95 (0-7933-0004-5); disk 29.95 (0-7933-0005-3) Gallopade Pub Group.

— A Kid's Book of Smarts: How to Think, Make Decisions, Figure Things Out, Budget Your Time, Money, Plan Your Day, Week, Life & Other Things Adults Wish They'd Learned When They Were Kids! (Quantum Leap Ser.). (Illus.). 68p. (J). (gr. 4-12). 1994. lib. bdg. 24.95 (1-55609-173-7); pap. 14.95 (0-935326-18-9) Gallopade Pub Group.

— The Kinky Sex Cookbook. (Naked Gourmet Ser.). (Orig.). 1994. 24.95 (1-55609-174-5); pap. 14.95 (1-55609-005-6) Gallopade Pub Group.

— The Kitchen House: How Yesterdays Black Women Created Todays American Foods. (Our Black Heritage Ser.). (J). (gr. 3-12). 1994. lib. bdg. 24.95 (1-55609-309-8); pap. 14.95 (1-55609-308-X); disk 29.95 (1-55609-310-1) Gallopade Pub Group.

— The Kudzu Cookbook: You Don't Eat It - It Eats You! (Naked Gourmet Ser.). (Orig.). 1994. 24.95 (1-55609-175-3); pap. 14.95 (1-55609-004-8) Gallopade Pub Group.

— Latin for Kids: Of All the Gaul. (Of All the Gaul Ser.). (Illus.). (J). (gr. 2-10). 1994. 24.95 (0-935326-17-0) Gallopade Pub Group.

— The Legend of the Devil's Hoofprints. (Carole Marsh Bks.). (Illus.). (Orig.). (J). (gr. 2 up). 1994. lib. bdg. 24.95 (1-55609-177-X); pap. 14.95 (0-935326-57-X) Gallopade Pub Group.

— Let's Find Out about Florida! In the Yellow Pages, Dictionary, Encyclopedia, Almanac, Atlas, Who's Who, Bartlett's Quotations & Other Reference Sources! 36p. (J). (gr. 3-5). 1994. lib. bdg. 24.95 (0-7933-7349-2); pap. 14.95 (0-7933-7350-6); disk 29.95 (0-7933-7351-4) Gallopade Pub Group.

— Let's Quilt Alabama & Stuff It Topographically! (Carole Marsh Alabama Bks.). (Illus.). (YA). (gr. 3-12). 1994. lib. bdg. 24.95 (1-55609-462-0); pap. 14.95 (1-55609-073-0); disk 29.95 (0-7933-1328-7) Gallopade Pub Group.

— Let's Quilt Alaska & Stuff It Topographically! (Carole Marsh Alaska Bks.). (Illus.). (YA). (gr. 3-12). 1994. lib. bdg. 24.95 (1-55609-475-2); pap. 14.95 (1-55609-094-3); disk 29.95 (0-7933-1344-9) Gallopade Pub Group.

— Let's Quilt Arizona & Stuff It Topographically! (Carole Marsh Arizona Bks.). (Illus.). (YA). (gr. 3-12). 1994. lib. bdg. 24.95 (1-55609-499-X); pap. 14.95 (1-55609-128-1); disk 29.95 (0-7933-1360-0) Gallopade Pub Group.

— Let's Quilt Arkansas & Stuff It Topographically! (Carole Marsh Arkansas Bks.). (Illus.). (YA). (gr. 3-12). 1994. lib. bdg. 24.95 (1-55609-486-8); pap. 14.95 (1-55609-078-1); disk 29.95 (0-7933-1376-7) Gallopade Pub Group.

— Let's Quilt California & Stuff It Topographically! (Carole Marsh California Bks.). (Illus.). (YA). (gr. 3-12). 1994. lib. bdg. 24.95 (1-55609-513-9); pap. 14.95 (1-55609-512-0); disk 29.95 (0-7933-1392-9) Gallopade Pub Group.

— Let's Quilt Colorado & Stuff It Topographically! (Carole Marsh Colorado Bks.). (Illus.). (YA). (gr. 3-12). 1994. lib. bdg. 24.95 (1-55609-526-0); pap. 14.95 (1-55609-126-5); disk 29.95 (0-7933-1408-9) Gallopade Pub Group.

— Let's Quilt Connecticut & Stuff It Topographically! (Carole Marsh Connecticut Bks.). (Illus.). (YA). (gr. 3-12). 1994. lib. bdg. 24.95 (1-55609-539-2); pap. 14.95 (0-685-45928-4); disk 29.95 (0-7933-1424-0) Gallopade Pub Group.

— Let's Quilt Delaware & Stuff It Topographically! (Carole Marsh Delaware Bks.). (Illus.). (YA). (gr. 3-12). 1994. lib. bdg. 24.95 (1-55609-552-X); pap. 14.95 (1-55609-063-3); disk 29.95 (0-7933-1440-2) Gallopade Pub Group.

— Let's Quilt Florida & Stuff It Topographically! (Carole Marsh Florida Bks.). (Illus.). (YA). (gr. 3-12). 1994. lib. bdg. 24.95 (1-55609-419-1); pap. 14.95 (1-55609-055-2); disk 29.95 (0-7933-1488-7) Gallopade Pub Group.

— Let's Quilt Georgia & Stuff It Topographically! (Carole Marsh Georgia Bks.). (Illus.). (YA). (gr. 3-12). 1994. lib. bdg. 24.95 (1-55609-382-9); pap. 14.95 (1-55609-054-4); disk 29.95 (0-7933-1507-7) Gallopade Pub Group.

— Let's Quilt Hawaii & Stuff It Topographically! (Carole Marsh Hawaii Bks.). (Illus.). (YA). (gr. 3-12). 1994. lib. bdg. 24.95 (1-55609-569-4); pap. 14.95 (1-55609-093-5); disk 29.95 (0-7933-1526-3) Gallopade Pub Group.

— Let's Quilt Idaho & Stuff It Topographically! (Carole Marsh Idaho Bks.). (Illus.). (YA). (gr. 3-12). 1994. lib. bdg. 24.95 (1-55609-584-8); pap. 14.95 (1-55609-139-7); disk 29.95 (0-7933-1545-X) Gallopade Pub Group.

— Let's Quilt Illinois & Stuff It Topographically! (Carole Marsh Illinois Bks.). (Illus.). (YA). (gr. 3-12). 1994. lib. bdg. 24.95 (1-55609-408-6); pap. 14.95 (1-55609-097-8); disk 29.95 (0-7933-1585-9) Gallopade Pub Group.

— Let's Quilt Indiana & Stuff It Topographically! (Carole Marsh Indiana Bks.). (Illus.). (YA). (gr. 3-12). 1994. lib. bdg. 24.95 (1-55609-429-9); pap. 14.95 (1-55609-096-X); disk 29.95 (0-7933-1604-9) Gallopade Pub Group.

— Let's Quilt Iowa & Stuff It Topographically! (Carole Marsh Iowa Bks.). (Illus.). (YA). (gr. 3-12). 1994. lib. bdg. 24.95 (1-55609-451-5); pap. 14.95 (1-55609-072-2); disk 29.95 (0-7933-1623-5) Gallopade Pub Group.

— Lets Quilt Kansas & Stuff It Topographically! (Carol Marsh Kansas Bks.). (J). (gr. 3-12). 1994. lib. bdg. 24.95 (1-55609-356-X); pap. 14.95 (1-55609-357-8); disk 29.95 (1-55609-358-6) Gallopade Pub Group.

— Let's Quilt Louisiana & Stuff It Topographically! (Carole Marsh Louisiana Bks.). (Illus.). (J). (gr. 3-8). 1994. lib. bdg. 24.95 (1-55609-397-7); pap. 14.95 (1-55609-075-7); disk 29.95 (0-7933-1664-2) Gallopade Pub Group.

— Let's Quilt Maine & Stuff It Topographically! (Carole Marsh Maine Bks.). (Illus.). (J). (gr. 3-8). 1994. lib. bdg. 24.95 (1-55609-599-6); pap. 14.95 (1-55609-068-4); disk 29.95 (1-55609-601-1) Gallopade Pub Group.

An Asterisk (*) at the beginning of an entry indicates that the title is appearing in BIP for the first time.

— Let's Quilt Maryland & Stuff It Topographically! (Carole Marsh Maryland Bks.). (Illus.). (J). (gr. 3-8). 1994. lib. bdg. 24.95 (1-55609-622-4); pap. 14.95 (1-55609-058-7); disk 29.95 (1-55609-623-2) Gallopade Pub Group.

— Let's Quilt Massachusetts & Stuff It Topographically! (Carole Marsh Massachusetts Bks.). (Illus.). (J). (gr. 3-8). 1994. lib. bdg. 24.95 (1-55609-684-4); pap. 14.95 (1-55609-685-2); disk 29.95 (1-55609-686-0) Gallopade Pub Group.

— Let's Quilt Michigan & Stuff It Topographically! (Carole Marsh Michigan Bks.). (Illus.). (J). (gr. 3 up). 1994. lib. bdg. 24.95 (1-55609-669-0); pap. 14.95 (1-55609-138-9); disk 29.95 (1-55609-670-4) Gallopade Pub Group.

— Let's Quilt Minnesota & Stuff It Topographically! (Carole Marsh Minnesota Bks.). (Illus.). (J). (gr. 3 up). 1994. lib. bdg. 24.95 (1-55609-645-3); pap. 14.95 (1-55609-099-4); disk 29.95 (1-55609-647-X) Gallopade Pub Group.

— Let's Quilt Mississippi & Stuff It Topographically! (Carole Marsh Mississippi Bks.). (Illus.). (J). (gr. 3 up). 1994. lib. bdg. 24.95 (1-55609-710-7); pap. 14.95 (1-55609-074-9); disk 29.95 (1-55609-716-6) Gallopade Pub Group.

— Let's Quilt Missouri & Stuff It Topographically! (Carole Marsh Missouri Bks.). (Illus.). (J). (gr. 3 up). 1994. lib. bdg. 24.95 (1-55609-733-6); pap. 14.95 (1-55609-734-4); disk 29.95 (1-55609-735-2) Gallopade Pub Group.

— Let's Quilt Montana & Stuff It Topographically! (Carole Marsh Montana Bks.). (Illus.). (J). (gr. 3 up). 1994. lib. bdg. 24.95 (1-55609-757-3); pap. 14.95 (1-55609-131-1); disk 29.95 (1-55609-759-X) Gallopade Pub Group.

— Let's Quilt Nebraska & Stuff It Topographically! (Carole Marsh Nebraska Bks.). (Illus.). (J). (gr. 3 up). 1994. lib. bdg. 24.95 (1-55609-781-6); pap. 14.95 (1-55609-779-4); disk 29.95 (1-55609-783-2) Gallopade Pub Group.

— Let's Quilt Nevada & Stuff It Topographically! (Carole Marsh Nevada Bks.). (Illus.). (J). 1994. lib. bdg. 24.95 (1-55609-805-7); pap. 14.95 (1-55609-130-3); disk 29.95 (1-55609-807-3) Gallopade Pub Group.

— Let's Quilt New Hampshire & Stuff It Topographically! (Carole Marsh New Hampshire Bks.). (Illus.). (J). 1994. lib. bdg. 24.95 (1-55609-829-4); pap. 14.95 (1-55609-067-6); disk 29.95 (1-55609-831-6) Gallopade Pub Group.

— Let's Quilt New Jersey & Stuff It Topographically! (Carole Marsh New Jersey Bks.). (Illus.). (J). 1994. lib. bdg. 24.95 (1-55609-853-7); pap. 14.95 (1-55609-069-2); disk 29.95 (1-55609-855-3) Gallopade Pub Group.

— Let's Quilt New Mexico & Stuff It Topographically! (Carole Marsh New Mexico Bks.). (Illus.). (J). 1994. lib. bdg. 24.95 (1-55609-877-4); pap. 14.95 (1-55609-127-3); disk 29.95 (1-55609-879-0) Gallopade Pub Group.

— Let's Quilt New York & Stuff It Topographically! (Carole Marsh New York Bks.). (Illus.). (J). 1994. lib. bdg. 24.95 (1-55609-904-5); pap. 14.95 (1-55609-060-9); disk 29.95 (1-55609-905-3) Gallopade Pub Group.

— Let's Quilt North Carolina & Stuff It Topographically! (Carole Marsh North Carolina Bks.). (Illus.). (J). 1994. lib. bdg. 24.95 (1-55609-925-8); pap. 14.95 (1-55609-050-1); disk 29.95 (1-55609-926-6) Gallopade Pub Group.

— Let's Quilt North Dakota & Stuff It Topographically! (Carole Marsh North Dakota Bks.). (Illus.). (J). 1994. lib. bdg. 24.95 (1-55609-946-0); pap. 14.95 (1-55609-135-4); disk 29.95 (1-55609-947-9) Gallopade Pub Group.

— Let's Quilt Ohio & Stuff It Topographically! (Carole Marsh Ohio Bks.). (Illus.). (J). 1994. lib. bdg. 24.95 (0-685-45975-6); pap. 14.95 (1-55609-095-1); disk 29.95 (1-55609-985-1) Gallopade Pub Group.

— Let's Quilt Oklahoma & Stuff It Topographically! (Carole Marsh Oklahoma Bks.). (Illus.). (J). 1994. lib. bdg. 24.95 (0-7933-1860-2); pap. 14.95 (0-7933-1861-0); disk 29.95 (0-7933-1862-9) Gallopade Pub Group.

— Let's Quilt Oregon & Stuff It Topographically! (Carole Marsh Oregon Bks.). (Illus.). (J). 1994. lib. bdg. 24.95 (0-7933-1893-9); pap. 14.95 (1-55609-132-X); disk 29.95 (0-7933-1894-7) Gallopade Pub Group.

— Let's Quilt Our Alabama County. (Carole Marsh Alabama Bks.). (J). 1994. lib. bdg. 24.95 (0-7933-6936-3); pap. text ed. 14.95 (0-7933-6935-5); disk 29.95 (0-7933-6937-1) Gallopade Pub Group.

— Let's Quilt Our Alabama Town. (Carole Marsh Alabama Bks.). (J). 1994. lib. bdg. 24.95 (0-7933-6933-9); pap. text ed. 14.95 (0-7933-6932-0); disk 29.95 (0-7933-6934-7) Gallopade Pub Group.

— Let's Quilt Our Alaska County. (Carole Marsh Alaska Bks.). (J). 1994. lib. bdg. 24.95 (0-7933-7116-3); pap. text ed. 14.95 (0-7933-7117-1); disk 29.95 (0-7933-7118-X) Gallopade Pub Group.

— Let's Quilt Our Alaska Town. (Carole Marsh Alaska Bks.). (J). 1994. lib. bdg. 24.95 (0-685-60854-9); pap. text ed. 14.95 (0-7933-6967-3); disk 29.95 (0-7933-6968-1) Gallopade Pub Group.

— Let's Quilt Our Arizona County. (Carole Marsh Arizona Bks.). (J). 1994. lib. bdg. 24.95 (0-7933-7119-8); pap. text ed. 14.95 (0-7933-7120-1); disk 29.95 (0-7933-7121-X) Gallopade Pub Group.

— Let's Quilt Our Arizona Town. (Carole Marsh Arizona Bks.). (J). 1994. lib. bdg. 24.95 (0-7933-6969-X); pap. text ed. 14.95 (0-7933-6970-3); disk 29.95 (0-7933-6971-1) Gallopade Pub Group.

— Let's Quilt Our Arkansas County. (Carole Marsh Arkansas Bks.). (J). 1994. lib. bdg. 24.95 (0-7933-7122-8); pap. text ed. 14.95 (0-7933-7123-6); disk 29.95 (0-7933-7124-4) Gallopade Pub Group.

— Let's Quilt Our Arkansas Town. (Carole Marsh Arkansas Bks.). (J). 1994. lib. bdg. 24.95 (0-7933-6972-X); pap. text ed. 14.95 (0-7933-6973-8); disk 29.95 (0-7933-6974-6) Gallopade Pub Group.

— Let's Quilt Our Black Heritage. (Our Black Heritage Ser.). 1994. 24.95 (1-55609-324-1); pap. 14.95 (1-55609-323-3); disk 29.95 (1-55609-325-X) Gallopade Pub Group.

— Let's Quilt Our California County. (Carole Marsh California Bks.). (J). 1994. lib. bdg. 24.95 (0-7933-7125-2); pap. text ed. 14.95 (0-7933-7126-0); disk 29.95 (0-7933-7127-9) Gallopade Pub Group.

— Let's Quilt Our California Town. (Carole Marsh California Bks.). (J). 1994. lib. bdg. 24.95 (0-7933-6975-4); pap. text ed. 14.95 (0-7933-6976-2); disk 29.95 (0-7933-6977-0) Gallopade Pub Group.

— Let's Quilt Our Colorado County. (Carole Marsh Colorado Bks.). (J). 1994. lib. bdg. 24.95 (0-7933-7128-7); pap. text ed. 14.95 (0-7933-7129-5); disk 29.95 (0-7933-7130-9) Gallopade Pub Group.

— Let's Quilt Our Colorado Town. (Carole Marsh Colorado Bks.). (J). 1994. lib. bdg. 24.95 (0-7933-6978-9); pap. text ed. 14.95 (0-7933-6979-7); disk 29.95 (0-7933-6980-0) Gallopade Pub Group.

— Let's Quilt Our Connecticut County. (Carole Marsh Connecticut Bks.). (J). 1994. lib. bdg. 24.95 (0-7933-7131-7); pap. text ed. 14.95 (0-7933-7132-5); disk 29.95 (0-7933-7133-3) Gallopade Pub Group.

— Let's Quilt Our Connecticut Town. (Carole Marsh Connecticut Bks.). (J). 1994. lib. bdg. 24.95 (0-7933-6981-9); pap. text ed. 14.95 (0-7933-6982-7); disk 29.95 (0-7933-6983-5) Gallopade Pub Group.

— Let's Quilt Our Delaware County. (Carole Marsh Delaware Bks.). (J). 1994. lib. bdg. 24.95 (0-7933-7134-1); pap. text ed. 14.95 (0-7933-7135-X); disk 29.95 (0-7933-7136-8) Gallopade Pub Group.

— Let's Quilt Our Delaware Town. (Carole Marsh Delaware Bks.). (J). 1994. lib. bdg. 24.95 (0-7933-6984-3); pap. text ed. 14.95 (0-7933-6985-1); disk 29.95 (0-7933-6986-X) Gallopade Pub Group.

— Let's Quilt Our Florida County. (Carole Marsh Florida Bks.). (J). 1994. lib. bdg. 24.95 (0-7933-7140-6); pap. text ed. 14.95 (0-7933-7141-4); disk 29.95 (0-7933-7142-2) Gallopade Pub Group.

— Let's Quilt Our Florida Town. (Carole Marsh Florida Bks.). (J). 1994. lib. bdg. 24.95 (0-7933-6990-8); pap. text ed. 14.95 (0-7933-6991-6); disk 29.95 (0-7933-6992-4) Gallopade Pub Group.

— Let's Quilt Our Georgia County. (Carole Marsh Georgia Bks.). (J). 1994. lib. bdg. 24.95 (0-7933-7143-0); pap. text ed. 14.95 (0-7933-7144-9); disk 29.95 (0-7933-7145-7) Gallopade Pub Group.

— Let's Quilt Our Georgia Town. (Carole Marsh Georgia Bks.). (J). 1994. lib. bdg. 24.95 (0-7933-6993-2); pap. text ed. 14.95 (0-7933-6994-0); disk 29.95 (0-7933-6995-9) Gallopade Pub Group.

— Let's Quilt Our Hawaii County. (Carole Marsh Hawaii Bks.). (J). 1994. lib. bdg. 24.95 (0-7933-7146-5); pap. text ed. 14.95 (0-7933-7147-3); disk 29.95 (0-7933-7148-1) Gallopade Pub Group.

— Let's Quilt Our Hawaii Town. (Carole Marsh Hawaii Bks.). (J). 1994. lib. bdg. 24.95 (0-7933-6996-7); pap. text ed. 14.95 (0-7933-6997-5); disk 29.95 (0-7933-6998-3) Gallopade Pub Group.

— Let's Quilt Our Idaho County. (Carole Marsh Idaho Bks.). (J). 1994. lib. bdg. 24.95 (0-7933-7149-X); pap. text ed. 14.95 (0-7933-7150-3); disk 29.95 (0-7933-7151-1) Gallopade Pub Group.

— Let's Quilt Our Idaho Town. (Carole Marsh Idaho Bks.). (J). 1994. lib. bdg. 24.95 (0-7933-6999-1); pap. text ed. 14.95 (0-7933-7000-0); disk 29.95 (0-7933-7001-9) Gallopade Pub Group.

— Let's Quilt Our Illinois County. (Carole Marsh Illinois Bks.). (J). 1994. lib. bdg. 24.95 (0-7933-7152-X); pap. text ed. 14.95 (0-7933-7153-8); disk 29.95 (0-7933-7154-6) Gallopade Pub Group.

— Let's Quilt Our Illinois Town. (Carole Marsh Illinois Bks.). (J). 1994. lib. bdg. 24.95 (0-7933-7002-7); pap. text ed. 14.95 (0-7933-7003-5); disk 29.95 (0-7933-7004-3) Gallopade Pub Group.

— Let's Quilt Our Indiana County. (Carole Marsh Indiana Bks.). (J). 1994. lib. bdg. 24.95 (0-7933-7155-4); pap. text ed. 14.95 (0-7933-7156-2); disk 29.95 (0-7933-7157-0) Gallopade Pub Group.

— Let's Quilt Our Indiana Town. (Carole Marsh Indiana Bks.). (J). 1994. lib. bdg. 24.95 (0-7933-7005-1); pap. text ed. 14.95 (0-7933-7006-X); disk 29.95 (0-7933-7007-8) Gallopade Pub Group.

— Let's Quilt Our Iowa County. (Carole Marsh Iowa Bks.). (J). 1994. lib. bdg. 24.95 (0-7933-7158-9); pap. text ed. 14.95 (0-7933-7159-7); disk 29.95 (0-7933-7160-0) Gallopade Pub Group.

— Let's Quilt Our Iowa Town. (Carole Marsh Iowa Bks.). (J). 1994. lib. bdg. 24.95 (0-7933-7008-6); pap. text ed. 14.95 (0-7933-7009-4); disk 29.95 (0-7933-7010-8) Gallopade Pub Group.

— Let's Quilt Our Kansas County. (Carole Marsh Kansas Bks.). (J). 1994. lib. bdg. 24.95 (0-7933-7161-9); pap. text ed. 14.95 (0-7933-7162-7); disk 29.95 (0-7933-7163-5) Gallopade Pub Group.

— Let's Quilt Our Kansas Town. (Carole Marsh Kansas Bks.). (J). 1994. lib. bdg. 24.95 (0-7933-7011-6); pap. text ed. 14.95 (0-7933-7012-4); disk 29.95 (0-7933-7013-2) Gallopade Pub Group.

— Let's Quilt Our Kentucky County. (Carole Marsh Kentucky Bks.). (J). 1994. lib. bdg. 24.95 (0-7933-7164-3); pap. text ed. 14.95 (0-7933-7165-1); disk 29.95 (0-7933-7166-X) Gallopade Pub Group.

— Let's Quilt Our Kentucky Town. (Carole Marsh Kentucky Bks.). (J). 1994. lib. bdg. 24.95 (0-7933-7014-0); pap. text ed. 14.95 (0-7933-7015-9); disk 29.95 (0-7933-7016-7) Gallopade Pub Group.

— Let's Quilt Our Louisiana Parish. (Carole Marsh Louisiana Bks.). (J). 1994. lib. bdg. 24.95 (0-7933-7167-8); pap. text ed. 14.95 (0-7933-7168-6); disk 29.95 (0-7933-7169-4) Gallopade Pub Group.

— Let's Quilt Our Louisiana Town. (Carole Marsh Louisiana Bks.). (J). 1994. lib. bdg. 24.95 (0-7933-7017-5); pap. text ed. 14.95 (0-7933-7018-3); disk 29.95 (0-7933-7019-1) Gallopade Pub Group.

— Let's Quilt Our Maine County. (Carole Marsh Maine Bks.). (J). 1994. lib. bdg. 24.95 (0-7933-7170-8); pap. text ed. 14.95 (0-7933-7171-6); disk 29.95 (0-7933-7172-4) Gallopade Pub Group.

— Let's Quilt Our Maine Town. (Carole Marsh Maine Bks.). (J). 1994. lib. bdg. 24.95 (0-7933-7020-5); pap. text ed. 14.95 (0-7933-7021-3); disk 29.95 (0-7933-7022-1) Gallopade Pub Group.

— Let's Quilt Our Maryland County. (Carole Marsh Maryland Bks.). (J). 1994. lib. bdg. 24.95 (0-7933-7173-2); pap. text ed. 14.95 (0-7933-7174-0); disk 29.95 (0-7933-7175-9) Gallopade Pub Group.

— Let's Quilt Our Maryland Town. (Carole Marsh Maryland Bks.). (J). 1994. lib. bdg. 24.95 (0-7933-7023-X); pap. text ed. 14.95 (0-7933-7024-8); disk 29.95 (0-7933-7025-6) Gallopade Pub Group.

— Let's Quilt Our Massachusetts County. (Massachuseets Bks.). (J). 1994. lib. bdg. 24.95 (0-7933-7176-7); pap. text ed. 14.95 (0-7933-7177-5); disk 29.95 (0-7933-7178-3) Gallopade Pub Group.

— Let's Quilt Our Massachusetts Town. (Massachuseets Bks.). (J). 1994. lib. bdg. 24.95 (0-7933-7026-4); pap. text ed. 14.95 (0-7933-7027-2); disk 29.95 (0-7933-7028-0) Gallopade Pub Group.

— Let's Quilt Our Michigan County. (Carole Marsh Michigan Bks.). (J). 1994. lib. bdg. 24.95 (0-7933-7179-1); pap. text ed. 14.95 (0-7933-7180-5); disk 29.95 (0-7933-7181-3) Gallopade Pub Group.

— Let's Quilt Our Michigan Town. (Carole Marsh Michigan Bks.). (J). 1994. lib. bdg. 24.95 (0-7933-7029-9); pap. text ed. 14.95 (0-7933-7030-2); disk 29.95 (0-7933-7031-0) Gallopade Pub Group.

— Let's Quilt Our Minnesota County. (Carole Marsh Minnesota Bks.). (J). 1994. lib. bdg. 24.95 (0-7933-7182-1); pap. text ed. 14.95 (0-7933-7183-X); disk 29.95 (0-7933-7184-8) Gallopade Pub Group.

— Let's Quilt Our Minnesota Town. (Carole Marsh Minnesota Bks.). (J). 1994. lib. bdg. 24.95 (0-7933-7032-9); pap. text ed. 14.95 (0-7933-7033-7); disk 29.95 (0-7933-7034-5) Gallopade Pub Group.

— Let's Quilt Our Mississippi County. (Carole Marsh Mississippi Bks.). (J). 1994. lib. bdg. 24.95 (0-7933-7185-6); pap. text ed. 14.95 (0-7933-7186-4); disk 29.95 (0-7933-7187-2) Gallopade Pub Group.

— Let's Quilt Our Mississippi Town. (Carole Marsh Mississippi Bks.). (J). 1994. lib. bdg. 24.95 (0-7933-7035-3); pap. text ed. 14.95 (0-7933-7036-1); disk 29.95 (0-7933-7037-X) Gallopade Pub Group.

— Let's Quilt Our Missouri County. (Carole Marsh Missouri Bks.). (J). 1994. lib. bdg. 24.95 (0-7933-7188-0); pap. text ed. 14.95 (0-7933-7189-9); disk 29.95 (0-7933-7190-2) Gallopade Pub Group.

— Let's Quilt Our Missouri Town. (Carole Marsh Missouri Bks.). (J). 1994. lib. bdg. 24.95 (0-7933-7038-8); pap. text ed. 14.95 (0-7933-7039-6); disk 29.95 (0-7933-7040-X) Gallopade Pub Group.

— Let's Quilt Our Montana County. (Carole Marsh Montana Bks.). (J). 1994. lib. bdg. 24.95 (0-7933-7191-0); pap. text ed. 14.95 (0-7933-7192-9); disk 29.95 (0-7933-7193-7) Gallopade Pub Group.

— Let's Quilt Our Montana Town. (Carole Marsh Montana Bks.). (J). 1994. lib. bdg. 24.95 (0-7933-7041-8); pap. text ed. 14.95 (0-7933-7042-6); disk 29.95 (0-7933-7043-4) Gallopade Pub Group.

— Let's Quilt Our Nebraska County. (Carole Marsh Nebraska Bks.). (J). 1994. lib. bdg. 24.95 (0-7933-7194-5); pap. text ed. 14.95 (0-7933-7195-3); disk 29.95 (0-7933-7196-1) Gallopade Pub Group.

— Let's Quilt Our Nebraska Town. (Carole Marsh Nebraska Bks.). (J). 1994. lib. bdg. 24.95 (0-7933-7044-2); pap. text ed. 14.95 (0-7933-7045-0); disk 29.95 (0-7933-7046-9) Gallopade Pub Group.

— Let's Quilt Our Nevada County. (Carole Marsh Nevada Bks.). (J). 1994. lib. bdg. 24.95 (0-7933-7197-X); pap. text ed. 14.95 (0-7933-7198-8); disk 29.95 (0-7933-7199-6) Gallopade Pub Group.

— Let's Quilt Our Nevada Town. (Carole Marsh Nevada Bks.). (J). 1994. lib. bdg. 24.95 (0-7933-7047-7); pap. text ed. 14.95 (0-7933-7048-5); disk 29.95 (0-7933-7049-3) Gallopade Pub Group.

— Let's Quilt Our New Hampshire County. (Carole Marsh New Hampshire Bks.). (J). 1994. lib. bdg. 24.95 (0-7933-7200-3); pap. text ed. 14.95 (0-7933-7201-1); disk 29.95 (0-685-60853-0) Gallopade Pub Group.

— Let's Quilt Our New Hampshire Town. (Carole Marsh New Hampshire Bks.). (J). 1994. lib. bdg. 24.95 (0-7933-7050-7); pap. text ed. 14.95 (0-7933-7051-5); disk 29.95 (0-7933-7052-3) Gallopade Pub Group.

— Let's Quilt Our New Jersey County. (Carole Marsh New Jersey Bks.). (J). 1994. lib. bdg. 24.95 (0-7933-7203-8); pap. text ed. 14.95 (0-7933-7204-6); disk 29.95 (0-7933-7205-4) Gallopade Pub Group.

— Let's Quilt Our New Jersey Town. (Carole Marsh New Jersey Bks.). (J). 1994. lib. bdg. 24.95 (0-7933-7053-1); pap. text ed. 14.95 (0-7933-7054-X); disk 29.95 (0-7933-7055-8) Gallopade Pub Group.

— Let's Quilt Our New Mexico County. (Carole Marsh New Mexico Bks.). (J). 1994. lib. bdg. 24.95 (0-7933-7206-2); pap. text ed. 14.95 (0-7933-7207-0); disk 29.95 (0-7933-7208-9) Gallopade Pub Group.

— Let's Quilt Our New Mexico Town. (Carole Marsh New Mexico Bks.). (J). 1994. lib. bdg. 24.95 (0-7933-7056-6); pap. text ed. 14.95 (0-7933-7057-4); disk 29.95 (0-7933-7058-2) Gallopade Pub Group.

— Let's Quilt Our New York County. (Carole Marsh New York Bks.). (J). 1994. lib. bdg. 24.95 (0-7933-7209-7); pap. text ed. 14.95 (0-7933-7210-0); disk 29.95 (0-7933-7211-9) Gallopade Pub Group.

— Let's Quilt Our New York Town. (Carole Marsh New York Bks.). (J). 1994. lib. bdg. 24.95 (0-7933-7059-0); pap. text ed. 14.95 (0-7933-7060-4); disk 29.95 (0-7933-7061-2) Gallopade Pub Group.

— Let's Quilt Our North Carolina County. (Carole Marsh North Carolina Bks.). (J). 1994. lib. bdg. 24.95 (0-7933-7212-7); pap. text ed. 14.95 (0-7933-7213-5); disk 29.95 (0-7933-7214-3) Gallopade Pub Group.

— Let's Quilt Our North Carolina Town. (Carole Marsh North Carolina Bks.). (J). 1994. lib. bdg. 24.95 (0-7933-7062-0); pap. text ed. 14.95 (0-7933-7063-9); disk 29.95 (0-7933-7064-7) Gallopade Pub Group.

— Let's Quilt Our North Dakota County. (Carole Marsh North Dakota Bks.). (J). 1994. lib. bdg. 24.95 (0-7933-7215-1); pap. text ed. 14.95 (0-7933-7216-X); disk 29.95 (0-7933-7217-8) Gallopade Pub Group.

— Let's Quilt Our North Dakota Town. (Carole Marsh North Dakota Bks.). (J). 1994. lib. bdg. 24.95 (0-7933-7065-5); pap. text ed. 14.95 (0-7933-7066-3); disk 29.95 (0-7933-7067-1) Gallopade Pub Group.

— Let's Quilt Our Ohio County. (Carole Marsh Ohio Bks.). (J). 1994. lib. bdg. 24.95 (0-7933-7218-6); pap. text ed. 14.95 (0-7933-7219-4); disk 29.95 (0-7933-7220-8) Gallopade Pub Group.

— Let's Quilt Our Ohio Town. (Carole Marsh Ohio Bks.). (J). 1994. lib. bdg. 24.95 (0-7933-7068-X); pap. text ed. 14.95 (0-7933-7069-8); disk 29.95 (0-7933-7070-1) Gallopade Pub Group.

— Let's Quilt Our Oklahoma County. (Oklahoma Bks.). (J). 1994. lib. bdg. 24.95 (0-7933-7221-6); pap. text ed. 14. 95 (0-7933-7222-4); disk 29.95 (0-7933-7223-2) Gallopade Pub Group.

— Let's Quilt Our Oklahoma Town. (Carole Marsh Oklahoma Bks.). (J). 1994. lib. bdg. 24.95 (0-7933-7071-X); pap. text ed. 14.95 (0-7933-7072-8); disk 29.95 (0-7933-7073-6) Gallopade Pub Group.

— Let's Quilt Our Oregon County. (Oregon Bks.). (J). 1994. lib. bdg. 24.95 (0-7933-7224-0); pap. text ed. 14.95 (0-7933-7225-9); disk 29.95 (0-7933-7226-7) Gallopade Pub Group.

— Let's Quilt Our Oregon Town. (Carole Marsh Oregon Bks.). (J). 1994. lib. bdg. 24.95 (0-7933-7074-4); pap. text ed. 14.95 (0-7933-7075-2); disk 29.95 (0-7933-7076-0) Gallopade Pub Group.

— Let's Quilt Our Pennsylvania County. (Pennsylvania Bks.). (J). 1994. lib. bdg. 24.95 (0-7933-7227-5); pap. text ed. 14.95 (0-7933-7228-3); disk 29.95 (0-7933-7229-1) Gallopade Pub Group.

— Let's Quilt Our Pennsylvania Town. (Carole Marsh Pennsylvania Bks.). (J). 1994. lib. bdg. 24.95 (0-7933-7077-9); pap. text ed. 14.95 (0-7933-7078-7); disk 29.95 (0-7933-7079-5) Gallopade Pub Group.

— Let's Quilt Our Rhode Island County. (Rhode Island Bks.). (J). 1994. lib. bdg. 24.95 (0-7933-7230-5); pap. text ed. 14.95 (0-7933-7231-3); disk 29.95 (0-7933-7232-1) Gallopade Pub Group.

— Let's Quilt Our Rhode Island Town. (Carole Marsh Rhode Island Bks.). (J). 1994. lib. bdg. 24.95 (0-7933-7080-9); pap. text ed. 14.95 (0-7933-7081-7); disk 29.95 (0-7933-7082-5) Gallopade Pub Group.

— Let's Quilt Our South Carolina County. (South Carolina Bks.). (J). 1994. lib. bdg. 24.95 (0-7933-7233-X); pap. text ed. 14.95 (0-7933-7234-8); disk 29.95 (0-7933-7235-6) Gallopade Pub Group.

— Let's Quilt Our South Carolina Town. (Carole Marsh South Carolina Bks.). (J). 1994. lib. bdg. 24.95 (0-7933-7083-3); pap. text ed. 14.95 (0-7933-7084-1); disk 29.95 (0-7933-7085-X) Gallopade Pub Group.

— Let's Quilt Our South Dakota County. (South Dakota Bks.). (J). 1994. lib. bdg. 24.95 (0-7933-7236-4); pap. text ed. 14.95 (0-7933-7237-2); disk 29.95 (0-7933-7238-0) Gallopade Pub Group.

— Let's Quilt Our South Dakota Town. (Carole Marsh South Carolina Bks.). (J). 1994. lib. bdg. 24.95 (0-7933-7086-8); pap. text ed. 14.95 (0-7933-7087-6); disk 29.95 (0-7933-7088-4) Gallopade Pub Group.

— Let's Quilt Our Tennessee County. (Tennessee Bks.). (J). 1994. lib. bdg. 24.95 (0-7933-7239-9); pap. text ed. 14. 95 (0-7933-7240-2); disk 29.95 (0-7933-7241-0) Gallopade Pub Group.

— Let's Quilt Our Tennessee Town. (Carole Marsh Tennessee Bks.). (J). 1994. lib. bdg. 24.95 (0-7933-7089-2); pap. text ed. 14.95 (0-7933-7090-6); disk 29.95 (0-7933-7091-4) Gallopade Pub Group.

— Let's Quilt Our Texas County. (Texas Bks.). (J). 1994. lib. bdg. 24.95 (0-7933-7242-9); pap. text ed. 14.95 (0-7933-7243-7); disk 29.95 (0-7933-7244-5) Gallopade Pub Group.

— Let's Quilt Our Texas Town. (Carole Marsh Texas Bks.). (J). 1994. lib. bdg. 24.95 (0-7933-7092-2); pap. text ed. 14.95 (0-7933-7093-0); disk 29.95 (0-7933-7094-9) Gallopade Pub Group.

— Let's Quilt Our Utah County. (Utah Bks.). (J). 1994. lib. bdg. 24.95 (0-7933-7245-3); pap. text ed. 14.95 (0-7933-7246-1); disk 29.95 (0-7933-7247-X) Gallopade Pub Group.

— Let's Quilt Our Utah Town. (Carole Marsh Utah Bks.). (J). 1994. lib. bdg. 24.95 (0-7933-7095-7); pap. text ed. 14.95 (0-7933-7096-5); disk 29.95 (0-7933-7097-3) Gallopade Pub Group.

— Let's Quilt Our Vermont County. (Vermont Bks.). (J). 1994. lib. bdg. 24.95 (*0-7933-7248-8*); pap. text ed. 14. 95 (*0-7933-7249-6*); disk 29.95 (*0-7933-7250-X*) Gallopade Pub Group.

— Let's Quilt Our Vermont Town. (Carole Marsh Vermont Bks.). (J). 1994. lib. bdg. 24.95 (*0-7933-7098-1*); pap. text ed. 14.95 (*0-7933-7099-X*); disk 29.95 (*0-7933-7100-7*) Gallopade Pub Group.

— Let's Quilt Our Virginia County. (Virginia Bks.). (J). 1992. lib. bdg. 24.95 (*0-7933-7251-8*); pap. text ed. 14. 95 (*0-7933-7252-6*); disk 29.95 (*0-7933-7253-4*) Gallopade Pub Group.

— Let's Quilt Our Virginia Town. (Carole Marsh Virginia Bks.). (J). 1994. lib. bdg. 24.95 (*0-7933-7101-5*); pap. text ed. 14.95 (*0-7933-7102-3*); disk 29.95 (*0-7933-7103-1*) Gallopade Pub Group.

— Let's Quilt Our Washington County. (Washington Bks.). (J). 1994. lib. bdg. 24.95 (*0-7933-7254-2*); pap. text ed. 14.95 (*0-7933-7255-0*); disk 29.95 (*0-7933-7256-9*) Gallopade Pub Group.

— Let's Quilt Our Washington Town. (Carol Marsh Washington Bks.). (J). 1994. lib. bdg. 24.95 (*0-7933-7104-X*); pap. text ed. 14.95 (*0-7933-7105-8*); disk 29.95 (*0-7933-7106-6*) Gallopade Pub Group.

— Let's Quilt Our West Virginia County. (West Virginia Bks.). (J). 1994. lib. bdg. 24.95 (*0-7933-7257-7*); pap. text ed. 14.95 (*0-7933-7258-5*); disk 29.95 (*0-7933-7259-3*) Gallopade Pub Group.

— Let's Quilt Our West Virginia Town. (Carole Marsh West Virginia Bks.). (J). 1994. lib. bdg. 24.95 (*0-7933-7107-4*); pap. text ed. 14.95 (*0-7933-7108-2*); disk 29.95 (*0-7933-7109-0*) Gallopade Pub Group.

— Let's Quilt Our Wisconsin County. (Wisconsin Bks.). (J). 1994. lib. bdg. 24.95 (*0-7933-7260-7*); pap. text ed. 14. 95 (*0-7933-7261-5*); disk 29.95 (*0-7933-7262-3*) Gallopade Pub Group.

— Let's Quilt Our Wisconsin Town. (Carole Marsh Wisconsin Bks.). (J). 1994. lib. bdg. 24.95 (*0-7933-7110-4*); pap. text ed. 14.95 (*0-7933-7111-2*); disk 29.95 (*0-7933-7112-0*) Gallopade Pub Group.

— Let's Quilt Our Wyoming County. (Wyoming Bks.). (J). 1994. lib. bdg. 24.95 (*0-7933-7263-1*); pap. text ed. 14. 95 (*0-7933-7264-X*); disk 29.95 (*0-7933-7265-8*) Gallopade Pub Group.

— Let's Quilt Our Wyoming Town. (Carole Marsh Wyoming Bks.). (J). 1994. lib. bdg. 24.95 (*0-7933-7113-9*); pap. text ed. 14.95 (*0-7933-7114-7*); disk 29.95 (*0-7933-7115-5*) Gallopade Pub Group.

— Let's Quilt Pennsylvania & Stuff It Topographically! (Carole Marsh Pennsylvania Bks.). (Illus.). (J). 1994. lib. bdg. 24.95 (*0-7933-1925-0*); pap. 14.95 (*1-55609-059-5*); disk 29.95 (*0-7933-1926-9*) Gallopade Pub Group.

— Let's Quilt Rhode Island & Stuff it Topographically! (Carole Marsh Rhode Island Bks.). (Illus.). (J). 1994. lib. bdg. 24.95 (*0-7933-1957-9*); pap. 14.95 (*1-55609-065-X*); disk 29.95 (*0-7933-1958-7*) Gallopade Pub Group.

— Let's Quilt South Carolina & Stuff It Topographically! (Carole Marsh South Carolina Bks.). (Illus.). (J). 1994. lib. bdg. 24.95 (*0-7933-1987-0*); pap. 14.95 (*1-55609-053-6*); disk 29.95 (*0-7933-1988-9*) Gallopade Pub Group.

— Let's Quilt South Dakota & Stuff It Topographically! (Carole Marsh South Dakota Bks.). (Illus.). (J). 1994. lib. bdg. 24.95 (*0-7933-2018-6*); pap. 14.95 (*1-55609-136-2*); disk 29.95 (*0-7933-2019-4*) Gallopade Pub Group.

— Let's Quilt Tennessee & Stuff It Topographically! (Tennessee Bks.). (Illus.). (J). 1994. lib. bdg. 24.95 (*0-7933-2048-8*); pap. 14.95 (*1-55609-079-X*); disk 29.95 (*0-7933-2049-6*) Gallopade Pub Group.

— Let's Quilt Texas & Stuff It Topographically! (Carole Marsh Texas Bks.). (Illus.). (J). 1994. lib. bdg. 24.95 (*0-7933-2078-X*); pap. 14.95 (*1-55609-077-3*); disk 29.95 (*0-7933-2079-8*) Gallopade Pub Group.

— Let's Quilt Utah & Stuff It Topographically! (Carole Marsh Utah Bks.). (Illus.). (J). 1994. lib. bdg. 24.95 (*0-7933-2109-3*); pap. 14.95 (*1-55609-129-X*); disk 29.95 (*0-7933-2110-7*) Gallopade Pub Group.

— Let's Quilt Vermont & Stuff It Topographically! (Carole Marsh Vermont Bks.). (Illus.). (J). 1994. lib. bdg. 24.95 (*0-7933-2141-7*); pap. 14.95 (*1-55609-066-8*); disk 29.95 (*0-7933-2142-5*) Gallopade Pub Group.

— Let's Quilt Virginia & Stuff It Topographically! (Carole Marsh Virginia Bks.). (Illus.). (J). 1994. lib. bdg. 24.95 (*0-7933-2171-9*); pap. 14.95 (*1-55609-051-X*); disk 29.95 (*0-7933-2172-7*) Gallopade Pub Group.

— Let's Quilt Washington & Stuff It Topographically! (Carole Marsh Washington Bks.). (Illus.). (J). 1994. lib. bdg. 24.95 (*0-7933-2204-9*); pap. 14.95 (*1-55609-133-8*); disk 29.95 (*0-7933-2205-7*) Gallopade Pub Group.

— Let's Quilt Washington, D.C. & Stuff it Topographically!. (Carole Marsh Washington, D.C. Bks.). (Illus.). (YA). (gr. 3-12). 1994. lib. bdg. 24.95 (*1-55609-564-3*); pap. 14.95 (*0-685-45930-6*); disk 29.95 (*0-7933-1461-5*) Gallopade Pub Group.

— Let's Quilt West Virginia & Stuff It Topographically! (Carole Marsh West Virginia Bks.). (Illus.). (J). 1994. lib. bdg. 24.95 (*0-7933-2236-7*); pap. 14.95 (*1-55609-052-8*); disk 29.95 (*0-7933-2237-5*) Gallopade Pub Group.

— Let's Quilt Wisconsin & Stuff It Topographically! (Carole Marsh Wisconsin Bks.). (Illus.). (J). 1994. lib. bdg. 24.95 (*0-7933-2268-5*); pap. 14.95 (*1-55609-098-6*); disk 29.95 (*0-7933-2269-3*) Gallopade Pub Group.

— Let's Quilt Wyoming & Stuff Topographically! (Carole Marsh Wyoming Bks.). (Illus.). (J). 1994. lib. bdg. 24.95 (*1-55609-290-3*); pap. 14.95 (*1-55609-134-6*); disk 29.95 (*1-55609-291-1*) Gallopade Pub Group.

— Life Isn't Fair: Murphy's Laws for Kids. (Quantum Leap Ser.). (Illus.). (J). (gr. 4-12). 1994. 14.95 (*0-935326-08-1*); lib. bdg. 24.95 (*0-7933-6916-9*) Gallopade Pub Group.

— Like a Virgin: How You Can Convince Your Child to Abstain from Sex. (Smart Sex Stuff Ser.). (Orig.). 1994. pap. 14.95 (*1-55609-223-7*) Gallopade Pub Group.

— The Little Known, Seldom Told Secrets of Book Distribution for Authors & Small Presses. (Lifewrite Ser.). (Illus.). 1994. 24.95 (*0-7933-2849-7*); pap. text ed. 14.95 (*0-7933-2850-0*); disk 29.95 (*0-7933-2851-9*) Gallopade Pub Group.

— The Lost Colony Classroom Gamebook. (Carole Marsh Bks.). (Illus.). (Orig.). (J). (gr. 3-12). 1994. pap. 19.95 (*0-935326-86-3*) Gallopade Pub Group.

— Louisiana! A(lligator) to Z(ydeco) (Carole Marsh Louisiana Bks.). (J). 1994. lib. bdg. 24.95 (*0-7933-7321-2*); pap. text ed. 14.95 (*0-7933-7320-4*); disk 29.95 (*0-7933-7322-0*) Gallopade Pub Group.

— Louisiana & Other State Greats (Biographies) (Carole Marsh Louisiana Bks.). (Illus.). (J). (gr. 3-8). 1994. lib. bdg. 24.95 (*1-55609-404-3*); pap. 14.95 (*1-55609-403-5*); disk 29.95 (*0-685-45939-X*) Gallopade Pub Group.

— Louisiana Bandits, Bushwackers, Outlaws, Crooks, Devils, Ghosts, Desperadoes & Other Assorted & Sundry Characters! (Carole Marsh Louisiana Bks.). (Illus.). (J). (gr. 3-8). 1994. lib. bdg. 24.95 (*0-7933-0502-0*); pap. 14. 95 (*0-7933-0501-2*); disk 29.95 (*0-7933-0503-9*) Gallopade Pub Group.

— The Louisiana Bookstore Book: A Surprising Guide to Our State's Bookstores & Their Specialties for Students, Teachers, Writers & Publishers. (Carole Marsh Louisiana Bks.). (Illus.). 1994. lib. bdg. 24.95 (*0-7933-2909-4*); pap. 14.95 (*0-7933-2910-8*); disk 29.95 (*0-7933-2911-6*) Gallopade Pub Group.

— Louisiana Classic Christmas Trivia: Stories, Recipes, Activities, Legends, Lore & More! (Carole Marsh Louisiana Bks.). (Illus.). (J). (gr. 3-8). 1994. lib. bdg. 24. 95 (*0-7933-0505-5*); pap. 14.95 (*0-7933-0504-7*); disk 29. 95 (*0-7933-0506-3*) Gallopade Pub Group.

— Louisiana Coastales. (Carole Marsh Louisiana Bks.). (J). 1994. lib. bdg. 24.95 (*0-7933-7283-6*) Gallopade Pub Group.

— Louisiana Coastales. (Carole Marsh Louisiana Bks.). (Illus.). (J). (gr. 3-8). 1994. lib. bdg. 24.95 (*1-55609-400-0*); pap. 14.95 (*1-55609-119-2*); disk 29.95 (*0-7933-1673-1*) Gallopade Pub Group.

— Louisiana "Crinkum-Crankum" A Funny Word Book about Our State. (Carole Marsh Louisiana Bks.). (Illus.). (J). 1994. lib. bdg. 24.95 (*0-7933-4862-5*); pap. 14.95 (*0-7933-4863-3*); disk 29.95 (*0-7933-4864-1*) Gallopade Pub Group.

— Louisiana Dingbats! Bk. 1: A Fun Book of Games, Stories, Activities & More about Our State That's All in Code! for You to Decipher. (Carole Marsh Louisiana Bks.). (Illus.). (J). (gr. 3-12). 1994. lib. bdg. 24.95 (*0-7933-3827-1*); pap. 14.95 (*0-7933-3828-X*); disk 29.95 (*0-7933-3829-8*) Gallopade Pub Group.

— Louisiana Festival Fun for Kids! (Carole Marsh Louisiana Bks.). (Illus.). (YA). (gr. 3-12). 1994. lib. bdg. 24.95 (*0-7933-3980-4*); pap. 14.95 (*0-7933-3981-2*); disk 29.95 (*0-7933-3982-0*) Gallopade Pub Group.

— The Louisiana Hot Air Balloon Mystery. (Carole Marsh Louisiana Bks.). (Illus.). (J). (gr. 2-9). 1994. 24.95 (*0-685-37850-0*); pap. 14.95 (*0-7933-2481-5*); disk 29.95 (*0-7933-2482-3*) Gallopade Pub Group.

— Louisiana Jeopardy! Answers & Questions about Our State! (Carole Marsh Louisiana Bks.). (Illus.). (J). (gr. 3-12). 1994. lib. bdg. 24.95 (*0-7933-4133-7*); pap. 14.95 (*0-7933-4134-5*); disk 29.95 (*0-7933-4135-3*) Gallopade Pub Group.

— Louisiana "Jography" A Fun Run Thru Our State! (Carole Marsh Louisiana Bks.). (Illus.). (J). (gr. 3-8). 1994. lib. bdg. 24.95 (*1-55609-396-9*); pap. 14.95 (*1-55609-108-7*); disk 29.95 (*0-7933-1663-4*) Gallopade Pub Group.

— Louisiana Kid's Cookbook: Recipes, How-to, History, Lore & More! (Carole Marsh Louisiana Bks.). (Illus.). (J). (gr. 3-8). 1994. lib. bdg. 24.95 (*0-7933-0514-4*); pap. 14.95 (*0-7933-0513-6*); disk 29.95 (*0-7933-0515-2*) Gallopade Pub Group.

— The Louisiana Library Book: A Surprising Guide to the Unusual Special Collections in Libraries Across Our State for Students, Teachers, Writers & Publishers - Includes Reproducible Mailing Labels Plus Activities for Young People! (Carole Marsh Louisiana Bks.). (Illus.). 1994. lib. bdg. 24.95 (*0-7933-3059-9*); pap. 14.95 (*0-7933-3060-2*); disk 29.95 (*0-7933-3061-0*) Gallopade Pub Group.

— The Louisiana Media Book: A Surprising Guide to the Amazing Print, Broadcast & Online Media of Our State for Students, Teachers, Writers & Publishers - Includes Reproducible Mailing Labels Plus Activities for Young People! (Carole Marsh Louisiana Bks.). (Illus.). 1994. lib. bdg. 24.95 (*0-7933-3215-X*); pap. 14.95 (*0-7933-3216-8*); disk 29.95 (*0-7933-3217-6*) Gallopade Pub Group.

— The Louisiana Mystery Van Takes Off! Book 1: Handicapped Louisiana Kids Sneak Off on a Big Adventure. (Carole Marsh Louisiana Bks.). (Illus.). (J). (gr. 3-12). 1994. 24.95 (*0-7933-5015-8*); pap. 14.95 (*0-7933-5016-6*); disk 29.95 (*0-7933-5017-4*) Gallopade Pub Group.

— Louisiana Quiz Bowl Crash Course! (Carole Marsh Louisiana Bks.). (Illus.). (J). (gr. 3-8). 1994. lib. bdg. 24. 95 (*1-55609-402-7*); pap. 14.95 (*1-55609-401-9*); disk 29. 95 (*0-7933-1672-3*) Gallopade Pub Group.

— Louisiana Rollercoasters! (Carole Marsh Louisiana Bks.). (Illus.). (YA). (gr. 3-12). 1994. lib. bdg. 24.95 (*0-7933-5278-9*); pap. 14.95 (*0-7933-5279-7*); disk 29.95 (*0-7933-5280-0*) Gallopade Pub Group.

— Louisiana School Trivia: An Amazing & Fascinating Look at Our State's Teachers, Schools & Students! (Carole Marsh Louisiana Bks.). (Illus.). (J). (gr. 3-8). 1994. lib. bdg. 24.95 (*0-7933-0511-X*); pap. 14.95 (*0-7933-0510-1*); disk 29.95 (*0-7933-0512-8*) Gallopade Pub Group.

— Louisiana Silly Basketball Sportsmysteries, Vol. I. (Carole Marsh Louisiana Bks.). (Illus.). (J). (gr. 3-8). 1994. lib. bdg. 24.95 (*0-7933-0508-X*); pap. 14.95 (*0-7933-0507-1*); disk 29.95 (*0-7933-0509-8*) Gallopade Pub Group.

— Louisiana Silly Basketball Sportsmysteries, Vol. II. (Carole Marsh Louisiana Bks.). (Illus.). (J). (gr. 3-8). 1994. lib. bdg. 24.95 (*0-7933-1678-2*); pap. 14.95 (*0-7933-1679-0*); disk 29.95 (*0-7933-1680-4*) Gallopade Pub Group.

— Louisiana Silly Football Sportsmysteries, Vol. I. (Carole Marsh Louisiana Bks.). (Illus.). (J). (gr. 3-8). 1994. lib. bdg. 24.95 (*1-55609-399-3*); pap. 14.95 (*1-55609-398-5*); disk 29.95 (*0-7933-1665-0*) Gallopade Pub Group.

— Louisiana Silly Football Sportsmysteries, Vol. II. (Carole Marsh Louisiana Bks.). (Illus.). (J). (gr. 3-8). 1994. lib. bdg. 24.95 (*0-7933-1666-9*); pap. 14.95 (*0-7933-1667-7*); disk 29.95 (*0-7933-1668-5*) Gallopade Pub Group.

— Louisiana Silly Trivia! (Carole Marsh Louisiana Bks.). (Illus.). (J). (gr. 3-8). 1994. lib. bdg. 24.95 (*1-55609-395-0*); pap. 14.95 (*1-55609-041-2*); disk 29.95 (*0-7933-0522-5*) Gallopade Pub Group.

— Louisiana Timeline: A Chronology of Louisiana History, Mystery, Trivia, Legend, Lore & More. (Carole Marsh Louisiana Bks.). (Illus.). (J). (gr. 3-12). 1994. lib. bdg. 24. 95 (*0-7933-5929-5*); pap. 14.95 (*0-7933-5930-9*); disk 29. 95 (*0-7933-5931-7*) Gallopade Pub Group.

— Louisiana's (Most Devastating!) Disasters & (Most Calamitous!) Catastrophies! (Carole Marsh Louisiana Bks.). (Illus.). (J). (gr. 3-8). 1994. lib. bdg. 24.95 (*0-7933-0499-7*); pap. 14.95 (*0-7933-0498-9*); disk 29.95 (*0-685-45940-3*) Gallopade Pub Group.

— Louisiana's Unsolved Mysteries (& Their "Solutions") Includes Scientific Information & Other Activities for Students. (Carole Marsh Louisiana Bks.). (Illus.). (J). (gr. 3-12). 1994. lib. bdg. 24.95 (*0-7933-5776-4*); pap. 14.95 (*0-7933-5777-2*); disk 29.95 (*0-7933-5778-0*) Gallopade Pub Group.

— The Magic & Sorcery Dingbats Book. (Carole Marsh Dingbats Book Ser.). (Illus.). (YA). (gr. 3-12). 1994. lib. bdg. 24.95 (*0-7933-5377-7*); pap. 14.95 (*0-7933-5378-5*); disk 29.95 (*0-7933-5379-3*) Gallopade Pub Group.

— Maine & Other State Greats (Biographies) (Carole Marsh Maine Bks.). (Illus.). (J). (gr. 3-8). 1994. lib. bdg. 24.95 (*1-55609-614-3*); pap. 14.95 (*1-55609-615-1*); disk 29.95 (*1-55609-616-X*) Gallopade Pub Group.

— Maine Bandits, Bushwackers, Outlaws, Crooks, Devils, Ghosts, Desperadoes & Other Assorted & Sundry Characters! (Carole Marsh Maine Bks.). (Illus.). (J). (gr. 3-8). 1994. lib. bdg. 24.95 (*0-7933-0527-6*); pap. 14.95 (*0-7933-0526-8*); disk 29.95 (*0-7933-0528-4*) Gallopade Pub Group.

— The Maine Bookstore Book: A Surprising Guide to Our State's Bookstores & Their Specialties for Students, Teachers, Writers & Publishers. (Carole Marsh Maine Bks.). (Illus.). 1994. lib. bdg. 24.95 (*0-7933-2912-4*); pap. 14.95 (*0-7933-2913-2*); disk 29.95 (*0-7933-2914-0*) Gallopade Pub Group.

— Maine Classic Christmas Trivia: Stories, Recipes, Activities, Legends, Lore & More! (Carole Marsh Maine Bks.). (Illus.). (J). (gr. 3-8). 1994. lib. bdg. 24.95 (*0-7933-0530-6*); pap. 14.95 (*0-7933-0529-2*); disk 29.95 (*0-7933-0531-4*) Gallopade Pub Group.

— Maine Coastales! (Carole Marsh Maine Bks.). (J). 1994. lib. bdg. 24.95 (*0-7933-7284-4*) Gallopade Pub Group.

— Maine Coastales! (Carole Marsh Maine Bks.). (Illus.). (J). (gr. 3-8). 1994. lib. bdg. 24.95 (*1-55609-608-9*); pap. 14. 95 (*1-55609-609-7*); disk 29.95 (*1-55609-610-0*) Gallopade Pub Group.

— Maine "Crinkum-Crankum" A Funny Word Book about Our State. (Carole Marsh Maine Bks.). (Illus.). (J). 1994. lib. bdg. 24.95 (*0-7933-4865-X*); pap. 14.95 (*0-7933-4866-8*); disk 29.95 (*0-7933-4867-6*) Gallopade Pub Group.

— Maine Dingbats! Bk. 1: A Fun Book of Games, Stories, Activities & More about Our State That's All in Code! for You to Decipher. (Carole Marsh Maine Bks.). (Illus.). (J). (gr. 3-12). 1994. lib. bdg. 24.95 (*0-7933-3830-1*); pap. 14.95 (*0-7933-3831-X*); disk 29.95 (*0-7933-3832-8*) Gallopade Pub Group.

— Maine Festival Fun for Kids! (Carole Marsh Maine Bks.). (Illus.). (YA). (gr. 3-12). 1994. lib. bdg. 24.95 (*0-7933-3983-9*); pap. 14.95 (*0-7933-3984-7*); disk 29.95 (*0-7933-3985-5*) Gallopade Pub Group.

— The Maine Hot Air Balloon Mystery. (Carole Marsh Maine Bks.). (Illus.). (J). (gr. 2-9). 1994. 24.95 (*0-7933-2489-0*); pap. 14.95 (*0-7933-2490-4*); disk 29.95 (*0-7933-2491-2*) Gallopade Pub Group.

— Maine Jeopardy! Answers & Questions about Our State! (Carole Marsh Maine Bks.). (Illus.). (J). (gr. 3-12). 1994. lib. bdg. 24.95 (*0-7933-4136-1*); pap. 14.95 (*0-7933-4137-X*); disk 29.95 (*0-7933-4138-8*) Gallopade Pub Group.

— Maine "Jography" A Fun Run Thru Our State! (Carole Marsh Maine Bks.). (Illus.). (J). (gr. 3-8). 1994. lib. bdg. 24.95 (*1-55609-596-1*); pap. 14.95 (*1-55609-597-X*); disk 29.95 (*1-55609-598-8*) Gallopade Pub Group.

— Maine Kid's Cookbook: Recipes, How-to, History, Lore & More! (Carole Marsh Maine Bks.). (Illus.). (J). (gr. 3-8). 1994. lib. bdg. 24.95 (*0-7933-0539-X*); pap. 14.95 (*0-7933-0538-1*); disk 29.95 (*0-7933-0540-3*) Gallopade Pub Group.

— The Maine Library Book: A Surprising Guide to the Unusual Special Collections in Libraries Across Our State for Students, Teachers, Writers & Publishers - Includes Reproducible Mailing Labels Plus Activities for Young People! (Carole Marsh Maine Bks.). (Illus.). 1994. lib. bdg. 24.95 (*0-7933-3062-9*); pap. 14.95 (*0-7933-3063-7*); disk 29.95 (*0-7933-3064-5*) Gallopade Pub Group.

— The Maine Media Book: A Surprising Guide to the Amazing Print, Broadcast & Online Media of Our State for Students, Teachers, Writers & Publishers - Includes Reproducible Mailing Labels Plus Activities for Young People! (Carole Marsh Maine Bks.). (Illus.). 1994. lib. bdg. 24.95 (*0-7933-3218-4*); pap. 14.95 (*0-7933-3219-2*); disk 29.95 (*0-7933-3220-6*) Gallopade Pub Group.

— The Maine Mystery Van Takes Off! Book 1: Handicapped Maine Kids Sneak Off on a Big Adventure. (Carole Marsh Maine Bks.). (Illus.). (J). (gr. 3-12). 1994. 24.95 (*0-7933-5018-2*); pap. 14.95 (*0-7933-5019-0*); disk 29.95 (*0-7933-5020-4*) Gallopade Pub Group.

— Maine Quiz Bowl Crash Course! (Carole Marsh Maine Bks.). (Illus.). (J). (gr. 3-8). 1994. lib. bdg. 24.95 (*1-55609-611-9*); pap. 14.95 (*1-55609-612-7*); disk 29.95 (*1-55609-613-5*) Gallopade Pub Group.

— Maine Rollercoasters! (Carole Marsh Maine Bks.). (Illus.). (YA). (gr. 3-12). 1994. lib. bdg. 24.95 (*0-7933-5281-9*); pap. 14.95 (*0-7933-5282-7*); disk 29.95 (*0-7933-5283-5*) Gallopade Pub Group.

— Maine School Trivia: An Amazing & Fascinating Look at Our State's Teachers, Schools & Students! (Carole Marsh Maine Bks.). (Illus.). (J). (gr. 3-8). 1994. lib. bdg. 24.95 (*0-7933-0536-5*); pap. 14.95 (*0-7933-0535-7*); disk 29.95 (*0-7933-0537-3*) Gallopade Pub Group.

— Maine Silly Basketball Sportsmysteries, Vol. I. (Carole Marsh Maine Bks.). (Illus.). (J). (gr. 3-8). 1994. lib. bdg. 24.95 (*0-7933-0533-0*); pap. 14.95 (*0-7933-0532-2*); disk 29.95 (*0-7933-0534-9*) Gallopade Pub Group.

— Maine Silly Basketball Sportsmysteries, Vol. II. (Carole Marsh Maine Bks.). (Illus.). (J). (gr. 3-8). 1994. lib. bdg. 24.95 (*0-7933-1684-7*); pap. 14.95 (*0-7933-1685-5*); disk 29.95 (*0-7933-1686-3*) Gallopade Pub Group.

— Maine Silly Football Sportsmysteries, Vol. I. (Carole Marsh Maine Bks.). (Illus.). (J). (gr. 3-8). 1994. lib. bdg. 24.95 (*1-55609-602-X*); pap. 14.95 (*1-55609-604-6*); disk 29.95 (*1-55609-606-2*) Gallopade Pub Group.

— Maine Silly Football Sportsmysteries, Vol. II. (Carole Marsh Maine Bks.). (Illus.). (J). (gr. 3-8). 1994. lib. bdg. 24.95 (*1-55609-603-8*); pap. 14.95 (*1-55609-605-4*); disk 29.95 (*1-55609-607-0*) Gallopade Pub Group.

— Maine Silly Trivia! (Carole Marsh Maine Bks.). (Illus.). (J). (gr. 3-8). 1994. lib. bdg. 24.95 (*1-55609-593-7*); pap. 14.95 (*1-55609-594-5*); disk 29.95 (*1-55609-595-3*) Gallopade Pub Group.

— Maine Timeline: A Chronology of Maine History, Mystery, Trivia, Legend, Lore & More. (Carole Marsh Maine Bks.). (Illus.). (J). (gr. 3-12). 1994. lib. bdg. 24.95 (*0-7933-5932-5*); pap. 14.95 (*0-7933-5933-3*); disk 29.95 (*0-7933-5934-1*) Gallopade Pub Group.

— Maine's (Most Devastating!) Disasters & (Most Calamitous!) Catastrophies! (Carole Marsh Maine Bks.). (Illus.). (J). (gr. 3-8). 1994. lib. bdg. 24.95 (*0-7933-0524-1*, 0-7933-0525-X); pap. 14.95 (*0-7933-0523-3*); disk 29.95 (*0-685-45941-1*) Gallopade Pub Group.

— Maine's Unsolved Mysteries (& Their "Solutions") Includes Scientific Information & Other Activities for Students. (Carole Marsh Maine Bks.). (Illus.). (J). (gr. 3-12). 1994. lib. bdg. 24.95 (*0-7933-5779-9*); pap. 14.95 (*0-7933-5780-2*); disk 29.95 (*0-7933-5781-0*) Gallopade Pub Group.

— Mariner's & More! Virginia People, Places & Things Everyone Should Know. (Carole Marsh Virginia Bks.). (Illus.). (YA). (gr. 9-12). 1994. lib. bdg. 24.95 (*0-7933-0000-2*); pap. 14.95 (*0-7933-0001-0*); disk 29.95 (*0-7933-0002-9*) Gallopade Pub Group.

— Maryland & Other State Greats (Biographies) (Carole Marsh Maryland Bks.). (Illus.). (J). (gr. 3-8). 1994. lib. bdg. 24.95 (*1-55609-636-4*); pap. 14.95 (*1-55609-637-2*); disk 29.95 (*1-55609-638-0*) Gallopade Pub Group.

— Maryland Bandits, Bushwackers, Outlaws, Crooks, Devils, Ghosts, Desperadoes & Other Assorted & Sundry Characters! (Carole Marsh Maryland Bks.). (Illus.). (J). (gr. 3-8). 1994. lib. bdg. 24.95 (*0-7933-0551-9*); pap. 14. 95 (*0-7933-0550-0*); disk 29.95 (*0-7933-0552-7*) Gallopade Pub Group.

— The Maryland Bookstore Book: A Surprising Guide to Our State's Bookstores & Their Specialties for Students, Teachers, Writers & Publishers. (Carole Marsh Maryland Bks.). (Illus.). 1994. lib. bdg. 24.95 (*0-7933-2915-9*); pap. 14.95 (*0-7933-2916-7*); disk 29.95 (*0-7933-2917-5*) Gallopade Pub Group.

— Maryland Classic Christmas Trivia: Stories, Recipes, Activities, Legends, Lore & More! (Carole Marsh Maryland Bks.). (Illus.). (J). (gr. 3-8). 1994. lib. bdg. 24. 95 (*0-7933-0554-3*); pap. 14.95 (*0-7933-0553-5*); disk 29. 95 (*0-7933-0555-1*) Gallopade Pub Group.

— Maryland Coastales! (Carole Marsh Maryland Bks.). (J). 1994. lib. bdg. 24.95 (*0-7933-7285-2*) Gallopade Pub Group.

— Maryland Coastales! (Carole Marsh Maryland Bks.). (Illus.). (J). (gr. 3-8). 1994. lib. bdg. 24.95 (*1-55609-630-5*); pap. 14.95 (*1-55609-631-3*); disk 29.95 (*1-55609-632-1*) Gallopade Pub Group.

— Maryland "Crinkum-Crankum" A Funny Word Book about Our State. (Carole Marsh Maryland Bks.). (Illus.). (J). 1994. lib. bdg. 24.95 (*0-7933-4868-4*); pap. 14.95 (*0-7933-4869-2*); disk 29.95 (*0-7933-4870-6*) Gallopade Pub Group.

— Maryland Dingbats! Bk. 1: A Fun Book of Games, Stories, Activities & More about Our State That's All in Code! for You to Decipher. (Carole Marsh Maryland Bks.). (Illus.). (J). (gr. 3-12). 1994. lib. bdg. 24.95 (*0-7933-3833-6*); pap. 14.95 (*0-7933-3834-4*); disk 29.95 (*0-7933-3835-2*) Gallopade Pub Group.

— Maryland Festival Fun for Kids! (Carole Marsh Maryland Bks.). (Illus.). (YA). (gr. 3-12). 1994. lib. bdg. 24.95 (*0-7933-3986-3*); pap. 14.95 (*0-7933-3987-1*); disk 29.95 (*0-7933-3988-X*) Gallopade Pub Group.

— The Maryland Hot Air Balloon Mystery. (Carole Marsh Maryland Bks.). (Illus.). (J). (gr. 2-9). 1994. 24.95 (*0-7933-2498-X*); pap. 14.95 (*0-7933-2499-8*); disk 29.95 (*0-7933-2500-5*) Gallopade Pub Group.

— Maryland Jeopardy! Answers & Questions about Our State! (Carole Marsh Maryland Bks.). (Illus.). (J). (gr. 3-12). 1994. lib. bdg. 24.95 (*0-7933-4139-6*); pap. 14.95 (*0-7933-4140-X*); disk 29.95 (*0-7933-4141-8*) Gallopade Pub Group.

— Maryland "Jography" A Fun Run Thru Our State! (Carole Marsh Maryland Bks.). (Illus.). (J). (gr. 3-8). 1994. lib. bdg. 24.95 (*1-55609-619-4*); pap. 14.95 (*1-55609-620-8*); disk 29.95 (*1-55609-621-6*) Gallopade Pub Group.

— Maryland Kid's Cookbook: Recipes, How-to, History, Lore & More! (Carole Marsh Maryland Bks.). (Illus.). (J). (gr. 3-8). 1994. lib. bdg. 24.95 (*0-7933-0563-2*); pap. 14.95 (*0-7933-0562-4*); disk 29.95 (*0-7933-0564-0*) Gallopade Pub Group.

— The Maryland Library Book: A Surprising Guide to the Unusual Special Collections in Libraries Across Our State for Students, Teachers, Writers & Publishers - Includes Reproducible Mailing Labels Plus Activities for Young People! (Carole Marsh Maryland Bks.). (Illus.). 1994. lib. bdg. 24.95 (*0-7933-3065-3*); pap. 14.95 (*0-7933-3066-1*); disk 29.95 (*0-7933-3067-X*) Gallopade Pub Group.

— The Maryland Media Book: A Surprising Guide to the Amazing Print, Broadcast & Online Media of Our State for Students, Teachers, Writers & Publishers - Includes Reproducible Mailing Labels Plus Activities for Young People! (Carole Marsh Maryland Bks.). (Illus.). 1994. lib. bdg. 24.95 (*0-7933-3221-4*); pap. 14.95 (*0-7933-3222-2*); disk 29.95 (*0-7933-3223-0*) Gallopade Pub Group.

— The Maryland Mystery Van Takes Off! Book 1: Handicapped Maryland Kids Sneak Off on a Big Adventure. (Carole Marsh Maryland Bks.). (Illus.). (J). (gr. 3-12). 1994. 24.95 (*0-7933-5021-2*); pap. 14.95 (*0-7933-5022-0*); disk 29.95 (*0-7933-5023-9*) Gallopade Pub Group.

— Maryland Quiz Bowl Crash Course! (Carole Marsh Maryland Bks.). (Illus.). (J). (gr. 3-8). 1994. lib. bdg. 24.95 (*1-55609-633-X*); pap. 14.95 (*1-55609-634-8*); disk 29.95 (*1-55609-635-6*) Gallopade Pub Group.

— Maryland Rollercoasters! (Carole Marsh Maryland Bks.). (Illus.). (YA). (gr. 3-12). 1994. lib. bdg. 24.95 (*0-7933-5284-3*); pap. 14.95 (*0-7933-5285-1*); disk 29.95 (*0-7933-5286-X*) Gallopade Pub Group.

— Maryland School Trivia: An Amazing & Fascinating Look at Our State's Teachers, Schools & Students! (Carole Marsh Maryland Bks.). (Illus.). (J). (gr. 3-8). 1994. lib. bdg. 24.95 (*0-7933-0560-8*); pap. 14.95 (*0-7933-0559-4*); disk 29.95 (*0-7933-0561-6*) Gallopade Pub Group.

— Maryland Silly Basketball Sportsmysteries, Vol. I. (Carole Marsh Maryland Bks.). (Illus.). (J). (gr. 3-8). 1994. lib. bdg. 24.95 (*0-7933-0557-8*); pap. 14.95 (*0-7933-0556-X*); disk 29.95 (*0-7933-0558-6*) Gallopade Pub Group.

— Maryland Silly Basketball Sportsmysteries, Vol. II. (Carole Marsh Maryland Bks.). (Illus.). (J). (gr. 3-8). 1994. lib. bdg. 24.95 (*0-7933-1696-0*); pap. 14.95 (*0-7933-1697-9*); disk 29.95 (*0-7933-1698-7*) Gallopade Pub Group.

— Maryland Silly Football Sportsmysteries, Vol. I. (Carole Marsh Maryland Bks.). (Illus.). (J). (gr. 3-8). 1994. lib. bdg. 24.95 (*1-55609-624-0*); pap. 14.95 (*1-55609-625-9*); disk 29.95 (*1-55609-626-7*) Gallopade Pub Group.

— Maryland Silly Football Sportsmysteries, Vol. II. (Carole Marsh Maryland Bks.). (Illus.). (J). (gr. 3-8). 1994. lib. bdg. 24.95 (*1-55609-627-5*); pap. 14.95 (*1-55609-628-3*); disk 29.95 (*1-55609-629-1*) Gallopade Pub Group.

— Maryland Silly Trivia! (Carole Marsh Maryland Bks.). (Illus.). (J). (gr. 3-8). 1994. lib. bdg. 24.95 (*1-55609-617-8*); pap. 14.95 (*1-55609-042-0*); disk 29.95 (*1-55609-618-6*) Gallopade Pub Group.

— Maryland Timeline: A Chronology of Maryland History, Mystery, Trivia, Legend, Lore & More. (Carole Marsh Maryland Bks.). (Illus.). (J). (gr. 3-12). 1994. lib. bdg. 24.95 (*0-7933-5935-X*); pap. 14.95 (*0-7933-5936-8*); disk 29.95 (*0-7933-5937-6*) Gallopade Pub Group.

— Maryland's (Most Devastating!) Disasters & (Most Calamitous!) Catastrophies! (Carole Marsh Maryland Bks.). (Illus.). (J). (gr. 3-8). 1994. lib. bdg. 24.95 (*0-7933-0548-9*); pap. 14.95 (*0-7933-0547-0*); disk 29.95 (*0-7933-0549-7*) Gallopade Pub Group.

— Maryland's Unsolved Mysteries (& Their "Solutions") Includes Scientific Information & Other Activities for Students. (Carole Marsh Maryland Bks.). (Illus.). (J). (gr. 3-12). 1994. lib. bdg. 24.95 (*0-7933-5782-9*); pap. 14.95 (*0-7933-5783-7*); disk 29.95 (*0-7933-5784-5*) Gallopade Pub Group.

— Massachusetts & Other State Greats (Biographies) (Carole Marsh Massachusetts Bks.). (Illus.). (J). (gr. 3-8). 1994. lib. bdg. 24.95 (*1-55609-699-2*); pap. 14.95 (*1-55609-700-X*); disk 29.95 (*1-55609-701-8*) Gallopade Pub Group.

— Massachusetts Bandits, Bushwackers, Outlaws, Crooks, Devils, Ghosts, Desperadoes & Other Assorted & Sundry Characters! (Carole Marsh Massachusetts Bks.). (Illus.). (J). (gr. 3-8). 1994. lib. bdg. 24.95 (*0-7933-0575-6*); pap. 14.95 (*0-7933-0574-8*); disk 29.95 (*0-7933-0576-4*) Gallopade Pub Group.

— The Massachusetts Bookstore Book: A Surprising Guide to Our State's Bookstores & Their Specialties for Students, Teachers, Writers & Publishers. (Massachuseets Bks.). (Illus.). 1994. lib. bdg. 24.95 (*0-7933-2918-3*); pap. 14.95 (*0-7933-2919-1*); disk 29.95 (*0-7933-2920-5*) Gallopade Pub Group.

— Massachusetts Classic Christmas Trivia: Stories, Recipes, Activities, Legends, Lore & More! (Carole Marsh Massachusetts Bks.). (Illus.). (J). (gr. 3-8). 1994. lib. bdg. 24.95 (*0-7933-0578-0*); pap. 14.95 (*0-7933-0577-2*); disk 29.95 (*0-7933-0579-9*) Gallopade Pub Group.

— Massachusetts Coastales. (Carole Marsh Massachusetts Bks.). (Illus.). (J). (gr. 3-8). 1994. lib. bdg. 24.95 (*1-55609-693-3*); pap. 14.95 (*1-55609-694-1*); disk 29.95 (*1-55609-695-X*) Gallopade Pub Group.

— Massachusetts Coastales! (Massachuseets Bks.). (J). 1994. lib. bdg. 24.95 (*0-7933-7286-0*) Gallopade Pub Group.

— Massachusetts "Crinkum-Crankum" A Funny Word Book about Our State. (Massachuseets Bks.). (Illus.). (J). 1994. lib. bdg. 24.95 (*0-7933-4871-4*); pap. 14.95 (*0-7933-4872-2*); disk 29.95 (*0-7933-4873-0*) Gallopade Pub Group.

— Massachusetts Dingbats! Bk. 1: A Fun Book of Games, Stories, Activities & More about Our State That's All in Code! for You to Decipher. (Massachuseets Bks.). (Illus.). (J). (gr. 3-12). 1994. lib. bdg. 24.95 (*0-7933-3836-0*); pap. 14.95 (*0-7933-3837-9*); disk 29.95 (*0-7933-3838-7*) Gallopade Pub Group.

— Massachusetts Festival Fun for Kids! (Massachuseets Bks.). (Illus.). (YA). (gr. 3-12). 1994. lib. bdg. 24.95 (*0-7933-3989-8*); pap. 14.95 (*0-7933-3990-1*); disk 29.95 (*0-7933-3991-X*) Gallopade Pub Group.

— The Massachusetts Hot Air Balloon Mystery. (Carole Marsh Massachusetts Bks.). (Illus.). (J). (gr. 2-9). 1994. 24.95 (*0-7933-2507-2*); pap. 14.95 (*0-7933-2508-0*); disk 29.95 (*0-7933-2509-9*) Gallopade Pub Group.

— Massachusetts Jeopardy! Answers & Questions about Our State! (Massachuseets Bks.). (Illus.). (J). (gr. 3-12). 1994. lib. bdg. 24.95 (*0-7933-4142-6*); pap. 14.95 (*0-7933-4143-4*); disk 29.95 (*0-7933-4144-2*) Gallopade Pub Group.

— Massachusetts "Jography" A Fun Run Thru Our State! (Carole Marsh Massachusetts Bks.). (Illus.). (J). (gr. 3-8). 1994. lib. bdg. 24.95 (*1-55609-682-8*); pap. 14.95 (*1-55609-111-7*); disk 29.95 (*1-55609-683-6*) Gallopade Pub Group.

— Massachusetts Kid's Cookbook: Recipes, How-to, History, Lore & More! (Carole Marsh Massachusetts Bks.). (Illus.). (J). (gr. 3-8). 1994. lib. bdg. 24.95 (*0-7933-0587-X*); pap. 14.95 (*0-7933-0586-1*); disk 29.95 (*0-7933-0588-8*) Gallopade Pub Group.

— The Massachusetts Library Book: A Surprising Guide to the Unusual Special Collections in Libraries Across Our State for Students, Teachers, Writers & Publishers - Includes Reproducible Mailing Labels Plus Activities for Young People! (Massachuseets Bks.). (Illus.). 1994. lib. bdg. 24.95 (*0-7933-3068-8*); pap. 14.95 (*0-7933-3069-6*); disk 29.95 (*0-7933-3070-X*) Gallopade Pub Group.

— The Massachusetts Media Book: A Surprising Guide to the Amazing Print, Broadcast & Online Media of Our State for Students, Teachers, Writers & Publishers - Includes Reproducible Mailing Labels Plus Activities for Young People! (Massachuseets Bks.). (Illus.). 1994. lib. bdg. 24.95 (*0-7933-3224-9*); pap. 14.95 (*0-7933-3225-7*); disk 29.95 (*0-7933-3226-5*) Gallopade Pub Group.

— Massachusetts' (Most Devastating!) Disasters & (Most Calamitous!) Catastrophies! (Carole Marsh Massachusetts Bks.). (Illus.). (J). (gr. 3-8). 1994. lib. bdg. 24.95 (*0-7933-0572-1*); pap. 14.95 (*0-7933-0571-3*); disk 29.95 (*0-7933-0573-X*) Gallopade Pub Group.

— The Massachusetts Mystery Van Takes Off! Book 1: Handicapped Massachusetts Kids Sneak Off on a Big Adventure. (Massachuseets Bks.). (Illus.). (J). (gr. 3-12). 1994. 24.95 (*0-7933-5024-7*); pap. 14.95 (*0-7933-5025-5*); disk 29.95 (*0-7933-5026-3*) Gallopade Pub Group.

— Massachusetts Quiz Bowl Crash Course! (Carole Marsh Massachusetts Bks.). (Illus.). (J). (gr. 3-8). 1994. lib. bdg. 24.95 (*1-55609-696-8*); pap. 14.95 (*1-55609-697-6*); disk 29.95 (*1-55609-698-4*) Gallopade Pub Group.

— Massachusetts Rollercoasters! (Massachuseets Bks.). (Illus.). (YA). (gr. 3-12). 1994. lib. bdg. 24.95 (*0-7933-5287-8*); pap. 14.95 (*0-7933-5288-6*); disk 29.95 (*0-7933-5289-4*) Gallopade Pub Group.

— Massachusetts School Trivia: An Amazing & Fascinating Look at Our State's Teachers, Schools & Students! (Carole Marsh Massachusetts Bks.). (Illus.). (J). (gr. 3-8). 1994. lib. bdg. 24.95 (*0-7933-0584-5*); pap. 14.95 (*0-7933-0583-7*); disk 29.95 (*0-7933-0585-3*) Gallopade Pub Group.

— Massachusetts Silly Basketball Sportsmysteries, Vol. I. (Carole Marsh Massachusetts Bks.). (Illus.). (J). (gr. 3-8). 1994. lib. bdg. 24.95 (*0-7933-0581-0*); pap. 14.95 (*0-7933-0580-2*); disk 29.95 (*0-7933-0582-9*) Gallopade Pub Group.

— Massachusetts Silly Basketball Sportsmysteries, Vol. II. (Carole Marsh Massachusetts Bks.). (Illus.). (J). (gr. 3-8). 1994. lib. bdg. 24.95 (*0-7933-1705-3*); pap. 14.95 (*0-7933-1706-1*); disk 29.95 (*0-7933-1707-X*) Gallopade Pub Group.

— Massachusetts Silly Football Sportsmysteries, Vol. I. (Carole Marsh Massachusetts Bks.). (Illus.). (J). (gr. 3-8). 1994. lib. bdg. 24.95 (*1-55609-687-9*); pap. 14.95 (*1-55609-688-7*); disk 29.95 (*1-55609-689-5*) Gallopade Pub Group.

— Massachusetts Silly Football Sportsmysteries, Vol. II. (Carole Marsh Massachusetts Bks.). (Illus.). (J). (gr. 3-8). 1994. lib. bdg. 24.95 (*1-55609-690-9*); pap. 14.95 (*1-55609-691-7*); disk 29.95 (*1-55609-692-5*) Gallopade Pub Group.

— Massachusetts Silly Trivia! (Carole Marsh Massachusetts Bks.). (Illus.). (J). (gr. 3-8). 1994. lib. bdg. 24.95 (*1-55609-680-1*); pap. 14.95 (*1-55609-110-9*); disk 29.95 (*1-55609-681-X*) Gallopade Pub Group.

— Massachusetts Timeline: A Chronology of Massachusetts History, Mystery, Trivia, Legend, Lore & More. (Massachuseets Bks.). (Illus.). (J). (gr. 3-12). 1994. lib. bdg. 24.95 (*0-7933-5938-4*); pap. 14.95 (*0-7933-5939-2*); disk 29.95 (*0-7933-5940-6*) Gallopade Pub Group.

— Massachusetts's Unsolved Mysteries (& Their "Solutions") Includes Scientific Information & Other Activities for Students. (Massachuseets Bks.). (Illus.). (J). (gr. 3-12). 1994. lib. bdg. 24.95 (*0-7933-5785-3*); pap. 14.95 (*0-7933-5786-1*); disk 29.95 (*0-7933-5787-X*) Gallopade Pub Group.

— Math for Boys: A Book with the Number or Getting Boys to Love & Excel in Math! (Quantum Leap Ser.). (Illus.). (J). (gr. 4-12). 1994. lib. bdg. 24.95 (*1-55609-806-5*); pap. 14.95 (*1-55609-830-8*); disk 29.95 (*1-55609-878-2*) Gallopade Pub Group.

— Math for Girls: The Book with the Number to Get Girls to Love & Excel in Math! (Quantum Leap Ser.). (Illus.). 60p. (J). (gr. 3-9). 1994. lib. bdg. 24.95 (*1-55609-343-8*); pap. 14.95 (*1-55609-344-6*); disk 29.95 (*1-55609-345-4*) Gallopade Pub Group.

— Meet in the Middle: The Parents Test - The Kids Test. (Quantum Leap Ser.). (Illus.). (J). (gr. 4 up). 1994. 24.95 (*0-935326-24-3*) Gallopade Pub Group.

— Meow! Alabama Cats in History, Mystery, Legend, Lore, Humor & More! (Carole Marsh Alabama Bks.). (Illus.). (J). (gr. 3-12). 1994. lib. bdg. 24.95 (*0-7933-3314-8*); pap. 14.95 (*0-7933-3315-6*); disk 29.95 (*0-7933-3316-4*) Gallopade Pub Group.

— Meow! Alaska Cats in History, Mystery, Legend, Lore, Humor & More! (Carole Marsh Alaska Bks.). (Illus.). (J). (gr. 3-12). 1994. lib. bdg. 24.95 (*0-7933-3317-2*); pap. 14.95 (*0-7933-3318-0*); disk 29.95 (*0-7933-3319-9*) Gallopade Pub Group.

— Meow! Arizona Cats in History, Mystery, Legend, Lore, Humor & More! (Carole Marsh Arizona Bks.). (Illus.). (J). (gr. 3-12). 1994. lib. bdg. 24.95 (*0-7933-3320-2*); pap. 14.95 (*0-7933-3321-0*); disk 29.95 (*0-7933-3322-9*) Gallopade Pub Group.

— Meow! Arkansas Cats in History, Mystery, Legend, Lore, Humor & More! (Carole Marsh Arkansas Bks.). (Illus.). (J). (gr. 3-12). 1994. lib. bdg. 24.95 (*0-7933-3323-7*); pap. 14.95 (*0-7933-3324-5*); disk 29.95 (*0-7933-3325-3*) Gallopade Pub Group.

— Meow! California Cats in History, Mystery, Legend, Lore, Humor & More! (Carole Marsh California Bks.). (Illus.). (J). (gr. 3-12). 1994. lib. bdg. 24.95 (*0-7933-3326-1*); pap. 14.95 (*0-7933-3327-X*); disk 29.95 (*0-7933-3328-8*) Gallopade Pub Group.

— Meow! Colorado Cats in History, Mystery, Legend, Lore, Humor & More! (Carole Marsh Colorado Bks.). (Illus.). (J). (gr. 3-12). 1994. lib. bdg. 24.95 (*0-7933-3329-6*); pap. 14.95 (*0-7933-3330-X*); disk 29.95 (*0-7933-3331-8*) Gallopade Pub Group.

— Meow! Connecticut Cats in History, Mystery, Legend, Lore, Humor & More! (Carole Marsh Connecticut Bks.). (Illus.). (J). (gr. 3-12). 1994. lib. bdg. 24.95 (*0-7933-3332-6*); pap. 14.95 (*0-7933-3333-4*); disk 29.95 (*0-7933-3334-2*) Gallopade Pub Group.

— Meow! Delaware Cats in History, Mystery, Legend, Lore, Humor & More! (Carole Marsh Delaware Bks.). (Illus.). (J). (gr. 3-12). 1994. lib. bdg. 24.95 (*0-7933-3335-0*); pap. 14.95 (*0-7933-3336-9*); disk 29.95 (*0-7933-3337-7*) Gallopade Pub Group.

— Meow! Florida Cats in History, Mystery, Legend, Lore, Humor & More! (Carole Marsh Florida Bks.). (Illus.). (J). (gr. 3-12). 1994. lib. bdg. 24.95 (*0-7933-3341-5*); pap. 14.95 (*0-7933-3342-3*); disk 29.95 (*0-7933-3343-1*) Gallopade Pub Group.

— Meow! Georgia Cats in History, Mystery, Legend, Lore, Humor & More! (Carole Marsh Georgia Bks.). (Illus.). (J). (gr. 3-12). 1994. lib. bdg. 24.95 (*0-7933-3344-X*); pap. 14.95 (*0-7933-3345-8*); disk 29.95 (*0-7933-3346-6*) Gallopade Pub Group.

— Meow! Hawaii Cats in History, Mystery, Legend, Lore, Humor & More! (Carole Marsh Hawaii Bks.). (Illus.). (J). (gr. 3-12). 1994. lib. bdg. 24.95 (*0-7933-3347-4*); pap. 14.95 (*0-7933-3348-2*); disk 29.95 (*0-7933-3349-0*) Gallopade Pub Group.

— Meow! Idaho Cats in History, Mystery, Legend, Lore, Humor & More! (Carole Marsh Idaho Bks.). (Illus.). (J). (gr. 3-12). 1994. lib. bdg. 24.95 (*0-7933-3350-4*); pap. 14.95 (*0-7933-3351-2*); disk 29.95 (*0-7933-3352-0*) Gallopade Pub Group.

— Meow! Illinois Cats in History, Mystery, Legend, Lore, Humor & More! (Carole Marsh Illinois Bks.). (Illus.). (J). (gr. 3-12). 1994. lib. bdg. 24.95 (*0-7933-3353-9*); pap. 14.95 (*0-7933-3354-7*); disk 29.95 (*0-7933-3355-5*) Gallopade Pub Group.

— Meow! Indiana Cats in History, Mystery, Legend, Lore, Humor & More! (Carole Marsh Indiana Bks.). (Illus.). (J). (gr. 3-12). 1994. lib. bdg. 24.95 (*0-7933-3356-3*); pap. 14.95 (*0-7933-3357-1*); disk 29.95 (*0-7933-3358-X*) Gallopade Pub Group.

— Meow! Iowa Cats in History, Mystery, Legend, Lore, Humor & More! (Carole Marsh Iowa Bks.). (Illus.). (J). (gr. 3-12). 1994. lib. bdg. 24.95 (*0-7933-3359-8*); pap. 14.95 (*0-7933-3360-1*); disk 29.95 (*0-7933-3361-X*) Gallopade Pub Group.

— Meow! Kansas Cats in History, Mystery, Legend, Lore, Humor & More! (Carole Marsh Kansas Bks.). (Illus.). (J). (gr. 3-12). 1994. lib. bdg. 24.95 (*0-7933-3362-8*); pap. 14.95 (*0-7933-3363-6*); disk 29.95 (*0-7933-3364-4*) Gallopade Pub Group.

— Meow! Kentucky Cats in History, Mystery, Legend, Lore, Humor & More! (Carole Marsh Kentucky Bks.). (Illus.). (J). (gr. 3-12). 1994. lib. bdg. 24.95 (*0-7933-3365-2*); pap. 14.95 (*0-7933-3366-0*); disk 29.95 (*0-7933-3367-9*) Gallopade Pub Group.

— Meow! Louisiana Cats in History, Mystery, Legend, Lore, Humor & More! (Carole Marsh Louisiana Bks.). (Illus.). (J). (gr. 3-12). 1994. lib. bdg. 24.95 (*0-7933-3368-7*); pap. 14.95 (*0-7933-3369-5*); disk 29.95 (*0-7933-3370-9*) Gallopade Pub Group.

— Meow! Maine Cats in History, Mystery, Legend, Lore, Humor & More! (Carole Marsh Maine Bks.). (Illus.). (J). (gr. 3-12). 1994. lib. bdg. 24.95 (*0-7933-3371-7*); pap. 14.95 (*0-7933-3372-5*); disk 29.95 (*0-7933-3373-3*) Gallopade Pub Group.

— Meow! Maryland Cats in History, Mystery, Legend, Lore, Humor & More! (Carole Marsh Maryland Bks.). (Illus.). (J). (gr. 3-12). 1994. lib. bdg. 24.95 (*0-7933-3374-1*); pap. 14.95 (*0-7933-3375-X*); disk 29.95 (*0-7933-3376-8*) Gallopade Pub Group.

— Meow! Massachusetts Cats in History, Mystery, Legend, Lore, Humor & More! (Massachuseets Bks.). (Illus.). (J). (gr. 3-12). 1994. lib. bdg. 24.95 (*0-7933-3377-6*); pap. 14.95 (*0-7933-3378-4*); disk 29.95 (*0-7933-3379-2*) Gallopade Pub Group.

— Meow! Michigan Cats in History, Mystery, Legend, Lore, Humor & More! (Carole Marsh Michigan Bks.). (Illus.). (J). (gr. 3-12). 1994. lib. bdg. 24.95 (*0-7933-3380-6*); pap. 14.95 (*0-7933-3381-4*); disk 29.95 (*0-7933-3382-2*) Gallopade Pub Group.

— Meow! Minnesota Cats in History, Mystery, Legend, Lore, Humor & More! (Carole Marsh Minnesota Bks.). (Illus.). (J). (gr. 3-12). 1994. lib. bdg. 24.95 (*0-7933-3383-0*); pap. 14.95 (*0-7933-3384-9*); disk 29.95 (*0-7933-3385-7*) Gallopade Pub Group.

— Meow! Mississippi Cats in History, Mystery, Legend, Lore, Humor & More! (Carole Marsh Mississippi Bks.). (Illus.). (J). (gr. 3-12). 1994. lib. bdg. 24.95 (*0-7933-3386-5*); pap. 14.95 (*0-7933-3387-3*); disk 29.95 (*0-7933-3388-1*) Gallopade Pub Group.

— Meow! Missouri Cats in History, Mystery, Legend, Lore, Humor & More! (Carole Marsh Missouri Bks.). (Illus.). (J). (gr. 3-12). 1994. lib. bdg. 24.95 (*0-7933-3389-X*); pap. 14.95 (*0-7933-3390-3*); disk 29.95 (*0-7933-3391-1*) Gallopade Pub Group.

— Meow! Montana Cats in History, Mystery, Legend, Lore, Humor & More! (Carole Marsh Montana Bks.). (Illus.). (J). (gr. 3-12). 1994. lib. bdg. 24.95 (*0-7933-3392-X*); pap. 14.95 (*0-7933-3393-8*); disk 29.95 (*0-7933-3394-6*) Gallopade Pub Group.

— Meow! Nebraska Cats in History, Mystery, Legend, Lore, Humor & More! (Carole Marsh Nebraska Bks.). (Illus.). (J). (gr. 3-12). 1994. lib. bdg. 24.95 (*0-7933-3395-4*); pap. 14.95 (*0-7933-3396-2*); disk 29.95 (*0-7933-3397-0*) Gallopade Pub Group.

— Meow! Nevada Cats in History, Mystery, Legend, Lore, Humor & More! (Carole Marsh Nevada Bks.). (Illus.). (J). (gr. 3-12). 1994. lib. bdg. 24.95 (*0-7933-3398-9*); pap. 14.95 (*0-7933-3399-7*); disk 29.95 (*0-685-41935-5*) Gallopade Pub Group.

— Meow! New Hampshire Cats in History, Mystery, Legend, Lore, Humor & More! (Carole Marsh New Hampshire Bks.). (Illus.). (J). (gr. 3-12). 1994. lib. bdg. 24.95 (*0-7933-3400-4*); pap. 14.95 (*0-7933-3401-2*); disk 29.95 (*0-7933-3402-0*) Gallopade Pub Group.

— Meow! New Jersey Cats in History, Mystery, Legend, Lore, Humor & More! (Carole Marsh New Jersey Bks.). (Illus.). (J). (gr. 3-12). 1994. lib. bdg. 24.95 (*0-7933-3404-7*); pap. 14.95 (*0-685-48034-8*); disk 29.95 (*0-7933-3406-3*) Gallopade Pub Group.

— Meow! New Mexico Cats in History, Mystery, Legend, Lore, Humor & More! (Carole Marsh New Mexico Bks.). (Illus.). (J). (gr. 3-12). 1994. lib. bdg. 24.95 (*0-7933-3407-1*); pap. 14.95 (*0-7933-3408-X*); disk 29.95 (*0-7933-3409-8*) Gallopade Pub Group.

— Meow! New York Cats in History, Mystery, Legend, Lore, Humor & More! (Carole Marsh New York Bks.). (Illus.). (J). (gr. 3-12). 1994. lib. bdg. 24.95 (*0-7933-3410-1*); pap. 14.95 (*0-7933-3411-X*); disk 29.95 (*0-7933-3412-8*) Gallopade Pub Group.

— Meow! North Carolina Cats in History, Mystery, Legend, Lore, Humor & More! (Carole Marsh North Carolina Bks.). (Illus.). (J). (gr. 3-12). 1994. lib. bdg. 24.95 (*0-7933-3413-6*); pap. 14.95 (*0-7933-3414-4*); disk 29.95 (*0-7933-3415-2*) Gallopade Pub Group.

— Meow! North Dakota Cats in History, Mystery, Legend, Lore, Humor & More! (Carole Marsh North Dakota Bks.). (Illus.). (J). (gr. 3-12). 1994. lib. bdg. 24.95 (*0-7933-3416-0*); pap. 14.95 (*0-7933-3417-9*); disk 29.95 (*0-7933-3418-7*) Gallopade Pub Group.

— Meow! Ohio Cats in History, Mystery, Legend, Lore, Humor & More! (Carole Marsh Ohio Bks.). (Illus.). (J). (gr. 3-12). 1994. lib. bdg. 24.95 (*0-7933-3419-5*); pap. 14.95 (*0-7933-3420-9*); disk 29.95 (*0-7933-3421-7*) Gallopade Pub Group.

— Meow! Oklahoma Cats in History, Mystery, Legend, Lore, Humor & More! (Carole Marsh Oklahoma Bks.). (Illus.). (J). (gr. 3-12). 1994. lib. bdg. 24.95 (*0-7933-3422-5*); pap. 14.95 (*0-7933-3423-3*); disk 29.95 (*0-7933-3424-1*) Gallopade Pub Group.

— Meow! Oregon Cats in History, Mystery, Legend, Lore, Humor & More! (Oregon Bks.). (Illus.). (J). (gr. 3-12). 1994. lib. bdg. 24.95 (*0-7933-3425-X*); pap. 14.95 (*0-7933-3426-8*); disk 29.95 (*0-7933-3427-6*) Gallopade Pub Group.

— Meow! Pennsylvania Cats in History, Mystery, Legend, Lore, Humor & More! (Pennsylvania Bks.). (Illus.). (J). (gr. 3-12). 1994. lib. bdg. 24.95 (*0-7933-3428-4*); pap. 14.95 (*0-7933-3429-2*); disk 29.95 (*0-7933-3430-6*) Gallopade Pub Group.

— Meow! Rhode Island Cats in History, Mystery, Legend, Lore, Humor & More! (Rhode Island Bks.). (Illus.). (J). (gr. 3-12). 1994. lib. bdg. 24.95 (*0-7933-3431-4*); pap. 14.95 (*0-7933-3432-2*); disk 29.95 (*0-7933-3433-0*) Gallopade Pub Group.

M

— Meow! South Carolina Cats in History, Mystery, Legend, Lore, Humor & More! (South Carolina Bks.). (Illus.). (J). (gr. 3-12). 1994. lib. bdg. 24.95 (0-7933-3434-9); pap. 14.95 (0-7933-3435-7); disk 29.95 (0-7933-3436-5) Gallopade Pub Group.

— Meow! South Dakota Cats in History, Mystery, Legend, Lore, Humor & More! (South Dakota Bks.). (Illus.). (J). (gr. 3-12). 1994. lib. bdg. 24.95 (0-7933-3437-3); pap. 14.95 (0-7933-3438-1); disk 29.95 (0-7933-3439-X) Gallopade Pub Group.

— Meow! Tennessee Cats in History, Mystery, Legend, Lore, Humor & More! (Tennessee Bks.). (Illus.). (J). (gr. 3-12). 1994. lib. bdg. 24.95 (0-7933-3440-3); pap. 14.95 (0-7933-3441-1); disk 29.95 (0-7933-3442-X) Gallopade Pub Group.

— Meow! Texas Cats in History, Mystery, Legend, Lore, Humor & More! (Texas Bks.). (Illus.). (J). (gr. 3-12). 1994. lib. bdg. 24.95 (0-7933-3443-8); pap. 14.95 (0-7933-3444-6); disk 29.95 (0-7933-3445-4) Gallopade Pub Group.

— Meow! Utah Cats in History, Mystery, Legend, Lore, Humor & More! (Utah Bks.). (Illus.). (J). (gr. 3-12). 1994. lib. bdg. 24.95 (0-7933-3446-2); pap. 14.95 (0-7933-3447-0); disk 29.95 (0-7933-3448-9) Gallopade Pub Group.

— Meow! Vermont Cats in History, Mystery, Legend, Lore, Humor & More! (Vermont Bks.). (Illus.). (J). (gr. 3-12). 1994. lib. bdg. 24.95 (0-7933-3449-7); pap. 14.95 (0-7933-3450-0); disk 29.95 (0-7933-3451-9) Gallopade Pub Group.

— Meow! Virginia Cats in History, Mystery, Legend, Lore, Humor & More! (Virginia Bks.). (Illus.). (J). (gr. 3-12). 1994. lib. bdg. 24.95 (0-7933-3452-7); pap. 14.95 (0-7933-3453-5); disk 29.95 (0-7933-3454-3) Gallopade Pub Group.

— Meow! Washington Cats in History, Mystery, Legend, Lore, Humor & More! (Washington Bks.). (Illus.). (J). (gr. 3-12). 1994. lib. bdg. 24.95 (0-7933-3455-1); pap. 14.95 (0-7933-3456-X); disk 29.95 (0-7933-3457-8) Gallopade Pub Group.

— Meow! Washington DC Cats in History, Mystery, Legend, Lore, Humor & More! (Washington, D.C. Bks.). (Illus.). (J). (gr. 3-12). 1994. lib. bdg. 24.95 (0-7933-3338-5); pap. 14.95 (0-7933-3339-3); disk 29.95 (0-7933-3340-7) Gallopade Pub Group.

— Meow! West Virginia Cats in History, Mystery, Legend, Lore, Humor & More! (West Virginia Bks.). (Illus.). (J). (gr. 3-12). 1994. lib. bdg. 24.95 (0-7933-3458-6); pap. 14.95 (0-7933-3459-4); disk 29.95 (0-7933-3460-8) Gallopade Pub Group.

— Meow! Wisconsin Cats in History, Mystery, Legend, Lore, Humor & More! (Wisconsin Bks.). (Illus.). (J). (gr. 3-12). 1994. lib. bdg. 24.95 (0-7933-3461-6); pap. 14.95 (0-7933-3462-4); disk 29.95 (0-7933-3463-2) Gallopade Pub Group.

— Meow! Wyoming Cats in History, Mystery, Legend, Lore, Humor & More! (Wyoming Bks.). (Illus.). (J). (gr. 3-12). 1994. lib. bdg. 24.95 (0-7933-3464-0); pap. 14.95 (0-7933-3465-9); disk 29.95 (0-7933-3466-7) Gallopade Pub Group.

— Michigan & Other State Greats (Biographies) (Carole Marsh Michigan Bks.). (Illus.). (J). (gr. 3 up). 1994. lib. bdg. 24.95 (1-55609-677-1); pap. 14.95 (1-55609-678-X); disk 29.95 (1-55609-679-8) Gallopade Pub Group.

— Michigan Bandits, Bushwackers, Outlaws, Crooks, Devils, Ghosts, Desperadoes & Other Assorted & Sundry Characters! (Carole Marsh Michigan Bks.). (Illus.). (J). (gr. 3 up). 1994. lib. bdg. 24.95 (0-7933-0599-3); pap. 14.95 (0-7933-0598-5); disk 29.95 (0-7933-0600-0) Gallopade Pub Group.

— The Michigan Bookstore Book: A Surprising Guide to Our State's Bookstores & Their Specialties for Students, Teachers, Writers & Publishers. (Carole Marsh Michigan Bks.). (Illus.). 1994. lib. bdg. 24.95 (0-7933-2921-3); pap. 14.95 (0-7933-2922-1); disk 29.95 (0-7933-2923-X) Gallopade Pub Group.

— Michigan Classic Christmas Trivia: Stories, Recipes, Activities, Legends, Lore & More! (Carole Marsh Michigan Bks.). (Illus.). (J). (gr. 3 up). 1994. lib. bdg. 24.95 (0-685-45942-X); pap. 14.95 (0-7933-0601-9); disk 29.95 (0-7933-0603-5) Gallopade Pub Group.

— Michigan Coastales. (Carole Marsh Michigan Bks.). (Illus.). (J). (gr. 3 up). 1994. lib. bdg. 24.95 (1-55609-671-2); pap. 14.95 (1-55609-672-0); disk 29.95 (1-55609-673-9) Gallopade Pub Group.

— Michigan Coastales! (Carole Marsh Michigan Bks.). (J). 1994. lib. bdg. 24.95 (0-7933-7287-9) Gallopade Pub Group.

— Michigan "Crinkum-Crankum" A Funny Word Book about Our State. (Carole Marsh Michigan Bks.). (Illus.). (J). 1994. lib. bdg. 24.95 (0-7933-4874-9); pap. 14.95 (0-7933-4875-7); disk 29.95 (0-7933-4876-5) Gallopade Pub Group.

— Michigan Dingbats! Bk. 1: A Fun Book of Games, Stories, Activities & More about Our State That's All in Code! for You to Decipher. (Carole Marsh Michigan Bks.). (Illus.). (J). (gr. 3-12). 1994. lib. bdg. 24.95 (0-7933-3839-5); pap. 14.95 (0-7933-3840-9); disk 29.95 (0-7933-3841-7) Gallopade Pub Group.

— Michigan Festival Fun for Kids! (Carole Marsh Michigan Bks.). (Illus.). (YA). (gr. 3-12). 1994. lib. bdg. 24.95 (0-7933-3992-8); pap. 14.95 (0-7933-3993-6); disk 29.95 (0-7933-3994-4) Gallopade Pub Group.

— The Michigan Hot Air Balloon Mystery. (Carole Marsh Michigan Bks.). (Illus.). (J). (gr. 2-9). 1994. 24.95 (0-7933-2516-1); pap. 14.95 (0-7933-2517-X); disk 29.95 (0-7933-2518-8) Gallopade Pub Group.

— Michigan Jeopardy! Answers & Questions about Our State! (Carole Marsh Michigan Bks.). (Illus.). (J). (gr. 3-12). 1994. lib. bdg. 24.95 (0-7933-4145-0); pap. 14.95 (0-7933-4146-9); disk 29.95 (0-7933-4147-7) Gallopade Pub Group.

— Michigan "Jography" A Fun Run Thru Our State. (Carole Marsh Michigan Bks.). (Illus.). (J). (gr. 3 up). 1994. lib. bdg. 24.95 (1-55609-666-6); pap. 14.95 (1-55609-667-4); disk 29.95 (1-55609-668-2) Gallopade Pub Group.

— Michigan Kid's Cookbook: Recipes, How-To, History, Lore & More! (Carole Marsh Michigan Bks.). (Illus.). (J). (gr. 3 up). 1994. lib. bdg. 24.95 (0-7933-0611-6); pap. 14.95 (0-7933-0610-8); disk 29.95 (0-7933-0612-4) Gallopade Pub Group.

— The Michigan Library Book: A Surprising Guide to the Unusual Special Collections in Libraries Across Our State for Students, Teachers, Writers & Publishers - Includes Reproducible Mailing Labels Plus Activities for Young People! (Carole Marsh Michigan Bks.). (Illus.). 1994. lib. bdg. 24.95 (0-7933-3071-8); pap. 14.95 (0-7933-3072-6); disk 29.95 (0-7933-3073-4) Gallopade Pub Group.

— The Michigan Media Book: A Surprising Guide to the Amazing Print, Broadcast & Online Media of Our State for Students, Teachers, Writers & Publishers - Includes Reproducible Mailing Labels Plus Activities for Young People! (Carole Marsh Michigan Bks.). (Illus.). 1994. lib. bdg. 24.95 (0-7933-3227-3); pap. 14.95 (0-7933-3228-1); disk 29.95 (0-7933-3229-X) Gallopade Pub Group.

— The Michigan Mystery Van Takes Off! Book 1: Handicapped Michigan Kids Sneak Off on a Big Adventure. (Carole Marsh Michigan Bks.). (Illus.). (J). (gr. 3-12). 1994. 24.95 (0-7933-5027-1); pap. 14.95 (0-7933-5028-X); disk 29.95 (0-7933-5029-8) Gallopade Pub Group.

— Michigan Quiz Bowl Crash Course! (Carole Marsh Michigan Bks.). (Illus.). (J). (gr. 3 up). 1994. lib. bdg. 24.95 (1-55609-674-7); pap. 14.95 (1-55609-675-5); disk 29.95 (1-55609-676-3) Gallopade Pub Group.

— Michigan Rollercoasters! (Carole Marsh Michigan Bks.). (Illus.). (YA). (gr. 3-12). 1994. lib. bdg. 24.95 (0-7933-5290-8); pap. 14.95 (0-7933-5291-6); disk 29.95 (0-7933-5292-4) Gallopade Pub Group.

— Michigan School Trivia: An Amazing & Fascinating Look at Our State's Teachers, Schools & Students! (Carole Marsh Michigan Bks.). (Illus.). (J). (gr. 3 up). 1994. lib. bdg. 24.95 (0-7933-0608-6); pap. 14.95 (0-7933-0607-8); disk 29.95 (0-7933-0609-4) Gallopade Pub Group.

— Michigan Silly Basketball Sportsmysteries, Vol. I. (Carole Marsh Michigan Bks.). (Illus.). (J). (gr. 3 up). 1994. lib. bdg. 24.95 (0-7933-0605-1); pap. 14.95 (0-7933-0604-3); disk 29.95 (0-7933-0606-X) Gallopade Pub Group.

— Michigan Silly Basketball Sportsmysteries, Vol. II. (Carole Marsh Michigan Bks.). (Illus.). (J). (gr. 3 up). 1994. lib. bdg. 24.95 (0-7933-1711-8); pap. 14.95 (0-7933-1712-6); disk 29.95 (0-7933-1713-4) Gallopade Pub Group.

— Michigan Silly Football Sportsmysteries, Vol. I. (Carole Marsh Michigan Bks.). (Illus.). (J). (gr. 3 up). 1994. lib. bdg. 24.95 (1-55609-702-6); pap. 14.95 (1-55609-703-4); disk 29.95 (1-55609-704-2) Gallopade Pub Group.

— Michigan Silly Football Sportsmysteries, Vol. II. (Carole Marsh Michigan Bks.). (Illus.). (J). (gr. 3 up). 1994. lib. bdg. 24.95 (1-55609-705-0); pap. 14.95 (1-55609-706-9); disk 29.95 (1-55609-707-7) Gallopade Pub Group.

— Michigan Silly Trivia! (Carole Marsh Michigan Bks.). (Illus.). (J). (gr. 3 up). 1994. lib. bdg. 24.95 (1-55609-663-1); pap. 14.95 (1-55609-664-X); disk 29.95 (1-55609-665-8) Gallopade Pub Group.

— Michigan Timeline: A Chronology of Michigan History, Mystery, Trivia, Legend, Lore & More. (Carole Marsh Michigan Bks.). (Illus.). (J). (gr. 3-12). 1994. lib. bdg. 24.95 (0-7933-5941-4); pap. 14.95 (0-7933-5942-2); disk 29.95 (0-7933-5943-0) Gallopade Pub Group.

— Michigan's (Most Devastating!) Disasters & (Most Calamitous!) Catastrophies! (Carole Marsh Michigan Bks.). (Illus.). (J). (gr. 3 up). 1994. lib. bdg. 24.95 (0-7933-0596-9); pap. 14.95 (0-7933-0595-0); disk 29.95 (0-7933-0597-7) Gallopade Pub Group.

— Michigan's Unsolved Mysteries (& Their "Solutions") Includes Scientific Information & Other Activities for Students. (Carole Marsh Michigan Bks.). (Illus.). (J). (gr. 3-12). 1994. lib. bdg. 24.95 (0-7933-5788-8); pap. 14.95 (0-7933-5789-6); disk 29.95 (0-7933-5790-X) Gallopade Pub Group.

— Minnesota & Other State Greats (Biographies) (Carole Marsh Minnesota Bks.). (Illus.). (J). (gr. 3 up). 1994. lib. bdg. 24.95 (1-55609-660-7); pap. 14.95 (1-55609-661-5); disk 29.95 (1-55609-662-3) Gallopade Pub Group.

— Minnesota Bandits, Bushwackers, Outlaws, Crooks, Devils, Ghosts, Desperadoes & Other Assorted & Sundry Characters! (Carole Marsh Minnesota Bks.). (Illus.). (J). (gr. 3 up). 1994. lib. bdg. 24.95 (0-7933-0623-X); pap. 14.95 (0-7933-0622-1); disk 29.95 (0-7933-0624-8) Gallopade Pub Group.

— The Minnesota Bookstore Book: A Surprising Guide to Our State's Bookstores & Their Specialties for Students, Teachers, Writers & Publishers. (Carole Marsh Minnesota Bks.). (Illus.). 1994. lib. bdg. 24.95 (0-7933-2924-8); pap. 14.95 (0-7933-2925-6); disk 29.95 (0-7933-2926-4) Gallopade Pub Group.

— Minnesota Classic Christmas Trivia: Stories, Recipes, Activities, Legends, Lore & More! (Carole Marsh Minnesota Bks.). (Illus.). (J). (gr. 3 up). 1994. lib. bdg. 24.95 (0-7933-0626-4); pap. 14.95 (0-7933-0625-6); disk 29.95 (0-7933-0627-2) Gallopade Pub Group.

— Minnesota Coastales. (Carole Marsh Minnesota Bks.). (Illus.). (J). (gr. 3 up). 1994. lib. bdg. 24.95 (1-55609-654-2); pap. 14.95 (1-55609-655-0); disk 29.95 (1-55609-656-9) Gallopade Pub Group.

— Minnesota Coastales! (Carole Marsh Minnesota Bks.). (J). 1994. lib. bdg. 24.95 (0-7933-7288-7) Gallopade Pub Group.

— Minnesota "Crinkum-Crankum" A Funny Word Book about Our State. (Carole Marsh Minnesota Bks.). (Illus.). (J). 1994. lib. bdg. 24.95 (0-7933-4877-3); pap. 14.95 (0-7933-4878-1); disk 29.95 (0-7933-4879-X) Gallopade Pub Group.

— Minnesota Dingbats! Bk. 1: A Fun Book of Games, Stories, Activities & More about Our State That's All in Code! for You to Decipher. (Carole Marsh Minnesota Bks.). (Illus.). (J). (gr. 3-12). 1994. lib. bdg. 24.95 (0-7933-3842-5); pap. 14.95 (0-7933-3843-3); disk 29.95 (0-7933-3844-1) Gallopade Pub Group.

— Minnesota Festival Fun for Kids! (Carole Marsh Minnesota Bks.). (Illus.). (YA). (gr. 3-12). 1994. lib. bdg. 24.95 (0-7933-3995-2); pap. 14.95 (0-7933-3996-0); disk 29.95 (0-7933-3997-9) Gallopade Pub Group.

— The Minnesota Hot Air Balloon Mystery. (Carole Marsh Minnesota Bks.). (Illus.). (J). (gr. 2-9). 1994. 24.95 (0-7933-2525-0); pap. 14.95 (0-7933-2526-9); disk 29.95 (0-7933-2527-7) Gallopade Pub Group.

— Minnesota Jeopardy! Answers & Questions about Our State! (Carole Marsh Minnesota Bks.). (Illus.). (J). (gr. 3-12). 1994. lib. bdg. 24.95 (0-7933-4148-5); pap. 14.95 (0-7933-4149-3); disk 29.95 (0-7933-4150-7) Gallopade Pub Group.

— Minnesota "Jography" A Fun Run Thru Our State. (Carole Marsh Minnesota Bks.). (Illus.). (J). (gr. 3 up). 1994. lib. bdg. 24.95 (1-55609-642-9); pap. 14.95 (1-55609-643-7); disk 29.95 (1-55609-644-5) Gallopade Pub Group.

— Minnesota Kid's Cookbook: Recipes, How-To, History, Lore & More. (Carole Marsh Minnesota Bks.). (Illus.). (J). (gr. 3 up). 1994. lib. bdg. 24.95 (0-7933-0635-3); pap. 14.95 (0-7933-0634-5); disk 29.95 (0-7933-0636-1) Gallopade Pub Group.

— The Minnesota Library Book: A Surprising Guide to the Unusual Special Collections in Libraries Across Our State for Students, Teachers, Writers & Publishers - Includes Reproducible Mailing Labels Plus Activities for Young People! (Carole Marsh Minnesota Bks.). (Illus.). 1994. lib. bdg. 24.95 (0-7933-3074-2); pap. 14.95 (0-7933-3075-0); disk 29.95 (0-7933-3076-9) Gallopade Pub Group.

— The Minnesota Media Book: A Surprising Guide to the Amazing Print, Broadcast & Online Media of Our State for Students, Teachers, Writers & Publishers - Includes Reproducible Mailing Labels Plus Activities for Young People! (Carole Marsh Minnesota Bks.). (Illus.). 1994. lib. bdg. 24.95 (0-7933-3230-3); pap. 14.95 (0-7933-3231-1); disk 29.95 (0-7933-3232-X) Gallopade Pub Group.

— The Minnesota Mystery Van Takes Off! Book 1: Handicapped Minnesota Kids Sneak Off on a Big Adventure. (Carole Marsh Minnesota Bks.). (Illus.). (J). (gr. 3-12). 1994. 24.95 (0-7933-5030-1); pap. 14.95 (0-7933-5031-X); disk 29.95 (0-7933-5032-8) Gallopade Pub Group.

— Minnesota Quiz Bowl Crash Course! (Carole Marsh Minnesota Bks.). (Illus.). (J). (gr. 3 up). 1994. lib. bdg. 24.95 (1-55609-657-7); pap. 14.95 (1-55609-658-5); disk 29.95 (1-55609-659-3) Gallopade Pub Group.

— Minnesota Rollercoasters! (Carole Marsh Minnesota Bks.). (Illus.). (YA). (gr. 3-12). 1994. lib. bdg. 24.95 (0-7933-5293-2); pap. 14.95 (0-7933-5294-0); disk 29.95 (0-7933-5295-9) Gallopade Pub Group.

— Minnesota School Trivia: An Amazing & Fascinating Look at Our State's Teachers, Schools & Students! (Carole Marsh Minnesota Bks.). (Illus.). (J). (gr. 3 up). 1994. lib. bdg. 24.95 (0-7933-0632-9); pap. 14.95 (0-7933-0631-0); disk 29.95 (0-7933-0633-7) Gallopade Pub Group.

— Minnesota Silly Basketball Sportsmysteries, Vol. I. (Carole Marsh Minnesota Bks.). (Illus.). (J). (gr. 3 up). 1994. lib. bdg. 24.95 (0-7933-0629-9); pap. 14.95 (0-7933-0628-0); disk 29.95 (0-7933-0630-2) Gallopade Pub Group.

— Minnesota Silly Basketball Sportsmysteries, Vol. II. (Carole Marsh Minnesota Bks.). (Illus.). (J). (gr. 3 up). 1994. lib. bdg. 24.95 (0-7933-1720-7); pap. 14.95 (0-7933-1721-5); disk 29.95 (0-7933-1722-3) Gallopade Pub Group.

— Minnesota Silly Football Sportsmysteries, Vol. I. (Carole Marsh Minnesota Bks.). (Illus.). (J). (gr. 3 up). 1994. lib. bdg. 24.95 (1-55609-648-8); pap. 14.95 (1-55609-649-6); disk 29.95 (1-55609-650-X) Gallopade Pub Group.

— Minnesota Silly Football Sportsmysteries, Vol. II. (Carole Marsh Minnesota Bks.). (Illus.). (J). (gr. 3 up). 1994. lib. bdg. 24.95 (1-55609-651-8); pap. 14.95 (1-55609-652-6); disk 29.95 (1-55609-653-4) Gallopade Pub Group.

— Minnesota Silly Trivia! (Carole Marsh Minnesota Bks.). (Illus.). (J). (gr. 3 up). 1994. lib. bdg. 24.95 (1-55609-639-9); pap. 14.95 (1-55609-640-2); disk 29.95 (1-55609-641-0) Gallopade Pub Group.

— Minnesota Timeline: A Chronology of Minnesota History, Mystery, Trivia, Legend, Lore & More. (Carole Marsh Minnesota Bks.). (Illus.). (J). (gr. 3-12). 1994. lib. bdg. 24.95 (0-7933-5944-9); pap. 14.95 (0-7933-5945-7); disk 29.95 (0-7933-5946-5) Gallopade Pub Group.

— Minnesota's (Most Devastating!) Disasters & (Most Calamitous!) Catastrophies! (Carole Marsh Minnesota Bks.). (Illus.). (J). (gr. 3 up). 1994. lib. bdg. 24.95 (0-7933-0620-5); pap. 14.95 (0-7933-0619-1); disk 29.95 (0-7933-0621-3) Gallopade Pub Group.

— Minnesota's Unsolved Mysteries (& Their "Solutions") Includes Scientific Information & Other Activities for Students. (Carole Marsh Minnesota Bks.). (Illus.). (J). (gr. 3-12). 1994. lib. bdg. 24.95 (0-7933-5791-8); pap. 14.95 (0-7933-5792-6); disk 29.95 (0-7933-5793-4) Gallopade Pub Group.

— The Missing Head Mystery. LC 79-55447. (History Mystery Ser.). (Illus.). (Orig.). (J). (gr. 3-9). 1994. 24.95 (1-55609-179-6); pap. 14.95 (0-935326-01-4) Gallopade Pub Group.

— The Missing Head Mystery Classroom Gamebook. (Carole Marsh Bks.). (Illus.). (Orig.). (J). (gr. 3-6). 1994. pap. 19.95 (0-935326-84-7) Gallopade Pub Group.

— The Missing Head Mystery Set. (Carole Marsh Mysteries Ser.). 1994. 125.00 (0-7933-6944-4) Gallopade Pub Group.

— Mississippi & Other State Greats (Biographies) (Carole Marsh Mississippi Bks.). (Illus.). (J). (gr. 3 up). 1994. lib. bdg. 24.95 (1-55609-725-5); pap. 14.95 (1-55609-726-3); disk 29.95 (1-55609-727-1) Gallopade Pub Group.

— Mississippi Bandits, Bushwackers, Outlaws, Crooks, Devils, Ghosts, Desperadoes & Other Assorted & Sundry Characters! (Carole Marsh Mississippi Bks.). (Illus.). (J). (gr. 3 up). 1994. lib. bdg. 24.95 (0-7933-0648-5); pap. 14.95 (0-7933-0647-7); disk 29.95 (0-7933-0649-3) Gallopade Pub Group.

— The Mississippi Bookstore Book: A Surprising Guide to Our State's Bookstores & Their Specialties for Students, Teachers, Writers & Publishers. (Carole Marsh Mississippi Bks.). (Illus.). 1994. lib. bdg. 24.95 (0-7933-2927-2); pap. 14.95 (0-7933-2928-0); disk 29.95 (0-7933-2929-9) Gallopade Pub Group.

— Mississippi Classic Christmas Trivia: Stories, Recipes, Activities, Legends, Lore & More. (Carole Marsh Mississippi Bks.). (Illus.). (J). (gr. 3 up). 1994. lib. bdg. 24.95 (0-7933-0651-5); pap. 14.95 (0-7933-0650-7); disk 29.95 (0-7933-0652-3) Gallopade Pub Group.

— Mississippi Coastales. (Carole Marsh Mississippi Bks.). (Illus.). (J). (gr. 3 up). 1994. lib. bdg. 24.95 (1-55609-720-4); pap. 14.95 (1-55609-122-2); disk 29.95 (1-55609-721-2) Gallopade Pub Group.

— Mississippi Coastales! (Carole Marsh Mississippi Bks.). (J). 1994. lib. bdg. 24.95 (0-7933-7289-5) Gallopade Pub Group.

— Mississippi "Crinkum-Crankum" A Funny Word Book about Our State. (Carole Marsh Mississippi Bks.). (Illus.). (J). 1994. lib. bdg. 24.95 (0-7933-4880-3); pap. 14.95 (0-7933-4881-1); disk 29.95 (0-7933-4882-X) Gallopade Pub Group.

— Mississippi Dingbats! Bk. 1: A Fun Book of Games, Stories, Activities & More about Our State That's All in Code! for You to Decipher. (Carole Marsh Mississippi Bks.). (Illus.). (J). (gr. 3-12). 1994. lib. bdg. 24.95 (0-7933-3845-X); pap. 14.95 (0-7933-3846-8); disk 29.95 (0-7933-3847-6) Gallopade Pub Group.

— Mississippi Festival Fun for Kids! (Carole Marsh Mississippi Bks.). (Illus.). (YA). (gr. 3-12). 1994. lib. bdg. 24.95 (0-7933-3998-7); pap. 14.95 (0-7933-3999-5); disk 29.95 (0-7933-4000-4) Gallopade Pub Group.

— The Mississippi Hot Air Balloon Mystery. (Carole Marsh Mississippi Bks.). (Illus.). (J). (gr. 2-9). 1994. 24.95 (0-7933-2534-X); pap. 14.95 (0-7933-2535-8); disk 29.95 (0-7933-2536-6) Gallopade Pub Group.

— Mississippi Jeopardy! Answers & Questions about Our State! (Carole Marsh Mississippi Bks.). (Illus.). (J). (gr. 3-12). 1994. lib. bdg. 24.95 (0-7933-4151-5); pap. 14.95 (0-7933-4152-3); disk 29.95 (0-7933-4153-1) Gallopade Pub Group.

— Mississippi "Jography" A Fun Run Thru Our State. (Carole Marsh Mississippi Bks.). (Illus.). (J). (gr. 3 up). 1994. lib. bdg. 24.95 (1-55609-709-3); pap. 14.95 (1-55609-091-9); disk 29.95 (1-55609-715-8) Gallopade Pub Group.

— Mississippi Kid's Cookbook: Recipes, How-To, History, Lore & More. (Carole Marsh Mississippi Bks.). (Illus.). (J). (gr. 3 up). 1994. lib. bdg. 24.95 (0-7933-0660-4); pap. 14.95 (0-7933-0659-0); disk 29.95 (0-7933-0661-2) Gallopade Pub Group.

— The Mississippi Library Book: A Surprising Guide to the Unusual Special Collections in Libraries Across Our State for Students, Teachers, Writers & Publishers - Includes Reproducible Mailing Labels Plus Activities for Young People! (Carole Marsh Mississippi Bks.). (Illus.). 1994. lib. bdg. 24.95 (0-7933-3077-7); pap. 14.95 (0-7933-3078-5); disk 29.95 (0-7933-3079-3) Gallopade Pub Group.

— The Mississippi Media Book: A Surprising Guide to the Amazing Print, Broadcast & Online Media of Our State for Students, Teachers, Writers & Publishers - Includes Reproducible Mailing Labels Plus Activities for Young People! (Carole Marsh Mississippi Bks.). (Illus.). 1994. lib. bdg. 24.95 (0-7933-3233-8); pap. 14.95 (0-7933-3234-6); disk 29.95 (0-7933-3235-4) Gallopade Pub Group.

— The Mississippi Mystery Van Takes Off! Book 1: Handicapped Mississippi Kids Sneak Off on a Big Adventure. (Carole Marsh Mississippi Bks.). (Illus.). (J). (gr. 3-12). 1994. 24.95 (0-7933-5033-6); pap. 14.95 (0-7933-5034-4); disk 29.95 (0-7933-5035-2) Gallopade Pub Group.

— Mississippi Quiz Bowl Crash Course! (Carole Marsh Mississippi Bks.). (Illus.). (J). (gr. 3 up). 1994. lib. bdg. 24.95 (1-55609-722-0); pap. 14.95 (1-55609-723-9); disk 29.95 (1-55609-724-7) Gallopade Pub Group.

— Mississippi Rollercoasters! (Carole Marsh Mississippi Bks.). (Illus.). (YA). (gr. 3-12). 1994. lib. bdg. 24.95 (0-7933-5296-7); pap. 14.95 (0-7933-5297-5); disk 29.95 (0-7933-5298-3) Gallopade Pub Group.

— Mississippi School Trivia: An Amazing & Fascinating Look at Our State's Teachers, Schools & Students! (Carole Marsh Mississippi Bks.). (Illus.). (J). (gr. 3 up). 1994. lib. bdg. 24.95 (0-7933-0657-4); pap. 14.95 (0-7933-0656-6); disk 29.95 (0-7933-0658-2) Gallopade Pub Group.

An Asterisk (*) at the beginning of an entry indicates that the title is appearing in BIP for the first time.

— Mississippi Silly Basketball Sports Mysteries, Vol. II. (Carole Marsh Mississippi Bks.). (Illus.). (J). (gr. 3 up). 1994. lib. bdg. 24.95 (*0-7933-1731-2*); pap. 14.95 (*0-7933-1732-0*); disk 29.95 (*0-685-45944-6*) Gallopade Pub Group.

— Mississippi Silly Basketball Sportsmysteries, Vol. I. (Carole Marsh Mississippi Bks.). (Illus.). (J). (gr. 3 up). 1994. lib. bdg. 24.95 (*0-7933-0654-X*); pap. 14.95 (*0-7933-0653-1*); disk 29.95 (*0-7933-0655-8*) Gallopade Pub Group.

— Mississippi Silly Football Sportsmysteries, Vol. I. (Carole Marsh Mississippi Bks.). (Illus.). (J). (gr. 3 up). 1994. lib. bdg. 24.95 (*1-55609-711-5*); pap. 14.95 (*1-55609-712-3*); disk 29.95 (*1-55609-713-1*) Gallopade Pub Group.

— Mississippi Silly Football Sportsmysteries, Vol. II. (Carole Marsh Mississippi Bks.). (Illus.). (J). (gr. 3 up). 1994. lib. bdg. 24.95 (*1-55609-717-4*); pap. 14.95 (*1-55609-718-2*); disk 29.95 (*1-55609-719-0*) Gallopade Pub Group.

— Mississippi Silly Trivia! (Carole Marsh Mississippi Bks.). (Illus.). (J). (gr. 3 up). 1994. lib. bdg. 24.95 (*1-55609-708-5*); pap. 14.95 (*1-55609-039-0*); disk 29.95 (*1-55609-714-X*) Gallopade Pub Group.

— Mississippi Timeline: A Chronology of Mississippi History, Mystery, Trivia, Legend, Lore & More. (Carole Marsh Mississippi Bks.). (Illus.). (J). (gr. 3-12). 1994. lib. bdg. 24.95 (*0-7933-5947-3*); pap. 14.95 (*0-7933-5948-1*); disk 29.95 (*0-7933-5949-X*) Gallopade Pub Group.

— Mississippi's (Most Devastating!) Disasters & (Most Calamitous!) Catastrophies! (Carole Marsh Mississippi Bks.). (Illus.). (J). (gr. 3 up). 1994. lib. bdg. 24.95 (*0-7933-0645-0*); pap. 14.95 (*0-7933-0643-4*); disk 29.95 (*0-7933-0646-9*) Gallopade Pub Group.

— Mississippi's Unsolved Mysteries (& Their "Solutions") Includes Scientific Information & Other Activities for Students. (Carole Marsh Mississippi Bks.). (Illus.). (J). (gr. 3-12). 1994. lib. bdg. 24.95 (*0-7933-5794-2*); pap. 14.95 (*0-7933-5795-0*); disk 29.95 (*0-7933-5796-9*) Gallopade Pub Group.

— Missouri & Other State Greats (Biographies) (Carole Marsh Missouri Bks.). (Illus.). (J). (gr. 3 up). 1994. lib. bdg. 24.95 (*1-55609-748-4*); pap. 14.95 (*1-55609-749-2*); disk 29.95 (*1-55609-750-6*) Gallopade Pub Group.

— Missouri Bandits, Bushwackers, Outlaws, Crooks, Devils, Ghosts, Desperadoes & Other Assorted & Sundry Characters! (Carole Marsh Missouri Bks.). (Illus.). (J). (gr. 3 up). 1994. lib. bdg. 24.95 (*0-7933-0672-8*); pap. 14.95 (*0-7933-0671-X*); disk 29.95 (*0-7933-0673-6*) Gallopade Pub Group.

— The Missouri Bookstore Book: A Surprising Guide to Our State's Bookstores & Their Specialties for Students, Teachers, Writers & Publishers. (Carole Marsh Missouri Bks.). (Illus.). 1994. lib. bdg. 24.95 (*0-7933-2930-2*); pap. 14.95 (*0-7933-2931-0*); disk 29.95 (*0-7933-2932-9*) Gallopade Pub Group.

— Missouri Classic Christmas Trivia: Stories, Recipes, Activities, Legends, Lore & More. (Carole Marsh Missouri Bks.). (Illus.). (J). (gr. 3 up). 1994. lib. bdg. 24.95 (*0-7933-0675-2*); pap. 14.95 (*0-7933-0674-4*); disk 29.95 (*0-7933-0676-0*) Gallopade Pub Group.

— Missouri Coastales. (Carole Marsh Missouri Bks.). (Illus.). (J). (gr. 3 up). 1994. lib. bdg. 24.95 (*1-55609-742-5*); pap. 14.95 (*1-55609-743-3*); disk 29.95 (*1-55609-744-1*) Gallopade Pub Group.

— Missouri Coastales! (Carole Marsh Missouri Bks.). (J). 1994. lib. bdg. 24.95 (*0-7933-7290-9*) Gallopade Pub Group.

— Missouri "Crinkum-Crankum" A Funny Word Book about Our State. (Carole Marsh Missouri Bks.). (Illus.). (J). 1994. lib. bdg. 24.95 (*0-7933-4883-8*); pap. 14.95 (*0-7933-4884-6*); disk 29.95 (*0-7933-4885-4*) Gallopade Pub Group.

— Missouri Dingbats! Bk. 1: A Fun Book of Games, Stories, Activities & More about Our State That's All in Code! for You to Decipher. (Carole Marsh Missouri Bks.). (Illus.). (J). (gr. 3-12). 1994. lib. bdg. 24.95 (*0-7933-3848-4*); pap. 14.95 (*0-7933-3849-2*); disk 29.95 (*0-7933-3850-6*) Gallopade Pub Group.

— Missouri Festival Fun for Kids! (Carole Marsh Missouri Bks.). (Illus.). (YA). (gr. 3-12). 1994. lib. bdg. 24.95 (*0-7933-4001-2*); pap. 14.95 (*0-7933-4002-0*); disk 29.95 (*0-7933-4003-9*) Gallopade Pub Group.

— The Missouri Hot Air Balloon Mystery. (Carole Marsh Missouri Bks.). (Illus.). (J). (gr. 2-9). 1994. 24.95 (*0-7933-2543-9*); pap. 14.95 (*0-7933-2544-7*); disk 29.95 (*0-7933-2545-5*) Gallopade Pub Group.

— Missouri Jeopardy! Answers & Questions about Our State! (Carole Marsh Missouri Bks.). (Illus.). (J). (gr. 3-12). 1994. lib. bdg. 24.95 (*0-7933-4154-X*); pap. 14.95 (*0-7933-4155-8*); disk 29.95 (*0-7933-4156-6*) Gallopade Pub Group.

— Missouri "Jography" A Fun Run Thru Our State. (Carole Marsh Missouri Bks.). (Illus.). (J). (gr. 3 up). 1994. lib. bdg. 24.95 (*1-55609-730-1*); pap. 14.95 (*1-55609-731-X*); disk 29.95 (*1-55609-732-8*) Gallopade Pub Group.

— Missouri Kid's Cookbook: Recipes, How-To, History, Lore & More. (Carole Marsh Missouri Bks.). (Illus.). (J). (gr. 3 up). 1994. lib. bdg. 24.95 (*0-7933-0684-1*); pap. 14.95 (*0-7933-0683-3*); disk 29.95 (*0-7933-0685-X*) Gallopade Pub Group.

— The Missouri Library Book: A Surprising Guide to the Unusual Special Collections in Libraries Across Our State for Students, Teachers, Writers & Publishers - Includes Reproducible Mailing Labels Plus Activities for Young People! (Carole Marsh Missouri Bks.). (Illus.). 1994. lib. bdg. 24.95 (*0-7933-3080-7*); pap. 14.95 (*0-7933-3081-5*); disk 29.95 (*0-7933-3082-3*) Gallopade Pub Group.

— The Missouri Media Book: A Surprising Guide to the Amazing Print, Broadcast & Online Media of Our State for Students, Teachers, Writers & Publishers - Includes Reproducible Mailing Labels Plus Activities for Young People! (Carole Marsh Missouri Bks.). (Illus.). 1994. lib. bdg. 24.95 (*0-7933-3236-2*); pap. 14.95 (*0-7933-3237-0*); disk 29.95 (*0-7933-3238-9*) Gallopade Pub Group.

— The Missouri Mystery Van Takes Off! Book 1: Handicapped Missouri Kids Sneak Off on a Big Adventure. (Carole Marsh Missouri Bks.). (Illus.). (J). (gr. 3-12). 1994. 24.95 (*0-7933-5036-0*); pap. 14.95 (*0-7933-5037-9*); disk 29.95 (*0-7933-5038-7*) Gallopade Pub Group.

— Missouri Quiz Bowl Crash Course! (Carole Marsh Missouri Bks.). (Illus.). (J). (gr. 3 up). 1994. lib. bdg. 24.95 (*1-55609-745-X*); pap. 14.95 (*1-55609-746-8*); disk 29.95 (*1-55609-747-6*) Gallopade Pub Group.

— Missouri Rollercoasters! (Carole Marsh Missouri Bks.). (Illus.). (YA). (gr. 3-12). 1994. lib. bdg. 24.95 (*0-7933-5299-1*); pap. 14.95 (*0-7933-5300-9*); disk 29.95 (*0-7933-5301-7*) Gallopade Pub Group.

— Missouri School Trivia: An Amazing & Fascinating Look at Our State's Teachers, Schools & Students! (Carole Marsh Missouri Bks.). (Illus.). (J). (gr. 3 up). 1994. lib. bdg. 24.95 (*0-7933-0681-7*); pap. 14.95 (*0-7933-0680-9*); disk 29.95 (*0-7933-0682-5*) Gallopade Pub Group.

— Missouri Silly Basketball Sportsmysteries, Vol. I. (Carole Marsh Missouri Bks.). (Illus.). (J). (gr. 3 up). 1994. lib. bdg. 24.95 (*0-7933-0678-7*); pap. 14.95 (*0-7933-0677-9*); disk 29.95 (*0-685-45947-0*) Gallopade Pub Group.

— Missouri Silly Basketball Sportsmysteries, Vol. II. (Carole Marsh Missouri Bks.). (Illus.). (J). (gr. 3 up). 1994. lib. bdg. 24.95 (*0-7933-1740-1*); pap. 14.95 (*0-7933-1741-X*); disk 29.95 (*0-7933-1742-8*) Gallopade Pub Group.

— Missouri Silly Football Sportsmysteries, Vol. I. (Carole Marsh Missouri Bks.). (Illus.). (J). (gr. 3 up). 1994. lib. bdg. 24.95 (*1-55609-736-0*); pap. 14.95 (*1-55609-737-9*); disk 29.95 (*0-685-45945-4*) Gallopade Pub Group.

— Missouri Silly Football Sportsmysteries, Vol. II. (Carole Marsh Missouri Bks.). (Illus.). (J). (gr. 3 up). 1994. lib. bdg. 24.95 (*1-55609-739-5*); pap. 14.95 (*1-55609-740-9*); disk 29.95 (*1-55609-741-7*) Gallopade Pub Group.

— Missouri Silly Trivia! (Carole Marsh Missouri Bks.). (Illus.). (J). (gr. 3 up). 1994. lib. bdg. 24.95 (*1-55609-728-X*); pap. 14.95 (*1-55609-100-1*); disk 29.95 (*1-55609-729-8*) Gallopade Pub Group.

— Missouri Timeline: A Chronology of Missouri History, Mystery, Trivia, Legend, Lore & More. (Carole Marsh Missouri Bks.). (Illus.). (J). (gr. 3-12). 1994. lib. bdg. 24.95 (*0-7933-5950-3*); pap. 14.95 (*0-7933-5951-1*); disk 29.95 (*0-7933-5952-X*) Gallopade Pub Group.

— Missouri's (Most Devastating!) Disasters & (Most Calamitous!) Catastrophies! (Carole Marsh Missouri Bks.). (Illus.). (J). (gr. 3 up). 1994. lib. bdg. 24.95 (*0-7933-0669-8*); pap. 14.95 (*0-7933-0668-X*); disk 29.95 (*0-7933-0670-1*) Gallopade Pub Group.

— Missouri's Unsolved Mysteries (& Their "Solutions") Includes Scientific Information & Other Activities for Students. (Carole Marsh Missouri Bks.). (Illus.). (J). (gr. 3-12). 1994. lib. bdg. 24.95 (*0-7933-5797-7*); pap. 14.95 (*0-7933-5798-5*); disk 29.95 (*0-7933-5799-3*) Gallopade Pub Group.

— The Monsters, Vampires & Werewolves Dingbats Book. (Carole Marsh Dingbats Book Ser.). (Illus.). (YA). (gr. 3-12). 1994. lib. bdg. 24.95 (*0-7933-5392-0*); pap. 14.95 (*0-7933-5393-9*); disk 29.95 (*0-7933-5394-7*) Gallopade Pub Group.

— Montana & Other State Greats (Biographies) (Carole Marsh Montana Bks.). (Illus.). (J). (gr. 3 up). 1994. lib. bdg. 24.95 (*1-55609-772-7*); pap. 14.95 (*1-55609-773-5*); disk 29.95 (*1-55609-774-3*) Gallopade Pub Group.

— Montana Bandits, Bushwackers, Outlaws, Crooks, Devils, Ghosts, Desperadoes & Other Assorted & Sundry Characters! (Carole Marsh Montana Bks.). (Illus.). (J). (gr. 3 up). 1994. lib. bdg. 24.95 (*0-7933-0697-3*); pap. 14.95 (*0-7933-0696-5*); disk 29.95 (*0-7933-0698-1*) Gallopade Pub Group.

— The Montana Bookstore Book: A Surprising Guide to Our State's Bookstores & Their Specialties for Students, Teachers, Writers & Publishers. (Carole Marsh Montana Bks.). (Illus.). 1994. lib. bdg. 24.95 (*0-7933-2933-7*); pap. 14.95 (*0-7933-2934-5*); disk 29.95 (*0-7933-2935-3*) Gallopade Pub Group.

— Montana Classic Christmas Trivia. (Carole Marsh Montana Bks.). (J). (gr. 3 up). 1994. lib. bdg. 24.95 (*0-7933-0700-7*); pap. 14.95 (*0-7933-0699-X*); disk 29.95 (*0-7933-0701-5*) Gallopade Pub Group.

— Montana Coastales. (Carole Marsh Montana Bks.). (Illus.). (J). (gr. 3 up). 1994. lib. bdg. 24.95 (*1-55609-766-2*); pap. 14.95 (*1-55609-767-0*); disk 29.95 (*1-55609-768-9*) Gallopade Pub Group.

— Montana Coastales! (Carole Marsh Montana Bks.). (J). 1994. lib. bdg. 24.95 (*0-7933-7291-7*) Gallopade Pub Group.

— Montana "Crinkum-Crankum" A Funny Word Book about Our State. (Carole Marsh Montana Bks.). (Illus.). (J). 1994. lib. bdg. 24.95 (*0-7933-4886-2*); pap. 14.95 (*0-7933-4887-0*); disk 29.95 (*0-7933-4888-9*) Gallopade Pub Group.

— Montana Dingbats! Bk. 1: A Fun Book of Games, Stories, Activities & More about Our State That's All in Code! for You to Decipher. (Carole Marsh Montana Bks.). (Illus.). (J). (gr. 3-12). 1994. lib. bdg. 24.95 (*0-7933-3851-4*); pap. 14.95 (*0-7933-3852-2*); disk 29.95 (*0-7933-3853-0*) Gallopade Pub Group.

— Montana Festival Fun for Kids! (Carole Marsh Montana Bks.). (Illus.). (YA). (gr. 3-12). 1994. lib. bdg. 24.95 (*0-7933-4004-7*); pap. 14.95 (*0-7933-4005-5*); disk 29.95 (*0-7933-4006-3*) Gallopade Pub Group.

— The Montana Hot Air Balloon Mystery. (Carole Marsh Montana Bks.). (Illus.). (J). (gr. 2-9). 1994. 24.95 (*0-7933-2552-8*); pap. 14.95 (*0-7933-2553-6*); disk 29.95 (*0-7933-2554-4*) Gallopade Pub Group.

— Montana Jeopardy! Answers & Questions about Our State! (Carole Marsh Montana Bks.). (Illus.). (J). (gr. 3-12). 1994. lib. bdg. 24.95 (*0-7933-4157-4*); pap. 14.95 (*0-7933-4158-2*); disk 29.95 (*0-7933-4159-0*) Gallopade Pub Group.

— Montana "Jography" A Fun Run Thru Our State. (Carole Marsh Montana Bks.). (Illus.). (J). (gr. 3 up). 1994. lib. bdg. 24.95 (*1-55609-754-9*); pap. 14.95 (*1-55609-755-7*); disk 29.95 (*1-55609-756-5*) Gallopade Pub Group.

— Montana Kid's Cookbook: Recipes, How-To, History, Lore & More. (Carole Marsh Montana Bks.). (Illus.). (J). (gr. 3 up). 1994. lib. bdg. 24.95 (*0-7933-0709-0*); pap. 14.95 (*0-7933-0708-2*); disk 29.95 (*0-7933-0710-4*) Gallopade Pub Group.

— The Montana Library Book: A Surprising Guide to the Unusual Special Collections in Libraries Across Our State for Students, Teachers, Writers & Publishers - Includes Reproducible Mailing Labels Plus Activities for Young People! (Carole Marsh Montana Bks.). (Illus.). 1994. lib. bdg. 24.95 (*0-7933-3083-1*); pap. 14.95 (*0-7933-3084-X*); disk 29.95 (*0-7933-3085-8*) Gallopade Pub Group.

— The Montana Media Book: A Surprising Guide to the Amazing Print, Broadcast & Online Media of Our State for Students, Teachers, Writers & Publishers - Includes Reproducible Mailing Labels Plus Activities for Young People! (Carole Marsh Montana Bks.). (Illus.). 1994. lib. bdg. 24.95 (*0-7933-3239-7*); pap. 14.95 (*0-7933-3240-0*); disk 29.95 (*0-7933-3241-9*) Gallopade Pub Group.

— The Montana Mystery Van Takes Off! Book 1: Handicapped Montana Kids Sneak Off on a Big Adventure. (Carole Marsh Montana Bks.). (Illus.). (J). (gr. 3-12). 1994. 24.95 (*0-7933-5039-5*); pap. 14.95 (*0-7933-5040-9*); disk 29.95 (*0-7933-5041-7*) Gallopade Pub Group.

— Montana Quiz Bowl Crash Course! (Carole Marsh Montana Bks.). (Illus.). (J). (gr. 3 up). 1994. lib. bdg. 24.95 (*1-55609-769-7*); pap. 14.95 (*1-55609-770-0*); disk 29.95 (*1-55609-771-9*) Gallopade Pub Group.

— Montana Rollercoasters! (Carole Marsh Montana Bks.). (Illus.). (YA). (gr. 3-12). 1994. lib. bdg. 24.95 (*0-7933-5302-5*); pap. 14.95 (*0-7933-5303-3*); disk 29.95 (*0-7933-5304-1*) Gallopade Pub Group.

— Montana School Trivia: An Amazing & Fascinating Look at Our State's Teachers, Schools & Students! (Carole Marsh Montana Bks.). (Illus.). (J). (gr. 3 up). 1994. lib. bdg. 24.95 (*0-7933-0706-6*); pap. 14.95 (*0-7933-0705-8*); disk 29.95 (*0-7933-0707-4*) Gallopade Pub Group.

— Montana Silly Basketball Sportsmysteries, Vol. I. (Carole Marsh Montana Bks.). (Illus.). (J). (gr. 3 up). 1994. lib. bdg. 24.95 (*0-7933-0703-1*); pap. 14.95 (*0-7933-0702-3*); disk 29.95 (*0-7933-0704-X*) Gallopade Pub Group.

— Montana Silly Basketball Sportsmysteries, Vol. II. (Carole Marsh Montana Bks.). (Illus.). (J). (gr. 3 up). 1994. lib. bdg. 24.95 (*0-7933-1749-5*); pap. 14.95 (*0-7933-1750-9*); disk 29.95 (*0-7933-1751-7*) Gallopade Pub Group.

— Montana Silly Football Sportsmysteries, Vol. I. (Carole Marsh Montana Bks.). (Illus.). (J). (gr. 3 up). 1994. lib. bdg. 24.95 (*1-55609-760-3*); pap. 14.95 (*1-55609-761-1*); disk 29.95 (*1-55609-762-X*) Gallopade Pub Group.

— Montana Silly Football Sportsmysteries, Vol. II. (Carole Marsh Montana Bks.). (Illus.). (J). (gr. 3 up). 1994. lib. bdg. 24.95 (*1-55609-763-8*); pap. 14.95 (*1-55609-764-6*); disk 29.95 (*1-55609-765-4*) Gallopade Pub Group.

— Montana Silly Trivia! (Carole Marsh Montana Bks.). (Illus.). (J). (gr. 3 up). 1994. lib. bdg. 24.95 (*1-55609-751-4*); pap. 14.95 (*1-55609-752-2*); disk 29.95 (*1-55609-753-0*) Gallopade Pub Group.

— Montana Timeline: A Chronology of Montana History, Mystery, Trivia, Legend, Lore & More. (Carole Marsh Montana Bks.). (Illus.). (J). (gr. 3-12). 1994. lib. bdg. 24.95 (*0-7933-5953-8*); pap. 14.95 (*0-7933-5954-6*); disk 29.95 (*0-7933-5955-4*) Gallopade Pub Group.

— Montana's (Most Devastating!) Disasters & (Most Calamitous!) Catastrophies! (Carole Marsh Montana Bks.). (Illus.). (J). (gr. 3 up). 1994. lib. bdg. 24.95 (*0-685-45943-8*); pap. 14.95 (*0-7933-0692-2*); disk 29.95 (*0-7933-0695-7*) Gallopade Pub Group.

— Montana's Unsolved Mysteries (& Their "Solutions") Includes Scientific Information & Other Activities for Students. (Carole Marsh Montana Bks.). (Illus.). (J). (gr. 3-12). 1994. lib. bdg. 24.95 (*0-7933-5800-0*); pap. 14.95 (*0-7933-5801-9*); disk 29.95 (*0-7933-5802-7*) Gallopade Pub Group.

— Multipreneur: How a Self-Published Writer Parlayed a Single Children's Mystery into 176 Companies. (MYOB Ser.). (Illus.). 1994. lib. bdg. 24.95 (*0-7933-4388-7*); pap. 14.95 (*0-7933-4389-5*); disk 29.95 (*0-685-49561-2*) Gallopade Pub Group.

— My First Book about Alabama. (Carole Marsh Alabama Bks.). (J). (gr. k-4). 1994. lib. bdg. 24.95 (*0-7933-5569-9*); pap. 14.95 (*0-7933-5570-2*); disk 29.95 (*0-7933-5571-0*) Gallopade Pub Group.

— My First Book about Alaska. (Carole Marsh Alaska Bks.). (J). (gr. k-4). 1994. lib. bdg. 24.95 (*0-7933-5572-9*); pap. 14.95 (*0-7933-5573-7*); disk 29.95 (*0-7933-5574-5*) Gallopade Pub Group.

— My First Book about Arizona. (Carole Marsh Arizona Bks.). (J). (gr. k-4). 1994. lib. bdg. 24.95 (*0-7933-5575-3*); pap. 14.95 (*0-7933-5576-1*); disk 29.95 (*0-7933-5577-X*) Gallopade Pub Group.

— My First Book about Arkansas. (Carole Marsh Arkansas Bks.). (J). (gr. k-4). 1994. lib. bdg. 24.95 (*0-7933-5578-8*); pap. 14.95 (*0-7933-5579-6*); disk 29.95 (*0-7933-5580-X*) Gallopade Pub Group.

— My First Book about California. (Carole Marsh California Bks.). (J). (gr. k-4). 1994. lib. bdg. 24.95 (*0-7933-5581-8*); pap. 14.95 (*0-7933-5582-6*); disk 29.95 (*0-7933-5583-4*) Gallopade Pub Group.

— My First Book about Colorado. (Carole Marsh Colorado Bks.). (J). (gr. k-4). 1994. lib. bdg. 24.95 (*0-7933-5584-2*); pap. 14.95 (*0-7933-5585-0*); disk 29.95 (*0-7933-5586-9*) Gallopade Pub Group.

— My First Book about Connecticut. (Carole Marsh Connecticut Bks.). (J). (gr. k-4). 1994. lib. bdg. 24.95 (*0-7933-5587-7*); pap. 14.95 (*0-7933-5588-5*); disk 29.95 (*0-7933-5589-3*) Gallopade Pub Group.

— My First Book about Delaware. (Carole Marsh Delaware Bks.). (J). (gr. k-4). 1994. lib. bdg. 24.95 (*0-7933-5590-7*); pap. 14.95 (*0-7933-5591-5*); disk 29.95 (*0-7933-5592-3*) Gallopade Pub Group.

— My First Book about Florida. (Carole Marsh Florida Bks.). (J). (gr. k-4). 1994. lib. bdg. 24.95 (*0-7933-5596-6*); pap. 14.95 (*0-7933-5597-4*); disk 29.95 (*0-7933-5598-2*) Gallopade Pub Group.

— My First Book about Georgia. (Carole Marsh Georgia Bks.). (J). (gr. k-4). 1994. lib. bdg. 24.95 (*0-7933-5599-0*); pap. 14.95 (*0-7933-5600-8*); disk 29.95 (*0-7933-5601-6*) Gallopade Pub Group.

— My First Book about Hawaii. (Carole Marsh Hawaii Bks.). (J). (gr. k-4). 1994. lib. bdg. 24.95 (*0-7933-5602-4*); pap. 14.95 (*0-7933-5603-2*); disk 29.95 (*0-7933-5604-0*) Gallopade Pub Group.

— My First Book about Idaho. (Carole Marsh Idaho Bks.). (J). (gr. k-4). 1994. lib. bdg. 24.95 (*0-7933-5605-9*); pap. 14.95 (*0-7933-5606-7*); disk 29.95 (*0-7933-5607-5*) Gallopade Pub Group.

— My First Book about Illinois. (Carole Marsh Illinois Bks.). (J). (gr. k-4). 1994. lib. bdg. 24.95 (*0-7933-5608-3*); pap. 14.95 (*0-7933-5609-1*); disk 29.95 (*0-7933-5610-5*) Gallopade Pub Group.

— My First Book about Indiana. (Carole Marsh Indiana Bks.). (J). (gr. k-4). 1994. lib. bdg. 24.95 (*0-7933-5611-3*); pap. 14.95 (*0-7933-5612-1*); disk 29.95 (*0-7933-5613-X*) Gallopade Pub Group.

— My First Book about Iowa. (Carole Marsh Iowa Bks.). (J). (gr. k-4). 1994. lib. bdg. 24.95 (*0-7933-5614-8*); pap. 14.95 (*0-7933-5615-6*); disk 29.95 (*0-7933-5616-4*) Gallopade Pub Group.

— My First Book about Kansas. (Carole Marsh Kansas Bks.). (J). (gr. k-4). 1994. lib. bdg. 24.95 (*0-7933-5617-2*); pap. 14.95 (*0-7933-5618-0*); disk 29.95 (*0-7933-5619-9*) Gallopade Pub Group.

— My First Book about Kentucky. (Carole Marsh Kentucky Bks.). (J). (gr. k-4). 1994. lib. bdg. 24.95 (*0-7933-5620-2*); pap. 14.95 (*0-7933-5621-0*); disk 29.95 (*0-7933-5622-9*) Gallopade Pub Group.

— My First Book about Louisiana. (Carole Marsh Louisiana Bks.). (J). (gr. k-4). 1994. lib. bdg. 24.95 (*0-7933-5623-7*); pap. 14.95 (*0-7933-5624-5*); disk 29.95 (*0-7933-5625-3*) Gallopade Pub Group.

— My First Book about Maine. (Carole Marsh Maine Bks.). (J). (gr. k-4). 1994. lib. bdg. 24.95 (*0-7933-5626-1*); pap. 14.95 (*0-7933-5627-X*); disk 29.95 (*0-7933-5628-8*) Gallopade Pub Group.

— My First Book about Maryland. (Carole Marsh Maryland Bks.). (J). (gr. k-4). 1994. lib. bdg. 24.95 (*0-7933-5629-6*); pap. 14.95 (*0-7933-5630-X*); disk 29.95 (*0-7933-5631-8*) Gallopade Pub Group.

— My First Book about Massachusetts. (Massachuseets Bks.). (J). (gr. k-4). 1994. lib. bdg. 24.95 (*0-7933-5632-6*); pap. 14.95 (*0-7933-5633-4*); disk 29.95 (*0-7933-5634-2*) Gallopade Pub Group.

— My First Book about Michigan. (Carole Marsh Michigan Bks.). (J). (gr. k-4). 1994. lib. bdg. 24.95 (*0-7933-5635-0*); pap. 14.95 (*0-7933-5636-9*); disk 29.95 (*0-7933-5637-7*) Gallopade Pub Group.

— My First Book about Minnesota. (Carole Marsh Minnesota Bks.). (J). (gr. k-4). 1994. lib. bdg. 24.95 (*0-7933-5638-5*); pap. 14.95 (*0-7933-5639-3*); disk 29.95 (*0-7933-5640-7*) Gallopade Pub Group.

— My First Book about Mississippi. (Carole Marsh Mississippi Bks.). (J). (gr. k-4). 1994. lib. bdg. 24.95 (*0-7933-5641-5*); pap. 14.95 (*0-7933-5642-3*); disk 29.95 (*0-7933-5643-1*) Gallopade Pub Group.

— My First Book about Missouri. (Carole Marsh Missouri Bks.). (J). (gr. k-4). 1994. lib. bdg. 24.95 (*0-7933-5644-X*); pap. 14.95 (*0-7933-5645-8*); disk 29.95 (*0-7933-5646-6*) Gallopade Pub Group.

— My First Book about Montana. (Carole Marsh Montana). (J). (gr. k-4). 1994. lib. bdg. 24.95 (*0-7933-5647-4*); pap. 14.95 (*0-7933-5648-2*); disk 29.95 (*0-7933-5649-0*) Gallopade Pub Group.

— My First Book about Nebraska. (Carole Marsh Nebraska Bks.). (J). (gr. k-4). 1994. lib. bdg. 24.95 (*0-7933-5650-4*); pap. 14.95 (*0-7933-5651-2*); disk 29.95 (*0-7933-5652-0*) Gallopade Pub Group.

— My First Book about Nevada. (Carole Marsh Nevada Bks.). (J). (gr. k-4). 1994. lib. bdg. 24.95 (*0-7933-5653-9*); pap. 14.95 (*0-7933-5654-7*); disk 29.95 (*0-7933-5655-5*) Gallopade Pub Group.

— My First Book about New Hampshire. (Carole Marsh New Hampshire Bks.). (J). (gr. k-4). 1994. lib. bdg. 24.95 (*0-7933-5656-3*); pap. 14.95 (*0-7933-5657-1*); disk 29.95 (*0-7933-5658-X*) Gallopade Pub Group.

— My First Book about New Jersey. (Carole Marsh New Jersey Bks.). (J). (gr. k-4). 1994. lib. bdg. 24.95 (*0-7933-5659-8*); pap. 14.95 (*0-7933-5660-1*); disk 29.95 (*0-7933-5661-X*) Gallopade Pub Group.

— My First Book about New Mexico. (Carole Marsh New Mexico Bks.). (J). (gr. k-4). 1994. lib. bdg. 24.95 (*0-7933-5662-8*); pap. 14.95 (*0-7933-5663-6*); disk 29.95 (*0-7933-5664-4*) Gallopade Pub Group.

— My First Book about New York. (Carole Marsh New York Bks.). (J). (gr. k-4). 1994. lib. bdg. 24.95 (*0-7933-5665-2*); pap. 14.95 (*0-7933-5666-0*); disk 29.95 (*0-7933-5667-9*) Gallopade Pub Group.

— My First Book about North Carolina. (Carole Marsh North Carolina Bks.). (J). (gr. k-4). 1994. lib. bdg. 24.95 (*0-7933-5668-7*); pap. 14.95 (*0-7933-5669-5*); disk 29.95 (*0-7933-5670-9*) Gallopade Pub Group.

— My First Book about North Dakota. (Carole Marsh North Dakota Bks.). (J). (gr. k-4). 1994. lib. bdg. 24.95 (*0-7933-5671-7*); pap. 14.95 (*0-7933-5672-5*); disk 29.95 (*0-7933-5673-3*) Gallopade Pub Group.

— My First Book about Ohio. (Carole Marsh Ohio Bks.). (J). (gr. k-4). 1994. lib. bdg. 24.95 (*0-7933-5674-1*); pap. 14.95 (*0-7933-5675-X*); disk 29.95 (*0-7933-5676-8*) Gallopade Pub Group.

— My First Book about Oklahoma. (Oklahoma Bks.). (J). (gr. k-4). 1994. lib. bdg. 24.95 (*0-7933-5677-6*); pap. 14.95 (*0-7933-5678-4*); disk 29.95 (*0-7933-5679-2*) Gallopade Pub Group.

— My First Book about Oregon. (Oregon Bks.). (J). (gr. k-4). 1994. lib. bdg. 24.95 (*0-7933-5680-6*); pap. 14.95 (*0-7933-5681-4*); disk 29.95 (*0-7933-5682-2*) Gallopade Pub Group.

— My First Book about Pennsylvania. (Pennsylvania Bks.). (J). (gr. k-4). 1994. lib. bdg. 24.95 (*0-7933-5683-0*); pap. 14.95 (*0-7933-5684-9*); disk 29.95 (*0-7933-5685-7*) Gallopade Pub Group.

— My First Book about Rhode Island. (Rhode Island Bks.). (J). (gr. k-4). 1994. lib. bdg. 24.95 (*0-7933-5686-5*); pap. 14.95 (*0-7933-5687-3*); disk 29.95 (*0-7933-5688-1*) Gallopade Pub Group.

— My First Book about South Carolina. (South Carolina Bks.). (J). (gr. k-4). 1994. lib. bdg. 24.95 (*0-7933-5689-X*); pap. 14.95 (*0-7933-5690-3*); disk 29.95 (*0-7933-5691-1*) Gallopade Pub Group.

— My First Book about South Dakota. (South Dakota Bks.). (J). (gr. k-4). 1994. lib. bdg. 24.95 (*0-7933-5692-X*); pap. 14.95 (*0-7933-5693-8*); disk 29.95 (*0-7933-5694-6*) Gallopade Pub Group.

— My First Book about Tennessee. (Tennessee Bks.). (J). (gr. k-4). 1994. lib. bdg. 24.95 (*0-7933-5695-4*); pap. 14.95 (*0-7933-5696-2*); disk 29.95 (*0-7933-5697-0*) Gallopade Pub Group.

— My First Book about Texas. (Texas Bks.). (J). (gr. k-4). 1994. lib. bdg. 24.95 (*0-7933-5698-9*); pap. 14.95 (*0-7933-5699-7*); disk 29.95 (*0-7933-5700-4*) Gallopade Pub Group.

— My First Book about Utah. (Utah Bks.). (J). (gr. k-4). 1994. lib. bdg. 24.95 (*0-7933-5701-2*); pap. 14.95 (*0-7933-5702-0*); disk 29.95 (*0-7933-5703-9*) Gallopade Pub Group.

— My First Book about Vermont. (Vermont Bks.). (J). (gr. k-4). 1994. lib. bdg. 24.95 (*0-7933-5704-7*); pap. 14.95 (*0-7933-5705-5*); disk 29.95 (*0-7933-5706-3*) Gallopade Pub Group.

— My First Book about Virginia. (Virginia Bks.). (J). (gr. k-4). 1994. lib. bdg. 24.95 (*0-7933-5707-1*); pap. 14.95 (*0-7933-5708-X*); disk 29.95 (*0-7933-5709-8*) Gallopade Pub Group.

— My First Book about Washington. (Washington Bks.). (J). (gr. k-4). 1994. lib. bdg. 24.95 (*0-7933-5710-1*); pap. 14.95 (*0-7933-5711-X*); disk 29.95 (*0-7933-5712-8*) Gallopade Pub Group.

— My First Book about Washington DC. (Washington, D.C. Bks.). (J). (gr. k-4). 1994. lib. bdg. 24.95 (*0-7933-5593-1*); pap. 14.95 (*0-7933-5594-X*); disk 29.95 (*0-7933-5595-8*) Gallopade Pub Group.

— My First Book about West Virginia. (West Virginia Bks.). (J). (gr. k-4). 1994. lib. bdg. 24.95 (*0-7933-5713-6*); pap. 14.95 (*0-7933-5714-4*); disk 29.95 (*0-7933-5715-2*) Gallopade Pub Group.

— My First Book about Wisconsin. (Wisconsin Bks.). (J). (gr. k-4). 1994. lib. bdg. 24.95 (*0-7933-5716-0*); pap. 14.95 (*0-7933-5717-9*); disk 29.95 (*0-7933-5718-7*) Gallopade Pub Group.

— My First Book about Wyoming. (Wyoming Bks.). (J). (gr. k-4). 1994. lib. bdg. 24.95 (*0-7933-5719-5*); pap. 14.95 (*0-7933-5720-9*); disk 29.95 (*0-7933-5721-7*) Gallopade Pub Group.

— My Lifetime of Sex & How to Handle It. (Smart Sex Stuff Ser.). (Orig.). (J). (ps-12). 1994. pap. 14.95 (*1-55609-211-3*) Gallopade Pub Group.

— The Mystery of Bat Cave Set. (Carole Marsh Mysteries Ser.). 1994. 125.00 (*0-7933-6956-8*) Gallopade Pub Group.

— Mystery of Old Salem Activity Book. (History Mystery Ser.). 12p. (Orig.). (J). (gr. 4-8). 1994. pap. 12.00 (*0-935326-67-7*) Gallopade Pub Group.

— Mystery of Old Salem Gamebook. (History Mystery Ser.). (Orig.). (J). (gr. 4-8). 1994. pap. 19.95 (*0-935326-66-9*) Gallopade Pub Group.

— Mystery of Old Salem S. P. A. R. K. Kit. (History Mystery Ser.). (Illus.). (Orig.). (J). (gr. 3-9). 1994. pap. 24.95 (*0-935326-74-X*) Gallopade Pub Group.

— The Mystery of Old Salem Set. (Carole Marsh Mysteries Ser.). 1994. 125.00 (*0-7933-6952-5*) Gallopade Pub Group.

— Mystery of Stone Mountain. (Real People-Real Places Ser.). (Orig.). (J). (gr. 3-7). 1994. lib. bdg. 24.95 (*1-55609-180-X*); pap. 14.95 (*0-935326-25-1*) Gallopade Pub Group.

— The Mystery of the Biltmore House. (History Mystery Ser.). (Illus.). (Orig.). (J). (gr. 3-9). 1994. 14.95 (*0-935326-07-3*) Gallopade Pub Group.

— The Mystery of the Biltmore House Set. (Carole Marsh Mysteries Ser.). 1994. 125.00 (*0-7933-6948-7*) Gallopade Pub Group.

— Mystery of the Lost Colony. (History Mystery Ser.). (Illus.). (J). (gr. 4-9). 1994. lib. bdg. 24.95 (*1-55609-182-6*); pap. 14.95 (*0-935326-05-7*) Gallopade Pub Group.

— The Mystery of the Lost Colony Set. (Carole Marsh Mysteries Ser.). 1994. 125.00 (*0-7933-6949-5*) Gallopade Pub Group.

— Mystery of the World's Fair. (Real People-Real Places Ser.). (Illus.). (Orig.). (J). (gr. 3-9). 1994. pap. 14.95 (*0-935326-04-9*) Gallopade Pub Group.

— Mystery of Tryon Palace Activity Book. (History Mystery Ser.). (Orig.). (J). (gr. 3-6). 1994. pap. 14.95 (*0-935326-69-3*) Gallopade Pub Group.

— Mystery of Tryon Palace Gamebook. (History Mystery Ser.). (Orig.). (J). (gr. 2-6). 1994. pap. 14.95 (*0-935326-70-7*) Gallopade Pub Group.

— Mystery of Tryon Palace S. P. A. R. K. Kit. (History Mystery Ser.). (Illus.). (Orig.). (J). (gr. 3-8). 1994. pap. 24.95 (*0-317-44654-1*) Gallopade Pub Group.

— The Mystery of Tryon Palace Set. (Carole Marsh Mysteries Ser.). 1994. 125.00 (*0-7933-6950-9*) Gallopade Pub Group.

— The Naked Gourmet. (Naked Gourmet Ser.). (Orig.). 1994. 24.95 (*1-55609-001-3*); pap. 14.95 (*0-685-43568-7*) Gallopade Pub Group.

— Natchez River Rogues! Pirates, Playboys & the Rest of the Cock-O'-the-Walk Crowd under-the-Hill & along the Natchez Trace. (Carole Marsh Mississippi Bks.). 1994. 24.95 (*0-7933-7369-7*); pap. 14.95 (*0-7933-7370-0*) Gallopade Pub Group.

— Nebraska & Other State Greats (Biographies) (Carole Marsh Nebraska Bks.). (Illus.). (J). (gr 3 up). 1994. lib. bdg. 24.95 (*1-55609-796-4*); pap. 14.95 (*1-55609-797-2*); disk 29.95 (*1-55609-798-0*) Gallopade Pub Group.

— Nebraska Bandits, Bushwackers, Outlaws, Crooks, Devils, Ghosts, Desperadoes & Other Assorted & Sundry Characters! (Carole Marsh Nebraska Bks.). (Illus.). (J). (gr. 3 up). 1994. lib. bdg. 24.95 (*0-7933-0721-X*); pap. 14.95 (*0-7933-0720-1*); disk 29.95 (*0-7933-0722-8*) Gallopade Pub Group.

— Nebraska Bandits, Bushwackers, Outlaws, Crooks, Devils, Ghosts, Desperadoes & Other Assorted & Sundry Characters. (Carole Marsh Nebraska Bks.). (YA). 1994. student ed 6.95 (*0-7933-6811-1*) Gallopade Pub Group.

— The Nebraska Bookstore Book: A Surprising Guide to Our State's Bookstores & Their Specialties for Students, Teachers, Writers & Publishers. (Carole Marsh Nebraska Bks.). (Illus.). 1994. lib. bdg. 24.95 (*0-7933-2936-1*); pap. 14.95 (*0-7933-2937-X*); disk 29.95 (*0-7933-2938-8*) Gallopade Pub Group.

— Nebraska Classic Christmas Trivia: Stories, Recipes, Activities, Legends, Lore & More! (Carole Marsh Nebraska Bks.). (Illus.). (J). (gr. 3 up). 1994. lib. bdg. 24.95 (*0-7933-0724-4*); pap. 14.95 (*0-7933-0723-6*); disk 29.95 (*0-7933-0725-2*) Gallopade Pub Group.

— Nebraska Coastales. (Carole Marsh Nebraska Bks.). (J). 1994. lib. bdg. 24.95 (*0-7933-7292-5*) Gallopade Pub Group.

— Nebraska Coastales. (Carole Marsh Nebraska Bks.). (Illus.). (J). (gr. 3 up). 1994. lib. bdg. 24.95 (*1-55609-790-5*); pap. 14.95 (*1-55609-791-3*); disk 29.95 (*1-55609-792-1*) Gallopade Pub Group.

— Nebraska "Crinkum-Crankum" A Funny Word Book about Our State. (Carole Marsh Nebraska Bks.). (Illus.). (J). 1994. lib. bdg. 24.95 (*0-7933-4889-7*); pap. 14.95 (*0-7933-4890-0*); disk 29.95 (*0-7933-4891-9*) Gallopade Pub Group.

— Nebraska Dingbats! Bk. 1: A Fun Book of Games, Stories, Activities & More about Our State That's All in Code! for You to Decipher. (Carole Marsh Nebraska Bks.). (Illus.). (J). (gr. 3-12). 1994. lib. bdg. 24.95 (*0-7933-3854-9*); pap. 14.95 (*0-7933-3855-7*); disk 29.95 (*0-7933-3856-5*) Gallopade Pub Group.

— Nebraska Festival Fun for Kids! (Carole Marsh Nebraska Bks.). (Illus.). (YA). (gr. 3-12). 1994. lib. bdg. 24.95 (*0-7933-4007-1*); pap. 14.95 (*0-7933-4008-X*); disk 29.95 (*0-7933-4009-8*) Gallopade Pub Group.

— The Nebraska Hot Air Balloon Mystery. (Carole Marsh Nebraska Bks.). (Illus.). (J). (gr. 2-9). 1994. 24.95 (*0-7933-2561-7*); pap. 14.95 (*0-7933-2562-5*); disk 29.95 (*0-7933-2563-3*) Gallopade Pub Group.

— Nebraska Jeopardy! Answers & Questions about Our State! (Carole Marsh Nebraska Bks.). (Illus.). (J). (gr. 3-12). 1994. lib. bdg. 24.95 (*0-7933-4160-4*); pap. 14.95 (*0-7933-4161-2*); disk 29.95 (*0-7933-4162-0*) Gallopade Pub Group.

— Nebraska "Jography" A Fun Run thru Our State. (Carole Marsh Nebraska Bks.). (Illus.). (J). (gr. 3 up). 1994. lib. bdg. 24.95 (*1-55609-778-6*); pap. 14.95 (*0-685-45948-9*); disk 29.95 (*1-55609-780-8*) Gallopade Pub Group.

— Nebraska Jography: Answers & Questions about Our State. (Carole Marsh Nebraska Bks.). (J). 1994. student ed 6.95 (*0-7933-6810-3*) Gallopade Pub Group.

— Nebraska Kid's Cookbook: Recipes, How-To, History, Lore & More! (Carole Marsh Nebraska Bks.). (Illus.). (J). (gr. 3 up). 1994. lib. bdg. 24.95 (*0-7933-0733-3*); pap. 14.95 (*0-7933-0732-5*); disk 29.95 (*0-7933-0734-1*) Gallopade Pub Group.

— The Nebraska Library Book: A Surprising Guide to the Unusual Special Collections in Libraries Across Our State for Students, Teachers, Writers & Publishers - Includes Reproducible Mailing Labels Plus Activities for Young People! (Carole Marsh Nebraska Bks.). (Illus.). 1994. lib. bdg. 24.95 (*0-7933-3086-6*); pap. 14.95 (*0-7933-3087-4*); disk 29.95 (*0-7933-3088-2*) Gallopade Pub Group.

— The Nebraska Media Book: A Surprising Guide to the Amazing Print, Broadcast & Online Media of Our State for Students, Teachers, Writers & Publishers - Includes Reproducible Mailing Labels Plus Activities for Young People! (Carole Marsh Nebraska Bks.). (Illus.). 1994. lib. bdg. 24.95 (*0-7933-3242-7*); pap. 14.95 (*0-7933-3243-5*); disk 29.95 (*0-7933-3244-3*) Gallopade Pub Group.

— The Nebraska Mystery Van Takes Off! Book 1: Handicapped Nebraska Kids Sneak off on a Big Adventure. (Carole Marsh Nebraska Bks.). (Illus.). (J). (gr. 3-12). 1994. 24.95 (*0-7933-5042-5*); pap. 14.95 (*0-7933-5043-3*); disk 29.95 (*0-7933-5044-1*) Gallopade Pub Group.

— Nebraska Quiz Bowl Crash Course! (Carole Marsh Nebraska Bks.). (Illus.). (J). (gr. 3 up). 1994. lib. bdg. 24.95 (*1-55609-793-X*); pap. 14.95 (*1-55609-794-8*); disk 29.95 (*1-55609-795-6*) Gallopade Pub Group.

— Nebraska Rollercoasters! (Carole Marsh Nebraska Bks.). (Illus.). (YA). (gr. 3-12). 1994. lib. bdg. 24.95 (*0-7933-5305-X*); pap. 14.95 (*0-7933-5306-8*); disk 29.95 (*0-7933-5307-6*) Gallopade Pub Group.

— Nebraska School Trivia: An Amazing & Fascinating Look at Our State's Teachers, Schools & Students! (Carole Marsh Nebraska Bks.). (Illus.). (J). (gr. 3 up). 1994. lib. bdg. 24.95 (*0-7933-0730-9*); pap. 14.95 (*0-7933-0729-5*); disk 29.95 (*0-7933-0731-7*) Gallopade Pub Group.

— Nebraska Silly Basketball Sportsmysteries, Vol. I. (Carole Marsh Nebraska Bks.). (Illus.). (J). (gr. 3 up). 1994. lib. bdg. 24.95 (*0-7933-0727-9*); pap. 14.95 (*0-7933-0726-0*); disk 29.95 (*0-7933-0728-7*) Gallopade Pub Group.

— Nebraska Silly Basketball Sportsmysteries, Vol. II. (Carole Marsh Nebraska Bks.). (Illus.). (J). (gr. 3 up). 1994. lib. bdg. 24.95 (*0-7933-1758-4*); pap. 14.95 (*0-7933-1759-2*); disk 29.95 (*0-7933-1760-6*) Gallopade Pub Group.

— Nebraska Silly Football Sportsmysteries, Vol. I. (Carole Marsh Nebraska Bks.). (Illus.). (J). (gr. 3 up). 1994. lib. bdg. 24.95 (*1-55609-784-0*); pap. 14.95 (*1-55609-785-9*); disk 29.95 (*1-55609-786-7*) Gallopade Pub Group.

— Nebraska Silly Football Sportsmysteries, Vol. II. (Carole Marsh Nebraska Bks.). (Illus.). (J). (gr. 3 up). 1994. lib. bdg. 24.95 (*1-55609-787-5*); pap. 14.95 (*1-55609-788-3*); disk 29.95 (*1-55609-789-1*) Gallopade Pub Group.

— Nebraska Silly Trivia! (Carole Marsh Nebraska Bks.). (Illus.). (J). (gr. 3 up). 1994. lib. bdg. 24.95 (*1-55609-775-1*); pap. 14.95 (*1-55609-776-X*); disk 29.95 (*1-55609-777-8*) Gallopade Pub Group.

— Nebraska Silly Trivia. (Carole Marsh Nebraska Bks.). (YA). 1994. student ed 6.95 (*0-7933-6809-X*) Gallopade Pub Group.

— Nebraska Timeline: A Chronology of Nebraska History, Mystery, Trivia, Legend, Lore & More. (Carole Marsh Nebraska Bks.). (Illus.). (J). (gr. 3-12). 1994. lib. bdg. 24.95 (*0-7933-5956-2*); pap. 14.95 (*0-7933-5957-0*); disk 29.95 (*0-7933-5958-9*) Gallopade Pub Group.

— Nebraska's (Most Devastating!) Disasters & (Most Calamitous!) Catastrophies! (Carole Marsh Nebraska Bks.). (Illus.). (J). (gr. 3 up). 1994. lib. bdg. 24.95 (*0-7933-0718-X*); pap. 14.95 (*0-7933-0717-1*); write for info. (*0-7933-0719-8*) Gallopade Pub Group.

— Nebraska's Unsolved Mysteries (& Their "Solutions") Includes Scientific Information & Other Activities for Students. (Carole Marsh Nebraska Bks.). (Illus.). (J). (gr. 3-12). 1994. lib. bdg. 24.95 (*0-7933-5803-5*); pap. 14.95 (*0-7933-5804-3*); disk 29.95 (*0-7933-5805-1*) Gallopade Pub Group.

— Nevada & Other State Greats (Biographies) (Carole Marsh Nevada Bks.). (Illus.). (J). 1994. lib. bdg. 24.95 (*1-55609-820-0*); pap. 14.95 (*1-55609-821-9*); disk 29.95 (*1-55609-822-7*) Gallopade Pub Group.

— Nevada Bandits, Bushwackers, Outlaws, Crooks, Devils, Ghosts, Desperadoes & Other Assorted & Sundry Characters! (Illus.). (J). 1994. lib. bdg. 24.95 (*0-7933-0745-7*); pap. 14.95 (*0-7933-0744-9*); disk 29.95 (*0-7933-0746-5*) Gallopade Pub Group.

— The Nevada Bookstore Book: A Surprising Guide to Our State's Bookstores & Their Specialties for Students, Teachers, Writers & Publishers. (Carole Marsh Nevada Bks.). (Illus.). 1994. lib. bdg. 24.95 (*0-7933-2939-6*); pap. 14.95 (*0-7933-2940-X*); disk 29.95 (*0-7933-2941-8*) Gallopade Pub Group.

— Nevada Classic Christmas Trivia: Stories, Recipes, Activities, Legends, Lore & More! (Carole Marsh Nevada Bks.). (Illus.). (J). 1994. lib. bdg. 24.95 (*0-7933-0748-1*); pap. 14.95 (*0-7933-0747-3*); disk 29.95 (*0-7933-0749-X*) Gallopade Pub Group.

— Nevada Coastales. (Carole Marsh Nevada Bks.). (Illus.). (J). 1994. lib. bdg. 24.95 (*1-55609-814-6*); pap. 14.95 (*1-55609-815-4*); disk 29.95 (*1-55609-816-2*) Gallopade Pub Group.

— Nevada Coastales! (Carole Marsh Nevada Bks.). (J). 1994. lib. bdg. 24.95 (*0-7933-7293-3*) Gallopade Pub Group.

— Nevada "Crinkum-Crankum" A Funny Word Book about Our State. (Carole Marsh Nevada Bks.). (Illus.). (J). 1994. lib. bdg. 24.95 (*0-7933-4892-7*); pap. 14.95 (*0-7933-4893-5*); disk 29.95 (*0-7933-4894-3*) Gallopade Pub Group.

— Nevada Dingbats! Bk. 1: A Fun Book of Games, Stories, Activities & More about Our State That's All in Code! for You to Decipher. (Carole Marsh Nevada Bks.). (Illus.). (J). (gr. 3-12). 1994. lib. bdg. 24.95 (*0-7933-3857-3*); pap. 14.95 (*0-7933-3858-1*); disk 29.95 (*0-7933-3859-X*) Gallopade Pub Group.

— Nevada Festival Fun for Kids! (Carole Marsh Nevada Bks.). (Illus.). (YA). (gr. 3-12). 1994. lib. bdg. 24.95 (*0-7933-4010-1*); pap. 14.95 (*0-7933-4011-X*); disk 29.95 (*0-7933-4012-8*) Gallopade Pub Group.

— The Nevada Hot Air Balloon Mystery. (Carole Marsh Nevada Bks.). (Illus.). (J). (gr. 2-9). 1994. 24.95 (*0-7933-2570-6*); pap. 14.95 (*0-7933-2571-4*); disk 29.95 (*0-7933-2572-2*) Gallopade Pub Group.

— Nevada Jeopardy! Answers & Questions about Our State! (Carole Marsh Nevada Bks.). (Illus.). (J). (gr. 3-12). 1994. lib. bdg. 24.95 (*0-7933-4163-9*); pap. 14.95 (*0-7933-4164-7*); disk 29.95 (*0-7933-4165-5*) Gallopade Pub Group.

— Nevada "Jography" A Fun Run Thru Our State! (Carole Marsh Nevada Bks.). (Illus.). (J). 1994. lib. bdg. 24.95 (*1-55609-802-2*); pap. 14.95 (*1-55609-803-0*); disk 29.95 (*1-55609-804-9*) Gallopade Pub Group.

— Nevada Kid's Cookbook: Recipes, How-to, History, Lore & More! (Carole Marsh Nevada Bks.). (Illus.). (J). 1994. lib. bdg. 24.95 (*0-7933-0757-0*); pap. 14.95 (*0-7933-0756-2*); disk 29.95 (*0-7933-0758-9*) Gallopade Pub Group.

— The Nevada Library Book: A Surprising Guide to the Unusual Special Collections in Libraries Across Our State for Students, Teachers, Writers & Publishers - Includes Reproducible Mailing Labels Plus Activities for Young People! (Carole Marsh Nevada Bks.). (Illus.). 1994. lib. bdg. 24.95 (*0-7933-3089-0*); pap. 14.95 (*0-7933-3090-4*); disk 29.95 (*0-7933-3091-2*) Gallopade Pub Group.

— The Nevada Media Book: A Surprising Guide to the Amazing Print, Broadcast & Online Media of Our State for Students, Teachers, Writers & Publishers - Includes Reproducible Mailing Labels Plus Activities for Young People! (Carole Marsh Nevada Bks.). (Illus.). 1994. lib. bdg. 24.95 (*0-7933-3245-1*); pap. 14.95 (*0-7933-3246-X*); disk 29.95 (*0-7933-3247-8*) Gallopade Pub Group.

— The Nevada Mystery Van Takes Off! Book 1: Handicapped Nevada Kids Sneak Off on a Big Adventure. (Carole Marsh Nevada Bks.). (Illus.). (J). (gr. 3-12). 1994. 24.95 (*0-7933-5045-X*); pap. 14.95 (*0-7933-5046-8*); disk 29.95 (*0-7933-5047-6*) Gallopade Pub Group.

— Nevada Quiz Bowl Crash Course! (Carole Marsh Nevada Bks.). (Illus.). (J). 1994. lib. bdg. 24.95 (*1-55609-817-0*); pap. 14.95 (*1-55609-818-9*); disk 29.95 (*1-55609-819-7*) Gallopade Pub Group.

— Nevada Rollercoasters! (Carole Marsh Nevada Bks.). (Illus.). (YA). (gr. 3-12). 1994. lib. bdg. 24.95 (*0-7933-5308-4*); pap. 14.95 (*0-7933-5309-2*); disk 29.95 (*0-7933-5310-6*) Gallopade Pub Group.

— Nevada School Trivia: An Amazing & Fascinating Look at Our State's Teachers, Schools & Students! (Carole Marsh Nevada Bks.). (Illus.). (J). 1994. lib. bdg. 24.95 (*0-7933-0754-6*); pap. 14.95 (*0-7933-0753-8*); disk 29.95 (*0-7933-0755-4*) Gallopade Pub Group.

— Nevada Silly Basketball Sportsmystereis, Vol. 2. (Carole Marsh Nevada Bks.). (Illus.). (J). 1994. lib. bdg. 24.95 (*0-7933-1767-3*); pap. 14.95 (*0-7933-1768-1*); disk 29.95 (*0-7933-1769-X*) Gallopade Pub Group.

— Nevada Silly Basketball Sportsmysteries, Vol. 1. (Carole Marsh Nevada Bks.). (Illus.). (J). 1994. lib. bdg. 24.95 (*0-7933-0751-1*); pap. 14.95 (*0-7933-0750-3*); disk 29.95 (*0-7933-0752-X*) Gallopade Pub Group.

— Nevada Silly Football Sportsmysteries, Vol. 1. (Carole Marsh Nevada Bks.). (Illus.). (J). 1994. lib. bdg. 24.95 (*1-55609-808-1*); pap. 14.95 (*1-55609-809-X*); disk 29.95 (*1-55609-810-3*) Gallopade Pub Group.

— Nevada Silly Football Sportsmysteries, Vol. 2. (Carole Marsh Nevada Bks.). (Illus.). (J). 1994. lib. bdg. 24.95 (*1-55609-811-1*); pap. 14.95 (*1-55609-812-X*); disk 29.95 (*1-55609-813-8*) Gallopade Pub Group.

— Nevada Silly Trivia! (Carole Marsh Nevada Bks.). (Illus.). (J). 1994. lib. bdg. 24.95 (*1-55609-799-9*); pap. 14.95 (*1-55609-800-6*); disk 29.95 (*1-55609-801-4*) Gallopade Pub Group.

— Nevada Timeline: A Chronology of Nevada History, Mystery, Trivia, Legend, Lore & More. (Carole Marsh Nevada Bks.). (Illus.). (J). (gr. 3-12). 1994. lib. bdg. 24.95 (*0-7933-5959-7*); pap. 14.95 (*0-7933-5960-0*); disk 29.95 (*0-7933-5961-9*) Gallopade Pub Group.

— Nevada's (Most Devastating!) Disasters & (Most Calamitous!) Castastrophies! (Carole Marsh Nevada Bks.). (Illus.). (J). 1994. lib. bdg. 24.95 (*0-7933-0742-2*); pap. 14.95 (*0-7933-0741-4*); disk 29.95 (*0-7933-0743-0*) Gallopade Pub Group.

— Nevada's Unsolved Mysteries (& Their "Solutions") Includes Scientific Information & Other Activities for Students. (Carole Marsh Nevada Bks.). (Illus.). (J). (gr. 3-12). 1994. lib. bdg. 24.95 (*0-7933-5806-X*); pap. 14.95 (*0-7933-5807-8*); disk 29.95 (*0-7933-5808-6*) Gallopade Pub Group.

— New Hampshire & Other State Greats (Biographies) (Carole Marsh New Hampshire Bks.). (Illus.). (J). 1994. lib. bdg. 24.95 (*0-685-45980-2*); pap. 14.95 (*1-55609-845-6*); disk 29.95 (*1-55609-846-4*) Gallopade Pub Group.

— New Hampshire Bandits, Bushwackers, Outlaws, Crooks, Devils, Ghosts, Desperadoes & Other Assorted & Sundry Characters! (Carole Marsh New Hampshire Bks.). (Illus.). (J). 1994. lib. bdg. 24.95 (*0-7933-0769-4*); pap. 14.95 (*0-7933-0768-6*); disk 29.95 (*0-7933-0770-8*) Gallopade Pub Group.

— The New Hampshire Bookstore Book: A Surprising Guide to Our State's Bookstores & Their Specialties for Students, Teachers, Writers & Publishers. (Carole Marsh New Hampshire Bks.). (Illus.). 1994. lib. bdg. 24.95 (*0-7933-2942-6*); pap. 14.95 (*0-7933-2943-4*); disk 29.95 (*0-7933-2944-2*) Gallopade Pub Group.

— New Hampshire Classic Christmas Trivia: Stories, Recipes, Activities, Legends, Lore & More! (Carole Marsh New Hampshire Bks.). (Illus.). (J). 1994. lib. bdg. 24.95 (*0-7933-0772-4*); pap. 14.95 (*0-7933-0771-6*); disk 29.95 (*0-7933-0773-2*) Gallopade Pub Group.

— New Hampshire Coastales. (Carole Marsh New Hampshire Bks.). (Illus.). (J). 1994. lib. bdg. 24.95 (*1-55609-838-3*); pap. 14.95 (*1-55609-839-1*); disk 29.95 (*1-55609-840-5*) Gallopade Pub Group.

An Asterisk (*) at the beginning of an entry indicates that the title is appearing in BIP for the first time.

— New Hampshire Coastales! (Carole Marsh New Hampshire Bks.). (J). 1994. lib. bdg. 24.95 (0-7933-7294-1) Gallopade Pub Group.

— New Hampshire "Crinkum-Crankum" A Funny Word Book about Our State. (Carole Marsh New Hampshire Bks.). (Illus.). (J). 1994. lib. bdg. 24.95 (0-7933-4895-1); pap. 14.95 (0-7933-4896-X); disk 29.95 (0-7933-4897-8) Gallopade Pub Group.

— New Hampshire Dingbats! Bk. 1: A Fun Book of Games, Stories, Activities & More about Our State That's All in Code! for You to Decipher. (Carole Marsh New Hampshire Bks.). (Illus.). (J). (gr. 3-12). 1994. lib. bdg. 24.95 (0-7933-3860-3); pap. 14.95 (0-7933-3861-1); disk 29.95 (0-7933-3862-X) Gallopade Pub Group.

— New Hampshire Festival Fun for Kids! (Carole Marsh New Hampshire Bks.). (Illus.). (YA). (gr. 3-12). 1994. lib. bdg. 24.95 (0-7933-4013-6); pap. 14.95 (0-7933-4014-4); disk 29.95 (0-7933-4015-2) Gallopade Pub Group.

— The New Hampshire Hot Air Balloon Mystery. (Carole Marsh New Hampshire Bks.). (Illus.). (J). (gr. 2-9). 1994. 24.95 (0-7933-2579-X); pap. 14.95 (0-7933-2580-3); disk 29.95 (0-7933-2581-1) Gallopade Pub Group.

— New Hampshire Jeopardy! Answers & Questions about Our State! (Carole Marsh New Hampshire Bks.). (Illus.). (J). (gr. 3-12). 1994. lib. bdg. 24.95 (0-7933-4166-3); pap. 14.95 (0-7933-4167-1); disk 29.95 (0-7933-4168-X) Gallopade Pub Group.

— New Hampshire "Jography" A Fun Run Thru Our State! (Carole Marsh New Hampshire Bks.). (Illus.). (J). 1994. lib. bdg. 24.95 (1-55609-826-X); pap. 14.95 (1-55609-827-8); disk 29.95 (1-55609-828-6) Gallopade Pub Group.

— New Hampshire Kid's Cookbook: Recipes, How-to, History, Lore & More! (Carole Marsh New Hampshire Bks.). (Illus.). (J). 1994. lib. bdg. 24.95 (0-7933-0781-3); pap. 14.95 (0-7933-0780-5); disk 29.95 (0-7933-0782-1) Gallopade Pub Group.

— The New Hampshire Library Book: A Surprising Guide to the Unusual Special Collections in Libraries Across Our State for Students, Teachers, Writers & Publishers - Includes Reproducible Mailing Labels Plus Activities for Young People! (Carole Marsh New Hampshire Bks.). (Illus.). 1994. lib. bdg. 24.95 (0-7933-3092-0); pap. 14.95 (0-7933-3093-9); disk 29.95 (0-7933-3094-7) Gallopade Pub Group.

— The New Hampshire Media Book: A Surprising Guide to the Amazing Print, Broadcast & Online Media of Our State for Students, Teachers, Writers & Publishers - Includes Reproducible Mailing Labels Plus Activities for Young People! (Carole Marsh New Hampshire Bks.). (Illus.). 1994. lib. bdg. 24.95 (0-7933-3248-6); pap. 14.95 (0-7933-3249-4); disk 29.95 (0-7933-3250-8) Gallopade Pub Group.

— The New Hampshire Mystery Van Takes Off! Book 1: Handicapped New Hampshire Kids Sneak Off on a Big Adventure. (Carole Marsh New Hampshire Bks.). (Illus.). (J). (gr. 3-12). 1994. 24.95 (0-7933-5048-4); pap. 14.95 (0-7933-5049-2); disk 29.95 (0-7933-5050-6) Gallopade Pub Group.

— New Hampshire Quiz Bowl Crash Course! (Carole Marsh New Hampshire Bks.). (Illus.). (J). 1994. lib. bdg. 24.95 (1-55609-841-3); pap. 14.95 (1-55609-842-1); disk 29.95 (1-55609-843-X) Gallopade Pub Group.

— New Hampshire Rollercoasters! (Carole Marsh New Hampshire Bks.). (Illus.). (YA). (gr. 3-12). 1994. lib. bdg. 24.95 (0-7933-5311-4); pap. 14.95 (0-7933-5312-2); disk 29.95 (0-7933-5313-0) Gallopade Pub Group.

— New Hampshire School Trivia: An Amazing & Fascinating Look at Our State's Teachers, Schools & Students! (Illus.). (J). 1994. lib. bdg. 24.95 (0-7933-0778-3); pap. 14.95 (0-7933-0777-5); disk 29.95 (0-7933-0779-1) Gallopade Pub Group.

— New Hampshire Silly Basketball Sportsmysteries, Vol. I. (Carole Marsh New Hampshire Bks.). (Illus.). (J). 1994. lib. bdg. 24.95 (0-7933-0775-9); pap. 14.95 (0-7933-0774-0); disk 29.95 (0-7933-0776-7) Gallopade Pub Group.

— New Hampshire Silly Basketball Sportsmysteries, Vol. II. (Carole Marsh New Hampshire Bks.). (Illus.). (J). 1994. lib. bdg. 24.95 (0-7933-1776-2); pap. 14.95 (0-7933-1777-0); disk 29.95 (0-7933-1778-9) Gallopade Pub Group.

— New Hampshire Silly Football Sportsmysteries, Vol. 1. (Carole Marsh New Hampshire Bks.). (Illus.). (J). 1994. lib. bdg. 24.95 (1-55609-832-4); pap. 14.95 (1-55609-833-2); disk 29.95 (1-55609-834-0) Gallopade Pub Group.

— New Hampshire Silly Football Sportsmysteries, Vol. 2. (Carole Marsh New Hampshire Bks.). (Illus.). (J). 1994. lib. bdg. 24.95 (1-55609-835-9); pap. 14.95 (1-55609-836-7); disk 29.95 (1-55609-837-5) Gallopade Pub Group.

— New Hampshire Silly Trivia! (Carole Marsh New Hampshire Bks.). (Illus.). (J). 1994. lib. bdg. 24.95 (1-55609-823-5); pap. 14.95 (1-55609-824-3); disk 29.95 (1-55609-825-1) Gallopade Pub Group.

— New Hampshire Timeline: A Chronology of New Hampshire History, Mystery, Trivia, Legend, Lore & More. (Carole Marsh New Hampshire Bks.). (Illus.). (J). (gr. 3-12). 1994. lib. bdg. 24.95 (0-7933-5962-7); pap. 14.95 (0-7933-5963-5); disk 29.95 (0-7933-5964-3) Gallopade Pub Group.

— New Hampshire's (Most Devastating!) Disasters & (Most Calamitous!) Catastrophies! (Carole Marsh New Hampshire Bks.). (Illus.). (J). 1994. lib. bdg. 24.95 (0-7933-0766-X); pap. 14.95 (0-7933-0765-1); disk 29.95 (0-7933-0767-8) Gallopade Pub Group.

— New Hampshire's Unsolved Mysteries (& Their "Solutions") Includes Scientific Information & Other Activities for Students. (Carole Marsh New Hampshire Bks.). (Illus.). (J). (gr. 3-12). 1994. lib. bdg. 24.95 (0-7933-5809-4); pap. 14.95 (0-7933-5810-8); disk 29.95 (0-7933-5811-6) Gallopade Pub Group.

— New Jersey & Other State Greats (Biographies) (Carole Marsh New Jersey Bks.). (Illus.). (J). 1994. lib. bdg. 24.95 (1-55609-868-5); pap. 14.95 (1-55609-869-3); disk 29.95 (1-55609-870-7) Gallopade Pub Group.

— New Jersey Bandits, Bushwackers, Outlaws, Crooks, Devils, Ghosts, Desperadoes & Other Assorted & Sundry Characters! (Carole Marsh New Jersey Bks.). (Illus.). (J). 1994. lib. bdg. 24.95 (0-7933-1788-6); pap. 14.95 (0-7933-1789-4); disk 29.95 (0-7933-1790-8) Gallopade Pub Group.

— The New Jersey Bookstore Book: A Surprising Guide to Our State's Bookstores & Their Specialties for Students, Teachers, Writers & Publishers. (Carole Marsh New Jersey Bks.). (Illus.). 1994. lib. bdg. 24.95 (0-7933-2945-0); pap. 14.95 (0-7933-2946-9); disk 29.95 (0-7933-2947-7) Gallopade Pub Group.

— New Jersey Classic Christmas Trivia: Stories, Recipes, Activities, Legends, Lore & More! (Carole Marsh New Jersey Bks.). (Illus.). (J). 1994. lib. bdg. 24.95 (0-7933-1791-6); pap. 14.95 (0-7933-1792-4); disk 29.95 (0-7933-1793-2) Gallopade Pub Group.

— New Jersey Coastales. (Carole Marsh New Jersey Bks.). (Illus.). (J). 1994. lib. bdg. 24.95 (1-55609-862-6); pap. 14.95 (1-55609-863-4); disk 29.95 (1-55609-864-2) Gallopade Pub Group.

— New Jersey Coastales! (Carole Marsh New Jersey Bks.). (J). 1994. lib. bdg. 24.95 (0-7933-7295-X) Gallopade Pub Group.

— New Jersey "Crinkum-Crankum" A Funny Word Book about Our State. (Carole Marsh New Jersey Bks.). (Illus.). (J). 1994. lib. bdg. 24.95 (0-7933-4898-6); pap. 14.95 (0-7933-4899-4); disk 29.95 (0-7933-4900-1) Gallopade Pub Group.

— New Jersey Dingbats! Bk. 1: A Fun Book of Games, Stories, Activities & More about Our State That's All in Code! for You to Decipher. (New Jersey Bks.). (Illus.). (J). (gr. 3-12). 1994. lib. bdg. 24.95 (0-7933-3863-8); pap. 14.95 (0-7933-3864-6); disk 29.95 (0-7933-3865-4) Gallopade Pub Group.

— New Jersey Festival Fun for Kids! (Carole Marsh New Jersey Bks.). (Illus.). (YA). (gr. 3-12). 1994. lib. bdg. 24.95 (0-7933-4016-0); pap. 14.95 (0-7933-4017-9); disk 29.95 (0-7933-4018-7) Gallopade Pub Group.

— The New Jersey Hot Air Balloon Mystery. (Carole Marsh New Jersey Bks.). (Illus.). (J). (gr. 2-9). 1994. 24.95 (0-7933-2588-9); pap. 14.95 (0-7933-2589-7); disk 29.95 (0-7933-2590-0) Gallopade Pub Group.

— New Jersey Jeopardy! Answers & Questions about Our State! (Carole Marsh New Jersey Bks.). (Illus.). (J). (gr. 3-12). 1994. lib. bdg. 24.95 (0-7933-4169-8); pap. 14.95 (0-7933-4170-1); disk 29.95 (0-7933-4171-X) Gallopade Pub Group.

— New Jersey "Jography" A Fun Run Thru Our State! (Carole Marsh New Jersey Bks.). (Illus.). (J). 1994. lib. bdg. 24.95 (1-55609-850-2); pap. 14.95 (1-55609-851-0); disk 29.95 (1-55609-852-9) Gallopade Pub Group.

— New Jersey Kid's Cookbook: Recipes, How-to, History, Lore & More. (Carole Marsh New Jersey Bks.). (Illus.). (J). 1994. lib. bdg. 24.95 (0-7933-1803-3); pap. 14.95 (0-7933-1804-1); disk 29.95 (0-7933-1805-X) Gallopade Pub Group.

— The New Jersey Library Book: A Surprising Guide to the Unusual Special Collections in Libraries Across Our State for Students, Teachers, Writers & Publishers - Includes Reproducible Mailing Labels Plus Activities for Young People! (Carole Marsh New Jersey Bks.). (Illus.). 1994. lib. bdg. 24.95 (0-7933-3095-5); pap. 14.95 (0-7933-3096-3); disk 29.95 (0-7933-3097-1) Gallopade Pub Group.

— The New Jersey Media Book: A Surprising Guide to the Amazing Print, Broadcast & Online Media of Our State for Students, Teachers, Writers & Publishers - Includes Reproducible Mailing Labels Plus Activities for Young People! (Carole Marsh New Jersey Bks.). (Illus.). 1994. lib. bdg. 24.95 (0-7933-3251-6); pap. 14.95 (0-7933-3252-4); disk 29.95 (0-7933-3253-2) Gallopade Pub Group.

— The New Jersey Mystery Van Takes Off! Book 1: Handicapped New Jersey Kids Sneak Off on a Big Adventure. (Carole Marsh New Jersey Bks.). (Illus.). (J). (gr. 3-12). 1994. 24.95 (0-7933-5051-4); pap. 14.95 (0-7933-5052-2); disk 29.95 (0-7933-5053-0) Gallopade Pub Group.

— New Jersey Quiz Bowl Crash Course! (Carole Marsh New Jersey Bks.). (Illus.). (J). 1994. lib. bdg. 24.95 (1-55609-865-0); pap. 14.95 (1-55609-866-9); disk 29.95 (1-55609-867-7) Gallopade Pub Group.

— New Jersey Rollercoasters! (Carole Marsh New Jersey Bks.). (Illus.). (YA). (gr. 3-12). 1994. lib. bdg. 24.95 (0-7933-5314-9); pap. 14.95 (0-7933-5315-7); disk 29.95 (0-7933-5316-5) Gallopade Pub Group.

— New Jersey School Trivia: An Amazing & Fascinating Look at Our State's Teachers, Schools & Students! (Carole Marsh New Jersey Bks.). (Illus.). (J). 1994. lib. bdg. 24.95 (0-7933-1800-9); pap. 14.95 (0-7933-1801-7); disk 29.95 (0-7933-1802-5) Gallopade Pub Group.

— New Jersey Silly Basketball Sportsmysteries, Vol. 1. (Carole Marsh New Jersey Bks.). (Illus.). (J). 1994. lib. bdg. 24.95 (0-7933-1794-0); pap. 14.95 (0-7933-1795-9); disk 29.95 (0-7933-1796-7) Gallopade Pub Group.

— New Jersey Silly Basketball Sportsmysteries, Vol. 2. (Carole Marsh New Jersey Bks.). (Illus.). (J). 1994. lib. bdg. 24.95 (0-7933-1797-5); pap. 14.95 (0-7933-1798-3); disk 29.95 (0-7933-1799-1) Gallopade Pub Group.

— New Jersey Silly Football Sportsmysteries, Vol. 1. (Carole Marsh New Jersey Bks.). (Illus.). (J). 1994. lib. bdg. 24.95 (1-55609-856-1); pap. 14.95 (1-55609-857-X); disk 29.95 (1-55609-858-8) Gallopade Pub Group.

— New Jersey Silly Football Sportsmysteries, Vol. 2. (Carole Marsh New Jersey Bks.). (Illus.). (J). 1994. lib. bdg. 24.95 (1-55609-859-6); pap. 14.95 (1-55609-860-X); disk 29.95 (1-55609-861-8) Gallopade Pub Group.

— New Jersey Silly Trivia! (Carole Marsh New Jersey Bks.). (Illus.). (J). 1994. lib. bdg. 24.95 (1-55609-847-2); pap. 14.95 (1-55609-848-0); disk 29.95 (1-55609-849-9) Gallopade Pub Group.

— New Jersey Timeline: A Chronology of New Jersey History, Mystery, Trivia, Legend, Lore & More. (Carole Marsh New Jersey Bks.). (Illus.). (J). (gr. 3-12). 1994. lib. bdg. 24.95 (0-7933-5965-1); pap. 14.95 (0-7933-5966-X); disk 29.95 (0-7933-5967-8) Gallopade Pub Group.

— New Jersey's (Most Devastating!) Disasters & (Most Calamitous!) Catastrophies! (Carole Marsh New Jersey Bks.). (Illus.). (J). 1994. lib. bdg. 24.95 (0-685-45981-0); pap. 14.95 (0-7933-1786-X); disk 29.95 (0-7933-1787-8) Gallopade Pub Group.

— New Jersey's Unsolved Mysteries (& Their "Solutions") Includes Scientific Information & Other Activities for Students. (Carole Marsh New Jersey Bks.). (Illus.). (J). (gr. 3-12). 1994. lib. bdg. 24.95 (0-7933-5812-4); pap. 14.95 (0-7933-5813-2); disk 29.95 (0-7933-5814-0) Gallopade Pub Group.

— New Mexico & Other State Greats (Biographies) (Carole Marsh New Mexico Bks.). (Illus.). (J). 1994. lib. bdg. 24.95 (1-55609-892-8); pap. 14.95 (1-55609-893-6); disk 29.95 (1-55609-894-4) Gallopade Pub Group.

— New Mexico Bandits, Bushwackers, Outlaws, Crooks, Devils, Ghosts, Desperadoes & Other Assorted & Sundry Characters! (Carole Marsh New Mexico Bks.). (Illus.). (J). 1994. lib. bdg. 24.95 (0-7933-0793-7); pap. 14.95 (0-7933-0792-9); disk 29.95 (0-7933-0794-5) Gallopade Pub Group.

— The New Mexico Bookstore Book: A Surprising Guide to Our State's Bookstores & Their Specialties for Students, Teachers, Writers & Publishers. (Carole Marsh New Mexico Bks.). (Illus.). 1994. lib. bdg. 24.95 (0-7933-2948-5); pap. 14.95 (0-7933-2949-3); disk 29.95 (0-7933-2950-7) Gallopade Pub Group.

— New Mexico Classic Christmas Trivia: Stories, Recipes, Activities, Legends, Lore & More! (Carole Marsh New Mexico Bks.). (Illus.). (J). 1994. lib. bdg. 24.95 (0-7933-0796-1); pap. 14.95 (0-7933-0795-3); disk 29.95 (0-7933-0797-X) Gallopade Pub Group.

— New Mexico Coastales. (Carole Marsh New Mexico Bks.). (Illus.). (J). 1994. lib. bdg. 24.95 (1-55609-886-3); pap. 14.95 (1-55609-887-1); disk 29.95 (1-55609-888-X) Gallopade Pub Group.

— New Mexico Coastales! (Carole Marsh New Mexico Bks.). (J). 1994. lib. bdg. 24.95 (0-7933-7296-8) Gallopade Pub Group.

— New Mexico "Crinkum-Crankum" A Funny Word Book about Our State. (Carole Marsh New Mexico Bks.). (Illus.). (J). 1994. lib. bdg. 24.95 (0-7933-4901-X); pap. 14.95 (0-7933-4902-8); disk 29.95 (0-7933-4903-6) Gallopade Pub Group.

— New Mexico Dingbats! Bk. 1: A Fun Book of Games, Stories, Activities & More about Our State That's All in Code! for You to Decipher. (Carole Marsh New Mexico Bks.). (Illus.). (J). (gr. 3-12). 1994. lib. bdg. 24.95 (0-7933-3866-2); pap. 14.95 (0-7933-3867-0); disk 29.95 (0-7933-3868-9) Gallopade Pub Group.

— New Mexico Festival Fun for Kids! (Carole Marsh New Mexico Bks.). (Illus.). (YA). (gr. 3-12). 1994. lib. bdg. 24.95 (0-7933-4019-5); pap. 14.95 (0-7933-4020-9); disk 29.95 (0-7933-4021-7) Gallopade Pub Group.

— The New Mexico Hot Air Balloon Mystery. (Carole Marsh New Mexico Bks.). (Illus.). (J). (gr. 2-9). 1994. 24.95 (0-7933-2597-8); pap. 14.95 (0-7933-2598-6); disk 29.95 (0-7933-2599-4) Gallopade Pub Group.

— New Mexico Jeopardy! Answers & Questions about Our State! (Carole Marsh New Mexico Bks.). (Illus.). (J). (gr. 3-12). 1994. lib. bdg. 24.95 (0-7933-4172-8); pap. 14.95 (0-7933-4173-6); disk 29.95 (0-7933-4174-4) Gallopade Pub Group.

— New Mexico "Jography" A Fun Run Thru Our State! (Carole Marsh New Mexico Bks.). (Illus.). (J). 1994. lib. bdg. 24.95 (1-55609-874-X); pap. 14.95 (1-55609-875-8); disk 29.95 (1-55609-876-6) Gallopade Pub Group.

— New Mexico Kid's Cookbook: Recipes, How-to, History, Lore & More! (Carole Marsh New Mexico Bks.). (Illus.). (J). 1994. lib. bdg. 24.95 (0-7933-0805-4); pap. 14.95 (0-7933-0804-6); disk 29.95 (0-7933-0806-2) Gallopade Pub Group.

— The New Mexico Library Book: A Surprising Guide to the Unusual Special Collections in Libraries Across Our State for Students, Teachers, Writers & Publishers - Includes Reproducible Mailing Labels Plus Activities for Young People! (Carole Marsh New Mexico Bks.). (Illus.). 1994. lib. bdg. 24.95 (0-7933-3098-X); pap. 14.95 (0-7933-3099-8); disk 29.95 (0-7933-3100-5) Gallopade Pub Group.

— The New Mexico Media Book: A Surprising Guide to the Amazing Print, Broadcast & Online Media of Our State for Students, Teachers, Writers & Publishers - Includes Reproducible Mailing Labels Plus Activities for Young People! (Carole Marsh New Mexico Bks.). (Illus.). 1994. lib. bdg. 24.95 (0-7933-3254-0); pap. 14.95 (0-7933-3255-9); disk 29.95 (0-7933-3256-7) Gallopade Pub Group.

— The New Mexico Mystery Van Takes Off! Book 1: Handicapped New Mexico Kids Sneak Off on a Big Adventure. (Carole Marsh New Mexico Bks.). (Illus.). (J). (gr. 3-12). 1994. 24.95 (0-7933-5054-9); pap. 14.95 (0-7933-5055-7); disk 29.95 (0-7933-5056-5) Gallopade Pub Group.

— New Mexico Quiz Bowl Crash Course! (Carole Marsh New Mexico Bks.). (Illus.). (J). 1994. lib. bdg. 24.95 (1-55609-889-8); pap. 14.95 (1-55609-890-1); disk 29.95 (1-55609-891-X) Gallopade Pub Group.

— New Mexico Rollercoasters! (Carole Marsh New Mexico Bks.). (Illus.). (YA). (gr. 3-12). 1994. lib. bdg. 24.95 (0-7933-5317-3); pap. 14.95 (0-7933-5318-1); disk 29.95 (0-7933-5319-X) Gallopade Pub Group.

— New Mexico School Trivia: An Amazing & Fascinating Look at Our State's Teachers, Schools & Students! (Carole Marsh New Mexico Bks.). (Illus.). (J). 1994. lib. bdg. 24.95 (0-7933-0802-X); pap. 14.95 (0-7933-0801-1); disk 29.95 (0-7933-0803-8) Gallopade Pub Group.

— New Mexico Silly Basketball Sportsmystereis, Vol. 1. (Carole Marsh New Mexico Bks.). (Illus.). (J). 1994. lib. bdg. 24.95 (0-7933-0799-6); pap. 14.95 (0-7933-0798-8); disk 29.95 (0-7933-0800-3) Gallopade Pub Group.

— New Mexico Silly Basketball Sportsmysteries, Vol. 2. (Carole Marsh New Mexico Bks.). (Illus.). (J). 1994. lib. bdg. 24.95 (0-7933-1818-1); pap. 14.95 (0-7933-1819-X); disk 29.95 (0-7933-1820-3) Gallopade Pub Group.

— New Mexico Silly Football Sportsmysteries. (Carole Marsh New Mexico Bks.). (Illus.). (J). 1994. lib. bdg. 24.95 (1-55609-880-4); pap. 14.95 (1-55609-881-2); pap. 14.95 (1-55609-884-7); disk 29.95 (1-55609-882-0); disk 29.95 (1-55609-885-5) Gallopade Pub Group.

— New Mexico Silly Trivia! (Carole Marsh New Mexico Bks.). (Illus.). (J). 1994. lib. bdg. 24.95 (1-55609-871-5); pap. 14.95 (1-55609-872-3); disk 29.95 (1-55609-873-1) Gallopade Pub Group.

— New Mexico Timeline: A Chronology of New Mexico History, Mystery, Trivia, Legend, Lore & More. (Carole Marsh New Mexico Bks.). (Illus.). (J). (gr. 3-12). 1994. lib. bdg. 24.95 (0-7933-5968-6); pap. 14.95 (0-7933-5969-4); disk 29.95 (0-7933-5970-8) Gallopade Pub Group.

— New Mexico's (Most Devastating!) Disasters & (Most Calamitous!) Catastrophies! (Carole Marsh New Mexico Bks.). (Illus.). (J). 1994. lib. bdg. 24.95 (0-7933-0790-2); pap. 14.95 (0-7933-0789-9); disk 29.95 (0-7933-0791-0) Gallopade Pub Group.

— New Mexico's Unsolved Mysteries (& Their "Solutions") Includes Scientific Information & Other Activities for Students. (Carole Marsh New Mexico Bks.). (Illus.). (J). (gr. 3-12). 1994. lib. bdg. 24.95 (0-7933-5815-9); pap. 14.95 (0-7933-5816-7); disk 29.95 (0-7933-5817-5) Gallopade Pub Group.

— New York & Other State Greats (Biographies) (Carole Marsh New York Bks.). (Illus.). (J). 1994. lib. bdg. 24.95 (1-55609-918-5); pap. 14.95 (1-55609-919-3); disk 29.95 (1-55609-920-7) Gallopade Pub Group.

— New York Bandits, Bushwackers, Outlaws, Crooks, Devils, Ghosts, Desperadoes & Other Assorted & Sundry Characters! (Carole Marsh New York Bks.). (Illus.). (J). 1994. lib. bdg. 24.95 (0-7933-0817-8); pap. 14.95 (0-7933-0816-X); disk 29.95 (0-7933-0818-6) Gallopade Pub Group.

— The New York Bookstore Book: A Surprising Guide to Our State's Bookstores & Their Specialties for Students, Teachers, Writers & Publishers. (Carole Marsh New York Bks.). (Illus.). 1994. lib. bdg. 24.95 (0-7933-2951-5); pap. 14.95 (0-7933-2952-3); disk 29.95 (0-7933-2953-1) Gallopade Pub Group.

— New York Classic Christmas Trivia: Stories, Recipes, Activities, Legends, Lore & More! (Carole Marsh New York Bks.). (Illus.). (J). 1994. lib. bdg. 24.95 (0-7933-0820-8); pap. 14.95 (0-685-45982-9); disk 29.95 (0-7933-0821-6) Gallopade Pub Group.

— New York Coastales. (Carole Marsh New York Bks.). (Illus.). (J). 1994. lib. bdg. 24.95 (1-55609-912-6); pap. 14.95 (1-55609-913-4); disk 29.95 (1-55609-914-2) Gallopade Pub Group.

— New York Coastales! (Carole Marsh New York Bks.). (J). 1994. lib. bdg. 24.95 (0-7933-7297-6) Gallopade Pub Group.

— New York "Crinkum-Crankum" A Funny Word Book about Our State. (Carole Marsh New York Bks.). (Illus.). (J). 1994. lib. bdg. 24.95 (0-7933-4904-4); pap. 14.95 (0-7933-4905-2); disk 29.95 (0-7933-4906-0) Gallopade Pub Group.

— New York Dingbats! Bk. 1: A Fun Book of Games, Stories, Activities & More about Our State That's All in Code! for You to Decipher. (Carole Marsh New York Bks.). (Illus.). (J). (gr. 3-12). 1994. lib. bdg. 24.95 (0-7933-3869-7); pap. 14.95 (0-7933-3870-0); disk 29.95 (0-7933-3871-9) Gallopade Pub Group.

— New York Festival Fun for Kids! (Carole Marsh New York Bks.). (Illus.). (YA). (gr. 3-12). 1994. lib. bdg. 24.95 (0-7933-4022-5); pap. 14.95 (0-7933-4023-3); disk 29.95 (0-7933-4024-1) Gallopade Pub Group.

— The New York Hot Air Balloon Mystery. (Carole Marsh New York Bks.). (Illus.). (J). (gr. 2-9). 1994. 24.95 (0-7933-2606-0); pap. 14.95 (0-7933-2607-9); disk 29.95 (0-7933-2608-7) Gallopade Pub Group.

— New York Jeopardy! Answers & Questions about Our State! (Carole Marsh New York Bks.). (Illus.). (J). (gr. 3-12). 1994. lib. bdg. 24.95 (0-7933-4175-2); pap. 14.95 (0-7933-4176-0); disk 29.95 (0-7933-4177-9) Gallopade Pub Group.

— New York "Jography" A Fun Run Thru Our State! (Carole Marsh New York Bks.). (Illus.). (J). 1994. lib. bdg. 24.95 (1-55609-897-9); pap. 14.95 (1-55609-898-7); disk 29.95 (1-55609-899-5) Gallopade Pub Group.

— New York Kid's Cookbook: Recipes, How-to, History, Lore & More! (Carole Marsh New York Bks.). (Illus.). (J). 1994. lib. bdg. 24.95 (0-7933-0829-1); pap. 14.95 (0-7933-0828-3); disk 29.95 (0-7933-0830-5) Gallopade Pub Group.

M

— The New York Library Book: A Surprising Guide to the Unusual Special Collections in Libraries Across Our State for Students, Teachers, Writers & Publishers - Includes Reproducible Mailing Labels Plus Activities for Young People! (Carole Marsh New York Bks.). (Illus.). 1994. lib. bdg. 24.95 (*0-7933-3101-3*); pap. 14.95 (*0-7933-3102-1*); disk 29.95 (*0-7933-3103-X*) Gallopade Pub Group.

— The New York Media Book: A Surprising Guide to the Amazing Print, Broadcast & Online Media of Our State for Students, Teachers, Writers & Publishers - Includes Reproducible Mailing Labels Plus Activities for Young People! (Carole Marsh New York Bks.). (Illus.). 1994. lib. bdg. 24.95 (*0-7933-3257-5*); pap. 14.95 (*0-7933-3258-3*); disk 29.95 (*0-7933-3259-1*) Gallopade Pub Group.

— The New York Mystery Van Takes Off! Book 1: Handicapped New York Kids Sneak Off on a Big Adventure. (Carole Marsh New York Bks.). (Illus.). (J). (gr. 3-12). 1994. 24.95 (*0-7933-5057-3*); pap. 14.95 (*0-7933-5058-1*); disk 29.95 (*0-7933-5059-X*) Gallopade Pub Group.

— New York Quiz Bowl Crash Course! (Carole Marsh New York Bks.). (Illus.). (J). 1994. lib. bdg. 24.95 (*1-55609-915-0*); pap. 14.95 (*1-55609-916-9*); disk 29.95 (*1-55609-917-7*) Gallopade Pub Group.

— New York Rollercoasters! (Carole Marsh New York Bks.). (Illus.). (YA). (gr. 3-12). 1994. lib. bdg. 24.95 (*0-7933-5320-3*); pap. 14.95 (*0-7933-5321-1*); disk 29.95 (*0-7933-5322-X*) Gallopade Pub Group.

— New York School Trivia: An Amazing & Fascinating Look at Our State's Teachers, Schools & Students! (Carole Marsh New York Bks.). (Illus.). (J). 1994. lib. bdg. 24.95 (*0-7933-0826-7*); pap. 14.95 (*0-7933-0825-9*); disk 29.95 (*0-7933-0827-5*) Gallopade Pub Group.

— New York Silly Basketball Sportsmysteries, Vol. 1. (Carole Marsh New York Bks.). (Illus.). (J). 1994. lib. bdg. 24.95 (*0-7933-0823-2*); pap. 14.95 (*0-7933-0822-4*); disk 29.95 (*0-7933-0824-0*) Gallopade Pub Group.

— New York Silly Basketball Sportsmysteries, Vol. 2. (Carole Marsh New York Bks.). (Illus.). (J). 1994. lib. bdg. 24.95 (*0-685-45983-7*); pap. 14.95 (*0-7933-1825-4*); disk 29.95 (*0-7933-1826-2*) Gallopade Pub Group.

— New York Silly Football Sportsmysteries, Vol. 1. (Carole Marsh New York Bks.). (Illus.). (J). 1994. lib. bdg. 24.95 (*1-55609-906-1*); pap. 14.95 (*1-55609-907-X*); disk 29.95 (*1-55609-908-8*) Gallopade Pub Group.

— New York Silly Football Sportsmysteries, Vol. 2. (Carole Marsh New York Bks.). (Illus.). (J). 1994. lib. bdg. 24.95 (*1-55609-909-6*); pap. 14.95 (*1-55609-910-X*); disk 29.95 (*1-55609-911-8*) Gallopade Pub Group.

— New York Silly Trivia! (Carole Marsh New York Bks.). (Illus.). (J). 1994. lib. bdg. 24.95 (*1-55609-895-2*); pap. 14.95 (*1-55609-103-6*); disk 29.95 (*1-55609-896-0*) Gallopade Pub Group.

— New York Timeline: A Chronology of New York History, Mystery, Trivia, Legend, Lore & More. (Carole Marsh New York Bks.). (Illus.). (J). (gr. 3-12). 1994. lib. bdg. 24.95 (*0-7933-5971-6*); pap. 14.95 (*0-7933-5972-4*); disk 29.95 (*0-7933-5973-2*) Gallopade Pub Group.

— New York's (Most Devasting!) Disasters & (Most Calamitous!) Catastrophies! (Carole Marsh New York Bks.). (Illus.). (J). 1994. lib. bdg. 24.95 (*0-7933-0814-3*); pap. 14.95 (*0-7933-0813-5*); disk 29.95 (*0-7933-0815-1*) Gallopade Pub Group.

— New York's Unsolved Mysteries (& Their "Solutions") Includes Scientific Information & Other Activities for Students. (Carole Marsh New York Bks.). (Illus.). (J). (gr. 3-12). 1994. lib. bdg. 24.95 (*0-7933-5818-3*); pap. 14.95 (*0-7933-5819-1*); disk 29.95 (*0-7933-5820-5*) Gallopade Pub Group.

— North Carolina & Other State Greats (Biographies) (Carole Marsh North Carolina Bks.). (Illus.). (J). 1994. lib. bdg. 24.95 (*1-55609-937-1*); pap. 14.95 (*1-55609-938-X*); disk 29.95 (*1-55609-939-8*) Gallopade Pub Group.

— North Carolina Bandits, Bushwackers, Outlaws, Crooks, Devils, Ghosts, Desperadoes & Other Assorted & Sundry Characters! (Carole Marsh North Carolina Bks.). (Illus.). (J). 1994. lib. bdg. 24.95 (*0-7933-0841-0*); pap. 14.95 (*0-7933-0840-2*); disk 29.95 (*0-7933-0842-9*) Gallopade Pub Group.

— The North Carolina Bookstore Book: A Surprising Guide to Our State's Bookstores & Their Specialties for Students, Teachers, Writers & Publishers. (Carole Marsh North Carolina Bks.). (Illus.). 1994. lib. bdg. 24.95 (*0-7933-2954-X*); pap. 14.95 (*0-7933-2955-8*); disk 29.95 (*0-7933-2956-6*) Gallopade Pub Group.

— North Carolina Classic Christmas Trivia: Stories, Recipes, Activities, Legends, Lore & More. (Carole Marsh North Carolina Bks.). (Illus.). (J). 1994. lib. bdg. 24.95 (*0-7933-0844-5*); pap. 14.95 (*0-7933-0843-7*); disk 29.95 (*0-7933-0845-3*) Gallopade Pub Group.

— North Carolina Coastales! (Carole Marsh North Carolina Bks.). (J). 1994. lib. bdg. 24.95 (*0-7933-7298-4*) Gallopade Pub Group.

— North Carolina "Crinkum-Crankum" A Funny Word Book about Our State. (Carole Marsh North Carolina Bks.). (Illus.). (J). (gr. 3-12). 1994. 24.95 (*0-7933-4907-9*); pap. 14.95 (*0-7933-4908-7*); disk 29.95 (*0-7933-4909-5*) Gallopade Pub Group.

— North Carolina Dingbats! Bk. 1: A Fun Book of Games, Stories, Activities & More about Our State That's All in Code! for You to Decipher. (Carole Marsh North Carolina Bks.). (Illus.). (J). (gr. 3-12). 1994. lib. bdg. 24. 95 (*0-7933-3872-7*); pap. 14.95 (*0-7933-3873-5*); disk 29. 95 (*0-7933-3874-3*) Gallopade Pub Group.

— North Carolina Festival Fun for Kids! (Carole Marsh North Carolina Bks.). (Illus.). (YA). (gr. 3-12). 1994. lib. bdg. 24.95 (*0-7933-4025-X*); pap. 14.95 (*0-7933-4026-8*); disk 29.95 (*0-7933-4027-6*) Gallopade Pub Group.

— The North Carolina Hot Air Balloon Mystery. (Carole Marsh North Carolina Bks.). (Illus.). (J). (gr. 2-9). 1994. 24.95 (*0-7933-2615-X*); pap. 14.95 (*0-7933-2616-8*); disk 29.95 (*0-7933-2617-6*) Gallopade Pub Group.

— North Carolina Jeopardy! Answers & Questions about Our State! (Carole Marsh North Carolina Bks.). (Illus.). (J). (gr. 3-12). 1994. lib. bdg. 24.95 (*0-7933-4178-7*); pap. 14.95 (*0-7933-4179-5*); disk 29.95 (*0-7933-4180-9*) Gallopade Pub Group.

— North Carolina Jography: A Fun Run Through the Tarheel State. (Statemeant Ser.). (Illus.). 50p. (Orig.). (J). (gr. 4-8). 1994. pap. 14.95 (*0-935326-81-2*) Gallopade Pub Group.

— North Carolina Kid's Cookbook: Recipes, How-to, History, Lore & More. (Carole Marsh North Carolina Bks.). (Illus.). (J). 1994. lib. bdg. 24.95 (*0-7933-0853-4*); pap. 14.95 (*0-7933-0852-6*); disk 29.95 (*0-7933-0854-2*) Gallopade Pub Group.

— The North Carolina Library Book: A Surprising Guide to the Unusual Special Collections in Libraries Across Our State for Students, Teachers, Writers & Publishers - Includes Reproducible Mailing Labels Plus Activities for Young People! (Carole Marsh North Carolina Bks.). (Illus.). 1994. lib. bdg. 24.95 (*0-7933-3104-8*); pap. 14.95 (*0-7933-3105-6*); disk 29.95 (*0-7933-3106-4*) Gallopade Pub Group.

— The North Carolina Media Book: A Surprising Guide to the Amazing Print, Broadcast & Online Media of Our State for Students, Teachers, Writers & Publishers - Includes Reproducible Mailing Labels Plus Activities for Young People! (Carole Marsh North Carolina Bks.). (Illus.). 1994. lib. bdg. 24.95 (*0-7933-3260-5*); pap. 14.95 (*0-7933-3261-3*); disk 29.95 (*0-7933-3262-1*) Gallopade Pub Group.

— The North Carolina Mystery Van Takes Off! Book 1: Handicapped North Carolina Kids Sneak Off on a Big Adventure. (Carole Marsh North Carolina Bks.). (Illus.). (J). (gr. 3-12). 1994. 24.95 (*0-7933-5060-3*); pap. 14.95 (*0-7933-5061-1*); disk 29.95 (*0-7933-5062-X*) Gallopade Pub Group.

— North Carolina Quiz Bowl Crash Course! (Carole Marsh North Carolina Bks.). (Illus.). (J). 1994. lib. bdg. 24.95 (*1-55609-934-7*); pap. 14.95 (*1-55609-935-5*); disk 29.95 (*1-55609-936-3*) Gallopade Pub Group.

— North Carolina Rollercoasters! (Carole Marsh North Carolina Bks.). (Illus.). (YA). (gr. 3-12). 1994. lib. bdg. 24.95 (*0-7933-5323-8*); pap. 14.95 (*0-7933-5324-6*); disk 29.95 (*0-7933-5325-4*) Gallopade Pub Group.

— North Carolina School Trivia: An Amazing & Fascinating Look at Our State's Teachers, Schools & Students! (Carole Marsh North Carolina Bks.). (Illus.). (J). 1994. lib. bdg. 24.95 (*0-7933-0850-X*); pap. 14.95 (*0-7933-0849-6*); disk 29.95 (*0-7933-0851-8*) Gallopade Pub Group.

— North Carolina Silly Basketball Sportsmysteries, Vol. 1. (Carole Marsh North Carolina Bks.). (Illus.). (J). 1994. lib. bdg. 24.95 (*0-7933-0847-X*); pap. 14.95 (*0-7933-0846-1*); disk 29.95 (*0-7933-0848-8*) Gallopade Pub Group.

— North Carolina Silly Basketball Sportsmysteries, Vol. 2. (Carole Marsh North Carolina Bks.). (Illus.). (J). 1994. lib. bdg. 24.95 (*0-7933-1836-X*); pap. 14.95 (*0-7933-1837-8*); disk 29.95 (*0-7933-1838-6*) Gallopade Pub Group.

— North Carolina Silly Football Sportmysteries, Vol. 2. (Carole Marsh North Carolina Bks.). (Illus.). (J). 1994. lib. bdg. 24.95 (*1-55609-930-4*); pap. 14.95 (*1-55609-931-2*); disk 29.95 (*1-55609-932-0*) Gallopade Pub Group.

— North Carolina Silly Football Sportsmysteries, Vol. 1. (Carole Marsh North Carolina Bks.). (Illus.). (J). 1994. lib. bdg. 24.95 (*1-55609-927-4*); pap. 14.95 (*1-55609-928-2*); disk 29.95 (*1-55609-929-0*) Gallopade Pub Group.

— North Carolina Silly Trivia! (Carole Marsh North Carolina Bks.). (Illus.). (J). 1994. lib. bdg. 24.95 (*1-55609-921-5*); pap. 14.95 (*0-685-45984-5*); disk 29.95 (*1-55609-922-3*) Gallopade Pub Group.

— North Carolina Timeline: A Chronology of North Carolina History, Mystery, Trivia, Legend, Lore & More. (Carole Marsh North Carolina Bks.). (Illus.). (J). (gr. 3-12). 1994. lib. bdg. 24.95 (*0-7933-5974-0*); pap. 14.95 (*0-7933-5975-9*); disk 29.95 (*0-7933-5976-7*) Gallopade Pub Group.

— North Carolina's (Most Devastating!) Disasters & (Most Calamitous!) Catastrophies! (Carole Marsh North Carolina Bks.). (Illus.). (J). 1994. lib. bdg. 24.95 (*0-7933-0838-0*); pap. 14.95 (*0-7933-0837-2*); disk 29.95 (*0-7933-0839-9*) Gallopade Pub Group.

— North Carolina's Scariest Swamp: The Great Dismal. (North Carolina Bks.). (Illus.). (J). (gr. 3 up). 1994. lib. bdg. 24.95 (*0-7933-1270-1*); pap. 14.95 (*0-7933-1271-X*); disk 29.95 (*0-7933-1272-8*) Gallopade Pub Group.

— North Carolina's Unsolved Mysteries (& Their "Solutions") Includes Scientific Information & Other Activities for Students. (Carole Marsh North Carolina Bks.). (Illus.). (J). (gr. 3-12). 1994. lib. bdg. 24.95 (*0-7933-5821-3*); pap. 14.95 (*0-7933-5822-1*); disk 29.95 (*0-7933-5823-X*) Gallopade Pub Group.

— The North Dakota Air Balloon Mystery. (Carole Marsh North Dakota Bks.). (Illus.). (J). (gr. 2-9). 1994. 24.95 (*0-7933-2624-9*); pap. 14.95 (*0-7933-2625-7*); disk 29.95 (*0-7933-2626-5*) Gallopade Pub Group.

— North Dakota & Other State Greats (Biographies) (Carole Marsh North Dakota Bks.). (Illus.). (J). 1994. lib. bdg. 24.95 (*1-55609-976-2*); pap. 14.95 (*1-55609-977-0*); disk 29.95 (*0-685-45973-X*) Gallopade Pub Group.

— North Dakota Bandits, Bushwackers, Outlaws, Crooks, Devils, Ghosts, Desperadoes & Other Assorted & Sundry Characters! (Carole Marsh North Dakota Bks.). (Illus.). (J). 1994. lib. bdg. 24.95 (*0-7933-0865-8*); pap. 14.95 (*0-7933-0864-X*); disk 29.95 (*0-7933-0866-6*) Gallopade Pub Group.

— The North Dakota Bookstore Book: A Surprising Guide to Our State's Bookstores & Their Specialties for Students, Teachers, Writers & Publishers. (Carole Marsh North Carolina Bks.). (Illus.). 1994. lib. bdg. 24.95 (*0-7933-2957-4*); pap. 14.95 (*0-7933-2958-2*); disk 29.95 (*0-7933-2959-0*) Gallopade Pub Group.

— North Dakota Classic Christmas Trivia: Stories, Recipes, Activities, Legends, Lore & More! (Carole Marsh North Dakota Bks.). (Illus.). (J). 1994. lib. bdg. 24.95 (*0-7933-0868-2*); pap. 14.95 (*0-7933-0867-4*); disk 29.95 (*0-7933-0869-0*) Gallopade Pub Group.

— North Dakota Coastales. (Carole Marsh North Dakota Bks.). (Illus.). (J). 1994. lib. bdg. 24.95 (*0-685-45972-1*); pap. 14.95 (*1-55609-971-1*); disk 29.95 (*1-55609-972-X*) Gallopade Pub Group.

— North Dakota Coastales! (Carole Marsh North Dakota Bks.). (J). 1994. lib. bdg. 24.95 (*0-7933-7299-2*) Gallopade Pub Group.

— North Dakota "Crinkum-Crankum" A Funny Word Book about Our State. (Carole Marsh North Dakota Bks.). (Illus.). (J). (gr. 3-12). 1994. 24.95 (*0-7933-4910-9*); pap. 14.95 (*0-7933-4911-7*); disk 29.95 (*0-7933-4912-5*) Gallopade Pub Group.

— North Dakota Dingbats! Bk. 1: A Fun Book of Games, Stories, Activities & More about Our State That's All in Code! for You to Decipher. (Carole Marsh North Dakota Bks.). (Illus.). (J). (gr. 3-12). 1994. lib. bdg. 24. 95 (*0-7933-3875-1*); pap. 14.95 (*0-7933-3876-X*); disk 29.95 (*0-7933-3877-8*) Gallopade Pub Group.

— North Dakota Festival Fun for Kids! (Carole Marsh North Dakota Bks.). (Illus.). (YA). (gr. 3-12). 1994. lib. bdg. 24.95 (*0-7933-4028-4*); pap. 14.95 (*0-7933-4029-2*); disk 29.95 (*0-7933-4030-6*) Gallopade Pub Group.

— North Dakota Jeopardy! Answers & Questions about Our State! (Carole Marsh North Dakota Bks.). (Illus.). (J). (gr. 3-12). 1994. lib. bdg. 24.95 (*0-7933-4181-7*); pap. 14.95 (*0-7933-4182-5*); disk 29.95 (*0-7933-4183-3*) Gallopade Pub Group.

— North Dakota "Jography" A Fun Run Thru Our State! (Carole Marsh North Dakota Bks.). (Illus.). (J). 1994. lib. bdg. 24.95 (*1-55609-943-6*); pap. 14.95 (*1-55609-944-4*); disk 29.95 (*1-55609-945-2*) Gallopade Pub Group.

— North Dakota Kid's Cookbook: Recipes, How-to, History, Lore & More! (Carole Marsh North Dakota Bks.). (Illus.). (J). 1994. lib. bdg. 24.95 (*0-7933-0877-1*); pap. 14.95 (*0-7933-0876-3*); disk 29.95 (*0-7933-0878-X*) Gallopade Pub Group.

— The North Dakota Library Book: A Surprising Guide to the Unusual Special Collections in Libraries Across Our State for Students, Teachers, Writers & Publishers - Includes Reproducible Mailing Labels Plus Activities for Young People! (Carole Marsh North Dakota Bks.). (Illus.). 1994. lib. bdg. 24.95 (*0-7933-3107-2*); pap. 14.95 (*0-7933-3108-0*); disk 29.95 (*0-7933-3109-9*) Gallopade Pub Group.

— The North Dakota Media Book: A Surprising Guide to the Amazing Print, Broadcast & Online Media of Our State for Students, Teachers, Writers & Publishers - Includes Reproducible Mailing Labels Plus Activities for Young People! (Carole Marsh North Dakota Bks.). (Illus.). 1994. lib. bdg. 24.95 (*0-7933-3263-X*); pap. 14. 95 (*0-7933-3264-8*); disk 29.95 (*0-7933-3265-6*) Gallopade Pub Group.

— The North Dakota Mystery Van Takes Off! Book 1: Handicapped North Dakota Kids Sneak Off on a Big Adventure. (Carole Marsh North Dakota Bks.). (Illus.). (J). (gr. 3-12). 1994. 24.95 (*0-7933-5063-8*); pap. 14.95 (*0-7933-5064-6*); disk 29.95 (*0-7933-5065-4*) Gallopade Pub Group.

— North Dakota Quiz Bowl Crash Course! (Carole Marsh North Dakota Bks.). (Illus.). (J). 1994. lib. bdg. 24.95 (*1-55609-973-8*); pap. 14.95 (*1-55609-974-6*); disk 29.95 (*1-55609-975-4*) Gallopade Pub Group.

— North Dakota Rollercoasters! (Carole Marsh North Dakota Bks.). (Illus.). (YA). (gr. 3-12). 1994. lib. bdg. 24.95 (*0-7933-5326-2*); pap. 14.95 (*0-7933-5327-0*); disk 29.95 (*0-7933-5328-9*) Gallopade Pub Group.

— North Dakota School Trivia: An Amazing & Fascinating Look at Our State's Teachers, Schools & Students! (Carole Marsh North Dakota Bks.). (Illus.). (J). 1994. lib. bdg. 24.95 (*0-7933-0874-7*); pap. 14.95 (*0-7933-0873-9*); disk 29.95 (*0-7933-0875-5*) Gallopade Pub Group.

— North Dakota Silly Basketball Sportsmysteries, Vol. 1. (Carole Marsh North Dakota Bks.). (Illus.). (J). 1994. lib. bdg. 24.95 (*0-7933-0871-2*); pap. 14.95 (*0-7933-0870-4*); disk 29.95 (*0-7933-0872-0*) Gallopade Pub Group.

— North Dakota Silly Basketball Sportsmysteries, Vol. 2. (Carole Marsh North Dakota Bks.). (Illus.). (J). 1994. lib. bdg. 24.95 (*0-685-45974-8*); pap. 14.95 (*0-7933-1846-7*); disk 29.95 (*0-7933-1847-5*) Gallopade Pub Group.

— North Dakota Silly Football Sportsmysteries, Vol. 1. (Carole Marsh North Dakota Bks.). (Illus.). (J). 1994. lib. bdg. 24.95 (*1-55609-948-7*); pap. 14.95 (*1-55609-949-5*); disk 29.95 (*0-685-45971-3*) Gallopade Pub Group.

— North Dakota Silly Football Sportsmysteries, Vol. 2. (Carole Marsh North Dakota Bks.). (Illus.). (J). 1994. lib. bdg. 24.95 (*1-55609-967-3*); pap. 14.95 (*1-55609-968-1*); disk 29.95 (*1-55609-969-X*) Gallopade Pub Group.

— North Dakota Silly Trivia! (Carole Marsh North Dakota Bks.). (Illus.). (J). 1994. lib. bdg. 24.95 (*1-55609-940-1*); pap. 14.95 (*1-55609-941-X*); disk 29.95 (*1-55609-942-8*) Gallopade Pub Group.

— North Dakota Timeline: A Chronology of North Dakota History, Mystery, Trivia, Legend, Lore & More. (Carole Marsh North Dakota Bks.). (Illus.). (J). (gr. 3-12). 1994. lib. bdg. 24.95 (*0-7933-5977-5*); pap. 14.95 (*0-7933-5978-3*); disk 29.95 (*0-7933-5979-1*) Gallopade Pub Group.

— North Dakota's (Most Devastating!) Disasters & (Most Calamitous!) Catastrophies! (Carole Marsh North Dakota Bks.). (Illus.). (J). 1994. lib. bdg. 24.95 (*0-7933-0862-3*); pap. 14.95 (*0-7933-0861-5*); disk 29.95 (*0-7933-0863-1*) Gallopade Pub Group.

— North Dakota's Unsolved Mysteries (& Their "Solutions") Includes Scientific Information & Other Activities for Students. (Carole Marsh North Dakota Bks.). (Illus.). (J). (gr. 3-12). 1994. lib. bdg. 24.95 (*0-7933-5824-8*); pap. 14.95 (*0-7933-5825-6*); disk 29.95 (*0-7933-5826-4*) Gallopade Pub Group.

— Ohio & Other State Greats (Biographies) (Carole Marsh Ohio Bks.). (Illus.). (J). 1994. lib. bdg. 24.95 (*1-55609-998-3*); pap. 14.95 (*1-55609-999-1*); disk 29.95 (*1-55609-854-5*) Gallopade Pub Group.

— Ohio Bandits, Bushwackers, Outlaws, Crooks, Devils, Ghosts, Desperadoes & Other Assorted & Sundry Characters! (Illus.). (J). 1994. lib. bdg. 24.95 (*0-7933-0889-5*); pap. 14.95 (*0-7933-0888-7*); disk 29.95 (*0-7933-0890-9*) Gallopade Pub Group.

— The Ohio Bookstore Book: A Surprising Guide to Our State's Bookstores & Their Specialties for Students, Teachers, Writers & Publishers. (Carole Marsh Ohio Bks.). (Illus.). 1994. lib. bdg. 24.95 (*0-7933-2960-4*); pap. 14.95 (*0-7933-2961-2*); disk 29.95 (*0-7933-2962-0*) Gallopade Pub Group.

— Ohio Classic Christmas Trivia: Stories, Recipes, Activities, Legends, Lore & More! (Carole Marsh Ohio Bks.). (Illus.). (J). 1994. lib. bdg. 24.95 (*0-7933-0892-5*); pap. 14.95 (*0-7933-0891-7*); disk 29.95 (*0-7933-0893-3*) Gallopade Pub Group.

— Ohio Coastales. (Carole Marsh Ohio Bks.). (Illus.). (J). 1994. lib. bdg. 24.95 (*1-55609-992-4*); pap. 14.95 (*1-55609-993-2*); disk 29.95 (*1-55609-994-0*) Gallopade Pub Group.

— Ohio Coastales! (Carole Marsh Ohio Bks.). (J). 1994. lib. bdg. 24.95 (*0-7933-7300-X*) Gallopade Pub Group.

— Ohio "Crinkum-Crankum" A Funny Word Book about Our State. (Carole Marsh Ohio Bks.). (Illus.). (J). (gr. 3-12). 1994. 24.95 (*0-7933-4913-3*); pap. 14.95 (*0-7933-4914-1*); disk 29.95 (*0-7933-4915-X*) Gallopade Pub Group.

— Ohio Dingbats! Bk. 1: A Fun Book of Games, Stories, Activities & More about Our State That's All in Code! for You to Decipher. (Carole Marsh Ohio Bks.). (Illus.). (J). (gr. 3-12). 1994. lib. bdg. 24.95 (*0-7933-3878-6*); pap. 14.95 (*0-7933-3879-4*); disk 29.95 (*0-7933-3880-8*) Gallopade Pub Group.

— Ohio Festival Fun for Kids! (Carole Marsh Ohio Bks.). (Illus.). (YA). (gr. 3-12). 1994. lib. bdg. 24.95 (*0-7933-4031-4*); pap. 14.95 (*0-7933-4032-2*); disk 29.95 (*0-7933-4033-0*) Gallopade Pub Group.

— The Ohio Hot Air Balloon Mystery. (Carole Marsh Ohio Bks.). (Illus.). (J). (gr. 2-9). 1994. 24.95 (*0-7933-2633-8*); pap. 14.95 (*0-7933-2634-6*); disk 29.95 (*0-7933-2635-4*) Gallopade Pub Group.

— Ohio Jeopardy! Answers & Questions about Our State! (Carole Marsh Ohio Bks.). (Illus.). (J). (gr. 3-12). 1994. lib. bdg. 24.95 (*0-7933-4184-1*); pap. 14.95 (*0-7933-4185-X*); disk 29.95 (*0-7933-4186-8*) Gallopade Pub Group.

— Ohio "Jography" A Fun Run Thru Our State! (Carole Marsh Ohio Bks.). (Illus.). (J). 1994. lib. bdg. 24.95 (*1-55609-981-9*); pap. 14.95 (*1-55609-982-7*); disk 29.95 (*1-55609-983-5*) Gallopade Pub Group.

— Ohio Kid's Cookbook: Recipes, How-to, History, Lore & More! (Carole Marsh Ohio Bks.). (Illus.). (J). 1994. lib. bdg. 24.95 (*0-7933-0901-8*); pap. 14.95 (*0-7933-0900-X*); disk 29.95 (*0-7933-0902-6*) Gallopade Pub Group.

— The Ohio Library Book: A Surprising Guide to the Unusual Special Collections in Libraries Across Our State for Students, Teachers, Writers & Publishers - Includes Reproducible Mailing Labels Plus Activities for Young People! (Carole Marsh Ohio Bks.). (Illus.). 1994. lib. bdg. 24.95 (*0-7933-3110-2*); pap. 14.95 (*0-7933-3111-0*); disk 29.95 (*0-7933-3112-9*) Gallopade Pub Group.

— The Ohio Media Book: A Surprising Guide to the Amazing Print, Broadcast & Online Media of Our State for Students, Teachers, Writers & Publishers - Includes Reproducible Mailing Labels Plus Activities for Young People! (Carole Marsh Ohio Bks.). (Illus.). 1994. lib. bdg. 24.95 (*0-7933-3266-4*); pap. 14.95 (*0-7933-3267-2*); disk 29.95 (*0-7933-3268-0*) Gallopade Pub Group.

— The Ohio Mystery Van Takes Off! Book 1: Handicapped Ohio Kids Sneak Off on a Big Adventure. (Carole Marsh Ohio Bks.). (Illus.). (J). (gr. 3-12). 1994. 24.95 (*0-7933-5066-2*); pap. 14.95 (*0-7933-5067-0*); disk 29.95 (*0-7933-5068-9*) Gallopade Pub Group.

— Ohio Quiz Crash Course! (Carole Marsh Ohio Bks.). (Illus.). (J). 1994. lib. bdg. 24.95 (*1-55609-995-9*); pap. 14.95 (*1-55609-996-7*); disk 29.95 (*1-55609-997-5*) Gallopade Pub Group.

— Ohio Rollercoasters! (Carole Marsh Ohio Bks.). (Illus.). (YA). (gr. 3-12). 1994. lib. bdg. 24.95 (*0-7933-5329-7*); pap. 14.95 (*0-7933-5330-0*); disk 29.95 (*0-7933-5331-9*) Gallopade Pub Group.

An Asterisk (*) at the beginning of an entry indicates that the title is appearing in BIP for the first time.

— Ohio School Trivia: An Amazing & Fascinating Look at Our State's Teachers, Schools & Students! (Carole Marsh Ohio Bks.). (Illus.). (J). 1994. lib. bdg. 24.95 (*0-7933-0898-4*); pap. 14.95 (*0-7933-0897-6*); disk 29.95 (*0-7933-0899-2*) Gallopade Pub Group.

— Ohio Silly Basketball Sportsmysteries, Vol. 1. (Carole Marsh Ohio Bks.). (Illus.). (J). 1994. lib. bdg. 24.95 (*0-7933-0895-X*); pap. 14.95 (*0-7933-0894-1*); disk 29.95 (*0-7933-0896-8*) Gallopade Pub Group.

— Ohio Silly Basketball Sportsmysteries, Vol. 2. (Carole Marsh Ohio Bks.). (Illus.). (J). 1994. lib. bdg. 24.95 (*0-685-45976-4*); pap. 14.95 (*0-7933-1854-8*); disk 29.95 (*0-7933-1855-6*) Gallopade Pub Group.

— Ohio Silly Football Sportsmysteries, Vol. 1. (Carole Marsh Ohio Bks.). (Illus.). (J). 1994. lib. bdg. 24.95 (*1-55609-986-X*); pap. 14.95 (*1-55609-987-8*); disk 29.95 (*1-55609-988-6*) Gallopade Pub Group.

— Ohio Silly Football Sportsmysteries, Vol. 2. (Carole Marsh Ohio Bks.). (Illus.). (J). 1994. lib. bdg. 24.95 (*1-55609-989-4*); pap. 14.95 (*1-55609-990-8*); disk 29.95 (*1-55609-991-6*) Gallopade Pub Group.

— Ohio Silly Trivia1. (Carole Marsh Ohio Bks.). (Illus.). (J). 1994. lib. bdg. 24.95 (*1-55609-979-7*); pap. 14.95 (*1-55609-112-5*); disk 29.95 (*1-55609-980-0*) Gallopade Pub Group.

— Ohio Timeline: A Chronology of Ohio History, Mystery, Trivia, Legend, Lore & More. (Carole Marsh Ohio Bks.). (Illus.). (J). (gr. 3-12). 1994. lib. bdg. 24.95 (*0-7933-5980-5*); pap. 14.95 (*0-7933-5981-3*); disk 29.95 (*0-7933-5982-1*) Gallopade Pub Group.

— Ohio's (Most Devastating!) Disasters & (Most Calamitous!) Catastrophies! (Carole Marsh Ohio Bks.). (Illus.). (J). 1994. lib. bdg. 24.95 (*0-7933-0886-0*); pap. 14.95 (*0-7933-0885-2*); disk 29.95 (*0-7933-0887-9*) Gallopade Pub Group.

— Ohio's Unsolved Mysteries (& Their "Solutions") Includes Scientific Information & Other Activities for Students. (Carole Marsh Ohio Bks.). (Illus.). (J). (gr. 3-12). 1994. lib. bdg. 24.95 (*0-7933-5827-2*); pap. 14.95 (*0-7933-5828-0*); disk 29.95 (*0-7933-5829-9*) Gallopade Pub Group.

— Oklahoma & Other State Greats (Biographies) (Carole Marsh Oklahoma Bks.). (Illus.). (J). 1994. lib. bdg. 24.95 (*0-7933-1878-5*); pap. 14.95 (*0-7933-1879-3*); disk 29.95 (*0-7933-1880-7*) Gallopade Pub Group.

— Oklahoma Bandits, Bushwackers, Outlaws, Crooks, Devils, Ghosts, Desperadoes & Other Assorted & Sundry Characters! (Carole Marsh Oklahoma Bks.). (Illus.). (J). 1994. lib. bdg. 24.95 (*0-7933-0914-X*); pap. 14.95 (*0-7933-0913-1*); disk 29.95 (*0-7933-0915-8*) Gallopade Pub Group.

— The Oklahoma Bookstore Book: A Surprising Guide to Our State's Bookstores & Their Specialties for Students, Teachers, Writers & Publishers. (Carole Marsh Oklahoma Bks.). (Illus.). 1994. lib. bdg. 24.95 (*0-7933-2963-9*); pap. 14.95 (*0-7933-2964-7*); disk 29.95 (*0-7933-2965-5*) Gallopade Pub Group.

— Oklahoma Classic Christmas Trivia: Stories, Recipes, Activities, Legends, Lore & More! (Carole Marsh Oklahoma Bks.). (Illus.). (J). 1994. lib. bdg. 24.95 (*0-7933-0917-4*); pap. 14.95 (*0-7933-0916-6*); disk 29.95 (*0-7933-0918-2*) Gallopade Pub Group.

— Oklahoma Coastales. (Carole Marsh Oklahoma Bks.). (Illus.). (J). 1994. lib. bdg. 24.95 (*0-7933-1872-6*); lib. bdg. 24.95 (*0-7933-7301-8*); pap. 14.95 (*0-7933-1873-4*); disk 29.95 (*0-7933-1874-2*) Gallopade Pub Group.

— Oklahoma "Crinkum-Crankum" A Funny Word Book about Our State. (Oklahoma Bks.). (Illus.). (J). (gr. 3-12). 1994. 24.95 (*0-7933-4916-8*); pap. 14.95 (*0-7933-4917-6*); disk 29.95 (*0-7933-4918-4*) Gallopade Pub Group.

— Oklahoma Dingbats! Bk. 1: A Fun Book of Games, Stories, Activities & More about Our State That's All in Code! for You to Decipher. (Carole Marsh Oklahoma Bks.). (Illus.). (J). (gr. 3-12). 1994. lib. bdg. 24.95 (*0-7933-3881-6*); pap. 14.95 (*0-7933-3882-4*); disk 29.95 (*0-7933-3883-2*) Gallopade Pub Group.

— Oklahoma Festival Fun for Kids! (Carole Marsh Oklahoma Bks.). (Illus.). (YA). (gr. 3-12). 1994. lib. bdg. 24.95 (*0-7933-4034-9*); pap. 14.95 (*0-7933-4035-7*); disk 29.95 (*0-7933-4036-5*) Gallopade Pub Group.

— The Oklahoma Hot Air Balloon Mystery. (Carole Marsh Oklahoma Bks.). (Illus.). (J). (gr. 2-9). 1994. 24.95 (*0-7933-2642-7*); pap. 14.95 (*0-7933-2643-5*); disk 29.95 (*0-7933-2644-3*) Gallopade Pub Group.

— Oklahoma Jeopardy! Answers & Questions about Our State! (Carole Marsh Oklahoma Bks.). (Illus.). (J). (gr. 3-12). 1994. lib. bdg. 24.95 (*0-7933-4187-6*); pap. 14.95 (*0-7933-4188-4*); disk 29.95 (*0-7933-4189-2*) Gallopade Pub Group.

— Oklahoma "Jography" A Fun Run Thru Our State! (Carole Marsh Oklahoma Bks.). (Illus.). (J). 1994. lib. bdg. 24.95 (*0-7933-1858-0*); pap. 14.95 (*1-55609-086-2*); disk 29.95 (*0-7933-1859-9*) Gallopade Pub Group.

— Oklahoma Kid's Cookbook: Recipes, How-to, History, Lore & More! (Carole Marsh Oklahoma Bks.). (Illus.). (J). 1994. lib. bdg. 24.95 (*0-7933-0926-3*); pap. 14.95 (*0-7933-0925-5*); disk 29.95 (*0-7933-0927-1*) Gallopade Pub Group.

— The Oklahoma Library Book: A Surprising Guide to the Unusual Special Collections in Libraries Across Our State for Students, Teachers, Writers & Publishers - Includes Reproducible Mailing Labels Plus Activities for Young People! (Carole Marsh Oklahoma Bks.). (Illus.). 1994. lib. bdg. 24.95 (*0-7933-3113-7*); pap. 14.95 (*0-7933-3114-5*); disk 29.95 (*0-7933-3115-3*) Gallopade Pub Group.

— The Oklahoma Media Book: A Surprising Guide to the Amazing Print, Broadcast & Online Media of Our State for Students, Teachers, Writers & Publishers - Includes Reproducible Mailing Labels Plus Activities for Young People! (Carole Marsh Oklahoma Bks.). (Illus.). 1994. lib. bdg. 24.95 (*0-7933-3269-9*); pap. 14.95 (*0-7933-3270-2*); disk 29.95 (*0-7933-3271-0*) Gallopade Pub Group.

— The Oklahoma Mystery Van Takes Off! Book 1: Handicapped Oklahoma Kids Sneak Off on a Big Adventure. (Oklahoma Bks.). (Illus.). (J). (gr. 3-12). 1994. 24.95 (*0-7933-5069-7*); pap. 14.95 (*0-7933-5070-0*); disk 29.95 (*0-7933-5071-9*) Gallopade Pub Group.

— Oklahoma Quiz Bowl Crash Course! (Carole Marsh Oklahoma Bks.). (Illus.). (J). 1994. lib. bdg. 24.95 (*0-7933-1881-5*); pap. 14.95 (*0-7933-1882-3*); disk 29.95 (*0-7933-1883-1*) Gallopade Pub Group.

— Oklahoma Rollercoasters! (Oklahoma Bks.). (Illus.). (YA). (gr. 3-12). 1994. lib. bdg. 24.95 (*0-7933-5332-7*); pap. 14.95 (*0-7933-5333-5*); disk 29.95 (*0-7933-5334-3*) Gallopade Pub Group.

— Oklahoma School Trivia: An Amazing & Fascinating Look at Our State's Teachers, Schools & Students! (Carole Marsh Oklahoma Bks.). (Illus.). (J). 1994. lib. bdg. 24.95 (*0-7933-0923-9*); pap. 14.95 (*0-7933-0922-0*); disk 29.95 (*0-7933-0924-7*) Gallopade Pub Group.

— Oklahoma Silly Basketball Sportsmysteries, Vol. 1. (Carole Marsh Oklahoma Bks.). (Illus.). (J). 1994. lib. bdg. 24.95 (*0-7933-0920-4*); pap. 14.95 (*0-7933-0919-0*); disk 29.95 (*0-7933-0921-2*) Gallopade Pub Group.

— Oklahoma Silly Basketball Sportsmysteries, Vol. 2. (Carole Marsh Oklahoma Bks.). (Illus.). (J). 1994. lib. bdg. 24.95 (*0-7933-1884-X*); pap. 14.95 (*0-7933-1885-8*); disk 29.95 (*0-7933-1886-6*) Gallopade Pub Group.

— Oklahoma Silly Football Sportsmysteries, Vol. 1. (Carole Marsh Oklahoma Bks.). (Illus.). (J). 1994. lib. bdg. 24.95 (*0-7933-1863-7*); pap. 14.95 (*0-7933-1864-5*); disk 29.95 (*0-7933-1865-3*) Gallopade Pub Group.

— Oklahoma Silly Football Sportsmysteries, Vol. 2. (Carole Marsh Oklahoma Bks.). (Illus.). (J). 1994. lib. bdg. 24.95 (*0-7933-1866-1*); pap. 14.95 (*0-7933-1867-X*); disk 29.95 (*0-7933-1868-8*) Gallopade Pub Group.

— Oklahoma Silly Trivia! (Carole Marsh Oklahoma Bks.). (Illus.). (J). 1994. lib. bdg. 24.95 (*0-685-45977-2*); pap. 14.95 (*1-55609-082-X*); disk 29.95 (*0-7933-1857-2*) Gallopade Pub Group.

— Oklahoma Timeline: A Chronology of Oklahoma History, Mystery, Trivia, Legend, Lore & More. (Oklahoma Bks.). (Illus.). (J). (gr. 3-12). 1994. lib. bdg. 24.95 (*0-7933-5983-X*); pap. 14.95 (*0-7933-5984-8*); disk 29.95 (*0-7933-5985-6*) Gallopade Pub Group.

— Oklahoma's (Most Devastating!) Disasters & (Most Calamitous!) Catastrophies! (Oklahoma Bks.). (Illus.). (J). 1994. lib. bdg. 24.95 (*0-7933-0911-5*); pap. 14.95 (*0-7933-0910-7*); disk 29.95 (*0-7933-0912-3*) Gallopade Pub Group.

— Oklahoma's Unsolved Mysteries (& Their "Solutions") Includes Scientific Information & Other Activities for Students. (Oklahoma Bks.). (Illus.). (J). (gr. 3-12). 1994. lib. bdg. 24.95 (*0-7933-5830-2*); pap. 14.95 (*0-7933-5831-0*); disk 29.95 (*0-7933-5832-9*) Gallopade Pub Group.

— Old Salem Mystery. (History Mystery Ser.). (Orig.). (J). (gr. 3-12). 1994. 24.95 (*1-55609-184-2*); pap. 14.95 (*0-935326-59-6*) Gallopade Pub Group.

— Oregon & Other State Greats (Biographies) (Carole Marsh Oregon Bks.). (Illus.). (J). 1994. lib. bdg. 24.95 (*0-7933-1913-7*); pap. 14.95 (*0-7933-1914-5*); disk 29.95 (*0-7933-1915-3*) Gallopade Pub Group.

— Oregon Bandits, Bushwackers, Outlaws, Crooks, Devils, Ghosts, Desperadoes & Other Assorted & Sundry Characters! (Carole Marsh Oregon Bks.). (Illus.). (J). 1994. lib. bdg. 24.95 (*0-7933-0938-7*); pap. 14.95 (*0-7933-0937-9*); disk 29.95 (*0-7933-0939-5*) Gallopade Pub Group.

— The Oregon Bookstore Book: A Surprising Guide to Our State's Bookstores & Their Specialties for Students, Teachers, Writers & Publishers. (Oregon Bks.). (Illus.). 1994. lib. bdg. 24.95 (*0-7933-2966-3*); pap. 14.95 (*0-7933-2967-1*); disk 29.95 (*0-7933-2968-X*) Gallopade Pub Group.

— Oregon Classic Christmas Trivia: Stories, Recipes, Activities, Legends, Lore & More! (Carole Marsh Oregon Bks.). (Illus.). (J). 1994. lib. bdg. 24.95 (*0-7933-0941-7*); pap. 14.95 (*0-7933-0940-9*); disk 29.95 (*0-7933-0942-5*) Gallopade Pub Group.

— Oregon Coastales. (Carole Marsh Oregon Bks.). (Illus.). (J). 1994. lib. bdg. 24.95 (*0-7933-1907-2*); pap. 14.95 (*0-685-45978-0*) Gallopade Pub Group.

— Oregon Coastales! (Oregon Bks.). (J). 1994. lib. bdg. 24.95 (*0-7933-7302-6*) Gallopade Pub Group.

— Oregon "Crinkum-Crankum" A Funny Word Book about Our State. (Oregon Bks.). (Illus.). (J). (gr. 3-12). 1994. 24.95 (*0-7933-4919-2*); pap. 14.95 (*0-7933-4920-6*); disk 29.95 (*0-7933-4921-4*) Gallopade Pub Group.

— Oregon Dingbats! Bk. 1: A Fun Book of Games, Stories, Activities & More about Our State That's All in Code! for You to Decipher. (Oregon Bks.). (Illus.). (J). (gr. 3-12). 1994. lib. bdg. 24.95 (*0-7933-3884-0*); pap. 14.95 (*0-7933-3885-9*); disk 29.95 (*0-7933-3886-7*) Gallopade Pub Group.

— Oregon Festival Fun for Kids! (Oregon Bks.). (Illus.). (YA). (gr. 3-12). 1994. lib. bdg. 24.95 (*0-7933-4037-3*); pap. 14.95 (*0-7933-4038-1*); disk 29.95 (*0-7933-4039-X*) Gallopade Pub Group.

— The Oregon Hot Air Balloon Mystery. (Carole Marsh Oregon Bks.). (Illus.). (J). (gr. 2-9). 1994. 24.95 (*0-7933-2651-6*); pap. 14.95 (*0-7933-2652-4*); disk 29.95 (*0-7933-2653-2*) Gallopade Pub Group.

— Oregon Jeopardy! Answers & Questions about Our State! (Oregon Bks.). (Illus.). (J). (gr. 3-12). 1994. lib. bdg. 24.95 (*0-7933-4190-6*); pap. 14.95 (*0-7933-4191-4*); disk 29.95 (*0-7933-4192-2*) Gallopade Pub Group.

— Oregon "Jography" A Fun Run Thru Our State. (Carole Marsh Oregon Bks.). (Illus.). (J). 1994. lib. bdg. 24.95 (*0-7933-1890-4*); pap. 14.95 (*0-7933-1891-2*); disk 29.95 (*0-7933-1892-0*) Gallopade Pub Group.

— Oregon Kid's Cookbook: Recipes, How-to, History, Lore & More! (Carole Marsh Oregon Bks.). (Illus.). (J). 1994. lib. bdg. 24.95 (*0-7933-0950-6*); pap. 14.95 (*0-7933-0949-2*); disk 29.95 (*0-7933-0951-4*) Gallopade Pub Group.

— The Oregon Library Book: A Surprising Guide to the Unusual Special Collections in Libraries Across Our State for Students, Teachers, Writers & Publishers - Includes Reproducible Mailing Labels Plus Activities for Young People! (Oregon Bks.). (Illus.). 1994. lib. bdg. 24.95 (*0-7933-3116-1*); pap. 14.95 (*0-7933-3117-X*); disk 29.95 (*0-7933-3118-8*) Gallopade Pub Group.

— The Oregon Media Book: A Surprising Guide to the Amazing Print, Broadcast & Online Media of Our State for Students, Teachers, Writers & Publishers - Includes Reproducible Mailing Labels Plus Activities for Young People! (Oregon Bks.). (Illus.). 1994. lib. bdg. 24.95 (*0-7933-3272-9*); pap. 14.95 (*0-7933-3273-7*); disk 29.95 (*0-7933-3274-5*) Gallopade Pub Group.

— The Oregon Mystery Van Takes Off! Book 1: Handicapped Oregon Kids Sneak Off on a Big Adventure. (Oregon Bks.). (Illus.). (J). (gr. 3-12). 1994. 24.95 (*0-7933-5072-7*); pap. 14.95 (*0-7933-5073-5*); disk 29.95 (*0-7933-5074-3*) Gallopade Pub Group.

— Oregon Quiz Bowl Crash Course! (Carole Marsh Oregon Bks.). (Illus.). (J). 1994. lib. bdg. 24.95 (*0-7933-1904-8*); pap. 14.95 (*0-7933-1905-6*); disk 29.95 (*0-7933-1906-4*) Gallopade Pub Group.

— Oregon Rollercoasters! (Oregon Bks.). (Illus.). (YA). (gr. 3-12). 1994. lib. bdg. 24.95 (*0-7933-5335-1*); pap. 14.95 (*0-7933-5336-X*); disk 29.95 (*0-7933-5337-8*) Gallopade Pub Group.

— Oregon School Trivia: An Amazing & Fascinating Look at Our State's Teachers, Schools & Students. (Carole Marsh Oregon Bks.). (Illus.). (J). 1994. lib. bdg. 24.95 (*0-7933-0947-6*); pap. 14.95 (*0-7933-0946-8*); disk 29.95 (*0-7933-0948-4*) Gallopade Pub Group.

— Oregon Silly Basketball Sportsmysteries, Vol. 1. (Carole Marsh Oregon Bks.). (Illus.). (J). 1994. lib. bdg. 24.95 (*0-7933-0944-1*); pap. 14.95 (*0-7933-0943-3*); disk 29.95 (*0-7933-0945-X*) Gallopade Pub Group.

— Oregon Silly Basketball Sportsmysteries, Vol. 2. (Carole Marsh Oregon Bks.). (Illus.). (J). 1994. lib. bdg. 24.95 (*0-7933-1916-1*); pap. 14.95 (*0-7933-1917-X*); disk 29.95 (*0-7933-1918-8*) Gallopade Pub Group.

— Oregon Silly Football Sportsmysteries, Vol. 1. (Carole Marsh Oregon Bks.). (Illus.). (J). 1994. lib. bdg. 24.95 (*0-7933-1895-5*); pap. 14.95 (*0-7933-1896-3*); disk 29.95 (*0-7933-1897-1*) Gallopade Pub Group.

— Oregon Silly Football Sportsmysteries, Vol. 2. (Carole Marsh Oregon Bks.). (Illus.). (J). 1994. lib. bdg. 24.95 (*0-7933-1898-X*); pap. 14.95 (*0-7933-1899-8*); disk 29.95 (*0-7933-1900-5*) Gallopade Pub Group.

— Oregon Silly Trivia! (Carole Marsh Oregon Bks.). (Illus.). (J). 1994. lib. bdg. 24.95 (*0-7933-1887-4*); pap. 14.95 (*0-7933-1888-2*); disk 29.95 (*0-7933-1889-0*) Gallopade Pub Group.

— Oregon Timeline: A Chronology of Oregon History, Mystery, Trivia, Legend, Lore & More. (Oregon Bks.). (Illus.). (J). (gr. 3-12). 1994. lib. bdg. 24.95 (*0-7933-5986-4*); pap. 14.95 (*0-7933-5987-2*); disk 29.95 (*0-7933-5988-0*) Gallopade Pub Group.

— Oregon's (Most Devastating!) Disasters & (Most Calamitous!) Catastrophies! (Carole Marsh Oregon Bks.). (Illus.). (J). 1994. lib. bdg. 24.95 (*0-7933-0935-2*); pap. 14.95 (*0-7933-0934-4*); disk 29.95 (*0-7933-0936-0*) Gallopade Pub Group.

— Oregon's Unsolved Mysteries (& Their "Solutions") Includes Scientific Information & Other Activities for Students. (Oregon Bks.). (Illus.). (J). (gr. 3-12). 1994. lib. bdg. 24.95 (*0-7933-5833-7*); pap. 14.95 (*0-7933-5834-5*); disk 29.95 (*0-7933-5835-3*) Gallopade Pub Group.

— Out of the Mouths of Slaves. (Our Black Heritage Ser.). (J). (gr. 3-12). 1994. lib. bdg. 24.95 (*1-55609-312-8*); pap. 14.95 (*1-55609-311-X*); disk 29.95 (*1-55609-313-6*) Gallopade Pub Group.

— Palm Fever. (Carole Marsh Short Story Ser.). (Illus.). (J). (gr. 4-12). 1994. 24.95 (*1-55609-185-0*); pap. 14.95 (*1-55609-237-7*) Gallopade Pub Group.

— Patch, the Pirate Dog: A California Pet Story. (Carole Marsh California Bks.). (J). (ps-4). 1994. lib. bdg. 24.95 (*0-7933-5428-5*); pap. 14.95 (*0-7933-5429-3*); disk 29.95 (*0-7933-5430-7*) Gallopade Pub Group.

— Patch, the Pirate Dog: A Colorado Pet Story. (Carole Marsh Colorado Bks.). (J). (ps-4). 1994. lib. bdg. 24.95 (*0-7933-5431-5*); pap. 14.95 (*0-7933-5432-3*); disk 29.95 (*0-7933-5433-1*) Gallopade Pub Group.

— Patch, the Pirate Dog: A Connecticut Pet Story. (Carole Marsh Connecticut Bks.). (J). (ps-4). 1994. lib. bdg. 24.95 (*0-7933-5434-X*); pap. 14.95 (*0-7933-5435-8*); disk 29.95 (*0-7933-5436-6*) Gallopade Pub Group.

— Patch, the Pirate Dog: A Delaware Pet Story. (Carole Marsh Delaware Bks.). (J). (ps-4). 1994. lib. bdg. 24.95 (*0-7933-5437-4*); pap. 14.95 (*0-7933-5438-2*); disk 29.95 (*0-7933-5439-0*) Gallopade Pub Group.

— Patch, the Pirate Dog: A Florida Pet Story. (Carole Marsh Florida Bks.). (J). (ps-4). 1994. lib. bdg. 24.95 (*0-7933-5443-9*); pap. 14.95 (*0-7933-5444-7*); disk 29.95 (*0-7933-5445-5*) Gallopade Pub Group.

— Patch, the Pirate Dog: A Georgia Pet Story. (Carole Marsh Georgia Bks.). (J). (ps-4). 1994. lib. bdg. 24.95 (*0-7933-5446-3*); pap. 14.95 (*0-7933-5447-1*); disk 29.95 (*0-7933-5448-X*) Gallopade Pub Group.

— Patch, the Pirate Dog: A Hawaii Pet Story. (Carole Marsh Hawaii Bks.). (J). (ps-4). 1994. lib. bdg. 24.95 (*0-7933-5449-8*); pap. 14.95 (*0-7933-5450-1*); disk 29.95 (*0-7933-5451-X*) Gallopade Pub Group.

— Patch, the Pirate Dog: A Kansas Pet Story. (Carole Marsh Kansas Bks.). (J). (ps-4). 1994. lib. bdg. 24.95 (*0-7933-5464-1*); pap. 14.95 (*0-7933-5465-X*); disk 29.95 (*0-7933-5466-8*) Gallopade Pub Group.

— Patch, the Pirate Dog: A Kentucky Pet Story. (Carole Marsh Kentucky Bks.). (J). (ps-4). 1994. lib. bdg. 24.95 (*0-7933-5467-6*); pap. 14.95 (*0-7933-5468-4*); disk 29.95 (*0-7933-5469-2*) Gallopade Pub Group.

— Patch, the Pirate Dog: A Louisiana Pet Story. (Carole Marsh Louisiana Bks.). (J). (ps-4). 1994. lib. bdg. 24.95 (*0-7933-5470-6*); pap. 14.95 (*0-7933-5471-4*); disk 29.95 (*0-7933-5472-2*) Gallopade Pub Group.

— Patch, the Pirate Dog: A Maine Pet Story. (Carole Marsh Maine Bks.). (J). (ps-4). 1994. lib. bdg. 24.95 (*0-7933-5473-0*); pap. 14.95 (*0-7933-5474-9*); disk 29.95 (*0-7933-5475-7*) Gallopade Pub Group.

— Patch, the Pirate Dog: A Maryland Pet Story. (Carole Marsh Maryland Bks.). (J). (ps-4). 1994. lib. bdg. 24.95 (*0-7933-5476-5*); pap. 14.95 (*0-7933-5477-3*); disk 29.95 (*0-7933-5478-1*) Gallopade Pub Group.

— Patch, the Pirate Dog: A Massachusetts Pet Story. (Massachuseets Bks.). (J). (ps-4). 1994. lib. bdg. 24.95 (*0-7933-5479-X*); pap. 14.95 (*0-7933-5480-3*); disk 29.95 (*0-7933-5481-1*) Gallopade Pub Group.

— Patch, the Pirate Dog: A Michigan Pet Story. (Carole Marsh Michigan Bks.). (J). (ps-4). 1994. lib. bdg. 24.95 (*0-7933-5482-X*); pap. 14.95 (*0-7933-5483-8*); disk 29.95 (*0-7933-5484-6*) Gallopade Pub Group.

— Patch, the Pirate Dog: A Minnesota Pet Story. (Carole Marsh Minnesota Bks.). (J). (ps-4). 1994. lib. bdg. 24.95 (*0-7933-5485-4*); pap. 14.95 (*0-7933-5486-2*); disk 29.95 (*0-7933-5487-0*) Gallopade Pub Group.

— Patch, the Pirate Dog: A Mississippi Pet Story. (Carole Marsh Mississippi Bks.). (J). (ps-4). 1994. lib. bdg. 24.95 (*0-7933-5488-9*); pap. 14.95 (*0-7933-5489-7*); disk 29.95 (*0-7933-5490-0*) Gallopade Pub Group.

— Patch, the Pirate Dog: A Missouri Pet Story. (Carole Marsh Missouri Bks.). (J). (ps-4). 1994. lib. bdg. 24.95 (*0-7933-5491-9*); pap. 14.95 (*0-7933-5492-7*); disk 29.95 (*0-7933-5493-5*) Gallopade Pub Group.

— Patch, the Pirate Dog: A Montana Pet Story. (Carole Marsh Montana Bks.). (J). (ps-4). 1994. lib. bdg. 24.95 (*0-7933-5494-3*); pap. 14.95 (*0-7933-5495-1*); disk 29.95 (*0-7933-5496-X*) Gallopade Pub Group.

— Patch, the Pirate Dog: A Nebraska Pet Story. (Carole Marsh Nebraska Bks.). (J). (ps-4). 1994. lib. bdg. 24.95 (*0-7933-5497-8*); pap. 14.95 (*0-7933-5498-6*); disk 29.95 (*0-7933-5499-4*) Gallopade Pub Group.

— Patch, the Pirate Dog: A Nevada Pet Story. (Carole Marsh Nevada Bks.). (J). (ps-4). 1994. lib. bdg. 24.95 (*0-7933-5500-1*); pap. 14.95 (*0-7933-5501-X*); disk 29.95 (*0-7933-5502-8*) Gallopade Pub Group.

— Patch, the Pirate Dog: A New Hampshire Pet Story. (Carole Marsh New Hampshire Bks.). (J). (ps-4). 1994. lib. bdg. 24.95 (*0-7933-5503-6*); pap. 14.95 (*0-7933-5504-4*); disk 29.95 (*0-7933-5505-2*) Gallopade Pub Group.

— Patch, the Pirate Dog: A New Jersey Pet Story. (Carole Marsh New Jersey Bks.). (J). (ps-4). 1994. lib. bdg. 24.95 (*0-7933-5506-0*); pap. 14.95 (*0-7933-5507-9*); disk 29.95 (*0-7933-5508-7*) Gallopade Pub Group.

— Patch, the Pirate Dog: A New Mexico Pet Story. (Carole Marsh New Mexico Bks.). (J). (ps-4). 1994. lib. bdg. 24.95 (*0-7933-5509-5*); pap. 14.95 (*0-7933-5510-9*); disk 29.95 (*0-7933-5511-7*) Gallopade Pub Group.

— Patch, the Pirate Dog: A New York Pet Story. (Carole Marsh New York Bks.). (J). (ps-4). 1994. lib. bdg. 24.95 (*0-7933-5512-5*); pap. 14.95 (*0-7933-5513-3*); disk 29.95 (*0-7933-5514-1*) Gallopade Pub Group.

— Patch, the Pirate Dog: A North Carolina Pet Story. (Carole Marsh North Carolina Bks.). (J). (ps-4). 1994. lib. bdg. 24.95 (*0-7933-5515-X*); pap. 14.95 (*0-7933-5516-8*); disk 29.95 (*0-7933-5517-6*) Gallopade Pub Group.

— Patch, the Pirate Dog: A North Dakota Pet Story. (Carole Marsh North Dakota Bks.). (J). (ps-4). 1994. lib. bdg. 24.95 (*0-7933-5518-4*); pap. 14.95 (*0-7933-5519-2*); disk 29.95 (*0-7933-5520-6*) Gallopade Pub Group.

— Patch, the Pirate Dog: A Ohio Pet Story. (Carole Marsh Ohio Bks.). (J). (ps-4). 1994. lib. bdg. 24.95 (*0-7933-5521-4*); pap. 14.95 (*0-7933-5522-2*); disk 29.95 (*0-7933-5523-0*) Gallopade Pub Group.

— Patch, the Pirate Dog: A Oklahoma Pet Story. (Oklahoma Bks.). (J). (ps-4). 1994. lib. bdg. 24.95 (*0-7933-5524-9*); pap. 14.95 (*0-7933-5525-7*); disk 29.95 (*0-7933-5526-5*) Gallopade Pub Group.

— Patch, the Pirate Dog: A Oregon Pet Story. (Oregon Bks.). (J). (ps-4). 1994. lib. bdg. 24.95 (*0-7933-5527-3*); pap. 14.95 (*0-7933-5528-1*); disk 29.95 (*0-7933-5529-X*) Gallopade Pub Group.

— Patch, the Pirate Dog: A Pennsylvania Pet Story. (Pennsylvania Bks.). (J). (ps-4). 1994. lib. bdg. 24.95 (*0-7933-5530-3*); pap. 14.95 (*0-7933-5531-1*); disk 29.95 (*0-7933-5532-X*) Gallopade Pub Group.

— Patch, the Pirate Dog: A Rhode Island Pet Story. (Rhode Island Bks.). (J). (ps-4). 1994. lib. bdg. 24.95 (*0-7933-5533-8*); pap. 14.95 (*0-7933-5534-6*); disk 29.95 (*0-7933-5535-4*) Gallopade Pub Group.

— Patch, the Pirate Dog: A South Carolina Pet Story. (South Carolina Bks.). (J). (ps-4). 1994. lib. bdg. 24.95 (*0-7933-5536-2*); pap. 14.95 (*0-7933-5537-0*); disk 29.95 (*0-7933-5538-9*) Gallopade Pub Group.

— Patch, the Pirate Dog: A South Dakota Pet Story. (South Dakota Bks.). (J). (ps-4). 1994. lib. bdg. 24.95 (*0-7933-5539-7*); pap. 14.95 (*0-7933-5540-0*); disk 29.95 (*0-7933-5541-9*) Gallopade Pub Group.

M

— Patch, the Pirate Dog: A Tennessee Pet Story. (Tennessee Bks.). (J). (ps-4). 1994. lib. bdg. 24.95 (0-7933-5542-7); pap. 14.95 (0-7933-5543-5); disk 29.95 (0-7933-5544-3) Gallopade Pub Group.

— Patch, the Pirate Dog: A Texas Pet Story. (Texas Bks.). (J). (ps-4). 1994. lib. bdg. 24.95 (0-7933-5545-1); pap. 14.95 (0-7933-5546-X); disk 29.95 (0-7933-5547-8) Gallopade Pub Group.

— Patch, the Pirate Dog: A Utah Pet Story. (Utah Bks.). (J). (ps-4). 1994. lib. bdg. 24.95 (0-7933-5548-6); pap. 14.95 (0-7933-5549-4); disk 29.95 (0-7933-5550-8) Gallopade Pub Group.

— Patch, the Pirate Dog: A Vermont Pet Story. (Vermont Bks.). (J). (ps-4). 1994. lib. bdg. 24.95 (0-7933-5551-6); pap. 14.95 (0-7933-5552-4); disk 29.95 (0-7933-5553-2) Gallopade Pub Group.

— Patch, the Pirate Dog: A Virginia Pet Story. (Virginia Bks.). (J). (ps-4). 1994. lib. bdg. 24.95 (0-7933-5554-0); pap. 14.95 (0-7933-5555-9); disk 29.95 (0-7933-5556-7) Gallopade Pub Group.

— Patch, the Pirate Dog: A Washington DC Pet Story. (Washington, D.C. Bks.). (J). (ps-4). 1994. lib. bdg. 24.95 (0-7933-5440-4); pap. 14.95 (0-7933-5441-2); disk 29.95 (0-7933-5442-0) Gallopade Pub Group.

— Patch, the Pirate Dog: A Washington Pet Story. (Washington Bks.). (J). (ps-4). 1994. lib. bdg. 24.95 (0-7933-5557-5); pap. 14.95 (0-7933-5558-3); disk 29.95 (0-7933-5559-1) Gallopade Pub Group.

— Patch, the Pirate Dog: A West Virginia Pet Story. (West Virginia Bks.). (J). (ps-4). 1994. lib. bdg. 24.95 (0-7933-5560-5); pap. 14.95 (0-7933-5561-3); disk 29.95 (0-7933-5562-1) Gallopade Pub Group.

— Patch, the Pirate Dog: A Wisconsin Pet Story. (Wisconsin Bks.). (J). (ps-4). 1994. lib. bdg. 24.95 (0-7933-5563-X); pap. 14.95 (0-7933-5564-8); disk 29.95 (0-7933-5565-6) Gallopade Pub Group.

— Patch, the Pirate Dog: A Wyoming Pet Story. (Wyoming Bks.). (J). (ps-4). 1994. lib. bdg. 24.95 (0-7933-5566-4); pap. 14.95 (0-7933-5567-2); disk 29.95 (0-7933-5568-0) Gallopade Pub Group.

— Patch, the Pirate Dog: An Alabama Pet Story. (Carole Marsh Alabama Bks.). (J). (ps-4). 1994. lib. bdg. 24.95 (0-7933-5416-1); pap. 14.95 (0-7933-5417-X); disk 29.95 (0-7933-5418-8) Gallopade Pub Group.

— Patch, the Pirate Dog: An Alaska Pet Story. (Carole Marsh Alaska Bks.). (J). (ps-4). 1994. lib. bdg. 24.95 (0-7933-5419-6); pap. 14.95 (0-7933-5420-X); disk 29.95 (0-7933-5421-8) Gallopade Pub Group.

— Patch, the Pirate Dog: An Arizona Pet Story. (Carole Marsh Arizona Bks.). (J). (ps-4). 1994. lib. bdg. 24.95 (0-7933-5422-6); pap. 14.95 (0-7933-5423-4); disk 29.95 (0-7933-5424-2) Gallopade Pub Group.

— Patch, the Pirate Dog: An Arkansas Pet Story. (Carole Marsh Arkansas Bks.). (J). (ps-4). 1994. lib. bdg. 24.95 (0-7933-5425-0); pap. 14.95 (0-7933-5426-9); disk 29.95 (0-7933-5427-7) Gallopade Pub Group.

— Patch, the Pirate Dog: An Idaho Pet Story. (Carole Marsh Idaho Bks.). (J). (ps-4). 1994. lib. bdg. 24.95 (0-7933-5452-8); pap. 14.95 (0-7933-5453-6); disk 29.95 (0-7933-5454-4) Gallopade Pub Group.

— Patch, the Pirate Dog: An Illinois Pet Story. (Carole Marsh Illinois Bks.). (J). (ps-4). 1994. lib. bdg. 24.95 (0-7933-5455-2); pap. 14.95 (0-7933-5456-0); disk 29.95 (0-7933-5457-9) Gallopade Pub Group.

— Patch, the Pirate Dog: An Indiana Pet Story. (Carole Marsh Indiana Bks.). (J). (ps-4). 1994. lib. bdg. 24.95 (0-7933-5458-7); pap. 14.95 (0-7933-5459-5); disk 29.95 (0-7933-5460-9) Gallopade Pub Group.

— Patch, the Pirate Dog: An Iowa Pet Story. (Carole Marsh Iowa Bks.). (J). (ps-4). 1994. lib. bdg. 24.95 (0-7933-5461-7); pap. 14.95 (0-7933-5462-5); disk 29.95 (0-7933-5463-3) Gallopade Pub Group.

— Pennsylvania & Other State Greats (Biographies) (Carole Marsh Pennsylvania Bks.). (Illus.). (J). 1994. lib. bdg. 24.95 (0-7933-1942-0); pap. 14.95 (0-7933-1943-9); disk 29.95 (0-7933-1944-7) Gallopade Pub Group.

— Pennsylvania Bandits, Bushwackers, Outlaws, Crooks, Devils, Ghosts, Desperadoes & Other Assorted & Sundry Characters! (Carole Marsh Pennsylvania Bks.). (Illus.). (J). 1994. lib. bdg. 24.95 (0-7933-0962-X); pap. 14.95 (0-7933-0961-1); disk 29.95 (0-7933-0963-8) Gallopade Pub Group.

— The Pennsylvania Bookstore Book: A Surprising Guide to Our State's Bookstores & Their Specialties for Students, Teachers, Writers & Publishers. (Pennsylvania Bks.). (Illus.). 1994. lib. bdg. 24.95 (0-7933-2969-8); pap. 14.95 (0-7933-2970-1); disk 29.95 (0-7933-2971-X) Gallopade Pub Group.

— Pennsylvania Classic Christmas Trivia: Stories, Recipes, Activities, Legends, Lore & More! (Carole Marsh Pennsylvania Bks.). (Illus.). (J). 1994. lib. bdg. 24.95 (0-7933-0965-4); pap. 14.95 (0-7933-0964-6); disk 29.95 (0-7933-0966-2) Gallopade Pub Group.

— Pennsylvania Coastales. (Carole Marsh Pennsylvania Bks.). (Illus.). (J). 1994. lib. bdg. 24.95 (0-7933-1936-6); lib. bdg. 24.95 (0-7933-7303-4); pap. 14.95 (0-7933-1937-4); disk 29.95 (0-7933-1938-2) Gallopade Pub Group.

— Pennsylvania "Crinkum-Crankum" A Funny Word Book about Our State. (Pennsylvania Bks.). (Illus.). (J). (gr. 3-12). 1994. 24.95 (0-7933-4922-2); pap. 14.95 (0-7933-4923-0); disk 29.95 (0-7933-4924-9) Gallopade Pub Group.

— Pennsylvania Dingbats! Bk. 1: A Fun Book of Games, Stories, Activities & More about Our State That's All in Code! for You to Decipher. (Pennsylvania Bks.). (Illus.). (J). (gr. 3-12). 1994. lib. bdg. 24.95 (0-7933-3887-5); pap. 14.95 (0-7933-3888-3); disk 29.95 (0-7933-3889-1) Gallopade Pub Group.

— Pennsylvania Festival Fun for Kids! (Pennsylvania Bks.). (Illus.). (YA). (gr. 3-12). 1994. lib. bdg. 24.95 (0-7933-4040-3); pap. 14.95 (0-7933-4041-1); disk 29.95 (0-7933-4042-X) Gallopade Pub Group.

— The Pennsylvania Hot Air Balloon Mystery. (Carole Marsh Pennsylvania Bks.). (Illus.). (J). (gr. 2-9). 1994. 24.95 (0-7933-2660-5); pap. 14.95 (0-7933-2661-3); disk 29.95 (0-7933-2662-1) Gallopade Pub Group.

— Pennsylvania Jeopardy! Answers & Questions about Our State! (Pennsylvania Bks.). (Illus.). (J). (gr. 3-12). 1994. lib. bdg. 24.95 (0-7933-4193-0); pap. 14.95 (0-7933-4194-9); disk 29.95 (0-7933-4195-7) Gallopade Pub Group.

— Pennsylvania "Jography" A Fun Run Thru Our State! (Carole Marsh Pennsylvania Bks.). (Illus.). (J). 1994. lib. bdg. 24.95 (0-7933-1922-6); pap. 14.95 (0-7933-1923-4); disk 29.95 (0-7933-1924-2) Gallopade Pub Group.

— Pennsylvania Kid's Cookbook: Recipes, How-to, History, Lore & More! (Carole Marsh Pennsylvania Bks.). (Illus.). (J). 1994. lib. bdg. 24.95 (0-7933-0974-3); pap. 14.95 (0-7933-0973-5); disk 29.95 (0-7933-0975-1) Gallopade Pub Group.

— The Pennsylvania Library Book: A Surprising Guide to the Unusual Special Collections in Libraries Across Our State for Students, Teachers, Writers & Publishers - Includes Reproducible Mailing Labels Plus Activities for Young People! (Pennsylvania Bks.). (Illus.). 1994. lib. bdg. 24.95 (0-7933-3119-6); pap. 14.95 (0-7933-3120-X); disk 29.95 (0-7933-3121-8) Gallopade Pub Group.

— The Pennsylvania Media Book: A Surprising Guide to the Amazing Print, Broadcast & Online Media of Our State for Students, Teachers, Writers & Publishers - Includes Reproducible Mailing Labels Plus Activities for Young People! (Pennsylvania Bks.). (Illus.). 1994. lib. bdg. 24.95 (0-7933-3275-3); pap. 14.95 (0-7933-3276-1); disk 29.95 (0-7933-3277-X) Gallopade Pub Group.

— The Pennsylvania Mystery Van Takes Off! Book 1: Handicapped Pennsylvania Kids Sneak Off on a Big Adventure. (Pennsylvania Bks.). (Illus.). (J). (gr. 3-12). 1994. 24.95 (0-7933-5075-1); pap. 14.95 (0-7933-5076-X); disk 29.95 (0-7933-5077-8) Gallopade Pub Group.

— Pennsylvania Quiz Bowl Crash Course! (Carole Marsh Pennsylvania Bks.). (Illus.). (J). 1994. lib. bdg. 24.95 (0-7933-1945-5); pap. 14.95 (0-7933-1946-3); disk 29.95 (0-7933-1947-1) Gallopade Pub Group.

— Pennsylvania Rollercoasters! (Pennsylvania Bks.). (Illus.). (YA). (gr. 3-12). 1994. lib. bdg. 24.95 (0-7933-5338-6); pap. 14.95 (0-7933-5339-4); disk 29.95 (0-7933-5340-8) Gallopade Pub Group.

— Pennsylvania School Trivia: An Amazing & Fascinating Look at Ou State's Teachers, Schools & Students! (Carole Marsh Pennsylvania Bks.). (Illus.). (J). 1994. lib. bdg. 24.95 (0-7933-0971-9); pap. 14.95 (0-7933-0970-0); disk 29.95 (0-7933-0972-7) Gallopade Pub Group.

— Pennsylvania Silly Basketball Sportsmysteries, Vol. 1. (Carole Marsh Pennsylvania Bks.). (Illus.). (J). 1994. lib. bdg. 24.95 (0-7933-0968-9); pap. 14.95 (0-7933-0967-0); disk 29.95 (0-7933-0969-7) Gallopade Pub Group.

— Pennsylvania Silly Basketball Sportsmysteries, Vol. 2. (Carole Marsh Pennsylvania Bks.). (Illus.). (J). 1994. lib. bdg. 24.95 (0-7933-1948-X); pap. 14.95 (0-7933-1949-8); disk 29.95 (0-7933-1950-1) Gallopade Pub Group.

— Pennsylvania Silly Football Sportsmysteries, Vol. 1. (Carole Marsh Pennsylvania Bks.). (Illus.). (J). 1994. lib. bdg. 24.95 (0-7933-1927-7); pap. 14.95 (0-7933-1928-5); disk 29.95 (0-7933-1929-3) Gallopade Pub Group.

— Pennsylvania Silly Football Sportsmysteries, Vol. 2. (Carole Marsh Pennsylvania Bks.). (Illus.). (J). 1994. lib. bdg. 24.95 (0-7933-1930-7); pap. 14.95 (0-7933-1931-5); disk 29.95 (0-7933-1932-3) Gallopade Pub Group.

— Pennsylvania Silly Trivia! (Carole Marsh Pennsylvania Bks.). (Illus.). (J). 1994. lib. bdg. 24.95 (0-7933-1919-6); pap. 14.95 (0-7933-1920-X); disk 29.95 (0-7933-1921-8) Gallopade Pub Group.

— Pennsylvania Timeline: A Chronology of Pennsylvania History, Mystery, Trivia, Legend, Lore & More. (Pennsylvania Bks.). (Illus.). (J). (gr. 3-12). 1994. lib. bdg. 24.95 (0-7933-5989-9); pap. 14.95 (0-7933-5990-2); disk 29.95 (0-7933-5991-0) Gallopade Pub Group.

— Pennsylvania's (Most Devastating!) Disasters & (Most Calamitous!) Catastrophies! (Carole Marsh Pennsylvania Bks.). (Illus.). (J). 1994. lib. bdg. 24.95 (0-7933-0959-X); pap. 14.95 (0-7933-0958-1); disk 29.95 (0-7933-0960-3) Gallopade Pub Group.

— Pennsylvania's Unsolved Mysteries (& Their "Solutions") Includes Scientific Information & Other Activities for Students. (Pennsylvania Bks.). (Illus.). (J). (gr. 3-12). 1994. lib. bdg. 24.95 (0-7933-5836-1); pap. 14.95 (0-7933-5837-X); disk 29.95 (0-7933-5838-8) Gallopade Pub Group.

— PG: He's Having Her Baby. 19.95 (1-877755-01-X) Six Hse.

— Phyzzics for Kids. (Quantum Leap Ser.). (J). (gr. 4-9). 1994. 24.95 (1-55609-258-X); pap. 14.95 (1-55609-245-8); disk 29.95 (1-55609-340-3) Gallopade Pub Group.

— The Pirate & Treasure Dingbats Book. (Carole Marsh Dingbats Book Ser.). (Illus.). (YA). (gr. 3-12). 1994. lib. bdg. 24.95 (0-7933-5407-2); pap. 14.95 (0-7933-5408-0); disk 29.95 (0-7933-5409-9) Gallopade Pub Group.

— Pirate's Cookbook. (Naked Gourmet Ser.). (Orig.). 1994. 24.95 (1-55609-002-1); pap. 14.95 (0-685-13574-8) Gallopade Pub Group.

— Publishing on Command: How to Publish & Print 1-1,000 Books at a Time! (ProPub Ser.). 1994. 24.95 (1-55609-960-6); lib. bdg. 19.95 (1-55609-958-4); pap. 14.95 (1-55609-959-2); disk 29.95 (1-55609-961-4) Gallopade Pub Group.

— Quiz Bowl Crash Course. (J). (gr. 5 up). 1994. 24.95 (1-55609-288-1); pap. 14.95 (1-55609-195-8); disk 29.95 (1-55609-289-X) Gallopade Pub Group.

— Rhode Island & Other State Greats (Biographies) (Carole Marsh Rhode Island Bks.). (Illus.). (J). 1994. lib. bdg. 24.95 (0-7933-1977-3); pap. 14.95 (0-7933-1978-1); disk 29.95 (0-7933-1979-X) Gallopade Pub Group.

— Rhode Island Bandits, Bushwackers, Outlaws, Crooks, Devils, Ghosts, Desperadoes & Other Assorted & Sundry Characters! (Carole Marsh Rhode Island Bks.). (Illus.). (J). 1994. lib. bdg. 24.95 (0-7933-0986-7); pap. 14.95 (0-7933-0985-9); disk 29.95 (0-7933-0987-5) Gallopade Pub Group.

— The Rhode Island Bookstore Book: A Surprising Guide to Our State's Bookstores & Their Specialties for Students, Teachers, Writers & Publishers. (Rhode Island Bks.). (Illus.). 1994. lib. bdg. 24.95 (0-7933-2972-8); pap. 14.95 (0-7933-2973-6); disk 29.95 (0-7933-2974-4) Gallopade Pub Group.

— Rhode Island Classic Christmas Trivia: Stories, Recipes, Activities, Legends, Lore & More! (Carole Marsh Rhode Island Bks.). (Illus.). (J). 1994. lib. bdg. 24.95 (0-7933-0989-1); pap. 14.95 (0-7933-0988-3); disk 29.95 (0-7933-0990-5) Gallopade Pub Group.

— Rhode Island Coastales. (Carole Marsh Rhode Island Bks.). (Illus.). (J). 1994. lib. bdg. 24.95 (0-7933-1971-4); pap. 14.95 (0-7933-1972-2); disk 29.95 (0-7933-1973-0) Gallopade Pub Group.

— Rhode Island Coastales! (Rhode Island Bks.). (J). 1994. lib. bdg. 24.95 (0-7933-7304-2) Gallopade Pub Group.

— Rhode Island "Crinkum-Crankum" A Funny Word Book about Our State. (Rhode Island Bks.). (Illus.). (J). (gr. 3-12). 1994. 24.95 (0-7933-4925-7); pap. 14.95 (0-7933-4926-5); disk 29.95 (0-7933-4927-3) Gallopade Pub Group.

— Rhode Island Dingbats! Bk. 1: A Fun Book of Games, Stories, Activities & More about Our State That's All in Code! for You to Decipher. (Rhode Island Bks.). (Illus.). (J). (gr. 3-12). 1994. lib. bdg. 24.95 (0-7933-3890-5); pap. 14.95 (0-7933-3891-3); disk 29.95 (0-7933-3892-1) Gallopade Pub Group.

— Rhode Island Festival Fun for Kids! (Rhode Island Bks.). (Illus.). (YA). (gr. 3-12). 1994. lib. bdg. 24.95 (0-7933-4043-8); pap. 14.95 (0-7933-4044-6); disk 29.95 (0-7933-4045-4) Gallopade Pub Group.

— The Rhode Island Hot Air Balloon Mystery. (Carole Marsh Rhode Island Bks.). (Illus.). (J). (gr. 2-9). 1994. 24.95 (0-7933-2669-9); pap. 14.95 (0-7933-2670-2); disk 29.95 (0-7933-2671-0) Gallopade Pub Group.

— Rhode Island Jeopardy! Answers & Questions about Our State! (Rhode Island Bks.). (Illus.). (J). (gr. 3-12). 1994. lib. bdg. 24.95 (0-7933-4196-5); pap. 14.95 (0-7933-4197-3); disk 29.95 (0-7933-4198-1) Gallopade Pub Group.

— Rhode Island "Jography" A Fun Run Thru Our State! (Carole Marsh Rhode Island Bks.). (Illus.). (J). 1994. lib. bdg. 24.95 (0-7933-1954-4); pap. 14.95 (0-7933-1955-2); disk 29.95 (0-7933-1956-0) Gallopade Pub Group.

— Rhode Island Kid's Cookbook: Recipes, How-to, History Lore & More! (Carole Marsh Rhode Island Bks.). (Illus.). (J). 1994. lib. bdg. 24.95 (0-7933-0998-0); pap. 14.95 (0-7933-0997-2); disk 29.95 (0-7933-0999-9) Gallopade Pub Group.

— The Rhode Island Library Book: A Surprising Guide to the Unusual Special Collections in Libraries Across Our State for Students, Teachers, Writers & Publishers - Includes Reproducible Mailing Labels Plus Activities for Young People! (Rhode Island Bks.). (Illus.). 1994. lib. bdg. 24.95 (0-7933-3122-6); pap. 14.95 (0-7933-3123-4); disk 29.95 (0-7933-3124-2) Gallopade Pub Group.

— The Rhode Island Media Book: A Surprising Guide to the Amazing Print, Broadcast & Online Media of Our State for Students, Teachers, Writers & Publishers - Includes Reproducible Mailing Labels Plus Activities for Young People! (Rhode Island Bks.). (Illus.). 1994. lib. bdg. 24.95 (0-7933-3278-8); pap. 14.95 (0-7933-3279-6); disk 29.95 (0-7933-3280-X) Gallopade Pub Group.

— The Rhode Island Mystery Van Takes Off! Book 1: Handicapped Rhode Island Kids Sneak Off on a Big Adventure. (Rhode Island Bks.). (Illus.). (J). (gr. 3-12). 1994. 24.95 (0-7933-5078-6); pap. 14.95 (0-7933-5079-4); disk 29.95 (0-7933-5080-8) Gallopade Pub Group.

— Rhode Island Quiz Bowl Crash Course! (Carole Marsh Rhode Island Bks.). (Illus.). (J). 1994. lib. bdg. 24.95 (0-7933-1968-4); pap. 14.95 (0-7933-1969-2); disk 29.95 (0-7933-1970-6) Gallopade Pub Group.

— Rhode Island Rollercoasters! (Rhode Island Bks.). (Illus.). (YA). (gr. 3-12). 1994. lib. bdg. 24.95 (0-7933-5341-6); pap. 14.95 (0-7933-5342-4); disk 29.95 (0-7933-5343-2) Gallopade Pub Group.

— Rhode Island School Trivia: An Amazing & Fascinating Look at Our State's Teachers, Schools & Students! (Carole Marsh Rhode Island Bks.). (Illus.). (J). 1994. lib. bdg. 24.95 (0-7933-0995-6); pap. 14.95 (0-7933-0994-8); disk 29.95 (0-7933-0996-4) Gallopade Pub Group.

— Rhode Island Silly Basketball Sportsmysteries, Vol. 1. (Carole Marsh Rhode Island Bks.). (Illus.). (J). 1994. lib. bdg. 24.95 (0-7933-0992-1); pap. 14.95 (0-7933-0991-3); disk 29.95 (0-685-45968-3) Gallopade Pub Group.

— Rhode Island Silly Basketball Sportsmysteries, Vol. 2. (Carole Marsh Rhode Island Bks.). (Illus.). (J). 1994. lib. bdg. 24.95 (0-7933-1980-3); pap. 14.95 (0-7933-1981-1); disk 29.95 (0-7933-1982-X) Gallopade Pub Group.

— Rhode Island Silly Football Sportsmysteries, Vol. 1. (Carole Marsh Rhode Island Bks.). (Illus.). (J). 1994. lib. bdg. 24.95 (0-7933-1959-5); pap. 14.95 (0-7933-1960-9); disk 29.95 (0-7933-1961-7) Gallopade Pub Group.

— Rhode Island Silly Football Sportsmysteries, Vol. 2. (Carole Marsh Rhode Island Bks.). (Illus.). (J). 1994. lib. bdg. 24.95 (0-7933-1962-5); pap. 14.95 (0-7933-1963-3); disk 29.95 (0-7933-1964-1) Gallopade Pub Group.

— Rhode Island Silly Trivia! (Carole Marsh Rhode Island Bks.). (Illus.). (J). 1994. lib. bdg. 24.95 (0-7933-1951-X); pap. 14.95 (0-7933-1952-8); disk 29.95 (0-7933-1953-6) Gallopade Pub Group.

— Rhode Island Timeline: A Chronology of Rhode Island History, Mystery, Trivia, Legend, Lore & More. (Rhode Island Bks.). (Illus.). (J). (gr. 3-12). 1994. lib. bdg. 24.95 (0-7933-5992-9); pap. 14.95 (0-7933-5993-7); disk 29.95 (0-7933-5994-5) Gallopade Pub Group.

— Rhode Island's (Most Devastating!) Disasters & (Most Calamitous!) Catastrophies! (Carole Marsh Rhode Island Bks.). (Illus.). (J). 1994. lib. bdg. 24.95 (0-7933-0983-2); pap. 14.95 (0-7933-0982-4); disk 29.95 (0-685-45966-7) Gallopade Pub Group.

— Rhode Island's Unsolved Mysteries (& Their "Solutions") Includes Scientific Information & Other Activities for Students. (Rhode Island Bks.). (Illus.). (J). (gr. 3-12). 1994. lib. bdg. 24.95 (0-7933-5839-6); pap. 14.95 (0-7933-5840-X); disk 29.95 (0-7933-5841-8) Gallopade Pub Group.

— River Rogues! Natchez Pirates, Playboys, & the Rest of the Cock-o-the-Walk Crowd under-the-Hill & along the Trace. (Carole Marsh Mississippi Bks.). (J). 1994. lib. bdg. 24.95 (0-7933-7584-3); pap. 14.95 (0-7933-7323-9) Gallopade Pub Group.

— Saturnalia. (Carole Marsh Short Story Ser.). (Illus.). (Orig.). (J). (gr. 4-12). 1994. 24.95 (1-55609-187-7); pap. 14.95 (1-55609-238-5) Gallopade Pub Group.

— School Trivia: Funny (& Not So Funny) Stuff about Schools, Teachers & Students. (Quantum Leap Ser.). (Illus.). 1994. 24.95 (0-7933-0007-X); pap. 14.95 (0-7933-0008-8) Gallopade Pub Group.

— The Secret Mysteries Dingbats Book. (Carole Marsh Dingbats Book Ser.). (Illus.). (YA). (gr. 3-12). 1994. lib. bdg. 24.95 (0-7933-5383-1); pap. 14.95 (0-7933-5384-X); disk 29.95 (0-7933-5385-8) Gallopade Pub Group.

— The Secret of Scotty's Castle Set. (Carole Marsh Mysteries Ser.). 1994. 125.00 (0-7933-6964-9) Gallopade Pub Group.

— The Secret of Somerset Place. (History Mystery Ser.). (Illus.). (Orig.). (gr. 3-9). 1994. pap. 4.95 (0-935326-02-2) Gallopade Pub Group.

— The Secret of Somerset Place S. P. A. R. K. Kit. (S. P. A. R. K. Ser.). (Illus.). (Orig.). (J). (gr. 3-9). 1994. pap. 24.95 (0-935326-20-0) Gallopade Pub Group.

— The Secret of Somerset Place Set. (Carole Marsh Mysteries Ser.). 1994. teacher ed 125.00 (0-7933-6946-0) Gallopade Pub Group.

— Self Publishing by the Seat of Your Pants! (ProPub Ser.). 1994. lib. bdg. 19.95 (1-55609-962-2); pap. text ed. 14.95 (1-55609-963-0); ring bd. 24.95 (1-55609-964-9); disk 29.95 (1-55609-965-7) Gallopade Pub Group.

— Sex Stuff for Boys: Sperm, Squirm & Other Squiggly Stuff. (Smart Sex Stuff Ser.). 1994. 24.95 (1-55609-189-3); pap. 14.95 (1-55609-207-5) Gallopade Pub Group.

— Sex Stuff for Girls: A Period Is More Than a Punctuation Mark. (Smart Sex Stuff Ser.). (Orig.). 1994. 24.95 (1-55609-190-7); pap. 14.95 (1-55609-206-7) Gallopade Pub Group.

— Sex Stuff for Kids 7-17: A Book of Practical Information & Ideas for Kids & Their Teachers & Parents, Contains Chapter on 'AIDS' (J). (gr. 2-12). 1994. 24.95 (1-55609-200-8); teacher ed 24.95 (1-55609-204-0); pap. 14.95 (1-55609-201-6) Gallopade Pub Group.

— Sex Stuff for Parents: The Painless, Foolproof, "Really Works!" Way to Teach 7-17-Year-Olds about Sex So They Won't Get AIDS, a Disease or a Baby (& You Won't Get Embarrassed!): For Alabama Parents. (Carole Marsh Alabama Bks.). (Illus.). 1994. lib. bdg. 29.95 (0-7933-2321-5); lib. bdg. 29.95 (0-7933-2330-4); lib. bdg. 29.95 (0-7933-2339-8); lib. bdg. 29.95 (0-7933-2357-6); lib. bdg. 29.95 (0-7933-2366-5); lib. bdg. 29.95 (0-7933-2375-4); lib. bdg. 29.95 (0-685-37842-X); lib. bdg. 29.95 (0-7933-2393-2); lib. bdg. 29.95 (0-7933-2402-5); lib. bdg. 29.95 (0-7933-2411-4); lib. bdg. 29.95 (0-7933-2420-3); lib. bdg. 29.95 (0-7933-2429-7); lib. bdg. 29.95 (0-7933-2438-6); lib. bdg. 29.95 (0-7933-2447-5); lib. bdg. 29.95 (0-7933-2456-4); lib. bdg. 29.95 (0-7933-2465-3); lib. bdg. 29.95 (0-7933-2474-2); lib. bdg. 29.95 (0-7933-2483-1); lib. bdg. 29.95 (0-7933-2492-0); lib. bdg. 29.95 (0-7933-2501-3); lib. bdg. 29.95 (0-7933-2510-2); lib. bdg. 29.95 (0-7933-2519-6); lib. bdg. 29.95 (0-7933-2528-5); lib. bdg. 29.95 (0-7933-2537-4); lib. bdg. 29.95 (0-7933-2546-3); lib. bdg. 29.95 (0-7933-2555-2); lib. bdg. 29.95 (0-7933-2564-1); lib. bdg. 29.95 (0-7933-2573-0); lib. bdg. 29.95 (0-7933-2582-X); lib. bdg. 29.95 (0-7933-2591-9); lib. bdg. 29.95 (0-7933-2600-1); lib. bdg. 29.95 (0-7933-2609-5); lib. bdg. 29.95 (0-7933-2618-4); lib. bdg. 29.95 (0-7933-2627-3); lib. bdg. 29.95 (0-7933-2636-2); lib. bdg. 29.95 (0-7933-2645-1); lib. bdg. 29.95 (0-7933-2654-0); lib. bdg. 29.95 (0-7933-2663-X); lib. bdg. 29.95 (0-7933-2672-9); lib. bdg. 29.95 (0-7933-2681-8); lib. bdg. 29.95 (0-7933-2690-7); lib. bdg. 29.95 (0-7933-2699-0); lib. bdg. 29.95 (0-7933-2708-3); lib. bdg. 29.95 (0-7933-2717-2); lib. bdg. 29.95 (0-7933-2726-1); lib. bdg. 29.95 (0-7933-2735-0); lib. bdg. 29.95 (0-7933-2744-X); lib. bdg. 29.95 (0-7933-2753-9); lib. bdg. 29.95 (0-7933-2762-8); lib. bdg. 29.95 (0-7933-2771-7) Gallopade Pub Group.

— Sign on the Dotted Line: Two Hundred Years of U. S. Constitution Silly Trivia. (Quantum Leap Ser.). (Illus.). (Orig.). (gr. 3-9). 1994. 24.95 (*1-55609-191-5*); pap. 14.95 (*0-935326-76-6*) Gallopade Pub Group.

— The Sinister Spies Dingbats Book. (Carole Marsh Dingbats Book Ser.). (Illus.). (YA). (gr. 3-12). 1994. lib. bdg. 24.95 (*0-7933-5389-0*); pap. 14.95 (*0-7933-5390-4*); disk 29.95 (*0-7933-5391-2*) Gallopade Pub Group.

— Six Puppy Feet: Bridge for Kids. (Quantum Leap Ser.). (Illus.). (J). (gr. k-12). 1994. 24.95 (*1-55609-157-5*); pap. 14.95 (*0-935326-13-8*) Gallopade Pub Group.

— Snowshoe & Earmuff Go North. (Serendipity Travel Series for Young People). (Illus.). (J). (ps-4). 1994. 24.95 (*1-55609-646-1*); pap. 14.95 (*1-55609-758-1*) Gallopade Pub Group.

— Snowshoe & Earmuff Go West. (Serendipity Travel Series for Young People). (Illus.). (J). (ps-3). 1994. 24.95 (*1-55609-304-7*); pap. 14.95 (*1-55609-303-9*) Gallopade Pub Group.

— Sorta Silly, Smart-Aleck Study Tips Even Teens Will Like. (Quantum Leap Ser.). (YA). (gr. 7-12). 1994. lib. bdg. 24.95 (*0-7933-7352-2*); pap. 14.95 (*0-7933-7353-0*); disk 29.95 (*0-7933-7354-9*) Gallopade Pub Group.

— South Carolina & Other State Greats (Biographies) (Carole Marsh South Carolina Bks.). (Illus.). (J). 1994. lib. bdg. 24.95 (*0-7933-2006-2*); pap. 14.95 (*0-7933-2007-0*); disk 29.95 (*0-7933-2008-9*) Gallopade Pub Group.

— South Carolina Bandits, Bushwackers, Outlaws, Crooks, Devils, Ghosts, Desperadoes & Other Assorted & Sundry Characters! (Carole Marsh South Carolina Bks.). (Illus.). (J). 1994. lib. bdg. 24.95 (*0-7933-1010-5*); pap. 14.95 (*0-7933-1009-1*); disk 29.95 (*0-7933-1011-3*) Gallopade Pub Group.

— The South Carolina Bookstore Book: A Surprising Guide to Our State's Bookstores & Their Specialties for Students, Teachers, Writers & Publishers. (South Carolina Bks.). (Illus.). 1994. lib. bdg. 24.95 (*0-7933-2975-2*); pap. 14.95 (*0-7933-2976-0*); disk 29.95 (*0-7933-2977-9*) Gallopade Pub Group.

— South Carolina Classic Christmas Trivia: Stories, Recipes, Activities, Legends, Lore & More! (Carole Marsh South Carolina Bks.). (Illus.). (J). 1994. lib. bdg. 24.95 (*0-7933-1013-X*); pap. 14.95 (*0-7933-1012-1*); disk 29.95 (*0-7933-1014-8*) Gallopade Pub Group.

— South Carolina Coastales. (Carole Marsh South Carolina Bks.). (Illus.). (J). 1994. lib. bdg. 24.95 (*0-7933-2001-1*); pap. 14.95 (*1-55609-115-X*); disk 29.95 (*0-7933-2002-X*) Gallopade Pub Group.

— South Carolina Coastales! (South Carolina Bks.). (J). 1994. lib. bdg. 24.95 (*0-7933-7305-0*) Gallopade Pub Group.

— South Carolina "Crinkum-Crankum" A Funny Word Book about Our State. (South Carolina Bks.). (Illus.). (J). (gr. 3-12). 1994. 24.95 (*0-7933-4928-1*); pap. 14.95 (*0-7933-4929-X*); disk 29.95 (*0-7933-4930-3*) Gallopade Pub Group.

— South Carolina Dingbats! Bk. 1: A Fun Book of Games, Stories, Activities & More about Our State That's All in Code! for You to Decipher. (South Carolina Bks.). (Illus.). (J). (gr. 3-12). 1994. lib. bdg. 19.95 (*0-7933-3893-X*); pap. 14.95 (*0-7933-3894-8*); disk 29.95 (*0-7933-3895-6*) Gallopade Pub Group.

— South Carolina Festival Fun for Kids! (South Carolina Bks.). (Illus.). (YA). (gr. 3-12). 1994. lib. bdg. 24.95 (*0-7933-4046-2*); pap. 14.95 (*0-7933-4047-0*); disk 29.95 (*0-7933-4048-9*) Gallopade Pub Group.

— The South Carolina Hot Air Balloon Mystery. (Carole Marsh South Carolina Bks.). (Illus.). (J). (gr. 2-9). 1994. 24.95 (*0-7933-2678-8*); pap. 14.95 (*0-7933-2679-6*); disk 29.95 (*0-7933-2680-X*) Gallopade Pub Group.

— South Carolina Jeopardy! Answers & Questions about Our State! (South Carolina Bks.). (Illus.). (J). (gr. 3-12). 1994. lib. bdg. 24.95 (*0-7933-4199-X*); pap. 14.95 (*0-7933-4200-7*); disk 29.95 (*0-7933-4201-5*) Gallopade Pub Group.

— South Carolina Jography: A Fun Run Through the Palmetto State. (Statemeant Ser.). (Illus.). 50p. (Orig.). (J). (gr. 3-9). 1994. pap. 14.95 (*0-935326-96-0*) Gallopade Pub Group.

— South Carolina "Jography" A Fun Run Thru Our State! (Carole Marsh South Carolina Bks.). (Illus.). (J). 1994. lib. bdg. 24.95 (*0-7933-1985-4*); pap. 14.95 (*1-55609-049-8*); disk 29.95 (*0-7933-1986-2*) Gallopade Pub Group.

— South Carolina Kid's Cookbook: Recipes, How-to, History, Lore & More! (Carole Marsh South Carolina Bks.). (Illus.). (J). 1994. lib. bdg. 24.95 (*0-7933-1022-9*); pap. 14.95 (*0-7933-1021-0*); disk 29.95 (*0-7933-1023-7*) Gallopade Pub Group.

— The South Carolina Library Book: A Surprising Guide to the Unusual Special Collections in Libraries Across Our State for Students, Teachers, Writers & Publishers - Includes Reproducible Mailing Labels Plus Activities for Young People! (South Carolina Bks.). (Illus.). 1994. lib. bdg. 24.95 (*0-7933-3125-0*); pap. 14.95 (*0-7933-3126-9*); disk 29.95 (*0-7933-3127-7*) Gallopade Pub Group.

— The South Carolina Media Book: A Surprising Guide to the Amazing Print, Broadcast & Online Media of Our State for Students, Teachers, Writers & Publishers - Includes Reproducible Mailing Labels Plus Activities for Young People! (South Carolina Bks.). (Illus.). 1994. lib. bdg. 24.95 (*0-7933-3281-8*); pap. 14.95 (*0-7933-3282-6*); disk 29.95 (*0-7933-3283-4*) Gallopade Pub Group.

— The South Carolina Mystery Van Takes Off! Book 1: Handicapped South Carolina Kids Sneak Off on a Big Adventure. (South Carolina Bks.). (Illus.). (J). (gr. 3-12). 1994. 24.95 (*0-7933-5081-6*); pap. 14.95 (*0-7933-5082-4*); disk 29.95 (*0-7933-5083-2*) Gallopade Pub Group.

— South Carolina Quiz Bowl Crash Course! (Carole Marsh South Carolina Bks.). (Illus.). (J). 1994. lib. bdg. 24.95 (*0-7933-1998-6*); pap. 14.95 (*0-7933-1999-4*); disk 29.95 (*0-7933-2000-3*) Gallopade Pub Group.

— South Carolina Rollercoasters! (South Carolina Bks.). (Illus.). (YA). (gr. 3-12). 1994. lib. bdg. 24.95 (*0-7933-5344-0*); pap. 14.95 (*0-7933-5345-9*); disk 29.95 (*0-7933-5346-7*) Gallopade Pub Group.

— South Carolina School Trivia: An Amazing & Fascinating Look at Our State's Teachers, Schools & Students! (Carole Marsh South Carolina Bks.). (Illus.). (J). 1994. lib. bdg. 24.95 (*0-7933-1019-9*); pap. 14.95 (*0-7933-1018-0*); disk 29.95 (*0-7933-1020-2*) Gallopade Pub Group.

— South Carolina Silly Basketball Sportsmysteries, Vol. 1. (Carole Marsh South Carolina Bks.). (Illus.). (J). 1994. lib. bdg. 24.95 (*0-7933-1016-4*); pap. 14.95 (*0-7933-1015-6*); disk 29.95 (*0-7933-1017-2*) Gallopade Pub Group.

— South Carolina Silly Basketball Sportsmysteries, Vol. 2. (Carole Marsh South Carolina Bks.). (Illus.). (J). 1994. lib. bdg. 24.95 (*0-7933-2009-7*); pap. 14.95 (*0-7933-2010-0*); disk 29.95 (*0-7933-2011-9*) Gallopade Pub Group.

— South Carolina Silly Football Sportsmysteries, Vol. 1. (Carole Marsh South Carolina Bks.). (Illus.). (J). 1994. lib. bdg. 24.95 (*0-7933-1989-7*); pap. 14.95 (*0-7933-1990-0*); disk 29.95 (*0-7933-1991-9*) Gallopade Pub Group.

— South Carolina Silly Football Sportsmysteries, Vol. 2. (Carole Marsh South Carolina Bks.). (Illus.). (J). 1994. lib. bdg. 24.95 (*0-7933-1992-7*); pap. 14.95 (*0-7933-1993-5*); disk 29.95 (*0-7933-1994-3*) Gallopade Pub Group.

— South Carolina Silly Trivia! (Carole Marsh South Carolina Bks.). (Illus.). (J). 1994. lib. bdg. 24.95 (*0-7933-1983-8*); pap. 14.95 (*0-685-54060-X*); disk 29.95 (*0-7933-1984-6*) Gallopade Pub Group.

— South Carolina Timeline: A Chronology of South Carolina History, Mystery, Trivia, Legend, Lore & More. (South Carolina Bks.). (Illus.). (J). (gr. 3-12). 1994. lib. bdg. 24.95 (*0-7933-5995-3*); pap. 14.95 (*0-7933-5996-1*); disk 29.95 (*0-7933-5997-X*) Gallopade Pub Group.

— South Carolina's (Most Devastating!) Disasters & (Most Calamitous!) Catastrophies! (Carole Marsh South Carolina Bks.). (Illus.). (J). 1994. lib. bdg. 24.95 (*0-7933-1007-5*); pap. 14.95 (*0-7933-1006-7*); disk 29.95 (*0-7933-1008-3*) Gallopade Pub Group.

— South Carolina's Unsolved Mysteries (& Their "Solutions") Includes Scientific Information & Other Activities for Students. (South Carolina Bks.). (Illus.). (J). (gr. 3-12). 1994. lib. bdg. 24.95 (*0-7933-5842-6*); pap. 14.95 (*0-7933-5843-4*); disk 29.95 (*0-7933-5844-2*) Gallopade Pub Group.

— South Dakota & Other State Greats (Biographies) (Carole Marsh South Dakota Bks.). (Illus.). (J). 1994. lib. bdg. 24.95 (*0-7933-2038-0*); pap. 14.95 (*0-7933-2039-9*); disk 29.95 (*0-7933-2040-2*) Gallopade Pub Group.

— South Dakota Bandits, Bushwackers, Outlaws, Crooks, Devils, Ghosts, Desperadoes & Other Assorted & Sundry Characters! (Carole Marsh South Dakota Bks.). (Illus.). (J). 1994. lib. bdg. 24.95 (*0-7933-1034-2*); pap. 14.95 (*0-7933-1033-4*); disk 29.95 (*0-7933-1035-0*) Gallopade Pub Group.

— The South Dakota Bookstore Book: A Surprising Guide to Our State's Bookstores & Their Specialties for Students, Teachers, Writers & Publishers. (South Dakota Bks.). (Illus.). 1994. lib. bdg. 19.95 (*0-7933-2978-7*); pap. 14.95 (*0-7933-2979-5*); disk 29.95 (*0-7933-2980-9*) Gallopade Pub Group.

— South Dakota Classic Christmas Trivia: Stories, Recipes, Activities, Legends, Lore & More! (Carole Marsh South Dakota Bks.). (Illus.). (J). 1994. lib. bdg. 24.95 (*0-7933-1037-7*); pap. 14.95 (*0-7933-1036-9*); disk 29.95 (*0-7933-1038-5*) Gallopade Pub Group.

— South Dakota Coastales. (Carole Marsh South Dakota Bks.). (Illus.). (J). 1994. lib. bdg. 24.95 (*0-7933-2032-1*); pap. 14.95 (*0-7933-2033-X*); disk 29.95 (*0-7933-2034-8*) Gallopade Pub Group.

— South Dakota Coastales! (South Dakota Bks.). (J). 1994. lib. bdg. 24.95 (*0-7933-7306-9*) Gallopade Pub Group.

— South Dakota "Crinkum-Crankum" A Funny Word Book about Our State. (South Dakota Bks.). (Illus.). (J). (gr. 3-12). 1994. 24.95 (*0-7933-4931-1*); pap. 14.95 (*0-7933-4932-X*); disk 29.95 (*0-7933-4933-8*) Gallopade Pub Group.

— South Dakota Dingbats! Bk. 1: A Fun Book of Games, Stories, Activities & More about Our State That's All in Code! for You to Decipher. (South Dakota Bks.). (Illus.). (J). (gr. 3-12). 1994. lib. bdg. 19.95 (*0-7933-3896-4*); pap. 14.95 (*0-7933-3897-2*); disk 29.95 (*0-7933-3898-0*) Gallopade Pub Group.

— South Dakota Festival Fun for Kids! (South Dakota Bks.). (Illus.). (YA). (gr. 3-12). 1994. lib. bdg. 19.95 (*0-7933-4049-7*); pap. 14.95 (*0-7933-4050-0*); disk 29.95 (*0-7933-4051-9*) Gallopade Pub Group.

— The South Dakota Hot Air Balloon Mystery. (Carole Marsh South Dakota Bks.). (Illus.). (J). (gr. 2-9). 1994. 24.95 (*0-7933-2687-7*); pap. 14.95 (*0-7933-2688-5*); disk 29.95 (*0-7933-2689-3*) Gallopade Pub Group.

— South Dakota Jeopardy! Answers & Questions about Our State! (South Dakota Bks.). (Illus.). (J). (gr. 3-12). 1994. lib. bdg. 24.95 (*0-7933-4202-3*); pap. 14.95 (*0-7933-4203-1*); disk 29.95 (*0-7933-4204-X*) Gallopade Pub Group.

— South Dakota "Jography" A Fun Run Thru Our State! (Carole Marsh South Dakota Bks.). (Illus.). (J). 1994. lib. bdg. 24.95 (*0-7933-2015-1*); pap. 14.95 (*0-7933-2016-X*); disk 29.95 (*0-7933-2017-8*) Gallopade Pub Group.

— South Dakota Kid's Cookbook: Recipes, How-to, History, Lore & More! (Carole Marsh South Dakota Bks.). (Illus.). (J). 1994. lib. bdg. 24.95 (*0-7933-1046-6*); pap. 14.95 (*0-7933-1045-8*); disk 29.95 (*0-7933-1047-4*) Gallopade Pub Group.

— The South Dakota Library Book: A Surprising Guide to the Unusual Special Collections in Libraries Across Our State for Students, Teachers, Writers & Publishers - Includes Reproducible Mailing Labels Plus Activities for Young People! (South Dakota Bks.). (Illus.). 1994. lib. bdg. 24.95 (*0-7933-3128-5*); pap. 14.95 (*0-7933-3129-3*); disk 29.95 (*0-7933-3130-7*) Gallopade Pub Group.

— The South Dakota Media Book: A Surprising Guide to the Amazing Print, Broadcast & Online Media of Our State for Students, Teachers, Writers & Publishers - Includes Reproducible Mailing Labels Plus Activities for Young People! (South Dakota Bks.). (Illus.). 1994. lib. bdg. 24.95 (*0-7933-3284-2*); pap. 14.95 (*0-7933-3285-0*); disk 29.95 (*0-7933-3286-9*) Gallopade Pub Group.

— The South Dakota Mystery Van Takes Off! Book 1: Handicapped South Dakota Kids Sneak Off on a Big Adventure. (South Dakota Bks.). (Illus.). (J). (gr. 3-12). 1994. 24.95 (*0-7933-5084-0*); pap. 14.95 (*0-7933-5085-9*); disk 29.95 (*0-7933-5086-7*) Gallopade Pub Group.

— South Dakota Quiz Bowl Crash Course! (Carole Marsh South Dakota Bks.). (Illus.). (J). 1994. lib. bdg. 24.95 (*0-7933-2029-1*); pap. 14.95 (*0-7933-2030-5*); disk 29.95 (*0-7933-2031-3*) Gallopade Pub Group.

— South Dakota Rollercoasters! (South Dakota Bks.). (Illus.). (YA). (gr. 3-12). 1994. lib. bdg. 24.95 (*0-7933-5347-5*); pap. 14.95 (*0-7933-5348-3*); disk 29.95 (*0-7933-5349-1*) Gallopade Pub Group.

— South Dakota School Trivia: An Amazing & Fascinating Look at Our State's Teachers, Schools & Students! (Carole Marsh South Dakota Bks.). (Illus.). (J). 1994. lib. bdg. 24.95 (*0-7933-1043-1*); pap. 14.95 (*0-7933-1042-3*); disk 29.95 (*0-7933-1044-X*) Gallopade Pub Group.

— South Dakota Silly Basketball Sportsmysteries, Vol. 1. (Carole Marsh South Dakota Bks.). (Illus.). (J). 1994. lib. bdg. 24.95 (*0-7933-1040-7*); pap. 14.95 (*0-7933-1039-3*); disk 29.95 (*0-7933-1041-5*) Gallopade Pub Group.

— South Dakota Silly Basketball Sportsmysteries, Vol. 2. (Carole Marsh South Dakota Bks.). (Illus.). (J). 1994. lib. bdg. 24.95 (*0-7933-2041-0*); pap. 14.95 (*0-7933-2042-9*); disk 29.95 (*0-7933-2043-7*) Gallopade Pub Group.

— South Dakota Silly Football Sportsmysteries, Vol. 1. (Carole Marsh South Dakota Bks.). (Illus.). (J). 1994. lib. bdg. 24.95 (*0-7933-2020-8*); pap. 14.95 (*0-7933-2021-6*); disk 29.95 (*0-7933-2022-4*) Gallopade Pub Group.

— South Dakota Silly Football Sportsmysteries, Vol. 2. (Carole Marsh South Dakota Bks.). (Illus.). (J). 1994. lib. bdg. 24.95 (*0-7933-2023-2*); pap. 14.95 (*0-685-45970-5*); disk 29.95 (*0-7933-2025-9*) Gallopade Pub Group.

— South Dakota Silly Trvia! (Carole Marsh South Dakota Bks.). (Illus.). (J). 1994. lib. bdg. 24.95 (*0-7933-2012-7*); pap. 14.95 (*0-7933-2013-5*); disk 29.95 (*0-7933-2014-3*) Gallopade Pub Group.

— South Dakota Timeline: A Chronology of South Dakota History, Mystery, Trivia, Legend, Lore & More. (South Dakota Bks.). (Illus.). (J). (gr. 3-12). 1994. lib. bdg. 24.95 (*0-7933-5998-8*); pap. 14.95 (*0-7933-5999-6*); disk 29.95 (*0-7933-6000-5*) Gallopade Pub Group.

— South Dakota's (Most Devastating!) Disasters & (Most Calamitous!) Catastrophies! (Carole Marsh South Dakota Bks.). (Illus.). (J). 1994. lib. bdg. 24.95 (*0-7933-1031-8*); pap. 14.95 (*0-7933-1030-X*); disk 29.95 (*0-7933-1032-6*) Gallopade Pub Group.

— South Dakota's Unsolved Mysteries (& Their "Solutions") Includes Scientific Information & Other Activities for Students. (South Dakota Bks.). (Illus.). (J). (gr. 3-12). 1994. lib. bdg. 24.95 (*0-7933-5845-0*); pap. 14.95 (*0-7933-5846-9*); disk 29.95 (*0-7933-5847-7*) Gallopade Pub Group.

— Stone Mountain Mystery Gamebook. (Carole Marsh Bks.). (Illus.). (Orig.). (J). (gr. 3-9). 1994. pap. 19.95 (*0-935326-80-4*) Gallopade Pub Group.

— The Stone Mountain Mystery Set. (Carole Marsh Mysteries Ser.). 1994. 125.00 (*0-7933-6957-6*) Gallopade Pub Group.

— The Super Silly Riddles Dingbats Book. (Carole Marsh Dingbats Book Ser.). (Illus.). (YA). (gr. 3-12). 1994. lib. bdg. 24.95 (*0-7933-5410-2*); pap. 14.95 (*0-7933-5411-0*); disk 29.95 (*0-7933-5412-9*) Gallopade Pub Group.

— The Super Silly Sports Trivia Dingbats Book. (Carole Marsh Dingbats Book Ser.). (Illus.). (YA). (gr. 3-12). 1994. lib. bdg. 24.95 (*0-7933-5380-7*); pap. 14.95 (*0-7933-5381-5*); disk 29.95 (*0-7933-5382-3*) Gallopade Pub Group.

— Teachers Guide to Silly Trivia Books. (Books for Teachers). (Illus.). (Orig.). 1994. teacher ed, pap. 14.95 (*0-935326-91-X*) Gallopade Pub Group.

— The Teddy Bear Company: Economics for Kids. (Quantum Leap Ser.). (Illus.). (J). (gr. 4-8). 1994. 14.95 (*0-935326-16-2*) Gallopade Pub Group.

— Teddy Bear's Annual Report. (Quantum Leap Ser.). (Illus.). (J). (gr. 4-8). 1994. 14.95 (*0-935326-26-X*) Gallopade Pub Group.

— Tennessee & Other State Greats (Biographies) (Carole Marsh Tennessee Bks.). (Illus.). (J). 1994. lib. bdg. 24.95 (*0-7933-1055-5*); pap. 14.95 (*0-7933-1054-7*); disk 29.95 (*0-7933-1056-3*) Gallopade Pub Group.

— Tennessee Bandits, Bushwackers, Outlaws, Crooks, Devils, Ghosts, Desperadoes & Other Assorted & Sundry Characters! (Carole Marsh Tennessee Bks.). (Illus.). (J). 1994. lib. bdg. 24.95 (*0-7933-1058-X*); pap. 14.95 (*0-7933-1057-1*); disk 29.95 (*0-7933-1059-8*) Gallopade Pub Group.

— The Tennessee Bookstore Book: A Surprising Guide to Our State's Bookstores & Their Specialties for Students, Teachers, Writers & Publishers. (Tennessee Bks.). (Illus.). 1994. lib. bdg. 24.95 (*0-7933-2981-7*); pap. 14.95 (*0-7933-2982-5*); disk 29.95 (*0-7933-2983-3*) Gallopade Pub Group.

— Tennessee Classic Christmas Trivia: Stories, Recipes, Activities, Legends, Lore & More! (Carole Marsh Tennessee Bks.). (Illus.). (J). 1994. lib. bdg. 24.95 (*0-7933-1061-X*); pap. 14.95 (*0-7933-1060-1*); disk 29.95 (*0-7933-1062-8*) Gallopade Pub Group.

— Tennessee Coastales. (Carole Marsh Tennessee Bks.). (Illus.). (J). 1994. lib. bdg. 24.95 (*0-7933-2062-3*); pap. 14.95 (*0-7933-2063-1*); disk 29.95 (*0-7933-2064-X*) Gallopade Pub Group.

— Tennessee Coastales! (Tennessee Bks.). (J). 1994. lib. bdg. 24.95 (*0-7933-7307-7*) Gallopade Pub Group.

— Tennessee "Crinkum-Crankum" A Funny Word Book about Our State. (Tennessee Bks.). (Illus.). (J). (gr. 3-12). 1994. 24.95 (*0-7933-4934-6*); pap. 14.95 (*0-7933-4935-4*); disk 29.95 (*0-7933-4936-2*) Gallopade Pub Group.

— Tennessee Dingbats! Bk. 1: A Fun Book of Games, Stories, Activities & More about Our State That's All in Code! for You to Decipher. (Tennessee Bks.). (Illus.). (J). (gr. 3-12). 1994. lib. bdg. 24.95 (*0-7933-3899-9*); pap. 14.95 (*0-7933-3900-6*); disk 29.95 (*0-7933-3901-4*) Gallopade Pub Group.

— Tennessee Festival Fun for Kids! (Tennessee Bks.). (Illus.). (YA). (gr. 3-12). 1994. lib. bdg. 24.95 (*0-7933-4052-7*); pap. 14.95 (*0-7933-4053-5*); disk 29.95 (*0-7933-4054-3*) Gallopade Pub Group.

— The Tennessee Hot Air Balloon Mystery. (Carole Marsh Tennessee Bks.). (Illus.). (J). (gr. 2-9). 1994. 24.95 (*0-7933-2696-6*); pap. 14.95 (*0-7933-2697-4*); disk 29.95 (*0-7933-2698-2*) Gallopade Pub Group.

— Tennessee Jeopardy! Answers & Questions about Our State! (Tennessee Bks.). (Illus.). (J). (gr. 3-12). 1994. lib. bdg. 24.95 (*0-7933-4205-8*); pap. 14.95 (*0-7933-4206-6*); disk 29.95 (*0-7933-4207-4*) Gallopade Pub Group.

— Tennessee "Jography" A Fun Run Thru Our State! (Carole Marsh Tennessee Bks.). (Illus.). (J). 1994. lib. bdg. 24.95 (*0-7933-2046-1*); pap. 14.95 (*1-55609-089-7*); disk 29.95 (*0-7933-2047-X*) Gallopade Pub Group.

— Tennessee Kid's Cookbook: Recipes, How-to, History, Lore & More! (Carole Marsh Tennessee Bks.). (Illus.). (J). 1994. lib. bdg. 24.95 (*0-7933-1070-9*); pap. 14.95 (*0-7933-1069-5*); disk 29.95 (*0-7933-1071-7*) Gallopade Pub Group.

— The Tennessee Library Book: A Surprising Guide to the Unusual Special Collections in Libraries Across Our State for Students, Teachers, Writers & Publishers - Includes Reproducible Mailing Labels Plus Activities for Young People! (Tennessee Bks.). (Illus.). 1994. lib. bdg. 24.95 (*0-7933-3131-5*); pap. 14.95 (*0-7933-3132-3*); disk 29.95 (*0-7933-3133-1*) Gallopade Pub Group.

— The Tennessee Media Book: A Surprising Guide to the Amazing Print, Broadcast & Online Media of Our State for Students, Teachers, Writers & Publishers - Includes Reproducible Mailing Labels Plus Activities for Young People! (Tennessee Bks.). (Illus.). 1994. lib. bdg. 24.95 (*0-7933-3287-7*); pap. 14.95 (*0-7933-3288-5*); disk 29.95 (*0-7933-3289-3*) Gallopade Pub Group.

— The Tennessee Mystery Van Takes Off! Book 1: Handicapped Tennessee Kids Sneak Off on a Big Adventure. (Tennessee Bks.). (Illus.). (J). (gr. 3-12). 1994. 24.95 (*0-7933-5087-5*); pap. 14.95 (*0-7933-5088-3*); disk 29.95 (*0-7933-5089-1*) Gallopade Pub Group.

— Tennessee Quiz Bowl Crash Course! (Carole Marsh Tennessee Bks.). (Illus.). (J). 1994. lib. bdg. 24.95 (*0-7933-2059-3*); pap. 14.95 (*0-7933-2060-7*); disk 29.95 (*0-7933-2061-5*) Gallopade Pub Group.

— Tennessee Rollercoasters! (Tennessee Bks.). (Illus.). (YA). (gr. 3-12). 1994. lib. bdg. 24.95 (*0-7933-5350-5*); pap. 14.95 (*0-7933-5351-3*); disk 29.95 (*0-7933-5352-1*) Gallopade Pub Group.

— Tennessee School Trivia: An Amazing & Fascinating Look at Our State's Teachers, Schools & Students! (Carole Marsh Tennessee Bks.). (Illus.). (J). 1994. lib. bdg. 24.95 (*0-7933-1067-9*); pap. 14.95 (*0-7933-1066-0*); disk 29.95 (*0-7933-1068-7*) Gallopade Pub Group.

— Tennessee Silly Basketball Sportsmysteries, Vol. 1. (Carole Marsh Tennessee Bks.). (Illus.). (J). 1994. lib. bdg. 24.95 (*0-7933-1064-4*); pap. 14.95 (*0-7933-1063-6*); disk 29.95 (*0-7933-1065-2*) Gallopade Pub Group.

— Tennessee Silly Basketball Sportsmysteries, Vol. 2. (Carole Marsh Tennessee Bks.). (Illus.). (J). 1994. lib. bdg. 24.95 (*0-7933-2071-2*); pap. 14.95 (*0-7933-2072-0*); disk 29.95 (*0-7933-2073-9*) Gallopade Pub Group.

— Tennessee Silly Football Sportsmysteries, Vol. 1. (Carole Marsh Tennessee Bks.). (Illus.). (J). 1994. lib. bdg. 24.95 (*0-7933-2050-X*); pap. 14.95 (*0-7933-2051-8*); disk 29.95 (*0-7933-2052-6*) Gallopade Pub Group.

— Tennessee Silly Football Sportsmysteries, Vol. 2. (Carole Marsh Tennessee Bks.). (Illus.). (J). 1994. lib. bdg. 24.95 (*0-7933-2053-4*); pap. 14.95 (*0-7933-2054-2*); disk 29.95 (*0-7933-2055-0*) Gallopade Pub Group.

— Tennessee Silly Trivia! (Carole Marsh Tennessee Bks.). (Illus.). (J). 1994. lib. bdg. 24.95 (*0-7933-2044-5*); pap. 14.95 (*1-55609-036-6*); disk 29.95 (*0-7933-2045-3*) Gallopade Pub Group.

— Tennessee Timeline: A Chronology of Tennessee History, Mystery, Trivia, Legend, Lore & More. (Tennessee Bks.). (Illus.). (J). (gr. 3-12). 1994. lib. bdg. 24.95 (*0-7933-6001-3*); pap. 14.95 (*0-7933-6002-1*); disk 29.95 (*0-7933-6003-X*) Gallopade Pub Group.

— Tennessee's (Most Devastating!) Disasters & (Most Calamitous!) Catastrophies! (Carole Marsh Tennessee Bks.). (Illus.). (J). 1994. lib. bdg. 24.95 (*0-7933-2068-2*); pap. 14.95 (*0-7933-2069-0*); disk 29.95 (*0-7933-2070-4*) Gallopade Pub Group.

— Tennessee's Unsolved Mysteries (& Their "Solutions") Includes Scientific Information & Other Activities for Students. (Tennessee Bks.). (Illus.). (J). (gr. 3-12). 1994. lib. bdg. 24.95 (*0-7933-5848-5*); pap. 14.95 (*0-7933-5849-3*); disk 29.95 (*0-7933-5850-7*) Gallopade Pub Group.

— The Terror & Tombstones Dingbats Book. (Carole Marsh Dingbats Book Ser.). (Illus.). (YA). (gr. 3-12). 1994. lib. bdg. 24.95 (*0-7933-5401-3*); pap. 14.95 (*0-7933-5402-1*); disk 29.95 (*0-7933-5403-X*) Gallopade Pub Group.

— Texas & Other State Greats (Biographies) (Carole Marsh Texas Bks.). (Illus.). (J). 1994. lib. bdg. 24.95 (*0-7933-2097-6*); pap. 14.95 (*0-7933-2098-4*); disk 29.95 (*0-7933-2099-2*) Gallopade Pub Group.

— Texas Bandits, Bushwackers, Outlaws, Crooks, Devils, Ghosts, Desperadoes & Other Assorted & Sundry Characters! (Carole Marsh Texas Bks.). (Illus.). (J). 1994. lib. bdg. 24.95 (*0-7933-1082-2*); pap. 14.95 (*0-7933-1081-4*); disk 29.95 (*0-7933-1083-0*) Gallopade Pub Group.

— The Texas Bookstore Book: A Surprising Guide to Our State's Bookstores & Their Specialties for Students, Teachers, Writers & Publishers. (Texas Bks.). (Illus.). 1994. lib. bdg. 24.95 (*0-7933-2984-1*); pap. 14.95 (*0-7933-2985-X*); disk 29.95 (*0-7933-2986-8*) Gallopade Pub Group.

— Texas Classic Christmas Trivia: Stories, Recipes, Activities, Legends, Lore & More! (Carole Marsh Texas Bks.). (Illus.). (J). 1994. lib. bdg. 24.95 (*0-7933-1085-7*); pap. 14.95 (*0-7933-1084-9*); disk 29.95 (*0-7933-1086-5*) Gallopade Pub Group.

— Texas Coastales. (Carole Marsh Texas Bks.). (Illus.). (J). 1994. lib. bdg. 24.95 (*0-7933-2092-5*); pap. 14.95 (*1-55609-121-4*); disk 29.95 (*0-7933-2093-3*) Gallopade Pub Group.

— Texas Coastales! (Texas Bks.). (J). 1994. lib. bdg. 24.95 (*0-7933-7308-5*) Gallopade Pub Group.

— Texas "Crinkum-Crankum" A Funny Word Book about Our State. (Texas Bks.). (Illus.). (J). (gr. 3-12). 1994. 24.95 (*0-7933-4937-0*); pap. 14.95 (*0-7933-4938-9*); disk 29.95 (*0-7933-4939-7*) Gallopade Pub Group.

— Texas Dingbats! Bk. 1: A Fun Book of Games, Stories, Activities & More about Our State That's All in Code! for You to Decipher. (Texas Bks.). (Illus.). (J). (gr. 3-12). 1994. lib. bdg. 24.95 (*0-7933-3902-2*); pap. 14.95 (*0-7933-3903-0*); disk 29.95 (*0-7933-3904-9*) Gallopade Pub Group.

— Texas Festival Fun for Kids! (Texas Bks.). (Illus.). (YA). (gr. 3-12). 1994. lib. bdg. 24.95 (*0-7933-4055-1*); pap. 14.95 (*0-7933-4056-X*); disk 29.95 (*0-7933-4057-8*) Gallopade Pub Group.

— The Texas Hot Air Balloon Mystery. (Carole Marsh Texas Bks.). (Illus.). (J). (gr. 2-9). 1994. 24.95 (*0-7933-2705-9*); pap. 14.95 (*0-7933-2706-7*); disk 29.95 (*0-7933-2707-5*) Gallopade Pub Group.

— Texas Jeopardy! Answers & Questions about Our State! (Texas Bks.). (Illus.). (J). (gr. 3-12). 1994. lib. bdg. 24.95 (*0-7933-4208-2*); pap. 14.95 (*0-7933-4209-0*); disk 29.95 (*0-7933-4210-4*) Gallopade Pub Group.

— Texas "Jography" A Fun Run Thru Our State! (Carole Marsh Texas Bks.). (Illus.). (J). 1994. lib. bdg. 24.95 (*0-7933-2076-3*); pap. 14.95 (*1-55609-087-0*); disk 29.95 (*0-7933-2077-1*) Gallopade Pub Group.

— Texas Kid's Cookbook: Recipes, How-To, History, Lore & More! (Carole Marsh Texas Bks.). (Illus.). (J). 1994. lib. bdg. 24.95 (*0-7933-1094-6*); pap. 14.95 (*0-7933-1093-8*); disk 29.95 (*0-7933-1095-4*) Gallopade Pub Group.

— The Texas Library Book: A Surprising Guide to the Unusual Special Collections in Libraries Across Our State for Students, Teachers, Writers & Publishers - Includes Reproducible Mailing Labels Plus Activities for Young People! (Texas Bks.). (Illus.). 1994. lib. bdg. 24.95 (*0-7933-3134-X*); pap. 14.95 (*0-7933-3135-8*); disk 29.95 (*0-7933-3136-6*) Gallopade Pub Group.

— The Texas Media Book: A Surprising Guide to the Amazing Print, Broadcast & Online Media of Our State for Students, Teachers, Writers & Publishers - Includes Reproducible Mailing Labels Plus Activities for Young People! (Texas Bks.). (Illus.). 1994. lib. bdg. 24.95 (*0-7933-3290-7*); pap. 14.95 (*0-7933-3291-5*); disk 29.95 (*0-7933-3292-3*) Gallopade Pub Group.

— The Texas Mystery Van Takes Off! Book 1: Handicapped Texas Kids Sneak Off on a Big Adventure. (Texas Bks.). (Illus.). (J). (gr. 3-12). 1994. 24.95 (*0-7933-5090-5*); pap. 14.95 (*0-7933-5091-3*); disk 29.95 (*0-7933-5092-1*) Gallopade Pub Group.

— Texas Quiz Bowl Crash Course! (Carole Marsh Texas Bks.). (Illus.). (J). 1994. lib. bdg. 24.95 (*0-7933-2089-5*); pap. 14.95 (*0-7933-2090-9*); disk 29.95 (*0-7933-2091-7*) Gallopade Pub Group.

— Texas Rollercoasters! (Texas Bks.). (Illus.). (YA). (gr. 3-12). 1994. lib. bdg. 24.95 (*0-7933-5353-X*); pap. 14.95 (*0-7933-5354-8*); disk 29.95 (*0-7933-5355-6*) Gallopade Pub Group.

— Texas School Trivia: An Amazing & Fascinating Look at Our State's Teachers, Schools & Students! (Carole Marsh Texas Bks.). (Illus.). (J). 1994. lib. bdg. 24.95 (*0-7933-1091-1*); pap. 14.95 (*0-7933-1090-3*); disk 29.95 (*0-7933-1092-X*) Gallopade Pub Group.

— Texas Silly Basketball Sportsmysteries, Vol. 1. (Carole Marsh Texas Bks.). (Illus.). (J). 1994. lib. bdg. 24.95 (*0-7933-1088-1*); pap. 14.95 (*0-7933-1087-3*); disk 29.95 (*0-7933-1089-X*) Gallopade Pub Group.

— Texas Silly Basketball Sportsmysteries, Vol. 2. (Carole Marsh Texas Bks.). (Illus.). (J). 1994. lib. bdg. 24.95 (*0-7933-2100-X*); pap. 14.95 (*0-7933-2101-8*); disk 29.95 (*0-7933-2102-6*) Gallopade Pub Group.

— Texas Silly Football Sportsmysteries, Vol. 1. (Carole Marsh Texas Bks.). (Illus.). (J). 1994. lib. bdg. 24.95 (*0-7933-2080-1*); pap. 14.95 (*0-7933-2081-X*); disk 29.95 (*0-7933-2082-8*) Gallopade Pub Group.

— Texas Silly Football Sportsmysteries, Vol. 2. (Carole Marsh Texas Bks.). (Illus.). (J). 1994. lib. bdg. 24.95 (*0-7933-2083-6*); pap. 14.95 (*0-7933-2084-4*); disk 29.95 (*0-7933-2085-2*) Gallopade Pub Group.

— Texas Silly Trivia! (Carole Marsh Texas Bks.). (Illus.). (J). 1994. lib. bdg. 24.95 (*0-7933-2074-7*); pap. 14.95 (*1-55609-081-1*); disk 29.95 (*0-7933-2075-5*) Gallopade Pub Group.

— Texas Timeline: A Chronology of Texas History, Mystery, Trivia, Legend, Lore & More. (Texas Bks.). (Illus.). (J). (gr. 3-12). 1994. lib. bdg. 24.95 (*0-7933-6004-8*); pap. 14.95 (*0-7933-6005-6*); disk 29.95 (*0-7933-6006-4*) Gallopade Pub Group.

— Texas's (Most Devastating!) Disasters & (Most Calamitous!) Catastrophies! (Carole Marsh Texas Bks.). (Illus.). (J). 1994. lib. bdg. 24.95 (*0-7933-1079-2*); pap. 14.95 (*0-7933-1078-4*); disk 29.95 (*0-7933-1080-6*) Gallopade Pub Group.

— Texas's Unsolved Mysteries (& Their "Solutions") Includes Scientific Information & Other Activities for Students. (Texas Bks.). (Illus.). (J). (gr. 3-12). 1994. lib. bdg. 24.95 (*0-7933-5851-5*); pap. 14.95 (*0-7933-5852-3*); disk 29.95 (*0-7933-5853-1*) Gallopade Pub Group.

— Thirty Days Has September: Calendar Trivia & Activities for Kids. (Quantum Leap Ser.). (J). (gr. 3-9). 1994. 24.95 (*0-7933-0015-0*); pap. 14.95 (*0-7933-0016-9*); disk 29.95 (*0-7933-0017-7*) Gallopade Pub Group.

— Thistle Worth: Poetry to Read Aloud. (Illus.). (Orig.). (gr. 2-12). 1994. pap. 14.95 (*0-935326-60-X*) Gallopade Pub Group.

— Those Whose Names Were Terrible. (Lost Colony Collection). (Illus.). (Orig.). (J). (gr. 4-8). 1994. pap. 14.95 (*0-935326-48-0*) Gallopade Pub Group.

— The Truth & Consequences of Sexually Transmitted Diseases. (Smart Sex Stuff Ser.). (Orig.). 1994. pap. 24.95 (*1-55609-212-1*) Gallopade Pub Group.

— Tryon Palace Mystery. (History Mystery Ser.). (Orig.). (J). (gr. 3-12). 1994. 24.95 (*1-55609-193-1*); pap. 14.95 (*0-935326-58-8*) Gallopade Pub Group.

— T'was the Night Before MacChristmas: A Christmas Tale for Macintosh Users. (Lifewrite Ser.). (Illus.). 1994. pap. 14.95 (*0-7933-0006-1*) Gallopade Pub Group.

— Typing in Ten Minutes: On Any Keyboard - At Any Age. (Quantum Leap Ser.). (Illus.). (J). (gr. k-12). 1994. 24.95 (*1-55609-194-X*); pap. 14.95 (*0-935326-12-X*) Gallopade Pub Group.

— Tyrannosaurus & Other Wrecks: Fossil Trivia for Kids. (Quantum Leap Ser.). (Illus.). (Orig.). (J). (gr. 2 up). 1994. 24.95 (*1-55609-166-4*); pap. 14.95 (*0-935326-56-1*) Gallopade Pub Group.

— U. S. A. Jography: A Fun Run Thru the United States, Vol. II. (Jography Ser.). (Illus.). 60p. (J). (gr. k-12). 1994. lib. bdg. 24.95 (*1-55609-301-2*); pap. 14.95 (*1-55609-300-4*); disk 29.95 (*1-55609-302-0*) Gallopade Pub Group.

— Uncle Rebus: Alabama Picture Stories for Computer Kids. (Carole Marsh Alabama Bks.). (Illus.). (J). (gr. k-3). 1994. lib. bdg. 24.95 (*0-7933-4504-9*); pap. 14.95 (*0-7933-4505-7*); disk 29.95 (*0-7933-4506-5*) Gallopade Pub Group.

— Uncle Rebus: Alaska Picture Stories for Computer Kids. (Carole Marsh Alaska Bks.). (Illus.). (J). (gr. k-3). 1994. lib. bdg. 24.95 (*0-7933-4507-3*); pap. 14.95 (*0-7933-4508-1*); disk 29.95 (*0-7933-4509-X*) Gallopade Pub Group.

— Uncle Rebus: Arizona Picture Stories for Computer Kids. (Carole Marsh Arizona Bks.). (Illus.). (J). (gr. k-3). 1994. lib. bdg. 24.95 (*0-7933-4510-3*); pap. 14.95 (*0-7933-4511-1*); disk 29.95 (*0-7933-4512-X*) Gallopade Pub Group.

— Uncle Rebus: Arkansas Picture Stories for Computer Kids. (Carole Marsh Arkansas Bks.). (Illus.). (J). (gr. k-3). 1994. lib. bdg. 24.95 (*0-7933-4513-8*); pap. 14.95 (*0-7933-4514-6*); disk 29.95 (*0-7933-4515-4*) Gallopade Pub Group.

— Uncle Rebus: California Picture Stories for Computer Kids. (Carole Marsh California Bks.). (Illus.). (J). (gr. k-3). 1994. lib. bdg. 24.95 (*0-7933-4516-2*); pap. 14.95 (*0-7933-4517-0*); disk 29.95 (*0-7933-4518-9*) Gallopade Pub Group.

— Uncle Rebus: Colorado Picture Stories for Computer Kids. (Carole Marsh Colorado Bks.). (Illus.). (J). (gr. k-3). 1994. lib. bdg. 24.95 (*0-7933-4519-7*); pap. 14.95 (*0-7933-4520-0*); disk 29.95 (*0-7933-4521-9*) Gallopade Pub Group.

— Uncle Rebus: Connecticut Picture Stories for Computer Kids. (Carole Marsh Connecticut Bks.). (Illus.). (J). (gr. k-3). 1994. lib. bdg. 24.95 (*0-7933-4522-7*); pap. 14.95 (*0-7933-4523-5*); disk 29.95 (*0-7933-4524-3*) Gallopade Pub Group.

— Uncle Rebus: Delaware Picture Stories for Computer Kids. (Carole Marsh Delaware Bks.). (Illus.). (J). (gr. k-3). 1994. lib. bdg. 24.95 (*0-7933-4525-1*); pap. 14.95 (*0-7933-4526-X*); disk 29.95 (*0-7933-4527-8*) Gallopade Pub Group.

— Uncle Rebus: Florida Picture Stories for Computer Kids. (Carole Marsh Florida Bks.). (Illus.). (J). (gr. k-3). 1994. lib. bdg. 24.95 (*0-7933-4528-6*); pap. 14.95 (*0-7933-4529-4*); disk 29.95 (*0-7933-4530-8*) Gallopade Pub Group.

— Uncle Rebus: Georgia Picture Stories for Computer Kids. (Carole Marsh Georgia Bks.). (Illus.). (J). (gr. k-3). 1994. lib. bdg. 24.95 (*0-7933-4531-6*); pap. 14.95 (*0-7933-4532-4*); disk 29.95 (*0-7933-4533-2*) Gallopade Pub Group.

— Uncle Rebus: Hawaii Picture Stories for Computer Kids. (Carole Marsh Hawaii Bks.). (Illus.). (J). (gr. k-3). 1994. lib. bdg. 24.95 (*0-7933-4534-0*); pap. 14.95 (*0-7933-4535-9*); disk 29.95 (*0-7933-4536-7*) Gallopade Pub Group.

— Uncle Rebus: Idaho Picture Stories for Computer Kids. (Carole Marsh Idaho Bks.). (Illus.). (J). (gr. k-3). 1994. lib. bdg. 24.95 (*0-7933-4537-5*); pap. 14.95 (*0-7933-4538-3*); disk 29.95 (*0-7933-4539-1*) Gallopade Pub Group.

— Uncle Rebus: Illinois Picture Stories for Computer Kids. (Carole Marsh Illinois Bks.). (Illus.). (J). (gr. k-3). 1994. lib. bdg. 24.95 (*0-7933-4540-5*); pap. 14.95 (*0-7933-4541-3*); disk 29.95 (*0-7933-4542-1*) Gallopade Pub Group.

— Uncle Rebus: Indiana Picture Stories for Computer Kids. (Carole Marsh Indiana Bks.). (Illus.). (J). (gr. k-3). 1994. lib. bdg. 24.95 (*0-7933-4543-X*); pap. 14.95 (*0-7933-4544-8*); disk 29.95 (*0-7933-4545-6*) Gallopade Pub Group.

— Uncle Rebus: Iowa Picture Stories for Computer Kids. (Carole Marsh Iowa Bks.). (Illus.). (J). (gr. k-3). 1994. lib. bdg. 24.95 (*0-7933-4546-4*); pap. 14.95 (*0-7933-4547-2*); disk 29.95 (*0-7933-4548-0*) Gallopade Pub Group.

— Uncle Rebus: Kansas Picture Stories for Computer Kids. (Carole Marsh Kansas Bks.). (Illus.). (J). (gr. k-3). 1994. lib. bdg. 24.95 (*0-7933-4549-9*); pap. 14.95 (*0-7933-4550-2*); disk 29.95 (*0-7933-4551-0*) Gallopade Pub Group.

— Uncle Rebus: Kentucky Picture Stories for Computer Kids. (Carole Marsh Kentucky Bks.). (Illus.). (J). (gr. k-3). 1994. lib. bdg. 24.95 (*0-7933-4552-9*); pap. 14.95 (*0-7933-4553-7*); disk 29.95 (*0-7933-4554-5*) Gallopade Pub Group.

— Uncle Rebus: Louisiana Picture Stories for Computer Kids. (Carole Marsh Louisiana Bks.). (Illus.). (J). (gr. k-3). 1994. lib. bdg. 24.95 (*0-7933-4555-3*); pap. 14.95 (*0-7933-4556-1*); disk 29.95 (*0-7933-4557-X*) Gallopade Pub Group.

— Uncle Rebus: Maine Picture Stories for Computer Kids. (Carole Marsh Maine Bks.). (Illus.). (J). (gr. k-3). 1994. lib. bdg. 24.95 (*0-7933-4558-8*); pap. 14.95 (*0-7933-4559-6*); disk 29.95 (*0-7933-4560-X*) Gallopade Pub Group.

— Uncle Rebus: Maryland Picture Stories for Computer Kids. (Carole Marsh Maryland Bks.). (Illus.). (J). (gr. k-3). 1994. lib. bdg. 24.95 (*0-7933-4561-8*); pap. 14.95 (*0-7933-4562-6*); disk 29.95 (*0-7933-4563-4*) Gallopade Pub Group.

— Uncle Rebus: Massachusetts Picture Stories for Computer Kids. (Massachuseets Bks.). (Illus.). (J). (gr. k-3). 1994. lib. bdg. 24.95 (*0-7933-4564-2*); pap. 14.95 (*0-7933-4565-0*); disk 29.95 (*0-7933-4566-9*) Gallopade Pub Group.

— Uncle Rebus: Michigan Picture Stories for Computer Kids. (Carole Marsh Michigan Bks.). (Illus.). (J). (gr. k-3). 1994. lib. bdg. 24.95 (*0-7933-4567-7*); pap. 14.95 (*0-7933-4568-5*); disk 29.95 (*0-7933-4569-3*) Gallopade Pub Group.

— Uncle Rebus: Minnesota Picture Stories for Computer Kids. (Carole Marsh Minnesota Bks.). (Illus.). (J). (gr. k-3). 1994. lib. bdg. 24.95 (*0-7933-4570-7*); pap. 14.95 (*0-7933-4571-5*); disk 29.95 (*0-7933-4572-3*) Gallopade Pub Group.

— Uncle Rebus: Mississippi Picture Stories for Computer Kids. (Carole Marsh Mississippi Bks.). (Illus.). (J). (gr. k-3). 1994. lib. bdg. 24.95 (*0-7933-4573-1*); pap. 14.95 (*0-7933-4574-X*); disk 29.95 (*0-7933-4575-8*) Gallopade Pub Group.

— Uncle Rebus: Missouri Picture Stories for Computer Kids. (Carole Marsh Missouri Bks.). (Illus.). (J). (gr. k-3). 1994. lib. bdg. 24.95 (*0-7933-4576-6*); pap. 14.95 (*0-7933-4577-4*); disk 29.95 (*0-7933-4578-2*) Gallopade Pub Group.

— Uncle Rebus: Montana Picture Stories for Computer Kids. (Carole Marsh Montana Bks.). (Illus.). (J). (gr. k-3). 1994. lib. bdg. 24.95 (*0-7933-4579-0*); pap. 14.95 (*0-7933-4580-4*); disk 29.95 (*0-7933-4581-2*) Gallopade Pub Group.

— Uncle Rebus: Nebraska Picture Stories for Computer Kids. (Carole Marsh Nebraska Bks.). (Illus.). (J). (gr. k-3). 1994. lib. bdg. 24.95 (*0-7933-4582-0*); pap. 14.95 (*0-7933-4583-9*); disk 29.95 (*0-7933-4584-7*) Gallopade Pub Group.

— Uncle Rebus: Nevada Picture Stories for Computer Kids. (Carole Marsh Nevada Bks.). (Illus.). (J). (gr. k-3). 1994. lib. bdg. 24.95 (*0-7933-4585-5*); pap. 14.95 (*0-7933-4586-3*); disk 29.95 (*0-7933-4587-1*) Gallopade Pub Group.

— Uncle Rebus: New Hampshire Picture Stories for Computer Kids. (Carole Marsh New Hampshire Bks.). (Illus.). (J). (gr. k-3). 1994. lib. bdg. 24.95 (*0-7933-4588-X*); pap. 14.95 (*0-7933-4589-8*); disk 29.95 (*0-7933-4590-1*) Gallopade Pub Group.

— Uncle Rebus: New Jersey Picture Stories for Computer Kids. (Carole Marsh New Jersey Bks.). (Illus.). (J). (gr. k-3). 1994. lib. bdg. 24.95 (*0-7933-4591-X*); pap. 14.95 (*0-7933-4592-8*); disk 29.95 (*0-7933-4593-6*) Gallopade Pub Group.

— Uncle Rebus: New Mexico Picture Stories for Computer Kids. (Carole Marsh New Mexico Bks.). (Illus.). (J). (gr. k-3). 1994. lib. bdg. 24.95 (*0-7933-4594-4*); pap. 14.95 (*0-7933-4595-2*); disk 29.95 (*0-7933-4596-0*) Gallopade Pub Group.

— Uncle Rebus: New York Picture Stories for Computer Kids. (Carole Marsh New York Bks.). (Illus.). (J). (gr. k-3). 1994. lib. bdg. 24.95 (*0-7933-4597-9*); pap. 14.95 (*0-7933-4598-7*); disk 29.95 (*0-7933-4599-5*) Gallopade Pub Group.

— Uncle Rebus: North Carolina Picture Stories for Computer Kids. (Carole Marsh North Carolina Bks.). (Illus.). (J). (gr. k-3). 1994. lib. bdg. 24.95 (*0-7933-4600-2*); pap. 14.95 (*0-7933-4601-0*); disk 29.95 (*0-7933-4602-9*) Gallopade Pub Group.

— Uncle Rebus: North Dakota Picture Stories for Computer Kids. (Carole Marsh North Dakota Bks.). (Illus.). (J). (gr. k-3). 1994. lib. bdg. 24.95 (*0-7933-4603-7*); pap. 14.95 (*0-7933-4604-5*); disk 29.95 (*0-7933-4605-3*) Gallopade Pub Group.

— Uncle Rebus: Ohio Picture Stories for Computer Kids. (Carole Marsh Ohio Bks.). (Illus.). (J). (gr. k-3). 1994. lib. bdg. 24.95 (*0-7933-4606-1*); pap. 14.95 (*0-7933-4607-X*); disk 29.95 (*0-7933-4608-8*) Gallopade Pub Group.

— Uncle Rebus: Oklahoma Picture Stories for Computer Kids. (Oklahoma Bks.). (Illus.). (J). (gr. k-3). 1994. lib. bdg. 24.95 (*0-7933-4609-6*); pap. 14.95 (*0-7933-4610-X*); disk 29.95 (*0-7933-4611-8*) Gallopade Pub Group.

— Uncle Rebus: Oregon Picture Stories for Computer Kids. (Oregon Bks.). (Illus.). (J). (gr. k-3). 1994. lib. bdg. 24.95 (*0-7933-4612-6*); pap. 14.95 (*0-7933-4613-4*); disk 29.95 (*0-7933-4614-2*) Gallopade Pub Group.

— Uncle Rebus: Pennsylvania Picture Stories for Computer Kids. (Pennsylvania Bks.). (Illus.). (J). (gr. k-3). 1994. lib. bdg. 24.95 (*0-7933-4615-0*); pap. 14.95 (*0-7933-4616-9*); disk 29.95 (*0-7933-4617-7*) Gallopade Pub Group.

— Uncle Rebus: Rhode Island Picture Stories for Computer Kids. (Rhode Island Bks.). (Illus.). (J). (gr. k-3). 1994. lib. bdg. 24.95 (*0-7933-4618-5*); pap. 14.95 (*0-7933-4619-3*); disk 29.95 (*0-7933-4620-7*) Gallopade Pub Group.

— Uncle Rebus: South Carolina Picture Stories for Computer Kids. (South Carolina Bks.). (Illus.). (J). (gr. k-3). 1994. lib. bdg. 24.95 (*0-7933-4621-5*); pap. 14.95 (*0-7933-4622-3*); disk 29.95 (*0-7933-4623-1*) Gallopade Pub Group.

— Uncle Rebus: South Dakota Picture Stories for Computer Kids. (South Dakota Bks.). (Illus.). (J). (gr. k-3). 1994. lib. bdg. 24.95 (*0-7933-4624-X*); pap. 14.95 (*0-7933-4625-8*); disk 29.95 (*0-7933-4626-6*) Gallopade Pub Group.

— Uncle Rebus: Tennessee Picture Stories for Computer Kids. (Tennessee Bks.). (Illus.). (J). (gr. k-3). 1994. lib. bdg. 24.95 (*0-7933-4627-4*); pap. 14.95 (*0-7933-4628-2*); disk 29.95 (*0-7933-4629-0*) Gallopade Pub Group.

— Uncle Rebus: Texas Picture Stories for Computer Kids. (Texas Bks.). (Illus.). (J). (gr. k-3). 1994. lib. bdg. 24.95 (*0-7933-4630-4*); pap. 14.95 (*0-7933-4631-2*); disk 29.95 (*0-7933-4632-0*) Gallopade Pub Group.

— Uncle Rebus: Utah Picture Stories for Computer Kids. (Utah Bks.). (Illus.). (J). (gr. k-3). 1994. lib. bdg. 24.95 (*0-7933-4633-9*); pap. 14.95 (*0-7933-4634-7*); disk 29.95 (*0-7933-4635-5*) Gallopade Pub Group.

— Uncle Rebus: Vermont Picture Stories for Computer Kids. (Vermont Bks.). (Illus.). (J). (gr. k-3). 1994. lib. bdg. 24.95 (*0-7933-4636-3*); pap. 14.95 (*0-7933-4637-1*); disk 29.95 (*0-7933-4638-X*) Gallopade Pub Group.

— Uncle Rebus: Virginia Picture Stories for Computer Kids. (Virginia Bks.). (Illus.). (J). (gr. k-3). 1994. lib. bdg. 24.95 (*0-7933-4639-8*); pap. 14.95 (*0-7933-4640-1*); disk 29.95 (*0-7933-4641-X*) Gallopade Pub Group.

— Uncle Rebus: Washington, DC Picture Stories for Computer Kids. (Washington, D.C. Bks.). (Illus.). (J). (gr. k-3). 1994. lib. bdg. 24.95 (*0-7933-4645-2*); pap. 14.95 (*0-7933-4646-0*); disk 29.95 (*0-7933-4647-9*) Gallopade Pub Group.

— Uncle Rebus: Washington Picture Stories for Computer Kids. (Washington Bks.). (Illus.). (J). (gr. k-3). 1994. lib. bdg. 24.95 (*0-7933-4642-8*); pap. 14.95 (*0-7933-4643-6*); disk 29.95 (*0-7933-4644-4*) Gallopade Pub Group.

— Uncle Rebus: West Virginia Picture Stories for Computer Kids. (West Virginia Bks.). (Illus.). (J). (gr. k-3). 1994. lib. bdg. 24.95 (*0-7933-4648-7*); pap. 14.95 (*0-7933-4649-5*); disk 29.95 (*0-7933-4650-9*) Gallopade Pub Group.

— Uncle Rebus: Wisconsin Picture Stories for Computer Kids. (Wisconsin Bks.). (Illus.). (J). (gr. k-3). 1994. lib. bdg. 24.95 (*0-7933-4651-7*); pap. 14.95 (*0-7933-4652-5*); disk 29.95 (*0-7933-4653-3*) Gallopade Pub Group.

— Uncle Rebus: Wyoming Picture Stories for Computer Kids. (Wyoming Bks.). (Illus.). (J). (gr. k-3). 1994. lib. bdg. 24.95 (*0-7933-4654-1*); pap. 14.95 (*0-7933-4655-X*); disk 29.95 (*0-7933-4656-8*) Gallopade Pub Group.

— Utah & Other State Greats (Biographies) (Carole Marsh Utah Bks.). (Illus.). (J). 1994. lib. bdg. 24.95 (*0-7933-2129-8*); pap. 14.95 (*0-7933-2130-1*); disk 29.95 (*0-7933-2131-X*) Gallopade Pub Group.

— Utah Bandits, Bushwackers, Outlaws, Crooks, Devils, Ghosts, Desperadoes & Other Assorted & Sundry Characters! (Carole Marsh Utah Bks.). (Illus.). (J). 1994. lib. bdg. 24.95 (*0-7933-1106-3*); pap. 14.95 (*0-685-45955-1*); disk 29.95 (*0-7933-1107-1*) Gallopade Pub Group.

— The Utah Bookstore Book: A Surprising Guide to Our State's Bookstores & Their Specialties for Students, Teachers, Writers & Publishers. (Utah Bks.). (Illus.). 1994. lib. bdg. 24.95 (*0-7933-2987-6*); pap. 14.95 (*0-7933-2988-4*); disk 29.95 (*0-7933-2989-2*) Gallopade Pub Group.

— Utah Classic Christmas Trivia: Stories, Recipes, Activities, Legends, Lore & More! (Carole Marsh Utah Bks.). (Illus.). (J). 1994. lib. bdg. 24.95 (*0-7933-1109-8*); pap. 14.95 (*0-7933-1108-X*); disk 29.95 (*0-7933-1110-1*) Gallopade Pub Group.

M

— Utah Coastales. (Carole Marsh Utah Bks.). (Illus.). (J). 1994. lib. bdg. 24.95 (0-7933-2123-9); pap. 14.95 (0-7933-2124-7); disk 29.95 (0-685-45954-3) Gallopade Pub Group.

— Utah Coastales! (Utah Bks.). (J). 1994. lib. bdg. 24.95 (0-7933-7309-3) Gallopade Pub Group.

— Utah "Crinkum-Crankum" A Funny Word Book about Our State. (Utah Bks.). (Illus.). (J). (gr. 3-12). 1994. 24.95 (0-7933-4940-0); pap. 14.95 (0-7933-4941-9); disk 29.95 (0-7933-4942-7) Gallopade Pub Group.

— Utah Dingbats! Bk. 1: A Fun Book of Games, Stories, Activities & More about Our State That's All in Code! for You to Decipher. (Utah Bks.). (Illus.). (J). (gr. 3-12). 1994. lib. bdg. 24.95 (0-7933-3905-7); pap. 14.95 (0-7933-3906-5); disk 29.95 (0-7933-3907-3) Gallopade Pub Group.

— Utah Festival Fun for Kids! (Utah Bks.). (Illus.). (YA). (gr. 3-12). 1994. lib. bdg. 24.95 (0-7933-4058-6); pap. 14.95 (0-7933-4059-4); disk 29.95 (0-7933-4060-8) Gallopade Pub Group.

— The Utah Hot Air Balloon Mystery. (Carole Marsh Utah Bks.). (Illus.). (J). (gr. 2-9). 1994. 24.95 (0-7933-2714-8); pap. 14.95 (0-7933-2715-6); disk 29.95 (0-7933-2716-4) Gallopade Pub Group.

— Utah Jeopardy! Answers & Questions about Our State! (Utah Bks.). (Illus.). (J). (gr. 3-12). 1994. lib. bdg. 24.95 (0-7933-4211-2); pap. 14.95 (0-7933-4212-0); disk 29.95 (0-7933-4213-9) Gallopade Pub Group.

— Utah "Jography" A Fun Run Thru Our State! (Carole Marsh Utah Bks.). (Illus.). (J). 1994. lib. bdg. 24.95 (0-7933-2106-9); pap. 14.95 (0-7933-2107-7); disk 29.95 (0-7933-2108-5) Gallopade Pub Group.

— Utah Kid's Cookbook: Recipes, How-to, History, Lore & More! (Carole Marsh Utah Bks.). (Illus.). (J). 1994. lib. bdg. 24.95 (0-7933-1118-7); pap. 14.95 (0-7933-1117-9); disk 29.95 (0-7933-1119-5) Gallopade Pub Group.

— The Utah Library Book: A Surprising Guide to the Unusual Special Collections in Libraries Across Our State for Students, Teachers, Writers & Publishers - Includes Reproducible Mailing Labels Plus Activities for Young People! (Utah Bks.). (Illus.). 1994. lib. bdg. 24.95 (0-7933-3137-4); pap. 14.95 (0-7933-3138-2); disk 29.95 (0-7933-3139-0) Gallopade Pub Group.

— The Utah Media Book: A Surprising Guide to the Amazing Print, Broadcast & Online Media of Our State for Students, Teachers, Writers & Publishers - Includes Reproducible Mailing Labels Plus Activities for Young People! (Utah Bks.). (Illus.). 1994. lib. bdg. 24.95 (0-7933-3293-1); pap. 14.95 (0-7933-3294-X); disk 29.95 (0-7933-3295-8) Gallopade Pub Group.

— The Utah Mystery Van Takes Off! Book 1: Handicapped Utah Kids Sneak Off on a Big Adventure. (Utah Bks.). (Illus.). (J). (gr. 3-12). 1994. 24.95 (0-7933-5093-X); pap. 14.95 (0-7933-5094-8); disk 29.95 (0-7933-5095-6) Gallopade Pub Group.

— Utah Quiz Bowl Crash Course! (Carole Marsh Utah Bks.). (Illus.). (J). 1994. lib. bdg. 24.95 (0-7933-2120-4); pap. 14.95 (0-7933-2121-2); disk 29.95 (0-7933-2122-0) Gallopade Pub Group.

— Utah Rollercoasters! (Utah Bks.). (Illus.). (YA). (gr. 3-12). 1994. lib. bdg. 24.95 (0-7933-5356-4); pap. 14.95 (0-7933-5357-2); disk 29.95 (0-7933-5358-0) Gallopade Pub Group.

— Utah School Trivia: An Amazing & Fascinating Look at Our State's Teachers, Schools & Students! (Carole Marsh Utah Bks.). (Illus.). (J). 1994. lib. bdg. 24.95 (0-7933-1115-2); pap. 14.95 (0-7933-1114-4); disk 29.95 (0-7933-1116-0) Gallopade Pub Group.

— Utah Silly Basketball Sportsmysteries, Vol. 1. (Carole Marsh Utah Bks.). (Illus.). (J). 1994. lib. bdg. 24.95 (0-7933-1112-8); pap. 14.95 (0-7933-1111-X); disk 29.95 (0-7933-1113-6) Gallopade Pub Group.

— Utah Silly Basketball Sportsmysteries, Vol. 2. (Carole Marsh Utah Bks.). (Illus.). (J). 1994. lib. bdg. 24.95 (0-7933-2132-8); pap. 14.95 (0-7933-2133-6); disk 29.95 (0-7933-2134-4) Gallopade Pub Group.

— Utah Silly Football Sportsmysteries, Vol. 1. (Carole Marsh Utah Bks.). (Illus.). (J). 1994. lib. bdg. 24.95 (0-7933-2111-5); pap. 14.95 (0-7933-2112-3); disk 29.95 (0-7933-2113-1) Gallopade Pub Group.

— Utah Silly Football Sportsmysteries, Vol. 2. (Carole Marsh Utah Bks.). (Illus.). (J). 1994. lib. bdg. 24.95 (0-7933-2114-X); pap. 14.95 (0-7933-2115-8); disk 29.95 (0-7933-2116-6) Gallopade Pub Group.

— Utah Silly Trivia! (Carole Marsh Utah Bks.). (Illus.). (J). 1994. lib. bdg. 24.95 (0-7933-2103-4); pap. 14.95 (0-7933-2104-2); disk 29.95 (0-7933-2105-0) Gallopade Pub Group.

— Utah Timeline: A Chronology of Utah History, Mystery, Trivia, Legend, Lore & More. (Utah Bks.). (Illus.). (J). (gr. 3-12). 1994. lib. bdg. 24.95 (0-7933-6007-2); pap. 14.95 (0-7933-6008-0); disk 29.95 (0-7933-6009-9) Gallopade Pub Group.

— Utah's (Most Devastating!) Disasters & (Most Calamitous!) Catastrophies! (Carole Marsh Utah Bks.). (Illus.). (J). 1994. lib. bdg. 24.95 (0-7933-1103-9); pap. 14.95 (0-7933-1102-0); write for info. (0-7933-1104-7) Gallopade Pub Group.

— Utah's Unsolved Mysteries (& Their "Solutions") Includes Scientific Information & Other Activities for Students. (Utah Bks.). (Illus.). (J). (gr. 3-12). 1994. lib. bdg. 24.95 (0-7933-5854-X); pap. 14.95 (0-7933-5855-8); disk 29.95 (0-7933-5856-6) Gallopade Pub Group.

— Vermont & Other State Greats (Biographies) (Carole Marsh Vermont Bks.). (Illus.). (J). 1994. lib. bdg. 24.95 (0-7933-2161-1); pap. 14.95 (0-7933-2162-X); disk 29.95 (0-7933-2163-8) Gallopade Pub Group.

— Vermont Bandits, Bushwackers, Outlaws, Crooks, Devils, Ghosts, Desperadoes & Other Assorted & Sundry Characters! (Carole Marsh Vermont Bks.). (Illus.). (J). 1994. lib. bdg. 24.95 (0-7933-1130-6); pap. 14.95 (0-7933-1129-2); write for info. (0-7933-1131-4) Gallopade Pub Group.

— The Vermont Bookstore Book: A Surprising Guide to Our State's Bookstores & Their Specialties for Students, Teachers, Writers & Publishers. (Vermont Bks.). (Illus.). 1994. lib. bdg. 24.95 (0-7933-2990-6); pap. 14.95 (0-7933-2991-4); disk 29.95 (0-7933-2992-2) Gallopade Pub Group.

— Vermont Classic Christmas Trivia: Stories, Recipes, Activities, Legends, Lore & More! (Carole Marsh Vermont Bks.). (Illus.). (J). 1994. lib. bdg. 24.95 (0-7933-1133-0); pap. 14.95 (0-7933-1132-2); disk 29.95 (0-7933-1134-9) Gallopade Pub Group.

— Vermont Coastales. (Carole Marsh Vermont Bks.). (Illus.). (J). 1994. lib. bdg. 24.95 (0-7933-2155-7); pap. 14.95 (0-7933-2156-5); disk 29.95 (0-7933-2157-3) Gallopade Pub Group.

— Vermont Coastales! (Vermont Bks.). (J). 1994. lib. bdg. 24.95 (0-7933-7310-7) Gallopade Pub Group.

— Vermont "Crinkum-Crankum" A Funny Word Book about Our State. (Vermont Bks.). (Illus.). (J). (gr. 3-12). 1994. 24.95 (0-7933-4943-5); pap. 14.95 (0-7933-4944-3); disk 29.95 (0-7933-4945-1) Gallopade Pub Group.

— Vermont Dingbats! Bk. 1: A Fun Book of Games, Stories, Activities & More about Our State That's All in Code! for You to Decipher. (Vermont Bks.). (Illus.). (J). (gr. 3-12). 1994. lib. bdg. 24.95 (0-7933-3908-1); pap. 14.95 (0-7933-3909-X); disk 29.95 (0-7933-3910-3) Gallopade Pub Group.

— Vermont Festival Fun for Kids! (Vermont Bks.). (Illus.). (YA). (gr. 3-12). 1994. lib. bdg. 24.95 (0-7933-4061-6); pap. 14.95 (0-7933-4062-4); disk 29.95 (0-7933-4063-2) Gallopade Pub Group.

— The Vermont Hot Air Balloon Mystery. (Carole Marsh Vermont Bks.). (Illus.). (J). (gr. 2-9). 1994. 24.95 (0-7933-2723-7); pap. 14.95 (0-7933-2724-5); disk 29.95 (0-7933-2725-3) Gallopade Pub Group.

— Vermont Jeopardy! Answers & Questions about Our State! (Vermont Bks.). (Illus.). (J). (gr. 3-12). 1994. lib. bdg. 24.95 (0-7933-4214-7); pap. 14.95 (0-7933-4215-5); disk 29.95 (0-7933-4216-3) Gallopade Pub Group.

— Vermont "Jography" A Fun Run Thru Our State! (Carole Marsh Vermont Bks.). (Illus.). (J). 1994. lib. bdg. 24.95 (0-7933-2138-7); pap. 14.95 (0-7933-2139-5); disk 29.95 (0-7933-2140-9) Gallopade Pub Group.

— Vermont Kids' Cookbook: Recipes, How-to, History, Lore & More! (Carole Marsh Vermont Bks.). (Illus.). (J). 1994. lib. bdg. 24.95 (0-7933-1142-X); pap. 14.95 (0-685-45957-8); disk 29.95 (0-7933-1143-8) Gallopade Pub Group.

— The Vermont Library Book: A Surprising Guide to the Unusual Special Collections in Libraries Across Our State for Students, Teachers, Writers & Publishers - Includes Reproducible Mailing Labels Plus Activities for Young People! (Vermont Bks.). (Illus.). 1994. lib. bdg. 24.95 (0-7933-3140-4); pap. 14.95 (0-7933-3141-2); disk 29.95 (0-7933-3142-0) Gallopade Pub Group.

— The Vermont Media Book: A Surprising Guide to the Amazing Print, Broadcast & Online Media of Our State for Students, Teachers, Writers & Publishers - Includes Reproducible Mailing Labels Plus Activities for Young People! (Vermont Bks.). (Illus.). 1994. lib. bdg. 24.95 (0-7933-3296-6); pap. 14.95 (0-7933-3297-4); disk 29.95 (0-7933-3298-2) Gallopade Pub Group.

— The Vermont Mystery Van Takes Off! Book 1: Handicapped Vermont Kids Sneak Off on a Big Adventure. (Vermont Bks.). (Illus.). (J). (gr. 3-12). 1994. 24.95 (0-7933-5096-4); pap. 14.95 (0-7933-5097-2); disk 29.95 (0-7933-5098-0) Gallopade Pub Group.

— Vermont Quiz Bowl Crash Course! (Carole Marsh Vermont Bks.). (Illus.). (J). 1994. lib. bdg. 24.95 (0-7933-2152-2); pap. 14.95 (0-7933-2153-0); disk 29.95 (0-7933-2154-9) Gallopade Pub Group.

— Vermont Rollercoasters! (Vermont Bks.). (Illus.). (YA). (gr. 3-12). 1994. lib. bdg. 24.95 (0-7933-5359-9); pap. 14.95 (0-7933-5360-2); disk 29.95 (0-7933-5361-0) Gallopade Pub Group.

— Vermont School Trivia: An Amazing & Fascinating Look at Our State's Teachers, Schools & Students! (Carole Marsh Vermont Bks.). (Illus.). (J). 1994. lib. bdg. 24.95 (0-7933-1139-X); pap. 14.95 (0-7933-1138-1); disk 29.95 (0-7933-1140-3) Gallopade Pub Group.

— Vermont Silly Basketball Sportsmysteries, Vol. 1. (Carole Marsh Vermont Bks.). (Illus.). (J). 1994. lib. bdg. 24.95 (0-7933-1136-5); pap. 14.95 (0-7933-1135-7); disk 29.95 (0-7933-1137-3) Gallopade Pub Group.

— Vermont Silly Basketball Sportsmysteries, Vol. 2. (Carole Marsh Vermont Bks.). (Illus.). (J). 1994. lib. bdg. 24.95 (0-7933-2164-6); pap. 14.95 (0-7933-2165-4); 29.95 (0-7933-2166-2) Gallopade Pub Group.

— Vermont Silly Football Sportsmysteries, Vol. 1. (Carole Marsh Vermont Bks.). (Illus.). (J). 1994. lib. bdg. 24.95 (0-7933-2143-3); pap. 14.95 (0-7933-2144-1); disk 29.95 (0-7933-2145-X) Gallopade Pub Group.

— Vermont Silly Football Sportsmysteries, Vol. 2. (Carole Marsh Vermont Bks.). (Illus.). (J). 1994. lib. bdg. 24.95 (0-7933-2146-8); pap. 14.95 (0-7933-2147-6); disk 29.95 (0-7933-2148-4) Gallopade Pub Group.

— Vermont Silly Trivia! (Carole Marsh Vermont Bks.). (Illus.). (J). 1994. lib. bdg. 24.95 (0-7933-2135-2); pap. 14.95 (0-7933-2136-0); disk 29.95 (0-7933-2137-9) Gallopade Pub Group.

— Vermont Timeline: A Chronology of Vermont History, Mystery, Trivia, Legend, Lore & More. (Vermont Bks.). (Illus.). (J). (gr. 3-12). 1994. lib. bdg. 24.95 (0-7933-6010-2); pap. 14.95 (0-7933-6011-0); disk 29.95 (0-7933-6012-9) Gallopade Pub Group.

— Vermont's (Most Devastating!) Disasters & (Most Calamitous!) Catastrophies! (Carole Marsh Vermont Bks.). (Illus.). (J). 1994. lib. bdg. 24.95 (0-7933-1127-6); pap. 14.95 (0-7933-1126-8); disk 29.95 (0-7933-1128-4) Gallopade Pub Group.

— Vermont's Unsolved Mysteries (& Their "Solutions") Includes Scientific Information & Other Activities for Students. (Vermont Bks.). (Illus.). (J). (gr. 3-12). 1994. lib. bdg. 24.95 (0-7933-5857-4); pap. 14.95 (0-7933-5858-2); disk 29.95 (0-7933-5859-0) Gallopade Pub Group.

— Virginia & Other State Greats (Biographies) (Carole Marsh Virginia Bks.). (Illus.). (J). 1994. lib. bdg. 24.95 (0-7933-2190-5); pap. 14.95 (0-7933-2191-3); disk 29.95 (0-7933-2192-1) Gallopade Pub Group.

— Virginia Bandits, Bushwackers, Outlaws, Crooks, Devils, Ghosts, Desperadoes & Other Assorted & Sundry Characters! (Carole Marsh Virginia Bks.). (Illus.). (J). 1994. lib. bdg. 24.95 (0-7933-1154-3); pap. 14.95 (0-7933-1153-5); disk 29.95 (0-7933-1155-1) Gallopade Pub Group.

— The Virginia Bookstore Book: A Surprising Guide to Our State's Bookstores & Their Specialties for Students, Teachers, Writers & Publishers. (Virginia Bks.). (Illus.). 1994. lib. bdg. 24.95 (0-7933-2993-0); pap. 14.95 (0-7933-2994-9); disk 29.95 (0-7933-2995-7) Gallopade Pub Group.

— Virginia Classic Christmas Trivia: Stories, Recipes, Activities, Legends, Lore & More. (Carole Marsh Virginia Bks.). (Illus.). (J). 1994. lib. bdg. 24.95 (0-7933-1157-8); pap. 14.95 (0-7933-1156-X); disk 29.95 (0-7933-1158-6) Gallopade Pub Group.

— Virginia Coastales. (Carole Marsh Virginia Bks.). (Illus.). (J). 1994. lib. bdg. 24.95 (0-685-45962-4); pap. 14.95 (1-55609-116-8); disk 29.95 (0-7933-2186-7) Gallopade Pub Group.

— Virginia Coastales! (Virginia Bks.). (J). 1994. lib. bdg. 24.95 (0-7933-7311-5) Gallopade Pub Group.

— Virginia "Crinkum-Crankum" A Funny Word Book about Our State. (Virginia Bks.). (Illus.). (J). (gr. 3-12). 1994. 24.95 (0-7933-4946-X); pap. 14.95 (0-7933-4947-8); disk 29.95 (0-7933-4948-6) Gallopade Pub Group.

— Virginia Dingbats! Bk. 1: A Fun Book of Games, Stories, Activities & More about Our State That's All in Code! for You to Decipher. (Virginia Bks.). (Illus.). (J). (gr. 3-12). 1994. lib. bdg. 24.95 (0-7933-3911-1); pap. 14.95 (0-7933-3912-X); disk 29.95 (0-7933-3913-8) Gallopade Pub Group.

— Virginia Festival Fun for Kids! (Virginia Bks.). (Illus.). (YA). (gr. 3-12). 1994. lib. bdg. 24.95 (0-7933-4064-0); pap. 14.95 (0-7933-4065-9); disk 29.95 (0-685-41938-X) Gallopade Pub Group.

— The Virginia Hot Air Balloon Mystery. (Carole Marsh Virginia Bks.). (Illus.). (J). (gr. 2-9). 1994. 24.95 (0-7933-2732-6); pap. 14.95 (0-7933-2733-4); disk 29.95 (0-7933-2734-2) Gallopade Pub Group.

— Virginia Jeopardy! Answers & Questions about Our State! (Virginia Bks.). (Illus.). (J). (gr. 3-12). 1994. lib. bdg. 24.95 (0-7933-4217-1); pap. 14.95 (0-7933-4218-X); disk 29.95 (0-7933-4219-8) Gallopade Pub Group.

— Virginia Jography: A Fun Run Through the Old Dominion State. (Statemeant Ser.). (Illus.). 50p. (Orig.). (J). (gr. 3-12). 1994. pap. 24.95 (0-935326-99-5) Gallopade Pub Group.

— Virginia "Jography" A Fun Run Thru Our State. (Carole Marsh Virginia Bks.). (Illus.). (J). 1994. lib. bdg. 24.95 (0-685-45960-8); pap. 14.95 (1-55609-057-9); disk 29.95 (0-7933-2170-0) Gallopade Pub Group.

— Virginia Kid's Cookbook: Recipes, How-to, History, Lore & More! (Carole Marsh Virginia Bks.). (Illus.). (J). 1994. lib. bdg. 24.95 (0-7933-1166-7); pap. 14.95 (0-7933-1165-9); disk 29.95 (0-7933-1167-5) Gallopade Pub Group.

— The Virginia Library Book: A Surprising Guide to the Unusual Special Collections in Libraries Across Our State for Students, Teachers, Writers & Publishers - Includes Reproducible Mailing Labels Plus Activities for Young People! (Virginia Bks.). (Illus.). 1994. lib. bdg. 24.95 (0-7933-3143-9); pap. 14.95 (0-7933-3144-7); disk 29.95 (0-7933-3145-5) Gallopade Pub Group.

— The Virginia Media Book: A Surprising Guide to the Amazing Print, Broadcast & Online Media of Our State for Students, Teachers, Writers & Publishers - Includes Reproducible Mailing Labels Plus Activities for Young People! (Virginia Bks.). (Illus.). 1994. lib. bdg. 24.95 (0-7933-3299-0); pap. 14.95 (0-7933-3300-8); disk 29.95 (0-7933-3301-6) Gallopade Pub Group.

— The Virginia Mystery Van Takes Off! Book 1: Handicapped Virginia Kids Sneak Off on a Big Adventure. (Virginia Bks.). (Illus.). (J). (gr. 3-12). 1994. 24.95 (0-7933-5099-9); pap. 14.95 (0-7933-5100-6); disk 29.95 (0-7933-5101-4) Gallopade Pub Group.

— Virginia Quiz Bowl Crash Courses! (Carole Marsh Virginia Bks.). (Illus.). (J). 1994. lib. bdg. 24.95 (0-7933-2182-4); pap. 14.95 (0-7933-2183-2); disk 29.95 (0-7933-2184-0) Gallopade Pub Group.

— Virginia Rollercoasters! (Virginia Bks.). (Illus.). (YA). (gr. 3-12). 1994. lib. bdg. 24.95 (0-7933-5362-9); pap. 14.95 (0-7933-5363-7); disk 29.95 (0-7933-5364-5) Gallopade Pub Group.

— Virginia School Trivia: An Amazing & Fascinating Look at Our State's Teachers, Schools & Students! (Carole Marsh Virginia Bks.). (Illus.). (J). 1994. lib. bdg. 24.95 (0-7933-1163-2); pap. 14.95 (0-7933-1162-4); disk 29.95 (0-7933-1164-0) Gallopade Pub Group.

— Virginia Silly Basketball Sportsmysteries, Vol. 1. (Carole Marsh Virginia Bks.). (Illus.). (J). 1994. lib. bdg. 24.95 (0-7933-1160-8); pap. 14.95 (0-7933-1159-4); disk 29.95 (0-7933-1161-6) Gallopade Pub Group.

— Virginia Silly Basketball Sportsmysteries, Vol. 2. (Carole Marsh Virginia Bks.). (Illus.). (J). 1994. lib. bdg. 24.95 (0-7933-2195-6); pap. 14.95 (0-7933-2196-4); disk 29.95 (0-7933-2197-2) Gallopade Pub Group.

— Virginia Silly Football Sportsmysteries, Vol. 1. (Carole Marsh Virginia Bks.). (Illus.). (J). 1994. lib. bdg. 24.95 (0-685-45961-6); pap. 14.95 (0-7933-2174-3); disk 29.95 (0-7933-2175-1) Gallopade Pub Group.

— Virginia Silly Football Sportsmysteries, Vol. 2. (Carole Marsh Virginia Bks.). (Illus.). (J). 1994. lib. bdg. 24.95 (0-7933-2176-X); pap. 14.95 (0-7933-2177-8); disk 29.95 (0-7933-2178-6) Gallopade Pub Group.

— Virginia Silly Trivia! (Carole Marsh Virginia Bks.). (Illus.). 60p. (Orig.). (J). (gr. 3-12). 1994. lib. bdg. 24.95 (0-7933-2167-0); pap. 14.95 (0-935326-94-4); disk 29.95 (0-7933-2168-9) Gallopade Pub Group.

— Virginia Timeline: A Chronology of Virginia History, Mystery, Trivia, Legend, Lore & More. (Virginia Bks.). (Illus.). (J). (gr. 3-12). 1994. lib. bdg. 24.95 (0-7933-6013-7); pap. 14.95 (0-7933-6014-5); disk 29.95 (0-7933-6015-3) Gallopade Pub Group.

— Virginia's (Most Devastating!) Disasters & (Most Calamitous!) Catastrophies! (Carole Marsh Virginia Bks.). (Illus.). (J). 1994. lib. bdg. 24.95 (0-7933-2193-X); pap. 14.95 (0-7933-1150-0); disk 29.95 (0-7933-2194-8) Gallopade Pub Group.

— Virginia's Unsolved Mysteries (& Their "Solutions") Includes Scientific Information & Other Activities for Students. (Virginia Bks.). (Illus.). (J). (gr. 3-12). 1994. lib. bdg. 24.95 (0-7933-5860-4); pap. 14.95 (0-7933-5861-2); disk 29.95 (0-7933-5862-0) Gallopade Pub Group.

— Washington & Other State Greats (Biographies!) (Carole Marsh Washington Bks.). (Illus.). (J). 1994. lib. bdg. 24.95 (0-7933-2224-3); pap. 14.95 (0-7933-2225-1); disk 29.95 (0-7933-2226-X) Gallopade Pub Group.

— Washington Bandits, Bushwackers, Outlaws, Crooks, Devils, Ghosts, Desperadoes & Other Assorted & Sundry Characters! (Carole Marsh Washington Bks.). (Illus.). (J). 1994. lib. bdg. 24.95 (0-7933-1178-0); pap. 14.95 (0-7933-1177-2); disk 29.95 (0-7933-1179-9) Gallopade Pub Group.

— The Washington Bookstore Book: A Surprising Guide to Our State's Bookstores & Their Specialties for Students, Teachers, Writers & Publishers. (Washington Bks.). (Illus.). 1994. lib. bdg. 24.95 (0-7933-2996-5); pap. 14.95 (0-7933-2997-3); disk 29.95 (0-7933-2998-1) Gallopade Pub Group.

— Washington Classic Christmas Trivia: Stories, Recipes, Activities, Legends, Lore & More! (Washington Bks.). (Illus.). (J). 1994. lib. bdg. 24.95 (0-7933-1181-0); pap. 14.95 (0-7933-1180-2); disk 29.95 (0-7933-1182-9) Gallopade Pub Group.

— Washington Coastales. (Carole Marsh Washington Bks.). (Illus.). (J). 1994. lib. bdg. 24.95 (0-7933-2218-9); pap. 14.95 (0-7933-2219-7); disk 29.95 (0-7933-2220-0) Gallopade Pub Group.

— Washington Coastales! (Washington Bks.). (J). 1994. lib. bdg. 24.95 (0-7933-7312-3) Gallopade Pub Group.

— Washington "Crinkum-Crankum" A Funny Word Book about Our State. (Washington Bks.). (Illus.). (J). (gr. 3-12). 1994. 24.95 (0-7933-4949-4); pap. 14.95 (0-7933-4950-8); disk 29.95 (0-7933-4951-6) Gallopade Pub Group.

— Washington, D. C. & Other State Greats (Biographies) (Washington, D.C. Bks.). (Illus.). (YA). (gr. 3-12). 1994. lib. bdg. 24.95 (0-7933-1480-1); pap. 14.95 (0-7933-1481-X); disk 29.95 (0-7933-1482-8) Gallopade Pub Group.

— Washington, D. C. Bandits, Bushwackers, Outlaws, Crooks, Devils, Ghosts, Desperadoes & Other Assorted & Sundry Characters! (Carole Marsh Washington, D.C. Bks.). (Illus.). (YA). (gr. 3-12). 1994. lib. bdg. 24.95 (0-7933-0262-5); pap. 14.95 (0-7933-0261-7); disk 29.95 (0-7933-0263-3) Gallopade Pub Group.

— The Washington, D. C. Bookstore Book: A Surprising Guide to Our State's Bookstores & Their Specialties for Students, Teachers, Writers & Publishers. (Washington, D.C. Bks.). (Illus.). 1994. lib. bdg. 24.95 (0-7933-2879-9); pap. 14.95 (0-7933-2880-2); disk 29.95 (0-7933-2881-0) Gallopade Pub Group.

— Washington, D. C. Classic Christmas Trivia: Stories, Recipes, Activities, Legends, Lore & More! (Carole Marsh Washington, D.C. Bks.). (Illus.). (YA). (gr. 3-12). 1994. lib. bdg. 24.95 (0-7933-0265-X); pap. 14.95 (0-7933-0264-1); disk 29.95 (0-7933-0266-8) Gallopade Pub Group.

— Washington, D. C. Coastales. (Carole Marsh Washington, D.C. Bks.). (Illus.). (YA). (gr. 3-12). 1994. lib. bdg. 24.95 (0-7933-1474-7); pap. 14.95 (0-7933-1475-5); disk 29.95 (0-7933-1476-3) Gallopade Pub Group.

— Washington, D. C. Coastales! (Washington, D.C. Bks.). (J). 1994. lib. bdg. 24.95 (0-7933-7273-9) Gallopade Pub Group.

— Washington D. C. "Crinkum-Crankum" A Funny Word Book about Our State. (Washington, D.C. Bks.). (Illus.). (J). (gr. 3-12). 1994. 24.95 (0-7933-4952-4); pap. 14.95 (0-7933-4953-2); disk 29.95 (0-7933-4954-0) Gallopade Pub Group.

— Washington, D. C. Dingbats! Bk. 1: A Fun Book of Games, Stories, Activities & More about Our State That's All in Code! for You to Decipher. (Washington, D.C. Bks.). (Illus.). (J). (gr. 3-12). 1994. lib. bdg. 24.95 (0-7933-3797-6); pap. 14.95 (0-7933-3798-4); disk 29.95 (0-7933-3799-2) Gallopade Pub Group.

— Washington, D. C. Festival Fun for Kids! Includes Reproducible Activities for Kids! (Washington, D.C. Bks.). (Illus.). (J). (gr. 3-12). 1994. lib. bdg. 24.95 (0-7933-3950-2); pap. 14.95 (0-7933-3951-0); disk 29.95 (0-7933-3952-9) Gallopade Pub Group.

M

— The Washington D. C. Hot Air Balloon Mystery. (Washington, D.C. Bks.). (Illus.). (J). (gr. 2-9). 1994. 24.95 (*0-7933-2390-8*); pap. 14.95 (*0-7933-2391-6*); disk 29.95 (*0-7933-2392-4*) Gallopade Pub Group.

— Washington, D. C. Jeopardy! Answers & Questions about Our State! (Washington, D.C. Bks.). (Illus.). (J). (gr. 3-12). 1994. lib. bdg. 24.95 (*0-7933-4103-5*); pap. 14.95 (*0-7933-4104-3*); disk 29.95 (*0-7933-4105-1*) Gallopade Pub Group.

— Washington, D. C. "Jography" A Fun Run Thru Our State! (Washington, D.C. Bks.). (Illus.). (YA). (gr. 3-12). 1994. lib. bdg. 24.95 (*1-55609-562-7*); pap. 14.95 (*1-55609-561-9*); disk 29.95 (*0-7933-1460-7*) Gallopade Pub Group.

— Washington, D. C. Kid's Cookbook: Recipes, How-to, History, Lore & More! (Carole Marsh Washington, D.C. Bks.). (Illus.). (YA). (gr. 3-12). 1994. lib. bdg. 24.95 (*0-7933-0274-9*); pap. 14.95 (*0-7933-0273-0*); disk 29.95 (*0-7933-0275-7*) Gallopade Pub Group.

— The Washington, D. C. Library Book: A Surprising Guide to the Unusual Special Collections in Libraries Across Our State for Students, Teachers, Writers & Publishers. (Washington, D.C. Bks.). (Illus.). 1994. lib. bdg. 24.95 (*0-7933-3029-7*); pap. 14.95 (*0-7933-3030-0*); disk 29.95 (*0-7933-3031-9*) Gallopade Pub Group.

— The Washington, D. C. Media Book: A Surprising Guide to the Amazing Print, Broadcast & Online Media of Our State for Students, Teachers, Writers & Publishers - Includes Reproducible Mailing Labels Plus Activities for Young People! (Washington, D.C. Bks.). (Illus.). 1994. lib. bdg. 24.95 (*0-7933-3185-4*); pap. 14.95 (*0-7933-3186-2*); disk 29.95 (*0-7933-3187-0*) Gallopade Pub Group.

— The Washington D. C. Mystery Van Takes Off! Book 1: Handicapped Washington D. C. Kids Sneak Off on a Big Adventure. (Washington, D.C. Bks.). (Illus.). (J). (gr. 3-12). 1994. 24.95 (*0-7933-5105-7*); pap. 14.95 (*0-7933-5106-5*); disk 29.95 (*0-7933-5107-3*) Gallopade Pub Group.

— Washington, D. C. Quiz Bowl Crash Course! (Carole Marsh Washington, D.C. Bks.). (Illus.). (YA). (gr. 3-12). 1994. lib. bdg. 24.95 (*0-7933-1471-2*); pap. 14.95 (*0-7933-1472-0*); disk 29.95 (*0-7933-1473-9*) Gallopade Pub Group.

— Washington, D. C. Rollercoasters! (Washington, D.C. Bks.). (Illus.). (YA). (gr. 3-12). 1994. lib. bdg. 24.95 (*0-7933-5248-7*); pap. 14.95 (*0-7933-5249-5*); disk 29.95 (*0-7933-5250-9*) Gallopade Pub Group.

— Washington, D. C. School Trivia: An Amazing & Fascinating Look at Our State's Teachers, Schools & Students! (Washington, D.C. Bks.). (Illus.). (YA). (gr. 3-12). 1994. lib. bdg. 24.95 (*0-7933-0271-4*); pap. 14.95 (*0-7933-0270-6*); disk 29.95 (*0-7933-0272-2*) Gallopade Pub Group.

— Washington, D. C. Silly Basketball Sportsmysteries, Vol. 1. (Washington, D.C. Bks.). (Illus.). (YA). (gr. 3-12). 1994. lib. bdg. 24.95 (*0-7933-0268-4*); pap. 14.95 (*0-7933-0267-6*); disk 29.95 (*0-7933-0269-2*) Gallopade Pub Group.

— Washington, D. C. Silly Basketball Sportsmysteries, Vol. 2. (Washington, D.C. Bks.). (Illus.). (YA). (gr. 3-12). 1994. lib. bdg. 24.95 (*0-7933-1483-6*); pap. 14.95 (*0-7933-1484-4*); disk 29.95 (*0-7933-1485-2*) Gallopade Pub Group.

— Washington, D. C. Silly Football Sportsmysteries, Vol. 1. (Washington, D.C. Bks.). (Illus.). (YA). (gr. 3-12). 1994. lib. bdg. 24.95 (*0-7933-1462-3*); pap. 14.95 (*0-7933-1463-1*); disk 29.95 (*0-7933-1464-X*) Gallopade Pub Group.

— Washington, D. C. Silly Trivia! (Washington, D.C. Bks.). (Illus.). (YA). (gr. 3-12). 1994. lib. bdg. 24.95 (*1-55609-560-0*); pap. 14.95 (*1-55609-559-7*); disk 29.95 (*0-7933-1459-3*) Gallopade Pub Group.

— Washington D. C. Timeline: A Chronology of Washington D. C. History, Mystery, Trivia, Legend, Lore & More. (Washington, D.C. Bks.). (Illus.). (J). (gr. 3-12). 1994. lib. bdg. 24.95 (*0-7933-5899-X*); pap. 14.95 (*0-7933-5900-7*); disk 29.95 (*0-7933-5901-5*) Gallopade Pub Group.

— Washington, D. C.'s (Most Devastating!) Disasters & (Most Calamitous!) Catastrophies! (Washington, D.C. Bks.). (Illus.). (YA). (gr. 3-12). 1994. lib. bdg. 24.95 (*0-7933-0259-5*); pap. 14.95 (*0-7933-0258-7*); disk 29.95 (*0-7933-0260-9*) Gallopade Pub Group.

— Washington D. C.'s Unsolved Mysteries (& Their "Solutions") Includes Scientific Information & Other Activities for Students. (Washington, D.C. Bks.). (Illus.). (J). (gr. 3-12). 1994. lib. bdg. 24.95 (*0-7933-5746-2*); pap. 14.95 (*0-7933-5747-0*); disk 29.95 (*0-7933-5748-9*) Gallopade Pub Group.

— Washington, D.C. Silly Football Sportsmysteries, Vol. 2. (Carole Marsh Washington, D.C. Bks.). (Illus.). (YA). (gr. 3-12). 1994. lib. bdg. 24.95 (*0-7933-1465-8*); pap. 14.95 (*0-7933-1466-6*); disk 29.95 (*0-7933-1467-4*) Gallopade Pub Group.

— Washington Dingbats! Bk. 1: A Fun Book of Games, Stories, Activities & More about Our State That's All in Code! for You to Decipher. (Washington Bks.). (Illus.). (J). (gr. 3-12). 1994. lib. bdg. 24.95 (*0-7933-3914-6*); pap. 14.95 (*0-7933-3915-4*); disk 29.95 (*0-7933-3916-2*) Gallopade Pub Group.

— Washington Festival Fun for Kids! Includes Reproducible Activities for Kids! (Washington Bks.). (Illus.). (J). (gr. 3-12). 1994. lib. bdg. 24.95 (*0-7933-4067-5*); pap. 14.95 (*0-7933-4068-3*); disk 29.95 (*0-7933-4069-1*) Gallopade Pub Group.

— The Washington Hot Air Balloon Mystery. (Carole Marsh Washington Bks.). (Illus.). (J). (gr. 2-9). 1994. 24.95 (*0-7933-2741-5*); pap. 14.95 (*0-7933-2742-3*); disk 29.95 (*0-7933-2743-1*) Gallopade Pub Group.

— Washington Jeopardy! Answers & Questions about Our State! (Washington Bks.). (Illus.). (J). (gr. 3-12). 1994. lib. bdg. 24.95 (*0-7933-4220-1*); pap. 14.95 (*0-7933-4221-X*); disk 29.95 (*0-7933-4222-8*) Gallopade Pub Group.

— Washington "Jography" A Fun Run Thru Our State! (Carole Marsh Washington Bks.). (Illus.). (J). 1994. lib. bdg. 24.95 (*0-7933-2201-4*); pap. 14.95 (*0-7933-2202-2*); disk 29.95 (*0-7933-2203-0*) Gallopade Pub Group.

— Washington Kid's Cookbook: Recipes, How-to, History, Lore & More! (Carole Marsh Washington Bks.). (Illus.). (J). 1994. lib. bdg. 24.95 (*0-7933-1190-X*); pap. 14.95 (*0-7933-1189-6*); disk 29.95 (*0-7933-1191-8*) Gallopade Pub Group.

— The Washington Library Book: A Surprising Guide to the Unusual Special Collections in Libraries Across Our State for Students, Teachers, Writers & Publishers - Includes Reproducible Mailing Labels Plus Activities for Young People! (Washington Bks.). (Illus.). 1994. lib. bdg. 24.95 (*0-7933-3146-3*); pap. 14.95 (*0-7933-3147-1*); disk 29.95 (*0-7933-3148-X*) Gallopade Pub Group.

— The Washington Media Book: A Surprising Guide to the Amazing Print, Broadcast & Online Media of Our State for Students, Teachers, Writers & Publishers - Includes Reproducible Mailing Labels Plus Activities for Young People! (Washington Bks.). (Illus.). 1994. lib. bdg. 24.95 (*0-7933-3302-4*); pap. 14.95 (*0-7933-3303-2*); disk 29.95 (*0-7933-3304-0*) Gallopade Pub Group.

— The Washington Mystery Van Takes Off! Book 1: Handicapped Washington Kids Sneak Off on a Big Adventure. (Washington Bks.). (Illus.). (J). (gr. 3-12). 1994. 24.95 (*0-7933-5102-2*); pap. 14.95 (*0-7933-5103-0*); disk 29.95 (*0-7933-5104-9*) Gallopade Pub Group.

— Washington Quiz Bowl Crash Course! (Carole Marsh Washington Bks.). (Illus.). (J). 1994. lib. bdg. 24.95 (*0-7933-2215-4*); pap. 14.95 (*0-7933-2216-2*); disk 29.95 (*0-7933-2217-0*) Gallopade Pub Group.

— Washington Rollercoasters! (Washington Bks.). (Illus.). (YA). (gr. 3-12). 1994. lib. bdg. 24.95 (*0-7933-5365-3*); pap. 14.95 (*0-7933-5366-1*); disk 29.95 (*0-7933-5367-X*) Gallopade Pub Group.

— Washington School Trivia: An Amazing & Fascinating Look at Our State's Teachers, Schools & Students! (Carole Marsh Washington Bks.). (Illus.). (J). 1994. lib. bdg. 24.95 (*0-685-45964-0*); pap. 14.95 (*0-7933-1186-1*); disk 29.95 (*0-7933-1188-8*) Gallopade Pub Group.

— Washington Silly Basketball Sportsmysteries, Vol. 1. (Carole Marsh Washington Bks.). (Illus.). (J). 1994. lib. bdg. 24.95 (*0-7933-1184-5*); pap. 14.95 (*0-7933-1183-7*); disk 29.95 (*0-7933-1185-3*) Gallopade Pub Group.

— Washington Silly Basketball Sportsmysteries, Vol. 2. (Carole Marsh Washington Bks.). (Illus.). (J). 1994. lib. bdg. 24.95 (*0-7933-2227-8*); pap. 14.95 (*0-7933-2228-6*); disk 29.95 (*0-7933-2229-4*) Gallopade Pub Group.

— Washington Silly Football Sportsmysteries, Vol. 1. (Carole Marsh Washington Bks.). (Illus.). (J). 1994. lib. bdg. 24.95 (*0-7933-2206-5*); pap. 14.95 (*0-7933-2207-3*); disk 29.95 (*0-7933-2208-1*) Gallopade Pub Group.

— Washington Silly Football Sportsmysteries, Vol. 2. (Carole Marsh Washington Bks.). (Illus.). (J). 1994. lib. bdg. 24.95 (*0-685-45963-2*); pap. 14.95 (*0-7933-2210-3*); disk 29.95 (*0-7933-2211-1*) Gallopade Pub Group.

— Washington Silly Trivia! (Carole Marsh Washington Bks.). (Illus.). (J). 1994. lib. bdg. 24.95 (*0-7933-2198-0*); pap. 14.95 (*0-7933-2199-9*); disk 29.95 (*0-7933-2200-6*) Gallopade Pub Group.

— Washington Timeline: A Chronology of Washington History, Mystery, Trivia, Legend, Lore & More. (Washington Bks.). (Illus.). (J). (gr. 3-12). 1994. lib. bdg. 24.95 (*0-7933-6016-1*); pap. 14.95 (*0-7933-6017-X*); disk 29.95 (*0-7933-6018-8*) Gallopade Pub Group.

— Washington's (Most Devastating!) Disasters & (Most Calamitous!) Catastrophies! (Carole Marsh Washington Bks.). (Illus.). (J). 1994. lib. bdg. 24.95 (*0-7933-1175-6*); pap. 14.95 (*0-7933-1174-8*); disk 29.95 (*0-7933-1176-4*) Gallopade Pub Group.

— Washington's Unsolved Mysteries (& Their "Solutions") Includes Scientific Information & Other Activities for Students. (Washington Bks.). (Illus.). (J). (gr. 3-12). 1994. lib. bdg. 24.95 (*0-7933-5863-9*); pap. 14.95 (*0-7933-5864-7*); disk 29.95 (*0-7933-5865-5*) Gallopade Pub Group.

— West Virginia & Other State Greats (Biographies) (Carole Marsh West Virginia Bks.). (Illus.). (J). 1994. lib. bdg. 24.95 (*0-7933-2256-1*); pap. 14.95 (*0-7933-2257-X*); disk 29.95 (*0-7933-2258-8*) Gallopade Pub Group.

— West Virginia Bandits, Bushwackers, Outlaws, Crooks, Devils, Ghosts, Desperadoes & Other Assorted & Sundry Characters! (Carole Marsh West Virginia Bks.). (Illus.). (J). 1994. lib. bdg. 24.95 (*0-7933-1202-7*); pap. 14.95 (*0-7933-1201-9*); disk 29.95 (*0-7933-1203-5*) Gallopade Pub Group.

— The West Virginia Bookstore Book: A Surprising Guide to Our State's Bookstores & Their Specialties for Students, Teachers, Writers & Publishers. (West Virginia Bks.). (Illus.). 1994. lib. bdg. 24.95 (*0-7933-2999-X*); pap. 14.95 (*0-7933-3000-9*); disk 29.95 (*0-7933-3001-7*) Gallopade Pub Group.

— West Virginia Classic Christmas Trivia: Stories, Recipies, Activities, Legends, Lore & More! (Carole Marsh West Virginia Bks.). (Illus.). (J). 1994. lib. bdg. 24.95 (*0-7933-1205-1*); pap. 14.95 (*0-7933-1204-3*); disk 29.95 (*0-7933-1206-X*) Gallopade Pub Group.

— West Virginia Coastales. (Carole Marsh West Virginia Bks.). (Illus.). (J). 1994. lib. bdg. 24.95 (*0-7933-2250-2*); pap. 14.95 (*0-7933-2251-0*); disk 29.95 (*0-7933-2252-9*) Gallopade Pub Group.

— West Virginia Coastales! (West Virginia Bks.). (J). 1994. lib. bdg. 24.95 (*0-7933-7313-1*) Gallopade Pub Group.

— West Virginia "Crinkum-Crankum" A Funny Word Book about Our State. (West Virginia Bks.). (Illus.). (J). (gr. 3-12). 1994. 24.95 (*0-7933-4955-9*); pap. 14.95 (*0-7933-4956-7*); disk 29.95 (*0-7933-4957-5*) Gallopade Pub Group.

— West Virginia Dingbats! Bk. 1: A Fun Book of Games, Stories, Activities & More about Our State That's All in Code! for You to Decipher. (West Virginia Bks.). (Illus.). (J). (gr. 3-12). 1994. lib. bdg. 24.95 (*0-7933-3917-0*); pap. 14.95 (*0-7933-3918-9*); disk 29.95 (*0-7933-3919-7*) Gallopade Pub Group.

— West Virginia Festival Fun for Kids! Includes Reproducible Activities for Kids! (West Virginia Bks.). (Illus.). (J). (gr. 3-12). 1994. lib. bdg. 24.95 (*0-7933-4070-5*); pap. 14.95 (*0-7933-4071-3*); disk 29.95 (*0-7933-4072-1*) Gallopade Pub Group.

— The West Virginia Hot Air Balloon Mystery. (Carole Marsh West Virginia Bks.). (Illus.). (J). (gr. 2-9). 1994. 24.95 (*0-7933-2750-4*); pap. 14.95 (*0-7933-2751-2*); disk 29.95 (*0-7933-2752-0*) Gallopade Pub Group.

— West Virginia Jeopardy! Answers & Questions about Our State! (West Virginia Bks.). (Illus.). (J). (gr. 3-12). 1994. lib. bdg. 24.95 (*0-7933-4223-6*); pap. 14.95 (*0-7933-4224-4*); disk 29.95 (*0-7933-4225-2*) Gallopade Pub Group.

— West Virginia "Jography" A Fun Run Thru Our State! (Carole Marsh West Virginia Bks.). (Illus.). (J). 1994. lib. bdg. 24.95 (*0-7933-2233-2*); pap. 14.95 (*0-7933-2234-0*); disk 29.95 (*0-7933-2235-9*) Gallopade Pub Group.

— West Virginia Kid's Cookbook: Recipes, How-to, History, Lore & More! (Carole Marsh West Virginia Bks.). (Illus.). (J). 1994. lib. bdg. 24.95 (*0-7933-1214-0*); pap. 14.95 (*0-7933-1213-2*); disk 29.95 (*0-7933-1215-9*) Gallopade Pub Group.

— The West Virginia Library Book: A Surprising Guide to the Unusual Special Collections in Libraries Across Our State for Students, Teachers, Writers & Publishers. (West Virginia Bks.). (Illus.). 1994. lib. bdg. 24.95 (*0-7933-3149-8*); pap. 14.95 (*0-7933-3150-1*); disk 29.95 (*0-7933-3151-X*) Gallopade Pub Group.

— The West Virginia Media Book: A Surprising Guide to the Amazing Print, Broadcast & Online Media of Our State for Students, Teachers, Writers & Publishers - Includes Reproducible Mailing Labels Plus Activities for Young People! (West Virginia Bks.). (Illus.). 1994. lib. bdg. 24.95 (*0-7933-3305-9*); pap. 14.95 (*0-7933-3306-7*); disk 29.95 (*0-7933-3307-5*) Gallopade Pub Group.

— The West Virginia Mystery Van Takes Off! Book 1: Handicapped West Virginia Kids Sneak Off on a Big Adventure. (West Virginia Bks.). (Illus.). (J). (gr. 3-12). 1994. 24.95 (*0-7933-5108-1*); pap. 14.95 (*0-7933-5109-X*); disk 29.95 (*0-7933-5110-3*) Gallopade Pub Group.

— West Virginia Quiz Bowl Crash Course! (Carole Marsh West Virginia Bks.). (Illus.). (J). 1994. lib. bdg. 24.95 (*0-7933-2247-2*); pap. 14.95 (*0-7933-2248-0*); disk 29.95 (*0-7933-2249-9*) Gallopade Pub Group.

— West Virginia Rollercoasters! (West Virginia Bks.). (Illus.). (YA). (gr. 3-12). 1994. lib. bdg. 24.95 (*0-7933-5368-8*); pap. 14.95 (*0-7933-5369-6*); disk 29.95 (*0-7933-5370-X*) Gallopade Pub Group.

— West Virginia School Trivia: An Amazing & Fascinating Look at Our State's Teachers, Schools & Students! (Carole Marsh West Virginia Bks.). (Illus.). (J). 1994. lib. bdg. 24.95 (*0-7933-1211-6*); pap. 14.95 (*0-7933-1210-8*); disk 29.95 (*0-7933-1212-4*) Gallopade Pub Group.

— West Virginia Silly Basketball Sportsmysteries, Vol. 1. (Carole Marsh West Virginia Bks.). (Illus.). (J). 1994. lib. bdg. 24.95 (*0-7933-1208-6*); pap. 14.95 (*0-7933-1207-8*); disk 29.95 (*0-7933-1209-4*) Gallopade Pub Group.

— West Virginia Silly Basketball Sportsmysteries, Vol. 2. (Carole Marsh West Virginia Bks.). (Illus.). (J). 1994. lib. bdg. 24.95 (*0-7933-2259-6*); pap. 14.95 (*0-7933-2260-X*); disk 29.95 (*0-7933-2261-8*) Gallopade Pub Group.

— West Virginia Silly Football Sportsmysteries, Vol. 1. (Carole Marsh West Virginia Bks.). (Illus.). (J). 1994. lib. bdg. 24.95 (*0-7933-2238-3*); pap. 14.95 (*0-7933-2239-1*); disk 29.95 (*0-7933-2240-5*) Gallopade Pub Group.

— West Virginia Silly Football Sportsmysteries, Vol. 2. (Carole Marsh West Virginia Bks.). (Illus.). (J). 1994. lib. bdg. 24.95 (*0-7933-2241-3*); pap. 14.95 (*0-7933-2242-1*); disk 29.95 (*0-685-45965-9*) Gallopade Pub Group.

— West Virginia Silly Trivia! (Carole Marsh West Virginia Bks.). (Illus.). (J). 1994. lib. bdg. 24.95 (*0-7933-2230-8*); pap. 14.95 (*0-7933-2231-6*); disk 29.95 (*0-7933-2232-4*) Gallopade Pub Group.

— West Virginia Timeline: A Chronology of West Virginia History, Mystery, Trivia, Legend, Lore & More. (West Virginia Bks.). (Illus.). (J). (gr. 3-12). 1994. lib. bdg. 24.95 (*0-7933-6019-6*); pap. 14.95 (*0-7933-6020-X*); disk 29.95 (*0-7933-6021-8*) Gallopade Pub Group.

— West Virginia's (Most Devastating!) Disasters & (Most Calamitous!) Catastrophies! (Carole Marsh West Virginia Bks.). (Illus.). (J). 1994. lib. bdg. 24.95 (*0-7933-1199-3*); pap. 14.95 (*0-7933-1198-5*); disk 29.95 (*0-7933-1200-0*) Gallopade Pub Group.

— West Virginia's Unsolved Mysteries (& Their "Solutions") Includes Scientific Information & Other Activities for Students. (West Virginia Bks.). (Illus.). (J). (gr. 3-12). 1994. lib. bdg. 24.95 (*0-7933-5866-3*); pap. 14.95 (*0-7933-5867-1*); disk 29.95 (*0-7933-5868-X*) Gallopade Pub Group.

— What the Heck Are Ethics? (Quantum Leap Ser.). (J). (gr. 4-9). 1994. 24.95 (*1-55609-342-X*); pap. 14.95 (*0-318-37388-2*) Gallopade Pub Group.

— Will Somebody Hold This Thing a Minute? Statue of Liberty Silly Trivia Book. (Quantum Leap Ser.). (Illus.). 60p. (Orig.). (J). (gr. 3-12). 1994. 24.95 (*1-55609-192-3*); pap. 14.95 (*0-935326-75-8*) Gallopade Pub Group.

— Wisconsin & Other State Greats (Biographies) (Carole Marsh Wisconsin Bks.). (Illus.). (J). 1994. lib. bdg. 24.95 (*0-7933-2288-X*); pap. 14.95 (*0-7933-2289-8*); disk 29.95 (*0-7933-2290-1*) Gallopade Pub Group.

— Wisconsin Bandits, Bushwackers, Outlaws, Crooks, Devils, Ghosts, Desperadoes & Other Assorted & Sundry Characters! (Carole Marsh Wisconsin Bks.). (Illus.). (J). 1994. lib. bdg. 24.95 (*0-7933-1226-4*); pap. 14.95 (*0-7933-1225-6*); disk 29.95 (*0-7933-1227-2*) Gallopade Pub Group.

— The Wisconsin Bookstore Book: A Surprising Guide to Our State's Bookstores & Their Specialties for Students, Teachers, Writers & Publishers. (Wisconsin Bks.). (Illus.). 1994. lib. bdg. 24.95 (*0-7933-3002-5*); pap. 14.95 (*0-7933-3003-3*); disk 29.95 (*0-7933-3004-1*) Gallopade Pub Group.

— Wisconsin Classic Christmas Trivia: Stories, Recipes, Activities, Legends, Lore & More. (Carole Marsh Wisconsin Bks.). (Illus.). (J). 1994. lib. bdg. 24.95 (*0-7933-1229-9*); pap. 14.95 (*0-7933-1228-0*); disk 29.95 (*0-7933-1230-2*) Gallopade Pub Group.

— Wisconsin Coastales. (Carole Marsh Wisconsin Bks.). (Illus.). (J). 1994. 24.95 (*0-7933-2282-0*); pap. 14.95 (*0-7933-2283-9*); disk 29.95 (*0-7933-2284-7*) Gallopade Pub Group.

— Wisconsin Coastales! (Wisconsin Bks.). (J). 1994. lib. bdg. 24.95 (*0-7933-7314-X*) Gallopade Pub Group.

— Wisconsin "Crinkum-Crankum" A Funny Word Book about Our State. (Wisconsin Bks.). (Illus.). (J). (gr. 3-12). 1994. 24.95 (*0-7933-4958-3*); pap. 14.95 (*0-7933-4959-1*); disk 29.95 (*0-7933-4960-5*) Gallopade Pub Group.

— Wisconsin Dingbats! Bk. 1: A Fun Book of Games, Stories, Activities & More about Our State That's All in Code! for You to Decipher. (Wisconsin Bks.). (Illus.). (J). (gr. 3-12). 1994. lib. bdg. 24.95 (*0-7933-3920-0*); pap. 14.95 (*0-7933-3921-9*); disk 29.95 (*0-7933-3922-7*) Gallopade Pub Group.

— Wisconsin Festival Fun for Kids! Includes Reproducible Activities for Kids! (Wisconsin Bks.). (Illus.). (J). (gr. 3-12). 1994. lib. bdg. 24.95 (*0-7933-4073-X*); pap. 14.95 (*0-7933-4074-8*); disk 29.95 (*0-7933-4075-6*) Gallopade Pub Group.

— The Wisconsin Hot Air Balloon Mystery. (Carole Marsh Wisconsin Bks.). (Illus.). (J). (gr. 2-9). 1994. 24.95 (*0-7933-2759-8*); pap. 14.95 (*0-7933-2760-1*); disk 29.95 (*0-7933-2761-X*) Gallopade Pub Group.

— Wisconsin Jeopardy! Answers & Questions about Our State! (Wisconsin Bks.). (Illus.). (J). (gr. 3-12). 1994. lib. bdg. 24.95 (*0-7933-4226-0*); pap. 14.95 (*0-7933-4227-9*); disk 29.95 (*0-7933-4228-7*) Gallopade Pub Group.

— Wisconsin "Jography" A Fun Run Thru Our State! (Carole Marsh Wisconsin Bks.). (Illus.). (J). 1994. lib. bdg. 24.95 (*0-7933-2265-0*); pap. 14.95 (*0-7933-2266-9*); disk 29.95 (*0-7933-2267-7*) Gallopade Pub Group.

— Wisconsin Kid's Cookbook: Recipes, How-To, History, Lore & More! (Carole Marsh Wisconsin Bks.). (Illus.). (J). 1994. lib. bdg. 24.95 (*0-7933-1238-8*); pap. 14.95 (*0-7933-1237-X*); disk 29.95 (*0-7933-1239-6*) Gallopade Pub Group.

— The Wisconsin Library Book: A Surprising Guide to the Unusual Special Collections in Libraries Across Our State for Students, Teachers, Writers & Publishers. (Wisconsin Bks.). (Illus.). 1994. lib. bdg. 24.95 (*0-7933-3152-8*); pap. 14.95 (*0-7933-3153-6*); disk 29.95 (*0-7933-3154-4*) Gallopade Pub Group.

— The Wisconsin Media Book: A Surprising Guide to the Amazing Print, Broadcast & Online Media of Our State for Students, Teachers, Writers & Publishers - Includes Reproducible Mailing Labels Plus Activities for Young People! (Wisconsin Bks.). (Illus.). 1994. lib. bdg. 24.95 (*0-7933-3308-3*); pap. 14.95 (*0-7933-3309-1*); disk 29.95 (*0-7933-3310-5*) Gallopade Pub Group.

— The Wisconsin Mystery Van Takes Off! Book 1: Handicapped Wisconsin Kids Sneak Off on a Big Adventure. (Wisconsin Bks.). (Illus.). (J). (gr. 3-12). 1994. 24.95 (*0-7933-5111-1*); pap. 14.95 (*0-7933-5112-X*); disk 29.95 (*0-7933-5113-8*) Gallopade Pub Group.

— Wisconsin Quiz Bowl Crash Course! (Carole Marsh Wisconsin Bks.). (Illus.). (J). 1994. lib. bdg. 24.95 (*0-7933-2279-0*); pap. 14.95 (*0-7933-2280-4*); disk 29.95 (*0-7933-2281-2*) Gallopade Pub Group.

— Wisconsin Rollercoasters! (Wisconsin Bks.). (Illus.). (YA). (gr. 3-12). 1994. lib. bdg. 24.95 (*0-7933-5371-8*); pap. 14.95 (*0-7933-5372-6*); disk 29.95 (*0-7933-5373-4*) Gallopade Pub Group.

— Wisconsin School Trivia: An Amazing & Fascinating Look at Our State's Teachers, Schools & Students! (Carole Marsh Wisconsin Bks.). (Illus.). (J). 1994. lib. bdg. 24.95 (*0-7933-1235-3*); pap. 14.95 (*0-7933-1234-5*); disk 29.95 (*0-7933-1236-1*) Gallopade Pub Group.

— Wisconsin Silly Basketball Sportsmysteries, Vol. 1. (Carole Marsh Wisconsin Bks.). (Illus.). (J). 1994. lib. bdg. 24.95 (*0-7933-1232-9*); pap. 14.95 (*0-7933-1231-0*); disk 29.95 (*0-7933-1233-7*) Gallopade Pub Group.

— Wisconsin Silly Basketball Sportsmysteries, Vol. 2. (Carole Marsh Wisconsin Bks.). (Illus.). (J). 1994. lib. bdg. 24.95 (*0-7933-2291-X*); pap. 14.95 (*0-7933-2292-8*); disk 29.95 (*0-7933-2293-6*) Gallopade Pub Group.

— Wisconsin Silly Football Sportsmysteries, Vol. 1. (Carole Marsh Wisconsin Bks.). (Illus.). (J). 1994. lib. bdg. 24.95 (*0-7933-2270-7*); pap. 14.95 (*0-7933-2271-5*); disk 29.95 (*0-7933-2272-3*) Gallopade Pub Group.

— Wisconsin Silly Football Sportsmysteries, Vol. 2. (Carole Marsh Wisconsin Bks.). (Illus.). (J). 1994. lib. bdg. 24.95 (*0-7933-2273-1*); pap. 14.95 (*0-7933-2274-X*); disk 29.95 (*0-7933-2275-8*) Gallopade Pub Group.

— Wisconsin Silly Trivia! (Carole Marsh Wisconsin Bks.). (Illus.). (J). 1994. lib. bdg. 24.95 (0-7933-2262-6); pap. 14.95 (0-7933-2263-4); disk 29.95 (0-7933-2264-2) Gallopade Pub Group.

— Wisconsin Timeline: A Chronology of Wisconsin History, Mystery, Trivia, Legend, Lore & More. (Wisconsin Bks.). (Illus.). (J). (gr. 3-12). 1994. lib. bdg. 24.95 (0-7933-6022-6); pap. 14.95 (0-7933-6023-4); disk 29.95 (0-7933-6024-2) Gallopade Pub Group.

— Wisconsin's (Most Devastating!) Disasters & (Most Calamitous!) Catastrophies! (Carole Marsh Wisconsin Bks.). (Illus.). (J). 1994. lib. bdg. 24.95 (0-7933-1223-X); pap. 14.95 (0-7933-1222-1); disk 29.95 (0-7933-1224-8) Gallopade Pub Group.

— Wisconsin's Unsolved Mysteries (& Their "Solutions") Includes Scientific Information & Other Activities for Students. (Wisconsin Bks.). (Illus.). (J). (gr. 3-12). 1994. lib. bdg. 24.95 (0-7933-5869-8); pap. 14.95 (0-7933-5870-1); disk 29.95 (0-7933-5871-X) Gallopade Pub Group.

— World's Fair Fun Trivia Book. (Quantum Leap Ser.). (Illus.). (Orig.). (J). (gr. 4 up). 1994. pap. 4.95 (0-935326-06-5) Gallopade Pub Group.

— Worlds Fair Kit S. P. A. R. K. (S. P. A. R. K. Ser.). (Illus.). (Orig.). (J). (gr. 3-12). 1994. pap. 24.95 (0-935326-85-5) Gallopade Pub Group.

— Write Your Own SportsMystery Kit. (Carole Marsh Bks.). (Illus.). (Orig.). (J). (gr. 3-12). 1994. pap. 24.00 (0-935326-11-1) Gallopade Pub Group.

— The Writer's Plan: Reproducible Forms to Organize Your Writing for Pleasure & Profit. (Lifewrite Ser.). (Orig.). 1994. lib. bdg. 24.95 (1-55609-950-9); pap. 14.95 (1-55609-951-7); ring bd. 39.95 (1-55609-952-5); Apple II 29.95 (1-55609-953-3) Gallopade Pub Group.

— Wyoming & Other State Greats (Biographies) (Carole Marsh Wyoming Bks.). (Illus.). (J). 1994. lib. bdg. 24.95 (0-7933-2312-6); pap. 14.95 (0-7933-2313-4); disk 29.95 (0-7933-2314-2) Gallopade Pub Group.

— Wyoming Bandits, Bushwackers, Outlaws, Crooks, Devils, Ghosts, Desperadoes & Other Assorted & Sundry Characters! (Carole Marsh Wyoming Bks.). (Illus.). (J). 1994. lib. bdg. 24.95 (0-7933-1250-7); pap. 14.95 (0-7933-1249-3); disk 29.95 (0-7933-1251-5) Gallopade Pub Group.

— The Wyoming Bookstore Book: A Surprising Guide to Our State's Bookstores & Their Specialties for Students, Teachers, Writers & Publishers. (Wyoming Bks.). (Illus.). 1994. lib. bdg. 24.95 (0-7933-3005-X); pap. 14.95 (0-7933-3006-8); disk 29.95 (0-7933-3007-6) Gallopade Pub Group.

— Wyoming Classic Christmas Trivia: Stories, Recipes, Activities, Legends, Lore & More! (Carole Marsh Wyoming Bks.). (Illus.). (J). 1994. lib. bdg. 24.95 (0-7933-1253-1); pap. 14.95 (0-7933-1252-3); disk 29.95 (0-7933-1254-X) Gallopade Pub Group.

— Wyoming Coastales. (Carole Marsh Wyoming Bks.). (Illus.). (J). 1994. lib. bdg. 24.95 (0-7933-2306-1); pap. 14.95 (0-7933-2307-X); disk 29.95 (0-7933-2308-8) Gallopade Pub Group.

— Wyoming Coastales! (Wyoming Bks.). (J). 1994. lib. bdg. 24.95 (0-7933-7315-8) Gallopade Pub Group.

— Wyoming "Crinkum-Crankum" A Funny Word Book about Our State. (Wyoming Bks.). (Illus.). (J). (gr. 3-12). 1994. 24.95 (0-7933-4961-3); pap. 14.95 (0-7933-4962-1); disk 29.95 (0-7933-4963-X) Gallopade Pub Group.

— Wyoming Dingbats! Bk. 1: A Fun Book of Games, Stories, Activities & More about Our State That's All in Code! for You to Decipher. (Wyoming Bks.). (Illus.). (J). (gr. 3-12). 1994. lib. bdg. 24.95 (0-7933-3923-5); pap. 14.95 (0-7933-3924-3); disk 29.95 (0-7933-3925-1) Gallopade Pub Group.

— Wyoming Festival Fun for Kids! Includes Reproducible Activities for Kids! (Wyoming Bks.). (Illus.). (J). (gr. 3-12). 1994. lib. bdg. 24.95 (0-7933-4076-4); pap. 14.95 (0-7933-4077-2); disk 29.95 (0-7933-4078-0) Gallopade Pub Group.

— The Wyoming Hot Air Balloon Mystery. (Carole Marsh Wyoming Bks.). (Illus.). (J). (gr. 2-9). 1994. 24.95 (0-7933-2768-7); pap. 14.95 (0-7933-2769-5); disk 29.95 (0-7933-2770-9) Gallopade Pub Group.

— Wyoming Jeopardy! Answers & Questions about Our State! (Wyoming Bks.). (Illus.). (J). (gr. 3-12). 1994. lib. bdg. 24.95 (0-7933-4229-5); pap. 14.95 (0-7933-4230-9); disk 29.95 (0-7933-4231-7) Gallopade Pub Group.

— Wyoming "Jography" A Fun Run Thru Our State! (Carole Marsh Wyoming Bks.). (Illus.). (J). (gr. 3-12). 1994. lib. bdg. 24.95 (1-55609-295-4); pap. 14.95 (1-55609-296-2); disk 29.95 (1-55609-297-0) Gallopade Pub Group.

— Wyoming Kid's Cookbook: Recipes, How-To, History, Lore & More. (Carole Marsh Wyoming Bks.). (Illus.). (J). 1994. lib. bdg. 24.95 (0-7933-1262-0); pap. 14.95 (0-7933-1261-2); 29.95 (0-7933-1263-9) Gallopade Pub Group.

— The Wyoming Library Book: A Surprising Guide to the Unusual Special Collections in Libraries Across Our State for Students, Teachers, Writers & Publishers. (Wyoming Bks.). (Illus.). 1994. lib. bdg. 24.95 (0-7933-3155-2); pap. 14.95 (0-7933-3156-0); disk 29.95 (0-7933-3157-9) Gallopade Pub Group.

— The Wyoming Media Book: A Surprising Guide to the Amazing Print, Broadcast & Online Media of Our State for Students, Teachers, Writers & Publishers - Includes Reproducible Mailing Labels Plus Activities for Young People! (Wyoming Bks.). (Illus.). 1994. lib. bdg. 24.95 (0-7933-3311-3); pap. 14.95 (0-7933-3312-1); disk 29.95 (0-7933-3313-X) Gallopade Pub Group.

— The Wyoming Mystery Van Takes Off! Book 1: Handicapped Wyoming Kids Sneak Off on a Big Adventure. (Wyoming Bks.). (Illus.). (J). (gr. 3-12). 1994. 24.95 (0-7933-5114-6); pap. 14.95 (0-7933-5115-4); disk 29.95 (0-7933-5116-2) Gallopade Pub Group.

— Wyoming Quiz Bowl Crash Course! (Carole Marsh Wyoming Bks.). (Illus.). (J). 1994. lib. bdg. 24.95 (0-7933-2303-7); pap. 14.95 (0-7933-2304-5); disk 29.95 (0-7933-2305-3) Gallopade Pub Group.

— Wyoming Rollercoasters! (Wyoming Bks.). (Illus.). (YA). (gr. 3-12). 1994. lib. bdg. 24.95 (0-7933-5374-2); pap. 14.95 (0-7933-5375-0); disk 29.95 (0-7933-5376-9) Gallopade Pub Group.

— Wyoming School Trivia: An Amazing & Fascinating Look at Our State's Teachers, Schools & Students! (Carole Marsh Wyoming Bks.). (Illus.). (J). 1994. lib. bdg. 24.95 (0-7933-1259-0); pap. 14.95 (0-7933-1258-2); disk 29.95 (0-7933-1260-4) Gallopade Pub Group.

— Wyoming Silly Basketball Sportsmysteries, Vol. 1. (Carole Marsh Wyoming Bks.). (Illus.). (J). 1994. lib. bdg. 24.95 (0-7933-1256-6); pap. 14.95 (0-7933-1255-8); disk 29.95 (0-7933-1257-4) Gallopade Pub Group.

— Wyoming Silly Basketball Sportsmysteries, Vol. 2. (Carole Marsh Wyoming Bks.). (Illus.). (J). 1994. lib. bdg. 24.95 (0-7933-2315-0); pap. 14.95 (0-7933-2316-9); disk 29.95 (0-7933-2317-7) Gallopade Pub Group.

— Wyoming Silly Football Sportsmysteries, Vol. 1. (Carole Marsh Wyoming Bks.). (Illus.). (J). 1994. lib. bdg. 24.95 (0-7933-2294-4); pap. 14.95 (0-7933-2295-2); disk 29.95 (0-7933-2296-0) Gallopade Pub Group.

— Wyoming Silly Football Sportsmysteries, Vol. 2. (Carole Marsh Wyoming Bks.). (Illus.). (J). 1994. lib. bdg. 24.95 (0-7933-2297-9); pap. 14.95 (0-7933-2298-7); disk 29.95 (0-7933-2299-5) Gallopade Pub Group.

— Wyoming Silly Trivia. (Carole Marsh Wyoming Bks.). (Illus.). (J). (gr. 3-12). 1994. lib. bdg. 24.95 (1-55609-292-X); pap. 14.95 (1-55609-293-8); disk 29.95 (1-55609-294-6) Gallopade Pub Group.

— Wyoming Timeline: A Chronology of Wyoming History, Mystery, Trivia, Legend, Lore & More. (Wyoming Bks.). (Illus.). (J). (gr. 3-12). 1994. lib. bdg. 24.95 (0-7933-6025-0); pap. 14.95 (0-7933-6026-9); disk 29.95 (0-7933-6027-7) Gallopade Pub Group.

— Wyoming's (Most Devastating!) Disasters & (Most Calamitous!) Catastrophies! (Carole Marsh Wyoming Bks.). (Illus.). (J). 1994. lib. bdg. 24.95 (0-7933-1247-7); pap. 14.95 (0-7933-1246-9); disk 29.95 (0-7933-1248-5) Gallopade Pub Group.

— Wyoming's Unsolved Mysteries (& Their "Solutions") Includes Scientific Information & Other Activities for Students. (Wyoming Bks.). (Illus.). (J). (gr. 3-12). 1994. lib. bdg. 24.95 (0-7933-5872-8); pap. 14.95 (0-7933-5873-6); disk 29.95 (0-7933-5874-4) Gallopade Pub Group.

— Yes, You Have to Wipe Your Feet! White House Trivia. (Quantum Leap Ser.). (J). 1994. lib. bdg. 24.95 (0-7933-6873-1); pap. text ed. 14.95 (0-7933-6872-3); disk 29.95 (0-7933-6874-X) Gallopade Pub Group.

— You'd Betters: The Rules Writers Break That Keep Them from Getting Published - (And How to Stop!) (Lifewrite Ser.). 1994. 24.95 (1-55609-346-2); pap. 14.95 (1-55609-347-0); ring bd. 39.95 (0-685-30783-2); disk 29.95 (1-55609-600-3) Gallopade Pub Group.

Marsh, Catherine. Exploring Data: An Introduction to Data Analysis for Social Scientists. (Illus.). 300p. 1988. text ed. 82.95 (0-7456-0171-5); pap. 34.95 (0-7456-0172-3) Blackwell Pubs.

— The Survey Method: The Contribution of Surveys to Sociological Explanation. (Contemporary Social Research Ser.: No. 6). 272p. (C). 1982. pap. text ed. 19.95 (0-04-310015-5) Routledge Chapman & Hall.

Marsh, Catherine & Arber, Sara, eds. Families & Households: Divisions & Change. 224p. 1992. text ed. 55.00 (0-312-06872-7) St Martin.

Marsh, Catherine, jt. ed. see Burrows, Roger.

Marsh, Charles. Reclaiming Dietrich Bonhoeffer: The Promise of His Theology. LC 93-30806. 208p. 1994. 29.95 (0-19-508723-2) OUP.

Marsh, Charles, jt. ed. see Floyd, Wayne W.

Marsh, Charles S. People of the Shining Mountains: The Ute Indians of Colorado. LC 81-21032. (Illus.). 190p. (Orig.). 1982. pap. 11.95 (0-87108-613-1) Pruett.

Marsh, Christine, jt. auth. see Duncan, Mary.

Marsh, Christopher C. The Theory & Practice of Bank Book-Keeping & Joint Stock Accounts: Exemplified & Elucidated in a Complete Set of Bank Account Books. Brief, Richard P., ed. LC 77-87278. (Development of Contemporary Accounting Thought Ser.). 1978. reprint ed. lib. bdg. 30.95 (0-405-10906-7) Ayer.

Marsh, Christopher W. The Family of Love in English Society, 1550-1630. LC 92-37006. (Studies in Early Modern British History). (Illus.). 285p. (C). 1994. 59.95 (0-521-44128-5) Cambridge U Pr.

Marsh, Chuck, ed. see Basow, Lynn.

Marsh, Clay B. & Mazzaferri, Ernest L. Internal Medicine Pearls. Sahn, Steven A. & Heffner, John E., eds. (Illus.). 276p. (Orig.). 1993. pap. text ed. 45.00 (1-56053-024-3) Hanley & Belfus.

Marsh, Clifton E. From Black Muslims to Muslims: The Transition from Separatism to Islam, 1930-1980. LC 84-5611. 159p. 1984. 24.00 (0-8108-1705-5) Scarecrow.

Marsh, Clive. Albrecht Ritschl & the Problem of the Historical Jesus. LC 92-3639. 248p. 1992. lib. bdg. 89.95 (0-7734-9822-2) E Mellen.

Marsh, Colin & Willis, George. Curriculum: Alternative Approaches, Ongoing Issues. LC 94-15871. 400p. (C). 1994. write for info. (0-02-428113-1, Merrill Pub Co) Macmillan.

Marsh, Colin J. Key Concepts for Understanding Curriculum. (Falmer Press Teachers' Library: No. 5). 284p. 1991. 71.00 (0-685-50667-3, Falmer Pr); pap. 27.00 (0-685-50668-1, Falmer Pr) Taylor & Francis.

— Reconceptualizing School-Based Curriculum Development. Day, Christopher W. et al, eds. 225p. 1990. 75.00 (1-85000-500-1, Falmer Pr); pap. 33.00 (1-85000-595-8, Falmer Pr) Taylor & Francis.

Marsh, Colin J. & Morris, Paul, eds. Curriculum Development in East Asia. 250p. 1991. 65.00 (1-85000-685-7, Falmer Pr); pap. 29.00 (1-85000-686-5, Falmer Pr) Taylor & Francis.

Marsh, Cynthia. File on Gorky. 96p. 1993. pap. 14.95 (0-413-65060-X, Pub. by Methuen UK) Heinemann.

Marsh, D. W. Marsh Genealogy, Giving Several Thousand Descendants of John Marsh of Hartford, Connecticut, 1636-1895. (Illus.). 585p. 1989. reprint ed. lib. bdg. 95.60 (0-8328-0852-0); reprint ed. pap. 87.60 (0-8328-0853-9) Higginson Bk Co.

Marsh, D. W., ed. see Hitchcock, E., Sr.

Marsh, Dale. The Way of the Painter. 64p. (C). 1990. 90.00 (0-86439-071-8, Pub. by Boolarong Pubns AT) St Mut.

Marsh, Dave. Before I Get Old: The Story of the Who. (Illus.). 592p. 1983. pap. 10.95 (0-312-07155-8) St Martin.

— Elvis. 272p. 1992. pap. 17.95 (1-56025-038-0) Thunders Mouth.

— Fifty Ways to Fight Censorship. (Illus.). 128p. (Orig.). 1991. pap. 5.95 (1-56025-011-9) Thunders Mouth.

— Fortunate Son: The Best of Dave Marsh. LC 84-42509. 1985. write for info. (0-394-53469-7) Random.

— Louie Louie: The History & Mythology of the World's Most Famous Rock n' Roll Song; Including the Full Details of Its Torture & Persecution at the Hands of the Kingsmen, J. Edgar Hoover's F. B. I., & a Cast of Millions; & Introducing, for the First Time Anywhere, the Actual Dirty Lyrics. (Illus.). 256p. 1993. 19.95 (1-56282-865-7) Hyperion.

— Louie, Louie: The History & Mythology of the World's Most Famous Rock 'n Roll Song Including the Full Details of Its Torture & Persecution at the Hands of the Kingsmen, J. Edgar Hoover's FBI & a Cast of Millions; & Introducing for the First Time Anywhere, the Actual Dirty Lyrics. (Illus.). 256p. 1994. pap. 12.95 (0-7868-8028-7) Hyperion.

— Mid-Life Confidential: The Rock Bottom Remainders Tour America with Three Chords & an Attitude. 224p. 1995. 11.95 (0-452-27459-1, Plume) NAL-Dutton.

Marsh, Dave, ed. Mid-Life Confidential: The Rock Bottom Remainders Tour America with Three Chords & an Attitude. (Illus.). 288p. 1994. 20.95 (0-670-85234-1, Viking) Viking Penguin.

Marsh, Dave & Propes, Steve. Merry Christmas, Baby: Holiday Music from Bing to Sting. LC 93-20372. 1993. 14.95 (0-316-54733-6) Little.

Marsh, Dave, jt. ed. see Henley, Don.

Marsh, David. The Germans: A People at the Crossroads. 364p. 1990. 22.95 (0-685-31269-0) St Martin.

— Lights! Camera! Celebrate! Hollywood Birthdays, Bashes & Blowouts. (Illus.). 64p. 1995. 16.95 (1-883318-26-2) Angel City Pr.

— The New Politics of British Trade Unionism: Union Power & the Thatcher Legacy. (Cornell International Industrial & Labor Relations Reports: No. 20). 288p. (Orig.). 1992. 42.00 (0-87546-704-0); pap. 17.95 (0-87546-705-9) ILR Pr.

— The World's Most Powerful Bank: Inside Germany's Bundesbank. LC 92-56830. 400p. 1993. 25.00 (0-8129-2158-5, Times Bks) Random.

Marsh, David, ed. Capital & Politics in Western Europe. (Illus.). 200p. 1983. 35.00 (0-7146-3225-2, Pub. by F Cass Pubs UK) Intl Spec Bk.

Marsh, David & Rhodes, R. A., eds. Implementing Thatcherite Policies: Audit of an Era. (Public Policy & Management Ser.). 192p. 1992. 90.00 (0-335-15683-5, Open Univ Pr); pap. 34.00 (0-335-15682-7, Open Univ Pr) Taylor & Francis.

— Policy Networks in British Government. (Illus.). 320p. 1992. 72.00 (0-19-827852-7) OUP.

Marsh, David, tr. see Alberti, Leon B.

Marsh, David, jt. auth. see Crawford, Michael.

Marsh, David C. The Welfare State: Concept & Development. 2nd ed. LC 79-41439. (Aspects of Modern Sociology: the Social Structure of Modern Britain Ser.). 120p. reprint ed. pap. 34.20 (0-685-20295-X, 2030329) Bks Demand.

Marsh, David C. & Read, Melvyn. Private Members' Bills. LC 87-15116. 1988. 59.95 (0-521-33051-3) Cambridge U Pr.

Marsh, David G. & Blumenthal, Malcolm N., eds. Genetic & Environmental Factors in Clinical Allergy. (Illus.). 209p. (C). 1990. text ed. 49.95 (0-8166-1736-8) U of Minn Pr.

Marsh, David G., et al, eds. The Genetics of Asthma. LC 92-17983. (Illus.). 384p. 1993. 135.00 (0-632-03191-3) Blackwell Sci.

Marsh, DeLoss L. Retirement Careers: Combining the Best of Work & Leisure. Williamson, Susan & Griffith, Roger, eds. LC 91-2036. 192p. (Orig.). 1991. pap. 10.95 (0-913589-55-1) Williamson Pub Co.

Marsh, Derek, jt. auth. see Cevc, Gregor.

Marsh, Diane T. Families & Mental Illness: New Directions in Professional Practice. LC 91-33605. 288p. 1992. text ed. 55.00 (0-275-94018-7, C4018, Praeger Pubs) Greenwood.

— Families & Mental Retardation: New Directions in Professional Practice. LC 91-38306. 272p. 1992. text ed. 55.00 (0-275-94014-4, C4014, Praeger Pubs) Greenwood.

Marsh, Diane T., ed. New Directions in the Psychological Treatment of Serious Mental Illness. LC 93-23930. 224p. 1993. text ed. 65.00 (0-275-94428-X, C4428, Praeger Pubs) Greenwood.

***Marsh, Donald J.** Renal Physiology. fac. ed. LC 83-11117. (Illus.). 163p. Date not set. pap. 46.50 (0-7837-7516-4, 2046989) Bks Demand.

— Renal Physiology. LC 83-11117. 163p. reprint ed. pap. 46.50 (0-7837-7111-8, 2046940) Bks Demand.

Marsh, Dottie, jt. auth. see Hanft, Barbara.

Marsh, E. G. The Old Man. 1990. reprint ed. pap. 2.99 (0-88019-265-8) Schmul Pub Co.

Marsh, Earle, jt. auth. see Brooks, Tim.

Marsh, Ed, jt. auth. see Newman, Steve.

Marsh, Edward, tr. see Fromentin, Eugene.

***Marsh, Elias J.** Sands of Yesteryear: Arabia Petraea. (Transactions of the Connecticut Academy of Arts & Sciences Ser.: Vol. 52, Pt. 1). 104p. 1994. pap. 16.00x (1-878508-08-3) CT Acad Arts & Sciences.

***Marsh, Ellen T.** Bed & Breakfast. (Special Edition Ser.). 1995. mass mkt. 3.75 (0-373-09978-9, 1-09978-7) Silhouette.

— Christmas Embrace Vol. 1. 1994. pap. 4.50 (0-312-92957-9) St Martin.

— The Enchanted Prince. 448p. (Orig.). 1995. mass mkt., pap. text ed. 5.99 (0-8439-3794-7) Dorchester Pub Co.

— Silk & Splendor. 432p. 1986. pap. 3.95 (0-380-89677-X) Avon.

— Tame the Wild Heart. 448p. 1988. pap. 3.95 (0-380-75219-0) Avon.

Marsh, F. E. Devotional Bible Studies. LC 79-2548. 304p. 1980. 14.99 (0-8254-3230-8) Kregel.

— Discipler's Manual: Thirty-Four Studies for Christian Life & Service. LC 79-2550. 344p. 1991. pap. 10.99 (0-8254-3238-3) Kregel.

— Emblems of the Holy Spirit. LC 63-11465. 268p. 1974. pap. 10.99 (0-8254-3222-7) Kregel.

— Five Hundred Bible Study Outlines. LC 79-2549. 382p. 1985. reprint ed. pap. 12.99 (0-8254-3248-0) Kregel.

— Illustrated Bible Study Outlines. LC 79-125116. 268p. 1979. pap. 9.99 (0-8254-3245-6) Kregel.

— Major Bible Truths. LC 79-2544. 442p. 1984. pap. 14.99 (0-8254-3246-4) Kregel.

— One Thousand Bible Study Outlines. LC 75-125115. 494p. 1970. pap. 16.99 (0-8254-3247-2) Kregel.

— Practical Truths from First Thessalonians. LC 86-2742. Orig. Title: Flashes from the Lighthouse of Truth. 272p. 1986. 12.99 (0-8254-3234-0) Kregel.

— Why Did Christ Die? LC 85-18093. Orig. Title: The Greatest Theme in the World. 204p. 1985. reprint ed. pap. 7.99 (0-8254-3249-9) Kregel.

Marsh, Fabienne. The Moralist of the Alphabet Streets. 252p. (YA). (gr. 10 up). 1991. 17.95 (0-945575-47-5) Algonquin Bks.

Marsh, Frank & Katz, Janet. Biology, Crime & Ethics: A Study of Biological Explanations for Criminal Behavior. (C). 1985. pap. 19.95 (0-87084-477-6) Anderson Pub Co.

Marsh, Frank H. & Yarborough, Mark. Medicine & Money: A Study of the Role of Beneficence in Health Care Cost Containment. LC 90-2718. (Contributions in Medical Studies: No. 30). 184p. 1990. text ed. 49.95 (0-313-26357-4, MMM/, Greenwood Pr) Greenwood.

Marsh, Frank H., jt. auth. see Abel, Charles F.

Marsh, Frank L. Life, Man & Time. 2nd ed. LC 66-21121. (Illus.). (YA). (gr. 7 up). 1967. 8.95 (0-911080-15-5) Outdoor Pict.

— Variation & Fixity in Nature. 150p. (Orig.). 1976. pap. 7.95 (0-940384-02-7) Creation Research.

Marsh, G. Barrie. Employer & Employee. (C). 1981. 210.00 (0-7219-0741-5, Scientific) St Mut.

Marsh, G. E., ed. The Local Plan Inquiry: The Role in Local Plan Preparation, Vol. 19/2. (Illus.). 80p. 1983. pap. 22.00 (0-08-030442-7, Pergamon Pr) Elsevier.

Marsh, G. N. Efficient Care in General Practice: How to Look after Even More Patients. (Oxford General Practice Ser.: No. 21). (Illus.). 176p. 1991. 32.50 (0-19-261953-5) OUP.

Marsh, G. P. The Origin & History of the English Language. 1972. 59.95 (0-8490-0774-7) Gordon Pr.

Marsh, G. P., et al. Corrosion of Carbon Steel Overpacks for the Geological Disposal of Radioactive, No. EUR 13671. 62p. 1991. pap. 8.00 (92-826-2910-4, CD-NA-13671-EN-C) UNIPUB.

Marsh, Geoffrey, jt. ed. see Keithley, Jane.

Marsh, George D., jt. auth. see Desberg, Peter.

Marsh, George E., II. Computers: Literacy & Learning: A Primer for Administrators. Herman, Jerry J. & Herman, Janice L., eds. (Road Maps to Success Ser.). 72p. 1993. 15.00 (0-8039-6073-5) Corwin Pr.

Marsh, George P. The Earth As Modified by Human Action. (American Environmental Studies). 1976. reprint ed. 36.95 (0-405-02677-3) Ayer.

— Earth As Modified by Human Action. LC 74-106906. 1970. reprint ed. 32.00 (0-403-00198-6) Scholarly.

— Man & Nature. Lowenthal, David, ed. LC 65-11591. (John Harvard Library). 496p. 1965. pap. 17.50 (0-674-54452-8) HUP.

Marsh, Glenda. Imaginative Collage. (Illus.). 100p. 1975. 22.95 (0-8464-1470-8) Beekman Pubs.

Marsh, Graham, ed. Blue Note: The Album Cover Art. (Illus.). 128p. (Orig.). 1991. pap. 24.95 (0-8118-0036-9) Chronicle Bks.

Marsh, Graham & Callingham, Glyn. New York Hot: East Coast Jazz of the 50s & 60s, the Album Cover Art. LC 93-12174. 112p. 1993. pap. 24.95 (0-8118-0416-X) Chronicle Bks.

Marsh, Graham & Callingham, Glyn, eds. California Cool: West Coast Jazz of the 50s & 60s, the Album Cover Art. LC 92-14118. (Illus.). 112p. 1992. 24.95 (0-8118-0275-2) Chronicle Bks.

Marsh, Harold, Jr. Marsh's California Corporation Law, 3 vols. 2nd ed. 1981. write for info. (0-318-65477-6, H39921) P-H.
Marsh, Harold, Jr. & Finkle, R. Roy. Marsh's California Corporation Law, 4 vols., Set. 3rd ed. 3730p. 1990. ring bd. 435.00 (0-13-564626-X) Aspen Law.
Marsh, Harold W. & Volk, Robert H. Practice under the California Corporate Securities Laws, 3 vols. 1972. Looseleaf updates avail. write for info. (0-8205-1552-3) Bender.
Marsh, Harry, et al. Introduction to Carbon Science. 321p. 1989. text ed. 94.95 (0-408-03837-3) Buttrwrth-Heinemann.
Marsh, Harry M., jt. auth. see Marsh, Matthew E.
Marsh, Helen C. & Marsh, Timothy R. Cemetery Records of Bedford County, Tennessee. rev. ed. (Illus.). 352p. 1986. pap. 25.00 (0-89308-569-3, TN 91) Southern Hist Pr.
— Davidson County, Tennessee, Wills & Inventories, 1817-1830, Vol. 2. 272p. 1989. 37.50 (0-89308-665-7, TN 118) Southern Hist Pr.
— Davidson County, Tennessee, Wills & Inventories, 1784-1817, Vol. 1. 272p. 1990. 37.50 (0-685-48908-6, TN 117) Southern Hist Pr.
— Earliest County Court Records of Bedford County, Tennessee. 184p. 1986. pap. 22.50 (0-89308-568-5, TN 90) Southern Hist Pr.
— Land Deed Genealogy of Bedford County, Tennessee. (Illus.). 484p. 1987. 40.00 (0-89308-610-X, TN 105) Southern Hist Pr.
— Mortality Schedule of Tennessee (Entire State), 1850. 368p. 1982. 30.00 (0-318-42548-3, TN 110) Southern Hist Pr.
— Tennesseans in Texas: As Found in the 1850 Census of Texas. 416p. 1986. 37.50 (0-89308-561-8, TN 94) Southern Hist Pr.
Marsh, Henri C. The New Bachelors Cookbook. Parker, Diane, ed. LC 92-56392. (Cooking Ser.). 72p. 1993. pap. 7.95 (0-88247-955-5, 955-5) R & E Pubs.
Marsh, Henry. Dark Age Britain. 1987. 22.50 (0-88029-156-7) Dorset Pr.
Marsh, Henry F., jt. auth. see Cadbury, Warder H.
Marsh, Howard C. Keeper's Reign. McGehee, Jean et al, eds. 180p. (Orig.). 1988. pap. 8.95 (0-9619178-0-6) Lookout Mountain.
Marsh, Hugh L., jt. auth. see Swanson, G. A.
*Marsh, Hugo. Miller's Antique Checklist: Toys & Games. (Illus.). 192p. 1995. 14.95 (1-85732-273-8, Pub. by Millers Pubns UK) Antique Collect.
*Marsh, Ian. Beyond the Two Party System: Political Representation, Economic Competitiveness & Australian Politics. (Reshaping Australian Institutions Ser.: No. 1). (Illus.). 448p. (C). 1995. write for info. (0-521-46223-1) Cambridge U Pr.
Marsh, Ian A. Policy Making in a Three-Party System: Committees, Coalitions & Parliament. 256p. 1986. text ed. 57.50 (0-416-92090-X, 1021) Routledge Chapman & Hall.
Marsh, Irving T. Best Sports Stories, 34 Vols. 989.00 (0-405-12042-7) Ayer.
— Best Sports Stories. 1980. 25.95 (0-405-12027-3) Ayer.
— Best Sports Stories, 1944. 1980. 25.95 (0-405-12039-7) Ayer.
— Best Sports Stories, 1945. 1980. 25.95 (0-405-12038-9) Ayer.
— Best Sports Stories, 1947. 1980. 25.95 (0-405-12037-0) Ayer.
— Best Sports Stories, 1948. 1980. 25.95 (0-405-12036-2) Ayer.
— Best Sports Stories, 1949. 1980. 25.95 (0-405-12035-4) Ayer.
— Best Sports Stories, 1950. 1980. 25.95 (0-405-12034-6) Ayer.
— Best Sports Stories, 1951. 1980. 25.95 (0-405-12033-8) Ayer.
— Best Sports Stories, 1952. 1980. 25.95 (0-405-12032-X) Ayer.
— Best Sports Stories, 1953. 1980. 25.95 (0-405-12031-1) Ayer.
— Best Sports Stories, 1954. 1980. 25.95 (0-405-12030-3) Ayer.
— Best Sports Stories, 1955. 1980. 25.95 (0-405-12029-X) Ayer.
— Best Sports Stories, 1956. 1980. 25.95 (0-405-12028-1) Ayer.
— Best Sports Stories, 1958. 1980. 25.95 (0-405-12026-5) Ayer.
— Best Sports Stories, 1959. 1980. 25.95 (0-405-12025-7) Ayer.
— Best Sports Stories, 1960. 1980. 25.95 (0-405-12074-5) Ayer.
— Best Sports Stories, 1961. 1980. 25.95 (0-405-12073-7) Ayer.
— Best Sports Stories, 1962. 1980. 25.95 (0-405-12072-9) Ayer.
— Best Sports Stories, 1963. 1980. 25.95 (0-405-12071-0) Ayer.
— Best Sports Stories, 1964. 1980. 25.95 (0-405-12070-2) Ayer.
— Best Sports Stories, 1965. 1980. 25.95 (0-405-12069-9) Ayer.
— Best Sports Stories, 1966. 1980. 25.95 (0-405-12068-0) Ayer.
— Best Sports Stories, 1967. 1980. 25.95 (0-405-12067-2) Ayer.
— Best Sports Stories, 1968. 1980. 25.95 (0-405-12066-4) Ayer.
— Best Sports Stories, 1969. 1980. 25.95 (0-405-12065-6) Ayer.
— Best Sports Stories, 1970. 1980. 25.95 (0-405-12064-8) Ayer.
— Best Sports Stories, 1973. 1980. 25.95 (0-405-12061-3) Ayer.
— Best Sports Stories, 1974. 1980. 25.95 (0-405-12060-5) Ayer.
— Best Sports Stories, 1975. 1980. 25.95 (0-405-12059-1) Ayer.
— Best Sports Stories, 1976. 1980. 25.95 (0-405-12058-3) Ayer.
— Best Sports Stories, 1978. 1980. 25.95 (0-405-12872-X) Ayer.
Marsh, Irving T. & Ehre, Edward. Best Sports Stories, 1977. 1980. 25.95 (0-405-12871-1) Ayer.
Marsh, J. B. Story of the Jubilee Singers with Their Songs. rev. ed. LC 72-165509. (Illus.). reprint ed. 31.50 (0-404-04189-2) AMS Pr.
*Marsh, James. Earth Alert. (Info Adventure Ser.). (Illus.). 32p. (J). (gr. 4-6). 1995. 12.95 (1-56847-473-3) Thomson Lrning.
— The Remains of the Rev. James Marsh, D.D., Late President, & Professor of Moral & Intellectual Philosophy, in the University of Vermont; with a Memoir of his Life. (American Biography Ser.). 642p. 1991. reprint ed. lib. bdg. 109.00 (0-7812-8269-1) Rprt Serv.
Marsh, James, intro. Selected Works of James Marsh, 3 vols. LC 76-42199. 2400p. 1976. lib. bdg. 200.00 (0-8201-1275-5) Schol Facsimiles.
Marsh, James, tr. see Herder, Johann G.
Marsh, James, et al. Modernity & Its Discontents. LC 91-46765. xiv, 219p. 1992. 32.50 (0-8232-1344-7); pap. 19.95 (0-8232-1345-5) Fordham.
Marsh, James B. Four Years in the Rockies: or, the Adventures of Isaac P. Rose. LC 72-9459. (Far Western Frontier Ser.). 266p. 1973. reprint ed. 23.95 (0-405-04987-0) Ayer.
Marsh, James B., ed. Resources & Environment in Asia's Marine Sector. 504p. 1992. 105.00 (0-8448-1708-2) Taylor & Francis.
Marsh, James G. Rediscovering Institutions. 1989. text ed. 29.95 (0-02-920115-2) Free Pr.
Marsh, James L. Critique, Action, & Liberation. LC 93-48999. (SUNY Series in the Philosophy of the Social Sciences). 352p. (C). 1994. text ed. 59.50 (0-7914-2169-4); pap. text ed. 19.95 (0-7914-2170-8) State U NY Pr.
— Post-Cartesian Meditations: An Essay in Dialectical Phenomenology. LC 88-82135. xvi, 279p. 1988. 40.00 (0-8232-1216-5) Fordham.
— Radical Fragments. LC 91-27578. (New Studies in Aesthetics: Vol. 9). 313p. (C). 1992. text ed. 55.95 (0-8204-1589-8) P Lang Pubs.
*Marsh, Jan. Christina Rossetti: A Literary Biography. 1995. 27.95 (0-670-83517-X, Viking) Viking Penguin.
— Edward Thomas: A Poet for His Country. (Illus.). 225p. 1978. text ed. 42.00 (0-06-494563-4, N6575) B&N Imports.
Marsh, Janet. A Child's Book of Flowers. (Illus.). 60p. (J). (ps-1). 1994. 19.95 (0-09-176231-6, Pub. by Hutchinson UK) Trafalgar.
*Marsh, Jayne D. & Boggis, Carol, eds. From the Heart: On Being the Mother of a Child with Special Needs. LC 95-2356. (Illus.). 150p. (C). 1995. pap. 14.95 (0-933149-79-4) Woodbine House.
— From the Heart: Stories by Mothers of Children with Special Needs. 152p. (Orig.). 1994. pap. text ed. 12.00 (0-939561-22-0) Univ South ME.
Marsh, Jean. The House of Eliott. 272p. 1994. 20.95 (0-312-10996-2) St Martin.
— The House of Eliott. large type ed. LC 94-14264. 403p. 1994. bds. 21.95 (0-7862-0230-0) Thorndike Pr.
— Love in Hazard. large type ed. (Linford Romance Library). 272p. 1993. pap. 14.95 (0-7089-7325-6, Linford) Ulverscroft.
— Shades of Aphrodite. large type ed. (Linford Romance Library). 272p. 1994. pap. 14.95 (0-7089-7515-1, Linford) Ulverscroft.
Marsh, Jeanne C., jt. auth. see Berlin, Sharon B.
Marsh, Jeanne C., et al. Rape & the Limits of Law Reform. LC 81-20621. 171p. 1982. text ed. 45.00 (0-86569-083-9, Auburn Hse) Greenwood.
Marsh, Jeffery L. Current Therapy in Plastic & Reconstructive Surgery, Vol. 1: Head & Neck. 800p. 1989. 89.50 (1-55664-083-8) Mosby Yr Bk.
Marsh, Jeffrey L. Decision Making in Plastic Surgery. 249p. 1992. 70.00 (0-8016-6675-9) Mosby Yr Bk.
Marsh, Jerry, ed. see Breakstone, Steve.
Marsh, Jessie. Chinook. (Indian Culture Ser.). 32p. (J). (ps-9). 1976. 4.95 (0-89992-041-1) Coun India Ed.
— Indian Folk Tales from Coast to Coast. (Indian Culture Ser.). (Illus.). (J). (gr. 3-6). 1978. pap. 1.95 (0-89992-068-3) Coun India Ed.
Marsh, Joan. Conflict of the Heart. large type ed. (Linford Romance Library). 240p. 1989. pap. 11.95 (0-7089-6658-6, Linford) Ulverscroft.
— Martha Washington. LC 92-24531. (First Bks.). (Illus.). 64p. (J). (gr. 5-8). 1993. lib. bdg. 13.93 (0-531-20145-7) Watts.
— The Truth about Janice Henderson. large type ed. (Linford Romance Library). 240p. 1993. pap. 14.95 (0-7089-7458-9, Trailtree Bookshop) Ulverscroft.
Marsh, Joan & Goode, Jamie, eds. Germline Development: Symposium on Germline Development Held at the Ciba Foundation, London, July 1993. LC 93-50785. (CIBA Foundation Symposia Ser.: Vol. 182). 1994. text ed. 76.00 (0-471-94264-2) Wiley.
— The GTPase Superfamily. LC 93-10294. (CIBA Foundation Symposia Ser.: Vol. 176). 289p. 1993. text ed. 72.00 (0-471-93914-5, Wiley-Interscience) Wiley.
*Marsh, Joan & Goode, Jamie A., eds. Cell Adhesion & Human Disease. (CIBA Foundation Symposium Ser.: Vol. 189). 1995. text ed. 79.95 (0-471-95279-6) Wiley.
Marsh, Joan, jt. ed. see Chadwick, Derek J.
Marsh, John. Managing Financial Services Marketing. 256p. (Orig.). 1988. pap. 38.00 (0-273-03700-5, Pub. by Pitman Pub Ltd UK) Trans-Atl Phila.
*Marsh, John, ed. The Changing Role of the Common Agricultural Policy: The Future of Farming in Europe. 1993. text ed. 74.95 (0-471-94712-1) Wiley.
Marsh, John, et al, eds. The Changing Role of the Common Agricultural Policy: The Future of Farming in Europe. 164p. 1992. text ed. 64.95 (0-470-21882-7) Halsted Pr.
Marsh, John H. & De La Rue, Richard M., eds. Waveguide Optoelectronics. LC 92-33757. (NATO Advanced Study Institutes Series E, Applied Sciences: Vol. 226). 1992. lib. bdg. 168.00 (0-7923-2033-6) Kluwer Ac.
Marsh, John O. & Blackwell, James A., Jr. Congressional Oversight of National Security: A Mandate for Change, the Final Report of the CSIS Project on Congressional Oversight of Defense. LC 92-18916. (CSIS Panel Report Ser.). 29p. (C). 1992. pap. text ed. 14.95 (0-89206-201-0) CSI Studies.
Marsh, Jordan. Jordan Marsh Illustrated Catalog of 1891: An Unabridged Reprint. 1991. pap. 8.95 (0-486-26738-5) Dover.
Marsh, K. J., ed. Full-Scale Fatigue Testing: Components & Structures. (Illus.). 331p. 1988. text ed. 72.95 (0-408-02244-2) Buttrwrth-Heinemann.
Marsh, Kate, ed. Writers & Their Houses. (Illus.). 544p. 1993. 30.00 (0-241-12769-6, H Hamilton) Viking Penguin.
*Marsh, Ken. Breakfast at Trout's Place. (Illus.). 192p. 1996. 29.00 (1-885106-29-7) Wild Adven Pr.
Marsh, Ken, ed. Battery Book One: Lead Acid Traction Batteries. LC 81-65733. (Illus.). 72p. (Orig.). 1981. pap. 7.95 (0-939488-00-0) Curtis Instruments.
Marsh, L. G. & Forde, L. A. Comprehension for the Caribbean - Pupil's Book. (C). 1984. text ed. 32.00 (0-7175-1253-3, Pub. by S Thornes Pubs UK) St Mut.
— Comprehension for the Caribbean - Teacher's Book. (C). 1984. text ed. 30.00 (0-7175-1254-1, Pub. by S Thornes Pubs UK) St Mut.
Marsh, L. G., jt. auth. see Forde, L. A.
Marsh, L. R., ed. see Stewart, Alvan.
Marsh, Linda. Jesus Is Coming. 24p. (Orig.). 1992. pap. 5.95 (0-687-19981-6) Abingdon.
Marsh, Lindell L., jt. ed. see Porter, Douglas R.
*Marsh, Lindell L., et al, eds. Mitigation Banking: Theory & Practice. 225p. (Orig.). (C). 1995. pap. text ed. 50.00 (1-55963-371-9) Island Pr.
Marsh, Lucius B. & Parker, Harriet F. Bronsdon & Box Families. (Illus.). 332p. 1989. reprint ed. lib. bdg. 63.00 (0-8328-0330-8); reprint ed. pap. 53.00 (0-8328-0331-6) Higginson Bk Co.
Marsh, M. N. Coeliac Disease. (Illus.). 352p. 1992. 175.00 (0-632-03097-6) Blackwell Sci.
Marsh, Mae. Screen Acting. 1976. lib. bdg. 59.95 (0-8490-2575-3) Gordon Pr.
*Marsh, Malcolm. Butterworths Road Traffic Handbook. 2nd ed. 1292p. 1993. pap. text ed. 78.00 (0-406-02348-4, UK) Butterworth Legal Pubs.
Marsh, Malcolm, et al. Butterworths Road Traffic Service. 1991. U.K. ring bd. 300.00 (0-406-11220-7, U.K.) Butterworth Legal Pubs.
Marsh, Margaret. Suburban Lives. LC 89-36060. (Illus.). 230p. (Orig.). (C). 1990. text ed. 35.00 (0-8135-1483-5); pap. text ed. 15.00 (0-8135-1484-3) Rutgers U Pr.
Marsh, Margaret C. Bankers in Bolivia: A Study in American Foreign Investment. LC 76-99250. reprint ed. 19.75 (0-404-04190-6) AMS Pr.
Marsh, Mary T. For Any Young Mother Who Lives in a Shoe. 110p. 1991. pap. 10.00 (0-8170-1170-6) Judson.
*Marsh, Mary V. & Rinehart, Carroll A. Zingers & Swingers. Busch, Brian, ed. (Illus.). 88p. (YA). 1994. pap. text ed. 10.95 (0-910957-58-4) CPP Belwin.
Marsh, Matthew E. & Marsh, Harry M. California Mechanics' Lien Law & Construction Industry Practice. 5th ed. 810p. 1993. ring bd. 125.00 (1-55943-160-1) Michie Butterworth.
— California Mechanics' Lien Law & Construction Industry Practice, No. 1. 5th suppl. ed. 1991. Suppl. 1 4/91. 30.50 (0-685-66102-4) Butterworth Legal Pubs.
— California Mechanics' Lien Law & Construction Industry Practice, No. 2. 5th suppl. ed. 1992. Suppl. 2, 6/92. 32.00 (0-685-66103-2) Butterworth Legal Pubs.
— California Mechanics' Lien Law & Construction Industry Practice, No. 3. 5th suppl. ed. 1993. 36.00 (0-685-74428-0) Butterworth Legal Pubs.
— California Mechanics' Lien Law Handbook. 4th ed. 1993. pap. 50.00 (1-55943-178-4) Butterworth Legal Pubs.
Marsh, Michael. Healing Through the Sacraments. 120p. 1989. pap. 5.95 (0-8146-1807-3) Liturgical Pr.
— A Matter of Personal Survival. LC 84-40514. (Illus.). 209p. (Orig.). 1985. pap. 7.50 (0-8356-0596-5, Quest) Theos Pub Hse.
— Philosophy of the Inner Light. LC 76-50674. (Orig.). 1976. pap. 3.00 (0-87574-209-2) Pendle Hill.
— Reaching Toward God. LC 81-81683. 27p. 1981. pap. 3.00 (0-87574-237-8) Pendle Hill.
— The Rudelstein Affair. LC 80-29323. 205p. 1981. 9.95 (0-918056-02-0) Ariadne Pr.
Marsh, Michael, jt. ed. see Gallagher, Michael.
Marsh, Michael, jt. ed. see Hill, Ronald J.
Marsh, Michael N., ed. Immunopathology of the Small Intestine. LC 86-5620. (Wiley-Medical Publication Ser.). 479p. reprint ed. pap. 136.60 (0-8357-3471-4, 2039733) Bks Demand.
*Marsh, Michael S. Carolina Hunting Adventures - Quest for the Limit. (Illus.). 262p. (Orig.). 1995. pap. 12.95 (0-937866-50-4) Atlantic Pub Co.
Marsh, Neville. Fibrinolysis. LC 80-42309. (Wiley-Medical Publication Ser.). (Illus.). 270p. reprint ed. pap. 77.00 (0-8357-6305-6, 2035578) Bks Demand.
*Marsh, Ngaio. Alleyn & Others. 1995. pap. 10.95 (1-55882-028-0) Intl Polygonics.
— Artists in Crime. 256p. 1994. pap. 4.50 (0-425-14331-7, Prime Crime) Berkley Pub.
— Artists in Crime. 1976. reprint ed. lib. bdg. 22.95 (0-88411-471-6, Aeonian Pr) Amereon Ltd.
— Black As He Is Painted. 1976. reprint ed. lib. bdg. 21.95 (0-88411-472-4, Aeonian Pr) Amereon Ltd.
— Black As He's Painted. (Mystery Ser.). 224p. 1984. pap. 3.99 (0-515-07627-9) Jove Pubns.
— Black As He's Painted. 1994. reprint ed. lib. bdg. 27.95 (1-56849-307-X) Buccaneer Bks.
— Clutch of Constables. 224p. 1986. pap. 3.99 (0-515-08775-0) Jove Pubns.
— Clutch of Constables. 1976. reprint ed. lib. bdg. 20.95 (0-88411-473-2, Aeonian Pr) Amereon Ltd.
— Clutch of Constables. 1994. reprint ed. lib. bdg. 27.95 (1-56849-308-8) Buccaneer Bks.
— Colour Scheme. 1976. reprint ed. lib. bdg. 22.95 (0-88411-474-0, Aeonian Pr) Amereon Ltd.
— Dead Water. 1976. reprint ed. lib. bdg. 21.95 (0-88411-475-9, Aeonian Pr) Amereon Ltd.
— Death & the Dancing Footman. 320p. 1992. pap. 3.99 (0-515-08610-X) Jove Pubns.
— Death & the Dancing Footman. 1976. reprint ed. lib. bdg. 25.95 (0-88411-477-5, Aeonian Pr) Amereon Ltd.
— Death at the Bar. (Ngaio Marsh Mystery Ser.). 272p. 1984. pap. text ed. 3.99 (0-515-07700-3) Jove Pubns.
— Death at the Bar. 1976. reprint ed. lib. bdg. 23.95 (0-88411-476-7, Aeonian Pr) Amereon Ltd.
— Death in a White Tie. 352p. 1994. pap. text ed. 4.50 (0-425-14408-9) Berkley Pub.
— Death in a White Tie. 1976. reprint ed. lib. bdg. 22.95 (0-88411-479-1, Aeonian Pr) Amereon Ltd.
— Death in Ecstasy. 256p. 1989. pap. 3.99 (0-515-08592-8) Jove Pubns.
— Death in Ecstasy. 1976. reprint ed. lib. bdg. 22.95 (0-88411-478-3, Aeonian Pr) Amereon Ltd.
— Death of a Fool. 288p. 1994. pap. 4.50 (0-425-14303-1, Prime Crime) Berkley Pub.
— Death of a Fool. 1976. reprint ed. lib. bdg. 21.95 (0-88411-480-5, Aeonian Pr) Amereon Ltd.
— Death of a Peer. 320p. 1994. pap. text ed. 4.99 (0-425-14353-8, Prime Crime) Berkley Pub.
— Death of a Peer. 1976. reprint ed. lib. bdg. 24.95 (0-88411-481-3, Aeonian Pr) Amereon Ltd.
— Died in the Wool. 256p. 1994. pap. 4.99 (0-425-14469-0, Prime Crime) Berkley Pub.
— Died in the Wool. (Ngaio Marsh Mystery Ser.). 256p. 1983. pap. 3.99 (0-515-07506-X) Jove Pubns.
— Died in the Wool. 1976. reprint ed. lib. bdg. 20.95 (0-88411-482-1, Aeonian Pr) Amereon Ltd.
— Enter a Murderer. 1976. reprint ed. lib. bdg. 20.95 (0-88411-483-X, Aeonian Pr) Amereon Ltd.
— Enter a Murderer. (Mystery Ser.). 192p. 1984. reprint ed. pap. text ed. 3.99 (0-515-07447-0) Jove Pubns.
— False Scent. (Ngaio Marsh Mystery Ser.). 224p. 1984. pap. 3.99 (0-515-08056-X) Jove Pubns.
— False Scent. 1976. reprint ed. lib. bdg. 21.95 (0-88411-484-8, Aeonian Pr) Amereon Ltd.
— Final Curtain. 1993. pap. 4.99 (0-425-14320-1) Berkley Pub.
— Final Curtain. 1976. reprint ed. lib. bdg. 24.95 (0-88411-485-6, Aeonian Pr) Amereon Ltd.
— Grave Mistake. 1976. 20.95 (0-8488-0577-1) Amereon Ltd.
— Grave Mistake. 1994. pap. 4.50 (0-425-14243-4) Berkley Pub.
— Grave Mistake. 256p. 1987. pap. 3.50 (0-515-08847-1) Jove Pubns.
— Hand in Glove. 240p. 1987. pap. 4.50 (0-515-07502-7) Jove Pubns.
— Hand in Glove. 1976. reprint ed. lib. bdg. 20.95 (0-88411-486-4, Aeonian Pr) Amereon Ltd.
— Killer Dolphin. (Ngaio Marsh Mystery Ser.). 256p. 1991. pap. 3.99 (0-515-08590-1) Jove Pubns.
— Killer Dolphin. 1976. reprint ed. lib. bdg. 23.95 (0-88411-487-2, Aeonian Pr) Amereon Ltd.
— Last Death. 1976. 21.95 (0-8488-0578-X) Amereon Ltd.
— Last Ditch. 288p. 1986. pap. 3.99 (0-515-08798-X) Jove Pubns.
— Light Thickens. 1976. 19.95 (0-8488-0579-8) Amereon Ltd.
— Light Thickens. 240p. 1994. pap. text ed. 4.99 (0-425-14529-8, Prime Crime) Berkley Pub.
— A Man Lay Dead. 1976. reprint ed. lib. bdg. 19.95 (0-88411-488-0, Aeonian Pr) Amereon Ltd.
— New Zealand. 1976. reprint ed. lib. bdg. 22.95 (0-88411-489-9, Aeonian Pr) Amereon Ltd.
— Ngaio Marsh: Five Complete Novels. 784p. 1990. 9.99 (0-517-41017-6) Random Hse Value.
— Night at the Vulcan. 1994. pap. 4.50 (0-425-14205-1) Berkley Pub.
— Night at the Vulcan. (Ngaio Marsh Mystery Ser.). 256p. 1983. pap. 4.50 (0-515-07507-8) Jove Pubns.
— Night at the Vulcan. 1976. reprint ed. lib. bdg. 22.95 (0-88411-490-2, Aeonian Pr) Amereon Ltd.
— The Nursing Home Murder. 240p. 1994. pap. text ed. 4.50 (0-425-14242-6, Prime Crime) Berkley Pub.
— Nursing Home Murder. 1976. reprint ed. lib. bdg. 20.95 (0-88411-491-0, Aeonian Pr) Amereon Ltd.
— Overture to Death. (Ngaio Marsh Mystery Ser.). 320p. 1984. pap. 3.99 (0-515-07606-6) Jove Pubns.
— Overture to Death. 1976. reprint ed. lib. bdg. 22.95 (0-88411-492-9, Aeonian Pr) Amereon Ltd.
— Photo Finish. 1976. 19.95 (0-8488-0580-1) Amereon Ltd.
— Photo Finish. (Ngaio Marsh Mystery Ser.). 224p. 1983. pap. 3.99 (0-515-07505-1) Jove Pubns.
— Scales of Justice. 1976. reprint ed. lib. bdg. 22.95 (0-88411-493-7, Aeonian Pr) Amereon Ltd.

An Asterisk (*) at the beginning of an entry indicates that the title is appearing in BIP for the first time.

— Singing in the Shrouds. 240p. 1984. pap. 3.99 (0-515-07735-6) Jove Pubns.

— Singing in the Shrouds. large type ed. LC 93-14421. 1993. pap. 20.95 (0-7927-1781-3, Curley Lrg Print) Chivers N Amer.

— Singing in the Shrouds. 1976. reprint ed. lib. bdg. 21.95 (0-88411-494-5, Aeonian Pr) Amereon Ltd.

— Spinsters in Jeopardy. 256p. 1986. pap. 3.99 (0-515-08718-1) Jove Pubns.

— Spinsters in Jeopardy. 1976. reprint ed. lib. bdg. 21.95 (0-88411-495-3, Aeonian Pr) Amereon Ltd.

— Surfeit of Lampreys. large type ed. 1983. 15.95 (0-7089-0990-6) Ulverscroft.

— Tied up in Tinsel. 288p. 1993. pap. 3.99 (0-515-07443-8) Jove Pubns.

— Tied up in Tinsel. 1976. reprint ed. lib. bdg. 21.95 (0-88411-496-1, Aeonian Pr) Amereon Ltd.

— Vintage Murder. 272p. 1987. pap. 3.99 (0-515-08084-5) Jove Pubns.

— Vintage Murder. 1976. reprint ed. lib. bdg. 20.95 (0-88411-497-X, Aeonian Pr) Amereon Ltd.

— When in Rome. 1976. lib. bdg. 21.95 (0-88411-498-8, Aeonian Pr) Amereon Ltd.

— When in Rome. 224p. 1987. pap. 3.99 (0-515-07504-3) Jove Pubns.

— A Wreath for Rivera. 336p. 1994. pap. 4.50 (0-425-14247-7) Berkley Pub.

— A Wreath for Rivera. 1976. reprint ed. lib. bdg. 23.95 (0-88411-499-6, Aeonian Pr) Amereon Ltd.

Marsh, Norma. The Chocolate Touch: A Study Guide. (Novel-Ties Ser.). (J). (gr. 2-4). 1989. student ed, teacher ed 15.95 (0-88122-043-4) Lrn Links.

— Follow My Leader: A Study Guide. Friedland, Joyce & Kessler, Rikki, eds. (Novel-Ties Ser.). 18p. (YA). (gr. 9-12). 1990. pap. text ed. 15.95 (0-88122-403-0) Lrn Links.

— A Gift for Mama: A Study Guide. (Novel-Ties Ser.). (J). (gr. 2-4). 1989. student ed, teacher ed 15.95 (0-88122-045-0) Lrn Links.

— Park's Quest: A Study Guide. Friedland, Joyce & Kessler, Rikki, eds. (Novel-Ties Ser.). (J). (gr. 5-8). 1991. pap. text ed. 15.95 (0-88122-581-9) Lrn Links.

— The Pushcart War: A Study Guide. (Novel-Ties Ser.). 1988. teacher ed 15.95 (0-88122-095-7) Lrn Links.

— Sarah, Plain & Tall: A Study Guide. (Novel-Ties Ser.). 1988. student ed, teacher ed 15.95 (0-88122-063-9) Lrn Links.

— The Secret Garden: A Study Guide. (Novel-Ties Ser.). 1989. student ed, teacher ed 15.95 (0-88122-057-4) Lrn Links.

Marsh, P. & Martin, M. Oral Microbiology. 3rd ed. (Illus.). 240p. (C). 1992. pap. text ed. 32.50 (0-412-43360-5, A6899) Chapman & Hall.

Marsh, P. D. Contract Negotiation Handbook. 424p. 1984. text ed. 78.95 (0-566-02403-9) Ashgate Pub Co.

— Contract Negotiation Handbook. 412p. (C). 1984. 475.00 (0-685-39921-4, Inst Pur & Supply) St Mut.

— Contract Negotiations Handbook. 412p. (C). 1988. 230.00 (0-685-29237-1, Inst Pur & Supply) St Mut.

— Contract Negotiations Handbook. 412p. (C). 1989. 525.00 (0-685-36156-X, Inst Pur & Supply) St Mut.

— Contracting for Engineering & Construction Projects. 315p. (C). 1988. 156.00 (0-685-29258-4, Inst Pur & Supply); 395.00 (0-685-39919-2, Inst Pur & Supply) St Mut.

— Contracting for Engineering & Construction Projects. 315p. (C). 1989. 375.00 (0-685-36153-5, Inst Pur & Supply) St Mut.

— Successful Bidding & Tendering. (Gower Business Enterprise Ser.). 179p. 1989. text ed. 25.95 (0-7045-0619-X, Pub. by Gower UK) Ashgate Pub Co.

Marsh, Patrick O. Messages That Work: A Guide to Communication Design. LC 83-1573. 460p. 1983. 38.95 (0-87778-184-2) Educ Tech Pubns.

Marsh, Paul, jt. auth. see Dimson, Elroy.

Marsh, Peter. Contracting for Engineering & Construction Projects. 3rd ed. 315p. 1989. text ed. 58.95 (0-566-02792-5, Pub. by Gower UK) Ashgate Pub Co.

Marsh, Peter, ed. The Conscience of the Victorian State. (C). 1979. 39.95 (0-8156-2195-7); pap. 16.95 (0-8156-2196-5) Syracuse U Pr.

— Contesting the Boundaries of Liberal & Professional Education: The Syracuse Experiment. (Illus.). 280p. (C). 1988. text ed. 39.95 (0-8156-2428-X) Syracuse U Pr.

— Human Behavior: The Marshall Cavendish Encyclopedia of Human Relationships, 19 vols. LC 90-36716. (Illus.). 2350p. 1991. lib. bdg. 499.95 (1-85435-331-4) Marshall Cavendish.

Marsh, Peter, jt. auth. see Doel, Mark.

Marsh, Peter, jt. ed. see Nicholls, David.

Marsh, Peter, jt. auth. see Triseliotis, John.

***Marsh, Peter D.** Contracting for Engineering & Construction Projects. 4th ed. 350p. 1995. 84.95 (0-566-07628-4) Ashgate Pub Co.

Marsh, Peter T. The Discipline of Popular Government: Lord Salisbury's Domestic Statecraft, 1881-1902. (Modern Revivals in History Ser.). 384p. (C). 1993. text ed. 63.95 (0-7512-0230-4, Pub. by Gregg Revivals UK) Ashgate Pub Co.

— Joseph Chamberlain: Entrepreneur in Politics. LC 93-47209. 720p. 1994. 45.00 (0-300-05801-2) Yale U Pr.

Marsh, Philip & Martin, Michael. Oral Microbiology. 2nd ed. (Aspects of Microbiology Ser.: No. 1). 128p. reprint ed. pap. 36.50 (0-7837-4043-3, 2043873) Bks Demand.

Marsh, Philip D., jt. ed. see Hill, Michael J.

Marsh, Philip M. Freneau's Published Prose: A Bibliography. (Author Bibliographies Ser.: No. 5). 1970. 22.50 (0-8108-0289-9) Scarecrow.

Marsh, R. B., ed. Organizational Change in Japanese Factories. (Monographs in Organizational Behavior & Industrial Relations: Vol. 9). 1988. 73.25 (0-89232-777-4) Jai Pr.

Marsh, R. E., jt. ed. see Jackson, W. B.

Marsh, R. W., jt. auth. see Olivo, C. T.

Marsh, Ralph, ed. see Emery, J. Gladston.

Marsh, Rebecca. Always in Her Heart. LC 93-20312. 1993. 18.95 (0-7927-1619-1, Curley Lrg Print) Chivers N Amer.

— Always in Her Heart. large type ed. LC 93-20312. 1993. pap. 16.95 (0-7927-1618-3, Curley Lrg Print) Chivers N Amer.

— Summer in Vermont. large type ed. LC 93-27184. 1994. 13.95 (0-7862-0048-0) Thorndike Pr.

Marsh, Reginald. Anatomy for Artists. LC 75-129078. (Illus.). 1970. reprint ed. pap. 7.95 (0-486-22613-1) Dover.

Marsh, Richard. The Beetle. 1976. 28.95 (0-405-08151-0, 18479) Ayer.

Marsh, Richard S. Reading & Understanding Technical Information. (Illus.). (J). (gr. 5). 1986. student ed 4.95 (0-89525-758-0) Ed Activities.

Marsh, Robert. Four Dialectical Theories of Poetry. LC 65-24432. 1965. lib. bdg. 19.00 (0-226-50689-4) U Ch Pr.

— We Are Not Alone: How ECK Masters Guide Our Spiritual Lives Today. 260p. 1994. pap. 11.00 (1-57043-062-4) ECKANKAR.

Marsh, Robert C., ed. see Russell, Bertrand.

Marsh, Robert M. The Mandarins: The Circulation of Elites in China, 1600 to 1900. Zuckerman, Harriet & Merton, Robert K., eds. LC 79-9013. (Dissertations on Sociology Ser.). 1980. lib. bdg. 31.95 (0-405-12981-5) Ayer.

Marsh, Robert M. & Mannari, Hiroshi. Modernization & the Japanese Factory. LC 75-3466. 560p. 1976. pap. 22.95 (0-691-10037-3) Princeton U Pr.

Marsh, Robin R. Development Strategies in Rural Colombia: The Case of Caqueta. LC 82-620032. (Latin American Studies: Vol. 55). 1983. text ed. 22.95 (0-87903-055-0) UCLA Lat Am Ctr.

***Marsh, Rosalind.** History & Literature in Contemporary Russia. 240p. 1995. 42.50 (0-8147-5527-5) NYU Pr.

Marsh, Rosalind J. Images of Dictatorship: Stalin in Literature. 304p. 1989. 45.00 (0-415-03796-4, A3493) Routledge.

— Soviet Fiction since Stalin: Science, Politics & Literature. LC 85-30610. 352p. 1986. 56.00 (0-389-20609-1, N8172) B&N Imports.

Marsh, S. B. & Soulsby, J. Business Law. 3rd ed. LC 85-11331. 6.50 (0-07-084876-9) McGraw.

— Outlines of English Law. 304p. 1982. write for info. (0-07-084655-3) McGraw.

Marsh, S. P., jt. ed. see Pande, C. S.

Marsh-Smith, David. The Phoney Club: Cleveland Club System. 80p. 1993. pap. 8.95 (0-8059-3307-7) Dorrance.

Marsh, Spencer. God, Man, & Archie Bunker. LC 74-25694. 128p. 1975. pap. 2.95i (0-06-065422-8, RD-96) Harper SF.

Marsh, Stephen. Computer Security: An Integrated Approach. 240p. (C). 1990. pap. text ed. 200.00 (0-273-03133-3, Pub. by Pitman Pubng UK) St Mut.

Marsh, Susan H., jt. ed. see Kau, Michael Y.

Marsh, T. F., et al, illus. Tom Kitten. (Classic Tales Ser.). 24p. (J). (gr. 2-4). 1992. lib. bdg. 10.50 (1-56674-010-X, HTS Bks) Forest Hse.

— Two Bad Mice. (Classic Tales Ser.). 24p. (J). (gr. 2-4). 1992. lib. bdg. 10.50 (1-56674-011-8, HTS Bks) Forest Hse.

Marsh, Terry. One-Hundred Walks in the French Pyrenees. (Illus.). 256p. 1992. pap. 24.95 (0-340-51517-1, Pub. by H & S UK) Trafalgar.

Marsh, Tess. The Children's Book of Embroidery. (Illus.). 64p. 1986. 22.95 (0-7134-5142-4, Pub. by Batsford UK) Trafalgar.

Marsh, Theron L., jt. ed. see Sweeney, Mary S.

***Marsh, Thomas.** The Triune God: A Biblical, Historical, & Theological Study. LC 94-78128. 208p. (Orig.). 1994. pap. 14.95 (0-89622-631-X) Twenty-Third.

Marsh, Thomas A. Gift of Community: Baptism & Confirmation. LC 83-80111. (Message of the Sacraments Ser.: Vol. 2). 200p. 1984. 13.95 (0-8146-5392-8); pap. 12.95 (0-8146-5228-X) Liturgical Pr.

Marsh, Thomas E. The Official Guide to Collecting Applied Color Label Soda Bottles. (Illus.). 104p. (Orig.). 1992. write for info. (0-9633682-0-6) T E Marsh.

— The Official Guide to Collecting Applied Color Soda Bottles, Vol. II. 105p. (YA). Date not set. per., pap. write for info. (0-9633682-1-4) T E Marsh.

Marsh, Thomas O. Roots of Crime: A Bio-Physical Approach to Crime Prevention & Rehabilitation. 208p. 1984. reprint ed. pap. text ed. 14.95 (0-8290-1570-1) Irvington.

Marsh, Timothy R., jt. auth. see Marsh, Helen C.

Marsh, Tracy, ed. Victorian Crafts: Over Forty Charming Projects to Make from the Victorian Era. (Illus.). 168p. 1993. 29.95 (0-943955-75-0, Trafalgar Sq Pub) Trafalgar.

***Marsh, Valerie.** Beyond Words: Sign Language Stories for Hand & Voice. (Illus.). 80p. (J). (ps-5). 1995. student ed 10.95 (0-917846-49-4, 33902, Alleyside) Highsmith Pr.

— Mystery Fold: Stories to Tell, Draw & Fold. (Illus.). 80p. (J). (ps-5). 1993. pap. 9.95 (0-913853-31-3, 32540, Alleyside) Highsmith Pr.

— Paper Cutting Stories for Holidays & Special Events. LC 94-26174. (J). (ps-5). 1994. 10.95 (0-917846-42-7, Alleyside) Highsmith Pr.

— Paper Cutting Stories from A to Z. (Illus.). 80p. (Orig.). (J). (ps-5). 1992. pap. 9.95 (0-913853-24-0, 32535, Alleyside) Highsmith Pr.

Marsh, W. D. Economics of Electric Utility Power Generation. (OESS Ser.). (Illus.). (C). 1980. text ed. 96.00 (0-19-856130-X) OUP.

***Marsh, W. Jeffrey.** Unto Us a Child Is Born. 1994. 10.95 (0-88494-937-0) Bookcraft Inc.

Marsh, W. Jeffrey & Munns, Ron R. Miracles & Blessings: Old Testament Stories with Present-Day Parallels. 1994. 9.95 (0-88494-915-X) Bookcraft Inc.

Marsh, William & Kuniansky, Harry R. Case Problems in Financial Management. 304p. (C). 1988. pap. text ed. write for info. (0-13-118944-1) P-H.

Marsh, William, tr. see Sakaiya, Taichi.

Marsh, William H. Basic Financial Management. LC 94-2856. 640p. 1994. 53.95 (0-538-84170-2) S-W Pub.

Marsh, William M. Earthscape a Physical Geography. LC 86-28209. 216p. (C). 1987. teacher ed 15.00 (0-471-85570-7); Net. text ed. write for info. (0-471-85055-1); trans. 27.50 (0-471-85571-5); sl. 145.00 (0-471-63018-7); disk 25.00 (0-471-53726-8); write for info. (0-471-62432-2) Wiley.

— Landscape Applications. LC 82-13889. (Earth Science Ser.). (Illus.). 225p. 1981. pap. text ed. write for info. (0-201-04102-2) Addison-Wesley.

— Landscape Planning: Environmental Applications. 2nd ed. 89p. 1991. teacher ed 23.00 (0-471-54740-9); Net. pap. text ed. write for info. (0-471-52506-5) Wiley.

Marsh, William M. & Dozier, Jeff. Landscape an Introduction to Physical Geography. 637p. 1986. Net. text ed. write for info. (0-471-85433-6) Wiley.

Marsh, William P., jt. auth. see Bamford, Christopher.

Marsha, M. & Soulsby, S. Business Law. 292p. (C). 1989. 115.00 (0-685-39840-4, Inst Pur & Supply) St Mut.

Marshak. Hail to Mail. Pervear, tr. (J). 1995. pap. 5.95 (0-8050-3124-3) H Holt & Co.

Marshak, Daniel, ed. see Tobin, Catherine.

***Marshak, Daniel, et al.** Strategies for Protein Purification & Characterization: A Laboratory Course Manual. (Illus.). 304p. (C). 1995. 110.00 (0-87969-449-1); pap. 75.00 (0-87969-385-1) Cold Spring Harbor.

Marshak, Daniel R. & Liu, Darrell T., eds. Therapeutic Peptides & Proteins: Assessing the New Technologies. (Banbury Report Ser.: No. 29). (Illus.). 288p. 1988. text ed. 77.00 (0-87969-229-4) Cold Spring Harbor.

— Therapeutic Peptides & Proteins: Formulation, Delivery & Targeting. (Current Communications in Molecular Biology Ser.). (Illus.). (Orig.). 1989. pap. text ed. 24.00 (0-87969-328-2) Cold Spring Harbor.

Marshak, David. HM Study Skills Program: Student Text Level II. rev. ed. Phipps, Paula et al, eds. 104p. 1986. teacher ed 5.95 (0-88210-100-5); pap. text ed. 5.95 (0-88210-099-8) Natl Assn Principals.

Marshak, David, ed. see Andrews, Barry & Hoertdoerfer, Pat.

Marshak, David, ed. see Arnason, W., et al.

Marshak, David, ed. see Branch, Robert C., et al.

Marshak, David, jt. auth. see Burkle, Candace R.

Marshak, David, ed. see Burkle, Frank.

Marshak, David, ed. see Fitzpatrick, Elaine M.

Marshak, David, ed. see Goldenberg, Samuel, et al.

Marshak, David, ed. see Hunting, Eleanor, et al.

Marshak, David, ed. see Keroack, Elizabeth C., et al.

Marshak, David, ed. see Tobin, Catherine D.

Marshak, David, ed. see Wilson, Carol & Krasnow, Gary.

Marshak, I. S. Pulsed Light Sources. LC 84-12669. 472p. 1984. 105.00 (0-306-10976-X, Consultants) Plenum.

Marshak, Laura E. & Seligman, Milton. Counseling Persons with Physical Disabilities: Theoretical & Clinical Perspectives. LC 92-35809. (Orig.). (C). 1993. pap. text ed. 27.00 (0-89079-580-0, 6594) PRO-ED.

Marshak, Laura E., jt. ed. see Nowell, Richard C.

Marshak, M. L., ed. High Energy Physics with Polarized Beams & Targets (Argonne, 1976) Proceedings. LC 76-50181. (AIP Conference Proceedings Ser., Subseries: Particle & Fields: No. 35, 12). 543p. 1977. 21.50 (0-88318-134-7) Am Inst Physics.

Marshak, R. E. Conceptual Foundations of Modern Particle Physics. 704p. 1993. text ed. 99.00 (981-02-1098-1); pap. text ed. 53.00 (981-02-1106-6) World Scientific Pub.

Marshak, Richard H., et al. Radiology of the Stomach. (Illus.). 656p. 1983. text ed. 155.00 (0-7216-6124-6) Saunders.

***Marshak, Robert E.** A Gift of Prophecy: Essays in Celebration of the Life of Robert Eugene Marshak. Sudarshan, E. C., ed. & comp. by. 584p. 1995. text ed. 109.00 (981-02-2075-8) World Scientific Pub.

Marshak, S., tr. see Milne, A. A.

Marshak, Samuel. Hail to Mail. Pevear, Richard, tr. LC 89-7605. (Illus.). 32p. (J). (ps-2). 1990. 14.95 (0-8050-1132-3, Bks Young Read) H Holt & Co.

— The Month Brothers: A Slavic Tale. Whitney, Thomas P., tr. LC 82-7927. (Illus.). 32p. (J). (gr. k up). 1983. lib. bdg. 15.93 (0-688-01510-7) Morrow Jr Bks.

— The Pup Grew Up! Pevear, Richard, tr. LC 88-28428. (Illus.). 32p. (J). (ps-2). 1989. 13.95 (0-8050-0952-3, Bks Young Read) H Holt & Co.

Marshak, Sondra. Prometheus Design. 1990. pap. 5.50 (0-671-72366-9) S&S Trade.

— Triangle. (Star Trek Ser.: No. 9). (Orig.). 1991. mass mkt. 5.50 (0-671-74351-1) PB.

Marshak, Sondra & Culbreath, Myrna. The Price of Phoenix. (Star Trek Ser.). 192p. (Orig.). 1993. mass mkt. 4.99 (0-553-24635-6) Bantam.

Marshak, Stephen. Structural Geology of Silurian & Devonian Strata in the Mid-Hudson Valley, New York: Fold-Thrust Belt Tectonics in Miniature. (New York State Museum Map & Chart Ser.: No. 41). (Illus.). 66p. (Orig.). 1990. pap. 15.00 (1-55557-200-6) NYS Museum.

Marshak, Stephen & Mitra, Gautam. Basic Methods of Structural Geology. 446p. (C). 1988. pap. text ed. write for info. (0-13-065178-8) P-H.

Marshak, Stephen, jt. auth. see Van Der Pluijm, Ben A.

Marshak, Suzanna. The Wizard's Promise. LC 92-36507. (Illus.). (J). 1994. pap. 15.00 (0-671-78431-5, S&S Bks Young Read) S&S Childrens.

Marshal, Edward. Four on the Shore. (J). (ps-3). 1993. pap. 4.99 (0-14-036186-3, Puffin) Puffin Bks.

Marshal, Maurice R. Your Food & Health: A Study Guide for Man's Food. 144p. (C). 1993. spiral bd. 19.95 (0-8403-9117-X) Kendall-Hunt.

Marshal, S. L. & Hackworth, David. Vietnam Primer. 58p. 1983. pap. 5.95 (0-318-36168-X) Lancer.

Marshal Sir Kenneth Bing Cross & Orange, Vincent. Straight & Level: The Autobiography of Air Chief Marshal Sir Kenneth "Bing" Cross, KCB, CBE, DSO, DFC, 1911-1945. 288p. 1993. 29.95 (0-948817-72-0, Pub. by Grub St Pubns UK) Seven Hills Bk.

Marshal, Walter G. Through America: Nine Months in the United States. LC 73-13143. (Foreign Travelers in America, 1810-1935 Ser.). (Illus.). 490p. 1974. reprint ed. 35.95 (0-405-05466-1) Ayer.

Marshalek, Kathy. Export Marketing & Sales. 154p. 1992. pap. 67.50 (1-883006-03-1) Intl Busn Pubns.

— Export Reference Glossary. 370p. 1992. pap. 67.50 (1-883006-04-X) Intl Busn Pubns.

Marshalek, Kathy & Ewert, Donald E. International Agents & Distributors. 228p. 1993. pap. 67.50 (1-883006-06-6) Intl Busn Pubns.

Marshall. Campylobacter Pylori. 1991. 65.00 (0-86542-108-0) Mosby Yr Bk.

— Catherine Marshall: Inspiration Writings. 1995. 12.98 (0-88486-118-X) Arrowood Pr.

— Goddess Disclosing Monologues for Gaia. 1993. per. 10.95 (1-55082-039-7, Pub. by Quarry Pr CN) InBook.

— Health Careers Today, Resource Kit. 192p. 1991. 51.95 (0-8016-3282-X) Mosby Yr Bk.

— Life Insurance Company Mergers & Consolidations. (C). 1972. 12.95 (0-256-00653-9) Irwin.

— Mammals from Pouches & Eggs. Graves, Jennifer A. et al, eds. (C). 1990. 60.00 (0-643-05020-5, Pub. by CSIRO AT) Intl Spec Bk.

— New International Commentary on the New Testament Epistles of John. 1994. (0-8028-2518-4) Eerdmans.

— Operative Urology. (Illus.). 656p. 1990. text ed. 147.00 (0-7216-6121-1) Saunders.

— Pulmonary Circulation. 1991. 37.50 (0-8151-5763-0, Yr Bk Med Pubs) Mosby Yr Bk.

— Telecommunications in the 1990s. 1995. 39.95 (0-8161-1974-0) G K Hall.

— Urologic Complications. 2nd ed. 600p. 1990. 86.00 (0-8151-5761-4, Yr Bk Med Pubs) Mosby Yr Bk.

Marshall, ed. The Four-Part Motets of Thomas Crecquillon, Pt. 1. (Wissenschaftliche Abhandlungen-Musicological Studies: Vol. 21). lib. bdg. 6.00 (0-912024-92-5) Inst Mediaeval Mus.

— The Four-Part Motets of Thomas Crecquillon, Pt. 2. (Wissenschaftliche Abhandlungen-Musicological Studies: Vol. 21). lib. bdg. 6.00 (0-912024-91-7) Inst Mediaeval Mus.

— The Four-Part Motets of Thomas Crecquillon, Pt. 3. (Wissenschaftliche Abhandlungen-Musicological Studies: Vol. 21). lib. bdg. 6.00 (0-912024-93-3) Inst Mediaeval Mus.

— The Four-Part Motets of Thomas Crecquillon, Pt. 4. (Wissenschaftliche Abhandlungen-Musicological Studies: Vol. 21). lib. bdg. 6.00 (0-912024-94-1) Inst Mediaeval Mus.

— Methods of Handling & Processing Imagery. 146p. 1987. 43.00 (0-89252-792-7, 757) SPIE.

Marshall & Briggs. Labor Economics. 6th ed. 656p. (C). 1988. text ed. 48.95 (0-256-07090-3) Irwin.

Marshall & Swift. Dodge Repair & Remodel Cost Book 1994. 8th ed. 300p. Date not set. per. 74.95 (1-56842-017-X) Marshall & Swift.

— Real Estate Repair & Remodel Cost Guide 1994. 4th ed. 224p. Date not set. per. 59.95 (1-56842-018-8) Marshall & Swift.

— Tenant Improvement Cost Book for Offices 1994. 336p. 1993. per. 89.95 (1-56842-012-9) Marshall & Swift.

Marshall & Wadsworth, eds. Rice Science & Technology. (Food Science & Technology Ser.: Vol. 59). 488p. 1994. 150.00 (0-8247-8887-7) Dekker.

***Marshall & Wood.** Services & Space: Key Aspects of Urban & Regional Development. Date not set. pap. text ed. write for info. (0-470-23511-X) Wiley.

Marshall, ed. see Boyle, Marie A. & Morris, Diane H.

Marshall, ed. see Boyle, Marie & Zyla, Gail.

Marshall, ed. see Cataldo, Corinne B., et al.

Marshall, ed. see Cohen, David C.

Marshall, ed. see Culver, Roger.

Marshall, ed. see DeBruyne, Linda K., et al.

Marshall, ed. see Devore, Jay & Peck, Roxy.

Marshall, ed. see Dintiman, George B., et al.

Marshall, ed. see Fadyn, Joseph N.

Marshall, ed. see Ferraro, Gary, et al.

Marshall, ed. see Ferraro, Gary.

Marshall, ed. see Flower, Phillip.

Marshall, ed. see Gould, Leroy C.

Marshall, ed. see Graham, Neill.

Marshall, ed. see Hamilton, Eva M., et al.

Marshall, ed. see Harrison, Frank.

Marshall, ed. see Havick, John J.

Marshall, ed. see Hepner, George F. & McKee, Jesse O.

Marshall, ed. see Hunt, Sara M. & Groff, James L.

Marshall, ed. see Jewell, Linda N. & Siegall, Marc.

Marshall, ed. see Kaplan, Paul S.

Marshall, ed. see Knox, David & Schacht, Caroline.

Marshall, ed. see Knox, David.

Marshall, ed. see Logsdon, Tom.

Marshall, ed. see McCammon, Susan L., et al.

Marshall, ed. see Napoli, Vince, et al.

Marshall, ed. see Rolfes, Sharon R., et al.

Marshall, ed. see Settle, Mickey G.

An Asterisk (*) at the beginning of an entry indicates that the title is appearing in BIP for the first time.

Marshall, ed. see Shiflet, Angela.

Marshall, ed. see Sizer, Frances S. & Whitney, Eleanor N.

Marshall, ed. see Steinlage, Ralph C.

Marshall, ed. see Territo, Leonard, et al.

Marshall, ed. see Turner, Lori, et al.

Marshall, ed. see Whitney, Eleanor N. & Rolfes, Sharon R.

Marshall, ed. see Whitney, Eleanor N., et al.

Marshall, et al. Neuroscience Critical Care: Pathophysiology & Patient Management. 464p. 1990. text ed. 76.50 (0-7216-2790-0) Saunders.

***Marshall & Swift Staff.** The Digest of Building Contract Awards. 26th ed. (Illus.). 450p. 1995. pap. 52.95 (1-56842-269-5) Marshall & Swift.

— Dodge Repair & Remodel Cost Book 1995. 9th ed. 300p. 1995. pap. 59.95 (1-56842-027-7) Marshall & Swift.

— Dodge Unit Cost Book 1995. 560p. (Orig.). 1995. pap. 59.95 (1-56842-029-3) Marshall & Swift.

— Dodge Unit Metric Cost Book 1995. (Orig.). 1995. pap. 59.95 (1-56842-028-5) Marshall & Swift.

— Home Repair & Remodel Cost Guide, 1995. 5th ed. (Illus.). 224p. Date not set. pap. 49.95 (1-56842-030-7) Marshall & Swift.

— Illustrated Guide to Houses: Terms, Definitions & Drawings. Cap, Cydney, ed. (Illus.). 132p. (Orig.). 1995. pap. 14.95 (1-56842-031-5) Marshall & Swift.

— Marshall Valuation Quarterly (MVS) Date not set. ring bd. 154.95 (1-56842-023-4) Marshall & Swift.

— Marshall Valuation Service. 1995. ring bd. 169.95 (1-56842-040-4) Marshall & Swift.

— Residential Cost Handbook. 1995. ring bd. 94.95 (1-56842-039-0) Marshall & Swift.

— Residential Cost Handbook (RCH) 1995. ring bd. 94.95 (1-56842-022-6) Marshall & Swift.

— Tenant Improvement Cost Book...for Offices 1995. 2nd ed. (Illus.). 258p. 1995. pap. 95.95 (1-56842-025-0) Marshall & Swift.

— Valuator Quarterly. 1995. ring bd. 99.95 (1-56842-041-2) Marshall & Swift.

Marshall, A. Marine Concrete. 1990. text ed. 145.00 (0-442-30297-5) Chapman & Hall.

— Principes D'Economie Politique, Vol. 1. xiv, 544p. 1971. pap. text ed. 124.00 (0-677-50515-9) Gordon & Breach.

— Principes D'Economie Politique, Vol. 2. 668p. 1971. pap. text ed. 124.00 (0-677-50525-6) Gordon & Breach.

— Principes d'Economique Politique, 2 vols., Vol. 2. 1156p. 1971. pap. text ed. 223.00 (0-677-50535-3) Gordon & Breach.

Marshall, A. C. Composites Basics. 4th ed. 200p. 1994. 45.00 (0-938648-35-7) T-C Pubns CA.

Marshall, A. D. & Martin, R. R. Computer Vision, Models & Inspection. (Series in Robotics & Automated Systems: Vol. 4). 300p. (C). 1992. text ed. 53.00 (981-02-0772-7) World Scientific Pub.

Marshall, A. G. The Ecology of Ectoparasitic Insects. LC 81-67916. 1982. text ed. 190.00 (0-12-474080-4) Acad Pr.

Marshall, A. G. & Verdun, F. R. Fourier Transforms in NMR, Optical, & Spectrometry: A User's Handbook. 440p. 1990. 113.00 (0-444-87360-0); pap. 49.95 (0-444-87412-7) Elsevier.

Marshall, A. L. Ambush. 256p. 1988. pap. 4.50 (0-515-09543-5) Jove Pubns.

Marshall, A. R. & Melling, P. J. Reduced Nox Emissions & Other Phenomena in Fluidized Bed Combustion, EUR 13876. 72p. 1992. pap. 9.00 (92-826-3366-7, CD-NA-13876-EN-C, Pub. by Europ Com) UNIPUB.

Marshall, A. Robert. Precalculus Functions & Graphs. (C). 1991. text ed. 53.75 (0-201-19095-8) Addison-Wesley.

Marshall, Alan. Classified Love: A Guide to Understanding Personal Ads. 100p. (Orig.). 1994. pap. 11.95 (0-9633029-8-1) Marshall MD.

— People in Pieces: Multiple Personality in Milder Forms & Greater Numbers. LC 92-32414. 124p. (Orig.). 1993. pap. 12.95 (0-935834-94-X) Rainbow Books.

— The Ruffian's Wage: Intelligence & Espionage in the Reign of Charles the Second, 1660-1685. LC 93-44477. (Cambridge Studies in Early Modern British History). (Illus.). 352p. (C). 1994. 59.95 (0-521-43180-8) Cambridge U Pr.

Marshall, Alan G., ed. Fourier, Hadamard, & Hilbert Transforms in Chemistry. LC 81-20984. 574p. (C). 1982. 125.00 (0-306-40904-6, Plenum Pr) Plenum.

Marshall, Alan J. The Black Musketeers. LC 75-35140. 344p. reprint ed. 49.50 (0-404-14156-0) AMS Pr.

— The Men & Birds of Paradise: Journeys Through Equatorial New Guinea. LC 75-35141. reprint ed. 25.50 (0-404-14157-9) AMS Pr.

Marshall, Albert & Olkin, Ingram. Inequalities: Theory of Majorization & Its Applications. LC 79-50218. (Mathematics in Science & Engineering Ser.). 1979. text ed. 99.00 (0-12-473750-1) Acad Pr.

Marshall, Alejandro & Bennett, Gordon H. La Salvacion y las Dudas de Algunas Personas. 2nd ed. Bautista, Sara, tr. (Serie Diamante). (Illus.). 36p. (ENG.). 1982. pap. 0.85 (0-942504-01-1) Overcomer Pr.

Marshall, Alexander, ed. Let's Travel Pathways Through Iowa: A Compilation of the Best in Iowa Travel. (Let's Travel Pathways Through America Ser.). (Illus.). 450p. (Orig.). 1995. reprint ed. pap. 16.95 (0-9626647-3-1) Clark & Miles.

— Let's Travel Pathways Through Wisconsin: A Compilation of the Best in Wisconsin Travel. (Let's Travel Pathways Through America Ser.). (Illus.). 640p. (Orig.). 1995. reprint ed. pap. 16.95 (0-9626647-2-3) Clark & Miles.

Marshall, Alfred. The Interlinear KJV - NIV Parallel: New Testament in Greek & English. LC 92-8493. (ENG & GRE.). 1991. 34.99 (0-310-95070-8) Zondervan.

— The Interlinear NASB-NIV Parallel New Testament in Greek & English. 784p. (ENG & GRE.). 1993. Printed caseside. 34.99 (0-310-40170-4) Zondervan.

— Memorials of Alfred Marshall. Pigou, A. C., ed. LC 66-24415. (Reprints of Economic Classics Ser.). 1925. 49.50 (0-678-00197-9) Kelley.

— Money, Credit & Commerce. LC 90-43794. (Reprints of Economic Classics Ser.). xvi, 369p. 1991. reprint ed. lib. bdg. 39.50 (0-678-01463-9) Kelley.

— NIV Interlinear Greek-English New Testament. 1976. 39.99 (0-310-28680-8, 6271) Zondervan.

— Official Papers. LC 78-10179. 428p. 1979. reprint ed. text ed. 35.00 (0-313-21110-8, MAOP, Greenwood Pr) Greenwood.

— Principles of Economics. 8th ed. (Illus.). xxxii, 731p. 1982. reprint ed. pap. 28.95 (0-87991-051-8) Porcupine Pr.

— Pure Theory of Foreign Trade & the Pure Theory of Domestic Values. LC 73-22013. (Reprints of Economic Classics Ser.). (Illus.). 1975. reprint ed. lib. bdg. 15.00 (0-678-01194-X) Kelley.

Marshall, Alice K. Pen Names of Women Writers. x, 181p. 1986. pap. 8.95 (0-9616387-0-2) A Marshall Collection.

Marshall, An. Aging in Action: A Dynamic Approach to Exercise. (Illus.). (Orig.). 1989. pap. write for info. (0-318-66585-9) Marshall Dynamics.

Marshall, Andrew W., jt. auth. see Goldhamer, Herbert.

Marshall, Ann E. Woven with Love. (Illus.). 36p. (Orig.). (J). (gr. 2-5). 1988. pap. 4.50 (0-934351-02-3) Heard Mus.

Marshall, Ann E. & Brennan, Mary H. The Heard Museum: History & Collections. LC 89-81003. (Illus.). 48p. (Orig.). 1989. pap. 8.95 (0-934351-04-X) Heard Mus.

Marshall, Anna, jt. auth. see Greenwood, Brian.

Marshall, Anne. The Complete Vegetarian Cookbook. (Illus.). 304p. 1993. 34.95 (0-8048-1974-2) C E Tuttle.

Marshall, Anne & Huston, James. Under the Double Cross. 295p. 1984. 10.95 (0-89697-214-3) Intl Univ Pr.

Marshall, Anthony. Don't Lose Your Hotel by Accident. LC 93-73107. 250p. (Orig.). 1995. pap. 39.95 (0-929870-17-4) Advanstar Commns.

— George's Story. LC 89-50143. (Great Adventure Tale Ser.). (J). (gr. 6-12). 1989. pap. 6.95 (0-932433-58-8) Windswept Hse.

Marshall, Anthony D. Zoos. LC 93-33984. 1994. 12.00 (0-679-74687-0) Random.

Marshall, Archibald. Clinton Twins, & Other Stories. LC 70-130062. (Short Story Index Reprint Ser.). 1977. 19.95 (0-8369-3661-2) Ayer.

— Clintons, & Others. LC 73-130063. (Short Story Index Reprint Ser.). 1977. 24.95 (0-8369-3662-0) Ayer.

Marshall, Arthur. Dictionary of Explosives. (Explosives Ser.). 1989. lib. bdg. 250.00 (0-8490-3967-3) Gordon Pr.

— Explosives: Their History, Manufacture, Properties & Tests, 3 vols. 1980. lib. bdg. 900.00 (0-8490-3151-6) Gordon Pr.

***Marshall, Arthur K. & Garb, Andrew S.** California Probate Procedure, 2 vols., Set. 5th ed. 480p. 1994. ring bd. 160.00 (1-55943-089-3) Michie Butterworth.

— California Probate Procedures, Suppl. 1, 4/91. Date not set. 71.50 (1-55943-087-7) Butterworth Legal Pubs.

— California Probate Procedures, Suppl. 2, 11/93. Date not set. 55.00 (1-55943-088-5) Butterworth Legal Pubs.

— California Probate Procedures, Vol. 1. Date not set. 71.50 (0-614-00282-6) Butterworth Legal Pubs.

Marshall, Atwood, jt. auth. see Lyman, Samuel.

Marshall, B. J., et al. Helicobacter Pylori in Peptic Ulcerations & Gastritis. (Illus.). 1991. 62.95 (0-685-52413-2) Blackwell Sci.

Marshall, Barbara. The Origins of Post-War German Politics. 256p. 1988. lib. bdg. 59.50 (0-7099-4690-2, Pub. by Croom Helm UK) Routledge Chapman & Hall.

Marshall, Barbara, jt. auth. see Hackman, Sue.

Marshall, Barbara K. & Clawson, Sharalee. Jesus Loves Me: Themes for Inspirational Children's Songs in Counted Cross-Stitch. 1985. 5.98 (0-88290-302-0) Horizon Utah.

Marshall, Barbara K. & Clawson, Sharalee S. Jesus Wants Me for a Sunbeam: Themes from Inspirational Children's Songs in Counted Cross-Stitch. 1985. 5.98 (0-88290-307-1) Horizon Utah.

Marshall, Barbara K., jt. auth. see Clawson, Sharalee S.

Marshall, Barbara L. Engendering Modernity: Feminism, Social Theory, & Social Change. 220p. 1994. text ed. 37.50 (1-55553-212-8); pap. text ed. 14.95 (1-55553-213-6) NE U Pr.

Marshall, Barbara S. The Shining Place of an Image. LC 88-37853. 168p. (C). 1989. lib. bdg. 36.00 (0-8191-7300-2) U Pr of Amer.

Marshall, Bette, jt. auth. see Lombardy, William.

Marshall, Bill. Angels, Bulldogs & Dragons: 355th Fighter Group in World War 2. 192p. 1985. pap. 14.95 (0-685-10425-7) Champlin Museum.

— Victor Serge: The Uses of Dissent. 240p. 1992. 49.95 (0-85496-766-4) Berg Pubs.

Marshall, Blaine, ed. see Lewis, Shari.

Marshall, Blaine, ed. see Time-Life Books Editors.

Marshall, Brenda. Teaching the Postmodern. 224p. 1991. 45.00 (0-415-90454-4, A5881, Routledge NY); pap. 14.95 (0-415-90455-2, A5885, Routledge NY) Routledge.

Marshall, Brian. Creating Graphical Programs in Visual C. 1995. pap. text ed. 42.95 (0-13-305145-5) P-H.

— The Secret of Getting Straight A's: Learn More in Less Time with Little Effort. (Illus.). 182p. (Orig.). (YA). (gr. 6 up). 1993. pap. 12.95 (0-9633357-9-0) Hathaway Intl.

Marshall, Brian & Ford, Wendy. The Secret of Getting Better Grades: Study Smarter, Not Harder. (Illus.). 160p. (Orig.). 1994. pap. 12.95 (1-57112-061-0, PA5027) JIST Works.

Marshall, Brian G. Bargains, Deals & Steals: How You Can Save up to 99 Percent on Almost Anything at Hidden Sales & Secret Auctions. Thomas, Bill, ed. 160p. (Orig.). 1991. pap. 14.95 (1-878969-21-8) Discovery UT.

Marshall, Bruce. A Foot in the Grave. large type ed. (Linford Mystery Library). 235p. 1988. pap. 11.95 (0-7089-6559-8, Linford) Ulverscroft.

— The White Rabbit. LC 87-8663. 256p. 1987. reprint ed. text ed. 59.75 (0-313-25322-6, MRWR, Greenwood Pr) Greenwood.

Marshall, Bruce D., ed. Theology & Dialogue: Essays in Conversation with George Lindbeck. LC 90-70847. 288p. (C). 1990. text ed. 29.95 (0-268-01873-1) U of Notre Dame Pr.

— Theology & Dialogue: Essays in Conversation with George Lindbeck. LC 90-70847. (C). 1992. pap. text ed. 14.95 (0-268-01874-X) U of Notre Dame Pr.

Marshall, Bruce T. A Holy Curiosity: Stories of a Liberal Religious Faith. 125p. (Orig.). 1990. pap. 7.95 (0-9626716-0-6) UUF Huntington.

Marshall, Bryce & Williams, Paul. Zero at the Bone. McCarthy, Paul, ed. 328p. (Orig.). 1991. mass mkt. 5.50 (0-671-68511-2, Pocket Star Bks) PB.

Marshall, Burke, ed. A Workable Government: The Constitution after 200 Years. (American Assembly Book Ser.). (Orig.). 1987. pap. 9.95 (0-393-30431-0) Norton.

Marshall, Burns. Automated Fabrication: Improving Productivity in Manufacturing. (Illus.). 400p. (C). 1993. text ed. 69.00 (0-13-119462-3) P-H.

— Chemical Engineering. 180p. Date not set. text ed. write for info. (0-13-131418-1) P-H.

Marshall, Byron K. Academic Freedom & the Japanese Imperial University, 1868-1939. (C). 1992. 40.00 (0-520-07821-7) U CA Pr.

— Capitalism & Nationalism in Prewar Japan: The Ideology of the Business Elite, 1868-1941. viii, 163p. 1967. 25.00 (0-8047-0325-6) Stanford U Pr.

— Learning to Be Modern: Japanese Political Discourse on Education. (New Perspectives on Asian History Ser.). (C). 1995. pap. text ed. 24.95 (0-8133-1892-0) Westview.

— Learning to Be Modern: Japanese Political Discourse on Education. (New Perspectives on Asian History Ser.). (C). 1995. text ed. 59.95 (0-8133-1891-2) Westview.

Marshall, Byron K., tr. see Sakae, Osugi.

Marshall, C. C. I. I. Life Assurance Law & Practice, No. 090. (C). 1984. 230.00 (0-685-33762-6, Pub. by Witherby & Co UK) St Mut.

— C. I. I. Life Assurance Law & Taxation, No. 130-071. (C). 1984. 230.00 (0-685-33761-8, Pub. by Witherby & Co UK) St Mut.

— The MacCormack Conspiracy. large type ed. (Linford Western Library). 1989. pap. 11.95 (0-7089-6783-3, Linford) Ulverscroft.

Marshall, C. & Grace, James B., eds. Fruit & Seed Production: Aspects of Development, Environmental Physiology & Ecology. (Society for Experimental Biology Seminar Ser.: No. 48). (Illus.). 250p. (C). 1992. 84.95 (0-521-37350-6) Cambridge U Pr.

Marshall, C. Alan. The Life & Times of Louis Farrakhan. 350p. 1992. pap. 21.95 (0-9633029-1-4) Marshall MD.

— The Seduction of Ministry: Everything You Wanted to Know about Ministry, but Nobody Had the Nerve to Tell You. 122p. 1992. pap. 14.95 (0-9633029-0-6) Marshall MD.

Marshall, C. B., jt. auth. see McIntosh, I. G.

Marshall, C. Edmund. The Physical Chemistry & Mineralogy of Soils: Soils in Place, Vol. II. LC 64-20074. 330p. 1977. 45.50 (0-471-02957-2, Wiley-Interscience) Krieger.

— The Physical Chemistry & Mineralogy of Soils: Volume 1: Soil Materials. LC 75-22180. 398p. 1975. reprint ed. 32.50 (0-88275-351-7) Krieger.

Marshall, Carol, tr. see Comte, Philippe.

Marshall, Carol, tr. see LeClezio, J. M.

Marshall, Caroline, jt. ed. see Cheuse, Alan.

Marshall, Catherine. Adventures in Prayer. 1987. mass mkt. 4.95 (0-345-34755-2) Ballantine.

— Adventures in Prayer. LC 75-15720. 112p. 1985. pap. 6.99 (0-8007-9105-3) Chosen Bks.

— Algo Mas. 171p. 1981. 5.95 (0-88113-001-X) Edit Betania.

— The Assistant Principal: Leadership Choices & Challenges. 144p. 1991. pap. 18.00 (0-8039-6110-3, D1478) Corwin Pr.

— Aventuras en la Oracion. 192p. 1976. 3.95 (0-88113-005-2) Edit Betania.

— The Best of Catherine Marshall. LeSourd, Leonard E., ed. LC 93-1606. 352p. 1993. 14.99 (0-8007-9209-2) Chosen Bks.

— Beyond Our Selves. (Catherine Marshall Library). 286p. 1994. reprint ed. pap. 8.99 (0-8007-9089-8) Revell.

— Beyond Ourselves. 272p. 1976. mass mkt. 4.99 (0-380-00246-9) Avon.

— Beyond Ourselves. 272p. 1994. pap. 8.00 (0-380-72202-X) Avon.

— The Bridge to Cutter Gap. LC 95-13127. (Christy Juvenile Fiction Ser.: Vol. 1). (J). 1995. pap. write for info. (0-8499-3686-1) Word Pub.

— Catherine Marshall's Story Bible. 200p. (J). (ps-5). 1985. pap. 10.95 (0-380-69961-3) Avon.

— Christy. 1976. mass mkt. 5.99 (0-380-00141-1) Avon.

— Christy. abr. ed. (Illus.). 160p. (J). (gr. 4-7). 1995. 10.99 (0-8007-1708-2) Revell.

— Christy. 1994. reprint ed. lib. bdg. 27.95 (1-56849-309-6) Buccaneer Bks.

— A Closer Walk. LeSourd, Leonard, ed. 251p. 1986. 12.99 (0-8007-9065-0) Chosen Bks.

— A Closer Walk. 224p. 1994. pap. 9.00 (0-380-72378-6) Avon.

— A Closer Walk: A Spiritual Lifeline to God. 224p. 1987. mass mkt. 4.99 (0-380-70390-4) Avon.

— Day by Day with Catherine Marshall. 382p. 1995. 10.99 (0-8007-9234-3) Chosen Bks.

— The Helper. 1979. pap. 3.95 (0-380-45583-8) Avon.

— The Helper. rev. ed. 192p. 1994. pap. 8.00 (0-380-72282-8) Avon.

— The Helper. (Catherine Marshall Library). 240p. 1994. reprint ed. pap. 9.99 (0-8007-9131-2) Revell.

— Inspirational Writings of Catherine Marshall. 1990. 12.98 (0-88486-025-6) Arrowood Pr.

— Inspirational Writings of Catherine Marshall. 1991. 12.98 (0-88486-048-5, Inspirational Pr) Arrowood Pr.

— Irish Art Masterpieces. 1995. 35.00 (0-88363-295-0) H L Levin.

— Julie. 448p. 1985. mass mkt. 5.99 (0-380-69891-9) Avon.

— Light in My Darkest Night. 1990. mass mkt. 4.99 (0-380-71023-4) Avon.

— Light in My Darkest Night. 256p. 1994. pap. 9.00 (0-380-72379-4) Avon.

— Light in My Darkest Night. 1989. 12.99 (0-8007-9146-0) Chosen Bks.

— Light in My Darkest Night. large type ed. 338p. 1991. text ed. 18.95 (0-8161-5247-0) G K Hall.

— Man Called Peter. 1976. mass mkt. 4.95 (0-380-00894-7) Avon.

— A Man Called Peter. 352p. 1994. pap. 8.00 (0-380-72204-6) Avon.

— A Man Called Peter: The Story of Peter Marshall. (Catherine Marshall Library). 288p. 1995. reprint ed. pap. 11.99 (0-8007-9230-0) Chosen Bks.

— Meeting God at Every Turn. large type ed. LC 80-28757. 447p. 1980. pap. 9.99 (0-8007-5335-6) Revell.

— Meeting God at Every Turn: A Spiritual Autobiography. (Catherine Marshall Library). (Illus.). 256p. 1995. pap. 9.99 (0-8007-9231-9) Chosen Bks.

— Midnight Rescue. LC 95-13160. (Christy Juvenile Fiction Ser.: Vol. 4). (J). 1995. pap. write for info. (0-8499-3689-6) Word Pub.

— Mr. Jones, Meet the Master. 1949. 8.99 (0-8007-5095-0) Revell.

— Personal Prayer Journal. 304p. 1988. 12.99 (0-8007-9135-5) Chosen Bks.

— Silent Superstitions. LC 95-13126. (Christy Juvenile Fiction Ser.: Vol. 2). (J). 1995. pap. write for info. (0-8499-3687-X) Word Pub.

— Something More. 1976. mass mkt. 4.50 (0-380-00601-4) Avon.

— Something More. rev. ed. 288p. 1994. pap. 8.00 (0-380-72203-8) Avon.

— To Live Again. 1976. mass mkt. 4.95 (0-380-01586-2) Avon.

— To Live Again. 336p. 1994. pap. 8.00 (0-380-72236-4) Avon.

— To Live Again. LC 57-13338. 335p. 1984. pap. 8.99 (0-8007-9156-8) Chosen Bks.

— The Unsung Role of the Career Assistant Principal. 68p. (Orig.). (C). 1993. pap. text ed. 8.00 (0-88210-272-9) Natl Assn Student.

Marshall, Catherine, ed. The Best of Peter Marshall. LC 83-7341. 340p. 1988. reprint ed. pap. 11.99 (0-8007-9123-1) Chosen Bks.

— The New Politics of Race & Gender: The 1992 Yearbook of the Politics of Education Association. (Education Policy Perspectives Ser.). 230p. 1993. 65.00 (0-7507-0176-5, Falmer Pr) Taylor & Francis.

— Research Dilemmas in Administration & Policy Settings. (Special Issues of the Anthropology & Education Quarterly Ser.: Vol. 15, No. 3). 1984. 7.50 (0-317-66345-3) Am Anthro Assn.

***Marshall, Catherine & Kasten, Katherine L.** The Administrative Career: A Casebook on Entry, Equity, & Endurance. (Illus.). 160p. 1994. 38.00 (0-8039-6088-3); pap. 18.00 (0-8039-6089-1) Corwin Pr.

Marshall, Catherine & Le Sourd, Leonard. My Personal Prayer Diary. (Epiphany Bks.). 1982. pap. 3.95 (0-345-30612-0) Ballantine.

Marshall, Catherine & Rossman, Gretchen B. Designing Qualitative Research. 172p. (C). 1989. text ed. 39.95 (0-8039-3157-3); pap. text ed. 17.95 (0-8039-3158-1) Sage.

— Designing Qualitative Research. 2nd ed. 188p. 1994. 39.95 (0-8039-5248-1); pap. 17.95 (0-8039-5249-X) Sage.

Marshall, Catherine, et al. Culture & Education Policy in the American States. 230p. 1989. 65.00 (1-85000-502-8, Falmer Pr); pap. 31.00 (1-85000-503-6, Falmer Pr) Taylor & Francis.

Marshall, Celia B. A Guide Through the New Testament. LC 93-45517. 176p. (Orig.). 1994. pap. 15.99 (0-664-25484-5) Westminster John Knox.

— A Guide Through the Old Testament. 120p. (Orig.). 1989. pap. 14.99 (0-8042-0124-2) Westminster John Knox.

Marshall, Charles. Planet of the Apes: Monkey Planet. 120p. (Orig.). 1991. pap. 9.95 (0-944735-89-4) Malibu Graphics.

Marshall, Charles B. The Exercise of Sovereignty: Papers on Foreign Policy. LC 65-11665. 296p. reprint ed. pap. 84.40 (0-317-28783-4, 2020546) Bks Demand.

— The Limits of Foreign Policy. enl. ed. LC 88-94. 162p. (Orig.). (C). 1988. reprint ed. pap. text ed. 18.00 (0-8191-6815-7) U Pr of Amer.

Marshall, Charles F. Discovering the Rommel Murder: Life & Death of the Desert Fox. (Illus.). 288p. 1994. 18.95 (0-8117-1480-2) Stackpole.

Marshall, Charles W. Vitamins & Minerals: Help or Harm. 206p. 1985. text ed. 11.95 (0-397-53060-9) Lippincott.

Marshall, Charlotte. Historic Houses of Athens. 64p. 1988. 10.00 (0-935265-15-5) Agee Pub.

***Marshall, Chester W. & Thompson, Warren.** Final Assault on the Rising Sun: Combat Diaries of B-29 Air Crews over Japan. (Illus.). 225p. 1995. 29.95 (0-933424-59-0) Specialty Pr.

Marshall, Chester. B-29 Superfortress. LC 93-24759. (Motorbooks International Warbird History Ser.). 1993. 24.95 (0-87938-785-8) Motorbooks Intl.

An Asterisk (*) at the beginning of an entry indicates that the title is appearing in BIP for the first time.

— Sky Giants over Japan. (Illus.). 214p. (Orig.). 1984. pap. 12.95 (*0-942397-15-0*) Buckeye Aviat Bk.
— Sky Giants over Japan. (Illus.). 220p. (Orig.). 1984. 12.95 (*0-9615206-0-4*) Global Press.
Marshall, Chester, ed. The Global Twentieth, Vol. II. (Anthology of Twentieth Air Force in World War II Ser.). (Illus.). 300p. 1987. 17.95 (*0-9615206-4-7*) Global Press.
Marshall, Chester & Silvester, Lindsey, eds. The Global Twentieth. (Anthology of Twentieth Air Force in World War II Ser.: Vol. III). (Illus.). 400p. 1988. 19.95 (*0-9615206-6-3*) Global Press.
Marshall, Chris. April Calls: The Sailing Adventure of a Lifetime. 144p. (Orig.). 1993. pap. 9.95 (*0-9637347-3-3*) C W Pub.
— I Ching: The Ancient Book of Chinese Wisdom for Divining the Future. LC 94-36523. 1995. pap. 20.00 (*0-684-80180-9*) S&S Trade.
— Life Assurance & Pensions Handbook: Taxbriefs. 4th ed. (C). 1988. 250.00 (*0-685-45046-5*, Pub. by Witherby & Co UK) St Mut.
Marshall, Christopher. Faith As a Theme in Mark's Narrative. (Society for New Testament Studies Monographs: No. 64). (C). 1989. 69.95 (*0-521-36507-4*) Cambridge U Pr.
— Physical Basis of Computed Tomography. 171p. 1982. 37.50 (*0-87527-314-9*) Green.
— Warfare in the Latin East, 1192-1291. 320p. (C). 1992. 59.95 (*0-521-39428-7*) Cambridge U Pr.
— Warfare in the Latin East, 1192-1291. (Studies in Medieval Life & Thought: No. 17). (Illus.). 308p. (C). 1994. pap. 22.95 (*0-521-47742-5*) Cambridge U Pr.
Marshall, Christopher D. & Duane, William, eds. Extracts from the Diary of Christopher Marshall Kept in Philadelphia & Lancaster, During the American Revolution. LC 77-79944. (Eyewitness Accounts of the American Revolution Ser., No. 1). 1969. reprint ed. 20.95 (*0-405-01162-8*) Ayer.
Marshall, Claudia E., jt. ed. see George, William R.
Marshall, Clifford & Solomon, Stephen S. Canadian Mortgage Payments. 2nd ed. 320p. 1993. pap. 8.95 (*0-8120-1617-3*) Barron.
Marshall, Connie. The Expectant Father: Helping the Father-to-Be Understand & Become a Part of the Pregnancy Experience. (Illus.). 180p. (Orig.). 1992. pap. 10.95 (*1-55958-219-7*) Prima Pub.
Marshall, Connie C. From Here to Maternity. 212p. 1986. pap. 9.95 (*0-9613784-1-7*) Conmar Pub.
— From Here to Maternity: Your Guide for the Nine-Month Journey Toward Motherhood. (Illus.). 225p. (Orig.). 1991. pap. 9.95 (*1-55958-077-1*) Prima Pub.
Marshall County Backboard Club Staff. Lady Marshalls, 1980-1990: The Decade of Howard Beth. LC 90-71725. 112p. 1990. 24.95 (*1-56311-016-4*) Turner Pub KY.
Marshall, Cynthia. Last Things & Last Plays: Shakespearean Eschatology. LC 90-9883. 176p. (C). 1991. 24.50 (*0-8093-1689-7*) S Ill U Pr.
Marshall, Cynthia, ed. Essays on C. S. Lewis & George MacDonald: Truth, Fiction, & the Power of Imagination. LC 90-21371. (Studies in British Literature: Vol. 11). 122p. 1991. lib. bdg. 59.95 (*0-88946-494-4*) E Mellen.
Marshall, D. & Tipton, Keith F., eds. Essays in Biochemistry, Vol. 23. (Serial Publication Ser.). 154p. 1988. pap. text ed. 49.00 (*0-12-158123-3*) Acad Pr.
Marshall, D. Bruce. The French Colonial Myth & Constitution-Making in the Fourth Republic. LC 71-99833. 376p. reprint ed. pap. 107.20 (*0-317-29281-1*, 2022019) Bks Demand.
Marshall, D. J. Cathodo-luminescence of Geological Materials. (Illus.). 128p. 1987. text ed. 125.00 (*0-04-552026-7*) Routledge Chapman & Hall.
— A Little Duck's Christmas Wish. (J). 1992. 6.95 (*0-533-08777-5*) Vantage.
Marshall, D. N. History of Libraries: Ancient & Mediaeval. 1986. 15.00 (*0-317-47434-0*, Pub. by Oxford IBH II) S Asia.
Marshall, Dale & Montgomery, Roger, eds. Housing Policy for the Eighties. (C). 1979. pap. 12.00 (*0-918592-36-4*) Pol Studies.
Marshall, Dale R., jt. ed. see Leonard, David K.
Marshall, Dale R., et al. Minority Perspectives: Papers. LC 78-186473. (Governance of Metropolitan Regions Ser.: No. 2). 76p. reprint ed. pap. 25.00 (*0-7837-3042-X*, 2023820) Bks Demand.
Marshall, Daniel, jt. ed. see Gregory, Judith.
Marshall, Daniel P., et al. Staying Healthy Without Medicine: A Manual of Home Prevention & Treatment. LC 83-2297. (Illus.). 312p. 1983. lib. bdg. 36.95 (*0-88229-635-3*) Nelson-Hall.
Marshall, Darrel R., jt. auth. see Strother, Judy A.
Marshall, David. The Figure of Theater: Shaftesbury, Defoe, Adam Smith, & George Eliot. 288p. 1986. text ed. 42.00 (*0-231-06084-X*) Col U Pr.
— Food. Young, Richard, ed. LC 91-20535. (First Technology Library). (Illus.). 32p. (J). (gr. 3-5). 1991. lib. bdg. 15.93 (*1-56074-011-6*) Garrett Ed Corp.
— The Surprising Effects of Sympathy: Marivaux, Diderot, Rousseau, & Mary Shelley. (Illus.). x, 286p. 1988. 27.50 (*0-226-50710-6*) U Ch Pr.
— Survey of Accounting: What the Numbers Mean. 2nd ed. 320p. (C). 1992. student ed, text ed. 23.95 (*0-256-11328-9*) Irwin.
Marshall, David, jt. auth. see Walker, Jane.
Marshall, David B. Secularizing the Faith: Canadian Protestant Clergy & the Crisis of Belief, 1850-1940. (Illus.). 288p. 1992. 55.00 (*0-8020-5938-4*); pap. 19.95 (*0-8020-6879-0*) U of Toronto Pr.
Marshall, David F., ed. Language Planning: Focusschrift in Honor of Joshua A. Fishman on the Occasion of His 65th Birthday, Vol. 3. LC 91-698. vii, 360p. 1991. 94.00x (*1-55619-118-9*) Benjamins North Am.
Marshall, David H. A Survey of Accounting: What the Numbers Mean. 2nd ed. LC 92-16798. 640p. (C). 1992. text ed. 65.95 (*0-256-11301-7*) Irwin.
Marshall, Deborah A., jt. auth. see Crispin, A. C.
Marshall, Don. Who Discovered the Straits of Juan de Fuca? 27p. 1991. pap. 6.95 (*0-87770-493-7*) Ye Galleon.
Marshall, Don B. Oregon Shipwrecks. LC 84-71477. (Illus.). 250p. 1984. 24.95 (*0-8323-0430-1*) Binford Mort.
Marshall, Don C., et al. Programmed Guide to Tax Research. 5th ed. LC 92-8445. (C). 1992. text ed. 36.95 (*0-538-82546-4*, AG70EA) S-W Pub.
Marshall, Don R. Successful Techniques for Solving Employees Compensation Problems. LC 77-17964. (Illus.). 212p. reprint ed. pap. 60.50 (*0-317-09588-9*, 2020189) Bks Demand.
Marshall, Donald G. Contemporary Critical Theory: A Selective Bibliography. LC 92-33515. 260p. 1993. text ed. 32.00 (*0-87352-963-4*, T126C); pap. text ed. 15.50 (*0-87352-964-2*, T126P) Modern Lang.
Marshall, Donald G., ed. see Gadamer, Hans-Georg.
Marshall, Donald R. The Enchantress of Crumbledown. LC 90-81830. 229p. (J). (gr. 3-6). 1990. 9.95 (*0-87579-352-5*) Deseret Bk.
Marshall, Dorothy. English People in the Eighteenth Century. LC 80-16871. (Illus.). xvi, 288p. 1980. reprint ed. text ed. 38.50 (*0-313-21080-2*, MAENP, Greenwood Pr) Greenwood.
— The Life & Times of Victoria. 224p. 1992. 24.95 (*1-55859-450-7*) Abbeville Pr.
Marshall, Duncan L. Dividend Potentials: A Productive Determinant for Investment Decision, 1990 Edition. 2nd ed. (Illus.). 68p. (Orig.). 1990. pap. text ed. 25.00 (*0-9626505-1-X*) D Marshall Pub.
Marshall, E. A., jt. auth. see Oliver, M. C.
Marshall, Ed & Lincoln Beta Club Staff. The Way It Is (un-RUSH-ed) Kyle, Jillian, ed. (Illus.). 120p. (Orig.). 1993. pap. 8.95 (*0-938041-15-0*) Arc Pr AR.
***Marshall Editions Staff.** Atlas of Dream Places. 1995. 39.95 (*0-528-83774-5*) Rand McNally.
— Vietnam: The Decisive Battles. (Illus.). 200p. 1990. text ed. 39.95 (*0-02-580171-6*) Macmillan.
Marshall, Edmund. Business & Society. LC 92-32042. (Elements of Business Ser.). 1993. write for info. (*0-415-06849-5*); pap. 26.00 (*0-415-06850-9*, B0109) Routledge.
Marshall, Edna M. Evaluation of Types of Student-Teaching. LC 73-177054. (Columbia University. Teachers College. Contributions to Education Ser.: No. 488). reprint ed. 37.50 (*0-404-55488-1*) AMS Pr.
Marshall, Edward. Four on the Shore. LC 84-1708. (Easy-to-Read Bks.). (Illus.). 48p. (J). (ps-3). 1985. 9.95 (*0-8037-0155-1*) Dial Bks Young.
— Four on the Shore. (Easy-to-Read Ser.: Level 3). (Illus.). (J). (gr. 1-4). 1994. pap. 3.25 (*0-14-037006-4*) Puffin Bks.
— Fox All Week. LC 84-1708. (Easy-to-Read Bks.). (Illus.). (J). (ps-3). 1984. 10.95 (*0-8037-0062-8*) Dial Bks Young.
— Fox All Week. LC 84-1708. (Easy-to-Read Paperback Ser.). (Illus.). 48p. (J). (ps-3). 1987. pap. 4.95 (*0-8037-0008-3*) Dial Bks Young.
— Fox All Week. (Easy-to-Read Program, Level 3 (Yellow) Ser.). (Illus.). 32p. (J). (gr. 1-4). 1995. 3.50 (*0-14-037708-5*) Puffin Bks.
— Fox & His Friends. LC 81-68769. (Easy-to-Read Bks.). 56p. (J). (ps-3). 1982. pap. 4.95 (*0-8037-2668-6*) Dial Bks Young.
— Fox & His Friends. (J). (ps-3). 1993. pap. 4.99 (*0-14-036188-X*) Puffin Bks.
— Fox & His Friends. (Easy-to-Read Ser.: Level 3). (Illus.). (J). (gr. 1-4). 1994. pap. 3.25 (*0-14-037007-2*) Puffin Bks.
— Fox at School. LC 82-45506. (Easy-to-Read Bks.). (Illus.). 48p. (J). (ps-3). 1983. lib. bdg. 9.89 (*0-8037-2675-9*); pap. 4.95 (*0-8037-2674-0*) Dial Bks Young.
— Fox at School. LC 93-2721. (Easy-to-Read Ser.: Level 3). (Illus.). (J). (gr. 1-4). 1993. reprint ed. pap. 3.25 (*0-14-036544-3*, Puffin) Puffin Bks.
— Fox in Love. LC 82-70190. (Easy-to-Read Bks.). (Illus.). 56p. (J). (ps-3). 1982. lib. bdg. 10.89 (*0-8037-2433-0*) Dial Bks Young.
— Fox on Wheels. LC 83-5254. (Easy-to-Read Bks.). (Illus.). 48p. (J). (ps-3). 1983. lib. bdg. 12.89 (*0-8037-0002-4*) Dial Bks Young.
— Fox on Wheels. (Easy-to-Read Ser.: Level 3). (Illus.). (J). (gr. 1-4). 1993. pap. 3.25 (*0-14-036541-9*, Puffin) Puffin Bks.
— La Pandilla en la Orilla - Four on the Shore. (Illus.). 52p. (SPA.). (J). (gr. 2-4). 1990. pap. write for info. (*84-204-4678-5*) Santillana.
— Space Case. LC 80-13369. (Illus.). 32p. (J). (ps-3). 1980. 14.99 (*0-8037-8005-2*); lib. bdg. 12.89 (*0-8037-8007-9*) Dial Bks Young.
— Space Case. (Pied Piper Bks.). (Illus.). 40p. (J). (gr. k-3). 1982. pap. 4.99 (*0-8037-8431-7*) Dial Bks Young.
— Three by the Sea. (Easy-to-Read Bks.). (Illus.). 48p. (J). (ps-3). 1981. lib. bdg. 12.89 (*0-8037-8687-5*) Dial Bks Young.
— Three by the Sea. (Easy-to-Read Ser.: Level 2). (Illus.). (J). (gr. k-3). 1994. pap. 3.25 (*0-14-037004-8*) Puffin Bks.
— Troll Country. LC 79-19324. (Easy-to-Read Bks.). (Illus.). 56p. (J). (ps-3). 1980. pap. 4.95 (*0-8037-6210-0*) Dial Bks Young.
***Marshall, Edward M.** Jump-Starting America: The Grass-Roots Revolution. Talcott, Margaret & Marshall, Jeff, eds. LC 94-96698. (Illus.). 264p. 1995. 17.95 (*0-9643618-0-9*) Grass-Rts.
— Transforming the Way We Work: The Power of the Collaborative Workplace. 1995. 22.95 (*0-8144-0255-0*) AMACOM.
Marshall, Edwin C., jt. auth. see Newcomb, Robert D.
Marshall, Eileen & Robinson, Colin. The Economics of Energy Self-Sufficiency: British Institute's Joint Energy Policy Programme; Energy Papers, No. 14. 149p. 1984. text ed. 52.95 (*0-435-84518-7*) Ashgate Pub Co.
Marshall, Eldon K., et al, eds. Interpersonal Helping Skills. LC 82-17275. (Jossey-Bass Social & Behavioral Science Ser.). (Illus.). 704p. reprint ed. pap. 180.00 (*0-8357-4907-X*, 2037837) Bks Demand.
Marshall, Eleanor & Carter, Anjean. Child Watch: New York City - Looking Out for America's Children. LC 85-105275. 30p. 1983. 5.00 (*0-88156-012-X*) Comm Serv Soc NY.
Marshall, Eliot. Legalization: A Debate. (Encyclopedia of Psychoactive Drugs Ser.: No. 2). (Illus.). 128p. (J). (gr. 5 up). 1988. lib. bdg. 19.95 (*1-55546-229-4*) Chelsea Hse.
Marshall, Eliot & Finn, Jeffrey. Medical Ethics. (Medical Issues Ser.). (Illus.). 128p. (YA). (gr. 6-12). 1990. 18.95 (*0-7910-0086-9*) Chelsea Hse.
Marshall, Elva, ed. see Resla, W. J.
Marshall, Eric & Hansen, Julie, eds. Children's Letters to God: The New Collection. LC 90-21211. (Illus.). 96p. (Orig.). 1991. pap. 6.95 (*0-89480-999-7*, 1999) Workman Pub.
Marshall, Evan P. & Sanow, Edwin J. Handgun Stopping Power: The Definitive Study. (Illus.). 240p. 1992. text ed. 39.95 (*0-87364-653-3*) Paladin Pr.
Marshall, F. Ray. Labor in the South. LC 67-22870. (Wertheim Publications in Industrial Relations). 420p. 1967. 29.95 (*0-674-50700-2*) HUP.
Marshall, F. Ray & Briggs, Vernon M., Jr. Equal Apprenticeship Opportunities: The Nature of the Issue & the New York Experience. LC 68-66987. (Policy Papers in Human Resources & Industrial Relations Ser.: No. 10). (Orig.). 1968. pap. 5.00 (*0-87736-110-X*) U of Mich Inst Labor.
— The Negro & Apprenticeship. LC 67-18561. 297p. reprint ed. pap. 84.70 (*0-317-39698-6*, 2023109) Bks Demand.
Marshall, F. Ray & Godwin, Lamond. Cooperatives & Rural Poverty in the South. LC 70-135534. (Policy Studies in Employment & Welfare: No. 7). 108p. reprint ed. pap. 30.80 (*0-317-19924-2*, 2023124) Bks Demand.
Marshall, Fiona. Losing a Parent. LC 93-36599. 168p. 1993. pap. 12.95 (*1-55561-056-0*) Fisher Bks.
Marshall, Florence. Life & Letters of Mary Wollstonecraft Shelley, 2 vols., Set. LC 70-115181. (Studies in Shelley: No. 25). 1970. reprint ed. lib. bdg. 99.95 (*0-8383-1011-7*) M S G Haskell Hse.
Marshall, Francine, jt. ed. see Gifford, Diane P.
Marshall, Francis. The Battle of Gettysburg. 337p. 1987. reprint ed. 30.00 (*0-942211-26-X*) Olde Soldier Bks.
Marshall, Frank, photos. Ladies & Gentle Men: Women Sharing with Women about the Art of Relating to Men. (Illus.). 134p. (Orig.). 1992. pap. 14.00 (*0-9634341-0-1*) Orphan Pr.
Marshall, Fray F. Cryptorchidism & Related Anomalies. Elder, Jack S., ed. LC 82-11302. 128p. 1982. text ed. 55.00 (*0-275-91374-0*, C1374, Praeger Pubs) Greenwood.
Marshall, G., ed. FLAX: Breeding & Utilisation: Proceedings of the EEC Flax Workshop Held in Brussels, Belgium, 4-5 May, 1988. (Advances in Agricultural Biotechnology Ser.). (C). 1988. lib. bdg. 71.50 (*0-7923-0065-3*) Kluwer Ac.
Marshall, G. A. Coleoptera - Rhynchophora - Curculionidae. (Fauna of British India Ser.). xvi, 370p. 1977. reprint ed. 30.00 (*0-88065-154-7*, Messers Today & Tomorrow) Scholarly Pubns.
Marshall, G. F., jt. auth. see Beiser, Leo.
Marshall, G. I., jt. auth. see Hanneman, L. J.
Marshall, Gail. The Challenge of Change: Questions & Resources for Computer-Using Educators. 129p. 1993. pap. text ed. 23.95 (*1-56484-030-1*) Intl Society Tech Educ.
Marshall, Garry. Students' Guide to Expert Systems. (Heinemann Newnes Informatics Ser.). (Illus.). 200p. 1990. pap. 24.95 (*0-434-91306-5*) Buttrwrth-Heinemann.
***Marshall, Garry & Marshall, Lori.** Wake Me When It's Funny: How to Break into Show Business & Stay There. LC 95-6630. 1995. write for info. (*1-55850-526-1*) Adams Pubng.
Marshall, Gene W. A Primer on Radical Christianity. LC 85-71566. 231p. 1985. pap. 10.00 (*0-9611552-1-3*) Realistic Living.
— To Be or Not to Be a Christian: Meditations & Essays on Authentic Christian Community. LC 94-65447. (Illus.). 336p. (Orig.). 1994. pap. 15.00 (*0-9611552-3-X*) Realistic Living.
Marshall, Gene W., jt. auth. see Marshall, Joyce.
Marshall, Geoffrey. Constitutional Conventions: The Rules & Forms of Political Accountability. 259p. 1987. pap. 19.95 (*0-19-876202-X*) OUP.
Marshall, Geoffrey, ed. Ministerial Responsibility. (Oxford Readings in Politics & Government Ser.). 186p. 1989. 39.95 (*0-19-827580-3*); pap. 14.95 (*0-19-827579-X*) OUP.
Marshall, George. Facing Death & Grief. LC 80-84402. (Library of Liberal Religion). 200p. 1981. 25.95x (*0-87975-140-1*); pap. 19.95 (*0-87975-169-X*) Prometheus Bks.
— Spirit of '69: A Skinhead Bible. (Illus.). 168p. (Orig.). 1991. pap. 19.95 (*0-9518497-0-0*, Pub. by S T Pubng UK) AK Pr Dist.
— Total Madness. (Illus.). (Orig.). 1993. pap. 19.95 (*0-9518497-4-3*, Pub. by S T Pubng UK) AK Pr Dist.
— The Two Tone Story. (Illus.). 111p. (Orig.). 1993. pap. 12.95 (*0-9518497-3-5*, Pub. by S T Pubng UK) AK Pr Dist.
Marshall, George & Poling, David. Albert Schweitzer: A Biography. 1990. 4.00 (*0-317-02831-6*) Albert Schweitzer.
— Schweitzer: A Biography. (Illus.). 346p. 1989. pap. 5.00 (*0-89129-020-6*) Albert Schweitzer.
— Schweitzer: A Biography. rev. ed. (Illus.). 346p. 1991. pap. text ed. 4.00 (*1-881815-26-9*) Albert Schweitzer.
Marshall, George, ed. see Marshall, Robert.
Marshall, George C. General Marshall's Victory Report on the Winning of World War II in Europe & the Pacific. (Illus.). 140p. 1989. reprint ed. 15.95 (*0-9624874-0-6*) A A Meverden.
— Marshall's Mission to China: December 1945 to January 1947, 2 vols., Vol. I: The Report. Van Slyke, Lyman P., ed. LC 76-43634. 465p. 1976. text ed. 65.00 (*0-313-26910-6*, U6910) Greenwood.
— Marshall's Mission to China: December 1945 to January 1947, 2 vols., Vol. 2. Van Slyke, Lyman P., ed. LC 76-43634. 522p. 1976. Vol. II: Appended Documents. text ed. 65.00 (*0-313-26911-4*, U6911) Greenwood.
— The Papers of George Catlett Marshall, Vol. 3: "The Right Man for the Job," December 7, 1941-May 31, 1943. Bland, Larry I. & Stevens, Sharon R., eds. (Illus.). 800p. 1991. text ed. 55.00x (*0-8018-2967-4*) Johns Hopkins.
— Selected Speeches & Statements of General of the Army George C. Marshall. DeWeerd, H. A., ed. LC 72-10365. (FDR & the Era of the New Deal Ser.). 1973. reprint ed. lib. bdg. 37.50 (*0-306-70556-7*) Da Capo.
Marshall, George N. A. Powell Davies & His Times. Wolff, Kathy, ed. 263p. 1990. 17.00 (*1-55896-172-0*, Skinner Hse Bks) Unitarian Univ.
— Buddha: His Quest for Serenity: A Biography. rev. ed. 264p. 1990. 29.95 (*0-87047-048-5*); pap. 15.95 (*0-87047-049-3*) Schenkman Bks Inc.
— Challenge of a Liberal Faith. 3rd ed. 224p. (Orig.). 1993. pap. 14.00 (*0-933840-31-4*, Skinner Hse Bks) Unitarian Univ.
Marshall, George R. & Friedman, Ken. The Manager's Guide to Desktop Electronic Publishing. (Illus.). 336p. 1991. 27.95 (*0-13-168584-8*) P-H.
Marshall, Gerald F., ed. Optical Scanning. (Optical Engineering Ser.: Vol. 31). 896p. 1991. 190.00 (*0-8247-8473-1*) Dekker.
Marshall, Gilbert. Safety Engineering. LC 94-10722. 1994. 29.95 (*0-939874-99-7*) ASSE.
Marshall, Gloria P. How to Be a Faerie Grandmother: A New Image for the 21st Century. LC 89-81010. (Illus.). 135p. (Orig.). 1990. pap. text ed. 8.95 (*1-878323-00-8*) Acronym Bks.
— Mimosa: A French Country Mystery. 242p. 1994. pap. 8.95 (*1-56901-147-8*) NW Pub.
Marshall, Gordian, ed. see Blue, Lionel.
Marshall, Gordian, jt. auth. see Hilton, Michael.
Marshall, Gordon. In Praise of Sociology. (Illus.). 274p. (C). 1990. text ed. 55.00 (*0-04-445687-5*) Routledge Chapman & Hall.
— In Search of the Spirit of Capitalism: An Essay on Max Weber's Protestant Ethic Thesis. (Modern Revivals in Sociology Ser.). 236p. 1993. 59.95 (*0-7512-0201-0*, Pub. by Gregg Revivals UK) Ashgate Pub Co.
— In Search of the Spirit of Capitalism: An Essay on Max Weber's Protestant Ethic Thesis. LC 81-18053. 233p. 1982. text ed. 42.00 (*0-231-05498-X*) Col U Pr.
— Presbyteries & Profits: Calvinism & the Development of Capitalism in Scotland, 1560 - 1707. 416p. 1992. pap. 25.00 (*0-7486-0333-6*, Pub. by Edinburgh U Pr UK) Col U Pr.
Marshall, Gordon, ed. The Concise Oxford Dictionary of Sociology. LC 93-37140. (Paperback Reference Ser.). (Illus.). 592p. (C). 1994. pap. 13.95 (*0-19-285237-X*) OUP.
Marshall, Gordon, et al. Social Class in Modern Britain. 336p. 1989. 49.95 (*0-09-167940-0*); pap. 19.95 (*0-04-445416-3*) Routledge Chapman & Hall.
Marshall-Graves, Jennifer A. & Sinclair, Andrew H. Mammalian Sex Chromosomes: An Evolutionary Perspective. (Molecular Biology Intelligence Unit Ser.). 118p. 1994. 89.95 (*1-879702-75-4*, LN0275) R G Landes.
Marshall, H. Diseases of Plants. 200p. 1991. 100.00 (*81-7158-246-X*, Pub. by Scientific Pubs II) St Mut.
Marshall, H., ed. see Mander, R. & Mitchinson, J.
Marshall, H. G. & Sorrells, M. E., eds. Oat Science & Technology. LC 92-19551. (Agronomy Ser.: No. 33). 1992. 48.00 (*0-89118-110-5*) Am Soc Agron.
Marshall, H. H. From Dependence to Statehood in Commonwealth Africa: Selected Documents, World War I to Independence, 2 vols., Set. LC 80-10407. 1982. lib. bdg. 150.00 (*0-379-20348-0*) Oceana.
— Like Father Like Son. 1981. 25.00 (*0-7223-1374-8*, Pub. by A H S Ltd UK) St Mut.
Marshall, Harry I. The Karen People of Burma: A Study in Anthropology & Ethnology. LC 77-87046. reprint ed. 47.50 (*0-404-16843-4*) AMS Pr.
Marshall, Helen E. Mary Adelaide Nutting: Pioneer of Modern Nursing. LC 72-174557. (Illus.). 396p. 1972. 49.50 (*0-8018-1365-4*) Johns Hopkins.
Marshall, Helen L. Bright Laughter-Warm Tears. LC 92-71916. 64p. 1990. reprint ed. pap. 3.95 (*1-881598-01-2*) Marshall Ent.
— A Faith That Smiles. LC 92-71917. Orig. Title: Inspirational Resources for Women's Groups. 64p. 1992. reprint ed. pap. 3.95 (*1-881598-00-4*) Marshall Ent.

— Quiet Power. LC 92-71918. 64p. (Orig.). 1992. reprint ed. pap. 3.95 (*1-881598-02-0*) Marshall Ent.
This book is superb as a gift, especially for those who need the touch of comforting & positive words. QUIET POWER is ideal for hospital patients & for those who have experienced, or now are in the midst of, situations of discouragement, grief or stress. These

An Asterisk (*) at the beginning of an entry indicates that the title is appearing in BIP for the first time.

soothing but challenging words - beautiful, sensitive & sometimes amusing - can bring inspiration & renewed joy to those you love. These reflections ring with the love of God & also prompt new ways of sharing & receiving human love. Some of the 58 inspirational poems include: May His Hand Be On Your Shoulder; A Faith To Live By; Walk The World Proudly; Dare To Be Happy. The inspirational poetry of HELEN LOWRIE MARSHALL has provided joy & comfort to thousands of people for over 40 years. She has gained nation-wide appreciation & acclaim through her books, friendship booklets & gift cards. She wrote many years for Doubleday & Hallmark Cards. Her ability to brighten the lives of others have made her one of America's most popular poets. Other books of poetry by HELEN LOWRIE MARSHALL: A FAITH THAT SMILES, 1-881598-00-4, $3.95; BRIGHT LAUGHTER - WARM TEARS, 1-881598-01-2, $3.95. Books are available from: Marshall Enterprises, 1645 W. Davies Ave., Littleton, CO 80120. (303) 798-7974.
Publisher Provided Annotation.

Marshall, Henry R. Pain, Pleasure & Aesthetics. LC 75-3281. reprint ed. 29.50 (*0-404-59269-4*) AMS Pr.

Marshall, Herbert. Masters of Soviet Cinema: Vsevolod Pudovkin, Dziga Vertov, Alexander Kovzhenko, Sergei Mikhailovich Eisenstein. (Illus.). 280p. 1983. 35.00 (*0-7100-9287-3*, RKP) Routledge.

Marshall, Herbert, ed. Hamlet Through the Ages. LC 70-148888. (Select Bibliographies Reprint Ser.). 1977. reprint ed. 30.95 (*0-8369-5677-X*) Ayer.

Marshall, Herbert & Stock, Mildred. Ira Aldridge: Negro Tragedian. LC 93-12937. Orig. Title: Ira Aldridge, the Negro Tragedian. 1993. 24.95 (*0-88258-150-3*) Howard U Pr.

Marshall, Herbert, tr. see Eisenstein, Sergei M.

Marshall, Herbert, tr. see Eisenstein, Sergei.

Marshall, Hermine H. Redefining Student Learning: Roots of Educational Change. 336p. (C). 1992. text ed. 55.00 (*0-89391-854-7*); pap. text ed. 22.50 (*0-89391-917-9*) Ablex Pub.

Marshall, Howard. Epistle to the Philippians. (Epworth Commentary Ser.). 176p. (Orig.). (C). 1993. pap. 15.95 (*0-7162-0485-1*, Epworth Pr) TPI PA.

Marshall, Howard, jt. ed. see Gasque, W. Ward.

Marshall, Howard W. Folk Architecture in Little Dixie: A Regional Culture in Missouri. LC 80-26064. (Illus.). 160p. 1981. text ed. 25.00 (*0-8262-0329-9*) U of Mo Pr.

— Paradise Valley, Nevada: The People & Buildings of an American Place. LC 94-26968. (Illus.). 165p. 1995. 55.00 (*0-8165-1310-4*) U of Ariz Pr.

Marshall, Howard W. & Ahlborn, Richard E. Buckaroos in Paradise: Cowboy Life in Northern Nevada. LC 81-10500. (Illus.). 112p. reprint ed. pap. 32.00 (*0-7837-6186-4*, 2045908) Bks Demand.

Marshall, Howard W., et al. Now That's a Good Tune: Masters of Traditional Missouri Fiddling. LC 89-50679. (Illus.). 64p. (Orig.). 1989. pap. 15.00 (*0-933842-12-0*) Extension Div.

Marshall, Hubert J. The Church or the Bible? LC 93-91524. 167p. (Orig.). 1993. 9.95 (*0-9636743-4-X*) Marshall Pub.

Marshall, Hugh. Art Directing Photography. (Illus.). 144p. 1989. 27.95 (*0-89134-259-1*, 30162) North Light Bks.

— Orestes Brownson & the American Republic: An Historical Perpective. LC 74-142187. 316p. reprint ed. pap. 90.10 (*0-317-55390-9*, 2029493) Bks Demand.

Marshall, I. H. Composite Structures Five: Proceedings of the Fifth International Conference on Composite Structures, Paisley College of Technology, Scotland, 24-26 July 1989. 902p. 1989. 252.00 (*1-85166-362-2*) Elsevier.

Marshall, I. H., ed. Composite Structures, Vol. 1. (Illus.). xvi, 732p. 1981. 187.25 (*0-85334-988-6*, Pub. by Elsevier Applied Sci UK) Elsevier.

— Composite Structures, Vol. 2. (Illus.). 592p. 1983. 183.75 (*0-85334-229-6*, Pub. by Elsevier Applied Sci UK) Elsevier.

— Composite Structures Six: Proceedings of the 6th International Conference, 9-11 September, 1991, Scotland, U.K. 848p. 1991. 297.50 (*1-85166-647-8*) Elsevier.

— Composite Structures Three: Proceedings of the Third International Conference on Composite Structures September 1985, Paisley, Scotland. (Illus.). 808p. 1985. 216.00 (*0-85334-378-0*, Pub. by Elsevier Applied Sci UK) Elsevier.

— Composite Structures 4, Vol. 1: Analysis & Design Studies: Proceedings of the Fourth International Conference, Paisley Colleg of Technology, Scotland, July 27-29, 1987. 616p. 1987. 180.00 (*1-85166-126-3*, Pub. by Elsevier Applied Sci UK) Elsevier.

— Composite Structures 4, Vol. 2: Damage Assessment & Material Evaluation: Proceedings of the Fourth International Conference, Paisley College of Technology, Scotland, July 27-29, 1987. 446p. 1987. 138.75 (*1-85166-127-1*, Pub. by Elsevier Applied Sci UK) Elsevier.

Marshall, I. H. & Demuts, E., eds. Optimum Design of Composite Structures: Proceedings of an International Workshop Sponsored by the U. S. Air Force & the Paisley College of Technology, Glasgow, Scotland, 27 July 1989. 281p. 1990. reprint ed. 86.50 (*1-85166-502-1*) Elsevier.

— Supportability of Composite Airframes: Proceedings of a Workshop, Sponsored by US Air Force European Office of Aerospace Research & Development, & Paisley College of Technology, Held in Glasgow, Scotland, 3-4 Aug., 1987. 120p. 1989. 54.00 (*1-85166-258-8*) Elsevier.

Marshall, I. H., jt. ed. see Brandt, A. M.

Marshall, I. H., ed. see European Mechanics Colloquium 204 Staff.

Marshall, I. H., jt. ed. see Fridlyander, J. N.

Marshall, I. Haen, jt. ed. see Leuw, Ed.

Marshall, I. Howard. Acts of the Apostles. (Tyndale New Testament Commentaries Ser.). (Orig.). 1980. pap. 9.99 (*0-8028-1423-9*) Eerdmans.

— Las Cartas de Juan. Padilla, C. Rene, ed. (Nueva Creacion Ser.). 320p. (Orig.). (SPA.). (C). 1991. pap. 16.99 (*0-8028-0911-1*) Eerdmans.

— First & Second Thessalonians. (New Century Bible Commentary Ser.). 240p. 1983. pap. 15.99 (*0-8028-1946-X*) Eerdmans.

— First Peter. Osborne, Grant R. et al, eds. LC 90-41306. (IVP New Testament Commentary Ser.). 180p. 1991. 15.99 (*0-8308-1817-0*, 1817) InterVarsity.

— The Gospel of Luke. (New International Greek Testament Commentary Ser.). 1978. 39.99 (*0-8028-3512-0*) Eerdmans.

— Last Supper & Lord's Supper. 191p. 1993. pap. 12.95 (*0-85364-313-X*, Pub. by Paternoster UK) Attic Pr.

— The New International Commentary on the New Testament: The Epistles of John. 1978. 24.99 (*0-8028-2189-8*) Eerdmans.

***Marshall, I. Howard, ed.** New Testament Interpretation: Essays on Principles & Methods. fac. ed. LC 77-9619. 406p. 1977. reprint ed. pap. 115.80 (*0-7837-7962-3*, 2047718) Bks Demand.

Marshall, I. Howard, jt. auth. see Donfried, Karl P.

Marshall, I. Howard, ed. see O'Brien, Peter T.

Marshall, Ian, illus. & text. Armored Ships. 180p. 1993. pap. 28.95 (*0-943231-63-9*) Howell Pr VA.

— Ironclads & Paddlers. 108p. 1993. 34.95 (*0-943231-62-0*) Howell Pr VA.

Marshall, Ian, jt. auth. see Zohar, Danah.

Marshall, Ian H. Armored Ships. Valenzi, Kathleen D., ed. LC 90-81634. (Illus.). 180p. 1990. 39.95 (*0-943231-34-5*) Howell Pr VA.

Marshall, J. A. Archaeological Guide to Taxila. 1987. reprint ed. 95.00 (*81-85046-15-8*, Scientific) St Mut.

Marshall, J. Dan, jt. auth. see Sears, James.

Marshall, J. Dan, jt. ed. see Sears, Jim.

Marshall, J. E. Control of Time-Delay Systems. (IEE Control Engineering Ser.: No. 10). 237p. 1979. boxed 69.00 (*0-906048-12-5*, CE010) Inst Elect Eng.

Marshall, J. E., et al. Integral Performance Criteria for Time-Delay Systems with Applications. 200p. 1993. text ed. 95.00 (*0-13-465923-6*) P-H.

Marshall, J. E., et al, eds. Third IMA Conference on Control Theory. LC 81-67923. 1982. text ed. 190.00 (*0-12-473960-1*) Acad Pr.

Marshall, J. Howard, II. Done in Oil: An Autobiography. LC 94-10098. (Illus.). 1994. 29.95 (*0-89096-533-1*) Tex A&M Univ Pr.

Marshall, J. Lawrence. Lightning Protection. LC 73-4415. (Illus.). 206p. reprint ed. pap. 58.80 (*0-317-10822-0*, 2006311) Bks Demand.

Marshall, J. M., ed. see International School on Condensed Matter Physics Staff.

Marshall, J. N., ed. Services & Uneven Development. (Illus.). 328p. 1988. 72.00 (*0-19-823285-3*) OUP.

Marshall, J. Paxton & De Voursney, Robert M., eds. Virginia Assembly on the Future of the Virginia Environment. 70p. 1986. pap. 8.50 (*0-318-20553-X*) U VA Ctr Pub Serv.

Marshall, J. R., jt. ed. see Fabb, W. E.

Marshall, J. T. Miles Expedition of Eighteen Seventy-Four-Eighteen Seventy-Five: An Eyewitness Account of the Red River Ear. White, Lonnie J., ed. (Narratives of the American West Ser.: Vol. 1). (Illus.). 1971. 20.00 (*0-88426-014-3*) Encino Pr.

— Miles Expedition of 1874-1875: An Eyewitness Account of the Red River War. (American Biography Ser.). 74p. 1991. reprint ed. lib. bdg. 59.00 (*0-7812-8270-5*) Rprt Serv.

Marshall, J. W., jt. auth. see Gillies, David.

Marshall, Jack. Arabian Nights. LC 86-19273. 101p. (Orig.). 1986. pap. 8.95 (*0-918273-28-5*) Coffee Hse.

— Chaos Comics. 32p. (Orig.). 1994. pap. 6.00 (*0-938631-25-X*) Pennywhistle Pr.

— Sesame. (Orig.). 1993. pap. 11.95 (*1-56689-015-2*) Coffee Hse.

Marshall, Jack, jt. ed. see Roberts, Howard.

Marshall, Jacqueline C. & Shepard-Moore, Marie. My Theory of Life A to Z. Incl. Straws Blowing in the Air. 1988. (*0-318-63146-6*); 99p. 1988. 8.95 (*0-318-35389-X*) Shepherd-Moore Ed Foun.

Marshall, Jacquelyn. Fundamental Skills for the Clinical Laboratory Professional Instructor's Guide. 79p. 1993. teacher ed 12.00 (*0-8273-4825-8*) Delmar.

— Microbiology: Clinical Laboratory Manual Ser. LC 93-38266. (Clinical Laboratory Manual Ser.). 160p. 1994. pap. text ed. 19.95 (*0-8273-5363-4*) Delmar.

Marshall, Jacquelyn R. Fundamental Skills for the Clinical Laboratory Professional. LC 92-49234. 698p. 1993. text ed. 32.95 (*0-8273-4823-1*) Delmar.

Marshall, James. The Cut-ups. (Illus.). 32p. (J). (gr. 3-8). 1984. pap. 14.99 (*0-670-25195-X*) Viking Child Bks.

— The Cut-Ups. (Picture Puffins Ser.). (Illus.). 32p. (J). (ps-3). 1986. pap. 4.99 (*0-14-050637-3*, Puffin) Puffin Bks.

— The Cut-ups at Camp Custer. (Illus.). 32p. (J). (ps-3). 1991. pap. 3.99 (*0-14-050817-1*, Puffin) Puffin Bks.

— The Cut-ups at Camp Custer. (Illus.). 32p. (J). (ps-3). 1989. pap. 12.95 (*0-670-82051-2*) Viking Child Bks.

— The Cut-ups Carry On. LC 92-40721. (Illus.). 32p. (J). (ps-3). 1993. pap. 4.99 (*0-14-050726-4*, Puffin) Puffin Bks.

— The Cut-ups Carry On. (Illus.). 32p. (J). (ps-2). 1990. pap. 12.95 (*0-670-81645-0*) Viking Child Bks.

— The Cut-ups Crack Up. (Illus.). 32p. (J). (ps-3). 1992. 14.00 (*0-670-84486-1*) Viking Child Bks.

— The Cut-Ups Crack Up. (Illus.). 32p. (J). (ps-3). 1994. pap. 4.99 (*0-14-055318-5*) Puffin Bks.

— The Cut-ups Cut Loose. (Illus.). 32p. (J). (ps-3). 1989. pap. 4.99 (*0-14-050672-1*, Puffin) Puffin Bks.

— The Cut-ups Cut Loose. (Illus.). 32p. (J). (ps-3). 1987. pap. 12.95 (*0-670-80740-0*) Viking Child Bks.

— Fox Be Nimble. Fogelman, Phyllis J., ed. LC 89-7933. (Easy-to-Read Bks.). (Illus.). 48p. (J). (ps-3). 1990. 12.99 (*0-8037-0760-6*); lib. bdg. 10.89 (*0-8037-0761-4*) Dial Bks Young.

— Fox Be Nimble. (Easy-to-Read Ser.: Level 3 (Yellow)). (Illus.). (J). (gr. 1-4). 1994. pap. 3.25 (*0-14-036842-6*) Puffin Bks.

— Fox in Love. (Easy-to-Read Ser.: Level 3 (Yellow)). (Illus.). (J). (gr. 1-4). 1994. pap. 3.25 (*0-14-036843-4*) Puffin Bks.

— Fox on Stage. LC 91-46740. (Dial Easy-to-Read Ser.). (Illus.). 48p. (J). (ps-3). 1993. 11.99 (*0-8037-1356-8*); lib. bdg. 11.89 (*0-8037-1357-6*) Dial Bks Young.

— Fox on the Job. LC 87-15589. (Easy-to-Read Ser.). (Illus.). 48p. (J). (gr. k-3). 1988. 10.99 (*0-8037-0350-3*); lib. bdg. 9.89 (*0-8037-0351-1*) Dial Bks Young.

— Fox on the Job. (J). 1990. pap. 4.99 (*0-8037-0746-0*, Dial Easy to Read) Puffin Bks.

— Fox Outfoxed. LC 91-21815. (Illus.). 48p. (J). (ps-3). 1992. 11.99 (*0-8037-1036-4*); lib. bdg. 11.89 (*0-8037-1037-2*) Dial Bks Young.

— Freedom to Be Free. LC 68-58804. (Essay Index Reprint Ser.). 1977. 20.95 (*0-8369-1043-5*) Ayer.

— George & Martha. LC 74-184250. (Illus.). 48p. (J). (gr. k-3). 1972. 14.95 (*0-395-16619-5*) HM.

— George & Martha. LC 74-184250. (Illus.). 48p. (J). (gr. k-3). 1974. pap. 4.95 (*0-395-19972-7*, Sandpiper) HM.

— George & Martha. (Book & Cassette Favorites Ser.). (J). (gr. 3 up). 1987. pap. 7.95 (*0-395-45739-4*) HM.

— George & Martha Back in Town. LC 83-22842. (Illus.). 32p. (J). (gr. k-3). 1984. 14.95 (*0-395-35386-6*, 5-90939); pap. 3.95 (*0-685-07886-8*) HM.

— George & Martha Encore. LC 73-5845. (Illus.). 48p. (J). (gr. k-3). 1973. 14.95 (*0-395-17512-7*) HM.

— George & Martha Encore. LC 73-5845. (Illus.). 48p. (J). (gr. k-3). 1977. pap. 5.95 (*0-395-25379-9*) HM.

— George & Martha One Fine Day. (Illus.). 48p. (J). (gr. k-3). 1978. 14.95 (*0-395-27154-1*) HM.

— George & Martha One Fine Day. (Illus.). 48p. (J). (gr. k-3). 1982. pap. 5.95 (*0-395-32921-3*) HM.

— George & Martha Rise & Shine. (Illus.). (J). (gr. k-3). 1976. 14.95 (*0-395-24738-1*) HM.

— George & Martha Rise & Shine. (Illus.). (J). (gr. k-3). 1979. pap. 5.95 (*0-395-28006-0*) HM.

— George & Martha Round & Round. LC 88-14739. (Illus.). 48p. (J). (gr. k-3). 1988. 13.95 (*0-395-46763-2*) HM.

— George & Martha Round & Round. (J). (ps-3). 1991. pap. 5.95 (*0-395-58410-8*) HM.

— George & Martha Tons of Fun. (Illus.). 48p. (J). (gr. k-3). 1980. 14.95 (*0-395-29524-6*) HM.

— George & Martha Tons of Fun. (Illus.). 48p. (J). (gr. k-3). 1986. pap. 5.95 (*0-395-42646-4*) HM.

— Goldilocks & the Three Bears. LC 87-32983. (Illus.). 32p. (J). (ps-3). 1988. 14.99 (*0-8037-0542-5*); lib. bdg. 13.89 (*0-8037-0543-3*) Dial Bks Young.

— Hansel & Gretel. LC 89-26011. (Illus.). 32p. (J). (ps-3). 1990. 12.95 (*0-8037-0827-0*); lib. bdg. 12.89 (*0-8037-0828-9*) Dial Bks Young.

— Hansel & Gretel. (Illus.). 32p. (J). (ps-3). 1994. pap. 4.99 (*0-14-050836-8*, Puff Pied Piper) Puffin Bks.

— Hey Diddle Diddle. (Illus.). 18p. (J). (ps). 1994. 5.95 (*0-374-33061-1*) FS&G.

— James Marshall's Mother Goose. LC 79-2574. (Sunburst Ser.). (Illus.). 40p. (J). (ps-6). 1986. pap. 6.95 (*0-374-43723-8*) FS&G.

— Merry Christmas, Space Case. LC 85-1664. (Illus.). 32p. (J). (ps-3). 1986. 11.95 (*0-8037-0215-9*) Dial Bks Young.

— Merry Christmas, Space Case. (J). 1994. pap. 4.99 (*0-14-054661-8*, Puff Pied Piper) Puffin Bks.

— The Night Before Christmas. (Illus.). (J). 1992. 4.95 (*0-590-45977-5*, Blue Ribbon Bks) Scholastic Inc.

— Old Mother Hubbard & Her Wonderful Dog. (J). (ps-3). 1991. 13.95 (*0-374-35621-1*) FS&G.

— Old Mother Hubbard & Her Wonderful Dog. (J). (ps-3). 1993. pap. 4.95 (*0-374-45611-9*) FS&G.

— Pocketful of Nonsense. (Little Golden Bks.). (Illus.). 24p. (J). (ps-00). 1992. write for info. (*0-307-00140-7*, 312-05, Golden Pr) Western Pub.

— Pocketful of Nonsense. LC 93-18297. (Illus.). 24p. (J). 1993. 12.95 (*0-307-17552-9*, Artsts Writrs) Western Pub.

— Rats on the Range & Other Stories. LC 92-28918. (J). (gr. 1-5). 1993. 12.99 (*0-8037-1384-3*); lib. bdg. 12.89 (*0-8037-1385-1*) Dial Bks Young.

— Rats on the Roof: And Other Stories. LC 90-44084. (Illus.). 80p. (J). (gr. 1-5). 1991. 13.00 (*0-8037-0834-3*); lib. bdg. 12.89 (*0-8037-0835-1*) Dial Bks Young.

— Red Riding Hood. LC 86-16722. (Illus.). 32p. (J). (ps-3). 1987. 14.99 (*0-8037-0344-9*); lib. bdg. 10.89 (*0-8037-0345-7*) Dial Bks Young.

— Red Riding Hood. (J). (ps-3). 1991. pap. 4.95 (*0-8037-1054-2*, Puff Pied Piper) Puffin Bks.

— Red Riding Hood. (J). 1993. pap. 4.99 (*0-14-054693-6*, Puff Pied Piper) Puffin Bks.

— Red Riding Hood. (Illus.). 32p. (J). (ps-3). 1993. pap. 17.99 (*0-14-054976-5*, Puff Pied Piper) Puffin Bks.

— Space Case. (J). 1992. pap. 4.99 (*0-14-054704-5*, Puff Pied Piper) Puffin Bks.

— Speedboat. (J). (ps-3). 1994. pap. 4.95 (*0-395-68977-5*) HM.

— Three up a Tree. LC 86-2163. (Easy-to-Read Bks.). (Illus.). 48p. (J). (ps-3). 1986. 9.95 (*0-8037-0328-7*); lib. bdg. 9.89 (*0-685-13452-0*) Dial Bks Young.

— Three up a Tree. (Puffin Easy-to-Read Level Two Ser.). (Illus.). (J). (gr. k-3). 1994. pap. 3.25 (*0-14-037003-X*) Puffin Bks.

— Tres en un Arbol - Three up a Tree. Baro, Ana B., tr. (Illus.). 48p. (SPA.). (J). (gr. 2-4). 1990. pap. write for info. (*84-204-4637-8*) Santillana.

— Troll Country. (J). 1992. pap. 4.99 (*0-14-036217-7*, Puff Pied Piper) Puffin Bks.

— What's the Matter with Carruthers? LC 72-75607. (Illus.). 32p. (J). (gr. k-3). 1972. 16.95 (*0-395-13895-7*) HM.

— Wings: A Tale of Two Chickens. (J). (ps up). 1988. pap. 4.99 (*0-14-050579-2*, Puffin) Puffin Bks.

— Wings: A Tale of Two Chickens. LC 85-40953. (Viking Kestrel Picture Bks.). (Illus.). 32p. (J). (ps-3). 1986. pap. 14.99 (*0-670-80961-6*) Viking Child Bks.

— Yummers! LC 72-5400. (Illus.). 32p. (J). (gr. k-3). 1973. 14.95 (*0-395-14757-3*) HM.

— Yummers! (Illus.). (J). (gr. 4-8). 1986. pap. 5.95 (*0-395-39590-9*, Sandpiper) HM.

— Yummers Too: The Second Course. (Illus.). 32p. (J). (gr. k-3). 1990. pap. 5.95 (*0-395-53967-6*) HM.

Marshall, James, ed. The Life & Times of Leith. 220p. (C). 1989. text ed. 36.00 (*0-85976-148-7*, Pub. by J Donald); pap. text ed. 26.00 (*0-85976-128-2*, Pub. by J Donald) St Mut.

Marshall, James, illus. Cinderella. 32p. (J). (ps-3). 1992. mass mkt. 4.95 (*0-316-48303-6*) Little.

— The Frog Prince. LC 92-25167. (Hello Reader! Ser.). 32p. (Orig.). (J). (ps-2). 1993. pap. 2.95 (*0-590-46571-6*) Scholastic Inc.

— James Marshall's Mother Goose. LC 79-2574. 40p. (J). (ps-3). 1979. 15.00 (*0-374-33653-9*) FS&G.

Marshall, James, illus. & ret. The Three Little Pigs. LC 88-33411. (J). (ps-3). 1989. 13.99 (*0-8037-0591-3*); lib. bdg. 12.89 (*0-8037-0594-8*) Dial Bks Young.

Marshall, James, jt. auth. see Allard, Harry.

Marshall, James D., jt. auth. see Beach, Richard W.

Marshall, James D., et al. The Language of Interpretation: Patterns of Discourse in Discussions of Literature. 270p. 1994. pap. write for info. (*0-318-72758-7*) NCTE.

— The Language of Interpretation: Patterns of Discourse in Discussions of Literature. 158p. 1995. pap. 19.95 (*0-8141-2709-6*) NCTE.

***Marshall, James H.** Abstracts of the Wills & Administrations of Northampton County, VA 1632-1802. 736p. 1994. 59.50 (*0-89725-163-6*, 1446) Picton Pr.

Marshall, James L. Carbon-Carbon & Carbon-Proton NMR Couplings: Applications to Organic Stereochemistry & Conformational Analysis. LC 82-16117. (Methods in Stereochemical Analysis Ser.: Vol. 2). (Illus.). 241p. 1983. lib. bdg. 80.00 (*0-89573-113-4*) VCH Pubs.

Marshall, James M. Land Fever: Dispossession & the Frontier Myth. LC 86-4030. 248p. 1986. 26.00 (*0-8131-1568-X*) U Pr of Ky.

Marshall, James N. William J. Fellner: A Bio-Bibliography. LC 92-15462. (Bio-Bibliographies in Economics Ser.: No. 1). 192p. 1992. text ed. 55.00 (*0-313-25856-2*, MWF, Greenwood Pr) Greenwood.

Marshall, James R. Shipwrecks of Lake Superior. (Illus.). 100p. (Orig.). 1987. pap. 18.95 (*0-942235-00-2*) LSPC Inc.

Marshall, James S. Noeth Leith Parish Church. 160p. 1993. 40.00 (*0-86153-161-2*, Pub. by St Andrew UK); pap. 21.00 (*0-86153-160-4*, Pub. by St Andrew UK) St Mut.

***Marshall, James V.** A River Ran Out of Eden. 124p. 1987. pap. 3.95 (*0-88741-026-X*) Sundance Pub.

— Walkabout. 1979. pap. 3.00 (*0-435-27062-1*) Heinemann.

— Walkabout. 158p. 1984. pap. 3.95 (*0-88741-099-5*) Sundance Pub.

Marshall, James W. Presbyterian Churches in Alabama 1811-1936: Sketches of Churches, Outposts, & Preaching Points in the Synod of Alabama, Pt. I: Abbeville-Butler, & Megargel. Foreman, Kenneth J., Jr., ed. (Illus.). 519p. (Orig.). 1985. 29.95 (*0-935883-01-0*); With computer-readable disk. disk 69.95 (*0-935883-02-9*); pap. 14.95 (*0-935883-00-2*) Cooling Spring.

Marshall, Jane. Grace, Noted. Heffley, Rosemary, ed. LC 92-70255. 168p. 1992. pap. 11.95 (*0-685-59167-0*) Hope Pub.

***Marshall, Janet.** Look Once, Look Twice. LC 94-27259. 64p. (J). 1995. 13.95 (*0-395-71644-6*) Ticknor & Flds Bks Yng Read.

Marshall, Janet P. My Camera: At the Zoo. (Illus.). 32p. (J). (ps-2). 1989. 12.95 (*0-316-54687-9*) Little.

— Ohmygosh My Pocket. (Illus.). 24p. (J). (ps-00). 1992. bds. 7.95 (*1-56397-044-9*) Boyds Mills Pr.

Marshall, Jay W. Israel & the Book of the Covenant: An Anthropological Approach to Biblical Law. LC 92-47446. (Dissertation Ser.: No. 140). 361p. 1993. 39.95 (*1-55540-831-1*); pap. 26.95 (*1-55540-832-X*) Scholars Pr GA.

***Marshall, Jeanie.** Energetic Meetings: Enhancing Personal & Group Energy & Handling Difficult Behavior. 134p. (Orig.). 1994. pap. 11.00 (*1-885893-00-0*) Jemel Pubng.

Marshall, Jeff, ed. see Marshall, Edward M.

Marshall, Jeffrey. Staying Ahead of CRA: What Financial Institutions Must Know to Win at Community Reinvestment. 276p. 1991. text ed. 45.00 (*1-55623-448-1*) Irwin Prof Pubng.

An Asterisk (*) at the beginning of an entry indicates that the title is appearing in BIP for the first time.

Marshall, Jeffrey D. Life & Legacy of the Reverend Phinehas Bailey. (Occasional Papers: No. 9). (Illus.). 32p. (Orig.). 1985. pap. text ed. 2.50 (*0-944277-14-4*, M37) U VT Ctr Rsch VT.

Marshall, Jeffrey L. & Davis, Bertha S. Wrightstown Township: A Tricentennial History. (Illus.). 96p. (Orig.). 1992. pap. 10.00 (*0-9624245-1-X*) Wrightstown Twp Hist Comm.

Marshall, Jeremy, jt. ed. see McDonald, Fred.

Marshall, Jerilynn, ed. see Arroyo, Stephen.

Marshall, Jimmie B. Anyone Can Write - Just Let It Come Out. 1995. 9.95 (*0-9625557-4-6*) Excelsior Cee.

— The Marshall Art of Creative Writing. 1995. write for info. (*0-9625557-3-8*) Excelsior Cee.

— Quilted Love: A Patchwork of Thoughts & Feelings. 50p. (Orig.). 1990. pap. 5.00 (*0-9625557-0-3*) Excelsior Cee.

***Marshall, Joan.** A Solitary Pillar: Montreal's Anglican Church & the Quiet Revolution. (McGill-Queen's Studies in Ethnic History). 232p. 1994. 34.95 (*0-7735-1224-1*, Pub. by McGill CN) U of Toronto Pr.

Marshall, Joan K. On Equal Terms: A Thesaurus for Nonsexist Indexing & Cataloging. LC 77-8987. 152p. 1977. 35.00 (*0-918212-02-2*) Neal-Schuman.

Marshall, Joanne G. The Impact of the Special Library on Corporate Decision Making. LC 93-12721. 121p. 1993. 28.00 (*0-87111-410-0*) SLA.

***Marshall, Jody.** In the Air & Everywhere: The Scientific American Pop-up Book of Birds. (Illus.). (J). (gr. 3 up). 1995. text ed. 15.95 (*0-7167-6547-0*, Sci Am Yng Rdrs) W H Freeman.

Marshall, Joe T. Systematics of Smaller Asian Night Birds Based on Voice. 58p. 1978. 7.00 (*0-943610-25-7*) Am Ornithologists.

Marshall, John. An Autobiographical Sketch. (History - United States Ser.). 48p. 1993. reprint ed. lib. bdg. 59.00 (*0-7812-4880-9*) Rprt Serv.

— An Autobiographical Sketch by John Marshall. Adams, John S., ed. LC 71-160849. (American Constitutional & Legal History Ser). (Illus.). 74p. 1973. reprint ed. lib. bdg. 19.50 (*0-306-70216-9*) Da Capo.

— An Autobiographical Sketch by John Marshall. (American Biography Ser.). 48p. 1991. reprint ed. lib. bdg. 59.00 (*0-7812-8271-3*) Rprt Serv.

— The Buddhist Art of Gandhara. (Illus.). 1981. reprint ed. text ed. 30.00 (*0-685-43580-6*) Coronet Bks.

— Energy at Work. LC 95-13499. (Energy & Action Ser.). (J). 1995. write for info. (*1-55916-153-1*) Rourke Bk Co.

— A Guide to Taxila. 154p. (C). 1990. 45.00x (*81-85453-50-0*, Pub. by Print Hse II) St Mut.

— John Locke: Resistance, Religion & Responsibility. LC 93-30796. 1993. 27.95 (*0-521-44280-X*) Cambridge U Pr.

— John Locke: Resistance, Religion & Responsibility. (Cambridge Studies in Early Modern British History). 480p. (C). 1994. pap. 34.95 (*0-521-46687-3*) Cambridge U Pr.

— Life of George Washington, 5 Vols. Washington, B., ed. 1807. write for info. (*0-318-50638-6*) AMS Pr.

— Life of George Washington, 5 Vols, 1. Washington, B., ed. LC 69-19159. 1807. 49.50 (*0-404-04251-1*) AMS Pr.

— Life of George Washington, 5 Vols, 2. Washington, B., ed. LC 69-19159. 1807. 49.50 (*0-404-04252-X*) AMS Pr.

— Life of George Washington, 5 Vols, 3. Washington, B., ed. LC 69-19159. 1807. 49.50 (*0-404-04253-8*) AMS Pr.

— Life of George Washington, 5 Vols, 4. Washington, B., ed. LC 69-19159. 1807. 49.50 (*0-404-04254-6*) AMS Pr.

— Life of George Washington, 5 Vols, 5. Washington, B., ed. LC 69-19159. 1807. 49.60 (*0-404-04255-4*) AMS Pr.

— Life of George Washington, 5 Vols, Set. Washington, B., ed. LC 69-19159. 1807. 495.00 (*0-404-04250-3*) AMS Pr.

— Make Your Own Japanese Clothes: Patterns & Ideas for Modern Wear. LC 87-82861. (Illus.). 136p. 1988. pap. 22.00 (*0-87011-865-X*) Kodansha.

— The Papers of John Marshall: Correspondence, Papers, & Selected Judicial Opinions, 1807-1813. Hobson, Charles, ed. LC 74-9575. (Institute of Early American History & Culture Ser.: Vol. 7). (Illus.). xxxviii, 446p. (C). 1993. 55.00 (*0-8078-2074-1*) U of NC Pr.

— The Papers of John Marshall, Vol. I: Correspondence & Papers, November 10, 1775-June 23, 1788, & Account Book, September 1783-June 1788. Johnson, Herbert A. et al, eds. LC 74-9575. (Institute of Early American History & Culture Ser.). (Illus.). xlvi, 448p. 1974. 50.00 (*0-8078-1233-1*) U of NC Pr.

— The Papers of John Marshall, Vol. II: Correspondence & Papers, July 1788-December 1795, & Account Book, July 1788-December 1795. Cullen, Charles T. & Johnson, Herbert A., eds. LC 74-9575. (Institute of Early American History & Culture Ser.). xxxvi, 547p. 1977. 50.00 (*0-8078-1302-8*) U of NC Pr.

— The Papers of John Marshall, Vol. III: Correspondence & Papers, January 1796-December 1798. Stinchcombe, William C. & Cullen, Charles T., eds. LC 74-9575. (Institute of Early American History & Culture Ser.). (Illus.). xxix, 553p. 1979. 50.00 (*0-8078-1337-0*) U of NC Pr.

— The Papers of John Marshall, Vol. IV: Correspondence & Papers, January 1799-October 1800. Cullen, Charles T. & Tobias, Leslie, eds. LC 74-9575. (Institute of Early American History & Culture Ser.). xxxii, 365p. 1984. 50.00 (*0-8078-1586-1*) U of NC Pr.

— The Papers of John Marshall, Vol. V: Selected Law Cases, 1784-1800. Hobson, Charles F. et al, eds. LC 74-9575. (Institute of Early American History & Culture Ser.). ixx, 583p. 1987. 50.00 (*0-8078-1746-5*) U of NC Pr.

— Papers of John Marshall, Vol. VI: Correspondence, Papers, & Selected Judicial Opinions, November 1800-March 1807. Hobson, Charles F., ed. LC 74-9575. (Institute of Early American History & Culture Ser.). (Illus.). xlvi, 568p. (C). 1990. 50.00 (*0-8078-1903-4*) U of NC Pr.

— The Structure of Urban Systems. 394p. 1989. text ed. 50.00 (*0-8020-5756-X*); pap. text ed. 24.95 (*0-8020-6735-2*) U of Toronto Pr.

— Taxila: An Illustrated Account of Archaeological Excavations, 1913-1934, 3 vols., Set. 1977. reprint ed. 90.00 (*0-8364-0022-4*, Pub. by Motilal Banarsidass II) S Asia.

Marshall, John, ed. Citizen Participation in Library Decision-Making: The Toronto Experience. LC 84-10617. (Dalhousie University School of Library Service Ser.: No. 1). 436p. 1984. 35.00 (*0-8108-1709-8*) Scarecrow.

Marshall, John, photos. Idaho. LC 85-71059. (Illus.). 160p. 1985. 39.95 (*0-912856-93-9*) Gr Arts Ctr Pub.

— Portrait of Washington. 80p. 1993. pap. 12.95 (*1-55868-154-X*) Gr Arts Ctr Pub.

— Washington. LC 88-80536. (Illus.). 160p. 1988. 39.95 (*0-932575-64-1*) Gr Arts Ctr Pub.

Marshall, John & Roberts, Jerry. Living (& Dying) in Avalanche Country. (Illus.). 200p. 1992. reprint ed. 24.95 (*0-9632028-0-4*) A Simple Way Bk.

Marshall, John, jt. ed. see Dickinson, Marquis F.

Marshall, John, tr. see Horace.

Marshall, John A. American Bastille. LC 71-121115. (Civil Liberties in American History Ser.). 1970. reprint ed. lib. bdg. 85.00 (*0-306-71963-0*) Da Capo.

— Find Your Perfect High. Roebuck, Scott & Williams, Brian, eds. LC 78-112715. (Illus.). (Orig.). 1978. pap. 5.95 (*0-933426-00-3*) Grassroots Ed Serv.

Marshall, John B., jt. auth. see Cornelius, Temple H.

Marshall, John C., jt. ed. see Morton, John.

Marshall, John D. Reconciliation Road: A Family Odyssey of War & Honor. (Illus.). 304p. Date not set. 29.95 (*0-8156-0274-X*) Syracuse U Pr.

Marshall, John D., ed. see Powell, Lawrence C.

Marshall, John F. A-Pack: Financial Analytics for the Business Student. LC 91-90545. 212p. 1991. pap. text ed. 44.00 (*1-878975-06-4*) Kolb Pub.

— By the Light of His Lamp. (Spirit & Life Ser.). 1967. 2.00 (*0-686-11574-0*) Franciscan Inst.

— Conferences on the Our Father. (Spirit & Life Ser.). 1967. 2.00 (*0-686-11573-2*) Franciscan Inst.

— Financial Engineering: A Guide to the Development & Use of Derivative Products. 1991. 65.00 (*0-13-312588-2*, Busn) P-H.

— In the Shadow of His Cross. (Spirit & Life Ser.). 1969. 2.00 (*0-686-11577-5*) Franciscan Inst.

— The Long Way Home, the Short Way of Love. (Spirit & Life Ser.). 1968. 3.50 (*0-686-11575-9*) Franciscan Inst.

Marshall, John F. & Bansul, Vipul K. Financial Engineering. 2nd ed. LC 92-78013. 1993. pap. 40.00 (*1-878975-33-1*) Kolb Pub.

Marshall, John F. & Ellis, M. E. Investment Banking & Brokerage. Date not set. pap. 37.50 (*1-878975-38-2*) Kolb Pub.

— Investment Banking & Brokerage: The New Rules of the Game. 325p. 1993. 55.00 (*1-55738-504-1*) Probus Pub Co.

Marshall, John F. & Kapner, Kenneth R. The Swaps Market. 2nd ed. LC 92-73929. 258p. 1993. pap. 24.00 (*1-878975-16-1*) Kolb Pub.

— Understanding Swaps. (Finance Editions Ser.). 270p. 1993. text ed. 59.50 (*0-471-30827-7*) Wiley.

Marshall, John F., jt. auth. see Kapner, Kenneth R.

Marshall, John F., jt. auth. see Weisz, Paul B.

***Marshall, John R.** Social Phobia: From Shyness to Stage Fright. 240p. 1995. pap. 13.00 (*0-465-07896-6*) Basic.

Marshall, John R. & Lipsett, Suzanne. Social Phobia: From Shyness to Stage Fright. LC 93-45449. 224p. 1994. 23.00 (*0-465-07214-3*) Basic.

Marshall, John R., jt. auth. see Jefferson, James W.

Marshall, John S. Hooker & the Anglican Tradition: An Historical & Theological Study of Hookers Ecclesiastical Polity. 187p. (Orig.). 1963. pap. 10.00 (*0-918769-20-5*) Univ South Pr.

— Hooker's Theology of Common Prayer. 194p. (Orig.). 1956. pap. 10.00 (*0-918769-19-1*) Univ South Pr.

Marshall, Jonaathan, jt. auth. see Scott, Peter D.

Marshall, Jonathan. Drug Wars. 1990. 14.95 (*1-56060-062-4*) Eclipse Bks.

— To Have & Have Not: Southeast Asia Raw Materials & the Origins of the Pacific War. LC 94-13367. 1994. 28.00 (*0-520-08823-9*) U CA Pr.

Marshall, Jonathan, jt. auth. see Scott, Peter D.

Marshall, Jonathan, et al. The Iran-Contra Connection: Secret Teams & Covert Operations in the Reagan Era. LC 87-13059. 330p. 1987. lib. bdg. 35.00 (*0-89608-292-X*); pap. 13.00 (*0-89608-291-1*) South End Pr.

Marshall, Joseph, III. On Behalf of the Wolf & the First Peoples. 1996. 19.95 (*1-878610-45-7*) Red Crane Bks.

Marshall, Joseph. Travels Through Germany, Russia & Poland in the Years 1769 & 1770. LC 77-135821. (Eastern Europe Collection Ser.). 1971. reprint ed. 19.95 (*0-405-02763-X*) Ayer.

Marshall, Joseph, III. Winter of the Holy Iron. 304p. 1994. 19.95 (*1-878610-44-9*) Red Crane Bks.

***Marshall, Joyce.** The Queen's Quest & Other Tales: Stories to Live By. (Illus.). 128p. 1994. pap. 13.50 (*0-9611552-6-4*) Realistic Living.

Marshall, Joyce & Marshall, Gene W. The Reign of Reality: A Fresh Start for the Earth. LC 87-90621. (Illus.). 267p. 1987. pap. 10.00 (*0-9611552-2-1*) Realistic Living.

Marshall, Joyce, tr. see Roy, Gabrielle.

Marshall, Judi. Women Managers: Travellers in a Male World. LC 83-23579. 250p. 1984. pap. text ed. 49.50 (*0-471-90419-8*) Wiley.

— Women Managers Moving On: Exploring Career & Life Choices. LC 95-1341. 1995. write for info. (*0-415-09738-X*); pap. write for info. (*0-415-09739-8*) Routledge.

Marshall, Judi & Cooper, Cary L. Executives under Pressure: A Psychological Study. LC 78-72594. (Praeger Special Studies). 160p. 1979. text ed. 49.95 (*0-275-90388-5*, C0388, Praeger Pubs) Greenwood.

Marshall, Judi & Cooper, Cary L., eds. Coping with Stress at Work. 256p. 1981. text ed. 59.95 (*0-566-02338-5*) Ashgate Pub Co.

Marshall, Judi, jt. auth. see Cooper, Cary L.

Marshall, Judi, jt. ed. see Cooper, Cary L.

Marshall, Judith. Medicate Me. 144p. 1987. pap. 10.00 (*0-934385-01-7*) Hlth Prof Inst.

— Medicate Me Again. 132p. 1994. pap. text ed. 10.00 (*0-934385-62-9*) Hlth Prof Inst.

— Other Side of the Mirror. 1991. mass mkt. 4.50 (*1-55817-503-2*, Pinnacle NY) Windsor NY.

— Shattered Silence. 352p. 1993. mass mkt. 4.50 (*1-55817-704-3*, Pinnacle NY) Windsor NY.

— When the Wind Blows. 1992. mass mkt. 4.50 (*1-55817-613-6*, Pinnacle NY) Windsor NY.

***Marshall, Judy.** Ride a Hole Through the Wind. 92p. (Orig.). (YA). (gr. 9-12). 1994. lib. bdg. 15.00 (*0-88092-148-X*); pap. 5.00 (*0-88092-147-1*) Royal Fireworks.

Marshall, Julian, jt. auth. see Pollock, Steve.

Marshall, K. C. Interfaces in Microbial Ecology. 131p. 1976. 25.00 (*0-674-45822-2*, MAIF) HUP.

Marshall, K. C., ed. Advances in Microbial Ecology, Vol. 6. LC 77-649698. 252p. 1982. 75.00 (*0-306-41064-8*, Plenum Pr) Plenum.

— Advances in Microbial Ecology, Vol. 7. LC 77-649698. 228p. 1984. 75.00 (*0-306-41458-9*, Plenum Pr) Plenum.

— Advances in Microbial Ecology, Vol. 8. LC 77-649698. 322p. 1985. 75.00 (*0-306-41877-0*, Plenum Pr) Plenum.

— Advances in Microbial Ecology, Vol. 9. LC 77-649698. 416p. 1986. 85.00 (*0-306-42184-4*, Plenum Pr) Plenum.

— Advances in Microbial Ecology, Vol. 10. LC 77-649698. 474p. 1988. 95.00 (*0-306-42710-9*, Plenum Pr) Plenum.

— Advances in Microbial Ecology, Vol. 11. (Illus.). 530p. 1989. 110.00 (*0-306-43340-0*, Plenum Pr) Plenum.

— Advances in Microbial Ecology, Vol. 12. (Illus.). 500p. (C). 1992. 97.50 (*0-306-44266-3*, Plenum Pr) Plenum.

Marshall Kaplan, Gans & Kahn. Children & the Urban Environment: Evaluation of the WGBH-TV Educational Project. LC 70-187397. (Special Studies in U. S. Economic, Social & Political Issues). 1973. 39.50 (*0-275-28687-8*) Irvington.

Marshall, Kathryn. My Sister Gone. LC 91-58685. 240p. 1992. reprint ed. pap. 9.95 (*0-944439-49-7*) Clark City Pr.

Marshall, Kay. The First Step: Guidelines on Care & Recovery Following Colostomy Surgery. 2nd ed. (Illus.). 1990. pap. text ed. write for info. (*0-916999-06-8*) HERC Inc.

— Moving Forward: A Book for Ileostomy Patients. (Illus.). 32p. 1990. pap. text ed. 3.95 (*0-916999-07-6*) HERC Inc.

— A New Beginning: A Book for Urostomy Patients. (Illus.). 1988. pap. text ed. write for info. (*0-916999-05-X*) HERC Inc.

Marshall, Kerry. A Boy, a Ball, & a Dream: The Marvin Wood Story. (Illus.). 192p. (Orig.). 1991. 19.95 (*0-9630362-0-3*); pap. 10.45 (*0-9630362-1-1*) Scott IN.

— The Ray Crowe Story: A Legend in High School Basketball. 185p. 1992. 20.00 (*0-9636873-0-1*) High Schl Bsktball.

— Two of a Kind: The Dick & Tom Vanarsdale Story. (Illus.). 224p. 1992. 18.95 (*0-9630362-2-X*) Scott IN.

Marshall, Kevin, jt. auth. see Characklis, William G.

Marshall, Kimball P., jt. auth. see Hall, Larry D.

Marshall, Kimberly, ed. Rediscovering the Muses: Women's Musical Traditions. (Illus.). 352p. 1993. text ed. 35.00 (*1-55553-173-3*) NE U Pr.

— Rediscovering the Muses: Women's Musical Traditions. (Illus.). 352p. 1993. pap. 15.95 (*1-55553-219-5*) NE U Pr.

Marshall, Kirk. Backboard Battle. (Hoops Ser.: No. 3). 144p. (J). (gr. 4 up). 1989. pap. 4.99 (*0-345-35910-0*) Ballantine.

— Fast Breaks. (Hoops Ser.: No. 1). (J). (gr. 4 up). 1989. mass mkt. 3.99 (*0-345-35908-9*) Ballantine.

— Longshot Center. (Hoops Ser.: No. 2). (J). (gr. 4 up). 1989. pap. 3.95 (*0-345-35909-7*) Ballantine.

— Tourney Fever. (Hoops Ser.: No. 5). 144p. 1989. pap. 3.95 (*0-345-35912-7*) Ballantine.

***Marshall, Kneale T. & Oliver, Robert M.** Decision Making & Forecasting: With Emphasis on Model Building & Policy Analysis. LC 95-869. 1995. write for info. (*0-07-048027-3*) McGraw.

Marshall, Lane. Landscape Architecture: Guidelines to Professional Practice. 160p. 1981. 28.95 (*0-941236-00-5*) Am Landscape Arch.

Marshall, Lauriston C. & Sahlin, Harry L., eds. Electrostatic & Electromagnetic Confinement of Plasmas & the Phenomenology of the Relativistic Electron Beam. (Annals Ser.: Vol. 251). 711p. 1975. 83.75 (*0-89072-005-3*) NY Acad Sci.

Marshall, Leisa L., jt. auth. see Arnett, Kirk P.

Marshall, Lenore. Latest Will. LC 68-56267. 1969. 6.00 (*0-393-04215-4*) Norton.

— Latest Will. LC 68-56267. (C). 1969. pap. text ed. 2.95 (*0-393-04178-6*) Norton.

Marshall, Leonie. Dressage: Training & Exercises for Competition. (Illus.). 176p. 1993. 27.50 (*0-7134-6958-7*, Pub. by Batsford UK) Trafalgar.

— Dressage Terms. 94p. 1990. pap. 21.00 (*0-85131-317-5*, Pub. by J A Allen & Co UK) St Mut.

— Novice to Advanced Dressage. 1990. pap. 21.00 (*0-85131-373-6*, Pub. by J A Allen & Co UK) St Mut.

— Questions on Dressage. 1990. pap. 21.00 (*0-85131-474-0*, Pub. by J A Allen & Co UK) St Mut.

Marshall, Leslie B., ed. Infant Care & Feeding in the South Pacific, Vol. 3. LC 85-12648. (Food & Nutrition in History & Anthropology Ser.). 368p. 1985. text ed. 99.00 (*2-88124-037-2*) Gordon & Breach.

Marshall, Leslie B., jt. auth. see Marshall, Mac.

Marshall, Linda. Befitting a Bride. (Illus.). 28p. (Orig.). 1987. pap. 5.95 (*0-933491-21-2*) Hot off Pr.

Marshall, Linda D. What Is a Step? LC 91-67511. (Illus.). 48p. (Orig.). (J). (ps-5). 1992. pap. 10.00 (*1-879289-00-8*) Native Sun Pubs.

Marshall, Lois, jt. auth. see Biggs, Bud.

Marshall, Loren, jt. auth. see LaFevers, Stephen.

Marshall, Loren, jt. auth. see Le Fevers, Stephen.

Marshall, Lori, jt. auth. see Marshall, Garry.

Marshall, Louise, jt. auth. see Bibus, Ethel.

Marshall, Lucie, ed. see Tarbell, Jim.

***Marshall, Lydie.** Chez Nous: Home Cooking from the South of France. (Illus.). 320p. 1995. 25.00 (*0-06-017203-7*) HarpC.

— A Passion for Potatoes: Two Hundred Recipes for Appetizers, Entrees, Side Dishes, Even Desserts. LC 91-50516. 304p. 1992. pap. 14.00 (*0-06-096910-5*, PL) HarpC.

***Marshall, Lyn.** Yogacise: The No-Sweat' Exercise Programme for the 90s. (Illus.). 95p. 1995. pap. 9.95 (*0-563-36279-0*, Pub. by BBC UK) Parkwest Pubns.

Marshall, Lyn, jt. auth. see Gosling, Ted.

Marshall, M. W., jt. auth. see Ferreira, Hugo G.

Marshall, Mac. Weekend Warriors: Alcohol in a Micronesian Culture. Edgerton, Robert B. & Langness, L. L., eds. LC 78-64597. 170p. (C). 1979. pap. 14.95 (*0-87484-455-X*) Mayfield Pub.

Marshall, Mac, ed. Beliefs, Behaviors, & Alcoholic Beverages: A Cross-Cultural Survey. 1979. pap. 24.95 (*0-472-08580-8*) U of Mich Pr.

— Siblingship in Oceania: Studies in the Meaning of Kin Relations. LC 83-14516. (ASAO Monograph: No. 8). (Illus.). 434p. (C). 1983. reprint ed. pap. text ed. 31.00 (*0-8191-3430-9*) U Pr of Amer.

Marshall, Mac & Marshall, Leslie B. Silent Voices Speak: Women & Prohibition in Truk. 190p. (C). 1990. pap. 17.95 (*0-534-12384-8*) Intl Thomson.

Marshall, Mac & Nason, James D. Micronesia 1944-1974: A Bibliography of Anthropological & Related Source Materials. LC 75-28587. (Bibliographies Ser.). 348p. 1975. 25.00 (*0-87536-215-X*) HRAFP.

Marshall, Madeleine. The Singer's Manual of English Diction. 208p. 1953. pap. 13.00 (*0-02-871100-9*) Schirmer Bks.

***Marshall, Madeleine F.** Common Hymnsense. LC 95-2774. 204p. 1995. 19.95 (*0-941050-69-6*, G-4023) GIA Pubns.

— The Poetry of Elizabeth Singer Rowe (1674-1737) LC 87-24399. (Studies in Women & Religion: Vol. 25). (Illus.). 380p. 1987. lib. bdg. 99.95 (*0-88946-524-X*) E Mellen.

Marshall, Madeleine F. & Todd, Janet M. English Congregational Hymns in the Eighteenth Century. LC 82-40176. 192p. 1982. 21.00 (*0-8131-1470-5*) U Pr of Ky.

Marshall, Margaret. Managing Library Provision for Handicapped Children. (Library Management in Context Ser.). 208p. 1993. pap. 22.50 (*0-7201-2198-1*, Mansell Pub) Cassell.

***Marshall, Margaret J.** Contesting Cultural Rhetorics: Public Discourse & Education 1890-1900. (Illus.). 288p. 1995. text ed. 39.50x (*0-472-10536-1*) U of Mich Pr.

Marshall, Margaret M. The Dialect of Notre-Dame-de-Sahilhac: A Natural Generative Phonology. (Stanford French & Italian Studies: Vol. 31). 160p. 1984. pap. 46.50 (*0-915838-06-0*) Anma Libri.

Marshall, Margaret R. An Introduction to the World of Children's Books. 2nd ed. 250p. 1988. text ed. 38.95 (*0-566-05461-2*, Pub. by Gower UK) Ashgate Pub Co.

— Managing Library Provision for Handicapped Children. 208p. 1991. text ed. 80.00 (*0-7201-2078-0*, Mansell Pub) Cassell.

Marshall, Marguerite M., et al. An Account of Afro-American in Southeast Kansas, 1884-1984. (Illus.). 106p. 1986. pap. 12.95 (*0-89745-091-4*) Sunflower U Pr.

Marshall, Marilyn, ed. People Chow: Favorite Recipes of the Famous & Almost Famous. (Illus.). 336p. 1985. spiral bd. 12.00 (*0-9616537-1-X*) Hays Humane Soc.

Marshall, Marion & Schapiro, Lorraine. Caring for Your Child: Questions Parents Ask. 1981. pap. 2.95 (*0-88409-042-6*) Borden.

Marshall, Marion B. & Wasserman, Paul, eds. Public Finance: An Information Sourcebook. (Sourcebook Series in Business & Management). 296p. 1987. 52.00 (*0-89774-276-1*) Oryx Pr.

Marshall, Marsh. Organizations & Growth in Rural China. LC 85-11884. 208p. 1985. text ed. 35.00 (*0-312-58768-6*) St Martin.

Marshall, Martha L. Pronouncing Dictionary of California Names in English & Spanish. (Shorey Historical Ser.). 44p. reprint ed. pap. 3.95 (*0-8466-0155-9*, S155) Shorey.

Marshall, Mary. Portraiture of Shakerism. LC 70-134420. reprint ed. 52.00 (*0-404-08461-3*) AMS Pr.

Marshall, Mary, jt. ed. see Chapman, Alan.

Marshall, Mary, jt. auth. see Foster, D. Glenn.

Marshall, Mary A. Music: Careers in Music. LC 93-14832. (Now Hiring Ser.). (Illus.). 48p. (J). (gr. 5-6). 1994. text ed. 14.95 (*0-89686-793-5*, Crstwood Hse) Silver Burdett Pr.

Marshall, Mary C., et al. The Future of Religious Life. Steinberg, Dolores & Coughlan, Helen, eds. 143p. 1990. pap. 5.95 (*0-8146-1908-8*) Liturgical Pr.

M

Marshall, Mary E., ed. see Sroufe, L. Alan, et al.
*Marshall, Maurice R. & Archer, Douglas L. Food & Health: Study Guide. 352p. (C). 1994. pap. text ed., spiral bd. 32.95 (0-7872-0406-4) Kendall-Hunt.
Marshall, Mel. How to Make Your Own Fishing Rods. 1982. pap. 4.50 (0-943822-12-2) Times Mir Mag Bk Div.
Marshall, Melinda. Good Enough Mothers: Changing Expectations for Ourselves. 352p. 1994. pap. 10.95 (1-56079-433-X) Petersons Guides.
Marshall, Melinda M. Good Enough Mothers: Changing Expectations for Ourselves. Colton, Kitty, ed. LC 93-5838. 344p. 1993. text ed. 18.95 (1-56079-253-1) Petersons Guides.
Marshall, Michael. The Freedom of Holiness: Biblical Reflections on the Witness of the Saints. LC 91-39692. 195p. (Orig.). 1992. pap. 11.95 (0-8192-1583-X) Morehouse Pub.
— The Gospel Connection: A Study in Evangelism for the 90s. LC 90-37965. 176p. (Orig.). 1990. pap. 8.95 (0-8192-1535-X) Morehouse Pub.
— Great Expectations? Preparing for Evangelism Through Bible Study. LC 91-6600. 160p. (Orig.). 1991. pap. 8.95 (1-56101-033-2) Cowley Pubns.
— Just Like Him. LC 88-38702. 112p. (Orig.). 1989. pap. 7.95 (0-8192-1433-7) Morehouse Pub.
— Long Waves of Regional Development. LC 86-15623. 246p. 1987. text ed. 39.95 (0-312-49674-5) St Martin.
— Tyne Waters: A River & Its Salmon. (Illus.). 224p. 1991. 45.00 (0-85493-195-3, Pub. by V Gollancz UK) Trafalgar.
Marshall, Michael E. The Anglican Church Today & Tomorrow. LC 83-62718. 176p. (Orig.). 1984. pap. 7.95 (0-8192-1341-1) Morehouse Pub.
Marshall, Michael P. & Walt, Henry J. Rio Abajo: Prehistory & History of a Rio Grande Province. (Illus.). 368p. 1984. pap. text ed. 19.95 (0-89013-180-5) Museum NM Pr.
Marshall, Michael P., jt. auth. see Hogan, Patrick.
*Marshall, Michael W. Ocean Traders: From the Portuguese Discoveries to the Present Day. fac. ed. LC 89-48361. (Illus.). 192p. 1990. reprint ed. pap. 54.80 (0-7837-8135-0, 2047942) Bks Demand.
Marshall, Mike, jt. ed. see Arestis, Philip.
Marshall, Mollie. Ready for Romance. (Leisure First Romance Ser.: No. 2). 192p. (Orig.). (J). (gr. 6-12). 1982. pap. 1.95 (0-8439-1129-8) Dorchester Pub Co.
Marshall, Molly. What It Means to Be Human. 176p. (Orig.). 1995. pap. 12.95 (1-880837-85-4) Smyth & Helwys.
Marshall, Molly T. No Salvation Outside the Church? A Critical Inquiry. LC 93-10803. 280p. 1993. text ed. 89.95 (0-7734-2854-2) E Mellen.
Marshall, Murdena, jt. auth. see Schmidt, David L.
Marshall, Muriel. Red Hole in Time. LC 87-21715. (Essays on the American West Ser.: No. 9). (Illus.). 312p. 1988. 29.50 (0-89096-316-9); pap. 12.95 (0-89096-332-0) Tex A&M Univ Pr.
— Uncompahgre. LC 80-11666. (Illus.). 211p. (Orig.). reprint ed. pap. 60.20 (0-8357-7939-4, 2057012) Bks Demand.
Marshall, N., jt. auth. see Brook, C.
Marshall, N. B. Aspects of Deep Sea Biology. 1977. lib. bdg. 250.00 (0-8490-1458-1) Gordon Pr.
— Explorations in the Life of Fishes. LC 75-129122. (Books in Biology: No. 7). 216p. 1971. 29.00 (0-674-27951-4) HUP.
Marshall-Nadel, Nathalie. Be Organized for College: A Basic Study Guide. 82p. 1995. pap. text ed. 19.95 (0-9632383-3-7) Intl Mgmt FL.
Marshall, Nancy T. & Vredevelt, Pam. Women Who Compete. LC 87-36018. (Illus.). 192p. (Orig.). 1988. pap. 7.99 (0-8007-5277-5) Revell.
Marshall, Nathaniel. Penitential Discipline of the Primitive Church. LC 74-172846. (Library of Anglo-Catholic Theology: No. 13). reprint ed. 44.00 (0-404-52105-3) AMS Pr.
Marshall, Nelson. The Scallop Estuary: The Natural History Features of the Niantic River. (Illus.). 150p. 1994. pap. write for info. (0-9628730-1-2) Th Anchorage.
— Understanding the Eastern Caribbean & the Antilles, with Checklists Appended. (Illus.). 252p. (Orig.). 1992. pap. write for info. (0-9628730-0-4) Th Anchorage.
*Marshall, Nina T. Gardener's Guide to Plant Conservation. 1993. 12.95 (0-942635-18-3) World Wildlife Fund.
Marshall, Nissim, tr. see Raabe, Marie.
Marshall-Noke, Dorothy. Feathers. Weinberger, Jane, ed. LC 88-51278. (Illus.). 64p. (J). (ps-4). 1990. pap. 5.95 (0-932433-52-9) Windswept Hse.
Marshall, Norm & Jones, Bill. The Great All-American Wooden Toy Book: More Than 40 Easy-to-Build Projects. LC 86-15568. (Illus.). 224p. 1986. pap. 12.95 (0-87857-628-2, 14-654-1) Rodale Pr Inc.
Marshall, Norman E. That Man Tate & Other Kindred Spirits: With Stories from the Allagash. LC 93-60020. (Orig.). 1993. pap. 12.95 (0-9636231-0-9) TreeTop MA.
Marshall, Norman F. & Ripamonti, Aldo. Leonardo da Vinci. (What Made Them Great Ser.). (Illus.). 104p. (J). (gr. 5-8). 1990. 12.95 (0-382-09982-6); pap. 5.95 (0-382-24007-3) Silver Burdett Pr.
Marshall, Norton, jt. auth. see Mason, William.
Marshall, Norton L., jt. auth. see Mason, William H.
Marshall, Oscar J., jt. auth. see Coddington, Edwin F.
Marshall, Oscar S. Journeyman Machinist En Route to the Stars. Douglas, Eva M., ed. LC 78-64614. (Illus.). 1979. 12.00 (0-88492-025-9) W S Sullwold.
Marshall, P. Geology of Mangaia. (BMB Ser.: No. 36). 1969. reprint ed. pap. 15.00 (0-527-02139-3) Periodicals Srv.
— Geology of Rarotonga & Atiu. (BMB Ser.: No. 72). 1969. reprint ed. 15.00 (0-527-02178-4) Periodicals Srv.
Marshall, P., ed. Austenitic Stainless Steels: Microstructure & Mechanical Properties. 444p. 1984. 106.25 (0-85334-277-6, I-262-84, Pub. by Elsevier Applied Sci UK) Elsevier.
Marshall, P. J. Bengal: The British Bridgehead. (New Cambridge History of India Ser.: II: 2). (Illus.). 200p. 1988. 44.95 (0-521-25330-6) Cambridge U Pr.
— Trade & Conquest: Studies on the Rise of British Dominance in India. (Collected Studies: No. CS 409). 320p. 1993. 82.50 (0-86078-373-1, Pub. by Variorum UK) Ashgate Pub Co.
Marshall, P. J. & Williams, Glyndwr. The Great Map of Mankind: Perceptions of New Worlds in the Age of Enlightenment. LC 82-80225. 320p. 1982. 37.50 (0-674-36210-1) HUP.
Marshall, P. J., ed. see Burke, Edmund E.
Marshall, P. K., ed. see Gellius, Aulus.
Marshall, P. W. Design of Welded Tubular Connections: Basis & Use of AWS Code Provisions. (Developments in Civil Engineering Ser.: Vol. 37). 412p. 1991. 131.25 (0-444-88201-4) Elsevier.
Marshall, Patricia T. & Hughes, George M. Physiology of Mammals & Other Vertebrates. 2nd ed. LC 78-73810. (Illus.). 1981. pap. 32.95 (0-521-29586-6) Cambridge U Pr.
Marshall, Paul, ed. Raparapa. 290p. (C). 1990. 90.00 (0-7316-3328-8, Pub. by Pascoe Pub AT) St Mut.
Marshall, Paul, jt. ed. see Chaplin, Jonathan.
Marshall, Paul A. & VanderVennen, Robert E., eds. Social Science in Christian Perspective. (Christian Studies Today). 357p. (Orig.). (C). 1988. lib. bdg. 55.00 (0-8191-7103-4, Inst Christ Stud) U Pr of Amer.
Marshall, Paul A., et al, eds. Stained Glass: Worldviews & Social Science. 188p. (Orig.). (C). 1989. lib. bdg. 40.00 (0-8191-7253-7, Inst Christ Stud); pap. text ed. 19.50 (0-8191-7254-5, Inst Christ Stud) U Pr of Amer.
*Marshall, Paula. The Captain's Lady. large type ed. (Legacy of Love Ser.). 1994. 18.95 (0-263-14011-3, Pub. by Mills & Boon Ltd UK) Chivers N Amer.
— The Cyprian's Sister. large type ed. 1994. 18.95 (0-263-14005-9, Pub. by Mills & Boon Ltd UK) Chivers N Amer.
— An Improper Duenna. (Regency Romance Ser.). 1993. mass mkt. 2.99 (0-373-31207-5, 1-31207-3) Harlequin Bks.
— Touch the Fire. large type ed. (Legacy of Love Ser.). 1994. 18.95 (0-263-14013-X, Pub. by Mills & Boon Ltd UK) Chivers N Amer.
*Marshall, Paula & Andrew, Sylvia. Reluctant Bridegrooms: My Lady Love; Darling Amazon. (Promo Ser.). 1995. mass mkt. 4.99 (0-373-31218-0, 1-31218-0) Harlequin Bks.
Marshall, Paula, jt. auth. see Hiatt, Brenda.
Marshall, Paule. Brown Girl, Brownstones. 336p. (C). 1981. reprint ed. pap. 10.95 (0-912670-96-7) Feminist Pr.
— The Chosen Place, the Timeless People. LC 84-40073. (Vintage Contemporaries Ser.). 480p. 1984. pap. 13.00 (0-394-72633-2, Vin) Random.
— Chosen Place, the Timeless People. LC 84-4007. 1992. pap. 13.00 (0-394-23987-3, Vin) Random.
— Daughters. LC 92-53558. (Contemporary Fiction Ser.). 416p. 1992. pap. 11.95 (0-452-26912-1, Plume) NAL-Dutton.
— Daughters. 416p. 1991. text ed. 19.95 (0-689-12139-3, Atheneum S&S) S&S Trade.
— Paule Marshall: For a Reading on the Occasion of a Reception in Honor of Her MacArthur Fellowship. (InterAmericas Ser.: No. 2). 16p. 1992. 5.00 (0-9633741-2-5) RI Study of Man.
— Praisesong for the Widow. (Contemporary Fiction Ser.). 256p. 1984. pap. 10.95 (0-452-26711-0, Plume) NAL-Dutton.
— Reena & Other Stories. LC 83-16592. 224p. 1983. pap. 11.95 (0-935312-24-2) Feminist Pr.
— Soul Clap Hands & Sing. (Howard University Press Library of Contemporary Literature). 208p. 1988. pap. 8.95 (0-88258-155-4) Howard U Pr.
Marshall, Peter. The Catholic Priesthood & the English Reformation. (Oxford Historical Monographs). 288p. 1994. 55.00 (0-19-820448-5) OUP.
— Enmity in Corinth: Social Conventions in Paul's Relations with the Corinthians. 460p. 1987. lib. bdg. 78.50 (3-16-145070-1, Pub. by J C B Mohr GW) Coronet Bks.
— The First Easter. rev. ed. LC 87-30876. (Illus.). 126p. 1995. 11.99 (0-8007-9120-7) Chosen Bks.
— His Hand on Your Shoulder. LC 89-48718. (Illus.). 88p. 1990. reprint ed. 9.99 (0-8007-9158-4) Chosen Bks.
— Let's Keep Christmas. 2nd ed. LC 53-10628. (Illus.). 48p. 1995. reprint ed. text ed. 9.99 (0-8007-9134-7) Chosen Bks.
— Nature's Web: Rethinking Our Place on Earth. LC 93-17233. 528p. 1993. reprint ed. 29.95 (1-55778-652-6) Paragon Hse.
— Now I Now Why Tigers Eat Their Young: How to Survive Your Teenagers - with Wisdom & a Little Humor. LC 93-48110. 1994. pap. write for info. (1-55958-499-8) Prima Pub.
— William Blake: Visionary Anarchist. (Illus.). 69p. (Orig.). Date not set. pap. 5.50 (0-900384-46-8) Left Bank.
Marshall, Peter, pref. The Prayers of Peter Marshall. LC 54-11762. 1989. 8.99 (0-8007-9141-X) Chosen Bks.
Marshall, Peter & Manuel, David. From Sea to Shining Sea. LC 85-20428. 448p. 1985. 16.99 (0-8007-1451-2) Revell.
— From Sea to Shining Sea. LC 85-20428. 448p. 1989. pap. 9.99 (0-8007-5308-9) Revell.
— The Light & the Glory. LC 77-23352. 352p. 1977. 16.99 (0-8007-0886-5); pap. 9.99 (0-8007-5054-3) Revell.
Marshall, Peter & Williams, Glyn, eds. British Atlantic Empire Before the American Revolution. 130p. 1980. 35.00 (0-7146-3158-2, Pub. by F Cass Pubs UK) Intl Spec Bk.
Marshall, Peter, ed. see Godwin, William.
Marshall, Peter, et al. From Sea to Shining Sea for Children: Discovering God's Plan for America in Her First Half-Century of Independence. LC 93-10801. 176p. (J). (gr. 3-6). 1993. pap. 9.99 (0-8007-5484-0) Revell.
— The Light & the Glory for Children. LC 92-11727. (Illus.). 160p. (Orig.). (J). (gr. 4-7). 1992. pap. 9.99 (0-8007-5448-4) Revell.
Marshall, Peter H. William Godwin: Philosopher, Novelist, Revolutionary. LC 83-19823. (Illus.). 498p. 1984. text ed. 50.00 (0-300-03175-0) Yale U Pr.
Marshall, Peter J., ed. The British Discovery of Hinduism in the 18th Century. LC 73-111132. (European Understanding of India Ser.). 320p. reprint ed. pap. 91.20 (0-8357-7422-8, 2024493) Bks Demand.
Marshall, Philip C., jt. ed. see Kelley, Stephen J.
Marshall, Philip H., jt. ed. see Elias, Jeffrey W.
Marshall, R. D. & Tipton, Keith F., eds. Essays in Biochemistry, Vol. 21. (Serial Publication Ser.). 176p. 1986. pap. text ed. 49.00 (0-12-158121-7) Acad Pr.
— Essays in Biochemistry, Vol. 24. (Serial Publication Ser.). 125p. 1989. pap. text ed. 49.00 (0-12-158124-1) Acad Pr.
Marshall, R. D., jt. ed. see Campbell, P. N.
Marshall, R. L. The Historical Criticism of Documents. 1977. lib. bdg. 59.95 (0-8490-1956-7) Gordon Pr.
Marshall, R. M. My Cook Book. 136p. 1985. 49.00 (0-906054-34-6) St Mut.
Marshall, Ralph O., et al. Alcohol & Marijuana Use in Texas. 24p. 1981. 2.00 (0-318-02511-6) S Houston Employ.
Marshall, Randall G., et al. La Fuente Hispana: Cuaderno de Ejercicios. 2nd ed. 1977. pap. text ed. write for info. (0-07-040582-4); Test replacements. pap. text ed. write for info. (0-07-040584-0) McGraw.
— La Fuente Hispana: Cuaderno de Ejercicios. 2nd ed. 1977. Tests. pap. text ed. write for info. (0-07-040583-2) McGraw.
Marshall, Ray. The Plane: Watch It Work! LC 85-3263. (Illus.). 10p. 1985. pap. 13.95 (0-670-80695-1) Viking Child Bks.
— State of Families Three: Losing Direction: Families, Human Resource Development, & Economic Performance. LC 87-24374. 160p. 1991. pap. 15.00 (0-87304-249-2) Families Intl.
Marshall, Ray & Christian, Virgil L., Jr., eds. Employment of Blacks in the South: A Perspective on the 1960s. LC 78-7331. (Illus.). 261p. reprint ed. pap. 74.40 (0-8357-3615-6, 2036109) Bks Demand.
Marshall, Ray & Osterman, Paul. Workforce Policies for the 1990s: A New Labor Market Agenda & The Possibilities of Employment Policy. LC 89-80284. 1989. 12.00 (0-944826-05-9) Economic Policy Inst.
Marshall, Ray & Tucker, Marc. Thinking for a Living: Education & the Wealth of Nations. LC 91-58596. 304p. 1993. reprint ed. pap. 13.00 (0-465-08557-1) Basic.
Marshall, Ray, jt. auth. see Glover, Robert.
Marshall, Ray, et al. Employment Discrimination: The Impact of Legal & Administrative Remedies. LC 78-17333. 176p. 1978. text ed. 42.95 (0-275-90306-0, C0306, Praeger Pubs) Greenwood.
Marshall, Ray, et al, contribs. Education, Technology, & the Texas Economy, 3 vols., Vol. 1. (Policy Research Project Report Ser.: No. 85). 130p. 1988. pap. 7.00 (0-89940-690-4) LBJ Sch Pub Aff.
— Education, Technology, & the Texas Economy, 3 vols., Vol. 2. (Policy Research Project Report Ser.: No. 85). 148p. 1988. pap. 7.00 (0-89940-691-2) LBJ Sch Pub Aff.
— Education, Technology, & the Texas Economy, 3 vols., Vol. 3. (Policy Research Project Report Ser.: No. 85). 50p. 1989. pap. 7.00 (0-89940-692-0) LBJ Sch Pub Aff.
Marshall, Renee, tr. see Luetke, Frederick.
Marshall, Richard. Edward Ruscha: Los Angeles Apartments. (Illus.). 64p. 1993. pap. 8.95 (0-8109-6808-8) Abrams.
— Fifty New York Artists: A Critical Selection of Painters & Sculptors Working in New York. (Illus.). 120p. (Orig.). 1986. pap. 18.95 (0-87701-397-7) Chronicle Bks.
— Jean-Michel Basquiat. (Illus.). 272p. 1995. 35.00 (0-8109-6814-2) Abrams.
Marshall, Richard, comp. Jean-Michel Basquiat. LC 92-19045. 1992. write for info. (0-87427-081-2) Whitney Mus.
Marshall, Richard & MacNamara, Mark. Strange, Amazing, & Mysterious Places. LC 93-8655. (Illus.). 1993. 45.00 (0-00-255109-8) Collins SF.
Marshall, Richard & Mapplethorpe, Robert. Robert Mapplethorpe. (Illus.). 1988. 65.00 (0-8212-1728-3) Bulfinch Pr.
— Robert Mapplethorpe. (Illus.). 1990. pap. 39.95 (0-8212-1786-0) Bulfinch Pr.
Marshall, Richard, jt. ed. see Merrick, David.
Marshall, Richard, jt. auth. see Rosenthal, Mark.
Marshall, Richard, ed. see Segar, E. C.
Marshall, Richard J. The Burning Bush Patrol. 1991. pap. 7.95 (0-88494-804-8) Bookcraft Inc.
— Home Teaching with Purpose & Power. LC 90-41525. 158p. (Orig.). 1990. pap. 9.95 (0-87579-371-1) Deseret Bk.
Marshall, Rick S., jt. auth. see Saling, Beverly M.
Marshall, Rita. I Hate to Read. (Illus.). (J). 1992. lib. bdg. 17.95 (0-88682-531-8) Creative Ed.
— I Hate to Read. (J). (gr. 4-7). 1995. pap. 9.95 (1-56846-100-3) Creative Ed.
Marshall, Robert. Alaska Wilderness: Exploring the Central Brooks Range. 2nd ed. Marshall, George, ed. & intro. by. LC 73-116025. (Illus.). 1970. pap. 13.00 (0-520-01711-0) U CA Pr.
— Arctic Village: A Nineteen Thirties Portrait of Wiseman, Alaska. LC 90-27265. (Illus.). xxviii, 399p. 1991. 28.00 (0-912006-47-1); pap. 20.00 (0-912006-51-X) U of Alaska Pr.
— In the Sewers of Lvov: An Heroic Story of Survival from the Holocaust. 208p. 1991. text ed. 22.95 (0-684-19320-5, Scribners) S&S Trade.
— Storm from the East: From Ghengis Khan to Khubilai Khan. LC 92-36544. (C). 1993. 28.50 (0-520-08300-8) U CA Pr.
Marshall, Robert, ed. see Hoagland, Loretta.
Marshall, Robert A. & Zubay, Eli A. The Debit System of Marketing Life & Health Insurance. LC 74-23820. 152p. 1975. 19.95 (0-13-197384-3) GA St U Busn Pr.
Marshall, Robert C. Collective Decision Making in Rural Japan. LC 84-3159. (Michigan Papers in Japanese Studies: No. 11). xiii, 178p. (Orig.). (C). 1984. pap. text ed. 9.95 (0-939512-17-3) U MI Japan.
Marshall, Robert G., ed. Short-Title Catalogue of Books Printed in Italy & of Books in Italian Printed Abroad, 1501-1600, Held in Selected North American Libraries, 3 Vols, Set. 1970. lib. bdg. 170.00 (0-8161-0852-8, Hall Library) G K Hall.
Marshall, Robert G. & Donovan, Charles A. Blessed Are the Barren: The Social Policy of Planned Parenthood. LC 90-84812. 381p. (Orig.). 1991. pap. 19.95 (0-89870-353-0) Ignatius Pr.
Marshall, Robert G. & St Aubyn, Frederic, eds. Trois Pieces Surrealistes: Les Maries de la Tour Eiffel; L'Armoire a Glace un Beau Soir; Victor ou les Enfants au Pouvoir. LC 75-89864. (Illus.). (FRE.). 1969. pap. text ed. 14.95 (0-89197-456-3) Irvington.
Marshall, Robert H. & Jacobs, Donald H. Physical Science: Investigating Matter & Energy. 2nd ed. (Illus.). 288p. 1992. teacher ed 12.99 (0-7916-0095-5); student ed 4.99 (0-7916-0096-3); text ed. 19.49 (0-7916-0094-7); student ed 9.99 (0-7916-0106-4) Media Materials.
Marshall, Robert J. & Marshall, Simone V. The Transference-Countertransference Matrix: Emotional-Cognitive Dialogue in Psychotherapy, Psychoanalysis, & Supervision. (Personality, Psychopathology & Psychotherapy: Theoretical & Clinical Perspectives Ser.). 388p. 1988. text ed. 45.00 (0-231-06166-8) Col U Pr.
Marshall, Robert L. The Compositional Process of J. S. Bach: A Study of the Autograph Scores of the Vocal Works, 2 vols. LC 76-113005. (Princeton Studies in Music: No. 4). (Illus.). 287p. reprint ed. Vol. 1, 287 p. pap. 81.80 (0-8357-4037-4, 2036729); reprint ed. Vol. 2, 195 p. pap. 55.60 (0-8357-4038-2, 2036729) Bks Demand.
— Mozart Speaks: Views on Music, Musicians, & the World. 446p. 1991. text ed. 35.00 (0-02-871385-0) Schirmer Bks.
— The Music of Johann Sebastian Bach: The Sources, the Style, the Significance. 375p. 1989. reprint ed. text ed. 36.00 (0-02-871781-3) Schirmer Bks.
— The Music of Johann Sebastian Bach: The Sources, the Style, the Significance. 375p. 1990. reprint ed. pap. 16.95 (0-02-871782-1) Schirmer Bks.
Marshall, Robert L., ed. Eighteenth Century Keyboard Music. (Studies in Musical Genres & Repertoires). 352p. 1994. text ed. 42.00 (0-02-871355-9, Scholarly) Schirmer Bks.
Marshall, Roger. Cruising Techniques Illustrated. (Illus.). 1989. 29.95 (0-393-03276-0) Norton.
— Designed to Cruise. (Illus.). 1990. 49.95 (0-393-03333-3) Norton.
— Marshall's Marine Sourcebook: Where to Find Absolutely Everything Nautical. LC 93-21623. (Illus.). 446p. (Orig.). 1994. pap. 19.95 (0-312-09871-5) St Martin.
Marshall, Roger & Larsen, Paul. A Sailor's Guide to Production Sailboats. LC 86-224. (Illus.). 304p. (Orig.). 1986. pap. 17.95 (0-688-05842-6, Hearst Marine Bks) Morrow.
Marshall, Ron. The Valley of Decision. 288p. 1993. pap. text ed. 5.99 (0-9638071-0-2) Eagle Pubns.
Marshall, Rosalind. Apes & Peacocks. LC 91-4232. (Orig.). 1990. pap. 7.00 (0-915541-79-3) Star Bks Inc.
— Mary I. 160p. 1993. pap. 19.95 (0-11-290509-9, HM05099, Pub. by HMSO UK) UNIPUB.
— Waterways. 32p. (Orig.). 1989. pap. 5.00 (0-918957-05-2) Pika Oregon.
Marshall, Rosalind K. Elizabeth I. (Great Periods of the British Monarchy Ser.). (Illus.). 160p. (Orig.). (C). 1992. pap. 19.95 (0-88045-119-X) Stemmer Hse.
— Henrietta Maria: The Intrepid Queen. (Great Periods of the British Monarchy Ser.). (Illus.). 157p. 1991. 29.95 (0-88045-118-1); pap. 19.95 (0-88045-117-3) Stemmer Hse.
— Virgins & Viragos: A History of Women in Scotland from 1080-1980. (Illus.). 340p. 1983. 22.00 (0-89733-074-9); pap. 10.00 (0-89733-075-7) Academy Chi Pubs.
Marshall, Roy K., jt. auth. see Levitt, J. M.
Marshall, Rush P. Control of Cedar-Apple Rust on Red Cedar. (CT Academy of Arts & Science Transactions Ser.: Vol. 34). 1941. pap. 39.50 (0-686-51364-9) Elliots Bks.
Marshall, Ruth, jt. auth. see Brackelsberg, Phyllis.
Marshall, S. L. American Heritage History of World War I. 1988. 19.99 (0-517-38555-4) Random Hse Value.
— Battle at Best. (Battery Classics Ser.). (Illus.). 257p. 1988. reprint ed. 22.50 (0-89839-115-6) Battery Pr.
— Bird: The Christmastide Battle. (Vietnam War Ser.: No. 4). (Illus.). 216p. 1983. reprint ed. 22.95 (0-89839-072-9) Battery Pr.
— Crimsoned Prairie: The Indian Wars. (Quality Paperbacks Ser.). (Illus.). 270p. (C). 1984. reprint ed. pap. 11.95 (0-306-80226-0) Da Capo.

An Asterisk (*) at the beginning of an entry indicates that the title is appearing in BIP for the first time.

— The Fields of Bamboo: Dong Tre, Trung Luong & Hoa Hui, Three Battles Just Beyond the South China Sea. (Vietnam War Ser.: No. 7). (Illus.). 242p. 1984. reprint ed. 22.95 (*0-89839-081-8*) Battery Pr.
— Men Against Fire: The Problem of Battle Command in Future War. 14.00 (*0-8446-4057-3*) Peter Smith.
— Pork Chop Hill: The American Fighting Man in Action: Korea, Spring 1953. (Combat Arms Ser.). (Illus.). 313p. 1986. reprint ed. 24.95 (*0-89839-090-7*) Battery Pr.
— The River & the Gauntlet. 14th ed. (Combat Arms Ser.). 400p. 1987. reprint ed. 24.95 (*0-89839-097-4*) Battery Pr.
— Sinai Victory: Command Decisions in History's Shortest War, Israel's Hundred Hour Conquest of Egypt East of Suez, Autumn 1956. (Combat Arms Ser.: 11th). (Illus.). 280p. 1958. reprint ed. 24.95 (*0-89839-085-0*) Battery Pr.
— The Soldier's Load. 120p. Date not set. reprint ed. 2.00 (*0-686-31001-2*) Marine Corps.
— Vietnam: Three Battles. (Quality Paperbacks Ser.). (Illus.). 242p. 1982. reprint ed. pap. 8.95 (*0-306-80174-4*) Da Capo.
— West to Cambodia. 256p. 1986. pap. 4.50 (*0-515-08890-0*) Jove Pubns.
— West to Cambodia. (Vietnam War Ser.: No. 6). (Illus.). 253p. 1984. reprint ed. 22.95 (*0-89839-078-8*) Battery Pr.
— World War I. LC 85-3968. (American Heritage Library). (Illus.). 384p. (Orig.). 1985. pap. 12.95 (*0-8281-0434-4*) HM.
— World War I. (Orig.). 1993. 21.00 (*0-8446-6712-9*) Peter Smith.

Marshall, S. L. & Atwood, Lyman. Island Victory: The Battle for Kwajalein. 1983. reprint ed. 17.95 (*0-89201-101-7*) Zenger Pub.
Marshall, S. L. & Davis, W. J. JFK Plus CIA Equals BOP (Bay of Pigs) The Inside Story of the Bay of Pigs. 172p. 1992. pap. 11.00 (*1-885541-01-5*) Marine Bks.
Marshall, S. L., et al. Bastogne: The Story of the First Eight Days in Which the 101st Airborne Division Was Closed Within the Ring of German Forces. (United States Army in Action Series. CMH Pub.: No. 22-2). (Illus.). 273p. 1988. reprint ed. pap. 8.50 (*0-16-001972-9*, S/N 008-029-00170-5) USGPO.
***Marshall, S. M. & Home, P. H., eds.** The Diabetes Annual, Vol. 8. 504p. 1994. text ed. 214.50 (*0-444-81788-3*) Elsevier.
Marshall, S. M., et al, eds. The Diabetes Annual 7. 384p. 1993. 185.75 (*0-444-89694-5*) Elsevier.
Marshall, Samuel L. Night Drop: The American Airborne Invasion of Normandy. (Airborne Ser.: No. 16). (Illus.). 425p. 1982. reprint ed. 27.50 (*0-89839-062-1*) Battery Pr.
***Marshall, Sandra P.** Schemas in Problem Solving. (Illus.). 350p. (C). 1995. 49.95 (*0-521-43072-0*) Cambridge U Pr.
Marshall, Shane A. & Ruedy, John. On Call: Principles & Protocols. 2nd ed. (Illus.). 480p. 1993. pap. text ed. 25.50 (*0-7216-3982-8*) Saunders.
Marshall, Sharon. Justin: Heaven's Baby. 120p. (Orig.). 1983. pap. 5.95 (*0-8341-0833-X*) Beacon Hill.
Marshall, Sharon G. When a Friend Gets a Divorce: What Can You Do? 128p. (Orig.). 1990. pap. 6.99 (*0-8010-6252-7*) Baker Bk.
Marshall, Sheila, jt. ed. see Marcuccio, Phyllis.
Marshall, Shelly. The Book of Karma. 246p. (Orig.). 1994. pap. 12.99 (*1-880197-99-5*) Gylantic Pub.
— Teenage Addicts Can Recover: Treating the Addict, Not the Age. 176p. 1992. pap. 12.95 (*1-880197-02-2*) Gylantic Pub.
— Your Dream of Recovery: Dream Interpretation & the Twelve Steps. 1995. pap. 14.95 (*0-87604-332-5*, 405) ARE Pr.
Marshall, Shelly, ed. Young, Sober, & Free. 137p. 1978. 9.00 (*0-89486-055-0*, 1116A) Hazelden.
Marshall, Sheri C. One Can Do It: A How-to-Guide for the Physically Handicapped. LC 93-22307. (Illus.). 192p. 1994. pap. 14.95 (*1-56825-002-9*) Rainbow Books.
Marshall, Sherrin D. The Dutch Gentry, Fifteen Hundred to Sixteen-Fifty: Family, Faith, & Fortune. LC 86-7647. (Contributions in Family Studies: No. 11). 252p. 1987. text ed. 59.95 (*0-313-25021-9*, WYD/, Greenwood Pr) Greenwood.
Marshall, Sherrin D., ed. Women in Reformation & Counter-Reformation Europe: Private & Public Worlds. LC 88-45758. (Illus.). 224p. 1989. 35.00 (*0-253-33678-3*); pap. 10.95 (*0-253-20527-1*, MB-527) Ind U Pr.
Marshall, Sherrin D., jt. ed. see Bebb, Phillip N.
Marshall, Sherrin D., ed. see Rabb, Theodore K.
Marshall, Sidney J. The King of Kor: Or, She's Promise Kept. Reginald, R. & Melville, Douglas, eds. LC 77-84255. (Lost Race & Adult Fantasy Ser.). (Illus.). 1978. reprint ed. lib. bdg. 24.95 (*0-405-10999-7*) Ayer.
Marshall, Simone V., jt. auth. see Marshall, Robert J.
Marshall, Stan, jt. auth. see Glass, Richard D.
Marshall, Stanley V. & Skitek, Gabriel G. Electromagnetic Concepts & Applications. 3rd ed. 542p. 1989. text ed. 75.00 (*0-13-250960-1*) P-H.
Marshall, Stephanie P., jt. pref. see Marzano, Robert J.
Marshall, Stephen E. Randax Education Guide to Colleges Seeking Students, 1990 Edition. 19th ed. (Illus.). 128p. (Orig.). 1990. pap. 12.95 (*0-914880-20-9*) Educ Guide.
— Randax Education Guide to Colleges Seeking Students, 1992. 21th ed. (Illus.). 128p. (Orig.). 1992. pap. 14.95 (*0-914880-22-5*) Educ Guide.
— Randax Education Guide to Colleges Seeking Students, 1993 Edition. 22th ed. (Illus.). 128p. 1993. pap. 15.95 (*0-914880-23-3*) Educ Guide.
— Randax Education Guide to Colleges Seeking Students, 1994. 23th ed. (Illus.). 128p. 1994. pap. 16.95 (*0-914880-24-1*) Educ Guide.

Marshall, Strome. Manual of Otolaryngology: Diagnosis & Therapy. 212p. 1985. 25.50 (*0-316-81967-0*) Little.
Marshall, Suzanne. Violence in the Black Patch of Kentucky & Tennessee. (Illus.). 232p. 1994. 34.95 (*0-8262-0971-8*) U of Mo Pr.
Marshall, Suzanne R. A Falling Leaf & Other Poetry Activities. LC 82-83777. 92p. 1983. pap. text ed. 19.95 (*0-918452-41-4*) Learning Pubns.
Marshall, Sybil. A Nest of Magpies. 476p. 1994. 24.95 (*0-312-11034-0*) St Martin.
Marshall, T. H. Class, Citizenship & Social Development: A Greenwood Archival Edition. LC 73-2879. 334p. 1973. reprint ed. text ed. 55.00 (*0-8371-6778-7*, MACL, Greenwood Pr) Greenwood.
Marshall, T. H. & Bottomore, Thomas B. Citizenship & Social Class. 101p. (C). 1991. text ed. 47.50 (*0-7453-0477-X*, Pub. by Pluto Pr UK); pap. text ed. 12.95 (*0-7453-0476-1*, Pub. by Pluto Pr UK) Westview.
Marshall, T. J. & Holmes, J. W. Soil Physics. 2nd ed. (Illus.). 350p. 1988. pap. 37.95 (*0-521-35817-5*) Cambridge U Pr.
Marshall, T. M. History of the Western Boundary of the Louisiana Purchase, 1819-1841. LC 73-87411. (American Scene Ser.). (Illus.). 1970. reprint ed. lib. bdg. 35.00 (*0-306-71554-6*) Da Capo.
Marshall-Taylor, Geoffrey, comp. The Complete Come & Praise: Words & Music Edition. 256p. 1990. pap. 21.95 (*0-563-34581-0*, Pub. by BBC UK) Parkwest Pubns.
Marshall, Terry. My Father's Hands. (Northway Ser.). vi, 193p. 1992. 19.95 (*0-89672-274-0*) Tex Tech Univ Pr.
— Whole World Guide to Language Learning. LC 88-45727. 176p. 1990. pap. 15.95 (*0-933662-75-0*) Intercult Pr.
Marshall, Terry V. Crater Lake. LC 23-939860. (Illus.). 70p. 1977. 16.95 (*0-939860-02-3*); pap. 6.95 (*0-939860-01-5*) Tremaine Graph & Pub.
Marshall, Thomas C. Free-Electron Lasers. 1985. text ed. 40.00 (*0-07-040609-X*) McGraw.
Marshall, Thomas F. An Analytical Index to American Literature: Vols. I-XXX, Mar. 1929-Jan. 1959, Vols. 1-30, Mar. 1929-Jan. 1959. LC 30-20216. ix, 253p. 1963. 31.95 (*0-8223-0114-8*) Duke.
Marshall, Thomas M., ed. The Life & Papers of Frederick Bates, 2 vols. in 1. LC 75-109. (Mid-American Frontier Ser.). 1975. reprint ed. 57.95 (*0-405-06876-X*) Ayer.
Marshall, Thomas R. Presidential Nominations in a Reform Age. LC 81-1684. 224p. 1981. text ed. 45.00 (*0-275-90677-9*, C0677, Praeger Pubs) Greenwood.
— Public Opinion & the Supreme Court. 256p. 1988. text ed. 39.95 (*0-04-497046-3*); pap. text ed. 14.95 (*0-04-497047-1*) Routledge Chapman & Hall.
Marshall, Thomas W., jt. auth. see Hinshaw, William W.
Marshall, Thurgood. Dream Makers, Dream Breakers: The World of Justice. 496p. 1993. 24.95 (*0-316-75918-X*) Little.
***Marshall, Tim.** Man's Greatest Fear: The Final Phase of Human Evolution. (Illus.). 180p. (Orig.). 1995. pap. 11.00 (*0-9645750-0-0*) Athena Bks.
— Murdering to Dissect: Graverobbing, Frankenstein & the Anatomy Literature. LC 95-1715. 1995. text ed. write for info. (*0-7190-4542-8*, Pub. by Manchester Univ Pr UK); text ed. write for info. (*0-7190-4543-6*, Pub. by Manchester Univ Pr UK) St Martin.
Marshall, Tom. Voices on the Brink: A Border Tale. 224p. 1989. pap. 9.95 (*0-571-12979-X*) Faber & Faber.
Marshall, Tom & Muccio, Tom. Leadership: Effective Spiritual Keys for Today's Leaders, 12 pts. 96p. (Orig.). 1993. audio 49.95 (*0-935779-16-7*); vhs 195.00 (*0-935779-17-5*) Crown Min.
— Leadership: Effective Spiritual Keys for Today's Leaders, 12 pts., Set. 96p. (Orig.). 1993. student ed 9.95 (*0-935779-15-9*) Crown Min.
Marshall, Tony. Community Disorders & Policing. 300p. 1992. 70.00 (*1-871177-25-1*, Pub. by Whiting & Birch UK); pap. text ed. 29.95 (*1-871177-26-X*, Pub. by Whiting & Birch UK) Paul & Co Pubs.
Marshall, Tony F. Alternatives to Criminal Courts: The Potential for Non-Judicial Dispute Settlements. 324p. 1985. 49.95 (*0-566-05002-1*) Ashgate Pub Co.
Marshall, Tony F., jt. auth. see Rose, Gordon.
Marshall, V. C. Consequences of Nuclear & Chemical Disasters. (Chemical Engineering Ser.). 350p. 1995. text ed. 115.95 (*0-13-170770-1*, 520805) P-H.
— Disaster at Flixborough. 1980. write for info. (*0-318-57467-5*, Pergamon Pr) Elsevier.
Marshall, Val & Tester, Bronwyn. And Grandpa Sat on Friday. LC 92-34159. (Voyages Ser.). (Illus.). (J). 1993. 4.25 (*0-383-03610-0*) SRA Schl Grp.
— The Cat's Whiskers. LC 93-11737. (Voyages Ser.). (Illus.). (J). 1994. 4.25 (*0-685-69328-7*) SRA Schl Grp.
— The Old Car. LC 92-27264. (Voyages Ser.). (Illus.). (J). 1993. 3.75 (*0-383-03644-5*) SRA Schl Grp.
Marshall, Verne M. The Roses of Geneva. LC 93-60765. (Illus.). 158p. 1993. write for info. (*1-55787-097-7*, Windswept Books) Hrt of the Lakes.
Marshall, Vernon C. & Royle, John. Multiple Choice Questions in Basic Surgical Sciences. 1991. pap. 37.50 (*0-409-30401-8*) Buttrwrth-Heinemann.
Marshall, Vernon C., jt. auth. see Ludbrook, John.
Marshall, Victor & McPherson, Barry, eds. Aging: Canadian Perspectives. 240p. 1994. pap. text ed. 19.95 (*1-55111-012-1*) Broadview Pr.
Marshall, W. G. Through America: Or, Nine Months in the United States. LC 72-3388. (Essay Index Reprint Ser.). 1977. reprint ed. 39.95 (*0-8369-2913-6*) Ayer.
Marshall, W. Gerald. A Great Stage of Fools: Theatricality & Madness in the Plays of William Wycherley. LC 91-11028. (Studies in the Seventeenth Century: No. 4). 125p. 1993. 37.50 (*0-404-61724-7*) AMS Pr.
Marshall, W. J. O Come, Emmanuel: Scripture Verses for Advent Worship. LC 94-12745. 100p. 1994. pap. 7.95 (*0-8192-1629-1*) Morehouse Pub.

Marshall, Walter. Gospel Mystery of Sanctification. 1981. pap. 11.99 (*0-85234-158-X*, Pub. by Evangel Pr UK) Presby & Reformed.
— Nuclear Power Technology, Vol 1: Reactor Technology. (Illus.). 1984. 95.00 (*0-19-851948-6*) OUP.
— Nuclear Power Technology, Vol. 2: Fuel Cycle. (Illus.). 1984. 75.00 (*0-19-851958-3*) OUP.
Marshall, Walter H. I've Met Them All. (Illus.). 186p. 1983. 12.95 (*0-317-00339-9*); pap. 8.95 (*0-317-00340-2*) W H Marshall.
Marshall, Will & Schram, Martin, eds. Mandate for Change. 1993. pap. 11.95 (*0-425-13964-6*) Berkley Pub.
Marshall, William. Adam's Island. (I Love to Read Collection). (Illus.). (J). (gr. 3-8). 1992. lib. bdg. 12.79 (*0-89565-889-5*) Childs World.
— Faces in the Crowd. 1991. 19.95 (*0-89296-367-0*) Mysterious Pr.
— Inches. 304p. 1994. 19.95 (*0-89296-368-9*) Mysterious Pr.
— Inches. 256p. 1995. mass mkt. 5.99 (*0-446-40455-1*, Mysterious Paperbk) Warner Bks.
— The New York Detective. 1989. 17.95 (*0-89296-366-2*) Mysterious Pr.
— Out of Nowhere. LC 88-40073. 224p. 1988. 15.95 (*0-89296-199-6*) Mysterious Pr.
— Review & Abstract of the County Reports to the Board of Agriculture, 5 vols., Set, Vols. 1-5. LC 69-11853. 1968. reprint ed. 250.00 (*0-678-05613-7*) Kelley.
— Rural Economy of the West of England: Including Devonshire, & Parts of Somersetshire, Dorsetshire & Cornwall, 2 vols. LC 78-85333. 1970. reprint ed. 87.50 (*0-678-05564-5*) Kelley.
— War Machine. 1988. 15.95 (*0-89296-198-8*) Mysterious Pr.
Marshall, William, tr. see Constantine I.
Marshall, William E. A Phrenologist Amongst the Todas or the Study of a Primitive Tribe in South India: History, Character, Customs, Religion, Infantcide, Polyandry, Language. (C). 1995. 34.00x (*81-206-0899-2*, Pub. by Asian Educ Servs II) S Asia.
Marshall, William L., et al, eds. Handbook of Sexual Assault: Issues, Theories, & Treatment of the Offender. LC 89-23174. (Applied Clinical Psychology Ser.). (Illus.). 424p. 1990. 65.00 (*0-306-43272-2*, Plenum Pr) Plenum.
Marshall, Wolf. Beginning Rock Bass Guitar. (Illus.). 24p. 1990. audio, pap. 14.95 (*0-8256-1150-4*, AM67430) Music Sales.
— Beginning Rock Lead Guitar. (Illus.). 24p. 1990. audio, pap. 14.95 (*0-8256-1149-0*, AM67422) Music Sales.
— Beginning Rock Rhythm Guitar. (Illus.). 24p. 1990. audio, pap. 14.95 (*0-8256-1151-2*, AM67448) Music Sales.
— Beginning Rock Riffs. (Illus.). 24p. 1990. audio, pap. 14.95 (*0-8256-1152-0*, AM67455) Music Sales.
— Classical Riffs for Rock Guitar. (Illus.). 24p. 1990. audio, pap. 14.95 (*0-8256-1155-5*, AM67463) Music Sales.
— Original Gary Moore. (Illus.). 48p. 1988. pap. 11.95 (*0-685-65798-1*, AM63868) Music Sales.
— Original Randy Rhoads. (Illus.). 48p. 1986. pap. 11.95 (*0-8256-1065-6*, AM63850) Music Sales.
Marshall, Wolf, ed. Ratt-Out of the Cellar: Recorded Versions. (Fretted Ser.). 120p. 1987. pap. 18.95 (*0-88188-764-1*, HL 00693911) H Leonard.
Marshall, Wolf, tr. Iron Maiden Collection. (Recorded Versions Ser.). 183p. 1987. 19.95 (*0-88188-768-4*, HL00693096) H Leonard.
Marshall, Wolf, jt. ed. see Phillips, Mark.
Marshallsay, Diana, et al, eds. Ford List of British Parliamentary Papers, 1974-1983. 700p. 1989. lib. bdg. 149.00 (*0-85964-188-0*) Chadwyck-Healey.
Marshand, La Mer. Awake Beloved: We've Slept Too Long. LC 91-73744. 312p. (Orig.). 1991. pap. 15.95 (*0-9630485-0-3*) In Print.
Marshbum, Sandra, jt. auth. see RanDelle, B. J.
Marshburn, Joseph H. & Velie, Alan R. Blood & Knavery: A Collection of English Renaissance Pamphlets & Ballads of Crime & Sin. LC 72-3523. (Illus.). 215p. 1973. 25.00 (*0-8386-1010-2*) Fairleigh Dickinson.
Marshburn, Sandra. Undertow. 21p. (Orig.). 1992. pap. 6.00 (*0-9624453-9-8*) March Street Pr.
Marshburn, Tom. Six-Moon Trail: Canada to Mexico along the Pacific Crest. Leishman, Robert K., ed. LC 85-50297. (Illus.). 224p. 1985. 15.95 (*0-9614526-0-9*) R Leishman.
Marshek, Kurt M. Design of Machine & Structural Parts. LC 87-6286. 222p. 1987. text ed. 79.95 (*0-471-84996-0*) Wiley.
Marshek, Kurt M., jt. auth. see Juvinall, Robert C.
***Marshel, Judy E. & Konner, Linda.** Trouble-Free Menopause: Every Woman's Guide to Living a Fit & Healthy Life. 336p. (Orig.). 1995. mass mkt. 5.50 (*0-380-77732-0*) Avon.
Marshell, Robin D. & Tipton, Keith F., eds. Essay in Biochemistry, Vol. 22. 200p. 1987. pap. text ed. 49.00 (*0-12-158122-5*) Acad Pr.
Marshment, Margaret, jt. ed. see Gamman, Lorraine.
Marshner, Connaught, jt. comp. see Weyrich, Paul.
Marshner, William, tr. see Crosby, John, et al.
Marsi, Rick. Once Around the Sun. LC 92-37300. (Illus.). 176p. 1992. pap. 14.50 (*0-935796-36-3*) Purple Mnt Pr.
Marsicano, Ed. No Satisfaction & the Happy Time: Two Novels. Collins, Patricia & Milazzo, Richard, eds. LC 93-85692. 229p. (Orig.). 1994. pap. 8.95 (*0-9631022-1-4*) Ridgefld Pr.
Marsick, Victoria J., ed. Enhancing Staff Development in Diverse Settings. LC 85-644750. (New Directions for Continuing Education Ser.: No. 38). 1988. 16.95 (*1-55542-917-3*) Jossey-Bass.
— Learning in the Workplace. 288p. 1987. lib. bdg. 30.00 (*0-7099-4659-7*, Pub. by Croom Helm UK) Routledge Chapman & Hall.

Marsick, Victoria J. & Baskett, H. K., eds. Professionals' Ways of Knowing: New Findings on How to Improve Professional Education. LC 85-644750. (New Directions for Adult & Continuing Education Ser.: No. ACE 55). 130p. 1992. student ed 16.95 (*1-55542-728-6*) Jossey-Bass.
Marsick, Victoria J. & Watkins, Karen E. Informal & Incidental Learning in the Workplace. 288p. 1990. 47.50 (*0-415-03141-9*, A4819) Routledge.
Marsick, Victoria J., jt. auth. see Watkins, Karen E.
***Marsiglio & Scanzoni.** Families & Friendships. (C). 1994. text ed. 6.00 (*0-673-99568-2*) HarpCollege.
Marsiglio of Padua. Defensor Minor & de Translatione Imperli. Nederman, Cary J., ed. LC 92-33311. (Cambridge Texts in the History of Political Thought Ser.). 120p. (C). 1993. 44.95 (*0-521-40277-8*); pap. 14.95 (*0-521-40846-6*) Cambridge U Pr.
***Marsiglio, William.** Fatherhood: Contemporary Theory, Research & Social Policy. (Research on Men & Masculinities Ser.). 320p. 1995. text ed. 49.95 (*0-8039-5782-3*); pap. text ed. 24.00 (*0-8039-5783-1*) Sage.
Marsili, Mario. Computer Chemistry. 192p. 1989. 144.00 (*0-8493-4554-5*, QD39) CRC Pr.
Marsilius of Padua. Defensor Pacis. Gewirth, Alan, tr. (Medieval Academy Reprints for Teaching Ser.). 1980. pap. 15.95 (*0-8020-6412-4*) U of Toronto Pr.
Marske, Charles E., ed. Communities of Fate: Readings in the Social Organization of Risk. 246p. (Orig.). (C). 1991. lib. bdg. 51.00 (*0-8191-8310-5*); pap. text ed. 23.00 (*0-8191-8311-3*) U Pr of Amer.
Marsland, Amy L., jt. auth. see Marsland, William D.
Marsland, Cora. Interpretive Reading. LC 78-86801. (Granger Index Reprint Ser.). 1977. 20.95 (*0-8369-6084-X*) Ayer.
Marsland, David. Neglect & Betrayal: War & Violence in Modern Sociology. (C). 1981. pap. 29.00 (*0-907967-65-5*, Inst Europ Def) St Mut.
— Neglect & Betrayal: War & Violence in Modern Sociology. (C). 1990. 60.00 (*0-685-52527-9*, Pub. by Inst Euro Def & Strat UK) St Mut.
Marsland, David, ed. Work & Employment in Liberal Democratic Societies. LC 93-46969. (Liberal Democratic Societies Ser.). 240p. (C). 1994. 34.95x (*0-943852-67-6*); pap. text ed. 17.95x (*0-943852-68-4*) Prof World Peace.
Marsland, Elizabeth A. The Nation's Cause: French, English & German Poetry of the First World War. 288p. 1991. 74.50 (*0-415-05460-5*, A4909) Routledge.
Marsland, Stephen. The Birth of the Japanese Labor Movement: Takano Fusataro & the Rodo Kumiai Kiseikai. LC 88-21622. (Illus.). 288p. 1989. text ed. 27.00 (*0-8248-1167-4*) UH Pr.
Marsland, T. A. & Schaeffer, J., eds. Computers, Chess, & Cognition. (Illus.). xii, 323p. 1990. 39.00 (*0-387-97415-6*) Spr-Verlag.
Marsland, T. Anthony, jt. auth. see Yang, Zhonghua.
Marsland, William D. & Marsland, Amy L. Venezuela Through Its History. LC 75-40919. (Illus.). 277p. 1976. reprint ed. text ed. 38.50 (*0-8371-8690-0*, MAVE, Greenwood Pr) Greenwood.
Marslen-Wilson, William, ed. Lexical Representation & Process. (Illus.). 592p. 1992. reprint ed. pap. 28.50 (*0-262-63142-3*) MIT Pr.
Marsmann, H., jt. auth. see Kintzinger, J. P.
Marsnik, Nadine C., jt. auth. see Wolff, Florence I.
Marso, Molly, jt. auth. see McCarthy, Gloria.
Marsoatsian, Armen, ed. see Buchler, Justus.
***Marsocci, Fred.** Weasel. Friedland, J. & Kessler, R., eds. (Novel-Ties Ser.). (J). (gr. 4-6). 1993. student ed, pap. text ed. 15.95 (*0-88122-901-6*) Lrn Links.
Marsolais, Ken. Broadway Day & Night. Grose, Bill, ed. 288p. 1992. 50.00 (*0-671-74637-5*) PB.
Marsoli, Lisa A. & Strong, Stacie. Jake & Jenny on the Farm. (Illus.). 18p. (J). (ps-2). 1990. 7.95 (*0-8431-2853-4*) Price Stern.
Marson, Charles M. & Giles, Paul R., eds. Synthesis Using Vilsmeier Reagents. 256p. 1994. 89.95 (*0-8493-7869-9*, 7869) CRC Pr.
Marson, Chuck. In Your Own Back Yard: A Guide for Great Plains Gardening. (Illus.). 160p. (Orig.). 1983. pap. 8.95 (*0-941974-01-4*) Baranski Pub Co.
Marson, E. L. The Ascetic Artist: Prefigurations in Thomas Mann's Der Tod in Venedig. (Australian & New Zealand Studies in German Language & Literature: Vol. 9). 165p. 1979. pap. 31.25 (*3-261-03120-4*) P Lang Pubs.
Marson, Iginio, ed. see International Gravity Commission & International Geoid Commission Staffs.
Marson, Peg, jt. auth. see Marson, Ron.
Marson, Ron. Balancing. LC 81-90443. (Science with Simple Things Ser.: No. 31). (Illus.). 80p. (YA). (gr. 5-10). 1981. teacher ed 15.00 (*0-941008-31-2*) Tops Learning.
— Balancing. (Task Cards Ser.: No. 4). (Illus.). 48p. (YA). (gr. 7-12). 1993. teacher ed 8.00 (*0-941008-74-6*) Tops Learning.
— Cohesion-Adhesion. (Task Cards Ser.: No. 13). (Illus.). 64p. (YA). (gr. 7-12). 1995. teacher ed 11.00 (*0-941008-83-5*) Tops Learning.
— The Earth Moon & Sun. (Science with Simple Things Ser.: No. 40). (Illus.). 72p. (J). (gr. 5-10). 1993. teacher ed 15.00 (*0-941008-40-1*) Tops Learning.
— Electricity. (Task Cards Ser.: No. 19). (Illus.). 88p. (YA). (gr. 7-12). 1990. teacher ed 16.00 (*0-941008-89-4*) Tops Learning.
— Electricity. LC 81-90444. (Science with Simple Things Ser.: No. 32). (Illus.). 80p. (YA). (gr. 5-10). 1983. teacher ed 15.00 (*0-941008-32-0*) Tops Learning.
— Floating & Sinking. (Task Cards Ser.: No. 9). (Illus.). 64p. (YA). (gr. 7-12). 1995. teacher ed 11.00 (*0-941008-79-7*) Tops Learning.

M

— Graphing. (Task Cards Ser.: No. 3). (Illus.). 56p. (YA). (gr. 7-12). 1990. teacher ed 9.50 (*0-941008-73-8*) Tops Learning.

— Green Thumbs: Corn & Beans. (Science with Simple Things Ser.: No. 39). (Illus.). 80p. (YA). (gr. 5-10). 1989. teacher ed 15.00 (*0-941008-39-8*) Tops Learning.

— Green Thumbs: Radishes. (Science wuth Simple Things Ser.: No. 38). (Illus.). 80p. (YA). (gr. 5-10). 1986. teacher ed 15.00 (*0-941008-38-X*) Tops Learning.

— Heat. (Task Cards Ser.: No. 15). (Illus.). 56p. (YA). (gr. 7-10). 1990. teacher ed 9.50 (*0-941008-85-1*) Tops Learning.

— Kinetic Model. (Task Cards Ser.: No. 14). (Illus.). 64p. (YA). (gr. 7-12). 1992. teacher ed 11.00 (*0-941008-84-3*) Tops Learning.

— Light. (Task Cards Ser.: No. 17). (Illus.). 88p. (YA). (gr. 7-12). 1991. teacher ed 16.00 (*0-941008-87-8*) Tops Learning.

— Machines. (Task Cards Ser.: No. 22). (Illus.). 48p. (YA). (gr. 7-12). 1989. teacher ed 8.00 (*0-941008-99-1*) Tops Learning.

— Magnetism. LC 81-90445. (Science with Simple Things Ser.: No. 33). (Illus.). 80p. (YA). (gr. 5-10). 1983. teacher ed 15.00 (*0-941008-33-9*) Tops Learning.

— Math Lab. (Task Cards Ser.: No. 7). (Illus.). 56p. (YA). (gr. 7-12). 1994. teacher ed 9.50 (*0-941008-77-0*) Tops Learning.

— Measuring Length. (Task Cards Ser.: No. 2). (Illus.). 48p. (YA). (gr. 7-12). 1991. teacher ed 8.00 (*0-941008-72-X*) Tops Learning.

— Metric Measure. (Task Cards Ser.: No. 6). (Illus.). 56p. (YA). (gr. 7-12). 1992. teacher ed 9.50 (*0-941008-76-2*) Tops Learning.

— Metric Measuring. LC 81-90446. (Science with Simple Things Ser.: No. 35). (Illus.). 80p. (YA). (gr. 5-10). 1984. teacher ed 15.00 (*0-941008-35-5*) Tops Learning.

— More Metrics. LC 81-90448. (Science with Simple Things Ser.: No. 36). (Illus.). 80p. (YA). (gr. 5-10). 1985. teacher ed 15.00 (*0-941008-36-3*) Tops Learning.

— Motion. (Task Cards Ser.: No. 21). (Illus.). 88p. (YA). (gr. 7-12). 1990. teacher ed 16.00 (*0-941008-98-3*) Tops Learning.

— Oxidation. (Task Cards Ser.: No. 11). (Illus.). 48p. (YA). (gr. 7-12). 1978. teacher ed 8.00 (*0-941008-81-9*) Tops Learning.

— Pendulums. (Task Cards Ser.: No. 1). (Illus.). 56p. (YA). (gr. 7-12). 1992. teacher ed 9.50 (*0-941008-71-1*) Tops Learning.

— Pendulums. LC 81-90447. (Science with Simple Things Ser.: No. 34). (Illus.). 80p. (YA). (gr. 5-10). 1983. teacher ed 15.00 (*0-941008-34-7*) Tops Learning.

— The Planets & Stars. (Science with Simple Things Ser.: No. 41). (Illus.). 80p. (J). (gr. 5-10). 1994. teacher ed 15.00 (*0-941008-41-X*) Tops Learning.

— Pressure. (Task Cards Ser.: No. 16). (Illus.). 80p. (YA). (gr. 7-12). 1992. teacher ed 14.50 (*0-941008-86-X*) Tops Learning.

— Solutions. (Task Cards Ser.: No. 12). (Illus.). 72p. (YA). (gr. 7-12). 1990. teacher ed 13.00 (*0-941008-82-7*) Tops Learning.

— Sound. (Task Cards Ser.: No. 18). (Illus.). 56p. (YA). (gr. 7-12). 1990. teacher ed 9.50 (*0-941008-88-6*) Tops Learning.

— Weighing. (Task Cards Ser.: No. 5). (Illus.). 56p. (YA). (gr. 7-12). 1990. teacher ed 9.50 (*0-941008-75-4*) Tops Learning.

***Marson, Ron & Marson, Peg.** Probability. (Task Cards Ser.: No. 8). (Illus.). 64p. (YA). (gr. 7-12). 1995. teacher ed 13.00 (*0-941008-78-9*) Tops Learning.

Marson, Ron, ed. see Balick, Don.

Marson, Ron, ed. see Fellers, Pat & Gritzmacher, Kathy.

Marson, Ron, ed. see Gritzmacher, Kathy.

Marson, Ron, jt. auth. see Metcalf, Doris.

***Marsonet, Michele.** Science, Reality, & Language. (Philosophy Ser.). 160p. (C). 1995. 44.50x (*0-7914-2475-8*); pap. 14.95x (*0-7914-2476-6*) State U NY Pr.

Marsot, Afaf L. Egypt in the Reign of Mohammad Ali. LC 83-5241. (Cambridge Middle East Library: No. 4). (Illus.). 320p. 1984. 69.95 (*0-521-24795-0*); pap. 27.95 (*0-521-28968-8*) Cambridge U Pr.

— A Short History of Modern Egypt. 168p. 1985. pap. 16.95 (*0-521-27234-3*) Cambridge U Pr.

Marsteller, William. Creative Management. 160p. 1988. pap. 14.95 (*0-8442-3171-1*, Crain Bks) NTC Pub Grp.

Marsteller, William A. Creative Management. 164p. 1992. pap. 11.95 (*0-8442-3119-3*, NTC Busn Bks) NTC Pub Grp.

Marsten, J. Sketches of Book Sellers of Other Days. 1976. lib. bdg. 99.95 (*0-8490-2612-1*) Gordon Pr.

Marsters, Bridget, jt. auth. see Marsters, Ted.

Marsters, James A. Fragments. Graves, Helen, ed. LC 89-52119. 69p. 1990. 8.95 (*1-55523-303-1*) Winston-Derek.

Marsters, Ted & Marsters, Bridget. The Big Ideas for Little People Book. (Illus.). (Orig.). 1981. pap. 4.00 (*0-939562-00-6*) Parker Pr.

Marsterson, William. Information Technology & the Role of the Librarian. (Information Technology Ser.). 208p. 1986. 37.50 (*0-7099-4610-4*, Pub. by Croom Helm UK) Routledge Chapman & Hall.

***Marston.** Annuals. 1994. pap. text ed. 12.99 (*0-517-13453-5*) Random Hse Value.

— Audio IC Circuits Manual. 1989. pap. 30.95 (*0-434-91210-7*, TK) CRC Pr.

— Cynthia & the Runaway Gazeb. 1994. pap. 4.99 (*0-517-13489-6*) Random Hse Value.

Marston, jt. auth. see Tindal.

Marston, et al. Splanchnic Ischemia. 1989. 79.00 (*0-8016-5523-4*) Mosby Yr Bk.

Marston, A., jt. auth. see Hostettmann, K.

Marston, A. T. The Swanscombe Skull. Bd. with Report on the Swanscombe Skull. LC 78-72701. LC 78-72701. reprint ed. 27.50 (*0-404-18271-2*) AMS Pr.

Marston, Adrian. Vascular Disease of the Gastrointestinal Tract. (Illus.). 186p. 1986. 52.95 (*0-683-05598-4*) Williams & Wilkins.

Marston, Bernice & Swiecki, Mark. In Plain English: A Game of Figurative Language. (J). 1991. teacher ed 34.95 (*1-55999-210-7*) LinguiSystems.

Marston, D. L. Law for Professional Engineers. xi, 243p. write for info. (*0-07-548073-5*) McGraw.

Marston, David A., jt. auth. see Burns, Stephen S.

Marston, David A., jt. ed. see Burns, Stephen S.

Marston, David W. Malice Aforethought: How Lawyers Use Our Secret Rules to Get Rich, Get Sex, Get Even...& Get Away with It. LC 90-46396. 240p. 1991. 19.95 (*0-688-07705-6*) Morrow.

Marston, Ed, ed. see High Country News Staff.

***Marston, Edmund.** Silent Woman. Date not set. pap. write for info. (*0-449-22375-2*) Fawcett.

Marston, Edward. The Mad Courtesan. 240p. 1992. 18.95 (*0-312-08259-2*) St Martin.

— The Mad Courtesan. large type ed. LC 92-46347. (General Ser.). 351p. 1993. reprint ed. lib. bdg. 17.95 (*1-56054-673-5*) Thorndike Pr.

— The Mad Courtesan. 1994. reprint ed. mass mkt. 4.99 (*0-449-22246-2*) Fawcett.

— The Merry Devils. (Elizabethan Mystery Ser.). 240p. 1991. pap. 3.95 (*0-449-21880-5*, Crest) Fawcett.

— The Nine Giants. 1993. mass mkt. 4.50 (*0-449-22128-8*, Crest) Fawcett.

— The Ravens of Blackwater. LC 94-3321. 1994. 20.95 (*0-312-11330-7*) St Martin.

— The Roaring Boy. LC 95-8568. 272p. 1995. 21.95 (*0-312-13155-0*) St Martin.

— The Silent Woman. 320p. 1994. 21.95 (*0-312-11115-0*) St Martin.

— The Wolves of Savernake. 256p. 1993. 19.95 (*0-312-09942-8*) St Martin.

— The Wolves of Savernake. 1995. mass mkt. 5.99 (*0-449-22310-8*, Crest) Fawcett.

Marston, Edwin H. The Dynamic Environment: Water, Transportation, & Energy. LC 74-82346. 432p. reprint ed. pap. 123.20 (*0-317-10809-3*, 2012461) Bks Demand.

***Marston, Elsa.** The Ancient Egyptians. (Cultures of the Past Ser.). 80p. (J). (gr. 5-8). 1995. lib. bdg. write for info. (*0-7614-0073-7*, Benchmark NY) Marshall Cavendish.

— Cynthia & the Runaway Gazebo. LC 91-32548. (Illus.). 32p. (J). (gr. k-4). 1992. 14.00 (*0-688-10282-4*, Tambourine Bks); lib. bdg. 13.93 (*0-688-10283-2*, Tambourine Bks) Morrow.

— The Fox Maiden. LC 95-1190. (Illus.). (J). 1996. 15.00 (*0-689-80107-6*, S&S Bks Young Read) S&S Childrens.

— A Griffin in the Garden. LC 92-35399. (Illus.). 32p. (J). (gr. k up). 1993. 15.00 (*0-688-10981-0*, Tambourine Bks); lib. bdg. 14.93 (*0-688-10982-9*, Tambourine Bks) Morrow.

— Lebanon: New Light in an Ancient Land. LC 93-5402. (Illus.). 128p. (J). (gr. 5 up). 1994. text ed. 14.95 (*0-87518-584-3*, Dillon Silver Burdett) Silver Burdett Pr.

Marston, Frank S. The Peace Conference of 1919: Organization & Procedure. LC 80-28997. xi, 276p. 1981. reprint ed. text ed. 45.00 (*0-313-22910-4*, MAPEC, Greenwood Pr) Greenwood.

— The Peace Conference of 1919, Organization & Procedure. LC 76-29412. reprint ed. 32.50 (*0-404-15349-6*) AMS Pr.

Marston, Gwen. American Beauties Rose-Tulip Quilt. 1988. pap. 14.95 (*0-89145-937-5*) Collector Bks.

— Twenty Little Amish Quilts: With Full-Size Templates. LC 93-9357. (Needlework Ser.). (Illus.). 1993. pap. 3.95 (*0-486-27582-5*) Dover.

— Twenty Little Patchwork Quilts. 1990. pap. 3.95 (*0-486-26131-X*) Dover.

— Twenty Little Pinwheel Quilts: With Full-Size Templates. (Illus.). 56p. (Orig.). 1994. pap. text ed. 4.95 (*0-486-28216-3*) Dover.

Marston, Gwen & Cunningham, Joe. Amish Quilting Patterns: Fifty-Six Full-Size Ready-to-Use Designs & Complete Instructions. 96p. (Orig.). 1987. pap. 4.95 (*0-486-25326-0*) Dover.

— Mary Schafer & Her Quilts. Fitzgerald, Ruth & Caltrider, Sue, eds. (Illus.). 64p. (Orig.). 1990. pap. 19.95 (*0-944311-04-0*) MSU Museum.

— Quilting with Style: Principles for Great Pattern Design. LC 93-7673. 1993. 19.95 (*0-89145-814-X*) Collector Bks.

— Sets & Borders. (Illus.). 104p. 1987. pap. 14.95 (*0-89145-923-5*, 1821) Collector Bks.

— Seventy Classic Quilting Patterns: Ready-to-Use Designs & Instructions. (Illus.). 96p. (Orig.). 1987. pap. 4.95 (*0-486-25474-7*) Dover.

***Marston, Hope.** By an Unfamiliar Path: The Story of David & Arlene Peters. (Junior Jaffray Ser.: Bk. 13). (Illus.). 32p. (J). (ps-2). 1995. 3.99 (*0-87509-581-X*) Chr Pubns.

— To Vietnam with Love. (Junior Jaffray Ser.: Bk. 12). (Illus.). 32p. (J). (ps-2). 1995. 3.99 (*0-87509-583-6*) Chr Pubns.

Marston, Hope I. Big Rigs. rev. ed. LC 92-39881. (Illus.). 48p. (J). (gr. 2-5). 1993. 14.99 (*0-525-65123-3*, Cobblehill Bks) Dutton Child Bks.

— Isaac Johnson: From Slave to Stonecutter. LC 94-32671. (Illus.). 1995. 14.99 (*0-525-65165-9*) NAL-Dutton.

— My Little Book of Wood Ducks. (Illus.). 32p. (Orig.). (J). (gr. 1-5). 1995. pap. write for info. (*1-55971-467-0*) NorthWord.

— To the Rescue. LC 90-2575. (Illus.). 48p. (J). (gr. 2-5). 1991. 14.95 (*0-525-65059-8*, Cobblehill Bks) Dutton Child Bks.

Marston, Jerrilyn G. King & Congress. 500p. 1987. text ed. 45.00 (*0-691-04745-6*) Princeton U Pr.

— King & Congress: The Transfer of Political Legitimacy, 1774-1776. LC 87-2439. Date not set. reprint ed. pap. 136.00 (*0-7837-9382-0*, 2060126) Bks Demand.

Marston, John. Antonio & Mellida. Gair, W. Reavley et al, eds. LC 90-13557. (Revels Plays Ser.). 192p. 1992. text ed. 49.95 (*0-7190-1547-2*, Pub. by Manchester Univ Pr UK) St Martin.

— Antonio & Mellida: The First Part. Hunter, G. K., ed. LC 64-17229. xxii, 88p. 1965. 12.95 (*0-8032-0272-5*) U of Nebr Pr.

— Antonio & Mellida: The First Part. Hunter, G. K., ed. LC 64-17229. (Regents Renaissance Drama Ser.). 110p. 1965. reprint ed. pap. 31.40 (*0-7837-8896-7*, 2049607) Bks Demand.

— The Dutch Courtesan. Wine, M. L., ed. LC 65-11519. (Regents Renaissance Drama Ser.). 156p. reprint ed. pap. 44.50 (*0-8357-7933-5*, 2057006) Bks Demand.

— The Fawn. Smith, Gerald A., ed. LC 65-11518. xx, 123p. 1965. pap. 5.95 (*0-8032-5275-7*, Bison Books) U of Nebr Pr.

— Histriomastix. LC 70-133706. (Tudor Facsimile Texts. Old English Plays Ser.: No. 128). reprint ed. 49.50 (*0-404-53428-7*) AMS Pr.

— Jack Drum's Entertainment. LC 74-133707. (Tudor Facsimile Texts. Old English Plays Ser.: No. 93). reprint ed. 49.50 (*0-404-53393-0*) AMS Pr.

— The Malcontent. 1976. 16.95 (*0-89190-098-5*, Am Repr) Amereon Ltd.

— The Malcontent. Harris, Bernard, ed. (New Mermaid Ser.). (C). 1976. pap. text ed. 4.95 (*0-393-90022-3*) Norton.

— The Malcontent. Wine, M. L., ed. LC 64-17228. (Regents Renaissance Drama Ser.). 151p. reprint ed. pap. 43.10 (*0-685-15565-X*, 2026710) Bks Demand.

— Parasitaster or the Fawn. Blostein, David A., ed. LC 78-60170. (Revels Plays Ser.). 256p. 1979. text ed. 44.00x (*0-8018-2161-4*) Johns Hopkins.

— The Plays of John Marston, 3 vols. reprint ed. 225.00 (*0-403-04206-2*) Somerset Pub.

— Plays of John Marston, 3 vols., Set. 1988. reprint ed. lib. bdg. 290.00 (*0-7812-0324-4*) Rprt Serv.

— Public Order: A Guide to the 1986 Public Order Act. 189p. 1987. 105.00 (*1-85190-024-1*, Pub. by Fourmat Pub UK) St Mut.

— The Scourge of Villanie. LC 73-21779. (English Literature Ser.: No. 33). 1974. lib. bdg. 57.95 (*0-8383-1828-2*) M S G Haskell Hse.

Marston, John & Nottridge, Robin E. Police Powers & Duties: A Practical Guide to the Pace Act, 1984. 168p. (C). 1985. 100.00 (*0-906840-82-1*, Pub. by Fourmat Pub UK) St Mut.

Marston, Leslie R. From Age to Age a Living Witness. 1960. 10.95 (*0-685-14209-4*) Light & Life.

Marston, Lloyd. Playground Equipment: Do-It-Yourself, Indestructible, Practically Free. LC 83-25565. (Illus.). 160p. 1984. pap. 20.95x (*0-89950-104-4*) McFarland & Co.

Marston, Luisa. La Abuelita: The Grandmother. (SPA.). 2.25 (*84-7228-321-6*, 220005, Pub. by Edit Clie SP) TSELF.

Marston, N. W. Marston Genealogy, 2 pts. (Illus.). 607p. 1989. reprint ed. lib. bdg. 99.00 (*0-8328-0856-3*); reprint ed. pap. 91.00 (*0-8328-0857-1*) Higginson Bk Co.

Marston, Nicholas. Beethoven's Piano Sonata in E, Op. 109. LC 94-10762. (Studies in Musical Genesis & Structure). (Illus.). 230p. 1995. 56.00 (*0-19-315332-7*) OUP.

— Schumann: "Fantasie, Op. 17" (Cambridge Music Handbooks Ser.). (Illus.). 136p. (C). 1992. 29.95 (*0-521-39284-5*); pap. 10.95 (*0-521-39892-4*) Cambridge U Pr.

Marston, Paul. First Principles of Card Play. 160p. (Orig.). 1990. pap. 9.95 (*0-571-14443-8*) Faber & Faber.

Marston, Paul, jt. auth. see Forster, Roger.

***Marston, Peter.** The Book of the Conservatory. (Illus.). 176p. 1995. pap. 19.95 (*0-297-83477-0*, Pub. by Weidenfeld) Trafalgar.

Marston, Philip B. Collected Poems. LC 72-148816. reprint ed. 49.50 (*0-404-04192-2*) AMS Pr.

Marston, Philip L., ed. Selected Papers on Geometrical Aspects of Scattering. LC 93-34227. (Milestone Ser.: Vol. MS89). 1993. write for info. (*0-8194-1405-0*); pap. write for info. (*0-8194-1404-2*) SPIE.

Marston, R. M. Diode, Transistor & FET Circuits Manual. (Illus.). 240p. 1991. pap. 26.95 (*0-7506-0228-7*) Buttrwrth-Heinemann.

— Modern TTL Circuits Manual. (Illus.). 224p. 1994. pap. 24.95 (*0-7506-2092-7*) Buttrwrth-Heinemann.

— Power Control Circuits Manual. (Illus.). 198p. 1990. pap. 29.95 (*0-434-91216-6*) Buttrwrth-Heinemann.

Marston, Ray. Instrumentation & Test-Gear Manual. (Illus.). 300p. 1993. pap. 34.95 (*0-7506-0758-0*) Buttrwrth-Heinemann.

— Integrated Circuit & Waveform Generator Handbook. (EDN Series for Design Engineers). (Illus.). 224p. 1991. pap. 24.95 (*0-7506-0409-3*) Buttrwrth-Heinemann.

— Newnes Electronic Circuit Pocketbook. (Illus.). 300p. 1991. 27.95 (*0-7506-0132-9*) Buttrwrth-Heinemann.

— Newnes Electronic Circuits Pocket Book, Vol. 2: Passive & Discrete Circuits. (Illus.). 367p. 1993. 21.95 (*0-7506-0857-9*) Buttrwrth-Heinemann.

Marston, Richard A. & Hasfurther, Victor, eds. Effects of Human-Induced Changes on Hydrologic Systems. LC 94-70721. (Technical Publication Ser.: No. 94-3). (Illus.). 1182p. (Orig.). 1994. pap. 66.00 (*1-882132-29-7*) Am Water Resources.

Marston, Richard A., jt. ed. see Miller, Maynard M.

***Marston, Richard C.** International Financial Integration: A Study of Interest Differentials Between the Major Industrial Countries. (Japan-U. S. Center Monographs on International Financial Markets: No. 1). (Illus.). 192p. (C). 1995. 39.95 (*0-521-47100-1*) Cambridge U Pr.

— Misalignment of Exchange Rates: Effects on Trade & Industry. (National Bureau of Economic Research Project Report Ser.). (Illus.). x, 318p. 1988. lib. bdg. 39.95 (*0-226-50723-8*) U Ch Pr.

Marston, Richard C., jt. ed. see Bilson, John F.

Marston, Richard C., jt. ed. see Buiter, Willem.

Marston, Richard C., jt. auth. see Herring, R. J.

Marston, Robert B. War, Famine & Our Food Supply. LC 75-26308. (World Food Supply Ser.). (Illus.). 1976. reprint ed. 23.95 (*0-405-07787-4*) Ayer.

Marston, Robert Q., ed. see Institute of Medicine Staff.

Marston, Sallie A., ed. Terminal Disasters: Computer Applications in Emergency Management. (Program on Environment & Behavior Monograph Ser.: No. 39). 218p. (Orig.). (C). 1986. pap. 10.00 (*0-685-28113-2*) Natural Hazards.

Marston, Shelby. Georgia for Children. (Illus.). 48p. 1986. pap. 2.95 (*0-87797-119-6*) Cherokee.

Marston, Stephanie. The Divorced Parent. LC 93-15847. 1994. 21.00 (*0-688-11323-0*) Morrow.

— The Divorced Parent: Success Strategies for Raising Happy Children after Separation. Rubenstein, Julie, ed. 352p. 1995. pap. 10.00 (*0-671-51128-9*) PB.

— The Magic of Encouragement. Rubenstein, Julie, ed. 252p. 1992. reprint ed. pap. 10.00 (*0-671-73273-0*) PB.

Marston, Thomas E., jt. auth. see Skelton, Raleigh A.

Marston, V. Paul, jt. auth. see Forster, Roger T.

Marszalek. Court Martial. 326p. 1994. pap. 12.00 (*0-02-034515-1*, Collier S&S) S&S Trade.

Marszalek-Gaucher, Ellen & Coffey, Richard J. Transforming Healthcare Organizations: How to Achieve & Sustain Organizational Excellence. LC 90-4777. (Health-Management Ser.). 308p. 1990. 35.95 (*1-55542-250-0*) Jossey-Bass.

Marszalek, Janet, ed. It's a Darne' Good Cookbook: From Darnestown, Maryland. LC 92-85354. (Illus.). 371p. 1992. ring bd. write for info. (*0-9634198-0-3*) Great Darnestwn.

Marszalek, John F. Court-Martial: A Black Man in America. LC 73-38282. 336p. reprint ed. pap. 95.80 (*0-317-29835-6*, 2051954) Bks Demand.

— Grover Cleveland: A Bibliography. LC 88-9096. (Bibliographies of the Presidents of the United States Ser.: No. 22). 268p. 1988. text ed. 65.00 (*0-313-28180-7*, AP22, Greenwood Pr) Greenwood.

— Sherman: A Soldier's Passion for Order. LC 92-24533. 1992. text ed. 29.95 (*0-02-920135-7*) Free Pr.

— Sherman: A Soldier's Passion for Order. 1994. pap. 15.00 (*0-679-74989-6*) Random.

Marszalek, John F., ed. Diary of Miss Emma Holmes, 1861-1866. (Library of Southern Civilization). (Illus.). 528p. 1994. reprint ed. pap. 16.95 (*0-8071-1940-7*) La State U Pr.

Marszalek, John F., jt. auth. see Conner, Douglas L.

Marszalek, John F., jt. ed. see Lowery, Charles D.

Mart, Maria, ed. see Storti-Storchi, Claudia, et al.

Marta-Dajka, Balazs, jt. auth. see Hronszky, Imre-feher.

Marta, Karen, ed. see Hickey, Dave.

Martanda, Acharya D., tr. Rigveda, Vol. 3. 816p. (ENG, HIN & SAN.). 1984. 17.00 (*0-685-72920-6*, Pub. by Sarvadeshik Arya II) Nataraj Bks.

— Rigveda, Vol. 1: With Maharishi Dayananda Sharaswati's Commentary. lx, 952p. 1974. 17.00 (*0-685-72918-4*, Pub. by Sarvadeshik Arya II) Nataraj Bks.

Martanda, Vidya, tr. see Snatak, Brahma D. & Hindi, Surendra K., eds.

Martchenko, Michael. Bird Feeder Banquet. (Illus.). 24p. (Orig.). (J). (gr. k-3). 1990. 14.95 (*1-55037-147-9*, Pub. by Annick CN); pap. 4.95 (*1-55037-146-0*, Pub. by Annick CN) Firefly Bks Ltd.

Martchenko, Michael, illus. Zoomerang a Boomerang: Poems to Make Your Belly Laugh. LC 92-26589. 32p. (J). (ps-3). 1993. pap. 4.99 (*0-14-054869-6*) Puffin Bks.

Martchenko, Michael, ed. see Munsch, Robert.

Martchenko, Michael, jt. auth. see Munsch, Robert.

Martchenko, Michael, ed. see Munsch, Robert.

Marte, L. F. Political Cycles in International Relations: The Cold War & Africa. 496p. 1994. 57.00 (*90-5383-280-7*, Pub. by VU Univ Pr NE) Paul & Co Pubs.

Marteau, Robert. Salamander: Selected Poems of Robert Marteau. LC 78-70307. (Lockert Library of Poetry in Translation). 127p. reprint ed. pap. 36.20 (*0-8357-7013-3*, 2052288) Bks Demand.

Marteau, Theresa, jt. ed. see Johnston, Marie.

Martei, Myles. Mastering the Art of Q & A. 228p. 1992. pap. 17.00 (*1-55623-686-7*) Irwin Prof Pubng.

Martel, Aimee. Secrets Not Shared. 1981. pap. 2.25 (*0-8439-0874-2*) Dorchester Pub Co.

***Martel, Alan.** Footprints. 205p. 1996. pap. 13.00 (*1-883721-16-4*) Silver Mtn Pr.

Martel, Gary. Taking Care of Your Back: A Guide for Healthcare Professionals. 90p. 1988. 11.95 (*0-318-35460-8*); pap. 26.97 (*0-942028-31-7*) R D Anderson.

Martel, Gordon. Imperial Diplomacy: Roseberry & the Failure of Foreign Policy. 320p. 1986. 44.95 (*0-7735-0442-7*, Pub. by McGill CN) U of Toronto Pr.

Martel, Gordon, ed. American Foreign Relations Reconsidered, 1890-1993. LC 93-36339. 280p. 1994. 59.95x (*0-415-10476-9*, B3803, Routledge NY); pap. 16.95 (*0-415-10477-7*, B3807, Routledge NY) Routledge.

— The Origins of the Second World War Reconsidered: The A. J. P. Taylor Debate after Twenty-Five Years. 292p. 1986. text ed. 75.00 (*0-04-940084-3*); pap. text ed. 19.95 (*0-04-940085-1*) Routledge Chapman & Hall.

An Asterisk (*) at the beginning of an entry indicates that the title is appearing in BIP for the first time.

— Studies in British Imperial History: Essays in Honor of A. P. Thornton. LC 85-8110. 256p. 1986. text ed. 29.95 (*0-312-77080-4*) St Martin.

Martel, Harry, jt. ed. see Selsam, Howard.

***Martel, John.** Conflicts of Interest. LC 94-45781. 464p. 1995. 23.00 (*0-671-89094-8*) PB.

Martel, Jose & Alpern, Hymen. Diez Comedias del Siglo de Oro. 2nd ed. (Illus.). 865p. (C). 1985. 25.95 (*0-88133-119-8*) Waveland Pr.

Martel, Laurence D., jt. auth. see Kline, Peter.

Martel, Leslie F. & Biller, Henry B. Stature & Stigma: A Biopsychosocial Perspective. 128p. 1987. text ed. 24.95 (*0-669-14632-3*) Free Pr.

Martel, Myles. Fire Away! Fielding Tough Questions with Finesse. LC 93-1265. 240p. 1993. text ed. 30.00 (*1-55623-976-9*) Irwin Prof Pubng.

Martel, Pierre, et al. Dictionnaire de Frequence des Mots du Francais Parle au Quebec. LC 91-5120. (American University Studies: Linguistics: Ser. XIII, Vol. 26). 768p. (Orig.). (C). 1992. pap. text ed. 110.95 (*0-8204-1740-8*) P Lang Pubs.

Martel, William C. & Savage, Paul L. Strategic Nuclear War: What the Superpowers Target & Why. LC 85-9869. (Contributions in Military Studies: No. 43). (Illus.). 280p. 1986. text ed. 55.00 (*0-313-24192-9*, SNU/, Greenwood Pr) Greenwood.

Martell, Alan R. & Long, Alton. The Wines & Wineries of the Hudson River Valley. LC 92-34361. (Illus.). 1993. pap. 14.95 (*0-88150-251-0*) Countryman.

Martell, Angela. Splendour in the Sun. (Rainbow Romances Ser.). 160p. 1993. 14.95 (*0-7090-4895-5*, Hale-Parkwest) Parkwest Pubns.

— Splendour in the Sun. large type ed. (Romance Library). 272p. 1995. pap. 14.95 (*0-7089-7663-8*, Linford) Ulverscroft.

Martell, Arthur E. Inorganic Chemistry in Biology & Medicine. LC 80-23248. (ACS Symposium Ser.: No. 140). 1980. 49.95 (*0-8412-0588-4*) Am Chemical.

Martell, Arthur E., ed. Coordination Chemistry, Vols. 1-2. LC 74-151255. (ACS Monograph: No. 168 & 174). Vol. 1 1971. 49.95 (*0-8412-0275-3*); Vol. 2 1978. 89.95 (*0-8412-0292-3*) Am Chemical.

Martell, Arthur E. & Motekaitis, Ramumas J. Determination & Use of Stability Constants. 2nd ed. LC 91-45076. 200p. 1993. 45.00 (*1-56081-516-7*) VCH Pubs.

Martell, Arthur E. & Sawyer, Donald T., eds. Oxygen Complexes & Oxygen Activation by Transition Metals. LC 87-32170. (Illus.). 352p. 1988. 85.00 (*0-306-42789-3*, Plenum Pr) Plenum.

Martell, Arthur E. & Smith, Robert M., eds. Critical Stability Constants, Vols. 1-4. Incl. Vol. 1. Amino Acids. LC 74-10610. 470p. 1974. 125.00 (*0-306-35211-7*); Vol. 2. Amines. LC 74-10610. 416p. 1975. 125.00 (*0-306-35212-5*); Vol. 3. Other Organic Ligands. LC 74-10610. 496p. 1977. 125.00 (*0-306-35213-3*); Vol. 4. Inorganic Complexes. LC 74-10610. 258p. 1976. 95.00 (*0-306-35214-1*); LC 74-10610. (Illus.). write for info. (*0-318-55315-5*, Plenum Pr) Plenum.

— Critical Stability Constants, Vol. 5: First Supplement. LC 74-10610. 622p. 1982. 135.00 (*0-306-41005-2*, Plenum Pr) Plenum.

Martell, Arthur E., jt. ed. see Sawyer, Donald T.

Martell, Arthur E., jt. auth. see Smith, R. M.

Martell, Charles A., Jr. The Client-Centered Academic Library: An Organizational Model. LC 82-9378. (Contributions in Librarianship & Information Science Ser.: No. 42). xii, 136p. 1983. text ed. 47.95 (*0-313-23213-X*, MLI/, Greenwood Pr) Greenwood.

***Martell, Hazel.** Food & Feasts with the Vikings. LC 94-5429. (Food & Feasts Ser.). (Illus.). (J). 1995. 14.95 (*0-02-726317-7*, Mac Bks Young Read) S&S Childrens.

Martell, Hazel M. The Age of Discovery, 1500-1650. LC 92-18621. (Illustrated History of the World Ser.). (Illus.). 80p. (J). (gr. 2-6). 1993. 17.95 (*0-8160-2789-7*) Facts on File.

— The Celts. (Illus.). 48p. (J). (gr. 3-7). 1995. 15.99 (*0-670-86558-3*) Viking Child Bks.

— Everyday Life in Viking Times. LC 93-36128. (Clues to the Past Ser.). (J). 1994. lib. bdg. 12.60 (*0-531-14287-6*) Watts.

— Native Americans & Mesa Verde. LC 92-27758. (Hidden Worlds Ser.). (Illus.). 32p. (J). (gr. 5 up). 1993. text ed. 13.95 (*0-87518-540-1*, Dillon Silver Burdett) Silver Burdett Pr.

— The Normans. LC 91-40970. (Worlds of the Past Ser.). (Illus.). 64p. (J). (gr. 6 up). 1992. text ed. 14.95 (*0-02-762428-5*, Mac Bks Young Read) S&S Childrens.

— Over Nine Hundred Years Ago: With the Vikings. LC 93-2647. (History Detectives Ser.). (Illus.). 32p. (YA). (gr. 6 up). 1993. text ed. 13.95 (*0-02-726325-8*, New Dscvry Bks) Silver Burdett Pr.

— Over Six Thousand Years Ago: In the Stone Age. LC 91-39458. (History Detectives Ser.). (Illus.). 32p. (J). (gr. 6 up). 1992. text ed. 13.95 (*0-02-762429-3*, Mac Bks Young Read) S&S Childrens.

— The Vikings. LC 91-507. (Worlds of the Past Ser.). (Illus.). 64p. (YA). (gr. 6 up). 1992. text ed. 14.95 (*0-02-762427-7*, Mac Bks Young Read) S&S Childrens.

— The Vikings & Jorvik. LC 92-25215. (Hidden Worlds Ser.). (Illus.). 32p. (J). (gr. 5 up). 1993. text ed. 13.95 (*0-87518-541-X*, Dillon Silver Burdett) Silver Burdett Pr.

— What Do We Know about the Celts? (What Do We Know about...? Ser.). (Illus.). 40p. (J). (gr. 3-6). 1993. 16.95 (*0-87226-363-0*) P Bedrick Bks.

***Martell, Hazel M. & Bahn, Paul.** The Kingfisher Book of the Ancient World. LC 94-46005. (J). 1995. write for info. (*1-85697-565-7*, Kingfisher LKC) LKC.

Martell, Helen M. What Do We Know about the Vikings? LC 92-7893. (What Do We Know about...? Ser.). (Illus.). 40p. (J). (gr. 3-6). 1992. lib. bdg. 16.95 (*0-87226-355-X*) P Bedrick Bks.

Martell, Jocelan. Money Watchers: The Four Week Money Management Makeover. 50p. (Orig.). 1989. pap. write for info. (*0-9623255-0-3*) J Martell.

Martell, John P. Brokers in Transportation: A Comprehensive History, Study & Guide on Motor Carrier Brokers of Property in the United States. rev. ed. 198p. 1988. pap. text ed. 29.95 (*0-9621540-0-8*) Transmart.

— Today's Highways: A Comprehensive History, Study & Guide on Motor Carriers of Property in the United States. LC 88-51766. 200p. (Orig.). (C). 1989. pap. text ed. 24.95 (*0-9621540-1-6*) Transmart.

Martell, Luke. Ecology & Society: An Introduction. LC 94-12254. 240p. (C). 1994. lib. bdg. 45.00 (*0-87023-945-7*); pap. 16.95 (*0-87023-946-5*) U of Mass Pr.

Martell, Mary H. The Ancient Chinese. LC 92-9052. (Worlds of the Past Ser.). (Illus.). 64p. (J). (gr. 6 up). 1993. text ed. 14.95 (*0-02-730653-4*, Mac Bks Young Read) S&S Childrens.

Martell, Paul, jt. auth. see Dupuy, Trevor N.

Martell, Ralph. Aesop's Fables in Song. (Illus.). 21p. (J). (gr. k-5). 1987. audio 9.95 (*0-941977-00-5*, RTB-1) Ralmar Enter.

— Memories of the Mato Grosso, Brazil. LC 89-61646. (Illus.). 96p. (Orig.). 1989. pap. 7.50 (*0-685-67696-X*) SCP Third.

Martell, Ralph G. Fish Tales & Other Stories to Get Hooked On. 1992. 24.95 (*0-9634828-0-7*) Pan Pr NY.

— Small Potatoes. 194p. Date not set. 19.95 (*0-9634828-1-5*) Pan Pr NY.

Martell, William A. Greco-Roman Wrestling. LC 92-28782. (Illus.). 176p. 1993. pap. 21.95 (*0-87322-408-6*, PMAR0408) Human Kinetics.

Martellaro, John, ed. see Zagat, Eugene H., Jr. & Zagat, Nina S.

Martellaro, Joseph A. Economic Development in Southern Italy, 1950-1960. LC 65-15549. 139p. reprint ed. pap. 39.70 (*0-685-17856-0*, 2029515) Bks Demand.

Martelli, A. & Valle, G., eds. Computational Intelligence: Proceedings of the International Conference, Milan Italy, 26-30 Sept., 1988, Vol. I. 284p. 1989. 77.00 (*0-444-87340-6*, North Holland) Elsevier.

Martelli, F., jt. ed. see Rodi, W.

Martelli, Fabrizio G. Twin Screw Extruders: A Basic Understanding. 128p. 1982. text ed. 67.95 (*0-442-26363-5*) Chapman & Hall.

— Twin-Screw Extruders: A Basic Understanding. (Illus.). 168p. 1983. 49.00 (*0-686-48173-9*, 0216) T-C Pubns CA.

Martelli, Len, et al. Going Places. (Our Nation, Our World Ser.). (gr. 2). 1983. text ed. 17.20 (*0-07-039942-5*) McGraw.

Martelli, Leonard J., et al. When Someone You Know Has AIDS: A Practical Guide. 256p. 1987. 15.97 (*0-317-52879-3*, Crown); pap. 12.00 (*0-517-56556-0*, Crown) Crown Pub Group.

— When Someone You Know Has AIDS: A Practical Guide. rev. ed. LC 93-2740. 1993. 16.00 (*0-517-88039-3*, Crown) Crown Pub Group.

Martelli, Mario. Discrete Dynamical Systems & Chaos. (Pitman Monographs & Surveys in Pure & Applied Mathematics). 282p. 1993. text ed. 197.00 (*0-470-22066-X*) Halsted Pr.

Martelli, Maurizio, ed. see Busenberg, Stavros N.

Martelli, Maurizio, ed. see Busenberg, Stavros N., et al.

Martelli, Maurizio, jt. ed. see Levi, Giorgio.

Martelli, Nancy N. Personnel Policy Manual. 125p. (Orig.). 1989. pap. 40.00 (*0-685-26074-7*) Park Pl Pubns.

Martello, Leo L. Reading the Tarot: Understanding the Cards of Destiny. LC 89-494121. (Illus.). 208p. (Orig.). 1990. pap. 8.95 (*0-89529-441-9*) Avery Pub.

— Witchcraft: The Old Religion. 1987. pap. 6.95 (*0-8065-1028-5*, Citadel Pr) Carol Pub Group.

Martello, Mary Ann, jt. auth. see Lesko, Matthew.

Martello, Silvano & Toth, Paolo. Knapsack Problems Algorithms & Computer Implementations. 296p. 1990. text ed. 179.00 (*0-471-92420-2*) Wiley.

Martello, Silvano, et al, eds. Surveys in Combinatorial Optimization. (North-Holland Mathematics Studies, No. 128; Lecture Notes in Numerical & Applied Analysis, No. 8). 384p. 1987. 95.00 (*0-444-70136-2*, North Holland) Elsevier.

Martells, Jack. Beer Can Collectors Bible. 1979. pap. 7.95 (*0-394-28918-8*, Ballantine Trade) Ballantine.

Martellucci, S. & Chester, A. N., eds. Optoelectronics for Environmental Science. LC 90-22278. (Ettore Majorana International Science Series, Life Sciences: Vol. 54). (Illus.). 290p. 1990. 85.00 (*0-306-43806-2*, Plenum Pr) Plenum.

— Phase Transitions in Liquid Crystals. (NATO ASI Series B, Physics: Vol. 290). (Illus.). 506p. (C). 1992. 125.00 (*0-306-44213-2*, Plenum Pr) Plenum.

— Progress in Microemulsions. (Ettore Majorana International Science Series, Life Sciences: Vol. 41). (Illus.). 302p. 1989. 85.00 (*0-306-43212-9*, Plenum Pr) Plenum.

***Martellucci, S., et al, eds.** Advances in Integrated Optics. (Illus.). 354p. 1994. 95.00 (*0-306-44833-5*, Plenum Pr) Plenum.

— Laser Applications for Mechanical Industry. LC 93-10592. (NATO Advanced Study Institutes Series E, Applied Sciences: Vol. 238). 448p. (C). 1993. lib. bdg. 166.00 (*0-7923-2303-3*) Kluwer Ac.

Marten, Elizabeth, jt. auth. see Crosby, Nina.

Marten, Elizabeth H. Work-a-Day: Your Classroom Employment Agency. 59p. 1979. pap. 9.50 (*0-914634-73-9*, 7919) DOK Pubs.

Marten, Elizabeth H. & Crosby, Nina. The Middle Ages: A Medieval Pageant for Your Classroom. (Illus.). 64p. (Orig.). 1981. pap. text ed. 9.95 (*0-914634-90-9*, 8109) DOK Pubs.

Marten, Elizabeth H., jt. auth. see Crobsy, Nina E.

Marten, Elizabeth H., jt. auth. see Crosby, Nina E.

Marten, Elizabeth H., jt. auth. see Crosby, Nina.

Marten, G. C. Grazing Research: Design, Methodlogy & Analysis. 148p. 1989. 20.00 (*0-89118-527-5*) Am Soc Agron.

Marten, G. C., et al. Near Infrared Reflectance Spectroscopy (NIRS) Analysis of Forage Quality. rev. ed. (Illus.). 110p. 1989. per., pap. 5.50 (*0-16-000098-X*, S/N 001-000-045) USGPO.

— Persistence of Forage Legumes. 596p. 1989. 19.00 (*0-89118-098-2*) Am Soc Agron.

Marten, H. & Seelinger, D., eds. Physics & Chemistry of Fission. 405p. (C). 1992. text ed. 112.00 (*1-56072-023-9*) Nova Sci Pubs.

Marten, Harry. The Art of Knowing: The Poetry & Prose of Conrad Aiken. LC 87-19840. 208p. 1988. text ed. 22.00 (*0-8262-0654-9*) U of Mo Pr.

— Understanding Denise Levertov. Bruccoli, Matthew J., ed. (Understanding Contemporary American Literature Ser.). 231p. 1989. text ed. 34.95 (*0-87249-578-7*); pap. 14.95 (*0-87249-579-5*) U of SC Pr.

Marten, Jacqueline. Dream Walker. 1987. pap. 3.95 (*0-317-56906-6*) PB.

— Glory in the Flower. 432p. 1988. pap. 3.95 (*0-317-67363-7*) PB.

— Just a Kiss Away. 448p. 1995. pap. 4.99 (*0-7860-0166-6*) Windsor NY.

— Moonshine & Glory. 544p. 1994. mass mkt. 4.99 (*0-7860-0079-1*) Windsor NY.

Marten, James. Chasing Rainbows: A Recollection of the Great Plains. LC 93-10389. (Illus.). 192p. 1993. 24.95 (*0-8138-1010-8*) Iowa St U Pr.

— Texas. LC 93-215090. (World Bibliographical Ser.). 229p. 1992. lib. bdg. 80.00 (*1-85109-184-X*) ABC-CLIO.

— Texas Divided: Loyalty & Dissent in the Lone Star State, 1856-1874. LC 89-48256. 256p. 1990. 28.00 (*0-8131-1700-3*) U Pr of Ky.

Marten, Janet L. & Todman, Allen. Lutheran Church Basement Women. LC 91-67641. 1992. 9.95 (*0-9613437-6-1*) Redbird Prods.

Marten, John, et al. Weird & Wonderful Wildlife. LC 82-25245. (Illus.). 224p. 1983. pap. 19.95 (*0-87701-295-4*) Chronicle Bks.

Marten, Kay, jt. auth. see Nunn, Ron.

***Marten, Neville.** Star Guitars: Guitars & Players That Have Helped Shape Modern Music. (Illus.). 106p. (Orig.). (YA). (gr. 9-12). 1995. pap. 24.95 (*0-931759-83-8*, HL00000168) Centerstream Pub.

Marten, Phyllis. Why Papa Went Away & Other Stories. 112p. (YA). (gr. 8 up). 1988. pap. 4.95 (*0-919797-45-8*) Kindred Prods.

Marten, Rainer. Existieren, Wahrsein, und Verstehen: Untersuchung zur ontologischen Basis sprachlicher Verstaendigung. 376p. (C). 1972. 97.70 (*3-11-003583-9*) De Gruyter.

***Martena, Maureen.** Bugger Bucharest. 192p. 1995. pap. 11.99 (*1-85594-126-0*) InBook.

Martens, Anne C. Home for Christmas. 59p. (Orig.). 1954. pap. 3.45 (*0-87129-167-3*, H24) Dramatic Pub.

— If Boys Wore the Skirts. 1958. 2.95 (*0-87129-497-4*, I11) Dramatic Pub.

— If Girls Asked Boys for Dates. 1952. 2.95 (*0-87129-394-3*, I12) Dramatic Pub.

— Never Trust a Man. 1935. 2.95 (*0-87129-443-5*, N12) Dramatic Pub.

— Pajama Party. 1983. 2.50 (*0-87129-289-0*, P12) Dramatic Pub.

— Whodunit. rev. ed. 1981. 2.50 (*0-87129-328-5*, W25) Dramatic Pub.

— You, the Jury. 1965. 2.50 (*0-87129-249-1*, Y12) Dramatic Pub.

Martens, Anne C., ed. see Spence, Hartzell.

Martens, Anne C., jt. auth. see Twain, Mark.

Martens, Bertin. Economic Development That Lasts: Labour Intensive Irrigation Projects in Nepal & the United Republic of Tanzania. xvii, 192p. 1989. pap. 22.00 (*92-2-106400-X*) Intl Labour Office.

Martens, Charles R. Emulsion & Water-Soluble Paints & Coatings. LC 64-22873. 168p. 1964. 19.50 (*0-442-15558-1*) Van Nos Reinhold.

Martens, Elmer A. Jeremiah. LC 86-9958. (Believers Church Bible Commentary Ser.). 328p. (Orig.). 1986. pap. 17.95 (*0-8361-3405-2*) Herald Pr.

Martens, Els, jt. ed. see Jaccarini, Victor.

Martens, Fred L. Basic Concepts of Physical Education: The Foundations in Canada. 474p. (Orig.). 1986. pap. text ed. 18.80x (*0-87563-280-7*) Stipes.

Martens, Frederick H. The Art of the Prima Donna & Concert Singer. Farkas, Andrew, ed. (Opera Biographies Ser.). (Illus.). 1977. reprint ed. lib. bdg. 30.95 (*0-405-09693-3*) Ayer.

— The Book of the Opera & the Ballet & the History of the Opera. LC 80-2289. reprint ed. 22.50 (*0-404-18857-5*) AMS Pr.

— Leo Ornstein: The Man, His Ideas, & His Work. LC 74-29505. (Modern Jewish Experiences Ser.). (Illus.). 1975. reprint ed. 16.95 (*0-405-06732-1*) Ayer.

— A Thousand & One Nights of Opera. LC 77-25416. (Music Reprint Ser.: 1978). 1978. reprint ed. lib. bdg. 49.50 (*0-306-77565-4*) Da Capo.

Martens, Frederick H., jt. auth. see Auer, Leopold.

Martens, Frederick H., tr. see Bachmann, Alberto.

Martens, Frederick H., tr. see Flesch, Carl.

Martens, Frederick H., tr. see Jeritza, Maria.

Martens, Hans. EC Direct: A Comprehensive Directory of EC Contacts. LC 92-24062. 248p. 1993. 34.95 (*0-631-18796-0*) Blackwell Pubs.

Martens, Harold & Naes, Tormod. Multivariate Calibration. 419p. 1992. pap. text ed. 79.95 (*0-471-93047-4*) Wiley.

Martens, Hinrich R. & Russwurm, H., Jr., eds. Food Research & Data Analysis: Proceedings of the IUFOST Symposium, Sept. 1982, Oslo, Norway. (Illus.). 535p. 1983. 117.00 (*0-85334-206-7*, Pub. by Elsevier Applied Sci UK) Elsevier.

Martens, Ione. The Savor of the Salt. LC 94-70089. 144p. 1994. pap. 9.95 (*0-9637515-1-4*) Dageforde Pub.

Martens, J., jt. ed. see Barth, E. M.

Martens, J. A., jt. auth. see Jacobs, P. A.

***Martens, Ken, ed.** Speciation in Ancient Lakes. (Advances in Limnology Ser.: No. 44). (Illus.). 508p. 1994. pap. 145.00 (*3-510-47045-1*, Pub. by Schweitzerbart'sche GW) Lubrecht & Cramer.

Martens, M., ed. see Weurman Flavour Research Symposium Staff.

Martens, M., Jr., et al, eds. Flavour Science & Technology: Proceedings of the 5th Weurman Flavour Research Symposium, 23-25 March 1987. LC 87-19019. 566p. 1987. text ed. 252.95 (*0-471-91743-5*) Wiley.

Martens, Marianne, tr. see De Beer, Hans.

Martens, Marianne, tr. see Moers, Herman.

Martens, Phyllis, ed. see Becker, Nancy, et al.

Martens, Phyllis, jt. ed. see Schertz, Mary H.

Martens, Rainer. Coaches Guide to Sport Psychology. LC 87-16814. (Illus.). 208p. 1987. pap. text ed. 22.00 (*0-87322-022-6*, BMAR0022) Human Kinetics.

— National Recreation & Park Association Special Edition of Youth Sport Director Guide. LC 94-39057. (Illus.). 180p. 1994. ring bd. write for info. (*0-87322-813-8*, ACEP0490) Human Kinetics.

— Parent Guide to U. S. A. Junior Field Hockey. 52p. 1982. 4.00 (*0-317-01164-2*) US Field Hockey.

— Successful Coaching. 2nd ed. LC 89-37573. (Illus.). 248p. 1990. pap. text ed. 18.00 (*0-88011-376-6*, PMAR0376) Human Kinetics.

— Successful Coaching: National Federation Interscholastic Coaches Education Program. LC 90-43427. (Illus.). 248p. 1990. pap. text ed. 18.00x (*0-88011-415-0*, ACEP0064) Human Kinetics.

— Youth Sport Director Guide. LC 94-28875. 224p. (Orig.). 1994. pap. 75.00x (*0-87322-751-4*, ACEP0480) Human Kinetics.

Martens, Rainer, ed. Joy & Sadness in Children's Sports. 376p. 1978. pap. text ed. 19.95 (*0-931250-15-3*, BMAR0015) Human Kinetics.

***Martens, Rainer, et al.** Competitive Anxiety in Sport. LC 89-38808. (Illus.). 288p. 1990. pap. text ed. 24.00x (*0-87322-935-5*, BMAR0935) Human Kinetics.

— Competitive Anxiety in Sport. rev. ed. LC 89-38808. (Illus.). 288p. 1990. text ed. 43.00x (*0-87322-264-4*, BMAR0264) Human Kinetics.

Martens, Richard A. & Martens, Sherlyn. Milk Sugar Dilemma: Living with Lactose Intolerance. 2nd rev. ed. LC 85-234985. (Illus.). 260p. 1987. pap. 13.95 (*0-936741-01-5*) Medi-Ed Pr.

Martens, Robert, ed. London Chronicles. 1992. pap. 2.50 (*0-932458-53-X*) Star Rover.

Martens, Robert W., jt. auth. see Sisson, James.

Martens, Sheri. Adam & Andrea Learn & Grow: Understanding Church Words from a Kid's Viewpoint. (Illus.). 80p. (J). (ps-5). 1989. pap. 7.95 (*0-919797-81-4*) Kindred Prods.

Martens, Sherlyn, jt. auth. see Martens, Richard A.

Martens, Tom, jt. auth. see Jeneid, Michael.

***Martensen, Daniel F., ed.** Concordat of Agreement: Supporting Essays. LC 94-44791. 1995. pap. 15.00 (*0-8066-2667-4*, Augsburg) Augsburg Fortress.

Martensen, Daniel F., jt. ed. see Griffiss, James F.

Martensen, Daniel F., jt. ed. see Rusch, William G.

Martensen, Kirk. The Chicago Used Car Seller's Guide, Vol. 1. (Orig.). 1989. pap. 6.95 (*0-685-30130-3*) Green Light Pr.

— Used Car Seller's Guide. 144p. (Orig.). 1990. pap. text ed. 6.95 (*0-9624853-0-6*) Green Light Pr.

Martenson. Myelin: Biology & Chemistry. 1992. 212.95 (*0-8493-8849-X*, QP752) CRC Pr.

Martenson, Dennis R. & Johnson, Walter K. Environmental Engineering. LC 82-72214. 763p. 1982. pap. 60.00 (*0-87262-311-4*) Am Soc Civil Eng.

Martensson, Alf. The Woodworker's Bible. LC 79-7355. (Illus.). 1979. 15.95 (*0-672-52607-7*, Bobbs) Macmillan.

— The Woodworker's Bible. LC 79-7355. 1982. pap. write for info. (*0-672-52717-0*) Macmillan.

— The Woodworkers Bible. 288p. 1985. pap. 17.95 (*0-02-011940-2*, Pub. by Gebrueder Borntraeger GW) Macmillan.

Martensson, Bent, jt. auth. see Hinrichsen, Diederich.

Martensson, Kerstin. Applique the Kwik-Sew Way. (Illus.). 1988. pap. write for info. (*0-913212-12-1*) Kwik Sew.

— Applique the Kwik-Sew Way. (Illus.). 77p. 1988. pap. write for info. (*0-913212-11-3*) Kwik Sew.

— Kwik-Sew's Beautiful Lingerie. (Illus.). 80p. (Orig.). 1990. pap. write for info. (*0-913212-14-8*) Kwik Sew.

— Kwik-Sew's Method for Easy Sewing. (Illus.). 80p. (Orig.). 1991. pap. 8.50 (*0-913212-15-6*) Kwik Sew.

— Kwik-Sew's Sewing for Baby. (Illus.). 94p. (Orig.). 1987. pap. write for info. (*0-913212-13-X*) Kwik Sew.

— Kwik Sew's Sewing for Children. (Illus.). 80p. (Orig.). (J). 1993. pap. write for info. (*0-913212-17-2*) Kwik Sew.

— Kwik-Sew's Sewing for Toddlers. (Illus.). 80p. (Orig.). 1992. pap. write for info. (*0-913212-16-4*) Kwik Sew.

— Kwik-Sew's Sweatshirt's Unlimited. (Illus.). 1989. pap. write for info. (*0-318-69464-6*) Kwik Sew.

— Kwik-Sew's Sweatshirts Unlimited. (Illus.). 79p. (Orig.). 1989. pap. write for info. (*0-318-72660-2*) Kwik Sew.

M

— Sew for Toddlers. (Illus.). 1979. pap. 8.95 (*0-913212-08-3*) Kwik Sew.
— Sewing for Baby. (Illus.). 128p. 1987. pap. 11.95 (*0-913212-10-5*) Kwik Sew.
Martenz, Arden. Fears Way Series, Set. 1994. 29.95 (*1-884063-20-9*) Mar Co Prods.
Martenz, Arden, jt. auth. see Cooper, JoAnn.
Marter, Ian. Doctor Who: The Invasion. 1993. pap. 5.95 (*0-426-20169-8*, Dr Who) Carol Pub Group.
Marter, Joan. Theodore Roszak: The Drawings. (Illus.). 96p. (Orig.). 1992. pap. 29.95 (*0-9633559-0-2*) Drawing Soc.
Marter, Joan M. Alexander Calder. (Monographs on American Artists). (Illus.). 288p. (C). 1992. 80.00 (*0-521-33038-6*) Cambridge U Pr.
— Dorothy Dehner: Sixty Years of Art. (Illus.). 64p. 1993. pap. 22.50 (*0-915171-29-5*) Katonah Gal.
— Theodore Roszak: The Drawings. (Illus.). 96p. 1993. pap. 29.95 (*0-295-97237-8*) U of Wash Pr.
Marter, Marilynn. Dining in Philadelphia. Hosner, Sheila, ed. (Dining in Ser.). 200p. (Orig.). 1988. pap. 8.95 (*0-89716-202-1*) P B Pubng.
Martey, Emmanuel. African Theology: Inculturation & Liberation. LC 93-16262. 184p. (Orig.). 1993. pap. 18.95 (*0-88344-861-0*) Orbis Bks.
Marth, jt. auth. see Ryser, Elliot T.
Marth, Del. Florida Almanac, 1988-89. 11.95 (*0-685-10121-5*) Trend Bk Div.
Marth, Del & Marth, Martha. Florida Almanac: 1992-1993 Edition. (Illus.). 416p. 1992. pap. 12.95 (*0-88289-886-8*) Pelican.
Marth, Del & Marth, Martha, eds. Florida Almanac, 1995-96. 10th ed. LC 74-76733. (Florida Almanac Ser.). (Illus.). 432p. (Orig.). (J). (gr. 4 up). 1995. pap. 14.95 (*0-88289-081-6*) Pelican.
***Marth, Del & Marth, Martha J.** The Florida Almanac, 1995. 11th ed. (Illus.). 448p. 1994. pap. 12.95 (*1-885034-01-6*) Suwannee River.
— The Florida Almanac, 1996. 12th ed. (Illus.). 512p. 1995. pap. 12.95 (*1-885034-03-2*) Suwannee River.
— Florida Guide, 1995 (Marth's) 5th ed. (Illus.). 188p. 1995. spiral bd. 34.95 (*1-885034-02-4*) Suwannee River.
— Florida Guide, 1996 (Marth's) 6th ed. (Illus.). 188p. 1996. spiral bd. 34.95 (*1-885034-04-0*) Suwannee River.
Marth, Del & Marth, Marty, eds. The Rivers of Florida. LC 89-49066. (Illus.). 168p. 1990. 24.95 (*0-910923-70-1*) Pineapple Pr.
Marth, Del, jt. auth. see Marth, Martha J.
Marth, E. H., jt. auth. see Minor, T.
Marth, Martha, jt. auth. see Marth, Del.
Marth, Martha, jt. ed. see Marth, Del.
Marth, Martha J. & Marth, Del. The Florida Almanac, 1994. 10th ed. (Illus.). 400p. 1994. pap. 12.95 (*1-885034-00-8*) Suwannee River.
Marth, Martha J., jt. auth. see Marth, Del.
Marth, Marty. Florida Cat Owner's Handbook. (Illus.). 176p. 1993. pap. 9.95 (*1-56164-008-5*) Pineapple Pr.
— Florida Dog Owner's Handbook. LC 89-49067. (Illus.). 175p. (Orig.). 1990. pap. 9.95 (*0-910923-72-8*) Pineapple Pr.
— Florida Horse Owner's Field Guide. LC 86-30672. (Illus.). 208p. (Orig.). 1987. 14.95 (*0-910923-32-9*) Pineapple Pr.
Marth, Marty, jt. ed. see Marth, Del.
Marth, Michael, et al. Four Valley Poets. LC 90-70715. 136p. (Orig.). 1990. pap. 10.95 (*0-9627031-0-9*) Stone & Scott Pubs.
Martha, J. The Jurisdiction to Tax in International Law: Theory & Practice of Legislative Fiscal Jurisdiction. (Series on International Taxation). 238p. 1989. 106.00 (*90-6544-416-5*) Kluwer Law Tax Pubs.
Martha, Stewart. Martha Stewart Writing Papers. 1992. 20.00 (*0-517-59193-6*, C P Pubs) Crown Pub Group.
Marthaler, Berard. The Creed: The Apostolic Faith in Contemporary Theology. rev. ed. LC 92-82595. 480p. (C). 1993. pap. 19.95 (*0-89622-537-2*) Twenty-Third.
Marthaler, Berard L., ed. Introducing the Catechism of the Catholic Church. LC 94-2648. 1994. pap. 11.95 (*0-8091-3495-0*) Paulist Pr.
Marthaler, Berard L., jt. ed. see Warren, Michael.
Marthaler, Bernard. The Catechism Yesterday & Today: A Short Story. 200p. (Orig.). 1995. pap. text ed. write for info. (*0-8146-2151-1*) Liturgical Pr.
Marthaler, L., jt. ed. see Berard.
Marthaler, Nancy. Promises in Poetry, Vol. 1. abr. ed. (Illus.). 100p. (C). 1989. reprint ed. pap. 8.50 (*0-9624310-9-5*) Words From the Heart Pub.
Marthas, Marya, jt. auth. see Sampson, Edward E.
Marthiel, tr. see Valery, Paul.
Marthilm, G., jt. auth. see Kass, E.
Marthinuss, George & Perry, Larry L. Bank Audit Manual, 3 vols., Vol. 1. (AICPA Integrated Practice System Ser.). 412p. 1992. reprint ed. pap. 117.50 (*0-7837-4864-7*, 2044397) Bks Demand.
— Bank Audit Manual, 3 vols., Vol. 2. (AICPA Integrated Practice System Ser.). 414p. 1992. reprint ed. pap. 118.00 (*0-7837-4865-5*, 2044397) Bks Demand.
— Bank Audit Manual, 3 vols., Vol. 3. (AICPA Integrated Practice System Ser.). 396p. 1992. reprint ed. pap. 112.90 (*0-7837-4866-3*, 2044397) Bks Demand.
— Bank Audit Manual Vol. 3. fac. ed. (AICPA Integrated Practice System Ser.). 396p. 1992. reprint ed. pap. 112.90 (*0-7837-8254-3*, 2049022) Bks Demand.
— Bank Audit Manual, 1992 Vol. 1. fac. ed. (AICPA Integrated Practice System Ser.). 448p. 1992. pap. 127.70 (*0-7837-8252-7*, 2049022) Bks Demand.
— Bank Audit Manual, 1992 Vol. 2. fac. ed. (AICPA Integrated Practice System Ser.). 438p. 1992. reprint ed. pap. 124.90 (*0-7837-8253-5*, 2049022) Bks Demand.
— Comprehensive Engagement Manual Vol. 1. fac. ed. (AICPA Integrated Practice System Ser.). 241p. 1992. pap. 68.70 (*0-7837-8242-X*, 2049009) Bks Demand.
— Comprehensive Engagement Manual Vol. 2. fac. ed. (AiCPA Integrated Practice Systems Ser.). 264p. 1992. pap. 75.30 (*0-7837-8243-8*, 2049009) Bks Demand.
— Comprehensive Engagement Manual Vol. 4. fac. ed. (AiCPA Integrated Practice Systems Ser.). 256p. 1992. pap. 73.00 (*0-7837-8244-6*, 2049009); pap. 67.90 (*0-7837-8245-4*, 2049009) Bks Demand.
— Comprehensive Engagement Manual Vol. 4, 4 vols. (AICPA Integrated Practice System Ser.). 265p. reprint ed. Vol. 1, 265p. pap. 75.60 (*0-7837-4872-8*, 2044400); reprint ed. Vol. 2, 318p. pap. 90.70 (*0-7837-4873-6*, 2044400); reprint ed. Vol. 3, 358p. pap. 102.10 (*0-7837-4874-4*); reprint ed. Vol. 4, 237p. pap. 67.60 (*0-7837-4875-2*, 2044400) Bks Demand.
— Small Business Audit Manual, 3 vols., Vol. 1. (AICPA Integrated Practice System Ser.). (Illus.). 234p. reprint ed. pap. 66.70 (*0-7837-4869-8*, 2044399) Bks Demand.
— Small Business Audit Manual, 3 vols., Vol. 2. (AICPA Integrated Practice System Ser.). (Illus.). 243p. reprint ed. pap. 69.30 (*0-7837-4870-1*, 2044399) Bks Demand.
— Small Business Audit Manual, 3 vols., Vol. 3. (AICPA Integrated Practice System Ser.). (Illus.). 368p. reprint ed. pap. 104.90 (*0-7837-4871-X*, 2044399) Bks Demand.
— Small Business Audit Manual Vol. 2. fac. ed. (AICPA Integrated Practice System Ser.). 610p. 1992. pap. 173.90 (*0-7837-8241-1*, 2049008) Bks Demand.
— Small Business Audit Manual Vol. 2, Vol. 1. fac. ed. (AICPA Integrated Practice System Ser.). 140p. 1992. pap. 39.90 (*0-7837-8240-3*, 2049008) Bks Demand.
Marthinuss, George, et al. Construction Contractors' Audit Manual: Nonauthoritative Practice Aids, Vol. 1. LC 91-208700. (Small Firm Library). 441p. reprint ed. pap. 125.70 (*0-7837-2434-9*, 2042583) Bks Demand.
— Construction Contractors' Audit Manual: Nonauthoritative Practice Aids, Vol. 2. LC 91-208700. (Small Firm Library). 217p. reprint ed. pap. 61.90 (*0-7837-2435-7*, 2042583) Bks Demand.
— Construction Contractors' Audit Manual Vol. 2. fac. ed. (AICPA Integrated Practice System Ser.). 442p. 1992. pap. 126.00 (*0-7837-8246-2*, 2049010); pap. 132.30 (*0-7837-8247-0*, 2049010) Bks Demand.
— Construction Contractors' Audit Manual Vol. 2, 2 vols. (AICPA Integrated Practice System Ser.). 442p. reprint ed. Vol. 1, 442p. pap. 126.00 (*0-7837-4862-0*, 2044396); reprint ed. Vol. 2, 434p. pap. 123.70 (*0-7837-4863-9*, 2044396) Bks Demand.
M'Arthur, John, ed. see Macpherson, James.
Marthy, H. J., ed. Experimental Embryology in Aquatic Plants & Animals. LC 90-43958. (NATO ASI Series A, Life Sciences: Vol. 195). (Illus.). 400p. 1990. 105.00 (*0-306-43678-7*, Plenum Pr) Plenum.
Marthy, T. K., et al, eds. Computers in Railways IV: Proceedings of the Fourth International Conference, 2 vols., Set. LC 94-72459. (Comprail Ser.: Vol. 4). 1074p. 1994. 379.00 (*1-56252-190-X*) Computational Mech MA.
Marti, A., et al. Pequeno Diccionario Espanol-Polaco, Polaco-Espanol. 707p. (POL & SPA.). 1991. 24.95 (*0-8288-5749-0*, S32367) Fr & Eur.
Marti, Donald B. Historical Directory of American Agricultural Fairs. LC 85-27145. 309p. 1986. text ed. 65.00 (*0-313-24188-0*, MDA/, Greenwood Pr) Greenwood.
— Women of the Grange: Mutuality & Sisterhood in Rural America, 1866-1920. LC 91-11328. (Contributions in Women's Studies: No. 124). 168p. 1991. text ed. 45.00 (*0-313-25723-X*, MSG/, Greenwood Pr) Greenwood.
Marti, Donald B., Jr., jt. auth. see Kouhoupt, Rudy.
Marti, Ed & Spano, Michael F. The Credit Saver: How to Protect Yourself from the Credit Bureaus. 108p. 1993. 69.95 (*1-883685-00-1*) Pincushion Pr.
Marti, Ernst. The Four Ethers. LC 83-20156. 64p. (Orig.). 1984. pap. 7.95 (*0-935690-02-6*) Schaumburg Pubns.
Marti, Fritz. Religion, Reason & Man. LC 74-9353. 127p. 1974. 6.30 (*0-87527-141-3*) Green.
— The Unconditional in Human Knowledge: Four Early Essays (1794-1796) by F. W. J. Schelling. Schelling, F. W., tr. LC 77-74407. 272p. 1980. 37.50 (*0-8387-2020-X*) Bucknell U Pr.
Marti, Heinrich. Rufin von Aquileia, De Ieiunio I, II, Zwei Predigten uber das Fasten nach Basileios von Kaisareia. LC 89-35687. (Supplements to Vigiliae Christianae Ser.: Vol. 6). xxxiii, 56p. (GER.). 1989. 27.50 (*90-04-08897-0*) E J Brill.
Marti-Ibanez, Felix. To Be a Doctor. Bd. with The Young PrincesLC 68-27688.; Race & the Runner. LC 68-27688. LC 68-27688. 1968. 4.95 (*0-910922-18-7*) MD Pubns.
Marti, J. RLISP '88: An Evolutionary Approach to Program Design. (Computer Science Ser.). 250p. 1993. text ed. 61.00 (*981-02-1479-0*) World Scientific Pub.
Marti, J. T. Konvexe Analysis. (Mathematische Reihe Ser.: No. 54). 286p. (GER.). 1980. 71.00 (*0-8176-0839-7*) Birkhauser.
— Die Toxizitat von Zink, Schwefel und Stickstoffverbindungen auf Flechten-Symbionten. (Bibliotheca Lichenologica Ser.: No. 21). (Illus.). 130p. 1985. pap. text ed. 30.00 (*3-7682-1426-5*) Lubrecht & Cramer.
Marti, J. T., ed. Introduction to Sobolov Spaces & Finite Element Solution of Elliptic Boundary Problems. Whiteman, John R., tr. 218p. 1987. text ed. 59.00 (*0-12-474510-5*) Acad Pr.
Marti, J. T., jt. ed. see Descloux, J.
***Marti, James.** The Alternative Health & Medicine Encyclopedia. LC 94-34460. 400p. 1994. 45.00 (*0-8103-9580-0*) Gale.
— Holistic Health & Medicine Encyclopedia. 650p. 1994. pap. 15.95 (*0-8103-8303-9*) Visible Ink Pr.
***Marti, Jed.** SEMINT: Seamless Model Integration. LC 94-27715. 1994. write for info. (*0-8330-1567-2*, MR403OSDA) Rand Corp.
Marti, Jorge L. El Periodismo Literario De Jorge Manach. LC 76-27678. (Coleccion Mente y Palabra). 333p. 1977. 5.00 (*0-8477-0542-0*); pap. 4.00 (*0-8477-0543-9*) U of PR Pr.
Marti, Jose. La Edad de Oro. 5th ed. (Clasicos Cubanos Ser.). (Illus.). 218p. (Orig.). (SPA.). 1983. reprint ed. pap. 7.95 (*0-89729-028-3*) Ediciones.
— Inside the Monster: Writings on the United States & American Imperialism. Randall, Elinor et al, trs. LC 74-21475. 384p. reprint ed. pap. 109.50 (*0-7837-3905-2*, 2043753) Bks Demand.
— Jose Marti: Major Poems. Foner, Philip S., ed. Randall, Elinor, tr. LC 81-20016. 200p. 1982. 29.50 (*0-8419-0761-7*); pap. 15.95 (*0-8419-0834-6*) Holmes & Meier.
— On Art & Literature: Critical Writings. Foner, Philip S., ed. Randall, Elinor, tr. LC 81-81697. 416p. 1982. 18.00 (*0-85345-589-9*); pap. 12.00 (*0-85345-590-2*) Monthly Rev.
— On Education: Articles on Educational Theory & Pedagogy, & Writings for Children from the Age of Gold. Foner, Philip, ed. Randall, Elinor, tr. LC 79-2326. 320p. 1979. 14.00 (*0-85345-483-3*); pap. 10.00 (*0-85345-565-1*) Monthly Rev.
— Our America: Writings on Latin America & the Struggle for Cuban Independence. Foner, Philip S., ed. Randall, Elinor, tr. LC 77-70967. 1979. pap. 10.00 (*0-85345-495-7*) Monthly Rev.
— Political Parties & Elections in the United States. Foner, Philip S., ed. Randall, Elinor, tr. 208p. (C). 1989. 24.95 (*0-87722-604-0*) Temple U Pr.
Marti, Jose, jt. ed. see Granma.
Marti, Jose M. Mujer de Ayer y Hoy. (Illus.). 28p. (Orig.). (SPA.). 1988. pap. 3.00 (*0-685-24433-4*) Editorial El Coqui.
Marti, Judith, jt. ed. see Womack, Mari.
Marti, K. Descent Directions & Efficient Solutions in Discretely Distributed Stochastic Programs. (Lecture Notes in Economics & Mathematical Systems Ser.: Vol. 299). 178p. 1988. pap. 32.00 (*0-387-18778-2*) Spr-Verlag.
Marti, K., ed. Stochastic Optimization: Numerical Methods & Technical Applications. (Lecture Notes in Economics & Mathematical Systems Ser.: Vol. 379). (Illus.). vii, 182p. 1992. pap. 39.00 (*0-387-55225-1*) Spr-Verlag.
Marti, Kevin. Body, Heart, & Text in the "Pearl"-Poet. LC 91-29879. (Studies in Mediaeval Literature: Vol. 12). 220p. 1991. lib. bdg. 89.95 (*0-7734-9764-1*) E Mellen.
Marti, Kurt, ed. see GAMM/IFIP-Workshop on "Stochastic Optimization: Numerical Techniques & Technical Applications" Staff.
Marti, Manuel, Jr. No Place to Hide: Crisis & Future of American Habitats. LC 83-22762. (Contributions in Sociology Ser.: No. 50). (Illus.). xviii, 245p. 1984. text ed. 55.00 (*0-313-24271-2*, MNO/, Greenwood Pr) Greenwood.
Marti, Noelia, jt. auth. see Grad, Frank P.
Marti-Olivella, Jaume, ed. see Castellet, George C.
Marti, Oscar A. Economic Causes of the Reformation in England. LC 83-45586. reprint ed. 32.50 (*0-404-19904-6*) AMS Pr.
Marti, Othmar & Amrein, Matthias. STM & SFM in Biology. (Illus.). 331p. 1993. text ed. 49.95 (*0-12-474500-8*) Acad Pr.
Marti, Peter. Plastic Analysis of Reinforced Concrete Shear Walls. (IBA Ser.: No. 87). 19p. 1980. pap. text ed. 10.50 (*0-8176-1065-0*) Birkhauser.
Marti, Tula. Un Azul Desesperado. LC 85-82349. 105p. (Orig.). (SPA.). 1985. pap. 7.95 (*0-89729-387-8*) Ediciones.
Martial. Epigrammata. Lindsay, W. M., ed. (Oxford Classical Texts Ser.). 1922. 32.95 (*0-19-814625-6*) OUP.
— The Epigrams. Michie, James, tr. 208p. 1988. mass mkt. 8.95 (*0-14-044350-9*, Penguin Classics) Viking Penguin.
— Epigrams, 2 Vols, 1. Shackleton-Bailey, D. R., ed. & tr. by. LC 92-8234. (Loeb Classical Library: No. 94). 416p. 1993. text ed. 18.95 (*0-674-99105-2*) HUP.
— Epigrams, 2 Vols, 2. (Loeb Classical Library: No. 94-95). text ed. 18.95 (*0-674-99106-0*) HUP.
— Epigrams, Vol. 1. Shackleton-Bailey, D. R., ed. & tr. by. LC 92-8234. (Loeb Classical Library: No. L094). 416p. (C). 1993. 18.95 (*0-674-99555-4*) HUP.
— Epigrams, Vol. 2. Shackleton-Bailey, D. R., ed. & tr. by. LC 92-8234. (Loeb Classical Library: No. L095). (C). 1993. text ed. 18.95 (*0-674-99556-2*) HUP.
— Epigrams, Vol. 3. Shackleton-Bailey, D. R., ed. & tr. by. (Loeb Classical Library: No. L480). 416p. 1993. text ed. 18.95 (*0-674-99529-5*) HUP.
Martialis, M. Valerius. Martialis, M. Valerius: Martial-Konkordanz. Siedschlag, Edgar, ed. (Alpha-Omega, Reihe A Ser.: Bd. XXXVIII). iv, 968p. 1979. write for info. (*3-487-06821-4*, Pub. by Georg Olms GW) Lubrecht & Cramer.
Martialis, Marcus V. Epigrams from Martial. O'Connell, Richard, ed. LC 76-3066. (Translation Ser.: No. 3). 1976. pap. 7.95 (*0-912288-07-8*) Perivale Pr.
Martian, M., ed. see Wood, Andrew.
Marticorena, Clodomiro. Bibliografia Botanica Taxonomica De Chile. (Monographs in Systematic Botany from the Missouri Botanical Garden: No. 41). 587p. 1992. 25.00 (*0-685-70546-3*) Miss Botan.
***Martien, Jerry.** Shell Game: A True Account of Beads & Money in North America. 224p. (Orig.). 1995. pap. 14.95 (*1-56279-080-3*) Mercury Hse Inc.
Martienssen, W., ed. see Goldmann, A., et al.
Martienssen, W., jt. auth. see Madelung, O.
Martig, Renee. Inspired by Nature. (Illus.). 56p. 1987. pap. 16.95 (*0-935133-20-8*) CKE Pubns.
— Vanishing Wildlife. (Illus.). (Orig.). 1989. pap. 9.95 (*0-9622625-0-1*) Timberline Colorado.
Martignoni & Schonenberger. Prosthodontic Reconstructions: Clinical & Laboratory Aspects. Pittwood & Rutter, trs. (Illus.). 579p. 1990. text ed. 182.00 (*0-86715-214-1*) Quint Pub Co.
Martijn, Jan K. Exchange-Rate Variability & Trade: Essays on the Impact of Exchange-Rate Variability on Trade Policy & Trade Flows. (Tinbergen Institute Research Ser.). 275p. 1993. pap. 27.00 (*90-5170-089-X*, Pub. by Thesis Pubs NE) IBD Ltd.
Martimort, A. G., ed. see Cabie, Robert, et al.
Martimort, A. G., et al. Church at Prayer: Principles of the Liturgy, Vol. 1. O'Connell, Matthew J., tr. 316p. 1987. pap. 15.95 (*0-8146-1363-2*) Liturgical Pr.
Martimort, Aime G., ed. The Church at Prayer: An Introduction to the Liturgy. LC 92-28775. 1992. 49.95 (*0-8146-2209-7*) Liturgical Pr.
Martin. America & Its People, 2 vols., 1. 2nd ed. (C). 1993. 43.00 (*0-673-46364-8*) HarpCollege.
— America & Its People, 2 vols., 2. (C). 1993. 43.00 (*0-673-46365-6*) HarpCollege.
— America & Its People, 2 vols., I. 2nd ed. (C). 1993. student ed 17.00 (*0-673-53825-7*) HarpCollege.
— America & Its People, 2 vols., II. 2nd ed. (C). 1993. student ed 17.00 (*0-673-53826-5*) HarpCollege.
— Billy's Brother. Date not set. per. 8.95 (*0-85449-109-0*, Pub. by Gay Mens Pr UK) InBook.
— The Blueberry Train. 1995. 14.00 (*0-689-80304-4*) Macmillan.
— British Game Shooting. (Illus.). 172p. 1988. 29.95 (*1-57157-008-X*) Safari Pr.
— But for the Grace of God.... (Orig.). 1984. pap. 1.00 (*0-914733-02-8*) Desert Min.
— Chicka Chicka Boom Boom. 1991. audio 19.99 (*0-671-74894-7*, S&S Bks Young Read) S&S Childrens.
— Claudia & the Recipe for Danger. (Baby-Sitters Club Mystery Ser.: No. 21). 1995. pap. (*0-590-48310-2*) Scholastic Inc.
— Confederate Monuments at Gettysburg. 1995. pap. text ed. 14.95 (*0-938289-48-9*) Combined Bks.
— Designer Kitchens: A Who's Who in Kitchen Design. 1995. 24.95 (*1-878667-05-X*) Amer Dist Serv.
— Devil's Prize. 1995. mass mkt. 5.50 (*0-312-95478-6*) St Martin.
— Doing Psychology Experiments. 3rd ed. (C). 1991. pap. 27.95 (*0-534-14490-X*) Brooks-Cole.
— Egyptian Administrative & Private Name Seals. 1971. 45.00 (*0-900416-01-7*, Pub. by Aris & Phillips UK) David Brown.
— Farewell, Dawn. (Baby-Sitters Club Ser.: No. 88). 1995. pap. (*0-590-22872-2*) Scholastic Inc.
— Great Divorce. 1995. mass mkt. (*0-553-57270-9*) Bantam.
— The Guide to the Foundations of Public Administration. (Public Administration & Public Policy Ser.: Vol. 37). 480p. 1989. 75.00 (*0-8247-8284-4*) Dekker.
— Handbook of Behavior Therapy. (C). 1991. 80.95 (*0-205-14412-8*, H4412) Allyn.
— Handbook Pharmacy Health Education. 1991. 83.50 (*0-85369-263-7*, Pub. by Pharmaceutical Pr UK) Rittenhouse.
— Handbook Pharmacy Health Education. 1992. pap. 75.00 (*0-685-56966-7*, Pub. by Pharmaceutical Pr UK) Rittenhouse.
— History & Power of Writing. 1994. 39.95 (*0-226-50835-8*) U Ch Pr.
— How to Help an Alcoholic. 22p. (Orig.). 1986. pap. 1.50 (*0-914733-05-2*) Desert Min.
— Karen's Lemonade Stand. (Baby-Sitters Little Sister Ser.: No. 64). 1995. pap. (*0-590-25997-0*) Scholastic Inc.
— Karen's Movie. (Baby-Sitters Little Sister Ser.: No. 63). 1995. pap. (*0-590-25996-2*) Scholastic Inc.
— Karen's New Bike. (Baby-Sitters Little Sister Ser.: No. 62). 1995. pap. (*0-590-48307-2*) Scholastic Inc.
— The Maestro Plays. (J). 1994. 15.95 (*0-8050-1746-1*) H Holt & Co.
— Mary Anne & Camp BSC. (Baby-Sitters Club Ser.: No. 86). 1995. pap. (*0-590-48227-0*) Scholastic Inc.
— Miss Manners Tells You. Date not set. write for info. (*0-517-70165-0*) Random Hse Value.
— Monkey Mothers. (J). Date not set. 15.00 (*0-06-023515-2*); lib. bdg. 14.89 (*0-06-023516-0*) HarpC Child Bks.
— National Fax Directory 1993. 1992. 85.00 (*0-8103-7638-5*) Gale.
— Neuroanatomy. 2nd ed. (C). 1995. text ed. 50.00 (*0-8385-6644-8*) Appleton & Lange.
— Pharmaceutical Design & Development. 300p. 1994. text ed. 95.00 (*0-13-553884-X*) P-H.
— Reaching Your Goal, 8 bks., Set I, Reading Level 2. (Illus.). 192p. (J). (gr. 1-4). 1987. 87.60 (*0-685-58796-7*); Set. lib. bdg. 116.80 (*0-86592-166-0*) Rourke Corp.
— Scarab Cylinders & Other Ancient Egyptian Seals: A Checklist of Publications. 1991. pap. write for info. (*0-85668-317-5*, Pub. by Aris & Phillips UK) David Brown.
— Small Animal Therapeutics. 1991. 75.00 (*0-7236-0930-6*) Blackwell Sci.
— Stacey & the Bad Girls. (Baby-Sitters Club Ser.: No. 87). 1995. pap. (*0-590-48237-8*) Scholastic Inc.
— Two Early Nineteenth-Century Bookbinding Manuals, Vol. 4. Cowie, ed. LC 90-39602. (History of Bookbinding & Design Ser.). 68p. 1990. reprint ed. 57.00 (*0-8240-4017-1*) Garland.
— Using Application Software. 192p. 1991. 11.25 (*0-87835-564-2*) Boyd & Fraser.
— Using Computers: Lab Manual. 2nd ed. 288p. 1991. 14.00 (*0-87835-689-4*) Boyd & Fraser.
Martin, ed. Functional Imaging in Movement Disorders. 1990. 179.00 (*0-8493-5837-X*, RM) CRC Pr.
Martin & Archambault. Boom Chicka Rock. (J). Date not set. 14.00 (*0-671-88689-4*, S&S Bks Young Read) S&S Childrens.

An Asterisk (*) at the beginning of an entry indicates that the title is appearing in BIP for the first time.

Martin & Ellis, Albert. Cage & Aviary Birds. 1980. pap. 16.95 (*0-685-43766-3*) Viking Penguin.

Martin & Gasparis. Medical-Surgical Nursing. (Nursetest: A Review Ser.). 1991. 19.95 (*0-87434-303-8*) Springhouse Pub.

***Martin & Knoohuizen.** Design Marketing Basics: A Sourcebook of Strategies & Ideas. Date not set. text ed. 34.95 (*0-471-11871-0*) Wiley.

Martin & Lumsden. Coaching: An Effective Behavioral Approach. (Illus.). 416p. (C). 1986. 31.95 (*0-8016-3152-1*) Mosby Yr Bk.

Martin & McDowell. Life & Works, 4 bks., Set. (Illus.). 448p. (J). (gr. 7 up). 1989. lib. bdg. 79.76 (*0-86592-295-0*) Rourke Corp.

— Life & Works, 4 bks., Set I, Reading Level 8. (Illus.). 448p. (J). (gr. 7 up). 1989. 59.80 (*0-685-58807-6*) Rourke Corp.

Martin & Raisz. Clinical Endocrinology of Calcium Metabolism. (Basic & Clinical Endocrinology Ser.: Vol. 9). 424p. 1987. 160.00 (*0-8247-7689-5*) Dekker.

Martin & Shell. Management of Professionals: Insights for Maximizing Cooperation. 348p. 1988. 55.00 (*0-8247-7847-2*) Dekker.

— WEESKA Human Resources Management. (What Every Engineer Should Know Ser.: Vol. 5). 192p. 1980. 49.75 (*0-8247-1130-0*) Dekker.

Martin & Steila. Atmospheric Interactions. 192p. (C). 1992. pap. text ed. 26.95 (*0-8403-8052-6*) Kendall-Hunt.

Martin & Tuaillon. Atlas Linguistique et Ethnographique du Jura et des Alpes du Nord, Tome I. (FRE.). 175.00 (*0-8288-9901-0*, F136320) Fr & Eur.

Martin & Whattam. The Early Days in Photographs: Automobiles. 16p. 1976. pap. 2.29 (*0-918146-06-2*) Peninsula WA.

— The Early Days in Photographs: Timber. 16p. 1976. pap. 2.29 (*0-918146-02-X*) Peninsula WA.

Martin & Youtsey. Respiratory Anatomy & Physiology. 288p. 1987. pap. 19.95 (*0-8016-3175-0*) Mosby Yr Bk.

Martin, jt. auth. see Clements.

Martin, jt. auth. see Fanaroff.

Martin, jt. auth. see Khan.

Martin, jt. auth. see Peacock.

Martin, et al. Basic Financial Management. 5th ed. 880p. 1990. text ed. 66.00 (*0-13-060807-6*) P-H.

— Modern Drug Research: Path to Better & Safer Drugs. (Medicinal Research Ser.: Vol. 12). 528p. 1989. 175.00 (*0-8247-7902-9*) Dekker.

Martin, A. & Cheung, F. Analytical Properties & Bounds of Scattering Amplitudes. 142p. 1970. text ed. 152.00 (*0-677-02290-5*) Gordon & Breach.

Martin, A. D. The Religion of Wordsworth. LC 72-8965. (Studies in Wordsworth: No. 29). 1973. reprint ed. lib. bdg. 42.95 (*0-8383-1680-8*) M S G Haskell Hse.

Martin, A. D., jt. auth. see Collins, P. D.

Martin, A. E., et al. Housing, the Housing Environment & Health. (Offset Publication Ser.: No. 27). 1976. pap. 7.20 (*92-4-170027-0*) World Health.

Martin, A. J. Sensors, Which Way Now? (C). 1988. 105.00 (*0-86022-211-X*, Pub. by Build Servs Info Assn UK) St Mut.

Martin, A. M. Bioconversion of Waste Materials to Industrial Products. 1991. 153.00 (*1-85166-571-4*) Elsevier.

***Martin, A. N.** A Life of Principled Obedience. 22p. 1992. pap. 1.95 (*0-85151-634-3*) Banner of Truth.

— Living the Christian Life. 32p. 1986. pap. 1.95 (*0-85151-493-6*) Banner of Truth.

Martin, A. S. & Grover, F., eds. Managing People. 142p. 1988. 30.00 (*0-7277-1354-X*, Pub. by T Telford UK) Am Soc Civil Eng.

Martin, A. S., jt. ed. see Rutter, P. A.

Martin, A. W. Essays in Australian Federalism. 1969. 29.95 (*0-522-83915-0*) Intl Spec Bk.

— Robert Menzies: A Life, Vol. 1: 1894-1943. 1993. 39.95 (*0-522-84442-1*) Intl Spec Bk.

Martin, A. W., ed. Letters from Menie: Sir Henry Parkes & His Daughter. (Illus.). 192p. 1983. 24.95 (*0-522-84222-4*) Intl Spec Bk.

Martin, Abigail. Tillie Olsen. LC 84-70253. (Western Writers Ser.: No. 65). 48p. (Orig.). 1984. pap. 3.95 (*0-88430-039-0*) Boise St U W Writ Ser.

Martin, Abigail A. Bess Streeter Aldrich. LC 92-52529. (Western Writers Ser.: No. 104). (Illus.). 46p. (Orig.). 1992. pap. 3.95 (*0-88430-103-6*) Boise St U W Writ Ser.

— An Irony of Fate: The Fiction of William March. Burgess, Mary A., ed. LC 93-6559. (Milford Series: Popular Writers of Today: Vol. 53). 136p. 1994. lib. bdg. 27.00x (*0-89370-182-3*); pap. 17.00x (*0-89370-282-X*) Borgo Pr.

Martin, Ace. Live the Good Life: World Traveling Harley Man. (Illus.). 257p. (Orig.). 1991. pap. 19.95 (*0-9631337-0-5*) A Martin Rd Ink.

***Martin-Acena, Pablo & Simpson, James, eds.** The Economic Development of Spain since 1870. LC 95-11860. (Economic Development of Modern Europe Since 1870 Ser.: Vol. 6). 1995. write for info. (*1-85278-793-7*, Pub. by E Elgar Pub UK) Ashgate Pub Co.

Martin-Achard, R. & Re'emi, P. The International Theological Commentary on Amos & Lamentations. (International Theological Commentary Ser.). 160p. (Orig.). (C). 1984. pap. 10.99 (*0-8028-1040-3*) Eerdmans.

Martin, Adrian R. Brothers from Bataan: POWs, 1942-1945. (Illus.). 334p. (Orig.). 1992. pap. 21.95 (*0-89745-142-2*) Sunflower U Pr.

Martin, Adrienne L. Cervantes & the Burlesque Sonnet. LC 90-39003. 312p. 1991. 40.00 (*0-520-07045-3*) U CA Pr.

Martin, Agnes. Agnes Martin: Writings. (Illus.). 176p. 1994. pap. 24.95 (*3-89322-375-4*, Pub. by Edition Cantz GW) Dist Art Pubs.

***Martin, Alan.** Tank Girl 2. (Illus.). 128p. 1995. pap. 17.95 (*1-56971-107-0*) Dark Horse Comics.

Martin, Alan & Hewlett, Jamie. Tank Girl Collection. (Illus.). 136p. 1993. pap. 14.95 (*1-878574-51-5*) Dark Horse Comics.

Martin, Alan D. & Gambrill, E. Geriatrics. (Management of Common Diseases in Family Practice Ser.). 1986. lib. bdg. 47.50 (*0-85200-755-8*) Kluwer Ac.

Martin, Alan D. & Harbison, S. A. An Introduction to Radiation Protection. 256p. 1986. 42.50 (*0-412-27800-6*, 9943); pap. 18.95 (*0-412-27810-3*, 9833) Chapman & Hall.

Martin, Alan D., jt. auth. see Halzen, Francis.

Martin, Albert N. A Bad Record & a Bad Heart. 16p. (Orig.). (C). 1989. pap. 1.25 (*0-9622508-1-3*) Simpson NJ.

— Practical Implications of Calvinism. 1979. pap. 1.95 (*0-85151-296-8*) Banner of Truth.

— What's Wrong with Preaching? 32p. 1992. pap. 1.95 (*0-85151-632-7*) Banner of Truth.

Martin, Albert N., frwd. Intercessory Prayer: A Ministerial Task. 42p. (Orig.). 1991. pap. 5.95 (*0-9622508-6-4*) Simpson NJ.

Martin, Albro. Enterprise Denied: Origins of the Decline of American Railroads, 1897-1917. LC 71-159673. 402p. 1978. text ed. 54.00 (*0-231-03508-X*) Col U Pr.

— James J. Hill & the Opening of the Northwest. LC 90-26749. (Illus.). xx, 676p. 1991. reprint ed. pap. 22.50 (*0-87351-261-8*, Borealis Book) Minn Hist.

— Railroads Triumphant: The Growth, Rejection, & Rebirth of a Vital American Force. (Illus.). 448p. 1992. 35.00 (*0-19-503853-3*) OUP.

Martin, Alex, jt. ed. see Grant, Igor.

Martin, Alexander C. Weeds. (Golden Guide Ser.). (Illus.). 160p. (J). (gr. 7 up). 1973. pap. write for info. (*0-307-24353-2*, Golden Pr) Western Pub.

Martin, Alexander C. & Zim, Herbert S. Flowers. (Golden Guide Ser.). (Illus.). 160p. (J). (gr. 6 up). 1987. pap. 4.95 (*0-307-24054-1*, Golden Bks) Western Pub.

Martin, Alexander C., jt. auth. see Zim, Herbert S.

Martin, Alexander C., et al. American Wildlife & Plants: A Guide to Wildlife Food Habits. 1951. pap. 8.95 (*0-486-20793-5*) Dover.

Martin, Alexander H. Introduction to Human Anatomy. (Illus.). 576p. (C). 1984. pap. text ed. 37.00 (*0-86577-087-5*) Thieme Med Pubs.

Martin, Alfred. Biblical Stewardship. LC 91-150. 1992. reprint ed. pap. 7.99 (*0-87213-645-0*) Loizeaux.

— Isaiah: The Salvation of Jehovah. (Everyman's Bible Commentary Ser.). (C). 1967. pap. 7.99 (*0-8024-2023-0*) Moody.

— Isaias: La Salvacion del Senor (Comentario Biblico Portavoz) Orig. Title: Isaiah: The Salvation of Jehovah (Everyman's Bible Commentary). 112p. (SPA.). 1979. pap. 5.99 (*0-8254-1455-5*) Kregel.

— Problem Solving, Physical Pharmacy IV. 1993. text ed. 19.50 (*0-8121-1642-9*) Williams & Wilkins.

— The Quest for Security. (Synthesis Ser.). 169p. 1979. pap. 1.95 (*0-8199-0371-X*, Frncscn Herld) Franciscan Pr.

Martin, Alfred, et al. Physical Pharmacy. 4th ed. (Illus.). 700p. 1993. text ed. 59.50 (*0-8121-1438-8*) Williams & Wilkins.

Martin, Alfred G. Hand-Taming Wild Birds at the Feeder: A Fascinating & Practical Guide to the World of Wild Birds...& How You Can Enter It. LC 63-13599. (Illus.). 144p. 1991. reprint ed. pap. 12.95 (*0-911469-07-9*) A C Hood.

Martin, Alice, ed. see Rest, Hillard C.

***Martin, Alice M.** The Algebra 1 Handbook: 1000 Problems Solved Simply & Clearly. 200p. 1995. pap. text ed. 12.95 (*0-9642188-8-7*) Four Seasns.

Martin, Alison, tr. see Irigaray, Luce.

Martin, Allan W. Henry Parkes: A Biography. 504p. 1980. 39.95 (*0-522-84174-0*) Intl Spec Bk.

Martin, Alson, et al. Kansas Corporation Law Practice & Procedure Including Tax Aspects, 2 vols. LC 88-82764. 1000p. 1988. 225.00 (*0-942357-23-X*) KS Bar CLE.

Martin, Alvin, jt. auth. see Lynx, David.

Martin, Alvin C. & Borteck, Robert D. New Jersey Estate Planning, Will Drafting & Estate Administration Forms, 2 vols. suppl. ed. 1993. ring bd. 82.00 (*0-685-74628-3*) Butterworth Legal Pubs.

— New Jersey Estate Planning, Will Drafting & Estate Administration Forms, Set. 1994. disk 75.00 (*0-685-74629-1*) Butterworth Legal Pubs.

— New Jersey Estate Planning, Will Drafting & Estate Administration Forms, 2 vols., Set. 1120p. 1988. disk, ring bd. 239.00 (*0-87189-072-0*) Michie Butterworth.

Martin, Ana. Prehistoric Stone Monuments. LC 93-756. (World Heritage Ser.). (Illus.). 36p. (ENG & SPA.). (J). (gr. 3 up). 1993. lib. bdg. 15.00 (*0-516-08386-4*); pap. 6.95 (*0-516-48386-2*) Childrens.

— Romanesque Art & Architecture. LC 93-3436. (World Heritage Ser.). (Illus.). 36p. (J). (gr. 3 up). 1993. lib. bdg. 15.00 (*0-516-08387-2*); pap. 6.95 (*0-516-48387-0*) Childrens.

Martin, Andre J. Distribution Resource Planning: The Gateway to True Quick Response & Continuous Improvement. 2nd rev. ed. LC 90-70333. 280p. 1993. 129.00 (*0-939246-17-1*) Oliver Wight.

— InfoPartnering: Using Quick Response to Create Ultimate Customer Delight. LC 93-61779. 256p. 1994. 68.00 (*0-939246-59-7*) Oliver Wight.

Martin, Andrew. Distribution Resource Planning. 329p. (C). 1990. 400.00 (*0-685-39892-7*, Inst Pur & Supply) St Mut.

— The Mask of the Prophet: The Extraordinary Fictions of Jules Verne. (Illus.). 240p. 1990. 59.00 (*0-19-815798-3*) OUP.

— Receptions of War: Vietnam in American Culture. LC 92-33825. (Project for Discourse & Theory Ser.: Vol. 10). 216p. 1994. pap. 12.95 (*0-8061-2540-3*) U of Okla Pr.

— Scotland's Weather: An Illustrated Anthology. (Illus.). 108p. (Orig.). 1995. pap. 14.95 (*0-948636-71-8*, Pub. by Natl Mus Scotland UK) A Schwartz & Co.

Martin, Andy. Blasting Cap Tin Catalog. LC 91-90085. (Illus.). 80p. (Orig.). 1991. pap. 8.00 (*0-9628762-0-8*) Old Adit.

— County High Points. 34p. (Orig.). 1994. pap. 6.00 (*0-9628762-1-6*) Old Adit.

***Martin, Angus.** Fish & Whaling. (Illus.). 88p. 1995. pap. 6.95 (*0-948636-67-X*, 667X, Pub. by Natl Mus Scotland UK) A Schwartz & Co.

— The Larch Plantation. (C). 1989. 39.00 (*0-86554-019-5*, Pub. by Saltire Soc) St Mut.

***Martin, Ann.** Building the New School: A Tonka Storybook. (J). (ps-3). 1995. pap. 2.50 (*0-590-20308-8*) Scholastic Inc.

— Dawn the School Spirit War. (Baby-Sitters Club Ser.: No. 84). (J). 1995. pap. 3.50 (*0-590-48228-9*) Scholastic Inc.

— Karen's Pony. (Baby-Sitters Little Sister Ser.: No. 60). (J). 1995. pap. 2.95 (*0-590-48305-6*) Scholastic Inc.

— Mary Anne & the Mystery at the Zoo. (Baby-Sitters Club Mystery Ser.: No. 20). (J). 1995. pap. 3.50 (*0-590-48309-9*) Scholastic Inc.

— Rachel Parker Kingergarten Show-Off. (Illus.). (J). 1993. pap. 6.95 (*0-8234-1067-6*) Holiday.

— Tonka Fire Truck to the Rescue. (Tonka Trucks Storybook Ser.). (J). (ps-3). 1994. pap. 2.50 (*0-590-48854-6*) Scholastic Inc.

Martin, Ann M. Baby-Sitters, Vols. 1-4. 1987. pap. 11.00 (*0-590-63296-5*); Boxed set. boxed 10.00 (*0-590-63218-3*) Scholastic Inc.

— Baby-Sitters, Vols. 5-8. 1987. pap. 10.00 (*0-590-63248-5*) Scholastic Inc.

— Baby-Sitters, Vols. 9-12. 1988. pap. 11.00 (*0-590-63288-4*) Scholastic Inc.

— Baby-Sitters, Vols. 13-16. 1988. pap. 11.00 (*0-590-63335-X*) Scholastic Inc.

— Baby-Sitters at Shadow Lake Super Special. (Baby-Sitters Club Ser.: No. 8). (J). 1992. pap. 3.50 (*0-590-44962-1*) Scholastic Inc.

— Baby-Sitters Club, Bks. 5-8. (J). (gr. 4-7). 1990. boxed, pap. 13.00 (*0-590-63672-3*) Scholastic Inc.

— The Baby-Sitters Club, Bks. 13-16. (J). (gr. 3-7). 1991. boxed, pap. 13.00 (*0-590-63705-3*) Scholastic Inc.

— The Baby-Sitters Club, Bks. 17-20. (J). (gr. 3-7). 1991. boxed, pap. 13.00 (*0-590-63704-5*) Scholastic Inc.

— The Baby-Sitters Club, Bks. 21-24. (J). (gr. 3-7). 1991. boxed, pap. 13.00 (*0-590-63703-7*) Scholastic Inc.

— Baby-Sitters Club, Bks. 29-32. (J). (gr. 4-7). 1990. boxed, pap. 13.00 (*0-590-63583-2*) Scholastic Inc.

— Baby-Sitters Club, 4 vols., Bks. 33-36. (J). (gr. 4-7). 1990. Boxed set. boxed 13.00 (*0-590-63669-3*) Scholastic Inc.

— Baby Sitters Club, Set, No. 2. 1987. Set no. 2. pap. 11.00 (*0-590-63351-1*) Scholastic Inc.

— Baby-Sitter's Club, Set, No. 5. (J). (gr. 4 up). 1989. Set no. 5. pap. 11.00 (*0-590-63344-9*) Scholastic Inc.

— Baby-Sitters Club, No. 45-48. (J). (gr. 4-7). 1991. boxed, pap. 13.00 (*0-590-63963-3*) Scholastic Inc.

— Baby-Sitters Club, 20 vols., Set. large type ed. 176p. (J). 1994. lib. bdg. 318.60 (*0-8368-1267-0*) Gareth Stevens Inc.

— Baby-Sitters Club - Set 2, 10 vols. large type ed. 176p. (J). 1994. lib. bdg. 159.30 (*0-8368-1241-7*) Gareth Stevens Inc.

— Baby-Sitters Club Guide to Baby-Sitting. (J). (gr. 4-7). 1993. pap. 3.25 (*0-590-47686-6*) Scholastic Inc.

— Baby-Sitter's Club, No. 26: Claudia & the Sad Good-Bye. 1989. pap. 3.50 (*0-590-42503-X*) Scholastic Inc.

— Baby Sitter's Club, No. 30: Mary Anne & the Great Romance. 1990. pap. 3.50 (*0-590-42498-X*) Scholastic Inc.

— Baby-Sitter's Club, No. 32: Kristy & the Secret of Susan. (J). (gr. 4-7). 1990. pap. 3.50 (*0-590-42496-3*) Scholastic Inc.

— Baby-Sitter's Club, No. 33: Claudia & the Great Search. (J). (gr. 4-7). 1990. pap. 3.25 (*0-590-42495-5*) Scholastic Inc.

— Baby-Sitters Club, No. 50: Dawn's Big Date. (J). (gr. 4-7). 1992. pap. 3.50 (*0-590-44969-9*) Scholastic Inc.

— Baby-Sitters Club Postcard Book. (J). (gr. 4-7). 1991. pap. 4.95 (*0-590-44783-1*) Scholastic Inc.

— The Baby-Sitters Club Super Summer Special, Bks. 1-3. (J). (gr. 3-7). 1991. boxed 10.50 (*0-590-63714-2*) Scholastic Inc.

— The Baby-Sitters Haunted House. (Baby-Sitters Club Super Mystery Ser.: No. 1). (J). (gr. 3-7). 1995. pap. 3.99 (*0-590-48311-0*) Scholastic Inc.

— The Baby-Sitters Little Sister, Bks. 5-8. (J). (gr. 2-4). 1990. boxed 11.00 (*0-590-63593-X*) Scholastic Inc.

— The Baby-Sitters Little Sister, Bks. 9-12. (J). (gr. 2-4). 1990. boxed, pap. 11.00 (*0-590-63668-5*) Scholastic Inc.

— The Baby-Sitters Little Sister, Bks. 17-20. (J). 1991. boxed, pap. 11.00 (*0-590-63950-1*) Scholastic Inc.

— The Baby-Sitters Little Sister: School Scrapbook. (J). (gr. 7-9). 1993. pap. 2.95 (*0-590-47677-7*) Scholastic Inc.

— Baby-Sitters Little Sister Boxed Set, 4 bks., Set. (J). 1992. 11.00 (*0-590-66125-6*) Scholastic Inc.

— Baby-Sitters Little Sister, No. 24: Karen's School Trip. (J). (gr. 4-7). 1992. pap. 2.95 (*0-590-44859-5*) Scholastic Inc.

— Baby-Sitters Little Sister No. 32: Karen's Pumpkin Patch. (Baby-Sitters Club Ser.). (J). 1992. 2.95 (*0-590-45647-4*) Scholastic Inc.

— Baby-Sitters Little Sisters: Secret Diary. (J). (gr. 4-7). 1991. pap. 2.50 (*0-590-45010-7*) Scholastic Inc.

— Baby-Sitters on Board! (Orig.). (YA). (gr. 3-6). 1988. pap. 3.95 (*0-590-44240-6*) Scholastic Inc.

— The Baby-Sitters Remember. (Baby-Sitters Club Super Special Ser.: no. 11). (J). (gr. 4-7). 1994. pap. 3.95 (*0-590-47015-9*) Scholastic Inc.

— Baby-Sitters' Summer Vacation Super Special, No. 2. (J). 1989. pap. 3.95 (*0-590-44239-2*) Scholastic Inc.

— Baby-Sitters' Winter Vacation Super Special, No. 3. (J). 1989. pap. 3.95 (*0-590-43973-1*) Scholastic Inc.

— The BabySitters Club, 10 titles, Set. large type ed. (J). (gr. 4 up). 1993. lib. bdg. 159.30 (*0-8368-1025-2*) Gareth Stevens Inc.

— Bethany Ann: A Mother's Difficult Choice. 98p. 1991. pap. 6.95 (*1-880153-36-X*) AmericaWORKS.

— Beware Dawn! (Baby-Sitters Club Mystery Ser.: No. 2). 160p. (J). 1991. pap. 3.50 (*0-590-44085-3*) Scholastic Inc.

— Boy-Crazy Stacey. (Baby-Sitters Club Ser.: No. 8). (Orig.). (J). (gr. 4-7). 1987. pap. 3.50 (*0-590-43509-4*) Scholastic Inc.

— Bummer Summer. (J). (gr. 4-7). 1990. pap. 3.50 (*0-590-43622-8*) Scholastic Inc.

— Calico Families. LC 76-20575. 48p. 1977. 9.95 (*0-88289-118-9*) Pelican.

— California Girls! (Baby-Sitters Club Super Special Ser.: No. 5). 240p. (J). (gr. 3-7). 1990. pap. 3.95 (*0-590-43575-2*) Scholastic Inc.

— Chain Letter. LC 92-44587. (J). 1993. 14.95 (*0-590-47151-1*) Scholastic Inc.

— Claudia: The Genius of Elm Street. (Baby-Sitters Club Ser.: No. 49). (YA). 1991. pap. 3.25 (*0-590-44970-2*) Scholastic Inc.

— Claudia & Crazy Peaches. (Baby-Sitters Club Ser.: No. 78). (J). (gr. 4-7). 1994. pap. 3.50 (*0-590-48222-X*) Scholastic Inc.

— Claudia & Mean Janine. (Baby-Sitters Club Ser.: No. 7). (Orig.). (J). (gr. 4-7). 1987. pap. 3.50 (*0-590-43719-4*) Scholastic Inc.

— Claudia & Middle School. (Baby-Sitters Club Ser.: No. 40). (J). (gr. 4-7). 1991. pap. 3.25 (*0-590-44082-9*) Scholastic Inc.

— Claudia & the Bad Joke. (Baby-Sitters Club Ser.: No. 19). 160p. (J). (gr. 3-7). 1988. pap. 3.50 (*0-590-43510-8*) Scholastic Inc.

— Claudia & the Bad Joke. large type ed. (Baby-Sitters Club Ser.). 176p. (J). (gr. 4 up). 1993. lib. bdg. 15.93 (*0-8368-1023-6*) Gareth Stevens Inc.

— Claudia & the Clue in the Photograph. (Baby-Sitters Club Ser.: No. 16). (J). (gr. 4-7). 1994. pap. 3.50 (*0-590-47054-X*) Scholastic Inc.

— Claudia & the Mystery at the Museum, No. 33. (J). 1993. pap. 3.50 (*0-590-47049-3*) Scholastic Inc.

— Claudia & the New Girl. large type ed. LC 93-15969. (Baby-Sitters Club Ser.). 176p. (J). (gr. 4 up). 1993. lib. bdg. 15.93 (*0-8368-1016-3*) Gareth Stevens Inc.

— Claudia & the New Girl, No. 12. (Baby-Sitters Club Ser.). (J). (gr. 4-7). 1988. pap. 3.50 (*0-590-43721-6*) Scholastic Inc.

— Claudia & the Perfect Boy. (Baby-Sitters Club Ser.: No. 71). (J). (gr. 5-7). 1994. pap. 3.50 (*0-590-47009-4*) Scholastic Inc.

— Claudia & the Phantom Phone Call. limited ed. (Baby-Sitters Club Ser.: No. 2). (J). (gr. 4-7). 1995. pap. 3.50 (*0-590-22763-7*) Scholastic Inc.

— Claudia & the Phantom Phone Calls. (Baby-Sitters Club Ser.: No. 2). 160p. (Orig.). (J). (gr. 3-7). 1986. pap. 3.50 (*0-590-43513-2*) Scholastic Inc.

— Claudia & the Sad Good-Bye. large type ed. (Baby-Sitters Club Ser.). 176p. (J). 1994. lib. bdg. 15.93 (*0-8368-1247-6*) Gareth Stevens Inc.

— Claudia's Book. (Baby-Sitters Club Portrait Collection). (J). (gr. 4-7). 1995. pap. 3.50 (*0-590-48400-1*) Scholastic Inc.

— Claudia's Friend. (Baby-Sitters Club Ser.: No. 63). (J). (gr. 4-7). 1993. pap. 3.50 (*0-590-45665-2*) Scholastic Inc.

— Dawn & the Big Sleepover. (Baby-Sitters Club Ser.: No. 44). (J). (gr. 4-7). 1991. pap. 3.50 (*0-590-43573-6*) Scholastic Inc.

— Dawn & the Disappearing Dogs. (Baby-Sitters Club Mystery Ser.: No. 07). (J). (gr. 4-7). 1993. pap. 3.50 (*0-590-44960-5*) Scholastic Inc.

— Dawn & the Halloween Mystery. (Baby-Sitters Club Mystery Ser.: No. 17). (J). (gr. 4-7). 1994. pap. 3.50 (*0-590-48232-7*) Scholastic Inc.

— Dawn & the Impossible Three. (Baby-Sitters Club Ser.: No. 5). 144p. (Orig.). (J). (gr. 4-6). 1987. pap. 3.50 (*0-590-43720-8*) Scholastic Inc.

— Dawn & the Impossible Three. 2nd ed. (Baby-Sitters Club Ser.: No. 5). (Orig.). 1988. pap. 3.50 (*0-590-42232-4*) Scholastic Inc.

— Dawn & the Older Boy. (Baby-Sitters Club Ser.: No. 37). (J). (gr. 4-7). 1990. pap. 3.25 (*0-590-43566-3*) Scholastic Inc.

— Dawn & the Surfer Ghost. (Baby-Sitters Club Mystery Ser.: No. 12). (J). (gr. 4-7). 1993. pap. 3.50 (*0-590-47050-7*) Scholastic Inc.

— Dawn & the We Kids Club. (Baby-Sitters Club Ser.: No. 72). (J). (gr. 4-7). 1994. pap. 3.50 (*0-590-47010-8*) Scholastic Inc.

— Dawn & Whitney: Friends Forever. (Baby-Sitters Club Ser.: No. 77). (J). (gr. 4-7). 1994. pap. 3.50 (*0-590-48221-1*) Scholastic Inc.

— Dawn on the Coast. (Baby-Sitters Club Ser.: No. 23). (J). 1989. pap. 3.25 (*0-590-43900-6*) Scholastic Inc.

— Dawn on the Coast. large type ed. (Baby-Sitters Club Ser.). 176p. (J). 1994. lib. bdg. 15.93 (*0-8368-1244-1*) Gareth Stevens Inc.

— Dawn Saves the Planet. (Baby-Sitters Club Ser.: No. 57). (J). 1992. 3.50 (*0-590-45658-X*, 052) Scholastic Inc.

— Dawn's Big Move. (Baby-Sitters Club Ser.: No. 67). (J). (gr. 4-7). 1993. pap. 3.50 (*0-590-47005-1*) Scholastic Inc.

M

An Asterisk (*) at the beginning of an entry indicates that the title is appearing in BIP for the first time.

— Dawn's Family Feud. (Baby-Sitters Club Ser.: No. 64). (J). (gr. 4-7). 1993. pap. 3.50 (*0-590-45666-0*) Scholastic Inc.

— Dawn's Wicked Stepsister. (Baby-Sitters Club Ser.: No. 31). (J). (gr. 4-7). 1990. pap. 3.50 (*0-590-42497-1*) Scholastic Inc.

— Eleven Kids, One Summer. LC 91-55025. 160p. (J). (gr. 3-7). 1991. 14.95 (*0-8234-0912-0*) Holiday.

— Eleven Kids, One Summer. (J). (gr. 4-7). 1993. pap. 2.95 (*0-590-45917-1*) Scholastic Inc.

— Enchanted Attic. (CYOA Skylark Ser.: No. 47). 64p. (Orig.). 1992. pap. 3.50 (*0-553-15636-5*) Bantam.

— Get Well Soon, Mallory. (Baby-Sitters Club Ser.: No. 69). (J). (gr. 4-7). 1993. pap. 3.50 (*0-590-47007-8*) Scholastic Inc.

— Ghost at Dawn's House, No. 9. (J). 1988. pap. 3.50 (*0-590-43508-6*) Scholastic Inc.

— Good-Bye, Stacy, Good-Bye. large type ed. LC 93-4345. (Baby-Sitters Club Ser.). 176p. (J). (gr. 4 up). 1993. lib. bdg. 15.93 (*0-8368-1017-1*) Gareth Stevens Inc.

— Goodbye Stacey, Goodbye. (J). 1988. pap. 3.50 (*0-590-43386-5*) Scholastic Inc.

— Hello, Mallory. large type ed. (Baby-Sitters Club Ser.). 176p. (Orig.). (J). (gr. 4 up). 1993. lib. bdg. 15.93 (*0-8368-1018-X*) Gareth Stevens Inc.

— Hello Mallory, No. 14. (J). 1988. pap. 3.50 (*0-590-43385-7*) Scholastic Inc.

— Here Come the Bridesmaids! (Baby-Sitters Club Super Special Ser.: No. 12). (J). (gr. 4-7). 1994. pap. 3.95 (*0-590-48308-0*) Scholastic Inc.

— Inside Out. LC 83-18631. 160p. (J). (gr. 4-9). 1984. 13.95 (*0-8234-0512-5*) Holiday.

— Island Adventure Super Special. (Baby-Sitters Club Ser.). (J). 1990. pap. 3.95 (*0-590-42493-9*) Scholastic Inc.

— Jessi & the Awful Secret. (Baby-Sitters Club Ser.: No. 61). (J). (gr. 4-7). 1993. pap. 3.50 (*0-590-45663-6*) Scholastic Inc.

— Jessi & the Bad Baby-Sitter, No. 68. (J). 1993. pap. 3.50 (*0-590-47006-X*) Scholastic Inc.

— Jessi & the Dance School Phantom. (Baby-Sitters Club Ser.: No. 42). 160p. (J). (gr. 3-7). 1991. pap. 3.50 (*0-590-44083-7*, Apple Paperbacks) Scholastic Inc.

— Jessi and the Jewel Thieves: Baby-sitters Club Mystery Ser., No. 8. (J). (gr. 4-7). 1993. pap. 3.50 (*0-590-44959-1*) Scholastic Inc.

— Jessi & the Superbrat. (Baby-Sitters Club Ser.: No. 27). (J). (gr. 5 up). 1989. pap. 3.50 (*0-590-42502-1*, Apple Paperbacks) Scholastic Inc.

— Jessi & the Superbrat. large type ed. (Baby-Sitters Club Ser.). 176p. (J). 1994. lib. bdg. 15.93 (*0-8368-1248-4*) Gareth Stevens Inc.

— Jessi & the Troublemaker. (Baby-Sitters Club Ser.: No. 82). (J). (gr. 4-7). 1995. pap. 3.50 (*0-590-48226-2*) Scholastic Inc.

— Jessi Ramsey, Pet-Sitter. large type ed. (Baby-Sitters Club Ser.). 176p. (J). 1994. lib. bdg. 15.93 (*0-8368-1243-3*) Gareth Stevens Inc.

— Jessi's Baby Sitter. (Baby-Sitters Club Ser.: No. 36). (J). (gr. 4-7). 1990. pap. 3.50 (*0-590-43565-5*) Scholastic Inc.

— Jessi's Gold Medal. (Baby-Sitters Club Ser.: No. 55). (J). 1992. pap. 3.25 (*0-590-44964-8*, Apple Paperbacks) Scholastic Inc.

— Jessi's Horrible Prank. (Baby-Sitters Club Ser.: No. 75). (J). (gr. 4-7). 1994. pap. 3.50 (*0-590-47013-2*) Scholastic Inc.

— Jessi's Secret Language. (Baby-Sitters Club Ser.: No. 16). (J). 1988. pap. 3.50 (*0-590-44234-1*) Scholastic Inc.

— Jessi's Secret Language. large type ed. LC 93-15971. (Baby-Sitters Club Ser.). 176p. (J). (gr. 4 up). 1993. lib. bdg. 15.93 (*0-8368-1020-1*) Gareth Stevens Inc.

— Jessi's Wish. (Baby-Sitters Club Ser.: No. 48). 160p. (J). 1991. pap. 3.50 (*0-590-43571-X*) Scholastic Inc.

— Jessi's Wish, No. 48. (J). (gr. 4 up). 1993. pap. 3.50 (*0-685-66003-6*) Scholastic Inc.

— Jump Rope Rhymes Pack. (Baby-sitters Little Sister Ser.). (J). (gr. 2-4). 1995. pap. 5.99 (*0-590-25995-4*) Scholastic Inc.

— Just a Summer Romance. LC 86-46201. 170p. (YA). (gr. 7 up). 1987. 13.95 (*0-8234-0649-0*) Holiday.

— Just a Summer Romance. (YA). 1988. pap. 2.95 (*0-590-43999-5*) Scholastic Inc.

— Karen, Hannie, & Nancy: The Three Musketeers. (Baby-Sitters Little Sister Super Special Ser.: No. 4). 128p. (J). (gr. 2-4). 1992. pap. 2.95 (*0-590-45644-X*, Little Apple) Scholastic Inc.

— Karen's Baby. (Baby-Sitters Little Sister Super Special Ser.: No. 5). (J). (gr. 4-7). 1992. pap. 3.25 (*0-590-45649-0*) Scholastic Inc.

— Karen's Baby-Sitter. (Baby-Sitters Little Sister Ser.: No. 46). (J). (gr. 4-7). 1994. pap. 2.95 (*0-590-47045-0*) Scholastic Inc.

— Karen's Big Joke. (Baby-Sitters Little Sister Ser.: No. 27). (J). 1992. pap. 2.95 (*0-590-44829-3*) Scholastic Inc.

— Karen's Big Lie. (Baby-Sitters Little Sister Ser.: No. 38). (J). (gr. 4-7). 1993. pap. 2.95 (*0-590-45655-5*) Scholastic Inc.

— Karen's Big Top. (Baby-Sitters Little Sister Ser.: No. 51). (J). (gr. 4-7). 1994. pap. 2.95 (*0-590-48229-7*) Scholastic Inc.

— Karen's Big Weekend. (Baby-Sitters Little Sister Ser.: No. 44). (J). (gr. 4-7). 1993. pap. 2.95 (*0-590-47043-4*) Scholastic Inc.

— Karen's Birthday. (J). (gr. 4-7). 1990. pap. 2.95 (*0-590-44257-0*) Scholastic Inc.

— Karen's Brothers. (Baby-Sitters Little Sister Ser.: No. 17). (J). (gr. 4-7). 1991. pap. 2.75 (*0-590-43643-0*) Scholastic Inc.

— Karen's Bully. (Baby-Sitters Little Sister Ser.: No. 31). (J). 1992. 2.95 (*0-590-45646-6*, 053) Scholastic Inc.

— Karen's Campout. (Baby-Sitters Little Sister Super Special Ser.: No. 6). (J). (gr. 3-7). 1993. pap. 3.25 (*0-590-46911-8*) Scholastic Inc.

— Karen's Candy. (Baby-Sitters Little Sister Ser.: No. 54). (J). (gr. 4-7). 1994. pap. 2.95 (*0-590-48301-3*) Scholastic Inc.

— Karen's Carnival. (Baby-Sitters Little Sister Ser.: No. 20). 112p. (J). (gr. 2-4). 1991. 2.75 (*0-590-44823-4*) Scholastic Inc.

— Karen's Cartwheel. (Baby-Sitters Little Sister Ser.: No. 29). (J). 1992. pap. 2.75 (*0-590-44825-0*) Scholastic Inc.

— Karen's Doll. (Baby-Sitters Little Sister Ser.: No. 23). 112p. (J). 1991. pap. 2.95 (*0-590-44832-3*) Scholastic Inc.

— Karen's Doll House. (Baby-Sitters Little Sister Ser.: No. 35). (J). (gr. 4-7). 1993. pap. 2.95 (*0-590-45652-0*) Scholastic Inc.

— Karen's Ducklings. (Baby-Sitters Little Sister Ser.: No. 26). 96p. (J). 1992. pap. 2.75 (*0-590-44830-7*) Scholastic Inc.

— Karen's Ghost. (Baby-Sitters Little Sister Ser.: No. 12). 96p. (J). (gr. 2-4). 1990. pap. 2.95 (*0-590-43649-X*) Scholastic Inc.

— Karen's Goldfish. (Baby-Sitters Little Sister Ser.: No. 16). 112p. (J). (gr. 2-4). 1991. pap. 2.75 (*0-590-43644-9*) Scholastic Inc.

— Karen's Good-Bye. (Baby-Sitters Little Sister Ser.: No. 19). (J). (gr. 4-7). 1991. pap. 2.95 (*0-590-43641-4*) Scholastic Inc.

— Karen's Grandmother. (Baby-Sitters Club Ser.: No. 10). (J). (gr. 4-7). 1990. pap. 2.95 (*0-590-43651-1*) Scholastic Inc.

— Karen's Haircut. (Baby-Sitters Little Sister Ser.: No. 8). (J). (gr. 4-7). 1990. pap. 2.95 (*0-590-42670-2*) Scholastic Inc.

— Karen's Home Run. (Baby-Sitters Little Sister Ser.: No. 18). (J). (gr. 4-7). 1991. pap. 2.75 (*0-590-43642-2*) Scholastic Inc.

— Karen's Ice Skates. (Baby-Sitters Little Sister Ser.: No. 56). (J). (gr. 4-7). 1994. pap. 2.95 (*0-590-48302-1*) Scholastic Inc.

— Karen's in Love. (Baby-Sitters Little Sister Ser.: No. 15). (J). (gr. 4-7). 1991. pap. 2.75 (*0-590-43645-7*) Scholastic Inc.

— Karen's Kite. (Baby-Sitters Little Sister Ser.: No. 47). (J). (gr. 4-7). 1994. pap. 2.95 (*0-590-46913-4*) Scholastic Inc.

— Karen's Kittens. (Baby-Sitters Little Sister Ser.: No. 30). (J). 1992. pap. 2.95 (*0-590-45645-8*) Scholastic Inc.

— Karen's Kittycat Club. (Baby-Sitters Little Sister Ser.: No. 4). 112p. (J). (gr. 2-4). 1989. pap. 2.95 (*0-590-44264-3*) Scholastic Inc.

— Karen's Leprechaun. (Baby-Sitters Little Sister Ser.: No. 59). (J). (gr. 4-7). 1995. pap. 2.99 (*0-590-48231-9*) Scholastic Inc.

— Karen's Little Sister. (Baby-Sitters Little Sister Ser.: No. 6). 96p. (J). (gr. 2-4). 1989. pap. 2.95 (*0-590-44298-8*) Scholastic Inc.

— Karen's Little Witch. (Baby-Sitters Little Sister Ser.: No. 22). 112p. (J). 1991. pap. 2.95 (*0-590-44833-1*) Scholastic Inc.

— Karen's Lucky Penny. (Baby-Sitters Little Sister Ser.: No. 50). (J). (gr. 4-7). 1994. pap. 2.95 (*0-590-47048-5*) Scholastic Inc.

— Karen's Magician. (Baby-Sitters Little Sister Ser.: No. 55). (J). (gr. 4-7). 1994. pap. 2.95 (*0-590-48230-0*) Scholastic Inc.

— Karen's Mermaid. (Baby-Sitters Little Sister Club Ser.: No. 52). (J). (gr. 4-7). 1994. pap. 2.95 (*0-590-48299-8*) Scholastic Inc.

— Karen's Mystery. (Baby-Sitters Little Sister Super Special Ser.: No. 3). 144p. (J). 1991. pap. 2.95 (*0-590-44827-7*) Scholastic Inc.

— Karen's New Friend. (Baby-Sitters Little Sister Ser.: No. 36). (J). (gr. 4-7). 1993. pap. 2.95 (*0-590-45651-2*) Scholastic Inc.

— Karen's New Teacher. (Baby-Sitters Little Sister Ser.: No. 21). (J). (gr. 4-7). 1991. pap. 2.95 (*0-590-44824-2*) Scholastic Inc.

— Karen's New Year. (Baby-Sitters Little Sister Ser.: No. 14). (J). (gr. 4-7). 1991. pap. 2.75 (*0-590-43646-5*) Scholastic Inc.

— Karen's Newspaper. (Baby-Sitters Little Sister Ser.: No. 40). (J). (gr. 4-7). 1993. pap. 2.95 (*0-590-47040-X*) Scholastic Inc.

— Karen's Pen Pal. (Baby-Sitters Little Sister Ser.: No. 25). 96p. (J). 1992. pap. 2.95 (*0-590-44831-5*) Scholastic Inc.

— Karen's Pizza Party, No. 42. (J). 1993. pap. 2.95 (*0-590-47042-6*) Scholastic Inc.

— Karen's Plane Trip. (Baby-Sitters Little Sister Ser.: No. 2). 144p. (J). (gr. 2-4). 1991. pap. 3.25 (*0-590-44834-X*) Scholastic Inc.

— Karen's Prize. (Baby-Sitters Club Ser.: No. 11). (J). 1990. pap. 2.95 (*0-590-43650-3*) Scholastic Inc.

— Karen's Roller Skates. (Baby-Sitters Little Sister Ser.: No. 2). 64p. (J). (gr. 2-4). 1988. pap. 2.95 (*0-590-44259-7*) Scholastic Inc.

— Karen's School. (Baby-Sitters Little Sister Ser.: No. 41). (J). (gr. 4-7). 1993. pap. 2.95 (*0-590-47041-8*) Scholastic Inc.

— Karen's School. (Baby-Sitters Little Sister Ser.: No. 53). (J). (gr. 4-7). 1994. pap. 2.95 (*0-590-48300-5*) Scholastic Inc.

— Karen's School Mystery. (Baby-Sitters Little Sister Ser.: No. 57). (J). (gr. 4-7). 1995. pap. 2.95 (*0-590-48303-X*) Scholastic Inc.

— Karen's School Picture. (Baby-Sitters Little Sister Ser.: No. 5). 112p. (J). (gr. 2-4). 1989. pap. 2.95 (*0-590-44258-9*) Scholastic Inc.

— Karen's Secret. (Baby-Sitters Little Sister Ser.: No. 33). (J). 1992. 2.95 (*0-590-45648-2*) Scholastic Inc.

— Karen's Ski Trip. (Baby-Sitters Little Sister Ser.: No. 58). (J). (gr. 4-7). 1995. pap. 2.95 (*0-590-48304-8*) Scholastic Inc.

— Karen's Sleepover. (Baby-Sitters Club Ser.: No. 9). (J). (gr. 4-7). 1990. pap. 2.95 (*0-590-43652-X*) Scholastic Inc.

— Karen's Snowy Day. (Baby-Sitters Little Sister Ser.: No. 34). (J). (gr. 4-7). 1993. pap. 2.95 (*0-590-45650-4*) Scholastic Inc.

— Karen's Stepmother. (Baby-Sitters Little Sister Ser.: No. 49). (J). (gr. 4-7). 1994. pap. 2.95 (*0-590-47047-7*) Scholastic Inc.

— Karen's Surprise. (Baby-Sitters Little Sister Ser.: No. 13). 112p. (J). (gr. 2-4). 1990. pap. 2.75 (*0-590-43648-1*) Scholastic Inc.

— Karen's Tea Party. (Baby-Sitters Little Sister Ser.: No. 28). 96p. (J). 1992. pap. 2.95 (*0-590-44828-5*) Scholastic Inc.

— Karen's Toothache. (Baby-Sitters Little Sister Ser.: No. 43). (J). (gr. 4-7). 1993. pap. 2.95 (*0-590-46912-6*) Scholastic Inc.

— Karen's Tuba. (Baby-Sitters Little Sister Ser.: No. 37). (J). (gr. 4-7). 1993. pap. 2.95 (*0-590-45653-9*) Scholastic Inc.

— Karen's Twin. (Baby-Sitters Little Sister Ser.: No. 45). (J). (gr. 5-7). 1994. pap. 2.95 (*0-590-47044-2*) Scholastic Inc.

— Karen's Two Families. (Baby-Sitters Little Sister Ser.: No. 48). (J). (gr. 4-7). 1994. pap. 2.95 (*0-590-47046-9*) Scholastic Inc.

— Karen's Wedding. (Baby-Sitters Little Sister Ser.: No. 39). (J). (gr. 4-7). 1993. pap. 2.95 (*0-590-45654-7*) Scholastic Inc.

— Karen's Wish. (Baby-Sitters Little Sister Super Special Ser.: No. 1). 128p. (J). (gr. 2-4). 1990. pap. 3.25 (*0-590-43647-3*) Scholastic Inc.

— Karen's Witch. (Baby-Sitters Little Sister Ser.: No. 1). 112p. (Orig.). (J). (gr. 2-4). 1988. pap. 2.95 (*0-590-44300-3*) Scholastic Inc.

— Karen's Worst Day, Vol. 1. (J). 1989. pap. 2.95 (*0-590-44299-6*) Scholastic Inc.

— Keep Out, Claudia! (Baby-Sitters Club Ser.: No. 56). 160p. (J). (gr. 3-7). 1992. pap. 3.50 (*0-590-45657-1*, Apple Paperbacks) Scholastic Inc.

— Kristy & Mr. Mom. (Baby-Sitters Club Ser.: No. 81). (J). (gr. 4-7). 1995. pap. 3.50 (*0-590-48225-4*) Scholastic Inc.

— Kristy & the Baby Parade. (Baby-Sitters Club Ser.: No. 45). 160p. (J). (gr. 3-7). 1991. pap. 3.50 (*0-590-43574-4*) Scholastic Inc.

— Kristy & the Baby Parade. braille ed. 154p. (J). 1992. vinyl bd. 12.32 (*1-56956-118-4*, BR8882) W A T Braille.

— Kristy & the Copycat. (Baby-Sitters Club Ser.: No. 74). (J). (gr. 4-7). 1994. pap. 3.50 (*0-590-47012-4*) Scholastic Inc.

— Kristy and the Haunted Mansion. (Baby-Sitters Club Mystery Ser.: No. 9). (J). (gr. 4-7). 1993. pap. 3.50 (*0-590-44958-3*) Scholastic Inc.

— Kristy & the Missing Child: Baby-Sitters Club Mystery, No. 4. 160p. (J). 1992. pap. 3.25 (*0-590-44800-5*) Scholastic Inc.

— Kristy & the Missing Fortune. (Baby-Sitters Club Mystery Ser.: No. 19). (J). (gr. 4-7). 1995. pap. 3.50 (*0-590-48234-3*) Scholastic Inc.

— Kristy & the Mother's Day Surprise. (Baby-Sitters Club Ser.: No. 24). (J). (gr. 4-7). 1989. pap. 3.50 (*0-590-43506-X*) Scholastic Inc.

— Kristy & the Mother's Day Surprise. large type ed. (Baby-Sitters Club Ser.). 176p. (J). 1994. lib. bdg. 15.93 (*0-8368-1245-X*) Gareth Stevens Inc.

— Kristy & the Snobs. large type ed. LC 93-15968. (Baby-Sitters Club Ser.). 176p. (J). (gr. 4 up). 1993. lib. bdg. 15.93 (*0-8368-1015-5*) Gareth Stevens Inc.

— Kristy & the Snobs, No. 11. (J). 1988. pap. 3.50 (*0-590-43660-0*) Scholastic Inc.

— Kristy & the Vampires. (Baby-Sitters Club Mystery Ser.: No. 15). (J). (gr. 4-7). 1994. pap. 3.50 (*0-590-47053-1*) Scholastic Inc.

— Kristy & the Walking Disaster. large type ed. (Baby-Sitters Club Ser.). 176p. (J). (gr. 4 up). 1993. lib. bdg. 15.93 (*0-8368-1024-4*) Gareth Stevens Inc.

— Kristy & the Walking Disaster, No. 20. (J). 1989. pap. 3.50 (*0-590-43722-4*) Scholastic Inc.

— Kristy and the Worst Kid Ever. (Baby-Sitters Club Ser.: No. 62). (J). (gr. 4-7). 1993. pap. 3.50 (*0-590-45664-4*) Scholastic Inc.

— Kristy for President. (Baby-Sitters Club Ser.: No. 53). 160p. (J). 1992. pap. 3.25 (*0-590-44967-2*) Scholastic Inc.

— Kristy's Big Day. (Baby-Sitters Club Ser.: No. 6). (Orig.). (J). (gr. 4-7). 1987. pap. 3.50 (*0-590-43899-9*) Scholastic Inc.

— Kristy's Great Idea, No. 1. (Orig.). (J). 1986. pap. 3.50 (*0-590-43388-1*) Scholastic Inc.

— Kristy's Great Idea: Collector's Edition. (Baby-Sitters Club Ser.: No. 01). (J). (gr. 4-7). 1995. pap. 3.50 (*0-590-22473-5*) Scholastic Inc.

— Kristy's Mystery Admirer. (Baby-Sitters Club Ser.: No. 38). (J). (gr. 4-7). 1990. pap. 3.25 (*0-590-43567-1*) Scholastic Inc.

— Little Miss Stoneybrook-- & Dawn. large type ed. LC 93-8100. (Baby-Sitters Club Ser.). 176p. (J). (gr. 4 up). 1993. lib. bdg. 15.93 (*0-8368-1019-8*) Gareth Stevens Inc.

— Little Miss Stoneybrook & Dawn. (Baby-Sitters Club Ser.: No. 15). 160p. (J). (gr. 3-7). 1988. pap. 3.25 (*0-590-43717-8*) Scholastic Inc.

— Logan Bruno, Boy Baby-Sitter. (Readers Special Request Ser.). (J). (gr. 3-7). 1993. pap. 3.50 (*0-590-47118-X*) Scholastic Inc.

— Logan Likes Mary Anne!, No. 10. (J). 1988. pap. 3.50 (*0-590-43387-3*) Scholastic Inc.

— Logan Likes Maryanne. (Baby-Sitters Club Ser.: No. 10). 160p. (Orig.). (J). (gr. 4-6). 1988. pap. 2.75 (*0-590-41124-1*, Apple Paperbacks) Scholastic Inc.

— Logan's Story (Special Edition Reader's Request) (Baby-Sitters Club Ser.). (J). 1992. pap. 3.25 (*0-590-45575-3*, Apple Paperbacks) Scholastic Inc.

— Ma & Pa Dracula. LC 89-2081. (Illus.). 128p. (J). (gr. 3-7). 1989. 14.95 (*0-8234-0781-0*) Holiday.

— Ma & Pa Dracula. 128p. (J). 1991. pap. 2.95 (*0-590-43828-X*) Scholastic Inc.

— Maid Mary Anne. (Baby-Sitters Club Ser.: No. 66). (J). (gr. 4-7). 1993. pap. 3.50 (*0-590-47004-3*) Scholastic Inc.

— Mallory & the Ghost Cat. (Baby-Sitters Club Mystery Ser.: No. 3). 160p. (J). 1992. pap. 3.25 (*0-590-44799-8*) Scholastic Inc.

— Mallory & the Mystery Diary. large type ed. (Baby-Sitters Club Ser.). 176p. (J). 1994. lib. bdg. 15.93 (*0-8368-1250-6*) Gareth Stevens Inc.

— Mallory & the Secret Diary. (Baby-Sitters Club Ser.: No. 29). (J). (gr. 5 up). 1989. pap. 3.25 (*0-590-42500-5*, Apple Paperbacks) Scholastic Inc.

— Mallory & the Trouble with Twins. (J). 1989. pap. 3.50 (*0-590-43507-8*) Scholastic Inc.

— Mallory & the Trouble with Twins. large type ed. (Baby-Sitters Club Ser.). 176p. (J). 1994. lib. bdg. 15.93 (*0-8368-1242-5*) Gareth Stevens Inc.

— Mallory Hates Boys (& Gym) (Baby-Sitters Club Ser.: No. 59). (J). 1992. 3.50 (*0-590-45660-1*) Scholastic Inc.

— Mallory on Strike. (Baby-Sitters Club Ser.: No. 47). (J). (gr. 4-7). 1991. pap. 3.50 (*0-590-44971-0*) Scholastic Inc.

— Mallory Pike No. 1: Fan. (Baby-Sitters Club Ser.: No. 80). (J). (gr. 4-7). 1994. pap. 3.50 (*0-590-48224-6*) Scholastic Inc.

— Mallory's Dream Horse. (Baby-Sitters Club Ser.: No. 54). 160p. (J). 1992. pap. 3.25 (*0-590-44965-6*) Scholastic Inc.

— Mary Anne & Miss Priss. (Baby-Sitters Club Ser.: No. 73). (J). (gr. 4-7). 1994. pap. 3.50 (*0-590-47011-6*) Scholastic Inc.

— Mary Anne & the Great Romance. large type ed. (Baby-Sitters Club Ser.). 176p. (J). 1994. lib. bdg. 15.93 (*0-8368-1251-4*) Gareth Stevens Inc.

— Mary Anne & the Library Mystery. (Baby-Sitters Club Mystery Ser.: No. 13). (J). (gr. 4-7). 1994. pap. 3.50 (*0-590-47051-5*) Scholastic Inc.

— Mary Anne & the Search for Tigger. (J). 1989. pap. 3.50 (*0-590-43347-4*) Scholastic Inc.

— Mary Anne & the Search for Tigger. large type ed. (Baby-Sitters Club Ser.). 176p. (J). 1994. lib. bdg. 15.93 (*0-8368-1246-8*) Gareth Stevens Inc.

— Mary Anne & the Secret in the Attic. (Baby-Sitters Club Mystery Club: No. 5). 160p. (J). (gr. 3-7). 1992. pap. 3.50 (*0-590-44801-3*, Apple Paperbacks) Scholastic Inc.

— Mary Anne & Too Many Babies. (Baby-Sitters Club Ser.: No. 52). 160p. (J). 1992. pap. 3.50 (*0-590-44966-4*) Scholastic Inc.

— Mary Anne & Too Many Boys. (Baby-Sitters Club Ser.: No. 34). (J). (gr. 4-7). 1990. pap. 3.50 (*0-590-42494-7*) Scholastic Inc.

— Mary Anne Breaks the Rules. (Baby-Sitters Club Ser.: No. 79). (J). (gr. 4-7). 1994. pap. 3.50 (*0-590-48223-8*) Scholastic Inc.

— Mary Anne Misses Logan. (Baby-Sitters Club Ser.: No. 46). 160p. (J). (gr. 3-7). 1991. pap. 3.50 (*0-590-43569-8*) Scholastic Inc.

— Mary Anne Saves the Day. (Orig.). (J). 1987. pap. 3.50 (*0-590-43512-4*) Scholastic Inc.

— Mary Anne vs. Logan. (Baby-Sitters Club Ser.: No. 41). (J). (gr. 4-7). 1991. pap. 3.50 (*0-590-43570-1*) Scholastic Inc.

— Mary Anne's Bad Luck Mystery. (Baby-Sitters Club Ser.: No. 17). 144p. (J). (gr. 3-7). 1988. 3.50 (*0-590-43659-7*) Scholastic Inc.

— Mary Anne's Bad-Luck Mystery. large type ed. LC 93-4346. (Baby-Sitters Club Ser.). 176p. (J). (gr. 4 up). 1993. lib. bdg. 15.93 (*0-8368-1021-X*) Gareth Stevens Inc.

— Mary Anne's Makeover. (Baby-Sitters Club Ser.: No. 60). (J). (gr. 4-7). 1993. pap. 3.50 (*0-590-45662-8*) Scholastic Inc.

— Me & Katie (the Pest) LC 85-5558. (Illus.). 160p. (J). (gr. 4-7). 1985. 13.95 (*0-8234-0580-X*) Holiday.

— Me & Katie the Pest. (J). 1990. pap. 3.25 (*0-590-43618-X*) Scholastic Inc.

— Missing since Monday. 176p. (YA). (gr. 7 up). 1987. pap. 2.95 (*0-590-43136-6*) Scholastic Inc.

— The Mystery at Claudia's House. (Baby-Sitters Club Ser.: No. 6). (J). 1992. 3.50 (*0-590-44961-3*) Scholastic Inc.

— New York, New York. (Baby-Sitters Club Super Special Ser.: No. 06). (J). (gr. 4-7). 1991. pap. 3.95 (*0-590-43576-0*) Scholastic Inc.

— Poor Mallory. (Baby-Sitters Club Ser.: No. 39). 160p. (J). 1990. pap. 3.25 (*0-590-43568-X*) Scholastic Inc.

— Rachel Parker, Kindergarten Show-Off. LC 91-25793. (Illus.). 40p. (J). (ps-3). 1992. lib. bdg. 15.95 (*0-8234-0935-X*) Holiday.

— Sea City, Here We Come! (Baby-Sitters Club Super Special Ser.: No. 10). (J). (gr. 3-7). 1993. pap. 3.95 (*0-590-45674-1*) Scholastic Inc.

— Secret Santa. LC 93-48981. (Baby-Sitters Club Ser.). (J). 1994. 14.95 (*0-590-48295-5*) Scholastic Inc.

— Shannon's Story. (Baby-Sitters Club Special Edition Ser.). (J). (gr. 4-7). 1994. pap. 3.50 (*0-590-47756-0*) Scholastic Inc.

— Slam Book. LC 87-45335. 160p. (YA). (gr. 7 up). 1987. 12.95 (*0-8234-0666-0*) Holiday.

— Slam Book. (J). 1989. pap. 2.75 (*0-590-41838-6*) Scholastic Inc.

— Snowbound. (Baby-Sitters Club Super Special Ser.: No. 7). 240p. (J). 1991. pap. 3.95 (*0-590-44963-X*) Scholastic Inc.

— Stacey & the Cheerleaders. (Baby-Sitters Club Ser.: No. 70). (J). (gr. 4-7). 1993. pap. 3.50 (*0-590-47008-6*) Scholastic Inc.
— Stacey & the Missing Ring. (Baby-Sitters Club Mystery Ser.: No. 1). 160p. (J). (gr. 3-7). 1991. pap. 3.50 (*0-590-44084-5*) Scholastic Inc.
— Stacey & the Mystery at the Empty House. (Baby-Sitters Club Mystery Ser.: No. 18). (J). (gr. 4-7). 1994. pap. 3.50 (*0-590-48233-5*) Scholastic Inc.
— Stacey & the Mystery at the Mall. (Baby-Sitters Club Mystery Ser.: No. 14). (J). (gr. 4-7). 1994. pap. 3.50 (*0-590-47052-3*) Scholastic Inc.
— Stacey & the Mystery Money. (Baby-Sitters Club Ser.: No. 10). (J). (gr. 4-7). 1993. pap. 3.50 (*0-590-45696-2*) Scholastic Inc.
— Stacey & the Mystery of Stoneybrook. (Baby-Sitters Club Ser.: No. 35). (J). (gr. 4-7). 1990. pap. 3.50 (*0-590-42508-0*) Scholastic Inc.
— Stacey vs. the BSC. (Baby-Sitters Club Ser.: No. 83). (J). (gr. 4-7). 1995. pap. 3.50 (*0-590-48235-1*) Scholastic Inc.
— Stacey's Big Crush. (Baby-Sitters Club Ser.: No. 65). (J). (gr. 4-7). 1993. pap. 3.50 (*0-590-45667-9*) Scholastic Inc.
— Stacey's Book. (Baby-Sitters Club Portrait Collection). (J). (gr. 4-7). 1994. pap. 3.50 (*0-590-48399-4*) Scholastic Inc.
— Stacey's Choice. (Baby-Sitters Club Ser.: No. 58). (J). 1992. 3.50 (*0-590-45659-8*) Scholastic Inc.
— Stacey's Emergency. (Baby-Sitters Club Ser.: No. 43). (J). (gr. 4-7). 1991. pap. 3.50 (*0-590-43572-8*) Scholastic Inc.
— Stacey's Ex-Best Friend. (Baby-Sitters Club Ser.: No. 51). 160p. (J). 1992. pap. 3.25 (*0-590-44968-0*) Scholastic Inc.
— Stacey's Lie. (Baby-Sitters Club Ser.: No. 76). (J). (gr. 4-7). 1994. pap. 3.50 (*0-590-47014-0*) Scholastic Inc.
— Stacey's Mistake. (J). 1988. pap. 3.50 (*0-590-43718-6*) Scholastic Inc.
— Stacey's Mistake. large type ed. (Baby-Sitters Club Ser.). 176p. (J). (gr. 4 up). 1993. lib. bdg. 15.93 (*0-8368-1022-8*) Gareth Stevens Inc.
— Stage Fright. (J). (gr. 5-7). 1990. pap. 2.95 (*0-590-43619-8*) Scholastic Inc.
— Starring the Baby-Sitters Club. (Baby-Sitters Club Super Special Ser.: No. 9). (J). (gr. 4-7). 1992. pap. 3.95 (*0-590-45661-X*) Scholastic Inc.
— Summer Fill-In Book. (Baby-sitters Little Sister Ser.). (J). (gr. 2-4). 1995. pap. 2.95 (*0-590-26467-2*) Scholastic Inc.
— Ten Kids, No Pets. LC 87-25206. 184p. (J). (gr. 3-7). 1988. 14.95 (*0-8234-0691-1*) Holiday.
— Ten Kids No Pets. (J). (gr. 5-7). 1990. pap. 3.25 (*0-590-43620-1*) Scholastic Inc.
— The Truth about Stacey. (Orig.). (J). 1986. pap. 3.50 (*0-590-43511-6*) Scholastic Inc.
— Welcome Back, Stacey. (Baby-Sitters Club Ser.: No. 28). (J). (gr. 5 up). 1989. pap. 3.50 (*0-590-42501-3*, Apple Paperbacks) Scholastic Inc.
— Welcome Back, Stacey! large type ed. (Baby-Sitters Club Ser.). 176p. (J). 1994. lib. bdg. 15.93 (*0-8368-1249-2*) Gareth Stevens Inc.
— With You & Without You. LC 85-21990. 192p. (J). (gr. 4-8). 1986. 14.95 (*0-8234-0601-6*) Holiday.
— With You & Without You. 1987. pap. 2.95 (*0-590-43625-2*) Scholastic Inc.
— Yours Turly, Shirley. LC 88-6460. 144p. (J). (gr. 3-7). 1988. 14.95 (*0-8234-0719-5*) Holiday.
Martin, Ann M., ed. see Cornell University, Programs for Employment & Workplace Systems Staff.
Martin, Anna, jt. auth. see Women's Co-operative Guild.
Martin, Anne. Quick & Easy Creative Art Lessons. LC 80-17558. 254p. 1981. 18.95 (*0-13-749663-X*, Parker Publishing Co) P-H.
— Reading Your Students: Their Writing & Their Selves. 64p. 1983. pap. 5.95 (*0-915924-32-3*) Tchrs & Writers Coll.
— Selected Writings of Anne Martin, Pioneer Nevada Feminist. Basso, Dave, ed. 1986. pap. 10.00 (*0-936332-25-5*) Falcon Hill Pr.
Martin, Annie-Claude. A Treasury of Fairy Tales. 400p. 1994. 14.98 (*0-8317-3398-5*) Smithmark.
Martin, Anthony & Camm, A. John, eds. Geriatric Cardiology: Principles & Practice. LC 93-40107. 1994. text ed. 150.00 (*0-471-94064-X*) Wiley.
— Heart Disease in the Elderly. LC 83-17058. (Wiley Series on Disease Management in the Elderly: No. 2). 285p. reprint ed. pap. 81.30 (*0-8357-3472-2*, 2039734) Bks Demand.
Martin, Antoinette T. Famous Seaweed Soup. Mathews, Judith, ed. LC 92-31612. (Illus.). 32p. (J). (ps-2). 1993. lib. bdg. 13.95 (*0-8075-2263-5*) A Whitman.
Martin, Anton. Handbuch der Gesammten Photographie. Bunnell, Peter C. & Sobieszek, Robert A., eds. LC 76-23057. (Sources of Modern Photography Ser.). (GER.). 1979. reprint ed. lib. bdg. 27.95 (*0-405-09621-6*) Ayer.
Martin, April. The Lesbian & Gay Parenting Handbook: Creating & Raising Our Families. LC 92-54782. 1993. pap. 15.00 (*0-06-096929-6*, PL) HarpC.
Martin, Aquinata. The Catholic Church on the Nebraska Frontier: 1854-1885. LC 73-3580. (Catholic University of America. Studies in Romance Languages & Literatures: No. 26). reprint ed. 39.50 (*0-404-57776-8*) AMS Pr.
Martin, Ariadna Y., tr. see Propp, Vladimir.
Martin, Arlan S. Vivaldi Violin Concertos: A Handbook. LC 76-169698. 278p. 1972. 20.00 (*0-8108-0432-8*) Scarecrow.
Martin, Arlene L. Complete Preschool Program. 143p. 1987. pap. text ed. 19.95 (*1-55691-008-8*) Learning Pubns.
Martin, Arthur, jt. auth. see Cahier, Charles.
Martin, Arthur E. Life in the Slow Lane. (Illus.). 304p. 1990. 25.00 (*0-914339-30-3*) P E Randall Pub.
Martin, Asa E. Pennsylvania History Told by Contemporaries. 1993. reprint ed. lib. bdg. 89.00 (*0-7812-5489-2*) Rprt Serv.
Martin, Augustine. W. B. Yeats. 1990. pap. 8.95 (*0-86140-325-8*) Dufour.
Martin, Augustine, intro. Forgiveness: Ireland's Best Contemporary Short Stories. LC 89-17014. 294p. 1989. 25.95 (*0-941423-32-8*); pap. 12.95 (*0-941423-33-6*) FWEW.
Martin, B. Atlas of Scrotal Ultrasound. 200p. 1993. 180.00 (*0-387-53309-5*) Spr-Verlag.
— Metabolic Regulation. 1987. pap. 44.95 (*0-632-01157-2*) Blackwell Sci.
— Tissue Culture Techniques: An Introduction. LC 94-6357. xi, 247p. 1994. pap. 39.00 (*0-8176-3643-9*) Birkhauser.
— Yo, Grocer. (J). (gr. 4 up). 1999. 12.95 (*0-8050-0329-0*) H Holt & Co.
Martin, B., jt. auth. see Ziegler, K.
Martin, B. Jay. Conundrum, Vol. 1: A Cartoon Collection of Concepts, College, & Confounded Connotations. (Illus.). 160p. (Orig.). (YA). (gr. 12 up). 1988. pap. 5.95 (*0-922073-00-7*) Thought Wave Pr.
Martin, B. R. & Shaw, G. Particle Physics. (Manchester Physics Ser.: No. 1173). 330p. 1992. text ed. 79.95 (*0-471-92358-3*); pap. text ed. 49.95 (*0-471-92359-1*) Wiley.
***Martin-Bagnaudez, Jacqueline.** Petit Dictionnaire de l'Architecture. 139p. (FRE.). 1990. pap. 22.95 (*0-7859-8629-4*, 222003139x) Fr & Eur.
***Martin, Barb.** The Haunted Pogo Stick. (Illus.). 23p. (J). 1995. text ed. 12.50 (*0-930329-92-9*) KABEL Pubs.
Martin, Barbara. Minimum Wage to Maximum Wealth: You Can Build a Fortune Starting with What You Have Right Now. 176p. (Orig.). (C). 1990. 19.95 (*0-9621499-7-7*); pap. 14.95 (*0-9621499-6-9*) Tangible Assets.
Martin, Barbara & Christie, Folla. Landlord & Tenant Law. 2nd ed. 448p. 1994. pap. 34.95 (*0-632-03469-6*) Blackwell Sci.
Martin, Barbara A. Social Studies Activities for the Gifted Student. (Illus.). 1977. 6.50 (*0-914634-47-X*, 7713) DOK Pubs.
***Martin, Barbara H.** When the East Wind Blows. 400p. (Orig.). Date not set. pap. 9.95 (*0-7610-0370-3*) NW Pub.
Martin, Barbara L. & Briggs, Leslie J. The Affective & Cognitive Domains: Integration for Instruction & Research. LC 85-16143. (Illus.). 500p. 1986. 39.95 (*0-87778-193-1*) Educ Tech Pubns.
Martin-Barbero, Jesus & Schlesinger, Philip. Communication, Culture & Hegemony: From Media to Mediations. (Communication & Human Values Ser.). (Illus.). 288p. (C). 1993. text ed. 65.00 (*0-8039-8488-X*); pap. text ed. 24.00 (*0-8039-8489-8*) Sage.
Martin-Barnes, Adrienne, jt. auth. see Paxson, Diana L.
***Martin-Baro, Ignacio.** Writings for a Liberation Psychology. Aron, Adrianne & Corne, Shawn, eds. LC 94-20987. (Illus.). 256p. 1994. text ed. 32.00 (*0-674-96246-X*, MARWRI) HUP.
Martin, Barry. Budgies As a New Pet. (Illus.). 64p. (Orig.). 1990. pap. 5.95 (*0-86622-611-7*, TU-004) TFH Pubns.
— Rabbits As a New Pet. (Illus.). 64p. (Orig.). 1990. pap. 5.95 (*0-86622-618-4*, TU-010) TFH Pubns.
Martin, Belinda B., intro. Pediatric Hospice Care: What Helps. (Illus.). 400p. (C). 1989. write for info. (*0-9623727-0-6*) Child Hosp LA.
Martin, Bengt. Olaf the Ship's Cat. (Illus.). 32p. (J). (ps-3). 1992. 7.95 (*1-56288-266-X*) Checkerboard.
Martin, Benjamin. The Agony of Modernization: Labor & Industrialization in Spain. LC 89-77909. (Cornell International Industrial & Labor Relations Reports: No. 16). 576p. 1990. 45.00 (*0-87546-165-4*) ILR Pr.
Martin, Benjamin & Kassalow, Everett M., eds. Labor Relations in Advanced Industrial Societies: Issues & Problems. LC 79-56777. 206p. 1980. pap. 6.00 (*0-87003-033-7*) Carnegie Endow.
Martin, Benjamin F. Crime & Criminal Justice under the Third Republic: The Shame of Marianne. LC 89-27334. 392p. 1990. text ed. 45.00 (*0-8071-1572-X*) La State U Pr.
— The Hypocrisy of Justice in the Belle Epouque. LC 83-16263. 267p. 1984. pap. 76.10 (*0-7837-8502-X*, 2049310) Bks Demand.
Martin, Bernard. The Existential Theology of Paul Tillich. (Masterworks of Literature Ser.). 1989. pap. 15.95 (*0-685-44682-4*) NCUP.
— The Existentialist Theology of Paul Tillich. 1963. pap. 15.95 (*0-8084-0400-8*) NCUP.
Martin, Bernard, tr. see Shestov, Lev.
***Martin, Bernd.** Japan & Germany in the Modern World. LC 94-42973. 256p. (C). 1995. text ed. 39.95 (*1-57181-858-8*) Berghahn Bks.
Martin, Bernice M. Tissue Culture Techniques: An Introduction. LC 94-6357. xi, 247p. 1994. 85.00 (*0-8176-3718-4*) Birkhauser.
Martin, Bessie. Desertion of Alabama Troops from the Confederate Army. LC 32-34110. (Columbia University. Studies in the Social Sciences: No. 378). reprint ed. 21.50 (*0-404-51378-6*) AMS Pr.
Martin, Bette. The Children's Material. (Illus.). 100p. (J). (gr. k-4). 1980. pap. write for info. (*1-880436-02-7*) Miracle Exper.
— Help Is on the Way. (Illus.). 61p. (J). (gr. 5-7). 1986. pap. write for info. (*1-880436-01-9*) Miracle Exper.
Martin, Bettina G., ed. The CLMA Guide to Managing a Clinical Laboratory. (Illus.). 95p. (Orig.). 1991. pap. text ed. 35.00 (*0-9625414-1-9*) Clinical Lab Mgmnt Assn.
Martin, Betty & Carson, Ben. The Principal's Handbook on the School Media Center. LC 81-801. 212p. 1981. reprint ed. pap. 26.00 (*0-208-01912-X*, Lib Prof Pubns) Shoe String.
Martin, Betty & Hatfield, Frances. The School District Library Media Director's Handbook. LC 81-14292. (Illus.). x, 236p. 1982. 33.50 (*0-208-01889-1*, Lib Prof Pubns); pap. 24.00 (*0-208-01890-5*, Lib Prof Pubns) Shoe String.
Martin, Betty & Sargent, Linda. The Teacher's Handbook on the School Library Media Center. LC 80-24542. 324p. 1980. 35.00 (*0-208-01854-9*, Lib Prof Pubns); pap. text ed. 26.00 (*0-208-01847-6*, LPP, Lib Prof Pubns) Shoe String.
Martin, Betty, jt. auth. see Martin, Don.
Martin, Betty, jt. ed. see Martin, Don.
***Martin, Betty D.** Orwell Remembered Vol. II: The Town of Orwell & America's Wars. 230p. 1993. pap. 12.50 (*1-886303-01-0*) Write to Print.
Martin, Betty W., jt. auth. see Martin, Don W.
Martin, Betty W., jt. ed. see Martin, Don W.
Martin, Betty W., ed. see Shockley, Bob & Mondavi, Robert.
Martin, Biddy. Women & Modernity: The (Life) Styles of Lou Andreas-Salome. LC 90-55718. (Reading Women Writing Ser.). (Illus.). 264p. 1991. 35.00 (*0-8014-2591-3*); pap. 13.95 (*0-8014-9907-0*) Cornell U Pr.
Martin, Bill, Jr. Brown Bear, Brown Bear, What Do You See? LC 83-12779. (Illus.). 32p. (Orig.). (J). (ps-k). 1983. 15.95 (*0-8050-0201-4*, Bks Young Read) H Holt & Co.
— Brown Bear, Brown Bear, What Do You See? 25th Anniversary Edition. LC 91-29115. (Illus.). 32p. (J). (ps-00). 1992. 15.95 (*0-8050-1744-5*, Bks Young Read) H Holt & Co.
Martin, Bill. Calendar Lion. (J). 1993. 15.95 (*0-8050-2417-4*) H Holt & Co.
Martin, Bill, Jr. Chicka Chicka ABC. (J). (ps-6). 1993. 4.95 (*0-671-87893-X*, Litl Simon S&S) S&S Childrens.
— Fire! Fire! Said Mrs. McGuire. LC 94-11258. (J). 1995. write for info. (*0-15-227562-2*) HarBrace.
Martin, Bill. Fit for the King. Haynes, Glenda, ed. (Illus.). 384p. (Orig.). (YA). (gr. 7 up). 1985. pap. 11.50 (*0-89114-154-5*) Baptist Pub Hse.
Martin, Bill, Jr. The Happy Hippopotami. Johnston, Allyn, ed. (Illus.). 32p. (J). (ps-3). 1991. 12.95 (*0-15-233380-0*) HarBrace.
— Happy Hippopotami. (Big Bks.). 30p. (J). (ps-3). 1991. pap. 19.95 (*0-15-233381-9*, HB Juv Bks) HarBrace.
— Happy Hippopotami. (J). (ps-3). 1992. pap. 4.95 (*0-15-233382-7*) HarBrace.
***Martin, Bill.** Humanism & Its Aftermath: The Shared Fate of Deconstruction & Politics. LC 94-39400. 216p. (C). 1995. text ed. 45.00 (*0-391-03893-1*); pap. 15.00 (*0-391-03894-X*) Humanities.
— The Joy of Drawing. LC 93-9265. (Illus.). 144p. 1993. pap. 22.50 (*0-8230-2370-2*, Watsn-Guptill) Watsn-Guptill.
— Knots on a Counting Rope. (Illus.). 32p. (J). (gr. k-3). 1993. pap. 19.95 (*0-8050-2955-9*, Bks Young Read) H Holt & Co.
— Little Woodland Books: The Bears & the Bees; The Doe & the Fawn; The Earthworm & the Underground; The Fox & the Fleas; The Gray Squirrel & the Red Intruder; The Owl & the Mouse; The Rabbit & the Cat; The Skunk & Its Swoosher; The Wild Turkey & Her Poults; The Bird & the Snake, 10 vols. (Illus.). (J). (gr. 1-6). 1979. audio 149.00 (*0-87827-322-0*) Ency Brit Ed.
— Matrix & Line: Derrida & the Possibilities of Postmodern Social Theory. LC 91-20980. (SUNY Series in Radical, Social & Political Theory). 255p. (C). 1992. 57.50 (*0-7914-1049-8*); pap. 18.95 (*0-7914-1050-1*) State U NY Pr.
Martin, Bill, Jr. Old Devil Wind. LC 92-37908. (Illus.). (J). 1993. 13.95 (*0-15-257768-8*) HarBrace.
— Polar Bear, Polar Bear, What Do You Hear? (Illus.). 32p. (J). (ps). 1991. 15.95 (*0-8050-1759-3*, Bks Young Read) H Holt & Co.
— Polar Bear, Polar Bear, What Do You Hear? (Illus.). 32p. (J). (ps-2). 1993. pap. 16.95 (*0-8050-2815-3*, Bks Young Read) H Holt & Co.
— Polar Bear, Polar Bear, What Do You Hear? Big Book. LC 91-13322. (Illus.). 32p. (J). (ps-2). 1992. pap. 19.95 (*0-8050-2346-1*, Bks Young Read) H Holt & Co.
***Martin, Bill.** Politics in the Impasse: Explorations in Postsecular Social Theory. (SUNY Series in Radical Social & Political Theory). 320p. (C). 1996. text ed. 59.50x (*0-7914-2793-5*); pap. 19.95x (*0-7914-2794-3*) State U NY Pr.
Martin, Bill, Jr. The Wizard. LC 93-15521. (Illus.). (J). 1994. 14.95 (*0-15-298926-9*) HarBrace.
— Words. (J). (ps-6). 1993. 4.95 (*0-671-87174-9*, Litl Simon S&S) S&S Childrens.
Martin, Bill, Jr. & Archambault, John. Barn Dance! LC 86-14225. (Illus.). 32p. (J). (ps-2). 1986. 14.95 (*0-8050-0089-5*, Bks Young Read) H Holt & Co.
— Barn Dance! LC 86-14225. (Illus.). 32p. (J). (ps-2). 1988. pap. 4.95 (*0-8050-0799-7*, Bks Young Read) H Holt & Co.
— Chicka Chicka Boom Boom. (Illus.). (J). (gr. 2-6). 1989. pap. 14.00 (*0-671-67949-X*, S&S Bks Young Read) S&S Childrens.
— The Ghost-Eye Tree. LC 85-8422. (Illus.). 32p. (Orig.). (J). (ps-2). 1985. 13.95 (*0-8050-0208-1*, Bks Young Read) H Holt & Co.
— The Ghost-Eye Tree. LC 85-8422. (Illus.). 32p. (Orig.). (J). (ps-2). 1988. pap. 5.95 (*0-8050-0947-7*, Bks Young Read) H Holt & Co.
— Here Are My Hands. LC 86-25842. (Illus.). 32p. (J). (ps-2). 1987. 14.95 (*0-8050-0328-2*, Bks Young Read) H Holt & Co.
— Here Are My Hands. LC 86-25842. (Illus.). 32p. (J). (ps-2). 1989. pap. 5.95 (*0-8050-1168-4*, Owlet BYR) H Holt & Co.
— Knots on a Counting Rope. LC 87-14832. (Illus.). 32p. (J). (ps-2). 1987. 14.95 (*0-8050-0571-4*, Bks Young Read) H Holt & Co.
— Listen to the Rain. LC 88-6502. (Illus.). 32p. (J). (ps-2). 1988. 15.95 (*0-8050-0682-6*, Bks Young Read) H Holt & Co.
— The Magic Pumpkin. LC 89-11162. (Illus.). 32p. (J). (ps-2). 1989. 14.95 (*0-8050-1134-X*, Bks Young Read) H Holt & Co.
— Up & down on the Merry-Go-Round. LC 87-28836. (Illus.). 32p. (J). (ps-2). 1988. 14.95 (*0-8050-0681-8*, Bks Young Read) H Holt & Co.
— Up & Down on the Merry-Go-Round. LC 87-28836. (Illus.). 32p. (J). (ps-2). 1991. pap. 4.95 (*0-8050-1638-4*, Bks Young Read) H Holt & Co.
— White Dynamite & Curly Kidd. LC 85-27214. (Illus.). 32p. (J). (ps-2). 1986. 12.95 (*0-8050-0658-3*, Bks Young Read) H Holt & Co.
— White Dynamite & Curly Kidd. LC 85-27214. (Illus.). 32p. (J). (ps-2). 1989. pap. 5.95 (*0-8050-1018-1*, Bks Young Read) H Holt & Co.
Martin, Bill & Martin, Bill. My Special Place. 136p. (gr. 4-9). 1980. pap. 8.95 (*0-89114-111-1*) Baptist Pub Hse.
Martin, Bill, Jr., jt. auth. see Archambault, John.
Martin, Bill, jt. auth. see Martin, Bill.
Martin, Bob. Hiking the Highest Passes. 2nd ed. LC 84-6893. (Illus.). 228p. 1988. pap. 12.95 (*0-87108-756-1*) Pruett.
— Hiking Trails of Central Colorado. 3rd ed. 225p. 1989. pap. 12.95 (*0-87108-787-1*) Pruett.
— Orlando & Disney World: A TravelVenture Guide. 3rd ed. (Illus.). 256p. 1991. pap. 9.95 (*0-937281-05-0*) Geotravel Res Ctr.
Martin, Bob & Martin, Dotty. Arizona's Mountains: A Hiking & Climbing Guide. 2nd ed. LC 87-15518. (Illus.). 208p. (Orig.). 1991. pap. 11.95 (*0-917895-37-1*) Cordillera CO.
Martin, Bob, jt. auth. see Garratt, Mike.
Martin, Bobi. All about Scarecrows. (Illus.). 64p. (Orig.). 1990. pap. 7.95 (*0-9617357-5-9*) Tomato Enter.
Martin, Brendan. In the Public Interest? Privatization & Public Sector Reform. LC 93-5391. 256p. (C). 1993. text ed. 49.95 (*1-85649-215-X*, Pub. by Zed Books UK); pap. 19.95 (*1-85649-216-8*, Pub. by Zed Books UK) Humanities.
Martin, Brian. Scientific Knowledge in Controversy: The Social Dynamics of the Fluoridation Debate. LC 90-34740. (SUNY Series in Science, Technology, & Society). 266p. 1991. 64.50 (*0-7914-0538-9*); pap. 21.95 (*0-7914-0539-7*) State U NY Pr.
— Strip the Experts. (Anarchist Discussion Ser.). 69p. 1991. pap. 5.00 (*0-900384-63-8*) Left Bank.
— Uprooting War. 298p. (Orig.). 1984. pap. 12.00 (*0-900384-26-3*) Left Bank.
***Martin, Brian, ed.** Confronting the Experts. 160p. (C). 1996. text ed. 44.50x (*0-7914-2913-X*); pap. 14.95x (*0-7914-2914-8*) State U NY Pr.
— The Nineteenth Century (Seventeen Ninety-Eight to Nineteen Hundred) LC 89-70174. (St. Martin's Anthologies of English Literature Ser.: Vol. No. 4.). 666p. 1990. text ed. 20.00 (*0-312-04476-3*) St Martin.
***Martin, Brian G.** The Shanghai Green Gang: Politics & Organized Crime, 1919-1937. LC 95-5017. 1996. write for info. (*0-520-20114-0*) U CA Pr.
Martin, Brigid. The Mische Technique: Painting Secrets of the Old Masters. (Illus.). 112p. 22.50 (*0-915829-59-2*) Chameleon Bks.
Martin, Buddy, jt. auth. see Bradshaw, Terry.
Martin, C. Brontes. (Life & Works). (Illus.). 112p. (J). (gr. 7 up). 1989. 14.95 (*0-685-58635-9*); lib. bdg. 19.94 (*0-86592-299-3*) Rourke Corp.
— H. G. Wells. (Life & Works). (Illus.). 112p. (J). (gr. 7 up). 1989. 14.95 (*0-685-58636-7*); lib. bdg. 19.94 (*0-86592-297-7*) Rourke Corp.
— Shakespeare. (Life & Works). (Illus.). 112p. (J). (gr. 7 up). 1989. 14.95 (*0-685-58633-2*); lib. bdg. 19.94 (*0-86592-296-9*) Rourke Corp.
Martin, C. Dianne, jt. ed. see Blomeyer, Robert L., Jr.
Martin, C. E., ed. see Institute of World Affairs Staff.
Martin, C. F., jt. auth. see Grosseteste, Robert.
Martin, C. F., jt. auth. see Hunt, L. R.
Martin, C. G. Maps & Surveys of Malawi. 280p. (C). 1980. text ed. 125.00 (*90-6191-092-7*, Pub. by A A Balkema NE) Ashgate Pub Co.
Martin, C. J., et al, eds. The Philosopher's Annual, 1985, Vol. VIII. vi, 271p. 1987. lib. bdg. 32.00 (*0-917930-90-8*); pap. text ed. 10.00 (*0-917930-70-3*) Ridgeview.
Martin, C. L. Down Dairy Farm Road. LC 92-42848. (Illus.). 32p. (J). (gr. k-3). 1994. text ed. 14.95 (*0-02-762450-1*, Mac Bks Young Read) S&S Childrens.
— The Dragon Nanny. LC 90-39985. (Illus.). 32p. (J). (gr. k-3). 1991. reprint ed. pap. 3.95 (*0-689-71451-3*, Aladdin Paperbacks) S&S Childrens.
Martin, C. L. G. Three Brave Women. LC 89-77770. (Illus.). 32p. (J). (gr. k-3). 1991. lib. bdg. 13.95 (*0-02-762445-5*, Mac Bks Young Read) S&S Childrens.
Martin, C. S., ed. see Applied Mechanics, Bioengineering, & Fluids Engineering Conference Staff.
Martin, Calvin. Keepers of the Game: Indian-Animal Relationship & the Fur Trade. LC 77-78381. 1978. pap. 15.00 (*0-520-04637-4*) U CA Pr.
Martin, Calvin, ed. The American Indian & the Problem of History. 320p. 1987. pap. 15.95 (*0-19-503856-8*) OUP.
Martin, Calvin L. In the Spirit of the Earth: Rethinking History & Time. 176p. 1992. 25.00x (*0-8018-4358-8*) Johns Hopkins.
— In the Spirit of the Earth: Rethinking History & Time. 160p. (C). 1993. reprint ed. pap. 12.95 (*0-8018-4709-5*) Johns Hopkins.

M

M

Martin, Carl R. Go Your Stations, Girl. 1991. pap. 17.50 (*0-685-51781-0*) Arion Pr.
— Go Your Stations, Girl. limited ed. 1991. 75.00 (*0-685-51780-2*) Arion Pr.
Martin, Carol. Dance Marathons: Performing American Culture in the 1920s & 1930s. (Performance Studies Ser.). (Illus.). 288p. 1994. 37.50 (*0-87805-673-4*); pap. 16.95 (*0-87805-701-3*) U Pr of Miss.
Martin, Carol, jt. auth. see Wattis, John.
Martin, Carol A. George Eliot's Serial Fiction. LC 93-34631. (Studies in Victorian Life & Literature). 312p. 1994. 49.50 (*0-8142-0625-5*) Ohio St U Pr.
Martin, Carol O. Exploring the California Missions. 2nd ed. (Illus.). 115p. (Orig.). 1989. pap. 7.95 (*0-317-93011-7*) Bay Area CA.
— Exploring the California Missions: Activity Cards. Margolin, Malcolm, ed. (Illus.). 94p. (Orig.). 1984. pap. 7.95 (*0-318-18397-8*) Bay Area CA.
Martin, Carolyn & Lewis, Gregg. I Can't Walk So I'll Learn to Dance. 256p. 1994. pap. 15.99 (*0-310-57600-8*) Zondervan.
Martin, Carolyn A. Games, Contest & Relays. (Illus.). 285p. 1981. pap. text ed. 13.95 (*0-89641-094-3*) American Pr.
Martin, Carter W. The True Country: Themes in the Fiction of Flannery O'Connor. LC 68-29047. 263p. 1994. reprint ed. pap. 16.95 (*0-8265-1249-6*) Vanderbilt U Pr.
Martin, Catherine. Kumihimo: Japanese Silk Braiding Technique. (Illus.). 96p. 1991. pap. 14.95 (*0-937274-59-3*) Lark Books.
— The Silent Sea. Foxton, Rosemary, ed. pap. 29.95 (*0-86840-373-3*, Pub. by New South Wales Univ Pr AT) Intl Spec Bk.
Martin, Cathie J. Shifting the Burden: The Struggle over Growth & Corporate Taxation. (American Politics & Political Economy Ser.). (Illus.). 256p. 1991. pap. text ed. 15.95 (*0-226-50833-1*) U Ch Pr.
— Shifting the Burden: The Struggle over Growth & Corporate Taxation. (American Politics & Political Economy Ser.). (Illus.). 256p. 1991. lib. bdg. 43.00 (*0-226-50832-3*) U Ch Pr.
Martin, Charles. Catullus. (Hermes Bks.). 192p. (Orig.). (C). 1992. text ed. 32.00 (*0-300-05199-9*); pap. text ed. 13.00 (*0-300-05200-6*) Yale U Pr.
— Letters from a Headmaster's Study (1949-1977) enl. rev. ed. Piazza, Louise D., ed. (Illus.). 302p. 1986. reprint ed. pap. text ed. 26.50 (*0-8191-5387-7*) U Pr of Amer.
— Letters from a Headmaster's Study (1949-1977) 2nd enl. rev. ed. Piazza, Louise D., ed. (Illus.). 302p. 1986. reprint ed. lib. bdg. 48.00 (*0-8191-5386-9*) U Pr of Amer.
— Passages from Friday: Poems. 1983. 17.50 (*0-317-40788-0*) Abattoir.
— Raw Passion. 1979. pap. 1.75 (*0-8439-0695-2*) Dorchester Pub Co.
— Steal the Bacon. LC 86-46285. (Johns Hopkins Poetry & Fiction Ser.). 88p. 1987. text ed. 14.95 (*0-8018-3493-7*); pap. 7.95 (*0-8018-3494-5*) Johns Hopkins.
— Your New Business: A Personal Plan for Success. Gerould, Philip, ed. LC 92-54374. (Small Business & Entrepreneurship Ser.). 200p. (Orig.). 1993. pap. 15.95 (*1-56052-170-8*) Crisp Pubns.
Martin, Charles, ed. Registrum Epistolarum Fratris Johannis Peckham, Archiepiscopi Cantuanriensis, 3 vols., Set. (Rolls Ser.: No. 77). 1974. reprint ed. 240.00 (*0-8115-1147-2*) Periodicals Srv.
Martin, Charles, illus. Wine Album. 160p. 1993. 20.00 (*0-517-59212-6*, Crown) Crown Pub Group.
Martin, Charles, tr. The Poems of Catullus. LC 89-45486. 208p. 1989. text ed. 35.00 (*0-8018-3925-4*); pap. 12.95 (*0-8018-3926-2*) Johns Hopkins.
Martin, Charles E. For Rent. LC 85-864. (Illus.). 32p. (J). (gr. k-3). 1986. 11.75 (*0-688-05716-0*); lib. bdg. 11.88 (*0-688-05717-9*) Greenwillow.
— Hollybush: Folk Building & Social Change in an Appalachian Community. LC 83-10201. (Illus.). 132p. (C). Date not set. pap. text ed. 16.00x (*0-87049-816-9*) U of Tenn Pr.
— Island Rescue. LC 84-13672. (Illus.). 32p. (J). (gr. k-3). 1985. 11.75 (*0-688-04257-0*); lib. bdg. 11.88 (*0-688-04258-9*) Greenwillow.
— Island Winter. LC 83-14098. (Illus.). 32p. (J). (gr. k-3). 1984. 13.95 (*0-688-02590-0*); lib. bdg. 13.88 (*0-688-02592-7*) Greenwillow.
— Policy of the United States As Regards Intervention. LC 21-3655. (Columbia University. Studies in the Social Sciences: No. 211). reprint ed. 21.50 (*0-404-51211-9*) AMS Pr.
— Sams Saves the Day. LC 86-19594. (Illus.). 32p. (J). (gr. k-3). 1987. 11.75 (*0-688-06814-6*); lib. bdg. 11.88 (*0-688-06815-4*) Greenwillow.
— Summer Business. LC 83-25422. (Illus.). 32p. (J). (gr. k-3). 1984. lib. bdg. 14.88 (*0-688-03864-6*) Greenwillow.
Martin, Charles H. The Angelo Herndon Case & Southern Justice. LC 73-91777. 256p. reprint ed. pap. 73.00 (*0-8357-5476-6*, 2051653) Bks Demand.
Martin, Charles H. & Craver, Rebecca M., eds. Diamond Days: An Oral History of the University of Texas at El Paso. 226p. 1991. pap. 10.00 (*0-87404-245-3*) Tex Western.
Martin, Charles L. A Sketch of Sam Bass, the Bandit: A Graphic Narrative of His Various Train Robberies, His Death, & Accounts of the Deaths of His Gang & Their History (with an Introduction by Ramon F. Adams) LC 56-5991. (Western Frontier Library: 6). 190p. reprint ed. pap. 54.20 (*0-317-42394-0*, 2052166) Bks Demand.
— Starting Your New Business: A Guide for Entrepreneurs. rev. ed. Crisp, Michael G., ed. LC 91-77079. (Fifty-Minute Ser.). (Illus.). 102p. 1992. pap. 8.95 (*1-56052-144-9*) Crisp Pubns.
Martin, Charles L. & Hackett, Donald. Facilitation Skills for Team Leaders. Gerould, Philip, ed. (Fifty-Minute Ser.). 90p. (Orig.). 1993. pap. 9.95 (*1-56052-199-6*) Crisp Pubns.
Martin, Charles T. The Record Interpreter: A Collection of Abbreviations, Latin Words & Names Used in English Historical Manuscripts & Records. xv, 464p. 1969. reprint ed. 76.70 (*0-685-66494-5*, 05102295, Pub. by Georg Olms GW) Lubrecht & Cramer.
Martin, Charles T., jt. ed. see Brewer, J. S.
Martin, Charles T., jt. ed. see Hardy, Thomas D.
Martin-Chauffier, Robert, ed. see La Rochefoucauld, Francois de.
*__Martin, Cheryl E.__ Governance & Society in Colonial Mexico: Chihuahua in the Eighteenth Century. LC 95-16036. 1996. write for info. (*0-8047-2547-0*) Stanford U Pr.
*__Martin, Cheryl L., comp.__ Matching Gift Details, 1994-95. 208p. 1994. 98.00 (*0-89964-306-X*) Coun Adv & Supp Ed.
Martin, Chester. Empire & Commonwealth. LC 74-9227. 385p. 1975. reprint ed. text ed. 75.00 (*0-8371-7626-3*, MAEC, Greenwood Pr) Greenwood.
Martin, Chester B. Lord Selkirk's Work in Canada. (BCL1 - History - Canada Ser.). 240p. 1991. reprint ed. lib. bdg. 79.00 (*0-7812-6374-3*) Rprt Serv.
Martin, Chester O. & Schmidly, David J. Taxonomic Review of the Pallid Bat: Antrozous Pallidus (Le Conte) (Special Publications: No. 18). (Illus.). 48p. 1982. pap. 7.00 (*0-89672-097-7*) Tex Tech Univ Pr.
*__Martin, Chia.__ The Art of Touch: A Massage Manual for Young People. (Illus.). (J). (gr. 4-12). 1995. pap. write for info. (*0-934252-57-2*) Hohm Pr.
— The Art of Touch: A Massage Manual for Young People. 50p. 1995. pap. 11.95 (*0-614-06937-8*) Hohm Pr.
— We Like to Nurse. LC 94-77052. (Illus.). 36p. (Orig.). (J). 1994. pap. 9.95 (*0-934252-45-9*) Hohm Pr.
Martin, Christine, ed. Children's Writer's & Illustrator's Market 1995. 384p. 1995. pap. 19.95 (*0-89879-679-2*) Writers Digest.
— 1996 Poet's Market. 552p. 1995. 22.99 (*0-89879-712-8*) Writers Digest.
— Poet's Market, 1995. 552p. 1994. 21.99 (*0-89879-677-6*) Writers Digest.
Martin, Christopher. Dickens. (Life & Works: Set II). (Illus.). 112p. (YA). (gr. 7 up). 1990. lib. bdg. 19.94 (*0-86593-016-3*); lib. bdg. 14.95 (*0-685-36352-X*) Rourke Corp.
— The Money Crop: Tobacco Culture in Calvert County, Maryland. McGuire, Patricia J. & McGrath, Sally V., eds. LC 92-30146. 64p. (Orig.). 1992. pap. 8.95 (*1-878399-60-8*) Div Hist Cult Progs.
— Policy in Love: Lyric & Public in Ovid, Petrarch & Shakespeare. LC 94-30961. (Duquesne Studies: Language & Literature Ser.: Vol. 17). 225p. (C). 1994. text ed. 44.95 (*0-8207-0260-9*) Duquesne.
— Prairie Patterns: Folk Arts in North Dakota. (Illus.). 126p. (Orig.). 1989. pap. 15.95 (*0-911205-03-9*) N Dak Coun Arts.
— Staying in or Dropping Out in Mexico: Educational Austerity in a Developing Country. 235p. 1994. 55.95 (*1-85628-665-7*, Pub. by Avebury Pub UK) Ashgate Pub Co.
Martin, Christopher, ed. The Ruralists: Art & Design Profile Twenty-Three. (Illus.). 96p. (Orig.). 1992. pap. 26.95 (*0-312-07264-3*, Academy Edits) St Martin.
Martin, Christopher, ed. see HRH the Prince of Wales.
Martin, Christopher, tr. see St. Thomas Aquinas.
Martin, Chuck. Bloody Kansas. 1993. 14.95 (*0-7451-4549-3*, Gunsmoke) Chivers N Amer.
— The Lobo Breed. (Gunsmoke Western Ser.). 172p. 1989. text ed. 12.95 (*0-86220-921-8*, Gunsmoke) Chivers N Amer.
— Rodeo Cowboy. 1979. pap. 1.75 (*0-8439-0696-0*) Dorchester Pub Co.
Martin, Claire. English - French Lexicon of Electricity. 51p. (ENG & FRE.). 1987. pap. 29.95 (*0-8288-9412-4*) Fr & Eur.
— I Can Be a Weather Forecaster. LC 86-31763. (I Can Be Bks.). (Illus.). 32p. (J). (gr. k-3). 1987. lib. bdg. 11.85 (*0-516-01908-2*); pap. 3.95 (*0-516-41908-0*) Childrens.
— The Race of the Golden Apples. LC 85-16290. (Illus.). 32p. (J). (ps-3). 1991. 14.95 (*0-8037-0248-5*) Dial Bks Young.
Martin, Claire & Martin, Steve. My Best Book: A Year-Long Record of "Personal Bests" (Illus.). 40p. (Orig.). (J). (gr. 3-5). 1988. pap. 7.95 (*0-929545-00-1*) Black Birch Bks.
Martin, Clarence L. God Is a Verb: Roots of a Rational Religion. LC 88-63981. 140p. (Orig.). 1989. pap. 8.95 (*0-88100-060-4*) Natl Writ Pr.
Martin-Clarke, Daisy E. Culture in Early Anglo-Saxon England. 1979. 18.95 (*0-405-10615-7*) Ayer.
Martin, Claude. Tropical Rain Forests of West Africa: Their Biology, Utilization, Destruction & Conservation. 235p. 1991. 19.50 (*0-8176-2380-9*) Birkhauser.
Martin, Claude, jt. ed. see Lesemann, Frederic.
Martin, Claudia J. & McQueen, David V., eds. Readings for a New Public Health. 250p. 1988. 37.50 (*0-85224-598-X*, Pub. by Edinburgh U Pr UK) Col U Pr.
— Readings for a New Public Health. 336p. 1991. pap. text ed. 29.00 (*0-85224-616-1*, Pub. by Edinburgh U Pr UK) Col U Pr.
Martin, Claudine. The Trekking Chef: Gourmet Recipes for the Great Outdoors. (Illus.). 192p. 1989. pap. 14.95 (*1-55821-005-9*) Lyons & Burford.
Martin, Clifford E. Math at Work. 1989. pap. 6.95 (*0-87813-924-9*) Christian Light.
Martin, Clyde F. & Hermann, Robert, eds. Ames Research Center (NASA) Conference on Geometric Control Theory, 1976. (Lie Groups: History, Frontiers & Applications Ser.: Vol. 7). 1977. 60.00 (*0-915692-21-X*) Math Sci Pr.
Martin, Clyde F., ed. see Byrnes, Christopher I.
Martin, Clyde F., jt. ed. see Byrnes, Christopher I.
Martin, Clyde F., ed. see NATO ASI & AMS Summer Seminar in Applied Mathematics Staff.
Martin, Colin & Parker, Geoffrey. The Spanish Armada. 288p. 1992. pap. 11.95 (*0-393-30926-6*) Norton.
Martin, Colin A., intro. Australian Aeronautical Conference, 1993, 2 vols. 5th ed. (National Conference Publication Ser.: No. 93-6). (Illus.). 610p. 1993. pap. text ed. 108.00 (*0-85825-576-6*, Pub. by Inst Engrs Aust-EA Bks AT) Accents Pubns.
Martin-Comin, J., et al, eds. Radiolabeled Blood Elements: Recent Advances in Techniques & Applications. (NATO ASI, Series A, Life Sciences: Vol. 262). (Illus.). 362p. 1994. 115.00 (*0-306-44700-2*, Plenum Pr) Plenum.
Martin, Connors. VideoHounds Pocket Movie Guide, Vol. 4. 1994. pap. 29.95 (*0-8103-9872-9*, 072444-M99348) Gale.
*__Martin, Constance.__ Search for the Blue Goose: J. Dewey Soper - the Arctic Adventures of a Canadian Naturalist. (Illus.). 96p. 1995. 22.00 (*1-896209-14-9*, Pub. by Bayeaux Arts CN) Trafalgar.
*__Martin, Constance R.__ Dictionary of Endocrinology & Related Biomedical Sciences. (Illus.). 800p. 1995. 59.95 (*0-19-506033-4*) OUP.
— Endocrine Physiology. (Illus.). 1985. 59.95 (*0-19-503359-0*) OUP.
Martin, Corinne. Earthmagic: Finding & Using Medicinal Herbs. LC 91-6330. 240p. 1991. pap. 15.00 (*0-88150-184-0*) Countryman.
— Earthmagic: Using New England Medicinal Herbs. Francis, Ed & Dovner, Sylvia, eds. (Illus.). 250p. (Orig.). 1990. pap. 12.95 (*0-9623199-1-0*) Dirigo Bks.
Martin, Cort. Bolt, No. 1: First Blood. (Orig.). 1981. pap. 2.25 (*0-89083-767-8*) Zebra.
— Bolt, No. 10: Bawdy House Showdown. 1983. pap. 2.25 (*0-8217-1176-8*) Zebra.
— Bolt, No. 14: Virginia City Virgin. pap. 2.25 (*0-8217-1360-4*) Zebra.
— Bolt, No. 15: Bordello Backshooter. 192p. 1984. pap. 2.25 (*0-8217-1411-2*) Zebra.
— Bolt, No. 2: Dead Man's Bounty. 1981. pap. 2.25 (*0-89083-783-X*) Zebra.
— Bolt, No. 20: Six-Guns & Silk. 1986. pap. 2.25 (*0-8217-1866-5*) Zebra.
— Bolt, No. 21: Deadly Withdrawal. 208p. 1986. pap. 2.25 (*0-8217-1956-4*) Zebra.
— Bolt, No. 22: Climax Mountain. 192p. 1987. pap. 2.25 (*0-8217-2024-4*) Zebra.
— Bolt, No. 25: Hot on the Warpath. 224p. 1988. pap. 2.50 (*0-8217-2265-4*) Zebra.
— Bolt, No. 26: Maverick Mistress. 224p. 1988. pap. 2.50 (*0-8217-2387-1*) Zebra.
— Bolt, No. 3: Showdown at Black Mesa. (Orig.). 1981. pap. 2.25 (*0-89083-812-7*) Zebra.
— Bolt, No. 4: The Guns of Taos. (Orig.). 1981. pap. 2.25 (*0-89083-873-9*) Zebra.
— Bolt, No. 5: Shootout at Santa Fe. (Orig.). 1982. pap. 2.25 (*0-89083-943-3*) Zebra.
— Bolt, No. 6: The Tombstone Honeypot. 1982. pap. 2.25 (*0-8217-1009-5*) Zebra.
— Bolt, No. 7: Rawhide Woman. (Orig.). 1982. pap. 2.25 (*0-8217-1057-5*) Zebra.
— Bolt, No. 8: Hard in the Saddle. 1982. pap. 2.25 (*0-8217-1095-8*) Zebra.
— Bolt, No. 9: Badman's Bordello. 1983. pap. 2.25 (*0-8217-1127-X*) Zebra.
— The Hangtown Harlots. (Bolt Ser.: No. 12). 1983. pap. 2.25 (*0-685-07876-0*) Zebra.
— The Last Bordello. (Bolt Ser.: No. 11). (Orig.). 1983. pap. 2.25 (*0-8217-1224-1*) Zebra.
— Lone-Star Stud. (Bolt Ser.: No. 17). 1985. pap. 2.25 (*0-8217-1632-8*) Zebra.
— Montana Mistress. (Bolt Ser.: No. 13). 1984. pap. 2.25 (*0-8217-1316-7*) Zebra.
Martin, Craig. Los Alamos Area Mountain Bike Trails. (Illus.). 84p. (Orig.). 1993. pap. 10.95 (*0-9639040-0-0*) All Seasons.
— Mountain Biking in Northern New Mexico: Historical & Natural History Rides. LC 93-49530. (Coyote Books Ser.). (Illus.). 205p. (Orig.). 1994. pap. 16.95 (*0-8263-1511-9*) U of NM Pr.
— Santa Fe Area Mountain Bike Trails. (Illus.). 110p. (Orig.). 1994. pap. 10.95 (*0-9639040-1-9*) All Seasons.
Martin, Craig, ed. Fly-Fishing in Northern New Mexico. LC 91-11440. (Coyote Books Ser.). (Illus.). 320p. (Orig.). 1991. pap. 14.95 (*0-8263-1290-X*) U of NM Pr.
Martin, Craig, jt. auth. see Lehr, Judy B.
Martin-Crosa, Ricardo & Lippard, Lucy R. Cesar Paternosto. (Illus.). (ENG & SPA.). 1981. pap. 5.00 (*0-89192-338-1*, Ctr Inter-Am Rel) Interbk Inc.
Martin, Curtis H. & Stronach, Bruce, eds. Politics East & West: A Comparison of Japanese & British Political Culture. LC 92-26273. 352p. (C). 1992. 51.95 (*0-87332-895-7*); pap. text ed. 18.95 (*1-56324-108-0*) M E Sharpe.
Martin, Cy. Men of the Twentieth: The Story of the 20th Aero Squadron. 127p. 1974. pap. text ed. 22.95 (*0-89126-006-4*) MA-AH Pub.
Martin, Cyd. A Yellowstone ABC. (Illus.). 16p. (J). 1992. pap. 5.95 (*1-879373-12-2*) R Rinehart.
Martin, Cynthia. Beating the Adoption Game. rev. ed. 544p. 1988. pap. 13.95 (*0-15-610930-1*) HarBrace.
— Lover's Knot Placemats. (Illus.). 24p. 1993. 6.95 (*0-922705-45-3*) Quilt Day.
Martin, Cynthia L., et al. The Russian Desk: A Listening & Conversation Course. x, 136p. (Orig.). (C). 1991. pap. text ed. 10.95 (*0-89357-218-7*) Slavica.
— The Russian Desk: Instructor's Manual. vi, 64p. (Orig.). (C). 1991. pap. text ed. 5.95 (*0-89357-219-5*) Slavica.
*__Martin, D.__ Bring Me Children. 1994. pap. 4.99 (*0-517-13036-X*) Random.
Martin, D., ed. see Schrag, Norm.
Martin, D. C., et al. Laparoscopic Appearance of Endometriosis, Vol. I. 2nd ed. Martin, Dan C., ed. LC 90-60383. (Illus.). 57p. 1990. pap. text ed. 14.00 (*0-9616747-3-3*) Resurge Pr.
— Laparoscopic Appearance of Endometriosis: Color Atlas, Vol. III. 2nd ed. Martin, Dan C., ed. LC 90-60393. (Illus.). 69p. 1990. pap. text ed. 38.00 (*0-9616747-6-8*) Resurge Pr.
Martin, D. E. Fabula Ranae. 56p. (ENG & LAT.). (YA). (gr. 6-12). 3.95 (*0-939507-07-2*, B705) Amer Classical.
Martin, D. G. Language, Truth & Poetry. 353p. 1975. pap. 14.50 (*0-85224-268-9*, Pub. by Edinburgh U Pr UK) Col U Pr.
Martin, D. Roger. No Dreams for Sale. 1983. pap. 6.00 (*0-938566-15-6*) Adastra Pr.
Martin, D. W., ed. Journal of the Acoustical Society of America, Vols. 75-84: Cumulative Index. 625p. 1989. 80.00 (*0-88318-615-2*) Acoustical Soc Am.
Martin, Dale. Into the Primitive: Advanced Trapping Techniques. (Illus.). 176p. 1989. pap. 15.00 (*0-87364-530-8*) Paladin Pr.
— The Trapper's Bible: Traps, Snares, & Pathguards. (Illus.). 72p. 1987. pap. 8.00 (*0-87364-406-9*) Paladin Pr.
*__Martin, Dale B.__ The Corinthian Body. LC 94-44947. 1995. write for info. (*0-300-06205-2*) Yale U Pr.
— Slavery as Salvation: The Metaphor of Slavery in Pauline Christianity. 272p. (C). 1990. text ed. 27.50 (*0-300-04735-5*) Yale U Pr.
Martin, Dale R., et al. Lotus 1-2-3 Applications for Intermediate Accounting. 224p. (C). 1990. write for info. (*0-13-539479-1*) P-H.
Martin, Dan, jt. auth. see Ahia, C. Emmanuel.
Martin, Dan C., ed. see Martin, D. C., et al.
Martin, Daniel C., jt. ed. see Adamson, G. David.
Martin, Daniel R., pref. The Order of Montaigne's Essays: Selected Papers from the Proceedings of the International Montaigne Colloquium Held at UMass-Amherst in Oct. 1988. 247p. 1989. 16.95 (*1-878417-00-2*) Hestia Pr.
Martin, Daniel R. & Cookerly, J. Richard. A Directory of Credentials in Counseling & Psychotherapy. (Reference Bks.). 270p. 1989. text ed. 35.00 (*0-8161-9062-3*, Hall Reference) Macmillan.
Martin, Daniel R., ed. see Moliere.
*__Martin, Dannie M.__ The Dishwasher: A Novel. LC 94-33733. 192p. 1995. 20.00 (*0-393-03790-8*) Norton.
Martin, Dannie M. & Sussman, Peter Y. Committing Journalism: The Prison Writings of Red Hog. LC 93-12569. 1993. 25.00 (*0-393-03574-3*) Norton.
— Committing Journalism: The Prison Writings of Red Hog. 352p. 1995. pap. 13.00 (*0-393-31322-0*, Norton Paperbks) Norton.
Martin, Darrel. Fly-Tying Methods. (Illus.). 320p. 1987. 35.00 (*0-941130-40-1*) Lyons & Burford.
Martin, Darrell. Micropatterns: Tying & Fishing the Small Fly. 408p. 1994. 40.00 (*1-55821-260-4*) Lyons & Burford.
Martin, Darwin J. Schipperkes. (Illus.). 160p. 1991. lib. bdg. 11.95 (*0-86622-161-1*, KW161) TFH Pubns.
Martin, David. Bring Me Children. Zion, Claire, ed. 352p. 1994. reprint ed. mass mkt. 5.99 (*0-671-88611-8*, Pocket Star Bks) PB.
— Camp Vredenburg in the Civil War. (Illus.). 28p. 1993. 6.00 (*0-944413-27-7*) Longstreet Hse.
— The Crying Heart Tattoo: A Novel. LC 93-44391. 320p. 1994. pap. 12.95 (*0-8118-0777-0*) Chronicle Bks.
— Dealing with Demanding Customers: How to Turn Complaints into Opportunities. (Institute of Management Ser.). 192p. (Orig.). 1994. pap. 39.50x (*0-273-60729-4*, Pub. by Pitman Pub Ltd UK) Trans-Atl Phila.
— The Dilemmas of Contemporary Religion. LC 78-17704. 1978. text ed. 29.95 (*0-312-21055-8*) St Martin.
— Europe: An Ever Closer Union. 101p. 1991. 57.50 (*0-85124-537-4*, Pub. by Spokesman Bks UK); pap. 26.50 (*0-85124-538-2*, Pub. by Spokesman Bks UK) Coronet Bks.
— Final Harbor. 320p. 1985. pap. 4.95 (*0-88184-215-X*) Carroll & Graf.
— Geographic Information Systems: Socioeconomic Applications. 2nd ed. LC 95-15958. 1995. write for info. (*0-415-12571-5*); pap. write for info. (*0-415-12572-3*) Routledge.
— Geographic Information Systems & Their Socioeconomic Applications. (Illus.). 224p. 1991. 87.50 (*0-415-05697-7*, A6200); pap. 22.50 (*0-415-05698-5*, A6204) Routledge.
— How to Be a Great Communicator: The Complete Guide to Mastering Internal Communications. (Institute of Management Ser.). 300p. 1995. pap. 43.50 (*0-273-61262-X*, Pub. by Pitman Pub Ltd UK) Trans-Atl Phila.
— Is My Child Gifted? A Guide for Caring Parents. 138p. 1986. pap. 16.95 (*0-398-06268-4*) C C Thomas.
— Is My Child Gifted? A Guide for Caring Parents. 138p. (C). 1986. 31.95x (*0-398-05248-4*) C C Thomas.
— Lie to Me. 288p. 1990. 18.95 (*0-394-58491-0*) Random.
— Lie to Me. 320p. 1991. reprint ed. mass mkt. 5.95 (*0-671-73876-3*, Pocket Star Bks) PB.
— Lizzie & Her Dolly. LC 92-54404. (Illus.). 24p. (J). (ps). 1993. 5.95 (*1-56402-060-6*) Candlewick Pr.
— Lizzie & Her Friend. LC 92-53009. (Illus.). 24p. (J). (ps). 1993. 5.95 (*1-56402-061-4*) Candlewick Pr.
— Lizzie & Her Kitty. LC 92-54405. (Illus.). 24p. (J). (ps). 1993. 5.95 (*1-56402-058-4*) Candlewick Pr.

An Asterisk (*) at the beginning of an entry indicates that the title is appearing in BIP for the first time.

— Lizzie & Her Puppy. LC 92-53008. (Illus.). 24p. (J). (ps). 1993. 5.95 (1-56402-059-2) Candlewick Pr.
— Manipulating Meetings: How to Get What You Want, When You Want It. (Institute of Management Foundation Ser.). 186p. (Orig.). 1994. pap. 42.50 (0-273-60521-6, Pub. by Pitman Pub Ltd UK) Trans-Atl Phila.
— Something Never Your Own. (Amelia Chapbooks Ser.). 90p. (Orig.). 1989. pap. 10.95 (0-936545-10-0) Amelia.
— Tap, Tap. LC 93-38838. 1994. 20.00 (0-679-41055-4) Random.
— Teaching English. 1977. pap. 1.80 (0-686-32333-5) Rod & Staff.
— Tongues of Fire: The Explosion of Protestantism in Latin America. 256p. 1991. 39.95 (0-631-17186-X) Blackwell Pubs.
— Tongues of Fire: The Explosion of Protestantism in Latin America. 254p. 1993. pap. 16.95 (0-631-18914-9) Blackwell Pubs.
— Tough Talking: How to Handle Awkward Situations. (Institute of Management Ser.). 192p. (Orig.). 1993. pap. 37.50x (0-273-60163-6, Pub. by Pitman Pub Ltd UK) Trans-Atl Phila.
— Web of Disinformation: Churchill's Yugoslav Blunder. 464p. 1990. 29.95 (0-15-180704-3) HarBrace.
Martin, David, ed. Anarchy & Culture: The Problem of the Contemporary University. LC 74-80271. 212p. 1969. text ed. 50.00 (0-231-03317-6) Col U Pr.
— Clara Barton & Hightstown. (Illus.). 32p. 1994. 6.00 (0-944413-30-7) Longstreet Hse.
Martin, David & Johnson, Phyllis. The Struggle for Zimbabwe. LC 81-84556. 400p. (Orig.). 1982. pap. 8.95 (0-85345-599-6) Monthly Rev.
***Martin, David & Taylor, Greg.** Recipes from an Adirondack Inn. (Recipes from Inn Ser.). 1995. pap. 14. 95 (1-56626-128-7) Country Rds.
Martin, David, jt. auth. see Barrett, Eric.
Martin, David, jt. auth. see Bernhardt, Roger.
Martin, David, jt. auth. see Johnson, Phyllis.
Martin, David, jt. ed. see Johnson, Phyllis.
Martin, David, ed. see Lehrer, Milton G.
Martin, David, ed. see Mahood, Wayne.
Martin, David, jt. auth. see Martin, Philip L.
Martin, David, tr. see Sepehry, Sohrab.
Martin, David, tr. see Soloukhin, Vladimir.
Martin, David, jt. auth. see Venables, Tony.
Martin, David, et al, eds. Sociology & Theology. 170p. 1980. text ed. 29.95 (0-312-74007-7) St Martin.
Martin, David A., ed. The New Asylum Seekers: Refugee Law in the 1980's. (Ninth Sokol Colloquium on International Law Ser.). (C). 1988. lib. bdg. 97.50 (90-247-3730-3) Kluwer Ac.
Martin, David A., jt. auth. see Aleinikoff, T. Alexander.
Martin, David C., jt. auth. see Bartol, Kathryn M.
Martin, David C., tr. see Farrokhzaad, Foroogh.
***Martin, David E. & Coe, Peter N.** Training Distance Runners. LC 90-33486. 312p. 1991. pap. text ed. 19.95 (0-87322-727-1, PMAR0727) Human Kinetics.
Martin, David E. & Rubinstein, David. Ideology & the Labour Movement: Essays Presented to John Saville. 276p. 1979. 36.00 (0-8476-6123-7) Rowman.
Martin, David G. Carl Bornemann's Regiment: The Forty-First New York Infantry (DeKalb Regt.) in the Civil War. LC 86-82998. (Illus.). 322p. (C). 1987. 24.00 (0-944413-03-X) Longstreet Hse.
— The Chancellorsville Campaign: November 1862-May 1863. (Great Campaigns Ser.). (Illus.). 176p. 1991. 24.95 (0-938289-06-3) Combined Bks.
— Confederate Monuments at Gettysburg: The Gettysburg Battle Monuments, Vol. 1. LC 85-82570. (Illus.). 295p. (C). 1986. 25.00 (0-944413-01-3) Longstreet Hse.
— Counseling & Therapy Skills. 289p. (C). 1989. reprint ed. pap. text ed. 16.95x (0-88133-409-X) Waveland Pr.
— Fluvanna Artillery. (Virginia Regimental Histories Ser.). (Illus.). 165p. 1992. 19.95 (1-56190-037-0) H E Howard.
— Gettysburg July First. (Illus.). 450p. 1994. 24.95 (0-938289-39-X, 7310) Stackpole.
— Jackson's Valley Campaign: November 1861 - June 1862. rev. ed. 256p. 1994. 22.95 (0-938289-40-3, 7316) Stackpole.
— OILSR Exemption Handbook. 200p. 45.00 (0-318-19278-0) Land Dev Inst.
— The Philadelphia Campaign. (Great Campaigns Ser.). (Illus.). 240p. 1993. 19.95 (0-938289-19-5) Combined Bks.
— The Vicksburg Campaign: April 1862-July 1863. rev. ed. (Illus.). 256p. 1994. 22.95 (0-938289-37-3, 7328) Combined Bks.
Martin, David G., ed. A Casualty at Gettysburg & Andersonville: Selections from the Civil War Diary of Private Austin A. Carr of the 82nd N.Y. Infantry. 36p. (Orig.). (C). 1990. pap. text ed. 6.00 (0-944413-15-3) Longstreet Hse.
— Hexamer's First New Jersey Battery in the Civil War. (Illus.). 36p. (C). 1992. 6.00 (0-944413-24-2) Longstreet Hse.
— The Monocacy Regiment: A Commemorative History of the Fourteenth New Jersey Infantry in the Civil War, 1862-1865. LC 87-81619. (Illus.). 352p. (C). 1987. 30.00 (0-944413-05-6) Longstreet Hse.
***Martin, David G. & Moore, Allan D.** First Steps in the Art of Intervention: A Guidebook for Trainees in the Helping Professions. LC 94-33769. 480p. 1995. text ed. 49.95 (0-534-22272-2) Brooks-Cole.
Martin, David G., ed. see Busey, John W.
Martin, David G., jt. auth. see Busey, John W.
Martin, David G., ed. see Marbaker, Thomas D.
Martin, David K. The Eighteenth Century Zimmerman Family of the Mohawk Valley. LC 93-80532. (Illus.). 1994. write for info. (0-9639300-1-X) Mouse Hse Bks.
Martin, David L. Alabama's State & Local Governments. 3rd ed. (Illus.). 256p. (C). 1994. pap. text ed. 17.95 (0-8173-0738-9) U of Ala Pr.
— Capital, Courthouse & City Hall. 7th ed. 360p. (C). 1988. pap. text ed. 24.95 (0-582-28686-7, 71699) Longman.
— Handbook for Creative Teaching. 1986. 18.50 (0-318-22869-6) Rod & Staff.
— Running City Hall: Municipal Administration in America. 2nd ed. 224p. 1990. pap. 17.95 (0-8173-0465-7) U of Ala Pr.
Martin, David N. Romancing the Brand: The Power of Advertising & How to Use It. 240p. 1989. 19.95 (0-8144-5949-8) AMACOM.
— Under a Lemon Moon: A Metaphysical Mystery. 288p. (Orig.). 1995. pap. 14.95 (0-9646601-7-2) Oaklea Pr.
Martin, David S., ed. Advances in Cognition, Education, & Deafness. LC 91-10693. (Illus.). 457p. 1991. 34.95 (0-930323-79-3) Gallaudet Univ Pr.
— Cognition, Education, & Deafness: Directions for Research & Instruction. LC 85-12992. 232p. 1985. text ed. 21.95 (0-930323-12-2) Gallaudet Univ Pr.
Martin, David S., jt. auth. see Gewirtz, Herman.
Martin, David S., et al. Curriculum Leadership: Case Studies for Program Practitioners. 89p. (Orig.). 1989. pap. 12.95 (0-87120-155-0, 611-89013) Assn Supervision.
***Martin, David W.** Doing Psychology Experiments. 4th ed. LC 94-47424. 1996. pap. 27.95 (0-534-33840-2) Brooks-Cole.
Martin, Dean F. Marine Chemistry, Vol. 1. 2nd ed. LC 76-169633. (Illus.). 401p. reprint ed. pap. 114.30 (0-317-07993-X, 2055069) Bks Demand.
— Marine Chemistry: Theory & Applications, Vol. 2. LC 68-27532. (Illus.). 463p. reprint ed. pap. 132.00 (0-685-24139-4, 2033011) Bks Demand.
***Martin, Deanna C. & Arendale, David R., eds.** Supplemental Instruction: Increasing Achievement & Retention. LC 85-644763. (New Directions for Teaching & Learning Ser.: No. 60). 110p. (Orig.). 1994. pap. 16.95 (0-7879-9999-7) Jossey-Bass.
Martin, Debbie. The Complete Weightloss Workbook: A Self-Help Guide to Permanent Weight Loss Including Food Journal, Weightloss Tips, Low Fat Recipes, Food Values. (Illus.). 220p. (Orig.). 1993. pap. 15.95 (0-9635558-0-4) Slender Visions.
Martin, Deborah. By Love Unveiled. 384p. (Orig.). 1993. pap. 4.99 (0-451-40362-2, Topaz) NAL-Dutton.
— Creole Nights. 400p. (Orig.). 1992. pap. 4.50 (0-8439-3368-2) Dorchester Pub Co.
— Dangerous Angel. 384p. (Orig.). 1994. pap. 4.99 (0-451-40528-5, Topaz) NAL-Dutton.
— Moonlight Enchantment. 448p. (Orig.). 1992. pap. 4.50 (0-8439-3229-5) Dorchester Pub Co.
— Silver Deceptions. 384p. 1994. 4.99 (0-451-40434-3, Topaz) NAL-Dutton.
— Storm Swept. 384p. 1995. pap. 4.99 (0-451-40529-3, Sig) NAL-Dutton.
Martin, Deborah L., jt. ed. see Gershuny, Grace.
Martin, Deborah S., jt. auth. see Wittlich, Gary E.
Martin, Debra L., et al. Black Mesa Anasazi Health: Reconstructing Life from Patterns of Death & Disease. LC 90-61289. (Center for Archaeological Investigations Research Paper Ser.: No. 14). (Illus.). xx, 314p. (Orig.). 1991. pap. 30.00 (0-88104-073-8) Center Archaeo.
***Martin, Del.** Battered Wives. 1990. mass mkt. 5.99 (0-671-72761-3) PB.
— Battered Wives. rev. ed. LC 81-12985. 288p. 1981. pap. 12.95 (0-912078-70-7) Volcano Pr.
Martin, Del & Lyon, Phyllis. Lesbian - Woman, 1991. enl. rev. ed. LC 91-15045. 384p. 1991. 25.00 (0-912078-91-X) Volcano Pr.
Martin del Campo, jt. auth. see Bogert.
Martin, Delores M., ed. Handbook of Latin American Studies, Vol. 46: Humanities. 768p. (ENG, FRE, GER, RUS & SER.). 1986. text ed. 65.00 (0-292-73035-7) U of Tex Pr.
Martin, Dennis. The Operas & Operatic Style of John Frederick Lampe. LC 85-14496. (Detroit Monographs in Musicology: No. 8). xx, 190p. 1985. 40.00 (0-89990-024-0) Info Coord.
Martin, Dennis, jt. ed. see Dyck, Cornelius J.
Martin, Dennis, jt. auth. see Martin, Kymberly.
Martin, Dennis, tr. see Von Balthasar, Hans U.
Martin, Dennis D. Fifteenth-Century Carthusian Reform: The World of Nicholas Kempf. LC 92-20135. (Studies in the History of Christian Thought: Vol. 49). xv, 415p. 1992. 103.00 (90-04-09636-1) E J Brill.
Martin, Derek. SWOT Revenue Law. 278p. (C). 1990. 80.00 (0-906322-91-X, Pub. by Blackstone Pr UK) St Mut.
***Martin, Diana, ed.** Graphic Design: Inspirations & Innovations. LC 94-43748. (Illus.). 144p. 1995. 28.99 (0-89134-640-6) North Light Bks.
Martin, Diana & Cropper, Mary. Fresh Ideas in Letterhead & Business Card Design. (Illus.). 144p. 1993. 29.99 (0-89134-505-1, 30481) Rockport Pubs.
Martin, Diana & White, Ed. How to Airbrush T-Shirts & Other Clothing. 128p. 1994. pap. 24.99 (0-89134-570-1) North Light Bks.
Martin, Diana, jt. auth. see Miller, David.
Martin, Diane. Artist's Pigments. 1987. write for info. (0-318-62760-4) Scriptorium Pr.
— Be Your Own Astrologer. 4th ed. (Illus.). 1987. pap. 9.95 (0-931485-27-4) Scriptorium Pr.
— Bring to the Boil & Simmer Gently: Secrets of Making Delicious, Simple Homemade Soup. 1988. pap. 9.95 (0-931485-10-X) Scriptorium Pr.
— Kill Bugs Dead: An Indoor Gardener's Guide to Eliminating Insects on Houseplants Without Using Harmful Pesticides. (Illus.). 40p. (Orig.). 1992. pap. 7.95 (0-931485-30-4) Scriptorium Pr.
— Seasons of the Sun, Phases of the Moon: Celestial Influences on Plants & Gardens. (Illus.). 50p. 1988. pap. 7.95 (0-931485-11-8) Scriptorium Pr.
Martin, Diane, ed. see Banta, Gordon.
Martin, Diane, ed. see Elgin, Suzette H.
Martin, Diane, ed. see O'Connor, Lois.
Martin, Dianne L., jt. auth. see Ruby, Clayton C.
Martin, Dick. Cut & Assemble the Emerald City. (J). 1980. pap. 5.95 (0-486-24053-3) Dover.
— Cut & Assemble Wizard of Oz Theatre. (J). 1985. pap. 4.95 (0-486-24799-6) Dover.
— The Executive's Guide to Handling a Press Interview. rev. ed. LC 77-593. 47p. 1994. pap. 5.95 (0-87576-058-9) Pilot Bks.
Martin, Didier. Il Serait un Fois. (FRE.). 1979. pap. 10.95 (0-7859-4116-9) Fr & Eur.
Martin, Dieter. Das Deutsche Versepos im 18. Jahrhundert: Studien & Kommentierte Gattungsbibliographie. (Quellen und Forschungen zur Sprach und Kulturgeschichte der Germanischen Voelker Ser.: Bd 103). xi, 450p. (GER.). (C). 1993. lib. bdg. 161.55 (3-11-013816-6) De Gruyter.
Martin, Dolores M. Handbook of Latin American Studies, Vol. 51: Social Sciences. LC 36-32633. 923p. (C). 1992. text ed. 65.00 (0-292-75149-4) U of Tex Pr.
— Handbook of Latin American Studies, Vol. 52: Humanities. 958p. (C). 1993. lib. bdg. 75.00 (0-292-75156-7) U of Tex Pr.
Martin, Dolores M., comp. Handbook of Latin American Studies, Vol. 50: Humanities. annot. ed. 825p. (ENG & SPA.). 1990. text ed. 65.00 (0-292-73058-6) U of Tex Pr.
Martin, Dolores M., ed. Handbook of Latin American Studies Vol. 53: Social Sciences. 960p. 1994. text ed. 75. 00 (0-292-75166-4) U of Tex Pr.
— Handbook of Latin American Studies, Humanities, Vol. 48. 784p. 1988. 65.00 (0-292-73041-1) U of Tex Pr.
— Handbook of Latin American Studies, Vol. 39: Social Sciences, 1977. LC 36-32633. (Handbook of Latin American Studies Ser.). 59.95 (0-8130-0600-7) U Press Fla.
— Handbook of Latin American Studies, Vol. 40: Humanities 1978. LC 36-32633. 59.95 (0-8130-0637-6) U Press Fla.
— Handbook of Latin American Studies, Vol. 41: Social Sciences. 814p. 1980. text ed. 65.00 (0-292-73013-6) U of Tex Pr.
— Handbook of Latin American Studies, Vol. 42: Humanities. 929p. 1981. text ed. 65.00 (0-292-73016-0) U of Tex Pr.
— Handbook of Latin American Studies, Vol. 43: Social Sciences. 969p. (C). 1982. text ed. 65.00 (0-292-73022-5) U of Tex Pr.
— Handbook of Latin American Studies, Vol. 44: Humanities. 795p. 1984. text ed. 65.00 (0-292-73023-3) U of Tex Pr.
— Handbook of Latin American Studies, Vol. 45: Social Sciences. 831p. 1985. text ed. 65.00 (0-292-73033-0) U of Tex Pr.
— Handbook of Latin American Studies, Vol. 47: Social Sciences. 832p. 1987. text ed. 65.00 (0-292-73038-1) U of Tex Pr.
— Handbook of Latin American Studies, Vol. 49: Social Sciences. 875p. 1989. text ed. 65.00 (0-292-73046-2) U of Tex Pr.
Martin, Dolores M. & Stewart, Donald E., eds. Handbook of Latin American Studies, Vol. 38: Humanities 1976. LC 36-32633. 1976. 59.95 (0-8130-0568-X) U Press Fla.
Martin, Dom. An Autobiography of Thoughts. 150p. (Orig.). 1994. pap. 15.00 (0-9616078-3-1) Trans Gala Pubns.
— The Day Before the Day After. (Illus.). 86p. 1985. pap. text ed. 4.95 (0-9616078-0-7) Trans Gala Pubns.
— The Principles of Zerometrics, Vol. I. 24p. (Orig.). 1989. pap. text ed. 5.00 (0-685-33290-X) Trans Gala Pubns.
— A Thousand Eyes for an Eye. (Illus.). 125p. (Orig.). 1994. pap. 15.00 (0-9616078-1-5) Trans Gala Pubns.
Martin, Don. Don Martin Sails Ahead. 192p. (Orig.). 1989. pap. 3.50 (0-446-35825-8) Warner Bks.
— Don Martin's Droll Book. Thorsland, Dan & Callahan, John, eds. (Illus.). 128p. (Orig.). 1992. pap. 9.95 (1-878574-37-X) Dark Horse Comics.
— Don Martin's Droll Book. limited ed. Thorsland, Dan & Callahan, John, eds. (Illus.). 128p. (Orig.). 1992. 39.95 (1-878574-69-8) Dark Horse Comics.
— Great Silver Bonanza. 1979. pap. 1.95 (0-449-14202-7, GM) Fawcett.
— Teamthink: Using the Sports Connection to Develop, Motivate, & Manage a Winning Business Team. Martin, Renee, ed. LC 93-47185. 320p. 1994. pap. 11.95 (0-452-27213-0, Plume) NAL-Dutton.
Martin, Don & Martin, Betty. The Best of San Francisco: An Insider's Guide. 3rd expanded rev. ed. LeBlond, Bill, ed. 208p. 1994. pap. 10.95 (0-8118-0611-1) Chronicle Bks.
Martin, Don & Martin, Betty, eds. Washington Discovery Guide: A Remarkably Useful Travel Companion for Motorists, RVers & Other Explorers. (Discovery Guide Ser.). (Illus.). 372p. (Orig.). 1994. pap. 13.95 (0-942053-16-8) Pine Cone Pr CA.
***Martin, Don, Jr. & Martin, Karen, eds.** Deployed, Not Disconnected. 128p. 1991. pap. 5.50 (0-913991-01-5) Off Christian Fellowship.
***Martin, Don & Martin, Kay.** Hiking Marin: One-Hundred-Twenty-One Great Hikes in Marin County. (Illus.). 304p. (Orig.). 1995. pap. 18.95 (0-9617044-5-4) Martin Press.
— MT Tam: A Hiking, Running & Nature Guide. (Illus.). 128p. 1994. pap. 9.95 (0-9617044-4-6) Martin Press.
— Point Reyes National Seashore: A Hiking & Nature Guide. (Illus.). 128p. (Orig.). 1992. pap. 9.95 (0-9617044-3-8) Martin Press.
Martin, Don & Martin, Maggie. Step by Step: A Guide to Stepfamily Living. LC 92-70822. 186p. (Orig.). 1992. pap. text ed. 9.95 (0-932796-38-9) Ed Media Corp.
Martin, Don, jt. auth. see Martin, Renee.
Martin, Don, et al. Is Your Family Making You Fat? How Your Family Affects Your Weight & What You Can Do about It. 208p. (Orig.). 1994. pap. 11.99 (0-945819-58-7) Sulzburger & Graham Pub.
— Stepfamilies in Therapy: Understanding Systems, Assessment, & Intervention. LC 92-12519. (Social & Behavioral Science Ser.). 288p. 1992. 31.95 (1-55542-453-8) Jossey-Bass.
Martin, Don W. & Martin, Betty W. The Best of the Wine Country: "A Witty, Opinionated & Remarkably Useful Guide to California's Vinelands" rev. ed. (Best of...Ser.: No. 4). (Illus.). 304p. (Orig.). 1995. pap. 13.95 (0-942053-17-6) Pine Cone Pr CA.
— Utah Discovery Guide: A Remarkably Useful Travel Companion for Motorists, RVers & Other Explorers. (Discovery Guide Ser.: No. 4). (Illus.). 352p. (Orig.). 1995. pap. 13.95 (0-942053-18-4) Pine Cone Pr CA.
Martin, Don W. & Martin, Betty W., eds. The Best of Arizona: A Witty, Definitive & Remarkably Useful Guide to the Grand Canyon State. rev. ed. (Best of... Ser.: No. 3). (Illus.). 336p. 1993. pap. 12.95 (0-942053-07-9) Pine Cone Pr CA.
— The Best of Nevada: A Witty, Difinitive & Remarkably Useful Guide to Las Vegas, Reno-Tahoe & Beyond. (Best of...Ser.: No. 5). (Illus.). 352p. (Orig.). 1992. pap. 12.95 (0-942053-13-3) Pine Cone Pr CA.
— The Best of the Gold Country: A Complete, Witty & Remarkably Useful Guide to California's Sierra Foothills & Historic Sacramento. rev. ed. (Best of...Ser.: No. 2). (Illus.). 240p. 1992. pap. 11.95 (0-942053-11-7) Pine Cone Pr CA.
— The Best of the Wine Country: A Witty, Opinionated, & Remarkably Useful Guide. (Illus.). 304p. 1995. pap. 12. 95 (0-942053-02-8) Pine Cone Pr CA.
— Coming to Arizona: The Complete Guide for Future Arizonans: Job-Seekers, Retirees & Snowbirds. (Illus.). 248p. (Orig.). 1993. pap. 12.95 (0-942053-09-5) Pine Cone Pr CA.
— Inside San Francisco: A Witty, Opinionated & Remarkably Useful Guide to Everybody's Favorite City. (Illus.). 248p. (Orig.). 1991. pap. 8.95 (0-942053-08-7) Pine Cone Pr CA.
— Northern California Discovery Guide: A Remarkably Useful Travel Companion for Motorists, RVers & Other Explorers Second in the "Discovery Guide" Series. LC 92-91153. (Illus.). 356p. (Orig.). 1993. pap. 12.95 (0-942053-12-5) Pine Cone Pr CA.
— Oregon Discovery Guide: A Remarkably Useful Travel Companion for Motorists, RVers & Other Explorers. x52p. (Orig.). 1995. pap. 12.95 (0-942053-10-9) Pine Cone Pr CA.
— San Francisco's Ultimate Dining Guide: A Survey of over 300 Bay Area Restaurants by the REAL Experts; Chefs, Concierges, Cafe Critics & Community Leaders. (Illus.). 224p. (Orig.). 1988. pap. 9.95 (0-942053-03-6) Pine Cone Pr CA.
Martin, Don W., ed. see Shocklely, Bob & Mondavi, Robert.
Martin, Donald. How to Be a Successful Student. 2nd ed. (Illus.). 48p. (Orig.). (J). (gr. 8-12). 1991. pap. text ed. 5.95 (0-9617044-2-X) Martin Press.
Martin, Donald & Martin, Renee. A Survival Kit for Wives. 1986. pap. 12.95 (0-394-74361-X, Villard Bks) Random.
Martin, Donald, tr. see Calvin, John.
Martin, Donald, jt. auth. see Prata, Stephen W.
Martin, Donald E., jt. ed. see Hensley, Frederick A., Jr.
Martin, Donald E., tr. see Theotokas, George.
***Martin, Donald J.** Designer Kitchens: A Who's Who in Kitchen Design. (Illus.). 176p. (C). 1995. pap. 15.00 (1-886378-01-0) Kasmar Pubns.
***Martin, Donald J., ed.** Designer Kitchens: A Who's Who in Kitchen Design. (Illus.). 176p. (C). 1995. 24.95 (1-886378-00-2) Kasmar Pubns.
Martin, Donald L. Tidbits for Young Doctors & Their Patients: Journal of a Country Doctor, Pt. II. (Orig.). 1993. pap. 9.95 (1-55673-528-6) CSS OH.
Martin, Donn D., et al. Anatomy of the Vertebrates: A Laboratory Guide. 112p. (C). 1988. spiral bd. write for info. (0-697-03159-4) Wm C Brown Pubs.
***Martin, Donna.** Classic Christmas Carols & Songs. 1994. 14.95 (0-8362-4514-8) Andrews & McMeel.
Martin, Donna R. Ephesians. LC 94-11717. (Covenant Bible Study Ser.). 1994. pap. 4.95 (0-87178-221-9) Brethren.
Martin, Doris. Corporate Productivity in Action: How Top American Firms Manage the Competitive Challenge. LC 85-90460. (Management Ser.). (Illus.). 92p. (Orig.). 1987. pap. 12.95 (0-9615541-1-8) Martin Mgmt.
— The Executive Life Style in Big Business. LC 90-91947. 102p. 1990. pap. 15.95 (0-9615541-7-7) Martin Mgmt.
— Global Players: Insights on Successful Corporate Management. LC 89-92309. 105p. 1990. pap. 15.95 (0-9615541-4-2) Martin Mgmt.
— Hot Buttons: Corporate Macro Issues in the 1990's. LC 88-90640. (Management Ser.). 101p. (Orig.). 1988. pap. 12.95 (0-9615541-2-6) Martin Mgmt.
— Management for Competitiveness: Maximize Productivity, Performance, & Profits. LC 91-90340. 101p. (Orig.). 1991. pap. 15.95 (0-9615541-8-5) Martin Mgmt.
— Managers at Risk: Reshaping the Manager's Job in Competitive & Productive Firms. LC 88-90641. (Management Ser.). (Illus.). 106p. (Orig.). 1989. pap. 13. 95 (0-9615541-3-4) Martin Mgmt.
— Managing in Tough Times: One Hundred One New Directions from Big Business. LC 92-90898. (Illus.). 101p. (Orig.). 1992. pap. 15.95 (1-878500-01-5) Martin Mgmt.

M

Martin, Dorothea A. The Making of a Sino-Marxist World View: Perceptions & Interpretations of World History in the People's Republic of China. LC 89-49161. (Studies on Contemporary China). 160p. 1990. 57.95 (*0-87332-656-3*) M E Sharpe.

Martin, Dorothy & Martin, L. C., trs. Sextette: Translations from the French Symbolists. LC 80-10539. (Symbolists Ser.). reprint ed. 34.50 (*0-404-16331-9*) AMS Pr.

Martin, Dotty, jt. auth. see Martin, Bob.

Martin, Douglas. Book Design. 1989. pap. 29.95 (*0-442-30513-3*) Van Nos Reinhold.

— Charles Keeping an Illustrator's Life. (Illus.). 224p. 1993. 65.00 (*1-85681-062-3*, Pub. by J MacRae UK) Trafalgar.

— An Outline of Book Design. 208p. 1991. 34.95 (*0-948905-40-9*) Chapman & Hall.

Martin, Douglas, tr. see Kapr, Robert.

***Martin, Douglas A.** My Gradual Demise & Honeysuckle. 84p. 1995. pap. 7.00 (*0-9641196-2-5*) Champion Bks.

Martin, Douglas C., jt. auth. see Gibson, Helen.

Martin, Douglas C., jt. auth. see Roth, Richard.

Martin, Douglas C., jt. auth. see White, Paul.

Martin, Douglas C., jt. auth. see Wolfe, Tom.

***Martin, Douglas D.** Yuma Crossing. fac. ed. LC 95-60255. (Illus.). 260p. 1995. pap. 9.95 (*0-9632228-1-3*) Yuma Crossing.

Martin du Gard, Roger. Confidence Africaine. 67p. (FRE.). 1991. pap. 19.95 (*0-7859-1583-4*, 29035344458) Fr & Eur.

Martin Du Gard, Roger. Confidence Africaine. Wainhouse, Austryn, tr. LC 83-60469. 48p. 1983. pap. 5.25 (*0-910395-08-X*) Marlboro Pr.

Martin du Gard, Roger. Maumort. (FRE.). 1983. lib. bdg. 110.00 (*0-8288-3555-1*, M5107) Fr & Eur.

— Oeuvres Completes, Vol. 1. (FRE.). 1955. lib. bdg. 105.00 (*0-8288-3556-X*, M5105) Fr & Eur.

— Oeuvres Completes, Vol. 2. (FRE.). 1955. lib. bdg. 95.00 (*0-7859-0642-8*, M5106) Fr & Eur.

Martin Du Gard, Roger, pseud. The Postman. Russell, John, tr. LC 74-13052. 156p. 1975. reprint ed. 29.50 (*0-86527-333-2*) Fertig.

Martin du Gard, Roger. Un Taciturne. 238p. (FRE.). 1932. pap. 12.95 (*0-7859-1285-1*, 2070242439) Fr & Eur.

Martin Du Gard, Roger. Thibault, 5 tomes, 1. (Folio Ser.: Nos. 788, 140, 164, 165, & 189). (FRE.). 1959. pap. 12.95 (*2-07-036788-6*) Schoenhof.

— Thibault, 5 tomes, 2. (Folio Ser.: Nos. 788, 140, 164, 165, & 189). (FRE.). 1959. pap. 10.95 (*2-07-036140-3*) Schoenhof.

— Thibault, 5 tomes, 3. (Folio Ser.: Nos. 788, 140, 164, 165, & 189). (FRE.). 1959. pap. 9.95 (*2-07-036164-0*) Schoenhof.

— Thibault, 5 tomes, 4. (Folio Ser.: Nos. 788, 140, 164, 165, & 189). (FRE.). 1959. 9.95 (*2-07-036165-9*) Schoenhof.

— Thibault, 5 tomes, 5. (Folio Ser.: Nos. 788, 140, 164, 165, & 189). (FRE.). 1959. pap. 10.95 (*2-07-036189-6*) Schoenhof.

Martin du Gard, Roger. Vieille France. (Folio Ser.: No. 540). 160p. (FRE.). 6.95 (*2-07-036540-9*) Schoenhof.

— Vielle France. (FRE.). 1974. pap. 8.95 (*0-7859-4025-1*) Fr & Eur.

Martin, Dyna, ed. see Bertch, David P.

Martin, Dyna, ed. see Bertch, David & Bertch, Barbara A.

Martin, Dyna, ed. see Bertch, David.

Martin, E. A Student's Notebook: A Cooking Manual for Teenagers Who Like to Cook. large type ed. 96p. (YA). (gr. 9 up). 1973. 24.00 (*0-317-01945-7*, J-24530-00) Am Printing Hse.

Martin, E. & Tapiz, L. Deaig Encyclopedic Dictionary of Arts & Industrial Graphics: Deaig Diccionario Enciclopedico de las Artes e Industrias Graficas. 651p. (SPA.). 1981. 75.00 (*0-8288-2227-1*, S39788) Fr & Eur.

Martin, E. C., et al. Indian Remains in Grundy County, Missouri. (Missouri Archaeologist Ser.: Vol. 11, No. 2). 1949. 1.50 (*0-943414-76-8*, 111102) MO Arch Soc.

***Martin, E. Davis, Jr. & Gandy, Gerald L.** Rehabilitation & Disability: Psychosocial Case Studies. 200p. 1990. pap. 24.95 (*0-398-06269-2*) C C Thomas.

— Rehabilitation & Disability: Psychosocial Case Studies. 200p. (C). 1990. text ed. 39.95x (*0-398-05698-6*) C C Thomas.

Martin, E. G. & Irving, John. Cruising & Ocean Racing: A Complete Manual on Yachting. 1977. lib. bdg. 99.95 (*0-8490-1687-8*) Gordon Pr.

Martin, E. N. Monoclinal Antibody Imaging & Treatment of Colon Cancer. (Medical Intelligence Unit Ser.). 120p. 1993. text ed. 89.95 (*1-879702-22-3*, LN0222) R G Landes.

***Martin, E. Osborn.** The Gods of India. 330p. (C). 1995. reprint ed. pap. text ed. 25.00 (*0-89341-762-9*) Hollowbrook.

Martin, E. T. Marketing. Vanhonacker, Wilfried R., ed. LC 83-1708. (Core Business Program Ser.). 127p. reprint ed. pap. 36.20 (*0-7837-2669-4*, 2043034) Bks Demand.

Martin, Earl & Martin, Pat H. World Winds: Meditations from the Blessed of the Earth. (Illus.). 88p. (Orig.). 1990. pap. 13.95 (*0-8361-3535-0*) Herald Pr.

Martin, Ed. Cost Containment Learning Module, No. 8. (Orig.). 1985. pap. text ed. 47.50 (*0-931369-10-X*) Southern IL Univ Sch.

— Stamford Street Railroad Co. (Transportation Bulletin Ser.: No. 83). (Illus.). 1978. 9.00 (*0-910506-19-1*) De Vito.

***Martin, Eddie.** The Crafton Manor Mystery. LC 92-91110. 64p. (Orig.). (J). (ps-8). 1994. pap. 7.00 (*1-56002-271-X*) Aegina Pr.

Martin, Edley W. Mathematics for Decision Making: A Programmed Basic Text, Vol. 1: Linear Mathematics. LC 69-17157. 669p. reprint ed. pap. 180.00 (*0-317-08612-X*, 2021671) Bks Demand.

Martin, Edley W. & Perkins, William C. Computers & Information Systems: An Introduction. LC 72-95392. (Irwin-Dorsey Information Processing Ser.). 654p. reprint ed. pap. 180.00 (*0-317-29612-4*, 2021665) Bks Demand.

Martin, Edley W., et al. Managing Information Technology: What Managers Need to Know. 2nd ed. 768p. (C). 1994. text ed. write for info. (*0-02-376751-0*) Macmillan.

Martin, Edmund F. & Morrison, David J. Bethlehem Steelmaker: My Ninety Years in Life's Loop. 168p. 1992. 19.98 (*0-9635251-0-7*) BMS Pr.

Martin, Edna, ed. see Southern Oregon Historical Society Staff, et al.

Martin, Edward. Why Be Shy? 128p. 1982. pap. 6.50 (*0-686-44148-6*) Martin Pubns.

Martin, Edward & Burstein, Jerome S. Computer Systems Fundamentals. 448p. (C). 1990. Text with BASIC. text ed. 41.25 (*0-03-032594-3*); pap. text ed. 39.00 (*0-03-031103-9*) Dryden Pr.

Martin, Edward A. Psychology of Funeral Service. 6th ed. text ed. 12.50 (*0-686-20530-8*) E A Martin.

***Martin, Edward A., ed.** In Defense of Marion: The Love of Marion Bloom & H.L. Mencken. LC 95-14155. 1996. write for info. (*0-614-05433-8*) U of Ga Pr.

Martin, Edward B. & Parker, Charles S. Mastering Today's Software: Spreadsheets with Lotus 1-2-3 Release 2.4 Module. 2nd ed. 231p. (C). 1994. pap. text ed. 17.50 (*0-03-098590-0*) Dryden Pr.

Martin, Edward C. Personal Injury Damages Law & Practice. (Trial Practice Library). 401p. 1990. text ed. 128.00 (*0-471-63604-5*) Wiley.

Martin, Edward C., Jr. & Melby, Pete. Home Landscapes: Planting, Design, & Management. LC 93-39302. (Illus.). 332p. 1994. 49.95 (*0-88192-282-X*) Timber.

Martin, Edward G. Using Application Software: Featuring DOS 5.0 & 6.0, WordPerfect 6.0, Lotus 1-2-3 2.4, & dBASE IV 2.0. LC 93-34932. 1993. write for info. (*0-87709-550-7*) Boyd & Fraser.

— Using Application Software: Featuring Windows 3.1, Wordperfect 6.0 for Windows, Excel for Windows 5.0, Paradox for Windows 4.5. LC 94-25499. 1994. write for info. (*0-87709-553-1*) Boyd & Fraser.

— Using Application Software, Alternate Edition: Alternate Edition Featuring DOS 5.0, WordPerfect 5.1, Lotus 1-2-3, Release 2.2-2.3, & dBASE IV, Version 1.1. LC 92-21995. 1992. write for info. (*0-87835-964-8*) Boyd & Fraser.

Martin, Edward G. & Parker, Charles S. Instructor's Manual with Test Bank to Accompany Mastering Today's Software: Microcomputer Concepts. 2nd ed. 208p. (C). 1994. pap. text ed. 28.50 (*0-03-003022-6*) Dryden Pr.

— Mastering Today's Software: Database Management with DBASE III Plus. 2nd ed. 191p. (C). 1994. pap. text ed. 17.50 (*0-03-098226-X*) Dryden Pr.

— Mastering Today's Software: Database Management with DBASE IV Version 1.5-2.0. 2nd ed. 232p. (C). 1993. pap. text ed. 17.50 (*0-03-098227-8*) Dryden Pr.

— Mastering Today's Software: DOS 5.0 Module. 2nd ed. 85p. (C). 1993. pap. text ed. 17.50 (*0-03-098588-9*) Dryden Pr.

— Mastering Today's Software: DOS 6.0. 2nd ed. 88p. (C). 1994. pap. text ed. 17.50 (*0-03-000638-4*) Dryden Pr.

— Mastering Today's Software: Extended Microcomputer Concepts Module. 2nd ed. 264p. (C). 1994. pap. text ed. 28.50 (*0-03-098587-0*) Dryden Pr.

— Mastering Today's Software: Spreadsheets with Lotus 1-2-3 Release 2.2-2.3 Module. 2nd ed. 216p. (C). 1994. pap. text ed. 17.50 (*0-03-098589-7*) Dryden Pr.

— Mastering Today's Software: Spreadsheets with lotus 1-2-3 2.2-2.3 & 2.4. 2nd ed. 132p. (C). 1994. pap. text ed. 28.50 (*0-03-003607-0*) Dryden Pr.

— Mastering Today's Software: With Concepts, DOS 6.0, WordPerfect 5.1, Quattro Pro 4.0, Paradox 4.0. 2nd ed. LC 93-32989. 800p. (C). 1994. pap. text ed. 51.25 (*0-03-098823-3*) Dryden Pr.

— Mastering Today's Software: With Concepts, DOS 6.0, WordPerfect 5.1, Quattro Pro 4.0, Paradox 4.0. 2nd ed. LC 93-32989. (C). 1994. 20.00 (*0-03-098884-5*); 21.50 (*0-03-098885-3*); 20.00 (*0-03-098886-1*) Dryden Pr.

— Mastering Today's Software: With DOS, WordPerfect, Lotus 1-2-3, & dBASE III Plus. LC 91-32925. 826p. (C). 1992. pap. text ed. 37.25 (*0-03-073603-X*) Dryden Pr.

— Mastering Today's Software: With DOS, WordPerfect, Lotus 1-2-3, & dBASE IV. 826p. (C). 1992. pap. text ed. 37.75 (*0-03-076541-2*) Dryden Pr.

— Mastering Today's Software: With DOS, WordPerfect, Lotus 1-2-3, dBASE III PLUS, & BASIC. LC 91-35016. 992p. (C). 1992. pap. text ed. 43.00 (*0-03-076707-5*); teacher ed. 5.25 hd 13.50 (*0-03-092684-X*) Dryden Pr.

— Mastering Today's Software: With DOS, WordPerfect, Lotus 1-2-3, dBASE IV, & BASIC. LC 91-34517. 992p. (C). 1992. pap. text ed. 43.00 (*0-03-076706-7*) Dryden Pr.

— Mastering Today's Software: Word Processing with WordPerfect 5.1 Module. 2nd ed. 208p. (C). 1993. pap. text ed. 17.50 (*0-03-098591-9*) Dryden Pr.

— Mastering Today's Software: Word Processing with WorkPerfect 5.2 for Windows Module. 2nd ed. 240p. (C). 1994. pap. text ed. 17.50 (*0-03-098592-7*) Dryden Pr.

— Mastering Today's Software, Database Management with DBase (III & IV) Instructor's Manual with Test Bank & Transparency Masters to Accompany. 2nd ed. 152p. (C). 1994. pap. text ed. 28.50 (*0-03-002699-7*) Dryden Pr.

— Mastering Today's Software, DOS (5.0 & 6.0) Instructor's Manual with Test Bank to Accompany. 2nd ed. 56p. (C). 1994. pap. text ed. 28.50 (*0-03-003017-X*) Dryden Pr.

— Mastering Today's Software, Windows 3.1. 189p. (C). 1994. pap. text ed. 17.50 (*0-03-004154-6*) Dryden Pr.

— Mastering Today's Software with Concepts, dB IV: With Concepts, DOS 5.0, WordPerfect 5.1, Lotus 1-2-3 (2.4), dBASE IV. 2nd ed. LC 93-33991. 900p. (C). 1994. pap. text ed. 42.25 (*0-03-098821-7*) Dryden Pr.

— Mastering Today's Software, Word Processing with Word Perfect 6.0. 247p. (C). 1994. pap. text ed. 17.50 (*0-03-000614-7*) Dryden Pr.

— Mastering Today's Software, Word Processing with WordPerfect 5.1: Instructor's Manual with Test Bank & Transparency Masters to Accompany. 2nd ed. 136p. (C). 1994. pap. text ed. 70.00 (*0-03-002907-4*) Dryden Pr.

Martin, Edward G., jt. auth. see Burstein, Jerome S.

Martin, Edward J. A History of the Iconclastic Controversy. LC 77-84711. reprint ed. 34.00 (*0-404-16117-0*) AMS Pr.

— The Trial of the Templars. LC 76-29845. reprint ed. 29.50 (*0-404-15424-7*) AMS Pr.

Martin, Edward J. & Johnson, James H. Hazardous Waste Management Engineering. (Illus.). 520p. 1986. text ed. 99.95 (*0-442-24439-8*, 128601) Chapman & Hall.

Martin, Edward J. & Martin, Edward T. Technologies for Small Water & Wastewater Systems. (Illus.). 376p. 1991. text ed. 64.95 (*0-442-23829-0*) Van Nos Reinhold.

Martin, Edward S. Courtship of a Careful Man, & a Few Other Courtships. LC 77-125232. (Short Story Index Reprint Ser.). 1977. 17.95 (*0-8369-3599-3*) Ayer.

— In a New Century. LC 73-142665. (Essay Index Reprint Ser.). 1977. reprint ed. 24.95 (*0-8369-2324-3*) Ayer.

— What's Ahead & Meanwhile. LC 74-156688. (Essay Index Reprint Ser.). 1977. reprint ed. 23.95 (*0-8369-2325-1*) Ayer.

Martin, Edward T., jt. auth. see Martin, Edward J.

Martin, Edwin M. Conference Diplomacy-A Case Study: The World Food Conference, Rome, 1974. LC 79-91018. 58p. (Orig.). 1979. pap. 5.00 (*0-934742-01-4*) Geo U Inst Diplmcy.

— Conference Diplomacy, A Case Study: The World Food Conference Rome, 1974. 72p. (C). 1985. reprint ed. pap. text ed. 12.50 (*0-8191-5054-1*, Inst Study Diplomacy) U Pr of Amer.

— Kennedy & Latin America. 476p. (C). Date not set. lib. bdg. 48.50 (*0-8191-9429-8*) U Pr of Amer.

— The United States & the Developing Countries. 150p. 1977. 14.00 (*0-317-33699-1*); pap. 5.95 (*0-317-33700-9*) Atl Coun US.

Martin, Edwin P. A Population Study of the Prairie Vole (Microtus ochrogaster) in Northeastern Kansas. (Museum Ser.: Vol. 8, No. 6). 56p. 1956. pap. 3.00 (*0-317-04886-4*) U of KS Mus Nat Hist.

Martin, Edwin W. Divided Counsel: The Anglo-American Response to Communist Victory in China. LC 86-1708. (Illus.). 288p. 1986. 31.00 (*0-8131-1591-4*) U Pr of Ky.

— The Hubbards of Sivas: A Chronicle of Love & Faith. LC 91-9794. 352p. (Orig.). 1991. pap. 11.95 (*0-931832-85-3*) Fithian Pr.

Martin, Edythe, ed. see Ancel, Martin.

Martin, Elaine. Baby Games. LC 87-43258. (Illus.). 224p. 1988. pap. 12.95 (*0-89471-617-4*) Running Pr.

Martin, Elaine, ed. Gender, Patriarchy, & Fascism in the Third Reich: The Response of Women Writers. LC 92-28667. 309p. (C). 1993. text ed. 39.95 (*0-8143-2420-7*); pap. 19.95 (*0-8143-2421-5*) Wayne St U Pr.

Martin, Elizabeth. Architecture as a Translation of Music. LC 94-22892. (Pamphlet Architecture Ser.: No. 16). (Illus.). 80p. (Orig.). 1994. pap. 11.95 (*1-56898-012-4*) Princeton Arch.

— CCL: Cl Pasta Sauces. 96p. 1994. 10.98 (*0-8317-1305-4*) Smithmark.

Martin, Elizabeth, jt. ed. see Turner, Charles F.

Martin, Elizabeth A., ed. A Dictionary of Law. 3rd ed. LC 93-36843. (Paperback Reference Ser.). 448p. (C). 1994. 29.95 (*0-19-211700-9*); pap. 13.95 (*0-19-280000-0*) OUP.

Martin, Ellen, ed. Favorite Country Cookbook, Vol. 2: From the Amish Mennonite Kitchens of Tampico, Illinois. (Illus.). 178p. (Orig.). 1990. spiral bd. 9.95 (*0-9623562-0-4*) Martin IL.

***Martin, Elmer P. & Martin, Joanne M.** Black Experience-Based Social Work. (C). 1995. lib. bdg. write for info. (*0-87101-257-X*, 257X) Natl Assn Soc Wkrs.

— The Black Extended Family. LC 77-17058. 1980. reprint ed. pap. text ed. 8.95 (*0-226-50797-1*, P872) U Ch Pr.

Martin, Elmer P., jt. auth. see Martin, Joanne M.

Martin, Elva. Seek Ye First. 1973. pap. 2.50 (*0-915374-32-3*, 32-3) Rapids Christian.

Martin, Emiliano. Words in Captivity. Gonzalez-Parker, Zulma, ed. 60p. (Orig.). 1990. pap. write for info. (*1-878255-06-1*) Heartfelt Pr.

Martin, Emily. Flexible Bodies: Tracking Immunity in American Culture from the Days of Polio to the Age of AIDS. LC 93-39065. (Illus.). 336p. 1994. 25.00 (*0-8070-4626-4*) Beacon Pr.

— Flexible Bodies: Tracking Immunity in American Culture from the Days of Polio to the Age of AIDS. 336p. (C). 1995. pap. 14.00 (*0-8070-4627-2*) Beacon Pr.

— The Woman in the Body: A Cultural Analysis of Reproduction. LC 92-7293. (Illus.). 304p. 1992. pap. 16.00 (*0-8070-4619-1*) Beacon Pr.

Martin, Eric R. & Langhorne, Karyn E. Cover Letters They Can't Forget. LC 92-38541. (Opportunities in...Ser.). 160p. 1993. pap. 8.95 (*0-8442-4139-3*, VGM Career Bks) NTC Pub Grp.

— How to Write Successful Cover Letters. LC 93-47489. 1994. 8.95 (*0-8442-4137-7*, VGM Career Bks) NTC Pub Grp.

Martin, Ernest, ed. Le Roman de Renart, 3 vols. 1476p. (C). 1973. reprint ed. 480.75 (*3-11-003337-2*) De Gruyter.

Martin, Ernest D. Colossians, Philemon. (Believers Church Bible Commentary Ser.). 304p. 1993. text ed. 17.95 (*0-8361-3621-7*) Herald Pr.

Martin, Ernest J. The Warlock. LC 82-61712. (Illus.). 296p. (Orig.). 1983. pap. 4.95 (*0-910759-00-6*) Mars Pubns.

***Martin, Ernest L.** The Biblical Manual: "The History of Doctrine in the New Testament. (Illus.). (Orig.). (YA). (gr. 10). Date not set. pap. write for info. (*0-945657-76-5*) Acad Scriptural Knowledge.

— 101 Bible Secrets That Christians Do Not Know. (Illus.). 226p. (Orig.). (C). 1993. pap. text ed. 14.95 (*0-945657-94-3*) Acad Scriptural Knowledge.

— The Original Bible Restored. 2nd ed. (Illus.). 336p. (YA). (gr. 10). 1991. pap. text ed. 14.95 (*0-945657-89-7*) Acad Scriptural Knowledge.

— The People That History Forgot. 2nd ed. (Illus.). 196p. (Orig.). (C). 1994. pap. 11.95 (*0-945657-82-X*) Acad Scriptural Knowledge.

— The Place of the New Third Temple. (Illus.). 136p. (Orig.). (C). 1994. pap. text ed. 10.95 (*0-945657-80-3*) Acad Scriptural Knowledge.

— Restoring the Original Bible. (Illus.). 512p. (Orig.). (C). 1994. pap. text ed. 19.95 (*0-945657-83-8*) Acad Scriptural Knowledge.

— The Star that Astonished the World. (Illus.). 220p. (Orig.). (YA). (gr. 10). 1991. pap. 14.95 (*0-945657-88-9*) Acad Scriptural Knowledge.

Martin, Ernst, ed. The Calculating Machine: Their History & Development. (Charles Babbage Institute Reprint Series for the History of Computing). (Illus.). 392p. 1992. 50.00 (*0-262-13278-8*) MIT Pr.

Martin, Esmond B., jt. auth. see De Blij, Harm J.

Martin, Etta P. Molly Anderson Pioneer Woman. LC 94-70292. 248p. (Orig.). Date not set. pap. 11.95 (*0-938041-20-7*) Arc Pr AR.

Martin, Eva. The Ring of Return. 306p. 1981. pap. 25.00 (*0-89540-109-6*, SB-109) Sun Pub.

Martin, Eva, jt. tr. see Shure, Edouard.

Martin, F. & Butler, J. Geography Skills for GCSE & Standard Grade. (C). 1989. 80.00 (*0-09-172995-5*, Pub. by S Thornes Pubs UK) St Mut.

Martin, F., jt. auth. see Bateman, R.

Martin, F. David. Art & the Religious Experience: The Language of the Sacred. LC 75-161508. (Illus.). 288p. 1975. 42.50 (*0-8387-7935-2*) Bucknell U Pr.

— Sculpture & Enlivened Space: Aesthetics & History. LC 79-4006. (Illus.). 352p. 1981. 38.00 (*0-8131-1386-5*) U Pr of Ky.

Martin, F. David & Jacobus, Lee A. The Humanities Through the Arts. 4th ed. 1991. pap. text ed. write for info. (*0-07-040723-1*) McGraw.

Martin, F. J., jt. ed. see Lasic, D. D.

Martin, F. J., Jr., jt. ed. see Poltzer, P.

***Martin, F. Lestar.** The Louisiana Architecture of William King Stubbs. (Illus.). 78p. 1994. 32.00 (*0-9644513-0-1*) LA Tech Univ.

***Martin, F. R.** Miniature Painting & Painters of Persia, India & Turkey, 2 vols. (C). 1993. 94.00 (*81-85557-13-6*) S Asia.

Martin, F. Raoul, ed. see Labbe, John T. & Replinger, Peter J.

Martin, F. X & Richmond, J. A., eds. From Augustine to Eriugena: Essays on Neoplatonism & Christianity in Honor of John O'Meara. LC 90-33250. 190p. 1991. text ed. 49.95 (*0-8132-0732-0*) Cath U Pr.

Martin, F. X., jt. ed. see Moody, T. W.

Martin, Fay C. Availing Prayer. 120p. reprint ed. pap. 1.50 (*0-686-29098-4*) Faith Pub Hse.

Martin, Fenton & Boehlert, Robert. How to Research the Supreme Court. 100p. 1992. 26.95 (*0-87187-697-3*); pap. 16.95 (*0-87187-633-7*) Congr Quarterly.

***Martin, Fenton S. & Goehlert, Robert.** Political Science Journal Information. 3rd ed. 111p. (Orig.). (C). 1990. pap. text ed. 25.00 (*1-878147-01-3*) Am Political.

Martin, Fenton S. & Goehlert, Robert U. The American Presidency: A Bibliography. 1987. 105.00 (*0-87187-415-6*) Congr Quarterly.

— American Presidents: A Bibliography. 756p. 1987. 155.00 (*0-87187-416-4*) Congr Quarterly.

— Supreme Court Bibliography. 564p. 1990. 215.00 (*0-87187-554-3*) Congr Quarterly.

***Martin, Fern & Woods, Paula.** Lafayette: A Pictorial History. (Indiana Pictorial History Ser.). (Illus.). 1994. write for info. (*0-943963-09-5*) G Bradley.

Martin, Fern, jt. auth. see Woods, Paula.

Martin, Fontaine. A History of the Bouligny Family & Allied Families. LC 89-81492. 366p. 1990. 30.00 (*0-940984-51-2*) U of SW LA Ctr LA Studies.

***Martin, Frances.** The Scarecrow & Santa Claus. (Illus.). 32p. (J). (ps-2). 1995. 19.95 (*0-370-31895-1*, Pub. by Bodley Head UK); write for info. (*0-614-04229-1*, Pub. by Bodley Head UK) Trafalgar.

Martin, Frances R. Manual for Nursing Care of Children. 352p. 1993. spiral bd. 27.99 (*0-8403-8616-8*) Kendall-Hunt.

Martin, Francesca, ret. The Honey Hunters. LC 91-58736. (Illus.). 32p. (J). (ps up). 1992. 14.95 (*1-56402-086-X*) Candlewick Pr.

— Honey Hunters. LC 91-58736. (Illus.). 32p. (J). (ps up). 1994. pap. 5.99 (*1-56402-276-5*) Candlewick Pr.

Martin, Francis. Baptism in the Holy Spirit: A Scriptural Foundation. 62p. (Orig.). 1986. pap. 3.95 (*0-940535-04-1*, UP105) Franciscan U Pr.

— The Feminist Question: Feminist Theology in the Light of Christian Tradition. 496p. (Orig.). 1994. pap. 29.99 (*0-8028-0794-1*) Eerdmans.

— The Life-Changer: How You Can Experience Power & Refreshment in the Holy Spirit. 170p. (Orig.). (C). 1990. pap. 8.99 (*0-89283-661-X*) Servant.

— Narrative Parallels to the New Testament. LC 88-38010. (Resources for Biblical Study Ser.). 325p. 1988. 33.95 (*1-55540-258-5*, 06 03 22); pap. 21.95 (*1-55540-259-3*, 06 03 22) Scholars Pr GA.

An Asterisk (*) at the beginning of an entry indicates that the title is appearing in BIP for the first time.

Martin, Francis, Jr., intro. Western & Wildlife: Selections from the Samuel B & Marion Lawrence Collection. (Illus.). 45p. (Orig.). 1987. pap. 10.00 (*0-9615828-1-2*) Cornell Fine Arts.
Martin, Francis, tr. see Bavarel, Michel.
Martin, Francis P. Hung by the Tongue. 1976. 4.99 (*0-89858-014-5*) Fill the Gap.
Martin, Francis X. Friar, Reformer, & Renaissance Scholar: The Life & Work of Giles of Viterbo, 1469-1532. Rotelle, John E. & O'Malley, John W., eds. LC 92-2863. (Augustinian Ser.: Vol. 18). 424p. 1993. 40.00 (*0-941491-51-X*); pap. 28.00 (*0-941491-50-1*) Augustinian Pr.
Martin, Francois. India in the Seventeenth Century, Vol. 2, Pt. 1. Varadarajan, Lotika, ed. 1985. 32.50 (*0-8364-1423-3*, Pub. by Manohar II) S Asia.
— India in the Seventeenth Century, Vol. 2, Pt. 2. Varadarajan, Lotika, ed. 1985. 38.00 (*0-8364-1424-1*, Pub. by Manohar II) S Asia.
— India in the Seventeenth Century: Social, Economic & Political Memoirs of Francois Martin, Vol. 1. Varadarajan, Lotika, tr. 1982. 36.00 (*0-8364-0818-7*, Pub. by Manohar II) S Asia.
Martin, Frank. The Kid-Friendly Dad: Connecting with Your Kids in a Chaotic World. LC 93-42737. (Saltshaker Bks.). 160p. (Orig.). 1994. pap. 8.99 (*0-8308-1632-1*, 1632, Saltshaker Bk) InterVarsity.
— Rogues' River: Crime on the River Thames in the Eighteenth Century. (Illus.). 200p. 1991. 15.00 (*0-86025-874-2*, Pub. by Ian Henry Pubns UK) Empire Pub Srvs.
— War in the Pews. 1995. pap. 9.99 (*0-8308-1640-2*) InterVarsity.
Martin, Frank, ed. Frank Martin: A Bio-Bibliography. LC 89-78255. (Bio-Bibliographies in Music Ser.: No. 26). 264p. 1990. text ed. 49.95 (*0-313-25418-4*, KFK/, Greenwood Pr) Greenwood.
Martin, Franklin W., ed. Handbook of Tropical Food Crops. 304p. 1984. 152.95 (*0-8493-0536-5*, SB176) CRC Pr.
Martin, Franklin W. & Ruberte, Ruth. Patiofarming: A Compendium of Useful Tables. (Studies in Tropical Agriculture). 1980. lib. bdg. 69.95 (*0-8490-3075-7*) Gordon Pr.
— The Round Garden: Plans for a Small Intensive Vegetable Garden for Year Round Production in the Tropics. (Studies in Tropical Agriculture). 1980. lib. bdg. 59.95 (*0-8490-3073-0*) Gordon Pr.
Martin, Franklin W. & Ruberte, Ruth M. Edible Leaves of the Tropics. (Tropical Agriculture Ser.). 1980. lib. bdg. 250.00 (*0-8490-3069-2*) Gordon Pr.
Martin, Franklin W., et al. Cultivation of Neglected Tropical Fruits with Promise. (Studies in Tropical Agriculture). 1980. lib. bdg. 59.95 (*0-8490-3074-9*) Gordon Pr.
— Vegetables for the Hot, Humid Tropics. (Studies in Tropical Agriculture). 1980. lib. bdg. 59.95 (*0-8490-3071-4*) Gordon Pr.
Martin, Fred W., Sr. & Willett, Albert J., Jr. The Martin Family of the Poquoson District of York County, Virginia. 317p. 1994. text ed. 25.00 (*1-55613-980-2*) Heritage Bk.
Martin, Frederick. Life of John Clare. 2nd ed. (Illus.). 319p. 1964. 27.50 (*0-7146-2070-X*, Pub. by F Cass Pubs UK) Intl Spec Bk.
— The Life of John Clare. (BCL1-PR English Literature Ser.). 301p. 1992. reprint ed. lib. bdg. 89.99 (*0-7812-7497-4*) Rprt Serv.
Martin, Frederick N. Clinical Audiometry & Masking. LC 74-183115. (Studies in Communicative Disorders). (C). 1972. pap. 3.25 (*0-672-61282-8*, Bobbs) Macmillan.
— Introduction to Audiology. 5th ed. LC 93-45317. 1994. text ed. 36.00 (*0-13-501057-8*) P-H.
— Introduction to Audiology: A Study Guide. 3rd ed. LC 93-46031. 1994. pap. text ed. write for info. (*0-13-035940-8*) P-H.
Martin, Frederick N., jt. ed. see Clark, John Greer.
Martin, Frederick T. The Passing of the Idle Rich. LC 75-1858. (Leisure Class in America Ser.). 1975. reprint ed. 20.95 (*0-405-06924-3*) Ayer.
— Things I Remember. LC 75-1859. (Leisure Class in America Ser.). (Illus.). 1975. reprint ed. 21.95 (*0-405-06925-1*) Ayer.
— Things I Remember. (American Biography Ser.). 255p. 1991. reprint ed. lib. bdg. 69.00 (*0-7812-8272-1*) Rprt Serv.
Martin, G., ed. Geographers, Vol. 13: Biobibliographical Studies. (Illus.). 198p. 1991. pap. text ed. 70.00 (*0-7201-2081-0*, Mansell Pub) Cassell.
— Geographers, Vol. 14: Biobibliographical Studies. (Illus.). 128p. 1992. text ed. 70.00 (*0-7201-2116-7*, Mansell Pub) Cassell.
Martin, G. & Kubin, L. P., eds. Non-Linear Phenomena in Materials Science. 600p. 1988. text ed. 138.00 (*0-87849-565-7*, Pub. by Trans Tech GW) LPS Dist Ctr.
— Non Linear Phenomena in Materials Science II. 520p. 1992. text ed. 146.00 (*0-87849-635-1*, Pub. by Trans Tech GW) LPS Dist Ctr.
Martin, G., jt. auth. see Brayne, H.
Martin, G. C. Martin Family, of Ireland, U. S. & Canada. 144p. 1993. reprint ed. lib. bdg. 35.00 (*0-8328-3715-6*); reprint ed. pap. 25.00 (*0-8328-3716-4*) Higginson Bk Co.
Martin, G. E. Foundations of Geometry & the Non-Euclidean Plane. (Undergraduate Texts in Mathematics Ser.). 509p. 1986. 32.00 (*0-387-90694-0*) Spr-Verlag.
— Transformation Geometry: An Introduction to Symmetry. (Undergraduate Texts in Mathematics Ser.). (Illus.). 240p. 1994. 39.95 (*0-387-90636-3*) Spr-Verlag.
Martin, G. F., jt. ed. see Kuypers, H. G.
Martin, G. H., ed. see Knighton, Henry.
Martin, G. M., jt. ed. see Esser, K.
Martin, G. R., jt. auth. see Craine, J. F.
Martin, G. R., jt. ed. see Holdsworth, B.
Martin, G. S., jt. auth. see Heap, N. W.
Martin, G. W. Revision of the North Central Tremellales. 1969. reprint ed. 24.00 (*3-7682-0636-X*) Lubrecht & Cramer.
Martin-Gaite, Carmen. From Fiction to Metafiction: Essays in Honor of Carmen Martin-Gaite. Servodidio, Mirella & Welles, Marcia L., eds. LC 82-61181. (Illus.). 223p. reprint ed. pap. 63.60 (*0-317-58192-9*, 2029716) Bks Demand.
Martin, Gale D. Introductory Physical Geology: Laboratory Handouts, GEO 101L. 72p. 1993. spiral bd. 6.95 (*0-8403-8748-2*) Kendall-Hunt.
Martin, Galen, jt. auth. see Fry, Gerald W.
***Martin, Garry.** Reflective Expressions. 36p. (Orig.). Date not set. pap. 4.98 (*0-9639912-1-3*) Southeast Pubns.
Martin, Garry L. & Osborne, J. Grayson. Psychology, Adjustment, & Everyday Living. 2nd ed. LC 92-22853. 688p. (C). 1992. text ed. write for info. (*0-13-735804-0*) P-H.
Martin, Garry L. & Pear, Joseph. Behavior Modification: What It Is & How to Do It. 4th ed. 528p. (C). 1991. pap. text ed. write for info. (*0-13-067166-5*) P-H.
— Behavior Modification & What It Is & How to Do It. 3rd ed. (Illus.). 576p. 1988. pap. text ed. 42.33 (*0-13-072315-0*) P-H.
Martin, Gary. Competitive Karting. LC 80-83189. (Illus.). 144p. 1980. pap. 12.95 (*0-9605068-0-2*) Martin Motorsports.
— Euchre: How to Play & Win. LC 82-90179. 64p. (Orig.). 1982. pap. 4.95 (*0-9605068-1-0*) Martin Motorsports.
— Four-Cycle Kart Engines. (Illus.). 88p. 1986. pap. 9.95 (*0-9605068-2-9*) Martin Motorsports.
— Karting Tools & Tips. (Illus.). 64p. 1992. pap. text ed. 9.95 (*0-9605068-3-7*) Martin Motorsports.
Martin, Gary E. & Zektzer, Andrew S. Two-Dimensional NMR Methods for Establishing Molecular Connectivity: A Chemist's Guide to Experiment Selection, Performance & Interpretation. LC 88-27705. 508p. 1988. 80.00 (*0-89573-703-5*) VCH Pubs.
Martin, Gary W. QBASIC: A Short Course in Structured Programming. 195p. (C). 1994. pap. text ed. 13.75 (*0-03-098845-4*) Dryden Pr.
— Turbo Pascal: Primer. 700p. (C). 1992. pap. text ed. 43.00 (*0-15-592375-7*) SCP.
Martin, Gay. Louisiana: Off the Beaten Path. 2nd ed. LC 93-1326. (Voyager Book Ser.). (Illus.). 160p. (Orig.). 1993. pap. 9.95 (*1-56440-233-9*) Globe Pequot.
Martin-Gay, K. Elayn. Beginning Algebra. 560p. (C). 1992. text ed. write for info. (*0-13-073784-4*) P-H.
— Beginning Algebra. LC 92-33973. 1993. write for info. (*0-13-086778-0*) P-H.
— Intermediate Algebra. LC 92-26907. 1993. teacher ed write for info. (*0-13-474123-4*) P-H.
— Intermediate Algebra. 576p. (C). 1993. text ed. write for info. (*0-13-468372-2*) P-H.
— Pre-Algebra. LC 92-26290. 648p. (C). 1992. pap. text ed. 31.50 (*0-13-062829-8*) P-H.
***Martin, Gay N.** Alabama. 2nd ed. LC 95-17675. (Off the Beaten Path Ser.). (Illus.). 160p. 1995. pap. 10.95 (*1-56440-731-4*) Globe Pequot.
Martin, Gene. Tidewater Bobber Fishing for Chinook Salmon. (Illus.). 32p. 1993. pap. 6.95 (*1-878175-54-8*) F Amato Pubns.
— Trail Dust. 1988. pap. 3.75 (*0-9606648-0-7*) Martin Assocs.
Martin, Gene L. & Boyd, Aaron. Bill Clinton: President from Arkansas. (Illus.). 104p. (YA). (gr. 7-12). 1993. lib. bdg. 17.95 (*0-936389-31-1*) Tudor Pubs.
Martin, Genevieve A. & Bertram, Theodor. Living English for German-Speaking People. 1988. Incl. cassettes. student ed, audio 18.95 (*0-517-51322-6*, Living Language); student ed, lp (*0-318-51563-6*, Living Language) Crown Pub Group.
Martin, Genevieve A. & Maiori, Rachel. Living English for Italian-Speaking People. 1988. Incl. cassettes. student ed, audio 20.00 (*0-517-51323-4*, Living Language); student ed, lp (*0-318-51564-4*, Living Language) Crown Pub Group.
Martin, Geoffrey J., ed. Geographers: Biobibliographical Studies, Vol. 15. (Illus.). 160p. 1994. 85.00 (*0-7201-2161-2*, Mansell Pub) Cassell.
Martin, Geoffrey J. & James, Preston E. All Possible Worlds: A History of Geographical Ideas. 3rd ed. 608p. 1993. Net. text ed. write for info. (*0-471-63414-X*) Wiley.
Martin, Geoffrey J., jt. auth. see James, Preston E.
Martin, Geoffrey T. A Bibliography of the Amarna Period: The Reigns of Akhenaten Smenkhkare, Tutankhamun & Ay. (Studies in Egyptology). 120p. (C). 1991. text ed. 55.00 (*0-7103-0413-7*, A5621, Pub. by Kegan Paul Intl UK) Routledge Chapman & Hall.
— Hidden Tombs of Memphis. 1992. pap. 19.95 (*0-500-27666-8*) Thames Hudson.
Martin, George. All You Need Is Ears. (Illus.). 288p. 1982. pap. 12.95 (*0-312-02044-9*) St Martin.
— The Companion to Twentieth Century Opera. 654p. 1992. pap. 24.95 (*0-7195-4767-9*, Pub. by John Murray UK) Trafalgar.
— The Opera Companion. 693p. 1989. pap. 24.95 (*0-7195-4110-7*, Pub. by John Murray UK) Trafalgar.
— Polyominoes: A Guide to Puzzles & Problems in Tiling. (Spectrum Ser.). (Illus.). 172p. 1991. pap. 24.50 (*0-88385-501-1*) Math Assn.
— Praying the Scriptures: A Guide to Talking with God. (Catholic Bible Study Guides Ser.). 76p. (Orig.). (C). 1990. pap. 4.99 (*0-89283-647-4*) Servant.
— Reading Scripture As the Word of God. 2nd ed. 201p. 1993. pap. 8.99 (*0-89283-152-9*, Charis) Servant.
— Wild Oakie. LC 92-85412. 76p. (J). (gr. 2-6). 1993. 6.95 (*1-55523-552-2*) Winston-Derek.
Martin, George, ed. Making Music: The Guide to Writing, Performing, & Recording. LC 82-63155. (Illus.). 352p. 1983. pap. 13.20 (*0-688-01466-6*, Quill) Morrow.
Martin, George, tr. Italian Folktales. LC 80-11879. (Helen & Kurt Wolff Bk.). (Illus.). 800p. 1990. reprint ed. 27.95 (*0-15-145770-0*) HarBrace.
Martin, George & Burren, Michael. The Obelisk Conspiracy. 224p. 1976. 7.95 (*0-8065-0513-3*, Citadel Pr) Carol Pub Group.
Martin, George & Hornsby, Jeremy. All You Need Is Ears. (Illus.). 288p. 1994. pap. 13.95 (*0-312-11482-6*) St Martin.
***Martin, George & Pearson, William.** With a Little Help from My Friends: The Making of Sgt. Pepper. (Illus.). 176p. 1995. 22.95 (*0-316-54783-2*) Little.
Martin, George A. Fences, Gates & Bridges: A Practical Manual. LC 92-18206. (Illus.). 192p. 1992. reprint ed. pap. 11.95 (*0-911469-08-7*) A C Hood.
— True Owners of the Soil. LC 90-80408. (Illus.). 92p. (Orig.). 1990. pap. 11.00 (*1-878515-13-6*) W S Dawson.
— Wausau in Nineteen Hundred. rev. ed. Janke, John & Johnson, Jane J., eds. (Illus.). 140p. 1987. 19.95 (*0-9617780-1-6*) Birch Lake Pr.
***Martin, George C., et al.** Castor Family of Pennsylvania, & the Castor Family of New York. (Illus.). 161p. 1994. reprint ed. lib. bdg. 36.00 (*0-8328-4305-9*); reprint ed. pap. 26.00 (*0-8328-4306-7*) Higginson Bk Co.
Martin, George H. Kinematics & Dynamics of Machines. 2nd ed. (Illus.). 544p. (C). 1982. text ed. write for info. (*0-07-040657-X*) McGraw.
Martin, George R. The Armageddon Rag. LC 83-13597. 335p. 1983. 25.00 (*0-89366-150-3*) Ultramarine Pub.
— Marked Cards. (Wild Cards Ser.: Vol. 2). 448p. (Orig.). 1994. mass mkt. 5.99 (*0-671-72212-3*) Baen Bks.
***Martin, George R., creator.** Black Trump: Wild Cards. 1995. mass mkt. 5.99 (*0-671-87679-1*) Baen Bks.
Martin, George R. & Tuttle, Lisa. Windhaven. 1980. 25.00 (*0-671-25277-1*) Ultramarine Pub.
Martin, George R., ed. see Zelazny, Roger, et al.
Martin, George R. R. Nightflyers. 304p. 1987. reprint ed. pap. 3.50 (*0-8125-4564-8*) Tor Bks.
Martin, George T. Social Policy in the Welfare State. 304p. (C). 1989. Casebound. text ed. write for info. (*0-13-816935-7*) P-H.
Martin, George T., Jr. & Zald, Mayer M., eds. Social Welfare in Society. LC 81-3837. 614p. reprint ed. pap. 175.00 (*0-8357-6866-X*, 2035564) Bks Demand.
Martin, George T. & Zald, Mayer N. Social Welfare in Society. LC 81-3837. (Illus.). 576p. 1981. text ed. 63.00 (*0-231-04922-6*) Col U Pr.
Martin, George W. Aspects of Verdi. LC 93-13748. (Illus.). 304p. 1993. reprint ed. pap. 15.95 (*0-87910-172-5*) Limelight Edns.
— Let's Communicate: A Self-Help Program on Writing Letters & Memos. LC 71-109516. (Supervisory Management Ser.). 1970. pap. text ed. write for info. (*0-201-04500-1*) Addison-Wesley.
— Verdi: His Music, Life & Times. LC 92-23999. (Illus.). 522p. 1992. reprint ed. pap. 22.95 (*0-87910-160-1*) Limelight Edns.
— Verdi at the Golden Gate: Opera & San Francisco in the Gold Rush Years. LC 92-18674. 1993. 30.00 (*0-520-08123-4*) U CA Pr.
— Verdi, His Music, Life & Times. LC 78-31783. (Music Reprint Ser.). 1979. reprint ed. 59.50 (*0-306-79549-3*) Da Capo.
Martin, George W. & Alexopoulos, C. J., eds. The Myxomycetes. LC 77-88357. (Illus.). 576p. (C). 1969. 75.00 (*0-87745-000-5*) U of Iowa Pr.
Martin, George W., et al, eds. The Genera of the Myxomycetes. LC 83-5092. (Illus.). 198p. (C). 1983. 42.95 (*0-87745-124-9*) U of Iowa Pr.
Martin, Gerald. Journeys Through the Labyrinth: Latin American Fiction in the Twentieth Century. (Critical Studies in Latin American Culture). 272p. 1989. 65.00 (*0-86091-238-8*, A3327, Pub. by Verso UK); pap. text ed. 19.95 (*0-86091-952-8*, A3331, Pub. by Verso UK) Routledge Chapman & Hall.
— Rusty Wallace: Racer. (Illus.). 128p. 1994. 49.95 (*0-89404-092-8*) Aztex.
— Rusty Wallace: Racer. deluxe limited ed. (Illus.). 128p. 1994. boxed 295.00 (*0-89404-093-6*) Aztex.
Martin, Gerald, tr. see Asturias, Miguel A.
Martin, Gerald, tr. see Aub, Max.
Martin, Gerald D. & Clay, William C., Jr. How to Win Maximum Awards for Lost Earnings: A Guide to Estimating Damages Fairly & Proving Them in Court. 1980. 89.50 (*0-13-440669-9*) Exec Reports.
Martin, Gerry, jt. auth. see Brayne, Hugh.
Martin, Glen. The Complete Guide to Starting or Evaluating a Singles Ministry, 3 cass., Set. 172p. 1993. audio, ring bd. 79.95 (*0-941005-93-3*) Chrch Grwth VA.
— Single, but Not Alone. 144p. (Orig.). 1993. pap. 8.95 (*0-941005-94-1*) Chrch Grwth VA.
Martin, Glen, jt. auth. see Ginter, Dian.
Martin, Glen, jt. auth. see McIntosh, Gary.
Martin, Glen, jt. auth. see Stuller, Jay.
***Martin, Glen S.** Beyond the Rat Race. LC 95-6451. 1995. write for info. (*0-8054-6151-5*) Broadman.
***Martin, Glen S. & Ginter, Dian.** Drawing Closer: A Step by Step Guide to Intimacy with God. LC 94-24526. 1995. 16.99 (*0-8054-6182-5*) Broadman.
***Martin, Glen S. & McIntosh, Gary L.** How to Minister in Changing Times: Understanding the Trends Confronting Your Church & Developing a Strategy for Success. 28p. 1995. audio, ring bd. 79.95 (*1-57052-004-6*) Chrch Grwth VA.
Martin, Glen S., jt. auth. see McIntosh, Gary L.
Martin, Glen T. From Nietzsche to Wittgenstein: The Problem of Truth & Nihilism in the Modern World. (Literature & the Sciences of Man Ser.: Vol. 1). 414p. (C). 1989. text ed. 60.00 (*0-8204-0917-0*) P Lang Pubs.
***Martin Gonzalez, J. J.** Historia de Escultura. 3rd ed. (Illus.). 326p. (SPA.). 1993. 100.00 (*84-249-3121-1*) Elliots Bks.
— Historia de la Arquitectura. 3rd ed. (Illus.). (SPA.). 1993. pap. 100.00 (*84-249-3117-3*) Elliots Bks.
— Historia de la Pintura. 3rd ed. (Illus.). 408p. (SPA.). 1993. 100.00 (*84-249-3119-X*) Elliots Bks.
— Historia Del Arte, 2 vols. 6th ed. (Illus.). 1410p. (SPA.). 1993. pap. 200.00 (*84-249-1022-2*) Elliots Bks.
Martin, Gotfried. Arithmetic & Combinatorics: Kant & His Contemporaries. Wubnig, Judy, ed. & tr. by. LC 84-5476. (Philosophical Explorations Ser.). 272p. 1985. text ed. 29.95 (*0-8093-1184-4*) S Ill U Pr.
Martin, Gottfried. Arithmetik und Kombinatorik bei Kant. 148p. (GER.). (C). 1972. 70.00 (*3-11-003593-6*) De Gruyter.
— Kant's Metaphysics & Theory of Science. Lucas, P. G., tr. LC 73-15053. 218p. 1974. reprint ed. text ed. 55.00 (*0-8371-7154-7*, MAKM, Greenwood Pr) Greenwood.
— Platons Ideenlehre. LC 72-81562. (C). 1973. 89.25 (*3-11-004135-9*) De Gruyter.
Martin, Gottfried & Loewisch, Dieter-Juergen, eds. Sachindex zu Kants Kritik der reinen Vernunft. (C). 1967. 29.25 (*3-11-005179-6*) De Gruyter.
Martin, Grace B. An Oregon Schoolma'am: From Rimrocks to Tidelands. (Illus.). 144p. 1981. pap. 7.95 (*0-934784-25-6*) Calapooia Pubns.
— Oregon Schoolma'am, Bk. 2: The Depression Years. (Illus.). 200p. pap. 7.95 (*0-934784-26-4*) Calapooia Pubns.
Martin, Graham. The Architecture of Experience. 201p. 1981. 25.00 (*0-85224-409-6*, Pub. by Edinburgh U Pr UK) Col U Pr.
— Birds by Night. (Illus.). 227p. 1990. text ed. 39.95 (*0-85661-059-3*, 784659, Pub. by Poyser UK) Acad Pr.
— Great Expectations. (Open Guides to Literature Ser.). 1985. 75.00 (*0-335-15089-6*, Open Univ Pr); pap. 22.00 (*0-335-15080-2*, Open Univ Pr) Taylor & Francis.
Martin, Graham, ed. see Hammond, Brean.
Martin, Graham, jt. auth. see Jefferson, Douglas.
Martin, Grant. The Hyperactive Child. (Orig.). 1992. pap. 9.99 (*0-89693-068-8*, Victor Books) SP Pubns.
— RCC, Vol. 6: Counseling in Cases of Family Violence & Abuse. 281p. 1987. write for info. (*0-8499-0587-7*) Word Inc.
— When Good Things Become Addictions. 192p. 1991. pap. 1.80 (*0-89693-933-2*) SP Pubns.
Martin, Grant L. Critical Problems in Children & Youth. (Contemporary Christian Counseling Ser.: Vol. 5). 1992. 15.99 (*0-8499-0886-8*) Word Inc.
Martin, Gregorio C., ed. Selected Proceedings of the Mountain Interstate Foreign Conference, 32nd. 415p. (Orig.). 1984. pap. text ed. write for info. (*0-918401-00-3*) U Wake Forest.
Martin, Gregory. Flemish School, 1600-1900. (National Gallery Publications). (Illus.). 1991. pap. 25.00 (*0-300-06140-4*) Yale U Pr.
***Martin, Guy & Laffort, Paul, eds.** Odors & Deodorization in the Environment. LC 94-5422. 1994. write for info. (*1-56081-666-X*) VCH Pubs.
Martin, H. J. Notices Genealogical & Historical of the Martin Family of New England, Who Settled at Weymouth & Hingham in 1635, with Some Account of Their Descendants. 358p. 1989. reprint ed. lib. bdg. 61.50 (*0-8328-0858-X*); reprint ed. pap. 53.50 (*0-8328-0859-8*) Higginson Bk Co.
Martin, H. R., jt. auth. see McCloy, Donaldson.
Martin, Hal. Even You Can Cook Book: Let's Start with Breakfast Go for Lunch Fine Dining Outdoor Cooking What to Do with Left Overs Banquets & Parties Hal Does Italian. 33p. (Orig.). 1988. write for info. (*0-318-64551-3*) Hal Martin.
Martin, Hans C., ed. Acidic Precipitation. 1987. lib. bdg. 411.50 (*1-55608-021-2*) Kluwer Ac.
Martin, Harold C. One Thousand Practical Show Card Layouts. 240p. 1984. reprint ed. 17.00 (*0-911380-64-7*) ST Pubns.
Martin, Harold H. Atlanta & Environs: A Chronicle of Its People & Events, Vol. 3: Years of Change & Challenge, 1940s-1970s. LC 86-16158. (Illus.). 632p. 1987. 39.95 (*0-8203-0913-3*) U of Ga Pr.
— Georgia. (States & the Nation Ser.). (Illus.). 1977. 14.95 (*0-393-05606-6*) Norton.
— William Berry Hartsfield: Mayor of Atlanta. LC 78-1550. (Illus.). 248p. 1978. 13.95 (*0-87797-115-3*) Cherokee.
Martin, Harold H., jt. ed. see O'Brien, Robert.
Martin, Harry. Farm Exports: What's Happening to Our Foreign Markets. (Illus.). 168p. (Orig.). 1983. pap. 3.95 (*0-9611416-0-3*) RRN Bks.
Martin, Harry, jt. auth. see Modlin, Dan.
Martin, Heather C. W. B. Yeats: Metaphysician As Dramatist. 136p. (C). 1986. text ed. 28.50 (*0-88920-192-7*, Pub. by Wilfrid Laurier CN) Humanities.
Martin, Helen R. Barnabetta. 1993. reprint ed. lib. bdg. 89.00 (*0-7812-5490-6*) Rprt Serv.
— Betrothal of Elypholate, & Other Tales of the Pennsylvania Dutch. LC 76-128739. (Short Story Index Reprint Ser.). (Illus.). 1977. 19.95 (*0-8369-3630-2*) Ayer.
— Yoked with a Lamb, & Other Stories. LC 76-152948. (Short Story Index Reprint Ser.). 1977. reprint ed. 21.95 (*0-8369-3807-0*) Ayer.
Martin, Helena F. On Some of Shakespeare's Female Characters. 5th ed. LC 75-111773. reprint ed. 49.50 (*0-404-04194-9*) AMS Pr.

M

Martin, Helene & Pelletier, Claire. Vocabulary of the Telephone. 39p. (ENG & FRE.). 1984. pap. 14.95 (*0-8288-9402-7*) Fr & Eur.

Martin, Helmut & Kinkley, Jeffrey, eds. Modern Chinese Writers: Self-Portrayals. LC 91-31578. (Studies on Modern China). 424p. 1992. 57.95 (*0-87332-816-7*); pap. text ed. 22.95 (*0-87332-817-5*) M E Sharpe.

***Martin, Henri-Jean.** The History & Power of Writing. (Illus.). 608p. 1995. pap. 18.95x (*0-226-50836-6*) U Ch Pr.

— Print, Power, & People in Seventeenth Century France. Gerard, David, tr. LC 91-39016. (Illus.). 758p. 1993. reprint ed. 82.50 (*0-8108-2477-9*) Scarecrow.

Martin, Henri-Jean, jt. auth. see Febvre, Lucien.

Martin, Henry. Enjoying Jazz. (Illus.). 300p. (Orig.). 1986. pap. 24.00 (*0-02-873130-1*) Schirmer Bks.

Martin, Henry, illus. World's Best Limericks. (Gift Editions Ser.). 64p. 1994. 7.99 (*0-88088-681-1*) Peter Pauper.

Martin, Henry, jt. auth. see Baruchello, Gianfranco.

Martin, Henry, jt. auth. see Glanvill, John.

Martin, Henry, tr. see Manganelli, Giorgio.

Martin, Henry, tr. see Ortese, Anna M.

Martin, Henry B. The Polynesian Journal of Henry Byam Martin. Dodd, Edward, ed. (Illus.). 200p. 1981. 16.95 (*0-87577-060-6*, Peabody Museum) Peabody Essex Mus.

Martin, Herbert W. The Forms of Silence. LC 79-88742. 61p. 1980. per. 4.00 (*0-916418-20-0*) Lotus.

Martin, Holger. Heat Exchangers. rev. ed. 160p. 1992. 49.50 (*1-56032-119-9*) Hemisp Pub.

Martin, Howard N. Myths & Folktales of the Alabama-Coushatta Indians. (Illus.). 1976. 20.00 (*0-88426-052-6*) Encino Pr.

***Martin, Hugh.** The Design of Hydraulic Components & Systems. LC 94-41388. (Fluid Power Technology Ser.). 1995. pap. write for info. (*0-13-297194-1*) Tavistock-E Horwood.

— Great Christian Books. LC 71-142666. (Essay Index Reprint Ser.). 1977. reprint ed. 16.95 (*0-8369-2242-5*) Ayer.

— Shadow of Calvary. 1983. pap. 8.95 (*0-85151-373-5*) Banner of Truth.

— Simon Peter. 1984. pap. 8.95 (*0-85151-427-8*) Banner of Truth.

Martin, Hugh, ed. Christian Social Reformers of the Nineteenth Century. LC 70-107725. (Essay Index Reprint Ser.). 1977. 20.95 (*0-8369-1526-7*) Ayer.

Martin, Hugh, ed. see Bernard de Clairvaux.

Martin, I. & Levey, A. B. Genesis of the Classical Conditioned Response. 164p. 1969. 70.00 (*0-08-013360-6*, Pub. by Pergamon Repr UK) Franklin.

Martin, I., jt. ed. see Eysenck, Hans J.

Martin, Ian, jt. auth. see Allen, Garth.

Martin, Ian, jt. auth. see Dummett, Ann.

Martin, Ian, jt. auth. see Grant, Lawrence.

Martin, Ian J. Accounting & Control in the Foreign Exchange Market. 2nd ed. 336p. 1993. boxed 130.00 (*0-406-01362-4*, UK) Butterworth Legal Pubs.

Martin, Ilse, ed. see Smith, George M.

Martin, Ilse, tr. see Wust, Klaus, ed.

Martin, Ilse, tr. see Wust, Klaus, et al, eds.

Martin, Inge, tr. see Groddeck, Marie.

Martin, Irene. Emerald Thorn. 300p. (Orig.). 1991. pap. 11.95 (*1-879366-20-7*) Hearthstone OK.

— Legacy & Testament: The Story of Columbia River Gillnetters. (Illus.). 224p. (Orig.). 1994. pap. 19.95 (*0-87422-109-9*) Wash St U Pr.

— Twentieth-Century Russian & East European Painting: The Thyssen-Bornemisza Collection. (Illus.). 1993. 175.00 (*0-302-00619-2*, Pub. by Zwemmer Bks UK) Sothebys Pubns.

Martin, Irene & Venables, Peter H., eds. Techniques in Psychophysiology. LC 79-42925. (Illus.). 711p. reprint ed. pap. 180.00 (*0-685-23760-5*, 2032834) Bks Demand.

Martin, Irene, jt. auth. see Boskovits, Miklos.

Martin, Irene, ed. see Vergo, Peter.

Martin, Isabella, ed. see Chesnut, Mary B.

Martin, J. General Relativity. 1995. pap. text ed. 35.00 (*0-13-291196-5*) P-H.

Martin, J. & Trowbridge, T., eds. Platelet Heterogeneity. (Illus.). 286p. 1990. 148.00 (*0-387-19602-1*) Spr-Verlag.

Martin, J. A. Voice, Speech, & Language in the Child: Development & Disorder. (Disorders of Human Communication Ser.: Vol. 4). (Illus.). 230p. 1981. 49.00 (*0-387-81629-1*) Spr-Verlag.

Martin, J. Campbell. The Successful Engineer: Personal & Professional Skills - A Sourcebook. LC 92-30123. 1993. text ed. write for info. (*0-07-040725-8*) McGraw.

Martin, J. Colby, jt. auth. see Lee, Ronald R.

Martin, J. F., ed. Signal Processing - A First Introduction. 272p. (C). 1990. pap. text ed. 130.00 (*0-273-03256-9*, Pub. by Pitman Pubng UK) St Mut.

Martin, J. G. Sharing Music: An Introductory Guide to Music Education. (Academic Ser.). 260p. (C). 1987. pap. 16.95 (*0-910075-06-9*) Hardin-Simmons.

Martin, J. J. Bayesian Decision Problems & Makrov Chains. LC 74-32489. 216p. 1975. reprint ed. 21.50 (*0-88275-277-4*) Krieger.

Martin, J. L. Basic Quantum Mechanics. (Oxford Physics Ser.). (Illus.). 1982. pap. 29.95 (*0-19-851816-1*) OUP.

Martin, J. L., et al, eds. Ultrafast Phenomena Eight: Proceedings of the Eight International Conference, Antibes Juan-les-Pins, France, June 8-12, 1992. LC 93-12330. (Chemical Physics Ser.: Vol. 55). 1993. Alk. paper. 99.00 (*0-387-56475-6*) Spr-Verlag.

Martin, J. M., jt. ed. see Lasserre, P.

Martin, J. M., jt. ed. see Mantoura, R. F.

Martin, J. Malcolm. Herrenrasse. LC 93-85730. 351p. 1993. 22.50 (*0-945319-01-0*) Spes Deo Pubns.

Martin, J. Michael. Life after CD's: How to Double the Return on Your Savings with Government-Backed Safety. (Illus.). 320p. (Orig.). 1993. pap. 19.95 (*0-7931-0609-5*, 5608-80) Fin Advantage.

***Martin, J. Michael & Martin, Mary E.** The Bill Payer by Homefile: Monthly Bill Organizer. Martin, Mary E., ed. (Financial Advantage Ser.). (Illus.). 96p. (Orig.). 1995. pap. 19.95 (*0-9628718-5-0*) Fin Advantage.

— Financial Planning Organizer by Homefile: A Complete Home Filing System. (Financial Advantage Ser.). (Illus.). 71p. 1995. reprint ed. pap. 19.95 (*0-9628718-4-2*) Fin Advantage.

— Home Filing Made Easy. (Illus.). 140p. (Orig.). 1993. pap. 15.95 (*0-7931-0610-9*, 560879) Fin Advantage.

— Homefile: A Complete Home Filing System. (HOMEFILE Home Management Ser.). (Illus.). 71p. (Orig.). 1990. pap. 29.95 (*0-9628718-1-8*) Fin Advantage.

Martin, J. Michael & Martin, Mary E., eds. Financial Planning Organizer Kit by HOMEFILE. rev. ed. (HOMEFILE Home Management Ser.). (Illus.). 61p. 1992. pap. 19.95 (*0-9628718-3-4*) Fin Advantage.

— Homefile: A Complete Home Management System. rev. ed. (HOMEFILE Home Management Ser.). (Illus.). 61p. 1991. pap. 19.95 (*0-9628718-2-6*) Fin Advantage.

Martin, J. Michael, jt. auth. see Martin, Mary E.

Martin, J. Peter. Adirondack Golf Courses: Past & Present. 2nd ed. (Illus.). 112p. 1987. reprint ed. pap. text ed. 14.95 (*0-685-48039-9*) Adirondack Golf.

— Adirondack Golf Courses Past & Present. 112p. (Orig.). 1987. pap. text ed. 14.95 (*0-9618820-0-X*) Adirondack Golf.

— Adirondack Golf Courses...Past & Present. (Illus.). 112p. (Orig.). 1987. pap. 14.95 (*0-685-19312-8*) Adirondack Golf.

Martin, J. R. English Text: System & Structure. LC 92-19652. xiv, 620p. 1992. 133.00x (*1-55619-115-4*); pap. 34.95 (*1-55619-485-4*) Benjamins North Am.

— Factual Writing: Exploring & Challenging Social Reality. 101p. (C). 1985. pap. 50.00x (*0-7300-0345-0*, ECS806, Pub. by Deakin Univ AT) St Mut.

Martin, J. R., jt. auth. see Halliday, M. A.

Martin, J. R., jt. ed. see Smith, M. E.

Martin, J. W. Religious Radicals in Tudor England. 256p. 1989. text ed. 55.00 (*1-85285-006-X*) Hambledon Press.

— Strong Materials. (Wykeham Science Ser.: No. 21). 124p. 1972. pap. 18.00 (*0-85109-260-8*) Taylor & Francis.

Martin, J. W. & Hull, R. A. Elementary Science of Metals. LC 73-75479. (Wykeham Science Ser.: No. 1). 148p. (C). 1974. 18.00 (*0-8448-1103-3*, Crane Russak) Taylor & Francis.

— Strong Materials. LC 72-189452. (Wykeham Science Ser.: No. 21). 124p. (C). 1972. 18.00 (*0-8448-1123-8*, Crane Russak) Taylor & Francis.

Martin, Jack. Border Boss: Captain John R. Hughes, Texas Ranger. limited ed. LC 89-48043. (Illus.). 252p. 1990. reprint ed. 60.00 (*0-938349-51-1*) State House Pr.

— Border Boss: Captain John R. Hughes, Texas Ranger. LC 89-48043. (Illus.). 252p. 1990. reprint ed. 21.95 (*0-938349-49-X*); reprint ed. pap. 14.95 (*0-938349-50-3*) State House Pr.

— The Construction & Understanding of Psychotherapeutic Change: Conversations, Memories, & Theories. LC 93-44505. (Counseling & Development Ser.). 160p. (C). 1994. text ed. 35.00 (*0-8077-3337-7*); pap. 18.95 (*0-8077-3336-9*) Tchrs Coll.

— Halloween II. (Orig.). 1987. pap. 2.95 (*0-8217-1080-X*) Zebra.

— Videodrome. pap. 2.95 (*0-8217-1166-0*) Zebra.

Martin, Jack & Hiebert, Bryan A. Instructional Counseling: A Method for Counselors. LC 84-19647. (Illus.). 232p. (C). 1985. 49.95 (*0-8229-3506-6*); pap. 19.95 (*0-8229-5367-6*) U of Pittsburgh Pr.

***Martin, Jack & Martin, Wyn.** Personal Development: Self-Instruction for Personal Agency. 200p. (Orig.). 1983. pap. 14.95 (*0-920490-29-8*) Temeron Bks.

***Martin, Jack & Sugarman, Jeff.** Models of Classroom Management: Principles, Applications, & Critical Perspectives. 184p. (Orig.). (C). 1993. pap. text ed. 19.95x (*1-55059-063-4*) Temeron Bks.

Martin, Jack, jt. auth. see Hoshmand, Lisa.

Martin, Jacky, jt. auth. see Harding, Wendy.

Martin, Jacqueline. The Voice of Modern Theatre. (Illus.). 256p. 1991. 54.00 (*0-415-01256-2*, A4858); pap. 17.95 (*0-415-04894-X*, A4862) Routledge.

Martin, Jacqueline, jt. auth. see Hewson, Lance.

Martin, Jacqueline B. Birdwashing Song: The Willow Tree Loon. LC 94-11787. (J). 1995. text ed. 15.95 (*0-02-762442-0*) Macmillan.

— Bizzy Bones & the Lost Quilt. LC 87-13577. (Illus.). (J). (ps-3). 1988. 16.00 (*0-688-07407-3*); lib. bdg. 12.88 (*0-688-07408-1*) Lothrop.

— Good Times on Grandfather Mountain. LC 91-17058. (Illus.). 32p. (J). (ps-1). 1992. 14.95 (*0-531-05977-4*); lib. bdg. 14.99 (*0-531-08577-5*) Orchard Bks Watts.

***Martin, Jacqueline Briggs.** Grandmother Bryant's Pocket. LC 94-31309. (Illus.). 1995. write for info. (*0-395-68984-8*) Ticknor & Flds Bks Yng Read.

Martin, Jacqueline M. The Second Street Gardens & the Green Truck Almanac. LC 94-10869. (Illus.). (J). 1995. text ed. 15.95 (*0-02-762460-9*, Four Winds Pr) S&S Childrens.

Martin, Jaime. Diccionario de Expresiones Malsonantes del Espanol. 2nd ed. 370p. (SPA.). 1974. pap. 17.95 (*0-8288-5978-7*, S31400) Fr & Eur.

Martin, James. Bobby. (C). 1990. pap. 24.00 (*0-85305-304-9*, Pub. by J Arthur Ltd UK) St Mut.

— A Breakthrough in Making Computers Friendly: The Macintosh Computer. write for info. (*0-318-59634-2*) S&S Trade.

— Ceaseless Talk, Which Never Stops, of Auschwitz from Our Bliss. (Illus.). 1978. pap. 1.50 (*0-914278-21-5*) Copper Beech.

— Chameleons: Dragons in the Trees. LC 91-8736. (Illus.). 36p. (J). (gr. 1-5). 1991. 13.00 (*0-517-58388-7*); lib. bdg. 13.99 (*0-517-58389-5*) Crown Bks Yng Read.

— Client Server Application Development. 400p. 1993. text ed. 48.00 (*0-13-138397-3*) P-H.

— Database Analysis & Design. 1989. 50.00 (*0-13-199688-6*) P-H.

— DB2: Concepts, Design, & Programming. 400p. 1989. text ed. 77.00 (*0-13-198581-7*) P-H.

— Design of Man-Computer Dialogues. (Illus.). 496p. 1973. pap. text ed. 60.00 (*0-13-201251-0*) P-H.

— Fourth Generation Languages, Vol. I. (Illus.). 432p. 1985. text ed. 64.00 (*0-13-329673-3*) P-H.

— Great White Sharks: The Ocean's Most Deadly Killers. (Animals & the Environment Ser.). 48p. (J). (gr. 3-4). 1994. lib. bdg. 13.35 (*1-56065-241-1*) Capstone Pr.

— Hiding Out: Camouflage in the Wild. LC 92-38211. (Illus.). 32p. (J). (gr. 2-6). 1993. 13.00 (*0-517-59392-0*); lib. bdg. 13.99 (*0-517-59393-9*) Crown Bks Yng Read.

— Hyperdocuments & How to Create Them. 224p. 1989. pap. 24.95 (*0-13-447905-X*) P-H.

— Information Engineering, Vol. I. 1989. text ed. 74.67 (*0-13-464462-X*) P-H.

— Information Engineering, Vol. II. 1989. text ed. 77.33 (*0-13-464885-4*) P-H.

— Information Engineering, Bk. III: Design. 1990. text ed. 80.00 (*0-13-465501-X*) P-H.

— An Information Systems Manifesto. (Illus.). 352p. (C). 1984. text ed. 92.00 (*0-13-464769-6*) P-H.

— It's My Belief. 96p. (C). 1989. pap. 40.00 (*0-685-60684-8*, Pub. by St Andrew UK) St Mut.

— It's My Belief. 96p. 1993. pap. 22.00 (*0-7152-0648-6*, Pub. by St Andrew UK) St Mut.

— Komodo Dragons: Giant Lizards of Indonesia. (Animals & the Environment Ser.). 48p. (J). (gr. 3-4). 1994. lib. bdg. 13.35 (*1-56065-238-1*) Capstone Pr.

— Lemurs & Other Animals of the Madagascar Rain Forest. (Animals & the Environment Ser.). 48p. (J). (gr. 3-4). 1994. lib. bdg. 13.35 (*1-56065-237-3*) Capstone Pr.

— Living Fossils. LC 94-7926. (J). 1995. write for info. (*0-517-59866-3*); lib. bdg. write for info. (*0-517-59867-1*) Crown Bks Yng Read.

— Managing the Data Base Environment. (Illus.). 752p. (C). 1983. text ed. 79.00 (*0-13-550582-8*) P-H.

— A Man's Life. LC 94-27683. 150p. 1995. pap. 5.95 (*0-9642188-9-5*) Four Seasns.

— Masters of Disguise: A Natural History of Chameleons. (Illus.). 192p. 1992. 24.95 (*0-8160-2618-1*) Facts on File.

— Non-Subscription to Texas Workers Comp: Lawyer's Edition. 110.00 (*0-685-52373-X*, B10) Sterling TX.

— Poisonous Lizards: Gila Monsters & Mexican Beaded Lizards. (Animals & the Environment Ser.). 48p. (J). (gr. 3-4). 1994. lib. bdg. 13.35 (*1-56065-240-3*) Capstone Pr.

— Principles of Data Base Management. (Illus.). 320p. 1976. Ref. Ed. text ed. 84.00 (*0-13-708917-1*) P-H.

— Rapid Application Development. 816p. (C). 1991. write for info. (*0-02-376775-8*) Macmillan.

— Recommended Diagramming Standards for Analysts & Programmers. (Illus.). 432p. 1986. text ed. 87.00 (*0-13-767377-9*) P-H.

— Reskilling the I.T. Professional. 1993. 29.99 (*0-9635336-0-6*) J Martin Insight.

— Reskilling the I.T. Professional. 300p. 1993. 35.95 (*0-13-090929-7*) P-H.

— A Reunion & Other Poems. 53p. 1975. pap. 3.50 (*0-914298-10-0*) Copper Beech.

— The Road to the Aisle. 1993. pap. 22.00 (*0-7152-0375-4*, Pub. by St Andrew UK) St Mut.

— The Spitting Cobras of Africa. (Animals & the Environment Ser.). 48p. (J). (gr. 3-4). 1994. lib. bdg. 13.35 (*1-56065-239-X*) Capstone Pr.

— Strategic Information Planning Methodologies. 2nd ed. 1989. text ed. 79.00 (*0-13-850538-1*) P-H.

— Systems Application Architecture: Common User Access. 1991. text ed. 74.00 (*0-13-785023-9*) P-H.

— Technology's Crucible. (Illus.). 192p. 1986. pap. 17.50 (*0-13-902024-1*) P-H.

— The Telematic Society: A Challenge for Tomorrow. (Illus.). 256p. (C). 1981. 35.95 (*0-13-902460-3*) P-H.

— Teleprocessing Network Organization. 1969. 38.00 (*0-13-902452-2*) P-H.

— Tentacles: Octopus, Squid, & Their Relatives. LC 92-22234. 32p. (J). (gr. 2-6). 1993. 14.00 (*0-517-59149-9*); lib. bdg. 14.99 (*0-517-59150-2*) Crown Bks Yng Read.

Martin, James, et al. VSAM: Services & Programming Techniques. (Illus.). 432p. (C). 1986. text ed. 79.00 (*0-13-944174-3*) P-H.

Martin, James, ed. It's My Belief. 96p. (C). 1991. pap. text ed. 39.00 (*86-15-30648-6*, Pub. by St Andrew UK) St Mut.

Martin, James & Chapman, Kathleen K. SNA: IBM's Networking Solution. (Illus.). 384p. 1987. text ed. 84.00 (*0-13-815143-1*) P-H.

Martin, James & Grant, Simon. Telecommunications & the Computer. 3rd ed. 640p. 1990. text ed. 65.00 (*0-13-902644-4*) P-H.

Martin, James & Keaveney, Timothy J. Readings & Cases in Labor Relations & Collective Bargaining. Allen, Robert, ed. LC 84-14484. 512p. 1985. teacher ed write for info. (*0-201-12354-1*); pap. text ed. 22.36 (*0-201-12353-3*) Addison-Wesley.

***Martin, James & Leben, Joe.** Client - Server Databases: Enterprise Computing. LC 95-10646. 1995. text ed. 48.00 (*0-13-305160-9*) P-H.

— DECnet Phase V: An OSI Implementation Networking. (Illus.). 572p. 1991. text ed. 49.95 (*1-55558-076-9*, EY-H882E-DP, Digital DEC) Buttrwrth-Heinemann.

— Network Application Support: Network Support Architecture for Open Systems. (Networking & Data Communications Ser.). (Illus.). 412p. 1993. pap. 34.95 (*1-55558-117-X*, EY-P950E-DP, Digital DEC) Buttrwrth-Heinemann.

— TCP/IP Networking: Architecture, Administration & Programming. 400p. 1994. text ed. 52.00 (*0-13-642232-2*) P-H.

Martin, James & McClure, Carma L. Action Diagrams: Clearly Structured Specifications, Programs & Procedures. 2nd ed. 176p. 1988. pap. text ed. 30.00 (*0-13-004268-4*) P-H.

— Diagramming Techniques for Analysts & Programmers. (Illus.). 416p. (C). 1984. text ed. 96.00 (*0-13-208794-4*) P-H.

— Software Maintenance: The Problems & Its Solutions. (Illus.). 512p. (C). 1983. text ed. 88.00 (*0-13-822361-0*) P-H.

— Structured Techniques: A Basis for CASE. rev. ed. (Illus.). 816p. (C). 1987. text ed. 89.00 (*0-13-854936-2*) P-H.

Martin, James & Norman, Adrian R. Computerized Society. (Automatic Computation Ser.). 1970. pap. text ed. 28.67 (*0-13-165977-4*) P-H.

Martin, James & Odell, James J. Object-Oriented Methods. 1994. text ed. 49.33 (*0-13-630856-2*) P-H.

— Principles of Object-Oriented Analysis & Design. 464p. 1992. text ed. 49.00 (*0-13-720871-5*) P-H.

Martin, James, jt. auth. see Arben Group, Inc. Staff.

Martin, James, jt. auth. see Arden Group Staff.

Martin, James, et al. Merging Colleges for Mutual Growth: A New Strategy for Academic Managers. LC 93-8380. 296p. (C). 1993. text ed. 35.95 (*0-8018-4666-8*) Johns Hopkins.

— Object-Oriented Analysis & Design. 400p. 1992. text ed. 55.00 (*0-13-630245-9*) P-H.

— SAA: Common Communications Support: Distributed Applications. 464p. 1991. text ed. 70.00 (*0-13-785908-2*) P-H.

— Systems Application Architecture: Common Programming Interface. LC 93-18129. 320p. 1993. text ed. 66.00 (*0-13-785916-3*) P-H.

Martin, James A., Jr. Beauty & Holiness: The Dialogue Between Aesthetics & Religion. (Illus.). 269p. 1990. text ed. 32.50 (*0-691-07357-0*) Princeton U Pr.

Martin, James A. Conflict of Law: Cases & Materials. 2nd ed. LC 83-82692. 720p. (C). 1984. 35.00 (*0-316-54856-1*) Little.

— Empirical Philosophies of Religion. LC 78-111850. (Essay Index Reprint Ser.). 1977. 19.95 (*0-8369-1618-2*) Ayer.

— Perspectives on Conflict of Laws: Choice of Law. 1980. 15.00 (*0-316-54853-7*) Little.

Martin, James A., jt. auth. see Landers, Jonathan M.

Martin, James A., Jr., jt. ed. see Wohlgelernter, Maurice.

Martin, James C., jt. auth. see Kennedy, Raoul D.

Martin, James C., jt. auth. see Martin, Robert S.

Martin, James D. Davidson's Introductory Hebrew Grammar. 224p. 1993. text ed. 29.95 (*0-567-09642-4*, Pub. by T & T Clark UK) Bks Intl VA.

Martin, James E. And Then You Die. 224p. 1993. mass mkt. 4.99 (*0-380-71696-8*) Avon.

— And Then You Die: A Novel. 1992. 18.00 (*0-688-11198-X*) Morrow.

— Ebbie's Newspaper Kite & Selected Stories. 1995. 9.95 (*0-8062-5303-7*) Carlton.

— A Fine & Private Place: A Gil Disbro Mystery. LC 93-41034. 1994. 23.00 (*0-688-11211-0*) Morrow.

— The Flip Side of Life. 256p. 1991. mass mkt. 3.99 (*0-380-71407-8*) Avon.

— The Mercy Trap. 256p. 1990. pap. 3.95 (*0-380-71041-2*) Avon.

— Towards a Theory of Text for Contrastive Rhetoric: An Introduction to Issues of Text for Students & Practitioners of Contrastive Rhetoric. LC 91-40824. (American University Studies: Linguistics: Ser. XIII, Vol. 19). 221p. (C). 1992. text ed. 38.95 (*0-8204-1855-2*) P Lang Pubs.

— Two-Tier Compensation Structures: Their Impact on Unions, Employers, & Employees. LC 89-48881. 280p. 1990. text ed. 25.00 (*0-88099-087-2*); pap. text ed. 15.00 (*0-88099-088-0*) W E Upjohn.

Martin, James G. Ancient Star. (Orig.). 1990. pap. 4.95 (*0-9627587-0-1*) Martin CA.

— The Tolerant Personality. LC 64-15881. (Wayne State University Studies - Sociology: No. 15). (Illus.). 182p. reprint ed. pap. 51.90 (*0-7837-3599-5*, 2043464) Bks Demand.

Martin, James H. A Computational Model of Metaphor Interpretation. (Perspectives in Artificial Intelligence Ser.: Vol. 8). 229p. 1990. text ed. 44.00 (*0-12-474730-2*) Acad Pr.

Martin, James J. An American Adventure in Bookburning in the Style of 1918. LC 89-3246. 1988. 8.50 (*0-87926-024-6*) R Myles.

— American Liberalism & World Politics, 1931-1941, 2 vol. set. 1963. 35.00 (*0-8159-5005-5*) Devin.

— Charles A. Beard: A Tribute. 1984. lib. bdg. 250.00 (*0-87700-602-4*) Revisionist Pr.

— The Man Who Invented Genocide: The Public Career & Consequences of Raphael Lemkin. LC 84-6682. 360p. 1984. 15.95 (*0-939484-14-5*); pap. 9.95 (*0-317-05144-X*) Inst Hist Rev.

— Men Against the State: The Expositors of Individualist Anarchism in America, 1827-1908. (Illus.). 1970. pap. 2.50 (*0-87926-006-8*) R Myles.

— Revisionist Viewpoints: Essays in a Dissident Historical Tradition. LC 75-187779. 1977. pap. 5.95 (*0-87926-008-4*) R Myles.

— The Saga of Hog Island & Other Essays in Inconvenient History. LC 76-62654. 1977. pap. 6.95 (*0-87926-021-1*) R Myles.

An Asterisk (*) at the beginning of an entry indicates that the title is appearing in BIP for the first time.

Martin, James J., ed. see Eltzbacher, Paul.
Martin, James J., jt. ed. see Liggio, Leonard P.
Martin, James J., ed. see Stirner, Max.
Martin, James K. In the Course of Human Events: An Interpretive Exploration of the American Revolution. LC 79-50878. (Illus.). 320p. (C). 1979. text ed. write for info. (*0-88295-794-5*); pap. text ed. write for info. (*0-88295-795-3*) Harlan Davidson.
— Men in Rebellion: Higher Governmental Leaders & the Coming of the American Revolution. LC 72-14142. 271p. reprint ed. pap. 77.30 (*0-7837-5675-5*, 2059102) Bks Demand.
Martin, James K., ed. The Human Dimensions of Nation Making: Essays on Colonial & Revolutionary America. LC 75-30821. 1976. 15.00 (*0-87020-158-1*) State Hist Soc Wis.
Martin, James K., intro. Ordinary Courage: The Life of Joseph Plumb Martin. 212p. (Orig.). (C). 1993. pap. text ed. 11.96 (*1-881089-12-6*) Brandywine Press.
Martin, James K. & Lender, Mark E. A Respectable Army: The Military Origins of the Republic, 1763-1789. Franklin, John H. & Eisenstadt, A. S., eds. LC 81-173990. (American History Ser.). (Illus.). 256p. (Orig.). (C). 1982. pap. text ed. write for info. (*0-88295-812-7*) Harlan Davidson.
Martin, James K. & Stubaus, Karen R. American Revolution: Whose Revolution? LC 76-18740. (American Problem Studies). 158p. 1981. reprint ed. pap. 10.50 (*0-88275-397-5*) Krieger.
Martin, James K., jt. auth. see Lender, Mark E.
Martin, James K., et al. America & Its People. 2nd ed. LC 92-18011. (C). 1993. 58.00 (*0-673-46363-X*) HarpCollege.
— America & Its People, 2 vols. 2nd ed. LC 92-28837. (C). 1995. Vol. 1, to 1877. 22.50 (*0-673-46781-3*); Vol. 2, from 1865. 22.50 (*0-673-46782-1*) HarpCollege.
— America & Its People, Vol. I. (C). 1988. text ed. 35.00 (*0-673-18302-5*); pap. text ed. 25.75 (*0-673-18315-7*) HarpCollege.
— America & Its People, Vol. II. (C). 1988. pap. text ed. 25.75 (*0-673-18316-5*) HarpCollege.
— A Concise History of America & Its People. LC 94-20138. (C). 1995. 30.00 (*0-673-46780-5*, HarpT) HarpC.
— A Concise History of America & Its People. 960p. 1995. reprint ed. pap. 30.00 (*1-886746-00-1*) Talman Pub.
Martin, James S. Scram: Relocating under a New Identity. LC 93-78605. 83p. (Orig.). 1993. pap. 12.00 (*1-55950-094-8*, 61138) Loompanics.
Martin, James T. Family Unit Method for Organizing Research & Publishing Genealogies. (Illus.). 74p. (Orig.). 1983. pap. write for info. (*0-9611862-0-8*) Martin Genealog.
Martin, James T., ed. Philosophies of Being & Mind: Ancient & Medieval. LC 91-27076. 1992. 50.00 (*0-88206-076-7*) Caravan Bks.
Martin, James W., et al. Surface Mining Equipment. LC 82-81951. (Illus.). 450p. 1982. 37.95 (*0-9609060-0-2*) Martin Consult.
Martin, Jan, ed. see Bulanda, Susan.
Martin, Jan, ed. see Gilbert, Ann.
Martin, Jan, ed. see Robinson, Jan.
Martin, Jane. Coup Clucks. 1984. pap. 4.75 (*0-8222-0245-X*) Dramatists Play.
— Jane Martin: Collected Works. 1995. pap. 14.95 (*1-880399-20-2*) Smith & Kraus.
— Screaming in the Wind. 1992. 14.95 (*0-533-09709-6*) Vantage.
Martin, Jane, ed. Milestones in Development: A Cumulative Index to Industrial Development, Site Selection Handbook & Related Publications Covering a Quarter-Century of Professional Contribution. 316p. 1981. 11.95 (*0-910436-16-9*) Conway Data.
Martin, Jane R. Changing the Educational Landscape: Philosophy, Women, & Curriculum. 256p. 1994. 49.95 (*0-415-90794-2*, B0660, Routledge NY); pap. 15.95 (*0-415-90795-0*, B0664, Routledge NY) Routledge.
— The Schoolhome: Rethinking Schools for Changing Families. 237p. (Orig.). (C). 1992. text ed. 24.95 (*0-674-79265-3*) HUP.
— The Schoolhome: Rethinking Schools for Changing Families. 248p. (Orig.). (C). 1995. pap. text ed. 14.95 (*0-674-79266-1*) HUP.
Martin, Jane R. & Marx, Patricia. Now Everybody Really Hates Me. LC 92-13075. (Illus.). 32p. (J). (ps-3). 1993. 14.95 (*0-06-021293-4*); lib. bdg. 14.89 (*0-06-021294-2*) HarpC Child Bks.
***Martin, Janet.** Medieval Russia, 980-1584. (Cambridge Medieval Textbooks Ser.). (Illus.). 336p. (C). 1995. write for info. (*0-521-36276-8*); pap. write for info. (*0-521-36832-4*) Cambridge U Pr.
Martin, Janet & Todnem, Allen. Cream & Bread. LC 84-60814. (Illus.). 124p. 1984. pap. 6.95 (*0-9613437-0-2*) Redbird Prods.
Martin, Janet L. Shirley Holmquist & Aunt Wilma, Who Dunit? Pearson, Eunice W., ed. (Illus.). 120p. (Orig.). 1988. pap. 7.95 (*0-9613437-2-9*, Martin Hse Pubns) Redbird Prods.
— Treasure of the Land of Darkness: The Fur Trade & Its Significance for Medieval Russia. (Illus.). 296p. 1987. 59.95 (*0-521-32019-4*) Cambridge U Pr.
***Martin, Janet L. & Nelson, Suzann J.** Cream Peas on Toast: Comfort Food for Norwegian Lutheran Farm Kids (& Others) (Illus.). 1994. 9.95 (*0-9613437-9-6*) Redbird Prods.
— They Glorified Mary: We Glorified Rice. 170p. 1994. pap. 6.95 (*0-9613437-4-5*) Redbird Prods.
— They Had Stores...We Had Chores. 274p. 1995. pap. 6.95 (*0-9613437-7-X*) Redbird Prods.
Martin, Janet L. & Todnem, Allen. Second Helpings of Cream & Bread. Pearson, Eunice W., ed. (Illus.). (Orig.). 1986. pap. 6.95 (*0-9613437-1-0*) Redbird Prods.
Martin, Janet M. Lessons from the Hill: The Legislative Journey of an Education Program. 222p. 1993. text ed. 35.00 (*0-312-10685-8*) St Martin.
— Lessons from the Hill: The Legislative Journey of an Education Program. 224p. 1993. pap. text ed. 10.50 (*0-312-07933-8*) St Martin.
Martin, Janice. Mostly Microwave. Toney, Kitty, ed. (Illus.). 130p. 1984. spiral bd. 6.50 (*0-9614072-0-4*) Mostly Micro.
Martin, Jay. Nathanael West: The Art of His Life. 435p. 1984. pap. 8.95 (*0-88184-030-0*) Carroll & Graf.
— Robert Lowell. LC 73-629878. (University of Minnesota Pamphlets on American Writers Ser.: No. 92). 48p. (Orig.). reprint ed. pap. 25.00 (*0-7837-2876-X*, 2057579) Bks Demand.
— Who Am I This Time? Uncovering the Fictive Personality. 1990. pap. 8.95 (*0-393-30634-8*) Norton.
Martin, Jean. Caribbean. 1990. 12.98 (*0-8317-1188-4*) Smithmark.
Martin, Jean-Baptiste. Dictionnaire du Francais Regional de Pilat. 280p. (FRE.). 1989. 59.95 (*0-8288-9486-8*) Fr & Eur.
Martin, Jean D. & Elmore, Robert C. Accounting Standards Complexity. 80p. 1994. 15.00 (*0-910586-99-3*) Finan Exec.
Martin, Jean-Hubert. Man Ray Photographs. (Illus.). 256p. 1991. reprint ed. pap. 29.95 (*0-500-27473-8*) Thames Hudson.
Martin, Jean L., et al, eds. The Sheldon Memorial Art Gallery Cookbook. LC 78-10588. (Illus.). 212p. 1978. pap. 13.95 (*0-9602018-1-5*) Nebraska Art.
Martin, Jeanne M., jt. auth. see Rona, Zoltan P.
Martin, Jeannette S., jt. auth. see Chaney, Lillian H.
Martin, JeanRead & Marx, Patricia. Now I Will Never Leave the Dinner Table. LC 94-3209. (Illus.). (J). (gr. 4 up). Date not set. 15.00 (*0-06-024794-0*); lib. bdg. 14.89 (*0-06-024795-9*) HarpC.
***Martin, Jeffery A.** The Complete Guide to Reiki. (Illus.). 236p. (Orig.). 1995. pap. 16.95 (*1-57242-578-4*) Integration Pr.
— The Complete Guide to Reiki. (Illus.). 112p. (Orig.). 1994. spiral bd., pap. 16.95 (*1-57242-592-X*) Integration Pr.
— The Complete Guide to Riki: Master Level Manual. (Illus.). 106p. (Orig.). 1995. pap. 14.95 (*1-57242-579-2*) Integration Pr.
— Reiki First Degree Manual. (Illus.). 78p. (Orig.). 1994. spiral bd., pap. 10.95 (*1-57242-594-6*) Integration Pr.
— Reiki Second Degree Manual. (Illus.). 73p. (Orig.). 1994. spiral bd., pap. 10.95 (*1-57242-586-5*) Integration Pr.
***Martin, Jeffery A., et al.** The Complete Guide to Reiki Vol. II: A Master's Toolbox. (Illus.). 124p. (Orig.). 1995. pap. 16.95 (*1-57242-258-0*) Integration Pr.
Martin, Jeffrey, jt. auth. see Stoops, Erik.
Martin, Jeffrey B. Ben Hecht: Hollywood Screenwriter. Kirkpatrick, Diane, ed. LC 84-16181. (Studies in Cinema: No. 27). 254p. reprint ed. 72.40 (*0-8357-1571-X*, 2070459) Bks Demand.
Martin, Jennifer. Open Summer. (Chapbook Series II: No. 4). 24p. 1980. pap. 2.50 (*1-880649-10-1*) Writ Ctr Pr.
***Martin, Jennifer & Dean, Rosemary.** The Angels Speak: Secrets from the Other Side. Gardner, Bud, ed. 332p. (Orig.). 1995. pap. 14.95 (*0-9646975-0-5*) Prairie Angel Pr.
Martin, Jerome. Carrot-Parrot. (J). (ps). 1991. pap. 9.95 (*0-671-69555-X*, S&S Bks Young Read) S&S Childrens.
— Mitten-Kitten. (J). (ps). 1991. pap. 9.95 (*0-671-69556-8*, S&S Bks Young Read) S&S Childrens.
Martin, Jerome L., ed. see Altug, Ziya & Hoffman, Janet L.
Martin, Jerry L. Henry L. Brunk & Brunk's Comedians, Tent Repoire Empire of the Southwest. LC 83-62703. 1984. 25.95 (*0-87972-268-1*); pap. 11.95 (*0-87972-269-X*) Bowling Green Univ.
Martin, Jim. A Bit of a Blue: The Life & Work of Frances Fuller Victor. LC 91-90607. (Illus.). 320p. (Orig.). 1992. pap. 14.95 (*0-9632066-0-5*) Deep Well Pub.
— Factual Writing: Exploring & Challenging Social Reality. (Language Education Ser.). 116p. 1989. pap. text ed. 12.95 (*0-19-437158-1*) OUP.
— Northern Man: The Victor. (Illus.). 256p. (Orig.). 1983. pap. 9.95 (*0-88839-979-0*) Hancock House.
— Palm Coast. (Illus.). 85p. (Orig.). 1991. pap. 8.00 (*0-918949-10-6*) Papier-Mache Press.
— Southwestern Cuisine. (Illus.). 64p. (Orig.). 1993. pap. 7.95 (*0-9624640-3-1*) Crow Canyon Archaeol.
— 1968 & Other Stories. 60p. 1984. pap. 6.00 (*1-878124-00-5*) Flatland.
Martin, Jo. Drugs & the Family. (Encyclopedia of Psychoactive Drugs Ser.: No. 2). (Illus.). 104p. (YA). (gr. 5 up). 1988. lib. bdg. 19.95 (*1-55546-220-0*); pap. 9.95 (*0-7910-0797-9*) Chelsea Hse.
***Martin, Joan.** Reading Quilts. Friedland, J. & Kessler, R., eds. (Novel-Ties Ser.). (J). (gr. k-3). 1992. student ed, pap. text ed. 20.95 (*0-88122-856-7*) Lrn Links.
— Urban Financial Stress: Why Cities Go Broke. LC 81-20659. 198p. 1982. text ed. 49.95 (*0-86569-084-7*, Auburn Hse) Greenwood.
Martin, Joan L., et al. Bowling. 7th ed. 128p. 1994. pap. write for info. (*0-697-12646-3*) Brown & Benchmark.
Martin, JoAnn, jt. auth. see Hutchins, Vickie L.
Martin, JoAnn, jt. auth. see Hutchins, Vickie.
Martin, Joanne. I Can Read Music (for Cello) 106p. 1991. pap. text ed. 12.95 (*0-87487-441-6*) Summy-Birchard.
— I Can Read Music (for Viola) 106p. 1991. pap. text ed. 12.95 (*0-87487-440-8*) Summy-Birchard.
— I Can Read Music (for Violin) 106p. 1991. pap. text ed. 12.95 (*0-87487-439-4*) Summy-Birchard.
Martin, Joanne, jt. auth. see Daniels, Stephen.
Martin, Joanne M. Cultures in Organizations: Three Perspectives. (Illus.). 256p. (C). 1992. pap. text ed. 19.95 (*0-19-507164-6*) OUP.
Martin, Joanne M. & Martin, Elmer P. The Helping Tradition in the Black Family & Community. LC 85-10511. 109p. 1985. pap. text ed. 16.95 (*0-87101-129-8*) Natl Assn Soc Wkrs.
Martin, Joanne M., jt. auth. see Martin, Elmer P.
Martin, Joanne M., jt. ed. see Nordstrom, Carolyn.
***Martin, Joe.** Mister Boffo Shrink Wrapped. (Illus.). 208p. 1995. pap. 10.95 (*0-8362-1777-2*) Andrews & McMeel.
Martin, Joe, tr. see Strindberg, August.
Martin, Joel. We Are Not Forgotten. 1992. mass mkt. 5.99 (*0-425-13288-9*) Berkley Pub.
Martin, Joel & Romanowski, Patricia. Our Children Forever: George Anderson's Message from Children on the Other Side. 336p. (Orig.). 1994. pap. 10.00 (*0-425-14138-1*, Berkley Trade) Berkley Pub.
— We Don't Die. 1989. mass mkt. 5.99 (*0-425-11451-1*) Berkley Pub.
Martin, Joel W. Sacred Revolt: The Muskogees' Struggle for a New World. (Illus.). 224p. 1993. pap. 14.00 (*0-8070-5403-8*) Beacon Pr.
— Screening the Sacred: Myth, Ritual, & Religion in Popular American Film. (C). 1995. pap. text ed. 17.95 (*0-8133-8830-9*) Westview.
***Martin, Joel W. & Ostwalt, Conrad E., Jr., eds.** Screening the Sacred: Religion, Myth & Ideology in Popular American Film. LC 94-40252. 1995. text ed. 55.00 (*0-8133-8829-5*) Westview.
Martin, Joel W., jt. auth. see Bauer, Raymond T.
Martin, John. Baroque. LC 76-12059. (Icon Editions Ser.). (Illus.). 288p. 1977. pap. text ed. 15.00i (*0-06-430077-3*, IN-77, Icon Edns) HarpC.
— Blessed Are the Addicts: The Spiritual Side of Alcoholism, Addiction & Recovery. 144p. 1991. 14.95 (*0-394-58401-5*, Villard Bks) Random.
— The Dance. LC 79-7776. (Dance Ser.). (Illus.). 1980. reprint ed. lib. bdg. 42.95 (*0-8369-9303-9*) Ayer.
— The Dance in Theory. LC 89-24192. 96p. 1989. pap. 12.95 (*0-916622-90-8*) Princeton Bk Co.
— Dictators & Democracies Today. LC 68-16953. (Essay Index Reprint Ser.). 1977. 19.95 (*0-8369-0680-2*) Ayer.
— Downing Street: The War Years. (Illus.). 200p. 1992. 39.95 (*0-7475-0838-0*, Pub. by Bloomsbury Pub Ltd UK) Trafalgar.
— In-Line Skating. LC 93-40644. (Action Sports Ser.). (J). (gr. 3-6). 1994. pap. 5.95 (*0-516-40202-1*) Childrens.
— In-Line Skating: Extreme Blading. (Action Sports Ser.). 48p. (J). (gr. 3-10). 1994. lib. bdg. 17.27 (*1-56065-202-0*) Capstone Pr.
— Jet Watercraft. (Cruisin' Ser.). 48p. (J). (gr. 3-10). 1994. lib. bdg. 17.27 (*1-56065-201-2*) Capstone Pr.
— Jet Watercraft. LC 93-45538. (Cruisin' Ser.). (J). (gr. 3-6). 1994. pap. 5.95 (*0-516-40201-3*) Childrens.
— Languages & the Theory of Computation. 672p. 1991. text ed. write for info. (*0-07-040659-6*) McGraw.
— Nara: A Cultural Guide to Japan's Ancient Capital. (Illus.). 208p. 1994. pap. 14.95 (*0-8048-1914-9*) C E Tuttle.
— Venice's Hidden Enemies: Italian Heretics in a Renaissance City. LC 92-19220. (Studies on the History of Society & Culture: Vol. 16). 1993. 42.50 (*0-520-07743-1*) U CA Pr.
— The World's Fastest Motorcycles. (Wheels Ser.). 48p. (J). (gr. 3-10). 1994. lib. bdg. 17.27 (*1-56065-208-X*) Capstone Pr.
— World's Fastest Motorcycles. (Wheels Ser.). (J). (gr. 3-6). 1994. pap. 5.95 (*0-516-40208-0*) Childrens.
— The World's Most Exotic Cars. (Wheels Ser.). 48p. (J). (gr. 3-10). 1994. lib. bdg. 17.27 (*1-56065-209-8*) Capstone Pr.
— World's Most Exotic Cars. (Wheels Ser.). (J). (gr. 3-6). 1994. pap. 5.95 (*0-516-40209-9*) Childrens.
Martin, John & Kensinger, John. New Realities for Stockholder-Management Relations. LC 94-70909. 100p. (Orig.). 1994. pap. text ed. 15.00 (*0-910586-91-8*) Finan Exec.
Martin, John, ed. see Bukowksi, Charles.
Martin, John, ed. see Bukowski, Charles.
Martin, John, jt. auth. see Kensinger, John.
Martin, John B. Call It North Country: The Story of Upper Michigan. LC 85-15923. (Great Lakes Bks.). (Illus.). 300p. 1986. reprint ed. pap. 14.95 (*0-8143-1869-X*) Wayne St U Pr.
— Indiana: An Interpretation. 352p. 1992. 29.95 (*0-253-33682-1*); pap. 12.95 (*0-253-20754-1*, MB-754) Ind U Pr.
— Indiana: An Interpretation. LC 72-5516. (Biography Index Reprint Ser.). 1977. reprint ed. 33.95 (*0-8369-8136-7*) Ayer.
Martin, John C. Labor Productivity Control: New Approaches for Industrial Engineers & Managers. LC 90-7449. 320p. 1990. text ed. 65.00 (*0-275-93663-5*, C3663, Praeger Pubs) Greenwood.
Martin, John C., ed. Nucleotide Analogues As Antiviral Agents. LC 89-15114. (Symposium Ser.: No. 401). (Illus.). xi, 175p. 1989. 44.95 (*0-8412-1659-2*) Am Chemical.
Martin, John D. Christopher Dock: Pioneer Schoolmaster on Skippack. 1971. pap. 3.85 (*0-87813-906-0*) Christian Light.
— Living Together on God's Earth. (Christian Day School Ser.). (J). (gr. 3). 1974. 16.25x (*0-87813-915-X*) Christian Light.
— Living Together on God's Earth. (Christian Day School Ser.). (J). (gr. 3). 1975. teacher ed 19.65 (*0-87813-910-9*) Christian Light.
Martin, John D. & Ferris, Frank D. I Can't Stop Crying: It's So Hard When Someone You Love Dies. 1992. pap. 7.95 (*1-55013-407-8*) U of Toronto Pr.
Martin, John D. & Kensinger, John W. Exploring the Controversy over Corporate Restructuring. LC 90-84429. 90p. (Orig.). 1990. pap. 12.00 (*0-910586-80-2*) Finan Exec.
Martin, John D. & Showalter, Lester E. Perspectives of Truth in Literature. (Christian Day School Ser.). (gr. 9). 1982. teacher ed 15.00 (*0-87813-922-2*) Christian Light.
— Perspectives of Truth in Literature. (Christian Day School Ser.). (YA). (gr. 9). 1983. 21.25x (*0-87813-921-4*) Christian Light.
Martin, John D., jt. auth. see Sanchack, A. J., Jr.
Martin, John D., II, et al. Basic Financial Management. 6th ed. 1008p. 1992. text ed. 66.00 (*0-13-059635-3*) P-H.
Martin, John D., et al. The Theory of Finance: Evidence & Applications. (Illus.). 656p. (C). 1988. text ed. 55.25 (*0-03-063854-2*) Dryden Pr.
Martin, John E., pref. Command Performance: The Art of Delivering Quality Service. LC 94-16423. (Harvard Business Review Book Ser.). 1994. 27.95 (*0-87584-562-2*) Harvard Busn.
Martin, John E., jt. ed. see Miller, William R.
Martin, John F. Profits in the Wilderness: Entrepreneurship & the Founding of New England Towns in the Seventeenth Century. LC 91-2945. xvi, 363p. (C). 1991. 37.50 (*0-8078-2001-6*); pap. 14.95 (*0-8078-4346-6*) U of NC Pr.
Martin, John G. It Began at Imphal: The Combat Cargo Story. (Illus.). 112p. 1988. pap. 18.95 (*0-89745-111-2*) Sunflower U Pr.
Martin, John H. A Day in the Life of a Ballet Dancer. LC 84-2424. (Day in the Life of...Ser.). (Illus.). 32p. (J). (gr. 4-8). 1985. lib. bdg. 11.79 (*0-8167-0089-3*); pap. text ed. 2.95 (*0-8167-0090-7*) Troll Assocs.
— A Day in the Life of a Carpenter. LC 84-2420. (Day in the Life of...Ser.). (Illus.). 32p. (J). (gr. 4-8). 1985. lib. bdg. 11.79 (*0-8167-0093-1*); pap. text ed. 2.95 (*0-8167-0094-X*) Troll Assocs.
— A Day in the Life of a High-Iron Worker. LC 84-2449. (Day in the Life of...Ser.). (Illus.). 32p. (J). (gr. 4-8). 1985. lib. bdg. 11.79 (*0-8167-0107-5*); pap. text ed. 2.95 (*0-8167-0108-3*) Troll Assocs.
— A Day in the Life of a Police Cadet. LC 84-2578. (Day in the Life of...Ser.). (Illus.). 32p. (J). (gr. 4-8). 1985. lib. bdg. 11.79 (*0-8167-0103-2*); pap. text ed. 2.95 (*0-8167-0104-0*) Troll Assocs.
— Historical Sketch of Bethlehem in Pennsylvania. LC 72-134382. reprint ed. 38.00 (*0-404-08479-6*) AMS Pr.
— Neuroanatomy: Text & Atlas. (Illus.). 483p. 1989. text ed. 49.50 (*0-8385-6691-X*, A6691-8) Appleton & Lange.
Martin, John H., ed. The Corning Flood: Museum Under Water. LC 77-73627. (Illus.). 72p. 1977. pap. 6.00 (*0-87290-063-0*) Corning.
Martin, John H., et al, eds. Journal of Glass Studies, Vol. 30. LC 59-12390. (Illus.). 190p. 1988. pap. 20.00 (*0-87290-030-4*) Corning.
Martin, John H. & Edwards, Charleen K., eds. Journal of Glass Studies, Vol. 25. LC 59-12390. (Illus.). 334p. 1983. pap. 30.00 (*0-87290-025-8*) Corning.
— Journal of Glass Studies, Vol. 27, 1985. LC 59-12390. (Illus.). 176p. 1985. pap. 20.00 (*0-87290-027-4*) Corning.
— Journal of Glass Studies, Vol. 26. LC 59-12390. (Illus.). 225p. 1984. pap. 20.00 (*0-87290-026-6*) Corning.
Martin, John H. & Friedberg, Ardy. Writing to Read. 224p. 1989. reprint ed. pap. 12.95 (*0-446-39051-8*) Warner Bks.
Martin, John H. & Martin, Phyllis G. Kyoto: A Cultural Guide. (Illus.). 280p. (Orig.). 1994. pap. 14.95 (*0-8048-1955-6*) C E Tuttle.
Martin, John H. & Price, Richard W., eds. Journal of Glass Studies, Vol. 28, 1986. LC 59-12390. (Illus.). 189p. 1986. pap. 20.00 (*0-87290-028-2*) Corning.
— Journal of Glass Studies, Vol. 29. LC 59-12390. (Illus.). 203p. (Orig.). 1987. pap. 20.00 (*0-87290-029-0*) Corning.
Martin, John H., jt. auth. see Irish, Michael W.
Martin, John J. Ruth Page: An Intimate Biography. LC 76-18427. (Dance Program Ser.: No. 4). (Illus.). 378p. reprint ed. pap. 107.80 (*0-7837-0981-1*, 2041288) Bks Demand.
Martin, John J., ed. see Schiller, Alexandra.
Martin, John L. Angel Food. LC 88-7978. 248p. 1989. 16.95 (*0-89407-092-4*) Strawberry Hill.
— Can We Control the Border? A Look at Recent Efforts in San Diego, El Paso & Nogales. (Illus.). 40p. (Orig.). 1995. pap. 6.95 (*1-881290-17-4*) Ctr Immigrat.
Martin, John L., jt. auth. see Bourier, Leon F.
Martin, John M. & Romano, Anne T. Multinational Crime: The Challenge of Terrorism, Espionage, Drug, & Arms Trafficking. (Studies in Crime, Law, & Justice: Vol. 9). (Illus.). 220p. 1992. 46.00 (*0-8039-4597-3*); pap. 19.95 (*0-8039-4598-1*) Sage.
Martin, John N. Elements of Formal Semantics. 1987. text ed. 105.00 (*0-12-474855-4*); pap. text ed. 52.00 (*0-12-474856-2*) Acad Pr.
Martin, John P., ed. Violence & the Family. LC 77-21846. 377p. reprint ed. pap. 107.50 (*0-8357-3110-3*, 2039366) Bks Demand.
Martin, John R. Divorce & Remarriage: A Perspective for Counseling. LC 73-18038. 144p. 1974. pap. 6.95 (*0-8361-1328-4*) Herald Pr.
— The Portrait of John Milton at Princeton. LC 61-14263. (Illus.). 42p. 1961. 15.00 (*0-87811-006-2*) Princeton Lib.
— Ventures in Discipleship. LC 84-19140. 304p. (Orig.). 1984. pap. 15.95 (*0-8361-3378-1*) Herald Pr.
Martin, John S., ed. see Hawthorne, Nathaniel.
Martin, John T. Positioning in Anesthesia & Surgery. 2nd ed. (Illus.). 368p. 1987. text ed. 64.95 (*0-03-012797-1*) Saunders.
Martin, John W. The Golden Age of French Cinema, Nineteen Twenty-Nine to Nineteen Thirty-Nine. (Filmmakers Ser.). 168p. 1983. lib. bdg. 23.95 (*0-8057-9292-9*, Twayne) Macmillan.

Martin, Jose M. Accounting Dictionary: Diccionario de Contabilidad. 4th ed. 270p. (SPA.). 1982. 29.95 (*0-8288-1289-6*, S50180) Fr & Eur.

— Diccionario de Contabilidad. 4th deluxe ed. (SPA.). 1982. 29.95 (*0-685-57710-4*, S-50180) Fr & Eur.

Martin, Josef. To Rise above Principle: The Memoirs of an Unreconstructed Dean. LC 87-27227. 200p. 1988. 24.95 (*0-252-01507-X*) U of Ill Pr.

Martin, Joseph. Chalk Talks on Alcohol. 1989. pap. 12.00 (*0-06-250593-9*) Harper SF.

Martin, Joseph B. & Barchas, Jack D., eds. Neuropeptides in Neurologic & Psychiatric Disease. (Association for Research in Nervous & Mental Disease Research Publications: Vol. 64). 382p. 1986. text ed. 110.00 (*0-88167-147-9*) Raven.

Martin, Joseph B. & Reichlin, Seymour. Clinical Neuroendocrinology. 2nd ed. LC 87-563. (Contemporary Neurology Ser.: No. 28). (Illus.). 759p. 1987. 79.00 (*0-8036-5886-9*) Davis Co.

Martin, Joseph B., ed. see Institute of Medicine, Committee on a National Neural Circuitry Database Staff.

Martin, Joseph B., jt. auth. see Tyler, Kenneth L.

Martin, Joseph F., ed. Foolish Wisdom: Stories, Activities, & Reflections from Ken Feit. LC 89-29108. 192p. (Orig.). (C). 1990. pap. 10.95 (*0-89390-174-1*) Resource Pubns.

Martin, Joseph H. & Steinberg, Eve P. Real Estate License Examinations: Salesperson & Broker. 4th ed. LC 93-4597. 1993. pap. 15.00 (*0-671-84835-6*) P-H Gen Ref & Trav.

Martin, Joseph P. Private Yankee Doodle. LC 67-29036. (Eyewitness Accounts of the American Revolution Ser., No. 1). 1980. reprint ed. 29.95 (*0-405-01137-7*) Ayer.

— Private Yankee Doodle. Scheer, George F., ed. 305p. 1979. reprint ed. pap. 2.25 (*0-915992-10-8*) Eastern Acorn.

— Yankee Doodle Boy. Scheer, George F., ed. (Illus.). (YA). (gr. 5 up). 1995. pap. 8.95 (*0-8234-1180-X*) Holiday.

— Yankee Doodle Boy: A Young Soldier's Adventures in the American Revolution Told by Himself. (American Biography Ser.). 190p. 1991. reprint ed. lib. bdg. 59.00 (*0-7812-8273-X*) Rprt Serv.

Martin, Joseph P., et al, eds. Hazardous & Industrial Waste: Proceedings of the 22nd Mid-Atlantic Industrial Waste Conference. 808p. 1990. 75.00 (*0-87762-781-9*) Technomic.

Martin, Joy R. Making Your Marriage Magnificent. (Joyful Living Ser.). 31p. 1983. pap. 2.00 (*0-912623-01-2*) Joyful Woman.

Martin, Joy R., jt. auth. see Handford, Elizabeth R.

Martin, Joyce L. Light Bright: A Bright Idea for Bright Minds in the Primary Grades. Mackellar, Thompson, ed. (Illus.). 212p. 1989. teacher ed 49.95 (*0-9621707-0-4*) Port Side Pub.

Martin, Juan. Hasta Que el Tiempo Estalle (Poesias) LC 86-81311. (Coleccion Espejo de Paciencia Ser.). 62p. (Orig.). (SPA.). 1987. pap. 9.00 (*0-89729-406-8*) Ediciones.

Martin, Judith. Dandelion. (Illus.). (Orig.). (J). (gr. 1-5). 1978. pap. 4.50 (*0-9606662-0-6*) Paper Bag.

— Everybody Everybody. (Illus.). 79p. 1987. pap. 4.50 (*0-526-67369-9*) Paper Bag.

— Gender-Related Behaviors of Children in Abusive Situations. LC 81-86006. 125p. (Orig.). 1983. pap. 16.95 (*0-88247-685-8*) R & E Pubs.

— I Won't Take a Bath. (Illus.). (Orig.). 1987. pap. write for info. (*0-318-62981-X*) Paper Bag.

— Miss Manner's Basics: Eat. Date not set. 10.00 (*0-517-88408-9*) Random.

— Miss Manners' Guide to Excruciatingly Correct Behavior. 1991. 12.98 (*0-88365-781-3*) Galahad Bks.

— Miss Manners' Guide to Excruciatingly Correct Behavior. 768p. 1988. pap. 16.99 (*0-446-38632-4*) Warner Bks.

— Miss Manners' Guide to Raising Perfect Children. 1993. 10.98 (*0-88365-838-0*) Galahad Bks.

— Miss Manner's Guide to the Turn of the Millenium. 1990. pap. 15.95 (*0-671-72228-X*) S&S Trade.

— Reasons to Be Cheerful. (Illus.). 80p. (J). (ps-4). 1985. pap. 4.50 (*0-9606662-1-4*) Paper Bag.

Martin, Judith & Ashwander, Donald. Christmas All over the Place. 22p. (Orig.). (J). (ps-12). 1977. 4.00 (*0-87602-113-5*) Anchorage.

— The Lost & Found Christmas. 14p. (Orig.). (J). (ps up). 1977. 4.00 (*0-87602-152-6*) Anchorage.

— The Runaway Presents. 16p. (Orig.). (J). (ps up). 1977. 4.00 (*0-87602-197-6*) Anchorage.

— Wiggle Worm's Surprise. 16p. (Orig.). (J). (ps up). 1977. 4.00 (*0-87602-218-2*) Anchorage.

Martin, Judith A., jt. auth. see Kadushin, Alfred.

Martin, Judy. Basic Airbrush Painting Techniques. (Illus.). 128p. (Orig.). 1994. pap. 19.95 (*0-89134-585-X*) North Light Bks.

— Color: How to See It & How to Use It. 1994. 19.98 (*0-7858-0053-0*) Bk Sales Inc.

— Complete Guide to Airbrushing Techniques & Materials. 1992. 14.98 (*1-55521-527-0*) Bk Sales Inc.

— The Complete Guide to Airbrushing Techniques & Materials. 1992. 14.98 (*0-685-60285-0*) Bk Sales Inc.

— Complete Guide to Calligraphy Techniques & Materials. 1993. 14.98 (*0-89009-675-9*) Bk Sales Inc.

— Designing with Type. (On the Spot Guide Ser.). (Illus.). 96p. 1994. 7.95 (*1-56970-506-2*, Nippan Pubns) Bks Nippan.

— The Encyclopedia of Colored Pencil Techniques. LC 92-53693. (Illus.). 192p. 1992. 24.95 (*1-56138-139-X*) Running Pr.

— Encyclopedia of Pastel Techniques. LC 91-51060. (Illus.). 192p. 1992. 24.95 (*1-56138-087-3*) Running Pr.

— The Encyclopedia of Printmaking Techniques. LC 93-83530. (Illus.). 176p. 1993. 24.95 (*1-56138-210-8*) Running Pr.

— High-Tech Illustration. (Illus.). 160p. 1989. 32.50 (*0-89134-311-3*, 30153) North Light Bks.

— Impressionism. LC 94-44415. (Art & Artists Ser.). 48p. (J). (gr. 6-10). 1995. 16.95 (*1-56847-355-9*) Thomson Lrning.

— Judy Martin's Ultimate Book of Quilt Block Patterns. LC 88-23700. (Illus.). 100p. (Orig.). 1988. pap. 15.95 (*0-929589-00-9*) Crosley-Griffith.

— 100 Keys to Great Acrylic Painting. (Illus.). 64p. 1995. 16.99 (*0-89134-694-5*) North Light Bks.

— Painting & Drawing. (First Guide Ser.). (Illus.). 96p. (J). (gr. 3-6). 1993. pap. 9.95 (*1-56294-709-5*) Millbrook Pr.

— Painting & Drawing. LC 92-18414. (First Guide Ser.). (Illus.). 96p. (J). (gr. 3-6). 1993. lib. bdg. 16.90 (*1-56294-203-4*) Millbrook Pr.

— Patchworkbook: Easy Lessons for Creative Quilt Design & Construction. (Illus.). 184p. 1994. reprint ed. pap. text ed. 7.95 (*0-486-27844-1*) Dover.

— The Rainbow Collection: Quilt Patterns for Rainbow Colors. 44p. (Orig.). 1987. pap. 10.95 (*0-9602970-2-2*) Leman Pubns.

— Scrap Quilts. LC 85-72392. (Illus.). 96p. (Orig.). 1985. pap. 12.95 (*0-9602970-9-X*) Leman Pubns.

— Scraps, Blocks & Quilts. (Illus.). 192p. (Orig.). 1990. pap. 19.95 (*0-929589-01-7*) Crosley-Griffith.

— Shining Star Quilts: Lone Star Variations. 144p. 1987. pap. 19.95 (*0-943721-00-8*) Leman Pubns.

— Sketching School. LC 91-25709. (Learn-As-You-Go Guides Ser.). (Illus.). 176p. 1992. 22.00 (*0-89577-405-4*, Random) RD Assn.

— Yes You Can! Make Stunning Quilts from Simple Patterns. (Illus.). 112p. (Orig.). 1992. pap. 15.95 (*0-929589-02-5*) Crosley-Griffith.

Martin, Judy & McCloskey, Marsha. Pieced Borders: The Complete Resource. (Illus.). 160p. (Orig.). 1994. pap. 21.95 (*0-929589-03-3*) Crosley-Griffith.

Martin, Judy & Strimbley, Miriam. Calligraphy Skills & Techniques. LC 94-15246. 1994. pap. 18.00 (*0-02-022655-1*) Macmillan.

Martin, Judy, jt. auth. see Leman, Bonnie.

Martin, Julia. Hellsgate. (Dark Conspiracy Ser.). 64p. (Orig.). (YA). 1992. pap. 10.00 (*1-55878-097-1*) Game Designers.

— Rotten to the Core. (Twenty-Three Hundred AD Ser.). (Illus.). 64p. (Orig.). (YA). 1990. pap. 8.00 (*1-55878-059-9*) Game Designers.

Martin, Julian. Francis Bacon, the State & the Reform of Natural Philosophy. (Illus.). 300p. (C). 1992. 64.95 (*0-521-38249-1*) Cambridge U Pr.

Martin, Juliet. A Puzzle. LC 93-18051. (J). 1994. write for info. (*0-383-03710-7*) SRA Schl Grp.

Martin, June H. Love's Fools: Aucassin, Troilus, Calisto & the Parody of the Courtly Lover. (Serie A: Monografias, XXI). 156p. (Orig.). (C). 1972. pap. 36.00 (*0-900411-33-3*, Pub. by Tamesis Bks Ltd UK) Boydell & Brewer.

***Martin, K. & Bastock, T. W., eds.** Waste Minimisation: A Chemist's Approach. 155p. 1994. 75.00 (*0-85186-585-2*, R6585) CRC Pr.

Martin, Kady. Let's Party. Martin, William, ed. (Illus.). 160p. (Orig.). 1986. pap. 7.95 (*0-942752-02-3*) C A M Co.

Martin, Karen. Healing the Forgotten Child: Support & Recovery for the Adult Children of Alcoholics (& Other Children of Dysfunctional Families) 60p. (Orig.). (C). 1989. student ed, pap. 79.95 (*0-9623925-0-2*) Resource Dynamics.

Martin, Karen, ed. Physical Therapy Practice in Educational Environments. 224p. 1990. ring bd. 65.00 (*0-912452-74-9*, P-67) Am Phys Therapy Assn.

Martin, Karen, jt. ed. see Martin, Don, Jr.

Martin, Kat. Bold Angel. 1994. mass mkt. 4.99 (*0-312-95303-8*) St Martin.

— Creole Fires. 1992. mass mkt. 4.99 (*0-440-20803-3*) Dell.

— Gypsy Lord. 1992. mass mkt. 4.99 (*0-312-92878-5*) St Martin.

— Lover's Gold. 1991. pap. 4.50 (*1-55773-505-0*) Diamond.

— Natchez Flame. 1994. mass mkt. 4.99 (*0-440-20805-X*) Dell.

— Savannah Heat. 1993. mass mkt. 4.99 (*0-440-20804-1*) Dell.

— Sweet Vengeance. 1993. mass mkt. 4.99 (*0-312-95095-0*) St Martin.

Martin, Kathy. Party Shakers. LC 82-21729. (Illus.). 47p. (J). (gr. k-8). 1982. pap. 3.95 (*0-942752-00-7*) C A M Co.

— Party Shakers. Martin, William, ed. (Illus.). 47p. 1982. pap. 3.95 (*0-942752-03-1*) C A M Co.

Martin, Kay, jt. auth. see Martin, Don.

Martin, Kellie S., et al. ACHIEV for Phonology: A Beginning Activity-Based Program for Phonological Remediation, 2 vols. (Illus.). (Orig.). (ps-2). 1990. Activities book, 260p.; Storybook 1, 193p.; Storybook 2, 200p. student ed, spiral bd. 49.95 (*1-55999-118-6*) LinguiSystems.

Martin, Kenneth R. Home Port - A History of the Navy Federal Credit Union. (Illus.). 136p. 1983. write for info. (*0-9610378-0-6*) Navy Fed Credit.

— Some Very Handsome Work: Scrimshaw at the Cape Cod National Seashore. (Illus.). 56p. (Orig.). 1991. pap. 6.95 (*0-915992-55-8*) Eastern Acorn.

— Whalemen's Paintings & Drawings: Selections from the Kendall Whaling Museum Collection. LC 81-50343. (Illus.). 172p. 1983. 30.00 (*0-87413-191-X*) Kendall Whaling.

— Whalemen's Paintings & Drawings: Selections from the Kendall Whaling Museum Collection. LC 81-50343. (Illus.). 176p. 1982. 30.00 (*0-685-07611-3*) U Delaware Pr.

Martin, Kenneth R. & Lipfert, Nathan R. Lobstering & the Maine Coast. LC 85-61988. (Illus.). 176p. 1985. 23.00 (*0-937410-03-9*); pap. 16.50 (*0-937410-04-7*) ME Maritime Mus.

Martin, Kenneth R. & Snow, Ralph L. Maine Odyssey: Good Times & Hard Times, Bath, 1936-1986. LC 88-61039. (Illus.). 320p. 1988. 30.00 (*0-9620401-0-X*) Patten Free Lib.

Martin, Kenneth R., ed. see Barnard, Edward C.

Martin, Kenneth R., jt. auth. see Thomas, P. R.

Martin, Kenneth R., jt. auth. see Thomas, Philip R.

Martin, Kenneth W., jt. auth. see Buckwald, Aaron.

Martin, Kerry, illus. The Little Mermaid: On Stage. LC 92-53439. (Tiny Changing Pictures Bks.). 10p. (J). (ps-00). 1993. 4.95 (*1-56282-375-2*) Disney Pr.

— The Little Mermaid Hunts for Treasure. LC 91-73811. (Surprise Lift-the-Flap Ser.). 18p. (J). (ps-1). 1992. 9.95 (*1-56282-146-6*) Disney Pr.

— One Hundred One Dalmatians Play Hide-&-Seek. LC 92-52972. (Surprise Life-the-Flap Ser.). 18p. (J). (ps-1). 1992. 9.95 (*1-56282-270-5*) Disney Pr.

Martin, Kerry & Marvin, Fred, illus. Disney's The Little Mermaid. (Little Nugget Bks.). 28p. (J). (ps). 1992. bds. write for info. (*0-307-12534-3*, 12534, Golden Pr) Western Pub.

Martin, Kerry & Wakeman, Diana, illus. Sleeping Beauty. LC 92-53435. (Pop-up Bk.). 12p. (J). (ps-00). 1993. 11.95 (*1-56282-369-8*) Disney Pr.

Martin, Kevin. Daniel & the Ivory Princess. LC 94-34556. (Illus.). 80p. (J). 1994. 14.95 (*0-942963-50-4*) Distinctive Pub.

Martin, Kimberly A., jt. auth. see Bertram, Dora R., Jr.

Martin, Kingsley. The Rise of French Liberal Thought: A Study of Political Ideas from Bayle to Condorcet. 2nd ed. Mayer, J. P., ed. LC 80-11662. xviii, 316p. 1980. reprint ed. text ed. 59.75 (*0-313-22368-8*, MARF, Greenwood Pr) Greenwood.

Martin, Knute, jt. auth. see Katz, Alfred H.

Martin, Kristine. Tried & True Art: Successful Projects for the Elementary Grades. LC 89-82079. (Illus.). 52p. 1990. pap. 6.95 (*0-9624597-8-X*) Aberdeen Pr.

***Martin-Kuri.** Living with Angels. Date not set. pap. write for info. (*0-345-39522-0*) Ballantine.

— Wisdom Book. Date not set. pap. write for info. (*0-345-39523-9*) Ballantine.

Martin, Kurt. Teaching of Development Economics. Knapp, John, ed. 238p. 1967. 30.00 (*0-7146-1014-3*, Pub. by F Cass Pubs UK) Intl Spec Bk.

Martin, Kurt, ed. Strategies of Economic Development: Readings in the Political Economy of Industrialization. LC 91-23306. 340p. 1991. text ed. 69.95 (*0-312-06800-X*) St Martin.

Martin, Kymberly & Martin, Dennis. Espresso Magic. 56p. 1989. pap. 5.95 (*0-9631850-0-4*) Shady Ln Ent.

Martin, L. Alligators. (Reptile Discovery Library). (Illus.). 24p. (J). (gr. k-5). 1989. lib. bdg. 11.94 (*0-86592-579-8*) Rourke Corp.

— Bird Eating Spiders. (Spider Discovery Library). (Illus.). 24p. (J). (gr. k-5). 1988. lib. bdg. 11.94 (*0-86592-966-1*) Rourke Corp.

— Black Widow Spiders. (Spider Discovery Library). (Illus.). 24p. (J). (gr. k-5). 1988. lib. bdg. 11.94 (*0-86592-965-3*) Rourke Corp.

— Chameleons. (Reptile Discovery Library). (Illus.). 24p. (J). (gr. k-5). 1989. lib. bdg. 11.94 (*0-86592-576-3*) Rourke Corp.

— Elephants. (Wildlife in Danger Ser.). (Illus.). 24p. (J). (gr. k-5). 1988. 8.95 (*0-685-58306-6*); lib. bdg. 11.94 (*0-86592-998-X*) Rourke Corp.

— Fishing Spiders. (Spider Discovery Library). (Illus.). 24p. (J). (gr. k-5). 1988. 8.95 (*0-685-58305-8*); lib. bdg. 11.94 (*0-86592-964-5*) Rourke Corp.

— Funnel Web Spiders. (Spider Discovery Library). (Illus.). 24p. (J). (gr. k-5). 1988. 8.95 (*0-685-58304-X*); lib. bdg. 11.94 (*0-86592-962-9*) Rourke Corp.

— Iguanas. (Reptile Discovery Library). (Illus.). 24p. (J). (gr. k-5). 1989. 8.95 (*0-685-58606-5*); lib. bdg. 11.94 (*0-86592-575-5*) Rourke Corp.

— Komodo Dragons. (Reptile Discovery Library). (Illus.). 24p. (J). (gr. k-5). 1989. 8.95 (*0-685-58604-9*); lib. bdg. 11.94 (*0-86592-574-7*) Rourke Corp.

— Lizards. (Reptile Discovery Library). (Illus.). 24p. (J). (gr. k-5). 1989. 8.95 (*0-685-58605-7*); lib. bdg. 11.94 (*0-86592-577-1*) Rourke Corp.

— Panda. (Wildlife in Danger Ser.). (Illus.). 24p. (J). (gr. k-5). 1988. lib. bdg. 11.94 (*0-86592-996-3*) Rourke Corp.

— The Probing Lance. (Illus.). 64p. 12.95 (*0-317-65041-6*) Pleasure Trove.

— Rhinoceros. (Wildlife in Danger Ser.). (Illus.). 24p. (J). (gr. k-5). 1988. lib. bdg. 11.94 (*0-86592-997-1*) Rourke Corp.

— Seals. (Wildlife in Danger Ser.). (Illus.). 24p. (J). (gr. k-5). 1988. lib. bdg. 11.94 (*0-86592-999-8*) Rourke Corp.

— Tarantulas. (Spider Discovery Library). (Illus.). 24p. (J). (gr. k-5). 1988. lib. bdg. 11.94 (*0-86592-967-X*); lib. bdg. 8.95 (*0-685-58302-3*) Rourke Corp.

— Tigers. (Wildlife in Danger Ser.). (Illus.). 24p. (J). (gr. k-5). 1988. lib. bdg. 11.94 (*0-86592-995-5*); lib. bdg. 8.95 (*0-685-58307-4*) Rourke Corp.

— Trapdoor Spiders. (Spider Discovery Library). (Illus.). 24p. (J). (gr. k-5). 1988. lib. bdg. 11.94 (*0-86592-963-7*); lib. bdg. 8.95 (*0-685-58303-1*) Rourke Corp.

— Turtles. (Reptile Discovery Library). (Illus.). 24p. (J). (gr. k-5). 1989. lib. bdg. 11.94 (*0-86592-578-X*); lib. bdg. 8.95 (*0-685-58607-3*) Rourke Corp.

— Whales. (Wildlife in Danger Ser.). (Illus.). 24p. (J). (gr. k-5). 1988. lib. bdg. 11.94 (*0-86592-988-2*); lib. bdg. 8.95 (*0-685-67679-X*) Rourke Corp.

Martin, L., jt. auth. see Berg, W.

Martin, L. C., ed. see Marlowe, Christopher.

Martin, L. C., jt. tr. see Martin, Dorothy.

Martin, L. Jay. Mojave Showdown. 256p. 1988. pap. 2.95 (*0-8217-2518-1*) Zebra.

— Tenkiller. 256p. 1988. pap. 2.95 (*0-8217-2415-0*) Zebra.

Martin, L. John. International Propaganda: Its Legal & Diplomatic Control. 11.25 (*0-8446-0788-6*) Peter Smith.

Martin, L. John & Hiebert, Ray E., eds. Current Issues in International Communication. 390p. (Orig.). (C). 1990. pap. text ed. 29.50 (*0-8013-0121-1*, 75785) Longman.

***Martin, L. Joyce.** Light in the Evening Time. 192p. 1995. pap. 6.99 (*1-56722-132-7*) Word Aflame.

Martin, L. L. Categorization & Differentiation. (Recent Research in Psychology Ser.). vii, 87p. 1985. pap. 30.00 (*0-387-96150-X*) Spr-Verlag.

Martin, L. R. & Gokcen, N. A. Thermodynamics, Solutions Manual. (Illus.). (C). 1978. pap. 8.95 (*0-918910-02-1*) Techscience Inc.

Martin, LaJoyce. Heart-Shaped Pieces. LC 90-22517. (Illus.). 160p. (Orig.). (YA). (gr. 9 up). 1991. pap. 6.99 (*0-932581-78-1*) Word Aflame.

— Love's Golden Wings. LC 87-17346. (Pioneer Trilogy Ser.). (Illus.). 256p. (Orig.). (YA). (gr. 7 up). 1987. pap. 6.99 (*0-932581-19-6*) Word Aflame.

— Love's Mended Wings. LC 86-33955. (Pioneer Trilogy Ser.: Bk. 2). (Illus.). 272p. (Orig.). 1987. pap. 6.99 (*0-932581-09-9*) Word Aflame.

— Love's Velvet Chains. LC 89-24983. (Illus.). 240p. (Orig.). 1989. pap. 6.99 (*0-932581-56-0*) Word Aflame.

— The Other Side of Jordan. LC 92-14091. 246p. (Orig.). 1992. pap. 6.99 (*0-932581-98-6*) Word Aflame.

— So Long the Night. 196p. (Orig.). (YA). 1995. pap. 6.99 (*1-56722-032-0*) Word Aflame.

— So Swift the Storm. LC 90-35201. (Illus.). 232p. (Orig.). 1990. pap. 6.99 (*0-932581-66-8*) Word Aflame.

— To Even the Score. LC 93-44338. 200p. (Orig.). 1994. pap. 6.99 (*1-56722-016-9*) Word Aflame.

— To Love a Bent Winged Angel. LC 86-7820. (Pioneer Trilogy Ser.: Bk. 1). (Illus.). 288p. (Orig.). 1986. pap. 6.99 (*0-912315-99-7*) Word Aflame.

— To Love a Runaway. LC 88-31620. 240p. (Orig.). 1989. pap. 6.99 (*0-932581-42-0*) Word Aflame.

— Two Scars Against One. LC 94-3763. 192p. (Orig.). 1995. pap. 6.99 (*1-56722-025-8*) Word Aflame.

— When Love Filled the Gap. LC 87-37241. 150p. (Orig.). 1988. pap. 6.99 (*0-932581-30-7*) Word Aflame.

— The Wooden Heart. LC 91-11965. 235p. (Orig.). 1991. pap. 6.99 (*0-932581-85-4*) Word Aflame.

Martin, Lance. Commandments for Relationships & Marriage. Cooper, Edythe, ed. (Illus.). 216p. 19.95 (*0-317-02260-1*) Pleasure Trove.

— The Healing Brain. 1978. 29.95 (*0-317-59098-7*); pap. 3.98 (*0-685-18300-9*) Pleasure Trove.

Martin, Lance & Aagre, Scott. Calligraphy & Related Ornamentation. (Illus.). 98p. (Orig.). 1982. lib. bdg. 12.95 (*0-317-57776-X*); pap. 5.95 (*0-685-18122-7*) Pleasure Trove.

Martin, Lance & Dicke, Robert, Jr. Calligraphy & Ornamental Lettering. Cooper, E., ed. (Illus.). 1979. 12.95 (*0-8024-9953-8*) Pleasure Trove.

Martin, Larry. Proven Profits from Pollution Prevention, Vol. II: Case Studies in Resource Conservation & Waste Reduction. White, Diana, ed. LC 85-82638. 130p. 1989. pap. text ed. 20.00 (*0-917582-40-3*) Inst Local Self Re.

Martin, Larry, jt. auth. see Rothschild, Bruce M.

Martin, Larry G. Youthful High School Noncompleters: Enhancing Opportunities for Employment & Education. 59p. 1987. 7.00 (*0-318-23415-7*, IN316) Ctr Educ Trng Employ.

Martin, Larry J. The Benicia Belle. large type ed. LC 92-32527. (General Ser.). 316p. 1993. 19.95 (*0-8161-5609-3*) G K Hall.

— The Devil's Bounty. large type ed. LC 92-18699. 342p. 1992. reprint ed. lib. bdg. 16.95 (*1-56054-480-5*) Thorndike Pr.

— Shadow of the Grizzly. 1994. pap. 3.99 (*0-553-56043-3*) Bantam.

— Shadow of the Grizzly. large type ed. LC 93-28535. 1993. 17.95 (*0-7862-0063-4*) Thorndike Pr.

— Write from History: Right from History. 131p. 1994. pap. 12.95 (*1-885339-06-2*) Buttonwillow.

Martin, Larry R., jt. auth. see Lewbel, George S.

Martin, Laura. Grandma's Garden. LC 90-61854. 176p. 1990. pap. 12.95 (*0-929264-41-X*) Longstreet Pr Inc.

— Life Without Fear: A Guide to Preventing Sexual Assault. LC 92-34239. (Illus.). 192p. (Orig.). 1992. pap. 9.95 (*1-55853-197-1*) Rutledge Hill Pr.

Martin, Laura, ed. Entre Lineas. 2nd ed. 1991. pap. 30.95 (*0-8384-1967-4*); pap. 30.95 (*0-8384-1962-3*) Heinle & Heinle.

Martin, Laura C. Folklore of Birds. LC 93-39582. 240p. (Orig.). 1993. 24.95 (*1-56440-216-9*) Globe Pequot.

— The Folklore of Trees & Shrubs. LC 91-12213. (Illus.). 240p. 1992. 24.95 (*1-56440-018-2*) Globe Pequot.

— Garden Flower Folklore: Paper Conversion. (Illus.). 272p. 1987. 19.95 (*0-87106-766-8*) Globe Pequot.

— Garden Flower Folklore: Paper Conversion. (Illus.). 272p. 1994. pap. 10.95 (*1-56440-611-3*) Globe Pequot.

— Handmade Gifts from a Country Garden. 1994. 29.95 (*1-55859-610-0*) Abbeville Pr.

— Precious Moments Last Forever. LC 94-27040. 1994. 35.00 (*1-55859-859-6*) Abbeville Pr.

— Southern Wildflowers. (Illus.). 272p. 1991. 12.99 (*0-517-05548-1*) Random Hse Value.

— The Wildflower Meadow Book: A Gardener's Guide. 2nd ed. LC 90-37510. (Illus.). 320p. 1990. pap. 16.95 (*0-87106-436-7*) Globe Pequot.

An Asterisk (*) at the beginning of an entry indicates that the title is appearing in BIP for the first time.

— Wildlife Folklore. LC 94-21560. (Illus.). 200p. 1994. 24.95 (*1-56440-499-4*) Globe Pequot.

***Martin, Laura M., et al, eds.** Sociocultural Psychology: Theory & Practice of Doing & Knowing. (Learning in Doing Ser.). (Illus.). 400p. (C). 1995. write for info. (*0-521-46278-9*) Cambridge U Pr.

Martin, Laurence, ed. The Management of Defense. LC 76-12233. 136p. (C). 1976. text ed. 29.95 (*0-312-51275-9*) St Martin.

Martin, Laurence W. Nuclear Warfare. (Modern Military Techniques Ser.). (Illus.). 48p. (J). (gr. 5 up). 1989. 14.95 (*0-8225-1384-6*, Lerner Publctns) Lerner Group.

Martin, Laurey K. & Berg, William J. Images. 240p. (FRE.). (C). 1990. pap. text ed. 22.00 (*0-03-013773-X*) HB Coll Pubs.

Martin, Laurie. Barron's French Vocabulary. 256p. 1990. pap. 5.95 (*0-8120-4496-7*) Barron.

Martin, Lawrence. All You Really Need to Know to Interpret Arterial Blood Gases. (Illus.). 224p. 1992. pap. 23.95 (*0-8121-1572-4*) Williams & Wilkins.

— Economics. 2nd ed. 1996. pap. write for info. (*0-393-96896-0*) Norton.

— Physical Geography of Wisconsin. 3rd ed. (Illus.). 636p. 1965. text ed. 30.00 (*0-299-03472-0*); pap. 12.95 (*0-299-03475-5*) U of Wis Pr.

— Pickwickian & Other Stories of Intensive Care: Medical & Ethical Challenges in the ICU. LC 91-61828. 247p. 1991. pap. 10.95 (*1-879653-04-4*) Lakeside Pr.

— Principles of Microeconomics. 1996. student ed, pap. write for info. (*0-393-96932-0*) Norton.

— Scuba Diving Explained: Questions & Answers on Physiology & Medical Aspects of Scuba Diving. LC 93-79817. (Illus.). 280p. (Orig.). 1995. pap. 20.00 (*1-879653-12-5*) Lakeside Pr.

Martin, Lawrence, tr. & intro. Commentary on the Acts of the Apostles by the Venerable Bede. 1989. 24.95 (*0-685-28779-3*); pap. 12.95 (*0-685-28780-7*) Cistercian Pubns.

Martin, Lawrence, et al. Scanning Microscopy of Vertebrate Mineralized Tissues: A Compilation in Memory of Edward J. Reith. (Illus.). viii, 384p. 1989. pap. text ed. 43.00 (*0-931288-41-X*) Scanning Microscopy.

Martin, Lawrence B., jt. ed. see Kimbel, William H.

Martin, Lawrence L. Total Quality Management in Human Service Organizations. (Human Services Guides Ser.: Vol. 67). (Illus.). 112p. (C). 1993. text ed. 39.95 (*0-8039-4949-9*); pap. text ed. 17.95 (*0-8039-4950-2*) Sage.

Martin, Lawrence L., jt. auth. see Kettner, Peter M.

Martin, Lawrence L., jt. ed. see Lynch, Thomas D.

Martin, Lawrence R., jt. auth. see Seldman, Neil N.

Martin, Lawrence T. & Hurst, Dom D., trs. Homilies on the Gospels by the Venerable Bede, 2 vols., CS110. (Cistercian Studies: Nos. CS110 & CS111). 1991. write for info. (*0-87907-610-0*); write for info. (*0-87907-710-7*) Cistercian Pubns.

— Homilies on the Gospels by the Venerable Bede, 2 vols., CS111. (Cistercian Studies: Nos. CS110 & CS111). 1991. write for info. (*0-87907-711-5*); write for info. (*0-87907-911-8*) Cistercian Pubns.

— Homilies on the Gospels by the Venerable Bede, 2 vols., Set. (Cistercian Studies: Nos. CS110 & CS111). 1991. 70.00 (*0-685-49216-8*); pap. 35.00 (*0-685-49217-6*) Cistercian Pubns.

Martin, Lawrence T., tr. see Bede.

***Martin, Lee.** Bird in a Cage. LC 95-14723. 1995. 20.95 (*0-312-13028-7*) St Martin.

— Black River. 1993. 13.95 (*0-8034-8998-6*) Bouregy.

— The Danger Trail. 192p. 1994. 17.95 (*0-8034-9058-5*, Avalon Bks) Bouregy.

— The Day that Dusty Died. 304p. 1994. 20.95 (*0-312-09779-4*) St Martin.

— Dead Man's Trail. 1993. 13.95 (*0-8034-9009-7*) Bouregy.

— Hacker. (Worldwide Library Mystery). 1994. mass mkt. 3.99 (*0-373-26135-7*, 1-26135-3) Harlequin Bks.

— Hacker: A Deb Ralston Mystery. 192p. 1992. 16.95 (*0-312-06990-1*) St Martin.

— Inherited Murder. (Deb Ralston Mystery Ser.). 304p. 1994. 19.95 (*0-312-11415-X*) St Martin.

— The Lone Rider. 1993. 13.95 (*0-8034-8988-9*) Bouregy.

— The Mensa Murders. 1993. mass mkt. 3.99 (*0-373-26115-2*, 1-26115-5) Harlequin Bks.

— The Mensa Murders. 192p. 1990. 15.95 (*0-312-05126-3*) St Martin.

— Track the Men Down. 1993. 13.95 (*0-8034-9029-1*) Bouregy.

— Trail of the Dangerous Gun. 1995. 17.95 (*0-8034-9099-2*, 094641) Bouregy.

— Traps. 32p. (Orig.). 1988. pap. 6.00 (*0-938507-17-6*) Ion Books.

— Valley of the Lawless. 1993. 13.95 (*0-8034-9018-6*) Bouregy.

Martin, Lee J. & Kroitor, Harry P. The Five-Hundred Word Theme. 4th ed. (Illus.). 352p. (C). 1984. pap. text ed. write for info. (*0-13-321639-X*) P-H.

Martin, Lee J., jt. auth. see Kroitor, Harry P.

Martin, Lee R., ed. Agriculture in Economic Development: 1940's to 1990's: A Survey of Agriculture Economics Literature, Vol. 4. (Illus.). 1064p. (C). 1991. text ed. 59.95 (*0-8166-1942-5*) U of Minn Pr.

— Economics of Welfare, Rural Development, & Natural Resources in Agriculture, 1940s-1970s. (Survey of Agricultural Ecomonics Literature Ser.: Vol. 3). 667p. 1981. text ed. 59.95 (*0-8166-0819-9*) U of Minn Pr.

— A Survey of Agricultural Economics Literature: Traditional Fields of Agricultural Economics, 1940s to 1970s, Vol. I. LC 76-27968. 1977. text ed. 59.95 (*0-8166-0801-6*) U of Minn Pr.

Martin, Lee R., et al, eds. A Survey of Agricultural Economics Literature: Quantitative Methods in Agricultural Economics, 1940's to 1970's, Vol. II. LC 76-27968. (Illus.). 1977. text ed. 59.95 (*0-8166-0818-0*) U of Minn Pr.

***Martin, Len.** Forbes Field: Build It Yourself: With An Introduction & History of Forbes Field by Dan Bonk. (Major League Baseball Parks Ser.: No. 2). (Illus.). 104p. (Orig.). 1995. pap. 19.95 (*0-9642887-0-2*) Pt Four Ltd.

Martin, Len D. The Allied Artists Checklist: The Feature Films & Short Subjects of Allied Artists Pictures Corporation, 1947-1978. LC 92-56665. (Illus.). 232p. 1993. lib. bdg. 45.00 (*0-89950-782-4*) McFarland & Co.

— The Columbia Checklist: The Feature Films, Serials, Cartoons & Short Subjects of the Columbia Pictures Corporation, 1922-1988. LC 90-53507. 647p. 1991. lib. bdg. 72.00x (*0-89950-556-2*) McFarland & Co.

Martin, Leonard G., illus. Build-Your-Own Cathedral of Learning. 44p. (Orig.). 1991. pap. 20.00 (*1-878242-00-8*) Fourth River Pr.

Martin, Leonard L. & Tesser, Abraham, eds. The Construction of Social Judgments. (Publication of the University of Georgia's Institute for Behavior Research Ser.). 368p. 1992. text ed. 79.95 (*0-8058-1149-4*) L Erlbaum Assocs.

— Striving & Feeling: Interactions Between Goals & Affect. 325p. 1995. text ed. 50.00 (*0-8058-1629-1*) L Erlbaum Assocs.

Martin, Leonide L. & Reeder, Sharon J. Clinical Manual for Essentials of Maternity Nursing: Family-Centered Care. (Illus.). 352p. 1991. text ed. 18.50 (*0-397-54897-4*) Lippincott.

— Essentials of Maternity Nursing: Family-Centered Care. (Illus.). 819p. 1990. text ed. 48.50 (*0-397-54791-9*) Lippincott.

Martin, Leonide L., et al. Comprehensive Rehabilitation Nursing. (Illus.). 816p. 1981. text ed. 44.95 (*0-07-040611-1*) McGraw.

Martin, Les. Prisoner of War. LC 92-56395. (Young Indiana Jones Chronicles Ser.). 136p. (Orig.). (J). (gr. 4-8). 1993. pap. 3.50 (*0-679-84389-2*) Random Bks Yng Read.

— Return of the Werewolf. LC 92-47289. (Bullseye Chillers Ser.). (Illus.). 96p. (Orig.). (J). (gr. 2-6). 1993. pap. 3.99 (*0-679-84189-X*) Random Bks Yng Read.

— The Shadow: Movie Adaptation. 128p. (Orig.). (J). (gr. 3-7). 1994. pap. 3.99 (*0-679-86863-1*, Silver Creek) Random Bks Yng Read.

— Young Indiana Jones & the Gypsy Revenge, Bk. 6. LC 90-52818. (Young Indiana Jones Ser.). 128p. (Orig.). (J). (gr. 3-7). 1991. pap. 2.95 (*0-679-81179-6*) Random Bks Yng Read.

— Young Indiana Jones & the Princess of Peril, Bk. 5. LC 90-52817. (Young Indiana Jones Ser.). 128p. (Orig.). (J). (gr. 3-7). 1991. pap. 2.95 (*0-679-81178-8*) Random Bks Yng Read.

— Young Indiana Jones & the Secret City, Bk. 4. LC 89-43391. (Young Indiana Jones Ser.). 112p. (Orig.). (J). (gr. 3-7). 1990. lib. bdg. 6.99 (*0-679-90580-4*); pap. 2.95 (*0-679-80580-X*) Random Bks Yng Read.

— Young Indiana Jones & the Titanic Adventure. (Young Indiana Jones Ser.). 132p. (Orig.). (J). (gr. 3-7). 1993. pap. 3.50 (*0-679-84925-4*, Bullseye Bks) Random Bks Yng Read.

— Young Indiana Jones & the Tomb of Terror, Bk. 2. LC 89-43389. (Young Indiana Jones Ser.). 112p. (Orig.). (J). (gr. 3-7). 1990. pap. 3.50 (*0-679-80581-8*) Random Bks Yng Read.

Martin, Les, jt. auth. see McCay, William.

Martin, Leslie J., jt. ed. see Jones, Mary M.

***Martin, Letty.** Straight Stitch Machine Applique: Patterns & Instructions for This Easy Technique. 1995. pap. 16.95 (*0-89145-839-5*) Collector Bks.

Martin, Liam C., illus. A Walking Tour of Dublin Churches. 64p. 1989. pap. 22.00 (*1-85390-945-9*, Pub. by Veritas IE) St Mut.

Martin, Lillien J. & De Grucy, Clare. Sweeping the Cobwebs. Kastenbaum, Robert, ed. LC 78-22209. (Aging & Old Age Ser.). 1979. reprint ed. lib. bdg. 17.95 (*0-405-11823-6*) Ayer.

Martin, Linda. Mesa Verde: The Story Behind the Scenery. LC 93-77024. (Illus.). 48p. 1993. pap. 6.95 (*0-88714-075-0*) KC Pubns.

— Watch Them Grow. LC 93-25426. (Illus.). 48p. (J). (ps-1). 1994. 14.95 (*1-56458-458-5*) Dorling Kindersley.

— When Dinosaurs Go Visiting. LC 93-10207. (J). 1993. 11.95 (*0-8118-0122-5*) Chronicle Bks.

Martin, Linda & Segrave, Kerry. Anti-Rock: The Opposition to Rock 'n' Roll. 382p. 1993. reprint ed. pap. 14.95 (*0-306-80502-2*) Da Capo.

— City Parks of Canada. (Illus.). 128p. 1995. lib. bdg. 33.00 (*0-8095-4913-1*) Borgo Pr.

— Women in Comedy. (Illus.). 312p. 1986. 19.95 (*0-8065-1000-5*, Citadel Pr) Carol Pub Group.

Martin, Linda, jt. auth. see Segrave, Kerry.

Martin, Linda, et al. Laboratory Exercises for Animal Sciences & Industry. rev. ed. 160p. (C). 1994. spiral bd. 21.95 (*0-8403-9248-6*) Kendall-Hunt.

Martin, Linda B., jt. auth. see Weidman, Bette S.

Martin, Linda C., et al. Laboratory Exercises for Animal Sciences & Industry. 128p. (C). 1993. spiral bd. 19.95 (*0-8403-8885-3*) Kendall-Hunt.

Martin, Linda G., ed. see National Research Council, Population Committee.

Martin, Lionel. The Early Fidel. 1978. 8.95 (*0-8184-0254-7*) Carol Pub Group.

Martin, Lisa L. Coercive Cooperation: Explaining Multilateral Economic Sanctions. (Illus.). 1992. text ed. 45.00 (*0-691-08624-9*) Princeton U Pr.

— Coercive Cooperation: Explaining Multilateral Economic Sanctions. (C). 1994. pap. 16.95 (*0-691-03476-1*) Princeton U Pr.

Martin, Lisa N., jt. ed. see Scroggins, Penelope.

Martin-Lof, Anders, ed. Harald Cramer: Selected Works. LC 93-25592. 1994. 89.00 (*0-387-56671-6*) Spr-Verlag.

Martin-Lof, Anders, ed. see Cramer, Harald.

Martin, Loren D. Isaiah: An Ensign to the Nations. LC 81-92840. (Isaiah Ser.: Vol. 1). (Illus.). 180p. 1982. 9.95 (*0-9608244-0-5*) Valiant Pubns.

— Isaiah: An Ensign to the Nations, Set. LC 81-92840. (Isaiah Ser.: Vol. 1). (Illus.). 180p. 1982. write for info. (*0-9608244-2-1*) Valiant Pubns.

— Utah Criminal Code. (Orig.). spiral bd. 12.50 (*0-9608244-3-X*) Valiant Pubns.

Martin, Lothar, jt. auth. see Fishman, Sterling.

Martin, Louise. Reptile Discovery Library, 6 bks., Set, Reading Level 2. (Illus.). 144p. (J). (gr. k-5). 1989. Set. lib. bdg. 71.60 (*0-86592-573-9*) Rourke Corp.

Martin, Lowell. Organizational Structure of Libraries. LC 84-4859. (Library Administration Ser.: No. 5). 304p. 1984. 20.00 (*0-8108-1696-2*) Scarecrow.

Martin, Lowell A. Library Personnel Administration. LC 94-6569. (Library Administration Ser.: No. 11). (Illus.). 214p. 1994. text ed. 29.50 (*0-8108-2839-1*) Scarecrow.

Martin, Loy D. Browning's Dramatic Monologues & the Post-Romantic Subject. LC 85-9796. 304p. 1985. text ed. 42.50 (*0-8018-2653-5*) Johns Hopkins.

Martin, Lucien T. & Martin, Melba B. Remember Us. (Illus.). 298p. 1987. 30.00 (*0-9620005-0-7*) Martin Pubs.

Martin, Lucy P., ed. see McCune, Shirley D., et al.

Martin, Lucy P., jt. ed. see Moyer, Joan.

Martin, Luis. Daughters of the Conquistadores: Women of the Viceroyalty of Peru. LC 89-42899. (Illus.). 368p. 1989. reprint ed. pap. text ed. 14.95 (*0-87074-297-3*) SMU Press.

— The Intellectual Conquest of Peru: The Jesuit College of San Pablo, 1568-1767. LC 67-26159. 208p. reprint ed. pap. 59.30 (*0-7837-5612-7*, 2045518) Bks Demand.

Martin, Luther, ed. Religious Transformations & Socio-Political Change: Eastern Europe & Latin America. LC 93-4333. (Religion & Society Ser.: No. 33). xiv, 457p. (C). 1993. lib. bdg. 152.35 (*3-11-013734-8*) Mouton.

Martin, Luther H. Hellenistic Religions: An Introduction. (Illus.). 192p. 1987. pap. 14.95 (*0-19-504391-X*) OUP.

Martin, Luther H., et al, eds. Technologies of the Self: A Seminar with Michel Foucault. LC 87-10756. 176p. (Orig.). (C). 1988. pap. 12.95x (*0-87023-593-1*) U of Mass Pr.

Martin, Lwey P., ed. see O'Brien, Shirley.

Martin, Lynda K. Maurice LeGrand LeSueur Sullins, Paintings, 1970-1986. (Illus.). x, 30p. (Orig.). 1988. pap. 10.00 (*0-89792-114-3*) Ill St Museum.

***Martin, Lynn.** Plague? Jesuit Accounts of Epidemic Diseases in the Sixteenth Century. LC 94-21215. (Sixteenth Century Essays & Studies: 28). 1995. write for info. (*0-940474-30-1*) Sixteenth Cent.

Martin, Lynn A. The Jesuit Mind: The Mentality of an Elite in Early Modern France. LC 87-47873. (Illus.). 288p. 1988. 36.50 (*0-8014-2147-0*) Cornell U Pr.

Martin, Lynn J., ed. Na Paniolo O Hawaii. (Illus.). 100p. (Orig.). 1987. pap. text ed. 15.95 (*0-937426-08-3*) Honolu Arts.

Martin, Lys, ed. see Rubin, David S.

Martin, M. How to Build the Ultimate Super Mopar. (How to Ser.). (Illus.). 110p. 1984. pap. 16.95 (*0-931472-20-2*, S-A Design Pub Co) Motorbooks Intl.

— Marketing. (Core Business Studies Ser.). 1990. 21.00 (*0-7463-0028-X*, Pub. by Northcote UK) St Mut.

— Wielki Slownik Techni Rosyjsko - Polski. 1151p. (POL & RUS.). 1980. 95.00 (*0-8288-2142-9*, M14452) Fr & Eur.

Martin, M. & Corcoran, B. Cardiology of the Dog & Cat. (Library of Veterinary Practice). (Illus.). 224p. 1994. pap. 39.95 (*0-632-03298-7*, Pub. by Blckwell Sci Pubns UK) Blackwell Sci.

Martin, M. & Firth, F. Statistics. (Core Business Studies Ser.). 1990. 35.00 (*0-7463-0048-4*, Pub. by Northcote UK) St Mut.

Martin, M. & Lockwood, Jill. Partnership Taxation Handbook. 528p. 1989. text ed. 79.95 (*0-13-651407-3*) P-H.

Martin, M. & Putinar, M. Lectures on Hyponormal Operators. (Operator Theory Ser.: No. 39). 304p. 1989. 108.50 (*0-8176-2329-9*) Birkhauser.

Martin, M. & Whittle, W. Core Geography: Leisure. (C). 1982. 50.00 (*0-09-144451-9*, Pub. by S Thornes Pubs UK) St Mut.

— Core Geography: Physical. (C). 1987. 55.00 (*0-09-164201-9*, Pub. by S Thornes Pubs UK) St Mut.

— Core Geography: The Developing World. (C). 1985. 55.00 (*0-09-156621-5*, Pub. by S Thornes Pubs UK) St Mut.

— Core Geography: United Kingdom. (C). 1986. 60.00 (*0-09-160691-8*, Pub. by S Thornes Pubs UK) St Mut.

— Core Geography Cities. (C). 1983. 50.00 (*0-09-147521-X*, Pub. by S Thornes Pubs UK) St Mut.

— Core Geography Work. (C). 1983. 50.00 (*0-09-144461-6*, Pub. by S Thornes Pubs UK) St Mut.

— Poverty & Progress. (Down to Earth Ser.). (C). 1987. 35.00 (*0-09-149161-4*, Pub. by S Thornes Pubs UK) St Mut.

Martin, M., jt. auth. see Marsh, P.

Martin, M. A., ed. see Menendez Pidal, Ramon.

Martin, M. C. & Hewett, C. A. Elements of Classical Physics. LC 73-3450. (C). 1975. 156.00 (*0-08-017098-6*, Pub. by Pergamon Repr UK) Franklin.

Martin, M. Dean & Adams, John. Professional Project Management. 154p. 1957. 28.00 (*0-317-54778-X*) Univ Tech.

Martin, M. H. & Coughtrey, P. J. Biological Monitoring of Heavy Metal Pollution: Land & Air. (Pollution Monitor Ser.: No. 5). (Illus.). x, 468p. 1982. 120.75 (*0-85334-136-2*, I-304-82, Pub. by Elsevier Applied Sci UK) Elsevier.

Martin, M. H., ed. see Applied Mathematics Symposium Staff.

Martin, M. J. Instructional Videotaping: A Teacher's Guide for Making Instructional Videotapes. 32p. 1992. teacher ed, pap. 5.00 (*0-9632211-0-8*) MTCI.

Martin, M. Jill. Partnership Taxation Handbook. LC 92-30819. 1992. write for info. (*0-13-016783-5*) P-H.

Martin, M. Kay & Voorhies, Barbara. Female of the Species. LC 74-23965. 432p. 1975. pap. text ed. 21.00 (*0-231-03876-3*) Col U Pr.

Martin, M. M. Inheritance: Lincoln's Public Buildings in the Historic District. (Illus.). 115p. (Orig.). 1988. pap. 15.00 (*0-944856-00-4*) Lincoln Hist Soc.

***Martin, M. P.** A Little Bit of Heaven. 220p. 1995. lib. bdg. 37.00 (*0-8095-4816-X*) Borgo Pr.

Martin, M. R. Historical Records Survey No. 2: Check List of Minnesota Imprints, 1849-1865. (Historical Records Survey Monographs). 1969. reprint ed. 20.00 (*0-527-01899-6*) Periodicals Srv.

Martin, Maggie, jt. auth. see Martin, Don.

Martin, Malachi. Hostage to the Devil: The Possession & Exorcism of Five Americans. LC 92-53900. 1992. pap. 13.00 (*0-06-065337-X*) Harper SF.

— Hostage to the Devil: The Possession of Exorcism of Five Living Americans. LC 86-46207. 488p. 1987. reprint ed. pap. 13.00 (*0-06-097103-7*, PL 7103, PL) HarpC.

— The Jesuits: The Society of Jesus & the Betrayal of the Roman Catholic Church. 1988. pap. 12.00 (*0-671-65716-X*, Touchstone Bks) S&S Trade.

— The Keys of This Blood: A Unique & Daring Portrait of Pope John Paul the Second. (Illus.). 300p. Date not set. write for info. (*0-688-07790-0*) Morrow.

— The Keys of This Blood: Pope John Paul II vs. Russia & the West for Control of the New World Order. 736p. 1991. pap. 15.00 (*0-671-74723-1*, Touchstone Bks) S&S Trade.

***Martin Management Books Staff, ed. & pref.** Great Vacations for You & Your Dog, U. S. A., 1995. 2nd rev. ed. LC 94-73097. (Illus.). 180p. (Orig.). 1995. pap. 17.95 (*1-878500-05-8*) Martin Mgmt.

Martin Management Editors. Managers Competitive Fitness Guide. LC 89-92299. 105p. 1989. pap. 7.95 (*0-9615541-6-9*) Martin Mgmt.

— Productive Meetings: How to Structure & Conduct Committee or Group Meetings in Competitive Firms. LC 90-91946. 59p. 1990. pap. 11.95 (*0-9615541-5-0*) Martin Mgmt.

Martin, Marcia. Riverbend. 384p. (Orig.). 1994. pap. 4.99 (*0-451-18053-4*, Onyx) NAL-Dutton.

— South of Paradise. 336p. (Orig.). 1993. mass mkt. 4.99 (*0-515-11123-6*) Jove Pubns.

— Southern Storms. 1992. mass mkt. 4.99 (*0-515-10870-7*) Jove Pubns.

Martin, Marcia, jt. auth. see Vinicoff, Eric.

***Martin, Margaret.** Husband in Waiting: (Debut Author) (Sil Romance Ser.). 1995. mass mkt. 2.99 (*0-373-19083-2*, 1-19083-4) Silhouette.

— The Illustrated Book of Pregnancy & Childbirth. (Illus.). 1991. 19.95 (*0-8160-2570-3*) Facts on File.

— Illustrated Book of Pregnancy & Childbirth. (Illus.). 128p. 1993. pap. 9.95 (*0-8160-2917-2*) Facts on File.

Martin, Margaret M., jt. auth. see Cratty, Bryant J.

Martin, Margaret M., jt. auth. see MacLean, John C.

Martin, Margaret R. Charleston Ghosts. LC 63-22508. (Illus.). xiv, 116p. 1963. 15.95 (*0-87249-091-2*) U of SC Pr.

Martin, Margery, ed. see Rich, Dorothy.

Martin, Maria R. Estructuras Imaginarias En la Poesia. Date not set. 47.50 (*0-685-69527-1*) Scripta.

Martin, Marian. Dangerous Stranger. 1981. pap. 1.75 (*0-8439-8024-9*) Dorchester Pub Co.

Martin, Marie, jt. ed. see Livingston, Donald.

Martin, Marie A. Cambodia: A Shattered Society. Mcleod, Mark W., tr. LC 93-31837. 383p. 1994. 40.00 (*0-520-07052-6*) U CA Pr.

Martin, Marie-Louise. Kimbangu: An African Prophet & His Church. Moore, D. M., tr. LC 75-45371. 222p. reprint ed. pap. 63.30 (*0-317-08451-8*, 2012735) Bks Demand.

Martin, Marie-Therese, tr. see Ladd, George E.

Martin Marietta Corporation Staff & Holst, Gerald C., eds. Infrared Imaging Systems: Design, Analysis, Modeling, & Testing: Proceedings of a Conference Held April 1990, Orlando. 322p. 1990. 62.00 (*0-8194-0360-1*, VOL. 1309) SPIE.

Martin, Marilyn. Pedro. 152p. (J). (gr. 3 up). 1980. 6.55 (*0-686-30765-8*) Rod & Staff.

Martin, Marilyn, ed. see Professional Truck Driving Institute of America (PTDIA) Staff.

Martin, Marilyn, et al. The Journal of Decorative & Propaganda Arts, No. 20. Duong Tuong, tr. (Illus.). 300p. (Orig.). 1994. pap. 19.00 (*0-9631601-3-3*) Wolfson Fnd D&P Arts.

Martin, Marilyn G. Shawn's Search for True Love. (Illus.). 24p. (J). (gr. k-6). 1991. 4.25 (*1-55976-154-7*) CEF Press.

Martin, Marilyn M., ed. see Calvin, Robert M.

Martin, Mark. Fishing Hot Spots Rhinelander Area. (North Central Wisconsin Area Ser.). (Illus.). 144p. 1988. pap. 9.95 (*0-939314-20-7*) Fishing Hot.

— The Ultimate Gnatrat. (Illus.). 120p. 1990. pap. 11.95 (*1-56097-027-8*) Fantagraph Bks.

Martin, Mark, ed. see Campbell, Eddie.

Martin, Mark, ed. see Frazetta, Frank.

Martin, Mark, ed. see McCloud, Scott.

Martin, Mark, ed. see Stark, Rolf & Stevens, Marlene.

Martin, Mark, ed. see Weiner, Jack & Rak, Charles.

Martin, Mark, ed. see Wrightson, Bernie.

Martin, Mark, et al. Strength Training for Performance Driving. LC 93-21106. (Illus.). 128p. 1994. pap. 14.95 (*0-87938-843-9*) Motorbooks Intl.

Martin, Marla. Birthday Friend. (Jewel Bks.). 1993. pap. 2.15 (*0-317-05266-7*) Rod & Staff.

An Asterisk (*) at the beginning of an entry indicates that the title is appearing in BIP for the first time.

— Caterpillar Green. 1977. 6.10 (*0-686-23330-1*) Rod & Staff.
— Kitten in the Well. 1978. 7.70 (*0-686-24051-0*) Rod & Staff.
— Little Church House by the River. 1994. 14.95 (*0-87813-552-9*) Christian Light.
— Locust Story. 62p. 1977. pap. 2.85 (*0-318-41779-0*) Rod & Staff.
— A Sweet Singer. (J). (gr. 2-4). 1976. 2.55 (*0-686-15487-8*) Rod & Staff.
Martin, Marlene. Practicing the Process: A Basic Text. (C). 1988. pap. text ed. 27.50 (*0-673-18759-4*) HarpCollege.
— Review & Revise. 320p. 1989. pap. text ed. write for info. (*0-07-040700-2*) McGraw.
Martin, Marlene & Girard, Maureen. Writing Wisely & Well. LC 92-37244. 1993. pap. text ed. write for info. (*0-07-023472-8*) McGraw.
Martin, Mart. The Voyeur's Guide to Men in the Movies - the Voyeur's Guide to Women in the Movies. (Illus.). 512p. 1994. pap. 15.95 (*0-8092-3642-7*) Contemp Bks.
Martin, Marta S., jt. auth. see Bonachea, Ramon L.
Martin, Martha. Home in the Bear's Domain. large type ed. 464p. 1987. 16.95 (*0-7089-1578-7*) Ulverscroft.
— O Rugged Land of Gold. (Illus.). 226p. 1989. pap. 12.95 (*0-940055-00-7*) Vanessapress.
Martin, Martha E. The Friendly Stars. rev. ed. Menzel, Donald H., ed. (Illus.). 147p. 1964. pap. 3.95 (*0-486-21099-5*) Dover.
Martin, Martin. A Description of the Western Isles of Scotland. 440p. (C). 1981. 52.00 (*0-901824-01-1*, Pub. by Mercat Pr Bks UK) St Mut.
— Voyage to St. Kilda Sixteen Ninety-Seven. 63p. (C). 1985. 50.00 (*0-685-30235-0*, Pub. by Mercat Pr Bks UK) St Mut.
Martin, Martin C. Elements of Thermodynamics. (Illus.). 224p. (C). 1986. text ed. write for info. (*0-13-273434-6*) P-H.
Martin Martinez, Juan M., ed. see De Rueda, Lope.
Martin Martinez, Juan M., ed. see Ruiz De Alarcon, Juan.
Martin, Marvin D., jt. auth. see Nachtigal, Chester.
Martin, Mary. Caress of Silk. 496p. 1986. pap. 3.95 (*0-8217-1842-8*) Zebra.
— Desire's Embrace. 448p. 1993. mass mkt. 4.50 (*0-8217-4187-X*) Zebra.
— Menopause: The Storm Before the Calm. LC 92-62008. 80p. 1993. pap. 8.95 (*1-56002-236-1*, Univ Edtns) Aegina Pr.
— Outlaw's Caress. 512p. 1988. pap. 3.95 (*0-8217-2349-9*) Zebra.
— Pirate's Conquest. 496p. 1987. pap. 3.95 (*0-8217-2036-8*) Zebra.
— Wild Texas Angel. 416p. 1992. mass mkt. 4.50 (*0-8217-3991-3*) Zebra.
Martin, Mary & Zorn, Steven. Start Exploring Masterpieces: A Fact-Filled Coloring Book. rev. ed. (Start Exploring Ser.). (Illus.). 128p. (J). (gr. 2 up). 1990. pap. 8.95 (*0-89471-801-0*) Running Pr.
Martin, Mary C. Blot the Spot: Tried & True Ways. Hubbard-Brown, Janet, ed. 175p. 1992. write for info. (*0-9611712-1-9*) Concepts Pub.
Martin, Mary E. & Martin, J. Michael. Home Filing Made Easy! Guide to Financial Organization. (Financial Organization Ser.). (Illus.). 140p. 1993. 19.95 (*0-9628718-7-7*) Fin Advantage.
Martin, Mary E., jt. auth. see Martin, J. Michael.
Martin, Mary E., ed. see Martin, J. Michael & Martin, Mary E.
Martin, Mary E., jt. ed. see Martin, J. Michael.
Martin, Mary L. & Lacy, Norris J. The Fables of Marie de France: An English Translation. 2nd ed. 259p. 1984. 23.95 (*0-917786-34-3*) Summa Pubns.
Martin, Mary L., jt. auth. see Palmer, Erskine L.
Martin, Mary P. Peace: A Thematic Unit. (Thematic Units Ser.). (Illus.). 80p. 1994. student ed 8.95 (*1-55734-248-2*) Tchr Create Mat.
Martin, MaryJoy. Suicide Legends, Homicide Rumors: The Griffin Mystery. LC 86-232434. (Illus.). 68p. (Orig.). 1986. pap. write for info. (*0-945319-00-2*) Spes Deo Pubns.
— Twilight Dwellers: Ghosts, Ghouls & Goblins of Colorado. LC 85-16716. (Illus.). 167p. (Orig.). 1985. pap. 11.95 (*0-87108-686-7*) Pruett.
Martin, Maryvonne L., et al. Practical NMR Spectroscopy. 492p. reprint ed. pap. 140.30 (*0-317-26326-9*, 2025202) Bks Demand.
Martin, Matthew. The Crumbling Facade of African Debt Negotiations: No Winners. LC 91-4014. (International Political Economy Ser.). 408p. 1992. text ed. 69.95 (*0-312-06734-8*) St Martin.
***Martin, Maurice A.** Urban Policing in Canada: Anatomy of an Aging Craft. 232p. 1995. 49.95 (*0-7735-1284-5*); pap. 17.95 (*0-7735-1294-2*) U of Toronto Pr.
Martin-McRae, Bettye. Brone in the Parlor. Boyd, Carol, ed. 120p. (Orig.). 1992. pap. 9.95 (*1-878162-03-9*) Unicorn Pr USA.
***Martin, Mel S.** How to Hire an Honest Lawyer...& Other Oxymorons. 182p. 1994. pap. text ed. 9.95 (*0-9642951-0-5*) Witty Bks.
Martin, Melanie. Itsy-Bitsy Giant. LC 88-1234. (Fiddlesticks Ser.). (Illus.). 48p. (Orig.). (J). (gr. 1-4). 1989. lib. bdg. 10.59 (*0-8167-1335-9*); pap. text ed. 3.50 (*0-8167-1336-7*) Troll Assocs.
— Madison Moves to the Country. LC 88-1313. (Fiddlesticks Ser.). (Illus.). 48p. (Orig.). (J). (gr. 1-4). 1989. lib. bdg. 10.59 (*0-8167-1345-6*); pap. text ed. 3.50 (*0-8167-1346-4*) Troll Assocs.
— Morris, the Millionaire Mouse. LC 88-1235. (Fiddlesticks Ser.). (Illus.). 48p. (Orig.). (J). (gr. 1-4). 1989. lib. bdg. 10.59 (*0-8167-1339-1*); pap. text ed. 3.50 (*0-8167-1340-5*) Troll Assocs.
Martin, Melba, ed. see Ruth-Heffelbower, Dwayne.
Martin, Melba B., jt. auth. see Martin, Lucien T.
Martin, Melissa & Smathers, James. Current Regulatory Issues in Medical Physics: Proceedings of an American College of Medical Physics Symposium, April 1992. 350p. 1992. pap. text ed. 55.00 (*0-944838-29-4*) Med Physics Pub.
Martin, Merle. Analysis & Design of Information Systems. 784p. (C). 1991. write for info. (*0-675-20852-1*, Merrill Pub Co) Macmillan.
Martin, Merle P. Analysis & Design of Business Information Systems. 2nd ed. LC 94-1357. 848p. (C). 1995. write for info. (*0-02-376741-3*) Macmillan.
Martin, Michael. Atheism: A Philosophical Justification. 1992. pap. 24.95 (*0-87722-943-0*) Temple U Pr.
— The Case Against Christianity. 1991. 44.95 (*0-87722-767-5*) Temple U Pr.
— The Case Against Christianity. 290p. 1993. pap. 22.95 (*1-56639-081-8*) Temple U Pr.
— Concepts of Science Education: A Philosophical Analysis. 184p. 1985. reprint ed. pap. text ed. 19.50 (*0-8191-4479-7*) U Pr of Amer.
— The Good Behavior Book. Harris, Stephen & Brower, Nancy, eds. (Illus.). (Orig.). (J). (ps up). 1988. pap. 10.95 (*0-9621191-7-2*) Behavior Products.
— The Team Behavior Board for Groups of 2 to 6. Harris, Steven & Brower, Nancy, eds. (Illus.). 23p. (Orig.). 1989. pap. text ed. 15.95 (*0-9621191-0-5*) Behavior Products.
Martin, Michael, ed. Speech Audiometry. 300p. 1987. 64.50 (*0-85066-641-4*); pap. 33.00 (*0-85066-638-4*) Singular Publishing.
— Streptokinase Treatment in Chronic Arterial Occlusions & Stenoses. 208p. 1982. 87.00 (*0-8493-5046-8*, RC694, CRC Reprint) Franklin.
Martin, Michael & Gelber, Leonard. Dictionary of American History. 728p. 1990. 19.95 (*0-88029-431-0*) Dorset Pr.
— Dictionary of American History. enl. rev. ed. (Quality Paperback Ser.: No. 124). 742p. 1981. reprint ed. pap. 16.95 (*0-8226-0124-9*) Littlefield.
***Martin, Michael & Greenwood, Cynthia W.** Solve Your Child's School-Related Problems. 1995. pap. 16.00 (*0-06-273366-4*, Harper Ref) HarpC.
Martin, Michael & McIntyre, Lee C., eds. Readings in the Philosophy of Social Science. 800p. 1993. 60.00 (*0-262-13296-6*, Bradford Bks); pap. 34.00 (*0-262-63151-2*, Bradford Bks) MIT Pr.
Martin, Michael, jt. auth. see Marsh, Philip.
Martin, Michael, jt. auth. see O'Hanlon, William H.
Martin, Michael A. The Booger Book. (Illus.). 80p. (Orig.). 1985. pap. 4.95 (*0-914245-00-7*) Martin Creatics.
***Martin, Michael C.** Drawing the Line: Reappraising Drawing Past & Present. (Illus.). 108p. Date not set. pap. 24.95 (*1-85332-133-8*) Dist Art Pubs.
Martin, Michael J. How to Outsmart the Sun: The Ultimate Guide to Healthy, Young-Looking Skin. 176p. 1993. pap. 14.95 (*1-883955-00-9*) Penmarin Bks.
— Managing Information & Entrepreneurship in Technology-Based Firms. LC 93-36588. 1994. text ed. 59.95 (*0-471-57219-5*) Wiley.
Martin, Michael J. & Denison, Raymond A., eds. Case Exercises in Operations Research. LC 75-146548. (Illus.). 228p. reprint ed. pap. 65.00 (*0-317-09630-3*, 2020328) Bks Demand.
Martin, Michael M. Basic Problems of Evidence. 6th ed. 498p. 1988. 105.00 (*0-8318-0525-0*, B525) Am Law Inst.
— Invertebrate-Microbial Interactions: Ingested Fungal Enzymes in Arthropod Biology (A Comstock Book) LC 87-47549. (Explorations in Chemical Ecology Ser.). (Illus.). 176p. (C). 1988. 37.50 (*0-8014-2055-5*); pap. 14.95 (*0-8014-9459-1*) Cornell U Pr.
Martin, Michael M., jt. auth. see Saltzburg, Stephen A.
***Martin, Michael N.** Angels in Red Hats: Paratroopers of the Second Indochina War. Strode, William, ed. (Illus.). 168p. 1995. 39.95 (*1-56469-025-3*) Harmony Hse Pub LO.
Martin, Michael R. & Lovett, Gabriel H. Encyclopedia of Latin-American History. rev. ed. Hoffman, Fritz L. & Hughes, Robert L., eds. LC 81-715. vi, 348p. 1981. reprint ed. text ed. 35.00 (*0-313-22881-7*, MAELA, Greenwood Pr) Greenwood.
***Martin, Michael T., ed.** Cinemas of the Black Diaspora: Diversity, Dependence, & Oppositionality. (Contemporary Film & Television Ser.). 560p. (C). 1996. 49.95 (*0-8143-2587-4*); pap. 19.95 (*0-8143-2588-2*) Wayne St U Pr.
Martin, Michael T. & Kandal, Terry R., eds. Studies of Development & Change in the Modern World. (Illus.). 480p. (C). 1989. pap. text ed. 21.00 (*0-19-505647-7*) OUP.
Martin, Michael W. & Schinzinger, Roland. Ethics in Engineering. 2nd ed. 364p. 1989. pap. text ed. write for info. (*0-07-040719-3*) McGraw.
Martin, Michel, jt. ed. see Greenfeld, Liah.
Martin, Michel L. Warriors to Managers: The French Military Establishment since 1945. LC 79-28114. 446p. reprint ed. pap. 127.20 (*0-7837-2456-X*, 2042609) Bks Demand.
Martin, Michele. Hello, Central? Gender, Technology, & Culture in the Formation of Telephone Systems. 1991. 42.95 (*0-7735-0830-9*, Pub. by McGill CN) U of Toronto Pr.
Martin, Michelle. The Hampshire Hoyden. (Orig.). 1993. mass mkt. 3.99 (*0-449-22202-0*, Crest) Fawcett.
— The Mad Miss Mathey. 1995. pap. 4.50 (*0-449-22339-6*) Fawcett.
— Pembroke Park. 256p. 1986. pap. 7.95 (*0-930044-77-0*) Naiad Pr.
Martin, Mick. Video Movie Guide for Family Viewing. 1992. mass mkt. 3.99 (*0-345-38224-2*) Ballantine.
— Video Movie Guide 1995. 1600p. (Orig.). 1994. pap. 16.00 (*0-345-39196-9*) Ballantine.
Martin, Mick & Porter, Marsha. Video Movie Guide 1994. (Orig.). 1993. pap. 7.99 (*0-345-38480-6*) Ballantine.
— Video Movie Guide 1995. (Orig.). 1994. pap. 7.99 (*0-345-39027-X*) Ballantine.
— Video Movie Guide 1996. 1600p. 1995. pap. 16.00 (*0-345-39777-0*) Ballantine.
Martin, Mickey. Woman's Missionary Union Manual. (SPA.). 1988. pap. text ed. 2.95 (*0-936625-48-1*) Womans Mission Union.
— Woman's Missionary Union Manual. rev. ed. (Illus.). 96p. 1988. pap. text ed. 2.95 (*0-936625-19-8*) Womans Mission Union.
Martin, Mickey J. Legacy of the Great Oklahoma Land Rush: A Photographic History of Hoffman Townsite & School in Okmulgee County. LC 93-72854. 489p. 1993. 88.00 (*0-9638279-0-1*) Fowble Pr.
Martin, Mike & Rea, Val. Creating Art, Creating Income: A Women's Textile Workshop in Bangladesh. (Illus.). 32p. (Orig.). 1994. 42.95 (*1-85339-213-8*, Pub. by Intermed Tech UK) Women Ink.
Martin, Mike & Valentine, Don. The Black Tigers: Elite Vietnamese Rangers & Their American Advisors. Strode, William & Butler, William, eds. (Illus.). 136p. 1993. 34.95 (*1-56469-016-4*) Harmony Hse Pub LO.
Martin, Mike W. Everyday Morality: An Introduction to Applied Ethics. 320p. (C). 1989. pap. 27.95 (*0-534-09738-3*) Intl Thomson.
— Everyday Morality: An Introduction to Applied Ethics. 2nd ed. 384p. 1995. pap. 27.95 (*0-534-20178-4*) Intl Thomson.
— Self-Deception & Morality. LC 86-5467. x, 182p. 1986. 19.95 (*0-7006-0297-6*); pap. 9.95 (*0-7006-0353-0*) U Pr of KS.
— Virtuous Giving: Philanthropy, Voluntary Service, & Caring. LC 93-8027. (Philanthropic Studies). (C). 1994. 24.95 (*0-253-33677-5*) Ind U Pr.
Martin, Mike W., ed. Self-Deception & Self-Understanding: New Essays in Philosophy & Psychology. LC 84-27013. x, 310p. 1985. pap. 12.95 (*0-7006-0396-4*) U Pr of KS.
Martin, Mildred. Half-Century of Eliot Criticism: Annotated Bibliography of Books & Articles in English, 1916-1965. LC 79-168814. 361p. 1975. 55.00 (*0-8387-7808-9*) Bucknell U Pr.
Martin, Mildred A. Missionary Stories & the Millers. (Miller Family Ser.). (Illus.). 208p. (J). (gr. 3 up). 1993. 9.50 (*0-9627643-7-X*) Green Psturs Pr.
— Missionary Stories & the Millers. (Miller Family Ser.). (Illus.). 208p. (J). (gr. 3 up). 1993. pap. 6.00 (*0-9627643-4-5*) Green Psturs Pr.
— Prudence & the Millers. (Miller Family Ser.). 190p. (Orig.). (J). (gr. 3-8). 1993. 9.50 (*0-9627643-9-6*); pap. 6.00 (*0-9627643-8-8*) Green Psturs Pr.
— School Days with the Millers. (Miller Family Ser.). (J). (gr. 3-8). 1995. pap. text ed. 6.00 (*1-884377-01-7*) Green Psturs Pr.
— Storytime with the Millers. 2nd ed. (Miller Family Ser.). (Illus.). 110p. (Orig.). (J). (ps-3). 1994. pap. 5.00 (*1-884377-00-9*) Green Psturs Pr.
— Wisdom & the Millers: Proverbs for Children. 2nd ed. (Miller Family Ser.). (Illus.). 159p. (J). (gr. 2-8). 1993. 9.50 (*0-685-68129-7*); pap. 6.00 (*0-9627643-5-3*) Green Psturs Pr.
— Working with Wisdom. (Miller Family Ser.). (J). (gr. 3-4). 1995. pap. text ed. write for info. (*1-884377-02-5*) Green Psturs Pr.
Martin, Mildred C. Chinatown's Angry Angel: The Story of Donaldina Cameron. LC 77-2151. (Illus.). 308p. 1986. pap. 10.95 (*0-87015-252-1*) Pacific Bks.
Martin, Minnie. Basutoland: Its Legends & Customs. LC 75-88997. 174p. 1969. reprint ed. text ed. 45.00 (*0-8371-1756-9*, MAK&, Negro U Pr) Greenwood.
Martin, Mircea, tr. see Khatskevich, Victor & Shoiykhet, David.
Martin, Molly, ed. Hard-Hatted Women: Stories of Struggle & Success in the Trades. LC 88-23850. 265p. (Orig.). 1988. pap. 12.95 (*0-931188-66-0*) Seal Pr Feminist.
Martin, Molly D., jt. auth. see Brain, Jean.
Martin, Murray S. Academic Library Budgets. LC 93-30103. (Foundations in Library & Information Science: Vol. 28). 1993. 73.25 (*1-55938-597-9*) Jai Pr.
— Budgetary Control in Academic Libraries. LC 76-5648. (Foundations in Library & Information Science: Vol. 5). 219p. 1978. lib. bdg. 73.25 (*0-89232-010-9*) Jai Pr.
— Collection Development & Finance: A Guide to Strategic Library-Materials Budgeting. Intner, Sheila S., ed. (Frontiers of Access Ser.). 130p. (Orig.). 1995. pap. text ed. 30.00x (*0-8389-0648-6*) ALA.
— Financial Planning for Libraries. LC 82-23346. (Journal of Library Administration: Vol. 3, Nos. 3-4). 131p. 1983. 39.95 (*0-86656-118-8*) Haworth Pr.
— Issues in Personnel Management. Stueart, Robert D., ed. LC 81-81649. (Foundations in Library & Information Science: Vol. 14). 226p. 1981. 73.25 (*0-89232-136-9*) Jai Pr.
Martin-Nagy, Rebecca, jt. auth. see Reynolds, Mike.
***Martin, Nancy.** Le Combat de Lorna. (Rouge Passion Ser.). (FRE.). 1994. pap. 3.50 (*0-373-37290-6*, 1-37290-3) Harlequin Bks.
— The Cop & the Chorus Girl: (Opposites Attract) (Desire Ser.). 1995. mass mkt. 3.25 (*0-373-05927-2*, 1-05927-8) Silhouette.
— Fortune's Cookie. (Silhouette Desire Ser.). 1993. mass mkt. 2.99 (*0-373-05826-8*, 5-05826-8) Silhouette.
— Mostly about Writing. 168p. (Orig.). (C). 1983. pap. text ed. 16.00 (*0-86709-069-3*) Boynton Cook Pubs.
— The Pauper & the Pregnant Princess: (Opposites Attract) (Desire Ser.). 1995. pap. 3.25 (*0-373-05916-7*, 1-05916-1) Silhouette.
— Prayers Through the Centuries. (C). 1988. 30.00 (*1-85219-018-3*, Pub. by Bishopsgate Pr Ltd UK) St Mut.
— TIPS: To Insure Perfect Spanish. (Illus.). 75p. Date not set. pap. 19.95 (*0-9643508-0-7*) MCL Pubs.
— Wish upon a Starr. 1994. mass mkt. 2.99 (*0-373-05858-6*) Silhouette.
Martin, Nancy, ed. see Colarusso, Ronald P. & Hammill, Donald D.
Martin, Nancy, jt. ed. see Lightfoot, Martin.
Martin, Nancy, ed. see Markoff, Annabelle.
Martin, Nancy, jt. auth. see McCloskey, Marsha.
Martin, Nancy, et al. Writing & Learning Across the Curriculum 11-16. 176p. 1976. pap. text ed. 17.00 (*0-86709-095-2*) Boynton Cook Pubs.
***Martin, Nancy A.** The Versatile Labrador Retriever. Foote, Marianne, ed. (Pure Breds Ser.). (Illus.). 320p. 1994. pap. 21.95 (*0-944875-43-2*) Doral Pub.
— The Versatile Labrador Retriever. Luther, Luana & Grossman, Alvin, eds. (Pure Breds Ser.). (Illus.). 320p. 1994. 26.95 (*0-944875-31-9*) Doral Pub.
Martin, Nancy J. Cathedral Window: A Fresh Look. McGehee, Liz & Tucker, Shellie, eds. LC 90-50783. (Illus.). 36p. 1991. pap. 8.95 (*0-943574-81-1*) That Patchwork.
— Fun with Fat Quarters. Reikes, Ursula, ed. LC 93-33013. (Illus.). 88p. (Orig.). 1994. pap. 16.95 (*1-56477-042-7*) That Patchwork.
— Houses, Cottages & Cabins Patchwork Quilts: With Full-Size Patterns. Orig. Title: Housing Projects. (Illus.). 68p. reprint ed. pap. 5.95 (*0-486-26907-8*) Dover.
— Make Room for Quilts: Beautiful Decorating Ideas. LC 94-3125. 1994. 29.95 (*1-56477-047-8*) That Patchwork.
— Ocean Waves. (Orig.). 1992. pap. 6.95 (*0-486-27200-1*) Dover.
— Tea Party Time: Romantic Quilts & Tasty Tidbits. Weiland, Barbara, ed. LC 92-44945. (Illus.). 64p. (Orig.). 1992. pap. 17.95 (*1-56477-008-7*) That Patchwork.
— Threads of Time. (Orig.). 1993. pap. 9.95 (*0-486-27418-7*) Dover.
Martin, Nancy J. & Hopkins, Judy. Rotary Riot: Forty Fast & Fabulous Quilts. LC 91-26050. (Illus.). 128p. 1992. pap. 21.95 (*0-943574-86-2*) That Patchwork.
Martin, Neil B., jt. auth. see Crawford, James E.
Martin, Netta. World to Win, Heart to Lose. 416p. (Orig.). 1993. pap. 4.99 (*0-451-17686-3*, Onyx) NAL-Dutton.
Martin, Nicholas. An Operator's Manual for Successful Living. LC 88-70784. (Illus.). 160p. (Orig.). 1988. pap. 12.95 (*0-87516-608-3*) DeVorss.
***Martin, Nora B.** The Federal Census of 1870 for Alleghany County, Virginia. viii, 122p. 1989. pap. 11.00x (*0-935931-42-2*) Borgo Pr.
— The Federal Census of 1870 for Alleghany County, Virginia. viii, 122p. (C). 1989. reprint ed. lib. bdg. 29.00x (*0-8095-8144-2*) Borgo Pr.
— The Federal Censuses of 1830, 1840 & 1850 for Alleghany County, Virginia. (Illus.). iv, 118p. 1988. pap. 11.00x (*0-935931-36-8*) Borgo Pr.
— The Federal Censuses of 1830, 1840 & 1850 for Alleghany County, Virginia. iv, 118p. (C). 1988. reprint ed. lib. bdg. 29.00x (*0-8095-8208-2*) Borgo Pr.
Martin, Norman M. Systems of Logic. (C). 1989. pap. 22.95 (*0-521-36770-0*) Cambridge U Pr.
Martin, Olga J. Hollywood's Movie Commandments, a Handbook for Motion Picture Writers & Reviewers. LC 77-124018. (Literature of Cinema, Ser. 1). 1970. reprint ed. 21.95 (*0-405-01624-7*) Ayer.
Martin, Olive. Dial a Christian Message. Oglethorpe, Jean, ed. (C). 1989. pap. 30.00 (*1-85072-022-3*, Pub. by W Sessions UK) St Mut.
***Martin, Oralisa.** ORACLE: A Text for African American Youth Ministry. 268p. (Orig.). 1994. pap. text ed. 39.95 (*0-9642067-0-6*) Maranatha Pr.
Martin, P. Doctor Who: Mind Warp. 1989. pap. 3.95 (*0-426-20335-6*, Univ Books) Carol Pub Group.
— Mexico of the Twentieth Century, 2 vols. 1976. lib. bdg. 200.00 (*0-8490-2249-5*) Gordon Pr.
Martin, P. A., jt. ed. see Wickham, Glynne W.
Martin, P. L. & Oughton, D. R. Faber & Kell's Heating & Air Conditioning of Buildings. 7th ed. 672p. 1989. text ed. 94.95 (*0-408-50032-8*) Buttrwrth-Heinemann.
Martin, P. L. & Oughton, D. R., revs. Faber & Kell's Heating & Air-Conditioning of Buildings. 8th ed. LC 94-16759. (Illus.). 704p. 1995. 125.00 (*0-7506-1858-2*, Butterwrth Archit) Buttrwrth-Heinemann.
Martin, P. S., ed. see International Association for Quaternary Research Staff.
Martin, Pam. Touch the Angel's Hand: A Family's Struggle With Depression. LC 87-62874. 96p. (Orig.). 1988. pap. 6.95 (*0-940989-21-2*) Meyer Stone Bks.
Martin, Pamela, ed. Telecommuting: The Ride of the Future. 100p. (Orig.). (C). 1992. pap. text ed. 24.95 (*0-941375-93-5*) Diane Pub.
Martin, Pat. Cherished Czech Recipes. 160p. 1988. spiral bd. 5.50 (*0-941016-46-3*) Penfield.
— Czechoslovak Culture: Recipes, History & Folk Arts. Liffring-Zug, Joan & Zug, John, eds. 176p. pap. 12.95 (*0-941016-61-7*) Penfield.
— Czechoslovak Wit & Wisdom. (Illus.). 40p. 1984. pap. 4.95 (*0-941016-12-9*) Penfield.
Martin, Pat, comp. The Czech Book: Recipes & Traditions. LC 81-80852. (Illus.). 60p. 1981. pap. 7.95 (*0-9603858-6-X*) Penfield.
Martin, Pat, et al. Rebuses for Readers. 130p. 1992. pap. text ed. 18.00 (*0-87287-920-8*) Teacher Ideas Pr.
Martin, Pat H., jt. auth. see Martin, Earl.
Martin, Patricia. Ancient Echoes: Native American Words of Wisdom. 64p. 1994. 5.95 (*1-56245-035-2*) Great Quotations.

An Asterisk (*) at the beginning of an entry indicates that the title is appearing in BIP for the first time.

— Glovebox Cookbook. (Illus.). 128p. (Orig.). 1993. pap. 12.95 (0-86417-515-9, Pub. by Kangaroo Pr AT) Seven Hills Bk.
— A Meadowlark Calling. (Orig.). 1981. pap. 2.25 (0-8439-8034-6) Dorchester Pub Co.
— Modern Woman: A Stress Relief Manual Just for Women. 78p. 1995. 7.95 (1-56245-195-2) Great Quotations.
Martin, Patricia P. Days of Plenty, Days of Want. LC 88-71438. x, 76p. 1988. pap. 7.00 (0-916950-88-3) Biling Rev-Pr.
— Songs My Mother Sang to Me: An Oral History of Mexican American Women. LC 92-6745. (Illus.). 250p. (Orig.). 1992. 35.00 (0-8165-1279-5); pap. 16.95 (0-8165-1329-5) U of Ariz Pr.
Martin, Patricia S. Beverly Clearly: She Makes Reading Fun. (Reaching Your Goal Bks.). (Illus.). 24p. (J). (gr. 1-4). 1987. 10.95 (0-685-67568-8); lib. bdg. 14.60 (0-86592-171-7) Rourke Corp.
— Bill Cosby: Superstar. (Reaching Your Goal Bks.). (Illus.). 24p. (J). (gr. 1-4). 1987. 10.95 (0-685-67569-6); lib. bdg. 14.60 (0-86592-169-5) Rourke Corp.
— Christine McAuliffe: Reach for the Stars. (Reaching Your Goal Bks.). (Illus.). 24p. (J). (gr. 1-4). 1987. lib. bdg. 14.60 (0-86592-172-5) Rourke Corp.
— Christine McAuliffe: Reach for the Stars, Set. (Reaching Your Goal Bks.). (Illus.). 24p. (J). (gr. 1-4). 1987. lib. bdg. 10.95 (0-685-67566-1) Rourke Corp.
— Dale Murphy: Baseball's Gentle Giant. (Reaching Your Goal Bks.). (Illus.). 24p. (J). (gr. 1-4). 1987. 10.95 (0-685-67567-X); lib. bdg. 14.60 (0-86592-167-9) Rourke Corp.
— Dr. Seuss: We Love You. (Reaching Your Goal Bks.). (Illus.). 24p. (J). (gr. 1-4). 1987. lib. bdg. 14.60 (0-86592-168-7) Rourke Corp.
— Dr. Seuss: We Love You, Set. (Reaching Your Goal Bks.). (Illus.). 24p. (J). (gr. 1-4). 1987. 10.95 (0-685-67570-X) Rourke Corp.
— Jesse Jackson: A Black Leader. (Reaching Your Goal Bks.). (Illus.). 24p. (J). (gr. 1-4). 1987. 10.95 (0-685-67565-3); lib. bdg. 14.60 (0-86592-170-9) Rourke Corp.
— Samantha Smith: Little Ambassador. (Reaching Your Goal Bks.). (Illus.). 24p. (J). (gr. 1-4). 1987. 10.95 (0-685-58131-4); lib. bdg. 14.60 (0-86592-173-3) Rourke Corp.
— Ted Kennedy Jr. He Faced His Challenge. (Reaching Your Goal Bks.). (Illus.). 24p. (J). (gr. 1-4). 1987. 10.95 (0-685-58129-2); lib. bdg. 14.60 (0-86592-174-1) Rourke Corp.
Martin, Patricia Y. & O'Connor, Gerald G. The Social Environment: Open Systems Applications. 320p. (C). 1989. pap. text ed. 27.50 (0-582-29014-7, 71713) Longman.
Martin, Patricia Y., jt. ed. see Ferree, Myra M.
***Martin, Patrick.** Tail Code: The Complete History of USAF Tactical Aircraft Tail Code Markings. (Illus.). 240p. 1994. 45.00 (0-88740-513-4) Schiffer.
Martin, Patrick, jt. auth. see Christie, George C.
Martin, Patrick E. The Mill Creek Site & Pattern Recognition in Historical Archaeology. (Archaeological Completion Report Ser.: No. 10). (Illus.). 265p. (Orig.). 1985. pap. 16.00 (0-911872-54-X) Mackinac Island.
***Martin, Paul.** Dictionnaire de Synonymes pour Mots Croises, Par Nombre de Lettres. 110p. (FRE.). 1986. pap. 12.95 (0-7859-8081-4, 2853191737) Fr & Eur.
— Family Fare. 79p. 1976. pap. 3.95 (0-8341-0403-2) Beacon Hill.
— The Floating World Cycle Poems. 5.00 (0-686-15307-3) Great Raven Pr.
— How to Find a Perfect Partner: The Original, Complete & Simplified Scientific Method for Comparing the Energies of Horoscopes for Compatibility. LC 90-83656. 280p. (Orig.). 1991. pap. 19.95 (1-878027-48-4) Channel Media.
— Potts Models & Related Problems in Statistical Mechanics. (Advanced Series in Stat Mechanics: Vol. 5). 360p. 1991. text ed. 36.00 (981-02-0075-7) World Scientific Pub.
— Songs Visions Traditions of Northwest Indian Tribes. 4.00 (0-686-15297-2) Great Raven Pr.
— Victorian Snapshots. LC 72-9219. (Literature of Photography Ser.). 1978. reprint ed. 13.95 (0-405-04926-9) Ayer.
— We Serve: A History of the Lions Clubs. LC 90-23618. (Illus.). 448p. 1991. 24.95 (0-89526-534-6) Regnery Pub.
Martin, Paul, intro. Twenty-Five Human Rights Documents. rev. ed. 228p. 1994. pap. 5.00 (1-881482-01-4) Columbia Ctr Stu Human Rts.
Martin, Paul & Bateson, Patrick. Measuring Behaviour: An Introductory Guide. 2nd ed. (Illus.). 232p. (C). 1993. pap. 16.95 (0-521-44614-7) Cambridge U Pr.
Martin, Paul & Brady, Peggy. Port Angeles-Washington: A History, Vol. I. LC 82-82187. (Illus.). 252p. 1983. pap. 18.95 (0-918146-23-2) Peninsula WA.
Martin, Paul, ed. see Schwengel, Robert.
Martin, Paul, jt. auth. see Sherring-Lucas, Michael.
Martin, Paul, ed. see Striner, Richard & Kennon, Donald.
Martin, Paul C. Measurements & Correlation Functions. 108p. 1968. text ed. 121.00 (0-677-02440-1) Gordon & Breach.
Martin, Paul D. Messengers to the Brain: Your Fantastic Five Senses. Crump, Donald J., ed. LC 82-45636. (Books for World Explorers Series 5: No. 3). 104p. (J). (gr. 3-8). 1984. 8.95 (0-87044-499-9); lib. bdg. 12.50 (0-87044-504-9) Natl Geog.
— Science: It's Changing Your World. Crump, Donald J., ed. LC 85-2936. (Books for World Explorers Series 6: No. 3). (Illus.). 104p. (J). (gr. 3-8). 1985. lib. bdg. 12.50 (0-87044-521-9) Natl Geog.
Martin, Paul K., ed. Airline Handbook. 9th ed. (Illus.). 608p. (Orig.). 1985. pap. 16.00 (0-914553-85-2) AeroTravel Res.
— Airline Handbook. 10th ed. (Illus.). 700p. (Orig.). 1987. pap. 17.50 (0-914553-86-0) AeroTravel Res.
— The Airline Handbook: 7th Annual. (Illus.). 476p. (Orig.). 1982. pap. 14.00 (0-686-32833-7) AeroTravel Res.
— Airline Handbook: 8th Annual. (Illus.). 500p. (Orig.). 1983. pap. 15.00 (0-914553-83-6) AeroTravel Res.
Martin, Paul R. Psychological Management of Chronic Headaches: A Functional Perspective. LC 92-48225. (Treatment Manuals for Practitioners Ser.). 266p. 1993. lib. bdg. 27.95 (0-89862-211-5) Guilford Pr.
— The Wall Street Journal Stylebook. 3rd ed. LC 92-73699. 200p. 1992. 18.00 (1-881944-00-X) Dow Jones & Co.
— The Wall Street Journal Stylebook. 4th ed. 1995. 18.00 (1-881944-03-4, Wall St Jrnl) Dow Jones & Co.
Martin, Paul S. Lowry Ruin in Southwestern Colorado. (Chicago Field Museum of Natural History Fieldiana Anthropology Ser.: Vol. 23). 1969. reprint ed. 66.00 (0-527-01883-X) Periodicals Srv.
— SU Site Excavations at a Mongollon Village, Western New Mexico, 1st, 2nd, & 3rd Seasons. (Field Museum of Natural History Ser.). (Illus.). 1974. reprint ed. 34.00 (0-527-01892-9) Periodicals Srv.
Martin, Paul S. & Klein, Richard G., eds. Quaternary Extinctions: A Prehistoric Revolution. LC 83-18053. 892p. 1989. reprint ed. pap. text ed. 40.00 (0-8165-1100-4) U of Ariz Pr.
Martin, Paul S. & Rinaldo, John B. Turkey Foot Ridge Site: A Mogollon Village, Pine Lawn Valley, Western New Mexico. LC 50-12533. (Chicago Natural History Museum. Fieldiana: Anthropology Ser.: Vol. 38, No. 2). 165p. reprint ed. pap. 47.10 (0-317-42395-9, 2056068) Bks Demand.
***Martin, Paula & Carss, Marjorie.** Giants. Aragon, Laurie W., ed. (Illus.). 83p. (J). (gr. k-3). 1993. pap. 8.99 (0-614-05561-X, 4002) COMAP Inc.
Martin, Paula K. Discovering the WHAT of Management: The Complete Guide to the Kenning Principles of Management. (Illus.). 204p. 1990. 29.95 (0-943811-01-5) Renai Educ Services.
Martin, Peggy, ed. see Fifth Period LEAP & Honors English Classes.
Martin, Percy F. Latin America & the War. 1925. 11.25 (0-8446-1301-0) Peter Smith.
— Latin America & World War I. 1976. lib. bdg. 59.95 (0-8490-2130-8) Gordon Pr.
— Mexico's Treasure House: Guanajuato. 1977. lib. bdg. 59.95 (0-8490-2255-X) Gordon Pr.
— Salvador of the Twentieth Century. 1977. lib. bdg. 59.95 (0-8490-2562-1) Gordon Pr.
Martin, Percy F., ed. see De Oliveira Lima, Manuel.
Martin, Pete, jt. auth. see Crosby, Bing.
***Martin, Peter.** Edmond Malone, Shakespearean Scholar: A Literary Biography. (Cambridge Studies in Eighteenth-Century English Literature & Thought: 25). (Illus.). 320p. (C). 1995. 59.95 (0-521-46030-1) Cambridge U Pr.
— The Pleasure Gardens of Virginia: From Jamestown to Jefferson. (Colonial Williamsburg Studies in Colonial Chesapeake History & Culture). (Illus.). 281p. 1991. text ed. 35.00 (0-691-04786-3) Princeton U Pr.
— Real Estate Bargains! 52p. (Orig.). 1990. pap. 7.95 (1-882066-01-4) Peters Pr.
— Sounds & Society: Themes in the Sociology of Music. LC 94-37797. (Music & Society Ser.). 1995. text ed. write for info. (0-7190-3223-7, Pub. by Manchester Univ Pr UK) St Martin.
Martin, Peter, ed. City Lights (Five Issues), Set. (Avant-Garde Magazines Ser.). 368p. 1974. reprint ed. 36.95 (0-405-01758-8) Ayer.
Martin, Peter & Nicholls, John. Creating a Committed Workforce. 224p. (C). 1987. 70.00 (0-85292-379-1) St Mut.
***Martin, Peter & Pierce, Robyn.** Elementary Applied Statistics: An Activity Based Approach. 186p. (C). 1993. 60.00x (0-7300-1387-1) St Mut.
Martin, Peter, jt. ed. see Frith, Simon.
Martin, Peter, et al. Shawcross & Beaumont Aviation Reports. 1990. U.K. boxed 650.00 (0-406-13030-2) Butterworth Legal Pubs.
Martin, Peter, et al, eds. Shawcross & Beaumont: Air Law, 3 vols. U.K. ring bd. 990.00 (0-406-37319-1) Butterworth Legal Pubs.
Martin, Peter A. A Marital Therapy Manual. LC 93-74555. 224p. 1994. pap. 30.00 (1-56821-171-6) Aronson.
Martin, Peter G. Dynamic Performance Management: The Path to World Class Manufacturing. LC 92-29989. (Competitive Manufacturing Ser.). 1993. text ed. 39.95 (0-442-01300-0) Van Nos Reinhold.
Martin, Peter G., jt. auth. see Hayman, David L.
***Martin, Peter J.** The VCE Mathematics Experiment: An Evaluation. 1993. pap. 45.00 (0-7300-0814-2, Pub. by Deakin Univ AT) St Mut.
Martin, Peter M. Index of Social Security Act Cases Decided by the United States Court of Appeals for the Fourth Circuit. 39p. 1986. pap. 4.00 (0-685-23188-7, 28, 947C) NCLS Inc.
Martin, Peter W., ed. see Donahue, Charles, Jr.
***Martin, Philip.** Farmhouse Fiddlers: Music & Dance Traditions in the Rural Midwest. LC 94-78042. (Illus.). 128p. (Orig.). 1994. pap. 19.95 (1-883953-06-5) Midwest Trad.
— Rosemaling in the Upper Midwest. LC 89-51941. (Illus.). 94p. (Orig.). 1989. pap. 21.50 (0-9624369-0-9) WI Folk Mus.
***Martin, Philip, ed.** Immigration Reform & U. S. Agriculture. 500p. 1995. pap. 40.00 (1-879906-20-1, 3358) ANR Pubns CA.
Martin, Philip, jt. auth. see Cornelius, Wayne.
Martin, Philip, jt. auth. see Gustafsson, Lars.
Martin, Philip L. & Martin, David. The Endless Quest: Helping America's Farmworkers. 258p. (C). 1993. pap. text ed. 47.50 (0-8133-1768-1) Westview.
Martin, Philip L., jt. auth. see Lee, James A.
Martin, Philip L., jt. ed. see Papademetriou, Demetrious G.
Martin, Philip R. Auto Mechanics for the Complete Dummy. 2nd ed. LC 82-62322. (Illus.). 192p. 1983. pap. 4.95 (0-930968-02-6) Motormatics.
Martin, Philip W. Mad Women in Romantic Writing. LC 87-20678. 240p. 1988. text ed. 39.95 (0-312-01246-2) St Martin.
Martin, Philip W. & Jarvis, Robin, eds. Reviewing Romanticism. LC 91-24823. 244p. 1992. text ed. 55.00 (0-312-06801-8) St Martin.
Martin, Phillip L. Trade & Migration: NAFTA & Agriculture. LC 93-2922. (Policy Analysis in International Economics Ser.: No. 38). 158p. 1993. pap. 15.00 (0-88132-201-6) Inst Intl Eco.
Martin, Phyllis. Job-Hunt Success Kit. rev. ed. (Illus.). 147p. 1981. pap. text ed. 13.50 (0-685-31062-0) Ctr Career Dev.
— Job-Hunt Success Plan, Adult Learner Edition. abr. rev. ed. (Illus.). 123p. 1989. pap. text ed. 8.50 (0-685-31059-0) Ctr Career Dev.
— Job-Hunt Success Plan, High School Edition. abr. rev. ed. (Illus.). 118p. (YA). (gr. 11-12). 1989. pap. text ed. 8.50 (0-685-31060-4) Ctr Career Dev.
— Martin's Magic Formula for Getting the Right Job. rev. ed. 192p. 1987. pap. 8.95 (0-312-01065-6) St Martin.
— Word Watcher's Handbook. 3rd ed. 1991. pap. 6.95 (0-312-05541-2) St Martin.
— Word Watcher's Handbook: A Deletionary of the Most Abused & Misused Words. 144p. 1982. pap. 4.95 (0-312-88938-0) St Martin.
Martin, Phyllis C., jt. auth. see Vincent, Elizabeth L.
Martin, Phyllis G., jt. auth. see Martin, John H.
***Martin, Phyllis M.** Lesiure & Society in Colonial Brazzaville. (African Studies: No. 87). (Illus.). 300p. (C). Date not set. write for info. (0-521-49551-2) Cambridge U Pr.
Martin, Phyllis M. & O'Meara, Patrick, eds. Africa. 2nd ed. LC 85-45413. (Illus.). 480p. 1986. 40.00 (0-253-30211-0); pap. 14.95 (0-253-20392-9, MB-392) Ind U Pr.
— Africa. 3rd ed. LC 95-5772. 1995. write for info. (0-253-32916-7); pap. write for info. (0-253-20984-6) Ind U Pr.
Martin, Phyllis M., jt. ed. see Birmingham, David.
Martin, Pierre-Marie. Introduction to International Relations. Johari, J. C., ed. 184p. 1987. text ed. 25.00 (81-207-0597-1, Pub. by Sterling Pubs II) Apt Bks.
Martin, Pol. Guide to Modern American Cooking. 1993. 17.99 (0-517-10327-3) Random Hse Value.
Martin, Pricilla C., jt. auth. see Martin, Steele W.
Martin, Priscilla. Chaucer's Women: Nuns, Wives & Amazons. LC 90-70034. 270p. (C). 1990. text ed. 33.95x (0-87745-293-8) U of Iowa Pr.
Martin, Priscilla, ed. Prayers New & Old. rev. ed. 94p. 1993. pap. 1.50 (0-88028-140-5, 375) Forward Movement.
Martin, Prisha. The Poor People of England & Other Works. (Orig.). (J). 1991. pap. write for info. (1-879019-04-3) Amer Edit Servs.
Martin, Prudence. Passion's Persuasion. 1990. pap. 2.95 (0-8217-3083-5) Zebra.
— Wager on Love. 1991. pap. 3.50 (0-8217-3548-9) Zebra.
Martin, Purvis, ed. Handbook of Office Gynecology. LC 79-2690. 320p. 1985. pap. 31.95 (0-685-42868-0, 792690, Grune) Saunders.
Martin, Purvis L. Ambulatory Gynecologic Surgery. LC 78-55286. (Illus.). 394p. 1979. 50.00 (0-88416-209-5, Yr Bk Med Pubs) Mosby Yr Bk.
Martin, R. Gel Electrophoresis: Nucleic Acids. (Introduction to Biotechniques Ser.). 160p. (Orig.). 1994. pap. 47.50x (1-872748-28-7, Pub. by Bios Scientific UK) Coronet Bks.
Martin, R., jt. ed. see Bergbreiter, D. E.
Martin, R. A. Syntactical & Critical Concordance to the Greek Text of Baruch & the Epistle of Jeremiah. (Computer Bible Ser.: Vol. XII). (GRE.). 1977. pap. 15.00 (0-935106-09-X) Biblical Res Assocs.
Martin, R. A. & Scorza, Sylvio. Syntactical Concordance to the Correlated Greek & Hebrew Text of Ruth. (Computer Bible Ser.: Vol. 30). 279p. (Orig.). 1988. 45.00 (0-935106-26-X) Biblical Res Assocs.
Martin, R. A., jt. auth. see Elliott, John H.
Martin, R. Bruce & Burr, David B. Structure, Function, & Adaptation of Compact Bone. 288p. 1989. 109.50 (0-88167-500-8) Raven.
Martin, R. C. The Cities & the Federal System. LC 77-74949. (American Federalism-the Urban Dimension Ser.). 1978. reprint ed. lib. bdg. 23.95 (0-405-10495-2) Ayer.
Martin, R. D. Primate Origins & Evolution: A Phylogenetic Reconstruction. (Illus.). 832p. 1990. text ed. 135.00 (0-691-08565-X) Princeton U Pr.
Martin, R. D., ed. New Quantitative Developments in Primatology & Anthropology, 1989. (Journal: Folia Primatologica: Vol. 53, No. 1-4). (Illus.). 248p. 1990. pap. 158.50 (3-8055-5121-5) S Karger.
Martin, R. D., tr. see Charles-Dominique, Pierre.
Martin, R. D., et al, eds. Paternity in Primates: Tests & Theories: Implications of Human DNA Fingerprint. (Illus.). xii, 288p. 1991. 198.50 (3-8055-5494-X) S Karger.
Martin, R. E. & Chapman, B. R., eds. Contributions in Mammalogy in Honor of Robert L. Packard. (Special Publications: No. 22). 234p. 1984. 50.00 (0-89672-124-8); pap. 25.00 (0-89672-123-X) Tex Tech Univ Pr.
Martin, R. G. Knight of the Snows (Willfred Grenfell) 1982. pap. 3.95 (0-87508-609-8) Chr Lit.
Martin, R. H. Applying Information Science & Consensus-Formation Technology Utilization to Do Zeitgeist-Sector Modeling, Scenario Reality Planning Bibliography, No. 3, Nos. 1172-1173. 1976. 12.50 (0-686-20416-6) CPL Biblios.
Martin, R. H., ed. see Tacitus.
Martin, R. H., ed. see Terence.
Martin, R. M. Logico-Linguistic Papers. (Publications in Language Sciences). xii, 202p. 1981. 67.70 (90-70176-39-4); pap. 50.00 (90-70176-93-9) Mouton.
— Peirce's Logic of Relations & Other Studies. 156p. 1980. pap. 34.60 (90-70176-17-3) Mouton.
Martin, R. M. & Teo, K. L. Optimal Control of Drug Administration in Cancer Chemotherapy. 204p. 1993. text ed. 61.00 (981-02-1428-6) World Scientific Pub.
Martin, R. N. Pierre Duhem. LC 91-26643. (C). 1991. 44.95 (0-8126-9159-8); pap. 19.95 (0-8126-9160-1) Open Court.
Martin, R. Niall, ed. see Leibniz, Gottfried W.
Martin, R. R., jt. auth. see Marshall, A. D.
Martin, Rafe. The Boy Who Lived with Seals. (Illus.). 32p. (J). (ps-3). 1993. lib. bdg. 14.95 (0-399-22413-0, Putnam) Putnam Pub Group.
— The Brave Little Parrot. LC 95-14194. (Illus.). (J). 1996. write for info. (0-399-22825-X, Putnam) Putnam Pub Group.
— The Hungry Tigress. 2nd rev. ed. LC 90-7993. 288p. 1990. per. 15.00 (0-938077-25-2) Parallax Pr.
— The Rough-Face Girl. (Illus.). 32p. (J). (ps-3). 1992. lib. bdg. 14.95 (0-399-21859-9, Putnam) Putnam Pub Group.
— The Snow Woman. LC 94-43464. (J). 1996. write for info. (0-399-22677-X, Putnam) Putnam Pub Group.
— A Storyteller's Story. LC 92-7794. (Meet the Author Ser.). (Illus.). 32p. (J). (gr. 2-5). 1992. 13.95 (0-913461-03-2) R Owen Pubs.
— Will's Mammoth. (Illus.). 32p. (J). (ps-3). 1989. 15.95 (0-399-21627-8, Putnam) Putnam Pub Group.
— Will's Mammoth. (Sandcastle Ser.). (Illus.). 32p. (J). (ps-1). 1993. pap. 4.95 (0-399-22603-6, Putnam) Putnam Pub Group.
***Martin, Rafe & Morimoto, Junko.** One Hand Clapping: Zen Stories for All Ages. LC 94-35257. (Illus.). 46p. 1995. 16.95 (0-8478-1853-5) Rizzoli Intl.
***Martin, Ralph.** Catholic Church at the End of an Age: What Is the Spirit Saying? 309p. (Orig.). 1994. pap. 12.95 (0-89870-524-X) Ignatius Pr.
Martin, Ralph, ed. The Mathematics of Surfaces II. (Institute of Mathematics & Its Applications Conference Series, New Ser.: New Series 11). 528p. 1987. 85.00 (0-19-853619-4) OUP.
***Martin, Ralph & Williamson, Peter, eds.** John Paul II & the New Evangelization. 288p. (Orig.). Date not set. pap. 12.95 (0-89870-536-3) Ignatius Pr.
Martin, Ralph, et al. Teaching Science for All Children. LC 93-31546. 1993. text ed. write for info. (0-205-14875-1) Allyn.
Martin, Ralph E., Jr. The Credibility Principle & Teacher Attitudes Toward Science. LC 83-49429. (American University Studies: Education: Ser. XIV, Vol. 3). 191p. (Orig.). (C). 1984. pap. text ed. 20.55 (0-8204-0101-3) P Lang Pubs.
Martin, Ralph G. A Hero for Our Time: An Intimate Story of the Kennedy Years. 1984. mass mkt. 6.99 (0-449-20604-1) Fawcett.
— Jennie: The Life of Lady Randolph Churchill, Vol. I: The Romantic Years 1854-1895. 1990. pap. 12.95 (0-13-511882-4) P-H.
— Seeds of Destruction: Joe Kennedy & His Sons. LC 94-48357. 1995. write for info. (0-399-14061-1) Putnam Pub Group.
Martin, Ralph P. Colossians: The Church's Lord & the Christian's Liberty. 192p. 1972. 12.50 (0-85364-125-0) Attic Pr.
— Colossians & Philemon. rev. ed. (New Century Bible Commentary Ser.). 192p. 1981. pap. 14.99 (0-8028-1908-7) Eerdmans.
— Commentary on Philippians. (New Century Bible Commentary Ser.). 192p. 1980. pap. 14.99 (0-8028-1840-4) Eerdmans.
— Ephesians, Colossians, & Philemon. (Interpretation: a Bible Commentary for Preaching & Teaching Ser.). 160p. (Orig.). 1992. text ed. 18.00 (0-8042-3139-7) Westminster John Knox.
— Epistle of Paul to the Philippians. rev. ed. (Tyndale Bible Commentaries Ser.). 1988. pap. 9.99 (0-8028-0310-5) Eerdmans.
— WBC, Vol. 40: Second Corinthians. 527p. 1985. write for info. (0-8499-0239-8) Word Inc.
— WBC, Vol. 48: James. 240p. 1988. write for info. (0-8499-0247-9) Word Inc.
— WBT: First & Second Corinthians. 131p. 1989. 9.99 (0-8499-0623-7) Word Inc.
— Worship in the Early Church. rev. ed. 144p. 1975. reprint ed. pap. 9.99 (0-8028-1613-4) Eerdmans.
— The Worship of God: Some Theological, Pastoral & Practical Reflections. 237p. (Orig.). 1982. pap. 13.99 (0-8028-1934-6) Eerdmans.
Martin, Ralph P., jt. auth. see Chester, Andrew.
Martin, Ramela. Out of Darkness. 1989. write for info. (0-916431-28-2) Zoryan Ins.
Martin, Randall. Edmund Ironside & Anthony Brewer's the Love-Sick King. rev. ed. LC 91-26246. (Renaissance Imagination Ser.). 488p. 1991. 96.00 (0-8153-0454-4) Garland.
Martin, Randy. Performance As Political Act: The Embodied Self. LC 89-33473. (Critical Perspectives in Social Theory Ser.). (Illus.). 223p. 1990. text ed. 47.95 (0-89789-174-0, H174, Greenwood Pr) Greenwood.

An Asterisk (*) at the beginning of an entry indicates that the title is appearing in BIP for the first time.

— Socialist Ensembles: Theater & State in Cuba & Nicaragua. 208p. 1994. text ed. 44.95x (*0-8166-2480-1*); pap. text ed. 19.95x (*0-8166-2482-8*) U of Minn Pr.

Martin, Randy, et al. Criminological Thought: Pioneers Past & Present. (Illus.). 380p. (C). 1989. text ed. write for info. (*0-02-376501-1*) Macmillan.

Martin, Raquel. Today's Health Alternative. (Illus.). 456p. (Orig.). (C). 1992. pap. text ed. 16.95 (*0-922356-45-9*) Amer West Pubs.

Martin, Ray. The Ninety-Nine Critical Shots in Pool: Everything You Need to Know to Learn & Master the Game. 240p. 1993. pap. 13.00 (*0-8129-2241-7*, Times Bks) Random.

Martin, Ray & Rankin, Lee. Building Garden Furniture: More Than Thirty Beautiful Outdoor Projects. (Illus.). 160p. 1994. pap. 15.95 (*0-8069-8375-2*) Sterling.

Martin, Ray & Reeves, Rosser. The Ninety-Nine Critical Shots in Pool. LC 75-36260. (Illus.). 256p. 1982. write for info. (*0-8129-0618-7*, Times Bks); pap. 12.00 (*0-8129-6313-X*, Times Bks) Random.

Martin, Raymond. An Introduction to New Testament Greek. 1980. text ed. 7.50 (*0-915948-07-9*) Bks Distinction.

— The Past Within Us: An Empirical Approach to Philosophy of History. 192p. (C). 1989. text ed. 29.95 (*0-691-07341-4*) Princeton U Pr.

Martin, Raymond, ed. Success Stories in American Electronics Industry. 106p. 1991. 20.00 (*1-55822-033-X*) Am Prod & Inventory.

Martin, Raymond & Scorza, Sylvio. Concordance to the Correlated Greek & Hebrew Text of Ruth, Part II: The Greek & Hebrew Syntactical Concordance. Baird, J. Arthur & Freedman, David N., eds. (Computer Bible Ser.: Vol. XXX-B). 209p. (Orig.). 1990. pap. 45.00 (*0-935106-30-8*) Biblical Res Assocs.

Martin, Raymond, jt. auth. see Kolak, Daniel.

Martin, Raymond, jt. ed. see Kolak, Daniel.

Martin, Raymond A. Studies in the Life & Ministry of the Early Paul & Related Issues. LC 93-20603. 264p. 1993. text ed. 89.95 (*0-7734-2368-0*, Mellen Biblical Pr) E Mellen.

— Studies in the Life & Ministry of the Historical Jesus. (Illus.). 172p. (C). 1995. lib. bdg. 39.00 (*0-8191-9772-6*); pap. text ed. 21.50 (*0-8191-9773-4*) U Pr of Amer.

— Syntax Criticism of Johannine Literature, the Catholic Epistles & the Gospel Passion Accounts. LC 89-13567. (Studies in the Bible & Early Christianity: Vol. 18). 200p. 1989. lib. bdg. 89.95 (*0-88946-618-1*) E Mellen.

— Syntax Criticism of the Synoptic Gospels. LC 87-5646. (Studies in Bible & Early Christianity: Vol. 10). 232p. 1987. lib. bdg. 99.95 (*0-88946-610-6*) E Mellen.

Martin, Rebecca R. Libraries & the Changing Face of Academia: Responses to Growing Multicultural Populations. LC 93-42118. 1993. 29.50 (*0-8108-2824-3*) Scarecrow.

Martin, Reed. Extraordinary Children, Ordinary Lives: Stories Behind Special Education Case Law. LC 91-62230. 180p. (Orig.). 1991. pap. text ed. 12.95 (*0-87822-332-0*, 4515) Res Press.

Martin, Reg. Making Wood Trucks & Construction Vehicles. LC 87-10260. (Illus.). 132p. (Orig.). 1987. pap. 10.95 (*0-8069-6570-3*) Sterling.

Martin, Reginald. Black Aesthetic Criticism: An Annotated Bibliography. (Bibliographies of Modern Critics & Critical Schools Ser.: Vol. 16). 250p. 37.00 (*0-8240-6890-4*, H1290) Garland.

Martin, Regis. Hope & Reality of Heaven. 28p. 1993. pap. 3.00 (*0-940535-62-9*) Franciscan U Pr.

— Images of Grace: 33 Christian Poems. 50p. 1994. pap. 4.95 (*0-940535-79-3*, UP179) Franciscan U Pr.

***Martin, Rene.** Dictionnaire Culturel de la Mythologie Greco-Romaine. 1992. write for info. (*0-7859-7721-X*, 2091800740) Fr & Eur.

Martin, Renee & Martin, Don. The Survival Guide for Women: Single - Married - Divorced Protecting Your Future. LC 91-8608. 224p. 1991. pap. 16.95 (*0-89526-737-3*) Regnery Pub.

Martin, Renee, ed. see Martin, Don.

Martin, Renee, jt. auth. see Martin, Donald.

***Martin, Renee J., ed.** Practicing What We Teach: Confronting Diversity in Teacher Education. (Social Context of Education Ser.). 288p. 1995. text ed. 59.50x (*0-7914-2549-5*); pap. text ed. 19.95x (*0-7914-2550-9*) State U NY Pr.

Martin, Rex. A System of Rights. 528p. 1993. 55.00 (*0-19-827374-6*) OUP.

Martin, Rex, ed. see MacCallum, Gerald C., Jr.

***Martin-Reynolds, Joanne & Pogacar, Timothy.** A Holistic View of Teaching Languages in Elementary & Middle Schools. 264p. (C). Date not set. pap. text ed. 30.00 (*1-57074-147-6*) Greyden Pr.

Martin, Rhona. Goodbye, Sally. large type ed. 640p. 1989. 17.95 (*0-7089-2015-2*) Ulverscroft.

— Writing Historical Fiction. 96p. 1988. 12.95 (*0-312-01848-7*) St Martin.

Martin, Rich. Designing Documents for Image Based Recognition. 1993. write for info. (*0-318-72173-2*) Assn Inform & Image Mgmt.

Martin, Richard. Dream of Long Headdresses: Poems from a Thousand Hospitals. LC 87-63356. 68p. (Orig.). 1988. pap. 8.00 (*0-936563-12-5*) Signpost.

— Fashion & Surrealism. LC 87-45490. (Illus.). 240p. 1987. pap. 35.00 (*0-8478-1073-9*) Rizzoli Intl.

— Ink in Her Blood: The Life & Crime Fiction of Margery Allingham. LC 88-27789. (Challenging the Literary Canon Ser.). 272p. 1991. 39.00 (*0-8357-1923-5*); pap. 29.00 (*0-8357-2028-4*) Univ Rochester Pr.

— K'aiiroondak: Behind the Willows. Pfisterer, Bill, ed. (Illus.). 321p. (Orig.). (C). 1993. pap. 19.00 (*1-877962-26-0*) Univ AK Ctr CCS.

— White Man Appears on Southern California Beach. LC 90-83254. 80p. (Orig.). 1991. pap. 9.95 (*0-9627420-0-7*) Bottom Fish.

***Martin, Richard, ed.** Contemporary Fashion. 850p. 1995. text ed. 135.00 (*1-55862-173-3*) St James Pr.

— The New Urban Landscape. LC 89-63218. (Illus.). 132p. 1990. pap. 29.95 (*0-9624916-0-8*) Drenttel Doyle.

Martin, Richard & Koda, Harold. Infra-Apparel. (Illus.). 132p. 1993. pap. 29.95 (*0-8109-6430-9*) Abrams.

— Jocks & Nerds: Men's Style in the Twentieth Century. LC 88-43418. (Illus.). 224p. 1989. pap. 29.95 (*0-8478-1046-1*) Rizzoli Intl.

— Orientalism: Vision of the East in Western Dress. (Illus.). 96p. 1995. pap. 29.95 (*0-8109-6490-2*) Abrams.

— Splash! A History of Swimwear. LC 89-43564. (Illus.). 144p. 1990. pap. 29.95 (*0-8478-1186-7*) Rizzoli Intl.

— Waist Not. (Illus.). 16p. 1994. 7.95 (*1-870997-12-3*) Metro Mus Art.

***Martin, Richard & Koda, Harols.** Orientalism: Visions of the East in Western Dress. 1994. write for info. (*0-87099-733-5*) Metro Mus Art.

Martin, Richard, jt. auth. see Friedman, Ellen J.

***Martin, Richard, et al.** Panfishing. LC 91-60047. (Complete Angler's Library). 278p. 1991. write for info. (*0-914697-37-4*) N Amer Outdoor Grp.

Martin, Richard C. Islam: A Cultural Perspective. (Illus.). 192p. (C). 1981. pap. text ed. 19.33 (*0-13-506345-0*) P-H.

— Islamic Studies: A History of Religions Approach. 2nd ed. LC 94-41956. 1995. pap. text ed. write for info. (*0-13-205543-0*) P-H.

Martin, Richard C., ed. Approaches to Islam in Reglious Studies. LC 85-1099. 243p. 1985. 30.00 (*0-8165-0868-2*) U of Ariz Pr.

Martin, Richard J., ed. Cardiorespiratory Disorders During Sleep. 2nd rev. ed. (Illus.). 408p. 1990. 55.00 (*0-87993-380-1*) Futura Pub.

— Nocturnal Asthma: Mechanisms & Treatment. LC 92-48725. (Illus.). 408p. 1993. 72.00 (*0-87993-546-4*) Futura Pub.

Martin, Richard M. Events, Reference, & Logical Form. LC 77-24685. 271p. reprint ed. pap. 77.30 (*0-317-55388-7*, 2029492) Bks Demand.

— Logical Semiotics & Mereology. LC 91-41368. (Foundations of Semiotics Ser.: No. 16). xiii, 282p. 1992. 89.00 (*90-272-3288-1*) Benjamins North Am.

— Metaphysical Foundations: Mereology & Metalogic. (Analytica Ser.). 387p. 1988. 92.00 (*3-88405-053-2*) Philosophia Pr.

— Pragmatics, Truth, & Language. (Boston Studies in the Philosophy of Science: No. XXXVIII). 1979. lib. bdg. 84.00 (*90-277-0992-0*); pap. text ed. 36.50 (*90-277-0993-9*) Kluwer Ac.

— Semiotics & Linguistic Structure: A Primer of Philosophic Logic. LC 78-6873. 321p. 1978. 59.50 (*0-87395-381-9*) State U NY Pr.

Martin, Richard M., jt. ed. see Eisele, Carolyn.

Martin, Richard P. The Language of Heroes: Speech & Performance in the "Iliad" LC 89-42889. (Myth & Poetics Ser.). 288p. 1989. 38.50 (*0-8014-2353-8*) Cornell U Pr.

— The Language of Heroes: Speech & Performance in the Iliad. LC 89-42889. (Myth & Poetics Ser.). 288p. 1993. pap. 14.95 (*0-8014-8070-1*) Cornell U Pr.

Martin, Richard P., ed. Bulfinch's Mythology: The Age of Fable, the Age of Chivalry, Legends of Charlemagne. LC 91-55002. (Illus.). 640p. 1991. 37.50 (*0-06-270025-1*, Harper Ref) HarpC.

Martin, Richard P., tr. see Propp, Vladimir.

Martin, Rick W., jt. ed. see Rivlin, Michel E.

***Martin, Riley L. & Wann, O-Qua T.** The Coming of Tan: Past, Present & Future of Humanity, Extraterrestrial Attention, Environmental Catastrophe. Cooperman, Curtis L., ed. (Illus.). 370p. (Orig.). Date not set. pap. 29.95 (*0-9645745-0-0*) Historicty Prodn.

Martin, Robert, jt. auth. see Fisher, Jeffrey.

Martin, Robert, jt. auth. see Laplante, Phillip.

Martin, Robert, jt. ed. see Winter, Robert.

Martin, Robert A., ed. The Writer's Craft: Hopwood Lectures, 1965-1981. 304p. 1982. pap. 14.95 (*0-472-06337-5*) U of Mich Pr.

Martin, Robert A. & Barnosky, Anthony D., eds. Morphological Change in Quaternary Mammals of North America. (Illus.). 400p. (C). 1993. 74.95 (*0-521-40450-9*) Cambridge U Pr.

Martin, Robert A. & Poland, Elizabeth Y. Learning to Change: A Self-Management Approach to Adjustment. 1980. text ed. write for info. (*0-07-040635-9*); Instr's. man. teacher ed, pap. text ed. write for info. (*0-07-040636-7*) McGraw.

Martin, Robert C. The Deep Sea Diver: Yesterday, Today & Tomorrow. LC 77-19076. (Illus.). 222p. 1979. text ed. 10.00 (*0-87033-238-4*) Cornell Maritime.

— Designing C Plus Plus Applications Using the Booch Notation. 1995. text ed. 45.00 (*0-13-203837-4*) P-H.

Martin, Robert C., et al. Practical Speech for Modern Business. LC 63-7333. 1963. 29.50 (*0-89197-353-2*) Irvington.

Martin, Robert D. Bankruptcy Forms. 1989. write for info. (*0-318-65474-1*, P05824) P-H.

Martin, Robert D. & Doud, Laurel M. Leslie Lewis Doud: His Family & Ancestors. LC 93-80964. (Illus.). 33p. reprint ed. pap. 25.00 (*0-7837-6970-9*, AU00448) Bks Demand.

Martin, Robert D., jt. auth. see Ginsberg, Robert E.

Martin, Robert D., tr. see Lorenz, Konrad.

Martin, Robert E., jt. auth. see DeBlase, Anthony F.

Martin, Robert E., jt. auth. see Williams, Wilson E.

Martin, Robert F. Howard Kester & the Struggle for Social Justice in the South, 1904-1977. (Minds of the New South Ser.). (Illus.). (C). 1991. text ed. 29.50 (*0-8139-1294-6*) U Pr of Va.

— National Income in the United States, 1799-1938. LC 75-22827. (America in Two Centuries Ser.). 1976. reprint ed. 18.95 (*0-405-07699-1*) Ayer.

Martin, Robert G., et al, eds. Foldable Intraoccular Lenses. LC 93-7927. 272p. 1993. 75.00 (*1-55642-219-9*) SLACK Inc.

Martin, Robert J. Professional Management of Housekeeping Operations. LC 85-6431. 224p. 1986. teacher ed write for info. (*0-471-82374-0*); Net. teacher ed, text ed. 26.25 (*0-471-84226-5*) Wiley.

— Wise Words to the Graduate. (Contempo Ser.). 1978. pap. 2.49 (*0-8010-6043-5*) Baker Bk.

Martin, Robert J. & Jones, Tom. Professional Management of Housekeeping Operations. 2nd ed. 480p. 1992. Net. text ed. write for info. (*0-471-54779-4*) Wiley.

Martin, Robert K. Hero, Captain, & Stranger: Male Friendship, Social Critique, & Literary Form in the Sea Novels of Herman Melville. LC 85-8674. xvi, 144p. 1986. 27.50 (*0-8078-1672-8*); pap. 10.95 (*0-8078-4146-3*) U of NC Pr.

Martin, Robert K., ed. The Continuing Presence of Walt Whitman: The Life after the Life. LC 91-44249. (Illus.). 282p. 1992. 28.95x (*0-87745-366-7*) U of Iowa Pr.

Martin, Robert L. The City Moves West: Economic & Industrial Growth in Central West Texas. LC 72-89807. 200p. reprint ed. pap. 57.00 (*0-685-20613-0*, 2030547) Bks Demand.

Martin, Robert L., ed. The Paradox of the Liar. xvi, 154p. (C). 1979. reprint ed. lib. bdg. 27.00 (*0-917930-30-4*); reprint ed. pap. text ed. 13.00 (*0-917930-10-X*) Ridgeview.

Martin, Robert M. Antique Maps of the Nineteenth Century World. 1989. 29.99 (*0-517-67881-0*) Random Hse Value.

— The Meaning of Language. 212p. 1987. pap. 12.95x (*0-262-63108-3*) MIT Pr.

— The Philosopher's Dictionary. 2nd ed. 1994. pap. 12.95 (*1-55111-044-X*) Broadview Pr.

— There Are Two Errors in the the Title of This Book: A Sourcebook of Philosophical Puzzles, Problems, & Paradoxes. 226p. (Orig.). 1992. pap. 15.95 (*0-921149-98-0*) Broadview Pr.

Martin, Robert P. The Death Penalty: God's Will or Man's Folly? 87p. (Orig.). (C). 1991. pap. 5.95 (*0-9622508-5-6*) Simpson NJ.

Martin, Robert S. Carnegie Denied: Communities Rejecting Carnegie Library Construction Grants, 1898-1925. LC 92-25741. (Beta Phi Mu Monograph: No. 3). 200p. 1993. text ed. 47.95 (*0-313-28609-4*, MNY, Greenwood Pr) Greenwood.

Martin, Robert S., ed. Scholarly Communication in an Electronic Environment: Issues for Research Libraries. 136p. 1993. 28.95 (*0-8389-7686-7*) Assn Coll & Res Libs.

Martin, Robert S. & Martin, James C. Contours of Discovery: Printed Maps Delineating the Texas & Southwestern Chapters in the Cartographic History of North America, 1513-1930. LC 82-83547. 1982. 39.95 (*0-87611-058-8*) Tex St Hist Assn.

Martin, Robert S., jt. auth. see Fisher, Jeffery.

Martin, Robert S., jt. auth. see Fisher, Jeffrey D.

Martin, Robert S., jt. auth. see Lovell, Douglas D.

Martin, Roberta, ed. Lesson Plans for a Unit on Japan. (Curriculum Project Ser.). 70p. 1989. pap. 19.50 (*0-913418-11-0*) Columbia U E Asian Inst.

Martin, Roberta, intro. National Review of Asia in American Textbooks in 1993: Secondary Level: World History, World Cultures, World Geography. LC 93-27198. 144p. (Orig.). 1993. pap. 15.00 (*0-924304-16-2*) Assn Asian Studies.

Martin, Roberta, jt. ed. see Keyser, Catherine.

Martin, Roberta, et al, eds. Contemporary Japan: A Teaching Workbook. 3rd rev. ed. (Illus.). 820p. 1988. teacher ed 45.00 (*0-685-21891-0*) Columbia U E Asian Inst.

Martin, Roberta P. To Walk with Jesus: A Guide Through Lent. LC 93-74039. 144p. (Orig.). 1994. pap. 6.95 (*0-87793-520-3*) Ave Maria.

Martin, Robin, ed. see Dare, Benjamin.

Martin, Robin B. & Krasnow, Erwin G. Radio Financing: A Guide to Lenders & Investors. 51p. (Orig.). 1990. pap. 40.00 (*0-89324-090-7*) Natl Assn Broadcasters.

Martin, Roderick. Bargaining Power. LC 92-13855. (Illus.). 208p. 1992. 49.95 (*0-19-827255-3*) OUP.

Martin, Rodney. The Making of a Picture Book. LC 88-42911. (Illus.). 32p. (J). (gr. 3-4). 1989. lib. bdg. 18.60 (*1-55532-958-6*) Gareth Stevens Inc.

— There's a Dinosaur in the Park! LC 86-42811. (Illus.). 31p. (J). (gr. 2-3). 1987. lib. bdg. 18.60 (*1-55532-151-8*) Gareth Stevens Inc.

— There's a Dinosaur in the Park! 32p. (C). 1995. 4.95 (*0-947212-18-3*, Pub. by ERA Pubns AT) Pubs Dist MI.

— Wise & Wacky Works by Anonymous. 32p. (J). 1995. 12.95 (*1-86374-039-2*, Pub. by ERA Pubns AT) Pubs Dist MI.

Martin, Roger. Pigs & Other Animals. LC 79-92628. 300p. (C). 1980. 10.95 (*0-936634-00-6*) Myco Pub Hse.

Martin, Roger, jt. auth. see Lee, Anthony.

Martin, Roger, et al. Cows Are Freaky When They Look at You: An Oral History of the Kaw Valley Hemp Pickers. (Illus.). 160p. 1991. pap. 15.00 (*0-922820-13-9*) Watermark Pr.

— Writing in the Design Disciplines. Bridwell-Bowles, Lillian et al, eds. (Monograph Ser.: Vol. 3). (Illus.). 108p. (Orig.). 1992. pap. 6.00 (*1-881221-02-4*) U Minn Ctr Interdis.

Martin, Roger A. John J. Zubly: Colonial Georgia Minister. 1981. 27.95 (*0-405-14095-9*) Ayer.

Martin, Roger H. Evangelicals United: Ecumenical Stirrings in Pre-Victorian Britain, 1795-1830. LC 82-10784. (Studies in Evangelicalism: No. 4). 244p. 1983. 25.00 (*0-8108-1586-9*) Scarecrow.

Martin, Roland. Greek Architecture. LC 88-42689. (History of World Architecture Ser.). (Illus.). 224p. 1988. pap. 29.95 (*0-8478-0968-4*) Rizzoli Intl.

— Roland Martin's One Hundred One Bass-Catching Secrets. Tucker, Tim, ed. 1988. 19.95 (*0-8329-0457-0*, Winchester Pr) New Win Pub.

Martin, Roland, jt. auth. see Ginouves, Rene.

Martin, Ron. Here Comes Barbell Brock, No. 1: America's Funniest Strongman. (Illus.). 64p. (Orig.). 1988. pap. 3.00 (*0-9621315-0-4*) Christian H & D Pubs.

Martin, Ron, jt. ed. see Townroe, Peter.

Martin, Ron G., ed. Libraries for the Future: Planning Buildings That Work: Proceedings of the Library Buildings Preconference, June 27 & 28, 1991, Atlanta, Georgia. LC 92-2252. (Illus.). 190p. (C). 1992. pap. text ed. 27.00 (*0-8389-0597-8*) ALA.

Martin, Ron G., jt. ed. see Hawthorne, Pat.

Martin, Ronald. Watch Out World...Here Comes Barbell Brock, Vol. 1: America's Funniest Strongman. (Illus.). 64p. (Orig.). 1988. pap. 3.00 (*0-685-22540-2*) Christian H & D Pubs.

Martin, Ronald E. American Literature & the Destruction of Knowledge: Innovative Writing in the Age of Epistemology. LC 90-21088. 416p. 1990. text ed. 31.95 (*0-8223-1125-9*) Duke.

— American Literature & the Universe of Force. LC 81-7806. xviii, 285p. 1983. pap. 19.50 (*0-8223-0579-8*) Duke.

Martin, Ronald L. Official Guide to Marvel Cave. 2nd ed. (Illus.). 1987. pap. 3.95 (*0-685-18052-2*) Ozark Mtn Pubs.

***Martin, Ronda J.** Stock Car Legends: The Laughs, Practical Jokes, & Fun Stories from Racing's Greats! 128p. 1994. reprint ed. pap. 5.95 (*0-9637733-5-6*) Premium Pr TN.

***Martin, Rosa M & Ellis, Martyn.** Pasos 1: A First Course in Spanish. 1995. audio 29.95 (*0-8120-8238-9*) Barron.

— Pasos 2: An Intermediate Course in Spanish. 1995. audio 29.95 (*0-8120-8240-0*) Barron.

Martin, Roscoe. The People's Party in Texas: A Study in Third-Party Politics. (Texas History Paperbacks Ser.: No. 7). 280p. 1970. reprint ed. pap. 7.95 (*0-292-70032-6*) U of Tex Pr.

Martin, Roscoe C. Water for New York: A Study in State Administration of Water Resources. LC 60-9946. 1960. 29.95x (*0-8156-2028-4*) Syracuse U Pr.

Martin, Roscoe C., et al. Decisions in Syracuse. LC 68-9709. 368p. 1968. reprint ed. text ed. 65.00 (*0-8371-0160-3*, MADS, Greenwood Pr) Greenwood.

Martin, Ross M. Trade Unionism: Purposes & Forms. (Illus.). 312p. 1989. 64.00 (*0-19-827710-5*) OUP.

Martin, Roy. Writing & Defending a Thesis or Dissertation in Psychology & Education. 120p. 1980. 19.95 (*0-398-03947-X*) C C Thomas.

Martin, Roy E. & Collete, Robert L., eds. Engineered Seafood Including Surimi. LC 89-71095. (Illus.). 721p. 1990. 72.00 (*0-8155-1228-7*) Noyes.

Martin, Roy E., jt. ed. see Flick, George J.

Martin, Roy F. & Flick, George J., Jr., eds. The Seafood Industry. 520p. 1990. text ed. 82.95 (*0-442-23915-7*) Chapman & Hall.

Martin, Roy P. Assessment of Personality & Behavior Problems: Infancy Through Adolescence. LC 88-19030. 399p. 1988. lib. bdg. 45.00 (*0-89862-727-3*) Guilford Pr.

— Assessment of Personality & Behavior Problems: Infancy Through Adolescence. 399p. 1992. reprint ed. pap. text ed. 21.95 (*0-89862-026-0*) Guilford Pr.

Martin, Roy S. Telling It Like It Is. LC 92-59946. 169p. 1993. 7.95 (*1-55523-568-9*) Winston-Derek.

Martin, Russell. Out of Silence: A Journey into language. LC 93-28434. 1994. 22.50 (*0-8050-1998-7*) H Holt & Co.

— Out of Silence: An Autistic Boy's Journey into Language & Communication. 320p. 1995. pap. 11.95 (*0-14-024701-7*, Penguin Bks) Viking Penguin.

— A Story That Stands Like a Dam: Glen Canyon & the Struggle for the Soul of the West. 368p. 1991. pap. 12.95 (*0-8050-1551-5*, Owl) H Holt & Co.

Martin, Russell, ed. New Writers of the Purple Sage: An Anthology of Contemporary Western Writing. 352p. (Orig.). 1992. pap. 12.95 (*0-14-016940-7*, Penguin Bks) Viking Penguin.

Martin, Russell & Barasch, Marc, eds. Writers of the Purple Sage: An Anthology of Recent Western Writing. 352p. 1984. pap. 12.00 (*0-14-007370-1*, Penguin Bks) Viking Penguin.

Martin, Ruth. Witchcraft & the Inquisition in Venice (1550-1650) (Illus.). 357p. 1989. text ed. 62.95 (*0-631-16118-X*) Blackwell Pubs.

Martin, Ruth & Brown, Walter. The Ruth Martin Story. LC 94-71237. (Illus.). 160p. (Orig.). 1995. reprint ed. pap. 15.95 (*0-923687-31-9*) Celo Valley Bks.

Martin, Ruth S. And They Built a Crooked House: An (Unlucky) Homeowner's Account of One of the Largest Residential Construction Cases Ever Tried in Court. LC 91-90070. (Illus.). 257p. (Orig.). 1991. pap. 12.95 (*1-879653-02-8*) Lakeside Pr.

— Crumbling Dreams: What You Must Know Before Building or Buying a New House (or Condo) LC 92-72164. 172p. 1993. pap. 8.00 (*1-879653-06-0*) Lakeside Pr.

Martin, Rux, jt. ed. see Cats-Baril, JoAnne B.

Martin, Rux, ed. see Foo, Susanna.

Martin, Rux, ed. see Gassenheimer, Linda.

Martin, Rux, ed. see Hodgman, Ann.

M

An Asterisk (*) at the beginning of an entry indicates that the title is appearing in BIP for the first time.

Martin, Rux, ed. see Kummer, Corby.
Martin, Rux, jt. auth. see Lawrence, James.
Martin, Rux, ed. see Simmons, Marie.
Martin, Rux, et al, eds. The Eating Well Cookbook: Favorite Recipes for Eating Well, the Magazine of Food & Health. LC 94-10042. 1994. 24.95 (1-884943-02-0) Eat Well Bks.
— The Eating Well Cookbook: Favorite Recipes from Eating Well - the Magazine of Food & Health. (Illus.). 256p. 1991. 24.95 (0-944475-19-1); pap. 17.95 (0-944475-22-1) Camden Hse Pub.
Martin, S. Wayne, et al. Veterinary Epidemiology: Principles & Methods. LC 87-3169. 356p. 1987. text ed. 41.95 (0-8138-1856-7) Iowa St U Pr.
Martin, Sadie E. The Life & Professional Career of Emma Abbott. LC 80-2290. reprint ed. 28.50 (0-404-18858-3) AMS Pr.
Martin, Sally. Fair Schemer. 224p. (Orig.). 1993. mass mkt. 3.99 (0-380-77397-X) Avon.
— Sweet Fancy. 224p. (Orig.). 1994. mass mkt. 3.99 (0-380-77398-8) Avon.
Martin, Samantha. Culturescope: The Princeton Review Guide to an Informed Mind, College. 1995. pap. 15.00 (0-679-75367-2, Villard Bks) Random.
Martin, Samuel. Basic Japanese Conversation Dictionary: English-Japanese & Japanese-English. LC 57-8797. 266p. (ENG & JPN.). 1957. pap. 6.95 (0-8048-0057-X) C E Tuttle.
— Martin's Comprehensive Japanese Dictionary: Fully Romanized with Complete Kanji & Kana. (Illus.). 768p. 1994. pap. 16.95 (0-8048-1912-2) C E Tuttle.
— Martins Pocket Dictionary: English-Japanese - Japanese-English. 700p. 1989. pap. 9.95 (0-8048-1588-7) C E Tuttle.
Martin, Samuel, jt. auth. see Chaplin, Hamako.
Martin, Samuel E., et al. Character Dictionary Accompanying "Japanese: A Manual of Reading & Writing" LC 86-50705. 378p. 1986. pap. 19.95 (0-8048-1511-9) C E Tuttle.
Martin, Samuel E. Easy Japanese: A Direct Approach to Immediate Conversation. LC 57-6763. 272p. (YA). (gr. 9 up). 1965. pap. 6.95 (0-8048-0157-6) C E Tuttle.
— Essential Japanese: An Introduction to the Standard Colloquial Language. rev. ed. LC 59-5072. 462p. 1962. pap. 14.95 (0-8048-1862-2) C E Tuttle.
— The Japanese Language Through Time. LC 87-50521. (Language Ser.). 964p. 1988. text ed. 65.00 (0-300-03729-5) Yale U Pr.
— Korean in a Hurry: A Quick Approach to Spoken Korean. rev. ed. LC 60-8363. 138p. 1954. pap. 6.95 (0-8048-0349-8) C E Tuttle.
— Reclaiming a Conversation. LC 85-2372. 221p. 1987. pap. 13.00 (0-300-03999-9, Y-684) Yale U Pr.
— Reference Grammar of Japanese. 1198p. 1988. 69.95 (0-8048-1550-X) C E Tuttle.
— Reference Grammar of Korean. 1040p. 1993. 74.95 (0-8048-1887-8) C E Tuttle.
Martin, Samuel E. & Chaplin, Hamako I. Japanese: A Manual of Reading & Writing, 2 vols. in 1. LC 86-50703. 700p. 1986. reprint ed. boxed 24.95 (0-8048-1508-9) C E Tuttle.
Martin, Samuel E. & Lee, Young-Sook C. Beginning Korean. LC 86-50701. 605p. 1986. reprint ed. pap. 24.95 (0-8048-1507-0) C E Tuttle.
Martin, Samuel E., jt. auth. see Gardner, Elizabeth F.
Martin, Samuel J. The Road to Glory: Confederate General Richard S. Ewell. 2nd ed. LC 91-58045. 420p. 1991. 24.95 (1-878208-07-1); pap. 19.95 (1-878208-08-X) Guild Pr IN.
Martin, Sandra. Programming for the Whole World: A Guide to Internationalization. 320p. 1994. pap. text ed. 40.00 (0-13-722190-8) P-H.
— UniForum Technology Guide: Internationalization Explored. 40p. 1992. pap. text ed. 10.00 (0-936593-18-0) UniForum.
Martin, Sandra & Hall, Roger. Rupert Brooke in Canada. 154p. 1978. 14.95 (0-88778-184-5, Pub. by Stoddart Pubng CN) Genl Dist Srvs.
Martin, Sandy D. Black Baptists & African Missions: The Origins of a Movement, 1880-1915. LC 89-39041. 180p. (C). 1990. 24.95 (0-86554-353-4, MUP/H287) Mercer Univ Pr.
Martin-Santos, Luis. Tiempo de Silencio. (SPA.). 1989. 19.95 (0-8288-2569-6) Fr & Eur.
— Time of Silence. Leeson, George, tr. 247p. 1989. text ed. 47.50 (0-231-06984-7); pap. text ed. 10.50 (0-231-06985-5) Col U Pr.
Martin, Sara H. Frente Al Cancer, Un Gigante a Mi Lado. 96p. (SPA.). 1987. reprint ed. pap. 3.25 (0-311-46101-8) Casa Bautista.
— Healing for Adult Children. 1989. pap. 4.99 (0-553-28246-8) Bantam.
— Healing for Adult Children of Alcoholics. LC 87-17342. 1991. 13.99 (0-8054-6002-0) Broadman.
— Meeting Needs Through Support Groups. McClain, Cindy, ed. 96p. (Orig.). 1992. pap. text ed. 5.95 (1-56309-053-8, New Hope) Womans Mission Union.
— Shame on You! LC 89-17425. 1991. 13.99 (0-8054-6010-1) Broadman.
martin, Sarah, tr. see Daeninckx, Didier.
***Martin, Scott C.** Killing Time: Leisure & Culture in Southwestern, Pennsylvania, 1800-1850. (Illus.). 280p. (C). 1995. 29.95x (0-8229-3916-9) U of Pittsburgh Pr.
***Martin, Scott V.** Guide to Evaluating Gold & Silver Objects for Appraisers, Collectors, Dealers. Soeffing, D. Albert, ed. 106p. 1995. pap. 24.95 (0-9645642-0-3) SM Pubns.
Martin, Sean. Scrapbook. (Orig.). 1994. pap. text ed. 4.95 (1-56333-224-8) Masquerade.
Martin, Sean, tr. see Stangerup, Henrik.
Martin, Sean, tr. see Strangerup, Henrik.
***Martin, Shannon E.** Bits, Bytes & Big Brother: Federal Information Control in the Technological Age. LC 94-32929. (Praeger Series in Political Communication). 184p. 1995. text ed. 52.95 (0-275-94900-1, Praeger Pubs) Greenwood.
***Martin, Sharron.** Murder Sings Out. 300p. 1995. pap. 8.95 (1-56901-690-9) NW Pub.
***Martin, Sheila A.** The Effectiveness of State Technology Incentives: Evidence from the Machine Tool Industry. (CARD Monograph Ser.: No. 94-M6). (Illus.). 228p. 1994. pap. text ed. 10.00 (0-936911-06-9) MATRIC.
Martin, Sheila A., jt. ed. see Johnson, Stanley R.
***Martin, Sheldon J.** Where I Come From. (Illus.). 150p. (Orig.). 1996. pap. 12.95 (0-9642188-7-9) Four Seasns.
Martin, Sherrill V., jt. ed. see Keck, George R.
***Martin, Sherry.** Having Fun with Alpha V: Tips Tricks & Techniques for Everyone. 272p. 1994. pap. 19.95 (0-13-346495-4) P-H.
Martin, Sheryl A. The Market Book: A Guide to the Pike Place Market in Seattle. (Illus.). 260p. 1986. pap. 12.95 (0-9616994-0-X) Mkt Bk Pubns.
Martin, Sidney & McMillan, Dana. Learning Ideas Through the Year. 112p. (J). (gr. 2-6). 1989. 9.95 (0-912107-91-X, MM1908) Monday Morning Bks.
Martin, Sidney W. Florida During the Territorial Days. LC 73-19815. (Perspectives in American History Ser.: No. 15). (Illus.). 308p. 1974. reprint ed. lib. bdg. 37.50 (0-87991-344-4) Porcupine Pr.
— Florida's Flagler. LC 49-8401. 292p. 1949. 19.95 (0-8203-0064-0) U of Ga Pr.
Martin, Sigur. History of Our Local Gov., Etc. 1966. 30.00 (0-685-42978-4) Claitors.
Martin, Simon, jt. auth. see Westell, Frank.
***Martin, Sophia S.** Smith: Complete Genealogy of the Descendants of Matthew Smith of East Haddam, Ct., with Mention of His Ancestors, 1637-1890. 269p. 1994. reprint ed. lib. bdg. 52.00 (0-8328-4380-6); reprint ed. pap. 42.00 (0-8328-4381-4) Higginson Bk Co.
Martin-Sperry, A. D., tr. see Laponce, J. A.
Martin-Sperry, Carol, tr. see Cocteau, Jean.
Martin-Sperry, Tony, tr. see Dube, Philippe.
Martin, Steele W. & Martin, Pricilla C. Blue Collar Ministry: Problems & Opportunities for Mainline "Middle" Congregations. LC 88-83757. 70p. (Orig.). 1989. pap. 10.25 (1-56699-064-5, OD83) Alban Inst.
Martin, Stella, jt. auth. see Walls, Dennis.
Martin, Stephen. Advanced Industrial Economics. LC 92-25471. 1993. pap. 34.95 (0-631-17852-X) Blackwell Pubs.
— Industrial Economics: Economic Analysis & Public Policy. MacLeod, Kenneth, ed. 560p. (C). 1988. write for info. (0-02-376780-4) Macmillan.
— Industrial Economics: Economic Analysis & Public Policy. 2nd ed. LC 93-427. (Illus.). 664p. (C). 1994. text ed. write for info. (0-02-376786-3) Macmillan.
Martin, Stephen, ed. The Construction of Europe: Essays in Honor of Emile Noel. LC 94-21318. (Diverse Ser.). 312p. (C). 1994. lib. bdg. 108.00 (0-7923-2969-4) Kluwer Ac.
Martin, Stephen & Battles, Thomas. Sold! The Professional's Guide to Real Estate Auctions. 304p. 1991. pap. 32.95 (0-7931-0211-1, 1903-31) Dearborn Finan.
***Martin, Stephen H.** Beyond Skepticism: All the Way to Enlightenment. 160p. (Orig.). 1995. pap. 11.95 (0-9646601-4-8) Oaklea Pr.
— Out of Body, into Mind: A Novel of Suspense. 252p. (Orig.). 1995. pap. 14.95 (0-9646601-6-4) Oaklea Pr.
— The Search for Nina Fletcher: A Metaphysical Adventure. 288p. (Orig.). 1995. pap. 14.95 (0-9646601-3-X) Oaklea Pr.
Martin, Stephen J., jt. auth. see Ritchie, Ingrid.
***Martin, Stephen P.** Things. (Illus.). 1991. pap. 4.95 (0-9623693-3-0) Heaven Bone Pr.
Martin, Stephen-Paul. Advancing Receding. 44p. (Orig.). 1989. pap. 3.00 (0-926935-21-6) Runaway Spoon.
— The Flood. rev. ed. 88p. 1992. pap. 7.00 (0-926935-70-4) Runaway Spoon.
— The Gothic Twilight. LC 92-70668. 100p. (Orig.). 1992. pap. 8.95 (1-878580-45-0) Asylum Arts.
— Invading Reagan. (Chapbook Ser.). (Illus.). 26p. (Orig.). 1990. pap. 4.00 (0-945112-09-2) Generator Pr.
— Open Form & the Feminine Imagination: The Politics of Reading in Twentieth-Century Innovative Writing. (Post Modern Positions Ser.: Vol. 2). 225p. (Orig.). 1988. lib. bdg. 22.95 (0-944624-02-2); pap. text ed. 11.95 (0-944624-03-0) Maisonneuve Pr.
— Tales. 24p. (Orig.). 1989. pap. 4.00 (0-945926-11-1) Paradigm RI.
— Until It Changes. 48p. 1988. pap. 3.00 (0-926935-07-0) Runaway Spoon.
Martin, Steve, jt. auth. see Martin, Claire.
Martin, Stoddard. The Great Expatriate Writers. LC 91-25431. 168p. 1992. text ed. 45.00 (0-312-06861-1) St Martin.
— Orthodox Heresy: The Rise of 'Magic' As Religion & Its Relation to Literature. LC 88-15863. 208p. 1989. text ed. 39.95 (0-312-02389-8) St Martin.
Martin, Stuart. Schur Algebras & Representation Theory. (Studies in Advanced Mathematics: No. 40). 200p. (C). 1994. 44.95 (0-521-41591-8) Cambridge U Pr.
Martin, Sue, jt. auth. see Green, Harriet.
Martin, Sue G., jt. auth. see Green, Harriet H.
Martin, Susan. Duran Duran. (J). 1984. 8.29 (0-685-09673-4) S&S Trade.
— I Sailed with Columbus: The Adventures of a Ship's Boy. (Illus.). 154p. (J). (gr. 5 up). 1991. 17.95 (0-87951-431-0) Overlook Pr.
Martin, Susan & Green, Harriet. Research Workout. (Illus.). 144p. (J). (gr. 4-9). 1984. student ed 12.95 (0-86653-194-7, GA 551) Good Apple.
Martin, Susan, ed. see De Meyer, Adolph.
Martin, Susan, ed. see Vahabzadeh, Mandy.
Martin, Susan B., ed. Notable Corporate Chronologies, 4 Vols., Set. 1994. 375.00 (0-8103-9217-8, M89334-007660) Gale.
— Notable Corporate Chronologies, Vol. 1. 800p. 1994. 95.00 (0-8103-9218-6, M89334-101945) Gale.
— Notable Corporate Chronologies, Vol. 2. 800p. 1994. 95.00 (0-8103-9219-4, M89334-101946) Gale.
— Notable Corporate Chronologies, Vol. 3. 800p. 1994. 95.00 (0-8103-9220-8, M89334-101947) Gale.
— Notable Corporate Chronologies, Vol. 4. 800p. 1994. 95.00 (0-8103-9221-6, M89334-101948) Gale.
— Worldwide Franchise Directory. 1300p. 1991. 129.50 (0-8103-7805-1, 100824-99854); pap. 129.50 (0-685-50197-3, 100824-M99348) Gale.
Martin, Susan E. On the Move: The Status of Women in Policing. LC 90-62667. 197p. (Orig.). 1990. pap. text ed. 20.95 (1-884614-06-X) Police Found.
Martin, Susan E., et al, eds. New Directions in the Rehabilitation of Criminal Offenders. LC 81-11287. 508p. reprint ed. pap. 144.80 (0-8357-3183-9, 2039452) Bks Demand.
Martin, Susan F., comp. Refugee Women. LC 92-5754. 256p. (C). 1991. text ed. 49.95 (1-85649-000-9, Pub. by Zed Books UK); pap. 15.95 (1-85649-001-7, Pub. by Zed Books UK) Humanities.
Martin, Susan K. Library Networks, 1986-1987: Libraries in Partnership. LC 86-7438. (Professional Librarian Ser.). 220p. 1986. text ed. 36.50 (0-86729-128-1, Hall Reference); pap. 28.50 (0-86729-127-3, Hall Reference) Macmillan.
Martin, Susan M. Palm Oil & Protest: An Economic History of the Ngwa Region, South-eastern Nigeria, 1800-1980. (African Studies: No. 59). (Illus.). 226p. 1988. 69.95 (0-521-34376-3) Cambridge U Pr.
***Martin, Suzanne.** Awesome Almanacs - Georgia. 1995. pap. 14.95 (1-880190-53-2) B&B Pub.
— Awesome Almanacs - Texas. 1995. pap. 14.95 (1-880190-22-2) B&B Pub.
Martin, Suzanne T., jt. auth. see Cech, Donna.
Martin, Sydney. Beacon Bible Expositions Vol. 10: Thessalonians, Timothy, Titus. Greathouse, William M & Taylor, Willard H., eds. 247p. 1977. 12.50 (0-8341-0321-4) Beacon Hill.
Martin, T. A Guide to Neophema & Psephotus Grass Parrots. (Illus.). 80p. 1989. pap. 22.95 (0-9587455-1-X) Avian Pubns.
— Metaphor & Composition in First Peter. (Society of Biblical Literature Dissertation Ser.). 396p. (C). 1992. 32.95 (1-55540-664-5, 062131); pap. 21.95 (1-55540-665-3) Scholars Pr GA.
Martin, T. C. Inventions, Researches & Writings of Nikola Tesla. (Nikola Tesla Ser.). 1986. lib. bdg. 250.00 (0-8490-3835-9) Gordon Pr.
Martin, T. E. Beacon Bible Expositions Vol. 12: John, Jude, Revelation. Greathouse, M., ed. 282p. 1983. 12.50 (0-8341-0809-7) Beacon Hill.
Martin, T. John, ed. see Cohn, David V.
Martin, T. John, jt. ed. see Mundy, Gregory R.
Martin, T. Patrick. Too Much of Nothing: The Nourishing Illusion of Hope. 235p. (Orig.). 1991. pap. write for info. (1-879019-02-7) Amer Edit Servs.
Martin, Terence. Nathaniel Hawthorne. rev. ed. (United States Authors Ser.: No. 75). 240p. 1983. text ed. 20.95 (0-8057-7384-3, Twayne) Macmillan.
— Parables of Possibility: The American Need for Beginnings. LC 94-17486. Date not set. 27.50 (0-231-07050-0) Col U Pr.
Martin, Teri. Junipero Serra: God's Pioneer. (Illus.). 64p. (J). (gr. 7-9). 1990. pap. 4.95 (0-8091-6589-9) Paulist Pr.
Martin, Terrell L. Prehistoric Settlement-Subsistence Relationships in the Fishing River Drainage, Western Missouri. Bray, Robert T., ed. (Missouri Archaeologist Ser.: Vol. 37). (Illus.). 170p. (Orig.). 1976. pap. 6.00 (0-943414-54-7) MO Arch Soc.
Martin, Terrence D. Santa Catalina: An Island Adventure. LC 83-83007. (Illus.). 48p. (Orig.). 1984. pap. 6.95 (0-916122-97-2) KC Pubns.
Martin, Terri & Lockhart, William J. Park Waters in Peril. (Illus.). 126p. (C). 1993. pap. text ed. write for info. (0-940091-33-X) Natl Parks & Cons.
Martin, Terry, ed. see Bertch, David P.
Martin, Terry, ed. see Bertch, David & Bertch, Barbara A.
Martin, Terry, ed. see Bertch, David.
Martin, Terry P., jt. auth. see Perret, Gene.
Martin, Thea, ed. Bibliography of Forth References. 3rd rev. ed. 1987. pap. 15.00 (0-914593-06-4) Inst Appl Forth.
— Rochester Conference on Data Bases & Process Control, 1982: Proceedings. 321p. 1982. pap. 25.00 (0-914593-03-X) Inst Appl Forth.
— Rochester Standards Conference, 1981: Proceedings. 374p. 1981. pap. 25.00 (0-914593-04-8) Inst Appl Forth.
Martin, Theodore, tr. see Dante Alighieri.
Martin, Thomas. Private High. 25p. (Orig.). (YA). (gr. 7 up). 1986. pap. 5.00 (0-87602-267-0) Anchorage.
Martin, Thomas C. The Inventions, Researches & Writings of Nikola Tesla. 496p. 1970. reprint ed. spiral bd. 16.50 (0-7873-0582-0) Mokelumne.
Martin, Thomas E. Military Aircraft Accidents Around Western Massachusetts 1941. LC 94-96095. 180p. 1995. pap. 18.95 (0-9641015-0-5) T E Martin.
***Martin, Thomas E. & Finch, Deborah M.** Ecology & Management of Neotropical Migratory Birds: A Synthesis & Review of Critical Issues. (Illus.). 416p. 1995. 65.00 (0-19-508440-3); pap. 35.00 (0-19-508452-7) OUP.
Martin, Thomas H. Etudes Sur le Timee De Platon, 2 vols. in 1. LC 75-13279. (History of Ideas in Ancient Greece Ser.). (FRE.). 1976. reprint ed. 60.95 (0-405-07319-4) Ayer.
— Memoire sur les Hypotheses Astronomiques des Plus Ancciens Philosophes de la Grece. Vlastos, Gregory, ed. (History of Ideas in Ancient Times Ser.). 1976. reprint ed. 39.95 (0-405-07320-8) Ayer.
***Martin, Thomas K.** A Call to Arms. 240p. (Orig.). 1995. pap. text ed. 4.99 (0-441-00242-0) Ace Bks.
— A Matter of Honor. 224p. (Orig.). 1994. pap. text ed. 4.99 (0-441-00107-6) Ace Bks.
— A Two-Edged Sword. 272p. (Orig.). 1994. mass mkt. 4.99 (0-441-83344-6) Ace Bks.
Martin, Thomas L., Jr. & Latham, Donald C. Strategy for Survival. LC 63-17720. (Illus.). 399p. reprint ed. 113.80 (0-8357-9624-8, 2011564) Bks Demand.
Martin, Thomas L., jt. auth. see Leonard, William F.
Martin, Thomas M. The Challenge of Christian Marriage: Marriage in Scripture, History & Contemporary Life. 1990. 9.95 (0-8091-3190-0) Paulist Pr.
— Country Auctioneer: Anecdotes, Admonitions, & Advice. Moore, Amy G., ed. (Illus.). 96p. (Orig.). 1994. pap. 12.95 (1-883912-00-8) Hamiltons.
— Images & the Imageless: A Study in Religious Consciousness & Film. 2nd ed. LC 90-48202. 208p. 1991. 29.50 (0-8387-5212-8) Bucknell U Pr.
Martin, Thomas M., jt. ed. see Voydanoff, Patricia.
Martin, Thomas R. Sovereignty & Coinage in Classical Greece. LC 84-26292. (Illus.). 300p. 1985. text ed. 49.50x (0-691-03580-6) Princeton U Pr.
Martin, Thomas W. French Military Adventures in Alabama 1818-1828. 1987. pap. 5.95 (0-317-68076-5) Southern U Pr.
Martin, Timothy. Joyce & Wagner: A Study of Influence. 300p. (C). 1992. 64.95 (0-521-39487-2) Cambridge U Pr.
Martin, Timothy, jt. ed. see Cheng, Vincent J.
Martin, Timothy P. Writers: Succeed. 63p. (Orig.). 1991. pap. write for info. (1-879019-00-0) Amer Edit Servs.
Martin, Tom. Rappelling: A Winter Adventure. 2nd rev. ed. LC 91-90423. (Illus.). 304p. 1995. 16.95 (0-930871-03-0) Search.
Martin, Tony. African Fundamentalism: A Literary & Cultural Anthology of Garvey's Harlem Renaissance. (New Marcus Garvey Library: No. 5). (Illus.). xviii, 363p. (Orig.). (C). 1991. pap. text ed. 14.95 (0-912469-09-9) Majority Pr.
— The Afro-Trinidadian: Reflections on an Endangered Species. LC 93-43662. 80p. (Orig.). (C). Date not set. pap. text ed. 9.95 (0-912469-31-5) Majority Pr.
— Amy Ashwood Garvey: Pan-Africanist, Feminist, & Wife, No. 1. (New Marcus Garvey Library: No. 4). (Illus.). (Orig.). Date not set. text ed. write for info. (0-912469-06-4); pap. text ed. write for info. (0-912469-07-2) Majority Pr.
— Illustrated Encyclopedia of Whales & Dolphins. 1990. 19.99 (0-517-02564-7) Random Hse Value.
— Insurance Direct Marketing. (C). 1989. 690.00 (0-685-32784-1, Pub. by Witherby & Co UK) St Mut.
— The Jewish Onslaught: Despatches from the Wellesley Battlefront. xii, 144p. (Orig.). (C). 1993. pap. text ed. 9.95 (0-912469-30-7) Majority Pr.
— Literary Garveyism: Garvey, Black Arts & the Harlem Renaissance. LC 83-60952. (New Marcus Garvey Library: No. 1). (Illus.). xii, 204p. (Orig.). 1983. text ed. 19.95 (0-912469-00-5); pap. text ed. 9.95 (0-912469-01-3) Majority Pr.
— Marcus Garvey, Hero: A First Biography. LC 83-61113. (New Marcus Garvey Library: No. 3). (Illus.). x, 179p. (Orig.). (YA). (gr. 9-12). 1983. pap. text ed. 8.95 (0-912469-05-6) Majority Pr.
— The Pan-African Connection: From Slavery to Garvey & Beyond. LC 82-19521. (New Marcus Garvey Library: No. 6). (Illus.). xii, 262p. (Orig.). (C). 1984. reprint ed. text ed. 22.95 (0-912469-10-2); reprint ed. pap. text ed. 10.95 (0-912469-11-0) Majority Pr.
— Race First: The Ideological & Organizational Struggles of Marcus Garvey & the Universal Negro Improvement Association. (New Marcus Garvey Library: No. 8). (Illus.). x, 421p. (Orig.). (C). 1986. reprint ed. text ed. 29.95 (0-912469-22-6); reprint ed. pap. text ed. 12.95 (0-912469-23-4) Majority Pr.
— The Strugglers: Working with Children Who Fail to Learn to Read. 160p. 1989. 75.00 (0-335-09512-7, Open Univ Pr); pap. 24.00 (0-335-09511-9, Open Univ Pr) Taylor & Francis.
Martin, Tony, ed. In Nobody's Backyard: The Grenada Revolution in Its Own Words, Vol. I: The Revolution at Home. (Illus.). xxiv, 264p. 1984. text ed. 22.95 (0-912469-12-9) Majority Pr.
— In Nobody's Backyard: The Grenada Revolution in Its Own Words, Vol. I: The Revolution at Home. (Illus.). xvi, 201p. 1985. 22.95 (0-912469-16-1) Majority Pr.
— The Poetical Works of Marcus Garvey. LC 83-61114. (New Marcus Garvey Library: No. 2). (Illus.). viii, 123p. (C). 1983. 17.95 (0-912469-02-1); pap. 9.95 (0-912469-03-X) Majority Pr.
Martin, Tony & Leather, Bob. Readers & Texts in the Primary Years. LC 94-12241. (Rethinking Reading Ser.). 1994. write for info. (0-335-19228-9, Open Univ Pr); pap. write for info. (0-335-19227-0, Open Univ Pr) Taylor & Francis.
Martin, Tony & Towell, Lisa. NewWave Agent Handbook. 1993. pap. 45.95 (0-201-56352-5) Addison-Wesley.
Martin, Tony, ed. see Garvey, Marcus.
Martin, Tovah. Essence of Paradise: Fragrant Plants for Indoor Gardens. 1991. 24.95 (0-316-54845-6) Little.
— Once upon a Windowsill: A History of Indoor Plants. LC 88-31499. (Illus.). 304p. 1989. 29.95 (0-88192-120-3) Timber.
— Well-Clad Windowsills: Houseplants for Four Exposures. LC 93-39565. 1994. 27.50 (0-671-85015-6, Horticulture Bk) P-H Gen Ref & Trav.

An Asterisk (*) at the beginning of an entry indicates that the title is appearing in BIP for the first time.

Martin, Tovah, ed. Greenhouses & Garden Rooms: (Plants & Gardens Ser.). (Illus.). 1990. per., pap. 6.95 (*0-945352-47-6*, Sterling) Bklyn Botanic.

Martin, Tovah, jt. auth. see Victoria Magazine Editors.

Martin, Troy K. Edge of Darkness. 350p. (Orig.). 1990. pap. 11.95 (*0-571-14194-3*) Faber & Faber.

Martin, Tyrone G., jt. auth. see Roach, John C.

Martin, Ursula & Wing, Jeannette M., eds. Proceedings of the First International Workshop on Larch, Dedham, U. S. A. 13-15 July 1992. LC 92-36174. (Workshops in Computing Ser.). 1993. 79.00 (*0-387-19804-0*) Spr-Verlag.

Martin, Val, ed. see Burt, Al.

Martin, Val, ed. see Ranson, Robert.

Martin, Valerie. Alexandria. Ng, Donna, ed. 192p. 1991. reprint ed. pap. 10.00 (*0-671-73688-4*, WSP) PB.

— The Great Divorce. LC 93-5227. 1994. 22.50 (*0-385-42125-7*, N A Talese) Doubleday.

— Love. (Illus.). 1976. pap. 4.50 (*0-89924-004-6*) Lynx Hse.

— Mary Reilly. large type ed. LC 90-38103. 343p. 1990. reprint ed. bds. 19.95 (*1-56054-031-1*) Thorndike Pr.

— Set in Motion. 224p. 1978. 8.95 (*0-374-26140-7*) FS&G.

— Set in Motion. Ng, Donna, ed. 224p. 1991. reprint ed. pap. 10.00 (*0-671-73687-6*, WSP) PB.

Martin, Van J. Coastal Georgia. (Illus.). 1985. 25.00 (*0-932958-02-8*); pap. 12.00 (*0-932958-03-6*) Golden Coast.

Martin, Van J., jt. auth. see Mitchell, William R., Jr.

Martin, Van J., jt. auth. see Mitchell, William R.

Martin, Vance, ed. For the Conservation of Earth: Proceedings of the 4th World Wilderness Congress. LC 88-16319. (Illus.). 418p. 1988. pap. 18.95 (*1-55591-026-2*) Fulcrum Pub.

Martin, Vance & Ingles, Mary, eds. Wilderness: The Way Ahead. (Illus.). 304p. 1984. pap. 10.50 (*0-936878-10-X*) Lorian Pr.

***Martin, Vance & Tyler, Nicholas, eds.** Arctic Wilderness: The 5th World Wilderness Congress. (Illus.). 320p. (Orig.). (C). 1995. pap. text ed. 32.00 (*1-55591-931-6*, North Amer Pr) Fulcrum Pub.

Martin, Vance, jt. ed. see Creedy, John.

Martin, Vanessa. Islam & Modernism: The Iranian Revolution of 1906. LC 89-5942. 242p. 1989. text ed. 45.00x (*0-8156-2473-5*, MAIM) Syracuse U Pr.

Martin, Vicky. Obey the Moon. large type ed. 545p. 1989. 17.95 (*0-7089-1963-4*) Ulverscroft.

— Seeds of the Sun. large type ed. 479p. 1981. 12.00 (*0-7089-0635-4*) Ulverscroft.

— Tigers of the Night. large type ed. 592p. 1986. 15.95 (*0-7089-1448-9*) Ulverscroft.

— The Windmill Years. large type ed. 590p. 1980. 12.00 (*0-7089-0465-3*) Ulverscroft.

Martin, Victor. La Vie Internationale Dans la Grece Des Cites. Vlastos, Gregory, ed. LC 78-19368. (Morals & Law in Ancient Greece Ser.). 1979. reprint ed. lib. bdg. 48.95 (*0-405-11559-8*) Ayer.

Martin-Vide, Carlos, ed. Current Issues in Mathematical Linguistics. LC 94-1198. (North-Holland Linguistic Ser.: Vol. 56). 1994. 165.75 (*0-444-81693-3*, North Holland) Elsevier.

***Martin, Vincent.** A House Divided: The Parting of the Ways Between Synagogue & Church. LC 95-3020. (Stimulus Book Ser.). 224p. (Orig.). 1995. pap. 11.95 (*0-8091-3569-8*) Paulist Pr.

Martin, Violet F., jt. auth. see Somerville, Edith A.

Martin, W. Women in the Visual Arts. 1992. pap. text ed. 22.00 (*2-88124-581-1*) Gordon & Breach.

Martin, W. & Aitken, I. Diseases of Sheep. 2nd ed. 1991. 160.00 (*0-632-02957-9*) Blackwell Sci.

Martin, W. & Macdonell, A. Canadian Education: A Sociological Analysis. 1978. pap. 13.33 (*0-13-113092-7*) P-H.

Martin, W. C. & Hutchins, R. Flora of New Mexico, 2 vols., Set. (Illus.). 3000p. 1980. lib. bdg. 600.00 (*3-7682-1263-7*) Lubrecht & Cramer.

Martin, W. Coda. A Matter of Life. 1965. 6.95 (*0-8159-6202-9*) Devin.

***Martin, W. K.** Marlene Dietrich. Duberman, Martin, ed. LC 94-23518. (Lives of Notable Gay Men & Lesbians Ser.). (Illus.). 168p. (YA). (gr. 9 up). 1995. lib. bdg. 19.95 (*0-7910-2862-3*); pap. 9.95 (*0-7910-2881-X*) Chelsea Hse.

Martin, W. L., jt. auth. see Chatto, James.

Martin, W. R., et al, eds. Tobacco Smoking & Nicotine: A Neurobiological Approach. LC 87-18513. (Advances in Behavioral Biology Ser.: Vol. 31). (Illus.). 534p. 1987. 120.00 (*0-306-42611-0*, Plenum Pr) Plenum.

Martin, W. W. Manual of Ecclesiastical Architecture. 1977. lib. bdg. 75.00 (*0-8490-2206-1*) Gordon Pr.

Martin, Wade E., ed. Environmental Economics & the Mining Industry. LC 93-32888. (Studies in Risk & Uncertainty). 136p. (C). 1993. lib. bdg. 49.95 (*0-7923-9404-6*) Kluwer Ac.

Martin, Waldo E., Jr. The Mind of Frederick Douglass. LC 84-5140. (Illus.). xii, 334p. 1986. reprint ed. 37.50 (*0-8078-1616-7*); reprint ed. pap. 13.95 (*0-8078-4148-X*) U of NC Pr.

Martin, Wallace. Recent Theories of Narrative. LC 85-22401. 248p. (C). 1986. 35.00 (*0-8014-1771-6*); pap. 12.95 (*0-8014-9355-2*) Cornell U Pr.

Martin, Wallace, ed. Language, Logic, & Genre: Papers from the Poetics & Literary Theory Section, Modern Language Association. 54p. 1974. 10.00 (*0-8387-1446-3*) Bucknell U Pr.

Martin, Wallace E., comp. Sail & Steam on the Northern California Coast, 1850-1900. LC 82-60604. 351p. 1983. bds. 27.50 (*0-9605182-0-7*) Natl Maritime.

Martin, Walter. Christian Science. 32p. 1957. pap. 3.50 (*0-87123-064-X*) Bethany Hse.

— Essential Christianity. LC 80-51625. 1985. reprint ed. pap. 6.99 (*0-8307-1029-9*, 5418458) Regal.

— Herbert W. Armstrong. 32p. 1969. pap. 3.99 (*0-87123-213-8*) Bethany Hse.

— Jehovah's Witnesses. 64p. 1969. pap. 3.99 (*0-87123-270-7*) Bethany Hse.

— The Kingdom of the Cults. rev. ed. LC 85-7410. 448p. 1985. 19.99 (*0-87123-796-2*) Bethany Hse.

— Martin Speaks Out on the Cults. LC 83-12368. 1983. pap. 5.95 (*0-88449-103-X*, A424367) Vision Hse.

— The Maze of Mormonism. LC 78-66067. (Orig.). (C). 1979. pap. 6.95 (*0-685-05259-1*, A424365) Vision Hse.

— Mormonism. 32p. 1968. pap. 3.99 (*0-87123-367-3*) Bethany Hse.

— Mormonismo. 112p. 1988. 3.95 (*0-88113-208-X*) Edit Betania.

— The New Age Cult. LC 89-6889. 128p. (Orig.). 1989. pap. text ed. 7.99 (*1-55661-077-7*) Bethany Hse.

— The New Cults. LC 80-52210. (Orig.). (C). 1980. pap. 8.95 (*0-88449-016-5*, A424378) Vision Hse.

— La Nueva Era. 144p. (Orig.). (SPA.). 1991. pap. 4.95 (*0-88113-055-9*) Edit Betania.

— Los Testigos de Jehova. 144p. 1988. 3.95 (*0-88113-285-3*) Edit Betania.

Martin, Walter & Klann, Norman H. Jehovah of the Watchtower. 192p. 1981. reprint ed. pap. 7.99 (*0-87123-267-7*) Bethany Hse.

Martin, Walter, jt. auth. see Moody, Dwight L.

Martin, Walter E. Laboratory Exercises for Atmospheric Interactions. 144p. (C). 1993. spiral bd. 10.95 (*0-8403-8389-4*) Kendall-Hunt.

Martin, Walter E. & Steila, Donald. Atmospheric Interactions. 192p. (C). 1993. per., pap. text ed. 26.95 (*0-8403-8717-2*) Kendall-Hunt.

Martin, Walter R. & Ober, Warren. Henry James' Apprenticeship: The Tales, 1864-1882. 240p. 1993. 48.00 (*0-88835-034-1*) P D Meany.

Martin, Warren B. A College of Character. LC 82-48392. (Jossey-Bass Series in Higher Education). 247p. reprint ed. pap. 70.40 (*0-8357-4689-5*, 2052344) Bks Demand.

— Conformity: Standards & Change in Higher Education. LC 72-92894. (Jossey-Bass Higher Education Ser.). 288p. reprint ed. 82.10 (*0-8357-9310-9*, 2013951) Bks Demand.

***Martin, Wayne F.** An Insight to Sports. (Illus.). 183p. (Orig.). 1993. pap. 14.95 (*0-9614895-3-7*) Sports Vision.

Martin, Wendy. An American Triptych: Anne Bradstreet, Emily Dickinson, & Adrienne Rich. LC 83-6864. x, 272p. 1983. pap. 11.95 (*0-8078-4112-9*) U of NC Pr.

— The Beacon Book of Essays by Contemporary American Women. 336p. (C). 1996. pap. 26.00 (*0-8070-6346-0*) Beacon Pr.

— Tune in for Murder. 1993. 13.95 (*0-8034-9026-7*) Bouregy.

Martin, Wendy, ed. New Essays on "The Awakening" (American Novel Ser.). 150p. 1988. 27.95 (*0-521-30712-0*); pap. 11.95 (*0-521-31445-3*) Cambridge U Pr.

— We Are Stories We Tell: The Best Short Stories by American Women since 1945. 1990. pap. 15.00 (*0-679-72881-3*) Pantheon.

Martin, Wendy, jt. auth. see Axton, W. F.

Martin, Werner, ed. Verzeichnis der Nobelpreistrager 1901-1987: Mit Preisbegundungen, Kurzkommentaren, Literarischen, Werkbibliographien und einer Biographie Alfred Nobel. 2nd ed. xi, 382p. 1988. lib. bdg. 60.00 (*3-598-10721-8*) K G Saur.

Martin, Werner, ed. see Agnon, Samuel J.

Martin, Werner, ed. see Heyse, Paul.

Martin, Werner, ed. see Solschenizyn, Alexander.

Martin, Willard E., Jr. Chaucer Bibliography, 1925-1933. LC 72-1042. reprint ed. 31.50 (*0-404-04195-7*) AMS Pr.

Martin, William. Back Bay. 1992. mass mkt. 5.99 (*0-446-36316-2*) Warner Bks.

— Cape Cod. 672p. 1991. 21.95 (*0-446-51510-8*) Warner Bks.

— Cape Cod. 736p. 1992. mass mkt. 5.99 (*0-446-36317-0*) Warner Bks.

— Classroom Management. 176p. (C). 1995. pap. text ed., spiral bd. 30.95 (*0-7872-1030-7*) Kendall-Hunt.

— Managing Quality Customer Service. Crisp, Michael G., ed. LC 88-92732. (Fifty-Minute Ser.). (Illus.). 96p. (Orig.). 1989. pap. 9.95 (*0-931961-83-1*) Crisp Pubns.

— Marra Familia. 64p. 1994. pap. 14.95 (*1-85224-221-3*, Pub. by Bloodaxe Bks UK) Dufour.

— My Prostate & Me: One Man's Experience with Prostate Cancer. LC 94-29594. 1994. 17.95 (*1-56977-888-4*) Cadell & Davies.

— A Prophet with Honor: The Billy Graham Story. (Illus.). 735p. 1991. 25.00 (*0-688-06890-1*) Morrow.

— A Prophet with Honor: The Billy Graham Story. (Illus.). 760p. 1992. pap. 12.00 (*0-688-11906-9*, Quill) Morrow.

— Quality Customer Service. 2nd rev. ed. Gerould, Philip, ed. 100p. (Orig.). 1993. pap. 9.95 (*1-56052-203-8*) Crisp Pubns.

— Restaurant Server's Guide to Quality Service. 1988. 6.95 (*0-685-44003-6*, 110) Am Bartenders.

— The Rising of the Moon. 544p. 1995. pap. 5.99 (*0-446-36418-5*) Warner Bks.

— Statesmen of the War in Retrospect, 1918-1928. LC 75-105029. (Essay Index Reprint Ser.). 1977. 23.95 (*0-8369-1675-1*) Ayer.

Martin, William, ed. see Martin, Kady.

Martin, William, ed. see Martin, Kathy.

Martin, William, et al. Hazardous Waste Handbook for Health & Safety. 2nd ed. 320p. 1992. 39.95 (*0-7506-9235-9*) Buttrwrth-Heinemann.

***Martin, William A.** A Martin Genealogy: Tied to the History of Germanna, Virginia. 382p. (Orig.). 1995. pap. text ed. 28.50 (*0-7884-0184-X*) Heritage Bk.

— The Siege in Peking: China Against the World. LC 72-79832. (China Library Ser.). 1972. reprint ed. lib. bdg. 23.00 (*0-8420-1376-8*) Scholarly Res Inc.

Martin, William B. Quality Service: The Restaurant Manager's Bible. 1986. 9.95 (*0-937056-05-7*, FB5) Cornell U Sch Hotel.

— Restaurant Server's Guide. rev. ed. LC 85-73177. (Fifty-Minute Ser.). (Illus.). 80p. (Orig.). 1987. pap. 9.95 (*0-931961-08-4*) Crisp Pubns.

— Spheres & Satellites. (Hi Map Ser.: No. 12). (Illus.). 60p. Date not set. pap. text ed. 11.99 (*0-614-05314-5*, HM 5612) COMAP Inc.

Martin, William B., ed. Texas Plays. LC 89-42893. (Southwest Life & Letters Ser.). (Illus.). 480p. 1990. text ed. 35.00 (*0-87074-300-7*); pap. 16.95 (*0-87074-301-5*) SMU Press.

***Martin, William C.** The Art of Pastoring: Contemplative Reflections. 92p. (Orig.). 1994. pap. 7.95 (*1-885121-00-8*) CTS Press.

— Christians in Conflict. LC 72-88018. (Studies in Religion & Society). 106p. 1972. 15.95 (*0-913348-01-5*); pap. 10.95 (*0-913348-10-4*) Ctr Sci Study.

Martin, William E., jt. auth. see Padfield, Harland.

Martin, William E., et al. Saving Water in a Desert City. LC 83-43263. 127p. reprint ed. pap. 36.20 (*0-7837-2180-3*, 2042518) Bks Demand.

Martin, William F. The Indissoluble Knot. LC 87-17927. 93p. (Orig.). 1987. lib. bdg. 31.00 (*0-8191-6604-9*) U Pr of Amer.

Martin, William F. & Levine, Steven P., eds. Protecting Personnel at Hazardous Waste Sites. 2nd ed. LC 93-28510. 450p. 1994. 94.95 (*0-7506-9457-2*) Buttrwrth-Heinemann.

Martin, William F., et al. Hazardous Waste Handbook for Health & Safety. 480p. 1987. text ed. 32.95 (*0-409-90070-2*) Buttrwrth-Heinemann.

Martin, William G., ed. Semiperipheral States in the World-Economy. LC 90-36779. (Contributions in Economics & Economic History Ser.: No. 113). 248p. 1990. text ed. 55.00 (*0-313-27489-4*, MGP, Greenwood Pr) Greenwood.

Martin, William H. & Martin, Wilma D. Captain Murrells Savory Seafood Recipes. (Illus.). 133p. 1990. spiral bd. 13.95 (*0-9630689-0-3*) Rum Gully.

Martin, William H., et al, eds. Biodiversity of the Southeastern United States: Lowland Terrestrial Communities, Vol. 2. LC 92-26503. 528p. 1993. text ed. 79.95 (*0-471-62883-2*) Wiley.

— Biodiversity of the Southeastern United States: Upland Terrestrial Communities, Vol. 3. LC 92-28863. (Bankruptcy Practice Library). 400p. 1993. text ed. 79.95 (*0-471-58594-7*) Wiley.

***Martin, William J.** The Global Information Society. 200p. 1995. 50.95 (*0-566-07715-9*, Pub. by Gower UK) Ashgate Pub Co.

Martin, William M., jt. auth. see Southard, Frank A., Jr.

Martin, William O. Metaphysics & Ideology. LC 59-9870. (Aquinas Lectures). 1959. 10.00 (*0-87462-124-0*) Marquette.

— Order & Integration of Knowledge. LC 68-54425. (Illus.). 355p. 1969. reprint ed. text ed. 65.00 (*0-8371-0161-1*, MAKN, Greenwood Pr) Greenwood.

Martin, William O., ed. Settlement of Shallow Foundations on Cohesionless Soils: Design & Performance. LC 86-70535. (Geotechnical Special Publication Ser.: No. 5). (Illus.). 98p. reprint ed. pap. 28.00 (*0-8357-6879-1*, 2056884) Bks Demand.

Martin, William R., jt. auth. see Duderstadt, James J.

Martin, William T. Franklin County, Ohio, History. 1969. reprint ed. 10.00 (*0-935057-48-X*) OH Genealogical.

— History of Franklin County. 480p. 1993. 25.00 (*0-9636036-0-4*) Bergman Bks.

— History of Franklin County, Ohio. 449p. 1993. reprint ed. lib. bdg. 47.50 (*0-8328-2793-2*) Higginson Bk Co.

— Motivation & Productivity in Public Sector Human Service Organizations. LC 88-3099. 161p. 1988. text ed. 55.00 (*0-89930-314-5*, MMV/, Quorum Bks) Greenwood.

— Problem Employees & Their Personalities: A Guide to Behaviors, Dynamics, & Intervention Strategies for Personnel Specialists. LC 89-3858. 200p. 1989. text ed. 55.00 (*0-89930-417-6*, MEY, Quorum Bks) Greenwood.

Martin, William T. & Reissner, Eric. Elementary Differential Equations. 331p. (C). 1986. reprint ed. pap. text ed. 8.95 (*0-486-65024-3*) Dover.

Martin, William T., et al. Elementary Differential Equations. 3rd ed. text ed. write for info. (*0-8162-5435-4*) Holden-Day.

Martin, William W. I ACCUSE! 350p. (C). 1989. 40.00 (*0-924932-01-5*); 100.00 (*0-924932-00-7*) Freedoms Herald.

Martin, Wilma D., jt. auth. see Martin, William H.

Martin, Wiltrud, jt. ed. see Bozarth, George S.

Martin, Wyn, jt. auth. see Martin, Jack.

***Martin, Yves, ed.** Selected Papers on Scanning Prove Microscopes: Design & Applications. LC 94-42035. (Milestone Ser.: No. 107). 1995. write for info. (*0-8194-1804-8*) SPIE.

Martin, Yves, tr. see Twitchell, Paul.

Martin, Yves D., tr. see Kemp, Harold.

Martin, Yves D., tr. see Twitchell, Paul.

Martin, Yvonne E. Marriages & Deaths from Steuben County, New York, Newspapers, 1797-1868. vi, 166p. (Orig.). 1988. pap. 12.50 (*1-55613-130-5*) Heritage Bk.

***Martin, Yvonne M. & Macpherson, R. J., eds.** Restructuring Administrative Policy in Public Schooling: Canadian & International Case Studies. 285p. (Orig.). (C). 1993. pap. text ed. 22.95x (*1-55059-054-5*) Temeron Bks.

***Martina, Aimee M.** Keeper of the Valley. 270p. 1995. pap. 8.95 (*0-7610-0126-3*) NW Pub.

Martina, Alan. Lectures on the Economic Theory of Taxation: Economic Reform, Socially Optimal Piecemeal Consumption Taxation Structures, & Information. LC 92-15323. (Lecture Notes in Economics & Mathematical Systems Ser.: Vol. 384). xii, 313p. 1992. pap. 59.00 (*0-387-55538-2*) Spr-Verlag.

Martina, Krissie, ed. see National Conference of State Legislatures Staff.

Martinac, Paula. Home Movies. LC 93-17841. 222p. (Orig.). 1993. pap. 10.95 (*1-878067-32-X*) Seal Pr Feminist.

— K. D. Lang. LC 95-14170. (Lives of Notable Gay Men & Lesbians Ser.). 1995. pap. write for info. (*0-7910-2899-2*) Chelsea Hse.

— K. D. Lang. LC 95-14170. (Lives of Notable Gay Men & Lesbians Ser.). (J). 1995. write for info. (*0-7910-2872-0*) Chelsea Hse.

— The One You Call Sister. 224p. 1990. pap. 11.95 (*0-946211-11-6*, Pub. by Attic IE) InBook.

— Out of Time. LC 90-36973. 224p. (Orig.). 1990. pap. 9.95 (*0-931188-91-1*) Seal Pr Feminist.

Martinac, Paula, ed. The One You Call Sister: New Women's Fiction. 216p. (Orig.). (C). 1989. 24.95 (*0-939416-30-1*); pap. 9.95 (*0-939416-31-X*) Cleis Pr.

Martinas, K., et al. Thermodynamics: History & Philosophy - Facts, Trends & Debates. 544p. 1991. text ed. 147.00 (*981-02-0464-7*) World Scientific Pub.

Martindale. Online Drug Information Thesaurus. 2nd ed. 1990. 133.00 (*0-85369-229-7*, Pub. by Pharmaceutical Pr UK) Rittenhouse.

Martindale, Andrew. Gothic Art. (World of Art Ser.). (Illus.). 288p. 1985. pap. 12.95 (*0-500-20058-0*) Thames Hudson.

— Simone Martini: Complete Edition. (Illus.). 240p. 1988. 210.00 (*0-8147-5444-9*) NYU Pr.

Martindale, C. C. The Sacraments. (Compact Study Ser.). 23p. (Orig.). 1993. pap. 1.95 (*0-685-70247-2*) Angelus Pr.

Martindale, Carolyn. The White Press & Black America. LC 85-27219. (Contributions in Afro-American & African Studies: No. 97). 215p. 1986. text ed. 49.95 (*0-313-25103-7*, MWP/, Greenwood Pr) Greenwood.

Martindale, Carolyn, ed. Pluralizing Journalism Education: A Multicultural Handbook. LC 92-35923. 264p. 1993. text ed. 55.00 (*0-313-28592-6*, MZG/) Greenwood.

Martindale, Charles. John Milton & the Transformation of Ancient Epic. LC 86-3408. 256p. 1986. 53.00 (*0-389-20624-5*, N8182) B&N Imports.

— Redeeming the Text: Latin Poetry & the Hermeneutics of Reception. (Roman Literature & Its Contexts Ser.). (Illus.). 140p. (C). 1993. 47.95 (*0-521-41717-1*); pap. 15.95 (*0-521-42719-3*) Cambridge U Pr.

Martindale, Charles, ed. Ovid Renewed: Ovidian Influences on Literature & Art from the Middle Ages to the Twentieth Century. (Illus.). 320p. 1988. 69.95 (*0-521-30771-6*) Cambridge U Pr.

— Ovid Renewed: Ovidian Influences on Literature & Art from the Middle Ages to the Twentieth Century. (Illus.). 320p. (C). 1990. pap. 24.95 (*0-521-39745-6*) Cambridge U Pr.

Martindale, Charles & Hopkins, David, eds. Horace Made New: Horatian Influences on British Writing from the Renaissance to the Twentieth Century. (Illus.). 326p. (C). 1993. 69.95 (*0-521-38019-7*) Cambridge U Pr.

Martindale, Charles & Martindale, Michelle. Shakespeare & the Uses of Antiquity: An Introductoy Essay on Shakespeare & English Renaissance Classicism. 240p. 1990. 45.00 (*0-415-02388-2*, A4634) Routledge.

Martindale, Colin. Cognitive Psychology: A Neural-Network Approach. 320p. (C). 1991. text ed. 23.95 (*0-534-14130-7*) Brooks-Cole.

Martindale, Cyril C. What Are Saints: Fifteen Chapters in Sanctity. LC 68-16954. (Essay Index Reprint Ser.). 1977. 17.95 (*0-8369-0681-0*) Ayer.

Martindale, Cyril C., tr. see Frisch, Hartvig.

Martindale, David. Perry Mason Casebook. 1991. pap. 14.95 (*1-55698-302-6*) Movie Pubs Servs.

— Rockford Phile. 1991. pap. 14.95 (*1-55698-288-7*) Movie Pubs Servs.

— Television Detective Shows of the 1970s: Credits, Storylines & Episode Guides for 109 Series. LC 90-53508. (Illus.). 576p. 1991. lib. bdg. 62.50x (*0-89950-557-0*) McFarland & Co.

Martindale, Don. The Nature & Types of Sociological Theory. 2nd ed. (Illus.). 656p. (C). 1988. reprint ed. pap. text ed. 28.95 (*0-88133-353-0*) Waveland Pr.

— Personality & Milieu: The Shaping of Social Science Culture. LC 82-72535. 216p. (C). 1983. text ed. 21.95 (*0-88105-001-6*) Cap & Gown.

Martindale, Don & Hanson, R. Galen. Small Town & the Nation: The Conflict of Local & Translocal Forces. LC 79-90793. (Contributions in Sociology Ser.: No. 3). 211p. 1970. text ed. 38.50 (*0-8371-1854-9*, MAT/, Greenwood Pr) Greenwood.

Martindale, Don & Martindale, Edith. Social Dimensions of Mental Illness, Alcoholism, & Drug Dependence. LC 72-133499. 332p. 1971. text ed. 59.95 (*0-8371-5175-9*, MAM/, Greenwood Pr) Greenwood.

Martindale, Don, jt. ed. see Mohan, Raj P.

Martindale, Don, ed. see Weber, Max M.

Martindale, Edith, jt. auth. see Martindale, Don.

Martindale, Hilda. Some Victorian Portraits & Others. LC 76-126324. (Biography Index Reprint Ser.). 1977. reprint ed. 17.95 (*0-8369-8030-1*) Ayer.

Martindale-Hubbell Staff, ed. Martindale-Hubbell Bar Register of Preeminent Lawyers 1994. 3000p. 1994. 145.00 (*1-56160-104-7*) Martindale-Hubbell.

—Martindale-Hubbell Bar Register of Preeminent Lawyers, 1995. 300p. 1995. 159.55 (*1-56160-138-1*) Martindale-Hubbell.

For 79 years, the MARTINDALE-HUBBELL BAR REGISTER OF PREEMINENT LAWYERS has listed only those select lawyers & law firms that have received the highest rating in the MARTINDALE-HUBBELL LAW DIRECTORY, & have been designated by their colleagues as preeminent in the field. This definitive roster of blue chip lawyers & firms in the U.S. & Canada provides over 21,000 listings for outstanding members of the bar in general practice as well as in 35 specific fields of law. The 1995 MARTINDALE-HUBBELL BAR REGISTER OF PREEMINENT LAWYERS is an essential tool for those needing a quick, reliable source of the latest information on today's leading attorneys & law firms. ***Publisher Provided Annotation.***

— Martindale-Hubbell Canadian Law Directory 1994. 1700p. 1994. 75.00 (*1-56160-105-5*) Martindale-Hubbell.

—Martindale-Hubbell Dispute Resolution Directory 1995. 2900p. 1994. 85.00 (*1-56160-109-8*) Martindale-Hubbell. More & more individuals & companies are turning to alternative methods--arbitration, mediation, minitrials, etc.--to resolve legal disputes involving everything from construction & labor contracts to insurance claims. More than 100,000 civil cases were resolved by alternative dispute resolution in the last year alone. To assist parties considering these litigation alternatives, Martindale-Hubbbell is proud to introduce our first new directory in over 75 years: the MARTINDALE-HUBBELL DISPUTE RESOLUTION DIRECTORY. The only directory of its kind, it provides accessible, state-by-state listings of professionals participating in dispute resolution. Published in cooperation with the American Arbitration Association, the MARTINDALE-HUBBELL DISPUTE RESOLUTION DIRECTORY is also an invaluable source of information on the dispute resolution field. It compiles valuable background information from many sources--from State Statutes to the American Arbitration Association Commercial Arbitration Rules--into a single convenient resource. A glossary of terms, Code of Professional Responsibility, profiles of principal non-profit dispute resolution organizations & government agency sources are included as well. Accurate & accessible, the MARTINDALE-HUBBELL DISPUTE RESOLUTION DIRECTORY will be an invaluable resource for people & companies looking for an arbitrator, mediator or other neutral, as well as an invaluable guide to the world of alternative dispute resolution. ***Publisher Provided Annotation.***

— Martindale-Hubbell Law Digest, 1994, 3. 1995. 195.00 (*1-56160-079-2*) Martindale-Hubbell.

— Martindale-Hubbell Law Directory 1994, 27 vols. 65000p. 1994. 645.00 (*1-56160-077-6*); CD-ROM - 795.00 for subscribers with listings in directory & 995.00 for all others. Discounted multi. cd-rom 995.00 (*0-318-69463-8*) Martindale-Hubbell.

—1995 Martindale-Hubbell Law Directory, 25 vols. 1995. 660.00 (*1-56160-112-8*) Martindale-Hubbell. Choosing an attorney can be one of the most important decisions your patrons will make. The 1995 MARTINDALE-HUBBELL LAW DIRECTORY will help them make an informed selection. This definitive resource has been the place to turn to for information on lawyers & law firms in the U.S., Canada, & other countries worldwide. The new 25- volume MARTINDALE HUBBELL LAW DIRECTORY makes finding the information you need easier than ever before. Organized alphabetically by state & city, the Biographical Volumes, are divided into three sections. The first part of each volume - the Practice Profiles section - provides a comprehensive listing of over 800,000 lawyers & law firms - virtually every active attorney in the U.S. The second section in each volume contains Professional Biographies, providing expanded information on lawyers & law firms. It includes not only a listing of each firm's attorneys & their backgrounds, but fields of law practiced, names of clients, & references. Services, Suppliers & Consultants, the third section in each volume, provides contact information for expert witnesses, title search companies, private detectives, & other specific legal- related services. The next volume features a Corporate Law Department section providing information on the in-house counsel of major corporations; a Law School section & a Government section. Next follows the Alphabetical Index Volume & the Areas of Practice Index Volume. The next three volumes, the International Law Directory, contains the most comprehensive listing available of international attorneys. It offers information on attorneys & law firms in over 130 countries worldwide. Finally, the Law Digest contains concise, up-to-date digests of the statutory laws of the 50 states, the District of Columbia, Puerto Rico & the Virgin Islands, the federal government, Canada, & 65 other countries. The MARTINDALE-HUBBELL LAW DIRECTORY is a definitive reference work for both the legal professional & the general public. ***Publisher Provided Annotation.***

Martindale, J. G. A Selective Bibliography of Textile Engineering. (C). 1973. pap. text ed. 70.00 (*0-685-36069-5*, Pub. by Textile Institue UK) St Mut.

Martindale, J. R., ed. The Prosopography of the Later Roman Empire, Vol. 2, A.D. 395-527. LC 77-118859. (Illus.). 1980. 275.00 (*0-521-20159-4*) Cambridge U Pr.

— The Prosopography of the Later Roman Empire, Vol. 3, A.D. 527-641. 1300p. (C). 1992. 375.00 (*0-521-20160-8*) Cambridge U Pr.

Martindale, Judith A. & Moses, Mary J. Creating Your Own Future: A Woman's Guide to Retirement Planning. LC 90-46484. 244p. 1991. 28.95 (*0-942061-08-X*, Sourcebooks Trade); pap. 14.95 (*0-942061-09-8*, Sourcebooks Trade) Sourcebks.

Martindale, Judith A., jt. auth. see Moses, Mary J.

Martindale, L. Craig. The Rise & Expansion of the Christian Church in the First Century. LC 93-60412. 500p. 1993. 12.95 (*0-910068-78-X*) Am Christian.

***Martindale, Meredith.** Lilla Cabot Perry. (Illus.). 164p. 1995. 29.95 (*0-7892-0045-7*) Abbeville Pr.

Martindale, Meredith & Mathews, Nancy M. Lilla Cabot Perry: An American Impressionist. LC 90-61820. (Illus.). 164p. 1991. pap. text ed. 29.95x (*0-940979-14-4*) Natl Museum Women.

Martindale, Michelle, jt. auth. see Martindale, Charles.

Martindale, Patrick, tr. see Patat, Jean-Pierre & Lutfalla, Michel.

***Martindale, Ruth.** Poems from the Heart. 2nd ed. 64p. 1994. reprint ed. pap. 7.95 (*1-885904-02-9*) Focus Pubng.

Martindale, T. Chris. The Voice in the Basement. Zion, Claire, ed. 288p. (Orig.). 1993. mass mkt. 4.99 (*0-671-76012-2*) PB.

Martindale, Wayne & Root, Jerry. The Quotable Lewis. (Illus.). 1989. 19.99 (*0-8423-5115-9*) Tyndale.

Martindale, William, ed. Extra Pharmacopoeia. 30th ed. 2363p. 1993. 275.00 (*0-85369-300-5*, Pub. by Pharmaceutical Pr UK) Rittenhouse.

Martindell, E. W. A Bibliography of the Works of Rudyard Kipling. LC 72-3118. (English Literature Ser.: No. 33). 1972. reprint ed. lib. bdg. 75.00 (*0-8383-1514-3*) M S G Haskell Hse.

Martine. Sexual Astrology. 1977. mass mkt. 4.99 (*0-440-18020-1*) Dell.

Martine-Barnes, Adrienne. The Crystal Sword. 224p. 1988. pap. 3.50 (*0-380-75454-1*) Avon.

— The Fire Sword. 384p. (Orig.). 1984. pap. 3.95 (*0-380-87718-X*) Avon.

— Rainbow Sword. 224p. 1988. pap. 3.50 (*0-380-75455-X*) Avon.

— The Sea Sword. 196p. (Orig.). 1989. pap. 3.50 (*0-380-75456-8*) Avon.

Martine-Barnes, Adrienne, jt. auth. see Paxson, Diana L.

Martine-Barnes, Adrienne, jt. auth. see Paxson, Diana.

Martine, Brian J. Indeterminacy & Intelligibility. LC 91-38674. (SUNY Series in Systematic Philosophy). 136p. (C). 1992. 49.50 (*0-7914-1173-7*); pap. 16.95 (*0-7914-1174-5*) State U NY Pr.

— Individuals & Individuality. LC 83-5094. (SUNY Series in Philosophy). 93p. 1984. 57.50 (*0-87395-829-2*); pap. 18.95 (*0-87395-828-4*) State U NY Pr.

Martine, Christine, tr. see Koike, Kazuo.

Martine, James J. Critical Essays on Arthur Miller. (Critical Essays on American Literature Ser.). 240p. 1979. text ed. 45.00 (*0-8161-8258-2*, Hall Reference) Macmillan.

— The Crucible: Politics, Property, & Pretense. LC 93-2843. (Masterwork Studies). 160p. 1993. text ed. 22.95 (*0-8057-8096-3*, Twayne); pap. 12.95 (*0-8057-8584-1*, Twayne) Macmillan.

Martine, James J., ed. American Novelists. (Contemporary Authors Bibliographical Ser.: Vol. 1). 300p. 1986. lib. bdg. 122.00 (*0-8103-2225-0*) Gale.

— American Novelists Nineteen Ten to Nineteen Forty-Five, 3 vols., Set. (Dictionary of Literary Biography Ser.: Vol. 9). (Illus.). 1056p. 1981. 367.00 (*0-8103-0931-9*) Gale.

Martine, Roberta. Basic Traffic Analysis. LC 93-8268. 1993. text ed. 76.00 (*0-13-335407-5*) P-H.

***Martine, Roddy.** Scotland: The Land & the Whisky. (Illus.). 224p. 1995. 50.00 (*0-7195-5351-2*, Pub. by John Murray UK) Trafalgar.

— Scottish Clan & Family Names: Their Arms, Origins & Tartans. (Illus.). 224p. 1993. pap. 22.95 (*1-85158-418-8*, Pub. by Mnstream UK) Trafalgar.

Martine, Roddy, jt. auth. see Astaire, Lesley.

Martine, Yvonne, jt. auth. see Clark, Linda.

Martineau, ed. see Stendhal.

***Martineau, Daniel L.** Mouse & the Terrible Flood. (Illus.). 30p. (J). 1994. text ed. 10.00 (*0-8059-3625-4*) Dorrance.

Martineau, Denise. Improv 2 for Windows Handbook. 1993. pap. text ed. 27.95 (*0-07-881974-1*) McGraw.

Martineau, Francis. The Sensitive Vein. LC 92-81538. 1992. 12.00 (*0-9633082-0-3*) Moon Dance.

Martineau, Harriet. Deerbrook: A Novel, 3 vols. in 2, Set. LC 79-8170. reprint ed. 84.50 (*0-404-62034-5*) AMS Pr.

— The Hour & the Man, 3 vols. in 1. LC 75-148341. reprint ed. 57.50 (*0-404-08890-2*) AMS Pr.

— How to Observe Morals & Manners. 239p. 1988. pap. 21.95 (*0-88738-751-9*) Transaction Pubs.

— Martyr Age of the United States. LC 73-82206. (Anti-Slavery Crusade in America Ser.). 1978. reprint ed. 18.95 (*0-405-00644-6*) Ayer.

— Miscellanies, 2 vols., Set. LC 79-148342. reprint ed. 71.00 (*0-404-08887-2*) AMS Pr.

— Retrospect of Western Travel, 2 Vols, LC 68-24988. (American History & Americana Ser.: No. 47). 1969. reprint ed. lib. bdg. 79.95 (*0-8383-0165-7*) M S G Haskell Hse.

— Retrospect of Western Travel, 3 vols., 1. LC 68-57623. (Illus.). 1970. reprint ed. text ed. 55.00 (*0-8371-1969-3*, MAWU) Greenwood.

— Retrospect of Western Travel, 3 vols., Set. LC 68-57623. (Illus.). 1970. reprint ed. text ed. 125.00 (*0-8371-0967-1*, MAWT) Greenwood.

— Retrospect of Western Travel, 3 vols., Set. (BCL1 - U. S. History Ser.). 1991. reprint ed. lib. bdg. 225.00 (*0-7812-6013-2*) Rprt Serv.

— Retrospect of Western Travel, 3 vols., Vol. 2. LC 68-57623. (Illus.). 1969. reprint ed. text ed. 55.00 (*0-8371-0968-X*, MAWV) Greenwood.

— Retrospect of Western Travel, 3 vols., Vol. 3. LC 68-57623. (Illus.). 1970. reprint ed. text ed. 55.00 (*0-8371-0969-8*, MAWX) Greenwood.

— Selected Letters. Sanders, Valerie, ed. 320p. 1991. 69.00 (*0-19-818604-5*) OUP.

— Society in America, 3 Vols. LC 01-27890. reprint ed. 145.00 (*0-404-04260-0*) AMS Pr.

— Society in America. Lipset, Seymour M., ed. LC 80-27647. (Social Science Classics Ser.). 357p. 1981. reprint ed. pap. 21.95x (*0-87855-853-5*) Transaction Pubs.

Martineau, Harriet, tr. see Comte, Auguste.

Martineau, Henri, ed. see Stendahl, pseud.

Martineau, Henri, ed. see Stendhal, pseud.

Martineau, Henri, ed. see Stendhal.

Martineau, Henri, ed. see Stendhal, pseud.

Martineau, Henri, ed. see Stendhal.

Martineau, Henri, ed. see Stendhal, pseud.

Martineau, Henri, ed. see Stendhal.

Martineau, James. A Study of Spinoza. 3rd ed. LC 78-152994. (Select Bibliographies Reprint Ser.). 1977. reprint ed. 25.95 (*0-8369-5746-6*) Ayer.

Martineau, LaVan. The Rocks Begin to Speak. LC 72-85137. (Illus.). 210p. 1973. 17.50 (*0-916122-30-1*) KC Pubns.

— Southern Paiutes. LC 92-74128. (Illus.). 327p. 1992. 24.95 (*0-88714-070-X*) KC Pubns.

Martineau, Louis, ed. see Stendahl, pseud.

Martineau, Robert J. Appellate Justice in England & the United States: A Comparative Analysis. LC 90-84310. xxii, 344p. 1990. lib. bdg. 60.00 (*0-89941-733-7*, 306710) W S Hein.

— Appellate Practice & Procedure, Cases & Materials On. (American Casebook Ser.). 565p. 1986. text ed. 38.00 (*0-314-30775-3*) West Pub.

— Drafting Legislation & Rules in Plain English. 155p. 1991. pap. text ed. 13.00 (*0-314-89023-8*) West Pub.

— Drafting Legislation & Rules in Plain English, Instructor's Manual of Drafting Exercises. (American Casebook Ser.). 88p. (C). 1991. pap. text ed. write for info. (*0-314-90368-2*) West Pub.

— Fundamentals of Modern Appellate Advocacy. LC 85-50347. 231p. 1985. pap. 25.00 (*0-318-11702-9*) Lawyers Cooperative.

— Modern Appellate Practice - Federal & State Civil Appeals. LC 83-80864. 1983. 95.00 (*0-318-00077-6*) Lawyers Cooperative.

— Modern Appellate Practice - Federal & State Civil Appeals. suppl. ed. LC 83-80864. 1993. Suppl. 1993. 71.00 (*0-317-04339-0*) Lawyers Cooperative.

Martinec, Jaroslav, jt. auth. see Hall, Dorothy.

Martinek, Thomas J. Psycho-Social Dynamics of Teaching Physical Education. (Illus.). 220p. 1991. pap. text ed. write for info. (*0-697-14846-7*) Brown & Benchmark.

Martinek, Thomas J. & Crowe, Patricia B. Pygmalion in the Gym. Rejeski, Walker J., ed. LC 81-81634. 160p. (Orig.). (C). 1982. pap. text ed. 17.00 (*0-918438-75-6*, PMAR0075) Human Kinetics.

Martinell, Patricia, et al. Study Guide & Manual for the National Certification Examinations for Nurse Practitioners & Other Primary Health Care Providers. 125p. 1989. pap. text ed. 19.95 (*0-8290-1279-6*) Irvington.

Martinelli, Alberto. International Markets & Global Firms: A Comparative Study of Organized Business in the Chemistry Industry. (Studies in Neo-Corporatism). 288p. 1991. text ed. 60.00 (*0-8039-8436-7*) Sage.

Martinelli, Alberto & Smelser, Neil J. Economy & Society: Overviews in Economic Sociology. (International Sociology Ser.). (Illus.). 304p. 1991. 60.00 (*0-8039-8416-2*); pap. 24.00 (*0-8039-8417-0*) Sage.

Martinelli, Franco, tr. see Cucchi, Enzo.

Martinelli, G. Standard Model, Hadron Phenomenology & Weak Decays on the Lattice: Dir in HEP, Vol. 8. 350p. 1994. pap. 37.00 (*981-02-0468-X*) World Scientific Pub.

— Standard Model, Hadron Phenomenology & Weak Decays on the Lattice: Dir in HEP, Vol. 8. 350p. 1995. text ed. 130.00 (*981-02-0467-1*) World Scientific Pub.

Martinelli, Jeanne E. Across the Spirituality Pole. 32p. (Orig.). 1989. pap. text ed. 5.00 (*0-685-29005-0*) J E Martinelli.

Martinelli, L. W., jt. auth. see Ladiges, P. Y.

Martinelli, Phylis C. Ethnicity in the Sunbelt: Italian-American Migrants in Scottsdale, Arizona. LC 87-45790. (Immigrant Communities & Ethnic Minorities in the U. S. & Canada Ser.: No. 25). 1987. 55.00 (*0-404-19435-4*) AMS Pr.

Martinelli, Phylis C., jt. auth. see Isolani, Paola A.

***Martinelli, S. D. & Kinghorn, J. R., eds.** Aspergillus: 50 Years On. (Progress in Industrial Microbiology Ser.: Vol. 29). 880p. 1994. text ed. 328.50 (*0-444-81762-X*) Elsevier.

Martinello, Marian & Cook, Gillian. Interdisciplinary Inquiry in Teaching & Learning. (Illus.). 300p. (Orig.). (C). 1994. pap. write for info. (*0-02-376502-X*) Macmillan.

Martinello, Marian, et al. Hopes, Prayers & Promises. (Texas Ser.: Vol. 2). (Illus.). 48p. (J). (gr. k-8). 1986. 12.95 (*0-935857-05-2*); pap. write for info. (*0-935857-06-0*) Texart.

Martinello, Marian L. Cedar Fever: Story of a German-Texan Girl During World War I. LC 92-73295. (Multicultural Texas Ser.). (Illus.). 212p. (YA). (gr. 7-9). 1992. 15.95 (*0-931722-90-X*); pap. 7.95 (*0-931722-95-0*) Corona Pub.

— The Search for Emma's Story: A Model For Humanities Detective Work. LC 86-30005. (Illus.). 224p. (Orig.). 1987. pap. 12.95 (*0-87565-070-8*) Tex Christian.

Martinello, Marian L. & Nesmith, Samuel P. With Domingo Leal in San Antonio, 1734. Institute of Texan Cultures Staff, ed. (University of Texas Institute of Texan Culture Young Readers Ser.). (Illus.). 78p. (Orig.). (J). (gr. 5-8). 1980. pap. 3.95 (*0-933164-40-8*) U of Tex Inst Tex Culture.

Martinengo-Cesaresco, Evelyn. Essays in the Study of Folksongs. 1976. lib. bdg. 59.95 (*0-8490-1785-8*) Gordon Pr.

Martinerie, Andree. Les Autres Jours. (FRE.). 1974. pap. 10.95 (*0-7859-4033-2*) Fr & Eur.

Martines, Julia, tr. see Brucker, Gene, ed.

Martines, Lauro. An Italian Renaissance Sextet: Six Tales in Historical Context. Baca, Murtha, tr. 280p. 1994. 28.00 (*1-56886-001-3*); pap. 18.95 (*1-56886-011-0*) Marsilio Pubs.

— Power & Imagination: City-States in Renaissance Italy. LC 87-29843. (Illus.). 400p. (C). 1988. reprint ed. pap. text ed. 15.95 (*0-8018-3643-3*) Johns Hopkins.

Martines, Melissa, jt. auth. see Moxley, Cynthia.

Martinet, Andre. From the Steppes to the Seas: Indo-European & the "Indo-Europeans" Weeks, David, tr. (Illus.). 272p. 1989. text ed. 60.00 (*0-89241-459-6*) Caratzas.

— Le Langage. (Methodique Ser.). 1544p. 46.95 (*0-686-56443-X*) Fr & Eur.

— Langage. deluxe ed. 1544p. (FRE.). 1968. 135.00 (*0-7859-4624-1*) Fr & Eur.

Martinet, Andre & Walter, Henriette. Dictionnaire de la Prononciation Francaise dans Son Usage Reel: Dictionary of French Pronunciation in Its Real Application. 932p. (FRE.). 1973. 125.00 (*0-7859-0729-7*, M-4739) Fr & Eur.

Martinet, Francoise. Ballet Center Work. Crist, Linda A., ed. (Illus.). 87p. (Orig.). (C). 1988. pap. 12.00 (*0-9620289-0-8*) Crist Pubns.

Martinet, Jacqueline. A Little Swiss Cookbook. (Little Book Ser.). (Illus.). 60p. 1991. 7.95 (*0-8118-0043-1*) Chronicle Bks.

Martinet, Jan. Hasidic Legends: A Suite by H. N. Werkman. (Illus.). 80p. (Orig.). (DUT & ENG.). 1985. 236.00 (*90-6243-048-1*, Pub. by Boumas Boekhuis NE) Benjamins North Am.

Martinet, Jeanne. The Art of Mingling: Easy, Proven Techniques for Mastering Any Room. 160p. (Orig.). 1992. pap. 8.95 (*0-312-08316-5*) St Martin.

— The Year You Were Born, 1981. (J). (gr. 4-7). 1994. 14.93 (*0-688-12874-2*, Tambourine Bks); pap. 7.95 (*0-688-12875-0*, Tambourine Bks) Morrow.

— The Year You Were Born, 1982. (J). (gr. 4-7). 1994. 14.93 (*0-688-12876-9*, Tambourine Bks); pap. 7.95 (*0-688-12877-7*, Tambourine Bks) Morrow.

— The Year You Were Born, 1983. LC 91-31605. (Year You Were Born Ser.). (Illus.). 56p. (J). 1992. lib. bdg. 13.93 (*0-688-11078-9*, Tambourine Bks); pap. 7.95 (*0-688-11077-0*, Tambourine Bks) Morrow.

— The Year You Were Born, 1984. LC 91-34577. (Year You Were Born Ser.). (Illus.). 56p. (J). 1992. lib. bdg. 13.93 (0-688-11080-0, Tambourine Bks); pap. 7.95 (0-688-11079-7, Tambourine Bks) Morrow.

— The Year You Were Born, 1985. LC 91-37439. (Year You Were Born Ser.). (Illus.). 56p. (J). 1992. lib. bdg. 13.93 (0-688-11082-7, Tambourine Bks); pap. 7.95 (0-688-11081-9, Tambourine Bks) Morrow.

— The Year You Were Born, 1986. (Illus.). 56p. (J). (gr. 2 up). 1993. lib. bdg. 13.93 (0-688-11969-7, Tambourine Bks); pap. 7.95 (0-688-11968-9, Tambourine Bks) Morrow.

— The Year You Were Born, 1987. (Illus.). 56p. (J). (gr. 2 up). 1993. lib. bdg. 13.93 (0-688-11971-9, Tambourine Bks); pap. 7.95 (0-688-11970-0, Tambourine Bks) Morrow.

*__Martinetti, Ronald.__ The James Dean Story: A Myth-Shattering Biography of an Icon. (Illus.). 256p. 1995. 19. 95 (1-55972-270-3, Birch Ln Pr) Carol Pub Group.

Martinez. Astrophotography II. (Illus.). 172p. 1987. text ed. 18.95 (0-943396-13-1) Willmann-Bell.

— Dictionary of Nautical Terms. 532p. (ENG, FRE & SPA.). 94.00 (84-7079-058-7) IBD Ltd.

— Modeling & Simulation on Microcomputers, 1983. 148p. 1983. pap. 24.00 (0-686-38790-2, MSM83) Soc Computer Sim.

— Zarela's Mexican Table. Date not set. 25.00 (0-06-016837-4, HarpT) HarpC.

Martinez-A, C., jt. ed. see Kroemer, G.

Martinez, A. Julio, ed. Free Living Amebas: Natural History, Preventions, Diagnosis, Pathology, & Treatment of Disease. 168p. 1985. 156.00 (0-8493-6631-3, QR201, CRC Reprint) Franklin.

Martinez, A. R. Venezuelan Oil: Development & Chronology. 242p. 1989. 79.25 (1-85166-276-6) Elsevier.

Martinez, A. R., ed. Solar Cooling & Dehumidifying: Proceedings of the First International Solar Cooling & Dehumidifying Conference (Solar 80), Held in Caracas, 3-6 August 1980. (Illus.). 260p. 1981. 113.00 (0-08-027571-0, Pub. by Pergamon Repr UK) Franklin.

Martinez, Adolfo, tr. see Brooks, B. David & Dalby, Rex K.

Martinez, Adolfo, et al. Agronomic & Economic Evaluation of Urea Placement & Sulfur-Coated Urea for Irrigated Paddy in Farmers' Fields in Eastern India, P-4. Frederick, Ernest D. & Roth, E. N., eds. LC 83-10874. (Paper Ser.). (Illus.). 36p. 1983. pap. text ed. 4.00 (0-88090-044-X) Intl Fertilizer.

— Fertilizer Use Statistics in Crop Production. LC 82-15856. (Technical Bulletin Ser.: No. T-24). (Illus.). 42p. (Orig.). 1982. pap. text ed. 4.00 (0-88090-042-3) Intl Fertilizer.

Martinez, Al. Ashes in the Rain. LC 89-4400. 256p. 1989. pap. 12.00 (0-89229-019-6) TQS Pubns.

Martinez, Albert B. Baedeker of the Argentine Republic. 1976. lib. bdg. 59.95 (0-87968-695-2) Gordon Pr.

Martinez, Alejandro C. The Woman Who Outshone the Sun: The Legend of Lucia Zenteno. LC 91-16646. (Illus.). 32p. (J). (gr. k-5). 1991. 13.95 (0-89239-101-4) Childrens Book Pr.

Martinez, Alicia. Feeling Fit. LC 90-10864. (Smart Talk Ser.). (Illus.). 128p. (J). (gr. 5-9). 1991. lib. bdg. 10.89 (0-8167-2140-8); pap. text ed. 2.95 (0-8167-2141-6) Troll Assocs.

Martinez-Alier. Marriage, Class, & Colour in Nineteenth-Century Cuba. 224p. 1989. pap. 13.95 (0-472-06405-3) U of Mich Pr.

Martinez-Alier, Juan. Ecological Economics: Energy, Environment & Society. 304p. (C). 1991. pap. 21.95 (0-631-17146-0) Blackwell Pubs.

Martinez Almoyna, Julio. Dicionario De Espanhol Portugues - Spanish - Portuguese Dictionary. 1068p. (POR & SPA.). 1990. 75.00 (0-8288-8541-9) Fr & Eur.

— Dicionario De Portugues Espanhol: Portuguese - Spanish Dictionary. 1332p. (POR & SPA.). 1990. 75.00 (0-8288-8540-0) Fr & Eur.

Martinez Alvarez, Antonio. El Tiempo y Yo: Articulos Ensayos, Cronicas. (UPREX, Ensayo Ser.: No. 5). 317p. (C). 1972. pap. 1.50 (0-8477-0005-4) U of PR Pr.

Martinez, Andrea P., ed. Planetary & Proto-Planetary Nebulae: From IRAS to ISO. (C). 1987. lib. bdg. 110.50 (90-277-2517-9) Kluwer Ac.

Martinez, Antonio J. Self-Instructional Modules in English As a Second Language for Spanish-Speaking Students, 2 vols., I. (Orig.). (C). 8.95 (0-8477-3323-8) U of PR Pr.

— Self-Instructional Modules in English As a Second Language for Spanish-Speaking Students, 2 vols., Set. (Orig.). (C). write for info. (0-8477-3330-0) U of PR Pr.

— Self-Instructional Modules in English As a Second Language for Spanish-Speaking Students, 2 vols., Vol. II. 88p. (Orig.). (C). 5.00 (0-8477-3329-7) U of PR Pr.

Martinez, Aquilina, tr. see Dussel, Enrique.

Martinez, Beatriz S., tr. see Hume, Maggie.

Martinez, Benjamin & Block, Jacqueline. Visual Forces: An Introduction to Design. 2nd ed. LC 93-29027. 228p. 1994. pap. text ed. write for info. (0-13-948290-3) P-H.

Martinez, Bob. Proverbial Poetry. LC 91-75210. 40p. 1993. pap. 6.95 (1-55523-467-4) Winston-Derek.

Martinez-Bonati, Felix. Don Quixote & the Poetics of the Novel. Fox, Dian, tr. LC 92-5913. 320p. 1992. 35.00 (0-8014-2359-7) Cornell U Pr.

— Fictive Discourse & the Structures of Literature: A Phenomenological Approach. exp. rev. ed. Silver, Philip W., tr. LC 80-23628. 200p. 1981. 32.50 (0-8014-1308-7) Cornell U Pr.

Martinez-Brawley, Emilia E. Perspectives on the Small Community: Humanistic Views for Practitioners. LC 90-6439. 261p. 1990. 24.95 (0-87101-183-2) Natl Assn Soc Wkrs.

— Rural Social & Community Work in the U. S. & U. K. A Cross-Cultural Perspective. LC 81-23464. 304p. 1982. text ed. 49.95 (0-275-90855-0, C0855, Praeger Pubs) Greenwood.

— Seven Decades of Rural Social Work: From Country Life Commission to Rural Caucus. LC 80-24185. 288p. 1981. text ed. 65.00 (0-275-90678-7, C0678, Praeger Pubs) Greenwood.

Martinez-Brawley, Emilia E. & Delevan, Sybil M. Transferring Technology in the Personal Social Services. LC 93-16123. 210p. (C). 1993. 24.95 (0-87101-226-X) Natl Assn Soc Wkrs.

Martinez Cachero, Jose M., ed. see Azorin.

Martinez Calvo, Lorenzo. Diccionario Ruso-Espanol. 2000p. (RUS & SPA.). 75.00 (0-7859-0884-6, S-50410) Fr & Eur.

Martinez, Carla, ed. see Punches, Laurie C.

Martinez, Carla, ed. see Punches, Laurie.

Martinez, Carlos G. New Mexico Workers' Compensation Manual. LC 93-27860. 710p. 1993. ring bd. 185.00 (0-250-42766-4) Michie Butterworth.

Martinez, Carol. Paco y Ana Aprenden Acerca de la Amabilidad. (Paco y Ana Aprenden Ser.). (Illus.). 32p. (Orig.). (SPA.). (J). (gr. 2-4). 1988. pap. 1.50 (0-311-38590-7, Edit Mundo) Casa Bautista.

— Paco y Ana Aprenden Acerca de la Amistad. (Paco y Ana Aprenden Ser.). (Illus.). (Orig.). (SPA.). (J). (gr. 2-4). 1988. pap. 1.50 (0-311-38589-3, Edit Mundo) Casa Bautista.

— Paco y Ana Aprenden Acerca de la Honradez. (Paco y Ana Aprenden Ser.). (Illus.). 32p. (Orig.). (SPA.). (J). (gr. 2-4). 1988. pap. 1.50 (0-311-38587-7, Edit Mundo) Casa Bautista.

— Paco y Ana Aprenden Acerca de la Obediencia. (Paco y Ana Aprenden Ser.). (Illus.). 32p. (Orig.). (SPA.). (J). (gr. 2-4). 1988. pap. 1.50 (0-311-38588-5, Edit Mundo) Casa Bautista.

Martinez, Carol, tr. see Cooper, Polly.

Martinez, Cathy L., jt. ed. see Long, Robert F.

Martinez, Cecelia, jt. auth. see Geist, Harold.

Martinez, Christopher D. Come the Dawn. 386p. 1994. pap. 9.95 (1-56901-248-2) NW Pub.

Martinez, Constantino F. Diccionario De la Mitologia Clasica, Vol. 2, I-Z. 8th ed. 304p. 1991. pap. 14.95 (0-7859-6447-9) Fr & Eur.

Martinez Cruz, Abelardo. Lexico de Antropologia. 3rd ed. 184p. (SPA.). 1975. pap. 9.95 (0-8288-5913-2, S50038) Fr & Eur.

Martinez Cuitino, Luis, ed. see Garcia Lorca, Federico.

Martinez, D. P., jt. ed. see van Bremen, Jan.

Martinez-Dacosta, Silvia. Los Personajes Obra de Eduardo Barrios. LC 87-61694. (Senda de Estudios y Ensayos Ser.). 176p. (Orig.). (SPA.). 1987. pap. 17.95 (0-918454-60-3) Senda Nueva.

Martinez Dalmau, Eduardo. Study on the Synoptic Gospels. 1964. 5.95 (0-8315-0013-1) Speller.

Martinez, Daniel. The Non-Lawyer Book to Form a Coporation in Guadalajara, Jalisco. 400p. (Orig.). 1994. pap. 49.99 (0-9642059-5-5) Infomex.

— The Non-Lawyer Book to Form a Corporation in Cd. Juarez, Chihuahua. 400p. (Orig.). 1994. pap. 49.99 (0-9642059-2-0) Infomex.

— The Non-Lawyer Book to Form a Corporation in Mexico City. 400p. (Orig.). 1994. pap. 49.99 (0-9642059-0-4) Infomex.

— The Non-Lawyer Book to Form a Corporation in Monterrey, N. L. 400p. (Orig.). 1994. pap. 49.99 (0-9642059-4-7) Infomex.

— The Non-Lawyer Book to Form a Corporation in Nuevo Laredo, Tamaulipas. 400p. (Orig.). 1994. pap. 49.99 (0-9642059-1-2) Infomex.

— The Non-Lawyer Book to Form a Corporation in Puebla, Puebla. (Orig.). 1994. pap. 49.99 (0-9642059-8-X) Infomex.

— The Non-Lawyer Book to Form a Corporation in Queretaro, Queretaro. 400p. (Orig.). 1994. pap. 49.99 (0-9642059-7-1) Infomex.

— The Non-Lawyer Book to Form a Corporation in San Luis Potosi. 400p. (Orig.). 1994. pap. 49.99 (0-9642059-6-3) Infomex.

— The Non-Lawyer Book to Form a Corporation in Tijuaha, B. C. 400p. (Orig.). 1994. pap. 49.99 (0-9642059-3-9) Infomex.

— The Non-Lawyer Book to Form a Corporation in Veracruz, Jalapa. 400p. (Orig.). 1994. pap. 49.99 (0-9642059-9-8) Infomex.

Martinez, David G., ed. P. Michigan, No. 16: A Greek Love Charm from Egypt. 176p. 1991. 44.95 (1-55540-547-9) Scholars Pr GA.

Martinez de Espinoza, Juan J. Diccionario Marino Espanol-Ingles, Ingles-Espanol Para Uso. 802p. 1989. 35.00 (0-7859-6218-2, 8473410483) Fr & Eur.

Martinez de Sousa, J. General Dictionary of Journalism: Diccionario General de Periodismo. 594p. (SPA.). 1981. pap. 75.00 (0-8288-1320-5, S40507) Fr & Eur.

Martinez de Sousa, Jose. Diccionario de Tipografia y del Libro. 2nd ed. (SPA.). 1981. write for info. (0-7859-3680-7, 8428311323) Fr & Eur.

Martinez de Toledo, Alfonso. Arcipreste de Talavera (Corbacho) Ciceri, Marcella, ed. (Nueva Austral Ser.: Vol. 95). (SPA.). 1991. pap. text ed. 24.95x (84-239-1895-5) Elliots Bks.

— Atalaya de las Coronicas. Larkin, James B., ed. (Spanish Ser.: No. 10). (Illus.). xvi, 157p. 1983. fiche 24.00 (0-942260-29-5) Hispanic Seminary.

Martinez de Velasco, Luis, ed. see Kant, Immanuel.

Martinez, Demetria. MotherTongue. LC 94-8664. 136p. (Orig.). 1994. 17.00 (0-927534-42-8) Biling Rev-Pr.

— MotherTongue. LC 94-8664. (Orig.). 1994. pap. 10.00 (0-927534-43-6) Biling Rev-Pr.

Martinez Diaz, Jose Luis, tr. see Thomas, I. D., et al.

Martinez, Dionisio D. History As a Second Language. LC 92-18049. (OSU Press - The Journal Award in Poetry Ser.). 88p. 1993. lib. bdg. 18.95 (0-8142-0591-7); pap. 9.95 (0-8142-0592-5) Ohio St U Pr.

Martinez, E. G., jt. auth. see Brumana, Fernando G.

Martinez, Edgar & Brown, Greg. Edgar Martinez: Patience Pays. (Illus.). 32p. (Orig.). 1992. pap. 3.50 (0-9634650-0-7) Pos for Kids.

Martinez, Edie, tr. see Apostles for Triumph Staff.

Martinez, Efrain. Classic Spanish Cooking with Chef Ef. LC 93-20469. (Illus.). 288p. 1993. 21.95 (1-56565-084-0) Lowell Hse.

— Classic Spanish Cooking with Chef Ef. (Illus.). 288p. 1994. pap. 15.00 (1-56565-119-7) Lowell Hse.

Martinez, Eliseo R. & Martinez, Irma C. French Readiness Skills, Vol. 1. Mahak, Francine T., tr. (Illus.). 87p. (J). 1987. student ed 9.50 (1-878300-02-4) Childrens Work.

— Spanish Readiness Skills, Vol. 1. (Illus.). 78p. (J). (ps-3). 1986. student ed 8.75 (1-878300-01-6) Childrens Work.

— Supplemental Studies in Math, Vol. 1. (Math Ser.). (Illus.). 73p. (J). (ps-1). 1985. student ed 8.75 (1-878300-00-8) Childrens Work.

Martinez, Eliud. The Art of Mariano Azuela: Modernism in la Malhora, el Desquite, la Luciernaga. Miller, Yvette E., ed. LC 79-29682. 101p. 1980. pap. 7.95 (0-935480-02-1) Lat Am Lit Rev Pr.

— Voice-Haunted Journey. LC 89-81825. 264p. 1990. 23.00 (0-927534-03-7); pap. 15.00 (0-927534-04-5) Biling Rev-Pr.

Martinez, Elizabeth, ed. The Art of Rini Templeton: Where There Is Life & Struggle, Bi-Lingual: English & Spanish. LC 88-60425. (Illus.). 284p. (Orig.). 1989. pap. 14.95 (0-941104-24-9) Real Comet.

— Five Hundred Years of Chicano History in Pictures: 500 Anos del Pueblo Chicano. rev. ed. (Illus.). (ENG & SPA.). 1991. 35.00 (0-9631123-1-7); pap. 16.00 (0-9631123-0-9) SW Organizing Proj.

Martinez, Elizabeth, ed. see Lopez y Rivas, Gilberto.

Martinez, Elizabeth A. Morpho-Syntactic Erosion Between Two Generational Groups of Spanish Speakers in the United States. LC 92-14656. (Theoretical Studies in Second Language Acquisition: Vol. 4). 136p. (C). 1993. text ed. 45.95 (0-8204-1944-3) P Lang Pubs.

Martinez, Elizabeth C. Edward James Olmos: Committed Actor. LC 93-37659. (Hispanic Heritage Ser.). 32p. (J). (gr. 2-4). 1994. lib. bdg. 13.40 (1-56294-410-X) Millbrook Pr.

— Henry Cisneros: Mexican-American Leader. LC 92-21384. (Hispanic Heritage Ser.). (Illus.). 32p. (J). (gr. 2-4). 1993. lib. bdg. 13.40 (1-56294-368-5); pap. 4.95 (1-56294-810-5) Millbrook Pr.

— The Mexican-American Experience. (Coming to America Ser.). (Illus.). 64p. (J). (gr. 4-6). 1995. lib. bdg. 15.90 (1-56294-515-7) Millbrook Pr.

— Sor Juana: A Trailblazing Thinker. (Hispanic Heritage Ser.). (Illus.). 32p. (J). (gr. 2-4). 1994. lib. bdg. 13.40 (1-56294-406-1) Millbrook Pr.

Martinez, Eluid L. & Smith, James C., Jr. What Is a New Mexico Santo? LC 77-78519. (Illus.). 1978. pap. 2.95 (0-913270-76-8) Sunstone Pr.

Martinez, Emilio. Julian y la Biblia: Julian's Bible. (SPA.). 4.95 (84-7645-043-5, 223109, Pub. by Edit Clie SP) TSELF.

— Recuerdos de Antano: Memories of the Spanish Inquisition. (SPA.). 7.95 (84-7228-317-8, 220751, Pub. by Edit Clie SP) TSELF.

Martinez, F., jt. ed. see Cabrera, E.

Martinez, F. Garcia, ed. Studies in Deuteronomy: In Honour of C. J. Labuschagne on the Occasion of His 65th Birthday. LC 94-4098. (Supplements to Vetus Testamentum Ser.: Vol. 53). 1994. 74.50 (90-04-10052-0) E J Brill.

Martinez, F. Garcia, et al. The Scriptures & the Scrolls: Studies in Honour of A. S. Van Der Woude on the Occasion of His 65th Birthday. LC 92-33127. (Supplements to Vetus Testamentum Ser.: Vol. 49). 1992. 65.75 (90-04-09746-5) E J Brill.

Martinez, F. J., tr. see Bulger, A. & Cherel, J. L.

*__Martinez-Falero, Eugenio & Gonzalez-Alonso, Santiago, eds.__ Quantitative Techniques in Landscape Planning. LC 95-2602. 1995. write for info. (1-56670-157-0) Lewis Pubs.

Martinez, Felix J. & Rosario, Benjamin. Manual Para Comites de Supervision. Bauza, Carmen M., ed. (Cooperatives Ser.). 84p. (Orig.). (SPA.). 1990. 5.95 (0-934885-03-6) Edit Nosotros.

Martinez-Fernandez, Luis. Torn Between Empires: Economy, Society, & Patterns of Political Thought in the Hispanic Caribbean, 1840-1878. LC 93-14972. 344p. (C). 1994. 50.00 (0-8203-1568-0) U of Ga Pr.

Martinez, Fernando V. Glossario Espanol-Arabe-Espanol de Terminos Economicos. 486p. (ARA & SPA.). 1986. pap. write for info. (0-7859-4939-9) Fr & Eur.

Martinez, Florentino G. Qumran & Apocalyptic: Studies on the Aramaic Texts from Qumran. LC 91-46425. (Studies on the Texts of the Desert of Judah: Vol. 9). 233p. 1992. 65.75 (90-04-09586-1) E J Brill.

Martinez, Florentino G., ed. & tr. The Dead Sea Scrolls Translated: The Qumran Texts in English. LC 94-17429. 1994. 80.00 (90-04-10088-1); pap. 30.00 (90-04-10048-2) E J Brill.

Martinez, Florentino G., jt. ed. see Brooke, George J.

Martinez, Francisco J., tr. see Bulger, Anthony.

Martinez, G., ed. Optical Properties of Semiconductors. 1992. lib. bdg. 140.00 (0-7923-2058-1) Kluwer Ac.

Martinez-Garcia, E., jt. ed. see Dallmeyer, R. D.

Martinez, Gayle R. Journey into Light: The Story of a Woman's Struggle to Heal, Love, & Forgive. 182p. (YA). 1992. pap. 10.95 (0-87604-292-2, 371) ARE Pr.

Martinez-Gil, Fernando, jt. ed. see Campos, Hector.

Martinez, Gloria C., ed. see Su Huei Huang.

Martinez, Guillermo. Regarding Roderer. Dail, Laura C., tr. 96p. 1994. 13.95 (0-312-11374-9) St Martin.

Martinez Hidalgo Teran, Jose M. Diccionario Nautico: Nautical Dictionary. deluxe ed. 540p. (ENG, FRE & SPA.). 1977. 125.00 (0-8288-5356-8, S50095) Fr & Eur.

*__Martinez, Homer T., Jr.__ The Rosary: A Child's Prayer (Coloring Book) (Illus.). 32p. (Orig.). (J). 1995. pap. 1.95 (0-8091-6622-4) Paulist Pr.

Martinez, Ines. To Know the Moon. LC 93-84222. 238p. (Orig.). 1993. pap. 14.95 (0-9636433-0-4) Sandia Pr.

Martinez, Irma C., jt. auth. see Martinez, Eliseo R.

Martinez, J. & Holland, C., eds. Ordered Algebraic Structures: The 1991 Conrad Conference. LC 93-18855. 1993. lib. bdg. 110.50 (0-7923-2258-4) Kluwer Ac.

Martinez, J., jt. ed. see Bali, J. P.

Martinez, J., jt. auth. see Kalman, R. E.

Martinez, J. D. Combat Mime: A Non-Violent Approach to Stage Violence. LC 82-3578. (Illus.). 224p. (C). 1982. pap. text ed. 24.95 (0-88229-809-7) Nelson-Hall.

— The Swords of Shakespeare: A Heavily Illustrated Guide to Stage Combat Choreography in the Plays of Shakespeare. (Illus.). 272p. 1995. lib. bdg. 45.00 (0-89950-959-2) McFarland & Co.

Martinez, J. L., tr. see Wiersbe, Warren W. & Wiersbe, David W.

Martinez, J. M. La Biblia Dice... According to the Bible. (SPA.). 5.50 (84-7645-054-0, 223116, Pub. by Edit Clie SP) TSELF.

— Los Cristianos En el Mundo Hoy: Christians in the Contemporary. (SPA.). 6.95 (84-7645-244-6, 223283, Pub. by Edit Clie SP) TSELF.

Martinez, J. M., ed. see Menendez Pidal, Ramon.

Martinez, J. R. & Barbero, B. J., eds. Animal Models for Cystic Fibrosis: The Reserpine-Treated Rat. (Illus.). 1985. 20.00 (0-911302-54-9) San Francisco Pr.

Martinez, Joe. The Business & Professional Communication Workbook. 96p. (C). 1992. pap. text ed. write for info. (0-8403-7563-8) Kendall-Hunt.

Martinez, Joe L., Jr. & Kesner, Raymond P. Learning & Memory: A Biological View. 1986. 35.00 (0-12-474990-9) Acad Pr.

Martinez, Joe L., Jr. & Kesner, Raymond P., eds. Learning & Memory: A Biological View. 2nd ed. (Illus.). 563p. 1991. text ed. 110.00 (0-12-474992-5); pap. text ed. 49. 95 (0-12-474993-3) Acad Pr.

Martinez, Joe L., Jr. & Mendoza, Richard H., eds. Chicano Psychology. 2nd ed. 1984. text ed. 50.00 (0-12-475660-3) Acad Pr.

Martinez, Jorge, ed. Ordered Algebraic Structures. (C). 1989. lib. bdg. 126.50 (0-7923-0489-6) Kluwer Ac.

Martinez, Jose. Novios: Conversemos Sobre Cosas Que Apenas Se Hablan. 80p. (SPA.). 1988. reprint ed. pap. 2.95 (0-311-46104-2) Casa Bautista.

Martinez, Jose & Trenchard, Ernesto. Escogidos en Cristo. 320p. (SPA.). 1987. pap. 9.99 (0-8254-1737-6) Kregel.

Martinez, Jose F. Los Del Camino. Cima Communications Staff, ed. (Orig.). (SPA.). 1991. write for info. (0-9628846-0-X) J F Martinez.

Martinez, Jose L. Antes de Dar el Si. 128p. (Orig.). (SPA.). 1990. pap. text ed. 4.25 (0-311-46118-2) Casa Bautista.

— Cuando el Dinero Causa Problemas. (Serie de la Familia). 96p. (SPA.). 1986. pap. 4.90 (0-311-46265-0) Casa Bautista.

— Mas Objetos Que Ensenan de Dios - More Objects That Teach about God. 96p. (Orig.). (SPA.). 1992. pap. 3.60 (0-311-44008-8) Casa Bautista.

Martinez, Jose L., comp. Bosquejos de Sermones para Bodas y Funerales. Orig. Title: Sermon Outlines for Weddings & Funerals. 112p. (Orig.). (SPA.). 1990. pap. 3.75 (0-311-43042-2) Casa Bautista.

— Bosquejos de Sermones Para Celebracion de Bautismo y Cena del Senor: Sermon Outlines on Baptism & The Lord's Supper. 112p. (Orig.). (SPA.). 1988. pap. 3.95 (0-311-43040-6) Casa Bautista.

— Ilustraciones Selectas, Tomo 1. 168p. (SPA.). 1992. reprint ed. pap. 5.30 (0-311-42074-5) Casa Bautista.

— Ilustraciones Selectas: Selected Illustrations, Vol. 2. 192p. (Orig.). (SPA.). 1990. pap. text ed. 5.50 (0-311-42077-X) Casa Bautista.

Martinez, Jose L., tr. see Amos, William E., Jr.

Martinez, Jose L., tr. see Hendricks, William.

Martinez, Jose L., tr. see McWilliams, Anne W.

Martinez, Jose L., tr. see Neighbour, Ralph W., Jr.

Martinez, Jose L., ed. see Neighbour, Ralph.

Martinez, Jose Luis, ed. see Haney, David.

Martinez, Jose M. Abba, Padre: Abba, Father. (SPA.). 9.95 (84-7645-383-3, 223533, Pub. by Edit Clie SP) TSELF.

— Biblia y Su Mensaje - Salmos: Bible & Its Message - Psalms, Vol. 6. (SPA.). 4.95 (84-7645-410-4, 223547, Pub. by Edit Clie SP) TSELF.

— Hermeneutica Biblica: Biblical Hermeneutics. (SPA.). 23. 95 (84-7228-833-1, 220453, Pub. by Edit Clie SP) TSELF.

— Job la Fe En Conflicto: Job: A Conflict of Faith. (SPA.). 6.95 (84-7228-211-2, 220514, Pub. by Edit Clie SP) TSELF.

— Manual de Instruccion para Nuevos: Instruction Manual for New. (SPA.). 5.50 (84-7228-683-5, 220566, Pub. by Edit Clie SP) TSELF.

— Ministros de Jesucristo: Ministers of Jesus Christ, Vol. 1. (SPA.). 6.50 (84-7228-329-1, 220244, Pub. by Edit Clie SP) TSELF.

— Ministros de Jesucristo: Ministers of Jesus Christ, Vol. 2. (SPA.). 5.95 (84-7228-330-5, 220245, Pub. by Edit Clie SP) TSELF.

— Por Que Aun soy Cristiano: Why Am I a Christian. (SPA.). 5.95 (84-7645-178-4, 223217, Pub. by Edit Clie SP) TSELF.

Martinez, Joseph, jt. auth. see Martinez, Nancy.

Martinez, Joseph G., jt. auth. see Martinez, Nancy C.

Martinez, Joseph U., jt. ed. see Martinez, Nancy C.

Martinez, Juan A. Cuban Art & National Identity: The Vanguardia Painters, 1927-1950. LC 94-7649. (Illus.). 216p. 1994. 34.95 (0-8130-1306-2) U Press Fla.

Martinez, Julio A., comp. Chicano Scholars & Writers: A Bio-Bibliographical Directory. LC 78-32076. 589p. 1979. 42.50 (0-8108-1205-3) Scarecrow.

Martinez, Julio A., ed. Dictionary of Twentieth-Century Cuban Literature. LC 88-35805. 537p. 1990. text ed. 75.00 (0-313-25185-1, MZC/, Greenwood Pr) Greenwood.

Martinez, Julio A. & Lomeli, Francisco A., eds. Chicano Literature: A Reference Guide. LC 83-22583. xiv, 576p. 1985. text ed. 75.00 (0-313-23691-7, MTL/, Greenwood Pr) Greenwood.

Martinez, Katherine, ed. American Cornucopia: Treasures of the Winterthur Library. LC 90-4115. (Illus.). 1990. pap. 19.50 (0-912724-20-X) Winterthur.

Martinez, Kerry A., ed. see Dorobiala, James F.

Martinez, L. S. & Kato, M. M. Spanish-Japanese Dictionary: Diccionario Espanol-Japones. 1103p. (JPN & SPA.). 1982. 150.00 (0-8288-1021-4, S40503) Fr & Eur.

Martinez, Larry. Communication Satellites: Power Politics in Space. LC 85-47746. (Artech House Telecom Library). 204p. reprint ed. pap. 58.20 (0-7837-3017-9, 2042923) Bks Demand.

Martinez, Larry, jt. auth. see Caggiano, Rosemary.

Martinez, Lionel. Gold Rushes of North America. 1990. 15.98 (1-55521-552-1) Bk Sales Inc.

— Murders in North America. 1991. 15.98 (1-55521-703-6) Bk Sales Inc.

Martinez-Lopez, Benjamin. Eduardo Barrios: Vida y Obra. LC 77-10946. (Coleccion Mente y Palabra). 163p. 1977. 5.00 (0-8477-0550-1); pap. 4.00 (0-8477-0551-X) U of PR Pr.

Martinez-Lopez, Enrique, jt. ed. see Belchior, Maria D.

Martinez-Lopez, Jorge I. A Casebook of Electrocardiographic Tracings. (Illus.). 168p. 1982. spiral bd. 35.00 (0-88416-307-5, Yr Bk Med Pubs) Mosby Yr Bk.

Martinez-Lopez, Jorge I., et al. A Casebook of Electrocardiographic Tracings. LC 81-16115. 167p. reprint ed. pap. 47.60 (0-8357-7873-8, 2036290) Bks Demand.

Martinez, Lorri. Where Eagles Fall. 1983. pap. 2.50 (0-942396-32-4) Blackberry ME.

Martinez, Lourdes, tr. see Kipling, Rudyard.

Martinez-Lucio, Miguel, jt. ed. see Kirkpatrick, Ian.

Martinez, Luis M. The Sanctifier. 1981. reprint ed. pap. 8.95 (0-8198-6804-3) Pauline Bks.

Martinez, M. E. Ayuda Para Predicadores: Help for Preachers. (SPA.). 6.95 (84-7645-035-4, 223104, Pub. by Edit Clie SP) TSELF.

Martinez, M. R. & Lev, M. C., eds. Computer Integrated Manufacturing. (PED Ser.: Vol. 8). 148p. 1983. pap. text ed. 30.00 (0-317-02557-0, H00288) ASME.

Martinez, Maldonado M. Hypertension & Renal Disease in the Elderly. (Illus.). 368p. 1992. 95.00 (0-86542-093-9) Blackwell Sci.

Martinez-Maldonado, Manuel, ed. Handbook of Renal Therapeutics. LC 82-24516. 588p. 1983. 95.00 (0-306-41096-6, Plenum Med Bk) Plenum.

***Martinez, Margaret.** 101 Great Lowfat Mexican Dishes: Hot, Spicy & Healthy! LC 95-5282. 1995. pap. write for info. (0-7615-0009-X) Prima Pub.

***Martinez, Mario.** Lady's Men: The Story of World War II's Mystery Bomber & Her Crew. (Illus.). 256p. 1995. 27.95 (1-55750-511-X) Naval Inst Pr.

— Lady's Men: The Story of World War II's Mystery Bomber & Her Crew. (Illus.). 256p. 1994. 39.50 (0-85052-378-8, Pub. by L Cooper Bks UK) Trans-Atl Phila.

Martinez, Mario, tr. see Lea, Thomas D. & Latham, Bill.

Martinez, Mario, tr. see Neighbour, Ralph W., Jr.

Martinez, Mario, tr. see Stacker, Joe R. & Wesley, Forbis.

Martinez, Max. The Adventures of the Chicano Kid & Other Stories. LC 81-601. 200p. (Orig.). (C). 1989. pap. 9.50 (0-934770-08-5) Arte Publico.

— A Red Bikini Dream. LC 89-35516. 144p. (Orig.). 1990. pap. 9.50 (1-55885-001-5) Arte Publico.

— Schoolland. LC 87-35127. 250p. (Orig.). 1988. pap. 9.50 (0-934770-87-5) Arte Publico.

Martinez-Miller, Orlando. La Etica Judia y la Celestina Como Alegoria. LC 77-89034. (Coleccion Polymita Ser.). 1978. 15.00 (0-89729-179-4) Ediciones.

Martinez-Miller, Orlando, tr. see Irvin, Judith L. & Downey, Joan M.

Martinez, Milton M. Espacio y Albedrio. LC 91-72886. 137p. 1991. 12.00 (0-89729-612-5) Ediciones.

— Sitio de Mascaras. LC 87-72348. (Coleccion Caniqui Ser.). (Illus.). 208p. (Orig.). (SPA.). 1987. pap. 9.95 (0-89729-460-2) Ediciones.

Martinez, Miriam, jt. ed. see Roser, Nancy L.

Martinez Moreno, Carlos. El Infierno. Wright, Ann, tr. LC 87-63467. (Readers International Ser.). 250p. (Orig.). 1988. 16.95 (0-930523-47-4); pap. 8.95 (0-930523-48-2) Readers Intl.

Martinez, Nancy & Martinez, Joseph. The Holt Workbook. 2nd ed. 416p. (C). 1989. pap. text ed. 15.00 (0-03-029809-1) HB Coll Pubs.

Martinez, Nancy C. Guide to British Poetry Explication: Restoration Through Romantic Period, Vol. 3. (Reference Ser.: Vol. 3). 576p. 1993. text ed. 50.00 (0-8161-1997-X) G K Hall.

Martinez, Nancy C. & Martinez, Joseph G. Basic College Writing: A Text with Readings. 320p. (C). 1990. pap. write for info. (0-318-68285-0) P-H.

— Guide to British Poetry Explication, Vol. I: Old English - Medieval. 225p. (C). 1991. text ed. 40.00 (0-8161-8921-8, Hall Reference) Macmillan.

Martinez, Nancy C. & Martinez, Joseph U., eds. Guide to British Poetry Explication, Vol. 2. (Guide to Poetry Explication Ser.). 400p. 1992. text ed. 45.00 (0-8161-8920-X, Hall Reference) Macmillan.

Martinez, Norma & Farrell, H. Clyde. Texas Routine Case Manual: Access to Attorneys. 66p. pap. 6.50 (0-685-23157-7, 41,575A) NCLS Inc.

Martinez, Oscar J. Border People: Life & Society in the U. S. - Mexico Borderlands. (Illus.). 375p. (Orig.). 1994. lib. bdg. 50.00 (0-8165-1396-1); pap. 24.95 (0-8165-1414-3) U of Ariz Pr.

— Troublesome Border. LC 87-34294. (PROFMEX Ser.). 177p. 1989. reprint ed. pap. 10.95 (0-8165-1104-7) U of Ariz Pr.

Martinez-Palomo, A., ed. Amebiasis: Human Parasitic Diseases, Vol. 2. 270p. 1986. 124.00 (0-444-80728-4) Elsevier.

Martinez-Palomo, Adolfo. The Biology of Entamoeba Histolytica. (Tropical Medicine Research Studies: No. 2). (Illus.). 173p. reprint ed. pap. 49.40 (0-685-27066-1, 2034230) Bks Demand.

Martinez, Patrick, ed. The Observer's Guide to Astronomy, 2 vols. Dunlop, Storm, tr. LC 93-29830. (Practical Astronomy Handbooks Ser.). (Illus.). (C). 1992. write for info. (0-521-38088-X); write for info. (0-521-38075-8) Cambridge U Pr.

— The Observer's Guide to Astronomy, Vol. 1. Dunlop, Storm, tr. (Practical Astronomy Handbooks Ser.: No. 4). (Illus.). 550p. (C). 1994. 79.95 (0-521-37068-X); pap. 34.95 (0-521-37945-8) Cambridge U Pr.

— The Observer's Guide to Astronomy, 2 vols., Vol. 2. Dunlop, Storm, tr. LC 93-29830. (Practical Astronomy Handbooks Ser.). (Illus.). (C). 1994. 79.95 (0-521-45265-1); pap. 34.95 (0-521-45898-6) Cambridge U Pr.

Martinez, Paul A. & Harbaugh, John W. Simulating Nearshore Environments. LC 93-29269. (Computer Methods in the Geosciences Ser.: Vol. 12). 1993. 130.00 (0-08-037937-0, Pergamon Pr) Elsevier.

Martinez, Paul H. Payment for Contractors, Subcontractors & Suppliers. (Construction Law Library). 1993. text ed. write for info. (0-471-54872-3) Wiley.

Martinez, R. Diccionario Biografico Historico Dominicano. (SPA.). write for info. (0-318-56669-9) Fr & Eur.

Martinez, Rafael B., jt. ed. see Barker, Thomas M.

***Martinez, Randolf.** A Matter of Survival - Burglary. (Illus.). 109p. (Orig.). 1994. write for info. (0-9644652-0-5) Chico Pub.

Martinez, Raul, tr. see Eubanks, David.

Martinez, Raul, tr. see Sharp, C. J.

Martinez, Raul, tr. see Sizemore, Denver.

Martinez, Raul, tr. see Winder, F. J.

Martinez, Ray P. Foreigners by Destiny. 1993. pap. write for info. (0-9636523-0-3) R P Martinez.

Martinez, Raymond J. Marie Laveau: Voodoo Queen & Folk Tales along the Mississippi. 96p. pap. 6.95 (0-911116-83-4) Pelican.

Martinez, Raymond J. & Holmes, Jack D. L. New Orleans: Facts & Legends. pap. 5.95 (0-911116-86-9) Pelican.

Martinez, Raymond J., jt. auth. see Hardy, Helen H.

***Martinez, Reuben & Cliff Staff.** Bless Me, Ultima Notes. Date not set. pap. text ed. 3.95 (0-8220-0249-3) Cliffs.

Martinez, Ricardo, jt. auth. see Berger, Bill.

Martinez, Ricardo A. The Healing Ritual. LC 83-51345. 174p. 1983. pap. 8.00 (0-89229-014-5) TQS Pubns.

Martinez, Richard. The Cranberry Tea Room Cookbook. Chavez, Gloria, ed. LC 92-35047. 144p. 1992. lib. bdg. 27.00x (0-8095-2950-5); pap. 17.00x (0-8095-3950-0) Borgo Pr.

Martinez, Robert E. Business & Democracy in Spain. LC 92-31845. 344p. 1993. text ed. 59.95 (0-275-94391-7, C4391, Praeger Pubs) Greenwood.

Martinez, Rodolfo V., jt. auth. see Duke, James A.

Martinez, Ronald L., tr. see Agamben, Giorgio.

Martinez, Ronald L., ed. see Alighieri, Dante.

Martinez, Ronald L., jt. auth. see Durling, Robert.

Martinez, Ruben. Other Side: Fault Lines, Guerilla Saints & the True Heart of Rock & Roll. 1992. 24.95 (0-86091-370-8, Pub. by Verso UK) Routledge Chapman & Hall.

— The Other Side: The Fault Lines, Guerrilla Saints & True Heart of Rock 'n' Roll. 1993. pap. 10.00 (0-679-74591-2, Vin) Random.

Martinez, Ruben G. Border Cafe. 1992. pap. 6.00 (0-685-62439-0) Pudding Hse Pubns.

Martinez, Ruben O., jt. auth. see Aguirre, Adalberto, Jr.

Martinez, Ruth. Mrs. McDockerty's Knitting. (Illus.). 32p. (J). (ps-3). 1990. 13.95 (0-395-51591-2) HM.

***Martinez, Samuel.** Peripheral Migrants: Haitians & Dominican Republic Sugar Plantations. LC 95-4359. 1995. write for info. (0-87049-901-7) U of Tenn Pr.

Martinez San Martin, Angel, ed. see Trigo, Felipe.

Martinez, Santiago. Diccionario Diplomatico. 252p. 1986. pap. 29.95 (0-7859-6199-2, 8472324095) Fr & Eur.

Martinez-Serros, Hugo. The Last Laugh & Other Stories. LC 88-6359. 120p. (Orig.). 1988. pap. 9.50 (0-934770-89-1) Arte Publico.

Martinez, Servet, jt. auth. see Goles, Eric.

Martinez, Servet, jt. ed. see Goles, Eric.

Martinez, Steve K. Material Testing & Biocompatibility--Index of New Information & Medical Research Bible. 150p. 1994. 44.50 (0-7883-0096-2); pap. 39.50 (0-7883-0097-0) ABBE Pubs Assn.

***Martinez, Susan E.** Angels & Dreams. Ilse, Sherokee, ed. (Gifts from the Universe Ser.). 116p. (Orig.). 1995. pap. 7.95 (0-9625379-4-2) Safe & Sound Prodns.

Martinez-Taboas, Alfonso. Multiple Personality Disorder: An Hispanic Psychological Perspective. rev. ed. Kluft, Richard, ed. Alvarado, Carlos S. & Kluft, Richard, trs. 150p. 1993. reprint ed. pap. text ed. 16.00 (0-9634501-0-7) Puente Pubns.

Martinez Tolentino, Jaime. Cuentos Fantasticos. LC 81-10292. (UPREX, Estudios Literarios Ser.: No. 62). 70p. 1983. pap. 2.00 (0-8477-0062-3) U of PR Pr.

Martinez, Tomas. The Human Marketplace: An Examination of Private Employment Agencies. LC 74-20196. 176p. 1975. text ed. 32.95 (0-87855-094-1) Transaction Pubs.

Martinez Torres, Augusto. Diccionario Nuevos Directores Franceses. 176p. (SPA.). 1976. pap. 9.95 (0-8288-5579-X, S50075) Fr & Eur.

Martinez, V. J., et al, eds. New Insights into the Universe: Proceedings of a Summer School, Held in Valencia, Spain, 23-27 September 1991. LC 92-27336. (Lecture Notes in Physics Ser.: Vol. 408). xi, 298p. 1992. 64.00 (0-387-55842-X); write for info. (3-540-55842-X) Spr-Verlag.

Martinez-Vergne, Teresita. Capitalism in Colonial Puerto Rico: Central San Vicente in the Late Nineteenth Century. (Illus.). 208p. (C). 1992. lib. bdg. 29.95 (0-8130-1110-8) U Press Fla.

***Martinez, Victor.** Caring for a House. 65p. 1992. pap. 10.00 (0-9624536-4-1) Chusma Hse.

Martinez, Violeta, ed. see Cowman, Charles E.

Martinez, Violeta, tr. see Wiersbe, Warren W. & Wiersbe, David W.

Martinez, Yasmin, ed. see Dounuts, Kevin.

Martinez, Zarela. Food from My Heart. 320p. 1992. text ed. 25.00 (0-02-580471-5) Macmillan.

Marting, Diane E. Clarice Lispector: A Bio-Bibliography. LC 93-28537. (Bio-Bibliographies in World Literature Ser.: Vol. 2). 368p. 1993. text ed. 85.00 (0-313-27803-2, Greenwood Pr) Greenwood.

Marting, Diane E., ed. Spanish American Women Writers: A Bio-Bibliographical Source Book. LC 89-27283. 656p. 1990. text ed. 89.50 (0-313-25194-0, MSA/, Greenwood Pr) Greenwood.

— Women Writers of Spanish America: An Annotated Bio-Bibliographical Guide. LC 86-33552. (Bibliographies & Indexes in Women's Studies Ser.: No. 5). 468p. 1987. text ed. 89.50 (0-313-24969-5, MWN/, Greenwood Pr) Greenwood.

Marting, Elizabeth. Invitation to Achievement: Your Career in Management. 35p. reprint ed. pap. 25.00 (0-317-20778-4, 2023908) Bks Demand.

Marting, Elizabeth, ed. see American Management Association, Research & Development Division Staff.

Marting, Janet, comp. Making a Living: A Real-World Reader. LC 92-12437. (C). 1992. 25.50 (0-06-500554-6) HarpCollege.

Marting, Janet, ed. The Voice of Reflection: A Writer's Reader. LC 94-1385. (C). 1995. 17.50 (0-673-46934-4) HarpCollege.

Martingale, Moira. Cannibal Killers: The History of Impossible Murders. 192p. 1994. pap. 10.95 (0-7867-0096-3) Carroll & Graf.

***Martini.** El Fantasma Imperfecto: The Imperfect Ghost. 1995. pap. 14.95 (0-679-76097-0, Villard Bks) Random.

— Practical Seal Design. (Mechanical Engineering Ser.: Vol. 29). 312p. 1984. 99.75 (0-8247-7166-4) Dekker.

Martini, Aemidius & Bassi, Domenicus. Catalogus Codicum Graecorum Bibliothecae Ambrosianae, 2 vols. in 1. li, 1297p. 1978. reprint ed. write for info. (3-487-06499-5, Pub. by Georg Olms GW) Lubrecht & Cramer.

Martini, Alberto. Renoir: Avenal Art Library. (Illus.). 1988. 6.99 (0-517-24955-3) Random Hse Value.

Martini, Carlo. Bread of the Word. 1989. 4.25 (0-685-28776-9) Catholic Bk Pub.

— Once More from Emmaus. 128p. (Orig.). 1995. pap. text ed. 7.95 (0-8146-2158-9) Liturgical Pr.

— What Am I That You Care for Me? 138p. (Orig.). 1992. pap. text ed. 9.95 (0-8146-2131-7) Liturgical Pr.

Martini, Carlo, ed. Ministers of the Gospel. (C). 1988. 39.00 (0-85439-220-3, Pub. by St Paul Pubns UK) St Mut.

— The Testimony of St. Paul. (C). 1988. 6.95 (0-8245-0958-7) Crossroad NY.

Martini, Carlo C. After Some Years: Reflection on the Ministry of the Priest. 125p. 1991. pap. 9.95 (1-85390-038-9, Pub. by Veritas Publns IE) Ignatius Pr.

— Drawn to the Lord: Six Stories of Vocation. Rogers, Patrick, tr. 80p. (Orig.). 1987. pap. 6.95 (0-86217-248-9, Pub. by Veritas Publns IE) Ignatius Pr.

— Praying with Saint Luke. 82p. 1989. pap. 22.00 (0-685-65153-3, Pub. by Veritas IE) St Mut.

— Reflections on the Church: Meditations on Vatican II. Griffin, Luke, tr. (Cathedral Ser.: No. 4). 93p. (Orig.). 1987. pap. 8.95 (1-85390-000-1, Pub. by Veritas Pubns IE) Irish Bks Media.

— Women & Reconciliation. Griffin, Luke, tr. (Cathedral Ser.: No. 3). 66p. (Orig.). 1987. pap. 7.95 (0-86217-239-X, Pub. by Veritas Publns IE) Ignatius Pr.

— Women & Reconciliation. 66p. (Orig.). 1989. pap. 30.00 (0-86217-293-4, Pub. by Veritas IE) St Mut.

Martini, Carlo M. Communicating Christ to the World. LC 93-35459. 212p. (Orig.). 1994. pap. 14.95 (1-55612-655-7) Sheed & Ward MO.

— In the Thick of His Ministry. 96p. 1992. pap. 24.95 (0-85439-336-6, Pub. by St Paul Pubns UK) St Mut.

— Jacob's Dream: Setting Out on a Spiritual Journey. 72p. (Orig.). 1992. pap. text ed. 4.95 (0-8146-2000-0) Liturgical Pr.

— Journeying with the Lord: Reflections for Everyday. 511p. 1987. pap. 14.95 (0-8189-0508-5) Alba.

— The Joy of the Gospel: Meditations for Young People. 119p. (Orig.). 1994. pap. text ed. 8.95 (0-8146-2126-0) Liturgical Pr.

— Letting God Free Us: Meditations on Ignatian Spiritual Exercises. Arnandez, Richard, tr. LC 93-15187. 128p. (Orig.). 1993. pap. 8.95 (1-56548-053-8) New City.

— Ministers of the Gospel. 1989. pap. 6.95 (0-8245-0959-5) Crossroad NY.

— The New Wine: Christian Witness of the Family. Berger, Mary J., tr. 232p. (Orig.). 1994. pap. 6.95 (0-8198-5131-0) Pauline Bks.

— Pilgrims, Not Strangers: Christian Witness in a Broken World. Berger, Mary J., tr. LC 93-6448. 176p. (Orig.). 1993. pap. 5.95 (0-8198-5888-9) Pauline Bks.

— The Spiritual Journey of the Apostles: Growth in the Gospel of Mark. Whitehead, K. D., tr. LC 91-31728. 190p. (Orig.). 1991. pap. 8.95 (0-8198-6910-4) Pauline Bks.

— Women in the Gospels. 136p. (Orig.). 1990. pap. 9.95 (0-8245-0986-2) Crossroad NY.

Martini, Carlo-Maria. David: Sinner & Believer. 187p. (C). 1990. 49.00 (0-85439-322-6, Pub. by St Paul Pubns UK) St Mut.

— In the Thick of His Ministry. 91p. (Orig.). 1991. pap. 6.95 (0-8146-1995-9) Liturgical Pr.

— Letting God Free Us. 128p. 1993. 26.00 (0-85439-452-4, Pub. by St Paul Pubns UK) St Mut.

— Promise Fulfilled. 176p. 1992. pap. 24.95 (0-85439-481-8, Pub. by St Paul Pubns UK) St Mut.

— The Testimony of St. Paul. 104p. (C). 1990. 39.00 (0-85439-221-1, Pub. by St Paul Pubns UK) St Mut.

— What Am I That You Care for Me? Praying with the Psalms. 138p. (C). 1990. 49.00 (0-85439-347-1, Pub. by St Paul Pubns UK) St Mut.

***Martini, Clem & Foreman, Kathleen, eds.** Something Like a Drug: An Unauthorized Oral History of Theatresports. LC 95-14873. 1995. pap. write for info. (0-88734-918-8) Players Pr.

***Martini, Elizabeth B., et al.** Long Term Care: Interpretation & Inspiration for Activity & Social Service Professionals. (Illus.). 400p. (Orig.). (C). 1994. pap. text ed. 35.00 (1-882883-11-X) Idyll Arbor.

***Martini, Frederic.** Fundamentals of Anatomy & Philsiology. 3rd ed. 1994. text ed. 72.25 (0-13-298952-2) P-H.

Martini, Frederic & Timmons, Michael J. Human Anatomy. LC 94-5082. 1994. text ed. 72.00 (0-13-444134-6) P-H.

Martini, Frederic H. Fundamentals of Anatomy & Physiology. 2nd ed. 1120p. (C). 1992. text ed. write for info. (0-13-334500-4) P-H.

Martini, Galen. The Heart's Slow Race: A Farewell to the Lands. LC 76-24956. (Illus.). 1976. 6.95 (0-87839-029-4) North Star.

Martini, Harold J. Athletic Injuries: Guidebook for Medicine & Research. LC 87-47678. 150p. 1987. 39.50 (0-88164-660-1); pap. 34.50 (0-88164-661-X) ABBE Pubs Assn.

Martini, I. P., ed. Canadian Inland Seas. 512p. 1986. 95.00 (0-444-42683-3) Elsevier.

Martini, James C. Basic Canoeing Workbook. (Illus.). 98p. (Orig.). 1992. 3.95 (1-881644-00-6) P E R Assocs.

Martini, Johannes. Four Chansons. (Renaissance Recorder Ser.: No. 1). 1970. 2.50 (0-913334-06-5, CM1005) Consort Music.

Martini, John. Fortress Alcatraz - Guardian of the Golden Gate. 1991. pap. 11.95 (0-9629227-0-6) Pacific Mono.

Martini, John A. Fort Point: Sentry at the Golden Gate. (Illus.). 48p. (Orig.). 1992. pap. 7.95 (0-9625206-5-9) Gldn Gate Natl Park Assoc.

Martini, Luciano & Ganong, William F., eds. Frontiers in Neuroendocrinology, Vol. 6. 428p. 1980. text ed. 112.00 (0-89004-404-X) Raven.

— Frontiers in Neuroendocrinology, Vol. 9. (Illus.). 294p. 1986. text ed. 99.50 (0-88167-168-1) Raven.

— Frontiers in Neuroendocrinology, Vol. 10. (Illus.). 358p. 1988. text ed. 155.00 (0-88167-379-X) Raven.

— Frontiers in Neuroendocrinology Vol. 4. fac. ed. LC 77-82030. (Illus.). 304p. Date not set. pap. 86.70 (0-7837-7146-0, 2047149) Bks Demand.

Martini, Luciano, jt. ed. see Ganong, William F.

Martini, Luciano, jt. ed. see International Symposium on Androgens & Antiandrogens Staff.

Martini, Luciano, jt. ed. see Molinatti, G. M.

Martini, Luciano, ed. see Motta, Marcella.

Martini, Luciano, jt. ed. see Serio, Mario.

Martini, Luciano, et al, eds. Research on Steroids, Vol. XI: Steroid Modulation of Neuroendocrine Function-Sterols, Steroids & Bone Metabolism. (International Congress Ser.: Vol. 633). 1985. 118.50 (0-444-80594-X) Elsevier.

Martini, M., ed. Tuberculosis of the Bones & Joints. (Illus.). 230p. 1988. 99.00 (0-387-18166-0) Spr-Verlag.

Martini, R., ed. Geometric Aspects of the Einstein Equation & Integrable Systems. (Lecture Notes in Physics Ser.: Vol. 239). 344p. 1985. pap. 35.00 (0-387-16039-6) Spr-Verlag.

Martini, R., jt. ed. see Bongaarts, P. J.

Martini, Steve. Compelling Evidence. 448p. 1993. mass mkt. 6.99 (0-515-11039-6) Jove Pubns.

— Compelling Evidence. large type ed. LC 92-18331. (General Ser.). 608p. 1992. lib. bdg. 23.95 (0-8161-5548-8) G K Hall.

— Compelling Evidence. large type ed. LC 92-18331. (General Ser.). 657p. 1993. pap. 16.95 (0-8161-5549-6) G K Hall.

— The Judge. 1995. 23.95 (0-399-14043-3) Putnam Pub Group.

— Prime Witness. 416p. 1994. mass mkt. 5.99 (0-515-11264-X) Jove Pubns.

— Prime Witness. 384p. 1993. 21.95 (0-399-13802-1, Putnam) Putnam Pub Group.

— Prime Witness. large type ed. LC 93-34152. 1993. 22.95 (0-8161-5869-X) Hall.

— Prime Witness. large type ed. LC 93-34152. 1994. pap. 17.95 (0-8161-5870-3) Hall.

— The Simeon Chamber. large type ed. 1994. 22.95 (0-7089-3151-0) Ulverscroft.

— Simeon Chamber. 320p. 1994. reprint ed. mass mkt. 5.99 (0-515-11371-9) Jove Pubns.

— Undue Influence. 400p. 1994. 22.95 (*0-399-13932-X*) Putnam Pub Group.
— Undue Influence. 480p. 1995. mass mkt. 6.99 (*0-515-11605-X*) Jove Pubns.
— Undue Influence. large type ed. LC 94-34499. 714p. 1994. 24.95 (*0-7838-1128-4*) Hall.
Martini, Steven P. The Simeon Chamber. 1988. 17.95 (*1-55611-103-7*) D I Fine.
Martini, Teri. Christmas for Andy. (J). (gr. 3 up). 1991. pap. 3.95 (*0-8091-6603-8*) Paulist Pr.
— Cowboys. LC 81-10049. (New True Bks.). (Illus.). 48p. (J). (gr. k-4). 1981. lib. bdg. 12.90 (*0-516-01611-3*) Childrens.
— Feliz Navidad, Pablo. (Illus.). (J). (gr. 4 up). 1990. pap. 2.95 (*0-8091-6597-X*) Paulist Pr.
— Secret Is Out. (J). (gr. 4-7). 1990. 14.95 (*0-316-54864-2*, Joy St Bks) Little.
— The Secret Is Out. 144p. (J). (gr. 5). 1992. pap. 2.99 (*0-380-71465-5*, Camelot) Avon.
Martinich, A. P. Communication & Reference. LC 84-14283. (Foundations of Communication & Cognition Ser.). xiii, 205p. 1984. lib. bdg. 76.15 (*3-11-010067-3*) De Gruyter.
— A Hobbes Dictionary. (The/Blackwell Philosopher Dictionaries Ser.). 400p. 1995. write for info. (*0-631-19261-1*); pap. write for info. (*0-631-19262-X*) Blackwell Pubs.
— Philosophical Writing. 144p. (C). 1988. pap. text ed. write for info. (*0-13-664103-2*) P-H.
— The Philosophy of Language. 2nd ed. 544p. (C). 1990. text ed. 35.00 (*0-19-506254-X*) OUP.
— The Philosophy of Language. 3rd ed. 576p. (C). 1995. text ed. 35.00 (*0-19-509368-2*) OUP.
— The Two Gods of Leviathan: Thomas Hobbes on Religion & Politics. 432p. (C). 1992. 69.95 (*0-521-41849-6*) Cambridge U Pr.
Martinich, A. P. & White, Michael, eds. Certainty & Surface in Epistemology & Philosophical Method: Essays in Honor of Avrum Stroll. LC 91-27368. (Problems in Contemporary Philosophy Ser.: Vol. 32). 228p. 1991. lib. bdg. 89.95 (*0-7734-9711-0*) E Mellen.
Martinich, Aloysius P., tr. Computatio Sive Logica: Thomas Hobbes, Pt. I. LC 77-86237. (Janus Ser.). 450p. 1981. 20.00 (*0-913870-36-6*) Abaris Bks.
***Martinie, Henri.** Art Deco Ornamental Ironwork. LC 94-47177. (Illus.). 1995. write for info. (*0-486-28535-9*) Dover.
Martinie, Louise & Glassman, Sallie A. New Orleans Voodoo Tarot. (Illus.). 256p. (Orig.). 1992. pap. 29.95 (*0-89281-363-6*) Inner Tradit.
Martinis, M., ed. Superstrings, Anomalies & Unification: Proceedings of the Adriatic Meeting on Particle Physics, 5th, Dubrovnik, Yugoslavia, June 16-28, 1986. 584p. 1987. pap. 47.00 (*9971-5-0233-X*) World Scientific Pub.
Martinis, M., et al, eds. Particle Physics. 400p. 1975. 36.00 (*0-444-10648-0*, North Holland) Elsevier.
Martinko, Mark. Attribution Theory: An Organizational Perspective. (Illus.). 260p. 1995. 39.95 (*1-884015-19-0*) St Lucie Pr.
Martinn, Chuck. Tall in the Saddle. 1993. 14.95 (*0-7451-4579-5*, Gunsmoke) Chivers N Amer.
Martino, Antonio A. Deontic Logic, Computational Linguistics & Legal Information Systems. 518p. 1982. 105.25 (*0-444-86415-6*, North Holland) Elsevier.
Martino, Antonio A., ed. Expert Systems in Law: Proceedings of the 3rd International Conference Logic, Informatics, Law: Legal Expert Systems, Held Nov. 2-5 in Florence, Italy. LC 92-15092. 1992. write for info. (*0-444-89333-4*, North Holland) Elsevier.
Martino, Antonio A. & Natali, F. Socci, eds. Automated Analysis of Legal Texts: Edited Versions of Selected Papers from the International Conference, 2nd, Florence, Italy, September, 1985. 938p. 1986. 166.75 (*0-444-70111-7*, North Holland) Elsevier.
***Martino, Joseph P.** R & D Project Selection. LC 94-30753. (Engineering Managment Ser.). 1995. text ed. 59.95 (*0-471-59537-3*) Wiley.
— Science Funding: Politics & Porkbarrel. 336p. (C). 1992. 39.95 (*1-56000-033-3*) Transaction Pubs.
— Technological Forcasting for Decision Making. 3rd ed. 1992. text ed. 65.00 (*0-07-040777-0*) McGraw.
Martino, Joseph P., ed. An Introduction to Technological Forecasting. (Futurist Library). 118p. 1973. text ed. 90.00 (*0-677-15050-4*) Gordon & Breach.
Martino, Lorenzo, jt. auth. see Bertino, Elisa.
Martino, Pierre. Naturalisme Francais 1870-95. 206p. 1969. 29.95 (*0-8288-7431-X*) Fr & Eur.
— Parnasse et Symbolisme. 191p. 1970. 29.95 (*0-8288-7432-8*) Fr & Eur.
Martino, R. L. Critical Path Networks. 176p. 1968. text ed. 158.00 (*0-677-61040-8*) Gordon & Breach.
— Dynamic Costing. 162p. 1968. text ed. 158.00 (*0-677-61060-2*) Gordon & Breach.
— Project Management. 108p. 1968. text ed. 158.00 (*0-677-61070-X*) Gordon & Breach.
Martino, Rocco L. Resources Management. 168p. 1968. text ed. 179.00 (*0-677-61050-5*) Gordon & Breach.
Martino, Teresa. Pizza! (Real Readers Ser.: Level Green). (Illus.). 32p. (J). (gr. 1-4). 1989. lib. bdg. 19.97 (*0-8172-3533-7*); pap. 3.95 (*0-8114-6730-9*) Raintree Steck-V.
Martinoff, James T., et al. Verbal Expression. (Language Rehabilitation Ser.). 352p. 1981. 84.00 (*0-88120-126-X*, 2366) PRO-ED.
Martinoli, Silvia. Men ... Wake Up! Date not set. 6.95 (*0-9634014-8-3*) S Martinoli.
— No More Detours. 102p. 1992. pap. write for info. (*0-9634014-7-5*) S Martinoli.
Martinovitch, Nicholas N. Turkish Theatre. LC 68-20241. (Illus.). 1972. reprint ed. 21.95 (*0-405-08761-6*, Pub. by Blom Pubns UK) Ayer.
Martins de Carvalho, J. L. Dynamical Systems & Automatic Control. LC 93-3829. 1993. 40.00 (*0-13-221755-4*) P-H.
***Martins, Helvecio & Grover, Mark.** The Autobiography of Elder Helvecio Martins. LC 94-37044. 131p. 1994. 12.95 (*1-56236-218-6*) Aspen Bks.
Martins, Herminio, ed. Knowledge & Passion: Essays in Sociology & Social Theory in Honour of John Rex. 256p. 1993. text ed. 70.00 (*1-85043-323-2*) St Martin.
Martins, Hermino, jt. ed. see Pickering, William S.
Martins, Isabel P., et al, eds. Acquired Aphasia in Children. 328p. 1991. lib. bdg. 112.50 (*0-7923-1315-1*) Kluwer Ac.
***Martins, J. A.** Diccionario Tecnico Ingles-Portuguese de Maquinas e Ferramentas. 229p. (ENG & POR.). 1983. 35.00 (*0-7859-7152-1*) Fr & Eur.
Martins, J. B., ed. Numerical Methods in Geomechanics. 1982. lib. bdg. 149.50 (*90-277-1461-4*) Kluwer Ac.
Martins, J. P. & Morgado, E. M., eds. EPIA 'Eighty-Nine. (Lecture Notes in Artificial Intelligence Ser.: Vol. 390). xii, 400p. 1989. pap. 47.00 (*0-387-51665-4*) Spr-Verlag.
Martins, J. P., et al, eds. Truth Maintenance Systems: ECAI-90 Workshop, Stockholm, Sweden, August 6, 1990 Proceedings. (Lecture Notes in Artificial Intelligence Ser.: Vol. 515). vii, 177p. 1991. pap. 25.00 (*0-387-54305-8*) Spr-Verlag.
Martins, James J. Critical Essays on Eugene O'Neill. (Critical Essays on American Literature Ser.). 224p. 1984. text ed. 45.00 (*0-8161-8683-9*) G K Hall.
Martins, Joao P. Introduction to Computer Science Using Pascal. 537p. (C). 1989. pap. 48.95 (*0-534-09402-3*) PWS Pubs.
Martins, M. Rui. An Organisational Approach to Regional Planning. 296p. 1986. text ed. 56.95 (*0-566-00515-8*, Pub. by Avebury Pub UK) Ashgate Pub Co.
Martins, Michael & Binette, Dennis A. The Commonwealth of Massachusetts vs. Lizzie A. Borden-The Knowlton Papers-1892-1893: A Collection of Previously Unpublished Letters from the Files of Prosecuting Attorney Hosea Morrill Knowlton. (Illus.). 400p. 1994. 49.95 (*0-9641248-3-1*) Fall River Hist Soc.
Martins, Pam. A Brush with Cats. (Illus.). 48p. 1995. 14.95 (*0-285-63087-3*, Pub. by Souvenir UK) Atrium Pubs.
Martins, Robyn. The Fun Book of Bible Trivia 2. 128p. (Orig.). 1993. pap. 5.95 (*1-55748-340-X*) Barbour & Co.
Martins, Robyn, ed. The Christian Bed & Breakfast Directory: 1992-1993 Edition. 1992. pap. 8.95 (*1-55748-289-6*) Barbour & Co.
Martins, Rui, ed. Recent Advances in Hydraulic Physical Modelling. (C). 1989. lib. bdg. 193.50 (*0-7923-0196-X*) Kluwer Ac.
Martins, Susanna W. A Great Estate at Work: The Holkham Estate & Its Inhabitants in the Nineteenth Century. LC 79-51827. 303p. reprint ed. pap. 86.40 (*0-317-55478-6*, 2029223) Bks Demand.
— Know the Landscape: Farms & Fields. (Illus.). 160p. 1995. pap. 34.95 (*0-7134-6790-8*, Pub. by Batsford UK) Trafalgar.
Martins-Swartz, Rosemarie A. Enter Quietly. 96p. (Orig.). 1993. 15.95 (*0-9636337-0-8*); pap. 9.95 (*0-9636337-1-6*) Intricate Lines.
Martins, Wilson. The Modernist Idea: A Critical Survey of Brazilian Writing in the Twentieth Century. Tomlins, Jack E., tr. LC 78-24232. 345p. 1979. reprint ed. text ed. 38.50 (*0-313-20811-5*, MAID, Greenwood Pr) Greenwood.
Martins, Wilson & Menton, Seymour, eds. Teatro Brasileiro Contemporaneo. rev. ed. LC 77-2753. (gr. 11-12). 1978. reprint ed. pap. text ed. 19.95 (*0-89197-640-X*) Irvington.
***Martinsen.** Using Visual Basic Special Edition. 1995. disk, pap. 39.99 (*1-56529-998-1*) Que.
Martinsen, Ella. Black Sand & Gold. LC 56-6862. (Illus.). 419p. 1974. pap. 14.95 (*0-8323-0189-2*) Binford Mort.
Martinsen, Ella L. Trail to North Star Gold: True Story of the Alaska-Klondike Gold Rush. 2nd ed. LC 70-98194. (Illus.). 378p. 1991. reprint ed. pap. 14.95 (*0-8323-0242-2*) Binford Mort.
Martinsen, Harald, jt. auth. see Von Tetzchner, Stephen.
Martinson. GMAT: Graduate Management Admissions Test. 1994. pap. 13.00 (*0-671-87463-2*, Arco Test) P-H Gen Ref & Trav.
— SAT Supercourse. 2nd ed. 1994. pap. 17.00 (*0-671-86402-5*, Arco Test) P-H Gen Ref & Trav.
Martinson & Widmer. Home Health Care Nursing. 432p. 1989. text ed. 51.95 (*0-7216-6148-3*) Saunders.
Martinson, A. D., jt. auth. see Magden, Ronald E.
Martinson, Arthur D. Wilderness above the Sound: The Story of Mount Rainier National Park. 2nd ed. 1994. pap. 11.95 (*1-879373-76-9*) R Rinehart.
Martinson, Denise. Forging a Foundation. (Illus.). 40p. (Orig.). 1992. pap. 6.00 (*1-879533-08-1*) Poetic Page.
Martinson, Denise, ed. see Cirino, Leonard J.
Martinson, Denise, ed. see Segall, Pearl B.
Martinson, Floyd M. Growing up in Norway, 800 to 1990. 264p. (C). 1992. 29.95 (*0-8093-1778-8*) S Ill U Pr.
— The Sexual Life of Children. LC 93-37847. 168p. 1994. text ed. 45.00 (*0-89789-376-X*, Bergin & Garvey) Greenwood.
Martinson, Harry. Wild Bouquet: Nature Poems. Smith, William J. & Sjoberg, Leif, trs. LC 84-73437. (International Ser.). (Illus.). 80p. 1985. 10.95 (*0-933532-48-2*) BkMk.
Martinson, Ida M. Home Care of the Dying Child: Professional Approaches. LC 76-29360. 345p. (Orig.). 1976. pap. 9.95 (*0-930194-09-8*) Ctr Thanatology.
Martinson, Ida M., jt. auth. see Moldow, D. Gay.
Martinson, Linda. New Directions in Financial Computing: Integrated Administrative Data Processing in Higher Education. LC 92-9622. 1992. 56.95 (*0-915164-81-7*) NACUBO.
— Simply Salmon: Fresh, Frozen & Canned. 138p. 1986. pap. 9.95 (*0-934363-02-1*) Lance Pubns.
— Simply Salmon, Fresh, Frozen & Canned. 2nd rev. ed. Lane, Jay, ed. (Illus.). 134p. 1988. reprint ed. spiral bd. 14.95 (*0-934363-03-X*) Lance Pubns.
— Simply Shrimp, Fresh, Frozen & Canned. Lane, Jay, ed. (Illus.). 130p. 1988. spiral bd. 14.95 (*0-934363-04-8*) Lance Pubns.
Martinson, Linda & O'Leary, Joanne. Don't Cut the Apron Strings: An Early Childhood Resource Featuring Integrated Curriculum & Theme Aprons. (Illus.). 114p. (Orig.). 1993. pap. 10.95 (*0-9637759-0-1*) Apron Strings.
Martinson, Moa. My Mother Gets Married. Lacy, Margaret S., tr. & aft. by. LC 88-21405. 304p. 1988. 35.00 (*0-935312-99-4*); pap. 9.95 (*0-935312-81-1*) Feminist Pr.
— Women & Appletrees. Lacy, Margaret S., tr. LC 85-6898. 224p. 1985. pap. 8.95 (*0-935312-38-2*) Feminist Pr.
***Martinson, Otto B.** Cost Accounting in the Service Industry: A Critical Assessment. Barth, Claire, ed. 125p. 1994. pap. 25.00 (*0-86641-228-X*, 94291) Inst Mgmt Account.
Martinson, Paul V., ed. Islam: An Introduction for Christians. Cox, Stefanie O., tr. LC 94-2356. (ENG.). 1994. pap. 15.99 (*0-8066-2583-X*, Augsburg) Augsburg Fortress.
Martinson, Robert, et al. Rehabilitation, Recidivism & Research. 96p. 1976. 6.00 (*0-318-15372-6*) Natl Coun Crime.
Martinson, Roland D. Effective Youth Ministry: A Congregational Approach. LC 88-6210. 160p. (Orig.). 1988. pap. 11.99 (*0-8066-2311-X*, 10-2030, Augsburg) Augsburg Fortress.
Martinson, Sue Ann. Changing Woman. 60p. 1985. 8.95 (*0-911051-15-5*) Plain View.
Martinson, T. L., ed. see Lee, T., et al.
Martinson, Thomas H. The Best Law Schools: In-Depth Profiles of 40 Top Schools by a Trusted Admissions Expert! 304p. 1993. pap. 17.00 (*0-671-84858-5*, Arco Test) P-H Gen Ref & Trav.
— Getting into Graduate Business School Today. 1995. pap. 11.95 (*0-02-860025-8*) Macmillan.
— Getting into Law School Today. 2nd ed. 1994. pap. 12.00 (*0-671-89033-6*, Arco Test) P-H Gen Ref & Trav.
— GMAT SuperCourse. 5th ed. LC 95-3266. 1995. 17.95 (*0-02-860318-4*) Macmillan.
— GRE: Graduate Record Examination. 4th ed. 624p. 1992. pap. 13.00 (*0-13-361775-0*, Arco Test) P-H Gen Ref & Trav.
— GRE: Graduate Record Examination: General Test. 6th ed. LC 95-793. 1995. 13.95 (*0-671-89965-1*) Macmillan.
— GRE Graduate Record Exam. 5th ed. 1994. pap. 13.00 (*0-671-88823-4*, Arco Test) P-H Gen Ref & Trav.
— LSAT, Law School Admission Test. 5th ed. LC 93-22326. 1993. 12.00 (*0-671-79972-X*) P-H Gen Ref & Trav.
— LSAT, Law School Admission Test. 6th ed. LC 95-7730. 1995. write for info. (*0-02-860326-5*) Macmillan.
— LSAT Supercourse. 4th rev. ed. LC 92-35392. Orig. Title: Supercourse for the LSAT. 1993. 18.00 (*0-671-84849-6*, Arco Test) P-H Gen Ref & Trav.
— SAT2 Subject Tests Supercourse. 2nd ed. 1994. pap. 17.00 (*0-671-86403-3*, Arco Test) P-H Gen Ref & Trav.
Martinson, Thomas H. & Crocetti, Gino. Graduate Record Examination General Test (GRE) 2nd ed. (Academic Test Preparation Ser.). 656p. (C). 1987. student ed 8.95 (*0-317-58457-X*, Arco Test) P-H Gen Ref & Trav.
Martinson, Thomas H. & Fazzone, Juliana. ACT SuperCourse. 3rd ed. Bosworth, Stefan et al, eds. LC 93-22327. 1993. 17.00 (*0-671-86604-4*, Arco Test) P-H Gen Ref & Trav.
— Supercourse for College Board Achievement Tests. 464p. 1991. pap. 16.95 (*0-13-876608-8*, Arco Test) P-H Gen Ref & Trav.
Martinson, Thomas H. & Waldherr, David P. Getting into Law School: Strategies for the 90s. 160p. 1991. pap. 12.00 (*0-13-351693-8*, Arco Test) P-H Gen Ref & Trav.
Martinson, Tom. The Christmas Loon. (Illus.). 48p. (J). (gr. 1-3). 1990. 14.95 (*1-55971-092-6*); pap. 6.95 (*1-55971-124-8*) NorthWord.
Martinson, Tom, jt. auth. see Gebhard, David.
Martinus. Opera Omnia. Barlow, Claude W., ed. LC 50-10338. (American Academy in Rome. Papers & Monographs: Vol. 12). 340p. reprint ed. pap. 96.90 (*0-685-15608-7*, 2026728) Bks Demand.
Martinus, Eivor, tr. see Jonsson, Reidar.
Martinus, Elivor, tr. see Soderbergh, Bengt.
Martinus, Norman & Reinker, Harry L. Warman's Paper. (Illus.). 432p. 1994. pap. 18.95 (*0-87069-672-6*) Chilton.
***Martinussen, John.** Democracy, Competition & Choice: Emerging Local Self-Government in Nepal. LC 94-45236. 188p. (C). 1995. 22.95 (*0-8039-9224-6*) Sage.
— Transnational Corporations in a Developing Country: The Indian Experience. 228p. (C). 1988. text ed. 24.00 (*0-8039-9584-9*) Sage.
Martinussen, Willy. The Distant Democracy: Social Inequality, Political Resources & Political Influence in Norway. LC 76-18748. 254p. reprint ed. pap. 72.40 (*0-317-28154-2*, 2024281) Bks Demand.
Martire, Joseph R. & Levinsohn, Mark E. Imaging of Athletic Injuries: Advanced Techniques. 368p. 1992. text ed. 110.00 (*0-07-040728-2*) Hlth Prof Div.
Martirena-Mantel, Ana M., ed. External Debt, Savings, & Growth in Latin America. LC 87-21422. xv, 207p. 1987. pap. 12.00 (*0-939934-95-7*) Intl Monetary.
Martis, Kenneth & Elmes, Gregory. The Historical Atlas of State Power in Congress, 1790-1990. 190p. 1993. 84.95 (*0-87187-742-2*) Congr Quarterly.
Martis, Kenneth C. Historical Atlas of Political Parties in the U. S. Congress: 1787-1988. 1988. 160.00 (*0-318-32915-8*, Scribners) S&S Trade.
— Historical Atlas of Political Parties in the United States Congress: 1789-1988. LC 88-675270. (Illus.). 518p. 1989. text ed. 195.00 (*0-02-920170-5*) Macmillan.
— The Historical Atlas of the Congresses of the Confederate States of America, 1861-1865. LC 93-40478. 1993. 65.00 (*0-13-389115-1*) S&S Trade.
— The Historical Atlas of United States Congressional Districts, 1789-1983. 302p. 1982. text ed. 195.00 (*0-02-920150-0*) Macmillan.
Martison, Thomas H. GMAT Supercourse. 4th ed. LC 92-38006. 1993. 18.00 (*0-671-84845-3*, Arco Test) P-H Gen Ref & Trav.
— GRE Supercourse. 3rd ed. LC 93-3537. 1993. 19.00 (*0-671-84848-8*, Arco Test) P-H Gen Ref & Trav.
Martius, jt. ed. see Elsner.
Martius, T. Dictionary of International Trade Fairs, 3 vols., Set. 1267p. 1980. 125.00 (*0-569-05140-1*, Pub. by Collets UK) St Mut.
Martiznez, Dionisio D. Bad Alchemy. 80p. 1995. 17.95 (*0-393-03733-9*) Norton.
Martland, Richard & Welsby. Basic Cookery. 3rd ed. 708p. 1993. 23.00 (*0-7506-0532-4*) Buttrwrth-Heinemann.
Martland, Thomas R. Religion As Art: An Interpretation. LC 80-27104. (Series in Philosophy). 221p. 1981. 49.50 (*0-87395-520-X*); pap. 16.95 (*0-87395-521-8*) State U NY Pr.
Martlew, Clive. Local Democracy in Practice: The Role & Working Environment of Councillors in Scotland. 184p. 1988. text ed. 53.95 (*0-566-05508-2*, Pub. by Dartmth Pub UK) Ashgate Pub Co.
Martlew, Gillian V. Electrolytes, Trace Minerals, the Spark of Life: The Keys to Quality of Life & Longevity. 112p. 1994. pap. text ed. 11.95 (*0-9640539-0-X*) Natures Pubng.
Martlew, Margaret, ed. The Psychology of Written Language: Developmental & Educational Perspectives. LC 82-21933. (Wiley Series in Developmental Psychology & Its Applications). (Illus.). 442p. reprint ed. pap. 126.00 (*0-8357-7544-5*, 2036266) Bks Demand.
Martley, Ed, jt. auth. see Hauer, Nancy.
Martling, Jackie. Just Another Dirty Joke Book. 1993. pap. 3.50 (*1-55817-736-1*, Pinnacle NY) Windsor NY.
— Only Dirty Joke Book You'll Ever Need. 160p. 1993. pap. 3.50 (*1-55817-710-8*, Pinnacle NY) Windsor NY.
— Raunchy Riddles. 192p. 1993. pap. 3.50 (*1-55817-771-X*, Pinnacle NY) Windsor NY.
Martna, Maret, ed. Arctic Bibliography, 2 vols., Vol. 15. LC 53-61783. 1633p. reprint ed. pap. 180.00 (*0-7837-1172-7*, 2041701) Bks Demand.
— Arctic Bibliography, 2 vols., Vol. 16. LC 53-61783. 1407p. reprint ed. pap. 180.00 (*0-7837-1173-5*, 2041701) Bks Demand.
Martner, Brooks E. Wyoming Climate Atlas. LC 86-675205. (Illus.). xiv, 432p. 1986. 45.00 (*0-8032-3112-1*) U of Nebr Pr.
Marto, P. J., ed. see National Heat Transfer Conference Staff.
Martof, Bernard S., et al. Amphibians & Reptiles of the Carolinas & Virginia. LC 79-11790. (Illus.). 264p. (C). 1989. reprint ed. pap. 16.95 (*0-8078-4252-4*) U of NC Pr.
Martome, Michael. Dark Light. LC 73-88291. (Illus.). (Orig.). 1973. pap. 6.95 (*0-912810-11-4*) Lustrum Pr.
Marton. A Flood of Sweet Fire. large type ed. 17.95 (*0-263-12940-3*, MB012, Pub. by Mills & Boon Ltd UK) Chivers N Amer.
Marton, Andrew. Andrew Marton: Interviewed by Joanne D'Antonio. LC 91-26801. (Directors Guild of merica Oral History Ser.: No. 12). (Illus.). 557p. 1991. 52.50 (*0-8108-2472-8*) Scarecrow.
Marton, Betty. Ruben Blades. (Hispanics of Achievement Ser.). (Illus.). (YA). (gr. 5 up). 1992. lib. bdg. 17.95 (*0-7910-1235-2*) Chelsea Hse.
Marton, Claire, ed. Methods of Experimental Physics: Fluid Dynamics, Vol. 18A. LC 79-26343. 1981. text ed. 151.00 (*0-12-475960-2*) Acad Pr.
— Methods of Experimental Physics: Fluid Dynamics, Vol. 18B. 1981. text ed. 179.00 (*0-12-475956-4*) Acad Pr.
Marton, Claire & Edmonds, Peter, eds. Methods of Experimental Physics: Ultrasonic, Vol. 19. LC 79-26343. 1981. text ed. 164.00 (*0-12-475961-0*) Acad Pr.
Marton, Claire & Lecar, Harold, eds. Methods of Experimental Physics: Biophysics, Vol. 20. 568p. 1982. text ed. 164.00 (*0-12-475962-9*) Acad Pr.
Marton, Claire & Septier, A., eds. Advances in Electronics & Electron Physics Supplement, No. 13C. (Serial Publication Ser.). 544p. 1983. text ed. 143.00 (*0-12-014576-6*) Acad Pr.
Marton, Claire, jt. auth. see Marton, L. L.
Marton, Claire, jt. ed. see Marton, L. L.
Marton, G. S. Tanker Operations: A Handbook for the Ship's Officer. 3rd ed. (Illus.). 328p. 1992. text ed. 35.00 (*0-87033-432-8*) Cornell Maritime.
Marton, Jirina. Amelia's Celebration. (Illus.). 24p. (J). (ps-3). 1992. lib. bdg. 15.95 (*1-55037-221-1*, Pub. by Annick CN); pap. 5.95 (*1-55037-220-3*, Pub. by Annick CN) Firefly Bks Ltd.
— Flores Para Mama (Flowers for Mom) (Illus.). 24p. (J). 1994. pap. 6.95 (*1-55037-970-4*, Pub. by Annick CN) Firefly Bks Ltd.
— Flowers for Mom. (Illus.). 24p. (J). (ps-3). 1991. lib. bdg. 15.95 (*1-55037-155-X*, Pub. by Annick CN); pap. 5.95 (*1-55037-158-4*, Pub. by Annick CN) Firefly Bks Ltd.
— I'll Do It Myself. (Illus.). (J). 1990. 14.95 (*1-55037-063-4*, Pub. by Annick CN); pap. 5.95 (*1-55037-062-6*, Pub. by Annick CN) Firefly Bks Ltd.
— Midnight Visit at Molly's House. (Illus.). 24p. (J). (ps-8). 1988. 12.95 (*0-920303-99-4*, Pub. by Annick CN); pap. 4.95 (*0-920303-98-6*, Pub. by Annick CN) Firefly Bks Ltd.
— You Can Go Home Again. (Illus.). 32p. (J). (gr. k-2). 1994. pap. 5.95 (*1-55037-990-9*, Pub. by Annick CN) Firefly Bks Ltd.

An Asterisk (*) at the beginning of an entry indicates that the title is appearing in BIP for the first time.

— You Can Go Home Again. (Illus.). 32p. (J). (gr. k-2). 1994. lib. bdg. 15.95 (*1-55037-991-7*, Pub. by Annick CN) Firefly Bks Ltd.

Marton, Joseph, tr. see Bergman, Gunnar.

Marton, Katherine. Multinationals, Technology, & Industrialization: Implications & Impact in Third World Countries. LC 86-7218. 320p. 1986. text ed. 45.00 (*0-669-13209-8*) Free Pr.

Marton, Katherine, ed. Multinationals, Technology & Industrialization: A Study of the Implications & Impact in Third World Countries. (Contemporary Studies in Economic & Financial Analysis: Vol. 61). 1987. 73.25 (*0-89232-839-8*) Jai Pr.

Marton, Kati. A Death in Jerusalem. 320p. 1994. 25.00 (*0-679-42083-5*) Pantheon.

— Polk Conspiracy: Murder & Cover up in the Case of CBS News. 1992. pap. 14.00 (*0-8129-2047-3*, Times Bks) Random.

— Polk Conspiracy: Murder & Cover-up in the Case of CBS News Correspondent George Polk. (Illus.). 369p. 1990. 22.95 (*0-374-13553-3*) FS&G.

Marton, L. & Hornyak, W. F., eds. Methods of Experimental Physics. Incl. Vol. 8. Problems & Solutions for Students. 1969. 60.00 (*0-12-475908-4*); write for info. (*0-318-50308-5*) Acad Pr.

Marton, L. L. Advances in Electronics & Electron Physics, Vol. 62. (Serial Publication Ser.). 1984. text ed. 151.00 (*0-12-014662-2*) Acad Pr.

Marton, L. L., ed. Advances in Electronics & Electron Physics, Vol. 60. (Serial Publication Ser.). 424p. 1983. text ed. 158.00 (*0-12-014660-6*) Acad Pr.

— Advances in Electronics & Electron Physics, Vol. 63. (Serial Publication Ser.). 1985. text ed. 151.00 (*0-12-014663-0*) Acad Pr.

Marton, L. L. & Fava, R. A., eds. Methods of Experimental Physics: Polymers Molecular Structure & Dynamics, Vol. 16A, Pt. A. 1980. Pt. A. text ed. 151.00 (*0-12-475916-5*) Acad Pr.

— Methods of Experimental Physics: Polymers Molecular Structure & Dynamics, Vol. 16A, Pt. B. 1980. Pt. B. text ed. 151.00 (*0-12-475917-2*) Acad Pr.

Marton, L. L. & Marton, Claire. Methods of Experimental Physics: Nuclear Methods in Solid State Physics, Vol. 21. 1983. text ed. 151.00 (*0-12-475963-7*) Acad Pr.

Marton, L. L. & Marton, Claire, eds. Advances in Electronics & Electron Physics, Vol. 52. (Serial Publication Ser.). 1980. text ed. 248.00 (*0-12-014652-5*) Acad Pr.

Marton, L. L. & Richard, Patrick, eds. Methods of Experimental Physics: Atomic Physics Accelerators, Vol. 17. (Serial Publication Ser.). 1980. text ed. 164.00 (*0-12-475959-9*) Acad Pr.

Marton, L. L., ed. see Harmuth, Henning F.

Marton, L. L., jt. ed. see Pratt, William K.

Marton, Laurence J., jt. ed. see Kabra, Pokar M.

Marton, Laurence J., jt. ed. see Kabra, Pokar.

Marton, Laurence J., jt. ed. see Morris, David R.

Marton, Ruchama, jt. ed. see Gordon, Neve.

***Marton, Sandra.** A Bride for the Taking. (Presents Ser.). 1995. mass mkt. 3.25 (*0-373-11751-5*, 1-11751-4) Harlequin Bks.

— By Dreams Betrayed. large type ed. 1991. reprint ed. lib. bdg. 18.95 (*0-263-12679-X*, Pub. by Mills & Boon UK) Thorndike Pr.

— The Corsican Gambit. (Presents Ser.). 1994. mass mkt. 2.99 (*0-373-11637-3*, 1-11637-5) Harlequin Bks.

— The Corsican Gambit. large type ed. 1992. lib. bdg. 18.95 (*0-263-13030-4*, Pub. by Mills & Boon UK) Thorndike Pr.

— Deal with the Devil. large type ed. LC 94-20151. 1995. pap. 15.95 (*0-8161-7454-7*) Hall.

— Eye of the Storm. large type ed. (Magna Large Print Ser.). 1994. 18.95 (*0-7505-0742-X*, Pub. by Magna Print Bks) Ulverscroft.

— Garden of Eden. large type ed. 291p. 1994. 18.95 (*0-7505-0662-8*) Ulverscroft.

— Hostage of the Hawk. 1995. pap. 3.25 (*0-373-11780-9*, 1-11780-3) Harlequin Bks.

— Lost in a Dream. large type ed. 1991. reprint ed. lib. bdg. 16.95 (*0-263-12685-4*, Pub. by Mills & Boon UK) Thorndike Pr.

— Lovescenes. large type ed. 298p. 1993. 21.95 (*0-7505-0439-0*, Pub. by Magna Print Bks) Ulverscroft.

— Night Fires. large type ed. 1991. reprint ed. lib. bdg. 16.95 (*0-263-12431-2*, Pub. by Mills & Boon UK) Thorndike Pr.

— No Need for Love. large type ed. (Harlequin Ser.). 1994. bds. 18.95 (*0-263-13715-5*) Thorndike Pr.

— Roarke's Kingdom. (Presents Ser.). 1993. mass mkt. 2.99 (*0-373-11574-1*, 1-11574-0) Harlequin Bks.

— Roarke's Kingdom. large type ed. (Harlequin Ser.). 1992. reprint ed. lib. bdg. 18.95 (*0-263-12983-7*, Pub. by Mills & Boon UK) Thorndike Pr.

— Roman Spring. 1994. mass mkt. 2.99 (*0-373-11660-8*, 1-11660-7) Harlequin Bks.

— That Long Ago Summer. large type ed. 285p. 1991. reprint ed. lib. bdg. 18.95 (*0-263-12806-7*) Thorndike Pr.

— A Woman Accused. (Presents Ser.). 1995. mass mkt. 3.25 (*0-373-11736-1*, 1-11736-5) Harlequin Bks.

— Yesterday & Forever. large type ed. 1993. reprint ed. lib. bdg. 18.95 (*0-263-13198-X*, Pub. by Mills & Boon UK) Thorndike Pr.

Marton, Sheila N. & Selick, Mimi B. Decorative Background Patterns for Needlepoint. (Embroidery, Needlepoint, Charted Designs Ser.). 96p. 1985. reprint ed. pap. 5.95 (*0-486-24798-8*) Dover.

Marton-Vas-Zoltan, Peter, jt. auth. see Tolnai.

Martone, John. Far Human Character. 20p. (Orig.). 1991. pap. 3.00 (*0-926935-56-9*) Runaway Spoon.

— In the Course of the Real. 1978. pap. 4.50 (*0-914278-18-5*) Copper Beech.

— Ocean Vows. 43p. (Orig.). 1983. pap. 4.50 (*0-914278-38-X*) Copper Beech.

— Primer. 56p. (Orig.). 1994. pap. 5.00 (*1-57141-008-2*) Runaway Spoon.

— Trousseau. 40p. (Orig.). 1991. pap. 3.00 (*0-926935-46-1*) Runaway Spoon.

Martone, Michael. Fort Wayne Is Seventh on Hitler's List: Indiana Stories. enl. ed. LC 93-8645. 1993. 22.50 (*0-253-33687-2*); pap. 14.95 (*0-253-20851-3*) Ind U Pr.

— Pensees: The Thoughts of Dan Quayle. 100p. (Orig.). 1994. pap. 8.95 (*0-9639885-0-6*) Broad Ripple.

— Return to Powers. 1985. 4.00 (*0-317-19728-2*) Windless Orchard.

— Safety Patrol. LC 87-26848. (Poetry & Fiction Ser.). 144p. 1988. 16.95 (*0-8018-3602-6*) Johns Hopkins.

— Seeing Eye: Short Stories. 192p. 1995. 20.95 (*0-944072-51-8*) Zoland Bks.

Martone, Michael, ed. A Place of Sense: Essays in Search of the Midwest. LC 88-15058. (Bur Oak Original Ser.). (Illus.). 170p. (Orig.). 1988. pap. 11.95 (*0-87745-217-2*) U of Iowa Pr.

— Townships. LC 91-25925. (Bur Oak Original Ser.). (Illus.). 243p. (Orig.). 1992. 32.95 (*0-87745-354-3*); pap. 14.95 (*0-87745-355-1*) U of Iowa Pr.

Martone, Mike. At a Loss. 1977. 2.00 (*0-685-67942-X*) Windless Orchard.

Martone, Robert L., ed. Renaissance Comic Tales of Love, Treachery, & Revenge. Martone, Valerie & Martone, Robert L., trs. LC 94-16287. (Illus.). 248p. (Orig.). 1994. pap. 15.00 (*0-934977-31-3*) Italica Pr.

Martone, Robert L., tr. see Martone, Robert L., ed.

Martone, Valerie, tr. see Manetti, Antonio.

Martone, Valerie, tr. see Martone, Robert L., ed.

Martonne, E., et al. The History of Geography: Translations of Some French & German Essays. LC 83-51533. 122p. 1983. pap. text ed. 13.75 (*0-89003-148-7*) Undena Pubns.

Martonosi, Anthony N., ed. The Enzymes of Biological Membranes, Vol. 1: Membrane Structure & Dynamics. 2nd ed. LC 84-8923. 474p. 1985. 95.00 (*0-306-41451-1*, Plenum Pr) Plenum.

— Enzymes of Biological Membranes, Vol. 2: Biosynthesis & Metabolism. 2nd ed. 472p. 1985. 95.00 (*0-306-41452-X*, Plenum Pr) Plenum.

— Enzymes of Biological Membranes, Vol. 3: Membrane Transport. 2nd ed. 700p. 1985. 130.00 (*0-306-41453-8*, Plenum Pr) Plenum.

— Enzymes of Biological Membranes, Vol. 4: Bioenergetics of Electron & Proton Transport. 2nd ed. LC 84-8423. 608p. 1985. 125.00 (*0-306-41454-6*, Plenum Pr) Plenum.

— Enzymes of Biological Membranes, Vol. 4: Bioenergetics of Electron & Proton Transport, Set, Vols. 1-4. 2nd ed. LC 84-8423. 608p. 1985. Set (Vols. 1-4). 265.00 (*0-685-09681-5*, Plenum Pr) Plenum.

— Membranes & Transport, Vol. 1. LC 82-3690. 722p. 1982. 110.00 (*0-306-40853-8*, Plenum Pr); Set price with Vol. 2:. 190.00 (*0-685-42428-6*, Plenum Pr) Plenum.

— Membranes & Transport, Vol. 2. LC 82-3690. 712p. 1982. Set price with Vol. 1: 190.00. 110.00 (*0-306-40854-6*, Plenum Pr) Plenum.

Martonyi, Csaba L., et al. Clinical Slit Lamp Biomicroscopy & Photo Slit Lamp Biomicrography. 2nd ed. (Illus.). 80p. (C). 1987. pap. 25.00 (*0-9625512-0-1*) Time One Ink.

Martorana, Barbara, jt. auth. see Kane, Andrea L.

Martorana, R. George. Your Pension & Your Spouse - The Joint & Survivor Dilemma. 3rd ed. Brzezinski, Mary J., ed. (Illus.). 24p. 1994. pap. 7.95 (*0-89154-474-7*) Intl Found Employ.

Martorana, R. George & Rowland, Susan. Your Pension & Your Spouse. (Illus.). 24p. (Orig.). 1991. pap. 7.25 (*0-89154-429-1*) Intl Found Employ.

Martorana, S. V. & Kuhns, Eileen. Managing Academic Change: Interactive Forces & Leadership in Higher Education. LC 74-27909. (Jossey-Bass Higher Education Ser.). 236p. reprint ed. pap. 67.30 (*0-317-42366-5*, 2052161) Bks Demand.

Martorana, S. V., jt. auth. see Kuhns, E.

Martorano, jt. auth. see Morgan.

Martorano, Joseph, et al. Unmasking PMS. 240p. 1993. 21.95 (*0-87131-692-7*); pap. 12.95 (*0-87131-704-4*) M Evans.

Martorano, Joseph T. & Kildahl, John P. Beyond Negative Thinking: Breaking the Cycle of Depressing & Anxious Thoughts. (Illus.). 314p. 1989. 20.95 (*0-306-43196-3*, Plenum Insight) Plenum.

— Beyond Negative Thinking: Reclaiming Your Life Through Optimism. 224p. 1992. mass mkt. 4.99 (*0-380-71606-2*) Avon.

Martorell, Joan, et al. The Olympic Village Barcelona 1992. (Illus.). 192p. (ENG & SPA.). 1992. 49.95 (*84-252-1485-8*) Rizzoli Intl.

Martorell, Joanot. Tirant Lo Blanc: The Complete Translation. La Fontaine, Ray, tr. LC 93-20108. (Catalan Studies: Vol. 1). 820p. (Orig.). (C). 1994. pap. text ed. 39.95 (*0-8204-1688-6*) P Lang Pubs.

Martorell, Luis F., jt. auth. see Liogier, Henri A.

Martorella, Peter H. Elementary Social Studies: Developing Reflective, Competant, & Concerned Citizens. (C). 1987. text ed. 46.00 (*0-673-39165-5*) HarpCollege.

— Elementary Social Studies: Developing Reflective, Competent, & Concerned Citizens. (C). 1985. text ed. 27.95 (*0-316-54870-7*) Little.

— Social Studies for Elementary School Children: Developing Young Citizens. 432p. (C). 1994. pap. write for info. (*0-02-376792-8*) Macmillan.

— Teaching Social Studies in Middle & Secondary Schools. 533p. (C). 1991. write for info. (*0-02-376791-X*) Macmillan.

Martorella, Rosanne. Corporate Art. LC 89-39325. (Illus.). 240p. 1990. 30.00 (*0-8135-1525-4*) Rutgers U Pr.

Martorella, Roseanne. The Sociology of Opera: Organization, Production & Performance. 288p. 1982. text ed. 59.95 (*0-275-90857-7*, C0857, Praeger Pubs) Greenwood.

Martorella, Roseanne, jt. ed. see Kamerman, Jack B.

Martori, Joe. Street Fights. Stein, Toby, ed. 1987. 17.95 (*0-915643-24-3*) Santa Barb Pr.

Martory, Pierre. The Landscape is Behind the Door. LC 94-11242. 1994. pap. 12.95 (*1-878818-30-9*) Sheep Meadow.

Martos, B. Economic Control Structures: Contributions of Economic Analysis, CEA 188, Vol. 188. 1990. 65.00 (*0-444-87411-9*) Elsevier.

Martos, Becky B., ed. Disappearances: A Workbook. 168p. (Orig.). 1981. pap. 4.95 (*0-939994-00-3*) Amnesty Intl USA.

Martos, Jean-Francois, tr. see Sanguinetti, Gianfranco.

Martos, Joseph. Doors to the Sacred: A Historical Introduction to Sacraments in the Catholic Church. LC 91-12298. 488p. 1991. reprint ed. pap. 15.95 (*0-89243-493-7*, Triumph Books) Liguori Pubns.

Martos, Joseph, jt. auth. see Rohr, Richard.

Martres, Laurent, tr. see Pellier, P.

Martres, Laurent R. Comment Creer une PME aux U. S. A. (Illus.). 144p. (Orig.). (FRE.). 1984. pap. 9.95 (*0-916189-00-7*) Graphie Intl.

— Sumo: Le Sport et le Sacre. (Illus.). 144p. (FRE.). 1985. pap. text ed. 12.95 (*0-916189-01-5*) Graphie Intl.

Martschenko, W. G. Deutsch-Russisches Meteorologisches Worterbuch: German - Russian Meteorological Dictionary. 392p. (GER & RUS.). 1973. 19.95 (*0-8288-6234-6*, M-9092) Fr & Eur.

Martsinkyavitshute, Victoria. Lithuanian-English English-Lithuanian Concise Dictionary. (Concise Dictionaries Ser.). 400p. (Orig.). 1993. pap. 11.95 (*0-7818-0151-6*) Hippocrene Bks.

Martucci, G., jt. auth. see Marathe, Kishore B.

Martucci, Roberto, jt. auth. see Giovannetti, Bruno.

Martuscelli, E. & Marchetta, C., eds. New Polymeric Materials: Reactive Processes & Physical Properties: Invited Papers Presented at a Symposium, Naples, Italy, June, 1986. 194p. 1987. lib. bdg. 85.00 (*90-6764-091-3*, Pub. by VSP NE) Coronet Bks.

Martuscelli, Ezio, et al, eds. Future Trends in Polymer Science & Technology--Polymers: Commodities or Specialties? LC 86-51370. 252p. 1987. pap. 49.00 (*0-87762-512-3*) Technomic.

***Martusewicz, Rebecca A. & Reynolds, William M.** Inside-Out: Contemporary Critical Perspectives in Education. 320p. 1994. pap. text ed. 20.00 (*0-312-08067-0*) St Martin.

Marty. Leaning on the Wind. Date not set. 22.00 (*0-06-258520-7*, HarpT) HarpC.

Marty, David R. The Ear Book: A Parent's Guide to Common Ear Disorders of Children. (Illus.). 132p. 1987. lib. bdg. 23.95 (*0-943023-11-4*); pap. 16.95 (*0-943023-12-2*) Lang E N T Pub.

Marty, G. Dictionnaire des Chansons de la Revolution. 1988. lib. bdg. 89.95 (*0-8288-2590-4*, 2235018009) Fr & Eur.

Marty, Jean-Pierre. The Tempo Indications of Mozart. LC 87-29571. 416p. (C). 1989. text ed. 47.00 (*0-300-03852-6*) Yale U Pr.

Marty-Laveaux, Charles J. Lexique De la Langue De Pierre Corneille. (Oeuvres De P. Corneille, Eleven - Les Grands Ecrivains De la France Ser.). xcvi, 1060p. 1971. reprint ed. write for info. (*3-487-04032-8*, Pub. by Georg Olms GW) Lubrecht & Cramer.

Marty, M. & Pappo, M., eds. Ondansetron & Chemotherapy Induced Emesis: 3rd International Congress on Neo-Adjuvant Chemotherapy. viii, 77p. 1992. pap. 40.00 (*0-387-54599-9*) Spr-Verlag.

Marty, Martin E. Baptism. LC 77-78653. 64p. (Orig.). 1977. pap. 6.00 (*0-8006-1317-1*, 1-1317, Fortress Pr) Augsburg Fortress.

— A Cry of Absence. 64p. 1993. pap. 5.00 (*0-06-065403-1*) Harper SF.

— A Cry of Absence: Reflections for the Winter of the Heart. LC 92-53217. 192p. 1993. reprint ed. pap. 12.00 (*0-06-065402-3*) Harper SF.

— Health & Medicine in the Lutheran Tradition. (Health & Medicine in Faith Tradition Ser.). 192p. 1983. 19.95 (*0-8245-0613-8*) Crossroad NY.

— Health Medicine & Faith Traditions: An Inquiry into Religion & Medicine. Vaux, Kenneth L., ed. LC 81-71383. 362p. reprint ed. pap. 103.20 (*0-685-16253-2*, 2026975) Bks Demand.

— The Lord's Supper. LC 79-6550. 80p. (Orig.). 1980. pap. 6.00 (*0-8006-1386-4*, 1-1386, Fortress Pr) Augsburg Fortress.

— Modern American Religion, Vol. 1: The Irony of It All, 1893-1919. LC 86-16524. (Illus.). 398p. (C). 1986. 24.95 (*0-226-50893-5*) U Ch Pr.

— Modern American Religion, Vol. 2: The Noise of Conflict, 1919-1941. LC 85-16524. (Illus.). 480p. 1991. 29.95 (*0-226-50895-1*) U Ch Pr.

— A Nation of Behavers. LC 76-7997. xii, 240p. 1980. pap. text ed. 9.95 (*0-226-50892-7*, P890) U Ch Pr.

— The New Shape of American Religion. LC 78-1576. 180p. 1978. reprint ed. text ed. 49.75 (*0-313-20353-9*, MANE, Greenwood Pr) Greenwood.

— Pilgrims in Their Own Land. 512p. 1985. pap. 13.95 (*0-14-008268-9*, Penguin Bks) Viking Penguin.

— Religion & Republic: The American Circumstance. LC 86-47755. 391p. 1989. pap. 17.00x (*0-8070-1207-6*) Beacon Pr.

— Religious Crises in Modern America. LC 81-80740. (Charles Edmondson Historical Lectures). 40p. (Orig.). 1981. pap. 4.50 (*0-918954-26-6*) Baylor Univ Pr.

— A Short History of American Catholicism. 256p. (Orig.). 1995. pap. 10.95 (*0-88347-320-8*) Thomas More.

— Short History of Christianity. 2nd enl. rev. ed. LC 80-8042. (Orig.). pap. 20.00 (*0-8006-1944-7*, 1-1944) Augsburg Fortress.

Marty, Martin E., ed. Modern American Protestantism & Its World, Set. Incl. Vol. 1. Writing of American Religious History. 351p. 1992. lib. bdg. 120.00 (*3-598-41531-1*); Vol. 2. Modern American Religion & the Protestant World. 294p. 1992. lib. bdg. 120.00 (*3-598-41532-X*); Vol. 3. Civil Religion, Church & State. 502p. 1992. lib. bdg. 120.00 (*3-598-41533-8*); Vol. 4. Theological Themes in the American Protestant World. 468p. 1992. lib. bdg. 120.00 (*3-598-41535-4*); Vol. 5. Varieties of Protestantism. 272p. 1992. lib. bdg. 120.00 (*3-598-41536-2*); Vol. 6. Protestanism & Social Christianity. 1993. lib. bdg. 120.00 (*3-598-41537-0*); Vol. 7. Protestantism & Regionalism. 248p. 1992. lib. bdg. 120.00 (*3-598-41538-9*); Vol. 8. Ethnic & Non-Protestant Themes. 311p. 1993. lib. bdg. 120.00 (*3-598-41539-7*); Vol. 9. Native American Religion & Black Protestantism. 344p. 1993. lib. bdg. 120.00 (*3-598-41540-0*); Vol. 10. Fundamentalism & Evangelicalism. 356p. 1993. lib. bdg. 120.00 (*3-598-41541-9*); Vol. 11. New & Intense Movements. 404p. 1993. lib. bdg. 120.00 (*3-598-41542-7*); Vol. 12. Women & Women's Issues. 380p. 1993. lib. bdg. 120.00 (*3-598-41543-5*); Vol. 13. Missions & Ecumenical Expressions. 222p. 1993. lib. bdg. 120.00 (*3-598-41544-3*); Vol. 14. Varieties of Religious Expression. 296p. 1993. lib. bdg. 120.00 (*3-598-41545-1*); 1993. Set lib. bdg. 1,525.00 (*3-598-41530-3*) U Pubns Amer.

— The Place of Bonhoeffer: Problems & Possibilities in His Thought. LC 79-8718. 224p. 1981. reprint ed. text ed. 55.00 (*0-313-20812-3*, MAPL, Greenwood Pr) Greenwood.

Marty, Martin E. & Appleby, R. Scott. The Glory & the Power: The Rapid Rise of Fundamentalism in the 1990's. (Illus.). 304p. 1992. text ed. 30.00 (*0-8070-1216-5*); pap. 16.00 (*0-8070-1217-3*) Beacon Pr.

Marty, Martin E. & Appleby, R. Scott, eds. Accounting for Fundamentalisms: The Dynamic Character of Movements. LC 93-36621. (Fundamentalism Project Ser.: Vol. 4). (C). 1994. 47.50 (*0-226-50885-4*) U Ch Pr.

— Fundamentalism Observed. xvi, 872p. (C). 1994. pap. text ed. 27.50 (*0-226-50878-1*) U Ch Pr.

— Fundamentalisms & Society: Reclaiming the Sciences, the Family, & Education. LC 92-10259. (Fundamentalism Project Ser.: Vol. 2). 560p. 1993. 45.00 (*0-226-50880-3*) U Ch Pr.

— Fundamentalisms & the State: Remaking Politics, Militance, & Economies. LC 92-14582. (Fundamentalism Project Ser.: Vol. 3). 496p. (C). 1993. 45.00 (*0-226-50883-8*) U Ch Pr.

— Fundamentalisms Comprehended. LC 94-45338. (Fundamentalism Project Ser.: Vol. 5). 1995. 45.00 (*0-226-50887-0*) U Ch Pr.

Marty, Martin E. & Brauer, Jerald, eds. The Unrelieved Paradox: Studies in the Theology of Franz Bibfeldt. (Illus.). 1994. pap. text ed. 14.99 (*0-8028-0745-3*) Eerdmans.

***Marty, Martin E. & Marty, Micah.** Places along the Way: Meditations on the Journey of Faith. LC 94-29532. (Illus.). 1994. pap. 11.99 (*0-8066-2746-8*, Augsburg) Augsburg Fortress.

Marty, Martin E. & Peerman, Dean G., eds. A Handbook of Christian Theologians. 736p. (Orig.). 1984. pap. 19.95 (*0-687-16563-6*) Abingdon.

Marty, Martin E., ed. see James, William.

Marty, Martin E., et al. The Religious Press in America. LC 72-6844. 184p. 1973. reprint ed. text ed. 49.75 (*0-8371-6500-8*, MARP, Greenwood Pr) Greenwood.

Marty, Micah, jt. auth. see Marty, Martin E.

***Marty, Michel E., ed.** New Directions in Anti-Cancer Chemotherapy. (Journal: Oncology: Vol. 51, Suppl. 1, 1994). (Illus.). iv, 40p. 1994. pap. 17.75 (*3-8055-6080-X*) S Karger.

Marty, Myron A., ed. see Kerr, K. Austin, et al.

Marty, Myron A., jt. auth. see Kyvig, David E.

Marty, Myron A., jt. auth. see Kyvig, David.

Marty, R. PISA Programming System for Interactive Production of Application Software. (Informatik-Fachberichte Ser.). 297p. 1981. pap. 32.00 (*0-387-10825-4*) Spr-Verlag.

Marty, Robert. L' Algebre Des Signes: Essai de Semiotique Scientifiqud'apres Charles Sanders Peirce. (Foundations of Semiotics Ser.: No. 24). xviii, 409p. (FRE.). 1990. 133.00x (*90-272-3296-2*) Benjamins North Am.

Marty, Sheree S. Chinese Jump Rope. LC 93-43812. (Illus.). 96p. (J). 1994. pap. 4.95 (*0-8069-0352-X*) Sterling.

Marty, Sid. Men for the Mountains. LC 81-80365. (Illus.). 272p. 1981. reprint ed. pap. 7.95 (*0-89886-027-X*) Mountaineers.

Marty, William. A Survey of the Old Testament: Student Notes. 228p. (C). 1994. pap. text ed., spiral bd. 18.50 (*0-8403-7603-0*) Kendall-Hunt.

— Surveying the New Testament. 208p. 1991. spiral bd. 17.95 (*0-8403-7025-3*) Kendall-Hunt.

***Martyn, Barrie.** Nicolas Medtner: His Life & Music. (Illus.). 500p. 1995. 68.95 (*0-85967-959-4*) Ashgate Pub Co.

— Rachmaninoff: Composer, Pianist, Conductor. (Illus.). 672p. 1990. text ed. 69.95 (*0-85967-809-1*, Pub. by Scolar Pr UK) Ashgate Pub Co.

Martyn, Barry, ed. see Bigard, Barney.

Martyn, Christopher N. Neurology. (Student Notes Ser.). (Illus.). 296p. 1989. pap. text ed. 19.95 (*0-443-03307-2*) Churchill.

Martyn, D., jt. auth. see Jones, Lloyd.

Martyn, David, tr. see Monbrun, Estelle.

M

An Asterisk (*) at the beginning of an entry indicates that the title is appearing in BIP for the first time.

M

Martyn, Dorothy. The Man in the Yellow Hat: Theology & Psychoanalysis in Child Therapy. (American Academy of Religion Academy Ser.). 197p. (C). 1992. 24.95 (1-55540-630-0, 010176); pap. 15.95 (1-55540-631-9) Scholars Pr GA.

Martyn, Elizabeth & Taylor, David. The Little Cat Behavior Book. LC 91-72736. (Little Cat Library). (Illus.). 64p. 1991. 6.95 (1-879431-63-7) Dorling Kindersley.

— The Little Cat Care Book. LC 91-72735. (Little Cat Library). (Illus.). 64p. 1991. 6.95 (1-879431-62-9) Dorling Kindersley.

— The Little Cat Facts Book. LC 92-56495. (Little Cat Library). (Illus.). 64p. 1993. 6.95 (1-56458-263-9) Dorling Kindersley.

— The Little Cat Vet Book. LC 92-56496. (Little Cat Library). (Illus.). 64p. 1993. 6.95 (1-56458-264-7) Dorling Kindersley.

— The Little Gray Cat Book. LC 92-56494. (Little Cat Library). (Illus.). 64p. 1993. 6.95 (1-56458-265-5) Dorling Kindersley.

— The Little Kitten Book. LC 91-72734. (Little Cat Library). (Illus.). 64p. 1991. 6.95 (1-879431-61-0) Dorling Kindersley.

— The Little Persian Cat Book. LC 92-56497. (Little Cat Library). (Illus.). 64p. 1993. 6.95 (1-56458-266-3) Dorling Kindersley.

— The Little Siamese Cat Book. LC 91-72733. (Little Cat Library). (Illus.). 64p. 1991. 6.95 (1-879431-60-2) Dorling Kindersley.

Martyn, J. R., ed. D. Iuni Iuvenalis: Satvrae. xxxii, 179p. (LAT.). 1987. pap. 42.00 (90-256-0923-6, Pub. by A M Hakkert NE) Benjamins North Am.

Martyn, John & Lancaster, F. Wilfrid. Investigative Methods in Library & Information Science: An Introduction. LC 81-80538. (Illus.). v, 260p. (C). 1981. text ed. 30.50 (0-87815-035-8) Info Resources.

Martyn, John, et al, eds. Information UK 2000. (British Library Research Ser.). 293p. 1990. 50.00 (0-86291-620-8) Bowker-Saur.

Martyn, John R. The Siege of Mazagao: A Perilous Moment in the Defence of Christendom Against Islam. LC 93-15019. (American University Studies). 264p. (C). 1994. text ed. 43.95 (0-8204-2210-X) P Lang Pubs.

Martyn, John R., tr. Antonio Ferreira: The Comedy of Bristo or the Pimp. 120p. 1985. 8.00 (0-919473-72-5, DH58, Pub. by Dovehouse CN) MRTS.

Martyn, Lois J., et al. Optic Fundus Signs of Developmental & Neurological Disorders in Children: A Manual for Clinicians. LC 65-80492. (Clinics in Developmental Medicine Ser.: No. 89). (Illus.). 80p. (C). 1991. 34.95 (0-521-41209-9, Pub. by Mc Keith Pr UK) Cambridge U Pr.

Martyn, Sean. How to Start & Run a Successful Mail Order Business. 1980. 14.95 (0-679-50259-9) McKay.

Martyn, Tim, jt. auth. see Hartley, Tim.

Martyn, Tim, et al. SQL 400: A Professional Programmer's Guide. 1995. text ed. 45.00 (0-07-040799-1) McGraw.

Martyn, W. Carlos. The Pilgrim Fathers of New England. 441p. (Orig.). 1992. reprint ed. pap. text ed. 28.00 (1-55613-673-0) Heritage Bk.

Martyna, Bobby, jt. auth. see Elbert, Bruce.

Martynau, V., ed. Etymological Dictionary of the Belorussian Language, Vol. 5. 320p. (C). 1989. 50.00 (0-685-46834-8, Pub. by Collets) St Mut.

Martynenko, O. G. & Zukauskas, A. A. Heat Transfer - Soviet Reviews, Vol. 1: Convective Heat Transfer. (Illus.). 200p. 1989. 116.00 (0-89116-632-7) Hemisp Pub.

— High Temperature Heat Transfer. 1991. 125.00 (0-89116-633-5) CRC Pr.

Martynenko, Oleg G., ed. see Idelchik, I. E.

Martynenko, Z., jt. auth. see Soane, David S.

Martynov, A. & Brix, V. Practical Aerodynamics. LC 63-10019. (International Series of Monographs in Aeronautics & Astronautics: Vol. 4). 1965. 167.00 (0-08-010137-2, Pub. by Pergamon Repr UK) Franklin.

Martynov, Anatoly I. The Ancient Art of Northern Asia. Shimkin, Demitri & Shimkin, Edith, eds. Shimkin, Edith, tr. (Illus.). 320p. 1991. 39.95 (0-252-01219-4) U of Ill Pr.

Martynov, G. A. Fundamental Theory of Liquids: Method of Distribution Functions. (Illus.). 492p. 1992. 134.00 (0-7503-0069-8) IOP Pub.

Martynov, G. A. & Salem, R. R. Electrical Double Layer at a Metal-dilute Electrolyte Solution Interface. (Lecture Notes in Chemistry Ser.: Vol. 33). 170p. 1983. pap. 25.00 (0-387-11995-7) Spr-Verlag.

Martynov, Ivan I. Dimitri Shostakovich, the Man & His Work: Music Book Index. 197p. 1993. reprint ed. lib. bdg. 69.00 (0-7812-9620-X) Rprt Serv.

— Dmitri Shostakovich, the Man & His Work. Guralsky, T., tr. LC 75-88903. 197p. 1969. reprint ed. text ed. 59.75 (0-8371-2100-0, MAS, Greenwood Pr) Greenwood.

Martyr, Anthony, jt. auth. see Plint, Michael A.

***Martyr, Justin.** Saint Justin Martyr: The First Apology, the Second Apology, Dialogue with Trypho, Exhortation to the Greeks, Discourse to the Greeks, the Monarchy, or the Rule of God. Falls, Thomas B., ed. LC 65-18317. (Fathers of the Church Ser.: Vol. 6). 486p. Date not set. reprint ed. pap. 138.60 (0-7837-9146-1, 2049946) Bks Demand.

Martyr, Justin, jt. auth. see Felix, Mark.

***Martyska, Barbara.** From Canyons to Highlands. 16p. 1995. pap. text ed. 4.95 (0-87487-747-4) Summy-Birchard.

Martz, Arnaud C. Philanthropy's Role in Civilization: Its Contribution to Human Freedom. 206p. (C). 1991. 34.95 (0-88738-405-6) Transaction Pubs.

Martz, C. W., ed. Solar Energy Source Book. 2nd ed. (Illus.). 1977. 30.00 (0-686-23456-1); pap. 15.00 (0-686-23457-X) SEINAM.

Martz, Clyde O. Cases & Materials on the Law of Natural Resources. Bruchey, Stuart, ed. LC 78-53553. (Development of Public Land Law in the U. S. Ser.). 1979. reprint ed. lib. bdg. 81.95 (0-405-11379-X) Ayer.

Martz, Edwine M., ed. see Walpole, Horace.

***Martz, Geoff.** Cracking the ACT with Sample Tests on Computer Disk, 1995-96 Edition: Mac Version. (Princeton Review Ser.). 1995. student ed, disk 29.95 (0-679-76024-5) Random.

— Princeton Review Cracking the Act with Sample Tests on Computer Disk 1995-96 Edition: Windows Version. 1995. student ed 29.95 (0-679-76025-3) Random.

— Princeton Review Cracking the Act, 1995-1996. 1995. student ed, pap. 17.00 (0-679-75912-3) Random.

***Martz, Geoff, et al.** Cracking the GMAT 1996. (Princeton Review Ser.). 1995. pap. 17.00 (0-679-76135-7, Villard Bks) Random.

— Cracking the GMAT 1996: With Sample Tests on Computer Disk (WIN) (Princeton Review Ser.). 1995. disk, pap. 29.95 (0-679-76137-3, Villard Bks) Random.

— Cracking the GMAT '96: With Sample Tests on Computer Disk (MAC) (Princeton Review Ser.). 1995. disk, pap. 29.95 (0-679-76138-1, Villard Bks) Random.

Martz, Geoffrey. The Princeton Review: Cracking the ACT, 1994. 1993. pap. 15.00 (0-679-74679-X, Villard Bks) Random.

— Princeton Review: Surviving Without Your Parents' Money. LC 92-38342. 1993. pap. 9.00 (0-679-74626-9, Villard Bks) Random.

— Princeton Review: The GMAT System, 1993. 1992. pap. 16.00 (0-679-74105-4, Villard Bks) Random.

— Princeton Review: The Student Access Financial Aid & Planning System. 1992. pap. 14.00 (0-679-73865-7, Villard Bks) Random.

— Princeton Review Cracking the ACT 1995 Edition. 1994. pap. 16.00 (0-679-75343-5, Villard Bks) Random.

— Princeton Review Cracking the GED, 1995. 1994. pap. 15.00 (0-679-75498-9, Villard Bks) Random.

— Princeton Review Cracking the GMAT Diagnostic Tests on Disk. 1994. pap. 29.95 (0-679-75371-0, Villard Bks) Random.

— Princeton Review Cracking the GMAT with Diagnostic Tests on Disk. 1994. pap. 29.95 (0-679-75351-6, Villard Bks) Random.

— Princeton Review Cracking the GMAT 1995 Edition. 1994. pap. 17.00 (0-679-75341-9, Villard Bks) Random.

Martz, Harry F. & Waller, Ray A. Bayesian Reliability Analysis. LC 89-6172. 768p. (C). 1991. reprint ed. lib. bdg. 69.50 (0-89464-395-9) Krieger.

Martz, Jim. Hurricane Warning: University of Miami Football. 1989. 17.95 (0-87397-315-1) Strode.

Martz, John, ed. see Bowling, David L. & Bowling, Patricia H.

Martz, John D. Accion Democratica: Evolution of a Modern Political Party in Venezuela. 1965. 69.50x (0-691-07500-X) Princeton U Pr.

— Accion Democratica: Evolution of a Modern Political Party in Venezuela. LC 65-17147. Date not set. reprint ed. pap. 130.30 (0-7837-9383-9, 2060127) Bks Demand.

— Colombia. LC 75-15694. (Illus.). 384p. 1975. reprint ed. text ed. 65.00 (0-8371-8215-8, MACOL, Greenwood Pr) Greenwood.

— Politics & Petroleum in Ecuador. 345p. 1987. 39.95 (0-88738-132-4) Transaction Pubs.

— United States Policy in Latin America: A Decade of Crisis & Challenge. 584p. (C). 1995. text ed. 55.00 (0-8032-3162-8); pap. text ed. 25.00 (0-8032-8189-7) U of Nebr Pr.

— Venezuela. 2nd ed. LC 85-28268. 489p. 1985. text ed. 65.00 (0-275-91815-7, C1815, Praeger Pubs); pap. text ed. 17.95 (0-275-92038-0, B2038, Praeger Pubs) Greenwood.

Martz, John D. & Myers, David J., eds. Venezuela: The Democratic Experience. LC 77-7509. (Praeger Special Studies). 432p. 1977. pap. 18.95 (0-275-91471-2, B1471, Praeger Pubs) Greenwood.

Martz, John D., jt. auth. see Baloyra, Enrique A.

Martz, John D., jt. auth. see Jorrin, Miguel.

Martz, Larry. Reclaiming Our Schools: Creating Classrooms That Work. 1992. 12.00 (0-8129-1939-4, Times Bks) Random.

Martz, Louis. The Paradise Within: Studies in Vaughan, Traherne, & Milton. 217p. (C). 1966. reprint ed. pap. 14.00 (0-300-00164-9) Yale U Pr.

Martz, Louis, ed. see Grassi, Carolyn.

Martz, Louis, ed. see Pound, Ezra.

Martz, Louis B., ed. Hero & Leander. (Facsimiles Ser.). 1978. 14.00 (0-918016-35-5) Folger Bks.

Martz, Louis L. From Renaissance to Baroque: Essays on Literature & Art. (Illus.). 298p. (C). 1991. text ed. 39.95 (0-8262-0796-0) U of Mo Pr.

— John Donne in Meditation: The Anniversaries. LC 70-99172. (English Literature Ser.: No. 33). 1970. reprint ed. lib. bdg. 49.95 (0-8383-0335-8) M S G Haskell Hse.

— Milton: Poet of Exile. 2nd ed. LC 86-7772. 356p. 1986. pap. text ed. 20.00 (0-300-03736-8) Yale U Pr.

— The Poetry of Meditation: A Study in English Religious Literature of the Seventeenth Century. rev. ed. LC 54-9520. 405p. reprint ed. pap. 115.50 (0-8357-8272-7, 2033814) Bks Demand.

— Thomas More: The Search for the Inner Man. (Illus.). 128p. (C). 1992. reprint ed. pap. 9.00x (0-300-05668-0) Yale U Pr.

Martz, Louis L., ed. George Herbert & Henry Vaughan. (Oxford Authors Ser.). 608p. 1986. pap. 18.95 (0-19-281342-0) OUP.

— George Herbert & Henry Vaughan. (Oxford Authors Ser.). 608p. 1986. 45.00 (0-19-254181-1) OUP.

Martz, Louis L. & Williams, Aubrey, eds. The Author in His Work: Essays on a Problem in Criticism. LC 77-16309. 427p. reprint ed. pap. 121.70 (0-8357-5899-0, 2032136) Bks Demand.

Martz, Louis L., ed. see Doolittle, Hilda.

Martz, Louis L., ed. see Herbert, George.

Martz, Louis L., tr. see More, Thomas.

Martz, Louis L., ed. see Vaughan, Henry.

Martz, Mary J. The Central American Soccer War: Historical Patterns & Internal Dynamics of OAS Settlement Procedures. LC 78-11595. (Papers in International Studies: Latin America Ser.: No. 4). 126p. reprint ed. pap. 36.00 (0-7837-1328-2, 2041476) Bks Demand.

Martz, Ron, jt. auth. see Bailey, Lawrence R.

Martz, Ron, jt. auth. see Malcom, Ben S.

Martz, Ron, jt. auth. see Terrell, Jack.

Martz, Sandra, ed. I Am Becoming the Woman I've Wanted. LC 94-19650. (Illus.). 218p. 1994. 16.00 (0-918949-50-5); pap. 10.00 (0-918949-49-1) Papier-Mache Press.

— If I Had a Hammer: Women's Work in Poetry, Fiction, & Photographs. LC 90-7580. (Illus.). 261p. (Orig.). 1990. pap. 11.00 (0-918949-09-2) Papier-Mache Press.

— The Tie That Binds: A Collection of Writings about Fathers & Daughters - Mothers & Sons. 2nd ed. (Illus.). 165p. 1992. 16.00 (0-918949-20-3); pap. 10.00 (0-918949-19-X) Papier-Mache Press.

— When I Am an Old Woman I Shall Wear Purple. 2nd ed. LC 91-13828. (Illus.). 181p. (Orig.). 1991. 16.00 (0-918949-15-7); pap. 10.00 (0-918949-16-5) Papier-Mache Press.

Martz, Sandra, frwd. If I Had My Life to Live over I Would Pick More Daisies. LC 92-34059. (Illus.). 205p. 1993. 16.00 (0-918949-25-4) Papier-Mache Press.

***Martz, Sandra H., ed.** If I Had My Life to Live over Reading Card. (Illus.). 24p. 1995. 5.00 (0-918949-71-8) Papier-Mache Press.

— When I Am an Old Woman Reading Card. (Illus.). 24p. 1995. 5.00 (0-918949-70-X) Papier-Mache Press.

Martz, Sandra H., frwd. If I Had My Life to Live over I Would Pick More Daisies. LC 92-34059. (Illus.). 205p. 1993. pap. 10.00 (0-918949-24-6) Papier-Mache Press.

Martz, Sandra K., ed. Atalanta: An Anthology of Creative Work Celebrating Women's Athletic Achievements. 54p. (Orig.). 1984. pap. 4.00 (0-918949-00-9) Papier-Mache Press.

— More Golden Apples: A Further Celebration of Women & Sport. 56p. (Orig.). 1986. pap. 5.95 (0-918949-01-7) Papier-Mache Press.

***Martz, Sheryl.** Basic Arrythmia Analysis. 168p. (C). 1994. per., pap. text ed. 14.95 (0-8403-9682-1) Kendall-Hunt.

Martz, William. The Place of the Tempest in Shakespeare's Universe of Comedy. 10.00 (0-87291-098-9) Coronado Pr.

Martz, William J. John Berryman. LC 70-628288. (University of Minnesota Pamphlets on American Writers Ser.: No. 85). 47p. (Orig.). reprint ed. pap. 25.00 (0-7837-2875-1, 2057580) Bks Demand.

— The Place of "Measure for Measure" in Shakespeare's Universe of Comedy. 150p. 1982. 12.50x (0-87291-159-4) Coronado Pr.

— The Place of the Merchant of Venice in Shakespeare's Universe of Comedy. 1976. lib. bdg. 250.00 (0-87700-233-9) Revisionist Pr.

— Shakespeare's Universe of Comedy. 1976. lib. bdg. 250.00 (0-87700-268-1) Revisionist Pr.

Martzilli, Richard. Homeowners Coverage, 1991. Date not set. 39.50 (1-56461-038-1, 46110) Rough Notes.

Martzolff, Clement L. Fifty Stories from Ohio History. 1993. reprint ed. lib. bdg. 89.00 (0-7812-5387-X) Rprt Serv.

Maru, Hans C., ed. see Symposium on Porous Electrodes, Theory & Practice Staff.

Maruani, J. Molecules in Physics, Chemistry & Biology, 4 vols., Set. (C). 1900. lib. bdg. 478.00 (90-277-2617-5) Kluwer Ac.

— Molecules in Physics, Chemistry & Biology, 4 vols., Vol. 1: General Introduction to Molecular Sciences. (C). 1988. lib. bdg. 96.00 (0-685-23151-8) Kluwer Ac.

— Molecules in Physics, Chemistry & Biology, 4 vols., Vol. 2: Physical Aspects of Molecular Systems. (C). 1900. lib. bdg. 199.00 (0-685-23152-6) Kluwer Ac.

— Molecules in Physics, Chemistry & Biology, 4 vols., Vol. 3: Electronic Structure & Chemical Reactivity. (C). 1900. lib. bdg. 133.00 (0-685-23153-4) Kluwer Ac.

— Molecules in Physics, Chemistry & Biology, 4 vols., Vol. 4: Molecular Phenomena in Biological Sciences. (C). 1988. lib. bdg. 113.00 (0-685-23154-2) Kluwer Ac.

Maruani, J. & Serre, Jean-Pierre, eds. Symmetries & Properties of Non-Rigid Molecules: A Comprehensive Survey. (Studies in Physical & Theoretical Chemistry: Vol. 23). 520p. 1983. 164.00 (0-444-42174-2) Elsevier.

***Marubini, Ettore & Grazia, Marai.** Analyzing Survival Data from Clinical Trials & Observational Studies. LC 94-30632. (Statistics in Practice Ser.). 1994. text ed. 63.95 (0-471-93987-0) Wiley.

Marucchi, Orazio. Christian Epigraphy. Willis, J. Armine, tr. LC 74-82057. 472p. 1975. 30.00 (0-89005-070-8) Ares.

Marucci, Ferdinando, jt. auth. see Weisz, Ilona.

Marucci, Franco. The Fine Delight That Fathers Thought: Rhetoric & Medievalism in Gerard Manley Hopkins. LC 92-39010. 288p. (C). 1994. 44.95 (0-8132-0778-9) Cath U Pr.

Marudanayagam, P. Celebrations & Distractions: Essays in Criticism. 1993. 22.50 (0-685-65105-3, Pub. by Reliance Pub Hse II) Apt Bks.

Maruf, Mohammad. Iqbal's Philosophy of Religion. 3rd ed. 267p. reprint ed. text ed. 29.00 (1-56744-027-4) Kazi Pubns.

Maruggi, Edward. Technical Graphics: Electronics Worktext. 2nd ed. 464p. (C). 1991. pap. write for info. (0-675-21378-9, Merrill Pub Co) Macmillan.

***Maruggi, Edward A.** Current Practices for Interpreting Engineering Drawings. 320p. 1995. spiral bd. 26.75 (0-314-04576-7) West Pub.

Maruhnich, John. Scoopy the Lop-Eared Rabbit. LC 93-93765. (Illus.). 64p. 1994. pap. 7.00 (1-56002-298-1, Univ Edtns) Aegina Pr.

Marui, Eiji, jt. ed. see Reich, Michael R.

Maruice, F. D., jt. auth. see Dunstan, G. R.

Maruish, Mark E., ed. The Use of Psychological Testing for Treatment Planning & Outcome Assessment. 624p. 1993. text ed. 135.00 (0-8058-1162-1) L Erlbaum Assocs.

Maruki, Toshi. Hiroshima No Pika. LC 82-15365. (Illus.). 48p. (J). (gr. 7 up). 1982. 16.00 (0-688-01297-3) Lothrop.

Marulli, L., ed. see World Symposium on International Documentation Staff.

Marulli, Luciana, tr. see Lunati, Rinaldo.

Marullo, Michael A. Supplier Profiles Directory of SCADA Products - Systems - Services: The Sourcebook of Products, Systems, & Services for Supervisory Control & Data Acquisition (SCADA) Professionals, 1988-89. 211p. 1988. pap. 40.00 (0-9622280-0-1) Tech-Marc.

— Supplier Profiles Directory of SCADA Products, Systems & Services: 1990-91 Edition. 259p. (Orig.). 1991. pap. 45.00 (0-685-48472-6) Tech-Marc.

Marullo, Michael A., pref. Supplier Profiles Directory of SCADA Products - Systems - Services, 1992-93. 265p. 1993. pap. 50.00 (0-9622280-2-8) Tech-Marc.

Marullo, Sam. Ending the Cold War at Home: From Militarism to a More Peaceful World Order. LC 93-29852. (Lexington Book Series on Social Issues). 1994. write for info. (0-669-24231-4) Free Pr.

Marullo, Sam & Lofland, John, eds. Peace Action in the 1980s: Social Science Perspectives. LC 89-49216. 300p. (C). 1990. text ed. 40.00 (0-8135-1560-2); pap. text ed. 15.00 (0-8135-1561-0) Rutgers U Pr.

***Marullo, Thomas G., ed. & intro.** Ivan Bunin: From the Other Shore, 1920-1933: A Portrait from Letters, Diaries, & Fiction. LC 94-46953. 1995. write for info. (1-56663-083-5) I R Dee.

Marullo, Thomas G., ed. Ivan Bunin: Russian Requiem, 1885-1920: A Portrait from Letters, Diaries, & Fiction. (Illus.). 416p. 1993. 30.00 (1-56663-012-6) I R Dee.

Marum, Andrew & Parise, Frank. Follies & Foibles: A View of 20th Century Fads. LC 82-2355. (Illus.). 238p. reprint ed. pap. 67.90 (0-7837-1565-X, 2041857) Bks Demand.

***Marum, Ed, ed.** Towards 2000: The Future of Childhood, Literacy, & Schooling. LC 95-7254. 1995. write for info. (0-7507-0420-9, Falmer Pr); pap. write for info. (0-7507-0421-7, Falmer Pr) Taylor & Francis.

Marumo, F., ed. Dynamic Processes of Material Transport & Transformation in the Earth's Interior. (C). 1991. lib. bdg. 254.50 (0-7923-1075-6) Kluwer Ac.

Marumoto, Claire, ed. Guide to Government in Hawaii. 9th ed. 1989. 3.00 (0-318-50041-8) HI Legis Ref.

Marun, Gioconda. Origenes del Costumbrismo Etico-Social, Addison y Steele: Antecedentes del Articulo Costumbrista Espanol y Argentino. LC 83-80966. (Coleccion Polymita Ser.). 167p. (Orig.). (SPA.). 1983. pap. 19.95 (0-89729-278-2) Ediciones.

Maruo, B. & Yoshikawa, Hiroyuki, eds. Bacillus Subtilis: Molecular Biology & Industrial Application. (Topics in Secondary Metabolism Ser.: Vol. 1). 268p. 1989. 138.50 (0-444-98852-1) Elsevier.

Maruo, H., jt. ed. see Horikawa, Kiyoshi.

Maruo, Suehiro. Mr. Arashi's Amazing Freak Show. 1991. pap. 10.95 (0-922233-06-3) Blast Bks.

***Maruri, Richard J.** Hundred & Five Investments for the Twenty-First Century. 1995. text ed. 22.95 (0-07-040939-0) McGraw.

Marus, Sheryl M. Kampus Kwestions: How to Bake a Potato & Other Great Mysteries. (Illus.). (Orig.). (C). 1994. pap. 9.99 (0-9641714-0-6) STS Instruct.

Maruska, Edward J. Amphibians: Creatures of the Land & Water. LC 93-29843. (Cincinnati Zoo Book Ser.). (Illus.). 56p. (J). (gr. 5-7). 1994. lib. bdg. 15.47 (0-531-11158-X); pap. 9.95 (0-531-15714-8) Watts.

Maruskin, Albert F. OCLC, Its Governance, Function, Financing, & Technology. LC 80-23417. (Books in Library & Information Science: No. 32). 157p. reprint ed. pap. 44.80 (0-7837-0761-4, 2041075) Bks Demand.

Marussi, A. Intrinsic Geodesy. Reilly, I, tr. (Illus.). 240p. 1985. 104.00 (0-387-15133-8) Spr-Verlag.

Marusyk, Raymond G., jt. ed. see Kurstak, Edouard.

Maruszewski, Mariusz. Language Communication & the Brain: A Neuropsychological Study. Shugar, Grace W., tr. (Janua Linguarum, Series Major: No. 80). (Illus.). 217p. 1975. text ed. 57.70 (90-279-3067-8) Mouton.

Marut, jt. auth. see Yu.

Marutollo, Frank. Organizational Behavior in the Marine Corps: Three Interpretations. LC 89-70913. 232p. 1990. text ed. 55.00 (0-275-93493-4, C3493, Greenwood Pr) Greenwood.

Maruya, Saiichi. A Mature Woman. Keene, Dennis, tr. 328p. 1994. 28.00 (4-7700-1864-9) Kodansha.

— Rain in the Wind: Four Stories. Keene, Dennis, tr. 190p. (YA). 1990. 18.95 (0-87011-940-0) Kodansha.

Maruya, Sancni. Rain in the Wind: Four Stories. Keene, Dennis, tr. 240p. 1992. pap. 8.00 (4-7700-1558-5) Kodansha.

Maruyama, et al, eds. Recent Advances in Coronary Circulation. 1994. 169.00 (0-387-70130-3) Spr-Verlag.

An Asterisk (*) at the beginning of an entry indicates that the title is appearing in BIP for the first time.

***Maruyama, E. & Watanabe, H., eds.** Physics & Industry: Proceedings of Academic Session of the XXI General Assembly of the International Union of Pure & Applied Physics Held at Nara, Japan, 22 & 23 September 1993. LC 94-30559. (Lecture Notes in Physics Ser.: Vol. 435). 1994. write for info. (*3-540-58376-9*) Spr-Verlag.

— Physics & Industry: Proceedings of Academic Session of the XXI General Assembly of the International Union of Pure & Applied Physics Held at Nara, Japan, 22 & 23 September 1993, 435. LC 94-30559. (Lecture Notes in Physics Ser.). 1994. write for info. (*0-387-58376-9*) Spr-Verlag.

Maruyama, Geoffrey & Deno, Stanley. Research in Educational Settings. (Applied Social Research Methods Ser.: Vol. 29). 160p. (C). 1992. text ed. 37.00 (*0-8039-4207-9*); pap. text ed. 16.95 (*0-8039-4208-7*) Sage.

Maruyama, K., jt. ed. see Kirchner, R.

Maruyama, M. & Reniker, S., eds. Context & Complexity: Cultivating Contextual Understanding. (Illus.). xii, 145p. 1991. 32.00 (*0-387-97542-X*) Spr-Verlag.

Maruyama, Magoroh. Management Reform in Eastern & Central Europe: Use of Pre-Communist Cultures. 192p. 1993. 29.95 (*1-85521-343-5*, Pub. by Dartmth Pub UK) Ashgate Pub Co.

— Mindscapes in Management: Use of Individual Differences in Multicultural Management. 160p. 1994. 39.95 (*1-85521-367-2*, Pub. by Dartmth Pub UK) Ashgate Pub Co.

Maruyama, Magoroh & Harkins, Arthur M., eds. Cultures of the Future. (World Anthropology Ser.). xxii, 668p. 1978. 100.00 (*90-279-7979-0*) Mouton.

Maruyama, Masakazu. Review of Clinical Research in Gastroenterology. LC 87-27379. 275p. 1988. 66.00 (*0-89640-134-0*) Igaku-Shoin.

Maruyama, Masao. Studies in the Intellectual History of Tokugawa Japan. Hane, Mikiso, tr. 424p. (C). 1989. pap. text ed. 23.95 (*0-691-00832-9*) Princeton U Pr.

— Studies in the Intellectual History of Tokugawa Japan. Hane, Mikiso, tr. 422p. 1994. pap. 34.50 (*0-86008-444-2*) Col U Pr.

Maruyama, Meredith E., et al. Japan Health Handbook. 320p. 1994. pap. 20.00 (*4-7700-1838-X*) Kodansha.

Maruyama, T. & Tsubokura, M. Current Investigations of the Microbiology of Yersiniae. Une, T. et al, eds. (Contributions to Microbiology & Immunology Ser.: Vol. 12). (Illus.). x, 316p. 1991. 252.00 (*3-8055-5370-6*) S Karger.

***Maruyama, Toru & Takahashi, Wataru, eds.** Nonlinear & Convex Analysis in Economic Theory. LC 94-39352. (Lecture Notes in Economics & Mathematical Systems: Vol. 419). 1995. write for info. (*0-387-58767-5*) Spr-Verlag.

Maruyama, Y., et al. CF-252 Neutron Brachytherapy & Fast Neutron Beam Therapy. 658p. 1986. text ed. 290.00 (*3-7186-0324-1*) Gordon & Breach.

Maruyama, Yosh. CF-252 Neutron Brachytherapy. (Nuclear Science Applications Ser.: Section B, Vol. 1, No. 8). 72p. 1984. pap. text ed. 39.00 (*3-7186-0208-3*) Gordon & Breach.

Maruzen. Student C Set: Organic Chemistry Model. (C). 1995. pap. text ed. write for info. (*0-7167-1972-X*) W H Freeman.

Maruzen, Benjamin. HGS Molecular Structure Models. (C). 1969. General Chemistry Set & Organic Chemistry Set. 22.75 (*0-8053-6971-6*) Benjamin-Cummings.

Maruzzi, Stefano. IBM OS - 2 2.1 Presentation Manual. 1994. pap. 44.00 (*0-679-79162-0*) Random.

Marvan, P., et al. Algal Assays & Monitoring Eutrophication. (Illus.). 253p. 1979. 33.50 (*3-510-65091-3*) Lubrecht & Cramer.

Marvano, jt. auth. see Haldeman, Joe.

Marvano, ed. see Haldeman, Joe.

Marvasti, F. A. Unified Approach to Zero-Crossings & Nonuniform Sampling of Single & Multidimensional Signals & Systems. (Illus.). 213p. 1987. pap. text ed. 35.00 (*0-9618167-0-8*) Nonuniform.

***Marvel, Bill.** Rock Island in Color Vol. 2: 1965-1980, Set. (Illus.). 1995. 49.95 (*1-878887-39-4*) Morning NJ.

Marvel, Bill, intro. Papers of the Military Historical Society of Massachusetts, 15 vols., Set. 1990. reprint ed. 500.00 (*0-916107-73-6*) Broadfoot.

***Marvel Comics Staff.** Pocahontas. (Illus.). 48p. 1995. pap. 4.95 (*0-7851-0108-X*) Marvel Entmnt.

Marvel Comics Staff, et al. Terminator II. 64p. 1991. 4.95 (*0-87135-756-9*) Marvel Entmnt.

Marvel Entertainment Group. X-Men X-tra Large Coloring & Activity Book. (Illus.). 64p. (Orig.). (J). (ps-3). 1994. pap. 3.99 (*0-679-86864-X*) Random Bks Yng Read.

***Marvel Entertainment Group, creator.** X-Men. (Postcard Bk.). (Illus.). 30p. 1995. pap. 8.95 (*1-56138-584-0*) Running Pr.

Marvel Entertainment Staff. The Uncanny X-Men. 128p. 1990. pap. 3.99 (*0-8125-1021-6*) Tor Bks.

Marvel, Richard. The New Oz: The Wizard Revisited. Schuck, Marjorie M., ed. 86p. (Orig.). 1992. pap. text ed. 10.00 (*0-934616-45-0*) Valkyrie Pub Hse.

Marvel Staff. Morlock Madness. (J). (gr. 4-7). 1993. pap. 2.50 (*0-679-85710-9*) Random Bks Yng Read.

— Night of the Sentinels Pt. 1: Meet the X-Men. (J). (gr. 4-7). 1993. pap. 2.50 (*0-679-85707-9*) Random Bks Yng Read.

— Night of the Sentinels, Pt. 2: Wolverine's Vengeance. (J). (gr. 4-7). 1993. pap. 2.50 (*0-679-85708-7*) Random Bks Yng Read.

— To Stop a Juggernaut. (J). (gr. 4-7). 1993. pap. 2.50 (*0-679-85709-5*) Random Bks Yng Read.

Marvel, Terrence L. Thirties America: Prints from the Milwaukee Art Museum. (Illus.). 30p. (Orig.). 1991. pap. 12.00 (*0-944110-30-4*) Milwauk Art Mus.

Marvel, Terrence L., jt. auth. see Bamberger, Tom.

Marvel, Thomas S. & Brooks, H. Allen. Antonin Nechodoma, Architect, 1877-1928: The Prairie School in the Caribbean. LC 93-32486. (Illus.). 256p. (C). 1994. lib. bdg. 44.95 (*0-8130-1269-4*) U Press Fla.

Marvel, William. Andersonville: The Last Depot. LC 93-40101. (Civil War America Ser.). (Illus.). xii, 338p. 1994. 29.95 (*0-8078-2152-7*) U of NC Pr.

— Burnside. LC 91-8419. (Illus.). xiv, 538p. (C). 1991. 32.50 (*0-8078-1983-2*) U of NC Pr.

— The First New Hampshire Battery, Eighteen Sixty-One to Eighteen Sixty-Five. (Illus.). 97p. (Orig.). 1985. pap. 6.95 (*0-9614826-0-5*) Lost Cemetery Pr.

— Race of the Soil: "The Ninth New Hampshire Regiment in the Civil War" (Illus.). 534p. 1988. 35.00 (*0-916107-67-1*) Broadfoot.

Marvel, William, contrib. Military Order of the Loyal Legion of the United States, 69 vols., 69 vols. (Illus.). 1991. reprint ed. Set. 2,400.00 (*1-56837-001-6*) Broadfoot.

Marvel, William, intro. Index. (Papers of the Military Historical Society of Massachusetts: Vol. 15). 412p. 1990. 100.00 (*1-56837-019-9*) Broadfoot.

Marvel, William, jt. auth. see Cavanaush, Michael A.

Marvell, Andrew. Andrew Marvell. Kermode, Frank & Walker, Keith, eds. (Oxford Authors Ser.). 384p. 1991. pap. 17.95 (*0-19-281347-1*) OUP.

— Andrew Marvell. Kermode, Frank & Walker, Keith, eds. LC 93-34646. (Oxford Poetry Library). 192p. 1994. pap. 7.95 (*0-19-282271-3*) OUP.

— The Complete Poems. Donno, Elizabeth S., ed. (Poets Ser.). 1977. pap. 9.95 (*0-14-042213-7*, Penguin Classics) Viking Penguin.

— Complete Works in Verse & Prose of Andrew Marvell, 4 vols., Set. LC 77-181955. (Fuller Worthies' Library). reprint ed. 345.00 (*0-404-04270-8*) AMS Pr.

— The Complete Works in Verse & Prose of Andrew Marvell, 4 vols., Set. (BCL1-PR English Literature Ser.). 1992. reprint ed. lib. bdg. 300.00 (*0-7812-7372-2*) Rprt Serv.

— Poems. LC 92-54301. 1993. 15.00 (*0-679-42038-X*, Everymans Lib) Knopf.

Marvell, Holt, jt. auth. see Gielgud, Val.

Marvell-Mell, Linaea. Basic Techniques, Bk. 1. rev. ed. Stephens, Lori, ed. (Skill Builder Ser.). (Illus.). 192p. 1989. reprint ed. student ed 12.95 (*1-55552-016-2*); reprint ed. audio, pap. 12.95 (*0-943920-02-7*) Metamorphous Pr.

Marvell, Thomas B. Appellate Courts & Lawyers: Information Gathering in the Adversary System. LC 77-94743. (Contributions in Legal Studies: No. 4). x, 391p. 1978. text ed. 75.00 (*0-313-20312-1*, MAA/, Greenwood Pr) Greenwood.

Marvick, Louis W. Mallarme & the Sublime. LC 85-27750. 211p. (C). 1986. 64.50 (*0-88706-278-4*); pap. 21.95 (*0-88706-279-2*) State U NY Pr.

Marvicsin, Dennis J. Maverick. 1991. pap. 5.50 (*0-515-10662-3*) Jove Pubns.

Marvin, A. P. History of the Town of Winchendon, Worcester County, Massachusetts. (Illus.). 528p. 1994. reprint ed. lib. bdg. 55.00 (*0-8328-3960-4*) Higginson Bk Co.

Marvin, Abijah P. History of the Town of Lancaster, Mass., from the First Settlement to the Present Time, 1643-1879. (Illus.). 798p. 1989. reprint ed. lib. bdg. 79.00 (*0-8328-0833-4*, MA0198) Higginson Bk Co.

— The Life & Times of Cotton Mather. LC 72-1979. (American Biography Ser.: No. 32). 1972. reprint ed. lib. bdg. 75.00 (*0-8383-1454-6*) M S G Haskell Hse.

Marvin, Bill. From Turnover to Teamwork: How to Build & Retain a Customer Oriented Foodservice Staff. 216p. 1994. text ed. 29.95 (*0-471-59077-0*) Wiley.

— Restaurant Basics: Why Guests Don't Come Back...& What You Can Do about It. 240p. 1991. text ed. 32.95 (*0-471-55174-0*) Wiley.

Marvin, Carolyn. When Old Technologies Were New. 272p. 1990. reprint ed. pap. 16.95 (*0-19-506341-4*) OUP.

Marvin, Charles T. The Region of Eternal Fire: An Account of a Journey to the Petroleum Region of the Caspian in 1883. LC 75-6481. (History & Politics of Oil Ser.). xviii, 413p. 1976. reprint ed. 31.85 (*0-88355-298-1*) Hyperion Conn.

— The Russians of Merv & Herat. 1990. reprint ed. 50.00 (*3-262-00043-4*) Periodicals Srv.

***Marvin, Elizabeth W. & Hermann, Richard, eds.** Concert Music, Rock, & Jazz since 1945: Essays & Analytical Studies. LC 94-30277. (Eastman Studies in Music: No. 2). (Illus.). 300p. (C). 1996. text ed. 79.00 (*1-878822-42-X*) Univ Rochester Pr.

Marvin, F. M. Shafer - Huston - Huston Family History. (Illus.). 470p. 1994. reprint ed. lib. bdg. 57.00 (*0-8328-4235-4*); reprint ed. pap. 47.00 (*0-8328-4236-2*) Higginson Bk Co.

— Shafer - Huston - Huston Family History. (Illus.). 470p. 1994. reprint ed. lib. bdg. 57.00 (*0-8328-4547-7*); reprint ed. pap. 47.00 (*0-8328-4548-5*) Higginson Bk Co.

Marvin, F. R. The Last Words of Distinguished Men & Women. 1972. 59.95 (*0-8490-0488-8*) Gordon Pr.

Marvin, Francis M. Van Horn Family History. (Illus.). 464p. 1992. reprint ed. lib. bdg. 77.50 (*0-8328-2464-X*); reprint ed. pap. 67.50 (*0-8328-2465-8*) Higginson Bk Co.

Marvin, Francis S., ed. Evolution of World-Peace: Essays. Unity Ser. 4. LC 68-20318. (Essay Index Reprint Ser.). 1977. 17.95 (*0-8369-0682-9*) Ayer.

— New World-Order: Essays. LC 67-30221. (Essay Index Reprint Ser.). 1977. 19.95 (*0-8369-0683-7*) Ayer.

— Progress & History: Essays. LC 78-84326. (Essay Index Reprint Ser.). 1977. 20.95 (*0-8369-1096-6*) Ayer.

— Recent Developments in European Thought. LC 71-111851. (Essay Index Reprint Ser.). 1977. 21.95 (*0-8369-1619-0*) Ayer.

— Science & Civilization. LC 70-105030. (Essay Index Reprint Ser.). 1977. 23.95 (*0-8369-1581-X*) Ayer.

— Unity of Western Civilization. LC 77-128277. (Essay Index Reprint Ser.). 1977. 21.95 (*0-8369-1889-4*) Ayer.

— Western Races & the World. Unity Ser. 5. LC 68-22929. (Essay Index Reprint Ser.). 1977. reprint ed. 19.95 (*0-8369-0684-5*) Ayer.

Marvin, Francis S. & Clutton-Brock, Alan F., eds. Art & Civilization: Essays. LC 67-26762. (Essay Index Reprint Ser.). 1977. 20.95 (*0-8369-0685-3*) Ayer.

Marvin, Frank. The Resurrectionist. 188p. 1994. pap. 8.95 (*1-56901-283-0*) NW Pub.

Marvin, Fred, illus. Bambi: The New Prince. LC 93-71377. (Tiny Changing Pictures Bks.). 10p. (J). (ps-00). 1994. 4.95 (*1-56282-601-8*) Disney Pr.

— Beauty & the Beast: The Friendship. LC 92-53440. (Tiny Changing Pictures Bks.). 10p. (J). (ps-00). 1993. 4.95 (*1-56282-376-0*) Disney Pr.

— Disney's The Little Mermaid: Tales from under the Sea. LC 90-85427. 80p. (J). (gr. 2-7). 1991. 10.95 (*1-56282-014-1*) Disney Pr.

— The Little Mermaid Novels, 4 bks., Set. (Little Mermaid Novels Ser.). (J). (gr. 1-4). 1993. Boxed set incl. Green-Eyed Pearl, Nefazia Visits the Palace, Reflections of Arsulu & The Same Old So. boxed, pap. 11.80 (*1-56282-562-3*) Disney Pr.

— Pinocchio: Geppetto's Surprise. LC 92-54877. (Tiny Changing Pictures Bks.). 10p. (J). (ps-00). 1993. 4.95 (*1-56282-397-3*) Disney Pr.

— Snow White & the Seven Dwarfs: Suppertime. LC 93-71376. (Tiny Changing Pictures Bks.). 10p. (J). (ps-00). 1994. 4.95 (*1-56282-600-X*) Disney Pr.

— Walt Disney's Pinocchio. (Little Nugget Bks.). 28p. (J). (ps). 1992. bds. write for info. (*0-307-12532-7*, 12532, Golden Pr) Western Pub.

— Walt Disney's Snow White & the Seven Dwarfs. LC 92-53430. (Illustrated Classics Ser.). 96p. (J). 1993. 14.95 (*1-56282-362-0*); lib. bdg. 14.89 (*1-56282-363-9*); pap. 5.95 (*0-7868-4020-X*) Disney Pr.

Marvin, Fred, jt. illus. see Cardona, Jose.

Marvin, Fred, jt. illus. see Martin, Kerry.

Marvin, Frederic R. Companionship of Books & Other Papers. LC 75-90662. (Essay Index Reprint Ser.). 1977. 23.95 (*0-8369-1227-6*) Ayer.

— The Excursions of a Book-Lover, Being Papers on Literary Themes. LC 77-92510. (Essay Index in Reprint Ser.). 1978. reprint ed. 25.00 (*0-8486-3004-1*) Roth Pub Inc.

— Fireside Papers. LC 68-8482. (Essay Index Reprint Ser.). 1977. 22.95 (*0-8369-0686-1*) Ayer.

Marvin, G. R., jt. ed. see Holman, M. L.

Marvin, Garry. Coping with Spain. (Coping with... Ser.). (Illus.). 192p. 1990. pap. 13.95 (*0-631-16832-X*) Blackwell Pubs.

Marvin, Gary. Bullfight. LC 94-15622. 1994. pap. write for info. (*0-252-06437-2*) U of Ill Pr.

Marvin, Isabel. Bridge to Freedom. 148p. (YA). (gr. 5-9). 1991. 14.95 (*0-8276-0377-0*) JPS Phila.

— The Tenth Rifle & the Jesse James Gang. 220p. (YA). 1994. pap. 5.00 (*0-614-06297-7*) Windswept Hse.

Marvin, Isabel R. A Bride for Anna's Papa. LC 93-41175. (Illus.). 152p. (J). 1994. pap. 6.95 (*0-915943-93-X*) Milkweed Ed.

— Green Fire. Whitaker, Kate, ed. 72p. (J). (gr. 5-8). 1994. pap. 6.95 (*0-932433-15-4*) Windswept Hse.

— Josefina & the Hanging Tree. LC 91-34501. (Chaparral Bks.). 128p. (YA). (gr. 6-9). 1992. pap. 9.95 (*0-87565-103-8*) Tex Christian.

— Mystery of the Ice Cream House. Whitaker, Kate, ed. LC 93-61532. 64p. (J). (gr. 5-8). 1994. pap. 6.95 (*0-932433-87-1*) Windswept Hse.

— Mystery of the Puerto Rican Penny. Weinberger, Jane, ed. (The Marisa Blake Mystery Ser.). 72p. (Orig.). (J). (gr. 5-8). 1995. pap. 6.95 (*1-883650-01-1*) Windswept Hse.

— Shipwrecked on Padre Island. (Illus.). 160p. (J). (gr. 4 up). 1993. 14.95 (*0-937460-83-4*) Hendrick-Long.

Marvin, J. G. Legal Bibliography or a Thesaurus of American, English, Irish & Scotch Law Books. (Marvin's Legal Bibliography Ser.). vii, 800p. 1992. reprint ed. lib. bdg. 75.00 (*0-89941-349-8*, 502150) W S Hein.

Marvin, John T. The Complete West Highland White Terrier. 4th ed. LC 76-58225. (Complete Breed Book Ser.). (Illus.). 256p. 1977. 25.95 (*0-87605-355-X*) Howell Bk.

— The New Complete Cairn Terrier. LC 86-282. (Illus.). 256p. 1986. 25.95 (*0-87605-097-6*) Howell Bk.

— The New Complete Scottish Terrier. 2nd rev. ed. LC 81-13416. (Illus.). 256p. 1982. 25.95 (*0-87605-306-1*) Howell Bk.

Marvin, Nathaniel. Big Deer. pap. 4.00 (*0-9622903-5-1*) DCHA.

Marvin, Patrice, jt. ed. see Vrooman, Nicholas.

Marvin, T. A. All I Really Needed to Know I Learned While Still in Diapers. 96p. 1991. mass mkt. 5.95 (*0-380-76432-6*) Avon.

Marvin, Ursula B. Field & Laboratory Investigations of Meteorites from Victoria Land, Antarctica. Mason, Brian, ed. LC 83-20087. (Smithsonian Contributions to the Earth Sciences Ser.: No. 26). 138p. reprint ed. pap. 39.40 (*0-317-20102-6*, 2023163) Bks Demand.

Marvin, Ursula B. & MacPherson, Glenn J., eds. Field & Laboratory Investigations of Meteorites from Victoria & the Thiel Mountains Region, Antarctica, 1982-1983 & 1983-1984. LC 88-600361. (Smithsonian Contributions to the Earth Sciences Ser.: No. 28). (Illus.). 150p. reprint ed. pap. 42.80 (*0-8357-6111-8*, 2034329) Bks Demand.

Marvin, Ursula B. & Mason, Brian, eds. Catalog of Meteorites from Victoria Land, Antarctica, 1978-1980. LC 81-607125. (Smithsonian Contributions to the Earth Sciences Ser.: No. 24). 101p. reprint ed. pap. 28.80 (*0-317-08558-1*, 2017827) Bks Demand.

Marvin, W. Commercial Foodservice Cleaning Manual. 1992. pap. write for info. (*0-442-00803-1*) Van Nos Reinhold.

Marvin, William R. The Foolproof Foodservice Selection System: The Complete Manual for Creating a Quality Staff. 352p. 1993. text ed. 54.95 (*0-471-57431-7*) Wiley.

Marvis, Barbara J. Contemporary American Success Stories: Famous People of Asian Ancestry. LC 93-78991. (Illus.). 96p. (J). (gr. 5-12). 1993. teacher ed 5.95 (*1-883845-05-X*) M Lane Pubs.

— Contemporary American Success Stories: Famous People of Asian Ancestry, Vol. 1. LC 93-78991. (Illus.). 96p. (J). (gr. 5-12). 1993. 15.95 (*1-883845-00-9*) M Lane Pubs.

— Contemporary American Success Stories: Famous People of Asian Ancestry, Vol. 1. LC 93-78991. 96p. (J). (gr. 5-12). 1994. pap. 8.95 (*1-883845-06-8*) M Lane Pubs.

— Contemporary American Success Stories: Famous People of Asian Ancestry, Vol. 2. LC 93-78991. (Illus.). 96p. (J). (gr. 5-12). 1993. 15.95 (*1-883845-01-7*) M Lane Pubs.

— Contemporary American Success Stories: Famous People of Asian Ancestry, Vol. 2. LC 93-78991. 96p. (J). (gr. 5-12). 1994. pap. text ed. 8.95 (*1-883845-07-6*) M Lane Pubs.

— Contemporary American Success Stories: Famous People of Asian Ancestry, Vol. 3. LC 93-78991. (Illus.). 96p. (J). (gr. 5-12). 1993. 15.95 (*1-883845-02-5*); pap. 8.95 (*1-883845-08-4*) M Lane Pubs.

— Contemporary American Success Stories: Famous People of Asian Ancestry, Vol. 4. LC 93-78991. (Illus.). 96p. (YA). (gr. 5 up). 1994. 15.95 (*1-883845-03-3*); pap. 8.95 (*1-883845-09-2*) M Lane Pubs.

— Contemporary American Success Stories: Famous People of Asian Ancestry, Vol 5. LC 93-78991. (Illus.). 96p. (YA). (gr. 5 up). 1994. pap. 8.95 (*1-883845-11-4*) M Lane Pubs.

— Contemporary American Success Stories: Famous People of Asian Ancestry, Vol. 5. LC 93-78991. (Illus.). 96p. (YA). (gr. 5 up). 1994. 15.95 (*1-883845-12-2*) M Lane Pubs.

— Contemporary American Success Stories Vol. I: Famous People of Hispanic Heritage. LC 95-75963. (Illus.). 128p. (J). (gr. 4-12). 1995. 16.95 (*1-883845-21-1*); pap. 9.95 (*1-883845-20-3*) M Lane Pubs.

— Contemporary American Success Stories Vol. II: Famous People of Hispanic Heritage. LC 95-75963. (Illus.). 128p. (J). (gr. 4-12). 1995. 16.95 (*1-883845-23-8*); pap. 9.95 (*1-883845-22-X*) M Lane Pubs.

— Contemporary American Success Stories Vol. III: Famous People of Hispanic Heritage. LC 95-75963. (Illus.). 128p. (J). (gr. 4-12). 1995. 16.95 (*1-883845-25-4*); pap. 9.95 (*1-883845-24-6*) M Lane Pubs.

Marvullo, Joe. Color Vision. (Illus.). 144p. 1989. 29.95 (*0-8174-3675-8*, Amphoto); pap. 22.50 (*0-8174-3676-6*, Amphoto) Watsn-Guptill.

Marvullo, Joseph. Improving Your Color Photography. (Illus.). 176p. 1984. pap. 8.95 (*0-685-08489-2*) P-H.

Marwah, Joe, ed. Neurobiology of Drug Use. (Monographs in Neural Sciences: Vol. 13). (Illus.). viii, 164p. 1987. 117.75 (*3-8055-4561-4*) S Karger.

Marwah, Raj. Buy This Book: Understanding Advertising & Making the Most Out of Your Advertising Dollar. (Illus.). 200p. 1991. reprint ed. pap. 24.95 (*0-87757-215-1*) Am Mktg.

Marwaha, J. & Anderson, W. J., eds. Neuroreceptors in Health & Disease. (Monographs in Neural Sciences: Vol. 10). (Illus.). viii, 256p. 1984. 119.25 (*3-8055-3715-8*) S Karger.

Marwak. Neural Transplantation, CNS Neuronal Injury & Regeneration. 1994. 95.00 (*0-8493-8683-7*, RD124) CRC Pr.

***Marwedel, Peter.** Code Generation for Embedded Processors. 340p. (C). 1995. lib. bdg. 97.50 (*0-7923-9577-8*) Kluwer Ac.

Marwell, Gerald & Oliver, Pamela. The Critical Mass in Collective Action: A Micro-Social Theory. LC 92-23162. (Studies in Rationality & Social Change). 1993. 49.95 (*0-521-30839-9*) Cambridge U Pr.

Marwick, Arthur. Beauty in History: Society, Politics & Personal Appearance, C. 1500 to the Present. LC 89-50598. (Illus.). 1989. 19.95 (*0-500-25101-0*) Thames Hudson.

— British Society since Nineteen Forty-Five. (Social History of Britain Ser.). 300p. 1983. mass mkt. 6.95 (*0-14-021906-4*, Penguin Bks) Viking Penguin.

— British Society Since Nineteen Forty-Five. (Pelican Social History of Britain Ser.). 302p. 1984. 15.95 (*0-317-00889-7*) Allen Lane.

— Class: Image & Reality in Britain, France & the U. S. A. since 1930. 1980. 29.95 (*0-19-520203-1*) OUP.

— Culture in Britain since Nineteen Forty-Five. 192p. 1991. pap. 12.95 (*0-631-17191-6*) Blackwell Pubs.

— The Nature of History. 3rd rev. ed. LC 89-2786. 442p. (C). 1989. pap. text ed. 29.95 (*0-925065-00-5*) Lyceum IL.

Marwick, Arthur, ed. The Arts, Literature, & Society. (Social History Society Ser.). (Illus.). 320p. 1990. 87.50 (*0-415-01445-X*, A4567) Routledge.

— Total War & Social Change. LC 88-14855. 256p. 1988. text ed. 45.00 (*0-312-02373-1*) St Martin.

Marwick, Arthur & Simpson. Documents, Nineteen Hundred to Nineteen Twenty-Nine. 1990. 80.00 (*0-335-09301-9*, Open Univ Pr); pap. 27.00 (*0-335-09300-0*, Open Univ Pr) Taylor & Francis.

An Asterisk (*) at the beginning of an entry indicates that the title is appearing in BIP for the first time.

Marwick, Arthur, et al. Europe on Eve of War, Nineteen Hundred to Nineteen Fourteen. 1990. 90.00 (0-335-09305-1, Open Univ Pr); pap. 32.00 (0-335-09304-3, Open Univ Pr) Taylor & Francis.
— War & Change in Twentieth Century Europe. (War, Peace & Social Change Series: Europe, 1900-1955). 144p. 1990. 90.00 (0-335-09313-2, Open Univ Pr); pap. 29.00 (0-335-09312-4, Open Univ Pr) Taylor & Francis.
Marwick, Arthur, et al, eds. The Illustrated Dictionary of British History. (Illus.). 320p. 1981. 19.95 (0-500-25072-3) Thames Hudson.
Marwick, Christine M. Your Right to Government Information. 2nd rev. ed. (ACLU Ser.). 284p. 1985. pap. 6.95 (0-8093-9960-1) S Ill U Pr.
Marwick, D. H., jt. auth. see Balfour, A.
Marwick, Hugh. The Orkney Norn. LC 78-72635. (Celtic Language & Literature Ser.: Goidelic & Brythonic). reprint ed. 22.50 (0-404-17568-6) AMS Pr.
Marwick, Lawrence. Biblical & Judaic Acronyms. 49.50 (0-87068-438-8) Ktav.
Marwick, Max G., ed. Witchcraft & Sorcery. 494p. 1987. pap. 7.95 (0-14-022678-8, Penguin Bks) Viking Penguin.
Marwick, Peat, jt. auth. see Russell, C. W.
Marwick, Thomas H. Stress Echocardiography: Its Role in the Diagnosis & Evaluation of Coronary Artery Disease. LC 93-41121. (Developments in Cardiovascular Medicine Ser.: No. 149). 192p. (C). 1994. lib. bdg. 83.00 (0-7923-2579-6) Kluwer Ac.
Marwick, William H. Economic Developments in Victorian Scotland. LC 77-95621. (Reprints of Economic Classics Ser.). 1973. reprint ed. lib. bdg. 39.50 (0-678-00739-X) Kelley.
— Scotland in Modern Times. (Illus.). 209p. 1964. 35.00 (0-7146-1342-8, Pub. by F Cass Pubs UK) Intl Spec Bk.
Marwil, Jonathan. Frederic Manning: An Unfinished Life. LC 87-15708. xx, 380p. (C). 1988. lib. bdg. 26.95 (0-8223-0803-7) Duke.
Marwil, Jonathan L. A History of Ann Arbor. LC 87-70981. (Illus.). (Orig.). 1987. pap. 9.95 (0-9618742-0-1) Ann Arbor Observer.
Marwil, Jonathon L. A History of Ann Arbor. (Illus.). 194p. (Orig.). (C). 1991. text ed. 24.95 (0-472-09463-7); pap. 13.95 (0-472-06463-0) U of Mich Pr.
Marwill, Anne. Northern Storm. 1995. 13.95 (0-8062-5014-3) Carlton.
Marwitt, John P. Median Village & Fremont Culture Regional Variation. (Utah Anthropological Papers: No. 95). reprint ed. 24.00 (0-404-60695-4) AMS Pr.
— Median Village & Fremont Culture Regional Variation. LC 73-623166. (University of Utah, Anthropological Papers: No. 95). (Illus.). 207p. reprint ed. pap. 59.00 (0-8357-6852-X, 2035548) Bks Demand.
— Pharo Village. (Utah Anthropological Papers: No. 91). reprint ed. 20.00 (0-404-60691-1) AMS Pr.
Marwood, J. F., jt. ed. see Stokes, G. S.
Marx. Gold Gloves. (Baseball Heroes Ser.). (J). 1991. 12.50 (0-86593-130-5); lib. bdg. 16.67 (0-685-59188-3) Rourke Corp.
— On Colonialism. Date not set. text ed. 15.00 (0-85315-129-6, Pub. by Lawrence & Wishart UK) Humanities.
— On Ireland & the Irish Question. Date not set. text ed. 19.95 (0-85315-247-0, Pub. by Lawrence & Wishart UK) Humanities.
— Relief Pitchers. (Baseball Heroes Ser.). (J). 1991. 12.50 (0-86593-131-3); lib. bdg. 16.67 (0-685-66096-6) Rourke Corp.
— Rookies. (Baseball Heroes Ser.). (J). 1991. 12.50 (0-86593-132-1); lib. bdg. 16.67 (0-685-66097-4) Rourke Corp.
— Vernunft und Welt. (Phaenomenologica Ser.: No. 36). 1970. lib. bdg. 37.50 (90-247-5042-3) Kluwer Ac.
***Marx & Engels.** On Historical Materialism. Date not set. text ed. 17.50 (0-85315-270-5, Pub. by Lawrence & Wishart UK) Humanities.
— Revolution of Eighteen Forty-Eight: Articles from the Neue Rheinische Zeitung. LC 77-188755. 240p. 1972. 7.50 (0-7178-0339-2) Intl Pubs Co.
Marx & Ledger. The Sisterhood of Steel. (Illus.). 1990. pap. 8.95 (0-913035-23-8) Eclipse Bks.
Marx, et al. German Essays on Socialism in the Nineteenth Century. Stassen, Manfred, ed. (German Library: Vol. 41). 300p. 1989. 29.50 (0-8264-0323-9); pap. text ed. 14.95 (0-8264-0324-7) Continuum.
Marx, Adolf B. Ludwig van Beethoven: Leben und Schaffen, 2 vols. in 1. 709p. 1979. reprint ed. write for info. (3-487-06720-X, Pub. by Georg Olms GW) Lubrecht & Cramer.
Marx, Alexander. Essays in Jewish Biography. LC 73-2217. (Jewish People; History, Religion, Literature Ser.). 1973. reprint ed. 28.95 (0-405-05281-2) Ayer.
— Essays in Jewish Biography. (Brown Classics in Judaica Ser.). 322p. 1986. reprint ed. pap. text ed. 28.00 (0-8191-5022-3) U Pr of Amer.
Marx, Alexander, jt. auth. see Finkelstein, Louis.
Marx, Alexander, ed. see Steinschneider, Moritz.
***Marx, Alfred.** Les Offrandes Vegetales Dans l'Ancien Testament: Du Trigut d'Hommage au Repas Eschatologique. 186p. (FRE.). 1994. text ed. 78.75 (90-04-10136-5) E J Brill.
***Marx, Allison.** The Clueless Gourmet. 160p. 1995. pap. 9.95 (0-8092-3443-2) Contemp Bks.
— Wok This Way. 208p. (Orig.). 1994. pap. text ed. 4.99 (0-425-14187-X) Berkley Pub.
Marx, Anne. A Further Semester: New Poems. 96p. 1985. 12.50 (0-87233-078-8) Bauhan.
— Love in Late Season: New Poems. LC 92-38177. 1992. 17.50 (0-87233-108-3) Bauhan.
Marx, Anthony W. Lessons of Struggle: South African Internal Opposition, 1960-1990. (Illus.). 352p. (C). 1992. pap. text ed. 17.95 (0-19-507348-7) OUP.
Marx, Arthur. My Life with Groucho. LC 91-41254. 1992. pap. 12.95 (0-942637-45-3) Barricade Bks.
— My Life with Groucho. large type ed. LC 92-25179. (General Ser.). 518p. 1993. pap. 16.95 (0-8161-5607-7) G K Hall.
— My Life with Groucho: A Son's Eye View. (Illus.). 287p. 1991. 26.95 (0-86051-494-3, Pub. by Robson UK) Parkwest Pubns.
— The Secret Life of Bob Hope. LC 92-35525. 1993. 21.99 (0-942637-74-7) Barricade Bks.
— Set to Kill. LC 92-33271. 1993. 17.95 (0-942637-80-1) Barricade Bks.
Marx-Aveline, Eleanor, ed. see Ibsen, Henrik.
Marx, Barry, ed. see Byrne, John.
Marx, Barry, ed. see Miller, Frank.
Marx, Barry, ed. see Moore, Alan.
Marx, C. E. Elsevier's Dictionary of Aquaculture. 454p. (ENG, FRE, GER, ITA, LAT & SPA.). 1991. 250.00 (0-8288-9212-1) Fr & Eur.
— Elsevier's Dictionary of Aquaculture: In English, French, Spanish, German, Italian & Latin. 460p. 1991. 141.00 (0-444-88663-X) Elsevier.
***Marx, C. W.** The Devil's Rights & the Redemption in the Literature of Medieval England. (Illus.). 242p. 1995. text ed. 53.00 (0-85991-455-0) Boydell & Brewer.
Marx, Daniel. International Shipping Cartels: A Study of Industrial Self-Regulation by Shipping Conferences. LC 69-13988. xvii, 323p. 1969. reprint ed. text ed. 59.75 (0-8371-1174-9, MASC, Greenwood Pr) Greenwood.
Marx, David, Jr., jt. ed. see Sneed, James H.
Marx, Doug. Homeless. (Troubled Society Ser.). (Illus.). 64p. (YA). (gr. 7 up). 1990. lib. bdg. 17.27 (0-86593-071-6); lib. bdg. 12.95 (0-685-36326-0) Rourke Corp.
— Mythical Beasts. (Unexplained Ser.). 48p. (J). (gr. 3-4). 1991. lib. bdg. 11.95 (1-56065-046-X) Capstone Pr.
— Running Backs. LC 92-8764. (Football Heroes Ser.). (J). 1992. 17.26 (0-86593-151-8); lib. bdg. 12.95 (0-685-59321-5) Rourke Corp.
— Track & Field. LC 93-27154. (J). 1993. write for info. (0-86593-345-6) Rourke Corp.
— Wrestling. LC 93-36544. (Pro-Am Sports Ser.). (J). 1993. write for info. (0-86593-347-2) Rourke Corp.
Marx, Eleanor, ed. see Engels, Friedrich.
Marx, Ellen. Optical Color & Simultaneity. 1983. pap. 45.95 (0-442-23864-9) Van Nos Reinhold.
Marx, Emanuel, ed. see Peters, Emrys.
Marx, Fred, jt. auth. see Cannel, Ward.
Marx, Frederic J. Mass Nonprofit Organizations. LC 92-85281. 1218p. 1992. ring bd. 125.00 (0-944490-48-4) Mass CLE.
Marx, Friedrich, ed. Incerti Auctoris de Ratione Dicendi Ad C. Herennium Libri IV. vi, 554p. 1966. reprint ed. write for info. (0-318-71153-2, Pub. by Georg Olms GW) Lubrecht & Cramer.
***Marx, G.** Nuclear Physics - Nuclear Power. 632p. (C). 1982. 119.00x (963-05-3105-4, Pub. by Akad Kiado HU) St Mut.
Marx, G. F. & Bassell, G. M. Obstetric Analgesia & Anesthesia. (Monographs in Anaesthesiology: Vol. 7). 416p. 1980. 137.00 (0-444-80137-5); pap. 30.00 (0-444-80228-2) Elsevier.
Marx, Gary. Disability Law Compliance Report. 130.00 (0-685-69659-6, ADAR) Warren Gorham & Lamont.
— Protest & Prejudice: A Study of Belief in the Black Community. (Patterns of American Prejudice Ser.). 352p. reprint ed. pap. 1.95 (0-686-95012-7) ADL.
Marx, Gary & Ordovensky, Pat. Working with the News Media. 32p. 1992. pap. 2.50 (0-87652-192-8) Am Assn Sch Admin.
Marx, Gary, et al. Public Relations for Administrators. 126p. (Orig.). 1985. pap. 7.95 (0-87652-101-4, 021-00146) Am Assn Sch Admin.
Marx, Gary S. & Goldberger, Gary G. Disability Law Compliance Manual. 1991. text ed. 135.00 (0-685-69658-8, DLCM) Warren Gorham & Lamont.
Marx, Gary T. Civil Disorder & the Agents of Social Control. (Reprint Series in Sociology). (C). 1993. reprint ed. pap. text ed. 2.90 (0-8290-2682-7, S-731) Irvington.
— Protest & Prejudice: A Study of Belief in the Black Community. LC 78-23898. 256p. 1979. reprint ed. text ed. 59.75 (0-313-20827-1, MAPT, Greenwood Pr) Greenwood.
— Undercover: Police Surveillance in America. (Twentieth Century Fund Book: No. 1). (Illus.). 280p. 1988. 35.00 (0-520-06286-8); pap. 14.00 (0-520-06969-2) U CA Pr.
Marx, Gary T., ed. Muckraking Sociology: Research As Social Criticism. LC 71-186711. 240p. 1972. 32.95 (0-87855-036-4); pap. text ed. 18.95 (0-87855-532-3) Transaction Pubs.
Marx, Gary T. & McAdam, Douglas. Collective Behavior & Collective Behavior Process. 208p. (C). 1993. pap. text ed. write for info. (0-13-142100-X) P-H.
Marx, George. Nuclear Physics-Nuclear Power. 632p. 1982. 225.00x (0-569-08722-8, Pub. by Collets UK) Pro-Am Music.
Marx, George, ed. Bioastronomy: The Next Steps. (C). 1988. lib. bdg. 157.50 (90-277-2714-7) Kluwer Ac.
Marx, Gretchen, jt. auth. see Kottas, John F.
Marx, Groucho. Groucho & Me. LC 83-46068. (Classics of Modern American Humor Ser.). reprint ed. 35.00 (0-404-19938-0) AMS Pr.
— The Groucho Letters: Letters from & to Groucho Marx. LC 94-15249. 319p. 1994. reprint ed. pap. 13.95 (0-306-80607-X) Da Capo.
— Letters of Groucho Marks. 1976. 22.95 (0-8488-1092-9) Amereon Ltd.
Marx, Hans J., jt. ed. see Buelow, George.
Marx, Harpo. Harpo Speaks. 1976. 28.95 (0-8488-0181-4) Amereon Ltd.
Marx, Harpo & Barber, Rowland. Harpo Speaks! LC 84-25038. 482p. 1985. pap. 16.95 (0-87910-036-2) Limelight Edns.
Marx, Ina. Fitness for the Unfit. (Illus.). 152p. 1991. reprint ed. pap. 9.95 (0-8065-1264-4, Citadel Pr) Carol Pub Group.
— Your Are in Charge: The IM Method Total Fitness for the Fit & Not So Fit. 148p. (Orig.). 1990. pap. text ed. 19.95 (0-9626194-0-X) Esperanza Pubns.
Marx, Ina B., et al. Professional Painted Finishes: A Guide to the Art & Business of Decorative Painting. (Illus.). 240p. 1991. 45.00 (0-8230-4418-1, Whitney Lib) Watsn-Guptill.
Marx, Jacqueline A., ed. see Arnoldt, Robert P.
Marx, Jacqueline A., jt. auth. see Arnoldt, Robert P.
Marx, Jean L., ed. A Revolution in Biotechnology. (Illus.). 256p. 1989. 49.95 (0-521-32749-0) Cambridge U Pr.
Marx, Jean L. & Kolata, Gina B. Combating the Number One Killer: The Science Report on Heart Research. LC 78-3626. (AAAS Publication Ser.: No. 78-3). (Illus.). 220p. reprint ed. pap. 62.70 (0-685-20798-6, 2030113) Bks Demand.
Marx, Jeffrey, jt. auth. see Lewis, Carl.
Marx, Jenifer. Pirates & Privateers of the Caribbean. 320p. (C). 1992. 32.50 (0-89464-483-1); pap. 21.50 (0-89464-633-8) Krieger.
Marx, Jenifer, jt. auth. see Marx, Robert.
Marx, Karl. Capital. Engels, Frederick, ed. 870p. (C). 1992. reprint ed. lib. bdg. 49.00 (1-877767-76-X) Univ Publng Hse.
— Capital, Vol. 1. Fowkes, Ben, tr. 1152p. 1992. 14.95 (0-14-044568-4, Penguin Classics) Viking Penguin.
— Capital, Vol. 2. Fernbach, David, tr. 624p. 1993. 13.95 (0-14-044569-2, Penguin Classics) Viking Penguin.
— Capital, Vol. 3. 1993. 14.95 (0-14-044570-6, Penguin Classics) Viking Penguin.
— Capital: A Critique of Political Economy, Vol. 1. Fowkes, Ben, tr. 1977. pap. 15.16 (0-394-72657-X, Vin) Random.
— Capital: A New Abridgment. McLellan, David, ed. (The World's Classics Ser.). (Illus.). 640p. 1995. pap. 14.95 (0-19-283122-4) OUP.
— Capital: Vol. 2-The Process of Circulation of Capital. Engels, Friedrich, ed. LC 67-19764. 558p. 1985. pap. text ed. 7.50 (0-7178-0622-7) Intl Pubs Co.
— Capital, Vol. 1: The Process of Capitalist Production. 820p. 1988. reprint ed. lib. bdg. 49.95 (0-89966-641-8) Buccaneer Bks.
— Capital, Vol. 2: The Process of Circulation of Capital. 558p. 1988. reprint ed. lib. bdg. 39.95 (0-89966-642-6) Buccaneer Bks.
— Capital, Vol. 3: The Process of Capitalist Production As a Whole. 960p. 1988. reprint ed. lib. bdg. 59.95 (0-89966-643-4) Buccaneer Bks.
— The Civil War in France. 144p. 1934. 19.95 (0-88286-035-6) C H Kerr.
— The Civil War in France. 91p. Date not set. pap. 5.00 (0-614-04202-X) Pathfinder NY.
— Class Struggles in France. 2nd ed. 220p. 1967. 3.50 (0-935534-07-5) NY Labor News.
— The Class Struggles in France, 1848-1850. LC 64-19792. 158p. 1964. pap. text ed. 3.95 (0-7178-0030-X) Intl Pubs Co.
— Communist Manifesto. 1992. pap. 3.95 (0-553-21406-3, Bantam Classics) Bantam.
— Contribution to the Critique of Political Economy. Dobb, Maurice, ed. LC 69-20357. 264p. 1989. pap. text ed. 5.95 (0-7178-0041-5) Intl Pubs Co.
— A Contribution to the Critique of Political Economy. 264p. (C). 1972. text ed. 19.95 (0-8464-1287-X) Beekman Pubs.
— Critique of the Gotha Program. LC 69-20357. 116p. (Orig.). 1938. pap. text ed. 3.45 (0-7178-0043-1) Intl Pubs Co.
— Early Political Writings. O'Malley, Joseph, ed. LC 93-31207. (Texts in the History of Political Thought Ser.). 336p. (C). 1994. 44.95 (0-521-34241-4); pap. 11.95 (0-521-34994-X) Cambridge U Pr.
— Early Writings. Hoare, Quintin, ed. Livingston, Rodney & Benton, Gregor, trs. LC 74-29156. 1975. pap. 14.00 (0-394-72005-9, Vin) Random.
— Early Writings. Livingstone, Rodney & Benton, Gregor, trs. 464p. 1992. 10.95 (0-14-044574-9, Penguin Classics) Viking Penguin.
— Economic & Philosophic Manuscripts of 1844. Struik, Dirk J., ed. Milligan, Martin, tr. LC 64-12877. 256p. (C). 1964. pap. text ed. 5.95 (0-7178-0053-9) Intl Pubs Co.
— The Eighteenth Brumaire of Louis Bonaparte. LC 63-23036. 128p. 1963. pap. text ed. 4.95 (0-7178-0056-3) Intl Pubs Co.
— The 18th Brumaire of Louis Bonaparte. 128p. Date not set. pap. write for info. (0-85315-594-1, Pub. by Lawrence & Wishart UK) Humanities.
— The First International & After: Political Writings, Vol. 3. 432p. 1993. 11.95 (0-14-044573-0, Penguin Classics) Viking Penguin.
— Genesis of Capital. 71p. Date not set. pap. 3.00 (0-614-04201-1) Pathfinder NY.
— Grundrisse: Foundations of the Critique of Political Economy. Nickolaus, Martin, tr. & frwd. by. 912p. 1993. 15.95 (0-14-044575-7, Penguin Classics) Viking Penguin.
— Das Kapital. Engels, Friedrich, ed. 356p. 1987. reprint ed. pap. 9.95 (0-89526-931-7) Regnery Pub.
— Karl Marx: A Reader. Elster, Jon, ed. 350p. 1986. pap. 15.95 (0-521-33832-8) Cambridge U Pr.
— Marx on China. 1973. lib. bdg. 250.00 (0-87968-352-X) Gordon Pr.
— Oeuvres, Vol. 1. (FRE.). 1963. lib. bdg. 110.00 (0-8288-3558-6, F16290) Fr & Eur.
— Oeuvres, Vol. 2. (FRE.). 1968. lib. bdg. 110.00 (0-8288-3559-4, F16300) Fr & Eur.
— Oeuvres, Vol. 3. (FRE.). 1982. lib. bdg. 125.00 (0-8288-3560-8, F16380) Fr & Eur.
— Oeuvres: Economie: Economie et Philosophie, Salaire, Principes d'un Critique de l'Economie Politique, Le Capital (Livre deuxieme e Livre Troisieme), Vol. 2. 2112p. 52.50 (0-686-56539-8) Fr & Eur.
— Oeuvres: Economie: Le Capital, Livre Premier (1867), Le Manifeste Communiste, Misere de la Philosophie, etc., Vol. 1. 2000p. 45.00 (0-686-56538-X) Fr & Eur.
— On Society & Social Change. Smelser, Neil J., ed. LC 73-78669. (Heritage of Sociology Ser.). xlii, 206p. 1975. reprint ed. pap. text ed. 12.95 (0-226-50918-4, P567) U Ch Pr.
— The Portable Karl Marx. Kamenka, Eugene, ed. 704p. 1983. pap. 13.95 (0-14-015096-X, Penguin Bks) Viking Penguin.
— Poverty of Philosophy. 205p. 1973. text ed. 22.95 (0-8464-1331-0) Beekman Pubs.
— Poverty of Philosophy. LC 63-10632. 160p. 1992. pap. text ed. 6.95 (0-7178-0701-0) Intl Pubs Co.
— The Poverty of Philosophy. 205p. Date not set. lib. bdg. 9.95 (0-614-04209-7) Pathfinder NY.
— The Poverty of Philosophy. Quelch, H., tr. LC 95-11391. (Great Books in Philosophy Ser.). 227p. 1995. pap. 7.95 (0-87975-977-1) Prometheus Bks.
— Pre-Capitalist Economic Formations. Cohen, Jack, tr. LC 65-16393. 160p. 1989. pap. text ed. 4.95 (0-7178-0165-9) Intl Pubs Co.
— The Revolutions of 1848: Political Writings, Vol. 1. 368p. 1993. 10.95 (0-14-044571-4, Penguin Classics) Viking Penguin.
— Selected Essays. Stenning, H. J., tr. LC 68-16955. (Essay Index Reprint Ser.). 1977. 18.95 (0-8369-0687-X) Ayer.
— Selected Writings. Simon, Lawrence H., ed. LC 94-362. 384p. (Orig.). (C). 1994. lib. bdg. 32.95 (0-87220-219-4); pap. text ed. 8.95 (0-87220-218-6) Hackett Pub.
— Selected Writings in Sociology & Social Philosophy. 1963. pap. text ed. write for info. (0-07-040672-3) McGraw.
— Surveys from Exile, Vol. 2: Political Writings. 384p. 1993. 10.95 (0-14-044572-2, Penguin Classics) Viking Penguin.
— Theories of Surplus Value, 3 vols., Set. 508p. 1970. 135.00 (0-8464-0920-8) Beekman Pubs.
— Value, Price & Profit. Aveling, Eleanor M., ed. Aveling, Edward, tr. 128p. 17.95 (0-88286-030-5); pap. 5.00 (0-88286-033-X) C H Kerr.
— Wage-Labor & Capital. Engels, Friedrich, tr. & intro. by. 59p. pap. 5.00 (0-88286-052-6) C H Kerr.
— Wage-Labour & Capital & Value, Price & Profit. LC 76-10456. 110p. (C). 1976. pap. text ed. 2.95 (0-7178-0470-4) Intl Pubs Co.
***Marx, Karl & Engels, Frederick.** The Collected Works, Vol. 47. 750p. Date not set. write for info. (0-85315-623-9, Pub. by Lawrence & Wishart UK) Humanities.
— The Cologne Communist Trial. Livingstone, Rodney, ed. & tr. by. LC 75-168986. 298p. 1971. 8.50 (0-7178-0240-X) Intl Pubs Co.
— The Communist Manifesto. 1976. 16.95 (0-89190-549-9, Am Repr) Amereon Ltd.
— The Communist Manifesto. (Illus.). 80p. Date not set. pap. write for info. (0-85315-732-4, Pub. by Lawrence & Wishart UK) Humanities.
— The Economic & Philosophic Manuscripts of 1844 & the Communist Manifesto. LC 88-60153. (Great Books in Philosophy). 243p. 1988. pap. 6.95 (0-87975-446-X) Prometheus Bks.
— The German Ideology. Arthur, C. J., ed. & intro. by. 166p. Date not set. pap. write for info. (0-85315-217-9, Pub. by Lawrence & Wishart UK) Humanities.
— Ireland & the Irish Question. 665p. Date not set. lib. bdg. 19.95 (0-614-04213-5) Pathfinder NY.
— El Manifiesto Comunista (The Communist Manifesto) Madrid, Luis, ed. 56p. (Orig.). (SPA.). (C). 1992. pap. 5.00 (0-87348-751-6) Pathfinder NY.
— Marx & Engels on the Trade Unions. LC 90-43327. xx, 240p. 1990. reprint ed. pap. text ed. 8.95 (0-7178-0676-6) Intl Pubs Co.
— Marx & Engels on the U. S. 391p. Date not set. lib. bdg. 15.95 (0-614-04212-7) Pathfinder NY.
— On Colonialism. 4th ed. 383p. Date not set. lib. bdg. 17.95 (0-614-04215-1) Pathfinder NY.
— On the Paris Commune. 356p. Date not set. lib. bdg. 15.95 (0-614-04216-X) Pathfinder NY.
— Selected Correspondence. 3rd rev. ed. 552p. Date not set. lib. bdg. 19.95 (0-614-04217-8) Pathfinder NY.
— Werke, 43 Vols. write for info. (0-318-50414-6) Adlers Foreign Bks.
Marx, Karl & Engels, Fredrich. Communist Manifesto. 1990. reprint ed. pap. 2.50 (0-87348-140-2) Pathfinder NY.
Marx, Karl & Engels, Friedric. Revolution in Spain: A Greenwood Archival Edition. LC 74-27667. 255p. 1975. reprint ed. text ed. 52.50 (0-8371-7909-2, MARS, Greenwood Pr) Greenwood.
— Selected Correspondence: Eighteen Forty-Six to Eighteen Ninety-Five. LC 75-25261. 551p. 1975. reprint ed. text ed. 38.50 (0-8371-8385-5, MAKMF, Greenwood Pr) Greenwood.
Marx, Karl & Engels, Friedrich. Articles on Britain. 466p. 1971. 25.00 (0-8464-0153-3) Beekman Pubs.
— Communist Manifesto. 1988. mass mkt. 4.99 (0-671-67881-7, WSP) PB.
— The Communist Manifesto. Beer, Samuel H., ed. LC 55-10808. (Crofts Classics Ser.). 128p. (C). 1955. pap. text ed. write for info. (0-88295-055-X) Harlan Davidson.
— The Communist Manifesto. 48p. (C). 1948. pap. text ed. 1.75 (0-7178-0241-8) Intl Pubs Co.
— The Communist Manifesto. McLellan, David, ed. (World's Classics Ser.). 128p. 1992. pap. 5.95 (0-19-282954-8) OUP.

An Asterisk (*) at the beginning of an entry indicates that the title is appearing in BIP for the first time.

— Communist Manifesto. Moore, Samuel, tr. 60p. 1978. reprint ed. pap. 3.95 (0-88286-043-7) C H Kerr.
— Communist Manifesto of Marx & Engels. 1985. mass mkt. 5.95 (0-14-044478-5, Penguin Classics) Viking Penguin.
— German Ideology, Pt. 1 & Selections From Pts 2 & 3. Arthur, C. J., ed. LC 71-148517. (C). 1970. pap. text ed. 4.95 (0-7178-0302-3) Intl Pubs Co.
— Karl Marx & Friedrich Engels on Literature & Art. Baxandall, Lee & Morawski, Stefan, eds. (Documents on Marxist Aesthetics Ser.: Vol.I). 192p. 1974. 29.95 (0-88477-000-1); pap. 11.95 (0-88477-001-X) Intl General.
— Manifesto of the Communist Party. 1965. pap. 3.95 (0-8351-2239-5) China Bks.
— Manifesto of the Communist Party. (Reprint Series in Social Sciences). (C). 1993. reprint ed. pap. text ed. 3.90 (0-8290-2655-X, S-455) Irvington.
— Marx & Engels on the Means of Communication. De La Haye, Yves, ed. 176p. (Orig.). 1980. pap. 11.95 (0-88477-013-3) Intl General.
— On Religion. LC 82-17032. (American Academy of Religion, Classics in Religious Studies). 384p. 1982. reprint ed. 24.95 (0-89130-599-8, 01 05 03) Scholars Pr GA.
Marx, Karl, jt. auth. see Engels, Friedrich.
Marx, Karl, tr. see Furet, Francois.
Marx, Karl, jt. auth. see Trotsky, Leon.
Marx, Karl, et al. Anarchism & Anarcho-Syndicalism. 387p. 1973. 25.00 (0-8464-0130-4) Beekman Pubs.
— Anarchism & Anarcho-Syndicalism. 414p. 1983. 23.00 (0-685-17083-7, Pub. by Collets UK) Pro-Am Music.
— The Civil War in France: The Paris Commune. rev. ed. LC 88-24454. 180p. (C). 1993. reprint ed. pap. text ed. 8.95 (0-7178-0666-9) Intl Pubs Co.
— On Historical Materialism. 751p. 1972. 34.95 (0-8464-0683-7) Beekman Pubs.
Marx, Karl T. Random Thoughts: Aphorisms, Reflections. 1956. 5.00 (0-686-31254-6) Freedom Univ-FS.
Marx, Kathryn. Right Brain - Left Brain Photography: The Art & Technique of 70 Modern Masters. LC 93-43031. (Illus.). 1994. 22.50 (0-8174-5717-8, Amphoto) Watsn-Guptill.
Marx, Laurie & Haskin, Joy. Nursing Quality Assurance Handbook: Developing - Updating Your Program for the 1990's. LC 90-63404. 251p. 1991. 39.95 (0-944496-19-9) Precept Pr.
Marx, Leo. Machine in the Garden: Technology & the Pastoral Ideal in America. (Illus.). 1967. pap. 12.95 (0-19-500738-7) OUP.
— The Pilot & the Passenger: Essays on Literature, Technology, & Culture in the United States. 384p. 1989. pap. 10.95 (0-19-504876-8) OUP.
Marx, Leo, ed. Mark Twain: Adventures of Hucklebery Finn. 391p. (C). 1967. pap. write for info. (0-02-376890-8) Macmillan.
Marx, Leo & Trachtenberg, Alan. Three on Technology: New Photographs by Robert Cumming. LC 88-2678. (Illus.). 72p. 1988. pap. 15.00 (0-938437-21-6) MIT List Visual Arts.
Marx, Leo, jt. ed. see Danly, Susan.
Marx, Leo, jt. ed. see Smith, Merritt R.
Marx, Leonie. Benny Anderson: A Critical Study. LC 83-12945. (Contributions to the Study of World Literature Ser.: No. 1). xvii, 161p. 1983. text ed. 45.00 (0-313-24168-6, MAN/, Greenwood Pr) Greenwood.
***Marx, Louis J.** Beyond Punishment. 200p. Date not set. pap. 8.95 (0-7610-0426-2) NW Pub.
Marx, Melvin H. Effects of Cumulative Training Upon Retroactive Inhibition & Transfer. (Comparative Psychology Monographs: No. 94). 1972. reprint ed. pap. 15.00 (0-527-24929-7) Periodicals Srv.
Marx, Melvin H. & Cronan-Hillix, W. A. Systems & Theories in Psychology. 4th ed. (Psychology Ser.). 576p. 1987. text ed. write for info. (0-07-040680-4); Instr's. man. teacher ed, pap. text ed. write for info. (0-07-040681-2) McGraw.
Marx Memorial Library, London Staff. Catalog of the Marx Memorial Library, 3 vols., Set. 1979. lib. bdg. 330.00 (0-8161-0280-5, Hall Library) G K Hall.
Marx, Milton. The Enjoyment of Drama. 2nd ed. LC 61-15689. 1961. pap. text ed. 9.95 (0-89197-609-4) Irvington.
Marx, Miriam. Armor & Ashes. Klein, Elizabeth, ed. (Chapbook Ser.: No. 13). 23p. 1983. pap. 3.00 (0-932884-12-1) Red Herring.
Marx, Mitchell. MVS Power Programming. 1992. text ed. 45.00 (0-07-040763-0) McGraw.
Marx, Morris L., jt. auth. see Larsen, Richard J.
Marx, Muxillo, jt. auth. see Baybn, Damidn.
Marx, Olga, tr. see George, Stefan.
Marx, P., jt. ed. see Dorndorf, W.
Marx, Pamela. Classroom Museums: Touchable Tables for Kids! Grades 3-6. (Illus.). 184p. (Orig.). (J). 1992. pap. 12.95 (0-673-36040-7) GdYrBks.
— Practical Plays. (Illus.). 128p. (Orig.). (J). (gr. 1-5). 1993. pap. 9.95 (0-673-36049-0) GdYrBks.
Marx, Pamela & Olson, Pamela. Exploring Contemporary Themes: Grades 4-6. (Illus.). 300p. (Orig.). 1994. pap. 18.95 (0-673-36010-5) GdYrBks.
Marx, Patricia & Stuart, Charlotte. How to Regain Your Virginity: And Ninety-Nine Other Recent Discoveries About Sex. LC 83-1341. (Illus.). 128p. 1983. pap. 5.95 (0-89480-365-4, 365) Workman Pub.
Marx, Patricia, jt. auth. see Martin, Jane R.
Marx, Patricia, jt. auth. see Martin, JeanRead.
Marx, Patty, jt. auth. see Hodgman, Ann.
Marx, Paul. The Apostle of Life. (Illus.). 204p. 1991. 12.95 (1-55922-028-7); pap. 6.95 (1-55922-029-5) Human Life Intl.
— Confessions of a Prolife Missionary. 1988. 12.95 (1-55922-020-1); pap. 6.95 (1-55922-021-X) Human Life Intl.
— Fighting for Life: The Further Journeys of Fr. Paul Marx. (Illus.). (Orig.). 1989. 12.95 (1-55922-026-0); pap. 6.95 (1-55922-027-9) Human Life Intl.
— The Warehouse Priest. (Illus.). 364p. 1994. 11.00 (1-55922-031-7); pap. 7.00 (1-55922-032-5) Human Life Intl.
Marx, Paul, jt. auth. see Byrne, Gary C.
***Marx, Paul L.** Meggan of Greenwood. 220p. 1995. pap. 8.95 (1-56901-863-4) NW Pub.
***Marx, Pearson.** On the Way to the Venus de Milo. LC 94-25976. 1995. 21.00 (0-671-88335-6) S&S Trade.
Marx, Peter, ed. Contracts in the Information Industry. 1988. 94.95 (0-942774-27-2) Info Indus.
Marx, R. J., jt. auth. see Franklin, Joe.
Marx, Robert. Buried Treasure You Can Find. LC 93-84521. (Illus.). 348p. (Orig.). 1993. pap. 14.95 (0-915920-82-4) Ram Pub.
— Sunken Teasure: How to Find It. Dawson, Hal, ed. LC 90-63186. (Illus.). 400p. 1990. pap. 14.95 (0-915920-74-3) Ram Pub.
Marx, Robert & Marx, Jenifer. New World Shipwrecks, 1492-1825: A Comprehensive Guide. LC 94-65593. (Illus.). 475p. 1994. 16.95 (0-915920-84-0) Ram Pub.
Marx, Robert, et al. Management Live! The Video Workbook. 400p. (C). 1991. pap. text ed. write for info. (0-13-946781-5) P-H.
Marx, Robert F. Following Columbus: The Voyage of the Nina II. (Illus.). 80p. (J). 1991. 17.95 (0-88415-004-6, 5004) Gulf Pub.
— History of Underwater Exploration. 1990. pap. 6.95 (0-486-26487-4) Dover.
— Shipwrecks in Florida Waters: A Billion Dollar Graveyard. LC 78-65775. (Illus.). ix, 147p. 1986. 12.50 (0-913122-55-6); pap. 7.95 (0-913122-51-3) Mickler Hse.
— Shipwrecks in the Americas. (Illus.). 1988. 21.00 (0-8446-6328-X) Peter Smith.
— Shipwrecks in the Americas. (Illus.). 544p. 1987. reprint ed. pap. 10.95 (0-486-25514-X) Dover.
— The Underwater Dig: Introduction to Marine Archaeology. 2nd ed. 252p. 1990. 19.95 (1-55992-031-9, Pisces Bks) Gulf Pub.
— The Voyage of the Nina II. (Illus.). 264p. 1991. 24.95 (0-88415-003-8, 5003) Gulf Pub.
***Marx, Robert W., ed.** The Census Bureau's TIGER System. (Cartography & Geographic Information Systems Journal Ser.: Vol. 17, No. 1). 107p. 1990. 20.00 (0-614-06094-X, AC171) Am Congrs Survey.
Marx, Russell. It's Not Your Fault: Overcoming Anorexia & Bulimia Through Biopsychiatry. 1991. 19.50 (0-394-57402-8, Villard Bks) Random.
Marx, Samuel. Mayer & Thalberg: The Make-Believe Saints. LC 88-31081. (Illus.). 274p. 1988. pap. 12.95 (0-573-60695-1) S French Trade.
Marx, Siegfried & Pfau, Werner. Astrophotography with the Schmidt Telescope. Lamble, Phillip, tr. (Illus.). 168p. (C). 1992. 59.95 (0-521-39549-6) Cambridge U Pr.
Marx, Trish. Echoes of World War Two. LC 92-47369. (YA). (gr. 5 up). 1993. 19.95 (0-8225-4898-4, Lerner Publctns) Lerner Group.
— Hanna's Cold Winter. LC 92-27143. (J). (ps-3). 1993. 18.95 (0-87614-772-4, Carolrhoda) Lerner Group.
Marx, Walter H. Claimed by Vesuvius. (Illus.). 164p. (C). 1975. pap. text ed. 8.25 (0-88334-069-0) Longman.
Marx, Werner. Hegel's Phenomenology of Spirit: A Commentary Based on the Preface & Introduction. Heath, Peter, tr. xxvi, 102p. 1988. pap. text ed. 9.95 (0-226-50923-0) U Ch Pr.
— Heidegger & the Tradition. LC 70-126901. (Studies in Phenomenology & Existential Philosophy). 275p. 1971. pap. 16.95 (0-8101-0656-6) Northwestern U Pr.
— Introduction to Aristotle's Theory of Being. Schine, Robert S., tr. 1977. pap. text ed. 37.50 (90-247-1941-0) Kluwer Ac.
— Is There a Measure on Earth? Foundations for a Non-Metaphysical Ethics. Nenon, Thomas J., Jr. & Lilly, Reginald, trs. 184p. (C). 1987. 22.95 (0-226-50921-4) U Ch Pr.
— Towards a Phenomenological Ethics: Ethos & the Life-World. LC 90-36907. (SUNY Series in Contemporary Continental Philosophy). 153p. (C). 1992. 57.50 (0-7914-0574-5); pap. 18.95 (0-7914-0575-3) State U NY Pr.
Marx, Werner, ed. Heidegger: The University of Freiburg Memorial Lectures. LC 82-5112. 108p. 1982. text ed. 12.50 (0-8207-0154-8) Duquesne.
Marx, Werner G. Proof Positive. pap. 8.95 (1-55673-462-X, 7915) CSS OH.
Marx, Wesley. Waste. LC 79-137805. (Man & His Environment Ser.). 189p. reprint ed. pap. 53.90 (0-317-11223-6, 2013235) Bks Demand.
Marxer, Donna, jt. auth. see Navaretta, Cynthia.
Marxhausen, Evelyn. Simeon & the Baby Jesus. (Arch Bks.). (Illus.). 24p. (J). (gr. k-4). 1986. pap. 1.99 (0-570-06202-0, 59-1425) Concordia.
— When God Laid Down the Law. LC 59-1259. (Arch Bks.). (J). (gr. k-4). 1981. pap. 1.99 (0-570-06142-3) Concordia.
Marxhausen, J. If I Should Die-If I Should Live. (Illus.). 48p. (J). (ps). 1987. pap. 4.99 (0-570-07793-1, 56HH1317) Concordia.
Marxhausen, Joanne. See His Banners Go. (Illus.). 32p. 1975. pap. 3.95 (0-570-03702-6, 12-2604) Concordia.
— Some of My Best Friends Are Trees. LC 56-1640. (Illus.). (Orig.). (J). (ps-4). 1990. pap. 7.99 (0-570-04182-1, 56-1640) Concordia.
Marxist-Leninist Party, U. S. A. Staff. Contra el Pensamiento Mao Zedong!, No. 5. National Executive Committee of the MLP, U. S. A., ed. 65p. (SPA.). 1981. pap. 1.00 (0-86714-017-8) Marxist-Leninist.
— Contra el Pensamiento Mao Zedong, No.1. National Executive Committee of the MLP, U. S. A., ed. (Contra el Pensamiento Mao Zedong Ser.). (Illus.). 49p. (Orig.). (SPA.). 1981. pap. 1.00 (0-86714-013-5) Marxist-Leninist.
— Contra el Pensamiento Mao Zedong!, Nos. 2 & 3. National Executive Committee of the MLP, U. S. A., ed. 61p. (SPA.). 1981. pap. 1.00 (0-86714-014-3) Marxist-Leninist.
Marxist-Leninist Party, USA & Marxist-Leninist Party, USA Staff. Zionism Is Racism in the Service of Imperialism. (Illus.). 112p. (Orig.). 1983. pap. 1.00 (0-86714-025-9) Marxist-Leninist.
Marxist-Leninist Party, USA Staff. Adelante Por el Camino Del Congreso Constituyente. National Executive Committee of the MLP, USA, ed. (Illus.). 52p. (Orig.). (SPA.). 1981. pap. 1.00 (0-86714-012-7) Marxist-Leninist.
— El Avance del Movimiento Revolucionario Require de una Enconada Lucha Contra la Socialdemocracia y el Liquidacionismo. 93p. (SPA.). 1982. pap. 1.00 (0-86714-023-2) Marxist-Leninist.
— Mao, Browder & Social-Democracy. National Executive Committee of Mlp, Usa, ed. 50p. (Orig.). 1980. pap. 1.00 (0-86714-001-1) Marxist-Leninist.
— Mao, Browder y la Social-Democracia. 75p. (Orig.). (SPA.). 1980. pap. 1.00 (0-86714-004-6) Marxist-Leninist.
— No to U. S. Imperialist War Preparations. National Executive Committee of the MLP, USA, ed. (Illus.). 81p. 1980. pap. 1.00 (0-86714-003-8) Marxist-Leninist.
— La Nueva Estrategia Browderiand del 'CPUSA-ML'de Weisberg. 52p. 1981. pap. 1.00 (0-86714-019-4) Marxist-Leninist.
— Songbook: Down with Ronald Reagan, Chieftain of Capitalist Reaction & Other Songs of Revolutionary Struggle & Socialism. (Illus.). 84p. 1982. pap. 1.00 (0-86714-024-0) Marxist-Leninist.
— The Struggle for the Party Versus Chinese Revisionism. National Executive Committee of the MLP, USA, ed. 73p. 1980. pap. 1.00 (0-86714-005-4) Marxist-Leninist.
— La Verdad sobre las Relaciones entre el Partido Marxista de los EUA y el Partido Communista del Canada (M-L) 86p. (SPA.). 1981. pap. 1.00 (0-86714-022-4) Marxist-Leninist.
Marxist-Leninist Party, USA Staff, jt. auth. see Marxist-Leninist Party, USA.
Marxsen, Willi. The Beginnings of Christology: Together with the Lord's Supper As a Christological Problem. LC 79-7384. 127p. reprint ed. pap. 36.20 (0-8357-7101-6, 2029295) Bks Demand.
— Jesus & the Church: The Beginnings of Christianity. Devenish, Philip E., tr. & intro. by. LC 92-33155. 1992. pap. 16.95 (1-56338-053-6) TPI PA.
— New Testament Foundations for Christian Ethics. Dean, O. C., Jr., tr. LC 92-47447. 1993. 17.00 (0-8006-2749-0, Fortress Pr) Augsburg Fortress.
Marxuach, Carmen I. Evaristo Ribera Chevremont: Voz de Vanguardia. 323p. 1987. pap. 15.00 (0-8477-3524-9) U of PR Pr.
Mary. All That You Are. 1959. pap. 8.95 (0-87516-055-7) DeVorss.
— Love. 1959. pap. 3.00 (0-87516-056-5) DeVorss.
Mary, A., ed. see Tristan et Iseut.
Mary, Andre. Tristan. (FRE.). 1973. pap. 11.95 (0-7859-4014-6) Fr & Eur.
Mary, Andre, ed. see Villon, Francois.
Mary B, ed. Stepping Stones to Recovery for Women. LC 89-17751. 240p. (Orig.). 1990. pap. 6.95 (0-934125-15-5) Hazelden.
Mary, Bevis, jt. auth. see Jeneanne, Sieck.
Mary da Bergamo, Cajetan. Humility of Heart. Vaughan, Herbert C., tr. 240p. 1978. reprint ed. pap. 7.00 (0-89555-067-9) TAN Bks Pubs.
Mary Eleanore. Certitudes. LC 68-16956. (Essay Index Reprint Ser.). 1977. 18.95 (0-8369-0688-8) Ayer.
Mary Francis. Right to Be Merry. LC 73-6850. 1973. reprint ed. pap. 6.50 (0-8199-0506-2, Frncscn Herld) Franciscan Pr.
Mary Ingraham Bunting Institute of Radcliffe College Staff. Collected Visions: Women Artist at the Bunting Institute, 1961-1986. 96p. 1986. pap. 7.95 (0-9601774-2-6) Radcliffe Coll.
Mary, J. Y. & Rigaut, J. P., eds. Quantitative Image Analysis in Cancer Cytology & Histology. 406p. 1987. 124.00 (0-444-80805-1) Elsevier.
Mary Louise, ed. Over the Bent World. LC 73-105031. (Essay Index Reprint Ser.). 1977. 44.95 (0-8369-1676-X) Ayer.
Mary, M. Family Relationships. 24p. (Orig.). 1985. pap. 1.55 (0-89486-334-7, 5285B) Hazelden.
Mary Of Agreda. Mystical City of God, 4 vols., 1. 2676p. 1971. write for info. (0-911988-27-0) AMI Pr.
— Mystical City of God, 4 vols., 2. 2676p. 1971. write for info. (0-911988-28-9) AMI Pr.
— Mystical City of God, 4 vols., 3. 2676p. 1971. write for info. (0-911988-29-7) AMI Pr.
— Mystical City of God, 4 vols., 4. 2676p. 1971. write for info. (0-911988-30-0) AMI Pr.
— Mystical City of God, 4 vols., Set. 2676p. 1971. 49.00 (0-911988-26-2) AMI Pr.
Mary of Agreda & Mary Of Agreda. Mystical City of God. abr. ed. 794p. 1981. pap. 12.50 (0-911988-31-9) AMI Pr.
Mary Of Agreda, jt. auth. see Mary of Agreda.
***Mary, Sylvia.** Pauline & Johannine Mysticism. 1964. 49.50 (0-614-00266-4) Elliots Bks.
Maryann, Barber, jt. auth. see Grauer, Robert T.
Maryanoff, Bruce E. & Maryanoff, Cynthia A., eds. Advances in Medicinal Chemistry, Vol. 1. 1991. 90.25 (1-55938-170-1) Jai Pr.
Maryanoff, Cynthia A., jt. ed. see Maryanoff, Bruce E.
Maryanov, Gerald S. Decentralization in Indonesia as a Political Problem. (Cornell University, Modern Indonesia Project, Monograph Ser.). 126p. reprint ed. pap. 36.00 (0-317-09553-6, 2010637) Bks Demand.
Maryanski, Alexandra & Turner, Jonathan H. The Social Cage: Human Nature & the Evolution of Society. LC 92-17311. 323p. (C). 1992. 39.50 (0-8047-2002-9); pap. 12.95 (0-8047-2003-7) Stanford U Pr.
Maryatt, Kitty, ed. see Zaitlin, Joyce.
Marydass, C. A Compendium of Shakespeare. 180p. (YA). (gr. 7 up). 1988. text ed. 25.00 (81-207-0713-3, Pub. by Sterling Pubs II) Apt Bks.
Marye, George T. Nearing the End in Imperial Russia. LC 71-115562. (Russia Observed, Series I). 1970. reprint ed. 24.95 (0-405-03048-7) Ayer.
Marygrove College, Detroit, Michigan Staff. Into Her Own: The Status of Woman from Ancient Times to the End of the Middle Ages. LC 76-38319. (Biography Index Reprint Ser.). 1977. reprint ed. 23.95 (0-8369-8123-5) Ayer.
Maryk, Denis, jt. auth. see Samson, Judith.
Maryland Department of Agriculture Staff. Maryland Seafood Cookbook, No. II. 72p. 1994. pap. 6.95 (1-885457-02-2) Eastwind MD.
— Maryland Seafood Cookbook, No. III. 72p. 1994. pap. 6.95 (1-885457-03-0) Eastwind MD.
***Maryland Head Injury Foundation Staff.** Why Did It Happen on a School Day? My Family's Experience with Brain Injury. (Illus.). 40p. (Orig.). (J). (gr. k-6). 1995. pap. 7.00 (0-927093-02-2) Natl Head Injury.
Maryland Historical Trust Staff. Assessment of Present Level of Historic Standing Structures Survey Coverage in Maryland Using U. S. Census of Housing Data. (White Papers Series on Preservation Planning: No. 5). 10p. 1987. 2.00 (1-878399-23-3) Div Hist Cult Progs.
— Historic Preservation & Affordable Housing in Maryland: A Summary. (White Papers Series on Preservation Planning: No. 8). 10p. 1987. 2.00 (1-878399-26-8) Div Hist Cult Progs.
— How to Use Historic Contexts in Maryland: A Guide for Survey, Registration, Protection & Treatment Projects. (White Papers Series on Preservation Planning: No. 9). 25p. 1987. 2.00 (1-878399-27-6) Div Hist Cult Progs.
— The Maryland Comprehensive Historic Preservation Plan: Planning the Future of Maryland's Past. 312p. 1986. 10.00 (1-878399-28-4) Div Hist Cult Progs.
— Recommended Research Issues for the Future Study of the State's Above-Ground Historic Resources. (White Papers Series on Preservation Planning: No. 4). 11p. 1987. 2.00 (1-878399-22-5) Div Hist Cult Progs.
— Regional & County-by-County Assessment of Archaeological Survey Coverage in Maryland. (White Papers Series on Preservation Planning: No. 1). 50p. 1987. 2.00 (1-878399-19-5) Div Hist Cult Progs.
— Regional & County-by-County Assessment of Historic Standing Structures Survey Coverage in Maryland. (White Papers Series on Preservation Planning: No. 2). 37p. 1987. 2.00 (1-878399-20-9) Div Hist Cult Progs.
Maryland House of Correction Writers' Club Staff. Hear My Cry! (Illus.). 64p. 1991. per. 8.95 (0-932616-36-4) New Poets Chestnut Hills.
Maryland-National Capital Park & Planning Commission Staff. Landmarks of Prince George's County: Architectural Photographs. LC 92-39873. (Illus.). 144p. 1993. 29.95 (0-8018-4628-5) Johns Hopkins.
Maryland State Dept. of Education, ed. see Cyzyk, Janet L.
***Maryniak.** A Hiking Guide to the National Parks & Historic Sites of Newfoundland. Date not set. per. 12.95 (0-86492-150-0, Pub. by Goose Ln Edits CN) InBook.
Maryon, Herbert. Metalwork & Enamelling. 4th ed. (Illus.). 1971. pap. 7.95 (0-486-22702-2) Dover.
Maryua, Saiichi. Singular Rebellion. Keene, Dennis, tr. 420p. 1990. pap. 6.95 (0-87011-989-3) Kodansha.
Marz, Eduard. Austrian Banking & Financial Policy: Creditanstalt at a Turning Point 1913-23. Kessler, Charles, tr. LC 84-15148. (Illus.). 672p. 1985. text ed. 39.95 (0-312-06124-2) St Martin.
— Joseph Schumpeter: Scholar, Teacher & Politician. 192p. (C). 1992. text ed. 35.00 (0-300-03876-3) Yale U Pr.
Marz, R. Franz Marc. (Illus.). (C). 1987. text ed. 80.00 (0-685-40273-8, Pub. by Collets) St Mut.
— Green Lantern: A New Start. Kahan, ed. (Illus.). 120p. Date not set. pap. 12.95 (1-56389-222-7) DC Comics.
— Green Lantern: Emerald Twilight. Kahan, B., ed. (Illus.). 80p. 1994. pap. 5.95 (1-56389-164-6) DC Comics.
— Marac, Franz. 72p. (C). 1987. 80.00 (0-685-34434-7, Pub. by Collets) St Mut.
***Marz, Reinhard.** Integrated Optics: Design & Modeling. 1994. write for info. (0-89006-665-5) Artech Hse.
— Integrated Optics: Design & Modeling. LC 94-37147. 336p. 1995. pap. 79.00 (0-89006-668-X) Artech Hse.
Marz, Roy. The Island-Maker. LC 82-17282. 100p. (Orig.). 1982. pap. 6.00 (0-87886-120-3, Greenfld Rev Pr) Greenfld Rev Lit.
Marz, Valerie, ed. see Capacchione, Lucia.
Marzahl, Peter. Town in the Empire: Government, Politics, & Society in Seventeenth-Century Popayan. LC 77-620062. (Latin American Monographs: No. 45). 242p. 1978. pap. text ed. 6.95 (0-292-78029-X) U of Tex Pr.
***Marzan, Julio.** The Numinous Site: The Poetry of Luis Pales Matos. LC 94-47234. 1995. write for info. (0-8386-3581-4) Fairleigh Dickinson.
— The Spanish American Roots of William Carlos Williams. LC 93-38636. 280p. (C). 1994. text ed. 30.00 (0-292-75160-5) U of Tex Pr.
— Translations Without Originals. 50p. 1986. pap. 3.95 (0-918408-23-7) Reed & Cannon.

An Asterisk (*) at the beginning of an entry indicates that the title is appearing in BIP for the first time.

Marzan, Julio, ed. Inventing a Word: An Anthology of Twentieth-Century Puerto Rican Poetry. LC 79-28472. 1980. text ed. 39.00 (*0-231-05010-0*); pap. text ed. 15.50 (*0-231-05011-9*) Col U Pr.

Marzano, Jana S., jt. auth. see Marzano, Robert J.

Marzano, Kathryn M. & Lyons, Pauline D. The Complete Review of Radiography. LC 86-9117. (Red Bks.). 252p. 1986. pap. text ed. 27.95 (*0-8273-4233-0*) Delmar.

Marzano, Robert, et al. Dimensions in Thinking: A Framework for Curriculum & Instruction. 176p. 1988. 10.00 (*0-8106-0230-X*) NEA.

Marzano, Robert J., et al. Assessing Student Outcomes: Performance Assessment Using the Dimensions of Learning Model. LC 93-41882. 1993. write for info. (*0-08-720225-5*, Pergamon Pr) Elsevier.

Marzano, Robert J. Cultivating Thinking in English & the Language Arts. (Illus.). 89p. 1991. pap. 9.95 (*0-8141-0991-8*) NCTE.

Marzano, Robert J. & Marshall, Stephanie P., prefs. A Different Kind of Classroom: Teaching with Dimensions of Learning. LC 92-9069. 191p. (Orig.). 1992. pap. 15.95 (*0-87120-192-5*, 611-92107) Assn Supervision.

Marzano, Robert J. & Marzano, Jana S. A Cluster Approach to Elementary Vocabulary Instruction. LC 88-2923. (Reading Aids Ser.). (Illus.). 270p. reprint ed. pap. 77.00 (*0-7837-4589-3*, 2044308) Bks Demand.

Marzano, Robert J. & Paynter, Diane E. New Approaches to Literacy: Helping Students Develop Reading & Writing Skills. (Psychology in the Classroom Ser.). 167p. (Orig.). 1994. pap. text ed. 17.95 (*1-55798-249-X*) Am Psychol.

Marzano, Robert J., et al. Assessing Student Outcomes: Performance Assessment Using the Dimensions of Learning Model. LC 93-41882. 138p. 1993. pap. 13.95 (*0-87120-225-5*, 611-93179) Assn Supervision.

Marzaroli & Grassie. Shades of Scotland 1956-1988. (By Appointment Only Ser.). 224p. 1989. 34.95 (*1-85158-213-4*, Pub. by Mnstream UK) Trafalgar.

Marzaroli, Oscar. Glasgow's People, 1956-1988. (Illus.). 192p. 1994. 34.95 (*1-85158-592-3*, Pub. by Mnstream UK) Trafalgar.

— One Man's World: Photographs 1955-1984. 112p. 1984. 40.00 (*0-906474-38-8*, Pub. by Third Eye Centre UK) St Mut.

Marze, Elaine H. Up from the Ashes. 1987. 11.75 (*0-318-40097-9*) Phoenix Soc.

Marzell. Woerterbuch der Deutschen Pflanzennamen. 59.95 (*0-8288-7889-7*, M7031) Fr & Eur.

— Woerterbuch der Deutschen Pflanzennamen, Nos. 1-22. fac. ed. (GER.). 550.00 (*0-686-56642-4*, M-7031) Fr & Eur.

Marzelli, Robert L. Massachusetts Real Estate. LC 83-82338. (Massachusetts Practice Systems Library). 1983. ring bd. 220.00 (*0-317-00786-6*) Lawyers Cooperative.

— Massachusetts Real Estate. suppl. ed. LC 83-82338. (Massachusetts Practice Systems Library). 1993. Suppl. 1993. 70.00 (*0-317-03242-9*) Lawyers Cooperative.

— Real Estate Taxes & Abatements Handbook. 301p. 1980. 34.00 (*0-318-03671-1*) Lawyers Weekly.

Marzen, Stephen, et al. Destruction of Evidence: 1992 Cumulative Supplement. 280p. 1992. pap. 65.00 (*0-471-57677-8*) Wiley.

Marzeno, Robert J., et al. Dimensions of Thinking: A Framework for Curriculum & Instruction. LC 87-72733. 162p. (Orig.). (C). 1988. pap. 10.00 (*0-87120-148-8*, 611-87040) Assn Supervision.

Marziali, Elsa & Munroe-Blum, Heather. Interpersonal Group Psychotherapy for Borderline Personality Disorder. LC 94-18148. 1994. text ed. 33.00 (*0-465-08893-7*) Basic.

Marzilli, Luigi G., jt. ed. see Eichhorn, Gunther L.

Marzilli, Richard. Understanding the Personal Auto Policy. 1991. 39.50 (*1-56461-039-X*, 46120) Rough Notes.

Marzilli, Vincent, II. Return of the Nighthawks. (Illus.). 56p. (Orig.). (J). (gr. k-6). 1987. pap. 7.95 (*0-9617809-1-6*) Vincent Marzilli.

— Where Ravens Fly. (Illus.). 64p. (Orig.). (J). (gr. k-6). 1987. reprint ed. pap. 7.95 (*0-9617809-0-8*) Vincent Marzilli.

Marzillier, John S. & Hall, John, eds. What Is Clinical Psychology? 2nd ed. (Illus.). 368p. 1992. 65.00 (*0-19-262169-6*); pap. 29.95 (*0-19-262168-8*) OUP.

Marzinotto, Paul J. The Connecticut Summary Process Manual. 259p. 1986. ring bd. 115.00 (*0-910051-04-6*) CT Law Trib.

— Connecticut Summary Process Manual - Second Supplement. 1991. ring bd. 15.00 (*0-910051-14-3*) CT Law Trib.

Marzio, Peter C. The Art Crusade. LC 75-20404. (Smithsonian Studies in History & Technology: No. 34). (Illus.). 102p. reprint ed. pap. 29.10 (*0-8357-5758-7*, 2004691) Bks Demand.

Marzio, Peter C., jt. auth. see Nygren, Edward J.

Marzio, Peter C., et al. The Museum of Fine Arts, Houston: A Permanent Legacy. LC 89-83701. (Illus.). 352p. 1989. 65.00 (*1-55595-022-1*) Hudson Hills.

Marzishevskaya, K., et al. Diccionario Espanol-Ruso, Ruso-Espanol. 2nd ed. 512p. (RUS & SPA.). 1992. pap. 29.95 (*0-7859-1087-5*, 5200021677) Fr & Eur.

Marzluff, John M. & Balda, Russell P. The Pinyon Jay: Behavioural Ecology of a Colonial & Cooperative Corvid. (Poyser Popular Bird Bks.). (Illus.). 344p. 1992. text ed. 39.95 (*0-85661-064-X*, 784664) Acad Pr.

Marzo, M. & Puigdefabergas, C., eds. Alluvial Sedimentation. LC 92-36455. (International Association of Sedimentologists Special Publication Ser.: No. 17). 1994. pap. write for info. (*0-632-03545-5*) Blackwell Sci.

Marzol, Gonzalo C. Aspectos Del Taller Poetico De Jaime Gil de Biedma. Date not set. 44.70 (*0-685-69529-8*) Scripta.

Marzola, Alessandra & Silva, Francesco, eds. John Maynard Keynes: Language & Methods. (Advances in Economic Methodology Ser.). 232p. 1994. 59.95 (*1-85278-923-9*, Pub. by E Elgar Pub UK) Ashgate Pub Co.

Marzolf, Marion T. The Danish-Language Press in America: Doctoral Dissertation, the University of Michigan, 1972. Scott, Franklyn D., ed. LC 78-15202. (Scandinavians in America Ser.). (Illus.). 1979. lib. bdg. 25.95 (*0-405-11650-0*) Ayer.

Marzoli, G. P. & Versontini, S. Warren's Operation. (Illus.). 90p. 1981. 63.00 (*0-387-10785-1*) Spr-Verlag.

Marzolllo, Jean. I Spy Fantasy: A Book of Picture Riddles. LC 93-44814. (J). 1994. 12.95 (*0-590-46295-4*) Scholastic Inc.

Marzollo, Claude, jt. auth. see Marzollo, Jean.

Marzollo, Claudio. Kenny & the Little Kickers. (Illus.). 32p. (J). 1992. pap. 2.95 (*0-590-45417-X*) Scholastic Inc.

Marzollo, Jean. Cannonball Chris. LC 86-31512. (Stepping into Reading Bks.). (Illus.). 48p. (J). (gr. 2-3). 1987. pap. 3.50 (*0-394-88512-0*) Random Bks Yng Read.

— Close Your Eyes. LC 76-42935. (Pied Piper Bks.). (Illus.). (J). (ps-2). 1978. lib. bdg. 12.89 (*0-8037-1610-9*) Dial Bks Young.

— Close Your Eyes. (Pied Piper Bks.). (Illus.). (J). (ps-00). 1981. 4.95 (*0-8037-1617-6*) Dial Bks Young.

— Fathers & Babies: How Babies Grow & What They Need from You from Birth to 18 Months. LC 92-53386. (Illus.). 192p. 1993. pap. 12.00 (*0-06-096908-3*, PL) HarpC.

— Fathers & Toddlers: How Toddlers Grow & What They Need from You, from 18 Months to Three Years. (Illus.). 192p. (Orig.). 1994. pap. 10.00 (*0-06-096907-5*, PL) HarpC.

— Feliz Cumpleanos, Martin Luther King: Happy Birthday, Martin Luther King. Romo, Alberto, tr. (Illus.). (SPA.). (J). (gr. 3-7). 1994. pap. 4.95 (*0-590-47507-X*) Scholastic Inc.

— Getting Your Period. (J). (gr. 4-7). 1993. pap. 6.99 (*0-14-036193-6*) Puffin Bks.

— Getting Your Period: A Book about Menstruation. LC 88-3986. (Illus.). 112p. (J). (gr. 4 up). 1989. 13.95 (*0-8037-0355-4*); 6.95 (*0-8037-0356-2*) Dial Bks Young.

— Halloween Cats. (J). (ps-3). 1992. pap. 2.50 (*0-590-46026-9*) Scholastic Inc.

— Happy Birthday, Martin Luther King. LC 91-42137. (Illus.). 32p. (J). (ps-3). 1993. 14.95 (*0-590-44065-9*) Scholastic Inc.

— Happy Birthday, Martin Luther King. (J). (ps-3). 1993. pap. 19.95 (*0-590-72828-8*) Scholastic Inc.

— I Am Water. LC 95-10528. (Hello Reader! Ser.: Level 1). (Illus.). (J). 1996. write for info. (*0-590-26587-3*) Scholastic Inc.

— I Spy Funhouse. LC 92-16425. (I Spy Ser.). (Illus.). 40p. (J). 1993. 12.95 (*0-590-46293-8*) Scholastic Inc.

— I Spy, Mystery: A Book of Picture Riddles. LC 92-40863. (Illus.). (J). 1993. 12.95 (*0-590-46294-6*) Scholastic Inc.

— I Spy School Days: A Book of Picture Riddles. LC 94-43629. (Illus.). (J). 1995. 12.95 (*0-590-48135-5*) Scholastic Inc.

— I'm a Seed. LC 95-13237. (Hello Reader! Ser.: Level 1). (Illus.). (J). 1996. write for info. (*0-590-26586-5*, Cartwheel) Scholastic Inc.

— I'm Tyrannosaurus! A Book of Dinosaur Rhymes. (Illus.). 32p. (J). (ps-1). 1993. pap. 2.50 (*0-590-44641-X*, Cartwheel) Scholastic Inc.

— In Fourteen Ninety-Two. (J). (ps-3). 1994. pap. 4.95 (*0-590-49442-2*) Scholastic Inc.

— My First Book of Biographies. LC 92-27623. (Illus.). (J). 1994. 14.95 (*0-590-45014-X*) Scholastic Inc.

— The Pizza Pie Slugger. LC 88-33379. (Stepping Stone Bks.). (Illus.). 64p. (Orig.). (J). (gr. 2-4). 1989. pap. 3.99 (*0-394-82881-X*) Random Bks Yng Read.

— The Pizza Pie Slugger. LC 88-33379. (Stepping Stone Bks.). (Illus.). 64p. (Orig.). (J). (gr. 2-4). 1989. lib. bdg. 6.99 (*0-394-92881-4*) Random Bks Yng Read.

— Pretend You're a Cat. Fogelman, Phyllis J., ed. LC 89-34546. (Illus.). 32p. (J). (ps-3). 1990. 14.99 (*0-8037-0773-8*); lib. bdg. 12.89 (*0-8037-0774-6*) Dial Bks Young.

— Rebus Treasure. 1986. 6.95 (*0-416-95530-4*) Routledge Chapman & Hall.

— Red Ribbon Rosie. LC 87-29641. (Stepping Stone Bks.). (Illus.). 64p. (Orig.). (J). (gr. 2-4). 1988. lib. bdg. 5.99 (*0-394-99608-9*); pap. 3.99 (*0-394-89608-4*) Random Bks Yng Read.

— Slam Dunk Saturday. (Stepping Stone Bks.). (Illus.). 64p. (Orig.). (J). (gr. 2-4). 1994. pap. 2.99 (*0-679-82366-2*) Random Bks Yng Read.

— Slam Dunk Saturday. (Stepping Stone Bks.). (Illus.). 64p. (Orig.). (J). (gr. 2-4). 1994. lib. bdg. 7.99 (*0-679-92366-7*) Random Bks Yng Read.

— The Snow Angel. LC 94-31997. (Illus.). (J). 1995. write for info. (*0-590-48748-5*) Scholastic Inc.

— Soccer Sam. LC 86-47533. (Step into Reading Bks.). (Illus.). 48p. (J). (gr. 1-3). 1987. pap. 3.50 (*0-394-88406-X*) Random Bks Yng Read.

— Soccer Sam. LC 86-47533. (Step into Reading Bks.). (Illus.). 48p. (J). (gr. 1-3). 1987. lib. bdg. 7.99 (*0-394-98406-4*) Random Bks Yng Read.

— Sun Song. (Illus.). 32p. (J). 1995. 14.95 (*0-06-020787-6*, HarpT) HarpC.

— Sun Song. (J). 1995. lib. bdg. 14.89 (*0-06-020788-4*, HarpT) HarpC.

— The Teddy Bear Book. LC 87-24538. (Illus.). 32p. (J). (ps-2). 1992. pap. 3.99 (*0-14-054546-8*, Puff Pied Piper) Puffin Bks.

— Ten Cats Have Hats. (J). (ps). 1994. 6.95 (*0-590-20656-7*) Scholastic Inc.

— Three Little Kittens. (Illus.). 32p. (Orig.). (J). (ps-00). 1986. pap. 2.50 (*0-590-43713-5*) Scholastic Inc.

— Valentine Cats. LC 94-47816. (Read with Me Paperbacks Ser.). (Illus.). (J). 1996. pap. write for info. (*0-590-47596-7*) Scholastic Inc.

— Veo: Un Libro de Adivinanzas Ilustradas. (Illus.). (J). (ps-3). 1994. 12.95 (*0-590-48635-7*, Cartwheel) Scholastic Inc.

Marzollo, Jean & Bjorkman, Steven. In 1492. (J). 1992. pap. 19.95 (*0-590-72737-0*) Scholastic Inc.

Marzollo, Jean & Carson, Carol D. I Spy: A Book of Picture Riddles. (Illus.). 48p. (J). 1992. 12.95 (*0-590-45087-5*, Cartwheel) Scholastic Inc.

Marzollo, Jean & Marzollo, Claude. Ruthie's Rude Friends. braille ed. 14p. (J). 1991. Braille. vinyl bd. 1.12 (*1-56956-311-X*, BR8065) W A T Braille.

Marzollo, Jean & Savage, Beth. Early Learning Mastery Masters. Incl. Letters & Sounds. (J). (ps-2). 1981. pap. 5.95 (*0-8224-4471-2*); Numbers & Number Values. (J). (ps-2). 1981. pap. 5.95 (*0-8224-4472-0*); Storytelling. (J). (ps-2). 1981. pap. 5.95 (*0-8224-4473-9*); Thinking Skills. (J). (ps-2). 1981. pap. 5.95 (*0-8224-4474-7*); Colors & Shapes. pap. 5.95 (*0-8224-4477-1*); Words. (J). (ps-2). pap. 5.95 (*0-8224-4480-1*); Concepts. (J). (ps-2). 1981. pap. 5.95 (*0-8224-4478-X*); Time. (J). (ps-2). 1981. pap. 5.95 (*0-8224-4479-8*); (Makemaster Bk.). (J). (ps-2). 1981. Set pap. write for info. (*0-318-55296-5*) Fearon Teach Aids.

Marzollo, Jean & Wick, Walter. I Spy Christmas. (J). 1992. bds. 12.95 (*0-590-45846-9*, Cartwheel) Scholastic Inc.

Marzollo, Jean, jt. auth. see Adams, Patricia.

Marzorati, Gerald, jt. ed. see Whittemore, Katharine.

Marzouk, M. A., et al. Operative Dentistry: Modern Theory & Practice. 477p. 1985. 47.50 (*0-912791-15-2*) Ishiyaku Euro.

Marzouk, Tobey. Protecting Your Proprietary Rights in the Computer & High-Technology Industries. LC 88-70782. 208p. 1988. 5.95 (*0-8186-8754-1*) IEEE Comp Soc.

Marzuez-Sterling, Manuel. Hondo Corre el Cauto. LC 90-81222. (Coleccion Caniqui Ser.). 404p. (Orig.). (SPA.). 1990. pap. 19.95 (*0-89729-554-4*) Ediciones.

Marzuki, S. & Dilts, R. Bintang Anda: A Game Process for Community Development. (Technical Notes Ser.: No. 18). 21p. (Orig.). (C). 1982. pap. 2.00 (*0-932288-63-4*) Ctr Intl Ed U of MA.

Marzulli, Francis N. & Maibach, Howard I., eds. Dermatotoxicology. 4th ed. 800p. 1991. 127.00 (*1-56032-055-9*) Hemisp Pub.

Marzullo & Snyder. Manual De Liberacion Para Obreros Cristianos (Manual for the Deliverance Worker) (SPA.). 1994. 3.75 (*958-95462-0-X*, 550061) Editorial Unilit.

Mas-Colell, Andreu. The Theory of General Economic Equilibrium. (Econometric Society Monographs). 369p. 1985. 64.95 (*0-521-26514-2*) Cambridge U Pr.

— The Theory of General Economic Equilibrium. (Econometric Society Monographs: No. 9). (Illus.). 398p. (C). 1990. pap. 29.95 (*0-521-38870-8*) Cambridge U Pr.

Mas-Colell, Andreu, ed. Noncooperative Approaches to the Theory of Perfect Competition. LC 82-13936. 1982. text ed. 66.00 (*0-12-476750-8*) Acad Pr.

Mas-Colell, Andreu, jt. ed. see Hildenbrand, W.

***Mas-Colell, Andreu, et al.** Microeconomic Theory. (Illus.). 1056p. 1995. text ed. 49.95 (*0-19-507340-1*) OUP.

Mas-Lopez, Edita, tr. & intro. The Last Poems of Miguel De Unamuno. LC 73-4295. 121p. 1974. 24.50 (*0-8386-1288-1*) Fairleigh Dickinson.

Mas Masumoto, David. Epitaph for a Peach: Four Seasons on My Family Farm. 240p. 1995. 20.00 (*0-06-251024-X*) Harper SF.

Masaaki Kitahara. Tinnitus. LC 99-12777. (Illus.). 140p. 1988. 66.00 (*0-89640-174-X*) Igaku-Shoin.

Masabuchi, M., jt. auth. see Yang Wen-Jei.

Masada, E, jt. ed. see Carli, A De.

Masafumi Shiomitsu. Dynamic Kicking Method. (Illus.). 130p. (Orig.). 1985. pap. 10.95 (*0-86568-069-8*, 540) Unique Pubns.

Masahiko, Aoki & Dore, Ronald, eds. The Japanese Firm: Sources of Competitive Strength. (Illus.). 424p. 1994. 49.95 (*0-19-828815-8*) OUP.

Masahiro Chatani. Origamic Architecture: Tour of Nara, Ancient Capital of Japan. 82p. 1993. pap. 32.95 (*4-395-27043-3*, Pub. by Shokokusha JA) Bks Nippan.

***Masahiro Tanimori.** A Handbook of Japanese Grammar. (Tuttle Language Library). 352p. (Orig.). (ENG & JPN.). 1994. pap. 14.95 (*0-8048-1940-8*) C E Tuttle.

Masakazu, Yamazaki, jt. tr. see Rimer, J. Thomas.

Masaki, I., ed. Vision-Based Vehicle Guidance. (Perception Engineering Ser.). (Illus.). 328p. 1992. 98.00 (*0-387-97553-5*) Spr-Verlag.

Masaki, Tomoh, ed. Endothelium-Derived Factors & Vascular Functions: Proceedings of the Fourth International Symposium on Endothelium-Derived Factors, Tokyo, 7-9 December 1993. LC 94-16819. (International Congress Ser.: No. 1051). 1994. 184.50 (*0-444-81669-0*, Excerpta Medica) Elsevier.

Masalha, Nur. Expulsion of the Palestinians: The Concept of 'Transfer' in Zionist Political Thought, 1882-1948. (C). 1992. text ed. 24.95 (*0-88728-235-0*); pap. 11.95 (*0-88728-242-3*) Inst Palestine.

Masalina, N. Andrei Riabushkin. (C). 1986. text ed. 50.00 (*0-569-08982-4*, Pub. by Collets) St Mut.

Masalski, William J. How to Use the Spreadsheet As a Tool in the Secondary School Mathematics Classroom. (Illus.). 76p. 1990. pap. 17.50 (*0-87353-303-8*) NCTM.

Masamba ma M'polo. Older Persons & Their Families in a Changing Village Society: A Perspective from Zaire. LC 84-591. 49p. 1984. pap. text ed. 5.00 (*0-910473-12-9*) Intl Fed Ageing.

Masani, Pesi. Norbert Wiener: Eighteen Ninety-Four to Nineteen Sixty-Four. (Vita Mathematica Ser.). 402p. 1989. 99.50 (*0-8176-2246-2*) Birkhauser.

Masani, Pesi, ed. see Wiener, Norbert.

Masani, Zareer. Indian Tales of the Raj. 165p. 1988. 22.00 (*0-520-06412-7*); pap. 14.00 (*0-520-07127-1*) U CA Pr.

Masanori Fujita & Michihiko Ike. Wastewater Treatment Using Genetically Engineered Microorganisms. LC 94-60490. 185p. 1994. pap. 55.00 (*1-56676-139-5*) Technomic.

Masanori, Nakamura. The Japanese Monarchy, 1931-1991: Ambassador Grew & the Making of the "Symbol Emperor System" Bix, Herbert P. et al, trs. LC 92-14157. (Illus.). 224p. (C). 1992. 47.50 (*1-56324-102-1*) M E Sharpe.

— The Japanese Monarchy, 1931-1991: Ambassador Grew & the Making of the "Symbol Emperor System" Bix, Herbert P. et al, trs. LC 92-14157. (Illus.). 224p. (C). 1992. pap. text ed. 12.95 (*1-56324-109-9*) M E Sharpe.

Masao Miyoshi. Off Center: Power & Culture Relations Between Japan & the United States. (Convergences Ser.). 289p. (C). 1991. 32.00 (*0-674-63175-7*) HUP.

Masao, Ten-Dan K. Kato's Attack & Kill. 1978. pap. 14.95 (*4-87187-027-8*, G27) Ishi Pr Intl.

Masaomi Kanzaki. Xenon, Vol. 2: Heavy Metal Warrior. Seiji Horibuchi, ed. Satoru Fujii, tr. (Illus.). 192p. (YA). 1991. pap. 14.95 (*0-929279-41-7*) Viz Commns Inc.

— Xenon, Vol. 2: Heavy Metal Warrior. Seiji Horibuchi, ed. Satoru Fujii, tr. (Illus.). 192p. 1992. pap. 14.95 (*0-929279-42-5*) Viz Commns Inc.

— Xenon, Vol. 3: Heavy Metal Warrior. Seiji Horibuchi, ed. Satoru Fujii, tr. (Illus.). 194p. 1992. pap. 14.95 (*0-929279-43-3*) Viz Commns Inc.

— Xenon, Vol. 4: Heavy Metal Warrior. Seiji Horibuchi, ed. Satoru Fujii, tr. (Illus.). 176p. (YA). 1992. pap. 14.95 (*0-929279-47-6*) Viz Commns Inc.

Masar, Stephen A., ed. Wisconsin Progressives: The Charles R. Van Hise Papers: Guide to a Microfilm Edition. 70p. 1986. pap. 25.00 (*0-87020-237-5*) Chadwyck-Healey.

Masar, Syed A. Schaum's Electric Power Systems. 1990. pap. text ed. 10.95 (*0-07-045917-7*) McGraw.

Masarik, Al. Excuses to Be Outside. Robertson, Kirk, ed. (Windriver Ser.). 64p. 1986. pap. 6.00 (*0-916918-32-7*) Duck Down.

— Excuses to Be Outside. deluxe limited ed. Robertson, Kirk, ed. (Windriver Ser.). 64p. 1986. 25.00 (*0-916918-33-5*) Duck Down.

— Nonesuch Creek: Selected Poems 1969 to 79. Robertson, Kirk, ed. LC 80-65779. (Windriver Ser.). 112p. (Orig.). 1980. pap. 4.50 (*0-916918-12-2*) Duck Down.

Masaru Takeuchi. Modern Spherical Functions. Toshinobu Nagura, tr. LC 93-24648. (Translations of Mathematical Monographs: Vol. 128). (ENG.). 1994. write for info. (*0-8218-4580-2*) Am Math.

Masaryk, Thomas G. Constructive Sociological Theory: The Forgotten Legacy of Thomas G. Masaryk. Imber, Jonathan B., ed. LC 93-45995. 347p. (C). 1994. 49.95 (*1-56000-164-X*) Transaction Pubs.

— Humanistic Ideals. Warren, W. Preston, tr. LC 79-124100. 132p. 1975. 25.00 (*0-8387-7664-7*) Bucknell U Pr.

— Ideals of Humanity, & How to Work. LC 79-90663. (Essay Index Reprint Ser.). 1977. 19.95 (*0-8369-1306-X*) Ayer.

— Ideals of Humanity & How to Work: Lectures Delivered in 1898 at the University of Prague. LC 72-135844. (Eastern Europe Collection Ser.). 1971. reprint ed. 16.95 (*0-405-02786-9*) Ayer.

— Masaryk on Marx. abr. ed. Kohak, Erazim V., ed. & tr. by. LC 70-168828. 444p. 1975. 35.00 (*0-8387-7951-4*) Bucknell U Pr.

— Modern Man & Religion. LC 74-107816. (Select Bibliographies Reprint Ser.). 1977. 26.95 (*0-8369-5216-2*) Ayer.

— The New Europe. LC 70-124580. 193p. 1975. 28.50 (*0-8387-7745-7*) Bucknell U Pr.

— On Thought & Life: Conversations with Karel Capek. Weatherall, Miles & Weatherall, R., trs. LC 78-156689. (Essay Index Reprint Ser.). 1971. reprint ed. 18.95 (*0-405-02782-6*) Ayer.

— Der Selbstmord als Sociale Massenerscheinung der Modernen Civilisation. Nyiri, J. C., ed. & intro. by. (Philosophia Resources Library Ser.). xvi, 245p. (GER.). 1982. lib. bdg. 66.00 (*3-88405-014-1*) Philosophia Pr.

— The Spirit of Thomas G. Masaryk, 1850 - 1937: An Anthology. Kovtun, George J., ed. LC 89-24053. 220p. 1990. text ed. 49.95 (*0-312-04017-2*) St Martin.

Masas, A. World Consumption of Wood, Trends & Prognoses. 130p. 1974. 40.00 (*0-569-08166-1*, Pub. by Collets UK) Pro-Am Music.

Masataka, Kasaka, ed. see Research Institute for Peace Studies Staff.

Masataka, Tokuda, jt. ed. see Khan, Akhtar S.

Masatomi, H., jt. ed. see Lewis, J. C.

Masatoshi. The Art of Netsuke Carving. (Illus.). 236p. 1992. reprint ed. 80.00 (*0-8348-0265-1*) Weatherhill.

Masavisut, Nitaya, et al, eds. Gender & Culture in Literature & Film East & West: Issues of Perception & Interpretation. (Literary Studies: East & West: No. 9). 320p. 1994. pap. text ed. 20.00 (*0-8248-1602-1*, Eastwest Ctr Pr) UH Pr.

Masaya Shiraishi. Japanese Relations with Vietnam: 1951-1987. (Southeast Asia Program Ser.: No. 5). 174p. (Orig.). (C). 1990. pap. text ed. 12.00 (*0-87727-122-4*) Cornell SE Asia.

Masayasu Nomura, et al, eds. Ribosomes. LC 74-83791. (Monograph Ser.: Vol. 4). (Illus.). 930p. 1974. 79.00 (*0-87969-110-7*) Cold Spring Harbor.

Masayesva, Victor & Younger, Erin, eds. Hopi Photographers-Hopi Images. LC 83-1301. (Sun Tracks Ser.: No. 8). 111p. 1983. pap. 19.95 (*0-8165-0804-6*) U of Ariz Pr.

Masayoshi Sato. The Shogun's Gold. Schilling, Mark, tr. 176p. 1991. 19.95 (*4-7700-1480-5*) Kodansha.

An Asterisk (*) at the beginning of an entry indicates that the title is appearing in BIP for the first time.

*Masayuki Hisataka. Essential Shorinji-Ryu Karate-Do. (Illus.). 304p. (Orig.). 1994. pap. 19.95 (0-8048-1953-X) C E Tuttle.

*Mascale, Deanna. This Golden Land. Ingram, tr. 350p. 1996. pap. 9.95 (0-7610-0437-8) NW Pub.

Mascall, E. L. The Triune God: An Ecumenical Study. LC 86-30327. (Princeton Theological Monograph Ser.: No. 10). 1986. pap. 12.90 (0-915138-96-4) Pickwick.

Mascall, Eric L. Importance of Being Human. LC 74-12849. 118p. 1974. reprint ed. text ed. 35.00 (0-8371-7761-8, MABH, Greenwood Pr) Greenwood.

Mascall, Leonard. A Booke of Fishing with Hooke & Line (Taken from the Treatise of Fishing with an Angle) LC 72-6017. (English Experience Ser.: No. 542). 92p. 1973. reprint ed. 25.00 (90-221-0542-3) Walter J Johnson.

— A Booke of the Arte & Manner How to Plant & Graffe All Sortes of Trees. LC 74-80200. (English Experience Ser.: No. 679). 90p. 1974. reprint ed. 25.00 (90-221-0679-9) Walter J Johnson.

Mascarelli, Gloria & Mascarelli, Robert. Warman's Oriental Antiques. LC 91-50680. (Illus.). 456p. 1992. pap. 21.95 (0-87069-573-8, Wallace-Hmestead) Chilton.

Mascarelli, Robert, jt. auth. see Mascarelli, Gloria.

Mascarenhas, Amyas & Sienkiewics, Teresa. Touche Ross: Accounts & Audit of Pension Schemes. 2nd ed. 1991. pap. 80.00 (0-406-00348-3, U.K.) Butterworth Legal Pubs.

Mascarenhas, Amyas & Turley, Stuart. Spicer's Practical Auditing. 18th ed. 1990. U.K. pap. 34.00 (0-406-12300-4) Butterworth Legal Pubs.

Mascarenhas, Ives, tr. see Suarez, Federico.

*Mascarenhas, Lambert. In the Womb of Saudade: Stories of Goan Life. (C). 1994. 9.00 (81-7167-239-6, Pub. by Rupa II) S Asia.

Mascarenhas, Oswald A. Towards Measuring the Technological Impact of Multinational Corporations in the Less Developed Countries. Bruchey, Stuart, ed. LC 80-583. (Multinational Corporations Ser.). 1980. lib. bdg. 44.95 (0-405-13375-8) Ayer.

Mascarenhas, R. C. A Strategy for Rural Development: Dairy Cooperatives in India. 288p. (C). 1988. text ed. 27.50 (0-8039-9548-2) Sage.

Mascarenhas, S. J., jt. auth. see Oswald, A. J.

Mascari, Claude J., ed. see Reid, Charles F., III.

Mascaro, Angelo, jt. auth. see Kowalewski, Kim J.

Mascaro, Francisco. Rita De Casia - Dios Hablara Esta Noche. 134p. (Orig.). (SPA.). 1991. pap. text ed. 10.00 (0-917049-55-1) Saeta.

Mascaro, Joan & Nespor, Marina, eds. Grammar in Progress: Glow Essays for Henk van Riemsdyk. (Studies in Generative Grammar). 300p. (Orig.). (C). 1990. pap. 123.10 (90-6765-417-5) Mouton.

Mascaro, Juan. Bhagavad Gita. 1962. mass mkt. 7.95 (0-14-044121-2, Penguin Classics) Viking Penguin.

— Upanishads. (Orig.). 1976. 16.95 (0-8488-0339-6) Amereon Ltd.

Mascaro, Juan, tr. The Dhammapada. (Classics Ser.). 1973. mass mkt. 7.95 (0-14-044284-7, Penguin Classics) Viking Penguin.

— Upanishads. (Classics Ser.). (Orig.). 1965. mass mkt. 6.95 (0-14-044163-8, Penguin Classics) Viking Penguin.

Mascaro Y Porcar, Jose M., prol. Diccionario Medico: De Bosillo. 2nd deluxe ed. 632p. (SPA.). 1974. 39.95 (0-8288-5997-3, S13673) Fr & Eur.

Mascaulay, Colman, ed. Sikkim: Report of a Mission to Sikkim & the Tibetan Frontier, with a Memoir on Our Relation with Tibet. (Illus.). 105p. (C). 1977. reprint ed. 55.00 (0-89771-100-9, Pub. by Ratna Pustak Bhandar) St Mut.

Mascenik, John, ed. Ports '80. LC 80-65719. 848p. 1980. pap. 55.00 (0-87262-108-1) Am Soc Civil Eng.

Mascetta, Joseph A. Barron's How to Prepare for the College Board Achievement Test - CBAT: Chemistry. 4th ed. 368p. 1990. pap. 10.95 (0-8120-4082-1) Barron.

— Chemistry the Easy Way. 2nd ed. (Easy Way Ser.). 350p. 1989. pap. 9.95 (0-8120-4198-4) Barron.

— How to Prepare for the SAT II: Chemistry. 5th ed. LC 93-21075. (SAT II: Subject Test Preparation Manuals Ser.). 1994. pap. 11.95 (0-8120-1702-1) Barron.

Mascetti, Daniela & Triossi, Amanda. Earrings: From Antiquity to the Present. LC 90-52600. (Illus.). 224p. 1990. 50.00 (0-8478-1230-8) Rizzoli Intl.

Mascetti, Daniela, jt. auth. see Bennett, David.

Mascetti, Manuela D. Song of Eve: An Enchanted Journey Into the Myths & Symbols of the Feminine. 1990. pap. 18.00 (0-671-68890-1) S&S Trade.

— Vampire: A Complete Guide to the World of the Undead. LC 92-53515. (Illus.). 224p. 1992. 20.00 (0-670-84664-3, Viking Studio) Studio Bks.

— Vampire: The Complete Guide to the World of the Undead. (Illus.). 224p. 1994. 14.95 (0-14-023801-8, Viking Studio) Studio Bks.

Mascetti, Manuela D., jt. auth. see Lorie, Peter.

Masch, M. Kathleen, jt. auth. see Wells, Carolyn C.

Maschal, Richard. Wet Wall Tattoos: Ben Long & the Art of Fresco. LC 93-13887. (Illus.). 1993. 25.95 (0-89587-105-X) Blair.

Maschio, G., et al, eds. Hypertension & Renal Disease. (Contributions to Nephrology Ser.: Vol. 54). (Illus.). viii, 232p. 1987. 142.50 (3-8055-4372-7) S Karger.

Maschio, Thomas. To Remember the Faces of the Dead: The Plenitude of Memory in Southwestern New Britain. LC 93-32388. 256p. 1994. 48.50 (0-299-14090-3); pap. 22.75 (0-299-14094-6) U of Wis Pr.

Maschke, Joachim. Moose Als Bioindikatoren Von Schwermetall-Immissionen. (Bryophytorum Bibliotheca Ser.: No. 22). (Illus.). 492p. (GER.). 1981. lib. bdg. 90.00 (3-7682-1320-X) Lubrecht & Cramer.

Maschke, Karen J. Litigation, Courts, Women Workers. LC 88-36993. 118p. 1989. text ed. 39.95 (0-275-93065-3, C3065, Praeger Pubs) Greenwood.

Maschke, Ruby. Bible Puzzles for Children, Vol. 2. 64p. (J). 1991. pap. 9.00 (0-8170-1165-X) Judson.

Maschke, Ruby A. Bible Puzzles for Children. 64p. (J). (gr. 4-6). 1986. pap. 8.00 (0-8170-1095-5) Judson.

Maschke, Thomas, jt. auth. see Burian, Peter K.

Maschko, Richard. Die Villdemslekre Im Griechischen Recht. Vlastos, Gregory, ed. LC 78-19369. (Morals & Law in Ancient Greece Ser.). 1979. reprint ed. lib. bdg. 18.95 (0-405-11560-1) Ayer.

*Maschler, Fay. Evening Standard London Restaurant Guide 1995. (Illus.). 224p. 1995. pap. 16.95 (1-85793-321-4, Pub. by Pavilion UK) Trafalgar.

Maschler, Michael B., jt. auth. see Aumann, Robert J.

Maschmeyer, Gloria, jt. photos see Crandall, Alissa.

*Maschmeyer, Gloria J. & Wedin, John. Paradise of the North: Alaska's Prince William Sound. (Illus.). 90p. 1995. pap. 19.95 (0-936425-35-0) Greatland Graphics.

*Maschner, Herbert D., ed. & pref. New Methods, Old Problems: Geographic Information Systems in Modern Archaeological Research. LC 95-68073. (Center for Archaeological Investigations Research Paper Ser.). (Illus.). 400p. (Orig.). 1996. pap. write for info. (0-88104-079-7, 89) Center Archaeo.

Masci, Barbara. Captured Heart. LC 89-34518. 160p. 1989. pap. 6.99 (0-8007-5331-3) Revell.

Masci, Joseph R. Primary & Ambulatory Care of the HIV-Infected Adult, No. 1. 328p. 1991. pap. 41.00 (0-8016-3159-9) Mosby Yr Bk.

Masci, Paul, jt. auth. see Kendall, Philip.

Mascia, L. Thermoplastics: Materials Engineering. 536p. 1989. 129.75 (1-85166-267-7) Elsevier.

Mascia-Lees, Frances E. Toward a Model of Women's Status. LC 83-48762. (American University Studies: Anthropology & Science: Ser. XI, Vol. 1). 146p. (Orig.). (C). 1984. pap. text ed. 14.60 (0-8204-0054-8) P Lang Pubs.

Mascia-Lees, Frances E. & Sharpe, Patricia, eds. Tattoo, Torture, Mutilation & Adornment: The Denaturalization of the Body in Culture & Text. LC 91-21296. (SUNY Series, The Body in Culture, History, & Religion). 172p. 1992. 57.50 (0-7914-1065-X); pap. 18.95 (0-7914-1066-8) State U NY Pr.

Mascia-Less, F. E., ed. Human Sexuality in Biocultural Perspective: A Special Issue of the Journal of Medical Anthropology. 103p. 1989. pap. text ed. 22.00 (2-88124-347-9) Gordon & Breach.

Masciandaro, Franco. Dante As Dramatist: The Myth of the Earthly Paradise & Tragic Vision in the "Divine Comedy" LC 91-2536. 224p. (C). 1991. text ed. 29.95 (0-8122-3069-8) U of Pa Pr.

Masciangelo, Bill, jt. auth. see Ninkovic, Tom.

Masciantonio, Rudolph. Greco Roman Sports & Games. 64p. (YA). (gr. 7-12). 1991. spiral bd. 4.50 (0-939507-28-5, B 314) Amer Classical.

— Latin, the Language of the Health Sciences. (Illus.). 42p. (Orig.). (J). (gr. 7-12). 1992. spiral bd. 3.10 (0-939507-43-9, B313) Amer Classical.

— Legal Latin. 82p. (Orig.). (ENG, GRE & LAT.). 1992. spiral bd. 5.65 (0-939507-22-6, B312) Amer Classical.

— Star Trek with Latin. 39p. (Orig.). 1991. spiral bd. 3.55 (0-939507-27-7, B 311) Amer Classical.

Mascie-Taylor, C. G., ed. Biosocial Aspects of Social Class. (Biosocial Society Ser.: No. 2). (Illus.). 160p. 1990. 45.00 (0-19-857724-9) OUP.

*Mascie-Taylor, C. G. & Bogin, Barry, eds. Human Variability & Plasticity. (Studies in Biological Anthropology: No. 15). (Illus.). 220p. (C). 1995. write for info. (0-521-45399-2) Cambridge U Pr.

Mascie-Taylor, C. G. & Lasker, G., eds. Biological Aspects of Human Migration. (Cambridge Studies in Biological Anthropology: No. 3). (Illus.). 250p. 1988. 74.95 (0-521-33109-9) Cambridge U Pr.

Mascie-Taylor, C. G. & Lasker, Gabriel W., eds. Applications of Biological Anthropology to Human Affairs. (Cambridge Studies in Biological Anthropology: No. 8). (Illus.). 240p. (C). 1991. 69.95 (0-521-38112-6) Cambridge U Pr.

Mascie-Taylor, C. G., jt. ed. see Lasker, G. W.

Mascie-Taylor, C. G., jt. ed. see Lasker, Gabriel W.

Mascie-Taylor, C. G., jt. ed. see Ulijaszek, S. J.

*Masciello, A. J. Mattino: An Intermediate Italian Grammar Book. 280p. 1995. lib. bdg. 41.00 (0-8095-4882-8) Borgo Pr.

*Masciotra, Patricia. Gentler Beginning. 191p. 1995. pap. 7.95 (1-56901-542-2) NW Pub.

— Nothing Perfect. abr. ed. 206p. 1994. pap. 7.95 (1-56901-305-5) NW Pub.

Mascitelli. Diccionario de Terminos Marxistos. 416p. (SPA.). 1979. pap. 19.95 (0-8288-4766-5, S50073) Fr & Eur.

Mascle, Alain, ed. Hydrocarbon & Petroleum Geology of France. LC 94-6892. (Special Publication of the European Association of Petroleum Geoscientists: Vol. 4). 1994. write for info. (3-540-57732-7) Spr-Verlag.

— Hydrocarbon & Petroleum Geology of France. LC 94-6892. (Special Publication of the European Association of Petroleum Geoscientists: Vol. 4). 1994. 229.00 (0-387-57732-7) Spr-Verlag.

Mascle, Deanna. The Golden Century. Van Treese, James B., ed. 364p. 1994. pap. 9.95 (1-56901-100-1) NW Pub.

Masco, Maisie. Between Two Worlds. 1993. mass mkt. 5.50 (0-06-100623-8, Harp PBks) HarpC.

Mascola. Charles Schulz, Reading Level 2. (Reaching Your Goal Bks.: Set II). (Illus.). 24p. (J). (gr. 1-4). 1989. lib. bdg. 14.60 (0-86592-429-5) Rourke Corp.

— Ray Kroc, Reading Level 2. (Reaching Your Goal Bks.: Set II). (Illus.). 24p. (J). (gr. 1-4). 1989. 10.95 (0-685-58802-5); lib. bdg. 14.60 (0-86592-433-3) Rourke Corp.

Mascola, et al. Reaching Your Goal, 8 bks., Set II, Reading Level 2. (Illus.). 192p. (J). (gr. 1-4). 1989. 87.60 (0-685-58797-5); Set. lib. bdg. 116.80 (0-86592-425-2) Rourke Corp.

Mascolini, Marcia & Freeman, Caryl. Objective Writing for Business & Industry. (C). 1984. write for info. (0-8359-8851-1, Reston) P-H.

Mascomm Associates Circle Education Staff, ed. see Donofrio, Phyllis.

Mascott, Trina. Palm Springs. 1990. pap. 4.95 (0-451-40173-5, Onyx) NAL-Dutton.

Mascrranahas, M. & Justa, H. R., eds. Value Education in Schools & Other Essays. 150p. 1989. text ed. 15.95 (81-220-0112-2, Pub. by Konark Pubs Pvt Ltd II) Advent Bks Div.

Mase, G. E. Continuum Mechanics. (Schaum's Outline Ser.). 1969. pap. text ed. 12.95 (0-07-040663-4) McGraw.

Mase, G. Thomas, jt. auth. see Mase, George E.

Mase, George E. & Mase, G. Thomas. Continuum Mechanics for Engineers. (Illus.). 176p. 1991. 59.95 (0-8493-8830-9, QA808) CRC Pr.

— Solutions Manual for Continuum Mechanics for Engineers. LC 92-42972. 1992. write for info. (0-8493-8862-7, CRC Reprint) Franklin.

*Mase, Thomas. What's Gnu? 32p. (J). (gr. 1-4). 1990. pap. 13.50 (0-8225-9581-8, Lerner Publctns) Lerner Group.

— What's Gnu? Riddles from the Zoo. (You Must Be Joking! Riddle Bks.). (Illus.). 32p. (J). (gr. 1-4). 1989. lib. bdg. 13.50 (0-8225-2330-2, Lerner Publctns) Lerner Group.

*Masear, Victoria R. Primary Care Orthopedics. (Illus.). 336p. 1995. text ed. write for info. (0-7216-5436-3) Saunders.

Masefield, Constance, jt. ed. see Masefield, John.

Masefield, Geoffrey B. A Short History of Agriculture in the British Colonies. LC 77-26015. 179p. 1978. reprint ed. text ed. 49.75 (0-313-20094-7, MAAG, Greenwood Pr) Greenwood.

Masefield, John. Jim Davis. 1976. 20.95 (0-8488-1093-7) Amereon Ltd.

— Sea Life in Nelson's Time. LC 75-75513. (Select Bibliographies Reprint Ser.). 1977. 24.95 (0-8369-5011-9) Ayer.

— Tarpaulin Muster. LC 73-132120. (Short Story Index Reprint Ser.). 1977. 17.95 (0-8369-3677-9) Ayer.

Masefield, John, ed. My Favourite English Poems. LC 75-76947. (Granger Index Reprint Ser.). 1977. 21.95 (0-8369-6028-9) Ayer.

— Sailor's Garland. LC 70-80376. (Granger Index Reprint Ser.). 1977. 25.95 (0-8369-6108-0) Ayer.

Masefield, John & Masefield, Constance, eds. Essays, Moral & Polite, Sixteen Sixty - Seventeen Fourteen. LC 78-157966. (Essay Index Reprint Ser.). 1977. reprint ed. 19.95 (0-8369-2243-3) Ayer.

Masefield, M. The Story of Fanny Burney. LC 73-21629. (English Biography Ser.: No. 31). 1974. lib. bdg. 51.95 (0-8383-1786-3) M S G Haskell Hse.

— Women Novelists. 1972. 59.95 (0-8490-1323-2) Gordon Pr.

Masefield, Muriel A. Women Novelists from Fanny Burney to George Eliot. LC 67-23244. (Essay Index Reprint Ser.). 1977. 19.95 (0-8369-0689-6) Ayer.

Masefield, P., tr. Vimana Stories. (C). 1988. 63.00 (0-86013-272-2, Pub. by Pali Text) Wisdom MA.

Masefield, P., jt. tr. see Kyaw, U Ba.

*Masefield, Peter. Divine Revelation in Pali Buddhism. 2nd ed. 187p. 1995. pap. 14.00 (955-9028-02-2) Paul & Co Pubs.

*Masefield, Peter, tr. The Udana. 218p. (C). 1994. 35.90 (0-86013-311-7) Wisdom MA.

Masefield, Peter & Wiebe, Donald, eds. Aspects of Religion Vol. 18: Essays in Honour of Ninian Smart. LC 94-15794. (Toronto Studies in Religion: Vol. 18). 417p. (C). 1994. text ed. 59.95 (0-8204-2237-1) P Lang Pubs.

Masefield, Peter, tr. see Dhammapala.

Masefield, Richard. Brimstone. large type ed. 544p. 1988. 15.95 (0-7089-1774-7) Ulverscroft.

— Chalkhill Blue. large type ed. 576p. 1985. 15.95 (0-7089-1269-9) Ulverscroft.

Masek, Carrie S., et al, eds. Proceedings: Papers from the Parasession on Language & Behavior. LC 81-82977. 274p. 1981. pap. 8.00 (0-914203-16-9) Chicago Ling.

Masek, Linda E. Mag-ni-fi-cat & the Christmas Tree Mystery. (J). 1992. 10.95 (0-533-10173-5) Vantage.

*Masel, Richard I. Principles of Adsorption & Reaction on Solid Surfaces. LC 95-17776. (Chemical Engineering Ser.). 1995. text ed. 74.95 (0-471-30392-5) Wiley.

Maseland, H., jt. ed. see Ortner, J.

Masellis, M., ed. The Management of Mass Burn Casualities & Fire Disasters. 352p. (C). 1993. lib. bdg. 125.00 (0-7923-8804-6) Kluwer Ac.

Masello, David. Architecture Without Rules: The Houses of Marcel Breuer & Herbert Beckhard. LC 92-32187. 1993. 35.00 (0-393-03491-7) Norton.

— Architecture Without Rules: The Houses of Marcel Breuer & Herbert Beckhard. (Illus.). 176p. 1995. pap. 19.95 (0-393-31375-1, Norton Paperbks) Norton.

Masello, Robert. Fallen Angels...& Spirits of the Dark: Demons, Fiends, & Spirits of the Dark. LC 94-16797. 240p. (Orig.). 1994. pap. 10.00 (0-399-51889-4, Perigee Bks) Berkley Pub.

— Proverbial Wisdom: A Treasury of the World's Greatest Proverbs. 1993. 9.95 (0-8092-3769-5) Contemp Bks.

— The Things Your Father Never Taught You. LC 95-12474. (Illus.). 1995. pap. write for info. (0-399-52168-2, Perigee Bks) Berkley Pub.

Maseo Doyama, et al, eds. Computer Aided Innovation of New Material, No. Two: Proceedings of the Second International Conference & Exhibition on Computer Applications to Materials & Molecular Science & Engineering - CAMSE '92, Pacifico Yokohama, Yokohama, Japan, September 22-25, 1992. LC 92-45915. 1993. write for info. (0-444-89778-X, North Holland) Elsevier.

Maser, Chris. Forest Primeval: The Natural History of an Ancient Forest. LC 89-31775. 1989. 25.00 (0-87156-683-4) Sierra.

— Forest Primeval: The Natural History of an Ancient Forest. LC 89-31775. (Illus.). 304p. 1994. reprint ed. pap. 12.00 (0-87156-548-X) Sierra.

— From the Forest to the Sea: A Story of Fallen Trees. (Illus.). 159p. 1990. per. 15.00 (0-16-000119-6, S/N 001-001-00642-4) USGPO.

— From the Forest to the Sea: The Ecology of Wood in Water. (Illus.). 250p. 1994. pap. 55.00 (1-884015-17-4) St Lucie Pr.

— The Global Imperative: Harmonizing Culture & Nature. 288p. 1992. pap. 12.95 (0-913299-90-1) Stillpoint.

— Sustainable Forestry. LC 94-5192. (Illus.). 400p. (Orig.). (C). 1994. pap. 39.95 (1-884015-14-X) St Lucie Pr.

Maser, Edward A. Drawings by Johann Michael Rottmayr. LC 80-53676. (Illus.). 124p. (Orig.). 1980. pap. 10.00 (0-935573-07-0) D & A Smart Museum.

Maser, Edward A., frwd. Alumni Who Collect I: Drawings from the Sixteenth Century to the Present, Vol. I. LC 82-70634. (Illus.). 78p. (Orig.). 1982. pap. text ed. 3.00 (0-935573-09-7) D & A Smart Museum.

Maser, Edward A., frwd. & intro. German & Austrian Painting of the Eighteenth Century. LC 78-55418. (Illus.). 56p. (Orig.). 1978. pap. 3.00 (0-935573-05-4) D & A Smart Museum.

Maser, Edward A. & Schiff, Gert. Adolf Hiremy-Hirschl: The Beauty of Decline. Taylor, Sue, ed. LC 84-60648. (Illus.). 32p. (Orig.). 1984. pap. 8.00 (0-9613449-0-3) R Ramsay Gallery.

Maser, Frederick E. How to Write a Local Church History. 10p. 1990. pap. 1.25 (1-880927-16-0) Gen Comm Arch.

— Richard Allen. 33p. 1976. pap. 0.50 (1-880927-07-1) Gen Comm Arch.

— The Story of John Wesley's Sisters: or Seven Sisters in Search of Love. LC 88-81533. (Illus.). 128p. (Orig.). 1988. 15.95 (0-914960-89-X); pap. 12.95 (0-914960-68-7) Academy Bks.

— Susanna Wesley. 4th ed. 31p. 1987. reprint ed. pap. 0.75 (1-880927-01-2) Gen Comm Arch.

Maser, H., tr. see Gauss, Karl.

Maser, Jack & Cloninger, C. Robert, eds. Comorbidity of Mood & Anxiety Disorders. LC 89-17681. 800p. 1990. text ed. 67.50 (0-88048-324-5) Am Psychiatric.

Maser, Jack D. Depression & Expressive Behavior. 128p. (C). 1987. text ed. 29.95 (0-89859-999-7) L Erlbaum Assocs.

— Treatment of Panic Disorder: A Consensus Development Conference. Wolfe, Barry E., ed. LC 93-17653. 358p. 1993. Alk. paper. text ed. 45.00 (0-88048-685-6) Am Psychiatric.

Maser, Jack D., jt. ed. see Rachman, S.

Maser, Jack D., jt. ed. see Tuma, Hussain A.

Maser, Kenneth R. Ground Penetrating Radar Surveys to Characterize Pavement Layer Thickness Variations at GPR Sites. 50p. (Orig.). (C). 1994. pap. text ed. 10.00 (0-309-05801-5, SHRP-P-397) SHRP.

Maser, Linda. EASYEST User's Manual. 84p. 1990. pap. write for info. (0-924729-16-3) Keithley Asyst.

Maser, Lou, jt. auth. see Raingruber, Bob.

Masera, Rainer S. An Increasing Role for the ECU: A Character in Search of a Script. LC 87-3747. (Essays in International Finance Ser.: No. 167). 1987. pap. text ed. 8.00 (0-88165-074-9) Princeton U Int Finan Econ.

Masereel, Frans. Passionate Journey: A Novel in One Hundred Sixty-Five Woodcuts. (Illus.). 160p. reprint ed. boxed 14.00 (0-87286-174-0) City Lights.

Maseri, Attilio, ed. Coronary Care Units. 292p. 1981. lib. bdg. 89.00 (90-247-2456-2) Kluwer Ac.

— Hammersmith Cardiology Workshop Series Vol. 2: 1985. LC 85-24360. (Illus.). 244p. Date not set. reprint ed. pap. 69.60 (0-7837-9247-6, 8524360) Bks Demand.

Maseri, Attilio & Goodwin, John F., eds. Hammersmith Cardiology Workshop. (Hammersmith Cardiology Workshop Ser.: Vol. 1). 348p. 1984. text ed. 81.50 (0-89004-291-8) Raven.

*Maseri, Attilio, et al, eds. Hammersmith Cardiology Workshop Series Vol. 3. fac. ed. LC 85-24360. (Illus.). 315p. Date not set. pap. 89.80 (0-7837-7141-X, 2047153) Bks Demand.

*Masey, Anthea. The Adventurers: A Year in the Life of a Venture Capital House. 184p. (Orig.). 1995. pap. 14.95 (0-563-36771-7, Pub. by BBC UK) Parkwest Pubns.

Mash, David S. Macintosh Multimedia Machine. LC 94-65686. 371p. 1994. pap. 39.99 (0-7821-1506-3) Sybex.

Mash, Eric J. & Barkley, Russell A., eds. Treatment of Childhood Disorders. LC 88-24464. 568p. 1989. lib. bdg. 52.00 (0-89862-743-5) Guilford Pr.

Mash, Eric J. & Terdal, Leif G., eds. Behavioral Assessment of Childhood Disorders. 2nd ed. LC 88-26928. (Guilford Behavioral Assessment Ser.). 824p. 1988. lib. bdg. 79.95 (0-89862-143-7) Guilford Pr.

— Behavioral Assessment of Childhood Disorders: Selected Core Problems. 2nd ed. LC 88-24684. (Guilford Behavioral Assessment Ser.). 456p. (C). 1988. pap. text ed. 30.95 (0-89862-512-2) Guilford Pr.

Masha, illus. Singing Words. LC 79-38605. (Granger Index Reprint Ser.). 1977. reprint ed. 18.95 (0-8369-6337-7) Ayer.

Mashat, Mazal, jt. auth. see Dvir, Azriel.

M

An Asterisk (*) at the beginning of an entry indicates that the title is appearing in BIP for the first time.

Mashaw, B. Programming Byte by Byte Structured FORTRAN. 3rd rev. ed. 550p. (C). 1992. pap. text ed. 37.45 (*0-934433-08-9*) Am Comp Pr.

Mashaw, Bijan. BASIC for IBM-PC Etc. 2nd ed. 420p. (C). 1990. pap. text ed. 29.95 (*0-934433-06-2*) Am Comp Pr.

— Programming Byte by Byte: Structured FORTRAN 77. 2nd rev. ed. 540p. (Orig.). (C). 1987. reprint ed. pap. 32. 20 (*0-934433-02-X*) Am Comp Pr.

Mashaw, Jerry L. Bureaucratic Justice. LC 82-17506. 242p. 1983. text ed. 45.00 (*0-300-02808-3*) Yale U Pr.

— Bureaucratic Justice: Managing Social Security Disability Claims. LC 82-17506. 242p. 1985. reprint ed. pap. 16.00 (*0-300-03403-2*, Y-526) Yale U Pr.

— Due Process in the Administrative State. LC 84-20948. 280p. 1985. text ed. 37.00 (*0-300-03258-7*) Yale U Pr.

Mashaw, Jerry L. & Harfst, David L. The Struggle for Auto Safety. 285p. 1990. 37.00 (*0-674-84530-7*) HUP.

Mashaw, Jerry L. & Merrill, Richard A. Administrative Law, the American Public Law System, Cases & Materials. 3rd ed. Shane, Peter M., ed. (American Casebook Ser.). 1187p. (C). 1993. reprint ed. text ed. 49. 00 (*0-314-00966-3*) West Pub.

Mashaw, Jerry L., jt. ed. see Marmor, Theodore R.

Mashaw, Jerry L., et al. Teacher's Manual to Accompany Administrative Law: The American Public Law System, Cases & Materials. 3rd ed. 271p. 1993. pap. text ed. write for info. (*0-318-70372-6*) West Pub.

Mashayekhi, Afsaneh, jt. auth. see Julius, DeAnne.

Mashayekhi, Mehrdad, jt. ed. see Farsoun, Samih K.

Mashburn. The Heart of Dixieland Combos. 1990. 4.95 (*0-685-32204-1*, B063); 4.95 (*0-685-47132-2*, B064) Hansen Ed Mus.

— How to Play Accordion Today. 1990. 4.95 (*0-685-32200-9*, H651) Hansen Ed Mus.

Mashburn, Emma H., ed. see Mashburn, J. L.

***Mashburn, J. L.** The Postcard Price Guide. 2nd ed. Mashburn, Emma H., ed. (Illus.). 464p. 1994. pap. 16.95 (*1-885940-00-9*) Colonial House.

Mashburn, William H. Managing Energy Resources in Times of Dynamic Change. LC 86-46135. 300p. 1988. text ed. 65.00 (*0-88173-035-1*) Fairmont Pr.

— Managing Energy Resources in Times of Dynamic Change. 224p. 1989. text ed. 65.00 (*0-13-551326-X*) P-H.

— Managing Energy Resources in Times of Dynamic Change. 2nd ed. LC 91-3451. 290p. 1993. 89.33 (*0-88173-136-6*) Fairmont Pr.

— A Mountain Summer. LC 88-11782. (Illus.). 140p. (Orig.). (YA). (gr. 9-12). 1990. reprint ed. pap. 8.95 (*0-936015-14-4*) Pocahontas Pr.

Mashburn, William H., jt. auth. see Fairmont Press Staff.

Masheck, Joseph. Building-Art: Modern Architecture under Cultural Construction. (Contemporary Artists & Their Critics Ser.). (Illus.). 256p. (C). 1993. 54.95 (*0-521-44013-0*); pap. 19.95 (*0-521-44785-2*) Cambridge U Pr.

— Historical Present: Essays of the 1970s. LC 83-24104. (Contemporary American Art Critics Ser.: No. 3). 316p. reprint ed. pap. 90.10 (*0-8357-1535-3*, 2070560) Bks Demand.

— Modernities: Art-Matters in the Present. (Illus.). 272p. 1992. 29.95 (*0-271-00808-3*) Pa St U Pr.

Masheck, Joseph, ed. Point One: Smart Art. (Illus.). (Orig.). 1984. pap. 7.95 (*0-930279-01-8*) Willis Locker & Owens.

***Masheck, Joseph D., ed.** Van Gogh One Hundred. LC 94-29206. (Contributions to the Study of Art & Architecture Ser.: No. 4). 416p. 1995. text ed. 75.00 (*0-313-29491-7*, Greenwood Pr) Greenwood.

Mashelkar, R. A., jt. ed. see Mujumdar, A. S.

Mashelkar, R. A., jt. ed. see Mujumdar, Arun S.

Mashelkar, R. A., jt. auth. see Rao, C. N. R.

Mashelkar, R. A., et al. Transport Phenomena in Polymeric Systems, No. I. (C). 1988. 52.50 (*0-85226-542-5*, Pub. by Wiley Eastern II) S Asia.

Mashiko, Ellen E. Japan. (World Education Ser.). (Illus.). 176p. (Orig.). 1989. pap. text ed. 25.00 (*0-910054-93-2*) Am Assn Coll Registrars.

Mashinini, Emma. Strikes Have Followed Me All My Life: A South African Autobiography. (Illus.). 1991. 39.95 (*0-415-90414-5*, A5579, Routledge NY); pap. 13.95 (*0-415-90415-3*, A5583, Routledge NY) Routledge.

Mashinksky, M. L., tr. see Schachnowitz, Selig.

Mashiro, N. Black Medicine I: The Dark Art of Death. LC 78-2210. (Illus.). 96p. 1978. pap. 12.00 (*0-87364-101-9*) Paladin Pr.

— Black Medicine II: Weapons at Hand. (Illus.). 88p. 1979. pap. 12.00 (*0-87364-168-X*) Paladin Pr.

— Black Medicine III: Low Blows. (Illus.). 128p. 1981. pap. 12.00 (*0-87364-214-7*) Paladin Pr.

Mashita. Niishima: The Life of a Samurai. Shimizu, H. & Terry, J., trs. 200p. 1988. pap. 9.95 (*0-933704-28-3*) Dawn Pr.

Mashiter, Rosa. A Little English Book of Teas. (Illus.). 1989. 7.95 (*0-87701-622-4*) Chronicle Bks.

— A Little English Cookbook. (Illus.). 60p. 1989. 7.95 (*0-87701-631-3*) Chronicle Bks.

Mashkova, E. S. & Molchanov, V. A. Medium-Energy Ion Reflection from Solids. (Modern Problems in Condensed Matter Sciences Ser.: Vol. 11). 434p. 1986. 154.00 (*0-444-86945-X*, North Holland) Elsevier.

Mashoor, S. M. Muslim Heroes of the Twentieth Century. 112p. (Orig.). 1985. pap. 6.95 (*1-56744-342-7*) Kazi Pubns.

Mashruwala, K. G. & Bhave, Vinoba. Gandhi & Marx. 119p. (Orig.). 1981. pap. 1.75 (*0-934676-30-5*) Greenlf Bks.

Mashuta, Mary. Story Quilts. Van Young, Sayre, ed. (Illus.). 96p. (Orig.). 1992. pap. 11.00 (*0-914881-47-7*) C & T Pub.

— Wearable Art for Real People. Van Young, Sayre, ed. LC 89-60484. (Illus.). 96p. (Orig.). 1989. pap. 9.00 (*0-914881-24-8*) C & T Pub.

Masi, Charles G. Digital Oscilloscope Handbook. (Test & Measurement Ser.). 250p. 1995. 29.95 (*0-7506-9434-3*) Buttrwrth-Heinemann.

Masi, Dale A. AIDS Issues in the Workplace: A Response Model for Human Resource Management. LC 90-8912. 232p. 1990. text ed. 55.00 (*0-89930-516-4*, MAQ/, Quorum Bks) Greenwood.

Masi, Dale A., ed. The AMA Handbook for Developing Employee Assistance & Counseling Programs. 464p. 1992. 59.95 (*0-8144-0107-4*) AMACOM.

Masi, Doris. Place Called Keeslers Corners. 1992. pap. 12.00 (*0-9628208-1-4*) Canal Side Pubs.

***Masi, Doris H.** Montgomery Hall. 1994. pap. text ed. 10. 00 (*0-9628208-9-X*) Canal Side Pubs.

— Pride O' the Hilltop. 180p. (J). 1992. pap. 12.00 (*0-9628208-6-5*) Canal Side Pubs.

Masi, Frank, intro. Radio Control Car How To's: Hot Tech from the Pros. (Illus.). 136p. (Orig.). 1993. pap. 14.95 (*0-911295-25-9*) Air Age.

Masi, Frank, ed. see Model Airplane News Editors Staff.

Masi, Joseph F., ed. see Thermophysical Properties Symposium Staff.

Masi, Oliviero. Incisioni - Etchings. (Illus.). 79p. 1987. pap. 25.00 (*0-936598-01-8*) J Szoke Graphics.

***Masi, Ralph, et al, eds.** Health & Cultures: Exploring the Relationships, Vol. 1. 1995. lib. bdg. 48.00 (*0-8095-4824-0*) Borgo Pr.

— Health & Cultures: Exploring the Relationships, Vol. 2. 1995. lib. bdg. 48.00 (*0-8095-4825-9*) Borgo Pr.

Masia, Seth. Alpine Ski Maintenance & Repair. rev. ed. (Illus.). 128p. 1987. pap. 10.95 (*0-8092-4718-6*) Contemp Bks.

— Insider's Guide to the Best Skiing in California & the West Coast. (Illus.). 192p. (Orig.). 1991. pap. 10.95 (*0-941283-10-0*) Western Eye Pr.

Masica, Colin P. Defining a Linguistic Area: South Asia. LC 74-16677. 256p. 1976. lib. bdg. 19.00 (*0-226-50944-3*) U Ch Pr.

— The Indo-Aryan Languages. (Language Surveys Ser.). (Illus.). 350p. (C). 1991. 130.00 (*0-521-23420-4*) Cambridge U Pr.

— The Indo-Aryan Languages. (Language Surveys Ser.). (Illus.). 555p. (C). 1993. pap. 42.95 (*0-521-29944-6*) Cambridge U Pr.

Masie, Elliott & Margulies, Dan. Computers for Non-Profit Organizations. 80p. (Orig.). 1985. pap. 8.95 (*0-913393-17-7*) Tools Trg.

Masie, Elliott & Stein, Michele. Using Computers in College Student Activities. (National Student Leadership Center Ser.). 104p. 1984. pap. 12.95 (*0-913393-16-9*) Tools Trg.

— Using Computers in High School Student Activities. (National Student Leadership Center Ser.). 104p. (Orig.). 1984. pap. 12.95 (*0-913393-15-0*) Tools Trg.

Masie, Elliott & Wolman, Rebekah. Computer Training Handbook: How to Teach People to Use Computers. Morris, David J., ed. 296p. 1989. text ed. 39.00 (*0-913393-26-6*) Tools Trg.

— The Computer Training Handbook: How to Teach People to Use Computers. 264p. 1988. 39.00 (*0-913393-25-8*) Tools Trg.

Masiello, A. Variational Methods in Lorentzian Geometry. 1994. write for info. (*0-318-72597-5*) Longman.

***Masiello, Antonio.** Variational Methods in Lorentzian Geometry. (Pitman Research Notes in Mathematics). 1994. pap. text ed. 54.00 (*0-470-23444-X*) Halsted Pr.

Masiello, Francine. Between Civilization & Barbarism: Women, Nation, & Literary Culture in Modern Argentina. LC 91-45603. (Engendering Latin America Ser.: Vol. 2). x, 246p. 1992. 40.00 (*0-8032-3158-X*) U of Nebr Pr.

Masih, Jeneen, ed. see Lawyers Committee for Human Rights.

Masih, Y. Comparative Study of Religions. (C). 1993. 22.00x (*81-208-0743-X*, Pub. by Motilal Banarsidass II) S Asia.

— Introduction to Religious Philosophy. (C). 1991. 21.00 (*81-208-0853-3*, Pub. by Motilal Banarsidass II) S Asia.

— Shankara's Universal Philosophy of Religion. viii, 163p. 1986. text ed. 24.00 (*81-215-0007-9*) Coronet Bks.

Masihi, Edwin. Trade Union Leadership in India: A Sociological Perspective. 1986. 19.00 (*0-8364-1530-2*, Pub. by Ajanta II) S Asia.

Masihi, K. N. & Lange, W., eds. Immunomodulators & Non-Specific Host Defence Mechanisms Microbial Infections: International Symposium, 6-8 May, 1987, West Berlin, FRG. (Advances in the Biosciences Ser.: Vol. 68). 480p. 1988. 185.00 (*0-08-036138-2*, Pub. by Pergamon Repr UK) Franklin.

— Immunotherapeutic Prospects of Infectious Diseases. (Illus.). 352p. 1991. 79.00 (*0-387-53214-5*) Spr-Verlag.

Masihi, K. Noel, ed. Immunotherapy of Infections. LC 94-16950. (Infectious Disease & Therapy Ser.: Vol. 15). 528p. 1994. 175.00 (*0-8247-9209-2*) Dekker.

Masihlall, Kamala. Drug Card. (Illus.). 13p. (J). (gr. k-3). 1993. pap. 12.95 (*1-895583-61-6*) MAYA Pubs.

— Rozan with Personnel. (Illus.). 16p. (J). (gr. k-3). 1993. pap. 9.95 (*1-895583-60-8*) MAYA Pubs.

Masin, Anton C. Incunabula Typographica: A Catalog of Fifteenth Century Books Held by the University of Notre Dame. 180p. 1979. 25.00 (*0-268-01144-3*) U of Notre Dame Pr.

Masin, Herman L. The Funniest Moments in Sports. LC 73-86219. (Illus.). 128p. (J). (gr. 4 up). 1973. 5.95 (*0-87131-133-X*) M Evans.

Masin, Sergio C., ed. Foundations of Perceptual Theory. LC 93-11012. (Advances in Psychology Ser.: Vol. 99). 1993. Alk. paper. write for info. (*0-444-89496-9*, North Holland) Elsevier.

Masing-Delic, Irene. Abolishing Death: A Salvation Myth of Russian Twentieth-Century Literature. LC 92-13992. 376p. (C). 1992. 42.50 (*0-8047-1935-7*) Stanford U Pr.

Masini, Donna. That Kind of Danger. LC 93-36956. 128p. 1994. 22.00 (*0-8070-6822-5*); pap. 12.00 (*0-8070-6823-3*) Beacon Pr.

Masini, E., ed. Visions of Desirable Societies. LC 82-18069. (Systems Science & World Order Library, Explorations of World Order Ser.) (Illus.). 260p. 1983. text ed. 121. 00 (*0-08-026089-6*, Pub. by Pergamon Repr UK) Franklin.

Masini, Gerald, et al, eds. Object-Oriented Languages. (APIC Ser.: No. 34). (Illus.). 483p. (C). 1991. boxed, text ed. 54.95 (*0-12-477390-7*) Acad Pr.

Masini, Lara-Vinca. Art Nouveau. (Illus.). 414p. 1991. 29.99 (*0-517-64175-5*) Random Hse Value.

Masini, Sergio. Complete Book of Firearms. 1988. 19.99 (*0-517-66947-1*) Random Hse Value.

Masino, Marcia. The Easy Tarot Guide. (Illus.). 288p. (Orig.). 1987. pap. 19.95 (*0-917086-59-7*) ACS Pubns.

Masironi, R., ed. Trace Elements in Relation to Cardiovascular Diseases: Status of the Joint WHO-IAEA Research Programme. (Offset Publication Ser.: No. 5). 1974. pap. 2.80 (*92-4-170005-X*) World Health.

Masius, Morton, tr. see Planck, Max.

Masjidjamei, Muhammad. The Revolution Which Islam Created. 64p. (Orig.). 1989. pap. text ed. 4.50 (*1-871031-16-8*) Abjad Bk.

Maskaleris, Thanasis, tr. see Kazantzakis, Nikos.

Maskall, Marty, ed. The Athena Treasury: One Hundred One Inspiring Quotations by Women. LC 93-70371. (Illus.). 128p. (Orig.). 1993. pap. 9.95 (*0-9627670-3-4*) Attitude Works.

— The Attitude Treasury: One Hundred One Inspiring Quotations. LC 90-84617. (Illus.). 128p. 1991. pap. 9.95 (*0-9627670-2-6*) Attitude Works.

***Maskarinec, Gregory G.** The Rulings of the Night: An Ethnography of Nepalese Shaman Oral Texts. LC 94-23024. (Illus.). 1995. 65.50 (*0-299-14490-9*); pap. 22.95 (*0-299-14494-1*) U of Wis Pr.

Maskawa, T., jt. ed. see Konuma, M.

***Maske, Alfred A.** Time, Space, & Man. 1995. 14.95 (*0-533-11438-1*) Vantage.

***Masked Basher.** The Corporate Victim's Guide to Executive Bashing! (Illus.). 160p. (Orig.). 1995. pap. 9.95 (*0-9645634-0-1*) R & O Pr.

Maskell, Brian H. New Performance Measure. (Management Master Ser.). 58p. (Orig.). 1994. 15.95 (*1-56327-062-5*) Prod Press.

— Performance Measurement for World Class Manufacturing: A Model for American Companies. (Illus.). 429p. 1991. 55.00 (*0-915299-99-2*) Prod Press.

— Software & the Agile Manufacturer: Computer Systems & World Class Manufacturing. LC 93-33282. (Illus.). 424p. 1994. 50.00 (*1-56327-046-3*) Prod Press.

Maskell, Duke. Coleridge's Prose. (C). 1989. 30.00 (*0-907839-09-6*, Pub. by Brynmill Pr Ltd UK) St Mut.

Maskell, William. The Ancient Liturgy of the Church of England. 1977. lib. bdg. 59.95 (*0-8490-1425-5*) Gordon Pr.

— Ancient Liturgy of the Church of England. 3rd ed. LC 71-172848. reprint ed. 62.50 (*0-404-04196-5*) AMS Pr.

Maskelyne, J. N. Locomotives I Have Known. 35.00 (*0-85242-636-4*) Apple Blossom.

Maskens, A. P., et al, eds. Concepts & Theories in Carcinogenesis: Proceedings of the 4th Annual Symposium on the European Organization for Cooperation in Cancer Prevention Studies, (ECP), Brugge, Belgium, June 11-13, 1986. (International Congress Ser.: No. 732). 332p. 1987. 106.25 (*0-444-80869-8*) Elsevier.

— Tobacco & Cancer - Perspective in Preventive Research: Proceedings of the Workshop of the European Organization for Cooperation in Cancer Prevention Studies, Brussels, Belgium, 29-30 Sept., 1988. (International Congress Ser.: No. 845). 172p. 1989. 92. 50 (*0-444-81093-5*, Excerpta Medica) Elsevier.

***Masker, John S.** Small States & Security Regimes: The International Politics of Nuclear Non-Proliferation in Nordic Europe & the South Pacific. LC 94-46781. 172p. (C). 1995. lib. bdg. 32.50 (*0-8191-9846-3*) U Pr of Amer.

Maskiell, Michelle. Women Between Cultures: The Lives of Kinnaird College Alumnae in British India. (Foreign & Comparative Studies Program, South Asian Ser.: No. 9). (Illus.). 1984. pap. text ed. 10.00 (*0-915984-86-5*) Syracuse U Foreign Comp.

Maskill, Howard. The Physical Basis of Organic Chemistry. (Illus.). (C). 1986. pap. 35.00 (*0-19-855199-1*) OUP.

Maskit, B. Kleinian Groups. (Grundlehren der Mathematischen Wissenschaften Ser.: Band 287). (Illus.). 287p. 1987. 87.00 (*0-387-17746-9*) Spr-Verlag.

Maskit, B., jt. ed. see Kra, I.

Maskow, Dietrich, jt. auth. see Enderlein, Fritz.

***Maskowitz, Daniel B.** Ranking Hospitals & Physicians Vol. III: The Use & Misuse of Performance Data. Vibbert, Spencer, ed. 224p. 1994. 125.00 (*1-881393-30-5*) Faulkner & Gray.

Maskowski, Alice, jt. auth. see Hauswald, Carol.

Maskrey, Andrew. Disaster Mitigation: A Community-Based Approach. 100p. (C). 1989. text ed. 80.00 (*0-85598-122-9*, Pub. by Oxfam Pubns UK); pap. text ed. 24.00 (*0-85598-123-7*, Pub. by Oxfam Pubns UK) St Mut.

Maskus, Keith E. The Changing Structure of Comparative Advantage in American Manufacturing. Bateman, Fred, ed. LC 83-9209. (Research in Business Economics & Public Policy Ser.: No. 4). 110p. reprint ed. 31.40 (*0-8357-1443-8*, 2070405) Bks Demand.

Maskus, Keith E., jt. ed. see Marks, Stephen V.

Maslach, Christina, jt. auth. see Pines, Ayala M.

Maslak, Paul. Strategy in Unarmed Combat. LC 80-130558. (Illus.). 136p. 1980. pap. 7.50 (*0-86568-000-0*, 101) Unique Pubns.

Masland, John W., jt. auth. see Lyons, Gene M.

Masland, Mary W., jt. ed. see Masland, Richard L.

Masland, R., et al, eds. Neuroplasticity: A New Therapeutic Tool in the CNS Pathology. (FIDIA Research Ser.: Vol. 12). 230p. 1988. 75.00 (*0-387-96620-X*) Spr-Verlag.

Masland, Richard L. & Masland, Mary W., eds. Preschool Prevention of Reading Failure. LC 88-50703. 240p. (Orig.). 1988. text ed. 35.00 (*0-912752-15-7*) York Pr.

***Masland, Skip.** William Willya & the Birthday Cake. (Misadventures of William Willya Ser.). (Illus.). 48p. (J). (gr. k-3). 1995. 14.95 (*1-883016-04-5*) Moonglow Pubns.

— William Willya & the Washing Machine. (Misadventures of William Willya Ser.). (Illus.). 40p. (J). (gr. k-5). 1993. 15.95 (*1-883016-01-0*) Moonglow Pubns.

Maslanka, Chris. The Guardian Book of Puzzles. 220p. 1992. pap. 11.95 (*1-872180-72-8*, Pub. by Fourth Estate UK) Trafalgar.

Maslanka, Michael P. Texas Employers' Guide. 1992. write for info. (*0-8205-1005-X*) Bender.

Maslansky, Carol J. & Maslansky, Steven P. Air Monitoring Instrumentation: A Manual for Emergency, Investigatory, & Remedial Responders. LC 92-10410. 1993. pap. 52.95 (*0-442-00973-9*) Van Nos Reinhold.

Maslansky, Steven P., jt. auth. see Maslansky, Carol J.

***Maslen, Bobby.** Bob Books Set No. 2. 1995. 14.95 (*0-615-00755-4*) Scholastic Inc.

***Maslen, Bobby L.** Bob Books No. 1: Even More Bob Books for Young Readers, 12 bks., Set 1. (Illus.). 144p. (J). (ps). 1983. pap. 14.95 (*0-590-20373-8*) Scholastic Inc.

— Bob Books No. 3: Even More Bob Books for Young Readers, 8 bks., Set 3. (Illus.). 144p. (J). (ps). 1987. pap. 14.95 (*0-590-20375-4*) Scholastic Inc.

— Bob Books, Beginning Readers, 12 bks., Set I. (Illus.). 144p. (J). (ps). 1983. reprint ed. pap. 14.95 (*0-9612104-0-0*) Bob Bks.

— Bob Books, Even More for Young Readers, 8 bks., Set III. (Illus.). 144p. (J). 1987. teacher ed, pap. 14.95 (*0-9612104-2-7*) Bob Bks.

— Bob Books, More for Young Readers, Set II. (Illus.). 144p. (YA). 1987. Set of 8 books & teaching guide. 14. 95 (*0-9612104-1-9*) Bob Bks.

— Bob Books Set No. 2, 8 bks., Set 2. (Illus.). 144p. (J). (ps). 1987. pap. 14.95 (*0-590-20374-6*) Scholastic Inc.

Maslen, Elizabeth. Doris Lessing. 1990. 40.00 (*0-7463-0700-4*, Pub. by Northcote House UK) St Mut.

— Doris Lessing. (Writers & Their Work Ser.). 96p. 1994. pap. text ed. 11.50 (*0-7463-0705-5*, Pub. by Northcote House UK) Trans-Atl Phila.

Maslen, Keith & Lancaster, John, eds. The Bowyer Ledgers: The Printing Accounts of William Bowyer Father & Son with a Checklist of Bowyer Printing 1699-1777, a Commentary, Indexes, & Appendixes. (Illus.). lxxv, 616p. 1991. 190.00 (*0-914930-13-3*, 12229) Biblio Soc Am.

Maslen, Keith, jt. auth. see Davis, Herbert.

Maslenikov, Oleg. Frenzied Poet: Andrey Biely & the Russian Symbolists. LC 68-54992. (Illus.). 234p. 1970. reprint ed. text ed. 59.75 (*0-8371-0163-8*, MAFR, Greenwood Pr) Greenwood.

Maslennikov, K. N. German & Russian Dictionary of the Textile Industry: Textilindustrie. 2nd ed. (GER & RUS.). 1981. 85.00 (*0-8288-2382-0*, M15355) Fr & Eur.

Maslennikov, M. V., ed. see Steklov Institute of Mathematics, Academy of Sciences, U. S. S. R. Staff.

Masler, Edward P., jt. ed. see Borkovec, A. B.

***Maslin.** Management in OT. 1991. 45.95 (*1-56593-009-6*, 0250) Singular Publishing.

Maslin, Bonnie. The Angry Marriage: Overcoming the Rage, Reclaiming the Love. LC 93-19272. 288p. 1994. 19.95 (*1-56282-806-1*) Hyperion.

— Angry Marriage: Overcoming the Rage, Reclaiming the Love. 288p. 1995. pap. 12.95 (*0-7868-8069-4*) Hyperion.

Maslin, Bonnie & Nir, Yehuda. Not Quite Paradise: Making Marriage Work. 256p. 1988. mass mkt. 4.95 (*0-449-21468-0*, Crest) Fawcett.

Maslin, Michael, jt. auth. see Donnelly, Liza.

Maslin, Michael, jt. ed. see Donnelly, Liza.

Maslin, Nicholas. HF Communications: A Systems Approach. 256p. (C). 1987. pap. text ed. 180.00 (*0-273-02675-5*, Pub. by Pitman Pubng UK) St Mut.

Maslin, Nicholas M. HF Communications: A Systems Approach. LC 87-42902. (Illus.). 256p. 1988. pap. 49.50 (*0-306-42757-5*, Plenum Pr) Plenum.

Maslin, Ruthie & Walter, Jeff. Insiders' Guide to Lexington & Kentucky's Bluegrass. 1994. pap. 12.95 (*0-912367-47-4*) Insiders Guide.

Maslin, Simeon J. What We Believe...What We Do... A Pocket Guide for Reform Jews. (Orig.). 1993. pap. 1.00 (*0-8074-0531-0*, 164030) UAHC.

Maslin, Simeon J., ed. Gates of Mitzvah: Shaarei Mitzvah: A Guide to the Jewish Life Cycle. LC 78-20790. (Illus.). 166p. 1979. pap. 9.95 (*0-916694-53-4*) Central Conf.

Maslin, Simeon J., et al. One God, Sixteen Houses: An Illustrated Introduction to the Churches & Synagogues of the Old York Road Corridor. (Illus.). 197p. (Orig.). 1990. pap. 25.00 (*0-9627062-0-5*) Cong Ken Israel.

Maslin, Zielfa. Management of Occupational Therapy. Campling, Jo, ed. (Therapy in Practice Ser.). 144p. 1990. pap. 23.00 (*0-412-33380-5*, A4414) Chapman & Hall.

Masline, Shelagh A. If We Knew Then What We Know Now: Planning for People with AIDS. (Paper Ser.: No. 15). 32p. 1991. 10.00 (*0-934459-64-9*) United Hosp Fund.

Masline, Shelagh R. The Concise Wine Guide. 192p. (Orig.). 1993. pap. 4.50 (*0-425-13633-7*) Berkley Pub.

Masline, Shelagh R., jt. auth. see Bergfeld, Wilma F.

Masline, Shelagh R., jt. auth. see Rooklin, Anthony R.

Masling, Joseph. Empirical Studies of Psychoanalytic Theories, Vol. 1. 320p. (C). 1983. text ed. 34.95 (*0-88163-000-4*) Analytic Pr.

An Asterisk (*) at the beginning of an entry indicates that the title is appearing in BIP for the first time.

— Empirical Studies of Psychoanalytic Theories, Vol. 2. 240p. 1986. text ed. 34.95 (0-88163-005-5) Analytic Pr.

Masling, Joseph M. Empirical Studies, Vol. 3. 250p. 1990. 34.95 (0-88163-108-6) Analytic Pr.

***Masling, Joseph M. & Bornstein, Robert F., eds.** Empirical Perspectives on Object Relations Theory, Vol. 5. LC 94-31989. (Empirical Studies of Psychoanalytic Theories Ser.: 5). 278p. 1994. 49.95 (1-55798-256-2, 431-6490) Am Psychol.

— Psychoanalytic Perspectives on Psychopathology. (Empirical Studies of Psychoanalytic Theories: Vol. 4). 340p. 1993. text ed. 49.95 (1-55798-211-2) Am Psychol.

Masloff, Jacqueline, jt. auth. see Lee, Kaiman.

Maslog, Crispin C., ed. Philippine Communication: An Introduction. 399p. (Orig.). (C). 1989. pap. 13.75 (971-11-0061-4, Pub. by New Day Pub PH) Cellar.

Maslon, Laurence, ed. The Arena Adventure: The First Forty Years. 108p. (Orig.). 1990. pap. 24.95 (1-55783-092-4) Applause Theatre Bk Pubs.

Maslon, Laurence, tr. see Slavkin, Viktor.

Maslov, N. Basic Engineering Geology & Soil Mechanics. 552p. (C). 1987. 90.00 (0-685-46652-3, Pub. by Collets) St Mut.

Maslov, Norman, jt. auth. see Bacon, David.

Maslov, S. Yu. Theory of Deductive Systems & Its Applications. Gelfond, Michael & Lifschitz, Vladimir, trs. 150p. 1987. 24.00 (0-262-13223-0) MIT Pr.

Maslov, V. P. & Nazaikinskii, V. E. Asymptotics of Operator & Pseudo-Differential Equations. LC 88-3984. (Monograph in Contemporary Mathematics). (Illus.). 320p. 1988. 95.00 (0-306-11014-8, Consultants) Plenum.

Maslov, V. P. & Samborskii, S. N., eds. Idempotent Analysis. LC 91-640741. (Advances in Soviet Mathematics Ser.: Vol. 13). 210p. 1992. 108.00 (0-8218-4114-9, ADVSOV/13C) Am Math.

Maslov, V. P., jt. auth. see Karasev, M. V.

***Maslova, N. & Pleshakova, T., eds.** The Roots of Russia: Paving the Way. 157p. (C). 1995. lib. bdg. 59.00 (1-56072-210-X) Nova Sci Pubs.

— The Russian Experience: Ideas in History. 137p. (C). 1995. lib. bdg. 59.00 (1-56072-211-8) Nova Sci Pubs.

Maslova, Niva B. Nonlinear Evolution Equations. LC 93-7001. (Series on Advances in Mathematics for Applied Sciences: Vol. 10). 208p. 1993. text ed. 74.00 (981-02-1162-7) World Scientific Pub.

Maslove, Allan M. & Winer, Stanley L., eds. Knocking on the Back Door: Canadian Perspectives on the Political Economy of Freer Trade with the United States. 1987. pap. text ed. 20.00 (0-88645-058-6, Pub. by Inst Res Pub CN) Ashgate Pub Co.

***Maslow.** Queer Birds. (J). Date not set. 16.00 (0-689-80249-8, Aladdin Paperbacks) S&S Childrens.

Maslow, Abraham H. The Farther Reaches of Human Nature. 1983. 22.00 (0-8446-6069-8) Peter Smith.

— The Farther Reaches of Human Nature. 1976. pap. 9.95 (0-14-004265-2, Penguin Bks) Viking Penguin.

— The Farther Reaches of Human Nature. 432p. 1993. pap. 13.95 (0-14-019470-3, Arkana) Viking Penguin.

— Religions: Values & Peak-Experiences. 1983. 20.00 (0-8446-6070-1) Peter Smith.

— Religions, Values, & Peak-Experiences. 1976. mass mkt. 6.00 (0-14-004262-8, Penguin Bks) Viking Penguin.

— Toward a Psychology of Being. 2nd ed. 1968. pap. 17.95 (0-442-03805-4) Van Nos Reinhold.

Maslow, Jonathan. Sacred Horses: The Memoirs of a Turkmen Cowboy. LC 93-11382. 1994. 25.00 (0-679-40875-4) Random.

— Torrid Zone: Seven Voices from the Gulf Coast. LC 95-3000. 1995. 22.00 (0-679-40876-2) Random.

***Maslow, Katie.** Hip Fracture Outcomes in People Age Fifty & Over. (Illus.). 95p. (Orig.). (C). 1994. pap. text ed. 45.00 (0-7881-1414-X) Diane Pub.

Maslowski, Peter. Armed with Cameras: The American Military Photographers of World War II. LC 93-7957. 1993. text ed. 29.95 (0-02-920265-5) Free Pr.

Maslowski, Peter, jt. auth. see Millet, Allan R.

Maslowski, Peter, jt. auth. see Millett, Allan R.

Maslowski, Raymond M. & Morgan, Lewis B. Interpersonal Growth & Self Actualization in Groups. LC 72-13775. (Illus.). (C). 1973. 29.50 (0-8422-5082-4) Irvington.

Maslowski, Raymond S. Eye Injuries: Medical Subject Survey with Bibliography. LC 87-47666. 150p. 1987. 39.50 (0-88164-614-8); pap. 34.50 (0-88164-615-6) ABBE Pubs Assn.

Maslowsky, Edward. Vibrational Spectra of Organometallic Compounds. LC 76-18694. (Illus.). 542p. reprint ed. pap. 154.50 (0-317-09212-X, 2013117) Bks Demand.

Masnick, George & Bane, Mary J. The Nation's Families: 1960-1990. LC 80-20531. (Illus.). 175p. (Orig.). (C). 1980. text ed. 21.00 (0-86569-050-2, Auburn Hse); pap. text ed. 15.00 (0-86569-051-0, Auburn Hse) Greenwood.

Masnick, George & Pitkin, John. The Changing Population of States & Regions: Analysis & Projections, 1970-2000. (Illus.). 250p. (Orig.). (C). 1982. pap. 12.00 (0-943142-01-6) St Local Inter.

***Masnik, Ann, comp.** The Jewish Woman Bibliography Supplement 1986-1993. 1995. write for info. (0-930395-25-5) Biblio NY.

Maso, Carole. The American Woman in the Chinese Hat. LC 93-36137. 200p. 1994. 19.95 (1-56478-045-7) Dalkey Arch.

— The American Woman in the Chinese Hat. 201p. 1995. 10.95 (0-452-27507-5, Plume) NAL-Dutton.

— The Art Lover: A Novel. LC 94-43655. 1995. write for info. (0-88001-410-5) Ecco Pr.

— AVA. LC 92-35600. 274p. 1993. 19.95 (1-56478-029-5) Dalkey Arch.

— Ava. 274p. (Orig.). 1995. pap. 12.95 (1-56478-074-0) Dalkey Arch.

— Ghost Dance. LC 94-43667. 1995. pap. 13.00 (0-88001-409-1) Ecco Pr.

Maso, J. C., ed. Interfaces in Cementitious Composites: Proceedings of the International Conference Held by RILEM (the International Union of Testing & Research Laboratories for Materials & Construction) at the Universite Paul Sabatier, Toulouse, & Organized by RILEM Technical Committee 108 & the Laboratory for Materials & Durability of Constructions (LMDC), INSA-UPS, Toulouse, France: Toulouse, October 21-23, 1992. LC 92-38104. 1992. write for info. (0-419-18230-6, E & FN Spon) Routledge Chapman & Hall.

Masoch, Count, jt. auth. see Pichard, Georges.

Masoliver, Juan A. Origins of Desire: Modern Spanish Short Stories. 1994. pap. 13.99 (1-85242-187-8) Serpents Tail.

Masolo, D. A. African Philosophy in Search of Identity. LC 93-15353. (African Systems of Thought Ser.). 1994. 35.00 (0-253-30271-4); pap. 14.95 (0-253-20775-4) Ind U Pr.

Mason. Comet Halley: Investigations, Results, Interpretation. 1990. text ed. 120.00 (0-13-171083-4) P-H.

— Comet Halley: Investigations, Results, Interpretations, Vol. 1. 1990. text ed. 130.00 (0-13-171075-3) P-H.

— Medicine for the Twenty-First Century. 1992. pap. 14.95 (1-85230-329-8) Element MA.

— Practice Tests for TOEFL. 2nd ed. 1989. pap. 15.95 (0-17-555731-4); audio 26.00 (0-17-555735-7) Heinle & Heinle.

— Practice Tests for TOEFL. 2nd ed. 1989. pap. 39.95 (0-17-555447-1) Heinle & Heinle.

— Saigon Singer. 1976. 22.95 (0-89190-352-6) Amereon Ltd.

Mason, IV. S.T.O.R.E.S. Structured Teaching of Research & Experimentation Skills (Middle School) 1991. pap. 15.00 (0-89824-504-4) Trillium Pr.

***Mason.** Summer of Love. 1995. mass mkt. (0-553-57241-5, Spectra) Bantam.

— Two Tickets for Tangier. 1976. 21.95 (0-89190-354-2) Amereon Ltd.

Mason, ed. see Corwin, Edward S.

Mason, jt. auth. see Vervoort.

Mason, et al. Cooperative Occupational Education & Work Experience in the Curriculum. 4th ed. 668p. 1989. 27.95 (0-8134-2752-5) Interstate.

Mason, A., jt. auth. see Beetham, P.

Mason, A. E. At the Villa Rose. 312p. 1984. pap. 3.50 (0-88184-111-0) Carroll & Graf.

— The Four Feathers. reprint ed. lib. bdg. 20.95 (0-88411-176-8, Aeonian Pr) Amereon Ltd.

— The Four Feathers. 1993. reprint ed. lib. bdg. 18.95 (1-56849-211-1) Buccaneer Bks.

— The House in Lordship Lane. 272p. 1985. pap. 3.50 (0-88184-140-4) Carroll & Graf.

— The House of the Arrow. 320p. 1984. pap. 3.50 (0-88184-066-1) Carroll & Graf.

— Murder at the Villa Rose. (Black Dagger Crime Ser.). 224p. 1992. reprint ed. 16.50 (0-86220-830-0, Black Dagger) Chivers N Amer.

— The Prisoner in the Opal. 356p. 1986. pap. 3.95 (0-88184-221-4) Carroll & Graf.

Mason, Abelle. Ports of Entry: Ethnic Impressions. 139p. (C). 1984. pap. text ed. 10.75 (0-15-570748-5) HB Coll Pubs.

— Ports of Entry: Scientific Concerns. 208p. (C). 1986. pap. text ed. 10.75 (0-15-570752-3) HB Coll Pubs.

— Ports of Entry: Social Concerns. 186p. (C). 1985. pap. text ed. 10.75 (0-15-570749-3) HB Coll Pubs.

Mason, Alexander. The Mexican Connection. 1977. pap. 1.50 (0-8439-0486-0) Dorchester Pub Co.

Mason, Alfred B., tr. see Von Holst, H.

Mason, Alfred E. Ensign Knightley & Other Stories. LC 70-103525. (Short Story Index Reprint Ser.). 1977. 21.95 (0-8369-3267-6) Ayer.

— Sir George Alexander & the St. James' Theatre. LC 72-84520. (Illus.). 1972. 24.95 (0-405-08762-4, Pub. by Blom Pubns UK) Ayer.

Mason, Alice L. Jolly Old Santa Claus. (Illus.). 24p. (J). (ps-12). 1985. pap. 2.95 (0-89542-448-7, Ideals Child) Hambleton-Hill.

— Jolly Old Santa Claus. rev. ed. (Illus.). 24p. (J). 1995. 5.95 (1-57102-081-0, Ideals Child); pap. 1.99 (1-57102-075-6, Ideals Child) Hambleton-Hill.

***Mason, Alistair, ed.** Religion in Leeds. LC 94-22149. 1994. 50.00 (0-7509-0581-6); pap. 24.00 (0-7509-0580-8) A Sutton Pub.

Mason, Alpheus T. Organized Labor & the Law. LC 73-89755. (American Labor, from Conspiracy to Collective Bargaining Ser., No. 1). 265p. 1972. reprint ed. 18.95 (0-405-02142-9) Ayer.

— The Supreme Court: Palladium of Freedom. LC 62-18443. 217p. reprint ed. pap. 61.90 (0-317-29150-5, 2055629) Bks Demand.

— The Supreme Court from Taft to Burger. enl. rev. ed. LC 78-19084. 352p. 1979. pap. text ed. 14.95 (0-8071-0469-8) La State U Pr.

— William Howard Taft: Chief Justice. LC 83-6461. 354p. (C). 1983. reprint ed. pap. text ed. 34.50 (0-8191-3091-5) U Pr of Amer.

Mason, Alpheus T. & Baker, Gordon E. Free Government in the Making: Readings in American Political Thought. 4th ed. 992p. 1985. 35.00 (0-19-503524-0) OUP.

Mason, Alpheus T. & Stephenson, D. Grier, Jr. American Constitutional Development. LC 74-32555. (Goldentree Bibliographies Series in American History). (C). 1977. pap. text ed. write for info. (0-88295-545-4) Harlan Davidson.

— American Constitutional Law: Introductory Essays & Selected Cases. 10th ed. LC 92-10942. 672p. (C). 1992. text ed. write for info. (0-13-033572-X) P-H.

— American Constitutional Law: Introductory Essays & Selected Cases. 11th ed. LC 95-6277. 1995. text ed. write for info. (0-13-341546-5) P-H.

Mason, Amelia R. Woman in the Golden Ages. 1977. lib. bdg. 250.00 (0-8490-2833-7) Gordon Pr.

Mason, Andrew. Explaining Political Disagreement. LC 92-39228. 192p. (C). 1993. 47.95 (0-521-43322-3) Cambridge U Pr.

— Homes - A Household Model for Economic & Social Studies: Reference Guide for Household Projections, Version 1.0. LC 87-22288. (Papers of the East-West Population Institute: No. 106). (Illus.). x, 114p. (Orig.). 1987. pap. 3.00 (0-86638-102-3) EW Ctr HI.

— Ward Lock Family Health Guide: First Aid. (Illus.). 80p. 1994. pap. 9.95 (0-7063-7254-9, Pub. by Ward Lock UK) Sterling.

Mason, Angela & Healey, Emma, eds. Stonewall Twenty-Five: The Making of the Lesbian & Gay Community in Britain. 224p. 1994. pap. 13.95 (1-85381-772-4, Pub. by Virago Pr UK) Trafalgar.

***Mason, Anita.** Reich Angel: A Novel. 373p. 1995. 24.00 (1-56947-033-2) Soho Press.

***Mason, Anthony.** Peary & Amundsen Race to the Poles. LC 94-36722. (Beyond the Horizons Ser.). (J). 1995. write for info. (0-8114-3977-1) Raintree Steck-V.

— Soccer. (Butterfly Bks.). (J). 1990. 7.95 (0-86685-475-4) Intl Bk Ctr.

Mason, Antony. Brussels: With Bruges, Ghent, & Antwerp. LC 93-47110. (Cadogan City Guides Ser.). (Illus.). 320p. (Orig.). 1995. pap. 14.95 (1-56440-273-8, Pub. by Cadogan Bks UK) Globe Pequot.

— Brussels, Bruges, Ghent & Antwerp. LC 93-47110. (Cadogan Guides Ser.). 1994. 10.99 (0-947754-55-5, Pub. by Cadogan Books UK) Macmillan.

— The Caribbean. (People & Places Ser.). (Illus.). 48p. (J). (gr. 4-8). 1989. lib. bdg. 12.95 (0-382-09823-4) Silver Burdett Pr.

— Cezanne. (Famous Artists Ser.). (Illus.). 32p. (J). (gr. 5 up). 1994. 10.95 (0-8120-6459-3); pap. 5.95 (0-8120-1293-3) Barron.

— The Children's Atlas of Civilizations. LC 93-23564. (Children's Atlases Ser.). (Illus.). 96p. (J). (gr. 2-6). 1994. lib. bdg. 18.90 (1-56294-494-0); pap. 12.95 (1-56294-733-8) Millbrook Pr.

— The Kingfisher First Picture Atlas. LC 93-46855. (Illus.). 40p. (J). (gr. 2-5). 1994. 12.95 (1-85697-836-2, Kingfisher LKC) LKC.

— Leonardo Da Vinci. (Famous Artists Ser.). (Illus.). 32p. (J). (gr. 5 up). 1994. 10.95 (0-8120-6460-7); pap. 5.95 (0-8120-1997-0) Barron.

— Middle East. LC 88-18312. (People & Places Ser.). (Illus.). 48p. (J). (gr. 4-8). 1988. lib. bdg. 12.95 (0-382-09514-6) Silver Burdett Pr.

— Monet. LC 94-22455. (Famous Artists Ser.). (Illus.). 1995. write for info. (0-8120-6494-1); pap. write for info. (0-8120-9174-4) Barron.

— Picasso. (Famous Artists Ser.). (Illus.). 32p. (YA). (gr. 5 up). 1995. 10.95 (0-8120-6496-8); pap. 5.95 (0-8120-9175-2) Barron.

— Southeast Asia. LC 91-24807. (World in View Ser.). (Illus.). 96p. (J). (gr. 6-12). 1992. lib. bdg. 24.26 (0-8114-2447-2) Raintree Steck-V.

— Southeast Asia. (People & Places Ser.). (Illus.). 48p. (J). (gr. 4-8). 1989. lib. bdg. 12.95 (0-382-09796-3) Silver Burdett Pr.

Mason, Antony & Lye, Keith. The Children's Atlas of Exploration. LC 92-28856. (Children's Atlases Ser.). (Illus.). 96p. (J). (gr. 2-6). 1993. pap. 12.95 (1-56294-711-7) Millbrook Pr.

— The Children's Atlas of Exploration. LC 92-28856. (Children's Atlases Ser.). (Illus.). 96p. (J). (gr. 2-6). 1993. lib. bdg. 18.90 (1-56294-256-5) Millbrook Pr.

Mason, Arthur. Cook & the Captain Bold. LC 70-128740. (Short Story Index Reprint Ser.). 1977. 17.95 (0-8369-3631-0) Ayer.

Mason, B. J., Jr. Elliott B. in Birds of a Feather. (Illus.). 66p. (Orig.). (J). (gr. 2-4). 1993. Incl. audio cass. audio 14.95 (0-9640707-0-7) Color-Me Storybks.

— Elliott B. in Birds of a Feather Teacher's Guide. (Illus.). 12p. (J). (ps-3). 1995. teacher ed. pap. 4.95 (0-9640707-1-5) Color-Me Storybks.

Mason, B. J., ed. The Surface Waters Acidification Programme. 400p. (C). 1991. 115.00 (0-521-39533-X) Cambridge U Pr.

Mason, Barry. Handing Over. 96p. 1992. pap. 16.95 (1-85575-018-X, Pub. by Karnac Bks UK) Brunner-Mazel.

Mason, Basil J. Clouds, Rain, & Rainmaking. 2nd ed. LC 74-16991. 197p. reprint ed. pap. 56.20 (0-317-20591-9, 2024497) Bks Demand.

Mason, Bernard S. The Book of Indian Crafts & Costumes. LC 46-6959. 128p. reprint ed. pap. 36.50 (0-8357-7341-8, 2055164) Bks Demand.

— Boomerangs: How to Make & Throw Them. (Illus.). (J). (gr. 5 up). 17.75 (0-8446-5062-5) Peter Smith.

— Boomerangs: How to Make & Throw Them. LC 73-94346. (Illus.). 99p. 1974. reprint ed. pap. 3.50 (0-486-23028-7) Dover.

— Dances & Stories of the American Indian. LC 44-516. (Illus.). 280p. reprint ed. pap. 79.80 (0-8357-9871-2, 2013407) Bks Demand.

— Drums, Tomtoms & Rattles: Primitive Percussion Instruments for Modern Use. (Illus.). (YA). (gr. 5 up). 18.75 (0-8446-5063-3) Peter Smith.

— How to Make Drums, Tom Toms & Rattles. (Illus.). 208p. 1974. reprint ed. pap. 5.95 (0-486-21889-9) Dover.

— Primitive & Pioneer Sports for Recreation Today: Rope Spinning, Lariat Throwing, Tumblesticks, Whip Cracking, Boomerangs, Log Rolling, Boomabirds, Tomahawks, Darts, Blowguns, & Many Others. (Illus.). 1995. reprint ed. 43.00 (1-55888-212-X) Omnigraphics Inc.

Mason, Bertha, ed. see Jackson, W. Francis.

Mason, Bessie M. Along the Creek. 72p. 1984. pap. 5.00 (0-916768-06-6) Sycamore Pr.

— On the Hill. 42p. 1984. 4.00 (0-916768-07-4) Sycamore Pr.

Mason, Bill. Bill Mason's No-Nonsense Guide to Fly Fishing Idaho. Banks, David et al, eds. (Illus.). 64p. (Orig.). 1994. pap. text ed. 14.95 (0-9637256-1-0) D Mktg Comm.

— The Path of the Paddle. (Illus.). 200p. 1991. pap. 19.95 (1-55971-004-7) NorthWord.

— Path of the Paddle: An Illustrated Guide to the Art of Canoeing. rev. ed. (Illus.). 200p. 1995. pap. 19.95 (1-55971-470-0) NorthWord.

— Song of the Paddle: An Illustrated Guide to Wilderness Camping. (Illus.). 208p. 1988. 29.95 (0-942802-83-7); pap. 19.95 (0-942802-84-5) NorthWord.

— Sports Illustrated Fly Fishing: Learn from a Master. (Orig.). 1994. pap. 11.95 (1-56800-033-2, Pub. by Sports Illus Bks) Natl Bk Netwk.

Mason, Bill, jt. auth. see Maisner, Larry.

Mason, Billy. Directory of Recyclable Wastes. (Illus.). 1976. pap. text ed. 11.95 (0-942140-01-X) Kelso.

— A Furniture Stripping Business for the Small Man. 1975. pap. text ed. 7.00 (0-942140-03-6) Kelso.

— Grandmaw Old Fashion Soap Making. 1978. 7.00 (0-942140-04-4) Kelso.

— Making Money with Vending Machine. pap. 7.00 (0-686-22698-4) Kelso.

— Outdoor Advertising. 1976. pap. 5.00 (0-686-22699-2) Kelso.

Mason, Billy, ed. Directory of Recyclable Wastes, Bk. 2. (Orig.). (C). 1981. pap. 11.95 (0-942140-00-1) Kelso.

Mason, Bim. Street Theatre & Other Outdoor Performance. LC 91-43615. (Illus.). 176p. 1992. 59.95 (0-415-07049-X, A7099); pap. 15.95 (0-415-07050-3, A7103) Routledge.

Mason, Bob. Gamblers, Grifters & Good Ol' Boys. 1986. 7.95 (0-89746-056-1) Gambling Times.

Mason, Bobbie A. Feather Crowns. 1994. pap. 13.00 (0-06-092549-3) HarpC.

— The Girl Sleuth. (Illus.). 160p. 1995. pap. 10.95 (0-8203-1739-X) U of Ga Pr.

— In Country. 256p. 1986. reprint ed. pap. 12.00 (0-06-091350-9, PL) HarpC.

— Love Life: Stories. LC 88-45535. 256p. 1990. reprint ed. pap. 11.00 (0-06-091668-0, PL) HarpC.

— Shiloh & Other Stories. 264p. 1995. 18.00 (0-8131-1948-0) U Pr of Ky.

— Shiloh & Other Stories. LC 82-47541. 256p. 1990. reprint ed. pap. 12.00 (0-06-091330-4, PL1330, PL) HarpC.

— Spence & Lila. LC 87-46155. (Illus.). 176p. 1989. reprint ed. pap. 9.00 (0-06-091559-5, PL 1559, PL) HarpC.

Mason, Bonnie N., jt. auth. see Southard, Edna C.

Mason, Brian. Handbook of Elemental Abundances in Meteorites: Reviews in Cosmochemistry & Allied Subjects. LC 71-148927. (Illus.). 576p. 1971. text ed. 415.00 (0-677-14950-6); pap. text ed. 237.00 (0-677-14955-7) Gordon & Breach.

— Victor Moritz Goldschmidt: Father of Modern Geochemistry. LC 91-78244. (Special Publication: No. 4). (Illus.). xii, 184p. 1992. 40.00 (0-941809-03-X) Geochemical Soc.

Mason, Brian, ed. see Marvin, Ursula B.

Mason, Brian, jt. ed. see Marvin, Ursula B.

Mason, Brian H. & Melson, William G. The Lunar Rocks. LC 73-129659. 185p. reprint ed. pap. 52.80 (0-317-08373-2, 2055128) Bks Demand.

Mason, Brian H. & Taylor, S. R. Inclusions in the Allende Meteorite. LC 82-600091. (Smithsonian Contributions to the Earth Sciences Ser.: No. 25). 34p. reprint ed. pap. 25.00 (0-317-08552-2, 2019305) Bks Demand.

Mason, Bruce, jt. auth. see Millham, Peter.

Mason, C. A., ed. International Symposium on Teleoperation & Control. (Illus.). 400p. 1988. 146.00 (0-387-50054-5) Spr-Verlag.

Mason, C. F. Biology of Freshwater Pollution. 2nd ed. 348p. 1991. pap. text ed. 51.95 (0-470-21698-0) Halsted Pr.

Mason, C. Russell. The Art & Science of Protective Relaying. LC 56-8964. (General Electric Series for the Advancement of Engineering Practice). 424p. reprint ed. pap. 120.90 (0-7837-2813-1, 2057659) Bks Demand.

Mason, Carol I. Introduction to Wisconsin Indians: Prehistory to Statehood. (Illus.). 327p. (Orig.). 1988. pap. text ed. 15.95 (0-88133-308-5) Sheffield WI.

***Mason, Caroline.** Simple Etiquette in China. 1989. pap. 6.95 (0-904404-70-6) St Mut.

— Very Simple Chinese. 1990. pap. 35.00 (0-904404-71-4, Pub. by Paul Norbury Pubns UK) Humanities.

Mason, Carolyn B. Deadly Impulse. 1989. pap. 3.95 (0-8217-2708-7) Zebra.

Mason, Charles. The Journal of Charles Mason & Jeremiah Dixon. LC 69-17273. (American Philosophical Society, Memoirs Ser.: Vol. 76). 243p. reprint ed. pap. 69.30 (0-317-29719-8, 2019710) Bks Demand.

— Meaning by All Means: A Vocabulary Text & Workbook for Students of ESL. 160p. (C). 1985. pap. text ed. 15.25 (0-13-567058-6) P-H.

***Mason, Charles, ed.** The Best of Sail Trim. (Illus.). 288p. Date not set. pap. 25.00 (0-7136-3594-0) Sheridan.

Mason, Charles, jt. auth. see Melges, Buddy.

Mason, Charles T., Jr. & Mason, Patricia B. A Handbook of Mexican Roadside Flora. LC 87-10890. (Illus.). 380p. 1987. pap. 19.95 (0-8165-0997-2) U of Ariz Pr.

Mason, Charles W. The Value-Philosophy of Alfred Edward Taylor: A Study in Theistic Implication. LC 79-52512. 1979. pap. text ed. 29.00 (0-8191-0772-7) U Pr of Amer.

Mason, Charlotte & Perreault, William D., Jr. The Marketing Game. 163p. (C). 1987. pap. text ed. 25.95 (0-256-06013-4) Irwin.

Mason, Cherie. Wild Fox: A True Story. LC 92-74622. (Illus.). 32p. (J). (gr. 2-5). 1993. 15.95 (0-89272-319-X) Down East.

Mason, Cheryl. Preparing & Directing a Teacher Institute. 32p. 1993. pap. text ed. 6.50 (0-87355-116-8) Natl Sci Tchrs.

Mason, Chris, jt. auth. see Macdonald, Sheila.

Mason, Colin, jt. ed. see Cobbett, Walter W.

Mason, Connie. Beyond the Horizon. 448p. (Orig.). 1990. pap. 4.50 (0-8439-3029-2) Dorchester Pub Co.

— Beyond the Horizon. (Women West Ser.). 448p. 1995. mass mkt., pap. text ed. 5.99 (0-8439-3798-X) Dorchester Pub Co.

— Bold Land, Bold Love. 480p. pap. 4.99 (0-8439-3327-5) Dorchester Pub Co.

— Brave Land, Brave Love. 448p. (Orig.). 1992. pap. 4.99 (0-8439-3281-3) Dorchester Pub Co.

— Caress & Conquer. 480p. (Orig.). 1993. pap. 4.99 (0-8439-3532-4) Dorchester Pub Co.

— Desert Ecstasy. 448p. (Orig.). 1988. pap. 4.50 (0-8439-2678-3) Dorchester Pub Co.

— For Honor's Sake. 400p. 1991. pap. 4.50 (0-8439-3166-3) Dorchester Pub Co.

— Ice & Rapture. 448p. (Orig.). 1993. pap. 4.99 (0-8439-3376-3) Dorchester Pub Co.

— My Lady Vixen. 448p. (Orig.). 1992. reprint ed. pap. 4.99 (0-8439-3370-4) Dorchester Pub Co.

— A Promise of Thunder. 448p. (Orig.). 1993. pap. 4.99 (0-8439-3444-1) Dorchester Pub Co.

— Promised Splendor. 448p. (Orig.). 1993. pap. 4.99 (0-8439-3438-7) Dorchester Pub Co.

— Sierra. 448p. (Orig.). 1995. mass mkt. 5.99 (0-8439-3815-3) Dorchester Pub Co.

— Tears Like Rain. 448p. (Orig.). 1994. mass mkt., pap. text ed. 4.99 (0-8439-3629-0) Dorchester Pub Co.

— Tempt the Devil. 448p. 1995. mass mkt. 4.99 (0-8439-3737-8) Dorchester Pub Co.

— Tender Fury. 400p. (Orig.). 1987. 3.95 (0-8439-2550-7) Dorchester Pub Co.

— Treasures of the Heart. 448p. (Orig.). 1993. pap. 4.99 (0-8439-3539-1) Dorchester Pub Co.

— Wild Is My Heart. 448p. (Orig.). 1993. reprint ed. pap. 4.99 (0-8439-3393-3) Dorchester Pub Co.

— Wild Land, Wild Love. 448p. (Orig.). 1992. pap. 4.99 (0-8439-3197-3) Dorchester Pub Co.

— Wind Rider. 448p. (Orig.). 1994. mass mkt. 4.99 (0-8439-3692-4) Dorchester Pub Co.

Mason, D. G., ed. see Moody, William V.

Mason, D. M. Development of Gaslight Emitters with Improved Durability. (Technical Reprint Ser.: No. 9). vi, 19p. 1964. 2.00 (0-317-56937-6) Inst Gas Tech.

Mason, D. M., jt. auth. see Janssen, A. J.

Mason, D. McA., et al. Identification & Determination of Organic Sulfur in Utility Gases. (Research Bulletin Ser.: No. 6). iv, 51p. 1959. 5.00 (0-685-43360-9) Inst Gas Tech.

Mason, Dale & Mason, Karen. Married to Television? Restructuring Your Prime Time. LC 89-82450. 1990. pap. 8.99 (0-89636-265-5, AC 216, LifeJourney) Chariot Family.

Mason, Dale T., ed. see Van Bebber, Mark & Taylor, Paul S.

Mason, Dan. Apache Thunder. (Ranger Ser.: No. 6). (Orig.). 1992. mass mkt. 3.50 (0-06-100415-4, Harp PBks) HarpC.

— The End of the Line. (Ranger Ser.: No. 8). 1993. mass mkt. 3.50 (0-06-100621-1, Harp PBks) HarpC.

— Range War. (Ranger Ser.: No. 4). (Orig.). 1991. mass mkt. 3.50 (0-06-100195-3, Harp PBks) HarpC.

— Ranger. 1990. mass mkt. 3.50 (0-06-100110-4, Harp PBks) HarpC.

— Ranger No. 2: Border Bandits. 1991. mass mkt. 3.50 (0-06-100156-2, Harp PBks) HarpC.

Mason, Daniel G. Beethoven & His Forerunners. LC 70-119653. reprint ed. 24.75 (0-404-04197-3) AMS Pr.

— Beethoven & His Forerunners. 352p. 1990. reprint ed. lib. bdg. 79.00 (0-7812-9038-4) Rprt Serv.

— Chamber Music of Brahms. LC 78-107817. (Select Bibliographies Reprint Ser.). 1977. 26.95 (0-8369-5209-X) Ayer.

— Chamber Music of Brahms. LC 70-119653. reprint ed. 17.50 (0-404-04198-1) AMS Pr.

— Contemporary Composers. LC 72-1726. reprint ed. 21.45 (0-404-08327-7) AMS Pr.

— The Dilemma of American Music & other Essays. 306p. 1990. reprint ed. lib. bdg. 79.00 (0-7812-9015-5) Rprt Serv.

— From Grieg to Brahms. enl. ed. LC 79-149689. reprint ed. 20.50 (0-404-04199-X) AMS Pr.

— From Grieg to Brahms: Studies of Some Modern Composers & Their Art. 259p. 1990. reprint ed. lib. bdg. 69.00 (0-7812-9039-2, 10,039) Rprt Serv.

— Great Modern Composers: Biographical Sections by M. L. Mason, Appreciation of Music Vol. 2. LC 68-20319. (Essay Index Reprint Ser.). 1977. 19.95 (0-8369-0690-X) Ayer.

— Music in My Time: And Other Reminiscences. (American Biography Ser.). 409p. 1991. reprint ed. lib. bdg. 89.00 (0-7812-8274-8) Rprt Serv.

— Music in My Time & Other Reminiscences. LC 71-107818. (Select Bibliographies Reprint Ser.). 1977. 36.95 (0-8369-5189-1) Ayer.

— Music in My Time & Other Reminiscences. LC 71-109784. 409p. 1970. reprint ed. text ed. 45.00 (0-8371-4274-1, MAMT, Greenwood Pr) Greenwood.

— The Orchestral Instruments & What They Do: A Primer for Concert-Goers. 104p. 1990. reprint ed. lib. bdg. 59.00 (0-7812-9155-0) Rprt Serv.

— Romantic Composers. LC 73-119654. reprint ed. 29.50 (0-404-04223-6) AMS Pr.

— Romantic Composers. LC 69-13990. 353p. 1970. reprint ed. text ed. 65.00 (0-8371-4096-X, MARC, Greenwood Pr) Greenwood.

— The Romantic Composers. 353p. 1990. reprint ed. lib. bdg. 79.00 (0-7812-9040-6) Rprt Serv.

— Tune in, America. LC 72-90664. (Essay Index Reprint Ser.). 1977. 19.95 (0-8369-1228-4) Ayer.

— Tune in America! A Study of Our Coming Musical Independence. LC 72-1720. reprint ed. 31.50 (0-404-08328-5) AMS Pr.

Mason, Daniel G., ed. The Art of Music, 14 vols., Set. LC 74-26067. reprint ed. 525.00 (0-404-13020-8) AMS Pr.

Mason, David. The Buried Houses. (Roerich Poetry Prize Winner Ser.). 95p. 1991. pap. 10.95 (0-934257-84-1) Story Line.

— Race & Ethnicity in Modern Britain. (Oxford Modern Britain Ser.). (Illus.). 144p. 1995. text ed. 39.95 (0-19-878098-2) OUP.

— Shadow over Babylon. 1995. pap. 5.99 (0-451-18063-1, Sig) NAL-Dutton.

— Shadow over Babylon. large type ed. LC 93-36957. 1994. 24.95 (0-7927-1894-1, Eagle Lrg Print) Chivers N Amer.

— Shadow over Babylon. large type ed. LC 93-36957. 1994. pap. 22.95 (0-7927-1893-3, Paragon Lrg Print) Chivers N Amer.

— Small Elegies. 1990. 2.50 (0-941127-09-5) Dacotah Terr Pr.

Mason, David & Enzmann, Alexander. Making Movies on Your PC: Dream up, Design, & Direct 3-D Movies. (Illus.). 210p. (Orig.). 1993. disk, pap. 34.95 (1-878739-41-7) Waite Group Pr.

***Mason, David & Willcocks, Leslie.** Systems Analysis, Systems Design. Date not set. pap. 22.00 (1-872474-09-8, Pub. by Alfred Waller UK) Paul & Co Pubs.

Mason, David, jt. auth. see Swindells, Philip.

***Mason, David E.** Managing the Expressive Dimension: How Nonprofit Managers Can Unleash the Human Potential of Their Organizations. (Nonprofit Sector Ser.). 1995. 26.95 (0-7879-0143-1) Jossey-Bass.

— Voluntary Nonprofit Enterprise Management. (Nonprofit Management & Finance Ser.). 206p. 1985. 49.50 (0-306-41582-8, Plenum Pr) Plenum.

Mason, David J., jt. auth. see Jurek, Zbigniew J.

Mason, David K. Morphing on Your PC. (Illus.). 200p. (Orig.). 1993. disk, pap. 29.95 (1-878739-53-0) Waite Group Pr.

***Mason, David P.** Massacre at Fort Mims. 196p. 1989. pap. 14.95 (0-926291-02-5) Greenberry Pub.

Mason, David S. Public Opinion & Political Change in Poland, 1980-1982. (Cambridge Russian, Soviet & Post-Soviet Studies: No. 46). (Illus.). 289p. 1985. 59.95 (0-521-30798-8) Cambridge U Pr.

— Revolution in East-Central Europe: The Rise & Fall of Communism & the Cold War. (Dilemmas in World Politics Ser.). 216p. (C). 1992. pap. text ed. 14.95 (0-8133-1341-4) Westview.

Mason, David S., jt. ed. see Rex, John.

***Mason, David T.** Japan, NAFTA, & Europe: Trilateral Cooperation of Confrontation? 1994. 49.95 (0-312-12393-0) St Martin.

***Mason, David V.** Hell High. 110p. 1995. pap. 7.95 (1-56901-812-X) NW Pub.

Mason, Diana J. & Ingersoll, Diane. Breastfeeding & the Working Mother: The Complete Guide for Today's Nursing Mother. (Illus.). 256p. 1986. pap. 11.95 (0-312-09527-9) St Martin.

Mason, Diana J. & Talbott, Susan W. The Political Action Handbook for Nurses. 640p. (C). 1985. pap. text ed. 29.75 (0-201-16368-3, Health Sci) Addison-Wesley.

Mason, Diana J., jt. auth. see Jones.

Mason, Diana J., et al, eds. Policy & Politics for Nurses: Action & Change in the Workplace, Government, Organizations & Community. 2nd ed. (Illus.). 728p. 1993. pap. text ed. 36.95 (0-7216-4668-9) Saunders.

Mason, Dorothy E. Music in Elizabethan England. LC 59-1448. (Folger Guides to the Age of Shakespeare Ser.). 1958. pap. 4.95 (0-918016-21-5) Folger Bks.

Mason, E. A. & Spurling, T. H. The Viral Equation of State. LC 69-17903. (C). 1970. 124.00 (0-08-013292-8, Pub. by Pergamon Repr UK) Franklin.

Mason, Edward A. & McDaniel, Earl W. Transport Properties of Ions in Gases. 560p. 1988. text ed. 120.00 (0-471-88385-9) Wiley.

Mason, Edward E. Fluid, Electrolyte & Nutrient Therapy in Surgery. LC 73-8805. (Illus.). 360p. reprint ed. 102.60 (0-8357-9403-2, 2014561) Bks Demand.

Mason, Edward S. Controlling World Trade: Cartels & Commodity Agreements. LC 72-4281. (World Affairs Ser.: National & International Viewpoints). 308p. 1972. reprint ed. 23.95 (0-405-04574-3) Ayer.

— The Economic & Social Modernization of the Republic of Korea. (East Asian Monographs: No. 92). 584p. 1981. 28.00 (0-674-23175-9) HUP.

— Economic Concentration & the Monopoly Problem. LC 57-6351. (Economic Studies: No. 100). (Illus.). 427p. 1957. 25.00 (0-674-22651-8) HUP.

— Economic Development in India & Pakistan. LC 77-38764. (Harvard University. Center for International Affairs. Occasional Papers in International Affairs: No. 13). reprint ed. 24.50 (0-404-54613-7) AMS Pr.

— Economic Planning in Underdeveloped Areas: Government & Business. LC 58-59763. (Moorhouse I.X. Millar Lecture Ser.: No. 2). 100p. reprint ed. pap. 28.50 (0-7837-0456-9, 2040779) Bks Demand.

— The Harvard Institute for International Development & Its Antecedents. 108p. (Orig.). (C). 1986. lib. bdg. 33.00 (0-8191-5552-7, Harvard Inst for Intl Dev); pap. text ed. 14.00 (0-8191-5553-5, Harvard Inst for Intl Dev) U Pr of Amer.

— On the Appropriate Size of a Development Program. LC 76-25007. (Harvard University. Center for International Affairs. Occasional Papers in International Affairs: No. 8). reprint ed. 24.50 (0-404-54608-0) AMS Pr.

Mason, Edward S. & Asher, Robert E. The World Bank Since Bretton Woods. LC 73-1089. 915p. 1973. 38.95 (0-8157-5492-2) Brookings.

Mason, Edward T. Samuel Johnson: His Words & His Ways. LC 72-2104. (Studies in Samuel Johnson: No. 97). 1972. reprint ed. lib. bdg. 49.95 (0-8383-1491-0) M S G Haskell Hse.

Mason, Eileen. Great Book of Funny Quotes: Witty Words for Every Day of the Year. (Illus.). 224p. 1993. pap. 7.95 (0-8069-8605-0) Sterling.

***Mason, Elisabeth & Eber, Eric.** Investing Tips Grampa Taught Us: A Guide for Financing College Costs & More. LC 94-37809. 1994. 13.95 (0-9643153-0-0) Finan Pr FL.

***Mason, Elizabeth.** The Rag Street Journal: The Ultimate Guide to Shopping Thrift & Consignment Stores Throughout the U. S. & Canada. 384p. (Orig.). 1995. pap. 14.95 (0-8050-3728-4, Owl) H Holt & Co.

Mason, Elizabeth B. & Starr, Louis M. The Oral History Collection of Columbia University. 4th ed. LC 79-11527. (Illus.). xxx, 306p. 1979. text ed. 22.50 (0-9602492-0-6) Columbia U Oral Hist Res.

Mason, Elizabeth J. How to Write Meaningful Nursing Standards. LC 84-13005. 261p. (C). 1984. pap. text ed. 39.95 (0-8273-4300-0) Delmar.

— How to Write Meaningful Standards of Care. LC 93-5210. Orig. Title: How to Write Meaningful Nursing Standards. 311p. 1994. pap. text ed. 39.95 (0-8273-5316-2) Delmar.

Mason, Elliott B. Human Physiology. 575p. 1983. teacher ed 12.95 (0-8053-6886-8); text ed. 52.75 (0-8053-6885-X) Benjamin-Cummings.

Mason, Elliott B., jt. auth. see Spence, Alexander P.

Mason, Ellsworth. The University of Colorado Library & Its Makers, 1876-1972. LC 93-33714. (Illus.). 401p. 1994. 42.50 (0-8108-2685-2) Scarecrow.

Mason, Ellsworth, ed. see Joyce, James.

Mason, Emma. St. Wulfstan of Worcester: C One Thousand Eight to One Thousand Ninety-Five. (Illus.). 288p. 1990. text ed. 59.95 (0-631-15041-2) Blackwell Pubs.

— Westminster Abbey & Its People c.1056 - c.1216. (Studies in History of Medieval Religion). 256p. 1996. text ed. 63.00 (0-85115-396-8) Boydell & Brewer.

Mason, Eudo C. Goethe's Faust: Its Genesis & Purport. LC 67-14969. 435p. reprint ed. pap. 124.00 (0-685-23556-4, 2029052) Bks Demand.

— Rilke, Europe, & the English-speaking World. LC 61-16153. 277p. reprint ed. pap. 79.00 (0-317-20596-X, 2024492) Bks Demand.

Mason, Eugene. Aucassin & Nicolette with Other Romances. LC 70-172850. (Illus.). reprint ed. 37.50 (0-404-07774-9) AMS Pr.

Mason, Eugene, tr. see Marie De France.

Mason, F. H., jt. auth. see Jensen, Cecil H.

Mason, F. V. Guns for Rebellion. 25.95 (0-89190-099-3, Am Repr) Amereon Ltd.

Mason, F. Van Wyck. At the Villa Rose. 1976. 22.95 (0-8488-0832-0) Amereon Ltd.

— The Rio Casino Intrigue. reprint ed. lib. bdg. 18.95 (0-89190-356-9, Rivercity Pr) Amereon Ltd.

***Mason, Felicia.** Body & Soul. 288p. 1995. pap. 4.99 (0-8217-0160-6) Zebra.

— Body & Soul. 288p. 1995. pap. 4.99 (0-7860-0160-7) Windsor NY.

— For the Love of You. 288p. 1994. mass mkt. 4.99 (0-7860-0071-6) Windsor NY.

Mason, Florence B. To Love Again: Intimate Relationships After 60. LC 89-1463. 132p. 1989. pap. 7.95 (0-933469-05-5) Gateway Bks.

Mason, Frances B. Great Design: Order & Progress in Nature. LC 72-156690. (Essay Index Reprint Ser.). 1977. reprint ed. 23.95 (0-8369-2562-9) Ayer.

Mason, Frances N., ed. John Norton & Sons, Merchants of London & Virginia: Being Papers from Their Counting House for the Years 1750-1795. LC 68-23839. (Illus.). xi, 573p. 1968. reprint ed. 49.50 (0-678-05614-5) Kelley.

Mason, Francis. I Remember Balanchine. 1992. pap. 15.00 (0-385-26611-1, Anchor NY) Doubleday.

Mason, Francis, jt. auth. see Balanchine, George.

Mason, Francis K. The British Bomber since 1914. (Illus.). 416p. 1994. 42.95 (1-55750-085-1) Naval Inst Pr.

— The British Fighter since Nineteen Twelve. (Putnam Aviation Ser.). (Illus.). 448p. 1993. 49.95 (1-55750-082-7) Naval Inst Pr.

— Hawker Aircraft since Nineteen Twenty. rev. ed. (Putnam Aviation Ser.). (Illus.). 512p. 1991. 47.95 (1-55750-351-6) Naval Inst Pr.

Mason, Francis K., jt. auth. see Windrow, Martin.

Mason, Franklin. Four Roses in Three Acts. LC 80-68007. 1981. pap. 5.95 (0-914590-65-0) Fiction Coll.

Mason, G. W. Mason: Ancestors & Descendants of Elisha Mason, Litchfield, Conn., 1759-1858, & His Wife Lucretia Webster, 1766-1853. 120p. 1992. reprint ed. lib. bdg. 33.00 (0-8328-2684-7); reprint ed. pap. 23.00 (0-8328-2685-5) Higginson Bk Co.

Mason, Gabriel R., ed. Great American Liberals. LC 76-156691. (Essay Index Reprint Ser.). 1977. reprint ed. 18.95 (0-8369-2413-4) Ayer.

Mason, Gene. Save Your License: A Driver's Survival Guide. LC 78-2218. (Illus.). 150p. 1978. text ed. 14.95 (0-87364-103-5) Paladin Pr.

Mason, Geoffrey, jt. ed. see Cooperstein, Bruce.

Mason, George. The Papers of George Mason, 1725-1792, 3 vols., Vol. 1. Rutland, Robert A., ed. LC 70-97016. 613p. reprint ed. pap. 165.60 (0-7837-0318-X, 2040640) Bks Demand.

— The Papers of George Mason, 1725-1792, 3 vols., Vol. 2. Rutland, Robert A., ed. LC 70-97016. 403p. reprint ed. pap. 114.90 (0-7837-0319-8) Bks Demand.

— The Papers of George Mason, 1725-1792, 3 vols., Vol. 3. Rutland, Robert A., ed. LC 70-97016. 477p. reprint ed. pap. 136.00 (0-7837-0320-1) Bks Demand.

Mason, George, jt. auth. see Alberti, Delbert.

Mason, George H. Life with the Zulus of Natal, South Africa. 232p. 1968. 35.00 (0-7146-1835-7, Pub. by F Cass Pubs UK) Intl Spec Bk.

Mason, Germaine. Concise Survey of French Literature. LC 75-94610. 344p. 1969. reprint ed. text ed. 65.00 (0-8371-2464-6, MAFL, Greenwood Pr) Greenwood.

Mason, Grace S. Women Are Queer. LC 77-37278. (Short Story Index Reprint Ser.). 1977. reprint ed. 23.95 (0-8369-4089-X) Ayer.

Mason, Grant W., et al. Physical Science Concepts. (Illus.). xiv, 370p. (Orig.). (C). 1989. pap. text ed. 20.00 (0-685-28123-X) Soundprint.

— Physical Science Concepts. (Illus.). xiv, 370p. (Orig.). (C). 1989. pap. text ed. 25.00 (0-9611938-1-6) Soundprint.

Mason, Gregory, jt. auth. see Mason, Ruth.

Mason, Griselda F. Sleigh Ride to Russia: The Quaker Mission to Russia to Try to Avert the Crimean War. (C). 1988. 60.00 (0-900657-99-5, Pub. by W Sessions UK) St Mut.

Mason, H. A. Sir Thomas Wyatt: A Literary Portrait. 352p. 1980. 36.95 (0-906515-65-3, Pub. by Brstl Class Pr UK) Focus Info Gr.

— The Tragic Plane. 200p. 1985. 45.00 (0-19-812843-6) OUP.

Mason, H. A., ed. Sir Thomas Wyatt: A Literary Portrait. 344p. 1987. 37.50 (0-8453-4512-5, Pub. by Brstl Class Pr UK) Assoc Univ Prs.

Mason, H. L. Toynbee's Approach to World Politics, Vol. 5. LC 60-202. 1958. 11.00 (0-930598-04-0) Tulane Stud Pol.

Mason, H. L., ed. see Oldenbourg, Rudolf C. & Sartorius, Hans.

Mason, H. Lee. Sermon Outlines for Evangelism. (Sermon Outline Ser.). (Orig.). 1981. pap. 2.99 (0-8010-6120-2) Baker Bk.

Mason, H. Lowell. Hymn-Tunes of Lowell Mason. LC 74-24144. reprint ed. 29.50 (0-404-13035-6) AMS Pr.

Mason, Hamilton. French Theatre in New York: 1899-1939. LC 40-14965. reprint ed. 19.45 (0-404-04224-4) AMS Pr.

Mason, Harry M. Life on the Dry Line: Working the Land, 1902-1944. LC 92-53038. 224p. 1992. 19.95 (1-55591-122-6) Fulcrum Pub.

Mason, Haydn. Candide: Optimism Demolished. (MWS Ser.). 170p. 1992. text ed. 21.95 (0-8057-8085-8, Twayne); pap. 12.95 (0-8057-8559-0, Twayne) Macmillan.

Mason, Heather L., jt. ed. see Etheridge, David T.

Mason, Helen. Great Careers for People Who Like Being Outdoors, 6 vols., Vol. 6. LC 93-78075. (Career Connections Ser.: Vol. 6). (Illus.). 48p. (J). (gr. 6-9). 1993. 17.95 (0-8103-9390-5, 102108, UXL) Gale.

— Life at the Seashore. (Illus.). 32p. (YA). (gr. 2-5). 1990. lib. bdg. 14.25 (0-88625-270-9); pap. 3.50 (0-88625-269-5) Durkin Hayes Pub.

— Life in a Forest. (Nature Ser.). (Illus.). 32p. (Orig.). (J). (gr. 3-6). 1992. pap. 3.50 (0-88625-260-1) Durkin Hayes Pub.

— Life in a Pond. (Nature Ser.). (Illus.). 32p. (Orig.). (J). (gr. 3-6). 1992. pap. 3.50 (0-88625-255-5) Durkin Hayes Pub.

Mason, Henry L. Mass Demonstrations Against Foreign Regimes, Vol. 10. LC 66-8068. 1966. 11.00 (0-930598-09-1) Tulane Stud Pol.

Mason, Henry M., tr. see Anjou, Lars A.

Mason, Herbert. The Death of Al-Hallaj: A Dramatic Narrative. LC 79-4403. (Illus.). 1979. pap. text ed. 6.95 (0-268-00843-4) U of Notre Dame Pr.

— A Legend of Alexander & the Merchant & the Parrot: Dramatic Poems. LC 86-40338. 128p. 1988. text ed. 18.95 (0-268-01281-4); pap. text ed. 9.95 (0-268-01282-2) U of Notre Dame Pr.

— Memoir of a Friend: Louis Massignon. LC 87-40349. 160p. 1988. text ed. 18.95 (0-268-01365-9) U of Notre Dame Pr.

— Two Statesmen of Mediaeval Islam: Vizir Ibn Hubayra (499-560 A. H., 1105-1165 A. D.) & Califh an-Nasir Li Din Allah (553-622 A. H., 1158-1225 A. D.) 146p. 1972. text ed. 44.65 (90-279-6979-5) Mouton.

Mason, Herbert, ed. & tr. Testimonies & Reflections: Essays of Louis Massignon. LC 88-40327. (C). 1989. text ed. 24.95 (0-268-01733-6) U of Notre Dame Pr.

Mason, Herbert, tr. Gilgamesh: A Verse Narrative. 128p. 1972. pap. 4.99 (0-451-62718-0, Ment) NAL-Dutton.

Mason, Herbert, ed. see Massignon, Louis.

Mason, Herbert B., ed. Encyclopedia of Ships & Shipping. 1977. lib. bdg. 250.00 (0-8490-1767-X) Gordon Pr.

Mason, Herbert L. A Flora of the Marshes of California. LC 57-7960. (Illus.). 1983. reprint ed. 60.00 (0-520-01433-2) U CA Pr.

***Mason, Herbert M.** Men at War: Great Pursuit. 320p. 1995. 12.98 (0-8317-5707-8) Smithmark.

— Men at War: Lafayette Escadrille. 352p. 1995. 12.98 (0-8317-5712-4) Smithmark.

Mason, Herbert W. Al-Hallaj. (Curzon Sufi Ser.: No. 2). 228p. (C). 1995. pap. 18.50 (0-7007-0311-X, Pub. by Curzon Pr UK) Humanities.

Mason, Howard S., jt. ed. see Florkin, Marcel.

Mason, I., ed. see International Congress of Animal Production Staff.

An Asterisk (*) at the beginning of an entry indicates that the title is appearing in BIP for the first time.

Mason, I. L. A World Dictionary of Livestock Breeds. 3rd ed. 348p. 1988. text ed. 49.00 (*0-85198-617-X*) CAB Intl.

Mason, I. L., jt. ed. see Hoffmann, B.

Mason, I. S., jt. auth. see Moriello, K. A.

Mason, Ian, jt. auth. see Hatim, Basil.

Mason, Ian A. The Semantics of Destructive Lisp. LC 86-72170. (Center for the Study of Language & Information-Lecture Notes Ser.: No. 5). 290p. 1986. 29.95 (*0-937073-05-9*); pap. 15.95 (*0-937073-06-7*) Ctr Study Language.

Mason, Irvin H. The Feasors, Vol. I. (Illus.). (Orig.). Date not set. 27.50 (*0-9635749-0-6*); pap. 15.00 (*0-685-63476-0*) Mason Eng.

Mason, Isaac. Life of Isaac Mason As a Slave. LC 72-89393. (Black Heritage Library Collection). 1977. 11.95 (*0-8369-8627-X*) Ayer.

Mason, J. Evolution Made Plain. 1992. lib. bdg. 250.95 (*0-8490-5567-9*) Gordon Pr.

— Methods of Functional Analysis for Application in Solid Mechanics. (Studies in Applied Mechanics: Vol. 9). 392p. 1985. 128.25 (*0-444-42436-9*) Elsevier.

— Variational, Incremental & Energy Methods in Solid Mechanics & Shell Theory: IFIP World Congress. (Studies in Applied Mechanics: Vol. 4). 368p. 1980. 115.50 (*0-444-41899-7*) Elsevier.

Mason, J., ed. Design for Manufacturability - 1994. LC 93-70158. (DE Ser.: Vol. 67). 132p. 1994. 32.50 (*0-7918-1269-3*, H00901) ASME.

Mason, J. & Davis, J. Fostering & Sustaining Mathematics: Thinking Through Problem Solving. 106p. (C). 1991. pap. 51.00x (*0-7300-1264-6*, ECT405, Pub. by Deakin Univ AT) St Mut.

— Modelling with Mathematics in Primary & Secondary Schools: Modelling with Mathematics in Primary & Secondary Schools. 78p. (C). 1991. pap. 60.00x (*0-7300-1265-4*, ECT404, Pub. by Deakin Univ AT) St Mut.

Mason, J., jt. ed. see Sutherland, R. J.

Mason, J. A. Archaeology of Santa Marta, Colombia: The Tairona Culture. (Chicago Field Museum of Natural History Fieldiana Anthropology Ser.: Vol. 20). 1972. reprint ed. 73.00 (*0-527-01880-5*) Periodicals Srv.

Mason, J. Alden. Puerto Rican Folklore. Espinosa, Aurelio M., ed. (Puerto Rico Ser.). 1979. lib. bdg. 59.95 (*0-8490-2989-9*) Gordon Pr.

Mason, J. Barry & Ezell, Hazel F. Marketing Management. (Illus.). 784p. (C). 1993. text ed. write for info. (*0-02-376921-1*) Macmillan.

Mason, J. Barry, et al. Cases & Problems in Contemporary Retailing. 3rd ed. LC 91-73501. 459p. 1992. 19.95 (*0-87393-139-4*) Dame Pubns.

— Retailing. 4th ed. (C). 1990. student ed, text ed. 21.95 (*0-256-09177-3*) Irwin.

— Retailing. 4th ed. 720p. (C). 1990. text ed. 60.95 (*0-256-08981-7*) Irwin.

— Retailing. 5th ed. LC 93-21286. (Series in Marketing). 704p. (C). 1993. text ed. 64.95 (*0-256-12002-1*) Irwin Prof Pubng.

— Retailing: Canadian Version. 448p. (C). 1990. text ed. 54.95 (*0-256-07865-3*) Irwin.

— Retailing, International. 4th ed. (C). 1992. student ed, text ed. 29.95 (*0-256-11410-2*) Irwin.

Mason, J. C., ed. Scientific Software Systems. 200p. 1990. 49.00 (*0-412-34570-6*, 836) Chapman & Hall.

Mason, J. C. & Cox, M. G. Algorithms for Approximation. 350p. 1990. 99.95 (*0-412-34580-3*, A3805) Chapman & Hall.

Mason, J. C. & Cox, M. G., eds. Algorithms for Approximation. (Institute of Mathematics & Its Applications Conference Series, New Ser.: New Series 10). (Illus.). 710p. 1987. 125.00 (*0-19-853612-7*) OUP.

Mason, J. C. & Stocks, D. C. BASIC Differential Equations. (Basic Ser.). (Illus.). 144p. 1987. pap. text ed. 24.95 (*0-408-01520-9*) Buttrwrth-Heinemann.

Mason, J. Day. Speaking to Strangers. (Illus.). 105p. 1987. 40.00 (*0-933858-22-1*) Kennebec River.

Mason, J. J. Coatings for Energy Efficiency & Solar Applications. (C). 1984. 100.00 (*0-685-33082-6*, Pub. by Interntl Solar Energy Soc UK) St Mut.

— Coatings for Energy Efficiency & Solar Applications (C38) 89p. (C). 1984. 95.00 (*0-685-30225-3*, Pub. by Interntl Solar Energy Soc UK) St Mut.

Mason, J. K. Forensic Medicine: An Illustrated Reference. LC 92-48550. (Illus.). 213p. 1993. 199.95 (*0-412-43300-1*) Chapman & Hall.

— Human Life & Medical Practice. 192p. 1988. 30.00 (*0-85224-560-2*, Pub. by Edinburgh U Pr UK) Col U Pr.

— Human Life & Medical Practice. 1990. pap. text ed. 15.00 (*0-85224-584-X*, Pub. by Edinburgh U Pr UK) Col U Pr.

— Mason: Forensic Medicine for Lawyers. rev. ed. 1983. pap. 47.95 (*0-407-01370-9*) Butterworth Legal Pubs.

Mason, J. K. & McCall Smith, R. Alexander. Law & Medical Ethics. 3rd ed. 1991. pap. 36.00 (*0-406-50078-9*, U.K.) Butterworth Legal Pubs.

Mason, J. K. & Smith, R. A. Butterworths Medico-Legal Encyclopaedia. 624p. 1991. boxed 175.00 (*0-407-00374-6*) Butterworth Legal Pubs.

Mason, J. K., jt. auth. see Gee, D. J.

Mason, J. M. Comments on the Last Edition of Shakespeare's Plays. LC 73-172851. reprint ed. 52.50 (*0-404-04225-2*) AMS Pr.

— Comments on the Several Editions of Shakespeare's Plays, Extended to Those of Malone & Steevens. LC 77-172852. reprint ed. 76.50 (*0-404-04226-0*) AMS Pr.

Mason, J. P., jt. ed. see Croall, I. F.

Mason, J. S. & Goldberg, A. S. Bulk Solids Handling: An Introduction to the Practice & Technology. 384p. 1986. text ed. 110.00 (*0-412-01251-0*, 9889, Chap & Hall NY) Chapman & Hall.

Mason, J. W. Creative Freedom & the Creative East. 1973. 59.95 (*0-87968-958-7*) Gordon Pr.

— Shinto, 2 vols. 1973. 500.00 (*0-8490-1050-0*) Gordon Pr.

Mason, J. W., & Co. Staff. Furniture Trade Catalog: Illustrated Catalog of Chairs & Furniture by Joel W. Mason. 116p. 1983. reprint ed. pap. 25.00 (*0-87556-653-7*) Saifer.

Mason, Jackie. Jackie Mason's "The World According to Me" 95p. 1991. 2.99 (*0-517-69432-8*) Random Hse Value.

Mason, Jackie & Berkow, Ira. How to Talk Jewish. 160p. 1991. pap. 8.95 (*0-312-07236-8*) St Martin.

Mason, Jackie & Gross, Ken. Jackie, Oy! The Birth & Rebirth of Jackie Mason. (Illus.). 224p. 1988. 16.95 (*0-316-54933-9*) Little.

Mason, James. Ancient Greece Resource Book. (Sense of History Ser.). 1991. pap. text ed. 13.32 (*0-582-06819-3*) Longman.

— Art of Chess. 3rd ed. Reinfeld, Fred & Bernstein, Sidney, eds. pap. 6.95 (*0-486-20463-4*) Dover.

— Medieval Realms. 1991. pap. text ed. 13.32 (*0-582-20735-5*) Longman.

— Roman Empire. 1991. pap. text ed. 13.32 (*0-582-20736-3*) Longman.

Mason, James D. Combat Handgun Shooting. (Illus.). 286p. 1980. 44.95 (*0-398-03461-3*) C C Thomas.

Mason, James H. The Dudley Genealogies. LC 82-62705. 216p. 1987. 35.00 (*0-9609032-1-6*) J H Mason.

Mason, James H. & Mason, Mary S. Our Dudley Heritage. LC 82-60822. 96p. 1982. 16.50 (*0-9609032-0-8*) J H Mason.

Mason, James J., ed. AIREA Financial Tables. 473p. 1981. 27.50 (*0-911780-54-8*) Appraisal Inst.

Mason, Jana M. & Au, Kathryn H. Reading Instruction for Today. 2nd ed. (C). 1990. text ed. 56.50 (*0-673-38774-7*) HarpCollege.

Mason, Jana M., jt. ed. see Allen, JoBeth.

Mason, Jana M., jt. auth. see McCormick, Christine E.

Mason, Jane. A Family Affair. (J). (gr. 4-8). 1993. pap. 2.50 (*0-448-40464-8*, G&D) Putnam Pub Group.

— Hello, Two-Wheeler! LC 94-28633. (All Aboard Reading). (Illus.). (J). 1995. 3.50 (*0-448-40854-6*, G&D); pap. write for info. (*0-448-40853-8*, G&D) Putnam Pub Group.

— The Mount People. (C). 1989. 70.00 (*1-85022-057-3*, Pub. by Dyllansow Truran UK) St Mut.

— River Day. LC 93-26573. (Illus.). 32p. (J). (gr. k-3). 1994. text ed. 14.95 (*0-02-762869-8*, Mac Bks Young Read) S&S Childrens.

— Theater. LC 93-5744. (Now Hiring Ser.). (J). 1994. text ed. 14.95 (*0-89686-792-7*, Crstwood Hse) Silver Burdett Pr.

***Mason, Jane B., adapt.** Apollo 13: The Movie Storybook. LC 95-13068. (J). 1995. write for info. (*0-448-41119-9*, G&D) Putnam Pub Group.

Mason, Janet. Abuse & Neglect of Children & Disabled Adults: North Carolina's Mandatory Reporting Laws. 51p. 1984. Including update, 1985-86. pap. 5.00 (*1-56011-000-7*); Update, 1985-86. pap. 2.00 (*1-56011-001-5*) Institute Government.

— North Carolina Juvenile Code & Termination of Parental Rights Statutes: As Amended by the 1993 Session of the General Assembly. 82p. (Orig.). (C). 1994. pap. text ed. 10.00 (*1-56011-272-7*, 94.04) Institute Government.

— North Carolina Marriage Laws & Procedures. 3rd ed. (C). 1994. pap. text ed. 2.50 (*1-56011-235-2*, 94.23) Institute Government.

***Mason, Janet, contrib.** North Carolina Juvenile Code & Termination of Parental Rights Statutes: As Amended by the 1994 General Assembly. (Orig.). (C). 1995. pap. text ed. write for info. (*1-56011-242-5*) Institute Government.

Mason, Janet, jt. auth. see Ennis, Trudy A.

Mason, Janet, jt. auth. see Thomas, Mason P., Jr.

Mason, Jeff. Philosophical Rhetoric: The Function of Indirection in Philosophical Writings. 192p. 1989. 45.00 (*0-415-03043-9*); pap. 13.95 (*0-415-03044-7*) Routledge.

Mason, Jeff & Washington, Peter. The Future of Thinking: Rhetoric & Liberal Arts Teaching. LC 92-7668. 160p. 1992. 69.95 (*0-415-07318-9*, A7869); pap. 13.95 (*0-415-07319-7*, A7873) Routledge.

Mason, Jeffrey. Wisecracks: The Farces of George S. Kaufman. Brockett, Oscar, ed. LC 88-11076. (Theater & Dramatic Studies: No. 53). 146p. reprint ed. 41.70 (*0-8357-1887-5*, 2070740) Bks Demand.

Mason, Jeffrey D. Melodrama & the Myth of America. LC 92-46375. (Drama & Performance Studies). 1993. 25.00 (*0-253-33686-4*) Ind U Pr.

***Mason, Jeffrey M. & McCarthy, Susan.** When Elephants Weep: The Emotional Lives of Animals. LC 94-23819. 1995. write for info. (*0-385-31425-6*) Delacorte.

Mason, Jennie. Introduction to Word Processing. 1979. teacher ed write for info. (*0-318-51114-2*); pap. write for info. (*0-672-97134-8*) Macmillan.

— Word Processing Skills & Simulations. LC 78-15761. 1979. teacher ed write for info. (*0-672-97135-6*); pap. write for info. (*0-672-97197-6*) Macmillan.

Mason, Jennifer, jt. auth. see Finch, Janet.

Mason, Jerry. The Family of Woman. (Ridge Press Bks.). (Illus.). 1979. 15.00 (*0-448-16268-7*, Perigree Bks); pap. 16.00 (*0-399-50966-6*, Perigree Bks) Berkley Pub.

Mason, Jerry, ed. Family of Children. LC 78-72515. (Illus.). 192p. 1979. pap. 14.95 (*0-399-50965-8*, Perigree Bks) Berkley Pub.

Mason, Jerry, intro. Financial Counseling. 450p. (C). Date not set. pap. text ed. 30.00 (*0-9639684-0-8*) Accred Finan.

Mason, Jesse D. History of Amador County California with Illustrations. Thompson & West, Publishers Oakland Staff, ed. (Illus.). 400p. 1986. reprint ed. 25.00 (*0-938121-01-4*) Cenotto Pubns.

Mason, Jesse D., ed. History of Amador County (CA) (Illus.). 400p. 1994. reprint ed. text ed. 44.95 (*0-938121-07-3*); reprint ed. pap. 29.95 (*0-938121-06-5*) Cenotto Pubns.

Mason, Jill, ed. see Chioffi, Nancy & Mead, Gretchen.

Mason, Jill, ed. see Mahnken, Jan.

Mason, Jill, ed. see Rupp, Rebecca.

Mason, Jill, ed. see Vargas, Pattie & Gulling, Rich.

Mason, Jill, ed. see Whitehead, Jeffrey.

Mason, Jim. Animal Factories Update. 1990. pap. 12.95 (*0-517-57751-8*, Harmony) Crown Pub Group.

— Unnatural Order. 1993. 24.00 (*0-671-76923-5*) S&S Trade.

Mason, Joan, ed. Multinuclear NMR. LC 87-12284. (Illus.). 660p. 1987. 135.00 (*0-306-42153-4*, Plenum Pr) Plenum.

Mason, John. Commercial Hydroponics. (Illus.). 172p. reprint ed. 24.95 (*0-86417-300-8*, Pub. by Kangaroo Pr AT) Seven Hills Bk.

— Don't Wait for Your Ship to Come in; Swim out & Meet It. 1994. pap. 5.95 (*1-56292-058-8*) Honor Bks OK.

— Four New World Yoruba Rituals. 3rd rev. ed. (Illus.). 200p. (C). 1993. pap. write for info. (*1-881244-03-2*) Yoruba Theol Arch.

— Growing Ferns. (Growing Ser.). (Illus.). 96p. (Orig.). 1990. reprint ed. pap. 11.95 (*0-86417-281-8*, Pub. by Kangaroo Pr AT) Seven Hills Bk.

— Growing Herbs. LC 93-42021. (Illus.). 116p. (Orig.). 1994. pap. 15.95 (*0-916638-50-2*) Meyerbooks.

— Nursery Management. (Illus.). 184p. 1994. 24.95 (*0-86417-603-1*, Pub. by Kangaroo Pr AT) Seven Hills Bk.

— Orin Orisa: Songs for Selected Heads. LC 92-80382. 416p. (Orig.). 1992. 50.00 (*1-881244-00-8*); pap. 25.00 (*1-881244-01-6*) Yoruba Theol Arch.

— Power Station Sun: The Story of Energy. (Discovering Science Ser.). (Illus.). 48p. (J). (gr. 1-4). 1987. 12.95 (*0-8160-1778-6*) Facts on File.

— Stress Passages: Surviving Life's Transitions Gracefully. LC 86-26904. (Illus.). 269p. (Orig.). 1988. pap. 11.95 (*0-89087-489-1*) Celestial Arts.

— The Turke: From Quartos of 1610 & 1632. Adams, J. Q., Jr., ed. (Material for the Study of the Old English Drama Ser.: No. 1, Vol. 37). 1974. reprint ed. pap. 21.00 (*0-8115-0286-4*) Periodicals Srv.

— Weather & Climate. (Our World Ser.). (Illus.). 48p. (J). (gr. 5-8). 1991. lib. bdg. 12.95 (*0-382-24225-4*) Silver Burdett Pr.

Mason, John & Lawrence, Rosemary. Growing Vegetables. (Growing Ser.). (Illus.). 110p. (Orig.). 1993. pap. 11.95 (*0-86417-377-6*, Pub. by Kangaroo Pr AT) Seven Hills Bk.

***Mason, John & Redmond, Tim.** Word of Promise. 1995. 12.99 (*0-88419-392-6*, Creation Hse) Strang Comms Co.

Mason, John, jt. auth. see Edwards, Gary.

Mason, John A. The Language of the Papago of Arizona. LC 52-81. (University of Pennsylvania, Museum Monographs). 88p. reprint ed. pap. 25.10 (*0-317-28360-X*, 2022382) Bks Demand.

Mason, John C. BASIC Matrix Methods. (Basic Ser.). (Illus.). 160p. 1984. pap. 24.95 (*0-408-01390-7*) Buttrwrth-Heinemann.

Mason, John F. & Dickey, Parke A., eds. Oil Field Development Techniques: Proceedings of the Daqing International Meeting, 1982. LC 88-35723. (AAPG Studies in Geology: No. 28). (Illus.). 255p. reprint ed. pap. 72.70 (*0-8357-3071-9*, 2039328) Bks Demand.

Mason, John H, ed. see Diderot, Denis.

Mason, John L. A Brief of the Pequot War. LC 71-152995. (Select Bibliographies Reprint Ser.). 1977. reprint ed. 11.95 (*0-8369-5747-4*) Ayer.

— An Enemy Called Average. 126p. (Orig.). 1990. pap. 5.95 (*0-89274-765-X*, HH765) Harrison Hse.

— The Identity Crisis Theme in American Feature Films, 1960-1969. 1977. 27.95 (*0-405-09896-0*, 11488) Ayer.

— Let Go of Whatever Makes You Stop. 1994. pap. 6.99 (*0-88419-373-X*, Creation Hse) Strang Comms Co.

— You're Born an Original Don't Die a Copy. 120p. 1993. pap. 6.99 (*0-88419-355-1*, Creation Hse) Strang Comms Co.

Mason, John M., Jr., jt. ed. see Smith, Bob L.

Mason, John O., Jr. Using IBM Microcomputers in Business: Decision Making with Lotus 1-2-3 & dBASE III Plus. 922p. (C). 1991. pap. text ed. 44.00 (*0-15-594489-4*) Dryden Pr.

Mason, John P. The Resurrection According to Paul. LC 92-47029. 168p. 1993. text ed. 79.95 (*0-7734-2358-3*) E Mellen.

Mason, John R. Reading & Responding to Mircea Eliade's History of Religious Ideas. LC 93-15344. 136p. 1993. text ed. 69.95 (*0-7734-9283-6*) E Mellen.

— Switch Engineering Handbook. 1992. text ed. 64.50 (*0-07-040769-X*) McGraw.

Mason, John T., Jr. The Atlantic War Remembered: An Oral History Collection. LC 90-43436. (Illus.). 380p. 1990. 36.95 (*0-87021-523-X*) Naval Inst Pr.

— The Pacific War Remembered: An Oral History Collection. LC 86-5438. (Illus.). 373p. 1986. 39.95 (*0-87021-522-1*) Naval Inst Pr.

Mason-John, Vakerie. Talking Black: African, Caribbean, & Asian Lesbians Speak Out. (Women on Women Ser.). 256p. 1994. pap. 14.95 (*0-304-32965-7*, Pub. by Cassell Pubng UK) InBook.

***Mason-John, Valerie.** Talking Black: African, Caribbean & Asian Lesbians Speak Out. (Women on Women Ser.). 256p. 1994. 55.00 (*0-304-32963-0*, Pub. by Cassell Pubng UK) InBook.

Mason-John, Valerie & Khambatta, Ann. Lesbians Talk Making Black Waves. 64p. 1994. pap. 8.50 (*1-85727-007-X*, Pub. by Scarlet Pr UK) InBook.

Mason, Joseph B., et al. Modern Retailing: Theory & Practice. 6th ed. LC 92-12011. 816p. (C). 1992. text ed. 64.95 (*0-256-10257-0*) Irwin.

Mason, Joseph J. Mirrorplay: A Novel. 1990. 14.95 (*0-533-08753-8*) Vantage.

***Mason, Joseph W.** A Heart Attack Can Save Your Life: The Complete Guide on How to Lose Weight & Reduce Your Risk of Heart Attack & Cancer Without Dieting. LC 95-67488. (Illus.). 256p. 1995. pap. 15.95 (*0-9646109-4-9*) Readers Choice.

Mason, Judy S. Mr. Farmer & His Animals. Scoggan, Nita, ed. (Illus.). 52p. (Orig.). (J). (gr. 3 up). 1987. pap. 3.95 (*0-910487-11-1*) Royalty Pub.

Mason, Julian D., Jr., ed. see Wheatley, Phillis.

Mason, Jutta, tr. see Poerksen, Uwe.

Mason, K. L. Advanced Spanish Course. 1967. 11.40 (*0-08-012272-8*, Pergamon Pr); pap. text ed. 9.80 (*0-08-012271-X*, Pergamon Pr) Elsevier.

Mason, K. L. & Sager, J. C. Spanish Oral Drill Book. 1969. pap. text ed. 7.80 (*0-08-013362-2*, Pergamon Pr) Elsevier.

Mason, K. O., et al, eds. The Physics of Accretion onto Compact Objects. (Lecture Notes in Physics Ser.: Vol. 266). viii, 421p. 1986. 53.00 (*0-387-17195-9*) Spr-Verlag.

Mason, Karen, jt. auth. see Mason, Dale.

***Mason, Karen O. & Jensen, An-Magritt, eds.** Gender & Family Change in Industrialized Countries. (International Studies in Demography). (Illus.). 320p. 1995. 65.00 (*0-19-828970-7*) OUP.

Mason, Kate. Make Your Own Cool Crafts. (J). (gr. 4-7). 1994. pap. 5.95 (*0-8167-3226-4*) Troll Assocs.

— My Friendship Bracelets. (J). (ps-3). 1994. pap. 5.95 (*0-8167-3227-2*) Troll Assocs.

Mason, Kathy. Going Beyond Words: The Art & Practice of Visual Thinking. 172p. (Orig.). (J). (gr. 4-8). 1991. pap. text ed. 19.95 (*0-913705-61-6*) Zephyr Pr AZ.

***Mason, Katrina R.** Children of Los Alamos: An Oral History of the Town Where the Atomic Age Began. LC 95-13825. (Twayne's Oral History Ser.). 1995. write for info. (*0-8057-9138-8*, Twayne); pap. write for info. (*0-8057-9139-6*, Twayne) Macmillan.

Mason, Keith. Constancy & Change: Moral & Religious Values in the Australian Legal System. 154p. 1990. pap. 33.00 (*0-685-51046-8*, Pub. by Federation Pr AU) W W Gaunt.

Mason, Kenneth. Abode of Snow. (Illus.). 384p. 1987. reprint ed. 22.95 (*0-89886-142-X*) Mountaineers.

Mason, Kermit R. The Roads Taken: A Country Lawyer Looks Back. Taylor, Carl B., ed. & intro. by. 152p. 1986. 12.95 (*0-9605948-2-5*) C B Taylor.

Mason, L. John. Guide to Stress Reduction. rev. ed. LC 79-2577. (Illus.). 207p. (Orig.). 1986. pap. 9.95 (*0-89087-452-2*) Celestial Arts.

Mason, Laura L. Lots of Ways to Win. LC 91-68087. (Illus.). 44p. (J). (gr. k-3). 1992. 7.95 (*1-55523-500-X*) Winston-Derek.

Mason, Lauris & Ludman, Joan. The Lithographs of George Bellows: A Catalogue Raisonne. rev. ed. (Illus.). 300p. 1992. 150.00 (*1-55660-141-7*) A Wofsy Fine Arts.

Mason, Leah. Making Connections: Adult Day Health Care for People with AIDS. LC 92-44741. (Practical Guide Ser.). 1993. 10.00 (*1-881277-14-3*) United Hosp Fund.

Mason, Leonard A. & Masson-Douglas, Jeanne. Come Set in the Warm: Twenty-or-So-Anecdotes of Rural Vermont. 2nd ed. (Illus.). 88p. 1982. pap. 4.95 (*0-940282-00-3*) Outermost Pr.

Mason, Leslie C., ed. see Levine, Leslie B.

Mason, Lisa. Arachne. 272p. 1992. mass mkt. 4.50 (*0-380-70911-2*, AvoNova) Avon.

— Cyberweb. LC 94-32026. 1995. 20.00 (*0-688-13987-6*) Morrow.

— Summer of Love. LC 94-7592. (Illus.). 1994. pap. 12.95 (*0-553-37330-7*) Bantam.

Mason, Lorna C., ed. see Means, Florence G.

Mason, Lowell. Musical Letters from Abroad. 2nd ed. LC 67-13035. (Music Ser.). 1967. reprint ed. lib. bdg. 37.50 (*0-306-70940-6*) Da Capo.

— The Pestalozzian Music Teacher. 1977. lib. bdg. 59.95 (*0-8490-2425-0*) Gordon Pr.

Mason, Lowell & Hitchcock, H. Wiley, eds. The Boston Handel & Haydn Society Collection of Church Music. LC 77-171078. (Earlier American Music Ser.: No. 15). 324p. 1973. reprint ed. lib. bdg. 37.50 (*0-306-77315-5*) Da Capo.

Mason, Lowell & Webb, George J. The Boston Glee Book. LC 76-52481. (Music Reprint Ser.: 1977). 1977. reprint ed. lib. bdg. 35.00 (*0-306-70860-4*) Da Capo.

***Mason, Lrvin.** The Feasors. 270p. 1996. pap. 8.95 (*0-7610-0462-9*) NW Pub.

Mason, Lynn, jt. auth. see Mason, Tim.

Mason, M. Elizabeth. Active Life & Contemplative Life: A Study of the Concepts from Plato to the Present. Ganss, George E., ed. 1961. pap. 10.00 (*0-87462-418-5*) Marquette.

Mason, Malcolm S., jt. auth. see Dembling, Paul G.

***Mason, Marco.** Point, Click & Learn Visual Basic X. 1995. pap. 34.99 (*1-56884-317-8*) IDG Bks.

Mason, Marcy, jt. auth. see Rubin, Bonnie M.

Mason, Margo C. Good Dog Rover. 1989. pap. 3.50 (*0-553-34724-1*) Bantam.

Mason, Marilyn. Intimacy. 24p. (Orig.). 1986. pap. 1.55 (*0-89486-365-7*, 5309B) Hazelden.

Mason, Marilyn G. The Federal Role in Library & Information Services. LC 83-11970. (Professional Librarian Ser.). 177p. 1983. lib. bdg. 37.50 (*0-86729-010-2*); pap. 30.50 (*0-86729-009-9*) G K Hall.

Mason, Marilyn J. Making Our Lives Our Own: A Woman's Guide to the Six Challenges of Personal Change. LC 90-55297. 1992. pap. 11.00 (*0-06-250634-X*) Harper SF.

Mason, Marilyn J., jt. auth. see Fossum, Merle A.

An Asterisk (*) at the beginning of an entry indicates that the title is appearing in BIP for the first time.

Mason, Marion, et al. The Dynamics of Clinical Dietetics. LC 81-16160. 354p. 1982. text ed. 30.95 (*0-8273-4298-5*) Delmar.
— Nutrition & the Cell: The Inside Story. LC 72-95734. (Illus.). 92p. reprint ed. 26.30 (*0-8357-9636-1*, 2013104) Bks Demand.
Mason, Mark. American Multinationals & Japan: The Political Economy of Japanese Capital Controls, 1899-1980. LC 92-9934. 373p. 1992. text ed. 35.00 (*0-674-02630-6*) HUP.
***Mason, Mark & Encarnation, Dennis, eds.** Does Ownership Matter? Japanese Multinationals in Europe. (Illus.). 488p. 1995. pap. 24.95 (*0-19-829026-8*) OUP.
Mason, Mark, jt. ed. see Encarnation, Dennis.
Mason, Mary, jt. auth. see Goldin, Stephen.
Mason, Mary A. From Father's Property to Children's Rights: The History of Child Custody in the United States. LC 93-34524. 1994. 29.50 (*0-231-08046-8*) Col U Pr.
Mason, Mary A. & Gambrill, Eileen, eds. Debating Children's Lives: Current Controversies. (C). 1993. text ed. 55.00 (*0-8039-5458-1*); pap. text ed. 25.95 (*0-8039-5459-X*) Sage.
Mason, Mary A. & Harris, Robert. Using Computers in the Law: Law Office Without Walls. 3rd ed. LC 93-41189. 275p. 1993. pap. text ed. 22.00 (*0-314-02396-8*) West Pub.
Mason, Mary-Claire. Male Infertility: Men Talking. LC 93-11986. 224p. 1993. 59.95 (*0-415-07289-1*, B2423); pap. 17.95 (*0-415-07290-5*, B2427) Routledge.
Mason, Mary G., jt. ed. see Green, Carol H.
Mason, Mary J. Toward My Father's House: Hope Filled Meditations for the Terminally Ill. 54p. (Orig.). 1993. pap. text ed. 3.95 (*0-89243-518-6*) Liguori Pubns.
Mason, Mary K. Laramie Community, Wyoming. (Illus.). 575p. 1987. 62.50 (*0-88107-093-9*) Curtis Media.
Mason, Mary S., jt. auth. see Mason, James H.
Mason, Marylee, ed. Sociology: Windows on Society. 3rd rev. ed. LC 93-38019. 274p. (C). 1994. pap. text ed. write for info. (*0-935732-53-5*) Roxbury Pub Co.
Mason, Matthew T. & Salisbury, J. Kenneth. Robot Hands & the Mechanics of Manipulation. (Artificial Intelligence Ser.). (Illus.). 275p. 1985. 39.95 (*0-262-13205-2*) MIT Pr.
Mason, Mervyn L. Human Sexuality: A Bibliography & Critical Evaluation of Recent Texts. LC 83-12688. iv, 207p. 1983. text ed. 42.95 (*0-313-23932-0*, MHU/, Greenwood Pr) Greenwood.
***Mason, Michael.** The Dream & the Awakening. 300p. (Orig.). 1995. pap. 9.95 (*0-7610-0064-X*) NW Pub.
— How to Write a Winning College-Application Essay. 250p. (Orig.). (YA). (gr. 10 up). 1991. pap. 8.95 (*1-55958-083-6*) Prima Pub.
— Lyrical Ballads. (Annotated Texts Ser.). 336p. (C). 1992. pap. text ed. 25.95 (*0-582-03303-9*) Longman.
— The Making of Victorian Sexual Attitudes, Vol. II. (Illus.). 272p. 1995. text ed. 29.95 (*0-19-812292-6*) OUP.
— The Making of Victorian Sexuality. (Illus.). 360p. 1995. pap. 14.95 (*0-19-285312-0*) OUP.
— The Making of Victorian Sexuality: Sexual Behaviour & Its Understanding. LC 93-28824. (Illus.). 364p. 1994. 27.50 (*0-19-812247-0*, Clarendon Pr) OUP.
Mason, Michael, ed. William Blake. LC 93-40488. (Oxford Poetry Library). 336p. 1994. pap. 7.95 (*0-19-282305-1*) OUP.
Mason, Michael, ed. see Blake, William.
Mason, Michael J. How to Write a Winning College Application Essay. 2nd rev. ed. LC 93-1741. 1993. pap. 9.95 (*1-55958-345-2*) Prima Pub.
Mason, Micheline. Creating Your Own Work. 108p. 1980. 35.00 (*0-905418-80-8*, Pub. by Gresham Bks UK) St Mut.
— Creating Your Own Work. 108p. 1983. 25.00 (*0-946095-04-3*, Pub. by Gresham Bks UK) St Mut.
Mason, Mike. The Gospel According to Job. LC 93-42371. 448p. 1994. 17.99 (*0-89107-786-3*) Crossway Bks.
— The Mystery of Marriage: As Iron Sharpens Iron. LC 85-3048. 185p. 1985. pap. 9.99 (*0-88070-296-6*, Multnomah Bks) Questar Pubs.
Mason, Mildred A. & Bates, Grace F. Basic Medical-Surgical Nursing. 5th ed. 915p. 1984. text ed. 36.95 (*0-07-105295-X*); Wkbk. student ed 15.95 (*0-07-105296-8*) Hlth Prof Div.
Mason, Miriam E. Mark Twain: Young Writer. LC 90-23768. (Childhood of Famous Americans Ser.). (Illus.). 192p. (J). (gr. 3-7). 1991. reprint ed. pap. 3.95 (*0-689-71480-7*, Aladdin Paperbacks) S&S Childrens.
Mason, Nancy. Oral History of West Southern Pines, North Carolina. 1982. 23.45 (*0-9617019-0-0*); pap. 14.95 (*0-9617019-1-9*) Southern Pines.
Mason, Nancy A. & Shimp, Leslie A. Building a Pharmacist's Patient Data Base. (Clinical Skills Program, Advancing Pharmaceutical Care Ser.). 96p. 1993. ring bd. 50.00 (*1-879907-32-1*) Am Soc Hlth-Syst.
Mason, Nancy A., jt. auth. see Shimp, Leslie A.
***Mason, Nicholas J. & Schwartz, Richard.** Following Your Treasure Map. 260p. 1995. pap. 8.95 (*1-56901-809-X*) NW Pub.
Mason, Nondita & Otte, George. Writers' Roles: Enactments of the Process. (Illus.). 768p. (Orig.). (C). 1993. pap. text ed. 24.00 (*0-15-500160-4*) HB Coll Pubs.
Mason, Otis T. Aboriginal American Indian Basketry: Studies in Textile Art Without Machinery. LC 71-112623. (Beautiful Rio Grande Classics Ser.). (Illus.). 688p. 1984. reprint ed. lib. bdg. 40.00 (*0-87380-012-5*) Rio Grande.
— Man's Knife Among the North American Indians. (Shorey Indian Ser.). 24p. reprint ed. pap. 1.95 (*0-8466-4051-1*, 151) Shorey.
— The Man's Knife Among the North American Indians: A Study in the Collections of the U. S. National Museum, 1897. 14.95 (*0-8488-0035-4*, J M C & Co) Amereon Ltd.
— North American Bows, Arrows & Quivers. (Illus.). 216p. 29.95 (*0-8488-0037-0*, J M C & Co) Amereon Ltd.
— The Origins of Invention: A Study of Industry Among Primitive Peoples. LC 77-38362. (Select Bibliographies Reprint Ser.). 1977. reprint ed. 29.95 (*0-8369-6779-8*) Ayer.
— Woman's Share in Primitive Culture. 1972. 250.00 (*0-87968-460-7*) Gordon Pr.
Mason, P. Maharishi. 1994. 24.95 (*1-85230-571-1*) Element MA.
Mason, Patrice G., jt. auth. see Rosenberg, Amye.
Mason, Patricia B., jt. auth. see Mason, Charles T., Jr.
***Mason, Paul N.** Circles of Grace. 1995. 5.00 (*0-87129-563-6*, C91) Dramatic Pub.
— The Discipline Committee. Date not set. 5.00 (*0-87129-564-4*, D63) Dramatic Pub.
Mason, Paul T., jt. ed. see Hunter, Jean E.
Mason, Penelope. History of Japanese Art. LC 92-28698. (Illus.). 432p. 1993. 60.00 (*0-8109-1085-3*) Abrams.
— History of Japanese Art. LC 92-34428. 1993. write for info. (*0-13-016395-3*) P-H Gen Ref & Trav.
Mason, Peter. Deconstructing America: Representations of the Other. (Illus.). 240p. 1990. 39.95 (*0-415-05260-2*, A4735) Routledge.
Mason, Philip. The Hammered Dulcimer's Companion. 1993. 8.95 (*0-87166-680-4*, 94019) Mel Bay.
Mason, Philip P. The Ambassador Bridge: A Monument to Progress. LC 87-18983. (Great Lakes Bks.). (Illus.). 272p. 1987. pap. 21.95 (*0-8143-1840-1*) Wayne St U Pr.
— The Birth of a Dilemma: The Conquest & Settlement of Rhodesia. LC 82-9162. (Illus.). xii, 367p. 1982. reprint ed. text ed. 65.00 (*0-313-23547-3*, MABI, Greenwood Pr) Greenwood.
— Call the Next Witness. LC 86-7122. xii, 208p. 1986. pap. 5.95 (*0-226-50955-9*) U Ch Pr.
— Detroit, Fort Lernoult, & the American Revolution. LC 64-18967. 34p. reprint ed. pap. 25.00 (*0-7837-3634-7*, 2043501) Bks Demand.
— Directory of Jewish Archival Institutions. LC 75-15504. 77p. reprint ed. pap. 25.00 (*0-7837-3652-5*, 2043523) Bks Demand.
— Rum Running & the Roaring Twenties: Prohibition on the Michigan-Ontario Waterway. (Illus.). 192p. 1995. 24.95 (*0-8143-2584-X*, Great Lks Bks) Wayne St U Pr.
Mason, Philip P., ed. After Tippecanoe. LC 73-7076. (Illus.). 106p. 1973. reprint ed. text ed. 38.50 (*0-8371-6903-8*, MAAT, Greenwood Pr) Greenwood.
Mason, Philip P., ed. see Hobart, Henry.
Mason, Philip P., jt. ed. see Leab, Daniel J.
Mason, Philip P., jt. ed. see Schoolcraft, Henry R.
Mason, Philip P., jt. auth. see Woodford, Frank B.
Mason, R. Petrology of the Metamorphic Rocks. (Textbook of Petrology Ser.). (Illus.). 1978. pap. text ed. 24.95 (*0-04-552014-3*) Routledge Chapman & Hall.
Mason, R. & Bacsich, P. D., eds. ISDN Applications in Education & Training. 256p. 1993. boxed 55.00 (*0-85296-860-4*, TE905) Inst Elect Eng.
Mason, R., jt. auth. see Brill, R.
Mason, R., jt. ed. see Churchman, C. W.
Mason, R., jt. auth. see Hoppe, W.
Mason, R. A. Air Power: An Overview of Roles. (Air Power: Aircraft, Weapons Systems & Technology Ser.: Vol. 1). (Illus.). 151p. 1987. 40.00 (*0-08-031195-4*, Pub. by Brasseys UK) Brasseys Inc.
— Air Power: An Overview of Roles. (Air Power: Aircraft, Weapons Systems & Technology Ser.: Vol. 1). (Illus.). 151p. 1987. pap. 15.95 (*0-08-031194-6*, Pub. by Brasseys UK) Brasseys Inc.
Mason, R. A., ed. War in the Third Dimension: Essays in Contemporary Air Power. 228p. 1986. 42.00 (*0-08-031187-3*, Pub. by Brasseys UK); 23.00 (*0-08-031188-1*, Pub. by Brasseys UK) Brasseys Inc.
Mason, R. A., jt. auth. see Armitage, M. J.
Mason, R. A., ed. see Armitage, Michael.
Mason, R. A., ed. see Knight, Michael.
Mason, R. A., ed. see Walker, J. R.
Mason, R. C. Diophantine Equations over Function Fields. LC 84-1900. (London Mathematical Society Lecture Note Ser.: No. 96). 126p. 1984. pap. 22.95 (*0-521-26983-0*) Cambridge U Pr.
Mason, R. D. Euro-American Pioneer Settlement Systems in the Central Salt River Valley of Northeast Missouri. (Illus.). xi, 99p. 1984. 10.00 (*0-917111-01-X*) Mus Anthro MO.
Mason, R. E., ed. Information Processing 83. (IFIP World Congress Ser.: Vol. 9). 1000p. 1984. 133.50 (*0-444-86729-5*, I-407-83, North Holland) Elsevier.
Mason, R. H. Japan's First General Election, Eighteen Ninety. LC 68-23915. (University of Cambridge Oriental Publications). 1969. 59.95 (*0-521-07147-X*) Cambridge U Pr.
Mason, R. Hal & Spich, Robert. Management: An International Perspective. 256p. (C). 1987. pap. text ed. 15.95 (*0-256-05631-5*) Irwin.
Mason, R. L., jt. auth. see Gunst, R. F.
Mason, Ralph E., et al. Marketing Practices & Principles. 3rd ed. (Illus.). 1980. text ed. 24.88 (*0-07-040693-6*) McGraw.
— Marketing Practices & Principles. 4th ed. 448p. 1985. text ed. 21.24 (*0-07-040705-3*) McGraw.
Mason, Ranier M. Jean Fautrier's Prints. (Illus.). 200p. (FRE.). 1986. pap. 75.00 (*1-55660-073-9*) A Wofsy Fine Arts.
— Kurt Seligmann's Graphic Work. (Illus.). 136p. 1982. pap. 150.00 (*1-55660-074-7*) A Wofsy Fine Arts.
Mason, Rex. Old Testament Pictures of God. LC 93-28067. 216p. 1993. pap. 14.95 (*1-880837-33-1*) Smyth & Helwys.
— Preaching the Tradition: Homily & Hermeneutics after the Exile. 320p. (C). 1990. 74.95 (*0-521-38304-8*) Cambridge U Pr.
Mason, Richard. Cambridge Minds. 240p. (C). 1994. 39.95 (*0-521-45405-0*); pap. 19.95 (*0-521-45625-8*) Cambridge U Pr.
— The Wind Cannot Read. large type ed. 1976. 12.00 (*0-85456-435-7*) Ulverscroft.
— The World of Suzie Wong. 23.95 (*0-8488-0052-4*, Amereon Hse) Amereon Ltd.
— The World of Suzie Wong. 1993. reprint ed. lib. bdg. 21.95 (*1-56849-097-6*) Buccaneer Bks.
Mason, Richard O., jt. ed. see Churchman, C. W.
Mason, Richard O., jt. auth. see Rowe, Alan J.
***Mason, Richard O., et al.** Information & Responsibility: The Ethical Challenge. (Series in Business Ethics: Vol. 2). 320p. (C). 1995. 52.00 (*0-8039-5755-6*); pap. 24.95 (*0-8039-5756-4*) Sage.
Mason, Rita A. A Guide to Dental Radiography. 3rd ed. (Dental Practitioners' Handbook Ser.: No. 27). (Illus.). 226p. 1988. pap. 45.00 (*0-7236-0974-8*, Pub. by John Wright UK) Buttrwrth-Heinemann.
Mason, Robert. Chickenhawk: Back in the World: Life after Vietnam. (Illus.). 400p. 1994. pap. 10.95 (*0-14-015876-6*, Penguin Bks) Viking Penguin.
— One of the Neighbors' Children. 230p. 1987. 14.95 (*0-912697-56-3*) Algonquin Bks.
— Solo. 320p. 1993. mass mkt. 4.99 (*0-425-13748-1*) Berkley Pub.
Mason, Robert C. Chickenhawk. 476p. 1984. pap. 10.00 (*0-14-007218-7*, Penguin Bks) Viking Penguin.
Mason, Robert C., ed. Basement Tectonics, No. 7. (C). 1992. lib. bdg. 200.00 (*0-7923-1582-0*) Kluwer Ac.
Mason, Robert C. & Young, William H., eds. Challenge & Change: Creating a New Era of Collaboration in Adult Continuing Education. LC 92-14850. 135p. 1993. pap. 18.95 (*1-879528-06-1*) LEPS Pr.
Mason, Robert C., ed. see Trollope, Anthony.
***Mason, Robert D.** Business & Economic Statistics. 1970. 4.50 (*0-256-01268-7*) Irwin Prof Pubng.
— Business & Economic Statistics. 4th ed. (Plaid Ser.). 166p. 1983. pap. 11.95 (*0-87094-334-0*) Irwin Prof Pubng.
Mason, Robert D. & Lind, Douglas A. Statistical Techniques in Business & Economics. 7th ed. 1024p. (C). 1989. text ed. 66.95 (*0-256-07696-0*) Irwin.
— Statistical Techniques in Business & Economics. 7th ed. (C). 1989. student ed 18.95 (*0-256-08054-2*) Irwin.
— Statistical Techniques in Business & Economics. 8th ed. LC 92-9933. 896p. (C). 1992. text ed. 66.95 (*0-256-10338-0*) Irwin.
Mason, Robert D., jt. auth. see Lind, Douglas A.
***Mason, Robert D., et al.** Statistical Techniques in Business & Economics & Computerized Business Statistics. 7th ed. (C). 1992. text ed., disk 64.00 (*0-256-09275-3*) Irwin.
— Statistics: An Introduction. 700p. (C). 1990. text ed. 52.00 (*0-15-583536-X*) SCP.
— Statistics: An Introduction. 4th ed. LC 93-80130. 778p. (C). 1993. text ed. 61.25 (*0-03-096917-4*) Saunders.
— Thinking Mathematically. 240p. (C). 1982. text ed. 9.95 (*0-201-10238-2*) Addison-Wesley.
Mason, Robert E. A Better School: Who Says So? (Occasional Paper: No. 9). 1976. pap. 3.00 (*0-933669-12-7*) Soc Profs Ed.
— Community of the Young. (Occasional Paper: No. 8). 1975. pap. 3.00 (*0-933669-11-9*) Soc Profs Ed.
Mason, Robert J. Contested Lands: Conflict & Compromise in New Jersey's Pine Barrens. (Conflicts in Urban & Regional Development Ser.). 256p. (C). 1992. 44.95 (*0-87722-925-2*) Temple U Pr.
Mason, Robert J. & Mattson, Mark T. Atlas of United States Environmental Issues. (Illus.). 192p. 1990. 80.00 (*0-685-38861-1*); text ed. 95.00 (*0-02-897261-9*) Macmillan.
Mason, Robert L., jt. auth. see Gunst, Richard F.
Mason, Robert L., et al. The Clergyman & the Psychiatrist: When to Refer. LC 77-22597. 248p. 1978. 29.95 (*0-88229-260-9*) Nelson-Hall.
— Statistical Design Analysis of Experiments with Applications to Engineering & Science. (Probability & Mathematical Statistics Ser.). 692p. 1989. text ed. 84.95 (*0-471-85364-X*) Wiley.
Mason, Robert M. Modern Methods of Music Analysis Using Computers. LC 85-26142. (Illus.). viii, 299p. 1985. lib. bdg. 39.50 (*0-9615669-0-6*) Schoolhouse Pr.
Mason, Robin. Using Communications Media in Open Learning. Lockwood, Fred, ed. (Open & Distance Learning Ser.). 160p. (Orig.). 1994. pap. 29.95 (*0-7494-1149-X*, Pub. by Kogan Page UK) Nichols Pub.
Mason, Robin, ed. Shotcrete for Underground Support, Vol. III. 346p. (Orig.). 1980. pap. 30.00 (*0-939204-04-5*, 78-14) Eng Found.
Mason, Roger & MacDougall, Norman, eds. People & Power in Scotland: Essays in Honour of T. C. Smout. 220p. (C). 1989. 90.00 (*0-85976-392-7*, Pub. by J Donald) St Mut.
Mason, Roger A., ed. Scots & Britons: Scottish Political Thought & the Union of 1603. LC 93-32399. 328p. (C). 1994. 59.95 (*0-521-42034-2*) Cambridge U Pr.
Mason, Roger A., ed. see Knox, John.
***Mason, Roger B.** Print & Be Damaged: or How I Put My Back Out Saving Letterpress for My Grandchildren's Children. 24p. 1994. pap. 20.00x (*0-930126-46-7*) Typographeum.
Mason, Ronald J. Rock Island: Historical Indian Archaeology in the Northern Lake Michigan Basin. LC 85-12661. (MCJA Special Paper Ser.: No. 6). 228p. reprint ed. pap. 65.00 (*0-7837-1341-X*, 2041489) Bks Demand.
Mason, Ronald M. Participatory & Workplace Democracy: A Theoretical Development in Critique of Liberalism. LC 81-16687. 268p. 1982. 29.95 (*0-8093-0992-0*) S Ill U Pr.
Mason, Rosalie. Beginners' Guide to Family Preparedness - Food Storage, Back to Basics & Survival Facts. LC 77-79750. (Illus.). 160p. 1977. pap. 10.98 (*0-88290-082-X*) Horizon Utah.
Mason, Rosemary A. Anaesthesia Databook: A Clinical Practice Compendium. 2nd ed. LC 94-7399. 1994. 79.95 (*0-443-04763-4*) Churchill.
Mason, Roy. Xanadu: The Computerized Home of Tomorrow & How It Can Be Yours Today. (Illus.). 208p. 1984. 18.95 (*0-87491-701-8*) Acropolis.
Mason, Russell E. Anxiety, Resolution, Relaxation, & Systematic, & Flexible Hierachy, & Tape Uses, Set-AH. 1975. Incl. Tape 1A, T-9, T-5A, T-10, T-8, T-11; Notes; Clinical Applications; Brief Outlines 3, Substitut. pap. 60.00 (*0-89533-009-1*) F I Comm.
— Basic, Advanced Systematic Substitution Training, Set-AS. 1975. pap. 35.00 (*0-89533-017-2*); Incl. Tape 12. T-13, T-14; H. E. S. T-a SET. write for info. (*0-89533-043-1*); Notes. write for info. (*0-89533-025-3*) F I Comm.
— Basic, Elementary Systematic Substitution Training, Set-ES. 1973. Incl. Brief Outlines 1, "Relaxation Trng."; Brief Outlines 3, "Substitution Trng."; Tape 1 (0-89533-. pap. 35.00 (*0-89533-015-6*) F I Comm.
— Basic, Intermediate Systematic Substitution Training, Set-IS. 1973. Incl.: Tape 3, T-10, T-11; Clinical Applications, rev. ed. 1979; Brief Outlines 2, Feeling Training. pap. 35.00 (*0-89533-016-4*) F I Comm.
— Brief Outlines for Relaxation Training (& Meditative Relaxation) (Brief Outlines SeR.: No. 1). 1973. pap. 15.00 (*0-89533-022-9*) F I Comm.
— Brief Outlines for Substitution Training & Positive Goal Achievement. (Brief Outlines SeR.: No. 3). 1973. pap. 15.00 (*0-89533-024-5*) F I Comm.
— Comprehensive Set: Purposeful Relaxation, Problem Solutions, Value Considerations & Communication, Set-A. 1975. Incl.: 18 Train-Ascendance C60 cassettes; Notes; Clinical Appllications, rev. ed., 1979; Brief Outli. pap. 150.00 (*0-89533-021-0*) F I Comm.
— Daily Growth for Broader Experiences or Awareness, Achievements, Purposeful Relaxation & Comfort, Set-DG. rev. ed. 1975. Incl. Brief Outlines 3, Substitution Training & Goal Achievement; Clinical Applications, rev. ed., 1. 60.00 (*0-89533-011-3*) F I Comm.
— De-Sensitization by Systematic Steps with Relaxation, Set-D. 1975. Incl. Notes; Clinical Applications (rev. 1979); Tape 9 (ISBN 0-89533-039-3); Tape 1A; Tape 2. pap. 35.00 (*0-89533-005-9*) F I Comm.
— Extended (Experiential) Awareness, Purposeful Relaxation, & Multiple (Differentiated Psychophysiological) Feeling States. 1975. Incl. Notes; Outlines 2, Feeling Trng.; Outlines 3, Substitution Trng.; Tape 1A, Tape 2, Tape 3, Tap. audio 60.00 (*0-89533-013-X*) F I Comm.
— Individual Uses of Positive Substitution & Problem Solutions, Set-IP. 1975. Incl. Notes; Clinical Applications (rev. 1979); Tape 1A, T-5A, T-10. pap. 35.00 (*0-89533-007-5*) F I Comm.
— Informational Guides for Groups, Communication, Living & Change, Set-GL. 1975. Incl. Tape 2, T-16, T-17; Notes; Clinical Applications (rev. 1979); H. E. S. T SET. pap. 35.00 (*0-89533-019-9*) F I Comm.
— Life-Extension, Purposeful Relaxation, Differential (Multiple) "Feeling" (Psychophysiological) Awareness & Communication, Set-Ta. 1975. Incl. Tape 1A, T-3, T-4, T-7, T-16, T-17; H. E. S. T-a SET; Positive Personalities: Joy, Significanc. 70.00 (*0-89533-018-0*) F I Comm.
— Multiple Uses: Positive Substitution, Problem Solutions, Relaxation, & Goal Achievements, Set-MS. 1975. Incl. Tape 1A, T-2, T-5A, T-10, T-16, T-17; Notes; Clinical Applications (rev. 1979); H. E. S. T-a S. pap. 60.00 (*0-89533-008-3*) F I Comm.
— Positive Awareness (Experiential Extension), Purposeful Relaxation, & (Differentiated Psychophysiological) "Feeling" States, Set-PA. 1975. Incl. Tape-1A, T-3, T-4; Notes; Brief Outlines 2, Feeling Training. pap. 35.00 (*0-89533-012-1*) F I Comm.
— Positive Personalities: Joy, Significance, & Sexual Feelings & Values. LC 70-167784. 1971. 16.00 (*0-89533-000-8*) F I Comm.
— Positive Personality Fulfillment, Set-PPF. 1975. Incl. Tape-1A, 1-5A; Positive Personalties: Joy Significance & Sexual Feeling & Values. 26.00 (*0-89533-048-2*) F I Comm.
— Positive Substitution, Purposeful Relaxation, & Goal Achievement Training: A Systematic Beginning, Set-PS. 1975. Incl.: Tape 1A, Tape 2, Tape 4, Tape 5, Tape 6 & Tape 10; Clinical Applications, rev. ed., 1979; Bri. 60.00 (*0-89533-014-8*) F I Comm.
— Relaxation & De-Sensitization Training, Set-RD. 1975. Incl. Tape-1A, T-1, T-2, T-6, T-5A, T-9; Brief Outlines 1, Relaxation Trng.; Hierarchy; Clinical App. pap. 60.00 (*0-89533-006-7*) F I Comm.
— SET, H. E. S. T-a Humanistic Endeavor & Surgent Train-Ascendance. 1975. Incl: Guides for Groups & Communication; Broad Considerations; Ways of Train-Ascendance. pap. 10.00 (*0-89533-028-8*) F I Comm.
— Simple Guides to Daily Growth, Problem Solving, or Purposeful Relaxation for Comfort or Effectiveness, Set-SG, Set-SG. 1975. Incl. Tape-1A, T-2, T-5A; Notes; Clinical Applications, Differential Criteria & Implications for Bio. pap. 30.00 (*0-89533-001-6*) F I Comm.

— Simplified Behavior & "Feeling" State Change & Goal Accomplishment, Set-SB. 1975. Incl. Tape 1A, T-2, T-5A, T-3, T-16, T-17; Notes; Cinical Applications (rev. 1979); Outlines 3, Subs. pap. 60.00 (*0-89533-002-4*) F I Comm.
— Simplified Extended, Deep, & or Meditative Relaxation, Set-R. 1975. Incl. Tape 1A, T-1, T-6; Clinical Applications (rev. 1979); Brief Outlines 1, Relaxation Trng. 35.00 (*0-89533-004-0*) F I Comm.
— Simplified Purposeful Relaxation for Comfort or Effectiveness, Set-PR. 1975. Incl. Tape 1A, T-2, T-6; Notes; Clinical Applications, rev. ed., 1979. pap. 35.00 (*0-89533-003-2*) F I Comm.
— Simplified Relaxation, Problem Solutions & Substitutions, & Value Considerations, Set-S. 1975. pap. 85.00 (*0-89533-020-2*) F I Comm.
— Solutions, Relaxation, or Understanding for Tense, Anxious, Depressive, Hostile (Irritated), & Disgusted States & Problems, Set-ST. 1975. pap. 60.00 (*0-89533-010-5*) F I Comm.
Mason, Ruth & Mason, Gregory. Danbury Curve. 13.95 (*0-8084-0370-2*) NCUP.
Mason, S. B. Danger Forward: The Story of the First Division in World War II. (Divisional Ser.: No. 14). (Illus.). 479p. 1980. reprint ed. 29.95 (*0-89839-033-8*) Battery Pr.
Mason, Sally & Scholtz, James. Video for Libraries: Special Interest Video for Small & Medium-Sized Public Libraries. LC 88-22235. 187p. reprint ed. pap. 53.30 (*0-7837-5921-5*, 2045720) Bks Demand.
Mason, Sammy. Stalls, Spins, & Safety. (Eleanor Friede Bks.). 192p. 1985. text ed. 25.95 (*0-02-581620-9*) Macmillan.
Mason, Sarah J. Corpse in the Kitchen. 224p. (Orig.). 1993. pap. 4.50 (*0-425-14006-7*) Berkley Pub.
— Dying Breath. 240p. (Orig.). 1994. pap. 4.50 (*0-425-14245-0*, Prime Crime) Berkley Pub.
— Frozen Stiff. 224p. (Orig.). 1993. pap. 3.99 (*0-425-13837-2*) Berkley Pub.
— Murder in the Maze. 224p. (Orig.). 1993. pap. 4.50 (*0-425-13795-3*) Berkley Pub.
Mason, Scott. No Dogs in Heaven. (Cleveland Poets Ser.: No. 24). 28p. 1980. pap. 2.50 (*0-914946-21-8*) Cleveland St Univ Poetry Ctr.
Mason, Scott, jt. auth. see Chartier, Lee.
***Mason, Scott, et al.** Cases in Financial Engineering: Applied Studies of Financial Innovation. LC 94-32273. 1994. text ed. 59.00 (*0-13-079419-8*) P-H.
— Diversification & Conversion Strategies for Rural Hospitals. 52p. (Orig.). 1989. pap. 35.00 (*0-87258-524-7*, 184207) Am Hospital.
Mason, Sharon, jt. ed. see Coman, Susan L.
Mason, Sharon R., ed. see Heyman, Barbara G.
Mason, Shirley L., jt. auth. see Mather, Kirtley F.
Mason, Simon. Secret Signals: The Euronumbers Mystery. 60p. 1991. pap. 12.95 (*0-936653-28-0*) Tiare Pubns.
Mason, Sophia. Art of Forecasting. 60p. 1977. 7.00 (*0-86690-330-5*, M1322-034) Am Fed Astrologers.
— Delineation of Progressions. 310p. 1985. 16.95 (*0-86690-280-5*, M2462-014) Am Fed Astrologers.
— Forecasting with New, Full & Quarter Moons. rev. ed. 126p. 1994. pap. 10.00 (*0-86690-362-3*, AFA) Am Fed Astrologers.
— From One House to Another. rev. ed. 64p. 1993. 9.00 (*0-86690-363-1*) Am Fed Astrologers.
— Lunations & Predictions. rev. ed. 66p. 1993. 9.00 (*0-86690-364-X*) Am Fed Astrologers.
— Understanding Planetary Placements. rev. ed. 86p. 1993. pap. 10.00 (*0-86690-365-8*) Am Fed Astrologers.
Mason, Stanley. Send Out the Dove. limited ed. (New Poetic Drama Ser.). 1986. pap. 5.00 (*0-934218-37-4*) Dragons Teeth.
Mason, Stephen F. History of the Sciences. Orig. Title: Main Currents of Scientific Thought. 640p. 1962. pap. 10.95 (*0-02-093400-9*, Pub. by Gebrueder Borntraeger GW) Macmillan.
— Molecular Optical Activity & the Chiral Discriminations. LC 82-1125. (Illus.). 250p. 1982. 59.95 (*0-521-24702-0*) Cambridge U Pr.
Mason, Stephen F., ed. Optical Activity & Chiral Discrimination. (NATO Advanced Study Institutes Series C, Mathematical & Physical Sciences: No. 48). 1979. lib. bdg. 89.00 (*90-277-0982-3*) Kluwer Ac.
Mason, Stephen T. Catecholamines & Behaviour. LC 83-7722. 400p. 1984. 84.95 (*0-521-24930-9*); pap. 34.95 (*0-521-27082-0*) Cambridge U Pr.
Mason, Steve. Flavius Josephus on the Pharisees. LC 90-19845. (Studia Post-Biblica Ser.: Vol. 39). xvi, 424p. 1990. 120.00 (*90-04-09181-5*) E J Brill.
Mason, Steven N. Josephus & the New Testament. LC 92-33067. (Illus.). 256p. (Orig.). 1992. pap. 9.95 (*0-943575-99-0*) Hendrickson MA.
Mason, Stuart. Bibliography of Oscar Wilde, 2 vols. LC 75-184647. (Reference Ser.: No. 44). 607p. 1972. reprint ed. lib. bdg. 150.00 (*0-8383-1378-7*) M S G Haskell Hse.
— Oscar Wilde: Art & Morality. LC 79-174694. (English Literature Ser.: No. 33). 1971. reprint ed. lib. bdg. 75.00 (*0-8383-1334-5*) M S G Haskell Hse.
— Oscar Wilde & the Aesthetic Movement. LC 75-119081. (English Literature Ser.: No. 33). 1970. reprint ed. lib. bdg. 75.00 (*0-8383-1077-X*) M S G Haskell Hse.
Mason, Stuart, jt. auth. see Swash, Michael.
Mason, Susan. Sbus Handbook. 176p. 1994. pap. text ed. 49.00 (*0-13-107210-2*) P-H.
Mason, T., jt. auth. see Alty, A.
Mason, T. David & Turay, Abdul M., eds. U. S. - Japan Trade Friction: Its Impact on Security Cooperation in the Pacific Basin. 208p. 1991. text ed. 49.95 (*0-312-05328-2*) St Martin.
Mason, T. J. Practical Sonochemistry. 150p. 1991. text ed. write for info. (*0-13-682642-3*) P-H.
Mason, T. J., ed. Chemistry with Ultrasound, Vol. 28: Critical Reports on Applied Chemistry. 196p. 1990. 83.00 (*1-85166-422-X*) Elsevier.
Mason, Ted, jt. auth. see Sutkamp, Jerry C.
Mason, Theodore. Battleship Sailor. LC 81-85440. (Bluejacket Paperback Ser.). 1994. pap. 12.95 (*1-55750-579-9*) Naval Inst Pr.
Mason, Theodore C. We Will Stand by You: Serving in the "Pawnee", 1942-1945. (Studies in Maritime History). (Illus.). 269p. 1990. 24.95 (*0-87249-709-7*) U of SC Pr.
***Mason, Thomas.** Governing Oregon. 272p. (C). 1994. per., pap. text ed. 29.95 (*0-7872-0005-0*) Kendall-Hunt.
— Serving God & Mammon: William Juxon, 1582-1663. LC 83-40507. (Illus.). 208p. 1985. 35.00 (*0-87413-251-7*) U Delaware Pr.
Mason, Thomas A., ed. see Madison, James.
***Mason, Tim.** Nazism, Fascism & the Working Class. Caplan, Jane, ed. 384p. (C). 1995. pap. 18.95 (*0-521-43787-3*) Cambridge U Pr.
— Nazism, Fascism & the Working Class. Caplan, Jane, ed. 384p. (C). 1995. 59.95 (*0-521-43212-X*) Cambridge U Pr.
— Social Policy & the Third Reich: The Working Class & the National Community, 1918-1939. Kaplan, Jane, ed. Bradwin, John A., tr. 432p. 1993. text ed. 69.95 (*0-85496-621-8*); pap. 22.95 (*0-85496-410-X*) Berg Pubs.
Mason, Tim & Mason, Lynn. Helen Hyde. Pulin, Carol, ed. (American Printmakers Ser.). 1991. pap. 19.95 (*1-56098-009-5*) Smithsonian.
Mason, Timothy. Ascension Day. 1991. pap. 4.75 (*0-8222-0068-6*) Dramatists Play.
— Babylon Gardens. 1993. 4.75 (*0-8222-1369-9*) Dramatists Play.
— Fiery Furnace. 1994. pap. 4.75 (*0-8222-1355-9*) Dramatists Play.
— In a Northern Landscape. 1985. pap. 4.75 (*0-8222-0558-0*) Dramatists Play.
— Levitation. 1984. pap. 4.75 (*0-8222-0654-4*) Dramatists Play.
— Only You. 73p. 1988. pap. 4.75 (*0-8222-0856-3*) Dramatists Play.
— Only You. Date not set. text ed. 4.75 (*0-8222-1488-1*) Dramatists Play.
Mason, Timothy J., ed. Advances in Sonochemistry, Vol. 1. 275p. 1990. 90.25 (*1-55938-178-7*) Jai Pr.
— Advances in Sonochemistry, Vol. 2. 1991. 90.25 (*1-55938-267-8*) Jai Pr.
Mason, Todd. Perot: An Unauthorized Biography. 300p. 1990. text ed. 17.00 (*1-55623-236-5*) Irwin Prof Pubng.
Mason, Tom. Dinosaurs for Hire, Vol. 1: Guns 'N Lizards. (Illus.). 88p. 1989. pap. 5.95 (*0-944735-21-5*) Malibu Graphics.
— Dinosaurs for Hire, Vol. 2: Dinosaurs Rule! (Illus.). 78p. 1990. pap. 5.95 (*0-944735-31-2*) Malibu Graphics.
— Robotech II, the Sentinels: Script Book, Vol. 2. 1992. pap. 9.95 (*1-56398-036-3*) Malibu Graphics.
Mason, Tom, ed. The Best of Spicy Tales. 104p. 1990. pap. 9.95 (*0-944735-71-1*) Malibu Graphics.
— I Love Lucy: A Comic Retrospect. 145p. 1990. pap. 19.95 (*0-685-60824-7*) Malibu Graphics.
— I Love Lucy: Authorized Collector's Edition. (Illus.). 48p. 1991. pap. 5.95 (*0-944735-88-6*) Malibu Graphics.
— I Love Lucy in Three-D! 32p. 1991. pap. 3.95 (*0-944735-90-8*) Malibu Graphics.
— Robotech II the Sentinels, Vol. 1: Scriptbook. 113p. 1991. pap. 9.95 (*1-56398-021-5*) Malibu Graphics.
— Spicy Horror Stories. 105p. 1990. pap. 9.95 (*0-944735-66-5*) Malibu Graphics.
— Spicy Mystery Stories: Classic Uncensored Tales of Mysteries & Horror. (Illus.). 112p. 1990. pap. 9.95 (*0-944735-23-1*) Malibu Graphics.
— Spicy Western Stories: Uncensored Tales of the Wild West. (Illus.). 107p. 1990. pap. 9.95 (*0-944735-53-3*) Malibu Graphics.
— The Three Stooges in Three-D! 32p. 1991. pap. 3.95 (*0-944735-91-6*) Malibu Graphics.
— The Three Stooges, Vol. 1: The Knuckleheads Return. (Illus.). 141p. 1989. pap. 14.95 (*0-944735-20-7*) Malibu Graphics.
— Video Classics, Vol. 1, Bk. 1: The Adventures of Mighty Mouse. (Illus.). 50p. 1989. pap. 3.50 (*0-944735-22-3*) Malibu Graphics.
— Video Classics, Vol. 2, Bk. 2: More Adventures of Mighty Mouse. (Illus.). 54p. 1989. pap. 3.50 (*0-944735-06-1*) Malibu Graphics.
Mason, Tom & Bennett, S. A., intros. Abbott & Costello: The Classic Comics. LC 89-32810. (Illus.). 138p. 1989. pap. 9.95 (*0-944735-17-7*) Malibu Graphics.
Mason, Tom & Korkis, Jim, intros. Teen Angst: A Treasury of '50s Romance. (Illus.). 154p. 1990. pap. 14.95 (*0-944735-35-5*) Malibu Graphics.
Mason, Tom & Ulm, Chris. Robotech II: The Sentinels, Vol. 2: The Marriage of Rick Hunter & Lisa Hayes. (Illus.). 124p. 1991. 19.95 (*0-944735-76-2*) Malibu Graphics.
— Robotech Two, Vol. 1: The Sentinels, Graphic Novel. (Illus.). 128p. 1990. 19.95 (*0-944735-28-2*) Malibu Graphics.
— Robotech 2: the Sentinels: A New Beginning. 129p. (Orig.). 1991. pap. 9.95 (*0-944735-83-5*) Malibu Graphics.
Mason, Tom & Villa, Mickie, eds. Vampyres: 13 Tales of Classic Horror. 109p. 1991. pap. 9.95 (*0-944735-16-9*) Malibu Graphics.
Mason, Tom & Wooley, John, intros. Spicy Tales. (Illus.). 128p. 1991. pap. 9.95 (*0-944735-32-0*) Malibu Graphics.
Mason, Tom, ed. see Bellem, Robert L.
Mason, Tom, ed. see Matsumoto, Leiji.
Mason, Tom, ed. see Meiser, Edith & Giacoia, Frank.
Mason, Tom, ed. see Rohmer, Sax.
Mason, Tony. Airpower: A Centennial Appraisal. 226p. 1994. 45.00 (*1-85753-069-1*) Macmillan.
— Football in South America: Passion of the People. (Critical Studies in Latin American Culture). 224p. 1994. 59.95x (*0-86091-403-8*, B3629, Pub. by Verso UK) Routledge Chapman & Hall.
— Only a Game? Sport in the Modern World. (Modern World Issues Ser.). (Illus.). 80p. (C). 1993. pap. 11.25 (*0-521-39992-0*) Cambridge U Pr.
— Soccer in Latin America. (Critical Studies in Latin American Culture). 224p. 1994. pap. 17.95 (*0-86091-667-7*, B3633, Pub. by Verso UK) Routledge Chapman & Hall.
— To Inherit the Skies: From Spitfire to Tornado: Britain's Air Defence Today. (Illus.). 102p. 1990. text ed. 19.95 (*0-08-040708-0*) Macmillan.
Mason, Tufton O. American Indian Basketry. 800p. 1988. pap. 16.95 (*0-486-25777-0*) Dover.
Mason, Valmari M., jt. auth. see Benson-von der Ohe, Elizabeth.
Mason, Victor. The Butterflies of Bali. 256p. 1992. pap. text ed. 19.95 (*0-945971-61-3*) Periplus.
Mason, Virgina, ed. see Mannering, Dennis E.
Mason, Virginia, ed. see Mannering, Dennis E.
Mason, Virginia, ed. see Mannering, Dennis E. & Wilde, Kevin.
Mason, W. & Richter, L. Reporting by Key Informants on Labour Markets: An Operational Manual. xi, 41p. (Orig.). 1985. pap. 10.00 (*92-2-105109-9*) Intl Labour Office.
Mason, W. H., et al. Laboratory Manual in Animal Biology. (Illus.). 156p. (Orig.). (C). 1986. pap. 9.95x (*0-89892-067-1*) Contemp Pub Co of Raleigh.
Mason, W. M. & Fienberg, Stephen E., eds. Cohort Analysis in Social Research: Beyond the Identification Problem. (Illus.). 250p. 1985. 69.00 (*0-387-96053-8*) Spr-Verlag.
Mason, W. S., et al, eds. Hepadnaviruses: Molecular Biololgy & Pathogenesis. (Current Topics in Microbiology & Immunology Ser.: Vol. 168). (Illus.). ix, 206p. 1991. 110.00 (*0-387-53060-6*) Spr-Verlag.
Mason, W. T. Fluorescent & Luminescent Probes for Biological Activity: A Practical Guide to Technology for Quantitative Analysis. (Biological Techniques Ser.). (Illus.). 464p. 1993. text ed. 112.00 (*0-12-477829-1*); spiral bd. 65.00 (*0-12-477830-5*) Acad Pr.
Mason, Warren P. & Thurston, Robert N., eds. Physical Acoustics, Vol. 17. 1984. text ed. 158.00 (*0-12-477917-4*) Acad Pr.
— Physical Acoustics Vol. 18: Principles & Methods. 502p. 1988. text ed. 169.00 (*0-12-477918-2*) Acad Pr.
Mason, William. Dagger. 352p. 1984. pap. 3.50 (*0-8217-1399-X*) Zebra.
— Memories of a Musical Life. LC 70-133825. 1970. reprint ed. 21.45 (*0-404-07216-X*) AMS Pr.
— Memories of a Musical Life. LC 70-125056. (Music Ser.). 1970. reprint ed. lib. bdg. 39.50 (*0-306-70021-2*) Da Capo.
— Memories of a Musical Life. (American Biography Ser.). 306p. 1991. reprint ed. lib. bdg. 79.00 (*0-7812-8275-6*) Rprt Serv.
Mason, William & Marshall, Norton. General Biology Laboratory Manual. 4th ed. 192p. (C). 1994. pap. text ed., spiral bd 17.95 (*0-8403-5104-6*) Kendall-Hunt.
Mason, William A. & Mendoza, Sally P., eds. Primate Social Conflict. LC 91-39372. 419p. 1993. 59.50 (*0-7914-1241-5*); pap. 19.95 (*0-7914-1242-3*) State U NY Pr.
Mason, William H. & Marshall, Norton L. The Human Side of Biology. 2nd ed. 642p. (C). 1990. text ed. 27.00 (*0-06-044245-X*); student ed 16.00 (*0-06-044256-5*) HarpCollege.
Masoner, Michael. An Audit of the Case Study Method. LC 87-29293. 250p. 1988. text ed. 55.00 (*0-275-92761-X*, C2761, Praeger Pubs) Greenwood.
Masonic Service Association of the U. S. Staff. Masonic Poems. 91p. 1992. reprint ed. pap. 12.95 (*1-56459-039-9*) Kessinger Pub.
— Masonry & Americanism. 145p. 1992. reprint ed. pap. 12.95 (*1-56459-038-0*) Kessinger Pub.
Masonry Society Codes & Standards Committee Staff. Commentary to Chapter Twenty-Four, Masonry, of the Uniform Building Code: 1991 Edition. Hogan, B., ed. (Illus.). 152p. (Orig.). 1992. pap. text ed. 25.00 (*0-9626074-1-X*) Masonry Soc.
Masood, Mukhtar. Eyewitnesses of History. 22.50 (*1-56744-001-0*) Kazi Pubns.
Masood, Rashid. Economic Diversification & Development in Saudi Arabia. (C). 1989. 24.00 (*0-86132-231-2*, Pub. by Popular Prakashan II) S Asia.
Masood, Shahla. Cytopathology of the Breast. (Illus.). 1995. write for info. (*0-89189-380-6*) Am Soc Clinical.
Masoro, E. J., ed. Pharmacology of Lipid Transport & Atherosclerotic Processes. 1975. 250.00 (*0-08-017762-X*, Pub. by Pergamon Repr UK) Franklin.
***Masoro, Edward J.** Handbook of Physiology Sect. 11: Aging. (Handbook of Physiology). (Illus.). 704p. 1995. 150.00 (*0-19-507722-9*) OUP.
Masoro, Edward J., ed. Handbook of Physiology in Aging. (Series in Clinical Laboratory Science). 520p. 1981. 146.00 (*0-8493-3143-9*, QP86) CRC Pr.
Masotta, Theodore, jt. auth. see Herubin, Charles A.
Masotti, L., jt. auth. see Collins, J. H.
Masotti, Louis, jt. ed. see Lineberry, Robert L.
Masotti, Louis H., jt. auth. see Lineberry, Robert L.
Masotti, Louis H., jt. ed. see Lineberry, Robert L.
Masouredis, Serafeim P. & Moulds, JoAnn M. Monoclonal Antibodies. LC 89-17576. (Illus.). (C). 1989. text ed. 28.00 (*0-915355-70-1*) Am Assn Blood.
MASP Professional Consulting Staff. Data Communication Networks Audit AP-03. (Audit Plan Ser.). 200p. 1990. student ed, ring bd. 899.00 (*0-940706-26-1*) Management Advisory Pubns.
— Local Area Network Security, Auditing & Controls (MAP-30) (Security, Audit & Control Ser.). (Illus.). 200p. Date not set. student ed, ring bd. 250.00 (*0-940706-51-2*) Management Advisory Pubns.
— Managing, Controlling & Auditing Purchased Software Packages. (Information Technologies Audit & Control Ser.). 200p. 1994. student ed, ring bd. 145.00 (*0-940706-54-7*) Management Advisory Pubns.
MASP Staff. Computer Viruses: Realities, Myths & Safeguards. (Illus.). 200p. 1990. 59.00 (*0-940706-24-5*) Management Advisory Pubns.
— EDI Management, Control, Security & Audit (MAP-29) (Audit, Security Plan Ser.). 200p. 1992. ring bd. 390.00 (*0-940706-27-X*) Management Advisory Pubns.
Maspero, Emilio. Los Trabajadores Frente a la Crisis. (Coleccion CLAT Ser.). 124p. (Orig.). (SPA.). 1986. pap. 6.00 (*0-917049-04-7*) Saeta.
Maspero, Francois. Cat's Grin. LC 88-34566. 295p. (C). 1989. reprint ed. pap. 9.95 (*0-941533-33-6*) New Amsterdam Bks.
— Roissy Express: A Journey Through the Paris Suburbs. Jones, Paul & Bellos, David, trs. LC 93-42235. (Illus.). 330p. 1994. 64.95 (*0-86091-373-2*, B2577, Pub. by Verso UK) Routledge Chapman & Hall.
Maspero, G. Popular Stories of Ancient Egypt. (African Studies). reprint ed. 40.00 (*0-938818-66-X*) ECA Assoc.
Maspero, Gaston. The Dawn of Civilization - Map & over Four Hundred Seventy Illustrations & Places. (African Studies). reprint ed. 75.00 (*0-938818-76-7*) ECA Assoc.
Maspero, Gaston, jt. auth. see Brugsch, Emile.
***Maspero, H., et al.** Asiatic Mythology: A Description & Explanation of the Mythologies of All the Great Nations of Asia. (C). 1995. reprint ed. 98.00x (*81-206-0920-4*, Pub. by Asian Educ Servs II) S Asia.
Maspero, Jean. L' Organisation Militaire de l'Egypt Byzantine. (Bibliotheque Des Hautes Etudes Ser.: No. 201). 157p. 1974. reprint ed. write for info. (*3-487-05282-2*, Pub. by Georg Olms GW) Lubrecht & Cramer.
Masquelet, Alain C. & Gilbert, Alain. Flaps in Limb Reconstruction. (Illus.). 256p. 1994. 135.00 (*0-397-51420-4*) Lippincott.
Masquelet, Alain C., et al. Atlas of Surgical Exposure of the Lower Extremities. 1992. text ed. 250.00 (*0-397-58325-7*) Lippincott.
Masquerier, Lewis. Sociology: Or, the Reconstruction of Society, Government, & Property. LC 76-88504. (Illus.). 213p. 1971. reprint ed. text ed. 55.00 (*0-8371-4967-3*, MASO) Greenwood.
— Sociology; or, the Reconstruction of Society, Government & Property. 1973. 59.95 (*0-8490-1073-X*) Gordon Pr.
Masquet, Georges. Dictionnaire des Grands Evenements de l'Histoire: Dictionary of the Great Events of History. 315p. (FRE.). 1973. pap. 15.95 (*0-8288-6260-5*, M-174) Fr & Eur.
Masrae, Mason. The Scarlet Saddle. large type ed. (Linford Western Library). 384p. 1986. pap. 11.95 (*0-7089-6204-1*) Ulverscroft.
Masri, Allan. The Golden Hills of California, Vol. 2. LC 78-65266. (Illus.). 131p. 1983. pap. 7.95 (*0-934136-21-1*) Western Tanager.
Masri, Sami F., ed. Proceedings of the U. S. National Workshop on Structural Control Research. LC 91-2839. 300p. 1991. 25.00 (*0-9628908-0-4*) USC Schl EDCE.
Masroor, Mehr N. Shadows of Time. (C). 1988. 31.00 (*81-7001-030-6*, Pub. by Chanakya II) S Asia.
Mass, Arthur A. Congress & Water Resources. (Reprint Series in Social Sciences). (C). 1993. reprint ed. pap. text ed. 1.00 (*0-8290-2735-1*, PS-176) Irvington.
***Mass, Jeffrey P.** Antiquity & Anachronism in Japanese History. 232p. 1995. pap. 14.95 (*0-8047-2592-6*) Stanford U Pr.
— Antiquity & Anachronism in Japanese History. 232p. (C). 1995. 37.50x (*0-8047-1974-8*) Stanford U Pr.
— The Development of Kamakura Rule, 1180-1250: A History with Documents. LC 78-62271. xvi, 312p. 1979. 39.50 (*0-8047-1003-1*) Stanford U Pr.
— The Kamakura Bakufu: A Study in Documents. LC 75-39335. (Illus.). 376p. 1976. 45.00 (*0-8047-0907-6*) Stanford U Pr.
— Lordship & Inheritance in Early Medieval Japan: A Study of the Kamakura Soryo System. 352p. 1989. 42.50 (*0-8047-1540-8*) Stanford U Pr.
— Warrior Government in Early Medieval Japan: A Study of the Kamakura Bakufu, Shugo & Jiteo. LC 74-75875. (Yale Historical Publications. Miscellany: No. 103). 269p. reprint ed. pap. 76.70 (*0-8357-8369-3*, 2033815) Bks Demand.
***Mass, Jeffrey P., ed.** Court & Bakufu in Japan: Essays in Kamakura History. 342p. (C). 1995. 49.50x (*0-8047-2532-2*); pap. 16.95 (*0-8047-2473-3*) Stanford U Pr.
Mass, Jeffrey P. & Hauser, William B., eds. The Bakufu in Japanese History. LC 84-51768. 288p. 1985. 37.50 (*0-8047-1278-6*) Stanford U Pr.
— The Bakufu in Japanese History. 282p. (C). 1993. pap. 15.95 (*0-8047-2210-2*) Stanford U Pr.
Mass, Jeffrey P., jt. ed. see Hall, John W.
Mass, Lawrence. Homosexuality & Sexuality: Dialogues of the Sexual Revolution, Vol. 1. LC 90-4985. (Gay & Lesbian Studies). 184p. 1990. text ed. 39.95 (*1-56024-045-8*) Haworth Pr.
— Homosexuality As Behavior & Identity: Dialogues of the Sexual Revolution, Vol. II. LC 90-4988. (Gay & Lesbian Studies Ser.). 268p. 1990. pap. 17.95 (*0-918393-90-6*) Harrington Pk.
— Homosexuality As Behavior & Identity: Dialogues of the Sexual Revolution, Vol. 2. LC 90-4986. (Gay & Lesbian Studies: Vol. 6). 268p. 1990. text ed. 39.95 (*1-56024-046-6*) Haworth Pr.

M

— Homsexuality & Sexuality: Dialogues of the Sexual Revolution, Vol. I. LC 90-4987. (Gay & Lesbian Studies Ser.). 184p. 1990. pap. text ed. 14.95 (*0-918393-89-2*) Harrington Pk.

Mass, Lawrence D. Confessions of a Jewish Wagnerite: Being Gay & Jewish in America. (Sexual Politics Ser.). 224p. 1994. pap. 15.95 (*0-304-33114-7*, Pub. by Cassell Pubng UK) InBook.

Mass, Lynne. Kids Working with Computers: The Texas Instruments LOGO Manual. (Illus.). 64p. (J). (gr. 4-7). 1983. pap. 4.99 (*0-89824-074-3*) Trillium Pr.

— Kids Working with Kids. 48p. 1980. pap. 10.00 (*0-89824-018-2*) Trillium Pr.

Mass, Lynne, jt. auth. see Kemnitz, T. M.

Mass, Lynne, jt. auth. see Kemnitz, Thomas M.

Mass, Lynne, jt. auth. see Kemntz, T. M.

Mass, Marc J., et al, eds. Cancer of the Respiratory Tract: Predisposing Factors. LC 85-1920. (Carcinogenesis: A Comprehensive Survey Ser.: Vol. 8). 496p. 1985. text ed. 129.00 (*0-88167-109-6*) Raven.

Mass, Nathaniel J., ed. Readings in Urban Dynamics, Vol. 1. LC 73-89545. (Illus.). 303p. (C). 1974. text ed. 45.00 (*0-262-13140-4*) Prod Press.

Mass Tech Times, Inc. Staff. Directory of Connecticut & Rhode Island High Technology Companies. 2nd ed. Lillie, Anne S., ed. 200p. 1991. pap. 125.00 (*0-927452-03-0*) Mass Tech Times.

— The Directory of Maine, New Hampshire & Vermont High Technology Companies. rev. ed. Lillie, Anne S., ed. 140p. 1989. pap. 125.00 (*0-927452-01-4*) Mass Tech Times.

— Directory of Maine, New Hampshire & Vermont High Technology Companies. 2nd ed. 1992. pap. write for info. (*0-927452-04-9*) Mass Tech Times.

— The Directory of Massachusetts High Technology Companies. rev. ed. Lillie, Anne S., ed. 324p. 1989. pap. write for info. (*0-927452-00-6*) Mass Tech Times.

— The Directory of Massachusetts High Technology Companies. 2nd ed. Lillie, Anne S., ed. 365p. 1990. pap. write for info. (*0-927452-02-2*) Mass Tech Times.

***Mass, Wendy.** Getting a Clue: Tammy. (Loop Ser.). 1995. mass mkt. 3.50 (*0-373-20209-1*, 1-20209-2) Harlequin Bks.

Mass, William, jt. ed. see Lazonick, William.

Massa, Ana. American Literature in Context, Vol. IV: 1900-1930. 220p. 1982. pap. 14.95 (*0-416-73930-X*, NO. 3616) Routledge Chapman & Hall.

Massa, Ann, ed. American Declarations of Love. LC 89-6106. 192p. 1990. text ed. 39.95 (*0-312-03190-4*) St Martin.

Massa, Ann & Stead, Alistair, eds. Forked Tongues: Comparing Twentieth-Century British & American Literature. LC 93-39018. (C). 1994. text ed. 63.95 (*0-582-07554-8*, Pub. by Longman UK) Longman.

— Forked Tongues: Comparing Twentieth-Century British & American Literature. LC 93-39018. (C). 1995. pap. text ed. 25.95 (*0-582-07555-6*, Pub. by Longman UK) Longman.

***Massa, Francoise.** Megalithes et Traditions Populaires Dictionnaire Illustre. 191p. (FRE.). 1991. pap. 38.95 (*0-7859-8177-2*, 2876240289) Fr & Eur.

***Massa, Louis R.** Regions of Infiltration. (Illus.). 32p. 1995. pap. 11.00 (*0-8059-3677-7*) Dorrance.

Massa, Mark, jt. ed. see Viladesau, Richard.

Massa, Mark S. Charles Augustus Briggs & the Crisis of Historical Criticism. (Harvard Dissertations in Religion Ser.). 232p. (Orig.). 1990. pap. 17.00 (*0-8006-7079-5*, 1-7079) Augsburg Fortress.

Massac County Historical Society Staff. History of Massac County, Illinois 1843-1987. LC 87-71196. 480p. 1987. 49.95 (*0-938021-20-6*) Turner Pub KY.

Massachi, Dalya & Cowan, Rich, eds. Guide to Uncovering the Right on Campus. (Study War No More Guidebook Ser.: No. 1). (Illus.). 52p. 1994. pap. 5.95 (*0-945210-03-5*) Public Search.

Massachusetts Art Commission Staff. Art in the Massachusetts State House. LC 86-63635. (Illus.). 78p. (Orig.). 1986. pap. write for info. (*0-9617851-0-1*) Mass Art Comm.

***Massachusetts BioTech Research Institute Staff.** BioTechnology. 352p. 1995. pap. text ed. 31.95 (*0-7872-0565-6*) Kendall-Hunt.

Massachusetts Board of Bar Overseers of the Supreme Court. Massachusetts Attorney Discipline Reports, 9 vols., Vol. 1. 420p. 55.00 (*0-685-42459-6*) Butterworth Legal Pubs.

— Massachusetts Attorney Discipline Reports, 9 vols., Vol. 5. 65.00 (*0-685-42460-X*) Butterworth Legal Pubs.

— Massachusetts Attorney Discipline Reports Vol. 2. 420p. 55.00 (*0-614-03140-0*) Butterworth Legal Pubs.

— Massachusetts Attorney Discipline Reports Vol. 3. 420p. 55.00 (*0-614-03143-5*) Butterworth Legal Pubs.

— Massachusetts Attorney Discipline Reports Vol. 4. 420p. 55.00 (*0-614-03144-3*) Butterworth Legal Pubs.

— Massachusetts Attorney Discipline Reports Vol. 6. 420p. 65.00 (*0-614-03145-1*) Butterworth Legal Pubs.

— Massachusetts Attorney Discipline Reports Vol. 7. 420p. 1993. 70.00 (*0-614-03147-8*) Butterworth Legal Pubs.

— Massachusetts Attorney Discipline Reports Vol. 8. 420p. 1993. 70.00 (*0-614-03148-6*) Butterworth Legal Pubs.

— Massachusetts Attorney Discipline Reports Vol. 9. 420p. 1994. 70.00 (*0-614-03149-4*) Butterworth Legal Pubs.

Massachusetts Colony Court of Assistants Staff. Records of the Court of Assistants of the Colony of the Massachusetts Bay, 1630-1692, 3 vols. reprint ed. write for info. (*0-318-50696-3*) AMS Pr.

— Records of the Court of Assistants of the Colony of the Massachusetts Bay, 1630-1692, 3 vols., 1. LC 70-172853. reprint ed. 75.00 (*0-404-07351-4*) AMS Pr.

— Records of the Court of Assistants of the Colony of the Massachusetts Bay, 1630-1692, 3 vols., 2. LC 70-172853. reprint ed. 75.00 (*0-404-07352-2*) AMS Pr.

— Records of the Court of Assistants of the Colony of the Massachusetts Bay, 1630-1692, 3 vols., 3. LC 70-172853. reprint ed. 75.00 (*0-404-07353-0*) AMS Pr.

— Records of the Court of Assistants of the Colony of the Massachusetts Bay, 1630-1692, 3 vols., Set. LC 70-172853. reprint ed. 247.50 (*0-404-07350-6*) AMS Pr.

Massachusetts Commission for Investigation of White Slave Traffic, tr. see New York Committee of Fifteen, et al.

Massachusetts Commission on Christian Unity Staff. Christian Understandings of Marriage: Ecumenical & Pastoral Directives: Roman Catholic, Protestant, Orthodox. 1990. pap. 4.95 (*0-9627112-0-9*) Divinitas Pr.

— Living the Faith You Share: Ten Ecumenical Guidelines for Couples in Roman Catholic - Protestant Marriages. 1990. 1.50 (*0-9627112-1-7*) Divinitas Pr.

Massachusetts Commission on Lunacy Staff. Insanity & Idiocy in Massachusetts: Report of the Commission on Lunacy, 1855. LC 72-134950. 309p. reprint ed. pap. 88.10 (*0-7837-2279-6*, 2057367) Bks Demand.

Massachusetts Commission on Old Age Pensions, Annuities & Insurance. Report of the Commission on Old Age Pensions, Annuities & Insurance. LC 75-17233. (Social Problems & Social Policy Ser.). (Illus.). 1976. reprint ed. 34.95 (*0-405-07502-2*) Ayer.

Massachusetts Commission on the Cost of Living. Report of the Commission on the Cost of Living. LC 75-17232. (Social Problems & Social Policy Ser.). (Illus.). 1976. reprint ed. 65.95 (*0-405-07501-4*) Ayer.

Massachusetts Continuing Legal Education-New England Law Institute, Inc. Staff. Massachusetts Corporation Laws: Reprinted from Massachusetts General Laws Annotated - Containing General Laws Enacted Through the 1982 Session of the General Court. iii, 377p. 1983. write for info. (*0-318-57764-X*) West Pub.

Massachusetts Continuing Legal Education, Inc. Staff, jt. auth. see Kantrowitz, R. Marc.

Massachusetts General Court Staff, jt. auth. see Philadelphia Board of Guardians Staff.

Massachusetts General Hospital, Department of Anesthesia Staff. Postoperative Critical Care of the Massachusetts General Hospital. 2nd ed. Hoffman, William et al, eds. LC 92-15625. 1992. 38.95 (*0-316-36838-5*) Little.

Massachusetts General Hospital Department of Dietetics Staff. Diet Reference Manual. Palombo, Ruth D. & Carey, Mary, eds. 240p. 1984. spiral bd. 17.50 (*0-316-54947-9*) Little.

Massachusetts General Hospital Department of Nursing Staff. Manual of Pediatric Nursing Practice. Pikl, Barbara H., ed. (Little, Brown Spiral Manual Ser.). 1981. pap. 16.00 (*0-316-54959-2*) Little.

— Massachusetts General Hospital Department of Nursing Teaching Guides for Patients with Neurologic Disorders. (C). 1984. pap. text ed. 27.95 (*0-8359-4342-9*, Reston) P-H.

Massachusetts General Hospital, Dept. of Anesthesia Staff & Harvard Medical School Staff. Clinical Anesthesia Procedures of the Massachusetts General Hospital. 4th ed. Davison, J. Kenneth et al, eds. LC 92-48517. (Handbook Ser.). (Illus.). 728p. 1993. pap. 34.95 (*0-316-17714-8*) Little.

Massachusetts General Hospital Organ Transplant Team & Pizer, H. F. Organ Transplants: A Patient's Guide. 243p. (C). 1991. text ed. 24.95 (*0-674-64235-X*) HUP.

Massachusetts Geographic Alliance Staff. Global Geography: Activities for Teaching the Five Themes of Geography. (Illus.). 172p. 1990. pap. 21.95 (*0-89994-356-X*) Soc Sci Ed.

Massachusetts Historical Society, Boston Staff. Catalog of Manuscripts of the Massachusetts Historical Society, Boston, 7 Vols, Set. 1970. lib. bdg. 805.00 (*0-8161-0822-6*, Hall Library) G K Hall.

Massachusetts Historical Society Staff. Catalog of Manuscripts of the Massachusetts Historical Society: First Supplement. 1980. lib. bdg. 255.00 (*0-8161-0850-1*, Hall Library) G K Hall.

— Warren-Adams Letters, Being Chiefly a Correspondence among John Adams, Samuel Adams, & James Warren, 2 Vols. LC 79-158225. reprint ed. Set. 125.00 (*0-404-06854-5*) AMS Pr.

— Warren-Adams Letters, Being Chiefly a Correspondence among John Adams, Samuel Adams, & James Warren, 2 Vols, 1. LC 79-158225. reprint ed. write for info. (*0-404-06855-3*) AMS Pr.

— Warren-Adams Letters, Being Chiefly a Correspondence among John Adams, Samuel Adams, & James Warren, 2 Vols, 2. LC 79-158225. 1925. reprint ed. write for info. (*0-404-06856-1*) AMS Pr.

— Witness to America's Past: Two Centuries of Collecting by the Massachusetts Historical Society. 208p. 1990. pap. text ed. 25.00 (*0-87846-334-8*) Mus Fine Arts Boston.

Massachusetts Horticultural Society, Boston Staff. Dictionary Catalog of the Library of the Massachusetts Horticultural Society, 3 Vols, Set. 1970. lib. bdg. 285.00 (*0-8161-0648-7*, Hall Library) G K Hall.

— Dictionary Catalog of the Library of the Massachusetts Horticultural Society, First Supplement. 1972. lib. bdg. 120.00 (*0-8161-1038-7*, Hall Library) G K Hall.

Massachusetts Horticultural Society Staff. Keeping Eden: A History of Gardening in America. Punch, Walter T., ed. (Illus.). 256p. 1992. 50.00 (*0-8212-1818-2*) Bulfinch Pr.

Massachusetts Institute of Technology, Conference on Advanced Research in VLSI Staff. Conference on Advanced Research in VLSI: Proceedings, January 25-27, 1982, Massachusetts Institute of Technology, Cambridge, MA, USA. Penfield, Paul, Jr., ed. LC 81-71335. (Illus.). 219p. reprint ed. pap. 62.50 (*0-8357-4191-5*, 2036969) Bks Demand.

Massachusetts Institute of Technology Library Staff. The MIT Catalog of Computer Science & Artificial Intelligence. 850p. 1988. lib. bdg. 215.00 (*0-8161-0480-8*, Hall Library) G K Hall.

Massachusetts Institute of Technology Library Staff & Stanford University Library Staff, eds. Bibliographic Guides to Computer Science: 1990. (Bibliographic Guides Ser.). 250p. (C). 1991. lib. bdg. 165.00 (*0-8161-7134-3*) G K Hall.

Massachusetts Institute of Technology Staff. Characterization of Copper-Binding Agents Released by Daphnia Magna. 31p. 1982. write for info. (*0-318-60400-0*) Intl Copper.

— Modeling the Interactions of Trace Metals & Aquatic Humic Materials. 150p. 1984. write for info. (*0-318-60404-3*) Intl Copper.

Massachusetts Institute of Technology Staff & Stanford University Staff. Bibliographic Guide to Computer Science, 1988. 250p. 1989. lib. bdg. 165.00 (*0-8161-7099-1*, Hall Reference) Macmillan.

Massachusetts Moderators Association Staff. Town Meeting Time: A Handbook of Parliamentary Law. 2nd ed. LC 84-4354. 202p. 1984. lib. bdg. 21.50 (*0-89874-754-6*) Krieger.

***Massachusetts Society of Mayflower Descendants Staff.** Index of Persons of the Mayflower Descendant, Vols. 1-34. 720p. 1995. text ed. 50.00 (*0-7884-0095-9*) Heritage Bk.

Massachusetts Special Commission on Investigation of the Judicial System. Report of the Special Commission on Investigation of the Judicial System, Commonwealth of Massachusetts: Under Chapter Sixty-Two of the Resolves of 1935. LC 74-3833. (Criminal Justice in America Ser.). 1974. reprint ed. 17.95 (*0-405-06153-6*) Ayer.

Massaguer, J., jt. auth. see Cabanellas, G.

Massalha, Omar. Towards the Long-Promised Peace: A History of the Israeli-Palestinian Conflict. 330p. 1994. 45.00 (*0-86356-057-1*, Pub. by Saqi Bks UK); pap. 16.95 (*0-86356-065-2*, Pub. by Saqi Bks UK) Interlink Pub.

Massalski, T. B., ed. Alloying Behavior & Effects in Concentrated Solid Solutions. LC 65-18398. (Metallurgical Society Conference Ser.: Vol. 29). 455p. reprint ed. pap. 129.70 (*0-8357-5322-0*, 2001517) Bks Demand.

Massalski, T. B., ed. see AIME Metallurgical Society Staff.

Massalski, T. B., jt. auth. see Barrett, C. S.

Massalski, T. B., jt. intro. see Okamoto, H.

Massam, Bryan H. The Right Place: Shared Responsibility & the Location of Public Facilities. LC 92-31995. 231p. 1993. text ed. 89.95 (*0-470-21991-2*) Halsted Pr.

— Spatial Search: Applications to Planning Problems in the Public Sector. (Urban & Regional Planning Ser.: Vol. 23). 1983. text ed. 66.00 (*0-08-024286-3*, Pub. by Pergamon Repr UK) Franklin.

Massam, J. A. Cliff Dwellers of Kenya. (Illus.). 268p. 1968. reprint ed. 35.00 (*0-7146-1697-4*, Pub. by F Cass Pubs UK) Intl Spec Bk.

Massanes, J. Horta. Diccionario de Sinonimos e Ideas Afines y de la Rima (Dictionary of Synonyms, Related Ideas & Rhyming) 4th ed. 363p. (SPA.). 1991. pap. 17.95 (*0-7859-3738-2*, S50243) Fr & Eur.

Massanet, Jules. Manon. John, Nicholas, ed. Edmund, Tracey, tr. (English National Opera Guide Series: Bilingual Libretto, Articles: No. 25). (Illus.). 1984. pap. 9.95 (*0-7145-4041-2*) Riverrun NY.

Massara. Design & Test Techniques for VLSI & WSI Circuits. 1990. 99.00 (*0-86341-165-7*, CM015) Inst Elect Eng.

Massara, Emily B. Que Gordita! A Study of Weight among Women in a Puerto Rican Community. LC 88-35144. (Immigrant Communities & Ethnic Minorities in the U. S. & Canada Ser.: No. 46). 1989. 57.50 (*0-404-19456-7*) AMS Pr.

Massardier-Kenney, Francoise, jt. ed. see Kadish, Doris Y.

Massare, Judy A. Prehistoric Marine Reptiles: Sea Monsters During the Age of Dinosaurs. LC 91-17057. (Non-Fiction Ser.). (Illus.). 64p. (J). (gr. 5-8). 1991. lib. bdg. 15.82 (*0-531-11022-2*) Watts.

Massarella, Derek. A World Elsewhere: Europe's Encounter with Japan in the Sixteenth & Seventeenth Centuries. LC 89-22639. 352p. (C). 1990. text ed. 35.00 (*0-300-04633-2*) Yale U Pr.

***Massarella, Derek & Bodart-Bailey, Beatrice M., eds.** The Furthest Goal: Englebert Kaempfer's Encounter with Tokugawa Japan. 192p. (C). 1995. text ed. 70.00 (*1-873410-37-9*, Pub. by Curzon Pr UK) Humanities.

Massarella, Gregory. How to Prepare a Results-Driven Business Plan. 185p. 1993. spiral bd. 65.00 (*0-8144-5136-5*) AMACOM.

Massarelli, Raphael, et al, eds. Phospholipids & Signal Transmission. LC 93-16726. (NATO ASI Series H: Cell Biology: Vol. 70). 1993. 198.00 (*0-387-54610-3*) Spr-Verlag.

Massari, U. & Miranda, M. Minimal Surfaces of Codimension One. (Mathematics Studies: Vol. 91). 1984. pap. 56.50 (*0-444-86873-9*, I-105-84, North Holland) Elsevier.

Massarik, Fred. Advances in Organization Development, Vol. 2. (Advances in Organization Development Ser.). 176p. (C). 1992. text ed. 65.00 (*0-89391-809-1*) Ablex Pub.

— Participative Management. (Studies in Productivity: Highlights of the Literature Ser.: Vol. 28). 40p. 1983. pap. 55.00 (*0-08-029509-6*) Work in Amer.

Massarik, Fred, comp. Bibliography on Human Relations Training & Related Subjects. 1985. pap. 8.00 (*0-9610392-3-X*) NTL Inst.

Massarik, Fred, ed. Advances in Organization Development, Vol. 1. LC 89-17852. 384p. 1990. text ed. 69.50 (*0-89391-242-5*) Ablex Pub.

Massarik, Fred & Kaback, Michael M. Genetic Disease Control: A Social Psychological Approach. LC 80-28219. (Sage Library of Social Research: No. 116). 168p. reprint ed. pap. 47.90 (*0-8357-8495-9*, 2034770) Bks Demand.

Massaro. Lung Cell Biology. (Lung Biology in Health & Disease Ser.: Vol. 41). 1464p. 1989. 275.00 (*0-8247-7962-2*) Dekker.

Massaro, Dominic R., et al, eds. Bicentennial Minutes: New York's Role in the Ratification of the Constitution. limited ed. (Illus.). 64p. reprint ed. boxed 30.00 (*0-318-35285-0*) NYS Bar.

Massaro, Dominic W. Experimental Psychology: An Information Processing Approach. 512p. (C). 1989. pap. text ed. 33.25 (*0-15-525851-6*) HB Coll Pubs.

— Speech Perception by Ear & Eye: A Paradigm for Psychological Inquiry. 336p. 1987. text ed. 59.95 (*0-8058-0061-1*); pap. text ed. 36.00 (*0-8058-0062-X*) L Erlbaum Assocs.

Massaro, Dominic W., jt. ed. see Solso, Robert L.

Massaro, John. Supremely Political: The Role of Ideology & Presidential Management in Unsuccessful Supreme Court Nominations. LC 89-21622. (SUNY Series in the Presidency: Contemporary Issues). 272p. 1990. 64.50 (*0-7914-0301-7*); pap. 21.95 (*0-7914-0302-5*) State U NY Pr.

Massaro, Jon F. Essentials of Elementary Statistics. 171p. (C). 1993. student ed 11.23 (*1-56870-068-7*) RonJon Pub.

Massaro, Toni M. Constitutional Literacy: A Core Curriculum for a Multicultural Nation. LC 93-10861. (Constitutional Conflicts Ser.). 208p. 1993. 24.95 (*0-8223-1364-2*) Duke.

Massart, C., tr. see Zarzycki, J.

Massart, D. L., et al. Chemometrics: A Textbook. 464p. 1988. 89.75 (*0-444-42660-4*) Elsevier.

— Evaluation & Optimization of Laboratory Methods & Analytical Procedures. (Techniques & Instrumentation in Analytical Chemistry Ser.: Vol. 1). 596p. 1978. 107.75 (*0-444-41743-5*) Elsevier.

Massart, D. L., et al, eds. Chemometrics Tutorials, Vols. 1-5: Collected from Chemometrics & Intelligent Laboratory Systems - an International Journal. 428p. 1990. pap. 66.75 (*0-444-88837-3*) Elsevier.

Massart, D. Luc & Kaufman, Leonard. Interpretation of Analytical Chemical Data by the Use of Cluster Analysis. LC 88-32691. 250p. (C). 1989. reprint ed. lib. bdg. 62.50 (*0-89464-358-4*) Krieger.

Massasati, Ahmad. Islamic Calligraphy Coloring Book. (Illus.). 57p. (Orig.). (J). (gr. 3-6). 1991. pap. 4.95 (*0-89259-120-X*) Am Trust Pubns.

***Massasoit Community College Staff.** Laboratory Exercises for Biological Principles. 176p. (C). 1994. spiral bd. 14.95 (*0-8403-9521-3*) Kendall-Hunt.

— Laboratory Exercises for Biology of Organisms. 204p. (C). 1991. spiral bd. 21.95 (*0-8403-7336-8*) Kendall-Hunt.

Massaux, Edouard. The Influence of the Gospel of Saint Matthew on Christian Literature Before Saint Irenaeus: Later Christian Writings. Bellinzoni, Arthur J., ed. Belval, Norman J. & Hecht, Suzanne, trs. (New Gospel Studies: No. 5/2). 1992. 25.00 (*0-86554-382-8*, H311) Mercer Univ Pr.

— The Influence of the Gospel of Saint Matthew on Christian Literature Before Saint Irenaeus: The First Ecclesiastical Writers. Bellinzoni, Arthur J., ed. Belval, Norman J. & Hecht, Suzanne, trs. LC 90-38747. xxvi, 172p. (C). 1991. 25.00 (*0-86554-381-X*, MUP/H309) Mercer Univ Pr.

— Influence of the Gospel of St. Matthew on Christian Literature Before St. Irenaeus. Bellinzoni, Arthur J., ed. Belval, Norman J. & Hecht, Suzanne, trs. (New Gospel Studies: No. 5/3). 285p. 1993. text ed. 25.00 (*0-86554-383-6*, MUP/H312) Mercer Univ Pr.

Masschelein, W. J., ed. Ozonization Manual for Water & Wastewater Treatment. LC 81-21986. (Illus.). 346p. reprint ed. pap. 98.70 (*0-8357-6650-0*, 2035319) Bks Demand.

Masschelein, Willy J. Unit Processes in Drinking Water Treatment. LC 92-20757. (Environmental Science & Pollution Ser.: Vol. 3). 656p. 1992. 190.00 (*0-8247-8678-5*) Dekker.

Masse, Anthony M. The Decline & Fall of the United States. 275p. 1985. pap. 8.95 (*0-9608294-0-7*) Bataan Bk Pubs.

Masse, Louis, ed. see Leaverton, Paul E.

Masse, Louis, jt. ed. see Leaverton, Paul E.

Masse, Michelle A. In the Name of Love: Women, Masochism, & the Gothic. LC 91-55552. (Reading Women Writing Ser.). 320p. 1992. 41.50 (*0-8014-2616-2*); pap. 15.95 (*0-8014-9918-6*) Cornell U Pr.

Masse, N. P., ed. see International Children's Center Conference Staff.

***Masse-Raimbault, Anne-Marie, et al, eds.** L' Alimentation des Femmes: Etape essentielle au Development de l'Enfant. 152p. (Orig.). (FRE.). 1994. pap. text ed. write for info. (*0-89492-107-X*) Acad Educ Dev.

Masse, Rolanda D. RV - Travel Leisurely Year Round. (U. S. A. Guides Ser.). 200p. (Orig.). 1991. pap. 14.95 (*0-87052-958-7*) Hippocrene Bks.

Massee, Robin, tr. see Evans, David & Hoxeng, James, eds.

An Asterisk (*) at the beginning of an entry indicates that the title is appearing in BIP for the first time.

Massel, S. R. Hydrodynamics of Coastal Zones. (Oceanography Ser.: No. 48). 336p. 1989. 102.75 (*0-444-87375-9*) Elsevier.

***Massel, Stanislaw R.** Ocean Waves; Their Physics & Prediction. (Advanced Series in Ocean Engineering). 350p. 1995. pap. text ed. 36.00 (*981-02-2109-6*) World Scientific Pub.

Masselin, Roselyne. Cuisine Imaginaire: Delicious Menus for Vegetarian Entertaining. (Illus.). 224p. 1994. 27.95 (*0-563-36413-0*, BBC-Parkwest) Parkwest Pubns.

***Massell, Gregory J.** The Surrogate Proletariat: Moslem Women & Revolutionary Strategies in Soviet Central Asia, 1919-1929. LC 73-16047. Date not set. reprint ed. pap. 140.00 (*0-7837-9384-7*, 2060128) Bks Demand.

Massell, Gregory L. Surrogate Proletariat: Moslem Women & Revolutionary Strategies in Soviet Central Asia, 1919-1929. (Center of International Studies). 452p. 1974. 67. 50 (*0-691-07562-X*) Princeton U Pr.

Masselos, Jim. Indian Nationalism: A History. rev. ed. 340p. (C). 1991. text ed. 35.00 (*81-207-1178-5*, Pub. by Sterling Pubs II); pap. text ed. 12.95 (*81-201-1405-1*, Pub. by Sterling Pubs II) Apt Bks.

Masselos, Jim, ed. India: Creating a Modern Nation. 1990. text ed. 45.00 (*81-207-1154-8*, Pub. by Sterling Pubs II) Apt Bks.

— Struggling & Ruling: The Indian National Congress, 1885-1985. (South Asian Publications: No. 2). 224p. 1987. text ed. 35.00 (*81-207-0691-9*, Pub. by Sterling Pubs II) Apt Bks.

Masselos, Jim, et al, eds. India: Rebellion to Republic. (Asian Studies Association of Austrlia South Asian Publications). 1990. text ed. 50.00 (*81-207-1107-6*, Pub. by Sterling Pubs II) Apt Bks.

Massen, Roy & Hodkinson, Dale. Does Not Compute: The Computer Users Guide. LC 84-50190. (Illus.). 96p. (Orig.). 1984. pap. 4.95 (*0-916437-00-0*) Sarcastic.

Massenet, Jules E. My Recollections. Barnett, H. Villiers, tr. LC 75-107819. (Select Bibliographies Reprint Ser.). 1977. 26.95 (*0-8369-5190-5*) Ayer.

— My Recollections (1848-1912) 304p. 1990. reprint ed. lib. bdg. 79.00 (*0-7812-9073-2*) Rprt Serv.

Massengale, Dee. The Guide to a Better Back. Mueller, Phyllis, ed. LC 87-31104. (Illus.). 104p. (Orig.). 1988. pap. 9.95 (*0-932419-12-7*) Cherokee.

Massengale, Eugene W. Fundamentals of Federal Contract Law. LC 90-40700. 264p. 1990. text ed. 59.95 (*0-89930-604-7*, MFK, Quorum Bks) Greenwood.

Massengale, Jean Montague, text. Fragonard. LC 92-21996. (Masters of Art Ser.). (Illus.). 1993. 22.95 (*0-8109-3313-6*) Abrams.

Massengale, John D., ed. Trends Toward the Future in Physical Education. LC 86-34282. (Illus.). 200p. 1987. text ed. 33.00x (*0-87322-103-6*, BMAS0103) Human Kinetics.

Massengale, Tim. Let My People Grow! LC 88-31269. (Illus.). 304p. (Orig.). 1989. pap. 7.99 (*0-932581-41-2*) Word Aflame.

Massengill, Paul K., ed. see Porter, Patrick K.

Massengill, Reed. Portrait of a Racist: The Man Who Killed Medgar Evers? (Illus.). 320p. 1993. 23.95 (*0-312-09365-9*) St Martin.

Massengill, Stephen E., ed. North Carolina Votes on the Constitution: A Roster of Delegates to the State Ratification Conventions of 1788 & 1789. (North Carolina & the Constitution Ser.). (Illus.). xii, 86p. (Orig.). 1988. pap. 5.00 (*0-86526-237-3*) NC Archives.

Massengill, Stephen E. & Topkins, Robert M. A North Carolina Postcard Album, 1905-1925. (Illus.). xii, 172p. 1988. 55.00 (*0-86526-236-5*) NC Archives.

Masser, Barry Z. Complete Handbook of All Purpose Telemarketing Scripts. 456p. 1990. 59.95 (*0-13-161068-6*) P-H.

— How to Make One Hundred Thousand Dollars a Year in Home Mail Order Business. 1992. pap. 12.95 (*0-13-397456-1*, Busn) P-H.

— How to Start & Run Your Home-Based Office. 1993. 16. 95 (*0-13-156548-6*) P-H.

— Power Selling by Telephone. 1983. pap. text ed. 10.95 (*0-13-687392-8*) P-H.

— Thirty-Six Thousand Dollars a Year in Your Own Home Merchandising Business. (Illus.). 1978. 14.95 (*0-13-918987-4*, Parker Publishing Co) P-H.

Masser, Barry Z. & Leeds, William M. Power Selling by Telephone. 240p. 1982. 19.95 (*0-13-686998-X*, Parker Publishing Co) P-H.

***Masser, Ian, et al.** The Geography of Europe's Futures. 1993. text ed. 69.95 (*0-471-94713-X*) Wiley.

Masser, Ian. Strategic Monitoring for Urban Planning in Developing Countries: Some Guidelines from British & Dutch Experience. (Working Papers Ser.: No. 85-7). 20p. (Orig.). 1986. pap. text ed. 5.00 (*0-318-21379-6*, CRD186) UNIPUB.

Masser, Ian & Blakemore, Michael. Handling Geographical Information: Methodology & Potential Applications. 317p. 1991. text ed. 125.00 (*0-470-21792-8*) Halsted Pr.

Masser, Ian & Brown, P. J. B. Spatial Representation & Spatial Interaction. (Studies in Applied Regional Science: Vol. 10). 1978. pap. text ed. 41.50 (*90-207-0717-5*) Kluwer Ac.

Masser, Ian & Onsrud, Harlan J., eds. Diffusion & Use of Geographic Information Technologies: Proceedings of the NATO Advanced Research Workshop on Modeling the Diffusion & Use of Geographic Information Technologies, Sounion, Greece, April 8-11, 1992. LC 93-9597. (NATO Advanced Study Institutes Series D, Behavioural & Social Sciences: No. 70). 364p. (C). 1993. Alk. paper. lib. bdg. 136.00 (*0-7923-2190-1*) Kluwer Ac.

Masser, Ian, jt. ed. see Friedrich, Peter.

***Masser, Ian, et al.** The Geography of Europe's Future. 1993. pap. text ed. 24.95 (*0-471-94714-8*) Wiley.

— The Geography of Europe's Futures. 225p. 1992. text ed. 64.95 (*0-470-21938-6*); pap. text ed. 21.95 (*0-470-21932-7*) Halsted Pr.

Masserman, Chris, jt. auth. see Masserman, Jules.

Masserman, J. H., ed. Current Psychiatric Therapies, Vols. I & II-XII. Incl. Vol. I. LC 61-9411. (Illus.). 256p. 1961. 47.00 (*0-8089-0280-6*); Vol V. LC 61-9411. 320p. 1965. text ed. 76.00 (*0-8089-0284-9*, 792705); Vol VI. LC 61-9411. 400p. 1966. text ed. 81.00 (*0-8089-0285-7*, 792706); Vol VII. LC 61-9411. (Illus.). 266p. 1967. text ed. 87.00 (*0-8089-0286-5*, 792707); Vol. VIII. LC 61-9411. 272p. 1968. text ed. 87.00 (*0-8089-0287-3*, 792708); Vol IX. LC 61-9411. (Illus.). 320p. 1969. text ed. 91.00 (*0-8089-0288-1*, 792709); LC 61-9411. write for info. (*0-318-52856-8*, Grune) Saunders.

Masserman, Jules & Masserman, Chris. Sexual Accusations & Social Turmoil. 160p. 1994. 34.95 (*0-916147-43-6*); pap. 17.95 (*0-916147-42-8*) Regent Pr.

Masserman, Jules H. Psychiatry & Health: A Comprehensive Integration. 253p. 1986. 35.95 (*0-89885-256-0*) Human Sci Pr.

— Theory & Therapy in Dynamic Psychiatry. LC 72-96926. 410p. 1986. 30.00x (*0-87668-067-8*) Aronson.

— Theory & Therapy in Dynamic Psychiatry. LC 72-96926. 240p. 1995. pap. 25.00 (*1-56821-511-8*) Aronson.

***Masserman, Jules H. & Uribe, Victor M.** Adolescent Sexuality. 118p. 1989. pap. 16.95 (*0-398-06270-6*) C C Thomas.

— Adolescent Sexuality. 118p. (C). 1989. text ed. 31.95x (*0-398-05629-3*) C C Thomas.

Masseron, Alexandre. Dante Alighieri: The Poet Who Loved St. Francis So Much. Aranadez, Richard, tr. (Tau Ser.). 1979. 2.95 (*0-8199-0757-X*, Frncscn Herld) Franciscan Pr.

***Masseron, Jean.** Petroleum Economics. 9000. pap. text ed. 74.00 (*2-7108-0597-9*) Technip.

Massey. Nursing Research. (Notes Ser.). 1991. 14.95 (*0-87434-317-8*) Springhouse Pub.

Massey, Andrew. Managing the Public Sector: A Comparative Analysis of Britain & the United States. 256p. 1992. 64.95 (*1-85278-333-8*, Pub. by E Elgar Pub UK) Ashgate Pub Co.

— Technocrats & Nuclear Politics: The Influence of Professional Experts in Policy-Making. 200p. 1988. text ed. 53.95 (*0-566-05644-5*, Pub. by Dartmth Pub UK) Ashgate Pub Co.

***Massey, Anne.** Blue Guide: Berlin & Eastern Germany. 1994. pap. 20.95 (*0-393-31197-X*, Norton Paperbks) Norton.

— The Independent Group: Modernism & Mass Culture in Britain, 1945-1959. LC 95-3509. 1995. text ed. write for info. (*0-7190-4244-5*, Pub. by Manchester Univ Pr UK) St Martin.

— Interior Design of the Twentieth Century. LC 89-52099. (World of Art Ser.). (Illus.). 216p. 1990. pap. 14.95 (*0-500-20247-8*) Thames Hudson.

Massey, B. Mechanics of Fluids. 6th ed. 704p. 1989. 39.95 (*0-278-00047-9*) Chapman & Hall.

Massey, Barbara, ed. Missions Adventures Resources for Leaders. 1991. pap. text ed. 6.95 (*1-56309-032-5*) Womans Mission Union.

Massey, Barbara, jt. auth. see McIndoo, Ethel.

Massey, Barbara, ed. see McIndoo, Ethel.

Massey, Burrows, tr. see Casteret, Norbert.

Massey, C. C. Thoughts of a Modern Mystic. 1972. 59.95 (*0-8490-1209-0*) Gordon Pr.

Massey, Calvin R. Missing Pieces. 280p. (C). 1995. lib. bdg. 49.95 (*1-56639-311-6*) Temple U Pr.

— Silent Rights: The Ninth Amendments & the Constitution's Unemurated Rights. (Orig.). (C). 1995. pap. text ed. 19.95 (*1-56639-312-4*) Temple U Pr.

Massey, Charles C., tr. see Du Prel, Carl.

Massey, Charles C., tr. see Zollner, Johann C.

Massey, Craig. Ajustarse o Autodestruirse. Orig. Title: Adjust or Self-Destruct. 144p. (SPA.). 1983. pap. 3.99 (*0-8254-1470-9*) Kregel.

Massey, David & Yousefzadeh, Behzad. The Banking System: Abstract Dimensions for the Next Few Centuries. 64p. (Orig.). 1993. pap. 9.95 (*0-9640970-0-1*) Hillside Pub GA.

Massey, David, jt. auth. see Shore, Graham.

Massey, Dennis. Doing Time in American Prisons: A Study of Modern Novels. LC 89-7512. (Contributions in Criminology & Penology Ser.: No. 24). 256p. 1989. text ed. 59.95 (*0-313-26635-2*, MDP/, Greenwood Pr) Greenwood.

Massey, Doreen. Nicaragua: Some Urban & Regional Issues in a Society in Transition. (Contemporary Issues in Social Sciences Ser.). 116p. 1987. pap. 17.00 (*0-335-15518-9*, Open Univ Pr) Taylor & Francis.

— Space, Place, & Gender. 290p. 1994. text ed. 44.95x (*0-8166-2616-2*); pap. 19.95 (*0-8166-2617-0*) U of Minn Pr.

— Spatial Divisions of Labour: Social Structures & the Geography of Production. 2nd ed. LC 94-44809. 432p. 1995. 65.00x (*0-415-91295-4*, B7275, Routledge NY); pap. 22.95 (*0-415-91296-2*, B7279, Routledge NY) Routledge.

***Massey, Doreen & Allen, John, eds.** Geographical Worlds. (Shape of the World Book Ser.: Vol. 1). (Illus.). 160p. (C). 1995. text ed. 34.00 (*0-19-874184-7*) OUP.

— Geographical Worlds. (Shape of the World Book Ser.: Vol. 1). (Illus.). 160p. (C). 1995. pap. text ed. 15.95 (*0-19-874185-5*) OUP.

Massey, Doreen & Meegan, Richard, eds. Politics & Method: Contrasting Studies in Industrial Geography. 200p. pap. 14.95 (*0-317-19448-8*, 9123) Routledge Chapman & Hall.

Massey, Doreen, et al. High-Tech Fantasies: Science Parks in Society, Science & Space. 272p. 1991. 79.50 (*0-415-01338-0*, A6538); pap. 23.50 (*0-415-01339-9*, A6542) Routledge.

Massey, Douglas S. & Denton, Nancy A. American Apartheid: Segregation & the Making of the Underclass. (Illus.). 292p. (C). 1993. 37.00 (*0-674-01820-6*) HUP.

— American Apartheid: Segregation & the Making of the Underclass. 292p. 1994. pap. text ed. 14.95 (*0-674-01821-4*, MASAMX) HUP.

Massey, Douglas S., jt. auth. see Durand, Jorge.

Massey, Douglas S., et al. Return to Aztlan: The Social Process of International Migration from Western Mexico. LC 87-5913. (Studies in Demography: Vol. 1). 354p. 1987. pap. 15.00 (*0-520-06970-6*) U CA Pr.

***Massey, Ed.** Milton. (Illus.). 44p. (J). (gr. k-5). 1995. 19.95 (*1-57143-047-4*, Wetlands Pr) RDR Bks.

Massey, Edwin, Jr. Fifty Cantos from the Land of Nod. (Mucho Somos Ser.: No. 15). 80p. (Orig.). (C). 1993. pap. 5.95 (*0-914370-61-8*) Mothers Hen.

Massey, Ellen G. The Bequest. 1993. 13.95 (*0-8034-8982-X*) Bouregy.

— Bittersweet Earth. LC 84-20991. (Illus.). 422p. 1985. 26. 95 (*0-8061-1927-6*) U of Okla Pr.

— Bittersweet Earth. LC 84-20991. (C). 1993. pap. 14.95 (*0-8061-2528-4*) U of Okla Pr.

— Candle Within Her Soul: Mary Elizabeth Mahnkey & Her Ozarks (1877-1948) (Illus.). 344p. 1996. lib. bdg. 42.95 (*0-944436-51-X*) Univ Central AR Pr.

— Equestricat. 1993. 13.95 (*0-8034-9035-6*) Bouregy.

Massey, Ellen G., ed. & intro. Bittersweet Country. LC 86-40091. (Illus.). 464p. (Orig.). 1986. reprint ed. pap. 14. 95 (*0-8061-2018-5*) U of Okla Pr.

Massey, Floyd, Jr. & McKinney, Samuel B. Church Administration in the Black Perspective. LC 76-9804. 176p. 1976. pap. 12.00 (*0-8170-0710-5*) Judson.

Massey, Frank J., Jr., jt. auth. see Dixon, Wilfred J.

Massey, Fred I., tr. see Najjar, Abdallah M.

Massey, Frederick R. Inside the Janitorial Business: How to Start from Scratch & Succeed in Professional Cleaning. 2nd ed. LC 89-2555. (Illus.). 220p. (Orig.). 1989. pap. 34.95 (*0-942144-02-3*) MBM Bks.

— The Professional Window Cleaning Manual: How to Make Money in Your Own Window Cleaning Business. (Illus.). 40p. (Orig.). 1983. pap. 14.95 (*0-942144-01-5*) MBM Bks.

Massey, G. A Book of the Beginnings, 2 vols., Set. 1991. lib. bdg. 119.95 (*0-8490-4294-1*) Gordon Pr.

— The Natural Genesis: The Lost Origins of Myths & Mysteries, Types & Symbols, Religion & Language, with Egypt As the Mouthpiece & Africa As the Birthplace, 2 vols., Set. 1991. lib. bdg. 119.95 (*0-8490-4297-6*) Gordon Pr.

Massey, Gale. Grief: Reminders for Healing. (Illus.). 24p. (Orig.). 1994. 1.95 (*0-9640883-0-4*, TX 3 390 733) Massey Pubng.

Massey, George V., II. Pennock: The Pennocks of Primitive Hall. (Illus.). 139p. 1991. reprint ed. lib. bdg. 32.50 (*0-8328-2227-2*); reprint ed. pap. 22.50 (*0-8328-2228-0*) Higginson Bk Co.

Massey, Gerald. Ancient Egypt. (African Heritage Classical Research Studies). 944p. reprint ed. 75.00 (*0-938818-57-0*) ECA Assoc.

— Ancient Egypt: The Light of the World, 2 vols. 944p. (Orig.). 1993. reprint ed. spiral bd. 82.50 (*0-7873-0586-3*) Mokelumne.

— Ancient Egypt: The Light of the World - A Work of Reclamation & Restitution, 2 vols., Set. 1992. lib. bdg. 555.95 (*0-8490-8829-1*) Gordon Pr.

— Ancient Egypt the Light of the World, Set. (Occultism (1897) Ser.: Vols. 1-2). 944p. (Orig.). 1992. pap. 60.00 (*1-56459-150-6*) Kessinger Pub.

— Ancient Egypt the Light of the World, Vol. 1. Obaba, Al I., ed. (Illus.). 220p. (Orig.). 1990. pap. text ed. 18.00 (*0-916157-53-9*) African Islam Miss Pubns.

— Ancient Egypt the Light of the World, Vol. 2. Obaba, Al I., ed. (Illus.). 236p. (Orig.). 1990. pap. text ed. 18.00 (*0-916157-54-7*) African Islam Miss Pubns.

— Ancient Egypt the Light of the World, Vol. 3. Obaba, Al I., ed. (Illus.). 236p. (Orig.). 1990. pap. text ed. 18.00 (*0-916157-55-5*) African Islam Miss Pubns.

— Ancient Egypt the Light of the World, Vol. 4. Obaba, Al I., ed. (Illus.). 248p. (Orig.). 1990. pap. text ed. 18.00 (*0-916157-56-3*) African Islam Miss Pubns.

— Ancient Egypt the Light of the World, Vol. 5. Obaba, Al I., ed. (Illus.). 190p. (Orig.). 1990. pap. text ed. 18.00 (*0-916157-57-1*) African Islam Miss Pubns.

— Ancient Egypt the Light of the World, Vol. I: A Work of Reclamation & Restitution. LC 91-74130. 1992. reprint ed. text ed. 42.47 (*0-933121-33-4*); reprint ed. pap. 29.95 (*0-933121-31-8*) Black Classic.

— Ancient Egypt the Light of the World, Vol II: A Work of Reclamation & Restitution. LC 91-74130. 1992. reprint ed. text ed. 42.57 (*0-933121-34-2*); reprint ed. pap. 29.95 (*0-933121-32-6*) Black Classic.

— The Book of Beginnings, Pt. 2: Natural Genesis, 2 vols., Set. 535p. 1989. reprint ed. spiral bd. 82.50 (*0-7873-1242-8*) Mokelumne.

— Book of the Beginnings. (African Heritage Classical Research Studies). 654p. reprint ed. 75.00 (*0-938818-58-9*) ECA Assoc.

— Book of the Beginnings, 2 vols., 1. reprint ed. write for info. (*0-933121-63-6*) Black Classic.

— Book of the Beginnings, 2 vols., 2. reprint ed. write for info. (*0-933121-64-4*) Black Classic.

— Book of the Beginnings, 2 vols., Set. 1187p. 1987. spiral bd. 82.50 (*0-7873-0585-5*) Mokelumne.

— Book of the Beginnings, 2 vols., Set. reprint ed. 75.00 (*0-685-72903-6*) Black Classic.

— A Book of the Beginnings: Egypt, Africa & the Cultural & Historic Heritage of the Black Race, African Origins of Mankind, 2 vols. 1991. lib. bdg. 199.75 (*0-8490-5040-5*) Gordon Pr.

— A Book of the Beginnings, Vols. 1-2: Containing an Attempt to Recover & Reconstitute the Lost Origins of the Myths & Mysteries, Types & Symbols, Religion & Language, with Egypt for the Mouthpiece & Africa as the Birthplace, Set. 1187p. 1992. pap. 57.00 (*1-56459-149-2*) Kessinger Pub.

— The Egyptian Book of the Dead & the Mysteries of Amenta. 126p. 1993. reprint ed. spiral bd. 6.60 (*0-7873-0583-9*) Mokelumne.

— Gerald Massey's Lectures. 287p. 1992. pap. 24.95 (*1-56459-174-3*) Kessinger Pub.

— Gerald Massey's Lectures. 287p. 1992. reprint ed. pap. text ed. write for info. (*1-881316-20-3*) A&B Bks.

— Gerald Massey's Lectures. (African Studies). reprint ed. 40.00 (*0-938818-46-5*) ECA Assoc.

— Gnostic & Historic Christianity. 1985. reprint ed. pap. 6.95 (*0-916411-51-6*, Sure Fire) Holmes Pub.

— The Hebrew & Other Creations. 1987. pap. 6.95 (*0-916411-64-8*, Sure Fire) Holmes Pub.

— The Historic Jesus & the Mythical Christ. 1991. pap. 6.95 (*1-55818-137-7*, Sure Fire) Holmes Pub.

— The Historical Jesus & the Mythical Christ. 224p. 1992. pap. text ed. 9.95 (*1-881316-04-1*) A&B Bks.

— The Historical Jesus & the Mythical Christ. 224p. 1993. reprint ed. spiral bd. 9.25 (*0-7873-0584-7*) Mokelumne.

— Moon Worship: Ancient & Modern. pap. 6.95 (*1-55818-136-9*) Holmes Pub.

— The Natural Genesis. (African Studies). reprint ed. 75.00 (*0-938818-80-5*) ECA Assoc.

— The Natural Genesis: or, The Second Part of a Book of the Beginnings, Set, Vols. 1-2. 1087p. 1992. Set. pap. 70. 00 (*1-56459-151-4*) Kessinger Pub.

— Secret Drama of Shakspeare's Sonnets Unfolded. 2nd enl. ed. LC 74-172854. reprint ed. 39.75 (*0-404-04237-6*) AMS Pr.

— Shakespeare's Sonnets Never Before Interpreted. LC 78-172855. reprint ed. 74.50 (*0-404-04238-4*) AMS Pr.

— World's Great Year: The Esoteric Time Cycle. 1988. reprint ed. pap. 7.95 (*1-55818-116-4*, Sure Fire) Holmes Pub.

Massey, Gerald J., jt. ed. see Horowitz, Tamara.

Massey, Gerard. Concerning Spiritualism. 130p. 1993. reprint ed. pap. 14.95 (*1-56459-395-9*) Kessinger Pub.

Massey, Grace C. Black Science: Old West, Transportation, Safety, Working Easier, Food, Communication, Black Women. Ethridge, Diedria & Davis, Deborah, eds. 56p. 1993. teacher ed 2.00 (*1-877804-07-X*) Chandler White.

— Black Science Activity Books Teacher's Guide. Ivery, Evelyn L., ed. (Illus.). (Orig.). (J). (gr. 1-6). 1988. pap. text ed. 2.95 (*0-685-26064-X*) Chandler White.

Massey, Grace C., jt. auth. see Howell, Ann C.

Massey, H. A Perspective of Physics: Vol. 3, Selections from 1978 Comments on Modern Physics, Vol. 3. (Perspective of Physics Ser.). 354p. 1979. text ed. 162.00 (*0-677-15970-6*) Gordon & Breach.

— A Perspective of Physics: Volume 4, Selections from Nineteen Seventy-Nine Comments on Modern Physics, Vol. 4. (Perspective of Physics Ser.). 384p. 1980. text ed. 171.00 (*0-677-16190-5*) Gordon & Breach.

Massey, H. & Robins, M. O. History of British Space Science. 544p. 1986. 130.00 (*0-521-30783-X*) Cambridge U Pr.

Massey, H., jt. auth. see Zorev, N.

Massey, H. S. Electronic & Ionic Impact Phenomena. 2nd ed. Incl. Vol. 2. Electron Collisions with Molecules & Photoionization. 1969. 135.00 (*0-19-851249-X*); 1969. write for info. (*0-318-54819-4*) OUP.

Massey, Harrie S., jt. auth. see Haug, A.

Massey, Howard. The Complete DX7. (Illus.). 288p. 1986. pap. 24.95 (*0-7119-0996-2*, AM63843) Music Sales.

— The Complete DX7II. (Illus.). 308p. 1987. pap. 29.95 (*0-8256-1119-9*, AM67109) Music Sales.

— The Complete Sound Blaster. (Illus.). 1993. pap. 12.95 (*0-8256-1351-5*) Music Sales.

— The MIDI Home Studio. (Illus.). 96p. 1988. pap. 14.95 (*0-8256-1127-X*, AM67182) Music Sales.

— A Synthesist's Guide to Acoustic Instruments. (Illus.). 228p. 1987. pap. 19.95 (*0-8256-1089-3*, AM65723) Music Sales.

Massey, Howard, jt. auth. see PASS Staff.

Massey, Howard C. Basic Plumbing with Illustrations. rev. ed. (Illus.). 384p. 1994. pap. 33.00 (*0-934041-99-7*) Craftsman.

— Estimating Plumbing Costs. LC 85-5010. 224p. (Orig.). 1982. pap. 22.50 (*0-910460-82-5*) Craftsman.

— Planning Drain, Waste & Vent Systems. 192p. (Orig.). 1990. pap. 19.25 (*0-934041-51-2*) Craftsman.

— Plumber's Exam Preparation Guide. LC 85-19050. 320p. (Orig.). 1985. pap. 24.00 (*0-934041-04-0*) Craftsman.

— Plumbers Handbook. rev. ed. LC 85-9668. (Illus.). 240p. 1985. pap. 18.00 (*0-910460-49-3*) Craftsman.

Massey, I. P. Administrative Law. 540p. 1985. 180.00 (*0-317-54571-X*) St Mut.

— Administrative Law. 3rd ed. (C). 1990. text ed. 80.00 (*0-89771-497-0*) St Mut.

Massey, Irving. Find You the Virtue: Ethics, Image & Desire in Literature. (Illus.). 288p. (Orig.). 1987. text ed. 59.00 (*0-8026-0008-5*, G Mason Univ Pr) Univ Pub Assocs.

— The Gaping Pig: Literature & Metamorphoses. LC 74-22967. 1976. 45.00 (*0-520-02887-2*) U CA Pr.

— Identity & Community: Reflections on English, Yiddish & French Literature in Canada. LC 94-20233. (Illus.). 206p. 1994. text ed. 26.95 (*0-8143-2518-1*) Wayne St U Pr.

M

An Asterisk (*) at the beginning of an entry indicates that the title is appearing in BIP for the first time.

Massey, Irving, contrib. Bodleian Manuscript Shelley Adds, No. d.7: A Notebook Containing 131 Transcripts by Mary Shelley of Poems & Fragments by Percy Bysshe Shelley. (Bodleian Shelley Manuscripts: Vol. II). 275p. 1987. 86.00 (0-8240-6262-0) Garland.

Massey, Irving, tr. see De Vigny, Alfred.

Massey, Irving J. Uncreating Word: Romanticism & the Object. LC 77-126213. 144p. reprint ed. 41.10 (0-8357-9250-1, 2013020) Bks Demand.

Massey, Isabel A. Interpreting the Sermon on the Mount in the Light of Jewish Tradition As Evidenced in the Palestinian Targums of the Pentateuch: Selected Themes. LC 90-21427. (Studies in the Bible & Early Christianity: Vol. 25). 232p. 1991. lib. bdg. 89.95 (0-88946-784-6) E Mellen.

Massey, James. Doctrine of Ultimate Reality in Sikh Religion. (C). 1991. 15.00 (81-85425-38-8, Pub. by Manohar II) S Asia.

Massey, James & Hayes, Lynne. Coleman vs. Block. 94p. 1986. pap. 5.00 (0-685-23186-0, 40,781) NCLS Inc.

Massey, James & Maxwell, Shirley. Gothic Revival. 1994. 12.95 (1-55859-823-5) Abbeville Pr.

Massey, James, jt. ed. see McCown, Wayne.

Massey, James A., tr. see Feuerbach, Ludwig.

Massey, James A., ed. see Gleason, Elisabeth G.

Massey, James A., ed. see Schleiermacher, Friedrich.

*Massey, James C. & Maxwell, Shirley. Arts & Crafts. LC 94-43397. (Stylebooks Ser.). (Illus.). 96p. 1995. 12.95 (0-7892-0010-4) Abbeville Pr.

Massey, James E. Designing the Sermon: Order & Movement in Preaching. LC 80-17920. (Abingdon Preacher's Library). 128p. (Orig.). 1980. pap. 11.95 (0-687-10490-4) Abingdon.

Massey, James G., et al. Butterflies & All That Jazz. 1992. 27.00 (0-536-58255-6) Ginn Pr.

Massey, James L. & Talarico, Susette M. Explorations in Crime & Justice: A Casebook. 150p. 1989. write for info. (0-318-66410-0, H21751); pap. text ed. 19.00 (0-205-12174-8, H21744) Allyn.

Massey, James O. Readiness for Kindergarten: A Coloring Book for Parents. 16p. 1975. pap. 5.25 (0-89106-014-6, 1281) Consulting Psychol.

Massey, Jamila, jt. auth. see Massey, Reginald.

Massey, John S., ed. see Isachenko, A. G.

Massey, Joseph G. MS-DOS, Lotus 1-2-3, & DBASE. 158p. (Orig.). 1987. pap. text ed. 26.00 (0-685-21222-X) Forest Res Syst.

Massey, Kay, ed. see Colorado Dietetic Association Staff.

Massey, Kay P., ed. see Colorado Dietetic Association, Staff.

*Massey, Kim & Baran, Stanley. Television Criticism: Reading, Writing & Analysis. 424p. (C). 1994. per., pap. text ed. 35.96 (0-8403-9809-3) Kendall-Hunt.

Massey, Kimberley K., jt. auth. see Adams, Michael H.

Massey, Lesly F. Women & the New Testament: An Analysis of Scripture in Light of New Testament Era Culture. LC 89-42735. 160p. 1989. lib. bdg. 27.50x (0-89950-438-8) McFarland & Co.

Massey, Linda. The TASP Test: Passing with Flying Colors. 257p. (Orig.). (C). 1989. pap. text ed. 11.95 (0-9624468-0-7) Acad Acad Excellence.

Massey, Linton R., jt. auth. see University of Virginia Library Staff.

Massey, Lorraine. Ashes of Roses. LC 90-70573. 200p. 1990. 6.95 (1-55523-348-1) Winston-Derek.

— Short Stories of the Twentieth Century. LC 94-90219. 128p. (Orig.). 1995. pap. 9.00 (1-56002-469-0, Univ Edtns) Aegina Pr.

*Massey, Margot G. Spring into Winter. (Orig.). 1994. pap. 12.95 (0-925917-01-X) Wyman Hse Pubns.

Massey, Marilyn C. Christ Unmasked: The Meaning of the Life of Jesus in German Politics. LC 82-8547. (Studies in Religion). 192p. reprint ed. pap. 54.80 (0-7837-2463-2, 2042616) Bks Demand.

Massey, Marilyn C., ed. In Defense of My Life of Jesus Against the Hegelians. xxxix, 72p. 1983. 59.50 (0-208-02017-9) Elliots Bks.

Massey, Mary. Testing: Where We Stand. 17p. 1989. pap. 2.75 (0-87652-141-3, 021-00253) Am Assn Sch Admin.

Massey, Mary E. Ersatz in the Confederacy: Shortages & Substitutes on the Southern Homefront. LC 92-23314. (Classics in Southern History Ser.). (Illus.). 185p. (C). 1993. reprint ed. 14.95 (0-87249-877-8) U of SC Pr.

— Women in the Civil War. LC 93-45580. (Illus.). xxix, 401p. 1994. pap. 14.95 (0-8032-8213-3, Bison Books) U of Nebr Pr.

Massey, Michael. Roman Religion. Hodge, Peter, ed. (Aspects of Roman Life Ser.). 48p. (Orig.). (gr. 7-12). 1979. pap. text ed. 9.00 (0-582-21573-0, 70846) Longman.

— Society in Imperial Rome: Selections from Juvenal, Martial, Petronius, Seneca, Tacitus & Pliny (Translations from Greek & Roman Authors) LC 81-15490. 96p. 1982. pap. 10.50 (0-521-28036-2) Cambridge U Pr.

— Women in Ancient Greece & Rome. (Illus.). 40p. (C). 1988. pap. 8.95 (0-521-31807-6) Cambridge U Pr.

Massey, Nancy J. Wistful Embers. LC 93-60414. 31p. 1994. pap. 5.95 (1-55523-630-8) Winston-Derek.

*Massey, Oliver T. Evaluating Human Resource Development Programs: A Practical Guide to Public Agencies. 1995. 41.95 (0-205-15713-0) Allyn.

*Massey, Patrick. New Zealand: Market Liberalization in a Developed Economy. LC 94-34878. 1995. write for info. (0-312-12486-4) St Martin.

Massey, Reginald & Massey, Jamila. The Dances of India: A General Guide & a Users' Handbook. (Illus.). xix, 164p. 1992. 20.00 (0-317-05152-0); pap. 13.00 (0-948725-05-2) Asia Pub Hse.

— The Immigrants. (Orient Paperbacks Ser.). 172p. (Orig.). 1973. pap. 2.50 (0-88253-243-X) Ind-US Inc.

Massey, Robert. Formulas for Painters. 224p. 1967. reprint ed. pap. 14.95 (0-8230-1877-6, Watsn-Guptill) Watsn-Guptill.

Massey, S. Jane, jt. ed. see Tyer, Charlie B.

Massey-Stewart, John, ed. The Soviet Environment: Problems, Policies & Politics. (International Council for Soviet & East European Studies). 280p. (C). 1992. 64.95 (0-521-41418-0) Cambridge U Pr.

Massey, Sue. Learning to Look: A Complete Art History & Appreciation Program for Grades K-8. 1991. pap. 89.95 (0-13-528795-2) P-H.

Massey, Truman. Christian Record Book: The Acivator's Calendar. rev. ed. 246p. 1992. student ed 15.99 (1-882844-01-7) TRU Pubns.

*Massey, Veta H. Nursing Research. 2nd ed. LC 94-29595. (Notes Ser.). 1994. write for info. (0-87434-742-4) Springhouse Pub.

Massey, Vincent. Good Neighbourhood, & Other Addresses in the United States. LC 69-17584. (Essay Index Reprint Ser.). 1977. 18.95 (0-8369-0087-1) Ayer.

Massey, W. S. Algebraic Topology: An Introduction. LC 77-22206. (Graduate Texts in Mathematics Ser.: Vol. 56). (Illus.). xxi, 261p. 1990. 39.00 (0-387-90271-6) Spr-Verlag.

— A Basic Course in Algebraic Topology. Ewing, J. H. et al, eds. (Graduate Texts in Mathematics Ser.: Vol. 127). (Illus.). 480p. 1993. 49.95 (0-387-97430-X) Spr-Verlag.

— Singular Homology Theory. LC 79-23309. (Graduate Texts in Mathematics Ser.: Vol. 70). (Illus.). 280p. 1980. 40.00 (3-540-90456-5) Spr-Verlag.

Massey Weddle, Linda. T. J. & the Big Trout River Vandals. LC 91-14678. 94p. (Orig.). (J). (gr. 4-7). 1991. pap. 3.95 (0-87227-148-X, RBP5180) Reg Baptist.

— T. J. & the Nobody House. LC 90-8702. 95p. (Orig.). (J). (gr. 3-7). 1990. pap. text ed. 3.95 (0-87227-145-5, RBP5174) Reg Baptist.

— T. J. & the Somebody Club. LC 92-5342. 108p. (J). 1992. 3.95 (0-87227-176-5, RBP5210) Reg Baptist.

Massey, William, ed. see Brown, Kay.

Massey, William S. & Peterson, F. P. The Mod Two Cohomology Structure of Certain Fibre Spaces. LC 52-42839. (Memoirs Ser.: No. 1/74). 97p. 1967. pap. 16.00 (0-8218-1274-2, MEMO 1/74) Am Math.

Masseyeff, Rene F., et al, eds. Methods of Immunological Analysis, Vol. 1. LC 92-49344. 500p. 1992. 265.00 (0-89573-902-X); 215.00 (0-685-61643-6) VCH Pubs.

Massi, Jeri. Abandoned. (Light Line Ser.). 136p. (Orig.). (J). (gr. 5-8). 1989. pap. 5.95 (0-89084-467-4) Bob Jones Univ Pr.

— The Bridge. (Pennant Ser.). (Illus.). 122p. (Orig.). (J). (gr. 2-4). 1986. pap. 5.95 (0-89084-348-1) Bob Jones Univ Pr.

— Courage by Darkness. (Light Line Ser.). 157p. (Orig.). (J). 1987. pap. 5.95 (0-89084-412-7) Bob Jones Univ Pr.

— Crown & Jewel. (Pennant Ser.). (Illus.). 160p. (Orig.). (J). (gr. 5). 1987. pap. 5.95 (0-89084-390-2) Bob Jones Univ Pr.

— A Dangerous Game. (Light Line Ser.). 121p. (Orig.). (J). (gr. 4-6). 1986. pap. 5.95 (0-89084-347-3) Bob Jones Univ Pr.

— Derwood, Inc. (English Skills for Christian Schools Ser.). 288p. (Orig.). (J). (gr. 4-6). 1986. pap. 7.72 (0-89084-323-6) Bob Jones Univ Pr.

— A Ghost at Horse Creek. 105p. (Orig.). 1989. pap. 5.95 (1-877778-01-X) Llama Bks.

— The Lesser Brother. 124p. (Orig.). (YA). (gr. 11). 1989. pap. 5.95 (1-877778-02-8) Llama Bks.

— Llamas on the Loose. (Light Line Ser.). 140p. (Orig.). 1988. pap. 5.95 (0-89084-452-6) Bob Jones Univ Pr.

— The Myth of the Llama. (Illus.). 118p. (Orig.). (J). (gr. 6). 1989. pap. 5.95 (1-877778-00-1) Llama Bks.

— Treasure in the Yukon. (Light Line Ser.). (Illus.). 136p. (Orig.). (J). (gr. 4-6). 1986. pap. 5.95 (0-89084-365-1) Bob Jones Univ Pr.

— Two Collars. (Pennant Ser.). 164p. (Orig.). 1988. pap. 5.95 (0-89084-441-0) Bob Jones Univ Pr.

Massiah, L., et al, eds. Women in Developing Economies: Making Visible the Invisible. 320p. 1993. 69.95 (0-85496-345-6); pap. 22.50 (0-85496-346-4) Berg Pubs.

Massialas, Byron G. & Zevin, Jack. Teaching Creatively: Learning Through Discovery. LC 81-19375. 270p. 1983. pap. 18.50 (0-89874-437-7) Krieger.

Massic, Barry M., jt. auth. see Abelmann, Walter H.

*Massicotte, Edouard Z. & Roy, Regis. Armorial Du Canada Francais: (Armorial of French-Canada), 2 vols., Set. (Illus.). 332p. 1994. pap. 28.50 (0-614-00921-9, 3790) Clearfield Co.

Massie, ed. Interferometric Metrology: Critical Reviews. 1987. 55.00 (0-89252-851-6, 816) SPIE.

Massie, Alan. Caesar. 228p. 1994. 20.00 (0-7867-0121-8) Carroll & Graf.

Massie, Allan. How Should Health Services Be Financed? A Patient's View. (David Hume Papers). 58p. 1988. pap. text ed. 14.00 (0-08-036585-X, Pub. by Aberdeen U Pr) Macmillan.

— The Novel Today: A Critical Guide to the British Novel, 1970-1989. (Illus.). 128p. (Orig.). (C). 1990. pap. text ed. 20.50 (0-582-00407-1, 78609) Longman.

— The Sins of the Father. 304p. 1992. 19.95 (0-88184-849-2) Carroll & Graf.

— These Enchanted Woods. 206p. 1994. 24.95 (0-09-177411-X, Pub. by Hutchinson UK) Trafalgar.

*Massie, Brigid M. & Waters, John. Not the World Oldest Profession: Everyday Selling Skills for Success at Work, at Home & in Your Life. Lee, Paula M., ed. 215p. (C). 1995. pap. 10.95 (0-614-04717-X) Eudemonia Pubns.

— What Do They Say When You Leave the Room? How to Increase Your Personal Effectiveness for Success at Work, at Home & in Your Life. Lee, Paula M., ed. LC 91-22182. 215p. (Orig.). (C). 1991. pap. 10.95 (0-9629850-0-7) Eudemonia Pubns.

*Massie, Elizabeth. Maryland: The Night the Harbor Lights Went Out. (American Chills Ser.: No. 1). 144p. 1995. pap. 3.50 (0-8217-5059-3) Zebra.

— SinEater. 352p. 1994. 21.00 (0-7867-0061-0) Carroll & Graf.

*Massie-Ferch, Kathleen M., et al, eds. Ancient Enchantresses. 352p. (Orig.). 1995. mass mkt. 5.50 (0-88677-677-5) DAW Bks.

Massie, James W. America: The Origin of Her Present Conflict, Her Prospect for the Slave & Her Claim for Anti-Slavery Sympathy. LC 75-83887. (Black Heritage Library Collection). 1977. 21.95 (0-8369-8628-8) Ayer.

Massie, Joseph L. Blazer & Ashland Oil: A Study in Management. LC 60-8519. 271p. reprint ed. pap. 77.30 (0-7837-5794-8, 2045460) Bks Demand.

Massie, Joseph L. & Douglas, John. Managing: A Contemporary Introduction. 5th ed. 544p. (C). 1992. pap. text ed. write for info. (0-13-544859-X) P-H.

Massie, Larry. Copper Trails & Iron Rails. 4th ed. LC 89-83953. (Illus.). 1990. pap. 11.95 (0-932212-60-3) Avery Color.

Massie, Larry B. Holland Area: Warm Friends & Wooden Shoes. 128p. 1988. 25.95 (0-89781-248-4, 5301) Preferred Mktg.

— Michigan Memories: True Stories from Two Peninsulas' Past. (Illus.). 288p. (Orig.). 1994. 18.95x (1-886167-01-X); pap. 10.95x (1-886167-00-1) Priscilla Pr.

— Potawatomi Tears & Petticoat Pioneers: More of the Romance of Michigan's Past. (Illus.). 296p. (Orig.). 1992. 18.95 (0-9626408-4-0); pap. 8.95 (0-9626408-3-2) Priscilla Pr.

— The Romance of Michigan's Past. (Illus.). 272p. (Orig.). 1991. pap. 8.95 (0-9626408-1-6) Priscilla Pr.

— Voyages into Michigan's Past. 6th ed. LC 88-70890. (Illus.). 1988. pap. 11.95 (0-932212-58-1) Avery Color.

Massie, Larry B., ed. Birchbark Belles. (Illus.). 310p. (Orig.). 1993. 18.95 (0-9626408-8-3); pap. 10.95 (0-9626408-7-5) Priscilla Pr.

Massie, Larry B. & Massie, Priscilla. Walnut Pickles & Watermelon Cake: A Century of Michigan Cooking. LC 89-16448. (Great Lakes Bks.). (Illus.). 354p. 1990. 29.95 (0-8143-1939-4) Wayne St U Pr.

Massie, Larry B., jt. auth. see Schmitt, Peter J.

Massie, Mariam. Soul Never Sleeps: Advanced Perceptions to a More Loving, Purposeful & Joyous Life. Mueller, Phyllis, ed. 200p. (Orig.). 1992. pap. 11.95 (0-9633140-2-5) Advanced Percept.

Massie, Paul. Programming IBM Assembly Language. (Illus.). 500p. 1985. pap. text ed. write for info. (0-8087-6405-5) Macmillan.

Massie, Priscilla, jt. auth. see Massie, Larry B.

Massie, Randall. When Godly Robes Unravel. 164p. (Orig.). 1990. pap. 5.99 (0-89900-386-9) College Pr Pub.

Massie, Rebecca. The Sydney & Frances Lewis Contemporary Art Fund Collection. LC 80-14914. (Illus.). 112p. (Orig.). 1980. pap. 5.00 (0-917046-09-9) Va Mus Arts.

Massie, Robert K. Dreadnought: Britain, Germany, & the Coming of the Great War. (Illus.). 1040p. 1992. pap. 17.50 (0-345-37556-4, Ballantine Trade) Ballantine.

— Nicholas & Alexandra. 608p. 1972. text ed. 35.00 (0-689-10177-5, Atheneum S&S) S&S Trade.

— Peter the Great. 1981. pap. 14.00 (0-345-29806-3, Ballantine Trade) Ballantine.

— Peter the Great. 924p. 1986. pap. 6.95 (0-345-33619-4) Ballantine.

— Peter the Great. (Illus.). 928p. 1993. reprint ed. 14.99 (0-517-06483-9) Random Hse Value.

— Peter the Great: His Life & His World. LC 80-7635. (Illus.). 864p. 1980. 40.00 (0-394-50032-6) Knopf.

Massie, Sonja. Carousel. 1990. mass mkt. 4.50 (1-55817-363-3, Pinnacle NY) Windsor NY.

— Dream Carver. 1989. mass mkt. 4.50 (1-55817-227-0, Pinnacle NY) Windsor NY.

— Far & Away. 1992. pap. 4.50 (0-425-13298-6) Berkley Pub.

Massie, Suzanne. Land of the Firebird. 1982. pap. 20.00 (0-671-46059-5, Touchstone Bks) S&S Trade.

— Land of the Firebird: The Beauty of Old Russia. LC 80-12860. (Illus.). 496p. (C). 1995. reprint ed. pap. 23.00 (0-9644184-1-X) HeartTree Pr.

— Pavlovsk: The Life of a Russian Palace. (Illus.). 416p. (C). 1995. pap. text ed. 21.00 (0-9644184-0-1) HeartTree Pr.

Massie, Wendy J. MuscleCar Resource Directory, 1990-91. (Illus.). 132p. (Orig.). 1990. pap. 17.00 (0-9626374-0-8) Best Auto Pubns.

Massignani, Alessandro, jt. auth. see Greene, Jack.

Massignon, Genevieve. Folktales of France. Hyland, Jacqueline, tr. LC 68-14008. (Folktales of the World Ser.). 363p. reprint ed. pap. 103.50 (0-685-23868-7, 2056652) Bks Demand.

Massignon, Louis. Essay on the Origins of the Technical Language of Islamic Mysticism. Clark, Benjamin, tr. LC 93-40284. (C). 1994. text ed. 34.95 (0-268-00928-7) U of Notre Dame Pr.

— The Passion of Al-Hallaj: Mystic & Martyr of Islam. abr. ed. Mason, Herbert, ed. & tr. by. LC 93-11410. (Bollingen Ser.: Vol. 98). 1994. reprint ed. pap. 16.95 (0-691-01919-3) Princeton U Pr.

Massil, Stephen, ed. Jewish Travel Guide, 1994. (Illus.). 360p. (Orig.). 1994. pap. 11.95 (0-85303-273-4, Pub. by Vallentine Mitchell UK) Intl Spec Bk.

— The Jewish Travel Guide, 1995. 400p. 1995. pap. 12.95 (0-85303-305-6, Pub. by M Vallentine UK) Hermon.

Massil, Stephen W., jt. ed. see Bossmeyer, Christine.

Massimo, L. Physics of High Temperature Reactors. 1976. 100.00 (0-08-019616-0, Pub. by Pergamon Repr UK) Franklin.

Massimo, L., et al, eds. Oncogenes in Pediatric Tumors. (Ettore Majorana International Life Sciences Ser.). 268p. 1988. text ed. 121.00 (3-7186-0469-8) Gordon & Breach.

*Massin. Fun with Numbers: Fascinating Facts about Numbers. Volk, Carol, tr. LC 94-6668. (Illus.). (J). 1995. write for info. (1-56846-111-9) Creative Ed.

Massina, Olivier, jt. auth. see Simon, Dominique.

Massinelli, Anna M. & Tuena, Filippo. Treasures of the Medici. LC 92-12965. 1992. 45.00 (0-86565-135-3) Vendome.

Massing, Andreas. Economic Anthropology of the Kru (West Africa) (Illus.). 289p. (Orig.). 1980. pap. 67.50x (3-515-03162-6) Coronet Bks.

Massinger, Philip. Believe As You List. LC 78-133708. (Folio - Tudor Facsimile Texts. Old English Plays Ser.: No. 139). reprint ed. 49.50 (0-404-53439-2) AMS Pr.

— The City Madam. fac. ed. Hoy, Cyrus, ed. LC 64-11357. (Regents Renaissance Drama Ser.). 127p. 1994. pap. 36.20 (0-7837-7338-2, 2047291) Bks Demand.

— New Way to Pay Old Debt. a Comedie. LC 76-25773. (English Experience Ser.: No. 262). 92p. 1970. reprint ed. 11.50 (90-221-0262-9) Walter J Johnson.

— New Way to Pay Old Debts. (New Mermaid Ser.). (C). 1984. pap. text ed. 6.95 (0-393-90009-6) Norton.

— Philip Massinger, 2 vols. (BCL1-PR English Literature Ser.). 1992. reprint ed. lib. bdg. 150.00 (0-7812-7251-3) Rprt Serv.

— Philip Massinger, 2 vols., Set. Symons, Arthur, ed. (BCL1-PR English Literature Ser.). 1992. reprint ed. lib. bdg. 150.00 (0-7812-7262-9) Rprt Serv.

— Philip Massinger: Roman Actor, Maid of Honour, New Way to Pay Old Debts, Believe As You List. (BCL1-PR English Literature Ser.). 416p. 1992. reprint ed. lib. bdg. 99.00 (0-7812-7263-7) Rprt Serv.

— Philip Massinger: The Roman Actor, the Maid of Honor, a New Way to Pay Old Debts, Believe As You List. (BCL1-PR English Literature Ser.). 416p. 1992. reprint ed. lib. bdg. 99.00 (0-7812-7252-1) Rprt Serv.

— Philip Massinger, 1887-1889. LC 72-108511. 59.00 (0-403-03683-6) Scholarly.

— Plays of Philip Massinger, 4 Vols, 1. 2nd ed. Gifford, William, ed. LC 12-36722. reprint ed. 40.00 (0-404-04281-3) AMS Pr.

— Plays of Philip Massinger, 4 Vols, 2. 2nd ed. Gifford, William, ed. LC 12-36722. reprint ed. 40.00 (0-404-04282-1) AMS Pr.

— Plays of Philip Massinger, 4 Vols, 3. 2nd ed. Gifford, William, ed. LC 12-36722. reprint ed. 40.00 (0-404-04283-X) AMS Pr.

— Plays of Philip Massinger, 4 Vols, 4. 2nd ed. Gifford, William, ed. LC 12-36722. reprint ed. 40.00 (0-404-04284-8) AMS Pr.

— Plays of Philip Massinger, 4 Vols, Set. 2nd ed. Gifford, William, ed. LC 12-36722. reprint ed. 160.00 (0-404-04280-5) AMS Pr.

Massingham, Betty. Gertrude Jekyll. 1989. pap. 25.00 (0-85263-304-1, Pub. by Shire UK) St Mut.

Massingham, Gordon, ed. see Richmond, Lee.

Massingham, Harold J. The Friend of Shelley; a Memoir of Edward John Trelawny. (BCL1-PR English Literature Ser.). 367p. 1992. reprint ed. lib. bdg. 89.00 (0-7812-7528-8) Rprt Serv.

— Letters to X. LC 67-26763. (Essay Index Reprint Ser.). 1977. 19.95 (0-8369-0691-8) Ayer.

Massingham, Harold J. & Massingham, Hugh, eds. Great Victorians. LC 70-156692. (Essay Index Reprint Ser.). 1977. reprint ed. 20.95 (0-8369-2284-0) Ayer.

Massingham, Hugh, jt. ed. see Massingham, Harold J.

Massingham, Lester, jt. auth. see Lancaster, Geoffrey.

Massini, Marcel. Ferrari by Vignale. (Illus.). 220p. 55.00 (88-7911-085-3, Pub. by Giorgio Nada Editore IT) Howell Pr VA.

Massion, Francois. Dictionnaire des Belgicismes, 2 vols., Set. 946p. (FRE.). 1987. write for info. (0-8288-9464-7) Fr & Eur.

Massion, J. & Lambin, H. Questions of Christians: Vol. 2: Matthew's Response. 144p. 1984. pap. 3.95 (0-914070-20-7, 224) ACTA Pubns.

— Questions of Christians: Vol. 3: Luke's Response. LC 85-71842. 144p. 1985. pap. 3.95 (0-914070-25-8, 225) ACTA Pubns.

Massion, J. & Sasaki, K., eds. Cerebro-Cerebellar Interactions. LC 79-18156. (Developments in Neuroscience Ser.: Vol. 6). 1979. 78.50 (0-444-80147-2) Elsevier.

Massion, J. C. & Lambin, H. R. Questions of Christians: Mark's Response, Vol. 1. LC 80-68045. 1980. pap. 3.95 (0-914070-15-0, 223) ACTA Pubns.

Massip, Josep M. Diccionari Catala de Falses Etimologies. 224p. (SPA.). 1984. pap. 19.95 (0-7859-5879-7, 8429722114) Fr & Eur.

Massip, Renee. La Bete Quaternaire. (FRE.). 1981. pap. 11.95 (0-7859-4145-2) Fr & Eur.

— Les Deesses. (FRE.). 1978. pap. 10.95 (0-7859-4072-3) Fr & Eur.

— La Regente. (FRE.). 1972. pap. 8.95 (0-7859-3998-9) Fr & Eur.

— Le Rire de Sara. (FRE.). 1975. pap. 10.95 (0-7859-4044-8) Fr & Eur.

Massirer, Mary. The Research Process in Technical & Professional Writing. 112p. (C). 1994. spiral bd. 17.56 (0-8403-9128-5) Kendall-Hunt.

Massisi. Hearts. 1982. pap. 4.95 (0-02-588340-2) Macmillan.

*Massler, Ina. Hanukkah Activities. (Holiday Activities Ser.). 1994. 2.95 (1-55734-783-2) Tchr Create Mat.

Massler, Maury & Schour, Isaac. Atlas of the Mouth. 2nd ed. (Illus.). (C). 22.40 (0-685-05572-8) Am Dental.

Massman, Virgil F., jt. ed. see Kathman, Michael D.

An Asterisk (*) at the beginning of an entry indicates that the title is appearing in BIP for the first time.

Massmann, H. F. Literatur der Totentanze. 162p. 1963. reprint ed. write for info. (*0-318-71844-8*, Pub. by Georg Olms GW) Lubrecht & Cramer.

Massolo, Maria, jt. auth. see Bernhardson, Wayne.

***Masson.** Acrylic Fiber Technology & Applications. 629p. 1995. 175.00 (*0-8247-8977-6*) Dekker.

Masson, ed. Optical Components & Systems. 178p. 1987. 43.00 (*0-89252-840-0*, 805) SPIE.

Masson, A. The Magic of Marionettes. (Illus.). 88p. (J). (gr. 6 up). 1989. pap. 9.95 (*1-55037-042-1*, Pub. by Annick CN) Firefly Bks Ltd.

Masson, A., et al, eds. Optical Design Methods, Applications & Large Optics, Vol. 1013. 1989. 51.00 (*0-8194-0048-3*) SPIE.

Masson, Andre, ed. see Flaubert, Gustave.

Masson, Andre, jt. auth. see Sartre, Jean-Paul.

Masson, C. R. Metallurgical Slags, Pt. 2. 1982. pap. 67.00 (*0-08-028684-4*, Pergamon Pr) Elsevier.

Masson, Charles. La Grenouille: A Feast of Flowers. LC 92-22149. 1994. 22.50 (*0-517-59057-3*, C P Pubs) Crown Pub Group.

— Nouveau Traite des Regles Pour la Composition de la Musique. 2nd ed. LC 67-25446. (Music Ser.). 1967. reprint ed. lib. bdg. 22.50 (*0-306-70941-4*) Da Capo.

Masson, Charles F. Secret Memoirs of the Court of Petersburg: Particularly Towards the End of the Reign of Catherine II & the Commencement of That of Paul I. LC 75-115563. (Russia Observed, Series I). 1970. reprint ed. 20.95 (*0-405-03049-5*) Ayer.

Masson, D. Drummond of Hawthornden: The Story of His Life & Writings. LC 68-24912. (English Biography Ser.: No. 31). 1969. reprint ed. lib. bdg. 59.95 (*0-8383-0282-3*) M S G Haskell Hse.

Masson, David. British Novelists & Their Styles. LC 72-10853. (Essay Index Reprint Ser.). 1977. reprint ed. 23.95 (*0-8369-7230-9*) Ayer.

— DeQuincey. Morley, John, ed. LC 68-58385. (English Men of Letters Ser.). reprint ed. lib. bdg. 12.50 (*0-404-51717-X*) AMS Pr.

— Drummond of Hawthornden: The Story of His Life & Writings. (BCL1-PR English Literature Ser.). 490p. 1992. reprint ed. lib. bdg. 99.00 (*0-7812-7207-6*) Rprt Serv.

— Three Devils: Luther's, Milton's & Goethe's. LC 78-128340. reprint ed. 36.00 (*0-404-04247-3*) AMS Pr.

— Wordsworth, Shelley, Keats, & Other Essays. LC 72-13205. (Essay Index Reprint Ser.). 1977. reprint ed. 21.95 (*0-8369-8168-5*) Ayer.

Masson, David, ed. see De Quincey, Thomas.

Masson-Douglas, Jeanne, jt. auth. see Mason, Leonard A.

Masson-Douglas, Jeanne, ed. see Sturm, John E.

***Masson, Dubos J. & Treasury Management Association Staff.** The Treasurer's Handbook of Financial Management: Applying the Theories, Concepts & Quantitative Methods of Corporate Finance. Oros, John G. et al, eds. (Illus.). 447p. 1995. 69.95 (*1-55738-884-9*) Probus Pub Co.

Masson, Elsie. The Story of a Marriage Vol. I: The Letters of Bronislaw Malinowski & Elsie Masson, 2 vols. Wayne, Helena, ed. LC 94-18587. (Illus.). 224p. 1995. 65.00 (*0-415-11758-5*, C0595) Routledge.

Masson, H. C. & O'Byrne, P. Applying Family Therapy: A Practical Guide for Social Workers. (Social Work Ser.). (Illus.). 134p. 1984. 68.00 (*0-08-030186-X*, 26-56, Pub. by Pergamon Repr UK) Franklin.

Masson, Herre. Dictionnaire Initiatique. rev. ed. 430p. (FRE.). 1984. 55.00 (*0-7859-4833-3*) Fr & Eur.

Masson, J., jt. auth. see Pender, J. A.

Masson, J. Moussaieff. The Oceanic Feeling: The Origins of Religious Sentiment in Ancient India. (Studies of Classical India: No. 3). 228p. 1980. lib. bdg. 70.00 (*90-277-1050-3*) Kluwer Ac.

Masson, Jean-Robert. The Great Indian Chiefs: Sitting Bull, Crazy Horse, Cochise, Geronimo. (Illus.). 80p. (J). (gr. 4 up). 1994. 14.95 (*0-8120-6468-2*) Barron.

Masson, Jeffrey M. Against Therapy. LC 93-26695. 1993. reprint ed. 29.95 (*1-56751-023-X*); reprint ed. pap. 15.95 (*1-56751-022-1*) Common Courage.

— Final Analysis: The Making & Unmaking of a Psychoanalyst. 1990. 18.22 (*0-201-52368-X*) Addison-Wesley.

— My Father's Guru: A Journey Through Spirituality & Disillusion. (Illus.). 256p. 1992. 19.23 (*0-201-56778-4*) Addison-Wesley.

— My Father's Guru: A Journey Through Spirituality & Disillusion. 1993. pap. 10.53 (*0-201-62619-5*) Addison-Wesley.

Masson, Jeffrey M., tr. see Freud, Sigmund.

Masson, Jeffrey M., ed. see Freud, Sigmund.

Masson, Joan, et al, eds. Warwick Valley Cooking. (Illus.). 160p. 1989. 7.50 (*0-9623003-0-6*) Frances A Wisner.

***Masson, L. R., ed.** Bourgeois de la Compagnie du Nord-Ouest, Recits de Voyages, Lettres et Rapports Inedits Relatifs au Nord-Ouest Canadien Avec une Esquisse Historique et des Annotations Series 1, Vol. 2: McDonald, John-Autobiographical Notes; Keith, George-Letters to Mr. Roderic McKenzie 1807-1817, Johnston, John-an Account of Lake Superior 1792-1807, Wilcooke, Samuel H.-Death of Mr. Benjamin Frobisher 1819, Duncan, Cameron-Nipigon Country 1804, Peter, Grant-Sauteaux Indians, 1804, McKenzie, James-Extracts from His Journal 1799-1800, Athabasca District, McKenzie, James-King's Posts & Journal of a. 499p. 1960. 100.00x (*0-614-01804-8*) Elliots Bks.

Masson, M. R., jt. auth. see Chalmers, R. A.

Masson, M. R., et al, eds. Sulfites, Selenites & Tellurites. (IUPAC Solubility Data Ser.). (Illus.). 451p. 1986. 155.00 (*0-08-032517-3*, E125, E120, Pergamon Pr); 130.00 (*0-08-032518-1*, Pergamon Pr) Elsevier.

Masson, Manju, jt. auth. see Kuenzel, Wayne J.

Masson, Marcelle. A Bag of Bones: Legends of the Wintu Indians of Northern California. LC 66-23398. 130p. (J). (gr. 4 up). 1967. pap. 8.95 (*0-911010-26-2*) Naturegraph.

Masson, Michael E., jt. ed. see Graf, Peter.

Masson, Mick. Surviving the Dole Years: The 1930s - a Personal Story. 200p. Date not set. pap. 24.95 (*0-86840-285-0*, Pub. by New South Wales Univ Pr AT) Intl Spec Bk.

Masson, Paul, et al. MULTIMOD Mark II: Revised & Extended Model. LC 90-37502. (Occasional Paper Ser.: No. 71). v, 50p. 1990. pap. 10.00 (*1-55775-141-2*) Intl Monetary.

Masson, Paul M. Berlioz. LC 74-24145. reprint ed. 15.50 (*0-404-13037-2*) AMS Pr.

Masson, Paul Marie. L' Opera de Rameau. LC 70-168675. (Music Ser.). (Illus.). 596p. 1972. reprint ed. lib. bdg. 75.00 (*0-306-70262-2*) Da Capo.

Masson, Paul R. & Taylor, Mark P., eds. Policy Issues in the Operation of Currency Unions. LC 92-20210. (Illus.). 275p. (C). 1993. 54.95 (*0-521-43455-6*) Cambridge U Pr.

Masson, Paul R., jt. auth. see Ghosh, A. R.

Masson, Pierre. Human Tumors: Histology, Diagnosis, & Techniques. 2nd rev. ed. LC 70-83489. (Illus.). 1360p. reprint ed. pap. 180.00 (*0-318-39777-3*, 2033179) Bks Demand.

Masson, Robert. The Charmed Circle: Theology for the Head, Heart, Hands & Feet. LC 86-61358. 260p. (Orig.). 1987. pap. 10.95 (*0-934134-40-5*) Sheed & Ward MO.

Masson, Robert L., ed. see Jacobs, Edward, et al.

Masson, Sophie. The House in the Rainforest. 1990. pap. 14.95 (*0-7022-2261-5*, Pub. by Univ Queensland Pr AT) Intl Spec Bk.

***Masson Staff.** Dictionnaire de Cardiologie. 352p. (FRE.). 1986. 135.00 (*0-7859-7827-5*, 2225802521) Fr & Eur.

Masson, Thomas L. Our American Humorists. LC 67-23245. (Essay Index Reprint Ser.). 1977. 26.95 (*0-8369-0692-6*) Ayer.

Masson, V. M. Altyn-Depe. Michael, Henry N., tr. (University Museum Monographs: No. 55). (Illus.). xx, 150p. 1989. text ed. 55.00 (*0-934718-54-7*) U PA Mus Pubns.

Masson, V. M., jt. auth. see Dani, A. H.

Masson, V. M., jt. ed. see Dani, A. H.

Masson-Zwaan, Tanja L. & Mendes de Leon, Pablo M., eds. Air & Space Law: De Lege Ferenda: Essays in Honour of Henri A. Wassenbergh. LC 92-18235. 344p. (C). 1992. lib. bdg. 122.00 (*0-7923-1626-6*) Kluwer Ac.

Massonnet, C., et al. Plasticity in Structural Engineering, Fundamentals & Applications. (CISM International Centre for Mechanical Sciences Ser.: Vol. 241). (Illus.). 302p. 1980. pap. 42.00 (*0-387-81350-0*) Spr-Verlag.

***Massopust, Peter R.** Fractal Functions, Fractal Surfaces, & Wavelets. LC 94-26551. (Illus.). 383p. 1995. boxed 49.95 (*0-12-478840-8*) Acad Pr.

Massosoit C. C. Biology Faculty Staff. Laboratory Exercises for Biological Principles. 4th ed. 176p. 1990. spiral bd. 11.95 (*0-8403-6169-6*) Kendall-Hunt.

Massot, R., jt. auth. see Cornu, Aymbe.

Massotty, Susan, tr. see Durlacher, Gerhard.

Massotty, Susan, tr. see Koppeschaar, Carl.

Massoud, H., jt. auth. see Middlesworth, E. M.

Massoud, Mary M. Translate to Communicate. 88p. 1988. pap. 9.95 (*1-55513-432-7*) D C Cook Fnd.

Massoudi, M. & Rajagopal, K. R., eds. Recent Advances in Mechanics of Structured Continua 1993. LC 93-71574. (AMD Series, Vol. 160; MD: Vol. 41). 159p. 1993. pap. 45.00 (*0-7918-1139-5*, G00783) ASME.

Massoudi, Robert & Julienne, Astrid. Rightsizing for Corporate Survival. 1995. pap. text ed. 32.00 (*0-13-123126-X*) P-H.

Massoulie, Jean, et al, eds. Cholinesterases: Structure, Function, Mechanism, Genetics, & Cell Biology. LC 91-12371. 414p. 1991. 89.95 (*0-8412-2008-5*) Am Chemical.

Massoum, Ahmed A., jt. ed. see Lieth, Helmut.

Massry, S. G., ed. The Charles R. Kleeman Festschrift. (Journal: Mineral & Electrolyte Metabolism: Vol. 12, Nos. 5-6, 1986). (Illus.). lv, 124p. 1987. pap. 56.00 (*3-8055-4454-5*) S Karger.

— Kidney in Systemic Diseases. (Contributions to Nephrology Ser.: Vol. 7). (Illus.). 1977. 78.50 (*3-8055-2445-5*) S Karger.

Massry, S. G., jt. ed. see Cinotti, G. A.

Massry, S. G., jt. ed. see Coburn, J. W.

Massry, S. G., jt. ed. see Gennari, C.

Massry, S. G., jt. ed. see Ritz, E.

Massry, Shaul G. & Fujita, T., eds. New Actions of Parathyroid Hormone. (Illus.). 494p. 1989. 110.00 (*0-306-43418-0*, Plenum Pr) Plenum.

Massry, Shaul G. & Glassock, Richard J. Textbook of Nephrology, 2 vols., Set. 2nd ed. (Illus.). 2024p. 1989. 229.00 (*0-683-05620-4*) Williams & Wilkins.

Massry, Shaul G. & Glassock, Richard J., eds. Textbook of Nephrology. 3rd ed. LC 94-904. 2104p. 1994. 295.00 (*0-683-05621-2*) Williams & Wilkins.

Massry, Shaul G., jt. ed. see Klahr, Saulo.

Massry, Shaul G., jt. ed. see Suki, Wadi N.

Massry, Shaul G., et al, eds. Phosphate & Mineral Homeostasis. LC 86-30431. (Advances in Experimental Medicine & Biology Ser.: Vol. 208). 568p. 1986. 110.00 (*0-306-42398-7*, Plenum Pr) Plenum.

— Phosphate & Mineral Metabolism. LC 83-13450. 500p. 1984. 95.00 (*0-306-41731-6*, Plenum Pr) Plenum.

Massumi, Brian. A User's Guide to Capitalism & Schizophrenia: Deviations from Deleuza & Guattari. 1992. 26.95 (*0-262-13282-6*); pap. 13.95 (*0-262-63143-1*) MIT Pr.

Massumi, Brian, ed. The Politics of Everyday Fear. (Illus.). 341p. (C). 1993. text ed. 49.95 (*0-8166-2162-4*); pap. 19.95 (*0-8166-2163-2*) U of Minn Pr.

Massumi, Brian, tr. see Attali, Jacques.

Massumi, Brian, tr. see De Certeau, Michel.

Massumi, Brian, tr. see Felman, Shoshana.

Massumi, Brian, tr. see Foucault, Michel & Blanchot, Maurice.

Massumi, Brian, tr. see Lyotard, Jean-Francois & Thebaud, Jean-Loup.

Massumi, Brian, tr. see Lyotard, Jean-Francois.

Massy, William F. & Meyerson, Joel W., eds. Strategy & Finance in Higher Education. LC 92-12863. 109p. 1992. 29.95 (*1-56079-178-0*) Petersons Guides.

Massy, William F., jt. auth. see Hopkins, David S.

Mast, Abe. Charm Countryview Favorites: Famous Recipes from the Inn. (Illus.). 160p. Date not set. 14.95 (*0-9637560-0-1*) Charm Cntryview Inn.

Mast, Ben V., tr. see Baumgart, Winfried.

Mast, Coleen K. Love & Life: A Christian Sexual Morality Guide for Teens. 155p. 1986. teacher ed, pap. 11.95 (*0-89870-108-2*) Ignatius Pr.

— Sex Respect: The Option of True Sexual Freedom: A Public Health Guide for Parents. (Illus.). 61p. (Orig.). (J). (gr. 7-9). 1986. pap. text ed. 8.95 (*0-945745-01-X*) Respect Inc.

— Sex Respect: The Option of True Sexual Freedom: A Public Health Guide for Parents. rev. ed. Forrestal, Julienne, ed. (Illus.). 180p. (Orig.). 1990. pap. text ed. 8.95 (*0-945745-04-4*) Respect Inc.

— Sex Respect: The Option of True Sexual Freedom: A Public Health Manual for Teachers. (Illus.). 61p. (Orig.). (J). (gr. 7-9). 1986. pap. 12.95 (*0-945745-00-1*) Respect Inc.

— Sex Respect: The Option of True Sexual Freedom: A Public Health Manual for Teachers. rev. ed. Forrestal, Julienne, ed. (Illus.). 182p. (Orig.). 1990. pap. text ed. 12.95 (*0-945745-03-6*) Respect Inc.

— Sex Respect: The Option of True Sexual Freedom: A Public Health Workbook for Students. (Illus.). 61p. (Orig.). (J). (gr. 7-9). 1986. pap. text ed. 7.95 (*0-945745-02-8*) Respect Inc.

— Sex Respect: The Option of True Sexual Freedom: A Public Health Workbook for Students. rev. ed. Forrestal, Julienne, ed. (Illus.). 118p. (Orig.). (YA). (gr. 7-9). 1990. pap. text ed. 8.95 (*0-945745-05-2*) Respect Inc.

Mast, Coleen K., et al. Love & Life: A Christian Sexual Morality Guide for Teens. LC 86-80693. 119p. 1986. pap. 8.95 (*0-89870-106-6*); teacher ed, pap. 6.95 (*0-89870-107-4*) Ignatius Pr.

Mast, Edward, adapt. Jungalbook. 60p. (Orig.). (J). 1990. Playscript. pap. 5.00 (*0-87602-291-3*) Anchorage.

Mast, Edward & Bensinger, Lenore. Dinosaurs. (Orig.). (J). 1994. 5.00 (*0-87602-327-8*) Anchorage.

Mast, Gerald. Can't Help Singin' The American Musical on Stage & Screen. LC 87-7986. (Illus.). 388p. 1987. 24.95 (*0-87951-283-0*) Overlook Pr.

— Can't Help Singing: The American Musical on Stage & Screen. 388p. 1987. pap. 15.95 (*0-87951-362-4*) Overlook Pr.

— The Comic Mind: Comedy & the Movies. LC 78-68546. (Illus.). 1979. pap. text ed. 16.95 (*0-226-50978-8*, P827) U Ch Pr.

— A Short History of the Movies. 3rd ed. LC 79-14309. 1981. pap. 19.96 (*0-317-00264-3*) Pegasus.

— A Short History of the Movies. 5th ed. 688p. (C). 1992. pap. write for info. (*0-02-377070-8*) Macmillan.

— Short History of the Movies. 5th ed. 688p. 1992. text ed. 35.00 (*0-02-580510-X*) Macmillan.

Mast, Gerald, ed. Bringing up Baby. (Films in Print Ser.). (Illus.). 233p. (Orig.). (C). 1988. text ed. 35.00 (*0-8135-1340-5*); pap. text ed. 16.00 (*0-8135-1341-3*) Rutgers U Pr.

Mast, Gerald, et al, eds. Film Theory & Criticism: Introductory Readings. 4th ed. 704p. (C). 1992. pap. text ed. 23.00 (*0-19-506398-8*) OUP.

Mast, J. W., et al. Planning & Reduction Technique in Fracture Surgery. (Illus.). 270p. 1993. 250.00 (*0-387-16283-6*) Spr-Verlag.

Mast, Jan, jt. auth. see Stoltzfus, Louise.

Mast, Jennifer A., ed. Ward's Private Company Profiles. 750p. 1993. 139.00 (*0-8103-9140-6*, 101789) Gale.

— Ward's Private Company Profiles, Vol. 2. 699p. 1994. 139.00 (*0-8103-9311-5*) Gale.

Mast, Joseph A. The Emerging Self: A Celtic Journey. LC 90-42538. (Illus.). 304p. (Orig.). 1991. 22.95 (*0-931832-77-2*) Fithian Pr.

Mast, Lois A. Mennonite Family History Ten-Year Index, 1982-1991. 1992. pap. 23.00 (*1-883294-05-3*) Olde Sprgfld.

— The Peter Leibundgutt Journal. 118p. 1991. pap. 9.00 (*1-883294-10-X*) Olde Sprgfld.

Mast, Lois A., jt. auth. see Lemar, J.

Mast, M. J., ed. County Agents Directory. 62th ed. 1977. 6.50 (*0-686-20517-0*) C L Mast.

Mast, Richard F., jt. ed. see Spencer, Charles W.

Mast, Robert H., comp. Detroit Lives. LC 93-51007. (Conflicts in Urban & Regional Development Ser.). 288p. 1994. 49.95 (*1-56639-225-X*); pap. 19.95 (*1-56639-226-8*) Temple U Pr.

Mast, Terrill A. User's Guide to Cost-Care. (Cost Containment Learning Modules Ser.). 59p. (Orig.). 1985. pap. text ed. 12.50 (*0-931369-17-7*) Southern IL Univ Sch.

Mast, Terrill A., ed. Book of Costs. (Cost Containment Learning Modules Ser.). 85p. (Orig.). 1985. pap. text ed. 12.50 (*0-931369-18-5*) Southern IL Univ Sch.

Mastaglia, F. L. & Walton, John, eds. Skeletal Muscle Pathology. 2nd ed. (Illus.). 803p. 1992. text ed. 225.00 (*0-443-04241-1*) Churchill.

Mastaglia, Frank L., jt. auth. see Kakulas, Byron A.

Mastai, Boleslaw. Star & Stripes. 1990. 14.70 (*0-685-33590-9*) S&S Trade.

Mastandrea, Paolo. De Fine Versus. Bd. CXXXII. Date not set. write for info. (*0-318-71172-9*, Pub. by Georg Olms GW) Lubrecht & Cramer.

— De Fine Versus: Repertorio Di Clausole Riccorenti Nella Poesia Dattilica Latina Dalle Origini a Sidonio Apollinare, 2 vols. (Alpha-Omega, Reihe A Ser.: Bd. CXXXII). xxiv, 1132p. (GER.). 1993. write for info. (*3-487-09693-5*, Pub. by Georg Olms GW) Lubrecht & Cramer.

— De Fine Versus Repertorio Di Clausole Ricorrenti Nella Poesia Dattilica Latina, Dalle Origini a Sidonio Apollinare. Bd. CXXXII. Date not set. write for info. (*0-318-70678-4*, Pub. by Georg Olms GW) Lubrecht & Cramer.

Mastanduno, Michael. Economic Containment: CoCom & the Politics of East-West Trade. LC 92-52766. (Cornell Studies in Political Economy). 376p. 1992. 48.50 (*0-8014-2709-6*); pap. 18.95 (*0-8014-9996-8*) Cornell U Pr.

Mastanduno, Michael, jt. ed. see Lyons, Gene M.

Mastascusa, E. J. Computer-Assisted Network & System Analysis. LC 87-29831. 318p. reprint ed. pap. 90.70 (*0-7837-2812-3*, 2057660) Bks Demand.

Masteler, R. A., tr. see Zharkov, V. N.

Mastella, G. & Quinton, P. M., eds. Cellular & Molecular Basis of Cystic Fibrosis. (Illus.). 1988. 40.00 (*0-911302-63-8*) San Francisco Pr.

Masteller, Richard N. Auto as Icon. (Illus.). (Orig.). (C). 1979. pap. 8.95 (*1-880269-02-3*) D H Sheehan.

— We, the People? Satiric Prints of the 1930s. LC 89-50444. (Illus.). 75p. (Orig.). (C). 1989. pap. 7.00 (*1-880269-05-8*) D H Sheehan.

Mastellone, L. Legal & Commercial Dictionary. 173p. (ENG & ITA.). 1980. write for info. (*0-8288-0397-8*, F 22010) Fr & Eur.

Masten. Maternal-Infant SR Outline. 1992. 18.95 (*0-944132-91-X*) Skidmore Roth Pub.

Masten & Goodner. Obstetric Survival Guide. (Nurse's Survival Guide Ser.). 1994. 14.95 (*0-944132-67-7*) Skidmore Roth Pub.

Masten, Arthur H. History of Cohoes, N.Y. (Illus.). 327p. 1993. reprint ed. lib. bdg. 39.50 (*0-8328-2877-7*) Higginson Bk Co.

Masten, Florence R. Across Time's Fence. 1978. pap. 2.00 (*0-911183-07-8*) Rockland County Hist.

Masten, M. K. & Stockum, L. A. Acquisition, Tracking, & Pointing V, Vol. 1482. 1991. 70.00 (*0-8194-0591-4*) SPIE.

Masten, Ric. Even As We Speak. LC 82-60705. 1982. pap. 5.50 (*0-931104-12-2*) Sunflower Ink.

— I Know It Isn't Funny but I Love to Make You Laugh. (Illus.). 176p. (Orig.). 1991. pap. 8.00 (*0-931104-31-9*) Sunflower Ink.

— Notice Me! LC 85-82615. 100p. 1986. pap. 6.00 (*0-931104-17-3*) Sunflower Ink.

— Ric Masten Speaking. LC 90-33891. (Illus.). 139p. (Orig.). 1990. pap. 8.00 (*0-918949-11-4*) Papier-Mache Press.

— Stark Naked. LC 80-51980. 1980. 10.00 (*0-931104-04-1*); pap. 5.50 (*0-686-77528-7*) Sunflower Ink.

— Voice of the Hive. rev. ed. LC 78-59786. (Orig.). 1978. pap. 6.00 (*0-931104-02-5*) Sunflower Ink.

***Masten, Scott E., ed.** Case Studies in Contracting & Organization. (Illus.). 368p. 1995. 39.95 (*0-19-509251-1*) OUP.

— Case Studies in Contracting & Organization. (Illus.). 368p. (C). 1995. pap. text ed. 19.95 (*0-19-509252-X*) OUP.

Masten, Scott E., jt. ed. see Williamson, Oliver E.

Masten, Yondell, jt. auth. see Goodner, Brenda.

Mastenbroek, Willem. Negotiate. (Illus.). 256p. 1989. text ed. 22.95 (*0-631-16348-4*) Blackwell Pubs.

Mastenbroek, Willem, ed. Management for Equality in the Service Sector. 256p. 1991. 47.95 (*0-631-17499-0*) Blackwell Pubs.

Mastenbroek, Willem F. Conflict Management & Organization Development. LC 87-10463. (Industrial Psychology & Organizational Behavior Ser.). 166p. 1987. text ed. 98.95 (*0-471-91415-0*) Wiley.

— Conflict Management & Organization Development. LC 93-17955. 228p. 1994. pap. text ed. 45.00 (*0-471-94141-7*) Wiley.

— Conflict Management & Organization Development. fac. ed. LC 87-10463. 176p. 1987. reprint ed. pap. 50.20 (*0-7837-8285-3*, 2049067) Bks Demand.

***Master.** Space Age. 9.99 (*0-517-13744-5*) Random Hse Value.

Master, Arthur M., et al. The Electrocardiogram & Chest X-Ray in Diseases of the Heart. LC 63-16703. (Illus.). 565p. reprint ed. 161.10 (*0-685-07752-7*, 2014563) Bks Demand.

Master Bob. The I AM Discourses, Vol. 12. LC 87-20624. (Illus.). 248p. 1987. 16.00 (*1-878891-52-9*); pap. 12.00 (*1-878891-53-7*) St Germain Pr.

Master, Chan & Chang, Sheng-yen. Getting the Buddha Mind. LC 82-73979. 147p. (Orig.). 1982. pap. text ed. 12.00 (*0-9609854-0-9*) Dharma Drum Pubs.

— Infinite Mirror. 1991. pap. 12.00 (*0-9609854-4-1*) Dharma Drum Pubs.

— Ox Herding at Morgan's Bay. Baldwin, Mark & Marano, Christopher, eds. LC 88-51571. 55p. (Orig.). 1988. pap. 8.00 (*0-9609854-3-3*) Dharma Drum Pubs.

— The Sword of Wisdom. 1991. pap. 12.00 (*0-9609854-5-X*) Dharma Drum Pubs.

— Zen Wisdom, Knowing & Doing: Thirty-Eight Conversations with Ch'an Master Sheng-Yen. 1994. pap. 15.00 (*0-9609854-6-8*) Dharma Drum Pubs.

Master Designer Staff. Modern Garment Design & Grading Clothing for Men & Boys: Designing Men's & Boys' Garments. 142p. (C). 1994. pap. text ed. 29.95 (*1-885646-02-X*) Master Design.

Master Designer Staff & Gebbia, A. Modern Method of Women's & Children's Garment Design: Designing Women's & Children's Garments. 163p. (C). 1994. pap. text ed. 29.95 (1-885646-00-3) Master Design.

Master Designer Staff & Waisman, A. Modern Custom Tailoring for Men: Tailoring & Repairing. 179p. (C). 1994. pap. text ed. 29.95 (1-885646-01-1) Master Design.

Master, Eileen, jt. auth. see Poley Rowan, Janice.

Master Hei Long. Twenty-One Techniques of Silent Killing. (Illus.). 104p. 1989. pap. 12.00 (0-87364-508-1) Paladin Pr.

Master Hua, Tripitaka. Great Compassion Dharma Transmission Verses of the 42 Hands & Eyes. Buddhist Text Translation Society, tr. (Illus.). 100p. (Orig.). (C). 1983. pap. 200.00 (0-88139-002-X) Buddhist Text.

— Listen to Yourself: Think Everything Over, Vol. II. Buddhist Text Translation Society, tr. 172p. 1983. pap. 7.00 (0-88139-010-0) Buddhist Text.

— Records of High Sanghans, Vol. I. Buddhist Text Translation Society, tr. 160p. (Orig.). 1983. pap. 7.00 (0-88139-012-7) Buddhist Text.

— Water Mirror Reflecting Heaven. Buddhist Text Translation Society, tr. (Illus.). 82p. (Orig.). 1982. pap. 4.00 (0-88139-501-3) Buddhist Text.

Master Hua, Triptaka. Herein Lies the Treasure-Trove, Vol. 1. Buddhist Text Translation Society, tr. (Illus.). 250p. (Orig.). (C). 1983. pap. 6.50 (0-88139-001-1) Buddhist Text.

Master Jackson. Sir! More Sir! The Joy of S&M. 192p. (Orig.). 1992. pap. 14.95 (0-943595-39-8) Leyland Pubns.

Master, Melvyn C., jt. auth. see Livingstone-Learmonth, John.

***Master Mind Staff.** Master Mind Goal Achiever's Journal, 1995. 213p. 1994. 24.95 (0-88152-100-0) Master Mind.

— Master Mind Goal Achievers Journal, 1996. 1995. 24.95 (0-88152-107-8) Master Mind.

Master, Myo-Bong. Gateway to Son (Ch'an) Hye-Am Choi, ed. LC 86-50750. 359p. (Orig.). (CHI & KOR.). 1986. 21.95 (0-938647-00-8) Western Son Acad.

Master Ni. The Footsteps of the Mystical Child. LC 86-60062. 180p. (C). 1986. pap. text ed. 9.50 (0-937064-11-4) SevenStar Comm.

Master, Peter A. Science, Medicine & Technology: English Grammar & Technical Writing. (Illus.). 320p. (C). 1986. pap. text ed. 16.00 (0-13-795469-7) P-H.

— Systems in English Grammar: An Introduction for Language Teachers. LC 95-15946. 1995. pap. 24.95 (0-13-156837-X) P-H.

Master Publishing, Inc. Staff. Installing Your Own Telephones. 2nd ed. (Illus.). 176p. 1986. pap. text ed. 1.75 (0-8359-3291-5, Reston) P-H.

— Installing Your Own Telephones. 2nd ed. (Illus.). 172p. 1986. 15.50 (0-8359-3292-3) P-H.

***Master, Rachel.** Cookies & Cakes. (You Can Do It! Ser.). (Illus.). 80p. (Orig.). (J). (ps up). Date not set. pap. 12.95 (1-56530-069-6) Summit TX.

— Jumping Rope. (You Can Do It! Ser.). (Illus.). 64p. (Orig.). (J). (ps up). Date not set. pap. 12.95 (1-56530-067-X) Summit TX.

Master, Roy. How to Survive Your Parents. LC 82-71162. 190p. 1982. pap. 12.95 (0-933900-10-4) Foun Human Under.

Master, T. W. Hairdressing in Theory & Practice. LC 84-23946. 280p. 1984. pap. 20.95 (0-291-39627-5) Ashgate Pub Co.

***Master Teacher Staff.** Lesson Plans & Modifications for Inclusion & Collaborative Classrooms. LC 95-79721. 203p. 1995. ring bd. 59.95 (0-914607-37-5) Master Tchr.

Master, Wakefield. The Complete Plays of the Wakefield Master. Brown, John R., ed. 1983. pap. 10.95 (0-87830-584-X, Theatre Arts Bks) Routledge Chapman & Hall.

***MasterCard International & College Students.** Mastering (& Succeeding With) the Job Hunt. 149p. (C). 1994. write for info. (0-9642751-0-4) Mstercard Intl.

Masterdy, E., ed. One Hundred Alive & Stay Alive! Double Your Life Expectancy. 162p. 1984. 12.95 (0-8159-6415-3) Devin.

Masterfield, Maxine. In Harmony with Nature. (Illus.). 144p. 1990. 29.95 (0-8230-3641-3, Watsn-Guptill) Watsn-Guptill.

— Painting the Spirit of Nature. (Illus.). 144p. 1984. 27.50 (0-8230-3861-0, Watsn-Guptill) Watsn-Guptill.

Masterman, A. H. & Boyce, R. M. Plumbing & Mechanical Services, Pt. 1. (Illus.). 246p. (C). 1984. pap. 33.00x (0-7487-0368-3, Pub. by S Thornes Pubs UK) St Mut.

— Plumbing & Mechanical Services, Pt. 2. (Illus.). 224p. (C). 1990. pap. 33.00x (0-7487-0232-6, Pub. by S Thornes Pubs UK) St Mut.

— Plumbing & Mechanical Services, Pt. 3. 232p. (C). 1990. pap. 33.00x (0-7487-0233-4, Pub. by S Thornes Pubs UK) St Mut.

Masterman, J. C. Case of the Four Friends. (Black Dagger Crime Ser.). 232p. 16.50 (0-86220-721-5, Black Dagger) Chivers N Amer.

Masterman, L. C. F. G. Masterman. (Illus.). 400p. 1968. 25.00 (0-7146-1565-X, Pub. by F Cass Pubs UK) Intl Spec Bk.

Masterman, Len. Teaching the Media. (Comedia Bk.). 220p. 1990. pap. 15.95 (0-415-03974-6, A4918) Routledge.

Masterman, Lucy B. C. F. G. Masterman: A Biography. LC 68-88329. (Illus.). 1968. reprint ed. 45.00 (0-678-05187-9) Kelley.

Masterman, M. & Boyce, B. Plumbing & Mechanical Services, Vol. 1. (C). 1989. 120.00 (0-09-154551-X, Pub. by S Thornes Pubs UK) St Mut.

Masterman-Smith, Virginia. The Treasure Trap. LC 91-45217. 208p. (J). (gr. 3-7). 1992. reprint ed. pap. 3.95 (0-689-71578-1, Aladdin Paperbacks) S&S Childrens.

Masterman, Sylvia. The Origins of International Rivalry in Samoa, 1845-1884. LC 75-35205. reprint ed. 19.00 (0-404-14228-1) AMS Pr.

Masterman, W. E. An Introduction to Building Procurement Systems. LC 92-17960. 1992. write for info. (0-442-31586-4, E & FN Spon) Routledge Chapman & Hall.

***Masteroff, Joe.** She Loves Me. (Illus.). 96p. 1995. 11.99 (1-56865-142-2, GuildAmerica) Dblday Bk Music.

Masters. Goddess Sekhmet. 1990. pap. 9.95 (0-916349-47-0, GOSEKP) Element MA.

— Serpent Mound. (J). Date not set. 14.00 (0-671-79976-2, S&S Bks Young Read) S&S Childrens.

Masters, jt. auth. see Masters, Roger D.

Masters, jt. auth. see Yee, Bernie.

Masters, Anthony. The Confessional. 240p. 1994. 19.95 (0-312-10956-3) St Martin.

— Klondyker. LC 92-351. (YA). 1992. pap. 15.00 (0-671-79173-7, S&S Bks Young Read) S&S Childrens.

— The Play of Personality in the Restoration Theatre. Trussler, Simon, ed. LC 92-25412. (Illus.). 112p. (C). 1992. text ed. 39.00 (0-85115-326-7, Boydell Pr) Boydell & Brewer.

Masters, B. R., ed. Noninvasive Diagnostic Techniques in Ophthalmology. (Illus.). 632p. 1990. 164.00 (0-387-96992-6) Spr-Verlag.

Masters, Brian. Killing for Company: Inside the Mind of a Mass Murderer. LC 92-56831. 384p. 1993. 24.00 (0-679-42425-3) Random.

— Killing for Company: The Story of a Man Addicted to Murder. 1994. pap. 4.99 (0-440-22043-2) Dell.

— The Life of E. F. Benson. (Illus.). 336p. 1994. pap. 16.95 (0-7126-5714-2, Pub. by Pimlico) Trafalgar.

Masters, Brien, ed. The Waldorf Song Book. (J). 1988. pap. 8.50 (0-86315-059-4, 20243) Gryphon Hse.

Masters, Bruce. The Origins of Western Economic Dominance in the Middle East: Mercantilism & the Islamic Economy in Aleppo, 1600-1750, No. 12. (Studies in Near Eastern Civilization). 320p. 1987. 55.00x (0-8147-5435-X) NYU Pr.

Masters, C. L. Amyloid Protein Precursor in Development, Aging, & Alzheimer's Disease. LC 94-4461. (Research & Perspectives in Alzheimer's Disease Ser.). 1994. 100.00 (0-387-57788-2) Spr-Verlag.

Masters, Carol. The Peace Terrorist: And Other Stories. LC 93-83979. (Minnesota Voices Project Ser.). 160p. (Orig.). 1994. pap. 9.95 (0-89823-156-6) New Rivers Pr.

***Masters, Charles J.** Glidermen of Neptune: The Neptune D-Day Glider Attack. LC 95-11452. (Illus.). 128p. (C). 1995. 39.95 (0-8093-2007-X); pap. 19.95 (0-8093-2008-8) S Ill U Pr.

***Masters, Christopher.** Dali. (Color Library). (Illus.). 128p. (C). 1995. pap. 14.95 (0-7148-3338-X, Pub. by Phaidon Press UK) Chronicle Bks.

— Dali. (Color Library). (Illus.). 128p. (C). 1995. 19.95 (0-7148-3339-8, Pub. by Phaidon Press UK) Chronicle Bks.

***Masters, Colin & Crane, Denis.** The Peroxisome: A Vital Organelle. (Illus.). 300p. (C). Date not set. write for info. (0-521-48212-7) Cambridge U Pr.

Masters, Colin & Stroud, Alan. Transfer Pricing. 1991. 170.00 (0-406-00112-X, U.K.) Butterworth Legal Pubs.

Masters, David. The Wonders of Salvage: Deep Sea Diving for Sunken Ships & Treasures. 1977. lib. bdg. 150.00 (0-8490-2839-6) Gordon Pr.

Masters, Dexter & Way, Katherine, eds. One World or None. LC 71-37858. (Essay Index Reprint Ser.). 1977. reprint ed. 25.95 (0-8369-2610-2) Ayer.

Masters, Diane. Magazine. 320p. 1984. pap. 3.25 (0-8439-2103-X) Dorchester Pub Co.

— Nothing but the Best. 384p. 1986. reprint ed. pap. 3.95 (0-8439-2389-X) Dorchester Pub Co.

Masters, Donald C. A Short History of Canada. LC 80-12913. (Anvil Ser.). 192p. 1980. reprint ed. pap. text ed. 10.50 (0-89874-201-3) Krieger.

— The Winnipeg General Strike. LC 51-5058. (Canadian University Paperbooks Ser.: No. 136). (Illus.). 179p. reprint ed. pap. 51.10 (0-8357-4160-5, 2036934) Bks Demand.

Masters, Edgar L. Across Spoon River. (Prairie State Bks.). pap. 14.95 (0-252-06051-2) U of Ill Pr.

— Across Spoon River: An Autobiography. (American Biography Ser.). 426p. 1991. reprint ed. lib. bdg. 89.00 (0-7812-8276-4) Rprt Serv.

— Along the Illinois. 86p. reprint ed. pap. text ed. 4.95 (1-877869-20-1) Mason Cnty Hist Proj.

— The Blood of Prophets. 1972. 59.95 (0-87968-761-4) Gordon Pr.

— A Book of Verses. 1972. 59.95 (0-87968-773-8) Gordon Pr.

— The Enduring River: Edgar Lee Masters' Uncollected Spoon River Poems. 104p. (C). 1991. 19.95x (0-8093-1685-4) S Ill U Pr.

— Mark Twain: A Portrait. LC 66-15216. 1938. 25.00 (0-8196-0171-3) Biblo.

— The New Spoon River. 1993. reprint ed. lib. bdg. 21.95 (1-56849-120-4) Buccaneer Bks.

— The Sangamon. LC 88-17510. (Prairie State Bks.). (Illus.). 296p. 1988. pap. 10.95 (0-252-06038-5) U of Ill Pr.

— Spoon River Anthology. 1976. 20.95 (0-8488-1430-4) Amereon Ltd.

— Spoon River Anthology. 1981. 14.95 (0-02-581730-2) Macmillan.

— Spoon River Anthology. 320p. 1992. pap. 4.95 (0-451-52530-2, Sig Classics) NAL-Dutton.

— Spoon River Anthology. 320p. 1962. pap. 7.00 (0-02-070010-5, Collier S&S) S&S Trade.

— Spoon River Anthology. 328p. 1987. text ed. 35.00 (0-02-581780-9, Scribners) S&S Trade.

— Spoon River Anthology. unabridged ed. 144p. 1992. reprint ed. pap. text ed. 1.00 (0-486-27275-3) Dover.

— Spoon River Anthology. 345p. 1983. reprint ed. lib. bdg. 21.95 (0-89966-456-3) Buccaneer Bks.

— Spoon River Anthology: An Annotated Edition. Hallwas, John E., ed. (Prairie State Bks.). (Illus.). 464p. 1992. 29.95 (0-252-01561-4); pap. 14.95 (0-252-06363-5) U of Ill Pr.

— Vachel Lindsay: A Poet in America. LC 68-56452. (Illus.). 1969. reprint ed. 25.00 (0-8196-0239-6) Biblo.

— Whitman. LC 68-22695. 1968. reprint ed. 25.00 (0-8196-0210-8) Biblo.

Masters, Elaine A. Those Women in White. (Illus.). 386p. 1989. 40.00 (0-685-26798-9) E A Masters.

Masters, Geofferey. Profiles of Learning. (C). 1992. 75.00 (0-86431-067-6, Pub. by Aust Council Educ Res AT) St Mut.

Masters, Geofferey N., jt. auth. see Wright, Benjamin D.

Masters, George M., ed. Medieval & Renaissance Studies: Proceedings of the Southeastern Institute of Medieval & Renaissance Studies, Summer 1979. LC 68-54949. (Medieval & Renaissance Monograph Ser.: No. 10). (Illus.). 132p. reprint ed. pap. 37.70 (0-7837-2467-5, 2042620) Bks Demand.

Masters, George R., jt. auth. see Allan, Francis C.

Masters, Gilbert M. Introduction to Environmental Engineering & Science. 512p. 1991. text ed. 70.00 (0-13-483066-0) P-H.

Masters, Hardin W. Edgar Lee Masters: A Biographical Sketchbook about a Great American Author. LC 76-20337. 1978. 28.50 (0-8386-2031-0) Fairleigh Dickinson.

Masters, Hilary. An American Marriage. LC 81-69038. 1982. reprint ed. 11.00 (0-941038-00-9) Coyne & Chenoweth.

— Clemmons. 1991. 6.00 (0-941038-05-X) Coyne & Chenoweth.

— Cooper. 1993. reprint ed. pap. text ed. 11.00 (0-941038-08-4) Coyne & Chenoweth.

— Hammertown Tales. LC 85-51667. 150p. 1986. 15.00 (0-913773-18-2) S Wright.

— Hammertown Tales. LC 85-51667. 128p. 1991. reprint ed. 6.00 (0-941038-02-5) Coyne & Chenoweth.

— Last Stands: Notes from Memory. 1991. 11.00 (0-941038-04-1) Coyne & Chenoweth.

— Strickland. 1991. reprint ed. 15.00 (0-941038-03-3) Coyne & Chenoweth.

Masters, J. G. Sarah Elizabeth: A Tale of Old Colorado. 208p. 1985. 13.95 (0-940672-29-4) Shearer Pub.

Masters, Jack. Masters Family History, Sixteen Ninety-One to Nineteen Eighty-Nine. (Illus.). 576p. 1989. 37.50 (0-9622761-0-3) J Masters.

— Smith & Allied Families History: Beaty - Bowers - Hull. (Illus.). 250p. 1991. 35.00 (0-9622761-1-1) J Masters.

Masters, James I., ed. The Hamptons Guidebook. LC 80-50137. (Illus.). 398p. (Orig.). 1980. 6.95 (0-89808-002-9, Blue Claw) Masters Pubns.

— North Fork & Shelter Island Guidebook. 3rd ed. LC 81-67384. (Illus.). 320p. (YA). (gr. 9-12). 1981. pap. 4.95 (0-89808-007-X, Blue Claw) Masters Pubns.

Masters, Jamie. Poetry & Civil War in Lucan's "Bellum Civile" (Classical Studies). (Illus.). 288p. (C). 1992. 59.95 (0-521-41460-1) Cambridge U Pr.

Masters, Jamie, jt. ed. see Elsner, Jas.

Masters, Janet F. & Smith, Joyce M. Art History: A Study Guide. 2nd ed. (Illus.). 304p. (C). 1987. pap. text ed. write for info. (0-13-047309-X) P-H.

Masters, Jesse & Johnston, Don. Sassy Sayin's & Mountain Badmouth. (Illus.). 80p. (Orig.). 1985. pap. 3.95 (0-9615347-0-2) Sassy Sayings.

Masters, John. Bhowani Junction. 450p. 1987. pap. 4.50 (0-88184-310-5) Carroll & Graf.

— Bhowani Junction. large type ed. 576p. 1983. 21.95 (0-7089-1056-4) Ulverscroft.

— The Deceivers. large type ed. 1980. 12.00 (0-7089-0433-5) Ulverscroft.

— The Himalayan Concerto. large type ed. 475p. 1982. 21.95 (0-7089-0839-X) Ulverscroft.

— The Lotus & the Wind. large type ed. 506p. 1980. 12.00 (0-7089-0443-2) Ulverscroft.

— Nightrunners of Bengal. large type ed. 1980. 12.00 (0-7089-0419-X) Ulverscroft.

***Masters, John A., ed.** Elmworth: Case Study of a Deep Basin Gas Field. (AAPG Memoir Ser.: No. 38). (Illus.). ix, 316p. 1984. 48.00 (0-89181-315-2) AAPG.

Masters, John C. & Smith, William P., eds. Social Comparison, Social Justice, & Relative Deprivation: Theoretical, Empirical, & Policy Perspectives. (Greenwald & Krauss Ser.). 320p. 1987. text ed. 59.95 (0-89859-632-7) L Erlbaum Assocs.

Masters, John C., et al. Behavior Therapy: Techniques & Empirical Findings. 3rd ed. 693p. (C). 1987. text ed. 45.25 (0-15-505376-0, RIMM 3) HB Coll Pubs.

Masters, John E., ed. Damage Detection in Composite Materials. LC 92-24755. (Special Technical Publication Ser.: No. 1128). (Illus.). 290p. 1992. text ed. 83.00 (0-8031-1474-5, 04-011280-33) ASTM.

Masters, John E. & Au, Joseph J., eds. Fractography of Modern Engineering Materials: Composites & Metals. LC 87-14970. (Special Technical Publication Ser.: No. 948). (Illus.). 459p. 1987. 59.00 (0-8031-0950-4, 04-948000-30) ASTM.

Masters, John E. & Gilbertson, Leslie N., eds. Fractography of Modern Engineering Materials, Vol. 2: Composites & Metals. (Special Technical Publication Ser.: No. STP 1203). (Illus.). 220p. 1993. text ed. 65.00 (0-8031-1866-X, 04-012030-30) ASTM.

Masters, John R., ed. Human Cancer in Primary Culture. (C). 1991. lib. bdg. 127.50 (0-7923-1088-8) Kluwer Ac.

Masters, Judith R., tr. see Rousseau, Jean-Jacques.

Masters, Kate. Turn Your Ideas into Millions: Selling & Marketing Your Idea or Product. LC 93-44225. 1994. 8.95 (0-8065-1525-2, Citadel Pr) Carol Pub Group.

Masters, Keith. Spray Drying Handbook. 5th ed. 725p. 1991. text ed. 220.00 (0-470-21743-X) Halsted Pr.

Masters, Kim J. The Angry Child: Sleeping Giant or Paper Tiger? 144p. (Orig.). 1991. pap. 8.95 (0-929162-49-8) PIA Pr.

Masters, Larry W., ed. Problems in Service Life Prediction of Building & Construction Materials. 1985. lib. bdg. 121.50 (90-247-3181-X) Kluwer Ac.

Masters, Lowell F. & Richardson, Howard D. Supervision for Successful Team Leadership: Your Personal Analysis with the Quesitons & Answers You Need to Know. Fish, S. A., ed. LC 91-38315. (Illus.). 128p. (Orig.). 1992. pap. 16.95 (0-9630748-0-6) Achieve Pr.

Masters, Lowell F., et al. Teaching Secondary Students with Mild Learning & Behavior Problems: Methods, Materials, Strategies. 2nd ed. LC 92-30450. (Illus.). 360p. (C). 1992. text ed. 38.00 (0-89079-570-3, 2073) PRO-ED.

Masters, Marcia L. Looking Across. 90p. (Orig.). 1990. pap. 7.95 (0-685-35764-3) Thorntree Pr.

Masters, Margaret D. Hartley Burr Alexander: Writer-in-Stone. (Illus.). 150p. (Orig.). 1992. 20.00 (0-9633322-0-1); pap. 10.00 (0-9633322-1-X) M D Masters.

Masters, Marie, jt. ed. see Olejnik, Renee M.

Masters, Nancy R. All My Downs Have Been Ups. (Illus.). 190p. 1992. 18.95 (0-9623563-2-8) J R Matthews.

Masters, Nanvy R. The Horrible, Homemade Halloween Costume. (Ups & Downs Book Ser.). (Illus.). 32p. (J). (gr. 2-4). 1993. 14.95 (0-9623563-3-6) J R Matthews.

Masters, Olga. The Home Girls. LC 82-2709. 194p. 1983. pap. 14.95 (0-7022-1821-9) Intl Spec Bk.

— Loving Daughters. LC 92-42487. 320p. 1993. 21.95 (0-393-03498-4) Norton.

— Loving Daughters. large type ed. LC 93-11696. (General Ser.). 1993. pap. 18.95 (0-7862-0032-4) Thorndike Pr.

Masters, P. M. Quarternary Coastlines & Marine Archaeology: Towards the Prehistory of Land Bridges & Continental Shelves. Fleming, N. C., ed. LC 82-45021. 1983. text ed. 118.00 (0-12-479250-2) Acad Pr.

Masters, Phil. Kingdom of Champions. Bell, Rob, ed. (Champions Ser.). (Illus.). 208p. (Orig.). (C). 1990. pap. text ed. 18.00 (1-55806-104-5, 410) Iron Crown Ent Inc.

Masters, R. E. Eros & Evil: The Sexual Psychopathology of Witchcraft. LC 79-8114. reprint ed. 36.50 (0-404-18427-8) AMS Pr.

Masters, Raymond. Social History of the Huntington Wildlife Forest: Which Includes Rich Lake & the Pendleton Settlement. LC 93-12342. 96p. 1993. pap. 9.95 (0-925168-13-0) North Country.

Masters, Richard & Oman, R. M. How to Convert Your Present Heater to Low-Cost Electric. (Illus.). 21p. 1978. pap. 7.95 (0-931660-00-9) R Oman Pub.

Masters, Robert. The Goddess Sekhmet: Psychospiritual Exercises of the Fifth Way. LC 90-45836. (Illus.). 266p. 1991. reprint ed. 22.95 (0-87542-495-3); reprint ed. pap. 12.95 (0-87542-485-6) Llewellyn Pubns.

— The Goddess Sekhmet. (Fifth Way Bks.). 224p. 1987. 18.95 (0-916349-33-0); pap. 9.95 (0-916349-39-X) Amity Hse Inc.

— Images of the Divine. (Soma Bks.). 176p. 1988. 18.95 (0-317-66017-9); pap. 9.95 (0-916349-50-0) Amity Hse Inc.

— The Masters Technique. (Soma Bks.). 192p. 1988. 18.95 (0-916349-64-0); pap. 9.95 (0-916349-63-2) Amity Hse Inc.

— Neurospeak. 107p. (Orig.). 1994. pap. 12.00 (0-8356-0707-0, Quest) Theos Pub Hse.

Masters, Robert & Houston, Jean. Mind Games: The Guide to Inner Space. 246p. 1990. 17.95 (0-88029-447-7) Dorset Pr.

Masters, Robert B. Vu-Calc & Vu-File (The Organizer) LC 83-22489. 176p. 1984. pap. 19.95 (0-89303-941-1) P-H.

Masters, Roberta, jt. auth. see Gottesman, Roberta.

Masters, Roger D. Beyond Relativism: Science & Human Values. LC 93-16925. (Illus.). 262p. 1993. 24.95 (0-87451-634-X) U Pr of New Eng.

— Machiavelli, Leonardo & the Science of Power. LC 94-40484. (Frank M. Covey, Jr., Loyola Lectures in Political Analysis). (C). 1995. text ed. 32.95x (0-268-01416-7) U of Notre Dame Pr.

— The Nature of Politics. LC 88-7652. 320p. (C). 1989. text ed. 37.00 (0-300-04169-1) Yale U Pr.

— The Political Philosophy of Rousseau. LC 67-12348. 488p. reprint ed. pap. 139.10 (0-685-44420-1, 2032638) Bks Demand.

Masters, Roger D. & Gruter, Margaret, eds. The Sense of Justice: Biological Foundations of Law. (Focus Editions Ser.: Vol. 136). 288p. (C). 1992. text ed. 49.95 (0-8039-4397-0); pap. text ed. 24.95 (0-8039-4398-9) Sage.

Masters, Roger D. & Masters. Rousseau's First & Second Discourses. 1969. write for info. (0-318-63175-X) St Martin.

Masters, Roger D., jt. ed. see Gruter, Margaret.

Masters, Roger D., ed. see McGuire, Michael T.

Masters, Roger D., ed. see Rousseau, Jean J.

Masters, Roger D., ed. see Rousseau, Jean-Jacques.

Masters, Roger D., jt. ed. see Schubert, Glendon.

Masters, Rogers D. Nature of Politics. 315p. 1991. pap. 15.00 (0-300-04981-1) Yale U Pr.

Masters, Roy. The Adam & Eve Sindrome. LC 85-80750. 266p. 1985. pap. text ed. 12.95 (0-933900-11-2) Foun Human Under.

— Beyond the Known. rev. ed. Baker, Dorothy, ed. LC 88-83553. 255p. (Orig.). 1989. reprint ed. pap. text ed. 12.95 (0-933900-03-1) Foun Human Under.

— Eat No Evil. LC 87-80407. 127p. (Orig.). 1987. pap. text ed. 12.95 (0-933900-12-0) Foun Human Under.

An Asterisk (*) at the beginning of an entry indicates that the title is appearing in BIP for the first time.

— How to Conquer Negative Emotions. Tappan, Melrose H., ed. & pref. by. LC 88-80163. 325p. 1988. pap. 12.95 (*0-933900-01-5*) Foun Human Under.

— How to Conquer Suffering Without Doctors. LC 76-489. 222p. 1976. pap. 12.95 (*0-933900-04-X*) Foun Human Under.

— How Your Mind Can Keep You Well. 15th ed. Baker, Dorothy, ed. 201p. 1978. pap. 12.95 (*0-933900-09-0*) Foun Human Under.

— The Hypnosis of Life. rev. ed. LC 88-80924. 259p. (Orig.). 1988. pap. 12.95 (*0-933900-05-8*) Foun Human Under.

— Secret Power of Words. Baker, Dorothy, ed. LC 88-81474. 213p. (Orig.). 1988. pap. text ed. 12.95 (*0-933900-14-7*) Foun Human Under.

— Secrets of a Parallel Universe: Why Our Deepest Problems Hold the Key to Ultimate Personal Success & Happiness. Baker, Dorothy, ed. LC 92-81343. 156p. (Orig.). 1992. pap. text ed. 12.95 (*0-933900-17-1*) Foun Human Under.

— Surviving the Comfort Zone. Baker, Dorothy, ed. LC 91-73149. 193p. (Orig.). 1991. pap. text ed. 12.95 (*0-933900-15-5*) Foun Human Under.

— Understanding Sexuality: The Mystery of Our Lost Identities. rev. ed. LC 87-83552. 361p. 1988. reprint ed. pap. 12.95 (*0-933900-13-9*) Foun Human Under.

Masters, Ruth & Roberson, Cliff. Inside Criminology. 432p. 1990. text ed. 49.33 (*0-13-463530-2*) P-H.

Masters, Ruth D. International Law in National Courts. LC 71-76631. (Columbia University. Studies in the Social Sciences: No. 370). reprint ed. 20.00 (*0-404-51370-0*) AMS Pr.

Masters, Ruth E. Counseling Criminal Justice Offenders. 264p. (C). 1994. text ed. 46.00 (*0-8039-5532-4*); pap. text ed. 19.95 (*0-8039-5533-2*) Sage.

Master's Seminary Faculty, jt. auth. see MacArthur, John, Jr.

Master's Seminary Faculty Staff & MacArthur, John, Jr. Rediscovering Expository Preaching. Mayhue, Richard L. & Thomas, Robert L., eds. LC 92-10804. 1992. 21.99 (*0-8499-0908-2*) Word Inc.

Masters Staff. The Rainbow Masters. (Phoenix Journals). 224p. 1993. pap. 6.00 (*1-56935-017-5*) Phoenix Source.

***Masters, Susan R.** Libby Bloom. LC 94-43898. (Redfeather Bks.). (Illus.). (J). 1995. 14.95 (*0-8050-3374-2*) H Holt & Co.

— Summer Song. LC 94-43684. 1995. 14.95 (*0-395-71127-4*, Clarion Bks) HM.

Masters, T. W. Salon Management: For Hairdressers & Beauty Therapists. 250p. 1987. text ed. 46.95 (*0-291-39709-3*, Pub. by Gower UK) Ashgate Pub Co.

***Masters, Timothy.** Advanced Algorithms for Neural Networks: A C++ Sourcebook. LC 94-43390. 1995. disk, pap. 44.95 (*0-471-10588-0*) Wiley.

— Practical Neural Network Recipes in C Plus Plus. (Illus.). 493p. 1993. disk 44.95 (*0-12-479040-2*) Acad Pr.

— Signal & Image Processing with Neural Networks: C Sourcebook. LC 94-6975. 1994. disk 44.95 (*0-471-04963-8*) Wiley.

Masters, W. Stuart, jt. auth. see Shackell, Dora.

Masters-Wicks, Karen. Victor Hugo's Les Miserables & the Novels of the Groteque Vol. 12. LC 92-25009. (Currents in Comparative Romance Languages & Literatures Ser.: Vol. 12). 248p. (C). 1994. text ed. 45.95 (*0-8204-2000-X*) P Lang Pubs.

Masters, William A. Government & Agriculture in Zimbabwe. LC 93-38884. 256p. 1994. text ed. 59.95 (*0-275-94755-6*, Praeger Pubs) Greenwood.

Masters, William H. & Johnson, L. Murphy. Human Sexuality. 4th ed. LC 94-36210. (C). 1991. text ed. 57.00 (*0-673-46362-1*) HarpCollege.

— Human Sexuality. 4th ed. LC 94-36210. (C). 1991. 22.00 (*0-673-46481-4*) HarpCollege.

Masters, William H. & Johnson, Virginia E. Human Sexual Response. 1966. 48.95 (*0-316-54987-8*) Little.

Masters, William H., et al. Biological Foundations of Human Sexuality. (C). 1993. 20.50 (*0-06-501517-7*) HarpCollege.

— Heterosexuality. LC 92-56197. (Illus.). 688p. 1994. 27.50 (*0-06-019041-8*, A Asher Bks) HarpC.

— Heterosexuality. 608p. 1995. pap. 16.00 (*0-06-092600-7*, PL) HarpC.

— Human Sexuality. 5th ed. LC 94-36210. (C). 1995. text ed. 55.50 (*0-673-46785-6*) HarpCollege.

— Masters & Johnson on Sex & Human Loving. 1988. pap. 19.95 (*0-316-50160-3*) Little.

Masters, Zeke. Ace in the Hole. (Faro Blake Ser.: No. 8). 176p. 1983. pap. 2.25 (*0-671-46485-X*) PB.

***Masterson & Klein.** Psychotherapy of the Disorders if the Self II: The Masterson Approach - Extending the Horizons. 1995. write for info. (*0-87630-786-1*) Brunner-Mazel.

Masterson, A. R. & Dieterich, Lana. Bibliography & Index of Texas Geology, 1981-1985. (Bibliography Ser.). 463p. 1990. 25.00 (*0-317-03129-5*) Bur Econ Geology.

Masterson, Audrey. The Day the Gypsies Came to Town. LC 83-7319. (Heritage Bks.). (Illus.). 32p. (J). (gr. 3-6). 1983. lib. bdg. 14.65 (*0-940742-22-5*) Raintree Steck-V.

Masterson, B. J. Manual of Gynecologic Surgery. 2nd ed. (Comprehensive Manuals of Surgical Specialties Ser.). (Illus.). 379p. 1986. 239.00 (*0-387-96193-3*) Spr-Verlag.

Masterson, B. L., jt. auth. see Moybridge, Eadweard.

Masterson, Dan. Those Who Trespass. LC 84-28075. 78p. 1985. pap. 5.95 (*0-938626-43-4*) U of Ark Pr.

— World Without End. LC 90-10890. 81p. 1991. 16.95 (*1-55728-177-7*); pap. 8.95 (*1-55728-178-5*) U of Ark Pr.

Masterson, Daniel, ed. Naval History: The Sixth Symposium of the U. S. Naval Academy. LC 86-29858. (Illus.). 376p. 1987. 60.00 (*0-8420-2278-3*) Scholarly Res Inc.

Masterson, Daniel M. Militarism & Politics in Latin America: Peru from Sanchez Cerro to Sendero Luminoso. LC 90-23010. (Contributions in Military Studies: No. 111). 360p. 1991. text ed. 65.00 (*0-313-27213-1*, MLM, Greenwood Pr) Greenwood.

Masterson, Dorothy, jt. auth. see Nash, Helen.

Masterson, James & Klein, eds. Disorders of the Self: New Therapeutic Horizons - The Masterson Approach. LC 83-3865. 400p. 1995. 48.95 (*0-87630-334-3*) Brunner-Mazel.

***Masterson, James, et al.** Robotics Technology. (Illus.). 300p. (Orig.). (C). 1995. pap. text ed. write for info. (*1-56637-046-9*) Goodheart.

Masterson, James F. The Emerging Self: A Developmental, Self, & Object Relations Approach to the Treatment of the Closet Narcissistic Disorder of the Self. LC 93-1604. 340p. 1993. 38.95 (*0-87630-721-7*) Brunner-Mazel.

— The Narcissistic & Borderline Disorders: An Integrated Developmental Approach. LC 81-38540. 260p. 1981. 35.95 (*0-87630-292-4*) Brunner-Mazel.

— The Psychiatric Dilemma of Adolescence. LC 83-24039. 232p. 1984. reprint ed. 35.95 (*0-87630-356-4*) Brunner-Mazel.

— Psychotherapy of the Borderline Adult: A Developmental Approach. LC 76-16564. 377p. 1976. 35.95 (*0-87630-127-8*) Brunner-Mazel.

— The Real Self: A Developmental, Self, & Object Relations Approach. LC 85-12824. 192p. 1985. 32.50 (*0-87630-400-5*) Brunner-Mazel.

— The Search for the Real Self: Unmasking the Personality Disorders of Our Age. 288p. 1988. text ed. 29.95 (*0-02-920291-4*) Free Pr.

— Search for the Real Self: Unmasking the Personality Disorders of Our Age. 1990. pap. 10.95 (*0-02-920292-2*) Free Pr.

— Treatment of the Borderline Adolescent: A Developmental Approach. LC 85-4236. 305p. 1985. reprint ed. 35.95 (*0-87630-394-7*) Brunner-Mazel.

Masterson, James F. & Costello, Jacinta L. From Borderline Adolescent to Functioning Adult: The Test of Time. LC 80-14270. 320p. 1980. 35.95 (*0-87630-234-7*) Brunner-Mazel.

Masterson, James F. & Klein, Ralph, eds. Psychotherapy of the Disorders of the Self: The Masterson Approach. LC 88-19341. 480p. 1988. 40.95 (*0-87630-533-8*) Brunner-Mazel.

Masterson, James F., et al. Comparing Psychoanalytic Psychotherapies: Developmental, Self, & Object Relations; Self Psychology; Short-Term Dynamic. LC 91-8288. 312p. 1991. 39.95 (*0-87630-640-7*) Brunner-Mazel.

Masterson, James J., jt. auth. see Gaetano, Ronald J.

Masterson, James R., comp. Writings on American History, 1962-73: A Subject Bibliography of Books & Monographs, 10 Vols. LC 82-49027. 6530p. 1985. lib. bdg. 1,300.00 (*0-527-98268-7*) Kraus Intl.

Masterson, James R. & Eberly, Joyce E., comps. Writings on American History: 1961, 2 vols., Set. LC 75-22257. (Writings on American History Ser.). 1978. lib. bdg. 65.00 (*0-527-98252-0*) Kraus Intl.

Masterson, Jane. Photographic Album of the Royal Family. 1991. 14.99 (*0-517-06607-6*) Random Hse Value.

***Masterson, John P. & Barlow, Paul M.** Effects of Simulated Ground-Water Pumping & Recharge on Ground-Water Flow in Cape Cod, Martha's Vineyard, & Nantucket Island Basins, Massaachusetts. LC 95-9823. (Water Supply Papers: Vol. 2447). Date not set. write for info. (*0-615-00643-4*) US Geol Survey.

Masterson, John T., jt. auth. see Beebe, Steven A.

Masterson, John T., et al. Invitation to Effective Speech Communication. (C). 1988. pap. text ed. 32.50 (*0-673-18565-6*) HarpCollege.

***Masterson, Josephine.** County Cork, Ireland, a Collection of 1851 Census Records. 117p. 1994. pap. 17.50 (*0-614-00923-5*, 9488) Clearfield Co.

Masterson, Karen A. Total Health: Designed for the HIV Challenged Individual. LC 91-66084. 156p. 1991. spiral bd. 29.95 (*0-942259-04-1*) Westerfield Enter.

Masterson, Linda. Summerhaven. (Illus.). 1979. pap. 1.95 (*0-89083-471-7*) Zebra.

Masterson, Marth G. One Woman's West: Recollections of the Oregon Trail & Settling the Northwest Country. 2nd rev. ed. Barton, Lois, ed. (Illus.). 222p. (Orig.). 1989. pap. 9.95 (*0-317-99836-6*) S Butte Pr.

Masterson, Michael. DBase Language Reference with Annotations. 1993. pap. 40.00 (*0-679-79173-6*) Random.

— FoxFASE Plus Simplified: Macintosh Edition. (Illus.). 480p. (Orig.). 1989. pap. 27.95 (*0-8306-3187-9*, Windcrest) TAB Bks.

— FoxPro Mac Handbook. (Illus.). 544p. 1993. pap. 26.95 (*0-8306-3856-3*, 4128, Windcrest) TAB Bks.

Masterson, Michael & Patterson, James. Mastering FoxPro 2.0. (Illus.). 400p. 1993. pap. 24.95 (*0-8306-4078-9*, 4203, Windcrest) TAB Bks.

Masterson, Michael P. FoxBase Plus Simplified: Macintosh. 1990. pap. text ed. 27.95 (*0-07-156554-X*) McGraw.

***Masterson, Patrick.** Port Orford, a History. (Illus.). 380p. 1994. 29.95 (*1-885221-08-8*) BookPartners.

Masterson, Thomas M. The Housestaff Book of Forms. 50p. (Orig.). (C). 1993. pap. text ed. 7.50 (*0-9634063-7-X*) Intl Med Pub.

— The Intern Pocket Admission Book. 78p. 1993. pap. text ed. 4.00 (*0-9634063-4-5*) Intl Med Pub.

— The Intern Pocket Survival Guide. 78p. (Orig.). (C). 1992. pap. text ed. 6.00 (*0-9634063-0-2*) Intl Med Pub.

— Owner's Manual: Young Adult. 50p. (Orig.). (C). Date not set. pap. text ed. 6.00 (*1-883205-01-8*) Intl Med Pub.

Masterson, Thomas M. & Rothenhaus, Todd C. The CCU Intern Pocket Survival Guide. 2nd ed. 78p. 1992. pap. text ed. 6.00 (*0-9634063-1-0*) Intl Med Pub.

— The ICU Intern Pocket Survival Guide. 78p. (Orig.). (C). 1992. pap. text ed. 6.00 (*0-9634063-3-7*) Intl Med Pub.

Masterson, Thomas M., jt. auth. see Rothenhaus, Todd C.

Masterson, Thomas M., jt. auth. see Tenner, Scott M.

Masterson, Thomas M., et al. The EKG Pocket Survival Guide. (Illus.). 54p. (Orig.). (C). 1993. pap. text ed. 6.00 (*0-9634063-8-8*) Intl Med Pub.

Masterson, Thomas R. & Nunan, J. Carlton. Ethics in Business. 240p. 1969. text ed. 18.50 (*0-8290-0288-X*) Irvington.

Masterson, V. V. The Katy Railroad & the Last Frontier. LC 87-19146. (Illus.). 354p. 1988. reprint ed. pap. 15.95 (*0-8262-0668-9*) U of Mo Pr.

Masterson, Whit. Touch of Evil. (Mystery Scene Book Ser.). 176p. 1992. pap. 3.95 (*0-88184-886-7*) Carroll & Graf.

Masterson, William B. Famous Gunfighters of the Western Frontier. Jones, William R., ed. (Illus.). 1978. reprint ed. pap. 5.95 (*0-89646-051-7*) Vistabooks.

Masterson, William H. William Blount. LC 79-88904. 378p. 1970. reprint ed. text ed. 59.75 (*0-8371-2308-9*, MABL, Greenwood Pr) Greenwood.

Masterton, Barbara. Island of Glass. large type ed. 448p. 1987. 16.95 (*0-7089-1644-9*) Ulverscroft.

— Late Harvest. large type ed. 384p. 1989. 17.95 (*0-7089-2043-8*) Ulverscroft.

— Orbs of Jade. large type ed. 1991. 21.95 (*0-7089-2372-0*) Ulverscroft.

Masterton, David S. Get Out of My Face. LC 90-24096. 160p. (J). (gr. 5-9). 1991. text ed. 13.95 (*0-689-31675-5*, Atheneum Bks Young) S&S Childrens.

Masterton, Graham. Burial. 384p. 1994. 22.95 (*0-312-85681-4*) Tor Bks.

— Burial. 1996. mass mkt. 4.99 (*0-614-05520-2*) Tor Bks.

— Drive Him Wild: The Ultimate Guide to Pleasing Your Man in Bed. 224p. (Orig.). 1993. pap. 5.99 (*0-451-17591-3*, Sig) NAL-Dutton.

— Feast. 1988. mass mkt. 4.50 (*1-55817-103-7*, Pinnacle NY) Windsor NY.

— Fortnight of Fear. 1994. lib. bdg. 22.00 (*0-7278-4438-5*) Severn Hse.

— How to Drive Women Wild in Bed. 1987. pap. 4.50 (*0-451-14781-2*, Sig) NAL-Dutton.

— How to Drive Your Man Even Wilder in Bed. 224p. (Orig.). 1995. mass mkt. 5.99 (*0-451-18151-4*, Sig) NAL-Dutton.

— How to Drive Your Man Wild in Bed. 224p. 1976. pap. 5.99 (*0-451-15277-8*, Sig) NAL-Dutton.

— How to Make Love Six Nights a Week. 224p. (Orig.). 1991. pap. 5.99 (*0-451-16941-7*, Sig) NAL-Dutton.

— Maiden Voyage. 1985. pap. 106.65 (*0-312-90226-3*) St Martin.

— Master of Lies. 336p. 1995. mass mkt. 4.99 (*0-8125-1166-2*) Tor Bks.

— More Ways to Drive Your Man Wild in Bed. 1985. pap. 5.99 (*0-451-16174-2*, Sig) NAL-Dutton.

— Night Plague. 1991. mass mkt. 4.50 (*0-8125-2204-4*) Tor Bks.

— Sex Secrets of Other Women. 1989. pap. 5.99 (*0-451-16227-7*, Sig) NAL-Dutton.

— Single, Wild, Sexy...& Safe. 256p. (Orig.). 1994. pap. 5.99 (*0-451-17364-3*, Sig) NAL-Dutton.

— The Sweetman Curve. 1991. reprint ed. 18.95 (*0-7278-4097-5*) Severn Hse.

— Wells of Hell. 320p. 1990. pap. 3.95 (*0-8125-2211-7*) Tor Bks.

— Wild in Bed Together. 256p. (Orig.). 1992. pap. 5.99 (*0-451-17212-4*, Sig) NAL-Dutton.

Masterton, Jack. Prayers for Use in Church. 152p. 1993. pap. 24.00 (*0-7152-0680-X*, Pub. by St Andrew UK) St Mut.

Masterton, Murray & Patching, Roger. Now the News in Detail. 2nd ed. 293p. (C). 1991. pap. 77.00x (*0-7300-1441-X*, Pub. by Deakin Univ AT) St Mut.

Masterton, R. B., jt. ed. see Syka, J.

Masterton, T. H., ed. Worldscapes. 2nd ed. 1987. pap. text ed. 13.05 (*0-05-004028-6*, 70094) Longman.

Masterton, William L. & Cherim, Stanley M. Introduction to Chemistry. LC 83-17244. 480p. (C). 1984. text ed. 47.00 (*0-03-059676-9*); student ed, pap. text ed. 28.50 (*0-03-069571-6*) SCP.

Masterton, William L. & Hurley, Cecile N. Chemistry: Principles & Reactions. 960p. (C). 1989. text ed. 61.25 (*0-03-013643-1*) SCP.

Masterton, William L. & Slowinski, Emil J. Mathematical Preparation for General Chemistry. 2nd ed. 260p. (C). 1982. pap. text ed. 21.50 (*0-03-060119-3*) SCP.

Masterton, William L., jt. auth. see Slowinski, Emil J.

Masterton, William L., et al. Chemical Principles, with Qualitative Analysis. 6th ed. 1168p. (C). 1986. student ed 17.50 (*0-685-43634-9*); teacher ed, pap. text ed. 14.00 (*0-03-008589-6*) SCP.

Masthay, Carl. Schmick's Mahican Dictionary. LC 86-90530. (Memoirs Ser.: Vol. 197). 188p. (C). 1992. 30.00 (*0-87169-197-3*, M197-MAC) Am Philos.

Mastice, Marjorie M., jt. ed. see Kopes, Jerome T.

Mastidoro, Maria R. Concordanza Dei Carmina Latina Epigraphica: Compresi Nella Silloge Di J. W. Zarker. (Classical & Byzantine Monographs: No. xxi). xxxi, 259p. (ITA.). 1991. pap. 46.00 (*90-256-1007-2*, Pub. by A M Hakkert SP) Benjamins North Am.

Mastin, Bettye L. Lexington Seventeen Seventy-Nine. LC 79-90522. 137p. 1979. 12.50 (*0-912839-00-7*) Lexington-Fayette.

Mastin, Emma D., ed. Daviess County, KY Marriages, 1815-1865: From Marriage in the Davies Co Courthouse. 268p. 22.00 (*0-318-24039-4*) West Cent KY Family Re Assoc.

Mastin, Emma Dunn, ed. Daviess County, KY, Marriages, 1815-1865. 268p. 1988. 22.00 (*0-318-23372-X*) West Cent KY Family Re Assoc.

Mastin, Fred & Miller, John G. Punching Out: Launching a Post-Military Career. 208p. 1994. 22.00 (*0-312-10527-4*) St Martin.

Mastin, Robert. Nine Hundred Know-How: How to Succeed with Your Own 900 Number Business. 2nd rev. ed. LC 93-74809. 336p. (Orig.). 1994. pap. 19.95 (*0-9632790-6-8*) Aegis Pub Grp.

Mastin, Robert, jt. auth. see Ginsburg, Carol M.

Mastini, Frank. Ship Modeling Simplified: Tips & Techniques for Model Construction from Kits. 1990. pap. text ed. 17.95 (*0-87742-272-9*) Intl Marine.

— Ship Modeling Simplified: Tips & Techniques for Model Construction from Kits. 1990. pap. text ed. 17.95 (*0-07-155867-5*) McGraw.

***Mastny, ed.** Turkey & Europe: Perspective. (C). 1995. text ed. 58.95 (*0-8133-2420-3*) Westview.

Mastny, Vojtech. Czechoslovakia: Crisis in World Communism. LC 70-166437. (Interim History Ser.). 400p. reprint ed. pap. 114.00 (*0-317-20498-X*, 2022915) Bks Demand.

— The Helsinki Process & the Reintegration of Europe: Analysis & Documentation, 1986-1990. 380p. (C). 1992. text ed. 65.00 (*0-8147-5476-7*); pap. text ed. 25.00 (*0-8147-5477-5*) NYU Pr.

— Italy & East-Central Europe: Dimensions of the Regional Relationship. LC 94-24013. 131p. (C). 1995. text ed. 44.95 (*0-8133-8885-6*) Westview.

— Russia's Road to the Cold War: Diplomacy, Strategy, & the Politics of Communism, 1941-1945. LC 78-13433. 384p. 1980. text ed. 50.50 (*0-231-04360-0*); pap. text ed. 19.50 (*0-231-04361-9*) Col U Pr.

Mastny, Vojtech, ed. Disarmament & Nuclear Tests, 1964-69. LC 72-122210. (Interim History Ser.). 264p. reprint ed. pap. 75.30 (*0-317-20496-3*, 2022917) Bks Demand.

— Helsinki, Human Rights, & European Security: Analysis & Documentation. LC 86-13560. xvi, 389p. 1986. text ed. 52.50 (*0-8223-0682-4*); pap. text ed. 26.95 (*0-8223-0763-4*) Duke.

— Power & Policy in Transition: Essays Presented on the Tenth Anniversary of the National Committee on American Foreign Policy in Honor of Its Founder, Hans J. Morgenthau. LC 84-15778. (Contributions in Political Science Ser.: No. 126). (Illus.). ix, 271p. 1985. text ed. 59.95 (*0-313-24498-7*, MAY/) Greenwood.

— Soviet-East European Survey, 1983-1984: Selected Research & Analysis from Radio Free Europe - Radio Liberty. LC 85-10281. (Duke Press Policy Studies). xvi, 436p. (C). 1985. 52.50 (*0-8223-0643-3*); pap. 26.95 (*0-8223-0650-6*) Duke.

— Soviet-East European Survey, 1984-1985: Selected Research & Analysis from Radio Free Europe-Radio Liberty. LC 85-10281. xii, 400p. (Orig.). 1986. text ed. 62.50 (*0-8223-0656-5*); pap. text ed. 26.95 (*0-8223-0699-9*) Duke.

— Soviet-East European Survey, 1985-1986: Selected Research & Analysis from Radio Free Europe-Radio Liberty. LC 85-10281. x, 451p. (C). 1987. 55.50 (*0-8223-0721-9*) Duke.

Mastny, Vojtech & Zielonka, Jan, eds. Human Rights & Security: Europe on the Eve of a New Era. 274p. 1991. text ed. 61.00 (*0-8133-8082-0*) Westview.

Maston, T. B. Biblical Ethics--A Survey: A Guide to the Ethical Message of the Scriptures from Genesis Through Revelation. LC 82-6470. 320p. 1982. pap. 14.95 (*0-86554-312-7*, P56) Mercer Univ Pr.

— Como Vivir en el Mundo de Hoy. Adams, Bob, tr. 110p. (SPA.). 1987. pap. 4.65 (*0-311-46084-4*) Casa Bautista.

— Consejos a la Juventud. Duffer, H. F., Jr., tr. Orig. Title: Advice to Youth. 60p. (SPA.). 1990. reprint ed. pap. 2.25 (*0-311-46005-4*) Casa Bautista.

— The Ethic of the Christian Life. Hogg, Gayle, ed. (Religious Education Ser.). 152p. (C). 1982. kivar 12.50 (*0-311-72605-4*) Casa Bautista.

— Etica de la Vida Cristiana Sus Principios Basicos. Ureta, Floreal, tr. 200p. (SPA.). 1987. reprint ed. pap. 5.50 (*0-311-46076-3*) Casa Bautista.

Mastrangelo, Judy. What Do Bunnies Do All Day? (Illus.). 32p. (J). (ps-1). 1991. per. 4.95 (*0-8249-8509-5*, Ideals Child) Hambleton-Hill.

Mastrangelo, Judy, illus. The Sandman: And Other Sleepy-Time Rhymes. LC 90-34513. (Through the Magic Window Ser.). 48p. (J). (ps-2). 1990. 4.95 (*0-88101-105-3*) Unicorn Pub.

Mastrangelo, R., ed. Central Nervous System Leukemia Prevention & Treatment. (Developments in Oncology Ser.). 1983. lib. bdg. 84.00 (*0-89838-570-9*) Kluwer Ac.

Mastrantonio, J. Louise, jt. ed. see Alden, John.

Mastrantonis, George. Augsburg & Constantinople: The Correspondence Between Patriarch Jeremiah II & the Tubingen Theologians. 424p. 1981. 22.95 (*0-916586-81-2*); pap. 14.95 (*0-916586-82-0*) Hellenic Coll Pr.

***Mastretta.** Arrancame la Vida: Mexican Bolero. 1995. pap. 14.95 (*0-679-76100-4*, Vin) Random.

Mastrianna, Frank & Hailstones, Thomas. Basic Economics. 10th ed. LC 94-13025. 1995. text ed. 41.95 (*0-538-84204-0*) S-W Pub.

Mastrianna, Frank V., jt. auth. see Hailstones, Thomas J.

Mastrianni, Steven J. Writing OS - 2 2.1 Device Drivers in Ck. 2nd ed. LC 93-2264. (OS-2 Ser.). 1993. pap. 39.95 (*0-442-01729-4*) Van Nos Reinhold.

Mastrich, James L. & Birnes, William J. Strong Enough for Two. 256p. 1989. pap. 10.95 (*0-02-040581-2*, Pub. by Gebrueder Borntraeger GW) Macmillan.

— Strong Enough for Two. 256p. 1991. pap. 9.95 (*0-02-034520-8*, Collier S&S) S&S Trade.

Mastro, Jim, jt. auth. see Westheimer, Patricia H.

Mastro, Joseph P. U. S. S. R. Calendar of Events Annual, 1987-1991. 72.00 (*0-685-27034-3*) Academic Intl.

— U. S. S. R. Calendar of Events Annual, 1987-1991, 5 vols., Set. 375.00 (*0-87569-113-7*) Academic Intl.

Mastrobuono, Antonio C. Dante's Journey of Sanctification. LC 90-35108. 260p. 1990. pap. 14.95 (0-89526-741-1) Regnery Pub.

Mastrofski, Stephen, jt. auth. see Klockars, Carl B.

Mastrofski, Stephen D., jt. ed. see Greene, Jack R.

Mastrogiannopoulos, Elias. The Byzantine Churches of Greece & Cyprus. 136p. 1984. 16.00 (0-917651-06-5); pap. 10.00 (0-917651-07-3) Holy Cross Orthodox.

***Mastrogiovanni, John L.** The Spirit of the Scorpion: Conquering the Power of Insurrection. 78p. (Orig.). 1995. pap. write for info. (1-885591-53-5) Morris Pubng.

Mastroianni, Anna C., ed. see Committee on the Ethical & Legal Issues Relating to the Inclusion of Women in Clinical Studies Staff.

Mastroianni, L., Jr., et al, eds. Gamete & Embryo Quality: The Proceedings of the Fourth Organon Round Table Conference, Thessaloniki, Greece, 24-25 June 1993. LC 93-40905. 1993. 98.00 (1-85070-543-7) Prthnon Pub.

Mastroianni, Luigi, Jr., et al, eds. Fertilization & Embryonic Development In Vitro. LC 81-13829. 382p. 1981. 85.00 (0-306-40783-3, Plenum Pr) Plenum.

Mastroianni, Luigi, Jr. & Paulsen, C. Alvin, eds. Aging, Reproduction, & the Climacteric. LC 85-28299. 332p. 1986. 69.50 (0-306-42142-9, Plenum Pr) Plenum.

Mastroianni, M. J., jt. auth. see Allied Chemical Corporation Staff.

***Mastroianni, Michael D. & Dasenbrook, Norman C.** Harnessing the Power of Conflict: Optimum Group Performance Through the Self Mediation Method. 170p. (Orig.). 1994. pap. text ed. 9.95 (0-9643949-0-1) Crysand Pr.

Mastrolorenzo, G., jt. auth. see Dvorak, J. J.

Mastromarco, G. The Public of Herondas. (London Studies of Classical Philology: Vol. 11). xiii, 122p. 1984. text ed. 35.00 (90-70265-94-X, Pub. by Gieben NE) Benjamins North Am.

Mastromarino, Anthony J., ed. Biology & Treatment of Colorectal Cancer Metastasis. (Developments in Oncology Ser.). 1986. lib. bdg. 80.50 (0-89838-786-8) Kluwer Ac.

Mastromarino, Anthony J. & Brattain, Michael G., eds. Large Bowel Cancer: Clinical & Basic Science Research. LC 84-15975. (Cancer Research Monographs: Vol. 3). 204p. 1985. text ed. 55.00 (0-275-91319-8, C1319, Praeger Pubs) Greenwood.

Mastromarino, Anthony J., jt. ed. see Wolman, Sandra R.

***Mastronarde, Donald.** Introduction to Attic Greek. LC 92-21731. 1995. 29.95 (0-520-20281-3) U CA Pr.

***Mastronarde, Donald J.** Contact & Discontinuity: Some Conventions of Speech & Action on the Greek Tragic Stage. LC 78-62877. (University of California Publications: No. 21). 153p. 1979. pap. 43.70 (0-7837-7491-5, 2049213) Bks Demand.

— Euripides: "Phoenissae" LC 93-3247. (Classical Texts & Commentaries Ser.: No. 29). (Illus.). 652p. (C). 1994. 90.00 (0-521-41071-1) Cambridge U Pr.

— Introduction to Attic Greek. LC 92-21731. (C). 1993. 35.00 (0-520-07843-8); pap. 17.00 (0-520-07844-6) U CA Pr.

Mastronarde, Donald J. & Bremer, Jan M. The Textual Tradition of Euripides' "Phoinissai" LC 82-13492. (UC Publications in Classical Studies: Vol. 27). 464p. (C). 1983. pap. 42.00 (0-520-09664-9) U CA Pr.

Mastronardi, G., ed. Mini & Microcomputers & Their Applications - MIMI '84: Proceedings, ISMM Symposium, Bari, Italy, June 5-8, 1984. 289p. 1984. 85.00 (0-88986-058-0, 065) Acta Pr.

Mastroni, Nick, jt. auth. see Pelz, Dave.

Mastronikola, Katerina. Yield Curves for Gilt-Edged Stocks: A New Model. (Bank of England. Discussion Papers. Technical Ser.: No. 49). 40p. reprint ed. pap. 25.00 (0-7837-3208-2, 2043204) Bks Demand.

Mastropasqua, S. The Banking System in the Countries of the EEC: Institutional & Structural Aspects. 170p. 1978. lib. bdg. 48.00 (90-286-0518-5) Kluwer Ac.

Mastropasqua, V. Dizionario Tecnico Nautico: Italiano-Inglese, Inglese-Italiano. 879p. (ENG & ITA.). 1967. pap. 75.00 (0-8288-6683-X, M-9297) Fr & Eur.

Mastropieri, Margo, jt. auth. see Scruggs, Thomas.

Mastropieri, Margo A. & Scruggs, Thomas E. Effective Instruction for Special Education. LC 90-34239. 419p. (Orig.). (C). 1987. pap. text ed. 34.00 (0-89079-368-9, 1736) PRO-ED.

— Effective Instruction for Special Education. 2nd ed. LC 93-41947. (Illus.). (Orig.). (C). 1994. pap. text ed. 35.00 (0-89079-572-X, 6694) PRO-ED.

— Guidelines for Effective Mainstreaming in Science. (Illus.). 371p. (C). 1994. pap. text ed. 29.00 (0-89079-611-4, 6817) PRO-ED.

— Teaching Students Ways to Remember: Strategies for Learning Mnemonically. 132p. 1990. pap. text ed. 21.95 (0-914797-67-0) Brookline Bks.

Mastrosimone, William. Burning Desire: A Play in Three Acts. 256p. Date not set. pap. 11.95 (1-880399-54-7) Smith & Kraus.

— William Mastrosimone: Collected Plays. (Plays for Actors Ser.). 360p. 1994. pap. 14.95 (1-880399-32-6) Smith & Kraus.

Masuba, Koh. Kenkyusha New Japanese-English Dictionary. 2119p. 1990. 495.00 (0-317-59317-X, Pub. by Collets UK) Pro-Am Music.

Masubuchi, M., jt. ed. see Broadbent, D. T.

Masuccio, et al. Romeo & Juliet - Original Text of Masuccio, Da Porto, Bandello, Shakespeare. Pinkerton, Percy & Jonas, Maurice, trs. 212p. 1992. 19.95 (0-937832-32-4) Dante U Am.

Masuch, Michael, ed. Organization, Management, & Expert Systems: Models of Automated Reasoning. (Studies in Organization: No. 23). x, 249p. (C). 1990. lib. bdg. 52.95 (3-11-011942-0) De Gruyter.

Masuch, Michael & Polos, Laszlo, eds. Knowledge Representation & Reasoning under Uncertainty: Logic at Work. LC 94-20068. 1994. 37.00 (0-387-58095-6) Spr-Verlag.

Masuch, Michael, jt. ed. see Polos, Laszlo.

Mas'Ud Ibn Umar Al-Taftazani. A Commentary on the Creed of Islam. LC 79-52565. (Islam Ser.). 1980. reprint ed. lib. bdg. 23.95 (0-8369-9268-7) Ayer.

Masud, M., jt. auth. see Khan, R.

Masud, Muhammad K. Islamic Legal Philosophy. 25.50 (1-56744-100-9) Kazi Pubns.

Masud, Muhammad K. & Liaqat, M. Muntaz, eds. Iqbal Through Western Eyes. 320p. 1993. text ed. 35.00 (81-207-0891-1, Pub. by Sterling Pubs II) Apt Bks.

Masud-Piloto, Felix. With Open Arms: Cuban Migration to the United States. LC 87-12809. 168p. 1988. 44.50 (0-8476-7566-1, R7566) Rowman.

***Masud-Piloto, Felix R.** With Open Arms: Cuban Migration to the United States. rev. ed. 200p. (C). 1995. lib. bdg. 49.50 (0-8476-8037-1) Rowman.

— With Open Arms: Cuban Migration to the United States. rev. ed. 200p. (C). 1995. pap. text ed. 19.95 (0-8476-8038-X) Rowman.

***Masuda.** Kenkyusha's New Pocket Japanese-English Dictionary. Date not set. 65.00 (0-7859-7130-0, F100790) Fr & Eur.

Masuda, Akiko. The Adventures of Kalakoa: A Hawaiian Rainbow Fantasy. (Illus.). 32p. (J). (gr. k-7). 1991. 7.95 (0-9629842-1-3) Stew & Rice.

Masuda, H., et al, eds. The Fishes of the Japanese Archipelago, 2 vols., Set. (Illus.). 842p. 1987. 325.00 (4-486-05054-1) OUP.

Masuda, Jiryo, tr. see Vasu-Mitra.

Masuda, K. & Mimura, M., eds. Recent Topics in Nonlinear PDE II. (North-Holland Mathematics Studies, No. 128; Lecture Notes in Numerical & Applied Analysis, No. 8). 228p. 1987. pap. 95.00 (0-444-87938-2, North Holland) Elsevier.

Masuda, K. & Suzuki, T., eds. Recent Topics in Nonlinear PDE III, Vol. 9. (Mathematics Studies: Lecture Notes in Numerical Applied Analysis: Vol. 148). 266p. 1988. pap. 107.75 (0-444-70317-9, North Holland) Elsevier.

Masuda, M. Dictionary of Marine Engineering Terms. 318p. (ENG & JPN.). 1980. 125.00 (0-8288-0420-6, M9339) Fr & Eur.

Masuda, S. & Takahashi, Koichiro, eds. Aerosols: Science, Industry, Health & Environment: Proceedings of the Third International Aerosol Conference, Kyoto, Japan, 24-27 September 1990, 2 vols., Set. (Illus.). 1388p. 1990. pap. 55.25 (0-08-037525-1, Pergamon Pr) Elsevier.

Masuda, Takashi, photos. The Design Heritage of Noren: Traditional Japanese Storefront Art. LC 88-80145. (Illus.). 200p. 1989. 55.00 (0-87040-770-8) Japan Pubns USA.

Masuda, Yoneji. The Information Society As Post-Industrial Society. 178p. (C). 1980. pap. 16.95 (0-930242-15-7) World Future.

Masuda, Yoshio, et al. Analytical Studies on Growing Plant Cell Walls. 50p. 1983. 5.00 (1-55528-084-6, Pub. by Today & Tomorrows P & P II) Scholarly Pubns.

Masuda, Yuji & Gill, K. S., eds. Human Centred Systems in the Global Economy: Proceedings from the International Workshop on Industrial Cultures & Human Centred Systems, Held by Tokyo Keizai University in Tokyo, May 1990. LC 92-10114. (Artificial Intelligence & Society Ser.). (Illus.). 272p. 1992. 69.00 (3-540-19745-1); 69.00 (0-387-19745-1) Spr-Verlag.

Masudi. The Meadows of Gold. Lunde, Paul & Stone, Catherine, trs. 320p. 1987. 65.00 (0-7103-0246-0, A0086, Routledge NY) Routledge Chapman & Hall.

***Masudi, H., ed.** Tribology Symposium: The Energy & Environmental Expo '95 - The Energy-Sources Technology Conference & Exhibition, Houston, Texas - January 29-February 1, 1995. (PD Ser.: Vol. 72). 184p. 1995. 86.00 (0-7918-1297-9, H00929) ASME.

— Tribology Symposium, 1994, Vol. 61. LC 93-74682. 140p. 1994. pap. 37.50 (0-7918-1189-1) ASME.

Masugi, Ken, ed. Interpreting Tocqueville's "Democracy in America" 548p. (C). 1991. pap. text ed. 29.50 (0-8476-7712-5) B&N Imports.

***Masugi, Ken & Hiraoka, Leona.** Japanese-American Internment: The Bill of Rights in Crisis. 1993. 29.95 (1-56696-004-5); student ed 37.00 (0-614-07314-6) Golden Owl NY.

Masuhara, Hiroshi, ed. see JRDC-KUL Joint International Symposium on "Spectroscopy & Chemistry in SmAll Domains" Staff, et al.

Masui, Mitsuko. Pandas of the World. Ooka, Diane, tr. (Illus.). 32p. (J). (gr. k-2). 1989. 11.95 (0-89346-314-0) Heian Intl.

Masuko, Noboru, et al, eds. New Trends & Approaches in Electrochemical Technology. LC 92-46440. 1993. 120.00 (1-56081-781-X) VCH Pubs.

Masulis, Ronald W. The Debt-Equity Choice. (Financial Management Survey & Synthesis Ser.). 1988. 34.95 (0-317-01474-9); pap. 24.95 (0-317-01475-7) Finan Mgmt Assn.

Masulli, F. & Morasso, P. G. Neural Networks in Biomedicine: Proceedings of the Course. 300p. 1994. text ed. 91.00 (981-02-1744-7) World Scientific Pub.

***Masumi, Junnosuke.** Contemporary Politics in Japan. Carlile, Lonny E., tr. LC 94-23660. 1995. 65.00 (0-520-05853-4); pap. 25.00 (0-520-05854-2) U CA Pr.

Masumi, Junnosuke, jt. auth. see Scalapino, Robert A.

Ma'sumi, M. H. Imam Razi's Ilm-al-Ikhlaq. 18.50 (1-56744-054-1) Kazi Pubns.

***Masumian, Farnaz.** Life after Death in World Religions. 1995. pap. 14.95 (1-85168-074-8) Onewrld Pubns.

Masumoto. Epitaph for a Peach: Four Seasons on My Family Farm. Date not set. pap. 12.00 (0-06-251025-8, PL) HarpC.

Masumoto, David M. Country Voices, the Oral History of a Japanese American Family Farm Community. LC 87-3126. (Illus.). 256p. (Orig.). 1987. pap. 14.95 (0-9614541-0-5) Inaka-Countryside Pubns.

— Silent Strength. 90p. (Orig.). 1985. pap. 5.95 (0-9614541-1-3, Pub. by New Currents Intl JA) Inaka-Countryside Pubns.

Masunaga, Reiho, tr. see Dogen.

Masunaga, Shizuto & Brown, Stephen. Zen Imagery Exercises: Meridian Exercises for Wholesome Living. LC 86-80220. (Illus.). 192p. (Orig.). 1987. pap. 15.95 (0-87040-669-8) Japan Pubns USA.

Masunaga, Shizuto & Ohashi, Wataru. Zen Shiatsu: How to Harmonize Yin & Yang for Better Health. (Illus.). 176p. 1977. pap. 18.00 (0-87040-394-X) Japan Pubns USA.

Masunaga, Yoshifumi, ed. see International Conference on Database Systems for Advanced Applications Staff.

Masuoka, Jitsuichi & Valien, P., eds. Race Relations. (New Reprints in Essay & General Literature Index Ser.). 1977. reprint ed. 26.95 (0-518-10205-X, 10205) Ayer.

***Masuoka, Susan N.** En Calavera: The Papier-Mache Art of the Linares Family. LC 94-36635. 1994. 40.00 (0-930741-40-4); pap. 27.00 (0-930741-41-2) UCLA Fowler Mus.

Masuol, M. & Kahn, R. The Long Wait & Other Psychoanalytic Narratives. 224p. 1989. 18.95 (0-685-22261-6) Summit Bks.

Masur, Gerhard. Imperial Berlin. (Reprints Ser.). (Illus.). 353p. 1990. reprint ed. 19.95 (0-88029-407-8) Dorset Pr.

Masur, Louis P. Rites of Execution: Capital Punishment & the Transformation of American Culture, 1776-1865. 224p. 1989. 42.00 (0-19-504899-7) OUP.

— Rites of Execution: Capital Punishment & the Transformation of America Culture, 1776-1865. (Illus.). 224p. 1991. reprint ed. pap. 15.95 (0-19-506663-4) OUP.

Masur, Louis P., ed. Heart-Shaped Leaves: American Writers During the Civil War. LC 92-24446. 1993. 25.00 (0-19-506868-8) OUP.

— The Real War Will Never Get in the Book: Selections from Writers During the Civil War. (Illus.). 320p. 1995. pap. 13.95 (0-19-509837-4) OUP.

Masur, Louis P., intro. The Autobiography of Benjamin Franklin. LC 92-72223. (Bedford Books in American History Ser.). 192p. (C). 1993. pap. text ed. 5.00 (0-312-08446-3, Bedford Bks) St Martin.

— The Autobiography of Benjamin Franklin. LC 92-72223. (Bedford Books in American History Ser.). 192p. (C). 1993. text ed. 35.00 (0-312-09665-8, Bedford Bks) St Martin.

***Masure, Bruno.** Dictionnaire Analphabetique. 202p. (FRE.). 1990. pap. 29.95 (0-7859-8102-0, 2855655986) Fr & Eur.

Masure, M. T. Eight Commandments for Political Reform: Power in the Elective Process. Goldstein, Wallace L., ed. (Illus.). 80p. (Orig.). 1993. pap. text ed. 10.00 (1-880836-02-5) Pine Isl Pr.

— Eight Commandments for Political Reform: Power in the Elective Process. 2nd ed. Goldstein, Wallace L. & Alward, Edgar C., eds. (Illus.). 80p. (Orig.). (YA). 1994. text ed. 11.00 (1-880836-05-X) Pine Isl Pr.

Masurel, Claire. Good Night! LC 93-30198. (Illus.). (J). 1994. 12.95 (0-8118-0644-8) Chronicle Bks.

Masurel, Edouard. L' Annee dans le Monde, 1990. (FRE.). 1991. pap. 11.95 (0-7859-3974-1) Fr & Eur.

Masuren-Matthies. Kunst Lerische Photographie. Sobieszek, Robert A. & Bunnell, Peter C., eds. LC 76-24675. (Sources of Modern Photography Ser.). (Illus.). (GER.). 1979. reprint ed. lib. bdg. 12.95 (0-405-09651-8) Ayer.

Masuya, Tomoko, jt. auth. see Carboni, Stefano.

Masuzawa, Tomoko. In Search of Dreamtime: The Quest for the Origin of Religion. LC 93-518. (Religion & Postmodernism Ser.). 264p. 1993. lib. bdg. 45.00 (0-226-50984-2); pap. text ed. 14.95 (0-226-50985-0) U Ch Pr.

***Maswell, et al.** Party Cakes. (Illus.). 96p. 1995. 12.98 (0-8317-6857-6) Smithmark.

Maswood, S. Javed. Japanese Defence: The Search for Political Power. 113p. 1990. pap. text ed. 16.00 (981-3035-39-0, Pub. by Inst SE Asian Studies SI) Ashgate Pub Co.

Maswood, Syed J. Japan & Protection: The Growth of Protectionist Sentiment & the Japanese Response. (Nissan Institute Japanese Studies). 224p. 1989. 57.95 (0-415-01030-6) Routledge.

Masyr, Caryl & Freifeld, Roberta. Space Planning in the Special Library. 1991. 41.00 (0-87111-356-2) SLA.

Maszynska, Maria, ed. see Szmielev, Wanda.

Mata, Alix. An English Odyssey. 1993. pap. 5.95 (1-56201-052-2) Blue Moon Bks.

Mata, Daya. Finding the Joy Within You. LC 90-63632. (Illus.). 336p. 1990. 10.00 (0-87612-288-8) Self Realization.

— Only Love. LC 75-44633. (Illus.). 295p. 1976. 9.00 (0-87612-215-2); pap. 14.00 (88-340-1025-6) Self Realization.

Mataga, Noboru & Kubota, Tanekazu. Molecular Interactions & Electronic Spectra. LC 71-107755. 520p. reprint ed. pap. 148.20 (0-685-15921-3, 2027821) Bks Demand.

Mataga, Noboru, et al, eds. Dynamics & Mechanisms of Photoinduced Electron Transfer & Related Phenomena: Proceedings of the Yamada Conference, XXIX, on Dynamics & Mechanisms of Photoinduced Electron Transfer & Related Phenomena, Senri, Osaka, Japan, May 12-16, 1991. LC 92-10487. (North-Holland Delta Ser.). 1992. write for info. (0-444-89191-9, North Holland) Elsevier.

Matahhari, Murtaza. Iqbal: Manifestation of the Islamic Spirit. Bakhtiar, Laleh, tr. 130p. (C). 1993. pap. 12.50 (1-871031-20-6) Abjad Bk.

Mataix Lord, Mariano. Diccionario de Electronica, Informatica y Centrales Nucleares. 660p. (ENG & SPA.). 1978. 175.00 (0-8288-4883-1, S30687) Fr & Eur.

Mataka, Laini. Never As Strangers. LC 88-82280. 60p. (Orig.). (YA). 1988. pap. 7.95 (0-933121-75-X) Black Classic.

— Restoring the Queen. LC 91-74131. 65p. (Orig.). 1991. pap. 8.95 (0-933121-80-6) Black Classic.

Mataka, S., et al. Sulphur Nitrides in Organic Chemistry. 32p. 1984. pap. text ed. 25.00 (3-7186-0263-6) Gordon & Breach.

Matalene, Carolyn B., ed. Worlds of Writing: Teaching & Writing in a Variety of Discourse Communities. 288p. (C). 1989. pap. text ed. 21.50 (0-394-38295-1) Random.

Matalin, Mary. Love, War & the Art of Politics. 1994. 24.00 (0-679-43103-9) Random.

***Matalin, Mary & Carville, James.** All's Fair: Love, War, & Running for President. 1995. pap. 13.00 (0-684-80133-7, Touchstone Bks) S&S Trade.

Matalon, David. Target: Hero. Bell, Robert, ed. (Champions Adventure Ser.). (Illus.). 32p. (Orig.). (YA). (gr. 10-12). 1988. pap. 6.00 (1-55806-004-9, 34) Iron Crown Ent Inc.

***Matalone, Ralph.** Feelings. 192p. (Orig.). 1994. pap. 12.50 (1-56167-181-9) Am Literary Pr.

Matanah. Love Bones. Ridge, Delores F., ed. 75p. (Orig.). (J). (gr. 9). 1974. pap. text ed. 4.95 (0-9600978-1-3) Knees Pbk.

Matanah, pseud. Private Thoughts. Ridge, Delores F., ed. 32p. (Orig.). (C). 1988. pap. text ed. 3.95 (0-9600978-0-5) Knees Pbk.

Matanah. Thoughts & Things. Ridge, Delores F., ed. LC 76-29534. 58p. (Orig.). 1976. pap. text ed. 4.95 (0-9600978-2-1) Knees Pbk.

Matanle, Ivor. Collecting & Using Classic Cameras. LC 91-75054. (Illus.). 224p. 1992. pap. 24.95 (0-500-27656-0) Thames Hudson.

— World War II. 1989. 19.99 (0-517-67605-2) Random Hse Value.

Matanovic, Milenko. Lightworks: Explorations in Art, Culture, & Creativity. LC 85-82035. (Illus.). 204p. (Orig.). 1986. pap. 11.95 (0-936878-11-8) Lorian Pr.

— Meandering Rivers & Square Tomatoes: The Art of Crafting Visions. (Illus.). 112p. (Orig.). (C). 1988. pap. text ed. 9.95 (0-929660-02-1) Morningtown.

Matanovich, et al. New in Chess Keybook,1970-1982. 1984. pap. 37.50 (0-917237-19-6) Chess Combi.

Matar, Joseph E., jt. auth. see Lochner, Robert H.

Matar, N. I., ed. Peter Sterry Vol. 60: Select Writings. LC 92-16212. (University of Kansas Humanistic Studies: Vol. 60). 225p. (C). 1994. text ed. 45.95 (0-8204-1953-2) P Lang Pubs.

Matar, Nabil I. Islam for Beginners. (Illus.). 160p. (Orig.). 1992. 19.95 (0-86316-156-1); pap. 9.00 (0-86316-155-3) Writers & Readers.

Matar, Sami & Hatch, Lewis F. Analysis & Simulations Fortran Programs: Applications in Process Design. LC 93-43441. 850p. 1994. 75.00 (0-88415-198-0) Gulf Pub.

Matar, Sami, jt. auth. see Hatch, Lewis F.

Matar, Sami, et al, eds. Catalysis in Petrochemical Processes. (C). 1988. lib. bdg. 114.50 (90-277-2721-X) Kluwer Ac.

Matarasso, P. M., tr. Quest of the Holy Grail. (Classics Ser.). 304p. 1969. pap. 9.95 (0-14-044220-0, Penguin Classics) Viking Penguin.

Matarasso, Pauline, ed. & tr. The Cistercian World: Monastic Writings of the Twelfth Century. 336p. 1993. 12.95 (0-14-043356-2, Penguin Classics) Viking Penguin.

Matarazzo, James. Corporate Library Excellence. 137p. 1990. 31.25 (0-87111-367-8) SLA.

Matarazzo, James M. Closing the Corporate Library: Case Studies on the Decision Making Process. LC 81-14452. 160p. reprint ed. pap. 45.60 (0-317-26315-3, 2025207) Bks Demand.

— Library Problems in Science & Technology. LC 70-164033. (Problem-Centered Approaches to Librarianship Ser.). 191p. reprint ed. 54.50 (0-8357-9043-6, 2017589) Bks Demand.

Matarazzo, James M. & Drake, Miriam A., eds. Information for Management: A Handbook. LC 94-21486. 196p. 1994. pap. 40.00 (0-87111-427-5) SLA.

Matarazzo, Jim, jt. auth. see Prusak, Larry.

Matarazzo, Joseph D. & Wechsler, David. Wechsler's Measurement & Appraisal of Adult Intelligence. 5th ed. (Illus.). 1972. 36.95 (0-19-502296-3) OUP.

Matarazzo, Ruth, jt. auth. see Greif, Elaine.

Matare, Herbert F. Energy: Facts & Future. 208p. 1988. 180.00 (0-8493-4616-9, TJ163) CRC Pr.

Matas, Carol. Adventure in Legoland. (J). (ps-3). 1992. pap. 2.50 (0-590-43875-1) Scholastic Inc.

— The Burning Time. LC 94-443. (YA). (gr. 6 up). 1994. 15.95 (0-385-32097-3) Delacorte.

— Code Name Kris. LC 90-32656. 160p. (YA). (gr. 7 up). 1990. text ed. 13.95 (0-684-19208-X, C Scribner Sons Young) S&S Childrens.

— Daniel's Story. 144p. (J). (gr. 4-7). 1993. pap. 3.95 (0-590-46588-0) Scholastic Inc.

— Daniel's Story. LC 92-27537. 144p. (J). (gr. 4-9). 1993. 13.95 (0-590-46920-7) Scholastic Inc.

— Kris's War. 176p. (YA). 1992. pap. 3.25 (0-590-45034-4, Point) Scholastic Inc.

— Lisa's War. (J). 1991. pap. 2.95 (0-590-43517-5) Scholastic Inc.

— Lisa's War. LC 88-29525. 128p. (YA). (gr. 7 up). 1989. text ed. 13.95 (0-684-19010-9, C Scribner Sons Young) S&S Childrens.

— Safari Adventure in Legoland. (J). (gr. 4-7). 1993. pap. 2.75 (0-590-45876-0) Scholastic Inc.

— Sworn Enemies. LC 92-6188. 148p. (YA). 1993. 16.00 (0-553-08326-0) Bantam.

An Asterisk (*) at the beginning of an entry indicates that the title is appearing in BIP for the first time.

— Sworn Enemies. (YA). 1994. mass mkt. 3.99 (*0-440-21900-0*) Dell.

Matas, Julio. El Extravio - La Cronica y el Sucesoaqui Cruza el Cirvo. LC 90-80368. (Coleccion Teatro). 205p. (Orig.). (SPA.). 1990. pap. 12.00 (*0-89729-563-3*) Ediciones.

— Juegos y Rejuegos. LC 91-76709. (Coleccion Teatro). 96p. (SPA.). 1992. pap. 12.00 (*0-89729-628-1*) Ediciones.

— Transiciones, Migraciones. LC 93-72085. (Coleccion Caniqui Ser.). 149p. (Orig.). (SPA.). 1993. pap. 16.00 (*0-89729-693-1*) Ediciones.

Matas, Julio, jt. tr. see Colecchia, Francesca.

Matasar, Ann B. Corporate PACs & Federal Campaign Financing Laws: Use or Abuse of Power? LC 85-12280. (Illus.). 171p. 1986. text ed. 55.00 (*0-89930-086-3*, MTP/, Quorum Bks) Greenwood.

Matassarin-Jacobs, Esther. Saunders Review for NCLEX-RN. 2nd ed. LC 93-22879. (Illus.). 800p. 1994. pap. text ed. 29.95 (*0-7216-4993-9*) Saunders.

Matassarin-Jacobs, Esther, jt. auth. see Black, Joyce M.

*__Mataya, Ewa.__ The Ewa Mataya Pool Guide: Hints, Tips & Championship Strategies from the Two-Time Women's Professional Billboard Association's Player of the Year. LC 94-23367. 128p. (Orig.). 1995. pap. 10.00 (*0-380-77645-6*) Avon.

Mataya, Geri. The Salon Biz: Tips for Success. LC 92-9492. 136p. 1992. pap. text ed. 18.95 (*1-56253-048-8*) Milady Pub.

Matcha, Jack, ed. see Dargan, James F.

Matchan, Don C., jt. auth. see Kaye, Anna.

Matchett, D., jt. ed. see Kilpatrick, F.

*__Matchett, Steve.__ Life in the Fast Lane. (Illus.). 224p. 1995. 19.95 (*0-7603-0026-7*) Motorbooks Intl.

Matchett, William, ed. see Shakespeare, William.

*__Matchette, Katharine E.__ Libby's Choice. 157p. 1995. pap. 8.75 (*0-9645045-0-2*) Deka Pr.

Matczak, S. A., ed. see Smith, William A.

Matczak, Sebastian A. Karl Barth on God: Our Knowledge of the Divine Existence. LC 62-15994. 358p. 1962. 25.25 (*0-912116-06-4*) Learned Pubns.

— Philosophy: A Select, Classified Bibliography of Ethics, Economics, Law, Politics, Sociology. LC 72-80678. (Philosophical Questions Ser.: No. 3). 1970. 45.00 (*0-912116-02-1*) Learned Pubns.

— Philosophy: Its Nature, Methods & Basic Sources. LC 70-183043. (Philosophical Questions Ser.: No. 4). 300p. 1976. 45.00 (*0-912116-09-9*) Learned Pubns.

— Le Probleme de Dieu dans la Pensee de Karl Barth. (Philosophical Questions Ser.: No. 1). 1968. pap. 25.00 (*0-912116-00-5*) Learned Pubns.

— Research & Composition in Philosophy. 2nd ed. (Philosophical Questions Ser.: No. 2). (C). 1971. pap. text ed. 35.00 (*0-912116-05-6*) Learned Pubns.

— Unificationism: A New Philosophy & Worldview. LC 81-86036. (Philosophical Questions Ser.: No. 11). 500p. 1982. 55.00 (*0-912116-14-5*) Learned Pubns.

Matczak, Sebastian A., ed. God in Contemporary Thought: A Philosophical Perspective. LC 75-31391. (Philosophical Questions Ser.: No. 10). 1977. 85.00 (*0-912116-12-9*) Learned Pubns.

Matczak, Sebastian A., ed. see Barral, R. M.

Matczak, Sebastian A., ed. see Van Treese, Glenn J.

Mate, Candace, jt. auth. see Mate, Ferenc.

Mate, Ferenc. Best Boats to Build or Buy. (Illus.). 1992. pap. 27.50 (*0-920256-24-4*) Norton.

— The Finely Fitted Yacht. (Illus.). 1979. Comp. ed. 27.95 (*0-920256-05-8*) Norton.

— Finely Fitted Yacht. 1994. pap. 25.00 (*0-920256-28-7*) Norton.

— From a Bare Hull: A Boat Building Manual. rev. ed. (Illus.). 1983. 29.95 (*0-920256-07-4*) Norton.

— From a Bare Hull: How to Build a Sailboat. (Illus.). 443p. 1995. pap. 25.00 (*0-920256-31-7*, Norton Paperbks) Norton.

— A Reasonable Life: Toward a Simpler, Secure, More Humane Existence. 1993. 17.95 (*0-920256-25-2*) Norton.

— A Reasonable Life: Toward a Simpler, Secure, More Humane Existence. 1994. pap. 9.95 (*0-920256-30-9*) Norton.

— Shipshape: The Art of Sailboat Maintenance. 1986. 29.95 (*0-920256-12-0*) Norton.

— The World's Best Sailboats. 1986. 50.00 (*0-920256-11-2*) Norton.

*__Mate, Ferenc & Mate, Candace.__ Autumn: A New England Journey. 1993. pap. 25.00 (*0-920256-27-9*) Norton.

Mate, L. Hilbert Space Methods in Science & Engineering. (Illus.). 200p. 1990. 75.00 (*0-85274-293-2*) IOP Pub.

Mateene, Kahombo C., jt. ed. see Biebuyck, Daniel.

Mateer, Catherine A., jt. auth. see Sohlberg, McKay M.

Mateer, Charlotte F. Let's Go to the Arctic: A Story & Activities Book about Arctic People & Animals. (Illus.). 64p. (J). (gr. 4-6). 1993. pap. text ed. 7.95 (*1-879373-24-6*) R Rinehart.

Mateer, Samuel. The Land of Charity: A Descriptive Account of Travancore & Its People. (C). 1991. reprint ed. 29.00 (*81-206-0319-2*, Pub. by Asian Educ Servs II) S Asia.

— Native Life in Travancore. 1991. reprint ed. text ed. 34.00 (*81-206-0514-4*, Pub. by Asian Educ Servs II) S Asia.

Mateja, Jim. Used Cars: Finding the Best Buy. rev. ed. 245p. 1988. pap. 6.95 (*0-933893-52-3*) Bonus Books.

Mateja, Wendy. Alana & the Dolphins. Orig. Title: Alana, Lady of Light. (Illus.). 16p. (Orig.). 1978. pap. text ed. 4.95 (*0-9601836-0-4*) Magic Unicorn Pubns.

Matejic, Mateja & Milivojevic, Dragan. An Anthology of Medieval Serbian Literature in English. (Illus.). 205p. 1978. pap. 14.95 (*0-89357-055-9*) Slavica.

Matejic, Mateja, jt. auth. see Mihailovich, Vasa D.

Matejic, Predrag & Thomas, Hannah. Manuscripts on Microform of the Hilandar Research Library (The Ohio State University) Resources in Medieval Slavic Studies, 2 vols., Set. xxix, 1196p. 1992. 79.95 (*0-89357-225-X*) Slavica.

Matejka, jt. ed. see Bailey.

Matejka, D. & Benko, B. Plasma Spraying of Metallic & Ceramic Materials. 280p. 1990. text ed. 275.00 (*0-471-91876-8*) Wiley.

Matejka, J. Kenneth. Handling Human Performance. 1983. pap. 29.95 (*0-8359-2767-9*, Reston) P-H.

Matejka, Ken. Why This Horse Won't Drink: How to Win - & Keep - Employee Commitment. LC 90-53215. 265p. 1990. 22.95 (*0-8144-5005-9*) AMACOM.

*__Matejka, Ken & Dunsing, Richard J.__ A Manager's Guide to the Millenium: Today's Strategies for Tomorrow's Success. LC 94-47650. 208p. 1995. 21.95 (*0-8144-0269-0*) AMACOM.

Matejka, L., et al, eds. Readings in Soviet Semiotics: Russian Texts. (Michigan Slavic Materials Ser.: No. 15). 1977. pap. 10.00 (*0-930042-08-5*) Mich Slavic Pubns.

Matejka, Ladislav, ed. Cross Currents, No. 7. (Michigan Slavic Materials Ser.: No. 29). 1988. pap. 15.00 (*0-930042-66-2*) Mich Slavic Pubns.

— Cross Currents, No. 8. (Michigan Slavic Materials Ser.: No. 30). 1989. pap. 15.00 (*0-930042-67-0*) Mich Slavic Pubns.

— Cross Currents, No. 11. (Illus.). 296p. (C). 1992. pap. 25.00 (*0-300-05242-1*) Yale U Pr.

— Cross Currents: A Yearbook of Central European Culture, No. 10. (Cross Current Yearbooks of Central European Culture Ser.). 272p. (Orig.). 1991. pap. 25.00 (*0-300-04326-0*) Yale U Pr.

— Cross Currents, No. 6. (Michigan Slavic Materials Ser.: No. 28). 1987. 15.00 (*0-930042-65-4*) Mich Slavic Pubns.

— Cross Currents 12. (Slavic Studies - Literature). (Illus.). 240p. (C). 1993. 25.00 (*0-300-05838-1*) Yale U Pr.

— Sound, Sign & Meaning: Quinquagenary of the Prague Linguistic Circle. (Michigan Slavic Contributions Ser.: No. 6). 1978. 25.00 (*0-930042-26-3*) Mich Slavic Pubns.

Matejka, Ladislav & Stolz, B. A., eds. Cross Currents, No. 3. (Michigan Slavic Materials Ser.: No. 24). 1984. pap. 15.00 (*0-930042-60-3*) Mich Slavic Pubns.

Matejka, Ladislav & Stolz, Benjamin A., eds. Cross Currents, No. 1. (Michigan Slavic Materials Ser.: No. 20). 1982. pap. 15.00 (*0-930042-43-3*) Mich Slavic Pubns.

Matejka, Ladislav & Titunik, Irwin R., eds. The Semiotics of Art: Prague School Contributions. 1984. reprint ed. pap. 14.95 (*0-262-63065-6*) MIT Pr.

Matejka, Ladislav, jt. ed. see Birnbaum, M. D.

Matejka, Ladislav, ed. see Jakobson, Roman.

Matejka, Ladislav, jt. ed. see Konigsberg, Ira.

Matejka, Ladislav, ed. see Reiner, Erica.

Matejka, Ladislav, ed. see Steiner, Wendy, et al.

Matejka, Ladislav, ed. see Veltrusky, Jarmila F.

Matejka, Ladislav, tr. see Volosinov, V. N.

Matejka, Mike & Koos, Greg, eds. Bloomington's C & A R. R. Shops: Our Lives Remembered. (Transactions of the Mclean County Historical Society Ser.). (Illus.). 161p. (Orig.). 1987. pap. 11.95 (*0-943788-04-8*) McLean County.

Matejko, Alexander J. A Christian Approach to Work & Industry. LC 88-13824. (Mellen Studies in Business: Vol. 4). 439p. 1989. lib. bdg. 109.95 (*0-88946-156-2*) E Mellen.

— Comparative Work Systems: Ideologies & Reality in Eastern Europe. LC 85-6354. 256p. 1985. text ed. 59.95 (*0-275-90216-1*, C0216, Praeger Pubs) Greenwood.

— In Search of New Organizational Paradigms. LC 86-9317. (Illus.). 366p. 1986. text ed. 65.00 (*0-275-92099-2*, C2099, Praeger Pubs) Greenwood.

— The Self Defeating Organization. LC 85-9524. 425p. 1986. text ed. 65.00 (*0-275-90026-6*, C0026, Praeger Pubs) Greenwood.

Matejko, Alexander J., jt. ed. see Jain, Ajit.

Matejski, Myrtle P., jt. auth. see Swonger, Alvin K.

Matela, Ray, jt. auth. see Ransom, Robert.

Matelic, Candace T. Cooperstown Conference on Professional Training: Needs, Issues & Opportunities for the Future. LC 90-1086. 138p. 1990. pap. 9.95 (*0-942063-08-2*) AASLH.

Mateljan, George. Baking Without Fat. Burns, Jim, ed. (Illus.). 175p. (Orig.). 1993. pap. 9.95 (*0-9633608-1-7*) Hlth Valley Foods.

— Cooking Without Fat. 416p. 1992. pap. 14.95 (*0-9633608-0-9*) Hlth Valley Foods.

— Healthy Meals in Minutes. Burns, Jim, ed. (Illus.). 128p. 1995. pap. 5.95 (*0-9633608-3-3*) Hlth Valley Foods.

Matelski, Marily J. & Thomas, David O. Variety Source, Bk. I: Broadcast-Video. 132p. 1990. pap. 22.95 (*0-240-80067-2*, Focal) Buttrwrth-Heinemann.

Matelski, Marilyn. Daytime Television Programming. (Electronic Media Guide Ser.). 112p. 1991. pap. 15.95 (*0-240-80087-7*, Focal) Buttrwrth-Heinemann.

— TV News Ethics. (Electronic Media Guide Ser.). (Illus.). 96p. 1991. pap. 15.95 (*0-240-80089-3*) Buttrwrth-Heinemann.

Matelski, Marilyn J. Broadcast Programming & Promotions Worktext. (Illus.). 202p. 1989. pap. 21.95 (*0-240-80025-7*, Focal) Buttrwrth-Heinemann.

— The Soap Opera Evolution: America's Enduring Romance with Daytime Drama. LC 87-43168. 224p. 1988. lib. bdg. 27.50x (*0-89950-324-1*) McFarland & Co.

— Variety - the Year in Review, 1991: TV Radio Film Video Theatre Music. 248p. 1992. pap. 27.95 (*0-240-80143-1*, Focal) Buttrwrth-Heinemann.

— Variety, 1990: The Year in Review. 173p. 1991. pap. 26.95 (*0-240-80074-5*, Focal) Buttrwrth-Heinemann.

— Vatican Radio: Propagation by the Airwaves. LC 94-22656. (Media & Society Ser.). 224p. 1995. text ed. 55.00 (*0-275-94760-2*, Praeger Pubs) Greenwood.

Maten, Franc, illus. Walt Disney's Alice in Wonderland. (J). (ps-2). 1991. write for info. (*0-307-12341-3*, Golden Pr) Western Pub.

Maten, Frenc, illus. Walt Disney Pictures Presents the Little Mermaid. (Golden Super Shape Bks.). (J). (ps-00). 1991. pap. write for info. (*0-307-10027-8*, Golden Pr) Western Pub.

Matenko, Percy. Ludwig Tieck & America. LC 54-62860. (North Carolina. University. Studies in the Germanic Languages & Literatures: No. 12). reprint ed. 27.00 (*0-404-50912-6*) AMS Pr.

Matens, Margaret H. Mandy & the Kookalocka. LC 93-77130. (Illus.). 32p. (J). (gr. k-5). 1993. 14.95 (*1-882959-53-1*) Foxglove TN.

— Wuzzy the Witch. LC 93-77128. (Illus.). 42p. (J). (gr. k-5). 1993. 14.95 (*1-882959-54-X*) Foxglove TN.

Mateo Diez, Luis. Relato de Babia. (Nueva Austral Ser.: Vol. 213). (SPA.). 1991. pap. text ed. 24.95x (*84-239-7213-5*) Elliots Bks.

Mateo, Franc, jt. illus. see Mateu, Franc.

Mateo, Mary A. Portraits of Native American Indians. (Illus.). 96p. (J). (gr. 4-7). 1992. 10.95 (*0-86653-669-8*, GA1322) Good Apple.

Mateo, N. Mountain Agriculture & Crop Genetics Resources. (C). 1989. 44.00 (*81-204-0472-6*) S Asia.

Mateos, Alvarez J. Vocabulario Teologico del Evangelio de San Juan. 310p. (SPA.). 1980. pap. 29.95 (*0-8288-2318-9*, S33107) Fr & Eur.

Mateos, Fernando. Diccionario Chino de la Lengua Espanola. 1200p. (CHI & SPA.). 1987. pap. 75.00 (*0-7859-3350-6*, 8429307621) Fr & Eur.

*__Mateos, Fernando, et al.__ Diccionario Espanol de la Lengua China. 1381p. (SPA.). 1990. 339.50x (*84-239-4771-8*) Elliots Bks.

Mater, Jean, et al. Marketing Forest Products: Gaining the Competitive Edge. (Illus.). 280p. 1992. 49.00 (*0-87930-193-7*, 412) Miller Freeman.

*__Mater, Rick & Wing, Kathy.__ Date to Win: How to Have More Dates, Find That Lasting Relationship, or Meet Your Ideal Marriage Partner. LC 94-96386. 256p. (Orig.). 1995. pap. 12.00 (*0-9643444-0-8*) Laurel Canyon.

*__Matera.__ Face Value. (Illus.). (J). 1995. mass mkt. 5.99 (*0-671-88840-4*) PB.

Matera, D. M. Strike Midnight. 350p. 1994. pap. 9.99 (*0-89283-859-0*, Vine Bks) Servant.

Matera, Frank. Galatians. (Sacra Pagina Ser.: No. 9). 266p. (Orig.). 1992. pap. text ed. 24.95 (*0-8146-5811-3*, M Glazier) Liturgical Pr.

Matera, Frank J. What Are They Saying about Mark? (What Are They Saying about...Ser.). 128p. (Orig.). 1987. pap. 7.95 (*0-8091-2885-3*) Paulist Pr.

*__Matera, Lia.__ Designer Crimes: A Laura Di Palma Mystery. LC 95-1701. 1995. 21.00 (*0-684-80312-7*) S&S Trade.

— Face Value: A Laura Di Palma Mystery. LC 93-27194. 1994. 20.00 (*0-671-74197-7*) S&S Trade.

— The Good Fight. 1991. mass mkt. 4.95 (*0-345-37107-0*) Ballantine.

— A Hard Bargain. (Northern California Mysteries Ser.). 1993. mass mkt. 4.99 (*0-345-38059-2*) Ballantine.

— Hidden Agenda. 1992. mass mkt. 5.99 (*0-345-37128-3*) Ballantine.

— Prior Convictions. (Northern California Mysteries Ser.). 1992. mass mkt. 4.99 (*0-345-37445-2*) Ballantine.

— A Radical Departure. 224p. (Orig.). 1991. mass mkt. 4.99 (*0-345-37126-7*) Ballantine.

— The Smart Money. 192p. (Orig.). 1991. mass mkt. 4.95 (*0-345-37127-5*) Ballantine.

— Where Lawyers Fear to Tread. 1991. mass mkt. 4.95 (*0-345-37125-9*) Ballantine.

*__Materer, Timothy.__ Modernist Alchemy: Poetry & the Occult. (Illus.). 240p. 1996. 29.95 (*0-8014-3146-8*) Cornell U Pr.

— Wyndham Lewis: The Novelist. LC 75-29310. 189p. reprint ed. pap. 53.90 (*0-7837-3666-5*, 2043539) Bks Demand.

Materer, Timothy, ed. The Selected Letters of Ezra Pound to John Quinn, 1915-1924. LC 90-23613. 252p. 1991. text ed. 39.50 (*0-8223-1132-1*) Duke.

Materer, Timothy, ed. see Pound, Ezra & Lewis, Wyndham.

Materials & Processes Congress. Process Modeling Tools: Proceedings of American Society for Metals Process Modeling Sessions Processes Congress 1980. LC 81-52303. (Materials-Metalworking Technology Ser.). 224p. reprint ed. pap. 63.90 (*0-685-15563-3*, 2027035) Bks Demand.

Materials Handling Conference Staff. Unit & Bulk Materials Handling: Presented at the Materials Handling Conference, ASME Century 2 - Emerging Technology Conferences, San Francisco, CA, August 19-21, 1980. Loeffler, F. J. & Proctor, C. R., eds. LC 80-66042. 297p. reprint ed. pap. 84.70 (*0-8357-8772-9*, 2033642) Bks Demand.

Materials Research Society Staff. Biomedical Materials & Devices: Symposium Held November 30-December 4, 1987, Boston, MA. Hanker, Jacob S. & Giammara, Beverly L., eds. LC 88-27355. (Material Research Society Symposium Proceedings Ser.: No. 110). (Illus.). 824p. reprint ed. pap. 180.00 (*0-7837-6760-9*, 2059159) Bks Demand.

— Comparison of Thin Film Transistor & SOI Technologies: Symposium Held February 1984 in Albuquerque, New Mexico, U. S. A. LC 84-24713. (Materials Research Society Symposia Proceedings Ser.: No. 33). (Illus.). 337p. reprint ed. pap. 96.10 (*0-7837-1925-6*, 2042140) Bks Demand.

— Optical Fiber Materials & Properties: Symposium Held December 3-5, 1986, Boston, Massachusetts, U. S. A. Nagel, Suzanne R., ed. LC 87-7852. (Materials Research Society Symposia Proceedings Ser.: No. 88). (Illus.). 261p. reprint ed. pap. 74.40 (*0-7837-1929-9*, 2042144) Bks Demand.

— Thin Films: The Relationship of Structure to Properties: Symposium Held April 15-17, 1985, San Francisco, California, U. S. A. Aita, Carolyn & SreeHarsha, K. S., eds. LC 85-21485. (Materials Research Society Symposia Proceedings Ser.: No. 47). (Illus.). 306p. reprint ed. pap. 87.30 (*0-7837-1927-2*, 2042142) Bks Demand.

Materials Research Society Staff, et al. Biomedical Materials: Symposium Held December 3-6, 1985, Boston, Massachusetts, U. S. A. Williams, J. M., ed. LC 86-23540. (Materials Research Society Symposia Proceedings Ser.: No. 55). (Illus.). 435p. reprint ed. pap. 124.00 (*0-7837-1928-0*, 2042143) Bks Demand.

— Fly Ash & Coal Conversion By-Products: Characterization, Utilization & Disposal IV: Symposium Held December 1-3, 1987, Boston, Massachusetts, U. S. A. McCarthy, Gregory J., ed. LC 88-9394. (Materials Research Society Symposium Proceedings Ser.: No. 113). 365p. reprint ed. pap. 104.10 (*0-7837-6803-6*, 2046635) Bks Demand.

— High-Temperature Ordered Intermetallic Alloys: Symposium Held November 26-28, 1984, Boston, Massachusetts, U. S. A. Koch, C. C. et al, eds. LC 85-11488. (Materials Research Society Symposia Proceedings Ser.: No. 39). (Illus.). 572p. reprint ed. pap. 163.10 (*0-7837-1926-4*, 2042141) Bks Demand.

— High-Temperature Superconductors: Symposium Held November 30-December 4, 1987, Boston, Massachusetts, U. S. A. Brodsky, Merwyn B., ed. LC 88-5130. (Materials Research Society Symposium Proceedings Ser.: No. 99). (Illus.). 1038p. reprint ed. pap. 180.00 (*0-7837-6802-8*, 2046634) Bks Demand.

— Specialty Cements with Advanced Properties: Symposium Held November 27-29, 1989, Boston, Massachusetts, U. S. A. Scheetz, Barry E., ed. LC 90-41629. (Materials Research Society Symposium Proceedings Ser.: No. 179). (Illus.). 317p. reprint ed. pap. 90.40 (*0-7837-6804-4*, 2046636) Bks Demand.

Materials Science Seminar, 1976, Metals Park, OH Staff. Metallic Glasses: Papers Presented at a Seminar of the Materials Science Division of the ASM, September 18 & 19, 1976. LC 77-24014. 360p. reprint ed. pap. 102.60 (*0-685-16027-0*, 2027037) Bks Demand.

Materials Science Seminar Staff. Fatigue & Microstructure: Papers Presented at the 1978 ASM. LC 79-4296. 543p. reprint ed. pap. 154.80 (*0-685-17059-4*, 2026994) Bks Demand.

Materials Transportation Bureau Staff, jt. auth. see U. S. Department of Transportation Staff.

Materka, Pat R. Time in, Time Out, Time Enough: A Time Management Guide for Women. 2nd ed. (Illus.). 1993. pap. 11.95 (*0-9635113-0-0*) Leap Frog.

— Workshops & Seminars: Planning, Producing & Profiting. write for info. (*0-318-59681-4*) S&S Trade.

— Workshops & Seminars: Planning, Promoting, Producing, Profiting. 224p. 1986. 15.95 (*0-13-967795-X*) P-H.

Materlik, G., et al, eds. Resonant Anomalous X-Ray Scattering: Theory & Applications. LC 94-20905. 1994. write for info. (*0-444-82025-6*, North Holland) Elsevier.

Matern, B. Spatial Variation. 2nd ed. (Lecture Notes in Statistics Ser.: Vol. 36). (Illus.). 155p. 1986. pap. 32.00 (*0-387-96365-0*) Spr-Verlag.

Matern, S., ed. Clinical Research in Gastroenterology, Vol. I. (C). 1987. lib. bdg. 78.00 (*0-85200-696-9*) Kluwer Ac.

— Clinical Research in Gastroenterology 2. (C). 1989. lib. bdg. 60.00 (*0-7923-8906-9*) Kluwer Ac.

*__Materne, Yves, ed.__ The Indian Awakening in Latin America. fac. ed. LC 80-11464. 128p. 1994. pap. 36.50 (*0-7837-7712-4*, 2047473) Bks Demand.

Maternity Center Association Staff. Birth Atlas. 6th rev. ed. (Illus.). 19p. 1993. reprint ed. 53.00 (*0-912758-00-7*) Maternity Ctr.

Maternity Center Association Staff & St. Vincent's Hospital & Medical Center of New York Staff. Las Necesidades del Recien Nacido: Una Guia para el Cuidad del Recien Nacido y la Madre en el Hogar. (Illus.). 40p. 1988. 4.00 (*0-912758-03-1*) Maternity Ctr.

Maternity Center Association Staff & St. Vincent's Hospital Maternity & Medical Center of New York. Newborn Needs: A Guide to Early Infant Care at Home. (Illus.). 48p. 1986. 4.00 (*0-912758-02-3*) Maternity Ctr.

Matero, Robert. Birth of A Humpback Whale. LC 94-10681. (Illus.). (J). 1995. text ed. 14.95 (*0-689-31931-2*, Atheneum S&S) S&S Trade.

— Eyes on Nature: Reptiles. (Illus.). 32p. (J). 1992. pap. 4.95 (*1-56156-151-7*) Kidsbks.

Materon, L. A., jt. auth. see Beck, D.

Mates, Benson. Elementary Logic. 2nd ed. (C). 1972. text ed. 22.00 (*0-19-501491-X*) OUP.

— The Philosophy of Leibniz: Metaphysics & Language. 280p. 1986. 49.95 (*0-19-503696-4*) OUP.

— The Philosophy of Leibniz: Metaphysics & Language. 288p. 1989. reprint ed. pap. 16.95 (*0-19-505946-8*) OUP.

— The Skeptic May: Sextus Empiricus's Outlines of Pyrrhonism. 352p. (C). 1995. text ed. 55.00 (*0-19-509212-0*); pap. text ed. 21.95 (*0-19-509213-9*) OUP.

— Skeptical Essays. LC 80-19553. xii, 176p. (C). 1981. 17.00 (*0-226-50986-9*) U Ch Pr.

— Stoic Logic. LC 53-9918. (California University Publications in Philosophy: Vol. 26). 156p. reprint ed. pap. 44.50 (*0-317-10250-8*, 2021174) Bks Demand.

Mates, Julian. The American Musical Stage Before Eighteen Hundred. LC 85-30497. 343p. 1986. reprint ed. text ed. 69.50 (*0-313-25324-2*, MAMUS, Greenwood Pr) Greenwood.

— America's Musical Stage: Two Hundred Years of Musical Theatre. LC 85-935. (Contributions in Drama & Theatre Studies: No. 18). (Illus.). xii, 252p. 1985. text ed. 55.00 (*0-313-23948-7*, MLY/, Greenwood Pr) Greenwood.

— America's Musical Stage: Two Hundred Years of Musical Theatre. (Illus.). 264p. 1987. pap. text ed. 15.95 (*0-275-92714-8*, B2714, Praeger Pubs) Greenwood.

Mates, Leo, jt. ed. see Friedmann, Wolfgang.

Mates, Michael, ed. The Secret Services: Is There a Case for Greater Openness? (C). 1990. 35.00 (*0-907967-07-8*, Pub. by Inst Euro Def & Strat UK) St Mut.

Mates, R. E., jt. ed. see Wod, S.

Mates, R. E., et al, eds. Mechanics of the Coronary Circulation. 94p. 1983. pap. text ed. 24.00 (*0-317-02632-1*, G00221) ASME.

Mates, Susan O. The Good Doctor. LC 94-18980. (John Simmons Short Fiction Award Ser.). 138p. 1994. 22.95x (*0-87745-467-1*) U of Iowa Pr.

Matesic, Josep. German - Serbocroatian Phraseological Dictionary: Hrvatsko-Njemacki I Frazeoloski Rjecnik. (GER & SER.). 1987. write for info. (*0-8288-1637-9*, F114950) Fr & Eur.

Matescu, Gheorghe D. & Valeriu, Adrian. Two Dimension NMR: A Density Matrix & Product Operator Treatment. 1992. text ed. 62.00 (*0-13-013368-X*) P-H.

Matesz, Clara, jt. auth. see Szekely, George.

Matesz, Don & Albert-Matesz, Rachel. The Nourishment for Life Cookbook. Williams, Danielle, ed. LC 94-66937. (Illus.). 500p. (Orig.). 1994. pap. 20.00 (*0-9641267-0-2*) Nourish For Life.

Mateu, illus. Disney's Aladdin. (Sound Story Books-Deluxe Editions Ser.). 24p. (J). (ps-4). 1992. 20.00 (*0-307-74026-9*, 64026, Golden Pr) Western Pub.

— Snow White & the Seven Dwarfs. (Golden Sound Story Book). 24p. (J). (ps up). 1991. write for info. (*0-307-74018-8*, 64018) Western Pub.

***Mateu, Franc, illus.** Cinderella: Pop-Up Book. LC 94-71482. 12p. (J). (ps-3). 1995. 12.95 (*0-7868-3025-5*) Disney Pr.

— The Jungle Book: Mowgli's Journey. LC 92-53438. (Surprise Lift-the-Flap Ser.). 18p. (J). (ps-1). 1993. 9.95 (*1-56282-374-4*) Disney Pr.

— Snow White & the Seven Dwarfs Whistle While You Work: A Musical Pop-up Book. LC 92-53432. 10p. (J). (ps-1). 1994. 11.95 (*1-56282-514-3*) Disney Pr.

— Walt Disney's Lady & the Tramp. LC 93-71378. (Illustrated Classics Ser.). 96p. (J). 1994. 14.95 (*1-56282-613-1*); lib. bdg. 14.89 (*1-56282-615-8*) Disney Pr.

Mateu, Franc & Mateo, Franc, illus. Snow White & the Seven Dwarfs. LC 92-53432. (Pop-up Bk.). 12p. (J). (ps-00). 1993. 11.95 (*1-56282-365-5*) Disney Pr.

Mateu Sancho, Pedro. Diccionario de la Astronomica y Astronautica. 350p. (SPA.). 1962. 49.95 (*0-8288-6806-9*, S-12334) Fr & Eur.

Matevski, Mateja. Footprints of the Wind. LC 87-827876. 1988. pap. 16.95 (*0-948259-41-8*) Dufour.

Matey, Maria. Labor Law & Industrial Relations in Poland. 178p. 1989. lib. bdg. 44.00 (*90-6544-401-7*) Kluwer Ac.

Matfield, Ron. Quality Assurance in Nuclear Power Plants, Vol. 6. (Ispra Courses on Nuclear Engineering & Technology Ser.). 316p. 1984. text ed. 114.00 (*3-7186-0151-6*) Gordon & Breach.

Math, Irwin. More Wires & Watts: Understanding & Using Electricity. LC 88-15767. (Illus.). 96p. (YA). (gr. 7 up). 1988. text ed. 14.95 (*0-684-18914-3*, C Scribner Sons Young) S&S Childrens.

— Tomorrow's Technology: Experimenting with the Science of the Future. LC 91-32341. (Illus.). 80p. (YA). (gr. 7 up). 1992. lib. bdg. 13.95 (*0-684-19294-2*, C Scribner Sons Young) S&S Childrens.

— Wires & Watts: Understanding & Using Electricity. LC 88-15767. (Illus.). 96p. (YA). (gr. 7 up). 1981. text ed. 15.95 (*0-684-16854-5*, C Scribner Sons Young) S&S Childrens.

— Wires & Watts: Using & Understanding Electricity. LC 81-2255. (Illus.). 96p. (YA). (gr. 7 up). 1989. reprint ed. pap. 4.95 (*0-689-71298-7*, Aladdin Paperbacks) S&S Childrens.

Mathabane, Mark. African Women. (Illus.). 320p. 1994. 23.00 (*0-06-016496-4*, HarpT) HarpC.

— African Women: Three Generations. 384p. 1995. pap. 13.00 (*0-06-092583-3*, PL) HarpC.

— Kaffir Boy. 1990. pap. 11.95 (*0-452-26471-5*, Plume) NAL-Dutton.

— Kaffir Boy: The True Story of a Black Youth's Coming of Age in Apartheid South Africa. 1987. pap. 9.95 (*0-452-25943-6*, Plume) NAL-Dutton.

— Kaffir Boy in America: An Encounter with Apartheid. (Illus.). 320p. 1990. pap. 10.00 (*0-02-034530-5*, Pub. by Gebrueder Borntraeger GW) Macmillan.

— Kaffir Boy in America: An Encounter with Apartheid. (Illus.). 288p. 1989. text ed. 19.95 (*0-684-19043-5*, Scribners) S&S Trade.

— Love in Black & White: The Triumph of Love over Prejudice & Taboo. LC 91-50454. (Illus.). 288p. 1993. pap. 11.00 (*0-06-092371-7*, PL) HarpC.

— Selected from Kaffir Boy. abr. ed. (Writers' Voices Ser.). 64p. (Orig.). 1991. pap. text ed. 3.50 (*0-929631-28-5*, Signal Hill) New Readers.

***Mathad, G. S. & Hess, D. E., eds.** Proceedings of the International Symposium on Plasma Processing, 9th. LC 92-82777. (Proceedings Ser.: Vol. 92-18). 670p. 1992. 60.00 (*1-56677-020-3*) Electrochem Soc.

***Mathad, G. S. & Hess, D. W., eds.** Proceedings of the International Symposium on Plasma Processing, 10th. LC 94-70852. (Processing Ser.: Vol. 94-20). 620p. 1994. 64.00 (*1-56677-077-7*) Electrochem Soc.

***Mathad, G. S. & Horiike, Y., eds.** Proceedings of the Symposium on Highly Selective Dry Etching & Damage Control. LC 93-70068. (Proceedings Ser.: Vol. 93-21). 440p. 1993. 60.00 (*1-56677-066-1*) Electrochem Soc.

Mathai, A. M. A Handbook of Generalized Special Functions for Statistical & Physical Sciences. (Illus.). 256p. 1993. 59.95 (*0-19-853595-3*) OUP.

Mathai, A. M., ed. Distributions of Test Statistics: Exact & Asymptotic, Null & Non-Null, Methods-Comparisons-Research Frontiers. LC 89-82198. (American Sciences Press Series in Mathematical & Management Sciences: Vol. 18). 1989. 110.00 (*0-935950-20-6*) Am Sciences Pr.

Mathai, Aleyamma, jt. auth. see Penland, Patrick R.

Mathai, M. O. My Days with Nehru. 270p. 1979. 14.95 (*0-7069-0823-6*) Asia Bk Corp.

Mathamatical Association Staff. Math Talk. 66p. 1990. pap. text ed. 14.50 (*0-435-08307-4*, 08307) Heinemann.

Mathan, Don C., jt. auth. see Kaye, Anna.

Mathas & Curland. Lernexpress II. 176p. (C). 1992. pap. text ed. 16.95 (*0-8403-7416-X*) Kendall-Hunt.

Mathas, Alexander. Der Kalte Krieg in der Deutschen Literaturkritik: Martin Walsers Narrative Prosa in der BRD und DDR. LC 91-48192. (German Life & Civilization Ser.: Vol. 12). 243p. (GER.). (C). 1993. text ed. 46.95 (*0-8204-1824-2*) P Lang Pubs.

Mathe, G. & Muggia, Franco M., eds. Cancer Chemo-& Immunopharmacology Part 1: Chemopharmacology. (Recent Results in Cancer Research Ser.: Vol. 74). (Illus.). 315p. 1980. 77.00 (*0-387-10162-4*) Spr-Verlag.

Mathe, G. & Reizenstein, P., eds. Pathophysiological Aspects of Cancer Epidemiology. (Advances in the Biosciences Ser.: No. 50). (Illus.). 276p. 1985. 99.00 (*0-08-030780-9*, Pergamon Pr) Elsevier.

Mathe, G., et al, eds. Lymphocytes, Macrophages, & Cancer. LC 76-26538. (Recent Results in Cancer Research Ser.: Vol. 56). 1976. 35.00 (*3-540-07902-5*) Spr-Verlag.

Mathe, Herve & Shapiro, Roy D. Total Service Management: Service Strategy for the Manufacturing Company. LC 92-42178. (Illus.). 336p. 1993. 49.95 (*0-412-46780-1*, A9464) Chapman & Hall.

Mathea-Foertsch, M., ed. see Andreade, B., et al.

Matheis, G. & Schandelmeier, H., eds. Current Research in African Earth Sciences: Extended Abstracts of the 14th Colloquium on African Geology, Berlin, 18-22 August 1987. 504p. (C). 1987. text ed. 105.00 (*90-6191-709-3*, Pub. by A A Balkema NE); pap. text ed. 60.00 (*90-6191-710-7*, Pub. by A A Balkema NE) Ashgate Pub Co.

Matheis, W., jt. auth. see Erb, Bruno.

Mathelitsch, L. & Plessas, W., eds. Substructures of Matter As Revealed with Electroweak Probes: Proceedings of the Thirty-Second Internationale Universit Atswochen fur Kern & Teilchenphysik, Schladming, Austria, 24 February-5 March 1993. LC 93-44976. (Lecture Notes in Physics Ser.: Vol. 426). 1994. 81.00 (*0-387-57575-8*) Spr-Verlag.

Mathema, Sudarshan B., jt. auth. see Farrington, John W.

Mathematical Institute of the Polish Academy of Sciences Staff & Institute of Mathematics of the Adam Mickiewicz University Staff. Approximation Theory: Proceedings of the Institute of Mathematics, Poznan, August 22-26, 1972. Ciesielski, Z. & Musielak, J., eds. LC 74-80524. 289p. 1975. lib. bdg. 103.00 (*90-277-0483-X*) Kluwer Ac.

Mathematical Sciences Education Board Staff. Measuring Up: Prototypes for Mathematics Assessment. LC 92-62904. (Illus.). 176p. (Orig.). 1993. pap. text ed. 10.95 (*0-309-04845-1*) Natl Res Coun.

***Mathematical Social Science Board Conference on the New Economic History of Britain Staff.** Essays on a Mature Economy: Britain after 1840. McCloskey, Donald N., ed. LC 73-170254. Date not set. reprint ed. pap. 129.70 (*0-7837-9500-9*, 2060247) Bks Demand.

Mathematical Society of Japan Staff. Functional Analysis & Related Topics, 1969: Proceedings of the International Conference. 423p. 1970. 42.50 (*0-86008-026-9*, Pub. by U of Tokyo JA) Col U Pr.

Mathematical Society of Japan Staff & Ito, Kiyosi, eds. Encyclopedic Dictionary of Mathematics, 2 vols. 2nd ed. LC 86-21092. (Illus.). 2148p. (C). 1993. reprint ed. pap. 70.00 (*0-262-59020-4*) MIT Pr.

Mathematical Society of Japan Staff & Kiyosi Ito, eds. Encyclopedic Dictionary of Mathematics, 4 vols., Set. 2nd ed. (Illus.). 2113p. 1987. 385.00 (*0-262-09026-0*) MIT Pr.

***Mathematics of Computation 50th Anniversary Symposium Staff.** Mathematics of Computation 1943-1993 3 Pts. Gautschi, Walter, ed. LC 94-31835. (Proceedings of Symposia in Applied Mathematics Ser.: Vol. 48). 1994. write for info. (*0-8218-0291-7*); write for info. (*0-8218-0353-0*) Am Math.

Matheny, Albert R., jt. auth. see Williams, Bruce A.

Matheny, Bradley L., jt. auth. see Wagner, Gary S.

Matheny, Emma R. & Yates, Helen K. Kingston Parish Register: Gloucester & Mathews Counties, Virginia, 1749-1827. 167p. 1991. reprint ed. pap. 17.50 (*0-685-60484-5*, 3800) Clearfield Co.

— Marriages of Lunenburg County, Virginia, 1746-1853. (Illus.). 177p. 1990. reprint ed. 21.75 (*0-685-60488-8*, 3805) Clearfield Co.

Matheny, Fred. Bicycling Magazine's Complete Guide to Riding & Racing Techniques. LC 88-31654. (Illus.). 256p. 1989. 19.95 (*0-87857-804-8*, 12-810-0); pap. 14.95 (*0-87857-805-6*, 12-810-1) Rodale Pr Inc.

Matheny, Fred, et al. Weight Training for Cyclists. LC 87-115125. (Illus.). 78p. (Orig.). 1986. pap. 9.95 (*0-941950-11-5*) Vitesse Pr.

Matheny, James F. & Matheny, Marjorie B. Collision Course: The Ram & the Goat of Daniel 8. Esolen, Debra, ed. (Illus.). 185p. (Orig.). 1993. pap. 8.95 (*0-939422-05-0*) Jay & Assocs.

— Come Thou Reign Over Us. 167p. (Orig.). (C). 1981. pap. 6.95 (*0-939422-00-X*) Jay & Assocs.

— The Four Beasts of Daniel Seven: Prophecy for the End Time. Esolen, Debra, ed. (Illus.). 190p. (Orig.). (C). 1992. pap. text ed. 8.95 (*0-939422-04-2*) Jay & Assocs.

— Gold, Silver, Brass, Iron: Rethinking the Kingdoms of Daniel 2. 175p. (Orig.). (C). 1988. pap. 6.95 (*0-939422-02-6*) Jay & Assocs.

— Is There a Russian Connection? An Exposition of Ezekiel 37 & 39. 76p. (Orig.). (J). 1987. pap. 3.95 (*0-939422-01-8*) Jay & Assocs.

Matheny, James F., jt. auth. see Matheny, Marjorie B.

Matheny, Kenneth B. & Riordan, Richard J. Stress & Strategies for Lifestyle Management. 250p. 1992. pap. 29.95 (*0-88406-250-3*) GA St U Busn Pr.

Matheny, Kenneth J., jt. auth. see Weston, J. Fred.

***Matheny, Marjorie B. & Matheny, James F.** A Kingdom Divided: An Exposition of Daniel 10-12. 195p. 1994. pap. text ed. 8.95 (*0-939422-06-9*) Jay & Assocs.

— The Mark of Blasphemy: An Exposition of Revelation 13:16-18. 108p. 1995. pap. text ed. 5.95 (*0-939422-08-5*) Jay & Assocs.

— The Seventy Weeks of Daniel: An Exposition of Daniel 9: 24-27. 133p. (Orig.). 1990. pap. 6.95 (*0-939422-03-4*) Jay & Assocs.

Matheny, Marjorie B., jt. auth. see Matheny, James F.

Matheny, Nelda & Clark, James. A Photographic Guide to the Evaluation of Hazard Trees in Urban Areas. 2nd ed. 85p. 1993. pap. text ed. 35.00 (*1-881956-04-0*) Int Soc Arboricult.

Matheny, Nelda, jt. auth. see Clark, James.

Matheny, Philip M. Critical Path Hiring: How to Employ Top-Flight Managers. LC 85-45472. (Illus.). 1986. text ed. 24.95 (*0-669-11789-7*) Free Pr.

***Matheny, Richard E.** Major Gifts: Solicitation Strategies. 1994. 41.50 (*0-89964-309-4*) Coun Adv & Supp Ed.

Matheopoulos, Helena. Diva: Great Sopranos & Mezzos Discuss Their Art. 352p. 1992. text ed. 29.95 (*1-55553-132-6*) NE U Pr.

***Mather & Chapman.** Environmental Resources. Date not set. pap. text ed. 34.95 (*0-470-23491-1*) Wiley.

Mather, A. S. Global Forest Resources. 351p. (C). 1991. text ed. 350.00 (*81-7089-137-X*, Pub. by Intl Bk Distr II) St Mut.

***Mather, Alexander, ed.** Afforestation: Policies, Planning & Progress. 1994. text ed. 79.95 (*0-471-94716-4*) Wiley.

Mather, Alexander S. Global Forest Resources. LC 84-22168. 341p. 1990. 45.00 (*0-88192-178-5*) Timber.

Mather, Anne. Alien Wife. large type ed. 357p. 1993. 21.95 (*0-7505-0412-9*, Pub. by Magna Print Bks) Ulverscroft.

— Apollo's Seed. large type ed. 278p. (Orig.). 1992. 21.95 (*0-7505-0385-8*, Pub. by Magna Print Bks) Ulverscroft.

— Betrayed. (Presents Ser.). 1992. pap. 2.89 (*0-373-11492-3*, 1-11492-5) Harlequin Bks.

— Betrayed. large type ed. 1992. reprint ed. lib. bdg. 18.95 (*0-263-12892-X*, Pub. by Mills & Boon UK) Thorndike Pr.

— Blind Passion. large type ed. 282p. 1991. reprint ed. lib. bdg. 18.95 (*0-263-12694-3*, Pub. by Mills & Boon UK) Thorndike Pr.

— Brittle Bondage. (Presents Ser.). 1995. pap. 3.25 (*0-373-11722-1*, 1-11722-5) Harlequin Bks.

— Dangerous Sanctuary. (Presents Ser.). 1993. pap. 2.89 (*0-373-11553-9*, 1-11553-4) Harlequin Bks.

— Dangerous Sanctuary. large type ed. 1993. reprint ed. lib. bdg. 18.95 (*0-263-13183-1*, Pub. by Mills & Boon UK) Thorndike Pr.

— Fever in the Blood. (Presents Ser.: No. 1251). 1990. pap. 2.50 (*0-373-11251-3*) Harlequin Bks.

— Guilty. (Presents Ser.). 1993. pap. 2.89 (*0-373-11542-3*, 1-11542-7) Harlequin Bks.

— Guilty. large type ed. 1992. reprint ed. lib. bdg. 18.95 (*0-263-13098-3*, Pub. by Mills & Boon UK) Thorndike Pr.

— Indiscretion. (Presents Ser.: No. 1354). 1991. pap. 2.75 (*0-373-11354-4*) Harlequin Bks.

— Legacy of the Past. large type ed. 316p. 1993. 21.95 (*0-7505-0551-6*, Pub. by Magna Print Bks) Ulverscroft.

— Monkshood. large type ed. 283p. 1994. 17.95 (*0-7505-0602-4*, Pub. by Magna Print Bks) Ulverscroft.

— Pale Orchid. large type ed. (Magna Romance Ser.). 1992. 11.95 (*0-7505-0226-6*, Pub. by Magna Print Bks) Ulverscroft.

— Raw Silk: (Too Hot to Handle) (Presents Ser.). 1995. mass mkt. 3.25 (*0-373-11731-0*, 1-11731-6) Harlequin Bks.

— A Relative Betrayal. 1990. pap. 2.50 (*0-373-11315-3*) Harlequin Bks.

— Rich As Sin. (Presents Ser.). 1993. mass mkt. 2.99 (*0-373-11567-9*, 1-11567-4) Harlequin Bks.

— Rich As Sin. large type ed. (Harlequin Ser.). 1993. 17.95 (*0-263-13412-1*) Thorndike Pr.

— A Secret Rebellion. (Presents Ser.). 1994. mass mkt. 2.99 (*0-373-11663-2*, 1-11663-1) Harlequin Bks.

— A Secret Rebellion. large type ed. (Harlequin Romance Ser.). 1994. 18.95 (*0-263-13822-4*) Thorndike Pr.

— Snowfire. (Presents Ser.). 1994. mass mkt. 2.99 (*0-373-11617-9*, 1-11617-7) Harlequin Bks.

— Strange Intimacy. 1994. mass mkt. 2.99 (*0-373-11697-7*, 1-11697-9) Harlequin Bks.

— Such Sweet Poison. large type ed. 285p. 1991. reprint ed. lib. bdg. 18.95 (*0-263-12807-5*) Thorndike Pr.

— Tender Assault. 1994. 2.99 (*0-373-11649-7*) Harlequin Bks.

— Tender Assault. large type ed. (Harlequin Ser.). 1994. 18.95 (*0-263-13716-3*) Thorndike Pr.

— Tidewater Seduction. (Presents Plus Ser.). 1993. mass mkt. 2.99 (*0-373-11591-1*, 1-11591-4) Harlequin Bks.

— Tidewater Seduction. large type ed. (Harlequin Ser.). 18.95 (*0-263-13356-7*, Pub. by Mills & Boon UK) Thorndike Pr.

— Treacherous Longings. (Presents Ser.). 1995. mass mkt. 3.25 (*0-373-11759-0*, 1-11759-7) Harlequin Bks.

— Wild Concerto. (Bestsellers Ser.). 384p. 1983. mass mkt. 4.95 (*0-373-97006-4*) Harlequin Bks.

Mather, Anne D. Just for Today: Thoughts to Live By. 190p. 1994. pap. 11.95 (*0-06-251062-2*) Harper SF.

Mather, Anne D. & Weldon, Louise B. Around the Year with the Cat at the Door: A Place for Me to Write My Thoughts. (Illus.). 96p. 1994. 14.95 (*1-56838-014-3*, 1476A) Hazelden.

— Around the Year with the Cat at the Door: Fifty Self-affirming Activities for the Classroom & Youth Groups. LC 93-4590. 96p. 1993. pap. 14.95 (*0-89486-937-X*, 1476A) Hazelden.

— The Cat at the Door: And Other Stories to Live By. (Illus.). 200p. (J). (ps-4). 1991. per., pap. 12.00 (*0-89486-758-X*, 5131A) Hazelden.

Mather, Berkely. The Pagoda Tree. large type ed. 576p. 1982. 15.95 (*0-7089-0892-6*) Ulverscroft.

Mather, Betty B. Interpretation of French Music from 1675-1775 for Woodwind & Other Performers. LC 74-168244. 1973. 20.00 (*0-941084-03-5*) McGinnis & Marx.

Mather, Betty B. & Karns, Dean M. Dance Rhythms of the French Baroque: A Handbook for Performance. LC 86-45991. (Music: Scholarship & Performance Ser.). (Illus.). 352p. 1988. 39.95 (*0-253-31606-5*) Ind U Pr.

Mather, Betty B. & Lasocki, David. Free Ornamentation in Woodwind Music. LC 87-753698. 1976. 22.00 (*0-941084-05-1*) McGinnis & Marx.

Mather, Betty B., jt. auth. see Lasocki, David.

Mather, Betty Bang & Lasocki, David. The Art of Preluding, 1700-1830. LC 84-758576. 1983. 12.00 (*0-941084-08-6*) McGinnis & Marx.

Mather, Carol. Aftermath of War: Everyone Must Go Home. (Illus.). 272p. 1992. 29.95 (*0-08-037708-4*, Pub. by Brasseys UK) Brasseys Inc.

Mather, Charlotte. Free to Good Home. 248p. 1991. pap. 9.99 (*1-879384-08-6*) Cypress Hse.

Mather, Christine. Colonial Frontiers: Art & Like in Spanish New Mexico. (Illus.). 120p. 1983. text ed. 29.95 (*0-89013-185-6*); pap. text ed. 19.95 (*0-89013-186-4*) Museum NM Pr.

— Native America: Arts, Traditions, & Celebrations. (Illus.). 1990. 40.00 (*0-517-57436-5*, C P Pubs) Crown Pub Group.

— Santa Fe Christmas. LC 93-2736. 1993. 16.00 (*0-517-59246-0*, C P Pubs) Crown Pub Group.

— True West. 1992. 40.00 (*0-517-58336-4*, C P Pubs) Crown Pub Group.

Mather, Christine & Woods, Sharon. Santa Fe Style. LC 86-42715. (Illus.). 256p. 1986. 40.00 (*0-8478-0734-7*) Rizzoli Intl.

Mather, Cotton. The Angel of Bethesda. Jones, Gordon W., ed. LC 72-185323. 384p. 1972. 30.00 (*0-8271-7220-6*, U Pr of Va) Am Antiquarian.

— Bonifacius: An Essay upon the Good. Levin, David, ed. LC 66-14448. 215p. reprint ed. pap. 61.30 (*0-8357-7340-X*, 2014654) Bks Demand.

— Bonifacius: An Essay...to Do Good. LC 67-18712. 1967. reprint ed. 50.00 (*0-8201-1032-9*) Schol Facsimiles.

— The Christian Philosopher. LC 92-32064. 630p. (C). 1993. 49.95 (*0-252-01952-0*) U of Ill Pr.

— Christian Philosopher: A Collection of the Best Discoveries in Nature, with Religious Improvements. LC 68-29082. 1968. reprint ed. 50.00 (*0-8201-1033-7*) Schol Facsimiles.

— Cotton Mather on Witchcraft. (Dorset Classic Reprints Ser.). (Illus.). 180p. 1991. 19.95 (*0-88029-672-0*) Dorset Pr.

— Day of Humiliation: Times of Affliction & Disaster. LC 68-24211. 1970. 60.00 (*0-8201-1067-1*) Schol Facsimiles.

— Great Works of Christ in America: Magnalia Christi Americana of the Ecclesiastical History of New England, 1620-1698, 2 vols., Set: Vol. 1, 650p.; Vol. 2, 680p. 1979. Set, Vol. 1, 650p.; Vol. 2, 680p. 69.95 (*0-85151-280-1*) Banner of Truth.

— Life of Sir William Phips. LC 75-137260. reprint ed. 31.50 (*0-404-04249-X*) AMS Pr.

— The Life of Sir William Phips. (BCL1 - United States Local History Ser.). 208p. 1991. reprint ed. lib. bdg. 79.00 (*0-7812-6266-6*) Rprt Serv.

— Magnalia Christi Americana, Bks. I & II. Murdock, Kenneth B. & Miller, Elizabeth W., eds. LC 73-76383. (John Harvard Library). (Illus.). 508p. reprint ed. pap. 146.00 (*0-7837-2496-9*, 2057459) Bks Demand.

— Magnalia Christi Americana, or the Ecclesiastical History of New-England from the Year 1620, Unto the Year 1698, 7 Bks, Set. LC 74-141092. (Research Library of Colonial Americana). (Illus.). 1972. reprint ed. 63.95 (*0-405-03297-8*) Ayer.

— Manuductio Administerium, Directions for a Candidate of the Ministry. LC 75-41190. reprint ed. 36.50 (*0-404-14685-6*) AMS Pr.

— Ornaments for the Daughters of Zion. LC 78-8588. 1978. 50.00 (*0-8201-1311-5*) Schol Facsimiles.

— Paterna: The Autobiography of Cotton Mather. Bosco, Ronald A., ed. LC 76-10595. (Center for Editions of American Authors). 504p. 1976. lib. bdg. 75.00 (*0-8201-1273-9*) Schol Facsimiles.

— Present State of New England. LC 68-24989. (American History & Americana Ser.: No. 47). 1969. reprint ed. lib. bdg. 69.95 (*0-8383-0214-9*) M S G Haskell Hse.

An Asterisk (*) at the beginning of an entry indicates that the title is appearing in BIP for the first time.

— The Present State of New England. (BCL1 - U. S. History Ser.). 52p. 1991. reprint ed. lib. bdg. 59.00 (*0-7812-6099-X*) Rprt Serv.

— Ratio Disciplinae Fratrum Novanglorum: A Faithful Account of the Discipline Professed & Practised, in the Churches of New-England. LC 71-141114. (Research Library of Colonial Americana). 1972. reprint ed. 25.95 (*0-405-03327-3*) Ayer.

— Selected Letters of Cotton Mather. Silverman, Kenneth, ed. LC 78-142338. 472p. reprint ed. pap. 134.60 (*0-317-29860-7*, 2019565) Bks Demand.

— The Threefold Paradise of Cotton Mather: An Edition of Triparadisus. Smolinski, Reiner, ed. LC 92-29850. 520p. 1995. 75.00 (*0-8203-1519-2*) U of Ga Pr.

Mather, Cotton & Karan, P. P. Beyond the Great Divide: Denver to the Grand Canyon. LC 92-10534. (Touring North America Ser.). (Illus.). 194p. 1992. 25.00 (*0-8135-1882-2*); pap. 9.95 (*0-8135-1883-0*) Rutgers U Pr.

***Mather, Cotton & Thompson, George F.** Registered Places of New Mexico: The Land of Enchantment. 1995. 19.95 (*0-9643841-0-8*) NMex Geograp.

Mather, Cotton, jt. ed. see De Souza, Anthony R.

Mather, Cotton, jt. auth. see Janeway, James.

Mather, Cotton, jt. ed. see Karan, P. P.

Mather, Cotton, jt. auth. see Mather, Increase.

Mather, Cynthia L. & Debye, Kristina E. How Long Does It Hurt? A Guide to Recovering from Incest for Teenagers, Their Friends, & Their Families. LC 94-12536. (Social & Behavioral Sciences Ser.). 178p. 1994. pap. 15.00 (*1-55542-674-3*) Jossey-Bass.

Mather, Eleanore P. Anna Brinton: A Study in Quaker Character. LC 74-152086. (Illus.). (Orig.). 1971. pap. 3.00 (*0-87574-176-2*) Pendle Hill.

— Barclay in Brief. (C). 1944. pap. 7.00 (*0-87574-028-6*) Pendle Hill.

— Edward Hicks, Primitive Quaker. LC 75-110287. (Illus.). (Orig.). 1970. pap. 3.00 (*0-87574-170-3*) Pendle Hill.

— Pendle Hill: A Quaker Experiment in Education & Community. LC 79-93378. 128p. 1980. 7.00 (*0-87574-954-2*) Pendle Hill.

Mather, Eleanore P. & Miller, Dorothy C. Edward Hicks: His Peaceable Kingdoms & Other Paintings. LC 81-71405. (Illus.). 224p. 1983. 40.00 (*0-8453-4760-8*, Cornwall Bks) Assoc Univ Prs.

Mather, Eleanore P., ed. see Fogelklou-Norlind, Emilia.

Mather, Eleanore P., ed. see Murphy, Carol.

Mather, Eleanore P., ed. see Robinson, Jo Ann.

Mather, F. C. High Church Prophet: Bishop Samuel Horsley (1733-1806) & the Caroline Tradition in the Later Georgian Church. (Illus.). 344p. 1992. 76.00 (*0-19-820227-X*) OUP.

Mather, F. C., ed. Chartism & Society. LC 80-15587. 488p. 1980. 54.50 (*0-8419-0625-4*) Holmes & Meier.

Mather, Frank A., Jr. Charles Herbert Moore, Landscape Painter. 1957. 29.95 (*0-691-03810-4*) Princeton U Pr.

Mather, Frank J. Estimates in Art. LC 79-137261. (Illus.). reprint ed. 39.50 (*0-404-04256-2*) AMS Pr.

— Estimates in Art, Ser. 2. LC 70-93356. (Essay Index Reprint Ser.). 1977. 23.95 (*0-8369-1527-5*) Ayer.

Mather, Frank J., Jr. Mahonri M. Young. (Illus.). 59p. (Orig.). 1940. pap. write for info. (*1-879886-05-7*) Addison Gallery.

Mather, Frank J. Western European Painting of the Renaissance. LC 65-28209. (Illus.). reprint ed. 72.00 (*0-8154-0148-5*) Cooper Sq.

Mather, Frederic G. The Refugees of Seventeen Seventy-Six from Long Island to Connecticut. (Illus.). 1206p. 1990. reprint ed. pap. 60.00 (*1-55613-342-1*) Heritage Bk.

Mather, George A. & Nichols, Larry A. Dictionary of Cults, Sects, Religions & the Occult. (Illus.). 384p. 1993. 24.99 (*0-310-53100-4*) Zondervan.

— Masonic Lodge. (Guide to Cults & Religious Movements Ser.). 64p. 1994. 4.99 (*0-310-70421-9*) Zondervan.

Mather, Gillian, ed. Halsbury's Statutory Instruments, 23 vols., Set. 2,300.00 (*0-406-04500-3*) Butterworth Legal Pubs.

Mather, Graham, intro. Europe's Constitutional Future. (Institute of Economic Affairs Book Ser.). 146p. 1991. text ed. 45.00x (*0-8147-3752-8*) NYU Pr.

Mather, H. E. Mather: Lineage of Rev. Richard Mather. (Illus.). 540p. 1990. reprint ed. lib. bdg. 89.00 (*0-8328-1612-4*); reprint ed. pap. 81.00 (*0-8328-1613-2*) Higginson Bk Co.

Mather, Hal. Bills of Materials. 200p. 1986. text ed. 45.00 (*0-87094-947-0*) Irwin Prof Pubng.

— Competitive Manufacturing. 272p. 1988. 29.95 (*0-13-155029-2*, Busn) P-H.

— Competitive Manufacturing. 1992. pap. 17.95 (*0-13-156753-5*) P-H.

— Competitive Manufacturing. 241p. (C). 1988. 310.00 (*0-685-39899-4*, Inst Pur & Supply) St Mut.

— Competitive Manufacturing. 241p. (C). 1989. 280.00 (*0-685-46419-9*, Inst Pur & Supply) St Mut.

Mather, Herb. Letters for All Seasons. LC 93-12892. 80p. (Orig.). 1993. pap. 6.95 (*0-687-39343-4*) Abingdon.

Mather, Herb & Hayes, Terrence. Collaborating in Ministry: Letters to Laity & Pastors of Smaller Churches. LC 93-72191. 112p. 1993. pap. 9.95 (*0-88177-126-0*, DR126) Discipleship Res.

Mather, Herbert. Becoming a Giving Church. LC 85-72879. 56p. (Orig.). 1985. pap. 4.95 (*0-88177-023-X*, DR023) Discipleship Res.

Mather, Increase. Departing Glory: Eight Jeremiads of Increase Mather. LC 86-31349. 1987. 50.00 (*0-8201-1415-4*) Schol Facsimiles.

— An Essay for the Recording of Illustrious Providences. LC 77-17526. 1977. reprint ed. lib. bdg. 60.00 (*0-8201-1299-2*) Schol Facsimiles.

— Relation of the Troubles Which Have Happened in New-England, by Reason of the Indians There from the Year 1614 to the Year 1675. LC 78-141093. (Research Library of Colonial Americana). 1972. reprint ed. 16.95 (*0-405-03298-6*) Ayer.

— Remarkable Providences Illustrative of the Earlier Days of American Colonisation. Dorsen, Richard M., ed. LC 77-70610. (International Folklore Ser.). 1977. reprint ed. lib. bdg. 26.95 (*0-405-10107-4*) Ayer.

Mather, Increase & Mather, Cotton. History of King Philip's War. 280p. 1991. reprint ed. pap. 20.00 (*1-55613-417-7*) Heritage Bk.

Mather, Increase & Stoddard, Solomon. Increase Mather Vs. Solomon Stoddard: Two Puritan Tracts. LC 72-141117. (Research Library of Colonial Americana). 1972. reprint ed. 25.95 (*0-405-03328-1*) Ayer.

Mather Jackson, Edward A. Nathaniel Hawthorne, a Modest Man. LC 77-110834. 356p. 1971. reprint ed. text ed. 35.00 (*0-8371-2594-4*, MANH, Greenwood Pr) Greenwood.

Mather, Jay & Maharidge, Dale. Yosemite - A Landscape of Life. Hennessy, Terry, ed. LC 90-41607. (Illus.). 120p. (Orig.). 1990. pap. 14.95 (*0-939666-56-1*) Yosemite Assn.

Mather, Jean. Fun of Grammar & Writing: English 301. 1992. pap. 22.60 (*1-56226-130-4*) CT Pub.

Mather, Jean, et al. Writing & Grammar: English 200. 1992. pap. 20.95 (*1-56226-131-2*) CT Pub.

Mather, Jennie P., ed. Mammalian Cell Culture: The Use of Serum-Free Hormone-Supplemented Media. LC 84-1985. 312p. 1984. 75.00 (*0-306-41584-4*, Plenum Pr) Plenum.

Mather, Jim, ed. see Green, Madge.

Mather, John R. Water Resources: Distribution, Use & Management. LC 83-21795. (Environmental Science & Technology Ser.: No. 1-121). 439p. 1983. text ed. 69.95 (*0-471-89401-X*) Wiley.

***Mather, John R. & Sanderson, Marie.** The Genius of C. Warren Thornthwaite, Climatologist-Geographer. LC 95-14239. 1995. write for info. (*0-8061-2787-2*) U of Okla Pr.

Mather, John R. & Sdasyuk, Galina V., eds. Global Change: Geographical Approaches. LC 91-14025. (Geographical Dialogue: Soviet & American Views Ser.). (Illus.). 289p. 1991. 45.00 (*0-8165-1272-8*) U of Ariz Pr.

***Mather, Karen T.** Silas, the Bookstore Cat. LC 94-72357. (Illus.). 32p. (J). (gr. 1-4). 1994. 14.95 (*0-89272-352-1*) Down East.

Mather, Kirtley F. & Mason, Shirley L. A Source Book in Geology, 1400-1900. LC 67-12100. (Source Books in the History of the Sciences). (Illus.). 726p. reprint ed. pap. 180.00 (*0-7837-3850-1*, 2043672) Bks Demand.

Mather, Linda. Blood of an Aries: A Zodiac Mystery. 208p. 1994. 18.95 (*0-312-10429-4*) St Martin.

Mather, Marshall. John Ruskin. LC 72-881. (English Biography Ser.: No. 31). 1972. reprint ed. lib. bdg. 58.95 (*0-8383-1425-2*) M S G Haskell Hse.

Mather, Mary. Pocket Guide to Outdoor Photography. (Illus.). 28p. 1993. spiral bd. 12.95 (*0-9633024-5-0*) Greycliff Pub.

Mather, Maurice W. & Hewitt, Joseph W. Xenophon's Anabasis, Bks. 1-4. LC 62-18051. (Illus.). 528p. (J). (gr. 12 up). 1976. reprint ed. pap. 22.95 (*0-8061-1347-2*) U of Okla Pr.

Mather, Melissa. Rough Road Home. LC 58-9537. 256p. (J). 1988. reprint ed. pap. 9.95 (*0-8397-7237-8*) Eriksson.

Mather, N. W. & Sutton, G. W. Engineering Aspects of Magnetohydrodynamics. 688p. 1964. text ed. 426.00 (*0-677-10320-4*) Gordon & Breach.

Mather, Nancy. Instructional Guide to the Woodcock-Johnson Psycho-Educational Battery. rev. ed. LC 90-82412. (Illus.). 305p. (C). 1990. pap. text ed. 42.50 (*0-88422-108-3*) Clinical Psych.

Mather, Nancy & Jaffe, Lynne E. The Woodcock-Johnson Psycho-Educational Battery: Recommendations & Reports. rev. ed. LC 91-75518. 396p. 1992. pap. text ed. 39.50 (*0-88422-115-6*) Clinical Psych.

***Mather, Nancy & Roberts, Rhia.** Informal Assessment & Remediation of Written Language: A Practitioner's Guide for Students with Learning Disabilities. LC 94-29759. 460p. 1995. 44.95 (*0-88422-153-9*) Clinical Psych.

Mather, Patricia, ed. A Coral Reef Handbook. 80p. (C). 1992. text ed. 100.00 (*0-949324-47-7*, Pub. by Surrey Beatty & Sons AT) St Mut.

Mather, Paul M. Computer Applications in Geography. 257p. 1991. pap. text ed. 49.95 (*0-471-92615-9*) Wiley.

— Computer Processing of Remotely-Sensed Images: An Introduction. 353p. 1992. pap. text ed. 46.95 (*0-471-92653-1*) Wiley.

Mather, Paul M., ed. Geographical Information Handling & Applications. LC 93-8835. 250p. 1994. text ed. 69.95 (*0-471-94060-7*) Wiley.

— TERRA-1: Understanding the Terrestrial Environment - The Role of Earth Observations from Space. LC 92-18705. 1992. 99.00 (*0-7484-0044-3*, Pub. by Tay Francis Ltd UK) Taylor & Francis.

— TERRA-2: Understanding the Terrestrial Environment: Remote Sensing Data Systems & Networks. LC 94-23083. 1995. text ed. 79.95 (*0-471-95405-5*) Wiley.

Mather, R. E. & Boswell, F. E. Gold Camp Desperadoes: A Study of Violence, Crime, & Punishment on the Mining Frontier. LC 92-50724. 1993. reprint ed. 11.95 (*0-8061-2521-7*) U of Okla Pr.

Mather, Richard. Church Covenant: Two Tracts. LC 75-141115. (Research Library of Colonial Americana). 1972. reprint ed. 25.95 (*0-405-03329-X*) Ayer.

Mather, Richard B. The Poet Shen Yueh (441-513) The Reticent Marquis. (Illus.). 192p. 1988. text ed. 45.00 (*0-691-06734-1*) Princeton U Pr.

***Mather, Robin.** A Garden of Unearthly Delights: Bioengineering & the Future of Food. 224p. 1995. 23.95 (*0-525-93864-8*) Facts on File.

Mather, Roger. The Art of Playing the Flute: Breath Control. LC 80-52140. (Series of Workbooks: Vol. 1). (Illus.). 88p. (Orig.). (C). 1980. pap. 8.95 (*0-9604640-0-X*) Romney Pr.

— The Art of Playing the Flute: Embouchure, Vol. 2. LC 80-52140. (Illus.). 112p. (Orig.). (C). 1981. pap. 9.95 (*0-9604640-1-8*) Romney Pr.

Mather, Ruth E. & Boswell, F. E. Hanging the Sheriff: A Biography of Henry Plummer. LC 87-2125. (Publications in the American West: No. 21). 208p. 1987. 19.95 (*0-87480-300-4*) U of Utah Pr.

— Hanging the Sheriff: A Biography of Henry Plummer. LC 87-2125. (University of Utah Publications in the American West: No. 21). 236p. reprint ed. pap. 67.30 (*0-8357-3271-1*, 2039492) Bks Demand.

— John David Borthwick: Artist of the Goldrush. LC 88-20671. (University of Utah Publications in the American West: No. 23). 230p. 1989. pap. 65.60 (*0-7837-8566-6*, 2049382) Bks Demand.

Mather, Ruth E. & Boswell, Fred E. Gold Camp Desperadoes: A Study of Violence, Crime & Punishment on the Mining Frontier. LC 89-77024. (Illus.). 224p. 1990. 23.95 (*0-9625069-0-7*) Hist West Pub.

— Vigilante Victims: Montana's Eighteen Sixty-Four Hanging Spree. LC 90-41114. (Illus.). 208p. 1991. 19.95 (*0-9625069-1-5*) Hist West Pub.

Mather, S. & Edbrooke, David. Pre-Hospital Emergency Care. 304p. 1983. pap. 19.95 (*0-7236-0701-X*, Pub. by John Wright UK) Buttrwrth-Heinemann.

Mather, Stephen J. & Hughes, David G., eds. A Handbook of Paediatric Anaesthesia. (Illus.). 320p. 1991. pap. 35.00 (*0-19-263011-3*) OUP.

Mather, Thomas M., jt. auth. see Sonenshine, Daniel E.

Matherly, Donna M., jt. auth. see Curtin, Dennis P.

Matherly, Sandra & Hodges, Shannon. Telephone Nursing: The Process. Pramik, Janice, ed. 132p. (Orig.). (C). 1990. pap. text ed. 44.00 (*0-933948-23-9*, 2550) Ctr Res Ambulatory.

Matherne, Beverly. Cajuns Images: Images Cadiennes. 36p. (Orig.). 1994. pap. text ed. 6.00x (*1-56439-032-2*) Ridgeway.

— Je Me Souviens de la Louisiane. Bixby, Robert, ed. 31p. 1993. pap. 6.00 (*1-882983-06-8*) March Street Pr.

Matheron, G. Estimating & Choosing. (Illus.). 170p. 1989. pap. 56.00 (*0-387-50087-1*) Spr-Verlag.

Mathers, et al. Principles of Clinical Anatomy. 800p. 1994. write for info. (*0-8016-6356-3*) Mosby Yr Bk.

Mathers, Douglas. Brain. LC 90-42883. (Illus.). 32p. (J). (gr. 4-6). 1992. lib. bdg. 11.89 (*0-8167-2090-8*); pap. 3.95 (*0-8167-2091-6*) Troll Assocs.

— Ears. LC 90-42176. (Illus.). 32p. (J). (gr. 4-6). 1992. lib. bdg. 11.89 (*0-8167-2092-4*); pap. text ed. 3.95 (*0-8167-2093-2*) Troll Assocs.

Mathers, E. P. Sung to Sharyar. 128p. 1987. 70.00 (*1-85077-146-4*, Darf Pubs Ltd) St Mut.

Mathers, E. Powys. The Book of the Thousand Nights & One Night, 4 vols. 1986. 12.95 (*0-685-73835-3*, A5329, RKP); 12.95 (*0-318-61561-4*, RKP); 12.95 (*0-318-61562-2*, RKP) Routledge.

— The Book of the Thousand Nights & One Night, 4 vols., Set. 1986. 37.50 (*0-7102-0869-3*, A5329, RKP) Routledge.

Mathers, Edward P., ed. Coloured Stars: Oriental Love Poetry. pap. 3.95 (*0-8283-1432-2*, 11) Branden Pub Co.

Mathers, James. The Motorist's Guide to the Law. 90p. 1986. 100.00 (*0-906840-95-3*, Pub. by Fourmat Pub UK) St Mut.

Mathers, James M. The Recovery Handbook. LC 90-86083. (Orig.). 1992. pap. 15.95 (*0-9628640-0-5*) Helion Pub.

Mathers, John C., jt. ed. see Widdowson, Elsie M.

Mathers, Lawrence J., Jr. The Peripheral Nervous System: Structure, Function, & Clinical Correlations. (Illus.). 227p. (C). 1984. reprint ed. pap. text ed. 26.95 (*0-409-90074-5*) Buttrwrth-Heinemann.

Mathers, MacGregor. The Kabbalah Unveiled. LC 71-16504. 388p. (Orig.). 1983. reprint ed. pap. 12.95 (*0-87728-557-8*) Weiser.

Mathers, Norm. The New Beyond: Predictions, Prophets & Psychics - A Global Issue. 160p. 1994. pap. write for info. (*0-9634654-1-4*) ATS Pubns.

***Mathers, Norman.** Beyond Desert Storm. 1993. pap. 9.95 (*0-916573-96-6*) LIFETIME.

Mathers, Norman W. Beyond Desert Storm: Hope for Days Ahead. (Illus.). 96p. 1993. pap. 12.95 (*0-9634654-0-6*) ATS Pubns.

***Mathers, Petra.** Kisses from Rosa. LC 94-32500. 1995. 16.00 (*0-679-82686-6*); pap. 15.99 (*0-679-82868-0*) Knopf Bks Yng Read.

— Maria Theresa. LC 84-48346. (Illus.). 32p. (J). (ps-3). 1985. lib. bdg. 13.89 (*0-06-024112-8*) HarpC Child Bks.

— Sophie & Lou. LC 90-37562. (Illus.). 32p. (J). (ps-3). 1991. lib. bdg. 14.89 (*0-06-024072-5*) HarpC Child Bks.

— Sophie & Lou. LC 90-37562. (Illus.). 32p. (J). (ps-3). 1991. 15.00 (*0-06-024071-7*) HarpC Child Bks.

— Victor & Christabel. LC 92-33468. (Illus.). 40p. (J). (ps-3). 1993. 15.00 (*0-679-83060-X*); lib. bdg. 15.99 (*0-679-93060-4*) Knopf Bks Yng Read.

Mathers, S. L. The Book of the Sacred Magic of Abramelin the Mage. LC 75-12248. 320p. 1975. reprint ed. pap. 6.95 (*0-486-23211-5*) Dover.

— The Kabbalah Unveiled. 359p. (Orig.). 1974. reprint ed. spiral bd. 13.25 (*0-7873-1270-3*) Mokelumne.

— The Tarot. 1973. 59.95 (*0-8490-1177-9*) Gordon Pr.

Mathers, S. L., tr. The Kabbala Unveiled: Books of the Zohar. 1973. lib. bdg. 250.00 (*0-87968-124-1*) Krishna Pr.

— The Kabbalah Unveiled. (Illus.). 400p. (Orig.). 1992. pap. 12.95 (*0-14-019310-3*, Arkana) Viking Penguin.

Mathers, S. L., tr. see Crowley, Aleister, ed.

***Mathers, William M.** Treasure of the Concepcion. (Illus.). 164p. (C). 1994. 34.95 (*0-931234-56-5*) Best Pub Co.

Matherson, Charles & Byrum, C. Stephen. A War Still Raging. (Illus.). 376p. 1991. 19.95 (*1-879908-01-8*) Milton Pub.

***Mathes, C. Hodge.** In the Shadow of Old Smoky: Stories of the Mountains & Their People. Maynard, Charles W., ed. (Illus.). 142p. 1994. text ed. 12.00 (*0-9630682-6-1*); pap. text ed. 8.95 (*0-9630682-5-3*) Panther TN.

— Tall Tales from Old Smoky. 252p. 1991. reprint ed. 14.95 (*0-932807-59-3*) Overmountain Pr.

Mathes, Eugene W. Jealousy: The Psychological Data. 218p. (C). 1992. lib. bdg. 36.50 (*0-8191-8521-3*) U Pr of Amer.

Mathes, J. C. Designing Technical Reports. 2nd ed. 528p. (C). 1991. pap. write for info. (*0-02-377095-3*) Macmillan.

Mathes, Jerry D., II. Power Focus: Reconstruction of Self Through Mental Imagery. 1994. 16.95 (*1-885018-04-5*); pap. 9.95 (*1-885018-05-3*) Logo Press.

Mathes, Michael, ed. see De Cardonda, Nicolas.

Mathes, P., ed. Secondary Prevention in Coronary Artery Disease & Myocardial Infarction. (Developments in Cardiovascular Medicine Ser.). 1985. lib. bdg. 178.00 (*0-89838-736-1*) Kluwer Ac.

Mathes, P. & Halhuber, M. J., eds. Controversies in Cardiac Rehabilitation. (Illus.). 240p. 1982. 35.50 (*0-387-11234-0*) Spr-Verlag.

Mathes, Patricia G. & Irby, Beverly J. Teen Pregnancy & Parenting Handbook. LC 92-85264. 440p. (Orig.). (YA). 1993. pap. text ed. 19.95 (*0-87822-333-9*, 4660) Res Press.

— Teen Pregnancy & Parenting Handbook: Discussion Guide. LC 92-85263. 64p. (Orig.). 1993. spiral bd. 6.95 (*0-87822-334-7*, 4661) Res Press.

Mathes, Stephen J. & Nahai, Foad. Clinical Applications for Muscle & Musculocutaneous Flaps. LC 81-18913. (Illus.). 752p. 1982. 199.00 (*0-8016-3164-5*) Mosby Yr Bk.

— Reconstructive Surgery. 1995. 375.00 (*0-942219-02-3*) Quality Med Pub.

Mathes, W. Michael. The America's First Academic Library: Santa Cruz de Tlatelolco. 101p. 1985. 8.95 (*0-929722-05-1*) CA State Library Fndtn.

— Cattle Brands of Baja California Sur: 1809-1885. LC 75-43217. (Baja California Travels Ser.: No. 40). 78p. 1978. 18.00 (*0-87093-240-3*) Dawsons.

Mathes, W. Michael, intro. Ethnology of the Baja California Indians. LC 92-4023. 525p. 1992. 78.00 (*0-8240-0793-X*) Garland.

Mathes, W. Michael, tr. Clemente Guillen, Explorer of the South: Diaries of the Overland Expeditions to Bahia Magdalena & La Paz, 1719, 1720-1721. LC 78-73364. (Baja California Travels Ser.: No. 42). (Illus.). 99p. 1979. 18.00 (*0-87093-242-X*) Dawsons.

Mathesius, Vilem. A Functional Analysis of Present Day English on a General Linguistic Basis. Vachek, Josef, ed. Duskova, Libuse, tr. (Janua Linguarum, Series Practica: No. 208). 228p. 1975. pap. text ed. 50.00 (*90-279-3077-5*) Mouton.

Matheson, Alva. Cedar City Reflections. 2nd rev. ed. LC 87-51370. (Illus.). 227p. Date not set. text ed. 24.95 (*0-935615-03-2*) S Utah St Coll.

Matheson, Andrew J. Molecular Acoustics. LC 73-147401. (Illus.). 308p. reprint ed. pap. 87.80 (*0-685-20597-5*, 2030531) Bks Demand.

Matheson, Ann. Theories of Rhetoric in the 18th-Century Scottish Sermon. LC 93-42728. 308p. 1994. text ed. 99.95 (*0-7734-9413-8*) E Mellen.

Matheson, B. S. Invented Personages in Shakespeare's Plays. LC 71-144656. reprint ed. 27.50 (*0-404-04258-9*) AMS Pr.

Matheson, Boyd C. A Champion Lives Within. Date not set. text ed. 16.95 (*1-882441-24-9*); pap. text ed. 10.95 (*1-882441-25-7*) InANutshell Bks.

— Elephants Don't Bite but Fleas Do. 200p. Date not set. text ed. 19.95 (*1-882441-75-3*); pap. text ed. 12.95 (*1-882441-76-1*) InANutshell Bks.

Matheson, Don. Stray Cat. 1988. pap. 3.50 (*0-671-66508-1*) PB.

Matheson, Douglas W. Experimental Psychology: Research, Design & Analysis. 3rd ed. LC 77-25185. 390p. (C). 1978. text ed. 43.25 (*0-03-089891-9*) HB Coll Pubs.

Matheson, Duncan. Legal Aid - the New Framework. 1988. U.K. pap. 32.00 (*0-406-50295-1*) Butterworth Legal Pubs.

Matheson, Elizabeth & McFee, Michael. To See. LC 91-62756. 80p. 1991. 24.95 (*0-933598-34-3*) NC Wesleyan Pr.

— To See. limited ed. LC 91-62756. 80p. 1991. 150.00 (*0-933598-35-1*) NC Wesleyan Pr.

Matheson, Elizabeth M., ed. see Hart, Robert.

***Matheson, Eve.** The Modeling Handbook: The Complete Guide to Breaking into Local, Regional & International Modeling. 3rd ed. 240p. 1995. pap. 12.00 (*0-8050-3830-2*, Owl) H Holt & Co.

Matheson, Ewing. The Depreciation of Factories, Mines & Industrial Undertakings & Their Valuation. 2nd ed. LC 75-18476. (History of Accounting Ser.). (Illus.). 1979. reprint ed. 18.95 (*0-405-07558-8*) Ayer.

Matheson-Ferrey, Juanita. One Hundred One Inexpensive Ways to Entertain Children. LC 88-72476. 125p. (Orig.). 1987. pap. write for info. (*0-317-59719-1*, 662-4685) AFCOM Pub.

Matheson, George. Portraits of Bible Men. LC 86-27221. (Second Series). 368p. 1987. reprint ed. pap. 9.99 (*0-8254-3252-9*); reprint ed. pap. 9.99 (*0-8254-3253-7*) Kregel.

— Portraits of Bible Women. LC 86-7429. 128p. 1993. reprint ed. pap. 8.99 (*0-8254-3250-2*) Kregel.

Matheson, John, jt. auth. see Kelsey, Hugh.

An Asterisk (*) at the beginning of an entry indicates that the title is appearing in BIP for the first time.

Matheson, John H. Publicly Traded Corporation Governance, Operation & Regulation, 1 vol. (Corporate Law Ser.). 1993. 110.00 (0-685-68838-0) Clark Boardman Callaghan.

— Publicly Traded Corporations: Governance, Operation & Regulation. 1993. 130.00 (0-318-72145-7) Clark Boardman Callaghan.

Matheson, John H. & Garon, Philip S. Minnesota Corporation Law & Practice. LC 92-32448. (National Corporation Law Ser.). 1992. 110.00 (0-13-145996-1) Aspen Law.

Matheson, Katy, jt. ed. see Cohen, Selma J.

Matheson, Lader D. Smoking among Secondary School Children in 1990. 136p. 1991. pap. 35.00 (0-11-691355-X, HM355X) UNIPUB.

Matheson, Lance A. Statistical Quality Control in High Reliability Systems. LC 93-34976. (Studies on Industrial Productivity). 120p. 1993. 35.00 (0-8153-1628-3) Garland.

Matheson, Lister M., ed. Popular & Practical Science of Medieval England. (Medieval Texts & Studies: No. 11). (Illus.). 438p. 1993. 68.00 (0-937191-30-2) Colleagues Pr Inc.

Matheson, M., tr. see Schuon, Frithjof.

Matheson, P. E., tr. see Moritz, Karl P.

***Matheson, Peter, ed. & tr.** Argula Von Grumbach: A Woman's Voice in the Reformation. 192p. 1995. text ed. 33.95 (0-567-09707-2, Pub. by T & T Clark UK) Bks Intl VA.

— The Collected Works of Thomas Muntzer. 544p. 1988. 59.95 (0-567-09495-2, Pub. by T & T Clark UK) Bks Intl VA.

— The Collected Works of Thomas Muntzer. 504p. 1994. pap. text ed. 39.95 (0-567-29252-5, Pub. by T & T Clark UK) Bks Intl VA.

Matheson, Peter, ed. The Third Reich & the Christian Churches. 128p. 1981. pap. 17.95 (0-567-29105-7, Pub. by T & T Clark UK) Bks Intl VA.

***Matheson, Richard.** The Beardless Warriors. 1994. lib. bdg. 24.95x (1-56849-431-9) Buccaneer Bks.

— Bid Time Return. 280p. 1986. reprint ed. lib. bdg. 35.95 (0-89966-514-4) Buccaneer Bks.

— By the Gun. 192p. 1994. pap. 4.50 (0-425-14099-7) Berkley Pub.

— By the Gun. 1994. 18.95 (0-87131-747-8) M Evans.

— Collected Stories. 920p. 1989. lib. bdg. 39.95 (0-910489-10-6, Dream Pr) Scream Pr.

— Darker: Three Novels of Suspense. 1989. lib. bdg. 30.00 (0-910489-05-X) Scream Pr.

— Earthbound. 224p. 1994. 19.95 (0-312-85712-8) Tor Bks.

— Earthbound. 224p. 1995. mass mkt. 4.99 (0-8125-4810-8) Tor Bks.

— Ghost Trilogy. 1988. lib. bdg. 30.00 (0-910489-16-5) Scream Pr.

— The Gun Fight. LC 93-19979. (Evans Novel of the West Ser.). 196p. 1993. 16.95 (0-87131-726-5) M Evans.

— The Gunfight. 256p. (Orig.). 1993. mass mkt. 4.99 (0-425-13901-8) Berkley Pub.

— The Gunfight. large type ed. LC 93-37092. (Orig.). 1993. 17.95 (0-7862-0002-2) Thorndike Pr.

— Hell House. 1994. lib. bdg. 24.95x (1-56849-435-1) Buccaneer Bks.

— I Am Legend. 1976. 27.95 (0-8488-1432-0) Amereon Ltd.

— I Am Legend. 400p. 1991. reprint ed. lib. bdg. 25.95x (0-89966-838-0) Buccaneer Bks.

— I Am Legend. 320p. 1995. reprint ed. mass mkt. 4.99 (0-8125-2300-8) Tor Bks.

— The Incredible Shrinking Man. 320p. 1995. mass mkt. 4.99 (0-8125-2299-0) Tor Bks.

— Journal of the Gun Years. 1992. pap. 4.50 (0-425-13207-2) Berkley Pub.

— Journal of the Gun Years. LC 91-27315. (Novel of the West Ser.). 192p. 1991. 16.95 (0-87131-689-7) M Evans.

— Journal of the Gun Years. large type ed. 340p. 1992. reprint ed. bds. 17.95 (1-56054-345-0) Thorndike Pr.

— Now You See It. 224p. 1995. 19.95 (0-312-85713-6) Tor Bks.

— Now You See It. 1996. mass mkt. write for info. (0-614-05531-8) Tor Bks.

— The Path: Metaphysics for the Nineties. 140p. (Orig.). 1993. 29.00x (0-8095-4120-3) Borgo Pr.

— The Path: Metaphysics for the Nineties. LC 93-13703. 140p. (Orig.). 1993. pap. 10.95 (0-88496-377-2) Capra Pr.

— 7 Steps to Midnight. 320p. 1993. 22.95 (0-312-85409-9) Forge NYC.

— 7 Steps to Midnight. 320p. 1995. pap. 5.99 (0-8125-5057-9) Tor Bks.

— Shadow on the Sun. 1994. 18.95 (0-87131-765-6) M Evans.

— Shadow on the Sun. 192p. 1994. pap. text ed. 4.50 (0-425-14461-5) Berkley Pub.

— The Shrinking Man. 1993. reprint ed. lib. bdg. 25.95x (0-89968-352-5, Lghtyr Pr) Buccaneer Bks.

— Somewhere in Time. 1976. 26.95 (0-8488-1094-5) Amereon Ltd.

— Somewhere in Time & What Dreams May Come. rev. ed. 512p. 1991. reprint ed. 25.00 (0-910489-06-8) Scream Pr.

***Matheson, Richard, ed.** Robert Bloch Tribute Anthology. 1995. 24.95 (0-614-03859-6) Tor Bks.

Matheson, Richard, et al. I Am Legend, Bk. 1. (Illus.). 1991. 5.95 (1-56060-096-9) Eclipse Bks.

— I Am Legend, Bk. 2. (Illus.). 1991. 5.95 (1-56060-097-7) Eclipse Bks.

— I Am Legend, Bk. 3. (Illus.). 1991. 5.95 (1-56060-098-5) Eclipse Bks.

— I Am Legend, Bk. 4. (Illus.). 1991. 5.95 (1-56060-106-X) Eclipse Bks.

Matheson, Richard, et al, eds. The Twilight Zone: The Original Stories. 576p. 1985. pap. 8.95 (0-380-89601-X) Avon.

Matheson, Richard C. Created By. 1994. mass mkt. 5.99 (0-553-56610-5) Bantam.

Matheson, Rob, jt. ed. see Smith, Dave.

Matheson, Robert E. Special Report on Surnames in Ireland: Together with Varieties & Synonymes of Surnames & Christian Names in Ireland, 2 vols. in 1. LC 68-54684. 172p. 1994. reprint ed. 18.50 (0-8063-0187-2, 3830) Genealog Pub.

Matheson, Ruth. Where to from Here: The Managerial Woman in Transition. 1993. pap. 18.95 (1-875680-07-1, Pub. by Busn & Prof Pubng AT) Pubs Dist MI.

***Matheson, Shirlee S.** Youngblood of the Peace. (Illus.). 235p. (Orig.). 1991. pap. 14.95 (1-55059-033-2) Temeron Bks.

Matheson, Shirley S., jt. auth. see Pollon, Earl K.

Matheson, Susan B. Ancient Glass in the Yale University Art Gallery. 1980. pap. 13.00 (0-89467-010-7) Yale Art Gallery.

— Dura-Europos: The Ancient City & the Yale Collection. LC 82-50113. (Illus.). 42p. (Orig.). 1983. pap. 6.50 (0-8143-1752-9) Wayne St U Pr.

— Dura-Europos: The Ancient City & the Yale Collection. (Illus.). 48p. (Orig.). 1982. pap. 3.75 (0-89467-022-0) Yale Art Gallery.

— Greek Vases: A Guide to the Yale Collection. LC 88-50027. (Illus.). 43p. (Orig.). 1988. pap. 6.00 (0-89467-048-4) Yale Art Gallery.

— Polygnotos & Vase Painting in Classical Athens. LC 95-9683. (Studies in Classics). 1995. write for info. (0-299-13870-4) U of Wis Pr.

Matheson, Sylvia. Rajasthan: Land of Kings. LC 84-7319. (Illus.). 200p. 1984. 50.00 (0-86565-046-2) Vendome.

Matheson, Tim. Traffic Tickets, Fines & Other Annoying Things. 72p. 1984. pap. 4.95 (0-8065-0883-3, Citadel Pr) Carol Pub Group.

Matheson, V. & Milner, A. C. Perceptions of the Haj: Five Malay Texts. 68p. 1986. pap. text ed. 10.00 (9971-902-83-4, Pub. by Inst SE Asian Studies SI) Ashgate Pub Co.

Matheson, Wayne, et al. Performance Evaluation in the Human Services. LC 93-23223. (Illus.). 145p. 1994. lib. bdg. 39.95 (1-56024-379-1) Haworth Pr.

Matheus, James & Scherger, Joseph. Patient Care Emergency Handbook. 650p. (C). 1991. text ed. 60.00 (1-878487-30-2) Practice Mgmt Info.

Mathew, Arnold H., tr. Old Catholic Missal & Ritual. LC 73-84708. reprint ed. 27.45 (0-404-01949-8) AMS Pr.

Mathew, Asha. Fair Sex in Unfair Society: Women & Crime. (Illus.). viii, 202p. 1992. 22.95 (1-881338-31-2) Nataraj Bks.

— Fair Sex in Unfair Society (Women & Crime) (C). 1992. 24.00 (81-7024-491-9, Pub. by Ashish II) S Asia.

Mathew, Brian. Iris. 2nd ed. (Illus.). 215p. 1990. 32.95 (0-88192-162-9) Timber.

— Lilies: A Romantic History with a Guide to Cultivation. LC 93-83528. (Flower Garden Ser.). (Illus.). 64p. 1993. 12.95 (1-56138-304-X) Running Pr.

— The Smaller Bulbs. 244p. 1988. 65.00 (0-7134-4922-5, Pub. by Batsford UK) Trafalgar.

Mathew, Brian & Swindells, Philip. Complete Book of Bulbs, Corms, Tubers, & Rhizomes. LC 93-13775. (Illus.). 240p. 1994. 30.00 (0-89577-546-8) RD Assn.

Mathew, Christopher G., ed. Protocols in Human Molecular Genetics. LC 91-25466. (Methods in Molecular Biology Ser.: Vol. 9). (Illus.). 472p. 1991. 69.50 (0-89603-205-1) Humana.

Mathew, David. Catholicism in England, 1535-1935. 1977. lib. bdg. 59.95 (0-8490-1587-1) Gordon Pr.

— Celtic Peoples & Renaissance Europe: A Study of the Celtic & Spanish Influences on Elizabethan History. (Illus.). 1975. reprint ed. 20.00 (0-685-00471-6) Appel.

Mathew, Frank. An Image of Shakespeare. LC 72-3654. (Studies in Shakespeare: No. 24). 1972. reprint ed. lib. bdg. 65.95 (0-8383-1550-X) M S G Haskell Hse.

Mathew, George. Communal Road to a Secular Kerala. 1989. 28.50 (81-7022-282-6, Pub. by Concept II) S Asia.

Mathew, George, ed. Dignity for All: Essays in Socialism & Democracy. (C). 1991. 25.00 (81-202-0318-6, Pub. by Ajanta II) S Asia.

— Panchayati Raj in Jammu & Kashmir. (C). 1990. text ed. 23.00 (81-7022-315-6, Pub. by Concept II) S Asia.

Mathew, Jan, ed. see Junior League of Sarasota FL, Inc. Staff.

Mathew, K. K. Democracy, Quality & Freedom. 468p. 1978. 235.00 (0-317-54570-1) St Mut.

— Three Lectures. 75p. 1983. 105.00 (0-317-54568-X) St Mut.

Mathew, K. M. History of the Portuguese Navigation in India. 352p. (C). 1987. 37.00 (81-7099-046-7, Pub. by Mittal II) S Asia.

Mathew, K. S. Portuguese Trade with India in the 16th Century. 1983. 24.00 (0-8364-0996-5, Pub. by Manohar II) S Asia.

Mathew, L. P. & Karikari, S. K. Horticulture: Principals & Practices. 202p. 1990. 13.95 (0-333-45306-9) Macmillan.

Mathew, Laura J., jt. ed. see Sloane, Philip D.

Mathew, Mohan. Dimensions of Dialogue. LC 84-17009. 145p. 1984. pap. 6.70 (0-918833-00-0) Comm Wholistic Growth.

Mathew, N. M., jt. ed. see Sethuraj, M. R.

Mathew, Ninan, ed. Cluster Headache. LC 84-4925. 176p. 1984. text ed. 40.00 (0-89335-204-7) PMA Pub Corp.

Mathew, P. M. Women's Organizations & Women's Interests. 177p. 1986. 25.00 (81-7024-036-0, Pub. by Ashish II) S Asia.

Mathew, P. M. & Philip, Omana. Studies in the Pollen Morphology of South Indian Rubiaceae. (Advances in Pollen Spore Research Ser.: Vol. 10). viii, 80p. 1983. 20.00 (1-55528-056-0, Pub. by Today & Tomorrows P & P II) Scholarly Pubns.

Mathew, R. J., ed. Treatment of Migraine: Pharmacological & Biofeedback Considerations. (Illus.). 170p. 1981. text ed. 27.50 (0-88331-209-3) Luce.

Mathew, Theobald. Forensic Fables by "O" 1985. reprint ed. 30.00 (0-406-20150-1, U.K.) Butterworth Legal Pubs.

Mathew, Vadakeparambil M. Due Process of Law - Fifth & Fourteenth Amendments of the U. S. Constitution. 49p. (Orig.). (C). 1980. lib. bdg. 5.00 (0-9614320-0-4) Mathew.

Mathew, William M. Edmund Ruffin & the Crisis of Slavery in the Old South: The Failure of Agricultural Reform. LC 87-25535. 304p. 1988. 35.00 (0-8203-1011-5) U of Ga Pr.

Mathew, William M., ed. see Ruffin, Edmund.

***Mathews.** Art History & Feminism. Date not set. 26.95 (0-8057-9779-3, Twayne); pap. 14.95 (0-8057-9780-7, Twayne) Macmillan.

— Clash of the Gods: A Reinterpretation of Early Christian Art. 1995. pap. (0-691-00159-6) Princeton U Pr.

Mathews & Van Holde, Kensal E. Biochemistry. Bowen, Diane, ed. 1100p. (C). 1990. text ed. 70.95 (0-8053-5015-2); trans. 215.25 (0-8053-5016-0); sl. 17.25 (0-8053-5017-9) Benjamin-Cummings.

Mathews, jt. auth. see Kramer, Janice.

Mathews, jt. auth. see Latourette, Jane.

Mathews, jt. auth. see MacLeod.

Mathews, jt. auth. see Warren, Mary P.

Mathews, Aidan. Lipstick on the Host. 1993. 21.95 (0-15-152575-7) HarBrace.

Mathews, Aidan C. Immediate Man: Cuimhni As Chearbhall o Dalaigh. 1983. pap. 21.00 (0-85105-416-1, Pub. by Colin Smythe Ltd UK) Dufour.

Mathews, Alfred. History of Wayne, Pike & Monroe Counties, PA. (Illus.). 1283p. 1994. reprint ed. lib. bdg. 119.50 (0-8328-3632-X) Higginson Bk Co.

Mathews, Alfred & Hungerford, Austin N. History of the Counties of Lehigh & Carbon, PA. (Illus.). 802p. 1993. reprint ed. lib. bdg. 81.00 (0-8328-2848-3) Higginson Bk Co.

Mathews, Alice. A Woman God Can Use. 1990. 8.99 (0-929239-30-X) Discovery Hse Pubs.

— A Woman Jesus Can Teach. 1991. 8.99 (0-929239-44-X) Discovery Hse Pubs.

Mathews, Alice & Sprintz, Alyse. Relationships: The Missing Link. McCombs, Maryglenn, ed. 58p. (Orig.). 1994. pap. 8.95 (0-9635026-7-0) Eggman Pub.

Mathews, Allison & Hardingham, Martin. Medical & Hygiene Textile Production: A Handbook. 56p. (Orig.). 1994. pap. 13.50 (1-85339-211-1, Pub. by Intermed Tech UK) Women Ink.

Mathews, Andrew & Steptoe, Andrew. Essential Psychology for Medical Practice. (Illus.). 186p. (C). 1988. pap. text ed. 22.00 (0-443-03423-0) Churchill.

Mathews, Andrew M., jt. ed. see Steptoe, Andrew.

Mathews, Andrew M., et al. Agoraphobia: Nature & Treatment. LC 80-29038. (Guilford Clinical Psychology & Psychotherapy Ser.). 233p. 1981. lib. bdg. 32.00 (0-89862-003-1) Guilford Pr.

Mathews, Anne J. Communicate: A Librarian's Guide to Interpersonal Relations. LC 83-2557. 88p. reprint ed. pap. 25.10 (0-7837-5972-X, 2045774) Bks Demand.

Mathews, Annette L., tr. see Perez, Ramon.

Mathews, Anthony, tr. see Adam, Jean-Pierre.

Mathews, Basil J., ed. East & West: Conflict or Cooperation. LC 67-26764. (Essay Index Reprint Ser.). 1977. 17.95 (0-8369-0694-2) Ayer.

Mathews, Binny, illus. Recipes: A Notebook for Cooks. 142p. 1988. 14.95 (0-948751-02-9) Interlink Pub.

Mathews, Boots, jt. auth. see Rieger, James.

Mathews, Chester O. The Grade Placement of Curriculum Materials in the Social Studies. LC 78-177058. (Columbia University. Teachers College. Contributions to Education Ser.: No. 241). reprint ed. 37.50 (0-404-55241-2) AMS Pr.

Mathews, Cleve, jt. auth. see Rivers, William L.

Mathews, Cornelius. Behemoth: A Legend of the Mound-Builders. 1972. reprint ed. 24.50 (0-8422-8138-X) Irvington.

— Big Abel & the Little Manhattan. 1972. reprint ed. 24.50 (0-8422-8093-6) Irvington.

— The Career of Puffer Hopkins. 1972. reprint ed. 28.00 (0-8422-8094-4) Irvington.

— The Various Writings of Cornelius Mathews. LC 72-144659. 370p. 1972. reprint ed. 47.50 (0-404-04265-1) AMS Pr.

— The Various Writings of Cornelius Mathews. (BCL1-PS American Literature Ser.). 370p. 1992. reprint ed. lib. bdg. 89.00 (0-7812-6791-9) Rprt Serv.

Mathews, Cornelius, ed. Enchanted Moccasins & Other Legends of the American Indians. LC 73-119646. reprint ed. 24.75 (0-404-04264-3) AMS Pr.

Mathews, Craig. Fishing Yellowstone Hatches. 144p. 1992. 19.95 (1-55821-178-0) Lyons & Burford.

Mathews, Craig & Juracek, John. Fly Patterns of Yellowstone. (Illus.). 88p. 1989. 17.95 (1-55821-030-X) Lyons & Burford.

Mathews, Daniel. Cascade-Olympic Natural History. LC 88-61494. (Illus.). 640p. (Orig.). 1988. pap. 22.50 (0-9620782-0-4) Raven Edit.

Mathews, David. Politics for People: Finding a Responsible Public Voice. LC 93-5794. 240p. 1994. 24.95 (0-252-02088-X); pap. 9.95 (0-252-06382-1) U of Ill Pr.

— The Promise of Democracy: A Source Book for Use with National Issues Forums. 162p. (Orig.). 1988. student ed (0-318-64412-6) Kettering Found.

Mathews, David, ed. see Mitchell, Donald.

Mathews, David M. Precalculus Investigations Using Derive. LC 93-33006. (C). 1993. 14.25 (0-673-99097-4) HarpCollege.

— Precalculus Investigations Using Maple. (C). 1994. 13.00 (0-673-99410-4) HarpCollege.

Mathews, David M. & Schwingendorf, Keith. Precalculus Investigations Using Maple V. LC 93-46030. 1994. write for info. (0-673-00410-4) HarpCollege.

Mathews-Deacon, Saundra. Magic Theatre I: Children's Musical. (J). 1977. 3.75 (0-87129-230-0, M12) Dramatic Pub.

— Magic Theatre II. 1981. 5.00 (0-87129-396-X, M45) Dramatic Pub.

Mathews, Diane L. New England Visitors' Guide to Botanical Gardens & Nature Centers. 20p. (Orig.). 1984. pap. 4.00 (0-917247-01-9) D L Mathews.

Mathews, Donald G. Religion in the Old South. LC 77-587. 1979. pap. text ed. 16.95 (0-226-51002-6, P819) U Ch Pr.

— Slavery & Methodism: A Chapter in American Morality, 1780-1845. LC 78-13249. 329p. 1978. reprint ed. text ed. 35.00 (0-313-21045-4, MASAM, Greenwood Pr) Greenwood.

Mathews, Donald G. & De Hart, Jane S. Sex, Gender & the Politics of ERA: A State & the Nation. (Illus.). 304p. 1990. 24.95 (0-19-503858-4) OUP.

— Sex, Gender, & the Politics of ERA: A State & the Nation. (Illus.). 304p. 1992. reprint ed. pap. 16.95 (0-19-507852-7) OUP.

Mathews, Dorothy, jt. auth. see Schaffter, Dorothy.

Mathews, E. Powys, tr. see Suikaku, Ilara.

Mathews, Eddie & Buege, Bob. Eddie Mathews & the National Pastime. LC 94-71074. (Illus.). 347p. 1994. 22.95 (1-882134-41-9); pap. 13.95 (1-882134-44-3) Douglas Amer Sports Pubns.

Mathews, Edward. Autobiography of Rev. E. Mathews, the Father Dickson of Mrs. Stowe's 'Dred' LC 79-89392. (Black Heritage Library Collection). 1977. 27.95 (0-8369-8629-6) Ayer.

Mathews, Edward G., Jr., tr. see St. Ephrem the Syrian.

Mathews, Edward H. Super-Endurance Paper Planes. (Illus.). 56p. (Orig.). 1992. pap. 13.95 (0-312-08314-9) St Martin.

Mathews, F. Neil. Entomology: Investigative Activities for Could-Be Bug Buffs. Smith, Linda H., ed. 1978. pap. 6.95 (0-936386-03-7) Creative Learning.

Mathews, F. X., ed. see Secundus, Joannes.

***Mathews, Francine.** Death in Rough Water: A Merry Folger Mystery. LC 95-13826. 1995. write for info. (0-688-13473-4) Morrow.

— Death in the Off-Season: A Merry Fogar Mystery. LC 94-8594. 1994. 23.00 (0-688-13443-2) Morrow.

Mathews, Freya. The Ecological Self. 200p. (C). 1991. text ed. 78.50 (0-389-20935-X) Rowman.

Mathews, George B. Theory of Numbers. 2nd ed. LC 61-17958. 18.95 (0-8284-0156-X) Chelsea Pub.

Mathews, Harry. Armenian Papers: Poems 1954-1984. 120p. 1987. 24.95 (0-691-06711-2); pap. 10.95 (0-691-01440-X) Princeton U Pr.

— Immeasurable Distances: The Collected Essays. (Illus.). 1991. 35.00 (0-932499-43-0) Lapis Pr.

— Immeasurable Distances: The Collected Essays. deluxe limited ed. (Illus.). 1991. 75.00 (0-932499-44-9) Lapis Pr.

— The Orchard. 48p. (Orig.). (C). 1988. pap. 7.00 (0-917453-18-2) Bamberger.

— Out of Bounds. (Burning Deck Poetry Chapbooks Ser.). 44p. (Orig.). 1989. pap. 5.00 (0-930901-61-4) Burning Deck.

— Singular Pleasures. LC 92-29478. (Illus.). 144p. 1993. 19.95 (1-56478-024-4) Dalkey Arch.

— Twenty Lines a Day. LC 87-73070. 134p. 1989. reprint ed. pap. 8.95 (0-916583-41-4) Dalkey Arch.

Mathews, Harry, tr. see Perec, Georges & Bober, Robert.

Mathews, Holly F., ed. Women in the South: An Anthropological Perspective. LC 88-4802. (Southern Anthropological Society Proceedings Ser.: No. 22). 166p. 1989. 25.00 (0-8203-1056-5) U of Ga Pr.

Mathews, Ian, jt. auth. see Fox, Russel.

Mathews, J. J. Life & Death of an Oilman: The Career of E. W. Marland. LC 89-70455. 1974. reprint ed. pap. 13.95 (0-8061-1238-7) U of Okla Pr.

Mathews, J. W., tr. see Legouis, Emile.

Mathews, Jackson, tr. The Collected Works of Paul Valery: Monsieur Teste. (Bollingen Ser.). 180p. 1989. pap. text ed. 9.95 (0-691-01879-0) Princeton U Pr.

Mathews, Jackson, tr. see Baudelaire, Charles.

Mathews, Jackson, ed. see Baudelaire, Charles.

Mathews, Jackson, jt. tr. see Folliot, Denise.

Mathews, Jackson, ed. see Valery, Paul.

Mathews, Jackson, tr. see Valery, Paul.

Mathews, Jacqueline E. Another Eighty Great Word Puzzles. 1992. mass mkt. 3.99 (0-8041-0674-6) Ivy Books.

Mathews, James, jt. auth. see Judge, Ken.

Mathews, James A. Barron's How to Prepare for the Air Traffic Controller Exam. 416p. 1990. pap. 10.95 (0-8120-3740-5) Barron.

Mathews, James K. The Matchless Weapon - Satyagraha. 210p. 1994. pap. 15.00 (0-934676-77-1) Greenlf Bks.

Mathews, James W., jt. ed. see Dameron, J. Lasley.

***Mathews, Jan & Eastaway, Nigel.** Tolley's Simplified Assessing. 250p. (C). 1994. 105.00 (0-614-00322-9) St Mut.

***Mathews, Jan & Eastaway, Nigel, eds.** Tolley's Simplified Assessing. 250p. (C). 1994. 150.00x (0-85459-925-8) St Mut.

***Mathews, Jane.** Not for Sadie. (Illus.). 48p. (Orig.). (J). (gr. k-3). 1993. pap. 9.95 (1-880812-05-3) S Ink WA.

An Asterisk (*) at the beginning of an entry indicates that the title is appearing in BIP for the first time.

Mathews, Jane G. & Mathews, Richard A. The Manor & Cottages: Albemarle Park, Asheville, North Carolina, a Historic Planned Residential Community. (Illus.). 112p. (Orig.). 1991. pap. 14.95 (*0-9630437-0-6*) Albemarle Pk.
Mathews, Jane S., ed. Practice Issues in Physical Therapy: Current Patterns & Future Directions. LC 86-42960. 193p. 1989. pap. 33.00 (*1-55642-006-4*) SLACK Inc.
Mathews, Jay. Escalante: The Best Teacher in America. LC 88-11960. 336p. 1989. pap. 12.95 (*0-8050-1195-1*, Owl) H Holt & Co.
Mathews, Jay, jt. auth. see Goldstein, Steven M.
Mathews, Jessica T., ed. Preserving the Global Environment: The Challenge of Shared Leadership. 362p. 1990. 22.95 (*0-393-02911-5*) Norton.
— Preserving the Global Environment: The Challenge of Shared Leadership. 384p. (C). 1990. pap. text ed. 10.95 (*0-393-96093-5*) Norton.
*__Mathews, Jo.__ I Remember Vietnam. LC 94-21854. 1994. lib. bdg. 19.97 (*0-8114-5605-6*) Raintree Steck-V.
Mathews, John. Complex Variables for Math & Engineering. 2nd ed. 368p. (C). 1988. text ed. write for info. (*0-697-06764-5*) Wm C Brown Pubs.
— Curriculum Exposed. 144p. (Orig.). 1990. pap. 26.95 (*0-8464-1486-4*) Beekman Pubs.
Mathews, John & Howell, Russ. Complex Analysis for Mathematics & Engineering. 3rd ed. 448p. (C). 1995. text ed. write for info. (*0-697-13548-9*) Wm C Brown Pubs.
Mathews, John, tr. see Gramsci, Antonio.
*__Mathews, John A.__ Catching the Wave: Workplace Reform in Australia. LC 94-25504. (Cornell International Industrial & Labor Relations Reports: No. 26). 359p. 1994. pap. 21.95 (*0-87546-706-7*) ILR Pr.
— Catching the Wave: Workplace Reform in Australia. LC 94-25504. (Cornell International Industrial & Labor Relations Reports: No. 36). 376p. 1994. 45.00 (*0-87546-707-5*) ILR Pr.
Mathews, John H. Numerical Methods for Computer Science, Engineering, & Mathematics. (Illus.). 512p. 1986. text ed. write for info. (*0-13-626656-8*) P-H.
— Numerical Methods for Mathematics, Science, & Engineering. 2nd ed. 592p. 1992. text ed. 68.00 (*0-13-624990-6*) P-H.
Mathews, John J. Osages: Children of the Middle Waters. LC 61-9006. (Civilization of the American Indian Ser.: No. 60). (Illus.). 848p. 1981. reprint ed. pap. 27.95 (*0-8061-1770-2*) U of Okla Pr.
— Sundown. LC 88-40214. 328p. 1988. pap. 14.95 (*0-8061-2160-2*) U of Okla Pr.
— Wah'Kon-Tah: The Osage & the White Man's Road. (Civilization of the American Indian Ser.: Vol. 3). (Illus.). 359p. 1981. pap. 15.95 (*0-8061-1699-4*) U of Okla Pr.
Mathews, John M. & Hart, James, eds. Essays in Political Science in Honor of Westel Woodbury Willoughby. LC 68-8458. (Essay Index Reprint Ser.). 1977. reprint ed. 21.95 (*0-8369-0428-1*) Ayer.
— Essays in Political Science in Honor of Westel Woodbury Willoughby. LC 68-8458. (Essay Index Reprint Ser.). 374p. 1982. reprint ed. lib. bdg. 18.00 (*0-8290-0831-4*) Irvington.
Mathews, Jon & Walker, Robert L. Mathematical Methods of Physics. 2nd ed. 501p. (C). 1970. text ed. 54.95 (*0-8053-7002-1*, Adv Bk Prog) Addison-Wesley.
Mathews, Joseph M. How to Succeed in the Practice of Medicine. LC 74-180582. (Medicine & Society in America Ser.). (Illus.). 244p. 1972. reprint ed. 19.95 (*0-405-03959-X*) Ayer.
Mathews, Judith. Knock-Knock Knees & Funny Bones: Riddles for Every Body. (J). (ps-3). 1993. 8.95 (*0-8075-4203-2*) A Whitman.
— Tuti, Blue Horse, & the Nipnope Man. LC 93-1. (Illus.). (J). 1993. write for info. (*0-8075-8130-5*) A Whitman.
Mathews, Judith & Robinson, Fay. Oh, How Waffle! Riddles You Can Eat. Levine, Abby, ed. LC 92-13478. (Illus.). 32p. (J). (gr. 1-4). 1992. 8.95 (*0-8075-5907-5*) A Whitman.
Mathews, Judith, ed. see Asher, Sandy.
Mathews, Judith, ed. see Baden, Robert.
Mathews, Judith, ed. see Berleth, Richard.
Mathews, Judith, ed. see Bernstein, Joanne E. & Fireside, Bryna.
Mathews, Judith, ed. see Bernstein, Joanne E. & Cohen, Paul.
Mathews, Judith, ed. see Brillhart, Julie.
Mathews, Judith, ed. see Coleman, Mary A.
Mathews, Judith, ed. see Green, Phyllis.
Mathews, Judith, ed. see Hamm, Diane J.
Mathews, Judith, ed. see Helfman, Elizabeth.
Mathews, Judith, ed. see Ketteman, Helen.
Mathews, Judith, ed. see Kroll, Virginia L.
Mathews, Judith, ed. see Lily Toy Hong.
Mathews, Judith, ed. see Martin, Antoinette T.
Mathews, Judith, ed. see Molnar, Dorothy E. & Fenton, Stephen H.
Mathews, Judith, ed. see Muldoon, Kathleen M.
Mathews, Judith, ed. see Nerlove, Miriam.
Mathews, Judith, ed. see Nims, Bonnie L.
Mathews, Judith, ed. see Nodar, Carmen M.
Mathews, Judith, ed. see Patneaude, David.
Mathews, Judith, ed. see Schlieper, Anne.
Mathews, Judith, ed. see Seltzer, Meyer.
Mathews, Judith, ed. see Shepard, Aaron.
Mathews, Judith, ed. see Stowe, Cynthia.
Mathews, Judith, ed. see Vigna, Judith.
Mathews, Judith, ed. see White, Laurence B., Jr. & Broekel, Ray.
Mathews, Judith, ed. see Zimelman, Nathan.
Mathews, K. A., jt. auth. see Freedman, D. N.
Mathews, Kate, ed. Fiberarts Design, Bk. Three. (Illus.). 208p. (Orig.). 1991. pap. 21.95 (*0-937274-61-5*) Lark Books.
Mathews, Kay. Hiking Trails of the Sandia & Manzano Mountains. (Illus.). 104p. (Orig.). 1985. pap. 7.50 (*0-910467-02-1*) Heritage Assocs.
Mathews, Kenneth E., jt. auth. see Stotland, Ezra.
Mathews, Larry. Norman Levine & His Works. 46p. (C). 1989. pap. text ed. 9.95 (*1-55022-034-9*, Pub. by ECW Press CN) Genl Dist Srvs.
Mathews-Larsen, Joan. Alcoholism the Biochemical Connection: A Breakthrough Seven-Week Self-Treatment Program. 1992. 22.50 (*0-679-41493-2*, Villard Bks) Random.
Mathews, Louise. Bunches & Bunches of Bunnies. (Illus.). 32p. (J). (gr. k-3). 1991. reprint ed. pap. 3.95 (*0-590-44766-1*) Scholastic Inc.
— The First Ladies. (Illus.). 40p. 1995. pap. 5.95 (*0-614-04033-7*) Sage Pr OK.
— Gator Pie. 38p. (J). (gr. 1-4). 1995. pap. 4.95 (*0-7608-0005-7*) Sundance Pub.
Mathews, Loulie A. Not Every Sea Hath Pearls. (Orig.). 1986. pap. 7.95 (*0-87961-165-0*) Naturegraph.
— Not Every Sea Hath Pearls. (Orig.). 1986. 15.95 (*0-87961-164-2*) Naturegraph.
Mathews, M. Cash. Strategic Intervention in Organizations: Resolving Ethical Dilemmas. (Library of Social Research: Vol. 169). 160p. (C). 1988. 49.95 (*0-8039-3303-7*); pap. 24.00 (*0-8039-3304-5*) Sage.
*__Mathews, M. R.__ An Introduction to Cost & Management Accounting. 280p. 1981. pap. 36.00 (*0-409-60105-5*, NZ) Butterworth Legal Pubs.
— Socially Responsible Accounting. LC 92-38135. 1993. write for info. (*0-412-47340-2*) Chapman & Hall.
Mathews, Marcia M. Henry Ossawa Tanner: American Artist. LC 69-10279. (Illus.). 280p. 1995. pap. 12.95 (*0-226-51006-9*) U Ch Pr.
Mathews, Marthiel, tr. see Baudelaire, Charles.
Mathews, Marthiel, ed. see Baudelaire, Charles.
Mathews, Marthiel, tr. see Male, Emile.
Mathews, Mary, jt. auth. see Gillespie, Patricia.
Mathews, Mary, et al, eds. Policing the Conflict in South Africa. LC 93-7218. 240p. 1993. lib. bdg. 34.95 (*0-8130-1224-4*) U Press Fla.
Mathews, Mary M. Ten Years in Nevada; or, Life on the Pacific Coast. LC 84-20813. (Illus.). vi, 343p. 1985. reprint ed. pap. 7.50 (*0-8032-8124-2*) U of Nebr Pr.
Mathews, Max V. & Pierce, John R., eds. Current Directions in Computer Music Research. (System Development Foundation, Benchmark Ser.). 400p. 1991. pap. 21.95 (*0-262-63139-3*) MIT Pr.
Mathews, Michael B., ed. Translational Control. (Current Communications in Molecular Biology Ser.). 192p. (Orig.). 1986. pap. text ed. 27.00 (*0-87969-191-3*) Cold Spring Harbor.
Mathews, Michelle, ed. see Baums, Roosevelt.
Mathews, N. Mowil, et al. Maurice Brazil Prendergast Charles Prendergast: A Catalogue Raisonne. Clark, C., ed. (Illus.). 812p. 1990. boxed 285.00 (*3-7913-0965-X*, Pub. by Prestel) TeNeues.
Mathews, Nancy. An American Perspective: Paintings from the Maier Museum of Art, Randolph-Macon Woman's College. LC 85-63217. (Illus.). 24p. (Orig.). 1985. pap. 4.00 (*0-88259-950-X*) NCMA.
— Mary Cassatt. LC 92-15548. (Rizzoli Art Ser.). (Illus.). 24p. 1992. 7.95 (*0-8478-1611-7*) Rizzoli Intl.
Mathews, Nancy M. The Art of Charles Prendergast from the Collections of the Williams College Museum of Art & Mrs. Charles Prendergast. LC 93-22826. (Exhibit Catalog Ser.). (Illus.). 120p. (Orig.). 1993. pap. 25.00 (*0-913697-16-8*) Williams Art.
— Cassatt & Her Circle: Selected Letters. LC 83-21449. (Illus.). 256p. 1984. 19.95 (*0-89659-421-1*) Abbeville Pr.
— Mary Cassatt. LC 86-17224. 160p. 1987. 39.95 (*0-8109-0793-3*) Abrams.
— A Passion for Line & Color: The Life of Mary Cassatt. LC 93-22148. 1994. 28.00 (*0-394-58497-X*, Villard Bks) Random.
— The Women of Impressionism. Date not set. pap. write for info. (*0-679-42582-9*) Random.
Mathews, Nancy M., ed. Maurice Prendergast. (Illus.). 196p. 1990. 60.00 (*3-7913-0966-8*, Pub. by Prestel) TeNeues.
Mathews, Nancy M. & Shapiro, Barbara S. Mary Cassatt: The Color Prints. (Illus.). 208p. 1989. 39.95 (*0-8109-1049-7*) Abrams.
— Mary Cassatt: The Color Prints. (Illus.). 208p. 1992. pap. 24.95 (*0-8109-2524-9*) Abrams.
Mathews, Nancy M., jt. auth. see Martindale, Meredith.
Mathews, Neal, Jr. The Nashville Numbering System. 64p. 1984. 6.95 (*0-88188-335-2*, HL 00704491) H Leonard.
Mathews, Oliver. The Album of Carte-de-Visite & Cabinet Portrait Photographs 1854-1914. (Illus.). 148p. 1987. 14.95 (*0-85945-002-3*, Pub. by Bishopsgte Pr UK) Intl Spec Bk.
Mathews, Patricia, tr. see Miro, Joan.
Mathews, Patricia T. Aurier's Symbolist Art Criticism & Theory. LC 85-20944. (Studies in the Fine Arts: Criticism: No. 18). (Illus.). 230p. reprint ed. pap. 65.60 (*0-8357-1686-4*, 2070610) Bks Demand.
*__Mathews, Peggy.__ Farmer Boy: (Hmong/English Edition) Vang, Va, tr. (Illus.). 30p. (MUL.). (J). (gr. 1-5). 1994. 15.95 (*1-879600-09-9*) Pac Asia Pr.
— Farmer Boy: (Tr. from Hmong) (Illus.). 30p. (J). (gr. 1-4). 1994. 14.95 (*1-879600-08-0*) Pac Asia Pr.
Mathews, Peter, jt. auth. see Houston, Stephen D.
Mathews, Peter, jt. auth. see Schele, Linda.
Mathews, Peter, jt. auth. see Willey, Gordon R.
Mathews, R. Arthur. Ready for Battle: Thirty One Studies on Christian Discipleship. LC 93-35784. 144p. 1993. pap. 7.99 (*0-87788-727-6*, OMF Books) Shaw Pubs.
Mathews, R. O. America: A View from Above. 240p. 1990. 24.99 (*0-517-69508-1*) Random Hse Value.
Mathews, Race. Australia's First Fabians: Middle-Class Radicals, Labour Activists, & the Early Labour Movement. LC 92-45211. (Illus.). 288p. (C). 1993. 59.95 (*0-521-44133-1*); pap. write for info. (*0-521-44678-3*) Cambridge U Pr.
Mathews, Richard. Aldiss Unbound: The Science Fiction of Brian W. Aldiss. LC 77-24582. (Milford Series: Popular Writers of Today: Vol. 9). 64p. 1977. lib. bdg. 20.00 (*0-89370-113-0*); pap. 10.00 (*0-89370-213-7*) Borgo Pr.
— The Clockwork Universe of Anthony Burgess. LC 78-14552. (Milford Ser.: Popular Writers of Today: Vol. 19). 63p. 1978. lib. bdg. 20.00 (*0-89370-127-0*); pap. 10.00 (*0-89370-227-7*) Borgo Pr.
— Lightning from a Clear Sky: Tolkien, the Trilogy & the Silmarillion. LC 78-922. (Milford Series: Popular Writers of Today: Popular Writers of Today: Vol. 15). 63p. 1978. lib. bdg. 21.00x (*0-89370-121-1*) Borgo Pr.
— Worlds Beyond the World: The Fantastic Vision of William Morris. LC 78-247. (Milford Series: Popular Writers of Today: Vol. 13). 63p. 1978. lib. bdg. 20.00 (*0-89370-118-1*); pap. 10.00 (*0-89370-218-8*) Borgo Pr.
Mathews, Richard & Wilber, Rick, eds. Subtropical Speculations: An Anthology of Florida Science Fiction. LC 90-37793. 304p. 1991. pap. 8.95 (*0-910923-82-5*) Pineapple Pr.
Mathews, Richard A., jt. auth. see Mathews, Jane G.
Mathews, Robert H. Chinese-English Dictionary: A Chinese-English Dictionary Compiled for the China Inland Mission. rev. ed. (Harvard-Yenching Institute Publications). 1250p. (C). 1943. 39.50 (*0-674-12350-6*) HUP.
Mathews, Sally S. The Sad Night: The Story of an Aztec Victory & a Spanish Loss. LC 92-25119. (Illus.). (J). (gr. 1-4). 1994. 16.95 (*0-395-63035-5*, Clarion Bks) HM.
*__Mathews, Sara.__ Share a Poem, a Thought & a Delicious Recipe with Sara. 1995. 9.95 (*0-8062-5350-9*) Carlton.
Mathews, Shailer. Faith of Modernism. LC 71-108117. reprint ed. 20.00 (*0-404-04266-X*) AMS Pr.
— Select Medieval Documents & Other Material Illustrative in the History of Church & Empire, 754 A.D.-1254 A.D. LC 70-178566. (LAT.). reprint ed. 34.50 (*0-404-56628-6*) AMS Pr.
— The Spiritual Interpretation of History. 1977. lib. bdg. 250.00 (*0-8490-2661-X*) Gordon Pr.
Mathews, Shailer, et al. Contributions of Science to Religion. LC 79-117822. (Essay Index Reprint Ser.). 1977. 30.95 (*0-8369-1763-4*) Ayer.
Mathews, Sibyl I. Charted Designs for Needlemade Rugs. LC 75-21350. (Illus.). 160p. 1976. reprint ed. pap. 6.95 (*0-486-23264-6*) Dover.
Mathews, Sue, jt. auth. see Hamilton, Peter.
Mathews, Thomas. La Politica Puertorriquena y el Nuevo Trato. Colorado, Antonio J., tr. 349p. (C). 1975. 4.00 (*0-8477-0831-4*); pap. 3.00 (*0-8477-0832-2*) U of PR Pr.
— Puerto Rican Politics & the New Deal. LC 76-1934. 345p. 1976. reprint ed. lib. bdg. 39.50 (*0-306-70752-7*) Da Capo.
Mathews, Thomas F. The Clash of Gods: A Reinterpretation of Early Christian Art. LC 93-19338. (Illus.). 208p. 1994. text ed. 49.50 (*0-691-03350-1*) Princeton U Pr.
— Early Churches of Constantinople: Architecture & Liturgy. LC 78-111972. (Illus.). 1971. 35.00 (*0-271-00108-9*) Pa St U Pr.
— Treasures in Heaven: Armenian Illuminated Manuscripts. 1994. pap. 35.00 (*0-691-03751-5*) Princeton U Pr.
Mathews, Thomas F. & Sanjian, Avedis K. Armenian Gospel Iconography: The Tradition of the Glajor Gospel. LC 90-2723. (Dumbarton Oaks Studies: No. 29). (Illus.). 440p. 1991. 50.00 (*0-88402-183-1*, MSAG) Dumbarton Oaks.
Mathews, Thomas F. & Wieck, Roger S., eds. Treasures in Heaven: Armenian Illuminated Manuscripts. LC 93-40269. 1994. write for info. (*0-87598-100-3*) Pierpont Morgan.
Mathews, Tom, jt. auth. see Wilkins, Roy.
Mathews, V., ed. see Arnold, Caroline.
Mathews, V., ed. see Liptak, Karen.
Mathews, V., ed. see Margolies, Jacob.
Mathews, V., ed. see Nourse, Alan E.
Mathews, Victor, jt. ed. see Coleson, Joseph.
*__Mathews, Virginia H., ed.__ Library Services for Children & Youth: Dollars & Sense. 68p. 1995. pap. 19.95 (*1-55570-176-0*) Neal-Schuman.
Mathews, Walter, Associates Inc. Staff, ed. see Finkbeiner-Zellmann, Peter & Michael-Rushmer, Jane.
Mathews, Wendell G., jt. ed. see Betts, Janice L.
Mathews, Wendell G., jt. auth. see Brown, Donald R.
Mathews, William S. How to Understand Music: A Concise Course in Musical Culture by Object Lessons & Essays, 2 Vols, 1. 5th ed. LC 75-144657. reprint ed. write for info. (*0-404-07214-3*) AMS Pr.
— How to Understand Music: A Concise Course in Musical Culture by Object Lessons & Essays, 2 Vols, 2. 5th ed. LC 75-144657. reprint ed. write for info. (*0-404-07215-1*) AMS Pr.
— How to Understand Music: A Concise Course in Musical Culture by Object Lessons & Essays, 2 Vols, Set. 5th ed. LC 75-144657. reprint ed. 65.00 (*0-404-07213-5*) AMS Pr.
— Masters & Their Music. LC 78-153364. reprint ed. 39.50 (*0-404-07209-7*) AMS Pr.
— Music: Its Ideals & Methods, a Collection of Essays for Young Teachers, Amateurs, & Students. LC 70-173057. reprint ed. 41.00 (*0-404-07211-9*) AMS Pr.
— Popular History of Music from the Earliest Times until the Present. rev. ed. LC 74-173058. reprint ed. 49.50 (*0-404-07212-7*) AMS Pr.
Mathews, William S., ed. Hundred Years of Music in America. LC 73-135725. reprint ed. 42.50 (*0-404-04259-7*) AMS Pr.
Mathews, William S. & Liebling, Emil. Pronouncing & Defining Dictionary of Music. LC 78-173059. reprint ed. 42.00 (*0-404-07210-0*) AMS Pr.
Mathews, Willis W. Atlas of Descriptive Embryology. 4th ed. 302p. (C). 1986. pap. write for info. (*0-02-377140-2*) Macmillan.
Mathews, Wilma K., jt. auth. see Howard, Carole M.
Mathews, Winifred. Dauntless Women: Stories of Pioneer Wives. LC 70-126325. (Biography Index Reprint Ser.). (Illus.). 1977. reprint ed. 18.95 (*0-8369-8031-X*) Ayer.
Mathewson. First Base Faulkner. 1976. 29.95 (*0-8488-1547-5*) Amereon Ltd.
— Pitching in a Pinch. 1976. 28.95 (*0-8488-1546-7*) Amereon Ltd.
Mathewson, C. H. Critical Shear Stress & Incongruent Shear in Plastic Deformation. (Connecticut Academy of Arts & Sciences Ser., Trans.: Vol. 38). 1951. pap. 39.50 (*0-685-22898-3*) Elliots Bks.
Mathewson, Champion H. Zinc, the Science & Technology of the Metal, Its Alloys & Compounds. LC 74-105708. 733p. reprint ed. pap. 180.00 (*0-317-10316-4*, 2015238) Bks Demand.
Mathewson, Christopher. Pitching in a Pinch: or, Baseball from the Inside. (American Biography Ser.). 306p. 1991. reprint ed. lib. bdg. 79.00 (*0-7812-8277-2*) Rprt Serv.
Mathewson, Christy. Pitching in a Pinch: or Baseball from the Inside. LC 93-42716. (Illus.). xxii, 320p. 1994. pap. 12.00 (*0-8032-8212-5*, Bison Books) U of Nebr Pr.
Mathewson, Dean. How Smart Are You? Test Your Baseball IQ. 64p. Date not set. pap. 2.95 (*0-9637056-5-2*) Blck Dog & Leventhal.
Mathewson, G. Bradley. Asking for Money: The Entrepreneur's Guide to the Financing Process. 261p. 1989. 24.95 (*0-9623770-0-7*) Fin Systs Assocs.
Mathewson, G. Frank. Fiscal Transfer Pricing in Multinational Corporations. LC 79-314786. (Ontario Economic Council Research Studies: No. 16). 170p. reprint ed. pap. 48.50 (*0-8357-3998-8*, 2036698) Bks Demand.
— Information, Entry, & Regulation in Markets for Life Insurance. LC 82-190622. (Ontario Economic Council Research Studies: No. 24). (Illus.). 125p. reprint ed. pap. 35.70 (*0-7837-4284-3*, 2043976) Bks Demand.
Mathewson, Kent, ed. Culture, Form & Place. LC 93-37168. (Geoscience & Man Ser.: Vol. 32). (Illus.). 356p. (C). 1994. pap. text ed. 24.95 (*0-938909-55-X*) Geosci Pubns LSU.
Mathewson, Kent & Neenan, William B., eds. Financing the Metropolis. LC 80-15718. 352p. 1980. text ed. 65.00 (*0-275-90518-7*, C0518, Praeger Pubs) Greenwood.
Mathewson-Kuhn, Merrily. Pharmacotherapeutics: A Nursing Process Approach. 3rd ed. LC 93-5695. (Illus.). 1696p. (C). 1994. text ed. 54.95 (*0-8036-5932-6*) Davis Co.
Mathewson, Mark, jt. auth. see Merrill, Gary.
Mathewson, Paul R. & Finley, John W., eds. Biosensor Design & Application. LC 92-31003. (ACS Symposium Ser.: No. 511). (Illus.). 230p. 1992. 54.95 (*0-8412-2494-3*) Am Chemical.
Mathewson, Rufus W., Jr. The Positive Hero in Russian Literature. 2nd ed. LC 72-97207. xviii, 366p. 1975. 47.50 (*0-8047-0836-3*); pap. 15.95 (*0-8047-0976-9*) Stanford U Pr.
Mathey, J. F. Hundertwasser. (CAL Art Ser.). 1988. 18.00 (*0-517-55872-6*, Crown) Crown Pub Group.
Mathey, K., ed. Housing Policies in the Socialist Third World. 342p. 1990. text ed. 90.00 (*0-7201-2049-7*, Mansell Pub) Cassell.
Mathey, Kosta, ed. Beyond Self-Help Housing. (Illus.). 432p. 1992. text ed. 90.00 (*0-7201-2047-0*, Mansell Pub) Cassell.
Mathez, E. A., ed. see Holden, Martin.
Mathhewman, Jim. HR Effectiveness. 176p. 1993. 75.00 (*0-85292-535-2*, Pub. by IPM Hse UK) St Mut.
Mathia, Myrna E. & Yamine, Lorena S., eds. Nursing Education in the Middle East: Community Health Needs & Curriculum Development. 244p. 1983. text ed. 24.95 (*0-8156-6066-9*, Am U Beirut) Syracuse U Pr.
Mathiak, K. Valuations of Skew Fields & Projective Hjelmslev Spaces. (Lecture Notes in Mathematics Ser.). vii, 116p. 1986. pap. 22.00 (*0-387-16099-X*) Spr-Verlag.
Mathiane, Nomavenda. South Africa: Diary of Troubled Times. Finn, James, ed. LC 88-33590. (Focus on Issues Ser.: No. 7). (Illus.). 189p. 1989. 23.95 (*0-932088-38-4*); pap. 12.95 (*0-932088-37-6*) Freedom Hse.
Mathias, A. R. Surveys in Set Theory. LC 83-10106. (London Mathematical Society Lecture Note Ser.: No. 87). 256p. 1983. pap. 44.95 (*0-521-27733-7*) Cambridge U Pr.
Mathias, Barbara. Between Sisters: Secret Rivals, Intimate Friends. 1992. 20.00 (*0-385-30450-1*) Delacorte.
— Between Sisters: Secret Rivals, Intimate Friends. 1994. pap. 11.95 (*0-385-31280-6*, Delta) Dell.
Mathias, Beverley. A Treasury of Christmas Stories. LC 93-50708. (Illus.). 160p. (J). (ps-3). 1994. pap. 5.95 (*1-85697-985-7*, Kingfisher LKC) LKC.
Mathias, Christopher J., jt. ed. see Bannister, Roger.
Mathias, Chuck & Puri, Bhaskar. The Danger of Walking on Water: And Other Cartoons. (Illus.). 102p. (Orig.). 1992. pap. 4.95 (*0-910303-36-3*) Writers Pub Serv.
*__Mathias, Don.__ Misuse of Drugs. 251p. 1988. pap. 54.00 (*0-409-78816-3*, NZ) Butterworth Legal Pubs.
Mathias, Dot & Floyd, Sally. Speedbuilding for Court Reporting, Vol. 1. Ritter, Beverly L., ed. 322p. (C). 1986. reprint ed. pap. 25.00 (*0-938643-03-7*) Stenotype Educ.
Mathias, Dot, jt. auth. see Floyd, Sally.

M

Mathias, Elizabeth & Raspa, Richard. Italian Folktales in America: The Verbal Art of an Immigrant Woman. LC 88-6598. (Illus.). 346p. 1985. 39.95 (*0-8143-1790-1*); pap. 18.95 (*0-8143-2122-4*) Wayne St U Pr.

Mathias, Frank F. G. I. Jive: An Army Bandsman in World War II. LC 82-4792. (Illus.). 256p. 1982. 26.00 (*0-8131-1462-4*) U Pr of Ky.

Mathias, Gerald B., jt. auth. see Habein, Yaeko.

Mathias, Harry & Patterson, Richard. Electronic Cinematography: Achieving Photographic Control over the Video Image. 251p. (C). 1985. text ed. 36.95 (*0-534-04281-3*) Intl Thomson.

Mathias, J. & Hixson, Sandra. A Compilation of Chinese Dictionaries. (CHI.). 1975. 8.95 (*0-88710-020-1*) Yale Far Eastern Pubns.

Mathias, Jack, jt. ed. see Li, Sifa.

Mathias, Jim, ed. Shanghai Common Expressions. LC 88-51589. 79p. 1989. 36.00 (*0-931745-38-1*); audio 30.00 (*0-931745-53-5*) Dunwoody Pr.

Mathias, Jim & Kennedy, Thomas L., eds. Computers, Language Reform & Lexicography in China: A Report by the CETA Delegation. LC 81-112015. 84p. reprint ed. pap. 25.00 (*0-685-24155-6*, 2033029) Bks Demand.

Mathias, John, jt. auth. see Jones, Jeff.

Mathias, Kay. Everyday English. 224p. (C). 1983. 50.00 (*0-85950-347-X*, Pub. by S Thornes Pubs UK) St Mut.

Mathias, L. J., ed. Solid State NMR of Polymers. (Illus.). 464p. 1991. 95.00 (*0-306-44015-6*, Plenum Pr) Plenum.

Mathias, Mildred E., ed. Flowering Plants in the Landscape. LC 81-16310. (Illus.). 215p. 1982. pap. 20.00 (*0-520-05414-8*) U CA Pr.

Mathias-Mundy, Evelyn & McCorkle, Constance M. Ethnoveterinary Medicine: An Annotated Bibliography. (Bibliographies in Technology & Social Change Ser.: No. 6). 209p. (C). 1989. pap. 18.00 (*0-945271-16-6*) ISU-TSCP.

Mathias-Mundy, Evelyn, et al. Indigenous Technical Knowledge of Private Tree Management: A Bibliographic Report. (Bibliographies in Technology & Social Change Ser.: No. 7). 175p. (C). 1992. pap. 18.00 (*0-945271-30-1*) ISU-TSCP.

Mathias, Peter. The Brewing Industry in England 1700-1830. (Modern Revivals in Economic & Social History Ser.). 63p. 1993. 92.95 (*0-7512-0150-2*, Pub. by Gregg Revivals UK) Ashgate Pub Co.

— The Transformation of England: Essays in the Economic & Social History of England in the Eighteenth Century. LC 80-10813. 302p. 1980. text ed. 43.00 (*0-231-05046-1*) Col U Pr.

Mathias, Peter, ed. Science & Society Sixteen Hundred to Nineteen Hundred. LC 76-172833. 174p. reprint ed. pap. 49.60 (*0-318-34821-7*, 2031688) Bks Demand.

Mathias, Peter & Davis, John A., eds. Innovation & Technology in Europe: From the Eighteenth Century to the Present Day. (Nature of Industrialization Ser.). 224p. 1991. 42.95 (*0-631-16797-8*) Blackwell Pubs.

Mathias, Peter, jt. ed. see Davis, John A.

Mathias, Robert. Beauty & the Beast. (J). 1991. 4.99 (*0-517-06693-9*) Random Hse Value.

Mathias, Robert & Steelman, Diane. Controlling Prison Populations: An Assessment of Current Mechanisms, 1982. 1982. 1.50 (*0-318-02050-5*) Natl Coun Crime.

Mathias, Roland. Anglo-Welsh Literature: An Illustrated History. LC 86-63547. (Illus.). 142p. 1987. pap. 16.95 (*0-907476-64-3*, Pub. by Poetry Wales Pr UK) Dufour.

— Burning Brambles: Selected Poems 1944-1979. 163p. (C). 1983. 22.00x (*0-85088-728-3*, Pub. by Gomer Pr UK) St Mut.

— A Ride Through the Wood: Essays on Anglo-Welsh Literature. LC 86-82057. 320p. 1986. 33.00 (*0-907476-50-3*, Pub. by Poetry Wales Pr UK) Dufour.

— Snipe's Castle. 89p. 1985. 25.00 (*0-317-54068-8*, Pub. by Gomer Pr UK) St Mut.

Mathias, Roland, ed. David Jones. 144p. (C). 1976. pap. 20.00x (*0-85088-372-5*, Pub. by Gomer Pr UK) St Mut.

Mathias, Roland, jt. auth. see Adams, Sam.

Mathias, Roland, jt. ed. see Adams, Sam.

Mathias, Roland, jt. ed. see Garlick, Raymond.

Mathias, Sara. Electing Justice: A Handbook of Judicial Election Reforms. LC 90-82925. 160p. (Orig.). 1990. pap. 6.00 (*0-938870-45-9*) Am Judicature.

Mathias, Sara, ed. Judicial Discipline & Disability Digest: 1989-1991 Supplement. LC 81-65601. 399p. 1993. 140.00 (*0-938870-61-0*) Am Judicature.

Mathias, Sara, et al, eds. Judicial Discipline & Disability Digest: July 1986 - December 1988 Supplement. LC 81-65601. 352p. 1990. 200.00 (*0-938870-48-3*); lib. bdg. 125.00 (*0-685-38274-5*) Am Judicature.

Mathias, Sheila F., jt. ed. see Franks, Felix.

Mathiasen, Carolyn, ed. How Institutions Voted on Social Policy Shareholder Resolutions in the Proxy Season, 1991. 144p. 1991. pap. 50.00 (*0-931035-92-9*) IRRC Inc DC.

Mathiasen, Carolyn, ed. see Booth, Helen E.

Mathiasen, Carolyn, ed. see Bradley, Adrienne.

Mathiasen, Carolyn, ed. see Ortigoza, Brenda.

Mathiasen, Carolyn, ed. see Shaw, Linda S., et al.

Mathiasen, Carolyn, ed. see Williams, Susan.

Mathiasen, Karen. Corporate Governance & Shareholder Rights: Voting by Institutional Investors & 1986 Annual Meeting Results. LC 86-230362. (Corporate Governance Service). 96p. 1986. pap. 50.00 (*0-931035-57-0*) IRRC Inc DC.

Mathiasen, Karl, III. Board Passages: Three Key Stages in a Nonprofit Board's Life Cycle. (Nonprofit Governance Ser.: No. 07). 20p. (Orig.). (C). 1992. pap. text ed. 10.00 (*0-925299-09-X*) Natl Ctr Nonprofit.

Mathiassen, L. Professional Systems Development: Experience, Ideas, & Action. 288p. 1990. boxed 41.00 (*0-13-725540-3*) P-H.

Mathiassen, Lars, jt. auth. see Dahlbom, Bo.

Mathiassen, Therkel. Archaeological Collections from the Western Eskimos. LC 76-21673. (Thule Expedition, 5th, 1921-1924 Ser.: Vol. 10, No. 1). reprint ed. 37.50 (*0-404-58325-3*) AMS Pr.

— Archaeology of the Central Eskimos, 2 pts. in 1 vol. LC 76-21669. (Thule Expedition, 5th, 1921-1924 Ser.: No. 4). reprint ed. 137.50 (*0-404-58315-6*) AMS Pr.

— Contributions to the Geography of Baffin Land & Melville Peninsula. LC 76-21640. (Thule Expedition, 5th, 1921-1924 Ser.: Vol. 1, No. 3). reprint ed. 32.00 (*0-404-58303-2*) AMS Pr.

— Contributions to the Physiography of Southampton Island. LC 76-21639. (Thule Expedition, 5th, 1921-1924 Ser.: Vol. 1, No. 2). reprint ed. 20.00 (*0-404-58302-4*) AMS Pr.

— Material Culture of the Iglulik Eskimos. LC 76-21671. (Thule Expedition. 5th. 1921-1924 Ser.: Vol. 6, No. 1). reprint ed. 67.50 (*0-404-58317-2*) AMS Pr.

— Report on the Expedition. LC 76-21664. (Thule Expedition, 5th, 1921-1924 Ser.: Vol. 1, No. 1). reprint ed. 32.50 (*0-404-58301-6*) AMS Pr.

Mathiasson, Sven & Dalhov, Goran. In the Wild: Wildlife in Great Britain & Europe. 280p. 1992. 37.95 (*1-85310-179-6*, Pub. by Airlife Pub Ltd UK) Voyageur Pr.

Mathie, Mellisa. Celebrating Oregon. Bishop, Janice, ed. (Illus.). 40p. 1993. pap. 30.00 (*0-9636258-0-2*) Will Creek W.

Mathie, R. T., et al. Principles of Surgical Research. (Illus.). 209p. 1990. text ed. 70.00 (*0-7236-0929-2*, Pub. by John Wright UK) Buttrwrth-Heinemann.

Mathie, Robert T. Blood Flow Measurement in Man. 250p. 1982. 44.50 (*0-7194-0078-3*) Raven.

Mathie, Vonne, jt. auth. see Brown, Hazel.

Mathien, Frances J. & McGuire, Randall H., eds. Ripples in the Chichimec Sea: New Considerations of Southwestern-Meso-American Interactions. LC 85-27862. (Publications in Archaeology). 318p. 1986. text ed. 34.95 (*0-8093-1247-6*) S Ill U Pr.

Mathies, Bonnie K., et al. Teaching with Computers: Yes You Can! 224p. (C). 1990. spiral bd. 19.95 (*0-8403-6428-8*) Kendall-Hunt.

Mathies, H., jt. ed. see Emre, M.

Mathiesen, Egon. Jungle in the Wheat Field. (Illus.). (J). (gr. k-3). 1960. 9.95 (*0-8392-3014-1*) Astor-Honor.

— Oswald the Monkey. (Illus.). (J). (gr. k-3). 1959. 9.95 (*0-8392-3025-7*) Astor-Honor.

Mathiesen, Hans E. Sculpture in the Parthian Empire, 2 vols., Set. (Illus.). 231p. (C). 1992. 87.50 (*87-7288-311-1*, Pub. by Aarhus Univ Pr DK) Coronet Bks.

Mathiesen, Michael. The New American Bible: Ecology of Mind, Pt. II. G. O. D., ed. (Collaboration Ser.). 500p. pap. 20.00 (*0-939887-87-8*) Millennium Sta Cruz.

***Mathiesen, Mike & Hoskins, Jim.** Marketing on the Internet: A Step-by-Step Guide for Planning Promoting, & Selling Your Products & Services to Millions over the Information Superhighway. 250p. (Orig.). 1995. pap. 39.95 (*1-885068-01-8*) Maximum Pr.

Mathiesen, Thomas. Law, Society & Political Action: Towards a Strategy under Late Capitalism. LC 80-49868. (Law, State & Society Ser.). 1981. text ed. 113.00 (*0-12-479940-X*); pap. text ed. 49.00 (*0-12-479942-6*) Acad Pr.

— Prison on Trial: A Critical Assessment. 192p. (C). 1990. text ed. 45.00 (*0-8039-8224-0*); pap. text ed. 17.95 (*0-8039-8225-9*) Sage.

***Mathiesen, Thomas J. & Rivera, Benito V., eds.** Festa Musicologica: Essays in Honor of George J. Buelow. LC 94-46264. (Festschrift Ser.: No. 14). 1995. 48.00 (*0-945193-70-X*) Pendragon NY.

Mathieson, A. C. Morphological Studies of the Marine Brown Alga Taonia Lennebackerae Farlow Ex. J. Agardh L. (Illus.). 1966. pap. 12.00 (*3-7682-0439-1*) Lubrecht & Cramer.

Mathieson, Alfred. Judson of Burma, Vol. 7. 1980. pap. 4.99 (*0-88019-075-2*) Schmul Pub Co.

Mathieson, Alistar & Wall, Geoffrey. Tourism: Economic, Physical & Social Impacts. (Illus.). 216p. 1986. pap. text ed. 37.95 (*0-470-20539-3*) Halsted Pr.

***Mathieson, D. L.** Cross on Evidence. 677p. 1989. pap. 87.00 (*0-409-78883-X*, NZ) Butterworth Legal Pubs.

— Cross on Evidence. 4th ed. 677p. 1989. boxed 108.00 (*0-409-78790-6*, NZ) Butterworth Legal Pubs.

Mathieson, Donald J. & Rojas-Suarez, Liliana. Liberalization of the Capital Account: Experiences & Issues. LC 93-16797. (Occasional Paper - International Fund Ser.: No. 103). 39p. 1993. 15.00 (*1-55775-280-X*) Intl Monetary.

Mathieson, Donald J., jt. auth. see Folkerts-Landau, David.

Mathieson, Donald J., et al. Managing Financial Risks in Indebted Developing Countries. (Occasional Paper Ser.: No. 65). 47p. 1989. pap. 10.00 (*1-55775-116-1*) Intl Monetary.

Mathieson, John A., jt. auth. see Sewell, John W.

Mathieson, Judy. Mariner's Compass: An American Quilt Classic. LC 87-71884. (Illus.). 72p. 1987. pap. 16.95 (*0-914881-11-6*) C & T Pub.

— Mariner's Compass Quilts - New Directions. Townsend, Louise, ed. (Illus.). 96p. 1995. pap. text ed. 21.95 (*0-914881-97-3*, 10119) C & T Pub.

Mathieson, Margaret, jt. auth. see McCulloch, Ros.

Mathieson, Raymond S. Japan's Role in Soviet Economic Growth: Transfer of Technology Since 1965. LC 78-19790. 304p. 1979. text ed. 65.00 (*0-275-90389-3*, C0389, Praeger Pubs) Greenwood.

Mathieson, Robert, ed. Japan & NAFTA. 128p. (Orig.). 1993. pap. 9.95 (*1-883223-01-6*) Pacific NY.

Mathieson, T. I., jt. auth. see Adams, J. S.

Mathieson, Yvonne. Simple Samplers. (Illus.). 128p. 1992. 29.95 (*0-7134-6703-7*, Pub. by Batsford UK) Trafalgar.

Mathieu, Aron. The Book Market: How to Write, Publish & Market Your Book. LC 80-71059. 474p. 1981. 19.95 (*0-939014-00-9*) Andover Pr.

Mathieu, Bertrand, tr. see Cendrars, Blaise.

Mathieu, Bertrand, tr. see Rimbaud, Arthur.

Mathieu, C., jt. auth. see Lozet, J.

Mathieu, Clement, jt. auth. see Lozet, Jean.

Mathieu, Corina S. Los Cuentos de Mario Benedetti. LC 83-48144. (American University Studies: Romance Languages & Literature: Ser. II, Vol. 3). 112p. 1983. pap. text ed. 12.65 (*0-8204-0015-7*) P Lang Pubs.

***Mathieu, David L.** All the Right Answers. 1995. 17.95 (*0-533-11111-0*) Vantage.

Mathieu, Deborah. Preventing Prenatal Harm: Should the State Intervene? 168p. 1991. lib. bdg. 58.00 (*0-7923-0984-7*) Kluwer Ac.

Mathieu, G., ed. Advances in the Teaching of Modern Languages, Vol. 2. 1966. 98.00 (*0-08-011840-2*, Pub. by Pergamon Repr UK) Franklin.

Mathieu, Gilbert. Vocabulaire de L'economie. (FRE.). pap. 35.00 (*0-686-57041-3*, M-6401) Fr & Eur.

— Vocabulaire de l'Economie. (FRE.). 35.00 (*0-8288-7890-0*, M6401) Fr & Eur.

Mathieu, Gustave. Introduction to German Poetry. 1991. pap. 3.95 (*0-486-26713-X*) Dover.

Mathieu, Gustave & Stern, Guy. Say It in German. (Orig.). 1957. pap. 2.95 (*0-486-20804-4*) Dover.

Mathieu, Gustave, tr. see Dover Staff.

Mathieu, Gustave B., jt. auth. see Haas, Werner.

Mathieu, Gustave B., ed. see Haas, Werner & Merrifield, Doris F.

Mathieu, J. & Fleury, P. Physics Dictionary: Dictionnaire de Physique. 3rd rev. ed. 567p. (FRE.). 1991. 135.00 (*0-8288-2233-6*, F23760) Fr & Eur.

Mathieu, J., jt. ed. see Comte-Bellot, G.

Mathieu, J. P., ed. Advances in Raman Spectoscopy: Proceedings of the Third International Conference on Raman Spectroscopy: University of Reims, France, September, 1972. LC 73-76120. 655p. reprint ed. pap. 180.00 (*0-8357-5182-1*, 2023996) Bks Demand.

Mathieu, J. P., jt. auth. see Poulet, H.

Mathieu, Jean, jt. auth. see Chevray, Rene.

Mathieu, Jean P. & Desnuelle, P. Selected Constants Optical Rotatory Power: Amino Acids. (Tables of Constants & Numerical Data Ser.: Vol. 10). 1959. 33.00 (*0-08-009202-0*, Pub. by Pergamon Repr UK) Franklin.

Mathieu, Jean P. & Jacques, J. Selected Constants Optical Rotary Power: IA Steroids. (Tables of Constants & Numerical Data Ser.: Vol. 14). 421.00 (*0-08-010982-9*, Pub. by Pergamon Repr UK) Franklin.

Mathieu, Jean P. & Janot, M. Selected Constants Optical Rotatory Power: Alkaloids. (Tables of Constants & Numerical Data Ser.). 1959. 96.00 (*0-08-009312-4*, Pub. by Pergamon Repr UK) Franklin.

Mathieu, Jean P. & Ourisson, G. Selected Constants Optical Rotatory Power: Triterpenoids. (Tables of Constants & Numerical Data Ser.: Vol. 9). 1958. 138.00 (*0-08-009201-2*, Pub. by Pergamon Repr UK) Franklin.

Mathieu, Jean P. & Petit, A. Constantes Selectionnees Pouvoir Rotatoire Naturel: Steroides. (Tables of Constants & Numerical Data Ser.: Vol. 6). 1956. 210.00 (*0-08-009716-2*, Pub. by Pergamon Repr UK) Franklin.

Mathieu, Joe. Big Bird's Big Book. (Illus.). 12p. (J). (ps-1). 1987. 29.95 (*0-394-89128-7*) Random Bks Yng Read.

— Elmo Wants a Bath. (Sesame Street R Bathtime Bks.). (Illus.). 10p. (J). (ps). 1992. vinyl bd. 3.95 (*0-679-83066-9*) Random Bks Yng Read.

— The Olden Days. (Pictureback Ser.). (Illus.). 32p. (J). (ps-3). 1981. lib. bdg. 4.99 (*0-394-94085-7*) Random Bks Yng Read.

— Sesame Street One Two Three: A Counting Book from 1 to 100. LC 91-1992. (Illus.). 32p. (J). (ps-1). 1991. 10.00 (*0-679-81230-X*) Random Bks Yng Read.

Mathieu, Joe, illus. Big Bird Visits the Dodos. LC 84-43051. (Pictureback Ser.). 32p. (J). (ps-3). 1985. lib. bdg. 5.99 (*0-394-97373-9*) Random Bks Yng Read.

— Sesame Street Fire Trucks. (Wheel Bks.). 14p. (J). (ps-00). 1988. bds. 4.99 (*0-394-89952-0*) Random Bks Yng Read.

— Sesame Street Stays up Late: Based on the Television Special by Lou Berger. LC 94-32232. (Pictureback Ser.). (J). 1995. 2.99 (*0-679-86743-0*) Random.

— Trucks in Your Neighborhood. (Wheel Bks.). 14p. (J). (ps-00). 1988. bds. 4.99 (*0-394-89951-2*) Random Bks Yng Read.

— Window on Sesame Street. (Magic Window Bks.). 9p. (J). (ps). 1995. 6.99 (*0-679-85312-X*) Random Bks Yng Read.

Mathieu, Joseph. Big Joe's Trailer Truck. LC 74-2538. (Pictureback Ser.). (Illus.). 32p. (Orig.). (J). (ps-1). 1993. pap. 2.25 (*0-394-82925-5*) Random Bks Yng Read.

Mathieu La Braque, Lily. Man from Mono. (Illus.). 196p. (Orig.). 1984. pap. text ed. 10.95 (*0-9613730-1-6*) L M LaBraque.

— Man from Mono. 5th ed. (Illus.). 196p. (Orig.). 1991. text ed. 15.00 (*0-9613730-0-8*) L M LaBraque.

Mathieu, M. Elementary Operators & Applications: In Memory of Domingo a Herroro. 300p. 1992. text ed. 86.00 (*981-02-0914-2*) World Scientific Pub.

***Mathieu, Mark.** New Drug Development: A Regulatory Overview. 3rd ed. 327p. 1994. 125.00 (*1-882615-01-8*) Parexel Intl.

***Mathieu, Mark, ed.** Biologics Development: A Regulatory Overview. 310p. 1993. 135.00 (*1-882615-00-X*) Parexel Intl.

— Parexel's Pharmaceutical R & D Statistical Sourcebook, 1995. 180p. 1995. spiral bd. 195.00 (*1-882615-10-7*) Parexel Intl.

Mathieu, Nicole, jt. ed. see Audouze, Jean.

Mathieu, Paul. The Druid's Lodge Confederacy. 224p. 1990. 60.00 (*0-85131-525-9*, Pub. by J A Allen & Co UK) St Mut.

Mathieu, Philippe. Teach Yourself Word 3.0. 189p. 1989. ring bd. 79.95 (*0-929533-10-0*) Tutorland.

Mathieu, Pierre L. The Symbolist Generation. LC 89-43610. (Illus.). 250p. 1990. 50.00 (*0-8478-1218-9*) Rizzoli Intl.

Mathieu, Renee. Diccionari Catala-Frances i Frances-Catala. 288p. 1990. pap. 11.95 (*0-7859-6037-6*, 8440461984) Fr & Eur.

— Diccionari Escolar Catala-Frances i Frances-Catala. 208p. 1988. pap. 19.95 (*0-7859-6197-6*, 8472111598) Fr & Eur.

Mathieu, Richard, jt. auth. see Letheren, Carole A.

***Mathieu-Rosay, Jean.** Dictionnaire du Christianisme. 316p. (FRE.). 1990. pap. 17.95 (*0-7859-7888-7*, 2501012887) Fr & Eur.

— Dictionnaire etymologique Marabout. 544p. (FRE.). 1985. pap. 17.95 (*0-7859-8641-3*, 250100664x) Fr & Eur.

Mathieu, W. A. The Listening Book: Discovering Your Own Music. LC 90-53384. 144p. (Orig.). 1991. pap. 13.00 (*0-87773-610-3*) Shambhala Pubns.

— The Musical Life: Reflections on What It Is & How to Live It. LC 93-39776. 1994. pap. 13.00 (*0-87773-670-7*) Shambhala Pubns.

Mathiez, Albert. Fall of Robespierre & Other Essays. LC 68-55329. 1968. reprint ed. lib. bdg. 37.50 (*0-678-00428-5*) Kelley.

Mathiopoulos, Margarita. History & Progress: In Search of European & American Identity. LC 89-8841. 459p. 1989. text ed. 69.50 (*0-275-92792-X*, C2792, Praeger Pubs) Greenwood.

Mathiot, Madeleine. A Dictionary of Papago Usage: Vol. I, B-K. (Language Science Ser.: No. 8-1). 504p. 1974. pap. text ed. 82.35 (*90-279-2677-8*) Mouton.

***Mathiprakasam, B. & Heenan, Patrick, eds.** Thirteenth International Conference on Thermoelectrics. (AIP Conference Proceedings Ser.: No. 316). (Illus.). 380p. 1995. text ed. 125.00 (*1-56396-444-9*, AIP Pr) Am Inst Physics.

Mathis, Andrew G., jt. auth. see Lillibridge, E. Michael.

Mathis, Averil. Antiques & Collectible Thimbles & Accessories. (Illus.). 184p. 1989. 19.95 (*0-89145-322-9*) Collector Bks.

Mathis, B. Claude, jt. auth. see Menges, Robert J.

Mathis, Carla M. & Connor, Helen V. The Triumph of Individual Style: A Guide to Dressing Your Body, Your Beauty, Your Self. (Illus.). 192p. (Orig.). 1992. pap. 28.95 (*0-9632223-0-9*) Timeless Edits.

Mathis, Cleopatra. Aerial View of Louisiana. LC 79-90841. 77p. 1979. 9.95 (*0-935296-00-X*) Sheep Meadow.

— The Bottom Land. LC 83-630. 58p. 1983. 13.95 (*0-935296-40-9*); pap. 7.95 (*0-935296-41-7*) Sheep Meadow.

— The Center for Cold Weather. LC 89-10838. 81p. 1990. 14.95 (*0-935296-84-0*); pap. 10.95 (*0-935296-85-9*) Sheep Meadow.

Mathis, Danny E., ed. see Mathis, Quincy D.

Mathis, Darlene. Women of Color: The Multicultural Guide to Fashion & Beauty. LC 94-15715. (Illus.). 160p. 1994. 23.00 (*0-345-38929-8*) Ballantine.

Mathis-Eddy, Darlene. Leaf Threads, Wind Rhymes. LC 84-71936. 64p. (Orig.). 1985. pap. 6.95 (*0-935306-31-5*) Barnwood Pr.

Mathis, Edward. The Fifth Level: A Dan Roman Mystery. 256p. 1992. text ed. 20.00 (*0-684-19386-8*, Scribners) S&S Trade.

— From a High Place. 1988. pap. 3.95 (*0-345-33370-5*) Ballantine.

Mathis, Emily D. & Doody, John E. Grant Proposals: A Primer for Writers. (Development Fastbacks Ser.). (Illus.). 56p. (Orig.). 1994. pap. 8.00 (*1-55833-129-8*) Natl Cath Educ.

Mathis, F. John, jt. ed. see Krause, Walter.

Mathis, F. John, jt. auth. see Taylor, Jon G.

***Mathis, Fred B.** Black Quotations of the South. 40p. 1995. text ed. 10.00 (*0-8059-3654-8*) Dorrance.

Mathis, Georgia A. How to Produce Your Own Videoconference. LC 86-21430. 165p. 1987. 37.95 (*0-86729-216-4*) Knowledge Indus.

Mathis, J. J. A Review of Russellism, Et Cetera, Et Cetera. 66p. 1988. reprint ed. pap. 2.95 (*1-883858-41-0*) Witness CA.

Mathis, Jack. Republic Confidential: The Players, Vol. 2. LC 92-90769. (Illus.). 270p. 1992. 60.00 (*0-9632878-0-X*) J Mathis Adv.

Mathis, James L. Clear Thinking about Sexual Deviations: A New Look at an Old Problem. LC 72-80165. 232p. 1972. 24.95 (*0-911012-40-0*) Nelson-Hall.

— Psychiatric Medicine: A Handbook. Gardner, James F., ed. (Allied Health Professions Monograph). 212p. (C). 1984. 22.50 (*0-87527-320-3*) Green.

Mathis, Judi, jt. ed. see Best, Anita.

Mathis, Mark A., ed. see Phelps, David S., et al.

Mathis, Mary, jt. auth. see Mathis, Ray.

Mathis, Michael J., jt. ed. see Dinchak, William G.

Mathis, Quincy D. Brudder & the Babe. Mathis, Danny E., ed. & comp. by. LC 93-60735. 92p. (Orig.). (J). (gr. 1-4). 1994. 8.95 (*1-55523-636-7*) Winston-Derek.

Mathis, Ray. John Horry Dent: South Carolina Aristocrat on the Alabama Frontier. LC 78-10693. (Illus.). 283p. 1979. 17.50 (*0-8173-5263-5*) U of Ala Pr.

***Mathis, Ray & Mathis, Mary.** Introduction & Index to the John Horry Dent Farm Journals & Account Books, 1840-1892. 206p. 1977. 11.00 (*0-614-04572-X*) Hist Chattahoochee.

***Mathis, Ray, et al, eds.** John Horry Dent Farm Journals & Account Books, 1840-1892. 5700p. 1976. mic. film 250.00 (*0-614-04571-1*) Hist Chattahoochee.

Mathis, Richard, jt. auth. see Coronado, Karen.

An Asterisk (*) at the beginning of an entry indicates that the title is appearing in BIP for the first time.

Mathis, Robert L. & Jackson, John H. Human Resource Management. 7th ed. Perlee, Simon, ed. LC 93-4430. 650p. (C). 1993. text ed. 63.25 (0-314-02529-4) West Pub.
— Personnel - Human Resource Management. 6th ed. Perlee, Clyde & Simon, eds. 635p. (C). 1991. text ed. 57.50 (0-314-77009-7) West Pub.
Mathis, Sharon B. The Hundred-Penny Box. (Newbery Library). (Illus.). 48p. (J). (gr. 1-4). 1986. pap. 3.99 (0-14-032169-1, Puffin) Puffin Bks.
— The Hundred-Penny Box. Dillon, Leo D., ed. (Illus.). 48p. (J). (gr. k-3). 1975. pap. 15.00 (0-670-38787-8) Viking Child Bks.
— Listen for the Fig Tree. 176p. (J). (gr. 7 up). 1990. pap. 4.99 (0-14-034364-4, Puffin) Puffin Bks.
— Red Dog - Blue Fly: Poems for a Football Season. (J). (ps-3). 1991. 13.95 (0-670-83623-0) Viking Child Bks.
— Red Dog, Blue Fly: Football Poems. (Illus.). 32p. (J). (gr. 1-5). 1995. 4.99 (0-14-054337-6) Puffin Bks.
— Sidewalk Story. (Novels Ser.). 64p. (J). (gr. 2-6). 1986. pap. 3.99 (0-14-032165-9, Puffin) Puffin Bks.
— Teacup Full of Roses. (J). (gr. 5-9). 1993. 16.75 (0-8446-6650-5) Peter Smith.
— Teacup Full of Roses. (Novels Ser.). (J). (gr. 3-7). 1987. pap. 4.99 (0-14-032328-7, Puffin) Puffin Bks.
Mathis, Stephen & Siegel, Lee. Quantitative Toolkit for Economics & Finance. LC 93-80417. 354p. 1993. pap. 20.00 (1-878975-14-5) Kolb Pub.
Mathis, Wayne N. Studies of Gymnomyzinae (Diptera: Ephydridae), IV: A Revision of the Shore-Fly Genus Hecamede Haliday. LC 91-14038. (Smithsonian Contributions to Zoology Ser.: No. 541). (Illus.). 50p. reprint ed. pap. 25.00 (0-7837-5896-0, 2045687) Bks Demand.
— Studies of Gymnomzinae (Diptera: Ephydridae) Pt. 6: A Revision of the Genus Glenanthe Haliday from the New World. LC 94-28014. (Smithsonian Contributions to Zoology Ser.: Vol. 567). 30p. 1994. reprint ed. pap. 25.00 (0-7837-8868-1, 2049579) Bks Demand.
— Studies of Parydrinae (Diptera: Ephydridae) Revision of the Shore Fly Genus Pelinoides Cresson, Pt. 2. LC 84-600299. (Smithsonian Contributions to Zoology Ser.: No. 410). 51p. reprint ed. pap. 25.00 (0-317-30174-8, 2025356) Bks Demand.
Mathis, Wayne N. & Ghorpade, Kumar D. Studies of Parydrinae (Diptera: Ephydridae) A Review of the Genus Brachydeutere Loew from the Oriental, Australian & Oceanian Regions, Pt. 1. LC 84-600345. (Smithsonian Contributions to Zoology Ser.: No. 406). 29p. reprint ed. pap. 25.00 (0-317-30040-7, 2025043) Bks Demand.
Mathis, Wayne N., jt. auth. see Baptitsta, Alessandra R.
Mathis, Wayne N., jt. auth. see Freidberg, Amnon.
Mathis, Wayne N., et al. Studies of Gymnomyzinae, Diptera, Ephydridae, Pt. 5: A Revision of the Shore-Fly Genus Mosillus Latreille. LC 93-24454. (Smithsonian Contributions to Zoology Ser.: No. 548). 42p. reprint ed. pap. 25.00 (0-7837-6416-2, 2046396) Bks Demand.
Mathis, William J., ed. Field Guide to Educational Renewal. (Illus.). 300p. (Orig.). (C). 1994. pap. text ed. 22.50 (0-9627232-5-8) Holistic Educ Pr.
Mathis, William R. Mustang Performance Handbook. LC 94-18029. 176p. (Orig.). 1994. pap. 15.00 (1-55788-193-6, HP Books) Berkley Pub.
— Mustang Performance Handbook Two: Chassis & Suspension Modifications for Street, Strip, & Road Racing Use for All Models of the Ford Mustand, 1979 to Present. LC 94-24719. 192p. (Orig.). 1995. pap. 15.00 (1-55788-202-9, HP Books) Berkley Pub.
Mathisen, Carl W. My Trusty Indian Guide: And Other Alaskan Tales. 256p. (Orig.). 1992. pap. 12.95 (1-882756-00-2) Alaska Eagle.
Mathisen, Marilyn. Apparel & Accessories. Lynch, Richard L., ed. (Career Competencies in Marketing Ser.). (Illus.). 1979. text ed. 12.04 (0-07-040905-6) McGraw.
Mathisen, Ralph W. Ecclesiastical Factionalism & Religious Controversy in Fifth-Century Gaul. LC 88-18922. 340p. 1989. 44.95 (0-8132-0658-8) Cath U Pr.
— Ecclesiastical Factionalism & Religious Controversy in Fifth-Century Gaul. LC 88-18922. reprint ed. pap. 104.60 (0-7837-9194-1, 2049895) Bks Demand.
— Roman Aristocrats in Barbarian Gaul: Strategies for Survival in an Age of Transition. LC 92-22725. (Illus.). 293p. 1993. text ed. 35.00x (0-292-77051-0) U of Tex Pr.
Mathisen, Robert R. The Role of Religion in American Life: An Interpretive Historical Anthology. 304p. (Orig.). (C). 1994. per. 30.36 (0-8403-9367-9) Kendall-Hunt.
Mathison, David L. Management Incidents & Cases: The Competitive Edge. 348p. (C). 1989. pap. write for info. (0-02-377141-0) Macmillan.
Mathison, John E. Tried & True. LC 92-71309. 128p. 1992. pap. 8.95 (0-88177-117-1, DR117) Discipleship Res.
***Mathison, Keith A.** Dispensationalism: Rightly Dividing the People of God. 176p. (Orig.). 1995. pap. 9.99 (0-87552-359-5) Presby & Reformed.
Mathison, Ruby L. Synthetic Fuels Research: A Bibliography. 4th ed. 218p. 1980. pap. 15.00 (0-318-12717-2, H01980) Am Gas Assn.
Mathison, Sheila R., ed. see Whippel, Frank W.
Mathley, Ian M. The Geography of International Tourism. 1987. reprint ed. 75.00 (0-317-62129-7, Scientific) St Mut.
Mathlouthi, Mohammed, ed. Food Packaging & Presentation: Procedure of Symposium Held at the University of Reims, France, 20-23 1985. 368p. 1986. 108.00 (0-85334-413-2) Elsevier.
Mathlouthi, Mohammed, et al, eds. Sweet-Taste Chemoreception. 1992. write for info. (0-318-69409-3) Elsevier.
***Mathog, Robert H., et al.** Trauma of the Nose & Paranasal Sinuses. Levine, Howard, ed. LC 94-26571. (Rhinology & Sinusology). (Illus.). 184p. 1994. 59.00 (0-86577-526-5) Thieme Med Pubs.
Mathon, Rudy, jt. auth. see Colbourn, D. V.
Mathon, Rudy, jt. ed. see Corneil, Derek.
Mathosian, Mark. First Byte: Taking the Mystery Out of Buying a Personal Computer. (Illus.). 16p. Date not set. pap. 2.95 (0-9631924-2-6) Inkwell Pubs.
— Prime Time Computing: A Seniors Guide to Home Computing. (Illus.). 164p. 1993. lib. bdg. 14.95 (0-9631924-1-8) Inkwell Pubs.
— Up & Running with Your Personal Computer: A Beginner's Guide to Buying, Using & Enjoying an IBM or Compatible Personal Computer. (Illus.). 168p. 1992. pap. 16.95 (0-9631924-0-X) Inkwell Pubs.
Mathot, Vincent B. F., ed. Calorimetry & Thermal Analysis of Polymers. LC 93-48558. 369p. 1994. write for info. (1-56990-126-0) Hanser-Gardner.
Mathre, D. E., ed. Compendium of Barley Diseases. LC 82-72159. 94p. 1982. pap. 30.00 (0-89054-047-0) Am Phytopathol Soc.
Mathru, Mali & Dries, David J. Right Ventricle: The Neglected Neighbor of the Left. (Medical Intelligence Unit Ser.). 275p. 1993. 159.95 (1-879702-80-0, R) R G Landes.
Mathson, Patricia. Burlap & Butterflies: One Hundred & One Religious Education Activities for Christian Holidays. LC 87-70841. (Illus.). 152p. (Orig.). 1987. pap. 7.95 (0-87793-359-6) Ave Maria.
— Celebrations: Prayers, Plays & Projects for the Church Year. (Illus.). 168p. (Orig.). 1995. teacher ed, pap. write for info. (0-87793-566-1) Ave Maria.
— Creativities: One Hundred One Creative Activities for Children to Celebrate God's Love. LC 92-71631. (Illus.). 152p. (Orig.). 1992. pap. 9.95 (0-87793-485-1) Ave Maria.
— Pray & Play: Twenty-Eight Prayer Services & Activities for Children in Kindergarten Through Sixth Grade. LC 88-83549. (Illus.). 128p. (Orig.). 1989. pap. 8.95 (0-87793-392-8) Ave Maria.
Mathur, A. P. Commentaries on Gambling Acts in India. 513p. 1973. 110.00 (0-317-54717-8) St Mut.
— Commentaries on Motor Vehicles Act. 9th ed. (C). 1990. 400.00 (0-685-37417-3) St Mut.
— Commentaries on Motor Vehicles Act, 2 vols., Set. 2000p. 1982. 720.00 (0-317-54714-3) St Mut.
— Commentaries on Prevention of Corruption Act, 1947. 699p. 1981. 240.00 (0-317-54712-7) St Mut.
— Commentaries on Prevention of Corruption Act, 1947: With Supplement of New Act. 3rd rev. ed. (C). 1990. 80.00 (0-685-39755-6) St Mut.
— Law Relating to Motor Vehicles. (C). 1990. text ed. 400.00 (0-89771-498-9) St Mut.
— Law Relating to Motor Vehicles. 9th ed. (C). 1993. 225.00 (81-7012-416-6, Pub. by Eastern Book II) St Mut.
— Prevention of Food Adulteration Act. 838p. 1983. 320.00 (0-317-54566-3) St Mut.
— Prevention of Food Adulteration Act, 1954. (C). 1990. 125.00 (0-685-39349-6) St Mut.
— Prevention of Food Adulteration Act, 1989, with Supplement. 9th ed. (C). 1990. text ed. 225.00 (0-685-52019-6) St Mut.
Mathur, A. P., ed. Commentaries on Gambling Acts in India, 1973: With Supplement. 2nd rev. ed. (C). 1990. 50.00 (0-685-39695-9) St Mut.
— Commentaries on Prevention of Corruption Act 1947. 3rd ed. (C). 1981. 130.00 (0-685-36422-4) St Mut.
Mathur, A. P., rev. Prevention of Food Adulteration Act, 1989, with Supplement. 9th rev. ed. (C). 1990. 225.00 (0-685-39702-5) St Mut.
Mathur, Anurag, jt. ed. see Suraiya, Jug.
***Mathur, B. B.** Women & Depressed Caste Population in India. (C). 1994. text ed. 32.00 (81-85613-79-6, Pub. by Chugh Pubns II) S Asia.
Mathur, B. P. Visual Information Processing, Vol. 1473: From Neurons to Chips. 1991. 53.00 (0-8194-0582-5) SPIE.
Mathur, D., ed. Physics of Ion Impact Phenomena. (Chemical Physics Ser.: Vol. 54). (Illus.). 304p. 1991. 72.00 (0-387-53429-6) Spr-Verlag.
Mathur, D. C. Contract Labour in India. (C). 1989. 105.00 (0-685-36496-8) St Mut.
— Naturalistic Philosophies of Experience: Studies in James, Dewey & Farber Against the Background of Husserl's Phenomenology. LC 79-117613. 170p. 1971. 10.20 (0-87527-052-2) Green.
Mathur, Deepa. Women, Family & Work. (C). 1992. 18.00 (81-7033-147-1, Pub. by Rawat II) S Asia.
***Mathur, G. C.** Low-Cost Housing in Developing Countries. (C). 1993. 24.00x (81-204-0774-1, Pub. by Oxford IBH II) S Asia.
Mathur, G. C., ed. Government Servants: Appointment, Promotion & Disciplinary Actions. (C). 1990. 200.00 (0-685-54205-X); 200.00 (0-685-39562-6) St Mut.
Mathur, G. C., rev. Prevention of Food Adulteration Act. 9th rev. ed. (C). 1989. 225.00 (0-685-37418-1) St Mut.
Mathur, G. C., ed. see Singh, S. D.
Mathur, H. C. Patanjali's Model of Human Mind. 345p. 1987. 59.95 (81-7071-065-0) Asia Bk Corp.
***Mathur, Hari M.** Anthropology & Development in Traditional Societies. (C). 1995. 28.00x (0-7069-8857-4, Pub. by Vikas II) S Asia.
— Improving Agricultural Administration. (C). 1989. 14.00 (81-204-0392-4, Pub. by Oxford IBH II) S Asia.
***Mathur, Hari M., ed.** Development, Displacement & Resettlement: Focus on Asian Experiences. (C). 1995. 29.00x (0-7069-8858-2, Pub. by Vikas II) S Asia.
Mathur, Ike, ed. Financial Management in Post-1992 Europe. LC 93-3802. (Journal of Multinational Financial Management: Vol. 2, Nos. 3-4). (Illus.). 219p. 1993. lib. bdg. 39.95 (1-56024-439-9) Haworth Pr.
Mathur, Ike & Jai-Sheng, Chen. Strategies for Joint Ventures in the People's Republic of China. LC 87-7033. 208p. 1987. text ed. 55.00 (0-275-92354-1, C2354, Praeger Pubs) Greenwood.
Mathur, Ike, jt. ed. see Doukas, John.
Mathur, J. S., ed. see Pyarelal, et al.
Mathur, Justice G. Amin & Sastri's Law of Easements. rev. ed. 839p. 1984. 360.00 (0-317-54827-1) St Mut.
— Government Servants - Appointment, Promotion & Disciplinary Actions. (C). 1990. text ed. 200.00 (0-89771-500-4) St Mut.
Mathur, K. M. Administration of Police Training in India. (C). 1987. 58.50 (81-212-0100-4, Pub. by Gian Publng Hse II) S Asia.
Mathur, Kamlesh, jt. auth. see Salkin, Harvey.
***Mathur, Krishna M.** Indian Police: Role & Challenges. 1994. 32.00 (81-212-0460-7, Pub. by Gian Publng Hse II) S Asia.
— Police, Law & Internal Security. (C). 1994. 32.00 (81-212-0455-0, Pub. by Gian Publng Hse II) S Asia.
Mathur, Kuldeep & Jayal, Niraja G. Drought, Policy & Politics in India: The Need for a Long-Term Perspective. (Illus.). 140p. (C). 1993. text ed. 26.00 (0-8039-9122-3) Sage.
Mathur, L. P. Indian Revolutionary Movement in the U. S. A. 1970. text ed. 20.00 (0-685-14077-6) Coronet Bks.
Mathur, Lalit M. Tree Plantation & Environment Awareness. (Illus.). xvi, 443p. 1993. 59.00 (81-7024-489-7, Pub. by Ashish Pub Hse II) Nataraj Bks.
***Mathur, M. V., et al, eds.** Indian University System: Revitalization & Reform. (C). 1994. text ed. 34.00 (81-224-0602-5, Pub. by Wiley Eastern II) S Asia.
Mathur, P. C. Government & Politics in South Asia, 22 vols., Set. (C). 1985. 390.00 (0-685-36473-9) St Mut.
— Water & Land Management in Arid Ecology: Policy & Socio-Scientific Perspectives on Soil-Crop-Water Synergy. 1991. 34.00 (81-7033-126-9, Pub. by Rawat II) S Asia.
Mathur, P. C., jt. auth. see Narain, Iqbal.
Mathur, P. L. Role of Governor in Non-Congress States. (C). 1988. 32.00 (81-7033-050-5, Pub. by Rawat II) S Asia.
***Mathur, Pushpa R.** Costumes of the Rulers of Mewar: With Patterns & Construction Techniques. (C). 1994. text ed. 82.00 (81-7017-293-4, Pub. by Abhinav II) S Asia.
Mathur, R. N. Quality of Working Life of Women Construction Workers. 1989. 26.50 (81-7169-000-9, Pub. by Commonwealth II) S Asia.
Mathur, Subbi & Fredericks, Christopher M., eds. Perspectives in Immunoreproduction: Conception & Contraception. (Reproductive Health Technology Ser.). 410p. 1988. 105.00 (0-89116-783-8) Hemisp Pub.
Mathur, Y. B. Growth of Muslim Politics in India. 296p. 1979. 25.95 (0-318-36575-8) Asia Bk Corp.
Mathureshwar das. Devotion at Home. 32p. (Orig.). 1988. pap. 2.00 (0-931889-08-1) Epistemology Pubs.
Mathurin, Owen C. Henry Sylvester Williams & the Origins of the Pan-African Movement, 1869-1911. LC 75-35348. (Contributions in Afro-American & African Studies: No. 21). 224p. 1976. text ed. 29.95 (0-8371-8594-7, MHW/, Greenwood Pr) Greenwood.
Mathus-Vliegen, Lisabeth M. The Role of Laser in Gastroenterology: Analysis of Eight Years' Experience. (Developments in Gastroenterology Ser.). (C). 1989. lib. bdg. 126.50 (0-7923-0425-X) Kluwer Ac.
***MathWorks Inc., Staff.** MATLAB: Version 4: User's Guide. LC 94-43322. (MATLAB Curriculum Ser.). 1995. student ed, pap. text ed. 45.00 (0-13-184979-4) P-H.
Mathworks, Inc. Staff. The Student Edition of MATLAB - Student User Guide. 304p. 1992. pap. text ed. 46.00 (0-13-856006-4) P-H.
— The Student Edition of MATLAB for Macintosh Computers. 304p. 1992. pap. text ed. 72.00 (0-13-855990-2) P-H.
— Student Edition of MATLAB for MS DOS Personal Computers 3.5 inch Disk. 304p. 1992. pap. text ed. 72.00 (0-13-855974-0) P-H.
— The Student Edition of MATLAB for MS DOS Personal Computers 5.25 inch Disk. 304p. 1992. pap. text ed. 72.00 (0-13-855982-1) P-H.
Mathy, Francis, tr. see Endo, Shusaku.
Mathy, Francis, tr. see Shusaku, Endo.
Mathy, Jean-Philippe. Extreme-Occident: French Intellectuals & America. LC 93-16456. 288p. (C). 1993. lib. bdg. 49.00 (0-226-51063-8); pap. 16.95 (0-226-51064-6) U Ch Pr.
Mathy, P., ed. Air Pollution & Ecosystems. (C). 1987. lib. bdg. 267.50 (90-277-2611-6) Kluwer Ac.
Mathy, Robin M., jt. auth. see Whitman, Frederick L.
Mathys, Nicholas J., jt. auth. see Burack, Elmer H.
Mathys, Robert, Sr., ed. Isoelastic Hip Prosthesis: Manual of Surgical & Operative Techniques. LC 92-1481. (Illus.). 110p. 1992. text ed. 56.00 (0-88937-094-X) Hogrefe & Huber Pubs.
Matias, Manuel. Las Chilenas. LC 91-73140. 128p. 1991. 13.00 (0-89729-611-7) Ediciones.
Matias, Tito & Petersen, Randy. Child of the City. 304p. pap. 4.99 (0-8423-7224-5) Tyndale.
***Matiasz, George.** Endtime: Notes on the Apocalypse. LC 93-74104. (Illus.). 308p. (Orig.). 1994. pap. 8.00 (1-873176-96-1, AK Pr San Fran) AK Pr Dist.
Matiasz, George Z. How to Survive on per Diem. 1974. pap. 1.00 (0-686-11777-8) Matiasz.
***Matick, Richard E.** Transmission Lines for Digital & Communication Networks: An Introduction to Transmission Lines, High-Frequency, & High-Speed Pulse Characteristics & Applications. LC 94-32639. 1994. write for info. (0-7803-1121-3) Inst Electrical.
— Transmission Lines for Digital & Communications Networks: An Introduction to Transmission Lines, High-Frequency & High-Speed Pulse Characteristics & Applications. LC 68-30561. 382p. reprint ed. pap. 108.90 (0-317-09847-0, 2052038) Bks Demand.
Matics, K. I. Introduction to the Thai Mural. (Illus.). 149p. (C). 1992. 35.00 (1-879155-08-7) Lotus WA.
— Introduction to the Thai Temple. (Illus.). 141p. (C). 1992. 35.00 (1-879155-09-5) Lotus WA.
Matiella, Ana C. Cultural Pride Curriculum Unit. (Latino Family Life Education Curriculum Ser.). 182p. (Orig.). 1988. teacher ed, pap. 17.95 (0-941816-67-2) ETR Assocs.
— Cultural Pride Student Workbook. (Latino Family Life Education Curriculum Ser.). (Illus.). 96p. (Orig.). (J). (gr. 5-8). 1988. pap. 7.95 (0-941816-68-0) ETR Assocs.
— La Familia Curriculum Unit. (Latino Family Life Education Curriculum Ser.). 188p. (Orig.). 1988. teacher ed, pap. 17.95 (0-941816-69-9) ETR Assocs.
— La Familia Student Workbook. (Latino Family Life Education Curriculum Ser.). (Illus.). 96p. (Orig.). (J). (gr. 5-8). 1988. pap. 7.95 (0-941816-70-2) ETR Assocs.
— The Multicultural Challenge in Health Education. LC 93-44540. 1994. write for info. (1-56071-355-0) ETR Assocs.
Matiella, Ana C., tr. see Stewart, Deborah D.
Matignon, Jeanne, jt. auth. see Montreynaud, Florence.
Matijasevich, Yuri. Hilbert's Tenth Problem. (Foundations of Computing Ser.). (Illus.). 225p. 1993. 45.00x (0-262-13295-8) MIT Pr.
Matijevic, Egon, ed. Surface & Colloid Science, Vol. 12. LC 67-29459. 484p. 1982. 110.00 (0-306-40616-0, Plenum Pr) Plenum.
— Surface & Colloid Science, Vol. 14. LC 67-29459. (Illus.). 404p. 1987. 105.00 (0-306-42421-5, Plenum Pr) Plenum.
— Surface & Colloid Science, Vol. 15. (Illus.). 325p. 1992. 89.50 (0-306-44150-0, Plenum Pr) Plenum.
Matijevic, Egon & Good, Robert J., eds. Surface & Colloid Science, Vol. 13. 288p. 1984. 95.00 (0-306-41322-1, Plenum Pr) Plenum.
Matik, Wendy-o. Love Like Rage. 64p. (Orig.). 1994. pap. 7.00 (0-916397-31-9) Manic D Pr.
Matilal, Bimal K. Language & Reality: An Introduction to Indian Philosophical Studies. 450p. 1986. 31.00 (0-317-53529-3, Pub. by Motilal Banarsidass II) S Asia.
— Navya-Nyaya Doctrine of Negation. LC 67-27088. (Oriental Ser.: No. 46). 219p. 1968. 15.00 (0-674-60650-7) HUP.
— Perception: An Essay on Classical Indian Theories of Knowledge. 456p. 1992. reprint ed. pap. 29.95 (0-19-823976-9) OUP.
— Philosophy of Indian Languages. 175p. 1991. 19.95 (0-19-562515-3) OUP.
Matilal, Bimal K., ed. Knowing from Words: Western & Indian Philosophical Analysis of Understanding & Testimony. LC 93-1731. (Synthese Library). 396p. (C). 1994. lib. bdg. 149.50 (0-7923-2345-9) Kluwer Ac.
— Moral Dilemmas in the Mahabharata. (C). 1989. 18.00 (81-208-0603-4, Pub. by Motilal Banarsidass II) S Asia.
Matilal, Bimal K. & Shaw, Jaysankar L., eds. Analytical Philosophy in Comparative Perspective. 1984. lib. bdg. 119.00 (90-277-1870-9) Kluwer Ac.
Matilal, Bimal K., jt. ed. see Evans.
Matile, P. The Lytic Compartment of Plant Cells. LC 75-5931. (Cell Biology Monographs: Vol. 1). (Illus.). xiii, 183p. 1975. 71.00 (0-387-81296-2) Spr-Verlag.
Matilsky, Barbara C. The Expressionist Surface: Contemporary Art in Plaster. (Illus.). 48p. 1990. pap. text ed. 9.25 (0-9604514-2-0) Queens Mus.
— Fragile Ecologies: Contemporary Artists' Interpretations & Solutions. LC 92-15771. (Illus.). 144p. 1992. pap. 24.95 (0-8478-1592-7) Rizzoli Intl.
Matinko-Wald, Ruth, ed. see Larsen, Susan C.
Matinko-Wald, Ruth, ed. see Van der Marck, Jan.
Matinko-Wald, Ruth A., ed. Three Decades of Exploration: Homage to Leo Castelli. LC 87-62753. 16p. (Orig.). 1987. pap. write for info. (0-942461-02-9) Mus Art Fl.
Matinko-Wald, Ruth A., ed. see Jones, Arthur F.
Matinuddin, Kamal, jt. ed. see Rose, Leo E.
Matis. Flotation Science & Engineering. 584p. 1995. 175.00 (0-8247-9264-5) Dekker.
Matis, Dave & Toole, Jobe H. Paint Contractor's Manual. LC 84-29315. (Illus.). 224p. (Orig.). 1985. pap. 24.00 (0-910460-46-9) Craftsman.
Matis, David. The Rising Stars' Guide for Show Biz Kids & their Parents. 1993. pap. 7.00 (0-517-88030-X, Crown) Crown Pub Group.
Matis, Herbert, ed. The Economic Development of Austria since 1870. (Economic Development of Modern Europe since 1870 Ser.: Vol. 4). (Illus.). 656p. 1994. 189.95 (1-85278-719-8, Pub. by E Elgar Pub UK) Ashgate Pub Co.
Matis, J. H., et al, eds. Compartmental Analysis of Ecosystem Models. (Statistical Ecology Ser.: Vol. 10). 1979. 45.00 (0-89974-007-3) Intl Co-Op.
Matis, K. A., jt. ed. see Mavros, P.
Matisoff, Bernard S. Wiring & Cable Designer's Handbook. 1987. 36.95 (0-07-156237-0) McGraw.
Matisoff, Bernard S. Wiring & Cable Designer's Handbook. (Illus.). 448p. 1986. 36.95 (0-8306-2720-0, NO. 2720, TAB/TPR) TAB Bks.
Matisoff, Bernard S., et al. Surface Mount Technology: The Handbook of Materials & Methods. (Illus.). 448p. 1989. 48.50 (0-8306-3130-5, 3130) TAB Bks.

Matisoff, James A. The Dictionary of Lahu. (Publications in Linguistics: Vol. III). 1989. 115.00 (0-520-09711-4) U CA Pr.
— The Grammar of Lahu. LC 81-85503. (Publications in Linguistics: Vol. 75). 752p. 1982. pap. 45.00 (0-520-09467-0) U CA Pr.
Matisoff, James A., ed. see LaPolla, Randy J. & Lowe, John B.
Matisoff, Susan. The Legend of Semimaru: Blind Musician of Japan. LC 77-24601. (Studies in Oriental Culture: No. 14). 290p. 1978. text ed. 43.00 (0-231-03947-6) Col U Pr.
Matison, Sumner, jt. ed. see Wiedeman, George H.
***Matisse, Henri.** Drawings: Themes & Variations. LC 94-40925. (Illus.). 168p. 1995. pap. text ed. 11.95 (0-486-28520-0) Dover.
— Jazz. Hawkes, Sophie, tr. LC 83-11934. (Illus.). 156p. 1983. reprint ed. pap. 29.50 (0-8076-1131-X) Braziller.
— Matisse. Faerna, Jose M., ed. Waldes, Teresa S., tr. LC 94-36573. (Great Modern Masters Ser.). 64p. 1995. 11.98 (0-8109-4685-8) Abrams.
— Matisse Line Drawings & Prints. (Fine Art Ser.). (Illus.). 48p. 1980. pap. 3.95 (0-486-23877-6) Dover.
— Matisse on Art. Flam, Jack D., ed. 1994. pap. 12.00 (0-520-08639-2) U CA Pr.
— Matisse on Art. Flam, Jack, ed. & intro. by. (Documents of Twentieth-Century Art Ser.). (Illus.). 300p. 1995. pap. 15.00 (0-520-20032-2) U CA Pr.
— Matisse on Art. rev. ed. Flam, Jack, ed. & intro. by. (Documents of Twentieth-Century Art Ser.). (Illus.). 300p. 1995. 25.00 (0-520-20037-3) U CA Pr.
— Portrait Drawings: Forty-Five Plates. 1990. pap. 3.95 (0-486-26438-6) Dover.
Matisse, Henri & Cartleman, Riva. Jazz. Hawkes, Sophie, tr. (Illus.). 96p. 1992. 11.95 (0-8076-1291-X) Braziller.
Matissek, R. & Wittkowski, R., eds. High Performance Liquid Chromatography in Food Control & Research. LC 92-62181. 384p. 1992. pap. text ed. 75.00 (0-87762-999-4) Technomic.
Matissek, R., jt. ed. see Wittkowski, R.
Matiyasevich, Y. V., jt. ed. see Nerode, A.
Matjasko, Jane & Katz, Jordan. Clinical Considerations in Neuroanesthesia & Neurosurgery. 288p. 1986. text ed. 59.95 (0-8089-1817-6, 792797, Grune) Saunders.
***Matkin, Gary W.** Managing & Using Financial Information in Continuing Education. Stern, Milton R., ed. 272p. 1996. 34.50 (0-89774-941-3, 2301) Oryx Pr.
— Technology Transfer & the University. (ACE-Oryx Series on Higher Education). (Illus.). 352p. 1990. 29.95 (0-02-897263-5, ACE-Oryx) Oryx Pr.
Matkin, Noel, jt. ed. see Roush, Jackson.
Matkin, R. E., jt. auth. see Riggar, T. F.
Matkin, Ralph E. Insurance Rehabilitation: Service Applications in Disability Compensation Systems. LC 85-593. 360p. 1985. pap. text ed. 32.00 (0-936104-55-4, 1279) PRO-ED.
Matkin, Ralph E. & Riggar, T. F. Persist & Publish: Helpful Hints for Academic Writing & Publishing. (Illus.). 176p. (Orig.). 1991. pap. text ed. 11.95 (0-87081-227-0) Univ Pr Colo.
Matko, Drago, et al. Simulation & Modelling of Continuous Systems: A Case Study Approach. 300p. 1992. pap. text ed. 38.40 (0-13-808064-X) P-H.
Matkov, Becky R., jt. auth. see O'Brien, Dawn.
Matkovics, B., et al. Radicals, Ions & Tissue Damage. (Illus.). 323p. (C). 1990. text ed. 39.00 (963-05-5879-3, Pub. by A K HU) Intl Spec Bk.
Matlack, Fred, jt. auth. see Hylton, Bill.
Matlack, Helena, ed. Brand Name & Trademark Guide: Jewelry & Kindred Trades: 1896, 1904, 1915, 1922, 1943, 1950, 1965, 1969, 1973, 1978. 11th ed. (Illus.). 1984. pap. 49.95 (0-931744-06-7, CR-010) Jewelers Bk Club.
Matlack, Lucius C. History of American Slavery & Methodism from 1780 to 1849. LC 77-138342. (Black Heritage Library Collection). 1977. 31.95 (0-8369-8734-9) Ayer.
— Life of Rev. Orange Scott. LC 70-138343. (Black Heritage Library Collection). 1977. 30.95 (0-8369-8735-7) Ayer.
Matlack, William F. Statistics for Public Managers. LC 91-68073. 536p. (Orig.). 1993. boxed 48.00 (0-87581-365-8) Peacock Pubs.
Matlak, Richard E., ed. Approaches to Teaching Coleridge's Poetry & Prose. LC 91-21906. (Approaches to Teaching World Literature Ser.: No. 38). x, 185p. 1991. text ed. 37.50 (0-87352-549-3, AP38C); pap. text ed. 18.00x (0-87352-700-3, AP38P) Modern Lang.
Matlaw, Myron. American Popular Entertainment: Paper & Proceedings of the Conference on the History of American Popular Entertainment. LC 78-74655. (Contributions in Drama & Theatre Studies: No. 1). (Illus.). 338p. 1979. text ed. 35.00 (0-313-21072-1, MEN/) Greenwood.
Matlaw, Myron, ed. & intro. Nineteenth-Century American Plays. rev. ed. Orig. Title: Black Crook & Other 19th Century American Plays. 262p. 1988. reprint ed. 24.95 (1-55783-017-7); reprint ed. pap. 8.95 (1-55783-018-5) Applause Theatre Bk Pubs.
Matlaw, Ralph E., ed. see Chekhov, Anton P.
Matlaw, Ralph E., ed. see Dostoyevsky, Fyodor.
Matlaw, Ralph E., tr. see Odoevsky, Vladimir F.
Matlaw, Ralph E., ed. see Turgenev, Ivan S.
Matlay, J., jt. auth. see Sharp.
Matley, Ben G. Principles of Elementary Algebra: A Language & Equations Approach Preliminary Edition. 960p. (C). 1992. pap. text ed. 54.95 (0-8403-7318-X) Kendall-Hunt.
Matley, Ben G. & McDannold, Thomas A. National Computer Policies. LC 87-72340. 172p. 1988. 5.95 (0-8186-8784-3, 784) IEEE Comp Soc.
Matley, I. M. The Geography of International Tourism. (C). 1987. text ed. 30.00 (81-85046-56-5, Pub. by Scientific Pubs II) St Mut.
Matley, Ian M. The Geography of International Tourism. (C). 1987. 50.00 (0-317-92354-4, Scientific) St Mut.
Matley, Jay, jt. auth. see Chemical Engineering Magazine Editors.
Matley, John F., jt. auth. see Fowler, Don D.
Matlick, Len. B.S.Ing: The Secrets of Success in the Business World. 120p. 1987. pap. 14.00 (0-87364-428-X) Paladin Pr.
Matlin, David. China Beach. 112p. (Orig.). 1989. pap. 8.95 (0-88268-066-8) Station Hill Pr.
— Dressed in Protective Fashion. (Illus.). 96p. (Orig.). 1990. pap. 8.00 (0-9626046-0-7) OtherWind Pr.
— Fontana's Mirror. LC 82-4341. (Boss Poets Ser.: No. 1). (Illus.). 32p. (Orig.). 1982. pap. 9.00 (0-932430-05-8) Boss Bks.
— How the Night Is Divided: A Novel. LC 93-12587. 201p. 1993. 20.00 (0-929701-33-X) McPherson & Co.
Matlin, Margaret. Cognition. 2nd ed. 448p. (C). 1989. text ed. 44.00 (0-03-021658-3) HB Coll Pubs.
— Psychology of Women. 608p. (C). 1987. pap. text ed. 24.75 (0-03-063409-1) HB Coll Pubs.
Matlin, Margaret & Stang, David. The Pollyanna Principle: Selectivity in Language, Memory, & Thought. LC 78-25548. 1979. text ed. 18.95 (0-87073-815-1) Schenkman Bks Inc.
Matlin, Margaret W. Cognition. 3rd ed. LC 92-75763. 554p. 1994. 46.25 (0-15-500571-5) HarBrace.
— Psychology. LC 91-27211. (Illus.). 800p. (C). 1992. text ed. 49.25 (0-03-029508-4) HB Coll Pubs.
— Sensation & Perception. 2nd ed. 550p. (C). 1988. pap. text ed. 49.33 (0-205-11125-4, H11257) Allyn.
— Sensation & Perception. 3rd ed. LC 91-26132. 533p. 1992. 55.00 (0-205-13519-6) Allyn.
Matlin, Margaret W. & Foley, Hugh J. Sensation & Perception. 3rd ed. 540p. (C). 1991. text ed. 55.00 (0-205-13313-4) Allyn.
Matlin, Myna L. Teachers & Research: Language Learning in the Classroom. 190p. 1989. pap. 7.00 (0-87207-350-5) Intl Reading.
Matlin, Samuel, jt. auth. see Neimark, Paul.
***Matlins, Antoinette L.** Pearls: The Buying Guide. (Illus.). 175p. 1995. 21.95 (0-943763-14-2) GemStone Pr.
— Pearls: The Buying Guide. (Illus.). 1995. pap. 16.95 (0-943763-15-0) Jewish Lights.
Matlins, Antoinette L. & Bonanno, A. C. Gem Identification Made Easy: A Hands-on Guide to More Confident Buying & Selling. LC 89-1611. (Illus.). 304p. 1989. 29.95 (0-943763-03-7) GemStone Pr.
— Jewelry & Gems: The Buying Guide, How to Buy Diamonds, Pearls, Colored Gemstones, Gold & Jewelry with Confidence & Knowledge. 3rd ed. (Illus.). 272p. 1993. pap. 16.95 (0-943763-11-8) GemStone Pr.
— Jewelry & Gems: The Buying Guide, How to Buy Diamonds, Pearls, Colored Gemstones, Gold & Jewelry with Confidence & Knowledge. 3rd ed. (Illus.). 272p. 1993. 23.95 (0-943763-12-6) GemStone Pr.
Matlins, Antoinette L., et al. Engagement & Wedding Rings: The Definitive Buying Guide for People in Love. (Illus.). 304p. 1990. pap. 14.95 (0-943763-05-3) GemStone Pr.
Matlis, Eben. Cotorsion Modules. (Memoirs of the American Mathematical Society Ser.: No. 49). 74p. reprint ed. pap. 25.00 (0-7837-1633-8, 2041926) Bks Demand.
— Torsion-Free Modules. (Chicago Lectures in Mathematics Ser.). (C). 1973. pap. text ed. 15.00 (0-226-51074-3) U Ch Pr.
Matlock, Bill J., jt. auth. see Schell, Frank R.
Matlock, Curtiss A. A Time & a Season. (Men Made in America Ser.). 1995. mass mkt. 3.99 (0-373-45186-5, 1-45186-3) Harlequin Bks.
— A Time to Keep. 1994. 3.59 (0-373-45166-0) Harlequin Bks.
— True Blue Hearts. 1993. mass mkt. 3.39 (0-373-09805-7, 5-09805-8) Silhouette.
— White Gold. (Historical Ser.). 1995. pap. 3.99 (0-373-28851-4, 1-28851-3) Harlequin Bks.
Matlock, D. K., jt. ed. see Krauss, G.
Matlock, David. Russiawalks. 1991. pap. 12.95 (0-8050-1204-4, Owl) H Holt & Co.
***Matlock, Gene D.** India Is the Real Jewish & 200p. 1996. pap. 8.95 (0-7610-0464-5) NW Pub.
— Jesus & Moses Are Buried in India. (Illus.). 100p. (Orig.). 1991. pap. 8.00 (0-9627739-0-5) Geo-Mind Pubns.
Matlock, Glen & Silverton, Pete. I Was a Teenage Sex Pistol. (Illus.). 192p. 1991. pap. 12.95 (0-571-12934-X) Faber & Faber.
— I Was a Teenage Sex Pistol. (Illus.). 160p. Date not set. pap. 25.95 (0-7119-1817-1) Omnibus NY.
***Matlock, J. W., Sr.** Be Fruitful & Multiply. 1994. 10.95 (0-533-10920-5) Vantage.
***Matlock, Jack, Jr.** Autopsy on an Empire: Observing the Collapse of the Soviet Union. LC 95-13833. 1995. 35.00 (0-679-41376-6) Random.
Matlock, Jann. Scenes of Seduction: Prostitution, Hysteria, & Reading Difference in Nineteenth-Century France. 1993. pap. 18.00 (0-231-07207-4) Col U Pr.
— Scenes of Seduction: Prostitution, Hysteria, & Reading Difference in Nineteenth-Century France. LC 93-13966. 422p. 1994. 60.00 (0-231-07206-6) Col U Pr.
Matlock, Paul. The Four Justifications in Fletcher's Theology. 1980. pap. 3.99 (0-88019-061-2) Schmul Pub Co.
Matlock, W. G. Realistic Planning for Arid Lands: Natural Resource Limitations to Agricultural Development, Vol. 2. (Advances in Desert & Arid Land Technology & Development Ser.). 284p. 1981. text ed. 145.00 (3-7186-0051-X) Gordon & Breach.
Matloff, Gregory L. Telescope Power: Fantastic Activities & Easy Projects for Young Astronomers. 128p. (Orig.). 1993. pap. text ed. 12.95 (0-471-58039-2) Wiley.
— The Urban Astronomer: A Practical Guide to Celestial Objects for Observers in Cities & Suburbs. (Science Editions Ser.: No. 1800). 224p. 1991. text ed. 34.95 (0-471-53142-1); pap. text ed. 16.95 (0-471-53143-X) Wiley.
Matloff, Gregory L., jt. auth. see Mallove, Eugene F.
Matloff, Jack M., ed. Cardiac Value Replacement: Current Status. 1985. lib. bdg. 107.00 (0-89838-722-1) Kluwer Ac.
Matloff, Jack M., jt. auth. see Gray, Richard J.
Matloff, Maurice, ed. World War One: Concise Military Histories of America's Major Wars. (Illus.). 1979. 7.95 (0-679-51450-3) McKay.
Matloff, Norman S. IBM Microcomputer Architecture & Assembly Language: A Look Under the Hood. 416p. 1991. text ed. 51.00 (0-13-451998-1) P-H.
— Probability Modeling & Computer Simulation: An Integrated Introduction with Applications to Engineering & Computer Science. 358p. (C). 1988. text ed. 53.95 (0-534-91854-9) Intl Thomson.
Matlon, Ronald J. Communication in the Legal Process. LC 87-16852. (Illus.). 400p. (C). 1988. text ed. 34.75 (0-03-062771-0) HB Coll Pubs.
— Opening Statements & Closing Arguments. LC 92-34211. (Trial Consultant Handbook Ser.: Vol. 1). 1992. 25.00 (0-9624181-2-9) Stuart Allen.
Matlon, Ronald J. & Ortiz, Syliva P., eds. Index to Journals in Communication Studies Through 1990, 2 vols., Set. LC 87-61574. (C). 1992. pap. text ed. 60.00 (0-944811-08-6, 110) Speech Commun Assn.
***Matloub, Ahmed.** Dictionary of Clothes from Lisan al-Arab. 142p. (ARA.). 1995. 18.95 (0-86685-652-8) Intl Bk Ctr.
***Matlzman, Stanley.** Drawing Nature. (Illus.). 144p. 1995. 24.99 (0-89134-579-5) North Light Bks.
Matney, Roy M., II & Roth, C. H., Jr. Parallel Computing Structures & Algorithms for Logic Design Problems. LC 72-133318. 124p. 1969. 19.00 (0-403-04518-5) Scholarly.
Mato. Phospholipid Metabolism in Cellular Signaling. 1990. 133.00 (0-8493-5978-3, QP752) CRC Pr.
Mato, Tataya. The Black Madonna Within: Drawings, Dreams, Reflections. LC 94-5690. (Dreamcatchers Ser.: Vol. 1). 217p. 1994. 44.95 (0-8126-9248-9); pap. 16.95 (0-8126-9249-7) Open Court.
Matocha, Linda & Sussman, Marvin B., eds. Publishing in Journals on the Family: Essays on Publishing. LC 93-9424. (Marriage & Family Review Ser.: Vol. 18, Nos. 1-2). (Illus.). 272p. 1993. lib. bdg. 39.95 (1-56024-341-4) Haworth Pr.
Matochik, Michael J., ed. The Civil War 1861-1865, Pt. 1. (Bibliographic Guide to the Microfiche Collection Ser.). ix, 144p. reprint ed. 40.00 (0-8357-0719-9) Univ Microfilms.
Matoesian, Gregory M. Reproducing Rape: Domination Through Talk in the Courtroom. LC 92-40155. (Language & Legal Discourse Ser.). viii, 256p. 1993. lib. bdg. 40.00 (0-226-51079-4); pap. text ed. 15.95 (0-226-51080-8) U Ch Pr.
Matolcsi, T. A Concept of Mathematical Physics: Models in Mechanics. 335p. (C). 1986. 102.00x (963-05-3627-7, Pub. by Akad Kiado HU) St Mut.
— A Concept of Mathematical Physics Models for Space Time. 236p. (C). 1984. 75.00x (963-05-3245-X, Pub. by Akad Kiado HU) St Mut.
Matolcsi, Tamas. Concept of Mathematical Physics: Models in Mechanics. 336p. (C). 1986. 250.00 (0-569-09012-1, Pub. by Collets) St Mut.
— Spacetime Without Reference Frames. (Illus.). 411p. (C). 1993. text ed. 50.00 (963-05-6433-5, Pub. by A K HU) Intl Spec Bk.
Matolcsi, Tomas. A Concept of Mathematical Physics: Models for Space-Time. 236p. 1984. 190.00 (0-569-08814-3, Pub. by Collets) St Mut.
Matolcsy, G., et al, eds. Pesticide Chemistry. (Studies in Environmental Science: No. 32). 800p. 1989. 254.00 (0-444-98903-X) Elsevier.
Matomors, Clemencia, jt. auth. see Horemis, George.
Maton, A., et al. Housing of Animals: Construction & Equipment of Animal Houses. (Developments in Agricultural Engineering Ser.: No. 8). 458p. 1985. 125.75 (0-444-42528-4) Elsevier.
Maton, Paul N., jt. auth. see Decker, John L.
Maton, Sonny. A Leaf Falls But Once. 1994. 11.95 (0-8062-4836-X) Carlton.
Matonis, A. T. & Melia, Daniel F., eds. Celtic Language - Celtic Culture: A Festschrift for Eric P. Hamp. xix, 415p. 1990. 45.00 (0-926689-01-0) Ford & Bailie Pubs.
Matonti, Charles. See All the People. 98p. (Orig.). 1990. pap. 6.95 (0-914544-79-9) Living Flame Pr.
***Matonti, Charles J.** I Call You Friend: Dialogues with Jesus. 144p. (Orig.). 1994. pap. 9.95 (1-883520-08-8) Jeremiah Pr.
Matore, Georges. Dictionnaire du Vocabulaire Essentiel: Dictionary of Essential Vocabulary. 6th ed. 360p. (FRE.). 1980. pap. 23.95 (0-8288-1945-9, M6652) Fr & Eur.
Matore, Georges, ed. see Gautier, Theophile.
Matoren, Gary M. The Clinical Research Process in the Pharmaceutical Industry. (Drugs & the Pharmaceutical Sciences Ser.: Vol. 19). 576p. 1984. 135.00 (0-8247-1914-X) Dekker.
Matory, J. Lorand. Sex & the Empire That Is No More: Gender & the Politics of Metaphor in Oyo Yoruba Religion. LC 93-37980. (C). 1994. text ed. 44.95 (0-8166-2226-4); pap. text ed. 19.95 (0-8166-2227-2) U of Minn Pr.
Matos, Gustavo P. Gustavo Pales Matos: Obras. LC 86-7094. 512p. 1986. 15.00 (0-8477-3235-5, 19865) U of PR Pr.
Matos, L., ed. Spectrum Management Engineering. LC 85-10721. (Reprint Ser.). 1985. 59.95 (0-87942-189-4, PC01834) Inst Electrical.
Matos, Luis P. Tuntun de Pasa y Griferia. (Puerto Rican Collection). 226p. 1993. pap. 6.95 (0-8477-0178-6) U of PR Pr.
Matos-Paoli, Francisco. Hacia el Hondo Vuelo. LC 80-26395. (UPREX, Poesia Ser.: No. 61). 200p. (Orig.). (SPA.). 1983. pap. 3.00 (0-8477-0061-5) U of PR Pr.
— Testigo de la Esperanza. (UPREX, Poesia Ser.: No. 29). 132p. (C). 1975. pap. 1.50 (0-8477-0029-1) U of PR Pr.
Matos, Paula C. California Decedent Estate Practice, No. 3: March 1992 Update. Dworin, Christopher D., ed. LC 86-70193. 480p. 1992. ring bd. 40.00 (0-88124-469-4, ES-30864) Cont Ed Bar-CA.
— California Decedent Estate Practice, Vol. 3: 1987. Dworin, Christopher D., ed. LC 86-70193. 850p. 1987. ring bd. 95.00 (0-88124-157-1, ES-30860) Cont Ed Bar-CA.
Matos, Ramiro, et al, eds. Andean Archaeology: Papers in Memory of Clifford Evans. LC 85-11854. (Monograph: No. 27). (Illus.). 238p. (Orig.). 1986. pap. text ed. 18.25 (0-917956-52-4) UCLA Arch.
Matossian, Mary K. Poisons of the Past: Molds, Epidemics, & History. LC 89-5345. 208p. (C). 1989. text ed. 27.50 (0-300-03949-2) Yale U Pr.
— Poisons of the Past: Molds, Epidemics, & History. (Illus.). 208p. (C). 1991. reprint ed. pap. 11.00 (0-300-05121-2) Yale U Pr.
Matossian, Mary K., jt. auth. see Villa, Susie H.
Matossian, Nouritza. Xenakis. 1991. pap. 19.95 (0-912483-35-0) Pro-Am Music.
Matousek, Clifford H., jt. auth. see Gray, Al.
Matousek, Mark & Harvey, Andrew. Dialogues with a Modern Mystic. (Illus.). 200p. (Orig.). 1994. pap. 12.00 (0-8356-0704-6, Quest) Theos Pub Hse.
Matov, G. Tales of Tzaddikim: Bereishis. Weinbach, Shaindel, tr. (ArtScroll Youth Ser.). (Illus.). 320p. (YA). (gr. 7-12). 1987. 15.95 (0-89906-825-1); pap. 11.95 (0-89906-826-X) Mesorah Pubns.
— Tales of Tzaddikim: Devarim. Weinbach, Shaindel, tr. (ArtScroll Youth Ser.). (Illus.). 320p. (YA). (gr. 7-12). 1988. 15.95 (0-89906-833-2); pap. 11.95 (0-89906-834-0) Mesorah Pubns.
— Tales of Tzaddikim: Sh'emos. Weinbach, Shaindel, tr. (ArtScroll Youth Ser.). (Illus.). 320p. (YA). (gr. 7-12). 1988. 15.95 (0-89906-827-8) Mesorah Pubns.
— Tales of Tzaddikim: Sh'emos. Weinbach, Shaindel, tr. (ArtScroll Youth Ser.). (Illus.). 320p. (YA). (gr. 7-12). 1988. pap. 11.95 (0-89906-828-6) Mesorah Pubns.
Matovcik, Gerard. Academic Sportfolio: Excuse Notes Are No Excuse. Pranzo, Donard, ed. (Sports Singles Ser.). (Illus.). (YA). (gr. 9-12). 1989. 50.00 (0-924086-11-4) Acad Sportfolio.
Matovich, Richard M. A Concordance to the Collected Poems of Sylvia Plath. LC 85-45126. 623p. 43.00 (0-8240-8664-3, H618) Garland.
***Matovina, Timothy M.** The Alamo Remembered: Tejano Accounts. LC 95-10131. 1995. write for info. (0-292-75185-0); pap. write for info. (0-292-75186-9) U of Tex Pr.
— Tejano Religion & Ethnicity: San Antonio, 1821-1860. 176p. 1995. 24.95 (0-292-75170-2) U of Tex Pr.
Matox, R. B. & Miller, W. D., eds. Ogallala Aquifer Symposium, 1979. (Special Report Ser.: No. 39). 242p. 1989. 20.00 (0-318-41146-6) Intl Ctr Arid & Semi-Arid.
Matozzi, Patricia R. God Is Love. LC 92-12769. (Illus.). (J). 1992. 3.99 (0-517-08143-1, Derrydale Bks) Random Hse Value.
Matranga, Frances C. I'm Glad I'm Me! Beegle, Shirley, ed. (Happy Day Bks.). (Illus.). 24p. (J). (ps-3). 1994. reprint ed. pap. 1.89 (0-7847-0259-4) Standard Pub.
— One Step at a Time. (Illus.). (J). (gr. 4-7). 1987. pap. 3.99 (0-570-03642-9, 39-1126) Concordia.
— The Perfect Friend. 80p. (Orig.). (J). (gr. 5-7). 1985. pap. 3.99 (0-570-04112-0, 56-1523) Concordia.
Matranga, Petrus, ed. Anecdota Graeca. 799p. 1971. reprint ed. write for info. (3-487-04163-4, Pub. by Georg Olms GW) Lubrecht & Cramer.
Matras, Christian. Seeing & Remembering. Johnston, George, tr. 48p. 1988. 7.95 (0-921254-09-1, Pub. by Penumbra Pr CN) U of Toronto Pr.
Matras, John. Illustrated Volvo Buyers Guide. (MBI Buyers Guides Ser.). (Illus.). 128p. 1993. pap. 16.95 (0-87938-713-0) Motorbooks Intl.
— Mazda RX-7. (Sports Car Color History Ser.). (Illus.). 128p. 1994. pap. 19.95 (0-87938-938-9) Motorbooks Intl.
Matras, John L. Illustrated Mazda Buyer's Guide. LC 93-32133. (Illustrated Buyer's Guide Ser.). (Illus.). 128p. 1994. pap. text ed. 16.95 (0-87938-842-0) Motorbooks Intl.
Matras, Judah. Dependency, Obligations, & Entitlements. 256p. (C). 1989. Casebound. text ed. write for info. (0-13-199316-X) P-H.
Matrau, Henry. Letters Home: Henry Matrau of the Iron Brigade. Reid-Green, Marcia, ed. LC 92-26862. (Illus.). xx, 170p. 1993. 22.50 (0-8032-3151-2) U of Nebr Pr.
Matravers, Hazel, jt. auth. see Kay, Thornton.
Matray, James A. The Reluctant Crusade: American Foreign Policy in Korea, 1941-1950. LC 85-1079. 368p. 1985. text ed. 30.00 (0-8248-0973-4) UH Pr.
Matray, James I., ed. Historical Dictionary of the Korean War. LC 90-22833. 662p. 1991. text ed. 85.00 (0-313-25924-0, MYK, Greenwood Pr) Greenwood.
Matray, James I., jt. ed. see Baum, Kim C.

An Asterisk (*) at the beginning of an entry indicates that the title is appearing in BIP for the first time.

Matreyek, Mary B. Rentsch: Herold Families in America. Bunkhouse Publishers, Inc. Staff, ed. 743p. 1986. 125.00 (*0-937594-10-5*) Stump Pub.

Matricardi, Connie. Preschool Puppet Plays. (Illus.). 36p. (Orig.). (J). (gr. k). 1993. pap. 9.95 (*1-884555-00-4*) P Depke Bks.

Matricon, J., jt. auth. see DeWitt, C.

Matrisciana, Caryl. The Pagan Invasion: Ancient Deceptions Repackaged for the Modern Mind. LC 93-31607. 1994. pap. 8.99 (*1-56507-138-7*) Harvest Hse.

Matrisciana, Caryl & Oakland, Roger. The Evolution Conspiracy. 1991. pap. 7.99 (*0-89081-939-4*) Harvest Hse.

Matrisciana, Caryl, jt. auth. see Decker, Ed.

***Matrisciana, Patrick.** The Clinton Chronicles. 320p. (Orig.). 1994. pap. 12.95 (*1-878993-63-1*) Jeremiah Pubs.

***Matriscrana, Patrick & Miller, Dorothy.** Dual Citizenship. 76p. (Orig.). Date not set. pap. 2.95 (*1-878993-66-6*) Jeremiah Pubs.

Matrone, Gennard, jt. auth. see Beeson, Kenneth C.

Matros, Y. S., ed. Unsteady State Processes in Catalysis. (Illus.). 724p. 1990. 245.00 (*90-6764-127-8*, Pub. by VSP NE) Coronet Bks.

Matros, Yu S. Catalytic Processes under Unsteady-State Conditions. (Studies in Surface Science & Catalysis: No. 43). 404p. 1989. 192.50 (*0-444-87116-0*) Elsevier.

— Unsteady Processes in Catalytic Reactors. (Studies in Surface Science & Catalysis: 22). 364p. 1985. 120.50 (*0-444-42523-3*) Elsevier.

Matrosov, V. M. Methods of Nonlinear Dynamical Analysis: Lecture Notes. (Soviet & East European Mathematics Ser.). 1993. text ed. 68.00 (*981-02-1112-0*) World Scientific Pub.

Matsagouras, E. The Early Church Fathers As Educators. 1977. pap. 7.95 (*0-937032-10-7*) Light&Life Pub Co MN.

Matsakis, Aphrodite. I Can't Get over It: A Handbook for Trauma Survivors. 400p. (Orig.). (C). 1992. text ed. 24.95 (*1-879237-26-1*); pap. 12.95 (*1-879237-25-3*) New Harbinger.

— Post-Traumatic Stress Disorder: A Complete Treatment Guide. LC 93-87082. 384p. 1994. text ed. 39.95 (*1-879237-68-7*) New Harbinger.

— When the Bough Breaks: A Helping Guide for Parents of Sexually Abused Children. 208p. (Orig.). 1991. 24.95 (*1-879237-01-6*); pap. 11.95 (*1-879237-00-8*) New Harbinger.

Matsch, C. L., jt. ed. see Goldthwait, R. P.

Matsch, Charles L., jt. auth. see Ojakangas, Richards W.

Matsch, Leander W. & Morgan, J. Derald. Electromagnetic & Electromechanical Machines. 3rd ed. 593p. 1986. Net. text ed. write for info. (*0-471-60364-3*); teacher ed 10.00 (*0-471-60421-6*) Wiley.

Matschat, Cecile H. Suwannee River: Strange Green Land. LC 79-5190. (Brown Thrasher Bks.). (Illus.). 308p. 1980. reprint ed. 25.00 (*0-8203-0508-1*) U of Ga Pr.

Matschoss, Conrad. Great Engineers. Hatfield, H. Stafford, tr. LC 70-128278. (Essay Index Reprint Ser.). 1977. 30.95 (*0-8369-1837-1*) Ayer.

***Matseiko, Youri & Miller, Steven E., eds.** Safeguarding Ukraine's Security: Dilemmas & Options. (CSIA Studies in International Security: No. 9). (Illus.). 350p. 1995. 39.95 (*0-262-93164-8*); 39.95 (*0-262-13310-5*) MIT Pr.

— Safeguarding Ukraine's Security: Dilemmas & Options. (CSIA Studies in International Security: Vol. No. 9). (Illus.). 350p. 1995. pap. text ed. 17.95 (*0-262-63164-4*) MIT Pr.

Matsen, Brad & Jay, Tom. Reaching Home: Pacific Salmon, Pacific People. Wheat, Ellen, ed. (Illus.). 144p. 1994. 37.95 (*0-88240-449-0*) Alaska Northwest.

***Matsen, Brad & Troll, Ray.** Planet Ocean. 144p. (Orig.). 1995. pap. 19.95 (*0-89815-778-1*) Ten Speed Pr.

Matsen, Brad, jt. auth. see Troll, Ray.

Matsen, F. A. & Pauncz, R. The Unitary Group in Quantum Chemistry. (Studies in Physical & Theoretical Chemistry: No. 44). 392p. 1987. 146.25 (*0-444-42730-9*) Elsevier.

Matsen, F. A. & Tajima, T., eds. Supercomputers: Algorithms, Architectures, & Scientific Computation. 488p. (C). 1986. text ed. 40.00 (*0-292-70388-0*) U of Tex Pr.

Matsen, Frederick, III, et al. Practical Evaluation & Management of the Shoulder. LC 93-41664. 1994. text ed. 75.00 (*0-7216-4819-3*) Saunders.

Matsen, Frederick A., III, et al, eds. The Shoulder: A Balance of Mobility & Stability. LC 93-30015. 653p. 1993. 105.00 (*0-89203-091-7*) Amer Acad Ortho Surg.

Matsen, Herbert S., ed. Alessandro Achillini (1463-1512) & His Doctrine of Universals & Transcendentals. LC 72-3521. 332p. 1975. 38.50 (*0-686-85741-0*) Bucknell U Pr.

Matsen, Jonn. Eating Alive: Prevention Thru Good Digestion. (Illus.). 305p. (Orig.). 1989. pap. 16.95 (*0-9693586-0-1*) Gordon Soules Bk.

Matsen, Kenneth, jt. auth. see Slocum, Robert.

Matsen, Patricia P., et al, eds. Readings from Classical Rhetoric. LC 89-36897. 400p. (C). 1990. 34.95 (*0-8093-1592-0*); pap. 19.95 (*0-8093-1593-9*) S Ill U Pr.

Matsen, William E. The Great War & the American Novel: Versions of Reality & the Writer's Craft in Selected Fiction of the First World War. LC 92-40772. (American University Studies: American Literature: Ser. XXIV, Vol. 48). 225p. (C). 1993. text ed. 39.95 (*0-8204-2093-X*) P Lang Pubs.

***Matsheru, M.** Income Tax Made Simple. 165p. 1991. pap. 20.00 (*0-409-10495-7*, SA) Butterworth Legal Pubs.

Matshikiza, Todd. Chocolates for My Wife. 128p. 1990. pap. 9.95 (*0-908396-83-X*, Pub. by D Philip SA) Interlink Pub.

Matshoba, Mtutuzeli. Call Me Not a Man. (African Classics Ser.). (C). 1979. pap. text ed. 9.95 (*0-582-00242-7*, 76386) Longman.

Matsikidze, Isabell P. Zimbabwean Collectibles. LC 90-60134. 72p. (Orig.). 1990. pap. 6.95 (*0-943512-34-4*) Linwood Pub.

***Matske.** Government in America. 2nd abr. ed. (C). 1995. student ed, text ed. write for info. (*0-673-99659-X*) HarpCollege.

Matsler, Franklin G. & Hines, Edward R. State Policy Formation in Illinois Higher Education. (Orig.). (C). 1987. pap. text ed. 7.50 (*0-944498-00-0*) ISU Ctr High Educ.

Matsner Gruenberg, Sidonie. Los Hijos: Enciclopedia Grafica Para Su Crianza y Educacion. 712p. (SPA.). 35.95 (*84-7082-016-8*, S-13986); 35.00 (*0-8288-7891-9*, S13986) Fr & Eur.

Matson. Giving Testimony. 1995. write for info. (*0-87371-400-8*) Lewis Pubs.

— Legal Risk Mitigation for the Environmental Professional. 1995. write for info. (*0-87371-299-4*) Lewis Pubs.

Matson, Alex, tr. see Kallas, Aino J.

Matson, Cathy D. & Onuf, Peter S. A Union of Interests: Political & Economic Thought in Revolutionary America. LC 89-16749. (American Political Thought Ser.). x, 238p. 1990. 25.00 (*0-7006-0417-0*) U Pr of KS.

Matson, Clive. Equal in Desire. 1989. pap. 4.50 (*0-914433-43-1*) Man-Root.

— Equal in Desire. deluxe ed. 1989. 20.00 (*0-686-37447-9*) Man-Root.

— On the Inside. LC 82-14621. (Illus.). 70p. (Orig.). 1982. pap. 4.00 (*0-916156-65-6*) Cherry Valley.

Matson, Daniel S. & Fontana, Bernard L., eds. Friar Bringas Reports to the King: Methods of Indoctrination on the Frontier of New Spain, 1796-97. LC 76-11987. 177p. 1977. 12.50 (*0-8165-0599-3*); pap. 9.95 (*0-8165-0524-1*) U of Ariz Pr.

Matson, Debra, ed. see Brannigan, Francis L.

Matson, Emerson N. Legends of the Great Chiefs. (Illus.). 144p. (YA). (gr. 8-12). 1984. reprint ed. pap. 5.95 (*0-9609940-0-9*) Storypole.

Matson, Floyd. Walking Alone & Marching Together: A History of the Organized Blind Movement in the United States, 1940-1990. (Illus.). 1117p. (Orig.). 1990. text ed. 30.00 (*0-9624122-1-X*) Natl Fed Blind.

Matson, Geoffrey. Golf Stories & Jokes for Speakers. 1993. pap. 5.95 (*0-572-01605-0*, Pub. by W Foulsham UK) Trans-Atl Phila.

Matson, Ghastgifvar E. The Middle East in Pictures, 4 vols. 1980. 192.95 (*0-405-12212-8*, 19456) Ayer.

— The Middle East in Pictures, Vol. 4. 1980. 49.95 (*0-405-18868-4*) Ayer.

Matson, Henrietta. The Mississippi Schoolmaster. LC 72-1511. (Black Heritage Library Collection). 1977. reprint ed. 25.95 (*0-8369-9035-8*) Ayer.

Matson, J. V. How to Fail Successfully: A Bold Approach to Meeting Your Goals Through Intelligent Fast Failure. 130p. 1991. pap. text ed. 15.00 (*0-9629789-0-6*) Dynamo Pub.

Matson, Jack V. Effective Expert Witnessing. 2nd ed. LC 94-15811. 1994. write for info. (*1-56670-002-7*) CRC Pr.

— Effective Expert Witnessing: A Handbook for Technical Professionals. (Illus.). 145p. 1990. 59.95 (*0-87371-297-8*, KF89) Lewis Pubs.

Matson, Johnny L. Enhancing Children's Social Skills. (C). 1988. pap. 19.95 (*0-205-14416-0*, H4416) Allyn.

— Handbook of Hyperactivity in Children. 368p. (C). 1993. boxed 49.95 (*0-205-14591-4*, H45917, Longwood Div) Allyn.

— Handbook of Mental Retardation. 2nd ed. (C). 1991. 100.95 (*0-205-14413-6*, H4413, Longwood Div) Allyn.

— Philosophy & Care of the Mentally Retarded: A Worldwide Status Report. 120p. 1983. pap. 15.25 (*0-08-028093-5*, Pergamon Pr) Elsevier.

***Matson, Johnny L., ed.** Autism in Children & Adults: Etiology, Assessment & Intervention. (Special Education Ser.). 420p. (C). 1993. text ed. 42.95 (*0-534-23826-2*) Sycamore Pub.

— Chronic Schizophrenia & Adult Autism: Issues in Diagnosis, Assessment & Psychological Treatment. LC 89-21631. 352p. 1989. 41.95 (*0-8261-6020-4*) Springer Pub.

— Handbook of Behavior Modification with the Mentally Retarded. 2nd ed. LC 89-23235. (Applied Clinical Psychology Ser.). (Illus.). 520p. 1990. 80.00 (*0-306-43309-5*, Plenum Pr) Plenum.

— Handbook of Treatment Approaches in Childhood Psychopathology. LC 88-19648. (Applied Clinical Psychology Ser.). (Illus.). 612p. 1988. 90.00 (*0-306-42844-X*, Plenum Pr) Plenum.

Matson, Johnny L. & Andrasik, Frank, eds. Treatment Issues & Innovations in Mental Retardation. (Applied Clinical Psychology Ser.). 666p. 1983. 95.00 (*0-306-40935-6*, Plenum Pr) Plenum.

Matson, Johnny L. & Barrett, Rowland P., eds. Psychopathology in the Mentally Retarded. 2nd ed. LC 92-49246. 1992. 50.95 (*0-205-13446-7*, Longwood Div) Allyn.

Matson, Johnny L. & DiLorenzo, Thomas M. Punishment & Its Alternatives: A New Perspective for Behavior Modification. (Behavior Therapy & Behavioral Medicine Ser.: Vol. 13). 288p. 1983. 29.95 (*0-8261-4560-4*) Springer Pub.

Matson, Johnny L. & Mulick, James A., eds. Handbook of Mental Retardation. (General Psychology Ser.: No. 121). (Illus.). 650p. 1983. 100.00 (*0-08-028060-9*, Pergamon Pr) Elsevier.

Matson, Johnny L., jt. ed. see Barrett, Rowland P.

Matson, Johnny L., jt. ed. see Frame, C. L.

Matson, Katinka. The Working Actor: A Guide to the Profession. (Handbook Ser.). 1978. mass mkt. 5.95 (*0-14-046343-7*, Penguin Bks) Viking Penguin.

Matson, Katinka & Katz, Judith. The Working Actor: A Guide to the Profession. rev. ed. LC 93-12324. 192p. 1993. pap. 12.00 (*0-14-014433-1*, Penguin Bks) Viking Penguin.

Matson, Katinka, jt. ed. see Brockman, John.

Matson, Madeline. Food in Missouri: A Cultural Stew. LC 93-50819. (Missouri Heritage Readers Ser.). (Illus.). 168p. 1994. pap. 7.95 (*0-8262-0960-2*) U of Mo Pr.

Matson, Mandy. Using Your Camcorder. (Illus.). 144p. 1989. pap. 18.95 (*0-8174-6349-6*, Amphoto) Watsn-Guptill.

Matson, Molly, ed. see Guerrier, Edith.

***Matson, N.** Reminiscences of Bureau County, Illinois. (Illus.). 406p. 1993. lib. bdg. 42.00 (*0-8328-3527-7*) Higginson Bk Co.

Matson, P. Trace Gases in Ecology. 1994. pap. write for info. (*0-632-03641-9*) Blackwell Sci.

Matson, R. G. The Origins of Southwestern Agriculture. LC 91-14054. (Illus.). 356p. 1991. 60.00 (*0-8165-1196-9*) U of Ariz Pr.

Matson, R. G. & Coupland, Gary. The Prehistory of the Northwest Coast. (Illus.). 364p. 1994. text ed. 69.00 (*0-12-480260-5*) Acad Pr.

Matson, Robert W. Neutrality & Navicerts: Britain, the United States, & Economic Warfare, 1939-1940. LC 93-43702. (Modern American History Ser.). 216p. 1994. lib. bdg. 54.00 (*0-8153-1651-8*) Garland.

Matson, Robert W., ed. see Paulaharju, Samuli.

Matson, Sue, ed. see Bowkett, Gerald E.

Matson, Suzanne. Durable Goods. LC 93-14958. 72p. (Orig.). 1993. pap. 9.95 (*1-882295-00-5*) Alicejamesbooks.

— Sea Level. LC 90-4952. 72p. (Orig.). 1990. pap. 9.95 (*0-914086-84-7*) Alicejamesbooks.

Matson, Ted & McDougall, Mark, eds. Information Systems for Ambulatory Care. LC 90-189. 299p. (Orig.). 1990. 49.95 (*1-55648-048-2*, 093100) AHPI.

Matson, Theodore A., ed. Restructuring for Ambulatory Care: A Guide to Reorganization. LC 90-18507. 312p. (Orig.). 1990. pap. 46.95 (*1-55648-045-8*, 016143) AHPI.

Matson, Theodore A. & McNamara, Peggy, eds. The Hospital Emergency Department: A Guide to Operational Excellence. LC 92-10498. 289p. 1992. 54.95 (*1-55648-088-1*, 052110) AHPI.

Matson, Theodore A., jt. ed. see Donovan, Michelle R.

Matson, Tim. Earth Ponds: The Country Pond Maker's Guide to Building, Maintenance & Restoration. 2nd rev. ed. LC 90-26957. 160p. 1991. pap. 17.00 (*0-88150-155-7*) Countryman.

Matson, Wallace I. A New History of Philosophy, Vol. 1: Ancient & Medieval. (Illus.). 249p. (C). 1987. pap. text ed. 18.75 (*0-15-565728-3*) HB Coll Pubs.

— A New History of Philosophy, Vol. 2: Modern. (Illus.). 236p. (C). 1987. pap. text ed. 18.75 (*0-15-565729-1*) HB Coll Pubs.

— Sentience. (Illus.). 200p. 1976. pap. 11.00 (*0-520-04776-1*) U CA Pr.

Matson, Wallace I., jt. auth. see Warren, Thomas B.

Matson, Wayne R., ed. Cosmonautics: a Colorful History: History of Soviet-Russian Space Programs. 212p. 1994. 49.95 (*1-885609-01-9*) Cosmos Books.

Matsoukas, G., jt. auth. see Sfekas, S.

Matsson, Per, et al, eds. Clinical Impact of the Monitoring of Allergic Inflammation. (Illus.). 272p. 1991. text ed. 72.00 (*0-12-480265-6*) Acad Pr.

Matsubaba, Tatsuo. Introduction to Water Color Painting, Set. (Easy Start Guide Ser.). (Illus.). 1991. 36.95 (*4-7661-0622-9*, Pub. by Graphic Sha JA) Bks Nippan.

***Matsubara, Mitsunori.** Pancaratra Samhitas & Early Vaisnava Theology. (C). 1995. 22.50x (*81-208-1221-2*, Pub. by Motilal Banarsidass II) S Asia.

***Matsubara, Naoko.** In Praise of Trees. (Illus.). 96p. 1995. lib. bdg. 37.00 (*0-8095-4917-4*) Borgo Pr.

Matsubara, T., ed. The Structure & Properties of Matter. (Solid-State Sciences Ser.: Vol. 28). (Illus.). 450p. 1982. 81.00 (*0-387-11098-4*) Spr-Verlag.

Matsubara, T. & Kotani, A., eds. Superconductiving in Magnetic & Exotic Materials: Proceedings of the Sixth Taniguchi International Symposium, Kashikojima, Japan, Nov. 14-18, 1983. (Solid-State Sciences Ser.: Vol. 52). (Illus.). 225p. 1984. 54.00 (*0-387-13324-0*) Spr-Verlag.

Matsuda, Fukumatsu, tr. see Tsuda, Sokichi.

Matsuda, K., jt. ed. see Sandford, Paul A.

Matsuda, Mari J., ed. Called from Within: Early Women Lawyers of Hawaii. LC 92-11002. (Biography Monographs). 400p. 1992. text ed. 45.00 (*0-8248-1430-4*); pap. 26.95 (*0-8248-1448-7*) UH Pr.

Matsuda, Mari J., et al. Words That Wound: Critical Race Theory, Assaultive Speech, & the First Amendment. (New Perspectives on Law, Culture, & Society Ser.). 160p. (C). 1993. pap. text ed. 17.95 (*0-8133-8428-1*) Westview.

Matsuda, Mitsugu, tr. see Yazaki, Takeo.

Matsuda, Ryuichi. Animal Evolution in Changing Environments: With Special Reference to Abnormal Metamorphosis. LC 86-15942. 355p. 1987. text ed. 74.95 (*0-471-87856-1*, Wiley-Interscience) Wiley.

Matsuda, S., et al, eds. Perspectives on Particle Physics: Festschrift in Honor of Prof. H. Miyazawa. 424p. (C). 1989. text ed. 99.00 (*9971-5-0589-4*) World Scientific Pub.

Matsuda, T. & Niitsuma, N. Collision Tectonics in the South Fossa Magna, Central Japan: A Special Issue of the Journal Modern Geoleogy. 152p. 1989. pap. text ed. 176.00 (*0-677-25920-4*) Gordon & Breach.

Matsuda, Tadayoshi, ed. Cancer Treatment by Hyperthermia, Radiation & Drugs. 380p. 1993. 160.00 (*0-85066-837-9*, Pub. by Tay Francis Ltd UK) Taylor & Francis.

Matsuda, Yoshiro, jt. auth. see Kurabayashi, Koshimasa.

Matsudaira, Paul, ed. A Practical Guide to Protein & Peptide Purification for Microsequencing. 2nd ed. (Illus.). 188p. 1993. 34.95 (*0-12-480282-6*) Acad Pr.

Matsudaira, Susumu, jt. auth. see Keyes, Roger.

Matsueda, Pat. The Fish Catcher. 1985. pap. 3.50 (*0-932136-08-7*) Petronium HI.

Matsuhashi, Ann. Writing in Real Time: Modelling Production Processes. Farr, Marcia, ed. LC 86-22214. (Writing Research Ser.: Vol. 16). 320p. (C). 1987. text ed. 47.50 (*0-89391-400-2*); pap. 27.50 (*0-89391-417-7*) Ablex Pub.

Matsui, Hideji & Kobayashi, Kando, eds. Biomechanics VIII, 2 Vols. (International Series on Biomechanics). 1983. text ed. 120.00 (*0-931250-42-0*, BMAT0042) Human Kinetics.

— Biomechanics VIII, Vol. B. LC 82-84703. (International Series on Biomechanics). 664p. (C). 1983. text ed. 67.00x (*0-931250-44-7*, BMAT0044) Human Kinetics.

Matsui, Isao. Theory & Practice of Eel Culture. Gopal, Alamelu, tr. 141p. 1980. text ed. 60.00 (*90-6191-036-6*, Pub. by A A Balkema NE) Ashgate Pub Co.

Matsui, K., jt. ed. see Eto, Hajime.

Matsui, Masato, jt. ed. see Song, Minako I.

Matsui, Susan, tr. see Akio, Terumasa.

Matsui, Susan, tr. see Nakawatari, Harutaka.

Matsui, Susan, tr. see Tejima, Keizaburo.

***Matsui, Tetsuo & Rosenblatt, Richard H.** Review of the Deep-Sea Fish Family Platytroctidae (Pisces: Salmoniformes) LC 86-25088. (Bulletin of the Scripps Institution of Oceanography, University of California, San Diego Ser.: No. 26). 169p. 1987. pap. 48.20 (*0-7837-7492-3*, 2049214) Bks Demand.

Matsui, Y., jt. auth. see Nariai, K.

Matsui, Yoshiichi. Goldfish Guide. 3rd ed. (Illus.). 325p. 1991. 19.95 (*0-86622-605-2*, PL2011) TFH Pubns.

Matsukata, Masayoshi. Report on the Adoption of the Gold Standard in Japan. Wilkins, Mira, ed. LC 78-3937. (International Finance Ser.). (Illus.). 1979. reprint ed. lib. bdg. 40.95 (*0-405-11238-6*) Ayer.

***Matsuki, Kenji.** Weyl Groups & Birational Transformations among Minimal Models. LC 95-15922. (Memoirs Ser.: No. 557). 1995. write for info. (*0-8218-0341-7*) Am Math.

Matsulenko, V. A. & Beketov, A. A. Camouflage: A Soviet View Pts. 1 & 2: Operational Camouflage of the Troops & Camouflage of Actions by Ground Force Subunits. LC 88-600452. (Soviet Military Thought Ser.: No. 22). (Illus.). 295p. (Orig.). 1989. pap. 12.00 (*0-16-002258-4*, S/N 008-070-006) USGPO.

Matsumoto, Akira & Ishii, Susumu, eds. Atlas of Endocrine Organs: Vertebrates & Invertebrates. Urano, A., tr. LC 92-28888. (Illus.). 320p. 1992. 200.00 (*0-387-53158-0*) Spr-Verlag.

Matsumoto, Brian, et al, eds. Methods in Cell Biology, Vol. 38: Cell Biological Applications of Confocal Microscopy. (Illus.). 380p. 1993. text ed. 95.00 (*0-12-564138-9*); spiral bd. 49.95 (*0-12-480430-6*) Acad Pr.

Matsumoto, David. Cultural Influences on Research Methods & Statistics. LC 93-41938. 1994. pap. 5.95 (*0-534-23766-5*) Brooks-Cole.

— Culture & Diversity. LC 95-8728. 1996. pap. 20.95 (*0-534-23220-5*) Brooks-Cole.

— People: Psychology from a Multicultural Perspective. LC 93-13916. 1994. pap. 15.95 (*0-534-19338-2*) Brooks-Cole.

Matsumoto, G., jt. auth. see Kaminuma, T.

Matsumoto, Gen & Kotani, Masao, eds. Nerve Membrane: Biochemistry & Function of Channel Protein & Cytoplasmic Structure. 250p. 1981. 62.50 (*0-86008-294-6*, Pub. by U of Tokyo JA) Col U Pr.

Matsumoto, H., ed. Modern Radio Science 1993. (Illus.). 264p. 1993. 37.50 (*0-19-856379-5*) OUP.

Matsumoto, H. & Sato, T. Computer Simulation of Space Plasmas. 1985. lib. bdg. 67.00 (*0-318-04239-8*) Kluwer Ac.

Matsumoto, Isamu, ed. Advances in Chemical Diagnosis & Treatment of Metabolic Disorders, Vol. 1: Updated Proceedings of the First & Second Symposia on Clinical Diagnosis of Metabolic Disorders, Kanazawa Medical University, Kanazawa, Japan: May 1989 & May 1990. 165p. 1993. text ed. 74.95 (*0-471-93889-0*) Wiley.

Matsumoto, Kenichi, jt. auth. see Ohtsuka, Yasunori.

Matsumoto, Kiiko & Birch, Stephen. Extraordinary Vessels. Felt, Robert L., ed. 220p. (Orig.). 1986. pap. 20.00 (*0-912111-35-6*) Paradigm Publns.

— Five Elements & Ten Stems: Nan-Ching Theory, Diagnosis, & Practice. Felt, Robert L., ed. (Illus.). 236p. 1989. reprint ed. pap. 16.95 (*0-912111-25-9*) Paradigm Publns.

— Hara Diagnosis: Reflections on the Sea. (Illus.). 496p. 1988. text ed. 59.95 (*0-912111-13-5*) Paradigm Publns.

Matsumoto, Kiyoshi & Acheson, Roy M. Organic Synthesis at High Pressures. 456p. 1991. text ed. 115.00 (*0-471-62761-5*) Wiley.

***Matsumoto, Koji.** Organizing for Higher Productivity: An Analysis of Japanese Systems & Practices. 2nd ed. (Illus.). 75p. 1986. reprint ed. text ed. 18.00 (*92-833-1065-9*, 310659, Pub. by APO JA); reprint ed. pap. text ed. 13.75 (*92-833-1066-7*, 310667, Pub. by APO JA) Qual Resc.

— The Rise of the Japanese Corporate System: The Inside View of a MITI Official. (Japanese Studies). 220p. (C). 1991. text ed. 89.95 (*0-7103-0407-2*, A5593, Pub. by Kegan Paul Intl UK) Routledge Chapman & Hall.

An Asterisk (*) at the beginning of an entry indicates that the title is appearing in BIP for the first time.

— The Rise of the Japanese Corporate System: The Inside View of a MITI Official. (Japanese Studies Ser.). 280p. 1994. pap. 25.50 (*0-7103-0488-9*, Pub. by Kegan Paul Intl UK) Routledge Chapman & Hall.

Matsumoto, Kunio, jt. ed. see Nakamura, Toshikazu.

Matsumoto, Leiji. Captain Harlock Television Scripts, Vol. 1. Villa, Mickie & Mason, Tom, eds. (Illus.). 135p. (YA). 1990. pap. 19.95 (*0-944735-63-0*) Malibu Graphics.

Matsumoto, Michihiro. The Unspoken Way: Haragei, or the Role of Silent Communication in Japanese Business & Society. LC 88-80138. 152p. 1988. pap. 8.00 (*0-87011-889-7*) Kodansha.

***Matsumoto, Pat, ed. & intro.** Chicago Designs: Fashion, Photography, Architecture. (Illus.). 16p. (Orig.). 1990. pap. 10.00 (*0-938903-11-X*) Chi Ofc Fine Arts.

Matsumoto, Pat, ed. see Bonesteel, Michael.

Matsumoto, Seicho. Inspector Imanishi Investigates. LC 89-34038. 310p. 1989. 18.95 (*0-939149-28-1*) Soho Press.

— Inspector Imanishi Investigates. LC 89-34089. 310p. 1994. pap. 11.00 (*1-56947-019-7*) Soho Press.

— Points & Lines. LC 72-117385. 160p. 1986. pap. 9.95 (*0-87011-456-5*) Kodansha.

— Points & Lines. Yamamoto, Makiko & Blum, Paul C., trs. 160p. Date not set. 9.00 (*4-7700-0937-2*) FS&G.

— The Voice & Other Stories. Kabat, Adam, tr. 192p. 1989. 17.95 (*0-87011-895-1*) Kodansha.

— The Voice & Other Stories. Kabat, Adam, tr. 180p. 1995. pap. 9.00 (*4-7700-1949-1*) Kodansha.

Matsumoto, Shigeru. Motoori Norinaga, 1730-1801. LC 77-95928. (Harvard East Asian Ser.: No. 44). 275p. reprint ed. pap. 78.40 (*0-317-08943-9*, 2005497) Bks Demand.

Matsumoto, Shoichi, ed. Electronic Display Devices. 380p. 1990. text ed. 190.00 (*0-471-92218-8*) Wiley.

— Recent Advances in Fertility Control: Proceedings of the 2nd International Symposium on Recent Advances in Fertility Control, Tokyo, Japan, Oct. 24, 1987, Vol. 2. (Current Clinical Practice Ser.: No. 50). 40p. 1989. 25.75 (*90-219-1676-2*, Excerpta Medica) Elsevier.

— Recent Advances in Fertility Control, Vol. 3: Proceedings of International Symposium on Recent Advances in Fertility Control, Tokyo, Japan, Nov. 27, 1988. (Current Clinical Practice Ser.: No. 53). 50p. 1990. 38.50 (*90-219-9857-2*, Excerpta Medica) Elsevier.

Matsumoto, Shoichi & Tamaki, N., eds. Hydrocephalus: Pathogenesis & Treatment. (Illus.). 720p. 1992. 225.00 (*0-387-70080-3*) Spr-Verlag.

Matsumoto, Shoichi, tr. see Sone, T.

Matsumoto, Shoichi, et al, eds. Annual Review of Hydrocephalus, 1988, Vol. 6. (Illus.). xvi, 171p. 1990. 104.00 (*0-387-52204-2*) Spr-Verlag.

— Annual Review of Hydrocephalus, 1989, Vol. 7. 176p. 1990. 104.00 (*0-387-52937-3*) Spr-Verlag.

— Annual Review of Hydrocephalus, 1990, Vol. 8. 192p. 1992. 125.00 (*0-387-54846-7*) Spr-Verlag.

Matsumoto, Shoji & Tabrah, Ruth. The Natural Way of Shin Buddhism. LC 93-43084. 176p. (Orig.). (C). 1993. pap. 9.95 (*0-938474-14-6*) Buddhist Study.

Matsumoto, Shoji & Tabrah, Ruth M. Ajatasatru: The Story of Who We Are. LC 88-16813. 84p. (Orig.). 1988. pap. 7.95 (*0-938474-08-1*) Buddhist Study.

Matsumoto, Shoji, tr. see Tabrah, Ruth M., ed.

Matsumoto, T. Age & Nature of the Circum-Pacific Orogenesis. 1967. 42.50 (*0-686-43415-3*) Elsevier.

***Matsumoto, T., et al, eds.** Computations, Glassy Materials & Non-Destructive Testing: Proceedings of a Symposia of the Third International Conference on Advanced Materials, Sunshine City, Ikebukuro, Tokyo, Japan, August 31-September 4, 1993. LC 95-3190. 1995. write for info. (*0-444-81993-2*) Elsevier.

Matsumoto, Teruo. Laser Disobstruction & Laser-Assisted Balloon Angioplasty: A Color Atlas. Hacke, Gregory, ed. (Illus.). 97p. 1991. 75.00 (*0-912791-66-7*) Ishiyaku Euro.

Matsumoto, Tomone, tr. see Mukoda, Kuniko.

Matsumoto, Toru. Beyond Prejudice. Daniels, Roger, ed. LC 78-54826. (Asian Experience in North America Ser.). 1979. reprint ed. lib. bdg. 15.95 (*0-405-11283-1*) Ayer.

Matsumoto, Valerie J. Farming the Home Place: A Japanese American Community in California, 1919-1982. LC 92-56774. (Illus.). 280p. 1993. 35.00 (*0-8014-2074-1*); pap. 14.95 (*0-8014-8115-5*) Cornell U Pr.

Matsumoto, Y. & Morita, S., eds. Aspects of Low Dimensional Manifolds. (Advanced Studies in Pure Mathematics: Vol. 20). 376p. 1992. 70.00 (*4-314-10077-X*, ASPM/20C, Pub. by Kinokuniya JA) Am Math.

Matsumoto, Y., jt. ed. see Ichimura, S.

Matsumoto, Yoshihio & Ohno, Yutaka. Japanese Perspectives in Software Engineering. (Illus.). 320p. (C). 1989. pap. text ed. 40.95 (*0-201-41629-8*) Addison-Wesley.

Matsumoto, Yukio, et al, eds. A Fete of Topology: Papers Dedicated to Etiro Tamura. 602p. 1988. text ed. 106.00 (*0-12-480440-3*) Acad Pr.

Matsumura & England. A Coloring Book of Embryology. (Illus.). 311p. 1992. 19.95 (*0-8151-5726-6*) Mosby Yr Bk.

Matsumura, Fumio, jt. ed. see Clark, J. Marshall.

Matsumura, Fumio, et al, eds. Biodegradation of Pesticides. LC 82-7570. 326p. 1982. 59.50 (*0-306-40857-0*, Plenum Pr) Plenum.

Matsumura, H., jt. auth. see Katsuyama, T.

Matsumura, Hideyuki. Commutative Ring Theory. (Cambridge Studies in Advanced Mathematics: No. 8). 300p. 1989. pap. 37.95 (*0-521-36764-6*) Cambridge U Pr.

Matsumura, Hideyuki, jt. ed. see Nagata, M.

Matsumura, K. N. & Hamilton, William L. After Fifteen Years: Artificial Liver & Artificial Pancreas. 2nd ed. LC 78-56092. (Illus.). 1978. 6.95 (*0-9606924-0-1*) Alin Found Pr.

Matsumura, Kenneth. Heterosexual AIDS: Myth or Fact? LC 88-70310. 1988. 7.95 (*0-9606924-3-6*) Alin Found Pr.

Matsumura, M., jt. auth. see Ruan, F. F.

Matsumura, Molleen, ed. see Komuta, Kensaburo.

Matsumura, Molleen, jt. auth. see Rogers, Judith.

Matsunaga, Alicia & Matsunaga, Daigan. Foundation of Japanese Buddhism: The Mass Movement, Vol. 2. LC 74-83654. 1976. 20.95 (*0-914910-27-2*); pap. 14.50 (*0-914910-28-0*) Buddhist Bks.

Matsunaga, Alicia, jt. auth. see Matsunaga, Daigan.

Matsunaga, Daigan & Matsunaga, Alicia. Foundation of Japanese Buddhism: The Aristocratic Age, Vol. I. LC 74-83654. 1974. 18.95 (*0-914910-25-6*); pap. 12.50 (*0-914910-26-4*) Buddhist Bks.

Matsunaga, Daigan, jt. auth. see Matsunaga, Alicia.

Matsunaga, Ichiro, et al. Encounter at Sea: And a Heroic Lifeboat Journey. LC 94-5792. (Illus.). 232p. 1994. pap. 15.95 (*1-879094-27-4*, Sabre Pr) Momentum Bks.

Matsunaga, Karen K. Japanese Country Quilting. (Illus.). 96p. (Orig.). 1990. pap. 19.00 (*0-87011-936-2*) Kodansha.

Matsunaga, Louella, tr. see Kobayashi, Shigenori.

Matsunami, Niichiro. Japanese Constitution & Politics. LC 78-78356. (Studies in Japanese Law & Government). 577p. 1979. text ed. 85.00 (*0-313-27028-7*, U7028, Greenwood Pr) Greenwood.

Matsuno, Koichiro. Protobiology: Physical Basis of Biology. 272p. 1989. 136.00 (*0-8493-6403-5*, QH505, CRC Reprint) Franklin.

Matsuno, Koichiro & Hartman, H. Origin & Evolution of Prokaryotic & Eukaryotic Cells. 442p. 1993. text ed. 106.00 (*981-02-1262-3*) World Scientific Pub.

Matsuno, Koichiro, et al, eds. Molecular Evolution & Protobiology. LC 83-24465. 480p. 1984. 110.00 (*0-306-41509-7*, Plenum Pr) Plenum.

Matsuno, T. Dynamics of the Middle Atmosphere. Holton, James S., ed. LC 84-8291. 550p. 1984. lib. bdg. 182.00 (*90-277-1758-3*) Kluwer Ac.

Matsuno, Yoshimasa. Bilinear Transformation Method: Monograph. (Mathematics in Science & Engineering Ser.). 1984. text ed. 91.00 (*0-12-480480-2*) Acad Pr.

Matsuo, Dorothy. Boyhood to War: History & Anecdotes of the 442nd Regimental Combat Team. (Illus.). 240p. 1992. boxed 35.00 (*1-56647-019-6*) Mutual Pub HI.

Matsuo, Hiro, ed. The Japan Business Study Program: Trade, Foreign Investment, & Competition. (Illus.). 100p. (Orig.). 1990. pap. 15.00 (*0-87755-321-1*) Bureau Busn UT.

Matsuo, HIro, ed. Japan Business Study Program: Understanding Japanese Business. (Illus.). 84p. (Orig.). 1989. pap. 15.00 (*0-87755-311-4*) Bureau Busn UT.

Matsuo, Hosaku. The Logic of Unity: The Discovery of Zero & Emptiness in Prajnaparamita Thought. Inada, Kenneth K., tr. LC 86-5916. (SUNY Series in Buddhist Studies). 148p. (C). 1987. 64.50 (*0-88706-391-8*); pap. 21.95 (*0-88706-392-6*) State U NY Pr.

Matsuo, T., et al. Biological Mass Spectrometry: Present & Future. LC 93-33841. 1994. text ed. 199.00 (*0-471-93896-3*) Wiley.

Matsuo, Y., et al, eds. Gastrointestinal Function: Regulation & Disturbances, Vol. 8: Proceedings of the 8th Symposium on the Regulation & Disturbances of Gastrointestinal Function, Tokyo, Japan, Sept. 30, 1989. (International Congress Ser.: No. 948). 116p. 1990. 85.50 (*0-444-81384-5*, Excerpta Medica) Elsevier.

Matsuo, Yukio. Ice Sculpture: Secrets of a Japanese Master. 200p. 1992. text ed. 79.95 (*0-471-55409-X*) Wiley.

***Matsuoka, Fumitaka.** Out of Silence: Emerging Themes in Asian American Churches. 152p. (Orig.). 1995. pap. 10.95 (*0-8298-1025-0*) Pilgrim OH.

Matsuoka, Kazuko, tr. see Seibu Museum of Art Staff.

Matsuoka, M., ed. Infrared Absorbing Dyes. LC 90-40052. (Topics in Applied Chemistry Ser.). (Illus.). 234p. 1990. 65.00 (*0-306-43478-4*, Plenum Pr) Plenum.

Matsuoka, Mikihiro & Rose, Brian. The DIR Guide to Japanese Economic Statistics. 304p. 1994. 37.50 (*0-19-828861-1*) OUP.

Matsuoka, Shiro. Relaxation Phenomena in Polymers. 322p. (C). 1992. text ed. 59.95 (*1-56990-060-4*) Hanser-Gardner.

Matsuoka, Yoko. Daughter of the Pacific. LC 72-12634. 245p. 1973. reprint ed. text ed. 35.00 (*0-8371-6683-7*, MADP, Greenwood Pr) Greenwood.

Matsurra. Synthetic Membranes & Membrane Separation Processes. 1993. 89.95 (*0-8493-4202-3*) CRC Pr.

Matsushima, Yozo. Differentiable Manifolds. Kobayashi, E. T., tr. LC 71-182215. (Pure & Applied Mathematics Ser.: No. 9). 315p. reprint ed. pap. 89.80 (*0-8357-6094-4*, 2034547) Bks Demand.

— Holomorphic Vector Fields on Compact Kahler Manifolds. LC 77-145641. (CBMS Regional Conference Series in Mathematics: No. 7). 38p. 1971. pap. 16.00 (*0-8218-1656-X*, CBMS-7) Am Math.

Matsushita, Konosuke. Not for Bread Alone. 176p. (Orig.). 1994. pap. 12.00 (*0-425-14133-0*, Berkley Trade) Berkley Pub.

Matsushita, Masatoshi. Japan in the League of Nations. LC 68-58606. (Columbia University. Studies in the Social Sciences: No. 314). reprint ed. 20.00 (*0-404-51314-X*) AMS Pr.

Matsushita, Mitsuo. International Trade & Competition Law in Japan. (Modern Japanese Law: No. 1). 368p. 1993. 45.00 (*0-19-825440-7*) OUP.

Matsushita, Mitsuo & Schoenbaum, Thomas J. Japanese International Trade & Investment Law. 240p. 1989. 54.50 (*0-86008-449-3*, Pub. by U of Tokyo JA) Col U Pr.

Matsushita, Shutaro. Economic Effects of Public Debts. LC 73-78012. (Columbia University. Studies in the Social Sciences: No. 309). reprint ed. 20.00 (*0-404-51309-3*) AMS Pr.

Matsutani, Toshio, ed. Excavations at Tell Kashkashok Two. 1991. text ed. 195.00 (*0-86008-472-8*, Pub. by U of Tokyo JA) Col U Pr.

Matsuura, Kumiko, et al. Annual Review of United Nations Affairs: Covering Years from 1949 Thru 1993, 40 vols., Set. annuals LC 50-548. 1949. lib. bdg. 1,995.00 (*0-379-12300-2*) Oceana.

— Annual Review of United Nations Affairs: Covering Years from 1980 Thru 1993, 22 vols., Set. annuals LC 50-548. 1949. 1,095.00 (*0-685-73396-3*) Oceana.

— Chronology & Factbook of the United Nations: 1941-1991. 8th ed. 598p. 1992. lib. bdg. 75.00 (*0-379-21200-5*) Oceana.

Matsuura, Nanshi F. International Business: A New Era. 576p. (C). 1991. text ed. 50.00 (*0-15-541336-8*) Dryden Pr.

Matsuura, T., jt. auth. see Anpo, M.

Matsuura, Takeshi, jt. ed. see Sourirajann, S.

Matsuya Piece-Goods Store Staff, ed. Japanese Design Motifs: 4260 Illustrations of Heraldic Crests. Adachi, Fumie, tr. & intro. by. (Pictorial Archive Ser.). (Illus.). 216p. 1973. reprint ed. pap. 8.95 (*0-486-22874-6*) Dover.

Matsuyama, Keisuke, jt. ed. see Matthews, Ron.

Matsuyama, Takashi & Hwang, S. S. SIGMA: A Knowledge-Based Aerial Image Understanding System. LC 89-29221. (Advances in Computer Vision & Machine Intelligence Ser.). (Illus.). 296p. 1990. 69.50 (*0-306-43301-X*, Plenum Pr) Plenum.

Matsuyama, Takashi, jt. ed. see Nagao, Makoto.

Matsuzaki, Yuji & Wada, Ben K., eds. Second Joint Japan - U. S. Conference on Adaptive Structures. LC 92-54123. 890p. 1992. text ed. 145.00 (*0-87762-932-3*) Technomic.

Matsuzawa, T. Clinical Pet on Oncology: Proceedings of the Second International Symposium. 452p. 1994. text ed. 109.00 (*981-02-1825-7*) World Scientific Pub.

Matt, Daniel C. Zohar, The Book of Enlightenment. (Classics of Western Spirituality Ser.). 320p. 1982. pap. 17.95 (*0-8091-2387-8*) Paulist Pr.

Matt, Daniel C., ed. Walking Humbly with God: The Life & Writings of Rabbi Hershel Jonah Matt. LC 92-26969. 1993. 25.00 (*0-88125-430-4*) Ktav.

***Matt, Daniel C., tr. & comp.** The Essential Kabbalah: The Heart of Jewish Mysticism. LC 94-40147. 1995. 18.00 (*0-06-251164-5*); pap. 12.00 (*0-06-251163-7*) Harper SF.

Matt, Dick, et al, illus. The EAA Air Adventure Museum: EAA Museum Guide Book. 48p. (Orig.). 1991. pap. 9.95 (*0-940000-42-3*) EAA Aviation.

Matt, Joe. Peep Show! The Cartoon Diary of Joe Matt. Schreiner, Dave, ed. (Illus.). 96p. 1992. pap. 10.95 (*0-87816-159-7*) Kitchen Sink.

— Peep Show! The Cartoon Diary of Joe Matt. deluxe ed. Schreiner, Dave, ed. (Illus.). 96p. 1992. 25.00 (*0-87816-160-0*) Kitchen Sink.

Matt, John. Crewdog: A Saga of a Young American. 512p. 1992. 24.95 (*1-881429-00-8*); pap. 16.95 (*1-881429-03-2*) Waterford Bks.

Matt, Pamela. A Kinesthetic Legacy: The Life & Works of Barbara Clark. (Illus.). 340p. (C). 1993. pap. 29.50 (*1-881914-25-9*) C Manuals Trust.

Matt, Paul. Aeronca, Best of Paul Matt. (Illus.). 96p. 1993. pap. text ed. 19.95 (*0-943691-02-8*) Aviation Heritage.

— Paul Matt Scale Airplane Drawings, Vol. 1. (Illus.). 160p. 1993. pap. text ed. 24.95 (*0-943691-04-4*) Aviation Heritage.

— Paul Matt Scale Airplane Drawings, Vol. 2. (Illus.). 158p. 1993. pap. text ed. 24.95 (*0-943691-05-2*) Aviation Heritage.

Matt, Stephen R. Electricity & Basic Electronics. (Illus.). 364p. 1994. 33.00 (*1-56637-017-5*) Goodheart.

Matta, Michael S. & Wilbraham, Antony C. General, Organic & Biological Chemistry. 2nd ed. LC 85-15765. (Illus.). 800p. (C). 1986. teacher ed 10.75 (*0-8053-9631-4*); text ed. 47.50 (*0-8053-9630-6*); student ed, pap. text ed. 17.25 (*0-8053-9632-2*); teacher ed 20.50 (*0-8053-9633-0*); trans. 10.75 (*0-8053-9635-7*) Benjamin-Cummings.

Matta, Paula, ed. Children's Books by Small Presses: An Exhibition, May 15-June 23, 1989, at the Small Press Center. 100p. (Orig.). 1989. pap. 5.00 (*0-9622769-1-X*) Small Pr Ctr.

— The Environment: Books by Small Presses: An Exhibition, April 22-May 31, 1990, at the Small Press Center. 64p. (Orig.). 1990. pap. 5.00 (*0-9622769-2-8*) Small Pr Ctr.

— Roots in Print: A Multicultural Exhibit of Small Press Books on Ethnic History, Culture, Customs & Neighborhoods: An Exhibition, May 15-June 25, 1992, at the Small Press Center. annot. ed. 208p. (Orig.). 1992. pap. 6.00 (*0-9622769-3-6*) Small Pr Ctr.

Mattachine Society Staff. The Mattachine Review, 5 vols., Set. LC 75-12336. (Homosexuality Ser.). 1975. reprint ed. 242.95 (*0-405-07373-9*) Ayer.

Mattai, Ravi J. The Rural University: The Jawaja Experiment in Educational Innovation. 1985. 27.50 (*0-8364-1406-3*, Pub. by Popular Prakashan II) S Asia.

Mattaini, Mark, jt. ed. see Meyer, Carol H.

Mattaini, Mark A. More Than a Thousand Words: Graphics for Clinical Practice. LC 93-6591. (Illus.). 297p. (C). 1993. 26.95 (*0-87101-224-3*); disk 60.95 (*0-87101-227-8*); disk 60.95 (*0-87101-229-4*) Natl Assn Soc Wkrs.

Mattaini, Mark A., jt. ed. see Mayer, Carol H.

Mattaj, I., jt. ed. see Nagai, K.

Mattalia, Sonia. La Figura En El Tapiz: Teoria y Practica Narrativa En Juan Carlos Onetti. (Series A: Monografias: No. CXXXVII). 240p. (Orig.). (C). 1990. pap. 45.00 (*0-7293-0295-4*, Pub. by Tamesis Bks Ltd UK) Boydell & Brewer.

Mattaliano, Jane & Omonde, Lois G. Milestones: A Pictorial History of Philippi, West Virginia 1844-1994. LC 94-17015. 1994. write for info. (*0-89865-902-7*) Donning Co.

Mattam, Donald. Vital Approach. 2nd ed. (C). 1973. 73.00 (*0-08-017700-X*, Pub. by Pergamon Repr UK) Franklin.

Mattar, Nabil. A Study in Bohairic Coptic. LC 90-33325. (Illus.). 641p. (Orig.). (ARA, COP & ENG.). (C). 1990. lib. bdg. 39.95 (*0-932727-42-5*); pap. text ed. 29.95 (*0-932727-41-7*) Hope Pub Hse.

— A Study of Bohairic Coptic. (Illus.). 725p. (Orig.). (ARA & ENG.). (C). 1989. pap. write for info. (*0-318-65809-7*) Holy Virgin Mary.

Mattar, Philip. The Mufti of Jerusalem. rev. ed. 176p. 1991. pap. text ed. 14.50 (*0-231-06463-2*) Col U Pr.

Mattausch, John. A Commitment to Campaign: A Sociological Study of CND. LC 88-32592. 256p. 1989. text ed. 69.95 (*0-7190-2908-2*, Pub. by Manchester Univ Pr UK) St Martin.

Mattavelli, L. & Novelli, L., eds. Advances in Organic Geochemistry, 1987: Organic Geochemistry in Petroleum Exploration & Analytical Geochemistry: Proceedings of the 13th International Meeting on Organic Geochemistry, Venice, September 21-25, 1987, Pts. 1 & 2. (Organic Geochemistry Ser.: No. 13). (Illus.). 1199p. 1989. 310.00 (*0-08-037236-8*, Pergamon Pr) Elsevier.

Mattax, Charlotte, tr. see Delair, Denis.

Mattay, J., ed. Electron Transfer I. (Topics in Current Chemistry Ser.: Vol. 169). (Illus.). 385p. 1994. 171.00 (*0-387-57565-0*) Spr-Verlag.

— Photoinduced Electron Transfer I. (Topics in Current Chemistry Ser.: Vol. 156). 256p. 1990. 106.00 (*0-387-52379-0*) Spr-Verlag.

— Photoinduced Electron Transfer III. (Topics in Current Chemistry Ser.: Vol. 159). (Illus.). xii, 259p. 1991. 90.00 (*0-387-53257-9*) Spr-Verlag.

— Photoinduced Electron Transfer IV. (Topics in Current Chemistry Ser.: Vol. 163). (Illus.). xiii, 250p. 1992. 124.00 (*0-387-55117-4*) Spr-Verlag.

— Photoinduced Electron Transfer V. (Topics in Current Chemistry Ser.: Vol. 168). (Illus.). 290p. 1993. 169.00 (*0-387-56746-1*) Spr-Verlag.

Matte-Blanco, Ignatio. Thinking, Feeling & Being. 300p. 1987. text ed. 37.50 (*0-415-00677-5*) Routledge.

Matte, Edouard J. Structures De la Pensee: Modes - Temps - Aspects - Modes De Proces En Anglais et En Francais. LC 92-15123. (American University Studies: Linguistics: Ser. XIII, Vol. 27). 420p. (FRE.). 1993. 62.95 (*0-8204-1880-3*) P Lang Pubs.

Matte, Edward. French & English Verbal Systems: A Descriptive & Contrastive Synthesis. (American University Studies: Linguistics: Ser. XIII, Vol. 7). 338p. (C). 1989. text ed. 44.95 (*0-8204-0756-9*) P Lang Pubs.

***Matte, James A.** The Art & Science of the Polygraph Technique. (Illus.). 296p. 1980. pap. 29.95 (*0-398-06271-4*) C C Thomas.

— The Art & Science of the Polygraph Technique. fac. ed. (Illus.). 296p. 1980. 45.95x (*0-398-04044-3*) C C Thomas.

Matte, Jaqueline A. The History of Washington County: First County in Alabama. LC 82-70721. (Illus.). 486p. 1982. 30.00 (*0-9608434-0-X*); 5.00 (*0-685-05992-8*) WA County Hist.

***Matte, Nancy L. & Henderson, Susan H.** Success, Your Style! Right & Left Brain Techniques for Learning. LC 94-41287. 1995. pap. 22.95 (*0-534-24468-8*) Intl Thomson.

Matte, Nicolas M. & Jakhu, Ram S. Law of International Telecommunications in Canada. (Law & Economics of International Telecommunications Ser.). 131p. 1987. 38.50 (*3-7890-1309-9*, Pub. by Nomos Verlags GW) Intl Bk Import.

Matte, Robert, Jr. Asylum Picnic. Robertson, Kirk, ed. LC 77-73205. 1980. pap. 3.00 (*0-916918-07-6*) Duck Down.

— Eating the English Army. 1975. 1.00 (*0-685-67935-7*) Windless Orchard.

Mattei, Carlos R. Ethical Self-Determination in Don Jose Ortega y Gasset. (American University Studies: Philosophy: Ser. V, Vol. 38). 271p. (C). 1987. text ed. 38.50 (*0-8204-0473-X*) P Lang Pubs.

Mattei, Janet A., et al. R Coronae Borealis Light Curves, 1843-1990. (AAVSO Monograph: No. 4). (Illus.). 40p. 1991. pap. text ed. 7.50 (*1-878174-03-7*) Am Assn Var Star.

— R Scuti Light Curves, 1985-1990. (AAVSO Monograph: No. 3, Supplement 1). (Illus.). 22p. 1991. pap. text ed. 7.50 (*1-878174-07-X*) Am Assn Var Star.

— RY Sagittarii Light Curves 1892-1990: AAVSO Monograph 5. (Illus.). 22p. 1994. pap. text ed. 10.00 (*1-878174-04-5*) Am Assn Var Star.

— SS Cygni Light Curves, 1985-1990. (AAVSO Monograph: No. 1, Supplement 1). (Illus.). 36p. 1991. pap. text ed. 7.50 (*1-878174-05-3*) Am Assn Var Star.

— U Geminorum Light Curves, 1985-1990. (AAVSO Monograph: No. 2, Supplement 1). (Illus.). 36p. 1991. pap. text ed. 7.50 (*1-878174-06-1*) Am Assn Var Star.

Mattei, Marie D., jt. ed. see Coll, Cynthia G.

Mattel, Jean-Francois, jt. auth. see Janicaud, Dominique.

Mattelart, Armand. Advertising International: The Globalisation of Consumer Culture. Chanan, Michael, tr. (Comedia Bk.). 208p. 1991. 49.95 (*0-415-05063-4*, A5739); pap. 15.95 (*0-415-05064-2*, A5767) Routledge.

— Mapping World Communication: War, Progress, Culture. Emanuel, Susan & Cohen, James A., trs. LC 93-32250. 1994. text ed. 49.95 (*0-8166-2261-2*); pap. text ed. 18.95 (*0-8166-2262-0*) U of Minn Pr.

— Transnationals & the Third World: The Struggle for Culture. (Illus.). 192p. 1985. text ed. 34.95 (*0-89789-030-2*, Bergin & Garvey); pap. text ed. 14.95 (*0-89789-100-7*, Bergin & Garvey) Greenwood.

Mattelart, Armand, ed. Communicating in Popular Nicaragua. (Illus.). 141p. 1986. pap. 13.95 (*0-88477-024-9*) Intl General.

— Communication & Class Struggle: New Historical Subjects, Vol. 3. (Illus.). 275p. (Orig.). 1995. pap. 30.00 (*0-88477-034-6*) Intl General.

Mattelart, Armand & Mattelart, Michele. Rethinking Media Theory: Signposts & New Directions. Cohen, James A. & Urquidi, Marina, trs. (Media & Society Ser.: Vol. 5). 208p. (C). 1992. text ed. 39.95 (*0-8166-1908-5*); pap. text ed. 16.95 (*0-8166-1910-7*) U of Minn Pr.

Mattelart, Armand & Schmucler, Hector. Communication & Information Technologies. Voigt, Melvin J., ed. Buxton, David, tr. (Communication & Information Science Ser.). 192p. 1985. text ed. 49.50 (*0-89391-214-X*) Ablex Pub.

Mattelart, Armand & Siegelaub, Seth, eds. Communication & Class Struggle: Capitalism, Imperialism, Vol. 1. 445p. (Orig.). 1979. pap. 45.00 (*0-88477-011-7*) Intl General.

— Communication & Class Struggle: Liberation, Socialism, Vol. 2. LC 80-110213. (Illus.). 438p. (Orig.). 1983. pap. 45.00 (*0-88477-018-4*) Intl General.

Mattelart, Armand & Stourdze, Y. Technology, Culture & Communication: A Report to the French Minister of Research & Industry. (Information Research & Resource Reports Ser.: Vol. 6). 244p. 1985. 66.75 (*0-444-87606-5*, North Holland) Elsevier.

Mattelart, Armand, jt. auth. see Dorfman, Ariel.

Mattelart, Armand, jt. auth. see Mattelart, Michele.

Mattelart, Michele & Mattelart, Armand. The Carnival of Images: Brazilian Television Fiction. LC 90-36026. 140p. 1990. text ed. 42.95 (*0-89789-212-7*, H212, Bergin & Garvey) Greenwood.

Mattelart, Michele, jt. auth. see Mattelart, Armand.

Matten, M. GCSE: A Parent's Guide. 1990. pap. 35.00 (*0-7463-0526-5*, Pub. by Northcote UK) St Mut.

Matteo, Anthony M. Quest for the Absolute: The Philosophical Vision of Joseph Marechal. LC 91-26367. 202p. 1992. lib. bdg. 30.00 (*0-87580-165-X*) N Ill U Pr.

Matteo, Michael A. How To Survive the Public School System: A Guide for Students, Parents & Teachers. LC 91-90383. 100p. (Orig.). 1991. pap. 8.50 (*0-9629771-9-5*) M&P Pub.

Matteo, Sante. Textual Exile: The Reader in Sterne & Foscolo. (American University Studies: Comparative Literature: Ser. III, Vol. 15). 283p. 1985. text ed. 35.00 (*0-8204-0168-4*) P Lang Pubs.

Matteo, Sante & Peer, Larry H. The Reasonable Romantic: Essays on Alessandro Manzoni. 274p. 1987. text ed. 49.50 (*0-8204-0372-5*) P Lang Pubs.

Matteo, Sherri, ed. American Women in the Nineties: Today's Critical Issues. 288p. 1993. text ed. 37.50 (*1-55553-150-4*); pap. text ed. 14.95 (*1-55553-151-2*) NE U Pr.

Matteoli, Enrico, jt. ed. see Mansoori, G. Ali.

Matteotti, Giacomo. The Fascist Exposed: A Year of Fascist Domination. LC 68-9637. 1969. reprint ed. 29.50 (*0-86527-064-3*) Fertig.

Matter, E. Ann. The Voice of My Beloved: The Song of Songs in Western Medieval Christianity. LC 89-28621. (Middle Ages Ser.). (Illus.). 268p. (C). 1990. pap. 15.95 (*0-8122-1420-X*) U of Pa Pr.

Matter, E. Ann & Coakley, John, eds. Creative Women in Medieval & Early Modern Italy: A Religious & Artistic Renaissance. (Middle Ages Ser.). (Illus.). 376p. (C). 1994. text ed. 36.95 (*0-8122-3236-4*) U of Pa Pr.

Matter, Ellen B. Picture This. 56p. (Orig.). 1993. pap. text ed. 9.95 (*0-913853-30-5*, 32541, Alleyside) Highsmith Pr.

Matter, Jacques. Saint-Martin, Vol. VIII. Amadou, Robert, ed. 329p. reprint ed. write for info. (*0-318-71419-1*, Pub. by Georg Olms GW) Lubrecht & Cramer.

Matter, William D. If It Takes All Summer: The Battle of Spotsylvania. LC 87-31950. (Illus.). xvi, 455p. (C). 1988. 32.50 (*0-8078-1781-3*) U of NC Pr.

Mattera, Christine B. Deadline for Danger. 1993. 13.95 (*0-8034-8995-1*) Bouregy.

Mattera, Don. Sophiatown: Coming of Age in South Africa. LC 88-47885. 176p. 1991. pap. 12.00 (*0-8070-0207-0*) Beacon Pr.

Mattera, Joanne, ed. Glamour Do's & Don'ts Hall of Fame: Fifty Years of Good Fun & Bad Taste. LC 92-53658. 1992. pap. 7.95 (*0-679-74233-6*, Villard Bks) Random.

Mattera, John. Abra Cadaver. 1982. 2.50 (*0-87129-202-5*, A28) Dramatic Pub.

— Restless in Peace. 82p. 1987. pap. 4.95 (*0-87129-000-6*, R49) Dramatic Pub.

— You Don't Have to Die. 71p. (Orig.). 1991. pap. 4.95 (*0-87129-083-9*, Y16) Dramatic Pub.

Mattera, Philip. Inside U.S. Business: A Concise Encyclopedia of Leading Industries. 3rd ed. LC 93-23940. 636p. 1993. text ed. 65.00 (*1-55623-731-6*) Irwin Prof Pubng.

— Prosperity Lost. 1990. 19.18 (*0-201-19897-5*) Addison-Wesley.

— World Class Business: A Guide to the 100 Most Powerful Global Corporations. 784p. 1992. 50.00 (*0-8050-1681-3*) H Holt & Co.

Mattera, Phillip. Inside U.S. Business: A Concise Encyclopedia of Leading Industries, 1991. 2nd ed. 588p. 1991. 60.00 (*1-55623-377-9*) Irwin Prof Pubng.

— Prosperity Lost. 1991. pap. 10.53 (*0-201-56772-5*) Addison-Wesley.

Mattern, Carolyn, jt. auth. see Behrnd-Klodt, Menzi L.

Mattern, Carolyn J., ed. The Papers of Nathaniel P. Tallmadge: Guide to a Microfilm Edition. 45p. 1973. pap. 55.00 (*0-685-48794-6*) Chadwyck-Healey.

— Papers of the International Workingmen's Association: Guide to a Microfilm Edition. (Guides to Historical Resources Ser.). 132p. 1972. pap. 1.00 (*0-87020-151-4*) State Hist Soc Wis.

— The Papers of the International Workingmen's Association, 1868-1877: Guide to a Microfilm Edition. 15p. 1972. pap. 55.00 (*0-685-48790-3*) Chadwyck-Healey.

Mattern, David B., ed. see Madison, James.

Mattern, Evelyn. Blessed Are You: The Beatitudes & Our Survival. LC 94-71728. 144p. (Orig.). 1994. pap. 7.95 (*0-87793-534-3*) Ave Maria.

Mattern, Joanne. Australian Animals. LC 92-41033. (Illus.). 24p. (J). (gr. k-2). 1993. 1.95 (*0-8167-3096-2*) Troll Assocs.

— Baby Animals. LC 91-40282. (Illus.). 24p. (J). (gr. 4-7). 1993. pap. text ed. 1.95 (*0-8167-2958-1*) Troll Assocs.

— Bears. LC 92-20176. (Illus.). 24p. (J). (gr. 4-7). 1992. pap. 1.95 (*0-8167-2952-2*) Troll Assocs.

— Lions & Tigers. LC 92-19053. (Illus.). 24p. (J). (gr. 4-7). 1992. pap. 1.95 (*0-8167-2956-5*) Troll Assocs.

— Monkeys & Apes. LC 92-28080. (Illus.). 24p. (J). (gr. 4-7). 1992. pap. text ed. 1.95 (*0-8167-2962-X*) Troll Assocs.

— A Picture Book of Butterflies & Moths. LC 92-5225. (Picture Book of...Ser.). (Illus.). 24p. (J). (gr. 1-4). 1992. lib. bdg. 9.59 (*0-8167-2796-1*); pap. 2.50 (*0-8167-2797-X*) Troll Assocs.

— Picture Book of Cats. LC 90-42548. (Picture Book of... Ser.). (Illus.). 24p. (J). (gr. 1-4). 1991. lib. bdg. 9.59 (*0-8167-2146-7*); pap. 2.50 (*0-8167-2147-5*) Troll Assocs.

— A Picture Book of Insects. LC 90-11211. (Picture Book of...Ser.). (Illus.). 24p. (J). (gr. 1-4). 1991. lib. bdg. 9.59 (*0-8167-2154-8*); pap. 2.50 (*0-8167-2155-6*) Troll Assocs.

— Reptiles & Amphibians. LC 92-20189. (Illus.). 24p. (J). (gr. 4-7). 1992. pap. 1.95 (*0-8167-2954-9*) Troll Assocs.

— Young Martin Luther King, Jr. I Have a Dream. LC 91-26478. (Illus.). 32p. (J). (gr. k-2). 1992. text ed. 11.59 (*0-8167-2544-6*); pap. text ed. 2.95 (*0-8167-2545-4*) Troll Assocs.

Mattern, Joanne, ed. see Montgomery, Lucy M.

Mattern, Joanne, ed. see Pyle, Howard.

Mattern, Johannes. Bavaria & the Reich: The Conflict over the Law for the Protection of the Republic. LC 78-64111. (Johns Hopkins University. Studies in the Social Sciences. Thirtieth Ser. 1912: 3). reprint ed. 11.50 (*0-404-61226-1*) AMS Pr.

— Geopolitik Doctrine of Self-Sufficiency & Empire. LC 78-64186. (Johns Hopkins University. Studies in the Social Sciences. Thirtieth Ser. 1912: 2). reprint ed. 16.00 (*0-404-61293-8*) AMS Pr.

Matters, C. Virginia, ed. Riding & Roping: The Memoirs of J. Will Harris. LC 74-78373. (Illus.). 211p. 1977. 20.00 (*0-913480-23-1*); pap. 6.00 (*0-913480-34-7*) Inter Am U Pr.

***Matters, Marion.** Introduction to the USMARC Format for Archival & Manuscripts Control. 24p. 1990. pap. 10.00 (*0-614-01638-X*) Soc Am Archivists.

***Matters, Marion, comp.** Oral History Cataloging Manual. LC 95-8672. 1995. write for info. (*0-931828-97-X*) Soc Am Archivists.

Matters, Marion, ed. Automated Records & Techniques in Archives: A Resource Directory. 75p. (C). 1990. pap. 16.00 (*0-931828-80-5*) Soc Am Archivists.

Matterson, Steven. Berryman & Lowell: The Art of Losing. LC 87-1824. 144p. 1987. 49.00 (*0-389-20730-6*, N8288) B&N Imports.

Mattes. Colter's Hell. 87p. 1962. 2.25 (*0-685-39940-0*) Yellowstone Assn.

Mattes, Eleanor B. In Memoriam: The Way of a Soul: A Study of Some Influences That Shaped Tennyson's Poem. 128p. (C). 1990. reprint ed. lib. bdg. 75.00 (*0-8383-0594-6*) M S G Haskell Hse.

Mattes, Jane. Single Mothers by Choice: A Guidebook for Single Women Who Are Considering or Have Chosen. 1994. pap. 14.00 (*0-8129-2246-8*, Times Bks) Random.

Mattes, Larry J. Bilingual Language, Speech, & Hearing Dictionary. 96p. (Orig.). 1985. pap. text ed. 9.00 (*0-930951-01-8*) Acad Comm.

— Criterion-Referenced Articulation Profile. 1986. pap. text ed. 45.00 (*0-930951-06-9*) Acad Comm.

— Handbook of Consonant Speech Drills. 175p. 1986. pap. text ed. 22.00 (*0-930951-04-2*) Acad Comm.

Mattes, Larry j. Spanish Language Assessment Procedures: A Communication Skills Inventory. (Illus.). 1985. pap. text ed. 38.00 (*0-930951-03-4*) Acad Comm.

Mattes, Larry J. & Eddo, Debe. Adventures in Pragmatic Problem-Solving: Stories & Language Activities for Children. (Illus.). 174p. 1989. pap. text ed. 22.95 (*0-930951-11-5*) Acad Comm.

Mattes, Larry J. & Santiago, George. Teaching Spanish Speech Sounds: Drills for Articulation Therapy. (Illus.). 122p. 1985. pap. text ed. 18.50 (*0-930951-02-6*) Acad Comm.

Mattes, Merrill J. The Great Platte River Road. LC 87-10844. (Illus.). xl, 600p. 1987. reprint ed. 40.00 (*0-8032-3124-5*); reprint ed. pap. 16.95 (*0-8032-8153-6*) U of Nebr Pr.

— Jackson Hole, Crossroads of the Western Fur Trade, 1807-1840. LC 94-37582. (Center Bks.: Vol. 1). 1994. pap. write for info. (*1-886402-00-0*) Jackson Hole Mus.

— Platte River Road Narratives: A Descriptive Bibliography of Travel over the Great Central Overland Route to Oregon, California, Utah, Colorado, Montana, & Other Western States & Territories, 1812-1866. LC 87-1668. (Illus.). 648p. 1988. 95.00 (*0-252-01342-5*) U of Ill Pr.

Mattesini, Fabrizio. Financial Markets, Asymmetric Information & Macroeconomic Equilibrium. 200p. 1993. 54.95 (*1-85521-177-7*, Pub. by Dartmth Pub UK) Ashgate Pub Co.

Matteson & Orr. Filtration: Principles & Practices. 2nd enl. rev. ed. (Chemical Industries Ser.: Vol. 27). 760p. 1987. 199.00 (*0-8247-7582-1*) Dekker.

Matteson, A. The Occult Family Physician & Botanic Guide to Health. 1992. lib. bdg. 89.95 (*0-8490-8744-9*) Gordon Pr.

Matteson, Antonette. The Occult Family Physician & Botanic Guide to Health. 317p. 1969. reprint ed. spiral bd. 11.00 (*0-7873-0587-1*) Mokelumne.

— The Occult Family Physician & Botanic Guide to Health: A Description of American & Foreign Plants & Their Medical Virtues. enl. rev. ed. (Illus.). 320p. 1993. reprint ed. pap. 12.50 (*0-916638-24-3*) Meyerbooks.

Matteson, Barbara J. Mystic Minerals: Wisdom of the Ancients. rev. ed. LC 86-71607. (Illus.). 64p. 1986. pap. 4.95 (*0-9620524-0-X*) Cosmic Resources.

Matteson, D. M. List of Manuscripts Concerning American History Preserved in European Libraries. (Carnegie Institute Ser.: Vol. 10). 1925. 25.00 (*0-527-00690-4*) Periodicals Srv.

Matteson, David M. Organization of the Government Under the Constitution. LC 72-118201. (American Constitutional & Legal History Ser). 1970. reprint ed. lib. bdg. 47.50 (*0-306-71935-5*) Da Capo.

Matteson, Edith M., jt. auth. see Matteson, Jean M.

Matteson, Esther, et al. Comparative Studies in Amerindian Languages. (Janua Linguarum, Ser. Practica: No. 127). 251p. (Orig.). 1972. pap. text ed. 70.80 (*90-279-2110-5*) Mouton.

***Matteson, Jean M. & Matteson, Edith M.** Blossoms of the Prairie: The History of the Danish Lutheran Churches in Nebraska. 247p. 1988. 30.95 (*0-9620787-0-0*) Blossoms Prairie.

Matteson, Marianna M. Manuel Diaz Rodriguez: Evolution & Dynamics of the Stylist, Vol. 107. LC 93-18340. 1993. 48.50 (*1-882528-02-6*) Scripta.

Matteson, Mary A. & McConnell, Eleanor S. Gerontological Nursing: Concepts & Practice. (Illus.). 873p. 1988. text ed. 52.50 (*0-7216-6183-1*) Saunders.

Matteson, Michael & Ivancevich, John M. Management & Organizational Behavior Classics. 5th ed. 464p. (C). 1992. text ed. 33.95 (*0-256-08750-4*) Irwin.

Matteson, Michael T. & Ivancevich, John M. Controlling Work Stress: Effective Human Resource & Management Strategies. LC 87-45503. (Management Ser.). 398p. 1987. 34.95 (*1-55542-062-1*) Jossey-Bass.

***Matteson, Michael T. & Ivancevich, John M., eds.** Management & Organizational Behavior Classics. 6th ed. LC 94-49391. 480p. (C). 1995. 33.95 (*0-256-16204-2*) Irwin.

Matteson, Michael T., jt. auth. see Invancevich, John M.

Matteson, Michael T., jt. auth. see Ivancevich, John M.

Matteson, Mollie Y. Vermont Backroads. (Vermont Geographic Ser.: No. 2). (Illus.). 104p. (Orig.). 1988. pap. 15.95 (*0-938314-50-5*) Am Wrld Geog.

Matteson, Mollie Y., jt. auth. see Wuerthner, George.

***Matteson, Peggy.** Advocating for Self: Women's Decisions Concerning Contraception. LC 95-14297. (Illus.). 146p. (C). 1995. lib. bdg. 29.95 (*1-56024-948-X*); pap. 12.95 (*1-56023-868-2*) Haworth Jrnl Co-Edits.

Matteson, Peggy, ed. Handbook in Prepared Childbirth. (Avery's Childbirth Education Ser.). (Illus.). 112p. 1983. pap. 5.95 (*0-89529-204-1*) Avery Pub.

Matteson, Richard. Early Hymns of America for Acoustic Guitar. 1993. 6.95 (*1-56222-414-X*, 94815); audio 9.98 (*0-685-64074-4*, 94815) Mel Bay.

— Folk Songs from the Appalachian Mountains for Acoustic Guitar. 1993. 6.95 (*1-56222-413-1*, 94739); audio 9.98 (*1-56222-414-X*, 94739) Mel Bay.

***Matteson, Ronald G.** Introduction to Document Image Processing Techniques. LC 95-15177. 1995. write for info. (*0-89006-492-X*) Artech Hse.

***Matteson, Rosemary.** Nothing Gold Can Stay. 350p. Date not set. pap. 9.95 (*0-7610-0288-X*) NW Pub.

Matteson, Stefanie. Murder at the Falls. 240p. (Orig.). 1993. pap. 4.50 (*0-425-14008-3*) Berkley Pub.

— Murder at the Spa. 1990. pap. 3.95 (*1-55773-411-9*, Charter Bks) Diamond.

— Murder on High. LC 94-8372. 1994. text ed. 18.95 (*0-425-14355-4*, Prime Crime) Berkley Pub.

— Murder on Silk Road. 240p. (Orig.). 1992. pap. 3.99 (*1-55773-814-9*) Diamond.

— Murder on the Cliff. 1991. pap. 3.99 (*1-55773-596-4*, Charter Bks) Diamond.

— Murder on the Silk Road. 1992. pap. 4.50 (*0-425-14820-3*) Berkley Pub.

Matteson, Stephen R., et al. Dental Radiology. 4th rev. ed. LC 87-16258. (Dental Assisting Manuals Ser.). (Illus.). viii, 155p. (C). 1988. pap. 20.00 (*0-8078-4205-2*) U of NC Pr.

***Matteson, Sumner.** Hawks for Kids. (Wildlife for Kids Ser.). (Illus.). 48p. (Orig.). (J). (gr. 3-7). 1995. pap. write for info. (*1-55971-462-X*) NorthWord.

Mattessich, Paul W. & Monsey, Barbara R. Collaboration: What Makes It Work: A Review of Research Literature on Factors Influencing Successful Collaboration. LC 92-72633. 53p. (Orig.). 1992. pap. 11.95 (*0-940069-02-4*) A H Wilder.

Mattessich, Richard. Instrumental Reasoning & Systems Methodology. (Theory & Decision Library: No. 15). 1978. pap. 20.00 (*0-686-28628-6*) Kluwer Ac.

***Mattessich, Richard V.** Critique of Accounting: Examination of the Foundations & Normative Structure of an Applied Discipline. LC 95-3776. 296p. 1995. text ed. 65.00 (*0-89930-863-5*, Quorum Bks) Greenwood.

Matteucci, Mario. Dictionnaire Juridique. (FRE & ITA.). 1963. write for info. (*0-7859-4892-9*) Fr & Eur.

Matteucci, N., jt. auth. see Bobbio, Norberto.

Mattews, Keith & Friedland, Jay. The MAC ROM Reference: A Programmer's Guide to Manintosh Macros. (Illus.). 650p. 1988. 29.95 (*0-685-18871-X*) P-H.

***Mattews, Patricia.** The Sound of Murder. large type ed. LC 94-33231. 1995. write for info. (*1-56054-335-3*) Thorndike Pr.

Mattey, Angela M. The Key to Spiritual & Psychic Development Table Tipping: An Exciting & Direct Communication Tool for Connecting with Your Spirit Guides & Higher Self for Personal & Universal Knowledge. LC 92-91268. (Illus.). 359p. (Orig.). 1993. pap. 13.95 (*1-882836-00-6*); The Meditation Tape to Use at the Beginning of Each Tipping Session. audio 11.95 (*1-882836-01-4*) TAM Ent.

Mattey, Joe P. The Timber Bubble That Burst: Government Policy & the Bailout of 1984. (Illus.). 120p. 1990. 35.00 (*0-19-506275-2*) OUP.

Mattfeld, Jacquelyn, ed. see M.I.T. Symposium Staff.

Mattfeld, Julius. A Hundred Years of Grand Opera in New York: 1825-1925. reprint ed. 21.50 (*0-404-13038-0*) AMS Pr.

Mattfeld, Victor. Georg Rhaw's Publications for Vespers. (Wissenschaftliche Abhandlungen-Musicological Studies: Vol. 11). 361p. 1967. lib. bdg. 40.00 (*0-912024-81-X*) Inst Mediaeval Mus.

Mattfield, Julius. The Folk Music of the Western Hemisphere: A List of References in the New York Public Library. Dorson, Richard M., ed. LC 80-796. (Folklore of the World Ser.). 1981. reprint ed. lib. bdg. 17.95 (*0-405-13335-9*) Ayer.

Matthaei, C. F., ed. see Emesenus, Nemesius.

Matthaei, G. L., et al. Microwave Filters, Impedance-Matching Networks, & Coupling Structures. LC 80-68976. (Artech Microwave Library). (Illus.). 1096p. 1980. reprint ed. 89.00 (*0-89006-099-1*) Artech Hse.

Matthaei, Gay, jt. auth. see Grutman, Jewel H.

Matthaei, Julie, jt. auth. see Amott, Teresa.

Matthaei, Sondra. The God We Worship. LC 93-8154. (We Believe Ser.). 144p. (Orig.). 1993. pap. 8.95 (*0-687-15203-8*) Abingdon.

Matthaeus, Antonius. De Criminibus on Crimes: A Commentary on Books XLVII & XLVIII of the Digest, Vol. 1. Hewett, M. L. & Stoop, B. C., eds. 313p. 1987. 38.00 (*0-7021-1854-0*, Pub. by Juta SA) W W Gaunt.

Matthai, William C. Microbiology: A Laboratory Textbook. 2nd ed. 348p. (C). 1991. pap. text ed. 29.00 (*0-89787-129-4*) Gorsuch Scarisbrick.

Matthais, Johnny, jt. auth. see Mancini, Henry.

Matthas, Ursula. Die Laubwerfenden Eichwaelder Kretas. (Dissertations Botanicae Ser.: Vol. 119). 174p. (GER.). 1988. pap. text ed. 63.00 (*3-443-64031-1*) Lubrecht & Cramer.

Matthau, Carol. Among the Porcupines: A Memoir. 1992. 22.50 (*0-394-58266-7*) Random.

***Matthay, Eileen.** Counseling for College. rev. ed. Pendleton, Erika, ed. 432p. 1995. pap. 29.95 (*1-56079-534-4*) Petersons Guides.

Matthay, Katherine, ed. see Isaacs, David.

Matthay, Michael A. & Wiedemann, Herbert P., eds. Annual Review of Pulmonary & Critical Care Medicine 93-94. (Annual Review Ser.). (Illus.). 365p. 1993. text ed. 55.00 (*1-56053-073-1*) Hanley & Belfus.

Matthay, Tobias A. Musical Interpretation: Its Laws & Principles, No. 3713. 1913. pap. text ed. 8.95 (*0-686-30014-9*) Boston Music.

— Musical Interpretation, Its Laws & Principles, & Their Application in Teaching & Performing. LC 70-107820. (Select Bibliographies Reprint Ser.). 1977. 17.95 (*0-8369-5191-3*) Ayer.

— Musical Interpretation, Its Laws & Principles, & Their Application in Teaching & Performing. LC 72-109787. 163p. 1970. reprint ed. text ed. 35.00 (*0-8371-4277-6*, MAMU, Greenwood Pr) Greenwood.

— Musical Interpretation, Its Laws & Principles, & Their Application in Teaching & Performing. 163p. 1990. reprint ed. lib. bdg. 59.00 (*0-7812-9152-6*) Rprt Serv.

Mattheck, G. C. Trees: The Mechanical Design. (Illus.). 125p. 1991. pap. 34.00 (*0-387-54276-0*) Spr-Verlag.

Matthee, Dalene. Fiela's Child. LC 92-12963. (Phoenix Fiction Ser.). x, 350p. (AFR & ENG.). 1992. pap. 10.95 (*0-226-51083-2*) U Ch Pr.

***Matthei, Wesley G.** (Mis)Managing the System. Jacob, Karen L., ed. LC 94-73196. 320p. 1995. pap. 19.95 (*0-936417-46-3*) Axelrod Pub.

Mattheisen, Paul F., ed. see Gissing, George, et al.

Mattheisen, Paul F., ed. see Gissing, George.

Mattheisen, Paul F., et al, eds. The Collected Letters of George Gissing, Vol. I: 1863-1880. LC 89-26577. 600p. (C). 1990. text ed. 70.00x (*0-8214-0955-7*) Ohio U Pr.

— The Collected Letters of George Gissing, Vol. 5: 1892-1895. LC 89-26577. 400p. (C). 1994. text ed. 60.00 (*0-8214-1067-9*) Ohio U Pr.

— The Collected Letters of George Gissing, 1881-1885, Vol. II. (Illus.). 429p. (C). 1991. text ed. 60.00 (*0-8214-0984-0*) Ohio U Pr.

— The Collected Letters of George Gissing, 1895-1897, Vol. 6. LC 89-26577. (Illus.). 390p. 1994. text ed. 60.00 (*0-8214-1098-9*) Ohio U Pr.

Matthen, M. & Linsky, B., eds. Philosophy & Biology. 267p. 1993. pap. 14.00 (*0-317-05547-X*, Pub. by Univ Calgary CN) Paul & Co Pubs.

Mattheou, Antonia S. Tracing Your Greek Ancestry Reference to Cyprus. (Illus.). 54p. (Orig.). 1992. pap. 6.50 (*0-9635648-0-3*) A S Mattheou.

Matthes, Chip, ed. see Banks, Michael A.

Matthes, Dieter, et al. Suctoria und Urceolariidae(Peritricha) (Protozoenfauna Ser.: Vol. 7-1). (Illus.). 309p. (GER.). 1988. lib. bdg. 118.80 (*3-437-30497-6*) Lubrecht & Cramer.

Matthes, Francois E. The Incomparable Valley: A Geologic Interpretation of the Yosemite. Fryxell, Fritiof, ed. (Illus.). 1950. pap. 14.00 (*0-520-00827-8*) U CA Pr.

Matthes, Gayle B. Discovering the Kingdom of Heaven. 157p. (C). 1988. reprint ed. pap. 5.95 (*0-944386-07-5*) SOM Pub.

Matthes, Georg. Die Beschaffenheit Des Grundwassers, 1990. 2nd ed. (Lehrbuch der Hydrobiologie Ser.: Vol. 2). (Illus.). 498p. (GER.). 1990. text ed. 97.50 (*3-443-01007-5*, Pub. by Gebrueder Borntraeger GW) Lubrecht & Cramer.

Matthes, Gertrud P. A Little German Cookbook. 60p. 1990. 7.95 (*0-87701-736-0*) Chronicle Bks.

Matthes, Joachim. Lebenswelt und Soziale Probleme. 561p. (GER.). 1982. 49.50 (*3-593-32695-7*) Irvington.

Matthes, William A., jt. ed. see Case, Charles W.

Matthess, G. & Ubell, K. Allgemeine Hydrogeologie. Grundwasserhaushalt. (Lehrbuch der Hydrogeologie Ser.: Vol. 1). (Illus.). 438p. (GER.). 1983. text ed. 77.00 (*3-443-01005-9*, Pub. by Gebrueder Borntraeger GW) Lubrecht & Cramer.

Matthess, G., et al, eds. Progress in Hydrogeochemistry: Organics - Carbonate Systems - Silicate Systems - Microbiology - Models. (Illus.). xxix, 544p. 1992. 139.00 (*0-387-54034-2*) Spr-Verlag.

Matthew & Sant'Ambrogio. Respiratory Function of the Upper Airway. (Lung Biology in Health & Disease Ser.: Vol. 35). 672p. 1988. 175.00 (*0-8247-7802-2*) Dekker.

Matthew, et al. Ligonier, Indiana: Memories of the First One Hundred Fifty Years, 1835-1985. Zimmerman, Ben, ed. 1985. 25.00 (*0-318-18809-0*) Ligonier Comm.

Matthew, Arnold H. Old Catholic Missal & Ritual. (Historical & Scholarly Resources Ser.). 300p. 1994. pap. 29.95 (*1-883938-09-0*) Dry Bones Pr.

Matthew Bender Staff. New Jersey Tax Service. LC 86-71789. 1986. Set plus one year service or two year service. write for info. (*0-8205-1499-3*) Bender.

Matthew Bender's Tax Staff. Bender's Federal Tax Forms. 1990. write for info. (*0-8205-1367-9*) Bender.

Matthew, Colin, jt. ed. see Garnett, Jane.

Matthew, D. J., tr. see Rorig, Fritz.

Matthew, Donald. Atlas of Medieval Europe. (Cultural Atlas Ser.). (Illus.). 240p. 45.00 (*0-87196-133-4*) Facts on File.

— The Norman Kingdom of Sicily. (Medieval Textbooks Ser.). 416p. (C). 1992. 79.95 (*0-521-26284-4*); pap. 24.95 (*0-521-26911-3*) Cambridge U Pr.

Matthew, H. C. Gladstone, Eighteen Nine to Eighteen Seventy-Four. (Illus.). 288p. 1989. reprint ed. pap. 21.50 (*0-19-282122-9*) OUP.

— Gladstone 1875-1898. (Illus.). 340p. 1995. 35.00 (*0-19-820405-1*) OUP.

Matthew, H. C. & Morgan, Kenneth O. The Oxford History of Britain, Vol. 5: The Modern Age. (Illus.). 192p. 1992. pap. 10.95 (*0-19-285267-1*) OUP.

Matthew, H. C., ed. see Gladstone, W. E.

Matthew, H. C., ed. see Gladstone, William E.

Matthew, Henry. The NIV Matthew Commentary in One Volume. 2000p. 1992. 29.99 (*0-310-26040-X*) Zondervan.

Matthew, James E. Literature of Music. LC 69-12688. (Music Ser.). 1969. reprint ed. lib. bdg. 37.50 (*0-306-71227-X*) Da Capo.

Matthew, James E., tr. see Borren, Charles V.

Matthew, Jean R. Testimony: Stories. LC 86-16126. 80p. 1987. pap. 9.95 (*0-8262-0623-9*, 83-36315) U of Mo Pr.

Matthew, John. The Quiet Corner. 96p. (C). 1991. pap. text ed. 39.00 (*86-15-30645-1*, Pub. by St Andrew UK) St Mut.

Matthew, John, ed. The Quiet Corner. 96p. (C). 1989. pap. 59.00 (*0-685-60675-9*, Pub. by St Andrew UK) St Mut.

Matthew, John & Matthew, Stewart. The Quiet Corner. 96p. 1993. pap. 22.00 (*0-7152-0645-1*, Pub. by St Andrew UK) St Mut.

Matthew, K. M. Illustration of the Flora of Tamilnadu Carnatic. (C). 1988. text ed. 60.00 (*0-685-22108-3*, Scientific) St Mut.

Matthew, Marlene. Double Trouble. (Road to Avonlea Ser.: No. 24). (J). (gr. 4-7). 1994. 3.99 (*0-553-48123-1*) Bantam.

Matthew of Westminster. Flowers of History, Especially Such As Relate to the Affairs of Britain, 2 Vols, Set. Yonge, C. D., tr. LC 68-57870. (Bohn's Antiquarian Library). reprint ed. 74.50 (*0-404-50030-7*) AMS Pr.

Matthew, Paris. The Holy City. LC 79-828. 1979. pap. 12.50x (*0-914140-05-1*) Carpenter Pr.

Matthew, R. G., jt. auth. see Falconer, R. A.

Matthew, Robert. Japanese Science Fiction: A View of a Changing Society. (Nissan Institute Japanese Studies). 272p. 1989. 57.95 (*0-415-01031-4*) Routledge.

Matthew, Sidney L. History of Bobby Jones Clubs. 300p. 1992. 49.95 (*0-9634887-0-8*) Impreg Quadrilat.

— The Life & Times of Bobby Jones. 400p. 1995. 29.95 (*1-886947-02-3*) Sleepng Bear.

— Life & Times of Bobby Jones: Portrait of a Gentleman. (Illus.). 454p. Date not set. text ed. write for info. (*0-9634887-1-6*) Impreg Quadrilat.

Matthew, Stewart. Session Matters: A Handbook for Elders. 88p. 1993. pap. 22.00 (*0-7152-0644-3*, Pub. by St Andrew UK) St Mut.

Matthew, Stewart, tr Session Matters: A Handbook for Elders. 88p. (C). 1989. 35.00 (*0-685-60673-2*, Pub. by St Andrew UK) St Mut.

Matthew, Stewart & Lawson, Ken. Caring for God's People: Handbook for Elders & Ministers on Pastoral Care. 128p. (C). 1988. pap. text ed. 35.00 (*0-7152-0634-6*) St Mut.

Matthew, Stewart & Scott, Kenneth. Leading God's People: A Handbook for Elders. 116p. (C). 1988. pap. text ed. 35.00 (*0-7152-0591-9*) St Mut.

— Leading God's People: A Handbook for Elders. 116p. (C). 1989. pap. 35.00 (*0-685-60683-X*, Pub. by St Andrew UK) St Mut.

— Leading God's People: A Handbook for Elders. 116p. 1993. pap. 30.00 (*0-7152-0696-6*, Pub. by St Andrew UK) St Mut.

Matthew, Stewart, jt. auth. see Matthew, John.

Matthew the Poor. Communion of Love. LC 84-10561. 234p. (Orig.). 1984. pap. text ed. 10.95 (*0-88141-036-5*) St Vladimirs.

Matthew, William D. Climate & Evolution. LC 73-17830. (Natural Sciences in America Ser.). (Illus.). 150p. 1974. reprint ed. 15.95 (*0-405-05748-2*) Ayer.

— Outline & General Principles of the History of Life: University of California Syllabus Series, No. 213. Gould, Stephen J., ed. LC 79-8335. (History of Paleontology Ser.). (Illus.). 1980. reprint ed. lib. bdg. 24.95 (*0-405-12719-7*) Ayer.

Matthewes-Green, Frederica. Giving Women Real Choices. 1994. 8.99 (*0-88070-678-3*, Multnomah Bks) Questar Pubs.

***Matthewman, Jim.** HR Effectiveness. 160p. (C). 1993. 50.00x (*0-614-03379-9*, Pub. by IPM Hse UK) St Mut.

— HR Effectiveness. 160p. (C). 1994. pap. 34.00x (*0-85292-570-0*, Pub. by IPM Hse UK) St Mut.

Matthewman, Jim, et al. Tolley's Social Security & State Benefits 1993-94. 580p. 1993. 105.00 (*0-85459-744-1*, Pub. by Tolley Pubng UK) St Mut.

Matthews. Diagnosis of Plant Virus Diseases. 1993. 99.50 (*0-8493-4284-8*, SB736) CRC Pr.

— Excel 5 for Windows Bundle. 1993. pap. 24.95 (*0-07-882022-7*) Osborne-McGraw.

— Financial Risk Management. Date not set. text ed. 60.00 (*0-471-94403-3*) Wiley.

— Guiness Book of Records 1995. 1995. mass mkt. 6.99 (*0-553-56942-2*) Bantam.

— Legumes: Chemistry, Technology, & Human Nutrition. (Food Science & Technology Ser.: Vol. 32). 408p. 1989. 125.00 (*0-8247-8042-6*) Dekker.

— Risk Management in Dentistry. 256p. 1995. text ed. 37.50 (*0-7236-1011-8*, Pub. by John Wright UK) Buttrwrth-Heinemann.

— Wisdom of Stones. 1995. mass mkt. 5.99 (*0-06-109030-1*, Harp PBks) HarpC.

Matthews, ed. Marx One Hundred Years On. (C). 1983. pap. 18.50 (*0-85315-566-6*, Pub. by Lawrence & Wishart UK) Humanities.

Matthews & Eidswick, Jack. HP 485X-285 Calculator: Calc Companion. (C). 1994. 25.00 (*0-06-500165-6*) HarpCollege.

Matthews, jt. auth. see Evans.

Matthews, jt. auth. see Fung.

Matthews, jt. auth. see Johnston.

Matthews, A., jt. ed. see Rickerby, D. S.

Matthews, Aidan. Muesli at Midnight. 288p. (C). 1991. pap. 9.95 (*0-7493-9135-9*, A0568) Heinemann.

***Matthews, Alfred W.** World Religions. 2nd ed. LC 94-26811. 500p. 1994. pap. text ed. 43.75 (*0-314-04598-8*) West Pub.

Matthews, Alison F., jt. auth. see Olsen, Margaret A.

Matthews, Allan, jt. auth. see Holmberg, Kenneth.

Matthews, Andrew. Being Happy. 1990. pap. 9.95 (*0-8431-2868-2*) Putnam Pub Group.

— Making Friends. (Illus.). 144p. 1991. pap. 9.95 (*0-8431-2969-7*) Putnam Pub Group.

— Mallory Cox & His Interstellar Socks. (Duckling Ser.). (Illus.). 96p. (J). (gr. 4-6). 1993. 18.95 (*0-460-88126-4*, J M Dent & Sons) Trafalgar.

Matthews, Andrew & Todd, Justin. The Jar of the Sun. (Illus.). 32p. (J). (gr. k-3). 1992. 16.95 (*0-09-176400-9*, Pub. by Hutchinson UK) Trafalgar.

Matthews, Anis. A Guide for Haj & Umra. pap. 14.50 (*1-56744-029-0*) Kazi Pubns.

Matthews, Anne. Vogue Dictionary of Crochet Stitches. (Illus.). 160p. 1988. 24.95 (*0-7153-9086-4*, Pub. by D & C Pub UK) Sterling.

— Vogue Dictionary of Knitting Stitches. LC 84-61900. (Illus.). 192p. 1985. pap. 14.95 (*0-688-04688-6*) Hearst Bks.

— Where the Buffalo Roam. 1992. pap. 9.95 (*0-8021-3339-8*) Grove-Atltic.

Matthews, Anne & Hooper, Nancy. Trade Secrets from a Three-Star Chef: Twenty Foolproof Menus & the Secrets of How to Prepare Them. LC 93-25594. (Illus.). 1994. 18.00 (*0-385-42614-3*) Doubleday.

Matthews, Arlene M. The Engaged Woman's Survival Guide. 160p. (Orig.). 1993. pap. 8.00 (*0-449-90756-2*, Columbine) Fawcett.

— Excited, Exhausted, Expecting: The Emotional Life of Mothers-to-Be. LC 94-27694. 224p. (Orig.). 1995. pap. 10.00 (*0-399-51885-1*, Perigree Bks) Berkley Pub.

— Your Money, Your Self: Understanding & Improving Your Relationship to Cash & Credit. 272p. 1993. pap. 11.00 (*0-671-78913-9*, Fireside) S&S Trade.

Matthews, Arlene M., jt. auth. see Cocola, Nancy W.

Matthews, Arline & Welan, Janet. In Charge of the Ward. 3rd ed. LC 93-25221. 1993. pap. 24.95 (*0-632-03448-3*) Blackwell Sci.

Matthews, Arthur D. & Emery, Clark M., eds. Studies in Shakespeare. LC 79-144658. reprint ed. 20.00 (*0-404-04267-8*) AMS Pr.

Matthews, Arthur H. Standing up, Standing Together: The Emergence of the National Association of Evangelicals. (Illus.). xiv, 187p. (Orig.). 1992. pap. 8.95 (*1-880844-00-1*) Nat Assn Evan.

— The Wall of Light: Nikola Tesla & the Venusian Space Ship, the X-12. 140p. 1973. reprint ed. spiral bd. 10.45 (*0-7873-0588-X*) Mokelumne.

Matthews, B., jt. auth. see Khan, M. A.

Matthews, B. A., et al. Sociology on a Disk: Interactive Activities for Sociology. 50p. 1988. IBM 5.25" disk version. disk 11.95 (*0-922077-00-2*); IBM 3.5" disk version. disk 11.95 (*0-922077-01-0*) CMS Sft.

Matthews, Bay. Laughter on the Wind. large type ed. (Special Edition Ser.). 1993. 17.95 (*0-373-58808-9*, Silhouette Lrg Print); pap. 16.95 (*0-373-58908-5*, Silhouette Lrg Print) Chivers N Amer.

— Sweet Lies, Satin Sighs. large type ed. (Silhouette Speical Edition Ser.). 1993. 17.95 (*0-373-58828-3*, Silhouette Lrg Print); pap. 16.95 (*0-373-58920-4*, Silhouette Lrg Print) Chivers N Amer.

— Worth Waiting For. (Silhouette Special Edition Ser.). 1993. mass mkt. 3.50 (*0-373-09825-1*, 5-09825-6) Silhouette.

Matthews, Beth, et al. I Only See My Dad on Weekends: Kids Tell Their Stories about Divorce & Blended Families. Norton, LoraBeth, ed. LC 94-4733. (Kids Helping Kids Ser.). 48p. (J). (gr. 3-8). 1994. pap. 2.99 (*0-7814-0110-0*, Chariot Bks) Chariot Family.

***Matthews, Betty.** English - Chinese Picture Dictionary. (Illus.). 48p. (CHI.). (J). (gr. 2-6). 1981. reprint ed. pap. 3.95 (*9971-947-00-5*) Heian Intl.

Matthews, Bill. Winning Big with Bargain Stocks. rev. ed. 224p. 1994. pap. 12.95 (*0-7931-0948-5*, 5680-0101) Dearborn Finan.

Matthews, Bill, ed. The English Boxing Champions (1872-1910) And Record Book. 176p. (C). 1989. pap. 29.00 (*0-7223-2413-8*, Pub. by A H S Ltd UK) St Mut.

***Matthews, Billie L. & Hurlburt, Virginia E.** Davy's Dawg. Welch, Karen E., ed. (Illus.). 64p. (J). (gr. 3-8). 1989. pap. 4.95 (*1-885777-02-7*) Hendrick-Long.

Matthews, Billie P. & Chichester, A. Lee. Secret of the Cibolo. Roberts, Melissa, ed. (Illus.). 104p. (J). (gr. 4-7). 1988. 9.95 (*0-89015-638-7*) Sunbelt Media.

***Matthews, Birch.** Wet Wings & Drop Tanks: Recollections of American Transcontinental Air Racing 1928-1970. (Illus.). 272p. 1993. 45.00 (*0-88740-530-4*) Schiffer.

Matthews, Birch J., jt. auth. see Carter, Dustin W.

Matthews, Bonnye L. Chemical Sensitivity: A Guide to Coping with Hypersensitivity Syndrome, Sick Building Syndrome & Other Environmental Illnesses. LC 92-54089. 292p. 1992. lib. bdg. 29.95 (*0-89950-731-X*) McFarland & Co.

Matthews, Boris, tr. The Herder Dictionary of Symbols: Symbols from Art, Archaeology, Mythology, Literature, & Religion. LC 93-17017. (Illus.). 228p. 1993. 14.95 (*0-933029-84-5*) Chiron Pubns.

Matthews, Boris, tr. see Barz, Ellynor.

Matthews, Boris, tr. see Neumann, Erich.

Matthews, Boris, tr. see Schellenbaum, Peter.

Matthews, Brander. American of the Future, & Other Essays. LC 68-57330. (Essay Index Reprint Ser.). 1977. 21.95 (*0-8369-0693-4*) Ayer.

— Bookbinding Old & New, Vol. 12. Huttner, Sidney F., ed. (History of Bookbinding & Design Ser.). (Illus.). 368p. 1990. 109.00 (*0-8240-4039-2*) Garland.

— Books & Play-Books: Essays on Literature & the Drama. LC 71-37795. (Essay Index Reprint Ser.). 1977. reprint ed. 19.95 (*0-8369-2612-9*) Ayer.

— Bookshelf of Brander Matthews. LC 79-134610. reprint ed. 31.50 (*0-404-04268-6*) AMS Pr.

— The Development of the Drama. LC 79-39199. (Select Bibliographies Reprint Ser.). 1977. reprint ed. 23.95 (*0-8369-6801-8*) Ayer.

— Essays on English. LC 73-156693. (Essay Index Reprint Ser.). 1977. reprint ed. 21.95 (*0-8369-2285-9*) Ayer.

— French Dramatists of the Nineteenth Century. LC 68-20240. 1972. reprint ed. 24.95 (*0-405-08782-9*, Pub. by Blom Pubns UK) Ayer.

— Gateways to Literature: And Other Essays. LC 70-142667. (Essay Index Reprint Ser.). 1977. reprint ed. 20.95 (*0-8369-2414-2*) Ayer.

— Historical Novel, & Other Essays. LC 68-20320. (Essay Index Reprint Ser.). 1977. reprint ed. 20.95 (*0-8369-0695-0*) Ayer.

— Inquiries & Opinions. LC 68-22930. (Essay Index Reprint Ser.). 1977. reprint ed. 20.95 (*0-8369-0696-9*) Ayer.

— Outlines in Local Color. LC 76-98584. (Short Story Index Reprint Ser.). 1977. 20.95 (*0-8369-3158-0*) Ayer.

— Parts of Speech. LC 68-54361. (Essay Index Reprint Ser.). 1977. 22.95 (*0-8369-0697-7*) Ayer.

— Pen & Ink. LC 73-37120. (Essay Index Reprint Ser.). 1977. reprint ed. 18.95 (*0-8369-2515-7*) Ayer.

— Playwrights on Playmaking - Other Studies of the Stage. LC 67-26765. (Essay Index Reprint Ser.). 1977. 23.95 (*0-8369-0698-5*) Ayer.

— Principles of Playmaking. LC 79-134113. (Essay Index Reprint Ser.). 1977. 23.95 (*0-8369-1989-0*) Ayer.

— Recreations of an Anthologist. LC 67-26766. (Essay Index Reprint Ser.). 1977. 19.95 (*0-8369-0699-3*) Ayer.

— Secret of the Sea & C. LC 74-160942. (Short Story Index Reprint Ser.). 1977. reprint ed. 19.95 (*0-8369-3921-2*) Ayer.

— Shakespere as a Playwright. LC 13-21467. reprint ed. 45.00 (*0-404-04269-4*) AMS Pr.

— Story of a Story & Other Stories. LC 70-98585. (Short Story Index Reprint Ser.). 1977. 20.95 (*0-8369-3159-9*) Ayer.

— Studies of the Stage. LC 72-294. (Essay Index Reprint Ser.). 1977. reprint ed. 20.95 (*0-8369-2806-7*) Ayer.

— Tales of Fantasy & Fact. LC 73-98586. (Short Story Index Reprint Ser.). 1977. 19.95 (*0-8369-3160-2*) Ayer.

— Vignettes of Manhattan. LC 70-90587. (Short Story Index Reprint Ser.). 1977. 20.95 (*0-8369-3070-3*) Ayer.

— Vistas of New York. LC 70-37279. (Short Story Index Reprint Ser.). 1977. reprint ed. 20.95 (*0-8369-4090-3*) Ayer.

— With My Friends: Tales Told in Partnership; with an Introductory Essay on the Art & Mystery of Collaboration, Vol. 1. LC 72-3372. (Short Story Index Reprint Ser.). 1977. reprint ed. 23.95 (*0-8369-4155-1*) Ayer.

Matthews, Brander, ed. Ballads of Books. LC 77-94814. (Granger Poetry Library). (Illus.). 1978. reprint ed. 16.50 (*0-89609-089-2*) Roth Pub Inc.

— Papers on Playmaking. LC 75-111852. (Essay Index Reprint Ser.). 1977. 21.95 (*0-8369-1890-8*) Ayer.

— Poems of American Patriotism. LC 70-133072. (Granger Index Reprint Ser.). 1977. 19.95 (*0-8369-6202-8*) Ayer.

Matthews, Brander, ed. see Bernard, John.

Matthews, Brander, et al. Stories of the Army. LC 76-113683. (Short Story Index Reprint Ser.). 1977. reprint ed. 19.95 (*0-8369-3412-1*) Ayer.

Matthews, Brian. Fundamentals of Autocad. Date not set. pap. 36.00 (*0-13-335456-3*) P-H.

Matthews, Bruce & Nagata, Judith, eds. Religion, Values & Development in Southeast Asia. 168p. 1986. pap. text ed. 14.75 (*9971-988-20-8*, Pub. by Inst SE Asian Studies SI) Ashgate Pub Co.

Matthews, Bryan. Multiple Sclerosis: The Facts. 3rd ed. (Facts Ser.). (Illus.). 120p. 1993. 19.95 (*0-19-262403-2*) OUP.

Matthews, Byron, ed. Current Municipal Problems: 1974-1990, 15 vols., Set. 160.00 (*0-317-12012-3*) Clark Boardman Callaghan.

Matthews, Byron, jt. auth. see Matthews, Thomas.

Matthews, C. Little Book of Celtic Blessings. 1994. 5.95 (*1-85230-564-9*) Element MA.

Matthews, C., jt. auth. see Matthews, J.

Matthews, C., jt. auth. see Topchiev, A.

Matthews, C. D. & Seamark, R. F., eds. Pineal Function. 272p. 1981. 102.75 (*0-444-80313-0*) Elsevier.

Matthews, C. S. & Russell, D. G. Pressure Buildup & Flow Tests in Wells. 163p. 1967. 35.00 (*0-89520-200-X*, 30401) Soc Petrol Engineers.

Matthews, Caitlin. Arthurian Tarot Course: A Quest for All Seasons. 1993. pap. 17.00 (*1-85538-258-X*, Pub. by Aquarian Pr UK) Thorsons SF.

— The Celtic Book of Days: A Guide to Celtic Spirituality & Wisdom. LC 95-11996. (Illus.). 128p. 1996. 19.95 (*0-89281-565-5*, Destiny Bks) Inner Tradit.

— Celtic Book of the Dead. 1992. 27.95 (*0-312-07241-4*) St Martin.

— Celtic Tradition. 1995. pap. 14.95 (*1-85230-709-9*) Element MA.

— Elements of Celtic Tradition. 1989. pap. 9.95 (*1-85230-075-2*) Element MA.

— Elements of the Goddess. 1990. pap. 9.95 (*1-85230-085-X*) Element MA.

— Hallowquest. 1990. pap. 12.95 (*0-85030-963-8*, Pub. by Aquarian Pr UK) Thorsons SF.

— Singing the Soul Back Home: Shamanism in Daily Life. 1995. pap. text ed. 14.95 (*1-85230-616-5*) Element MA.

— Sophia - Goddess of Wisdom: The Divine Feminine from Black Goddess to World Soul. (Illus.). 1993. reprint ed. pap. 15.00 (*1-85538-275-X*, Pub. by Mandala UK) Thorsons SF.

— Sophia - Goddess of Wisdom: The Divine Wisdom from Black Goddess to World Soul. (Illus.). 224p. 1991. 27.95 (*0-04-440590-1*, Pub. by Mandala UK) Thorsons SF.

Matthews, Caitlin & Matthews, John. Ladies of the Lake. 1992. pap. 14.00 (*1-85538-045-5*, Pub. by Aquarian Pr UK) Thorsons SF.

— The Western Way. 480p. 1995. pap. 12.95 (*0-14-019462-2*, Arkana) Viking Penguin.

Matthews, Caitlin, jt. auth. see Matthews, John.

Matthews, Candace. Business Interactions. (Illus.). 224p. (C). 1987. pap. text ed. 17.25 (*0-13-100876-5*) P-H.

Matthews, Candace & Edmondson, Phillip. Speaking Solutions: Interaction, Presentation, Listening, & Pronunciation. 240p. 1994. pap. text ed. 18.75 (*0-13-701229-2*) P-H.

Matthews, Carey. Strike From Mariel. LC 83-81519. 254p. (Orig.). 1983. 14.95 (*0-912709-00-6*); pap. 7.95 (*0-912709-01-4*) First Commonwealth.

Matthews, Cari P. Federal Civil Trialbook. 240p. 1991. ring bd. 70.00 (*0-314-00815-2*) West Pub.

Matthews, Carol L. Marine Biology & Oceanography: Experiments & Activities. 4th ed. Matthews, Douglas L., ed. & illus. by. 208p. 1991. 14.95 (*0-9629357-0-0*); teacher ed 50.00 (*0-9629357-2-7*); student ed 11.95 (*0-9629357-1-9*) Water Pr.

Matthews, Carole B. Q & A 4.0 Made Easy. 2nd ed. 1991. pap. text ed. 19.95 (*0-07-881697-1*) Osborne-McGraw.

Matthews, Carole B. & Shepard, Patricia. Paradox 4: The Complete Reference. 896p. 1992. pap. text ed. 29.95 (*0-07-881794-3*) Osborne-McGraw.

Matthews, Carrie D. Your Paper Chase to Employment. 94p. (Orig.). 1989. student ed 11.95 (*0-913956-37-6*) EBSCO.

Matthews, Catherine, jt. ed. see McGee, Kate.

Matthews, Cecily. Captain Orinoco's Onion. LC 93-2802. (J). 1994. write for info. (*0-383-03680-1*) SRA Schl Grp.

— Mr. Clutterbus. LC 92-34257. (Voyages Ser.). (Illus.). (J). 1993. 4.25 (*0-383-03642-9*) SRA Schl Grp.

— My Dog Ben. LC 92-31946. (Voyages Ser.). (Illus.). (J). 1993. 3.75 (*0-383-03585-6*) SRA Schl Grp.

— Why Not? LC 93-9280. (Voyages Ser.). (Illus.). (J). 1994. write for info. (*0-383-03727-1*) SRA Schl Grp.

***Matthews, Charles.** The Oscar Encyclopedia. LC 94-47288. 1995. write for info. (*0-385-47312-5*); pap. write for info. (*0-385-47364-8*) Doubleday.

Matthews, Charles, ed. see Ibn Al-Firkah & Ibrahim ibn Abd Al-Rahman.

Matthews, Charles W. Shoot Better II: Ballistics Tables. (Illus.). 521p. (Orig.). 1989. pap. 18.95 (*0-9613734-1-5*) B Matthews Inc.

— Shoot Better Three-Ballistics Tables. (Illus.). (Orig.). (YA). 1994. pap. 19.45 (*0-9613734-3-1*) B Matthews Inc.

— Shoot Better with Centerfire Rifle Cartridges-Ballistics Tables. LC 84-90636. (Illus.). 560p. (Orig.). 1984. pap. 16.45 (*0-9613734-0-7*) B Matthews Inc.

An Asterisk (*) at the beginning of an entry indicates that the title is appearing in BIP for the first time.

— The Sporting Ballistics Book. (Illus.). 184p. (Orig.). 1991. pap. 19.95 (*0-9613734-2-3*) B Matthews Inc.

Matthews, Cherian K., jt. auth. see Borgstedt, Hans U.

Matthews, Cheryl & Hailey, Karen, eds. Mixed with Love. 250p. (Orig.). 1985. pap. 11.00 (*0-685-08482-5*) Chattanooga Christ.

Matthews, Christopher. Hardball: How Politics Is Played - Told by One Who Knows the Game. LC 88-45940. 240p. 1989. reprint ed. pap. 12.00 (*0-06-097233-5*, PL 7233, PL) HarpC.

Matthews, Christopher K., ed. see American Society for Microbiology Staff.

Matthews, Cindy B. Marketing Speech-Language Pathology & Audiology Services: A How-to-Guide. LC 92-27489. (Illus.). 212p. (Orig.). (C). 1992. pap. text ed. 42.50x (*1-879105-85-3*) Singular Publishing.

Matthews, Clayton, jt. auth. see Matthews, Patricia.

Matthews, Clifford N. & Varghese, Roy A., eds. Cosmic Beginnings & Human Ends: Where Science & Religion Meet. 442p. 1994. 41.95 (*0-8126-9269-1*); pap. 17.95 (*0-8126-9270-5*) Open Court.

Matthews, D. E. & Farewell, V. T. Using & Understanding Medical Statistics. 2nd rev. ed. (Illus.). xii, 228p. 1988. 32.00 (*3-8055-4719-6*) S Karger.

***Matthews, D. J.** Iqbal: A Selection of the Urdu Verse-Text & Translation. (C). 1993. pap. 38.00x (*0-7286-0215-6*) S Asia.

Matthews, Dakin, tr. see Moreto, Augustin.

Matthews, Dan. Force Option. (Slam Ser.). 1993. mass mkt. 3.50 (*0-373-63407-2*, 1-63407-0) Harlequin Bks.

— Shadow Warriors. (Slam Ser.). 1993. mass mkt. 3.50 (*0-373-63409-9*, 1-63409-6) Harlequin Bks.

— White Powder, Black Death. (Slam Ser.). 1993. mass mkt. 3.50 (*0-373-63408-0*, 1-63408-8) Harlequin Bks.

Matthews, David. A Course in Nepali. 1984. pap. 42.50 (*0-8364-1061-0*, Pub. by Sch Orient & African Stud UK) S Asia.

— I Saw the Welsh Revival: An Eyewitness Account of the 1904 Revival in Wales. 144p. 1992. reprint ed. pap. 5.95 (*0-9626908-2-1*) Pioneer Kimmell.

Matthews, David, ed. Urdu Verse in English. 144p. (ENG & URD.). 1995. 15.95 (*0-19-563462-4*) OUP.

***Matthews, David, tr.** Battle of Karbala: Marsiya of Anis. (C). 1994. 16.00 (*81-7167-213-2*, Pub. by Rupa II) S Asia.

Matthews, David, jt. auth. see Krehbiel, Anthony.

Matthews, David A. & Murtha, Steve. M S Basic: A Concise Introduction. (Illus.). 160p. pap. 16.95 (*0-938661-01-9*) Franklin Beedle.

Matthews, David A. & Picken, Fiona M. Medical Librarianship. LC 79-40833. (Outlines of Modern Librarianship Ser.: No. 12). 173p. reprint ed. pap. 49.40 (*0-7837-5317-9*, 2045056) Bks Demand.

Matthews, David J., tr. see Siddiqi, Shaukat.

***Matthews, David L., 3rd.** The Richest Man There Ever Was or Ever Will Be: The Financial Laws of Your Future. Collins, Mike, ed. LC 94-69820. 106p. 1994. pap. 14.95 (*0-9644282-0-2*) Stick To The Word.

Matthews, David M., jt. auth. see Ford, Michael J.

Matthews, David O. Managing Collegiate Sport Clubs. LC 86-27633. (Illus.). 256p. 1987. text ed. 31.00 (*0-88011-284-0*, PMAT0284) Human Kinetics.

— Managing the Intramural-Recreational Sports Program. Zeigler, Earle F., ed. (Stipes Monograph Series on Sport & Physical Education Management). 62p. (Orig.). 1984. pap. text ed. 4.00 (*0-87563-255-6*) Stipes.

Matthews, David R. Controlling Common Property Regulating Canada's East Coast Fishery. LC 93-93870. 277p. 1993. 55.00 (*0-8020-2932-9*) U of Toronto Pr.

Matthews, Donald N., jt. ed. see Gorman, Lyn.

Matthews, Donald R. U. S. Senators & Their World. LC 80-17163. (Illus.). xvi, 303p. 1980. reprint ed. text ed. 59.75 (*0-313-22664-4*, MASE, Greenwood Pr) Greenwood.

Matthews, Donald R., ed. Perspectives on Presidential Selection. LC 73-1078. (Brookings Insitution Studies in Presidential Selection). 258p. reprint ed. pap. 73.60 (*0-317-26737-X*, 2025390) Bks Demand.

Matthews, Donald R. & Prothro, James W. Negro Political Participation Study, 1961-1962. 2nd ed. 1975. write for info. (*0-89138-112-0*) ICPSR.

Matthews, Donald R. & Stimson, James A. Yeas & Nays: Normal Decision-Making in the U. S. House of Representatives. LC 75-16124. (Wiley-Interscience Publication Ser.). (Illus.). 106p. reprint ed. pap. 30.30 (*0-317-09266-9*, 2012589) Bks Demand.

Matthews, Donald R., jt. auth. see Keech, William R.

Matthews, Douglas L., ed. see Matthews, Carol L.

Matthews, Downs. Arctic Foxes. LC 94-6012. (YA). (gr. 5 up). 1995. write for info. (*0-671-86563-3*, S&S Bks Young Read) S&S Childrens.

— Arctic Summer. LC 92-25376. (Illus.). 40p. (J). (gr. 2-5). 1993. pap. 14.00 (*0-671-79539-2*, S&S Bks Young Read) S&S Childrens.

— Harp Seal Pups. LC 95-2314. (Illus.). (J). 1996. 15.00 (*0-689-80014-2*, S&S Bks Young Read) S&S Childrens.

— How to Manage Employee Publications. (Illus.). 129p. 1988. 21.95 (*0-944607-00-4*) J W Comm.

— Polar Bear Cubs. (Illus.). (J). (gr. 2 up). 1989. pap. 13.95 (*0-671-66757-2*, S&S Bks Young Read) S&S Childrens.

— Polar Bear Cubs. LC 88-10284. (Illus.). 32p. (J). (gr. 2-5). 1991. pap. 4.00 (*0-671-74493-3*, S&S Bks Young Read) S&S Childrens.

— Wetlands. LC 93-3439. (J). 1994. pap. 15.00 (*0-671-86562-5*, S&S Bks Young Read) S&S Childrens.

Matthews, E., jt. auth. see Fraser, P. M.

Matthews, E. G. & Kitching, R. L. Insect Ecology. 2nd ed. LC 83-7015. (Australian Ecology Ser.). (Illus.). 212p. 1988. pap. text ed. 24.95 (*0-7022-1812-X*, Pub. by Univ Queensland Pr AT) Intl Spec Bk.

Matthews, Edith V., tr. see Halevy, Ludovic.

Matthews, Edward, jt. auth. see Brusselmans, Christiane.

Matthews, Edward M. The Ancient Path. 56p. 1989. reprint ed. pap. 1.75 (*0-935461-23-X*) St Alban Pr CA.

— Deceptio, Falsum et Dissimulatio: A Critique. 96p. 1984. reprint ed. pap. 5.00 (*0-935461-09-4*) St Alban Pr CA.

— A Means of Grace. 58p. 1946. pap. 1.50 (*0-935461-08-6*) St Alban Pr CA.

— Principles or Expediency? 64p. 1989. reprint ed. pap. 2.00 (*0-935461-17-5*) St Alban Pr CA.

Matthews, Elizabeth W. Access Points to the Law Library: Card Catalog Interpretation. LC 82-80900. vi, 66p. 1982. lib. bdg. 30.00 (*0-89941-156-8*, 302290) W S Hein.

— Lincoln As a Lawyer: An Annotated Bibliography. LC 90-39143. 272p. (C). 1991. 29.95 (*0-8093-1644-7*) S Ill U Pr.

Matthews, Elizabeth W., intro. Law Library Reference Shelf: Annotated Subject Guide. 2nd rev. ed. LC 92-2275. 206p. 1992. 42.50 (*0-89941-796-5*, 305600) W S Hein.

Matthews, Elmora M. Neighbor & Kin: Life in a Tennessee Ridge Community. LC 66-15287. 216p. reprint ed. pap. 61.60 (*0-8357-3259-2*, 2039480) Bks Demand.

Matthews, Eric & Menlown, Michael, eds. Philosophy & Health Care. 237p. 1992. 68.95 (*1-85628-325-9*, Pub. by Avebury Pub UK) Ashgate Pub Co.

Matthews, Eric, tr. see Bubner, Rudiger.

Matthews, Eric, jt. ed. see Dalgarno, Melvin.

Matthews, Eric, tr. see Weber, Max.

Matthews, Fred H. Quest for an American Sociology: Robert E. Park & the Chicago School. LC 77-373940. 288p. reprint ed. pap. 82.10 (*0-7837-1029-1*, 2041340) Bks Demand.

Matthews, Frederick. American Merchant Ships Eighteen Fifty to Nineteen Hundred, 2 Vols., I. (Illus.). 960p. 1987. reprint ed. pap. 11.95 (*0-486-25538-7*) Dover.

— American Merchant Ships Eighteen Fifty to Nineteen Hundred, 2 Vols., II. (Illus.). 960p. 1987. reprint ed. pap. 11.95 (*0-486-25539-5*) Dover.

Matthews, Frederick C., jt. auth. see Howe, Octavius T.

Matthews, G. Power in the Blood. 1994. mass mkt. 5.99 (*0-06-109086-7*, Harp PBks) HarpC.

— PVC: Production, Properties & Uses. 512p. 1994. 90.00 (*0-901716-59-6*) Ashgate Pub Co.

Matthews, G. & Tunstall, J. Insect Pests of Cotton. 590p. 1994. 125.00 (*0-85198-724-9*) CAB Intl.

Matthews, G., jt. auth. see Kelly, P.

Matthews, G. A. Pesticide Application Methods. 2nd ed. 405p. 1992. pap. text ed. 48.95 (*0-470-21818-5*) Halsted Pr.

Matthews, G. A. & Hislop, E. C., eds. Application Technology for Crop Protection. 359p. 1993. 99.50 (*0-85198-834-2*) CAB Intl.

***Matthews, G. A. & Thronhill, E. W.** Pesticide Application Equipment for Use in Agriculture: Manually Carried. (Agricultural Services Bulletins Ser.: No. 112-1). (Illus.). 163p. 1994. pap. 25.00 (*92-5-103582-2*, F35822, Pub. by FAO IT) UNIPUB.

Matthews, G. Peter. Experimental Physical Chemistry. (Illus.). 400p. 1986. 59.95 (*0-19-855162-2*); pap. 29.95 (*0-19-855212-2*) OUP.

Matthews, Gareth B. Dialogues with Children. 136p. 1984. 17.95 (*0-674-20282-1*) HUP.

— Dialogues with Children. 136p. 1992. pap. 10.95 (*0-674-20284-8*) HUP.

— Philosophy & the Young Child. LC 80-14494. 123p. 1980. 19.95 (*0-674-66605-4*) HUP.

— Philosophy & the Young Child. 123p. 1982. pap. text ed. 8.95 (*0-674-66606-2*) HUP.

— The Philosophy of Childhood. LC 94-16178. 144p. 1994. 18.95 (*0-674-66480-9*, MATPHC) HUP.

— Thought's Ego in Augustine & Descartes. LC 92-52767. 240p. (C). 1992. 28.95 (*0-8014-2775-4*) Cornell U Pr.

Matthews, Gareth B., tr. see Ammonius.

Matthews, Gary. Cellular Physiology of Nerve & Muscle. 2nd ed. LC 85-15727. (Illus.). 224p. (C). 1991. pap. text ed. 29.95 (*0-86542-159-5*) Blackwell Sci.

Matthews, Gary L. The Challenge of Baha'u'llah. 284p. (Orig.). 1993. pap. 9.95 (*0-85398-360-7*) G Ronald Pub.

Matthews, Geoff. Museums & Art Galleries: Design & Development Guides. 168p. 1991. text ed. 69.95 (*0-7506-1227-4*) Buttrwrth-Heinemann.

Matthews, Geoffery. The Reconquest of Burma: 1943-1945. pap. 3.95 (*0-685-56071-6*) Beachcomber Bks.

Matthews, Geoffrey V. Bird Navigation. 2nd ed. LC 68-23181. (Cambridge Monographs in Experimental Biology: Vol. 3). 207p. reprint ed. pap. 59.00 (*0-8357-7270-5*, 2027236) Bks Demand.

Matthews, George, jt. ed. see King, Francis.

Matthews, Glen P. Water Resources Geography & Law. 1987. reprint ed. 60.00 (*81-85046-45-X*, Scientific) St Mut.

Matthews, Glenice L. Enamels, Enameling, Enamelists. LC 83-70776. (Illus.). 192p. 1984. 29.95 (*0-8019-7285-X*) Chilton.

Matthews, Glenna. Just a Housewife: The Rise & Fall of Domesticity in America. LC 86-33318. 305p. 1987. 25. 00 (*0-19-503859-2*) OUP.

— Just a Housewife: The Rise & Fall of Domesticity in America. 304p. 1989. reprint ed. pap. 10.95 (*0-19-505925-5*) OUP.

— The Rise of Public Woman. (Illus.). 316p. 1994. reprint ed. pap. 11.95 (*0-19-509045-4*) OUP.

— The Rise of Public Woman: Woman's Power & Woman's Place in the United States, 1630-1970. (Illus.). 320p. 1992. 25.00 (*0-19-505460-1*) OUP.

Matthews, Gordon. Dire Straits. (Orig.). 1987. pap. 2.95 (*0-345-33885-5*) Ballantine.

— Madonna. (Illus.). 64p. (J). (gr. 3-7). 1985. lib. bdg. 8.79 (*0-685-11123-7*, Julian Messner) Silver Burdett Pr.

— Madonna. Arico, Diane, ed. LC 85-10587. (Hot Rock Ser.). (Illus.). 64p. (J). (gr. 8-12). 1985. pap. 3.50 (*0-685-10385-4*) S&S Trade.

Matthews, Graeme & Bellamy, David, photos. Trees: A Celebration in Photography. LC 94-4807. 1994. 60.00 (*0-517-59963-5*, C P Pubs) Crown Pub Group.

Matthews, Graham P., Jr. Children's Bible Stories with Questions. LC 93-19623. (Illus.). (J). (gr. 3 up). 1993. write for info. (*0-910683-18-2*) Townsnd-Pr.

Matthews, Grant J., ed. Strong, Weak, & Electromagnetic Interactions in Nuclei, Atoms, & Astrophysics: A Workshop in Honor of Stewart D. Bloom's Retirement. LC 91-76876. (AIP Conference Proceedings Ser.: No. 242). 248p. 1992. 88.00 (*0-88318-943-7*) Am Inst Physics.

***Matthews, Greg.** Heart of the Country. 704p. 1988. pap. 5.99 (*0-8217-4677-4*) Zebra.

— One True Thing. 320p. 1992. reprint ed. mass mkt. 4.99 (*0-8217-3994-8*) Zebra.

— The Wisdom of Stones: A Novel. 384p. 1994. 23.00 (*0-06-017738-1*, A Asher Bks) HarpC.

Matthews, Guy, jt. auth. see James, David.

Matthews, H. R., jt. auth. see Gould, H.

Matthews, Harry. The Journalist. 240p. 1994. 21.95 (*1-56792-007-1*) Godine.

Matthews, Harry, tr. see Bataille, Georges.

Matthews, Harry G. International Tourism: A Political & Social Analysis. LC 77-24764. (Illus.). 100p. 1978. text ed. 18.95 (*0-87073-944-1*); pap. 11.95 (*0-87073-945-X*) Schenkman Bks Inc.

— Multinational Corporations & Black Power. 136p. 1976. text ed. 27.95 (*0-87073-776-7*) Transaction Pubs.

Matthews, Hellen, ed. A Hairst o' Words: New Writing from the North East of Scotland. (Aberdeen University Press Bks.). (Illus.). 160p. 1991. pap. text ed. 13.90 (*0-08-041198-3*, Pub. by Aberdeen U Pr) Macmillan.

Matthews, Henry, jt. auth. see Linton, Harold.

Matthews, Herbert, ed. Surface Wave Filters: Design, Construction & Use. LC 77-3913. 535p. reprint ed. pap. 152.50 (*0-317-09163-8*, 2019522) Bks Demand.

Matthews, Herbert L. The Education of a Correspondent. LC 76-106672. 550p. 1970. reprint ed. text ed. 75.00 (*0-8371-3369-6*, MACO, Greenwood Pr) Greenwood.

— The Fruits of Fascism. LC 78-63694. (Studies in Fascism: Ideology & Practice). 352p. 1983. reprint ed. 34.50 (*0-404-16955-4*) AMS Pr.

Matthews, Herbert L., ed. The United States & Latin America. rev. ed. LC 59-15330. 1963. reprint ed. pap. 1.95 (*0-317-02968-1*, 93840-C) Am Assembly.

***Matthews, Heyward.** Oceanography Text Flash Card. 320p. (C). 1995. pap. text ed., spiral bd. 18.95 (*0-7872-1120-6*) Kendall-Hunt.

Matthews, Hugoe, jt. auth. see Miller, George.

Matthews, Irene, tr. see Campobello, Nellie.

Matthews, Irene, tr. see Felinto, Marilene.

Matthews, J. Arthurian Tradition. 1994. 19.95 (*1-85230-567-3*) Element MA.

— Little Book of Arthurian Wisdom. 1994. 5.95 (*1-85230-565-7*) Element MA.

— Outline of Clinical Diagnosis in the Goat. 1991. pap. 65. 00 (*0-7236-1475-X*) Blackwell Sci.

Matthews, J., ed. The Chester Plays, Vol. II. Incl. 1916. (*0-318-54811-9*); (Early English Text Society Extra Ser.: No. 115). 1916. write for info. (*0-318-54810-0*) OUP.

Matthews, J. & Matthews, C. Encyclopedia of Celtic Wisdom. 1994. 39.95 (*1-85230-561-4*) Element MA.

Matthews, J. E. The Art of Grill & Smoker Cooking. Van Treese, James B., ed. 280p. 1993. pap. 9.95 (*1-56901-052-8*) NW Pub.

Matthews, J. F. Andre Breton. LC 67-16892. (Columbia Essays on Modern Writers Ser.: No. 26). 48p. (Orig.). (C). 1967. pap. text ed. 7.50 (*0-231-02910-1*) Col U Pr.

Matthews, J. H. Andre Breton: Sketch for an Early Portrait. LC 86-20741. (Purdue University Monographs in Romance Languages: No. 22). xii, 176p. (Orig.). 1986. pap. 46.00x (*0-915027-71-2*) Benjamins North Am.

— Benjamin Peret. LC 74-30229. (Twayne's World Authors Ser.). 176p. (C). 1975. lib. bdg. 17.95 (*0-8057-2691-8*) Irvington.

— Eight Painters: The Surrealist Context. (Illus.). 160p. 1983. pap. text ed. 18.95x (*0-8156-2302-X*) Syracuse U Pr.

— Imagery of Surrealism. (Illus.). 320p. 1977. 39.95 (*0-8156-2183-3*) Syracuse U Pr.

— The Inner Dream: Celine As Novelist. 1978. 39.95x (*0-8156-2197-3*) Syracuse U Pr.

— Surrealism & Film. LC 75-163624. 226p. reprint ed. pap. 64.50 (*0-685-16170-6*, 2056146) Bks Demand.

— Surrealism, Insanity, & Poetry. LC 82-3165. (Illus.). 168p. 1982. 39.95x (*0-8156-2273-2*) Syracuse U Pr.

— The Surrealist Mind. LC 88-43398. 240p. 1991. 40.00 (*0-945636-06-7*) Susquehanna U Pr.

— Surrealist Poetry in France. LC 71-96815. 254p. reprint ed. pap. 72.40 (*0-8357-3125-1*, 2039386) Bks Demand.

— Theatre in Dada & Surrealism. LC 73-16286. 300p. reprint ed. pap. 85.50 (*0-8357-7052-4*, 2033443) Bks Demand.

— Toward the Poetics of Surrealism. 244p. 1976. 39.95x (*0-8156-0120-4*) Syracuse U Pr.

Matthews, J. H., tr. The Custom-House of Desire: A Half-Century of Surrealist Stories. LC 74-16712. 375p. 1976. pap. 12.00 (*0-520-03274-8*) U CA Pr.

***Matthews, J. Rosser.** Quantification & the Quest for Medical Certainty. LC 94-24091. 1995. write for info. (*0-691-03794-9*) Princeton U Pr.

Matthews, J. W., ed. Epitaxial Growth, Pt. A. (Materials Science & Technology Ser). 1975. text ed. 143.00 (*0-12-480901-4*) Acad Pr.

— Epitaxial Growth, Pt. B. (Materials Science & Technology Ser). 1975. text ed. 143.00 (*0-12-480902-2*) Acad Pr.

Matthews, Jack. An Almanac for Twilight. (Classic Contemporaries Ser.). 1992. reprint ed. pap. 10.95 (*0-88748-143-4*) Carnegie-Mellon.

— Booking in the Heartland. LC 86-7150. 176p. 1986. 16.95 (*0-8018-3332-9*) Johns Hopkins.

— Booking Pleasures. 150p. 1995. 24.95 (*0-8214-1129-2*) Ohio U Pr.

— Crazy Women. LC 84-25112. (Poetry & Fiction Ser.). 176p. 1987. reprint ed. pap. 9.95 (*0-8018-3469-4*) Johns Hopkins.

— Crazy Women: Short Stories. LC 84-25112. (Poetry & Fiction Ser.). 176p. (C). 1985. 17.50 (*0-8018-2633-0*) Johns Hopkins.

— Dirty Tricks. LC 90-30832. (Poetry & Fiction Ser.). 168p. 1990. 26.00 (*0-8018-4053-8*); pap. 10.95 (*0-8018-4054-6*) Johns Hopkins.

— Dubious Persuasions: Short Stories by Jack Matthews. LC 81-47591. (Poetry & Fiction Ser.). 168p. 1981. 16.50 (*0-8018-2692-6*) Johns Hopkins.

— Ghostly Populations. LC 86-45439. (Poetry & Fiction Ser.). 192p. 1986. 16.95 (*0-8018-3391-4*) Johns Hopkins.

— An Interview with the Sphinx. 52p. 1992. 2.50 (*0-87129-149-5*, I48) Dramatic Pub.

— Memoirs of a Bookman. LC 89-37615. 220p. 1989. 24.95 (*0-8214-0937-9*) Ohio U Pr.

— Memoirs of a Bookman. LC 89-37615. 1991. pap. 14.95 (*0-8214-0974-3*) Ohio U Pr.

— On the Shore of That Beautiful Shore. 1991. pap. 2.50 (*0-87129-082-0*, O46) Dramatic Pub.

— Storyhood As We Know It & Other Tales. (Poetry & Fiction Ser.). 208p. 1993. text ed. 32.50 (*0-8018-4622-6*); pap. 12.95 (*0-8018-4623-4*) Johns Hopkins.

— Tales of the Ohio Land. (Illus.). 186p. 1978. 11.95 (*0-87758-011-1*) Ohio Hist Soc.

— Toys Go to War: World War II Military Toys, Games Puzzles & Books. Chenoweth, Candace, ed. LC 94-73995. (Illus.). 272p. (Orig.). (C). 1995. pap. 27.95 (*0-929521-95-1*) Pictorial Hist.

Matthews, Jack, ed. see Wessen, Ernest J.

Matthews, Jack L. Hunt-Kill Selling: Sales Secrets of the Professional Persuaders. 1993. pap. 9.99 (*1-56171-243-4*, S P I Bks) Sure Sellers.

— Hunt-Kill Selling: Sales Secrets of the Professional Persuaders. 278p. 1993. reprint ed. 18.95 (*0-944007-78-3*, S P I Bks); reprint ed. pap. 9.99 (*1-56171-226-4*, S P I Bks) Sure Sellers.

— Outsell Them All: Two Hundred Twenty-Seven Selling Strategies. 276p. 1995. 18.95 (*1-56171-002-4*) Sure Sellers.

— The Sales-Driven Company: Transforming Your Company--from the Mail Room to the Board Room--into a Marketing Machine. 275p. 1995. 19.95 (*1-55738-894-6*) Probus Pub Co.

Matthews, Jackson, ed. see Valery, Paul.

Matthews, James. Frank O'Connor. LC 75-125470. (Irish Writers Ser.). 94p. 1975. pap. 1.95 (*0-8387-7609-4*) Bucknell U Pr.

— Statutes at Large of the Provisional Government of the Confederate States of America. LC 87-83739. 922p. 1988. reprint ed. lib. bdg. 95.00 (*0-89941-629-2*, 305500) W S Hein.

Matthews, James, ed. High Energy Gamma-Ray Astronomy. LC 91-70876. (AIP Conference Proceedings Ser.: No. 220). (Illus.). 360p. 1991. 85.00 (*0-88318-812-0*) Am Inst Physics.

Matthews, James M. High Energy Astrophysics: Theory & Observations from MeV to TeV. 296p. 1994. text ed. 86. 00 (*981-02-1680-7*) World Scientific Pub.

Matthews, James R., ed. Acoustic Emission. LC 82-20928. (Nondestructive Testing Monographs & Tracts: Vol. 2). (Illus.). viii, 167p. 1983. text ed. 105.00 (*0-677-16490-4*) Gordon & Breach.

Matthews, Jana, jt. auth. see Botkin, James.

Matthews, Janet S. Edge of Wilderness: A Settlement History of Manatee River & Sarasota Bay, 1528-1885. LC 83-72562. (Illus.). 464p. 1984. reprint ed. 21.50 (*0-914381-00-8*) Pine Level Pr.

— Venice: Journey from Horse & Chaise. LC 89-60490. (Illus.). 394p. 1989. 20.00 (*0-9621986-0-9*) Pine Level Pr.

Matthews, Janet S., ed. Sarasota: Journey to Centennial: A Pictorial & Entertaining Commentary on the Growth & Development of Sarasota, Florida. 1989. reprint ed. 29. 95 (*0-9621986-1-7*) Pine Level Pr.

Matthews, Jason, jt. auth. see Guttman, Michael.

Matthews, Jay, ed. Business Focus: Newspaper Travel & Entertainment Expense Policies & Guidelines. (Illus.). 68p. (Orig.). (C). 1990. pap. 39.95 (*1-877888-12-5*) Intl Newspaper.

Matthews, Jay & Rozak, Chester. Newspaper Financial Management: An Introduction. 72p. (Orig.). 1988. pap. 49.95 (*1-877888-05-2*) Intl Newspaper.

Matthews, Jay, jt. auth. see Pew, David.

Matthews, Jaymie M., jt. ed. see Nemec, James M.

Matthews, Jean, jt. auth. see Kymlicka, B. B.

Matthews, Jean, tr. see Rodinson, Maxime.

Matthews, Jean V. Toward a New Society: American Thought & Culture, 1800-1830. (Illus.). 208p. 1990. text ed. 26.95 (*0-8057-9052-7*, Pub. by Royal Botanic Garden UK); pap. 14.95 (*0-8057-9057-8*, Pub. by Royal Botanic Garden UK) Macmillan.

Matthews, Jerry. Motorcycling: A Beginner's Manual. 64p. (C). 1990. text ed. 59.00 (*0-906754-53-4*, Pub. by Fernhurst Bks UK) St Mut.

Matthews, Jessie. Over My Shoulder. large type ed. 1990. 21.95 (*0-7089-2241-4*) Ulverscroft.

Matthews, Jill. The Lives & Loves of New Kids on the Block. 1990. pap. 3.95 (*0-685-33337-X*) PB.

***Matthews, Jo.** I Remember Somalia. LC 94-25547. (Why We Left Ser.). (J). 1994. lib. bdg. 19.97 (*0-8114-5606-4*) Raintree Steck-V.

Matthews, Joan. Mindy Mouse & the A-Frame House. (J). 1994. 7.95 (*0-533-10683-4*) Vantage.

An Asterisk (*) at the beginning of an entry indicates that the title is appearing in BIP for the first time.

Matthews, Joan M., et al, eds. From Politics to Policy: A Case Study in Educational Reform. LC 91-8074. 336p. 1991. text ed. 55.00 (*0-275-93736-4*, C3736, Praeger Pubs) Greenwood.

***Matthews, John.** Arthurian Tradition. 1995. pap. 14.95 (*1-85230-713-7*) Element MA.

— The Beginning Entrepreneur. LC 93-1466. 1994. 12.95 (*0-8442-4141-5*, VGM Career Bks) NTC Pub Grp.

— Celtic Reader: Selections from Celtic Legend, Scholarship, & Story. 1991. 25.95 (*0-85030-935-2*, Pub. by Aquarian Pr UK) Thorsons SF.

— The Celtic Shaman: A Handbook. (Illus.). 224p. 1991. pap. 14.95 (*1-85230-245-3*) Element MA.

— The Celtic Shaman's Pack: Exploring the Inner Worlds. LC 94-22046. (Illus.). 1995. pap. 24.95 (*1-85230-481-2*) Element MA.

— Elements of the Arthurian Tradition. 1989. 9.95 (*1-85230-074-4*) Element MA.

— Elements of the Grail Tradition. 1990. pap. 9.95 (*1-85230-077-9*) Element MA.

— Gawain: Knight of the Goddess - Restoring an Archetype. 1990. 19.95 (*0-85030-783-X*, Pub. by Aquarian Pr UK) Thorsons SF.

— The Grail: Quest for the Eternal. LC 90-71439. (Art & Imagination Ser.). (Illus.). 96p. 1991. pap. 14.95 (*0-500-81027-3*) Thames Hudson.

— King Arthur & the Grail Quest: Myth & Vision from Celtic Times to the Present. (Illus.). 160p. 1995. 19.95 (*0-7137-2437-4*, Pub. by Blandford Pr UK) Sterling.

— The Restoration of Organs. (Music Ser.). (Illus.). 170p. 1981. reprint ed. lib. bdg. 27.50 (*0-306-76098-3*) Da Capo.

— Roman Empire of Ammianus. LC 89-45756. 622p. 1990. text ed. 65.00 (*0-8018-3965-3*) Johns Hopkins.

— The Song of Taliesin: Stories & Poems from the Books of Broceliande. 1992. pap. 14.00 (*1-85538-114-1*, Pub. by Aquarian Pr UK) Thorsons SF.

— Taliesin: Shamanism & the Bardic Mysteries in Britain & Ireland. (Illus.). 256p. 1990. pap. 13.95 (*0-04-440586-3*) Routledge Chapman & Hall.

— Taliesin: Shamanism & the Bardic Mysteries in Britain & Ireland. (Illus.). 256p. 1991. pap. 14.95 (*1-85538-109-5*, Pub. by Aquarian Pr UK) Thorsons SF.

Matthews, John, ed. A Celtic Reader: Selections from Celtic Legend, Scholarship, & Story. (Illus.). 1992. reprint ed. pap. 16.00 (*1-85538-228-8*, Pub. by Aquarian Pr UK) Thorsons SF.

— From Isles of Dream: Visionary Stories from the Celtic Renaissance. 304p. (Orig.). 1993. pap. 17.95 (*0-940262-61-4*) Lindisfarne Pr.

— The Household of the Grail. 1990. pap. 12.95 (*0-85030-883-6*) Thorsons SF.

— Progress in Agricultural Physics & Engineering. 350p. 1991. 95.00 (*0-85198-705-2*) CAB Intl.

— World Atlas of Divination. (Illus.). 224p. 1992. 24.95 (*0-8212-1950-2*) Bulfinch Pr.

***Matthews, John, intro.** Within the Hollow Hills: An Anthology of New Celtic Writing. 288p. (Orig.). 1995. pap. 17.95 (*0-940262-70-3*) Lindisfarne Pr.

Matthews, John & Matthews, Caitlin. A Fairy Tale Reader: A Collection of Story, Lore & Vision. 1993. pap. 16.00 (*1-85538-283-0*, Pub. by Aquarian Pr UK) Thorsons SF.

— The Little Book of Celtic Wisdom. (Little Book Ser.). (Illus.). 64p. 1993. 5.95 (*1-85230-435-9*) Element MA.

Matthews, John & Stewart, Bob. Celtic Warrior Chiefs. (Illus.). 192p. 1994. pap. 14.95 (*1-85314-116-X*, Pub. by Firebird Bks UK) Sterling.

— Warriors of Arthur. (Illus.). 192p. 1989. pap. 16.95 (*0-7137-2146-4*, Pub. by Blandford Pr UK) Sterling.

— Warriors of Medieval Times. (Illus.). 192p. 1993. pap. 14.95 (*1-85314-115-1*, Pub. by Firebird Bks UK) Sterling.

Matthews, John, ed. see Burch, Monte.

Matthews, John, jt. auth. see Cornell, Tim.

Matthews, John, jt. tr. see Heather, Peter.

Matthews, John, jt. auth. see Matthews, Caitlin.

Matthews, John, jt. auth. see Stewart, Bob.

Matthews, John, jt. ed. see Stewart, R. J.

Matthews, John A. The Ecology of Recently-Deglaciated Terrain: A Geoecological Approach to Glacier Forelands Succession. (Studies in Ecology). (Illus.). 400p. (C). 1992. 120.00 (*0-521-36109-5*) Cambridge U Pr.

— Quantitative & Statistical Approaches to Geography: A Practical Manual. (Pergamon Oxford Geography Ser.). (Illus.). 224p. 1981. text ed. 90.00 (*0-08-024296-0*, Pub. by Pergamon Repr UK) Franklin.

Matthews, John B., et al. Policies & Persons: A Casebook in Ethics. 2nd ed. 512p. (C). 1991. teacher ed write for info. (*0-318-72116-3*); text ed. write for info. (*0-07-040999-4*) McGraw.

Matthews, John Charles. Fundamentals of Receptor, Enzyme, & Transport Kinetics. 1993. 39.95 (*0-8493-4426-3*, QP517) CRC Pr.

Matthews, John D. Silvicultural Systems. (Illus.). 304p. 1991. reprint ed. pap. 29.95 (*0-19-854670-X*) OUP.

Matthews, John F. George Bernard Shaw. LC 72-92031. (Columbia Essays on Modern Writers Ser.: No. 45). 48p. (Orig.). 1970. pap. text ed. 7.50 (*0-231-03145-9*) Col U Pr.

Matthews, John H. Introduction to the Design & Analysis of Building Electrical Systems. LC 92-26279. 1993. text ed. 59.95 (*0-442-00874-0*) Van Nos Reinhold.

Matthews, John M. Legislative & Judicial History of the Fifteenth Amendment. LC 77-129081. (American Constitutional & Legal History Ser.). 1971. reprint ed. 22.50 (*0-306-70063-8*) Da Capo.

Matthews, John O. Struggle & Survival on Wall Street: The Economics of Competition Among Securities Firms. LC 93-98. 1994. Alk. paper. 35.00 (*0-19-505063-0*) OUP.

Matthews, John R. Eating Disorders. (Library in a Book Ser.). (Illus.). 240p. (YA). (gr. 9-12). 1990. 21.95 (*0-8160-1911-8*) Facts on File.

Matthews, John T. The Sound & the Fury: Faulkner & the Lost Cause. Lecker, Robert, ed. (Twayne's Masterwork Studies). 152p. 1990. text ed. 21.95 (*0-8057-7965-5*, MWS 61, Pub. by Royal Botanic Garden UK); pap. 12.95 (*0-8057-8018-1*, MWS 61, Pub. by Royal Botanic Garden UK) Macmillan.

Matthews, Joseph. Beat the Nursing Home Trap: A Consumer's Guide to Choosing-Financing Long-Term Care. 2nd ed. (Illus.). 400p. 1993. pap. 18.95 (*0-87337-230-1*) Nolo Pr.

— How to Win Your Personal Injury Claim: First National Edition. 224p. 1992. pap. 24.95 (*0-87337-189-5*) Nolo Pr.

Matthews, Joseph L. Social Security, Medicare & Pensions. large type ed. 300p. 1991. reprint ed. lib. bdg. 22.95 (*1-56054-034-6*) Thorndike Pr.

— Social Security, Medicare & Pensions. large type ed. 288p. 1991. pap. 14.95 (*1-56054-989-0*) Thorndike Pr.

***Matthews, Joseph L. & Berman, Dorothy M.** Social Security, Medicare, & Pensions. 6th ed. 1995. pap. 19.95 (*0-87337-289-1*) Nolo Pr.

Matthews, Joseph R., ed. The Impact of Online Catalogs. LC 85-32014. 146p. 1986. pap. text ed. 35.00 (*0-918212-84-7*) Neal-Schuman.

Matthews, Judith & Robinson, Fay. Nathaniel Willy, Scared Silly. LC 92-4052. (Illus.). 32p. (J). (gr. k-3). 1994. text ed. 15.00 (*0-02-765285-8*, Bradbury S&S) S&S Childrens.

Matthews, Judy G., et al. Clipart & Dynamic Designs for Libraries & Media Centers: Books & Basics, Vol. 1. 193p. 1987. lib. bdg. 28.00 (*0-87287-636-5*) Libs Unl.

— Clipart & Dynamic Designs for Libraries & Media Centers, Vol. 2: Computers & Audiovisual. (Illus.). 191p. 1989. pap. text ed. 26.50 (*0-87287-750-7*) Libs Unl.

Matthews, Julian G., tr. see Legrand, B.

Matthews, Kathy, jt. auth. see Galloway, Diane.

Matthews, Kathy, jt. auth. see Giller, Robert M.

Matthews, Kathy, jt. auth. see Vartabedian, Roy E.

Matthews, Kay. An Anasazi Welcome. LC 92-796. (Illus.). 40p. (J). (gr. 1-6). 1992. pap. 6.95 (*1-878610-27-9*) Red Crane Bks.

— Cross-Country Skiing in Northern New Mexico: An Introduction & Trail Guide. rev. ed. (Illus.). 165p. 1993. pap. 10.95 (*0-940875-00-4*) Acequia Madre.

— Hiking the Wilderness: A Backpacking Guide to the Wheeler Peak, Pecos, & San Pedro Parks Wilderness Areas. (Illus.). 139p. (Orig.). 1992. pap. 10.95 (*0-940875-02-0*) Acequia Madre.

— Hiking Trails of the Sandia & Manzano Mountains. rev. ed. (Illus.). 86p. 1991. reprint ed. pap. 9.95 (*0-940875-01-2*) Acequia Madre.

— I'm Glad You Asked. (Illus.). 36p. (Orig.). (J). (ps-3). 1994. pap. 7.50 (*0-940875-03-9*) Acequia Madre.

Matthews, Ken. The Gulf Conflict & International Relations. LC 92-47343. (Illus.). 352p. 1993. 59.95 (*0-415-07518-1*, A7691, Routledge NY); pap. 16.95 (*0-415-07519-X*, A7695, Routledge NY) Routledge.

Matthews, Kent, jt. auth. see Benjamin, Dan.

Matthews, Kermit D. Matthews, Page, Wilson, Dean, Bartlett & Related Families. (Illus.). 290p. 1993. lib. bdg. 55.00 (*0-8328-3615-X*); pap. 45.00 (*0-8328-3616-8*) Higginson Bk Co.

Matthews, L. Cowboys. (Wild West in American History Ser.). (Illus.). 32p. (J). (gr. 3-8). 1989. lib. bdg. 18.00 (*0-86625-363-7*); lib. bdg. 13.50 (*0-685-58277-9*) Rourke Corp.

— Gunfighters. (Wild West in American History Ser.). (Illus.). 32p. (J). (gr. 3-8). 1989. 13.50 (*0-685-58278-7*); lib. bdg. 18.00 (*0-86625-361-0*) Rourke Corp.

— Indians. (Wild West in American History Ser.). (Illus.). 32p. (J). (gr. 3-8). 1989. 13.50 (*0-685-58279-5*); lib. bdg. 18.00 (*0-86625-364-5*) Rourke Corp.

— Pioneers. (Wild West in American History Ser.). (Illus.). 32p. (J). (gr. 3-8). 1989. 13.50 (*0-685-73975-9*); lib. bdg. 18.00 (*0-86625-362-9*) Rourke Corp.

— Railroaders. (Wild West in American History Ser.). (Illus.). 32p. (J). (gr. 3-8). 1989. 13.50 (*0-685-67677-3*); lib. bdg. 18.00 (*0-86625-366-1*) Rourke Corp.

— Soldiers. (Wild West in American History Ser.). (Illus.). 32p. (J). (gr. 3-8). 1989. 13.50 (*0-685-67678-1*); lib. bdg. 18.00 (*0-86625-365-3*) Rourke Corp.

Matthews, L. Harrison. The Natural History of the Whale. LC 78-2328. (Illus.). 219p. 1980. text ed. 52.50 (*0-231-04588-3*); pap. text ed. 18.50 (*0-231-04589-1*) Col U Pr.

Matthews, L. R. Cardiopulmonary Anatomy & Physiology. (Illus.). 352p. (C). 1994. pap. text ed. 24.95 (*0-397-54954-7*, Lippincott Medical) Lippincott.

Matthews, Larry E. Cumberland Caverns. 316p. 1989. pap. 9.95 (*0-9615093-4-1*) Natl Speleological.

***Matthews, Larryl & Garcia, Gabe.** Laser & Eye Safety in the Laboratory. LC 94-27878. 156p. 1994. pap. 19.95 (*0-7803-1037-3*) Inst Elect Eng.

Matthews, Laura. Alicia. (Regency Romance Ser.). 256p. (Orig.). 1992. pap. 3.99 (*0-451-17197-7*, Sig) NAL-Dutton.

— A Curious Courting. large type ed. LC 93-37450. 1994. 18.95 (*0-7862-0095-2*) Thorndike Pr.

— In My Lady's Chamber. large type ed. LC 93-33460. 334p. (Orig.). 1994. bds. 18.95 (*0-7862-0096-0*) Thorndike Pr.

— The Lady Next Door. (Regency Romance Ser.). 224p. 1993. pap. 3.99 (*0-451-17526-3*, Sig) NAL-Dutton.

— Lord Clayborne's Fancy. (Regency Romance Ser.). 256p. 1991. pap. 3.99 (*0-451-17065-2*, Sig) NAL-Dutton.

— The Nomad Harp. (Regency Romance Ser.). 224p. (Orig.). 1993. pap. 3.99 (*0-451-17590-5*, Sig) NAL-Dutton.

— The Village Spinster. 224p. (Orig.). 1993. pap. 3.99 (*0-451-17568-9*, Sig) NAL-Dutton.

— The Village Spinster. LC 93-1107. (Orig.). 1993. 17.95 (*1-56054-742-1*) Thorndike Pr.

Matthews, Leah S., sel. Words of Love. 64p. 1992. 8.95 (*0-312-07235-X*, Pub. by Thomas Dunne Bks) St Martin.

Matthews, Leonard J. Pioneers & Trailblazers: Adventures of the Old West. 6 vols. (J). 1990. 9.99 (*0-517-02537-X*) Random Hse Value.

Matthews, Lewis. Proteas of the World. (Illus.). 256p. 1993. 45.00 (*0-88192-235-8*) Timber.

Matthews, Linda, jt. auth. see Trojan, Penelope A.

Matthews, Liz. Teeny Witch & Christmas Magic. LC 90-11206. (Teeny Witch Ser.). (Illus.). 48p. (J). (gr. k-1). 1991. lib. bdg. 11.89 (*0-8167-2270-6*); pap. 3.50 (*0-8167-2271-4*) Troll Assocs.

— Teeny Witch & the Great Halloween Ride. LC 90-11207. (Teeny Witch Ser.). (Illus.). 48p. (J). (gr. k-1). 1991. lib. bdg. 11.89 (*0-8167-2274-9*); pap. text ed. 3.50 (*0-8167-2275-7*) Troll Assocs.

— Teeny Witch & the Perfect Valentine. LC 90-11204. (Teeny Witch Ser.). (Illus.). 48p. (J). (gr. k-1). 1991. lib. bdg. 11.89 (*0-8167-2280-3*); pap. text ed. 3.50 (*0-8167-2281-1*) Troll Assocs.

— Teeny Witch & the Terrible Twins. LC 90-11139. (Illus.). 48p. (J). (gr. k-1). 1991. lib. bdg. 11.89 (*0-8167-2266-8*); pap. text ed. 3.50 (*0-8167-2267-6*) Troll Assocs.

— Teeny Witch & the Tricky Easter Bunny. LC 90-11205. (Teeny Witch Ser.). (Illus.). 48p. (J). (gr. k-1). 1991. lib. bdg. 11.89 (*0-8167-2272-2*); pap. text ed. 3.50 (*0-8167-2273-0*) Troll Assocs.

— Teeny Witch Goes on Vacation. LC 90-11141. (Teeny Witch Ser.). (Illus.). 48p. (J). (gr. k-1). 1991. lib. bdg. 11.89 (*0-8167-2278-1*); pap. text ed. 3.50 (*0-8167-2279-X*) Troll Assocs.

— Teeny Witch Goes to School. LC 90-11208. (Teeny Witch Ser.). (Illus.). 48p. (J). (gr. k-1). 1991. lib. bdg. 11.89 (*0-8167-2276-5*); pap. 3.50 (*0-8167-2277-3*) Troll Assocs.

— Teeny Witch Goes to the Library. LC 90-11140. (Illus.). 48p. (J). (gr. k-1). 1991. lib. bdg. 11.89 (*0-8167-2268-4*); pap. text ed. 3.50 (*0-8167-2269-2*) Troll Assocs.

Matthews, Lydia. The Voice of Citizenry: Artists & Communities in Collaboration. (Illus.). 36p. (Orig.). 1993. pap. write for info. (*0-930495-22-5*) San Fran Art Inst.

Matthews, M. H. Making Sense of Place: Children's Understanding of Large-Scale Environments. (Illus.). 352p. (C). 1992. text ed. 68.00 (*0-389-20987-2*) B&N Imports.

Matthews, M. H., jt. ed. see Bondi, L.

Matthews, M. H., jt. auth. see Hepple, B. A.

Matthews, M. M. The Beginners of American English. 1972. 59.95 (*0-87968-717-7*) Gordon Pr.

Matthews, Margery I., et al. Churches of Foster: A History of Religious Life in Rural Rhode Island. (Illus.). 169p. (Orig.). 1978. pap. 5.00 (*0-917012-20-8*) N Foster Baptist.

Matthews, Marian. New Mexico Creditor - Debtor Law, 1989-1992. 300p. 1994. disk, ring bd. 115.00 (*0-409-25140-2*) Michie Butterworth.

— New Mexico Creditor - Debtor Law, 1989-1992. suppl. ed. 300p. 1993. 53.50 (*1-56257-976-2*) Butterworth Legal Pubs.

***Matthews, Mark.** The Horseman: Obsessions of a Zoophiliac. 208p. (C). 1994. 27.95 (*0-87975-902-X*) Prometheus Bks.

Matthews, Marlene. But When She Was Bad, Pt. 1. (Road to Avonlea Ser.: No. 23). (J). (gr. 4-7). 1994. mass mkt. 3.99 (*0-553-48122-3*) Bantam.

Matthews, Marti. Pain: The Challenge & the Gift. 256p. 1991. pap. 12.95 (*0-913299-80-4*) Stillpoint.

Matthews, Martin. Access 2.0 from the Ground Up. 1994. pap. 19.95 (*1-55958-511-0*) Prima Pub.

— Windows 95 Instant Reference. 1995. 9.99 (*0-7821-1489-X*) Sybex.

Matthews, Martin H., jt. auth. see Beatson, Jack.

Matthews, Martin S. Access: From the Ground Up. (Illus.). 400p. (Orig.). 1993. pap. 19.95 (*1-55958-303-7*) Prima Pub.

— Coleldraw 5 Made Easy: The Basics Beyond. 1994. pap. 29.95 (*0-07-882066-9*) McGraw.

— Excel for Windows: The Complete Reference. 2nd ed. 1994. pap. text ed. 34.95 (*0-07-881975-X*) McGraw.

— Excel Make Easy. 4th ed. 1994. pap. text ed. 24.95 (*0-07-881973-3*) McGraw.

— Excel 3 Made Easy, IBM PC Version. 550p. 1991. pap. text ed. 19.95 (*0-07-881723-4*) Osborne-McGraw.

— Excel 4 for Windows Made Easy: IBM PC Version. 2nd ed. 464p. 1992. pap. text ed. 19.95 (*0-07-881807-9*) Osborne-McGraw.

— The MAC Made Easy. 545p. 1992. pap. text ed. 19.95 (*0-07-881773-0*) Osborne-McGraw.

— PageMaker 4 for Macintosh Made Easy. 1990. pap. text ed. 19.95 (*0-07-881650-5*) Osborne-McGraw.

— Using PageMaker Five for Windows. 4th ed. 1993. pap. text ed. 39.95 (*0-07-881852-4*) Osborne-McGraw.

— Windows X.0 Power Tools. 3rd ed. (Power Tools Ser.). 1995. pap. 40.00 (*0-679-75587-X*) Random.

— Windows 95 Answers. (Certified Tech Support Ser.). Date not set. pap. text ed. 19.95 (*0-07-882128-2*) Osborne-McGraw.

— Your FoxPro for Windows Consultant: From the Ground Up. (Illus.). 400p. (Orig.). 1993. pap. 39.95 (*1-55958-305-3*) Prima Pub.

Matthews, Martin S. & Dobson, Bruce. The Power of Windows & DOS Together: Work Faster & Smarter by Combining the Strengths of Both. LC 93-3791. 1993. 24.95 (*1-55958-339-8*) Prima Pub.

Matthews, Mary Jo, ed. see Ramsay, Linda M.

Matthews, Merrill. BG129 Managed Competition. Date not set. 5.00 (*0-685-67208-5*) Natl Ctr Pol.

Matthews, Merrill, jt. auth. see Goodman, John C.

Matthews, Merrill, Jr.

Matthews, Mervyn. Education in the Soviet Union: Policies & Institutions since Stalin. LC 82-6656. 239p. reprint ed. pap. 68.20 (*0-317-20055-0*, 2023274) Bks Demand.

— The Passport Society: Controlling Movement in Russia & the U. S. S. R. LC 93-6054. (C). 1993. text ed. 49.95 (*0-8133-8570-9*) Westview.

— Patterns of Deprivation in the Soviet Union under Brezhnev & Gorbachev. (P-383 Ser.). 158p. (C). 1989. pap. text ed. 18.95 (*0-8179-8832-7*) Hoover Inst Pr.

— Poverty in the Soviet Union. (Illus.). 260p. 1986. 54.95 (*0-521-32544-7*); pap. 18.95 (*0-521-31059-8*) Cambridge U Pr.

— Privilege in the Soviet Union. (Illus.). 1978. pap. text ed. 16.95 (*0-04-323021-0*) Routledge Chapman & Hall.

Matthews, Mervyn, ed. Party, State & Citizen in the Soviet Union: A Collection of Documents. LC 89-34446. 428p. 1990. 67.95 (*0-87332-430-7*) M E Sharpe.

Matthews, Michael D. Money Clips (Mini) The Little Book of Big Money Ideas. LC 94-15351. 160p. 1994. pap. 5.99 (*0-88070-687-2*) Questar Pubs.

Matthews, Michael R. History, Philosophy, & Science Teaching. LC 93-32237. (Philosophy of Education Research Library). 1994. write for info. (*0-415-90282-7*, Routledge NY); pap. write for info. (*0-415-90899-X*, Routledge NY) Routledge.

— History, Philosophy, & Science Teaching: Selected Readings. 240p. (C). 1990. pap. 23.95 (*0-8077-3094-7*) Tchrs Coll.

Matthews, Michael R., ed. The Scientific Background to Modern Philosophy: Selected Readings. LC 88-32012. 174p. (C). 1989. 24.50 (*0-87220-075-2*); pap. 4.95 (*0-87220-074-4*) Hackett Pub.

Matthews, Mildred S., jt. ed. see Black, David C.

Matthews, Mildred S., jt. ed. see Burns, Joseph A.

Matthews, Mildred S., jt. ed. see Gehrels, Tom.

Matthews, Morgan. The Big Race. LC 88-1287. (Fiddlesticks Ser.). (Illus.). 48p. (Orig.). (J). (gr. 1-4). 1989. lib. bdg. 10.59 (*0-8167-1329-4*); pap. text ed. 3.50 (*0-8167-1330-8*) Troll Assocs.

— Brave Sir Laughalot. LC 85-14010. (Illus.). 48p. (Orig.). (J). (gr. 1-3). 1986. lib. bdg. 10.59 (*0-8167-0594-1*); pap. text ed. 3.50 (*0-8167-0595-X*) Troll Assocs.

— Chuck, the Unlucky Duck. LC 88-1284. (Fiddlesticks Ser.). (Illus.). 48p. (Orig.). (J). (gr. 1-4). 1989. lib. bdg. 10.59 (*0-8167-1333-2*); pap. text ed. 3.50 (*0-8167-1334-0*) Troll Assocs.

— Fish for Supper. LC 85-14056. (Illus.). 48p. (Orig.). (J). (gr. 1-3). 1986. lib. bdg. 10.59 (*0-8167-0588-7*); pap. text ed. 3.50 (*0-8167-0589-5*) Troll Assocs.

— Houdini, the Vanishing Hare. LC 88-1286. (Fiddlesticks Ser.). (Illus.). 48p. (Orig.). (J). (gr. 1-4). 1989. lib. bdg. 10.59 (*0-8167-1343-X*); pap. text ed. 3.50 (*0-8167-1344-8*) Troll Assocs.

— Icky, Sticky Gloop. LC 85-14013. (Illus.). 48p. (Orig.). (J). (gr. 1-3). 1986. lib. bdg. 10.59 (*0-8167-0616-6*); pap. text ed. 3.50 (*0-8167-0617-4*) Troll Assocs.

— One Hundred Two Goofy Jokes. LC 91-35176. (Illus.). 64p. (J). (gr. 2-6). 1992. pap. text ed. 2.95 (*0-8167-2697-3*) Troll Assocs.

— One Hundred Two Out of This World Jokes. LC 91-45021. (Illus.). 64p. (J). (gr. 2-6). 1992. pap. text ed. 2.95 (*0-8167-2789-9*) Troll Assocs.

— One Hundred Two School Cafeteria Jokes. LC 91-30055. (Illus.). 64p. (J). (gr. 2-6). 1991. pap. text ed. 2.95 (*0-8167-2611-6*) Troll Assocs.

— Silly Sidney. LC 85-14063. (Illus.). 48p. (Orig.). (J). (gr. 1-3). 1986. lib. bdg. 10.59 (*0-8167-0610-7*); pap. text ed. 3.50 (*0-8167-0611-5*) Troll Assocs.

— Squeaky Shoes. LC 85-14014. (Illus.). 48p. (Orig.). (J). (gr. 1-3). 1986. lib. bdg. 10.59 (*0-8167-0642-5*); pap. text ed. 3.50 (*0-8167-0643-3*) Troll Assocs.

— Tricky Alex. LC 85-14018. (Illus.). 48p. (Orig.). (J). (gr. 1-3). 1986. lib. bdg. 10.59 (*0-8167-0598-4*); pap. text ed. 3.50 (*0-8167-0599-2*) Troll Assocs.

— What's It Like to Be a Farmer. LC 89-34386. (What's It Like to Be a...Ser.). (Illus.). 32p. (J). (gr. k-3). 1990. lib. bdg. 10.89 (*0-8167-1803-2*); pap. text ed. 2.95 (*0-8167-1804-0*) Troll Assocs.

— What's It Like to Be a Postal Worker. LC 89-34385. (What's It Like to Be a...Ser.). (Illus.). 32p. (J). (gr. k-3). 1990. lib. bdg. 10.89 (*0-8167-1813-X*); pap. text ed. 2.95 (*0-8167-1814-8*) Troll Assocs.

— What's It Like to Be a Railroad Worker. LC 89-34389. (What's It Like to Be a...Ser.). (Illus.). 32p. (J). (gr. k-3). 1989. lib. bdg. 10.89 (*0-8167-1815-6*); pap. text ed. 2.95 (*0-8167-1816-4*) Troll Assocs.

— Which Way, Hugo? LC 85-14132. (Illus.). 48p. (Orig.). (J). (gr. 1-3). 1986. lib. bdg. 10.59 (*0-8167-0648-4*); pap. text ed. 3.50 (*0-8167-0649-2*) Troll Assocs.

— Whoo's Too Tired? LC 88-1285. (Fiddlesticks Ser.). (Illus.). 48p. (Orig.). (J). (gr. 1-4). 1988. lib. bdg. 10.59 (*0-8167-1331-6*); pap. text ed. 3.50 (*0-8167-1332-4*) Troll Assocs.

Matthews, Nancy. Easter - The Beginning. 1974. 4.25 (*0-685-68681-7*, ME-19) Lillenas.

— Wilderness Preservation. (Earth at Risk Ser.). (Illus.). 112p. (YA). (gr. 5 up). 1991. lib. bdg. 19.95 (*0-7910-1580-7*); pap. write for info. (*0-7910-1605-6*) Chelsea Hse.

Matthews, Nancy A. Managing Rape: The Feminist Anti-Rape Movement & the State. LC 93-49037. (International Library of Sociology). 224p. 1994. 59.95x (*0-415-06491-0*, B3816, Routledge NY); pap. 17.95 (*0-415-11401-2*, B3820, Routledge NY) Routledge.

Matthews, Nancy L. William Sheppard: Cromwell's Law Reformer. (Studies in English Legal History). 320p. 1985. 69.95 (*0-521-26483-9*) Cambridge U Pr.

Matthews, Nathan. Municipal Charters: A Discussion of the Essentials of a City Charter with Forms or Models for Adoption. 18.95 (*0-405-19037-9*) Ayer.

An Asterisk (*) at the beginning of an entry indicates that the title is appearing in BIP for the first time.

Matthews, Olen P. Water Resources, Geography & Law. LC 84-70006. 1984. pap. 10.00 (*0-89291-174-3*) Assn Am Geographers.
Matthews, P. Choosing & Using ECL. 1984. text ed. 40.00 (*0-07-040949-8*) McGraw.
Matthews, P. & MacLean, R. Working with Children. 116p. (C). 1986. 50.00 (*0-7300-0389-2*, Pub. by Deakin Univ AT) St Mut.
Matthews, P. H. Grammatical Theory in the United States: From Bloomfield to Chomsky. LC 92-41067. (Studies in Linguistics: Vol. 67). 296p. (C). 1993. 64.95 (*0-521-43351-7*); pap. 27.95 (*0-521-45847-1*) Cambridge U Pr.
— Morphology. 2nd ed. (Cambridge Textbooks in Linguistics Ser.). 272p. (C). 1991. 59.95 (*0-521-41043-6*); pap. 18.95 (*0-521-42256-6*) Cambridge U Pr.
Matthews, Pamela R. Ellen Glasgow & a Woman's Traditions. 288p. (C). 1994. text ed. 29.50 (*0-8139-1539-2*) U Pr of Va.
Matthews, Pamela R., ed. see Glasgow, Ellen.
Matthews, Patricia. Love, Forever More. 1989. pap. 3.95 (*1-55817-244-0*, Pinnacle NY) Windsor NY.
— Love's Avenging Heart. 1989. pap. 3.95 (*1-55817-302-1*, Pinnacle NY) Windsor NY.
— Love's Bold Journey. 1990. mass mkt. 4.50 (*1-55817-421-4*, Pinnacle NY) Windsor NY.
— Love's Daring Dream. 1990. mass mkt. 4.50 (*1-55817-372-2*, Pinnacle NY) Windsor NY.
— Love's Golden Destiny. 1990. mass mkt. 4.50 (*1-55817-393-5*, Pinnacle NY) Windsor NY.
— Love's Magic Moment. 1990. mass mkt. 4.50 (*1-55817-409-5*, Pinnacle NY) Windsor NY.
— Loves Pagan Heart. 1990. pap. 3.95 (*1-55817-344-7*, Pinnacle NY) Windsor NY.
— Love's Raging Tide. 1990. mass mkt. 4.50 (*1-55817-381-1*, Pinnacle NY) Windsor NY.
— Love's Wildest Promise. 1990. mass mkt. 4.50 (*1-55817-356-0*, Pinnacle NY) Windsor NY.
— Mirrors. (Worldwide Library). 1988. pap. 4.50 (*0-317-70120-7*) S&S Trade.
— Mist of Evil. 1991. 17.95 (*0-7278-4110-6*) Severn Hse.
— Oasis. large type ed. LC 88-36823. 503p. (Orig.). 1989. reprint ed. lib. bdg. 7.95 (*0-89621-857-0*) Thorndike Pr.
— Sapphire. large type ed. LC 90-48876. 431p. 1991. reprint ed. lib. bdg. 19.95 (*1-56054-095-8*) Thorndike Pr.
— Sapphire. 1991. reprint ed. 19.95 (*0-7278-4255-2*) Severn Hse.
— Sound of Murder. 1994. 20.00 (*0-7278-4594-2*) Severn Hse.
— Taste of Evil. large type ed. LC 93-42206. 1994. 20.95 (*1-56054-334-5*) Thorndike Pr.
— The Unquiet. 1991. 19.95 (*0-7278-4219-6*) Severn Hse.
Matthews, Patricia & Matthews, Clayton. The Scent of Fear. large type ed. LC 92-23099. 351p. 1992. reprint ed. lib. bdg. 19.95 (*1-56054-336-1*) Thorndike Pr.
— Vision of Death. 256p. 1993. lib. bdg. 19.00 (*0-7278-4397-4*) Severn Hse.
— Vision of Death. large type ed. LC 93-21868. (Basic Ser.). 353p. 1993. reprint ed. lib. bdg. 20.95 (*1-56054-333-7*) Thorndike Pr.
Matthews, Paul. Forty Years With .45-70. (Illus.). 148p. (Orig.). 1989. pap. 11.50 (*0-935632-84-0*) Wolfe Pub Co.
— Loading the Black Powder Rifle Cartridge. 1993. 22.50 (*1-879356-20-1*) Wolfe Pub Co.
— The Paper Jacket. 1991. 13.50 (*1-879356-02-3*) Wolfe Pub Co.
— Sixty Years of Rifles. 1991. 19.50 (*1-879356-03-1*) Wolfe Pub Co.
***Matthews, Paul & Millichap, Denzil.** Guide to Leasehold Reform, Housing & Urban Development Act 1993. 400p. 1993. pap. text ed. 48.00 (*0-406-02650-5*, UK) Butterworth Legal Pubs.
***Matthews, Paul A.** Shooting the Black Powder Cartridge Rifle. 129p. 1994. 22.50 (*1-879356-38-4*) Wolfe Pub Co.
Matthews, Paul C. How to Try a Federal Criminal Case, 2 vols. & supplement. LC 60-8096. lxxii, 1347p. 1960. lib. bdg. 68.00 (*0-89941-601-2*, 500450) W S Hein.
— How to Try a Federal Criminal Case, 2 vols. & supplement. suppl. ed. LC 60-8096. lxxii, 1347p. 1972. lib. bdg. 25.00 (*0-685-73945-7*) W S Hein.
Matthews, Paul M. & Arnold, Douglas R. Diagnostic Tests in Neurology. (Illus.). 372p. 1990. pap. text ed. 44.95 (*0-443-08621-4*) Churchill.
***Matthews, Penny.** Hair-Raising: Ten Horror Stories. (YA). 1995. pap. 3.50 (*0-590-48403-6*) Scholastic Inc.
Matthews, Peter. User's Guide: Front & Tools. 1991. pap. text ed. 37.33 (*0-13-463720-8*) P-H.
Matthews, Philip S. Quantum Chemistry of Atoms & Molecules. (Illus.). 200p. (C). 1987. pap. 27.95 (*0-521-27025-1*) Cambridge U Pr.
Matthews, Phoebe. The Boy on the Cover. (YA). (gr. 7 up). 1988. pap. 2.75 (*0-380-75407-X*, Flare) Avon.
— Switchstance. 176p. (Orig.). (YA). (gr. 7 up). 1989. pap. 2.95 (*0-380-75729-X*, Flare) Avon.
Matthews, R., jt. auth. see Aizerman, M.
Matthews, R. Arthur. Born for Battle. 9th ed. 1988. pap. 7.95 (*9971-972-36-0*) OMF Bks.
— Born for Battle: Thirty-One Studies on Spiritual Warfare. 190p. 1993. pap. 7.99 (*0-87788-090-5*, OMF Books) Shaw Pubs.
— Nascido para a Batalha. Orig. Title: Born for Battle. 192p. (POR.). 1987. write for info. (*0-8297-1606-8*) Life Pubs Intl.
Matthews, R. C., ed. Economic Growth & Resources: Trends & Factors, Vol. II. LC 79-4430. 1980. text ed. 45.00 (*0-312-23315-9*) St Martin.
— Economy & Democracy: Proceedings of the Section F (Economics) of the British Association for the Advancement of Science, Norwich, 1984. LC 85-11869. 260p. 1985. text ed. 35.00 (*0-312-23679-4*) St Martin.
— Slower Growth in the Western World. (NIESR-PSI-RIIA Joint Studies in Public Policy Ser.: No. 6). vi, 176p. 1982. pap. text ed. 26.95 (*0-435-84516-0*) Ashgate Pub Co.
Matthews, R. C. & Stafford, B. The Grants Economy & Collective Consumption. LC 81-18289. 1982. text ed. 39.95 (*0-312-34274-8*) St Martin.
Matthews, R. C., et al. British Economic Growth, 1856-1973. LC 80-53222. (Studies of Economic Growth in Industrialized Countries). 736p. 1982. 79.50 (*0-8047-1110-0*) Stanford U Pr.
Matthews, R. E. A Critical Appraisal of Viral Taxonomy. 264p. 1983. 156.00 (*0-8493-5648-2*, QR394, CRC Reprint) Franklin.
— Fundamentals of Plant Virology. (Illus.). 403p. 1992. text ed. 39.95 (*0-12-480558-2*) Acad Pr.
— Plant Virology. 3rd ed. (Illus.). 835p. 1991. text ed. 49.95 (*0-12-480553-1*) Acad Pr.
Matthews, R. E., ed. Classification & Nomenclature of Viruses. (Journal: Intervirology: Vol. 17, No. 1-3, 1982). (Illus.). 200p. 1982. 29.00 (*3-8055-3557-0*) S Karger.
— Classification & Nomenclature of Viruses: Report of the International Committee on Taxonomy of Viruses, 3rd. (Intervirology Ser.: Vol. 12, Nos. 3-5, 1979). 1980. pap. 8.00 (*3-8055-0523-X*) S Karger.
Matthews, R. H. Reliability, 1991. 1991. 190.00 (*1-85166-643-5*) Elsevier.
Matthews, R. K., jt. auth. see Halley, R. B.
Matthews, Ralph. The Creation of Regional Dependency. 336p. 1983. 40.00 (*0-8020-5617-2*); pap. 15.95 (*0-8020-6510-4*) U of Toronto Pr.
Matthews, Rex, ed. see Copeland, Warren R.
Matthews, Richard & Hoyle, Mark. Injunctions. 1300p. 1993. 80.00 (*0-85459-823-5*, Pub. by Tolley Pubng UK) St Mut.
Matthews, Richard, jt. auth. see Ingersoll, David.
Matthews, Richard, ed. see Tenhover, Gregory R.
Matthews, Richard E. The 149th Pennsylvania Volunteer Infantry Unit in the Civil War. (Illus.). 346p. 1994. lib. bdg. 42.00 (*0-89950-993-2*) McFarland & Co.
Matthews, Richard K. If Men Were Angels: James Madison & the Heartless Empire of Reason. (American Political Thought Ser.). 256p. 1994. 25.00 (*0-7006-0643-2*) U Pr of KS.
— Radical Politics of Thomas Jefferson. LC 84-5240. xii, 172p. 1984. reprint ed. pap. 7.95 (*0-7006-0293-3*) U Pr of KS.
Matthews, Richard K., ed. Virtue, Corruption, & Self-Interest: Political Values in the Eighteenth Century. LC 93-55063. 1994. write for info. (*0-934223-26-2*) Lehigh Univ Pr.
Matthews, Rob. Beyond Two Thousand: A Minimum Model for the Global Future. (Illus.). 230p. (Orig.). (C). 1989. pap. 16.00 (*0-9622962-0-1*) Global Dynamics.
Matthews, Robert J. A Bible! A Bible! 12.95 (*0-88494-727-0*) Bookcraft Inc.
— A Plainer Translation: Joseph Smith's Translation of the Bible, a History & Commentary. LC 75-5937. 1975. 9.95 (*0-8425-2237-9*) BYU Scholarly.
Matthews, Robert J. & Demopoulos, William, eds. Learnability & Linguistic Theory. (C). 1989. lib. bdg. 91. 50 (*0-7923-0247-8*) Kluwer Ac.
Matthews, Robert O. & Pratt, Cranford, eds. Human Rights in Canadian Foreign Policy. 320p. (C). 1988. pap. text ed. 24.95 (*0-7735-0683-7*, Pub. by McGill CN) U of Toronto Pr.
Matthews, Robert O., et al. International Conflict & Conflict Management. 2nd ed. 624p. (C). 1990. pap. text ed. write for info. (*0-13-471665-5*) P-H.
Matthews, Robert W., jt. ed. see Ross, Kenneth G.
***Matthews, Robin, photos.** Travels with Queen Victoria: HRH the Duchess of York & Benita Stoney. (Illus.). 208p. 1995. 34.95 (*0-297-83195-X*, Pub. by Weidenfeld) Trafalgar.
Matthews, Roger. Informal Justice. (Contemporary Criminology Ser.). 224p. (C). 1988. text ed. 45.00 (*0-8039-8148-1*); pap. text ed. 16.95 (*0-8039-8149-X*) Sage.
Matthews, Roger, ed. Privatizing Criminal Justice. (Contemporary Criminology Ser.). 224p. (C). 1989. text ed. 45.00 (*0-8039-8240-2*); pap. text ed. 18.95 (*0-8039-8241-0*) Sage.
Matthews, Roger & Young, Jock, eds. Confronting Crime. LC 85-62748. 256p. (Orig.). (C). 1986. text ed. 39.95 (*0-8039-9731-0*); pap. text ed. 16.95 (*0-8039-9732-9*) Sage.
— Issues in Realist Criminology: A Reader. (Contemporary Criminology Ser.). (Illus.). 176p. 1992. 49.95 (*0-8039-8624-6*); pap. 19.95 (*0-8039-8625-4*) Sage.
— Rethinking Criminology: The Realist Debate. (Contemporary Criminology Ser.). (Illus.). 176p. 1992. 49.95 (*0-8039-8620-3*); pap. 19.95 (*0-8039-8485-5*) Sage.
Matthews, Ron. European Armaments Collaboration: Policy Problems & Prospects. LC 92-17039. 1992. text ed. 60. 00 (*3-7186-5244-7*) Gordon & Breach.
Matthews, Ron & Matsuyama, Keisuke, eds. Japan's Military Renaissance? LC 92-37814. 264p. 1993. text ed. 65.00 (*0-312-09150-8*) St Martin.
Matthews, Ronald. English Messiahs: Studies of Six English Religious Pretenders, 1656-1927. LC 76-172553. 1972. reprint ed. 15.95 (*0-405-18187-6*, Pub. by Blom Pubns UK) Ayer.
Matthews, Roy & Burstein, Nancy. Thirty Days to a Flatter Stomach for Men. 1983. pap. 4.99 (*0-553-34337-8*) Bantam.
***Matthews, Roy T. & Platt, F. Dewitt.** Instructor's Manual to Accompany The Western Humanities, Complete Volume. 2nd ed. 1994. teacher ed, pap. write for info. (*1-55934-413-X*) Mayfield Pub.
— The Western Humanities. 2nd ed. 1994. sl., vhs write for info. (*0-614-02479-X*) Mayfield Pub.
— The Western Humanities, 2 vols., 1. LC 92-12550. 368p. 1992. pap. 34.95 (*1-55934-122-X*) Mayfield Pub.
— The Western Humanities, 2 vols., 2. LC 92-12550. 285p. 1992. pap. 34.95 (*1-55934-123-8*) Mayfield Pub.
— The Western Humanities, Complete Volume. 2nd ed. 1994. vhs write for info. (*0-614-03281-4*) Mayfield Pub.
— The Western Humanities, Complete Volume. 2nd ed. LC 94-16373. 648p. (C). 1994. pap. text ed. 43.95 (*1-55934-412-1*) Mayfield Pub.
— The Western Humanities, Complete Volume: Test Bank. 2nd ed. 1994. disk write for info. (*0-614-03280-6*) Mayfield Pub.
***Matthews, Roy T. & Platt, F. DeWitt.** The Western Humanities, Vol. II. 376p. (C). 1994. pap. text ed. 36.95 (*1-55934-421-0*) Mayfield Pub.
***Matthews, Roy T. & Platt, F. Dewitt.** The Western Humanities Vol. 1: Beginnings Through the Renaissance, Vol. I. LC 94-25909. (Illus.). 360p. (C). 1994. pap. text ed. 36.95x (*1-55934-418-0*) Mayfield Pub.
— The Western Humanities (Complete Volume) 590p. (C). 1992. teacher ed, pap. write for info. (*1-55934-165-3*); vhs write for info. (*0-318-68884-0*); sl. write for info. (*0-318-68883-2*); cd-rom write for info. (*0-318-68885-9*); disk write for info. (*0-318-68882-4*) Mayfield Pub.
***Matthews, Rupert.** Dictionnaire des Dinosaures. 48p. (FRE.). 1990. 22.95 (*0-7859-7960-3*, 2719215236) Fr & Eur.
— Explorer. LC 91-8428. (Eyewitness Bks.). (Illus.). 64p. (J). (gr. 5 up). 1991. 17.00 (*0-679-81460-4*) Knopf Bks Yng Read.
— Explorer. LC 91-8428. (Eyewitness Bks.). (Illus.). 64p. (J). (gr. 5 up). 1991. lib. bdg. 16.99 (*0-679-91460-9*) Knopf Bks Yng Read.
— The Power Brokers: Kingmakers & Usurpers Throughout History. (Illus.). 336p. 1989. 27.95 (*0-8160-2156-2*) Facts on File.
— Record Breakers of the Air. LC 89-5212. (Illus.). 32p. (J). (gr. 2-6). 1990. lib. bdg. 9.59 (*0-8167-1921-7*); pap. text ed. 2.50 (*0-8167-1922-5*) Troll Assocs.
— Record Breakers of the Land. LC 89-5202. (Illus.). 32p. (J). (gr. 2-6). 1990. lib. bdg. 9.59 (*0-8167-1923-3*); pap. text ed. 2.50 (*0-8167-1924-1*) Troll Assocs.
— Record Breakers of the Sea. LC 89-35503. (Illus.). 32p. (J). (gr. 2-6). 1990. lib. bdg. 9.59 (*0-8167-1925-X*); pap. text ed. 2.50 (*0-8167-1926-8*) Troll Assocs.
Matthews, Rupert O. The Atlas of Natural Wonders. (Illus.). 240p. 1988. 35.00 (*0-8160-1993-2*) Facts on File.
— Germany: A Photographic Journey. 1990. 14.99 (*0-517-00179-9*) Random Hse Value.
***Matthews, Ruth.** Heat Shock Proteins in Fungal Infections. Burnie, James P., ed. (Molecular Biology Intelligence Unit Ser.). 170p. 1995. write for info. (*1-57059-275-6*) R G Landes.
Matthews, Ruth C., jt. ed. see Burnie, James P.
Matthews, Ruth H., jt. auth. see Gebhardt, Susan E.
Matthews, Ruth H., jt. auth. see Gebhardt, Susane.
Matthews, S., jt. auth. see Thomson, J.
Matthews, Sallie R. Interwoven: A Pioneer Chronicle. LC 81-48373. (Illus.). 248p. 1982. reprint ed. 18.95 (*0-89096-123-9*) Tex A&M Univ Pr.
Matthews, Sarah, tr. see Bombarde, Odile & Moatti, Claude.
Matthews, Sarah, tr. see Braudel, Fernand.
Matthews, Sarah, tr. see Brice, Raphaelle.
Matthews, Sarah, tr. see De Sairigne, Catherine.
Matthews, Sarah, tr. see Farre, Marie.
Matthews, Sarah, tr. see Jobin, Claire.
Matthews, Sarah, tr. see Limousin, Odile.
Matthews, Sarah, tr. see Pfeffer, Pierre.
Matthews, Sarah, tr. see Planche, Bernard.
Matthews, Sarah, tr. see Ruffault, Charlotte.
Matthews, Sarah, tr. see Segalen, Martine.
Matthews, Sarah, tr. see Singh, Anne.
***Matthews, Scott & Alpert, Barbara.** Santa's Little Instruction Book: His Checklist to See Who's Been Naughty or Nice. 96p. 1994. pap. 4.99 (*0-7860-0129-1*) Windsor NY.
Matthews, Scott & Nikuradse, Tamara. Dear Dad: Thank You for Being Mine. LC 92-40270. 1993. pap. 5.99 (*0-553-37198-3*) Bantam.
— Dear Mom: Thank You For Being Mine. LC 92-41689. 1993. pap. 5.99 (*0-553-37197-5*) Bantam.
— To the Woman I Love, Thank You for Being Mine. 160p. (Orig.). 1994. mass mkt. 5.99 (*0-449-90915-8*, Columbine) Fawcett.
Matthews, Scott, jt. auth. see Nikuradse, Tamara.
Matthews, Scott, et al. Stuck in the Seventies: One Hundred Thirteen Things That Screwed up the Twentysomething Generation. (Illus.). 196p. (Orig.). 1991. pap. 9.95 (*0-929387-35-X*) Bonus Books.
Matthews, Stanley L., jt. ed. see Powell, Frank J.
Matthews, Stephen & Yip, Virginia. Cantonese: A Comprehensive Grammar. LC 93-36173. 1994. pap. write for info. (*0-415-08945-X*, Routledge NY) Routledge.
Matthews, Stewart & Lawson, Ken. Caring for God's People: A Handbook for Elders & Ministers on Pastoral Care. 128p. (C). 1992. pap. 39.00 (*0-685-60690-2*, Pub. by St Andrew UK) St Mut.
Matthews, T. W., tr. see Legouis, Emile.
Matthews, Tanya S. War in Algeria: Background for Crisis. LC 62-10305. 165p. reprint ed. pap. 47.10 (*0-7837-0457-7*, 2040780) Bks Demand.
Matthews, Thomas. A Village in the Vineyards. LC 93-17262. 1993. 23.00 (*0-374-28381-8*) FS&G.
Matthews, Thomas & Matthews, Byron. Matthews Municipal Ordinances: 1963-1992, 7 Vols. LC 72-80615. 700.00 (*0-685-09238-0*) Clark Boardman Callaghan.
Matthews, Tom. The African Mural. 168p. (C). 1989. 250.00 (*1-85368-062-1*, Pub. by New Holland Pubs UK) St Mut.
Matthews, Tony. Shadows Dancing: Japanese Espionage Against the West, 1939-1945. LC 93-42720. (Illus.). 192p. 1994. 20.95 (*0-312-10544-4*, Pub. by Thomas Dunne Bks) St Martin.
— This Dawning Land. 116p. (C). 1990. 45.00 (*0-86439-010-6*, Pub. by Boolarong Pubns AT) St Mut.
Matthews, V. J. St. Philip Neri. LC 84-50406. 120p. 1984. reprint ed. pap. 4.50 (*0-89555-237-X*) TAN Bks Pubs.
Matthews, Valerie, ed. see Kirk, Douglas.
Matthews, Velda & Beard, Ray. Basic Bible Dictionary. Korth, Bob, ed. (Illus.). 128p. (Orig.). (J). (gr. 4-12). 1984. pap. 13.99 (*0-87239-720-3*, 2770) Standard Pub.
Matthews, Victor H. Manners & Customs in the Bible. rev. ed. (Illus.). 320p. 1991. 17.95 (*0-943575-77-X*); pap. 9.95 (*0-943575-81-8*) Hendrickson MA.
Matthews, Victor H. & Benjamin, Don C. Old Testament Parallels: Documents from the Ancient Near East. 1991. pap. 14.95 (*0-8091-3182-X*) Paulist Pr.
— Social World of Ancient Israel. LC 93-34183. 1993. 24.95 (*0-913573-89-2*) Hendrickson MA.
Matthews, Victoria E. Black-Belt Diamonds of Booker T. Washington. LC 73-83901. 1990. reprint ed. 13.00 (*1-56675-021-0*); reprint ed. pap. 10.00 (*1-56675-022-9*) Mnemosyne.
Matthews, Vincent, ed. Laramide Folding Associated with Basement Block Faulting in the Western United States. LC 78-54346. (Geological Society of America, Memoir Ser.: No. 151). 400p. reprint ed. pap. 114.00 (*0-317-28993-4*, 2023731) Bks Demand.
Matthews, Virginia, ed. Library Services for Children Youth: Dollars Sense. 1994. write for info. (*0-318-72917-2*) Neal-Schuman.
Matthews, W. Cockney, Past & Present. 1972. 150.00 (*0-87968-881-5*) Gordon Pr.
Matthews, W. B., et al. McAlpine's Multiple Sclerosis. 2nd ed. (Illus.). 401p. 1991. text ed. 110.80 (*0-443-04047-8*) Churchill.
Matthews, W. H., III. The Geologic Story of Longhorn Cavern. (Guidebook Ser.: GB 4). (Illus.). 50p. 1991. reprint ed. 3.00 (*0-686-29313-4*) Bur Econ Geology.
— The Geologic Story of Palo Duro Canyon. (Guidebook Ser.: GB 8). (Illus.). 51p. 1989. reprint ed. 2.00 (*0-686-29316-9*) Bur Econ Geology.
Matthews, W. H. Mazes & Labyrinths: Their History & Development. (Illus.). 1970. reprint ed. pap. 5.95 (*0-486-22614-X*) Dover.
Matthews, W. H., III. Texas Fossils: An Amateur Collector's Handbook. (Guidebook Ser.: GB 2). (Illus.). 123p. 1991. reprint ed. 3.50 (*0-686-29311-8*) Bur Econ Geology.
Matthews, W. R., ed. Christian Faith: Essays in Explanation & Defence. LC 73-152162. (Essay Index Reprint Ser.). 1977. reprint ed. 23.95 (*0-8369-2348-0*) Ayer.
Matthews, Warren. World Religions. Baxter, ed. 491p. (C). 1991. pap. text ed. 42.50 (*0-314-78261-3*) West Pub.
Matthews, Washington. Grammar & Dictionary of the Language of the Hidatsa. LC 76-44080. (Shea's American Linguistics, Ser. 2: Nos. 1 & 2). reprint ed. 49. 50 (*0-404-15787-4*) AMS Pr.
— Navajo Weavers & Silversmiths. LC 70-97218. (Wild & Woolly West Ser., No. 7). (Illus.). 1968. pap. 3.00 (*0-910584-07-9*) Filter.
— The Night Chant: A Navaho Ceremony. LC 74-7991. reprint ed. 94.50 (*0-404-11880-1*) AMS Pr.
— The Night Chant: A Navaho Ceremony. (Illus.). 376p. 1995. reprint ed. text ed. 45.00x (*0-87480-490-6*); reprint ed. pap. 19.95x (*0-87480-491-4*) U of Utah Pr.
Matthews, Washington, tr. & comp. Navaho Legends. (Illus.). 320p. 1993. reprint ed. pap. 19.95 (*0-87480-424-8*) U of Utah Pr.
***Matthews, Wendy.** The Gift of a Traveler. LC 94-35307. (Illus.). 32p. (J). (gr. k-3). 1995. lib. bdg. 14.95 (*0-8167-3656-1*) BridgeWater.
Matthews, Wendy L., jt. auth. see McClay, John B.
Matthews, William. Blues If You Want. 72p. 1989. pap. 9.95 (*0-395-51756-7*) HM.
— British Autobiographies: An Annotated Bibliography of British Autobiographies Published or Written Before 1951. (California Library Reprint Edition). 390p. reprint ed. pap. 111.20 (*0-7837-4836-1*, 2044483) Bks Demand.
— British Diaries: An Annotated Bibliography of British Diaries Written Between 1442-1942. 11.25 (*0-8446-1304-5*) Peter Smith.
— British Diaries: An Annotated Bibliography of British Diaries Written Between 1442-1942. (California Library Reprint). 373p. reprint ed. pap. 106.40 (*0-7837-4838-8*, 2044485) Bks Demand.
— Canadian Diaries & Autobiographies. LC 50-62732. 144p. reprint ed. pap. 41.10 (*0-8357-7994-7*, 2052054) Bks Demand.
— Cowboys & Images. LC 94-1187. (Illus.). 136p. 1994. 40. 00 (*0-8118-0768-1*) Chronicle Bks.
— Curiosities. LC 89-5127. 200p. 1989. 39.50 (*0-472-09388-6*); pap. 13.95 (*0-472-06388-X*) U of Mich Pr.
— A Happy Childhood. LC 84-803. 71p. 1984. 12.95 (*0-316-55073-6*) Little.
— Modern Bookbinding Practically Considered. Huttner, Sidney F., ed. (History of Bookbinding & Design Ser.). (Illus.). 120p. 1990. reprint ed. 43.00 (*0-8240-4023-6*) Garland.
— The Mortal City One-Hundred Epigrams from Martial. 128p. (Orig.). 1995. pap. 15.00 (*0-942148-17-7*) Ohio Review.
— Selected Poems & Translations, 1969-1991. 256p. 1992. 19.95 (*0-395-63121-1*) HM.
— Selected Poems & Translations, 1969-1991. 224p. 1993. 12.95 (*0-395-66993-6*) HM.
— Sleek for the Long Flight. 1988. 8.00 (*0-934834-22-9*) White Pine.

An Asterisk (*) at the beginning of an entry indicates that the title is appearing in BIP for the first time.

— Time & Money: New Poems. 69p. 1995. 19.95 (*0-395-71134-7*) HM.

— Words: Their Use & Abuse. LC 70-37792. (Essay Index Reprint Ser.). 1977. reprint ed. 25.95 (*0-8369-2611-0*) Ayer.

Matthews, William, ed. Later Medieval English Prose. LC 63-9439. (Goldentree Books in English Literature). (Orig.). 1963. pap. text ed. 14.95 (*0-89197-270-6*) Irvington.

Matthews, William, ed. see Pepys, Samuel.

Matthews, William, jt. ed. see Spisak, James W.

Matthews, William H., III, ed. Man's Impact on the Global Environment: Assessment & Recommendations for Action. (Study of Critical Environmental Problems). 1970. pap. 6.95 (*0-262-69027-6*) MIT Pr.

Matthews, William K. Structure & Development of Russian. LC 77-90152. 224p. 1969. reprint ed. text ed. 55.00 (*0-8371-2246-5*, MARU, Greenwood Pr) Greenwood.

Matthews, Z. K. Freedom for My People. 264p. 1990. pap. 9.95 (*0-908396-84-8*, Pub. by D Philip SA) Interlink Pub.

***Matthewson, Audrey.** Blue Rose-Year 2094. 300p. Date not set. pap. 9.95 (*0-7610-0340-1*) NW Pub.

***Matthiae, Paolo, et al, eds.** Resurrecting the Past: A Joint Tribute to Adnan Bounni. xxxvi, 407p. 1990. pap. text ed. 87.00 (*90-6258-067-X*, Pub. by Netherlands Inst NE) Eisenbrauns.

Matthias, Catherine. Arriba y Abajo (Over-Under) LC 83-21005. (Rookie Reader Ser.). (Illus.). 32p. (SPA.). (J). (ps-2). 1989. lib. bdg. 10.35 (*0-516-32048-3*); pap. 2.95 (*0-516-52048-2*) Childrens.

— Demasiados Globos (Too Many Balloons) LC 81-15520. (Rookie Reader Ser.). (Illus.). 32p. (SPA.). (J). (ps-2). 1990. pap. 2.95 (*0-516-53633-8*) Childrens.

— Los Gatos Me Gustan Mas (I Love Cats) LC 83-7215. (Rookie Readers - Spanish Ser.). (Illus.). 32p. (SPA.). (J). (ps-2). 1988. pap. 2.95 (*0-516-52041-5*) Childrens.

— I Can Be a Computer Operator. LC 84-23281. (I Can Be Bks.). (Illus.). 32p. (J). (gr. k-3). 1985. lib. bdg. 11.85 (*0-516-01838-8*); pap. 3.95 (*0-516-41838-6*) Childrens.

— I Can Be a Police Officer. LC 84-12106. (I Can Be Bks.). (Illus.). 32p. (J). (gr. k-3). 1984. lib. bdg. 11.85 (*0-516-01840-X*); pap. 3.95 (*0-516-41840-8*) Childrens.

— I Love Cats. LC 83-7215. (Rookie Reader Ser.). (Illus.). 32p. (J). (ps-2). 1983. lib. bdg. 10.35 (*0-516-02041-2*); pap. 2.95 (*0-516-42041-0*) Childrens.

— Out the Door. LC 81-17060. (Rookie Reader Ser.). (Illus.). 32p. (J). (ps-2). 1982. lib. bdg. 10.35 (*0-516-03560-6*); pap. 2.95 (*0-516-43560-4*) Childrens.

— Over-Under. LC 83-21005. (Rookie Reader Ser.). (Illus.). 32p. (J). (ps-2). 1984. lib. bdg. 10.35 (*0-516-02048-X*); pap. 2.95 (*0-516-42048-8*) Childrens.

— Puedo Ser un Policia (I Can Be a Police Officer) LC 84-12106. (Spanish--I Can Be Bks.). (Illus.). 32p. (SPA.). (J). (gr. k-3). 1987. pap. 3.95 (*0-516-51840-2*) Childrens.

— Sal y Entra (Out the Door) LC 81-17060. (Rookie Reader Ser.). (Illus.). 32p. (SPA.). (J). (ps-2). 1989. pap. 2.95 (*0-516-53560-9*) Childrens.

— Too Many Balloons. LC 81-15520. (Rookie Reader Ser.). (Illus.). 32p. (J). (ps-2). 1982. lib. bdg. 10.35 (*0-516-03633-5*); pap. text ed. 2.95 (*0-516-43633-3*) Childrens.

Matthias, Christopher, jt. ed. see Bannister, Roger.

Matthias, Dody. Working for Life. 1990. 12.00 (*1-55673-191-4*, 7693) CSS OH.

Matthias, Howard. The Korean War: Reflections of a Young Combat Platoon Leader. (Illus.). 1992. 15.95 (*0-942407-17-2*) Father & Son.

***Matthias, John.** Beltane at Aphelion: Longer Poems. 203p. 1995. text ed. 32.95x (*0-8040-0983-X*) Swallow.

— A Gathering of Ways. LC 90-20684. 136p. 1991. 19.95 (*0-8040-0941-4*); pap. 10.95 (*0-8040-0945-7*) Swallow.

— North Dakota Statewide Court Automation Plan, Vol. I: Report. 50p. 1991. 3.00 (*0-685-50604-5*, MWRO010) Natl Ctr St Courts.

— North Dakota Statewide Court Automation Plan, Vol. II: Appendices. 295p. 1991. 18.00 (*0-685-50605-3*, MWRO012) Natl Ctr St Courts.

— Northern Summer: New & Selected Poems, 1963-1983. LC 83-18199. 224p. 1984. 24.95 (*0-8040-0852-3*); pap. 12.95 (*0-8040-0853-1*) Swallow.

— Reading Old Friends: Essays, Reviews, & Poems on Poetics 1975-1990. LC 90-28980. (SUNY Series, The Margins of Literature). 348p. (C). 1992. 59.50 (*0-7914-0879-5*); pap. 19.95 (*0-7914-0880-9*) State U NY Pr.

— Swimming at Midnight: Selected Shorter Poems. 132p. 1995. text ed. 26.95x (*0-8040-0984-8*); pap. text ed. 11.95x (*0-8040-0985-6*) Swallow.

Matthias, John, ed. David Jones: Man & Poet. (Man & Poet Ser.). 580p. 1989. 55.00 (*0-943373-03-4*); pap. 30.00 (*0-943373-04-2*) Natl Poet Foun.

— Selected Works of David Jones. (Poetry & Literature Ser.). 237p. 1993. pap. 12.00 (*0-943373-19-0*) Natl Poet Foun.

— Selected Works of David Jones. (Poetry & Literature Ser.). 237p. 1993. 18.00 (*0-943373-18-2*) Natl Poet Foun.

Matthias, John & Vuckovic, Vladeta, trs. The Battle of Kosovo. LC 87-10061. (Illus.). 76p. 1988. pap. 12.95 (*0-8040-0897-3*) Swallow.

Matthias, John & Yeh, Chang-ming. Management Review of the Court of Appeals, Fifth District of Texas at Dallas. 280p. 1990. 17.00 (*0-685-50601-0*, MWRO006) Natl Ctr St Courts.

Matthias, John P. On the Edge. LC 90-71984. 190p. (Orig.). 1992. pap. text ed. 7.50 (*1-56002-044-X*, Univ Edtns) Aegina Pr.

Matthias, Kurt E. Citizen "M" Speaks, Vol. 1. LC 82-74183. (Illus.). 125p. 1983. pap. 5.00 (*0-9609110-0-6*) Creative Lit.

Matthias, Margaret, jt. ed. see Thiessen, Diane.

Matthiasson, John. Living on the Land: Change among the Inuit of Northern Baffin Island. 180p. 1992. pap. 13.95 (*0-921149-93-X*) Broadview Pr.

Matthies, H., ed. Learning & Memory: Mechanisms of Information Storage in the Nervous System. 413p. 1986. 120.00 (*0-08-034186-1*, H222, H223, Pergamon Pr) Elsevier.

Matthies, H., jt. ed. see Ajmone-Marsan, Cosimo.

Matthies, S., et al. Standard Distribution in Texture Analysis: Maps for the Case of Cubic - Orthorhombic Symmetry, Vol. 1. 442p. 1987. lib. bdg. 105.00 (*3-05-500247-4*, Pub. by Akademie GW) VCH Pubs.

— Standard Distribution in Texture Analysis: Maps for the Case of Cubic - Orthorhombic Symmetry, Vol. 2. 256p. 1988. lib. bdg. 66.00 (*3-05-500248-2*, Pub. by Akademie GW) VCH Pubs.

— Standard Distribution in Texture Analysis: Maps for the Case of Cubic - Orthorhombic Symmetry, Vol. 3. 480p. 1990. lib. bdg. 103.00 (*3-05-500249-0*, Pub. by Akademie GW) VCH Pubs.

Matthies, Susanna. Egyptians, Maya, Minoans. (Enrichment & Gifted Ser.). (Illus.). 112p. (J). (gr. 4-6). 1986. 9.95 (*0-88160-122-5*, LW 906) Learning Wks.

Matthiesen, Peter. Killing Mr. Watson. large type ed. LC 90-21129. 635p. 1991. reprint ed. bds. 21.95 (*1-56054-099-0*) Thorndike Pr.

Matthiesen, Steven J. Essential Words for the TOEFL. 192p. 1993. pap. 8.95 (*0-8120-1470-7*) Barron.

Matthiessen, Christian & Strohmeier, K. Peter. Innovation & Urban Population Dynamics: A Multi-Level Process. (Urban Europe Ser.). 320p. 1992. 68.95 (*1-85628-143-4*, Pub. by Avebury Pub UK) Ashgate Pub Co.

Matthiessen, F. O. American Renaissance: Art & Expression in the Age of Emerson & Whitman. (C). 1968. reprint ed. pap. 19.95 (*0-19-500759-X*) OUP.

— Theodore Dreiser. LC 72-7876. (American Men of Letters Ser.). (Illus.). 267p. 1973. reprint ed. text ed. 35.00 (*0-8371-6550-4*, MATD, Greenwood Pr) Greenwood.

Matthiessen, F. O., ed. Oxford Book of American Verse. (YA). (gr. 9 up). 1950. 49.95 (*0-19-500049-8*) OUP.

Matthiessen, F. O. & Murdock, Kenneth B., eds. The Notebooks of Henry James. xxviii, 426p. 1981. pap. 10.95 (*0-226-51104-9*) U Ch Pr.

Matthiessen, Francis. American Renaissance. (BCL1-PS American Literature Ser.). 678p. 1993. reprint ed. lib. bdg. 109.00 (*0-7812-6577-0*) Rprt Serv.

Matthiessen, Francis O. Sarah Orne Jewett. 1929. 11.25 (*0-8446-1305-3*) Peter Smith.

— Sarah Orne Jewett. (BCL1-PS American Literature Ser.). 159p. 1992. reprint ed. lib. bdg. 69.00 (*0-7812-6775-7*) Rprt Serv.

— Translation, an Elizabethan Art. (BCL1-PR English Literature Ser.). 232p. 1992. reprint ed. lib. bdg. 79.00 (*0-7812-7034-0*) Rprt Serv.

Matthiessen, Peter. African Silences. 1991. 21.00 (*0-679-40021-4*) Random.

— African Silences. 1992. pap. 11.00 (*0-679-73102-4*, Vin) Random.

— At Play in the Fields of the Lord. 1992. 23.25 (*0-8446-6636-X*) Peter Smith.

— At Play in the Fields of the Lord. LC 86-40559. 1987. pap. 10.95 (*0-394-75083-7*, Vin) Random.

— At Play in the Fields of the Lord. LC 91-50228. 384p. 1991. pap. 11.00 (*0-679-73741-3*, Vin) Random.

— Baikal: Sacred Sea of Siberia. LC 92-3057. (Illus.). 128p. 1992. 25.00 (*0-87156-584-6*) Sierra.

— The Cloud Forest. 1992. 19.50 (*0-8446-6605-X*) Peter Smith.

— The Cloud Forest: A Chronicle of the South American Wilderness. (Illus.). 320p. 1987. pap. 11.00 (*0-14-009549-7*, Penguin Bks) Viking Penguin.

— East of Lo Monthang: In the Land of Mustang. LC 95-204. (Illus.). 192p. 1995. 35.00 (*1-57062-131-4*) Shambhala Pubns.

— East of Lo Monthang: In the Land of Mustang. limited ed. (Illus.). 192p. 1995. 150.00 (*1-57062-159-4*) Shambhala Pubns.

— Far Tortuga. LC 87-40154. 416p. 1988. pap. 14.00 (*0-394-75667-3*, Vin) Random.

— In the Spirit of Crazy Horse. (Illus.). 688p. 1992. pap. 15.95 (*0-14-014456-0*, Penguin Bks) Viking Penguin.

— Indian Country. 1993. 20.75 (*0-8446-6677-7*) Peter Smith.

— Indian Country. 352p. 1992. pap. 12.00 (*0-14-013023-3*, Penguin Bks) Viking Penguin.

— Killing Mister Watson. 384p. 1990. 21.95 (*0-394-55400-0*) Random.

— Killing Mister Watson. LC 90-50631. 384p. 1991. pap. 13.00 (*0-679-73405-8*, Vin) Random.

— Men's Lives: Surfmen & Baymen of the South Fork. LC 85-24482. (Illus.). 352p. 1986. 29.95 (*0-394-55280-6*) Random.

— Men's Lives: Surfmen & Baymen of the South Fork. LC 87-40095. 352p. 1988. pap. 10.00 (*0-394-75560-X*, Vin) Random.

— Men's Lives: The Surfmen & Baymen of the South Fork, 2 vols. LC 85-24482. (Illus.). 408p. 1986. Boxed set. boxed 200.00 (*0-295-96605-X*) U of Wash Pr.

— Midnight Turning Gray. LC 83-82381. 96p. 1984. pap. 5.50 (*0-9604740-5-6*) Ampersand RI.

— Nine-Headed Dragon River: Zen Journals 1969-1982. LC 85-27918. (Dragon Ser.). 288p. 1987. pap. 19.00 (*0-87773-401-1*) Shambhala Pubns.

— On the River Styx & Other Stories. 1989. 17.95 (*0-394-55399-3*) Random.

— On the River Styx & Other Stories. LC 89-40508. 224p. 1990. pap. 8.95 (*0-685-29463-3*, Vin) Random.

— On the River Styx & Other Stories. LC 89-40508. 224p. 1991. 11.00 (*0-679-72852-X*, Vin) Random.

— Partisans. LC 86-40558. 1987. 5.95 (*0-394-75342-9*, Vin) Random.

— Race Rock. LC 87-40096. 320p. 1988. pap. 8.95 (*0-394-74538-8*, Vin) Random.

— Raditzer. LC 86-40557. 1987. 5.95 (*0-394-75343-7*, Vin) Random.

— The Snow Leopard. 352p. 1987. pap. 11.00 (*0-14-010266-3*, Penguin Bks) Viking Penguin.

— The Tree Where Man Was Born. (Nature Classics Ser.). 448p. 1995. 12.95 (*0-14-023934-0*, Penguin Bks) Viking Penguin.

— Under the Mountain Wall. 1987. pap. 10.00 (*0-14-009548-9*, Penguin Bks) Viking Penguin.

— Wildlife in America. 1978. mass mkt. 12.95 (*0-14-004793-X*, Penguin Bks) Viking Penguin.

— The Wind Birds: Shorebirds of North America. LC 93-48005. (Curious Naturalist Ser.). (Illus.). 168p. 1994. reprint ed. pap. 12.95 (*1-881527-37-9*) Chapters Pub.

Matthiessen, Peter & Frank, Mary. Shadows of Africa. (Illus.). 120p. 1992. 34.95 (*0-8109-3828-6*) Abrams.

Matthieu, Carol Y., ed. see Coleman, Craig S.

Matthieu, Carol Y., jt. ed. see Coleman, Craig S.

***Matthioulus, P. A.** Compendium. 921p. (C). 1992. 810.00x (*963-05-0200-3*, Pub. by Akad Kiado HU) St Mut.

Matthys, E., jt. ed. see Kushner, B. G.

Matthys, E. F., ed. Melt-Spinning & Strip Casting - Research & Implementation. (Illus.). 287p. 1992. 108.00 (*0-87339-183-7*, 444) Minerals Metals.

Matthys, H., ed. see International Titisee Conference Staff.

Matthys, Heinrich, jt. ed. see Barnes, Peter J.

Matthys, John H., ed. Masonry: Components to Assemblages. LC 90-36037. (Special Technical Publication (STP) Ser.: STP 1063). (Illus.). 450p. 1990. text ed. 42.00 (*0-8031-1453-2*, 04-010630-60) ASTM.

Matthys, Robert J. Crystal Oscillator Circuits. rev. ed. 266p. (C). 1992. lib. bdg. 44.50 (*0-89464-552-8*) Krieger.

Matthysee, J. G. & Colbo, M. H. Ixodid Ticks of Uganda. (Illus.). 426p. 1987. 45.00 (*0-938522-31-0*) Entomol Soc.

Matthysse, S., jt. ed. see Van Ree, J. M.

Matthysse, Steven & Kety, Seymour S. Catecholamines & Their Enzymes in the Neuropathology of Schizophrenia. LC 75-4093. (Illus.). 382p. 1975. 163.00 (*0-08-018242-9*, Pub. by Pergamon Repr UK) Franklin.

Matti, Jonathan C., jt. auth. see Murphy, Michael A.

Matti, Jonathan C., et al. Silurian & Lower Devonian Basin & Basin-Slope Limestones, Copenhagen Canyon, Nevada. LC 74-19734. (Geological Society of America, Special Paper Ser.: No. 159). 56p. reprint ed. pap. 25.00 (*0-317-28377-4*, 2025458) Bks Demand.

***Mattia, Jan B. & Marler, Patti.** Resumes Made Easy. Kennedy, Sarah, ed. (Orig.). 1995. pap. 6.95 (*0-8442-4348-5*, VGM Career Bks) NTC Pub Grp.

***Mattia, Jan B. & Morler, Patty.** Job Interviews Made Easy. Kennedy, Sarah, ed. (Orig.). 1995. pap. 6.95 (*0-8442-4349-3*, VGM Career Bks) NTC Pub Grp.

Mattiasson & Holst, eds. Extractive Bioconversions. (Bioprocess Technology Ser.: Vol. 11). 352p. 1991. 125.00 (*0-8247-8272-0*) Dekker.

Mattiasson, Bo, ed. Immobilized Cells & Organelles, Vol. I. 152p. 1983. 115.00 (*0-8493-6440-X*, QH585) Franklin.

— Immobilized Cells & Organelles, Vol. II. 168p. 1983. 119.00 (*0-8493-6441-8*, QH585) Franklin.

Mattiasson, K., et al, eds. Numiform 86: Proceedings of the International Conference on Numerical Methods in Industrial Forming Processes, Gothenburg, 25-29 August 1986. 404p. (C). 1986. text ed. 170.00 (*90-6191-659-3*, Pub. by A A Balkema NE) Ashgate Pub Co.

Mattiat, Oskar E., ed. Ultrasonic Transducer Materials. LC 71-131885. 186p. 1971. 59.50 (*0-306-30501-1*, Plenum Pr) Plenum.

Mattice, Wayne L. & Suter, Ulrich W. Conformational Theory of Large Molecules: The Rotational Isomeric State Model in Macromolecular Systems. LC 93-40718. 1994. text ed. 74.95 (*0-471-84338-5*) Wiley.

Mattick, Hans W. A Selected Bibliography on the American Jail with Special Emphasis on Illinois Jails, No. 821. 1975. 8.50 (*0-686-20357-7*) CPL Biblios.

Mattick, Paul. Economic Crisis & Crisis Theory. LC 80-5459. 235p. reprint ed. pap. 67.00 (*0-685-16334-2*, 2027622) Bks Demand.

— Economics, Politics & the Age of Inflation. LC 78-68044. 151p. reprint ed. pap. 43.10 (*0-317-41962-5*, 2026131) Bks Demand.

— Marx & Keynes: The Limits of the Mixed Economy. LC 69-15526. (Extending Horizons Ser.). 350p. (C). 1973. 6.95 (*0-87558-045-9*); pap. 3.45 (*0-87558-069-6*) Porter Sargent.

Mattick, Paul, Jr., ed. Eighteenth-Century Aesthetics & the Reconstitution of Art. LC 92-26692. 256p. (C). 1993. 49.95 (*0-521-43106-9*) Cambridge U Pr.

— Marxism: Last Refuge of the Bourgeoisie? LC 83-620. 336p. 1983. pap. text ed. 22.95 (*0-87332-261-4*) M E Sharpe.

Matties, Gordon H. Ezekiel Eighteen & the Rhetoric of Moral Discourse. 256p. 1990. 24.95 (*1-55540-458-8*); pap. 14.95 (*1-55540-459-6*) Scholars Pr GA.

Mattiessen, Peter. The Tree Where Man Was Born. 353p. 1983. reprint ed. pap. 8.95 (*0-525-48032-3*, Obelisk) NAL-Dutton.

Mattila, John M., jt. auth. see Thompson, Wilbur R.

Mattila, M. Clinical Pharmacology. LC 75-33069. (Proceedings Sixth International Congress of Pharmacology Ser.: Vol. 5). 1976. 109.00 (*0-08-020543-7*, Pub. by Pergamon Repr UK) Franklin.

Mattila, M., ed. see Satellite Symposium on Alcohol, Drugs & Driving Staff.

Mattila, Markku & Karwowski, Waldemar, eds. Computer Applications in Ergonomics, Occupational Safety, & Health: Proceedings of the International Conference on Computer-Aided Ergonomics & Safety '92: CAES '92, Tampere, Finland, 18-20 May 1992. LC 92-10527. 1992. write for info. (*0-444-89605-8*, North Holland) Elsevier.

***Mattila, Pertti.** Geometry of Sets & Measures in Euclidean Spaces: Fractals & Rectifiability. (Cambridge Studies in Advanced Mathematics: 44). 350p. (C). 1995. 49.95 (*0-521-46576-1*) Cambridge U Pr.

Mattill, A. J., Jr. Luke & the Last Things. 1979. pap. 8.95 (*0-915948-03-6*) Bks Distinction.

Mattill, A. J., Jr., jt. auth. see Schweitzer, Albert.

Mattimore, Bryan W. Ninety-Nine Percent Inspiration: Tips, Tales & Techniques for Liberating Your Business. 176p. 1993. pap. 17.95 (*0-8144-7788-7*) AMACOM.

Mattina, Anthony, ed. The Golden Woman: The Colville Narrative of Peter J. Seymour. DeSautel, Madeline, tr. LC 85-1156. 357p. 1985. 29.95 (*0-8165-0915-8*) U of Ariz Pr.

Mattina, Anthony & Montler, Timothy, eds. American Indian Linguistics & Ethnography in Honor of Laurence C. Thompson. (Occasional Papers in Linguistics: No. 10). xi, 497p. 1993. 35.00 (*1-879763-50-8*); pap. 20.00 (*1-879763-10-9*) U MT UMOPL.

Mattingley, Christobel. The Miracle Tree. LC 86-4541. (Illus.). 28p. (J). (gr. 3 up). 1986. 11.95 (*0-15-200530-7*, Gulliver Bks) HarBrace.

Mattingley, Jason B., jt. auth. see Bradshaw, John L.

Mattingly, Anna. Artie's Big Surprise. 1994. 8.95 (*0-8062-5034-8*) Carlton.

Mattingly, Cheryl & Fleming, Maureen H. Clinical Reasoning: Forms of Inquiry in Occupational Therapy. (Illus.). 378p. (C). 1993. text ed. 29.00 (*0-8036-5937-7*) Davis Co.

Mattingly, David, jt. auth. see Jones, Barri.

***Mattingly, David J.** Tripolitania. LC 94-46968. 1995. 49.50 (*0-472-10658-9*) U of Mich Pr.

Mattingly, David M. & Seward, Charles. Seward's Bedside Diagnosis. 13th ed. (Illus.). 373p. 1989. pap. text ed. 45.00 (*0-443-04077-X*) Churchill.

Mattingly, Garrett. The Armada. 464p. 1974. pap. 11.95 (*0-395-08366-4*, 17, SenEd) HM.

— Catherine of Aragon. LC 83-45808. reprint ed. 32.50 (*0-404-20169-5*) AMS Pr.

— The Invincible Armada & Elizabethean England. LC 79-65984. (Folger Guides to the Age of Shakespeare Ser.). 1979. pap. 4.95 (*0-918016-11-8*) Folger Bks.

— Renaissance Diplomacy. 284p. 1988. reprint ed. pap. 8.95 (*0-486-25570-0*) Dover.

Mattingly, George. Breathing Space. LC 75-5515. (Illus.). (Orig.). 1975. pap. 19.95 (*0-912652-11-X*) Blue Wind.

Mattingly, H. AES & PECVNIA: Records of Roman Currency Down to 269 B.C. 19p. 1979. pap. 5.00 (*0-916710-51-3*) Obol Intl.

— The Various Styles of the Roman Republican Coinage. 18p. 1977. 5.00 (*0-916710-31-9*) Obol Intl.

Mattingly, H. & Robinson, E. S. The Date of the Roman Denarius & Other Landmarks in Early Roman Coinage. (Illus.). 59p. 1974. pap. 8.00 (*0-916710-17-3*) Obol Intl.

Mattingly, Harold. The Coinage of the Civil Wars of 68-69 A.D. 1977. 3.75 (*0-915018-21-7*) Attic Bks.

— Fel Temp Reparatio. (Illus.). 1977. 3.75 (*0-915018-22-5*) Attic Bks.

— Man in the Roman Street. 1966. pap. 7.95 (*0-393-00337-X*) Norton.

Mattingly, Harold, tr. see Alfoldi, Andras.

Mattingly, Hugh, tr. see Tacitus.

Mattingly, I. G. & Studdert-Kennedy, M., eds. Modularity & the Motor Theory of Speech Perception: Proceedings of a Conference to Honor Alvin M. Liberman. 480p. 1990. text ed. 89.95 (*0-8058-0331-9*) L Erlbaum Assocs.

Mattingly, J., et al. Aircraft Engine Design. (Educ Ser.). 600p. 1987. Book. 61.95 (*0-930403-23-1*); Disks. disk 27.00 (*0-930403-31-2*) AIAA.

— Aircraft Engine Design, Set. (Educ Ser.). 600p. 1987. 86.95 (*0-685-73870-1*) AIAA.

***Mattingly, Jack D.** Elements of Gas Turbine Propulsion. LC 95-897. (Mechanical Engineering Series; Aeronautical & Aerospace Engineering Ser.). 1995. write for info. (*0-07-912196-9*) McGraw.

Mattingly, James, et al. Connecticut's Saltwater Fishing & Shoreline Recreation Guide. 1992. pap. text ed. 3.95 (*1-881514-02-1*) Red Bk Atlas.

Mattingly, Jennie, ed. see Nelson, Theresa M.

Mattingly, Jennie, ed. see Stueart, Robert.

Mattingly, Jennie, ed. see Tyler, Jan.

Mattingly, Jim, et al. Connecticut's Bass Fishing: Guides to the Best Bass Lakes & Ponds. 60p. 1992. pap. 3.95 (*1-881514-00-5*) Red Bk Atlas.

— Connecticut's Trout Fishing: Guides to the Best Lakes & Ponds, Rivers & Streams. 64p. 1992. pap. 3.95 (*1-881514-01-3*) Red Bk Atlas.

Mattingly, John, ed. see Branfield, Wilfred.

Mattingly, M. R. The Catholic Church on the Kentucky Frontier: 1785-1812. LC 73-3579. (Catholic University of America. Studies in Romance Languages & Literatures: No. 25). reprint ed. 40.00 (*0-404-57775-X*) AMS Pr.

Mattingly, Mary, ed. see Dickhoner, Elaine M.

Mattingly, Rick, ed. see Pinksterboer, Hugo.

Mattinson, Jan, ed. Index to Well Logging Literature, 1965-1984. 405p. (Orig.). 1985. 75.00 (*0-932602-07-X*) Pet Abstracts.

Mattioli, Leone, jt. ed. see Miller, Herbert C.

Mattioli, Maria, tr. see Swart, Susan.

Mattioli, Massimo. Squeak the Mouse. (Illus.). (Orig.). 1989. pap. 10.95 (*0-87416-070-7*) Catalan Communs.

— Squeak the Mouse Two. 1993. pap. 10.95 (*1-56163-064-0*, Eurotica) NBM.

An Asterisk (*) at the beginning of an entry indicates that the title is appearing in BIP for the first time.

— Superwest. Metz, Bernd, ed. Leighton, Tom, tr. (Illus.). 48p. 1987. 12.95 (*0-87416-035-9*) Catalan Communs.
Mattione, Richard P. OPEC's Investments & the International Financial System. LC 84-23242. 201p. 1985. 32.95 (*0-8157-5510-4*); pap. 12.95 (*0-8157-5509-0*) Brookings.
Mattione, Richard P., jt. auth. see Dale, Richard S.
Mattione, Richard P., jt. auth. see Enders, Thomas O.
Mattioni, et al. Pennsylvania Environmental Law Handbook. 3rd ed. 426p. 1991. pap. 79.00 (*0-86587-273-2*) Gov Insts.
***Mattioni, Mattioni, & Mattioni Ltd. Staff.** Pennsylvania Environmental Law Handbook. 4th ed. 426p. 1994. pap. text ed. 95.00 (*0-86587-399-2*) Gov Insts.
Mattis, Ann, ed. A Society for International Development: Prospectus 1984. LC 83-16550. (Duke Press Policy Studies). xxi, 249p. (C). 1983. text ed. 31.95 (*0-8223-0561-5*); pap. text ed. 17.00 (*0-8223-0562-3*) Duke.
Mattis, D. C. The Many-Body Problem: An Encyclopedia of Exactly Solved Models. 984p. 1993. pap. text ed. 74.00 (*981-02-1476-6*) World Scientific Pub.
— Theory of Magnetism I. (Solid-State Sciences Ser.: Vol. 17). (Illus.). xv, 300p. 1988. pap. 47.00 (*0-387-18425-2*) Spr-Verlag.
— The Theory of Magnetism II. (Solid-State Sciences Ser.: Vol. 55). (Illus.). 190p. 1985. 69.00 (*0-387-15025-0*) Spr-Verlag.
Mattis, D. C., jt. ed. see Lieb, Elliott H.
Mattis, Mary C. Flexible Work Arrangements for Managers & Professionals: Findings from a Catalyst Study. 1990. 25.00 (*0-89584-161-4*) Catalyst.
***Mattison.** Flight of Andy Burns. Date not set. pap. 3.99 (*0-517-13444-6*) Random Hse Value.
Mattison, Alice. Animals. LC 79-54884. 72p. 1979. pap. 9.95 (*0-914086-29-4*) Alicejamesbooks.
— Field of Stars: A Novel. 256p. 1992. 19.00 (*0-688-11119-X*) Morrow.
— The Flight of Andy Burns. LC 92-21641. 1993. 20.00 (*0-688-11118-1*) Morrow.
— Hilda & Pearl. large type ed. 426p. 1995. reprint ed. 21.95 (*0-7862-0494-X*) Hall.
— Hilda & Pearl: A Novel. LC 94-2634. 288p. 1994. write for info. (*0-688-13127-1*) Morrow.
Mattison, Andrew M., jt. auth. see McWhirter, David P.
Mattison, Chris. The Care of Reptiles & Amphibians in Captivity. (Illus.). 336p. 1992. pap. 17.95 (*0-7137-2338-6*, Pub. by Blandford Pr UK) Sterling.
— A Complete Guide to Exotic Pets. LC 93-85543. (Illus.). 128p. 1994. 15.98 (*1-56138-370-8*) Courage Bks.
— Frogs & Toads of the World. (Illus.). 192p. 1987. 25.95 (*0-8160-1602-X*) Facts on File.
— Keeping & Breeding Amphibians. (Illus.). 224p. 1993. 24.95 (*0-7137-2328-9*, Pub. by Blandford Pr UK) Sterling.
— Keeping & Breeding Lizards. (Illus.). 224p. 1991. 29.95 (*0-7137-2188-X*, Pub. by Blandford Pr UK) Sterling.
— Lizards of the World. (Of the World Ser.). (Illus.). 192p. 1989. 25.95 (*0-8160-1900-2*) Facts on File.
— Snakes of the World. (Illus.). 192p. 1986. 25.95 (*0-8160-1082-X*) Facts on File.
***Mattison, Chris, ed.** The Encyclopedia of Snakes. LC 95-2501. (Illus.). 288p. 1995. 35.00 (*0-8160-3072-3*) Facts on File.
***Mattison, D. R. & Olshan, A. F., eds.** Male-Mediated Developmental Toxicity. (Reproductive Biology Ser.: 1). (Illus.). 298p. 1994. 115.00 (*0-306-44815-7*, Plenum Pr) Plenum.
Mattison, Georgia & Storey, Sandra. Women in Citizen Advocacy: Stories of 28 Shapers of Public Policy. LC 91-50950. 312p. 1992. lib. bdg. 32.50x (*0-89950-700-X*) McFarland & Co.
Mattison, H. Impending Crisis of Eighteen Sixty: The Present Connection of the Methodist Episcopal Church with Slavery. LC 75-149870. (Black Heritage Library Collection). 1977. 20.95 (*0-8369-8750-0*) Ayer.
Mattison, Harry, et al, eds. El Salvador. 1983. 29.95 (*0-86316-063-8*); pap. 14.95 (*0-86316-064-6*) Writers & Readers.
Mattison, Judith. Delight in the Gift: Meditations for Mothers. LC 90-47105. 80p. (Orig.). 1991. pap. 4.99 (*0-8066-2503-1*, 9-2503, Augsburg) Augsburg Fortress.
— Divorce-The Pain & the Healing: Personal Mediations When Marriage Ends. LC 85-11140. 96p. (Orig.). 1985. pap. 8.99 (*0-8066-2128-1*, 10-1905, Augsburg) Augsburg Fortress.
— The Seven Last Words of Christ: The Message of the Cross for Today. LC 92-19355. 80p. 1992. pap. 7.99 (*0-8066-2628-3*, 9-2628) Augsburg Fortress.
Mattison, Mark. The Prophecies of Daniel: Concerning the Antichrist. (Orig.). (C). 1988. pap. 45.00 (*0-945517-05-X*) Ministry Schl Pubns.
Mattison, Mark & Gallagher, Michael. Old Testament Role-Playing. (Illus.). 106p. 1991. ring bd. 19.95 (*0-945517-17-3*) Ministry Schl Pubns.
Mattison, Mark M. The Making of a Tradition. 152p. (Orig.). 1991. pap. 5.95 (*0-945517-16-5*) Ministry Schl Pubns.
Mattison, Phillip E. Practical Digital Video Programming with Examples in C. LC 93-49734. 1994. pap. text ed. 39.95 (*0-471-31015-8*); disk 54.95 (*0-471-31016-6*) Wiley.
Mattison, Rob & Sipolt, Michael J. The Object-Oriented Enterprise: Making Corporate Information Systems Work. 1994. text ed. 45.00 (*0-07-041031-3*) McGraw.
Mattison, Robert. Understanding Database Management: An Insider's Guide to Architectures, Products, & Design. LC 92-25971. 1992. text ed. 50.00 (*0-07-040973-0*) McGraw.
Mattison, Robert S. Grace Hartigan: A Painter's World. LC 90-80947. (Illus.). 156p. 1990. 50.00 (*1-55595-041-8*) Hudson Hills.
— Robert Motherwell: The Formative Years. Foster, Stephen C., ed. LC 87-10742. (Studies in the Fine Arts: The Avant-Garde: No. 56). (Illus.). 256p. reprint ed. pap. 73.00 (*0-8357-1810-7*, 2070741) Bks Demand.
Mattison, Robert S. & Kraus, Jerelle. X=T: The Art of X-Ray Photography. (Illus.). 200p. 1995. 50.00 (*1-55595-081-7*) Hudson Hills.
***Mattison, Wendy & Scareth, Thomas, eds.** Hmong Lives: From Laos to La Crosse. Lo, Laotou, tr. (Illus.). 232p. (Orig.). 1994. pap. text ed. 12.95 (*0-9647337-0-6*) Pump Hse Regional Ctr.
Mattiza, Dorothy B. One Hundred Texas Wildflowers. Foreman, Ronald J., ed. LC 93-84561. (Illus.). 72p. (Orig.). (C). 1993. pap. 7.95 (*1-877856-35-5*) SW Pks Mnmts.
Mattler, Leon E. Facial Improvement Therapy. 45p. 1961. reprint ed. spiral bd. 4.40 (*0-7873-1195-2*) Mokelumne.
Mattlews, Edward. St. Stephen's Handbook for Altar Servers. 1994. pap. 4.95 (*0-85244-277-7*, Pub. by Gracewing UK) Morehouse Pub.
Mattlin, Everett, jt. auth. see Stolper, Michael.
Mattman. Cell Wall Deficient Forms. 2nd ed. 1992. 49.95 (*0-8493-4405-0*, QR77) CRC Pr.
Mattman, Jurg W. & Kaufer, Steve, eds. The Complete Workplace Violence Prevention Manual. (Illus.). 400p. 1994. student ed 149.00 (*0-9637790-5-2*) Inter-Act Assocs.
Matto de Turner, Clorinda. Birds Without a Nest: A Story of Indian Life in Peru. 1977. lib. bdg. 59.95 (*0-8490-1508-1*) Gordon Pr.
Matto, Edward A. A Manager's Guide to the Antitrust Laws. LC 79-54843. 207p. reprint ed. pap. 59.00 (*0-317-20775-X*, 2023907) Bks Demand.
Matto, Michele S. Twelve Steps in the Bible: A Path to Wholeness for Adult Children. LC 91-24872. 184p. 1991. pap. 7.95 (*0-8091-3264-8*) Paulist Pr.
***Mattock, et al.** SBS: Roses. (Illus.). 112p. 1995. 14.98 (*0-8317-7791-5*) Smithmark.
Mattock, John. Growing Roses. (Ward Lock Master Gardener Ser.). (Illus.). 96p. 1994. pap. 10.95 (*0-7063-7132-1*, Pub. by Ward Lock UK) Sterling.
— Identifying Guide to Roses. 1994. 6.98 (*0-7858-0052-2*) Bk Sales Inc.
Mattock, John, jt. auth. see Guy, Vincent.
Mattock, John, et al. The Complete Book of Roses. (Illus.). 256p. 1994. 29.95 (*0-7063-7163-1*, Pub. by Ward Lock UK) Sterling.
— The Complete Book of Roses. (Illus.). 240p. 1995. pap. 16.95 (*0-7063-7359-6*, Pub. by Ward Lock UK) Sterling.
***Mattock, Michael.** New Capabilities for Strategic Mobility Analysis Using Mathematical Programming. LC 94-42766. 1995. write for info. (*0-8330-1610-5*) Rand Corp.
Mattocks, A. R. Chemistry & Toxicology of Pyrrolizidine Alkloids. 1986. text ed. 129.00 (*0-12-480570-1*) Acad Pr.
***Mattogno, Carlo.** Auschwitz: The End of a Legend: A Critique of Jean-Claude Pressac. Granata, Russ, tr. (Illus.). xiii, 138p. (Orig.). (C). 1994. pap. 12.95 (*0-939484-50-1*) Inst Hist Rev.
— Auschwitz: The End of a Legend: How Was Such Mass Murder Technically Possible? (Critique on Pressac's Auschwitz Bks.). 150p. 1994. pap. 20.00 (*0-9640716-0-6*) Granata Pubng.
Matton, Mary-Ann, ed. Berlin 1986: The Archetype of Shadow in a Split World. 456p. 1987. 35.00 (*3-85630-514-9*, Pub. by Daimon Verlag SZ) Atrium Pubs.
— Berlin 1986: The Archetype of Shadow in a Split World. 456p. 1995. pap. 19.95 (*3-85630-506-8*, Pub. by Daimon Verlag SZ) Atrium Pubs.
Mattone, John G. Coal Miner's Son. LC 93-92783. 104p. (Orig.). 1994. pap. 8.00 (*1-56002-374-0*, Univ Edtns) Aegina Pr.
Mattoni, Rudi. Butterflies of Greater Los Angeles. (Illus.). (Orig.). (C). 1990. pap. text ed. 8.00 (*0-9611464-4-3*) Lepidoptera.
Mattoo, Anita. Reform Movements & Social Transformation in India. 134p. 1991. text ed. 25.00 (*81-85047-72-3*, Pub. by Reliance Pub Hse II) Apt Bks.
Mattoo, Autar K. & Suttle, Jeffrey C. The Plant Hormone Ethylene. (Illus.). 344p. 1991. 225.00 (*0-8493-4566-9*, QK898) CRC Pr.
***Mattoo, Neerga.** The Stranger Beside Me: Short Stories from Kashmir. (C). Date not set. pap. 8.50 (*81-86112-14-6*, Pub. by UBS Pubs Dist II) S Asia.
Mattoon, John S., jt. auth. see Nyland, Thomas G.
Mattoon, Mary A. Chicago 1992. 550p. 1995. 35.00 (*3-85630-538-6*, Pub. by Daimon Verlag SZ); pap. 25.00 (*3-85630-537-8*, Pub. by Daimon Verlag SZ) Atrium Pubs.
— Jungian Psychology after Jung. LC 93-45880. 64p. (Orig.). 1994. pap. 7.95 (*1-882275-03-9*) Rnd Table Pr.
— Paris Eighty-Nine: Personal & Archetypal Dynamics in the Analytical Relationship. 530p. 1995. 35.00 (*3-85630-529-7*, Pub. by Daimon Verlag SZ); pap. 25.00 (*3-85630-524-6*, Pub. by Daimon Verlag SZ) Atrium Pubs.
— Understanding Dreams. LC 84-5523. Orig. Title: Applied Dream Analysis: A Jungian Approach. vii, 248p. 1978. pap. 17.00 (*0-88214-326-3*) Spring Pubns.
Mattoon, Mary-Ann. Jungian Psychology in Perspective. 352p. 1985. pap. 16.95 (*0-02-920650-2*) Free Pr.
Mattoon, Richard W., jt. ed. see Forman, Donald T.
Mattoon, Steven. S. W. A. T. Training & Employment. (Illus.). 152p. 1987. pap. 14.00 (*0-87364-439-5*) Paladin Pr.
Mattos, N. M. An Approach to Knowledge Base Management. Siekmann, Joerg H., ed. (Lecture Notes in Artificial Intelligence Ser.: Vol. 513). xi, 247p. 1991. pap. 31.00 (*0-387-54268-X*) Spr-Verlag.
Mattotti & Kramsky. Murmur. (Illus.). 56p. (Orig.). 1993. pap. 10.00 (*0-14-016782-X*, Penguin Bks) Viking Penguin.
Mattotti, Lorenzo. Fires. Metz, Bernd, ed. Leighton, Tom, tr. (Illus.). 64p. (Orig.). 1988. 35.00 (*0-87416-064-2*); pap. 12.95 (*0-87416-048-0*) Catalan Communs.
Mattox. Techniques in Vascular Trauma. 1991. 75.00 (*0-8151-5797-5*, Yr Bk Med Pubs) Mosby Yr Bk.
Mattox, Cheryl. My Play a Tune Book: Shake It to the One That You Love the Best. (Sing a Song, Play along Series with Electronic Keyboard). (J). 1991. 14.95 (*0-938971-11-5*) JTG Nashville.
Mattox, Cheryl W. Let's Get the Rhythm of the Band. (J). (ps-3). 1993. pap. 8.95 (*0-938971-97-2*) JTG Nashville.
Mattox, Cheryl W., ed. Shake It to the One That You Love the Best: Play Songs & Lullabies from Black Musical Traditions. (Illus.). (Orig.). (J). (ps-6). 1990. pap. 7.95 (*0-9623381-0-9*) Warren-Mattox.
Mattox, D. M., et al, eds. Adhesion in Solids. (Symposium Proceedings Ser.: Vol. 119). 1988. text ed. 42.00 (*0-931837-89-8*) Materials Res.
Mattox, Gale A. & Shingleton, Bradley, eds. Germany at the Crossroads: Foreign & Domestic Policy Issues. 217p. (C). 1992. text ed. 54.00 (*0-8133-1251-5*) Westview.
Mattox, Gale A., jt. ed. see Kelleher, Catherine M.
Mattox, Henry E. Army Football in 1945: Anatomy of a Championship Season. LC 89-43659. (Illus.). 254p. 1990. lib. bdg. 43.50x (*0-89950-502-3*) McFarland & Co.
— The Twilight of Amateur Diplomacy: The American Foreign Service & Its Senior Officers in the 1890s. LC 88-29022. (American Diplomatic History Ser.: No. 2). 228p. 1989. 21.00 (*0-87338-375-3*) Kent St U Pr.
Mattox, Karl R. & Bold, Harold C. Phycological Studies, Vol. 3: The Taxonomy of Certain Ulotrichacean Algae. 66p. 1975. reprint ed. pap. 28.00 (*3-87429-098-0*) Koeltz Sci Bks.
Mattox, Kenneth L., ed. Complications of Trauma. (Illus.). 616p. 1993. text ed. 139.95 (*0-443-08851-9*) Churchill.
Mattox, Mary A. The Nurses Role in Recognizing Chemical Dependency. 16p. (Orig.). 1986. pap. 2.55 (*0-89486-364-9*, 5403B) Hazelden.
Mattox, Phil, jt. auth. see Giammatteo, Mike.
***Mattox, Rick E.** Minnesota Legal Forms: Criminal Law Forms. 240p. 1993. disk, ring bd. 69.95 (*0-614-05902-X*) Michie Butterworth.
— Minnesota Legal Forms, 1981-1993: Criminal Law Forms. (Minnesota Legal Forms Ser.). 240p. disk, ring bd. 69.95 (*0-917126-83-1*) Butterworth Legal Pubs.
— Minnesota Legal Forms, 1981-1993: Criminal Law Forms. suppl. ed. (Minnesota Legal Forms Ser.). 240p. 1993. 28.50 (*0-86678-030-0*) Butterworth Legal Pubs.
Mattox, Robert. The Christian Employee. LC 77-20588. 220p. 1978. pap. 5.95 (*0-88270-263-7*) Bridge Pub.
Mattozzi, Patricia. Little Lessons for Little Learners: Birthdays Are Special. 1993. 4.50 (*0-8378-5315-X*) Gibson.
Mattozzi, Patricia R. Eastertime. (Little Lessons for Little Learners Ser.). (Illus.). (J). 1992. 4.50 (*0-8378-2459-1*) Gibson.
— The Greatest Gift. (Little Lessons for Little Learners Ser.). (J). 1990. 4.50 (*0-8378-1887-7*) Gibson.
— Little Lessons for Little Lerners: The New Baby. (Illus.). 24p. 1994. 4.50 (*0-8378-7689-3*) Gibson.
— My Father's World: Inspirational Treasures. LC 92-12782. 1992. 3.99 (*0-517-08144-X*, Derrydale Bks) Random Hse Value.
Mattozzi, Patti. Little Lessons for Little Learners: Angels. 32p. (J). (gr. 2 up). 1989. pap. 4.50 (*0-8378-1843-5*) Gibson.
— Little Lessons for Little Learners: Heaven. (J). (gr. 3 up). 1991. 4.50 (*0-8378-1986-5*) Gibson.
— Little Lessons for Little Learners: Prayer. 32p. (J). (gr. 1 up). 1989. 4.50 (*0-8378-1844-3*) Gibson.
Matts & Sperling. Reasons for Jewish Customs & Traditions. LC 68-31711. 310p. 1989. pap. 10.95 (*0-8197-0184-X*) Bloch.
***Mattson.** Atlas of the States. Date not set. 70.00 (*0-13-324708-2*) P-H.
— Statistics: Difficult Concepts Understandable Explanations. LC 80-24947. 1984. 24.00 (*0-86516-056-2*) Bolchazy-Carducci.
Mattson, jt. auth. see Mark.
Mattson, Catherine & Mattson, Mark T. Contemporary Atlas of the United States. (Illus.). 160p. 1990. text ed. 95.00 (*0-02-897281-3*) Macmillan.
Mattson, Donald E., et al. Old Fort Snelling Instruction Book for Fife, with Music of Early America. 2nd ed. LC 74-7298. (Minnesota Historic Sites Pamphlet Ser: No. 11). 112p. 1976. pap. 8.95 (*0-87351-090-9*) Minn Hist.
Mattson, Elmer W. Professionalism: How to Enhance & Enrich Your Profession. LC 82-99894. (Illus.). (Orig.). 1982. pap. 4.95 (*0-9609084-0-4*) Motiv Unltd.
Mattson, Francis O. Edna St. Vincent Millay, 1892-1950. (Illus.). 48p. 1991. pap. 6.00 (*0-87104-429-3*) NY Pub Lib.
— Walt Whitman: In Life or Death Forever Highlights from the Library's Collections. (Illus.). 45p. 1992. pap. 10.00 (*0-87104-431-5*) NY Pub Lib.
***Mattson, Francis O., ed.** E. E. Cummings at 100. (Illus.). 80p. 1994. pap. 14.95 (*0-87104-436-6*) NY Pub Lib.
— New in the Berg Collection, 1991-1993: Manuscripts, Books, & Images from the Berg Collection. (Illus.). 31p. 1994. pap. 8.95 (*0-87104-435-8*) NY Pub Lib.
— Virginia Woolf & Her Circle: Manuscripts, Books, & Images from the Berg Collection. (Illus.). 72p. 1993. pap. 11.95 (*0-87104-434-X*) NY Pub Lib.

Mattson, Frank K. A Search for Wellness: How to Turn Back Your Biological Clock. LC 90-70585. (Search for Wellness Ser.: Vol. 1). (Illus.). 218p. 1990. 12.95 (*0-9625584-7-8*) Super G Pub Co.
When a concerned secretary volunteered how her own father had been healed of prostate problems without surgery, Mattson, a marketing executive, listened. Besides being scheduled for prostate surgery, Mattson was nursing his wife through a losing battle with lung cancer & was supporting his adult son's efforts in combating colitis. The executive's overall health was in shambles. The account of Mattson's return to exuberant health is chronicled in his new book, A SEARCH FOR WELLNESS. He shrugged off the "No known cure" philosophy & discovered valid therapies that are not widely known that resulted in improved: energy levels, mental alertness, cardiovascular function & cosmetic appearance. The author achieved dramatic changes in his health, ridding himself of a number of "Aging disorders." This work is a gold mine of information on ailments that plague us all. It answers questions like these: What are alternatives for bypass surgery? Is there any hope for people with acute circulatory problems in their legs or feet other than surgical intervention (amputation)? How does a man avoid prostate problems? What are the toxic metals? How do they affect a person? What are preventive-corrective measures? We need doctors' help, but when we take responsibility for our own health the prospect of "Growing old" can take on a different meaning. ***Publisher Provided Annotation.***

Mattson, George E. Black Belt Test Guide. LC 88-92266. (Illus.). 300p. (Orig.). 1988. pap. 20.00 (*0-930559-01-0*) Peabody Pub.
— Uechiryu Karate Do. LC 75-5978. (Illus.). 492p. (Orig.). 1974. 40.00 (*0-686-10569-9*); pap. 25.00 (*0-685-03984-6*) Peabody Pub.
— Way of Karate. 200p. 1992. pap. 16.95 (*0-8048-1852-5*) C E Tuttle.
— Way of Karate. 21.95 (*0-685-22157-1*) Wehman.
Mattson, Hans. Reminiscences: Story of an Emigrant. Scott, Franklyn D., ed. LC 78-15201. (Scandinavians in America Ser.). (Illus.). 1979. reprint ed. lib. bdg. 28.95 (*0-405-11651-9*) Ayer.
— Reminiscences: The Story of an Emigrant. (American Biography Ser.). 314p. 1991. reprint ed. lib. bdg. 79.00 (*0-7812-8278-0*) Rprt Serv.
Mattson, Harold F. Discrete Mathematics with Applications to Computer Science. LC 92-33772. 672p. 1993. Net. text ed. write for info. (*0-471-60672-3*) Wiley.
Mattson, Harold F., et al, eds. Applied Algebra, Algebraic Algorithms & Error-Correcting Codes: 9th International Symposium, AAECC-9 New Orleans, LA, U. S. A., October 7-11, 1991 Proceedings. (Lecture Notes in Computer Science Ser.: Vol. 539). xi, 489p. 1991. pap. 44.00 (*0-387-54522-0*) Spr-Verlag.
***Mattson, Heidi.** Ivy League Stripper. LC 94-23871. (Illus.). 288p. 1995. 21.95 (*1-55970-290-7*) Arcade Pub Inc.
Mattson, Ivar T. Simon. King, Ella M., ed. 188p. (Orig.). 1992. pap. 6.99 (*0-9625584-5-1*) Super G Pub Co.
Mattson, J., et al, eds. Spectroscopy & Kinetics. (Computers in Chemistry & Instrumentation Ser.: Vol. 3). 352p. 1973. 165.00 (*0-8247-6058-1*) Dekker.
***Mattson, James S.** Computer-Assisted Instruction in Chemistry Part A: General Approach. LC 73-89669. (Computers in Chemistry & Instrumentation Ser.: No. 4). 287p. 1974. reprint ed. pap. 81.80 (*0-7837-8641-7*, 2041000) Bks Demand.
Mattson, James S. & Mark, Harry B., Jr. Activated Carbon: Surface Chemistry & Adsorption from Solution. LC 74-138502. (Illus.). 247p. reprint ed. pap. 70.40 (*0-8357-6004-9*, 2034548) Bks Demand.
Mattson, James S., et al, eds. Computer-Assisted Instruction in Chemistry, Pt. B: Applications. LC 73-89669. (Computers in Chemistry & Instrumentation Ser.: No. 4). (Illus.). 1974. reprint ed. pap. 75.10 (*0-7837-0664-2*, 2041000) Bks Demand.
— Computer Fundamentals for Chemists. LC 72-91432. (Computers in Chemistry & Instrumentation Ser.: No. 1). (Illus.). 380p. reprint ed. pap. 108.30 (*0-7837-3377-1*, 2043335) Bks Demand.
— Computers in Polymer Sciences. LC 75-40603. (Computers in Chemistry & Instrumentation Ser.: No. 6). (Illus.). 390p. reprint ed. pap. 111.20 (*0-7837-0732-0*, 2041056) Bks Demand.
— Infrared, Correlation, & Fourier Transform Spectroscopy. LC 77-9460. (Computers in Chemistry & Instrumentation Ser.: No. 7). (Illus.). 247p. reprint ed. pap. 70.40 (*0-7837-0862-9*, 2041170) Bks Demand.
— Laboratory Systems & Spectroscopy. LC 75-32388. (Computers in Chemistry & Instrumentation Ser.: No. 5). (Illus.). 300p. reprint ed. pap. 85.50 (*0-7837-0729-0*, 2041053) Bks Demand.
Mattson, Jerauld, jt. ed. see Fossum, John.
Mattson, Lloyd. The Apples in a Seed. 80p. 1983. pap. 3.50 (*0-942684-04-4*) Camp Guidepts.

M

— Build Your Church Through Camping. 48p. (Orig.). 1984. pap. 1.95 (*0-942684-06-0*) Camp Guidepts.
— The Camp Counselor. (Illus.). 192p. 1984. pap. 3.95 (*0-942684-02-8*) Camp Guidepts.
— New Life in Alaska. 224p. (Orig.). 1984. pap. 7.95 (*0-942684-05-2*) Camp Guidepts.
Mattson, Lloyd, ed. God's Good Earth. (Illus.). 224p. (Orig.). 1985. pap. 25.00 (*0-942684-09-5*) Camp Guidepts.
Mattson, Lloyd & Graendorf, Werner. Introduction to Christian Camping. rev. ed. (Illus.). (C). reprint ed. pap. 7.95 (*0-942684-07-9*) Camp Guidepts.
Mattson, Margaret E., jt. auth. see Donovan, Dennis M.
Mattson, Mark. The Scholastic Environmental Atlas of the United States. LC 92-46757. 1993. 14.95 (*0-590-49354-X*, Scholastic Ref) Scholastic Inc.
Mattson, Mark T., comp. Factbook on Elementary, Middle and Secondary Schools. LC 92-34283. 1995. 39.95x (*0-590-49225-X*, 2846m3985 1993) Scholastic Inc.
Mattson, Mark T., jt. auth. see Asante, Molefi K.
Mattson, Mark T., jt. auth. see Cuff, David J.
Mattson, Mark T., jt. auth. see Mason, Robert J.
Mattson, Mark T., jt. auth. see Mattson, Catherine.
Mattson, Marylu, et al. Help Yourself: A Guide to Writing & Rewriting. 3rd ed. 320p. (C). 1983. pap. write for info. (*0-675-20027-X*, Merrill Pub Co) Macmillan.
Mattson, Patrick R. Air Traffic Control Test Prep Study Guide. (Illus.). 210p. 1991. pap. text ed. 19.95 (*0-89100-388-6*, EA-388) IAP.
Mattson, Paul. The Real American Quarter Horse: Versatile Athletes Who Proved Supreme. LC 91-90201. (Illus.). 160p. 1991. 26.00 (*1-879984-77-6*) Premier KS.
Mattson, Ralph. Visions of Grandeur: Leadership That Creates Positive Change. 1994. pap. 9.99 (*0-8024-4640-X*) Moody.
Mattson, Ralph & Black, Thom. Discovering Your Child's Design. LC 89-32705. 256p. 1989. 14.99 (*1-55513-226-X*, LifeJourney) Chariot Family.
Mattson, Ralph T., jt. auth. see Miller, Arthur F.
Mattson, Robert A. The Living Ocean. LC 89-25791. (Living World Ser.). (Illus.). 64p. (J). (gr. 6 up). 1991. lib. bdg. 15.95 (*0-89490-277-6*) Enslow Pubs.
Mattson, Susan, ed. see Organization for Obstetric, Gynecologic & Neonatal Nurses Staff.
Mattson, Ted. The Eye of the Rainbow: An Alaskan Dream & Other Tales. (Illus.). 206p. (Orig.). 1993. pap. 11.95 (*0-9605388-5-2*) Tern Pr.
Mattson, Thomas. Small Town: Reflections on People, History, Religion & Nature in Central New England. (Illus.). 366p. 1992. pap. 12.95 (*0-9633929-0-5*) Northfld Pr.
***Mattson, Timothy G., ed.** Parallel Computing in Computational Chemistry. LC 95-1232. (ACS Symposium Ser.: No. 592). (Illus.). 232p. 1995. 69.95 (*0-8412-3166-4*) Am Chemical.
Mattson, W. J., et al, eds. Mechanisms of Woody Plant Defenses Against Insects. (Illus.). 435p. 1987. 96.00 (*0-387-96673-0*) Spr-Verlag.
***Mattsson, Han & Kalbro, Thomas.** Urban Land & Property Markets in Sweden. 256p. 1995. 75.00x (*1-85728-052-0*, Pub. by UCL Pr UK) Taylor & Francis.
Mattsson, L., jt. auth. see Bennett, J. M.
Mattsson, L. G. & Stymne, B., eds. Corporate & Industry Strategies for Europe: Adaptations to the European Single Market in a Global Industrial Environment. (Advanced Series in Management: Vol. 15). 380p. 1995. 98.00 (*0-444-89182-X*, North Holland) Elsevier.
Mattsson, Lars-Goran, jt. ed. see Johansson, Borge.
Mattuck, Richard D. A Guide to Feynman Diagrams in the Many-Body Problem. (Illus.). 444p. 1992. reprint ed. pap. 1.95 (*0-486-67047-3*) Dover.
Matturro, Richard. Troy. 252p. 1989. 19.95 (*0-8027-1079-4*) Walker & Co.
— Troy. braille ed. 1991. vinyl bd. 31.68 (*1-56956-323-3*, BR8357) W A T Braille.
Mattusch, Carol C. Bronzeworkers in the Athenian Agora. (Excavations of the Athenian Agora Picture Bks.: No. 20). (Illus.). 32p. 1982. pap. 3.00 (*0-87661-624-4*) Am Sch Athens.
— Greek Bronze Statuary: From the Beginnings Through the Fifth Century B. C. LC 88-47737. (Illus.). 288p. 1988. 48.50 (*0-8014-2148-9*) Cornell U Pr.
***Mattutat, Heinrich.** Harrap's Compact Dictionary: German-French, French-German. rev. ed. 646p. (FRE & GER.). 1992. 49.95 (*0-7859-8591-3*, 055053783X) Fr & Eur.
Mattutat, Heinrich, jt. auth. see Weis, E.
Mattutat, Heinrich, jt. auth. see Weis, Erich.
Matty, Paul. Planning Publications: An Annotated Bibliography & Reference Guide. (CPL Bibliographies Ser.: No. 68). 100p. 1981. 15.00 (*0-86602-068-3*) Coun Plan Librarians.
Matual, David. Tolstoy's Translation of the Gospels: A Critical Study. LC 92-6906. 212p. 1992. lib. bdg. 89.95 (*0-7734-9502-9*) E Mellen.
Matula, Joyce. A Friend in Winter. LC 91-68091. (Illus.). 44p. (J). (gr. k-4). 1992. pap. 6.95 (*1-55523-504-2*) Winston-Derek.
Matula, Richard A., ed. see American Society of Mechanical Engineers Staff.
Matula, Susan, ed. see Goldberg, Mark.
Matulic, Rusko. Bibliography of Sources on Yugoslavia. LC 80-53861. 260p. 1981. per. 18.00 (*0-918660-13-0*) Ragusan Pr.
Matulich, Loretta K. A Cross-Disciplinary Study of the European Immigrants of 1870 to 1925. Corasco, Francesco, ed. LC 80-878. (American Ethnic Groups Ser.). 1981. lib. bdg. 30.95 (*0-405-13439-8*) Ayer.
Matulich, Serge. Financial Accounting. LC 92-64249. 870p. (C). 1993. text ed. 49.95 (*1-881934-00-4*) Unicorn Res.
— Financial Accounting. 2nd ed. LC 94-5626. (Illus.). 876p. (C). 1994. text ed. 55.45 (*1-881934-14-4*) Unicorn Res.
Matulich, Serge, et al. Financial Accounting. 2nd ed. 912p. 1985. student ed 15.95 (*0-07-040914-5*); text ed. 43.95 (*0-07-040912-9*) McGraw.
Matulich, Serge. Financial Accounting Computer Assignments. 50p. (C). 1993. student ed 9.95 (*1-881934-05-5*) Unicorn Res.
— Financial Accounting Examination Questions. 460p. (C). 1993. teacher ed write for info. (*1-881934-03-9*) Unicorn Res.
— Financial Accounting Instructor's Lecture Notes. 90p. (Orig.). (C). 1993. teacher ed write for info. (*1-881934-09-8*) Unicorn Res.
— Financial Accounting Lecture Notes. 90p. (C). 1993. student ed 7.75 (*1-881934-06-3*) Unicorn Res.
— Financial Accounting Manual. 170p. (C). 1993. teacher ed write for info. (*1-881934-04-7*) Unicorn Res.
— Financial Accounting Merchandising Practice Set. 32p. 1993. 8.50 (*1-881934-12-8*) Unicorn Res.
— Financial Accounting Solutions. 650p. (C). 1993. teacher ed write for info. (*1-881934-02-0*) Unicorn Res.
— Financial Accounting Solutions to Computer Assignments. 32p. 1993. write for info. (*1-881934-08-X*) Unicorn Res.
— Financial Accounting Study Guide. 266p. (C). 1993. student ed 17.75 (*1-881934-01-2*) Unicorn Res.
— Financial Accounting Study Guide. 2nd ed. 266p. (C). 1993. student ed 17.50 (*1-881934-13-6*) Unicorn Res.
— Financial Accounting Transparencies. 500p. (C). 1993. teacher ed write for info. (*1-881934-10-1*) Unicorn Res.
— Financial Accounting Working Papers. 50p. (C). 1993. student ed write for info. (*1-881934-07-1*) Unicorn Res.
Matulich, Serge, jt. auth. see Heitger, Lester E.
Matulionis, Raymond C. Preventive Maintenance of Building. 1991. text ed. 49.95 (*0-442-31866-9*) Van Nos Reinhold.
Matulonis, Frank. Corporate Battleground: How to Find Your Ideal Civilian Job. LC 85-90256. 164p. 1985. pap. 12.95 (*0-9623256-0-0*) F Matulonis.
Matunas, Edward. Handbook of Metallic Cartridge Reloading. LC 80-20098. (Illus.). 272p. 1981. 19.95 (*0-8329-3206-X*, Winchester Pr) New Win Pub.
Matunas, Edward A. Metallic Cartridge Reloading. 2nd ed. LC 81-70996. (Illus.). 320p. (Orig.). 1988. pap. 18.95 (*0-87349-024-X*) DBI.
— Reloading for Shotgunners. 3rd ed. LC 81-65119. (Illus.). 288p. (Orig.). 1993. pap. 16.95 (*0-87349-151-3*) DBI.
Matunde, Nwandu S. Makini's Coming of Age. (Illus.). 40p. (Orig.). (gr. 8-12). 1981. pap. text ed. 3.00 (*0-936868-01-5*) Freeland Pubns.
Matunde, Nwandu S., ed. see Brooks, Robert F.
Matunde, Skobi. Crossing the Great River: A Glimpse into the Funeral Rites of African-Americans. (Illus.). 72p. (Orig.). (C). 1990. pap. 7.00 (*0-936868-20-1*) Freeland Pubns.
— Rites of African-American People: A Glimpse into Rites of Passage of African-American People. (Illus.). (Orig.). 1990. pap. write for info. (*0-936868-21-X*) Freeland Pubns.
Matunis, Joe, jt. auth. see Hammond, Anna.
Matura, Mustapha. The Coup: A Play of Revolutionary Dreams. (Methuen Modern Plays Ser.). 69p. (Orig.). 1991. pap. 9.95 (*0-413-65260-2*, AO563, Pub. by Methuen UK) Heinemann.
— Matura: Six Plays. 374p. 1992. pap. 13.95 (*0-413-66070-2*, A0631, Pub. by Methuen UK) Heinemann.
Matura, Thaddbee. Gospel Radicalism: The Hard Sayings of Jesus. Despot, Maggi & Lachance, Paul, trs. LC 83-6249. 208p. reprint ed. pap. 59.30 (*0-8357-2684-3*, 2040220) Bks Demand.
Matura, Thadee, jt. auth. see Flood, David.
Maturano, Humberto R. & Varela, Francisco J. The Tree of Knowledge: The Biological Roots of Human Understanding. rev. ed. LC 91-50781. (Illus.). 264p. 1992. pap. 25.00 (*0-87773-642-1*) Shambhala Pubns.
Maturi, Richard J. Divining the Dow: One Hundred of the World's Most Widely Followed Stock Market Prediction Systems. 200p. 1993. 22.95 (*1-55738-475-4*) Probus Pub Co.
— Main Street Beats Wall Street: How the Top Investment Clubs Are Outperforming the Investment. 1994. 22.95 (*1-55738-804-0*) Probus Pub Co.
— Money Making Investments Your Broker Doesn't Tell You About. 1993. 22.95 (*1-55738-537-8*) Probus Pub Co.
— Stock Picking: The Eleven Best Tactics for Beating the Market. LC 93-36. 1993. text ed. 23.00 (*0-07-040937-4*); pap. text ed. 14.95 (*0-07-040938-2*) McGraw.
— Wall Street Words: From Annuities to Zero Coupon Bonds. rev. ed. 150p. 1995. 14.95 (*1-55738-865-2*) Probus Pub Co.
***Maturin, B. W.** Self-Knowledge & Self-Discipline. vi, 276p. 1995. text ed. 18.95 (*0-912141-16-6*) Roman Cath Bks.
Maturin, Charles R. The Albigenses: A Romance, 4 vols., Set. LC 73-22768. (Gothic Novels II Ser.). 1979. reprint ed. 96.95 (*0-405-06017-3*) Ayer.
— Bertram. LC 92-36902. 110p. 1992. reprint ed. 40.00 (*1-85477-120-5*, Pub. by Woodstock Bks UK) Cassell.
— The Fatal Revenge: The Family of Montorio, 3 vols., Set. LC 73-22767. (Gothic Novels II Ser.). 1979. reprint ed. 94.95 (*0-405-06018-1*) Ayer.
— Melmoth the Wanderer. Grant, Douglas & Baldick, Chris, eds. (World's Classics Ser.). 584p. 1989. pap. 9.95 (*0-19-282199-7*) OUP.
— Melmoth the Wanderer: A Tale. LC 61-5561. 434p. reprint ed. pap. 123.70 (*0-318-39742-0*, 2033114) Bks Demand.
— The Milesian Chief: A Romance, 4 vols. in 2, Set. LC 79-8172. reprint ed. 84.50 (*0-404-62038-8*) AMS Pr.
— The Wild Irish Boy. Varma, Devendra P., ed. LC 77-2043. (Gothic Novels Ser.: No. III). 1977. lib. bdg. 72.95 (*0-405-10141-4*) Ayer.
— Women, or Pour et Contre, 3 vols. in 2, Set. LC 79-8173. reprint ed. 84.50 (*0-404-62043-4*) AMS Pr.
Maturo, Cathy, ed. see Maturo, Jeffrey.
***Maturo, Jeffrey.** The ABCs of Handguns & Shooting. Maturo, Cathy, ed. (Illus.). 41p. 1995. pap. 8.95 (*0-9645196-0-7*) Ambass Pub.
Matus, Irvin L. Shakespeare: The Living Record. LC 90-8113. 192p. 1991. text ed. 45.00 (*0-312-04704-5*) St Martin.
— Shakespeare, in Fact. LC 93-16327. (Illus.). 331p. 1989. pap. text ed. 15.95 (*0-8264-0624-6*) Continuum.
***Matus, Irwin.** Wrestling with Parenthood: Contemporary Dilemmas. LC 94-41833. 180p. (Orig.). 1995. pap. 12.95 (*1-880197-12-X*) Gylantic Pub.
***Matus, Jill L.** Unstable Bodies: Victorian Representations of Sexuality & Maternity. LC 94-22957. 1995. text ed. 69.95 (*0-7190-4347-6*, Pub. by Manchester Univ Pr UK); text ed. 19.95 (*0-7190-4348-4*) St Martin.
Matus, Joel. Leroy & the Caveman. LC 92-24647. 144p. (J). (gr. 3-7). 1993. text ed. 13.95 (*0-689-31812-X*, Atheneum Bks Young) S&S Childrens.
Matus, Thomas, et al. Mystery of Master Romuald: History of Camaldolese Benedictines. 220p. (Orig.). 1994. pap. 12.00 (*0-940147-33-5*) Source Bks CA.
Matuschak. Multiple Systems Organ Failure: Hepatic Regulation of Systemic Host Defense. 408p. 1993. 165.00 (*0-8247-9059-6*) Dekker.
Matusita, K., ed. Statistical Theory & Data Analysis: Proceedings of the Pacific Area Statistical Conference, 1985. 812p. 1985. 164.00 (*0-444-87665-0*, North Holland) Elsevier.
— Statistical Theory & Data Analysis: Proceedings of the 2nd Pacific Area Statistical Conference, Tokyo, Japan, 10-12 December, 1986, Vol. II. 566p. 1988. 148.75 (*0-444-70387-X*, North Holland) Elsevier.
Matusita, K., et al, eds. Statistical Sciences & Data Analysis: Proceedings of the Third Pacific Area Statistical Conference. x, 570p. 1993. 295.00 (*90-6764-150-2*) Coronet Bks.
Matusky, Greg & Freudberg, Frank. Fifty Things You Can Do to Save American Jobs. LC 92-38090. 1993. pap. 8.95 (*0-8065-1414-0*, Citadel Pr) Carol Pub Group.
Matusky, Gregory. Hussein. (World Leaders - Past & Present Ser.). (Illus.). 112p. (J). (gr. 5 up). 1987. lib. bdg. 17.95 (*0-87754-533-2*) Chelsea Hse.
Matusky, Gregory & Hayes, John P. The U. S. Secret Service. (Know Your Government Ser.). (Illus.). 96p. (J). (gr. 5 up). 1988. lib. bdg. 14.95 (*1-55546-130-1*) Chelsea Hse.
Matusky, Gregory, jt. auth. see Raab, Steven S.
Matusky, Patricia. Malaysian Shadow Play & Music: Continuity of an Oral Tradition. (South-East Asian Social Science Monographs). (Illus.). 188p. 1994. 49.95 (*967-65-3048-4*) OUP.
Matusmoto, J. & Matusuo, T., eds. Treatment, Disposal & Management of Human Wastes: Proceedings of an IAWPRC Conference Held in Tokyo, Japan, 30 September-4 October 1985. LC 82-645900. (Water Science & Technology Ser.: No. 18). (Illus.). 428p. 1987. pap. 105.00 (*0-08-035192-1*, Pergamon Pr) Elsevier.
Matusmura, Fumio. Toxicology of Insecticides. 2nd ed. LC 85-12371. 618p. 1985. 59.50 (*0-306-41979-3*, Plenum Pr) Plenum.
Matusov, A. L. Medical Research on Arctic & Antarctic Expeditions. 216p. 1972. text ed. 56.00 (*0-7065-1282-0*, Pub. by Keter Pub IS) Coronet Bks.
Matusov, Joseph, jt. auth. see Statnikov, Roman B.
Matusow, Allen J. Farm Policies & Politics in the Truman Years. LC 67-12101. (Historical Studies: No. 80). 279p. 1967. 17.50 (*0-674-29500-5*) HUP.
— Joseph R. McCarthy. 1970. 8.95 (*0-13-566729-1*, Spectrum Bks) P-H.
— Unraveling of America: A History of Liberalism in the 1960s. LC 83-48019. (New American Nation Ser.). 560p. 1986. pap. text ed. 16.00 (*0-06-132058-7*, TB2058, Torch) HarpC.
Matusow, Allen J., jt. ed. see Bernstein, Barton J.
Matussek, N., jt. ed. see Hippius, H.
Matustik, Martin J. Postnational Identity: Critical Theory & Existential Philosophy in Habermas, Kierkegaard & Havel. LC 92-42692. (Critical Perspectives Ser.). 300p. 1993. lib. bdg. 36.95 (*0-89862-420-7*); pap. text ed. 18.95 (*0-89862-270-0*) Guilford Pr.
***Matustik, Martin J. & Westphal, Merold, eds.** Kierkegaard in Post/Modernity. LC 94-46241. (Studies in Continental Thought). 1995. write for info. (*0-253-32888-8*); pap. write for info. (*0-253-20967-6*) Ind U Pr.
Matusuo, T., jt. ed. see Matusmoto, J.
Matuszak, David F. Nelson Point: Portrait of a Northern Gold Rush Town. large type ed. LC 92-64297. (Illus.). 270p. (Orig.). 1993. pap. 19.95 (*0-9633582-0-0*) Pacific Sunset.
Matuszewki, Barbara B. Bounty on the Brandywine. (Illus.). 324p. 1988. 35.00 (*0-912608-56-0*); pap. 24.95 (*0-912608-63-3*) Mid Atlantic.
Matuszewski, Bohdan. Animal Cytogenetics, Vol. 3: Insecta, Pt. 3: Diptera I -- Cecidomyiidae. (Illus.). 144p. 1982. text ed. 54.00 (*3-443-26011-X*, Pub. by Gebruder Borntraeger GW) Lubrecht & Cramer.
Matuszewski, Daniel, jt. ed. see Thambipillai, Pushpa.
Matuszewski, James, jt. auth. see Matuszewski, Robert.
Matuszewski, Robert & Matuszewski, James. Playin' the Game: A Man's Guide to Understanding Women & Dating. A Women's Guide to Understanding the Men They Date. (Illus.). 125p. (Orig.). (YA). Date not set. pap. 8.95 (*0-9641105-6-3*) RJ Pubng.
Matutano, Jose R. Diccionario Terminologico de Quimica. 2nd ed. 786p. (ENG, GER & SPA.). 1982. pap. 105.00 (*0-7859-5095-8*) Fr & Eur.
Matute, Ana M. El Arrepentido y Otras Narraciones. (SPA.). 1989. 13.50 (*0-8288-2570-X*, S2295) Fr & Eur.
— The Heliotrope Wall & Other Stories. Doyle, Michael S., tr. 160p. 1989. text ed. 34.00 (*0-231-06556-6*) Col U Pr.
— School of the Sun. 256p. 1989. text ed. 47.50 (*0-231-06916-2*); pap. text ed. 13.00 (*0-231-06917-0*) Col U Pr.
— Soldiers Cry by Night. Miller, Yvette E., ed. Nugent, Robert & De la Camara, Maria, trs. LC 94-25087. (Discoveries Ser.). 160p. 1994. pap. 16.95 (*0-935480-67-6*) Lat Am Lit Rev Pr.
Matuz, Roger. Contemporary Literary Criticism, Vol. 45. Marowski, Daniel G., ed. 792p. 1987. 122.00 (*0-8103-4419-X*) Gale.
— Contemporary Literary Criticism, Vol. 64. 1991. 122.00 (*0-8103-4438-6*) Gale.
— Contemporary Literary Criticism, Vol. 65. 1991. 122.00 (*0-8103-4439-4*) Gale.
— Contemporary Literary Criticism, Vol. 66. 1991. 122.00 (*0-8103-4440-8*) Gale.
— Contemporary Literary Criticism, Vol. 67. 1991. 122.00 (*0-8103-4975-2*) Gale.
— Contemporary Literary Criticism, Vol. 68. 1992. 104.00 (*0-8103-4442-4*) Gale.
— Contemporary Literary Criticism, Vol. 69. 1992. 122.00 (*0-8103-4446-7*) Gale.
— Contemporary Literary Criticism, Vol. 70. 1992. 122.00 (*0-8103-4447-5*) Gale.
— Contemporary Literary Criticism, Vol. 71. 1992. 122.00 (*0-8103-4448-3*) Gale.
— Contemporary Literary Criticism, Vol. 72. 1992. 122.00 (*0-8103-4976-0*) Gale.
— Contemporary Literary Criticism, Vol. 72. 1992. 122.00 (*0-8103-4977-9*) Gale.
— Contemporary Literary Criticism, Vol. 74. 1993. write for info. (*0-8103-4978-7*); 122.00 (*0-8103-4980-9*) Gale.
— Contemporary Literary Criticism, Vol. 75. 1993. 122.00 (*0-8103-4981-7*) Gale.
— Contemporary Literary Criticism, Vol. 76. 1993. 122.00 (*0-8103-4982-5*) Gale.
— Contemporary Literary Criticism, Vol. 77. 1993. 122.00 (*0-8103-4983-3*) Gale.
— Contemporary Literary Criticism, Vol. 78. 1993. 122.00 (*0-8103-4986-8*) Gale.
— Contemporary Literary Criticism, Vol. 79. 1994. 122.00 (*0-8103-4987-6*) Gale.
— Contemporary Literary Criticism, Vol. 79. 1994. write for info. (*0-8103-4984-1*) Gale.
— Contemporary Literary Criticism, 2 Vols., Vol. 80. 1994. 122.00 (*0-8103-4988-4*) Gale.
— Contemporary Literary Criticism, Vol. 82. 1994. 122.00 (*0-8103-4990-6*) Gale.
— Contemporary Literary Criticism & Index, Vol. 68. 1992. 122.00 (*0-8103-4445-9*) Gale.
— Contemporary Literary Criticism, Vol. 63: In, Vol. 63. 1991. 122.00 (*0-8103-4437-8*) Gale.
— Contemporary Literary Criticism, Vol. 81: Yb 93, Vol. 81. 8th ed. 1994. 122.00 (*0-8103-4989-2*) Gale.
Matuz, Roger, ed. Contemporary Literary Criticism, Vol. 55. 600p. 1989. 122.00 (*0-8103-4429-7*) Gale.
— Contemporary Literary Criticism, Vol. 56. 535p. 1989. 122.00 (*0-8103-4430-0*) Gale.
— Contemporary Literary Criticism, Vol. 58. 435p. 1990. 122.00 (*0-8103-4432-7*) Gale.
— Contemporary Literary Criticism & Index, Vol. 57. 1990. 122.00 (*0-8103-4449-1*) Gale.
— Contemporary Literary Criticism Cumulative Index, Vol. 1-68. 1992. write for info. (*0-8103-4444-0*) Gale.
— Contemporary Literary Criticism, Vol. 60, Vol. 60. (Illus.). 525p. 1990. text ed. 122.00 (*0-8103-4434-3*) Gale.
— Contemporary Literary Criticism, Vol. 61, Vol. 61. (Illus.). 525p. 1990. text ed. 122.00 (*0-8103-4435-1*) Gale.
Matuz, Roger, jt. auth. see Marowski, Daniel G.
Matuz, Roger, jt. ed. see Marowski, Daniel G.
Matveev, L. T. Cloud Dynamics. 1984. lib. bdg. 162.50 (*90-277-1737-0*) Kluwer Ac.
— Fundamentals of General Meteorology: Physics of the Atmosphere. 668p. 1967. text ed. 149.50 (*0-7065-0515-8*, Pub. by Keter Pub IS) Coronet Bks.
Matveev, V. A., et al. Particles & Cosmology: International School, Bakson Valley, Moscow, 6-12 May 1991. Alexeev, E. N. et al, eds. 400p. 1992. text ed. 109.00 (*981-02-1002-7*) World Scientific Pub.
Matveev, V. B. & Salle, M. A. Darboux Transformations & Solitons. (Nonlinear Dynamics Ser.). (Illus.). 144p. 1991. 89.50 (*0-387-50660-8*) Spr-Verlag.
Matveev, Vladimir. The Commissar of the Gold Express: An Episode in the Civil War. LC 74-10088. (Soviet Literature in English Translation Ser.). (Illus.). 212p. 1974. reprint ed. 18.15 (*0-88355-174-8*) Hyperion Conn.
Matveeva, N., jt. ed. see Makarov, V.
Matwiyoff, N. A. Magnetic Resonance Workbook. 133p. 1990. 40.00 (*0-88167-558-X*) Raven.
Matxner, Egon & Streck, Wolfgang, eds. Beyond Keynesianism: The Socio-Economics of Production & Full Employment. 288p. 1994. pap. 24.95 (*1-85898-072-0*, Pub. by E Elgar Pub UK) Ashgate Pub Co.
***Matya, Marla.** Young & Naive. 350p. 1995. pap. 9.95 (*1-56901-883-9*) NW Pub.
Matyas, Antal. History of Modern Non-Marxian Economics: From Marginalist Revolution Through the Keynesian Revolution to Contemporary Monetarist Counter-Revolution. 2nd ed. LC 84-40658. 592p. 1986. text ed. 45.00 (*0-312-38166-2*) St Martin.
Matyas, C., jt. ed. see Giertych, M.

An Asterisk (*) at the beginning of an entry indicates that the title is appearing in BIP for the first time.

Matyas, Marsha L. & Malcom, Shirley M. Investing in Human Potential: Science & Engineering at the Crossroads. 165p. 1991. 9.95 (*0-87168-430-6*, 91-39S) AAAS.

Matyas, Marsha L., ed. see National Research Council, Committee on Women in Science & Engineering, Ad Hoc Panel on Interventions Staff.

Matyas, Stephen M., jt. auth. see Meyer, Carl H.

Matyi, Robert. My God - They're Real! LC 78-32013. 1979. 22.95 (*0-87949-150-7*) Ashley Bks.

Matz. Cookie, Snack, Bakery, Chemical Set. 1992. text ed. 383.80 (*0-442-30902-3*) Van Nos Reinhold.

Matz, B. W. The Inns & Taverns of Pickwick. LC 72-6748. (Studies in Dickens: No. 52). (Illus.). 261p. 1972. reprint ed. lib. bdg. 75.00 (*0-8383-1644-1*) M S G Haskell Hse.

Matz, Dale, jt. auth. see Edgar, Pamela.

***Matz, David.** Ancient World Lists & Numbers: Numerical Phrases & Rosters in Greco-Roman & Near Eastern Civilizations. 320p. 1995. lib. bdg. 44.50x (*0-7864-0039-0*) McFarland & Co.

— Greek & Roman Sport: A Dictionary of Athletes & Events from the Eighth Century B.C. to the Third Century A.D. LC 90-53509. 175p. 1991. lib. bdg. 32.50x (*0-89950-558-9*) McFarland & Co.

Matz, David E., jt. auth. see Hoffman, David A.

***Matz, Karl A.** Themes Across the Curriculum: Ready-to-Use Activities & Projects for the Elementary Classroom. 1994. spiral bd. 27.95 (*0-87628-907-3*) Ctr Appl Res.

Matz, Mary J. The Many Lives of Otto Kahn: A Biography. LC 83-26326. 320p. 1984. reprint ed. 18.00 (*0-918728-36-3*) Pendragon NY.

Matz, Onas P. History of the Second Ferrying Group Ferrying Division, Air Transport Command: New Castle Army Air Base, Wilmington, Delaware. LC 92-63231. (Illus.). 431p. 1993. lib. bdg. 49.95 (*0-9635652-0-6*) Modet Ent.

Matz, Ruth G., jt. auth. see Botsford, Margot.

Matz, S. Cookie & Cracker Technology. 3rd ed. 1992. text ed. 79.95 (*0-442-30892-2*) Chapman & Hall.

— Snack Food Technology. 3rd ed. 1992. text ed. 74.95 (*0-442-30893-0*) Chapman & Hall.

Matz, Samuel A. Administering Technical Functions in the Food Industry. (Illus.). 300p. 1995. text ed. 69.00 (*0-942849-12-4*) Pan Tech Intl.

— Bakery Technology: Nutrition, Packaging, Product Development, QA. LC 88-33634. (Illus.). 384p. 1989. text ed. 79.00 (*0-942849-03-5*) Pan Tech Intl.

— Bakery Technology & Engineering. 3rd ed. (Illus.). 853p. 1992. text ed. 129.95 (*0-442-30855-8*) Chapman & Hall.

— Bakery Technology & Engineering. 3rd ed. (Illus.). 850p. 1991. text ed. 129.00 (*0-942849-07-8*) Pan Tech Intl.

— The Chemistry & Technology of Cereals As Food & Feed. 2nd ed. (Illus.). 650p. 1991. text ed. 98.00 (*0-942849-06-X*) Pan Tech Intl.

— The Chemistry & Technology of Cereals As Food & Feed. 2nd rev. ed. (Illus.). 700p. 1991. text ed. 105.00 (*0-442-30830-2*) Chapman & Hall.

— Cookie & Cracker Technology. 3rd ed. (Illus.). 420p. 1992. 79.00 (*0-942849-09-4*) Pan Tech Intl.

— Designing Foods to Meet Special Dietary Needs. (Illus.). 300p. 1995. text ed. 69.00 (*0-942849-13-2*) Pan Tech Intl.

— Equipment for Bakers. LC 88-9747. (Illus.). 494p. (C). 1988. 69.00 (*0-942849-02-7*) Pan Tech Intl.

— Formulas & Processes for Bakers. LC 87-20607. (Illus.). 407p. 1987. 69.00 (*0-942849-01-9*) Pan Tech Intl.

— Glossary of Cereal Science & Technology. LC 94-48585. 1995. write for info. (*0-942849-14-0*) Pan Tech Intl.

— Glossary of Milling & Baking Terms. 120p. (C). 1993. lib. bdg. 29.00 (*0-942849-10-8*) Pan Tech Intl.

— Ingredients for Bakers. LC 87-8938. (Illus.). 11p. (C). 1990. text ed. 59.00 (*0-942849-00-0*) Pan Tech Intl.

— Snack Food Technology. 3rd rev. ed. LC 92-31152. (Illus.). 450p. (C). 1993. text ed. 74.00 (*0-942849-08-6*) Pan Tech Intl.

— Technology of Food Product Development. 300p. 1993. 79.00 (*0-942849-11-6*) Pan Tech Intl.

— Technology of the Materials of Baking. (Illus.). 296p. (C). 1990. text ed. 79.00 (*0-942849-04-3*) Pan Tech Intl.

***Matz, Terry.** Lost in God: Rediscovering Modern Prayer Form in Traditional Saints. LC 94-76023. 64p. (Orig.). 1994. pap. 2.95 (*0-89243-674-3*) Liguori Pubns.

***Matza, Aleks.** The Video Producer's Notebook: A Guide for Businesses, Schools, Agencies, & Professional Organizations. LC 94-44269. (Illus.). 224p. 1995. pap. 29.95 (*0-240-80229-2*, Focal) Buttrwrth-Heinemann.

Matza, David. Delinquency & Drift. 224p. 1989. pap. 18.95x (*0-88738-804-3*) Transaction Pubs.

Matza, David, jt. auth. see Sykes, Gresham M.

Matzat, Don. Christ-Esteem. LC 89-27039. 144p. 1990. pap. 7.99 (*0-89081-784-7*) Harvest Hse.

— The Lord Told Me...I Think. (Orig.). 1995. pap. 8.99 (*1-56507-370-3*) Harvest Hse.

Matzen-Lang. Clinical Preventive Medicine. 1312p. 1993. 85.00 (*0-8016-3176-9*) Mosby Yr Bk.

Matzen, Richard N., Jr. The Artist's Album. (Illus.). 48p. (Orig.). 1985. pap. 5.95 (*0-9619926-2-X*) A Mann Enterps.

Matzen, Richard N., ed. see Curzen, Leo M.

Matzen, Robert D. Carole Lombard: A Bio-Bibliography. LC 88-15429. (Bio-Bibliographies in the Performing Arts Ser.: No. 4). 181p. 1988. text ed. 45.00 (*0-313-26286-1*, MZL/, Greenwood Pr) Greenwood.

Matzer, John, Jr., ed. Advanced Supervisory Practices. LC 92-15124. (Municipal Management Ser.). 1992. pap. 29.95 (*0-87326-087-2*) Intl City-Cnty Mgt.

— Capital Financing Strategies for Local Governments. (Practical Management Ser.). (Illus.). 208p. (Orig.). 1983. pap. 23.95 (*0-87326-037-6*) Intl City-Cnty Mgt.

— Capital Projects: New Strategies for Planning, Management, & Finance. LC 89-27321. (Practical Management Ser.). 230p. 1989. pap. 23.95 (*0-87326-059-7*) Intl City-Cnty Mgt.

— Pay & Benefits: New Ideas for Local Government. (Practical Management Ser.). (Orig.). 1988. pap. text ed. 23.95 (*0-87326-056-2*) Intl City-Cnty Mgt.

— Personnel Practices for the Nineties: A Local Government Guide. (Practical Management Ser.). (Orig.). 1988. pap. text ed. 23.95 (*0-87326-055-4*) Intl City-Cnty Mgt.

— Practical Financial Management: New Techniques for Local Governments. (Practical Management Ser.). (Illus.). 207p. 1984. pap. text ed. 23.95 (*0-87326-043-0*) Intl City-Cnty Mgt.

Matzer, John, ed. Productivity Improvement Techniques: Creative Approaches for Local Government. (Practical Management Ser.). (Illus.). 180p. 1986. pap. text ed. 23.95 (*0-87326-049-X*) Intl City-Cnty Mgt.

Matzer, M., et al. Eine Revision der Lichenologischen Arten der Sammelgattung Rosellinia (Ascomycetes) (Bibliotheca Lichenologica Ser.: Vol. 37). (Illus.). 146p. 1990. pap. 56.00 (*3-443-58016-5*, Pub. by Cramer-Borntraeger GW) Lubrecht & Cramer.

Matzerath, Horst, jt. ed. see Engeli, Christian.

***Matzeu, Michele & Vignoli, Alfonso, eds.** Topological Nonlinear Analysis: Degree, Singularity, & Variations. LC 94-5251. (Progress in Nonlinear Differential Equations & Their Applications Ser.: 15). ix, 531p. 1994. 95.00 (*0-8176-3742-7*) Birkhauser.

Matzinger-Tchakerian, Margit & Odell, John. European Community Enlargement & the United States. (Pew Case Studies in International Affairs). 54p. (C). 1992. pap. text ed. 2.50 (*1-56927-130-5*) Geo U Inst Dplmcy.

Matzke, Eric. Greenberg's Guide to Marx Trains, Vol. I. Denzene, Georges, ed. (Illus.). 128p. 1989. text ed. 29.95 (*0-89778-131-7*, 10-7200) Greenberg Bks.

— Greenberg's Guide to Marx Trains, Vol. II. Denzene, Georges, ed. LC 89-16979. (Illus.). 136p. 1990. text ed. 32.95 (*0-89778-132-5*, 10-7205) Greenberg Bks.

Matzke, H., ed. Indentation Fracture & Mechanical Properties of Ceramic Fuels & Glasses. (Applied Research Reports Ser.). 246p. 1987. pap. text ed. 149.00 (*3-7186-0443-4*) Gordon & Breach.

***Matzke, H. & Schumacher, G., eds.** Nuclear Materials for Fission Reactors: Proceedings of Symposium E of the 1991 E-MRS Fall Conference, Strasbourg, France, 4-7 November 1991. (European Materials Research Society Symposia Proceedings Ser.: 29). 348p. 1992. 200.00 (*0-444-89571-X*) Elsevier.

Matzke, Hj. Science & Technology of Advanced LMFBR Fuels: A Monograph on Solid State Physics, Chemistry & Technology of Carbides, Nitrides & Carbonitrides of Uranium & Plutonium. 755p. 1986. 215.50 (*0-444-86997-2*, North Holland) Elsevier.

Matzke, Howard A. & Foltz, Floyd M. Synopsis of Neuroanatomy. 4th ed. (Illus.). 1983. pap. 14.95 (*0-19-503244-6*) OUP.

Matzke, Shirley, jt. auth. see Conroy, Dennis.

Matzler, C. Applications of the Interaction of Microwaves with the Natural Snow Cover. Becker, F., ed. (Remote Sensing Reviews Ser.: Vol. 2, No. 2). ii, 132p. 1987. pap. text ed. 113.00 (*3-7186-0416-7*) Gordon & Breach.

Matzner-Bekerman, Shoshana. The Jewish Child: Halakhic Perspectives. LC 83-19950. 314p. 1984. 20.00 (*0-88125-017-1*); pap. 14.95 (*0-88125-024-4*) Ktav.

Matzner, Egon & Streeck, Wolfgang. Beyond Keynesianism: The Socio-Economics of Production & Full Employment. 256p. 1991. text ed. 69.95 (*1-85278-424-5*, Pub. by E Elgar Pub UK) Ashgate Pub Co.

Matzner, Egon & Wagner, Michael, eds. The Employment Impact of New Technology: The Case of West Germany. 327p. 1990. text ed. 79.95 (*0-566-07177-0*, Pub. by Avebury Pub UK) Ashgate Pub Co.

Matzner, Joseph. She Loves Me, She Loves Me Knot. (Illus.). 32p. (Orig.). 1993. pap. 8.95 (*0-317-05730-8*) J Matzner.

Matzner, Richard, jt. auth. see Shepley, Lawrence.

Matzo, Marianne, jt. ed. see Fulmer, Terry.

Matzulewitsch, Leonid. Byzantinische Antike: Studien auf Grund der Silbergefaesse der Ermitage. (Archaeologische Mitteilungen aus Russischen Sammlungen Ser.: Vol. 2). (Illus.). xi, 150p. (GER.). (C). 1974. reprint ed. 542.30 (*3-11-002245-1*) De Gruyter.

Mau, August. Pompeii: Its Life & Art. 2nd ed. Kelsey, Francis W., tr. (Illus.). xxv, 557p. (C). 1982. reprint ed. lib. bdg. 60.00 (*0-89241-346-8*) Caratzas.

Mau, Jacob, jt. auth. see Kepler, Kay.

Mau, James. Social Change & Images of the Future. 192p. 1968. 18.95 (*0-87073-048-7*) Schenkman Bks Inc.

Mau, James, jt. ed. see Bell, Wendell.

Mau, Renni, jt. auth. see Wheeler, Eugene D.

Mau, Rennie, ed. see Bunas, Charlene.

Mau, Rennie, ed. see Lee, Grant S.

Mau, Rennie, ed. see Nagano, Paul.

Mau, Rennie, jt. auth. see Wheeler, Eugene D.

Mau, S. T., jt. auth. see Hsieh, Yuan-Yu.

Mau-sang Ng. The Russian Hero in Modern Chinese Fiction. LC 88-2165. 332p. 1988. 64.50 (*0-88706-880-4*); pap. 21.95 (*0-88706-881-2*) State U NY Pr.

Maubrey, Pierre. L' Expression de la Passion Interieure dans le Style de Bernanos Romancier. LC 70-94195. (Catholic University of America. Studies in Romance Languages & Literatures: No. 59). (FRE.). reprint ed. 37.50 (*0-404-50359-4*) AMS Pr.

Mauceri, Joseph. The Great Break: A Short History of the Separation of Medical Science from Religion. 156p. 1987. pap. 9.95 (*0-940170-13-2*, Pulse Bks) Station Hill Pr.

Mauch & Birch, eds. Guide to the Successful Thesis & Dissertation: A Handbook for Students & Faculty. 3rd ed. (Books in Library & Information Science: Vol. 55). 368p. 1993. 59.75 (*0-8247-8972-5*) Dekker.

Mauch, jt. auth. see Ehrenkranz, David.

***Mauch, Jack.** Competitive Writing Handbook: Five Steps To. 130p. (Orig.). 1995. pap. 7.95 (*0-614-02688-1*) NW Pub.

Mauch, James E. & Birch, Jack W. Guide to the Successful Thesis & Dissertation: Conception to Publication: A Handbook for Students & Faculty. LC 83-2112. (Books in Library & Information Science: No. 43). (Illus.). 252p. reprint ed. pap. 71.90 (*0-8357-6135-5*, 2034549) Bks Demand.

***Mauch, James E. & Sabloff, Paula L., eds.** Reform & Change in Higher Education: International Perspectives. LC 94-31729. (Garland Studies in Higher Education: No. 2). (Illus.). 308p. 1994. 46.00 (*0-8153-1706-9*, SS961) Garland.

Mauch, James E., et al. The Emeritus Professor: Old Rank - New Meaning. LC 90-60888. (ASHE-ERIC Higher Education Report Ser.: No. 2, 1990). 88p. (Orig.). (C). 1990. pap. 17.00 (*0-9623882-9-7*) GWU Schl E&HD.

Mauch, Janet L. Mauch's Sailboat Guides, 2 Vols. (Illus.). 976p. 1994. pap. 44.90 (*0-9642621-9-3*) Mauchs Sailboat. A set of two of the most comprehensive sailboat references available including specifications, interiors & illustrations on almost 800 sailboat designs by over 100 manufacturers. An invaluable tool for yacht brokers, surveyors, marine lenders, yards & an especially valuable guide for sailboat buyers. Users may review different designs on today's new or used boat market from the privacy of their own homes or offices. MAUCH'S SAILBOAT GUIDES are published as a set of two volumes (Vol. I & Vol. II) & were written & developed by a yacht broker to help eliminate confusion in the sailboat marketplace. Hundreds of different models are treated in the two volumes. The volumes are designed to help users save priceless time needed to evaluate sailboats in both the new or used boat markets. They also help users avoid wasted trips. Order this set of two volumes (books may be also ordered separately) from Mauch's Sailboat Guides, P.O. Box 24, Ortega Station, Jacksonville, FL 32210. 800-772-2460.** ***Publisher Provided Annotation.

Mauch, John J., jt. auth. see Ehrenkranz, David.

Mauch, K., jt. auth. see Lawrence, P.

Mauch, Peter & Loeffler, Jay, eds. Radiation Oncology: Technology & Biology. LC 93-31650. 1994. text ed. 110.00 (*0-7216-6724-4*) Saunders.

Mauch, Peter D. A Basic Approach to Quality Control & SPC. LC 92-44597. 61p. 1993. pap. 14.95 (*0-87389-243-7*) ASQC Qual Pr.

Mauch, Thomas, ed. see Boccaccio, Giovanni.

Mauch, Thomas, tr. see Boccaccio, Giovanni.

Mauch, Thomas, ed. see Boccaccio, Giovanni.

Mauch, Thomas, tr. see Boccaccio, Giovanni.

Mauche, Christopher W., ed. Accretion-Powered Compact Binaries. (Illus.). 496p. (C). 1990. 69.95 (*0-521-40212-3*) Cambridge U Pr.

Maucher, Helmut. Leadership in Action: Tough-Minded Strategies from the Global Giant. 1994. text ed. 19.95 (*0-07-041041-0*) McGraw.

Mauchline, J. & Nemoto, T. Marine Biology: Its Accomplishment & Future Prospect. 300p. 1991. 115.50 (*0-444-98696-0*) Elsevier.

Mauck, Christine K., et al, eds. Barrier Contraceptives: Current Status & Future Prospects. LC 93-34517. 1994. text ed. 99.95 (*0-471-30440-9*, Wiley-Liss) Wiley.

Mauck, Dave, ed. see Herrick, Rodney.

Mauck, Diane & Jenkins, Janet. Teaching Primaries. 1983. pap. 4.95 (*0-89137-610-0*); student ed, pap. 3.95 (*0-89137-612-7*) Quality Pubns.

Mauck, Marchita. Places for Worship: A Guide to Constructing & Renovating Worship Spaces. LC 94-7252. (American Essays in Liturgy Ser.). 72p. (Orig.). 1995. pap. text ed. 4.95 (*0-8146-2283-6*) Liturgical Pr.

— Shaping a House for the Church. 105p. (Orig.). 1990. pap. 9.95 (*0-929650-06-9*) Liturgy Tr Pubns.

Mauck, Scott, jt. auth. see Haynes, J. H.

Mauck, Sue I., jt. auth. see Clapp, Steve.

Mauck, Sue I., ed. see Herrick, Rodney.

Mauck, Sue I., jt. auth. see Schriner, Chris.

Mauclair, Camille. Turner. Shaw, E. B., tr. (Illus.). 168p. 1939. lib. bdg. 35.00 (*0-8288-3930-1*) Fr & Eur.

***Maud, Peter J. & Foster, Carl, eds.** Physiological Assessment of Human Fitness. LC 94-40072. (Illus.). 362p. 1995. text ed. write for info. (*0-87322-776-X*, BMAU0776) Human Kinetics.

Maud, R. R., jt. ed. see Heine, K.

***Maud, Ralph.** Charles Olson's Reading: A Biography. LC 94-44403. 1995. write for info. (*0-8093-1995-0*) S Ill U Pr.

— Charles Olson's Reading: A Biography. LC 94-44403. 448p. (C). 1995. 44.95x (*0-614-07244-1*) S Ill U Pr.

— Dylan Thomas in Print: A Bibliographical History. LC 78-101190. 273p. reprint ed. 77.90 (*0-8357-9753-8*, 2017793) Bks Demand.

Maud, Ralph, tr. & anno. The Porcupine Hunter: And Other Stories. 112p. 1994. pap. 13.95 (*0-88922-333-5*, Pub. by Talonbooks CN) InBook.

Maudadi, A. A. Tafhimul - Quran: Urdu Translation & Commentary, 6 vols., Set. 150.00 (*0-933511-70-1*) Kazi Pubns.

Maude, tr. see Tolstoy, Leo.

Maude, Angus. South Asia. LC 66-18564. 1966. 16.95 (*0-8023-1076-1*) Dufour.

Maude, Aylmer. Peculiar People, the Dukhobors. LC 72-131033. reprint ed. 24.50 (*0-404-04275-9*) AMS Pr.

— Tolstoy & His Problems. 1973. 250.00 (*0-8490-1220-1*) Gordon Pr.

Maude, Aylmer & Tomas, Vincent. What Is Art? Tolstoy. 232p. (C). 1960. pap. write for info. (*0-02-377400-2*) Macmillan.

Maude, Aylmer, tr. see Tolstoy, Leo.

Maude, Aylmer, ed. see Tolstoy, Leo.

Maude, Aylmer, tr. see Tolstoy, Leo.

Maude, Aylmer. Leo Tolstoy. LC 75-20491. (Studies in Tolstoy: No. 62). 1974. lib. bdg. 55.95 (*0-8383-2001-5*) M S G Haskell Hse.

— Leo Tolstoy & His Works. LC 74-6377. (Studies in Tolstoy: No. 62). 1974. lib. bdg. 49.95 (*0-8383-2009-0*) M S G Haskell Hse.

— Tolstoy & His Problems. LC 74-7137. (Studies in Tolstoy: No. 62). 1974. lib. bdg. 75.00 (*0-8383-1999-8*) M S G Haskell Hse.

— Tolstoy on Art. LC 72-2134. (Studies in European Literature: No. 56). 1972. reprint ed. lib. bdg. 75.00 (*0-8383-1459-7*) M S G Haskell Hse.

***Maude, George.** Historical Dictionary of Finland. LC 95-1497. (European Historical Dictionaries Ser.: No. 8). 1995. write for info. (*0-615-00498-9*) Scarecrow.

Maude, H. E. Slavers in Paradise: The Peruvian Slave Trade in Polynesia, 1862-1864. LC 81-51203. (Illus.). 264p. 1981. 35.00 (*0-8047-1106-2*) Stanford U Pr.

Maude, H. E., ed. see Grimble, Arthur F.

Maude, Jenny M. The Life of Jenny Lind. Farkas, Andrew, ed. LC 76-29953. (Opera Biographies Ser.). (Illus.). 1977. reprint ed. lib. bdg. 21.95 (*0-405-09694-1*) Ayer.

— The Life of Jenny Lind: Briefly Told by Her Daughter. LC 74-24149. (Illus.). reprint ed. 32.50 (*0-404-13041-0*) AMS Pr.

Maude, Louise, tr. see Tolstoy, Leo.

Maude, Louise, ed. see Tolstoy, Leo.

Maude, Louise, tr. see Tolstoy, Leo.

Maudgal, D. P., ed. Hypothermia: Medical & Social Aspects. LC 86-25508. (Illus.). 70p. 1987. text ed. 52.00 (*0-08-034188-8*, Pub. by Pergamon Repr UK) Franklin.

Maudgal, P. C. & Missotten, L., eds. Herpetic Eye Diseases. (Documenta Ophthalmologicia Proceedings Ser.). 1985. lib. bdg. 162.50 (*90-6193-527-X*) Kluwer Ac.

— Superficial Keratitis. 1981. lib. bdg. 94.00 (*90-6193-801-5*) Kluwer Ac.

Maudlin, John H. Prospects for Interstellar Travel. LC 57-43769. (Science & Technology Ser.: Vol. 80). (Illus.). 390p. 1992. lib. bdg. 50.00x (*0-87703-344-7*, Pub. by Am Astro Soc); pap. text ed. 27.00x (*0-87703-346-3*, Pub. by Am Astro Soc) Univelt Inc. This book shows the problem of interstellar travel to be more than just the most complex technical problem ever conceived by humans, but also a problem of astronomy, biology, psychology, sociology, politics, economics, philosophy & education - in short, it bears on almost all fields of human interest & opens profound questions about the existence of other beings & mutual searches for them & their possible travel. The book reviews most of the serious published literature on interstellar travel & is a source book for professional & amateur scientists & engineers, educators & students seeking to study a problem that integrates many fields. The book also advances the literature with new ideas & findings & provides novel tools for understanding the scope of the problem. The main text is non-mathematical, introduces all relevant principles, & is accessible to anyone wanting a contemplative journey through modern hard & soft sciences as well as a mental journey to the stars. The appendices have mathematical & physical tools, including computer programs needed for technical study of interstellar travel & related subjects. Extensive bibliography. Index. ***Publisher Provided Annotation.***

Maudlin, Tim. Quantum Non-Locality & Relativity: Metaphysical Intimations of Modern Physics. (Aristotelian Society Monograph Ser.). (Illus.). 336p. 1994. text ed. 59.95 (*0-631-18609-3*) Blackwell Pubs.

Maudoodi, Syed A. An Introduction to Understanding the Quaran. Ansari, Zafar I., tr. 48p. 1990. pap. write for info. (1-882837-21-5) Wamy Intl.

Maudslay, A. P. Archaeology: Biologia Centrali-America or, Contibutions to the Knowledge of the Fauna & Flora of Mexico & Central America. Godman, F. Ducane & Salvin, Osbert, eds. LC 74-30688. (Illus.). 907p. 1983. 285.00 (0-8061-9919-9, Milpatron Publishing Corp) U of Okla Pr.

Maudslay, A. P., tr. see Del Castillo, Bernal.

Maudslay, Alfred P., jt. auth. see Maudslay, Anne C.

Maudslay, Anne C. & Maudslay, Alfred P. A Glimpse at Guatemala: And Some Notes on the Ancient Monuments of Central America. LC 92-85006. (Illus.). 289p. 1992. reprint ed. 40.00 (0-9633895-0-5) F Silver Bks.

Maudslay, Robert. Texas Sheepman. Kupper, Winifred, ed. LC 78-157347. (Select Bibliographies Reprint Ser.). (Illus.). 1977. reprint ed. 20.95 (0-8369-5808-X) Ayer.

Maudsley, Henry. The Physiology & Pathology of Mind, 2 vols., Set. 3rd enl. rev. ed. LC 78-72810. reprint ed. 75.00 (0-404-60878-7) AMS Pr.

— Physiology & Pathology of the Mind, Vol. 4. LC 77-72191. (Contributions to the History of Psychology Ser.: Pt. C, Vol. IV, Medical Psychology). 496p. 1977. reprint ed. text ed. 75.00 (0-313-26943-2, U6943, Greenwood Pr) Greenwood.

— Responsibility in Mental Disease, Vol. 3. Bd. with Treatise on Insanity. LC 77-72191. LC 77-72191. (Contributions to the History of Psychology Ser.: Vol. III, Pt. C, Medical Psychology). 603p. 1977. reprint ed. Set text ed. 85.00 (0-313-26942-4, U6942, Greenwood Pr) Greenwood.

Maududi, A. A. Economic Problems of Man & Its Islamic Solution. pap. 3.00 (0-935782-84-2) Kazi Pubns.

— Ethical Viewpoint of Islam. pap. 2.00 (0-935782-99-0) Kazi Pubns.

— First Principles of Islamic State. pap. 3.00 (1-56744-008-8) Kazi Pubns.

— Fundamentals of Islam (Khutabat) 14.50 (0-935782-09-5) Kazi Pubns.

— Islamic Law & Constitution. 16.95 (1-56744-099-1) Kazi Pubns.

— Islamic Way of Life. pap. 4.50 (1-56744-107-6) Kazi Pubns.

— The Meaning of the Quran, 6 vols., Set. (ARA & ENG.). 160.00 (1-56744-134-3) Kazi Pubns.

— Political Theory of Islam. pap. 3.00 (1-56744-189-0) Kazi Pubns.

— Process of Islamic Revolution. pap. 3.00 (1-56744-195-5) Kazi Pubns.

— Purdah & the Status of Women in Islam. pap. 12.00 (1-56744-200-5) Kazi Pubns.

— The Religion of Truth. pap. 3.00 (0-933511-36-1) Kazi Pubns.

— Rights of Non-Muslims in Islamic State. pap. 3.00 (0-933511-41-8) Kazi Pubns.

— The Road to Salvation. pap. 3.00 (0-933511-42-6) Kazi Pubns.

— Towards Understanding Islam. pap. 4.95 (0-933511-79-5) Kazi Pubns.

Maududi, Abul A. Human Rights in Islam. 39p. (Orig.). 1981. pap. 1.95 (0-9503954-9-8, Pub. by Islamic Fnd UK) New Era Publns MI.

— Towards Understanding Islam. Ahmad, Khurshid, tr. 116p. pap. 5.95 (0-86037-053-4, Pub. by Islamic Fnd UK) New Era Publns MI.

Maududi, S. A. Economic System of Islam. 230p. (Orig.). 1993. pap. 12.50 (1-56744-263-3) Kazi Pubns.

— Islam & Ignorance. 42p. (Orig.). 1992. pap. 2.50 (1-56744-468-7) Kazi Pubns.

— Islamic Sermons (Khutabat) 262p. 1992. 12.50 (1-56744-312-5) Kazi Pubns.

Maududi, S. Abul. Holy Quran Arabic English Translation & Brief Footnotes. 29.95 (1-56744-041-X) Kazi Pubns.

Maududi, Sayyid A. Towards Understanding Islam. Ahmad, Khurshid, tr. 126p. 1977. pap. 4.00 (0-89259-151-X) Am Trust Pubns.

Mauduit, Caroline. An Architect in Italy. (Illus.). 112p. 1988. 4.99 (0-517-05595-3) Random Hse Value.

Mauduit, Israel. Observations upon the Conduct of Sir William Howe at the White Plains: As Related in the Gazette of December 30, 1776. LC 71-140874. (Eyewitness Accounts of the American Revolution Ser., No. 1). 1971. reprint ed. 14.95 (0-405-01219-5) Ayer.

Maue-Dickson, Wilma, jt. auth. see Dickson, David.

Maue-Dickson, Wilma, et al. Computed Tomographic Atlas of the Head & Neck. 453p. 1983. 145.00 (0-316-55081-7) Little.

***Mauelshagen, Carl.** The Salzburg Lutheran Expulsion & Its Impact. (Illus.). 167p. 1994. pap. text ed. 17.50 (0-7884-0002-9) Heritage Bk.

Mauer, Alison K. & Mauer, Edgar F., eds. George Dock, M.D. A Bibliography of His Writings. 2nd ed. (Illus.). 36p. 1991. pap. text ed. 20.00 (0-9631270-0-4) Fr Lib LA Cty Med.

Mauer, Alvin M., ed. The Biology of Human Leukemia. LC 89-45457. (Series in Contemporary Medicine & Public Health). (Illus.). 274p. 1990. text ed. 65.00 (0-8018-3907-6) Johns Hopkins.

Mauer, Edgar F., jt. ed. see Mauer, Alison K.

Mauer, Friedrich, ed. see Hartmann Von Aue.

Mauer, Shelley M., jt. auth. see Morford, Ted R.

Mauermayer, W. Transurethral Surgery. (Illus.). 477p. 1982. 432.00 (0-387-11869-1) Spr-Verlag.

Mauet, Thomas. United States v. William Hill: Casefile. (Illus.). 214p. 1984. 14.95 (1-55681-091-1) Natl Inst Trial Ad.

Mauet, Thomas A. Fundamentals of Litigation for Paralegals. 1991. 42.00 (0-316-55095-7) Little.

Maufort, Marc. Songs of American Experience: The Vision of O'Neill & Melville. LC 90-41225. (American University Studies: American Literature: Ser. XXIV, Vol. 24). 226p. (C). 1991. text ed. 35.00 (0-8204-1407-7) P Lang Pubs.

Maufrrij-Sherower, T. S., ed. see Sherower, Abbott W.

Maugans, Jayne E. Aging Parents, Ambivalent Baby Boomers: A Critical Approach to Gerontology. LC 93-79472. 192p. (Orig.). 1994. text ed. 34.95 (0-930390-49-0); pap. text ed. 18.95 (0-930390-23-7) Gen Hall.

Mauge, Clarence A. The Buffalo Soldier. 1993. 8.75 (0-8062-4754-1) Carlton.

***Mauge, Conrad E.** ODU IFA Bk. 1: Sacred Scriptures of IFA. 48p. 1994. pap. 6.95 (0-9637516-2-X) Hse of Providence.

— ODU IFA Bk. 2: Sacred Scriptures of IFA. 48p. 1995. pap. 6.95 (0-9637516-3-8) Hse of Providence.

—The Yoruba Religion: Introduction to its Practice. 112p. (Orig.). 1993. pap. text ed. 12.95 (0-9637516-0-3) Hse of Providence.

An intellectually stimulating & informative introduction to the practice of the fastest growing African religion in the Americas. Every journey must begin with a first step. Mauge successfully takes you through the Yoruba metaphysical & spiritual journey from heaven to earth & return. He skillfully blends the knowledges & practices of the old world with that of the New World, offering explanations that few have offered before. His chapter on Divination can be considered a textbook of classical knowledge by itself. Ancestor reverence is explained in such a way that the reader will want to communicate with his or her ancestors right away. The reader meets the Yoruba people & acknowledges their belief system which is based on the belief in a Supreme Being. His philosophical treatment of the manifold & often misunderstood subject of reincarnation explains the Yoruba perspective of non-destructible energy & life everlasting. *Publisher Provided Annotation.*

—The Yoruba World of Good & Evil. (Illus.). 180p. (Orig.). 1994. pap. 12.95 (0-9637516-1-1) Hse of Providence.

Expanding of his earlier work, Mauge takes us past the foundation of basic beliefs into the creative arena of IFA theological discourse. Spiritual concepts of America's fastest growing religion are presented by tracing their origins, showing their development & suggesting ways in which they impact upon our current personal & social conditions. The author has accepted the task of reinterpreting the eternal light of a religious tradition in the light of contemporary issues. He begins by giving a detailed account of IFA descriptions of Creation, & those Spiritual Forces that sustain the World we live in. Throughout his presentation, the reader is given access to some of the wisdom that was previously unavailable to the Western reader. The material on ORI further establishes the wisdom of IFA as the early predecessor of contemporary psychology. It is obvious to the reader that the structure of human consciousness were known to the African observers of human behaviour long before they were "discovered" by Western science. We eventually take a journey through turbulent waters in a human effort to understand the principles of male & female forces & the forces of good & evil. Mauge's writing is both an effort to reclaim lost ideas of our ancestors & an effort to relearn lost forms of social interaction. *Publisher Provided Annotation.*

Maugel, T. K., jt. auth. see Pierce, S. K.

Mauger. Cours de Langue et de Civilisation Francaise a L'usage des Etrangers, 4 tomes. Incl. Tome I. 18.95 (0-8288-9904-5, F138130); Tome II. 19.95 (0-8288-9905-3, F138131); Tome III. 24.95 (0-8288-9906-1, F138132); Tome IV. 29.95 (0-8288-9907-X, F138133); (FRE.). write for info. (0-318-51975-5) Fr & Eur.

— Grammaire Pratique du Francais d Aujourd Hui, Lanque Parlee, Laugue Ecrite. (Coll. F). 19.95 (0-685-36653-7) Fr & Eur.

— Grammaire Pratique du Francais d'Aujourd Hui, Lanque Parlee, Laugue Ecrite. 8th ed. (FRE.). 1978. pap. 25.95 (0-7859-4728-0) Fr & Eur.

— Havener's Ocular Pharmacology. 6th ed. 700p. 1994. 85.00 (0-8016-6767-4) Mosby Yr Bk.

— Scenes de la Vie Francaise. 6.95 (0-685-36697-9) Fr & Eur.

Mauger, G. Francais Accelere. 186p. (FRE.). 1964. 14.95 (0-8288-7497-2) Fr & Eur.

Mauger, Gaston. Cours De Langue et De Civilisation Francaise, 4 Vols, 1. 16.95 (2-01-008054-8) Schoenhof.

— Cours De Langue et De Civilisation Francaise, 4 Vols, 2. 15.95 (2-01-007944-2) Schoenhof.

— Cours De Langue et De Civilisation Francaise, 4 Vols, 3. 16.95 (2-01-001554-1) Schoenhof.

— Cours De Langue et De Civilisation Francaise, 4 Vols, 4. 24.95 (2-01-007945-0) Schoenhof.

Mauger, Marie-Lucie, jt. auth. see Allen-Weber, Kathleen.

Mauger, Thierry. The Ark of the Desert. (Illus.). 160p. 1991. 49.95 (0-7103-0436-6, A6715, Pub. by Kegan Paul Intl UK) Routledge Chapman & Hall.

— The Bedouins of Arabia. (Illus.). 139p. 1990. 45.00 (0-7103-0366-1, A4185, Pub. by Kegan Paul Intl UK) Routledge Chapman & Hall.

— Flowered Men & Green Slopes of Arabia. (Illus.). 189p. 1990. 45.00 (0-7103-0365-3, A4188, Pub. by Kegan Paul Intl UK) Routledge Chapman & Hall.

Maugeri, A., jt. ed. see Giannessi, Franco.

Maugham, Frederick H. The Tichborne Case. LC 74-10430. (Classics of Crime & Criminology Ser.). (Illus.). 384p. 1975. reprint ed. 19.80 (0-88355-197-7) Hyperion Conn.

Maugham, M., jt. auth. see Peace, P.

Maugham, Robin. Enemy! 1994. pap. 12.95 (1-873741-18-9, Pub. by Millvres Bks UK) InBook.

— Somerset & All the Maughams. LC 75-22759. (Illus.). 270p. 1977. reprint ed. text ed. 59.75 (0-8371-8236-0, MASOM, Greenwood Pr) Greenwood.

Maugham, S. Somerset. Gentleman in the Parlour. braille ed. 372p. 1992. vinyl bd. 29.56 (1-56956-240-7, BR8352) W A T Braille.

***Maugham, Somerset.** The Moon & Sixpence. large type ed. 390p. 1995. lib. bdg. 22.00 (0-939495-78-3) North Bks.

Maugham, Somerset W. Don Fernando. 1994. pap. 10.95 (1-56924-902-4) Marlowe & Co.

Maugham, W. S. Ten Novels & Their Authors. 301p. 1978. 6.95 (0-330-25497-9) Academy Chi Pubs.

Maugham, W. Somerset. Ah King. LC 75-26127. (Works of W. Somerset Maugham Ser.). 1977. reprint ed. 23.95 (0-405-07850-1) Ayer.

— Andalusia: The Land of the Blessed Virgin. LC 75-25381. (Works of W. Somerset Maugham Ser.). 1977. reprint ed. 23.95 (0-405-07833-1) Ayer.

— Appointment. LC 92-391. (Illus.). (J). (ps-3). 1993. 16.00 (0-671-75887-X, Green Tiger S&S) S&S Childrens.

— Ashenden. 256p. 1976. pap. 8.00 (0-14-017431-1, Penguin Classics) Viking Penguin.

— Ashenden, or, the British Agent. 22.95 (0-89190-213-9, Am Repr) Amereon Ltd.

— Ashenden, or The British Agent. large type ed. 512p. 1992. 22.95 (1-85290-034-2, Pub. by ISIS UK) Transaction Pubs.

— Ashenden, or, The British Agent. LC 76-178451. (Short Story Index Reprint Ser.). reprint ed. 14.50 (0-8369-4052-0) Ayer.

— Ashenden, or, The British Agent. LC 75-25348. (Works of W. Somerset Maugham Ser.). 1977. reprint ed. 27.95 (0-405-07805-6) Ayer.

— Cakes & Ale. 208p. 1993. 9.95 (0-14-018588-7, Penguin Classics) Viking Penguin.

— Catalina: A Romance. LC 75-25350. (Works of W. Somerset Maugham Ser.). 1977. reprint ed. 23.95 (0-405-07808-0) Ayer.

— Christmas Holiday. LC 75-25351. (Works of W. Somerset Maugham Ser.). 1977. reprint ed. 23.95 (0-405-07809-9) Ayer.

— Collected Short Stories. 448p. 1992. pap. 9.95 (0-14-018589-5, Penguin Classics) Viking Penguin.

— Collected Short Stories, Vol. 2. 1991. mass mkt. 4.95 (0-14-001872-7, Penguin Bks) Viking Penguin.

— Collected Short Stories, Vol. 2. 256p. 1992. 10.95 (0-14-018590-9, Penguin Classics) Viking Penguin.

— Collected Short Stories, Vol. 3. 256p. 1984. mass mkt. 5.95 (0-14-001873-5, Penguin Bks) Viking Penguin.

— Collected Short Stories, Vol. 4. 464p. 1993. 11.95 (0-14-018592-5, Penguin Classics) Viking Penguin.

— Creatures of Circumstance. LC 75-26130. (Works of W. Somerset Maugham Ser.). 1977. reprint ed. 23.95 (0-405-07853-6) Ayer.

— Don Fernando: Or Variations on Some Spanish Themes. LC 75-25382. (Works of W. Somerset Maugham Ser.). 1977. reprint ed. 23.95 (0-405-07834-X) Ayer.

— East of Suez: A Play in Seven Scenes. LC 75-25386. (Works of W. Somerset Maugham Ser.). 1977. reprint ed. 23.95 (0-405-07838-2) Ayer.

— The Explorer: With Four Illustrations by F. Graham Cootes. LC 75-25353. (Works of W. Somerset Maugham Ser.). 1977. reprint ed. 23.95 (0-405-07810-2) Ayer.

— First Person Singular. LC 75-26133. (Works of W. Somerset Maugham Ser.). 1977. reprint ed. 23.95 (0-405-07854-4) Ayer.

— For Services Rendered: A Play in Three Acts. LC 75-25388. (Works of W. Somerset Maugham Ser.). 1977. reprint ed. 23.95 (0-405-07839-0) Ayer.

— France at War. LC 75-25373. (Works of W. Somerset Maugham Ser.). 1977. reprint ed. 23.95 (0-405-07835-8) Ayer.

— Gentleman in the Parlour. 1994. pap. 10.95 (1-56924-903-2) Marlowe & Co.

— The Letter: A Play in Three Acts. LC 75-25389. (Works of W. Somerset Maugham Ser.). 1977. reprint ed. 23.95 (0-405-07841-2) Ayer.

— Liza of Lambeth. 126p. 1992. 8.95 (0-14-018593-3, Penguin Classics) Viking Penguin.

— The Magician. 1978. mass mkt. 5.95 (0-14-002668-1, Penguin Bks) Viking Penguin.

— The Magician. 233p. 1974. reprint ed. spiral bd. 6.60 (0-7873-0589-8) Mokelumne.

— The Making of a Saint: A Romance of Mediaeval Italy. LC 75-30388. (Works of W. Somerset Maugham Ser.). 1977. reprint ed. 26.95 (0-405-07815-3) Ayer.

— The Merry-Go-Round. 352p. 1994. 9.95 (0-14-018596-8, Penguin Classics) Viking Penguin.

— The Mixture As Before. LC 75-26134. (Works of W. Somerset Maugham Ser.). 1977. reprint ed. 23.95 (0-405-07855-2) Ayer.

— The Moon & Sixpence. 288p. 1993. pap. 4.95 (0-451-52567-1, Sig Classics) NAL-Dutton.

— Moon & Sixpence. 1995. pap. 4.95 (0-553-21441-1, Bantam Classics) Bantam.

— Mrs. Craddock. 256p. 1992. 9.95 (0-14-018594-1, Penguin Classics) Viking Penguin.

— Mrs. Craddock. LC 75-25358. (Works of W. Somerset Maugham Ser.). 1977. reprint ed. 26.95 (0-405-07817-X) Ayer.

— The Narrow Corner. 224p. 1993. 8.95 (0-14-018598-4, Penguin Classics) Viking Penguin.

— The Narrow Corner. LC 75-25359. (Works of W. Somerset Maugham Ser.). 1977. reprint ed. 23.95 (0-405-07818-8) Ayer.

— Of Human Bondage. 1976. 29.95 (0-8488-1095-3) Amereon Ltd.

— Of Human Bondage. 1991. mass mkt. 5.50 (0-553-21392-X, Bantam Classics) Bantam.

— Of Human Bondage. 704p. 1991. pap. 5.50 (0-451-52556-6, Sig Classics) NAL-Dutton.

— Of Human Bondage. 1978. mass mkt. 6.00 (0-14-001861-1, Penguin Bks) Viking Penguin.

— Of Human Bondage. (Twentieth-Century Classics Ser.). 608p. 1992. pap. 9.95 (0-14-018522-4, Penguin Classics) Viking Penguin.

— Of Human Bondage. 1981. reprint ed. lib. bdg. 41.95 (0-89966-386-9) Buccaneer Bks.

— Of Human Bondage. (Illus.). 684p. 1992. reprint ed. 33.95 (1-877767-71-9) Univ Publng Hse.

— On a Chinese Screen. braille ed. 287p. 1992. vinyl bd. 22.96 (1-56956-079-X, BR8671) W A T Braille.

— The Painted Veil. 240p. 1992. 9.95 (0-14-018599-2, Penguin Classics) Viking Penguin.

— The Painted Veil. large type ed. 1974. 15.95 (0-85456-255-9) Ulverscroft.

— Points of View: Five Essays. LC 75-25374. (Works of W. Somerset Maugham Ser.). 1977. reprint ed. 23.95 (0-405-07827-7) Ayer.

— The Razor's Edge. 1978. mass mkt. 5.95 (0-14-001860-3, Penguin Bks) Viking Penguin.

— The Razor's Edge. (Twentieth-Century Classics Ser.). 320p. 1992. pap. 8.95 (0-14-018523-2, Penguin Classics) Viking Penguin.

— The Sacred Flame: A Play in Three Acts. LC 75-25390. (Works of W. Somerset Maugham Ser.). 1977. reprint ed. 23.95 (0-405-07847-1) Ayer.

— Selected Prefaces & Introductions. LC 75-25375. (Works of W. Somerset Maugham Ser.). 1977. reprint ed. 23.95 (0-405-07828-5) Ayer.

— Sheppey: A Play in Three Acts. LC 75-30396. (Works of W. Somerset Maugham Ser.). 1977. reprint ed. 23.95 (0-405-07848-X) Ayer.

— Six Comedies. LC 75-25391. (Works of W. Somerset Maugham Ser.). 1977. reprint ed. 35.95 (0-405-07849-8) Ayer.

— Strictly Personal. LC 75-25376. (Works of W. Somerset Maugham Ser.). 1977. reprint ed. 23.95 (0-405-07829-3) Ayer.

— The Summing Up. 208p. 1992. 8.95 (0-14-018600-X, Penguin Classics) Viking Penguin.

— The Summing up. LC 75-25377. (Works of W. Somerset Maugham Ser.). 1978. reprint ed. 23.95 (0-405-07830-7) Ayer.

— Theatre. LC 75-25365. (Works of W. Somerset Maugham Ser.). 1977. reprint ed. 23.95 (0-405-07823-4) Ayer.

— Then & Now. LC 75-25364. (Works of W. Somerset Maugham Ser.). 1977. reprint ed. 25.95 (0-405-07822-6) Ayer.

— The Trembling of a Leaf. 302p. 1985. reprint ed. pap. 4.95 (0-935180-21-4) Mutual Pub HI.

— Up at the Villa. LC 75-25366. (Works of W. Somerset Maugham Ser.). 1977. reprint ed. 23.95 (0-405-07824-2) Ayer.

— The Vagrant Mood: Six Essays. LC 75-25378. (Works of W. Somerset Maugham Ser.). 1977. reprint ed. 23.95 (0-405-07831-5) Ayer.

— A Writer's Notebook. 336p. (C). 1984. mass mkt. 6.95 (0-14-002644-4, Penguin Bks) Viking Penguin.

— A Writer's Notebook. 336p. 1993. 10.95 (0-14-018601-8, Penguin Classics) Viking Penguin.

Maugham, W. Somerset, ed. see Kipling, Rudyard.

Maughan, Jackie & Maughan, Ralph. Hiker's Guide to Idaho. rev. ed. LC 84-80089. (Falcon Guide Ser.). (Illus.). 352p. 1991. pap. 12.95 (1-56044-049-X) Falcon Pr MT.

***Maughan, Jackie J., et al.** Go Tell It on the Mountain: Fire Lookout Stories & Dispatches. 256p. 1996. 19.95 (0-8117-0738-5) Stackpole.

Maughan, James T. Ecological Assessment of Hazardous Waste Sites. LC 92-27826. 1993. text ed. 69.95 (0-442-01091-5) Van Nos Reinhold.

Maughan, Ralph, jt. auth. see Maughan, Jackie.

Maughon, Martha. Why Am I Crying? 1989. 7.99 (0-929239-17-2) Discovery Hse Pubs.

An Asterisk (*) at the beginning of an entry indicates that the title is appearing in BIP for the first time.

Maugin, Gerard A. Continuum Mechanics of Electromagnetics Solids. (Applied Mathematical & Mechanics Ser.: Vol. 33). 598p. 1988. 179.50 (*0-444-70399-3*, North Holland) Elsevier.

— Material Inhomogeneities in Elasticity. LC 93-6887. (Applied Mathematics & Mathematical Computation Ser.: Vol. 3). 1993. write for info. (*0-412-49520-1*) Chapman & Hall.

— Nonlinear Electromechanical Effects & Applications. (Series in Theoretical & Applied Mechanics: Vol. 1). 184p. 1986. text ed. 47.00 (*9971-978-43-1*); pap. text ed. 28.00 (*9971-5-0096-5*) World Scientific Pub.

— The Thermomechanics of Plasticity & Fracture. (Cambridge Texts in Applied Mathematics Ser.: No. 7). (Illus.). 400p. (C). 1992. 94.95 (*0-521-39476-7*); pap. 37.95 (*0-521-39780-4*) Cambridge U Pr.

Maugin, Gerard A., ed. The Mechanical Behavior of Electromagnetic Solid Continua. 428p. 1983. 87.25 (*0-444-86818-6*, I-445-83, North Holland) Elsevier.

Maugin, Gerard A., jt. auth. see Eringen, A. Cemal.

Maugin, Gerard A., et al. Nonlinear Electromechanical Couplings. 424p. 1992. text ed. 229.00 (*0-471-93575-1*) Wiley.

Mauguiere, F., jt. auth. see Rossini, P. M.

Maui Cooks Inc. Staff. Maui Cooks. 1985. pap. 11.95 (*0-910501-30-0*) U of Missouri Mus Art Arch.

Mauila, A., et al. Dictionnaire Francais de Medicine et de Biologie, Vol. 3. 1200p. (FRE.). 1972. 195.00 (*0-7859-0746-7*, M-6394) Fr & Eur.

Mauk, A. Grant, jt. auth. see Scott, Robert A.

Mauk, Barbara, jt. auth. see Fatooh, Audrey.

***Mauk, David & Oakland, John.** American Civilization: An Introduction. LC 95-13129. 1995. write for info. (*0-415-10171-9*, Routledge NY) Routledge.

***Maul, ed.** Climatic Change in the Intra-Americas Sea. 1995. text ed. 99.95 (*0-470-24973-0*) Wiley.

Maul, Armand, et al. Microbiological Analysis in Water Distribution Networks. (Water & Waste Water Technology Ser.). 108p. 1991. text ed. 39.00 (*0-13-791039-8*, 520703) P-H.

Maul, George A. Introduction to Satellite Oceanography. 1984. lib. bdg. 178.00 (*90-247-3096-1*) Kluwer Ac.

Maul, George A., ed. Climatic Change in the Intra-Americas Sea. LC 93-6852. 1993. write for info. (*0-340-58981-7*, Pub. by E Arnold UK) Routledge Chapman & Hall.

Maul, George A., ed. see Kumar, M.

Maul, Lyle R. & Mayfield, Dianne C. The Entrepreneur's Road Map. 320p. (Orig.). 1990. pap. 12.95 (*0-929382-06-4*) Saxtons River Pubns.

— The Entrepreneur's Road Map to Business Success. rev. ed. 350p. 1992. pap. 14.95 (*0-929382-60-9*) Saxtons River Pubns.

Maul, Richard W. An Analysis of the Constitutional Provisions Pertaining to Legislative Organization in South Dakota. 1952. 5.00 (*1-55614-019-3*) U of SD Gov Res Bur.

Maul, Susan K. & Adams, Jeanette N. Childhood Cancer: A Nursing Overview. (C). 1987. boxed 59.95 (*0-86720-381-1*) Jones & Bartlett.

Maul, Terry, jt. auth. see Conrad, Eva.

Maulana Abdul Majid Daryabadi. Tafsir ul-Quran, 4 vol. set. 2800p. (C). 1985. text ed. 59.00 (*1-56744-216-1*) Kazi Pubns.

Maulana Ashraf Ali Thanawi. Khutubat-i-Jumu'ah. 110p. (Orig.). 1985. pap. 7.50 (*1-56744-317-6*) Kazi Pubns.

Maulana Muhammad Ali. A Manual of Hadith. LC 88-17974. 408p. (ARA & ENG.). 1989. reprint ed. 19.95 (*0-940793-20-2*, Olive Branch Pr) Interlink Pub.

— The New World Order. 4th ed. 86p. 1989. pap. 4.95 (*0-913321-33-8*) Ahmadiyya Anjuman.

—The Religion of Islam. 617p. 1992. reprint ed. 20.95 (*0-913321-32-X*) Ahmadiyya Anjuman.
A comprehensive discussion of the sources, principles & practices of Islam. Containing over 2000 references & analysis to 50 authoritative sources. PART I: SOURCES -- The Holy Qur'an, Hadith, Ijtihad. PART II: PRINCIPLES -- Belief in God, Angels, Revealed Books, Prophets, Life after death, Taqdir. PART III: PRACTICES -- Prayer, Zakat, Fasting, Pilgrimage, Jihad, Marriage, Property, Penal Laws, The State, Ethics etc. DETAILED INDEX including index of Arabic words & phrases. "Probably no man living has done longer or more valuable service for the cause of Islamic revival than Maulana Muhammad Ali of Lahore...THE PRESENT VOLUME IS HIS FINEST WORK...Without moving a hair's breadth from the traditional position with regard to worship & religious duties, the author shows a wide field in which changes are lawful & may be desirable because here the rules & practices are not based on an ordinance of the Qur'an or on an edict of the Prophet...we recommend it as a stimulus to Islamic thought"--(Marmaduke Pickthall, translator of Qur'an into English) "...deeply engrossing...reflects the author's scholarship & sincerity in every line."--(Times of Ceylon), "... extremely useful work almost indispensable to the students of Islam"--(M. Iqbal poet philosopher). Available from: AAII 1315 Kingsgate Rd, Columbus, OH 43221. (614) 457-8504; FAX (614) 457-4455, Baker & Taylor & Ingram Books. ***Publisher Provided Annotation.***

— The Religions of Islam. 808p. 1986. 90.00 (*0-317-52151-9*, Pub. by S Chand II) St Mut.

Maulana Muhammad Kandhlawi. Hayatus Sahabah: The Lives of the Sahabah, 2 vol. set. Majiid Ali Khan, tr. 450p. (C). 1991. text ed. 69.00 (*1-56744-287-0*) Kazi Pubns.

— Hayatus Sahabah: The Lives of the Sahabah, Vol. 1. Majid Ali Khan, tr. 430p. (C). 1991. text ed. write for info. (*1-56744-288-9*) Kazi Pubns.

Maulana Muhammad Zaigham, tr. see Shaikh Wali-ud-Din Khatab.

Maulana Muhammed Ali. Holy Qur'an. rev. ed. vi, 1256p. (ARA & ENG.). 1991. reprint ed. 19.95 (*0-913321-01-X*) Ahmadiyya Anjuman.
A highly acclaimed work, first published in 1917, the first generally available English rendering by a Muslim. Revised by the translator & re-published in 1951. Contains the Arabic text & English translation in parallel columns, with explanatory notes underneath. The translation is idiomatic, yet more faithful to the Arabic original than other translations. Detailed notes discuss meanings of all important words, review previous explanations of various passages & reach an interpretation with scholarly integrity. All conclusions are based on sound principles & strong arguments. There are extensive references to standard authorities. Modern criticism is fully dealt with & misconceptions about Islam are cleared. Comprehensive introduction deals with Islamic teachings & the collection of the Qur'an. Extensive index of subjects & of Arabic words. "..a work of which any scholar might be proud, & as a translator the author has always had the reputation of being accurate & reliable." --(Times of Ceylon). "The skillful presentation of the research shows that he has been an apt scholar in the school of Western methodology."--(The Quest, London). "Among human productions of literary masterpieces,...undoubtedly claims a position of distinction & pre-eminence...deserves to be extensively read."--(United India & Indian States). ***Publisher Provided Annotation.***

Maulana S. Tilmiz H. Rizvi. Guide Book of Qur'an. 1990. pap. 3.95 (*0-685-66726-X*, 126) Tahrike Tarsile Quran.

Maulbetsch, J. S., et al. Basic Research in Heat Transfer. 158p. 1977. pap. 7.25 (*0-318-12589-7*, M60177) Am Gas Assn.

***Mauldin.** Up Front. 50th fac. ed. 240p. 1995. 19.95 (*0-393-03816-5*) Norton.

Mauldin, Bill. Back Home. 23.95 (*0-89190-856-0*, Am Repr) Amereon Ltd.

— Bill Mauldin's Army: Bill Mauldin's Greatest World War II Cartoons. (Illus.). 384p. 1983. reprint ed. 30.00 (*0-89141-180-1*); reprint ed. pap. 14.95 (*0-89141-159-3*) Presidio Pr.

— Up Front. 19.95 (*0-89190-896-X*, Am Repr) Amereon Ltd.

— Up Front. 1994. lib. bdg. 24.95x (*1-56849-444-0*) Buccaneer Bks.

— Up Front: A Fiftieth Anniversary Edition. (Illus.). 240p. 1991. 21.95 (*0-393-03053-9*) Norton.

Mauldin, Christopher A. Honor Bound: The Life of Harvey P. Everest. (Oklahoma Commerce & Industry Hall of Honor Ser.). (Illus.). 149p. (Orig.). (C). 1989. text ed. 24.95 (*0-9623357-0-3*); pap. text ed. 12.95 (*0-685-26157-3*) Okla City Univ Pr.

Mauldin, D., ed. The Scottish Book. 320p. (C). 1982. 32.50 (*0-8176-3045-7*) Birkhauser.

Mauldin, John H. Light, Lasers & Optics. (Illus.). 240p. 1988. 22.95 (*0-8306-9038-7*, 3038); pap. 16.95 (*0-8306-9338-6*, 3038) TAB Bks.

— Particles in Nature: The Chronological Discovery of the New Physics. (Illus.). 288p. 1986. 23.95 (*0-8306-0416-2*, 2616); pap. 16.95 (*0-8306-0516-9*, 2616P) TAB Bks.

— Sun Spaces-Home Additions for Year-Round Natural Living. LC 87-21913. (Illus.). 256p. 1987. 21.95 (*0-8306-7816-6*, 2816) TAB Bks.

Mauldin, Michael L. Conceptual Information Retrieval: A Case Study in Adaptive Partial Parsing. 240p. (C). 1991. lib. bdg. 68.00 (*0-7923-9214-0*) Kluwer Ac.

Mauldin, Pam, ed. see Hagglund, Howard E.

Mauldin, R., et al. Measure & Measurable Dynamics. LC 89-14914. (CONM Ser.: Vol. 94). 326p. 1989. pap. 57.00 (*0-8218-5099-7*, CONM-94) Am Math.

Mauldin, W. P., jt. ed. see Ross, J. A.

Mauldon, Margaret, tr. see Zola, Emile.

Maule, A. J., jt. ed. see Svenson, Olga.

Maule, Elizabeth M. Bird's Eye Views of Wisconsin Communities: A Preliminary Checklist. LC 77-24430. 1977. pap. 2.00 (*0-87020-168-9*) State Hist Soc Wis.

Maule, H. G. & Weiner, J. S., eds. Design for Work & Use: Case Studies in Ergonomics Practice, Vol. 2. LC 81-139177. 150p. 1981. 51.00 (*0-85066-208-7*) Taylor & Francis.

Maule, Harry E., ed. Great Tales of the American West. reprint ed. lib. bdg. 25.95 (*0-88411-875-4*, Aeonian Pr) Amereon Ltd.

Maule, Helen L., ed. see Hastings, Diana.

Maule, Henry. Caen: The Brutal Battle & Breakout from Normandy. LC 89-893. (Battle Standards Ser.). (Illus.). 176p. (C). 1989. reprint ed. lib. bdg. 25.00x (*0-8095-7502-7*) Borgo Pr.

Maule, James E. S Corporations: State Law & Taxation, 2 vols., Set. 1990. 250.00 (*0-685-28165-5*) Clark Boardman Callaghan.

Maule, James E., jt. auth. see Clay, Alvin A., III.

Maule, Jeremy, jt. ed. see Poole, Adrian.

***Maule, Magie.** Contemporary Stencils. 1994. pap. 14.00 (*0-207-18291-4*, Pub. by Angus & Robertson AT) HarpC.

Maule, Magie M. Decorative Stencils for Interior Design: More Than 150 Stencil Motifs, from Classical... 1992. pap. 17.00 (*0-207-17095-9*, Pub. by Angus & Robertson AT) HarpC.

— Floral Stencils: For Interior Design. 120p. 1993. pap. 15.00 (*0-207-17501-2*, Pub. by Angus & Robertson AT) HarpC.

Mauleon, Rebeca. The Salsa Guidebook for Piano & Ensemble. (Illus.). 259p. (C). 1993. pap. 20.00 (*0-9614701-9-4*) Sher Music.

Maulik, D. & McNellis, D., eds. Doppler Ultrasound Measurement of Maternal-Fetal Hemodynamics. LC 87-29083. (Reproductive & Perinatal Medicine Ser.: No. VIII). 1987. 77.50 (*0-916859-29-0*) Perinatology.

Maulik, S. Coleoptera - Phytophaga - Chrysomelidae: Chrysomelinae & Halticinae. (Fauna of British India Ser.). (Illus.). xiv, 442p. 1977. reprint ed. 30.00 (*0-88065-156-3*, Messers Today & Tomorrow) Scholarly Pubns.

— Coleoptera - Phytophaga - Chrysomelidae: Galerucinae. (Fauna of British India Ser.). (Illus.). xiv, 658p. 1979. reprint ed. 30.00 (*0-88065-157-1*, Messers Today & Tomorrow) Scholarly Pubns.

— Coleoptera - Phytophaga - Chrysomelidae: Hispinae & Cossidinae. (Fauna of British India Ser.). xii, 442p. 1973. reprint ed. 16.00 (*0-88065-155-5*, Messers Today & Tomorrow) Scholarly Pubns.

Maulitz, Russell C. Morbid Appearances: The Anatomy of Pathology in the Early Ninetenth Century. (Cambridge History of Medicine Ser.). (Illus.). 272p. 1987. 59.95 (*0-521-32828-4*) Cambridge U Pr.

Maulitz, Russell C., ed. Unnatural Causes: The Three Leading Killer Diseases in America. 210p. 1989. text ed. 37.00 (*0-8135-1405-3*); pap. text ed. 16.00 (*0-8135-1406-1*) Rutgers U Pr.

Maulitz, Russell C., tr. see Grmek, Mirko D.

Maull. Advances in Trauma, Vol. 3. 288p. 1988. 69.95 (*0-8151-5787-8*, Yr Bk Med Pubs) Mosby Yr Bk.

— Advances in Trauma, Vol. 4. 352p. 1989. 69.95 (*0-8151-5789-4*, Yr Bk Med Pubs) Mosby Yr Bk.

— Advances in Trauma, Vol. 5. 256p. 1990. 69.95 (*0-8151-5788-6*, Yr Bk Med Pubs) Mosby Yr Bk.

— Advances in Trauma, Vol. 6. 257p. 1991. 69.95 (*0-8151-5782-7*) Mosby Yr Bk.

— Advances in Trauma, Vol. 7. 236p. 1992. 69.95 (*0-8151-5783-5*) Mosby Yr Bk.

— Advances in Trauma, Vol. 8. 300p. 1993. 69.95 (*0-8151-6200-6*, Yr Bk Med Pubs) Mosby Yr Bk.

— Advances in Trauma, Vol. 9. 270p. 1994. 69.95 (*0-8151-6201-4*, Yr Bk Med Pubs) Mosby Yr Bk.

— Advances in Trauma, Vol. 10. 270p. 1995. 69.95 (*0-8151-6202-2*, Yr Bk Med Pubs) Mosby Yr Bk.

— Advances in Trauma, Vol. 11. 270p. 1996. 69.95 (*0-8151-6203-0*, Yr Bk Med Pubs) Mosby Yr Bk.

Maull, B. Maull. Bailey, R. F., ed. 241p. 1991. reprint ed. lib. bdg. 53.00 (*0-8328-2053-9*); reprint ed. pap. 43.00 (*0-8328-2054-7*) Higginson Bk Co.

Maull, Diana, jt. auth. see Carmicheal, David W.

Maull, Hanns & Pick, Otto, eds. The Gulf War: Regional & International Dimensions. 350p. 1990. text ed. 49.95 (*0-312-03738-4*) St Martin.

Maull, Hanns W. Energy, Minerals, & Western Security. LC 84-15410. 431p. reprint ed. pap. 122.90 (*0-7837-2190-0*, 2042528) Bks Demand.

— Natural Gas & Economic Security. (Atlantic Papers: No. 43). 60p. (Orig.). 1981. pap. text ed. 10.50 (*0-86598-082-9*) Rowman.

Maull, Kimball, et al. Trauma Update for the EMT. 272p. 1992. pap. 24.00 (*0-89303-889-X*, 740503) P-H.

Maulmier, Thierrey. Diccionario Terminologia Politica. 340p. (SPA.). 1977. pap. 19.95 (*0-8288-5366-5*, S50250) Fr & Eur.

Maultsby, Maxie C., Jr. Coping Better, Anytime, Anywhere: The New Handbook of Rational Self-Counseling. (Illus.). 1990. reprint ed. pap. 12.95 (*0-932838-05-7*) Ratnl Self-Help Aids.

— Guia Ilustrada del Medico Para Auto-Tratemiento Emocional. Munoz, Gabriela & Maultsby, Rossnilda O., trs. (Illus.). 109p. (SPA.). 1990. reprint ed. pap. 7.95 (*0-932838-06-5*) Ratnl Self-Help Aids.

— Help Yourself to Happiness. LC 75-15057. 1975. pap. 9.95 (*0-917476-06-9*) Inst Rational-Emotive.

— Rational Behavior Therapy. (Illus.). 288p. (C). 1984. pap. 28.95 (*0-13-752907-4*) P-H.

— Rational Behavior Therapy: The Self-Help Psychotherapy. (Illus.). 1990. reprint ed. pap. 16.95 (*0-932838-08-1*) Ratnl Self-Help Aids.

— Relapse Prevention Treatment for Alcoholics & Other Addicted People. (Illus.). 233p. 1990. reprint ed. pap. 9.95 (*0-932838-03-0*) Ratnl Self-Help Aids.

— You & Your Emotions. (Illus.). 109p. 1990. reprint ed. pap. 7.95 (*0-932838-01-4*) Ratnl Self-Help Aids.

Maultsby, Rossnilda O., tr. see Maultsby, Maxie C., Jr.

***Maulucci, Anthony.** The Discovery of Luminous Being. LC 94-96880. 112p. 1995. pap. 7.95 (*0-9645226-0-8*) Lorenzo Pr.

Maum, Ima G., pseud. Beyond Ramen Noodles: How to Feed Yourself When You Don't Have the Time, the Space, or the Equipment, & You Can't Afford to Eat Every Meal Out. (Illus.). 132p. (Orig.). 1993. pap. 9.95 (*1-883770-00-9*, El Moro Pr) El Moro Pub.

***Maumee Valley Herb Society Staff, et al.** There's More to Life Than Parsley. (Illus.). 192p. (Orig.). 1994. pap. 12.95 (*0-9644350-0-4*) Maumee Vall Herb Soc.

Maumela, T. N. Mafangambiti: The Story of a Bull. (Staffrider Ser.: No. 38). 112p. (C). 1986. pap. 8.95 (*0-86975-284-7*, Pub. by Ravan Pr ZA) Ohio U Pr.

***Maumenee, A. Edward.** A. Edward Maumenee, M. D. The Wilmer Ophthalmological Institute at the Johns Hopkins University & the Stanford Medical School. (Ophthalmology Oral History Ser.). (Illus.). xxx, 267p. 1994. pap. 45.00 (*1-56055-068-6*) FAAO.

Maun, Clint & Haacker, Robert W. Power Tools. 85p. (Orig.). 1992. per. 169.00 (*0-929442-15-6*) Publicare Pr.

Maun, Clint & Thorson, James A. Are You Still Working at the Home? A Book for Human Service Professionals. (Long Term Care Ser.). 96p. 1992. pap. 7.95 (*0-9631371-1-5*) Longterm Pr.

Maun, Clint, jt. auth. see Haacker, Robert W.

***Maund, Barry.** Colours: Their Nature & Representation. (Studies in Philosophy). 272p. (C). Date not set. 49.95 (*0-521-47273-3*) Cambridge U Pr.

Maund, K. L. Ireland, Wales & England in the Eleventh Century. (Studies in Celtic History: Vol. 12). (Illus.). 240p. (C). 1991. text ed. 71.00 (*0-85115-533-2*) Boydell & Brewer.

Maunder, Allen, ed. Agriculture in a Turbulent World Economy: Proceedings of the 19th International Conference of Agricultural Economists. 740p. 1986. text ed. 62.95 (*0-566-05225-3*, Pub. by Avebury Pub UK) Ashgate Pub Co.

Maunder, Aller & Ohkawa, Kazushi, eds. Growth & Equity in Agricultural Development: Proceedings of the Eighteenth International Conference of Agricultural Economists. 619p. 1984. text ed. 99.95 (*0-566-00636-7*) Ashgate Pub Co.

Maunder, Colin. The Designer's Guide to Testable Logic Circuits. (Illus.). 208p. (C). 1992. pap. text ed. 35.50 (*0-201-56513-7*) Addison-Wesley.

Maunder, Colin & Tulloss, Rodham. Test Access Port & Boundary-Scan Architecture. LC 90-39682. 400p. 1990. text ed. 55.00 (*0-8186-9070-4*, 2070) IEEE Comp Soc.

Maunder, Elwood R. & Davidson, Margaret, eds. First National Colloquium on the History of Forest Products Industry. vii, 221p. 1967. pap. 16.00 (*0-8223-0266-7*) Duke.

Maunder, Elwood R., jt. auth. see Clepper, Henry E.

***Maunder, John W.** Dictionary of Global Climate Change. 2nd ed. LC 92-19059. 257p. 1995. pap. 24.95 (*0-412-99581-6*) Chapman & Hall.

Maunder, Leonard. Machines in Motion. (Illus.). 192p. 1987. 34.95 (*0-521-30034-7*) Cambridge U Pr.

Maunder, Richard. Mozart's Requiem: On Preparing a New Edition. (Illus.). 240p. 1988. 55.00 (*0-19-316413-2*) OUP.

***Maunder, Richard, ed.** Domenico Corri's a Select Collection of the Most Admired Songs, Duetts, &C., Volume 4, & the Singer's Preceptor, Vols. 1-2. LC 93-8550. (Domenico Corri's Treatises on Singing Ser.: Vol. 3). 328p. 1995. 115.00 (*0-8153-0681-4*) Garland.

— Domenico Corri's, Vols. 1-3: A Select Collection of the Most Admired Songs, Duetts, & C. LC 93-8550. (Domenico Corri's Treatises on Singing Ser.: No.1). 364p. 1993. 119.00 (*0-8153-0679-2*) Garland.

— The Musical Sources for Domenico Corri's: A Select Collection of the Most Admired Songs, Duets, & C., 1-3, Set. LC 93-8550. (Domenico Corri's Treatises on Singing Ser.: No. 2). 608p. 1994. 150.00 (*0-8153-0680-6*) Garland.

— The Musical Sources for Domenico Corri's a Select Collection of the Most Admired Songs, Duetts, & C., the Singer's Preceptor. LC 93-8550. (Domenico Corri's Treatises on Singing Ser.: Vol. 4). 272p. 1995. 115.00 (*0-8153-0845-0*) Garland.

Maunder, W., jt. auth. see Bosworth, D. L.

Maunder, W., jt. auth. see Lock, G.

Maunder, W., jt. auth. see Walker, M. A.

Maunder, W. F. Employment in an Underdeveloped Area. LC 73-19566. (Caribbean Ser.). 215p. 1974. reprint ed. text ed. 55.00 (*0-8371-7296-9*, MAUA, Greenwood Pr) Greenwood.

Maunder, W. F. & Coppock, J. T., eds. Land Use & Town & Country Planning. 1978. 100.00 (*0-08-022451-2*, Pub. by Pergamon Repr UK) Franklin.

Maunder, W. F., ed. see Baxter, R. E. & Phillips, C.

Maunder, W. F., jt. auth. see Bishop, C. F.

Maunder, W. F., ed. see Buckley, P. & Pearce, R. D.

Maunder, W. F., ed. see Mark, J., et al.

Maunder, W. F., ed. see Wilson, R. A. & Bosworth, D. L.

Maunder, W. J. The Human Impact of Climate Uncertainty: Weather Information, Economic Planning, & Business Management. 240p. 1989. 49.95 (*0-415-04076-0*, A3673); pap. 14.95 (*0-415-04077-9*, A3677) Routledge.

— The Uncertainty Business. 1987. 55.00 (*0-416-36100-5*) Routledge Chapman & Hall.

Maunder, W. John, comp. Dictionary of Global Climate Change. LC 92-19059. 256p. 1992. 45.00 (*0-412-03901-X*, A9802, Chap & Hall NY) Chapman & Hall.

Maunders, Keith, jt. auth. see Foley, Bernard.

Mauner, George. Three Swiss Painters: Cuno Amiet, Giovanni Giacometti, Augusto Giacometti: Exhibition Catalogue. (Illus.). 166p. 1973. pap. 7.50 (*0-911209-02-6*) Palmer Mus Art.

Mauner, George, et al, eds. Paris: Center of Artistic Enlightenment. (Papers in Art History: Vol. IV). (Illus.). 250p. (Orig.). 1988. pap. 22.00 (*0-915773-03-1*) Penn St Univ Dept Art Hist.

Maung, M. Ismael. Estimates of Burma's Mortality, Age Structure, & Fertility, 1973-83. (Papers of the East-West Population Institute: No. 116). vii, 66p. (Orig.). 1990. pap. 3.00 (*0-86638-128-7*) EW Ctr HI.

Maung, Mya. The Burma Road to Poverty. LC 90-27555. 360p. 1991. text ed. 69.50 (*0-275-93613-9*, C3613, Praeger Pubs) Greenwood.

Maung Tin, tr. see Buddhaghosa.

Maung, U. Maung. Burmese Nationalist Movements, 1940-1949. LC 90-11053. 416p. (C). 1991. text ed. 39.00 (*0-8248-1342-1*) UH Pr.

Maunuhal Singh. Strategy of International Business. 240p. 1986. 19.00 (*81-7003-069-2*, Pub. by S Asia Pubs II) S Asia.

Maupas, P. & Guesry, P., eds. Hepatitis B Vaccine. (INSERM Symposium Ser.: No. 18). 318p. 1981. 112.00 (*0-444-80325-4*) Elsevier.

Maupas, P., jt. ed. see Melnick, J. L.

Maupertius, Pierre L. Oeuvres, 4 vols., Set. liii, 1590p. 1974. reprint ed. write for info. (*3-487-01056-9*, Pub. by Georg Olms GW) Lubrecht & Cramer.

Maupin, Armistead. Back to Barbary Lane: The Final Tales of the City Omnibus. LC 90-56366. 720p. 1991. 27.50 (*0-06-016649-5*, HarpT) HarpC.

— Maybe the Moon: A Novel. LC 92-52596. 320p. 1993. reprint ed. pap. 12.00 (*0-06-092434-9*, PL) HarpC.

— More Tales of the City. LC 92-52596. (Tales of the City Ser.). 320p. 1992. 11.00 (*0-685-60778-X*, PL) HarpC.

— More Tales of the City. 1994. pap. 12.00 (*0-06-092479-9*, PL) HarpC.

— Tales of the City. 371p. 1994. 31.00x (*0-8095-9139-1*) Borgo Pr.

— Tales of the City. LC 77-11781. 384p. 1994. reprint ed. pap. 12.00 (*0-06-092480-2*, PL) HarpC.

— Twenty-Eight Barbary Lane: The Tales of the City Omnibus. 1990. 27.50 (*0-06-016466-2*, HarpT) HarpC.

Maupin, B. Blood Platelets in Man & Animals, 2 vols., Set. 1969. 427.00 (*0-08-006405-1*, Pub. by Pergamon Repr UK) Franklin.

Maupin, G. W., Jr., et al, eds. Extending the Life of Bridges. LC 90-40769. (Special Technical Publication (STP) Ser.: STP 1100). (Illus.). 140p. 1990. text ed. 35.00 (*0-8031-1402-8*) ASTM.

Mauquoy-Hendrickx, Marie. Van Dyck's Prints (L'Iconographie d'Antoine van Dyck), Catalogue Raisonne, 2 vols. 2nd ed. (Illus.). 450p. (FRE.). 1991. pap. 120.00 (*1-55660-226-X*) A Wofsy Fine Arts.

— Wierix Family Prints (Les Estampes des Wierix), Catalogue Raisonne, 4 vols. (Illus.). 1983. pap. 295.00 (*1-55660-225-1*) A Wofsy Fine Arts.

Maura. What We Women Know. 3rd ed. (Vagrom Chap Book Ser.: No. 15). 41p. 1981. 3.95 (*0-935552-05-7*) Sparrow Pr.

Maura, P. Roderick. Dr. Morgan's Guide to North American Wild Life: 1992-1993 Edition. 258p. 1992. pap. 16.95 (*0-9630814-7-0*) Dr Morgans.

Maurais, Jacques. Lexicon of Carbonated Beverages: Lexiques des Boissons Gazeuses. 40p. (ENG & FRE.). 1980. pap. 14.95 (*0-8288-4818-1*, M9241) Fr & Eur.

— Lexicon of Food Chemistry: Lexique de la Chimie Alimentaire. 10th ed. 119p. (ENG & FRE.). 1981. pap. 9.95 (*0-8288-0837-6*, M6656) Fr & Eur.

— Lexicon of Spices & Seasonings: Lexique des Epices et Assaisonnements. 44p. (ENG & FRE.). 1980. pap. 14.95 (*0-8288-4817-3*, M9236) Fr & Eur.

Maurais, Jacques & Villa, T. Guide de Redaction des Menus Anglais-Francais: English-French Menu Translation Guide. 10th ed. 153p. (ENG & FRE.). 1980. pap. 9.95 (*0-8288-0838-4*, M9237) Fr & Eur.

Maurais, Jacques, et al. Lexicon of Pasta, 1982. 3rd ed. 43p. (ENG & FRE.). 1980. pap. 14.95 (*0-8288-0839-2*, M9243) Fr & Eur.

Mauran, J. E. & Stockbridge, J. C. Memorials of the Mauran Family. 171p. 1993. reprint ed. lib. bdg. 39.50 (*0-8328-3799-7*); reprint ed. pap. 29.50 (*0-8328-3800-4*) Higginson Bk Co.

Maurande, G., jt. auth. see Pierre, C.

Maure, Erin. Wanted Alive. 111p. (Orig.). 1983. pap. 8.95 (*0-88784-097-3*, Pub. by Hse of Anansi Pr CN) Genl Dist Srvs.

Maureau, Paul M. The Masardis Saga: Nineteenth Century Life in Aroostook County, Maine. LC 83-50686. (Illus.). 160p. (Orig.). 1985. pap. 10.95 (*0-931474-28-0*) TBW Bks.

Maurel, Victor. Dix Ans de Carriere, 1887-1897. Farkas, Andrew, ed. LC 76-29954. (Opera Biographies Ser.). (Illus.). (FRE.). 1977. reprint ed. lib. bdg. 35.95x (*0-405-09695-X*) Ayer.

Maurello, S. Ralph. Commercial Art Techniques. (Illus.). 10. 95 (*0-8148-0612-0*); pap. 7.95 (*0-8148-0056-4*) L Amiel Pub.

Mauren, Mary L. Creating Communities of Good News: A Handbook for Small-Group Facilitators. LC 92-64035. 80p. (Orig.). 1992. pap. 8.95 (*1-55612-473-2*, LL1473) Sheed & Ward MO.

Maurenbrecher, Berthold. Forschungen Zur Lateinischen Sprachgeschichte und Metrik. 269p. (GER.). 1979. reprint ed. write for info. (*3-487-06049-3*, Pub. by Georg Olms GW) Lubrecht & Cramer.

Maurens, Jacques, ed. see Voltaire, Francois-Marie de.

Maurer. Aviation in the U. S. Army, 1919-1939. (Illus.). 626p. 1987. 29.00 (*0-912799-38-2*); pap. 29.00 (*0-912799-40-4*) Off Air Force.

— Combat Squadrons of the Air Force in World War II: History & Insignia. 1983. reprint ed. 29.95 (*0-89201-097-5*) Zenger Pub.

Maurer & Gilbert, James B., eds. Air Force Combat Units of World War II. LC 79-7285. (Flight: Its First Seventy-Five Years Ser.). 1980. reprint ed. lib. bdg. 44.95 (*0-405-12194-6*) Ayer.

Maurer, A. E., et al, eds. The Works of John Dryden: Prose, 1691-1698, De Arte Graphica & Shorter Works, Vol. XX. LC 55-7149. (Illus.). 546p. 1990. 60.00 (*0-520-02133-9*) U CA Pr.

Maurer, Adah. Corporal Punishment Handbook. (Illus.). 32p. 1981. 3.50 (*0-932141-01-3*) End Violence.

— Instead of Spanking: 1001 Alternatives, Vol. 2. (Illus.). 1986. 6.50 (*0-932141-06-4*) End Violence.

— One-Thousand-One Alternatives to Corporal Punishment, Vol. 1. (Illus.). 58p. 1984. 5.95 (*0-932141-03-X*) End Violence.

Maurer, Adah, jt. auth. see Taylor, Leslie.

Maurer, Armand A. About Beauty: A Thomistic Interpretation. LC 83-70939. 141p. (Orig.). 1983. pap. text ed. 6.95 (*0-9605456-1-1*, 85-06065) U of St Thomas.

— St. Thomas & Historicity. LC 79-84278. (Aquinas Lectures). 1979. 10.00 (*0-87462-144-5*) Marquette.

Maurer, B. B., ed. Mountain Heritage. 4th ed. (Illus.). 352p. 1989. reprint ed. pap. 12.00 (*0-87012-279-7*) McClain.

Maurer, Bonnie. Old Thirty Seven: The Mason Cows. (Illus.). 32p. (Orig.). 1981. pap. 6.00 (*0-935306-09-9*) Barnwood Pr.

Maurer, Charles B. Call to Revolution: The Mystical Anarchism of Gustav Landauer. LC 75-14827. 219p. reprint ed. pap. 62.50 (*0-8357-7976-9*, 2027659) Bks Demand.

Maurer, Christopher, ed. see Garcia Lorca, Federico.

Maurer, Christopher, tr. see Gracian, Baltazar.

Maurer, Christopher, tr. see Hernandez, Mario.

Maurer, Christopher, ed. see Lorca, Federico G.

Maurer, Christopher, tr. see Lorca, Francisco G.

Maurer, D. W. The Argot of the Racetrack. (Publications of the American Dialect Society: No. 16). 70p. 1951. pap. 7.15 (*0-8173-0616-1*) U of Ala Pr.

***Maurer, David W.** The American Confidence Man. 316p. 1974. pap. 24.95 (*0-398-06272-2*) C C Thomas.

— The American Confidence Man. 316p. 1974. 39.95 (*0-398-02974-1*) C C Thomas.

— Whiz Mob. 1964. 21.95 (*0-8084-0321-4*) NCUP.

Maurer, David W. & Pearl, Quinn. Kentucky Moonshine. LC 74-7880. (Kentucky Bicentennial Bookshelf Ser.). (Illus.). 162p. reprint ed. pap. 46.20 (*0-8357-4295-4*, 2037094) Bks Demand.

***Maurer, Debra K.** Taffy for the Tooth Fairy. (Illus.). (J). (ps-4). 1996. 13.95 (*1-880092-29-8*) Bright Bks TX.

Maurer, Diane. Marbling: Creating Beautiful Patterned Papers & Fabrics. 1991. 15.99 (*0-517-02019-X*) Random Hse Value.

***Maurer, Diane V.** Marbling: A Complete Guide to Creating Beautiful Patterned Papers & Fabrics. 1994. pap. 11.95 (*1-56799-113-0*, Friedman-Fairfax) M Friedman Pub Grp Inc.

Maurer, Donna. Annie, Bea, & Chi Chi Dolores: A School Day Alphabet. LC 92-25104. (Illus.). 32p. (J). (ps-k). 1993. 14.95 (*0-531-05467-5*); lib. bdg. 14.99 (*0-531-08617-8*) Orchard Bks Watts.

***Maurer, Donna & Sobal, Jeffery.** Food, Eating, & Nutrition As Social Problems. (Social Problems & Social Issues Ser.). 352p. 1995. pap. 26.95 (*0-202-30508-2*) Aldine de Gruyter.

— Food, Eating, & Nutrition As Social Problems. (Social Problems & Social Issues Ser.). 352p. 1995. lib. bdg. 51. 95 (*0-202-30507-4*) Aldine de Gruyter.

Maurer, Edward L. Selected Ethics & Protocols in Chiropractic. 270p. 1991. 54.00 (*0-8342-0277-8*) Aspen Pub.

Maurer, Edward S. Perfumes & Their Production. LC 59-17885. 328p. reprint ed. pap. 93.50 (*0-317-26615-2*, 2025424) Bks Demand.

Maurer, Ernest W. The Dream Is Alive: Space Flight & Operations in Earth Orbit. (Illus.). 320p. (Orig.). (C). 1991. pap. text ed. 29.95 (*0-9628591-0-9*) Geosync Pubns.

Maurer, Evan E. Gerome Kamrowski: A Retrospective Exhibition. (Illus.). 120p. 1983. pap. 7.95 (*0-912303-27-1*) Michigan Mus.

Maurer, Evan E., intro. Sculpture of Africa: Selections from a Private Collection. (Illus.). 52p. 1984. 5.00 (*0-912303-41-7*) Michigan Mus.

Maurer, Evan M., pref. Mignonette Yin Cheng. (Illus.). 46p. (Orig.). (C). 1988. pap. 5.00 (*0-912303-40-9*) Michigan Mus.

Maurer, Evan M. & Roberts, Allen F. The Rising of a New Moon: A Century of Tabwa Art. (Illus.). 288p. (Orig.). (C). 1986. pap. 39.95 (*0-912303-32-8*) Michigan Mus.

Maurer, Evan M., jt. ed. see Roberts, Allen F.

Maurer, Frances A., jt. auth. see Smith, Claudia M.

Maurer, Friedrich & Rupp, Heinz, eds. Deutsche Wortgeschichte, Vol. 1. 3rd ed. LC 73-88302. (Grundriss der Germanischen Philologie Ser.: Vol. 17, Pt. 1). 581p. (C). 1974. 157.70 (*3-11-003627-4*) De Gruyter.

— Deutsche Wortgeschichte, Vol. 2. 3rd rev. ed. (Grundriss der Germanischen Philologie Ser.: Vol. 17, Pt. 2). vi, 698p. (GER.). (C). 1974. 169.25 (*3-11-003619-3*) De Gruyter.

— Deutsche Wortgeschichte, Vol. 3. 3rd ed. (Grundriss der Germanischen Philologie Ser.: Vol. 17, Pt. 3). (C). 1978. 113.10 (*3-11-003620-7*) De Gruyter.

Maurer, Friedrich, ed. see Gottfried, Strassburg.

Maurer, George, jt. auth. see Uncle Hyggly.

Maurer, Gerald. Echocardiography & Doppler in Cardiac Surgery. LC 89-11154. (Illus.). 376p. 1989. 115.00 (*0-89640-161-8*) Igaku-Shoin.

— Transesophageal Echocardiography. (Illus.). 304p. 1994. text ed. 149.00 (*0-07-040988-9*) Hlth Prof Div.

Maurer, H. A., ed. Automata, Languages & Programming: Sixth Colloquium. (Lecture Notes in Computer Science Ser.: Vol. 71). 1979. pap. 48.00 (*0-387-09510-1*) Spr-Verlag.

— New Results & New Trends in Computer Science: Graz, Austria, June 20-21, 1991 Proceedings. (Lecture Notes in Computer Science Ser.: Vol. 555). viii, 403p. 1991. pap. 48.00 (*0-387-54869-6*) Spr-Verlag.

Maurer, Hans W., jt. ed. see Kearney, Robert L.

Maurer, Hans W., jt. ed. see Kearny, Robert L.

Maurer, Harold M., ed. Pediatrics. LC 82-9423. 1097p. reprint ed. pap. 180.00 (*0-7837-6247-X*, 2045959) Bks Demand.

Maurer, Harold M. & Ruymann, Frederick B. Rhabdomyosarcoma & Related Tumors in Children & Adolescents. (Illus.). 504p. 1991. 156.00 (*0-8493-6902-9*, RC281) CRC Pr.

Maurer, Harry. Sex: An Oral History. LC 93-27432. 544p. 1994. 22.95 (*0-670-84564-7*, Viking) Viking Penguin.

— Sex: Real People Talk about What They Really Do. 560p. 1995. pap. 12.95 (*0-14-017145-2*, Penguin Bks) Viking Penguin.

— Strange Ground: Americans in Vietnam, 1945-1975. 656p. 1990. reprint ed. pap. 12.95 (*0-380-70931-7*) Avon.

Maurer, Heinz F., jt. auth. see Mange, Maria A.

Maurer, Hermann, ed. Educational Multimedia & Hypermedia Annual 1993. (Illus.). 662p. (Orig.). 1993. pap. 45.00 (*1-880094-06-1*) Assn Advan Comput Educ.

Maurer, Herrymon. The Power of Truth. (C). 1950. pap. 3.00 (*0-87574-053-7*) Pendle Hill.

Maurer, Herrymon, ed. Pendle Hill Reader. LC 74-142668. (Essay Index Reprint Ser.). 1977. reprint ed. 20.95 (*0-8369-2415-0*) Ayer.

Maurer, J. R. Developments in the Power Industry: Heat Exchanger Technologies & Materials Improvements. LC 93-73003. (PWR Ser.: Vol. 23). 124p. 1993. 35.00 (*0-7918-0998-6*, H00830) ASME.

***Maurer, Jack R., ed.** Heat Exchanger Technology for the Global Environment: International Joint Power Generation Conference, Phoenix, AZ, 1994. 173p. 1994. pap. 40.00 (*0-7918-1381-9*) ASME.

Maurer, Janet R. Building a New Dream: A Family Guide to Coping with Chronic Illness & Disability. 1990. pap. 9.57 (*0-201-55098-9*) Addison-Wesley.

***Maurer, Jay.** Focus on Grammar: An Advanced Course for Reference & Practice. 1995. write for info. (*0-201-65693-0*) Addison-Wesley.

— Focus on Grammar Advanced. 176p. 1995. teacher ed, pap. write for info. (*0-201-65694-9*) Addison-Wesley.

— Focus on Grammar Advanced, Vol. B. 208p. 1995. student ed, pap. write for info. (*0-201-82585-6*) Addison-Wesley.

— Focus on Grammar Advanced Students Book Vol. A. 224p. (J). Date not set. pap. text ed. write for info. (*0-201-82584-8*) Addison-Wesley.

Maurer, Jay, jt. auth. see LaPorte, Penny.

Maurer, Joan H. Curly: An Illustrated Biography of the Superstooge. (Illus.). 256p. 1985. 19.95 (*0-8065-0979-1*, Citadel Pr) Carol Pub Group.

— CURLY: An Illustrated Biography of the Superstooge. (Illus.). 224p. 1988. pap. 14.95 (*0-8065-1086-2*, Citadel Pr) Carol Pub Group.

— The Three Stooges Book of Scripts. LC 84-17614. (Illus.). 256p. 1984. 19.95 (*0-8065-0933-3*) Carol Pub Group.

Maurer, Joan H. & Maurer, Norman. The Three Stooges Book of Scripts, Vol. II. (Illus.). 256p. 1987. 19.95 (*0-8065-1018-8*, Citadel Pr) Carol Pub Group.

Maurer, Joan H., et al. The Three Stooges Scrapbook. (Illus.). 256p. 1985. reprint ed. pap. 16.95 (*0-8065-0946-5*, Citadel Pr) Carol Pub Group.

Maurer, John, jt. ed. see Goldstein, Erik.

Maurer, John H. & Porth, Richard H. Military Intervention in the Third World: Threats, Constraints, & Options. LC 84-11685. (Foreign Policy Issues Ser.). 1984. text ed. 59. 95 (*0-275-91223-X*, C1223, Praeger Pubs) Greenwood.

Maurer, Judy A., tr. see Sandberg, Inger.

***Maurer, Karl.** Evidence of Interpolation in the Text of Thucydides. LC 95-10386. (Mnemosyne, Bibliotheca Classica Batava: Supplementum Ser.: Vol. 150). 1995. write for info. (*90-04-10300-7*) E J Brill.

Maurer, Katharine. Intellectual Status at Maturity As a Criterion for Selecting Items in Preschool Tests, Vol. 21. LC 46-5115. (Illus.). ix, 166p. 1970. reprint ed. text ed. 45.00 (*0-8371-7895-9*, CWMP, Greenwood Pr) Greenwood.

Maurer, Katharine, jt. auth. see Goodenough, Florence L.

Maurer, Kent L., jt. auth. see Locke, David R.

Maurer, Konrad, ed. Imaging of the Brain in Psychiatry & Related Fields. LC 92-49551. 1993. 145.00 (*0-387-54785-1*) Spr-Verlag.

Maurer, Konrad & Dierks, T. Atlas of Brain Mapping: Topographic Mapping of EEG & Evoked Potentials. (Illus.). xi, 103p. 1991. 70.00 (*0-387-53090-8*) Spr-Verlag.

Maurer, Konrad, et al, eds. Alzheimer's Disease Epidemiology, Neuropathology, Neurochemistry, & Clinics: Proceedings, International Congress on Alzheimer's Disease, Wurzburg, June 1989. (Key Topics in Brain Research Ser.). (Illus.). 600p. 1990. pap. 114.00 (*0-387-82197-X*) Spr-Verlag.

Maurer, Linda K. I Don't Know How to Help Them. 48p. 1993. pap. 5.95 (*0-9636977-0-6*) L K Maurer.

***Maurer-Mathison, Diane.** Make Your Own Spectacular Valentines. (Illus.). (J). (ps-5). 1995. 12.95 (*0-316-54557-0*) Little.

***Maurer-Mathison, Diane V. & Philippoff, Jennifer.** Papercraft: Making & Decorating Paper. LC 94-27976. 1995. write for info. (*1-56799-151-3*, Friedman-Fairfax) M Friedman Pub Grp Inc.

Maurer, Maurer. Air Force Combat Units of World War II. reprint ed. 29.95 (*0-89201-092-4*) Zenger Pub.

Maurer, Maurer, ed. Air Force Combat Units of World War II. LC 94-13389. 1994. 12.98 (*0-7858-0194-4*, Chrtwell) Bk Sales Inc.

— Air Force Combat Units of World War II. (Illus.). 506p. (C). 1984. reprint ed. 14.00 (*0-685-09259-3*) Off Air Force.

Maurer, Norman, jt. auth. see Maurer, Joan H.

Maurer, Pierre, jt. auth. see Milivojevic, Marko.

Maurer, Richard. Junk in Space. (J). (gr. 3 up). 1989. pap. 14.95 (*0-671-67768-3*, S&S Bks Young Read); pap. 5.95 (*0-671-67747-0*, S&S Bks Young Read) S&S Childrens.

— The NOVA Space Explorer's Guide: Where to Go & What to See. LC 90-20074. (Illus.). 128p. (J). (gr. 3-7). 1991. 20.00 (*0-517-57758-5*, Clarkson Potter) Crown Bks Yng Read.

— Rocket! How a Toy Launched the Space Age. LC 94-19243. (J). 1995. write for info. (*0-517-59628-8*); lib. bdg. write for info. (*0-517-59629-6*) Crown Bks Yng Read.

***Maurer, Richard E.** Designing Alternative Assessments for Interdisciplinary Curriculum. LC 95-15017. 1996. write for info. (*0-205-17393-4*) Allyn.

— Managing Conflict: Tactics for School Administrators. 272p. 1991. text ed. 35.95 (*0-205-12668-5*, H26685, Longwood Div) Allyn.

***Maurer, Rick.** Beyond the Wall of Resistance: Unconventional Strategies That Build Support for Change. (Illus.). 208p. 1995. 24.95 (*1-885167-07-5*) Bard & Stephen.

— Caught in the Middle: A Leadership Guide for Partnership in the Workplace. LC 91-23238. 258p. 1992. 30.00 (*1-56327-004-8*) Prod Press.

— The Feedback Toolkit: 16 Tools for Better Communication in the Workplace. LC 94-11842. (Illus.). 50p. (Orig.). 1994. pap. 12.00 (*1-56327-056-0*) Prod Press.

Maurer, Robert J. Drug-Free Workplace. 198p. (Orig.). 1989. Employer's handbook, 198 p. pap. 85.00 (*0-317-93916-5*); Supervisor's guide, 24 p. pap. 40.00 (*0-317-93917-3*) ACET NY.

— Drug-Free Workplace Employer's Handbook. 198p. (Orig.). 1989. pap. 85.00 (*0-685-25974-9*) ACET NY.

Maurer, Ruth A., jt. auth. see Parker, Joni M.

Maurer, Stephen, ed. Guide to Wild & Scenic Rio Chama. (Illus.). 32p. 1991. pap. 5.95 (*1-879343-05-3*) SW NCH Assn.

***Maurer, Stephen B. & Ralston, A.** Discrete Algorithmic Mathematics. 720p. (C). 1991. text ed. 58.25 (*0-201-15585-0*) Addison-Wesley.

Maurer, Stephen G., ed. Grand Canyon by Stage. (Illus.). 24p. (Orig.). 1982. reprint ed. pap. 3.85 (*0-910467-00-5*) Heritage Assocs.

— Trail Guide to Pecos Wilderness: Santa Fe National Forest. (National Forest Visitors Guide Ser.). (Illus.). 192p. 1991. pap. 9.95 (*1-879343-01-0*) SW NCH Assn.

— Visitors Guide to Kaibab National Forest: Chalender, Williams & Tusayan Ranger Districts. (National Forest Visitors Guide Ser.). (Illus.). 128p. (Orig.). 1990. pap. 6.95 (*1-879343-00-2*) SW NCH Assn.

Maurer, Steve. Wild Dogs. 24p. (Orig.). 1981. pap. 3.50 (*0-940846-01-2*) Hastings Bks.

Maurer, Thomas. Contact & Photocontact Allergens: A Manual of Predictive Test Methods. (Dermatology Ser.: Vol. 3). (Illus.). 192p. 1983. 99.75 (*0-8247-7013-7*) Dekker.

***Maurer, Tracy M. & Woolf, Joni W.** Macon: An American Enterprise Book. Putz, Robyn & Turner, James E., eds. (Illus.). 240p. 1995. 39.00 (*1-885352-20-4*) Community Comm.

Maurer, Virginia G. Business Law: Text & Cases. 2nd ed. 1228p. (C). 1987. text ed. 59.00 (*0-15-505648-4*); student ed, pap. text ed. 20.50 (*0-15-505649-2*) Dryden Pr.

Maurer, W. C. Novel Drilling Techniques. 1968. 56.00 (*0-08-012734-7*, Pub. by Pergamon Repr UK) Franklin.

Maurer, W. D. The Programmer's Introduction to SNOBOL. LC 75-26837. (Elsevier Computer Science Library Ser.: No. 3). 142p. 1976. pap. 29.75 (*0-444-00172-7*, North Holland) Elsevier.

***Maurer, Walter.** The Sanskrit Language: An Introductory Grammar & Reader, 2 vols., Set. 838p. (C). 1995. text ed. 120.00 (*0-7007-0352-7*, Pub. by Curzon Pr UK) Humanities.

Maurer, Ward D. The Programmer's Introduction to SNOBOL. LC 75-26837. (Programming Languages Series Elsevier Computer Science Library). 151p. reprint ed. pap. 43.10 (*0-685-15469-6*, 2026270) Bks Demand.

— Programming: An Introduction to Computer Techniques. 2nd rev. ed. LC 70-188126. (Illus.). (C). 1972. text ed. 32.95 (*0-8162-5453-2*) Holden-Day.

Maurer, Warren R. Understanding Gerhart Hauptmann. Hardin, James N., ed. LC 92-14308. (Understanding Modern European & Latin American Literature Ser.). 196p. (C). 1992. text ed. 34.95 (*0-87249-823-9*) U of SC Pr.

Maurer, Wilhelm. Historical Commentary on the Augsburg Confession. Anderson, H. George, tr. LC 86-45214. 464p. 1986. 35.00 (*0-8006-0781-3*, 1-781, Fortress Pr) Augsburg Fortress.

An Asterisk (*) at the beginning of an entry indicates that the title is appearing in BIP for the first time.

Maurette, Michel. Hunting for Stars. Leonard, Isabel A., tr. LC 93-23978. (McGraw-Hill Horizons of Science Ser.). 1994. pap. text ed. 11.95 (*0-07-041029-1*) McGraw.

Maurey, B, jt. auth. see Ghoussoub, N.

Maurey, Eugene. Exorcism: How to Clear at a Distance a Spirit Possessed Person. LC 88-51882. (Illus.). 176p. 1989. pap. 12.95 (*0-914918-88-5*) Midwest Bks.

— Forward Observer. (YA). 1994. write for info. (*0-9626906-1-9*); pap. write for info. (*0-9626906-0-0*) Midwest Bks.

— Power of Thought: How to Control What Happens to You. (Illus.). 96p. (Orig.). 1990. pap. write for info. (*0-318-68473-X*) Midwest Bks.

— Power of Thought: How to Control What Happens to You. (Illus.). 95p. (Orig.). 1992. pap. text ed. 5.95 (*0-9626906-2-7*) Midwest Bks.

Mauri, C. Biological & Clinical Aspects of Phagocyte Function: (International Congress, Pavia, Italy, Sept. 1986) Roath, S. & Corn, M., eds. (Hematology Reviews & Communications Ser.: Vol. 1). vii, 182p. 1986. pap. text ed. 145.00 (*3-7186-0354-3*) Gordon & Breach.

Mauri, C., et al, eds. The Biology of Phagocytes in Health & Disease: Proceedings of the International Congress on the Biological & Clinical Aspects of Phagocyte Function, 7-10 September, 1986, Pavia, Italy. 651p. 1988. 120.00 (*0-08-036133-1*, Pergamon Pr) Elsevier.

Mauriac, Claude. Le Diner en Ville. (FRE.). 1985. pap. 13. 95 (*0-7859-4229-7*) Fr & Eur.

— La Marquise Sortit a Cinq Heures. (FRE.). 1984. pap. 13. 95 (*0-7859-4201-7*) Fr & Eur.

Mauriac, Francois. L' Adieu a l'Adolescence: Poeme. 19.95 (*0-8288-6081-5*, F112530) Fr & Eur.

— Un Adolescent d'Autrefois. 10.95 (*0-8288-6083-1*, F113000) Fr & Eur.

— L' Agneau. 12.95 (*0-685-73251-7*, F112540) Fr & Eur.

— L' Agneau. (FRE.). 1985. pap. 10.95 (*0-7859-2986-X*, F112540) Fr & Eur.

— Les Anges Noirs. 17.95 (*0-686-55449-3*, F112950) Fr & Eur.

— Les Anges Noirs. (FRE.). 1960. pap. 17.95 (*0-8288-9855-3*, F113020) Fr & Eur.

— Asmodee: Theatre. 1938. write for info. (*0-7859-5260-8*) Fr & Eur.

— Le Baillon Denoue: Chronique. 1945. 13.95 (*0-7859-5267-5*) Fr & Eur.

— Le Baiser au Lepreux. (FRE.). 1963. pap. 10.95 (*0-8288-9865-0*, F113030) Fr & Eur.

— Le Baiser au Lepreux. 9.95 (*0-686-55450-7*) Fr & Eur.

— Ce que Je Crois. 1962. 24.95 (*0-7859-5268-3*) Fr & Eur.

— Les Chemins de la Mer. 1939. write for info. (*0-7859-5269-1*) Fr & Eur.

— Les Chemins de la Mer: Avec: Le Mal. (Illus.). 12.50 (*0-686-55455-8*) Fr & Eur.

— Commencements d'une Vie. 1932. 15.95 (*0-7859-5273-X*) Fr & Eur.

— D'autres et Moi. (FRE.). 1966. pap. 17.95 (*0-7859-5303-5*) Fr & Eur.

— De Gaulle. (FRE.). 1964. 24.95 (*0-8288-9861-8*, F112660) Fr & Eur.

— Le Dernier Bloc-Notes (V, 1968-1970) 360p. (FRE.). 1971. pap. 34.95 (*0-7859-4610-1*) Fr & Eur.

— Desert de l'Amour. (Coll. Diamant). 1961. 13.50 (*0-685-11132-6*) Fr & Eur.

— La Desert de l'Amour. (FRE.). 1971. 10.95 (*0-8288-9862-6*, F112671) Fr & Eur.

— The Desert of Love. 214p. 1989. pap. 7.95 (*0-88184-485-3*) Carroll & Graf.

— Destins. 126p. (FRE.). 1928. pap. 9.95 (*0-7859-1453-6*, 2246144817) Fr & Eur.

— Destins. (Coll. Diamant). 1965. 11.95 (*0-685-11133-4*) Fr & Eur.

— Dieu et Mammon. (FRE.). 1958. pap. 17.95 (*0-7859-5304-3*) Fr & Eur.

— Discours de Reception a l'Academie Francaise. (FRE.). 1934. pap. 10.95 (*0-7859-5305-1*) Fr & Eur.

— L' Enfant Charge de Chaines: Avec: Commencement d'un Via, Bordeaux ou l'Adolescencwe, Orages, Blaise Pascal et sa soeur Jacqueline, L'Affaire Fabre-Butte. (Illus.). 12. 50 (*0-686-55459-0*) Fr & Eur.

— Le Fils de l'Homme. (FRE.). 1958. pap. 15.95 (*0-7859-4882-1*) Fr & Eur.

— Fin de la Nuit. 1962. pap. 9.95 (*0-685-11185-7*) Fr & Eur.

— Le Fleuve de Feu. (Coll. Diamant). 19.95 (*0-685-34293-X*) Fr & Eur.

— La Fleuve de Feu. 1970. pap. write for info. (*0-7859-5270-5*) Fr & Eur.

— Galigai. pap. 9.95 (*0-685-34294-8*) Fr & Eur.

— Genitrix. 1964. pap. 9.95 (*0-685-11212-8*) Fr & Eur.

— Holy Thursday: An Intimate Remembrance. LC 88-34643. 120p. 1991. reprint ed. 16.95 (*0-918477-08-5*) Sophia Inst Pr.

— Journal: Coll. Diamant. (FRE.). 19.15 (*0-685-34295-6*) Fr & Eur.

— Journal d'un Homme de Treinte Ans. 135p. 1948. 19.95 (*0-8288-7434-4*) Fr & Eur.

— Le Mal. Aufort, Jean, ed. (FRE.). 1952. 14.95 (*0-8288-9753-0*, F100590) Fr & Eur.

— Les Mal-Aimes. (FRE.). 1945. pap. 15.95 (*0-7859-5488-0*) Fr & Eur.

— Maltaverne. 22.50 (*0-685-34296-4*) Fr & Eur.

— Memoires Interieurs. 9.95 (*0-686-55468-X*) Fr & Eur.

— Memoires Interieurs. 384p. (FRE.). 1959. 24.95 (*0-8288-7444-1*) Fr & Eur.

— Memoires Interieurs. 520p. (FRE.). 1985. pap. 29.95 (*0-7859-4611-X*) Fr & Eur.

— Memoires Politiques. (FRE.). 1967. 12.95 (*0-8288-9864-2*, F112800); 24.95 (*0-8288-7442-5*) Fr & Eur.

— Mystere Frontenac. (Coll. Diamant). (FRE.). 1957. 7.95 (*0-8288-9869-3*, F113200) Fr & Eur.

— Le Mystere Frontenac. 9.95 (*0-686-55470-1*) Fr & Eur.

— Le Noeud de Viperes. (Coll. Diamant). 9.50 (*0-685-23904-7*); pap. 3.95 (*0-686-55471-X*) Fr & Eur.

— Le Noeud de Viperes. (FRE.). 1979. pap. 12.95 (*0-7859-3057-4*) Fr & Eur.

— Le Nouveau Bloc-Notes (II, 1958-1960) 11.50 (*0-685-34281-6*) Fr & Eur.

— Le Nouveau Bloc-Notes (III, 1961-1964) 15.95 (*0-685-34282-4*) Fr & Eur.

— Le Nouveau Bloc-Notes (IV, 1965-1967) 22.50 (*0-685-34283-2*) Fr & Eur.

— Nouveaux Memoires Interieurs. 13.50 (*0-685-34297-2*) Fr & Eur.

— Nouveaux Memoirs Interieurs - More Reflections from the Soul. Kimbrough, Mary, tr. LC 91-33023. 228p. 1992. lib. bdg. 89.95 (*0-7734-9616-5*) E Mellen.

— Noveaux Memoires Interieurs. (Folio Ser.: No. 566). (FRE.). pap. 8.95 (*2-07-036566-2*) Schoenhof.

— Oeuvres Romanesques et Theatrales Completes, 2. deluxe ed. Petit, Jacques, ed. (Pleiade Ser.). 1978. 75.95 (*2-07-010957-7*) Schoenhof.

— Oeuvres Romanesques et Theatrales Completes, 3. deluxe ed. Petit, Jacques, ed. (Pleiade Ser.). 1978. 74.95 (*2-07-010990-9*) Schoenhof.

— Oeuvres Romanesques et Theatrales Completes, 4. deluxe ed. Petit, Jacques, ed. (Pleiade Ser.). 1978. 93.95 (*2-07-011091-5*) Schoenhof.

— Oeuvres Romanesques et Theatrales Completes, I. deluxe ed. Petit, Jacques, ed. (Pleiade Ser.). 1978. 77.95 (*2-07-010931-3*) Schoenhof.

— Oeuvres Romanesques Illustrees, 2 tomes, Set. (FRE.). 1949. 59.95 (*2-253-05511-5*) Fr & Eur.

— Oeuvres Romanesques, 1911-1951. (FRE.). 1992. pap. 56. 95 (*0-7859-3160-0*, 2253055115) Fr & Eur.

— Orages: Poemes. 9.50 (*0-685-34298-0*) Fr & Eur.

— La Pharisienne. pap. 9.95 (*0-686-55475-2*) Fr & Eur.

— Le Pharisienne. (FRE.). 1985. pap. 19.95 (*0-7859-3047-7*) Fr & Eur.

— Preseances. pap. 9.95 (*0-685-34300-6*) Fr & Eur.

— Preseances; Galigai. (FRE.). 1990. pap. 18.95 (*0-7859-3422-7*) Fr & Eur.

— Reponses a Paul Claudel: Avec: Lettres Ouvertes. (Illus.). 12.50 (*0-686-55476-0*) Fr & Eur.

— La Robe Pretexte. pap. 9.95 (*0-685-34301-4*) Fr & Eur.

— Le Roman. pap. 9.50 (*0-685-34302-2*) Fr & Eur.

— Le Roman. LC 75-41191. (FRE.). reprint ed. 27.50 (*0-404-14766-6*) AMS Pr.

— Le Romancier et Ses Personnages. Bd. with Education des Filles. (FRE.). 1990. Set pap. 10.95 (*0-7859-3230-5*, 2266033859) Fr & Eur.

— Les Sagouin. (FRE.). 1963. pap. 10.95 (*0-8288-9867-7*, F113150) Fr & Eur.

— La Sagouin. 9.95 (*0-686-55477-9*) Fr & Eur.

— Sainte Marguerite de Cortone. pap. 9.95 (*0-685-34304-9*) Fr & Eur.

— Second Thoughts: Reflections on Literature & on Life. LC 72-13201. (Essay Index Reprint Ser.). 1977. reprint ed. 15.95 (*0-8369-8169-3*) Ayer.

— Souffrances et Bonheur du Chretien. pap. 9.50 (*0-685-34305-7*) Fr & Eur.

— Theatre. Asmodee: Avec: Les Mal Aimes. (Illus.). 12.50 (*0-686-55478-7*) Fr & Eur.

— Therese. Hopkins, Gerard, tr. 400p. 1995. 10.95 (*0-14-018153-9*, Penguin Classics) Viking Penguin.

— Therese Desqueyroux. pap. 9.95 (*0-686-55479-5*) Fr & Eur.

— Therese Desqueyroux. (Coll. Diamant). (FRE.). 1955. 10. 95 (*0-8288-9868-5*, F113170) Fr & Eur.

— Trois Recits. 1992. pap. 12.95 (*0-7859-3174-0*, 2253062073) Fr & Eur.

— La Vie de Jean Racine: Avec: Le Romancier et ses Personnages, L'Education ces Filles, Mes Grandes Hommes, Recontre avec Barres, Pascal. (Illus.). 12.50 (*0-686-55480-9*) Fr & Eur.

— Vie de Jesus. 9.95 (*0-685-34307-3*) Fr & Eur.

— La Vie et la Mort d'un Poete. pap. 9.50 (*0-685-34308-1*) Fr & Eur.

— Viper's Tangle. 208p. 1987. pap. 8.95 (*0-88184-305-9*) Carroll & Graf.

— Woman of the Pharisees. (Thomas More Books to Live Ser.). 500p. 1986. reprint ed. 13.95 (*0-88347-203-1*) Thomas More.

— The Woman of the Pharisees. Hopkins, Gerard M., tr. 284p. 1988. reprint ed. pap. 8.95 (*0-88184-371-7*) Carroll & Graf.

Mauriac, Francois & Blanche, Jacques-Emile. Correspondance 1916-1942. Collet, Georges-Paul, ed. 256p. (FRE.). 1976. 13.95 (*0-7859-0108-6*, M3746) Fr & Eur.

Mauriac, Francois & Goesch, Keith. Lacordaire. 148p. (FRE.). 1976. 29.95 (*0-8288-9752-2*, F100580) Fr & Eur.

Mauriac, Francois, jt. auth. see Gide, Andre.

Mauriac, L. Oeuvres Autobiographiques. (FRE.). 1990. lib. bdg. 125.00 (*0-8288-3561-6*, F89430) Fr & Eur.

— Oeuvres Romanesques et Theatrales, Vol. 1. (FRE.). 1978. lib. bdg. 95.00 (*0-8288-3562-4*, M5109) Fr & Eur.

— Oeuvres Romanesques et Theatrales, Vol. 2. (FRE.). 1987. lib. bdg. 95.00 (*0-8288-3563-2*, M5635) Fr & Eur.

— Oeuvres Romanesques et Theatrales, Vol. 3. (FRE.). 1981. lib. bdg. 95.00 (*0-8288-3564-0*, F16630) Fr & Eur.

— Oeuvres Romanesques et Theatrales, Vol. 4. (FRE.). 1985. lib. bdg. 140.00 (*0-8288-3565-9*, F16810) Fr & Eur.

***Maurice.** BusinessWatch. (ABC News Intermediate ESL Video Library). (Illus.). 160p. 1993. pap. text ed. 15.50 (*0-13-501164-7*) P-H.

— The Lion's Roar. 4.95 (*0-8065-0323-8*, Citadel Pr) Carol Pub Group.

Maurice, A. B. New York in Fiction. 1972. 59.95 (*0-8490-0728-3*) Gordon Pr.

— The Paris of the Novelists. 1972. 59.95 (*0-8490-0801-8*) Gordon Pr.

Maurice, A. B., jt. auth. see Cooper, F. T.

Maurice, Arthur B. Fifth Avenue. LC 75-1860. (Leisure Class in America Ser.). (Illus.). 1975. reprint ed. 26.95 (*0-405-06926-X*) Ayer.

Maurice, C. E. Revolutionary Movement of Eighteen Forty-Eight to Forty-Nine in Italy, Austria-Hungary, & Germany. LC 68-25250. (World History Ser.: No. 48). (Illus.). 1969. reprint ed. lib. bdg. 59.95 (*0-8383-0215-7*) M S G Haskell Hse.

Maurice, Catherine. Let Me Hear Your Voice: A Family's Triumph over Autism. LC 92-2471. 1993. 24.00 (*0-679-40863-0*) Knopf.

— Let Me Hear Your Voice: A Family's Triumph over Autism. 1994. reprint ed. pap. 12.00 (*0-449-90664-7*, Columbine) Fawcett.

Maurice, Charles & Smithson, Charles W. The Doomsday Myth: Ten Thousand Years of Economic Crises. (Publication Ser.: No. 296). (Illus.). xx, 142p. (C). 1984. pap. 11.95 (*0-8179-7962-X*) Hoover Inst Pr.

Maurice, Charles E. Revolutionary Movement in Italy, Austria, Hungary & Germany, 1848-49. LC 03-13471. 1968. reprint ed. 14.00 (*0-403-00075-0*) Scholarly.

***Maurice, Charles S. & Thomas, Christopher R.** Managerial Economics: Applied Microeconomics for Decision Making. 5th ed. LC 94-26272. 752p. (C). 1994. text ed. 63.95 (*0-256-16055-4*) Irwin.

Maurice, Clyde F. Private Sector Involvement with the Vocational Community: An Analysis of Policy Options. 106p. 1984. 8.75 (*0-318-22180-2*, IN281) Ctr Educ Trng Employ.

Maurice, Dick, jt. auth. see Newton, Wayne.

***Maurice, Duke.** Chesapeake Bay Voices: Narratives of Four Centuries. 1993. pap. 19.95 (*0-615-00185-8*) Dietz.

Maurice, F. Path to Parnassus. 4th ed. 1956. pap. 4.00 (*0-522-83804-9*) Intl Spec Bk.

Maurice, Frederick. Robert E. Lee: The Soldier. LC 70-37898. (Select Bibliographies Reprint Ser.). 1977. reprint ed. 35.95 (*0-8369-6736-4*) Ayer.

Maurice, Frederick D. The Gospel of the Kingdom of Heaven. 416p. 1977. reprint ed. 14.00 (*0-87921-037-0*) Attic Pr.

— The Prayer Book & the Lord's Prayer. 416p. 1977. reprint ed. 14.00 (*0-87921-038-9*) Attic Pr.

— Sketches of Contemporary Authors, 1828. Hartley, A. J., ed. LC 74-106555. 182p. reprint ed. 51.90 (*0-8357-9585-3*, 2011080) Bks Demand.

— What Is Revelation? LC 76-173061. reprint ed. 49.50 (*0-404-04276-7*) AMS Pr.

— Workman & the Franchise: Chapters from English History on the Representation & Education of the People. LC 68-18601. xvi, 244p. 1970. reprint ed. 35.00 (*0-678-00592-3*) Kelley.

Maurice, J. F. Military History of the Campaigns of 1882 in Egypt Prepared in the Intelligence Branch of the War Office. 228p. (C). 1987. reprint ed. 110.00 (*0-317-90439-6*, Pub. by Picton UK) St Mut.

Maurice, Klaus & Heuer, Peter. European Pendulum Clocks. LC 88-61468. (Illus.). 248p. 1988. 59.95 (*0-88740-144-9*) Schiffer.

Maurice, Marc, et al. The Social Foundations of Industrial Powers: A Comparison of France & Germany. Goldhammer, Arthur, tr. 400p. 1986. pap. 42.50 (*0-262-13213-3*) MIT Pr.

Maurice Price, Ira. Compendio De la Historia Del A. T. An Outline of Old Testament. (SPA.). 5.25 (*84-7645-425-2*, 223331, Pub. by Edit Clie SP) TSELF.

Maurice, S. Charles & Hobson, Jane. Series on Public Issues, No. 2. Pejovich, Svetozar, ed. Orig. Title: Minimum Wage Law: Who Benefits, Who Loses?. 1983. pap. 2.00 (*0-86599-009-3*) PERC.

Maurice, S. Charles & Pejovich, Svetozar, eds. Texas Yesterday, Today & Tomorrow. (Series on Public Issues: No. 22). 1986. pap. 2.00 (*0-86599-026-3*) PERC.

Maurice, S. Charles & Phillips, Owen R. Economic Analysis: Theory & Application. 6th ed. 704p. (C). 1992. text ed. 64.95 (*0-256-08209-X*, 05-0188-06) Irwin.

Maurice, S. Charles & Smithson, Charles W. Are We Running Out of Everything?, No. 1. Pejovich, Svetozar & Joyce, Janet G., eds. (Series on Public Issues). 1983. pap. 2.00 (*0-86599-008-5*) PERC.

— Managerial Economics: Applied Microeconomics for Decision Making. 4th ed. 784p. (C). 1992. text ed. 63.95 (*0-256-08268-5*) Irwin.

— Pollution in America: The Trouble with Trash. Pejovich, Steve & Dethloff, Henry, eds. (Series on Public Issues: No. 7). (Illus.). 27p. (Orig.). (C). 1984. pap. 2.00 (*0-86599-017-4*) PERC.

Maurice, Thomas. The History of Hindostan. Feldman, Burton & Richardson, Robert D., eds. LC 78-60888. (Myth & Romanticism Ser.). 1359p. 1984. lib. bdg. 20.00 (*0-8240-3566-6*) Garland.

Maurice-Williams, R. S. Spinal Degenerative Disease. (Illus.). 356p. 1981. 48.00 (*0-685-24837-2*, Yr Bk Med Pubs) Mosby Yr Bk.

— Subarachnoid Haemorrhage: Aneurysms & Vascular Malformations of the Central Nervous System. (Illus.). 448p. 1987. 131.50 (*0-685-24836-4*, Yr Bk Med Pubs) Mosby Yr Bk.

Maurice, Yvon T., ed. International Association on the Genesis of Ore Deposits, Papers Presented at the 8th Symposium, Ottawa, 1990. (Illus.). 894p. 1993. lib. bdg. 218.00 (*3-510-65153-7*, Pub. by Schweitzerbart'sche GW) Lubrecht & Cramer.

Mauriceau, A. M. The Married Woman's Private Medical Companion. LC 73-20635. (Sex, Marriage & Society Ser.). 256p. 1974. reprint ed. 23.95 (*0-405-05811-X*) Ayer.

Mauricio, Rufino, jt. auth. see Fry, Gerald W.

Mauricio, Victoria. The Return of Chief Black Foot. LC 81-2769. (Illus.). 140p. (Orig.). 1981. pap. 5.95 (*0-89865-053-4*) Donning Co.

Mauriel, John J. Strategic Leadership for Schools: Creating & Sustaining Productive Change. LC 89-45592. (Education-Higher Education Ser.). 373p. 1989. 32.95x (*1-55542-184-9*) Jossey-Bass.

Mauriello, Sally M., et al. Dental Radiology. (Illus.). 400p. (C). 1994. text ed. 35.00 (*0-397-55020-0*, Lippincott Medical) Lippincott.

Mauriello, Thomas, jt. auth. see Ingraham, Barton I.

Maurier, Anina, ed. see Pascal, Alana & VanderKar, Lynne.

Mauries, Patrick. Fornasetti: Designer of Dreams. (Illus.). 288p. 1991. 95.00 (*0-8212-1872-7*) Bulfinch Pr.

— Jewelry by Chanel, Vol. 1. (Illus.). 144p. 1993. 75.00 (*0-8212-1960-X*) Bulfinch Pr.

— Shell Shock. LC 93-61598. (Illus.). 112p. 1994. 19.95 (*0-500-01609-7*) Thames Hudson.

Mauries, Patrick, jt. auth. see Vautrin, Line.

Maurin, Jacques. Virologie Medicale. (Collection Traites). (Illus.). 930p. (FRE.). 1985. 150.00 (*2-257-10435-8*) S M P F Inc.

Maurin, Krzysztof. Analysis: Integration, Distributions, Holomorphic Functions, Tensor & Harmonic Analysis, Pt. 2. 1980. lib. bdg. 149.50 (*90-277-0865-7*) Kluwer Ac.

— Analysis, Part 1: Elements. Lepa, Eugene, tr. LC 74-80525. 672p. 1976. lib. bdg. 117.00 (*90-277-0484-8*) Kluwer Ac.

Maurin, Krzysztof & Raczka, R., eds. Mathematical Physics & Physical Mathematics. LC 74-34289. (Mathematical Physics & Applied Mathematics Ser: No. 2). 1976. lib. bdg. 117.00 (*90-277-0537-2*) Kluwer Ac.

Maurin, Mario. Henri de Regnier: Le Labyrinthe et le Double. LC 72-339689. 301p. (FRE.). reprint ed. pap. 85.80 (*0-7837-6942-3*, 2046771) Bks Demand.

Maurin, Peter. Easy Essays. pap. 2.95 (*0-89979-015-1*) British Am Bks.

— Easy Essays. 1977. pap. 9.95 (*0-8199-0681-6*, Frncscn Herld) Franciscan Pr.

Maurin, Vladimir M., tr. see Okladnikov, Aleksei P.

Maurin, Vladimir M., tr. see Oshanin, L. V.

Maurin, Vladimir M., tr. see Tretiakov, P. N. & Mongait, A. L.

Maurine, jt. auth. see Moon, Margaret.

Maurino, Ferdinando D. Salvatore Di Giacomo & Neapolitan Dialectal Literature. 1951. 8.95 (*0-913298-30-1*) S F Vanni.

Maurizi, Vincenzo. History of Seyd Said: Sultan of Muscat; Together with an Account of the Countries & People on the Shores of the Persian Gulf, by Sheik Mansur. (Arabia Past & Present Ser.: Vol. 13). 208p. 1984. 35.00 (*0-906672-33-3*) Oleander Pr.

***Mauro, Alexander, ed.** Muscle Regeneration. fac. ed. LC 77-90593. (Illus.). 576p. Date not set. pap. 164.20 (*0-7837-7263-7*, 2047042) Bks Demand.

Mauro, Bob. College Athletic Scholarships: A Complete Guide. LC 87-43210. 157p. 1988. lib. bdg. 18.95x (*0-89950-328-4*) McFarland & Co.

Mauro-Cochrane, Jeanette. Self-Respect & Sexual Assault. LC 92-38938. 1993. pap. 12.60 (*0-8306-4289-7*) TAB Bks.

— Self Respect & Sexual Assault: Before, During & After. 1993. pap. 12.95 (*0-07-041040-2*) McGraw.

Mauro, Francesco, jt. auth. see Gledhill, Barton.

Mauro, John B. Statistical Deception at Work. (Communication Textbook Ser.). 128p. (C). 1992. pap. 17.50 (*0-8058-1232-6*) L Erlbaum Assocs.

Mauro, Joseph V. & Meyrowitz, Michael R. Oral Pathology: Mucous Membrane Lesions. 64p. 1984. 30.00 (*0-318-17795-1*); write for info. (*0-318-17796-X*) Am Dental Hygienists.

Mauro, Philip. Baptism: A Bible Defense of Believer's Immersion. pap. 3.99 (*0-87377-046-3*) GAM Pubns.

— Champion of Kingdom. pap. 2.99 (*0-87377-047-1*) GAM Pubns.

— Chronology of the Bible. 1980. lib. bdg. 49.95 (*0-8490-3140-0*) Gordon Pr.

— Church Churches & Kingdom. pap. 12.99 (*0-87377-048-X*) GAM Pubns.

— Evolution. pap. 2.99 (*0-87377-050-1*) GAM Pubns.

— Hope of Israel. pap. 11.99 (*0-87377-052-8*) GAM Pubns.

— Kingdom Heresies. pap. 1.99 (*0-87377-009-9*) GAM Pubns.

— The Last Call to the Godly Remnant. pap. 3.99 (*0-87377-053-6*) GAM Pubns.

— More Than a Prophet: On John the Baptist. pap. 1.99 (*0-87377-054-4*) GAM Pubns.

— Never Man Spake Like This Man. 32p. 1974. pap. 0.99 (*0-87377-055-2*) GAM Pubns.

— Ruth. pap. 9.99 (*0-87377-057-9*) GAM Pubns.

— Seventy Weeks & the Great Tribulation. 285p. 1975. pap. 11.99 (*0-87377-058-7*) GAM Pubns.

— Speaking in Tongues. 1978. pap. 0.79 (*0-87377-059-5*) GAM Pubns.

— Things Which Soon Must Come to Pass: Commentary on Revelation. 1984. reprint ed. 17.99 (*0-87377-056-0*) GAM Pubns.

— Wonders of Bible Chronology. 1974. pap. 5.99 (*0-87377-060-9*) GAM Pubns.

— The World & Its God. 95p. 1981. reprint ed. pap. 2.95 (*0-89084-151-9*) Bob Jones Univ Pr.

***Mauro, Raf.** Fitting In. 64p. (Orig.). (J). (gr. 1-3). 1995. pap. 8.95 (*0-940669-31-5*) Dramaline Pubns.

— Modern Monologues for Modern Kids. 64p. 1994. pap. 8.95 (*0-940669-29-3*) Dramaline Pubns.

Mauro, Robert. Engineering Electronics: A Practical Approach. 1120p. 1989. text ed. 81.00 (*0-13-278029-1*) P-H.

— Finding Love & Intimacy. Garee, Betty, ed. 200p. 1994. pap. 8.95 (*0-915708-37-X*) Cheever Pub.

M

— On Stage! Zapel, Arthur L., ed. LC 90-52982. 257p. (Orig.). 1990. pap. text ed. 10.95 (*0-916260-67-4*, B165) Meriwether Pub.
— Two-Character Plays for Student Actors: A Collection of 15 One-Act Plays. Zapel, Arthur L., ed. LC 88-60078. 192p. 1988. pap. text ed. 10.95 (*0-916260-53-4*, B-174) Meriwether Pub.
Mauro, Robert, jt. auth. see Becker, Elle.
Mauro, Robert, jt. auth. see Gross, Samuel R.
Maurois, Andre. Adrienne ou la Vie de Madame de La Fayette. (FRE.). 1968. pap. 29.95 (*0-7859-5109-1*) Fr & Eur.
— Ariel on la Vie de Shelley. (Coll. Diamant). 1970. pap. write for info. (*0-7859-5275-6*) Fr & Eur.
— Un Art de Vivre. 256p. (FRE.). 1973. 6.95 (*0-7859-0110-8*, M3759) Fr & Eur.
— Aspects de la Biographie. 1930. 13.95 (*0-7859-5271-3*) Fr & Eur.
— Aux Innocents les Mains Pleines. (FRE.). pap. 9.95 (*0-7859-5571-2*) Fr & Eur.
— Balzac. (Illus.). (FRE.). 1976. 49.95 (*0-8288-9740-9*, 2080607464) Fr & Eur.
— Bernard Quesnay. 1963. pap. 17.50 (*0-685-11045-1*) Fr & Eur.
— Bernard Quesnay. 192p. (FRE.). 1973. pap. 10.95 (*0-7859-0109-4*, M3757) Fr & Eur.
— Cercle De Famille. (Coll. Diamant). 1959. 23.25 (*0-685-11071-0*) Fr & Eur.
— Le Cercle de Famille. 437p. (FRE.). 1977. 10.95 (*0-8288-9882-0*, F114050) Fr & Eur.
— Chantiers Americains. (FRE.). pap. 6.95 (*0-8288-9872-3*, F113470) Fr & Eur.
— Choses Nues. (Coll. Soleil). 284p. (FRE.). 1963. pap. 15. 95 (*0-7859-1286-X*, 2070243125) Fr & Eur.
— Climates of Love. Levien, Michael, ed. Schiff, Violet & Cook, Esme, trs. LC 87-60486. (Modern Romance Classics Ser.). 214p. 1986. reprint ed. 25.00 (*0-7206-0671-3*, Pub. by P Owen Ltd UK) Dufour.
— Climats. 9.95 (*0-686-55489-2*) Fr & Eur.
— Climats. (Coll. Diamant). (FRE.). 1955. 39.95 (*0-7859-0049-7*, FC1394) Fr & Eur.
— La Conquete de l'Angleterre par les normands. (Coll. Le Memorial des Siecles). (FRE.). 19.95 (*0-8288-9873-1*, F113500) Fr & Eur.
— Le Cote de Chelsea. 144p. 1967. pap. 21.95 (*0-7859-5272-1*) Fr & Eur.
— Cours De Bonheur Conjugal. (FRE.). pap. 10.95 (*0-8288-9875-8*, F113530) Fr & Eur.
— D'Aragon a Montherlant et De Shakespeare a Churchill. (FRE.). 12.95 (*0-8288-9876-6*, F113540) Fr & Eur.
— De Gide a Sartre. (FRE.). 12.95 (*0-8288-9877-4*, F113550) Fr & Eur.
— De la Bruyere a Proust: Lecture Mon Doux Plaisir. (Coll. Les Grands Evenements Litteraires). (FRE.). 11.95 (*0-8288-9878-2*, F113560) Fr & Eur.
— Dialogues sur le Commandement. (FRE.). 1924. pap. 13. 95 (*0-7859-5316-7*) Fr & Eur.
— Les Discours du Docteur O'Grady. (FRE.). 1968. pap. 26. 95 (*0-7859-5549-6*) Fr & Eur.
— Don Juan ou la Vie de Byron. (Coll. Diamant). 1969. pap. write for info. (*0-7859-5274-8*) Fr & Eur.
— France. (Illus.). 37.50 (*0-686-55492-2*) Fr & Eur.
— Histoire d'Angleterre. 26.25 (*0-685-36938-2*) Fr & Eur.
— Histoire de la France. 34.90 (*0-685-36939-0*) Fr & Eur.
— Histoire des Etats-Unis, 2 vols. 48.25 (*0-685-36940-4*) Fr & Eur.
— Illusions. LC 68-29043. 101p. 1968. text ed. 29.50 (*0-231-03171-8*) Col U Pr.
— Les Illusions. (Coll. Les Soirees du Luxembourg). 26.95 (*0-685-36941-2*) Fr & Eur.
— L' Instinct du Bonheur. pap. 8.95 (*0-685-36942-0*) Fr & Eur.
— Lelia ou la Vie de George Sand. 22.95 (*0-685-36943-9*) Fr & Eur.
— Lettre Ouverte a un Jeune Homme sur la Conduite de la Vie. (Coll. Lettre Ouverte). pap. 9.95 (*0-685-36944-7*) Fr & Eur.
— Lyautey. 17.95 (*0-685-36945-5*) Fr & Eur.
— Memoires I: Les Annees d'Apprentissage. 19.95 (*0-685-36946-3*) Fr & Eur.
— Mes Songes Que Voici. pap. 17.50 (*0-685-36948-X*) Fr & Eur.
— Les Mondes Imaginaires. pap. 18.50 (*0-685-36949-8*) Fr & Eur.
— Ni Ange, Ni Bete. (FRE.). 1927. 10.95 (*0-8288-9883-9*, F114080) Fr & Eur.
— Nico le Petit Garcon Change en Chien. 9.95 (*0-686-55495-7*) Fr & Eur.
— Nouveaux Discours du Docteur O'Grady. pap. 9.95 (*0-685-36950-1*) Fr & Eur.
— Olympio ou La Vie de Victor Hugo. 28.50 (*0-685-36951-X*) Fr & Eur.
— Le Pays des 36000 Volontes. 94p. (FRE.). 1990. pap. 11. 95 (*0-7859-4614-4*) Fr & Eur.
— Le Poeme de Versailles. pap. 9.50 (*0-685-36952-8*) Fr & Eur.
— Portrait d'un Ami qui s'appelait Moi. (Coll. Les Auteurs Juges par leurs Oeuvres). pap. 17.50 (*0-685-36953-6*) Fr & Eur.
— Pour Piano Seul. pap. 19.50 (*0-685-36954-4*) Fr & Eur.
— Private Universe. Miles, Hamish, tr. LC 70-177963. (Essay Index Reprint Ser.). 1977. reprint ed. 22.95 (*0-8369-2564-5*) Ayer.
— Promethee ou la vie de Balzac. 27.50 (*0-685-36955-2*) Fr & Eur.
— Promethee ou la Vie de Balzac; Olympio ou la Vie de Victor Hugo. (FRE.). 1993. pap. 60.00 (*0-7859-3406-5*) Fr & Eur.
— Prometheus: The Life of Balzac. 573p. 1983. pap. 11.95 (*0-88184-023-8*) Carroll & Graf.
— Proust: Portrait of a Genius. 336p. 1984. pap. 10.95 (*0-88184-104-8*) Carroll & Graf.
— Quatre Etudes Anglaises. pap. 17.95 (*0-685-36956-0*) Fr & Eur.
— Rene ou La Vie de Chateaubriand. (Coll. Diamant). 25.50 (*0-685-36957-9*) Fr & Eur.
— Rene ou la Vie de Chateaubriand. 315p. (FRE.). 1985. pap. 39.95 (*0-7859-4613-6*) Fr & Eur.
— Ricochets: Miniature Tales of Human Life. Miles, Hamish, tr. LC 73-150551. (Short Story Index Reprint Ser.). 1977. reprint ed. 16.95 (*0-8369-3848-8*) Ayer.
— Robert et Elizabeth Browning. pap. 17.50 (*0-685-36958-7*) Fr & Eur.
— Les Roses de Septembre. 123.50 (*0-685-36968-4*) Fr & Eur.
— Sentiments et Coutumes. pap. 17.50 (*0-685-36959-5*) Fr & Eur.
— Seven Faces of Love. 1977. reprint ed. 20.95 (*0-518-10169-X*) Ayer.
— Les Silences de Colonel Bramble. Dicours. Nouveau Discours du Dr. O'Grady. (FRE.). 1992. pap. 12.95 (*0-7859-3085-X*, 2253012769) Fr & Eur.
— Les Silences du Colonel Bramble. Bd. with Discours et Nouveaux discours ou Docteur O'Grady. Set pap. 6.50 (*0-685-23886-5*, 90) Fr & Eur.
— Les Silences du Colonel Bramble: Avec: Discours, Nouveaux Discours du Dr. O'Grady. 14.50 (*0-686-55498-1*) Fr & Eur.
— Soixante Ans de Ma Vie Litteraire. Incl. Role de l'ecrivain dans le monde d'aujourd'hui. 9.95 (*0-685-36961-7*); write for info. (*0-318-52265-9*) Fr & Eur.
— Terre Promise. 340p. 9.95 (*0-686-55499-X*); pap. 16.50 (*0-685-36962-5*) Fr & Eur.
— Les Titans ou les Trois Dumas. pap. 12.50 (*0-685-36963-3*) Fr & Eur.
— Tourgueniev. (Coll. Grandes Figures Litteraires). pap. 16. 50 (*0-685-36964-1*) Fr & Eur.
— Les Trois Dumas. 25.95 (*0-685-36969-2*) Fr & Eur.
— Trois Portraits de Femme: La Duchesse de Devonshire, la Comtesse D'Albany, Henriette de France. (Coll. Les Soirees du Luxembourg). 21.50 (*0-685-36965-X*) Fr & Eur.
— La Vie de Disraeli. (Coll. Leurs Figures). pap. 32.50 (*0-685-36967-6*) Fr & Eur.
Maurois, Andre, tr. see Hopkins, Gerard Manley.
Mauron, Jean, ed. Nutrition Adequacy: Nutrients Available & Needs. (Experientia Supplementa Ser.: Vol. 44). 384p. (C). 1983. text ed. 52.95 (*3-7643-1479-6*) Birkhauser.
Maurus, Rhabanus. The Life of Saint Mary Magdalene & of Her Sister Saint Martha. Mycoff, David, tr. (Cistercian Studies: No. 108). 166p. 31.95 (*0-87907-608-9*); pap. 15. 95 (*0-87907-908-8*) Cistercian Pubns.
Maurus, Terentianus. Concordantia in Terentianum Maurum. Beck, Jan-Wilhelm, ed. (Alpha-Omega, Reihe A Ser.: Bd. CXXXVI). 268p. (GER.). 1993. write for info. (*3-487-09723-0*, Pub. by Georg Olms GW) Lubrecht & Cramer.
Maurus, Walt. A Complete Introduction to Bettas. (Complete Introduction to...Ser.). (Illus.). 128p. 1987. pap. 5.95 (*0-86622-288-X*, CO-005S) TFH Pubns.
Maury, Ann, ed. see Fontaine, James.
Maury, C. J. Recent Mollusks of the Gulf of Mexico: With Pleistocene & Pliocene Species from the Gulf States. 282p. 1971. reprint ed. 8.00 (*0-87710-361-5*) Paleo Res.
Maury, E. A. Drainage in Homoeopathy. (C). 1980. text ed. 8.95 (*0-8464-1007-9*) Beekman Pubs.
*__Maury, Emmerick-Armand.__ Dictionnaire Familial D'Homeopathie. 1982. write for info. (*0-7859-7938-7*, 2-7113-0026-9) Fr & Eur.
— Dictionnaire Familial D'Homeopathie. 1991. write for info. (*0-7859-7896-8*, 2-501-01456-0) Fr & Eur.
Maury, Emmerick-Armand & De Rudder, Chantal. Dictionnaire Familial des Medecines Naturelles. (FRE.). 1982. 105.00 (*0-8288-9523-6*, M6832) Fr & Eur.
Maury, Emmerick-Armand & Rudder, C. Diccionario Familiar de Medicina Natural: Colloquial Dictionary of Natural Medicine. 441p. (SPA.). 1981. 19.95 (*0-8288-1867-3*, S37815) Fr & Eur.
Maury, Inez. My Mother & I Are Growing Strong. 4th ed. (Illus.). (ENG & SPA.). (J). (ps-4). 1978. pap. 6.95 (*0-938678-06-X*) New Seed.
— My Mother the Mail Carrier - Mi Mama la Cartera. Alemany, Norah, tr. LC 76-14275. (Illus.). 32p. (Orig.). (ENG & SPA.). (J). (gr. k-4). 1976. pap. 7.95 (*0-935312-23-4*) Feminist Pr.
Maury, Jean-Pierre. The Atmosphere. (Focus on Science Ser.). 80p. (YA). (gr. 8 up). 1989. pap. 4.95 (*0-8120-4213-1*) Barron.
— Heat & Cold. (Focus on Science Ser.). 80p. (YA). (gr. 8 up). 1989. pap. 4.95 (*0-8120-4211-5*) Barron.
— Newton: The Father of Modern Astronomy. Paris, I. Mark, tr. (Discoveries Ser.). (Illus.). 144p. 1992. pap. 12. 95 (*0-8109-2835-3*) Abrams.
— The Turtleons Are Coming. (I Love to Read Collection). (Illus.). 48p. (J). (gr. 3-8). 1990. lib. bdg. 12.79 (*0-89565-810-0*) Childs World.
Maury, Jean-Pierre, jt. auth. see Balibar, Francoise.
Maury, Louis F. La Magie Et l'Astrologie Dans l'Antiquite Et au Moyen-Age. (Volkskundliche Quellen Ser.: Reihe II). iv, 484p. 1980. reprint ed. write for info. (*3-487-06956-3*, Pub. by Georg Olms GW) Lubrecht & Cramer.
Maury, Pierre. Two Hundred Examples of Letters: Two Hundred Modeles de Lettres. 285p. (FRE.). 1986. pap. 17.95 (*0-8288-1557-7*, F113580) Fr & Eur.
Maury, Richard. Saga of Cimba. (Illus.). 1973. 7.25 (*0-8286-0063-5*) J De Graff.
Maury, V. & Fourmaintraux, D., eds. Rock at Great Depth: Rock Mechanics & Rock Physics at Great Depth - Proceedings of an International Symposium, Pau, 28 - 31 August 1989, 3 vols., Set. (Illus.). 1620p. (C). 1989. text ed. 250.00 (*90-6191-975-4*, Pub. by A A Balkema NE) Ashgate Pub Co.
Maurya, Abhay. Confluence: Historico-Comparative & Other Literary Studies. 160p. 1988. text ed. 27.50 (*81-207-0781-8*, Pub. by Sterling Pubs II) Apt Bks.
Maurya, S. D. Population & Housing Problems in India, 2 vols., Set. (C). 1989. 76.00 (*81-85076-79-0*, Pub. by Chugh Pubns II) S Asia.
— Women in India. (C). 1988. 31.00 (*81-85076-49-9*, Pub. by Chugh Pubns II) S Asia.
Maurya, S. D. & Devi, Gayatri. Social Environment of India. (C). 1989. 34.00 (*81-85076-65-0*, Pub. by Chugh Pubns II) S Asia.
Maus, Cynthia P. Puerto Rico in Pictures & Poetry. 1976. lib. bdg. 250.00 (*0-8490-1385-2*) Gordon Pr.
Maus, Janet, ed. see Jordan, Joe.
*__Maus, Katharine, ed.__ Four Revenge Tragedies: (The Spanish Tragedy, by Thomas Kyd; The Revenger's Tragedy, by Thomas Middleton; The Revenge of Bussy D'Ambois, by George Chapman; & The Atheist's Tragedy, by Cyril Tourneur) (World's Classics Ser.). 352p. 1995. pap. 10.95 (*0-19-282633-6*) OUP.
— Four Revenge Tragedies: (The Spanish Tragedy, by Thomas Kyd; The Revenger's Tragedy, by Thomas Middleton; The Revenge of Bussy D'Ambois, by George Chapman; & The Atheist's Tragedy, by Cyril Tourneur) (World's Classics Ser.). 352p. 1995. 55.00 (*0-19-812170-9*) OUP.
Maus, Katharine E. Ben Jonson & the Roman Frame of Mind. LC 84-17691. 224p. 1985. text ed. 35.00 (*0-691-06629-9*) Princeton U Pr.
— Ben Jonson & the Roman Frame of Mind. LC 84-17691. 223p. reprint ed. pap. 63.60 (*0-7837-6767-6*, 2046597) Bks Demand.
— Inwardness & Theater in the English Renaissance. LC 94-43099. 1995. lib. bdg. 37.50 (*0-226-51123-5*); pap. text ed. 14.95 (*0-226-51124-3*) U Ch Pr.
Maus, Katharine E., jt. ed. see Harvey, Elizabeth D.
Maus, Rex & Huggard, Susan. The CAP GEMINI Reference to Expert Systems. (CAP GEMINI America Ser.). 256p. 1990. text ed. 24.95 (*0-07-040981-1*) McGraw.
Maus, Rex & Keyes, Jessica. Handbook of Expert Systems in Manufacturing. 480p. 1991. text ed. 59.50 (*0-07-040984-6*) McGraw.
Mauser, Ferdinand F. & Schwartz, David J. American Business: An Introduction. 6th ed. 729p. (C). 1986. pap. text ed. 32.00 (*0-15-502315-2*) Dryden Pr.
Mauser, Gary A. Political Marketing: An Approach to Campaign Strategy. Permut, Steven E., ed. LC 82-25973. (Praeger Series in Public & Nonprofit Sector Marketing). 320p. 1983. text ed. 57.95 (*0-275-91721-5*, C1721, Praeger Pubs) Greenwood.
Mauser, Gary A., jt. auth. see Margolis, Michael.
Mauser, Pat R. A Bundle of Sticks. (J). 1994. 17.50 (*0-8446-6770-6*) Peter Smith.
— A Bundle of Sticks. LC 87-1074. (Illus.). 176p. (J). (gr. 3-6). 1987. reprint ed. pap. 3.95 (*0-689-71169-7*, Aladdin Paperbacks) S&S Childrens.
— How I Found Myself at the Fair. LC 90-30630. (Illus.). 64p. (J). (gr. 1-4). 1990. reprint ed. pap. 2.95 (*0-689-71414-9*, Aladdin Paperbacks) S&S Childrens.
— Love Is for the Dogs. (J). 1989. pap. 2.50 (*0-380-75723-0*, Flare) Avon.
— Patti's Pet Gorilla. 64p. (J). 1991. pap. 2.95 (*0-380-71039-0*, Camelot) Avon.
— Rip-Off. LC 90-31543. 160p. (YA). (gr. 7 up). 1990. reprint ed. pap. 3.95 (*0-02-044471-0*, Collier Bks Young) S&S Childrens.
Mauser, Ulrich. The Gospel of Peace: A Scriptural Message for Today's World. 192p. (Orig.). 1992. pap. 16.99 (*0-664-25349-0*) Westminster John Knox.
Mausert, O. Herbs for Health. (Longevity Ser.). 1991. lib. bdg. 75.00 (*0-8490-4195-3*) Gordon Pr.
Mausert, Otto. Herbs for Health. 200p. 1976. reprint ed. spiral bd. 16.50 (*0-7873-0590-1*) Mokelumne.
Mauseth, James D. Botany: An Introduction to Plant Biology. 1138p. (C). 1991. text ed. 61.25 (*0-03-030222-6*) SCP.
— Plant Anatomy. 600p. (C). 1988. text ed. 61.25 (*0-8053-4570-1*) Benjamin-Cummings.
Maushard, Lawrence J. Made in Managua: A Nonfiction Account of One Journalist's Trip Through a Telling Place & Time. (Illus.). 162p. (Orig.). 1990. pap. 5.95 (*0-9626912-0-8*) Quimby Archives.
Mauskopf, Norman, photos. Dark Horses: Photographs by Norman Mauskopf. (Illus.). 112p. 1988. 50.00 (*0-944092-04-7*) Twin Palms Pub.
Mauskopf, Seymour H., ed. Chemical Sciences in the Modern World. (Chemical Sciences in Society Ser.). (Illus.). 448p. (C). 1994. text ed. 39.95 (*0-8122-3156-2*) U of Pa Pr.
Mauskopf, Seymour H. & McVaugh, Michael R. The Elusive Science: Origins of Experimental Psychical Research. LC 80-7991. (Illus.). 392p. 1981. text ed. 48. 50 (*0-8018-2331-5*) Johns Hopkins.
Mausner, Judith S. & Kramer, Shira. Mausner & Bahn Epidemiology: An Introductory Text. 2nd ed. (Illus.). 361p. 1985. pap. text ed. 35.50 (*0-7216-6181-5*) Saunders.
Mauss, Armand L. The Angel & the Beehive: The Mormon Struggle with Assimilation. LC 93-11328. 296p. 1994. 29.95 (*0-252-02071-5*) U of Ill Pr.
Mauss, Marcel. A General Theory of Magic. Brain, Robert, tr. 152p. 1972. 19.95 (*0-7100-7338-0*, RKP) Routledge.
— Gift: The Form & Reason for Exchange in Archaic Societies. 1990. pap. 9.95 (*0-393-30698-4*) Norton.
Mauss, Marcel, jt. auth. see Durkheim, Emile.
Mauss, Marcel, jt. auth. see Hubert, Henri.
*__Mausser, Wayne.__ Chicago Bears Facts & Trivia. (Illus.). 128p. (Orig.). 1995. pap. 7.99 (*0-938313-10-X*) E B Houchin.
Maust, John. New Song in the Andes. LC 89-35170. (Illus.). 173p. (Orig.). 1992. pap. 9.95 (*0-87808-219-0*, WCL219-0) William Carey Lib.
Mautner, Helen, tr. see Niemtschek, Franz X.
*__Mautner, Thomas, ed. & intro.__ A Dictionary of Philosophy. 640p. Date not set. text ed. write for info. (*0-631-18459-7*) Blackwell Pubs.
Mautner, Thomas, ed. see Hutcheson, Francis.
Mautor, Claudette, jt. auth. see Pulleyn, Rob.
*__Mautz, Carl, et al.__ Biographies of Western Photographers: A Reference Tool for Historians & Collectors. (Illus.). 500p. 1995. 85.00 (*0-9621940-7-7*) C Mautz Pubng.
— Biographies of Western Photographers: A Reference Tool for Historians & Collectors. (Illus.). 500p. 1995. pap. 50. 00 (*0-9621940-8-5*) C Mautz Pubng.
Mautz, R. K. & Sharaf, Hussein A. The Philosophy of Auditing. (Monograph No. 6). 248p. 1961. 12.00 (*0-86539-002-9*) Am Accounting.
Mautz, Robert K. Financial Reporting for Nonprofit Organizations: A Fresh Look. LC 93-40062. 136p. 1994. 35.00 (*0-8153-1718-2*) Garland.
— Fundamentals of Auditing. 2nd ed. LC 64-20075. 593p. reprint ed. pap. 169.10 (*0-317-10032-7*, 2012587) Bks Demand.
Mauvais-Jarvis, P. & Labrie, F. Medecine de la Reproduction, Tome 1: Gynecologie Endocrinienne. (Illus.). 520p. 1982. 58.00 (*0-318-04526-5*) S M P F Inc.
— Medecine de la Reproduction Masculine. (Illus.). 1984. 65.00 (*0-318-04527-3*) S M P F Inc.
Mauver, Judy A., tr. see Sandberg, Inger.
Mauw, S. & Veltink, G. J. Algebraic Specification of Communication Protocols. (Tracts in Theoretical Computer Science Ser.: No. 36). 200p. (C). 1993. 42.95 (*0-521-41883-6*) Cambridge U Pr.
Mavalankar, Damodar K. The Service of Humanity. (Sangam Texts Ser.). 132p. 1986. pap. 8.75 (*0-88695-025-2*) Concord Grove.
Mavalwala, Jamshed, ed. Dermatoglyphics: An International Bibliography (World Anthropology) xvi, 306p. 1978. text ed. 53.85 (*90-279-7999-5*) Mouton.
— Dermatoglypics: An International Perspective. (World Anthropology Ser.). (Illus.). xxii, 382p. 1978. text ed. 61. 55 (*90-279-7580-9*) Mouton.
Mavaridis, L. N., ed. see NATO Advanced Study Institute Staff.
Mavbank, Burnet, III, et al. The Law of Workers' Compensation in South Carolina. 1991. ring bd. 125.00 (*0-943856-30-2*, 431) SC Bar CLE.
MaVeciana, Jose, ed. SME's: Internationalization, Networks & Strategy. 736p. 1994. 105.95 (*1-85628-696-7*, Pub. by Avebury Pub UK) Ashgate Pub Co.
Maveety, Nancy. Representation Rights & the Burger Years. 280p. (C). 1991. text ed. 42.50 (*0-472-10227-3*) U of Mich Pr.
Mavel, Alain. Dictionnaire De Gynecologie et D'Obstetrique: Termes Usuels S'Hier et D'Aujourd'Hui. 592p. (FRE.). 1990. pap. write for info. (*0-7859-0499-9*, 2718404957) Fr & Eur.
Maver, T. & Wagter, H., eds. CAAD Futures '87: Proceedings of the 2nd International Conference on Computer-Aided Architectural Design Futures, Eindhoven, the Netherlands, 20-22 May, 1987. 262p. 1988. 87.25 (*0-444-42916-6*) Elsevier.
Maverick, Augustus. Henry J. Raymond & the New York Press: The Progress of American Journalism from 1840-1870. LC 78-125708. (American Journalists Ser.). 1971. reprint ed. 29.95 (*0-405-01689-1*) Ayer.
Maverick, Mary. Memoirs. LC 88-31141. (Illus.). xviii, 158p. 1989. pap. 5.95 (*0-8032-8159-5*) U of Nebr Pr.
— Memoirs. 1993. reprint ed. lib. bdg. 75.00 (*0-7812-5944-4*) Rprt Serv.
Maverick, Maury. Maverick American. 1993. reprint ed. lib. bdg. 75.00 (*0-7812-5969-X*) Rprt Serv.
Maves, Carolyn, jt. auth. see Maves, Paul.
Maves, Paul & Maves, Carolyn. Finding Your Way Through the Bible: Revised NRSV Edition. 176p. (Orig.). (J). (gr. 2-5). 1992. pap. 4.95 (*0-687-13046-8*) Abingdon.
Maves, Paul B. Understanding Ourselves As Adults. LC 59-4795. reprint ed. pap. 54.30 (*0-317-10345-8*, 2001254) Bks Demand.
Mavi, H. S. Introduction to Agrometeorology. (C). 1986. 14. 00 (*81-204-0122-0*, Pub. by Oxford IBH II) S Asia.
Mavian, Vahram. Selected Writings of Vahram Mavian, 1926-1983: A Unique Voice in Armenian Diaspora Literature. Hacikyan, Agop J., ed. & tr. by. Mamourian, Arsene, tr. LC 92-21428. 296p. 1992. text ed. 89.95 (*0-7734-9198-8*) E Mellen.
*__Maviglia, Joseph.__ A God Hangs Upside Down. 128p. 1994. pap. 10.00 (*1-55071-014-1*) Guernica Editions.
Mavigliano, George J. & Lawson, Richard A. The Federal Art Project in Illinois, 1939-1943. LC 89-6172. (Illus.). 192p. (C). 1990. 24.95 (*0-8093-1580-7*) S Ill U Pr.
Mavigliano, George J., jt. auth. see Lawson, Richard A.
Mavis, David G. The Fisherman's Edge: Your Personal Guide to the 1994 Peak Fishing Times. (Illus.). 128p. (Orig.). 1994. pap. 19.95 (*0-9640741-0-9*) Techno Leisure.
Mavissakalian, Matig & Barlow, David H., eds. Phobia: Psychological & Pharmacological Treatment. LC 80-15306. 256p. 1981. lib. bdg. 32.00 (*0-89862-602-1*) Guilford Pr.
Mavissakalian, Matig, et al, eds. Obsessive-Compulsive Disorder: Psychological & Pharmacological Treatment. 274p. 1985. 49.50 (*0-306-41850-9*, Plenum Pr) Plenum.
Mavituna, F., jt. auth. see Atkinson, B.

An Asterisk (*) at the beginning of an entry indicates that the title is appearing in BIP for the first time.

Mavlin, George J. & Mygak, Joe. The Guidebook to Municipal Bonds: The History, the Industry, the Mechanics. (Illus.). 228p. 1991. 29.95 (*0-9618162-7-9*) Thomson Financial.

Mavor, Anne S., ed. see Commission on Behavioral & Social Sciences & Education, National Research Council Staff.

Mavor, Anne S., ed. see National Research Council, Committee on Vision Staff.

***Mavor, Carol.** Pleasures Taken: Performances of Sexuality & Loss in Victorian Photographs. (Illus.). 208p. 1995. lib. bdg. 47.95 (*0-8223-1603-X*); pap. 17.95 (*0-8223-1619-6*) Duke.

Mavor, Elizabeth. The Captain's Wife: The South American Journals of Mario Graham 1821-23. 208p. 1993. 39.95 (*0-297-81296-3*) Trafalgar.

Mavor, J., ed. M.O.S.T. Integrated Circuit Engineering. LC 73-87027. (Illus.). 172p. reprint ed. pap. 49.10 (*0-685-23329-4*, 2032255) Bks Demand.

Mavor, James W., Jr. Voyage to Atlantis: A Firsthand Account of the Scientific Expedition to Solve the Riddle of the Ages. rev. ed. (Illus.). 320p. 1990. reprint ed. pap. 14.95 (*0-89281-269-9*) Inner Tradit.

Mavor, James W. & Dix, Byron E. Manitou. (Illus.). 392p. 1992. pap. 18.95 (*0-89281-078-5*) Inner Tradit.

Mavor, Michael B. Joseph Andrews Notes. 1971. pap. 3.75 (*0-8220-0682-0*) Cliffs.

Mavor, W. Ferrier. English for Business. 186p. 1980. pap. 14.95 (*0-8464-1318-3*) Beekman Pubs.

Mavragis, Edward. Writing: The Essay. 91p. 1991. student ed 4.95 (*1-56078-025-8*) Comp Pr.

Mavragis, Edward P., jt. auth. see Craz, Albert G.

Mavrich, Dorothy L. Rialto Square Theatre. (Illus.). 16p. 1993. 8.00 (*0-9635264-0-5*) D Mavrich.

Mavrides, Marios. Triangular Arbitrage in the Foreign Exchange Market: Inefficiencies, Technology, & Investment Opportunities. LC 91-47075. 200p. 1992. text ed. 55.00 (*0-89930-718-3*, Quorum Bks) Greenwood.

Mavrocordatos, Nicolas. Les Loisirs De Philothee. LC 90-189048. (Illus.). 253p. (FRE & GRE.). reprint ed. pap. 72.20 (*0-7837-6949-0*, 2046778) Bks Demand.

Mavrodes, George I. Revelation in Religious Belief. LC 87-26697. 168p. (C). 1988. 32.95 (*0-87722-545-1*) Temple U Pr.

Mavrodineanu, Radu. & Boiteux, Henri. Flame Spectroscopy. LC 64-20088. (Wiley Series in Pure & Applied Spectroscopy). 741p. reprint ed. pap. 180.00 (*0-317-08746-0*, 2007476) Bks Demand.

Mavrogordato, Alice, tr. see Hadamovsky, Eugen.

Mavrogordato, J. P. Hawk for the Bush. (Illus.). 224p. 1988. 45.00 (*0-87556-654-5*) Saifer.

Mavroiudis, Constantine. Pediatric Cardiac Surgery. 2nd ed. 512p. 1994. 149.00 (*0-8016-7045-4*) Mosby Yr Bk.

Mavrolas, Pamela & Schechtman, Michael. Coal Mine Subsidence: Proceedings from a Citizens' Conference. 2nd ed. Henderson, Harold, ed. 46p. 1982. reprint ed. 4.00 (*0-943724-01-5*) Illinois South.

Mavrolas, Pamela, ed. see Boulding, Russell.

Mavromatis, Andreas. Hypnagogia: The Unique State of Consciousness Between Wakefulness & Sleep. 360p. 1991. pap. 25.00 (*0-415-05794-9*, A4929) Routledge.

Mavromatis, Andreas, ed. Hypnogogia: The Unique State of Consciousness Between Wakefullness & Sleep. 353p. 1987. text ed. 70.00 (*0-7102-0282-2*, RKP) Routledge.

Mavromatis, Harry A. Exercises in Quantum Mechanics: A Collection of Illustrative Problems & Their Solutions. 1986. lib. bdg. 80.50 (*90-277-2288-9*) Kluwer Ac.

Mavrommatis, P. D. & Reichmeider, P. F. Precalculus Mathematics for Technical Students. (Technical Mathematics Ser.). (Illus.). 416p. 1976. write for info. (*0-13-695163-5*) P-H.

Mavros, P. & Matis, K. A., eds. Innovations in Flotation Technology. (C). 1991. lib. bdg. 174.00 (*0-7923-1560-X*) Kluwer Ac.

Mavrovitis, Basil P. Cashflow Credit & Collection: Over 100 Proven Techniques for Protecting & Strengthening. 1993. pap. 27.50 (*1-55738-522-X*) Probus Pub Co.

Mavrovouniotis, Michael L., ed. Artificial Intelligence in Process Engineering. 367p. 1990. text ed. 73.00 (*0-12-480575-2*) Acad Pr.

Maw, G. A. Biochemistry of S-Methyl-L-Cysteine & Its Principal Derivatives. (Sulfur Report Ser.). 31p. (Orig.). 1982. pap. text ed. 65.00 (*3-7186-0112-5*) Gordon & Breach.

Maw, Joan E. Twende! A Practical Swahili Course. (Illus.). 352p. 1985. 37.50 (*0-19-713605-2*) OUP.

***Maw, Mary & Patterson, Radha.** A Little Tuscan Cookbook. Brunesteyn, Lesley, ed. (Illus.). 60p. 1994. 7.95 (*0-8118-0803-3*) Chronicle Bks.

Maw, Nigel G., et al. Maw on Corporate Governance. Alsbury, Alison, ed. LC 93-41372. 206p. (C). 1994. 39.95 (*1-85521-378-8*, Pub. by Dartmth Pub UK) Ashgate Pub Co.

Maw, Roland, jt. auth. see Butler, James.

Mawby, Janet. Writers & Politics in Modern Scandinavia. LC 78-18931. (Writers & Politics Ser.). 53p. 1978. 15.95 (*0-8419-0414-6*); pap. text ed. 10.50 (*0-8419-0417-0*) Holmes & Meier.

Mawby, Larry, ed. see Sisson, Linda & Sisson, John.

Mawby, R. I. Comparative Policing Issues: The British & American Experience in International Perspective. 240p. 1992. text ed. 67.50 (*0-04-445545-3*, A7480); pap. text ed. 17.95 (*0-04-445544-5*, A7484) Routledge Chapman & Hall.

Mawby, R. I. & Gill, M. L. Crime Victims: Needs, Services, & the Voluntary Sector. (Illus.). 272p. (C). 1987. pap. text ed. 25.00 (*0-422-61450-5*, Pub. by Tavistock UK) Routledge Chapman & Hall.

Mawby, R. I. & Walklate, Sandra. Critical Victimology: International Perspectives. 240p. (C). 1994. text ed. 65.00 (*0-8039-8511-8*); pap. text ed. 19.95 (*0-8039-8512-6*) Sage.

Mawby, R. I., jt. auth. see Gill, M. L.

Mawby, R. I., jt. auth. see Gill.

Mawdesley-Thomas, Lionel E., et al. Diseases of Fish. 277p. (C). 1974. text ed. 24.50 (*0-8422-7178-3*) Irvington.

Mawdsley. Academic Misconduct: Cheating & Plagiarism. (Monograph Ser.: No. 51). 122p. (Orig.). 1993. pap. 26.95 (*1-56534-082-5*) NOLPE.

Mawdsley, et al. Yearbook of Education Law, 1993. Stephen, B. Thomas, ed. 360p. 1993. text ed. 45.95 (*1-56534-059-0*) NOLPE.

Mawdsley, Alice L., jt. auth. see Mawdsley, Ralph D.

Mawdsley, Andres A., pref. Palau: A Challenge to the Rule of Law in Micronesia: Report of a Mission by William J. Butler, Esq., The Hon. George C. Edwards, The Hon. Michael D. Kirby, C.M.G. 58p. (Orig.). (C). 1988. pap. text ed. 5.00 (*0-916265-04-8*) Am Assn Intl Comm Jurists.

Mawdsley, Dean L. The America of Eric Sloane: A Collector's Bibliography. 1990. write for info. (*0-918676-24-X*) Conn Hist Com.

— Cruise Books of the United States Navy in World War II: A Bibliography. LC 92-41498. 162p. 1993. 6.00 (*0-945274-13-0*) Naval Hist Ctr.

Mawdsley, Evan. Moscow & Leningrad. 2nd ed. 1991. pap. 22.50 (*0-393-30773-5*) Norton.

— The Russian Civil War. (Illus.). 320p. (C). 1987. text ed. 55.00 (*0-04-947024-8*); pap. text ed. 18.95 (*0-04-947025-6*) Routledge Chapman & Hall.

Mawdsley, Evan & Munck, Thomas. Computing for Historians: An Introductory Guide. (Illus.). 200p. 1993. pap. 19.95 (*0-7190-3454-X*, Pub. by Manchester Univ Pr UK) St Martin.

— Computing for Historians: An Introductory Guide. LC 92-38789. 1993. text ed. 59.95 (*0-7190-3547-3*, Pub. by Manchester Univ Pr UK); text ed. 19.95 (*0-7190-3548-1*, Pub. by Manchester Univ Pr UK) St Martin.

Mawdsley, R. Legal Problems of Religious & Private Schools. 1989. 15.50 (*1-56534-016-7*) NOLPE.

Mawdsley, Ralph D. Legal Aspects of Plagiarism. 1985. 9.95 (*1-56534-007-8*) NOLPE.

— Legal Aspects of Pupil Transportation. 1984. 9.95 (*1-56534-004-3*) NOLPE.

— Pupil Transportation & the Law. 73p. (Orig.). 1992. pap. 25.95 (*1-56534-077-9*) NOLPE.

Mawdsley, Ralph D. & Mawdsley, Alice L. Free Expression & Censorship: Public Policy & the Law. 1988. 12.95 (*1-56534-013-2*) NOLPE.

Mawdudi, Sayyid A. Towards Understanding Islam. Ahmad, Khurshid, tr. 179p. (Orig.). 1980. pap. 5.95 (*0-939830-22-1*, Pub. by IIFSO KW) New Era Publns MI.

Mawe, Sheelagh M. Dandelion: The Triumphant Life of a Misfit, a Story for All Ages. 165p. (Orig.). (J). (gr. 4). 1994. pap. 6.95 (*0-9642168-0-9*) Totally Unique.

***Mawer, Mick.** The Effective Teaching of Physical Education. LC 94-38241. (Effective Teacher Ser.). 1995. write for info. (*0-582-09522-0*, Pub. by Longman UK) Longman.

Mawhin, J. L. & Willem, M. Critical Point Theory & Hamiltonian Systems. (Applied Mathematical Sciences Ser.: Vol. 74). (Illus.). xiv, 277p. 1989. 59.00 (*0-387-96908-X*) Spr-Verlag.

Mawhin, Jean. Topological Degree Methods in Non-Linear Boundary Value Problems. LC 78-31906. (CBMS Regional Conference Series in Mathematics: No. 40). 122p. 1981. reprint ed. pap. 18.00 (*0-8218-1690-X*, CBMS-40) Am Math.

Mawhiney, Anne-Marie. Towards Aboriginal Self-Government: Relations Between Status Indian Peoples & the Government of Canada. LC 93-18018. (Reference Library of Social Science: Vol. 773). 160p. 1993. 23.00 (*0-8153-0823-X*, 93-18018) Garland.

Mawhinney, Brian & Wells, Ronald. Conflict & Christianity in Northern Ireland. LC 75-8948. (Illus.). 126p. reprint ed. pap. 36.00 (*0-317-09250-2*, 2012891) Bks Demand.

Mawhinney, Bruce. Preaching with Freshness. 1991. pap. 12.99 (*0-89081-898-3*) Harvest Hse.

Mawhinney, Charles H. A Modular Approach to dBASE IV: IBM Version. 96p. (C). 1992. spiral bd. write for info. (*0-697-13252-8*) Bus & Educ Tech.

Mawhinney, M. H., jt. auth. see Trinks, Willibald.

Mawhinney, Paul C. Musicmaster: The 45RPM: Singles Directory - Supplement Artist. 200p. (Orig.). 1992. pap. text ed. 50.00 (*0-910925-03-8*) Record-Rama.

— Musicmaster: The 45RPM: Singles Directory - Supplement Title. 200p. (Orig.). 1992. pap. text ed. 50.00 (*0-910925-04-6*) Record-Rama.

Mawhinney, Paul C., ed. Music Master: The CD-Five Singles Directory, 1994, Vol. One. 2nd ed. 194p. reprint ed. pap. 30.00 (*0-910925-07-0*) Record-Rama.

— Music Master: The Forty-Five RPM Christmas Singles Directory, 1994, Vol. One. 2nd ed. 142p. reprint ed. pap. 30.00 (*0-910925-08-9*) Record-Rama.

— Musicmaster: The 45 R.P.M. Record Directory, 2 vols., Set. 2500p. (Orig.). 1983. pap. 49.99 (*0-910925-02-X*) Record-Rama.

Mawhinney, Thomas C., ed. Organizational Behavior Management & Statistical Process Control: Theory, Technology & Research. LC 87-32520. (Journal of Organizational Behavior Management: Vol. 9, No. 1). (Illus.). 159p. 1988. text ed. 49.95 (*0-86656-751-8*) Haworth Pr.

— Pay for Performance: History, Controversy, & Evidence. LC 91-41350. (Journal of Organizational Behavior Management: Vol. 12, No. 1). 1992. text ed. 39.95 (*1-56024-254-X*); pap. text ed. 19.95 (*1-56024-255-8*) Haworth Pr.

Mawhinney, Thomas C., intro. Organizational Culture, Rule-Governed Behavior & Organizational Behavior Management: Theoretical Foundations & Implications for Research & Practice. LC 92-30026. (Journal of Organizational Behavior Management: Vol. 12, No. 2, 1992). (Illus.). 168p. 1993. lib. bdg. 32.95 (*1-56024-359-7*) Haworth Pr.

Mawhood, Philip, ed. Local Government in the Third World: The Experience of Tropical Africa. LC 82-11176. (Wiley Series on Public Administration in Developing Countries). (Illus.). 275p. reprint ed. pap. 78.40 (*0-8357-2954-0*, 2039210) Bks Demand.

Mawley, Edward, jt. auth. see Jekyll, Gertrude.

Mawson, Anthony R. Guide to Area Schools & Day Care Centers: New Orleans Region. 168p. (Orig.). 1989. pap. 9.95 (*0-9622274-0-4*) S & DCIS Inc.

— Transient Criminality: A Model of Stress-Induced Crime. LC 87-11741. 352p. 1987. text ed. 65.00 (*0-275-92552-8*, C2552, Praeger Pubs) Greenwood.

Mawson, C. O. Roget's Thesaurus: A Treasury of Synonyms & Antonyms. 1991. mass mkt. 4.99 (*0-06-100267-4*, Harper Ref) HarpC.

Mawson, C. O., ed. Roget's Pocket Thesaurus. pap. 3.95 (*0-317-56742-X*) PB.

Mawson, Thomas. The Imperial Obligation: Industrial Villages for the Partialy Disabled Soldiers & Sailors. Phillips, William R. & Rosenberg, Janet, eds. LC 79-6918. (Physically Handicapped in Society Ser.). 1980. reprint ed. lib. bdg. 17.95 (*0-405-13125-9*) Ayer.

Mawson, Timothy. Garden Rooms. LC 93-19680. (Illus.). 1994. 35.00 (*0-517-59015-8*, C P Pubs) Crown Pub Group.

Mawton, ed. Du Bellay: Poems. (Bristol French Texts Ser.). (FRE.). 1992. 13.95 (*0-685-49974-X*, Pub. by Brstl Class Pr UK) Focus Info Gr.

***Mawyer, Martin.** Defending the American Family. 224p. (Orig.). 1995. pap. 9.95 (*0-89221-296-9*) New Leaf.

— Pathways to Success: First Steps for Becoming a Christian in Action. LC 94-68852. 200p. (Orig.). 1994. pap. 9.95 (*0-89221-270-5*) New Leaf.

Max. Ignorance Almanac 1986: What You Know Ain't So. 14.95 (*0-911505-15-6*) Lifecraft.

— Peter Pank. Metz, Bernd, ed. (Illus.). 56p. (Orig.). 1991. pap. 10.95 (*0-87416-119-3*) Catalan Communs.

Max, Gerry. Concerto for Ten Broken Fingers. 162p. 1978. pap. 9.95 (*0-686-38100-9*, 101) William of Orange.

— Ixion's Wheel. 118p. 1979. pap. 9.95 (*0-686-38099-1*, 102) William of Orange.

Max, H., intro. Gay(s) Language: A Dic (k) tionary of Gay Slang. 50p. (Orig.). 1988. pap. 4.95 (*0-934411-15-8*, Banned Bks) Edward-William Austin.

Max, Herbert B. Business Investment & Loan Agreements: Forms & Authorities. suppl. ed. 1985. Supplements avail. 75.00 (*0-317-29386-9*, #H43902) HarBrace.

Max, Herbert B., jt. auth. see Frome, Robert L.

***Max, Ingolf & Stelzner, Werner, eds.** Logik und Mathematik: Frege-Kolloquium 1993. (Perspektiven der Analytischen Philosophie - Perspectives in Analytical Philosophy Ser.: Bd. 5). xi, 553p. (GER.). (C). 1995. lib. bdg. 207.70 (*3-11-014545-6*) De Gruyter.

Max, Jill, ed. see Bohlke, Dorothee.

Max, Jill, ed. see Mann, Marek.

Max, Mitchell B., et al. The Design of Analgesic Clinical Trials. (Advances in Pain Research & Therapy Ser.: Vol. 18). 752p. 1991. 135.00 (*0-88167-736-1*) Raven.

Max Mueller, F. Keshub Chunder Sen. rev. ed. Mookerjee, Nanda, ed. 1976. 6.00 (*0-88386-862-8*) S Asia.

Max-Muller, F. & Fleet, J. F. Indian Paleography from about B.C. 350 to about A.D. 1300: With a Life Sketch of Buhler. (Illus.). 140p. 1987. reprint ed. 20.00 (*0-88065-073-7*, Messers Today & Tomorrow) Scholarly Pubns.

Max-Neef, Manfred. From the Outside Looking In: Experiences in "Barefoot Economics" (Illus.). 208p. (C). 1992. text ed. 49.95 (*1-85649-187-0*, Pub. by Zed Books UK); pap. 17.50 (*1-85649-188-9*, Pub. by Zed Books UK) Humanities.

Max-Neef, Manfred, jt. ed. see Ekins, Paul.

Max-Neef, Manfred A. Human Scale Development: Conception, Application & Further Reflections. LC 91-12713. (Illus.). 128p. (Orig.). 1991. pap. 12.95 (*0-945257-35-X*) Apex Pr.

Max-Planck-Institut fuer Geschichte Staff, ed. Germania Sacra Neue Folge: Historisch-Statistische Bechreibung der Kirche des Alten Reiches, No. 31. (Illus.). xii, 560p. (GER.). (C). 1993. lib. bdg. 203.10 (*3-11-013657-0*) De Gruyter.

Max-Planck-Institut Fur Geschichte Staff, ed. Germania Sacra: Historisch-Statistische Beschreibung der Kirche Des Alten Reiches. (Illus.). xvii, 768p. (GER.). (C). 1991. lib. bdg. 252.35 (*3-11-012927-2*) De Gruyter.

— Germania Sacra: Historische-statistische Beschreibung der Kirche Des Alten Reiches. xii, 358p. (GER.). (C). 1992. lib. bdg. 144.65 (*3-11-013223-0*) De Gruyter.

***Max Planck Institute for Foreign & International Patent, Copyright & Competition Law Staff.** The Experimental Use Exemption from Patent Infringement Liability. LC 94-42982. 1995. write for info. (*3-527-28660-8*, Pub. by Vlg Chemie) VCH Pubs.

Max Planck Institute Staff. Justification & Excuse, Set. 1989. Vol. 1. 135.00 (*0-929179-22-6*) Transnatl Juris Pubns.

***Max-Planck-Society for the Advancement of Science, Gmelin Institute for Inorganic Chemistry Staff.** Gmelin: Handbook of Inorganic & Organometallic Chemistry. 8th ed. Incl. U Uranium Suppl Vol. B, Pt. 3: Alloys of Uranium with Transition Metals of Groups 1B to IVB. 8th ed. (Illus.). xviii, 304p. 1994. text ed. 1,267.00 (*0-387-93702-1*); B Boron - Boron Compounds Suppl Vol. 4, Pt. 1/a: Boron & Noble Gases, Hydrogen. (Illus.). xi, 157p. 1994. text ed. 665.00 (*0-387-93704-8*); write for info. (*0-615-00701-5*) Spr-Verlag.

***Max Plank Institute for History Staff & Theil, Bernhard, eds.** Germania Sacra: Historisch-Statistische Beschreibung der Kirche des Alten Reiches. xii, 224p. (GER.). (C). 1994. lib. bdg. 169.25 (*3-11-014214-7*) De Gruyter.

Max, Robert R. & Cerny, Sarah P. Power Writing. 167p. 1988. teacher ed 75.00 (*1-55678-008-7*) Learn Inc.

— Power Writing. rev. ed. 167p. 1988. reprint ed. digital audio 120.00 (*1-55678-006-0*) Learn Inc.

Max, Stanley M. The United States Great Britain & the Sovietization of Hungary 1945-1948. 1985. text ed. 42.00 (*0-88033-069-4*, 177) Col U Pr.

***Max, Tung A.** Preserving World's Cities. Date not set. write for info. (*0-517-70148-0*) Random.

Maxa, Kathleen, jt. auth. see Pulitzer, Roxanne.

Maxa, Kathy, jt. auth. see Pulitzer, Roxanne.

Maxam, Donald, Jr., ed. see Khedr, Sam & Maxam, Mark.

Maxam, Mark, jt. auth. see Khedr, Sam.

Maxcy, Kenneth F., ed. see Frost, Wade H.

***Maxcy, Spencer J.** Democracy, Chaos, & the New School Order. 240p. 1994. 45.95 (*0-8039-6198-7*) Corwin Pr.

— Democracy, Chaos, & the New School Order. 240p. 1994. pap. 22.95 (*0-8039-6199-5*) Corwin Pr.

— Educational Leadership: A Critical Pragmatic Perspective. LC 91-4637. (Critical Studies in Education & Culture). 240p. 1991. text ed. 55.00 (*0-89789-258-5*, H258, Bergin & Garvey); pap. text ed. 16.95 (*0-89789-259-3*, G259, Bergin & Garvey) Greenwood.

Maxcy, Spencer J., ed. Postmodern School Leadership: Meeting the Crisis in Educational Administration. LC 93-2868. 200p. 1993. text ed. 55.00 (*0-275-94565-0*, C4565, Praeger Pubs) Greenwood.

Maxeiner, James R. Policy & Methods in German & American Antitrust Law: A Comparative Study. LC 86-8108. 188p. 1986. text ed. 55.00 (*0-275-92113-1*, C2113, Praeger Pubs) Greenwood.

Maxes, Anna. Dead to Rights. 256p. 1994. 20.95 (*0-312-10449-9*) St Martin.

Maxewell, Joe, jt. auth. see Coen, Patricia.

Maxey, Gary S. The Latent Power of Mammon. pap. 3.99 (*0-88019-159-7*) Schmul Pub Co.

Maxey, I. Parker. The Cornerstone of Living. 1991. pap. 8.99 (*0-88019-276-3*) Schmul Pub Co.

— Man's Ascent to God. 1993. pap. 12.99 (*0-88019-306-9*) Schmul Pub Co.

— Ministerial Ethics & Etiquette. 1987. pap. 12.99 (*0-88019-222-4*) Schmul Pub Co.

Maxey, Julia, jt. auth. see Shillingburg, Peter L.

Maxey, M., jt. auth. see Park, M. E.

Maxey, Margaret N. & Kuhn, Robert L. Regulatory Reform: New Vision or Old Curse. LC 84-26261. 254p. 1985. text ed. 40.95 (*0-275-90145-9*, C0145, Praeger Pubs) Greenwood.

Maxey, Ron, jt. auth. see Harrison, Joyce M.

Maxey, Russell. Airports of Columbia: A Photographic History. (Illus.). 300p. 1987. 19.50 (*0-317-56064-6*) Palmetto Pub.

— Columbia's Bicentennial Seventeen Eighty-Six to Nineteen Eighty-Six. LC 86-60217. (Illus.). 180p. 1986. pap. 16.00 (*0-317-45809-4*) Palmetto Pub.

Maxfield. Charitable Organizations of the U. S. 2nd ed. 1991. 150.00 (*0-8103-8081-1*) Gale.

— Charitable Organizations of the U. S. 3rd ed. 1995. 150.00 (*0-8103-8511-2*) Gale.

— Taxation of Mining Operations. 1981. write for info. (*0-8205-1418-7*, 418) Bender.

***Maxfield, Albert & Brady, Robert.** Company D, Eleventh Regiment Maine Infantry Volunteers. 85p. 1995. reprint ed. pap. 9.95 (*0-9642029-5-6*) Union Pubng.

***Maxfield, Clive.** Bebop to the Boolean Boogie: An Unconventional Guide to Electronics Fundamentals, Components & Processes. 460p. 1995. pap. 35.00 (*1-878707-22-1*) HighText.

Maxfield, John E. & Maxfield, Margaret W. Abstract Algebra & Solution by Radicals. (Illus.). 224p. 1992. reprint ed. pap. 7.95 (*0-486-67121-6*) Dover.

Maxfield, Kathryn E. & Bucholz, Sandra. A Social Maturity Scale for Blind Preschool Children: A Guide to Its Use. 57p. 1957. pap. 9.95 (*0-89128-059-6*) Am Foun Blind.

Maxfield, Margaret W., jt. auth. see Maxfield, John E.

Maxfield, Michael & Maxfield, Myrica. The Sound of Success: Musical Motivation. 32p. (YA). 1992. 19.95 (*0-9634682-1-9*, 232822) Myrichael Way.

***Maxfield, Michael G. & Babbie, Earl.** Research Methods for Criminal Justice & Criminology. LC 94-37944. 395p. 1995. text ed. 52.95 (*0-534-23154-3*) Intl Thomson.

Maxfield, Myrica, jt. auth. see Maxfield, Michael.

Maxfield, Peter C. & Houghton, James L. Federal Income Taxation of Oil & Gas & Natural Resources Transactions, Cases & Materials on The. Garr, James R., ed. 335p. 1990. pap. text ed. 22.95 (*0-88277-781-5*) Foundation Pr.

Maxfield, Sylvia. Governing Capital: International Finance & Mexican Politics. LC 90-55137. 208p. 1990. 26.50 (*0-8014-2458-5*) Cornell U Pr.

Maxfield, Sylvia & Anzaldua, Ricardo, eds. Government & Private Sector in Contemporary Mexico. (Monograph Ser.: No. 20). 146p. (Orig.). (C). 1987. pap. 12.50 (*0-935391-71-1*, MN-20) UCSD Ctr US-Mex.

Maxham, Mintcy D., jt. auth. see Houck, Peter W.

Maxham, Robert, tr. see Tarrasch, S.

M

***Maxian, Bruce, ed.** ASIS '94: The Economics of Information-Proceedings of the 57th Annual Meeting of the American Society for Information Science. 115p. (1-56870-...) 1994. pap. 47.50 (*0-938734-93-8*) Learned Info.

Maxim, A. & Coppage. Wulfeck's Virginia Marriages. (Second Ser.). 280p. 1990. 42.50 (*0-317-02847-2*) A M Coppage.

Maxim, Bruce B., jt. auth. see Koffman, Elliot B.

Maxim, Bruce R., jt. auth. see Koffman, Elliot B.

Maxim, Daniel, et al. Covert German Rearmament, 1919-1939: Deception & Misperception. LC 84-11891. 160p. 1984. text ed. 45.00 (*0-313-27012-0*, U7012, Greenwood Pr) Greenwood.

Maxim, George W. Social Studies & the Elementary School Child. 4th ed. 528p. (C). 1990. write for info. (*0-675-21271-5*, Merrill Pub Co) Macmillan.

— Social Studies & the Elementary School Child. 5th ed. LC 94-11830. 528p. (C). 1994. write for info. (*0-02-377940-3*) Macmillan.

— The Sourcebook: Activities for Infants & Young Children. 2nd ed. 336p. (C). 1990. pap. write for info. (*0-675-21055-0*, Merrill Pub Co) Macmillan.

— The Very Young: Guiding Children from Infancy Through the Early Years. 4th ed. (Illus.). 576p. (C). 1993. pap. write for info. (*0-02-378171-8*) Macmillan.

Maxim, Jane & Bryan, Karen. Language & the Elderly: A Clinical Perspective. (Illus.). 278p. (Orig.). (C). 1994. pap. text ed. 54.00x (*1-56593-254-4*) Singular Publishing.

Maxim, John R. Bannerman's Law. 1991. pap. 4.99 (*0-553-29326-5*) Bantam.

Maxim, L. Daniel & Cook, Frank X. Financial Risk Analysis. LC 72-182226. (AMA Management Briefing Ser.). (Illus.). 70p. reprint ed. pap. 25.00 (*0-317-09128-X*, 2050386) Bks Demand.

Maxim, Silas P., jt. auth. see Lapham, William B.

Maximilian, C. Encyclopedic Dictionary of Genetics: Dictionar Enciclopedic de Genetica. (RUM.). 1984. write for info. (*0-8288-1445-7*, M15835) Fr & Eur.

Maximin, Daniel. Lone Sun. LC 89-30992. (CARAF Bks.). 352p. 1989. 35.00 (*0-8139-1224-5*); pap. 14.95 (*0-8139-1245-8*) U Pr of Va.

Maximoff, G. P. The Guillotine at Work: Twenty Years of Terror in Soviet Russia, 2 vols., Set. 1973. 600.00 (*0-87700-203-7*) Revisionist Pr.

Maximoff, G. P., ed. see Bakunin, Mikhail A.

Maximoff, Gregory P. The Guillotine at Work. Nowlin, William G., Jr., ed. 1979. pap. 13.00 (*0-932366-06-6*) Black Thorn Bks.

Maximov, Vladimir, ed. see Solzhenitsyn, et al.

Maximova, M. Global Problems & Peace Among Nations. 80p. 1982. 20.00 (*0-317-53759-8*, Pub. by Collets) St Mut.

Maximova, T. A., tr. see Gogotsi, Yu & Lavrenko, V. A.

Maximovitch, John. The Orthodox Veneration of Mary the Birthgiver of God: Orthodox Theological Texts. 4th rev. ed. St. Herman of Alaska Brotherhood Staff, ed. Rose, Seraphim, tr. & intro. by. LC 94-66189. (Illus.). 80p. 1994. pap. 7.00 (*0-938635-68-9*) St Herman AK.

Maximus, Valerius. Factorum et Dictorum Memorabilium Libri IX. Cum Inserti Auctoris Fragmento de Paraenominibus. Recensuit et Emendavit. vi, 792p. (LAT.). 1976. reprint ed. lib. bdg. 137.95 (*3-487-06117-1*) Lubrecht & Cramer.

Maxine, Cassin. Turnip's Blood. Maddox, Everette et al, eds. (Illus.). 112p. (Orig.). 1985. pap. 5.00 (*0-9614371-0-3*) Sisters Grim Pr.

Maxine, David, ed. see Baum, L. Frank.

Maxine, Mitchel. Blood on the Unicorn. abr. ed. 370p. 1995. pap. 9.95 (*1-56901-452-3*) NW Pub.

Maxmanian, Paul E., jt. auth. see Fox, Robert D.

Maxmen, Jerrold S. Essential Psychopathology. (Professional Bks.). 1986. 29.95 (*0-393-70029-1*) Norton.

— The Post-Physician Era: Medicine in the Twenty-First Century. LC 76-2442. 312p. reprint ed. pap. 89.00 (*0-317-07738-4*, 2016471) Bks Demand.

— Psychotropic Drugs: Fast Facts. 1991. pap. 29.95 (*0-393-70118-2*) Norton.

Maxmen, Jerrold S. & Ward, Nicholas G. Essential Psychopathology & Its Treatment. 2nd ed. 400p. (C). 1994. 40.00 (*0-393-70173-5*) Norton.

— Psychotropic Drugs: Fast Facts. 2nd ed. 320p. 1995. pap. 35.00 (*0-393-70181-6*) Norton.

Maxmin, Jody. The Painter of Berlin, 1686. (Illus.). 320p. 1988. text ed. 75.00 (*0-89241-404-9*) Caratzas.

Maxner, Joyce. Lady Bugatti. LC 90-19127. (Illus.). 32p. (J). (gr. k up). 1991. 13.95 (*0-688-10340-5*); lib. bdg. 13.88 (*0-688-10341-3*) Lothrop.

— Lady Bugatti. (Illus.). 32p. (J). (ps-3). 1993. pap. 4.99 (*0-14-054832-7*) Puffin Bks.

— Nicholas Cricket. LC 88-33076. (Illus.). 32p. (J). (gr. k-3). 1989. 14.00 (*0-06-024216-7*); lib. bdg. 13.89 (*0-06-024222-1*) HarpC Child Bks.

— Nicholas Cricket. LC 88-33076. (Trophy Picture Bk.). (Illus.). 28p. (J). (gr. k-3). 1991. pap. 4.95 (*0-06-443275-0*, Trophy) HarpC Child Bks.

Maxon, Antonia B. & Brackett, Diane. The Hearing-Impaired Child. 208p. 1992. 39.95 (*1-56372-013-2*, Andover Med Pubs) Buttrwrth-Heinemann.

Maxon, Dianne, jt. auth. see Patton, Sally J.

Maxon, Gayle. Douglas Johnson, "Birds of Magic" LC 90-60857. (Illus.). 32p. 1990. text ed. 9.00 (*0-935037-31-4*) G Peters Gallery.

— Edward Borein: Artist of the Old West. LC 84-61996. 48p. 1984. pap. 18.00 (*0-935037-02-0*) G Peters Gallery.

— A Selection of Paintings from the Gerald Peters Collection. LC 83-62810. (Illus.). 94p. 1987. pap. 18.00 (*0-935037-05-5*) G Peters Gallery.

Maxon, Gayle, ed. Beverly Pepper, Small Scale Sculpture & Drawings. LC 89-83479. (Illus.). 21p. 1989. 8.00 (*0-935037-28-4*) G Peters Gallery.

Maxon, Gayle & Hopkins, Quincie, eds. Carol Mothner. LC 86-60902. (Illus.). 15p. 1986. 10.00 (*0-935037-09-8*) G Peters Gallery.

Maxon, Gayle, ed. see Campbell, Lawrence.

Maxon, Gayle, ed. see Carlson, George A.

Maxon, Gayle, jt. intro. see Peters, Gerald P.

Maxon, Helen. D. Howard Hitchcock. 1986. 39.95 (*0-914916-63-7*) Ku Paa.

Maxon, James C. Lake Mead-Hoover Dam: The Story Behind the Scenery. LC 79-87573. (Illus.). 48p. 1980. pap. 6.95 (*0-916122-61-1*) KC Pubns.

Maxon, Robert M. Conflict & Accommodation in Western Kenya: The Gusii & the British, 1907-1963. LC 88-45734. (Illus.). 216p. 1989. 37.50 (*0-8386-3350-1*) Fairleigh Dickinson.

— East Africa: An Introductory History. 289p. 1986. 27.50 (*0-937058-24-6*) West Va U Pr.

— Struggle for Kenya: The Loss & Reassertion of Imperial Initiative, 1912-1923. LC 91-58952. (Illus.). 352p. 1993. 47.50 (*0-8386-3486-9*) Fairleigh Dickinson.

Maxon, Yale C. Control of Japanese Foreign Policy. LC 72-12330. 286p. 1973. reprint ed. text ed. 59.75 (*0-8371-6728-0*, MACJ, Greenwood Pr) Greenwood.

Maxson, Charles H. The Great Awakening in the Middle Colonies. 12.00 (*0-8446-1306-1*) Peter Smith.

Maxson, J. Robin, jt. auth. see Friesen, Garry.

Maxson, Linda & Daugherty, Charles. Genetics: A Human Perspective. 3rd ed. 448p. (C). 1992. pap. text ed. write for info. (*0-697-09918-0*) Wm C Brown Pubs.

Maxted, Traci & Tomsic, Melinda S. Don't Just Bake Cookies: A Handbook to Creative Volunteering in the Elementary School. (Illus.). 146p. 1990. pap. text ed. 18.00 (*0-87287-791-4*) Libs Unl.

***Maxton, Graeme.** Driving over a Cliff? Strategy & Analysis of the World's Car Industry. (C). 1994. pap. text ed. 29.25 (*0-201-59392-0*) Addison-Wesley.

Maxton, Hugh. At the Protestant Museum. 1986. pap. 10.95 (*0-85105-443-9*, Pub. by Colin Smythe Ltd UK) Dufour.

— The Engraved Passion: (New & Selected Poems) 120p. (C). 1991. 24.00 (*0-948268-96-4*, Pub. by Dedalus Pr IE); pap. 18.00 (*0-948268-95-6*, Pub. by Dedalus Pr IE) St Mut.

— Jubilee for Renegades. 1982. pap. 10.95 (*0-85105-392-0*, Pub. by Colin Smythe Ltd UK) Dufour.

— The Puzzle Tree Ascendant. (C). 1988. pap. 22.00 (*0-948268-34-4*, Pub. by Dedalus Pr IE) St Mut.

Maxton, Hugh, tr. Between: Selected Poems of Agnes Nemes Nagy. (C). 1988. pap. 15.00 (*0-948268-39-5*, Pub. by Dedalus Pr IE) St Mut.

Maxton, Hugh, ed. see Clarke, Austin.

***Maxton, Julie.** Nevill's Law of Trusts, Wills & Administration in New Zealand. 8th ed. 450p. 1985. pap. 54.00 (*0-409-70185-8*, NZ) Butterworth Legal Pubs.

Maxtone-Graham, John. Crossing & Cruising: From the Decline of Yesterday's Ocean Liners to the Rise of the Cruise Ships of Today. (Illus.). 320p. 1992. text ed. 30.00 (*0-684-19154-7*, Scribners) S&S Trade.

— From Song to Sovereign. (Illus.). 96p. 1987. 15.00 (*0-945335-00-8*) Intl Voyage.

— From Song to Sovereign. rev. ed. (Illus.). 112p. 1987. 15.00 (*0-945335-01-6*); pap. 10.95 (*0-945335-02-4*) Intl Voyage.

— The Only Way to Cross. (Illus.). 448p. 1978. pap. 26.00 (*0-02-096010-7*, Collier S&S) S&S Trade.

Maxtone-Graham, Katrina. An Adopted Woman. 1982. write for info. (*0-318-56975-2*) Eleventh Hour.

— An Adopted Woman. LC 82-71563. 1983. 21.95 (*0-943362-00-8*) Remi Bks.

— Pregnant by Mistake: The Stories of Seventeen Women. rev. ed. 456p. 1990. reprint ed. 21.95 (*0-943362-01-6*); reprint ed. pap. 12.95 (*0-943362-02-4*) Remi Bks.

***Maxwell.** Billie Dyer & Other Stories. 2.99 (*0-517-13584-1*) Random Hse Value.

— Diamond Tiger. 1994. pap. 2.99 (*0-06-108260-0*, PL) HarpC Child Bks.

— Just Dial a Number. (J). 1990. pap. 2.99 (*0-671-72867-9*) PB.

— Leadership, 101. 1994. pap. text ed. 5.95 (*1-56292-077-4*) Honor Bks OK.

— An Outline of Psychotherapy for Medical Students & Practitioners. 107p. 1986. 22.95 (*0-7236-0849-0*, Pub. by John Wright UK) Buttrwrth-Heinemann.

— Plastic Surgery of the Breast. (Illus.). 900p. 1991. 250.00 (*0-8016-5821-7*) Mosby Yr Bk.

— Plastic Surgery of the Breast. 900p. 1995. 250.00 (*0-8016-7507-3*) Mosby Yr Bk.

— Psychotherapy. 2nd ed. 1991. 43.95 (*1-56593-574-8*, 0304) Singular Publishing.

— Scandinavian Cooking. 1995. (*0-7858-0186-3*) Bk Sales Inc.

— Tarot. 1995. pap. 17.95 (*0-85207-206-6*) Atrium Pubs.

— Women in Ministry: An Historical & Biblical Look at the Role of Women in Christian Leadership. 1995. pap. text ed. 7.99 (*0-87509-587-9*) Chr Pubns.

Maxwell & Satake, Eiki. Theory of Probability for Clinical Diagnostic Testing. 123p. (C). 1993. teacher ed 12.95 (*1-56870-062-8*) RonJon Pub.

Maxwell, A. King of Nothing. 1994. mass mkt. 5.50 (*0-06-104230-7*, Harp PBks) HarpC.

Maxwell, A. E. Art of Survival. 1993. mass mkt. 4.99 (*0-06-104115-7*, Harp PBks) HarpC.

— Frog & the Scorpion. 1993. mass mkt. 4.99 (*0-06-104113-0*, Harp PBks) HarpC.

— Gatsby's Vineyard. 1993. mass mkt. 4.99 (*0-06-104112-2*, Harp PBks) HarpC.

— The Golden Empire. (Orig.). 1979. pap. 2.50 (*0-449-14267-1*, GM) Fawcett.

— Just Another Day in Paradise. 1993. mass mkt. 4.99 (*0-06-104114-9*, Harp PBks) HarpC.

— Just Enough Light to Kill. 1993. mass mkt. 4.99 (*0-06-104111-4*, Harp PBks) HarpC.

— The King of Nothing. large type ed. 1993. reprint ed. lib. bdg. 17.95 (*1-56054-594-1*) Thorndike Pr.

— Money Burns. 1993. mass mkt. 5.50 (*0-06-104123-8*, Harp PBks) HarpC.

— Money Burns. 1991. 17.50 (*0-394-58873-8*, Villard Bks) Random.

— Multivariate Analysis in Behavioral Research: For Medical & Social Science Students. 2nd ed. 1977. 19.95 (*0-412-14300-3*, NO. 6193) Chapman & Hall.

— Murder Always Hurts: A Fiddler Novel. LC 92-46654. 1993. 18.00 (*0-679-41817-2*, Villard Bks) Random.

— Murder Hurts. 1994. pap. 4.99 (*0-06-104318-4*, Harp PBks) HarpC.

— Redwood Empire. (Historical Ser.). 1995. mass mkt. 4.50 (*0-373-28867-0*, 1-28867-9) Harlequin Bks.

Maxwell, Aileen & Maxwell, Thomas. Canyonlands of Utah: A Pictorial of the Needles District. (Illus.). 32p. (Orig.). 1985. pap. 4.95 (*0-9614389-0-8*) Rigelle Pubns.

Maxwell, Alice. The Gift of Laughter & Nineteen Other Short Stories. 1974. 10.00 (*0-685-41736-0*) Fountainhead.

Maxwell, Alice S. & Dunlevy, Marion B. Virago! The Story of Anne Newport Royall 1769-1854. LC 84-42731. 1991. pap. 19.98 (*0-9629706-0-3*) Dunwell Pr.

Maxwell, Allen, jt. ed. see Hudson, Wilson M.

***Maxwell, Ann.** Fire Dancer. 288p. 1995. pap. 5.99 (*0-7860-0155-0*) Windsor NY.

— Fire Dancer. 288p. 1995. pap. 5.99 (*0-8217-0155-X*) Zebra.

— Ruby. 1994. pap. 5.50 (*0-06-104269-2*, Harp PBks) HarpC.

— The Secret Sisters. large type ed. LC 94-2975. 1994. 18.95 (*0-7862-0202-5*) Thorndike Pr.

Maxwell, Anne. The Diamond Tiger. (Orig.). 1992. mass mkt. 4.99 (*0-06-104079-7*, Harp PBks); mass mkt. 4.99 (*0-06-104181-5*, Harp PBks) HarpC.

— The Secret Sisters. 1993. mass mkt. 5.50 (*0-06-104236-6*, Harp PBks) HarpC.

Maxwell, Anthony, jt. auth. see Bates, Andrew D.

Maxwell, Arthur S. & Holloway, Cheryl W. Uncle Arthur's Storytime. (Children's True Adventures Classic Edition Ser.: Vol. 3). (Illus.). 128p. (J). 1989. 29.90 (*1-877773-03-4*) Fam Media.

— Uncle Arthur's Storytime, Vol. 1. (Children's True Adventures Classic Edition Ser.). (Illus.). 128p. (J). 1989. lib. bdg. 29.90 (*1-877773-01-8*) Fam Media.

— Uncle Arthur's Storytime, Vol. 2. (Children's True Adventures Classic Edition Ser.). (Illus.). 128p. (YA). 1989. lib. bdg. 29.90 (*1-877773-02-6*) Fam Media.

Maxwell, Baldwin, ed. see Shakespeare, William.

Maxwell, Bernard J., et al. Easter for Fifty Days. LC 88-51302. 96p. (Orig.). 1989. pap. 12.95 (*0-89622-367-1*) Twenty-Third.

***Maxwell, Bruce.** How to Access the Federal Government on the Internet 1995: Washington Online. 250p. 1995. pap. 19.95 (*1-56802-034-1*) Congr Quarterly.

Maxwell, Bruce & Jacobson, Michael F. Marketing Disease to Hispanics. (Illus.). 100p. (Orig.). 1989. per., pap. 6.95 (*0-89329-020-3*) Ctr Sci Public.

Maxwell, Bruce, jt. auth. see Jacobson, Michael F.

Maxwell, C. The Pergamon Dictionary of Perfect Spelling. 2nd ed. LC 78-40291. 335p. 1978. pap. 11.75 (*0-08-022865-8*, Pergamon Pr) Elsevier.

Maxwell, C. Bede. The New German Shorthaired Pointer. 4th ed. LC 82-3059. (Illus.). 320p. 1982. 29.95 (*0-87605-157-3*) Howell Bk.

Maxwell, C. J. Minear, Descendants of John Minear (1732-1781) 232p. 1993. reprint ed. lib. bdg. 46.50 (*0-8328-3243-X*); reprint ed. pap. 36.50 (*0-8328-3244-8*) Higginson Bk Co.

Maxwell, C. Mervyn. God Cares, Vol. 1. 1981. pap. 12.95 (*0-8163-0390-8*) Pacific Pr Pub Assn.

— Magnificent Disappointment: A Restored View of What Really Happened in 1844 & What It Teaches Us about Jesus & the Adventist Church Today. LC 93-27338. 1994. pap. 9.95 (*0-8163-1180-3*) Pacific Pr Pub Assn.

Maxwell, Carolyn, ed. Haydn: Solo Piano Literature-A Comprehensive Guide Annotated & Evaluated with Thematics. (Maxwell Music Evaluation Bks.). (Illus.). 200p. (Orig.). (C). 1983. pap. 7.95 (*0-912531-00-2*) Maxwell Mus Eval.

— Mozart: Solo Piano Literature - A Comprehensive Guide: Annotated & Evaluated with Thematics. (Maxwell Music Evaluation Bks.). (Illus.). 347p. (Orig.). 1987. pap. 13.95 (*0-912531-04-5*) Maxwell Mus Eval.

— Scarlatti: Solo Piano Literature-A Comprehensive Guide Annotated & Evaluated with Thematics. (Maxwell Music Evaluation Bks.). (Illus.). 412p. (Orig.). 1985. pap. 13.95 (*0-912531-02-9*) Maxwell Mus Eval.

— Schubert: Solo Piano Literature-A Comprehensive Guide: Annotated & Evaluated with Thematics. (Maxwell Music Evaluation Bks.). (Illus.). (Orig.). 1986. pap. 12.95 (*0-912531-03-7*) Maxwell Mus Eval.

Maxwell, Carolyn & DeVan, William, eds. Schumann: Solo Piano Literature-A Comprehensive Guide: Annotated & Evaluated with Thematics. (Maxwell Music Evaluation Bks.). (Illus.). 339p. (Orig.). 1984. pap. 11.95 (*0-912531-01-0*) Maxwell Mus Eval.

Maxwell, Carolyn, ed. see Owens, Vivian W.

Maxwell, Cassandre. Bright Star, Bright Star, What Do You See? LC 89-82551. (Illus.). 32p. (J). (ps-00). 1990. pap. 5.99 (*0-8066-2462-0*, 9-2462) Augsburg Fortress.

— Yosef's Gift of Many Colors: An Easter Story. LC 92-44189. 32p. (J). (ps-3). 1993. 14.99 (*0-8066-2627-5*, 9-2627) Augsburg Fortress.

Maxwell, Cathy. All Things Beautiful. 1994. mass mkt. 4.50 (*0-06-108278-3*, Harp PBks) HarpC.

Maxwell, Charles E. Financial Markets & Institutions: The Global View. Bruckner, ed. LC 93-36889. 700p. (C). 1993. text ed. 61.50 (*0-314-02821-8*) West Pub.

Maxwell, Christine & Gregory, O. B. Spelling Basics. 128p. (C). 1993. pap. text ed. 11.95 (*1-56118-091-2*); teacher ed, pap. text ed. 8.00 (*1-56118-092-0*) Paradigm MN.

— Spelling Basics, Set 2. (C). 1993. digital audio 36.00 (*1-56118-090-4*) Paradigm MN.

***Maxwell, Christine & Grycz, Czeslaw J.** New Riders' Official Internet Yellow Pages. 2nd ed. LC 94-34785. 800p. 1994. pap. 29.99 (*1-56205-408-2*) New Riders Pub.

Maxwell, Colin. Model Making. (Fresh Start Ser.). (Illus.). 48p. (J). (gr. 5-8). 1992. lib. bdg. 12.95 (*0-531-14195-0*) Watts.

Maxwell-Cook, John C. Fundamental Structural Diagrams. (Viewpoint Publication Ser.). (Illus.). 1978. text ed. 45.00 (*0-7210-1073-3*, Pub. by C & CA UK) Scholium Intl.

— Structural Notes & Details. (C & CA Viewpoint Publication Ser.). (Illus.). 1976. text ed. 40.00 (*0-7210-1006-7*, Pub. by C & CA UK) Scholium Intl.

Maxwell, D. E. Brian Friel. LC 76-125299. (Irish Writers Ser.). 110p. 1975. pap. 1.95 (*0-8387-7666-3*) Bucknell U Pr.

***Maxwell, D. R.** EC Study-Lessons Learnt from Emergencies after Accidents in Ireland Involving Dangerous Substances. 98p. 1994. pap. 25.00 (*92-826-7516-5*, CLNA15565ENC, Pub. by Europ Com) UNIPUB.

Maxwell, Dan & Schubert, Klaus, eds. Metataxis in Practice: Dependency Syntax for Multilingual Machine Translation. (Distributed Language Translation Ser.). 323p. (Orig.). (C). 1989. 98.60 (*90-6765-422-1*, Pinnacle NY); pap. 80.00 (*90-6765-421-3*, Pinnacle NY) Mouton.

Maxwell, Dan, jt. ed. see Schubert, Klaus.

Maxwell, Dan, et al, eds. New Directions in Machine Language. (Distributed Language Translation Ser.). 259p. (C). 1988. 90.80 (*90-6765-377-2*); pap. 61.55 (*90-6765-378-0*) Mouton.

Maxwell, David. Private Security Law Case Studies: Torts, Agency, Contracts, Damages. 480p. 1993. 54.95 (*0-7506-9034-8*) Buttrwrth-Heinemann.

Maxwell, David, jt. auth. see Barefoot, J. Kirk.

***Maxwell, Donald.** Economics. 3rd ed. 736p. (C). 1993. student ed, text ed. 19.95 (*0-256-11808-6*) Irwin.

— Macroeconomics. 3rd ed. 432p. (C). 1993. student ed, text ed. 18.95 (*0-256-11811-6*) Irwin.

— Microeconomics. 3rd ed. 488p. (C). 1993. student ed, text ed. 18.95 (*0-256-11810-8*) Irwin.

Maxwell, Donald W. Literature of the Great Lakes Region: An Annotated Bibliography. LC 91-14663. 502p. 1991. 62.00 (*0-8240-7027-5*, H1252) Garland.

Maxwell, Dorothy B. A Florida Guidebook . . . Five Hundred Free or Exceptionally Low-Cost Places to Go and Things to Do in Florida (Nothing over 2.50) 112p. (Orig.). 1988. per., pap. 6.95 (*0-929731-00-X*) Ariel Publishing.

Maxwell, E. Mind of My Own. Date not set. 23.00 (*0-685-69284-1*, HarpT) HarpC.

Maxwell, Edwin A. Fallacies in Mathematics. 1959. 24.95 (*0-521-05700-0*) Cambridge U Pr.

Maxwell, Elisabeth. A Mind of My Own. 1994. 25.00 (*0-06-017104-9*, HarpT) HarpC.

Maxwell, Emily. An Easter Disguise. 320p. 1994. mass mkt. 3.99 (*0-8217-4515-8*) Zebra.

— Queen of Hearts. 1992. pap. 3.50 (*0-8217-3639-6*) Zebra.

— Wicked Count. 1990. pap. 2.95 (*0-8217-2994-2*) Zebra.

Maxwell, Ernest, illus. Trees of the San Jacinto Mountains. 32p. 1976. pap. 1.75 (*0-913612-02-2*) Strawberry Valley.

***Maxwell, Evan.** All the Winters That Have Been: A Novel. 192p. 1995. 15.00 (*0-06-017633-4*) HarpC.

***Maxwell, Fay.** Carroll & Harrison County, Ohio: Eckley & Perry 1921 Ohio History Index. 24p. 1983. 10.00 (*1-885463-01-4*) Ohio Genealogy.

— The 1880 Franklin & Pickaway Counties, Ohio: History Illustrations Index. (Illus.). 4p. 1984. 3.00 (*1-885463-12-X*) Ohio Genealogy.

— Fairfield County, Ohio: Hervey Scott's 1795-1876 History Index & C. M. L. Wiseman History Index Plus Fairfield County 1806 Taxables & Fairfield County, Lancaster 1803-1865 Will Index. 102p. 1971. 15.00 (*1-885463-02-2*) Ohio Genealogy.

— Franklin County, Ohio: Columbus 1843 City Directory Indexed Including Important Events in Columbus 1797-1843 Plus Franklin County Death Records 1811-1832 from Area Newspapers. 55p. 1977. 10.00 (*1-885463-03-0*) Ohio Genealogy.

— Franklin County, Ohio: Franklinton Cemetary Records. 14p. 1985. 3.00 (*1-885463-10-3*) Ohio Genealogy.

— Franklin County, Ohio: German Village & Brewery History Including Index. 57p. 1971. 8.00 (*1-885463-07-3*) Ohio Genealogy.

— Franklin County, Ohio: Living in a Landmark, a Pictorial of German Village. 54p. 1971. 4.00 (*1-885463-08-1*) Ohio Genealogy.

— Franklin County, Ohio: Scotch-Irish Accadian Nova Scotia Refugee Tract History Traces Them Back to Scotland, a First. 160p. 1974. 30.00 (*1-885463-11-1*) Ohio Genealogy.

— Franklin County, Ohio: Taxables of 1806, 1810 & 1814 Plus Franklin County 1803-1865 Will Index. 43p. 1976. 10.00 (*1-885463-04-9*) Ohio Genealogy.

— Franklin County, Ohio: 1826, 1832 & 1842 Chattels. 120p. 1978. 30.00 (*1-885463-05-7*) Ohio Genealogy.

— Franklin County, Ohio: 1860 Mortality Schedules, Complete Death Records. 24p. 1977. 5.00 (*1-885463-09-X*) Ohio Genealogy.

— Franklin County, Ohio: 1864 Civil War Military Roster Index. 98p. 1984. 25.00 (*1-885463-06-5*) Ohio Genealogy.

— Jackson County, Ohio: Romain Aten Jones 1842 History Index. 14p. 1976. 4.00 (*1-885463-13-8*) Ohio Genealogy.

— Lake County, Ohio: 1940 WPA History Index. 7p. 1975. 3.00 (*1-885463-14-6*) Ohio Genealogy.

An Asterisk (*) at the beginning of an entry indicates that the title is appearing in BIP for the first time.

— Laws & Religions 4713 B. C. to 1948 A. D. First Facts in World Order. 23p. 1968. 15.00 (1-885463-15-4) Ohio Genealogy.

— Licking County, Ohio: Records Indexes to Licking County 1808-1822 Marriages & Isaac Smucker's Centennial History Index. 117p. 1984. 20.00 (1-885463-16-2) Ohio Genealogy.

— Maxwell History & Genealogies Many Lines: 1970 to Northern Ireland Then Back to 12th Century Scotland. 165p. 1977. 30.00 (1-885463-17-0) Ohio Genealogy.

— Muskingum County, Ohio: J. F. Everhart History Index & Muskingum County Duplicate Tax Lists of 1807. 53p. 1976. 10.00 (1-885463-19-7) Ohio Genealogy.

— Muskingum County, Ohio: Marriages 1804-1818 & Some of 1818-1835. 86p. 1977. 15.00 (1-885463-18-9) Ohio Genealogy.

— Northwest Territory 1800 Census: Index of Washington County, Ohio 1791-1803 Marriages & Thomas Summers History of Marietta Index Plus Wm. P. Cutlers List of Signers of July 13, 1787 Ordinance. 51p. 1973. 10.00 (1-885463-20-0) Ohio Genealogy.

— Ohio Charles Galbreath's History of Ohio Index: Leaders of 1900's. 7p. 1973. 5.00 (1-885463-23-5) Ohio Genealogy.

— Ohio Genealogical Helper Covers Ohio Sources, Excellent for Out of State Searchers: Covering Available Record Locations. 53p. 1975. 5.00 (1-885463-21-9) Ohio Genealogy.

— Ohio Indian, Revolutionary War & War of 1812 Trails. 59p. 1974. 7.00 (1-885463-22-7) Ohio Genealogy.

— Ohio Revolutionary War Soldiers 1840 Census: Also Grave Locations. 69p. 1985. 10.00 (1-885463-24-3) Ohio Genealogy.

— Ohio's Virginia Military Tract Settlers: Also 1801 Tax List. 25p. 1991. 10.00 (1-885463-25-1) Ohio Genealogy.

— Perry County, Ohio: Clement L. Martzolff 1902 History Index. 18p. 1983. 7.00 (1-885463-26-X) Ohio Genealogy.

— Virginia, Augusta County: Rev. John Craig, D.D., Baptistmal Records 1740-1749 Scotch-Irish Father-Child Name Lists, Incomplete, Many Came to Ohio. 21p. 1975. 5.00 (1-885463-28-6) Ohio Genealogy.

— Washington County, Ohio: Marriages 1804-1823. 26p. 1974. 6.00 (1-885463-29-4) Ohio Genealogy.

Maxwell, Fowden G. & Jennings, Peter R., eds. Breeding Plants Resistant to Insects. LC 79-13462. (Environmental Science & Technology Ser.). 700p. reprint ed. pap. 180.00 (0-7837-2811-5, 2057661) Bks Demand.

Maxwell, G., jt. auth. see Hanson, W.

Maxwell, G. W., jt. auth. see Giordano, Albert G.

Maxwell, Gavin. Raven Seek Thy Brother. large type ed. 1970. 15.95 (0-85456-001-7) Ulverscroft.

— A Reed Shaken by the Wind: A Journey Through the Unexplored Marshlands of Iraq. large type ed. 283p. 1990. 19.95 (1-85089-272-5, Pub. by ISIS UK) Transaction Pubs.

— Ring of Bright Water. 236p. 1987. pap. 9.95 (0-14-003923-6, Penguin Bks) Viking Penguin.

— Ring of Bright Water. large type ed. 292p. 1991. 11.47 (1-85089-591-0, Pub. by ISIS UK) Transaction Pubs.

— The Rocks Remain. large type ed. 1976. 12.00 (0-85456-404-7) Ulverscroft.

Maxwell, Georgia, ed. see Holmes, Ernest.

***Maxwell, Geraldine Boldt.** Royal Matron's Treasury of Addresses & Ceremonies. pap. 2.00 (0-88053-319-6, S-295) Wilson Pub.

Maxwell, Gilbert S. Navajo Rugs: Past, Present & Future. (Illus.). 95p. (Orig.). 1995. reprint ed. 8.95 (0-918080-35-5, 20962) Treas Chest Bks.

Maxwell, Gleyn. Out of the Rain. 1992. pap. 16.95 (1-85224-193-4) Dufour.

— Tale of the Mayor's Son. LC 90-80810. 96p. 1990. pap. 14.95 (1-85224-098-9, Pub. by Bloodaxe Bks UK) Dufour.

***Maxwell, Glyn.** Blue Burneau. 288p. 1995. pap. 16.95 (0-7011-6071-3, Pub. by Chatto & Windus UK) Trafalgar.

— Gnyss the Magnificent: Three Verse Plays. 312p. 1994. pap. 19.95 (0-7011-5723-2, Pub. by Chatto & Windus UK) Trafalgar.

Maxwell, Gordon. The Romans in Scotland. 250p. (C). 1989. 90.00 (0-901824-76-3, Pub. by Mercat Pr Bks UK) St Mut.

Maxwell, Gordon S. A Battle Lost: Romans & Caledonians at Mons Graupius. (Illus.). 112p. 1988. 20.00 (0-85224-490-8, Pub. by Edinburgh U Pr UK) Col U Pr.

Maxwell, Graham. Servants or Friends? Another Look at God. LC 92-15397. (Illus.). 224p. 1992. 15.95 (1-56652-000-2); pap. 9.95 (1-56652-001-0); digital audio 15.95 (0-685-59396-7) Pine Knoll Pubns.

Maxwell, Grant T. Music for Three or More Pianists: A Historical Survey & Catalogue. LC 92-37842. 387p. 1992. 42.50 (0-8108-2631-3) Scarecrow.

Maxwell, Grover, jt. ed. see Feyerabend, Paul K.

Maxwell, Grover, et al. The Nature & Function of Scientific Theories: Essays in Contemporary Science & Philosophy. Colodny, Robert G., ed. LC 70-123094. (Pittsburg University Series in Philosophy of Science: Vol. 4). 379p. reprint ed. pap. 108.10 (0-317-26634-9, 2025434) Bks Demand.

Maxwell, H. Douglas: A History of the House of Douglas, from the Earliest Times to the Legislative Union of England & Scotland, 2 vols. in 1, Set. (Illus.). 1992. reprint ed. lib. bdg. 109.50 (0-8328-2472-0); reprint ed. pap. 99.50 (0-8328-2473-9) Higginson Bk Co.

Maxwell, H. V. History of Randolph County, West Virginia. 531p. 1993. reprint ed. lib. bdg. 55.00 (0-8328-3122-0) Higginson Bk Co.

Maxwell, Helen & Maxwell, Michael. Home Safe Home: How to Safeguard Your Home & Family Against Break-Ins. LC 92-60612. 288p. (Orig.). 1992. pap. 13.95 (0-88282-113-X) New Horizon NJ.

Maxwell, Herbert E. Robert the Bruce & the Struggle for Scottish Independence. LC 73-14456. (Heroes of the Nations Ser.). reprint ed. 30.00 (0-404-58274-5) AMS Pr.

Maxwell, Hu. The History of Barbour County, West Virginia. (Illus.). 517p. 1994. reprint ed. lib. bdg. 52.50 (0-8328-3922-1) Higginson Bk Co.

— History of Randolph County. 531p. 1991. reprint ed. pap. 20.00 (0-87012-051-4) McClain.

— The History of Randolph County, West Virginia. (Illus.). 531p. 1994. reprint ed. lib. bdg. 55.00 (0-8328-3921-3) Higginson Bk Co.

Maxwell, Hudson C. Complete Book of Massage. 1988. pap. 17.00 (0-394-75975-3) Random.

Maxwell-Hudson, Clare. Massaging with Essential Oils: The Complete Illustrated Guide to Aromatherapy. LC 94-16051. (Illus.). 112p. 1994. 19.95 (1-56458-642-1) Dorling Kindersley.

Maxwell-Hyslop, A. R., tr. see Grimal, Pierre.

Maxwell-Hyslop, A. R., tr. see Montet, Pierre.

Maxwell, I. & Phillips, A. A. In Fealty to Apollo. 6th ed. 1966. 14.95 (0-522-83671-2) Intl Spec Bk.

Maxwell, J. B. Data Book on Hydrocarbons: Application to Process Engineering. LC 74-30163. 268p. 1975. reprint ed. text ed. 34.50 (0-88275-257-X) Krieger.

Maxwell, J. C., ed. see Shakespeare, William.

Maxwell, J. C., ed. see Wordsworth, William.

Maxwell, J. R., jt. ed. see Douglas, A G.

Maxwell, J. W., ed. Applications of Information Technology in Construction. 346p. 1991. text ed. 97.00 (0-7277-1653-0, Pub. by T Telford UK) Am Soc Civil Eng.

Maxwell, Jack M. Worship & Reformed Theology: The Liturgical Lessons of Mercersburg. LC 75-45492. (Pittsburgh Theological Monographs: No. 10). 1976. pap. 12.00 (0-915138-12-3) Pickwick.

Maxwell, James. Narrative of Charles Prince of Wales' Expedition to Scotland in the Year 1745. LC 73-173063. (Maitland Club, Glasgow. Publications: No. 53). reprint ed. 20.00 (0-404-53035-4) AMS Pr.

— Plastics in the Automobile Industry. (Authored (Royalty) Ser.). 200p. 1994. 69.00 (1-56091-527-7, R-147) Soc Auto Engineers.

Maxwell, James A. Federal Grants & the Business Cycle. (Fiscal Studies Ser.: No. 4). 138p. 1952. reprint ed. 35. 90 (0-87014-120-1); reprint ed. mic. film 20.00 (0-685-61288-0) Natl Bur Econ Res.

— Fiscal Policy, Its Techniques & Institutional Setting. LC 68-9710. (Illus.). 218p. 1969. reprint ed. text ed. 55.00 (0-8371-0165-4, MAFP, Greenwood Pr) Greenwood.

— Maxwell Macmillan Federal Tax Handbook: Professional and Business Reference Division. 1991. pap. 27.95 (0-02-081141-1) Macmillan.

— Recent Developments in Dominion-Provincial Fiscal Relations in Canada. (Occasional Papers: No. 25). 64p. 1948. reprint ed. 20.00 (0-87014-340-9); reprint ed. mic. film 20.00 (0-685-61274-0) Natl Bur Econ Res.

— Tax Credits & Intergovernmental Fiscal Relations. LC 86-22731. 216p. 1987. reprint ed. text ed. 59.75 (0-313-25279-3, MATX, Greenwood Pr) Greenwood.

Maxwell, James C. Electricity & Magnetism, 2 Vols, 1. (Illus.). 1891. pap. text ed. 9.95 (0-486-60636-8) Dover.

— Electricity & Magnetism, 2 Vols, 2. (Illus.). 1891. pap. text ed. 9.95 (0-486-60637-6) Dover.

— Matter & Motion. 176p. reprint ed. pap. 6.95 (0-486-66895-9) Dover.

— Maxwell on Molecules & Gases. Garber, Elizabeth et al, eds. (Illus.). 650p. 1986. 65.00 (0-262-07094-4) MIT Pr.

— The Scientific Letters & Papers of James Clerk Maxwell, Vol. 2: 1862-1873, Vol. 2. Harman, P. M., ed. (Illus.). 1056p. (C). 1995. 285.00 (0-521-25626-7) Cambridge U Pr.

— The Scientific Letters & Papers, Vol. 1: 1846-1862. Harman, P. M., ed. (Illus.). 750p. (C). 1990. 215.00 (0-521-25625-9) Cambridge U Pr.

— Theory of Heat. 3rd ed. LC 77-173064. reprint ed. 29.50 (0-404-04277-5) AMS Pr.

— Theory of Heat. 3rd ed. LC 69-13993. 318p. 1970. reprint ed. text ed. 65.00 (0-8371-4097-8, MATH, Greenwood Pr) Greenwood.

Maxwell, James C., ed. Electrical Researches of the Honourable Henry Cavendish. 454p. 1967. reprint ed. 45.00 (0-7146-1057-7, BHA-01057, Pub. by F Cass Pubs UK) Intl Spec Bk.

Maxwell, James C., et al. Maxwell on Saturn's Rings. Brush, Stephen G. et al, eds. 240p. 1983. 37.50 (0-262-13190-0) MIT Pr.

***Maxwell, Jan, pseud.** Baptism by Murder. 224p. (Orig.). 1995. mass mkt. 4.99 (0-380-77621-9) Avon.

Maxwell, Jane. Getting Away with Murder: A True Story of Love & Death. 1994. 18.95 (0-533-10799-7) Vantage.

***Maxwell, Jessica.** Madonna. (Illus.). 76p. (Orig.). (YA). (gr. 7-12). 1986. pap. 3.95 (0-89872-201-2) Turman Pub.

Maxwell, Jessica, jt. auth. see Maxwell, Judith.

Maxwell, Jim. Carving Characters with Jim Maxwell: Twelve Designs. 2nd ed. (Illus.). 1994. pap. 6.95 (1-56523-035-3) Fox Chapel Pub.

— Making Collectible Santas & Christmas Ornaments in Wood. 2nd ed. (Illus.). 40p. 1994. pap. 6.95 (1-56523-034-5) Fox Chapel Pub.

— Woodcarving Adventure Movie Caricatures in Wood: 1-2-3 Step-by-Step Techniques. (Illus.). 128p. 1994. pap. 12.95 (1-56523-051-5) Fox Chapel Pub.

Maxwell, John. Be a People Person. 156p. 1994. pap. 5.99 (1-56476-264-5, Victor Books) SP Pubns.

— CC, OT, Vol. 5: Deuteronomy. 351p. 1987. write for info. (0-8499-0410-2) Word Inc.

— Your Family Time with God: A Weekly Plan for Family Devotions. Lewis, Brad, ed. 320p. 1995. 19.99 (0-7814-0240-9) Chariot Family.

Maxwell, John & Friedberg, James. Human Rights in Western Civilization: 1600 to the Present. 2nd ed. 328p. (C). 1994. per. 29.95 (0-8403-9243-5) Kendall-Hunt.

Maxwell, John, jt. auth. see Towns, Elmer.

Maxwell, John A., jt. auth. see Johnson, Wesley M.

Maxwell, John A., et al. An Introduction to the Study of History. 112p. (C). 1993. per. 8.95 (0-8403-8707-5) Kendall-Hunt.

Maxwell, John C. Be a People Person. 180p. 1989. 18.99 (0-89693-715-1) SP Pubns.

— Be All You Can Be. 180p. 1995. text ed. 14.99 (1-56476-516-4, 6-3516, Victor Books) SP Pubns.

Maxwell, Jordan. Jordan Maxwell: On Religion & Politics. 23p. 1994. pap. 3.95 (1-885395-01-9) Book Tree.

Maxwell, Joseph. The Tarot. Powell, Ivor, tr. 224p. (Orig.). Date not set. pap. 26.95 (0-8464-4297-3) Beekman Pubs.

Maxwell, Joseph R., Sr. Commodity Futures Trading Orders. LC 74-84265. 84p. 1975. pap. 10.50 (0-917832-10-8) Speer Bks.

— Commodity Futures Trading with Moving Averages. LC 74-75760. 80p. 1975. pap. 12.75 (0-917832-09-4) Speer Bks.

— Commodity Futures Trading with Point & Figure Charts. LC 78-62217. 1978. pap. 10.75 (0-917832-16-7) Speer Bks.

— Commodity Futures Trading with Stops. LC 76-42905. 1977. pap. 10.75 (0-917832-13-2) Speer Bks.

***Maxwell, Josie G.** Joy Is to Know Him. 180p. (Orig.). 1994. pap. 12.95 (0-9638758-1-7) Brockton Pubng.

Maxwell, Judith. Full Circle: The Phase II Manual: A Support Group Guidebook for Battered Women. Farias, Helen G. & Janezic, Shirley, eds. LC 92-83703. 230p. 1993. reprint ed. pap. text ed. 12.95 (0-9632698-0-1) Veda Vangarde.

***Maxwell, Judith & Maxwell, Jessica.** The Feminist Revised Mother Goose: A 21st-Century Children's Edition. 2nd ed. (Illus.). 1995. pap. text ed. 7.95 (0-9632698-7-9) Veda Vangarde.

— The Feminist Revised Mother Goose Rhymes: A 21st Century Children's Edition. LC 92-81770. 32p. (J). (gr. 1-9). 1992. pap. 7.95 (0-9632698-1-X) Veda Vangarde.

Maxwell, Judith M. & Hanson, Craig A. Of the Manners of Speaking That the Old Ones Had: The Andres de Olmos Metaphors in the TULAL Manuscript. LC 91-37822. (Illus.). 356p. 1992. 40.00 (0-87480-369-1) U of Utah Pr.

Maxwell, K. The Sex Imperative: An Evolutionary Tale of Sexual Survival. (Illus.). 300p. (C). 1994. 24.95 (0-306-44649-9, Plenum Pr) Plenum.

Maxwell, Kathryn & Maxwell, Shami. International Price Guide of Old & Unusual Playing Cards. (Illus.). 120p. (Orig.). 1988. pap. 14.95 (0-940649-00-4) Parnell Pub.

Maxwell, Kathryn, jt. auth. see Maxwell, Shami.

Maxwell, Kathryn, et al. Richer Than You Dreamed: How to Take Control of Your Two-Income Family's Finances. 192p. 1992. 18.00 (0-517-57432-2, C P Pubs) Crown Pub Group.

Maxwell, Kathryn S. Pioneer Cooking. (Illus.). 184p. (Orig.). 1987. pap. 4.95 (0-940649-02-0) Parnell Pub.

Maxwell, Katie. Bedside Manners: A Practical Guide to Visiting the Ill. 112p. (Orig.). 1990. pap. 5.99 (0-8010-6265-9) Baker Bk.

— Orientaciones Practicas para Visitar Enfermos: Bedside Manners - A Practical Guide to Visiting the Ill. De Gaydou, Nelda B., tr. 96p. (Orig.). (SPA.). 1992. pap. 4.35 (0-311-46131-X) Casa Bautista.

***Maxwell, Kenneth.** The Making of Portuguese Democracy. 220p. (C). 1995. write for info. (0-521-46077-8) Cambridge U Pr.

— Pombal, Paradox of the Enlightenment. (Illus.). 192p. (C). 1995. 44.95 (0-521-45044-6) Cambridge U Pr.

Maxwell, Kenneth, ed. Portugal in the Nineteen Eighties: Dilemmas of Democratic Consolidation. LC 85-9872. (Contributions in Political Science Ser.: No. 138). (Illus.). 268p. 1986. text ed. 59.95 (0-313-24889-3, MPG/, Greenwood Pr) Greenwood.

— The Press & the Rebirth of Iberian Democracy. LC 82-24201. (Contributions in Political Science Ser.: No. 99). (Illus.). xvi, 198p. 1983. text ed. 55.00 (0-313-23100-1, MPI/, Greenwood Pr) Greenwood.

Maxwell, Kenneth & Clark, Susan. Soviet Dilemmas in Latin America. (Critical Issues 1989 Ser.: No. 3). 32p. 1989. pap. 4.95 (0-87609-070-6) Coun Foreign.

Maxwell, Kenneth & Haltzel, Michael H., eds. Portugal: Ancient Country, Young Democracy. (Illus.). 136p. (C). 1990. lib. bdg. 25.25 (0-943875-20-X, Johns Hopkins) W Wilson Ctr Pr.

Maxwell, Kenneth & Spiegel, Steven. The New Spain: From Isolation to Influence. LC 93-44751. 120p. 1994. pap. text ed. 14.95 (0-87609-163-X) Coun Foreign.

Maxwell, Kenneth R. Conflicts & Conspiracies: Brazil & Portugal, 1750-1808. LC 72-89813. (Cambridge Latin American Studies: No. 16). 301p. reprint ed. pap. 85.80 (0-685-44043-5, 2030608) Bks Demand.

Maxwell, Kimberly. Peer to Peer Networking. 1993. pap. 24.95 (1-56529-324-X) Que.

Maxwell, L. E. Born Crucified. (Moody Classics Ser.). 1984. pap. 3.99 (0-8024-0038-8) Moody.

***Maxwell, L. E. & Dearing, Ruth C.** Women in Ministry: An Historical & Biblical Look at the Role of Women in Christian Leadership. 1995. pap. 7.99 (0-87509-592-5) Chr Pubns.

Maxwell, L. S., jt. ed. see Darby, H. C.

Maxwell, Larry. Becoming a Dynamic Youth Leader: A Guide for Equipping Volunteer Youth Workers. Spear, Cindy G., ed. 208p. (Orig.). 1993. pap. 9.95 (0-941005-88-7) Chrch Grwth VA.

— The Complete Guide to Starting or Evaluating a Dynamic Youth Ministry. Johnson, Tamara & Spear, Cindy, eds. 164p. 1993. Resource pkt. incl. 3 audiotapes & 208p. textbk. ring bd. 79.95 (0-941005-87-9) Chrch Grwth VA.

— Gaining Personal Financial Freedom: Through the Biblical Principles of Finances. Spear, Cindy G. & Johnson, Tamara, eds. 162p. (Orig.). 1992. pap. 8.95 (0-941005-55-0); pap. 3.95 (0-941005-54-2); student ed, pap. 2.95 (0-941005-53-4); 69.95 (0-941005-56-9) Chrch Grwth VA.

— How to Start a Local Church Bible Institute. 127p. 1994. ring bd., vinyl bd. 69.95 (1-57052-020-8) Chrch Grwth VA.

— Relationships: Living in a World Full of People. Spear, Cindy G., ed. 99p. 1993. ring bd., vinyl bd. 29.95 (0-941005-89-5) Chrch Grwth VA.

Maxwell, Lawrence. Another Chance. LC 93-1415. 1993. 1.99 (0-8163-1165-X) Pacific Pr Pub Assn.

— Pathfinder Field Guide. rev. ed. 1980. 10.95 (0-8280-0053-0, 16070-5); pap. 9.95 (0-686-62242-1, 16071-3) Review & Herald.

Maxwell, Lee M. & Reed, Myril B. The Theory of Graphs: A Basis for Network Theory. LC 77-106387. 181p. 1971. text ed. 78.00 (0-08-016321-1, Pub. by Pergamon Repr UK) Franklin.

Maxwell, Leslie E. & Dearing, Ruth C. La Mujer en el Servicio Cristiano. Almanza, Francisco, tr. 144p. (Orig.). (SPA.). 1990. pap. text ed. 5.25 (0-311-42078-8) Casa Bautista.

***Maxwell, Lisa.** The Berserker's House. 256p. (Orig.). 1995. pap. text ed. 4.99 (0-441-00199-8) Ace Bks.

Maxwell, M. H. A Christmas Song of Old Boston. Junghanns, George, ed. & intro. by. (Illus.). 40p. 1973. reprint ed. 3.50 (0-686-05469-5) Gauntlet Bks.

— A Christmas Song of Old Boston: A String of Pearls, 1852 Replica. 31p. 1973. 10.00 (1-881946-04-5) Gauntlet Bks.

Maxwell, Maltz. Psycho-Cybernetics: A New Way to Get More Living out of life. 1975. pap. 8.95 (0-671-22150-7, Fireside) S&S Trade.

Maxwell, Margaret. Handbook for AACR2, 1988 Revision: Explaining & Illustrating the Anglo-American Cataloguing Rules. 1989. pap. text ed. 37.00 (0-8389-0505-6) ALA.

— Narodniki Women: Russian Women Who Sacrificed Themselves for the Dream of Freedom. (Athene Ser.). 310p. 1990. text ed. 36.00 (0-08-037462-X, Pergamon Pr); pap. text ed. 14.50 (0-08-037461-1, Pergamon Pr) Elsevier.

— Narodniki Women: Russian Women Who Sacrificed Themselves for the Dream of Freedom. (Athene Ser.). 360p. (C). text ed. 36.00 (0-8077-6247-4); pap. text ed. 16.95 (0-8077-6246-6) Tchrs Coll.

***Maxwell, Margaret F.** A Passion for Freedom: The Life of Sharlot Hall. LC 82-4866. (Illus.). 234p. 1995. pap. 17. 95 (0-8165-1506-9) U of Ariz Pr.

Maxwell, Margaret J. Listening Games: Ninety-Two Listening & Thinking Activities. pap. 9.95 (0-87491-619-4) Acropolis.

Maxwell, Margaret M., ed. see Kriplen, Nancy.

Maxwell, Marilyn. Missing Pieces: Mending Head Injury Families. 200p. (Orig.). 1988. pap. 24.95 (0-945822-01-4) Brain Technologies.

Maxwell, Marilyn C., ed. see Newell, Coke.

***Maxwell, Marion.** A Little Irish Baking Book. (Little Irish Book Ser.). (Illus.). 60p. 1995. 7.95 (0-86281-534-7, Pub. by Appletree Pr IE) Irish Bks Media.

— Perfectly Simple Pies & Tarts. (Perfectly Simple Cookbooks Ser.). (Illus.). 60p. 1993. 6.95 (0-399-13837-4, Putnam) Putnam Pub Group.

Maxwell, Martha. Improving Student Learning Skills. LC 79-83582. (Jossey-Bass Series in Higher Education). (Illus.). 538p. reprint ed. pap. 153.40 (0-7837-6518-5, 2045630) Bks Demand.

Maxwell, Martha, ed. When Tutor Meets Student. 2nd ed. 226p. (C). 1993. text ed. 32.50 (0-472-09532-3); pap. text ed. 16.95 (0-472-06532-7) U of Mich Pr.

Maxwell, Mary. Human Evolution: A Philosophical Anthropology. 288p. 1984. text ed. 55.00 (0-231-05946-9, King's Crown Paperbacks) Col U Pr.

— Moral Inertia: Ideas for Social Action. 232p. (Orig.). (C). 1991. text ed. 24.95 (0-87081-196-7); pap. text ed. 12.95 (0-87081-197-5) Univ Pr Colo.

— Morality among Nations: An Evolutionary View. LC 89-27881. (SUNY Series in Bio-politics). 198p. 1990. 59.50 (0-7914-0349-1); pap. 19.95 (0-7914-0350-5) State U NY Pr.

— Playing with Fire. (Silhouette Desire Ser.). 1993. mass mkt. 2.99 (0-373-05825-X, 5-05825-0) Silhouette.

Maxwell, Mary, ed. The Sociobiological Imagination. LC 90-10336. (Philosophy & Biology Ser.). 376p. 1991. 59. 50 (0-7914-0767-5); pap. 19.95 (0-7914-0768-3) State U NY Pr.

Maxwell, Mary E. The Doctor's Wife, 3 vols. in 2, Set. LC 79-8426. reprint ed. 84.50 (0-404-62047-7) AMS Pr.

Maxwell, Mary L. & Savage, C. Wade, eds. Science, Mind, & Psychology: Essays in Honor of Grover Maxwell. LC 89-36360. 476p. (Orig.). (C). 1989. lib. bdg. 65.00 (0-8191-7557-9) U Pr of Amer.

***Maxwell, Maxwell.** Chateau. 1995. pap. 13.00 (0-679-76156-X) Random.

***Maxwell, Michael.** Manual of Policy & Procedure for Your Internal Security Force. 1992. pap. 149.50 (0-614-05762-0) Abbott Langer Assocs.

Maxwell, Michael, jt. auth. see Maxwell, Helen.

Maxwell, Moreau S., ed. Eastern Arctic Prehistory: Paleoeskimo Problems. (Memoir Ser.: No. 31). 176p. 1976. 8.00 (0-932839-01-0) Soc Am Arch.

Maxwell Museum of Anthropology Staff. Seven Families in Pueblo Pottery. LC 75-17376. (Illus.). 115p. 1975. reprint ed. pap. 9.95 (0-8263-0388-9) U of NM Pr.

M

Maxwell, Nan L. Income Inequality in the United States, 1947-1985. LC 89-11971. (Contributions in Economics & Economic History Ser.: No. 101). 227p. 1989. text ed. 55.00 (*0-313-26411-2*, MIQ/, Greenwood Pr) Greenwood.

Maxwell, Nancy. Washington County, Arkansas, Sheriff's Census for 1865. 67p. (Orig.). 1994. pap. text ed. 16.50 (*1-55613-885-7*) Heritage Bk.

Maxwell, Neal A. All These Things Shall Give Thee Experience. LC 79-26282. 138p. 1979. 10.95 (*0-87747-796-5*) Deseret Bk.

— The Christmas Scene. 1994. pap. write for info. (*0-88494-962-1*) Bookcraft Inc.

— Lord, Increase Our Faith. 1994. 10.95 (*0-88494-919-2*) Bookcraft Inc.

— Meek & Lowly. LC 86-32784. xii, 127p. 1994. pap. 6.95 (*0-87579-945-0*) Deseret Bk.

— Men & Women of Christ. 1991. 9.95 (*0-88494-785-8*) Bookcraft Inc.

— Neal A. Maxwell, Set. 1992. reprint ed. Boxed set of 4 incls. Wherefore, Ye Must Press Forward, All These Things Shall Give Thee Experience,. boxed 24.95 (*0-87579-607-9*) Deseret Bk.

— Not My Will, But Thine. 9.95 (*0-88494-672-X*) Bookcraft Inc.

— That Ye May Believe. 1992. 11.95 (*0-88494-843-9*) Bookcraft Inc.

— Things As They Really Are. LC 78-26077. 138p. 1992. reprint ed. boxed 7.95 (*0-87579-615-X*) Deseret Bk.

— A Wonderful Flood of Light. 9.95 (*0-88494-728-9*) Bookcraft Inc.

Maxwell, Nicole. Witch-Doctor's Apprentice: Hunting for Medicinal Plants in the Amazon. 1990. pap. 12.95 (*0-8065-1174-5*, Citadel Pr) Carol Pub Group.

Maxwell, Patricia. How to Become a Christian & Stay One. LC 79-4603. (Waymark Ser.). 1979. pap. 3.50 (*0-8127-0221-2*) Review & Herald.

Maxwell, Peter B. On the Interpretation of Statutes. xxxii, 458p. 1991. reprint ed. lib. bdg. 42.50 (*0-8377-2440-6*) Rothman.

Maxwell, R. & Erdei, F. Information Hungary. LC 68-15951. (Countries of the World Information Ser.: Vol. 2). 1968. 466.00 (*0-08-012095-4*, Pub. by Pergamon Repr UK) Franklin.

Maxwell, R. A. The Big Bend of the Rio Grande, a Guide to the Rocks, Landscape, Geologic History, & Settlers of the Area of Big Bend National Park. 5th ed. (Guidebook Ser.: GB 7). (Illus.). 138p. 1990. reprint ed. 5.00 (*0-686-29315-0*) Bur Econ Geology.

— Mineral Resources of South Texas: Region Served Through the Port of Corpus Christi. (Report of Investigations Ser.: RI 43). (Illus.). 140p. 1962. 3.50 (*0-686-29333-9*) Bur Econ Geology.

Maxwell, R. A., et al. Geology of Big Bend National Park, Brewster County, Texas. (Publication Ser.: PUB 6711). (Illus.). 320p. 1967. 12.00 (*0-318-03320-8*) Bur Econ Geology.

Maxwell, R. M. Jimmie Stewart - Frontiersman. 116p. (C). 1989. text ed. 59.00 (*1-872795-53-6*, Pub. by Pentland Pr UK) St Mut.

— Villiers-Stuart Goes to War. 349p. (C). 1989. text ed. 69.00 (*0-946270-85-6*, Pub. by Pentland Pr UK) St Mut.

— Villiers-Stuart on the Frontier. 209p. (C). 1989. text ed. 50.00 (*0-946270-57-0*, Pub. by Pentland Pr UK) St Mut.

Maxwell, Rachel R., et al. Susan Rothenberg - The Prints: A Catalogue Raisonne. (Illus.). 104p. (Orig.). (C). 1987. pap. 20.00 (*0-944751-00-8*) Maxwells Busn.

*__Maxwell, Randy.__ If My People Pray: An Eleventh Hour Call to Prayer & Revival. 1995. pap. 10.95 (*0-8163-1246-X*) Pacific Pr Pub Assn.

Maxwell, Rhoda J. Images of Mothers in Literature for Young Adults. LC 93-9534. (American University Studies, XXIV, American Literature: Vol. 51). 139p. (C). 1994. text ed. 36.95 (*0-8204-2175-8*) P Lang Pubs.

Maxwell, Rhoda J. & Meiser, Mary J. Teaching English in the Middle & Secondary School. LC 92-27515. 352p. (C). 1993. pap. write for info. (*0-02-377960-8*) Macmillan.

Maxwell, Richard. The Mysteries of Paris & London. (Victorian Literature & Culture Ser.). (Illus.). 416p. 1992. 37.50 (*0-8139-1341-1*) U Pr of Va.

— The Spectacle of Democracy: Spanish Television, Nationalism, & Political Transition. 1994. text ed. 44.95 (*0-8166-2357-0*) U of Minn Pr.

Maxwell, Richard C., et al. California Cases on Security Transactions in Land. 4th ed. (American Casebook Ser.). 778p. (C). 1991. text ed. 46.00 (*0-314-89955-3*) West Pub.

— California Cases on Security Transactions in Land, Teacher's Manual to Accompany. 4th ed. (American Casebook Ser.). 194p. (C). 1992. pap. text ed. write for info. (*0-314-01383-0*) West Pub.

— Cases & Materials on the Law of Oil & Gas. 6th ed. LC 92-5650. (University Casebook Ser.). 1060p. 1992. text ed. 45.95 (*0-88277-983-4*) Foundation Pr.

— Law of Oil & Gas: Teacher's Manual for Cases & Materials on The. 6th ed. (University Casebook Ser.). 177p. (C). 1992. pap. text ed. write for info. (*1-56662-030-9*) Foundation Pr.

Maxwell, Robert. Desperate Encounters: The Fifth Royal Gurkha Rifles (the Punjab Frontier Force) 264p. (C). 1989. text ed. 65.00 (*0-946270-35-X*, Pub. by Pentland Pr UK) St Mut.

— Sweet Disorder & the Carefully Careless. LC 93-32943. (Princeton Papers on Architecture: No. 2). (Illus.). 336p. (Orig.). 1994. pap. 18.95 (*1-56898-005-1*) Princeton Arch.

Maxwell, Robert, ed. Reshaping the National Health Service, Vol. II. (Reshaping the Public Sector Ser.). 256p. 1987. 32.95 (*0-946967-18-0*); pap. 18.95 (*0-946967-30-X*) Transaction Pubs.

Maxwell, Robert & Muirhead, Thomas. James Stirling & Michael Wilford: Buildings & Projects 1975-1992. LC 93-60420. (Illus.). 320p. 1994. 80.00 (*0-500-34126-5*) Thames Hudson.

Maxwell, Robert A. & Eckhardt, Shohreh B. Drug Discovery: A Casebook & Analysis. LC 90-4915. 448p. 1990. 79.50 (*0-89603-180-2*) Humana.

Maxwell, Robert S. Texas Economic Growth, 1890 to World War II: From Frontier to Industrial Giant. (Texas History Ser.). (Illus.). 42p. 1982. pap. text ed. 3.95x (*0-89641-099-4*) American Pr.

Maxwell, Robert S. & Baker, Robert D. Sawdust Empire: The Texas Lumber Industry, 1830-1940. LC 82-40442. (Illus.). 256p. 1983. 24.95 (*0-89096-148-4*) Tex A&M Univ Pr.

*__Maxwell, Robert W.__ Maxwell Quick Medical Reference. (Illus.). 32p. (Orig.). (C). 1995. pap. text ed. 7.95 (*0-9645191-0-0*) Mxwll Pub.

Maxwell, Ross A. The Big Bend Country. Pearson, John R., ed. (Illus.). 88p. 1986. 14.95 (*0-912001-13-5*); pap. 9.95 (*0-912001-12-7*) Big Bend.

Maxwell, Ross A., et al. Geology of Big Bend National Park, Brewster County, Texas. LC 68-65757. (University of Texas Publication Ser.: No. 6711). 621p. reprint ed. pap. 177.00 (*0-7837-3157-4*, 2042828) Bks Demand.

Maxwell, Ruth. Beyond the Booze Battle. 1988. mass mkt. 4.95 (*0-345-35474-5*) Ballantine.

— The Booze Battle. 1986. mass mkt. 5.99 (*0-345-33851-0*) Ballantine.

Maxwell, S. Emotionally Disturbed Children: Proceedings of the Conference Assc Workers for Maladjusted Children, Edinburg, Aug. 1965. LC 66-27640. 1966. 27.00 (*0-08-012041-5*, Pub. by Pergamon Repr UK) Franklin.

Maxwell, Sarah. Greek Meze Cooking. 1992. 12.98 (*1-55521-774-5*) Bk Sales Inc.

— Show Me How I Can Cook. (Illus.). 48p. (J). 1995. 7.98 (*0-8317-7684-6*) Smithmark.

— Vegetarian Pasta. 1994. 12.98 (*0-7858-0092-1*) Bk Sales Inc.

*__Maxwell, Sarah & Nilsen, Angela.__ Fabulous Cakes. (CCL Ser.). 96p. 1994. 10.98 (*0-8317-7786-9*) Smithmark.

Maxwell, Scott E. & Delaney, Harold D. Designing Experiments & Analyzing Data: A Model Comparison Perspective. 902p. (C). 1990. text ed. 73.95 (*0-534-10374-X*) Brooks-Cole.

Maxwell, Scott E., jt. auth. see Bray, James H.

Maxwell, Shami & Maxwell, Kathryn. Playing Card Price Guide. (Illus.). 128p. 1992. lib. bdg. 12.95 (*0-940649-11-X*) Parnell Pub.

— Self Publish to Success: Make Money Publishing. (Illus.). 128p. (Orig.). 1988. pap. 9.95 (*0-940649-03-9*) Parnell Pub.

Maxwell, Shami, jt. auth. see Maxwell, Kathryn.

Maxwell, Shirley, jt. auth. see Massey, James C.

Maxwell, Shirley, jt. auth. see Massey, James.

Maxwell, Sidney D. The Suburbs of Cincinnati: Sketches, Historical & Descriptive. LC 73-2907. (Metropolitan America Ser.). 190p. 1977. reprint ed. 15.95 (*0-405-05402-5*) Ayer.

*__Maxwell, Stanley.__ The Man Who Couldn't be Killed: An Incredible Story of Faith & Courage During China's Cultural Revolution. LC 94-26486. 1995. pap. 10.95 (*0-8163-1235-4*) Pacific Pr Pub Assn.

Maxwell, Steve & Hall, Bruce, intros. Conference on Railway Engineering, 1993: Contracting Railways-Safety, Standards & the Surroundings. (National Conference Publication Ser.: No. 93-12). (Illus.). 288p. (Orig.). 1993. pap. text ed. 54.00 (*0-85825-582-0*, Pub. by Inst Engrs Aust-EA Bks AT) Accents Pubns.

*__Maxwell, T. G. & Bates, David.__ Luxford's Police Law in New Zealand. 4th ed. 675p. 1991. boxed 144.00 (*0-409-78728-0*, NZ) Butterworth Legal Pubs.

Maxwell, T. S. Visvarupa. (Illus.). 382p. 1989. 24.95 (*0-19-562117-4*) OUP.

Maxwell, T. S., ed. Eastern Approaches: Essays on Asian Art & Archaeology. (Illus.). 340p. 1993. 35.00 (*0-19-562925-6*) OUP.

Maxwell, Taylor & Scott, Bryon. Visual BASIC Super Bible. (Illus.). 744p. (Orig.). 1992. pap. 39.95 (*1-878739-12-3*) Waite Group Pr.

Maxwell, Terry B. & Hughes, Joan E. The CompuResource Book: A Collection of Activities to Integrate Curriculum & Computers. (Illus.). 146p. (C). 1994. Tchr.'s ed. teacher ed 24.95 (*1-885401-00-0*) Maxwell Grp.

Maxwell, Terry G. Diversified Mutual Fund Investment Strategies: How to Build a High-Return, Low-Risk Portfolio of Mutual Funds. Stankiewicz, Ilene, ed. LC 91-75315. (Illus.). 165p. 1991. 19.95 (*0-9630625-0-6*) Capital MI.

Maxwell, Thomas. The Suspense Is Killing Me. 272p. 1990. 19.95 (*0-89296-167-8*) Mysterious Pr.

Maxwell, Thomas, jt. auth. see Maxwell, Aileen.

Maxwell, Timothy T. & Jones, Jesse C. Alternative Fuels: Emissions, Economics & Performance. 243p. 1994. 49.00 (*1-56091-523-4*, R143) Soc Auto Engineers.

Maxwell, Vicky. The Other Side of Summer. large type ed. 305p. 1980. 15.95 (*0-7089-0480-7*) Ulverscroft.

— The Way of Tamarisk. large type ed. 318p. 1980. 12.00 (*0-7089-0593-5*) Ulverscroft.

Maxwell, W. Andrew & Nordan, Lee, eds. Current Concepts of Multifocal Intraocular Lenses. LC 90-53271. 239p. 1990. 85.00 (*1-55642-167-2*) SLACK Inc.

Maxwell, W. H., jt. ed. see Beard, Leo R.

Maxwell, Will N., ed. The Country Music Guide to Life. 176p. 1994. pap. 3.99 (*0-451-17955-2*, Sig) NAL-Dutton.

*__Maxwell, William.__ All Days & Nights. 1995. pap. write for info. (*0-679-76102-0*) Random.

— All the Days & Nights: The Collected Stories of William Maxwell. LC 94-27509. 415p. 1995. 25.00 (*0-679-43829-7*) Knopf.

— Ancestors: A Family History. LC 94-31109. 1995. pap. 12.00 (*0-679-75929-8*, Vin) Random.

— Billie Dyer: And Other Stories. 1992. 17.50 (*0-679-40832-0*) Knopf.

— Billie Dyer & Other Stories. large type ed. LC 92-45885. (General Ser.). 187p. 1993. pap. 16.95 (*0-8161-5572-0*, Large Print Bks) Hall.

— Bun. LC 93-42390. (J). 1995. 16.00 (*0-679-86053-3*); lib. bdg. 17.99 (*0-679-96053-8*) Knopf Bks Yng Read.

— The Folded Leaf. LC 78-63992. (Gay Experience Ser.). 320p. reprint ed. 45.00 (*0-404-61510-4*) AMS Pr.

— The Folded Leaf. LC 80-67031. 288p. 1981. reprint ed. pap. 11.95 (*0-87923-351-6*) Godine.

— Heavenly Tenants. (J). (gr. 4-7). 1992. 13.95 (*0-930407-25-3*) Parabola Bks.

— The Old Man at the Railroad Crossing: And Other Tales. LC 86-46248. 192p. (Orig.). 1987. pap. 10.95 (*0-87923-676-0*) Godine.

— Over by the River. LC 76-30608. 256p. 1984. pap. 10.95 (*0-87923-541-1*) Godine.

— So Long See You Tomorrow. LC 88-45294. 174p. 1988. pap. 9.95 (*0-87923-754-6*) Godine.

— They Came Like Swallows. LC 86-46249. (Non Pareil Ser.). 192p. 1995. pap. 10.95 (*0-87923-677-9*) Godine.

— Time Will Darken It. LC 82-81311. 320p. 1983. pap. 11.95 (*0-87923-448-2*) Godine.

Maxwell, William, ed. Thinking: The Expanding Frontier. (Problem Solving Ser.). 304p. 1983. text ed. 59.95 (*0-89859-731-5*) L Erlbaum Assocs.

Maxwell, William E. & Crain, Ernest. Texas Politics Today. 6th ed. Simon, ed. 416p. (C). 1992. pap. text ed. 36.50 (*0-314-89956-1*) West Pub.

— Texas Politics Today. 7th ed. LC 94-3694. 500p. 1994. pap. text ed. 35.50 (*0-314-04324-1*) West Pub.

Maxym, L. Russian Lacquer, Legends & Fairy Tales, Vol. II. 80p. (C). 1986. 275.00 (*0-685-34470-3*, Pub. by Collets) St Mut.

Maxym, Lucy. The Lucy Maxym Collection of Russian Lacquer. (Illus.). 50p. (Orig.). 1989. write for info. (*0-940202-10-7*) Siamese Imports.

— Russian Lacquer, Legends & Fairy Tales. LC 81-51492. (Illus.). 80p. 1981. 35.00 (*0-940202-01-8*) Siamese Imports.

— Russian Lacquer, Legends & Fairy Tales, Vol. II. (Illus.). 80p. 1986. 35.00 (*0-940202-03-4*) Siamese Imports.

— Russian Lacquer, Legends & Fairy Tales, Vol. II. deluxe limited ed. (Illus.). 80p. 1986. ring bd. 150.00 (*0-940202-04-2*) Siamese Imports.

Maxym, Lucy, ed. see Vorobyev, Nicolai.

May. De Swiet Medical Disorders in OB Practice. 2nd ed. 1989. 134.95 (*0-632-01974-3*, Yr Bk Med Pubs) Mosby Yr Bk.

— Drug Information. 300p. 1993. 39.95 (*0-8016-6486-1*) Mosby Yr Bk.

— Epoxy Resins: Chemistry & Technology. 2nd expanded rev. ed. 1288p. 1988. 299.00 (*0-8247-7690-9*) Dekker.

— Halloween, Reading Level 4. (Holidays & Festivals Ser.: Set II). (Illus.). 48p. (J). (gr. 3-8). 1989. 11.95 (*0-685-58773-8*); lib. bdg. 15.94 (*0-86592-983-1*) Rourke Corp.

— Voices of Denver: Speaking Out from the Mile-High City. 1995. pap. text ed. 11.00 (*0-06-258583-5*) Harper SF.

May, ed. Ethics in the Accounting Curriculum: Cases & Readings. 1990. 45.00 (*0-86539-074-6*) Am Accounting.

May & Mehlmeister. Student Workbook for Comprehensive Maternity Nursing: Nursing Process & the Childbearing Family. 2nd ed. 272p. 1990. text ed. 15.95 (*0-397-54754-4*) Lippincott.

May & Youtsey. Rehabilitation & Continuity of Care in Pulmonary Disorders. (Illus.). 224p. 1990. 31.95 (*0-8016-5679-6*) Mosby Yr Bk.

*__May, A. David, et al, eds.__ Spectral Line Shapes: 12th ICSLS. (Conference Proceedings Ser.: No. 328). (Illus.). 448p. (C). 1995. text ed. 125.00 (*1-56396-326-4*, AIP Pr) Am Inst Physics.

May, A. J., jt. auth. see Bird, J. O.

May, A. R. Mental Health Services in Europe. (Offset Publication Ser.: No. 23). 1976. pap. 4.80 (*92-4-170023-8*) World Health.

May, Adolf D. Traffic Flow Fundamentals. 726p. 1989. text ed. 79.00 (*0-13-926072-2*) P-H.

May, Alex & May, Nancy. Bed, Breakfast & Bike - Mid-Atlantic: A Cycling Guide to Country Inns. LC 92-60539. (Illus.). 256p. (Orig.). 1992. pap. 12.95 (*0-933855-06-0*) White Meadow.

— Bed, Breakfast & Bike New England: A Cycling Guide to Country Inns. LC 91-65376. (Illus.). 205p. (Orig.). 1991. pap. 12.95 (*0-933855-05-2*) White Meadow.

— Ride Guide: South Jersey. LC 91-65375. (Illus.). 86p. (Orig.). 1991. pap. 9.95 (*0-933855-04-4*) White Meadow.

May, Alf. Out of Grimsby. 161p. (C). 1989. text ed. 42.00 (*0-902662-86-4*, Pub. by R K Pubns UK); pap. text ed. 21.00 (*0-902662-87-2*, Pub. by R K Pubns UK) St Mut.

May, Alice G., jt. auth. see May, Angelo M.

May, Angelo M. & May, Alice G. The Two Lions of Lyons: The Tale of Two Surgeons, Alexis Carrel & Rene Leriche. rev. ed. (Illus.). 323p. (C). 1994. 39.50 (*0-930329-45-7*); pap. text ed. 34.50 (*0-685-71138-2*) KABEL Pubs.

May, Annabelle, jt. auth. see Light, Donald.

May, Anne. Epidurals for Childbirth. LC 94-8975. (Oxford Medical Publications Ser.). (Illus.). 200p. 1994. 59.95 (*0-19-262439-3*); pap. 26.00 (*0-19-262438-5*) OUP.

May, Anne C. Manipulatives for Keyboard Capers. 40p. 1993. 37.95 (*1-884098-03-7*); 20.00 (*1-884098-02-9*) Elijah Co.

May, Antionette. Free Spirit. Hickman, Irene, ed. 196p. (Orig.). 1985. pap. 5.95 (*0-915689-07-3*) Hickman Systems.

— Psychic Women. 1984. pap. 6.95 (*0-915689-03-0*) Hickman Systems.

May, Antoinette. The Annotated Ramona. LC 88-27696. 256p. (Orig.). 1989. pap. 14.95 (*0-933174-52-7*) Wide World-Tetra.

— Haunted Houses of California. 2nd ed. (Illus.). 208p. 1993. pap. 10.95 (*0-933174-91-8*) Wide World-Tetra.

— Mexico for Lovers. (Illus.). 200p. (Orig.). 1994. pap. 12.95 (*0-933174-96-9*) Wide World-Tetra.

— Passionate Pilgrim: The Extraordinary Life of Alma Reed. (Illus.). 320p. (C). 1994. pap. 10.00 (*1-56924-887-7*) Marlowe & Co.

— The Yucatan: A Guide to the Land of Maya Mysteries. 3rd ed. (Illus.). 296p. (Orig.). 1993. pap. text ed. 10.95 (*0-933174-90-X*) Wide World-Tetra.

*__May, Antoinette & Appleby, Vernon, eds.__ Voices of Seattle: Speaking Out from the Emerald City. LC 94-34980. 1995. 11.00 (*0-06-258584-3*) Harper SF.

May, Antoinette, jt. auth. see Brown, Sylvia.

May, Arthur J. Hapsburg Monarchy, 1867-1914. LC 51-7368. 544p. reprint ed. 155.10 (*0-8357-9162-9*, 2003780) Bks Demand.

*__May, B. Roxanne.__ Friends, Lovers, Husbands. Stones, Pamela M., ed. 84p. (Orig.). 1994. pap. 25.00 (*0-9641426-0-0*) Triangle Pubns.

May, Beatrice. Sister to Jane. large type ed. (Historical Romance Ser.). 320p. 1992. 21.95 (*0-7089-2696-7*) Ulverscroft.

May, Bella J., ed. Home Health & Rehabilitation: Concepts of Care. LC 92-49433. (Illus.). 381p. 1993. 65.00 (*0-8036-5939-3*) Davis Co.

May, Bess R. Starting & Operating a Business after You Retire: What You Need to Know to Succeed. LC 93-23063. 246p. 1993. pap. 9.95 (*0-89529-567-9*) Avery Pub.

May, Betty. Tiger Woman. (Illus.). reprint ed. 35.00 (*1-55818-225-X*, First Impress) Holmes Pub.

May, Betty M. Best Little Hors d'oeuvres in Kansas. (Illus.). 81p. (Orig.). 1987. pap. 9.95 (*0-9619522-0-2*) B M May.

*__May, Bob.__ 9th Inning Wedding. (Illus.). 19p. (Orig.). 1994. pap. 3.00 (*0-88680-401-9*) I E Clark.

May, Bob & Tibbetts, Cristopher. The Andrew Is Dead Story. 26p. (Orig.). (YA). (gr. 7-12). 1991. pap. 3.00 (*0-88680-345-4*) I E Clark.

May, C. Epoxy Resins. 1288p. 1988. 200.00 (*0-318-37730-6*) T-C Pubns CA.

May, C. E. Thomas Hardy: An Agnostic & a Romantic. LC 92-73938. 412p. (Orig.). 1993. pap. 24.50 (*1-55618-125-6*) Brunswick Pub.

May, Caroline, ed. The American Female Poets. reprint ed. 29.50 (*0-8422-8095-2*) Irvington.

*__May, Charles.__ The Short Story. (Studies in Genre). 1994. lib. bdg. 23.95x (*0-8057-0953-3*, Twayne) Macmillan.

May, Charles E. Edgar Allan Poe: A Study of the Short Fiction. (Twayne's Studies in Short Fiction: No. 28). 192p. 1991. text ed. 22.95 (*0-8057-8337-7*, Pub. by Royal Botanic Garden UK) Macmillan.

— Fiction's Many Worlds. 766p. (C). 1993. pap. text ed. write for info. (*0-669-27762-2*); Instr.'s guide. teacher ed write for info. (*0-669-27765-7*) Heath.

May, Charles E., ed. The New Short Story Theories. LC 94-7037. 368p. (Orig.). (C). 1994. pap. text ed. 16.95 (*0-8214-1087-3*) Ohio U Pr.

— Short Story Theories. LC 75-36982. xiv, 251p. 1977. pap. 9.95 (*0-8214-0221-8*) Ohio U Pr.

May, Cheryl. Cattle Management. 350p. (C). 1981. teacher ed write for info. (*0-8359-0722-8*) P-H.

— Legacy: Engineering at Kansas State University. (Illus.). 105p. (Orig.). 1983. pap. text ed. 5.00 (*0-9609342-0-0*) College Engineering KS.

May, Chris. Bob Geldof. (Profiles Ser.). (Illus.). 64p. (J). (gr. 5-9). 1991. 11.95 (*0-237-60031-5*, Pub. by Evans Bros Ltd UK) Trafalgar.

— Bob Marley. (Profiles Ser.). (Illus.). 64p. (J). (gr. 5-9). 1991. 11.95 (*0-237-60017-X*, Pub. by Evans Bros Ltd UK) Trafalgar.

— The Horse Care Manual: How to Keep Your Horse Healthy, Fit & Happy. 160p. 1989. 21.95 (*0-8120-5795-3*) Barron.

May, Christopher N. In the Name of War: Judicial Review & the War Powers since 1918. LC 88-9444. 370p. 1989. 39.95 (*0-674-44549-X*) HUP.

May, Claire, jt. auth. see Braine, George.

May, Claire A. Effective Writing: A Handbook for Accountants. 3rd ed. 224p. 1991. pap. text ed. 24.80 (*0-13-244864-5*) P-H.

May, Clayton A., ed. Chemorheology of Thermosetting Polymers. LC 83-12280. (ACS Symposium Ser.: No. 227). 338p. 1983. lib. bdg. 49.95 (*0-8412-0794-1*) Am Chemical.

— Resins for Aerospace. LC 80-15342. (ACS Symposium Ser.: No. 132). 1980. 54.95 (*0-8412-0567-1*) Am Chemical.

May, D., jt. ed. see Kunii, T. L.

May, D. J. Mr. Marble's Moose. LC 93-1494. (J). 1993. 9.99 (*0-8499-1068-4*) Word Pub.

May, Dan. There's an Old Southern Saying: The Wit & Wisdom of Dan May. 130p. (Orig.). 1995. pap. 13.95 (*0-9638911-0-3*) Crabby Keys.

May, Darcy. Elves & Fairies Stickers. (Illus.). (J). (gr. 4-7). 1993. pap. 1.00 (*0-486-27717-8*) Dover.

— Twelve Days of Christmas. 12p. (J). 1993. 9.95 (*1-55670-336-8*) Stewart Tabori & Chang.

May, Darcy, illus. The Nutcracker Ballet. (Read with Me Ser.). 32p. (J). (ps-3). 1994. pap. 2.50 (*0-590-48197-5*, Cartwheel) Scholastic Inc.

May, Daryl & Bansemer, Roger. Rachael's Splendifilous Adventure. Little, Carl, ed. LC 91-66032. (Illus.). 40p. (Orig.). (J). (ps-4). 1992. 10.95 (*0-932433-83-9*) Windswept Hse.

May, David, jt. ed. see Horobin, Gordon.

An Asterisk (*) at the beginning of an entry indicates that the title is appearing in BIP for the first time.

May, Dawn. Aboriginal Labour & the Cattle Industry: Queensland from White Settlement to the Present. (Studies in Australian History: No. 13). (Illus.). 288p. (C). 1994. 59.95 (0-521-46506-0) Cambridge U Pr.

May, Dean. Utah: A People's History. LC 87-17898. (Bonneville Bks.). (Illus.). 1987. pap. 15.95 (0-87480-284-9) U of Utah Pr.

May, Dean L. Three Frontiers: Family, Land, & Society in the American West, 1850-1900. LC 93-43560. (Interdisciplinary Perspectives on Modern History Ser.). (Illus.). 352p. (C). 1994. 44.95 (0-521-43499-8) Cambridge U Pr.

May, Deborah C., jt. auth. see Marozas, Donald S.

***May, Derwent.** The New Times Nature Diary. (Illus.). 127p. 1995. 18.95 (0-86051-850-7, Robson-Parkwest) Parkwest Pubns.

***May, Dorothy.** Codependency: PowerLoss, SoulLoss. 320p. 1994. pap. 12.95 (0-8091-3532-9) Paulist Pr.

— Codependency: PowerLoss SoulLoss. 300p. 1994. pap. 12.95 (1-882195-02-7) Whales Tale Pr.

May Dugan Center Staff & Horton, Charlene. Raising Money & Having Fun (Sort of) A "How-to" Book for Small Non-Profit Groups. LC 91-66345. (Illus.). 132p. 1991. pap. text ed. 18.95 (0-9630760-0-0) M Dugan Ctr.

May, Ed, ed. Contemporary Authors, Vol. 109. 552p. 1983. 122.00 (0-8103-1909-8) Gale.

May, Edgar. The Wasted Americans: Cost of Our Welfare Dilemma. LC 80-19500. (Illus.). xi, 227p. 1980. reprint ed. text ed. 59.75 (0-313-22674-1, MAWAM, Greenwood Pr) Greenwood.

May, Edward, jt. auth. see Staufer, Alvin F.

May, Edward L., jt. auth. see Staufer, Alvin E.

May, Elaine. Adaptation. 1970. pap. 2.75 (0-8222-0009-0) Dramatists Play.

***May, Elaine T.** Barren in the Promised Land: Childless Americans & the Pursuit of Happiness. LC 94-41427. 288p. 1995. 24.00 (0-465-00609-4) Basic.

— Great Expectations: Marriage & Divorce in Post-Victorian America. LC 80-10590. (Illus.). 1983. pap. text ed. 11.95 (0-226-51170-7) U Ch Pr.

— Homeward Bound. 1990. pap. text ed. 15.00 (0-465-03055-6) Basic.

— Young Oxford History of Women in the United States, Vol. 9: Pushing the Limits: American Women 1940-1961. (Illus.). 144p. (J). 1994. lib. bdg. 20.00 (0-19-508084-X) OUP.

May, Elizabeth, ed. Musics of Many Cultures: An Introduction. LC 76-50251. (Illus.). 454p. 1980. 65.00 (0-520-03393-0); pap. 22.50 (0-520-04778-8) U CA Pr.

May, Ernest, jt. ed. see Feidel, Frank.

May, Ernest, jt. ed. see Stauffer, George B.

May, Ernest R. American Imperialism: A Speculative Essay. 1991. 14.95 (1-879176-03-3) Imprint Pubns.

— Imperial Democracy: The Emergence of America As a Great Power. 1991. 15.95 (1-879176-04-1) Imprint Pubns.

— The Lessons of the Past: The Use & Misuse of History in American Foreign Policy. LC 73-82670. 1975. reprint ed. pap. 8.95 (0-19-501890-7) OUP.

— The Making of the Monroe Doctrine. (Illus.). 328p. (C). 1992. pap. 14.95 (0-674-54341-6) Belknap Pr.

May, Ernest R., ed. Knowing One's Enemies: Intelligence Assessment Before the Two World Wars. LC 84-42573. 577p. reprint ed. pap. 164.50 (0-7837-0239-6, 2040547) Bks Demand.

— NSC Sixty-Eight: Blueprint for American Strategy in the Cold War. 176p. 1993. text ed. 35.00 (0-312-09445-0); pap. text ed. 7.00 (0-312-06637-6) St Martin.

May, Ernest R. & Fairbank, John K., eds. America's China Trade in Historical Perspective: The Chinese & American Performance. (Studies in American-East Asian Relations: No. 11). 390p. 1986. 25.00 (0-674-03075-3) HUP.

May, Ernest R. & Fraser, Janet. Campaign Seventy-Two: The Managers Speak. LC 73-85182. 224p. 1973. 25.00 (0-674-09141-8); pap. 13.50 (0-674-09143-4) HUP.

May, Ernest R. & Thomson, James C., Jr., eds. American-East Asian Relations: A Survey. LC 70-188970. (Harvard Studies in American-East Asian Relations: No. 1). 440p. reprint ed. pap. 125.40 (0-7837-4141-3, 2057964) Bks Demand.

May, Ernest R., jt. auth. see Neustadt, Richard E.

May, F. J. The Book of Acts & Church Growth. 1990. 7.99 (0-87148-113-8) Pathway Pr.

May, F. L. Catalogue of Laces & Embroideries in the Collection. (Illus.). 1936. 10.00 (0-87535-038-0) Hispanic Soc.

May, Fiona, jt. auth. see Manias, Paul.

May, Florence. The Life of Johannes Brahms, 2 vols., Set. 1976. lib. bdg. 79.00 (0-403-03630-5) Scholarly.

— The Life of Johannes Brahms, 2 vols., Set. 1988. reprint ed. lib. bdg. 99.00 (0-7812-0192-6) Rprt Serv.

May, Florence L. Hispanic Lace & Lace Making. (Illus.). 417p. 1936. 12.00 (0-317-00622-3, Hispanic Soc) Interbk Inc.

— Hispanic Lace & Lacemaking. 1980. reprint ed. 12.00 (0-87535-048-8) Hispanic Soc.

— Silk Textiles of Spain, Eighth-Fifteenth Century. (Illus.). 296p. 1957. 14.00 (0-317-00613-4, Hispanic Soc) Interbk Inc.

***May, Frances.** The Poets' Cat. 69p. 1990. pap. 7.00 (1-878660-09-8) Fireweed WI.

May, Frank B. Reading as Communication: An Interactive Approach. 4th ed. 640p. (C). 1994. text ed. write for info. (0-02-378242-0, Merrill Pub Co) Macmillan.

May, Frank P., jt. auth. see Tyner, Mack.

May, Gabriele S. Tradition im Umbruch: Zur Sophokles-Rezeption im Deutschen Vormarz. (American University Studies: Germanic Languages & Literature: Ser. I, Vol. 76). 163p. (C). 1989. text ed. 32.95 (0-8204-1007-1) P Lang Pubs.

May, Gary. China Scapegoat: The Diplomatic Ordeal of John Carter Vincent. 370p. (C). 1982. reprint ed. pap. 13.95 (0-917974-98-0) Waveland Pr.

— Un-American Activities: The Trials of William Remington. LC 93-25321. (Illus.). 416p. (C). 1994. 30.00 (0-19-504980-2) OUP.

***May, Gayle L., et al, eds.** Space: A Vital Stimulus to Out National Well-Being, 31st Goddard Memorial Sumposium, & World Space Programs & Fiscal Reality, 30th Goddard Memorial Symposium. (Science & Technology Ser.: 83). (Illus.). 334p. 1994. lib. bdg. 70.00 (0-87703-389-7, Pub. by Am Astro Soc) Univelt Inc.

— Space Exploitation & Utilization Symposium. LC 57-43769. (Advances in the Astronautical Sciences Ser.: Vol. 60). (Illus.). 740p. 1986. lib. bdg. 70.00 (0-87703-254-8, Pub. by Am Astro Soc); pap. text ed. 55.00 (0-87703-255-6, Pub. by Am Astro Soc) Univelt Inc.

— Space Exploitation & Utilization Symposium. suppl. ed. LC 57-43769. (Advances in the Astronautical Sciences Ser.: Vol. 60). (Illus.). 740p. 1986. fiche 10.00 (0-87703-256-4, Pub. by Am Astro Soc) Univelt Inc.

— World & National Space Programs: Proceedings of the 30th & 31st Goddard Memorial Symposia, Arlington & Alexandria, VA, 1992 & 1993. LC 57-43769. (Science & Technology Ser.: 83). (Illus.). 334p. 1994. pap. text ed. 50.00x (0-87703-390-0, Pub. by Am Astro Soc) Univelt Inc.

May, Georg. Das Recht des Gottesdienstes in der Diozese Mainz zur Zeit von Bischof Joseph Ludwig Colmar, Vol. 1. (Kanonistische Studien und Texte Ser.: No. 36). xiv, 762p. 1987. 71.00 (0-685-53316-6, Pub. by B R Gruener NE) Benjamins North Am.

— Das Recht des Gottesdienstes in der Diozese Mainz zur Zeit von Bischof Joseph Ludwig Colmar (1802-1818), Band 2. (Kanonistische Studien und Texte Ser.: Vol. 37). xii, 692p. (GER.). 1987. 60.00 (90-6032-290-8, Pub. by B R Gruener NE) Benjamins North Am.

May, George. Doctor's Secret Journal. (Illus.). 47p. 1960. pap. 3.00 (0-911872-30-2) Mackinac Island.

— Stewards of the State: The Governors of Michigan. Kirk, Robert, ed. (Illus.). 193p. 1987. 20.95 (0-9614344-2-2) Historical Soc MI.

— War Eighteen Twelve. (Illus.). 43p. (Orig.). 1962. pap. 3.00 (0-911872-28-0) Mackinac Island.

May, George O. Financial Accounting: A Distillation of Experience. 1972. reprint ed. text ed. 20.00 (0-914348-05-1) Scholars Bk.

— Twenty-Five Years of Accounting Responsibility 1911-1936, Vols. I & II. Hunt, Carleton, ed. 1971. reprint ed. text ed. 25.00 (0-914348-03-5) Scholars Bk.

May, George S. A Most Unique Machine: The Michigan Origins of the American Automobile Industry. LC 74-19230. (Illus.). 406p. reprint ed. pap. 115.80 (0-317-09723-7, 2012736) Bks Demand.

May, George S., ed. Automobile Industry, 1896-1920. 1989. 85.00 (0-8160-2084-1) Facts on File.

— Automobile Industry, 1920-1980. (Encyclopedia of American Business History & Biography Ser.). (Illus.). 544p. 1989. 85.00 (0-8160-2083-3) Facts on File.

— Michigan Civil War History: An Annotated Bibliography. LC 61-14050. 140p. reprint ed. pap. 39.90 (0-7837-3670-3, 2043544) Bks Demand.

May, George S., jt. auth. see Dunbar, Willis F.

May, George W. Down Illinois Rivers. (Illus.). 400p. 1981. 16.00 (0-9605566-5-6) G W May.

— History of Massac County, Illinois. (Illus.). 232p. 1983. reprint ed. 6.00 (0-9605566-4-8) G W May.

— History Papers on Massac County, Illinois. (Illus.). 200p. 1990. 12.00 (0-9605566-7-2) G W May.

— Massac County, Nineteen Fifty-Five to Nineteen Eighty-Two: Accompanies History of Massac County. 1983. 1.00 (0-9605566-6-4) G W May.

— Walter West's Probation: The Birth of Massac County, a Novel of the Regulator-Flathead War. (Illus.). 322p. 1993. 12.00 (0-9605566-8-0) G W May.

May, Gerald & Gardiner, Richard. Clinical Imaging of the Pancreas. (Clinical Imaging of the Gastrointestinal Tract Ser.). (Illus.). 192p. 1987. text ed. 66.00 (0-88167-265-3) Raven.

May, Gerald G. Addiction & Grace: Love & Spirituality in the Healing of Addictions. LC 88-45147. (Illus.). 208p. 1991. reprint ed. pap. 11.00 (0-06-065537-2) Harper SF.

— The Awakened Heart: Living Beyond Addiction. LC 91-55086. 272p. 1993. reprint ed. pap. 12.00 (0-06-065473-2) Harper SF.

— Care of Mind-Care of Spirit: A Psychiatrist Explores Spiritual Direction. 192p. 1992. reprint ed. pap. 11.00 (0-06-065567-4) Harper SF.

— Simply Sane: The Spirituality of Mental Health. enl. ed. LC 93-2581. 166p. 1993. pap. 11.95 (0-8245-1366-5) Crossroad NY.

— Will & Spirit. LC 82-47751. (Illus.). 368p. 1987. pap. 20.00 (0-06-250582-3) Harper SF.

***May, Gerhard.** Creatio Ex Nihilo: The Doctrine of 'Creation Out of Nothing' in Early Christian Thought. Worral, A. S., tr. 216p. 1994. text ed. 39.95 (0-567-09695-5, Pub. by T & T Clark UK) Bks Intl VA.

— Schoepfung aus dem Nichts: Die Entstehung der Lehre von der Creatio Ex Nihilo. (Arbeiten zur Kirchengeschichte Ser.: Vol. 48). (C). 1978. 86.95 (3-11-007204-1) De Gruyter.

May, Gita. Madame Roland & the Age of Revolution. LC 70-108418. (Illus.). 360p. 1970. text ed. 50.50 (0-231-03379-6) Col U Pr.

May, Glenn A. Battle for Batangas: A Philippine Province at War. (Illus.). 352p. (C). 1991. text ed. 35.00 (0-300-04850-5) Yale U Pr.

— A Past Recovered. 267p. (Orig.). (C). 1987. pap. 14.50 (971-10-0260-4, Pub. by New Day Pub PH) Cellar.

— Social Engineering in the Philippines: The Aims, Execution & Impact of American Colonial Policy, 1900-1913. LC 79-7467. (Contributions in Comparative Colonial Studies: No. 2). 268p. 1980. text ed. 59.95 (0-313-20978-2, MAE, Greenwood Pr) Greenwood.

May, Hal, ed. Contemporary Authors, Vol. 119. 600p. 1986. 122.00 (0-8103-1919-5) Gale.

— Contemporary Authors, Vol. 120. 760p. 1987. 122.00 (0-8103-1920-9) Gale.

— Contemporary Authors, Vol. 121. 475p. 1987. 122.00 (0-8103-1921-7) Gale.

— Contemporary Authors, Vol. 122. 500p. 1987. 122.00 (0-8103-1922-5) Gale.

May, Hal & Evory, Ann, eds. Contemporary Authors, Vol. 108. 824p. 1983. 122.00 (0-8103-1908-X) Gale.

— Contemporary Authors, Vol. 110. LC 62-52046. 833p. 1984. 122.00 (0-8103-1910-1) Gale.

— Contemporary Authors, Vol. 111. LC 62-52046. 528p. 1984. 122.00 (0-8103-1911-X) Gale.

— Contemporary Authors, Vol. 112. LC 62-52046. 528p. 1984. 122.00 (0-8103-1912-8) Gale.

— Contemporary Authors, Vol. 113. LC 65-52046. 536p. 1985. 122.00 (0-8103-1913-6) Gale.

— Contemporary Authors, Vol. 114. 792p. 1985. 122.00 (0-8103-1914-4) Gale.

— Contemporary Authors, Vol. 115. LC 62-52046. 492p. 1985. 122.00 (0-8103-1915-2) Gale.

— Contemporary Authors, Vol. 116. 600p. 1986. 122.00 (0-8103-1916-0) Gale.

— Contemporary Authors, Vol. 117. 800p. 1986. 122.00 (0-8103-1917-9) Gale.

— Contemporary Authors, Vol. 118. 500p. 1986. 122.00 (0-8103-1918-7) Gale.

May, Hal & Lesniak, James. Contemporary Authors, Vol. 35: Index, Vol. 35. rev. ed. 1991. 122.00 (0-8103-1996-9) Gale.

— Contemporary Authors, Vol. 36, Vol. 36. (New Revision Ser.). 1992. 122.00 (0-8103-1990-X) Gale.

— Contemporary Authors, Vol. 37: Index, Vol. 37. rev. ed. 1992. 122.00 (0-8103-1997-7) Gale.

May, Hal & Lesniak, James, eds. Contemporary Authors, Vol. 27. (New Revision Ser.). 1989. 122.00 (0-8103-1981-0) Gale.

— Contemporary Authors, Vol. 28. (New Revision Ser.). 510p. 1989. 122.00 (0-8103-1982-9) Gale.

— Contemporary Authors, Vol. 29. (New Revision Ser.). 1990. 122.00 (0-8103-1983-7) Gale.

May, Hal & Straub, Deborah A., eds. Contemporary Authors, Vol. 25, Vol. 25. (New Revision Ser.). 600p. 1988. 122.00 (0-8103-1979-9) Gale.

May, Hal & Trosky, Susan M. Contemporary Authors, Vol. 124. 1988. 122.00 (0-8103-1924-1) Gale.

May, Hal & Trosky, Susan M., eds. Contemporary Authors, Vol. 123. 488p. 1988. 122.00 (0-8103-1923-3) Gale.

— Contemporary Authors, Vol. 125. 1988. 122.00 (0-8103-1950-0) Gale.

May, Hal, ed. see Gale Research Inc. Staff.

***May, Harriett J.** Enterostomal Therapy. fac. ed. LC 76-19894. (Illus.). 286p. Date not set. pap. 81.60 (0-7837-7195-9, 2047104) Bks Demand.

***May-Hayes, Gila.** Effective Defense: The Woman, the Plan, the Gun. (Illus.). 200p. (Orig.). 1994. pap. 13.95 (1-885036-01-9) FAS Bks.

May, Helen K., ed. see Klukowski, Zygmunt.

May, Henry F. The Divided Heart: Essays on Protestantism & the Enlightment in America. 240p. 1991. 35.00 (0-19-505899-2) OUP.

— The End of American Innocence: A Study of the First Years of Our Own Time, 1912-1917. LC 93-33225. 439p. 1993. 49.00 (0-231-09652-6); pap. 17.50 (0-231-09653-4) Col U Pr.

— The Enlightenment in America. LC 75-32349. 1978. pap. 16.95 (0-19-502367-6) OUP.

— Ideas, Faiths, & Feelings: Essays on American Intellectual & Religious History, 1952-1982. 1983. pap. 9.95 (0-19-503236-5) OUP.

— Three Faces of Berkeley: Competing Ideologies in the Wheeler Era, 1899-1919. Brentano, Carroll & Rothblatt, Sheldon, eds. LC 93-30444. (Chapters in the History of the University of California Ser.: No. 1). 53p. (Orig.). 1994. pap. 10.00 (0-87772-342-7) UCB IGS.

May, Herbert G., ed. Oxford Bible Atlas. 1985. pap. 16.95 (0-19-143451-5) OUP.

— Oxford Bible Atlas. 3rd ed. 1985. 30.00 (0-19-143452-3) OUP.

May, Irvin M., Jr. Marvin Jones: The Public Life of an Agrarian Advocate. LC 79-5282. (Centennial Series of the Association of Former Students: No. 8). (Illus.). 312p. 1980. 22.95 (0-89096-093-3) Tex A&M Univ Pr.

May, Isobel. English-Italian, Italian-English Dictionary. 672p. (ENG & ITA.). 1988. 39.50 (0-87557-045-3, 045-3) Saphrograph.

May, J. George Eliot: A Study. 1973. 250.00 (0-8490-0221-4) Gordon Pr.

— Orion Arm. Date not set. pap. write for info. (0-345-39519-0) Ballantine.

— Sagattarius Whirl. Date not set. pap. write for info. (0-345-39518-2) Ballantine.

May, J. A., ed. see Franklin, Benjamin, et al.

May, J. C. & Brown, F., eds. Biological Product Freeze-Drying & Formulation. (Developments in Biological Standardization Ser.: Vol. 74). (Illus.). x, 382p. 1992. pap. 224.00 (3-8055-5466-4) S Karger.

May, J. J. Danforth Genealogy: Nicholas Danforth of Framingham, England & Cambridge, Mass. (1589-1638) & William of Newbury, Mass. (1640-1771) & Their Descendants. 492p. 1989. reprint ed. lib. bdg. 72.00 (0-8328-0452-5); reprint ed. pap. 62.00 (0-8328-0453-3) Higginson Bk Co.

May, J. L., ed. see France, Anatole.

May, J. Lewis, tr. see Hazard, Paul.

May, J. P. E-Zero-Zero Ring Spaces & F-Zero-Zero Ring Spectra. (Lecture Notes in Mathematics Ser.: Vol. 577). 1977. pap. 24.00 (0-387-08136-4) Spr-Verlag.

— The Geometry of Iterated Loop Spaces. LC 72-85090. (Lecture Notes in Mathematics Ser.: Vol. 271). ix, 175p. 1972. pap. 31.20 (0-387-05904-0) Spr-Verlag.

May, J. P., jt. auth. see Greenlees, J. P.

May, J. Peter. Classifying Spaces & Fibrations. (Memoirs Ser.: No. 1/155). 98p. 1989. reprint ed. pap. 19.00 (0-8218-1855-4, MEMO 1/155) Am Math.

— Simplicial Objects in Algebraic Topology. LC 82-51078. (Chicago Lectures in Mathematics Ser.). viii, 162p. (C). 1992. pap. text ed. 23.95 (0-226-51181-2) U Ch Pr.

May, J. Peter & Thomas, Charles B., eds. The Selected Works of J. Frank Adams, Vol. 1. 1992. 79.95 (0-521-41063-0) Cambridge U Pr.

May, J. Peter, ed. see Adams, J. Frank.

May, J. Peter, jt. auth. see Gugenheim, V. M.

***May, Jack Q.** Clyde. 1994. 15.95 (0-533-11140-4) Vantage.

May, James. Circles of Care & Understanding: Support Groups for Fathers of Children with Special Needs. 1992. pap. 6.95 (0-937821-86-1) Assn Care Child.

— Fathers of Children with Special Needs: New Horizons. 51p. (Orig.). 1991. pap. 4.95 (0-937821-73-X, R-3266-1) Assn Care Child.

May, James L. John Lane & the Nineties. LC 79-8070. reprint ed. 30.00 (0-404-18380-8) AMS Pr.

May, James M. Trials of Character: The Eloquence of Ciceronian Ethos. LC 87-13884. viii, 216p. (C). 1988. 34.95 (0-8078-1759-7) U of NC Pr.

May, James M., jt. auth. see Groton, Anne H.

May, James M., tr. see Groton, Anne H. & May, James M.

May, James V. Mental Diseases: A Public Health Problem. Grob, Gerald N., ed. LC 78-22574. (Historical Issues in Mental Health Ser.). 1980. reprint ed. lib. bdg. 40.95 (0-405-11927-5) Ayer.

May, Janis S. Lacey. 192p. 1987. 16.95 (0-8027-0955-9) Walker & Co.

— Where Shadows Linger. large type ed. LC 93-2488. 1993. 19.95 (0-7927-1767-8, Curley Lrg Print); pap. 18.95 (0-7927-1766-X, Curley Lrg Print) Chivers N Amer.

May, Jayne & Murdock, Dick. Love Lines. 4th ed. 130p. 1978. pap. 5.00 (0-932916-01-5) May-Murdock.

May, Jeffrey A., jt. ed. see Abbott, Patrick L.

May, Jerry, jt. auth. see Muir, Roy.

May, Jerry R. & Asken, Michael J., eds. Sport Psychology: The Psychological Health of the Athlete. LC 87-787361. 315p. 1987. 35.00 (0-89335-304-3) PMA Pub Corp.

May, Jill. A Reference Manual for Teachers of Dance Exercise. (Illus.). 128p. (Orig.). 1988. pap. 28.50 (0-572-01472-4, Pub. by W Foulsham UK) Trans-Atl Phila.

***May, Jill P.** Children's Literature & Critical Theory: Reading & Writing for Understanding. 288p. (C). 1995. text ed. 30.00 (0-19-509584-7); pap. text ed. 16.95 (0-19-509585-5) OUP.

— Lloyd Alexander. (Twayne's United States Authors Ser.: No. 576). 200p. 1991. text ed. 21.95 (0-8057-7622-2, Twayne) Macmillan.

May, Jill P., jt. ed. see Nodelman, Perry.

May, Jim. The Boo Baby Girl Meets the Ghost of Mable's Gable. LC 92-72702. (Illus.). 32p. (J). (ps-5). 1992. lib. bdg. 14.95 (1-878925-03-2) Brotherstone Pubs.

— The Farm on Nippersink Creek. 192p. 1993. 18.95 (0-87483-339-6) August Hse.

May, John. A Declaration of the Estate of Clothing Now Used Within This Realme of England. LC 71-171775. (English Experience Ser.: No. 400). 60p. 1971. reprint ed. 8.00 (90-221-0400-1) Walter J Johnson.

— Reference Wales. 300p. 1994. pap. 19.95 (0-7083-1234-9, Pub. by Univ Wales Pr UK) Paul & Co Pubs.

— The RIF Survival Handbook: How to Manage Your Money if You're Unemployed. LC 82-80357. 132p. (Orig.). 1982. pap. 4.95 (0-905750-2-2) Tilden Pr.

— Symantec C Plus Plus for Windows, the Basics. 1994. pap. 29.95 (1-55828-327-7) MIS Press.

May, John, ed. The Greenpeace Book of Dolphins. LC 90-38836. (Illus.). 160p. (YA). (gr. 10-12). 1992. pap. 21.95 (0-8069-7485-0) Sterling.

May, John, jt. auth. see Brown, Michael.

May, John C. Extending the Macintosh Programming Menus: Windows, Dialogs, & More. 1991. pap. 24.95 (0-201-57722-4) Addison-Wesley.

***May, John C. & Whittle, Judith B.** Programming Primer for the MacIntosh. 352p. 1994. disk 1.95 (0-12-480623-6) Acad Pr.

— Programming Primer for the MacIntosh, Vol. 1. (Illus.). 287p. 1994. disk, pap. 37.95 (0-12-480621-X, AP Prof) Acad Pr.

May, John G., comp. Historical Studies in the Physical Sciences: A Subject Index to Vols. 1-10. LC 84-51371. 50p. (Orig.). 1984. pap. 3.00 (0-918102-11-1) U Cal Hist Sci Tech.

May, John L. With Staff & Pen. LC 92-72597. 344p. (Orig.). 1992. pap. text ed. 14.95 (0-89243-460-0) Liguori Pubns.

May, John R. The Pruning Word: The Parables of Flannery O'Connor. LC 75-19878. 204p. reprint ed. pap. 58.20 (0-317-29674-4, 2022075) Bks Demand.

May, John R., ed. Image & Likeness: Religious Visions in American Film Classics. 1991. pap. 14.95 (0-8091-3286-9) Paulist Pr.

— The New Age of Religious Film. 514p. (Orig.). Date not set. pap. 24.95 (1-55612-761-8) Sheed & Ward MO.

May, John R. & Bird, Michael, eds. Religion in Film. LC 81-23983. (Illus.). 276p. 1982. text ed. 29.00x (0-87049-352-3); pap. text ed. 16.00 (0-87049-368-X) U of Tenn Pr.

May, John W. The Law of Crimes. xxii, 239p. 1985. reprint ed. lib. bdg. 26.50 (0-8377-0823-0) Rothman.

May, Judith V. & Wildavsky, Aaron B., eds. The Policy Cycle. LC 78-15351. (Sage Yearbooks in Politics & Public Policy Ser.: No. 5). (Illus.). 332p. reprint ed. pap. 94.70 (*0-8357-4775-1*, 2037712) Bks Demand.

May, Judy. Programming in Symantec C Plus Plus for the Macintosh. 1993. pap. 29.95 (*1-55828-276-9*) MIS Press.

May, Julian. The Adversary. (Saga of Pliocene Exile Ser.: Vol. IV). 512p. 1987. mass mkt. 4.95 (*0-345-35244-0*, Del Rey) Ballantine.

— Blood Trillium. 1993. mass mkt. 5.99 (*0-553-56198-7*) Bantam.

— Diamond Mask. (Galactic Milieu Ser.: Bk. 2). 1995. mass mkt., pap. 5.99 (*0-345-36248-9*, Del Rey) Ballantine.

— Diamond Mask: A Novel. LC 93-37802. (Galactic Milieu Trilogy Ser.: Vol. 2). 1994. 22.00 (*0-679-43310-4*) Knopf.

— The Golden Torc. (Saga of Pliocene Exile Ser.: Vol. II). 416p. 1985. mass mkt. 4.95 (*0-345-32419-6*, Del Rey) Ballantine.

— Intervention, Vol. 1: The Surveillance. 1988. mass mkt. 5.99 (*0-345-35523-7*, Del Rey) Ballantine.

— Jack the Bodiless. (Galactic Milieu Trilogy Ser.: Book 1). 1993. mass mkt. 5.99 (*0-345-36247-0*, Del Rey) Ballantine.

— Magnification. Date not set. pap. 23.00 (*0-679-44177-8*) Random.

— The Many-Colored Land. 1985. mass mkt. 4.95 (*0-345-32444-7*, Del Rey) Ballantine.

— The Metaconcert. (Intervention Ser.: Bk. 2). 1989. mass mkt. 4.95 (*0-345-35524-5*, Del Rey) Ballantine.

— The Nonborn King. 1987. mass mkt. 5.95 (*0-345-34749-8*, Del Rey) Ballantine.

— Perseus Spur. Date not set. pap. write for info. (*0-345-39510-7*) Ballantine.

May, Kara. Big Brave Brother Ben. LC 91-530234. (Illus.). (J). (ps-3). 1992. 14.00 (*0-688-11234-X*); lib. bdg. 13.93 (*0-688-11235-8*) Lothrop.

— Creepy Crawly Caterpillar. LC 94-32713. (Illus.). (J). 1995. write for info. (*0-385-32166-X*) Doubleday.

May, Karl. Jubilaums-Bildband. 305p. (GER.). 1992. write for info. (*3-487-08169-5*, Pub. by Georg Olms GW) Lubrecht & Cramer.

— Mein Leben und Streben. xiii, 570p. 1975. reprint ed. write for info. (*3-487-08084-2*, Pub. by Georg Olms GW) Lubrecht & Cramer.

May, Katharyn A. & Mahlmeister, Laura R. Pocket Guide to Maternal & Neonatal Nursing. LC 93-30921. 1993. write for info. (*0-397-55125-8*) Lippincott.

May, Kathryn A. & Mahlmeister, Laura R. Maternal & Neonatal Nursing: Family-Centered Care. 3rd ed. (Illus.). 1232p. (C). 1994. text ed. 55.95 (*0-397-54953-9*, Lippincott Nursing) Lippincott.

May, Kathryn E., jt. auth. see Messer, Ellen.

May, Keith M. Nietzsche & Modern Literature. LC 87-20741. 172p. 1988. text ed. 39.95 (*0-312-01548-8*) St Martin.

— Nietzsche & the Spirit of Tragedy. LC 89-24057. 370p. 1990. text ed. 45.00 (*0-312-04028-8*) St Martin.

***May, Kenneth M., ed.** Electronic Underwriter: Artificial Intelligence & Insurance. 183p. 1991. pap. 35.00 (*0-614-05733-7*) Charter Prop Underwriters Soc.

***May, Kerry P.** Test Flights. 71p. (Orig.). 1995. pap. 8.95 (*0-931122-79-1*) West End.

May, L. & Gardner, C. M. Gardner History & Genealogy. 407p. 1989. reprint ed. lib. bdg. 62.50 (*0-8328-0583-1*); reprint ed. pap. 52.50 (*0-8328-0584-X*) Higginson Bk Co.

May, L., et al, eds. Rotifer Symposium, No. IV. (C). 1987. lib. bdg. 213.50 (*90-6193-645-4*) Kluwer Ac.

May, Larry. The Morality of Groups: Collective Responsibility, Group-Based Harm & Corporate Rights. LC 87-40350. (Soundings: A Series in Ethics, Economics & Business: Vol. 1). 216p. (C). 1989. pap. text ed. 10.95 (*0-268-01378-0*) U of Notre Dame Pr.

— Screening out the Past: The Birth of Mass Culture & the Motion Picture Industry. LC 83-4927. (Illus.). (C). 1983. reprint ed. pap. text ed. 14.95 (*0-226-51173-1*) U Ch Pr.

— Sharing Responsibility. LC 92-12658. 208p. 1992. 31.95 (*0-226-51168-5*) U Ch Pr.

May, Larry, ed. Recasting America: Culture & Politics in the Age of Cold War. LC 88-21618. (Illus.). 328p. 1988. pap. text ed. 15.95 (*0-226-51176-6*) U Ch Pr.

— Recasting America: Culture & Politics in the Age of Cold War. LC 88-21618. (Illus.). 328p. 1989. lib. bdg. 49.95 (*0-226-51175-8*) U Ch Pr.

May, Larry, et al, eds. Rethinking Masculinity: Philosophical Explorations in Light of Feminism. LC 92-22430. (New Feminist Perspectives Ser.). 244p. (C). 1992. 50.00 (*0-8476-7773-7*); pap. 12.95 (*0-8226-3021-4*) Rowman.

May, Larry & Hoffman, Stacey. Collective Responsibility. 320p. (C). 1991. text ed. 54.50 (*0-8476-7691-9*); pap. text ed. 20.00 (*0-8476-7692-7*) Rowman.

May, Larry & Sharratt, Shari C., eds. Applied Ethics: A Multicultural Approach. LC 93-5395. 1993. pap. text ed. write for info. (*0-13-068842-8*) P-H.

***May, Larry, et al, eds.** Mind & Morals: Essays on Ethics & Cognitive Science. (Illus.). 344p. 1995. 40.00x (*0-262-13313-X*, Bradford Bks); pap. 18.00x (*0-262-63165-2*, Bradford Bks) MIT Pr.

May, Lawrence, tr. see Groth, Lynn.

***May, Lee.** In My Father's Garden: Estranged for 39 Years, a Father & Son Find Common Ground in the Garden. 208p. 1995. 19.45 (*1-56352-192-X*) Longstreet Pr Inc.

May, Leland C. Parodies of the Gothic Novel. Varma, Devendra P., ed. LC 79-8464. (Gothic Studies & Dissertations). 1980. lib. bdg. 19.95 (*0-405-12654-9*) Ayer.

May, Lewis, tr. see De Pourtales, Guy.

May, Lola J. Teaching Mathematics in the Elementary School. 2nd ed. LC 73-18285. (Illus.). (C). 1974. 21.95 (*0-02-920380-5*); pap. text ed. 14.95 (*0-02-920370-8*) Free Pr.

***May, Lowell A.** Camp Concordia. (Illus.). 140p. 1995. pap. 20.95 (*0-89745-192-9*) Journal of the West.

May, Lynn, ed. Encyclopedia of Southern Baptists, Vol. IV. LC 81-66989. 1982. 19.99 (*0-8054-6556-1*) Broadman.

— Encyclopedia of Southern Baptists: Index to Vols. I-IV. 1982. pap. 1.75 (*0-8054-6562-6*) Broadman.

May, Lynn E. Church History Committee Handbook. Deweese, Charles W., ed. (Resource Kit for Your Church's History Ser.). 20p. 1984. pap. 2.95 (*0-317-61214-X*) Hist Comm S Baptist.

May, M., jt. auth. see James, D.

May, M. D., et al. Networks, Routers & Transputers. LC 93-77461. (Transputer & Occam Engineering Ser.: Vol. 32). 221p. 1993. 80.00 (*90-5199-129-0*, Pub. by IOS Pr NE) IOS Press.

— Networks, Routers & Transputers. LC 93-77461. (Transputer & Occam Engineering Ser.: Vol. 32). 221p. 1994. pap. 50.00 (*90-5199-185-1*) IOS Press.

May, Marge & Hall, John, eds. Memories of Little Traverse Bay. (Illus.). 112p. (Orig.). 1989. pap. 10.00 (*0-685-26072-0*) Little Traverse.

May, Marianne, jt. auth. see Apple, Loyal E.

May, Mark, jt. auth. see Hartshorne, Hugh.

May, Mark, jt. auth. see Levine, Howard L.

May, Mark A. A Social Psychology of War & Peace. 1943. 79.50 (*0-686-51314-2*) Elliots Bks.

May, Marsha, ed. see Wegner, Oscar.

May, Marshall, tr. see Blond, George.

May, Matthew. Admissions Guide to Selective Business Schools. 1990. pap. 16.95 (*0-8442-8556-0*, VGM Career Bks) NTC Pub Grp.

— Admissions Guide to Selective Business Schools. 192p. 1991. 29.95 (*0-8442-8550-1*, Passport Bks) NTC Pub Grp.

May, Maurice I., et al. Managing Institutional Long-Term Care for the Elderly. 336p. 1991. 67.00 (*0-8342-0275-1*) Aspen Pub.

May, Melanie. Bonds of Unity. LC 88-37682. (American Academy of Religion Academy Ser.). 196p. 1989. 23.95 (*1-55540-308-5*, 01 01 65); pap. 15.95 (*1-55540-309-3*) Scholars Pr GA.

***May, Melanie A.** A Body Knows: A Theopoetics of Death & Resurrection. 128p. 1995. 16.95 (*0-8264-0849-4*) Continuum.

May, Melvyn, jt. auth. see Letman, Sloan T.

May, Michael M., et al. Strategic Arms Reductions. 73p. 1988. pap. 8.95 (*0-8157-5525-2*) Brookings.

May, Michael W. Building with the Basics...Radio Personality Development. (Illus.). 169p. 1983. pap. text ed. 11.95 (*0-9612074-0-X*) M May Ent.

May, Nancy, jt. auth. see May, Alex.

May, Nola. Classic Earring Designs. (Illus.). 96p. (Orig.). 1994. pap. 9.95 (*0-943604-43-5*) Eagles View.

May, Peter. The Big Three. 1994. 22.00 (*0-671-79955-X*) S&S Trade.

May, Peter J. Recovering from Catastrophes: Federal Disaster Relief Policy & Politics. LC 84-19731. (Contributions in Political Science Ser.: No. 128). (Illus.). x, 186p. 1985. text ed. 55.00 (*0-313-24698-X*, MYR/, Greenwood Pr) Greenwood.

May, Peter J. & Williams, Walter. Disaster Policy Implementation: Managing Programs under Shared Governance. LC 86-22653. (Disaster Research in Practice Ser.). 210p. 1986. 42.50 (*0-306-42179-8*, Plenum Pr) Plenum.

May, Peter J., jt. ed. see Leiggi, Patrick.

May, Philip R. Origins of Hydraulic Mining in California. limited ed. (Illus.). 88p. 1970. 6.95 (*0-910740-17-8*) Holmes.

May, Phillip T., jt. auth. see Spiller, Earl A., Jr.

May, R., Jr. The Urbanization Revolution: Planning a New Agenda for Human Settlements. (Urban Innovation Abroad Ser.). (Illus.). 288p. 1989. 70.00 (*0-306-43222-6*, Plenum Pr) Plenum.

May, R. & Weber, J., eds. Pelvic & Abdominal Veins. (International Congress Ser.: No. 550). 374p. 1981. 112.50 (*0-444-90215-5*, Excerpta Medica) Elsevier.

May, R., jt. auth. see Gottlob, R.

May, R., jt. ed. see Noye, J.

May, R. A., ed. see Beit-Arie, Malachi.

***May, Rachel.** The Translator in the Text: On Reading Russian Literature in English. LC 94-22792. (Studies in Russian Literature & Theory). 209p. 1994. pap. text ed. 15.95 (*0-8101-1158-6*) Northwestern U Pr.

— The Translator in the Text: On Reading Russian Literature in English. LC 94-22792. (Studies in Russian Literature & Theory). 220p. (C). 1994. text ed. 49.95 (*0-8101-1157-8*) Northwestern U Pr.

May, Rachel, tr. see Tertz, Abram.

May, Rachel, tr. see Xi Xi.

May, Rachel, tr. see Yu Luojin.

May, Raoul M., jt. ed. see Anderson, R. C.

May, Raoul M., tr. see DeFelipe, Javier & Jones, Edward G., eds.

May, Richard B., et al. Application of Statistics in Behavioral Research. 618p. (C). 1990. text ed. 49.00 (*0-06-044311-1*) HarpCollege.

May, Richard D. Self-Concept: Background & Sixty-Seven Collected Activities. 1985. write for info. (*0-931802-01-6*) Prof Assocs.

May, Richard E., jt. auth. see Wolfe, Susan M.

May, Richard L. Reducing New Home Costs As Much As 30,000 Dollars. rev. ed. LC 90-70961. (Orig.). 1990. 23.00 (*0-9627119-0-X*) J Zachary Pub.

May, Richard M. The Shreek of Wagons. 154p. 1993. 29.95 (*1-883543-00-2*); pap. 19.95 (*1-883543-01-0*) Rigel Pubns.

— A Sketch of a Migrating Family to California in 1848. 66p. 1991. 14.95 (*0-685-47920-X*); pap. 9.95 (*0-87770-494-5*) Ye Galleon.

May, Robert. Logical Form: Its Structure & Derivation. 280p. 1985. pap. 18.95 (*0-262-63102-4*) MIT Pr.

— Rudolph the Red Nosed Reindeer. LC 91-156221. (J). (ps-3). 1990. 9.95 (*1-55709-139-0*) Applewood.

May, Robert, ed. Psychoanalytic Psychotherapy in a College Context. LC 87-2836. 216p. 1988. text ed. 49.95 (*0-275-92733-4*, C2733, Praeger Pubs) Greenwood.

May, Robert & Koster, Jan, eds. Levels of Syntactic Representation. (Studies in Generative Grammar). 350p. 1981. pap. 69.25 (*90-70176-30-0*) Mouton.

May, Robert, jt. auth. see Fiengo, Robert.

May, Robert, jt. auth. see Huang, C. T.

May, Robert, jt. ed. see Huang, C. T.

***May, Robert, et al.** Accounting. LC 94-31231. (AB-Accounting Principles Ser.). (Illus.). 1200p. 1995. text ed. 60.95 (*0-538-83062-X*) S-W Pub.

May, Robert E. How Billy Joe Bobtail Met Texas Slim. (Bobtail Chronicles Ser.). (Illus.). 32p. (J). (gr. k-7). 1987. lib. bdg. 11.89 (*0-87397-303-8*); pap. 5.95 (*0-87397-300-3*) Strode.

— John A. Quitman: Old South Crusader. LC 84-10019. (Southern Biography Ser.). (Illus.). 465p. 1995. pap. 19.95 (*0-8071-1207-0*) La State U Pr.

— Poppa & Elizabeth: A Bobtail Romance. (Bobtail Chronicles Ser.). (Illus.). 32p. (Orig.). (J). (ps-3). 1988. lib. bdg. 11.89 (*0-87397-314-3*); pap. 5.95 (*0-87397-313-5*) Strode.

— The Southern Dream of a Caribbean Empire, 1854-1861. LC 88-29608. (Illus.). 318p. 1989. reprint ed. pap. 15.00 (*0-8203-1136-7*) U of Ga Pr.

May, Robert E., ed. see Jones, Howard, et al.

***May, Robert G., et al.** Accounting. LC 94-31231. 1995. text ed. 60.95 (*0-538-83074-3*) S-W Pub.

May, Robert L. Rudolph the Red-Nosed Reindeer. 32p. 1993. audio, spiral bd. 5.95 (*1-55709-137-4*) Applewood.

— Rudolph the Red-Nosed Reindeer. LC 94-20997. (Illus.). 32p. (J). (ps-3). 1994. 9.95 (*1-55709-294-X*) Applewood.

— Rudolph the Red-Nosed Reindeer. (J). (ps). 1993. 4.95 (*0-307-12396-0*, Golden Pr) Western Pub.

— Rudolph's Second Christmas. LC 92-18416. (Illus.). (J). (ps-3). 1992. 9.95 (*1-55709-192-7*) Applewood.

May, Robert M. Cosmic Consciousness Revisited: The Modern Origins & Development of Western Spiritual Psychology. rev. ed. 276p. 1993. pap. 19.95 (*1-85230-280-1*) Element MA.

— Physicians of the Soul. (Chrysalis Bks.). 160p. 1988. 18.95 (*0-916349-53-5*); pap. 9.95 (*0-317-66000-4*) Amity Hse Inc.

— Physicians of the Soul: The Psychologies of the World's Great Spiritual Teachers. 248p. 1991. pap. 13.95 (*1-85230-257-7*) Element MA.

— Stability & Complexity in Model Ecosystems. (Population Biology Monographs: No. 6). 150p. 1973. 49.50x (*0-691-08125-5*); pap. 18.95 (*0-691-08130-1*) Princeton U Pr.

May, Robert M., ed. see Karlin, Samuel & Lessard, Sabin.

May, Robert M., jt. ed. see Lawton, John H.

May, Robert M., ed. see Lomnicki, Adam.

May, Robert M., ed. see Tilman, David.

May, Robin. The British Army in North America. (Men-at-Arms Ser.: No. 39). (Illus.). 48p. pap. 11.95 (*0-85045-195-7*, 9161, Pub. by Osprey UK) Stackpole.

— Looking at Theater. LC 89-17255. (Exploring the Arts Ser.). 48p. (J). (gr. 4-8). 1990. 13.95 (*1-85435-103-6*) Marshall Cavendish.

— Plains Indians of North America. (Original People Ser.). (Illus.). 48p. (J). (gr. 4-8). 1987. 12.50 (*0-685-67607-2*); lib. bdg. 16.67 (*0-86625-258-4*) Rourke Corp.

— Wolfe's Army. (Men-at-Arms Ser.: No. 48). (Illus.). 48p. pap. 11.95 (*0-85045-193-0*, 9163, Pub. by Osprey UK) Stackpole.

May, Robin & Ross, David. Royal Canadian Mounted Police. (Men-at-Arms Ser.: No. 197). (Illus.). 48p. pap. 11.95 (*0-85045-834-X*, 9130, Pub. by Osprey UK) Stackpole.

May, Robin, jt. auth. see Rosa, Joseph G.

May, Roger J., jt. auth. see Chopra, Sanjiv.

May, Rollo. The Art of Counseling. rev. ed. LC 88-30155. 1990. text ed. 23.95 (*0-89876-156-5*) Gardner Pr.

— The Courage to Create. 1995. 20.50 (*0-8446-6854-0*) Peter Smith.

— The Courage to Create. LC 93-43718. 144p. 1994. pap. 9.95 (*0-393-31106-6*) Norton.

— Cry for Myth. 1992. pap. 12.95 (*0-385-30685-7*, Delta) Dell.

— The Discovery of Being. 1995. 22.75 (*0-8446-6855-9*) Peter Smith.

— Existential Psychology. 1990. pap. 9.95 (*0-394-30743-7*) Random.

— Freedom & Destiny. 1989. pap. 10.95 (*0-385-29207-4*, Delta) Dell.

— Freedom & Destiny. 1981. 14.95 (*0-393-01477-0*) Norton.

— Love & Will. 1989. pap. 12.95 (*0-385-28590-6*) Doubleday.

— Love & Will. LC 66-12799. 1969. 19.95 (*0-393-01080-5*) Norton.

— Man's Search for Himself. 1973. pap. 12.95 (*0-385-28617-1*, Delta) Dell.

— My Quest for Beauty. LC 85-61687. (Illus.). 244p. 1987. reprint ed. pap. 9.95 (*0-933071-13-2*) Saybrook Pub Co.

— Paulus: The Dimensions of a Teacher. 1988. reprint ed. pap. 6.95 (*0-933071-18-3*) Saybrook Pub Co.

— Paulus - Tillich As Spiritual Teacher. 1992. 18.50 (*0-8446-6500-2*) Peter Smith.

— Politics & Innocence. 1986. 15.95 (*0-933071-09-4*) Saybrook Pub Co.

— Power & Innocence: A Search for the Sources of Violence. 288p. 1972. 14.95 (*0-393-01065-1*) Norton.

— Psychology & the Human Dilemma. 240p. 1980. reprint ed. pap. 9.95 (*0-393-00978-5*) Norton.

May, Rollo, ed. Existential Psychology. 2nd ed. 1969. pap. text ed. write for info. (*0-07-553578-5*) McGraw.

May, Rollo, jt. auth. see Schneider, Kirk J.

May, Rollo, et al, eds. Existence. LC 94-71311. 456p. 1994. pap. 40.00 (*1-56821-271-2*) Aronson.

May, Ron, jt. auth. see Barnes, Mark.

May, Ronald V. An Evaluation of Mexican Majolica in Alta California. 1980. reprint ed. 4.95 (*0-686-31787-4*) Acoma Bks.

May, Ronald V. Mexican Majolica in Northern New Spain: A Model for Interpreting Ceramic Change. (Illus.). 147p. 1975. pap. text ed. 12.50 (*1-55567-031-8*) Coyote Press.

May, Roy H., Jr. The Poor of the Land: A Christian Case for Land Reform. LC 90-46980. 1991. pap. 14.95 (*0-88344-729-0*) Orbis Bks.

May, S. Case Studies in Business. 146p. (C). 1984. 83.00 (*0-685-39810-2*, Inst Pur & Supply) St Mut.

— Costa Rica. 1976. lib. bdg. 59.95 (*0-8490-1677-0*) Gordon Pr.

— The Descendants of Richard Sares (Sears) of Yarmouth, Mass., 1638-1888, with Some Notices of Other Families by the Name of Sears. 676p. 1989. reprint ed. lib. bdg. 108.00 (*0-685-25064-4*); reprint ed. pap. 98.00 (*0-8328-1053-3*) Higginson Bk Co.

May, S., et al. Grading of Continuously Cast Material Via the Image Analysis of Macro Etched EN, No. EUR 12958. 78p. 1990. pap. 11.00 (*92-826-1685-1*, CD-NA-12958-EN-C) UNIPUB.

***May, S. Beville.** Sexual Harassment: Litigating, Preventing & Resolving Claims. 1994. 35.00 (*0-614-06019-2*, 4923); audio 135.00 (*0-614-06020-6*) Natl Prac Inst.

May, S. R. & Dogo, G., eds. Care of the Burn Wound. (Illus.). xiv, 246p. 1985. 176.00 (*3-8055-3991-6*) S Karger.

May, Samuel. Some Recollections of Our Anti-Slavery Conflict. pap. 15.00 (*1-56675-043-1*, N160P) Mnemosyne.

May, Samuel J. Fugitive Slave Law & Its Victims. LC 77-133161. (Black Heritage Library Collection). 1977. 15.95 (*0-8369-8716-0*) Ayer.

— Some Recollections of Our Anti-Slavery Conflict. LC 79-83888. (Black Heritage Library Collection). 1977. 17.95 (*0-8369-8630-X*) Ayer.

— Some Recollections of Our Anti-Slavery Conflict. LC 68-29010. (American Negro: His History & Literature, Ser. No. 1). 1968. reprint ed. 17.95 (*0-405-01829-0*) Ayer.

May, Sarton. Magnificent Spinster. 384p. 1995. pap. 11.00 (*0-393-31249-6*) Norton.

— Shower of Summer Days. 256p. 1995. pap. 10.00 (*0-393-31250-X*) Norton.

May, Sheila. Case Studies in Business. 146p. (C). 1989. 73.00 (*0-685-36147-0*, Inst Pur & Supply) St Mut.

May, Simon, jt. ed. see Creasey, Pauline.

May, Stacy, jt. auth. see Hamilton, Walton H.

May, Stacy, jt. auth. see Keezer, Dexter M.

May, Stephen. Fire from the Skies. LC 90-71976. 158p. (Orig.). 1991. pap. 8.95 (*1-56002-036-9*) Aegina Pr.

— Footloose on the Santa Fe Trail. (Illus.). 144p. 1993. 19.95 (*0-87081-294-7*); pap. 12.95 (*0-87081-295-5*) Univ Pr Colo.

— Making Multicultural Education Work. LC 94-9690. (Language & Education Library Ser.: Vol. 7). 1994. write for info. (*1-85359-237-4*, Pub. by Multilingual Matters UK) Taylor & Francis.

— Making Multicultural Education Work. LC 94-9690. (Language & Education Library: Vol. 7). 223p. 1994. pap. 24.95 (*1-85359-236-6*) Taylor & Francis.

— Pilgrimage: A Journey Through Colorado's History & Culture. LC 82-76537. (Illus.). 200p. 1986. text ed. 18.95 (*0-8040-0882-5*); pap. 8.95 (*0-8040-0883-3*) Swallow.

May, Steven W. Sir Walter Raleigh. (Twayne's English Authors Ser.: No. 469). 400p. 1989. text ed. 21.95 (*0-8057-6983-8*, Pub. by Royal Botanic Garden UK) Macmillan.

May, Suzanne D., jt. auth. see Ashby, Clifford.

May, Theodore W. & Dana, Richard H., eds. Internship Training in Professional Psychology. 527p. 1987. 68.00 (*0-89116-580-0*); pap. 34.00 (*0-89116-773-0*) Hemisp Pub.

May, Theresa, jt. auth. see Fried, Larry K.

May, Thomas. Tragedy of Julia Agrippina, Empresse of Rome, with an Essay on Thomas May & the Tragedy of Nero. Schmid, F. E., ed. (Material for the Study of the Old English Drama Ser.: No. 1, Vol. 43). 1974. reprint ed. pap. 30.00 (*0-8115-0292-9*) Periodicals Srv.

May, Thomas, ed. Philosophy Books, 1982-1986. (Philosophical Bibliographies Ser.). 211p. 1990. 19.00 (*0-912632-89-5*) Philos Document.

May, Thomas E. The Constitutional History of England since the Accession of George Third 1760-1860, 2 vols., Set. 1080p. 1986. reprint ed. lib. bdg. 75.00 (*0-8377-2429-5*) Rothman.

May, Thomas G. Leader's Guide for Friends under Construction. 64p. 1990. teacher ed 2.99 (*0-87403-609-7*, 39951) Standard Pub.

May, Thornton A. Electronic Image Management: Case Studies. 43p. 1994. pap. 33.00 (*0-89258-255-3*, R056) Assn Inform & Image Mgmt.

May, Timothy. Probation: Politics, Policy & Practice. 176p. 1990. 85.00 (*0-335-09378-7*, Open Univ Pr); pap. 29.00 (*0-335-09377-9*, Open Univ Pr) Taylor & Francis.

— Social Research: Issues, Methods, & Process. LC 92-43089. 1993. pap. 23.00 (*0-335-19054-5*, Open Univ Pr) Taylor & Francis.

May, Timothy, jt. auth. see Barberis, Peter.

May, Timothy, jt. auth. see Hobbs, Dick.

An Asterisk (*) at the beginning of an entry indicates that the title is appearing in BIP for the first time.

May, Todd. Between Genealogy & Epistemology: Psychology, Politics, & Knowledge in the Thought of Michel Foucault. LC 92-29112. 144p. (C). 1993. 27.50 (0-271-00905-5) Pa St U Pr.

— The Moral Theory of Poststructuralism. LC 94-45435. 152p. 1995. 27.50 (0-271-01468-7); pap. 13.95 (0-271-01469-5) Pa St U Pr.

— The Political Philosophy of Poststructuralist Anarchism. LC 93-30551. 1994. 28.50 (0-271-01045-2); pap. 13.95 (0-271-01046-0) Pa St U Pr.

May, Tom, jt. auth. see McAllister, Dawson.

May, Tony, jt. auth. see Timings, Roger.

May, V. Riverbend. 105p. 1984. 4.95 (0-89697-131-7) Intl Univ Pr.

May, W., jt. auth. see Lawler, R.

May, W. Samuel, Jr., et al. Capnography in the Operating Room: An Introductory Directory. LC 85-18261. (Illus.). 64p. 1985. spiral bd. 18.00 (0-88167-128-2) Raven.

May, William & Harvey, John. On Understanding Human Sexuality. (Synthesis Ser.). 1978. pap. 1.95 (0-8199-0720-0, Frncscn Herld) Franciscan Pr.

May, William E. An Introduction to Moral Theology. rev. ed. LC 90-60638. 240p. (Orig.). (C). 1991. pap. 9.95 (0-87973-453-1, 453) Our Sunday Visitor.

— Moral Absolutes, Catholic Traditions, Current Trends & the Truth. LC 88-44163. (Pere Marquette Lectures). 1989. text ed. 10.00 (0-87462-544-0, PM-20) Marquette.

— Sex & the Sanctity of Human Life. 141p. (Orig.). 1984. pap. 6.95 (0-931888-17-4) Christendom Pr.

— The Unity of the Moral & Spiritual Life. (Synthesis Ser.). 1978. pap. 1.95 (0-8199-0745-6, Frncscn Herld) Franciscan Pr.

May, William E., tr. see De Haro, Ramon G.

May, William F. The Patient's Ordeal. LC 90-45841. (Medical Ethics Ser.). 234p. 1991. 24.95 (0-253-33717-8); pap. 10.95 (0-253-20870-X) Ind U Pr.

— The Physician's Covenant: Images of the Healer in Medical Ethics. LC 83-16992. 204p. 1983. pap. 12.99 (0-664-24497-1, Westminster) Westminster John Knox.

May, William V., et al. World's Greatest Music Teacher's Guide. (Orig.). (C). 1989. teacher ed, pap. 47.00 (0-685-37980-9, 3021/3021A) Music Ed Natl.

May, William W. Business Ethics & the Law: Beyond Compliance. LC 91-23017. (Rockwell Lecture Ser.: Vol. 2). 100p. (C). 1992. text ed. 16.95 (0-8204-1728-9) P Lang Pubs.

— Ethics & Higher Education. (ACE-Oryx Series on Higher Education). 408p. 1991. 27.95 (0-02-897267-8, ACE-Oryx) Oryx Pr.

May, William W., ed. Vatican Authority & American Catholic Dissent: The Curran Case & Its Consequences. 160p. 1987. 16.95 (0-8245-0840-8) Crossroad NY.

May, Willie & Sahadi, Lou. Say Hey: The Autobiography of Willie Mays. 1989. mass mkt. 4.50 (0-671-67836-1) PB.

Mayadas, Azim L. NGCSA: A Retrospective. 14p. 1985. 9.00 (0-318-21719-8) NGCSA.

Mayadas, Azim L., jt. auth. see Intermarkon Inc. Staff.

Mayaguez Institute of Tropical Agriculture Staff. The Mayaguez Institute of Tropical Agriculture, Puerto Rico: A Bibliography of Publications. (Studies in Tropical Agriculture). 1980. lib. bdg. 59.95 (0-8490-3072-2) Gordon Pr.

Mayakovsky, Stanislaw, pseud. & Geary, Rick. Cyberantics. (Illus.). 56p. (Orig.). (J). 1992. 14.95 (1-878574-29-9) Dark Horse Comics.

Mayakovsky, Vladimir. The Bedbug & Selected Poetry. Blake, Patricia, ed. Hayward, Max & Reavey, George, trs. LC 75-10805. 320p. 1975. reprint ed. pap. 12.95 (0-253-20189-6, MB-189) Ind U Pr.

— Legends! Early Poems. Enzensberger, Maria, tr. 64p. (Orig.). 1991. pap. 5.95 (0-87286-255-0) City Lights.

Mayali, Laurent & Tibbetts, Stephanie J., eds. The Two Laws: Studies in Medieval Legal History Dedicated to Stephan Kuttner. LC 90-1686. 248p. 1990. 39.95 (0-8132-0725-8) Cath U Pr.

Mayali, Laurent, ed. see Storti-Storchi, Claudia, et al.

Mayall, jt. auth. see Maze, Marilyn.

***Mayall, Berry, ed.** Children's Childhoods: Observed & Experienced. LC 94-36526. 192p. 1994. 75.00 (0-7507-0369-5, Falmer Pr); pap. 24.95 (0-7507-0370-9, Falmer Pr) Taylor & Francis.

Mayall, David. Gypsy-Travellers in Nineteenth Century Society. (Illus.). 320p. 1988. 74.95 (0-521-32397-5) Cambridge U Pr.

Mayall, Don, comp. The Worker Traits Data Book: Specific Details on the 12,741 Jobs Listed in the Dictionary of Occupational Titles. LC 93-33412. 344p. 1994. pap. 49.95 (1-56370-110-3, WTDB) JIST Works.

Mayall, Donald. Careers in Banking & Finance: How to Achieve Your Professional Goal. American Institute of Banking Staff & Lubow, Joseph, eds. LC 85-18691. 143p. (Orig.). 1985. pap. 10.50 (0-935183-00-0) Amer Inst Bank.

Mayall, Donald, jt. auth. see Maze, Marilyn.

Mayall, James. Nationalism & International Society. (Cambridge Studies in International Relations: No. 10). 176p. (C). 1990. pap. 16.95 (0-521-38961-5) Cambridge U Pr.

Mayall, James & Payne, Anthony J., eds. The Fallacies of Hope: The Post-Colonial Record of the Commonwealth Third World. LC 90-40820. 224p. 1991. text ed. 59.95 (0-7190-1760-2, Pub. by Manchester Univ Pr UK) St Martin.

Mayall, James, jt. ed. see Goodwin, Geoffrey.

***Mayall, Jan K. & Desharnais, Guylaine.** Positioning in a Wheelchair: A Guide for Professional Caregivers of the Disabled Adult. 2nd ed. LC 94-27090. 140p. 1995. pap. text ed. 22.00 (1-55642-251-2, 42512) SLACK Inc.

— Positioning in a Wheelchair: A Guide for the Professional Caregivers of the Disabled Adult. LC 89-43139. (Illus.). 110p. (Orig.). (C). 1990. pap. text ed. 18.00 (1-55642-147-8, 30599) SLACK Inc.

Mayall, Margaret W., jt. auth. see Mayall, R. Newton.

Mayall, Margaret W., jt. auth. see Mayall, Robert N.

Mayall, Margaret W., ed. see Webb, Thomas W.

Mayall, R. Newton & Mayall, Margaret W. Sundials: Their Construction & Use. 3rd ed. LC 73-76242. 320p. 1994. 14.95 (0-933346-71-9) Sky Pub.

Mayall, R. Newton, et al. Sky Observer's Guide. rev. ed. (Golden Guide Ser.). (Illus.). (J). (gr. 9 up). 1985. pap. write for info. (0-307-24009-6, Golden Pr) Western Pub.

Mayall, Robert N. & Mayall, Margaret W. Skyshooting: Photography for Amateur Astronomers. rev. ed. reprint ed. pap. 5.95 (0-486-21854-6) Dover.

Mayan, Wayne W. Is It Possible to Be a Christian & Modern? LC 93-11069. 90p. (Orig.). (C). 1993. lib. bdg. 29.50 (0-8191-9158-2); pap. text ed. 18.50 (0-8191-9159-0) U Pr of Amer.

Mayanathan, Saha D., jt. auth. see Salleh, Ismail.

Mayans, Ernesto. Haddock: A Painter's Life. Mikesell, Susan & Langan, Bernie, eds. (Illus.). 193p. (C). 1989. text ed. 45.00 (0-685-62654-7) E Mayans Gallery.

— Haddock: A Painter's Life. LC 88-83277. (Illus.). 210p. 1990. 45.00 (0-295-96921-0) U of Wash Pr.

— Haddock: A Painter's Life. limited ed. Mikesell, Susan & Langan, Bernie, eds. LC 88-83277. 210p. 1989. boxed 250.00 (0-937723-04-5, Dolp) Doubleday.

Mayants, Lazar. Beyond the Quantum Paradox: Probability Riddles... Quantum Riddles... Other Riddles... LC 94-1214. 102p. 1994. write for info. (0-7484-0206-3, Pub. by Tay Francis Ltd UK); pap. 49.50 (0-7484-0207-1, Pub. by Tay Francis Ltd UK) Taylor & Francis.

— The Enigma of Probability & Physics. 392p. 1984. lib. bdg. 145.00 (90-277-1674-9) Kluwer Ac.

Mayaram, Kartikeya, jt. auth. see Pederson, Donald O.

Mayard. Ghosts. (World of Unkown Ser.). 32p. (J). (gr. k-6). 1977. pap. 5.95 (0-86020-148-1) EDC.

Mayasandra, Venogopal. Chemical Characterization of Liquefaction Products of an Inertinite Enriched Northern Alaska Coal. (MIRL Report Ser.: No. 86). (Illus.). 56p. (Orig.). (C). 1989. pap. 7.00 (0-911043-10-1) UAKF Min Ind Res Lab.

Mayaud, P. N. Derivation, Meaning, & Use of Geomagnetic Indices. (Geophysical Monograph Ser.: Vol. 22). 154p. 1980. 26.00 (0-87590-022-4, GM2200) Am Geophysical.

Maybank, Burnet R., et al. The Law of Automobile Insurance in South Carolina. 1989. ring bd. 90.00 (0-943856-16-7, 436) SC Bar CLE.

Maybank, Stephen. Theory of Reconstruction from Image Motion. Huang, T. S. et al, eds. LC 92-17979. (Information Sciences Ser.: Vol. 28). (Illus.). 264p. 1992. 69.00 (0-387-55537-4) Spr-Verlag.

Maybaum, Klaus. Fachhochschulen in the Federal Republic of Germany: Material Concerning Functions & Organization. 431p. 1989. pap. 35.50 (3-7890-1790-6, Pub. by Nomos Verlags GW) Intl Bk Import.

Maybeck, Jacomena. People & Places: A Memoir. (Illus.). 152p. (Orig.). 1992. pap. 9.95 (1-879042-01-0) Stonegarden Pr.

Maybeck, Peter S. Stochastic Models, Estimation & Control, Vol. 3. (Mathematics in Science & Engineering Ser.). 270p. 1982. text ed. 75.00 (0-12-480703-8) Acad Pr.

***Maybee, Rolland H.** Michigan's White Pine Era. 56p. Date not set. write for info. (0-935719-07-5) MI Hist Mag.

— Railroad Competition & the Oil Trade: 1855-1873. LC 73-16234. (Perspectives in American History Ser.: No. 16). (Illus.). 451p. 1974. reprint ed. lib. bdg. 49.50 (0-87991-341-X) Porcupine Pr.

Mayberry, B. D. A Century of Agriculture in the 1890 Land-Grant Institutions & Tuskegee University - 1890-1990. 1991. 22.95 (0-533-09510-7) Vantage.

Mayberry, Bob. Theatre of Discord: Dissonance in Beckett, Albee, & Pinter. LC 88-45786. 96p. 1989. 22.50 (0-8386-3353-6) Fairleigh Dickinson.

Mayberry, Claude. Discovering Seeds of Change. (YA). 1993. pap. 4.95 (0-201-49003-X) Addison-Wesley.

— Discovering Seeds of Change. (J). (gr. 4-7). 1993. pap. 4.95 (0-201-49002-1) Addison-Wesley.

— Discovering Seeds of Change. (J). (ps-3). 1993. pap. 4.95 (0-201-49001-3) Addison-Wesley.

Mayberry, Jodine. Business Leaders Who Built Financial Empires. (Twenty Events Ser.). (Illus.). 48p. (J). (gr. 4-8). 1994. lib. bdg. 22.80 (0-8114-4934-3) Raintree Steck-V.

— Chinese. LC 90-17223. (Recent American Immigrants Ser.). (Illus.). 64p. (J). (gr. 5-8). 1990. lib. bdg. 14.21 (0-531-10977-1) Watts.

— Eastern Europeans. Cullerton, P., ed. LC 90-12995. (Recent American Immigrants Ser.). (Illus.). 64p. (J). (gr. 5-8). 1991. lib. bdg. 14.21 (0-531-11109-1) Watts.

— Filipinos. LC 90-12274. (Recent American Immigrants Ser.). (Illus.). 64p. (J). (gr. 5-8). 1990. lib. bdg. 14.21 (0-531-10978-X) Watts.

— Koreans. LC 90-12987. (Recent American Immigrants Ser.). (Illus.). 64p. (J). (gr. 5-10). 1991. lib. bdg. 14.21 (0-531-11106-7) Watts.

— Leaders Who Changed the Twentieth Century. LC 93-19032. (Twenty Events Ser.). (Illus.). 48p. (J). (gr. 5-7). 1993. lib. bdg. 22.80 (0-8114-4926-2) Raintree Steck-V.

— Mexicans. LC 90-32095. (Recent American Immigrants Ser.). (Illus.). 64p. (J). (gr. 5-8). 1990. lib. bdg. 14.21 (0-531-10979-8) Watts.

Mayberry, John P. Game-Theoretic Models of Cooperation & Conflict. 212p. (C). 1992. pap. text ed. 48.00 (0-8133-1524-7) Westview.

Mayberry, Katherine J. Christina Rossetti & the Poetry of Discovery. LC 89-33163. 160p. 1989. text ed. 27.50 (0-8071-1529-0) La State U Pr.

***Mayberry, Katherine J. & Golden, Robert E.** For Argument's Sake: A Guide to Writing Effective Arguments. 2nd ed. LC 95-15722. 1995. write for info. (0-673-52459-0) HarpCollege.

Mayberry, Katherine J., jt. auth. see Golden, Robert.

***Mayberry, Maralee, et al.** Home Schooling: Parents As Educators. (Illus.). 160p. 1995. 38.00 (0-8039-6075-1); pap. 18.00 (0-8039-6076-X) Corwin Pr.

Mayberry, Nancy, jt. auth. see Mayberry, Robert.

Mayberry, R. J. Zillah Pickett. 1992. 8.95 (0-533-09124-1) Vantage.

Mayberry, Richard. Handprinting Workshops in the U. S. A. A Directory. 200p. (Orig.). 1993. ring bd., vinyl bd. 20.00 (0-915427-13-3) Spirit Sq Ctr.

Mayberry, Robert & Mayberry, Nancy. Francisco Martinez de la Rosa. (Twayne World Authors Ser.: No. 618). 176p. (C). 1988. text ed. 27.95 (0-8057-6460-7, TWAS 618, Pub. by Royal Botanic Garden UK) Macmillan.

Mayberry, Robert W. Wines of the Rhone Valley: A Guide to Origins. LC 87-16516. 224p. 1987. 53.50 (0-8476-7430-4, R7430) Rowman.

Mayberry, Susanah. My Amiable Uncle: Recollections about Booth Tarkington. LC 82-81021. (Illus.). 160p. 1983. 16.95 (0-911198-66-0) Purdue U Pr.

Mayberry, Tom. Coleridge & Wordsworth in the West Country. (Illus.). 224p. (YA). (gr. 11-12). 1992. 30.00 (0-86299-896-4) A Sutton Pub.

— Coleridge & Wordsworth in the West Country. (Illus.). 224p. 1994. pap. 26.00 (0-7509-0628-6) A Sutton Pub.

Maybery, Paul, ed. see Line, Lorie.

Maybin, Harry B. Low Voltage Wiring Handbook. 1994. text ed. 59.50 (0-07-041083-6) McGraw.

Maybin, Janet, ed. Langauge & Literacy in Social Practice. LC 93-29932. 264p. 1993. 69.95 (1-85359-216-1, Pub. by Multilingual Matters UK); pap. 24.95 (1-85359-215-3, Pub. by Multilingual Matters UK) Taylor & Francis.

Maybin, Janet, jt. ed. see Stierer, Barry.

Maybon, Charles B. & Fredet, Jean. Histoire de la Concession Francaise de Changhai. LC 78-38077. reprint ed. 75.00 (0-404-56941-2) AMS Pr.

Maybury, Anne. Dark Star. large type ed. LC 90-36324. 482p. 1990. reprint ed. lib. bdg. 19.95 (1-56054-025-7) Thorndike Pr.

— I Am Gabriella! large type ed. 1983. 15.95 (0-7089-0979-5) Ulverscroft.

— Midnight Dancers. large type ed. LC 91-8483. 498p. 1991. reprint ed. bds. 19.95 (1-56054-160-1) Thorndike Pr.

— The Moonlit Door. large type ed. 448p. 1995. 23.95 (0-7089-3222-3) Ulverscroft.

— Radiance. large type ed. 467p. 1981. 21.95 (0-7089-0648-6) Ulverscroft.

— The Terracotta Palace. large type ed. LC 89-27151. 475p. (YA). 1989. lib. bdg. 19.95 (0-89621-898-8) Thorndike Pr.

— Walk in the Paradise Garden. large type ed. 1983. 15.95 (0-7089-1004-1) Ulverscroft.

Maybury-Lewis, Biorn. The Politics of the Possible: The Brazilian Rural Workers' Trade Union Movement, 1964-1985. LC 93-26985. 320p. 1994. 49.95 (1-56639-166-0); pap. 19.95 (1-56639-167-9) Temple U Pr.

Maybury-Lewis, David. The Savage & the Innocent. rev. ed. LC 87-42850. (Illus.). 292p. (C). 1988. pap. 14.00 (0-8070-4603-5, BP 774) Beacon Pr.

Maybury-Lewis, David, ed. Dialectical Societies: The Ge & Bororo of Central Brazil. LC 79-10689. (Harvard Studies in Cultural Anthropology: No. 1). 354p. 1979. 37.50 (0-674-20285-6) HUP.

— The Prospects for Plural Societies, 1982. (Proceedings of the American Ethnological Society Ser.). 1984. 16.00 (0-942976-04-5) Am Anthro Assn.

Maybury-Lewis, David & Almagor, Uri, eds. The Attraction of Opposites: Thought & Society in a Dualistic Mode. 50p. 1989. 52.50 (0-472-10094-7); pap. 21.95 (0-472-08086-5) U of Mich Pr.

Maybury, Mark T., ed. Intelligent Multimedia Interfaces. (AAAI Press Ser.). (Illus.). 450p. 1993. pap. 42.00 (0-262-63150-4) MIT Pr.

***Maybury, Richard J.** Ancient Rome: How It Affects You Today. (Uncle Eric Book Ser.). 1995. pap. 8.95 (0-942617-22-3) Blstckng Pr.

— Are You Liberal? Conservative? or Confused? (Uncle Eric Book Ser.). 1995. pap. 8.95 (0-942617-23-1) Blstckng Pr.

— Evaluating Books - What Would Thomas Jefferson Think about This? Guidelines for Selecting Books: Consistent with the Principles of America's Founders. 1994. 8.95 (0-942617-14-2) Blstckng Pr.

— Uncle Eric Talks about Personal, Career & Financial Security. LC 94-11733. (Uncle Eric Book Ser.). 1994. write for info. (0-942617-20-7) Blstckng Pr.

— Whatever Happened to Justice? Williams, Jane A., ed. (Illus.). 256p. (Orig.). (J). (gr. 7 up). 1993. pap. 14.95 (0-942617-10-X) Blstckng Pr.

Maybury, Richard J., see Uncle Eric, pseud..

Maychick, Diana. Audrey Hepburn: An Intimate Portrait. (Illus.). 304p. 1993. 21.95 (1-55972-195-2, Birch Ln Pr) Carol Pub Group.

— Audrey Hepburn: An Intimate Portrait. large type ed. LC 93-42995. 1994. 22.95 (0-7862-0103-7); pap. 13.95 (0-7862-0104-5) Thorndike Pr.

Mayck, Arthur & Waddell, Gene. Charleston in Eighteen Eighty-Three. (Illus.). 176p. 1984. reprint ed. pap. 15.00 (0-89308-428-X) Southern Hist Pr.

Maycock, A. L. Nicholas Ferrar of Little Gidding. LC 80-16684. 334p. reprint ed. pap. 95.20 (0-8357-9131-9, 2019345) Bks Demand.

Maycock, Susan E. An Architectural History of Carbondale, Illinois. LC 82-19189. (Illus.). 256p. 1983. pap. 15.95 (0-8093-1120-8) S Ill U Pr.

***Mayda, Jaro.** Francois Geny & Modern Jurisprudence. fac. ed. LC 78-17864. 288p. 1978. reprint ed. pap. 82.10 (0-7837-7930-5, 2047686) Bks Demand.

Mayden, Richard L. Phylogenetic Studies of North American Minnows, with Emphasis on the Genus Cyprinella (Teleostei: Cypiniformes) (Miscellaneous Publications: No. 80). (Illus.). 189p. 1989. pap. text ed. 15.00 (0-89338-029-6) U of KS Mus Nat Hist.

Mayden, Richard L., ed. Systematics, Historical Ecology, & North American Freshwater Fishes. LC 92-19781. 1992. 69.50 (0-8047-2162-9) Stanford U Pr.

Mayden, Richard L. & Burr, Brooks M. Life History of the Slender Madtom, Noturus Exilis, in Southern Illinois: (Pisces: Ictaluridae) (Occasional Papers: No. 93). 64p. 1981. 1.00 (0-317-04827-9) U of KS Mus Nat Hist.

Mayden, Richard L., jt. auth. see Burr, Brooks M.

Maydew. Agribusiness Accounting & Taxation: (Including '86 TRA Supplement) 368p. 1986. 39.50 (0-318-33074-1, 5421) Commerce.

— Small Business Taxaton: Planning & Practice. 464p. 1992. 50.00 (0-685-67145-3, 4975) Commerce.

Maye, Patricia. Fieldbook of Nature Photography. LC 73-86880. (Totebook Ser.). (Illus.). 210p. 1974. pap. 10.95 (0-87156-085-2) Sierra.

Mayeda, Noriko & Brown, W. Norman. Tawi Tales: Folktales from Jammu. (American Oriental Ser.: Vol. 57). 1974. pap. 10.00 (0-940490-57-9) Am Orient Soc.

Mayeda, Sengaku, tr. A Thousand Teachings: The Upadesasahasri of Sankara. 265p. 1979. 40.00 (0-86008-242-3, Pub. by U of Tokyo JA) Col U Pr.

Mayeda, Sengaku & Koller, John M., eds. A Thousand Teachings: The Upadesasahasri of Sankara. Koller, John M., tr. LC 91-9641. 265p. (C). 1992. 44.50 (0-7914-0943-0); pap. 14.95 (0-7914-0944-9) State U NY Pr.

Mayeda, Wataru. Digital Signal Processing. 352p. 1992. text ed. 74.00 (0-13-211301-5) P-H.

Mayeell, Mark, jt. auth. see Natural Health Magazine Editors.

***Mayell, Mark & Natural Health Magazine Editors Staff.** 52 Simple Steps to Natural Health: A Week-by-Week Guide to More Healthful Living. Zion, Claire, ed. 448p. 1995. pap. 14.00 (0-671-88061-6) PB.

***Mayer.** Alien. (J). 1995. pap. text ed. 3.50 (0-307-16661-9, Golden Pr) Western Pub.

— Golden Eagle. (J). 1995. pap. text ed. 3.50 (0-307-16662-7, Golden Pr) Western Pub.

— Handbook of Insect Phermones & Sex Attractants. 1990. 314.95 (0-8493-2934-5, QD557) CRC Pr.

— I Am Helping. LC 94-68287. 1995. 4.99 (0-679-87348-1) Random.

— I Am Hiding. LC 94-68290. 1995. 4.99 (0-679-87347-3) Random.

— I Am Playing. LC 94-68289. 1995. 4.99 (0-679-87350-3) Random.

— I Am Sharing. LC 94-68288. 1995. 4.99 (0-679-87349-X) Random.

— International Auction Records, 1993. (Illus.). 2130p. 1993. 179.00 (1-56466-053-2) Archer Fields.

— Jaguar Paw. (J). 1995. pap. text ed. 3.50 (0-307-16663-5, Golden Pr) Western Pub.

— Little Critter's Jack & the Beanstalk: Little Critter Chunky Flap Book. LC 94-68285. 1995. 3.50 (0-679-87345-7) Random.

— Little Critter's Little Red Riding Hood: Little Critter Chunky Flap Book. LC 94-68286. 1995. 3.50 (0-679-87346-5) Random.

— Octopus Island. (J). 1995. pap. text ed. 3.50 (0-307-16664-3, Golden Pr) Western Pub.

— Prince. (J). 1995. pap. text ed. 3.50 (0-307-16665-1, Golden Pr) Western Pub.

— Swamp Thing. (J). 1995. pap. text ed. 3.50 (0-307-16660-0, Golden Pr) Western Pub.

— Where's My Frog. 1995. 3.50 (0-679-87344-9) Random.

— Where's My Kitty. 1995. 3.50 (0-679-87343-0) Random.

Mayer, jt. auth. see Fleming.

Mayer, ed. see Lucan.

Mayer, et al. Perspectives on the Educational Use of Animals. (Illus.). 77p. 1980. pap. 3.00 (0-913098-38-8) Myrin Institute.

Mayer, A. M. & Poljakoff-Mayber, A. The Germination of Seeds. 3rd ed. (Illus.). 212p. 1982. text ed. 51.00 (0-08-028854-5, Pergamon Pr); pap. text ed. 35.00 (0-08-028853-7, Pergamon Pr) Elsevier.

— The Germination of Seeds. 4th ed. (Illus.). 240p. 1989. text ed. 70.00 (0-08-035723-7, Ed Skills Dallas); pap. text ed. 37.00 (0-08-035722-9, Pergamon Pr) Elsevier.

Mayer, Adele. Child Sexual Abuse & the Courts: A Manual for Therapists. 1990. pap. 19.95 (1-55691-046-0, 460) Learning Pubns.

— Incest. 2nd ed. 1993. 24.95 (1-55691-054-1, 541) Learning Pubns.

— Repressed Memories of Sexual Abuse. 1995. 22.95 (1-55691-117-3) Learning Pubns.

— Sex Offenders: Perspectives & Approaches to Understanding & Management. LC 86-45796. 300p. 1988. pap. 19.95 (0-918452-95-3) Learning Pubns.

— Sexual Abuse: Causes, Consequences & Treatment of Incestuous & Pedophilic Acts. LC 84-80657. 176p. 1985. 19.95 (1-55691-059-2) Learning Pubns.

— Women Sex Offenders: Treatment & Dynamics. 1991. 16.95 (1-55691-063-0, 41X) Learning Pubns.

Mayer, Adrian C. Land & Society in Malabar. LC 73-13032. 158p. 1974. reprint ed. text ed. 49.75 (0-8371-7103-2, MASM, Greenwood Pr) Greenwood.

Mayer, Albert, et al. Pilot Project, India. LC 72-12332. (Illus.). 367p. 1973. reprint ed. text ed. 69.50 (0-8371-6729-9, MAPI, Greenwood Pr) Greenwood.

Mayer, Albert I. Mystery at Seabreeze. (J). (gr. 6-10). 1965. lib. bdg. 7.19 (0-8313-0077-9) Lantern.

An Asterisk (*) at the beginning of an entry indicates that the title is appearing in BIP for the first time.

Mayer, Albert I., Jr. Olympiad. LC 61-12875. (Illus.). (YA). (gr. 7 up). 1938. 18.00 (0-8196-0115-2) Biblo.

Mayer, Albert J., III. Real Estate Office Management: People, Functions Systems. 2nd ed. LC 88-31636. (Illus.). 350p. 1988. reprint ed. pap. 23.00 (0-913652-64-4, 113) Realtors Natl.

Mayer, Alfred, comp. Annals of European Civilization, 1501-1900. LC 83-45811. reprint ed. 42.00 (0-404-20172-5) AMS Pr.

Mayer, Andrew, et al, eds. Protect the President: Outrageous Editorials from the Ultra-Right Newspaper Publisher William Loeb. LC 79-87929. (Illus.). 1979. pap. 7.25 (0-932400-01-9) Intervale Pub Co.

Mayer, Andy. Good Dog, Millie: A Day in the Life of America's Most Influential Canine. 30p. 1992. pap. 8.95 (0-02-508201-9) Macmillan.

Mayer, Andy & Becker. Let's Look at Animals. (Let's Look Board Bks.). (Illus.). 12p. (J). 1993. 5.95 (0-590-45700-4) Scholastic Inc.

— Let's Look at My World. (Let's Look Board Bks.). (Illus.). 12p. (J). 1993. 5.95 (0-590-45699-7) Scholastic Inc.

Mayer, Andy & Becker, Jim. Fire Trucks. LC 92-61195. (Look & Listen Board Books Ser.). (Illus.). 12p. (J). (ps). 1993. bds. 6.95 (0-590-46298-9, Cartwheel) Scholastic Inc.

— Official Book of Thumb Wrestling. LC 80-51513. 1983. 5.95 (0-89480-363-8, 363) Workman Pub.

— The Supreme Court: A Paper Doll Book. (Illus.). 40p. (Orig.). 1993. pap. 9.99 (0-312-09397-7) St Martin.

— Work Trucks. LC 92-61194. (Look & Listen Board Books Ser.). (Illus.). 12p. (J). (ps). 1993. bds. 6.95 (0-590-46299-7, Cartwheel) Scholastic Inc.

Mayer, Andy, jt. auth. see Beckel, Jim.

Mayer, Andy, jt. auth. see Becker, Jim.

Mayer, Anita L. Clothing from the Hands That Weave. LC 84-81051. (Illus.). 168p. 1986. spiral bd., pap. 18.00 (0-934026-14-9) Interweave.

— Handwoven Clothing Felted to Wear. LC 87-63347. (Illus.). 100p. 1988. pap. 16.95 (0-916658-45-7) Shuttle Craft.

***Mayer, Ann E.** Islam & Human Rights: Tradition & Politics. 2nd ed. LC 94-41412. 1995. text ed. 64.95 (0-8133-2130-1) Westview.

— Islam & Human Rights: Tradition & Politics. 2nd ed. LC 94-41412. (C). 1995. pap. text ed. 23.95 (0-8133-2131-X) Westview.

Mayer, Ann E., ed. Property, Social Structure, & Law in the Modern Middle East. LC 85-2786. (SUNY Series in Near Eastern Studies). 274p. 1985. 64.50 (0-87395-988-4); pap. 21.95 (0-87395-987-6) State U NY Pr.

Mayer, Anne. How to Stay Lovers While Raising Your Children. 1992. mass mkt. 4.99 (0-312-92715-0) St Martin.

Mayer, August L. Francisco de Goya. LC 70-15338. reprint ed. 34.50 (0-404-07954-7) AMS Pr.

Mayer, Augusto. El Estilo Gotico en Espana. 3rd ed. (Illus.). 307p. (SPA.). 1960. lib. bdg. 35.00 (0-8288-3937-9, S16754) Fr & Eur.

Mayer, B. Mexico: Aztec, Spanish & Republican, 2 vols. 1976. lib. bdg. 250.00 (0-8490-2246-0) Gordon Pr.

Mayer, Barbara. The College Survival Guide. (Illus.). 160p. 1981. pap. 6.95 (0-8442-6674-4, VGM Career Bks) NTC Pub Grp.

— Complete Book of Home Decorating. 1994. pap. 19.95 (1-56799-063-0, Friedman-Fairfax) M Friedman Pub Grp Inc.

— The High School Survival Guide. (Illus.). 160p. 1986. pap. 6.95 (0-8442-6670-1, VGM Career Bks) NTC Pub Grp.

— How to Succeed in College. 2nd ed. LC 92-15710. 1992. 9.95 (0-8442-4166-0, VGM Career Bks) NTC Pub Grp.

— How to Succeed in High School. 160p. 1992. pap. 7.95 (0-8442-8121-2, Natl Textbk) NTC Pub Grp.

— In the Arts & Crafts Style. (Illus.). 224p. 1992. 35.00 (0-8118-0202-7) Chronicle Bks.

Mayer, Barbara & Lu, Monica M. Guidelines for Formal Verification Systems. (NCSC TG Ser.: No. 014). (Orig.). 1989. pap. 2.00 (0-16-001531-6, S/N 008-000-00540-1) USGPO.

Mayer, Ben, jt. auth. see Liller, William.

Mayer, Bernadette. A Bernadette Mayer Reader. LC 91-43995. 144p. (Orig.). 1992. pap. 11.95 (0-8112-1203-3, NDP739) New Directions.

— The Desires of Mothers to Please Others in Letters. 350p. 1994. pap. 12.95 (0-9638433-1-1) Hard Pr MA.

— The Formal Field of Kissing. 32p. 1990. pap. 6.00 (0-685-56988-8) SPD-Small Pr Dist.

— Memory. 150p. 1975. pap. 4.00 (0-913028-39-8) North Atlantic.

— Poetry. 1976. 7.00 (0-686-16289-7); pap. 3.50 (0-686-16290-0) Kulchur Foun.

— Studying Hunger. (Orig.). 1975. 3.00 (0-929844-02-5) Big Sky Bolinas.

Mayer, Bernadette, jt. auth. see Worsley, Dale.

***Mayer, Bernard.** Entombed: My True Story: How Forty-Five Jews Lived Underground & Survived the Holocaust. (Illus.). 206p. (Orig.). (YA). (gr. 8-12). 1994. pap. 9.95 (0-9641508-0-8) Aleric Pr.

Mayer, Bill. Longing. 90p. (Orig.). 1993. pap. 9.95 (0-9636556-0-4) Pangaea Bks.

Mayer, Bill, illus. Golf-o-Rama: The Wacky Nine-Hole Pop-up Mini-Golf Book. 8p. (J). 1994. 17.95 (1-56282-635-2) Hyprn Child.

Mayer, Bob. Cut-Out: A Novel. 312p. 1995. 19.95 (0-89141-508-4) Presidio Pr.

— Eyes of the Hammer. 1992. mass mkt. 4.99 (0-312-92862-9) St Martin.

— Operation Dragon-Sim. 1994. mass mkt. 4.99 (0-312-95233-3) St Martin.

— Operation Synbat Vol. 1. 1995. mass mkt. 4.99 (0-312-95363-1) St Martin.

— Synbat: A Novel. LC 93-28062. 1994. 19.95 (0-89141-416-9, Lyford Bks) Presidio Pr.

Mayer, Brantz, ed. Captain Canot, or Twenty Years of an African Slaver. LC 68-29011. (American Negro: His History & Literature, Ser. No. 1). 1969. reprint ed. 32.95 (0-405-01830-4) Ayer.

Mayer, Brantz, ed. see Carroll, Charles H.

Mayer, C. H. The Continuing Struggle: Autobiography of a Labor Activist. LC 89-62399. 187p. 1989. pap. 11.95 (0-938875-20-5) Pittenbruach Pr.

Mayer, C. P., jt. auth. see Davis, E. P.

Mayer, Carl, jt. auth. see Meringer, Rudolf.

***Mayer, Carol A.** My Thumb & I. Brown, Barbara E., ed. & illus. by. 92p. (J). (gr. 1-4). 1995. student ed, pap. 30.00 (0-9645256-0-7) ABC Thumb.

Mayer, Carol H. & Mattaini, Mark A., eds. Foundations of Social Work Practice. 1994. write for info. (0-318-72322-0) Natl Assn Soc Wkrs.

Mayer, Charles S., jt. auth. see Adler, Lee.

Mayer, Charles W., jt. ed. see Logsdon, Loren.

Mayer, Christine A., jt. auth. see Cummings, Kevin S.

***Mayer, Colin & Vives, Xavier, eds.** Capital Markets & Financial Intermediation. (Illus.). 384p. (C). 1995. pap. write for info. (0-521-55853-0) Cambridge U Pr.

— Financial Intermediation. 290p. (C). 1993. 59.95 (0-521-44397-0) Cambridge U Pr.

Mayer, Colin, jt. auth. see Franks, Julian.

Mayer, Colin, jt. ed. see Giovannini, Alberto.

Mayer, Colin, jt. auth. see Jenkinson, Tim.

Mayer, Cynthia, jt. auth. see Liggett, Twila C.

Mayer, D. P. & Kemper, F. H., eds. Acesulfame-K. (Food Science & Technology Ser.: Vol. 47). 256p. 1991. 115.00 (0-8247-8530-4) Dekker.

Mayer, Dale C. Dining with the Hoover Family: A Collection of Reminiscences & Recipes. (Illus.). 96p. (Orig.). 1991. pap. 5.00 (0-938469-11-8) Hoover Lib.

Mayer, Dale C., ed. Lou Henry Hoover: Essays on a Busy Life. LC 93-78297. (Illus.). 160p. 1994. 23.50 (1-881019-04-7) High Plns WY.

Mayer, Daniel F., jt. auth. see Johansen, Carl A.

Mayer, David. Harlequin in His Element: The English Pantomine, 1806-1836. LC 79-88809. 417p. reprint ed. pap. 118.90 (0-7837-2297-4, 2057385) Bks Demand.

— Playing Out the Empire: Ben-Hur & Other Toga Plays & Films, 1883-1908. A Critical Anthology. (Illus.). 336p. 1994. 55.00 (0-19-811990-9) OUP.

— Sergei M. Eisenstein's Potemkin: A Shot-by-Shot Presentation. (Quality Paperbacks Ser.). (Illus.). 256p. 1990. reprint ed. pap. 12.95 (0-306-80388-7) Da Capo.

Mayer, David, ed. see Fraser, Neil.

Mayer, David, ed. see Hawkins, Terry & Menear, Pauline.

Mayer, David, ed. see Holt, Michael.

Mayer, David, ed. see McCaffery, Michael.

Mayer, David, jt. ed. see Melanson, Richard A.

Mayer, David C., jt. auth. see Mullins, Charles E.

Mayer, David N. The Constitutional Thought of Thomas Jefferson. LC 93-29649. 1994. 39.50 (0-8139-1484-1) U Pr of Va.

— The Constitutional Thought of Thomas Jefferson. LC 93-29649. 416p. (C). 1995. pap. text ed. 18.50 (0-8139-1485-X) U Pr of Va.

Mayer, David P., et al. Foot & Ankle: A Sectional Imaging Atlas. LC 93-9264. (Illus.). 228p. 1993. text ed. 105.00 (0-7216-3199-1) Saunders.

Mayer, Debby, ed. Literary Agents: A Writer's Guide. LC 83-617350. 92p. 1988. pap. 6.95 (0-913734-17-9) Poets & Writers.

Mayer, Debby, jt. ed. see Wallace, Ainslie.

***Mayer, Dianne S.** Rush Hour Times Two! 1994. write for info. (0-9611584-0-9) Deanne Inc.

Mayer, Dorothy M. Angelica Kauffmann R. A. 1741-1807. 192p. 1972. 50.00 (0-900675-68-3, Pub. by Colin Smythe Ltd UK) Dufour.

— The Forgotten Master: The Life & Times of Louis Spohr. LC 80-27659. (Music Reprint Ser.). 208p. 1981. reprint ed. 29.50 (0-306-76099-1) Da Capo.

Mayer, Doug. The Slightly Skewed Computer Dictionary. LC 94-19285. 1994. 8.95 (1-55958-432-7) Prima Pub.

Mayer, E., jt. ed. see Bolton, R.

Mayer, Edgar N. Structure of French: A Programmed Course on the Linguistic Structure of French. (C). 1969. pap. text ed. 9.75 (0-89197-429-6) Irvington.

Mayer, Egon. Children of Intermarriage: A Study in Pattern of Identification & Family Life. LC 83-82077. 56p. 1983. pap. 2.50 (0-87495-055-4) Am Jewish Comm.

— Love & Tradition: Marriage Between Jews & Christians. LC 85-6588. 312p. 1985. 19.95 (0-306-42043-0, Plenum Pr) Plenum.

Mayer, Egon & Avgar, Amy. Conversion among the Intermarried: Choosing to Become Jewish. LC 87-70999. 44p. (Orig.). 1987. pap. 5.00 (0-87495-091-0) Am Jewish Comm.

Mayer, Egon & Sheingold, Carl. Intermarriage & the Jewish Future. LC 79-63378. 46p. 1980. pap. 2.00 (0-87495-031-7) Am Jewish Comm.

Mayer, Elise, ed. see Barley, Chris S.

Mayer, Elizabeth, tr. see Goethe, Johann Wolfgang Von.

Mayer, Elizabeth, tr. see Goethe, Johann Wolfgang von.

Mayer, Elizabeth, tr. see Goethe, Johann Wolfgang Von.

Mayer, Elizabeth, tr. see Goethe, Johann Wolfgang von.

Mayer, Elizabeth, tr. see Junger, Ernst.

Mayer, Elizabeth, tr. see Von Goethe, Johann W.

***Mayer, Elizabeth L.** Basic Learning Skills Bk. II: How Music Can Contribute, Bk. II. (Music Makes a Difference Ser.). 12p. 1994. pap. 1.95 (1-886380-01-5) Langstaff Vid.

— Making Music in the Classroom. (Making Music with John Langstaff Ser.). 24p. (J). (ps-2). 1994. per., pap. 3.50 (1-886380-07-4) Langstaff Vid.

— Making Music in the Classroom. (Making Music with John Langstaff Ser.). 24p. (J). (gr. 2-6). 1994. pap. 3.50 (1-886380-08-2) Langstaff Vid.

— Making Music with Children. (Making Music with John Langstaff Ser.). 24p. (J). (gr. 2-7). 1994. pap. 3.50 (1-886380-06-6) Langstaff Vid.

— Making Music with Children. (Making Music with John Langstaff Ser.). 24p. (J). (ps-2). 1994. pap. 3.50 (1-886380-05-8) Langstaff Vid.

— Making Music with Children Bk. I: Why It Matters, Bk. I. (Music Makes a Difference Ser.). 12p. 1994. per., pap. text ed. 1.95 (1-886380-00-7) Langstaff Vid.

— Making Music with John Langstaff Series. 96p. (J). (ps). 1994. pap. 10.95 (1-886380-09-0) Langstaff Vid.

— The Whole Child Bk. III: How Music Fits In, Bk. III. (Music Makes a Difference Ser.). 12p. 1994. pap. 1.95 (1-886380-02-3) Langstaff Vid.

***Mayer, Elizabeth L. & Langstaff, John.** Music Makes a Difference Ser. Bks. I - IV. 48p. 1994. pap. 5.95 (1-886380-04-X) Langstaff Vid.

Mayer, Emeran A. & Raybould, Helen, eds. Basic & Clinical Aspects of Chronic Abdominal Pain. LC 93-11488. (Pain Research & Clinical Management Ser.: Vol. 9). 1993. write for info. (0-444-89437-3) Elsevier.

Mayer, Emilio. International Lending: Country Risk Analysis. (C). 1985. text ed. 73.13 (0-8359-3182-X, Reston) P-H.

***Mayer, Enrique.** Dictionnaire des Meubles et Objets D'Art: 8,000 Prix En Ventes Publiques. 720p. (FRE.). 1993. 450.00 (0-7859-7836-4, 2226059601) Fr & Eur.

Mayer, F. E. The Religious Bodies of America. 616p. 1987. 20.95 (0-570-03294-6, 15-1714) Concordia.

Mayer, F. L. & Hamelink, J. L., eds. Aquatic Toxicology & Hazard Evaluation: First Conference- STP 634. 315p. 1977. 30.75 (0-8031-0278-X, 04-634000-16) ASTM.

Mayer, Fanny H. Ancient Tales in Modern Japan: An Anthology of Japanese Folk Tales. LC 84-47746. (Illus.). 381p. reprint ed. pap. 108.90 (0-8357-3940-6, 2057035) Bks Demand.

Mayer, Fanny H., ed. & tr. The Yanagita Kunio Guide to the Japanese Folk Tale. LC 85-45291. (Illus.). 392p. (C). 1986. 29.95 (0-253-36812-X) Ind U Pr.

Mayer, Fanny H & Kenichi, Mizusawa. Where Folk Tales Are Treasured: Fifteen Tales from the Japanese of Mizusawa Kenichi. LC 84-81974. (Illus.). iv, 63p. 1984. pap. 8.50 (0-910913-01-3) Laughing B P.

Mayer, Fanny H., tr. see Yanagita, Kunio.

Mayer, Frank. Cytology & Morphogenesis of Bacteria, Vol. VI, Pt. 2. (Encyclopedia of Plant Anatomy Ser.: Part 2, Vol. VI). (Illus.). 290p. 1986. lib. bdg. 96.30 (3-443-14017-3) Lubrecht & Cramer.

Mayer, Frank & Norris, John R., eds. Methods in Microbiology, Vol. 20: Electron Microscopy in Microbiology. 431p. 1988. text ed. 113.00 (0-12-521520-7) Acad Pr.

Mayer, Frank A. The Opposition Years: Winston Churchill & the Conservative Party, 1945- 1951. LC 91-4348. (American University Studies: History: Ser. IX, Vols. 116). 187p. (C). 1992. text ed. 36.95 (0-8204-1661-4) P Lang Pubs.

Mayer, Frank B. With Pen & Pencil on the Frontier in 1851: The Diary & Sketches of Frank Blackwell Mayer. LC 75-103. (Mid-American Frontier Ser.). (Illus.). 1975. reprint ed. 15.95 (0-405-06871-9) Ayer.

— With Pen & Pencil on the Frontier in 1851: The Diary & Sketches of Frank Blackwell Mayer. Heilbron, Bertha L., ed. LC 86-717. xvii, 256p. 1986. reprint ed. pap. 9.95 (0-87351-195-6, Borealis Book) Minn Hist.

Mayer, Fred. Forgotten Peoples of Siberia. 1993. 50.00 (1-881616-08-8, Pub. by Scalo Pubs) Dist Art Pubs.

Mayer, Frederick. Creative Universities. 1961. pap. 13.95 (0-8084-0094-0) NCUP.

— Man, Morals & Education. 1962. 16.95x (0-8084-0206-4) NCUP.

Mayer, G. Roy, jt. auth. see Sulzer-Azaroff, Beth.

Mayer, Garry F., ed. Ecological Stress & the New York Bight: Science & Management. LC 82-71795. (Illus.). x, 717p. (Orig.). (C). 1982. pap. text ed. 10.00 (0-9608990-0-6) Estuarine Res.

Mayer, Geoff, jt. auth. see McFarlane, Brian.

Mayer, George H. The Political Career of Floyd B. Olson. LC 86-33332. xxi, 329p. 1987. reprint ed. pap. 10.95 (0-87351-206-5, Borealis Book) Minn Hist.

***Mayer, Gerald S.** The Divorced Dad Dilemma: A Father's Guide to Understanding, Grieving, & Growing Beyond the Losses of Divorce & to Developing a Deeper, Ongoing Relationship to His Children. 100p. 1994. pap. 9.95 (0-9642504-0-3) Desert City Pr.

Mayer, Gertrude T. Women of Letters, 2 vols. LC 73-1197. (Essay Index Reprint Ser.). 1977. reprint ed. 53.95 (0-518-10059-6) Ayer.

Mayer, Gina. Just Lost! (Golden Look-Look Bks.). (Illus.). 24p. (J). 1994. write for info. (0-307-12844-X, Golden Bks) Western Pub.

— Just Me in the Tub. (J). (ps-3). 1994. pap. 2.25 (0-307-12816-4, Golden Pr) Western Pub.

— Trick or Treat, Little Critter. (J). (ps-3). 1993. pap. 2.25 (0-307-12791-5, Golden Pr) Western Pub.

Mayer, Gina & Mayer, Mercer. Just a Thunderstorm. (Little Look-Look Bks.). (Illus.). 24p. (J). (ps-00). 1993. pap. 1.45 (0-307-11540-2, 11540, Golden Pr) Western Pub.

— The New Potty. (Golden Little Look Look Book Ser.). (Illus.). 24p. (J). (ps-00). 1992. write for info. (0-307-11523-2, 11523) Western Pub.

— This Is My Family. (Little Golden Bks.). (Illus.). 24p. (J). (ps-00). 1992. write for info. (0-307-00137-7, 312-02, Golden Pr) Western Pub.

— A Very Special Critter. (Look-Look Bks.). (Illus.). 24p. (J). (ps-3). 1993. pap. 1.95 (0-307-12763-X, 12763, Golden Pr) Western Pub.

Mayer, Gladys. Behind the Veils of Death & Sleep. 1973. lib. bdg. 250.00 (0-87968-541-7) Krishna Pr.

— Color & Healing. 1973. lib. bdg. 250.00 (0-87968-309-0) Krishna Pr.

— Color & the Human Soul. 1973. lib. bdg. 250.00 (0-87968-542-5) Krishna Pr.

— Colour & Healing: How Color Affects Us. 29p. 1963. reprint ed. spiral bd. 3.30 (0-7873-0591-X) Mokelumne.

Mayer, Gloria G., jt. ed. see Barnett, Albert E.

Mayer, Gloria G., et al. Patient Care Delivery Models. 360p. (C). 1990. 53.00 (0-8342-0097-X, 20097) Aspen Pub.

Mayer-Gross, W., et al. Clinical Psychiatry. 3rd ed. (Illus.). 1969. text ed. 115.00 (0-7020-0001-9, Bailliere-Tindall) Saunders.

Mayer, Guenter. Index Philoneus. LC 73-81702. 312p. (C). 1974. text ed. 211.55 (3-11-004536-2) De Gruyter.

Mayer, H. M. & Brock, M., eds. Percutaneous Lumbar Discectomy. (Illus.). 225p. 1989. 70.00 (0-387-51032-X) Spr-Verlag.

Mayer, Hans. Outsiders: A Study in Life & Letters. Sweet, Denis, tr. 422p. 1982. 45.00 (0-262-13175-7) MIT Pr.

Mayer, Hans, jt. auth. see Stewart, Bruce W.

Mayer, Hans E. The Crusades. 2nd ed. Gillingham, John, tr. (Illus.). 368p. 1988. pap. text ed. 19.95 (0-19-873097-7) OUP.

— Kings & Lords in the Latin Kingdom of Jerusalem. (Collected Studies: No. CS 437). 352p. 1994. 95.00 (0-86078-416-9, Pub. by Variorum UK) Ashgate Pub Co.

— Kreuzzuge und Lateinischer Osten. (Collected Studies: No. CS171). 332p. (GER.). (C). 1983. reprint ed. lib. bdg. 105.00 (0-86078-119-4, Pub. by Variorum UK) Ashgate Pub Co.

— Probleme des Lateinischen Konigreichs Jerusalem. (Collected Studies: No. CS178). (Illus.). 356p. (GER.). (C). 1983. reprint ed. lib. bdg. 105.00 (0-86078-126-7, Pub. by Variorum UK) Ashgate Pub Co.

Mayer, Hans-Georg. German Trucks & Cars in World War II: VW "Beetle" at War, Vol. 6. Force, Edward, tr. (Illus.). 48p. 1992. pap. 7.95 (0-88740-400-6) Schiffer.

Mayer, Harold M. & Hayes, Charles R. Land Uses in American Cities. LC 82-81036. (Illus.). 200p. (Orig.). (C). 1983. pap. text ed. 9.95 (0-941226-02-6) Park Pr Co.

Mayer, Harold M. & Kohn, Clyde F., eds. Readings in Urban Geography. LC 59-11973. (Illus.). 625p. reprint ed. pap. 180.00 (0-8357-7002-8, 2056776) Bks Demand.

Mayer, Harold M. & Wade, Richard C. Chicago: Growth of a Metropolis. LC 68-54054. (Illus.). 1969. 50.00 (0-226-51273-8) U Ch Pr.

— Chicago: Growth of a Metropolis. LC 68-54054. (Illus.). 1973. pap. 24.95 (0-226-51274-6, P546) U Ch Pr.

Mayer, Harry, ed. Modern Reader's Book of Psalms. (Black & Gold Library). 1968. 6.95 (0-87140-879-1) Liveright.

***Mayer, Henry.** Mayer on the Media: Issues & Arguments. Tiffen, Rod, ed. 208p. 1995. pap. 22.95 (1-86373-625-5, Pub. by Allen Unwin AT) Paul & Co Pubs.

— A Son of Thunder: Patrick Henry & the American Republic. 544p. 1992. reprint ed. pap. 18.95 (0-8139-1376-4) U Pr of Va.

Mayer, Herbert. Advanced C Programming on the IBM PC. (Orig.). 1991. 24.95 (0-8306-8694-0); 24.95 (0-8306-8695-9) TAB Bks.

Mayer, Herbert A., jt. auth. see Meyer, Daniel P.

Mayer, Herbert G. Advanced C Programming on the IBM PC. (Illus.). 400p. (Orig.). 1989. 33.95 (0-8306-9163-4, Windcrest) TAB Bks.

— Programming in Modula-2: The Art & the Craft. 582p. (C). 1987. pap. write for info. (0-02-378160-2) Macmillan.

Mayer, J. Equilibrium Statistical Mechanics. LC 68-21387. (International Encyclopedia of Physical Chemistry & Chemical Physics Ser.: No. 1). 1968. 109.00 (0-08-012647-2, Pub. by Pergamon Repr UK) Franklin.

— Equilibrium Statistical Mechanics. LC 68-21387. (International Encyclopedia of Physical Chemistry & Chemical Physics Ser.: Vol. 1: TP8). 1968. 101.00 (0-08-018989-X, Pub. by Pergamon Repr UK) Franklin.

Mayer, J., jt. ed. see Zirm, K. L.

Mayer, J. E. The Herbalist. (Alternative Medicine Ser.). 1992. lib. bdg. 79.99 (0-8490-5409-5) Gordon Pr.

Mayer, J. P. Alexis de Tocqueville. LC 78-67399. (European Political Thought Ser.). (GER.). 1980. reprint ed. lib. bdg. 17.95 (0-405-11716-7) Ayer.

— British Cinemas & Their Audiences. Jowett, Garth S., ed. LC 77-11387. (Aspects of Film Ser.). (Illus.). 1978. lib. bdg. 20.95 (0-405-11141-X) Ayer.

— Max Weber & German Politics. 3rd rev. ed. LC 78-67371. (European Political Thought Ser.). 1979. reprint ed. lib. bdg. 17.95 (0-405-11717-5) Ayer.

— Political Thought in France. LC 78-67367. (European Political Thought Ser.). 1980. reprint ed. lib. bdg. 17.95 (0-405-11718-3) Ayer.

— Sociology of Film: Studies & Documents. LC 73-169334. (Literature of Cinema, Ser. 2). (Illus.). 398p. 1976. reprint ed. 26.95 (0-405-03901-8) Ayer.

Mayer, J. P., ed. Considerations sur les Principaux Evenemens de la Revolution Francoise, Madame la Baronne Stael, 3 vols. in 2, 1. LC 78-67391. (European Political Thought Ser.). (FRE.). 1980. reprint ed. lib. bdg. 47.95 (0-405-11743-4) Ayer.

— Considerations sur les Principaux Evenemens de la Revolution Francoise, Madame la Baronne Stael, 3 vols. in 2, 2. LC 78-67391. (European Political Thought Ser.). (FRE.). 1980. reprint ed. lib. bdg. 47.95 (0-405-11744-2) Ayer.

— Considerations sur les Principaux Evenemens de la Revolution Francoise, Madame la Baronne Stael, 3 vols. in 2, Set. LC 78-67391. (European Political Thought Ser.). (FRE.). 1980. reprint ed. lib. bdg. 94.95 (0-405-11742-6) Ayer.

An Asterisk (*) at the beginning of an entry indicates that the title is appearing in BIP for the first time.

— European Political Thought Series: Traditions & Endurance, 67 bks., Set. (Illus.). 1979. lib. bdg. 2,593.00 (*0-405-11670-5*) Ayer.
— European Political Thought Series: Traditions & Endurance, 67 bks., Vols. 1-20. (Illus.). 1979. lib. bdg. 662.00 (*0-685-00508-9*) Ayer.
— European Political Thought Series: Traditions & Endurance, 67 bks., Vols. 21-35. (Illus.). 1979. lib. bdg. 724.00 (*0-405-18995-8*) Ayer.
— European Political Thought Series: Traditions & Endurance, 67 bks., Vols. 36-67. (Illus.). 1979. lib. bdg. 858.00 (*0-405-18996-6*) Ayer.
— Fundamental Studies of Jean Bodin: An Original Anthology. LC 78-67314. (European Political Thought Ser.). (FRE & GER.). 1979. lib. bdg. 50.95 (*0-405-11671-3*) Ayer.
— The Impact of the Eighteenth Brumaire: An Original Anthology. LC 78-67322. (European Political Thought Ser.). (ENG & GER.). 1979. lib. bdg. 40.95 (*0-405-11672-1*) Ayer.
Mayer, J. P., ed. see Althusius, Johannes.
Mayer, J. P., ed. see Bagge, Dominique.
Mayer, J. P., ed. see Baudrillart, Henri.
Mayer, J. P., ed. see Bayle, Francis & Rohden, Peter R.
Mayer, J. P., ed. see Beer, Max.
Mayer, J. P., ed. see Bluntschli, Johann C.
Mayer, J. P., ed. see Bodin, Jean.
Mayer, J. P., ed. see Bougle, Celestin C.
Mayer, J. P., ed. see Burchhardt, Jacob.
Mayer, J. P., ed. see Chaix-Ruy, Jules.
Mayer, J. P., ed. see Chalres, Celestin, et al.
Mayer, J. P., ed. see Chinard, Gilbert.
Mayer, J. P., ed. see Constant de Rebecque, Henri B.
Mayer, J. P., ed. see Cortes, Juan D. & Schramm, Edmund.
Mayer, J. P., ed. see Cotta, Sergio.
Mayer, J. P., ed. see Cottu, Charles.
Mayer, J. P., ed. see Cranston, Maurice W.
Mayer, J. P., ed. see De Lolme, J. L. & Machelon, Jean-Pierre.
Mayer, J. P., ed. see De Remusat, Charles F.
Mayer, J. P., ed. see De Tocqueville, Alexis C.
Mayer, J. P., ed. see De Tocqueville, Alexis.
Mayer, J. P., ed. see Dempf, Alois.
Mayer, J. P., ed. see Dolleans, Edouard.
Mayer, J. P., ed. see Flint, Robert.
Mayer, J. P., ed. see Gadave, Renne.
Mayer, J. P., ed. see Gewirth, Alan.
Mayer, J. P., ed. see Guizot, Francois P.
Mayer, J. P., ed. see Hubert, Rene.
Mayer, J. P., ed. see Huit, C.
Mayer, J. P., ed. see Jannet, Claudio.
Mayer, J. P., ed. see Jefferson, Thomas.
Mayer, J. P., ed. see Lanson, Gustave.
Mayer, J. P., ed. see Lehmann, William C.
Mayer, J. P., ed. see Leroy, Andre L.
Mayer, J. P., ed. see Luccioni, Jean.
Mayer, J. P., ed. see MacCunn, John.
Mayer, J. P., ed. see Martin, Kingsley.
Mayer, J. P., ed. see McIlwain, Charles H.
Mayer, J. P., ed. see Mommsen, Theodor.
Mayer, J. P., ed. see Morley, John M.
Mayer, J. P., ed. see Moulinie, Henri.
Mayer, J. P., ed. see Pellissier, Georges.
Mayer, J. P., ed. see Perthes, Clemens T.
Mayer, J. P., jt. auth. see Pierson.
Mayer, J. P., ed. see Remond, Gabriel.
Mayer, J. P., ed. see Reybaud, Louis.
Mayer, J. P., ed. see Robin, Leon.
Mayer, J. P., ed. see Rommen, Heinrich A.
Mayer, J. P., ed. see Saresberiensis, Ioannis.
Mayer, J. P., ed. see Schemann, Ludwig.
Mayer, J. P., ed. see See, Henri E.
Mayer, J. P., ed. see Sidney, Algernon.
Mayer, J. P., ed. see Sieyes, Emmanuel & Sainte-Beuve, Charles Augustin.
Mayer, J. P., ed. see Sorel, Georges.
Mayer, J. P., ed. see Troeltsch, Ernst.
Mayer, J. P., ed. see Vinet, Alexandre R.
Mayer, J. P., ed. see Von Ulrich & Wiliamovitz-Moellendorff, B. Niese.
Mayer, J. P., ed. see Vorlander, Franz.
Mayer, J. P., ed. see Waitz, Georg.
Mayer, J. W., jt. auth. see Feldman, L. C.
Mayer, Jack, ed. see Schwartz, Bob & Schwartz, Leah.
Mayer, Jacob, et al. Political Thought. LC 72-134114. (Essay Index Reprint Ser.). 1977. 29.95 (*0-8369-1932-7*) Ayer.
Mayer, James M., jt. auth. see Nugent, William A.
Mayer, Jan, jt. auth. see Ada, Alma F.
Mayer, Jan, tr. see Evans, Joy & Moore, Jo E.
Mayer, Jane. Strange Justice: The Selling of Clarence Thomas. 1994. 24.95 (*0-395-63318-4*) HM.
***Mayer, Jane & Abramson, Jill.** Strange Justice: The Selling of Clarence Thomas. LC 95-13311. 1995. write for info. (*0-452-27499-0*, Plume) NAL-Dutton.
Mayer, Jean, ed. Bringing Jobs to People: Employment Promotion at Regional & Local Levels. vi, 211p. (Orig.). 1988. 32.00 (*92-2-106326-7*); pap. 20.00 (*92-2-106325-9*) Intl Labour Office.
Mayer, Jean, jt. ed. see Moss, N. Henry.
***Mayer, Jeffrey.** Act! for Windows for Dummies. 1995. pap. 19.99 (*1-56884-902-8*) IDG Bks.
— Time Management for Dummies. 1995. pap. 16.99 (*1-56884-360-7*) IDG Bks.
— Time Management Survival Guide for Dummies. 1995. pap. 12.99 (*1-56884-972-9*) IDG Bks.
Mayer, Jeffrey J. Find the Job You've Always Wanted in Half the Time with Half the Effort. 144p. 1993. pap. 7.95 (*0-8092-3816-0*) Contemp Bks.
— If You Haven't Got the Time to Do It Right, When Will You Find the Time to Do It Over? (Illus.). 157p. 1990. 17.95 (*0-671-94303-0*) S&S Trade.
— If You Haven't Got the Time to Do It Right, When Will You Find the Time to Do It Over? (Illus.). 160p. 1991. pap. 10.00 (*0-671-73364-8*, Fireside) S&S Trade.
— Winning the Fight Between You & Your Desk: Use Your Computer to Get Organized, Become More Productive, & Make More Money. (Illus.). 272p. 1995. pap. 10.00 (*0-88730-718-3*) Harper Busn.
— Winning the Fight Between You & Your Desk, Your Office, & Your Computer. (Illus.). 160p. 1994. 18.00 (*0-88730-674-8*) Harper Busn.
Mayer, Jill S., ed. Space: The Next Renaissance: Proceedings of the 7th Annual International Space Development Conference. 518p. 1991. pap. 30.00 (*0-912183-06-3*) Univelt Inc.
Mayer, John E. Jewish-Gentile Courtships: An Exploratory Study of a Social Process. LC 80-16130. x, 240p. 1980. reprint ed. text ed. 55.00 (*0-313-22465-X*, MAJG, Greenwood Pr) Greenwood.
Mayer, John E. & Timms, Noel. The Client Speaks: Working Class Impressions of Casework. 193p. 1970. 19.50 (*0-932400-03-5*) Intervale Pub Co.
Mayer, John J. & Brisbin, I. Lehr, Jr. Wild Pigs in the United States: Their History, Comparative Morphology, & Current Status. LC 90-10945. (Illus.). 336p. 1991. 40.00 (*0-8203-1239-8*) U of Ga Pr.
***Mayer, John R., ed.** The Alloway Strange: Alva Extranea de Virginia. 2nd ed. LC 90-148997. (Extraneus Ser.: Vol. III, Bk. X). (Illus.). xxiv, 256p. (C). 1994. pap. 22.00 (*0-9638665-3-2*) Arapacana Pr.
— Strange of Blisland: Extraneus De Terra Felicitas. 2nd ed. (Extraneus Ser.: Vol. IV, Bk. XI). (Illus.). xxxii, 368p. (C). 1993. pap. 44.00 (*0-9638665-1-6*) Arapacana Pr.
— Strange of Eastern America: Extraneus De America Orientalis. 2nd rev. ed. (Extraneus Ser.: Vol. I, Bk. V). (Illus.). xviii, 380p. (Orig.). (C). 1993. pap. 36.00 (*0-9638665-0-8*) Arapacana Pr.
— Strange of the Carolinas: Extraneus de Carolina. 2nd ed. (Extraneus Ser.: Vol. IV, Bk. XII). (Illus.). xxvi, 548p. (C). 1993. pap. 58.00 (*0-9638665-2-4*) Arapacana Pr.
Mayer, John T. T. S. Eliot's Silent Voices. 368p. 1990. 45.00 (*0-19-505668-X*) OUP.
Mayer, K. F. Thunder Rising: Chief Joseph of the Nez Perce. 173p. (Orig.). (C). 1994. pap. 13.95 (*0-932863-17-5*) Clarity Pr.
Mayer, Karl H. Maya Monuments: Sculptures of Unknown Provenance in Europe. Brizee, Sandra L., tr. (Illus.). 1978. pap. 20.00 (*0-916552-11-X*) Acoma Bks.
— Maya Monuments: Sculptures of Unknown Provenance in the U. S. (Illus.). 1980. pap. 30.00 (*0-916552-16-0*) Acoma Bks.
— Mushroom Stones of Meso-America. (Illus.). 1977. pap. 4.95 (*0-916552-09-8*) Acoma Bks.
Mayer, Karl U. & Tuma, Nancy B., eds. Event History Analysis in Life Course Research. LC 89-40261. (Life Course Studies). 320p. (C). 1990. text ed. 50.00 (*0-299-12200-X*); pap. text ed. 18.75 (*0-299-12204-2*) U of Wis Pr.
Mayer, Karl U., ed. see Blossfeld, Hans-Peter & Hamerle, Alfred M.
Mayer, Karl U., jt. ed. see Mueller, Walter.
Mayer, Kathy, jt. auth. see Szifra, Birke.
Mayer, Ken. Real Women Don't Diet! One Man's Praise of Large Women & His Outrage at the Society That Rejects Them. LC 93-36312. (Illus.). 1993. 18.95 (*0-910155-27-5*) Bartleby Pr.
Mayer, Kenneth R. The Politics of Defense Contracting. 240p. 1991. text ed. 32.50 (*0-300-04524-7*) Yale U Pr.
— Well Spoken: Oral Communication Skills for Business. 246p. (C). 1989. pap. text ed. 19.00 (*0-15-595154-8*) Dryden Pr.
Mayer, Kurt B. & Goldstein, Sidney. Migration & Economic Development in Rhode Island. LC 58-10480. reprint ed. 20.00 (*0-685-15746-6*) Bks Demand.
Mayer, L. A. A Bibliography of Jewish Numismatics, 1966. 15.00 (*0-87068-796-4*) Ktav.
Mayer, Lance, et al. The Devotion Family: The Lives & Possessions of Three Generations in Eighteenth-Century Connecticut. (Illus.). 64p. (Orig.). 1991. pap. 14.95 (*1-878541-03-X*) Lyman Allyn.
Mayer, Larry. Introduction to Quantitative Geomorphology: An Exercise Manual. 384p. (C). 1990. pap. text ed. write for info. (*0-13-488263-6*) P-H.
— Montana from the Big Sky. (Illus.). 144p. 1990. 29.95 (*0-9627618-1-8*) Billings Gazette.
Mayer, Larry, ed. Extensional Tectonics of the Southwestern United States: A Perspective on Processes & Kinematics. (Special Paper Ser.: No. 208). (Illus.). 130p. 1986. pap. 6.60 (*0-8137-2208-X*) Geol Soc.
— Extensional Tectonics of the Southwestern United States: A Perspective on Processes & Kinematics. fac. ed. LC 86-22853. (Geological Society of America Special Paper Ser.: No. 208). (Illus.). 130p. 1986. reprint ed. pap. 37.10 (*0-7837-8039-7*, 2047795) Bks Demand.
Mayer, Larry, photos. Wisconsin from the Sky. (Illus.). 120p. (Orig.). 1994. 29.95 (*1-56037-057-2*) Am Wrld Geog.
Mayer, Larry, jt. photos see Sample, Michael.
Mayer, Lawrence C. Redefining Comparative Politics: Promise Versus Performance. (Library of Social Research). 320p. (C). 1989. text ed. 49.95 (*0-8039-3463-7*); pap. text ed. 24.00 (*0-8039-3464-5*) Sage.
Mayer, Lawrence C. & Burnett, John A. Politics in Industrial Societies: A Comparative Perspective. LC 76-54694. 399p. reprint ed. pap. 113.80 (*0-317-09456-4*, 2055491) Bks Demand.
Mayer, Lawrence C., et al. Comparative Politics: Nations & Theories in a Changing World. LC 92-25889. 368p. 1992. text ed. write for info. (*0-13-151572-1*) P-H.
Mayer, Lene, jt. auth. see Gipson, Morrell.
***Mayer, Leonard.** Design & Planning of Research & Clinical Laboratory Facilities. LC 94-28955. 1995. text ed. 75.00 (*0-471-30623-1*) Wiley.
Mayer, Levy, ed. see Rorer, David.
Mayer, Lorenzo, jt. auth. see Aldrich, Daniel G., Jr.
Mayer, Louis B., jt. auth. see Higham, Charles.
***Mayer, Lyle V.** Fundamentals of Voice & Articulation. 352p. (C). 1995. pap. write for info. (*0-697-27066-1*); audio write for info. (*0-697-27068-8*) Brown & Benchmark.
— Fundamentals of Voice & Diction. 10th ed. 352p. 1994. pap. write for info. (*0-697-13932-8*) Brown & Benchmark.
Mayer, M. Diploma: International Schools & University Entrance. LC 68-26129. (Twentieth Century Fund Ser.). 1968. reprint ed. pap. 10.00 (*0-527-02828-2*) Periodicals Srv.
Mayer, Marc, jt. auth. see Brutvan, Cheryl.
***Mayer, Margaret M. & Castagner, Claude.** The American Dream: American Popular Music. rev. ed. (Illus.). 218p. (C). 1994. pap. text ed. write for info. (*0-9640120-3-0*) Front Desk LLC.
Mayer, Margarita. Breathing & Relaxation: In Theory & Practice. Callender, Vesta & Clark, Winifred, eds. Mayer, Thomas, tr. (Illus.). 45p. (Orig.). (C). 1988. pap. text ed. write for info. (*0-318-62904-6*) W Clark.
Mayer, Marianna. Beauty & the Beast. LC 78-54679. (Illus.). 48p. (J). (gr. k up). 1984. text ed. 15.95 (*0-02-765270-X*, Four Winds Pr) S&S Childrens.
— Beauty & the Beast. LC 87-1095. (Illus.). 48p. (J). (ps up). 1987. reprint ed. pap. 5.95 (*0-689-71151-4*, Aladdin Paperbacks) S&S Childrens.
— Boy, a Dog, a Frog, & a Friend. 1993. pap. 3.99 (*0-14-054610-3*) Puffin Bks.
— Iduna & the Magic Apples. LC 88-2494. (Illus.). 40p. (J). (gr. k-4). 1988. text ed. 16.95 (*0-02-765120-7*, Mac Bks Young Read) S&S Childrens.
— Turandot. LC 93-27033. (Illus.). (J). 1995. 16.00 (*0-688-09073-7*); lib. bdg. 15.93 (*0-688-09074-5*) Morrow Jr Bks.
— Twelve Dancing Princess. LC 83-1034. (Illus.). 40p. (J). (ps up). 1989. 16.00 (*0-688-08051-0*); lib. bdg. 15.93 (*0-688-02026-7*) Morrow Jr Bks.
— The Unicorn Alphabet. (Illus.). 32p. (J). (gr. 1 up). 1989. lib. bdg. 14.89 (*0-8037-0373-2*) Dial Bks Young.
— The Unicorn Alphabet. (Illus.). 32p. (J). 1993. pap. 5.99 (*0-14-054922-6*, Puff Pied Piper) Puffin Bks.
— Unicorn & the Lake. LC 81-5469. (Pied Piper Bks.). (Illus.). 32p. (J). (gr. k up). 1987. pap. 4.95 (*0-8037-0436-4*) Dial Bks Young.
— Unicorn & the Lake. (J). (ps-3). 1990. 17.99 (*0-8037-0844-0*) Dial Bks Young.
Mayer, Marianna & McDermott, Gerald. The Brambleberrys Animal Alphabet. LC 91-70420. (Illus.). 32p. (J). (ps up). 1991. 3.95 (*1-878093-78-9*) Boyds Mills Pr.
— The Brambleberrys Animal Book of Colors. LC 91-70418. (Illus.). 32p. (J). (ps up). 1991. 3.95 (*1-878093-76-2*) Boyds Mills Pr.
— The Brambleberrys Animal Book of Counting. LC 91-70419. (Illus.). 32p. (J). (ps up). 1991. 3.95 (*1-878093-75-4*) Boyds Mills Pr.
— The Brambleberrys Animal Book of Shapes. LC 91-70421. (Illus.). 32p. (J). (ps up). 1991. 3.95 (*1-878093-77-0*) Boyds Mills Pr.
Mayer, Marianna, jt. auth. see Mayer, Mercer.
***Mayer, Marion.** History of a Family Dispersed. (Illus.). 300p. 1995. 35.00 (*0-9644869-0-3*) Mayer Pr.
Mayer, Martha H. Poetry Is Made to Be Loved: Poems. LC 91-66917. 120p. 1991. pap. 4.50 (*0-938875-28-0*) Pittenbruach Pr.
Mayer, Martin. The Greatest Ever Bank Robbery: The Collapse of the Savings & Loan Industry. 384p. 1992. reprint ed. pap. 12.95 (*0-02-012620-4*, Pub. by Gebrueder Borntraeger GW) Macmillan.
— The Lawyers. LC 79-26324. 586p. 1980. reprint ed. text ed. 42.50 (*0-313-22222-3*, MALY, Greenwood Pr) Greenwood.
— Madison Avenue, U. S. A. (NTC's Business Classics Ser.). 304p. 1992. pap. 11.95 (*0-8442-3247-5*, NTC Busn Bks) NTC Pub Grp.
— Making News. rev. ed. 336p. 1993. pap. 16.95 (*0-87584-371-9*) Harvard Busn.
— Making News. rev. ed. 1993. pap. text ed. 16.95 (*0-07-103389-0*) McGraw.
— Markets. 1990. pap. 8.95 (*0-393-30652-6*) Norton.
— Nightmare on Wall Street: Salomon Brothers & the Corruption of the Marketplace. LC 93-14703. (Illus.). 304p. 1993. 23.00 (*0-671-78187-1*) S&S Trade.
— Stealing the Market: How the Giant Brokerage Firms, with Help from the SEC, Stole the Stock Market from Small Investors. LC 91-55600. 224p. 1993. pap. 13.00 (*0-465-08224-6*) Basic.
Mayer, Martin & Finn, David. Children of the World: Learning Together at the United Nations International School. (Illus.). 160p. 1990. 34.95 (*0-8191-7681-8*) Madison Bks UPA.
Mayer, Martin & Young, James W. How to Become an Advertising Man. (NTC's Business Classics Ser.). 96p. 1991. pap. 11.95 (*0-8442-3002-2*, NTC Busn Bks) NTC Pub Grp.
Mayer, Martin, jt. auth. see Linowtiz, Sol M.
Mayer-Martin, Donna. Thematic Catalogue of Troubadour & Trouvere Melody. (Thematic Catalogues Ser.: No. 18). (Illus.). 1994. lib. bdg. 76.00 (*0-918728-82-7*) Pendragon NY.
Mayer, Martin P. Gay, Lesbian, & Heterosexual Teachers: An Investigation of Acceptance of Self, Acceptance of Others, Affectional & Lifestyle Orientation: Their Rightful Place. LC 93-26785. 196p. 1993. text ed. 79.95 (*0-7734-2236-6*, Mellen Univ Pr) E Mellen.
Mayer, Mary H., tr. see Fitzpatrick, Edward A., ed.
Mayer, Melanie J. Klondike Women: True Tales of the 1897-1898 Gold Rush. LC 89-33517. (Illus.). 280p. 1989. 34.95 (*0-8040-0926-0*); pap. 18.95 (*0-8040-0927-9*) Swallow.
Mayer, Mercer. Ah-Choo. (Pied Piper Bks.). (Illus.). (J). (gr. k-2). 1977. lib. bdg. 4.58 (*0-8037-4895-7*) Dial Bks Young.
— All By Myself. (Golden Look-Look Bks.). (Illus.). 24p. (J). (ps-3). 1985. reprint ed. pap. write for info. (*0-307-11938-6*, Golden Bks) Western Pub.
— Appelard & Liverwurst. LC 89-13803. (Illus.). 40p. (J). (gr. k up). 1990. 13.95 (*0-688-09659-X*); lib. bdg. 13.88 (*0-688-09660-3*) Morrow Jr Bks.
— Baby Sister Says No. LC 86-82368. (Golden Look-Look Bks.). (Illus.). 24p. (J). (gr. 4-8). 1987. pap. write for info. (*0-307-11949-1*, Golden Bks) Western Pub.
— A Boy, a Dog, a Frog & a Friend. LC 70-134857. (J). (ps-2). 1971. reprint ed. 8.95 (*0-8037-0754-1*) Dial Bks Young.
— A Boy, a Dog, a Frog & a Friend. LC 70-134857. (J). (ps-2). 1978. reprint ed. lib. bdg. 8.89 (*0-8037-0755-X*); reprint ed. pap. 2.95 (*0-8037-0804-1*) Dial Bks Young.
— A Boy, a Dog & a Frog. LC 67-22254. (Pied Piper Bks.). (Illus.). (J). (ps-3). 1985. lib. bdg. 9.89 (*0-8037-0767-3*) Dial Bks Young.
— A Boy, a Dog & a Frog. LC 67-22254. (Pied Piper Bks.). (Illus.). 32p. (J). (ps-2). 1985. reprint ed. pap. 3.50 (*0-8037-0769-X*) Dial Bks Young.
— Bubble Bubble. rev. ed. (Illus.). 48p. (J). 1992. reprint ed. pap. 5.95 (*1-879920-03-4*) Rain Bird Prods.
— The Cat's Meow. (School Time Readers Ser.). (Illus.). 48p. (J). 1994. write for info. (*0-307-15984-1*, Golden Bks) Western Pub.
— De Comprns Con Mama - Just Shopping with Mom. (Spanish Language Look-Look Bks.). (Illus.). 24p. (SPA.). (J). 1994. write for info. (*0-307-71972-3*, Golden Bks) Western Pub.
— Dog, & a Frog. (J). (ps-3). 1992. pap. 3.99 (*0-14-054611-1*) Viking Child Bks.
— East of the Sun & West of the Moon. LC 80-11496. (Illus.). 48p. (J). (gr. k up). 1984. text ed. 15.95 (*0-02-765190-8*, Four Winds Pr) S&S Childrens.
— East of the Sun & West of the Moon. LC 86-20578. (Illus.). 48p. (J). (ps-3). 1987. reprint ed. pap. 5.95 (*0-689-71113-1*, Aladdin Paperbacks) S&S Childrens.
— Eight Favorite Little Critter Books Just for You. (Look-Look Bks.). (Illus.). (J). (ps-3). 1993. Incls. Just for You, Just Me & My Dad, Just Grandma & Me, When I Get Bigger, Just Go to Bed, I Was S. boxed 15.95 (*0-307-16205-2*, 16205-0, Golden Pr) Western Pub.
— Frog Goes to Dinner. LC 74-2881. (Pied Piper Bks.). (Illus.). 32p. (J). (ps-2). 1974. lib. bdg. 8.89 (*0-8037-3381-X*) Dial Bks Young.
— Frog Goes to Dinner. (J). (ps). 1992. 3.99 (*0-14-054633-2*) Puffin Bks.
— Frog Goes to Dinner. (Pied Piper Bks.). (Illus.). (J). (gr. k-2). 1977. reprint ed. pap. 2.95 (*0-8037-2733-X*) Dial Bks Young.
— Frog on His Own. LC 73-6018. (Pied Piper Bks.). (Illus.). 32p. (J). (ps-2). 1973. 8.95 (*0-8037-2701-1*); lib. bdg. 8.89 (*0-8037-2695-3*) Dial Bks Young.
— Frog on His Own. LC 73-6018. (Pied Piper Bks.). (Illus.). 32p. (J). (ps-2). 1980. pap. 2.95 (*0-8037-2716-X*) Dial Bks Young.
— Frog, Where Are You? LC 72-85544. (Illus.). (J). (ps-3). 1969. 9.95 (*0-8037-2737-2*); lib. bdg. 9.89 (*0-8037-2732-1*) Dial Bks Young.
— Frog, Where Are You? LC 72-85544. (Pied Piper Bks.). (Illus.). 32p. (J). (ps-2). 1980. reprint ed. pap. 2.95 (*0-8037-2729-1*) Dial Bks Young.
— Great Cat Chase. (J). (ps-3). 1994. pap. 5.95 (*1-879920-07-7*) Rain Bird Prods.
— Happy Easter, Little Critter. LC 87-81759. (Golden Look-Look Bks.). (Illus.). 24p. (J). (ps-3). 1988. pap. write for info. (*0-307-11723-5*, Golden Bks) Western Pub.
— Hiccup. (J). (gr. 4-7). 1993. pap. 3.99 (*0-14-054641-3*) Puffin Bks.
— Hiccup. LC 76-2284. (Pied Piper Bks.). (Illus.). (J). (ps-2). 1978. reprint ed. pap. 3.95 (*0-8037-3590-1*, 0383-120) Dial Bks Young.
— I Just Forgot. LC 87-81779. (Golden Look-Look Bks.). (Illus.). 24p. (Orig.). (J). (ps-3). 1988. pap. write for info. (*0-307-11975-0*) Western Pub.
— If I Had a Gorilla. (J). (ps-3). 1994. pap. 5.95 (*1-879920-06-9*) Rain Bird Prods.
— Just a Daydream. (Golden Look-Look Book Ser.). (Illus.). 24p. (J). (ps-3). 1989. pap. write for info. (*0-307-11973-4*, Golden Bks) Western Pub.
— Just a Mess. LC 86-82369. (Golden Look-Look Bks.). (Illus.). 24p. (J). (gr. 4-8). 1987. pap. write for info. (*0-307-11948-3*, Golden Bks) Western Pub.
— Just a Nap. (Golden Little Look-Look Book Ser.). (Illus.). 24p. (J). (ps-00). 1989. pap. write for info. (*0-307-11713-8*, Golden Bks) Western Pub.
— Just a Rainy Day. (J). (ps). 1990. pap. write for info. (*0-307-11682-4*) Western Pub.
— Just a Snowy Day. (Golden Touch & Feel Bks.). (Illus.). 20p. (J). (gr. k). 1983. spiral bd. write for info. (*0-307-12156-9*, 12156, Golden Bks) Western Pub.
— Just Camping Out. (Golden Little Look-Look Book Ser.). (Illus.). 24p. (J). (ps-00). 1989. pap. write for info. (*0-307-11714-6*, Golden Bks) Western Pub.

M

An Asterisk (*) at the beginning of an entry indicates that the title is appearing in BIP for the first time.

— Just for You. (Golden Look-Look Bks.). (Illus.). 24p. (J). (ps-3). 1975. pap. write for info. (0-307-11838-X, Golden Bks) Western Pub.
— Just Go to Bed. rev. ed. (Golden Look-Look Bks.). (Illus.). 24p. (J). (ps-3). 1985. reprint ed. pap. write for info. (0-307-11940-8, 11940, Golden Bks) Western Pub.
— Just Going to the Dentist. (J). (ps-3). 1990. pap. write for info. (0-307-12583-1) Western Pub.
— Just Grandma & Me. (Golden Look-Look Bks.). (Illus.). 24p. (J). (ps-3). 1985. reprint ed. pap. write for info. (0-307-11893-2, Golden Bks) Western Pub.
— Just Grandpa & Me. (Golden Look-Look Bks.). (Illus.). 24p. (J). (ps-3). 1985. pap. write for info. (0-307-11936-X, Golden Bks) Western Pub.
— Just Me & My Babysitter. (Golden Look-Look Bks.). (Illus.). 24p. (Orig.). (J). (ps-3). 1986. pap. write for info. (0-307-11945-9, Golden Bks) Western Pub.
— Just Me & My Cousin. (Golden Look-Look Bks.). (Illus.). 24p. (J). (ps-3). 1992. pap. write for info. (0-307-12688-9, 12688, Golden Pr) Western Pub.
— Just Me & My Dad. (Look-Look Ser.). (Illus.). 24p. (J). (ps-3). 1977. pap. write for info. (0-307-11839-8, Golden Bks) Western Pub.
— Just Me & My Little Sister. (Golden Look-Look Bks.). (Illus.). 24p. (Orig.). (J). (ps-3). 1986. pap. write for info. (0-307-11946-7, Golden Bks) Western Pub.
— Just Me & My Mom. (J). (ps-3). 1990. pap. write for info. (0-307-12584-X) Western Pub.
— Just Me & My Puppy. (Golden Look-Look Bks.). (Illus.). 24p. (J). (ps-3). 1985. pap. write for info. (0-307-11937-8, Golden Bks) Western Pub.
— Just My Friend & Me. (Golden Look-Look Bks.). (J). 1988. write for info. (0-307-11947-5, 11947, Golden Bks) Western Pub.
— Just Shopping with Mom. (Golden Look-Look Book Ser.). (Illus.). 24p. (J). (ps-3). 1989. pap. write for info. (0-307-11972-6, Golden Bks) Western Pub.
— Little Critter's Day at the Farm Sticker Book. (Little Critter Sticker Books Ser.). (Illus.). 16p. (J). (ps-1). 1994. pap. 4.95 (0-590-48641-1, Cartwheel) Scholastic Inc.
— Little Critter's Holiday Fun. (Peel 'n Press Sticker Bks.). (Illus.). 24p. (Orig.). (J). (ps-3). 1984. pap. 3.95 (0-590-33658-4) Scholastic Inc.
— Little Critter's Holiday Fun Sticker Book. (Illus.). 16p. (J). (ps-1). 1994. pap. 4.95 (0-590-48640-3, Cartwheel) Scholastic Inc.
— Little Critter's Joke Book. (J). (ps-3). 1993. pap. 2.25 (0-307-12790-7, Golden Pr) Western Pub.
— Little Critter's Read-It-Yourself Storybook: Six Funny Easy-to-Read Stories. (Illus.). 196p. (J). (gr. k-2). 1993. 11.95 (0-307-16840-9, 16840, Golden Pr) Western Pub.
— Little Critter's: This Is My School. (ps-3). 1990. write for info. (0-307-11589-5) Western Pub.
— Little Critter's This Is My School. (Golden Softcover Fast Start Readers Ser.: Level 2). (Illus.). 32p. (J). (ps-2). 1992. pap. write for info. (0-307-15963-9, 15963) Western Pub.
— Little Critter's This Is My Town. (J). (ps-3). 1993. pap. 3.50 (0-307-11567-4, Golden Pr) Western Pub.
— Little Monster's Moving Day. (Little Monster Sticker Bks.). (Illus.). 16p. (J). (ps-1). 1995. pap. 4.95 (0-590-48643-8, Cartwheel) Scholastic Inc.
— Little Monster's Sports Fun. (Little Monster Sticker Bks.). (Illus.). 16p. (Orig.). (J). (ps-1). 1995. pap. 4.95 (0-590-48644-6, Cartwheel) Scholastic Inc.
— Liverwurst Is Missing. LC 90-5435. (Illus.). 32p. (J). (gr. k up). 1990. 16.00 (0-688-09657-3); lib. bdg. 15.93 (0-688-09658-1) Morrow Jr Bks.
— Liza Lou & the Yeller Belly Swamp. LC 80-16605. (Illus.). 48p. (J). (gr. k-3). 1984. reprint ed. text ed. 14.95 (0-02-765220-3, Four Winds Pr) S&S Childrens.
— Me Too! (Golden Look-Look Bks.). (Illus.). 24p. (J). (ps-3). 1985. reprint ed. pap. write for info. (0-307-11941-6, Golden Bks) Western Pub.
— Mercer Mayer's Super Critter to the Rescue. (Golden Sound Story Books - Classics Ser.). (Illus.). 20p. (J). (ps up). 1992. write for info. (0-307-74708-5, 64708, Golden Pr) Western Pub.
— Mercer Mayer's What a Bad Dream. (Golden Look Look Book Ser.). (Illus.). 24p. (J). (ps-3). 1992. write for info. (0-307-12685-4, 12685) Western Pub.
— Merry Christmas Mom & Dad. (Golden Look-Look Bks.). (Illus.). 24p. (J). (ps-3). 1982. pap. write for info. (0-307-11886-X, Golden Bks) Western Pub.
— Mi Abueln y Yo - Just Grandma & Me. (Spanish Language Look-Look Bks.). (Illus.). 24p. (SPA.). (J). 1994. write for info. (0-307-71893-X, Golden Bks) Western Pub.
— Mi Mimo y Yo - Just Me & My Cousin. (Spanish Language Look-Look Bks.). (Illus.). 24p. (SPA.). (J). 1994. write for info. (0-307-72688-6, Golden Bks) Western Pub.
— The Mummy's Curse. (School Time Readers Ser.). (Illus.). 48p. (J). 1994. write for info. (0-307-15959-0, Golden Bks) Western Pub.
— My Teacher Is a Vampire. (School Time Readers Ser.). (Illus.). 48p. (J). 1994. write for info. (0-307-15957-4, Golden Bks) Western Pub.
— The New Baby. (Golden Look-Look Bks.). (Illus.). 24p. (J). (ps-3). 1985. reprint ed. pap. write for info. (0-307-11942-4, Golden Bks) Western Pub.
— No Howling in the House. LC 95-13690. (Step into Reading Ser., Step 2 Bks.). (J). 1996. pap. 3.99 (0-679-87365-1) Random.
— El Nuevo Bibi - The New Baby. (Spanish Language Look-Look Bks.). (Illus.). 24p. (SPA.). (J). 1994. write for info. (0-307-71942-1, Golden Bks) Western Pub.
— One Monster after Another. (J). (ps-3). 1993. pap. 5.95 (1-879920-05-0) Rain Bird Prods.
— The Pied Piper of Hamlin. LC 87-1607. (Illus.). 48p. (J). (gr. k up). 1987. lib. bdg. 16.95 (0-02-765361-7, Mac Bks Young Read) S&S Childrens.
— Professor Wormbog in Search for the Zipperump-a-Zoo. (Illus.). 48p. (J). (ps up). 1992. pap. 5.95 (1-879920-04-2) Rain Bird Prods.
— The Purple Kiss. (LC & the Critter Kids Mini-Novels Ser.). (Illus.). 72p. (J). 1994. write for info. (0-307-15980-9, Golden Bks) Western Pub.
— Purple Pickle Juice. 3.99 (0-679-87366-X) Random.
— Se Me Olvido - I Just Forgot. (Spanish Language Look-Look Bks.). (Illus.). 24p. (SPA.). (J). 1994. write for info. (0-307-71975-8, Golden Bks) Western Pub.
— The Secret Code. (LC & the Critter Kids Mini-Novels Ser.). (Illus.). 72p. (J). 1994. write for info. (0-307-15983-3, Golden Bks) Western Pub.
— Showdown at the Aracade. (School Time Readers Ser.). (Illus.). 48p. (J). 1994. write for info. (0-307-15958-2, Golden Bks) Western Pub.
— A Silly Story: Nothing Less Nothing More. (Illus.). 48p. (J). 1992. reprint ed. pap. 5.95 (1-879920-02-6) Rain Bird Prods.
— Surf's Up. (LC & the Critter Kids Mini-Novels Ser.). (Illus.). 72p. (J). 1994. write for info. (0-307-15982-5, Golden Bks) Western Pub.
— There's a Nightmare in My Closet. LC 68-15250. (Illus.). (J). (ps-3). 1968. 14.99 (0-8037-8682-4) Dial Bks Young.
— There's a Nightmare in My Closet. LC 68-15250. (Illus.). (J). (ps-3). 1985. lib. bdg. 13.89 (0-8037-8683-2); pap. 4.95 (0-8037-8574-7); student ed 17.99 (0-8037-0843-2) Dial Bks Young.
— There's a Nightmare in My Closet. (J). 1992. pap. 4.99 (0-14-054712-6, Puffin) Puffin Bks.
— There's a Nightmare in My Closet. (J). 1992. pap. 18.99 (0-14-054713-4) Puffin Bks.
— There's a Nightmare in My Closet - Una Pesadilla En Mi Armario. (SPA.). (J). 7.50 (84-372-1754-7) Santillana.
— There's an Alligator under My Bed. LC 86-19944. (Illus.). 32p. (J). (ps-3). 1987. 14.99 (0-8037-0374-0); lib. bdg. 14.89 (0-8037-0375-9) Dial Bks Young.
— There's Something in My Attic. LC 86-32875. (Illus.). 32p. (J). (ps-3). 1988. 11.95 (0-8037-0414-3); lib. bdg. 11.89 (0-8037-0415-1) Dial Bks Young.
— There's Something in My Attic. (Illus.). 32p. (J). (ps-3). 1992. pap. 4.99 (0-14-054813-0, Puffin) Puffin Bks.
— These Are My Pets, Level 2. (Little Critters Ser.). (Illus.). 32p. (J). (gr. 1-2). 1992. pap. 3.00 (0-307-15962-0, 15962, Golden Pr) Western Pub.
— This Is My Friend. (Golden Easy Reader Ser.: Level 2). (Illus.). 40p. (J). (gr. k-2). 1989. write for info. (0-307-11685-9, Golden Bks) Western Pub.
— Top Dog. (LC & the Critter Kids Mini-Novels Ser.). (Illus.). 72p. (J). 1994. write for info. (0-307-15981-7, Golden Bks) Western Pub.
— What Do You Do with a Kangaroo. (J). (ps-3). 1987. pap. 3.95 (0-590-44850-1) Scholastic Inc.
— When I Get Bigger. (Golden Look-Look Bks.). (Illus.). 24p. (J). (ps-3). 1985. reprint ed. pap. write for info. (0-307-11943-2, Golden Bks) Western Pub.
— Whinnie the Lovesick Dragon. LC 85-18886. (Illus.). 32p. (J). (gr. k-3). 1986. text ed. 14.95 (0-02-765180-0, Mac Bks Young Read) S&S Childrens.
— The Wizard Comes to Town. (Illus.). 40p. (J). 1991. reprint ed. pap. 5.95 (1-879920-00-X) Rain Bird Prods.
— Yo Colite - All By Myself. (Spanish Language Look-Look Bks.). (Illus.). 24p. (SPA.). (J). 1994. write for info. (0-307-71938-3, Golden Bks) Western Pub.
— You're the Scaredy-Cat. (Illus.). 40p. (J). 1991. reprint ed. pap. 5.95 (1-879920-01-8) Rain Bird Prods.

Mayer, Mercer, illus. & abr. A Christmas Carol: Being a Ghost Story of Christmas. LC 86-12651. 48p. (J). (ps up). 1986. lib. bdg. 16.95 (0-02-730310-1, Mac Bks Young Read) S&S Childrens.
Mayer, Mercer, ret. The Sleeping Beauty. LC 84-7195. (Illus.). 48p. (J). (gr. k up). 1984. lib. bdg. 14.95 (0-02-765340-4, Mac Bks Young Read) S&S Childrens.
Mayer, Mercer & Mayer, Marianna. One Frog Too Many. LC 75-6325. (Pied Piper Bks.). (Illus.). (J). (ps-2). 1977. pap. 3.50 (0-8037-6734-X) Dial Bks Young.
— One Frog Too Many. LC 75-6325. (Pied Piper Bks.). (Illus.). 32p. (J). (ps-2). 1985. 9.95 (0-8037-4838-8); lib. bdg. 9.89 (0-8037-4858-2) Dial Bks Young.
Mayer, Mercer, jt. auth. see Mayer, Gina.
Mayer, Michael. Limits of the Heart. 1993. pap. 12.95 (0-89087-700-9) Celestial Arts.
Mayer, Michael F. Foreign Films on American Screens. LC 82-49212. (Cinema Classics Ser.). 126p. 1985. lib. bdg. 27.00 (0-8240-5769-4) Garland.
— The Libel Revolution: A New Look at Defamation & Privacy. 28.75 (0-317-67926-0) Law Arts.
— Rights of Privacy. 251p. (C). 1972. text ed. 7.95 (0-317-67878-7) Law Arts.
Mayer, Michael J. How to Love, Understand & Cope with Teenagers. LC 78-61586. 1979. 10.95 (0-87212-123-2) Libra.
— The Re-Creation of a Nation Through Real Parenting. Parker, Diane, ed. LC 92-54174. 125p. 1992. pap. 9.95 (0-88247-929-6) R & E Pubs.
Mayer, Milton. Biodegradable Man: Selected Essays by Milton Mayer. Stein, Leone, ed. LC 90-30058. 320p. 1990. 24.95 (0-8203-1244-4) U of Ga Pr.
— The Nature of the Beast. Gustafson, W. Eric, ed. LC 74-21243. 376p. 1975. 37.50x (0-87023-176-6) U of Mass Pr.
— Robert Maynard Hutchins: A Memoir. Hicks, John H., ed. LC 92-16512. 1993. 35.00 (0-520-07091-7) U CA Pr.
— They Thought They Were Free: The Germans 1933-45. 2nd ed. LC 55-5137. 1966. pap. text ed. 14.95 (0-226-51192-8, P222) U Ch Pr.
Mayer, Milton, jt. auth. see Boulding, Kenneth E.
Mayer, Milton S. What Can a Man Do? A Selection of His Most Challenging Writings. Gustafson, W. Eric, ed. LC 64-15801. 320p. reprint ed. pap. 91.20 (0-317-09760-1, 2020118) Bks Demand.
Mayer, Mordecai. Israel's Wisdom in Modern Life: Essays & Interpretations of Religious & Cultural Problems Based on the Talmudic & Midrashic Literature. 32.50 (0-87559-147-7) Shalom.
***Mayer, Morris & Melancon, Richard.** The University of Alabama: College of Commerce & Business Administration. (First 75 Years Ser.). 250p. 1995. 49.95 (0-9644291-0-1) U Ala Coll of C & B A.
Mayer, Morris F. A Guide for Child Care Workers. LC 58-10171. 184p. 1958. pap. 16.95 (0-87868-066-7) Child Welfare.
Mayer, Musa. Examining Myself: One Woman's Story of Breast Cancer Treatment & Recovery. 180p. 1993. 19.95 (0-571-19828-7) Faber & Faber.
— Examining Myself: One Woman's Story of Breast Cancer Treatment & Recovery. 180p. 1994. pap. 10.95 (0-571-19845-7) Faber & Faber.
Mayer, Nancy. The Male Mid-Life Crisis: Fresh Starts After 40. 1979. pap. 4.95 (0-451-14847-9, AE2178, Sig) NAL-Dutton.
Mayer, Nancy K. Rainy Day Activities for the Commodore 64. write for info. (0-318-58231-7) P-H.
Mayer, Nathan. Beyond a Reasonable Doubt. (Orig.). 1992. 4.95 (0-87129-166-5, B71) Dramatic Pub.
Mayer, Nonna, jt. ed. see Boy, Daniel.
Mayer, O. B., et al. The Dutch Fork. Holcomb, Brent, ed. (Illus.). 155p. (C). 1982. 20.00 (0-9611610-0-0) Dutch Fork Pr.
Mayer-Oakes, Thomas F., ed. see Kumao, Harada.
Mayer-Oakes, William J. El Inga, a Paleo-Indian Site in the Sierra of Northern Ecuador. LC 86-71457. (Transactions Ser.: Vol. 76, Pt. 4). 1986. pap. 30.00 (0-87169-764-5, T764-MAW) Am Philos.
***Mayer, Oliver.** Blade to the Heat. Date not set. 4.75 (0-8222-1473-3) Dramatists Play.
Mayer, Patricia E., ed. see Holden, William M.
Mayer, Paul. Fresh Vegetable Cookbook. rev. ed. (Illus.). 192p. 1982. pap. 5.95 (0-911954-34-1) Bristol Pub Ent CA.
Mayer, Peter, jt. ed. see Rittberger, Volker.
Mayer, Philip. The Lineage Principle in Gusii Society. LC 79-320820. (International African Institute Ser.: No. 24). 35p. reprint ed. pap. 25.00 (0-8357-3020-4, 2057106) Bks Demand.
Mayer, Philip F. The Mature Spirit: Religion Without Supernatural Hopes. LC 87-6134. 173p. 1987. pap. 10.95 (0-938875-08-6) Pittenbruach Pr.
Mayer, R., jt. auth. see Hoepleman, J.
Mayer, R., jt. auth. see Thiel, W.
Mayer, R. J. & Brown, I. R., eds. Heat Shock Proteins in the Nervous System. (Neuroscience Perspectives Ser.). (Illus.). 297p. 1994. text ed. 67.50 (0-12-480960-X) Acad Pr.
Mayer, R. J. & Walker, J. H., eds. Immunochemical Methods in Cell & Molecular Biology. (Biological Techniques Ser.). 325p. 1988. text ed. 76.00 (0-12-480855-7) Acad Pr.
Mayer, R. John, jt. auth. see Doherty, Fergus J.
Mayer, Ralph. The Artist's Handbook of Materials & Techniques. 5th rev. ed. LC 90-50357. (Illus.). 800p. 1991. 40.00 (0-670-83701-6) Viking Penguin.
— The HarperCollins Dictionary of Art Terms & Techniques: In-Depth Explanations & Examples Covering More Than 3,200 Entries with Extensive Line Drawings. 2nd ed. LC 91-55395. (Illus.). 480p. 1992. pap. 15.00 (0-06-461012-8, PL) HarpC.
— Making CAD-CAM Data Transfer Work: IGES & Other Solutions (a Hands-On Guide) Linden, Jonathan, ed. (Illus.). 250p. 1987. 295.00 (0-932007-13-9) Mgmt Roundtable.
— The Painter's Craft: An Introduction to Artists' Methods & Materials. (Handbook Ser.). (Illus.). 1979. pap. 12.95 (0-14-046369-0, Penguin Bks) Viking Penguin.
Mayer, Rayner M., ed. Design with Reinforced Plastics: A Guide for Engineers & Designers. (Illus.). 212p. (C). 1993. pap. 42.95x (0-85072-294-2, Pub. by Design Council Bks UK) Ashgate Pub Co.
Mayer, Rayner M., jt. auth. see Hancox, Neil.
Mayer, Richard E. Educational Psychology: A Cognitive Approach. (C). 1987. pap. text ed. 59.50 (0-673-39187-6) HarpCollege.
— The Promise of Cognitive Psychology. (Illus.). 136p. (C). 1990. reprint ed. pap. text ed. 17.50 (0-8191-7653-2) U Pr of Amer.
— Thinking, Problem Solving, Cognition. 2nd ed. (C). 1995. pap. text ed. 28.95 (0-7167-2215-1) W H Freeman.
Mayer, Richard E., ed. Teaching & Learning Computer Programming: Multiple Research Perspectives. 336p. 1988. 59.95 (0-8058-0073-5) L Erlbaum Assocs.
Mayer, Richard J. Conflict Management: The Courage to Confront. LC 89-38236. 152p. 1990. 24.50 (0-935470-51-4) Battelle.
— Conflict Management: The Courage to Confront. 2nd ed. LC 94-30934. 1995. 24.50 (0-935470-82-4) Battelle.
Mayer, Richard T., jt. ed. see Bailey, Mary T.
Mayer, Richard T., jt. ed. see Fisher, Joseph L.
Mayer, Richard T., jt. auth. see Soufi, Wahib A.
Mayer, Robern N. The Consumer Movement: Guardians of the Marketplace. (Social Movements Past & Present Ser.). 216p. 1989. pap. 13.95 (0-8057-9719-X, Twayne) Macmillan.
— The Consumer Movement: Guardians of the Marketplace. (Social Movements Past & Present Ser.). 216p. 1989. text ed. 26.95 (0-8057-9718-1, Twayne) Macmillan.
Mayer, Robert. Baseball & Men's Lives: The True Confessions of a Skinny Marink. LC 93-26750. 1994. 12.95 (0-385-30926-0, Delta) Dell.
— The Dreams of Ada: A True Story of Murder, Obsession, & a Small Town. (Illus.). 544p. 1991. pap. 5.99 (0-451-16981-6) NAL-Dutton.
— Minolta Classic Cameras. (Illus.). 170p. (Orig.). (C). 1995. pap. 19.95 (1-883403-17-0, Silver Pixel Pr) Saunders Photo.
— Sweet Salt, A Novel. 132p. (Orig.). 1984. 14.95 (0-933553-02-1); pap. 9.95 (0-933553-03-X) Mariposa Print Pub.
Mayer, Robert & Shuster, Tillie. Developing Shelter Models for the Homeless: Three Program Design Options. 107p. (Orig.). 1985. pap. 10.00 (0-88156-028-6) Comm Serv Soc NY.
Mayer, Robert, et al. Opportunities in Photography Careers. rev. ed. LC 90-50737. (Opportunities in...Ser.). 160p. (YA). (gr. 7 up). 1991. 13.95 (0-8442-8152-2, VGM Career Bks); pap. 10.95 (0-8442-8153-0, VGM Career Bks) NTC Pub Grp.
Mayer, Robert A., intro. Blacks in America: A Photographic Record. LC 86-80319. (Illus.). 60p. (Orig.). 1986. pap. 12.50 (0-935398-12-0, 030) G Eastman Hse.
Mayer, Robert E., et al. Photography Careers. (Opportunities in...Ser.). (Illus.). 160p. 1991. 13.95 (0-8442-6180-7, VGM Career Bks) NTC Pub Grp.
Mayer, Robert G. Embalming: History, Theory & Practice. (Illus.). 475p. (C). 1990. boxed 70.00 (0-8385-2185-1, A2185-5) Appleton & Lange.
Mayer, Robert J. & Griswold, Millie H., eds. Advent Christian Catechism. 70p. 1987. student ed write for info. (1-881909-02-6) Advent Christ Gen Conf.
Mayer, Robert N., ed. Enhancing Consumer Choice: Proceedings, Second International Conference on Research in the Consumer Interest. (Orig.). 1991. pap. text ed. 15.00 (0-945857-01-2) Am Coun Consumer.
Mayer, Robert R. Policy & Program Planning: A Developmental Perspective. (Illus.). 224p. (C). 1985. text ed. write for info. (0-13-684473-1) P-H.
— Social Science & Institutional Change. LC 81-2705. 202p. 1982. text ed. 32.95 (0-87855-432-7) Transaction Pubs.
Mayer, Robert S. Satan's Children. 272p. 1992. mass mkt. 4.99 (0-380-71830-8) Avon.
— Through Divided Minds. 304p. 1992. mass mkt. 4.99 (0-380-71920-7) Avon.
— Through Divided Minds: Probing the Mysteries of Multiple Personalites - A Doctor's First-Person Story. 304p. 1990. pap. 8.95 (0-380-70905-8) Avon.
Mayer, Robert T., tr. Bernard of Clairvaux: The Irishman. LC 78-768. (Cistercian Fathers Ser.). 1978. 7.95 (0-685-87078-2); pap. 4.00 (0-87907-910-X) Cistercian Pubns.
Mayer, Roland, ed. see Horace.
Mayer, Ronald A. Christy Mathewson: A Game-by-Game Profile of a Legendary Pitcher. LC 92-50890. (Illus.). 380p. 1993. lib. bdg. 29.95 (0-89950-821-9) McFarland & Co.
— The Nineteen Thirty-Seven Newark Bears: A Baseball Legend. (Illus.). 300p. (C). 1994. reprint ed. pap. 14.95 (0-8135-2153-X) Rutgers U Pr.
— Perfect! Biographies & Lifetime Statistics of 14 Pitchers of "Perfect" Baseball Games, with Summaries & Boxscores. LC 90-53510. 239p. 1991. lib. bdg. 28.50x (0-89950-571-6) McFarland & Co.
Mayer, Rosemary. Pontormo's Diary. (Illus.). 200p. (C). 1983. 26.95 (0-915570-17-3); pap. 16.95 (0-686-86541-3) Oolp Pr.
***Mayer, S. Suzanne.** Celebrating the Woman You Are. LC 94-49164. (Illumination Bks.). (Illus.). 80p. (Orig.). 1995. pap. 3.95 (0-8091-3559-0) Paulist Pr.
Mayer, Sandy, ed. see Knott, Tara D.
***Mayer, Shelly.** Preparing Dairy Cattle for Show. (Illus.). 48p. (C). 1995. pap. text ed. 4.00 (0-932147-25-9) Hoard & Sons Co.
Mayer, Sigrid, jt. auth. see Eggers, Walter.
Mayer-Skumanz, Lene. Caroline Moves In. (Illus.). 96p. (J). (gr. 1-3). 1988. pap. 2.95 (0-8120-3938-6) Barron.
— The Tower. (J). (gr. 2-5). 1993. 12.95 (965-465-000-2) Pitspopany.
Mayer-Spitzweck, E., jt. auth. see Hussain, Maria.
Mayer, Stefan & Weber, Michael. Bibliographie Zur Linguistischen Gesprachsforschung. (Germanistische Linguistik Ser.). 216p. 1983. write for info. (3-487-07399-4, Pub. by Georg Olms GW) Lubrecht & Cramer.
Mayer, Stephen J., jt. ed. see Mench, Joy A.
***Mayer, Steve.** The Sultis Variation of the Yugoslav Attack. (Studies in Contemporary Opening Theory). 280p. (Orig.). 1994. pap. 22.95 (1-886040-13-3) Hypermodern Pr.
Mayer, Steven E. & Scheie, David. Supporting Low Income Neighborhood Organizations: A Guide for Community Foundations. Lilya, Mary, ed. (Illus.). 1989. write for info. (0-318-65778-3) Rainbow Research.
Mayer, Susan, ed. The Best in Sales & Marketing Strategies for Point-of-Use Water Treatment Professionals. (Illus.). 130p. 1993. 59.95 (0-9609052-7-8) Clean Mgmt Inst.
Mayer, Susan B., jt. auth. see Rogers, Donna C.
Mayer, Susan M. & Reese, Becky D. American Images: Selections from the James & Mari Michener Collection of 20th Century American Art. 2nd ed. (Illus.). 28p. 1981. pap. 12.95 (0-935213-06-6) A M Huntington Art.
— A Woman's Place. (Illus.). 20p. 1977. pap. 4.95 (0-935213-05-8) A M Huntington Art.
Mayer, T. F., ed. Thomas Starkey: A Dialogue Between Pole & Lupset. (Royal Historical Society: Camden Fourth Ser.: No. 37). 176p. 1989. 30.00 (0-86193-119-X) Boydell & Brewer.
***Mayer, T. W.** The Caribbean & Its People. (People & Places Ser.). (Illus.). 48p. (J). (gr. 5-8). 1995. 15.95 (1-56847-338-9) Thomson Lrning.

An Asterisk (*) at the beginning of an entry indicates that the title is appearing in BIP for the first time.

Mayer, Tamar. Women & the Israeli Occupation: The Politics of Change. LC 94-3886. (International Studies of Women & Places). (Illus.). 240p. 1994. 59.95x (*0-415-09545-X*, B0129); pap. 16.95 (*0-415-09546-8*, B0133) Routledge.

Mayer, Thom. Emergency Management of Pediatric Trauma. (Illus.). 531p. 1985. text ed. 115.00 (*0-7216-6189-0*) Saunders.

Mayer, Thom, ed. see Schwartz, George & Cayten, C. Gene.

Mayer, Thomas. The Changing Past: Egyptian Historiography of the Urabi Revolt, 1882-1983. LC 87-25410. 117p. 1988. pap. text ed. 17.95 (*0-8130-0889-1*) U Press Fla.

— Doing Economic Research: Essays on the Applied Methodology of Economics. (Economists of the Twentieth Century Ser.). 200p. 1995. 69.95 (*1-85278-939-5*, Pub. by E Elgar Pub UK) Ashgate Pub Co.

— Monetarism & Macroeconomic Policy. 256p. 1990. text ed. 69.95 (*1-85278-088-6*, Pub. by E Elgar Pub UK) Ashgate Pub Co.

— Monetary Theory. 416p. 1990. text ed. 109.95 (*1-85278-180-7*, Pub. by E Elgar Pub UK) Ashgate Pub Co.

***Mayer, Thomas, et al.** Money, Banking, & the Economy. 1996. student ed, pap. text ed. write for info. (*0-393-96849-9*) Norton.

Mayer, Thomas. Truth Versus Precision in Economics. 192p. 1992. 49.95 (*1-85278-546-2*, Pub. by E Elgar Pub UK); pap. 12.95 (*1-85278-552-7*, Pub. by E Elgar Pub UK) Ashgate Pub Co.

Mayer, Thomas, ed. The Political Economy of American Monetary Policy. (Illus.). 314p. (C). 1993. pap. 18.95 (*0-521-44651-1*) Cambridge U Pr.

***Mayer, Thomas & Duesenberry, James.** Money, Banking, & the Economy. 1996. teacher ed, pap. text ed. write for info. (*0-393-96850-2*) Norton.

***Mayer, Thomas & Sheffrin, Steven M., eds.** Fiscal & Monetary Policy. LC 94-46730. (International Library of Critical Writings in Economics: Vol. 52). 1995. 140.00 (*1-85898-009-7*, Pub. by E Elgar Pub UK) Ashgate Pub Co.

Mayer, Thomas & Spinelli, Franco. Macroeconomics & Macroeconomic Policy Issues. 271p. 1991. text ed. 68.95 (*1-85628-219-8*, Pub. by Avebury Pub UK) Ashgate Pub Co.

Mayer, Thomas, jt. ed. see Fideler, Paul.

Mayer, Thomas, tr. see Mayer, Margarita.

Mayer, Thomas, et al. Money, Banking, & the Economy. (C). 1993. pap. text ed. write for info. (*0-393-96302-0*) Norton.

— Money, Banking, & the Economy. 4th ed. (Illus.). (C). 1990. text ed. 49.95 (*0-393-95927-9*) Norton.

— Money, Banking, & the Economy. 5th ed. (C). 1993. text ed. 57.95 (*0-393-96300-4*) Norton.

— Money, Banking, & the Economy. 5th ed. (C). 1993. pap. text ed. 14.95 (*0-393-96301-2*) Norton.

— Money, Banking, & the Economy. 6th ed. LC 95-13313. (C). 1995. text ed. write for info. (*0-393-96848-0*) Norton.

Mayer, Thomas F. Analytical Marxism. LC 94-4601. (Contemporary Social Theory Ser.). 1994. 48.00 (*0-8039-4680-5*); pap. 24.95 (*0-8039-4681-3*) Sage.

— Mathematical Models of Group Structure. LC 74-1031. (Studies in Sociology). (C). 1975. pap. text ed. 3.00 (*0-672-61212-7*, Bobbs) Macmillan.

— Thomas Starkey & the Commonweal: Humanist Politics & Religion in the Reign of Henry VIII. (Cambridge Studies in Early Modern British History). 328p. (C). 1989. 69.95 (*0-521-36104-4*) Cambridge U Pr.

Mayer, Toby G., jt. auth. see Fleming, Richard W.

Mayer, Tom G. & Gatchel, Robert J. Functional Restoration for Spinal Disorders: The Sports Medicine Approach. LC 87-29859. (Illus.). 321p. 1988. text ed. 55.00 (*0-8121-1137-0*) Williams & Wilkins.

Mayer, Tom G., et al. Contemporary Conservative Care for Painful Spinal Disorders. LC 91-9298. (Illus.). 588p. 1991. text ed. 99.00 (*0-8121-1344-6*) Williams & Wilkins.

Mayer, Virginia. Festival Marketplaces: The Formula for Success. Murphy, Jenny & Kailo, Andrea, eds. 28p. (Orig.). 1986. pap. 17.00 (*0-317-04910-0*) Natl Coun Econ Dev.

Mayer, Walter G., jt. ed. see Alippi, Adriano.

Mayer, William G. The Changing American Mind: How & Why American Public Opinion Changed Between 1960 & 1988. LC 92-26578. 400p. (C). 1992. text ed. 52.50 (*0-472-09498-X*); pap. 18.95 (*0-472-06498-3*) U of Mich Pr.

***Mayer, William G., et al.** In Pursuit of the White House: How We Choose Our Presidential Nominees. (Illus.). 480p. (Orig.). (C). 1995. pap. text ed. 24.95x (*1-56643-027-5*) Chatham Hse Pubs.

Mayer-Wolf, Eddy, et al, eds. Stochastic Analysis: Liber Amicorum for Moshe Zakai. (Illus.). 532p. 1991. text ed. 83.00 (*0-12-481005-5*) Acad Pr.

***Mayerchak, Patrick M.** East Asia & the Western Pacific 1995. 28th ed. 168p. 1995. pap. 9.50 (*0-943448-91-3*) Stryker-Post.

— Scholars' Guide to Washington, D. C., for Southeast Asian Studies: Brunei, Burma, Cambodia, Indonesia, Laos, Malaysia, Philippines, Singapore, Thailand, & Vietnam. David, Zdenek V., ed. LC 82-19454. 412p. 1983. 29.95 (*0-87474-626-4*, Johns Hopkins); pap. text ed. 12.95 (*0-87474-625-6*, Johns Hopkins) W Wilson Ctr Pr.

Mayerchak, Patrick N., jt. auth. see Indorf, Hans H.

Mayergoyz, I. D. Mathematical Models of Hysteresis. (Illus.). 248p. 1990. 59.50 (*0-387-97352-4*) Spr-Verlag.

Mayerik, Val, jt. auth. see Gerber, Steve.

Mayeroff, Milton. On Caring. LC 90-55052. 128p. 1990. reprint ed. pap. 10.00 (*0-06-092024-6*, PL) HarpC.

Mayers, D. F., jt. auth. see Morton, K. W.

Mayers, David. The Ambassadors & America's Soviet Policy. (Illus.). 352p. 1995. 35.00 (*0-19-506802-5*) OUP.

— George Kennan & the Dilemmas of U. S. Foreign Policy. 416p. 1990. reprint ed. pap. 12.95 (*0-19-506318-X*) OUP.

Mayers, David A. Cracking the Monolith: U. S. Policy Against the Sino-Soviet Alliance, 1949-1955. LC 86-40. (Political Traditions in Foreign Policy Ser.). xiii, 176p. 1986. text ed. 27.50 (*0-8071-1287-9*) La State U Pr.

Mayers, Florence C. ABC: National Museum of American History. (ABC Ser.). (Illus.). 32p. (J). 1989. 12.95 (*0-8109-1875-7*) Abrams.

— ABC: The Wild West Buffalo Bill Historical Center, Cody, Wyoming. LC 90-440. (Illus.). 32p. (J). 1990. 12.95 (*0-8109-1903-6*) Abrams.

— ABC; Egyptian Art from the Brooklyn Museum. (ABC Ser.). (Illus.). 32p. 1988. 12.95 (*0-8109-0888-3*) Abrams.

— ABC Museum of Fine Arts, Boston. (Illus.). 32p. 1986. 12.95 (*0-8109-1847-1*) Abrams.

— The ABC Museum of Modern Art, New York. (ABC Ser.). (Illus.). 32p. 1986. 12.95 (*0-8109-1849-8*) Abrams.

— The ABC National Air & Space Museum. (ABC Ser.). (Illus.). 32p. 1987. 12.95 (*0-8109-1859-5*) Abrams.

— ABC: the Alef-Bet Book: The Israel Museum, Jerusalem. LC 88-27501. (ABC Ser.). (Illus.). 32p. (J). (gr. k up). 1989. 12.95 (*0-8109-1885-4*) Abrams.

— Baseball ABC. LC 94-1167. (J). 1994. write for info. (*0-8109-1938-9*) Abrams.

— A Russian ABC: Featuring Masterpieces from the Hermitage, St. Petersburg. (ABC Ser.). (Illus.). 36p. (J). 1992. 12.95 (*0-8109-1919-2*) Abrams.

Mayers, Harry R. & Brunsvold, Brian G. Drafting Patent License Agreements. 3rd ed. LC 90-48874. 292p. 1991. text ed. 68.00 (*0-87179-674-0*, 0674) BNA.

Mayers, Jeff, jt. auth. see Hughes, John.

Mayers, Lewis. The American Legal System: The Administration of Justice in the United States by Judicial, Administrative, Military, & Arbitral Tribunals. rev. ed. xi, 594p. 1981. reprint ed. lib. bdg. 42.50 (*0-8377-0839-7*) Rothman.

— Federal Service: A Study of the System of Personnel Administration of the United States Government. (Brookings Institution Reprint Ser.). reprint ed. lib. bdg. 36.50 (*0-697-00165-2*) Irvington.

— The Machinery of Justice: An Introduction to Legal Structure & Process. (Quality Paperback Ser.: No. 261). 115p. 1976. reprint ed. pap. 10.00 (*0-8226-0261-X*) Littlefield.

— Shall We Amend the Fifth Amendment? LC 78-6206. 341p. 1978. reprint ed. text ed. 65.00 (*0-313-20394-6*, MASH, Greenwood Pr) Greenwood.

Mayers, Marlene. Clinical Care Plans: Surgical Nursing. 157p. (Orig.). (C). 1989. pap. text ed. 19.95 (*0-939605-02-3*) Markham-McKenzie.

Mayers, Marlene, jt. auth. see Watson, Annita.

Mayers, Marlene G. Clinical Care Plans: Medical Nursing. 141p. (Orig.). (C). 1989. pap. text ed. 19.95 (*0-939605-01-5*) Markham-McKenzie.

— Clinical Care Plans: Orthopedic & Neurologic Nursing. 119p. (C). 1989. pap. text ed. 19.95 (*0-939605-03-1*) Markham-McKenzie.

— Clinical Care Plans: Pediatric Nursing. 340p. (Orig.). (C). 1991. pap. 32.50 (*0-939605-04-X*) Markham-McKenzie.

— Clinical Care Plans: Perinatal Nursing. (Illus.). 280p. (Orig.). (C). 1991. pap. 32.50 (*0-939605-05-8*) Markham-McKenzie.

Mayers, Marlene G. & Jacobson, Annette L., eds. Clinical Care Plans for Perinatal-Neonatal Nursing. (McGraw-Hill Clinical Care Plans Ser.). 298p. 1995. pap. 22.00 (*0-07-105463-4*) Hlth Prof Div.

— McGraw-Hill Clinical Care Plans for Medical-Surgical. (McGraw-Hill Clinical Care Plans Ser.). 362p. 1995. pap. 22.00 (*0-07-105464-2*) Hlth Prof Div.

Mayers, Marlene G. & Pankratz, Carol, eds. McGraw-Hill Clinical Care Plans for Pediatric Nursing. (McGraw-Hill Clinical Care Plans Ser.). 330p. 1995. pap. 22.00 (*0-07-105462-6*) Hlth Prof Div.

Mayers, Marvin, ed. Languages of Guatemala. (Janua Linguarum, Ser. Practica: No. 23). (Orig.). 1966. pap. text ed. 58.70 (*90-279-0642-4*) Mouton.

Mayers, Marvin K. Christianity Confronts Culture. enl. rev. ed. 1987. 22.99 (*0-310-28901-7*) Zondervan.

— A Look at Latin American Lifestyles. 2nd ed. (Museum of Anthropology Publications: No. 2). 120p. 1981. pap. 8.00 (*0-88312-170-0*); fiche 8.00x (*0-88312-238-3*) Summer Instit Ling.

Mayers, Marvin K. & Rath, Daniel D., eds. Nucleation in Papua New Guinea Cultures. LC 88-81188. (International Museum of Cultures Publications: No. 23). 120p. (Orig.). 1988. pap. 4.00 (*0-88312-177-8*) Summer Instit Ling.

— Nucleation in Papua New Guinea Cultures, 2 fiche, Set. LC 88-81188. (International Museum of Cultures Publications: No. 23). 120p. (Orig.). 1988. fiche 8.00 (*0-88312-262-6*) Summer Instit Ling.

Mayers, Marvin K., jt. auth. see Grunlan, Stephen A.

Mayers, Marvin K., jt. auth. see Lingenfelter, Sherwood G.

Mayers, Phil D. Give Us This Day Our Daily Bread: Spiritual-Simple-Educational, a Step-by-Step Guide to Baking Bread. (Illus.). 32p. 1993. 14.99 (*0-9635606-1-1*) P D Mayers.

***Mayers, Raymond S.** Financial Management for Nonprofit Human Service Agencies: Text - Cases - Readings. (Illus.). 358p. 1989. pap. 37.95 (*0-398-06273-0*) C C Thomas.

— Financial Management for Nonprofit Human Service Agencies: Text - Cases - Readings. (Illus.). 358p. (C). 1989. text ed. 67.95x (*0-398-05571-8*) C C Thomas.

Mayers, Raymond S., et al. Dilemmas in Human Service Management. LC 93-50540. (Social Work Ser.: Vol. 23). 184p. (C). 1994. text ed. 31.95 (*0-8261-7740-9*) Springer Pub.

Mayers, Raymond S., et al, eds. Hispanic Substance Abuse. LC 92-43848. (Illus.). 258p. (C). 1993. text ed. 51.95x (*0-398-05849-0*) C C Thomas.

— Hispanic Substance Abuse. LC 92-43848. (Illus.). 258p. 1993. pap. 30.95 (*0-398-06274-9*) C C Thomas.

Mayers, Ronald B. Evangelical Perspectives: Toward a Biblical Balance. LC 86-28966. 204p. (Orig.). 1987. lib. bdg. 44.00 (*0-8191-6062-8*); pap. text ed. 21.00 (*0-8191-6063-6*) U Pr of Amer.

Mayers, Susan, jt. ed. see Berry, Nancy.

Mayers, T. K. Understanding Weapons & Arms Control: A Guide to the Issues. 4th rev. ed. (Illus.). 157p. 1991. text ed. 9.95 (*0-08-037438-7*) Brasseys Inc.

Mayers, W. E. The Chinese Reader's Manual: A Handbook of Biographical, Historical, Mythological, & General Literary Reference. 1972. 250.00 (*0-87968-855-6*) Gordon Pr.

Mayers, William F., ed. Treaties Between the Empire of China & Foreign Powers. 1976. lib. bdg. 59.95 (*0-8490-2761-6*) Gordon Pr.

Mayersberg, Paul. Homme Fatale. 1994. mass mkt. 4.99 (*0-312-95177-9*) St Martin.

— The Siege. 1999. pap. write for info. (*0-670-81367-2*) Viking Penguin.

Mayerski, Kathy, ed. see Moreno, Richard.

Mayerski, Kathy, ed. see Tegeler, Dorothy.

Mayerson, Arlene B. Americans with Disabilities Act Annotated: Legislative History, Regulations & Commentary. 1994. 350.00 (*0-318-72575-4*) Clark Boardman Callaghan.

Mayerson, Evelyn W. The Cat Who Escaped from Steerage. LC 90-32890. 80p. (J). (gr. 4-6). 1990. text ed. 13.95 (*0-684-19209-8*, C Scribner Sons Young) S&S Childrens.

— Dade County Pine. 464p. 1994. 22.95 (*0-525-93646-7*, Dutton) NAL-Dutton.

— Miami. 496p. 1995. pap. 5.99 (*0-451-18147-6*, Sig) NAL-Dutton.

— Miami: A Saga. large type ed. LC 94-17035. 778p. Date not set. bds. 22.95 (*0-7862-0267-X*) Thorndike Pr.

— Well & Truly. 400p. 1991. pap. 5.50 (*0-451-16988-3*, Sig) NAL-Dutton.

— Well & Truly. large type ed. LC 90-22548. 622p. 1991. reprint ed. lib. bdg. 19.95 (*1-56054-084-2*) Thorndike Pr.

Mayerson, Philip. Classic Mythology in Literature, Art, & Music. (C). 1971. text ed. 63.50 (*0-673-15690-7*) HarpCollege.

Mayes. The Perfect Guide to Learning WordPerfect 5.1. 192p. (C). 1992. pap. text ed. 18.00 (*0-87835-899-4*) Boyd & Fraser.

— Supervision for Midwives. 1995. pap. 24.95 (*1-898507-14-7*, Focal) Buttrwrth-Heinemann.

Mayes, A. D. Deuteronomy. (New Century Bible Ser.). 352p. 1979. 15.95 (*0-551-00804-0*) Attic Pr.

— Deuteronomy. Clements, Ronald E., ed. (New Century Bible Commentary Ser.). 1981. pap. 19.99 (*0-8028-1882-X*) Eerdmans.

Mayes, A. D., ed. see Lindars, Barnabas.

Mayes, Andrew R. Human Organic Memory Disorders. (Problems in the Behavioral Sciences Ser.: No. 7). (Illus.). 324p. 1988. pap. 29.95 (*0-521-34879-X*) Cambridge U Pr.

Mayes, Ann S., jt. ed. see Kerry, Trevor.

Mayes, Ann S., jt. ed. see Moon, Bob.

Mayes, Anne C. & Mayes, David G. Introductory Economic Statistics. LC 75-15838. 233p. reprint ed. pap. 66.50 (*0-685-20353-0*, 2029801) Bks Demand.

Mayes, Catherine S., contrib. Bill Viola: The City of Man. (Illus.). 10p. 1989. 5.00 (*0-934358-24-9*) Fuller Mus Art.

Mayes, Dave, jt. auth. see Davis, Kathleen.

Mayes, David, jt. auth. see Britton, Andrew.

Mayes, David, et al. Public Interest & Market Pressures: Problems Posed by Europe, 1992. LC 92-32754. 220p. 1993. text ed. 65.00 (*0-312-09102-8*) St Martin.

Mayes, David G., ed. The European Challenge: Industry's Response to the 1992 Programme. 464p. (C). 1992. text ed. 62.50 (*0-472-10372-5*) U of Mich Pr.

— The External Implications of European Integration. 224p. text ed. 75.00 (*0-472-10452-7*) U of Mich Pr.

Mayes, David G. & Hart, Peter. The Single Market Programme As Stimulus to Change: Britain & Germany. (National Institute of Economic & Social Research Occasional Papers: No. 47). (Illus.). 250p. (C). 1994. 54.95 (*0-521-47156-7*) Cambridge U Pr.

Mayes, David G., jt. auth. see Mayes, Anne C.

Mayes, Dianne S. & Stafford, Dorothy D. It's Christmas! Welcome to Our House! Easy & Elegant Holiday Menus. (Illus.). 256p. (Orig.). 1989. pap. text ed. 12.95 (*0-685-25968-4*) Deanne Inc.

Mayes, Donald S. Managed Dental Care: A Guide to Dental HMOs. Brennan, Mary, ed. LC 93-78068. 248p. (Orig.). 1993. pap. 47.00 (*0-89154-464-X*) Intl Found Employ.

Mayes, Edward. Lucius Q. C. Lamar: His Life, Times & Speeches, 1825-1893. LC 70-173065. reprint ed. 47.50 (*0-404-04613-4*) AMS Pr.

Mayes, Frances. After Such Pleasures. LC 79-14984. 1979. 9.95 (*0-913282-20-0*); pap. 4.75 (*0-913282-21-9*) Seven Woods Pr.

— Climbing Aconcagua. (Sansfolio Ser.: No. 1). 8p. 1977. pap. 1.75 (*0-913282-11-1*) Seven Woods Pr.

— The Discovery of Poetry. 583p. (C). 1987. pap. text ed. 22.75 (*0-15-517678-1*) HB Coll Pubs.

— The Discovery of Poetry. 2nd ed. 600p. (C). 1993. pap. text ed. write for info. (*0-15-500162-0*) HB Coll Pubs.

— Ex Voto. (Lost Road Ser.: No. 42). 64p. (Orig.). 1995. pap. 10.95 (*0-918786-47-9*) Lost Roads.

— January Sixth, Quarter of Four. (Flowering Quince Poetry Ser.: No. 1). (Illus.). 20p. (Orig.). 1978. pap. 7.50 (*0-940592-02-9*) Heyeck Pr.

Mayes, Gary, jt. auth. see Spader, Dann.

***Mayes, Gary R.** Now What! Resting in the Lord When Life Doesn't Make Sense. 176p. (Orig.). 1995. pap. 9.99 (*0-89107-856-8*) Crossway Bks.

***Mayes, Herb.** Why Sue: A Journey Through Life's Darkest Days. 142p. (Orig.). 1995. pap. write for info. (*1-885591-93-4*) Morris Pubng.

Mayes, Herbert R. Alger: A Biography Without a Hero. (Illus.). 247p. 1978. reprint ed. 33.00 (*0-686-35758-2*) G K Westgard.

Mayes, J. T., jt. ed. see Kibby, Michael R.

Mayes, James R. Small Favors. LC 94-19573. 303p. 1994. 19.95 (*1-55583-258-X*) Alyson Pubns.

Mayes, Janis, tr. see Dadie, Bernard B.

Mayes, Janis A., jt. ed. see Adams, Anne V.

Mayes, John A. Quantum Velocity of Light: The Unification of Quantum & Classical Physics. LC 83-61674. (C). 1984. text ed. 35.00 (*0-9611548-0-2*) Quantum Pubns.

***Mayes, John B. & Thurston, Rosemary P.** Instructor-Student Workbook & Study Guide: For Anatomy & Physiology Text Book. (Illus.). 118p. 1994. 16.50 (*0-916973-06-9*) Burnell Co.

Mayes, Joseph R., ed. Virginia Lawyer: A Basic Practice Handbook. suppl. ed. 1991. 50.00 (*0-87473-907-1*) Michie Butterworth.

Mayes, Joseph R., ed. see Virginia Bar Association, Virginia Lawyer Committee of Young Lawyers Staff.

Mayes, Karen. One Hundred One Ways to Love a Black Man! LC 93-86782. 72p. (Orig.). 1994. pap. 7.95 (*1-882368-03-7*) Quantum Christ.

— One Hundred-One Ways to Love a Black Woman! (Illus.). 72p. (Orig.). 1994. pap. 7.95 (*1-882368-04-5*) Quantum Christ.

Mayes, Karen, ed. see Barkley, Zelphia.

Mayes, Karen, ed. see Service, Ron.

Mayes, Kathleen. Muffin Magic...& More: Baking Secrets Your Mother Never Told You. LC 93-25105. (Illus.). 208p. (Orig.). 1993. 12.95 (*0-88007-201-6*) Woodbridge Pr.

Mayes, Kathleen & Gottfried, Sandra. Boutique Bean Pot: Exciting Bean Varieties in Superb New Recipes! LC 92-7572. (Illus.). 208p. (Orig.). 1992. pap. 12.95 (*0-88007-196-6*) Woodbridge Pr.

— Roots: A Vegetarian Bounty. large type ed. LC 94-48213. (Illus.). 208p. (Orig.). 1995. pap. 14.95 (*0-88007-206-7*) Woodbridge Pr.

Mayes, Kathleen L. The Perfect Guide to WordPerfect 5.1 for Windows. LC 92-29046. 1992. write for info. (*0-87835-968-0*) Boyd & Fraser.

— WordPerfect 5.1 for Windows. 656p. 1993. write for info. (*0-87835-966-4*) Boyd & Fraser.

Mayes, Linda, tr. see Rustow, Hanns-Joachim.

Mayes, M. A. & Barrow, M. G., eds. Aquatic Toxicology & Risk Assessment: Fourteenth Volume. (Special Technical Publication Ser.: No. 1124). (Illus.). 385p. 1992. text ed. 89.00 (*0-8031-1425-7*, 04-011240-16) ASTM.

Mayes, Mary E. Nurse's Aide Study Manual. 3rd ed. LC 75-28796. (Illus.). 283p. 1976. text ed. 24.95 (*0-7216-6191-2*) Saunders.

Mayes, Philip E., jt. ed. see Bentz, Valerie M.

***Mayes, S.** Baby Animals. (Young Nature Ser.). (Illus.). 32p. (J). (ps-1). 1995. pap. 5.95 (*0-7460-1652-2*, Usborne) EDC.

— Baby Animals. (Young Nature Ser.). (Illus.). 32p. (J). (ps-1). 1995. lib. bdg. 13.96 (*0-88110-725-5*, Usborne) EDC.

— Baby Animals Board Book. (Young Nature Board Book Ser.). (Illus.). 12p. (J). (ps up). 1995. 4.50 (*0-7460-1976-9*, Usborne) EDC.

— How Do Animals Talk? (Starting Point Science Ser.). (Illus.). 24p. (J). (gr. 1 up). 1991. lib. bdg. 11.96 (*0-88110-549-X*, Usborne); pap. 3.95 (*0-7460-0600-4*, Usborne) EDC.

— How Does a Bird Fly? (Starting Point Science Ser.). (Illus.). 24p. (J). (gr. 1 up). 1991. lib. bdg. 11.96 (*0-88110-546-5*, Usborne); pap. 3.95 (*0-7460-0694-2*, Usborne) EDC.

— Life on Earth. (Starting Point Science Ser.). (Illus.). 144p. (J). (gr. k up). 1995. pap. 17.95 (*0-7460-1793-6*, Usborne); pap. 17.95 (*0-7460-1973-4*, Usborne) EDC.

— What Makes a Flower Grow? (Starting Point Science Ser.). (Illus.). 24p. (J). (gr. 1-4). 1989. lib. bdg. 11.96 (*0-88110-381-0*, Usborne); pap. 3.95 (*0-7460-0275-0*, Usborne) EDC.

— What Makes It Rain? (Starting Point Science Ser.). (Illus.). 24p. (J). (gr. 1-4). 1989. lib. bdg. 11.96 (*0-88110-379-9*, Usborne); pap. 3.95 (*0-7460-0274-2*, Usborne) EDC.

— What's Inside You? (Starting Point Science Ser.). (Illus.). 24p. (J). (gr. 1 up). 1991. lib. bdg. 11.96 (*0-88110-550-3*, Usborne); pap. 3.95 (*0-7460-0602-0*, Usborne) EDC.

— What's Out in Space? (Starting Point Science Ser.). (Illus.). 24p. (J). (gr. 1-4). 1990. lib. bdg. 11.96 (*0-88110-443-4*, Usborne); pap. 3.95 (*0-7460-0430-3*, Usborne) EDC.

— What's under the Ground? (Starting Point Science Ser.). (Illus.). 24p. (J). (gr. 1-4). 1989. pap. 3.95 (*0-7460-0357-9*, Usborne) EDC.

— Where Do Babies Come From? (Starting Point Science Ser.). (Illus.). 24p. (J). (gr. 1 up). 1992. lib. bdg. 11.96 (*0-88110-547-3*, Usborne); pap. 3.95 (*0-7460-0690-X*, Usborne) EDC.

— Where Does Electricity Come From? (Starting Point Science Ser.). (Illus.). 24p. (J). (gr. 1-4). 1989. pap. 3.95 (*0-7460-0358-7*, Usborne) EDC.

An Asterisk (*) at the beginning of an entry indicates that the title is appearing in BIP for the first time.

— Where Does Rubbish Go? (Starting Point Science Ser.). (Illus.). 24p. (J). (gr. 1 up). 1992. lib. bdg. 11.96 (*0-88110-551-1*, Usborne); pap. 3.95 (*0-7460-0627-6*, Usborne) EDC.

— Why Is Night Dark? (Starting Point Science Ser.). (Illus.). 24p. (J). (gr. 1-4). 1990. lib. bdg. 11.96 (*0-88110-442-6*, Usborne); pap. 3.95 (*0-7460-0428-1*, Usborne) EDC.

Mayes, S., et al. Starting Point Science, Vol. 2. (J). (gr. 4-7). 1992. 12.95 (*0-7460-0655-1*, Usborne) EDC.

Mayes, Sean, jt. auth. see Cann, Kevin.

Mayes, Sharon. Immune. 1987. 16.95 (*0-89823-096-9*); pap. 9.95 (*0-89823-109-4*) New Rivers Pr.

***Mayes, Stephen, ed.** The Critical Mirror: A History of Postwar Journalism. LC 95-60603. (Illus.). 240p. (Orig.). 1995. pap. 29.95 (*0-500-27848-2*) Thames Hudson.

Mayes, Stephen & Stein, Lyndall, eds. Positive Lives - Responses to HIV: A Photodocumentary. LC 93-40472. 1993. 29.95 (*0-304-32846-4*, InBook) Cassell.

Mayes, Sue. Dinosaurs. (Young Nature Ser.). (Illus.). 32p. (J). (gr. k-1). 1993. lib. bdg. 13.96 (*0-88110-641-0*, Usborne); pap. 5.95 (*0-7460-1020-6*, Usborne) EDC.

***Mayes, Susan.** Earth & Space. (Starting Point Science Ser.). (Illus.). 144p. (J). (gr. 1 up). 1995. 17.95 (*0-7460-1971-8*, Usborne) EDC.

— What's the Earth Made Of? (Starting Point Science Ser.). (Illus.). 24p. (J). (ps up). 1995. lib. bdg. 11.96 (*0-88110-752-2*, Usborne); pap. 3.95 (*0-7460-1709-X*, Usborne) EDC.

Mayes, Thorn L. Wireless Communication in the United States: The Early Development of American Radio Operating Companies. Goodnow, Arthur C. et al, eds. (Illus.). 248p. 1989. pap. text ed. 29.95 (*0-9625170-0-3*) NE Wireless & Steam Mus.

Mayes, Vernon O. Nanise: A Navajo Herbal. 1990. pap. 27.00 (*0-912586-62-1*) Navajo Coll Pr.

***Mayes, Vernon O. & Rominger, James M.** Navajoland Plant Catalog. viii, 72p. (Orig.). (C). 1994. pap. 7.00 (*0-9628075-5-9*) Natl Woodlands Pub.

Mayeski, Marie A. Women: Models of Liberation. LC 87-62399. 256p. (Orig.). (C). 1989. pap. 12.95 (*1-55612-086-9*) Sheed & Ward MO.

Mayeski, Marie A., ed. A Rocking-Horse Catholic: A Caryll Houselander Reader. LC 90-62084. 224p. (Orig.). (C). 1991. pap. 12.95 (*1-55612-401-5*) Sheed & Ward MO.

***Mayesky.** Creative Activities for Young Children IG. 5th ed. 1995. teacher ed 14.00 (*0-8273-5887-3*) Delmar.

Mayesky, Mary. Creative Activities for Young Children. 5th ed. LC 94-21328. 720p. 1994. pap. text ed. 29.95 (*0-8273-5886-5*) Delmar.

Mayesky, Mary E. Creative Activities for Children in the Early Primary Grades. 250p. 1986. pap. text ed. 19.95 (*0-8273-2573-8*) Delmar.

Mayesky, Mary E. & Nueman, Donald. Creative Activities for Young Children. 4th ed. Wlodkowski, Raymond J., ed. LC 94-21328. 560p. 1989. teacher ed 14.00 (*0-8273-3959-3*); pap. text ed. 29.95 (*0-8273-3958-5*) Delmar.

Mayeur, Jean-Marie & Hilaire, Yves-Marie. Dictionnaire du Monde Religieux dans la France Contemporaine, Vol. 1: Les Jesuites. Duclos, Paul, ed. 272p. (FRE.). 1985. 125.00 (*0-8288-9489-2*) Fr & Eur.

— Dictionnaire du Monde Religieux dans la France Contemporaine, Vol. 2: L'Alsace. Vogler, Bernard, ed. 483p. (FRE.). 1987. 125.00 (*0-8288-9490-6*) Fr & Eur.

— Dictionnaire du Monde Religieux dans la France Contemporaine, Vol. 3: La Bretagne. Lagree, Michel, ed. 428p. (FRE.). 1985. pap. write for info. (*0-7859-5243-8*) Fr & Eur.

— Dictionnaire du Monde Religieux dans la France Contemporaine, Vol. 4: Lille-Flandres. Caudron, Andre, ed. 504p. (FRE.). 1990. 125.00 (*0-8288-9492-2*) Fr & Eur.

Mayeur, Jean-Marie & Reberioux, Madeleine. The Third Republic from Its Origins to the Great War, 1871-1914. (Cambridge History of Modern France Ser.: No. 4). (Illus.). 412p. 1988. pap. 19.95 (*0-521-35857-4*) Cambridge U Pr.

Mayeux, Peter. Broadcast News: Writing & Reporting. 432p. (C). 1991. pap. write for info. (*0-697-05573-6*) Brown & Benchmark.

— Broadcast News: Writing & Reporting. 432p. (C). 1995. pap. write for info. (*0-697-20151-1*) Brown & Benchmark.

— Writing for the Electronic Media. 2nd ed. 464p. 1994. pap. write for info. (*0-697-14399-6*) Brown & Benchmark.

Mayeux, Richard & Rosen, Wilma G., eds. The Dementias. (Advances in Neurology Ser.: Vol. 38). 288p. 1983. text ed. 80.00 (*0-89004-696-4*) Raven.

***Mayfield.** How to Control Your Destiny. 160p. 1994. per., pap. text ed. 15.95 (*0-8403-9687-2*) Kendall-Hunt.

Mayfield, Barbara J. Kid's Club: Nutrition Learning Activities for Young Children. 400p. 1992. 150.00 (*1-883983-00-2*); 60.00 (*1-883983-01-0*) Noteworthy Creat.

— The Kid's Club Cubs & the Search for the Treasures of the Pyramid. (Illus.). 40p. (Orig.). (J). (ps-2). 1994. pap. 24.95 (*1-883983-15-0*) Noteworthy Creat.

— Nutrition Notes: Musical Nutrition Education to Sing & Color, Set. (Illus.). 80p. (J). (ps-2). 1992. audio, pap. 12.00 (*1-883983-02-9*) Noteworthy Creat.

— Teaching for a Lifetime: Nutrition Education for Young Children. 70p. 1994. vhs 45.95 (*1-883983-25-8*) Noteworthy Creat.

Mayfield, Carl. Sandia Mountain Sequence. 20p. 1982. pap. 2.00 (*0-913719-57-9*) High-Coo Pr.

Mayfield, Carl P. & Courtney, Richard. The Life & Times of Bubba Skynyrd: Speedbumps & Other Obstacles. Hines, Emily, ed. 128p. (Orig.). 1993. pap. 9.95 (*0-9635026-2-X*) Eggman Pub.

Mayfield, Craig K. Reading Skills for Law Students. 170p. 1980. pap. 14.00 (*0-87215-313-4*) Michie Butterworth.

Mayfield, Dianne C., jt. auth. see Maul, Lyle R.

Mayfield, Helen, illus. The Enchanted Deer. 77p. (Orig.). (J). (gr. 6 up). Date not set. pap. 4.00 (*1-884993-03-6*) Koldarana.

Mayfield, James. Discovering Grace in Grief. 112p. 1994. pap. 7.95 (*0-8358-0696-0*) Upper Room Bks.

Mayfield, James B. Go to the People: Releasing the Rural Poor Through the People's School System. 204p. 1985. 16.00 (*0-931816-35-1*) Intl Inst Rural.

Mayfield, Janis B., ed. see Zuber, William P.

Mayfield, Julian. The Hit & the Long Night. (Northeastern Library of Black Literature). 310p. 1989. reprint ed. pap. text ed. 14.95 (*1-55553-065-6*) NE U Pr.

***Mayfield, Karen & Whitlow, Robert, eds.** Equals Investigations: Flea-Sized Surgeons: A Middle-School Mathematics Unit Focusing on Surface Area, Volume & Scale. Coates, Grace & Franco, Jose, trs. (Equals Ser.). (Illus.). 140p. (Orig.). (J). (gr. 7-9). 1995. pap. 22.00 (*0-912511-25-7*) Lawrence Science.

— Equals Investigations: Growth Patterns: A Middle-School Mathematics Unit Focusing on Linear & Exponential Growth Functions. Coates, Grace & Franco, Jose, trs. (Equals Ser.). (Illus.). 154p. (Orig.). (J). (gr. 7-9). 1995. pap. 22.00 (*0-912511-57-5*) Lawrence Science.

— Equals Investigations: Remote Rulers: A Middle-School Mathematics Unit Focusing on the Relationship Between Algebraic Graphs & Graphs from Real Data Involving Direct & Inverse Variation. Coates, Grace & Franco, Jose, trs. (Equals Ser.). (Illus.). 134p. (Orig.). (J). (gr. 7-9). 1995. pap. 22.00 (*0-912511-58-3*) Lawrence Science.

— Equals Investigations: Telling Someone Where to Go: A Middle-School Mathematics Unit Focusing on Measurement of Distance & Angle. Coates, Grace & Franco, Jose, trs. (Equals Ser.). (Illus.). 140p. (Orig.). (J). (gr. 7-9). 1995. pap. 22.00 (*0-912511-59-1*) Lawrence Science.

***Mayfield, Karen, et al, eds.** Equals Investigations: Scatter Matters: A Middle-School Mathematics Unit Focusing on Scatterplots, Correlation, & Cause & Effect. Coates, Grace & Franco, Jose, trs. (Equals Ser.). (Illus.). 76p. (Orig.). (J). (gr. 7-9). 1995. pap. 22.00 (*0-912511-56-7*) Lawrence Science.

Mayfield, Larry. All Men Praise. 1978. 5.25 (*0-685-74865-0*, MB-449) Lillenas.

— God's Power. (Illus.). (J). (gr. k-6). 1980. 5.99 (*3-901170-17-0*) CEF Press.

— Jesus Is Caring for You. (Illus.). 20p. (J). (gr. k-6). 1982. 5.99 (*3-901170-26-X*) CEF Press.

Mayfield, Larry, jt. auth. see Hawthorne, Grace.

Mayfield, Margie I., jt. auth. see Ollila, Lloyd O.

Mayfield, Marlys. Thinking for Yourself: Developing Critical Thinking Skills Through Reading & Writing. 3rd ed. LC 93-9950. 440p. 1994. pap. 28.95 (*0-534-20334-5*) Intl Thomson.

— Thinking for Yourself: Developing Critical Thinking Skills Through Writing. 2nd ed. 424p. (C). 1991. pap. 27.95 (*0-534-13812-8*) Intl Thomson.

Mayfield, Marlys, jt. auth. see Bothwell, Dorr.

Mayfield, Michael W. & Gallo, Raphael E. The Rivers of Costa Rica: A Canoeing, Kayaking, & Rafting Guide. LC 88-22783. (Illus.-Latin). 123p. 1988. pap. 10.95 (*0-89732-083-2*) Menasha Ridge.

Mayfield, Peggy, et al. Health Assessment: A Modular Approach. Browning, Martha, ed. (Illus.). 1980. text ed. 29.95 (*0-07-041027-5*) McGraw.

Mayfield, R. J. Mothproofing, Vol. 11, No. 4. (C). 1982. pap. text ed. 75.00 (*0-900739-47-9*, Pub. by Textile Institue UK) St Mut.

***Mayfield, Signe.** Christopher Brown: Works on Paper. Date not set. pap. text ed. write for info. (*0-9636922-3-2*) Palo Alto Cult.

Mayfield, Sue. I Carried You on Eagles' Wings. LC 90-28554. 128p. (J). (gr. 6 up). 1991. 12.95 (*0-688-10597-1*) Lothrop.

Mayfield, Susan. Timeline: Women & Power. (Weighing up the Evidence Ser.). (Illus.). 64p. (YA). (gr. 7-9). 1989. 19.95 (*0-85219-768-3*, Pub. by Batsford UK) Trafalgar.

Mayfield, Terry, jt. auth. see Hale, Michael W.

Mayfield, Thomas J. Indian Summer: Traditional Life among the Choinumne Indians of California's San Joaquin Valley. (Illus.). 144p. 1993. pap. 16.00 (*0-930588-64-9*) Heyday Bks.

— Indian Summer: Traditional Life among the Choychimni Indians of California's San Joaquin Valley. (Illus.). 144p. (C). 1993. reprint ed. lib. bdg. 39.00x (*0-8095-4979-4*) Borgo Pr.

Mayfield, Wendy M., jt. auth. see Jazzar, Bernard N.

Mayforth, Ruth D. Designing Antibodies. (Illus.). 207p. 1993. 49.95 (*0-12-481025-X*) Acad Pr.

Mayglothing, Rosie. Rowing. (Skills of the Game Ser.). (Illus.). 144p. Date not set. pap. text ed. 15.95 (*1-85223-753-8*, Pub. by Crowood Pr UK) Trafalgar.

***Mayhall, C. Glen, ed.** Hospital Epidemiology & Infection Control. LC 94-42059. 1995. write for info. (*0-683-05660-3*) Williams & Wilkins.

Mayhall, Carole. Help Lord My Whole Life Hurts. LC 88-62595. 192p. 1988. pap. 9.00 (*0-89109-371-0*) NavPress.

— When God Whispers: Glimpses of an Extraordinary God by an Ordinary Woman. LC 93-48513. 144p. 1994. 12.00 (*0-89109-771-6*, NavPr) NavPress.

— Words That Hurt, Words That Heal. LC 86-61136. 112p. 1986. pap. 6.00 (*0-89109-179-3*) NavPress.

Mayhall, Carole, jt. auth. see Mayhall, Jack.

Mayhall, Jack & Mayhall, Carole. Marriage Takes More Than Love. LC 77-85736. 240p. 1978. pap. 9.00 (*0-89109-426-1*) NavPress.

Mayhall, Jane. Givers & Takers 2. LC 68-55445. 78p. 1973. 10.00 (*0-87130-032-X*); pap. 7.50 (*0-87130-033-8*) Eakins.

— Ready for the Ha Ha. LC 66-23198. 102p. 1966. 30.00 (*0-87130-014-1*) Eakins.

Mayhall, Mildred P. The Kiowas. 2nd ed. LC 62-16477. (Civilization of the American Indian Ser.: Vol. 63). (Illus.). 384p. 1972. pap. 17.95 (*0-8061-0987-4*) U of Okla Pr.

Mayhall, Pamela D. Police-Community Relations & the Administration of Justice. 3rd ed. LC 84-7551. 438p. 1985. text ed. 41.50 (*0-471-06044-5*) P-H.

Mayhall, Pamela D., et al. Child Abuse & Neglect: Sharing Responsibility. LC 82-24799. 400p. (C). 1983. pap. write for info. (*0-02-378290-0*) Macmillan.

— Police-Community Relations & the Administration of Justice. 4th ed. LC 94-5158. 448p. 1994. text ed. 59.00 (*0-13-097791-8*) P-H.

Mayhall, Yolanda. The Sumi-E Book. (Illus.). 128p. 1989. pap. 14.95 (*0-8230-5022-X*, Watsn-Guptill) Watsn-Guptill.

Mayhan, Robert J. Discrete-Time & Continuous-Time Linear Systems. LC 83-5999. (Electrical Engineering Ser.). (Illus.). 640p. 1984. write for info. (*0-201-05597-X*) Addison-Wesley.

— Discrete-Time & Continuous-Time Linear Systems. LC 83-5999. (Electrical Engineering Ser.). (Illus.). 640p. (C). 1984. text ed. 72.25 (*0-201-05596-1*) Addison-Wesley.

***Mayhar, Ardath.** Hunters of the Plains. 224p. (Orig.). 1995. pap. text ed. 4.99 (*0-425-14645-6*) Berkley Pub.

— Island in the Lake. 272p. (Orig.). 1993. mass mkt. 4.99 (*1-55773-903-X*) Diamond.

— People of the Mesa. 1992. mass mkt. 4.99 (*1-55773-674-X*) Diamond.

— A Place of Silver Silence. (Millennium Science Fiction Ser.). (Illus.). (YA). (gr. 7 up). 1988. 15.95 (*0-8027-6825-3*) Walker & Co.

— Slewfoot Sally & the Flying Mule: And Other Tales from Cotton County. (Illus.). (Orig.). 1995. pap. text ed. 12.00 (*1-887303-00-6*) Blu Lantern Pub.

— Through a Stone Wall: A Writer's Handbook & Literary Autobiography. (Illus.). 200p. Date not set. pap. write for info. (*1-887303-07-3*) Blu Lantern Pub.

— Towers of the Earth. 272p. (Orig.). 1994. mass mkt. 4.99 (*1-55773-980-3*) Diamond.

— The Wall. LC 86-31453. (Illus.). 136p. (Orig.). 1987. pap. 6.95 (*0-917053-06-0*) Space And.

Mayhar, Ardath & Fortier, Ron. Monkey Station. LC 88-51729. (TSR Bks.). 320p. (Orig.). (J). 1989. pap. 3.95 (*0-88038-743-2*) TSR Inc.

Mayhead, Robin. Walter Scott. LC 72-88622. (British Authors-Introductory Critical Studies). 142p. reprint ed. pap. 40.50 (*0-685-15593-5*, 2026348) Bks Demand.

Mayher, John S. Uncommon Sense: Theoretical Practice in Language Education. 302p. (Orig.). 1989. pap. text ed. 20.00 (*0-86709-247-5*, 0247) Boynton Cook Pubs.

Mayher, John S., jt. ed. see Brause, Rita S.

Mayher, John S., et al. Learning to Write Writing to Learn. 152p. (Orig.). 1983. pap. text ed. 17.00 (*0-86709-073-1*) Boynton Cook Pubs.

Mayher, Philip J., jt. auth. see Abernathy, William B.

Mayhew, A. L., ed. Promptorium Parvulorum: The First English-Latin Dictionary. (EETS. ES Ser.: No. 102). 1974. reprint ed. 65.00 (*0-527-00306-9*) Periodicals Srv.

Mayhew, A. L., ed. see Skeat, Walter W.

Mayhew, Alan. Subcontracting Terminology: Textile & Clothing Sectors. 633p. 1990. pap. 65.00 (*92-826-0147-1*, CB-58-90-223-9A-C) UNIPUB.

Mayhew, Anthony L., ed. see Skeat, Walter W.

Mayhew, Arthur B. Christianity in India. (C). 1988. 32.50 (*81-212-0143-8*, Pub. by Gian Publng Hse II) S Asia.

Mayhew, Augustus. Paved with Gold: The Romance & Reality of the London Street. 2nd ed. (Illus.). 408p. 1971. reprint ed. 25.00 (*0-7146-1412-2*, BHA-01412, Pub. by F Cass Pubs UK) Intl Spec Bk.

Mayhew, Bob & Birdsall, John. The Art of Western Riding. Frawley, Sean, ed. 160p. 1990. 24.00 (*0-87605-886-1*) Howell Bk.

Mayhew, Catherine M. Genealogical Periodical Annual Index, Vol. 18, 1979. Towle, Laird C., ed. xiv, 179p. 1982. 20.00 (*0-917890-24-8*) Heritage Bk.

— Genealogical Periodical Annual Index: 1977, Vol. 16. Towle, Laird C., ed. 175p. (Orig.). 1979. 20.00 (*0-917890-17-5*) Heritage Bk.

— Genealogical Periodical Annual Index: 1978, Vol.17. Towle, Laird C., ed. xii, 167p. (Orig.). 1980. 20.00 (*0-917890-23-X*) Heritage Bk.

— Genealogical Periodical Annual Index, 1980, Vol. 19. Towle, Laird C., ed. 191p. (Orig.). 1984. 20.00 (*0-917890-38-8*) Heritage Bk.

— Genealogical Periodical Annual Index, 1981, Vol. 20. Towle, Laird C., ed. ivx, 176p. (Orig.). 1985. 20.00 (*0-917890-57-4*) Heritage Bk.

Mayhew, Catherine M. & Towle, Laird C. Genealogical Periodical Annual Index, 1983, Vol. 22. 240p. (Orig.). 1985. 20.00 (*0-917890-69-8*) Heritage Bk.

Mayhew, Catherine M., jt. auth. see New England Historic Genealogical Society Staff.

Mayhew, David R. Congress: The Electoral Connection. LC 74-78471. (Studies in Political Science: No. 26). (Illus.). 192p. 1975. pap. 12.00 (*0-300-01809-6*) Yale U Pr.

— Divided We Govern: Party Control, Lawmaking & Investigations, 1946-1990. 192p. (Orig.). 1991. text ed. 27.50 (*0-300-04835-1*) Yale U Pr.

— Divided We Govern: Party Control, Lawmaking & Investigations, 1946-1990. 192p. (Orig.). 1993. pap. 14.00 (*0-300-04837-8*) Yale U Pr.

— Placing Parties in American Politics: Organization, Electoral Settings, & Government Activity in the Twentieth Century. LC 85-43298. (Illus.). 1986. text ed. 59.50x (*0-691-07707-X*); pap. 15.95x (*0-691-02249-6*) Princeton U Pr.

Mayhew, Deborah J. Principles & Guidelines in Software User Interface Design. 544p. 1991. text ed. 75.00 (*0-13-721929-6*) P-H.

Mayhew, Deborah J., jt. ed. see Bias, Randolph G.

Mayhew, Dianne V. Secret Passions. 150p. 1993. pap. 3.79 (*0-9634431-0-0*) C Y Pub Grp.

Mayhew, Elisabeth. The Dark Mountain. large type ed. 352p. 1985. 15.95 (*0-7089-1285-0*) Ulverscroft.

Mayhew, Eugene J., ed. Shalom: Essays in Honor of Dr. Charles H. Shaw. 231p. 1983. pap. 11.95 (*0-912407-01-8*) William Tyndale Col Pr.

Mayhew, Henry. London Labour & the London Poor. (Classics Ser.). 544p. 1986. pap. 10.95 (*0-14-043241-8*, Penguin Classics) Viking Penguin.

— London Labour & the London Poor, 4 vols., 1. (Illus.). 1968. pap. 9.95 (*0-486-21934-8*) Dover.

— London Labour & the London Poor, 4 vols., 2. (Illus.). 1968. pap. 9.95 (*0-486-21935-6*) Dover.

— London Labour & the London Poor, 4 vols., 3. (Illus.). 1968. pap. 9.95 (*0-486-21936-4*) Dover.

— London Labour & the London Poor, 4 vols., 4. (Illus.). 1968. pap. 9.95 (*0-486-21937-2*) Dover.

— Mormons: Or, Latter Day Saints. LC 71-134398. reprint ed. 45.00 (*0-404-08440-0*) AMS Pr.

— Voices of the Poor: Selections from the "Morning Chronicle" & "Labour & the Poor", 1849-1950. Humphreys, Anne, ed. (Illus.). 280p. 1971. 37.50 (*0-7146-2929-4*, Pub. by F Cass Pubs UK) Intl Spec Bk.

Mayhew, Henry & Binny, John. Criminal Prisons of London: And Scenes of Prison Life. LC 68-18227. (Illus.). xii, 634p. 1968. reprint ed. 49.50 (*0-678-05072-4*) Kelley.

— Criminal Prisons of London & Scenes of Prison Life. (Illus.). 634p. 1968. 35.00 (*0-7146-1411-4*, Pub. by F Cass Pubs UK) Intl Spec Bk.

Mayhew, Ian G. Large Animal Neurology: A Handbook for Veterinary Clinicians. LC 88-34037. 380p. 1989. pap. text ed. 58.00 (*0-8121-1183-4*) Williams & Wilkins.

Mayhew, Isabel, ed. see Smith, Charles W.

Mayhew, James. Dare You! LC 92-18862. (J). 1993. 13.95 (*0-395-65013-5*, Clarion Bks) HM.

— Koshka's Tales: Stories from Russia. LC 92-41185. (Illus.). 80p. (J). (gr. k up). 1993. 16.95 (*1-85697-943-1*, Kingfisher LKC) LKC.

***Mayhew, Jayne N. & Wheeler, Nicki.** Animals in Cross Stitch. (Illus.). 128p. 1995. 24.95 (*0-7153-0199-3*, Pub. by D & C Pub UK) Sterling.

Mayhew, John E. & Frisby, John P., eds. Three-D Model Recognition from Stereoscopic Cues. (Artificial Intelligence Ser.). (Illus.). 350p. 1991. 50.00 (*0-262-13243-5*) MIT Pr.

Mayhew, Jonathan. Claudio Rodriguez & the Language of Poetic Vision. LC 89-42931. 160p. 1990. 32.50 (*0-8387-5174-1*) Bucknell U Pr.

— Observations on the Charter & Conduct of the Society for the Propagation of the Gospel in Foreign Parts; Designed to Show Their Non-Conformity to Each Other. LC 72-38456. (Religion in America, Ser. 2). 180p. 1972. reprint ed. 18.95 (*0-405-04077-6*) Ayer.

— The Poetics of Self-Consciousness: Twentieth-Century Spanish Poetry. LC 92-56608. 1994. write for info. (*0-8387-5256-X*) Bucknell U Pr.

— Sermons. LC 76-83429. (Religion in America, Ser. 1). 1975. reprint ed. 21.95 (*0-405-00254-8*) Ayer.

Mayhew, Lenore & McNaughton, William. As Though Dreaming: The Tz'u of Pure Jade. (Illus.). 1977. 5.95 (*0-685-50392-5*) SPD-Small Pr Dist.

Mayhew, Lenore, tr. see Akhmatova, Anna.

Mayhew, Lenore, tr. see Basho, et al.

Mayhew, Leon H., ed. see Parsons, Talcott.

Mayhew, Leonard, tr. see Truffaut, Francois.

Mayhew, Leslie. Urban Hospital Location. LC 85-15820. (London Research Series in Geography: No. 4). (Illus.). 176p. 1985. text ed. 60.00 (*0-04-362054-X*) Routledge Chapman & Hall.

Mayhew, Lewis B. Colleges Today & Tomorrow. LC 74-75939. (Jossey-Bass Higher Education Ser.). 272p. reprint ed. 77.60 (*0-8357-9308-7*, 2013952) Bks Demand.

— Literature of Higher Education 1971. LC 74-155167. (Higher Education Ser.). 176p. reprint ed. 50.20 (*0-8357-9332-X*, 2013818) Bks Demand.

— The Literature of Higher Education 1972. LC 74-155167. (Jossey-Bass Higher Education Ser.). 198p. reprint ed. 56.50 (*0-8357-9333-8*, 2013859) Bks Demand.

— Surviving the Eighties. LC 79-88773. (Jossey-Bass Series in Higher Education). 366p. reprint ed. pap. 104.40 (*0-7837-0183-7*, 2040479) Bks Demand.

Mayhew, Lewis B. & Ford, Patrick J. Changing the Curriculum. LC 79-159265. (Jossey-Bass Higher Education Ser.). 206p. reprint ed. pap. 58.80 (*0-8357-9302-8*, 2017237) Bks Demand.

— Reform in Graduate & Professional Education. LC 73-20968. (Jossey-Bass Higher Education Ser.). 270p. reprint ed. pap. 77.00 (*0-685-16184-6*, 2027762) Bks Demand.

Mayhew, Lewis B., jt. auth. see Dressel, Paul L.

Mayhew, Lewis B., et al. The Quest for Quality: The Challenge for Undergraduate Education in the 1990s. LC 90-34307. (Higher & Adult Education Ser.). 320p. 1990. 34.95 (*1-55542-254-3*) Jossey-Bass.

Mayhew, Margaret. The Flame & the Furnace. large type ed. 432p. 1982. 15.95 (*0-7089-0888-8*) Ulverscroft.

— The Master of Aysgarth. large type ed. 368p. 1983. 15.95 (*0-7089-1058-0*) Ulverscroft.

An Asterisk (*) at the beginning of an entry indicates that the title is appearing in BIP for the first time.

— The Railway King. large type ed. 423p. 1980. 12.00 (*0-7089-0558-7*) Ulverscroft.
— Regency Charade. 192p. 1987. pap. 2.50 (*0-449-21370-6*, Crest) Fawcett.
— Regency Charade. LC 86-9110. 192p. 1986. 15.95 (*0-8027-0912-5*) Walker & Co.
*__Mayhew, Mary.__ Your Star Child: Birthing an Evolved Soul. Charles, Rodney, ed. (Illus.). 400p. (Orig.). 1995. pap. 17.95 (*0-9638502-2-9*) Sunstar Pubng.
__Mayhew, Miriam, jt. auth. see Carver, John.__
__Mayhew, Nicholas.__ Coinage in France from the Dark Ages to Napoleon. (Illus.). 163p. (YA). (gr. 10 up). 1988. 39. 95 (*0-900652-87-X*, Pub. by Seaby UK) Trafalgar.
__Mayhew, Nicholas, jt. auth. see Gemmill, Elizabeth.__
__Mayhew, Peter.__ A Theology of Force & Violence. LC 89-4491. 1989. pap. 8.95 (*0-334-02360-2*) TPI PA.
__Mayhew, Susan.__ Minidictionary of Geography. LC 93-46664. (Oxford Minireference Ser.). 1994. pap. write for info. (*0-19-211692-4*) OUP.
__Mayhew, Susan & Penny, Anne.__ The Concise Oxford Dictionary of Geography. 256p. 1992. pap. 8.95 (*0-19-282565-8*) OUP.
__Mayhew, Terry M., jt. ed. see Reith, Albrecht.__
__Mayhew, Y., jt. auth. see Rogers, G. F.__
__Mayhill, R. Thomas.__ Lancaster County, Pa. Deed Abstracts 1729 to 1770 & Oaths of Allegiance. enl. rev. ed. 277p. 1979. 24.00 (*0-686-27817-8*) Bookmark.
__Mayhue, Richard.__ Como Interpretar la Biblia Uno Mismo. Orig. Title: How to Interpret the Bible for Yourself. 112p. (SPA.). 1994. pap. 6.99 (*0-8254-1471-7*) Kregel.
— Divine Healing Today. 1983. pap. 8.99 (*0-88469-154-3*) BMH Bks.
— The Healing Promise. LC 94-6870. 1994. pap. 8.99 (*1-56507-182-4*) Harvest Hse.
— La Promesa de Sanidad. 288p. (SPA.). 1995. pap. 8.99 (*0-8254-1472-5*) Kregel.
— Snatched Before the Storm! 1980. pap. 1.50 (*0-88469-124-1*) BMH Bks.
— Spiritual Maturity. LC 92-476. (Orig.). 1992. pap. 1.60 (*0-89693-887-5*, Victor Books) SP Pubns.
— Unmasking Satan. 168p. 1988. pap. 1.60 (*0-89693-603-1*, Victor Books) SP Pubns.
__Mayhue, Richard L.__ How to Interpret the Bible for Yourself. (Orig.). 1986. pap. 5.99 (*0-88469-178-0*) BMH Bks.
__Mayhue, Richard L., ed. see Master's Seminary Faculty Staff & MacArthur, John, Jr.__
__Mayinger, Franz, ed.__ Optical Measurements: Techniques & Applications. LC 94-20066. 1994. 99.00 (*0-387-56765-8*) Spr-Verlag.
__Maykapar, Samuel.__ Pedal Preludes. 32p. (gr. 4-12). 1974. pap. text ed. 5.95 (*0-87487-650-8*) Summy-Birchard.
__Maykovich, Minako, jt. auth. see Lee, Ivy.__
__Maykrantz, Scott P.__ Invaders from Below. Bell, Rob, ed. (Champions Ser.). (Illus.). 64p. (Orig.). (C). 1990. pap. 10.00 (*1-55806-103-7*, 409) Iron Crown Ent Inc.
__Maykut, M. O.__ Health Consequences of Acute & Chronic Marijuana Use. (Illus.). 320p. 1984. 42.00 (*0-08-031984-X*, Pergamon Pr) Elsevier.
*__Maykut, Pamela & Morehouse, Richard.__ Beginning Qualitative Research: A Philosophic & Practical Guide. LC 94-26385. (Teachers' Library Ser.). 194p. 1994. pap. 24.95x (*0-7507-0273-7*, Falmer Pr) Taylor & Francis.
__Maylam, Paul.__ Rhodes, the Tswana, & the British: Colonialism, Collaboration, & Conflict in the Bechuanaland Protectorate, 1885-1899. LC 79-8582. (Contributions in Comparative Colonial Studies: No. 4). (Illus.). x, 245p. 1980. text ed. 79.50 (*0-313-20885-9*, MTB/) Greenwood.
__Mayland, H.__ Adventures with Discus. (Illus.). 256p. 1994. 29.95 (*0-7938-0081-1*, TS218) TFH Pubns.
__Mayland, Paul F.__ Bank Operating Credit Risk: Assessing & Controlling Credit Risk in Bank Operating. 1993. 60.00 (*1-55738-346-4*) Probus Pub Co.
__Mayle.__ Congratulations, You're Not Pregnant. 1981. 10.95 (*0-02-582540-2*) Macmillan.
— Divorce Can Happen to Nice People. 1980. 9.95 (*0-02-582500-3*) Macmillan.
— Grown-Ups & Other Problems. 1983. 12.95 (*0-02-582550-X*) Macmillan.
— Worse Than His Bite. Date not set. pap. write for info. (*0-679-76267-1*) Random Hse Value.
__Mayle, Jan.__ Standard Securities Calculation Methods: Fixed Income Securities Formulas for Analytic Measures, Vol. 2. 1994. write for info. (*0-318-72505-3*) Securities Industry.
__Mayle, Mark A.__ The Veganza Plot. 320p. 1994. pap. 9.95 (*1-56901-289-X*) NW Pub.
__Mayle, Paul D.__ Eureka Summit: Agreement in Principle & the Big Three at Tehran, 1943. LC 85-40879. (Illus.). 216p. 1987. 38.50 (*0-87413-295-9*) U Delaware Pr.
__Mayle, Peter.__ Acquired Tastes. 1993. pap. 9.95 (*0-553-37183-5*) Bantam.
— Acquired Tastes. large type ed. 300p. 1992. reprint ed. lib. bdg. 20.95 (*1-56054-543-7*) Thorndike Pr.
— Anything Considered. Date not set. pap. write for info. (*0-679-44123-9*) Random.
— A Dog's Life. 1995. 20.00 (*0-679-44122-0*) Knopf.
— Hotel Pastis. 1994. pap. 12.00 (*0-679-75111-4*, Vin) Random.
— Hotel Pastis: A Novel of Provence. LC 93-14641. 1993. 23.00 (*0-679-40229-2*) Knopf.
— Hotel Pastis: A Novel of Provence. LC 93-41323. 557p. 1994. pap. 14.95 (*0-7862-0123-1*); bds. 22.95 (*0-7862-0122-3*) Thorndike Pr.
— How to Be a Pregnant Father? (Illus.). 1977. 12.00 (*0-8184-0245-8*) Carol Pub Group.
— How to Be a Pregnant Father. (Illus.). 56p. (Orig.). 1986. pap. 6.95 (*0-8184-0399-3*) Carol Pub Group.
— Is There Life After Lunch. Date not set. pap. write for info. (*0-679-44124-7*) Random.
— Provence. LC 94-16914. 1994. 35.00 (*0-679-43564-6*) Random.
— Sweet Dreams & Monsters: A Beginner's Guide to Dreams & Nightmares & Things That Go Bump under the Bed. (Illus.). (J). (gr. k up). 1986. 9.95 (*0-517-55972-2*, Harmony) Crown Pub Group.
— Toujours Provence. 1991. pap. 21.00 (*0-679-40253-5*) Knopf.
— Toujours Provence. 1992. pap. 10.00 (*0-679-73604-2*, Vin) Random.
— Toujours Provence. large type ed. 336p. 1991. reprint ed. lib. bdg. 20.95 (*1-56054-262-4*) Thorndike Pr.
— Up the Agency: The Funny Business of Advertising. 160p. 1993. 18.95 (*0-312-09930-4*) St Martin.
— Up the Agency: The Funny Business of Advertising. 1994. pap. 8.95 (*0-312-11911-9*) St Martin.
— What's Happening to Me? LC 75-14410. (Illus.). 56p. (J). (gr. 3 up). 1975. 12.00 (*0-8184-0221-0*); pap. 6.95 (*0-8184-0312-8*) Carol Pub Group.
— Where Did I Come From. (Illus.). 48p. (J). (gr. 3 up). 1973. 12.00 (*0-8184-0161-3*); pap. 8.95 (*0-8184-0253-9*) Carol Pub Group.
— Why Are We Getting a Divorce? LC 87-12105. (Illus.). 32p. (J). (gr. k-3). 1988. 15.00 (*0-517-56527-7*, Harmony) Crown Pub Group.
— Wicked Willie's Guide to Women: A Worm's-Eye View of the Fair Sex. (Illus.). 64p. 1987. pap. 8.95 (*0-517-56652-4*, CPT Corp) Crown Pub Group.
— A Year in Provence. 1990. 23.00 (*0-394-57230-0*) Knopf.
— A Year in Provence. LC 90-50623. 224p. 1991. pap. 10. 00 (*0-679-73114-8*, Vin) Random.
— A Year in Provence. large type ed. 1992. 21.95 (*0-7089-2485-9*) Ulverscroft.
— Year in Provence: Toujours Provence, 2 vols., Set. 1993. Boxed set. boxed 21.00 (*0-679-74943-8*) Knopf.
__Mayle, Peter, jt. auth. see Fletcher, Raffaella.__
__Mayle, Peter, jt. auth. see Jolliffe, Gray.__
__Mayleas, Davidyne S.__ By Appointment Only. 448p. 1989. mass mkt. 4.50 (*0-380-75362-6*) Avon.
— The Gardiner Women. 480p. (Orig.). 1993. mass mkt. 5.99 (*0-380-75690-0*) Avon.
— A Man of Property. 592p. 1988. mass mkt. 4.50 (*1-55817-099-5*, Pinnacle NY) Windsor NY.
— Naked Call. 672p. (Orig.). 1991. mass mkt. 5.50 (*0-380-75688-9*) Avon.
— The Woman Who Had Everything. 1987. mass mkt. 4.50 (*0-380-75327-8*) Avon.
__Maylin, George A., jt. auth. see Krook, Lennart.__
__Mayman, Martin & Schlesinger, Herbert J., eds.__ Psychoanalytic Research: Three Approaches to the Experimental Study of Subliminal Processes. LC 73-2848. (Psychological Issues Monograph: 30, Vol. 8, No. 2). 116p. (C). 1975. text ed. 26.00 (*0-8236-4490-1*) Intl Univs Pr.
__Maymon, Gilbert W., jt. auth. see Cave, William C.__
__Maynadier, G. H.__ The Wife of Bath's Tale, Its Sources & Analogues. 1972. 200.00 (*0-8490-1299-6*) Gordon Pr.
__Maynadier, Gustavus.__ Wife of Bath's Tale: Its Sources & Analogues. LC 71-144526. (Grimm Library: No. 13). reprint ed. 27.50 (*0-404-53556-9*) AMS Pr.
__Maynadier, Gustavus H.__ The First American Novelist. LC 79-175703. (Select Bibliographies Reprint Ser.). 1977. reprint ed. 17.95 (*0-8369-6618-X*) Ayer.
__Maynadier, Howard.__ The Arthur of the English Poets. 454p. (C). 1966. text ed. 75.00 (*0-8383-0670-5*) M S G Haskell Hse.
__Maynar-Moliner, Manuel, et al, eds.__ Percutaneous Revascularization Techniques. LC 92-49670. 1993. 139. 00 (*0-86577-441-2*) Thieme Med Pubs.
__Maynard.__ Stars & Planets. (Young Scientist Ser.). (Illus.). 32p. (J). (gr. 4-8). 1976. lib. bdg. 13.96 (*0-88110-313-6*); pap. 6.95 (*0-86020-094-9*) EDC.
__Maynard, ed. see Arden.__
__Maynard, et al.__ Alabama Environmental Law Handbook. 2nd ed. (State Environmental Law Ser.). 120p. 1992. pap. 69.00 (*0-86587-320-8*) Gov Insts.
__Maynard, Alan & Tether, Philip, eds.__ Preventing Alcohol & Tobacco Problems, Vol. 1: The Addiction Market: Consumption, Production & Policy Development. (Illus.). 270p. 1990. text ed. 63.95 (*0-566-05701-8*) Ashgate Pub Co.
__Maynard, Arthur H.__ Understanding the Gospel of John. LC 91-37589. 100p. 1991. lib. bdg. 59.95 (*0-7734-9640-8*) E Mellen.
__Maynard, Barbara.__ Modern Basketry Techniques. (Illus.). 1993. pap. 29.95 (*0-7134-6160-8*, Pub. by Batsford UK) Trafalgar.
__Maynard, Bill.__ Time Out for the Family-1989. 1989. pap. 6.25 (*0-89137-119-2*) Quality Pubns.
__Maynard, Charles.__ Murmansk Venture. LC 79-115564. (Russia Observed Ser.). (Illus.). 1971. reprint ed. 23.95 (*0-405-03085-1*) Ayer.
— Yellowstone & Grand Teton Waterfall Guide: A Scenic Guide to 50 Favorite Waterfalls & Cascades. (Illus.). 112p. (Orig.). 1995. pap. 14.95 (*1-55566-139-4*) Johnson Bks.
__Maynard, Charles, ed. see Beeson, D. R.__
__Maynard, Charles W.__ Where the Rhododendrons Grow: A History of Camping & Leisure Ministries in the Holston Conference. (Illus.). 130p. 1988. 14.95 (*0-932807-31-3*); pap. 9.95 (*0-932807-32-1*) Overmountain Pr.
__Maynard, Charles W., ed. see Beeson, D. R.__
__Maynard, Charles W., ed. see Mathes, C. Hodge.__
__Maynard, Chris.__ Amazing Animal Babies. LC 92-23736. (Eyewitness Juniors Ser.: Vol. 25). 32p. (Orig.). (J). (gr. 1-5). 1993. lib. bdg. 10.99 (*0-679-93924-5*); pap. 7.99 (*0-679-83924-0*) Knopf Bks Yng Read.
— I Wonder Why Planes Have Wings & Other Questions about Transport. LC 92-42373. (Illus.). 32p. (J). (gr. k-3). 1993. 8.95 (*1-85697-877-X*, Kingfisher LKC) LKC.
— I Wonder Why Stars Twinkle & Other Questions about Space: And Other Questions about Space. LC 92-44259. (I Wonder Why Ser.). (Illus.). 32p. (J). (gr. k-3). 1993. 8.95 (*1-85697-881-8*, Kingfisher LKC) LKC.
__Maynard, Chris & Scheller, Bill.__ The Bad-for-You Cookbook. 1992. pap. 10.00 (*0-679-73545-3*, Villard Bks) Random.
— Manifold Destiny: The One! The Only! Guide to Cooking on Your Car Engine. LC 89-40194. (Illus.). 1989. pap. 7.95 (*0-679-72337-4*, Villard Bks) Random.
__Maynard, Christopher.__ Castles. LC 92-32844. 32p. (J). (gr. 1-4). 1993. 3.95 (*1-85697-891-5*, Kingfisher LKC) LKC.
— The Deepsea Sub. LC 93-41691. (Fold Out...Find Out Ser.). (J). 1995. 8.95 (*1-85697-510-X*, Kingfisher LKC) LKC.
— Jungle Animals. LC 92-32845. (Little Library). 32p. (J). (gr. 1-4). 1993. 3.95 (*1-85697-896-6*, Kingfisher LKC) LKC.
— Questions & Answers about Explorers. LC 94-31067. (Questions & Answers about Ser.). (J). 1995. 12.90 (*1-85697-556-8*, Kingfisher LKC); pap. 5.95 (*1-85697-555-X*, Kingfisher LKC) LKC.
— Space. LC 92-32266. (Little Library). (Illus.). 32p. (J). (gr. 1-4). 1993. 3.95 (*1-85697-897-4*, Kingfisher LKC) LKC.
— The Space Shuttle. LC 93-416970. (Fold Out...Find Out Ser.). (J). 1994. 8.95 (*1-85697-514-2*, Kingfisher LKC) LKC.
— Submarines. LC 94-640. (Little Library). (Illus.). 32p. (J). (gr. 2-5). 1994. 3.95 (*1-85697-508-8*, Kingfisher LKC) LKC.
__Maynard, Christopher & Verdet, Jean-Pierre.__ The Universe. LC 94-9085. (First Facts Ser.). (Illus.). 128p. (J). (gr. k-4). 1994. pap. 5.95 (*1-85697-527-4*, Kingfisher LKC) LKC.
__Maynard, Christopher, jt. auth. see Joly, Dominique.__
__Maynard, D., jt. ed. see Prior, P.__
*__Maynard, Dennis R.__ Forgiven, Healed, & Restored. LC 94-92276. 80p. 1994. pap. 7.50 (*1-885985-01-0*) Dionysus Pubns.
— The Money Book: A Christian Perspective. LC 94-92275. 64p. (Orig.). 1994. pap. 7.50 (*1-885985-00-2*) Dionysus Pubns.
— Those Episkopols. rev. ed. LC 94-92277. Orig. Title: Episcopalians: Following in the Way of Jesus. 70p. (Orig.). 1994. pap. 7.50 (*1-885985-02-9*) Dionysus Pubns.
__Maynard, Donald N., jt. auth. see Lorenz, Oscar A.__
__Maynard, Douglas W.__ Inside Plea Bargaining: The Language of Negotiation. LC 84-9809. 270p. 1984. 49.50 (*0-306-41577-1*, Plenum Pr) Plenum.
__Maynard, Edward S., jt. auth. see Ellison, Craig W.__
__Maynard, Edwin H.__ Keeping up with a Revolution: The Story of United Methodist Communications. Purdue, Joretta, ed. 216p. 1990. write for info. (*1-878946-01-3*) United Meth Comm.
__Maynard, Edwin S.__ Bureaucracy & Diplomacy. (Nineteen Eighty-Eight Project Ser.: No. 4). 96p. 1989. pap. text ed. 5.00 (*0-934143-28-5*) Lawyers Comm Human.
__Maynard, Frankie.__ A Tree! For Me! (Illus.). 60p. 1985. 15. 00 (*0-912783-02-8*) Upton Sons.
— A Tree! for Me! LC 86-51132. (Illus.). 68p. (J). 15.00 (*0-912783-07-9*) Upton Sons.
__Maynard, Geoffrey.__ Economic Development & the Price Level. LC 72-85018. (Reprints of Economic Classics Ser.). (Illus.). viii, 295p. 1972. reprint ed. lib. bdg. 37.50 (*0-678-07016-4*) Kelley.
__Maynard, Harold B.__ Methods-Time Measurement. LC 48-7173. (McGraw-Hill Industrial Organization & Management Ser.). (Illus.). 302p. reprint ed. pap. 86.10 (*0-317-10748-8*, 2055405) Bks Demand.
__Maynard, Herman B., Jr. & Mehrtens, Susan E.__ The Fourth Wave: Business in the Twenty-First Century. LC 93-2705. 235p. 1993. 24.95 (*1-881052-15-X*) Berrett-Koehler.
__Maynard, J.__ Craft Practice in Wood: An Introduction to Basic Techniques. 96p. (C). 1979. 50.00 (*0-7175-0825-0*, Pub. by S Thornes Pubs UK) St Mut.
— Woodwork Designing, Constructions & Workshop Practice. 2nd rev. ed. Jones, D., ed. 166p. (C). 1981. reprint ed. 55.00 (*0-7175-0696-7*, Pub. by S Thornes Pubs UK) St Mut.
__Maynard, J. Barry.__ Geochemistry of Sedimentary Ore Deposits. (Illus.). 305p. 1983. 72.00 (*0-387-90783-1*) Spr-Verlag.
__Maynard, James.__ Some Microeconomics of Higher Education: Economics of Scale. LC 76-139371. (Illus.). 202p. reprint ed. pap. 57.60 (*0-8357-3806-X*, 2036534) Bks Demand.
__Maynard, Joan.__ Mud Pies. 8p. (J). (gr. 1). 1988. pap. text ed. 2.50 (*1-882225-09-0*) Tott Pubns.
— Mud Puddles. 7p. (J). (gr. 1). 1989. pap. text ed. 2.50 (*1-882225-06-6*) Tott Pubns.
__Maynard, Joe & Miles, Barry, eds.__ William S. Burroughs, Nineteen Fifty-Three to Nineteen Seventy-Three: A Bibliography. LC 77-2663. (Illus.). 243p. 1978. 27.50 (*0-8139-0710-1*) U Pr of Va.
__Maynard, John.__ Russia in Flux. Guest, S. Haden, ed. LC 83-45812. reprint ed. 48.50 (*0-404-20173-3*) AMS Pr.
— Victorian Discourses on Sexuality & Religion. LC 92-12820. (Illus.). 352p. (C). 1993. 59.95 (*0-521-33254-0*) Cambridge U Pr.
__Maynard, John & Auslander Munich, Adrienne, eds.__ Victorian Literature & Culture, 1992-1993, Set. rev. ed. (Illus.). 1993. Vol. 19. write for info. (*0-318-70345-9*) AMS Pr.
— Victorian Literature & Culture, 1992-1993, Vol. 20. rev. ed. (Illus.). 1993. 57.50 (*0-404-64220-9*) AMS Pr.
— Victorian Literature & Culture, 1992-1993, Vol. 21. rev. ed. (Illus.). 1993. Set. 52.25 (*0-404-64221-7*) AMS Pr.
__Maynard, John & Munich, Adrienne A., eds.__ An Annual of Victorian Literature & Cultural History, Vol. 19: Victorian Literature & Culture, Vol. 19. (Browning Institute Studies Ser.). 1991. 57.50 (*0-404-64219-5*) AMS Pr.
__Maynard, John, jt. ed. see Bloom, Abigail B.__
__Maynard, John A.__ Venice West: The Beat Generation in Southern California. LC 90-45114. 264p. (C). 1991. 22. 95 (*0-8135-1653-6*) Rutgers U Pr.
— Venice West: The Beat Generation in Southern California. LC 90-45114. 264p. 1993. pap. 14.95 (*0-8135-1965-9*) Rutgers U Pr.
__Maynard, John L.__ Writing about Computers. (Illus.). (C). 1989. disk 14.95 (*0-929739-00-0*) Maynard Desktop Pubs.
__Maynard, John R.__ Browning's Youth. (Illus.). 512p. 1977. 42.50 (*0-674-08441-1*) HUP.
__Maynard, John T. & Peters, Howard M.__ Understanding Chemical Patents: A Guide for the Inventor. 2nd ed. LC 91-24124. 1991. 39.95 (*0-8412-1997-4*); pap. 29.95 (*0-8412-1998-2*) Am Chemical.
__Maynard, Joseph E.__ Healing Hands: The Story of the Palmer Family - Discoverers & Developers of Chiropractic. 4th ed. LC 59-14319. 432p. 1992. 34.95 (*0-9630413-0-4*) Jonorm Pubs.
__Maynard, Joyce.__ Domestic Affairs: Enduring the Pleasures of Motherhood & Family. 1987. 17.95 (*0-8129-1244-6*, Times Bks) Random.
— To Die For. 368p. 1993. pap. 5.99 (*0-451-17327-9*, Sig) NAL-Dutton.
— Where Love Goes. 352p. 1995. 23.00 (*0-517-70177-4*) Random Hse Value.
__Maynard, Katherine K.__ Thomas Hardy's Tragic Poetry: The Lyrics & "The Dynasts" LC 91-15975. 247p. 1991. text ed. 32.95 (*0-87745-344-6*) U of Iowa Pr.
__Maynard, Kitty & Maynard, Lucian.__ The American Country Inn & Bed & Breakfast Cookbook, Vol. I. LC 87-10105. (Illus.). 528p. 1987. 24.95 (*0-934395-50-0*) Rutledge Hill Pr.
— The American Country Inn & Bed & Breakfast Cookbook, Vol. I. 2nd ed. Pitkin, Julie M., ed. LC 87-10105. (Illus.). 511p. (C). 1990. reprint ed. pap. 17.95 (*1-55853-064-9*) Rutledge Hill Pr.
— The American Country Inn & Bed & Breakfast Cookbook, Vol. II. LC 87-10105. (Illus.). 628p. 1990. 24. 95 (*1-55853-059-2*) Rutledge Hill Pr.
— The American Country Inn & Bed & Breakfast Cookbook, Vol. II. LC 87-10105. (Illus.). 640p. 1993. pap. 16.95 (*1-55853-218-8*) Rutledge Hill Pr.
__Maynard, Kitty, et al.__ Cooking for Diabetics: A Complete Guide to Easy Menu Planning & Enjoyable Eating for Healthy Living. LC 88-32374. (Illus.). 1989. 17.95 (*1-55853-000-2*) Rutledge Hill Pr.
__Maynard, Leonard A., et al.__ Animal Nutrition. 7th ed. (Illus.). 1979. text ed. write for info. (*0-07-041049-6*) McGraw.
__Maynard, Lucian, jt. auth. see Maynard, Kitty.__
__Maynard, Margaret.__ Fashioned from Penury: Dress As Cultural Practice in Colonial Australia. LC 93-37953. (Studies in Australian History). (Illus.). 200p. (C). 1994. pap. write for info. (*0-521-45925-7*) Cambridge U Pr.
— Fashioned from Penury: Dress As Cultural Practice in Colonial Australia. LC 93-37953. (Studies in Australian History). (Illus.). 200p. (C). 1994. 54.95 (*0-521-45310-0*) Cambridge U Pr.
__Maynard, Mary.__ Houses with Stories: From Cottages to Castles, Landmarks to Literary Sites, 50 Tours of New England's Most Fascinating Homes. LC 93-24180. (Travel Guide Ser.). (Illus.). 1994. pap. write for info. (*0-89909-370-1*) Yankee Bks.
— Open Houses in New England. (Travel Guide Ser.). (Illus.). 320p. (Orig.). 1992. pap. 16.95 (*0-89909-347-7*, 80-651-3) Yankee Bks.
*__Maynard, Mary & Purvis, June, eds.__ (Hetero)sexual Politics. LC 95-14661. 1995. pap. write for info. (*0-7484-0295-0*, Pub. by Tay Francis Ltd UK); pap. write for info. (*0-7484-0296-9*, Pub. by Tay Francis Ltd UK) Taylor & Francis.
— Researching Women's Lives from a Feminist Perspective. LC 93-38801. 1994. write for info. (*0-7484-0152-0*, Pub. by Tay Francis Ltd UK); pap. write for info. (*0-7484-0153-9*, Pub. by Tay Francis Ltd UK) Taylor & Francis.
__Maynard, Mary, jt. ed. see Afshar, Haleh.__
__Maynard, Mary, jt. ed. see De Groot, Joanna.__
__Maynard, Mary, jt. ed. see Hanmer, Jalna.__
*__Maynard, Meredy.__ Dreamcatcher. 160p. (Orig.). (J). 1995. pap. 7.50 (*1-896095-01-1*) Orca Bk Pubs.

__*Maynard, Michael. A History of the Debate over 1 John 5: 7-8: A Tracing of the Longevity of the Comma Johannuem, with Evaluations of Arguments Against Its Authenticity. LC 95-67775. (Illus.). 382p. (Orig.). 1995. pap. 19.00 (*1-886971-05-6*) Comma Pubns.__

__Is the celebrated passage 1 John 5: 7-8 (KJV) authentic or spurious? This question once raised so much interest, that even Sir Isaac Newton, & later the historian Edward Gibbon wrote about it. (1784). The librarian T. H. Horne (d. 1862) listed over 50 bibliographic items, each devoted to the disputed verse. This forthcoming book expands Horne's list, fills in gaps, & provides a history of the debate, with details gleaned from__

primary readings taken from items in this first update of Horne's bibliography in over a century. The author, himself a librarian (ALA/M.L.S.), compiled 137 items (37 journal articles, 50 essays from books, & 50 books). Journal articles on 1 John 5: 7-8 were published in no less than six different languages. In the late 1800's some boasted that the debate was over. However, interest in the verse grew. Of the journal articles, 75% were written after 1900! History indicates the verse attracts the interest of librarians, such as LaCroze (d. 1739, Berlin), LeLong (d. 1721, Paris), Horne (d. 1862, British Museum), E. Abbot (d. 1884, Harvard), von Harnack (d. 1930, director Prussian State Library), & Kenyon (d. 1952, British Museum) were all librarians, who published their views on this verse. A scholar said in 1947 that one could write a huge tome relating to the history of this disputed verse. But no one attempted to, until now. Order from: Comma Publications, P.O. Box 1625, Tempe, AZ 85281-1625.
Publisher Provided Annotation.

Maynard, Michael, jt. auth. see Leigh, Andrew.

***Maynard-Moody, Steven.** Dilemma of the Fetus: Fetal Research, Medical Progress, & Moral Politics. 1995. 23.95 (*0-312-11785-X*) St Martin.

Maynard-Moody, Steven W., jt. auth. see Palumbo, Dennis J.

***Maynard, Nan.** The Dancing Willows. large type ed. 384p. 1995. 23.95 (*0-7089-3360-2*) Ulverscroft.

— Rise up My Love. large type ed. (General Ser.). 400p. 1993. 21.95 (*0-7089-2789-0*) Ulverscroft.

Maynard, P., ed. see University of Western Ontario Conference Staff.

Maynard, Paul, jt. ed. see Greenberg, Noah.

Maynard, Randall, et al. Brainwaves: Mental Training for Martial Artists. 140p. (Orig.). 1993. pap. 8.95 (*0-9633737-4-9*) Nordique Pub.

Maynard, Randall L. Mind Games for Consenting Adults. 128p. 1992. pap. text ed. 11.95 (*0-9633737-6-5*) Nordique Pub.

Maynard-Reid, Pedrito U. Poverty & Wealth in James. LC 86-23506. 128p. (Orig.). 1987. pap. 14.95 (*0-88344-417-8*) Orbis Bks.

Maynard, Richard. The Return. LC 87-46267. 240p. 1988. 17.95 (*1-55611-083-9*) D I Fine.

— The Return. 240p. 1989. pap. 3.95 (*0-8439-2852-2*) Dorchester Pub Co.

***Maynard, Robert C.** Letters to My Children. (Illus.). 1995. 16.95 (*0-8362-7027-4*) Andrews & McMeel.

Maynard, Robert W. English to Spanish Vocabulary Conversion. 487p. (Orig.). (C). 1990. pap. 14.95 (*0-9626879-0-1*) Convocab Pub.

Maynard, Roger. Advanced Bowhunting Guide. (Illus.). 224p. (Orig.). 1984. pap. 14.95 (*0-88317-115-5*) Stoeger Pub Co.

Maynard, Roy. The Old Man. LC 93-43218. (Emerson Dunn Mystery Ser.). 192p. (Orig.). 1994. pap. 7.99 (*0-89107-772-3*) Crossway Bks.

— A Quick Thirty Seconds. LC 93-10829. (Emerson Dunn Mystery Ser.). 192p. (YA). 1993. pap. 7.99 (*0-89107-745-6*) Crossway Bks.

— Thirty-Eight Caliber. LC 92-6024. (Emerson Dunn Mystery Ser.). 192p. (Orig.). 1992. pap. 7.99 (*0-89107-674-3*) Crossway Bks.

— Twenty-Two Automatic. LC 92-21559. (Emerson Dunn Mystery Ser.). 192p. (Orig.). 1993. pap. 7.99 (*0-89107-696-4*) Crossway Bks.

Maynard, Russell. Tanto: Japanese Knives & Knife Fighting. LC 86-50440. 160p. (Orig.). 1986. pap. 7.95 (*0-86568-078-7*, 110) Unique Pubns.

Maynard, Senko K. Discourse Modality: Subjectivity, Emotion & Voice in the Japanese Language. LC 92-36878. (Pragmatics & Beyond New Series (P&BNS): No. 24). x, 315p. 1993. 65.00x (*1-55619-292-4*) Benjamins North Am.

— Japanese Conversation: Self-Contextualization Through Structure & Interactional Management. Freedle, Roy O., ed. (Advances in Discourse Processes Ser.: Vol. 35). 264p. (C). 1989. text ed. 55.00 (*0-89391-509-2*) Ablex Pub.

— One Hundred One Japanese Idioms: "Packed Like Sushi" & Other Popular Japanese Phrases: For All Students of Japanese. (Illus.). 240p. (JPN.). 1993. pap. 7.95 (*0-685-62853-1*, Natl Textbk) NTC Pub Grp.

Maynard-Smith, John. Evolution & the Theory of Games. 200p. 1982. pap. 21.95 (*0-521-28884-3*) Cambridge U Pr.

— Evolutionary Genetics. (Illus.). 344p. (C). 1989. pap. text ed. 35.00 (*0-19-854215-1*) OUP.

— The Theory of Evolution. 3rd ed. LC 93-20358. (Canto Book Ser.). (Illus.). 368p. 1993. pap. 11.95 (*0-521-45128-0*) Cambridge U Pr.

Maynard, Thane. Animal Olympians. LC 93-30769. (Cincinnati Zoo Ser.). (Illus.). (J). (gr. 5-7). 1994. lib. bdg. 15.47 (*0-531-11159-8*); pap. 9.95 (*0-531-15715-6*) Watts.

— Endangered Animal Babies: Saving Species One Birth at a Time. LC 92-33220. (Cincinnati Zoo Book Ser.). (Illus.). 56p. (J). (gr. 5-8). 1993. 15.95 (*0-531-15257-X*); lib. bdg. 15.47 (*0-531-11077-X*) Watts.

— Giant Animals. (Cincinnati Zoo Bks.). (Illus.). 64p. (J). (gr. 4-6). 1995. lib. bdg. 15.47 (*0-531-11208-X*) Watts.

— Giant Animals: The Struggles & Successes of Nature's Biggest Creatures. (Cincinnati Zoo Bks.). (Illus.). 64p. (J). (gr. 5-8). 1995. pap. 9.95 (*0-531-15742-3*) Watts.

— Primates: Apes, Monkeys, Prosimians. (Cincinnati Zoo Bks.). (Illus.). 64p. (J). (gr. 4-7). 1994. lib. bdg. 15.47 (*0-531-11169-5*) Watts.

— A Rhino Comes to America. (Illus.). 40p. (J). (gr. 4-8). 1993. 15.95 (*0-531-15258-8*); lib. bdg. 15.47 (*0-531-11173-3*) Watts.

— Saving Endangered Birds: Ensuring a Future in the Wild. (Illus.). 56p. (J). (gr. 5-7). 1993. 15.95 (*0-531-15260-X*); lib. bdg. 15.47 (*0-531-11094-X*) Watts.

— Saving Endangered Mammals: A Field Guide to Some of the Earth's Rarest Animals. LC 92-14439. (Cincinnati Zoo Book Ser.). 1992. 15.95 (*0-531-15253-7*) Watts.

— Saving Endangered Mammals: A Field Guide to Some of the Earth's Rarest Animals. (Illus.). 64p. (J). (gr. 5-8). 1992. lib. bdg. 15.47 (*0-531-11076-1*) Watts.

Maynard, Theodore. Carven from the Laurel Tree, Essays. LC 67-23246. (Essay Index Reprint Ser.). 1977. 15.95 (*0-8369-0700-0*) Ayer.

— Il Mondo E' Troppo Piccolo: Vita Di Francesca Cabrini. Santi, M., tr. (Orig.). (ITA.). (C). 1987. reprint ed. pap. text ed. 5.00 (*0-9619397-0-2*) MSSH.

— Pillars of the Church. LC 76-136763. (Essay Index Reprint Ser.). 1977. 21.95 (*0-8369-1940-8*) Ayer.

Maynard, Trisha, jt. auth. see Furlong, John.

***Maynard, Ursula K.** Performing Postmodernity. 1995. write for info. (*0-8204-2661-X*) P Lang Pubs.

Maynard, Winifred. Elizabethan Lyric Poetry & Its Music. (Illus.). 256p. 1986. 65.00 (*0-19-812844-4*) OUP.

Maync, Harry. Conrad Ferdinand Meyer und Sein Werk. LC 76-100522. (GER.). reprint ed. 49.50 (*0-404-00597-7*) AMS Pr.

Mayne, jt. auth. see Hopkins.

Mayne, Alan. The Imagined Slum: Newspaper Representations in the English Speaking World, 1870-1914. 256p. 1993. 59.00 (*0-7185-1389-4*, Pub. by Leicester Univ Pr) St Martin.

— Imagined Slum Vol. 1: Newspaper Representations in the English Speaking World, 1870-1914. 1994. pap. 20.00 (*0-7185-2134-X*, Pub. by Leicester Univ Pr) St Martin.

Mayne, Alan J. Resources for the Future: An International Annotated Bibliography. LC 92-35820. (Bibliographies & Indexes in Economics & Economic History Ser.: No. 13). 288p. 1993. text ed. 75.00 (*0-313-28911-5*, GR8911) Greenwood.

Mayne, Anne. Annie's Cottage Crafts. (Illus.). 56p. 1993. pap. 7.95 (*0-86417-406-3*, Pub. by Kangaroo Pr AT) Seven Hills Bk.

— Annie's Country Crafts. (Illus.). 48p. 1993. reprint ed. pap. 7.95 (*0-86417-307-5*, Pub. by Kangaroo Pr AT) Seven Hills Bk.

— Annie's Creative Crafts. (Illus.). 56p. (Orig.). 1993. pap. 7.95 (*0-86417-537-X*, Pub. by Kangaroo Pr AT) Seven Hills Bk.

— Annie's Easy Crafts. (Annie's Ser.). (Illus.). 72p. (Orig.). 1995. pap. 10.95 (*0-86417-583-3*) Seven Hills Bk.

***Mayne, Anne & Simmonds, Diane.** Annie's Easy Treats. (Annie's Ser.). (Illus.). 64p. (Orig.). 1995. pap. 10.95 (*0-86417-618-X*) Seven Hills Bk.

Mayne, Cora. Romance at Perristone. large type ed. 1990. 21.95 (*0-7089-2127-2*) Ulverscroft.

— Romance in Norway. large type ed. (Linford Romance Library). 255p. 1984. pap. 11.95 (*0-7089-6019-7*, Trailtree Bookshop) Ulverscroft.

— Romance on Lizard Island. large type ed. (Linford Romance Library). 215p. 1984. pap. 11.95 (*0-7089-6021-9*, Trailtree Bookshop) Ulverscroft.

— Romantic Legacy. large type ed. (Linford Romance Library). 304p. 1984. pap. 11.95 (*0-7089-6008-1*, Trailtree Bookshop) Ulverscroft.

— The Roylake Ruby. large type ed. 1991. 21.95 (*0-7089-2373-9*) Ulverscroft.

— The Sanborne Beguest. large type ed. (Linford Romance Library). 304p. 1985. pap. 11.95 (*0-7089-6105-3*, Trailtree Bookshop) Ulverscroft.

Mayne, E. Byron, 2 vols., Set. 1972. 200.00 (*0-87968-807-6*) Gordon Pr.

***Mayne, Elizabeth.** All That Matters: (March Madness) (Historical Ser.). 1995. pap. 4.50 (*0-373-28859-X*, 1-28859-6) Harlequin Bks.

— Heart of the Hawk. 1995. mass mkt. 4.50 (*0-373-28891-3*) Harlequin Bks.

Mayne, Ethel C. Byron. LC 76-117883. (Select Bibliographies Reprint Ser.). 1977. reprint ed. 26.95 (*0-8369-5336-3*) Ayer.

— Byron. (BCL1-PR English Literature Ser.). 474p. 1992. reprint ed. lib. bdg. 99.00 (*0-7812-7480-X*) Rprt Serv.

— Byron. LC 72-108511. (Illus.). xvi, 474p. 1972. reprint ed. 22.00 (*0-403-01098-5*) Scholarly.

Mayne, Ethel C., tr. see Haller, Johannes.

Mayne, Gilles. Eroticism in Georges Bataille & Henry Miller. LC 93-85167. 206p. (Orig.). 1993. pap. 24.95 (*0-917786-93-9*) Summa Pubns.

Mayne, J., jt. auth. see Carr, T. L.

Mayne, J., et al, eds. Advancing Public Policy Evaluation: Learning from International Experiences. LC 92-40625. 1992. write for info. (*0-444-89810-7*, North Holland) Taylor & Francis.

Mayne, Jonathan, ed. see Baudelaire, Charles P.

Mayne, Jonathan, ed. see Baudelaire, Charles.

Mayne, Jonathan, ed. see Leslie, C. R.

Mayne, Judith. Cinema & Spectatorship. LC 92-24927. (Sightlines Ser.). 192p. 1993. 49.95 (*0-415-03415-9*, A1707, Routledge NY); pap. 16.95 (*0-415-03416-7*, Routledge NY) Routledge.

— Directed by Dorothy Arzner. LC 93-51496. 1995. 29.95 (*0-253-33716-X*); pap. 15.95 (*0-253-20896-3*) Ind U Pr.

— Kino & the Woman Question: Feminism & Soviet Silent Film. (Illus.). 211p. 1989. text ed. 35.00 (*0-8142-0481-3*) Ohio St U Pr.

— Private Novels, Public Films. LC 87-19239. 200p. 1988. 25.00 (*0-8203-1007-7*) U of Ga Pr.

— The Woman at the Keyhole: Feminism & Women's Cinema. LC 90-34125. (Illus.). 270p. 1990. 35.00 (*0-253-33719-4*); pap. 12.95 (*0-253-20606-5*, MB-606) Ind U Pr.

Mayne, Lynette K. A Glimpse of Our Society Through Poetry. 1987. 39.00 (*0-7223-2072-8*, Pub. by A H S Ltd UK) St Mut.

Mayne, Peter. A Year in Marrakesh. 1993. reprint ed. pap. 14.95 (*0-907871-30-5*) Hippocrene Bks.

Mayne, R. & Margolis, S. Introduction to Engineering. 1982. text ed. write for info. (*0-07-041137-9*) McGraw.

Mayne, R. W., ed. see American Society of Mechanical Engineers Staff.

Mayne, Richard, comp. Operation 'Nestegg: The Liberation of Jersey, 1945. (Illus.). 80p. (C). 1987. pap. 21.00 (*0-317-90376-4*, Pub. by Picton UK) St Mut.

Mayne, Richard & Burgeson, Robert E., eds. Structure & Function of Collagen Types. (Biology of Extracellular Matrix Ser.). 274p. 1987. text ed. 105.00 (*0-12-481280-5*) Acad Pr.

***Mayne, Richard J., ed.** Western Europe. fac. rev. ed. LC 85-29242. (Handbooks to the Modern World Ser.). 786p. 1986. pap. 180.00 (*0-7837-8613-1*, 2059168) Bks Demand.

***Mayne, Seymour.** Children of Abel. 80p. 1995. lib. bdg. 27.00 (*0-8095-4531-4*) Borgo Pr.

— Diasporas: Poems 1973-1977. 128p. 1995. lib. bdg. 27.00 (*0-8095-4538-1*) Borgo Pr.

— The Impossible Promised Land: Poems New & Selected. 128p. 1995. lib. bdg. 27.00 (*0-8095-4555-1*) Borgo Pr.

— Killing Time. 80p. 1995. lib. bdg. 33.00 (*0-8095-4800-3*) Borgo Pr.

***Mayne, Seymour, ed. & tr.** Generations: Selected Poems of Rachel Korn. 96p. 1995. lib. bdg. 25.00 (*0-8095-4947-6*) Borgo Pr.

Mayne, Seymour, ed. see Dor, Moshe.

Mayne, Seymour, tr. see Ravitch, Melech.

Mayne, Seymour, tr. see Sutzkever, Abraham.

Mayne, Seymour, tr. see Vinner, Shlomo.

Mayne, Sharon. Winner Takes All. (Temptation Ser.). 1993. mass mkt. 2.99 (*0-373-25535-7*, 1-25535-5) Harlequin Bks.

Mayne, Thom. Morphosis Connected Isolation: Architectural Monograph. No. 23. 1993. 55.00 (*0-312-08687-3*, Academy Edits) St Martin.

Mayne, Tracy J., et al. Insiders Guide to Graduate Programs in Clinical Psychology: 1994-1995 Edition. 1994. pap. 18.95 (*0-89862-650-1*) Guilford Pubns.

Mayne, W. Harry. Fifty Years of Geophysical Ideas. 104p. 1989. pap. 17.00 (*0-931830-73-7*, 571) Soc Expl Geophys.

Mayne, William. Drift. 1992. 16.00 (*0-8446-6547-9*) Peter Smith.

— Earthfasts. (J). (gr. 4-7). 19.75 (*0-8446-6430-8*) Peter Smith.

— Hob & the Goblins. LC 94-7029. (Illus.). 144p. (J). (gr. 3-6). 1994. 12.95 (*1-56458-713-4*) Dorling Kindersley.

— Lady Muck. LC 95-14009. (J). 1996. write for info. (*0-395-75281-7*) HM.

— Low Tide. (J). (gr. 4-7). 1995. pap. 3.99 (*0-440-41055-X*) Dell.

— A Year & a Day. (J). (gr. 4-7). 18.75 (*0-8446-6431-6*) Peter Smith.

Mayne, Xavier, pseud. Imre: A Memorandum. LC 75-12337. (Homosexuality Ser.). 1975. reprint ed. 17.95 (*0-405-07388-7*) Ayer.

Mayne, Xavier. The Intersexes: A History of Similsexualism As a Problem in Social Life. LC 75-12338. (Homosexuality Ser.). 1975. reprint ed. 48.95 (*0-405-07364-X*) Ayer.

Maynell, Everard. The Life of Francis Thompson. 1988. reprint ed. lib. bdg. 75.00 (*0-317-90165-6*) Rprt Serv.

***Maynes, C. William & Williamson, Richard S., eds.** United States Foreign Policy & the United Nations System. 352p. 1995. 27.50 (*0-393-03907-2*) Norton.

Maynes, Florence J., jt. auth. see Ross, John A.

Maynes, Judah L. Pioneer & Prophet on Two Continents: A Pictorial Biography. (Illus.). 56p. 1977. 6.00 (*0-685-49190-0*) Magnes Mus.

Maynes, Mary J. Schooling in Western Europe: A Social History. LC 84-8847. (SUNY Series in Interdisciplinary Perspectives in Social History). 177p. 1985. 64.50 (*0-87395-978-7*); pap. 21.95 (*0-87395-977-9*) State U NY Pr.

— Taking the Hard Road: Life Course & Class Identity in Nineteenth-Century French & German Workers' Autobiographies. LC 94-27197. (Illus.). 300p. 1995. lib. bdg. 39.95x (*0-8078-2187-X*); pap. text ed. 16.95x (*0-8078-4497-7*) U of NC Pr.

Maynes, Mary Jo. Schooling for the People: Comparative Local Studies of Schooling History in France & Germany, 1750-1850. LC 84-10929. 272p. 1985. 49.75 (*0-8419-0966-0*) Holmes & Meier.

Maynes, Mary Jo, jt. ed. see Joeres, Ruth-Ellen B.

Maynial, ed. see Flaubert, Gustave.

Maynor, Beth & Johnson, Norman. Everyday Flowers. LC 90-60750. 160p. 1990. 34.95 (*0-929264-39-8*) Longstreet Pr Inc.

Mayo. Women's Bodybuilding for Beginners. 1984. pap. 2.95 (*0-02-499890-7*) Macmillan.

Mayo, A., et al. Inquiry on Cost Efficiency & Mechanisms Towards a Systematic Evaluation. 102p. 1992. pap. 12.00 (*92-826-3271-7*, CD-NA-13992-EN-C, Pub. by Europ Com) UNIPUB.

Mayo, Allen. Contract at Mount Horeb. LC 75-13402. (Illus.). 1977. 10.95 (*0-918268-01-X*) Tex-Mex.

— The Fortress of Miguel. 2nd ed. LC 57-12987. (Illus.). 1974. 10.95 (*0-918268-00-1*) Tex-Mex.

***Mayo, Amory D.** Southern Women in the Recent Educational Movement in the South. fac. ed. Carter, Dan T. & Friedlander, Amy, eds. LC 78-1554. (Library of Southern Civilization Ser.). 333p. 1978. reprint ed. pap. 95.00 (*0-7837-7807-4*, 2047563) Bks Demand.

Mayo, Andrew. Managing Careers. 320p. (C). 1991. pap. 100.00 (*0-85292-481-X*, Pub. by IPM Hse UK) St Mut.

***Mayo, Andrew & Lank, Elizabeth.** The Power of Learning: A Guide to Gaining Competitive Advantage. 280p. (C). 1994. pap. 60.00x (*0-85292-565-4*, Pub. by IPM Hse UK) St Mut.

Mayo, Bernard. Jefferson Himself: The Personal Narrative of a Many-Sided American. LC 70-87871. (Illus.). 384p. 1970. reprint ed. pap. 14.95 (*0-8139-0310-6*) U Pr of Va.

— The Philosophy of Right & Wrong. 176p. 1986. 25.00 (*0-7102-0851-0*, 08510, RKP); pap. 13.95 (*0-7102-0859-6*, 08596, RKP) Routledge.

Mayo, Bernard, ed. Instructions to the British Ministers to the United States, 1791-1812. LC 70-75280. (Law, Politics & History Ser.). 1971. lib. bdg. 55.00 (*0-306-71303-9*) Da Capo.

Mayo, Bernard & Bear, James A., eds. Thomas Jefferson & His Unknown Brother. LC 80-25272. 59p. 1981. 7.95 (*0-8139-0890-6*) U Pr of Va.

Mayo, Buddy. Finance: An Introduction. 4th ed. 700p. (C). 1992. pap. text ed. 56.00 (*0-03-055018-1*) Dryden Pr.

Mayo, C. & Henley, N. H., eds. Gender & Nonverbal Behavior. (Social Psychology Ser.). (Illus.). 288p. 1981. 64.00 (*0-387-90601-0*) Spr-Verlag.

***Mayo, C. M.** Sky over El Nido. LC 95-9961. 1995. write for info. (*0-8203-1766-7*) U of Ga Pr.

Mayo, Clark. Kurt Vonnegut: The Gospel from Outer Space: or Yes We Have No Nirvanas. LC 77-24460. (Milford Ser.: Popular Writers of Today Vol. 7). 64p. 1977. lib. bdg. 20.00 (*0-89370-111-4*); pap. 10.00 (*0-89370-211-0*) Borgo Pr.

Mayo Clinic Staff. Clinical Examinations in Neurology. 6th ed. 536p. 1991. 39.95 (*0-8151-2216-0*, Yr Bk Med Pubs) Mosby Yr Bk.

— Mayo Clinic Heart Book. 1993. 25.00 (*0-688-09972-6*) Morrow.

Mayo, Cynthia R. Developing Tomorrow's Leaders Today: A Global Perspective: Leadership Development for Youths. 200p. (J). (gr. 8 up). 1991. pap. 25.00 (*0-9630519-0-3*) M&M Pub.

Mayo, Dana W., et al. Microscale Organic Laboratory. 2nd ed. 522p. 1989. Net. text ed. write for info. (*0-471-63629-0*) Wiley.

— Microscale Organic Laboratory with Selected Macroscale Experiments. 3rd ed. 768p. 1994. text ed. write for info. (*0-471-57505-4*) Wiley.

— Techniques of Microscale Organic Chemistry. 285p. 1991. Net. pap. text ed. write for info. (*0-471-62192-7*) Wiley.

Mayo, DeBarra. Runner's World Yoga, Bk. II. 180p. (Orig.). 1983. pap. 9.95 (*0-89037-274-8*) Anderson World.

Mayo, Deborah G. & Hollander, Rachelle D., eds. Acceptable Evidence: Science & Values in Risk Management. (Environmental Ethics & Science Policy Ser.). (Illus.). 304p. 1991. 49.95 (*0-19-506372-4*) OUP.

Mayo, Deborah G., et al, eds. Acceptable Evidence: Science & Values in Risk Management. (Environmental Ethics & Science Policy Ser.). (Illus.). 304p. 1994. reprint ed. pap. 19.95 (*0-19-508929-4*) OUP.

Mayo, Diane. Murder at Bean & Beluga. (Illus.). 64p. 1983. pap. 5.95 (*0-932966-33-0*) Permanent Pr.

Mayo, Dorothy O., jt. auth. see Whitcomb, Esther K.

Mayo, E. L. Collected Poems. Ray, David, ed. LC 80-84519. (New Letters Ser.). 272p. (Orig.). 1981. pap. text ed. 20.00 (*0-938652-00-1*) New Letters MO.

Mayo, Edith. American Material Culture. LC 84-71338. 255p. 1984. 30.95 (*0-87972-303-3*); pap. 13.95 (*0-87972-304-1*) Bowling Green Univ.

Mayo, Edith P. & Meringolo, Denise D. First Ladies: Political Role & Public Image. LC 94-14470. 1994. 8.95 (*0-929847-06-7*) Natl Mus Am.

Mayo, Elton. The Human Problems of an Industrial Civilization. Stein, Leon, ed. LC 77-70515. (Work Ser.). 1977. reprint ed. lib. bdg. 28.95 (*0-405-10184-8*) Ayer.

— The Social Problems of an Industrial Civilization. Stein, Leon, ed. LC 77-70516. (Work Ser.). 1977. reprint ed. lib. bdg. 22.95 (*0-405-10185-6*) Ayer.

Mayo Foundation for Medical Education & Research. Mayo Clinic Book of Pregnancy & Baby's First Year. LC 94-7264. 1994. 30.00 (*0-688-11761-9*) Morrow.

Mayo, Gael E. A Man in a Panther Skin. 112p. 1985. 42.00 (*0-946041-36-9*, Pub. by Kensal Pr UK) St Mut.

Mayo, Gretchen W. Earthmaker's Tales: North American Indian Stories about Earth Happenings. LC 88-20515. (Illus.). 96p. (J). (gr. 5 up). 1989. 12.95 (*0-8027-6839-3*); lib. bdg. 13.85 (*0-8027-6840-7*) Walker & Co.

— Meet Tricky Coyote! LC 92-12424. (Native American Trickster Tales Ser.). (Illus.). 35p. (J). (gr. 6-10). 1993. 12.95 (*0-8027-8198-5*); lib. bdg. 13.85 (*0-8027-8199-3*) Walker & Co.

— North American Indian Stories, 4 vols., Set. (Illus.). 256p. (J). (gr. 5 up). 1990. pap. 23.80 (*0-8027-7341-9*) Walker & Co.

— North American Indian Stories: Earthmaker's Tales. (Illus.). 48p. (J). (gr. 5 up). 1990. pap. 5.95 (*0-8027-7343-5*) Walker & Co.

— North American Indian Stories: More Earthmaker's Tales. (Illus.). 48p. (J). (gr. 5 up). 1990. pap. 5.95 (*0-8027-7344-3*) Walker & Co.

— North American Indian Stories: More Star Tales. (Illus.). 48p. (J). (gr. 5 up). 1990. pap. 5.95 (*0-8027-7347-8*) Walker & Co.

— North American Indian Stories: Star Tales. (Illus.). 48p. (J). (gr. 5 up). 1990. pap. 5.95 (*0-8027-7345-1*) Walker & Co.

An Asterisk (*) at the beginning of an entry indicates that the title is appearing in BIP for the first time.

— Star Tales: North American Indian Stories about the Stars. 96p. (J). (gr. 5 up). 1987. 12.95 (*0-8027-6672-2*); lib. bdg. 13.85 (*0-8027-6673-0*) Walker & Co.

— That Tricky Coyote! LC 92-12440. (Native American Trickster Tales Ser.). (Illus.). 32p. (J). (gr. 1-5). 1993. 12.95 (*0-8027-8200-0*); lib. bdg. 13.85 (*0-8027-8201-9*) Walker & Co.

Mayo, Gretchen W., illus. & ret. Big Trouble for Tricky Rabbit! LC 93-29749. (Native American Trickster Tales Ser.). 48p. (J). (gr. 2-3). 1994. 12.95 (*0-8027-8275-2*); lib. bdg. 13.85 (*0-8027-8276-0*) Walker & Co.

— Here Comes Tricky Rabbit. LC 93-29763. (Native American Trickster Tales Ser.). 48p. (J). (gr. 2-3). 1994. 12.95 (*0-8027-8273-6*); lib. bdg. 13.85 (*0-8027-8274-4*) Walker & Co.

Mayo, Herbert B. Finance: An Introduction. 3rd ed. LC 88-7146. (Illus.). 797p. (C). 1989. text ed. 54.75 (*0-03-026723-4*) Dryden Pr.

— Investments: An Introduction. 3rd rev. ed. (Illus.). 750p. (C). 1991. text ed. 57.25 (*0-03-032668-0*) Dryden Pr.

— Investments: An Introduction. 4th ed. LC 92-76104. 1993. text ed. 59.00 (*0-03-097647-2*) Dryden Pr.

Mayo, Hope, ed. Descriptive Inventories of Manuscripts Microfilmed for the Hill Monastic Manuscript Library, Austrian Libraries, Vol. III: Herzogenburg. (Orig.). 1985. pap. 50.00 (*0-940250-03-9*) Hill Monastic.

Mayo, James M. The American Grocery Store: The Business Evolution of an Architectural Space. LC 92-45072. (Contributions in American History Ser.: No. 150). 304p. 1993. text ed. 59.95 (*0-313-26520-8*, MGS, Greenwood Pr) Greenwood.

— War Memorials As Political Landscape: The American Experience & Beyond. LC 87-22328. 219p. 1988. text ed. 52.95 (*0-275-92812-8*, C2812, Praeger Pubs) Greenwood.

***Mayo, Jeff.** Astrology: A Key to Personality. 384p. 1995. 13.95 (*0-14-019489-4*, Arkana) Viking Penguin.

— The Planets & Human Behavior. LC 85-22367. 182p. 1986. pap. 9.95 (*0-916360-27-X*) CRCS Pubns CA.

— Teach Yourself Astrology. (Teach Yourself Ser.). (Orig.). 1980. pap. 6.95 (*0-679-12001-7*) McKay.

Mayo-Jefferies, Deborah. Equal Educational Opportunity for All Children: A Research Guide to Discrimination in Education, 1950-1992. LC 93-43237. xiv, 90p. 1994. 35.00 (*0-89941-859-7*, 308050) W S Hein.

— Religious Freedom in the Education Process: A Research Guide to Religion in Education (1950-1992) LC 94-8623. (Legal Research Guides Ser.). 1994. 32.50 (*0-89941-871-6*, 308170) W S Hein.

Mayo, Jeffrey K. Angel of My Heart. abr. ed. 180p. 1995. pap. 7.95 (*1-56901-348-9*) NW Pub.

Mayo, John K., et al. Educational Reform with Television: The El Salvador Experience. LC 75-7484. (Illus.). 232p. 1976. 29.50 (*0-8047-0896-7*) Stanford U Pr.

Mayo, Jon, jt. auth. see Accrocco, Joseph O.

Mayo, Jonathan L. Optical Disks. (Illus.). 208p. 1990. 24.95 (*0-8306-8372-0*, 3372, Windcrest); pap. 15.95 (*0-8306-3372-3*, 3372, Windcrest) TAB Bks.

— The Packet Radio Handbook. (Illus.). 224p. 1987. pap. 14.95 (*0-8306-2722-7*, NO. 2722) TAB Bks.

— The Packet Radio Handbook. 2nd ed. (Illus.). 240p. 1989. pap. 16.95 (*0-8306-3222-0*) TAB Bks.

— The Radio Amateur's Digital Communications Handbook. 1992. pap. text ed. 14.95 (*0-07-156007-6*) McGraw.

— The Radio Amateur's Digital Communications Handbook. (Illus.). 224p. 1992. 22.95 (*0-8306-8362-3*, 3362); pap. 14.95 (*0-8306-3362-6*) TAB Bks.

— Superconductivity: The Threshold of a New Technology. (Illus.). 160p. 1988. 18.95 (*0-317-67252-5*); pap. 12.95 (*0-317-67253-3*) TAB Bks.

— Superconductivity - The Threshold of a New Technology. 1988. pap. 12.95 (*0-8306-9322-X*, 3022P) TAB Bks.

Mayo, Jonathan L., jt. auth. see Traister, Robert J., Sr.

Mayo, Katherine. Justice to All: The Story of the Pennsylvania State Police. LC 70-154576. (Police in America Ser.). 1971. reprint ed. 24.95 (*0-405-03374-5*) Ayer.

— Mother India. LC 76-88906. 440p. 1970. reprint ed. text ed. 65.00 (*0-8371-2309-7*, MAMO, Greenwood Pr) Greenwood.

Mayo, Laurence S. John Endecott: A Biography. 1988. reprint ed. lib. bdg. 49.00 (*0-7812-0166-7*) Rprt Serv.

— John Endecott: A Biography. (Illus.). 1971. reprint ed. 49.00 (*0-403-01099-3*) Scholarly.

***Mayo, Lawrence S.** Jeffrey Amherst: A Biography. (Illus.). 344p. 1995. reprint ed. lib. bdg. 45.00 (*0-8328-4505-1*) Higginson Bk Co.

Mayo, Louise A. The Ambivalent Image: Nineteenth-Century America's Perception of the Jew. LC 87-45572. 224p. 1988. 32.50 (*0-8386-3318-8*) Fairleigh Dickinson.

Mayo, M. J., et al, eds. Superplasticity in Metals, Ceramics, & Intermetallics: Symposium Proceedings Ser., Vol. 196. 1990. text ed. 52.00 (*1-55899-085-2*) Materials Res.

Mayo, Margaret. Dangerous Journey. large type ed. 1991. pap. 8.95 (*0-7451-9483-4*, 265, Atlantic Lrg Print) Chivers N Amer.

— An Impossible Situation. large type ed. 1991. reprint ed. lib. bdg. 18.95 (*0-263-12565-3*) Thorndike Pr.

— Intrigue. (Romance Ser.). 1995. pap. 2.99 (*0-373-17216-8*, 1-17216-2) Harlequin Bks.

— Intrigue. large type ed. 1993. reprint ed. lib. bdg. 18.95 (*0-263-13185-8*, Pub. by Mills & Boon UK) Thorndike Pr.

— Our Fate & the Zodiac. 135p. 1967. reprint ed. spiral bd. 5.50 (*0-7873-0592-8*) Mokelumne.

— Reluctant Hostage. large type ed. 1992. lib. bdg. 18.95 (*0-263-13126-2*, Pub. by Mills & Boon UK) Thorndike Pr.

— Stormy Relationship. 1994. 2.99 (*0-373-11652-7*) Harlequin Bks.

— Tortoise's Flying Lesson: Animal Stories. LC 94-19752. (Illus.). (J). 1995. 17.00 (*0-15-200332-0*) HarBrace.

— Wild Injustice. large type ed. Date not set. 18.95 (*0-263-14041-5*) Thorndike Pr.

Mayo, Marjorie. Communities & Caring: The Mixed Economy of Welfare. LC 93-37356. 1994. text ed. 45.00 (*0-312-12027-3*) St Martin.

Mayo, Marjorie, jt. ed. see Craig, Gary.

Mayo, Martha, ed. Comunidade: The Portuguese Community in Lowell, 1905-1930. (Illus.). 84p. (Orig.). 1994. pap. 8.95 (*0-9631604-2-7*) Lowell Hist Soc.

***Mayo, Marti.** Robert Helm: 1981-1993. (Illus.). 144p. 1995. pap. 25.00 (*0-295-97452-4*) U of Wash Pr.

Mayo, Marti, ed. Painters: Jones, Smith, Stack, Utterback. (Illus.). 28p. 1981. pap. 9.00 (*0-936080-04-3*) Cont Arts Museum.

Mayo, Marti, text. Robert Morris: Selected Works, 1970-1980. (Illus.). 60p. 1981. pap. 8.00 (*0-936080-06-X*) Cont Arts Museum.

Mayo, Marti & Ward, Elizabeth. Houston Area Exhibition, 1988. (Illus.). 28p. 1988. pap. 3.00 (*0-941193-03-9*) U Houst Sarah.

Mayo, Marti, jt. ed. see Schnabel, Julian.

Mayo, Mary A. God's Good Gift: Teaching Your Kids about Sex--Ages 8 to 11. 48p. 1991. pap. 5.99 (*0-310-53470-4*) Zondervan.

— In the Beginning: Teaching Your Children about Sex--Ages 4-7. 32p. 1991. pap. 5.99 (*0-310-53480-1*) Zondervan.

— Looking Good, but Feeling Bad: How a Healthy Body Image Can Set You Free to Enjoy the Way You Look. 216p. 1994. pap. 8.99 (*0-89283-867-1*, Vine Bks) Servant.

Mayo, Melanie. The Directory of Stained Glass: Books & Patterns Thru 1988. 2nd ed. Stained Glass Images Inc. Staff, ed. 208p. 1989. text ed. write for info. (*0-936459-10-7*) Stained Glass.

Mayo, Michael A. & Harrap, K. A., eds. Vectors in Virus Biology. (Society for General Microbiology Special Publications: No. 12). 1984. text ed. 85.00 (*0-12-481480-8*) Acad Pr.

Mayo, Morrow. Los Angeles. 1992. reprint ed. lib. bdg. 75.00 (*0-7812-5064-1*) Rprt Serv.

Mayo, Oliver. Agriculture: The Theory of Plant Breeding. 2nd ed. (Illus.). 320p. 1987. 52.50 (*0-19-854172-4*) OUP.

— Wines of Australia. (Books on Wine Ser.). 246p. 1991. pap. 13.95 (*0-571-13869-1*) Faber & Faber.

— Wines of Australia: New Edition. (Faber Books on Wine Ser.). 246p. 1991. 24.95 (*0-571-16395-5*) Faber & Faber.

Mayo, Oliver, jt. ed. see Brock, D. J.

Mayo, P., jt. auth. see Gajewski, N.

Mayo, Patrick. You're Entitled! Browne, Thomas P., ed. LC 89-80335. 144p. (Orig.). 1989. pap. 9.95 (*0-926991-00-0*) Linmar Assocs.

Mayo, Patty & Gajewski, Nancy. SSS: Social Skill Strategies, Book B: A Curriculum for Adolescents. (Illus.). 350p. (Orig.). (YA). (gr. 5-12). 1989. pap. 33.00 (*0-930599-52-7*) Thinking Pubns.

— Transfer Activities: Thinking Skill Vocabulary Development. (Illus.). 202p. (YA). (gr. 5-12). 1987. pap. text ed. 31.00 (*0-930599-13-6*) Thinking Pubns.

Mayo, Patty & Waldo, Pattii. Communicate. (Educational Game Activity Ser.). (Orig.). (YA). (gr. 5-12). 1986. 39.00 (*0-930599-04-7*) Thinking Pubns.

— Communicate Expansion Cards. (Educational Game Activity Ser.). (YA). (gr. 5-12). 1988. 25.00 (*0-930599-22-5*) Thinking Pubns.

— Scripting: Social Communication for Adolescents. 292p. (YA). (gr. 5-12). 1994. spiral bd. 31.00 (*0-930599-08-X*) Thinking Pubns.

Mayo, Patty, jt. auth. see Gajewski, Nancy.

Mayo, Patty, et al. Communicate Junior. (Illus.). 60p. (J). (gr. 1-4). 1991. bds. 35.00 (*0-930599-68-3*) Thinking Pubns.

— Social Star: General Interaction Skills, Bk. 1. LC 92-39097. 485p. (J). (gr. 2-5). 1993. pap. 35.00 (*0-930599-79-9*) Thinking Pubns.

— Study Smart. (Illus.). 59p. (YA). (gr. 5-12). 1990. 39.00 (*0-930599-64-0*) Thinking Pubns.

Mayo, Peg E. Blind Raftery: Seven Nights of a Wake. 166p. 1991. pap. 14.95 (*1-880797-00-3*) RiverVoice Pr.

— Heroes in the Seaweed: A Therapist's View of the Resilent Human Spirit. 408p. 1991. pap. 14.95 (*1-880797-02-X*) RiverVoice Pr.

Mayo, Peg E., jt. auth. see Feinstein, David.

Mayo, Peter J. The Morphology of Aspect in Seventeenth-Century Russian: (Based on Texts of the Smutnoe Vremja) xi, 234p. (Orig.). 1985. pap. 19.95 (*0-89357-145-8*) Slavica.

Mayo, Roy F. Gold Mines of Southwest Oregon. (Illus.). 63p. (Orig.). 1987. pap. 10.95 (*0-931461-04-9*) Nugget Ent.

— Gold, Yours for the Digging. 52p. 1985. spiral bd. 9.95 (*0-931461-01-4*) Nugget Ent.

— A Journey with Roy Mayo: Liberty & Blewett. (Illus.). 50p. 1986. pap. 5.95 (*0-931461-02-2*) Nugget Ent.

— Washington State Gold Mines. 92p. 1983. boxed 10.95 (*0-931461-00-6*) Nugget Ent.

Mayo, S. T., jt. auth. see Kurtz, A. K.

Mayo-Santana, Raul, jt. auth. see Negron-Portillo, Mariano.

***Mayo-Smith, Ian.** Poems, Essays & Comments for Everyone. LC 94-39164. 92p. (Orig.). 1994. pap. 9.95 (*1-56549-043-6*) Kumarian Pr.

— Reports That Get Results: Guidelines for Executives. fac. ed. LC 89-24716. (Illus.). 45p. 1994. pap. 25.00 (*0-7837-7582-2*, 2047335) Bks Demand.

Mayo-Smith, Ian & Ruther, Nancy L. Achieving Improved Performance in Public Organizations: A Guide for Managers. LC 86-7327. (Guideline Ser.). 128p. (Orig.). 1986. pap. 14.95 (*0-931816-04-1*) Kumarian Pr.

Mayo, Virginia. Dont' Forget Me Santa Claus. (J). (ps). 1993. 12.95 (*0-8120-6391-0*) Barron.

— The Swan. (Illus.). 32p. (J). (ps-3). 1994. 12.95 (*0-8120-6408-9*); pap. 5.95 (*0-8120-1938-5*) Barron.

Mayo, W. E., ed. Processing & Applications of High Tc Superconductors. LC 88-62259. (Illus.). 257p. 1988. 95.00 (*0-87339-075-X*, 335) Minerals Metals.

Mayo, Wally, contrib. Praise for Two. 1988. 8.95 (*0-685-68331-1*, MB-597) Lillenas.

Mayo, William E. & Cwiakala, Martin. The FORTRAN 90 Workbook. 1991. pap. text ed. write for info. (*0-07-041148-4*) McGraw.

— Introduction to Computing for Engineers. 1991. text ed. write for info. (*0-07-041139-5*) McGraw.

— Schaum's Outline of Programming with FORTRAN. (Schaum's Outline Ser.). 1994. pap. text ed. write for info. (*0-07-041155-7*) McGraw.

— Schaum's Outline of Programming with Fortran 90. LC 95-15657. (Schaum's Outline Ser.). 1995. pap. text ed. 13.95 (*0-07-041156-5*) McGraw.

Mayo, William E., ed. see Metallurgical Society Staff.

Mayo, William S. Kaloolah; or, Journeyings to the Djebel Kumri: An Autobiography of Jonathan Romer. LC 72-2071. (Black Heritage Library Collection). 1977. reprint ed. 43.95 (*0-8369-9059-5*) Ayer.

Mayoh, B., et al, eds. Constraint Programming. (NATO ASI, Series F, Computer & Systems Sciences: Vol. 131). vii, 452p. 1994. 98.00 (*0-387-57859-5*) Spr-Verlag.

Mayoh, B. H. Problem Solving with ADA. LC 81-14675. (Wiley Series in Computing). 243p. reprint ed. pap. 69.30 (*0-685-44424-4*, 2032658) Bks Demand.

Mayoh, Brian, ed. Scandinavian Conference on Artificial Intelligence '91: Proceedings of the SCAI '91, Roskilde, Denmark, 21-24 May, 1991. (Frontiers in Artificial Intelligence & Applications Ser.: Vol. 12). 350p. 1991. 66.00 (*90-5199-056-1*, Pub. by IOS Pr NE) IOS Press.

Mayor, A. Hyatt. Artists & Anatomists. 1994. 19.95 (*0-8109-6447-3*) Abrams.

— Prints & People: A Social History of Printed Pictures. LC 80-7817. (Illus.). 496p. 1980. pap. 29.50 (*0-691-00326-2*) Princeton U Pr.

Mayor, A. Hyatt, ed. Fifteenth & Sixteenth Century European Drawings. (Illus.). 1967. pap. 7.95 (*0-8079-0101-6*) October.

Mayor, A. Hyatt, intro. A Century of American Sculpture: Treasures from Brookgreen Gardens. LC 80-22762. (Illus.). 132p. 1988. 49.95 (*0-89659-877-2*) Abbeville Pr.

Mayor, Andreas, tr. see Proust, Marcel.

Mayor, Archer. Borderlines. 320p. 1991. mass mkt. 4.50 (*0-380-71600-3*) Avon.

— Borderlines. 320p. 1994. mass mkt. 5.50 (*0-446-40443-8*, Mysterious Paperbk) Warner Bks.

— Borderlines. large type ed. LC 91-2310. 398p. 1991. reprint ed. lib. bdg. 19.95 (*1-56054-162-8*) Thorndike Pr.

— The Dark Root. 1995. write for info. (*0-89296-558-4*) Mysterious Pr.

— Fruits of the Poisonous Tree. 1994. 19.95 (*0-89296-557-6*) Mysterious Pr.

— Fruits of the Poisonous Tree. 304p. 1995. mass mkt. 5.50 (*0-446-40374-1*, Mysterious Paperbk) Warner Bks.

— Open Season. 320p. 1989. pap. 3.95 (*0-380-70756-X*) Avon.

— Open Season. 336p. 1994. mass mkt. 5.99 (*0-446-40414-4*, Mysterious Paperbk) Warner Bks.

— Scent of Evil. 368p. 1992. 18.95 (*0-89296-471-5*) Mysterious Pr.

— Scent of Evil. 384p. 1993. mass mkt. 5.99 (*0-446-40335-0*, Mysterious Paperbk) Warner Bks.

— The Skeleton's Knee. 320p. 1993. 18.95 (*0-89296-470-7*) Mysterious Pr.

— The Skeleton's Knee. 320p. 1994. mass mkt. 5.50 (*0-446-40099-8*, Mysterious Paperbk) Warner Bks.

— The Skeleton's Knees. large type ed. LC 94-5669. 1994. lib. bdg. 20.95 (*0-7862-0227-0*) Thorndike Pr.

Mayor, Barbara & Pugh, A. K., eds. Language, Communication & Education. 480p. (Orig.). 1986. pap. 16.95 (*0-7099-3590-0*, Pub. by Croom Helm UK) Routledge Chapman & Hall.

***Mayor, David G., ed. & comp.** The Saga of a Quiet Birdman: The Autobiography of Paul B. Jackson, Colonel USAF (Ret.) (Illus.). 320p. (Orig.). 1994. pap. 19.95 (*1-877633-20-8*) Luthers.

Mayor, F., ed. Scientific Research & Social Goals: Toward a New Development Model. 248p. 1982. 107.00 (*0-08-028118-4*, Pub. by Pergamon Repr UK) Franklin.

Mayor, F. M. The Rector's Daughter. 224p. 1992. 9.95 (*0-14-018265-9*, Penguin Classics) Viking Penguin.

— The Rector's Daughter. large type ed. 1993. 39.95 (*0-7066-1030-X*, Pub. by Remploy Pr CN) St Mut.

***Mayor, Federico.** The New Page. (UNESCO Ser.). 100p. 1995. text ed. 39.95 (*1-85521-652-3*, Pub. by Dartmth Pub UK) Ashgate Pub Co.

— Patterns. Wiltshire, Rosemary, tr. 89p. 1994. pap. 14.95 (*1-85610-034-0*, Pub. by Forest Bks UK) Dufour.

Mayor, G., ed. International Continence Society, Annual Meeting, 7th, Portoroz, 1977. (Urologia Internationalis Ser.: Vol. 33, No. 5). (Illus.). 1978. pap. 31.25 (*3-8055-2974-0*) S Karger.

Mayor, Georges & Zingg, Ernst J. Urologic Surgery: Diagnosis, Techniques, & Postoperative Treatment. LC 75-36660. 643p. reprint ed. pap. 180.00 (*0-317-07965-4*, 2016475) Bks Demand.

Mayor, J. B. Classification of Shelley's Metre. LC 75-116796. (Studies in Shelley: No. 25). 1970. reprint ed. lib. bdg. 50.95 (*0-8383-1038-9*) M S G Haskell Hse.

Mayor, J. E., ed. see Ascham, Roger.

Mayor, J. E., ed. see Fisher, John.

Mayor, John E. Ricardi di Cirenscestria Speculum Historiale de Gestis Regum Angliae, 2 vols. (Rolls Ser.: No. 30). 1974. reprint ed. Vol. 1, 447-871. write for info. (*0-8115-1059-X*); reprint ed. Vol. 2, 872-1066. write for info. (*0-318-58897-8*) Periodicals Srv.

— Ricardi di Cirenscestria Speculum Historiale de Gestis Regum Angliae, 2 vols., Set. (Rolls Ser.: No. 30). 1974. reprint ed. 110.00 (*0-8115-1058-1*) Periodicals Srv.

Mayor, Joseph B. Chapters on English Metre. LC 73-100516. reprint ed. 29.50 (*0-404-04285-6*) AMS Pr.

— The Epistle of James. 3rd ed. LC 90-36539. 402p. 1990. reprint ed. lib. bdg. 24.99 (*0-8254-3256-1*); reprint ed. pap. 19.99 (*0-8254-3255-3*) Kregel.

Mayor la Guardia's Commission on the Harlem Riot. Complete Report of Mayor La Guardia's Commission on the Harlem Riot of March 19, 1935. LC 76-90204. (Mass Violence in America Ser.). 1977. reprint ed. 20.95 (*0-405-01328-0*) Ayer.

Mayor Marsan, Maricel. Rostro Cercano: (Antologia Poetica) LC 86-82717. 62p. (SPA.). 1986. pap. 8.00 (*0-935318-12-7*) Edins Hispamerica.

Mayor, Michael, jt. ed. see Duquennoy, Antoine.

***Mayor, Susan & Fowle, Diane.** Samplers. Calloway, Stephen, ed. (Illus.). 64p. 1995. pap. 9.95 (*1-55921-154-7*) Moyer Bell.

M

Mayoral, Jorge. Ayuda y Esperanza para el Toxicomano: Help & Hope for the Addict. (SPA.). 5.95 (*84-7645-251-9*, 223249, Pub. by Edit Clie SP) TSELF.

Mayorga, Dolores. David Plays Hide-&-Seek in Celebrations: David Juega Al Escondite y Celebra. (David Bks.). (Illus.). 24p. (ENG & SPA.). (J). (gr. 2-5). 1992. lib. bdg. 18.95 (*0-8225-2001-X*, Lerner Publctns) Lerner Group.

— David Plays Hide-&-Seek in Folktales: David Juega Al Escondite En Cuentos Folkloricos. (David Bks.). (Illus.). 24p. (ENG & SPA.). (J). (gr. 2-5). 1992. lib. bdg. 18.95 (*0-8225-2003-6*, Lerner Publctns) Lerner Group.

— David Plays Hide-&-Seek in the City: David Juega Al Escondite En la Ciudad. (David Bks.). (Illus.). 24p. (ENG & SPA.). (J). (gr. 2-5). 1992. lib. bdg. 18.95 (*0-8225-2002-8*, Lerner Publctns) Lerner Group.

— David Plays Hide-&-Seek on Vacation: David Juega Al Escondite En Vacaciones. (David Bks.). (Illus.). 24p. (ENG & SPA.). (J). (gr. 2-5). 1992. lib. bdg. 18.95 (*0-8225-2004-4*, Lerner Publctns) Lerner Group.

***Mayorga, Margaret, ed.** Best Short Plays of 1957-58. LC 38-8006. 316p. 1958. 16.95 (*0-910278-84-9*) Boulevard.

***Mayorga, Nancy.** Hunger of the Soul. 144p. Date not set. pap. 5.95 (*0-940698-00-5*) Vedanta Ctr.

***Mayorga, Roberto & Montt, Luis.** Foreign Investment in Chile: The Legal Framework for Business, the Foreign Investment Regime in Chile, Environmental System in Chile, Documents. LC 95-4054. 1995. lib. bdg. 114.00 (*0-7923-3359-4*, Pub. by M Nijhoff) Kluwer Ac.

Mayorova, K. V. Teach Yourself Russian. 318p. (C). 1988. 19.95 (*0-8285-3927-8*) Firebird NY.

Mayors Commission for Women of Philadelphia, et al. Guide to Women's History Resources in the Delaware Valley Area. (Illus.). 224p. (Orig.). 1984. pap. 23.95 (*0-8122-1168-5*) U of Pa Pr.

Mayott, Clarence W. & Milano, Geraldine B. Solid Modelling with Pro-Engineer. 336p. (C). 1993. ring bd. 36.95 (*0-8403-8729-6*) Kendall-Hunt.

Mayotte, Georgia. Ten Poems. (Illus.). 32p. 1994. pap. 10.00 (*1-883862-05-1*) Bks Beyond Brdrs.

Mayotte, Judy. Disposable People? The Plight of Refugees. LC 92-29489. 300p. 1992. 23.95 (*0-88344-839-4*) Orbis Bks.

Mayper. Come & See. (J). Date not set. 15.00 (*0-06-023526-8*); lib. bdg. 14.89 (*0-06-023527-6*) HarpC Child Bks.

Mayper, Monica. Oh Snow. LC 90-42088. (Illus.). 32p. (J). (ps-1). 1991. lib. bdg. 14.89 (*0-06-024204-3*) HarpC Child Bks.

Mayper, Stuart, ed. General Semantics Bulletin: Official Annual Journal of the Institute of General Semantics. 15.00 (*0-910780-00-5*) Inst Gen Seman.

Mayr, D. & Sussmann, G. Space, Time, & Mechanics. 1982. lib. bdg. 74.50 (*90-277-1525-4*) Kluwer Ac.

Mayr, E. W., ed. Graph-Theoretic Concepts in Computer Science: Eighteenth International Workshop, Wiesbaden-Naurod, Germany, June 18-20, 1992, Proceedings. LC 92-46173. (Lecture Notes in Computer Science Ser.: Vol. 657). 1993. 53.00 (*0-387-56402-0*) Spr-Verlag.

***Mayr, E. W. & Schmidt, G., eds.** Graph-Theoretic Concepts in Computer Science. (Lecture Notes in Computer Science: Vol. 903). 414p. 1995. pap. 68.00 (*3-540-59071-4*) Spr-Verlag.

Mayr, Ernst. Animal Species & Evolution. LC 63-9552. (Illus.). 811p. 1963. text ed. 56.00 (*0-674-03750-2*) Belknap Pr.

— Evolution & the Diversity of Life: Selected Essays. 709p. 1976. 50.00 (*0-674-27104-1*) HUP.

— The Growth of Biological Thought: Diversity, Evolution & Inheritance. 992p. 1990. pap. text ed. 18.95 (*0-674-36446-5*) Belknap Pr.

— One Long Argument: Charles Darwin & the Genesis of Modern Evolutionary Thought. (Illus.). 195p. (C). 1991. text ed. 19.95 (*0-674-63905-7*) HUP.

— One Long Argument: Charles Darwin & the Genesis of Modern Evolutionary Thought. (Questions of Science Ser.). (Illus.). 195p. (C). 1993. pap. text ed. 14.00 (*0-674-63906-5*) HUP.

— Populations, Species, & Evolution: An Abridgment of Animal Species & Evolution. abr. ed. LC 79-111486. 453p. 1970. pap. 16.95 (*0-674-69013-3*) Belknap Pr.

— Principles of Systematic Zoology. 2nd ed. 1991. text ed. write for info. (*0-07-041144-1*) McGraw.

An Asterisk (*) at the beginning of an entry indicates that the title is appearing in BIP for the first time.

— Systematics & the Origin of Species. Eldridge, Niles & Gould, Stephen J., eds. LC 82-4215. (Classics in Evolution Ser.). 384p. 1982. reprint ed. pap. text ed. 21.00 (*0-231-05449-1*) Col U Pr.
— Toward a New Philosophy of Biology: Observations of an Evolutionist. (Illus.). 640p. 1989. pap. text ed. 16.95 (*0-674-89666-1*) HUP.
Mayr, Ernst, ed. The Species Problem. LC 73-17831. (Natural Sciences in America Ser.). (Illus.). 410p. 1974. reprint ed. 28.95 (*0-405-05749-0*) Ayer.
Mayr, Ernst & Provine, William B. The Evolutionary Synthesis: Perspectives on the Unification of Biology. LC 80-13973. 498p. 1980. 42.50 (*0-674-27225-0*) HUP.
Mayr, Ernst & Short, Lester L. Species Taxa of North American Birds: A Contribution to Comparative Systematics. (Publications of the Nuttall Ornithological Club: No. 9). (Illus.). 127p. 1970. 7.00 (*1-877973-19-X*, 9) Nuttall Ornith.
Mayr, Ernst, jt. auth. see Kohler, Rolf.
Mayr, Giovanni S. Adelasia Ed Aleramo & Excerpts from Other Operas. LC 90-754562. (Italian Opera Ser., 1810-1840). 368p. 1991. text ed. 119.00 (*0-8240-6560-3*) Garland.
Mayr, Giovanni S., ed. Medea in Corinto. (Italian Opera Ser., 1810-1840: Vol. 12). 250p. 1987. 97.00 (*0-8240-6561-1*) Garland.
Mayr, Grace A., jt. auth. see Holtje, Adrienne K.
Mayr-Harting, Henry. The Coming of Christianity to Anglo-Saxon England. 3rd ed. 336p. 1991. 35.00 (*0-271-00806-7*); pap. 14.95 (*0-271-00769-9*) Pa St U Pr.
Mayr-Harting, Henry, ed. St. Hugh of Lincoln. (Illus.). 144p. 1987. 39.00 (*0-19-820120-6*) OUP.
Mayr-Harting, Henry & Moore, R. I., eds. Studies in Medieval History. (Illus.). 330p. 1985. text ed. 60.00 (*0-907628-68-0*) Hambledon Press.
Mayr, Helmut. A Guide to Fossils. Dinalay, D. & Windsor, A. G., trs. LC 92-15856. (Illus.). 256p. (C). 1992. text ed. 24.95 (*0-691-08789-X*) Princeton U Pr.
Mayr, Marlene, ed. Does the Church Really Want Religious Education? LC 87-35592. 267p. (C). 1988. pap. 17.95 (*0-89135-062-4*) Religious Educ.
— Modern Masters of Religious Education. LC 82-25009. 380p. (Orig.). 1983. pap. 16.95 (*0-89135-033-0*) Religious Educ.
Mayr, Otto. Authority, Liberty, & Automatic Machinery in Early Modern Europe. LC 85-15460. (Studies in the History of Technology). (Illus.). 304p. 1986. text ed. 38.00 (*0-8018-2843-0*) Johns Hopkins.
— Authority, Liberty & Automatic Machinery in Early Modern Europe. LC 85-15460. (Illus.). 288p. 1989. reprint ed. pap. text ed. 17.95 (*0-8018-3939-4*) Johns Hopkins.
— Deutsches Museum, Munich. (Illus.). 160p. 1990. 29.95 (*1-870248-29-5*) Scala Books.
Mayr, Otto, ed. The Clockwork Universe. 1980. lib. bdg. 55.00 (*0-88202-188-5*); write for info. (*0-686-77549-X*) Watson Pub Intl.
— Philosophers & Machines. LC 75-39528. 1975. lib. bdg. 15.00 (*0-88202-044-7*); pap. text ed. 6.95 (*0-685-52444-2*) Watson Pub Intl.
Mayr, Otto & Post, Robert C., eds. Yankee Enterprise: The Rise of the American System of Manufactures. LC 81-607315. (Illus.). 236p. (Orig.). (C). 1982. pap. text ed. 13.95 (*0-87474-631-0*, MAYEP) Smithsonian.
Mayr, Otto & Stephens, Carlene. American Clocks: Highlights from the Collections of the National Museum of American History. (Illus.). 48p. (Orig.). 1989. pap. 6.95 (*0-929847-03-2*) Natl Mus Am.
Mayr, P., ed. Surface Engineering. 595p. 1993. lib. bdg. 108.00 (*3-88355-189-9*, Pub. by DGM Metallurgy Info GW) IR Pubns.
Mayr-Pletschen, Heide, illus. A Christmas Carol Book. (J). (gr. 3 up). 2.75 (*0-685-24603-5*) Merry Thoughts.
Mayr, Robert. Vocabularium Codicis Justiniani, 2 vols. 1552p. 1986. reprint ed. Bd. I: Pars Latina. write for info. (*0-318-70781-0*, Pub. by Georg Olms GW); reprint ed. Bd. II: Pars Graeca. write for info. (*0-318-70782-9*, Pub. by Georg Olms GW) Lubrecht & Cramer.
— Vocabularium Codicis Justiniani, 2 vols., Set. 1965. reprint ed. write for info. (*0-318-72048-5*, Pub. by Georg Olms GW) Lubrecht & Cramer.
— Vocabularium Codicis Justiniani, 2 vols., Set. 1552p. 1986. reprint ed. write for info. (*3-487-00835-1*, Pub. by Georg Olms GW) Lubrecht & Cramer.
***Mayr, Troy.** Southern California Sport Crags. 2nd ed. (Illus.). 200p. 1995. pap. write for info. (*0-614-05457-5*) Chockstone Pr.
Mayr, W. R., ed. Advances in Forensic Haemogenetics, No. 2. 670p. 1988. pap. 87.60 (*0-387-18765-0*) Spr-Verlag.
Mayr, Werner. The Cinderella Tree: The Story of Mayr Bros. Logging. (Illus.). 208p. (Orig.). 1992. pap. 14.95 (*1-879628-01-5*) Keokee ID.
Mayrand, jt. auth. see Goodner.
***Mayrand, Albert.** Dictionnaire de Maximes et Locutions Latines Utilisees en Droit Quebecois. 235p. (FRE & LAT.). 1972. 39.95 (*0-7859-8020-2*, 2760107787) Fr & Eur.
Mayreder, Rosa. A Survey of the Woman Problem. Herman, Scheffauer, tr. LC 79-2944. 275p. 1994. reprint ed. 30.00 (*0-8305-0108-8*) Hyperion Conn.
Mayrhofer, H. Monographie der Flechtengattung Thelenella. (Bibliotheca Lichenologica Ser.: Vol. 26). (Illus.). 116p. (GER.). 1987. pap. 36.60 (*3-443-58005-X*) Lubrecht & Cramer.
Mayrhofer, H. & Poelt, J. Die Saxicolen Arten der Flechtengattung Rinodina in Europa. (Bibliotheca Lichenologica Ser.: No. 12). (Illus.). (GER.). 1979. lib. bdg. 30.00 (*3-7682-1237-8*) Lubrecht & Cramer.
Mayrhofer, Manfred. Kurzgefasstes Etymologisches Woerterbuch des Altindischen, 4 vols., Set. (GER & SAN.). 1976. 995.00 (*0-8288-5722-9*, M7529) Fr & Eur.
Mayrhofer, Michaela. Studien ueber die saxicolen Arten der Flechtengattung Lecania II. Lecania s. Str. (Bibliotheca Lichenologica Ser.: Vol. 28). (Illus.). 134p. (GER.). 1988. pap. text ed. 39.00 (*3-443-58007-6*) Lubrecht & Cramer.
Mayrides, Paul, jt. auth. see Shelton, Gilbert.
***Mayrocker, Friederike.** Heiligenanstalt. Waldrop, Rosmarie, tr. (Dichten Ser.: No. 1). 96p. (Orig.). 1994. pap. 7.00 (*0-930901-95-9*) Burning Deck.
— Night Train. Bjorklund, Beth, tr. & aft. by. (Studies in Austrian Literature, Culture, & Thought. Translation Ser.). 126p. 1992. 17.00 (*0-929497-53-8*) Ariadne CA.
***Mays.** Pet Owners Rabbits. 1995. 8.00 (*0-87605-995-7*) Macmillan.
— Your First Mouse. 1995. pap. text ed. (*0-7938-0179-6*) TFH Pubns.
Mays & Valentine. Virginia Environmental Law Handbook. 2nd ed. (State Environmental Law Ser.). 342p. 1992. pap. text ed. 74.00 (*0-86587-315-1*) Gov Insts.
Mays & Valentine Staff. Virginia OSHA Compliance Handbook. 140p. (Orig.). 1992. pap. text ed. 72.00 (*0-86587-304-6*) Gov Insts.
Mays, Benjamin E. Born to Rebel: An Autobiography by Benjamin E. Mays. LC 86-19308. (Brown Thrasher Bks.). (Illus.). 440p. 1986. reprint ed. pap. 14.95 (*0-8203-0881-1*) U of Ga Pr.
— Negro's God As Reflected in His Literature. LC 69-16578. (Illus.). 269p. 1970. reprint ed. text ed. 59.50 (*0-8371-1139-0*, MAG&, Negro U Pr) Greenwood.
— Quotable Quotes of Benjamin E. Mays. LC 82-91028. 20p. 1983. 11.95 (*0-533-05685-3*) Vantage.
Mays, Benjamin E. & Nicholson, Joseph W. Negro's Church. LC 70-83430. (Religion in America, Ser. 1). 1973. reprint ed. 30.95 (*0-405-00255-6*) Ayer.
Mays, Bruce & Maltbie, Cynthis. Arenas, Stages & Spaces: A Guide to Theatres in Chicago & Vicinity. (Illus.). 117p. (Orig.). 1982. pap. 6.95 (*0-941906-00-0*) Diversity Pr.
Mays, Buddy. Ancient Cities of the Southwest. LC 81-21732. 1990. pap. 9.95 (*0-87701-696-8*) Chronicle Bks.
— Guide to Western Wildlife. 2nd ed. LC 77-22043. (Illus.). (Orig.). 1988. pap. 8.95 (*0-87701-504-X*) Chronicle Bks.
— Indian Villages of Southwest. 1990. pap. 9.95 (*0-87701-735-2*) Chronicle Bks.
***Mays, Carl.** Prayers from the Heart. (Illus.). 128p. (Orig.). 1995. pap. 9.95 (*1-879111-49-7*) Lincoln-Bradley.
— A Strategy for Winning: Winning...in Business, in Sports, in Family, in Life. LC 90-62803. (Illus.). 272p. 1991. 21.95 (*1-879111-75-6*) Lincoln-Bradley.
— Winning Thoughts: A Very Special Gift Book. 96p. (Orig.). 1994. pap. 5.95 (*1-879111-23-3*) Lincoln-Bradley.
Mays, D. A., ed. Forage Fertilization. (Illus.). 621p. 1974. 12.50 (*0-89118-006-0*) Am Soc Agron.
Mays, Daniel T. & Franks, Cyril M. Negative Outcome in Psychotherapy & What to Do about It. 384p. 1985. 39.95 (*0-8261-4030-0*) Springer Pub.
Mays, David, ed. see Forrest, Thomas.
Mays, E. C., tr. see Kung, Guido.
Mays, E. G., tr. see Hasenjaeger, G.
***Mays, Elaine & Midgley, Jon.** CompuCat. 85p. Date not set. pap. text ed. 7.95 (*0-9640463-1-8*) Compucat Ptrns.
Mays, G. C., ed. Durability of Concrete Structures: Investigation, Repair, Protection. 264p. 1991. 59.95 (*0-419-15620-8*, E & FN Spon) Routledge Chapman & Hall.
Mays, G. C. & Hutchinson, A. R. Adhesives in Civil Engineering. (Illus.). 342p. (C). 1992. 120.00 (*0-521-32677-X*) Cambridge U Pr.
Mays, G. Larry, jt. auth. see Champion, Dean J.
Mays, G. Larry, jt. ed. see Thompson, Joel A.
***Mays, Harriet A.** Daring Hearts & Spirits Free: History of the United Methodist Women of the South Carolina Conference. 256p. 1995. 16.95 (*1-881576-53-1*) Providence Hse.
***Mays, Harry R.** The History of Main Street United Methodist Church, Greenwood, South Carolina. (Illus.). 224p. 1993. 19.95 (*1-881576-09-4*) Providence Hse.
Mays, Howard L. Raising Fishworms with Rabbits. rev. ed. 1981. pap. 5.00 (*0-914116-10-X*) Shields.
Mays, J. C., intro. & notes. The Collected Poems of Denis Devlin. 366p. (C). 1989. 63.00 (*0-948268-50-6*, Pub. by Dedalus Pr IE) St Mut.
Mays, J. C., ed. see Devlin, Denis.
Mays, James L. Amos: A Commentary. LC 79-76885. (Old Testament Library). 176p. 1969. 20.00 (*0-664-20863-0*, Westminster) Westminster John Knox.
— Hosea: A Commentary. LC 75-79618. (Old Testament Library). 202p. 1969. 20.00 (*0-664-20871-1*, Westminster) Westminster John Knox.
— The Lord Reigns: A Theological Handbook of the Psalms. LC 94-10407. (Interpretation). 228p. (Orig.). 1994. pap. 14.99 (*0-664-25558-2*) Westminster John Knox.
— Micah: A Commentary. LC 76-2599. (Old Testament Library). 180p. 1976. 20.00 (*0-664-20817-7*, Westminster) Westminster John Knox.
— Psalms. LC 93-32887. (Interpretation, A Bible Commentary for Teaching & Preaching Ser.). 432p. 1994. 29.00 (*0-8042-3115-X*) Westminster John Knox.
Mays, James L., ed. Harper's Bible Commentary. LC 88-45148. 1988. 40.00 (*0-06-065541-0*); 42.50 (*0-06-065542-9*) Harper SF.
— Interpreting the Gospels. LC 80-8057. 317p. reprint ed. pap. 90.40 (*0-685-17050-0*, 2027872) Bks Demand.
Mays, James L. & Achtemeier, Paul J., eds. Interpreting the Prophets. LC 86-45223. 336p. 1987. pap. 20.00 (*0-8006-1932-3*, 1-1932, Fortress Pr) Augsburg Fortress.
Mays, James L., ed. see Clements, R. E.
Mays, James L., ed. see Janzen, J. Gerald.
Mays, James L., ed. see Japhet, Sara.
Mays, James L., ed. see Limburg, James.
Mays, James L., ed. see Seitz, Christopher.
***Mays, James L., et al.** Old Testament Interpretation: Past, Present & Future Essays in Honor of Gene M. Tucker. 400p. (Orig.). 1995. pap. 19.95 (*0-687-13871-X*) Dimen for Liv.
Mays, Jeanne, jt. auth. see Mays, John.
Mays, Jimmy W., jt. ed. see Barth, Howard G.
***Mays, John & Mays, Jeanne.** Worth Remembering: Ten Year Family Diary. (Illus.). 1994. pap. 20.00 (*1-880994-33-X*) Mt Olive Coll Pr.
— Worth Remembering: Ten Year Family Diary. (Illus.). 274p. 1994. 20.00 (*1-880994-22-4*) Mt Olive Coll Pr.
Mays, John B. Crime & Its Treatment. 2nd ed. LC 76-357144. (Aspects of Modern Sociology: the Social Structure of Modern Britain Ser.). 183p. reprint ed. pap. 52.20 (*0-685-43699-3*, 2027708) Bks Demand.
Mays, Ken. Harly Weaver & the Race across America. 128p. (YA). (gr. 6-12). 1994. pap. 5.00 (*0-88092-089-0*) Royal Fireworks.
— Harly Weaver & the Race across America. 128p. (YA). (gr. 6-12). 1994. lib. bdg. 15.00 (*0-88092-090-4*) Royal Fireworks.
Mays, Larry, jt. ed. see Thompson, Joel.
Mays, Larry W., ed. Reliability Analysis of Water Distribution Systems. 544p. 1989. pap. text ed. 36.00 (*0-87262-712-8*, 712) Am Soc Civil Eng.
Mays, Larry W. & Tung, Yeo-Koung. Hydrosystems Modeling for Engineering & Modeling. 1992. text ed. write for info. (*0-07-041146-8*) McGraw.
Mays, Larry W., jt. ed. see Chaudhry, M. Hanif.
Mays, Marianne. Proper Care of Hamsters. (Illus.). 256p. 1993. 14.95 (*0-86622-370-3*, TW125) TFH Pubns.
Mays, Mark H. CERCLA Enforcement Policy Manual. LC 93-8578. (Environmental Law Ser.). 1993. text ed. 95.00 (*0-07-172506-7*) Shepards-McGraw.
Mays, Melinda, jt. auth. see Grierson, Philip.
Mays, Nick. Proper Care of Fancy Rats. (Illus.). 256p. 1993. 14.95 (*0-86622-340-1*, TW122) TFH Pubns.
Mays, Ricard H., jt. auth. see Steinberg, Robert E.
Mays, Richard H. CERCLA Litigation. LC 93-4325. (Environmental Law Ser.). 1993. text ed. 190.00 (*0-07-172443-5*) Shepards-McGraw.
— Environmental Law Forms Guide. 2nd ed. LC 94-32775. (Environmental Law Ser.). 1994. write for info. (*0-07-172542-3*) Shepards-McGraw.
— Environmental Laws: Impact on Business Transactions: A Practice Guide with Forms. 538p. 1992. 98.00 (*0-87179-711-9*) BNA.
Mays, Robert E. Laboratory Experiences at USI. 60p. (C). 1986. pap. text ed. 6.00 (*0-89917-468-X*) Tichenor Pub.
Mays, Sted. A Kitten a Week. 112p. (Orig.). 1994. mass mkt. 4.00 (*0-345-38704-X*, Ballantine Trade) Ballantine.
***Mays, Terry.** Historical Dictionary of Multinational Peacekeeping. LC 95-14695. (International Organizations Ser.: No. 9). 1995. write for info. (*0-615-00714-7*) Scarecrow.
Mays, Terry M., jt. auth. see DeLancey, Mark W.
Mays, Vickie M., et al, eds. Primary Prevention of AIDS. (Primary Prevention of Psychopathology Ser.: Vol. 13). (Illus.). 400p. (C). 1989. 49.95 (*0-8039-3600-1*) Sage.
Mays, William E. Sublette Revisited: Stability & Change in a Rural Kansas Community After a Quarter of a Century. 142p. 1968. pap. 4.95 (*0-912598-03-4*) Florham.
Mays, Wolfe, jt. ed. see Brown, S. C.
Mayse, Susan W. Merlin's Web. 368p. 1989. mass mkt. 4.50 (*0-380-70624-5*) Avon.
Mayshack, John L. One Hundred & Seventy-Five Sermon Outlines. (Sermon Outline Ser.). 1979. pap. 2.99 (*0-8010-6085-0*) Baker Bk.
— One Hundred Sixty-Five Dynamic Sermon Outlines. (Sermon Outline Ser.). 80p. (Orig.). 1991. pap. 3.99 (*0-8010-6277-2*) Baker Bk.
Mayson, Cedric. A Certain Sound: The Struggle for Liberation in South Africa. LC 85-13678. 160p. (Orig.). reprint ed. pap. 45.60 (*0-8357-8546-7*, 2034884) Bks Demand.
Mayson, Stephen. Personal Management. 112p. (C). 1992. 31.00 (*1-85431-166-2*, Pub. by Blackstone Pr UK) W W Gaunt.
Mayson, Stephen & Blake, Susan. Mayson on Revenue Law. 728p. (C). 1991. 90.00 (*1-85431-146-8*, Pub. by Blackstone Pr UK) W W Gaunt.
— Revenue Law. 710p. (C). 1990. 225.00 (*1-85431-052-6*, Pub. by Blackstone Pr UK) St Mut.
— Revenue Law. 13th ed. 1993. 64.00 (*1-85431-269-3*, Pub. by Blackstone Pr UK) W W Gaunt.
Mayson, Stephen, et al. Company Law. 6th rev. ed. 744p. (C). 1990. 220.00 (*1-85431-076-3*, Pub. by Blackstone Pr UK) St Mut.
Mayson, Stephen, et al, eds. Mayson, French & Ryan on Company Law. 704p. (C). 1991. 58.00 (*1-85431-145-X*, Pub. by Blackstone Pr UK) W W Gaunt.
Mayson, Stephen W. & Blake, Susan. Revenue Law, 1992-93. 13th ed. 606p. 1993. pap. 58.00 (*1-85431-226-X*, Pub. by Blackstone Pr UK) W W Gaunt.
Mayson, Stephen W., et al. Company Law. 10th ed. 709p. 1994. pap. 54.00 (*1-85431-270-7*, Pub. by Blackstone Pr UK) W W Gaunt.
— Company Law, 1992-93. 9th ed. 704p. 1993. pap. 58.00 (*1-85431-225-1*, Pub. by Blackstone Pr UK) W W Gaunt.
Maystre, D. & Dainty, J. C., eds. Modern Analysis of Scattering Phenomena. (Illus.). 208p. 1991. 108.00 (*0-7503-0156-2*) IOP Pub.
Maystre, Daniel, ed. Selected Papers on Diffraction Gratings. LC 93-27724. (Milestone Ser.: Vol. MS83). 1993. write for info. (*0-8194-1371-2*); pap. write for info. (*0-8194-1370-4*) SPIE.
Maytag Staff. Maytag Handbook of Good Cooking. Settel, Trudy, ed. (Illus.). (Orig.). 1985. pap. 3.95 (*0-932523-00-5*) Briarcliff Pr.
Maytas, Antal. History of Modern Non-Marxian Economics. 592p. 1980. 117.50 (*0-685-17043-8*, Pub. by Collets UK) Pro-Am Music.
Mayton, William T., jt. auth. see Aman, Alfred C., Jr.
Mayura. Sanskrit Poems of Mayura. Quackenbos, George P., tr. LC 77-181072. (Columbia University. Indo-Iranian Ser.: No. 9). reprint ed. 28.50 (*0-404-50479-5*) AMS Pr.
Mayuranathan, P. V. The Flowering Plants of Madras City & Its Immediate Neighbourhood. 345p. 1981. 360.00 (*0-685-21851-1*, Pub. by Intl Bk Distr II) St Mut.
— Flowering Plants of Madras City & Its Immediate Neighbourhood. 345p. (C). 1981. text ed. 350.00 (*0-89771-584-5*, Pub. by Intl Bk Distr II) St Mut.
Maywald, Henry. The Backbone of American Passenger Trains: "E" Units. (Illus.). 72p. (Orig.). 1988. pap. 25.95 (*0-934088-19-5*) NJ Intl Inc.
***Maywald, Henry, ed.** Classic Freight Cars Vol. 6: Loaded Flats & Gondolas. (Illus.). 64p. (Orig.). 1994. pap. text ed. 24.95 (*1-882608-06-2*) H & M Prods.
— Classic Freight Cars Vol. 7: More 40 Ft. Boxcars. (Illus.). 64p. (Orig.). 1994. pap. text ed. 24.95 (*1-882608-08-9*) H & M Prods.
Mayyasi, Kim A. Inside Cellular: An Operating Manual for Dealers, Carriers, & Investors. LC 89-9687. 200p. 1989. ring bd. 95.00 (*0-931790-88-3*) Brick Hse Pub.
Mayz, Eusebio, et al. Mercury Poisoning, No. 1. LC 72-13563. (Illus.). 220p. (C). 1972. text ed. 29.50 (*0-8422-7072-8*) Irvington.
Maza, Bernard. With Fury Poured Out: The Power of the Powerless During the Holocaust. 256p. 1988. 24.95 (*0-944007-23-6*); pap. 12.95 (*0-944007-13-9*) Sure Sellers.
Maza, Sarah. Private Lives & Public Affairs: The Causes Celebres of Prerevolutionary France. LC 93-4518. (Studies on the History of Society & Culture: No. 18). 341p. 1993. 35.00 (*0-520-08144-7*) U CA Pr.
— Private Lives & Public Affairs: The Causes Celebres of Prerevolutionary France. (Studies on the History of Society & Culture: Vol. 18). (Illus.). 354p. 1995. pap. 15.00 (*0-520-20163-9*) U CA Pr.
Maza, Sarah C. Servants & Masters in 18th Century France: The Uses of Loyalty. LC 83-42566. (Illus.). 320p. 1983. 52.50 (*0-691-05394-4*) Princeton U Pr.
Mazak, Lisa. One, Two, Three, Jesus Loves Me. (Illus.). (J). (gr. k-6). 1982. 3.99 (*3-901170-18-9*) CEF Press.
Mazal-Cami, Charles. Twenty Thousand Words in Spanish, in Twenty Minutes! LC 91-91298. 198p. (Orig.). (C). 1991. pap. 14.95 (*0-9630572-2-7*) Palabra Pr.
***Mazal-Cami, Charles, ed.** 20,000 Words in Spanish, in 20 Minutes! 2nd ed. 198p. (Orig.). (C). 1995. pap. 14.95 (*0-9630572-3-5*) Palabra Pr.
Mazar, Amihai. Archaeology of the Land of the Bible: 10,000-586 B. C. E. (Anchor Bible Reference Library). 1990. 37.50 (*0-385-23970-X*, Anchor Bible) Doubleday.
— Archeology of the Land of the Bible: 10,000-586 B.C.E. 1992. pap. 20.00 (*0-385-42590-2*) Doubleday.
Mazar, Amihai, jt. auth. see Kelm, George L.
Mazar, Benjamin. Biblical Israel: State & People. Ahituv, Shmuel, ed. 175p. 1992. text ed. 25.00 (*0-685-72549-9*, Pub. by Magnes Press IS) Eisenbrauns.
***Mazar, Peter.** Clip Art for Bulletins. (Illus.). 85p. (Orig.). 1995. pap. write for info. (*1-56854-086-8*) Liturgy Tr Pubns.
— Clip Art for Year A. 84p. 1992. pap. 25.00 (*0-929650-59-X*, CLIP/A) Liturgy Tr Pubns.
— Liturgy & Appointment Calendar, 1995. Huck, Gabe, ed. (Illus.). 112p. (Orig.). 1994. pap. 12.95 (*1-56854-020-5*, APPCA5) Liturgy Tr Pubns.
— To Crown the Year: Decorating the Church Through the Seasons. 220p. (Orig.). 1995. pap. 9.95 (*1-56854-041-8*, CROWN) Liturgy Tr Pubns.
Mazar, Peter, ed. Take-Me-Home: Notes on the Church Year for Children. (Illus.). 128p. (Orig.). (J). (gr. 1-8). 1991. pap. 15.00 (*0-929650-52-2*) Liturgy Tr Pubns.
***Mazar, Peter & Piercy, Robert.** A Guide to the Lectionary for Masses with Children. 128p. (Orig.). 1994. pap. 8.95 (*1-56854-043-4*, GLmc) Liturgy Tr Pubns.
Mazar, Peter, ed. see Hynes, Mary E.
Mazar, Peter, et al, eds. A Lent Sourcebook, 2 vols., Set. (Orig.). 1990. spiral bd. 23.95 (*0-929650-36-0*) Liturgy Tr Pubns.
— A Lent Sourcebook, Vol. 1. (Seasonal Sourcebook Ser.). 232p. (Orig.). 1991. spiral bd. 12.95 (*0-929650-20-4*) Liturgy Tr Pubns.
— A Lent Sourcebook, Vol. 2: The Forty Days. (Seasonal Sourcebook Ser.). 229p. 1991. spiral bd. 12.95 (*0-929650-35-2*) Liturgy Tr Pubns.
Mazaris. Mazaris' Journey to Hades. (Arethusa Monographs: No. 5). xxxviii, 134p. (C). 1975. pap. 8.00 (*0-930881-02-8*) Dept Classics.
Mazaroff, Stanley. Maryland Employment Law. 767p. 1990. 70.00 (*0-87473-658-7*) Michie Butterworth.
— Maryland Employment Law. suppl. ed. 767p. 1992. 20.00 (*0-87473-857-1*) Michie Butterworth.
Mazarr, Michael J. Missile Defenses & Asian-Pacific Security. 173p. 1989. text ed. 49.95 (*0-312-02775-3*) St Martin.
— North Korea & the Bomb: A Case Study in Nonproliferation. LC 94-34868. 1995. text ed. 35.00 (*0-312-12443-0*) St Martin.
— Semper Fidel: America & Cuba, Seventeen Seventy-Six to Nineteen Eighty-Eight. LC 88-22537. 580p. 1988. 24.95 (*0-933852-74-6*) Nautical & Aviation.
— START & the Future of Deterrence. LC 90-8881. 208p. 1991. text ed. 65.00 (*0-312-05330-4*) St Martin.

An Asterisk (*) at the beginning of an entry indicates that the title is appearing in BIP for the first time.

Mazarr, Michael J. & Lennon, Alexander T., eds. Toward a Nuclear Peace: The Future of Nuclear Weapons. LC 93-28019. 224p. 1994. text ed. 39.95 (*0-312-10404-9*) St Martin.

Mazarr, Michael J., et al. Desert Storm: The Gulf War & What We Learned. LC 92-29687. 207p. (C). 1992. text ed. 37.00 (*0-8133-1598-0*) Westview.

Mazars, J., ed. Cracking & Damage - Strain Localization & Size Effects: Proceedings of the France - U. S. Workshop Held at the Laboratoire de Mechanique et Technolgie, ENS de Cachan, France, 6-9 September 1988. 552p. 1989. 108.00 (*1-85166-347-9*) Elsevier.

Mazat, Alberta. Questions You've Asked about Sexuality. (Lifeline Ser.). 127p. 1991. pap. 1.99 (*0-8163-1038-6*) Pacific Pr Pub Assn.

Mazauskas, Joan L. Mayday! Mayday! Eastern Airlines in a Tailspin! LC 89-84208. (Illus.). 352p. 1990. pap. 9.95 (*0-9623740-0-8*) Mazauskas Pubns.

Mazda, F. F. Discrete Electronic Components. 200p. 1981. 59.95 (*0-521-23470-0*) Cambridge U Pr.

— Electronics Engineer's Reference Book. 6th ed. 1032p. 1989. text ed. 160.00 (*0-408-00590-4*) Buttrwrth-Heinemann.

— Integrated Circuits: Technology & Applications. LC 77-71418. 218p. reprint ed. pap. 62.20 (*0-685-44044-3*, 2030609) Bks Demand.

— Power Electronics: Components, Circuits & Applications. 417p. 1990. text ed. 85.00 (*0-408-03004-6*, Pub. by John Wright UK) Buttrwrth-Heinemann.

— Power Electronics Handbook: Components, Circuits & Applications. (Illus.). 415p. 1993. pap. 45.00 (*0-7506-1633-4*) Buttrwrth-Heinemann.

Mazda, Fraidoon, ed. Telecommunications Engineer's Reference Book. (Illus.). 1000p. 1993. 125.00 (*0-7506-1162-6*) Buttrwrth-Heinemann.

Mazda, Maideh. In a Persian Kitchen: Favorite Recipes from the Near East. LC 60-6926. 176p. 1960. pap. 12.95 (*0-8048-1619-0*) C E Tuttle.

Mazdiyasni, K. S., ed. Fiber-Reinforced Ceramic Composites: Materials, Processing & Technology. LC 89-70989. (Illus.). 515p. 1990. 78.00 (*0-8155-1233-3*) Noyes.

Maze, C. Norman Glossary: Glossaire Normand. 124p. (FRE.). 1984. pap. 39.95 (*0-8288-1716-2*, F52940) Fr & Eur.

Maze, Carol M. Mexican Microwave Cookery. Lark, Virginia & Medina, Robert C., eds. LC 84-72508. 116p. (Orig.). 1984. pap. text ed. 6.00 (*0-933196-03-2*) Bilingue Pubns.

— Mexican Microwave Cookery. rev. ed. LC 90-46439. (Illus.). 164p. (Orig.). 1990. pap. 9.95 (*1-55561-039-0*) Fisher Bks.

Maze Carter, K. Holly. The Asian Dilemma in U. S. Foreign Policy: National Interest versus Strategic Planning. LC 88-3416. 250p. (C). 1989. 62.95 (*0-87332-512-5*); pap. text ed. 25.95 (*0-87332-544-3*) M E Sharpe.

Maze, Dessie L., ed. see Michelson, Maureen R.

Maze, John, jt. auth. see White, Graham.

***Maze, Marilyn & Mayall.** The Enhanced Guide for Occupational Exploration: Descriptions for the 2,500 Most Important Jobs. 2nd rev. ed. LC 91-8830. 704p. 1995. pap. 34.95 (*1-56370-207-X*) JIST Works.

Maze, Marilyn & Mayall, Donald. The Enhanced Guide for Occupational Exploration: Descriptions for the 2,500 Most Important Jobs. LC 91-8830. 608p. 1991. pap. 29.95 (*0-942784-76-6*, EGOE) JIST Works.

***Maze-Sencier, Genevieve.** Dictionnaire des Matechaux de France du Moyen Age a nos Jours. 452p. (FRE.). 1988. 115.00 (*0-7859-8637-5*, 226200546x) Fr & Eur.

Maze, T. H., jt. ed. see Maggio, Margk.

Mazei, Louis M. Practical Spreadsheet Statistics & Curve Fitting For Scientists & Engineers. 1990. text ed. 70.00 (*0-13-519877-1*) P-H.

Mazel, Charles. Heave Ho: My Little Green Book of Seasickness. 128p. 1992. pap. 7.95 (*0-87742-324-5*, 60313) Intl Marine.

— Heave Ho: My Little Green Book of Seasickness. (J). 1992. pap. 7.95 (*0-07-041165-4*) McGraw.

— Side Scan Sonar Record Interpretation. 146p. 1985. 46.95 (*0-932146-50-3*) Peninsula CA.

Mazel, David. Arizona Trails. 3rd ed. LC 89-50191. (Illus.). 320p. 1989. pap. 12.95 (*0-89997-104-0*) Wilderness Pr.

— My Heart's World: Stories by David Mazel. Adam-Casimiro, Niki, ed. & illus. by. LC 84-62148. 144p. 1985. pap. 9.95 (*0-931762-02-2*) Phunn Pubs.

Mazel, David, intro. Mountaineering Women: Stories by Early Climbers. LC 94-11260. (Illus.). 200p. 1994. 27.50 (*0-89096-616-8*); pap. 14.95 (*0-89096-617-6*) Tex A&M Univ Pr.

Mazel, Judy. Beverly Hills Diet. 1981. 10.95 (*0-02-582600-X*) Macmillan.

— The Beverly Hills Diet. 1994. reprint ed. lib. bdg. 24.95x (*1-56849-542-0*) Buccaneer Bks.

— Beverly Hills Diet Lifetime. 1982. 13.95 (*0-02-582630-1*) Macmillan.

Mazelev, L. Ye. Borate Glasses: Thermochemical Processes in Glass Formation, Crystallo-Optics, Technology, Physicochemical Properties, & Structure of Glasses with the Composition B203-Li20-MeO. LC 60-8719. 159p. reprint ed. pap. 45.40 (*0-8357-7349-3*, 2055799) Bks Demand.

Mazella, Annemarie, tr. see Consolata, Germana.

Mazen, Abu, jt. auth. see Abbas, Mahmoud.

Mazen, Thomas L., jt. auth. see Ratner, David L.

Mazenko, G., jt. ed. see Grinstein, G.

***Mazenod, Lucienne.** Dictionnaire des Femmes Celebres. 940p. (FRE.). 1992. pap. 59.95 (*0-7859-7803-8*, 2221052927) Fr & Eur.

Mazepa, S. C. Mazepa the Cossack: Mazepa Hetman of the Ukraine. (Illus.). 250p. Date not set. 19.95 (*0-9636099-0-4*) S C Mazepa.

***Mazer, Anne.** The Accidental Witch. LC 94-44284. (Illus.). 128p. (J). (gr. 3-7). 1995. 13.95 (*0-7868-0088-7*); lib. bdg. 13.89 (*0-7868-2073-X*) Hyprn Child.

— The Oxboy. LC 92-37199. 112p. (J). (gr. 3-7). 1993. 13.00 (*0-679-84191-1*) Knopf Bks Yng Read.

— The Salamander Room. LC 90-33301. (Illus.). 32p. (J). (ps-3). 1991. 15.00 (*0-394-82945-X*) Knopf Bks Yng Read.

— The Salamander Room. LC 90-33301. (Illus.). 32p. (J). (ps-3). 1991. lib. bdg. 14.99 (*0-394-92945-4*) Knopf Bks Yng Read.

— The Salamander Room. (Dragonfly Bks.). (Illus.). 32p. (J). (ps-3). 1994. pap. 5.99 (*0-679-86187-4*) Knopf Bks Yng Read.

Mazer, Anne, intro. America Street: A Multicultural Anthology of Stories. (YA). 1993. 14.95 (*0-89255-190-9*); pap. 4.95 (*0-89255-191-7*) Persea Bks.

— Going Where I'm Coming From: Personal Narrative of American Youth. (YA). (gr. 6 up). 1995. 15.95 (*0-89255-205-0*); pap. 6.95 (*0-89255-206-9*) Persea Bks.

***Mazer, Ben.** White Cities. LC 95-75261. (Illus.). 52p. (Orig.). 1995. pap. 10.00 (*0-9645516-0-8*) B Matteau.

Mazer, Bill. Bill Mazer's Amazin' Baseball Book. 1990. 19.95 (*0-8217-2947-0*) Zebra.

— Bill Mazer's Amazin' Baseball Book. 416p. 1991. pap. 8.95 (*0-8217-3361-3*) Zebra.

Mazer, Harry. Cave under the City. LC 86-45008. (Trophy Bk.). 160p. (J). (gr. 3-7). 1989. pap. 3.95 (*0-06-440303-3*, Trophy) HarpC Child Bks.

— The Dollar Man. (Orig.). (J). (gr. 6-12). 16.00 (*0-8446-6415-4*) Peter Smith.

— The Girl of His Dreams. 1988. pap. 2.95 (*0-380-70599-0*, Flare) Avon.

— Hey Kid! Does She Love Me? 176p. 1986. pap. 2.95 (*0-380-70025-5*, Flare) Avon.

— I Love You, Stupid! 192p. 1983. pap. 3.50 (*0-380-61432-4*, Flare) Avon.

— The Island Keeper. 176p. (J). (gr. k-12). 1982. pap. 3.50 (*0-440-94774-X*, LFL) Dell.

— The Last Mission. 192p. (J). (gr. 7 up). 1981. mass mkt. 3.99 (*0-440-94797-9*, LE) Dell.

— Snow Bound. 144p. (J). (gr. 5 up). 1975. mass mkt. 3.99 (*0-440-96134-3*, LFL) Dell.

— Snow Bound. 1987. 17.25 (*0-8446-6240-2*) Peter Smith.

— Someone's Mother Is Missing. (YA). 1991. pap. 3.50 (*0-440-21097-6*, YB) Dell.

— When the Phone Rang. 192p. (YA). (gr. 7 up). 1986. pap. 3.50 (*0-590-44773-4*) Scholastic Inc.

— Who Is Eddie Leonard? LC 93-22114. (J). (gr. 4 up). 1993. 14.95 (*0-385-31136-2*) Delacorte.

— Who Is Eddie Leonard? (YA). 1995. pap. 3.99 (*0-440-21922-1*) Dell.

Mazer, Harry, jt. auth. see Mazer, Norma F.

Mazer, Harvey, jt. ed. see Rako, Susan.

Mazer, Milton. People & Predicaments. 332p. 1976. 29.50 (*0-674-66075-7*) HUP.

Mazer, Norma F. A, My Name Is Ami. 160p. (Orig.). (J). (gr. 3-7). 1994. pap. 3.25 (*0-590-43896-4*, Apple Paperbacks) Scholastic Inc.

— After the Rain. 240p. 1987. mass mkt. 3.99 (*0-380-75025-2*, Flare) Avon.

— After the Rain. LC 86-33270. 304p. (YA). (gr. 7 up). 1987. 15.00 (*0-688-06867-7*) Morrow Jr Bks.

— After the Rain. large type ed. 408p. (J). (gr. 7 up). 1989. 14.95 (*0-8161-4807-4*, Large Print Bks) Hall.

— B, My Name Is Bunny. (J). (gr. 4-7). 1994. pap. 3.25 (*0-590-43895-6*) Scholastic Inc.

— Babyface. 176p. (YA). 1991. mass mkt. 3.99 (*0-380-75720-6*, Flare) Avon.

— Babyface. LC 90-6485. 176p. (YA). (gr. 7 up). 1990. 15.00 (*0-688-08752-3*) Morrow Jr Bks.

— Bright Days, Stupid Nights. 1993. mass mkt. 3.99 (*0-440-21594-3*) Dell.

— Bright Days, Stupid Nights. (YA). 1993. pap. 3.50 (*0-553-56253-3*) Bantam.

— C My Name Is Cal. 144p. (YA). 1990. 13.95 (*0-590-41833-5*, Point); pap. 2.95 (*0-685-49598-1*, Point) Scholastic Inc.

— D: My Name Is Danita. (J). (gr. 4-7). 1994. pap. 3.25 (*0-590-43656-2*) Scholastic Inc.

— D, My Name Is Danita. (J). (gr. 7 up). 1991. 13.95 (*0-590-43655-4*) Scholastic Inc.

— Downtown. 208p. 1984. pap. 3.50 (*0-380-88534-4*, Flare) Avon.

— Downtown. LC 84-91105. 192p. (YA). (gr. 7 up). 1984. 15.00 (*0-688-03859-X*) Morrow Jr Bks.

— E, My Name is Emily. 176p. (J). 1991. 13.95 (*0-590-43653-8*, Scholastic Hardcover) Scholastic Inc.

— Missing Pieces. 208p. (YA). (gr. 7 up). 1995. 15.00 (*0-688-13349-5*) Morrow Jr Bks.

— Mrs. Fish, Ape & Me, the Dump Queen. 144p. (Orig.). (J). (gr. 4 up). 1981. pap. 3.50 (*0-380-69153-1*, Flare) Avon.

— Out of Control. 224p. (J). (gr. 5 up). 1994. mass mkt. 3.99 (*0-380-71347-0*) Avon.

— Out of Control. LC 92-32516. 224p. (YA). (gr. 7 up). 1993. 15.00 (*0-688-10208-5*) Morrow Jr Bks.

— Out of Control. large type ed. LC 93-47266. (J). 1994. pap. write for info. (*0-7862-0159-2*) Thorndike Pr.

— Silver. 208p. (J). 1989. mass mkt. 3.99 (*0-380-75026-0*, Flare) Avon.

— Silver. LC 88-18652. 272p. (YA). (gr. 7 up). 1988. 15.00 (*0-688-06865-0*) Morrow Jr Bks.

— Silver. braille ed. 293p. (J). 1994. text ed. 23.44 (*1-56956-516-3*, BR9376) W A T Braille.

— Taking Terri Mueller. 192p. (J). (gr. 8 up). 1981. pap. 3.99 (*0-380-79004-1*, Flare) Avon.

— Taking Terri Mueller. LC 82-18849. 224p. (J). (gr. 7 up). 1983. 16.00 (*0-688-01732-0*) Morrow Jr Bks.

Mazer, Norma F. & Grey, Zane. The Shortstop. LC 88-18652. 272p. (YA). (gr. 7 up). 1988. pap. 4.95 (*0-688-11261-7*) Morrow Jr Bks.

Mazer, Norma F. & Mazer, Harry. Bright Days, Stupid Nights. 1992. 16.00 (*0-553-08126-8*) Bantam.

— Heartbeat. (YA). (gr. 7 up). 1990. mass mkt. 3.99 (*0-553-28779-6*, Starfire) Bantam.

— The Solid Gold Kid. (YA). (gr. 7 up). 1989. pap. 3.50 (*0-553-27851-7*, Starfire) Bantam.

Mazer, William M. Electrical Accident Investigation Handbook: Includes 1983-95 Supplements. LC 82-72167. (Illus.). 1300p. (C). 1995. 295.00 (*0-943890-03-9*, NA) Electrodata.

— Electrical Accident Investigation Handbook: 1983 Supplement. LC 82-72167. (Illus.). 100p. 1983. ring bd. write for info. (*0-943890-04-7*) Electrodata.

— Electrical Accident Investigation Handbook: 1984 Supplement. LC 82-72167. (Illus.). 150p. 1984. ring bd. 45.00 (*0-943890-05-5*) Electrodata.

— Electrical Accident Investigation Handbook: 1985 Supplement. LC 82-72167. (Illus.). 175p. 1985. ring bd. 55.00 (*0-943890-06-3*) Electrodata.

— Electrical Accident Investigation Handbook: 1986 Supplement. LC 82-72167. (Illus.). 200p. 1987. ring bd. 60.00 (*0-943890-07-1*) Electrodata.

— Electrical Accident Investigation Handbook: 1995 Supplement. suppl. ed. 350p. 1995. ring bd. 70.00 (*0-943890-10-1*) Electrodata.

— The Electrical Accident Investigation Handbook, 1987. suppl. ed. 300p. (C). 1990. 65.00 (*0-943890-08-X*) Electrodata.

Mazet, P. Analytic Sets in Locally Convex Spaces. (Mathematics Studies: Vol. 89). 1984. pap. 54.00 (*0-444-86867-4*, I-088-84, North Holland) Elsevier.

Mazey, Mary E., jt. auth. see Center for Urban.

Mazey, Mary E., et al. Her Space, Her Place: A Geography of Women. LC 83-22289. (Resource Publications in Geography). 90p. (C). 1983. pap. text ed. 10.00 (*0-89291-172-7*) Assn Am Geographers.

Mazey, Sonia & Newman, Michael, eds. Mitterrand's France. 256p. 1987. lib. bdg. 67.50 (*0-7099-4648-1*, Pub. by Croom Helm UK) Routledge Chapman & Hall.

Mazey, Sonia & Richardson, Jeremy J., eds. Lobbying in the European Community. (Nuffield European Studies, New Ser.). (Illus.). 280p. 1993. 49.95 (*0-19-827789-X*) OUP.

Mazey, Sonia, jt. ed. see Rhodes, Carolyn.

Mazgaj, Paul. The Action Francaise & Revolutionary Syndicalism. LC 79-4229. 293p. reprint ed. pap. 83.60 (*0-8357-4422-1*, 2037242) Bks Demand.

Maziar, A., tr. see Trakl, Georg.

Maziarka, Cynthia, ed. see Hemingway, Ernest.

Maziarka, Robert F., jt. auth. see Scott, Terrence J.

Maziarz, E. Value & Values in Evolution: A Symposium. (Current Topics of Contemporary Thought Ser.). 208p. 1979. text ed. 76.00 (*0-677-15240-X*) Gordon & Breach.

Maziarz, Edward A. You: Become a Full Person. (Illus.). 132p. (Orig.). 1983. pap. text ed. 6.95 (*0-9611274-0-6*) Shaman Bks.

Maziasz, Robert L. & Hayes, John P. Layout Minimization of CMOS Cells. (C). 1991. lib. bdg. 71.00 (*0-7923-9182-9*) Kluwer Ac.

Mazidi, Janice, jt. auth. see Mazidi, Muhammad A.

Mazidi, Janicer G., jt. auth. see Mazidi, Muhammad A.

Mazidi, Muhammad A. & Mazidi, Janice. Eighty x Eighty-Six IBM - Compatible Computers, Vol. 1: Assembly Language Programming. 480p. (C). 1993. text ed. 67.00 (*0-13-036286-7*) P-H.

***Mazidi, Muhammad A. & Mazidi, Janicer G.** Design & Interacting of the IBM PC, PS & Compatible. LC 94-29197. (Eighty X Eighty-Six IBM PC & Compatible Computers Ser.). 448p. 1994. text ed. 69.00 (*0-13-098567-8*) P-H.

Mazie, Sara M., jt. ed. see Hawley, Amos H.

Mazier, W. Patrick, et al. Surgery of the Colon, Rectum, & Anus. LC 93-40034. (Illus.). 992p. 1994. text ed. 225.00 (*0-7216-4689-1*) Saunders.

Mazik, James M., jt. auth. see Parsons, Bonnie.

Mazique, Mignon, jt. auth. see Kaplan, Robert E.

Mazis, Glen. Trickster, Magician & Grieving Man: Reconnecting Men with Earth. 324p. (Orig.). 1994. pap. 12.95 (*1-879181-11-8*) Bear & Co.

Mazis, Glen A. Emotion & Embodiment: Fragile Ontology. LC 93-3083. (Studies in Contemporary Continental Philosophy: Vol. 3). 1993. 39.95 (*0-8204-2171-5*) P Lang Pubs.

Mazja, W. G., jt. auth. see Gelman, I. W.

Mazlakh, Serhifi & Shakhrai, Vasyl. On the Current Situation in the Ukraine. Potichnyj, Peter J., ed. LC 76-107976. 254p. reprint ed. pap. 72.40 (*0-317-29148-3*, 2055631) Bks Demand.

Mazliak, P. Biogenesis & Function of Plant Lipids: Proceedings of the Paris Meeting, June 1980. (Developments in Plant Biology Ser.: Vol. 6). 1980. 106.75 (*0-444-80273-8*) Elsevier.

Mazliak, Paul, ed. see Eleventh International Meeting on Plant Lipids Staff.

Mazlish, Bruce. The Fourth Discontinuity: The Co-Evolution of Humans & Machines. LC 92-38075. (Illus.). 272p. 1993. 30.00 (*0-300-05411-4*) Yale U Pr.

— James & John Stuart Mill: Father & Son in the Nineteenth Century. 475p. (Orig.). 1988. pap. 24.95 (*0-88738-727-6*) Transaction Pubs.

— The Leader, the Led, & the Psyche: Essays in Psychohistory. LC 90-35351. 333p. 1990. 35.00 (*0-8195-5220-8*, Wesleyan Univ Pr) U Pr of New Eng.

— A New Science: The Breakdown of Connections & the Birth of Sociology. LC 93-3773. 348p. 1993. reprint ed. pap. 14.95 (*0-271-01092-4*) Pa St U Pr.

Mazlish, Bruce & Buultjens, Ralph, eds. Conceptualizing Global History. LC 93-25123. (Global History Ser.). 253p. 1993. text ed. 63.00 (*0-8133-1683-9*) Westview.

— Conceptualizing Global History. LC 93-25123. (Global History Ser.). 253p. (C). 1993. pap. text ed. 14.85 (*0-8133-1684-7*) Westview.

Mazlish, Bruce, jt. auth. see Bronowski, Jacob.

Mazlish, Bruce H. A New Science: The Breakdown of Connections & the Birth of Sociology. 352p. 1989. 39.95 (*0-19-505846-1*) OUP.

Mazlish, Elaine, jt. auth. see Faber, Adele.

Mazmanian, D. A., jt. auth. see Sabatier, Paul A.

Mazmanian, Daniel & Morell, David. Beyond Superfailure: America's Toxics Policy for the 1990s. 278p. (C). 1992. pap. text ed. 20.95 (*0-8133-1467-4*) Westview.

— Beyond Superfailure: America's Toxics Policy for the 1990s. 278p. 1992. text ed. 61.00 (*0-8133-1466-6*) Westview.

Mazmanian, Daniel A. Third Parties in Presidential Elections. LC 74-281. (Studies in Presidential Selection). (Illus.). 175p. reprint ed. pap. 49.90 (*0-685-23664-1*, 2027969) Bks Demand.

Mazmanian, Daniel A. & Nienaber, Jeanne. Can Organizations Change? Environmental Protection, Citizen Participation, & the Army Corps of Engineers. LC 78-27767. 232p. reprint ed. pap. 66.20 (*0-8357-8823-7*, 2033589) Bks Demand.

Mazmanian, Daniel A. & Trzyna, Thaddeus C. Issues & Alternatives: Reasons & Methods for Protecting California Farmlands. (California Farmlands Project Working Paper Ser.: No. 3). 24p. (Orig.). 1983. pap. 5.00 (*0-912102-64-0*) Cal Inst Public.

Mazmanian, Daniel A., et al. Breaking Political Gridlock: California's Experiment in Public-Private Cooperation for Hazardous Waste Policy. LC 88-15342. (Environmental Studies: No. 8). (Illus.). 104p. (Orig.). 1988. pap. 20.00 (*0-912102-86-1*) Cal Inst Public.

Mazo-Calf, Karyn, et al. Among Us: A Collection of Writings. (Illus.). 53p. (Orig.). 1989. pap. 7.00 (*0-929848-00-4*) Peace Ventures Pr.

Mazo, Joseph H. Dance Is a Contact Sport. LC 76-6557. (Paperback Ser.). 1976. pap. 9.95 (*0-306-80044-6*) Da Capo.

Mazo, Judith F., et al, eds. Providing Health Care Benefits in Retirement. LC 94-13655. (Pensions Ser.). 280p. (C). 1994. text ed. 39.95 (*0-8122-3270-4*) U of Pa Pr.

Mazo, R. & McCoubrey, J. Statistical Mechanical Theories of Transport Processes. LC 66-26595. (International Encyclopedia of Physical Chemistry & Chemical Physics Ser.: Vol. 1, TP 9). 1967. 74.00 (*0-08-011942-5*, Pub. by Pergamon Repr UK) Franklin.

Mazollier, J., jt. auth. see Daumas, Eugene.

Mazon, Mauricio. The Zoot-Suit Riots: The Psychology of Symbolic Annihilation. (Mexican American Monographs: No. 8). (Illus.). 179p. 1984. reprint ed. pap. 9.95 (*0-292-79803-2*) U of Tex Pr.

Mazonowicz, Douglas. Cave Art. (Shorewood Art Programs for Education Ser.). 8p. (Orig.). 1984. pap. 57.50 (*0-88185-025-X*); 75.50 (*0-685-09477-4*) Shorewood Fine Art.

Mazor, Emanuel. Applied Chemical & Isotopic Groundwater Hydrology. 274p. 1991. text ed. 79.95 (*0-471-93242-6*) Wiley.

Mazor, L. Analytical Chemistry of Organic Halogen Compounds. LC 75-5934. 400p. 1975. 120.00 (*0-08-017903-7*, Pub. by Pergamon Repr UK) Franklin.

Mazor, M., jt. ed. see Svehla, Gyula I.

Mazor, Michel. The Vanished City: Everyday Life in the Warsaw Ghetto. Jacobson, David, tr. LC 92-62367. 208p. 1994. 24.00 (*0-941419-93-2*) Marsilio Pubs.

Mazor, Miriam & Simons, Harriet. Infertility: Medical, Emotional & Social Considerations. 264p. 1984. 36.95 (*0-89885-140-8*); pap. 22.95 (*0-89885-177-7*) Human Sci Pr.

Mazor, Stanley & Langstraat, Patricia. A Guide to VHDL. LC 92-17444. 336p. (C). 1992. lib. bdg. 78.00 (*0-7923-9255-8*) Kluwer Ac.

— A Guide to VHDL. 2nd ed. LC 93-23132. 1993. lib. bdg. 85.00 (*0-7923-9387-2*) Kluwer Ac.

Mazoue, Jo A. Queen of the Island. 260p. (Orig.). 1993. pap. 11.95 (*0-923568-30-1*) Wilderness Adventure Bks.

Mazour, A., et al. People & Nations: A World History, 7 vols., Set. large type ed. 2000p. (YA). (gr. 9-12). 1984. reprint ed. 417.50 (*0-317-01920-1*, J-21590-00) Am Printing Hse.

Mazour, Anatole G. Finland Between East & West. LC 75-31771. (Illus.). 298p. 1975. reprint ed. text ed. 35.00 (*0-8371-8495-9*, MAFEW, Greenwood Pr) Greenwood.

— The First Russian Revolution, 1825: The Decembrist Movement. (Illus.). xvi, 328p. 1937. 42.50 (*0-8047-0081-8*) Stanford U Pr.

— Modern Russian Historiography. rev. ed. LC 75-16962. (Illus.). 224p. 1976. text ed. 55.00 (*0-8371-8285-9*, MRH/, Greenwood Pr) Greenwood.

— Rise & Fall of the Romanovs. (Anvil Ser.). 190p. (Orig.). 1960. reprint ed. pap. 10.50 (*0-685-07020-4*) Krieger.

— Women in Exile: Wives of the Decembrists. LC 74-22111. (Illus.). 134p. 1975. 15.00 (*0-910512-19-1*) Diplomatic IN.

Mazow, Julia W., ed. The Woman Who Lost Her Names: Selected Writings by American Jewish Women. LC 79-2986. 240p. 1981. pap. text ed. 10.00 (*0-06-250567-X*, CN 4017) Harper SF.

Mazower, Mark. Greece & the Inter-War Economic Crisis. (Oxford Historical Monographs). 352p. 1991. 69.00 (*0-19-820205-9*) OUP.

— Inside Hitler's Greece: The Experience of Occupation, 1941-1944. (Illus.). 352p. 1993. 30.00 (*0-300-05804-7*) Yale U Pr.

M

*Mazower, Mark, ed. The Policing of Politics in the Twentieth Century: Historical Perspectives. 256p. 1996. 49.95 (*1-57181-873-1*) Berghahn Bks.

Mazoyer, B. M., ed. PET Studies on Amino Acid Metabolism & Protein Synthesis. (Developments in Nuclear Medicine Ser.). 288p. (C). 1993. lib. bdg. 109.00 (*0-7923-2076-X*) Kluwer Ac.

Mazrui, A. A., ed. UNESCO General History of Africa Vol. VIII: Africa since 1935. 1994. 45.00 (*0-520-03920-3*) U CA Pr.

Mazrui, Alamin M. & Shariff, Ibrahim N. The Swahili: Idiom & Identity of an African People. LC 93-9903. 1994. 45.95 (*0-86543-310-0*); pap. 14.95 (*0-86543-311-9*) Africa World.

Mazrui, Ali. The Political Sociology of the English Language: An African Perspective. (Contributions to the Sociology of Language Ser.: No. 7). 232p. 1975. text ed. 29.35 (*90-279-7821-2*) Mouton.

— The Trial of Christopher Okigbo. (African Writers Ser.). 1971. pap. 8.95 (*0-435-90097-8*) Heinemann.

Mazrui, Ali A. The African Condition. LC 79-9657. 192p. 1980. 42.95 (*0-521-23265-1*); pap. 14.95 (*0-521-29884-9*) Cambridge U Pr.

— The Barrel of the Gun & the Barrel of Oil in the North-South Equation. 33p. 1978. pap. 18.95 (*0-87855-759-8*) Transaction Pubs.

— Cultural Forces in World Politics. 262p. (C). 1990. pap. 24.95 (*0-435-08047-4*, 08047) Heinemann.

— The Moving Cultural Frontier of World Order: From Monotheism to North-South Relations. 20p. 1982. pap. 10.95 (*0-911646-11-6*) Transaction Pubs.

— The Trial of Cristopher Okigbo. LC 78-180662. 160p. 1972. 15.95 (*0-89388-024-8*) Okpaku Communications.

Mazrui, Ali A. & Kleban, Toby, eds. The Africans: A Reader. LC 85-28166. 366p. 1986. text ed. 29.95 (*0-275-92066-6*, C2066, Praeger Pubs); pap. text ed. 17.95 (*0-275-92073-9*, B2073, Praeger Pubs) Greenwood.

Mazrui, Ali A. & Patel, Hasu H. Africa in World Affairs: The Next Thirty Years. LC 72-80184. 286p. (C). 1973. 25.00 (*0-89388-046-9*) Okpaku Communications.

Mazru'i, Ali A., jt. auth. see Al-Amin, Shaykh.

Mazuka, Reiko & Nagai, Noriko, eds. Japanese Sentence Processing. 368p. 1994. text ed. 89.95 (*0-8058-1125-7*) L Erlbaum Assocs.

Mazumdar, Dipak. Microeconomic Issues of Labor Markets in Developing Countries: Analysis & Policy Implications. (EDI Seminar Paper Ser.: No. 40). 128p. 1989. 7.95 (*0-8213-1183-2*, 11183) World Bank.

Mazumdar, J. Biofluid Mechanics. 200p. 1992. text ed. 43.00 (*981-02-0927-4*) World Scientific Pub.

— An Introduction to Mathematical Physiology & Biology. (Australian Mathematical Society Lecture Ser.: No. 4). (Illus.). (C). 1989. pap. 22.95 (*0-521-37901-6*) Cambridge U Pr.

Mazumdar, Pauline. Eugenics, Human Genetics & Human Failings. (Illus.). 304p. 1991. 74.50 (*0-415-04424-3*, A5873) Routledge.

Mazumdar, Pauline M. Species & Specificity: An Interpretation of the History of Immunology. LC 93-31219. (Illus.). 530p. (C). 1994. 64.95 (*0-521-43172-7*) Cambridge U Pr.

*Mazumdar, Shudha. Memoirs of an Indian Woman. Forbes, Geraldine H., ed. LC 89-10272. (Foremother Legacies Ser.). 248p. 1989. pap. 19.95 (*1-56324-552-3*, East Gate Bk) M E Sharpe.

— Memoirs of an Indian Woman. Forbes, Geraldine H., ed. LC 89-10272. (Foremother Legacies Ser.). 248p. 1989. 46.50 (*0-87332-520-6*) M E Sharpe.

— Ramayana. 542p. 1974. 12.95 (*0-318-37159-6*) Asia Bk Corp.

Mazumdar, V., ed. Role of Rural Women in Development. 373p. 1979. 11.95 (*0-318-37072-7*) Asia Bk Corp.

Mazumdar, Vina, ed. Symbols of Power. 373p. 1979. 19.95 (*0-318-37080-8*) Asia Bk Corp.

Mazumdar, Vina, jt. ed. see Kasturi, Leela.

Mazumder. Laser Doppler Velocitometry & Its Applications. 1995. write for info. (*0-8493-5215-0*) CRC Pr.

Mazumder, J. & Mukherjee, K. N., eds. Laser Materials Processing, No. III. (Illus.). 435p. 1990. 20.00 (*0-87339-104-7*, 376) Minerals Metals.

Mazumder, J., jt. ed. see Mukherjee, K.

*Mazumder, J., et al, eds. Laser Materials Processing IV: Proceedings. 307p. 1994. 82.00 (*0-87339-233-7*) Minerals Metals.

*Mazumder, Jyoti & Kar, Aravinda. Theory & Application of Laser Chemical Vapor Deposition. (Lasers, Photonics, & Electro-Optics Ser.). 400p. 1995. 89.50 (*0-306-44936-6*) Plenum.

Mazur, Allan. Global Social Problems. 240p. (C). 1990. pap. text ed. write for info. (*0-13-357013-4*) P-H.

Mazur, Allan & Robertson, Leon S. Biology & Social Behavior. LC 72-169236. 1974. 19.95 (*0-02-920450-X*) Free Pr.

Mazur, Amy, jt. ed. see Stetson, Dorothy M.

Mazur, B., jt. ed. see Artin, M.

Mazur, B., jt. auth. see Artin, Michael.

Mazur, B. W. Colloquial Polish. (Colloquial Ser.). 224p. 1983. pap. 14.95 (*0-7100-9030-7*, RKP); audio 14.95 (*0-7100-9387-X*, RKP) Routledge.

— Colloquial Polish. (Colloquial Ser.). 282p. 1988. audio 24.95 (*0-415-00078-5*, A2583) Routledge.

Mazur, Barry, jt. auth. see Friedlander, Eric M.

Mazur, Barry, jt. auth. see Hirsch, Morris W.

Mazur, Cynthia S. & Bullis, Ronald K. Legal Guide for Day-to-Day Church Matters: A Handbook for Pastors & Church Members. LC 94-7401. 148p. (Orig.). 1994. pap. 4.95 (*0-8298-0990-2*) Pilgrim OH.

Mazur, Cynthia S., jt. auth. see Bullis, Ronald K.

Mazur, Edward H. Minyans for a Prairie City: The Politics of Chicago Jewry, 1850-1940. LC 90-3294. (European Immigrants & American Society Ser.). 456p. 1990. reprint ed. 30.00 (*0-8240-0297-0*) Garland.

Mazur, G. A., jt. auth. see Proctor, Thomas E.

Mazur, G. A., jt. auth. see Rockis, G.

*Mazur, Gail. The Common. LC 94-33930. (Phoenix Poets Ser.). 1995. lib. bdg. 22.50 (*0-226-51438-2*) U Ch Pr.

— The Common. LC 94-33930. (Phoenix Poets Ser.). 1995. pap. 11.95 (*0-226-51439-0*) U Ch Pr.

— Pose of Happiness. LC 85-45963. 96p. 1986. pap. 8.95 (*0-87923-616-7*) Godine.

Mazur, Glen A. & Proctor, Thomas E. Troubleshooting Electrical - Electronic Systems. LC 94-10801. (Illus.). 476p. 1993. pap. text ed. 30.96 (*0-8269-1775-5*) Am Technical.

Mazur, James E. Learning & Behavior. 3rd ed. LC 93-6858. 1993. text ed. write for info. (*0-13-131814-4*) P-H.

Mazur, Joseph C. How to Study Calculus. 48p. (C). 1993. pap. write for info. (*0-697-20197-X*) Wm C Brown Pubs.

Mazur, Laura, jt. auth. see White, Jon.

Mazur, Laurie, jt. auth. see Jacobson, Michael F.

Mazur, Laurie A., ed. Beyond the Numbers: A Reader on Population & Consumption Issues. LC 94-75842. 1994. text ed. 40.00 (*1-55963-298-4*); pap. text ed. 19.95 (*1-55963-299-2*) Island Pr.

Mazur, Michael T. & Kurman, Robert J. Diagnosis of Endometrial Biopsies & Curetting: A Practical Approach. LC 94-10428. 1994. 79.00 (*0-387-94230-0*) Spr-Verlag.

— Diagnosis of Endometrial Biopsies & Curetting: A Practical Approach. LC 94-10428. 1994. 158.00 (*3-540-94230-0*) Spr-Verlag.

*Mazur, Norma F. E, My Name Is Emily. (J). (gr. 4-7). 1994. pap. 3.25 (*0-590-43654-6*) Scholastic Inc.

Mazur, P., jt. auth. see DeGroot, S. R.

Mazur, Robert E., ed. Breaking the Links: Development Theory & Practice in Southern Africa - a Festschrift for Ann W. Seidman. 321p. 1990. 45.00 (*0-86543-178-7*); pap. 14.95 (*0-86543-179-5*) Africa World.

Mazur, T., ed. Classical Analysis: Proceedings of 6th Symposium, Kazimierz Dolny, Poland, 23-29 September 1991. 400p. 1992. text ed. 109.00 (*981-02-0983-5*) World Scientific Pub.

*Mazure, Carolyn M. Does Stress Cause Psychiatric Illness?, 46. LC 94-22178. (Progress in Psychiatry Ser.: Vol. 46). 1994. boxed write for info. (*0-88048-482-9*) Am Psychiatric.

Mazurek, Kas & Winzer, Margret A., eds. Comparative Studies in Special Education. LC 94-212. 504p. 1994. 55.95 (*1-56368-027-0*) Gallaudet Univ Pr.

Mazurek, Kas, jt. ed. see Kach, Nick.

Mazurin, Oleg V., et al. Handbook of Glass Data: Ternary Silicate Glasses, Part C. (Physical Sciences Data Ser.: Vol. 15C). 1110p. 1987. 338.50 (*0-444-42889-5*) Elsevier.

— Single-Component, Binary, & Ternary Oxide Glasses. LC 93-27810. (Handbook of Glass Data Ser., Pt. E, Physical Sciences Data Ser.: Vol. 15). 1993. write for info. (*0-444-81635-6*) Elsevier.

Mazurin, Oleg V. & Poraikoshits, E. A., eds. Phase Separation in Glass. 1985. 120.50 (*0-444-86810-0*) Elsevier.

Mazurin, Oleg V., et al. Handbook of Glass Data, Part B: Single-Component & Binary Non-Silicate Oxide Glasses: Physical Sciences Data, Pt. 15B. 806p. 1985. 251.50 (*0-444-42484-9*) Elsevier.

— Handbook of Glass Data, Pt. D: Ternary Non-Silicate Glasses. (Physical Sciences Data Ser.: No. 15D). 992p. 1991. 360.00 (*0-444-88955-8*) Elsevier.

Mazurkiewicz, A., ed. Mathematical Foundations of Computer Science 1976. (Lecture Notes in Computer Science Ser.: Vol. 45). (Illus.). 1976. 31.00 (*0-387-07854-1*) Spr-Verlag.

Mazurkiewicz, B. K. Design & Consruction of Dry Docks. (Illus.). 500p. (C). pap. 15.00 (*0-87849-036-1*, Pub. by Trans Tech GW) LPS Dist Ctr.

— Offshore Platforms & Pipelines: Selected Contributions. (Series on Rock & Soil Mechanics: Vol. 13). 390p. 1987. text ed. 48.00 (*0-87849-058-2*, Pub. by Trans Tech GW) LPS Dist Ctr.

*Mazurkiewicz, Ludwik. Human Geography in Eastern Europe & the Former Soviet Union. 1993. text ed. 64.95 (*0-471-94719-9*) Wiley.

— Human Geography in Eastern Europe & the Soviet Union. LC 92-19942. 163p. 1992. text ed. 53.95 (*0-470-21905-X*) Wiley.

Mazurkiewicz, Z. E. & Nagorski, R. T. Shells of Revolution: Developments in Civil Engineering, No. 30. 640p. 1991. 225.75 (*0-444-98779-7*) Elsevier.

Mazursky, Alan D. & Dlugoss, Eileen B. The dBASE IV: A Practical Learning Guide. 448p. (C). 1990. teacher ed 8.00 (*1-56118-347-4*); pap. text ed. 29.95 (*1-56118-346-6*) Paradigm MN.

— Lotus 1-2-3: A Practical Learning Guide. 500p. (C). 1988. teacher ed 7.30 (*1-56118-087-4*); pap. text ed. 25.95 (*1-56118-086-6*) Paradigm MN.

— Lotus 1-2-3: Short Course. 208p. (C). pap. text ed. 19.95 (*1-56118-089-0*) Paradigm MN.

Mazursky, Paul & Capetanos, Leon. Tempest: A Screenplay. LC 82-81975. (Illus.). 1982. 13.95 (*0-933826-40-0*); pap. 8.95 (*0-933826-41-9*) PAJ Pubns.

Mazuski, Paula R., jt. auth. see Bynum, Robert C.

Mazuzan, George T. Warren R. Austin at the U. N., 1946-1953. LC 76-52990. 245p. reprint ed. pap. 69.90 (*0-7837-0504-2*, 2040828) Bks Demand.

Mazuzan, George T. & Walker, J. Samuel. Controlling the Atom: The Beginnings of Nuclear Regulation, 1946-1962. LC 84-2485. (Illus.). 500p. (C). 1985. 55.00 (*0-520-05182-3*) U CA Pr.

Mazuzan, George T., jt. ed. see Fausold, Martin L.

Maz'ya, V. G. Sobolev Spaces. Saposhnikova, T. O., tr. (Soviet Mathematics Ser.). (Illus.). 510p. 1985. 89.00 (*0-387-13589-8*) Spr-Verlag.

Maz'ya, V. G. & Nikol'skij, S. M. Analysis IV: Linear & Boundary Integral Equations. Gamkrelidze, G. V., ed. Bottcher, A. & Prossdorf, S., trs. (Encyclopaedia of Mathematical Sciences Ser.: Vol. 27). (Illus.). 248p. 1991. 65.00 (*0-387-51997-1*) Spr-Verlag.

Mazya, V. G., jt. auth. see Burago, Iurii D.

Mazza. Anthocyanins of Food Crops. 1992. 188.95 (*0-8493-0172-6*, QK898) CRC Pr.

Mazza, jt. auth. see Pasolini.

*Mazza, Antonino. The Way I Remember It. (Essential Poets Ser.: No. 56). 64p. 1994. pap. 10.00 (*0-920717-74-8*) Guernica Editions.

Mazza, Antonino, tr. see Duliani, Mario.

Mazza, Antonino, tr. see Montale, Eugenio.

Mazza, Cris. Animal Acts. 163p. (Orig.). 1989. 18.95 (*0-932511-15-5*); pap. 8.95 (*0-932511-16-3*) Fiction Coll.

— Exposed. 256p. (Orig.). 1994. pap. 11.95 (*1-56689-019-5*) Coffee Hse.

— How to Leave a Country. LC 92-4005. 179p. (Orig.). 1992. pap. 11.95 (*0-918273-96-X*) Coffee Hse.

— Is It Sexual Harassment Yet? 1991. 18.95 (*0-932511-33-3*); pap. 8.95 (*0-932511-34-1*) Fiction Coll.

— Your Name Here: 288p. (Orig.). 1995. pap. 12.95 (*1-56689-031-4*) Coffee Hse.

Mazza, Cris & Orland, Ted. Revelation Countdown: Stories by Cris Mazza. (Black Ice Books Ser.). (Illus.). 151p. 1993. pap. 7.00 (*0-932511-73-2*) Fiction Coll.

Mazza, Enrico. Eucharist Prayers of the Roman Rites. 376p. 1992. pap. 19.50 (*0-8146-6078-9*, Pueblo Bks) Liturgical Pr.

— Mystagogy: A Theology of Liturgy in the Patristic Age. 228p. 1992. pap. 14.50 (*0-8146-6093-2*, Pueblo Bks) Liturgical Pr.

— The Origins of the Eucharistic Prayer. 300p. (Orig.). 1995. pap. text ed. 19.95 (*0-8146-6119-X*, Pueblo Bks) Liturgical Pr.

*Mazza, Joseph J., ed. Manual of Clinical Hematology. 2nd ed. LC 94-26649. 1994. 32.95 (*0-316-55220-8*) Little.

Mazza, Karen A., jt. comp. see Franzosa, Susan D.

*Mazza, Michael J. The Truth Will Set You Free: A Presentation of the Catholic Faith for Young Adults Based on the Catechism of the Catholic Church. 85p. 1995. teacher ed 20.00 (*0-9646214-1-X*) Veritas Pr SD.

— The Truth Will Set You Free: A Presentation of the Catholic Faith for Young Adults Based on the Catechism of the Catholic Church. (Illus.). 128p. (YA). (gr. 9-12). 1995. pap. 6.95 (*0-9646214-0-1*) Veritas Pr SD.

Mazza, Samuele. Brahaus. LC 93-5515. 192p. (ITA.). 1994. pap. 16.95 (*0-8118-0593-X*) Chronicle Bks.

— Cinderella's Revenge. Jensen, Jack, ed. (Illus.). 192p. 1994. pap. text ed. 16.95 (*0-8118-0681-2*) Chronicle Bks.

Mazzaferri. Advances in Endocrinology & Metabolism, Vol. 2. 329p. 1991. 64.95 (*0-8151-5709-6*) Mosby Yr Bk.

— Advances in Endocrinology & Metabolism, Vol. 3. 316p. 1992. 64.95 (*0-8151-5710-X*) Mosby Yr Bk.

— Advances in Endocrinology & Metabolism, Vol. 4. 325p. 1993. 64.95 (*0-8151-6150-6*, Yr Bk Med Pubs) Mosby Yr Bk.

— Advances in Endocrinology & Metabolism, Vol. 5. 325p. 1994. 64.95 (*0-8151-6151-4*, Yr Bk Med Pubs) Mosby Yr Bk.

— Advances in Endocrinology & Metabolism, Vol. 6. 325p. 1995. 64.95 (*0-8151-6152-2*, Yr Bk Med Pubs) Mosby Yr Bk.

— Advances in Endocrinology & Metabolism, Vol. 7. 300p. 1996. 64.95 (*0-8151-6153-0*, Yr Bk Med Pubs) Mosby Yr Bk.

Mazzaferri, E. L., jt. ed. see Bowen, J. M.

Mazzaferri, Ernest L., jt. auth. see Marsh, Clay B.

Mazzaferri, Ernest L., ed. see Samaan, Naguib A.

Mazzaferri, Frederick D. The Genre of the Book of Revelation from a Source-Critical Perspective. xix, 486p. (C). 1989. lib. bdg. 134.65 (*0-89925-460-8*) De Gruyter.

*Mazzalongo, Michael, ed. Gay Rights or Wrongs: A Christian's Guide to Homosexual Issues & Ministry. LC 95-8743. 1995. write for info. (*0-89900-731-7*) College Pr Pub.

Mazzaoui, Maureen F., jt. ed. see Blomquist, Thomas W.

Mazzaoui, Michel M. & Millward, William G., eds. Social & Cultural Selections from Contemporary Persian. LC 73-569. 128p. (C). 1973. text ed. 15.00 (*0-88206-100-3*) Caravan Bks.

Mazzaoui, Michel M. & Moreen, Vera B., eds. Intellectual Studies on Islam. LC 90-52746. (Illus.). 288p. 1990. lib. bdg. 27.50 (*0-87480-342-X*) U of Utah Pr.

Mazzara, Richard A., tr. see Lispector, Clarice.

Mazzarella, Mimi. Alphabatty Animals & Funny Foods. LC 83-81449. (Illus.). 96p. (Orig.). (J). (gr. k-3). 1984. pap. 5.95 (*0-89709-045-4*) Liberty Pub.

Mazzarins, Laimdota, tr. see Beck-Gernsheim, Elisabeth.

Mazzarins, Laimdota, tr. see Bolz, Norbert & Van Reijen, Willem.

Mazzaro, Jerome. The Figure of Dante: An Essay on the Vita Nuova. LC 81-47146. (Princton Essays in Literature Ser.). 173p. reprint ed. pap. 49.40 (*0-8357-4671-2*, 2037617) Bks Demand.

— Postmodern American Poetry. fac. ed. LC 79-11119. 215p. 1980. reprint ed. pap. 61.30 (*0-7837-8079-6*, 2047832) Bks Demand.

Mazzatinti, Guiseppe. Gli Archivi Della Storia d'Italia, 9 vols. in 5. xxxviii, 3498p. 1988. reprint ed. Set. write for info. (*3-487-09043-0*, Pub. by Georg Olms GW) Lubrecht & Cramer.

Mazze, R. S., jt. ed. see Alberti, K. G.

*Mazze, Roger, et al. Staged Diabetes Management: DecisionPaths. 1995. ring bd. write for info. (*1-885115-03-2*) Intl Diabetes.

— Staged Diabetes Management: Guide. 1995. write for info. (*1-885115-02-4*) Intl Diabetes.

Mazzei, George, jt. auth. see Morella, Joseph.

Mazzei, Philip. Researches on the United States. Sherman, Constance D., ed. & tr. by. LC 75-20037. (Illus.). 436p. reprint ed. 124.30 (*0-8357-9814-3*, 2016965) Bks Demand.

Mazzeno, Laurence W. Herman Wouk. LC 93-29926. (Twayne's United States Authors Ser.: No. 639). 160p. 1994. text ed. 22.95 (*0-8057-3982-3*, Pub. by Royal Botanic Garden UK) Macmillan.

— Victorian Poetry: An Annotated Bibliography. annot. ed. LC 95-5328. (Magill Bibliographies Ser.). 261p. 1995. 32.50 (*0-8108-3008-6*) Scarecrow.

Mazzeo, Guido. Abate Juan Andres, Literary Historian & Defender of Spanish & Medieval Hispano-Arab Learning, Literature & Culture, 1740-1917. 228p. 1965. 5.00 (*0-318-22340-6*) Hispanic Inst.

Mazzeo, Joseph A., jt. ed. see Henderson, Katherine U.

Mazzeo, Karen. Fitness Through Aerobics & Step Training. (Illus.). 160p. (Orig.). (C). 1993. pap. text ed. 14.95x (*0-89582-253-9*) Morton Pub.

Mazzeo, Karen & Mangili, Lauren. Step Training Plus. (Illus.). (Orig.). (C). 1993. pap. text ed. 13.95x (*0-89582-255-5*) Morton Pub.

Mazzeo, Karen S. Aerobics: The Way to Fitness. (Illus.). 200p. (C). 1992. pap. text ed. 14.95x (*0-89582-221-0*) Morton Pub.

Mazzetti, P., jt. ed. see D'Amico, A.

Mazzilli, Luiqui, jt. auth. see Eichhorn, Gunther.

Mazzini, Giuseppe. The Living Thoughts of Mazzini Presented by Ignazio Silone. LC 79-138163. (Illus.). 130p. 1972. reprint ed. text ed. 49.50 (*0-8371-5620-3*, MALI, Greenwood Pr) Greenwood.

Mazzio, Joann. Leaving Eldorado. LC 92-13853. 176p. (J). (gr. 5-9). 1993. 13.95 (*0-395-64381-3*) HM.

— The One Who Came Back. 208p. (J). (gr. 5-9). 1992. 13.95 (*0-395-59506-1*) HM.

Mazziotta, John C. & Gilman, Sid, eds. Clinical Brain Imaging: Principles & Applications. (Contemporary Neurology Ser.: No. 39). iii, 480p. (C). 1992. text ed. 120.00 (*0-8036-5944-X*) Davis Co.

Mazziotti, Maria. Luce d'Inverno: English & Italian Poetry. Scammacca, Nina & Scammacca, Nat, trs. (Illus.). 67p. (ENG & ITA.). 1988. pap. 7.50 (*0-89304-524-1*) Cross-Cultrl NY.

— Luce d'Inverno: English & Italian Poetry. Scammacca, Nina & Scammacca, Nat, trs. (Illus.). 67p. 1988. 15.00 (*0-89304-525-X*) Cross-Cultrl NY.

Mazzo, William L. A Business Plan & Evaluation: Simple As One-Two-Three - Three Easy Steps for a Do-It-Yourself Business Plan - Just Fill in the Blanks. rev. ed. LC 85-62990. 254p. (C). 1986. reprint ed. pap. text ed. 19.95 (*0-936257-00-8*) Busn Plan Pub.

A business plan guidebook in three easy steps, just fill in the blanks. This guidebook marks the first time a step-by-step guide on creating a business plan for new & expanding businesses & their owners has been developed. Combining "what-to" with "how-to," the guidebook is designed to give "hands-on" guidance that will help readers prepare an effective business plan. It is already in its third edition. "If you want lenders to take you seriously, but you don't know how to write a business plan, Mazzo's book makes it as easy as 1-2-3." New Business Opportunities. "Unpretentious & direct, it's actually more of a detailed outline than a book, but that's where its beauty lies. It's simple."--The Security Traders Handbook. A BUSINESS PLAN & EVALUATION is distributed by Baker & Taylor, Ingram. ***Publisher Provided Annotation.***

*Mazzocchi, Dorothy. Organic Chemistry LM, Vol. I. 128p. (C). 1994. pap. text ed., spiral bd. 5.95 (*0-7872-0383-1*) Kendall-Hunt.

— Organic Chemistry LM, Vol. II. 112p. (C). 1994. pap. text ed., spiral bd. 5.95 (*0-7872-0402-1*) Kendall-Hunt.

Mazzocco, Angelo. Linguistic Theories in Dante & the Humanists: Studies of Language & Intellectual History in Late Medieval & Early Renaissance Italy. LC 93-21469. (Studies in Intellectual History: No. 38). xvi, 270p. 1993. 71.50 (*90-04-09702-3*) E J Brill.

Mazzocco, Dennis W. Networks of Power: Corporate TV's Threat to Democracy. 200p. (Orig.). (C). 1994. lib. bdg. 30.00 (*0-89608-473-6*); pap. text ed. 14.00 (*0-89608-472-8*) South End Pr.

Mazzola, Claude J. Active Sound Absorption. LC 92-93587. (Illus.). 113p. (Orig.). (C). 1993. pap. text ed. 49.50 (*0-9636316-0-8*) NAMLAK.

Mazzola, Claudio, jt. auth. see Capek-Habekovic, Romana.

Mazzola, Claudio, jt. auth. see Habekovic, Romana.

Mazzola, Claudio, jt. auth. see Olken, Ilene T.

Mazzola, M. L. Proto-Romance & Sicilian. 142p. 1976. pap. 20.00 (*90-316-0088-1*, Pub. by B R Gruener NE) Benjamins North Am.

An Asterisk (*) at the beginning of an entry indicates that the title is appearing in BIP for the first time.

Mazzola, Michael L., ed. Issues & Theory in Romance Linguistics: Selected Papers from the Linguistic Symposium on Romance Languages XXIII. LC 93-36991. (C). 1994. 60.00 (0-87840-243-8) Georgetown U Pr.

Mazzola, Toni & Guten, Mimi. Wally Koala & Friends. Cohen, Keri, ed. LC 93-94001. (Wally Koala Ser.). (Illus.). 24p. (J). (ps-3). 1993. 9.95 (1-883747-00-7) WK Prods.

— Wally Koala & the Little Green Peach. Cohen, Keri, ed. LC 93-94002. (Wally Koala Ser.). (Illus.). 22p. (J). (ps-3). 1993. 9.95 (1-883747-01-5) WK Prods.

Mazzolani, F., ed. Testing of Metals for Structures: Proceedings of the International Workshop. (RILEM Proceedings Ser.: No. 12). (Illus.). 500p. 1991. write for info. (0-412-42650-1, E & FN Spon) Routledge Chapman & Hall.

Mazzoldi, P. From Galileo's "Occhialino" to Optoelectronics. 750p. 1993. text ed. 135.00 (981-02-1332-8) World Scientific Pub.

Mazzoldi, P., ed. Modifications Induced by Irradiation in Glasses: Proceedings of the Symposium of the E-MRS Fall Conference, Strasbourg, France, 4-7 November 1991. LC 92-16779. 1992. write for info. (0-444-89572-8, North Holland) Elsevier.

Mazzoldi, P. & Arnold, G. W., eds. Ion Beam Modifications of Insulators. 1987. 187.25 (0-444-42816-X, North Holland) Elsevier.

Mazzoldi, Paolo, jt. ed. see Draper, Clifton W.

Mazzoleni, Mario. A Catholic Priest Meets Sai Baba. Moevs, Christian, tr. LC 93-86227. 296p. (Orig.). 1994. pap. 12.00 (0-9629835-1-9) Leela Pr.

Mazzolini, Renato. Government Controlled Enterprises: International Strategic & Policy Decisions. LC 78-10961. 424p. reprint ed. pap. 120.90 (0-8357-8892-X, 2033349) Bks Demand.

Mazzone, Domenico. Sculpturing. (Artist's Library). (Illus.). 64p. (Orig.). 1994. pap. 6.95 (1-56010-124-5, AL21) W Foster Pub.

Mazzone, Jaures & Taylor, Robert G., eds. A Guide for Foreign Investors to the Brazilian Stock Market. 2nd ed. (Illus.). 68p. 1992. pap. 95.00 (1-880506-01-7) Intl Reports.

Mazzoni, A., ed. see European Skull Base Society Staff.

Mazzoni, Steve. Safety Considerations of Energy Saving Materials & Devices. 1978. 3.25 (0-686-12080-9, TR 78-6) Society Fire Protect.

Mazzoni, Tim L., Jr., jt. auth. see Campbell, Roald F.

Mazzotta, Giuseppe. Critical Essays on Dante. (Critical Essays in World Literature Ser.). 232p. 1991. text ed. 45.00 (0-8161-8849-1, Hall Reference) Macmillan.

— Dante, Poet of the Desert: History & Allegory in the Divine Comedy. LC 78-27468. 360p. 1987. pap. text ed. 18.95 (0-691-10233-3) Princeton U Pr.

— Dante's Vision & the Circle of Knowledge. 352p. 1993. text ed. 39.50 (0-691-06966-2) Princeton U Pr.

— The World at Play in Boccaccio's "Decameron" LC 85-43299. 310p. 1986. text ed. 45.00x (0-691-06677-9) Princeton U Pr.

— The Worlds of Petrarch. LC 93-19793. (Monographs in Medieval & Renaissance Studies: Vol. 14). 248p. 1993. lib. bdg. 35.00 (0-8223-1363-4); pap. text ed. 15.95 (0-8223-1396-0) Duke.

Mazzotta, Giuseppe, jt. ed. see Spariosu, Mihai.

Mazzotta, Lawrence A. Education Profile: Omaha & the State. 34p. (Orig.). 1973. pap. 3.00 (1-55719-056-9) U NE CPAR.

Mazzucchelli, David, jt. auth. see Miller, Frank.

Mazzucchelli, R. H., jt. ed. see Davy, R.

Mazzucchi-Ballard, Lois, jt. auth. see Torres, Hazel O.

Mazzucchi, Lois E., jt. auth. see Torres, Hazel O.

Mazzuchelli, Samuel. The Memoirs of Father Samuel Mazzuchelli, O.P. (American Biography Ser.). 329p. 1991. reprint ed. lib. bdg. 79.00 (0-7812-8279-9) Rprt Serv.

Mazzula, Jo. Al Packer: A Colorado Cannibal. 3.50 (0-686-16037-1) F&J Mazzulla.

Mazzullo, jt. auth. see Harder.

MBA Ethics Task Force Staff. Combating Fraud & Unethical Practices in Real Estate Transactions. Linthicum, Bob, ed. 60p. (Orig.). 1991. pap. 25.00 (0-945359-09-8) Mortgage Bankers.

Mba, Nina E. Nigerian Women Mobilized: Women's Political Activity in Southern Nigeria, 1900-1965. LC 82-15477. (Research Ser.: No. 48). (Illus.). xii, 348p. 1982. pap. 12.95 (0-87725-148-7) U of Cal IAS.

MBA Staff. Building a Mortgage Banking Team. 160p. 1992. per. 40.00 (0-8403-8227-8) Kendall-Hunt.

— Foreclosure Management. Powell, Lynn S., ed. (Illus.). 100p. (C). 1993. pap. text ed. 40.00 (0-945359-08-X) Mortgage Bankers.

Mbabuike, Michael C. Notes (on the Poems of) Leopold Sedar Senghor, Poet of Lost Villages: Reflections on Selected Poems of L. S. Senghor. (Illus.). 150p. (C). 1989. text ed. 25.00 (0-318-42042-2) Andres & Co.

Mbaeyi, Paul M. British Military & Naval Forces in West African History 1807-1874. LC 77-23627. (Library of African Affairs). (Illus.). 263p. 1978. 21.95 (0-88357-029-7) NOK Pubs.

***Mbah, Samuel & Igariwey, I. G.** African Anarchism: The History of a Movement. 1995. pap. 12.95 (1-884365-05-1) See Sharp Pr.

Mbali, Zolile. The Churches & Racism. 240p. (C). 1987. pap. text ed. 17.95 (0-334-01923-0, SCM Pr) TPI PA.

Mbalia, Doreatha D. Toni Morrison's Developing Class Consciousness. LC 90-50402. 144p. 1991. 32.50 (0-945636-17-2) Susquehanna U Pr.

***Mbalia, Doreatha D.** John Edgar Wideman: Reclaiming the African Personality. LC 94-47088. 1995. write for info. (0-945636-78-4) Susquehanna U Pr.

M'Baye, A. A., jt. ed. see Mun, J.

Mbeki, Govan. Learning from Robben Island: Govan Mbeki's Prison Writings. LC 91-3198. 232p. 1991. text ed. 24.95 (0-8214-1006-7); pap. 15.95 (0-8214-1007-5) Ohio U Pr.

— South Africa: The Peasant's Revolt. 12.00 (0-8446-0791-6) Peter Smith.

Mbele, Cosbie. Freedom Now. LC 94-65525. 150p. 1994. write for info. (1-884921-10-8) Pheko & Assocs.

Mbele, Cosbie, ed. Lady Africa in America. LC 94-65535. 150p. 1994. 17.00 (1-884921-19-1) Pheko & Assocs.

Mbella, Mokeba H., jt. auth. see Delancey, Mark W.

Mbengue, Demba, illus. Aesop: Tales of Aethiop the African, Vol. 1. 64p. (J). (gr. 2-9). 1991. 6.95 (1-877610-03-8); audio 6.95 (0-685-50185-X) Sea Island.

Mberi, Antar S. A Song Out of Harlem. LC 80-12500. (Vox Humana Ser.). 96p. 1980. 9.95 (0-89603-018-0); pap. 4.95 (0-89603-021-0) Humana.

Mberia, M., et al. Examination Mathematics. (C). 1990. text ed. 50.00 (0-7487-0509-0, Pub. by S Thornes Pubs UK) St Mut.

***Mbiba, Beacon.** Urban Agriculture in Zimbabwe: Implications for Urban Management, Urban Economy, Urban Poverty, the Environment & Gender. 238p. 1995. boxed, pap. 54.95 (1-85628-857-9, Pub. by Avebury Pub UK) Ashgate Pub Co.

Mbiti, John S. African Religions & Philosophy. 2nd ed. LC 89-48596. 288p. (C). 1990. pap. 21.50 (0-435-89591-5, 89591) Heinemann.

— Afrikanische Religion und Weltanschauung. Feuser, W. F., tr. xvi, 375p. (GER.). (C). 1974. 36.95 (3-11-002498-5) De Gruyter.

— Introduction to African Religion. 2nd rev. ed. (Illus.). 216p. (Orig.). 1992. pap. 18.50 (0-435-94002-3, 94002) Heinemann.

Mboya, Susan. Ambulatory Externship Manual. (C). 1993. 9.50 (1-56870-066-0) RonJon Pub.

Mboya, Tom. The Challenge of Nationhood. (African Writers Ser.). 1970. pap. 9.95 (0-435-90081-1) Heinemann.

***Mbugua, Judy.** Our Time Has Come: African Christian Women Address the Issues of Today. LC 94-41369. (World Evangelical Fellowship Ser.). 154p. (Orig.). 1995. pap. 10.99 (0-8010-2018-2) Baker Bk.

***Mbulu, Mba.** Black-Smart. 1995. pap. 10.00 (1-883885-09-4) The People.

— Not to Be. 105p. 1995. pap. 8.00 (1-883885-10-8) The People.

— Ten Lessons: An Introduction to Black History. 2nd ed. Sekou, Bomani, ed. 230p. 1993. reprint ed. pap. 12.00 (1-883885-06-X) The People.

Mbulu, Mba & Sekou, Bomani. Spotlight on Male Female Relations. 29p. 1993. pap. 3.00 (1-883885-00-0) The People.

Mburu, F. M. Ocular Needs in Africa. 147p. 1984. pap. 25.00 (0-08-031299-3, Pergamon Pr) Elsevier.

Mburugu, Edward, ed. see Himmelstrand, Ulf, et al.

Mbuy-Beya, Bernadette, jt. ed. see Abraham, K. C.

Mbuyi, Dennis M. Beyond Policy & Language Choice: An Analysis of Texts in Four Instructional Contexts in East Africa. LC 87-6362. (Special Studies in Comparative Education: No. 18). 1987. pap. text ed. 10.00 (0-937033-08-1) SUNY GSE Pubns.

Mc Allister, Lee & Ochman, Myron S. Hiking the Catskills: A How-to-Do-It Manual for Librarians & Archivists. LC 83-3129. (Illus.). 192p. 1989. pap. 13.95 (0-9603966-6-7) NY-NJ Trail Confer.

Mc Burney, Gene H., Jr. The Yellow Book: One Thousand One Ideas So Individuals & Institutions Can Become Part of the Solution & Not the Problem. Willis, Tracy & Christiansen, Beth, eds. 107p. (Orig.). 1990. pap. 7.00 (0-9626209-0-4) Power Pr Chico.

Mc Clean, Vernon & Lyles, Lois. Solutions to Problems of Race, Class & Gender. 464p. (C). 1993. per. 28.95 (0-8403-8785-7) Kendall-Hunt.

Mc Clure, Lewis. The Mc Clure Press. limited ed. (Illus.). 32p. 1984. 95.00 (0-915998-21-1) Lime Rock Pr.

Mc Cormac, B. M., ed. see Summer Advanced Study Institute Staff.

Mc Coy, Dell A. Artistic Reflections of Women. 19.50 (0-913582-41-7) Sundance.

Mc Coy, Ronald. Archaeoastronomy. (Plateau Ser.). 32p. 1992. pap. 6.95 (0-89734-109-0) Mus Northern Ariz.

Mc Craw, David R. Chinese Lyricists of the Seventeenth Century. LC 90-10899. 192p. 1990. text ed. 24.00 (0-8248-1279-4) UH Pr.

— Du Fu's Laments from the South. LC 92-24973. 296p. (C). 1992. text ed. 42.00 (0-8248-1422-3); pap. text ed. 18.95 (0-8248-1455-X) UH Pr.

Mc Cutchan, Robert. Hymn Tune Names: Their Sources & Significance. reprint ed. 49.00 (0-403-03608-9) Scholarly.

Mc Diarmid, Finley. Letters to My Wife. Date not set. write for info. (0-87770-472-4) Ye Galleon.

Mc Donald. International Marketing Digest. 1990. 54.95 (0-434-91293-X) Buttrwrth-Heinemann.

Mc Donald, Archie. When the Corn Grows Tall in Texas. (Illus.). 96p. (J). (gr. 4-8). 1991. 11.95 (0-89015-808-8) Sunbelt Media.

***Mc Donald, Lucile & Mc Donald, Richard.** A Foot in the Door: The Reminiscences of Lucile McDonald. (Illus.). 302p. (Orig.). 1995. pap. 19.95 (0-87422-120-X) Wash St U Pr.

Mc Donald, Richard, jt. auth. see Mc Donald, Lucile.

Mc Gill, Daniel J. Forty Nights: Creation Centered Night Prayer. LC 93-21386. 288p. (Orig.). 1994. pap. 12.95 (0-8091-3437-3) Paulist Pr.

Mc Glashan, Alan. The Savage & Beautiful Country: The Secret Life of the Mind. 208p. 1995. pap. 15.95 (3-85630-517-3, Pub. by Daimon Verlag SZ) Atrium Pubs.

Mc Gonnagle, Warren J., ed. International Advances in Nondestructive Testing, Vol. 12. 371p. 1986. text ed. 119.00 (2-88124-182-4) Gordon & Breach.

Mc Hose, Andre. Manufacturing Development Applications: Guidelines for Attaining Quality & Productivity. 1992. 29.95 (0-89806-122-9) Ind Eng Mgmt Pr.

Mc Kibbin, L. S. Vadecum del Cuidador de Caballos. (SPA.). pap. 56.95 (84-200-0435-9) Fr & Eur.

Mc Kinnon, Isiah. Vision: God's Gift to Joseph & You. 140p. (Orig.). 1994. pap. 7.99 (1-56043-771-5) Destiny Image.

Mc Lelland, Joseph C. Prometheus Rebound: The Irony of Athens. (Editions SR Ser.: Vol. 10). (C). 1988. pap. 19.95 (0-88920-974-X, Pub. by Wilfrid Laurier CN) Humanities.

***Mc Michael, Calvin R.** Slingshot, Bouncy & the Magpies. 600p. 1996. pap. 12.95 (0-7610-0505-6) NW Pub.

Mc Nulty, K. K., Sr. Proper-T-Care: How to Win at Real Estate! (One of the Answers Ser.). (Illus.). 320p. 1989. 19.95 (0-935025-02-2) Data & Res Tech.

MC Productions Staff, ed. see Dellavalle, Charles & Mulhern, Tom.

MC Publishing Co. Staff. Candy Buyers Directory 1992. Allurd, Allen R., ed. 322p. 1992. pap. 35.00 (0-685-34782-6) MC Pub Co NJ.

— Candy Buyers Directory 1993. Allured, Allen R., ed. 335p. 1993. pap. 35.00 (0-944254-19-5) MC Pub Co NJ.

— McCutcheon's Functional Materials: North American Edition & International Edition. rev. ed. Allured, Michael, ed. LC 82-644577. 475p. 1992. 135.00 (0-944254-18-7) MC Pub Co NJ.

— McCutcheon's, Vol. 1: Emulsifiers & Detergents: International Edition. rev. ed. Allured, Michael, ed. LC 82-644576. 1992. pap. 60.00 (0-944254-14-4) MC Pub Co NJ.

— McCutcheon's, Vol. 1: Emulsifiers & Detergents: North American Edition. rev. ed. Allured, Michael, ed. LC 82-644576. 328p. 1992. pap. 60.00 (0-944254-13-6) MC Pub Co NJ.

— McCutcheon's, Vol. 2: Functional Materials: International Edition. Allured, Michael, ed. LC 82-644577. 125p. 1992. pap. 55.00 (0-944254-17-9) MC Pub Co NJ.

— McCutcheon's, Vol. 2: North American Edition: Functional Materials. rev. ed. Allured, Michael, ed. LC 82-644577. 325p. 1992. pap. 60.00 (0-944254-16-0) MC Pub Co NJ.

McA. Mason, D. & Eakin, B. E. Calculation of Heating & Specific Gravity of Fuel Gases. (Research Bulletin Ser.: No. 32). iv, 18p. 1961. 3.50 (0-685-18037-9) Inst Gas Tech.

McA. Mason, D., et al. Investigation of Factors Affecting Gas Mantle Life. (Technical Reports: No. 6). vi, 33p. 1962. 1.00 (0-317-56936-8) Inst Gas Tech.

McAally, Mary, ed. We Sing Our Struggle: A Tribute to Us All. (Illus.). 82p. (Orig.). 1982. pap. 5.00 (0-943594-03-0) Cardinal Pr.

McAbee, Harold v., jt. auth. see Grunwald, Bernice B.

McAdam, Douglas. Freedom Summer. (Illus.). 368p. 1990. reprint ed. pap. 12.95 (0-19-506472-0) OUP.

— Political Process & the Development of Black Insurgency, 1930 to 1970. LC 82-2712. (Illus.). viii, 304p. (C). 1985. pap. text ed. 12.95 (0-226-55552-6) U Ch Pr.

McAdam, Douglas, jt. auth. see Marx, Gary T.

McAdam, Douglas, et al. The Politics of Privacy: Planning for Personal Data Systems As Powerful Technologies. LC 80-13788. 212p. 1981. text ed. 35.00 (0-444-99074-7, RPP/) Greenwood.

McAdam, E. L., Jr., ed. see Johnson, Samuel.

McAdam, John M., jt. auth. see Scharer, Lawrence L.

McAdam, K. P., jt. ed. see Behrens, R. H.

***McAdam, R.** History of Insects. (Illus.). 160p. 1995. pap. 20.00 (0-87556-787-8) Saifer.

McAdam, Roger W. Floating Palaces: New England to New York on the Old Fall River Line. LC 72-85203. (Illus.). 207p. 1972. 20.00 (0-917218-03-5) A Mowbray.

McAdam, S. Asymptotic Prime Divisors. (Lecture Notes in Mathematics Ser.: Vol. 1023). 118p. 1983. pap. 22.00 (0-387-12722-4) Spr-Verlag.

— Primes Associated to an Ideal. LC 89-27624. 167p. 1989. pap. 37.00 (0-8218-5108-X, CONM-102) Am Math.

McAdam, Stuart, jt. auth. see Pinder, Mark.

McAdam, Terry W. Doing Well by Doing Good: The Complete Guide to Careers in the Nonprofit Sector. 199p. 1991. 27.95 (0-930807-21-9, 600300) Fund Raising.

McAdams, A. James. East Germany & Detente: Building Authority after the Wall. (Cambridge Russian, Soviet & Post-Soviet Studies: No. 49). 245p. 1985. 59.95 (0-521-26835-4) Cambridge U Pr.

— Germany Divided: From the Wall to Reunification. LC 92-15654. (Studies in International History & Politics). 272p. 1993. text ed. 39.50 (0-691-07892-0) Princeton U Pr.

— Germany Divided: From the Wall to Reunification. 1994. pap. 14.95 (0-691-00108-1) Princeton U Pr.

McAdams, Audrey, ed. see Hampton, Aubrey.

McAdams, C. Michael. Croatia: Myth & Reality. 89p. 1992. pap. 10.00 (0-9633625-1-8) CIS Monographs.

— Croatia: Myth & Reality. 2nd ed. (Illus.). 93p. 1994. pap. 12.95 (0-9633625-2-6) CIS Monographs.

McAdams, Cliff. Grand Teton National Park: Guide & Reference Book. LC 83-7228. (Illus.). 90p. (Orig.). 1983. pap. text ed. 7.95 (0-87004-300-5) Caxton.

McAdams, Dan P. The Person: An Introduction to Personality Psychology. 677p. (C). 1989. text ed. 46.75 (0-15-569320-4) HB Coll Pubs.

— The Person: An Introduction to Personality Psychology. (Illus.). 704p. (C). 1994. text ed. 56.00 (0-15-501274-6) HB Coll Pubs.

— Power, Intimacy, & the Life Story: Personological Inquiries into Identity. LC 88-5285. 336p. 1988. pap. text ed. 19.95 (0-89862-506-8) Guilford Pr.

— The Stories We Live By: Personal Myths & the Making of the Self. LC 92-27051. 1993. 22.00 (0-688-10866-0) Morrow.

McAdams, Dan P., ed. see Ochberg, Richard L.

McAdams, Elizabeth & Bayless, Raymond. The Case for Life After Death. LC 80-29289. 168p. 1981. 23.95 (0-88229-592-6) Nelson-Hall.

McAdams, Heather. Cartoon Girl: The Best of Heather McAdams. LC 93-81142. (Illus.). 96p. 1994. pap. 8.95 (1-56352-130-X) Longstreet Pr Inc.

***McAdams, Laurel & Skindzier, James.** Pennsylvania Continuing Education for Real Estate Salespersons & Brokers: Elective Course. 2nd ed. 88p. (C). 1994. pap. text ed. write for info. (0-7931-0938-8, 152008-01, Real Estate Ed) Dearborn Finan.

***McAdams, Laurel & Skindzier, Jim.** Pennsylvania Continuing Education for Real Estate Salespersons & Brokers: Required Course. 2nd ed. 112p. (C). 1994. pap. text ed. write for info. (0-7931-1144-7, 152004-02, Real Estate Ed) Dearborn Finan.

McAdams, Laurel D. & Skindzier, James J. Pennsylvania Continuing Education for Real Estate Salespersons & Brokers. LC 92-42135. 1993. pap. 14.95 (0-7931-0638-9, 1520-04, Real Estate Ed) Dearborn Finan.

McAdams, Richard. Lessons from Abroad: How Other Countries Educate Their Children. LC 93-60192. 340p. 1993. text ed. 29.00 (0-87762-986-2) Technomic.

McAdams, Richard, jt. auth. see Langlois, Donald.

McAdams, S. Music & Psychology: A Mutual Regard. (Contemporary Music Review Ser.). 319p. 1987. pap. text ed. 38.00 (3-7186-0382-9) Gordon & Breach.

McAdams, S. & Deilege, I., eds. Music & the Cognitive Sciences: Proceedings from the "Symposium on Music & the Cognitive Sciences," 14-18 March 1988 Paris, France. (Contemporary Music Review Ser.: Vol. 4). x, 468p. 1989. pap. text ed. 50.00 (3-7186-4953-5) Gordon & Breach.

McAdams, Stephen & Bigand, Emmanuel, eds. Thinking in Sound: The Cognitive Psychology of Human Audition. LC 92-26340. (Illus.). 368p. 1993. pap. 26.95 (0-19-852257-6) OUP.

McAdams, Tony, et al. Law, Business & Society. 3rd ed. 912p. (C). 1991. text ed. 67.95 (0-256-08744-X) Irwin.

— Law, Business & Society. 4th ed. LC 94-21204. (Legal Studies in Business). 876p. (C). 1994. text ed. 67.95 (0-256-14166-5) Irwin.

McAden, Ann, jt. auth. see Saunders, Boyd.

McAden, Anthony E. Sing a Message to Freedom: The Freedom Man. Satchell, Alexis, ed. (Illus.). 50p. (Orig.). 1986. pap. 6.25 (0-931841-07-0) Satchells Pub.

McAdie, Alexander G. Making the Weather. LC 77-10233. reprint ed. 20.00 (0-404-16213-4) AMS Pr.

McAdoo, David. The Dragon of Ord. LC 85-81417. (Books for Students by Students Ser.). 1985. lib. bdg. 14.95 (0-933849-23-0) Landmark Edns.

McAdoo, Harriette & McAdoo, John L. Black Children. (Focus Editions Ser.: Vol. 72). 1985. 49.95 (0-8039-2461-5); pap. 24.95 (0-8039-2462-3) Sage.

McAdoo, Harriette P. Black Families. 2nd ed. (Focus Editions Ser.: Vol. 41). 320p. 1988. text ed. 49.95 (0-8039-3179-4); pap. 24.95 (0-8039-3180-8) Sage.

— Family Ethnicity: Strength in Diversity. (Illus.). 320p. (C). 1993. text ed. 52.00 (0-8039-3736-9); pap. text ed. 26.00 (0-8039-3737-7) Sage.

McAdoo, Henry R. The Unity of Anglicanism: Catholic & Reformed. LC 82-62392. 48p. (Orig.). 1983. pap. 4.95 (0-8192-1324-1) Morehouse Pub.

McAdoo, John L., jt. auth. see McAdoo, Harriette.

McAdoo, William. Guarding a Great City. LC 73-154577. (Police in America Ser.). 1971. reprint ed. 24.95 (0-405-03373-7) Ayer.

— Pre-Civil War Black Nationalism. LC 83-60956. (Illus.). 96p. (Orig.). (C). 1983. 12.95 (0-912135-01-8); pap. 5.95 (0-912135-00-X) D Walker Pr.

McAdow, Ron. The Charles River: Exploring Nature & History on Foot & by Canoe. LC 91-21450. (Illus.). 224p. (Orig.). 1992. pap. 13.95 (0-9625144-1-1) Bliss Pub Co.

— The Concord, Sudbury, & Assabet Rivers: A Guide to Canoeing, Wildlife, & History. LC 90-38. (Illus.). 232p. (Orig.). 1990. pap. 13.95 (0-9625144-0-3) Bliss Pub Co.

— New England Time Line. 2nd ed. LC 92-80179. 96p. 1992. pap. write for info. (1-880644-01-0) Nutshell Bks.

— New England Time Line: A Concise Guide to the Region's History. (McAdow's Time Lines Ser.). 48p. 1991. pap. 4.95 (1-880644-00-2) Nutshell Bks.

McAdow, Ron, jt. auth. see Stier, Maggie.

McAfee, Bruce & Ricks, Betty. License Plate Trivia Book. Friedman, Robert S., ed. 200p. (Orig.). 1988. pap. 7.95 (0-89865-553-6) Donning Co.

Mcafee, Carol. The Climbing Tree. large type ed. 1991. 21.95 (0-7089-2502-2) Ulverscroft.

McAfee, Gage, ed. Energy Laws of Asia. 260p. 1985. 69.00 (0-87201-261-1) Gulf Pub.

McAfee, Helen, ed. see Pepys, Samuel.

McAfee, James W. Power to Live Through Nutrition. LC 80-82331. (Illus.). 196p. (Orig.). 1980. pap. 6.95 (0-9604592-0-0) Image Awareness.

McAfee, John & Haynes, Colin. Computer Viruses, Worms, Data Diddlers, Killer Programs, & Other Threats to Your System: What They Are, How They Work, & How to Defend Your PC or Mainframe. 240p. 1989. pap. 16.95 (0-312-02889-X) St Martin.

— Computer Viruses, Worms, Data Diddlers, Killer Programs, & Other Threats to Your System: What They Are, How They Work, & How to Defend Your PC or Mainframe. enl. rev. ed. 265p. 1992. pap. 18.95 (0-312-08164-2) St Martin.

M

McAfee, John P. Slow Walk in a Sad Rain. (Fresh Voices Ser.). 224p. 1994. mass mkt. 5.99 (*0-446-36500-9*) Warner Bks.

McAfee, Julie G., jt. auth. see Shipley, Kenneth G.

McAfee, Kathy. Storm Signals: Structural Adjustment & Development Alternatives in the Caribbean. 240p. (Orig.). 1991. 30.00 (*0-89608-421-3*); pap. 15.00 (*0-89608-420-5*) South End Pr.

McAfee, Michael J. Zouaves: The First & the Bravest. (Illus.). 124p. (C). 1991. text ed. 16.95 (*0-939631-37-7*) Thomas Publications.

— Zouaves: The First & the Bravest. (Illus.). 124p. (C). 1994. pap. text ed. 12.95 (*0-939631-80-6*) Thomas Publications.

McAfee, Michael J., jt. auth. see Elting, John.

McAfee, Norman, tr. see De Beauvoir, Simone, ed.

McAfee, Oralie & Leong, Deborah. Assessing & Guiding Young Children's Development & Learning. LC 93-19943. 1993. pap. text ed. write for info. (*0-205-14018-1*) Allyn.

McAfee, Paul C., jt. auth. see Long, Donlin M.

McAfee, Paul K. Bonner. large type ed. (Linford Western Library). 256p. 1993. pap. 14.95 (*0-7089-7439-2*, Linford) Ulverscroft.

McAfee, R. Bruce & Champagne, Paul J. Organizational Behavior: A Manager's View. LC 86-24745. (Illus.). 489p. (C). 1987. text ed. 61.50 (*0-314-93201-1*); teacher ed, pap. text ed. write for info. (*0-314-35226-0*) West Pub.

McAfee, R. Bruce, jt. auth. see Champagne, Paul J.

McAfee, R. Preston & McMillan, John, eds. Incentives in Government Contracting. (Economic Council Research Ser.). 168p. 1989. pap. text ed. 17.95 (*0-8020-6638-0*) U of Toronto Pr.

***McAfee, Robert B.** History of the Late War in the Western Country, Comprising a Full Account of All the Transactions in That Quarter... 549p. 1995. pap. text ed. 34.00 (*0-7884-0130-0*) Heritage Bk.

***McAfee, Virginia T.** A Season of the Heart. (Illus.). 96p. (Orig.). 1995. pap. 12.95 (*0-9647323-0-0*) Home Place Bks.

McAfee, W. R. The Cattlemen. 228p. 1989. 29.95 (*0-9623394-0-7*) Davis Mntn Pr.

— The Cattlemen. 270p. 1991. reprint ed. 27.95 (*0-9623394-1-5*) Davis Mntn Pr.

McAfee, Ward. A History of the World's Great Religions. 240p. (Orig.). (C). 1983. lib. bdg. 50.50 (*0-8191-3394-9*) U Pr of Amer.

McAffee, Cheryl W. The U. S. Postal Service. (Know Your Government Ser.). (Illus.). 96p. (YA). (gr. 5 up). 1987. lib. bdg. 14.95 (*0-87754-826-9*) Chelsea Hse.

McAffee, M. Clayton. Demise of the Stars & Stripes. 1994. 13.95 (*0-8062-4826-2*) Carlton.

McAffee, Michael, ed. Apple Access: Users' Guide to Apple Computer-Related Periodical Literature (Jan.-June 1984) (Apple Access of Semi-Annual Ser.: Vol. 1). (Illus.). 256p. (Orig.). 1985. pap. 19.95 (*0-931293-00-6*) Stony Point Pubns.

McAffee, R. Bruce & Champagne, Paul J. Effectively Managing Troublesome Employees. LC 93-49029. 200p. 1994. text ed. 55.00 (*0-89930-773-6*, Quorum Bks) Greenwood.

McAlarv, Florence & Cohen, Judith L. You Can Be a Woman Marine Biologist. (Illus.). 40p. (Orig.). (J). (gr. 4-7). 1992. pap. 6.00 (*1-880599-06-6*) Cascade Pass.

McAlary, Florence & Cohen, Judith L. Tu Puedes Ser Bióloga Marina. Yanez, Juan, tr. (Illus.). 40p. (SPA.). (J). (gr. 4-7). 1992. pap. 6.00 (*1-880599-07-4*) Cascade Pass.

McAlary, Mike. Cop Shot: The True Story of a Murder That Shocked the Nation. 288p. (Orig.). 1992. mass mkt. 4.99 (*0-515-10992-4*) Jove Pubns.

McAlary, Mike, jt. auth. see Trimboli, Joseph.

McAlear, Robert. Name Index to the Eighteen Eighty-Five History of Warren County, NY. 58p. 1981. 10.00 (*0-932334-49-0*) Hrt of the Lakes.

McAleavey. Evidence of Community: Writing from the Jenny McKean Moore Workshops at George Washington University. 1984. 7.00 (*0-318-21781-3*) G Washington Univ.

McAleavey, David. The Forty Days. LC 75-328954. 40p. 1975. 3.50 (*0-87886-071-1*, Greenfld Rev Pr) Greenfld Rev Lit.

— Holding Obsidian. LC 84-52605. (Series Nine). 53p. 1985. pap. 7.00 (*0-931846-26-9*) Wash Writers Pub.

— Shrine, Shelter, Cave. LC 80-19572. 72p. 1980. 4.00 (*0-87886-110-6*, Greenfld Rev Pr) Greenfld Rev Lit.

McAleavey, David, ed. Evidence of Community: Writings from the Jenny McKean Moore Workshops at the George Washington University, Vol. M11. 1984. 7.00 (*0-317-01777-2*) GWU CWAS.

— Washington & Washington Writing, Vol. M12. 1986. 7.00 (*0-317-01829-9*) GWU CWAS.

McAleavy, Tony. Agricultural Change. (C). 1988. 40.00 (*0-7157-2769-9*) St Mut.

— Medieval Britain: Conquest, Power & People. (Cambridge History Programme Ser.). (Illus.). 80p. (C). 1993. pap. 10.25 (*0-521-40708-7*) Cambridge U Pr.

McAleavy, Tony, jt. auth. see Kernaghan, Pamela.

McAleer, Beth D., ed. Directory of North American Fisheries & Aquatic Scientists. 2nd ed. LC 86-72933. 1987. pap. 13.00 (*0-913235-40-7*) Am Fisheries Soc.

McAleer, Dave. The Fab British Rock'n'Roll Invasion of 1964. (Illus.). 160p. 1994. pap. 13.95 (*0-312-10191-0*) St Martin.

— The Omnibus Book of British & American Hit Singles: 1960-1990. (Illus.). 160p. 1990. pap. 19.95 (*0-7119-2180-6*, OP45889) Omnibus NY.

McAleer, Dave, comp. The All Music Book of Hit Singles: Top Twenty Charts from 1954 to the Present Day. LC 94-11272. (Illus.). 432p. (Orig.). 1994. pap. 22.95 (*0-87930-330-1*) Miller Freeman.

McAleer, E. C., ed. see Browning, Robert.

McAleer, Edward C. The Brownings of Casa Guidi. LC 78-56858. (Illus.). 112p. 1979. 12.00 (*0-930252-04-7*); pap. 6.25 (*0-930252-03-9*) Browning Inst.

McAleer, Edward C., ed. see Browning, Robert.

McAleer, G. A Study in the Etymology of the Indian Place Name. 1977. 59.95 (*0-8490-2709-8*) Gordon Pr.

McAleer, Jill, jt. auth. see Gunter, Barrie.

McAleer, John J. Rex Stout: A Biography. LC 93-335. (Brownstone Mystery Guides Ser.: Vol. 6). (Illus.). x, 622p. 1994. lib. bdg. 57.00x (*0-941028-09-7*, Brownstone Bks); pap. 47.00x (*0-941028-10-0*, Brownstone Bks) Borgo Pr.

McAleer, Joseph. Popular Reading & Publishing in Britain, 1914-1950. LC 92-19004. (Oxford Historical Monographs). (Illus.). 304p. 1993. 62.00 (*0-19-820329-2*, Clarendon Pr) OUP.

McAleer, Kevin. Dueling: The Cult of Honor in Fin-de-siecle Germany. LC 94-4401. 1994. 24.95 (*0-691-03462-1*) Princeton U Pr.

McAleer, Neil. Arthur C. Clarke: The Authorized Biography. 448p. 1993. pap. 12.95 (*0-8092-3720-2*) Contemp Bks.

— The Cosmic Mind-Boggling Book. 320p. (Orig.). 1989. pap. 11.95 (*0-446-39046-1*) Warner Bks.

McAleese, Dermot, et al. Africa & the European Community after Nineteen Ninety-Two. LC 92-43305. (EDI Seminar Report Ser.). 108p. 1993. 7.95 (*0-8213-2368-7*, 12368) World Bank.

McAleese, Frank G. The Laser Experimenter's Handbook. (Illus.). 1979. 11.95 (*0-8306-9770-5*); pap. 10.95 (*0-8306-1123-1*, 1123) TAB Bks.

McAleese, Ray. Hpertext: Theory into Practice. 160p. (Orig.). 1993. pap. text ed. 22.95 (*1-871516-04-8*, Pub. by Intellect Bks UK) Cromland.

— Hypertext, No. I. LC 89-238. 192p. (C). 1989. text ed. 32.50 (*0-89391-575-0*) Ablex Pub.

— Hypertext, No. II. text ed. 39.50 (*0-89391-672-2*) Ablex Pub.

McAleese, Ray, jt. ed. see Unwin, Derek.

McAleese, Tama. Get Rich Slow. rev. ed. 224p. 1992. pap. 9.95 (*1-56414-046-6*) Career Pr Inc.

— Get Rich Slow. 3rd ed. 288p. 1995. pap. 16.99 (*1-56414-157-8*) Career Pr Inc.

— Money: How to Get It, Keep It & Make It Grow. 256p. (Orig.). 1992. pap. 9.95 (*1-56414-013-X*) Career Pr Inc.

— Money Power for Families. (Money Power Ser.). 96p. (Orig.). 1993. pap. 6.95 (*1-56414-049-0*) Career Pr Inc.

— Money Power for Retirement. (Money Power Ser.). 96p. (Orig.). 1993. pap. 6.95 (*1-56414-051-2*) Career Pr Inc.

— Money Power for Singles. (Money Power Ser.). 96p. (Orig.). 1993. pap. 6.95 (*1-56414-048-2*) Career Pr Inc.

— Money Power Through Mutual Funds. (Money Power Ser.). 96p. (Orig.). 1993. pap. 6.95 (*1-56414-050-4*) Career Pr Inc.

McAlester, A. Lee. Earth: An Introduction to the Geological & Geophysical Sciences. 1973. 29.95 (*0-685-03849-1*); teacher ed 1.95 (*0-685-03850-5*) P-H.

— The History of Life. 2nd ed. (Illus.). 1977. 11.95 (*0-13-390146-7*); pap. text ed. write for info. (*0-13-390120-3*) P-H.

McAlester, A. Lee & Hay, Edward A. Physical Geology: Principles & Perspectives. (Illus.). 448p. 1975. 26.95 (*0-685-03894-7*) P-H.

McAlester, A. Lee, jt. auth. see Hay, Edward A.

McAlester, Lee, jt. auth. see McAlester, Virginia.

McAlester, Virginia. Great American Houses & Their Architectural Styles. 1994. 55.00 (*1-55859-750-6*) Abbeville Pr.

McAlester, Virginia & McAlester, Lee. A Field Guide to American Houses. LC 82-48740. (Illus.). 525p. 1984. pap. 21.95 (*0-394-73969-8*) Knopf.

— A Field Guide to American Houses. LC 82-48740. (Illus.). 525p. 1984. 35.00 (*0-394-51032-1*) Knopf.

McAlexander, Hubert H. Critical Essays on Peter Taylor. (Critical Essays on American Literature Ser.). 200p. 1993. text ed. 45.00 (*0-8161-7322-2*, Twayne) Macmillan.

McAlexander, Hubert H., ed. Conversations with Peter Taylor. LC 87-13679. (Literary Conversations Ser.). 178p. 1987. 37.50 (*0-87805-324-7*); pap. 15.95 (*0-87805-325-5*) U Pr of Miss.

McAlexander, Patricia J., jt. auth. see Hayes, Christopher G.

McAlexander, Patricia J., et al. Beyond the "SP" Label: Improving the Spelling of Learning Disabled & Basic Writers. LC 92-11633. 90p. 1992. 12.95 (*0-8141-0289-1*) NCTE.

McAlindon, Harold. Management Magic. Anderson, Mac, ed. 77p. 1991. pap. 7.50 (*1-880461-05-6*) Celebrat Excell.

— What Motivates People. Anderson, Mac, ed. 77p. (Orig.). 1988. pap. 7.50 (*1-880461-11-0*) Celebrat Excell.

McAlindon, T. Shakespeare's Tragic Cosmos. 328p. (C). 1991. 64.95 (*0-521-39041-9*) Cambridge U Pr.

McAlindon, Thomas. Doctor Faustus: Divine in Show. (Twayne's Masterwork Studies Ser.: No. 134). 125p. 1994. text ed. 22.95x (*0-8057-4453-3*, Twayne); pap. 12.95 (*0-8057-8388-1*, Twayne) Macmillan.

McAliskey, Bernadette D. On the Irish Freedom Struggle. 16p. 1986. reprint ed. 2.00 (*0-87348-478-9*) Pathfinder NY.

McAlister, George A. Alamo...the Price of Freedom. (Illus.). 230p. (Orig.). 1988. pap. text ed. 7.95 (*0-924307-00-5*) Docutex Inc.

— A Time to Love...a Time to Die. (Illus.). 216p. (Orig.). (YA). (gr. 10). 1988. pap. 7.95 (*0-924307-01-3*) Docutex Inc.

McAlister, George A. & McLeod, Lloyd. Dominoes Texas Style. (Illus.). 164p. (Orig.). (YA). (gr. 9). 1977. pap. 5.95 (*0-924307-02-1*) Docutex Inc.

McAlister, H., ed. Complementary Approaches to Double & Multiple Star Research. (ASP Conference Series Publications: Vol. 32). 598p. 1992. 40.00 (*0-937707-51-1*) Astron Soc Pacific.

McAlister, Jeffrey G., ed. see Richardson, Jessica.

McAlister, Joan M. Radionuclide Techniques in Medicine. LC 78-68348. (Techniques of Measurement in Medicine Ser.: No. 3). 239p. reprint ed. pap. 68.20 (*0-685-15640-0*, 2026349) Bks Demand.

McAlister, John & McAlister, Marcia. McAlister's Car Care Organizer. 12p. (Orig.). 1985. pap. 2.99 (*0-9615587-0-9*) M McAlister Enterps.

McAlister, Katsy, jt. auth. see Crim, Lottie.

McAlister, Leigh, ed. Choice Models for Buyer Behavior: Supplement, 1. (Research in Marketing Ser.). 350p. 1982. 73.25 (*0-89232-267-5*) Jai Pr.

McAlister, Linda L., tr. see Wittgenstein, Ludwig.

McAlister, Lyle N. Spain & Portugal in the New World, 1492-1700. LC 83-21745. (Europe & the World in the Age of Expansion Ser.: Vol. 3). (Illus.). 612p. 1984. text ed. 44.95 (*0-8166-1216-1*); pap. text ed. 17.95 (*0-8166-1218-8*) U of Minn Pr.

McAlister, Marcia. With House in Hand: Organize Your Decorating. A Step-by-Step Planner for Home or Office. 54p. 1992. reprint ed. pap. 11.95 (*0-9615587-1-7*) M McAlister Enterps.

McAlister, Marcia, jt. auth. see McAlister, John.

McAlister, Martha K., jt. auth. see McAlister, Wayne H.

McAlister, Micheal J. The Language of Visual Effects. (Illus.). 176p. 1993. 18.95 (*0-943728-47-9*) Lone Eagle Pub.

McAlister, Roy E. Precision Spark Injection (PSI) System. 1986. pap. 4.95 (*0-685-24740-6*) Research Analysts.

McAlister, Wayne H. & McAlister, Martha K. Guidebook to the Arkansas National Wildlife Refuge. LC 94-41619. (Illus.). 304p. (Orig.). 1987. pap. 10.95 (*0-9618448-0-9*) Mince Country.

— Guidebook to the Arkansas National Wildlife Refuge. LC 94-41619. (Illus.). 400p. (Orig.). 1995. text ed. 45.00x (*0-292-75171-0*); pap. 19.95x (*0-292-75172-9*) U of Tex Pr.

— Matagorda Island: A Naturalist's Guide. LC 92-13024. (Illus.). 380p. (Orig.). 1993. text ed. 40.00 (*0-292-75150-8*); pap. 19.95 (*0-292-75151-6*) U of Tex Pr.

McAll, Christopher. Class, Ethnicity, & Social Inequality. (McGill-Queen's Studies in Ethnic History). 320p. (C). 1990. pap. 19.95 (*0-7735-0923-2*, Pub. by McGill CN) U of Toronto Pr.

McAll, Frances. For God's Sake Doctor. 96p. (Orig.). 1986. pap. 3.95 (*0-901269-82-4*) Grosvenor USA.

McAllan, Andrew. Fanfare. 608p. 1992. pap. 13.95 (*0-7472-3823-5*, Pub. by Headline UK) Trafalgar.

McAllen, Audrey E. The Listening Ear: The Development of Speech as a Creative Influence in Education. 192p. 1990. pap. 16.95 (*1-869890-18-3*, 1477, Pub. by Hawthorn Press UK) Anthroposophic.

— Sleep: An Unobserved Element in Education. 68p. 1990. pap. 14.95 (*1-869890-03-5*, 619, Pub. by Hawthorn Press UK) Anthroposophic.

McAllen, Jack B. The Boss Should Be a Woman: How Women Can Manage Their Way to the Top & Compromise Nothing; How to Succeed Because You Are a Woman. LC 93-28066. (Illus.). 208p. 1993. pap. 12.95 (*0-931892-56-2*) B Dolphin Pub.

McAllen, John B. The Boss Should Be a Woman: How Women Can Manage Their Way to the Top & Compromise Nothing; How to Succeed Because You Are a Woman. 264p. 1992. pap. text ed. 38.95 (*0-9634510-4-9*) Castlerock Pub.

McAllester, David P., ed. Becoming Human Through Music. 144p. 1985. 15.50 (*0-940796-51-1*, 1035) Music Ed Natl.

McAllester, David P., ed. & tr. Hogans: Navajo Houses & House Songs. LC 79-25075. (Wesleyan Poetry in Translation Ser.). (Illus.). 115p. 1987. pap. 14.95 (*0-8195-6185-1*, Wesleyan Univ Pr) U Pr of New Eng.

McAllester, David P., ed. see Mitchell, Frank.

McAllester, Mary, ed. The Philosophy & Poetics of Gaston Bachelard. LC 89-33901. (Current Continental Research Ser.: No. 011). 192p. (C). 1989. lib. bdg. 42.00 (*0-8191-7471-8*, Ctr Adv Res) U Pr of Amer.

McAllester, Melanie. The Lessons. LC 94-2770. 240p. 1994. pap. 9.95 (*0-933216-99-8*) Spinsters Ink.

McAllister. Steven Spielberg, Reading Level 2. (Reaching Your Goal Bks.: Set II). (Illus.). 24p. (J). (gr. 1-4). 1989. 10.95 (*0-685-58803-3*); lib. bdg. 14.60 (*0-86592-427-9*) Rourke Corp.

McAllister & Robbins, eds. True Three-Dimensional Imaging Techniques & Display Technologies. 192p. 1987. 43.00 (*0-89252-796-X*, 761) SPIE.

***McAllister, A.** Jessie's Journey. Date not set. pap. 4.99 (*0-517-13328-8*) Random.

McAllister, A. S. Thomson: Descendants of John Thomson, Pioneer Scotch Covenanter: Genealogical Notes on All Known Descendants of John Thomson of Scotland, Ireland & Pennsylvania, with Biographical Sketches. (Illus.). 357p. 1993. reprint ed. lib. bdg. 69.50 (*0-8328-3422-X*); reprint ed. pap. 59.50 (*0-8328-3423-8*) Higginson Bk Co.

McAllister, Angela. The Babies of Cockle Bay. (Illus.). 32p. (J). (ps-3). 1994. 13.95 (*0-8120-6424-0*); pap. 5.95 (*0-8120-1952-0*) Barron.

— The Honey Festival. LC 92-46079. (J). (gr. 1-8). 1999. 13.99 (*0-8037-1240-5*) Dial Bks Young.

— The Ice Palace. LC 93-45255. (J). 1994. 15.95 (*0-399-22784-9*, Putnam) Putnam Pub Group.

— The Ice Palace. (Illus.). 32p. (J). (ps-3). 1994. 15.95 (*0-399-22874-8*) Putnam Pub Group.

— The King Who Sneezed. LC 88-6858. (Illus.). 32p. (J). (gr. k-3). 1988. 12.95 (*0-688-08327-7*); lib. bdg. 12.88 (*0-688-08328-5*) Morrow Jr Bks.

— Midnight At the Oasis. (Illus.). 32p. (J). (ps-2). 1995. 19.95 (*0-370-31884-6*, Pub. by Bodley Head UK) Trafalgar.

— Nesta, the Little Witch. (Illus.). 32p. (J). (ps-3). 1999. pap. 4.99 (*0-14-054266-3*, Puffin) Puffin Bks.

— One Breeze-Scented, Sun-Sparkling Morning. (Illus.). 32p. (J). (ps-1). 1993. 17.95 (*0-09-176363-0*, Pub. by Hutchinson UK) Trafalgar.

— Paradise Park. (Illus.). 32p. (J). (ps-2). 1992. 16.95 (*0-370-31576-6*, Pub. by Bodley Head UK) Trafalgar.

— The Snow Angel. LC 92-44155. (Illus.). (J). 1993. write for info. (*0-688-04569-3*) Lothrop.

— The Wind Garden. LC 93-37435. (J). 1994. write for info. (*0-688-13280-4*) Lothrop.

McAllister, Angus. McAllister: Scottish Law of Leases. 1989. 42.00 (*0-406-10589-8*) Butterworth Legal Pubs.

McAllister, Angus & Guthrie, T. G. McAllister & Guthrie: Scottish Property Law - an Introduction. 232p. 1992. pap. 42.00 (*0-406-00105-7*) Butterworth Legal Pubs.

***McAllister, Angus & McMaster, Raymond.** Scottish Planning Law. 230p. 1994. pap. text ed. 51.00 (*0-406-02012-4*, UK) Butterworth Legal Pubs.

***McAllister, Anne.** The Alexakis Bride. 1995. mass mkt. 3.25 (*0-373-11769-8*, 1-11769-6) Harlequin Bks.

— Call up the Wind. (Presents Ser.). 1994. mass mkt. 2.99 (*0-373-11620-9*, 1-11620-1) Harlequin Bks.

— Call up the Wind. large type ed. (Harlequin Ser.). 1993. reprint ed. lib. bdg. 18.95 (*0-263-13268-4*, Pub. by Mills & Boon UK) Thorndike Pr.

— Cowboy's Don't Cry. (Desire Ser.). 1995. pap. 3.25 (*0-373-05907-8*, 1-05907-0) Silhouette.

— Cowboys Don't Quit. (Desire Ser.). 1995. mass mkt. 3.25 (*0-373-05944-2*, 1-05944-3) Silhouette.

— Cowboys Don't Stay. 1995. pap. 3.25 (*0-373-05969-8*, 1-05969-0) Silhouette.

— The Eight-Second Wedding. (American Romance Ser.). 1994. mass mkt. 3.50 (*0-373-16533-1*) Harlequin Bks.

— I Thee Wed. (American Romance Ser.: No. 387). 1991. mass mkt. 3.25 (*0-373-16387-8*) Harlequin Bks.

Mcallister, Anne. Imagine. (American Romance Ser.: No. 341). 1990. pap. 2.95 (*0-373-16341-X*) Harlequin Bks.

McAllister, Anne. Island Interlude. large type ed. 285p. 1992. reprint ed. lib. bdg. 18.95 (*0-263-12840-7*) Thorndike Pr.

— Starstruck. (Men Made in America Ser.). 1994. pap. 3.99 (*0-373-45199-7*, 1-45199-6) Harlequin Bks.

— To Tame a Wolfe. 1994. 3.59 (*0-373-45172-5*) Harlequin Bks.

McAllister, Becky. Justin. 32p. 1987. pap. 0.75 (*0-88144-101-5*) Christian Pub.

McAllister, Bill. History of Inverness. 200p. (C). 1989. pap. text ed. 50.00 (*0-85976-369-2*, Pub. by J Donald) St Mut.

McAllister, Bruce. Dream Baby. 448p. 1994. pap. 13.95 (*0-312-89025-7*) Orb NYC.

— North American Horse Travel Guide. (Illus.). 312p. (Orig.). 1993. pap. 19.95 (*0-9638817-2-8*) Roundup Pr.

— North American Horse Travel Guide. 2nd ed. (Illus.). 448p. (Orig.). 1995. pap. 19.95 (*0-9638817-3-6*) Roundup Pr.

McAllister, Bruce, jt. ed. see Harrison, Harry.

McAllister, Carol H., jt. auth. see Nogales, Patti D.

McAllister, Casey. Catch Me If You Can. 288p. (Orig.). 1993. mass mkt. 4.50 (*0-380-76571-3*) Avon.

McAllister, Constance. Creative Writing Activities, 2-6. 32p. (J). (gr. 2-6). 1980. pap. 2.95 (*0-87534-176-4*) Highlights.

— Creative Writing for Beginners. 32p. (Orig.). (J). (gr. 1-3). 1976. pap. 2.95 (*0-87534-165-9*) Highlights.

McAllister, D. Electric Cables Handbook. 2nd ed. (Illus.). 896p. 1990. text ed. 150.00 (*0-632-02299-X*) Sheridan.

McAllister, D., et al. Computer Modelling in Electrostatics. LC 85-14479. (Electrostatics & Electrostatic Applications Ser.). 130p. 1985. text ed. 125.00 (*0-471-90882-7*) Wiley.

McAllister, D. E., ed. On Lampreys & Fishes: A Memorial Anthology in Honor of Vadim D. Vladykov. (Developments in Environmental Biology of Fishes Ser.). (C). 1988. lib. bdg. 117.50 (*90-6193-661-6*) Kluwer Ac.

McAllister, David, et al. From Custody to Community: Thoroughcare for Young Offenders. 183p. 1992. 55.95 (*1-85628-265-1*, Pub. by Avebury Pub UK) Ashgate Pub Co.

McAllister, David F. Ontic: A Knowledge Representation System for Mathematics. (Artificial Intelligence Ser.). 375p. 1989. 27.50 (*0-262-13235-4*) MIT Pr.

McAllister, David F., ed. Stereo Computer Graphics & Other True 3D Technologies. LC 93-16642. (Computer Science Ser.). (Illus.). 328p. 1993. text ed. 75.00 (*0-691-08741-5*) Princeton U Pr.

McAllister, Dawson. Discussion Manual for Student Relationships, Vol. 2. (Illus.). (J). (gr. 5-12). 1976. pap. 8.75 (*0-923417-07-9*) Shepherd Minst.

— Discussion Manual for Student Relationships, Vol. 3. (Illus.). (J). (gr. 5-12). 1978. pap. 8.75 (*0-923417-08-7*) Shepherd Minst.

Mcallister, Dawson. Great War. 1991. pap. 8.99 (*0-923417-21-4*) Shepherd Minst.

McAllister, Dawson. How to Know If You're Really in Love. LC 93-40906. (YA). 1994. 8.99 (*0-8499-3312-9*) Word Pub.

— Please Don't Tell My Parents. 176p. (YA). 1992. pap. 8.99 (*0-8499-3311-0*) Word Inc.

— Self Esteem & Loneliness. (Illus.). (J). (gr. 5-12). 1989. pap. 3.95 (*0-923417-02-8*) Shepherd Minst.

An Asterisk (*) at the beginning of an entry indicates that the title is appearing in BIP for the first time.

— Student Conference Follow-Up Manual. (Illus.). (J). (gr. 5-12). 1989. pap. 2.95 (*0-923417-10-9*) Shepherd Minst.

— Student Relationships, Vol. 1. (J). (gr. 5-12). 1981. teacher ed, pap. 6.95 (*0-923417-18-4*) Shepherd Minst.

— A Walk with Christ Through the Resurrection. (Illus.). (J). (gr. 5-12). 1981. pap. 8.95 (*0-923417-14-1*) Shepherd Minst.

— A Walk with Christ to the Cross. (Illus.). (J). (gr. 5-12). 1980. pap. 8.95 (*0-923417-09-5*) Shepherd Minst.

— Who Are You, Jesus? (Illus.). (J). (gr. 5-12). 1986. pap. 7.95 (*0-923417-05-2*) Shepherd Minst.

McAllister, Dawson & Altman, Tim. Preparing Your Teenager for Sexuality. Peterson, Wayne, ed. (Illus.). 1988. pap. 6.95 (*0-923417-00-1*) Shepherd Minst.

— You, God & Your Sexuality. Peterson, Wayne, ed. (Illus.). (J). (gr. 5-12). 1988. pap. 3.95 (*0-923417-01-X*) Shepherd Minst.

McAllister, Dawson & Kimmel, Tim. Student Relationships, Vol. 2. (J). (gr. 5-12). 1981. teacher ed, pap. 6.95 (*0-923417-04-4*) Shepherd Minst.

— Walk with Christ to the Cross. (J). (gr. 5-12). 1981. teacher ed, pap. 5.95 (*0-923417-20-6*) Shepherd Minst.

McAllister, Dawson & May, Tom. Who Are You Jesus? (J). (gr. 5-12). 1986. teacher ed, pap. 7.95 (*0-923417-03-6*) Shepherd Minst.

McAllister, Dawson & McGee, Robert S. Search for Significance: Youth Edition. 1990. pap. 7.95 (*0-923417-12-5*) Shepherd Minst.

McAllister, Dawson & Miller, John. Discussion Manual for Student Discipleship, Vol. 2. (Illus.). (J). (gr. 5-12). 1978. pap. 8.50 (*0-923417-16-8*) Shepherd Minst.

McAllister, Dawson & Miller, Rich. Who Are You, God? (Illus.). (J). (gr. 5-12). 1988. pap. 7.95 (*0-923417-11-7*) Shepherd Minst.

— Who Are You God? (J). (gr. 5-12). 1990. teacher ed, pap. 5.95 (*0-923417-13-3*) Shepherd Minst.

McAllister, Dawson & Sharp, Floyd. Handbook for Financial Faithfulness. (Illus.). (J). (gr. 5-12). 1974. pap. 6.95 (*0-923417-17-6*) Shepherd Minst.

McAllister, Dawson & Webster, Dan. Discussion Manual for Student Discipleship, Vol. 1. (Illus.). (J). (gr. 5-12). 1975. pap. 8.50 (*0-923417-15-X*) Shepherd Minst.

— Discussion Manual for Student Relationships, Vol. 1. (Illus.). (J). (gr. 5-12). 1975. pap. 8.75 (*0-923417-06-0*) Shepherd Minst.

McAllister, Donald. Evaluation in Environmental Planning: Assessing Environmental, Social, Economic & Political Tradeoffs. 1980. pap. 18.95x (*0-262-63087-7*) MIT Pr.

***McAllister, Donald & Naas, Lucille, eds.** Marriage Returns of Oxford County, Maine, Prior to 1892. rev. ed. 352p. 1993. 37.50 (*0-89725-141-5*) Picton Pr.

McAllister, E. W., ed. Pipe Line Rules of Thumb. 3rd ed. (Illus.). 528p. 1993. pap. 59.00 (*0-88415-094-1*, 5094) Gulf Pub.

***McAllister, Elizabeth.** Peer Teaching & Collaborative Learning in the Language Arts. Lewis, Warren, ed. (Illus.). 68p. 1990. pap. 15.95 (*0-927516-21-7*) ERIC-REC.

***McAllister, Elizabeth A.** Learning Together: Collaboration for Active Learning in the Early Language Arts. (TRIED, Teaching Resources in the ERIC Database Ser.). (Illus.). 110p. (Orig.). 1995. pap. write for info. (*1-883790-12-3*, EDINFO Pr) Grayson Bernard Pubs.

— Learning Together: Collaborative Activities for Elementary Language Arts Students. LC 94-12655. (Teaching Resources in the ERIC Database, TRIED Ser.). 1994. 14.95 (*0-927516-42-X*) ERIC-REC.

***McAllister, Elizabeth A. & Neubert, Gloria A.** New Teachers Helping New Teachers: Preservice Peer Coaching. LC 94-49407. 1995. write for info. (*1-883790-14-X*, EDINFO Pr) Grayson Bernard Pubs.

McAllister, Eugene. Words about Birds in Rhyme Time. (Illus.). 80p. (Orig.). 1985. pap. 4.95 (*0-933380-27-5*) Olive Pr Pubns.

McAllister, Fran, jt. auth. see McAllister, Frank.

McAllister, Frank. Tooth Fairy Legend. LC 90-28136. (Illus.). 40p. (J). (gr. k-6). 1992. 12.95 (*0-915677-54-7*) Roundtable Pub.

McAllister, Frank & McAllister, Fran. The Tooth Fairy Legend. LC 76-9595. (J). (gr. k-4). 1976. 9.95 (*0-916864-01-4*) Block.

McAllister, Greg & McAllister, Jim. Leading Questions: A Free Will Baptist Discipleship Manual. 145p. 1988. ring bd. 12.95 (*0-89265-133-4*) Randall Hse.

***McAllister, Heather.** Jilt Trip. (Temptation Ser.). 1995. mass mkt. 3.25 (*0-373-25643-4*, 1-25643-7) Harlequin Bks.

McAllister, Hugh A., Jr. & Fenoglio, John J., Jr. Atlas of Tumor Pathology: Tumors of the Cardiovascular System. (Second Ser.: Fascicle 15). (Illus.). 157p. 1990. per., pap. 8.00 (*0-16-001839-0*, S/N 008-023-000) USGPO.

McAllister, Ian. Sustaining Relief with Development: Strategic Issues for the Red Cross & Red Crescent. LC 93-75. 280p. (C). 1993. Alk. paper. lib. bdg. 105.00 (*0-7923-2163-4*) Kluwer Ac.

McAllister, Ian, jt. auth. see Graetz, Brian.

McAllister, Ian, jt. auth. see Rose, Richard.

McAllister, J. Gray. McAllister Family Records: Compiled for the Descendants of Abraham Addams McAllister & His Wife Julia Ellen Stratton McAllister of Covington, Virginia. (Illus.). 88p. 1994. reprint ed. lib. bdg. 27.50 (*0-8328-4226-5*); reprint ed. pap. 17.50 (*0-8328-4227-3*) Higginson Bk Co.

— McAllister Family Records, Comp. for the Descendants of Abraham Addams McAllister & His Wife Julia Ellen (Stratton) McAllister of Covington, Va. (Illus.). 88p. 1994. reprint ed. lib. bdg. 27.50 (*0-8328-4539-6*); reprint ed. pap. 17.50 (*0-8328-4540-X*) Higginson Bk Co.

McAllister, J. M. & Tandy, L. B. Genealogy of the Lewis & Kindred Families. (Illus.). 416p. 1989. reprint ed. lib. bdg. 70.00 (*0-8328-0769-9*); reprint ed. pap. 62.00 (*0-8328-0770-2*) Higginson Bk Co.

McAllister, J. T. Virginia Militia in the Revolutionary War. 338p. 1990. reprint ed. pap. 21.50 (*1-55613-266-2*) Heritage Bk.

McAllister, James, jt. auth. see Kanski, Jack J.

McAllister, James A. The Government of Edward Schreyer: Democratic Socialism in Manitoba. 224p. 1984. pap. 24.95 (*0-7735-0437-0*, Pub. by McGill CN) U of Toronto Pr.

— The Government of Edward Schreyer: Democratic Socialism in Manitoba. LC 85-160930. (Illus.). 224p. reprint ed. pap. 63.90 (*0-7837-6904-0*, 2046734) Bks Demand.

McAllister, Jim, jt. auth. see McAllister, Greg.

McAllister, Lee. Squaw Dance. Seginski, John, ed. 245p. 1991. write for info. (*1-879586-00-2*) TJE NV.

McAllister, Leigh. The Winds of Rome. LC 87-42908. 200p. 1988. 9.95 (*1-55523-119-5*) Winston-Derek.

McAllister, Lester G. An Alexander Campbell Reader. 128p. (Orig.). 1988. pap. 10.99 (*0-8272-0017-X*) Chalice Pr.

McAllister, Lester G. & Tucker, William E. Journey in Faith: A History of the Christian Church. LC 75-11738. 512p. 1975. 18.99 (*0-8272-1703-X*) Chalice Pr.

McAllister, Mimi. Christmas at Gump's. LC 90-60435. (Illus.). 48p. (J). 1990. 16.95 (*0-9624887-4-7*) C Salway Pr.

***McAllister, P. K.** Maia's Veil: The Cloudships of Orion. 288p. (Orig.). 1995. mass mkt. 4.99 (*0-451-45320-4*, ROC) NAL-Dutton.

— Siduri's Net. (Cloudships of Orion Ser.: No. 1). 336p. (Orig.). 1994. pap. 4.99 (*0-451-45319-0*, ROC) NAL-Dutton.

McAllister, Pam. This River of Courage: Generations of Women's Resistance & Action. (Barbara Deming Memorial Ser.). 240p. 1991. 39.95 (*0-86571-197-6*); pap. 16.95 (*0-86571-198-4*) New Soc Pubs.

— You Can't Kill the Spirit. (Barbara Deming Memorial Series: Stories of Women & Nonviolence: Pt. 1). 240p. (Orig.). 1988. 39.95 (*0-86571-130-5*); pap. 14.95 (*0-86571-131-3*) New Soc Pubs.

McAllister, Pam, jt. ed. see Riley, Dick.

McAllister, Pam, ed. see Waisbrooker, Lois.

McAllister, Patricia. Gypsy Jewel. 416p. 1993. mass mkt. 4.50 (*0-8217-4306-6*) Zebra.

— Mountain Angel. 416p. 1995. mass mkt. 4.99 (*0-8217-4806-8*) Windsor NY.

McAllister, Patrick A., jt. ed. see Spiegel, Andrew D.

McAllister, Robert M., et al. Cancer. (Illus.). 352p. 1994. pap. 13.00 (*0-465-00846-1*) Basic.

McAllister, Samuel W. Society As I Have Found It. LC 75-1855. (Leisure Class in America Ser.). 1975. reprint ed. 34.95 (*0-405-06921-9*) Ayer.

— Society As I Have Found It. (American Biography Ser.). 469p. 1991. reprint ed. lib. bdg. 89.00 (*0-7812-8280-2*) Rprt Serv.

McAllister, Shawn R. Columbus in Black & White. (Illus.). 114p. (Orig.). 1993. pap. 5.95 (*0-9637286-0-1*) Remmington Pr.

***McAllister, Ted V.** Revolt Against Modernity: Leo Strauss, Eric Voegelin, & the Search for a Post-Liberal Order. (American Political Thought Ser.). 304p. (C). 1995. 29.95x (*0-7006-0740-4*) U Pr of KS.

McAllister, V. L., jt. auth. see Sengupta, R. P.

McAllister, Warren A., jt. auth. see Clemens, Donald F.

McAlmon, Robert. Miss Knight & Others. Lorusso, Edward N., ed. LC 92-4323. 159p. 1992. pap. 15.95 (*0-8263-1353-1*) U of NM Pr.

— North America: Continent of Conjecture, An Archetype Edition. (Illus.). 44p. (Orig.). (C). 1983. reprint ed. pap. 10.00 (*0-932139-02-7*) Dark Child Pr.

— Post-Adolescence: A Selection of Short Fiction. Lorusso, Edward N., ed. LC 91-18987. 294p. 1991. pap. 19.95 (*0-8263-1310-8*) U of NM Pr.

McAlmon, Robert, jt. auth. see Boyle, Kay.

McAlpin, Anne B. Pack-It-Up! Hundreds of Ways to Save Time, Money & Space When You Travel. LC 90-82758. (Illus.). 74p. (Orig.). 1991. pap. 7.95 (*0-9627263-0-3*) Flying Cloud.

***McAlpin, Jon, ed.** Stopover in Kansas. (Illus.). 156p. 1995. pap. text ed. 9.95 (*1-57166-014-3*) Quixote Pr IA.

***McAlpin, Michelle B.** Subject to Famine: Food Crises & Economic Change in Western India, 1860-1920. LC 82-61376. Date not set. reprint ed. pap. 86.70 (*0-7837-9385-5*, 2060129) Bks Demand.

— Subject to Famine: Food Crisis & Economic Change in Western India, 1860-1920. LC 82-61376. 320p. 1983. 49.50x (*0-691-05385-5*) Princeton U Pr.

McAlpine, A., et al, eds. New Challenges for Teachers & Teacher Education. vi, 174p. 1988. 29.50 (*90-265-0884-0*, Pub. by Swets Pub Serv NE) Taylor & Francis.

***McAlpine, Alistair.** Journal of a Collector. (Illus.). 192p. 1995. 34.95 (*1-85793-433-4*, Pub. by Pavilion UK) Trafalgar.

— Servant. 112p. 1993. 18.95 (*0-571-16886-8*) Faber & Faber.

McAlpine, Barbara, jt. auth. see Art Gallery California State University, Fullerton Staff.

McAlpine, Barbara, ed. see California-International Arts Foundation Staff.

McAlpine, Campbell. Alone with God: A Manual of Biblical Meditation. 1981. reprint ed. pap. 7.99 (*0-87123-000-3*) Bethany Hse.

***McAlpine, Dave, et al.** Para Empezar - Interacciones: Beginning Spanish. 1995. text ed. write for info. (*0-07-044978-3*) McGraw.

McAlpine, Frank. Popular Poetic Pearls & Biographies of Poets. LC 74-15745. (Popular Culture in America Ser.). (Illus.). 384p. 1975. reprint ed. 33.95 (*0-405-06380-6*) Ayer.

McAlpine, Janet. Play Guide Two: Travel Through Time & Space. (Illus.). 1990. teacher ed 10.00 (*1-879616-01-7*, 34892) Brio Scanditoy.

McAlpine, Ken, jt. auth. see Tinley, Scott.

McAlpine, Monica E. Chaucer's Knight's Tale: An Annotated Bibliography 1894-1984. (Chaucer Bibliographies Ser.). 496p. 1991. text ed. 85.00 (*0-8020-5913-9*) U of Toronto Pr.

— The Genre of Troilus & Criseyde. LC 77-12511. 256p. 1978. 34.95 (*0-8014-0962-4*) Cornell U Pr.

McAlpine, R. W. The Life & Times of Col. James Fisk, Jr. Bruchey, Stuart, ed. LC 80-1329. (Railroads Ser.). (Illus.). 1981. reprint ed. lib. bdg. 35.95 (*0-405-13803-2*) Ayer.

McAlpine, T. S. The Process of Management. 1973. 26.95 (*0-8464-0765-5*) Beekman Pubs.

— Profit Planning & Control. (Illus.). 164p. 1969. 24.95 (*0-8464-1122-9*) Beekman Pubs.

McAlpine, Thomas H. Facing the Powers. 103p. 1991. pap. 7.95 (*0-912552-72-7*) MARC.

Mcalpine, William, ed. Japanese Tales & Legends. (Oxford Myths & Legends Ser.). (Illus.). 218p. (J). 1989. pap. 10.95 (*0-19-274140-3*) OUP.

***McAlvany, Don.** The Coming Persecution of the Church. 64p. (Orig.). 1992. pap. 2.50 (*1-879366-36-3*) Hearthstone OK.

— Confronting Our Nation's Problems. 30p. (Orig.). 1994. pap. 2.50 (*1-879366-47-9*) Hearthstone OK.

— The Fourth Reich. 70p. (Orig.). 1994. pap. 2.50 (*1-879366-86-X*) Hearthstone OK.

***McAlvany, Don & Hutchings, Noah W.** Five Years to World Government & the Cashless Society. 60p. (Orig.). 1995. pap. 2.50 (*1-879366-91-6*) Hearthstone OK.

McAlvany, Donald S. Toward a New World Order: The Countdown to Armageddon. 250p. (Orig.). (C). 1990. pap. 8.95 (*0-9624517-9-7*) Hearthstone OK.

McAlvay, Nora & Chorpenning, Charlotte B. The Elves & the Shoemaker. (J). 1946. 5.00 (*0-87602-124-0*) Anchorage.

— Flibbertygibbet. (J). 1952. 5.00 (*0-87602-127-5*) Anchorage.

***McAnallen, Rachel & Frye, Ellen.** Action Fractions. (Ms. Math Presents Ser.). 40p. (YA). 1993. 6.00 (*1-886915-02-4*) Koplow Games.

—Action Fractions with Hexadrons & Pattern Blocks. (Ms. Math Presents Ser.). 40p. (J). (gr. 2 up). 1995. 20.00 (*1-886915-00-8*) Koplow Games. ACTION FRACTIONS demonstrates a concrete approach to fractions. It is written for children ages seven & up as well as for teachers & parents of those children. The book offers you some tools for learning fractions - a pretend gold mine & a bag of gold! Using pattern blocks & dice, you'll add & subtract fractions by adding & subtracting pieces of gold. Math is a language that should be spoken & an art that should be seen & touched. ACTION FRACTIONS encourages learners to speak fractionese, to visualize fractions & to feel fractions. Publisher: Koplow Games, Box 965, Hull, MA 02045. 671-482-4011. ***Publisher Provided Annotation.***

— Action Fractions with Hexahedron. (Ms. Math Presents Ser.). 40p. (YA). 1993. 8.50 (*1-886915-01-6*) Koplow Games.

McAnally, D. R., Jr. Irish Wonders. LC 92-46307. (Illus.). 224p. 1994. pap. 7.95 (*0-8069-0299-X*, Sterling-Main St) Sterling.

McAnally, Don. Kisses, Dime-On Pins, Twins, Celebrities, & Humor Are My Life! (Illus.). 132p. 1991. pap. 14.95 (*0-9630282-0-0*) McAnally & Assocs.

— Thoroughbred Hookers I Have Known (Items to Make You Chuckle) 72p. 1991. pap. 5.95 (*0-9630282-1-9*) McAnally & Assocs.

McAnally, Mary, ed. Warning: Anthology of Poetry from Prisoners of Oklahoma. 1980. pap. 5.00 (*0-931350-03-4*) Moonlight Pubns.

McAnally, Mary E. The Absence of the Father & the Dance of Zygotes. Dochniak, Jim, ed. (U. S. A. Poetry Chapbook Ser.: No. 1). 20p. (C). 1982. pap. 1.95 (*0-937724-00-9*) Shadow Pr.

McAnally, Patricia L., et al. Language Learning Practices with Deaf Children. Quigley, Stephen P., ed. LC 90-20956. (Illus.). 238p. (C). 1987. pap. text ed. 35.00 (*0-89079-372-7*, 1738) PRO-ED.

— Language Learning Practices with Deaf Children. 2nd ed. LC 93-39470. (C). 1994. text ed. 36.00 (*0-89079-597-5*, 6667) PRO-ED.

***McAnally, Tom.** Questions & Answers about the United Methodist Church. 24p. (Orig.). 1995. pap. 1.95 (*0-687-01670-3*) Abingdon.

McAnaney, Kate D. I Wish... Dreams & Realities of Parenting a Special Needs Child. 96p. (Orig.). 1992. pap. 8.95 (*0-9632338-0-7*) United Cereb Palsy.

McAnaney, Pat. Dear Psychic: A New Perspective on Life's Everyday Problems. LC 92-31487. 167p. (Orig.). 1993. 9.95 (*1-878217-07-0*) Victory Press.

McAnany, Emile G., ed. Communications in the Rural Third World: The Role of Information in Development. LC 79-21406. (Praeger Special Studies). 240p. 1980. text ed. 39.95 (*0-275-90519-5*, C0519, Praeger Pubs) Greenwood.

McAnany, Emile G., jt. ed. see Atwood, Rita.

McAnany, Emile G., et al, eds. Communication & Social Structure: Critical Studies in Mass Media Research. 348p. 1981. text ed. 37.95 (*0-275-90679-5*, C0679, Praeger Pubs); pap. write for info. (*0-275-91459-3*, B1459, Praeger Pubs) Greenwood.

McAnany, Kathleen, jt. auth. see Schavitz, Peter.

McAnany, Patricia A. Living with the Ancestors: Kinship & Kingship in Ancient Maya Society. LC 94-5469. (Illus.). 248p. (C). 1995. text ed. 27.50x (*0-292-75165-6*) U of Tex Pr.

McAnarney, Elizabeth R., jt. ed. see Levine, Melvin D.

McAnarney, Elizabeth R., et al. Textbook of Adolescent Medicine. (Illus.). 1269p. 1992. text ed. 132.50 (*0-7216-3077-4*) Saunders.

McAndrew, Bill, jt. auth. see Copp, Terry.

McAndrew, Francis. Environmental Psychology. 320p. (C). 1993. text ed. 47.95 (*0-534-19308-0*) Brooks-Cole.

McAndrew, Ian. On Poultry & Game. 1990. text ed. 24.98 (*0-442-30274-6*) Chapman & Hall.

McAndrew, Toni. Seasons of Myself. (Illus.). 21p. (Orig.). 1990. pap. 5.00 (*0-910147-86-8*) World Poetry Pr.

McAndrews, Anita. Conquistador's Lady. LC 90-30127. 240p. (Orig.). 1990. pap. 10.95 (*0-931832-48-9*) Fithian Pr.

McAndrews, Laurence J. Broken Ground: John F. Kennedy & the Politics of Education. LC 91-14284. (Modern American History Ser.). 248p. 1991. 62.00 (*0-8240-1897-4*) Garland.

McAndrews, Lynn. My Father Forgets. LC 90-91658. 110p. (Orig.). 1991. pap. 8.95 (*0-9626683-0-3*) Northern Maple.

McAnelly, James R. & McAnelly, Patricia L. Business Mathematics for College. LC 86-26670. (Illus.). 534p. (Orig.). (C). 1987. teacher ed, pap. text ed. 52.00 (*0-314-26207-5*) West Pub.

McAnelly, Patricia L., jt. auth. see McAnelly, James R.

McAnelly, Vera P., ed. see Easley, Barbara P.

McAnelly, Verla P., ed. see Easley, Barbara P.

McAnelly, Verla P., jt. ed. see Easley, Barbara P.

***McAneny, Daniel T.** So You're "On Disability"...& You Think You Might Want to Get Back Into Action: Thoughts & Stories That May Help Some People Who Are Receiving "Long Term Disability" Benefits. 124p. (Orig.). 1995. pap. 7.95 (*0-9646490-0-4*) D T McAneny.

McAniff, Edward. Strategic Concepts in Fire Fighting. (Illus.). 1974. 37.75 (*0-912212-02-0*) Fire Eng.

McAninch, Amy R. Teacher Thinking & the Case Method: Theory & Future Directions. LC 93-18207. 160p. (C). 1993. text ed. 23.00 (*0-8077-3243-5*) Tchrs Coll.

***McAninch, Jack W., ed.** Traumatic & Reconstructive Urology. LC 95-10055. 1995. text ed. write for info. (*0-7216-3886-4*) Saunders.

McAninch, Jack W., jt. auth. see Tanagho, Emil A.

McAninch, Sandra, comp. Sun Power: A Bibliography of United States Government Documents on Solar Energy. LC 80-29037. xx, 944p. 1981. text ed. 135.00 (*0-313-20992-8*, MSU/, Greenwood Pr) Greenwood.

McAninch, William S. & Fairey, W. Gaston. The Criminal Law of South Carolina. 2nd ed. 1989. text ed. 75.00 (*0-943856-06-X*, 414) SC Bar CLE.

McAninch, William S., jt. auth. see Watson, Patricia S.

McAnulty, Richard D., jt. ed. see Diamant, Louis.

McAra, Duncan. Sir James Gowans: Romantic Rationalist. 1977. 14.95 (*0-8464-0851-1*) Beekman Pubs.

McArdle, A. D. International Ship Arrest. 1990. 100.00 (*1-85044-190-1*) Lloyds London Pr.

McArdle, C. B., ed. Applied Photochromic Polymer Systems. 320p. 1991. 119.95 (*0-412-02971-5*, A5310, Blackie & Son-Chapman NY) Routledge Chapman & Hall.

— Side Chain Liquid Crystal Polymers. (Illus.). 416p. 1989. 150.00 (*0-412-01761-X*, Chap & Hall NY) Chapman & Hall.

McArdle, Frank B., ed. The Changing Health Care Market. LC 87-619. (EBRI-ERF Policy Forum Ser.). 292p. (Orig.). (C). 1987. text ed. 61.00 (*0-8191-6510-7*, Pub. by Employee Benefit Rsch Inst); pap. text ed. 31.00 (*0-8191-6511-5*, Empl Benefit Res Inst) U Pr of Amer.

McArdle, Geri. Delivering Effective Training Sessions. Gerould, Philip, ed. (Fifty-Minute Ser.). 100p. (Orig.). 1993. pap. 9.95 (*1-56052-193-7*) Crisp Pubns.

— Developing Instructional Design. Crisp, Michael G., ed. LC 90-83479. (Fifty-Minute Ser.). (Illus.). 80p. (Orig.). 1991. pap. 9.95 (*1-56052-076-0*) Crisp Pubns.

McArdle, Gilbert C. Modelling the USF Constellation. LC 84-46108. (Illus.). 160p. (Orig.). 1985. pap. 9.95 (*0-87033-334-8*) Cornell Maritime.

McArdle, H. & Suggitt, G. Per Saecula, Pt. 1. 1974. pap. text ed. 10.84 (*0-582-36727-1*, 72516) Longman.

— Per Saecula, Pt. 2. 1974. pap. text ed. 10.84 (*0-582-36728-X*, 72517) Longman.

McArdle, J. Functional Morphology of the Hip & Thigh of the Lorisiformes. (Contributions to Primatology Ser.: Vol. 17). (Illus.). viii, 132p. 1981. pap. 25.75 (*3-8055-1767-X*) S Karger.

McArdle, J. L., et al. Treatment of Hazardous Waste Leachate: Unit Operations & Costs. LC 87-34715. (Pollution Technology Review Ser.: No. 151). (Illus.). 111p. 1988. 36.00 (*0-8155-1160-4*) Noyes.

McArdle, Jack. The Higher Power. 62p. (Orig.). 1988. pap. 5.95 (*0-948183-63-2*, Pub. by Columba Pr IE) Twenty-Third.

— It's Really Very Simple: Uncomplicating the Message. 144p. (Orig.). 1994. pap. 9.95 (*1-85607-093-X*, Pub. by Columba Pr IE) Twenty-Third.

M

— One Hundred-Fifty More Stories for Preachers & Teachers. LC 92-82675. 96p. (Orig.). 1993. pap. 7.95 (*0-89622-540-2*) Twenty-Third.

— Simple Steps to Spiritual Living. 128p. (Orig.). 1993. pap. 7.95 (*1-85607-080-8*, Pub. by Columba Pr IE) Twenty-Third.

— Twelve Simple Words. 134p. (Orig.). 1994. pap. 7.95 (*1-85607-119-7*, Pub. by Columba Pr IE) Twenty-Third.

***McArdle, Nora.** Internet Security: From Basics to Beyond. 1995. pap. 34.95 (*1-55958-747-4*) Prima Pub.

McArdle, William D., jt. auth. see Katch, Frank I.

McArdle, William D., et al. Essentials of Exercise Physiology. (Illus.). 589p. 1994. pap. text ed. 47.95 (*0-8121-1724-7*) Williams & Wilkins.

— Exercise Physiology: Energy, Nutrition & Home Performance. 3rd ed. 853p. 1991. text ed. 57.95 (*0-8121-1351-9*) Williams & Wilkins.

McAroy, Hazel, jt. ed. see Powell, Alice.

***McArthur.** The Economics of Money & Banking. 4th ed. (C). 1994. student ed, text ed. 15.00 (*0-673-52402-7*) HarpCollege.

McArthur, jt. auth. see Eakins.

McArthur, Bruce. Your Life: Why It Is the Way It Is & What You Can Do About It: An Exploration of the Universal Laws That Govern all of Us. 273p. (Orig.). 1993. pap. 12.95 (*0-87604-300-7*, 375) ARE Pr.

McArthur, C. Operations Analysis in the United States Army Eighth Air Force in World War II. (HMATH Ser.: Vol. 4). 349p. 1990. text ed. 36.00 (*0-8218-0158-9*, HMATH-4) Am Math.

***McArthur, C. Dan & Womack, Larry.** Outcome Management: Redesigning Your Business Systems to Achieve Your Vision. LC 95-5100. 1995. write for info. (*0-527-76292-X*) Qual Resc.

McArthur, Colin. The Big Heat. (BFI Film Classics Ser.). 1993. pap. 9.95 (*0-85170-342-9*, Pub. by British Film Inst UK) Ind U Pr.

McArthur, Colin & Barnard, Ian. A Director's Guide. (Waterlow Practitioner's Library). 144p. 1990. pap. 26.00 (*0-08-040121-X*, Pergamon Pr) Elsevier.

McArthur, Dalton R. The First Snowflake. (Illus.). 32p. (Orig.). (J). (ps-4). 1991. pap. 4.95 (*0-9626111-0-7*) McArthur UT.

***McArthur, Dan & Womack, Larry.** Outcome Management: Redesigning Your Business Systems to Achieve Your Visions. 224p. 1995. 24.95 (*0-8144-0289-5*) AMACOM.

McArthur, Dorothea S. The Birth of a Self in Adulthood. LC 87-33337. 250p. 1988. 30.00 (*0-87668-909-8*) Aronson.

McArthur, Edith K. Language Characteristics & Schooling in the United States, a Changing Picture: 1979 & 1989. (Illus.). 67p. (Orig.). (C). 1994. pap. text ed. 34.95 (*0-7881-0696-1*) Diane Pub.

McArthur, Edwin. Flagstad: A Personal Memoir. LC 79-28361. (Music Reprint Ser.: 1980). (Illus.). 1980. reprint ed. lib. bdg. 39.50 (*0-306-76028-2*) Da Capo.

McArthur, Erna, tr. see Steiner, Rudolf.

McArthur, Harvey K. Understanding the Sermon on the Mount. LC 78-16404. 192p. 1978. reprint ed. text ed. 42.50 (*0-313-20569-8*, MCUS, Greenwood Pr) Greenwood.

McArthur, Ian. Reading Japanese Signs: Deciphering Daily Life in Japan. Kuromachi-san & Ikeda, Megumi, eds. (Illus.). 138p. 1993. pap. 10.00 (*4-7700-1671-9*) Kodansha.

McArthur, Jill. Dissolution. (Illus.). 96p. (Orig.). 1991. pap. 15.95 (*0-9629518-0-3*) J McArthur.

McArthur, Lewis. Oregon Geographic Names. 6th ed. 1992. pap. 19.95 (*0-87595-237-2*) Oregon Hist.

McArthur, Lewis L. Oregon Geographic Names. 6th ed. 920p. 1992. 29.95 (*0-87595-236-4*); pap. 19.95 (*0-685-58928-5*) Oregon Hist.

***McArthur, Loretta & Clark, Tim.** Yoga Cards, Create Your Own Yoga Program. 1994. pap. 14.95 (*0-89087-740-8*) Celestial Arts.

McArthur, M. S. Report on Brunei in Nineteen Hundred Four. LC 87-11218. (Monographs in International Studies, Southeast Asia Ser.: No. 74). 216p. 1986. pap. text ed. 15.00 (*0-89680-135-7*, Ohio U Ctr Intl) Ohio U Pr.

***McArthur, Margaret.** Earth Magic. Date not set. pap. 19.95 (*1-898307-01-6*, Pub. by Capall Bann Pubng UK) Holmes Pub.

McArthur, Margie. WiccaCraft for Families. (Illus.). 266p. (Orig.). 1994. pap. 14.95 (*0-919345-52-2*) Phoenix WA.

McArthur, Micky. I'd Rather Be Wanted Than Had: The Memoirs of an Unrepentant Bank Robber. 272p. 1990. 24.95 (*0-7737-2340-4*, Pub. by Stoddart Pubng CN) Genl Dist Srvs.

McArthur, Murray. Stolen Writings: Blake's "Milton", Joyce's "Ulysses", & the Nature of Influence. Litz, A. Walton, ed. LC 87-28566. (Studies in Modern Literature: No. 87). 188p. reprint ed. 53.60 (*0-8357-1846-8*, 2070742) Bks Demand.

McArthur, Nancy. The Adventure of the Backyard Sleepout. 80p. (J). 1992. pap. 2.95 (*0-590-45033-6*) Scholastic Inc.

— The Escape of the Plant That Ate Dirty Socks. 128p. (Orig.). (J). 1992. pap. 3.50 (*0-380-76756-2*, Camelot) Avon.

— How to Do Theatre Publicity. 1978. spiral bd. 19.50 (*0-9603940-0-1*) Good Ideas.

— More Adventures of the Plant That Ate Dirty Socks. 128p. (Orig.). (J). 1994. pap. 3.50 (*0-380-77663-4*, Camelot) Avon.

— The Plant That Ate Dirty Socks. 128p. (Orig.). (J). 1988. pap. 3.99 (*0-380-75493-2*, Camelot) Avon.

— The Plant That Ate Dirty Socks Goes up in Space. 160p. (Orig.). (J). (gr. 4-5). 1995. pap. 3.99 (*0-380-77664-2*, Camelot) Avon.

— The Return of the Plant That Ate Dirty Socks. 128p. (Orig.). (J). (gr. 5-6). 1990. pap. 3.50 (*0-380-75873-3*, Camelot) Avon.

— The Secret of the Plant That Ate Dirty Socks. 128p. (Orig.). (J). 1993. pap. 3.50 (*0-380-76757-0*, Camelot) Avon.

McArthur, Robert, jt. auth. see Payne, Edmund C.

McArthur, Robert P. From Logic to Computing. 511p. (C). 1991. text ed. 41.95 (*0-534-13320-7*) Intl Thomson.

— Tense Logic. 1976. lib. bdg. 45.50 (*90-277-0697-2*) Kluwer Ac.

McArthur, Shirley D. Frank Lloyd Wright: American System Built Homes in Milwaukee. LC 83-61201. (Illus.). 186p. (Orig.). 1985. pap. text ed. 20.00 (*0-9606072-1-8*) N Point Hist Soc.

— North Point Historic Districts - Milwaukee. LC 80-83990. (Illus.). 260p. (Orig.). 1981. pap. 25.00 (*0-9606072-0-X*) N Point Hist Soc.

McArthur, Shirley H. Raising Your Hearing-Impaired Child: Guideline for Parents. 256p. 1982. pap. 12.95 (*0-88200-150-7*) Alexander Graham.

McArthur, Simon, jt. ed. see Hall, C. Michael.

McArthur, Thomas. Oxford Companion to the English Language. (Illus.). 1216p. 1992. 49.95 (*0-19-214183-X*) OUP.

McArthur, Thomas G. Longman Lexicon of Contemporary English. 910p. 1981. text ed. 34.95 (*0-582-55636-8*, 74430) Longman.

McArthur, Tom. Beyond Logic & Mysticism: Guide to Developing a More Integrative Mind Through Unitive Thinking. (Illus.). 144p. (Orig.). (C). 1990. pap. 8.95 (*0-8356-0659-7*, Quest) Theos Pub Hse.

McArthur, William G. & Crawley, J. Winston. Structuring Data with Pascal: A Practical Introduction to Abstract Data Types. 896p. 1991. pap. text ed. 61.00 (*0-13-853060-2*) P-H.

— Structuring Data with Turbo Pascal: A Practical Introduction to Abstract Data Types. 960p. 1991. pap. text ed. 56.00 (*0-13-853052-1*, 270803) P-H.

McArtor, Judith. Life...an Event! LC 89-90275. (Illus.). 80p. (Orig.). 1989. pap. 6.95 (*0-9623782-0-8*) Cynosure Self Discovery.

McArtot, Marion, jt. auth. see Goss, Louise.

McAsey, Christopher. How to Live in Australia: A Guide for the Japanese. 176p. 1993. pap. 12.95 (*4-89684-756-3*, Pub. by Yohan Pubns JA) Weatherhill.

McAshan, H. H. Competency-Based Education & Behavioral Objectives. LC 78-31160. (Illus.). 280p. 1979. 33.95 (*0-87778-132-X*) Educ Tech Pubns.

McAshan, Hildreth. Comprehensive Planning for School Administrators. (Orig.). (C). 1983. pap. text ed. 11.95 (*0-89894-000-1*) Advocate Pub Group.

McAshan, M., ed. Supercollider 1. (Illus.). 840p. 1989. 145.00 (*0-306-43365-6*, Plenum Pr) Plenum.

— Supercollider 2. LC 90-49839. (Illus.). 790p. 1990. 145.00 (*0-306-43801-1*, Plenum Pr) Plenum.

McAshan, Marie P. A Houston Legacy. Bell, Mary J., ed. LC 85-21926. (Illus.). 296p. 1985. 19.95 (*0-87201-407-X*) Gulf Pub.

McAtee, Robert E. Facilitated Stretching. LC 92-36778. (Illus.). 120p. 1993. pap. 15.95 (*0-87322-420-5*, PMCA0420) Human Kinetics.

McAthie, jt. auth. see Lindeman.

McAtlee, Eric G. One Hundred Seventy-Five Plus Uses for the Dremel Moto-Tool & Cordless Freewheeler. (Illus.). 96p. (Orig.). 1989. pap. 5.10 (*0-685-26823-3*) Dremel.

McAughey, Patricia. Calculated Risk. (Rainbow Romances Ser.). 160p. 1993. 14.95 (*0-7090-4919-6*, Hale-Parkwest) Parkwest Pubns.

— Calculated Risk. large type ed. (Romance Library). 272p. 1995. pap. 14.95 (*0-7089-7662-X*, Linford) Ulverscroft.

McAughtry, Sam. Belfast Stories. 157p. 1993. pap. 10.95 (*0-85640-520-5*, Pub. by Blackstaff Pr IE) Dufour.

— Touch & Go: A Novel. 233p. 1994. pap. 11.95 (*0-85640-503-5*, Pub. by Blackstaff Pr IE) Dufour.

Mcaulay. Optical Computer Architectures: The Application of Optical Concepts to Next Generation Computers. 1991. text ed. 89.95 (*0-471-63242-2*) Wiley.

McAulay, John D. Carbines of the Civil War, 1861-1865. 1981. 8.95 (*0-913150-45-2*) Pioneer Pr.

— Civil War Breech Loading Rifles: A Survey of the Innovative Infantry Arms of the American Civil War. LC 87-60724. (Illus.). 144p. 1987. pap. 15.00 (*0-917218-29-9*) A Mowbray.

— Civil War Pistols. (Illus.). 1992. pap. 24.00 (*0-685-59082-8*) A Mowbray.

McAuley. God Hears Everything. LC 91-72357. (J). 1992. 4.99 (*1-55513-715-6*, Chariot Bks) Chariot Family.

— God Made Fireflies. LC 91-72356. (J). 1992. 4.99 (*1-55513-716-4*, Chariot Bks) Chariot Family.

McAuley, A., ed. Inorganic Reaction Mechanisms, Vols. 1-6. Incl. Vol. 1. 1969-70 Literature. LC 73-642977. 1971. 38.00 (*0-85186-255-1*); Vol. 3. 1972-73 Literature. LC 73-642977. 1974. 47.00 (*0-85186-275-6*); Vol. 4. 1973-74 Literature. LC 73-642977. 1976. 59.00 (*0-85186-285-3*); Vol. 5. 1975-76 Literature. LC 73-642977. 1977. 73.00 (*0-85186-295-0*); Vol. 6. LC 73-642977. 1979. 86.00 (*0-85186-305-1*); Vol. 2. 1970-71 Literature. LC 73-642977. 1972. 38.00 (*0-85186-265-9*). LC 73-642977. write for info. (*0-318-50472-3*) Am Chemical.

McAuley, Alastair. Economic Welfare in the Soviet Union: Poverty, Living Standards, & Inequality. LC 78-53290. 400p. 1979. 40.00 (*0-299-07640-7*) U of Wis Pr.

McAuley, Alastair, ed. Soviet Federalism: Nationalism & Economic Decentralisation. LC 91-28124. 210p. 1991. text ed. 55.00 (*0-312-07191-4*) St Martin.

McAuley, Finbarr. Insanity, Psychiatry & Criminal Responsibility. 248p. 1993. text ed. 49.50 (*1-85800-011-4*, Pub. by Round Hall); pap. text ed. 30.00 (*1-85800-019-X*, Pub. by Round Hall) Intl Spec Bk.

McAuley, Helen & Jackson, Peter. Educating Young Children: A Structural Approach. 144p. 1992. 27.50 (*1-85346-195-4*, Pub. by D Fulton UK) Taylor & Francis.

M'Cauley, I. H. Historical Sketch of Franklin County, PA. 294p. 1994. reprint ed. lib. bdg. 29.50 (*0-8328-3976-0*) Higginson Bk Co.

McAuley, Ian. Guide to Ethnic London. (C). 1990. pap. 100.00 (*0-902743-46-5*, Pub. by IMMEL Pubng UK) St Mut.

McAuley, James. Coming & Going: New & Selected Poems. LC 88-29576. 161p. 1989. 18.95 (*1-55728-072-X*); pap. 10.95 (*1-55728-073-8*) U of Ark Pr.

— Versification: A Short Introduction. 88p. 1986. reprint ed. pap. 6.00 (*0-87013-096-X*) Mich St U Pr.

McAuley, James J. After the Blizzard: Poems. LC 74-84571. (Breakthrough Bks). 72p. 1975. text ed. 14.95 (*0-8262-0170-9*) U of Mo Pr.

— The Exiles Book of Hours: A Sequence. 1982. pap. 4.00 (*0-917652-29-0*) Confluence Pr.

McAuley, James W. Protestant Working Class Politics & Culture in Belfast: The Politics of Identity. 204p. 1993. 54.95 (*1-85628-537-5*, Pub. by Avebury Pub UK) Ashgate Pub Co.

McAuley, John. Hazardous Renaissance. 1978. pap. 3.00 (*0-916696-06-5*) Cross Country.

— Mattress Testing. 1979. pap. 3.00 (*0-916696-09-X*) Cross Country.

McAuley, John J., jt. auth. see Young, Philip K. Y.

McAuley, Karen. Eleanor Roosevelt. (World Leaders - Past & Present Ser.). (Illus.). 112p. (YA). (gr. 5 up). 1987. lib. bdg. 17.95 (*0-87754-574-X*) Chelsea Hse.

— Golda Meir. (World Leaders - Past & Present Ser.). (Illus.). 112p. 1985. lib. bdg. 17.95 (*0-87754-568-5*) Chelsea Hse.

McAuley, Kathleen A. Edgar Allan Poe Cottage. 36p. 1988. teacher ed, pap. text ed. 10.00 (*0-941980-23-5*) Bronx County.

McAuley, Liam. The Musicians. LC 94-60618. 90p. (J). (gr. 6-11). 1995. pap. 6.95 (*1-55523-704-5*) Winston-Derek.

McAuley, Marilyn, jt. auth. see Lockwood, Barbara.

McAuley, Mary. Bread & Justice: State & Society in Petrograd, 1917-1922. (Illus.). 488p. 1991. 85.00 (*0-19-821982-2*) OUP.

— Soviet Politics, Nineteen Seventeen to Nineteen Ninety-One. LC 92-7517. 160p. (C). 1992. 25.00 (*0-19-878066-4*); pap. 10.95 (*0-19-878067-2*) OUP.

McAuley, Milt. Guide to the Backbone Trail: Santa Monica Mountains. LC 90-83558. (Illus.). 144p. (Orig.). 1990. pap. 7.95 (*0-942568-23-0*) Canyon Pub Co.

— Hiking in Topanga State Park. 3rd rev. ed. LC 81-67940. (Illus.). 160p. 1991. pap. 7.95 (*0-942568-24-9*) Canyon Pub Co.

— Hiking Trails of Malibu Creek State Park (Santa Monica Mountains) LC 82-74274. (Illus.). 112p. 1983. pap. 5.95 (*0-942568-04-4*) Canyon Pub Co.

— Hiking Trails of the Santa Monica Mountains. 5th ed. LC 80-67568. (Illus.). 320p. 1991. pap. 9.95 (*0-942568-25-7*) Canyon Pub Co.

— Hiking Trails of the Santa Monica Mountains. 6th ed. LC 80-67568. (Illus.). 1996. pap. write for info. (*0-942568-28-1*) Canyon Pub Co.

— Wildflower Walks in the Santa Monica Mountains, Vol. 1. LC 87-72856. (Illus.). 128p. (Orig.). 1988. pap. 5.95 (*0-942568-16-8*) Canyon Pub Co.

— Wildflowers of the Santa Monica Mountains. 2nd ed. LC 84-73487. (Illus.). 544p. (YA). (gr. 8-12). 1995. pap. write for info. (*0-942568-27-3*) Canyon Pub Co.

McAuley, Paul J. Eternal Light. 1993. pap. 22.00 (*0-380-97227-1*, AvoNova) Avon.

— Eternal Light. 432p. 1994. mass mkt. 4.99 (*0-380-76623-X*, AvoNova) Avon.

— Eternal Light. 1993. 22.00 (*0-688-12757-6*) Morrow.

— Four Hundred Billion Stars. 288p. 1988. pap. 3.50 (*0-345-35175-4*, Del Rey) Ballantine.

— Of the Fall. 352p. 1989. pap. 3.95 (*0-345-36056-7*, Del Rey) Ballantine.

— Red Dust: A Novel. 1994. 22.00 (*0-688-13793-8*) Morrow.

McAuley, Paul J. & Newman, Kim, eds. In Dreams. 447p. 1993. pap. 11.95 (*0-575-05201-5*, Pub. by V Gollancz UK) Trafalgar.

McAuley, Skeet. Sign Language: Contemporary Southwest Native America. (Illus.). 80p. 1989. 29.95 (*0-89381-333-8*) Aperture.

McAuley, Susie. STATS for Those in the Know! LC 88-90536. 76p. (Orig.). 1988. pap. text ed. write for info. (*0-9619964-0-4*) S McAuley.

McAuley, Tanya, jt. auth. see Townsend, Charles E.

McAuley, William J. Applied Research in Gerontology. (Illus.). 288p. (C). 1987. text ed. 44.95 (*0-442-26468-2*) Van Nos Reinhold.

McAuliffe. Patient Workbook. 176p. 1992. pap. text ed. 12.95 (*0-8403-7717-7*) Kendall-Hunt.

McAuliffe, Amy, ed. Guide to Federal Funding for Volunteer Programs & Community Service. 317p. 1993. 85.00 (*0-933544-66-9*) Gov Info Srvs.

McAuliffe, C. A. & Levason, W. Phosphine, Arsine & Stibine Complexes of the Transition Elements. (Studies in Inorganic Chemistry: Vol. 1). 564p. 1978. 172.00 (*0-444-41749-4*) Elsevier.

McAuliffe, C. A. & Mackie, A. Chemistry of Arsenic. 350p. 1994. text ed. 57.00 (*0-13-126368-4*) P-H.

McAuliffe, Dan, jt. auth. see Androvich, Bob.

McAuliffe, Daniel J. Arizona Civil Rules Handbook. 1120p. (C). 1993. pap. text ed. 43.50 (*0-314-02418-2*) West Pub.

— Arizona Civil Rules Handbook: 1994-1995 Edition. 1125p. 1994. pap. text ed. write for info. (*0-314-05641-6*) West Pub.

McAuliffe, Dennis. Deaths of Sybil Bolton: An American History. 1994. 23.00 (*0-8129-2150-X*, Times Bks) Random.

McAuliffe, Garrett. Outcomes of a Group Career Planning Process. 1988. 3.00 (*0-318-40010-3*, OC 126) Ctr Educ Trng Employ.

McAuliffe, Jane & Stoskin, Laura. What Color Is Saturday? Using Analogies to Enhance Creative Thinking in the Classroom. LC 93-8575. 142p. 1993. 25.00 (*0-913705-87-X*) Zephyr Pr AZ.

McAuliffe, Jane D. Qur'anic Christians: An Analysis of Classical & Modern Exegesis. 370p. (C). 1991. 64.95 (*0-521-36470-1*) Cambridge U Pr.

McAuliffe, Jane D., tr. The History of Al-Tabari Vol. XXVIII: Cabbasid Authority Affirmed: The Early Years of Al-Mansur, A.D. 753-763 - A.H. 136-145. (SUNY Series in Near Eastern Studies). 288p. 1994. 64.50x (*0-7914-1895-2*); pap. 19.95x (*0-7914-1896-0*) State U NY Pr.

McAuliffe, Jody, ed. Plays, Movies, & Critics. LC 93-17308. (Illus.). 304p. 1993. lib. bdg. 42.50 (*0-8223-1404-5*); pap. text ed. 16.95 (*0-8223-1418-5*) Duke.

McAuliffe, Lindsay, jt. auth. see Robinson, Sandra R.

McAuliffe, Mary B. & McAuliffe, Robert M. The Essentials of Chemical Dependency, Vol. I. LC 75-13362. 1975. 9.95 (*0-317-00368-2*) Am Chem Dep Soc.

McAuliffe, Mary B., jt. auth. see McAuliffe, Robert M.

McAuliffe, Mary S. Crisis on the Left: Cold War Politics & American Liberals, 1947-1954. LC 77-73479. 224p. 1978. 27.50 (*0-87023-241-X*) U of Mass Pr.

McAuliffe, Patricia. Fundamental Ethics: A Liberationist Approach. LC 93-11108. 320p. 1993. 35.00 (*0-87840-541-0*) Georgetown U Pr.

McAuliffe, Robert E. Advertising, Competition, & Public Policy Theories & New Evidence. 128p. 1986. text ed. 32.95 (*0-669-12391-9*) Free Pr.

McAuliffe, Robert M. & McAuliffe, Mary B. Diagnostic Manual: Essentials for the Diagnosis of Chemical Dependency, Vol. II. LC 75-13360. 1975. 6.95 (*0-317-00369-0*) Am Chem Dep Soc.

— Essentials of Chemical Dependency, Vol. III: Patient Work Book. 1986. 9.95 (*0-318-33040-7*) Am Chem Dep Soc.

McAuliffe, Robert M., jt. auth. see McAuliffe, Mary B.

McAuliffe, Thomas P. & Shamlin, Carolyn S. Critical Information Network: The Next Generation of Executive Information Systems. (Illus.). 130p. 1992. pap. 29.95 (*0-9633121-7-0*) McAuliffe & Co.

McAuliffe, William E. & Albert, Jeffrey. Clean Start: An Outpatient Program for Initiating Cocaine Recovery. LC 92-1528. (Substance Abuse Ser.). 234p. 1992. lib. bdg. 35.00 (*0-89862-190-9*) Guilford Pr.

— Clean Start: An Outpatient Program for Initiating Cocaine Recovery. LC 92-1528. (Substance Abuse Ser.). 234p. 1993. pap. text ed. 18.95 (*0-89862-194-1*) Guilford Pr.

McAulyfe, William E., jt. auth. see Zackon, Fred.

McAuslan, Ian & Walcot, Peter, eds. Greek Tragedy. LC 92-26819. (Greece & Rome Studies). 240p. 1993. 49.95 (*0-19-920300-8*); pap. 19.95 (*0-19-920301-6*) OUP.

— Virgil. (Greece & Rome Studies). 208p. 1990. 55.00 (*0-19-920166-8*); pap. 22.50 (*0-19-920170-6*) OUP.

McAuslan, J. P., jt. ed. see Kanyeihamba, G. W.

McAuslan, Patrick. The Ideologies of Planning Law. (Urban & Regional Planning Ser.: Vol. 22). 1980. 116.00 (*0-08-023696-0*, Pub. by Pergamon Repr UK) Franklin.

McAuslan, Patrick, jt. auth. see Farvacque, Catherine.

McAveeney, David C. Gloucester & Rockport: A Curious Traveller Guide. (Illus.). 96p. (Orig.). 1990. pap. 9.95 (*0-9625660-0-4*) Curious Traveller Pr.

McAvin, Margaret, ed. Landscape & Architecture: Sharing Common Ground, Defining Turf, Charting New Paths: Proceedings, Council of Educators in Landscape Architecture Annual Conference, August 13-15, 1987. (Illus.). 831p. (Orig.). 1988. pap. 14.00 (*0-9621050-0-7*) CELA.

McAvin, Margaret, ed. see Council of Educators in Landscape Architecture, Conference Staff.

McAvinn, Douglas, jt. auth. see Opie, Brenda.

McAvity, Helen. Everybody Has to Be Somebody. 1971. pap. 4.75 (*0-8222-0366-9*) Dramatists Play.

McAvity, Helen, jt. auth. see Howard, Eleanor H.

McAvoy, Brian R., ed. Caring for Asians in General Practice. (Oxford General Practice Ser.: No. 18). (Illus.). 344p. 1990. pap. 35.00 (*0-19-261733-8*) OUP.

McAvoy, George E. And Then There Was One: A History of the Hotels of the Summit & the West Side of Mount Washington. 356p. 1988. 34.95 (*0-9630647-0-3*) Crawford Pr.

— And Then There Was One: A History of the Hotels of the Summit & the West Side of Mount Washington. limited ed. 356p. 1988. 100.00 (*0-9630647-1-1*) Crawford Pr.

— A Citizen-Soldier Remembers 1942-1946: 149th Armored Signal Company of the 9th Armored Division. (Illus.). 238p. 1991. 32.50 (*0-9630647-2-X*) Crawford Pr.

McAvoy, Jane E., ed. Table Talk: Resources for the Communion Meal. 112p. (Orig.). 1993. pap. 8.99 (*0-8272-3632-8*) Chalice Pr.

McAvoy, Joseph M. Nottoway River Survey Pt. 1: Clovis Settlement Patterns, Vol. 28. 171p. 1923. pap. 32.95 (*1-884626-01-7*) Archeolog Soc.

McAvoy, K. T. Stories & Activities for Articulation Reinforcement, No. 803118. 128p. (gr. k-6). 1990. student ed 19.50 (*0-86703-216-2*) Opportunities Learn.

McAvoy, T. J., jt. ed. see Morari, M.

McAvoy, Thomas T. Catholic Church in Indiana, Seventeen Eighty-Nine to Eighteen Thirty-Four. LC 41-6425. (Columbia University. Studies in the Social Sciences: No. 471). reprint ed. 20.00 (*0-404-51471-5*) AMS Pr.

An Asterisk (*) at the beginning of an entry indicates that the title is appearing in BIP for the first time.

McAvoy, Thomas T., ed. Roman Catholicism & the American Way of Life. LC 72-13177. (Essay Index Reprint Ser.). 1977. reprint ed. 18.95 (*0-8369-8167-7*) Ayer.

McAvoy, Thomas T. & Nye, Russel B. The Midwest: Myth or Reality? a Symposium. LC 61-10848. 104p. reprint ed. pap. 29.70 (*0-317-55788-2*, 2029311) Bks Demand.

McAvoy, William C., comp. Twelfth Night, or What You Will: A Bibliography to Supplement the New Variorum Edition of 1901. LC 84-6546. (New Variorum Edition of Shakespeare Ser.). vi, 57p. 1984. pap. 10.00 (*0-87352-285-0*) Modern Lang.

***M'Caw & Co. Staff.** A User's Guide to Patents. 1995. pap. text ed. write for info. (*0-406-01307-1*, UK) Butterworth Legal Pubs.

McBain. Another Part of the City. 1987. mass mkt. 3.95 (*0-445-40584-8*) Warner Bks.

McBain, A. G. The Private Secretary. (C). 1982. pap. write for info. (*0-7219-0500-5*, Scientific) St Mut.

McBain, Donald J., jt. auth. see Graves, Barbara F.

McBain, Ed. And All Through the House. 48p. 1994. 12.95 (*0-446-51845-X*) Warner Bks.

— Ax. 160p. 1977. pap. 4.50 (*0-451-16407-5*, Sig) NAL-Dutton.

— Ax. 1989. pap. 2.95 (*0-451-14599-2*) NAL-Dutton.

— Beauty & the Beast. 224p. 1994. mass mkt. 5.99 (*0-446-60131-4*) Warner Bks.

McBain, Ed, pseud. Beauty & the Beast. 256p. 1992. mass mkt. 3.99 (*1-55817-662-4*, Pinnacle NY) Windsor NY.

McBain, Ed. Big Man. 176p. 1991. mass mkt. 4.50 (*0-380-71123-0*) Avon.

— Bread. 176p. 1987. mass mkt. 4.50 (*0-380-70368-8*) Avon.

— Calypso. 208p. 1988. mass mkt. 4.99 (*0-380-70591-5*) Avon.

— Cinderella. 272p. 1994. mass mkt. 5.99 (*0-446-60134-9*) Warner Bks.

— The Con Man. (Eighty-Seventh Precinct Mysteries Ser.). 160p. 1987. pap. 3.99 (*0-451-15085-6*, Sig) NAL-Dutton.

— The Con Man. deluxe ed. LC 91-8405. 168p. 1991. 25.00 (*0-922890-94-3*) Armchair Detective.

— The Con Man. limited ed. LC 91-8405. 168p. 1991. 75.00 (*0-922890-95-1*) Armchair Detective.

— The Con Man. LC 91-8405. 168p. 1991. reprint ed. 17.95 (*0-922890-93-5*) Armchair Detective.

— Cop Hater. (Eighty-Seventh Precinct Mysteries Ser.). 160p. 1987. pap. 3.99 (*0-451-15079-1*, Sig) NAL-Dutton.

— Cop Hater. deluxe ed. LC 89-18327. 184p. 1990. reprint ed. Collector edition. 25.00 (*0-922890-12-9*) Armchair Detective.

— Cop Hater. limited ed. LC 89-18327. 184p. 1990. reprint ed. Limited edition. 75.00 (*0-922890-13-7*) Armchair Detective.

— Cop Hater. LC 89-18327. 184p. 1990. reprint ed. 17.95 (*0-922890-06-4*) Armchair Detective.

— Death of a Nurse. 192p. 1991. mass mkt. 4.50 (*0-380-71125-7*) Avon.

— Death of a Nurse. limited ed. (Armchair Detective Library). 192p. 1994. reprint ed. 75.00 (*1-56287-062-9*) Armchair Detective.

— Death of a Nurse. (Armchair Detective Library). 192p. reprint ed. 22.00 (*1-56287-061-0*) Armchair Detective.

— Doors. 256p. 1988. pap. 3.50 (*0-380-70371-8*) Avon.

— Doors. 288p. (Orig.). 1995. mass mkt. 5.99 (*0-446-60148-9*) Warner Bks.

— Downtown. 302p. 1991. 20.00 (*0-688-08736-1*) Morrow.

— Downtown. braille ed. 495p. 1993. text ed. 39.60 (*1-56956-500-7*, BR8899) W A T Braille.

— Downtown. large type ed. 1992. 18.95 (*0-7927-1112-2*, E0032, Eagle Lrg Print) Chivers N Amer.

— Downtown. large type ed. 1992. pap. 17.95 (*0-7927-1111-4*, Paragon Lrg Print) Chivers N Amer.

— Downtown. 352p. 1993. reprint ed. mass mkt. 5.99 (*0-380-70761-6*) Avon.

— Ed McBain: Three Complete Novels. 1992. 11.99 (*0-517-06499-5*) Random Hse Value.

— Eight Black Horses. (Eighty-Seventh Precinct Novel Ser.). 256p. 1986. mass mkt. 4.99 (*0-380-70029-8*) Avon.

— Eighty Million Eyes. 176p. 1987. mass mkt. 4.50 (*0-380-70367-X*) Avon.

— The Eighty-Seventh Precinct Companion. (Orig.). 1995. pap. write for info. (*0-89296-989-X*, Mysterious Paperbk) Warner Bks.

— Even the Wicked. 128p. 1991. mass mkt. 3.99 (*0-380-71122-2*) Avon.

— Fuzz. (Eighty-Seven Precinct Mystery Ser.). 192p. 1978. pap. 3.99 (*0-451-15554-8*, E8399, Sig) NAL-Dutton.

— Gangs! 208p. 1989. reprint ed. pap. 3.50 (*0-380-70757-8*) Avon.

— Give the Boys a Great Big Hand. 240p. 1981. pap. 4.50 (*0-451-15921-7*, Sig) NAL-Dutton.

McBain, Ed, pseud. Goldilocks. 224p. 1988. pap. 3.95 (*1-55817-108-8*, Pinnacle NY) Windsor NY.

McBain, Ed. Guns. 224p. 1988. mass mkt. 3.99 (*0-380-70373-4*) Avon.

— Hail, Hail, the Gang's All Here: An 87th Precinct Mystery. 160p. 1972. pap. 3.99 (*0-451-15609-9*, Sig) NAL-Dutton.

— He Who Hesitates. (Eighty-Seventh Precinct Novel Ser.). 160p. 1986. mass mkt. 4.50 (*0-380-70084-0*) Avon.

— He Who Hesitates. 1996. mass mkt. write for info. (*0-446-60147-0*) Warner Bks.

— Heat. (Eighty-Seventh Precinct Mystery Ser.). 208p. 1995. mass mkt. 4.99 (*0-451-17078-4*, Sig) NAL-Dutton.

— The Heckler. 176p. 1982. pap. 4.50 (*0-451-15970-5*, Sig) NAL-Dutton.

— The House That Jack Built. 256p. 1994. mass mkt. 5.99 (*0-446-60136-5*) Warner Bks.

— Ice. 320p. 1984. mass mkt. 5.99 (*0-380-67108-5*) Avon.

— Jack & the Beanstalk. 256p. 1994. mass mkt. 5.99 (*0-446-60132-2*) Warner Bks.

McBain, Ed, pseud. Jack & the Beanstalk. 288p. 1992. mass mkt. 3.99 (*1-55817-663-2*, Pinnacle NY) Windsor NY.

McBain, Ed. Jigsaw. (Eighty-Seventh Precinct Mysteries Ser.). 144p. 1970. pap. 4.50 (*0-451-15480-0*, Sig) NAL-Dutton.

— Killer's Choice. 160p. 1992. 18.95 (*1-56287-008-4*); 25.00 (*1-56287-016-5*) Armchair Detective.

— Killer's Choice. (Eighty-Seventh Precinct Novel Ser.). 160p. 1986. mass mkt. 4.50 (*0-380-70083-2*) Avon.

— Killer's Choice. 1996. mass mkt. write for info. (*0-446-60144-6*) Warner Bks.

— Killer's Choice. limited ed. 160p. 1992. 75.00 (*1-56287-009-2*) Armchair Detective.

— Killer's Payoff. (Armchair Detective Library). 160p. 1994. 20.00 (*1-56287-054-8*) Armchair Detective.

— Killer's Payoff. limited ed. (Armchair Detective Library). 160p. 1994. 75.00 (*1-56287-053-X*) Armchair Detective.

— King's Ransom: An 87th Precinct Mystery. 176p. 1981. pap. 4.50 (*0-451-15933-0*, Draft Horse & Mule) NAL-Dutton.

— Kiss: A Novel of the Eighty-Seventh Precinct. 384p. 1992. mass mkt. 5.99 (*0-380-71382-9*) Avon.

— Kiss: A Novel of the Eighty-Seventh Precinct. braille ed. 562p. 1992. vinyl bd. 44.96 (*1-56956-065-X*, BR8753) W A T Braille.

— Kiss: A Novel of the Eighty-Seventh Precinct. large type ed. LC 92-22860. (General Ser.). 458p. 1993. lib. bdg. 21.95 (*0-8161-5588-7*); pap. 16.95 (*0-8161-5589-5*) G K Hall.

— Lady Killer. (Eighty-Seventh Precinct Mysteries Ser.). 160p. 1987. pap. 4.50 (*0-451-15082-1*, Sig) NAL-Dutton.

— Lady Killer: An Eighty-Seventh Precinct Mystery. limited ed. 160p. 1994. 75.00 (*1-56287-101-3*) Armchair Detective.

— Lady Killer: An Eighty-Seventh Precinct Mystery. limited ed. 160p. 1994. reprint ed. text ed. 22.00 (*1-56287-100-5*) Armchair Detective.

— Lady, Lady, I Did It! 256p. 1982. pap. 4.50 (*0-451-15841-5*, Sig) NAL-Dutton.

— Lightning. (Eighty-Seventh Precinct Novel Ser.). 304p. 1985. mass mkt. 4.95 (*0-380-69974-5*) Avon.

— Like Love. 176p. 1982. pap. 4.50 (*0-451-13903-8*, Sig); pap. 4.50 (*0-451-16383-4*, Sig) NAL-Dutton.

— Like Love: An Eighty-Seventh Precinct Mystery. large type ed. LC 92-40908. (Nightingale Ser.). 1993. write for info. (*0-8161-5705-7*) G K Hall.

— Long Time, No See. 272p. 1987. mass mkt. 4.99 (*0-380-70369-6*) Avon.

— Lullaby. 352p. 1990. mass mkt. 5.99 (*0-380-70384-X*) Avon.

— Mary, Mary. 384p. 1994. mass mkt. 5.99 (*0-446-60054-7*) Warner Bks.

— Mary, Mary. large type ed. LC 93-3870. 1993. 24.95 (*0-7927-1662-0*, Eagle Lrg Print); pap. 22.95 (*0-7927-1661-2*, Eagle Lrg Print) Chivers N Amer.

— Mischief. 352p. 1994. mass mkt. 5.99 (*0-380-71384-5*) Avon.

— Mischief: A Novel of the Eighty-Seventh Precinct. 1993. 20.00 (*0-688-10221-2*) Morrow.

— Mischief: A Novel of the 87th Precinct. large type ed. LC 93-49514. 1994. 25.95 (*0-7927-2015-6*, Eagle Lrg Print) Chivers N Amer.

— Mischief: A Novel of the 87th Precinct. large type ed. LC 93-49514. 1995. pap. 23.95 (*0-7927-2014-8*, Paragon Lrg Print) Chivers N Amer.

— Mugger. (Eighty-Seventh Precinct Novel Ser.). 160p. 1986. pap. 3.50 (*0-380-70081-6*) Avon.

— The Mugger. 160p. 1996. mass mkt. 5.99 (*0-446-60143-8*) Warner Bks.

— Mugger. limited ed. LC 90-32352. 160p. 1990. reprint ed. 75.00 (*0-922890-28-5*) Armchair Detective.

— Mugger. LC 90-32352. 160p. 1990. reprint ed. 17.95 (*0-922890-29-3*); reprint ed. 25.00 (*0-922890-27-7*) Armchair Detective.

— Poison. 256p. 1988. mass mkt. 4.99 (*0-380-70030-1*) Avon.

— Pusher. (Eighty-Seventh Precinct Mysteries Ser.). 160p. 1987. pap. 3.99 (*0-451-15080-5*, Sig) NAL-Dutton.

— The Pusher. limited ed. LC 90-47709. 160p. 1991. 75.00 (*0-922890-71-4*) Armchair Detective.

— The Pusher. LC 90-47709. 160p. 1991. reprint ed. 17.95 (*0-922890-69-2*); reprint ed. 25.00 (*0-922890-70-6*) Armchair Detective.

— Puss in Boots. 1988. mass mkt. 4.95 (*0-445-40621-6*, Mysterious Paperbk) Warner Bks.

— Puss in Boots. 224p. 1994. mass mkt. 5.99 (*0-446-60135-7*) Warner Bks.

— Romance. 352p. 1996. mass mkt. 6.50 (*0-446-60280-9*) Warner Bks.

— Romance: A Novel of the 87th Precinct. 336p. 1995. 22.95 (*0-446-51804-2*) Warner Bks.

— Rumpelstiltskin. 240p. 1985. mass mkt. 4.95 (*0-345-33149-4*) Ballantine.

— Rumpelstiltskin. 1992. mass mkt. 4.99 (*0-446-40167-6*, Mysterious Paperbk) Warner Bks.

— Rumpelstiltskin. 240p. 1994. mass mkt. 5.99 (*0-446-60130-6*) Warner Bks.

— Sadie When She Died. 1973. pap. 3.99 (*0-451-15366-9*, Sig) NAL-Dutton.

— See Them Die. 1989. pap. 2.95 (*0-451-14596-8*) NAL-Dutton.

— See Them Die: An 87th Precinct Mystery. 160p. 1982. reprint ed. pap. 4.50 (*0-451-16426-1*, Sig) NAL-Dutton.

— The Sentries. 304p. 1988. pap. 3.50 (*0-380-70489-7*) Avon.

— The Sentries. 288p. 1995. mass mkt. 5.99 (*0-446-60145-4*) Warner Bks.

— Shotgun. 1970. pap. 4.50 (*0-451-15674-9*, Sig) NAL-Dutton.

— Shotgun. 1982. pap. 2.50 (*0-451-11971-1*, Sig) NAL-Dutton.

— Snow White & Rose Red. 256p. 1994. mass mkt. 5.99 (*0-446-60133-0*) Warner Bks.

— Snow White & Rose Red. 256p. 1986. reprint ed. mass mkt. 4.99 (*0-445-40513-9*, Mysterious Paperbk) Warner Bks.

— Ten Plus One. 272p. 1982. pap. 4.50 (*0-451-16367-2*, Sig) NAL-Dutton.

— Ten Plus One. 1989. pap. 2.95 (*0-451-14598-4*) NAL-Dutton.

— There Was a Little Girl. 336p. 1994. 21.95 (*0-446-51739-9*) Warner Bks.

— There Was a Little Girl. 384p. 1995. mass mkt. 6.50 (*0-446-60214-0*) Warner Bks.

— There Was a Little Girl. large type ed. 1995. 23.95 (*0-7838-1180-2*) Hall.

— There Was a Little Girl. large type ed. 1995. pap. 18.95 (*0-7838-1181-0*) Hall.

— Three Blind Mice. 1990. 18.95 (*0-685-36235-3*) Little.

— Three Blind Mice. 1991. mass mkt. 4.99 (*0-446-40035-1*, Mysterious Paperbk) Warner Bks.

— Three Blind Mice. 304p. 1994. mass mkt. 5.99 (*0-446-60137-3*) Warner Bks.

— Three Blind Mice. braille ed. 484p. 1992. vinyl bd. 38.72 (*1-56956-096-X*, BR8767) W A T Braille.

— Three Blind Mice. large type ed. (General Ser.). 396p. 1991. text ed. 20.95 (*0-8161-5169-5*, Large Print Bks) Hall.

— Til Death. (Eighty-Seventh Precinct Mystery Ser.). 176p. 1995. mass mkt. 4.50 (*0-451-15891-1*, Sig) NAL-Dutton.

— Tricks. 256p. 1989. reprint ed. mass mkt. 5.99 (*0-380-70383-1*) Avon.

— Vanishing Ladies. 160p. 1991. reprint ed. mass mkt. 4.50 (*0-380-71121-4*) Avon.

— Vespers. 352p. 1991. mass mkt. 4.95 (*0-380-70385-8*) Avon.

— Vespers. 288p. 1991. 6.98 (*1-56865-122-8*, GuildAmerica) Dblday Bk Music.

— Where There's Smoke. 192p. 1987. pap. 3.50 (*0-380-70372-6*) Avon.

— Widows. large type ed. (General Ser.). 454p. 1992. text ed. 20.95 (*0-8161-5311-6*) G K Hall.

— Widows. 336p. 1992. reprint ed. mass mkt. 5.99 (*0-380-71383-7*) Avon.

McBain, Ed, ed. Doll. (Eighty-Seventh Precinct Novel Ser.). 160p. 1986. mass mkt. 4.50 (*0-380-70082-4*) Avon.

McBain, Graham, ed. Butterworths Banking Law Handbook. 1989. U.K. pap. 84.00 (*0-406-18130-6*) Butterworth Legal Pubs.

McBain, Graham S. Butterworths Banking Law Handbook. 2nd ed. 730p. 1993. pap. 110.00 (*0-406-02005-1*, UK) Butterworth Legal Pubs.

McBain, Howard L. De Witt Clinton & the Origin of the Spoils System in New York. LC 07-36153. (Columbia University. Studies in the Social Sciences: No. 75). reprint ed. 12.50 (*0-404-51075-2*) AMS Pr.

— Prohibition Legal & Illegal. LC 72-67. (Select Bibliographies Reprint Ser.). 1977. reprint ed. 15.95 (*0-8369-9963-0*) Ayer.

McBain, J. The Merrick & the Neighbouring Hills. 340p. 1985. 20.00 (*0-317-43645-7*, Alloway Pub) St Mut.

McBain, Laurie. Chance the Winds of Fortune. 512p. 1980. mass mkt. 4.95 (*0-380-75796-6*) Avon.

— Dark Before the Rising Sun. 528p. 1982. mass mkt. 4.50 (*0-380-79848-4*) Avon.

— Devil's Desire. 1976. mass mkt. 5.50 (*0-380-00295-7*) Avon.

— Moonstruck Madness. 408p. 1977. mass mkt. 4.95 (*0-380-00871-8*) Avon.

— Tears of Gold. 576p. 1979. mass mkt. 5.50 (*0-380-41475-9*) Avon.

— When the Splendor Falls. 1985. mass mkt. 4.95 (*0-380-89826-8*) Avon.

— Wild Bells to the Wild Sky. 592p. 1984. mass mkt. 4.95 (*0-380-87387-7*) Avon.

McBaine, Robert. Student Workbook for Sentence Combining with Exercises & Key. 135p. (Orig.). (YA). (gr. 8 up). 1984. pap. 8.90 (*0-89420-244-8*, 261000) Natl Book.

McBaine, Susan. Miniature Needlepoint Rugs for Dollhouses Charted for Easy Use. (Illus.). (Orig.). 1976. pap. 3.50 (*0-486-23388-X*) Dover.

McBane, S. Keeping Horses: The Working Owner's Guide to Saving Time & Money. 2nd ed. (Illus.). 192p. 1993. pap. 22.95 (*0-632-03443-2*) Blackwell Sci.

— Poor Richards Horse Keeper. 1993. 27.95 (*0-914327-52-6*) Breakthrgh NY.

McBane, Susan. Grooming. (Threshold Picture Guides Ser.). (Illus.). 24p. (Orig.). 1992. pap. 10.00 (*1-872082-29-7*, Pub. by Kenilworth Pr UK) Half Halt Pr.

— How to Cure Behavior Problems in Horses. 1991. pap. 15.00 (*0-87980-429-7*) Wilshire.

— The Illustrated Guide to Horse Tack. (Illus.). 208p. 1993. 29.95 (*0-7153-9947-0*, Pub. by David & Charles UK) Trafalgar.

— Know Your Pony. (Riding School Ser.). (Illus.). 114p. 1992. pap. 14.95 (*0-7063-6978-5*, Pub. by Ward Lock UK) Sterling.

— A Natural Approach to Horse Management. (Illus.). 240p. 1992. 34.95 (*0-413-62370-X*, Pub. by W Heinemann Ltd) Trafalgar.

— The Outdoor Pony. (Threshold Picture Guides Ser.). (Illus.). 24p. (Orig.). 1992. pap. 10.00 (*1-872082-30-0*, Pub. by Kenilworth Pr UK) Half Halt Pr.

— Tack & Clothing. (Riding School Ser.). (Illus.). 112p. 1993. 14.95 (*0-7063-7145-3*, Pub. by Ward Lock UK) Sterling.

— Ward Lock Riding School: Modern Stable Management. (Illus.). 112p. 1994. 14.95 (*0-7063-7196-8*, Pub. by Ward Lock UK) Sterling.

McBarnet, Gill. Fountain of Fire. (Illus.). 32p. (J). (gr. k-2). 1987. 8.95 (*0-9615102-3-4*) Ruwanga Trad.

— Gecko Hide & Seek. (Illus.). 24p. (J). (gr. k-2). 1993. 8.95 (*0-9615102-7-7*) Ruwanga Trad.

— The Goodnight Gecko. (Illus.). 32p. (J). (gr. k-2). 1991. 8.95 (*0-9615102-6-9*) Ruwanga Trad.

— The Pink Parrot. (Illus.). 40p. (J). (gr. k-2). 1986. 8.95 (*0-9615102-1-8*) Ruwanga Trad.

— The Shark Who Learned a Lesson. (Illus.). 32p. (J). (gr. k-2). 1990. 8.95 (*0-9615102-5-0*) Ruwanga Trad.

— The Whale Who Wanted to Be Small. (Illus.). 32p. (J). (gr. k-2). 1985. 8.95 (*0-9615102-0-X*) Ruwanga Trad.

— A Whale's Tale. (Illus.). 32p. (J). (gr. k-2). 1988. 8.95 (*0-9615102-4-2*) Ruwanga Trad.

— The Wonderful Journey. (Illus.). 32p. (J). (gr. k-2). 1986. 8.95 (*0-9615102-2-6*) Ruwanga Trad.

***McBarnet, Gill, illus.** The Brave Little Turtle. 32p. (J). (gr. k-2). 1994. 8.95 (*0-9615102-8-5*) Ruwanga Trad.

McBarron, E. J. Poisonous Plants: Handbook for Farmers & Graziers. (Illus.). 160p. 1983. pap. 22.95 (*0-909605-29-7*, Pub. by Inkata Pr AT) Intl Spec Bk.

McBath, James H., jt. auth. see Dickens, Milton.

***McBay, Marian Y.** First Do No Harm: Leader's Guide. 1994. pap. 5.95 (*0-687-00264-8*) Abingdon.

McBean, D. M. Drying & Processing Tree Fruits. (Illus.). 20p. 1976. pap. 10.00 (*0-643-00181-6*, Pub. by CSIRO AT) Intl Spec Bk.

McBean, Edward A., jt. ed. see Unny, T. E.

McBean, Edward A., et al. Solid Waste Landfill Engineering & Design. LC 94-10676. 544p. 1994. text ed. 65.00 (*0-13-079187-3*) P-H.

McBean, Edward A., et al, eds. Reliability in Water Resources Management. LC 79-64191. 1979. 22.00 (*0-918334-30-6*) WRP.

McBean, Eleanor. The Hidden Dangers in Polio Vaccine. 86p. 1993. reprint ed. spiral bd. 4.40 (*0-7873-0593-6*) Mokelumne.

McBean, Eleanora. The Poisoned Needle. 230p. 1993. reprint ed. spiral bd. 8.25 (*0-7873-0594-4*) Mokelumne.

McBean, G. A. & Hantel, M., eds. Interactions Between Global Climate Subsystems: The Legacy of Hann. LC 93-13345. (Geophysical Monograph Ser.: Vol. 75). 1993. 28.00 (*0-87590-466-1*) Am Geophysical.

McBean, Jean. Marriage & Family Law in Alberta: The Rights of Husbands, Wives, Children & Common Law Spouses. 3rd ed. (Legal Ser.). 248p. 1987. Canadian Edition. 8.95 (*0-88908-245-6*) Self-Counsel Pr.

McBeath, et al. Patterns of Control: Executive Summary. 14p. 1984. (*0-318-68989-8*) Univ AK Ctr CCS.

McBeath, Gerald, et al. Parental Involvement in Rural Alaska Education. 78p. (Orig.). 1994. pap. 8.00 (*1-877962-29-5*) Univ AK Ctr CCS.

McBeath, Gerald A. North Slope Borough Government & Policymaking. (ISER Reports: No. 51). (Illus.). 94p. 1981. pap. 7.50 (*0-88353-028-7*) U Alaska Inst Res.

McBeath, Gerald A. & Morehouse, Thomas A. Alaska Politics & Government. LC 93-5390. (Politics & Governments of the American States Ser.). (Illus.). xxx, 367p. 1994. 47.50 (*0-8032-3120-2*); pap. 17.95 (*0-8032-8149-8*) U of Nebr Pr.

McBeath, Gerald A. & Morehouse, Thomas A., eds. Alaska State Government & Politics. LC 86-51368. (Illus.). 357p. 1986. 27.00 (*0-912006-20-X*); pap. 17.00 (*0-912006-21-8*) U of Alaska Pr.

McBeath, Gordon. The Handbook of Human Resource Planning. LC 92-13157. 1992. pap. 36.95 (*0-631-18686-7*) Blackwell Pubs.

— Practical Management Development: Strategies for Management Resourcing & Development in the 1990s. (Illus.). 350p. 1990. pap. text ed. write for info. (*0-631-19346-4*) Blackwell Pubs.

— Salary Administration. 4th ed. 192p. 1989. text ed. 49.95 (*0-566-02811-5*, Pub. by Gower UK) Ashgate Pub Co.

McBeath, Norman. Photographer's Britain: Oxfordshire. (Illus.). 150p. 1992. pap. 20.00 (*0-7509-0072-5*) A Sutton Pub.

McBeath, Ron, et al, eds. Trends & Practices. (Instructional Media & Technology Ser.: Vol. 1). 210p. (Orig.). (C). 1983. pap. text ed. 11.50 (*0-89503-041-1*) Baywood Pub.

McBeath, Ron J., ed. Instructing & Evaluating in Higher Education: A Guidebook for Planning Learning Outcomes. LC 91-40486. (Illus.). 365p. (Orig.). 1992. 34.95 (*0-87778-242-3*) Educ Tech Pubns.

McBee. Strategies for Waste Minimization. 1995. write for info. (*0-87371-521-7*) Lewis Pubs.

McBee, Alice F. From Utopia to Florence: The Story of a Transcendentalist Community in Northampton, Massachusetts, 1830-1852. LC 74-31281. (American Utopian Adventure Ser.). (Illus.). ix, 93p. 1975. reprint ed. lib. bdg. 25.00 (*0-87991-027-5*) Porcupine Pr.

McBee, Bob, jt. auth. see Hines, Ben.

***McBee, May W.** Mississippi County Court Records. 94p. 1994. pap. 13.50 (*0-614-00917-0*) Clearfield Co.

— The Nachez Court Records, 1767-1805. 635p. 1994. pap. 47.50 (*0-614-00919-7*, 3490) Clearfield Co.

McBee, Rick. Kalahari. abr. ed. 210p. 1995. pap. 8.95 (*1-56901-326-8*) NW Pub.

McBee, Robert, et al, eds. Coaches' Guide to Championship Baseball Drills & Fundamentals. LC 82-45643. 294p. 1982. pap. 15.95 (*0-9609500-0-1*) McBee Sports.

McBee, Shar. To Lead Is to Serve: How to Attract Volunteers & Keep Them. 208p. 1994. pap. 14.95 (*0-9638560-0-6*) S McBee.

McBee, Wanda N. Get It Together. 300p. (Orig.). pap. text ed. 29.95 (*0-317-91112-0*) W McBee.

McBeth, B. S. British Oil Policy, 1919-1939. (Illus.). 190p. 1985. 35.00 (*0-7146-3229-5*, Pub. by F Cass Pubs UK) Intl Spec Bk.

M

An Asterisk (*) at the beginning of an entry indicates that the title is appearing in BIP for the first time.

— Juan Vicente Gomez & the Oil Companies in Venezuela, 1908-1935. LC 82-14667. (Cambridge Latin American Studies: No. 43). (Illus.). 256p. 1983. 74.95 (*0-521-24717-9*) Cambridge U Pr.

McBeth, H. Leon. English Baptist Literature on Religious Liberty to Sixteen Eighty Nine: Doctoral Dissertation. Gaustad, Edwin S., ed. LC 79-52575. (Baptist Tradition Ser.). 1980. lib. bdg. 42.95 (*0-405-12443-0*) Ayer.

— A Sourcebook for Baptist Heritage. LC 89-33091. 1992. 29.99 (*0-8054-6589-8*) Broadman.

McBeth, Kate. The Nez Perce since Lewis & Clark. (Idaho Yesterdays Ser.). (Illus.). 288p. (C). 1993. reprint ed. pap. 15.95 (*0-89301-160-6*) U of Idaho Pr.

McBeth, Leon. Baptist Heritage. LC 86-31667. 1987. 29.99 (*0-8054-6569-3*) Broadman.

— Hombres Claves en las Misiones. Orig. Title: Men Who Made Missions. 128p. 1986. reprint ed. pap. 4.60 (*0-311-01070-9*) Casa Bautista.

McBeth, Muhammad A. Combinatorial Number-Theory: A Treatise on Growth, Based on the Goodstein-Skolem Hierarchy, Including a Critique of Non-Constructive or First-Order Logic. LC 94-13953. 430p. 1994. text ed. 109.95 (*0-7734-9085-X*) E Mellen.

McBeth, Robert W. & Ferguson, J. Robert. IBM Assembler: An Intuitive Approach. LC 86-32468. 650p. 1987. Net. text ed. write for info. (*0-471-82424-0*) Wiley.

McBeth, Sally J. Ethnic Identity & the Boarding School Experience of West-Central Oklahoma American Indians. LC 82-21983. (Illus.). 184p. (Orig.). 1983. pap. text ed. 22.50 (*0-8191-2896-1*) U Pr of Amer.

McBirney, A. R., jt. auth. see Williams, Howel.

McBirney, Alexander R. Igneous Petrology. 2nd ed. 512p. 1992. boxed 52.50 (*0-86720-175-4*) Jones & Bartlett.

McBirney, Alexander R. & Williams, Howell. Geology & Petrology of the Galapagos Islands. LC 79-98018. (Geological Society of America, Memoir Ser.: No. 118). 223p. reprint ed. pap. 63.60 (*0-317-28365-0*, 2025468) Bks Demand.

McBirnie, S. C. & Fox, W. J. Marine Steam Engines & Turbines. 4th ed. (Illus.). 672p. 1980. text ed. 80.00 (*0-408-00387-1*) Buttrwrth-Heinemann.

McBirnie, Stewart. Retorno a la Iglesia Primitiva: Search for the Early Church. (SPA.). 5.25 (*84-7228-733-5*, 220775, Pub. by Edit Clie SP) TSELF.

McBirnie, William S. The Search for the Twelve Apostles. 1979. pap. 5.99 (*0-8423-5839-0*) Tyndale.

McBogg, Bruce. Ropeless Jumping: The Conversion of a Jogger. (Illus.). 71p. 1981. 3.45 (*0-686-32863-9*) B McBogg.

***McBratney, Sam.** The Dark at the Top of the Stairs. LC 94-48921. (Illus.). 1995. write for info. (*1-56402-640-X*) Candlewick Pr.

— The Ghastly Gertie Swindle: With the Ghosts of Hungryhouse Lane. (Illus.). 128p. (J). (gr. 3-6). 1994. 14. 95 (*0-8050-2614-2*, Bks Young Read) H Holt & Co.

— Guess How Much I Love You. LC 94-1599. (Illus.). 32p. (J). (ps up). 1995. 13.95 (*1-56402-473-3*) Candlewick Pr.

McBrayer, Brenda. Mom, I Don't Want to Get My Hair Washed: And Other Poems. (Illus.). 43p. (Orig.). (J). (gr. 2 up). 1992. pap. 7.95 (*0-910303-40-1*) Writers Pub Serv.

***McBrayer, James D., Jr.** Escape! Memoir of a World War II Marine Who Broke Out of a Japanese POW Camp & Linked up with Chinese Communist Guerillas. LC 94-24528. (Illus.). 232p. 1995. lib. bdg. 25.95 (*0-7864-0058-7*) McFarland & Co.

***McBrayer, Peggy.** Howell's Pond. 1994. 7.95 (*0-533-11041-6*) Vantage.

McBrayer, Robert, jt. auth. see Wysocki, Donald C.

McBrayer, William D., jt. auth. see Goodwin, Charles D.

McBrearty, James C. American Labor History & Comparative Labor Movements: A Selected Bibliography. LC 78-190624. 272p. reprint ed. pap. 77. 60 (*0-8357-5378-6*, 2022750) Bks Demand.

McBrearty, Kathleen. Caribbean Pink. large type ed. 1991. pap. 13.95 (*0-7089-6983-6*) Ulverscroft.

***McBreen, Joan.** A Walled Garden in Moylough. 80p. 1995. pap. text ed. 10.95 (*1-885266-07-3*) Story Line.

— The Wind Beyond the Wall. 2nd ed. 64p. (Orig.). (C). 1991. pap. 8.95 (*0-934257-33-7*) Story Line.

McBriar, A. M. Fabian Socialism & English Politics, 1884-1918. LC 66-70570. 398p. reprint ed. pap. 113.50 (*0-685-16087-4*, 2027245) Bks Demand.

McBriarty, Douglas. Snowshot. LC 88-14406. 192p. 1989. 17.95 (*0-8027-5717-0*) Walker & Co.

— Whitewater VI. 1987. 16.95 (*0-8027-5686-7*) Walker & Co.

McBriarty, J. P. & Henry, N., III, eds. Performance of Protective Clothing, Vol. 4. (Special Technical Publication Ser.: No. STP 1133). (Illus.). 1025p. 1992. text ed. 83.00 (*0-8031-1430-3*, 04-011330-55) ASTM.

McBride. SuperCalc 5.0 - 3D Spreadsheets. 320p. 1990. pap. 67.95 (*0-434-91308-1*) Buttrwrth-Heinemann.

McBride, jt. auth. see Tracy.

McBride, A., jt. ed. see Roach, G. F.

McBride, Alfred. Essentials of the Faith: A Guide to the Catechism of the Catholic Church. LC 93-87231. 224p. (Orig.). 1994. pap. 9.95 (*0-87973-740-9*, 740) Our Sunday Visitor.

— The Ten Commandments: Sounds of Love from Sinai. 158p. 1990. 6.95 (*0-86716-109-4*) St Anthony Mess Pr.

McBride, Alfred & Praem, O. Invitation: A Catholic Learning Guide for Adults: The Search for God, Self & Church. (Illus.). 124p. 1984. ring bd. 9.95 (*0-918951-00-3*) Paulist Natl Catholic.

— The Second Coming of Jesus: Meditation & Commentary on the Book of Revelation. LC 92-61979. (Popular Bible Study Ser.). 180p. (Orig.). 1993. pap. 5.95 (*0-87973-526-0*, 526) Our Sunday Visitor.

McBride, Angela B. How to Enjoy a Good Life with Your Teenager. LC 89-7714. 218p. 1989. reprint ed. pap. 9.95 (*1-55561-023-4*) Fisher Bks.

***McBride, Angela B. & Austin, Joan K., eds.** Psychiatric-Mental Health Nursing: Integrating the Behavioral & Biological Sciences. LC 95-10059. 480p. 1995. text ed. write for info. (*0-7216-4038-9*) Saunders.

McBride, Angus. The Zulu War. (Men-at-Arms Ser.: No. 57). (Illus.). 48p. pap. 11.95 (*0-85045-256-2*, 9009, Pub. by Osprey UK) Stackpole.

McBride, Angus, jt. illus. see Chappell, Michael.

McBride, Betty, ed. see Fisher, James N.

***McBride, Bunny.** Molly Spotted Elk: A Penobscot in Paris. LC 95-6891. 1995. 24.95 (*0-8061-2756-2*) U of Okla Pr.

— Our Lives in Our Hands: Micmac Indian Basketmakers. (Illus.). 96p. (Orig.). 1991. pap. 10.95 (*0-88448-084-4*) Tilbury Hse.

McBride, Caitlin. Journey of the Heart. 1994. mass mkt. 4.99 (*0-7865-0003-4*) Diamond.

McBride, Carmen. Silent Victory. LC 73-84602. 224p. 1969. 21.95 (*0-911012-03-6*) Nelson-Hall.

***McBride, Carolyn.** Bobbing for Apples - with Success! Practical How-to's for Congregational Leaders. Hermanson, Renee, ed. (Illus.). 1995. pap. 13.95 (*1-880292-09-2*) LangMarc.

McBride, Charles C. Mission Failure & Survival. (Illus.). 192p. (Orig.). 1989. pap. 17.95 (*0-89745-125-2*) Sunflower U Pr.

McBride, Christy, ed. see Dungan, F. Alvin.

McBride, Clifford. Napolean: An Original Compilation. First Collection of the Complete First Year of the Daily Script,1932-33. Blackbeard, Bill, ed. LC 76-53047. (Classic American Comic Strips Ser.). (Illus.). 1977. 16. 00 (*0-88355-649-9*); pap. 10.00 (*0-88355-648-0*) Hyperion Conn.

McBride, Colleen. Irish Cooking. 1991. 10.99 (*0-517-05919-3*) Random Hse Value.

McBride, David. From TB to AIDS: Epidemics among Urban Blacks since 1900. LC 90-9758. (SUNY Series in Afro-American Studies). (C). 1991. 64.50 (*0-7914-0528-1*); pap. 21.95 (*0-7914-0529-X*) State U NY Pr.

— Integrating the City of Medicine: Blacks in Philadelphia Health Care, 1910-1965. LC 88-15924. 320p. (C). 1988. 39.95 (*0-87722-546-X*) Temple U Pr.

McBride, David N. & McBride, Jane N. Common Pleas Court Records of Highland County, Ohio 1805-1860. (Vital Records of Highland County, Ohio Ser.). 306p. 1984. lib. bdg. 32.50 (*0-941000-02-8*) S Ohio Genealog.

— Marriage Records of Highland County, Ohio (1805-1880) (Vital Records of Highland County, Ohio Ser.). 416p. 1982. reprint ed. lib. bdg. 37.00 (*0-931000-01-7*) S Ohio Genealog.

— Records of the Recorder's Office of Highland County, Ohio, 1805-1850. (Vital Records of Highland County, Ohio Ser.). 570p. reprint ed. lib. bdg. 45.00 (*0-941000-03-6*) S Ohio Genealog.

McBride, Dean, ed. see Wolff, Hans W., Jr.

McBride, Delbert J. One Hundred Years of Native American Arts: Six Washington Cultures. Loucas, Penelope, ed. (Illus.). 16p. (Orig.). 1989. pap. 1.00 (*0-924335-07-6*) Tacoma Art Mus.

McBride, Denis. Impressions of a Life: Stories of Jesus. LC 93-36055. 224p. (Orig.). 1994. 15.95 (*0-89243-642-5*, Triumph Books) Liguori Pubns.

McBride, Dennis. How to Do Architectural Ink Renderings. (Illus.). 1980. 5.95 (*0-910158-68-1*) Art Dir.

— How to Make Visual Presentations. rev. ed. LC 85-7201. (Illus.). 80p. (C). 1981. pap. 6.95 (*0-910158-86-X*) Art Dir.

McBride, Dennis, jt. auth. see Dunar, Andrew.

McBride, Dick. Cometh with Clouds, (Memory: Allen Ginsberg) LC 81-12272. 64p. 1982. 15.00 (*0-916156-54-0*); pap. 5.00 (*0-916156-51-6*) Cherry Valley.

McBride, Don, jt. ed. see Bray, Donald E.

McBride, Donna, ed. see McDaniel, Nello & Thorn, George.

McBride, Duane C., jt. auth. see Inciardi, James A.

McBride, E. F. Sedimentary Petrology & History of the Haymond Formation (Pennsylvanian), Marathon Basin, Texas. (Report of Investigations Ser.: RI 57). 101p. 1966. 2.50 (*0-686-29339-8*) Bur Econ Geology.

McBride, E. F., et al. Lithology & Petrology of the Gueydan (Catahoula) Formation in South Texas. (Report of Investigations Ser.: RI 63). (Illus.). 122p. 1968. 2.00 (*0-318-03163-9*) Bur Econ Geology.

McBride, Elizabeth. Addresses by Worthy Matron & Worthy Patron. 44p. 1983. pap. 3.50 (*0-88053-359-5*, S 306) Macoy Pub.

McBride, Erle F., ed. Silica in Sediments: Nodular & Bedded Chert. (Reprint Ser.: No. 8). 184p. 1979. 14.00 (*0-918985-34-X*) SEPM.

McBride, Gary P. A Gold Medal Family. 200p. 1985. reprint ed. 9.95 (*0-938696-01-7*, 8999) Pubs Bk Sales.

McBride, Genevieve G. On Wisconsin Women: Working for Their Rights from Settlement to Suffrage. LC 93-846. (History of American Thought & Culture Ser.). (Illus.). 304p. (Orig.). (C). 1993. lib. bdg. 43.00 (*0-299-14000-8*); pap. 19.95 (*0-299-14004-0*) U of Wis Pr.

McBride, Glenn & Westfall, Peggy. Shiftwork Safety & Performance: A Manual for Managers & Trainers. 270p. 1992. 99.50 (*0-9638482-0-8*) McBride Pubns.

McBride, Glynn. Agricultural Cooperatives: Their Why & Their How. (Illus.). 1986. text ed. 62.95 (*0-87055-534-0*) AVI.

McBride, H. W. The Emma Gees. (Illus.). 240p. 1988. reprint ed. 18.95 (*0-935856-03-X*) Lancer.

McBride, Henry, et al. John Marin. LC 66-26650. (Museum of Modern Art Publications in Reprint). reprint ed. 17. 95 (*0-405-01520-8*) Ayer.

McBride, Herbert W. A Rifleman Went to War. 425p. 1987. reprint ed. 24.95 (*0-935856-01-3*) Lancer.

McBride, Jack, ed. see United States Catholic Conference Staff.

McBride, James. Pioneer Biography: Sketches of the Lives of Some of the Early Settlers of Butler County, Ohio. 660p. 1991. reprint ed. pap. 37.50 (*1-55613-487-8*) Heritage Bk.

— War, Battering, & Other Sports: The Gulf Between American Men & Women. LC 94-39404. (Religion-Society - Society-Religion Ser.). (Illus.). 192p. (C). 1995. text ed. 45.00 (*0-391-03881-8*); pap. 15.00 (*0-391-03882-6*) Humanities.

McBride, Jane N., jt. auth. see McBride, David N.

***McBride, Jere J. Quiet-Time Messages: Training for Believers. Rodriguez, Maria et al, trs. 375p. (Orig.). (ENG & SPA.). 1995. pap. 12.95 (*0-9645310-0-3*) LPC Pub.**

If readers are familiar with GOD CALLING (Dodd, Mead & Co., 1945), they will love QUIET-TIME MESSAGES. This book is a set of prophesies (Each prophesy has been judged for accuracy & agreement with the Holy Bible) (366) that have been made into a yearly devotional for believers. Each message is accompanied by: (1) Scriptures with which the reader can verify the message for the day. (2) A corresponding daily short prayer for guidance or inspiration. The author is: * a SPIRIT-FILLED Christian since 1972 * a CERTIFIED Counselor in Texas Public Schools for 20-plus years * a charter member of AMERICAN ASSOCIATION OF CHRISTIAN COUNSELORS * a member of CHRISTIAN COUNSELORS OF TEXAS * an officer of BIG BEND WOMEN'S AGLOW for 10-plus years. The author believes that: *God is preparing his CHURCH for the end-time harvest. *The gifts of the Holy Spirit are active today. *The name of Jesus is still the most powerful force in the universe. *Faith must be developed for the work of the CHURCH. To order contact: LPC Publishing, P.O. Box 725, 100 McBride Ln., Alpine, TX 79831. Also available in Spanish. ***Publisher Provided Annotation.***

McBride, Joe E., Jr. Turnaround Tactics. 76p. (Orig.). 1990. pap. 7.95 (*0-9625668-0-2*) First Renaissance.

McBride, John C. & Wachtel, Isadore H. Government Contracts: Law Administration & Procedure, 16 vols., Set. 1962. Looseleaf set with updating service for a year. ring bd. write for info. (*0-8205-1326-1*) Bender.

McBride, Joseph. Albert Camus: Philosopher & Litterateur. LC 92-12753. 1993. text ed. 35.00 (*0-312-07597-9*) St Martin.

— American Madness: The Life of Frank Capra. 1989. 29.95 (*0-394-54417-X*) Knopf.

— Frank Capra: The Catastrophe of Success. (Illus.). 768p. 1993. pap. 16.00 (*0-671-79788-3*, Touchstone Bks) S&S Trade.

— Hawks on Hawks. LC 81-362. (Illus.). 172p. 1982. pap. 13.00 (*0-520-04552-1*) U CA Pr.

McBride, Joseph & Wilmington, Michael. John Ford. LC 75-19281. (Theatre, Film & the Performing Arts Ser.). (Illus.). 234p. 1975. lib. bdg. 29.50 (*0-306-70750-0*); pap. 10.95 (*0-306-80016-0*) Da Capo.

McBride, Jule. The Baby & the Bodyguard. (American Romance Ser.). 1994. mass mkt. 3.50 (*0-373-16562-5*, 1-16562-0) Harlequin Bks.

— Baby Trap. (American Romance Ser.). 1994. mass mkt. 3.50 (*0-373-16519-6*, 1-16519-0) Harlequin Bks.

— Bride of the Badlands. (American Romance Ser.). 1995. mass mkt. 3.50 (*0-373-16577-3*, 1-16577-8) Harlequin Bks.

— Wild Card Wedding. (American Romance Ser.). 1993. mass mkt. 3.50 (*0-373-16500-5*, 1-16500-0) Harlequin Bks.

— The Wrong Wife? (American Romance Ser.). 1994. mass mkt. 3.50 (*0-373-16546-3*, 1-16546-3) Harlequin Bks.

McBride, Kate, ed. see Cummings, E. E.

McBride, Kathleen. Tips for Working Parents: Creative Solutions to Everyday Problems. Burns, Deborah, ed. LC 88-62787. (Illus.). 144p. 1989. pap. 7.95 (*0-88266-546-4*, Storey Pub) Storey Comm Inc.

McBride, L. R. About Hawaii's Volcanoes. (Illus.). 48p. (JPN.). 1990. pap. 4.95 (*0-912180-47-1*) Petroglyph.

— About Hawaii's Volcanoes. rev. ed. (Illus.). 48p. 1986. pap. 4.95 (*0-912180-43-9*) Petroglyph.

— Kahuna: Versatile Mystics of Old Hawaii. 1972. pap. 6.95 (*0-912180-18-8*) Petroglyph.

— Petroglyphs of Hawaii. (Illus.). 1969. pap. 5.95 (*0-912180-12-9*) Petroglyph.

— Practical Folk Medicine of Hawaii. (Illus.). 1975. pap. 7.95 (*0-912180-27-7*) Petroglyph.

McBride, Lawrence W. The Greening of Dublin Castle: The Transformation of Bureaucratic & Judicial Personnel in Ireland, 1892-1922. LC 89-38830. (Illus.). 337p. 1991. text ed. 44.95 (*0-8132-0715-0*) Cath U Pr.

McBride, Lydia. Exmoor & Dartmoor. (Classic Country Companions Ser.). (Illus.). 1993. 34.95 (*1-85145-977-4*, Pub. by Pavilion UK) Trafalgar.

McBride, M. M. Constance Bennett. 1976. lib. bdg. 59.95 (*0-8490-1667-3*) Gordon Pr.

— The Story of Dwight W. Morrow. 1972. 59.95 (*0-8490-1131-0*) Gordon Pr.

McBride, M. W. & Dobbs, A. L. Nonpetroleum Mineral Producers in Texas--1983. (Mineral Resource Circular Ser.: MRC 74). (Illus.). 94p. 1983. 3.50 (*0-318-17364-6*) Bur Econ Geology.

McBride, Mary. The Empty Nest Symphony. LC 88-31821. 120p. 1989. pap. 4.95 (*0-88166-160-0*) Meadowbrook.

— Fly Away Home. (Historical Ser.). 1993. mass mkt. 3.99 (*0-373-28789-5*, 1-28789-5) Harlequin Bks.

— Forever & a Day. 1995. mass mkt. 4.50 (*0-373-28894-8*) Harlequin Bks.

— The Fourth of Forever. 1994. 3.99 (*0-373-28821-2*) Harlequin Bks.

— Grandma Knows Best, but No One Ever Listens! LC 87-1575. 132p. 1987. pap. 6.00 (*0-88166-094-9*) Meadowbrook.

— Grandma Knows Best, but No One Ever Listens! 1987. 5.00 (*0-671-63622-7*) S&S Trade.

— The Gunslinger. (Historical Ser.). 1995. pap. 4.50 (*0-373-28856-5*, 1-28856-2) Harlequin Bks.

— The Sugerman. (Historical Ser.). 1994. mass mkt. 3.99 (*0-373-28837-9*, 1-28837-2) Harlequin Bks.

McBride, Mary & McBride, Veronica. Don't Call Mommy at Work Today, Unless the Sitter Runs Away. Duffy, Helen, ed. (Illus.). 98p. 1991. reprint ed. pap. 4.95 (*0-9627601-2-9*) Bros Grinn.

— Empty Nest Symphony. (Illus.). 96p. 1991. reprint ed. pap. 4.95 (*0-9627601-3-7*) Bros Grinn.

— Grandma's Guide to a Happy Marriage. (Illus.). 84p. (Orig.). 1991. pap. 4.95 (*0-9627601-1-0*) Bros Grinn.

— Grandma's Guide to Child Care. Duffy, Helen, ed. (Illus.). 112p. (Orig.). 1990. pap. 4.95 (*0-9627601-0-2*) Bros Grinn.

— Grandpa Knows Best, but No One Ever Listens! Hilarious Helpful Hints for Grandpas. Duffy, Helen, ed. (Illus.). 75p. (Orig.). 1992. pap. 4.95 (*0-9627601-4-5*) Bros Grinn.

— Take This Book & Call Me in the Morning! Duffy, Helen, ed. (Illus.). 104p. (Orig.). 1993. pap. 4.95 (*0-9627601-5-3*) Bros Grinn.

McBride, Mary M. & Whiteman, Paul. Jazz. LC 74-15753. (Popular Culture in America Ser.). (Illus.). 298p. 1978. reprint ed. 21.95 (*0-405-06387-3*) Ayer.

McBride, Mekeel. The Going under of the Evening Land. LC 82-71662. 1983. 16.95 (*0-915604-76-0*); pap. 6.95 (*0-915604-77-9*) Carnegie-Mellon.

— Red Letter Days. (Poetry Ser.). 1988. 16.95 (*0-88748-064-0*); pap. 9.95 (*0-88748-065-9*) Carnegie-Mellon.

— Wind of the White Dresses. LC 94-70465. (Poetry Ser.). 80p. 1995. 16.95 (*0-88748-184-1*); pap. 11.95 (*0-88748-185-X*) Carnegie-Mellon.

McBride-Mellinger, Maria. The Wedding Dress. LC 93-17435. 1993. 40.00 (*0-679-41884-9*) Random.

McBride-Mellinger, Maria & Stites, William. Bridal Flowers: Arrangements for a Perfect Wedding. (Illus.). 96p. 1992. 24.95 (*0-8212-1917-0*) Bulfinch Pr.

McBride, Murray B. Environmental Chemistry of Soils. (Illus.). 416p. (C). 1994. text ed. 45.00 (*0-19-507011-9*) OUP.

McBride, Neal F. How to Build a Small-Group Ministry. 200p. (Orig.). 1995. pap. 20.00 (*0-89109-769-4*, NavPr) NavPress.

— How to Lead Small Groups. LC 90-61778. 144p. 1990. pap. 6.00 (*0-89109-303-6*) NavPress.

McBride, O. Praem. The Seven Last Words of Jesus. 87p. 1990. 4.95 (*0-86716-149-3*) St Anthony Mess Pr.

— The Story of the Church: Peak Moments from Pentecost to the Year 2000. (Illus.). 168p. (gr. 7-11). 1984. pap. text ed. 7.95 (*0-86716-029-2*) St Anthony Mess Pr.

McBride, P. K. C Clearly. (Computer Studies Ser.). (Illus.). 256p. 1993. pap. 28.00 (*0-632-03395-9*) Blackwell Sci.

— Lotus Improv 2 for Windows: Step by Step. 300p. 1994. pap. 24.95 (*0-7506-1873-6*) Buttrwrth-Heinemann.

— UNIX by Example: A Handbook for New Users. 240p. 1993. pap. 27.50 (*0-7506-0637-1*) Buttrwrth-Heinemann.

— Using Quattro Pro 3: Step-by-Step. 256p. 1992. pap. 32. 95 (*0-7506-0358-5*) Buttrwrth-Heinemann.

McBride, Peter. Paradox for Windows: Step-by-Step. 256p. 1993. pap. 29.95 (*0-7506-0610-X*) Buttrwrth-Heinemann.

McBride, R. Bruce, jt. auth. see Brearley, K.

McBride, R. Bruce, jt. auth. see Gordon, Gary R.

McBride, R. L. & Macfie, H. J. Psychological Basis of Sensory Evaluation. 1990. 72.00 (*1-85166-453-X*) Elsevier.

McBride, Rachael, jt. auth. see Adler, Katie.

McBride, Regina. Yarrow Field. Iddings, Kathleen, ed. LC 90-60171. (American Book Ser.). 91p. (Orig.). 1990. per. 10.00 (*0-931289-04-1*) San Diego Poet Pr.

McBride, Rob, ed. The In-Service Training of Teachers: Some Issues & Perspectives. 250p. 1989. 55.00 (*1-85000-583-4*, Falmer Pr); pap. 30.00 (*1-85000-584-2*, Falmer Pr) Taylor & Francis.

McBride, Robert. The Triumph of Ballet in Moliere's Theatre. LC 92-19477. 380p. 1992. text ed. 99.95 (*0-7734-9567-3*) E Mellen.

McBride, Robert E., ed. Mexico & the United States. LC 81-5171. 312p. 1981. 11.95 (*0-13-579565-6*) Am Assembly.

An Asterisk (*) at the beginning of an entry indicates that the title is appearing in BIP for the first time.

McBride, Robert W. Cooking with Tofu: For Those Who Hate Tofu but Don't Know Any Better. LC 91-76659. 66p. 1991. pap. 7.95 (*1-880197-01-4*) Gylantic Pub.

McBride, Robert W., jt. auth. see Hicks, Margerie.

***McBride, Roger L.** In the Land of the Big Red Apple. LC 94-33646. (Illus.). 256p. (J). (gr. 3-7). 1995. 3.95 (*0-06-440574-5*, Trophy) HarpC Child Bks.

McBride, Ronald, jt. auth. see Jones, Louis.

***McBride, Roy, ed.** My Heart Is a Glowing Sunset: My Voice Is a Warming Song. (Illus.). 177p. (Orig.). 1990. pap. 8.00 (*0-927663-15-5*) COMPAS.

McBride, Shannon. Writing Proposals for Contract Training. 67p. Date not set. 39.95 (*0-914951-76-9*) LERN.

McBride, Simon. The Spirit of Scotland. (Illus.). 128p. 1992. 29.00 (*0-86350-371-3*, Webb & Bowr) Viking Penguin.

McBride, Stephen. Not Working: State, Unemployment, & Neo-Conservatism in Canada. (State & Economic Life Ser.: No. 16). 272p. (Orig.). 1992. 50.00 (*0-8020-5998-8*); pap. 19.95 (*0-8020-6929-0*) U of Toronto Pr.

McBride, Tammy. The Mouldings Recipe Book: Recipes, Ideas, Instructions, Hints & Other Stuff. 20p. 1993. pap. write for info. (*0-9639921-0-4*) Mouldings.

— The Mouldings Recipe Book: Recipes, Ideas, Instructions, Hints, & Other Stuff Book II. 2nd ed. (Illus.). 32p. Date not set. pap. 1.50 (*0-9639921-1-2*) Mouldings.

McBride, Travis & Sieber, Mary. Initiative & Referendum: Direct Democracy in the American States. (Illus.). 6p. 1980. pap. text ed. 0.50 (*0-915757-09-5*) League Women Voters TX.

***McBride, Vaughn.** Echoes. 1988. 5.00 (*0-87129-514-8*, E25) Dramatic Pub.

— Pass My Imperfections Lightly By. 1991. 5.00 (*0-87129-144-4*, P69) Dramatic Pub.

McBride, Veronica, jt. auth. see McBride, Mary.

McBride, Virginia L. Think It Through. 112p. (C). 1991. pap. text ed. 11.95 (*0-8403-7000-8*) Kendall-Hunt.

McBride, W. Blan, jt. auth. see Burton, E. James.

McBride, W. Blan, jt. auth. see Burton, James.

McBride, Walter J. Computer Troubleshooting & Maintenance. 306p. (C). 1988. pap. text ed. 2.25 (*0-15-512664-4*) SCP.

— Computer Troubleshooting & Maintenance. 306p. (C). 1988. text ed. 37.25 (*0-15-512663-6*) SCP.

McBride, Wesley D., jt. auth. see Jackson, Robert K.

McBride, William. Gambling Times Guide to Greyhound Racing, 1990. (Illus.). (Orig.). 1984. pap. text ed. 9.95 (*0-89746-007-3*) Gambling Times.

McBride, William, ed. see Lipper Analytical Services International Corporation Staff.

McBride, William L. Fundamental Change in Law & Society: Hart & Sartre on Revolution. LC 77-118280. (Studies in the Social Sciences: No. 6). (Orig.). 1971. pap. text ed. 26.95 (*3-10-800276-7*) Mouton.

— Sartre's Political Theory. LC 90-25291. (Studies in Continental Thought). 260p. 1991. 37.50 (*0-253-33621-X*); pap. 12.95 (*0-253-20655-3*, MB-655) Ind U Pr.

McBride, William L. Social & Political Philosophy. LC 92-44094. (Issues in Philosophy Ser.). 144p. (C). 1993. pap. text ed. 16.95 (*1-55778-220-2*) Paragon Hse.

McBride, William L. & Schrag, Calvin O., eds. Phenomenology in a Pluralistic Context. LC 82-19609. (Selected Studies in Phenomenology & Existential Philosophy: No. 9). 317p. 1984. 74.50 (*0-87395-730-X*); pap. 24.95 (*0-87395-731-8*) State U NY Pr.

McBride, William M. Mark Twain: A Bibliography of the Collections of the Mark Twain Memorial & the Stowe-Day Foundation. (Illus.). 512p. 1984. 60.00 (*0-930313-00-3*) McBride Pub.

McBride, William M., ed. Good Night Officially: The Pacific War Letters of a Destroyer Sailor. LC 93-28239. (History & Warfare Ser.). 328p. 1994. text ed. 26.50 (*0-8133-1950-1*) Westview.

— A Pocket Guide to the Identification of First Editions. 5th ed. 100p. 1995. pap. 9.95 (*0-685-45324-3*) McBride Pub.

— Points of Issue: A Compendium of Points of Issue of Books by 20th Century Authors. 2nd ed. 104p. 1987. pap. 6.75 (*0-317-89906-6*) McBride Pub.

McBrien, David C. & Slater, Trevor F. Biomedical & Clinical Aspects of Cancer of the Uterine Cervix. (NFCR Cancer Research Association Symposium Ser.: No. 3). 1984. text ed. 88.00 (*0-12-481760-2*) Acad Pr.

McBrien, David C. & Slater, Trevor F., eds. Protective Agents in Cancer. (NFCR Symposium Ser.). 1983. text ed. 90.00 (*0-12-481770-X*) Acad Pr.

McBrien, Judith, et al. The EDY Course: Behavioural Teaching for Children & Adults Who Have Severe Learning Difficulties. 2nd ed. LC 92-29964. (Illus.). 112p. (C). 1992. text ed. 40.00 (*0-7190-3522-8*, Pub. by Manchester Univ Pr UK); student ed, text ed. 25.00 (*0-7190-3521-X*, Pub. by Manchester Univ Pr UK) St Martin.

McBrien, Philip. How to Teach with the Lectionary: Conversations. LC 92-81717. 176p. (Orig.). 1992. pap. 9.95 (*0-89622-522-4*) Twenty-Third.

— How to Teach with the Lectionary: Guide. 80p. (Orig.). 1992. pap. 12.95 (*0-89622-523-2*) Twenty-Third.

— The Word of the Lord: Reflections on the Sunday Readings. 176p. (Orig.). 1995. pap. 9.95 (*0-89622-659-X*) Twenty-Third.

McBrien, Richard. What Is Sacrament? Guide. 20p. 1987. pap. 4.95 (*0-89505-557-0*) Tabor Pub.

McBrien, Richard P. Catholicism. rev. ed. LC 93-21328. 1328p. 1994. 60.00 (*0-06-065404-X*); pap. 35.00 (*0-06-065405-8*) Harper SF.

— HarperCollins Encyclopedia of Catholicism. 1995. 45.00 (*0-06-065338-8*, HarpT) HarpC.

— Inside Catholicism. 1995. pap. 20.00 (*0-00-649052-2*) Collins SF.

— Ministry: A Theological, Pastoral Handbook. LC 86-43011. 128p. 1988. pap. 10.00 (*0-06-065324-8*) Harper SF.

McBrien, Vincent O. Introductory Analysis. LC 61-6044. (Century Mathematics Ser.). (Illus.). 1969. 39.00 (*0-89197-248-X*); pap. text ed. 19.50 (*0-89197-804-6*) Irvington.

McBrien, William, jt. auth. see Barbera, Jack.

McBrier, E. M. Loucks: Genealogy of the Loucks Family, Beginning with Johann Dietrich Loucks & His Descendants in Direct Line to Joseph Louck, & All His Known & Traceable Descendants to Date. (Illus.). 317p. 1991. reprint ed. lib. bdg. 58.50 (*0-8328-1726-0*); reprint ed. pap. 48.50 (*0-8328-1727-9*) Higginson Bk Co.

McBrier, Michael. Getting Oliver's Goat. LC 87-13870. (Illus.). 96p. (J). (gr. 3-6). 1988. lib. bdg. 9.89 (*0-8167-1145-3*); pap. text ed. 2.95 (*0-8167-1146-1*) Troll Assocs.

— Oliver & the Amazing Spy. LC 87-13793. (Oliver & Company Ser.). (Illus.). 96p. (J). (gr. 3-6). 1988. lib. bdg. 9.89 (*0-8167-1143-7*); pap. text ed. 2.95 (*0-8167-1144-5*) Troll Assocs.

— Oliver & the Runaway Alligator. LC 86-7120. (Oliver & Company Ser.). (Illus.). 96p. (Orig.). (J). (gr. 3-6). 1987. lib. bdg. 9.89 (*0-8167-0818-5*); pap. text ed. 2.95 (*0-8167-0819-3*) Troll Assocs.

— Oliver Smells Trouble. LC 87-13954. (Illus.). 96p. (J). (gr. 3-6). 1988. lib. bdg. 9.89 (*0-8167-1149-6*); pap. text ed. 2.95 (*0-8167-1150-X*) Troll Assocs.

— Oliver's Back-Yard Circus. LC 86-40378. (Oliver & Company Ser.). (Illus.). 96p. (Orig.). (J). (gr. 3-6). 1987. lib. bdg. 9.89 (*0-8167-0822-3*); pap. text ed. 2.95 (*0-8167-0823-1*) Troll Assocs.

— Oliver's Barnyard Blues. LC 87-13864. (Illus.). 96p. (J). (gr. 3-6). 1988. lib. bdg. 9.89 (*0-8167-1147-X*); pap. text ed. 2.95 (*0-8167-1148-8*) Troll Assocs.

— Oliver's High-Flying Adventure. LC 86-16038. (Oliver & Company Ser.). (Illus.). 96p. (Orig.). (J). (gr. 3-6). 1987. lib. bdg. 9.89 (*0-8167-0820-7*); pap. text ed. 2.95 (*0-8167-0821-5*) Troll Assocs.

McBrier, Page. Adventure in the Haunted House. LC 85-8436. (Oliver & Company Ser.). (Illus.). 96p. (J). (gr. 3-6). 1986. lib. bdg. 9.89 (*0-8167-0539-9*); pap. text ed. 2.95 (*0-8167-0540-2*) Troll Assocs.

— Confessions of a Reluctant Elf. LC 94-68006. 144p. (J). (gr. 3-7). 1995. pap. 3.95 (*0-7868-1010-6*) Hyprn Ppbks.

— Daphne Takes Charge. (Treehouse Times Ser.: No. 5). (J). 1990. pap. 2.95 (*0-380-75899-7*, Camelot) Avon.

— First Course: Trouble. (Treehouse Times Ser.: No. 4). 128p. (J). 1990. pap. 2.50 (*0-380-75783-4*, Camelot) Avon.

— The Great Rip-Off. (Treehouse Times Ser.: No. 8). 128p. (J). 1990. pap. 2.95 (*0-380-75902-0*, Camelot) Avon.

— The Kickball Crisis. (Treehouse Times Ser.: No. 2). 96p. (J). 1989. pap. 2.50 (*0-380-75781-8*, Camelot) Avon.

— Oliver & the Lucky Duck. LC 85-8417. (Oliver & Company Ser.). (Illus.). 96p. (J). (gr. 3-6). 1986. lib. bdg. 9.89 (*0-8167-0541-0*); pap. text ed. 2.95 (*0-8167-0542-9*) Troll Assocs.

— Oliver's Lucky Day. LC 85-8437. (Oliver & Company Ser.). (Illus.). 96p. (J). (gr. 3-6). 1986. lib. bdg. 9.89 (*0-8167-0537-2*); pap. text ed. 2.95 (*0-8167-0538-0*) Troll Assocs.

— The Press Mess. (Treehouse Times Ser.: No. 6). 128p. (Orig.). (J). (gr. 4-5). 1990. pap. 2.95 (*0-380-75900-4*, Camelot) Avon.

— Rats. (Treehouse Times Ser.: No. 7). 128p. (J). 1990. pap. 2.95 (*0-380-75901-2*, Camelot) Avon.

— Secret of the Missing Camel. LC 86-887. (Oliver & Company Ser.). (Illus.). 96p. (Orig.). (J). (gr. 3-6). 1987. lib. bdg. 9.89 (*0-8167-0816-9*); pap. text ed. 2.95 (*0-8167-0817-7*) Troll Assocs.

— Secret of the Old Garage. LC 85-16505. (Oliver & Company Ser.). (Illus.). 96p. (J). (gr. 3-6). 1986. lib. bdg. 9.89 (*0-8167-0543-7*); pap. text ed. 2.95 (*0-8167-0544-5*) Troll Assocs.

— Spaghetti Breath. (Treehouse Times Ser.: No. 3). 128p. (J). (gr. 4). 1989. pap. 2.50 (*0-380-75782-6*, Camelot) Avon.

— Stinky Business. (Treehouse Times Ser.: No. 9). 128p. (Orig.). (YA). 1991. pap. 2.95 (*0-380-76269-2*, Camelot) Avon.

— Under Twelve Not Allowed. (Treehouse Times Ser.: No. 1). 128p. (J). (gr. 4). 1989. pap. 2.50 (*0-380-75780-X*, Camelot) Avon.

McBrier, Vivian F. R. Nathaniel Dett: His Life & Works (1882-1943) (YA). 1990. 15.95 (*0-87498-092-5*) Assoc Pubs DC.

McBrierty, Vincent J. & Packer, Kenneth J. Nuclear Magnetic Resonance in Solid Polymers. LC 92-45158. (Solid State Science Ser.). (Illus.). 300p. (C). 1993. 89.95 (*0-521-30140-8*) Cambridge U Pr.

McBroom. Third Sex. 1994. pap. 14.95 (*1-56924-908-3*) Marlowe & Co.

McBroom, Amanda. Amanda McBroom Songbook. Okun, Milton, ed. pap. 14.95 (*0-89524-583-3*) Cherry Lane.

McBroom, Louise H. Bits & Pieces of Eighty Years. 1993. 12.95 (*0-533-10381-9*) Vantage.

***McBroom, Michael.** McBrooms Camera Bluebook 1995: 1995-1996 Edition. (Illus.). 232p. 1995. pap. 24.95 (*0-936262-35-4*) Amherst Media.

McBrown, Gertrude P. Picture Poetry Book. (Illus.). (J). 1990. 4.25 (*0-87498-007-0*) Assoc Pubs DC.

McBryde, W., intro. Erskine: An Institute of the Law of Scotland, 1871, 2 vols., Set. (Scottish Legal Classics Ser.). 1990. 210.00 (*0-406-17897-6*) Butterworth Legal Pubs.

McBryde, W. A., ed. A Critical Review of Equilibrium Data for Proton & Metal Complexes of 1,10-Phenanthroline, 2,2'-Bipyridyl & Related Compounds: Critical Evaluation of Equilibrium Construction in Solution; Part A: Stability Construction of Metal Complexes, Vol. 17. 1978. pap. 43.00 (*0-08-022344-3*, Pub. by Pergamon Repr UK) Franklin.

McBurney, Charles, ed. Reformed Presbyterian Ministers: 1950-1993. 225p. 1994. 25.00 (*1-884527-05-1*) Crown & Covenant.

— Reformed Presbyterian Ministers: 1950-1993. LC 93-74257. 225p. 1994. pap. 15.00 (*1-884527-09-4*) Crown & Covenant.

McBurney, Charles B. The Haua Fteah (Cyrenaica) & the Stone Age of the South-East Mediterranean. LC 67-10257. 457p. reprint ed. pap. 130.30 (*0-317-20593-5*, 2024495) Bks Demand.

McBurney, Donald H. Experimental Psychology. 2nd ed. 410p. (C). 1989. text ed. 49.95 (*0-534-12084-9*) Brooks-Cole.

— Research Methods. 3rd ed. LC 93-5651. 1994. text ed. 50.95 (*0-534-17646-1*) Brooks-Cole.

McBurney, James H. Discussions in Human Affairs. LC 75-109296. 432p. (C). 1971. reprint ed. text ed. 59.75 (*0-8371-3839-6*, MCHA, Greenwood Pr) Greenwood.

McBurney, Jim. Technopoly. Kraven, Mae, ed. (Technology Education Ser.). (Illus.). 96p. (J). (gr. 4-5). 1991. text ed. 19.95 (*0-9629471-0-5*) J McBurney.

McBurney, Louis. RCC, Vol. 2: Counseling Christian Workers. 291p. 1986. write for info. (*0-8499-0586-9*) Word Inc.

McBurney, Margaret & Byers, Mary. Tavern in the Town: Early Inns & Taverns of Ontario. (Illus.). 259p. 1987. 35.00 (*0-8020-5732-2*) U of Toronto Pr.

McBurney, Margaret, jt. auth. see Byers, Mary.

McBurney, Melissa. Key Guide to Electronic Resources: Engineering. Ensor, Pat, ed. 150p. 1994. pap. text ed. 35.00 (*0-88736-963-4*) Learned Info.

McBurney, Stuart. Ecology into Economics Won't Go: Or Life Is Not a Concept. (Illus.). 208p. (Orig.). 1993. pap. 11.95 (*1-870098-28-5*, Pub. by Green Bks UK) Seven Hills Bk.

McBurney, William H. A Check List of English Prose Fiction: 1700-1739. LC 60-13292. 164p. reprint ed. pap. 46.80 (*0-317-10464-0*, 2001585) Bks Demand.

— Four Before Richardson: Selected English Novels, 1720-1727. LC 63-9095. (Illus.). 411p. reprint ed. pap. 117.20 (*0-318-39764-1*, 2033138) Bks Demand.

McBurney, William H., jt. auth. see Lillo, George.

McBurnie, Grant & Polack, Michael. Aunt Wilhelmina's Will. LC 93-6570. (J). 1994. write for info. (*0-383-03676-3*) SRA Schl Grp.

***McCabe.** Introduction to Oxygen Therapies. 1995. 12.00 (*1-879323-08-7*) Sound Horizons AV.

McCabe, jt. auth. see Moore.

McCabe, A. & Peterson, C., eds. Developing Narrative Structure. 376p. (C). 1991. text ed. 75.00 (*0-8058-0475-7*); pap. 32.50 (*0-8058-0476-5*) L Erlbaum Assocs.

McCabe, Alice S. Supplement to Gwinnett County, Georgia, Families, 1818-1968. 32p. (Orig.). 1988. pap. write for info. (*0-914923-08-0*) Gwinnett Hist.

McCabe, Alice S., ed. Gwinnett County, Georgia, Families 1818-1968 with 1987 Supplement. 686p. 1988. reprint ed. write for info. (*0-914923-02-1*) Gwinnett Hist.

— Gwinnett County, Georgia, Inferior Court Minutes for Ordinary Purposes, 1819-1861. 104p. 1987. pap. write for info. (*0-914923-07-2*) Gwinnett Hist.

McCabe, Alice S. & Garrett, Franklin M. Gwinnett County, Georgia, Deaths 1818-1989. 810p. 1991. 60.00 (*0-914923-10-2*) Gwinnett Hist.

McCabe, Alice S., jt. auth. see Baughman, John W.

McCabe, Alice S., ed. see Cates, Donald W.

McCabe, Allyssa. Language Games to Play with Your Child: Enhancing Communication from Infancy Through Late Childhood. 2nd ed. (Illus.). 255p. (C). 1992. 24.95 (*0-306-44320-1*, Plenum Insight) Plenum.

McCabe, Allyssa, jt. auth. see Peterson, Carole.

McCabe, Ann C. & Fairbanks, Eugene B. English Writing: Fifteen-Day Competency Review Text. Gamsey, Wayne H., ed. (Illus.). 160p. (Orig.). (YA). (gr. 7-12). 1992. pap. text ed. 4.95 (*0-935487-56-5*) N & N Pub Co.

McCabe, Bernard. Bottle Rabbit & Friends. (Illus.). 136p. (J). (gr. 3-7). 1991. 14.95 (*0-571-15318-6*) Faber & Faber.

McCabe, Bernard, ed. see Yeats, William Butler.

McCabe, Brendan & Tremayne, Andrew. Elements of Modern Asymptotic Theory with Statistical Applications. 272p. (C). 1993. text ed. 79.95 (*0-7190-3052-8*, Pub. by Manchester Univ Pr UK); text ed. 24.95 (*0-7190-3053-6*, Pub. by Manchester Univ Pr UK) St Martin.

McCabe, Brian. One Atom to Another. LC 87-63148. 76p. (Orig.). 1988. pap. 10.95 (*0-948275-22-7*) Dufour.

McCabe, Brian F., jt. ed. see Veldman, Jan E.

McCabe, Brian F., et al, eds. Immunobiology in Otology, Rhinology & Laryngology. LC 92-10311. (Illus.). 407p. 1992. lib. bdg. 116.00 (*90-6299-083-5*, Pub. by Kugler NE) Kugler Pubns.

McCabe, Cameron. The Face on the Cutting-Room Floor. 348p. 1981. 19.95 (*0-8398-2738-5*) Boulevard.

McCabe, Charles R., ed. see Scripps, Edward W.

McCabe, Chuck. Uncle Rhythm's Cosmic Riff & Gig Guide: The First How-Not-to Book for a Career in Music. LC 93-60729. 164p. 1993. pap. 12.95 (*0-9636869-6-8*) Woodshed Prods.

McCabe, Colin, ed. TVEI: The Organisation of the Early Years. 68p. 1984. pap. 19.95 (*0-905028-62-7*, Pub. by Multilingual Matters UK) Taylor & Francis.

McCabe, Constance, jt. auth. see McCabe, Neal.

McCabe, Cynthia J. Artistic Collaboration in the Twentieth Century. LC 84-3090. (Illus.). 224p. 1984. pap. text ed. 29.95 (*0-87474-687-6*, MCACP) Smithsonian.

McCabe, David A. Standard Rate in American Trade Unions. LC 70-156435. (American Labor Ser., No. 2). 1971. reprint ed. 19.95 (*0-405-02932-2*) Ayer.

McCabe, David A., jt. auth. see Barnett, George E.

McCabe, David J., jt. auth. see Schmidt, Peter W.

McCabe, Don. AVKO Spelling "Difficulty" Dictionary. Webb, James E., ed. 204p. 1988. pap. 19.95 (*1-56400-211-X*) AVKO Educ Res.

— AVKO Student Response Book for Sequential Spelling. 60p. 1980. student ed 5.95 (*1-56400-360-4*) AVKO Educ Res.

— Helping Anyone Overcome Their Reading-Spelling Problems: A Handbook for Volunteer Tutors. 86p. 1991. teacher ed 8.95 (*1-56400-730-8*) AVKO Educ Res.

— Helping Volunteers Become Reading-Spelling Tutors: Lesson Plans for an Adult Community Education Course for Volunteer Tutors. 72p. 1991. pap. text ed. 7.95 (*1-56400-750-2*) AVKO Educ Res.

— If It Is to Be, It Is up to Me: Overcoming My Reading-Spelling Problems Not in One Day but in 180 Days. 112p. 1991. pap. text ed. 11.95 (*1-56400-740-5*) AVKO Educ Res.

— Sequential Spelling Examination Set. 240p. 1990. pap. text ed. 27.95 (*1-56400-300-0*) AVKO Educ Res.

— Sequential Spelling I. 36p. (Orig.). 1990. pap. text ed. 5.95 (*1-56400-310-8*) AVKO Educ Res.

— Sequential Spelling II. 36p. 1990. pap. text ed. 5.95 (*1-56400-320-5*) AVKO Educ Res.

— Sequential Spelling III. 36p. 1990. pap. text ed. 5.95 (*1-56400-330-2*) AVKO Educ Res.

— Sequential Spelling IV. 36p. 1990. pap. text ed. 5.95 (*1-56400-340-X*) AVKO Educ Res.

— Sequential Spelling V. 36p. 1990. pap. text ed. 5.95 (*1-56400-350-7*) AVKO Educ Res.

McCabe, Donald F. The Prose-Rhythm of Demosthenes. rev. ed. Connor, W. R., ed. LC 80-2658. (Monographs in Classical Studies). 1981. lib. bdg. 35.95 (*0-405-14044-4*) Ayer.

McCabe, Douglas M. Corporate Nonunion Complaint Procedures & Systems: A Strategic Human Resources Management Analysis. LC 88-11758. 220p. 1988. text ed. 55.00 (*0-275-93059-9*, C3059, Praeger Pubs) Greenwood.

McCabe, Ed. Against Gravity. 1991. pap. 15.95 (*0-446-39239-1*) Warner Bks.

— Oxygen Ozone Home Companions: The Complete Story of Combating Disease with Oxygen & Oxygen Related Products & Devices. 2nd rev. ed. (Energy Publications Alternatives: No. OT2). (Illus.). 250p. (C). 1996. pap. 15.00 (*0-9620527-1-X*) Energy Pubns.

— Oxygen Therapies: A New Way of Approaching Disease. (Energy Publications Alternatives). (Illus.). 224p. (Orig.). (C). 1988. pap. 12.00 (*0-9620527-0-1*) Energy Pubns.

McCabe, Edith, ed. see Ruchhoft, Robert H.

McCabe, Eugene. Cancer. (Adaptations Ser.). 1980. pap. 2.95 (*0-912262-68-0*) Proscenium.

— Cyril: Quest of an Orphaned Squirrel. 72p. (J). (ps-8). 1987. 13.95 (*0-86278-116-7*, Pub. by OBrien Pr IE); pap. 7.95 (*0-86278-131-0*, Pub. by OBrien Pr IE) Dufour.

— Heritage. 156p. 1985. pap. 8.95 (*0-86278-079-9*, Pub. by OBrien Pr IE) Dufour.

— King of the Castle. 1978. pap. 2.95 (*0-912262-50-8*) Proscenium.

— King of the Castle. deluxe ed. 1978. 7.50 (*0-912262-49-4*) Proscenium.

McCabe, Francis G. Logic & Objects. 180p. 1992. pap. text ed. 28.00 (*0-13-536079-X*) P-H.

McCabe, Frank. High Level Programmers Guide to the 68000. 300p. 1991. pap. text ed. 34.00 (*0-13-388034-6*) P-H.

McCabe, G., et al. Advances in Library Administration & Organization, Vol. 3. 320p. 1984. 73.25 (*0-89232-386-8*) Jai Pr.

McCabe, George A. Catch the Vision on Prayer in the Last Days. (Illus.). 152p. 1988. pap. 6.95 (*0-317-90967-3*) Vision Ministry Pr.

McCabe, George P., jt. auth. see Moore, David S.

McCabe, Gerard B. Advances in Library Administration & Organization, Vol. 5. 307p. 1986. 73.25 (*0-89232-674-3*) Jai Pr.

McCabe, Gerard B., ed. Academic Libraries in Urban & Metropolitan Areas: A Management Handbook. LC 91-21182. (Library Management Collection). 288p. 1991. text ed. 55.00 (*0-313-27536-X*, MLZ, Greenwood Pr) Greenwood.

— Operations Handbook for the Small Academic Library. LC 88-34811. (Library Management Collection). 360p. 1989. text ed. 59.95 (*0-313-26474-0*, MOB/, Greenwood Pr) Greenwood.

— The Smaller Academic Library: A Management Handbook. LC 87-23655. (Library Management Collection). (Illus.). 400p. 1988. text ed. 59.95 (*0-313-25027-8*, MMH/, Greenwood Pr) Greenwood.

McCabe, Gerard B. & Kreissman, Bernard, eds. Advances in Library Administration & Organization, Vol. 2. 373p. 1983. 73.25 (*0-89232-214-4*) Jai Pr.

— Advances in Library Administration & Organization, Vol. 4. 233p. 1985. 73.25 (*0-89232-566-6*) Jai Pr.

— Advances in Library Administration & Organization, Vol. 6. 1987. lib. bdg. 73.25 (*0-89232-724-3*) Jai Pr.

— Advances in Library Administration & Organization, Vol. 7. 1988. 73.25 (*0-89232-817-7*) Jai Pr.

— Advances in Library Administration & Organization: A Research Annual. 302p. 1989. 73.25 (*0-89232-967-X*) Jai Pr.

M

An Asterisk (*) at the beginning of an entry indicates that the title is appearing in BIP for the first time.

M

*McCabe, Gerard B. & Person, Ruth J. Academic Libraries: Their Rationale & Role in American Higher Education. LC 94-40319. (Contributions in Librarianship & Information Science Ser.: Vol. 84). 248p. 1995. text ed. 55.00 (0-313-28597-7, Greenwood Pr) Greenwood.

McCabe, Gerard B., jt. ed. see Head, John W.

McCabe, Herbert. God Matters. 1991. pap. 14.95 (0-87243-190-8) Templegate.

— The Teaching of the Catholic Church. LC 86-45875. 80p. 1986. pap. 3.95 (0-8146-5608-0) Liturgical Pr.

McCabe, Ian. A Diplomatic History of Ireland, 1948-49: The Republic, the Commonwealth & NATO. 212p. 1992. text ed. 39.50 (0-7165-2461-9, Pub. by Irish Acad Pr IE) Intl Spec Bk.

McCabe, J. Applied Dental Materials. 7th ed. 1990. pap. 55. 00 (0-632-02826-2) Blackwell Sci.

McCabe, J., jt. auth. see Eckenfelder, W. Wesley.

McCabe, J. L. Algebra & Practical Applications. rev. ed. (Illus.). 133p. 1994. reprint ed. pap. text ed. 13.95 (0-942465-03-2, 2-038-778) Summertree Bks.

— Geometry & Practical Applications. rev. ed. (Illus.). 140p. 1994. reprint ed. pap. text ed. 13.95 (0-942465-02-4, 2-009-496) Summertree Bks.

— Getting Started As a Contractor. Orig. Title: How to Get Started As a Contractor. (Illus.). 65p. 1994. reprint ed. pap. text ed. 8.95 (0-942465-16-4) Summertree Bks.

— Mathematics in Review. rev. ed. Orig. Title: Everyday Mathematics, a Study Guide. (Illus.). 168p. 1994. pap. text ed. 13.95 (0-942465-15-6, 2-323-279) Summertree Bks.

— Word Problems Made Easy. rev. ed. Orig. Title: Word Problems Simplified. (Illus.). 127p. 1994. pap. text ed. 13.95 (0-942465-18-0, 1-972-966) Summertree Bks.

McCabe, James, jt. auth. see Murray, Stuart.

McCabe, James D., Jr. Behind the Scenes in Washington. LC 73-19158. (Politics & People Ser.). (Illus.). 548p. 1974. reprint ed. 41.95 (0-405-05880-2) Ayer.

— Great Fortunes & How They Were Made: Or, the Struggles & Triumphs of Our Selfmade Men. LC 70-37895. (Select Bibliographies Reprint Ser.). (Illus.). 1977. reprint ed. 44.95 (0-8369-6732-1) Ayer.

McCabe, James D. History of the Grange Movement: Or the Farmer's War Against Monopolies. LC 68-18600. (Library of Early American Business & Industry: No. 37). 1969. reprint ed. 49.50 (0-678-00514-1) Kelley.

McCabe, James P. A Critical Guide to Catholic Reference Books. 3rd rev. ed. (Research Studies in Library Science: No. 20). 323p. 1989. lib. bdg. 47.00 (0-87287-621-7) Libs Unl.

McCabe, Janet, jt. auth. see Kochen, Cinda L.

McCabe, John. Babe: The Life & Times of Oliver Hardy. 1990. 16.95 (0-8065-1187-7, Citadel Pr) Carol Pub Group.

— Charlie Chaplin. (Illus.). 298p. (Orig.). 1993. pap. 13.95 (0-86051-791-8, Robson-Parkwest) Parkwest Pubns.

— The Comedy World of Stan Laurel: Centennial Edition. rev. ed. (Vintage Comedy Ser.). 288p. 1990. reprint ed. 19.95 (0-940410-23-0, Moonstone Pr); reprint ed. pap. 14.95 (0-940410-22-2, Moonstone Pr) Past Times.

— George M. Cohan: The Man Who Owned Broadway. (Quality Paperbacks Ser.). (Illus.). 1980. reprint ed. pap. 6.95 (0-306-80118-3) Da Capo.

— Plastic Surgery Hopscotch: A Resource Guide for Those Considering Cosmetic Surgery. Ingersoll, Miriam, ed. LC 93-74927. 384p. 1995. pap. 19.95 (1-884702-32-5) Carmania Bks.

— Surgery Electives: What to Know Before the Doctor Operates. Ingersol, Miriam, ed. LC 93-74926. 330p. 1994. pap. 14.95 (1-884702-14-7) Carmania Bks.

McCabe, John L. The Budget Book. 2nd ed. 45p. (Orig.). 1987. pap. 3.95 (0-945326-06-8) Intrawest Pub.

McCabe, Joseph. Biographical Dictionary of Modern Rationalists. 1977. lib. bdg. 75.95 (0-8490-1506-5) Gordon Pr.

— A Candid History of the Jesuits. 1977. lib. bdg. 59.95 (0-8490-1567-7) Gordon Pr.

— Crises in the History of the Papacy. 1977. lib. bdg. 59.95 (0-8490-1684-3) Gordon Pr.

— The Forgery of the Old Testament, & Other Essays. LC 93-27365. (Freethought Library). 150p. 1994. pap. 14.95 (0-87975-850-3) Prometheus Bks.

— George Bernard Shaw. LC 74-30406. (George Bernard Shaw Ser.: No. 92). 1974. lib. bdg. 75.00 (0-8383-1749-9) M S G Haskell Hse.

— George Bernard Shaw: A Critical Study. 1972. 59.95 (0-8490-0219-2) Gordon Pr.

— Handel's Messiah: A Devotional Commentary. large type ed. (Large Print Inspirational Ser.). 144p. 1986. pap. 14. 95 (0-8027-2556-2) Walker & Co.

— History's Greatest Liars. 2nd ed. LC 84-141646. 175p. 1985. reprint ed. pap. 6.50 (0-911826-81-5, 5524) Am Atheist.

— The Myth of the Resurrection & Other Essays. LC 92-46038. (Freethought Library). 168p. (Orig.). (C). 1993. pap. 14.95 (0-87975-833-3) Prometheus Bks.

— Peter Abelard. LC 74-148889. (Select Bibliographies Reprint Ser.). 1977. reprint ed. 24.95 (0-8369-5655-9) Ayer.

— Spain in Revolt, 1814-1931. 1976. lib. bdg. 59.95 (0-8490-2642-3) Gordon Pr.

— Vice in German Monasteries. 35p. 1993. reprint ed. pap. 3.00 (0-911826-93-9) Am Atheist.

McCabe, Joseph, tr. see Carrere, Jean.

McCabe, Joseph, tr. see Denis, Pierre.

McCabe, Joseph, tr. see Drews, Arthur.

McCabe, Joseph, tr. see Ferrer Y Guardia, Francisco.

McCabe, Joseph, tr. see Haeckel, Ernst.

McCabe, Joseph, tr. see Iorga, Nicolae.

McCabe, Kendall K. The Path of the Phoenix. Sherer, Michael L., ed. (Orig.). 1986. pap. 7.60 (0-89536-818-8, 6827) CSS OH.

McCabe, Larry. Blues Band Rhythm Guitar. 1993. 15.00 (1-56222-566-9, 94825); audio 9.98 (1-56222-795-5, 94825) Mel Bay.

— Blues, Boogie & Rock Guitar. 1993. 8.95 (0-685-63953-3, 93996); audio 9.98 (1-56222-614-2, 93996) Mel Bay.

— Country Lead Guitar. 1993. 8.95 (0-87166-935-8, 94079); audio 9.98 (1-56222-623-1, 94079) Mel Bay.

McCabe, Margaret E. & Rhoades, Jacqueline. Cooperative Meeting Management. 40p. (Orig.). (YA). (gr. 8 up). 1986. pap. 3.95 (0-933935-03-X) ITA Pubns.

— How to Say What You Mean. 31p. (Orig.). 1986. pap. 3.95 (0-933935-05-6) ITA Pubns.

— The Nurturing Classroom: Developing Thinking Skills, Self-Esteem, Responsibility through Simple Cooperation. LC 85-80102. (Illus.). 363p. (Orig.). (ps up). 1989. pap. 26.00 (0-933935-09-9) ITA Pubns.

McCabe, Margaret E., jt. auth. see Rhoades, Jacqueline.

McCabe, Marla. The Creative Spiral: PS-6 to PS-12. LC 91-71011. 208p. 1991. teacher ed 24.95 (0-932881-14-9) Greenpl Bks.

— Homestyle Creativity: PS-6. LC 91-71010. 64p. 1991. teacher ed 14.95 (0-932881-12-2) Greenpl Bks.

— Opening the Corners to Creativity & Self-Esteem: PS-6 to PS-12. LC 90-82431. 128p. 1990. teacher ed 16.95 (0-685-40133-2) Greenpl Bks.

McCabe, Mary. Clara Sipprell. LC 90-80190. (Illus.). 150p. 1990. 39.95 (0-88360-064-1) Amon Carter.

— Everwinding Times. 416p. (C). 1994. pap. 32.00x (1-874640-55-6, Pub. by Argyll Pubng UK) St Mut.

McCabe, Mary J. Learn to See: Symbols in Daily Life. 128p. 1994. pap. 9.95 (0-931892-86-4) B Dolphin Pub.

McCabe, Mary M. Plato's Individuals. LC 93-42370. 1994. 45.00 (0-691-07351-1) Princeton U Pr.

McCabe, Michael. Arizona: Studies. (Illus.). 46p. (J). (gr. 4-6). 1994. student ed 5.75 (0-911981-59-4) Cloud Pub.

— Arizona: Su Origen. (Illus.). (SPA.). (J). (gr. 4-6). 1987. pap. 14.95 (0-911981-54-3) Cloud Pub.

— Arizona: Studies: Blackline Masters. (Illus.). 41p. 1990. teacher ed 27.95 (0-911981-64-0) Cloud Pub.

— Colorado: Grassroots. (Illus.). 48p. (J). (gr. 4-6). 1984. student ed 5.65 (0-911981-13-6) Cloud Pub.

— Colorado: Grassroots Blackline Masters. (Illus.). 34p. 1983. teacher ed 27.95 (0-911981-18-7) Cloud Pub.

McCabe, Michael & Brew, Virginia. California: Roots. (Illus.). 59p. (J). (gr. 4-6). 1983. student ed 5.25 (0-911981-05-5) Cloud Pub.

— California: Roots. 28p. (J). (gr. 4-6). 1991. reprint ed. teacher ed 7.95 (0-911981-07-1) Cloud Pub.

— Colorado: Grassroots. 20p. (J). (gr. 4-6). 1983. teacher ed 8.95 (0-911981-14-4) Cloud Pub.

McCabe, Michael, jt. auth. see Brew, Virginia.

McCabe, Michael, jt. auth. see Stacy, Darryl.

McCabe, Neal & McCabe, Constance. Baseball's Golden Age: The Photographs of Charles M. Conlon. LC 93-187. (Illus.). 1993. 29.95 (0-8109-3130-3) Abrams.

*McCabe, Neil & Burnett, Catherine. State Constitutional Criminal Procedure. LC 94-78748. 630p. 1994. 60.00 (0-916081-34-6) J Marshall Pub Co.

McCabe, P. J. & Parrish, J. Totman, eds. Controls on the Distribution & Quality of Cretaceous Coals. (Special Paper Ser.: No. 267). (Illus.). 1992. pap. 80.00 (0-8137-2267-5) Geol Soc.

*McCabe, P. J., et al. The Future of Energy Gases. (Illus.). 58p. (Orig.). (C). 1995. pap. text ed. 40.00 (0-7881-1651-7) Diane Pub.

McCabe, Pat. Music on Clinton Street. 152p. 1986. pap. 8.95 (1-85186-012-6) Dufour.

McCabe, Patrick. The Butcher Boy. LC 93-2831. 224p. 1993. 19.95 (0-88064-147-9) Fromm Intl Pub.

Mccabe, Patrick. Butcher Boy. 1994. mass mkt. 9.95 (0-385-31237-7) Doubleday.

*McCabe, Patrick. The Dead School: A Novel. LC 94-44636. 1995. 21.95 (0-385-31420-5, Dial) Doubleday.

*McCabe, Paul. The Hidden Hand. 1995. 17.95 (0-533-11157-9) Vantage.

McCabe, Peter. City of Lies: A Novel. LC 92-16733. 1993. 20.00 (0-688-12118-7) Morrow.

— Wasteland: A Novel. LC 93-2238. 258p. 1994. text ed. 20.00 (0-684-19681-6, Scribners) S&S Trade.

McCabe, Peter J., et al. The Future of Energy Gases. Carter, L. M. H., ed. Vol. 1115. 1994. write for info. (0-318-72281-X) US Geol Survey.

McCabe, Philip M. & Schneiderman, N. Stress, Coping & Disease. Field, Tiffany & Skyler, Jay, eds. 264p. 1991. 39.95 (0-8058-0408-0) L Erlbaum Assocs.

McCabe, R., jt. auth. see Hegedus, L.

McCabe, R. K. The Accountant's Guide to Peer & Quality Review. LC 92-34946. 248p. 1993. text ed. 55.00 (0-89930-685-3, MGQ, Quorum Bks) Greenwood.

McCabe, Richard. The Pillars of Eternity: Time & Providence in The Faerie Queene. 256p. 1989. 39.50 (0-7165-2428-7, Pub. by Irish Acad Pr IE) Intl Spec Bk.

McCabe, Richard A. Incest, Drama, & Nature's Law, 1550-1700. LC 92-44182. (Illus.). 354p. (C). 1993. 59.95 (0-521-43173-5) Cambridge U Pr.

McCabe, Richard A., jt. ed. see Erskine-Hill, Howard.

McCabe, Richard E. The Unique Wood Duck: Tableau of a Field Trip with Frank Bellrose & Scott Nielsen. LC 92-46903. (Illus.). 136p. 1993. pap. 24.95 (0-8117-3099-9) Stackpole.

McCabe, Robert, et al. Metering Pump Handbook. 280p. 1984. 29.95 (0-8311-1157-7) Indus Pr.

McCabe, Robert K. International Herald Tribune Guide to Business Travel in Asia. 208p. 1988. pap. 14.95 (0-8442-9625-2, Natl Textbk) NTC Pub Grp.

McCabe, Sandra. Monstergrams: Twelve Spooky Pop-Up Greeting Cards to Make Yourself. (Illus.). 24p. (J). (gr. k-5). 1996. 5.95 (0-8037-1647-8) Dial Bks Young.

McCabe, Sarah, et al, eds. The Police, Public Order & Civil Liberties: Legacies of Miners' Strike. 256p. (C). 1988. lib. bdg. 45.00 (0-415-00724-0) Routledge.

McCabe, Susan. Elizabeth Bishop: Her Poetics of Loss. LC 93-30390. 1994. 45.00 (0-271-01047-9); pap. 16.95 (0-271-01048-7) Pa St U Pr.

McCabe, Thomas R. Supervictim Syndrome: How to Break the Cycle. 64p. 1992. pap. 4.95 (1-56246-008-0, P168) Johnsn Inst.

— Victims No More. LC 77-94792. 104p. (Orig.). 1978. pap. 9.00 (0-89486-049-6, 1112) Hazelden.

McCabe, Timothy L. Atlas of Adirondack Caterpillars. (Bulletin Ser.: No. 470). (Illus.). 114p. (Orig.). (C). 1991. pap. text ed. 19.95 (1-55557-185-9) NYS Museum.

McCabe, Vickie & Balzano, Gerald J., eds. Event Cognition: An Ecological Perspective. (Ecological Psychology Ser.). 304p. (C). 1986. text ed. 59.95 (0-89859-811-7) L Erlbaum Assocs.

*McCabe, Victoria, ed. John Keats's Porridge: Favorite Recipes of American Poets. 1975. pap. 9.95 (0-87745-058-7) U of Iowa Pr.

McCabe, Warren L., et al. Unit Operations in Chemical Engineering. 5th ed. LC 92-36218. (McGraw-Hill Chemical Engineering Ser.). 1993. text ed. write for info. (0-07-044844-2) McGraw.

McCabe, William H. An Introduction to the Jesuit Theater. LC 83-81114. (Original Studies Composed in English Series III: No. 6). xiv, 346p. 1983. pap. 19.00 (0-912422-62-9) Inst Jesuit.

McCadden, Charlene S. The Masterbuilder. (Illus.). 14p. (Orig.). 1988. pap. 3.00 (0-9620794-0-5) King Realm Pubns.

McCadden, Joseph J. Education in Pennsylvania, 1801-1835 & Its Debt to Robert Vaux. LC 78-89199. (American Education: Its Men, Institutions & Ideas, Ser. 1). 1978. reprint ed. 19.95 (0-405-01438-4) Ayer.

McCaddin, Joe. Duck Stamps & Prints. 1990. 19.99 (0-517-01780-6) Random Hse Value.

McCaffer, Ronald, jt. auth. see Harris, Frank.

*McCafferty. Hanky Panky. 1995. mass mkt. 5.50 (0-671-51049-5) PB.

McCafferty, Dermot, jt. auth. see Woolfson, David.

McCafferty, Donald N. Successful Field Service Management. LC 79-54842. 191p. reprint ed. pap. 54.50 (0-317-26903-8, 2023561) Bks Demand.

McCafferty, James. Human & Computer Vision: Perceptual Organization. 1990. text ed. 79.00 (0-13-445396-4) P-H.

McCafferty, Jane. Director of the World & Other Stories. LC 92-11734. (Drue Heinz Literature Prize Ser.). 160p. (C). 1992. text ed. 22.50 (0-8229-3729-8) U of Pittsburgh Pr.

McCafferty, Jeanne. Star Gazer. 208p. 1994. 19.95 (0-312-11074-X) St Martin.

McCafferty, Jim. Holt & the Cowboys. LC 93-16618. (Illus.). 40p. (J). (gr. 4-8). 1993. 12.95 (0-88289-985-6) Pelican.

— Holt & the Teddy Bear. LC 90-44060. (Illus.). 40p. (J). (gr. 4-8). 1991. 12.95 (0-88289-823-X) Pelican.

*McCafferty, Lawrence. The Heart of the Mystery. LC 94-75863. (Art of Meditation Ser.). 152p. (Orig.). 1995. pap. 11.95 (1-884884-04-0) La Chevre dOr Pr.

McCafferty, Mell, jt. auth. see Murphy, Pat.

McCafferty, Michael D. & Meyer, Steven M. Medical Malpractice: Bases of Liability. LC 84-23580. 494p. 1985. text ed. 125.00 (0-07-044837-X) Shepards-McGraw.

McCafferty, Nell. The Best of Nell: A Selection of Writings Over 14 Years. 128p. (C). 1987. pap. 9.99 (0-946211-06-X, Pub. by Attic IE) InBook.

— Goodnight Sisters Vol. 2: Selected Writings. 160p. (C). 1994. pap. 15.99 (0-946211-36-1, Pub. by Attic IE) InBook.

— In the Eyes of the Law. 185p. 1987. pap. 8.95 (0-905169-95-6, Pub. by Poolbeg Pr IE) Dufour.

— Peggy Deery: A Derry Family at War. 144p. (Orig.). (C). 1988. pap. 11.95 (0-946211-55-8, Pub. by Attic IE) InBook.

— Peggy Deery: A Derry Family at War. 1992. 25.00 (0-946211-58-2, Pub. by Attic Pr IE) St Mut.

— Peggy Deery: An Irish Family at War. 144p. (Orig.). 1989. 21.95 (0-939416-29-8); pap. 9.95 (0-939416-28-X) Cleis Pr.

— A Woman to Blame: The Kerry Babies Case. 176p. (Orig.). (C). 1985. pap. 7.95 (0-946211-21-3, Pub. by Attic IE) InBook.

McCafferty, Owen, jt. ed. see Sheridan, John.

McCafferty, Stephen. Macroeconomic Theory. 448p. (C). 1990. text ed. 70.50 (0-06-044324-3) HarpCollege.

McCafferty, Taylor. Bed Bugs. Chelius, Jane, ed. 256p. (Orig.). 1993. mass mkt. 5.50 (0-671-75468-8) PB.

— Pet Peeves. Chelius, Jane, ed. 224p. (Orig.). 1990. pap. 4.99 (0-671-72802-4) PB.

— Ruffled Feathers. Chelius, Jane, ed. 224p. (Orig.). 1992. mass mkt. 4.50 (0-671-72803-2) PB.

— Thin Skins. 1994. mass mkt. 4.99 (0-671-79977-0) PB.

McCafferty, Thomas A. In House Telemarketing: The Masterplan for Starting & Managing a Profitable. rev. ed. 1993. 27.50 (1-55738-529-7) Probus Pub Co.

— Winning with Managed Futures: How to Select a Top Performing Commodity Trading Advisor. 1994. 47.50 (1-55738-587-4) Probus Pub Co.

McCafferty, Thomas A. & Wasendorf, Russell R. All about Futures: From the Inside Out. 300p. 1992. 19.95 (1-55738-296-4) Probus Pub Co.

— All about Options: From the Inside Out. 225p. 1993. pap. 19.95 (1-55738-434-7) Probus Pub Co.

McCafferty, Thomas A., jt. auth. see Wasendorf, Russell R.

McCafferty, W. Patrick. Aquatic Entomology: The Fisherman's & Ecologists Illustrated Guide to Insects & Their Relatives. (Illus.). 448p. (C). 1982. pap. 50.00 (0-86720-017-0) Jones & Bartlett.

— Aquatic Entomology: The Fisherman's & Ecologists Illustrated Guide to Insects & Their Relatives. deluxe ed. (Illus.). 448p. (C). 1982. 300.00 (0-86720-010-3) Jones & Bartlett.

McCaffery, A. R. & Wilson, I. D., eds. Chromatography & Isolation of Insect Hormones & Pheromones. (Chromatographic Society Symposium Ser.). (Illus.). 360p. 1990. 95.00 (0-306-43707-4, Plenum Pr) Plenum.

McCaffery, Anne. Killashandra. LC 85-6193. 303p. 1985. 25. 00 (0-89366-187-2) Ultramarine Pub.

McCaffery-Beebe. Pain: Clinical Manual for Nursing Practice. (Illus.). 376p. 1989. spiral bd. 29.95 (0-8016-3248-X) Mosby Yr Bk.

McCaffery, Janet & Lindemeyer, Nancy. A Show of Hands: Needlepoint Designs. LC 94-13327. (Illus.). 1994. 27.00 (0-688-11297-8) Morrow.

McCaffery, Jerry L., jt. auth. see Jones, L. R.

McCaffery, Larry. The Metafictional Muse: The Work of Robert Coover, Donald Barthelme, & William H. Gass. LC 82-1872. (Critical Essays in Modern Literature Ser.). xi, 256p. 1982. 49.95 (0-8229-3462-0) U of Pittsburgh Pr.

McCaffery, Larry, ed. Across the Wounded Galaxies: Interviews with Contemporary American Science Fiction Writers. (Illus.). 280p. 1990. 29.95 (0-252-01692-0) U of Ill Pr.

— Across the Wounded Galaxies: Interviews with Contemporary American Science Fiction Writers. (Illus.). 300p. 1991. pap. 12.95 (0-252-06140-3) U of Ill Pr.

— After Yesterday's Crash: The Avant-Pop Anthology. LC 94-48772. 1995. write for info. (0-01-402485-3, Penguin Bks) Viking Penguin.

*McCaffery, Larry, ed. & intro. After Yesterday's Crash: The Avant-Pop Anthology. 320p. (Orig.). 1995. pap. 12. 95 (0-14-024085-3, Penguin Bks) Viking Penguin.

McCaffery, Larry, ed. Avant-Pop: Fiction for a Daydream Nation. (Black Ice Books Ser.). (Illus.). 247p. 1993. pap. 7.00 (0-932511-72-4) Fiction Coll.

— Storming the Reality Studio: A Casebook of Cyberpunk & Postmodern Science Fiction. LC 91-14316. (Illus.). 405p. 1991. lib. bdg. 52.95 (0-8223-1158-5); pap. 19.95 (0-8223-1168-2) Duke.

McCaffery, Larry & Gregory, Sinda, eds. Alive & Writing: Interviews with American Authors of the 1980s. LC 86-25075. (Illus.). 296p. (C). 1987. 29.95 (0-252-01385-9) U of Ill Pr.

McCaffery, Larry, jt. ed. see Jaffe, Harold.

McCaffery, Larry, jt. ed. see Jeffe, Harold.

McCaffery, Lawrence F., ed. Postmodern Fiction: A Bio-Bibliographical Guide. LC 85-17723. (Movements in the Arts Ser.: No. 2). 632p. 1986. text ed. 85.00 (0-313-24170-8, MML/, Greenwood Pr) Greenwood.

McCaffery, M. A. Irish Trivia. 1990. 6.99 (0-685-33412-0); pap. 7.99 (0-517-69909-5) Random Hse Value.

*McCaffery, Michael. Directing a Play. rev. ed. (Theater Manuals Ser.). (Illus.). 128p. 1995. reprint ed. pap. 14.95 (0-7148-2513-1, Pub. by Phaidon Press UK) Chronicle Bks.

— Directing a Play, Vol. 1. Mayer, David, ed. (Theatre Manuals Ser.). 1991. pap. 8.95 (0-02-871342-7) Schirmer Bks.

McCaffery, Peter. When Bosses Ruled Philadelphia: The Emergence of the Republican Machine, 1867-1933. LC 92-42467. (Illus.). 304p. 1993. 35.00 (0-271-00923-3) Pa St U Pr.

McCaffery, Robert M. Employee Benefit Programs: A Total Compensation Perspective. 2nd ed. 250p. 1992. pap. 20. 95 (0-534-92814-5) Intl Thomson.

McCaffery, Steve. North of Intention. LC 86-63324. (Roof Bks.). 240p. (Orig.). 1987. pap. 12.95 (0-937804-23-1) Segue NYC.

— Theory of Sediment. 160p. 1991. pap. 11.95 (0-88922-299-1) SPD-Small Pr Dist.

McCaffery, Steve, ed. The Toronto Research Group Reports. 320p. 1991. pap. 18.95 (0-88922-300-9) SPD-Small Pr Dist.

McCaffery, Steve & Nichol, B. P. Rational Geomancy, the Kids of the Book Machine: The Collected Research Reports of the Toronto Research Group, 1973-1982. (Illus.). 320p. (Orig.). 1993. pap. 16.95 (0-317-05589-5, Pub. by Talonbooks CN) InBook.

McCaffray, Susan P., ed. see Fenin, Aleksandr I.

*McCaffree, Maryjane & Innis, Pauline. Protocol: The Complete Handbook of Diplomatic Official & Social Usage. rev. ed. LC 85-71131. (Illus.). 414p. 1989. reprint ed. pap. text ed. 20.00 (0-941402-08-8) Devon Pub.

McCaffree, R., ed. Critical Care in Internal Medicine. (Progress in Critical Care Medicine Ser.: Vol. 2). (Illus.). viii, 352p. 1985. 76.00 (3-8055-3900-2) S Karger.

McCaffrey, A. & Scarborough. The Powers That Be. 1994. mass mkt. 5.99 (0-345-38779-1, Del Rey) Ballantine.

McCaffrey, Anne. Alchemy & Academe. 1987. mass mkt. 4.95 (0-345-34419-7, Del Rey) Ballantine.

— All the Weyrs of Pern. 1992. mass mkt. 5.99 (0-345-36893-2, Del Rey) Ballantine.

— The Chronicles of Pern: First Fall. 1994. mass mkt. 5.99 (0-345-36899-1, Del Rey) Ballantine.

— The Chronicles of Pern: The First Fall. 1992. 22.00 (0-345-36898-3, Del Rey) Ballantine.

— Coelura. 176p. 1989. pap. 3.95 (0-8125-0297-3) Tor Bks.

— Crisis on Doona. 1992. mass mkt. 4.99 (0-441-23194-2) Ace Bks.

— Crystal Line. 1993. mass mkt. 5.99 (0-345-38491-1, Del Rey) Ballantine.

— Crystal Singer. 320p. (Orig.). 1985. mass mkt. 4.95 (0-345-32786-1, Del Rey) Ballantine.

— Damia. 352p. 1993. mass mkt. 5.99 (0-441-13556-0) Ace Bks.

— Damia's Children. 336p. 1994. 5.99 (0-441-00007-X) Ace Bks.

An Asterisk (*) at the beginning of an entry indicates that the title is appearing in BIP for the first time.

— Damia's Children. LC 92-31601. 272p. 1993. 22.95 (0-399-13817-X, Ace-Putnam) Putnam Pub Group.

— Damia's Children. limited ed. LC 92-31601. 272p. 1993. 100.00 (0-399-13836-6, Ace-Putnam) Putnam Pub Group.

— Decision at Doona. 256p. 1987. mass mkt. 4.95 (0-345-35377-3, Del Rey) Ballantine.

— Dinosaur Planet. 1984. mass mkt. 5.99 (0-345-31995-8, Del Rey) Ballantine.

— The Dinosaur Planet Survivors. 304p. 1984. mass mkt. 4.95 (0-345-27246-3, Del Rey) Ballantine.

— The Dolphins of Pern. 416p. 1994. 22.00 (0-345-36894-0, Del Rey) Ballantine.

— Dragondrums. 208p. 1980. mass mkt. 5.99 (0-553-25855-9, Spectra) Bantam.

— Dragondrums. LC 78-11318. (Illus.). 256p. (YA). (gr. 6 up). 1979. text ed. 16.95 (0-689-30685-7, Atheneum Bks Young) S&S Childrens.

— Dragonflight. 1978. 8.95 (0-345-27749-X, Del Rey) Ballantine.

— Dragonflight. 1986. mass mkt. 4.95 (0-345-33546-5, Del Rey) Ballantine.

— Dragonflight Graphic Novel. 1993. pap. 12.99 (0-06-105003-2, PL) HarpC.

— Dragonquest, Vol. 2. 1979. 8.95 (0-345-28030-X, Del Rey) Ballantine.

— Dragonquest, Vol. 2. 1986. mass mkt. 5.95 (0-345-33508-2, Del Rey) Ballantine.

— The Dragonriders of Pern, 3 vols., Set. 1986. Boxed set. boxed 23.80 (0-345-34045-0, Del Rey) Ballantine.

— The Dragonriders of Pern: Dragonflight, Dragonquest, The White Dragon. 832p. 1988. pap. 16.00 (0-345-34024-8, Del Rey) Ballantine.

— Dragonsdawn. (Dragonriders of Pern Ser.). 1989. mass mkt. 5.99 (0-345-36286-1, Del Rey) Ballantine.

— Dragonsdawn. 431p. 1988. 25.00 (0-89366-213-5) Ultramarine Pub.

— Dragonsdawn. braille ed. 804p. 1991. vinyl bd. 64.32 (1-56956-222-9, BR7601) W A T Braille.

— Dragonsinger. 256p. 1983. mass mkt. 5.99 (0-553-25854-0, Spectra) Bantam.

— Dragonsinger. LC 76-40988. 276p. (J). (gr. 5-9). 1977. text ed. 16.95 (0-689-30570-2, Atheneum Bks Young) S&S Childrens.

— Dragonsong. 176p. 1977. mass mkt. 5.99 (0-553-25852-4, Bantam Classics) Bantam.

— Dragonsong. LC 75-30530. 224p. (J). (gr. 5-9). 1976. text ed. 16.95 (0-689-30507-9, Atheneum Bks Young) S&S Childrens.

— Freedom's Landing. LC 94-43820. 1995. write for info. (0-399-14062-X, Putnam) Putnam Pub Group.

— The Girl Who Heard Dragons. 352p. 1994. 22.95 (0-312-93173-5) Tor Bks.

— The Girl Who Heard Dragons. 416p. 1995. mass mkt. 5.99 (0-8125-1099-2) Tor Bks.

— THe Harper Hall of Pern, 3 vols. in 1. 512p. 1984. 12.98 (1-56865-017-5, GuildAmerica) Dblday Bk Music.

— Killashandra. 1986. mass mkt. 5.99 (0-345-31600-2, Del Rey) Ballantine.

— The Lady. 1988. mass mkt. 4.95 (0-345-35674-8, Del Rey) Ballantine.

— The Lady. 461p. 1987. 25.00 (0-89366-214-3) Ultramarine Pub.

— Lyon's Pride. 272p. 1994. 22.95 (0-399-13907-9, Ace-Putnam) Putnam Pub Group.

— Lyon's Pride. 336p. (Orig.). 1995. pap. text ed. 5.99 (0-441-00141-6) Ace Bks.

— Lyon's Pride. limited ed. 272p. 1994. 100.00 (0-399-13953-2, Ace-Putnam) Putnam Pub Group.

— Moreta: Dragonlady of Pern. 1984. mass mkt. 5.95 (0-345-29873-X, Del Rey) Ballantine.

— Moreta: Dragonlady of Pern. LC 83-4630. 286p. 1983. 25.00 (0-89366-251-8) Ultramarine Pub.

— Nerilka's Story. 1987. mass mkt. 5.99 (0-345-33949-5, Del Rey) Ballantine.

— Pegasus in Flight. 304p. 1991. mass mkt. 5.99 (0-345-36897-5, Del Rey) Ballantine.

— The Renegades of Pern. LC 89-6694. 448p. 1989. 19.95 (0-345-34096-5, Del Rey) Ballantine.

— The Renegades of Pern. 384p. 1989. text ed. 25.00 (0-89366-284-4) Ultramarine Pub.

— Renegades of Pern. 1990. mass mkt. 5.95 (0-345-36933-5, Del Rey) Ballantine.

— Restoree. 1987. mass mkt. 5.99 (0-345-35187-8, Del Rey) Ballantine.

— Rowan. 1991. mass mkt. 5.99 (0-441-73576-2) Ace Bks.

— The Ship Who Sang. 1985. mass mkt. 4.95 (0-345-33431-0) Ballantine.

— Three Women. 1992. mass mkt. 5.99 (0-8125-0587-5) Tor Bks.

— To Ride Pegasus. 256p. 1986. mass mkt. 5.99 (0-345-33603-8, Del Rey) Ballantine.

— Treaty at Doona. Nye, Jody L., ed. 352p. (Orig.). 1994. pap. text ed. 5.99 (0-441-00089-4) Ace Bks.

— The White Dragon, No. 3. 1986. mass mkt. 5.95 (0-345-34167-8, Del Rey) Ballantine.

— Year of the Lucy. 320p. 1987. pap. 3.95 (0-8125-8565-8) Tor Bks.

McCaffrey, Anne & Ball, Margaret. PartnerShip. 336p. 1992. mass mkt. 5.99 (0-671-72109-7) Baen Bks.

McCaffrey, Anne & Lackey, Mercedes. The Ship Who Searched. 320p. 1992. mass mkt. 5.99 (0-671-72129-1) Baen Bks.

McCaffrey, Anne & Moon, Elizabeth. Generation Warriors. 1991. mass mkt. 5.99 (0-671-72041-4) Baen Bks.

— Sassinak. (Planet Pirate Ser.). 352p. 1990. mass mkt. 5.99 (0-671-69863-X) Baen Bks.

McCaffrey, Anne & Nye, Jody L. The Death of Sleep. (Orig.). 1990. mass mkt. 5.99 (0-671-69884-2) Baen Bks.

— The Ship Who Won. (Brain-Brawn Ser.). 336p. 1994. 21.00 (0-671-87595-7) Baen Bks.

— The Ship Who Won. 336p. 1995. mass mkt. 5.99 (0-671-87657-0) Baen Bks.

McCaffrey, Anne & Scarborough, Elizabeth A. Power Lines. 272p. 1994. 20.00 (0-345-38174-2, Del Rey) Ballantine.

— Power Lines. 1995. mass mkt. 5.99 (0-345-38780-5, Del Rey) Ballantine.

— Power Play. 304p. 1995. 22.00 (0-345-38826-7) Ballantine.

— Powers That Be. LC 92-54992. 272p. 1993. 20.00 (0-345-38173-4, Del Rey) Ballantine.

McCaffrey, Anne & Stirling, S. M. The City Who Fought. LC 93-2651. 432p. 1993. 19.00 (0-671-72166-6) Baen Bks.

— The City Who Fought. (Brain-Brawn Ser.). 448p. 1994. mass mkt. 5.99 (0-671-87599-X) Baen Bks.

McCaffrey, Anne, jt. auth. see Nye, Jody L.

McCaffrey, Anne, et al. Dragonflight, Bk. 1. (Illus.). 1991. 4.95 (1-56060-074-8) Eclipse Bks.

— Dragonflight, Bk. 2. (Illus.). 1991. 4.95 (1-56060-075-6) Eclipse Bks.

— Dragonflight, Bk. 3. (Illus.). 1991. 4.95 (1-56060-076-4) Eclipse Bks.

— The Planet Pirates. 864p. (Orig.). 1993. 12.00 (0-671-72187-9) Baen Bks.

McCaffrey, David P. The Politics of Nuclear Power: A History of the Shoreham Nuclear Power Plant. (Technology, Risk & Society Ser.). 276p. 1991. lib. bdg. 102.50 (0-7923-1035-7) Kluwer Ac.

McCaffrey, David P., ed. OSHA & the Politics of Health Regulation: Organizational & Political Changes in a Regulatory Agency. LC 82-11201. 210p. 1982. 42.50 (0-306-41050-8, Plenum Pr) Plenum.

McCaffrey, Donald W. Assault on Society: Satirical Literature to Film. LC 92-4040. (Illus.). 293p. 1992. 35.00 (0-8108-2507-4) Scarecrow.

— Assault on Society: Satirical Literature to Film. LC 92-4040. (Illus.). 293p. 1992. reprint ed. pap. 19.50 (0-8108-2594-5) Scarecrow.

— Three Classic Silent Screen Comedies Starring Harold Lloyd. LC 74-4993. (Illus.). 264p. 1976. 35.00 (0-8386-1455-8) Fairleigh Dickinson.

McCaffrey, Eugene V. & McCaffrey, Roger A. Players Choice. LC 86-19705. (Illus.). 240p. reprint ed. pap. 68.40 (0-7837-1567-6, 2041859) Bks Demand.

McCaffrey, Hugh, tr. see Isaac Of Stella.

McCaffrey, James. Thirsting for God in Scripture. 96p. 1984. pap. 4.95 (0-914544-55-1) Living Flame Pr.

McCaffrey, James M. Army of Manifest Destiny: The American Soldier in the Mexican War, 1846-1848. (American Social Experience Ser.). (Illus.). 275p. (C). 1992. 50.00 (0-8147-5468-6); pap. 17.95 (0-8147-5505-4) NYU Pr.

McCaffrey, James M., jt. auth. see Kinney, John F.

McCaffrey, Judy B., ed. see Harris, Brenda.

McCaffrey, Larry, jt. ed. see Jaffe, Harold.

***McCaffrey, Lawrence J.** The Irish Diaspora in America. LC 83-25280. reprint ed. pap. 63.90 (0-7837-9102-X, 2049904) Bks Demand.

— The Irish Question: Two Centuries of Conflict. 2nd ed. LC 95-6860. 240p. 1996. text ed. 34.95 (0-8131-1928-6); pap. 15.95 (0-8131-0855-1) U Pr of Ky.

— Textures of Irish America. (Irish Studies). (Illus.). 300p. 1992. 29.95 (0-8156-0267-7) Syracuse U Pr.

McCaffrey, Lawrence J., ed. Irish Nationalism & the American Contribution. LC 76-6354. (Irish Americans Ser.). 1976. 23.95 (0-405-09347-0) Ayer.

McCaffrey, Lawrence J., jt. ed. see Hachey, Thomas E.

McCaffrey, Lawrence J., et al. The Irish in Chicago. LC 86-24977. (Ethnic History of Chicago Ser.). (Illus.). 184p. (C). 1987. 24.95 (0-252-01397-2) U of Ill Pr.

McCaffrey, Lawrence J., et al, eds. Ideas, Concepts, Doctrine: A History of Basic Thinking in the United States Air Force, 1907-1964. LC 79-7255. (Flight: Its First Seventy-Five Years Ser.). 1980. reprint ed. lib. bdg. 52.95 (0-405-12166-0) Ayer.

McCaffrey, Margot K., tr. To the Chukchi Peninsula & to the Tlingit Indians, 1881-1882: Journals & Letters by Aurel & Arthur Krause. LC 92-47100. (Rasmuson Library Historical Translation Ser.: Vol. VIII). (Illus.). xiii, 230p. (ENG & GER.). 1993. pap. 17.50 (0-912006-66-8) U of Alaska Pr.

McCaffrey, Moira, et al. Wrapped in the Colours of the Earth: Cultural Heritage of the First Nations. (Illus.). 128p. 1992. pap. 34.95 (0-7735-0968-2, Pub. by McGill CN) U of Toronto Pr.

McCaffrey, Patrick, jt. auth. see Flanagan, Richard W.

McCaffrey, R. J., jt. ed. see Puente, A. E.

McCaffrey, Roger A., jt. auth. see McCaffrey, Eugene V.

McCaffrey, Rosanne, ed. see Platou, Dode.

McCaffrey, Thomas V., ed. System Disease & the Nasal Airway. LC 92-49198. (Rhinology & Sinusology Ser.). 1993. 49.00 (0-86577-466-8) Thieme Med Pubs.

McCaffrey, Thomas V. & Kern, Eugene B. The Obstructed Nasal Airway: Evaluation & Treatment. 1995. write for info. (0-7817-0193-7) Raven.

McCaffry, Annie. Journey to My Self: The Healing & Transformation of Family Patterns. 196p. 1992. pap. 12.95 (1-85230-362-X) Element MA.

McCagg, William O., Jr. A History of Habsburg Jews, 1670-1918. LC 88-544. (Illus.). 304p. 1992. 29.95 (0-253-33189-7); pap. 12.95 (0-253-20649-9, MB-649) Ind U Pr.

— Jewish Nobles & Geniuses in Modern Hungary. LC 73-189944. (East European Monographs: No. 3). 256p. 1972. text ed. 44.00 (0-88033-092-9) East Eur Quarterly.

McCagg, William O. Stalin Embattled, Nineteen Forty-Three to Nineteen Forty-Eight. LC 77-28286. 424p. reprint ed. pap. 120.90 (0-685-20906-7, 2032034) Bks Demand.

McCagg, William O. & Siegelbaum, Lewis, eds. The Disabled in the Soviet Union: Past & Present, Theory & Practice. LC 89-40206. (Series in Russian & East European Studies). 310p. 1989. 49.95 (0-8229-3622-4) U of Pittsburgh Pr.

McCagg, William O., Jr. & Silver, Brian D., eds. Soviet Asian Ethnic Frontiers. LC 77-11796. (Policy Studies). (Illus.). 1979. 96.00 (0-08-024637-0, Pergamon Pr) Elsevier.

McCaghy, Charles H. Deviant Behavior: Crime, Conflict, & Interest Groups. 2nd ed. LC 84-14390. (C). 1985. pap. write for info. (0-02-378450-4) Macmillan.

McCaghy, Charles H. & Capron, Timothy H. Deviant Behavior: Crime, Conflict, & Interest Groups. 3rd ed. LC 93-24352. (Illus.). 512p. (C). 1993. pap. write for info. (0-02-378462-8, Maxwell Macmillan) Macmillan.

McCaghy, Charles H. & Cernkovich, Stephen A. Crime in American Society. 2nd ed. 496p. (C). 1987. text ed. write for info. (0-02-378340-0) Macmillan.

McCague, James P. The Ivory Legend. (Orig.). 1979. pap. 2.25 (0-89083-459-8) Zebra.

***McCahery, Joseph, et al, eds.** Corporate Control & Accountability: Changing Structures & Dynamics of Regulation. (Illus.). 272p. 1995. pap. 32.00 (0-19-825990-5) OUP.

— Corporate Control & Accountability: Changing Structures & the Dynamics of Regulation. LC 92-19420. 1994. 45.00 (0-19-825827-5, Clarendon Pr) OUP.

***McCahrey, James R.** What Evil Lurks: A Lavina London Mystery. 304p. 1995. 16.95 (0-8217-4797-5) Zebra.

McCaig & Boyce. Alabama State Parks. 100p. (Orig.). 1989. pap. text ed. 5.95 (0-935201-62-9) Affordable Adven.

— Maine State Parks. (Illus.). 100p. (Orig.). 1989. pap. text ed. 5.95 (0-935201-64-5) Affordable Adven.

— Maryland State Parks. (Illus.). 100p. (Orig.). 1989. pap. text ed. 5.95 (0-935201-63-7) Affordable Adven.

— Massachusetts State Park. (Illus.). 100p. (Orig.). 1989. pap. text ed. 5.95 (0-935201-67-X) Affordable Adven.

— Minnesota State Parks. (Illus.). 100p. (Orig.). 1989. pap. text ed. 5.95 (0-935201-68-8) Affordable Adven.

— New Mexico State Parks. (Illus.). 100p. (Orig.). 1989. pap. text ed. 5.95 (0-935201-66-1) Affordable Adven.

— North Carolina State Parks. (Illus.). 100p. (Orig.). 1989. pap. text ed. 5.95 (0-935201-65-3) Affordable Adven.

— Wisconsin State Parks. (Illus.). 100p. (Orig.). 1989. pap. text ed. 5.95 (0-935201-69-6) Affordable Adven.

McCaig, Barb. Alabama Biking Guide. Boyce, Chris, ed. (Illus.). 80p. (Orig.). 1989. pap. text ed. 5.95 (0-935201-81-5) Affordable Adven.

— Minnesota Biking Guide. Vanderboom, Gretchen, ed. 100p. (Orig.). 1989. pap. text ed. 5.95 (0-935201-78-5) Affordable Adven.

— New York Biking Guide. Vanderboom, Gretchen, ed. 100p. (Orig.). 1989. pap. text ed. 5.95 (0-935201-83-1) Affordable Adven.

— Wisconsin Biking Guide. Vanderboom, Cary, ed. (Illus.). 100p. (Orig.). 1989. pap. text ed. 5.95 (0-935201-77-7) Affordable Adven.

McCaig, Barb, ed. see Boyce, Chris.

McCaig, Barb, ed. see McCaig, Margie & Boyce, Chris.

McCaig, Barb, jt. auth. see Soli, Lynn.

McCaig, Barbara. Dakota's Parks Guide. Boyce, Chris, ed. (Illus.). 120p. (Orig.). 1989. pap. text ed. 5.95 (0-935201-82-3) Affordable Adven.

— Dining Out Milwaukee. 3rd rev. ed. Boyce, Chris, ed. 150p. 1988. pap. 4.95 (0-935201-42-4) Affordable Adven.

— Door Country Family Fun & Adventure Guide. Bussler, Rod, ed. 120p. (Orig.). 1987. pap. text ed. 7.95 (0-935201-21-1) Affordable Adven.

— Illinois Biking Guide. Vanderboom, Gretchen, ed. 100p. (Orig.). 1989. pap. text ed. 5.95 (0-935201-80-7) Affordable Adven.

— Oregon Parks Guide. Boyce, Chris, ed. 100p. (Orig.). 1988. pap. text ed. 5.95 (0-935201-41-6) Affordable Adven.

— Texas Parks Guide. Boyce, Chris, ed. 100p. (Orig.). 1988. pap. text ed. 5.95 (0-935201-40-8) Affordable Adven.

McCaig, Barbara & Boyce, Chris. California Parks Guide. 130p. 1988. pap. 5.95 (0-935201-36-X) Affordable Adven.

McCaig, Barbara, ed. see Boyce, Chris.

McCaig, Barbara, ed. see Jones, Penny.

McCaig, Barbara, ed. see Powers, William H.

McCaig, Barbara, jt. auth. see Soli, Lynn D.

McCaig, Barbara, jt. auth. see Soli, Lynn.

McCaig, Donald. American Homeplace. (Illus.). 224p. 1992. 20.00 (0-517-58487-5, Crown) Crown Pub Group.

— Eminent Dogs - Dangerous Men. large type ed. 1992. 22.95 (0-7927-1198-X, CH0253, Curley Lrg Print) Chivers N Amer.

— Eminent Dogs - Dangerous Men. large type ed. 1992. pap. 20.95 (0-7927-1199-8, Curley Lrg Print) Chivers N Amer.

— Eminent Dogs, Dangerous Men: Searching Through Scotland for a Border Collie. LC 90-55055. (Illus.). 224p. 1992. reprint ed. pap. 11.00 (0-06-098114-8, E Burlingame Bks) HarpC.

— The Man Who Made the Devil Glad. 1987. pap. 3.95 (0-685-19193-1) St Martin.

— Nop's Hope. 1994. 20.00 (0-517-58488-3, Crown) Crown Pub Group.

— Nop's Trials. 336p. 1992. pap. 13.95 (1-55821-185-3) Lyons & Burford.

McCaig, Margie & Boyce, Chris. Indiana Parks Guide. McCaig, Barb, ed. (Illus.). 100p. (Orig.). 1988. pap. text ed. 5.95 (0-935201-52-1) Affordable Adven.

McCaig, Robert. The Devil's Band. (Orig.). 1986. pap. 2.25 (0-8217-1903-3) Zebra.

McCain. Diagnostic & Operative Arthroscopy of the Temporomandibular Joint. (Illus.). 300p. 1993. 129.00 (0-8016-6074-2) Mosby Yr Bk.

McCain, Garvin & Segal, Erwin M. The Game of Science. 5th ed. LC 87-22396. 211p. (Orig.). (C). 1988. pap. 19.95 (0-534-09072-9) Brooks-Cole.

McCain, J. D. & Floyd, J. M., eds. Converting, Fire Refining & Casting: Proceedings. LC 94-81060. 381p. 1994. 42.00 (0-87339-263-9) Minerals Metals.

McCain, James. The Root of His Evil. large type ed. LC 93-697. (Large Print Bks.). 256p. 1993. pap. 16.95 (0-8161-5715-4) Hall.

McCain, John, et al. Deterrence in Decay: The Future of the U. S. Defense Industrial Base. (CSIS Panel Report). 67p. 1989. 24.95 (0-89206-139-1) CSI Studies.

McCain, John C., jt. auth. see Sadiq, Muhammad.

McCain, Liliane Q. & Strauss, Larry. What Do You Mean You Don't Want to Go to College? Turning Crisis into Opportunity for You & Your Child. 160p. 1990. 17.95 (0-929923-16-2) Lowell Hse.

— What Do You Mean You Don't Want to Go to College? Turning Crisis into Opportunity for You & Your Child. 156p. 1991. pap. 9.95 (0-929923-36-7) Lowell Hse.

McCain, Mic. Inflation: Its Real Causes. LC 82-90210. 126p. (Orig.). 1982. pap. 6.95 (0-9608314-0-1) McCain Pub.

McCain, Mollie Helen. Collector's Encyclopedia of Pattern Glass. (Illus.). 544p. 1990. pap. 12.95 (0-89145-211-7, 1380) Collector Bks.

McCain, Paul M. County Court in North Carolina Before Seventeen Fifty. LC 70-115996. (Duke University. Trinity College Historical Society. Historical Papers: No. 31). reprint ed. 30.00 (0-404-51781-1) AMS Pr.

McCain, R. Markets, Decisions & Organizations: Intermediate Microeconomic Theory. 1981. text ed. write for info. (0-13-557884-1) P-H.

McCain, Roger A. A Framework for Cognitive Economics. LC 91-44446. 336p. 1992. text ed. 62.50 (0-275-94142-6, C4142, Praeger Pubs) Greenwood.

McCain, Ron, jt. auth. see Garrett, Kyle.

McCain, Rych. Let's Get Rich! The Pre-Millionaire's Guide to Music & Business. Smith, Janeska, ed. (Illus.). 175p. (Orig.). 1984. pap. text ed. 6.95 (0-9611904-1-8) Highest Joy.

— Make It Go Right! 14p. 1990. 3.00 (0-9611904-2-6) Highest Joy.

McCain, Ted D. & Ekelund, Mark. Computer Networking for Educators. (Illus.). 244p. 1993. pap. text ed. 28.95 (1-56484-039-5) Intl Society Tech Educ.

McCain, Thomas A. & Shyles, Leonard, eds. The One Thousand Hour War: Communication in the Gulf. LC 93-12979. (Contributions in Military Studies: No. 148). 232p. 1993. text ed. 52.95 (0-313-28747-3, GM8747, Greenwood Pr) Greenwood.

McCain, W. Calvin. Pieces of Peace. LC 74-25235. 80p. 1983. reprint ed. pap. text ed. 5.95 (0-931680-01-8) Dunbar Pub.

— Soul in the Opera House. LC 82-229693. 80p. 1982. pap. 5.00 (0-931680-02-6) Dunbar Pub.

McCain, William D., Jr. Properties of Petroleum Fluids. 2nd ed. 596p. 1990. 84.95 (0-87814-335-1, P4465) PennWell Bks.

McCain, William D. United States & the Republic of Panama. LC 72-111724. (American Imperialism: Viewpoints of United States Foreign Policy, 1898-1941 Ser.). 1970. reprint ed. 21.95 (0-405-02036-8) Ayer.

***McCairen, Pat.** River Runner's Recipes. 127p. (Orig.). 1994. pap. 12.95 (0-89732-109-X) Menasha Ridge.

***McCaleb, Joseph.** How Do Teachers Communicate? Review & Critique of Assessment Practice. 1987. 9.50 (0-89333-046-9) AACTE.

***McCaleb, Sudia P.** Building Communities of Learners: A Collaboration Among Students, Teachers, Families & Community. 240p. 1994. pap. text ed. 13.00 (0-312-09163-X) St Martin.

McCaleb, Walter F. The Aaron Burr Conspiracy. Bd. with New Light on Aaron Burr. 476p. 1966. reprint ed. 20.00 (0-87266-021-4) Argosy.

McCaleb, Walter F., ed. see Reagan, John H.

McCall, Andrew. Medieval Underworld. 1992. 24.95 (0-88029-714-X) Marboro Bks.

McCall, Anne. The Last Survivors. LC 87-42909. 114p. 1988. pap. 7.95 (1-55523-117-9) Winston-Derek.

McCall, Anne B. Larger Vision: Tower-Room Talks. LC 77-156686. (Essay Index Reprint Ser.). 1977. reprint ed. 20.95 (0-8369-2283-2) Ayer.

McCall, B. The Cherokee. (Native American People Ser.). (Illus.). 32p. (J). (gr. 5-8). 1989. lib. bdg. 15.94 (0-86625-376-9); lib. bdg. 11.95 (0-685-58583-2) Rourke Corp.

— The Iroquois. (Native American People Ser.). (Illus.). 32p. (J). (gr. 5-8). 1989. 11.95 (0-685-58582-4); lib. bdg. 15.74 (0-86625-378-5) Rourke Corp.

McCall, Barbara. Apache. (Native American People Ser.). (Illus.). 32p. (J). (gr. 5-8). 1990. lib. bdg. 15.94 (0-86625-384-X); lib. bdg. 11.95 (0-685-36387-2) Rourke Corp.

— Daily Life. LC 94-5528. (Native American Culture Ser.). (J). 1994. write for info. (0-86625-534-6) Rourke Corp.

— The European Invasion. LC 94-5530. (Native American Culture Ser.). (J). (gr. 5 up). 1994. write for info. (0-86625-535-4) Rourke Pubns.

McCall, Barbara, et al. Native American People, 6 bks., Reading Level 4. (Illus.). 192p. (J). (gr. 5-8). 1989. lib. bdg. 71.70 (0-685-58768-1) Rourke Corp.

— Native American People, 6 bks., Set. (Illus.). 192p. (J). (gr. 5-8). 1989. lib. bdg. 95.64 (0-86625-375-0) Rourke Corp.

McCall, Barbara A. Los Apache. Marcuse, Aida E., tr. LC 92-12177. (J). 1992. 17.26 (0-86625-454-4); 12.95 (0-685-59386-X) Rourke Pubns.

McCall, Bevode C., jt. auth. see Maddox, George L.

M

McCall, Bruce F. Survival: The Ten Rules for Success in Petroleum Marketing. 145p. 15.00 (*0-685-65573-3*) Petro Mktg Ed Found.

McCall, Carlos, ed. see Zorotovich, Betty.

McCall, Catherine. Concepts of Person: An Analysis of Concepts of Person, Self & Human Being. 210p. 1990. text ed. 55.95 (*1-85628-039-X*, Pub. by Avebury Pub UK) Ashgate Pub Co.

McCall, Chester H., Sr. Action Guide to Sure-Sale Real Estate Listings. 1979. 49.50 (*0-13-003111-9*) Exec Reports.

McCall, Clare M. Captain John McCall, Seventeen Twenty-Six to Eighteen Twelve: His Ancestors & His Descendants. LC 85-18767. (Illus.). 185p. 1985. lib. bdg. 40.00 (*0-88082-012-8*) New Eng Hist.

McCall, Dan. Messenger Bird. 192p. 1993. 19.95 (*0-15-159284-5*) HarBrace.

— Messenger Bird. 1994. pap. 9.95 (*0-15-600042-3*) HarBrace.

— The Silence of Bartleby. LC 89-627. 240p. 1989. 33.50 (*0-8014-2320-1*); pap. 10.95 (*0-8014-9593-8*) Cornell U Pr.

McCall, David. Heart Failure. (Current Topics in Cardiology Ser.). 1994. 79.00 (*0-412-04441-2*) Chapman & Hall.

McCall, David, ed. Acute Myocardial Infarction. (Contemporary Management in Internal Medicine Ser.: Vol. 2, No. 2). (Illus.). 213p. 1992. text ed. 36.00 (*0-443-08838-1*) Churchill.

*__McCall, David E.__ Crimes Against Children: A Guide to Child Protection for Parents & Professionals. LC 95-68229. 200p. (Orig.). 1995. 19.95 (*1-884570-27-5*) Research Triangle.

McCall, Dewitt C., III. California Artists, Nineteen Thirty-Five to Nineteen Fifty-Six. McCall, Ruth, ed. LC 81-65529. (Illus.). 212p. 1981. lib. bdg. 50.00 (*0-939370-02-6*) DeRu's Fine Art.

McCall, Dorothy. The Theatre of Jean Paul Sartre. 1969. text ed. 46.00 (*0-231-03180-7*) Col U Pr.

— The Theatre of Jean Paul Sartre. 1971. pap. text ed. 16.50 (*0-231-08657-1*) Col U Pr.

McCall, Dorothy L. Copper King's Daughter: From Cape Cod to Crooked River. LC 74-188836. (Illus.). 200p. 1972. pap. 9.95 (*0-8323-0203-1*) Binford Mort.

McCall, Douglas L. Monty Python: A Chronological Listing of the Troupe's Creative Output, & Articles & Reviews about Them, 1969-1989. LC 91-52638. 222p. 1991. lib. bdg. 32.50x (*0-89950-559-7*) McFarland & Co.

McCall, Edith. Better Than a Brother. (Illus.). 1988. 13.95 (*0-8027-6782-6*); 14.85 (*0-8027-6783-4*) Walker & Co.

— Biography of a River: The Mississippi. (Illus.). (YA). (gr. 7 up). 1990. 16.95 (*0-8027-6914-4*); lib. bdg. 17.85 (*0-8027-6915-2*) Walker & Co.

— Message from the Mountains. Nankin, Fran, ed. LC 85-3142. (Walker's American History Series for Young People). (Illus.). 122p. (J). (gr. 6-9). 1985. 11.95 (*0-8027-6582-3*) Walker & Co.

— Mississippi Steamboatman: The Story of Henry Miller Shreve. LC 85-13795. (Walker's American History Series for Young People). (Illus.). 115p. (J). (gr. 5-8). 1986. 11.95 (*0-8027-6597-1*) Walker & Co.

— Sometimes We Dance Alone. large type ed. LC 94-41433. 236p. 1995. 19.95 (*0-7838-1190-X*, Large Print Bks) Hall.

— Sometimes We Dance Alone: Your Next Years Can Be Your Best Years. LC 93-23419. 192p. 1994. 16.95 (*0-9636620-0-7*) Brett Bks.

McCall, Elizabeth B. Old Philadelphia Houses on Society Hill, 1750-1840. (Illus.). 1966. 22.50 (*0-8038-0194-7*) Archit CT.

McCall, Emmanuel L. Black Church Life-Styles. LC 86-17591. 1986. pap. 5.99 (*0-8054-5665-1*) Broadman.

McCall, Francis X., Jr., jt. auth. see Keeler, Patricia A.

McCall, G. J. & Marker, B. R., eds. Earth Science Mapping for Planning, Development & Conservation. (C). 1989. lib. bdg. 169.50 (*0-86010-989-5*, Pub. by Graham & Trotman UK) Kluwer Ac.

McCall, G. J., et al. Geohazards: Natural & Man-Made. Lamming, D. & Scott, S., eds. (Illus.). 236p. (C). 1992. text ed. 99.95 (*0-412-43920-4*, A6979); pap. text ed. 39.95 (*0-412-43930-1*, A6983) Chapman & Hall.

McCall, George A. Letters from the Frontiers: A Facsimile Reproduction of the 1868 Edition with an Introduction & Index by John K. Mahon. LC 74-22038. (Bicentennial Floridian Facsimile Ser.). (Illus.). 591p. reprint ed. pap. 168.50 (*0-7837-0596-4*, 2040944) Bks Demand.

McCall, George J., jt. auth. see Weber, George H.

McCall, Grant. Rapanui: Tradition & Survival on Easter Island. 2nd ed. LC 93-48273. 1994. pap. text ed. 14.95 (*0-8248-1641-2*) UH Pr.

McCall, Grant, ed. see Young Nations Conference, Sidney, 1976 Staff.

McCall, Helen. French Flower Beading, No. One: A Guide for Beginners. Spears, Therese, ed. (Illus.). 28p. (Orig.). 1993. pap. 12.95 (*0-932255-04-3*) Promenade Pub.

McCall, Henrietta. Mesopotamian Myths. (Legendary Past Ser.). (Illus.). 80p. 1991. pap. 9.95 (*0-292-75130-3*) U of Tex Pr.

McCall, I. Communication Problem Solving: The Language of Effective Management. 1990. text ed. 71.50 (*0-471-92026-6*) Wiley.

McCall, J. B. & Warrington, M. B. Marketing by Agreement: A Cross Cultural Approach to Business Negotiations. 2nd ed. 330p. 1989. text ed. 49.95 (*0-471-92151-3*) Wiley.

McCall, J. L. & Steele, J. H., Jr., eds. Practical Applications of Quantitative Metallography - STP 839. LC 83-73230. 190p. 1984. text ed. 34.00 (*0-8031-0220-8*, 04-839000-28) ASTM.

McCall, Jack. The Principal's Edge. LC 94-4121. (Illus.). 250p. 1994. 34.95 (*1-883001-08-0*) Eye On Educ.

— The Small Town Survival Guide: Help for Changing the Economic Future of Your Town. 1993. 17.00 (*0-688-10021-X*) Morrow.

McCall, James. Antitrust. 2nd ed. (Sum & Substance Ser.). 1984. 15.95 (*0-940366-00-2*) Sum & Substance.

McCall, James L., et al, eds. Metallography & Interpretation of Weld Microstructures: Proceedings of a Symposium Co-Sponsored by the International Metallographic Society, ASM International, & the American Welding Society. LC 87-71104. (Illus.). 399p. reprint ed. pap. 113.80 (*0-8357-4091-9*, 2036857) Bks Demand.

*__McCall, James P.__ The Stallion: A Breeding Guide for Owners & Handlers. 1995. 29.95 (*0-87605-987-6*) Howell Bk.

McCall, Jeffrey J., et al. Marketing in the U. S. - Marketing in den USA. 153p. 1990. 30.00 (*0-86640-035-4*) German Am Chamber.

McCall, Jim. The Construction & Processing of Criterion Referenced Assessment. (C). 1989. 100.00 (*1-85098-016-0*, Pub. by Jordanhill College UK) St Mut.

— Influencing Horse Behavior: A Natural Approach to Training. LC 88-956. (Illus.). 98p. 1988. text ed. 14.95 (*0-931866-37-5*) Alpine Pubns.

McCall, Jody, ed. see Reuther, Ruth E.

McCall, John. Interactions with Ancestors in Everyday Life. 29p. 1989. 2.00 (*0-941934-54-3*) Indiana Africa.

McCall, John E., jt. auth. see Barnhill, J. B.

McCall, John J. Search, Symmetry & Arbitrage: A Unified Approach to the Social & Biological Sciences. 256p. 1929. text ed. 22.00 (*0-8133-0806-2*) Westview.

McCall, John J., ed. The Economics of Information & Uncertainty. LC 81-15930. (Conference Report - Universities - National Bureau Committee for Economic Research Ser.: No. 32). 346p. reprint ed. pap. 98.70 (*0-8357-3237-1*, 2057131) Bks Demand.

McCall, John J., jt. ed. see DesJardins, Joseph R.

McCall, Karen. Cougar: Ghost of the Rockies. LC 92-3691. (Illus.). 160p. 1993. reprint ed. pap. 20.00 (*0-87156-463-7*) Sierra.

McCall, Kathleen. Ivory Rose. 448p. 1988. pap. 3.75 (*0-8217-2269-7*) Zebra.

McCall, Linda, tr. see Waquet, Jean-Claude.

*__McCall, Linda L.__ If I Had a Hammer. 256p. 1995. 5.95 (*0-87067-748-9*) Holloway.

McCall, Malcolm & Ramsbotham, Oliver. Just Deterrence. 126p. 1990. 35.00 (*0-08-040704-8*, Pub. by Brasseys UK) Brasseys Inc.

McCall, Michael. Garth Brooks. 1991. mass mkt. 4.99 (*0-553-29823-2*) Bantam.

McCall, Michael K. Indigenous Technical Knowledge in Farming Systems of Eastern Africa: A Bibliography. (Bibliographies in Technology & Social Change Ser.: No. 9). 101p. (Orig.). (C). 1994. pap. 12.00 (*0-945271-34-4*) ISU-TSCP.

*__McCall, Michael W.__ The Worldwide Guide to Cheap Airfares: How to Travel the World without Breaking the Bank. 5th ed. White, Sue, ed. LC 94-77556. (Illus.). 256p. 1995. pap. 14.95 (*0-9633512-1-4*) Insider Pubns.

McCall, Michal M., jt. ed. see Becker, Howard S.

McCall, Morgan W., Jr. & Kaplan, Robert K. Whatever It Takes: Decision Makers at Work. (Illus.). 144p. 1985. text ed. 27.00 (*0-13-952086-4*) P-H.

McCall, Morgan W., Jr. & Lombardo, Michael M. Off the Track: Why & How Successful Executives Get Derailed. (Technical Report Ser.: No. 121G). 14p. 1983. pap. 10.00 (*0-912879-19-X*) Ctr Creat Leader.

McCall, Morgan W., Jr., ed. see Lindsey, Esther H. & Homes, Virginia.

McCall, Morgan W., Jr., jt. auth. see Lombardo, Michael M.

McCall, Morgan W., Jr., et al. The Lessons of Experience: How Successful Executives Develop on the Job. LC 87-46405. 224p. 1988. text ed. 22.95 (*0-669-18095-5*) Free Pr.

McCall, Nancy & Mix, Lisa A., eds. Designing Archival Programs to Advance Knowledge in the Health Fields. LC 93-40454. 256p. 1994. 38.50 (*0-8018-4761-3*) Johns Hopkins.

McCall, Nathan. Makes Me Wanna Holler: A Young Black Man in America. LC 93-30654. 1994. 23.00 (*0-679-41268-9*) Random.

— Makes Me Wanna Holler: A Young Black Man in America. 1995. pap. 12.00 (*0-679-74070-8*, Vin) Random.

— Makes Me Wanna Holler: A Young Black Man in America. 1995. 12.00 (*0-615-00496-2*, Vin) Random.

McCall, Peter & Lacy, Maryanne. Rise & Be Healed. 239p. (Orig.). 1992. pap. 15.00 (*0-936269-01-4*) Hse of Peace.

McCall, Peter L., jt. ed. see Tevesz, Michael J.

McCall, Randy & Siembieda, Kevin. Beyond the Supernatural. Marciniszyn, Alex & Siembieda, Florence, eds. (Illus.). 256p. (Orig.). (YA). (gr. 8 up). 1988. pap. 19.95 (*0-916211-18-5*, 700) Palladium Bks.

McCall, Raymond J. Phenomenological Psychology: An Introduction. LC 83-47764. 136p. 1983. text ed. 22.50 (*0-299-09410-3*); pap. 12.95 (*0-299-09414-6*) U of Wis Pr.

*__McCall, Robert.__ Study Guide Psychology. 7th ed. (C). 1992. pap. text ed. 20.00 (*0-15-572648-X*) HarBrace.

McCall, Robert B. Fundamental Statistics for the Behavioral Sciences. 5th ed. 464p. (C). 1990. pap. text ed. 20.00 (*0-15-529477-6*) HB Coll Pubs.

— Fundamental Statistics for the Behavioral Sciences. 5th ed. 464p. (C). 1990. text ed. 47.25 (*0-15-529476-8*) HB Coll Pubs.

— Infants. (Illus.). 185p. 1979. 23.00 (*0-674-45265-8*) HUP.

McCall, Robert B., et al. High School Underachievers. (Individual Differences & Development Ser.: Vol. 1). (Illus.). 160p. (C). 1992. 42.95 (*0-8039-4604-X*); pap. 18.95 (*0-8039-4605-8*) Sage.

McCall, Ruth, ed. see McCall, Dewitt C., III.

McCall, Ruth E. Phlebotomy. (Illus.). 256p. 1993. text ed. 27.95 (*0-397-54929-6*) Lippincott.

McCall, Samuel W. Business of Congress. LC 11-13147. reprint ed. 16.45 (*0-404-04101-9*) AMS Pr.

— Thaddeus Stevens. Morse, John T., Jr., ed. LC 78-128951. (American Statesmen Ser.: No. 31). reprint ed. 32.50 (*0-404-50881-2*) AMS Pr.

— Thomas B. Reed. Morse, John T., Jr., ed. LC 74-128950. (American Statesmen Ser.: No. 35). reprint ed. 32.50 (*0-404-50885-5*) AMS Pr.

McCall Smith, R. Alexander, jt. auth. see Mason, J. K.

McCall, Storrs. A Model of the Universe: Space-Time, Probability, & Decision. (Clarendon Library of Logic & Philosophy). (Illus.). 344p. 1994. 45.00 (*0-19-824053-8*) OUP.

McCall, Thomas. Beyond Ice, Beyond Death. LC 94-12713. 304p. 1995. 21.95 (*0-7868-6022-7*) Hyperion.

McCall, Thomas S. & Levitt, Zola. Coming: The End: Russia & Israel in Prophecy. 1992. pap. 8.99 (*0-8024-4007-X*) Moody.

*__McCall, Timothy B.__ Examining Your Doctor: A Patient's Guide to Avoiding Harmful Medical Care. 224p. 1995. 18.95 (*1-55972-282-7*, Birch Ln Pr) Carol Pub Group.

McCall, Vicki B., jt. auth. see Lowenkamp, William.

McCall, Virginia. Sunrise: A Support Program for Children of Divorced Parents. LC 92-26329. 160p. 1992. pap. 12.95 (*0-8091-3330-X*) Paulist Pr.

McCall, Walter M. Eighty Years of Cadillac LaSalle. LC 92-26171. (Motorbooks International Crestline Ser.). 1992. 34.95 (*0-87938-676-2*) Motorbooks Intl.

McCall, Walter P. American Fire Engines since 1900. LC 93-13160. (Crestline Ser.). 384p. 1993. 34.95 (*0-87938-829-3*) Motorbooks Intl.

McCall, Wayne, ed. see Andree, Herb, et al.

McCall, William A. & Crabbs, Lelah M. Standard Test Lessons in Reading. 3rd ed. 1979. pap. text ed. write for info. (*0-318-64746-X*); pap. text ed. 2.95 (*0-8077-5550-8*); pap. text ed. 2.95 (*0-8077-5552-4*); Book A, Grades 2-4. write for info. (*0-318-64747-8*) Tchrs Coll.

— Standard Test Lessons in Reading, Bk. C. 3rd ed. (J). (gr. 4-6). 1979. Book C, Grades 4-6. pap. text ed. 2.95 (*0-8077-5542-7*) Tchrs Coll.

— Standard Test Lessons in Reading, Bk. D. 3rd ed. (J). (gr. 5-7). 1979. Book D, Grades 5-7. pap. text ed. 2.95 (*0-8077-5544-3*) Tchrs Coll.

— Standard Test Lessons in Reading, Bk. B. 3rd ed. (J). (gr. 3-5). 1979. Book B, Grades 3-5. pap. text ed. 2.95 (*0-8077-5540-0*) Tchrs Coll.

— Standard Test Lessons in Reading, Bk. E. 3rd ed. (J). (gr. 6-8). 1979. Book E, Grades 6-8. pap. text ed. 2.95 (*0-8077-5546-X*) Tchrs Coll.

— Standard Test Lessons in Reading, Bk. F. 3rd ed. (YA). (gr. 7-12). 1979. Book F, Grades 7-12. pap. text ed. 2.95 (*0-8077-5548-6*) Tchrs Coll.

McCall, William A. & Harby, Mary L. Test Lessons in Primary Reading. 2nd ed. (J). (gr. 2-3). 1980. pap. text ed. 3.50 (*0-8077-5965-1*); 2.95 (*0-8077-5966-X*) Tchrs Coll.

McCall, William A., et al. Test Lessons in Reading Figurative Language. (gr. 9-12). 1980. pap. text ed. 6.95 (*0-8077-5970-8*); teacher ed 1.95 (*0-8077-5971-6*) Tchrs Coll.

McCall, Yvonne H. The Story of Jacob, Rachel & Leah. (Arch Bks.). (Illus.). 24p. (J). (gr. k-4). 1986. pap. 1.99 (*0-570-06205-5*, 59-1428) Concordia.

*__McCalla.__ Twentieth Century Music. 1995. pap. 42.00 (*0-02-871348-6*) Macmillan.

McCalla, Alex F. & Josling, Timothy E. Agricultural Policies of the World Markets. 1985. text ed. 43.00 (*0-07-044795-0*) McGraw.

McCalla, Douglas. The Upper Canada Trade, Eighteen Thirty-Four to Seventy-Two: A Study of the Buchanans' Business. LC 79-323032. 239p. reprint ed. pap. 68.20 (*0-8357-8361-8*, 2034006) Bks Demand.

McCalla, Gord & Greer, Jim, eds. Student Modelling: The Key to Individualized Knowledge-Based Instruction. LC 94-2917. (NATO ASI Series F: Computer & Systems Sciences, Special Programme AET: Vol. 125). 1994. 95.00 (*0-387-57510-3*) Spr-Verlag.

McCalla, James. Jazz: A Listener's Guide. (Illus.). 192p. 1982. 17.50 (*0-13-510172-7*) P-H.

— Jazz, a Listener's Guide. LC 93-24078. 1994. write for info. (*0-13-097940-6*) P-H.

McCalla, Robert B. Uncertain Perceptions: U. S. Cold War Crisis Decision Making. 250p. (C). 1992. text ed. 39.50 (*0-472-10228-1*) U of Mich Pr.

McCallen, Brian. Golf Resorts of the World: The Best Places to Stay & Play: A Golf Magazine Book. LC 93-21854. 1993. 45.00 (*0-8109-3372-1*) Abrams.

McCallen, James. Stand & Deliver: Stories of Irish Highwaymen. 128p. 1993. pap. 13.95 (*1-85635-036-3*, Pub. by Mercier Pr IE) Dufour.

McCalley, Bruce W. Model T Ford. LC 93-80697. (Illus.). 400p. 1994. 39.95 (*0-87341-293-1*) Krause Pubns.

McCalley, John. Nantucket Yesterday & Today. (Illus.). 176p. (Orig.). 1981. pap. 9.95 (*0-486-24059-2*) Dover.

McCalley, John W. Nantucket, Yesterday & Today. 18.00 (*0-8446-5902-9*) Peter Smith.

McCalley, Russell W. Marketing Channel Development & Management. LC 92-15768. 300p. 1992. text ed. 49.95 (*0-89930-780-9*, MKB, Quorum Bks) Greenwood.

McCalley, Stuart W. & Neeson, Francis J. Photographic Case Studies in Cardiopulmonary Disease: Diagnostic Tests for the Practitioner. (Photographic Case Studies). 1993. pap. text ed. write for info. (*0-9633775-6-6*) Clinical Comms.

McCallion, Barry. Art Maxims in a Bronx Fedora. 1973. pap. 1.75 (*0-911856-06-4*) Abyss.

McCallion, H. Vibration of Linear Mechanical Systems. LC 73-181235. 316p. reprint ed. pap. 90.10 (*0-317-11053-5*, 2006380) Bks Demand.

McCallion, Jean. Tough Roots. 78p. 1987. 9.95 (*0-920806-94-5*, Pub. by Penumbra Pr CN) U of Toronto Pr.

*__McCallion, Kenneth F.__ Shoreham & the Rise & Fall of the Nuclear Power Industry. LC 94-32930. 240p. 1995. text ed. 55.00 (*0-275-94299-6*, Praeger Pubs) Greenwood.

McCallion, Michael. The Voice Book: For Actors, Public Speakers, & Everyone Who Wants to Make Best Use of Their Voice. 256p. 1988. 45.00 (*0-87830-986-1*, Theatre Arts Bks); pap. 15.95 (*0-87830-987-X*, Theatre Arts Bks) Routledge Chapman & Hall.

McCallister, Linda. I Wish I'd Said That: How to Talk Your Way Out of Trouble & into Success. 336p. 1992. text ed. 29.95 (*0-471-55551-7*) Wiley.

— I Wish I'd Said That: How to Talk Your Way Out of Trouble & Into Success. 1994. pap. text ed. 14.95 (*0-471-00857-5*) Wiley.

McCall's Magazine Staff. McCall's Best One-Dish Meals. LC 94-1808. 1994. 21.95 (*0-316-55351-4*) Little.

McCall's Needlework & Crafts Editors. Cross-Stitch from a Country Garden. (Illus.). 168p. 1988. write for info. (*0-02-496900-1*) Macmillan.

McCall's Needlework & Crafts Staff. Xmas At Home. 1986. 22.95 (*0-02-609160-7*) Macmillan.

McCallum. Franchising in Canada: An Accounting, Auditing & Tax Analysis. 256p. 1991. pap. 34.00 (*0-409-89713-2*) Butterworth Legal Pubs.

— Idiom Drills. 2nd ed. 1982. pap. 17.95 (*0-8384-2853-3*) Heinle & Heinle.

— Words People Use. 1982. pap. 18.95 (*0-8384-2852-5*) Heinle & Heinle.

McCallum & Whitlow. Linking Mathematics & Language: Practical Classroom Activities. 140p. 1994. pap. text ed. 16.00 (*0-88751-038-8*, 00765) Heinemann.

*__McCallum, Barbara.__ More Than Beans & Cornbread: Traditional West Virginia Cooking. LC 93-86404. (Illus.). 200p. 1993. pap. text ed. 12.95 (*0-929521-81-1*) Pictorial Hist.

*__McCallum, Bennett T.__ International Monetary Economics. 224p. (C). 1995. 39.95 (*0-19-509494-8*) OUP.

— Monetary Economics: Theory & Policy. 352p. 1988. write for info. (*0-02-948981-4*) Macmillan.

— Monetary Economics: Theory & Practice. 480p. (C). 1989. text ed. write for info. (*0-02-378471-7*) Macmillan.

McCallum, Brian K. Breaking the Bread of Revelation, Vol. 1. 150p. (Orig.). (C). 1988. pap. text ed. 4.95 (*0-9620883-0-7*) McCallum Ministries.

— Israel: God's Glory, Vol. 3: Breaking the Bread of Revelation. 160p. (Orig.). 1990. pap. text ed. 4.95 (*0-9620883-2-3*) McCallum Ministries.

McCallum, Christine, jt. auth. see McCallum, Paul.

McCallum, Christine L., jt. auth. see McCallum, Paul.

McCallum, D. S. C. I. I. Liability Insurance, No. 220. (C). 1981. 230.00 (*0-685-33763-4*, Pub. by Witherby & Co UK) St Mut.

McCallum, David. The Social Production of Merit: Education, Psychology & Politics in Australia, 1900-1950. 224p. 1990. 55.00 (*1-85000-859-0*, Falmer Pr); pap. 26.00 (*1-85000-864-7*, Falmer Pr) Taylor & Francis.

— The Social Production of Merit: Education, Psychology & Politics in Australia 1900-1950. 224p. 1990. 50.00 (*1-85000-922-8*, Falmer Pr); pap. 22.00 (*1-85000-923-6*, Falmer Pr) Taylor & Francis.

McCallum, Dennis. Christianity: Faith That Makes Sense. 208p. 1992. pap. text ed. 3.99 (*0-8423-0525-4*) Tyndale.

— The Summons. LC 93-38603. 352p. (Orig.). 1993. pap. 11.00 (*0-89109-768-6*, NavPr) NavPress.

— Walking in Victory: Experiencing the Power of Your Identity. LC 94-19548. 240p. (Orig.). 1994. pap. 11.00 (*0-89109-835-6*, NavPr) NavPress.

McCallum, Donald F. Zenkoji & Its Icon: A Study in Medieval Japanese Religious Art. LC 93-41543. 1994. 39.50 (*0-691-03203-3*) Princeton U Pr.

McCallum, Frances T., jt. auth. see Bohlender, Dorothy G.

McCallum, Frances T., jt. auth. see McCallum, Henry D.

McCallum, George P. One Hundred & One Word Games. 1980. pap. text ed. 10.75 (*0-19-502742-6*) OUP.

— Visitor from Another Planet & Other Plays. (J). (gr. 4-6). 1982. student ed 7.95 (*0-19-502743-4*) OUP.

McCallum, George P., adapt. Seven Plays from American Literature. rev. ed. 1977. pap. 3.75 (*0-87789-062-5*); audio 39.50 (*0-87789-126-5*) ELS Educ Servs.

McCallum, Henry D. & McCallum, Frances T. The Wire That Fenced the West. LC 65-11234. (Illus.). 1985. pap. 15.95 (*0-8061-1559-9*) U of Okla Pr.

McCallum, Jack. Dream Team: The Inside Story of the Nineteen Ninety-Two U. S. Olympic Basketball Team. 1992. 19.95 (*0-316-55370-0*) Little.

McCallum, James. History of Giles County, Tennessee. 135p. 1983. reprint ed. pap. 15.00 (*0-89308-326-7*, TN 27) Southern Hist Pr.

— Trial by Fire. 1994. mass mkt. 4.99 (*0-553-29716-3*) Bantam.

McCallum, James D. Eleazar Wheelock. LC 78-89200. (American Education: Its Men, Institutions & Ideas, Ser. 1). 1975. reprint ed. 24.95 (*0-405-01439-2*) Ayer.

McCallum, John. The Complete Keys to Progress. Strossen, Randall J., ed. LC 93-80635. (Orig.). 1993. pap. 17.95 (*0-926888-01-3*) IronMind Enterprises.

— Unequal Beginnings: Agriculture & Economic Development in Quebec & Ontario until 1870. (State & Economic Life Ser.). 1980. pap. 15.95 (*0-8020-6362-4*) U of Toronto Pr.

— Unequal Beginnings: Agriculture & Economic Development in Quebec & Ontario until 1870. LC 80-501832. (State & Economic Life Ser.: No. 2). 159p. reprint ed. pap. 45.40 (*0-8357-4026-9*, 2036718) Bks Demand.

An Asterisk (*) at the beginning of an entry indicates that the title is appearing in BIP for the first time.

McCallum, Karen, ed. see Cohen, Larry.

McCallum, Karen T. & Granovetter, Pamela. The Copperfield Checklist of Mystery Authors. 2nd ed. (Copperfield Collection Ser.: Vol. 2). 160p. (Orig.). 1992. reprint ed. pap. 6.95 (*0-9617037-1-7*) Copperfld NY.

— A Shopping List of Mystery Classics. (Copperfield Collection Ser.: Vol. 1). 96p. (Orig.). 1986. pap. 6.95 (*0-9617037-0-9*) Copperfld NY.

McCallum, Paul. The Parent's Guide to Teaching Self-Defense. 144p. 1994. 12.95 (*1-55870-346-2*) Betterway Bks.

— A Practical Self-Defense Guide for Women. (Illus.). 200p. (Orig.). 1991. pap. 16.95 (*1-55870-203-2*) Betterway Bks.

— Spinning: A Guide to the World of Cycling. (Illus.). 192p. (Orig.). 1993. pap. 14.95 (*1-55870-286-5*) Betterway Bks.

— Underwater Adventures: Fifty of the World's Greatest! (Illus.). 160p. (Orig.). 1992. pap. 19.95 (*1-55870-255-5*) Betterway Bks.

McCallum, Paul & McCallum, Christine. A Parent's Guide to Teaching Skiing. (Parent's Guide Ser.). (Illus.). 144p. (Orig.). 1993. pap. 8.95 (*1-55870-309-8*) Betterway Bks.

McCallum, Paul & McCallum, Christine L. The Downhill Skiing Handbook. (Illus.). 192p. (Orig.). 1992. pap. 17.95 (*1-55870-254-7*) Betterway Bks.

McCallum, R. B. & Readman, Alison. British General Election of 1945. 311p. 1964. 35.00 (*0-7146-1566-8*, Pub. by F Cass Pubs UK) Intl Spec Bk.

***McCallum, R. C.** Australian Labour Law: Cases & Materials. Date not set. boxed write for info. (*0-409-30781-5*, Austral) Butterworth Legal Pubs.

— Australian Labour Law: Cases & Materials. 3rd ed. 1994. pap. 138.00 (*0-409-30731-9*, Austral) Butterworth Legal Pubs.

McCallum, Richard W., jt. ed. see Chen, Jiande Z.

McCallum, Rod, des. Plotting Sheets & Sight Forms for Yachtsmen. (C). 1989. 35.00 (*0-685-40424-2*, Pub. by Imray Laurie Norie & Wilson UK) St Mut.

***McCallum, Ron, et al, eds.** Employment Security. 1994. pap. 49.00 (*1-86287-146-9*, Pub. by Federation Pr AU) W W Gaunt.

McCallum, Ross A. Franchising: An Accounting, Auditing, & Income Tax Guide. LC 92-31967. 416p. 1993. text ed. 115.00 (*0-471-59119-X*) Wiley.

***McCallum, Sally & Ertel, Monica, eds.** Automated Systems for Access to Multilingual & Multiscript Library Materials: Proceedings of the Second IFLA Satelite Meeting, Madrid, August 18-19, 1993, 70. (IFLA Publications: vol. 70). 185p. 1994. 65.00 (*3-598-21797-8*) K G Saur.

***McCallum, Scott.** The Christian Life: An Owner's Manual. 128p. 1995. pap. 7.99 (*0-8254-3194-8*, 95-027) Kregel.

McCallum, Sheila & Strong, Anne. Starting Work in Sales. 128p. (C). 1987. 80.00 (*0-946139-27-X*, Pub. by Elm Pubns UK) St Mut.

McCallum, Taffy, told to. White Woman Witchdoctor: Tales from the African Life of Rae Graham. LC 92-72451. 1993. 22.95 (*0-933031-76-9*) Coun Oak Bks.

McCallum, Taffy G. White Woman Witch Doctor: Tales from the African Life of Rae Graham. LC 92-72451. (Illus.). 248p. (Orig.). 1994. pap. 12.95 (*0-933031-63-7*) Coun Oak Bks.

McCallum, Taffy G., told to. White Woman Witchdoctor: Tales of the African Life of Rae Graham. LC 92-72451. 248p. 1992. 22.95 (*0-9633721-8-1*, Coun Oak Bks) Fielden Bks.

McCallum, Toshiko M., text. Containing Beauty: Japanese Bamboo Flower Baskets. LC 88-50730. (Illus.). 96p. 1988. 35.00 (*0-930741-15-3*); pap. 21.00 (*0-930741-16-1*) UCLA Fowler Mus.

McCallum, Tracy. Fast Associations: A Guide to the Appearance of Butterflies & Moths. (Illus.). 65p. 1982. pap. 4.95 (*0-935684-03-4*) Plumbers Ink Bks.

McCallum, W. Cheyne & Curry, S. Hutch, eds. Slow Potential Changes in the Human Brain. LC 93-26280. (NATO ASI Series A, Life Sciences: Vol. 254). 1994. 95.00 (*0-306-44596-4*, Plenum Pr) Plenum.

McCallum, W. Cheyne, et al, eds. Cerebral Psychophysiology: Studies in Event-Related Potentials. 592p. 1987. 244.00 (*0-444-80741-1*) Elsevier.

***McCallum, William & Hughes-Hallet, Deborah.** Multivariable Calculus, Draft Version. 1994. pap. text ed. write for info. (*0-471-30450-6*) Wiley.

McCallun, Sheila & Strong, Anne. Starting Work in the Salon. 132p. (C). 1989. 69.00 (*0-946139-32-6*, Pub. by Elm Pubns UK) St Mut.

***McCally, John F.** The Gatekeeper: A Guide to Capitation for the Primary Care Physician. 200p. 1995. 40.00 (*1-55738-634-X*) Probus Pub Co.

McCally, Regina W. The Secret of Mojo: The Story of the Odessa, Texas, Permian High School Football Team. Baldwin, James, ed. LC 86-90445. 236p. 1986. 20.00 (*0-9619703-0-8*) R W McCally.

McCalman, Iain. Radical Underworld: Prophets, Revolutionaries & Pornographers in London, 1795-1840. (Illus.). 352p. 1988. 69.95 (*0-521-30755-4*) Cambridge U Pr.

— Radical Underworld: Prophets, Revolutionaries, & Pornographers in London, 1795-1840. 354p. 1993. pap. 19.95 (*0-19-812286-1*) OUP.

McCalman, James. The Electronics Industry in Britain: Coping with Change. 176p. 1989. 59.95 (*0-415-00031-9*) Routledge.

McCalman, James & Paton, Robert A. Change Management: A Guide to Effective Implementation. 256p. 1992. pap. 35.00 (*1-85396-155-8*, Pub. by Paul Chapman UK) Taylor & Francis.

McCalman, James, jt. auth. see Buchanan, David A.

McCalman, Janet. Journeyings: Biography of a Middle-Class 1920-1990. 348p. 1993. 39.95 (*0-522-84569-X*) Intl Spec Bk.

— Struggle Town: Public & Private Life in Richmond, Australia, 1900-1965. 338p. (Orig.). pap. 19.95 (*0-522-84303-4*) Intl Spec Bk.

McCalpin, Deborah J., et al, eds. Health Media Review Index, Nineteen Eighty-Four to Nineteen Eighty-Six: A Guide to Reviews & Descriptions of Commercially Available Nonprint Material for the Medical, Mental, Allied Healthy Human Service, & Related Counseling Professions. LC 88-18452. 771p. 1988. 52.50 (*0-8108-2172-9*) Scarecrow.

McCalpin, James P. Quaternary Geology & Neotectonics of the West Flank of the Northern Sangre de Cristo Mountains, South-Central Colorado. Raese, Jon W. & Goldberg, J. H., eds. LC 82-17899. (Colorado School of Mines Quarterly Ser.: Vol. 77, No. 3). 97p. 1983. pap. text ed. 12.00 (*0-686-82132-7*) Colo Sch Mines.

McCalvin, Jaki. Harlem's Daughter. 1993. 6.00 (*0-9636757-0-2*) McCalvin Pub.

McCamant, Kathryn & Durrett, Charles. Cohousing. rev. ed. 1993. pap. 29.95 (*0-89815-539-8*) Ten Speed Pr.

— Cohousing: A Contemporary Approach to Housing Ourselves. (Illus.). 208p. (Orig.). 1989. reprint ed. pap. 21.95 (*0-89815-306-9*) Ten Speed Pr.

McCamant, Kathryn M. & Durrett, Charles R. Cohousing: A Contemporary Approach to Housing Ourselves. LC 88-80988. (Illus.). 208p. (Orig.). (C). 1988. pap. 19.95 (*0-945929-29-3*) Habitat Pr.

McCambley, Casimir, comment. The Commentary on the Song of Songs by St. Gregory of Nyssa. (Archbishop Iakovos Library of Ecclesiastical & Historical Sources: No. 12). 300p. 1987. 22.95 (*0-917653-17-3*); pap. 14.95 (*0-917653-18-1*) Hellenic Coll Pr.

McCamey, Randy B. Journeys: Writings & Poetry in Search of a Dream. LC 92-73079. 100p. 1992. pap. 8.00 (*0-9635423-0-3*) Four Dots.

McCammon, A. L. Currencies of the Anglo Norman Isles. (Illus.). 1984. lib. bdg. 45.00 (*0-907605-13-3*) S J Durst.

McCammon, J. A. & Harvey, S. C. Dynamics of Proteins & Nucleic Acids. (Illus.). 220p. 1988. pap. 32.95 (*0-521-35652-0*) Cambridge U Pr.

McCammon, Robert R. Baal. Peters, Sally, ed. 1988. mass mkt. 5.99 (*0-671-73774-0*) PB.

— Bethany's Sin. Peters, Sally, ed. 1988. mass mkt. 5.99 (*0-671-73775-9*) PB.

— Blue World. Peters, Sally, ed. 464p. 1990. mass mkt. 5.99 (*0-671-69518-5*) PB.

— Boy's Life. large type ed. 644p. 1992. reprint ed. lib. bdg. 21.95 (*1-56054-326-4*) Thorndike Pr.

— Boy's Life. large type ed. 644p. 1992. reprint ed. pap. 14.95 (*1-56054-938-6*) Thorndike Pr.

— Boy's Life. Peters, Sally, ed. 592p. 1992. reprint ed. pap. 6.50 (*0-671-74305-8*) PB.

— Gone South. large type ed. 1993. 22.95 (*1-56895-018-7*) Wheeler Pub.

— Gone South. 400p. 1993. reprint ed. mass mkt. 5.99 (*0-671-74307-4*, Pocket Star Bks) PB.

— Mine. Grose, Bill, ed. 496p. 1991. reprint ed. mass mkt. 5.99 (*0-671-73944-1*) PB.

— Mystery Walk. Peters, Sally, ed. 432p. 1992. reprint ed. mass mkt. 5.99 (*0-671-76991-X*) PB.

— Night Boat. Peters, Sally, ed. 1988. mass mkt. 5.99 (*0-671-73281-1*) PB.

— Stinger. Peters, Sally, ed. 512p. 1988. pap. 6.50 (*0-671-73776-7*) PB.

— Swan Song. Peters, Sally, ed. 1987. pap. 7.50 (*0-671-74103-9*) PB.

— They Thirst. 1991. 22.95 (*0-913165-60-3*) Dark Harvest.

— They Thirst. Peters, Sally, ed. 1988. mass mkt. 5.99 (*0-671-73563-2*) PB.

— Usher's Passing. Peters, Sally, ed. 416p. 1992. reprint ed. mass mkt. 5.99 (*0-671-76992-8*) PB.

— The Wolf's Hour. (Orig.). 1990. pap. 6.50 (*0-671-73142-4*) PB.

McCammon, Susan L., et al. Choices in Sexuality. Marshall, ed. LC 92-38235. 675p. (C). 1993. text ed. 54.50 (*0-314-01267-2*) West Pub.

McCampbell, B. Harrison. Problems in Roofing Design. 256p. 1991. pap. text ed. 39.95 (*0-7506-9162-X*) Buttrwrth-Heinemann.

McCampbell, Coleman. Saga of a Frontier Seaport. 1993. reprint ed. lib. bdg. 75.00 (*0-7812-5945-2*) Rprt Serv.

McCampbell, Darlene Z., jt. sel. see Rochman, Hazel.

McCamy, James L. The Quality of the Environment. LC 72-80576. 1972. 19.95 (*0-02-920480-1*) Free Pr.

McCan, Robert L. World Economy & World Hunger: The Response of the Churches. 119p. (C). 1982. text ed. 42.95 (*0-313-27078-3*, U7078) Greenwood.

McCance & Huether. Pathophysiology: The Biologic Basis of Disease in Adults & Children. (Illus.). 1520p. 1989. 55.95 (*0-8016-3360-5*) Mosby Yr Bk.

McCance, Kathryn L. & Huether, Sue E. Pathophysiology: The Biologic Basis for Diseases in Adults & Children. 2nd ed. LC 93-31475. 1410p. 1993. 57.95 (*0-8016-6902-2*) Mosby Yr Bk.

McCance, M. E., jt. ed. see Harrigan, W. F.

McCance, Robert M., ed. see Andreas, Barbara, et al.

McCandless, Barbara. Equal Before the Lens: Jno. Trlica's Photographs of Granger, Texas. LC 91-26693. (Charles & Elizabeth Prothro Texas Photography Ser.: No. 3). 208p. 1992. 34.50 (*0-89096-486-6*) Tex A&M Univ Pr.

***McCandless, Barbara, et al.** New York to Hollywood: The Photography of Karl Struss. LC 95-4977. (Illus.). 256p. 1995. 60.00 (*0-8263-1637-9*); pap. 35.00 (*0-8263-1638-7*) U of NM Pr.

McCandless, Boyd R. & Trotter, Robert J. Children: Behavior & Development. 3rd ed. LC 76-54683. 512p. (C). 1977. text ed. 34.75 (*0-03-089750-5*) HB Coll Pubs.

McCandless, D. W., ed. Cerebral Energy Metabolism & Metabolic Encephalopathy. 478p. 1985. 125.00 (*0-306-41797-9*, Plenum Pr) Plenum.

McCandless, George T., Jr. Macroeconomic Theory. 336p. (C). 1990. text ed. write for info. (*0-13-543323-1*) P-H.

McCandless, George T., Jr. & Wallace, Neil. Introduction to Dynamic Macroeconomic Theory: An Overlapping Generations Approach. 372p. (C). 1992. 42.50 (*0-674-46111-8*) HUP.

McCandless, N. Jane & Cintron, Myrna, eds. Women: Contemporary Issues & Perspectives. (Studies in the Social Sciences). 100p. (Orig.). 1993. pap. text ed. 5.00 (*1-883199-01-8*) W GA College.

McCandless, Perry & Foley, William E. Missouri: Then & Now. rev. ed. LC 90-32545. (Illus.). 328p. (J). (gr. 4). 1992. text ed. 19.95 (*0-8262-0825-8*) U of Mo Pr.

McCandless, Stanley. Method of Lighting the Stage. 4th ed. LC 56-10331. 1958. 14.95 (*0-87830-082-1*, Theatre Arts Bks) Routledge Chapman & Hall.

McCandless, Susan K., tr. see Namikoshi, Toru.

McCandless, W., jt. auth. see Campbell, B.

McCandlish, David B. McCandlish Family History. (Illus.). 1991. 50.00 (*0-9619300-0-4*) D McCandlish.

— McCandlish Family History. 3rd ed. (Illus.). 1993. 49.00 (*0-9619300-2-0*) D McCandlish.

McCandlish, L. E., et al, eds. Multicomponent Ultrafine Microstructures: Materials Research Society Symposium Proceedings, Vol. 132. 1989. text ed. 50.00 (*1-55899-005-4*) Materials Res.

McCandliss, Bill & Watson, Albert. Problemoids: Math Challenge, Grade 5. 1982. student ed, pap. 4.99 (*0-89824-033-6*) Trillium Pr.

— Problemoids: Math Challenge, Grade 5. 1984. teacher ed, pap. 10.00 (*0-89824-070-0*) Trillium Pr.

— Problemoids: Math Challenge, Grade 5. 1986. teacher ed, pap. 25.00 (*0-89824-044-1*) Trillium Pr.

— Problemoids: Math Challenge, Grade 5. suppl. ed. 1984. pap. 1.00 (*0-89824-069-7*) Trillium Pr.

— Problemoids: Math Challenge, Grade 6. student ed 4.99 (*0-685-56826-1*) Trillium Pr.

— Problemoids: Math Challenge, Grade 6. 1983. teacher ed, pap. 25.00 (*0-89824-039-5*); pap. 4.99 (*0-89824-038-7*) Trillium Pr.

— Problemoids: Math Challenge, Grade 6. suppl. ed. 1983. pap. 1.00 (*0-89824-071-9*) Trillium Pr.

— Problemoids: Math Challenge, Grade 6, Cards. 1983. teacher ed 10.00 (*0-89824-072-7*) Trillium Pr.

McCane, Bryon R. & VanLoon, Preston C. Building a Faith to Live By: Programs for Youth (Foundation for Discipleship) 128p. 1987. pap. 11.00 (*0-8170-1107-2*) Judson.

McCaney, Kevin, ed. see Eveland, Thomas.

McCanles, Michael. The Discourse of "Il Principe" LC 83-51532. (Humana Civilitas Ser.: Vol. 8). 162p. 1983. pap. 25.50 (*0-89003-141-X*) Undena Pubns.

— Jonsonian Discriminations: The Humanist Poet & the Praise of True Nobility. 352p. 1992. text ed. 65.00 (*0-8020-5955-4*) U of Toronto Pr.

— The Text of Sidney's Arcadian World. LC 88-26742. 224p. (C). 1989. lib. bdg. 38.50 (*0-8223-0797-9*) Duke.

McCanless, Christel L. Faberge & His Works: An Annotated Bibliography of the First Century of His Art. LC 93-46653. (Illus.). 454p. 1994. 49.50 (*0-8108-2836-7*) Scarecrow.

McCanlies, Tim. Harlem. (Orig.). (J). (ps-12). 1984. pap. 2.25 (*0-87067-245-2*, BH245) Holloway.

***McCann.** God's Answers to the Mystery of Life. 1990. pap. text ed. 3.97 (*1-55748-360-4*) Barbour & Co.

— Heritage Book Nineteen Eighty-Five. 1984. 5.95 (*0-02-582880-0*) Macmillan.

McCann, jt. auth. see Albertyn.

McCann, tr. see So, Chongju.

McCann, Anna M. Roman Sarcophagi in The Metropolitan Museum of Art. LC 77-28089. (Illus.). 152p. 1978. 25.00 (*0-87099-173-6*) Metro Mus Art.

McCann, Anna M., et al. The Roman Port & Fishery of Cosa: A Center of Ancient Trade. LC 85-42693. (Illus.). 750p. 1985. text ed. 180.00x (*0-691-03581-4*) Princeton U Pr.

McCann, Annes, ed. Fundamental Principles of Gas Turbines. (Illus.). 88p. 1980. 14.00 (*0-88698-147-6*, 1. 76010) PETEX.

McCann, Annes, jt. ed. see Reynolds, Jeanette.

McCann, Annes, jt. auth. see Whalen, Bruce.

McCann, Brian, jt. ed. see Robinson, Jeffrey.

McCann, C. Trees of India, a Popular Handbook. (C). 1988. text ed. 85.00 (*0-685-44243-8*, Scientific) St Mut.

McCann, C., jt. auth. see Blatter, E.

McCann, Carole R. Birth Control Politics in the United States, 1916-1945. 256p. 1994. 29.95 (*0-8014-2490-9*) Cornell U Pr.

McCann, Charles R., Jr. Probability Foundations of Economic Theory. LC 93-43881. 192p. 1994. 59.95x (*0-415-10867-5*, B3926, Routledge NY) Routledge.

McCann, Cheryl, ed. see Host, Atley.

McCann, David R., ed. Black Crane, No. 1: An Anthology of Korean Literature. (Cornell East Asia Ser.: No. 14). 153p. 1977. 9.00 (*0-939657-14-7*) Cornell East Asia Pgm.

McCann, David R. & Salee, Hyun-jae Y., trs. Selected Poems by Kim Namjo. (East Asia Papers: No. 63). (C). 1993. 18.00 (*0-939657-05-8*, 63); pap. 10.00 (*0-939657-63-5*, 63) Cornell East Asia Pgm.

McCann, David R., tr. see Chi Ha, Kim.

McCann, David R., tr. see Chongju, So.

McCann, David R., tr. see Kim Dae Jung.

McCann, David R., et al, eds. Studies on Korea in Transition. LC 78-67859. (Occasional Papers: No. 9). 245p. 1979. pap. 8.00 (*0-917536-13-4*) UH Manoa CKS.

***McCann, Debbie.** A House in Order. (Illus.). 120p. (Orig.). 1994. pap. 10.00 (*1-883968-03-8*) Blinking Yellow.

McCann, Dennis. The Art & Science of Resort Sales. 144p. (Orig.). 1990. pap. 14.95 (*0-942645-07-3*) Hampton Hse Pub.

McCann, Dennis P. & Strain, Charles R. Polity & Praxis: A Program for American Practical Theology. 252p. (C). 1990. reprint ed. pap. text ed. 26.50 (*0-8191-7847-0*) U Pr of Amer.

***McCann, Dennis P., et al, eds.** On Moral Business: Classical Contemporary Resources for Ethics in Economic Life. LC 94-21941. 944p. (Orig.). 1995. pap. text ed. 34.99 (*0-8028-0626-0*) Eerdmans.

McCann, Dick. How to Influence Others at Work. 2nd ed. 152p. 1993. pap. 19.95 (*0-7506-0990-7*) Buttrwrth-Heinemann.

***McCann, E. Armitage.** How to Make a Clipper Ship Model. LC 94-46480. (Illus.). 176p. 1995. pap. text ed. 5.95 (*0-486-28580-4*) Dover.

McCann, Eamonn. War & an Irish Town. (C). 1980. pap. text ed. 17.00 (*0-86104-302-2*, Pub. by Pluto Pr UK) Westview.

— War & an Irish Town. 2nd rev. ed. LC 93-36051. 176p. (C). 1994. pap. text ed. 15.95 (*0-7453-0725-6*) Westview.

— War & an Irish Town. 2nd rev. ed. LC 93-36051. 176p. (C). 1994. text ed. 54.00 (*0-7453-0830-9*, Pub. by Pluto Pr UK) Westview.

McCann, Eamonn & Shiels, Maureen, eds. Bloody Sunday in Derry: What Really Happened. (Illus.). 256p. (Orig.). 1992. pap. 11.95 (*0-86322-139-4*, Pub. by Brandon Bk Pubs IE) Irish Bks Media.

McCann, Eileen. The Two-Step: Dancing Toward Intimacy. LC 85-14764. (Illus.). 160p. 1989. pap. 12.95 (*0-8021-3032-1*) Grove-Atltic.

McCann, Forrest. Great Songs of the Church. LC 85-82565. 673p. 1986. 8.95 (*0-915547-90-2*) Abilene Christ U.

McCann, Frank, jt. auth. see Collins, Neil.

McCann, Frank D., jt. ed. see Conniff, Michael L.

McCann, Garth. Edward Abbey. LC 77-76321. (Western Writers Ser.: No. 29). 47p. 1977. pap. 3.95 (*0-88430-053-6*) Boise St U W Writ Ser.

McCann, Gordon, jt. auth. see Randolph, Vance.

McCann, Graham. Marilyn Monroe: The Body in the Library. (Illus.). 220p. (C). 1988. text ed. 35.00 (*0-8135-1302-2*); pap. 11.95 (*0-8135-1303-0*) Rutgers U Pr.

— Rebel Males: Clift, Brando, & Dean. LC 92-33768. (Illus.). 235p. (C). 1993. text ed. 38.00 (*0-8135-1952-7*); pap. 14.95 (*0-8135-1953-5*) Rutgers U Pr.

— Woody Allen: New Yorker. 1992. pap. 17.95 (*0-7456-0890-6*) Blackwell Pubs.

McCann, H. Gilman. Chemistry Transformed: The Paradigmatic Shift from Phlogiston to Oxygen. LC 78-19173. (Modern Sociology Ser.). 1978. 37.50 (*0-89391-004-X*) Ablex Pub.

McCann, Heather. Whispers in the Dark. (Intrigue Ser.). 1993. mass mkt. 2.99 (*0-373-22236-X*, 1-22236-3) Harlequin Bks.

***McCann, Helen.** The Coward. LC 94-79393. (Ten-Minute Mysteries Ser.). 32p. (YA). (gr. 6-12). 1994. pap. 2.49 (*1-56103-804-0*) Lake Pub Co.

— The Coward Readalong. LC 94-79393. (Ten-Minute Mysteries Ser.). 32p. (YA). (gr. 6-12). 1994. pap. 12.39 (*1-56103-806-7*) Lake Pub Co.

— I Dare You. LC 94-79395. (Ten-Minute Mysteries Ser.). 32p. (YA). (gr. 6-12). 1995. pap. 2.49 (*1-56103-810-5*) Lake Pub Co.

— I Dare You Readalong. LC 94-79395. (Ten-Minute Mysteries Ser.). 32p. 1995. audio, pap. 12.39 (*1-56103-812-1*) Lake Pub Co.

— What Do We Do Now, George? LC 91-2329. (Illus.). 160p. (J). (gr. 4-7). 1993. pap. 2.95 (*0-671-86691-5*, Half Moon Paper) S&S Childrens.

— What's French for Help, George? LC 91-41563. (Illus.). 460p. (J). (gr. 5-9). 1993. pap. 13.00 (*0-671-74689-8*, S&S Bks Young Read) S&S Childrens.

McCann, I. Lisa & Pearlman, Laurie A. Psychological Trauma & the Adult Survivor: Theory, Therapy, & Transformation. LC 90-2336. (Psychosocial Stress Ser.: No. 21). 320p. 1990. 40.95 (*0-87630-594-X*) Brunner-Mazel.

***McCann, Ian, contrib.** Complete Guide to the Music of Bob Marley. (Illus.). (Orig.). 1995. pap. 7.95 (*0-7119-3550-5*, OP 47384, Pub. by Omnibus Press UK) Omnibus NY.

McCann, J. Clinton. A Theological Introduction to the Book of Psalms: The Psalms As Torah. 224p. (Orig.). 1993. pap. 16.95 (*0-687-41468-7*) Abingdon.

McCann, J. E. Thomas Howell & the School at Llandaff. 260p. (C). 1989. 39.00 (*0-685-61445-X*, Pub. by D Brown & Sons Ltd UK) St Mut.

McCann, James. From Poverty to Famine in Northeast Ethiopia: A Rural History, 1900-1935. LC 86-14680. (Ethnohistory Ser.). (Illus.). 256p. 1987. text ed. 42.95 (*0-8122-8038-5*) U of Pa Pr.

***McCann, James C.** People of the Plow: An Agricultural History of Ethiopia. LC 94-37124. (Illus.). 304p. 1994. pap. text ed. 24.95 (*0-299-14614-6*) U of Wis Pr.

— People of the Plow: An Agricultural History of Ethiopia. LC 94-37124. (Illus.). 304p. 1995. text ed. 54.00 (*0-299-14610-3*) U of Wis Pr.

McCann, James Z. Aftershock: The Loma Prieta Earthquake & Its Impact on San Benito County. Churchill, Adele, ed. LC 90-63594. (Illus.). 80p. (Orig.). 1990. pap. 14.95 (*0-9628177-0-8*) J Churchill.

McCann, Jan. Sarasota's Chef du Jour: Chef Recipes. 3rd ed. 190p. 1994. pap. 12.00 (*0-9640198-0-9*) Strawbry Press.

McCann, Janet. Dialogue with the Dogcatcher. 50p. (Orig.). 1987. 10.95 (*0-941720-52-7*); pap. 3.95 (*0-941720-53-5*) Slough Pr TX.

— How They Got Here. 1984. pap. 4.00 (*0-318-04456-0*) Pudding Hse Pubns.

M

An Asterisk (*) at the beginning of an entry indicates that the title is appearing in BIP for the first time.

— Wallace Steven Revisited. (Twayne's United States Author Ser.). 1995. lib. bdg. 22.95x (*0-8057-7644-3*, Twayne) Macmillan.

McCann, Janet, jt. ed. see Craig, David.

***McCann, Janice.** Fort Myers Chef du Jour: Chef Recipes from Popular Ft. Myers Area Restaurants. 152p. 1994. pap. 12.00 (*0-9640198-4-1*) Strawbry Press.

***McCann, Janice & Shand, Betsy.** Surviving Natural Disasters: How to Prepare for Earthquakes, Hurricanes, Tornados, Floods, Wildfires, Thunderstorms, Blizzards, Tsunamis, Volcanic Eruptions, & Other Calamities. LC 94-25256. (Illus.). 170p. (Orig.). 1995. pap. 14.95 (*0-931625-26-2*) DIMI Pr.

McCann, Jennifer, jt. auth. see Kuzmier, Kerrie.

McCann, Joachim. Monks in the Modern World: The Monks of Mount Angel Abbey. (Illus.). 105p. (Orig.). 1993. pap. 15.95 (*1-884563-00-7*) Canyon Creat.

McCann, John. NetWare Performance & Tuning. 1993. disk, pap. 34.95 (*0-672-30314-0*) Sams.

McCann, John & Segal, Rick. Netware LAN Management Toolkit. (Illus.). (Orig.). 1992. pap. 34.95 (*0-672-30170-9*) Sams.

McCann, John A., jt. auth. see Safford, Edward L., Jr.

McCann, John D. Find 'em Fast: A Private Investigator's Workbook. 168p. 1984. pap. 20.00 (*0-87364-301-1*) Paladin Pr.

McCann, John D., jt. auth. see Hoyer, Frederick C., Jr.

McCann, John M. Expert Systems for a Scanner Data Environment: The Marketing Workbench Experience. (C). 1990. lib. bdg. 64.00 (*0-7923-9076-8*) Kluwer Ac.

— The Marketing Workbench: Using Computers for Better Performance. 250p. 1986. pap. 30.00 (*0-87094-763-X*) Irwin Prof Pubng.

McCann, John T. Netware Programmer's Guide. 1990. pap. 34.95 (*1-55851-152-0*) M&T Bks.

— Netware Programmer's Guide with Disk. 1990. pap. 44.95 (*1-55851-154-7*) M&T Bks.

— NetWare 4.1 Supervisor's Guide. 1995. disk, pap. 39.95 (*1-55851-402-3*) M&T Bks.

— Supervisor's Guide to Netware X OS. 2nd ed. 1992. pap. 32.95 (*1-55851-284-5*) M&T Bks.

McCann, John T., et al. Netware Supervisor's Guide. (Illus.). 510p. (Orig.). 1989. pap. 29.95 (*1-55851-111-3*) M&T Bks.

McCann, Joseph E. Sweet Success: How NutraSweet Created a Billion Dollar Business. 300p. 1990. text ed. 30.00 (*1-55623-268-3*) Irwin Prof Pubng.

McCann, Joseph E. & Gilkey, Roderick. Joining Forces: Creating & Managing Successful Mergers & Acquisitions. (Illus.). 1988. 38.95 (*0-13-510538-2*) P-H.

McCann, Joseph F. Church & Organization: A Sociological & Theological Inquiry. LC 91-68568. (Illus.). 256p. 1993. 39.50 (*0-940866-19-6*) U Scranton Pr.

***McCann, Karen K.** Take Charge of Your Hospital Stay: A "Start Smart" Guide for Patients & Care Partners. LC 94-26399. 341p. 1994. 24.95 (*0-306-44765-7*, Plenum Insight) Plenum.

McCann, Kelly, jt. auth. see Griffin, Lynne.

***McCann, Kenyon.** Ride into Darkness. LC 94-90229. 232p. (Orig.). 1995. pap. 10.95 (*1-56002-470-4*, Univ Edtns) Aegina Pr.

McCann, Lee. Nostradamus: The Man Who Saw Through Time. (Illus.). 421p. 1982. pap. 9.95 (*0-374-51754-1*) FS&G.

— Nostradamus: The Man Who Saw Through Time. (Illus.). 432p. 1994. reprint ed. 9.99 (*0-517-43693-0*) Random Hse Value.

McCann Lucas, Jerri. Christianity: A Growing Experience. 1983. pap. 6.25 (*0-89137-429-9*) Quality Pubns.

McCann, Margaret, jt. auth. see Brewer, Richard.

***McCann, Mark.** Relational Youth Ministry. Stamschror, Robert, ed. (Illus.). (Orig.). 1995. pap. 27.95 (*0-88489-351-0*) St Marys.

McCann, Mary A., jt. auth. see Lampe, Kenneth F.

McCann, Mat. Money Mad. LC 87-40248. 132p. 1987. 8.95 (*1-55523-107-1*) Winston-Derek.

McCann, Michael. Artist Beware. 2nd ed. (Illus.). 480p. 1992. pap. 29.95 (*1-55821-175-6*) Lyons & Burford.

— Artists Health Hazards Manual. 80p. 1985. 7.95 (*0-685-43406-0*) Foun Commun Artists.

— Health Hazards. 4th ed. (Illus.). 128p. 1994. pap. 11.95 (*1-55821-306-6*, Focal) Buttrwrth-Heinemann.

— Health Hazards Manual for Artists. rev. ed. LC 78-70898. (Illus.). 48p. 1978. pap. 3.50 (*0-685-01622-6*) Foun Commun Artists.

McCann, Michael J. & Thomas, Mason P., Jr. The Law & the Elderly in North Carolina. 2nd ed. (C). 1992. pap. text ed. write for info. (*1-56011-202-6*, 92.01) Institute Government.

McCann, Michael L. The Ultimate Secrets of Knowing God, Vol. 1. Cotton, Irene, ed. 94p. (Orig.). Date not set. pap. text ed. 6.00 (*0-9638195-0-X*) M L McCann.

McCann, Michael W. Rights at Work: Pay Equity Reform & the Politics of Legal Mobilization. LC 93-21278. (Language & Legal Discourse Ser.). 1994. pap. text ed. 18.95 (*0-226-55572-0*) U Ch Pr.

— Rights at Work: Pay Equity Reform & the Politics of Legal Mobilization. LC 93-21278. (Language & Legal Discourse Ser.). 1994. lib. bdg. 65.00 (*0-226-55571-2*) U Ch Pr.

— Taking Reform Seriously: Perspectives on Public Interest Liberalism. LC 86-47647. 348p. 1986. 42.50 (*0-8014-1952-2*); pap. 17.95 (*0-8014-9415-X*) Cornell U Pr.

McCann, Michael W. & Houseman, Gerald L. Judging the Constitution: Critical Essays on Judicial Lawmaking. (C). 1989. pap. text ed. 25.50 (*0-673-39897-8*) HarpCollege.

***McCann, Mike.** Creative Groups Guide: Find Us Faithful. Mack, Michael, ed. 160p. (Orig.). 1995. student ed, pap. 14.99 (*0-7847-0308-6*, 11-40308) Standard Pub.

— Give Me the Hudson or the Yukon. 1991. 5.95 (*0-9627530-0-9*) Ridgetop Pr.

McCann, Nancy D. & McGinn, Thomas A. Harassed: One Hundred Women Define Inappropriate Behavior in the Workplace. 150p. 1992. 17.00 (*1-55623-796-0*) Irwin Prof Pubng.

McCann, Peter P., et al, eds. Inhibition of Polyamine Metabolism: Biological Significance & Basis for New Therapies. 352p. 1987. text ed. 124.00 (*0-12-481835-8*) Acad Pr.

McCann, Rebecca. Complete Cheerful Cherub. 514p. 1990. reprint ed. lib. bdg. 35.95 (*0-89966-662-0*) Buccaneer Bks.

McCann, Richard. A Dream of the Traveler. LC 76-17642. 68p. 1976. 3.50 (*0-87886-070-3*, Greenfld Rev Pr) Greenfld Rev Lit.

— Ghost Letters: Poems. LC 94-26245. (Orig.). 1994. pap. 9.95 (*1-882295-04-8*) Alicejamesbooks.

— Nights of 1990. (Illus.). 22p. 1994. pap. 6.00 (*1-879294-08-7*) Warm Spring Pr.

McCann, Ron & Vitale, Joe. The Joy of Service! Bring Service Excellence to the World Through Your Work. (Illus.). 135p. (Orig.). 1989. pap. 10.95 (*0-9617549-2-3*) Awareness Pubns.

McCann, S. M., ed. Endocrinology. (People & Ideas Ser.). (Illus.). 476p. 1988. 75.00 (*0-19-520718-1*) OUP.

McCann, S. M. & Weiner, R. I., eds. Integrative Neuroendocrinology: Molecular, Cellular & Clinical Aspects. (Illus.). viii, 244p. 1987. 144.00 (*3-8055-4467-7*) S Karger.

McCann, S. M., jt. ed. see Doerner, G.

McCann, Sean. Growing Things. LC 89-51018. 138p. (Orig.). (J). 1989. pap. 5.95 (*1-85371-029-6*, Pub. by Poolbeg Pr IE) Dufour.

— Irish Wit: Religion, the Law, Literature, Love, Drink, Wisdom & Proverbs. (Illus.). 144p. (Orig.). 1990. pap. 8.95 (*0-86278-227-9*, Pub. by OBrien Pr IE) Dufour.

— The Rose: An Encyclopedia of North American Roses, Rosarians, & Rose Lore. LC 93-9589. (Illus.). 224p. 1993. 24.95 (*0-8117-1490-X*) Stackpole.

— World of Brendan Behan. 1976. 18.95 (*0-8488-0572-0*) Amereon Ltd.

McCann, Stephen, jt. auth. see Vaughn, Dean.

McCann, Timothy J. West Sussex Probate Inventories, Fifteen Twenty-One to Eighteen Thirty-Four. 1981. 95.00 (*0-86260-005-7*) St Mut.

McCann, Tom. The Droll Troll: A View from under the Bridge. (Illus.). 112p. 1994. pap. 10.00 (*0-943389-15-1*) Snow Lion-SLG Bks.

McCann, W. P., jt. auth. see Stewart, W. A.

***McCann, Will.** Mano Grande. 220p. (Orig.). Date not set. pap. 8.95 (*0-7610-0171-9*) NW Pub.

McCann, William, ed. see Bierce, Ambrose.

McCann, Yvette B. Eddie Pasghetti. Damerest, Nancy & Lea, Judy, eds. (Eddie Pasghetti Collection: Bk. 1). (Illus.). 64p. (J). (gr. 4 up). 1994. 14.95 (*0-9639486-5-2*) Rhyme Tyme.

McCannon, Doris D. Buried Alive in the State of Nevada: Innnocent Until Fabricated Guilty. 1995. 29.95 (*1-887297-51-0*) Last Chnce Pub. In 1991, Doris McCannon met Harold "Pete" Guyette, a man released in 1972 on a Writ of Habeas Corpus. Three years later, their travels led to the discovery of new & suppressed evidence showing how he was convicted for a crime in Nevada he did not commit. This book tells the story of Pete's early childhood to the day he was delivered, a convicted man, to the gates of the Nevada State Prison at the age of nineteen. It was April 1, 1966, April Fool's Day, in Elkhart, Indiana when Pete was arrested on a year old traffic warrant, & taken to jail, only to be questioned about a double murder that had occurred on March 12, 1966 in Fallon, Nevada. Pete thought it was a joke! This is the first of three books detailing what the Nevada & Indiana officials did to fabricate evidence, because there was no evidence linking him to the crime scene. Presently, a lawsuit is pending in the Reno Federal Court, documenting the contents of the book. Order from "A Last Chance Publisher", P.O. Box 279, Pleasant Garden, NC 27313, Tel. 800-990-9502.** ***Publisher Provided Annotation.

McCanny, J., et al. Systolic Arrays. 720p. 1989. boxed 61.60 (*0-13-473422-X*) P-H.

McCanny, J. V. & White, John. VLSI Technology & Design. (Microelectronics & Signal Processing Ser.). 388p. 1987. text ed. 117.00 (*0-12-481840-4*) Acad Pr.

McCanse, Anne E., jt. auth. see Blake, Robert R.

McCant, Jerry. Teens & Self Esteem: Helping Christian Youth Discover Their Worth. 152p. (Orig.). 1985. pap. 6.95 (*0-8341-1055-5*) Beacon Hill.

McCants, David A. Patrick Henry, the Orator. LC 90-33274. (Great American Orators: Critical Studies, Speeches & Sources: No. 8). 176p. 1990. text ed. 47.95 (*0-313-26210-1*, MPX, Greenwood Pr) Greenwood.

McCants, Dorothea O., ed. They Came to Louisiana: Letters of a Catholic Mission, 1854-1882. LC 72-96258. (Illus.). 287p. reprint ed. 81.80 (*0-8357-9392-3*, 2020997) Bks Demand.

McCants, Gary J. Can We As Black Men & Women Really Trust Each Other? 1994. 10.95 (*0-533-10888-8*) Vantage.

McCants, Louise & Robert, Cavett. Retire to Fun & Freedom. 192p. 1990. pap. 12.95 (*0-446-39139-5*) Warner Bks.

McCants, William D. Anything Can Happen in High School: And It Usually Does. LC 92-32982. (YA). 1993. 10.95 (*0-15-276604-9*); pap. 3.95 (*0-15-276605-7*) HarBrace.

— Much Ado about Prom Night. LC 94-43349. 192p. (YA). (gr. 7 up). 1995. 11.00 (*0-15-200083-6*, Red Wagon Bks); mass mkt. 5.00 (*0-15-200081-X*, Red Wagon Bks) HarBrace.

McCants, William R. War Patrols of the USS Flasher. Turner, Ginny, ed. 480p. 1994. 27.00 (*1-57087-054-3*) Prof Pr NC.

McCardell, John M., Jr. The Idea of a Southern Nation: Southern Nationalists & Southern Nationalism, 1830-1860. 432p. (C). 1981. pap. text ed. 6.95 (*0-393-95203-7*) Norton.

McCardell, Lee. Ill-Starred General: Braddock of the Cold-Stream Guards. LC 86-7015. (Illus.). viii, 335p. 1986. reprint ed. pap. 14.95 (*0-8229-5903-8*) U of Pittsburgh Pr.

McCardell, Marion, ed. see Ellsworth, Barry A.

McCardle. Surgical Oncology. 332p. 1990. text ed. 165.00 (*0-407-01700-3*) Buttrwrth-Heinemann.

McCardle, Arthur W. Friedrich Schiller & Swabian Pietism. (American University Studies: Germanic Languages & Literature: Ser. I, Vol. 36). 236p. 1986. text ed. 40.65 (*0-8204-0196-X*) P Lang Pubs.

McCardle, Arthur W. & Boenau, A. Bruce, eds. East Germany: A New German Nation under Socialism? LC 84-7476. 284p. (Orig.). (C). 1984. lib. bdg. 55.50 (*0-8191-3997-1*); pap. text ed. 30.00 (*0-8191-3998-X*) U Pr of Amer.

McCardle, Ellen S. Nonverbal Communication for Media, Library, & Information. Penland, Patrick R., ed. LC 73-90766. (Communications Science & Technology Ser.: No. 5). (Illus.). 111p. reprint ed. pap. 31.70 (*0-7837-0650-2*, 2040989) Bks Demand.

McCardle, William H., jt. auth. see Lowry, Robert.

McCarey-Laird, M. Martin. Lester Dent: The Man, His Craft & His Market. LC 94-76268. 120p. (Orig.). 1994. pap. 11.95 (*0-9641004-9-5*) Hidalgo Pubng.

McCarg, Barbara. Georgia Parks Guide. Boyer, Chris, ed. 100p. (Orig.). 1988. pap. text ed. 4.95 (*0-935201-31-9*) Affordable Adven.

McCarg, Barbara, ed. see Boyer, Chris.

McCarg, Barbara, ed. see McCarg, Margie.

McCarg, Margie. Virginia Parks Guide. McCarg, Barbara & Boyer, Chris, ed. 100p. (Orig.). 1988. pap. text ed. 5.95 (*0-935201-30-0*) Affordable Adven.

McCargar, David J., jt. ed. see Shrimpton, Gordon S.

McCarl, Robert. The District of Columbia Fire Fighter's Project: A Case Study in Occupational Folklore. LC 84-600291. (Smithsonian Folklore Studies: No. 4). 244p. reprint ed. pap. 69.60 (*0-317-41993-5*, 2025682) Bks Demand.

McCarl, Robert & Vennum, Thomas, Jr. The District of Columbia Fire Fighters' Project: A Case Study in Occupational Folklife. LC 84-600291. (Illus.). 244p. (Orig.). 1985. pap. 15.95 (*0-87474-651-5*, MCDFP) Smithsonian.

McCarley, J. Britt, et al. The Atlanta Campaign: A Civil War Driving Tour of Atlanta-Area Battlefields with a Reader's Guide to the Atlanta Campaign. Rice, Bradley R. & Weldon, Jane P., eds. LC 88-18941. (Illus.). 112p. (Orig.). 1989. reprint ed. pap. 9.95 (*0-87797-160-9*) Cherokee.

McCarley, R. W., jt. auth. see Steriade, Mircea.

McCarn, Ellen D. Ellen McCarn on English Smocking. (Illus.). 32p. (Orig.). 1986. pap. 9.95 (*0-9618066-0-5*) McCarn Enterp.

— Picture Smocking with Ellen McCarn. (Illus.). 48p. 1990. pap. 10.00 (*0-9618066-2-1*) McCarn Enterp.

McCarney, Joseph. Social Theory & the Crisis of Marxism. 200p. 1990. 50.00 (*0-86091-231-0*, A3762, Pub. by Verso UK); pap. 17.95 (*0-86091-948-X*, Pub. by Verso UK) Routledge Chapman & Hall.

McCarney-Muldoon, Eileen & O'Brien, Mary B. Fun with Colors. LC 91-42672. (Illus.). 24p. (J). (ps). 1992. pap. 6.95 (*0-689-71610-9*, Aladdin Paperbacks) S&S Childrens.

— Fun with Numbers. LC 91-39592. (Illus.). 24p. (J). (ps). 1992. pap. 6.95 (*0-689-71609-5*, Aladdin Paperbacks) S&S Childrens.

McCarney, Stephen B. Adaptive Behavior Intervention Manual. 168p. 1987. pap. 20.00 (*1-878372-08-4*) Hawthorne Educ Servs.

— The At Risk Student in Our Schools: A Model Intervention Program for the At Risk Student's Most Common Learning & Behavior Problems. 470p. (Orig.). 1991. pap. 30.00 (*1-878372-03-3*) Hawthorne Educ Servs.

— The Attention Deficit Disorders Intervention Manual. 200p. (Orig.). 1990. pap. 22.00 (*0-685-29445-5*) Hawthorne Educ Servs.

— Attention Deficit Disorders Intervention Manual. 167p. (Orig.). 1989. pap. 22.00 (*1-878372-06-8*) Hawthorne Educ Servs.

— Early Childhood Behavior Intervention Manual. 130p. (Orig.). 1992. pap. 20.00 (*1-878372-15-7*) Hawthorne Educ Servs.

— Emotional & Behavior Problem Scale IEP & Intervention Manual. 205p. (Orig.). 1989. pap. 22.00 (*0-685-29444-7*) Hawthorne Educ Servs.

— Emotional Behavior Disorder Intervention Manual. 202p. (Orig.). 1992. pap. 22.00 (*1-878372-10-6*) Hawthorne Educ Servs.

— The Student Teacher's Guide: Intervention Strategies for the Most Common Learning & Behavior Problems Encountered by Student Teachers in Our Schools. 470p. (Orig.). 1989. pap. 20.00 (*1-878372-12-2*) Hawthorne Educ Servs.

— The Transition Behavior Scale IEP & Intervention Manual. 230p. (Orig.). 1989. pap. 20.00 (*1-878372-14-9*) Hawthorne Educ Servs.

— Work Adjustment Intervention Manual. 171p. (Orig.). 1992. pap. 16.00 (*1-878372-16-5*) Hawthorne Educ Servs.

McCarney, Stephen B., intro. The Learning Disability Intervention Manual. rev. ed. 234p. reprint ed. pap. 22.00 (*1-878372-07-6*) Hawthorne Educ Servs.

McCarney, Stephen B. & Bauer, Angela M. The Parent's Guide to Attention Deficit Disorders: Intervention Strategies for the Home. 157p. (Orig.). 1990. pap. 13.00 (*1-878372-01-7*, 840) Hawthorne Educ Servs.

— Parent's Guide to Learning Disabilities. 200p. (Orig.). 1991. pap. 15.00 (*1-878372-05-X*) Hawthorne Educ Servs.

McCarney, Stephen B. & Tucci, Janet. Study Skills for Students in Our Schools. 206p. (Orig.). 1991. pap. 16.00 (*1-878372-04-1*) Hawthorne Educ Servs.

McCarney, Stephen B. & Wunderlicht, Kathy K. Pre-Referral Intervention Manual: The Most Common Learning & Behavior Problems Encountered in the Educational Environment. 470p. (Orig.). 1988. pap. 30.00 (*1-878372-11-4*) Hawthorne Educ Servs.

McCarney, Stephen B., et al. The Parent's Guide: Solutions to Today's Most Common Behavior Problems in the Home. 247p. (Orig.). 1989. pap. 14.95 (*1-878372-00-9*) Hawthorne Educ Servs.

***McCarr, Dorothy.** Multiple Meanings for the Young Adult. (C). 1995. pap. text ed. 9.00 (*0-89079-670-X*, 6972) PRO-ED.

McCarr, Ken. The Kentucky Harness Horse. LC 75-3548. (Kentucky Bicentennial Bookshelf Ser.). (Illus.). 152p. 1979. 10.00 (*0-8131-0213-8*) U Pr of Ky.

McCarra, Kevin. Scottish Football: A Pictorial History from 1867 to the Present Day. 132p. 1984. 29.00 (*0-685-17024-1*, Pub. by Third Eye Centre UK) St Mut.

McCarren, Felicia, tr. see Serres, Michel.

McCarren, Vincent P., ed. see Michigan Papyri Staff.

McCarrick, Chris S. Now You See Her. 1993. mass mkt. 4.99 (*0-515-11236-4*) Jove Pubns.

***McCarrick, Theodore, intro.** Pope John Paul II: An American Celebration. (Illus.). 128p. 1994. pap. 17.95 (*0-9642957-0-9*) Jersey Photo Project.

McCarriston, Linda. Eva-Mary. (TriQuarterly Bks.). 80p. (C). 1994. reprint ed. pap. 10.95 (*0-8101-5008-5*) Northwestern U Pr.

— Talking Soft Dutch. LC 83-51718. 71p. (Orig.). 1984. 10.95 (*0-89672-116-7*); pap. 6.95 (*0-89672-115-9*) Tex Tech Univ Pr.

McCarroll, John. Before You Go to Asia: A Primer for Personal Adventure Without Spending a Lot of Money. (Illus.). 120p. (Orig.). 1988. pap. 8.95 (*0-929220-01-3*) Laurel CA.

— Cheap Eats San Francisco: Good Meals Under Six Dollars. (Illus.). 192p. (Orig.). 1989. pap. 8.95 (*0-929220-02-1*) Laurel CA.

McCarroll, Tolbert. Child Song, Monk Song: A Spiritual Journey. 1994. 13.95 (*0-312-11253-X*) St Martin.

— Notes from the Song of Life: A Spiritual Companion. rev. ed. LC 77-7135. (Illus.). 144p. (Orig.). 1990. reprint ed. pap. 8.95 (*0-89087-200-7*) Celestial Arts.

McCarron, David A., jt. ed. see Bennett, William A.

McCarron, David A., jt. ed. see Bennett, William M.

McCarron, Kevin. William Golding. 1990. 60.00 (*0-7463-0730-6*, Pub. by Northcote House UK) St Mut.

— William Golding. (Writers & Their Work Ser.). 96p. 1994. pap. text ed. 11.50 (*0-7463-0735-7*, Pub. by Northcote House UK) Trans-Atl Phila.

***McCarron, Paul.** The Prints of Martin Lewis: A Catalogue Raisonne. LC 95-76596. (Illus.). 256p. 1995. 120.00x (*0-9628234-1-4*) M Hausberg.

McCarron, Robert J., jt. auth. see Leavitt, Christine.

Mccarron, S. Developing Portable Applications for Posix. 1990. pap. 31.80 (*0-13-204173-1*) P-H.

***McCarron, Shane.** Open Systems Standards. UniForum Staff, ed. (Illus.). 32p. (C). 1995. pap. text ed. write for info. (*0-936593-31-8*) UniForum.

McCarron, William E. Lesser Metaphysical Poets: A Bibliography, 1961-1980. LC 83-448. (Checklists in the Humanities & Education Ser.: No. 7). 64p. reprint ed. pap. 25.00 (*0-8357-6351-X*, 2035626) Bks Demand.

McCarry, Charles. Double Eagle. large type ed. 441p. 1982. 15.95 (*0-7089-0812-8*) Ulverscroft.

— The Great Southwest. LC 78-21450. (Special Publications Series 15: No. 3). (Illus.). 1980. lib. bdg. 12.95 (*0-87044-288-0*) Natl Geog.

— The Last Supper. large type ed. 624p. 1986. 23.95 (*0-7089-8322-7*, Charnwood) Ulverscroft.

— The Miernik Dossier. 1977. pap. write for info. (*0-345-29116-6*) Ballantine.

— Shelley's Heart: A Novel. 1995. 23.00 (*0-679-41533-5*) Random.

McCarry, Charles, jt. auth. see Haig, Alexander M., Jr.

McCarry, D. C., jt. ed. see Wightman, W. D.

McCarry, G. J. Aspects of Public Sector Employment Law. xxi, 254p. 1988. pap. 49.50 (*0-455-20794-1*, Pub. by Law Bk Co) W W Gaunt.

An Asterisk (*) at the beginning of an entry indicates that the title is appearing in BIP for the first time.

McCarry, John & O'Leary, Brendan, eds. The Future of Northern Ireland. (Illus.). 400p. 1991. 89.00 (*0-19-827329-0*) OUP.

McCart, Alice, ed. Automated Medical Payments Directory: 1993 Edition. 1992. 295.00 (*1-881393-07-0*) Faulkner & Gray.

— Automated Medical Payments Directory, 1994. 424p. 1993. pap. 325.00 (*1-881393-17-8*) Faulkner & Gray.

McCart, Dennie D. The Hope Truck Line & Seventy-Five Miles of Women. LC 83-72535. 101p. 1983. 5.95 (*0-8323-0420-4*) Binford Mort.

— Memories of Edenbrook Farm: Twenty-One Years of Farm Life. (Illus.). 1984. pap. 7.95 (*0-8323-0432-8*) Binford Mort.

McCart, Gerald D., jt. auth. see Welch, Charles D.

***McCart, Linda.** Changing Systems for Children & Families. Glass, Karen, ed. 60p. (Orig.). 1994. pap. text ed. 15.00 (*1-55877-224-3*) Natl Governor.

— Developing Innovative Programs to Support Families. Glass, Karen, ed. 56p. (Orig.). 1992. pap. text ed. 15.00 (*1-55877-147-6*) Natl Governor.

— Investing in Family Self-Sufficiency. Glass, Karen, ed. 51p. (Orig.). 1992. pap. text ed. 15.00 (*1-55877-149-2*) Natl Governor.

***McCart, Linda & Heller, Anne.** Putting Families First. Glass, Karen, ed. 56p. (Orig.). 1993. pap. text ed. 15.00 (*1-55877-211-1*) Natl Governor.

McCartan, Anne-Marie, jt. auth. see Cross, K. Patricia.

McCartan, Marie, jt. auth. see McGarvey, Carol.

McCarter, C. One Minute Reference: Lotus 1-2-3. (Illus.). 200p. (Orig.). 1993. pap. 6.99 (*1-56761-189-3*) Alpha Bks IN.

McCarter, M. K., ed. see Society of Mining Engineers of AIME Staff.

McCarter, Neely D., jt. ed. see Long, Thomas G.

McCarter, P. Kyle, Jr. Samuel I: Volume Eight, a New Translation with Introduction & Commentary. LC 79-7201. (Anchor Bible Ser.). 1980. 34.00 (*0-385-06760-7*) Doubleday.

McCarter, P. Kyle, Jr., ed. Samuel II. LC 81-43919. (Anchor Bible Ser.: Vol. 9). (Illus.). 576p. 1984. pap. 35.00 (*0-385-06808-5*, Anchor NY) Doubleday.

McCarter, P. Kyle, Jr., et al. Ancient Israel: A Short History from Abraham to the Roman Destruction of the Temple. Shanks, Hershel, ed. LC 88-42996. (Illus.). 267p. (C). 1991. reprint ed. 23.95 (*0-9613089-4-X*, 7H70); reprint ed. pap. 16.95 (*1-880317-13-3*) Biblical Arch Soc.

McCarter, P. S., jt. auth. see Greaves, A.

***McCarter, R. William.** 1200 Art Appreciation SG. 176p. (C). 1995. per., pap. text ed. 19.95 (*0-7872-1099-4*) Kendall-Hunt.

***McCarter, Rob.** Optimistic Thinking: The Key to Success. 96p. 1994. pap. 9.95 (*1-57087-073-X*) Prof Pr NC.

***McCarter, Robert.** Fallingwater: Bear Run, Pennsylvania, 1935, Frank Lloyd Wright. (Architecture in Detail Ser.). (Illus.). 60p. (Orig.). (C). 1994. pap. 29.95 (*0-7148-2995-1*, Pub. by Phaidon Press UK) Chronicle Bks.

McCarter, Robert, ed. Abstract, 1988-89. (Illus.). 120p. (Orig.). (C). 1989. pap. write for info. (*0-9623829-0-6*) CUGSA.

— Abstract, 1989-90. (Illus.). 136p. (Orig.). 1990. pap. write for info. (*0-9623829-1-4*) CUGSA.

— Abstract, 1990-91. (Illus.). 128p. (Orig.). (C). 1991. pap. 19.95 (*0-9623829-2-2*) CUGSA.

— Frank Lloyd Wright: A Primer on Architectural Principles. LC 91-8534. (Illus.). 304p. (Orig.). 1991. pap. 29.95 (*0-910413-86-X*) Princeton Arch.

McCarter, Robert, et al, eds. Building; Machines. (Pamphlet Architecture Ser.: No. 12). (Illus.). 64p. (Orig.). 1987. pap. 10.95 (*0-910413-40-1*) Princeton Arch.

McCarter, Steve. Guide to the Milwaukee Road in Montana. LC 92-23233. (Illus.). 104p. (Orig.). 1992. pap. 5.95 (*0-917298-27-6*) Falcon Pr MT.

McCartey, W., Jr., jt. auth. see Hill, Levi L.

McCarthy. A Charmed Life. 1992. pap. 10.95 (*0-15-616774-3*, Harvest Bks) HarBrace.

— Color Atlas of Surgery for the Removal of Melanoma, Vol. 40. (Illus.). 1991. write for info. (*0-8151-5859-9*, Yr Bk Med Pubs) Mosby Yr Bk.

— Essentials of Safe Dentistry for the Medical Compromised Patient. 272p. 1989. text ed. 39.50 (*0-7216-6233-1*) Saunders.

— Materials Characterization Applied to Utilization, Immobilization & Disposal of Solid Wastes. write for info. (*0-444-00870-5*) Elsevier.

— Plastic Surgery, 8 vols. (Illus.). 6448p. 1989. 850.00 (*0-685-45055-4*) Saunders.

— Plastic Surgery, 8 vols., Set. (Illus.). 6448p. 1989. text ed. 895.00 (*0-7216-1514-7*) Saunders.

— The Stonemason. 1995. pap. write for info. (*0-679-76280-9*) Random Hse Value.

McCarthy & Cambron-McCabe, Nelda H. Public School Law. 2nd ed. 1987. text ed. 40.95 (*0-205-10489-4*, H04898) Allyn.

McCarthy, ed. see Wiggershaus, Rolf.

McCarthy, Aine. Body Matters for Women. (Attic Handbooks Ser.). (Illus.). 128p. (Orig.). (C). 1989. pap. 7.95 (*0-946211-86-8*, Pub. by Attic IE) InBook.

— Get Up & Go: A Travel Survival Kit for Women. (Illus.). 160p. (Orig.). (C). 1992. pap. 13.99 (*1-85594-037-X*, Pub. by Attic IE) InBook.

McCarthy, Albert, jt. auth. see Hentoff, Nat.

McCarthy, Albert J., ed. see Hentoff, Nat.

***McCarthy, Alice R. Healthy Preschoolers: At School - At Home. 2nd ed. McCarthy, Jim, ed. LC 94-72479. (Illus.). 93p. 1995. pap. 7.98 (*0-9621645-2-6*) Bridge Commns Inc. First book to describe what preschoolers are learning about health & to encourage families to build on these lessons. Primer on nutrition, safety, sexual abuse, immunization, violence, conflict resolution, disease prevention, & mental health-issues treated with openness, awareness, & hope. Extensive listings of resources. McCarthy is uniquely qualified to write HEALTHY PRESCHOOLERS. Trained in early childhood education at Cornell University, she understands the importance of the family in contributing to the progress of children in school. She called upon the finest experts in the health & education fields to assist her. Dr. Kit Payne, Professor, MI State University says, "I applaud Dr. McCarthy for this valuable offering!" Dr. Eli Saltz, Director, Merrill Palmer Institute, Wayne State University, says, "This truly delightful book is full of good advice & is wonderfully interesting to read. Parents will love it." Dr. Charles J. Barone II, M.D., pediatrician at Henry Ford Medical Center, adds, "WHILE THE BOOK LOOKS DECEPTIVELY SIMPLE, IT IS CRAMMED WITH IMPORTANT HEALTH INFORMATION YOUNG FAMILIES NEED TO KNOW." Foreword by Patricia Nichols, Supervisor, MI Dept. of Ed. Order from Bridge Communications, Inc., 1450 Pilgrim Road, Birmingham, MI 48009 (810) 646-1020; FAX (810) 644-8546.**
Publisher Provided Annotation.

McCarthy, Ann. Minnesota: A Photographic Journey. 1990. 14.99 (*0-517-00177-2*) Random Hse Value.

— North Carolina: A Photographic Journey. 1990. 14.99 (*0-517-00172-1*) Random Hse Value.

McCarthy, Anne. Recognition Technologies: An Introduction. 1994. write for info. (*0-318-72182-1*) Assn Inform & Image Mgmt.

McCarthy, Anne S. Recognition Technologies & Users' Needs - Closing the Gap: An Industry Study & Source Book. McCarthy, Leonard D., Jr., ed. (Illus.). 160p. 1992. 195.00 (*0-9634923-0-6*) Imagine MA.

McCarthy-Arnolds, Eileen, et al, eds. Africa, Human Rights, & the Global System: The Political Economy of Human Rights in a Changing World. LC 93-1643. 288p. 1993. text ed. 57.95 (*0-313-29007-5*, Greenwood Pr) Greenwood.

McCarthy, B. G. The Female Pen: Women Writer's & Novelists, 1621-1818. LC 94-10446. 448p. 1994. 55.00 (*0-8147-5519-4*); pap. 18.50 (*0-8147-5518-6*) NYU Pr.

McCarthy, Barbara, tr. see Verkhovsky, Abbess V.

McCarthy, Barry. Male Sexual Awareness: Increasing Sexual Pleasure. 242p. (Orig.). 1988. pap. 9.95 (*0-88184-348-2*) Carroll & Graf.

McCarthy, Barry & McCarthy, Emily. Confronting the Victim Role: Healing from an Abusive Childhood. 224p. 1993. pap. 11.95 (*0-7867-0011-4*) Carroll & Graf.

— Couple Sexual Awareness: Building Sexual Happiness. (Illus.). 274p. 1990. pap. 9.95 (*0-88184-592-2*) Carroll & Graf.

— Female Sexual Awareness: Achieving Sexual Fulfillment. (Illus.). 320p. 1989. pap. 9.95 (*0-88184-479-9*) Carroll & Graf.

— Intimate Marriage: Developing a Life Partnership. (Illus.). 256p. 1992. pap. 10.95 (*0-88184-824-7*) Carroll & Graf.

— Sexual Awareness. enl. rev. ed. (Illus.). 272p. 1993. pap. 11.95 (*0-7867-0015-7*) Carroll & Graf.

McCarthy, Barry W. & McCarthy, Emily. Sexual Awareness. LC 84-9502. 320p. 1984. pap. 9.95 (*0-88184-100-5*) Carroll & Graf.

McCarthy, Belinda & Langworthy, Robert J., eds. Older Offenders: Perspectives in Criminology & Criminal Justice. LC 87-7147. 256p. 1988. text ed. 65.00 (*0-275-92734-2*, C2734, Praeger Pubs) Greenwood.

McCarthy, Belinda R., ed. Intermediate Punishments: Intensive Supervision, Home Confinement & Electronic Surveillance. LC 87-5069. (Issues in Crime & Justice Ser.). 216p. (Orig.). 1987. pap. text ed. 25.00 (*0-9606960-4-0*) Willow Tree NY.

McCarthy, Belinda R. & McCarthy, Bernard J., Jr. Community-Based Corrections. 2nd ed. LC 90-47532. 431p. (C). 1991. pap. 23.95 (*0-534-15510-3*) Intl Thomson.

McCarthy, Bernard J., Jr., jt. auth. see McCarthy, Belinda R.

McCarthy, Bernice. FourMat in Action: 1982. rev. ed. LC 80-70421. 1990. 19.95 (*0-9608992-1-9*) Excel.

— The FourMat System: Teaching to Learning Styles with Right-Left Mode Techniques. rev. ed. LC 80-70421. 1987. 25.95 (*0-9608992-0-0*) Excel.

***McCarthy, Bernice & Morris, Susan.** 4mat in Action: Sample Units for Grades K-6. 3rd ed. (Illus.). Date not set. 15.95 (*0-9608992-4-3*) Excel.

— 4mat in Action: Sample Units for Grades 7-12. 3rd ed. (Illus.). Date not set. 15.95 (*0-9608992-5-1*) Excel.

McCarthy, Bernice, et al. The FourMat Workbook: Guided Pratice in FourMat Lesson & Unit Planning. 160p. 1987. pap. 12.50 (*0-9608992-3-5*) Excel.

McCarthy, Betty. Utah. LC 89-35083. (America the Beautiful Ser.). 144p. (J). (gr. 4 up). 1989. lib. bdg. 20.55 (*0-516-00490-5*) Childrens.

— Utah. braille ed. 199p. (J). 1993. vinyl bd. 15.40 (*1-56956-176-1*, BR9045) W A T Braille.

McCarthy, Bill & Mallowe, Mike. Vice Cop. 352p. 1993. mass mkt. 5.99 (*0-8217-4025-3*) Zebra.

McCarthy, Bobette. Dreaming. LC 93-2882. (Illus.). 32p. (J). (ps up). 1994. 12.95 (*1-56402-184-X*) Candlewick Pr.

— Happy Hiding Hippos. LC 92-32599. (Illus.). 32p. (J). (ps-1). 1994. text ed. 13.95 (*0-02-765446-X*, Bradbury S&S) S&S Childrens.

— See You Later, Alligator. (Illus.). (J). (ps-1). 1995. 15.00 (*0-02-765447-8*, Mac Bks Young Read) S&S Childrens.

— Ten Little Hippos: A Counting Book. LC 91-17175. (Illus.). 32p. (J). (ps-2). 1992. lib. bdg. 13.95 (*0-02-765445-1*, Bradbury S&S) S&S Childrens.

***McCarthy, Brian.** Au-dela des Mots: Authentic Texts for Advanced Students of French. 96p. (C). 1989. pap. 9.95 (*0-521-31964-1*) Cambridge U Pr.

McCarthy, Bridget B. Cultural Tourism: How the Arts Can Help Market Tourism Products; How Tourism Can Help Provide Markets for the Arts. (Illus.). 200p. (Orig.). 1992. pap. 59.00 (*0-9616696-7-5*) B B McCarthy.

— Where to Find the Oregon in Oregon, 1989-1990. 5th rev. ed. (Illus.). 128p. (Orig.). 1989. pap. 6.95 (*0-9616696-3-2*) B B McCarthy.

McCarthy, Bridget-Beattie. Where to Find the Oregon in Oregon: A Guide to Oregon's Local, Natural, & Cultural Resources. 8th rev. ed. (Illus.). 182p. 1994. pap. 10.95 (*0-9616696-6-7*) B B McCarthy.

McCarthy, Brigid, tr. see Bishop Seraphim Joanta.

McCarthy, C., jt. auth. see Evans, A.

McCarthy, Callum, jt. auth. see Davies, Duncan.

McCarthy, Cameron. Race & Curriculum: Social Inequality & the Theories & Politics of Difference in Contemporary Research on Schooling. 224p. 1990. 60.00 (*1-85000-682-2*, Falmer Pr); pap. 28.00 (*1-85000-683-0*, Falmer Pr) Taylor & Francis.

McCarthy, Cameron & Crichlow, Warren, eds. Race, Identity & Representation in Education. (Critical Social Thought Ser.). 416p. 1993. 55.00 (*0-415-90557-5*, A6865, Routledge NY); pap. 17.95 (*0-415-90558-3*, A6869, Routledge NY) Routledge.

***McCarthy, Candace.** Heaven's Fire. 384p. 1995. mass mkt. 4.99 (*0-8217-4834-3*) Zebra.

— Rapture's Betrayal. 384p. 1993. mass mkt. 4.25 (*0-8217-4108-X*) Zebra.

— Sea Mistress. 384p. 1993. mass mkt. 4.50 (*0-8217-4304-X*) Zebra.

— Smuggler's Woman. 1991. mass mkt. 4.25 (*0-8217-3483-0*) Zebra.

— Warrior's Caress. 384p. 1992. mass mkt. 4.25 (*0-8217-3916-6*) Zebra.

McCarthy, Caritas. The Spirituality of Connelly. LC 86-21718. (Studies in Women & Religion: Vol. 19). 280p. 1986. lib. bdg. 89.93 (*0-88946-530-4*) E Mellen.

McCarthy, Carlton. Detailed Minutiae of Soldier Life in the Army of Northern Virginia, 1861-1865. LC 93-26190. (Illus.). xix, 224p. 1993. pap. 9.95 (*0-8032-8197-8*, Bison Books) U of Nebr Pr.

McCarthy, Carmel, ed. Saint Ephrem's Commentary on Tatian's "Diatessaron" An English Translation of Chester Beatty Syriac MS 709 with Introduction & Notes. (Journal of Semetic Studies: Suppl. No. 2). (Illus.). 388p. 1994. 55.00 (*0-19-922163-4*) OUP.

McCarthy, Carmel & Riley, William. The Old Testament Short Story: Explorations into Narrative Spirituality. (Message of Biblical Spirituality Ser.: Vol. 7). 229p. 1986. 12.95 (*0-8146-5557-2*); pap. 12.95 (*0-8146-5573-4*) Liturgical Pr.

McCarthy, Charles. Doing Business in Ireland. 1987. Looseleaf. ring bd. write for info. (*0-8205-1111-0*) Bender.

McCarthy, Charles H. Lincoln's Plan of Reconstruction. LC 01-26549. reprint ed. 18.45 (*0-404-04105-1*) AMS Pr.

McCarthy, Chris. The Somme: The Day-by-Day Account. (Illus.). 176p. 1994. 29.95 (*1-85409-206-5*) Sterling.

McCarthy, Claire. Learning How the Heart Beats: The Making of a Pediatrician. LC 94-11596. 1995. 21.95 (*0-670-83874-8*, Viking) Viking Penguin.

McCarthy, Claire, jt. auth. see Peterson, Craig A.

McCarthy, Clarence F., et al. The Federal Income Tax: Its Sources & Applications, 1985 Edition. 1,985th ed. (Illus.). 912p. (C). 1984. pap. text ed. 39.33 (*0-13-309220-8*) P-H.

— The Federal Income Tax, 1983: Its Sources & Applications. 32.95 (*0-685-05834-4*) P-H.

McCarthy, Clifford, jt. auth. see Ringgold, Gene.

McCarthy, Colin & Arnold, Nick. Reptile. LC 90-4890. (Eyewitness Bks.: No. 27). (Illus.). 64p. (J). (gr. 5 up). 1991. 16.00 (*0-679-80783-7*); lib. bdg. 16.99 (*0-679-90783-1*) Knopf Bks Yng Read.

McCarthy, Colleen, ed. see Hujsak, Edward.

McCarthy, Colleen, jt. auth. see Ohlinger, John.

McCarthy, Colman. All of One Peace. LC 93-45521. 256p. (C). 1994. text ed. 37.00 (*0-8135-2096-7*); pap. text ed. 15.00 (*0-8135-2097-5*) Rutgers U Pr.

McCarthy, Colman, jt. auth. see Regan, Tom.

McCarthy, Cormac. All the Pretty Horses. 1992. 21.00 (*0-394-57474-5*) Random.

— All the Pretty Horses. LC 92-50836. 1993. pap. 12.00 (*0-679-74439-8*, Vin) Random.

— All the Pretty Horses. large type ed. LC 93-7017. 1993. pap. 22.95 (*0-7927-1575-6*, Curley Lrg Print) Chivers N Amer.

— Blood Meridian. 1994. 21.50 (*0-8446-6793-5*) Peter Smith.

— Blood Meridian. 1992. pap. 11.00 (*0-679-72875-9*, Vin) Random.

— Child of God. 1994. 21.00 (*0-8446-6750-1*) Peter Smith.

— Child of God. LC 92-50587. 1993. pap. 10.00 (*0-679-72874-0*, Vin) Random.

— Crossing. 1994. 23.00 (*0-394-57475-3*) Knopf.

— Crossing. 1995. pap. 5.99 (*0-679-76434-8*, Vin) Random.

— The Crossing. 1995. pap. 13.00 (*0-679-76084-9*, Vin) Random.

— Crossing. 1995. pap. 7.00 (*0-679-76086-5*) Random.

— Crossing. large type ed. 1994. pap. 22.00 (*0-679-75434-2*) Random.

— The Orchard Keeper. 1994. 21.50 (*0-8446-6751-X*) Peter Smith.

— The Orchard Keeper. LC 92-56360. 1993. pap. 11.00 (*0-679-72872-4*) Vintage NY.

— Outer Dark. 1994. 21.00 (*0-8446-6749-8*) Peter Smith.

— Outer Dark. LC 92-50588. 1993. pap. 10.00 (*0-679-72873-2*, Vin) Random.

— The Stonemason: A Play in Five Acts. LC 93-41252. 1994. 19.95 (*0-88001-359-1*) Ecco Pr.

— Suttree. 1994. 22.00 (*0-8446-6792-7*) Peter Smith.

— Suttree. 1992. pap. 12.00 (*0-679-73632-8*, Vin) Random.

McCarthy, D. D. & Carter, W. E., eds. Variations in Earth Rotation. (Geophysical Monograph Ser.: Vol. 59/IUGG 9). 205p. 1990. write for info. (*0-87590-459-9*) Am Geophysical.

McCarthy, Daniel. Computer Industry Advertising & Marketing Forecast, 1990-91. 194p. 1990. ring bd. 1, 395.00 (*0-88709-023-0*) Simba Info Inc.

— Computer Industry Advertising & Marketing Forecast, 1991-92. 206p. 1991. ring bd. 1,495.00 (*0-88709-051-6*) Simba Info Inc.

— Computer Industry Advertising & Marketing Forecast, 1992-93. 250p. ring bd. 295.00 (*0-88709-053-2*) Simba Info Inc.

— Pick the Right Wine: The Only Comprehensive & Foolproof Guide to Matching Specific Foods. 1991. mass mkt. 10.00 (*0-385-41986-4*) Doubleday.

McCarthy, Daniel, ed. Computer Industry Advertising & Marketing Forecast, 1989-90. 135p. 1989. ring bd. 1, 095.00 (*0-88709-019-2*) Simba Info Inc.

McCarthy, David. Golden Age of Rock. 1990. 12.98 (*1-55521-559-9*) Bk Sales Inc.

McCarthy, David A. Fear No More: A B-17 Navigator's Journey. LC 91-73262. (Illus.). 254p. (Orig.). 1991. pap. 12.95 (*0-9624155-3-7*) Cottage Wordsmiths.

McCarthy, David F. Essentials of Soil Mechanics & Foundations. 2nd ed. 640p. (C). 1982. teacher ed write for info. (*0-8359-1782-7*, Reston) P-H.

— Essentials of Soil Mechanics & Foundations: Basic Geotechnics. 4th ed. LC 92-12532. 1992. 69.00 (*0-13-287814-3*) P-H.

McCarthy, David J., Jr. Local Government Law in a Nutshell. 3rd ed. (Nutshell Ser.). 435p. 1990. pap. text ed. 17.50 (*0-314-74486-X*) West Pub.

McCarthy, David J., Jr., jt. auth. see Valente, William D.

McCarthy, David S. That Unforgettable Encounter. 108p. (Orig.). 1983. pap. 4.95 (*0-8341-0834-8*) Beacon Hill.

McCarthy, Dennis. Across the Thlassa Mey. 1991. mass mkt. 4.95 (*0-345-35310-2*, Del Rey) Ballantine.

McCarthy, Dennis D. & Pilkington, John D., eds. Time & the Earth's Rotation. (International Astronomical Union Symposia Ser.: No. 82). 1979. lib. bdg. 84.00 (*90-277-0892-4*); pap. text ed. 56.50 (*90-277-0893-2*) Kluwer Ac.

McCarthy, Dennis M. International Business History: A Contextual & Case Approach. LC 92-31844. 304p. 1994. text ed. 59.95 (*0-275-94413-1*, C4413, Praeger Pubs); pap. text ed. 18.95 (*0-275-94414-X*, B4414, Praeger Pubs) Greenwood.

McCarthy, Dermot. A Poetics of Place: The Poetry of Ralph Gustafson. 352p. (C). 1991. text ed. 49.95 (*0-7735-0815-5*, Pub. by McGill CN) U of Toronto Pr.

— Ralph Gustafson & His Works. (Canadian Author Studies). 86p. (C). 1989. pap. text ed. 9.95 (*1-55022-009-8*, Pub. by ECW Press CN) Genl Dist Srvs.

***McCarthy, Desmond F.** Reconstructing the Family in Contemporary American Fiction. LC 94-38218. (Studies in Themes & Motifs in Literature: Vol. 6). 1995. write for info. (*0-8204-2306-8*) P Lang Pubs.

McCarthy, Dianne, jt. auth. see Davison, Michael.

McCarthy, Donald. Fun with Math-E-Magic. Cooper, William H., ed. (Illus.). 65p. (J). (gr. 4-9). 1984. pap. 3.60 (*0-914127-01-2*) Univ Class.

— More Fun with Science Magic. LC 91-75095. (Illus.). 80p. (Orig.). (J). 1991. pap. 7.33 (*0-914127-12-8*) Univ Class.

McCarthy, Donald G. The New Technologies of Birth & Death: Medical, Legal & Moral Dimensions. LC 80-83425. xvi, 196p. (Orig.). 1980. pap. 8.95 (*0-935372-07-5*) Pope John Ctr.

McCarthy, Donald G., ed. The Family Today & Tomorrow: The Church Addresses Her Future. 291p. 1985. pap. 17.95 (*0-935372-17-2*) Pope John Ctr.

— Moral Theology Today: Certitudes & Doubts. LC 84-11714. 355p. (Orig.). 1984. pap. 17.95 (*0-935372-14-8*) Pope John Ctr.

McCarthy, Donald G. & Leies, John A., eds. Human Sexuality & Personhood: Proceedings of the 1981 Bishops' Workshop. rev. ed. 280p. 1990. pap. text ed. 9.95 (*0-935372-28-8*) Pope John Ctr.

McCarthy, Donald G., ed. see Pope John XXIII Medical-Moral Research & Education Center.

McCarthy, Donald W. Fun with Science Magic. Cooper, William H., ed. LC 84-50893. (Illus.). 80p. (J). (gr. 4-9). 1984. pap. 6.27 (*0-914127-15-2*) Univ Class.

— More Fun with Math-E-Magic. LC 94-61919. (Illus.). 83p. (J). (gr. 5-8). 1995. pap. 7.33 (*0-914127-45-4*, M005) Univ Class.

McCarthy, Dorothea. The Language Development of the Preschool Child, Vol. 4. LC 74-141549. (University of Minnesota Institute of Child Welfare Monographs: No. 4). (Illus.). 174p. 1975. reprint ed. text ed. 45.00 (*0-8371-5896-6*, CWML, Greenwood Pr) Greenwood.

***McCarthy, E. Jerome & Perreault, William.** Basic Marketing Learning Aid. 11th ed. 448p. (C). 1993. text ed. 23.50 (*0-256-12010-2*) Irwin.

— Essentials of Marketing. 4th ed. (C). 1988. text ed. 56.95 (*0-256-06009-6*) Irwin.

McCarthy, E. Jerome, Jr. & Perreault, William D. Essentials of Marketing. 5th ed. 544p. (C). 1990. text ed. 56.95 (*0-256-09323-7*) Irwin.

— Essentials of Marketing: A Global-Managerial Approach. 6th ed. LC 93-29973. (Marketing Ser.). 576p. (C). 1993. text ed. 61.95 (*0-256-12746-8*) Irwin.

McCarthy, E. Jerome & Perreault, William D., eds. Applications in Basic Marketing: Clippings from the Popular Business Press, 1991-1992. 2nd ed. 208p. (C). 1991. pap. text ed. 14.95 (*0-256-10116-7*) Irwin Prof Pubng.

***McCarthy, E. Jerome, et al.** Basic Marketing: Canadian Version. 6th ed. 850p. (C). 1992. text ed. 56.95 (*0-256-09963-4*) Irwin.

— Basic Marketing: Computer-Aided Problems: Canadian Version. 5th ed. 40p. (C). 1989. text ed. 14.00 (*0-256-07387-2*) Irwin.

— Essentials of Marketing: Canadian Version. 3rd ed. 672p. (C). 1990. text ed. 46.95 (*0-256-09420-9*) Irwin.

McCarthy, Edward H. Speechwriting: A Professional Step-by-Step Guide for Executives. LC 89-83450. 121p. 1989. pap. 19.95 (*0-930255-01-1*) Exec Speaker Co.

McCarthy, Emily, jt. auth. see McCarthy, Barry W.

McCarthy, Emily, jt. auth. see McCarthy, Barry.

McCarthy, Eugene & McGaughey, William. Nonfinancial Economics: The Case for Shorter Hours of Work. LC 88-28833. 244p. 1989. text ed. 55.00 (*0-275-92514-5*, C2514, Praeger Pubs) Greenwood.

McCarthy, Eugene, et al. Second Opinion Elective Surgery. LC 81-3471. 193p. 1981. text ed. 55.00 (*0-86569-079-0*, Auburn Hse) Greenwood.

McCarthy, Eugene J. And Time Began. (Illus.). 1993. 10.00 (*0-9627860-6-3*) Lone Oak MN.

— Complexities & Contraries: Essays of Mild Discontent. LC 81-48016. 192p. 1982. 10.95 (*0-15-121202-3*) HarBrace.

— Ground Fog & Night. LC 78-11437. 64p. 1979. 8.95 (*0-15-137261-6*) HarBrace.

— Mr. Raccoon & His Friends. (Illus.). 112p. (J). 1992. reprint ed. 16.00 (*0-89733-377-2*); reprint ed. pap. 6.95 (*0-89733-374-8*) Academy Chi Pubs.

— Required Reading: A Decade of Political Wit & Wisdom. 256p. 1988. 17.95 (*0-15-176880-3*) HarBrace.

— The Ultimate Tyranny: The Majority Over the Majority. LC 79-3530. 256p. 1980. 12.95 (*0-15-192581-X*) HarBrace.

— The View from Rappahannock, No. II. 2nd ed. LC 89-1640. (Illus.). 96p. 1989. pap. 12.95 (*0-939009-19-6*) EPM Pubns.

McCarthy, F. & Hayes, M., eds. Elastic Wave Propagation: Proceedings of the IUTAM-IUPAP Symposium, Galway, Ireland, 20-25 March, 1988. (Applied Mathematics & Mechanics Ser.: No. 35). 638p. 1989. 161.75 (*0-444-87272-8*, North Holland) Elsevier.

McCarthy, F. Desmond, ed. Problems of Developing Countries in the 1990s: Country Studies. (Discussion Paper Ser.: No. 98). 280p. 1990. 15.95 (*0-8213-1633-8*, 11633) World Bank.

— Problems of Developing Countries in the 1990s Vol. 2: Country Studies. (Discussion Paper Ser.: No. 98). 280p. 1990. 15.95 (*0-614-02836-1*, 11633) World Bank.

McCarthy, Flor. Windows on the Gospel: Stories & Reflections. LC 92-61742. 176p. (Orig.). 1992. pap. 9.95 (*0-89622-545-3*) Twenty-Third.

McCarthy, Francis B. & Carr, James G. Juvenile Law & Its Processes. 2nd ed. (Contemporary Legal Education Ser.). 822p. 1989. text ed. 40.00 (*0-87473-435-5*) Michie Butterworth.

McCarthy, Frank C. Frank C. McCarthy: The Old West. deluxe ed. LC 81-80256. (Illus.). 168p. 1981. ring bd. 850.00 (*0-86713-001-6*) Greenw Pr Ltd.

McCarthy, G. J., ed. Fly Ash & Coal Conversion By-Products Characterization, Utilization & Disposal III. (MRS Symposium Proceedings Ser.: Vol. 86). 1987. text ed. 42.00 (*0-931837-51-0*) Materials Res.

McCarthy, G. J. & Roy, D. M. Fly Ash & Coal Conversion By-Products: Characterization, Utilization & Disposal II. (Materials Research Society Symposium Proceedings Ser.: Vol. 65). 1986. text ed. 36.00 (*0-931837-30-8*) Materials Res.

McCarthy, G. Michael. Hour of Trial: The Conservation Conflict in Colorado & the West 1891-1907. LC 75-29410. 1977. 22.95 (*0-8061-1320-0*) U of Okla Pr.

McCarthy, Gary. American River. (RW Ser.: No. 7). 1992. mass mkt. 4.99 (*0-553-29532-2*, Bantam Domain) Bantam.

— Cherokee Lighthorse. (Horsemen Ser.: Bk. 2). 192p. (Orig.). 1992. pap. 3.99 (*1-55773-797-5*) Diamond.

— Colorado. (Rivers West Ser.: No. 3). 1990. 4.99 (*0-553-28451-7*) Bantam.

— The Comstock Camels. LC 92-31938. 1993. 15.00 (*0-385-41990-2*) Doubleday.

— Gila River. 1993. mass mkt. 4.99 (*0-553-29769-4*, Bantam Domain) Bantam.

— The Horseman: Texas Mustangers, Bk. 3. 208p. (Orig.). 1993. pap. 3.99 (*1-55773-857-2*) Diamond.

— The Horsemen, Bk. 1. 1992. pap. 3.99 (*1-55773-733-9*) Diamond.

— The Horsemen Book 5: Stallion Valley. 192p. (Orig.). 1994. pap. text ed. 3.99 (*0-515-11434-0*) Jove Pubns.

— The Russian River. (Rivers West Ser.: No. 5). 1991. mass mkt. 4.50 (*0-553-28844-X*) Bantam.

— Yosemite. 384p. 1995. pap. 5.99 (*0-8217-0144-4*) Zebra.

— Yosemite: A Sweeping Epic Novel of the American Wilderness in the Bestselling Tradition of James Michener... 476p. 1995. pap. 5.99 (*0-7860-0144-5*) Windsor NY.

McCarthy, George. Marx & the Ancients. 356p. (C). 1990. lib. bdg. 51.00 (*0-8476-7641-2*) Rowman.

McCarthy, George & Rhodes, Royal. Eclipse of Justice: Ethics, Economics & the Lost Traditions of American Catholicism. LC 91-34527. 1992. pap. 24.95 (*0-88344-806-8*) Orbis Bks.

McCarthy, George D. Acquisitions & Mergers. LC 63-15017. 361p. reprint ed. pap. 102.90 (*0-8357-5081-7*, 2016632) Bks Demand.

McCarthy, George E. Marx' Critique of Science & Positivism. (C). 1988. lib. bdg. 93.00 (*90-277-2702-3*) Kluwer Ac.

McCarthy, George E., ed. Dialectics & Decadence: Echoes of Antiquity in Marx & Nietzsche. LC 93-49607. 250p. (C). 1994. lib. bdg. 54.50 (*0-8476-7920-9*); pap. text ed. 22.95 (*0-8476-7921-7*) Rowman.

— Marx & Aristotle: Nineteenth-Century German Social Theory & Classical Antiquity. 260p. (C). 1992. text ed. 65.00 (*0-8476-7713-3*); pap. text ed. 24.95 (*0-8476-7714-1*) Rowman.

McCarthy, Gerald. The Ethics of Belief Debate. (American Academy of Religion, Studies in Religion). (C). 1986. 23.95 (*0-89130-892-X*, 01-00-41); pap. 18.95 (*0-89130-893-8*) Scholars Pr GA.

— Shoetown: Poems by Gerald McCarthy. LC 92-71673. (Annual Prize for Poetry (1992) Ser.). 64p. (Orig.). (C). 1992. pap. text ed. 24.95 (*1-55605-207-3*) Wyndhall Pr.

McCarthy, Gillian T., ed. Physical Disability in Childhood. (Interdisciplinary Approach to Management Ser.). (Illus.). 594p. 1992. text ed. 59.95 (*0-443-04288-8*) Churchill.

McCarthy, Gloria & Marso, Molly. Classroom Museums. (Illus.). 56p. (gr. 3-6). 1983. 7.50 (*0-88047-027-5*, 8317) DOK Pubs.

McCarthy, Gregor J. Debt Collection: A Manual for Queensland. 100p. (C). 1990. pap. 65.00 (*1-875114-09-2*, Blckstone AT) W W Gaunt.

McCarthy, Gregory J. & Lauf, Robert J., eds. Fly Ash & Coal Conversion By-Products: Characterization, Utilization & Disposal, Vol. 43. LC 85-7248. 1985. text ed. 30.00 (*0-931837-08-1*) Materials Res.

McCarthy, Gregory J., ed. see Materials Research Society Staff, et al.

McCarthy, Harold T. The Expatriate Perspective: American Novelists & the Idea of America. LC 72-418. 320p. 1973. 35.00 (*0-8386-1150-8*) Fairleigh Dickinson.

McCarthy, Henry, ed. Complete Guide to Employing Persons With Disabilities. LC 84-43093. 1985. 15.00 (*0-318-19037-0*) Human Res Ctr.

McCarthy, Henry & Smart, Lana. Affirmative Action in Action: Strategies for Enchancing Employment Prospects of Qualified Handicapped Individuals. LC 79-90291. 40p. 1979. 3.75 (*0-686-38808-9*) Human Res Ctr.

McCarthy, I. E. Nuclear Reactions. 1970. 143.00 (*0-08-006630-5*, Pub. by Pergamon Repr UK); pap. 120.00 (*0-08-006629-1*, Pub. by Pergamon Repr UK) Franklin.

***McCarthy, Ian E. & Weigold, Erich.** Electron-Atom Collisions. (Cambridge Monographs on Atomic, Molecular, & Chemical Physics: 5). (Illus.). 385p. (C). 1995. 89.95 (*0-521-41359-1*) Cambridge U Pr.

Mccarthy, J. Allan. Transition Equation: A Proven Strategy for Organizational Change. 1995. text ed. 23.00 (*0-02-920485-2*) Free Pr.

McCarthy, J. E. & Shapiro, Stanley J. Basic Marketing: A Managerial Approach. 5th ed. 864p. (C). 1989. text ed. 52.95 (*0-256-07386-4*) Irwin.

McCarthy, J. E. & Tuite, Mick F., eds. Post-Transcriptional Control of Gene Expression. (NATO ASI Series H: Cell Biology: Vol. 49). xix, 652p. 1991. 195.00 (*0-387-51774-X*) Spr-Verlag.

McCarthy, J. M., ed. Kinematics of Robot Manipulators. 200p. 1986. pap. 25.00 (*0-262-63105-9*) MIT Pr.

McCarthy, J. Thomas. McCarthy on Trademarks & Unfair Competition. 3rd ed. LC 92-33247. (IP Ser.). 1992. ring bd. 625.00 (*0-87632-900-8*) Clark Boardman Callaghan.

— McCarthy's Desk Encyclopedia of Intellectual Property. LC 91-8747. 402p. 1991. pap. text ed. 66.00 (*0-87179-682-1*, 0682) BNA.

— The Rights of Publicity & Privacy. LC 86-21543. (Entertainment & Communications Law Ser.). 1987. ring bd. 145.00 (*0-87632-524-X*) Clark Boardman Callaghan.

McCarthy, Jack. Joyce's Dublin: A Walking Guide to 'Ulysses' (Illus.). 80p. 1986. pap. 9.95 (*0-86327-115-4*, Pub. by Wolfhound Pr IE) Dufour.

McCarthy, Jack & Rose, Danis. Joyce's Dublin: A Walking Guide to Ulysses. (Illus.). 96p. 1992. pap. 8.95 (*0-312-07844-7*) St Martin.

McCarthy, Jack, jt. ed. see Lyon, John G.

McCarthy, James. Papago Traveler: The Memories of James McCarthy. Westover, John G., ed. LC 85-14138. (Sun Tracks Ser.: Vol. 13). 200p. 1985. pap. 12.95 (*0-8165-0942-5*) U of Ariz Pr.

— A Pocket Guide to Great Relationships. 96p. 1995. pap. 6.95 (*1-883697-37-9*) Hara Pub.

McCarthy, James B. Adolescence & Character Disturbance. LC 94-16770. 218p. (Orig.). (C). reprint ed. lib. bdg. 48.50 (*0-8191-9582-0*); reprint ed. pap. text ed. 24.50 (*0-8191-9583-9*) U Pr of Amer.

— Death Anxiety: The Loss of the Self. 1980. text ed. 27.95 (*0-89876-069-0*) Gardner Pr.

McCarthy, James D. Deduction Allowed! Challenge the IRS & Win. 1989. pap. 19.95 (*0-13-199134-5*) P-H.

McCarthy, James F., ed. Making Trial Objections. LC 86-5488. (Trial Practice Library Ser.). 240p. 1986. text ed. 128.00 (*0-471-84791-7*) Wiley.

***McCarthy, James G.** The Gospel According to Rome. LC 94-41023. (Orig.). 1995. pap. 11.99 (*1-56507-107-7*) Harvest Hse.

McCarthy, James R. & Allison, George B. Linebacker II: A View from the Rock. (USAF Southeast Asia Monograph Ser.: Vol. 6, Monograph 8). (Illus.). 208p. 1986. reprint ed. pap. write for info. (*0-912799-31-5*) Off Air Force.

McCarthy, Jane & Shorett, Alice. Negotiating Settlements - A Guide to Environmental Mediation. LC 84-70963. 120p. 1984. pap. 10.00 (*0-318-43199-8*) Am Arbitration.

McCarthy, Jane, jt. auth. see Ladimer, Irving.

McCarthy, Jane E., et al. Managing Faculty Disputes. LC 84-47991. (Jossey-Bass Higher Education Ser.). 292p. reprint ed. pap. 83.30 (*0-8357-4909-6*, 2037839) Bks Demand.

McCarthy, Jay, jt. auth. see Walsh, Robb.

***McCarthy, Jim.** Dynamics of Software Development. 1995. 24.95 (*1-55615-823-8*) Microsoft.

— Introduction to Theoretical Kinematics. 160p. 1990. 31.50 (*0-262-13252-4*) MIT Pr.

— Vintage Racing!! Start to Finish: A Complete Guide to the Exciting World of Vintage Racing. LC 90-60140. (Illus.). 150p. (Orig.). 1990. pap. 19.95 (*0-9625532-0-4*, Bruce Michael Assoc) Motorsport Intl.

McCarthy, Jim, ed. see McCarthy, Alice R.

McCarthy, John, Jr. Baseball's All-Time Dream Team. 240p. (Orig.). 1994. pap. 12.95 (*1-55870-329-2*) Betterway Bks.

McCarthy, John. Fantasy & Reality: An Epistemological Approach to Wieland. (European University Studies: German Language & Literature: Ser. 1, Vol. 97). 166p. 1974. pap. 26.70 (*3-261-01357-5*) P Lang Pubs.

— LISP One-Point-Five Programmer's Manual. 1962. text ed. 8.95 (*0-262-13011-4*) MIT Pr.

— The Modern Horror Film: Fifty Contemporary Classics from Curse of Frankenstein to the Lair of the White Worm. (Illus.). 256p. (Orig.). (gr. 9-12). 1990. pap. 15.95 (*0-8065-1164-8*, Citadel Pr) Carol Pub Group.

McCarthy, John, ed. Irish Humor: The Book for All Seasons. LC 68-15417. 384p. 1993. reprint ed. pap. text ed. 14.95 (*0-8264-0622-X*) Continuum.

— Planning Your Veterinary Career. 115p. 1987. 15.00 (*0-941451-00-3*) Am Animal Hosp Assoc.

McCarthy, John & Lifschitz, Vladimir, eds. Formalizing Common Sense: Papers by John McCarthy. LC 89-17660. (Ablex Series in Artificial Intelligence: Vol. 5). 272p. (C). 1990. text ed. 59.50 (*0-89391-535-1*) Ablex Pub.

McCarthy, John, jt. auth. see Akbulat, Selman.

McCarthy, John, jt. ed. see Eid, Mushira.

McCarthy, John, jt. auth. see Hines, Edward R.

McCarthy, John, jt. auth. see Robertson, John.

McCarthy, John A. Crossing Boundaries: A Theory & History of Essay Writing in German, 1680-1815. LC 88-26834. 360p. (C). 1989. text ed. 43.95 (*0-8122-8148-9*) U of Pa Pr.

McCarthy, John C. Punitive Damages in Bad Faith Cases. LC 87-81538. 718p. 1987. 80.00 (*0-915544-18-0*) Lawpress CA.

— Punitive Damages in Wrongful Discharge Cases. LC 85-50568. 543p. 1985. 75.00 (*0-915544-16-4*) Lawpress CA.

— Recovery of Damages for Bad Faith, 2 vols., Set. 5th ed. LC 83-81290. 530p. 1992. 150.00 (*0-915544-46-6*) Lawpress CA.

McCarthy, John D., jt. auth. see Zald, Mayer N.

McCarthy, John F. The Beauty of Golf in New York State. (Illus.). 104p. 1989. 24.95 (*0-685-27011-4*) Summerfield Hse.

— The Science of Historical Theology: Elements of a Definition. LC 91-65352. 195p. (Orig.). 1991. reprint ed. pap. 10.00 (*0-89555-441-0*) TAN Bks Pubs.

McCarthy, John F. & Shugart, Lee R., eds. BioMarkers of Environmental Contamination. (Illus.). 487p. 1990. 79.95 (*0-87371-284-6*, QH541) Lewis Pubs.

McCarthy, John F. & Wright, John. The Science of Historical Theology: Elements of a Definition, Vol. 1. 195p. (Orig.). 1976. pap. 6.00 (*0-912103-01-9*) Stella Maris Bks.

McCarthy, John F., et al, eds. Concepts in Manipulation of Groundwater Colloids for Environmental Restoration. 1993. 79.95 (*0-87371-828-3*, TD426) Lewis Pubs.

McCarthy, John J. John J. McCarthy's Secrets of Super Selling. LC 82-9533. 320p. 1983. pap. 50.00 (*0-932648-43-6*) Boardroom.

***McCarthy, John L., ed.** For Matters of Greater Moment: The First Thirty Jesuit General Congregations. O'Keefe, Martin D., tr. (Series I: No. 12). (Illus.). xix, 788p. 1994. 47.95 (*1-880810-06-9*) Inst Jesuit.

***McCarthy, John P., Jr.** Coaching Youth Football. 2nd rev. ed. LC 95-14391. (Coaching Kids Ser.). Orig. Title: A Parent's Guide to Coaching Football. (Illus.). 160p. 1995. pap. 12.99 (*1-55870-395-0*) Betterway Bks.

McCarthy, John P. Dissent from Irish America. LC 92-45195. 1993. 39.50 (*0-8191-9048-9*) U Pr of Amer.

— Hilaire Belloc: Edwardian Radical. LC 78-5635. (Illus.). 1979. pap. 3.00 (*0-913966-44-4*) Liberty Fund.

McCarthy, John P., Jr. A Parent's Guide to Coaching Baseball. (Parent's Guide Ser.). (Illus.). 128p. 1989. pap. 7.95 (*1-55870-124-9*) Betterway Bks.

— A Parent's Guide to Coaching Basketball. (Parent's Guide Ser.). (Illus.). 136p. (Orig.). 1990. pap. 8.95 (*1-55870-170-2*) Betterway Bks.

— A Parent's Guide to Coaching Soccer. (Parent's Guide Ser.). (Illus.). 136p. (Orig.). 1991. pap. 12.99 (*1-55870-144-3*) Betterway Bks.

McCarthy, John T. Financial Planning for a Secure Retirement. Brennan, Mary E., ed. LC 90-84145. 138p. (Orig.). 1991. pap. 9.95 (*0-89154-412-7*) Intl Found Employ.

McCarthy, Joseph M., ed. see Fenwick, Benedict J.

McCarthy, Joseph M., ed. see Hines, Edward R. & McCarthy, John.

McCarthy, Joseph P., Sr. Twenty-One Bottles of Beer on the Wall: If One Should Happen to Fall. (Illus.). 24p. (Orig.). 1989. pap. text ed. write for info. (*0-318-66434-8*) J P McCarthy.

McCarthy, Joseph R. Major Speeches & Debates of Senator McCarthy. 1975. 250.00 (*0-87968-308-2*) Gordon Pr.

— McCarthyism: The Fight for America. LC 76-46087. (Anti-Movements in America Ser.). 1977. lib. bdg. 22.95 (*0-405-09960-6*) Ayer.

McCarthy, Justin. British Political Portraits. LC 68-22924. (Essay Index Reprint Ser.). 1977. 23.95 (*0-8369-0641-1*) Ayer.

— Death & Exile: The Ethnic Cleansing of Ottoman Muslims, 1821-1922. 384p. 1995. 35.00 (*0-87850-094-4*) Darwin Pr.

— If I Were King. 265p. 1977. reprint ed. lib. bdg. 14.75 (*0-89966-272-2*) Buccaneer Bks.

— The Population of Palestine: Population Statistics of the Late Ottoman Period & the Mandate. (Institute for Palestine Studies). 496p. 1990. text ed. 55.00 (*0-231-07110-8*) Col U Pr.

— Portraits of the Sixties. LC 79-142661. (Essay Index Reprint Ser.). 1977. reprint ed. 25.95 (*0-8369-2061-9*) Ayer.

***McCarthy, Karin & Lashman, Rebekah.** Workforce Development: Building Statewide Systems. 24p. 1994. 15.00 (*1-55516-342-4*, 3123) Natl Conf State Legis.

McCarthy, Kathleen D. Noblesse Oblige: Charity & Cultural Philanthropy in Chicago, 1849-1929. LC 81-21849. (Illus.). (C). 1982. 20.00 (*0-226-55580-1*) U Ch Pr.

— Philanthropy & Culture: The International Foundation Perspective. LC 84-2356. 190p. 1984. pap. 22.95 (*0-8122-1173-1*) U of Pa Pr.

— Women's Culture: American Philanthropy & Art, 1830-1930. LC 91-16632. (Illus.). xviii, 324p. (C). 1992. pap. text ed. 16.95 (*0-226-55584-4*) U Ch Pr.

McCarthy, Kathleen D., ed. Lady Bountiful Revisited: Women Philanthropy, & Power. LC 90-32549. 250p. (C). 1990. text ed. 40.00 (*0-8135-1598-X*); pap. text ed. 15.00 (*0-8135-1611-0*) Rutgers U Pr.

McCarthy, Kathleen D. & Hodgkinson, Virginia A. The Nonprofit Sector in the Global Community: Voices from Many Nations. LC 91-26280. (Nonprofit Sector-Public Administration Ser.). 552p. 1992. 52.95 (*1-55542-397-3*) Jossey-Bass.

***McCarthy, Kevin.** Black Florida. (Illus.). 317p. (Orig.). 1995. pap. 16.95 (*0-7818-0291-1*) Hippocrene Bks.

— Florida Lighthouses. 144p. 1990. pap. 12.95 (*0-8130-0993-6*) U Press Fla.

— Freudian Slips... And Other Childhood Misconcneptions. (Childhood Misconceptions Ser.). (Illus.). 80p. 1995. pap. 6.95 (*1-880925-08-7*) Equitable Media.

— Gorilla Warfare... And Other Childhood Misconceptions. LC 94-76198. (Illus.). 80p. 1994. pap. 6.95 (*1-880925-05-2*) Equitable Media.

— Saudi Arabia: A Desert Kingdom. LC 85-6941. (Discovering Our Heritage Ser.). (Illus.). 128p. (J). (gr. 5 up). 1986. text ed. 14.95 (*0-87518-295-X*, Dillon Silver Burdett) Silver Burdett Pr.

McCarthy, Kevin, ed. Florida Stories. 300p. 1989. pap. 17.95 (*0-8130-0910-3*) U Press Fla.

McCarthy, Kevin M. Grammar & Usage: A Rapid Review. 199p. (C). 1980. pap. text ed. 18.75 (*0-15-529680-9*); teacher ed, pap. text ed. 1.50 (*0-15-529681-7*) HB Coll Pubs.

— Thirty Florida Shipwrecks. LC 91-47020. (Illus.). 128p. 1992. pap. 17.95 (*1-56164-007-7*) Pineapple Pr.

— Twentieth-Century Florida Authors. LC 95-8691. (Studies in American Literature: Vol. 17). (Illus.). 260p. 1996. text ed. 89.95 (*0-7734-8902-9*) E Mellen.

— Twenty Florida Pirates. LC 93-48310. (Illus.). 96p. 1994. pap. 17.95 (*1-56164-050-6*) Pineapple Pr.

McCarthy, Kevin M., ed. The Book Lover's Guide to Florida: Authors, Books & Literary Sites. LC 92-20483. (Illus.). 512p. 1992. 27.95 (*1-56164-012-3*); pap. 18.95 (*1-56164-021-2*) Pineapple Pr.

McCarthy, Kevin M. & Jones, James P. The Gators & the Noles: Honor, Guts, & Glory. (Illus.). 256p. 1993. boxed 22.95 (*0-929895-11-8*) Maupin Hse.

McCarthy, Kevin M., ed. see Douglas, Marjory S.

McCarthy, Kevin M., jt. auth. see Jones, Maxine D.

McCarthy, Kevin W. The On-Purpose Person: How to Discover, Clarify, & Achieve Your Life Purpose. LC 92-61234. 144p. 1992. 12.00 (*0-89109-705-8*) Pinon Press.

McCarthy, Kieran. A Spanish Frontier in the Enlightened Age: Franciscan Beginnings in Sonora & Arizona, 1767-1770. (Monograph Ser.). 1981. 30.00 (*0-88383-063-9*) AAFH.

McCarthy, Kieran & Christensen, Maj-Britt. Cobh's Contribution to the Fight for Irish Freedom: 1913-1990. 223p. (Orig.). 1992. pap. 13.95 (*0-685-67431-2*, Pub. by Oileann Mor IR) Irish Bks Media.

McCarthy, L. T., et al, eds. Chemical Dispersants for the Control of Oil Spills - STP 659. 328p. 1978. 30.00 (*0-8031-0299-2*, 04-659000-24) ASTM.

***McCarthy, Laura F.** Everywoman's Beauty Basics. 224p. 1993. 12.95 (*1-56865-057-4*, GuildAmerica) Dblday Bk Music.

McCarthy, Laura J., et al. Nurse Leadership Development: A Training Program for Developing Nurse Entrepreneurs. LC 91-75022. (Illus.). 346p. 1991. 149.00 (*1-880254-00-X*) Vista.

McCarthy, Lee. Combing Hair with a Seashell. 32p. 1992. pap. 7.50 (*0-938507-20-6*) Ion Books.

An Asterisk (*) at the beginning of an entry indicates that the title is appearing in BIP for the first time.

— Desire's Door. (Roerich Poetry Prize Winner Ser.). 83p. 1991. pap. 10.95 (*0-934257-85-X*) Story Line.

McCarthy, Leo J. & Baldwin, Michael J. Controversies of Leukocyte-Poor Blood & Components. LC 89-17732. (Illus.). (C). 1989. text ed. 22.00 (*0-915355-68-X*) Am Assn Blood.

McCarthy, Leonard D., Jr., ed. see McCarthy, Anne S.

McCarthy, Lillian, tr. see Rohlfs, Gerhard.

McCarthy, M. Dianne. The Maple Leaf. LC 92-91176. 168p. (J). (gr. 3 up). 1994. pap. 9.00 (*1-56002-280-9*, Univ Edtns) Aegina Pr.

***McCarthy, M. J.** To Lay down One's Life for You, Brother. 450p. (Orig.). 1994. pap. 12.95 (*1-885689-00-4*) Spread the Wrd.

McCarthy, M. J. & Carter, Ronald A. Language As Discourse: Perspectives for Language Teaching. LC 92-40126. (Applied Linguistics & Language Study Ser.). 1993. 27.95 (*0-582-08424-5*, 79593) Longman.

McCarthy, M. P. Plain Talk about Prostate Problems: Questions & Answers about Benign Prostatism. LC 90-50889. 1991. pap. 3.95 (*0-88247-857-5*) R & E Pubs.

***McCarthy, Margaret.** Letter Writing Made Easy! Featuring Sample Letters for Hundreds of Common Occasions. 224p. (Orig.). 1995. pap. 12.95 (*0-9639946-2-X*) Snta Monica.

McCarthy, Margaret E. & Owens, John R., Jr. Physics Review Manual for Radiology, Diagnostic, Therapy & Nuclear Medicine. (C). 1984. pap. text ed. 36.25 (*0-534-04452-2*) Jones & Bartlett.

***McCarthy, Margaret W.** Amy Fay: Pioneering American Woman Musician. LC 95-10196. (Detroit Monographs in Musicology/Studies in Music: No. 17). 1995. write for info. (*0-89990-074-7*) Info Coord.

McCarthy, Margaret W., ed. More Letters of Amy Fay: The American Years, 1879-1916. LC 86-2852. xx, 168p. 1986. 40.00 (*0-89990-028-3*) Info Coord.

McCarthy, Marianthy. Readings in English, Bk. 3: Careers. (Readings in English Ser.). 105p. (gr. 9-12). 1987. pap. text ed. write for info. (*0-13-756032-X*, 18884) Prentice ESL.

McCarthy, Marie, ed. Winds of Change: A Colloquium in Music Education with Charles Fowler & David J. Elliott. LC 94-6524. (State-of-the-Arts Ser.). 1994. write for info. (*1-879903-19-9*) Am Council Arts.

McCarthy, Marilyn. They Came to Appomattox. 1993. 9.95 (*0-8062-4694-4*) Carlton.

McCarthy, Martha M. Discrimination in Public Employment: The Evolving Law. 1983. 8.95 (*1-56534-003-5*) NOLPE.

— How Can I Best Manage My Classroom? (Teachers Education Ser.: No. 2). (Orig.). 1980. pap. 1.50 (*0-934402-05-1*) BYLS Pr.

McCarthy, Martha M. & Cambron-McCabe, Nelda H. Public School Law: Teachers' & Students' Rights. 3rd ed. 560p. (C). 1992. text ed. 60.00 (*0-205-13500-5*) Allyn.

McCarthy, Martha M. & Hall, Gayle C. The Emergence of University-Based Education Policy Centers. (Trends & Issues Ser.). vi, 22p. (Orig.). 1989. 7.00 (*0-86552-098-4*) U of Oreg ERIC.

McCarthy, Martha M., et al. Under Scrutiny: The Educational Administration Professoriate. 1988. 13.95 (*0-922971-01-3*) Univ Council Educ Admin.

***McCarthy, Mary.** Birds of America. 1994. lib. bdg. 24.95x (*1-56849-426-2*) Buccaneer Bks.

— Birds of America. 1992. pap. 10.95 (*0-15-612630-3*) HarBrace.

— Cannibals & Missionaries. LC 79-4869. 384p. 1979. 10.95 (*0-15-115387-6*, Harvest Bks) HarBrace.

— Cannibals & Missionaries. 1991. pap. 10.95 (*0-15-615386-6*) HarBrace.

— Cast a Cold Eye. LC 50-9761. 212p. 1950. 12.95 (*0-15-115941-6*) HarBrace.

— Cast a Cold Eye. LC 92-21660. 1992. pap. 10.95 (*0-15-615444-7*, Harvest Bks) HarBrace.

— A Charmed Life. LC 55-10153. 318p. 1955. 15.95 (*0-15-116907-1*) HarBrace.

— The Company She Keeps. 1994. lib. bdg. 24.95x (*1-56849-400-9*) Buccaneer Bks.

— The Company She Keeps. LC 60-3858. 304p. 1901. pap. 7.95 (*0-15-620085-6*, Harvest Bks) HarBrace.

— The Group. 1980. mass mkt. 4.95 (*0-380-52134-2*) Avon.

— The Group. (Modern Classic Ser.). 1989. 15.95 (*0-15-137281-0*) HarBrace.

— Group. 1991. pap. 9.95 (*0-15-637208-8*) HarBrace.

— The Group. 400p. 1991. reprint ed. lib. bdg. 28.95 (*0-89966-856-9*) Buccaneer Bks.

— Le Groupe. (FRE.). 1983. pap. 17.95 (*0-7859-4181-9*) Fr & Eur.

— Groves of Academe. LC 92-21659. 1992. pap. 12.95 (*0-15-637211-8*, Harvest Bks) HarBrace.

— How I Grew. (Illus.). 272p. 1988. pap. 8.95 (*0-15-642185-2*) HarBrace.

— Ideas & the Novel. LC 80-82344. 128p. 1980. 7.95 (*0-15-143682-7*) HarBrace.

— Intellectual Memoirs: New York 1936-1938. 1992. 15.95 (*0-15-144820-5*) HarBrace.

— Intellectual Memoirs: New York, 1936-1938. LC 93-12571. (Harvest Book Ser.). 1993. pap. 9.95 (*0-15-644787-8*) HarBrace.

— The Mask of State: Watergate Portraits Including a Postscript on the Pardons. LC 74-26953. 183p. 1975. pap. 2.65 (*0-15-657302-4*, Harvest Bks) HarBrace.

— Memories of a Catholic Girlhood. LC 57-8842. 245p. 1972. reprint ed. pap. 8.95 (*0-15-658650-9*, Harvest Bks) HarBrace.

— Occasional Prose: Essays. LC 85-765. 352p. 1985. 17.95 (*0-15-167810-3*) HarBrace.

— The Seventeenth Degree. LC 74-1065. 451p. 1974. reprint ed. pap. 3.95 (*0-15-680680-0*, Harvest Bks) HarBrace.

— The Stones of Florence. LC 64-49015. 230p. 1963. pap. 8.95 (*0-15-685080-X*, Harvest Bks) HarBrace.

— The Stones of Florence. LC 59-10257. (Illus.). 138p. 1976. 49.95 (*0-15-185079-8*) HarBrace.

— The Stones of Florence. (Illus.). 1987. text ed. 49.95 (*0-317-64159-X*, Harvest Bks); pap. 19.95 (*0-15-685081-8*, Harvest Bks) HarBrace.

— Venice Observed. LC 64-49016. 158p. 1963. pap. 8.00 (*0-15-693521-X*, Harvest Bks) HarBrace.

— The Writing on the Wall & Other Literary Essays. LC 70-100498. Orig. Title: Hanging by a Thread & Other Literary Essays. 213p. 1971. reprint ed. pap. 4.95 (*0-15-698390-7*, HB207, Harvest Bks) HarBrace.

McCarthy, Mary, jt. auth. see Arendt, Hannah.

McCarthy, Mary E., jt. auth. see Cundiff, David.

McCarthy, Mary F., tr. see Ciria, Alberto.

McCarthy, Mary F., tr. see Ratzinger, Joseph C.

McCarthy, Mary F., tr. see Von Balthasar, Hans U.

McCarthy, Mary F., tr. see Von Speyr, Adrienne.

McCarthy, Mary J. Elk Grove: The Peony Village. Wagner, Roswita M., ed. (Illus.). 167p. 1981. pap. 6.95 (*0-9605940-0-0*) Elk Grove Vill.

McCarthy, Mary-Jane, et al. Reading & Learning Across the Disciplines. 424p. (C). 1993. pap. 27.95 (*0-534-12817-3*) Intl Thomson.

McCarthy, Maureen. Catching the Spirit: Songs of Light & Shadow. LC 94-12991. 67p. 1994. 6.95 (*1-879007-12-6*) St Bedes Pubns.

McCarthy, Maureen E. & Rosenberg, Gail S. Work Sharing Case Studies. LC 81-15943. 277p. 1981. pap. 14.00 (*0-911558-88-8*) W E Upjohn.

McCarthy, Max R. The Last Chance Canal Company. LC 86-23295. 131p. 1987. pap. 7.95 (*0-941214-53-2*) Signature Bks.

McCarthy, Michael. Dark Continent: Africa As Seen by Americans. LC 83-8878. (Contributions in Afro-American & African Studies: No. 75). (Illus.). xxx, 192p. 1983. text ed. 55.00 (*0-313-23828-6*, MDK/, Greenwood Pr) Greenwood.

— Discourse Analysis for Language Teachers. (Language Teaching Library). (Illus.). 224p. (C). 1991. 42.95 (*0-521-36541-4*); pap. 16.95 (*0-521-36746-8*) Cambridge U Pr.

— The Gothic Revival. LC 86-28119. 214p. 1987. text ed. 45.00 (*0-300-03723-6*) Yale U Pr.

McCarthy, Michael, ed. The New Politics of Welfare: An Agenda for the 1990s. LC 89-12855. 274p. (Orig.). (C). 1989. pap. text ed. 25.95 (*0-925065-23-4*) Lyceum IL.

McCarthy, Michael, jt. auth. see Carter, Ronald A.

McCarthy, Michael, jt. auth. see Monnett, John H.

McCarthy, Michael H. The Crisis of Philosophy. LC 89-30040. (SUNY Series in Philosophy). 383p. 1989. 64.50 (*0-7914-0152-9*); pap. 21.95 (*0-7914-0153-7*) State U NY Pr.

McCarthy, Michael J. Introducing Art History: A Guide for Teachers. LC 78-319686. (Ontario Institute for Studies in Education, Symposium Ser.: No. 33). 128p. reprint ed. pap. 36.50 (*0-317-26527-X*, 2023974) Bks Demand.

— Magnetic Resonance Imaging for Food Research & Technology. LC 92-34008. 1992. text ed. 69.95 (*0-442-01021-4*) Chapman & Hall.

— Magnetic Resonance Imaging in Foods. LC 93-48653. 110p. 1994. 79.95 (*0-412-98811-9*) Chapman & Hall.

— Mastering the Information Age. 240p. 1990. pap. 12.95 (*0-87477-575-2*) J P Tarcher.

McCarthy, Michael P. Typhoid & the Politics of Public Health in Nineteenth Century Philadelphia. LC 86-72881. (Memoirs Ser.: Vol. 179). (Illus.). 150p. (Orig.). (C). 1988. pap. 10.00 (*0-87169-179-5*, M179-MCM) Am Philos.

McCarthy, Michael R. Carlisle, History & Guide. LC 93-33707. 1993. pap. 16.00 (*0-7509-0236-1*) A Sutton Pub.

McCarthy, Mignon, jt. auth. see Abdul-Jabbar, Kareem.

McCarthy, Mike, ed. see Redman, Stuart & Ellis, Robert.

McCarthy, Miriam J., jt. auth. see Herman, David.

McCarthy, Muriel Q. David R. Williams: Pioneer Architect. LC 82-17002. (Illus.). 192p. 1984. 35.00 (*0-87074-182-9*) SMU Press.

***McCarthy, Nancy.** Quark Design. 144p. 1995. pap. 34.95 (*0-201-88376-7*) Peachpit Pr.

McCarthy, Nancy W., ed. see Heideman, Carol.

McCarthy, P. Critical Essays on James Joyce's "Finnegans Wake." (Critical Essays on British Literature Ser.). 250p. 1992. text ed. 45.00 (*0-8161-8870-X*, Hall Reference) Macmillan.

McCarthy, P. J. Introduction to Arithmetical Functions. (Universitext Ser.). (Illus.). 375p. 1985. pap. 54.00 (*0-387-96262-X*) Spr-Verlag.

McCarthy, Padraig. A Wedding of Your Own. 108p. 1989. pap. 22.00 (*0-86217-107-5*, Pub. by Veritas IE) St Mut.

McCarthy, Pat. Secrets of Classical Karate. Lee, Mike, ed. LC 87-61100. (Japanese Arts Ser.). 256p. (Orig.). 1987. pap. 19.95 (*0-89750-113-6*, 453) Ohara Pubns.

McCarthy, Patricia A., jt. auth. see Alpiner, Jerome G.

***McCarthy, Patrick.** The Bible of Karate: The Bubishi. (Illus.). 248p. (Orig.). 1995. pap. 16.95 (*0-8048-2015-5*) C E Tuttle.

— Camus: "The Stranger" (Landmarks of World Literature Ser.). 128p. 1988. pap. 10.95 (*0-521-33851-4*) Cambridge U Pr.

— The Crisis of the Italian State: From the Origins of the Cold War to the Fall of Berlusconi. LC 95-11890. 1995. text ed. 35.00 (*0-312-12667-0*) St Martin.

— Saxicolous Species of PorinaMuell. Aeg., Trichotheliae, in the Southern Hemisphere. (Bibliotheca Lichenologica Ser.: Vol. 52). (Illus.). 134p. 1993. pap. 48.00 (*3-443-58031-9*, Pub. by Cramer-Borntraeger GW) Lubrecht & Cramer.

McCarthy, Patrick, ed. France-Germany, 1983-1993: The Struggle to Cooperate. LC 93-12551. 1993. text ed. 45.00 (*0-312-08524-9*) St Martin.

McCarthy, Patrick, jt. ed. see Pasquino, Gianfranco.

McCarthy, Patrick, jt. auth. see Spector, Robert.

McCarthy, Patrick A. Critical Essays on Samuel Beckett. (Critical Essays on British Literature Ser.). 240p. 1986. lib. bdg. 40.00 (*0-8161-8760-6*) G K Hall.

— Forests of Symbols: World, Text, & Self in Malcolm Lowry's Fiction. LC 93-5337. 216p. 1994. 40.00 (*0-8203-1609-1*) U of Ga Pr.

— The Riddles of Finnegans Wake. LC 79-24075. 184p. 1970. 29.50 (*0-8386-3005-7*) Fairleigh Dickinson.

— Ulysses: Portals of Discovery. (Masterwork Studies: No. 41). 130p. 1989. text ed. 21.95 (*0-8057-7976-0*, MWS-41, Pub. by Royal Botanic Garden UK); pap. 12.95 (*0-8057-8026-2*, Pub. by Royal Botanic Garden UK) Macmillan.

McCarthy, Patrick A., ed. The French Socialists in Power, 1981-1986. LC 86-33569. (Contributions in Political Science Ser.: No. 174). 226p. 1987. text ed. 55.00 (*0-313-25407-9*, MFH/, Greenwood Pr) Greenwood.

— Malcolm Lowry's "La Mordida" LC 95-12606. 1996. write for info. (*0-8203-1763-2*) U of Ga Pr.

McCarthy, Patrick A., et al, eds. The Legacy of Olaf Stapledon: Critical Essays & an Unpublished Manuscript. LC 88-25097. (Contributions to the Study of Science Fiction & Fantasy Ser.: No. 34). 140p. 1989. text ed. 45.00 (*0-313-26114-8*, MLC/, Greenwood Pr) Greenwood.

***McCarthy, Paul.** Postmodern Desire Learning from India. (C). 1995. 32.00x (*81-85002-41-X*, Pub. by Promilla) S Asia.

— The Twisted Mind: Madness in Herman Melville's Fiction. LC 90-10754. 192p. (C). 1990. text ed. 26.95x (*0-87745-284-9*) U of Iowa Pr.

McCarthy, Paul & Schroeder, Roger. Woodcarving Illustrated, Bk. 2: Eight Useful Projects You Can Carve Out of Wood. LC 85-10081. (Illus.). 256p. (Orig.). 1985. pap. 12.95 (*0-8117-2285-6*) Stackpole.

McCarthy, Paul, ed. see Ahmed, Saleem.

McCarthy, Paul, ed. see Blackburn, Tom.

McCarthy, Paul, ed. see Brady, James P.

McCarthy, Paul, jt. ed. see Brennan, Matthew.

McCarthy, Paul, ed. see Camp, R. D.

McCarthy, Paul, ed. see Carroll, Gerry.

McCarthy, Paul, ed. see Coonts, Stephen.

McCarthy, Paul, ed. see Costello, John.

McCarthy, Paul, ed. see Coyle, Harold.

McCarthy, Paul, ed. see Cussler, Clive.

McCarthy, Paul, ed. see Davis, Bart.

McCarthy, Paul, ed. see Dickson, Paul.

McCarthy, Paul, ed. see Edelman, Bernard.

McCarthy, Paul, ed. see Foss, Joe & Brennan, Matthew.

McCarthy, Paul, ed. see Galantin, I. J.

McCarthy, Paul, ed. see Goddard, Donald.

McCarthy, Paul, ed. see Hackworth, David H. & Sherman, Julie.

McCarthy, Paul, ed. see Hinshaw, Arned L.

McCarthy, Paul, ed. see Holtz, L.

McCarthy, Paul, ed. see Hynes, Samuel.

McCarthy, Paul, ed. see Joseph, Mark.

McCarthy, Paul, ed. see Kessler, Ronald.

McCarthy, Paul, ed. see Ketwig, John.

McCarthy, Paul, ed. see Krause, Moose & Singular, Stephen.

McCarthy, Paul, ed. see Krulak, Victor H.

McCarthy, Paul, ed. see Kurzman, Dan.

McCarthy, Paul, ed. see Lust, John & Tierra, Michael.

McCarthy, Paul, ed. see Marcinko, David & Weisman, John.

McCarthy, Paul, ed. see Marcinko, Richard & Weisman, John.

McCarthy, Paul, ed. see Marshall, Bryce & Williams, Paul.

McCarthy, Paul, ed. see Miller, F. D. & Kureth, E. C.

McCarthy, Paul, ed. see Miller, John G.

McCarthy, Paul, ed. see Norman, Geoffrey.

McCarthy, Paul, ed. see Norman, Michael.

McCarthy, Paul, ed. see Peters, Ralph.

McCarthy, Paul, ed. see Ruggero, Ed.

McCarthy, Paul, ed. see Sasser, Charles W.

McCarthy, Paul, jt. auth. see Schroeder, Roger.

McCarthy, Paul, ed. see Sellers, Con.

McCarthy, Paul, ed. see Slap, Gail B. & Jablow, Martha M.

McCarthy, Paul, ed. see Stauth, Cameron.

McCarthy, Paul, tr. see Tanizaki, Junichiro.

McCarthy, Paul, tr. see Tanizaki, Jun'ichiro.

McCarthy, Paul, ed. see Taylor, Charles D.

McCarthy, Paul, ed. see Wastermann, John.

McCarthy, Paul, ed. see Westerman, John.

McCarthy, Paul, ed. see Westermann, John.

McCarthy, Paul, ed. see Wilcox, Robert K.

McCarthy, Paul, ed. see Wilson, George C.

McCarthy, Paul, ed. see Zumbro, Ralph.

McCarthy, Paul A. Operation Sea Angel: A Case Study. LC 93-42926. 1994. 13.00 (*0-8330-1492-7*, MR-374) Rand Corp.

McCarthy, Paul A., jt. auth. see Childress, Michael T.

McCarthy, Paul E., jt. auth. see Szilard, Paula.

McCarthy, Paul H., ed. Archives Assessment & Planning Workbook. 86p. 1989. ring bd. 24.00 (*0-931828-72-4*) Soc Am Archivists.

McCarthy, Paul J. Algebraic Extensions of Fields. 1991. pap. 6.95 (*0-486-66651-4*) Dover.

***McCarthy, Paul L.** General Pediatrics: Gastroenterology & Nutrition. Hyams, Jeffrey S., ed. (Current Opinion in Pediatrics Ser.). (Illus.). 620p. (Orig.). 1994. pap. text ed. 34.95 (*1-85922-640-X*) Current Science.

McCarthy, Paul L., et al. General Pediatrics, Gastroenterology & Nutrition, Cardiovascular Medicine, Office Pediatrics. (Current Opinion in Pediatrics, 1993 Ser.). (Illus.). 118p. (Orig.). 1993. pap. text ed. 34.95 (*1-85922-017-7*) Current Science.

McCarthy, Pearl. Leo Smith: A Biographical Sketch. LC 76-383510. 64p. reprint ed. pap. 25.00 (*0-317-09912-4*, 2014277) Bks Demand.

McCarthy, Peter & Simpson, Bob. Issues in Post-Divorce Housing: Family Policy or Housing Policy? 159p. 1991. text ed. 55.95 (*1-85628-202-3*, Pub. by Avebury Pub UK) Ashgate Pub Co.

McCarthy, Philip J. Introduction to Statistical Reasoning. LC 78-1044. 416p. 1978. reprint ed. lib. bdg. 32.50 (*0-88275-661-3*) Krieger.

McCarthy, Philip J., jt. auth. see Stephen, Fredrick F.

McCarthy, Philip L. & Shklar, Gerald. Diseases of the Oral Mucosa. 2nd ed. LC 80-10335. (Illus.). 589p. reprint ed. pap. 167.90 (*0-8357-8687-0*, 2056844) Bks Demand.

***McCarthy, R. L.** Hollywood Squares on Round Mountain. 152p. (Orig.). 1994. pap. 14.95 (*0-9645308-1-3*) Benchtree Pub.

McCarthy, Ralph, tr. see Dazai, Osamu.

McCarthy, Ralph F. The Adventures of Momotaro, the Peach Boy. Ogawa & Pockell, eds. LC 93-18501. (Children's Classics Ser.). (Illus.). 48p. (J). 1994. 13.00 (*4-7700-1755-3*) Kodansha.

— Click-Clack Mountain. Ogawa, ed. (Children's Classics Ser.). (Illus.). 48p. (J). 1994. 14.95 (*4-7700-1850-9*) Kodansha.

— Click-Clack Mountain. (Children's Classic Ser.). (Illus.). 48p. (J). 1994. 14.95 (*4-7700-1856-8*) Kodansha.

— The Monkey & the Crab. (Children's Classics Ser.). (Illus.). 48p. (J). 1994. pap. 14.95 (*4-7700-1844-4*) Kodansha.

— The Sparrow's Inn. (Children's Classics Ser.). (Illus.). 48p. (J). 1994. 14.95 (*4-7700-1849-5*) Kodansha.

— Urashima & the Kingdom Beneath the Sea. Ogawa & Pockell, eds. LC 93-18500. (Children's Classics Ser.). (Illus.). 48p. (J). 1994. 13.00 (*4-7700-1757-X*) Kodansha.

McCarthy, Ralph F., tr. see Dazai, Osamu.

McCarthy, Ralph F., tr. see Murakami, Ryu.

McCarthy, Raymond G., ed. Drinking & Intoxication: Selected Readings in Social Attitudes & Controls. 1959. pap. 23.95x (*0-8084-0409-1*) NCUP.

— Drinking & Intoxication: Selected Readings in Social Attitudes & Controls. LC 59-5289. 1963. pap. 13.95 (*0-911290-28-1*) Rutgers Ctr Alcohol.

McCarthy, Rebecca, ed. see Hodler, Thomas W. & Schretter, Howard A.

McCarthy, Richard. Designing Better Libraries: Selecting & Working with Architects & Related Specialists. 100p. 1995. pap. 15.00 (*0-917846-36-2*, 95612) Highsmith Pr.

McCarthy, Rick. Spymaster. (YA). (gr. 6-10). 1991. write for info. (*0-9629205-0-9*) Develop Solutions.

McCarthy, Rita E. & White, Olivia M. Eighteenth-Century English Pottery: Selections from the Collection of Harry A. Root. (Illus.). 48p. 1991. pap. 14.95 (*0-86559-093-1*) Art Inst Chi.

McCarthy, Robert A. Vinyl Plastics: A World View of the Industry & Market. LC 85-20410. (Series of Special Reports: No. 14). (Illus.). 392p. reprint ed. pap. 111.80 (*0-7837-0859-9*, 2041167) Bks Demand.

McCarthy, Robert E. Secrets of Hollywood Special Effects. 208p. 1992. pap. 39.95 (*0-240-80108-3*, Focal) Buttrwrth-Heinemann.

— Special Effects Sourcebook. 82p. 1992. pap. 31.95 (*0-240-80147-4*, Focal) Buttrwrth-Heinemann.

McCarthy, Robert J. Initiating Restructuring at the School Site. (Fastback Ser.: No. 324). 1991. 1.25 (*0-87367-324-7*) Phi Delta Kappa.

McCarthy, Robert J., ed. see Howard, Sheldon.

McCarthy, Rockne M., jt. ed. see Skillen, James W.

McCarthy, Rockne M., et al. Disestablishment a Second Time: Genuine Pluralism for American Schools. LC 82-9409. 183p. reprint ed. pap. 52.20 (*0-317-30153-5*, 2025335) Bks Demand.

McCarthy, Ron. Building Plank-on-Frame Ship Models. LC 94-68317. (Illus.). 192p. 1994. 34.95 (*1-55750-091-6*) Naval Inst Pr.

McCarthy, Ronald M. & Kruegler, Christopher. Toward Research & Theory Building in the Study of Nonviolent Action. (Monograph Ser.). 35p. (Orig.). 1993. pap. 3.00 (*1-880813-08-4*) A Einstein Inst.

McCarthy, Rosaleen A. & Warrington, Elizabeth K. Cognitive Neuropsychology: A Clinical Introduction. 428p. 1990. text ed. 79.95 (*0-12-481845-5*); pap. text ed. 39.95 (*0-12-481846-3*) Acad Pr.

***McCarthy, Ruth.** By the Seat of Your Pants. 60p. 1994. per., pap. text ed. 4.95 (*0-7872-0054-9*) Kendall-Hunt.

McCarthy, Scott. Celebrating the Earth: An Earth-Centered Theology of Worship with Blessings, Prayers, & Rituals. enl. rev. ed. Orig. Title: Creation Liturgy. (Illus.). 360p. 1991. pap. text ed. 19.95 (*0-89390-199-7*) Resource Pubns.

McCarthy, Sean. Hengler's Circus. 36p. 1981. 39.00 (*0-906474-21-3*, Pub. by Third Eye Centre UK) St Mut.

McCarthy, Sharon, jt. ed. see Stern, Robert N.

McCarthy, Sharon M., jt. auth. see Stern, Robert N.

McCarthy, Sharon M., jt. auth. see Yocom, John E.

McCarthy, Shawn P. Engineer Your Way to Success: America's Top Engineers Share Their Personal Advice on What They Look for in Hiring & Promoting. 112p. (Orig.). 1989. pap. text ed. 18.95 (*0-915409-03-8*) Natl Soc Prof Engrs.

McCarthy, Sherri. Personal Filing Systems: Creating Information Retrieval Systems on Microcomputers. (Orig.). 1988. pap. text ed. 22.40 (*0-8108-2428-0*) Med Lib Assn.

***McCarthy, Sheryl.** Why are the Heroes Always White? 150p. 1995. pap. 8.95 (*0-8362-7049-5*) Andrews & McMeel.

McCarthy, Shirley & Haseltine, Florence P. Magnetic Resonance of the Reproductive System. 180p. 1986. 68.95 (*0-316-55374-3*) Little.

M

An Asterisk (*) at the beginning of an entry indicates that the title is appearing in BIP for the first time.

McCarthy, Stephen. Africa: The Challenge of Transformation. 256p. 1994. text ed. 55.00 (*1-85043-821-8*, Pub. by I B Tauris UK) St Martin.

McCarthy, Susan. Ethnobotany & Medicinal Plants Bibliography: July 1991-July 1992. 134p. (Orig.). (C). 1993. pap. text ed. 50.00 (*1-56806-620-1*) Diane Pub.

McCarthy, Susan, jt. auth. see Cavanaugh, Michael.

McCarthy, Susan, jt. auth. see Mason, Jeffrey M.

***McCarthy, Susanne.** A Candle for the Devil. (Presents Ser.). 1995. mass mkt. 3.25 (*0-373-11748-5*, 1-11748-0) Harlequin Bks.

— Love Is for the Lucky. large type ed. 1990. lib. bdg. 18.95 (*0-263-12347-2*, Pub. by Mills & Boon UK) Thorndike Pr.

— Satan's Contract. (Presents Ser.). 1995. pap. 2.99 (*0-373-11717-5*, 1-11717-5) Harlequin Bks.

McCarthy, T. AutoCAD Express. (Illus.). xiii, 312p. (C). 1991. pap. 29.00 (*0-387-19590-4*, 3781) Spr-Verlag.

— AutoCAD Express. 2nd rev. ed. (Illus.). xvi, 335p. 1993. pap. 39.00 (*0-387-19748-6*) Spr-Verlag.

— AutoCAD of Windows Express. 328p. 1994. pap. text ed. 29.95 (*0-387-19865-2*) Spr-Verlag.

McCarthy, T. L., jt. auth. see Bia, Fred.

McCarthy, Tara. Multicultural Fables & Fairy Tales: Stories & Activities & Promote Literacy. 1994. pap. 12.95 (*0-590-49231-4*) Scholastic Inc.

McCarthy, Tara, jt. auth. see Staton, Hilarie N.

McCarthy, Taylor G. Black Rage. LC 93-93782. (Illus.). 104p. 1994. text ed. 7.95 (*1-56002-317-1*, Univ Edtns) Aegina Pr.

McCarthy, Terence. An Introduction to Malory. Orig. Title: Reading the Morte Darthur. 192p. 1991. reprint ed. text ed. 63.00 (*0-85991-328-7*) Boydell & Brewer.

— An Introduction to Malory. Orig. Title: Reading the Morte Darthur. 192p. 1994. reprint ed. pap. text ed. 25.00 (*0-85991-325-2*) Boydell & Brewer.

McCarthy, Theresa, et al, eds. The Nursing Assistant. LC 93-3671. 1993. pap. 14.50 (*0-13-035924-6*) P-H.

McCarthy, Thomas. Asya & Christine. 217p. 1993. pap. 13.95 (*1-85371-175-6*, Pub. by Poolbeg Pr IE) Dufour.

— The Critical Theory of Jurgen Habermas. 1978. pap. 20.00 (*0-262-63073-7*) MIT Pr.

— Ideals & Illusions: On Reconstruction & Deconstruction in Contemporary Critical Theory. (Illus.). 264p. (C). 1993. pap. 17.50 (*0-262-63145-8*) MIT Pr.

— Ideals & Illusions on Reconstruction & Deconstruction in Contemporary Critical Theory. 315p. 1991. 30.00 (*0-262-13268-0*) MIT Pr.

— Seven Winters in Paris. (C). 1990. 22.00 (*0-948268-61-1*, Pub. by Dedalus Pr IE) St Mut.

McCarthy, Thomas, tr. see Habermas, Jurgen.

McCarthy, Thomas, jt. auth. see Hoy, David.

McCarthy, Thomas A., jt. ed. see Dallmayr, Fred R.

***McCarthy, Tim.** AutoCad for Windows Express. 1994. pap. 39.00 (*3-540-19865-2*) Spr-Verlag.

McCarthy, Timothy. Marx & the Proletariat: A Study in Social Theory. LC 78-4025. (Contributions in Political Science Ser.: No. 18). 102p. 1978. text ed. 49.95 (*0-313-20412-8*, MPL/, Greenwood Pr) Greenwood.

***McCarthy, Timothy G.** The Catholic Tradition: Before & after Vatican II 1878-1993. LC 93-44446. 427p. 1994. 23.95 (*0-8294-0803-7*) Loyola.

— The Catholic Tradition: Before & after Vatican II 1878-1993. LC 93-44446. 427p. 1994. pap. 13.95 (*0-8294-0776-6*) Loyola Univ Pr.

McCarthy, Tom. The King's Men. 256p. (C). 1990. text ed. 31.95 (*0-7453-0310-2*, Pub. by Pluto Pr UK); pap. text ed. 12.50 (*0-7453-0414-1*, Pub. by Pluto Pr UK) Westview.

***McCarthy, Tony.** The Ancestral Album: Record Your Family Tree for Living Memory. (Illus.). 64p. (Orig.). 1994. pap. 9.95 (*1-874675-45-7*, Pub. by Lilliput Pr Ltd IE) Irish Bks Media.

— The Irish Roots Guide. 128p. (Orig.). 1991. pap. 7.95 (*0-946640-77-7*, Pub. by Lilliput Pr Ltd IE) Irish Bks Media.

McCarthy-Tucker, Sherri N. Coping with Special-Needs Classmates. LC 92-40662. 1993. 15.95 (*0-8239-1598-0*) Rosen Group.

McCarthy, Victoria, jt. ed. see Sword, Elizabeth H.

McCarthy, Vincent A. The Phenomenology of Moods in Kierkegaard. 1978. pap. text ed. 51.50 (*90-247-2008-7*) Kluwer Ac.

— Quest for a Philosophical Jesus: Christianity & Philosophy in Rousseau, Kant, Hegel, & Schelling. LC 86-2521. xv, 240p. 1986. 28.95 (*0-86554-210-4*, MUP-H190) Mercer Univ Pr.

McCarthy, Wil. Aggressor Six. 256p. (Orig.). 1994. pap. 4.99 (*0-451-45405-7*, ROC) NAL-Dutton.

— Files from the Amber. 304p. (Orig.). 1995. mass mkt., pap. 4.99 (*0-451-45406-5*, ROC) NAL-Dutton.

McCarthy, Willard. Machine Tool Technology, No. 5. 1986. 29.32 (*0-02-671570-8*) Macmillan.

McCarthy, William. Bible, Church & God. 50.00 (*0-936128-46-1*) De Young Pr.

— Bible, Church & God. 2nd ed. LC 70-169211. (Atheist Viewpoint Ser.). (Illus.). 736p. 1972. reprint ed. 45.95 (*0-405-03805-4*) Ayer.

— Hester Thrale Piozzi: Portrait of a Literary Woman. LC 85-1097. xvi, 306p. 1985. 39.95 (*0-8078-1659-0*) U of NC Pr.

— A Police Administrator Looks at Police Corruption. (Criminal Justice Center Monographs). 1978. pap. text ed. 3.50x (*0-318-37488-9*) John Jay Pr.

McCarthy, William, ed. Legal Intervention in Industrial Relations: Gains & Losses. LC 92-25468. (Warwick Studies in Industrial Relations). 1992. 64.95 (*0-631-18591-7*) Blackwell Pubs.

McCarthy, William & Kraft, Elizabeth, eds. The Poems of Anna Letitia Barbauld. LC 92-39712. (Illus.). 448p. 1994. 65.00 (*0-8203-1528-1*) U of Ga Pr.

McCarthy, William & Mallowe, Mike. Vice Cop: My Twenty Year Battle with New York's Dark Side. LC 90-13365. 320p. 1991. 19.95 (*0-688-08451-6*) Morrow.

McCarthy, William, jt. ed. see Rogers, Katherine M.

McCarthy, William B. The Ballad Matrix: Personality, Mileu, & the Oral Tradition. LC 89-46012. 192p. 1990. 27.95 (*0-253-33718-6*) Ind U Pr.

McCarthy, William B., et al, eds. Jack in Two Worlds: Contemporary North American Tales & Their Tellers. LC 93-35592. (Publications of the American Folklore Society, Bibliographical & Special Ser.). (Illus.). xlvi, 290p. (C). lib. bdg. 45.00 (*0-8078-2135-7*); pap. 16.95 (*0-8078-4443-8*) U of NC Pr.

***McCartin.** From the Street. Date not set. 50.00 (*0-85449-195-3*, Pub. by Gay Mens Pr UK) InBook.

McCartin, James T. The Crazy Aunt & Other Stories. LC 87-26256. 1988. pap. 7.95 (*0-9617589-2-9*) Lincoln Springs Pr.

McCartney. An Embassy to China: Being the Journal Kept by Lord Macartney During His Embassy to the Emperor Ch'ien-lung. LC 70-166618. xv, 241p. 1950. lib. bdg. 49.00 (*0-403-02250-9*) Scholarly.

McCartney, Bill, et al. What Makes a Man? Twelve Promises That Will Change Your Life. LC 92-61235. 240p. 1992. 17.00 (*0-89109-707-4*) NavPress.

McCartney, Brenna. Passion's Blossom. 1982. pap. 3.50 (*0-8217-1109-1*) Zebra.

McCartney, Dan & Clayton, Charles. Let the Reader Understand. 300p. (C). 1994. 16.99 (*1-56476-266-1*, Victor Books) SP Pubns.

McCartney, Donal. Parnell: The Politics of Power. (Illus.). 191p. 1992. 39.95 (*0-86327-317-3*, Pub. by Wolfhound Pr IE); pap. 25.00 (*0-86327-321-1*, Pub. by Wolfhound Pr IE) Dufour.

McCartney, Eugene S. Recurrent Maladies in Scholarly Writing. LC 77-90361. 141p. (C). 1969. reprint ed. 40.00 (*0-87752-068-2*) Gordian.

McCartney, Eugene S., ed. see Campbell, Oscar J., et al.

McCartney, George. Confused Roaring: Evelyn Waugh & the Modernist Tradition. LC 86-46166. 206p. (C). 1987. 25.00 (*0-253-31411-9*) Ind U Pr.

McCartney, James L., ed. see Galliher, John E.

McCartney, Jenny. Grandma's Hospital. LC 92-29958. (Voyages Ser.). (Illus.). (J). 1993. 4.25 (*0-383-03570-8*) SRA Schl Grp.

McCartney, Joan M. The Other Side Makes Chocolate. (Illus.). 88p. (Orig.). 1981. pap. 2.95 (*0-9609788-0-1*) J M McCartney.

McCartney, John T. Black Power Ideologies: An Essay in African-American Political Thought. 256p. (C). 1992. 44.95 (*0-87722-914-7*); pap. 18.95 (*1-56639-145-8*) Temple U Pr.

McCartney, Kathleen, ed. Child Care & Maternal Employment: A Social Ecology Approach. LC 85-644581. (New Directions for Child Development Ser.: No. CD 49). 1990. 17.95 (*1-55542-805-3*) Jossey-Bass.

McCartney, Kathleen, jt. ed. see Pillemer, Karl.

McCartney, Linda. Linda McCartney's Home Cooking: Quick, Easy & Economical Dishes for Today. (Illus.). 176p. 1992. pap. 17.95 (*1-55970-160-9*) Arcade Pub Inc.

— Linda McCartney's Home Cooking: Quick, Easy, & Economical Vegetarian Dishes for Today. (Illus.). 176p. 1990. 24.95 (*1-55970-097-1*) Arcade Pub Inc.

— Linda McCartney's Sixties: Portrait of an Era. (Illus.). 176p. 1992. 50.00 (*0-8212-1959-6*) Bulfinch Pr.

— Linda McCartney's Sixties: Portrait of an Era, Vol. 1. (Illus.). 176p. 1993. pap. 19.95 (*0-8212-2056-X*) Bulfinch Pr.

— Linda's Kitchen: Simple & Inspiring Recipes for Meatless Meals. 192p. 1995. 25.95 (*0-8212-2123-X*) Bulfinch Pr.

McCartney, Marion & Van der Meer, Antonia. Midwife's Pregnancy & Childbirth Book: Having Your Baby Your Way. LC 90-56093. 256p. 1991. pap. 11.00 (*0-06-097360-9*, PL) HarpC.

McCartney, Paul, jt. auth. see Lennon, John.

***McCartney, Rae.** The Crossing. Friedland, J. & Kessler, R., eds. (Novel-Ties Ser.). (J). (gr. 5-7). 1994. student ed, pap. text ed. 15.95 (*1-56982-066-X*) Lrn Links.

McCartney, Robert, jt. ed. see Lowry, Michael.

McCartney, Scott. Defying the Gods: Inside the New Frontiers of Organ Transplants. LC 93-38976. 298p. 1994. text ed. 22.00 (*0-02-582820-7*) Macmillan.

McCartney, Scott, jt. auth. see Bartimus, Tad.

McCartney, Susan. Active Learning in a Family Day Care Setting: Preschool. (Illus.). 184p. (Orig.). 1991. pap. 9.95 (*0-673-46401-6*) GdYrBks.

— Nature & Wildlife Photography: A Practical Guide to How to Shoot & Sell. LC 93-71919. 256p. (Orig.). 1994. pap. 18.95 (*1-880559-12-9*) Allworth Pr.

— Travel Photography: A Complete Guide to How to Shoot & Sell. LC 91-77926. (Illus.). 384p. 1992. pap. 22.95 (*1-880559-00-5*) Allworth Pr.

McCartney, William. The Jungleers: A History of the 41st Infantry Division. (Divisional Ser.). (Illus.). 208p. 1988. reprint ed. 32.50 (*0-89839-120-2*) Battery Pr.

McCartney, Wilma M. Ring the Doorbell with Your Elbow: A Cookbook of "Portables" rev. ed. LC 80-84349. (Illus.). 136p. 1981. pap. 8.95 (*0-933050-07-0*) New Eng Pr VT.

McCartor, Robert & Tyner, George. Eye of the Storm. (Instant Doctor Ser.: Vol. 1). (Illus.). viii, 208p. 1986. 24.95 (*0-89672-141-8*) Tex Tech Univ Pr.

McCarty. Bogey: The Films of Humphrey Bogart. (Illus.). 1970. pap. 16.95 (*0-8065-0001-8*, Citadel Pr) Carol Pub Group.

— English Springer Spaniel. 1994. (*0-7938-1072-8*) TFH Pubns.

McCarty & Young. The Cruise of the Dancer. 1994. pap. 15.95 (*1-881116-29-8*) Black Forrest Pr.

McCarty, Bernie. All-America: The Complete Roster of Football's Heroes. 300p. 1991. pap. 19.95 (*0-685-48956-6*) B McCarty.

— All-America: the Complete Roster of Football's Heroes, Vol. 1: 1889-1945. (Illus.). 300p. (Orig.). 1991. pap. 19.95 (*0-9629969-0-4*) B McCarty.

McCarty, Burke. The Suppressed Truth About the Assassination of Abraham Lincoln. 255p. 1960. reprint ed. 20.00 (*0-686-29301-0*, Chedney) A-albionic Res.

— The Suppressed Truth about the Assassination of Abraham Lincoln. 272p. 1993. reprint ed. spiral bd. 8.25 (*0-7873-0595-2*) Mokelumne.

— The Suppressed Truth About the Assassination of Lincoln. 1972. 250.00 (*0-87968-169-1*) Gordon Pr.

McCarty, C. Barry. A Parliamentary Guide for Church Leaders. 1987. pap. 9.99 (*0-8054-3116-0*) Broadman.

McCarty, Cara. Information Art: Diagramming Microchips. (Illus.). 48p. 1991. pap. 14.95 (*0-87070-310-2*, 0-8109-6087-7) Mus of Modern Art.

— Mario Bellini, Designer. (Illus.). 80p. (Orig.). 1987. pap. 9.95 (*0-87070-224-6*, 0-8109-6014-1) Mus of Modern Art.

McCarty, Cheryll S., see Ima G. Maum, pseud..

Mccarty, Clifford. Complete Films of Humphrey Bogart. 1985. pap. 16.95 (*0-8065-0955-4*, Citadel Pr) Carol Pub Group.

McCarty, Clifford. Film Composers in America: A Checklist of Their Work. LC 72-4448. (Music Ser.). 196p. 1972. reprint ed. lib. bdg. 29.50 (*0-306-70495-1*) Da Capo.

— Published Screenplays: A Checklist. LC 73-138656. (Serif Series: Bibliographies & Checklists: No. 18). 141p. reprint ed. pap. 40.20 (*0-8357-5574-6*, 2035201) Bks Demand.

McCarty, Clifford, ed. Film Music, No. I. LC 88-31035. (Illus.). 300p. 1989. 49.00 (*0-8240-1939-3*) Garland.

McCarty, Clifford, et al. Films of Errol Flynn. 1971. pap. 14.95 (*0-8065-0237-1*, Citadel Pr) Carol Pub Group.

Mccarty, Clifford, et al. Films of Errol Flynn. 1971. 15.95 (*0-685-03372-4*, Citadel Pr) Carol Pub Group.

McCarty, Collin. For You, Just Because You're Very Special to Me. LC 91-73570. (Illus.). 64p. 1991. pap. 7.95 (*0-88396-347-7*) Blue Mtn Pr CO.

McCarty, Daine. Labrador Retriever. 1989. 11.95 (*0-86622-119-0*, KW040) TFH Pubns.

McCarty, Daniel. Arthritis & Allied Conditions: A Textbook of Rheumatology, 2 vols. 12th ed. LC 91-33513. (Illus.). 2151p. 1992. text ed. 198.50 (*0-8121-1430-2*) Williams & Wilkins.

McCarty, Daniel E. & Osteryoung, Jerome S. Analysis of Working Capital Decisions. write for info. (*0-318-57698-8*, Reston) P-H.

McCarty, Dennis. The Birth of the Blade. 1993. mass mkt. 4.99 (*0-345-37713-3*, Del Rey) Ballantine.

McCarty, Dennis, jt. auth. see Argerion, Milton.

***McCarty, Diane.** Basset Hounds. 1994. 11.95 (*0-7938-1088-4*) TFH Pubns.

— German Shorthaired Pointer. (Illus.). 160p. 1991. 11.95 (*0-86622-224-3*, KW-086) TFH Pubns.

— Great Danes. (Illus.). 125p. 1981. 11.95 (*0-86622-508-0*, KW-082) TFH Pubns.

— Lhasa Apsos. 1991. 11.95 (*0-86622-222-7*, KW076) TFH Pubns.

McCarty, Diane & Henneberry, Janet. English Springer Spaniels. (Illus.). 1980. 11.95 (*0-87666-687-X*, KW-081) TFH Pubns.

McCarty, Diane & Kattell, Ted. Collies. (Illus.). 128p. 1980. 11.95 (*0-86622-862-4*, KW-078) TFH Pubns.

McCarty, Diane & Look, Travis. Basset Hounds. (Illus.). 125p. 1979. 11.95 (*0-86622-809-8*, KW-069) TFH Pubns.

McCarty, Donald E. & Hooper, Glynn. The Fine Art of Fault Locating. (ABC of the Telephone Ser.: Vol. 16). (Illus.). 90p. 1989. pap. 24.95 (*1-56016-041-1*) ABC TeleTraining.

McCarty, Donald J. New Perspectives on Teacher Education. LC 73-1852. (Jossey-Bass Higher Education Ser.). 271p. reprint ed. pap. 77.30 (*0-317-41801-7*, 2025662) Bks Demand.

McCarty, Donald J., et al. The School Managers: Power & Conflict in American Public Education. LC 70-105975. (Illus.). 281p. 1971. text ed. 65.00 (*0-8371-3299-1*, MSM/, Greenwood Pr) Greenwood.

McCarty, Doran C. Leading the Small Church. (Orig.). 1991. pap. 7.99 (*0-8054-6039-X*, 4260-39) Broadman.

McCarty, Dwight G. Psychology for the Lawyer. (Historical Foundations of Forensic Psychiatry & Psychology Ser.). 1980. lib. bdg. 59.50 (*0-306-76068-1*) Da Capo.

McCarty, Elizabeth, jt. auth. see Michaels, Bonnie.

McCarty, F. William & Bagby, John W. The Legal Environment of Business. 2nd ed. LC 92-19956. 816p. (C). 1992. text ed. 67.95 (*0-256-10628-2*) Irwin.

— Legal Environment of Business. 2nd ed. 176p. (C). 1992. student ed, text ed. 24.95 (*0-256-11600-8*) Irwin.

McCarty, George. Topology: An Introduction with Application to Topological Groups. (Illus.). 288p. 1988. reprint ed. pap. text ed. 6.95 (*0-486-65633-0*) Dover.

McCarty, Hanoch & McCarty, Melodee. Acts of Kindness: How to Join the Kindness Revolution. 200p. (Orig.). 1994. pap. 10.00 (*1-55874-295-6*, 2956) Health Comm.

McCarty, Hanoch, jt. auth. see McCarty, Meladee.

McCarty, Hanoch, jt. auth. see Simon, Sidney.

McCarty, Harold H., et al. The Measurement of Association in Industrial Geography. LC 81-23752. v, 143p. 1982. reprint ed. text ed. 59.75 (*0-313-23442-6*, MCME, Greenwood Pr) Greenwood.

McCarty, J. W., tr. see Wyrick, D.

McCarty, Jeanne. The Struggle for Sobriety: Protestants & Prohibition in Texas, 1919-1935. (Southwestern Studies: No. 62). 1980. pap. 10.00 (*0-87404-121-X*) Tex Western.

McCarty, Jeannette H. Flowers & Fantasies in the Garden: A Guide for Gardeners & Stories for Romantics. Shea, Jim, ed. LC 92-63257. (Illus.). 186p. (Orig.). 1993. pap. text ed. 16.95 (*0-9635434-0-7*) J H McCarty.

McCarty, John. The Complete Films of John Huston. 1990. pap. 15.95 (*0-8065-1190-7*, Citadel Pr) Carol Pub Group.

— The Fearmakers: The Screen's Directorial Masters of Suspense & Terror. (Illus.). 224p. 1994. pap. 14.95 (*0-312-11272-6*) St Martin.

— The Films of John Huston. (Illus.). 256p. 1987. 19.95 (*0-8065-1020-X*, Citadel Pr) Carol Pub Group.

— Hollywood Gangland: The Movies' Love Affair with the Mob. (Illus.). 288p. 1993. 24.95 (*0-312-09306-3*) St Martin.

— Official Splatter Movie Guide. 1989. pap. 10.95 (*0-312-02958-6*) St Martin.

— The Official Splatter Movie Guide, Vol. II. (Illus.). 208p. (Orig.). 1992. pap. 12.95 (*0-312-07046-2*) St Martin.

— Psychos: Ninety Years of Mad Movies, Maniacs, & Murderous Deeds. LC 92-37552. 1993. 14.95 (*0-8065-1392-6*) Carol Pub Group.

— Sleaze Merchants: Adventures in Exploitation Filmmaking. 1995. pap. 16.95 (*0-312-11893-7*) St Martin.

— Splatter Movies: Breaking the Last Taboo of the Screen. LC 83-19134. (Illus.). 192p. 1984. pap. 13.95 (*0-312-75257-1*) St Martin.

— Thrillers: Seven Decades of Classic Film Suspense. (Illus.). 256p. 1992. pap. 17.95 (*0-8065-1339-X*, Citadel Pr) Carol Pub Group.

McCarty, John L. Maverick Town: The Story of Old Tascosa. LC 87-5946. (Illus.). 320p. (YA). (gr. 6-12). 1968. pap. 13.95 (*0-8061-2089-4*) U of Okla Pr.

McCarty, Maclyn. The Transforming Principle: Discovering That Genes Are Made of DNA. LC 84-20544. (Illus.). 288p. 1986. pap. 5.95 (*0-393-30450-7*) Norton.

McCarty, Marilu H. Dollars & Sense: An Introduction to Economics. 7th ed. 372p. (C). 1993. pap. 34.25 (*0-673-46806-2*) HarpCollege.

— Dollars & Sense: An Introduction to Economics. 7th ed. 372p. (C). 1993. Study guide. student ed 15.00 (*0-673-46807-0*) HarpCollege.

— Introductory Economics. (C). 1987. text ed. 42.75 (*0-673-18320-3*) HarpCollege.

— Introductory Macroeconomics. (C). 1987. pap. text ed. 26.25 (*0-673-18432-3*) HarpCollege.

— Introductory Microeconomics. (C). 1987. pap. text ed. 27.50 (*0-673-18433-1*) HarpCollege.

— Money & Banking: Financial Institutions & Economic Policy. (Economics Ser.). (Illus.). 544p. (C). 1982. teacher ed write for info. (*0-201-05099-4*); text ed. write for info. (*0-201-05098-6*) Addison-Wesley.

McCarty, Marilu H. & Galambos, Eva C. Supply & Demand for College Graduates in the South, 1985. 1978. pap. text ed. 2.50 (*0-686-23907-5*) S Regional Ed.

McCarty, Meladee & McCarty, Hanoch. A Year of Kindness (Perpetual) Three Hundred Sixty-Five Ways to Spread Sunshine: Three Hundred Sixty-Five Ways to Spread Sunshine. 380p. (Orig.). 1994. pap. 8.95 (*1-55874-324-3*, 3243) Health Comm.

McCarty, Melodee, jt. auth. see McCarty, Hanoch.

McCarty, Michael. Michael's Cookbook. 256p. 1989. text ed. 29.95 (*0-02-583111-9*) Macmillan.

McCarty, Michelle, ed. see O'Connor, Sifu R.

McCarty, Patrick, jt. auth. see Yamamoto, Shizuko.

McCarty, Perry L. & Roberts, P. V., eds. Contaminants in the Subsurface Environment: Proceedings of the International Symposium on Processes Governing the Movement & Fate of Contaminants in the Subsurface Environment, Held at Stanford University, California, U. S. A., 23-26 July 1989. (Water Science & Technology Ser.: Vol. 22). (Illus.). 120p. 1990. pap. 86.00 (*0-08-040768-4*, Pergamon Pr) Elsevier.

McCarty, Perry L., jt. auth. see Sawyer, Clair.

McCarty, Raymond. Trumpet in the Twilight of Time. LC 80-53734. (Illus.). 144p. (Orig.). 1981. 10.95 (*0-938310-00-3*); pap. 6.95 (*0-938310-01-1*) Volunteer Pubns.

***McCarty, Robert.** Breaking Ground in Youth Ministry: A Manual for Developing a Parish Youth Ministry. 64p. Date not set. write for info. (*0-89944-322-2*) Don Bosco Multimedia.

— Meeting the Challenge: Resources for Catholic Youth Evangelization. Stamschror, Robert, ed. (Illus.). 46p. (Orig.). 1993. pap. 9.95 (*0-88489-312-X*) St Marys.

***McCarty, Robert J.** Survival in Youth Ministry. Stamschror, Robert, ed. 120p. (Orig.). 1994. pap. 6.95 (*0-88489-317-0*) St Marys.

McCarty, Robert J. & Tooma, Lynn. Training Adults for Youth Ministry. Stamschror, Robert P., ed. 131p. (Orig.). 1990. Training manual. spiral bd. 14.95 (*0-88489-238-7*) St Marys.

McCarty, Skip. The Jehovahs Witnesses. (Discovery Ser.). 31p. 1987. pap. 0.79 (*0-8163-0725-3*) Pacific Pr Pub Assn.

— Mormans, What They Believe. (Discovery Ser.). 31p. 1989. pap. 0.15 (*0-8163-0852-7*) Pacific Pr Pub Assn.

McCarty, William. History of the American War of 1812. 2nd ed. LC 75-126242. (Select Bibliographies Reprint Ser.). 1977. reprint ed. 20.95 (*0-8369-5469-6*) Ayer.

McCarus, et al. Contemporary Arabic Readers: Essays in 2 Parts, Vol. 2. 1976. 18.00 (*0-86685-363-4*) Intl Bk Ctr.

— Contemporary Arabic Readers: Formal Arabic in 2 Parts, Vol. 3. 1987. pap. 19.95 (*0-86685-364-2*) Intl Bk Ctr.

— Contemporary Arabic Readers: Modern Arabic Poetry, 2 Pts., Vol. 5. 1987. 19.95 (*0-86685-366-9*) Intl Bk Ctr.

— Contemporary Arabic Readers: Newspaper Arabic, Vol. 1. 1967. pap. 15.00 (*0-86685-362-6*) Intl Bk Ctr.

— Contemporary Arabic Readers: Short Stories in 2 Parts, Vol. 4. 1992. pap. 19.95 (*0-86685-365-0*) Intl Bk Ctr.

An Asterisk (*) at the beginning of an entry indicates that the title is appearing in BIP for the first time.

— Course in Levantine Arabic. 1979. 22.00x (0-86685-385-5) Intl Bk Ctr.
McCarus, E., et al. First Lessons in Literary Arabic. vi, 90p. 1972. 5.00 (0-916798-08-9, International Academy of Preventive Medicine) Intl Bk Ctr.
— First Lessons in Literary Arabic. 1972. 9.95x (0-86685-383-9) Intl Bk Ctr.
McCarus, E. N., jt. auth. see Abdulla, Jamal.
McCarus, Ernest, ed. The Development of Arab-American Identity. 200p. 1994. text ed. 45.00 (0-472-10439-X) U of Mich Pr.
McCarus, Ernest & Rammuny, Raji. Programmed Course in Modern Literary Arabic Phonology & Script. 1974. 14. 95x (0-86685-384-7) Intl Bk Ctr.
McCarus, Ernest N. Kurdish-English Dictionary. x, 194p. 1967. 16.00 (0-916798-64-X) UM Dept NES.
McCarus, Ernest N. & Rammuny, Raji. A Programmed Course in Modern Literary Arabic Phonology & Script. rev. ed. vi, 175p. 1974. 8.00 (0-916798-02-X) Intl Bk Ctr.
— A Programmed Course in Modern Literary Arabic Phonology & Script. rev. ed. vi, 175p. 1974. audio write for info. (0-318-51707-8) UM Dept NES.
McCarus, Ernest N. & Yacoub, Adil I., eds. Newspaper Arabic. (Contemporary Arabic Readers Ser.: Vol. I). viii, 280p. 1962. 6.00 (0-916798-11-9) Intl Bk Ctr.
McCarus, Ernest N., jt. ed. see Abdulla, Jamal.
McCarus, Ernest N., et al. A Course in Levantine Arabic. rev. ed. 333p. 1978. 15.00 (0-916798-07-0, International Academy of Preventive Medicine) Intl Bk Ctr.
— A Course in Levantine Arabic. rev. ed. 333p. 1978. audio write for info. (0-318-51701-9, International Academy of Preventive Medicine) UM Dept NES.
McCarus, Ernest N., et al, eds. Formal Arabic, 2 pts., Set. (Contemporary Arabic Readers Ser.: Vol. III). 1963. 8.00 (0-916798-13-5) Intl Bk Ctr.
— Formal Arabic Pt. 1: Texts, 2 pts. vii, 118p. 1963. write for info. (0-318-51703-5) UM Dept NES.
— Formal Arabic Pt. 2: Notes & Glossaries, 2 pts. iv, 219p. 1963. write for info. (0-318-51704-3) UM Dept NES.
McCarver, Tim & Levenson, Bob. Oh, Baby I Love It! Baseball Summers, Hot Pennant Races, Grand Salamis, Jellylegs, el Swervos, Dingers, & Dunkers. LC 86-40381. 1987. 16.95 (0-394-55691-7, Villard Bks) Random.
McCary, Ben C. Indians in Seventeenth Century Virginia. (Illus.). 93p. 1980. reprint ed. pap. 6.95 (0-8139-0142-1) U Pr of Va.
— John Smith's Map of Virginia: With a Brief Account of Its History. LC 81-138846. (Jamestown Three Hundred Fiftieth Anniversary Historical Booklets Ser.: No. 3). 26p. reprint ed. pap. 25.00 (0-7837-3568-5, 2043426) Bks Demand.
McCary, James L., jt. auth. see McCary, Stephen P.
McCary, P. K. Black Bible Chronicles, Book I: From Genesis to the Promised Land. LC 93-71549. 208p. (Orig.). 1993. pap. 14.95 (1-56977-000-X) Af Am Family Pr.
— Rappin with Jesus: The Good News According to the Four Brothers. (Black Bible Chronicle Ser.). 208p. 1993. pap. 14.95 (1-56977-005-0) Af Am Family Pr.
McCary, Stephen P. & McCary, James L. Human Sexuality. 3rd ed. 344p. (C). 1984. pap. 32.95 (0-534-02980-9) Intl Thomson.
McCash, Elaine, jt. auth. see Banwell, Colin.
McCash, June H., ed. The Cultural Patronage of Medieval Women. LC 94-13063. 352p. 1995. 60.00 (0-8203-1701-2); pap. 25.00 (0-8203-1702-0) U of Ga Pr.
McCash, June H., jt. auth. see McCash, William B.
McCash, William B. & McCash, June H. The Jekyll Island Club: Southern Haven for America's Millionaires. LC 88-17520. (Illus.). 256p. 1989. 34.95 (0-8203-1070-0) U of Ga Pr.
McCaskey, Glen. The View from Sterling Bluff. LC 88-83080. (Illus.). 56p. 1989. 24.95 (0-929264-13-4) Longstreet Pr Inc.
McCaskey, J. P. Lincoln Literary Collection. LC 71-108586. (Granger Index Reprint Ser.). 1977. 29.95 (0-8369-6114-5) Ayer.
McCaskey, John P. Christmas in Song, Sketch & Story: Nearly Three Hundred Christmas Songs, Hymns & Carols. 1980. lib. bdg. 67.95 (0-8490-3175-3) Gordon Pr.
***McCaskie, T. C.** State & Society in Pre-Colonial Asante. (African Studies: No. 79). (Illus.). 512p. (C). 1995. 69.95 (0-521-41009-6) Cambridge U Pr.
McCaskie, T. C., jt. ed. see Henige, David.
McCaskill, Agnes, tr. see Aliotta, Antonio.
McCaskill, Barbara, jt. ed. see Miller, Suzanne M.
McCaskill, Mizzy & Gilliam, Dona. Flute Handbook. (Building Excellence Ser.). 1993. 7.95 (0-87166-414-3, 94110); audio 16.95 (0-87166-416-X, 94110); 9.98 (0-87166-415-1, 94110) Mel Bay.
— The Flutist's Companion: A Comprehensive Method. 1993. 8.95 (0-87166-764-9, 93886) Mel Bay.
— Fun with the Fife. (Fun Bks.). 1993. 3.95 (1-56222-448-4, 94811); audio 9.98 (1-56222-449-2, 94811) Mel Bay.
— Fun with the Melody Flute. (Fun Bks.). 1993. 3.95 (1-56222-450-6, 94812); audio 9.98 (1-56222-451-4, 94812); audio 12.95 (0-685-74547-3, 94812) Mel Bay.
— Sacred Solos for the Flute, Vol. I. 1993. 6.95 (0-87166-003-2, 94014); audio 9.98 (0-87166-082-2, 94014) Mel Bay.
— Sacred Solos for the Flute, Vol. II. 1993. 6.95 (0-87166-239-6, 94246); audio 9.98 (0-87166-889-0, 94246) Mel Bay.
— Solo Pieces for the Intermediate Flutist. 1993. 6.95 (1-56222-811-0, 94878) Mel Bay.
McCaskill, Mizzy, jt. auth. see Gilliam, Dona.
McCasland, David. Oswald Chambers: Abandoned to God. LC 93-9528. 1993. 19.99 (0-929239-75-X) Discovery Hse Pubs.
— Pinstripe Parables. 144p. (Orig.). (YA). (gr. 10). 1994. pap. 8.99 (0-929239-91-1) Discovery Hse Pubs.
McCasland, David, jt. auth. see Irwin, Bill.
McCasland, Selby V. By the Finger of God: Demon Possession & Exorcism in Early Christianity in the Light of Modern Views of Mental Illness. LC 79-8111. reprint ed. 23.50 (0-404-18425-1) AMS Pr.
McCaslin, Keith. What the Bible Says about Miracles. LC 88-70493. (What the Bible Says Ser.). 426p. 1988. text ed. 13.95 (0-89900-259-5) College Pr Pub.
McCaslin, Mary J. Royal Bayreuth: A Collector's Guide. (Illus.). 150p. 1994. 42.95 (0-915410-97-4); pap. 34.95 (0-915410-96-6) Antique Pubns.
McCaslin, Nellie. Angel of the Battlefield. LC 93-2604. 20p. (J). 1993. pap. 4.00 (0-88734-430-5) Players Pr.
— Bluebonnets. LC 93-5271. 20p. (J). 1993. pap. 4.00 (0-88734-439-9) Players Pr.
— Brave New Banner. 20p. (J). 1993. pap. 4.00 (0-88734-436-4) Players Pr.
— Cold Face - Warm Heart. LC 93-5273. 20p. (J). 1993. pap. 4.00 (0-88734-440-2) Players Pr.
— Creative Drama in the Classroom. 5th ed. 448p. (C). 1990. text ed. 41.95 (0-8013-0380-X, 78160) Longman.
— Creative Drama in the Classroom. 5th rev. ed. LC 89-63227. (Illus.). 520p. 1990. pap. 24.00 (0-88734-604-9) Players Pr.
— Creative Drama in the Classroom: And Beyond. 6th ed. LC 95-15411. (C). 1996. pap. text ed. 36.95 (0-8013-1585-9) Longman.
— Creative Drama in the Intermediate Grades. LC 89-63228. (Illus.). 346p. 1990. pap. 24.00 (0-88734-605-7) Players Pr.
— Creative Drama in the Primary Grades. LC 89-63229. (Illus.). 276p. 1990. pap. 24.00 (0-88734-606-5) Players Pr.
— Daring, Darling Dolly. LC 93-14392. 20p. 1993. pap. 4.00 (0-88734-435-6) Players Pr.
— Historical Guide to Children's Theatre in America. LC 85-12684. 365p. 1987. text ed. 79.50 (0-313-24466-9, Greenwood Pr) Greenwood.
— The Last Horizon. LC 93-5270. 24p. (J). 1993. pap. 4.00 (0-88734-431-3) Players Pr.
— Leading Lady. LC 93-14391. 20p. 1993. pap. 4.00 (0-88734-432-1) Players Pr.
— The Legend of Minna Lamourrie. LC 93-2603. 20p. (J). 1993. pap. 4.00 (0-88734-438-0) Players Pr.
— Legends in Action: Ten Plays of Ten Lands. LC 93-22161. (J). 1995. pap. 15.95 (0-88734-633-2) Players Pr.
— Little Snow Girl. 33p. 1963. pap. 3.45 (0-87129-070-7, L66) Dramatic Pub.
— Mercy in Moccasins. LC 93-14393. 16p. 1993. pap. 4.00 (0-88734-441-0) Players Pr.
— A Miracle in the Christmas City. LC 93-2602. 16p. (J). 1993. pap. 4.00 (0-88734-437-2) Players Pr.
— Pioneers in Petticoats. (Illus.). 206p. (YA). 1993. 20.00 (0-88734-625-1) Players Pr.
— Prelude to Fame. LC 93-14390. 24p. (Orig.). 1993. pap. 4.00 (0-88734-433-X) Players Pr.
— Rabbit Who Wanted Red Wings. 28p. 1963. reprint ed. pap. 3.45 (0-87129-023-5, R44) Dramatic Pub.
— Shows on a Shoestring. 106p. 1979. 9.95 (0-679-20952-2) New Plays Inc.
— A Straight Shooter. LC 93-5252. 16p. (J). 1993. pap. 4.00 (0-88734-429-1) Players Pr.
— Too Many Cooks. LC 93-5250. 20p. (J). 1993. pap. 4.00 (0-88734-434-8) Players Pr.
McCaslin, Richard B. Andrew Johnson: A Bibliography. LC 92-31761. (Bibliographies of the Presidents of the United States Ser.: No. 17). 352p. 1992. text ed. 75.00 (0-313-28175-0, AP17, Greenwood Pr) Greenwood.
— Portraits of Conflict: A Photographic History of South Carolina in the Civil War, No. 4. (Illus.). 416p. 1994. 68. 00 (1-55728-363-X) U of Ark Pr.
— Tainted Breeze: The Great Hanging at Gainesville, Texas 1862. LC 93-15835. (Illus.). 264p. (C). 1993. text ed. 29. 95 (0-8071-1825-7) La State U Pr.
McCaslin, Rosemary, ed. The Older Person As a Mental Health Worker. LC 82-25632. 176p. 1983. 21.95 (0-8261-4290-7) Springer Pub.
***McCaslin, Susan.** Into the Open. 64p. (Orig.). 1995. pap. 9.00 (0-944920-15-2) Bellowing Ark Pr.
— Thinking about God. (Illus.). 24p. (J). 1994. 7.95 (0-89622-615-8) Twenty-Third.
McCaslin, Thomas E. Study Guide to Accompany Guy-Alderman-Winters, Auditing. 3rd ed. 173p. (C). 1993. student ed, pap. text ed. 21.00 (0-03-096536-5) Dryden Pr.
McCaughan, Ed, jt. auth. see Baird, Peter.
McCaughan, Edward J., jt. auth. see Jonas, Susanne.
McCaughan, Edward J., jt. auth. see Jonas, Suzanne.
McCaughan, Jill A., jt. ed. see Kaminski, John P.
McCaughan, Nano & McDougall, Kay, eds. Group Work: A Guide for Teachers & Practitioners. 1978. 23.00 (0-317-05788-X, Pub. by Natl Inst Soc Work) St Mut.
***McCaughan, Nano & Palmer, Barry.** Systems Thinking for Harassed Managers. 160p. 1994. pap. 26.50 (1-85575-055-4) Brunner-Mazel.
McCaughan, Richard. Socks on a Rooster - Louisiana's Earl K. Long. 1967. 15.00 (0-87511-081-9) Claitors.
McCaughey, Davis, et al. Victoria's Colonial Governors, 1839-1900. (Illus.). 453p. 1993. 49.95 (0-522-84509-6) Intl Spec Bk.
McCaughey, Donald G., Jr. Graphic Design for Corrugated Packaging. LC 94-7885. (Illus.). 290p. 1995. 86.00 (1-885067-00-3) Jelmar Pub.
McCaughey, Elizabeth P. From Loyalist to Founding Father. 1980. text ed. 52.00 (0-231-04506-9) Col U Pr.
McCaughey, Robert A. International Studies & Academic Enterprise. 1984. text ed. 47.00 (0-231-05054-2) Col U Pr.
— Josiah Quincy, Seventeen Seventy-Two to Eighteen Sixty-Four: The Last Federalist. LC 73-89506. (Historical Studies: No. 90). 288p. 1974. 20.00 (0-674-48375-8) HUP.
McCaughey, W. T. Atlas of Tumor Pathology: Tumors & Pseudotumors of the Serous Membranes. (Second Ser.: Fascicle 20). (Illus.). 136p. 1990. per., pap. 10.00 (0-16-001857-9, S/N 008-023-000) USGPO.
McCaughrean, Geraldine. El Cid. (Oxford Myths & Legends Ser.). (Illus.). 128p. (YA). (gr. 5 up). 1989. 19. 95 (0-19-276077-7) OUP.
— A Little Lower than the Angels. 144p. (YA). (gr. 6-9). 1987. 15.00 (0-19-271561-5) OUP.
— The Odyssey. (Illus.). 100p. (J). (gr. 4 up). 1993. 14.95 (1-56288-433-6) Checkerboard.
— The Odyssey. (Oxford Illustrated Classics Ser.). (Illus.). 96p. (J). (gr. 2 up). 1995. 19.95 (0-19-274130-6) OUP.
— A Pack of Lies. 168p. (J). (gr. 5-8). 1989. 15.00 (0-19-271612-3) OUP.
McCaughrean, Geraldine, ret. Greek Myths. LC 92-61748. (Illus.). 96p. (J). (gr. 4 up). 1993. text ed. 18.95 (0-689-50583-3, McElderry) S&S Childrens.
McCaughrean, Geraldine, tr. see Ikeda, Daisaku.
McCaughren, Tom. Rainbows of the Moon. 160p. (YA). (gr. 9-12). 1989. 13.95 (0-947962-45-X, Pub. by Childrens Pr IE) Irish Bks Media.
— Run Swift, Run Free. 191p. (J). (ps-8). 1987. 14.95 (0-86327-111-1); pap. 7.95 (0-685-25877-7) Dufour.
— Run Swift Run Free. 1987. pap. 8.95 (0-86327-106-5) Dufour.
— Run to Earth. (Illus.). 144p. (J). (ps-8). 1988. pap. 8.95 (0-86327-116-2, Pub. by Wolfhound Pr IE) Dufour.
— Run to the Ark. (Wildlife Adventure Ser.: Bk. 4). (Illus.). 208p. (J). (gr. 4-8). 1993. 13.95 (0-86327-304-1, Pub. by Wolfhound Pr IE); pap. 9.95 (0-86327-342-4, Pub. by Wolfhound Pr IE) Dufour.
— Run with the Wind. (Illus.). 160p. (J). (ps-8). 1987. pap. 8.95 (0-86327-071-9, Pub. by Wolfhound Pr IE) Dufour.
— The Silent Sea. (Illus.). 111p. (Orig.). (YA). 1988. reprint ed. pap. 7.95 (0-947962-20-4, Pub. by Childrens Pr IE) Irish Bks Media.
— Wildlife Gift Pack. 1990. pap. 27.00 (0-86327-278-9, Pub. by Wolfhound Pr IE) Dufour.
McCaul, Robert L. The Black Struggle for Public Schooling in Nineteenth-Century Illinois. LC 86-26004. 208p. 1987. text ed. 24.95 (0-8093-1335-9) S Ill U Pr.
McCauley. Object Affection. 1991. pap. 10.00 (0-671-74350-3) S&S Trade.
McCauley, Anna K. Miles from Home. 108p. 1984. pap. 3.95 (0-9612430-0-7) A K L M Pubns.
McCauley, Anne. Nineteenth-Century French Caricatures & Comic Illustrations. (Illus.). 40p. 1986. pap. 6.00 (0-935213-02-3) A M Huntington Art.
McCauley, Barbara. Her Kind of Man. (Silhouette Desire Ser.). 1993. pap. 2.89 (0-373-05771-7, 5-05771-6) Silhouette.
— A Man Like Cade. (Silhouette Desire Ser.). 1994. mass mkt. 2.99 (0-373-05832-2, 5-05832-6) Silhouette.
— Texas Heat: (Hearts of Stone) (Desire Ser.). 1995. mass mkt. 3.25 (0-373-05917-5, 1-05917-9) Silhouette.
— Texas Pride. 1995. pap. 3.25 (0-373-05971-X, 1-05971-6) Silhouette.
— Texas Temptation. (Desire Ser.). 1995. mass mkt. 3.25 (0-373-05948-5, 1-05948-4) Silhouette.
— Whitehorn's Woman. (Silhouette Desire Ser.). 1993. mass mkt. 2.99 (0-373-05803-9, 5-05803-7) Silhouette.
McCauley, Carol S. Happenthing in Travel On. 288p. (Orig.). 1990. pap. 10.95 (0-7043-4212-X, Pub. by Womens Pr UK) Interlink Pub.
McCauley, Carole S. The Honesty Tree. LC 84-25905. 224p. (Orig.). 1986. pap. 6.95 (0-9603628-6-X) Frog in Well.
— Pregnancy after Thirty-Five. 224p. 1987. pap. 3.95 (0-317-59883-X) PB.
McCauley, Clark, ed. Terrorism Research & Public Policy. 168p. 1991. 35.00 (0-7146-3429-8, Pub. by F Cass Pubs UK) Intl Spec Bk.
***McCauley, Cleyburn L.** A Brief Bible Outline. Foley, Lucy, ed. (Illus.). 245p. (Orig.). 1995. pap. text ed. 15.95 (0-910531-21-8) Wolcotts.
— Messiah. Foley, Lucy, ed. 198p. (Orig.). 1995. pap. text ed. 9.95 (0-910531-20-X) Wolcotts.
McCauley, Cleyburn L., jt. auth. see Gabriel, Michael L.
McCauley, Cleyburn L., jt. auth. see Gabrile, Michael L.
McCauley, Cynthia D. Effective School Principals: Competencies for Meeting the Demands of Educational Reform. (Technical Report Ser.: No. 146G). 52p. 1990. pap. 15.00 (0-912879-43-2) Ctr Creat Leader.
***McCauley, Cynthia J. & Hughes-James, Martha W.** An Evaluation of the Outcomes of a Leadership Development Program. 84p. 1994. pap. text ed. 35.00 (1-882197-03-8) Ctr Creat Leader.
McCauley, Daniel & McCauley, Kathryn. Decorative Arts of the Amish of Lancaster County. LC 88-81264. (Illus.). 160p. 1988. 29.95 (0-934672-66-0); pap. 19.95 (0-934672-69-5) Good Bks PA.
McCauley, Daniel J. Audit Committees. (Corporate Practice Ser.: No. 49). 1986. 92.00 (1-55871-255-0) BNA.
McCauley, Deborah V. Appalachian Mountain Religion: A History. LC 94-18247. Date not set. write for info. (0-252-02129-0); pap. write for info. (0-252-06414-3) U of Ill Pr.
McCauley, Denis M., tr. see Boguslavsky, M. M. & Smirnov, P. S.
McCauley, Elizabeth A. A. A. E. Disderi & the Carte de Viste Portrait Photograph. LC 84-17281. (Publications in the History of Art: No. 31). (Illus.). 262p. 1985. text ed. 42.50 (0-300-03169-6) Yale U Pr.
— Industrial Madness: Commercial Photography in Paris, 1840-1870. LC 93-30016. (Publications in the History of Art). (Illus.). 456p. 1994. 45.00 (0-300-03854-2) Yale U Pr.
McCauley, George. Aces. 78p. (Orig.). 1991. pap. 8.95 (0-9622889-2-6) Something More.
— Night Air Dancing. 80p. (Orig.). 1990. pap. 8.95 (0-9622889-1-8) Something More.
— No Bright Shield. 80p. (Orig.). 1989. pap. text ed. 8.95 (0-9622889-0-X) Something More.
McCauley, James E. A Stove-up Cowboy's Story. LC 65-4439. (Illus.). 100p. 1965. reprint ed. 9.95 (0-87074-093-8) SMU Press.
***McCauley, James F.** The Steam Trap Handbook. LC 95-13399. 1995. write for info. (0-88173-187-0) Fairmont Pr.
McCauley, James R., jt. auth. see Buchanan, Rex.
McCauley, James W. & Weiss, Volker, eds. Materials Characterization for Systems Performance & Reliability. LC 85-19118. (Sagamore Army Materials Research Conference Proceedings Ser.: Vol. 31). 618p. 1986. 125. 00 (0-306-42095-3, Plenum Pr) Plenum.
***McCauley, Jane.** Phoenix Baby Resource Guide. 2nd rev. ed. (Illus.). 300p. Date not set. pap. 9.95 (0-9637868-1-4) AZ Baby Res.
McCauley, Jane & National Geographic Society Staff. Africa's Animal Giants. Crump, Donald J., ed. (Books for Young Explorers Ser.: Set 14, No. 4). (Illus.). 32p. (J). (ps-3). 1993. pap. 8.00 (0-87044-680-0) Natl Geog.
— National Geographic Society Field Guide of Birds in North America. 2nd ed. LC 86-33249. (Illus.). 464p. 1993. pap. 21.20 (0-87044-692-4) Natl Geog.
— Why on Earth? LC 88-25486. (Books for World Explorers Ser.). (Illus.). 96p. (J). (gr. 3-6). 1993. pap. 12.50 (0-87044-701-7) Natl Geog.
— Wild Animals of North America. rev. ed. (Illus.). 406p. 1988. pap. 35.00 (0-87044-699-1) Natl Geog.
McCauley, Janet, jt. auth. see Olson, Joyce A.
McCauley, Joseph L. Chaos, Dynamics, & Fractals: An Algorithmic Approach to Deterministic Chaos. (Nonlinear Science Ser.: No. 2). (Illus.). 320p. (C). 1993. 94.95 (0-521-41658-2) Cambridge U Pr.
— Chaos, Dynamics, & Fractals: An Algorithmic Approach to Deterministic Chaos. (Nonlinear Science Ser.: No. 2). (Illus.). 320p. (C). 1994. pap. 27.95 (0-521-46747-0) Cambridge U Pr.
***McCauley, Joyce K., et al, eds.** Evolving Issues in the Pacific: Educational Challenges for the 21st Century. (MARC Educational Ser.: No. 16). 143p. 1993. 10.00 (1-878453-16-5) Univ Guam MAR Ctr.
McCauley, Kathryn, jt. auth. see McCauley, Daniel.
McCauley, Kirby, ed. Dark Forces. 1989. pap. 5.99 (0-451-16221-8, Sig) NAL-Dutton.
McCauley, Leo P., tr. see Cyril Of Jerusalem.
***McCauley, Mark.** Interior Design for Idiots. 168p. (Orig.). 1995. pap. 5.95 (1-56245-186-3) Great Quotations.
McCauley, Marlene. Adventures with a Saint: Kateri Tekawitha, "Lily of the Mohawks" McCauley, R. Allan, ed. (Illus.). 208p. (Orig.). 1992. pap. text ed. 8.00 (0-9633633-0-1) Grace House Pub.
McCauley, Martin. The German Democratic Republic since 1945. LC 83-3410. 296p. 1986. pap. 14.95 (0-312-32554-1) St Martin.
— The Khrushchev Era, 1954-1964. LC 95-10405. (Seminar Studies in History). (C). 1995. pap. text ed. 11.95 (0-582-27776-0, Pub. by Longman UK) Longman.
— The Origins of the Cold War 1941-1948. 2nd ed. LC 95-9846. (Seminar Studies in History). 128p. (C). 1996. pap. text ed. 11.95 (0-582-27659-4) Longman.
— Russia's Leading Commercial Banks. LC 94-70632. 178p. Date not set. 69.00 (0-9639807-0-X) CEBIS.
— The Soviet Union: 1917-1991. 2nd ed. LC 92-25942. (Longman History of Russia Ser.). 440p. (C). 1994. pap. text ed. 28.50 (0-582-01323-2, 79637) Longman.
— Stalin & Stalinism. 2nd ed. LC 95-10104. (Seminar Studies in History). 128p. (C). 1996. pap. text ed. 11.95 (0-582-27658-6) Longman.
McCauley, Martin, ed. Gorbachev & Perestroika. LC 89-70320. 240p. 1990. text ed. 49.95 (0-312-04510-7) St Martin.
— Khrushchev & Khrushchevism. LC 86-33896. (Illus.). 254p. (C). 1988. 29.95 (0-253-33142-0) Ind U Pr.
— The Soviet Union after Brezhnev. LC 83-12956. (Illus.). 160p. (C). 1983. 19.95 (0-8419-0918-0); pap. 13.95 (0-8419-0919-9) Holmes & Meier.
— The Soviet Union under Gorbachev. LC 87-9537. 259p. 1987. pap. 14.95 (0-312-00903-8) St Martin.
McCauley, Martin, jt. auth. see Carter, Stephen.
McCauley, Michael. Jim Thompson: Sleep with the Devil. 1991. 19.95 (0-89296-392-1) Mysterious Pr.
McCauley, Patrick B., et al. Michigan Civil Trial Guide. LC 93-16361. 1993. write for info. (0-8205-1915-4) Bender.
McCauley, R. Allan, ed. see McCauley, Marlene.
McCauley, R. W. Marxist Ideology & Soviet Criminal Law. 319p. 1980. 44.00 (0-389-20099-9, 06873) B&N Imports.
McCauley, Robert N., jt. auth. see Lawson, E. Thomas.
McCauley, Rosemarie. Mini Sims Temporaries: Modern Office Simulations, 2 vols. 232p. (Orig.). 1979. teacher ed write for info. (0-672-97168-2) Macmillan.
— Mini Sims Temporaries: Modern Office Simulations, 2 vols., 1. 232p. (Orig.). 1979. pap. text ed. write for info. (0-672-97167-4) Macmillan.
— Mini Sims Temporaries: Modern Office Simulations, 2 vols., 2. 232p. (Orig.). 1979. pap. text ed. write for info. (0-672-97424-X) Macmillan.
McCauley, Rosemarie & Slocum, Keith. Business Spelling & Word Power. 2nd ed. 336p. (C). 1983. teacher ed write for info. (0-672-97976-4); pap. text ed. write for info. (0-672-97975-6) Macmillan.

An Asterisk (*) at the beginning of an entry indicates that the title is appearing in BIP for the first time.

McCauley, Stephen. The Easy Way Out. Rosenman, Jane, ed. LC 92-42590. 1993. reprint ed. pap. 10.00 (*0-671-78738-1*, WSP) PB.

McCaull, Charlene. The Weekend Galley. (Illus.). 56p. 1984. pap. 6.95 (*0-916669-01-7*) Alcyone Pubns.

McCaull, Julian. The Hinge: A Novel on the Mind of War. LC 84-70570. 361p. 1984. 16.95 (*0-916669-00-9*) Alcyone Pubns.

— Train No. 8. LC 87-30756. 1989. 22.95 (*0-87949-279-1*) Ashley Bks.

McCausland, et al. Speech Through Pictures. 1973. text ed. 2.50 (*0-686-09390-9*) Expression.

McCausland, Clare. An Element of Love. Mobium Corporation Staff & Ineman, K., eds. (Illus.). 140p. (Orig.). 1981. pap. 10.00 (*0-9607400-0-7*) Childrens Memorial.

McCausland, Cynthia M., jt. tr. see McCausland, Robert R.

McCausland, Elizabeth. George Inness. LC 76-42705. reprint ed. 26.00 (*0-404-15365-8*) AMS Pr.

— Life & Work of Edward Lamson Henry N. A. LC 74-100614. (Library of American Art Ser.). (Illus.). 1970. reprint ed. lib. bdg. 55.00 (*0-306-71866-9*) Da Capo.

McCausland, M. A., jt. auth. see Calvert, Jack M.

McCausland, Robert R. & McCausland, Cynthia M., trs. The Diary of Martha Ballard, 1785-1812. LC 92-67980. 992p. 1992. 59.95 (*0-929539-62-1*) Picton Pr.

***McCauslin, Mark.** AIDS. LC 94-27798. (Update). (J). 1995. 13.95 (*0-89686-812-5*, Mac Bks Young Read) S&S Childrens.

— The Homeless. LC 93-24106. (Update Ser.). (J). 1994. text ed. 13.95 (*0-89686-805-2*, Crstwood Hse) Silver Burdett Pr.

— Lesbian & Gay Rights. LC 91-40863. (Facts About Ser.). (Illus.). 48p. (J). (gr. 5-6). 1992. text ed. 12.95 (*0-89686-751-X*, Crstwood Hse) Silver Burdett Pr.

— Sexually Transmitted Diseases. LC 91-18445. (Facts About Ser.). (Illus.). 48p. (J). (gr. 5-6). 1992. text ed. 12.95 (*0-89686-720-X*, Crstwood Hse) Silver Burdett Pr.

McCavitt, William E. Radio & Television: A Selected, Annotated Bibliography Supplement One: 1977-1981. LC 82-5743. 167p. 1982. 20.00 (*0-8108-1556-7*) Scarecrow.

— Television & Technology: Alternative Communication Systems. LC 83-10428. (Illus.). 152p. (Orig.). (C). 1983. pap. text ed. 20.00 (*0-8191-3330-2*) U Pr of Amer.

McCaw, Barbara. The Tea Leaf Island. 80p. 1976. 6.50 (*0-87881-029-3*) Mojave Bks.

McCaw, John B. & Arnold, Phillip G. Lower Extremity Reconstruction. LC 87-82108. (Illus.). 246p. 1987. 163.50 (*0-939789-04-3*) Raven.

McCaw, Larry. See You Sunday! Sixty-Two Pastor's Letters to Children. 1992. pap. 3.95 (*1-55673-512-X*, 9304) CSS OH.

McCaw, Mabel. What Is Loving? (Good Little Books for Good Little Children). (Illus.). 12p. (J). (ps). 1987. 3.25 (*0-8378-5208-0*) Gibson.

McCawley, Chris. The First Thing in the Field. LC 82-12061. (Kestrel Chapbks.). 32p. (Orig.). 1982. pap. 3.00 (*0-914974-33-5*) Holmgangers.

McCawley, James D. Everything That Linguists Have Always Wanted to Know about Logic: But Were Ashamed to Ask. LC 80-345. (Illus.). 528p. 1980. pap. text ed. 22.95 (*0-226-55618-2*) U Ch Pr.

— Everything That Linguists Have Always Wanted to Know about Logic but Were Ashamed to Ask. 2nd ed. LC 92-30744. 592p. (C). 1993. lib. bdg. 100.00 (*0-226-55610-7*); pap. text ed. 34.95 (*0-226-55611-5*) U Ch Pr.

— The Syntactic Phenomena of English, Vol. 1. (Illus.). 416p. 1988. pap. text ed. 22.50 (*0-226-55624-7*) U Ch Pr.

— Syntactic Phenomena of English, Vol. 2. (Illus.). 464p. 1988. pap. text ed. 22.50 (*0-226-55626-3*) U Ch Pr.

— Thirty Million Theories of Grammar. LC 82-40319. 240p. (C). 1982. 23.00 (*0-226-55619-0*) U Ch Pr.

McCawley, Patrick. Guide to Civil War Records in the South Carolina Department of Archives & History. Andrews, Judith M., ed. 84p. 1994. pap. write for info. (*1-880067-23-4*) SC Dept of Arch & Hist.

McCawley, Patrick J. Artificial Limbs for Confederate Soldiers. Brimelow, Judith M., ed. 40p. 1992. pap. write for info. (*1-880067-15-3*) SC Dept of Arch & Hist.

McCawley, Rosemary, jt. auth. see Dobrot, Nancy L.

***McCay.** Ellen Gilchrist. 1997. text ed. 22.95 (*0-8057-4029-5*) Macmillan.

— The Eye of the Tiger. (Young Indiana Jones Ser.: No. 15). 1995. pap. 3.99 (*0-679-86992-1*) Random.

McCay, Bill. Stan Lee's Riftworld: Crossover. 256p. 1993. pap. 4.50 (*0-451-45274-7*, ROC) NAL-Dutton.

— Stargate: Rebellion. 272p. 1995. pap. 4.99 (*0-451-45502-9*, ROC) NAL-Dutton.

McCay, Bonnie J. & Acheson, James M., eds. The Question of the Commons: The Culture & Ecology of Communal Resources. LC 87-19833. (Arizona Studies in Human Ecology). 439p. (C). 1990. reprint ed. pap. text ed. 16.95 (*0-8165-1205-1*) U of Ariz Pr.

McCay, Clive M. & McCay, Jeannette B. The Cornell Bread Book: Fifty-Four Recipes for Nutritious Loaves, Rolls & Coffee Cakes. rev. ed. (Illus.). 52p. 1980. reprint ed. pap. 2.95 (*0-486-23995-0*) Dover.

McCay, James T. The Management of Time. 1986. 14.95 (*0-13-548909-1*, Reward); 7.95 (*0-13-548891-5*, Reward) P-H.

McCay, Jeanette B. Clive McCay, Nutrition Pioneer: Biographical Memoirs by His Wife. LC 94-10013. 1994. write for info. (*1-881539-04-0*) Tabby Hse Bks.

McCay, Jeannette B., jt. auth. see McCay, Clive M.

McCay, Mary A. Rachel Carson. (Twayne's United States Authors Ser.). 160p. 1993. text ed. 21.95 (*0-8057-3988-2*, Twayne) Macmillan.

McCay, T. D. & Roux, J. A., eds. Combustion Diagnostics by Nonintrusive Methods, PAAS92. LC 84-12425. (Illus.). 347p. 1984. 74.95 (*0-915928-86-8*) AIAA.

McCay, T. D., jt. ed. see Roux, J. A.

McCay, W. A. & Flood, E. L. The Chains of Command. Stern, David, ed. (Star Trek: The Next Generation Ser.: No. 21). 288p. (Orig.). 1992. mass mkt. 5.50 (*0-671-74264-7*) PB.

McCay, William. Animals in Danger: A Pop-up Book. (Illus.). 12p. (J). (gr. 1-7). 1990. pap. 12.95 (*0-689-71408-4*, Aladdin Paperbacks) S&S Childrens.

— Shoot the Works. LC 89-37749. (Three Investigators Crimebusters Ser.: No. 8). 144p. (J). (gr. 5 up). 1990. pap. 2.95 (*0-679-80157-X*) Random Bks Yng Read.

— Young Indiana Jones & the Circle of Death, Bk. 3. LC 89-43390. (Young Indiana Jones Ser.). 112p. (Orig.). (J). (gr. 3-7). 1990. lib. bdg. 6.99 (*0-679-90578-2*); pap. 2.95 (*0-679-80578-8*) Random Bks Yng Read.

— Young Indiana Jones & the Curse of the Ruby Cross, Bk. 8. LC 90-53242. (Young Indiana Jones Ser.). 128p. (Orig.). (J). (gr. 3-7). 1991. pap. 2.95 (*0-679-81181-8*) Random Bks Yng Read.

— Young Indiana Jones & the Face of the Dragon. (Young Indiana Jones Ser.: No. 11). 132p. (J). (gr. 3-7). 1994. pap. 3.50 (*0-679-85092-9*) Random Bks Yng Read.

— Young Indiana Jones & the Ghostly Riders, Bk. 7. LC 90-53241. (Young Indiana Jones Ser.). 128p. (Orig.). (J). (gr. 3-7). 1991. pap. 3.50 (*0-679-81180-X*) Random Bks Yng Read.

— Young Indiana Jones & the Mountain of Fire. LC 93-46118. (Young Indiana Jones Bks.: Vol. 13). 132p. (Orig.). (J). (gr. 3-7). 1994. pap. 3.99 (*0-679-86384-2*, Bullseye Bks) Random Bks Yng Read.

— Young Indiana Jones & the Plantation Treasure, Bk. 1. LC 89-43388. (Young Indiana Jones Ser.). 112p. (Orig.). (J). (gr. 3-7). 1990. pap. 3.50 (*0-679-80579-6*) Random Bks Yng Read.

McCay, William & Martin, Les. Young Indiana Jones, 4 vols., Set. (J). (gr. 3-7). 1992. Boxed set incls. Young Indiana Jones & The Plantation Treasure, The Gypsy Revenge, The Tomb of Terro. boxed 11.80 (*0-679-83866-X*) Random Bks Yng Read.

McCay, Winsor. Complete Little Nemo, Vol. 1. Marschall, Rick, ed. (Illus.). 112p. 1989. 35.00 (*0-930193-63-6*) Fantagraph Bks.

— The Complete Little Nemo, Vol. 2. (Illus.). 95p. 1990. 29.95 (*0-930193-64-4*) Fantagraph Bks.

— Complete Little Nemo, Vol. 3. Marschall, Richard, ed. (Illus.). 96p. 1990. 35.00 (*1-56097-025-1*) Fantagraph Bks.

— The Complete Little Nemo, Vol. 4. Marschall, Richard, ed. (Illus.). 96p. 1990. 35.00 (*1-56097-045-6*) Fantagraph Bks.

— Complete Little Nemo in Slumberland, Vol. II. Marschall, Richard, ed. & intro. by. (Illus.). 96p. (J). (gr. 6 up). 1989. 34.95 (*0-924359-02-1*) Remco Wrldserv Bks.

— The Complete Little Nemo in Slumberland: In the Land of Wonderful Dreams, Part 2 - 1913-1914, Vol. VI. Marschall, Richard, ed. (Illus.). 96p. (J). (gr. 6 up). 1992. 34.95 (*0-924359-36-6*) Remco Wrldserv Bks.

— Complete Little Nemo in Slumberland: In the Land of Wonderful Dreams, Pt. 1, 1911-1912, Vol. V. (Illus.). 96p. 1991. 39.95 (*0-924359-35-8*) Remco Wrldserv Bks.

— The Complete Little Nemo in Slumberland, Vol. III: 1908-1910. (Illus.). 96p. (YA). (gr. 6 up). 1990. 34.95 (*0-924359-03-X*) Remco Wrldserv Bks.

— The Complete Little Nemo in Slumberland, Vol. IV: 1910-1911. (Illus.). 96p. (YA). (gr. 6 up). 1990. 34.95 (*0-924359-04-8*) Remco Wrldserv Bks.

— The Complete Little Nemo in Slumberland, Vols. I-IV: 1905-1911. (Illus.). 96p. (YA). (gr. 6 up). 1991. 139.80 (*0-924359-00-5*) Remco Wrldserv Bks.

— Dreams of the Rarebit Fiend. (Illus.). 80p. 1973. reprint ed. pap. 4.95 (*0-486-21347-1*) Dover.

— Little Nemo, in the Land of Wonderful Dreams, Vol. 1: 1911-1912. 1991. pap. 19.95 (*1-56060-125-6*) Eclipse Bks.

— Little Nemo in the Palace of Ice, & Further Adventures. LC 75-19834. (Illus.). 32p. (Orig.). 1976. pap. 6.95 (*0-486-23234-4*) Dover.

McCelland, Doug. Blackface to Blacklist: Al Jolson, Larry Parks, & "The Jolson Story" LC 86-29797. (Illus.). 298p. 1987. 29.50 (*0-8108-1965-1*) Scarecrow.

McCelland, Mike. Crankbaits: A Guide to Trolling & Casting Depths of 200 Popular Lures. (Illus.). 84p. 1990. spiral bd. write for info. (*0-318-66847-5*) Fishing Enterprises.

McCGwire, Michael. Military Objectives in Soviet Foreign Policy. LC 86-24932. 530p. 1987. 39.95 (*0-8157-5552-X*); pap. 18.95 (*0-8157-5551-1*) Brookings.

— Perestroika & Soviet National Security. LC 87-17657. 481p. 1991. 39.95 (*0-8157-5554-6*); pap. 18.95 (*0-8157-5553-8*) Brookings.

McCheever, Ted. Eddy Current. Schreck, Bob & Prosser, Jerry, eds. (Illus.). 360p. 1992. 24.95 (*1-878574-20-5*) Dark Horse Comics.

***McChesney, Debbie.** Once Upon a Child: Writing Your Child's Special Story. (Illus.). 1995. 19.95 (*1-56145-100-2*) Peachtree Pubs.

McChesney, Fred S. & Shughart, William F., II, eds. The Causes & Consequences of Antitrust: The Public-Choice Perspective. (Illus.). 392p. 1994. pap. text ed. 32.95 (*0-226-55635-2*) U Ch Pr.

— The Causes & Consequences of Antitrust: The Public-Choice Perspective. (Illus.). 392p. 1995. lib. bdg. 66.00 (*0-226-55634-4*) U Ch Pr.

***McChesney, James.** Picture Oregon: Portraits of the University of Oregon. 1994. 59.95 (*0-87114-287-2*) U of Oreg Bks.

McChesney, Jim. Best Choices on Oregon I-5. 1992. pap. 12.95 (*1-879881-01-2*) Global Pub OR.

McChesney, Kathryn, jt. auth. see Rogers, A. R.

McChesney, Malcolm. Thermodynamics of Electrical Processes. LC 75-166417. 286p. reprint ed. pap. 81.60 (*0-317-10940-5*, 2016147) Bks Demand.

McChesney, R. D. War in Central Asia: Four Hundred Years in the History of a Muslim Shrine, 1480-1889. 347p. 1991. text ed. 55.00 (*0-691-05584-X*) Princeton U Pr.

McChesney, Roberet W. The Battle for the Control of U. S. Broadcasting, 1930-1935. LC 92-15440. (C). 1993. 49.95 (*0-19-507174-3*) OUP.

McChesney, Robert, jt. ed. see Solomon, William.

McChesney, Robert W. Telecommunications, Mass Media, & Democracy: The Battle for the Control of U. S. Broadcasting, 1928-1935. 416p. 1995. reprint ed. pap. 17.95 (*0-19-509394-1*) OUP.

McChesney, Robert W., ed. see Berry, William E.

McCheyne, Murray. Siete Iglesias de Asia: Seven Churches of Asia. (SPA.). 3.25 (*84-7645-114-8*, 223168, Pub. by Edit Clie SP) TSELF.

McCheyne, Robert M. Mensajes Biblicos. 284p. (SPA.). 1988. reprint ed. pap. 9.95 (*0-85151-541-X*) Banner of Truth.

***McChristian, Douglas C.** The U. S. Army in the West, 1870-1880: Uniforms, Weapons, & Equipment. LC 94-48216. (Illus.). 384p. 1995. 34.95 (*0-8061-2705-8*) U of Okla Pr.

McChristian, Douglas C., ed. Garrison Tangles in the Friendless Tenth: The Journal of First Lieutenant John Bigelow, Jr., Fort Davis, Texas. (Guidon Monograph Ser.). (Illus.). 1985. 13.95 (*0-8488-0238-1*, J M C & Co) Amereon Ltd.

***McChrystal, Karen.** A Garden of Light. 50p. (Orig.). 1995. pap. 11.95 (*0-9644183-4-7*) Earthly Delights.

McChrystal, Karen, jt. auth. see Ross, Steven L.

MccKay, Sandra L. Verbs for a Specific Purpose. (Illus.). 256p. (C). 1982. pap. text ed. 11.75 (*0-13-941617-X*) P-H.

MccKay, Sandra L. & Petitt, Dorothy. At the Door: Selected Literature for ESL Students. (Illus.). 208p. (C). 1983. pap. text ed. 16.95 (*0-13-049676-6*) P-H.

McClain, Alva J. Bible Truths. 1981. pap. 1.75 (*0-88469-013-X*) BMH Bks.

— Daniel's Prophecy of the Seventy Weeks. pap. 5.99 (*0-88469-076-8*) BMH Bks.

— Daniel's Prophecy of the Seventy Weeks. 1985. pap. 6.99 (*0-310-29011-2*, 10177P) Zondervan.

— Freemasonry & Christianity. 1979. pap. 1.25 (*0-88469-012-1*) BMH Bks.

— The Greatness of the Kingdom. 16.99 (*0-88469-011-3*) BMH Bks.

— The Inspiration of the Bible. 1980. pap. 1.50 (*0-88469-115-2*) BMH Bks.

— The Jewish Problem. 1979. pap. 1.00 (*0-88469-014-8*) BMH Bks.

— Law & Grace. pap. 3.95 (*0-88469-001-6*) BMH Bks.

— The "Problems" of Verbal Inspiration. 1968. pap. 0.75 (*0-88469-116-0*) BMH Bks.

— Romans Outlined & Summarized. 1979. pap. 3.50 (*0-88469-015-6*) BMH Bks.

— Romans, the Gospel of God's Grace. 1979. 12.99 (*0-88469-080-6*) BMH Bks.

McClain, Bebe F. Super Eight Filmaking from Scratch. (Illus.). 1978. pap. 19.95 (*0-13-876110-8*) P-H.

McClain, Carol S., ed. Women As Healers: Cross-Cultural Perspectives. LC 88-16896. 272p. (C). 1989. pap. text ed. 15.00 (*0-8135-1370-7*) Rutgers U Pr.

***McClain, Charles.** The Mass Internment of Japanese Americans & the Quest for Legal Redress. LC 94-22630. (Asian Americans & the Law Ser.: No. 3). (Illus.). 485p. 1994. 76.00 (*0-8153-1866-9*) Garland.

***McClain, Charles, ed.** Asian Indians, Filipinos, Other Asian Communities & the Law. LC 94-22629. (Asian Americans & the Law Ser.: No. 4). (Illus.). 424p. 1994. 63.00 (*0-8153-1851-0*) Garland.

— Chinese Immigrants & American Law. LC 94-26787. (Asian Americans & the Law Ser.: No. 1). (Illus.). 479p. 1994. 75.00 (*0-8153-1849-9*) Garland.

— Japanese Immigrants & American Law: The Alien Land Laws & Other Issues. LC 94-29033. (Asian Americans & the Law Ser.: No. 2). (Illus.). 448p. 1994. 63.00 (*0-8153-1850-2*) Garland.

McClain, Charles J. Building Systems Evaluation Handbook. (Illus.). 260p. 1991. pap. text ed. 69.00 (*0-86587-266-X*) Gov Insts.

— In Search of Equality: The Chinese Struggle Against Discrimination in Nineteenth-Century America. LC 93-4942. 317p. 1994. 35.00 (*0-520-08337-7*) U CA Pr.

***McClain, Cindy, ed.** Mission Friends Planbook. (Illus.). 39p. (Orig.). 1995. pap. text ed. 2.95 (*1-56309-134-8*) Womans Mission Union.

McClain, Cindy, ed. see Appling, Mary Ann, et al.

McClain, Cindy, ed. see Bishop, Gary.

McClain, Cindy, ed. see Brunt, Deborah.

McClain, Cindy, ed. see Burns, Kathy.

McClain, Cindy, ed. see Causey, Carol.

McClain, Cindy, ed. see Causey, Carol & Johnson, Trudy.

McClain, Cindy, ed. see Corley, Marion.

McClain, Cindy, ed. see DeLoach, Sylvia.

McClain, Cindy, ed. see Faughn, Jackie & McQueen, Marcia.

McClain, Cindy, ed. see Kent, Renee.

McClain, Cindy, ed. see Martin, Sara H.

McClain, Cindy, ed. see McCoy, Leighann.

McClain, Cindy, ed. see McCullough, Mary F.

McClain, Cindy, ed. see Strawn, Kathy.

McClain, Cindy, ed. see Tapp, Sandra.

McClain, Clifford H. Fluid Flow in Pipes: A Clear-Sut Summary of Modern Theory in the Flow of Liquids & Gases Through Piping & Ducts, with Practical Applications & Detailed Worked-Out Examples. 2nd ed. LC 63-2059. 132p. reprint ed. pap. 37.70 (*0-317-10965-0*, 2001910) Bks Demand.

McClain, Ellen J. No Big Deal. 160p. (J). (gr. 5-9). 1994. 14.99 (*0-525-67483-7*, Lodestar Bks) Dutton Child Bks.

McClain, Ernest G. Meditations Through the Quran: Tonal Images in an Oral Culture. LC 81-82124. (Illus.). 180p. 1981. 16.95 (*0-89254-009-5*) Nicolas-Hays.

— Myth of Invariance: The Origins of the Gods, Mathematics & Music from the Rg Veda to Plato. LC 76-28411. (Illus.). 216p. 1985. pap. 8.95 (*0-89254-012-5*) Nicolas-Hays.

— Pythagorean Plato: Prelude to the Song Itself. (Illus.). 192p. (Orig.). 1984. pap. 8.95 (*0-89254-010-9*) Nicolas-Hays.

McClain, Florence W. A Practical Guide to Past Life Regression. LC 84-45285. 160p. (Orig.). 1985. pap. 7.95 (*0-87542-510-0*) Llewellyn Pubns.

— The Truth about Past Life Regression. (Vanguard Ser.). (Illus.). 32p. (Orig.). 1986. pap. 2.00 (*0-87542-359-0*) Llewellyn Pubns.

— Visions of Murder. 336p. 1995. pap. 5.99 (*1-56718-452-9*) Llewellyn Pubns.

McClain, Frank, et al. F. D. Maurice: A Study. LC 82-70636. 93p. 1982. pap. 8.95 (*0-936384-05-0*) Cowley Pubns.

McClain, Gary. Handbook of International Connectivity Standards. 1992. text ed. 59.95 (*0-442-30851-5*) Van Nos Reinhold.

— OLTP Handbook. 1994. text ed. 49.50 (*0-07-044985-6*) McGraw.

McClain, Gary R. Open Systems Interconnection Handbook. (Communications Skills Ser.). 480p. 1991. text ed. 49.50 (*0-07-044969-4*) McGraw.

— VM & Departmental Computing. (Computing That Works Ser.). 1988. pap. 29.95 (*0-07-044939-2*) McGraw.

McClain, Gary R., ed. The Handbook of Networking & Connectivity. (Illus.). 415p. 1994. pap. 39.95 (*0-12-482080-8*, AP Prof) Acad Pr.

— VM Applications Handbook. 320p. 1989. text ed. 44.50 (*0-07-044948-1*) McGraw.

McClain, Heidi, jt. auth. see Benegar, Cynthia.

McClain, J. Dudley. Political Profiles of Black College Students in the South: Socio-Political Attitudes, Preferences, Personality & Characteristics. LC 77-82709. 1977. 14.95 (*0-89583-002-7*); pap. 7.95 (*0-89583-003-5*) Resurgens Pubns.

— Political Profiles of College Students in Southern Appalachia: Socio-Political Attitudes, Preferences, Personality & Characteristics. LC 77-84178. 1978. 14.95 (*0-89583-006-X*); pap. 7.95 (*0-89583-007-8*) Resurgens Pubns.

— Political Profiles of College Students in the South: Socio-Political Attitudes, Preferences, Personality & Characteristics. LC 77-82715. 1977. 14.95 (*0-89583-000-0*); pap. 9.95 (*0-89583-001-9*) Resurgens Pubns.

— Political Profiles of Female College Students in the South: Socio-Political Attitudes, Preferences, Personality & Characteristics. LC 77-84179. 1978. 14.95 (*0-89583-008-6*); pap. 9.95 (*0-89583-009-4*) Resurgens Pubns.

— Political Profiles of Male College Students in the South: Socio-Political Attitudes, Preferences, Personality & Characteristics. LC 79-65787. 1979. 14.95 (*0-89583-012-4*); pap. 9.95 (*0-89583-013-2*) Resurgens Pubns.

— Political Profiles of White College Students in the South: Socio-Political Attitudes, Preferences, Personality & Characteristics. LC 77-84177. 1977. 14.95 (*0-89583-004-3*); pap. 9.95 (*0-89583-005-1*) Resurgens Pubns.

McClain, James L., et al, eds. Edo & Paris: Urban Life & the State in the Early Modern Era. (Illus.). 512p. 1994. 42.50 (*0-8014-2987-0*) Cornell U Pr.

McClain, John O., et al. Operations Management: Production of Goods & Services. 3rd ed. 736p. (C). 1991. text ed. write for info. (*0-13-636135-8*) P-H.

McClain, Lamar. The God of the Valley: Moving from Tragedy to Triumph. LC 92-60933. 76p. (Orig.). 1992. pap. text ed. 4.95 (*1-880679-01-9*) Mtn MD.

McClain, Leanita. A Foot in Each World: Articles & Essays. Page, Clarence, ed. 181p. 1986. 29.95 (*0-8101-0741-4*); pap. 12.95 (*0-8101-0742-2*) Northwestern U Pr.

***McClain, Leanita & Page, Clarence.** What Killed Leanita McClain? Essays on Living in Both Black & White Worlds. 1995. 21.95 (*1-879360-38-1*) Noble Pr.

McClain, Margaret S. Bellboy: A Muletrain Journey. LC 89-61681. (Illus.). 154p. (J). (gr. 5 up). 1990. 14.95 (*0-9622468-1-6*) NM Pub Co.

McClain, Mary. Baby's Pockets. (Illus.). 8p. (J). (ps). 1981. pap. 3.95 (*0-671-43204-4*, Litl Simon S&S) S&S Childrens.

McClain, Maureen E. & Polsky, Jeffrey D. Preparing for Trial: Summer 1992, Action Guide. Tindel, Kay E., ed. 86p. 1992. pap. text ed. 47.00 (*0-88124-555-0*, CP-11132) Cont Ed Bar-CA.

McClain, Michael, ed. see International Conference on Carcinogenesis & Risk Assessment Staff.

McClain, Paula, ed. Agenda Setting, Public Policy, & Minority Group Influence. (Orig.). 1989. pap. 12.00 (*0-944285-19-8*) Pol Studies.

***McClain, Paula D.** Why Can't We Just All Get Along. (Dilemmas in American Politics Ser.). (C). 1995. text ed. 45.00 (*0-8133-1968-4*); pap. text ed. 13.95 (*0-8133-1969-2*) Westview.

An Asterisk (*) at the beginning of an entry indicates that the title is appearing in BIP for the first time.

McClain, Paula D., ed. Minority Group Influence: Agenda Setting, Formulation, & Public Policy. LC 93-7707. (Contributions in Political Science Ser.: No. 333). 232p. 1993. text ed. 55.00 (*0-313-29036-9*, GM9036, Greenwood Pr) Greenwood.

McClain, Paula D., jt. ed. see Karnig, Albert K.

McClain, Paula D., jt. auth. see Rose, Harold M.

McClain Printing Co., Staff, ed. see Long, Roy C.

McClain Printing Staff, ed. see Clagg, Sam E.

McClain, S. Navajo Weapon. Kristiansson, Jan, ed. (Illus.). 336p. 1994. 29.95 (*1-883862-07-8*) Bks Beyond Brdrs.

McClain, Sandra L., jt. auth. see Morgan, Kathy J.

McClain, Theresa. Forever After: Couples Committed to God & Each Other. 81p. (Orig.). 1990. pap. text ed. 4.95 (*0-936625-80-5*, New Hope AL) Womans Mission Union.

McClain, Wallace, jt. auth. see Westlein, Pat.

***McClain, Wallis E., Jr.** U. S. Environmental Laws: 1994 Edition. LC 90-36685. 1292p. 1994. pap. text ed. 60.00 (*0-87179-836-0*) BNA.

McClain, William B. Black People in the Methodist Church: Whither Thou Goest? 160p. (Orig.). 1985. pap. 8.95 (*0-687-03588-0*) Abingdon.

— Come Sunday: The Liturgy of Zion. 1990. pap. 12.95 (*0-687-08884-4*) Abingdon.

McClain, William H. Between Real & Ideal: Course of Otto Ludwig's Development As a Narrative Writer. LC 72-181951. (North Carolina. University. Studies in the Germanic Languages & Literatures: No. 40). reprint ed. 27.00 (*0-404-50940-1*) AMS Pr.

McClam, Tricia & Woodside, Marianne. Problem Solving in the Helping Professions. LC 93-19783. 1994. pap. 24.95 (*0-534-20454-6*) Brooks-Cole.

McClam, Tricia, jt. auth. see Woodside, Marianne.

McClamrock, Ron. Existential Cognition: Computational Minds in the World. LC 93-48967. (Illus.). 1995. 28.95 (*0-226-55641-7*) U Ch Pr.

McClanahan, Alexandra J. Our Stories, Our Lives. (Illus.). 243p. (Orig.). 1986. pap. 15.95 (*0-938227-01-7*) CIRI Found.

McClanahan, Bill. Scenery for Model Railroads. LC 67-14545. (Illus.). 104p. (Orig.). 1967. pap. 9.95 (*0-89024-508-8*) Kalmbach.

McClanahan, Carl, jt. auth. see Arman, Mike.

McClanahan, Clarence. European Romanticism: Literary Societies, Poets, & Poetry. LC 89-12632. (American University Studies: Comparative Literature: Ser. III, Vol. 31). 170p. (C). 1990. text ed. 48.95 (*0-8204-1167-1*) P Lang Pubs.

McClanahan, Dave. FoxPro for Windows Developer's Workshop: Tools & Techniques for Rapid Application. 1993. pap. 49.99 (*1-56686-071-7*) Brady Compu Bks.

***McClanahan, David.** Mastering Visual Basic X. 1995. pap. write for info. (*0-7821-1605-1*) Sybex.

— Oracle Developer's Guide. 1995. pap. text ed. 29.95 (*0-07-882087-1*) McGraw.

— Powerbuilder 4.0: Developer's Guide. 1994. pap. 39.95 (*1-55851-417-1*) M&T Bks.

McClanahan, Ed. Famous People I Have Known. LC 85-13137. 196p. 1985. 13.95 (*0-374-15329-9*) FS&G.

— Famous People I Have Known. rev. ed. Date not set. pap. 12.50 (*0-917788-58-3*) Gnomon Pr.

— The Natural Man. LC 93-77697. 240p. 1993. reprint ed. pap. 12.50 (*0-917788-56-7*) Gnomon Pr.

McClanahan, Elaine & Wicks, Carolyn. Future Force: Kids That Want to, Can & Do. 1993. pap. 19.95 (*1-882180-09-7*) Griffin CA.

— Future Force - Kids That Want to, Can, & Do! A Teacher's Handbook for Using TQM in the Classroom. (Illus.). 158p. 1993. reprint ed. pap. text ed. 19.95 (*0-9646935-0-X*) Pact Pubng.

McClanahan, Frank. Christmas with Grandma. (Storytime Christmas Bks.). (Illus.). 24p. (Orig.). (J). (gr. k-1). 1990. pap. 0.99 (*1-878624-46-6*) McClanahan Bk.

— The Little Policeman. (Storytime Bks.). (Illus.). 24p. (Orig.). (J). (gr. k-1). 1990. pap. 0.99 (*1-878624-38-5*) McClanahan Bk.

McClanahan, Grant V. Diplomatic Immunity. 290p. 1989. pap. 15.95 (*0-312-02832-6*) St Martin.

McClanahan, John H. El Hombre Como Pecador. Robleto, Adolfo, tr. (Layman's Library of Christian Doctrine). 155p. (SPA.). 1988. pap. 5.25 (*0-311-09117-2*) Casa Bautista.

***McClanahan, Kip.** PowerPC Program for Intel Programmers. 1995. pap. 49.99 (*1-56884-306-2*) IDG Bks.

McClanahan, Rebecca. One Word Deep: Lectures & Readings. (Writers-in-Residence Ser.). 112p. 1993. pap. 7.00 (*0-912592-34-6*) Ashland Poetry.

McClanahan Staff. Doll Books: A Boy for All Seasons. (Illus.). 10p. (J). (ps-1). 1994. bds. 4.95 (*1-56293-493-7*) McClanahan Bk.

— Doll Books: Let's Dress Puppy Dog. (Illus.). 10p. (J). (ps-1). 1994. bds. 4.95 (*1-56293-491-0*) McClanahan Bk.

— Doll Books: My Baby Doll. (Illus.). 10p. (J). (ps-1). 1994. bds. 4.95 (*1-56293-492-9*) McClanahan Bk.

— Doll Books: When Teddy Grows Up. (Illus.). 10p. (J). (ps-1). 1994. bds. 4.95 (*1-56293-490-2*) McClanahan Bk.

— I Can Learn: Colors & Numbers. (Illus.). 24p. (J). (ps). 1994. 1.95 (*1-56293-511-9*) McClanahan Bk.

— I Can Learn: First Numbers. (Illus.). 24p. (J). (ps). 1994. 1.95 (*1-56293-514-3*) McClanahan Bk.

— I Can Learn: First Words. (Illus.). 24p. (J). (ps). 1994. 1.95 (*1-56293-509-7*) McClanahan Bk.

— I Can Learn: Little Red Riding Hood. (Illus.). 24p. (J). (ps). 1994. 1.95 (*1-56293-513-5*) McClanahan Bk.

— I Can Learn: Old MacDonald's Farm. (Illus.). 24p. (J). (ps). 1994. 1.95 (*1-56293-512-7*) McClanahan Bk.

— I Can Learn: Shapes & Sizes. (Illus.). 24p. (J). (ps). 1994. 1.95 (*1-56293-510-0*) McClanahan Bk.

— The Nutcracker. (Illus.). 24p. (J). (ps-2). 1994. 0.99 (*1-56293-497-X*) McClanahan Bk.

— The Story of Santa Claus. (Illus.). 24p. (J). (ps-2). 1994. bds. 0.99 (*1-56293-496-1*) McClanahan Bk.

— The Twelve Days of Christmas. (Illus.). 24p. (J). (ps-2). 1994. bds. 0.99 (*1-56293-495-3*) McClanahan Bk.

McClane, A. North American Fish Cookery. 1991. 27.95 (*0-8050-1065-3*) H Holt & Co.

McClane, A. J. The Encyclopedia of Fish Cookery. LC 77-72781. 512p. 1977. 65.00 (*0-8050-1046-7*) H Holt & Co.

— McClane's Field Guide to Freshwater Fishes of North America. LC 77-11967. (Illus.). 232p. 1978. pap. 15.95 (*0-8050-0194-8*, Owl) H Holt & Co.

— McClane's Field Guide to Saltwater Fishes of North America. LC 77-14417. (Illus.). 304p. 1978. pap. 15.95 (*0-8050-0733-4*, Owl) H Holt & Co.

— McClane's New Standard Fishing Encyclopedia & International Angling Guide. rev. ed. LC 74-6108. (Illus.). 1176p. 1974. 75.00 (*0-8050-1117-X*) H Holt & Co.

— McClane's Secrets of Successful Fishing. LC 78-24367. (Owl Bks.). (Illus.). 288p. 1980. pap. 11.95 (*0-8050-0707-5*, Owl) H Holt & Co.

— The Practical Fly Fisherman. 240p. 1983. pap. 7.95 (*0-13-689380-5*, Reward) P-H.

McClane, A. J. & Gardner, Keith. McClane's Game Fish of North America. (Illus.). 384p. 1989. 22.99 (*0-517-68852-2*) Random Hse Value.

— McClane's Game Fish of North America: The Best Fishing in the United States, Canada, Mexico & the Bahamas. LC 84-40105. (Illus.). 376p. 1984. 50.00 (*0-8129-1134-2*, Times Bks) Random.

McClane, Kenneth A. Take Five: Collected Poems. LC 87-23699. (Contributions in Afro-American & African Studies: No. 109). 296p. 1988. text ed. 49.95 (*0-313-25761-2*, MTA/, Greenwood Pr) Greenwood.

— Walls: Essays, 1985-1990. LC 90-22624. (African American Life Ser.). 121p. 1991. 12.95 (*0-8143-2134-8*) Wayne St U Pr.

McClaney, Eula. God I Listened. 277p. 1988. write for info. (*0-9621422-0-4*) McClaney.

McClaran, Don, jt. auth. see Moore, Greg.

McClaran, Jeanne L., ed. see Stopke, Judy & Staley, Chip.

McClard, Megan. Harriet Tubman: Slavery & the Underground Railroad. (History of the Civil War Ser.). (Illus.). 160p. (J). (gr. 5 up). 1990. lib. bdg. 12.95 (*0-382-09938-9*); pap. 7.95 (*0-382-24047-2*) Silver Burdett Pr.

McClard, Megan & Ypsilantis, George. Hiawatha. Furstinger, Nancy, ed. (Alvin Joseph's Biography of the American Indians Ser.). (Illus.). 138p. (J). (gr. 5-7). 1989. lib. bdg. 12.95 (*0-382-09568-5*); pap. 7.95 (*0-382-09757-2*) Silver Pr.

McClary, Ben H. Samuel Lorenzo Knapp & Early American Biography. 30p. 1985. reprint ed. pap. 4.50 (*0-912296-80-1*) Am Antiquarian.

McClary, Ben H., ed. The Lovingood Paper, 1964. LC 63-22059. 51p. reprint ed. pap. 25.00 (*0-8357-6543-1*, 2035906) Bks Demand.

— The Lovingood Papers, 1965. LC 63-22059. 77p. reprint ed. pap. 25.00 (*0-8357-6544-X*, 2035907) Bks Demand.

McClary, Ben H., ed. see Irving, Washington.

McClary, Cheryl & Ray, Keith. Wellness & the Liberal Arts: Preliminary Edition. 92p. (C). 1994. spiral bd. 10.95 (*0-8403-9362-8*) Kendall-Hunt.

McClary, Cheryl, jt. auth. see Ray, Keith.

***McClary, Clebe & Barker, Diane.** Living Proof. 230p. 1978. pap. write for info. (*0-614-00604-X*) C McClary Evang.

McClary, D., jt. auth. see Lumpkin, T.

***McClary, Deanna & Jenkins, Jerry.** Commitment to Love. 220p. 1989. pap. 12.95 (*0-9640666-0-2*) C McClary Evang.

McClary, Susan. Feminine Endings: Music, Gender, & Sexuality. (Illus.). 224p. (Orig.). (C). 1991. text ed. 39.95 (*0-8166-1898-4*); pap. text ed. 14.95 (*0-8166-1899-2*) U of Minn Pr.

— Georges Bizet: "Carmen" (Cambridge Opera Handbooks Ser.). (Illus.). 190p. (C). 1992. pap. 15.95 (*0-521-39897-5*) Cambridge U Pr.

McClary, Susan, jt. ed. see Leppert, Richard D.

McClary, Thomas C. Rebirth: When Everyone Forgot. (Classics of Science Fiction Ser.). 187p. 1976. reprint ed. 15.00 (*0-88355-373-2*); reprint ed. pap. 10.00 (*0-88355-459-3*) Hyperion Conn.

McClaskey, Marilyn H. What Kind of Name Is Juan? Rosen, Roger, ed. (Flipside Fiction Ser.). (YA). (gr. 7 up). 1989. lib. bdg. 12.95 (*0-8239-0830-5*) Rosen Group.

McClatchey, Kenneth D. Clinical Laboratory Medicine. (Illus.). 1984p. 1994. 95.00 (*0-683-05755-3*) Williams & Wilkins.

McClatchy, J. D. The Rest of the Way. 1992. pap. 10.00 (*0-679-74059-7*) McKay.

— Stars Principal. 80p. 1986. pap. 9.95 (*0-02-070030-X*, Collier S&S) S&S Trade.

— White Paper: On Contemporary American Poetry. 256p. 1990. text ed. 44.00 (*0-231-06944-8*); pap. text ed. 14.50 (*0-231-06945-6*) Col U Pr.

McClatchy, J. D., ed. Poets on Painters: Essays on the Art of Painting by Twentieth-Century Poets. (Illus.). 228p. 1988. pap. 15.00 (*0-520-06971-4*) U CA Pr.

— Vintage Book of Contemporary American Poetry. LC 90-50119. 400p. (Orig.). 1990. pap. 15.00 (*0-679-72858-9*, Vin) Random.

McClatchy, Valentine S. Four Anti-Japanese Pamphlets: An Original Anthology. Daniels, Roger, ed. LC 78-7080. (Asian Experience in North America Ser.). 1979. lib. bdg. 23.95 (*0-405-11282-3*) Ayer.

McClaughry, C. C. McClaughry. Genealogy of the MacClaughry Family: A Scoto-Irish Family from Galloway, Scotland, Appearing in Ireland about 1600, & Emigrants to N.Y. in 1765. 459p. 1991. reprint ed. lib. bdg. 81.00 (*0-8328-1993-X*); reprint ed. pap. 71.00 (*0-8328-1994-8*) Higginson Bk Co.

McClaughry, John, jt. auth. see Bryan, Frank.

***McClave, James T.** First Course in Business Statistics. 6th ed. 1995. 70.00 (*0-02-379175-6*) Macmillan.

— A First Course in Statistics. 5th ed. LC 94-41307. 1995. text ed. 63.00 (*0-02-379195-0*) P-H.

McClave, James T., II. Statistics. 5th ed. 1991. write for info. (*0-02-379185-3*) Dellen Pub.

McClave, James T. & Benson, George. Statistics for Business & Economics. 6th ed. LC 93-33416. (Illus.). 935p. (C). 1994. text ed. write for info. (*0-02-379201-9*) Dellen Pub.

McClave, James T. & Dietrich, Frank H., II. Statistics. 6th ed. LC 93-33415. 992p. (C). 1994. write for info. (*0-02-379211-6*) Dellen Pub.

McClave, James T., II, jt. auth. see Conlon, Michael.

McClave, James T., jt. auth. see Scheaffer, Richard L.

McClave, James T., II, et al. Statistics for Business & Economics. 5th ed. (Illus.). 1248p. (C). 1991. text ed. write for info. (*0-02-379182-9*) Macmillan.

***McClave, Kevin.** Darkness & Light: A Collection of Poems. 1995. 8.95 (*0-533-11129-3*) Vantage.

***McClay, Gail.** Past, Present, & Future Perspectives in Education. 663p. 1995. 55.00 (*0-911541-34-9*) Gregory Pub.

***McClay, John B. & Matthews, Wendy L.** Corpus Juris Humorous: In Brief: A Compilation of Outrageous, Unusual, Infamous & Witty Judicial Opinions from 1256 A.D. to the Present. 288p. 1994. 9.95 (*0-9631488-1-8*) Mac-Mat.

McClay, K. R. The Mapping of Geological Structures. (Geological Society of London Professional Handbook Ser.: No. 1572). 161p. 1991. pap. text ed. 29.95 (*0-471-93243-4*) Wiley.

***McClay, Michael.** I Love Lucy: The Complete Picture History of the Popular TV Show Ever. (Illus.). 320p. 1995. 34.95 (*0-446-51750-X*) Warner Bks.

McClay, R. Fundamentals of System Safety. 1990. text ed. write for info. (*0-442-23843-6*) Van Nos Reinhold.

McClay, Shirley Atwater & Miech, Marilyn. Trim & Thin 4-Ingredient Cookbook. 328p. (Orig.). 1988. pap. 6.95 (*0-89586-724-9*, HP Books) Berkley Pub.

McClay, Wilfred M. The Masterless: Self & Society in Modern America. LC 93-9673. 380p. (C). 1994. lib. bdg. 45.00 (*0-8078-2117-9*); pap. 16.95 (*0-8078-4419-5*) U of NC Pr.

McClean, Andrew, comp. Security, Arms Control, & Conflict Reduction in East Asia & the Pacific. LC 93-18142. (Bibliographies & Indexes in Law & Political Science Ser.: No. 19). 576p. 1993. text ed. 105.00 (*0-313-27539-4*, MNB, Greenwood Pr) Greenwood.

McClean, Cheryl, ed. see Butherus, Cindy.

McClean, David. International Judicial Assistance. LC 92-5648. 430p. 1992. 110.00 (*0-19-825224-2*) OUP.

McClean, J. R. The Origin of Weight. (Illus.). 1979. pap. 5.00 (*0-916710-46-7*) Obol Intl.

McClean, June. Groovy Granny. 1989. pap. 10.95 (*0-932298-71-0*) Tri-State Pr Corp.

McClean, Mary. Creating Jobs by Creating New Businesses: The Role of Business Incubators. 72p. (Orig.). 1985. pap. 20.00 (*0-317-04904-6*) Natl Coun Econ Dev.

— Establishing & Operating Private Sector Development Organizations. Kailo, Andrea, ed. 72p. (Orig.). 1984. pap. 20.00 (*0-317-04824-4*) Natl Coun Econ Dev.

— Private Sector Development Organizations: A Directory. 84p. (Orig.). 1987. pap. 20.00 (*0-317-04816-3*) Natl Coun Econ Dev.

— Special Improvement Districts: Business Self-Help. Murphy, Jenny, ed. 52p. (Orig.). 1988. pap. 18.00 (*0-317-04850-3*) Natl Coun Econ Dev.

McClean, Mary, ed. see Nutter, David.

McClean, Mervyn, jt. auth. see Firth, Raymond.

McClean, R. J. Teach Yourself Swedish. (Teach Yourself Ser.). 1978. 10.95 (*0-679-10226-4*) McKay.

— Teach Yourself Swedish. (Teach Yourself Ser.). 1992. 15.95 (*0-8288-8406-4*) Fr & Eur.

McClean, Tom. Rough Passage. large type ed. 336p. 1985. 15.95 (*0-7089-1301-6*) Ulverscroft.

McClean, William J. ASIC Outlook 1994: An Application Specific IC Report & Directory. (Illus.). 260p. 1993. per., pap. 485.00 (*1-877750-23-9*) ICE Corp.

— Status 1989: A Report in the IC Industry. (Illus.). 223p. (Orig.). (C). 1989. pap. 350.00 (*1-877750-05-0*) ICE Corp.

McClean, William J., ed. see Bowman, Ron.

McClear, Johanna, jt. auth. see Appleman, Diane.

***McClearen, H. Addison & Sheetz, S. Owen.** St. Thaddeus of Aiken: A Church & Its City. LC 94-7187. (Illus.). 308p. 1994. 37.50 (*0-87152-481-3*) Reprint.

***McClearin, Veronica.** Children of the New Amazon. 40p. (J). Date not set. pap. 9.95 (*0-7610-0389-4*) NW Pub.

McClearn, Gerald E., jt. ed. see Plomin, Robert.

McCleary, Dick. The Logic of Imaginative Education: Research Understanding. (Advances in Contemporary Educational Thought Ser.). 192p. (C). 1993. text ed. 43.00 (*0-8077-3302-4*); pap. text ed. 18.95 (*0-8077-3301-6*) Tchrs Coll.

McCleary, John. Geometry from a Differential Viewpoint. (Illus.). 250p. (C). 1995. 54.95 (*0-521-41430-X*); pap. 22.95 (*0-521-42480-1*) Cambridge U Pr.

— User's Guide to Spectral Sequences. LC 85-63230. (Mathematics Lecture Ser.: No. 12). xvi, 423p. 1985. 40.00 (*0-914098-21-7*) Publish or Perish.

McCleary, John, jt. ed. see Rowe, David.

McCleary, Ken W., jt. ed. see Stevens, Peter J.

McCleary, Rachel M. The Ethics of Intervention: The United States & Nicaragua, 1978-1979. (Pew Case Studies in International Affairs). 52p. (C). 1988. pap. text ed. 2.50 (*1-56927-347-2*) Geo U Inst Dplmcy.

— New International Economic Order. (Pew Case Studies in International Affairs). 81p. (C). 1988. pap. text ed. 2.50 (*1-56927-149-6*) Geo U Inst Dplmcy.

McCleary, Rachel M., ed. Seeking Justice: Ethics & International Affairs. (Case Studies in International Affairs). 165p. (C). 1992. pap. text ed. 14.95 (*0-8133-8059-6*) Westview.

McCleary, Richard C., tr. see Merleau-Ponty, Maurice.

McCleary, Rita W. Conversing with Uncertainty: Practicing Psychotherapy in a Hospital Setting. 160p. 1992. text ed. 26.95 (*0-88163-148-5*) Analytic Pr.

McCleary, Sheila C., jt. auth. see Scott, Janet M.

McCleary, William J. Writing All the Way. 350p. (C). 1988. pap. 26.95 (*0-534-08604-7*) Intl Thomson.

McCleave, Kathe, ed. see Paulson, Pat A., et al.

McCleery, Alistair, ed. Landscape & Light: Essays by Neil M. Gunn. 264p. 1987. text ed. 30.00 (*0-08-035060-7*, Pub. by Aberdeen U Pr); pap. text ed. 19.95 (*0-08-035061-5*, Pub. by Aberdeen U Pr) Macmillan.

McCleery, Patsy R. Mattie Monkey Mouth. LC 94-60619. (Illus.). 44p. (J). (gr. 3-7). 1995. 7.95 (*1-55523-705-3*) Winston-Derek.

***McCleeve, Carol.** Christmas Crafts. LC 95-16921. (Illus.). 128p. 1995. 24.95 (*0-8069-4214-2*) Sterling.

McClellan, Andrew. Inventing the Louvre: Art, Politics, & the Origins of the Modern Museum in 18th-Century Paris. (Illus.). 304p. (C). 1994. 65.00 (*0-521-45065-9*) Cambridge U Pr.

McClellan, B. Edward & Reese, William J., eds. The Social History of American Education. LC 87-5893. 381p. 1988. pap. 15.95 (*0-252-01462-6*) U of Ill Pr.

McClellan, Bill. Evidence of Murder. 352p. (Orig.). 1993. pap. 5.99 (*0-451-40347-9*, Onyx) NAL-Dutton.

McClellan, Catharine. My Old People Say: An Ethnographic Survey of Southern Yukon Territory, 2 vols., Pt. 1. (Illus.). ixii, 324p. 1983. Part 1, ixii, 324p. pap. 10.00 (*0-660-00064-4*, 56437-1, Pub. by Natl Mus Sci Tech CN) U Ch Pr.

— My Old People Say: An Ethnographic Survey of Southern Yukon Territory, 2 vols., Pt. 2. (Illus.). 320p. 1983. Part 2, 320 pp. pap. 10.00 (*0-686-88482-5*, 56439-8, Pub. by Natl Mus Sci Tech CN) U Ch Pr.

McClellan, Dorien S. Paralegal Drafting Guide. LC 93-1378. (Paralegal Law Library). 288p. 1993. Alk. paper. text ed. 93.00 (*0-471-58797-4*) Wiley.

***McClellan, Doris.** Baxter Badger's Home. LC 95-9774. (Illus.). 32p. (J). (gr. k up). 1995. 14.95 (*1-885777-03-5*) Hendrick-Long.

McClellan, Douglas. Wayne Thiebaud, Paintings & Works on Paper. (Illus.). 8p. (Orig.). 1976. pap. 5.00 (*0-939982-00-5*) Sesnon Art Gall.

McClellan, Douglas, et al, frwds. Albert Stewart: The Artist, Teacher & Friend. (Illus.). 125p. 1966. 30.00 (*0-915478-05-6*) Galleries Coll.

McClellan, Edwin. Two Japanese Novelists: Soseki & Toson. LC 76-81223. 180p. reprint ed. pap. 51.30 (*0-317-10055-6*, 2007276) Bks Demand.

McClellan, Edwin, tr. see Shiga, Naoya.

McClellan, Edwin, tr. see Soseki, Natsume.

McClellan, Edwin, tr. see Yoshikawa, Eiji.

McClellan, Elisabeth. Historic Dress in America Sixteen Seven to Eighteen Seventy, 2 vols., Set. LC 70-81515. (Illus.). 1972. reprint ed. 82.95 (*0-88143-077-3*) Ayer.

— Historic Dress in America Sixteen Seven to Eighteen Seventy, 2 vols., Vol. 1: 1607-1800. LC 70-81515. (Illus.). 1988. reprint ed. Vol. 1, 1607-1800. 38.95 (*0-88143-075-7*) Ayer.

— Historic Dress in America Sixteen Seven to Eighteen Seventy, 2 vols., Vol. 2: 1800-1870. LC 70-81515. (Illus.). 1988. reprint ed. Vol. 2, 1800-1870. 44.95 (*0-88143-076-5*) Ayer.

McClellan, Frank M. Medical Malpractice: Law, Tactics, & Ethics. 296p. (C). 1993. text ed. 49.95 (*1-56639-065-6*); pap. 24.95 (*1-56639-066-4*) Temple U Pr.

McClellan, George B. The Armies of Europe: The Military Systems of England, France, Russia, Prussia, Austria, & Sardinia. 1976. lib. bdg. 59.95 (*0-8490-1450-6*) Gordon Pr.

— The Civil War Papers of George B. McClellan: Selected Correspondence 1860-1865. Sears, Stephen W., ed. 669p. 1992. reprint ed. pap. 17.95 (*0-306-80471-9*) Da Capo.

— Report of the Organization & Campaigns of the Army of the Potomac: To Which Is Added an Account of the Campaign in Western Virginia, with Plans of Battle-Fields. LC 78-109629. (Select Bibliographies Reprint Ser.). 1977. 35.95 (*0-8369-5238-3*) Ayer.

McClellan, George M. Old Greenbottom Inn & Other Stories. LC 74-144654. reprint ed. 17.45 (*0-404-00199-8*) AMS Pr.

— Path of Dreams. LC 70-152925. (Black Heritage Library Collection). 1977. 19.95 (*0-8369-8769-1*) Ayer.

— Poems of George Marion M'Clellan. LC 79-133159. (Black Heritage Library Collection). 1895. 12.00 (*0-8369-8714-4*) Ayer.

McClellan, Grant, ed. Canada in Transition. (Reference Shelf Ser.). 1977. 15.00 (*0-8242-0603-7*) Wilson.

***McClellan, Gregory.** Ideology. 2nd ed. LC 95-16276. (Concepts in Social Thought Ser.). 1995. text ed. 37.95 (*0-8166-2802-5*) U of Minn Pr.

— Ideology. 2nd ed. LC 95-16276. (Concepts in Social Thought Ser.). 1995. pap. text ed. 14.95 (*0-8166-2803-3*) U of Minn Pr.

McClellan, H. B. Campaigns of Stuart's Cavalry. 1993. 9.98 (*1-55521-971-3*) Bk Sales Inc.

An Asterisk (*) at the beginning of an entry indicates that the title is appearing in BIP for the first time.

— I Rode with Jeb Stuart: The Life & Campaigns of Major General J.E.B. Stuart. (Illus.). 475p. 1994. reprint ed. pap. 15.95 (*0-306-80605-3*) Da Capo.

McClellan, Hassell H. Managing One-Bank Holding Companies. LC 81-4351. 314p. 1981. text ed. 42.95 (*0-275-90680-9*, C0680, Praeger Pubs) Greenwood.

McClellan, Henry B. I Rode with Jeb Stuart: The Life & Campaigns of Major General J. E. B. Stuart. LC 58-12208. (Indiana University Civil War Centennial Ser.). (Illus.). 1968. reprint ed. 40.00 (*0-527-59100-9*) Periodicals Srv.

McClellan, James. Joseph Story & the American Constitution: A Study in Political & Legal Thought. LC 75-160499. (Illus.). 448p. (C). 1990. reprint ed. 32.50 (*0-8061-0971-8*); reprint ed. pap. 16.95 (*0-8061-2290-0*) U of Okla Pr.

McClellan, James E., III. Colonialism & Science: Saint Domingue in the Old Regime. (Illus.). 416p. 1992. text ed. 55.00x (*0-8018-4270-0*) Johns Hopkins.

McClellan, James F. Science Reorganized. 1985. text ed. 65.00 (*0-231-05996-5*) Col U Pr.

McClellan, Jim. Great Moments in American History, Vol. I. (Illus.). 384p. (Orig.). (C). 1995. pap. text ed. 14.95 (*1-56134-114-2*) Dushkin Pub.

McClellan, Jim R. Great Moments in American History, Vol. II. (Illus.). 464p. (Orig.). (C). 1995. pap. text ed. 14.95 (*1-56134-115-0*) Dushkin Pub.

McClellan, Keith. Prayer Therapy. LC 89-82664. (Illus.). 76p. (Orig.). 1990. pap. 3.95 (*0-87029-225-0*, 20206-9) Abbey.

McClellan, Keith & Corneil, Wayne, eds. Alcohol in Employment Settings: The Results of the WHO-ILO International Review. LC 87-35998. (Employee Assistance Quarterly Ser.: Vol. 3, No. 2). (Illus.). 119p. 1988. text ed. 32.95 (*0-86656-713-5*) Haworth Pr.

McClellan, Keith & Miller, Richard E., eds. EAPs & the Information Revolution: The Dark Side of Megatrends. LC 86-33519. (Employee Assistance Quarterly Ser.: Vol. 2, No. 2). 106p. 1987. text ed. 39.95 (*0-86656-606-6*) Haworth Pr.

McClellan, Maggie. Artist's Express: Secrets of the Obedient Brush. (Illus.). 117p. 1990. pap. 21.50 (*0-9623952-0-X*) DAVCO.

McClellan, Marian, jt. auth. see McClellan, Sherman.

McClellan, Marian A. Seeds of Stillness: Opening to the Self. (Illus.). 64p. (Orig.). 1994. pap. 8.50 (*1-56474-074-9*) Fithian Pr.

McClellan, Mary Elizabeth. Felt-Silk-Straw Handmade Hats: Tools & Processes, Vol. III. (Illus.). 23p. 1978. pap. 3.50 (*0-910302-04-9*) Bucks Co Hist.

***McClellan, Pam.** Don't Be a Slave to Housework. 176p. 1995. pap. 10.99 (*1-55870-356-X*) Betterway Bks.

— The Organization Map. (Illus.). 208p. (Orig.). 1993. pap. 12.95 (*1-55870-316-0*) Betterway Bks.

McClellan, Phyllis I. The Artillerymen of Historic Fort Monroe, Virginia. (Illus.). 264p. (Orig.). 1992. pap. text ed. 20.00 (*1-55613-529-7*) Heritage Bk.

— Silent Sentinel on the Potomac, Fort McNair 1791-1991. (Illus.). 280p. (Orig.). 1993. pap. text ed. 24.00 (*1-55613-848-2*) Heritage Bk.

McClellan, Randall. The Healing Forces of Music. (Chrysalis Bks.). (Illus.). 1987. pap. 12.95 (*0-916349-34-9*) Amity Hse Inc.

— The Healing Forces of Music: History, Theory & Practice. 224p. 1991. pap. 14.95 (*1-85230-255-0*) Element MA.

McClellan, Robert W. & Usher, Carolyn E. Claiming a Frontier: Ministry & Older People. LC 77-85413. 1977. 10.00 (*0-88474-040-4*, 05741-X) Free Pr.

McClellan, Roger O. & Henderson, Rogene F. Concepts in Inhalation Toxicology. 560p. 1988. 121.00 (*0-89116-805-2*) Hemisp Pub.

***McClellan, Roger O. & Henderson, Rogene F., eds.** Concepts in Inhalation Toxicology. 2nd ed. LC 95-13914. 1995. write for info. (*1-56032-368-X*) Taylor & Francis.

McClellan, Sherman & McClellan, Marian. Patterns for Profit. 2nd ed. 54p. 1989. reprint ed. pap. 50.00 (*1-879192-07-1*) Fndtn Study Cycles.

***McClellan, Tierney.** Closing Statement: A Schuyler Ridgway Mystery. 288p. (Orig.). 1995. mass mkt. 4.99 (*0-451-18464-5*, Sig) NAL-Dutton.

— Heir Condition. 256p. (Orig.). 1995. 3.99 (*0-451-18144-1*, Sig) NAL-Dutton.

McClellan, Tim, ed. see Biasiotto, Judd.

McClellan, Val J. This Is Our Land, Vol. 1. (Illus.). 902p. 1977. 12.50 (*0-685-49214-1*) Western Pubns.

— This Is Our Land, Vol. 1. LC 77-151749. (Illus.). 902p. 1977. 17.95 (*0-533-02248-7*, 77-151749) Western Pubs FL.

— This Is Our Land, Vol. 2. LC 77-151749. (Illus.). 1979. 17.95 (*0-9602218-0-8*) Western Pubs FL.

McClellan, Woodford. Revolutionary Exiles: The Russians in the First International & the Paris Commune. (Illus.). 266p. 1979. 35.00 (*0-7146-3115-9*, Pub. by F Cass Pubs UK) Intl Spec Bk.

— Russia: The Soviet Period & After. 3rd ed. LC 93-5364. 1993. pap. text ed. 42.00 (*0-13-035965-3*) P-H.

McClelland. Small Animals of America Coloring Book. (Illus.). (J). (gr. k-3). 1976. pap. 2.95 (*0-486-24217-X*) Dover.

McClelland, jt. auth. see King.

McClelland, Allen. Virginian & Ohio Story. (Illus.). 104p. 1983. pap. 19.95 (*0-911868-47-X*, C47) Carstens Pubns.

***McClelland, Atha.** Heavenly Ways of Earths Graduates. Hanson, Jenet, ed. 160p. (Orig.). 1994. pap. 10.00 (*0-9636435-4-1*) M A P.

McClelland, Averil E. The Education of Women in the United States: A Guide to Theory, Teaching, & Research. LC 92-14495. (Source Books on Education: Vol. 23). 228p. 1992. 35.00 (*0-8240-4842-3*, SS551) Garland.

McClelland, Ben W. The New American Rhetoric: A Multicultural Approach. LC 92-15012. (C). 1992. text ed. 21.25 (*0-673-38605-8*) HarpCollege.

McClelland, Ben W. & Donovan, Timothy R., eds. Perspectives on Research & Scholarship in Composition. LC 85-15401. ix, 266p. 1985. 37.50 (*0-87352-144-7*); pap. text ed. 19.75 (*0-87352-145-5*) Modern Lang.

McClelland, Bramlette & Reifel, Michael, eds. Planning & Design of Fixed Offshore Platforms. LC 84-27078. (Illus.). 1056p. 1985. text ed. 125.95 (*0-442-25223-4*) Van Nos Reinhold.

McClelland, Bruce. The Marchen Cycle. LC 80-10183. (Illus.). 50p. 1980. pap. 4.00 (*0-930794-25-7*) Station Hill Pr.

McClelland, Bruce, tr. Tristia: Poems by Osip Mandelstam. LC 86-32305. (Illus.). 120p. 1987. 13.95 (*0-88268-041-2*) Station Hill Pr.

McClelland, Bryan L., ed. Fruit of the Vine. LC 85-72071. (Illus.). 392p. (Orig.). 1985. pap. 5.95 (*0-913342-50-5*) Barclay Pr.

McClelland, C. Ivor, ed. see Gacy, John W.

McClelland, Carol L. Nature's Wisdom: A Powerfully Insightful Guide for Exploring Life's Changes. (Illus.). 80p. 1993. pap. 28.95 (*0-9635123-3-1*) Transition Dyn.

McClelland, Charles E. The German Experience of Professionalization: Modern Learned Professions & Their Organizations from the Early Nineteenth Century to the Hitler Era. 256p. (C). 1991. 64.95 (*0-521-39457-0*) Cambridge U Pr.

— The German Historians & England: A Study in Nineteenth-Century Views. LC 79-154514. 311p. reprint ed. pap. 88.70 (*0-317-09512-9*, 2013895) Bks Demand.

McClelland, D. E., et al, eds. Gravitational Astronomy: Instrument Design & Astrophysical Prospects. 468p. (C). 1991. text ed. 104.00 (*981-02-0688-7*) World Scientific Pub.

McClelland, David C. Achievement Motive. LC 75-34465. (Illus.). Date not set. 42.50 (*0-8290-1167-6*) Irvington.

— Achieving Society. LC 69-11373. 1967. pap. 18.95 (*0-02-920510-7*) Free Pr.

— The Achieving Society: With a New Introduction. 520p. (C). Date not set. 50.50 (*0-8290-0870-5*) Irvington.

— Human Motivation. 663p. 1988. pap. 39.95 (*0-521-36951-7*) Cambridge U Pr.

— Motives, Personality & Society. LC 84-2033. (Centennial Psychology Ser.). 502p. 1984. text ed. 65.00 (*0-275-91224-8*, C1224, Praeger Pubs) Greenwood.

— Personality. rev. ed. 672p. reprint ed. text ed. write for info. (*0-318-53722-2*) Irvington.

— Power: The Inner Experience. LC 75-35603. (Illus.). 441p. 1979. 39.50 (*0-8290-0686-9*); pap. text ed. 19.95 (*0-8290-0101-8*) Irvington.

— Roots of Consciousness. enl. ed. (Illus.). text ed. write for info. (*0-8290-0124-7*) Irvington.

— Some Social Consequences of Achievement Motivation. (Reprint Series in Social Sciences). (C). 1993. reprint ed. pap. text ed. 2.30 (*0-8290-2669-X*, S-457) Irvington.

McClelland, David C., ed. Development of Social Maturity. 260p. 1982. 29.50 (*0-8290-0089-5*) Irvington.

— Development of Social Maturity. 260p. 1984. pap. text ed. 12.95 (*0-8290-1556-6*) Irvington.

— Education for Values. 220p. 1982. 29.50 (*0-8290-0090-9*) Irvington.

— Education for Values. 220p. 1984. pap. text ed. 12.95 (*0-8290-1557-4*) Irvington.

McClelland, Deke. CorelDraw! for Dummies. 424p. 1993. pap. 19.95 (*1-56884-042-X*) IDG Bks.

— CorelDraw! 5 for Dummies. 1994. pap. 19.95 (*1-56884-157-4*) IDG Bks.

— Drawing on the Macintosh: A Non-Artist's Guide to MacDraw, Illustrator, FreeHand, & Many Others. 2nd rev. ed. LC 92-16052. 384p. 1992. 26.00 (*1-55623-909-2*) Irwin Prof Pubng.

— Drawing on the PC: A Non-Artist's Guide to CorelDRAW!, Micrografx Designer, & Many Others. 2nd rev. ed. (Desktop Publishing Library). 350p. 1992. pap. 26.00 (*1-55623-911-4*) Irwin Prof Pubng.

— First Book of PC Paintbrush 5 Plus. (First Bks.). (Illus.). (Orig.). 1992. pap. 19.95 (*0-672-27416-7*) Alpha Bks IN.

— Illustrator 5 Book. (Illus.). 668p. 1993. pap. 29.95 (*1-56609-090-3*) Peachpit Pr.

— Illustrator 5.0 5.5 Book. 1994. pap. 29.95 (*1-56609-163-2*) Peachpit Pr.

— Mac Multimedia & CD-ROMS for Dummies. 1995. pap. 19.99 (*1-56884-910-9*) IDG Bks.

— The Macintosh Bible Guide to MacDraw Pro. (Illus.). 416p. (Orig.). 1993. pap. 22.00 (*1-56609-039-3*) Peachpit Pr.

— Macintosh System 7.1: Everything You Need to Know. 2nd ed. LC 93-83102. 496p. 1993. 26.95 (*0-7821-1278-1*) Sybex.

— Macworld Freehand 4.0 Bible. 1994. pap. 29.95 (*1-56884-170-1*) IDG Bks.

— Macworld Photoshop 2.5 Bible. (Illus.). 720p. 1993. pap. 29.95 (*1-56884-022-5*) IDG Bks.

— Macworld Photoshop 3.0 Bible. 1994. pap. 39.95 (*1-56884-158-2*) IDG Bks.

— Mastering Adobe Illustrator: Macintosh Version 3.0. 592p. 1990. pap. 26.00 (*1-55623-442-2*) Irwin Prof Pubng.

— MW Freehand 5 Bible. 2nd ed. 1995. pap. 29.99 (*1-56884-492-1*) IDG Bks.

— PageMaker 5 for Windows for Dummies. 1994. pap. 19.95 (*1-56884-160-4*) IDG Bks.

— Painting on the Macintosh: A Non-Artist's Guide to Superpaint, Pixelpaint, Painter, & Many More. rev. ed. (Desktop Publishing Library). 1993. pap. 25.00 (*1-55623-910-6*) Irwin Prof Pubng.

— Painting on the Macintosh & Painting on the PC. 250p. 1989. Macintosh. pap. 26.00 (*1-55623-265-9*) Irwin Prof Pubng.

— Painting on the Macintosh & Painting on the PC. 250p. 1989. IBM. pap. 26.00 (*1-55623-266-7*) Irwin Prof Pubng.

— Painting on the PC: A Non-Artist's Guide to Popular Painting Programs. rev. ed. 1993. pap. 25.00 (*1-55623-912-2*) Irwin Prof Pubng.

— Photoshop 3 for Macs for Dummies. 1995. pap. 19.99 (*1-56884-208-2*) IDG Bks.

— QR-Photoshop 3 for Macs for Dummies. 1995. pap. 9.99 (*1-56884-968-0*) IDG Bks.

McClelland, Deke & Danuloff, Craig. Desktop Publishing - Type & Graphics: A Comprehensive Handbook. 1987. pap. 29.95 (*0-15-625298-8*, Harvest Bks) HarBrace.

— Mastering Adobe Illustrator PC. 300p. 1989. pap. 28.00 (*1-55623-158-X*) Irwin Prof Pubng.

— Mastering Aldus Freehand: Version 2.0. 464p. 1989. pap. 28.00 (*1-55623-288-8*) Irwin Prof Pubng.

— Mastering Aldus Freehand: Version 3.0. 608p. 1991. pap. 28.00 (*1-55623-443-0*) Irwin Prof Pubng.

— The Micrografx Designer Companion: Featuring Version 3.0. Glinert, Susan, ed. 450p. 1992. 29.00 (*1-55623-410-4*) Irwin Prof Pubng.

— The PageMaker Companion. 566p. 1989. Macintosh Version 3.0. disk 30.00 (*1-55623-190-3*) Irwin Prof Pubng.

— The PageMaker Companion. 608p. 1989. IBM PC Version 3.0. disk 30.00 (*1-55623-189-X*) Irwin Prof Pubng.

McClelland, Deke, jt. auth. see Danuloff, Craig.

McClelland, Donald, jt. intro. see Keaveney, Raymond.

McClelland, Donna & McDonald, Bettye. Head Start Program Manager's Guide to the Basic Educational Skills Project. 34p. (Orig.). 1984. pap. 8.95 (*0-931114-25-X*) High-Scope.

McClelland, Donna, jt. auth. see Donnan, Christopher B.

McClelland, Doug. Eleanor Parker, Woman of a Thousand Faces: A Bio-Bibliography & Filmography. LC 89-10292. (Illus.). 291p. 1989. 32.50 (*0-8108-2242-3*) Scarecrow.

— Forties Film Talk: Oral Histories of Hollywood, with 120 Lobby Posters. LC 92-54087. 469p. 1992. lib. bdg. 49.95 (*0-89950-672-0*) McFarland & Co.

— Hollywood Talks Turkey: The Screen's Greatest Flops. (Illus.). 300p. 1990. pap. 14.95 (*0-571-12901-3*) Faber & Faber.

McClelland, Douglas. Down the Yellow Brick Road: The Making of the Wizard of Oz. (Illus.). 160p. 1989. 9.99 (*0-517-69911-7*) Random Hse Value.

McClelland, Eleanor, et al, eds. Continuity of Care: Advancing the Concept of Discharge Planning. 256p. 1985. text ed. 54.50 (*0-8089-1765-X*, 792822, Grune) Saunders.

***McClelland, Eliza.** Traditional Beadwork: 20 Glorious Projects for Beading on Canvas. (Illus.). 112p. 1995. 29.95 (*1-85470-198-3*, Pub. by Anaya Pubs UK) Trafalgar.

McClelland, Elizabeth. William Sommer: Cleveland's Early Modern Master. LC 92-74017. (John Carroll University Cleveland Artists Ser.). 120p. 1992. pap. 24.00 (*1-882470-12-5*) J C Univ Gallery.

McClelland, Fleming, jt. ed. see Tarr, Rodger L.

McClelland, Gary H., jt. auth. see Judd, Charles M.

McClelland, Gordon, jt. auth. see Lovoos, Janice.

McClelland, Gordon T. Emil Kosa, Jr. (Illus.). 80p. 1990. 27.50 (*0-914589-06-7*) Hillcrest Pr.

— George Post. (Illus.). 82p. 1992. 27.50 (*0-914589-08-3*) Hillcrest Pr.

McClelland, Gordon T. & Last, Jay T. California Orange Box Labels. (Illus.). 136p. 1984. 37.50 (*0-914589-01-6*) Hillcrest Pr.

— Fruit Box Labels: An Illustrated Price Guide to Citrus Labels. (Illus.). 144p. (C). 1995. 35.00 (*0-914589-09-1*) Hillcrest Pr.

McClelland, Gordon T. & Zornes, Milford. Milford Zornes. (Illus.). 70p. 1992. 27.50 (*0-914589-07-5*) Hillcrest Pr.

McClelland, Hamish, jt. ed. see Kerr, Alan.

McClelland, Herbert L. 'SThe Secret Flower of Ranatan. LC 82-71949. (Illus.). 60p. (J). (gr. 3-5). 1984. pap. 3.50 (*0-943864-09-7*) Davenport.

McClelland, I. L. Benito Jeronimo Feijoo. LC 68-17230. (Twayne's World Authors Ser.). 1969. lib. bdg. 17.95 (*0-8057-2308-0*) Irvington.

— Diego de Torres Villarroel. LC 76-6548. (Twayne's World Authors Ser.). 162p. (C). 1976. lib. bdg. 17.95 (*0-317-38185-7*) Irvington.

McClelland, Ivy L. Spanish Drama of Pathos, 1750-1808, Vol. 2. LC 70-504666. 300p. reprint ed. pap. 85.50 (*0-8357-3767-5*, 2036496) Bks Demand.

— Spanish Drama of Pathos, 1750-1808, Vol. 1: High Tragedy. LC 70-504666. 360p. reprint ed. pap. 102.60 (*0-7837-0039-3*, 2036496) Bks Demand.

— Tirso De Molina. LC 76-28272. (Liverpool Studies in Spanish Literature 3rd Ser.). reprint ed. 32.50 (*0-404-15033-0*) AMS Pr.

McClelland, J. B. & Gibson, B. F. New Vistas in Physics with High-Energy Pion Beams: Preconference Workshop. 180p. 1993. text ed. 95.00 (*981-02-1275-5*) World Scientific Pub.

McClelland, James L. Parallel Distributed Processing: Explorations in the Microstructure of Cognition, Vol. 2: Psychological & Biological Models. (Illus.). 550p. 1987. 47.50 (*0-262-13218-4*, Bradford Bks); pap. 24.95 (*0-262-63110-5*, Bradford Bks) MIT Pr.

McClelland, James L. & Rumelhart, David E. Explorations in Parallel Distributed Processing: A Handbook of Models, Programs & Exercises. 1988. IBM Version. pap. 45.00x (*0-262-63113-X*); Macintosh Version. pap. 45.00x (*0-262-63129-6*) MIT Pr.

McClelland, John. The Bravest of Bears. (Illus.). 32p. (J). (ps-1). 1994. bds. 12.95 (*0-86264-389-9*, Pub. by Andersen Pr UK) Trafalgar.

McClelland, John, Jr. Window to the Past: The Washington State Historical Society's First Century. LC 92-13738. 1993. pap. 19.00 (*0-917048-69-5*) Wash St Hist Soc.

— Wobbly War: The Centralia Story. LC 87-51095. (Illus.). 256p. 1987. 15.00 (*0-917048-62-8*) Wash St Hist Soc.

McClelland, John J., et al. An Evaluation & Forecasting Model for Metal-Nonmetal Mining Research Needs: Model Development for Computer-Assisted Technology. 1994. write for info. (*0-318-72569-X*) US Interior.

McClelland, Joseph C., jt. ed. see Donnelly, John P.

McClelland, Julia. This Baby. LC 92-43756. (J). 1994. 13.95 (*0-395-66613-9*) HM.

McClelland, Kate M. The Mouth of Witnesses: Biblical Exegesis & the Dead Sea Scrolls. LC 76-48407. 1978. 10.00 (*0-916620-09-3*) Portals Pr.

McClelland, Keith, jt. ed. see Kaye, Harvey J.

McClelland, L. & Hale, P. English Grammar Through Guided Writing: Parts of Speech. 1978. pap. text ed. 15.75 (*0-13-281089-1*) P-H.

— English Grammar Through Guided Writing: Verbs. 1978. pap. text ed. 15.75 (*0-13-281097-2*) P-H.

McClelland, L., et al. English Sounds & Spelling. 1978. pap. text ed. 16.50 (*0-13-282954-1*) P-H.

McClelland, Lindsay, et al. Global Volcanism (1975-1985) 672p. 1989. text ed. 49.20 (*0-13-357203-X*) Am Geophysical.

Mcclelland, Mike, jt. auth. see Murray, Jeff.

McClelland, Nina I. & Evans, Joe L., eds. Individual Onsite Wastewater Systems, Vol. 7: Proceedings of the Seventh National Conference, 1980. LC 76-50983. (Illus.). 355p. 1981. 30.00 (*0-940006-00-6*) Natl Sanit Foun.

McClelland, Peter D. The American Search for Economic Justice. (Interpretive Economics Ser.). (Illus.). 400p. 1990. text ed. 42.95 (*1-55786-068-8*) Blackwell Pubs.

— Causal Explanation & Model Building in History, Economics, & the New Economic History. LC 74-25372. (Illus.). 296p. 1975. 38.95 (*0-8014-0929-2*) Cornell U Pr.

— Introduction to Microeconomics: Readings on Contemporary Issue, 86-87. 240p. 1987. pap. text ed. write for info. (*0-07-044860-4*) McGraw.

— Readings in Introductory Macroeconomics-Annual, 87-88. 768p. 1987. pap. text ed. write for info. (*0-318-62550-4*) McGraw.

McClelland, Ralph A. The Law of Corporate Mortgage Bond Issues. Reams, Bernard D., Jr., ed. LC 38-7784. (Historical Reprints in Jurisprudence & Classical Legal Literature Ser.). xiii, 1077p. 1984. reprint ed. lib. bdg. 84.00 (*0-89941-251-3*, 303230) W S Hein.

McClelland, Robert W. Architects of Worship. 1990. pap. 18.40 (*1-55673-216-3*) CSS OH.

McClelland, Robyn. Bibliography: Social Networks, Social Planning & Community Needs, No. 1135. 1976. 5.00 (*0-686-20409-3*) CPL Biblios.

McClelland, S. Surface Mount Technology: The Future for Electronics Assembly. (Illus.). 200p. 1987. pap. 173.00 (*0-387-17430-3*) Spr-Verlag.

***McClelland, Samuel B.** Organizational Needs Assessment: Design, Facilitation & Analysis. LC 95-14606. 1995. text ed. write for info. (*0-89930-950-X*, Quorum Bks) Greenwood.

McClelland, Sharon. A Clinical Manual for Nursing Assistants. LC 84-11985. 440p. (C). 1985. pap. text ed. 32.50 (*0-86720-365-X*) Jones & Bartlett.

***McClelland, Stephen, ed.** Intelcom '94: The Outlook for Mediterranean Communications. 1994. write for info. (*0-89006-811-9*) Artech Hse.

McClelland, V. Alan. Christian Education in Pluralist Society. 224p. (C). 1988. lib. bdg. 47.50 (*0-415-00540-X*, A1841) Routledge.

McClelland, W. Robert. Fire in the Hole. 1991. pap. 8.25 (*1-55673-315-1*, 9136) CSS OH.

— The Scandal & the Star. 128p. (Orig.). 1988. pap. 8.99 (*0-8272-3430-9*) Chalice Pr.

— Worldly Spirituality. 176p. (Orig.). 1990. pap. 10.99 (*0-8272-4227-1*) Chalice Pr.

McClelland, Whitney. Nineteen Ninety-Three Viewer's Guide to Professional Golf. 1992. pap. 24.95 (*0-9631259-1-5*) Golfguide.

— Nineteen Ninety-Three Viewer's Guide to Professional Golf. 1992. pap. 24.95 (*1-56683-022-2*) Mstr Artists.

— Viewer's Guide to Professional Golf, 1993. 1992. pap. 24.95 (*0-9631259-0-7*) Golfguide.

— The Viewers Guide to Professional Golf, 1993. (Illus.). 192p. 1993. write for info. (*0-9631259-2-3*) Golfguide.

— Viewers Guide to Professional Golf, 1995. 1994. pap. 24.95 (*0-9631259-3-1*) Golfguide.

McClellanville Arts Council. The McClellanville Coast Cookbook: Recipes, Oral Histories, Poetry, Prose, Prints, Photographs & Paintings. 1992. pap. 11.95 (*1-882966-00-7*) McClellanville Arts.

McClenaghan, Leroy R. & Gaines, Michael S. Reproduction in Marginal Populations of the Hispid Cotton Rat (Sigmodon hispidus) (Occasional Papers: No. 74). 16p. 1978. pap. 1.00 (*0-317-04888-0*) U of KS Mus Nat Hist.

McClenahan, Carolyn, jt. auth. see Getzoff, Ann.

McClenahan, Kelly L., jt. ed. see Belous, Richard S.

McClenahan, Pat & Jaqua, Ida. Cool Cooking for Kids. LC 75-32841. (J). (ps-00). 1976. pap. 9.99 (*0-8224-1614-X*) Fearon Teach Aids.

McClenathan, DayAnn K., jt. ed. see Monson, Dianne L.

McClendon. Wild Days. LC 89-62912. pap. 12.95 (*0-916990-23-0*) META Pubns.

McClendon, Bruce. Customer Service in Local Government: Challenges for Planners & City Managers. LC 91-75139. 250p. (Orig.). 1992. lib. bdg. 45.95 (*0-918286-76-X*); pap. 34.95 (*0-918286-75-1*) Planners Pr.

An Asterisk (*) at the beginning of an entry indicates that the title is appearing in BIP for the first time.

McClendon, Bruce W. & Quay, Ray. Mastering Change: Winning Strategies for Effective City Planning. LC 87-70796. (Illus.). 300p. 1988. lib. bdg. 44.95 (0-685-18403-X); pap. 27.95 (0-918286-48-4) Planners Pr.

McClendon, Charles B. The Imperial Abbey of Farfa. LC 86-3466. 318p. 1987. text ed. 42.00 (0-300-03333-8) Yale U Pr.

McClendon, Charles B., et al. Rome & the Provinces: Studies in the Transformation of Art & Architecture in the Mediterranean World. LC 86-18234. (Illus.). 83p. (Orig.). 1986. pap. 13.00 (0-89467-043-3) Yale Art Gallery.

McClendon, Dennis E. The Lady be Good: Mystery Bomber of World War II. (Illus.). 208p. 1982. pap. 12.95 (0-8168-6624-4, 26624, TAB-Aero) TAB Bks.

*McClendon, Dennis E. & Richards, Wallace F. The Legend of Colin Kelley: America's First Hero of WWII. LC 94-67868. (Illus.). 72p. (Orig.). 1994. pap. 8.95 (0-929521-93-5) Pictorial Hist.

McClendon, Garrard O. The African-American Guide to Better English: A Speaking & Writing Survival Manual for African-Americans. 2nd ed. LC 93-80308. (Illus.). 79p. (Orig.). 1995. pap. 7.95 (0-9639329-0-X) Positive People.

McClendon, James W., Jr. Biography As Theology: How Life Stories Can Remake Today's Theology. rev. ed. LC 90-49778. 224p. (C). 1990. pap. 13.95 (0-334-02482-X) TPI PA.

— Doctrine: Systematic Theology, Vol. 2. 496p. (Orig.). 1994. pap. 24.95 (0-687-11021-1) Abingdon.

McClendon, James W. Ethic: Systematic Theology, Vol. 1. 384p. 1988. pap. 16.95 (0-687-12016-0) Abingdon.

*McClendon, James W., Jr. Making Gospel Sense: To a Troubled Church. 176p. 1995. pap. 14.95 (0-8298-1072-2) Pilgrim OH.

*McClendon, James W., Jr. & Smith, James M. Convictions: Defusing Religious Relativism. rev. ed. LC 94-30851. 1994. pap. 18.00 (1-56338-106-0) TPI PA.

*McClendon, Lise. Painted Truth: An Alix Thorssen Mystery. 1995. 19.95 (0-8027-3271-2) Walker & Co.

*McClendon, Marion W. & Grelle, June R. Cee Vee, Our Home on the Range. 500p. 1991. text ed. 58.50 (0-9629112-0-8) Cee Vee Hist.

McClendon, McKee. Multiple Regression & Causal Analysis. LC 93-86171. 380p. 1994. boxed 48.00 (0-87581-384-4) Peacock Pubs.

McClendon, Patience. Under a Tyler Moon. (Illus.). 50p. (Orig.). 1988. pap. write for info. (0-941402-06-1) Devon Pub.

McClendon, Stewart & Goodman, Rosabel E., eds. International Commercial Arbitration in New York. 326p. 1986. lib. bdg. 35.00 (0-941320-41-3); pap. text ed. 25.00 (0-941320-45-6) Transnatl Pubs.

*McClendon, Theodore. How to Find a Good Black Man: Find Yourself. LC 94-74085. 85p. 1995. pap. 10.00 (0-9639329-1-8) Positive People.

McClennan. AP4 & Other Dinucleoside Polyphosphates. 1992. 173.00 (0-8493-5918-X, QP625) CRC Pr.

*McClennan, Bardi. On Good Behavior: Questions & Answers on Solving & Preventing Dog Problems. 240p. 1995. pap. 9.95 (0-87605-667-2) Macmillan.

McClennen, Crane. Arizona Courtroom Evidence Manual. 2nd ed. 1990. ring bd. 90.00 (0-88726-006-3) AZ St Bar.

McClennen, Edward F. Rationality & Dynamic Choice: Foundational Explorations. 320p. (C). 1990. 54.95 (0-521-36047-1) Cambridge U Pr.

McClennen, Sandra. Cognitive Skills for Community Living: Teaching Students with Moderate to Severe Disabilities. LC 90-27494. (Illus.). 402p. (C). 1991. pap. text ed. 34.00 (0-89079-459-6, 1591) PRO-ED.

McClennen, Sandra E., et al. Social Skills for Adults with Severe Retardation: An Inventory & Training Program. LC 80-51546. 284p. (C). 1980. ring bd. 49.95 (0-87822-220-0, 2200) Res Press.

McClenney, Byron N. Management for Productivity. LC 80-134596. 128p. reprint ed. pap. 36.50 (0-685-16375-X, 2027294) Bks Demand.

McClenney, Earl H., Jr. How to Supervise Black, Minorities & Women: A Guide for White & Japanese Males. 200p. (Orig.). 1990. pap. text ed. 10.95 (0-9618835-3-7) First Assocs Pub.

— How to Survive When You're the Only Black in the Office: What They Can't Teach You at White Business Schools. 212p. (Orig.). 1988. pap. 7.95 (0-9618835-0-2) First Assocs Pub.

McClenney, Kay, et al. Building Communities Through Strategic Planning: A Guidebook for Community Colleges. 88p. 1991. 20.00 (0-87117-230-5) Am Assn Comm Coll.

McClenon, James. Wondrous Events: Foundations of Religious Belief. LC 94-20228. (Illus.). 296p. (Orig.). (C). 1994. text ed. 39.95 (0-8122-3074-4); pap. text ed. 18.95 (0-8122-1355-6) U of Pa Pr.

McCleod, Carol, ed. see Barton, Charles D.

McClernan, James. Change Your Mind, Change Your Weight. LC 85-24890. 254p. 1986. pap. 10.95 (0-932090-15-X) Health Plus.

— Hugs from the Refrigerator. LC 93-24657. 192p. (Orig.). 1994. pap. 12.00 (0-933701-61-6) Westport Pubs.

McClernand, Edward J. On Time for Disaster: The Rescue of Custer's Command. LC 89-4931. (Illus.). x, 176p. 1989. reprint ed. pap. 6.95 (0-8032-8166-8, Bison Books) U of Nebr Pr.

McCleskey, Clifton. Political Power & American Democracy. 247p. (C). 1989. pap. 19.95 (0-534-11069-X) Intl Thomson.

McCleskey, F. David, Jr. Crane Operation & Preventive Maintenance. (Illus.). 104p. 1983. pap. text ed. 20.00 (0-934114-43-9, BK-101) Marine Educ.

McClester, Cedric. Kwanzaa: Everything You Always Wanted to Know But Didn't Know Where to Ask. 56p. 1993. pap. 5.95 (0-936073-08-X) Gumbs & Thomas.

McCleverty, J. A., jt. ed. see Pombeiro, A. J.

Mcclimans, Fred J. Communications Wiring & Interconnection. 352p. 1992. text ed. 40.00 (0-07-044847-7) McGraw.

*McClincy, William D. Instructional Methods in Emergency Services: A Resource Text Designed for EMS, Fire, & Rescue Instructors. LC 94-37817. 352p. 1994. pap. 27.00 (0-89303-541-6) P-H.

McClinn, Patricia. Not a Family Man. (Silhouette Special Edition Ser.). 1994. mass mkt. 3.50 (0-373-09864-2, 5-09864-5) Silhouette.

McClinte, Paige. Buyer Beware: Step-by-Step Guide for the First Time Home Buyer. LC 94-65053. 320p. (Orig.). 1997. 29.95 (1-884573-01-0); pap. 19.95 (1-884573-18-5) S-By-S Pubns.

— In Search of Success: Step-by-Step Guide for the Entrepreneur. LC 94-65051. 320p. (Orig.). 1996. 29.95 (1-884573-03-7); pap. 19.95 (1-884573-16-9) S-By-S Pubns.

— Life Styles of the Fittest: Step-by-Step Guide to Living Longer & Healthier. LC 94-65055. 320p. (Orig.). 1997. 29.95 (1-884573-21-5); pap. 19.95 (1-884573-20-7) S-By-S Pubns.

— Yes, There Is Life after Bankruptcy: Step-by-Step Guide to Getting Your Life Back on Track. LC 94-65049. 320p. (Orig.). 1996. 29.95 (1-884573-05-3); pap. 19.95 (1-884573-14-2) S-By-S Pubns.

McClintic, Miranda, jt. auth. see Fry, Edward F.

*McClintick, David. Indecent Exposure: A True Story of Hollywood & Wall Street. 1994. pap. 15.00 (0-688-13227-8, Quill) Morrow.

— Stealing from the Rich: The Home Stake Oil Swindle. LC 77-22103. 336p. 1977. 10.00 (0-87131-240-9) M Evans.

— Swordfish. 1995. pap. 5.99 (0-517-11687-1) Random.

— Swordfish: A Story of Ambition, Savagery & Betrayal. LC 92-50777. (Illus.). 512p. 1993. 25.00 (0-679-42019-3) Pantheon.

McClintick, Kyle. Koala & Me: Classroom Computer Activities for the Elementary School Year Using a Touchtablet, Joystick, or Mouse. (Illus.). 68p. (Orig.). 1986. 11.95 (0-9617571-0-8) Robertson Pubns.

McClintick, Malcolm. Death of an Old Flame. 208p. 1989. pap. 3.50 (0-380-70817-5) Avon.

— The Key. 256p. 1990. pap. 3.50 (0-380-70819-1) Avon.

— Mary's Grave. 224p. 1990. pap. 3.50 (0-380-70818-3) Avon.

*McClintock, Alexander, ed. The Convergence of Machine & Human Nature: A Critique of the Computer Metaphor of Mind & Artificial Intelligence. 152p. 1995. 55.95 (1-85628-997-4, Pub. by Avebury Pub UK) Ashgate Pub Co.

McClintock, Ann, jt. auth. see Ellis, Richard.

McClintock, Anne. Imperial Leather: Race, Gender & Sexuality in the Colonial Conquest. LC 94-7593. 1994. 55.00 (0-415-90889-2); pap. 18.95 (0-415-90890-6) Routledge.

— Sex Workers & Sex Work, Vol. 11, No. 4. 1994. pap. 8.00 (0-8223-6412-3) Duke.

McClintock, Barbara. Animal Fables from Aesop. 1991. 18.95 (0-87923-913-1) Godine.

— The Battle of Luke & Longnose. LC 93-12815. (J). 1994. 14.95 (0-395-65751-2) HM.

— The Fantastic Drawings of Danielle. LC 94-48842. (J). 1996. write for info. (0-395-73980-2) HM.

McClintock, C. Peasant Cooperatives & Political Change in Peru. 1981. 65.00x (0-691-07627-8); pap. 18.95x (0-691-02202-X) Princeton U Pr.

*McClintock, Cynthia. Peasant Cooperatives & Political Change in Peru. LC 80-8563. Date not set. reprint ed. pap. 124.60 (0-7837-9386-3, 2060130) Bks Demand.

McClintock, Dalene & Holmes, Carolyn. Communication Skillbook 3: New Worlds in English. (Communication Skillbooks Ser.). 64p. 1991. pap. text ed. 9.25 (0-8325-0656-7, Natl Textbk) NTC Pub Grp.

McClintock, David L. Formula Budgeting: An Approach to Facilities Funding. 50p. 5.00 (0-913359-05-X); 3.50 (0-685-43340-4) APPA VA.

McClintock, Elizabeth & Leiser, Andrew T. An Annotated Checklist of Woody Ornamental Plants of California, Oregon, & Washington. LC 78-73983. 134p. 1979. pap. 6.00 (0-931876-28-1, 4091) ANR Pubns CA.

McClintock, Elizabeth, jt. auth. see Fuller, Thomas C.

McClintock, Elizabeth, et al. An Annotated Checklist of Ornamental Plants of Coastal Southern California. LC 82-71105. 172p. (Orig.). 1982. pap. text ed. 12.00 (0-931876-58-3, 3276) ANR Pubns CA.

— A Flora of the San Bruno Mountains. (Special Publication Ser.: No. 8). 192p. (Orig.). 1990. pap. 14.95 (0-317-99709-2) Calif Native.

McClintock, F. A. & Argon, A. S. Mechanical Behavior of Materials. 1966. write for info. (0-201-04545-1) Addison-Wesley.

McClintock, F. H., jt. auth. see Odgers, F. J.

*McClintock, Grant & Crockett, Michael. Flywater. LC 94-25931. (Illus.). 144p. 1995. 39.95 (1-55821-339-2) Lyons & Burford.

McClintock, Hugh. The Bicycle & City Traffic: Principle & Practice. LC 92-20664. 224p. 1992. text ed. 51.95 (0-470-21928-9) Halsted Pr.

*McClintock, Hugh, ed. Bicycle & City Traffic: Principles & Practices. 1993. text ed. 59.95 (0-471-94720-2) Wiley.

McClintock, Jack & Helgren, David. Everything Is Somewhere: The Geography Quiz Book. LC 86-580. (Illus.). 160p. (Orig.). 1986. pap. 12.95 (0-688-05873-6, Quill) Morrow.

— Everything Is Somewhere in the U. S. A. The Geography Quiz Book. LC 93-49458. 1994. 12.95 (0-688-12733-9) Morrow.

McClintock, James. Mormon Settlement in Arizona. LC 78-134397. reprint ed. 42.50 (0-404-08439-7) AMS Pr.

— Nature's Kindred Spirits: Aldo Leopold, Joseph Wood Krutch, Edward Abbey, Annie Dillard, & Gary Snyder. 180p. 1994. 39.50 (0-299-14170-5); pap. 12.95 (0-299-14174-8) U of Wis Pr.

McClintock, James A. Clint. 1991. 8.95 (0-533-09260-4) Vantage.

McClintock, James C. & Caroline, Nancy L. Workbook for Emergency Care in the Streets. 3rd ed. 1987. 17.50 (0-316-55437-5) Little.

McClintock, James H. Mormon Settlement in Arizona. LC 85-8458. (Illus.). 384p. 1985. reprint ed. pap. 17.95 (0-8165-0953-0) U of Ariz Pr.

McClintock, James I. White Logic: Jack London's Short Stories. LC 74-84862. (Monograph Ser: No. 2). (Illus.). 208p. 1976. 15.00 (0-915046-22-9) Wolf Hse.

McClintock, John & Strong, James. Cyclopaedia of Biblical, Theological, & Ecclesiastical Literature: Cyclopaedia of Biblical Literature, Vol. 1-10. 250.00 (0-405-00020-0, 11917) Ayer.

— Cyclopedia of Biblical, Theological, & Ecclesiastical Literature, 12 vols. 12400p. (C). 1981. text ed. 395.00 (0-8010-6123-7) Baker Bk.

McClintock, Lorene. The McClintock Piano Course: A New Experience in Learning, 11 vols., Set. 2198p. (YA). 1992. boxed, spiral bd. 388.00 (1-880556-70-7) McClintock Ent.

McClintock, Margery, jt. auth. see Bean, Wiliam.

McClintock, Marian & Simms, Michael, eds. O. Henry's Texas Stories. LC 85-27951. 320p. (J). (ps-12). 1986. 19.95 (0-933841-03-5) Still Point TX.

McClintock, Michael. The American Connection: Vol. I: State Terror & Popular Resistance in El Salvador. 400p. (C). 1985. text ed. 35.00 (0-86232-240-5, Pub. by Zed Books UK); pap. 12.50 (0-86232-241-3, Pub. by Zed Books UK) Humanities.

— The American Connection: Vol. II: State Terror & Popular Resistance in Guatemala. 327p. (C). 1985. text ed. 35.00 (0-86232-258-8, Pub. by Zed Books UK); pap. 12.50 (0-86232-259-6, Pub. by Zed Books UK) Humanities.

McClintock, Mike. Alternative Housebuilding. LC 88-38140. (Popular Science Ser.). (Illus.). 299p. 1989. pap. 19.95 (0-8069-6995-4) Sterling.

— Alternative Housebuilding. (Illus.). 384p. (C). 1989. reprint ed. lib. bdg. 45.00x (0-8095-7530-2) Borgo Pr.

— Fly Went By. LC 58-9018. (Illus.). (J). (gr. 1-3). 1958. 7.99 (0-394-80003-6); lib. bdg. 9.99 (0-394-90003-0) Beginner.

— Lalique for Collectors. 1986. pap. 17.50 (0-684-14101-9, Scribners) S&S Trade.

— Mike McClintock's Home Sense Car & Repair Almanac. 1989. 28.95 (0-318-41623-9); pap. 14.60 (0-318-41624-7) TAB Bks.

— Mike McClintock's Home Sense Care & Repair Almanac. (Illus.). 416p. (Orig.). 1989. 28.95 (0-8306-0449-9); pap. 19.95 (0-8306-0349-2) TAB Bks.

— Stop That Ball! LC 59-9741. (Illus.). (J). (gr. 1-2). 1959. 7.99 (0-394-80010-9) Beginner.

McClintock, P. V., jt. ed. see Moss, Frank.

McClintock, Robert, ed. Computing & Education: The Second Frontier. (Special Issues for the Teachers College Record Ser.). 128p. 1988. reprint ed. pap. text ed. 15.95 (0-8077-2943-4) Tchrs Coll.

McClintock, Walter. Old Indian Trails. 1992. pap. 12.95 (0-395-61155-5) HM.

— The Old North Trail: Life, Legends & Religion of the Blackfeet Indians. LC 92-16001. (Illus.). xxiv, 539p. (C). 1992. reprint ed. pap. 14.95 (0-8032-8188-9, Bison Books) U of Nebr Pr.

— The Tragedy of the Blackfoot. (Illus.). 53p. 1970. reprint ed. pap. 5.00 (0-916561-63-1) Southwest Mus.

*McClinton, Joe, tr. Men's Hats. LC 94-43850. (Bella Cosa Library). (Illus.). (ENG & ITA.). 1995. pap. 12.95 (0-8118-1059-3) Chronicle Bks.

McClinton, Katharine M. Art Deco. 1986. pap. 14.95 (0-517-54599-3, C P Pubs) Crown Pub Group.

McClish, Glen, jt. auth. see Walker, Jeffrey.

McCloghrie, Keith, jt. auth. see Rose, Marshall T.

*McClory, Robert. Turning Point: The Inside Story of the Papal Birth Control Commission, & How Humanae Vitae Changed the Life of Patty Crowley & the Future of the Church. (Illus.). 192p. 1995. 19.95 (0-8245-1458-0) Crossroad NY.

McCloskey. Current Issues in Nursing. 3rd ed. (Illus.). 672p. 1989. pap. 35.95 (0-8016-5525-0) Mosby Yr Bk.

— Current Issues in Nursing. 4th ed. 744p. 1994. pap. write for info. (0-8016-6954-5) Mosby Yr Bk.

McCloskey & Orr. Textbook of Pediatric Transport Medicine. 900p. 1994. 99.00 (0-8016-7817-X) Mosby Yr Bk.

McCloskey & Stack. Voices in Literature, Bk. 1. 1993. pap. 24.95 (0-8384-2264-0) Heinle & Heinle.

— Voices in Literature, Bk. 1. 1993. text ed. 28.95 (0-8384-2258-6); teacher ed, pap. 12.95 (0-8384-2260-8) Heinle & Heinle.

— Voices in Literature, Bk. 2. 1994. teacher ed, pap. 12.95 (0-8384-2261-6) Heinle & Heinle.

— Voices in Literature, Bk. 2. 1996. pap. 24.95 (0-8384-2265-9) Heinle & Heinle.

McCloskey, jt. auth. see Ehrlich.

McCloskey, jt. auth. see Johnson, Joyce Y.

McCloskey, jt. auth. see Johnson.

McCloskey, A. L., jt. ed. see Steinberg, H.

McCloskey, Amanda H. & Luehrs, John. State Initiatives to Improve Rural Health Care. Glass, Karen, ed. 129p. (Orig.). 1990. pap. text ed. 15.00 (1-55877-081-X) Natl Governor.

*McCloskey, Burr. Novella Trio: Little Girl, What Now?; Dreams Under Fire; Afterwards. 288p. 1994. boxed, pap. 32.00 (0-8059-3610-6) Dorrance.

McCloskey, Donald N. The Applied Theory of Price. 2nd ed. LC 84-5621. 624p. (C). 1985. text ed. write for info. (0-02-378520-9) Macmillan.

— Economic Maturity & Entrepreneurial Decline: British Iron & Steel, 1870-1913. LC 72-92131. (Economic Studies: No. 142). 192p. 1973. 12.00 (0-674-22875-8) HUP.

— Enterprise & Trade in Victorian Britain: Essays in Historical Economics. (Modern Revivals in Economic History Ser.). 232p. (C). 1993. reprint ed. text ed. 59.95 (0-7512-0176-6, Pub. by Gregg Revivals UK) Ashgate Pub Co.

— If You're So Smart: The Narrative of Economic Expertise. LC 90-33041. 192p. 1990. 17.95 (0-226-55670-0) U Ch Pr.

— If You're So Smart: The Narrative of Economic Expertise. LC 90-33041. ix, 180p. 1992. pap. 9.95 (0-226-55671-9) U Ch Pr.

— Knowledge & Persuasion in Economics. LC 93-12078. (Illus.). 416p. (C). 1994. 59.95 (0-521-43475-0); pap. 17.95 (0-521-43603-6) Cambridge U Pr.

— The Rhetoric of Economics. LC 85-40373. (Rhetoric of the Human Sciences Ser.). 232p. 1987. reprint ed. pap. 14.95 (0-299-10384-6) U of Wis Pr.

— The Writing of Economics. 97p. (C). 1987. pap. write for info. (0-02-379520-4) Macmillan.

McCloskey, Donald N., ed. Essays on a Mature Economy: Britain after 1840. LC 73-170254. (Quantitative Studies in History). 453p. 1972. 69.50 (0-691-05198-4) Princeton U Pr.

— Second Thoughts: Myths & Morals of U. S. Economic History. 224p. 1995. pap. 15.95 (0-19-510118-9) OUP.

— Second Thoughts: The Uses of Economic History. 256p. 1993. 28.00 (0-19-506633-2) OUP.

McCloskey, Donald N. & Hersh, George K., Jr., eds. A Bibliography of Historical Economics to 1980. 1991. 64.95 (0-521-40327-8) Cambridge U Pr.

McCloskey, Donald N., jt. ed. see Floud, Roderick.

McCloskey, Donald N., ed. see Mathematical Social Science Board Conference on the New Economic History of Britain Staff.

McCloskey, J. A., jt. ed. see Burlingame, A. L.

McCloskey, James. Transformational Syntax & Model Theoretic Semantics. (Synthese Language Library: No. 9). 1979. lib. bdg. 80.00 (90-277-1025-2); pap. text ed. 36.50 (90-277-1026-0) Kluwer Ac.

McCloskey, Jenny. Your Sexual Health: What Every Teen Should Know about Sex. LC 92-35228. 336p. 1993. 15.95 (1-879904-08-X) Halo Bks.

McCloskey, Joanne C. Classification of Nursing Interventions. 581p. 1992. spiral bd. 24.95 (0-8016-6701-1) Mosby Yr Bk.

— Toward an Educational Model of Nursing Effectiveness. LC 83-9288. (Studies in Nursing Management: No. 11). 187p. reprint ed. pap. 53.30 (0-685-20811-7, 2070025) Bks Demand.

McCloskey, John W. America's Federal Gold Coinage, 1793-1933, No. 8: Handbook. 36p. 1989. pap. 9.50 (0-685-72021-7); boxed, sl. 30.00 (0-685-72022-5) Am Numismatic.

— America's Silver Coinage, 1794-1891, No. 6: Handbook. 38p. 1986. 6.00 (0-685-72023-3); boxed, sl. 25.00 (0-685-72024-1) Am Numismatic.

McCloskey, Kevin. Mrs. Fitz's Flamingos. LC 90-2278. (Illus.). (J). (ps-3). 1992. 14.00 (0-688-10474-6); lib. bdg. 13.93 (0-688-10475-4) Lothrop.

*McCloskey, Larry A. & Wirth, Bryan. Selling with Excellence: A Quality Approach for Sales Professionals. LC 94-37982. 1994. pap. 15.00 (0-87389-322-0) ASQC Qual Pr.

McCloskey, M. C., jt. auth. see Enright, D. Scott.

McCloskey, Maris, ed. see Welles, Laura & Welles, Ted.

McCloskey, Mark. The Secret Documents of America. 1976. pap. 1.50 (0-88031-032-4) Invisible-Red Hill.

McCloskey, Mark, tr. see Herbert, George.

McCloskey, Marsha. Christmas Quilts. 1990. pap. 6.95 (0-486-26406-8) Dover.

— Dozen Variables. 1992. pap. 5.95 (0-486-27201-X) Dover.

— Feathered Star Quilts. (Illus.). 128p. (Orig.). 1995. pap. 22.95 (0-9635422-3-0) Feathered Star.

— Feathered Star Sampler. 24p. 1994. pap. 7.95 (0-9635422-2-2) Feathered Star.

— Guide to Rotary Cutting. 24p. 1990. pap. 5.95 (0-9635422-1-4) Feathered Star.

— Lessons in Machine Piecing. McGehee, Liz, ed. LC 89-20597. (Illus.). 96p. (Orig.). 1990. pap. 9.95 (0-943574-63-3) That Patchwork.

— On to Square Two. Weiland, Barbara, ed. LC 91-48158. (Illus.). 80p. 1992. pap. 18.95 (0-943574-97-8, B138) That Patchwork.

— One Hundred Pieced Patterns for Eight Inch Quilt Blocks. 64p. 1993. pap. 9.95 (0-9635422-0-6) Feathered Star.

— Rotary Cutting Companion for Feathered Star Quilts. 24p. 1995. pap. 6.95 (0-9635422-4-9) Feathered Star.

— Stars & Stepping Stones. (Orig.). 1993. pap. 6.95 (0-486-27416-0) Dover.

— Wall Quilts. 1990. pap. 5.95 (0-486-26370-3) Dover.

*McCloskey, Marsha & Martin, Nancy. Variable Star Quilts & How to Make Them. LC 94-41222. (Illus.). 64p. 1995. pap. text ed. 7.95 (0-486-28595-2) Dover.

McCloskey, Marsha, jt. auth. see Martin, Judy.

McCloskey, Mary A. Kant's Aesthetic. LC 86-14479. 184p. 1987. 64.50 (0-88706-424-8); pap. 21.95 (0-88706-423-X) State U NY Pr.

An Asterisk (*) at the beginning of an entry indicates that the title is appearing in BIP for the first time.

McCloskey, Michael. The Formative Years of the Missionary College of Santa Cruz of Queretaro: 1683-1733. (Monograph Ser.). 1955. 25.00 (0-88382-051-X) AAFH.

McCloskey-Padgett, Patty. The Real Mother Goose ABC's. (Illus.). 32p. (J). 1993. pap. 5.95 (1-56565-090-5) Lowell Hse.

***McCloskey-Padgett, Patty, et al, illus.** The Real Mother Goose Book of American Rhymes. LC 94-48663. (J). 1995. 8.95 (0-590-50955-1) Scholastic Inc.

McCloskey, Pat. Naming Your God: The Search for Mature Images. LC 90-85157. 192p. (Orig.). 1991. pap. 7.95 (0-87793-452-5) Ave Maria.

McCloskey, Patrick. St. Anthony of Padua: Wisdom for Today. 120p. 1977. 3.95 (0-912228-36-9) St Anthony Mess Pr.

McCloskey, Patrick & Schoenberg, Ronald. Criminal Law Deskbook. 1984. Looseleaf Updates Avail. write for info. (0-8205-1217-6) Bender.

McCloskey, Patty, illus. Find the Real Mother Goose. 32p. (J). (ps-1). 1993. reprint ed. pap. 5.95 (1-56565-054-9) Lowell Hse.

McCloskey, Paul N., Jr. The Taking of Hill 610: And Other Essays on Friendship. 220p. 1992. 12.95 (0-9635186-0-7) Eaglet Bks.

McCloskey, Richard G., jt. auth. see Beavis, Bill.

McCloskey, Robert. Blueberries for Sal. LC 48-4955. (Illus.). (J). (ps-1). 1976. pap. 4.99 (0-14-050169-X, Puffin) Puffin Bks.

— Blueberries for Sal. (Story Tapes Ser.). (Illus.). (J). (ps-3). 1989. pap. 6.95 (0-14-095032-X, Puffin) Puffin Bks.

— Blueberries for Sal. (Illus.). (J). 1993. audio, pap. 6.99 (0-14-095110-5, Puffin) Puffin Bks.

— Blueberries for Sal. LC 48-4955. (Illus.). 56p. (J). (ps-1). 1948. pap. 14.95 (0-670-17591-9) Viking Child Bks.

— Burt Dow: Deep-Water Man. LC 68-364. (Illus.). 64p. (J). (gr. 4-6). 1963. pap. 16.99 (0-670-19748-3) Viking Child Bks.

— Burt Dow, Deep-Water Man. (Illus.). 64p. (J). (ps-3). 1989. pap. 4.99 (0-14-050978-X, Puffin) Puffin Bks.

— Centerburg Tales. (Illus.). (J). (gr. 1-3). 1977. pap. 4.99 (0-14-031072-X, Puffin) Puffin Bks.

— Centerburg Tales. LC 51-10675. (Illus.). 192p. (J). (gr. 4-6). 1951. pap. 15.99 (0-670-20977-5) Viking Child Bks.

— Homer Price. (Storybooks Ser.). (Illus.). (J). (gr. 3-7). 1976. pap. 3.99 (0-14-030927-6, Puffin) Puffin Bks.

— Homer Price. (Illus.). (J). (gr. 4-6). 1943. pap. 14.99 (0-670-37729-5) Viking Child Bks.

— Homer Price. braille ed. 124p. 1993. text ed. 9.92 (1-56956-503-1, BR9232) W A T Braille.

— Lentil. (J). (ps-3). 1978. pap. 4.99 (0-14-050287-4, Puffin) Puffin Bks.

— Lentil. (Illus.). (J). (gr. k-3). 1940. pap. 14.95 (0-670-42357-2) Viking Child Bks.

— Make Way for Ducklings. (Picture Puffins Ser.). (Illus.). (J). (gr. 1-3). 1976. pap. 4.99 (0-14-050171-1, Puffin) Puffin Bks.

— Make Way for Ducklings. (Illus.). (J). 1993. audio, pap. 6.99 (0-14-095118-0, Puffin) Puffin Bks.

— Make Way for Ducklings. (Illus.). (J). (gr. k-3). 1941. pap. 14.99 (0-670-45149-5) Viking Child Bks.

— Make Way for Ducklings: A Giant Book. (J). (ps-3). 1991. pap. 18.99 (0-14-054434-8, Puffin) Puffin Bks.

— One Morning in Maine. (Picture Puffins Ser.). (J). (ps-3). 1976. pap. 4.99 (0-14-050174-6, Puffin) Puffin Bks.

— One Morning in Maine. (Illus.). (J). (gr. k-3). 1952. pap. 14.99 (0-670-52627-4) Viking Child Bks.

— Time of Wonder. (Illus.). 64p. (J). (gr. k-3). 1989. pap. 5.99 (0-14-050201-7, Puffin) Puffin Bks.

— Time of Wonder. (Illus.). (J). (gr. k-3). 1957. pap. 16.00 (0-670-71512-3) Viking Child Bks.

McCloskey, Robert G. American Supreme Court. LC 60-14235. (Chicago History of American Civilization Ser.). 1961. pap. text ed. 10.95 (0-226-55675-1, CHAC13) U Ch Pr.

— The American Supreme Court. Levinson, Sanford, ed. LC 94-10905. 352p. 1994. pap. text ed. 12.95 (0-226-55678-6) U Ch Pr.

— The American Supreme Court. 2nd ed. Levinson, Sanford, ed. LC 94-10905. 352p. 1994. lib. bdg. 45.00 (0-226-55677-8) U Ch Pr.

— The Modern Supreme Court. LC 70-173408. 376p. reprint ed. pap. 110.60 (0-7837-6079-5, 2059125) Bks Demand.

***McCloskey, Seosamh.** Irish Language Books: A Reader's Guide. rev. ed. 72p. 1995. pap. 9.95 (0-9635738-2-9) Irish Bks NY.

— A Reader's Guide to Books in the Irish Language. 59p. (C). 1993. pap. 6.95 (0-9635738-0-2) Irish Bks NY.

***McCloskey, William.** Highliners: The Classic Novel of Alaska & Its Fishermen. 416p. 1995. pap. 16.95 (1-55821-375-9) Lyons & Burford.

McClosky, Herbert. Consensus & Ideology in American Politics. (Reprint Series in Social Sciences). (C). 1993. reprint ed. pap. text ed. 1.00 (0-8290-3149-9, P-403) Irvington.

McClosky, Herbert & Brill, Alida. Dimensions of Tolerance: What Americans Believe about Civil Liberties. LC 82-72959. 525p. 1983. 45.00 (0-87154-591-8) Russell Sage.

— Dimensions of Tolerance: What Americans Believe about Civil Liberties. 512p. (C). 1986. pap. 17.95 (0-87154-592-6) Russell Sage.

McClosky, Herbert & Zaller, John R. The American Ethos: Public Attitudes Toward Capitalism & Democracy. LC 84-12793. (Twentieth Century Fund Study). 360p. 1988. pap. 17.50 (0-674-02331-5) HUP.

McCloud. Zot: Book 1. (Illus.). 1990. 29.95 (0-913035-03-3); pap. 14.95 (0-913035-04-1) Eclipse Bks.

McCloud, Aminah B. African American Islam. LC 94-18313. 200p. 1995. 49.95 (0-415-90785-3, B0634); pap. 16.95 (0-415-90786-1, B0638) Routledge.

***McCloud, Barry.** Definite Country: The Ultimate Encyclopedia of Country Music & Its Performers. LC 94-28400. 1994. pap. 19.00 (0-399-52144-5, Perigee Bks); pap. text ed. 40.00 (0-399-51890-8, Perigee Bks) Berkley Pub.

McCloud, Bill. What Should We Tell Our Children about Vietnam? 176p. 1992. pap. 4.50 (0-425-13361-3) Berkley Pub.

— What Should We Tell Our Children about Vietnam? LC 89-40218. 144p. 1989. 18.95 (0-8061-2229-3) U of Okla Pr.

***McCloud, Cornie B.** Cumberland Gap's Hillbilly Preacher: Hugh Vancel. 128p. 1995. pap. 12.95 (1-881576-55-8) Providence Hse.

***McCloud, Donald G.** Southeast Asia: Tradition & Modernity in the Contemporary World. 2nd ed. LC 95-5014. (C). 1995. text ed. 59.95 (0-8133-1897-1); pap. text ed. 19.95 (0-8133-1896-3) Westview.

Mccloud, Kevin. Decorative Style Most Original. 1990. 40.00 (0-671-69142-2) S&S Trade.

McCloud, Kevin. Lighting Style: The Complete Visual Sourcebook for Every Room in Your House. LC 94-13676. 1995. 25.00 (0-671-88706-8) S&S Trade.

***McCloud, Linda.** Do You Take This Man. 140p. 1995. pap. 7.95 (1-56901-680-1) NW Pub.

McCloud, Mac, jt. auth. see Barrett, R.

***McCloud, Melody T.** Medical Bloopers!! Amusing & Amazing Stories of Health Care Workers. 72p. (Orig.). 1994. pap. 6.95 (0-9643554-0-X) New Life GA.

McCloud, Scott. Understanding Comics. Martin, Mark, ed. (Illus.). 216p. (Orig.). 1993. pap. 19.95 (1-56862-019-5) Tundra MA.

— Understanding Comics. 2nd deluxe limited ed. Martin, Mark, ed. (Illus.). 224p. (Orig.). (J). (gr. 4 up). 1993. 34.95 (0-87816-245-3) Kitchen Sink.

— Understanding Comics. 2nd ed. Martin, Mark, ed. (Illus.). 224p. (Orig.). (J). (gr. 4 up). 1993. reprint ed. 27.95 (0-87816-244-5); reprint ed. pap. 19.95 (0-87816-243-7) Kitchen Sink.

— Understanding Comics: The Invisible Art. 1994. pap. 20.00 (0-06-097625-X) HarpC.

McCloud, Susan E. A. A. Seagull. (J). pap. 4.95 (0-88494-721-1) Bookcraft Inc.

— Abide the Dark Dawn. LC 91-76003. 251p. 1991. 6.95 (1-56236-302-6) Aspen Bks.

— Anna. 1992. pap. 4.95 (0-88494-855-2) Bookcraft Inc.

— By All We Hold Dear. 1994. pap. 6.95 (0-88494-929-X) Bookcraft Inc.

— A Face in the Shadows. 1993. 10.95 (0-88494-898-6) Bookcraft Inc.

— For Love of Ivy. 1993. pap. 5.95 (0-88494-873-0) Bookcraft Inc.

— The Heart That Truly Loves. 1994. 12.95 (0-88494-952-4) Bookcraft Inc.

— I'm Going to Be Baptized. (J). 5.95 (0-88494-512-X) Bookcraft Inc.

— Jennie. pap. 5.95 (0-88494-736-X) Bookcraft Inc.

— Joseph Smith: A Photobiography. LC 91-76005. (Illus.). 169p. (YA). (gr. 4-12). 1992. 12.95 (1-56236-400-6) Aspen Bks.

— Ravenwood. 1992. 10.95 (0-88494-852-8) Bookcraft Inc.

McCloud, Tom, jt. auth. see Benner, Bob.

***McCloy.** Some Girls. 1995. pap. (0-452-27273-4, Plume) NAL-Dutton.

McCloy, Charles H. & Young, Norma D. Tests & Measurements in Health & Physical Education. 3rd ed. (Illus.). 1979. reprint ed. text ed. 29.50 (0-89197-448-2) Irvington.

McCloy, Donaldson & Martin, H. R. Control of Power Analysis & Design. 2nd rev. ed. 1988. pap. text ed. 52.95 (0-470-21091-5) Wiley.

McCloy, Helen. A Change of Heart. 224p. 1994. 16.95 (0-7451-8634-3, Black Dagger) Chivers N Amer.

— Cruel As the Grave. large type ed. 1979. 12.00 (0-7089-0260-X) Ulverscroft.

— Minotaur Country. large type ed. 1979. 12.00 (0-7089-0275-8) Ulverscroft.

— Mr. Splitfoot. large type ed. (Keating's Choice Ser.). 287p. 1992. 24.95 (1-85089-493-0, Pub. by ISIS UK) Transaction Pubs.

— A Question of Time. large type ed. 1973. 15.95 (0-85456-222-2) Ulverscroft.

— The Sleepwalker. large type ed. 320p. 1982. 15.95 (0-7089-0857-8) Ulverscroft.

McCloy, James F. & Miller, Ray, Jr. The Jersey Devil. (Illus.). 121p. (YA). (gr. 5 up). 1987. pap. 9.95 (0-912608-11-0) Mid Atlantic.

McCloy, John J., et al. The Great Oil Spill, the Inside Report: Gulf Oil's Bribery & Political Chicanery. LC 76-424. 340p. (Orig.). 1976. pap. 2.25 (0-87754-044-6) Chelsea Hse.

McCloy, Kristin. Some Girls. 320p. 1994. 20.95 (0-525-93837-0) NAL-Dutton.

— Velocity. 272p. 1990. pap. 7.95 (0-671-68920-7, WSP) PB.

McCloy, Peter. Smart Selling: The Consultative Approach. 1993. pap. 16.95 (1-875680-04-7, Pub. by Busn & Prof Pubng AT) Pubs Dist MI.

McCloy, Shelby T. French Inventions of the Eighteenth Century. LC 52-5903. 255p. reprint ed. pap. 72.70 (0-317-10751-8, 2000284) Bks Demand.

— Government Assistance in Eighteenth Century France. LC 77-23743. (Perspectives in European History Ser.: No. 14). xi, 496p. 1977. reprint ed. lib. bdg. 49.50 (0-87991-621-4) Porcupine Pr.

— Humanitarianism in 18th Century. LC 72-5476. (World History Ser.: No. 48). 1972. reprint ed. lib. bdg. 61.95 (0-8383-1600-X) M S G Haskell Hse.

— The Negro in France. LC 72-5545. (Studies in Black History & Culture: No. 54). 1972. reprint ed. lib. bdg. 75.00 (0-8383-1601-8) M S G Haskell Hse.

McCluer, Eric, ed. Kansas Craft Register 1993. (Illus.). 160p. 1992. pap. 13.95 (1-880652-16-1) Wichita Eagle.

— Kansas Craft Register, 1994: A Directory of Artisans & Craft Shows for 1994. 140p. 1993. pap. 13.95 (1-880652-27-7) Wichita Eagle.

— Kansas Craft Register 1995: A Directory of Artisans & Craft Shows for 1995. 144p. 1994. pap. 13.95 (1-880652-39-0) Wichita Eagle.

— Kansas Directory of Commerce 1993. 880p. 1993. pap. 62.00 (1-880652-18-8) Wichita Eagle.

— Kansas Directory of Commerce, 1994: A Guide to Manufacturers & Other Major Employers Throughout the State. 880p. Date not set. pap. 62.00 (1-880652-28-5) Wichita Eagle.

— The Kansas Directory of Commerce 1995: A Guide to Manufacturers & Other Major Employees Throughout the State. 860p. 1994. pap. 67.00 (1-880652-40-4) Wichita Eagle.

— Missouri Craft Register 1993. (Illus.). 132p. 1992. pap. 13.95 (1-880652-17-X) Wichita Eagle.

— Missouri Craft Register, 1994: A Directory of Artisans & Craft Shows for 1994. 120p. 1993. pap. 13.95 (1-880652-29-3) Wichita Eagle.

— Missouri Craft Register 1995: A Directory of Artisans & Craft Shows for 1995. 120p. 1994. pap. 13.95 (1-880652-41-2) Wichita Eagle.

***McCluggage, Denise.** By Brooks Too Broad for Leaping: Selections from Autoweek. 288p. 1994. pap. 17.95 (0-9642309-0-9) Fulcorte Pr.

— Centered Skier. (Illus.). 230p. 1992. reprint ed. pap. 14.95 (0-9632484-0-5) Tempest Bk.

McCluggage, Robert W., ed. Selected Papers in Illinois History, 1982. LC 85-14310. 1984. pap. 7.50 (0-912226-15-3) Ill St Hist Soc.

— Selected Papers in Illinois History, 1983. LC 86-116885. 1985. pap. 7.50 (0-912226-17-X) Ill St Hist Soc.

McCluhan, Michael, ed. see Owl, Michael W.

McClun, Diana & Nownes, Laura. Quilts Galore! Quiltmaking Styles & Techniques. LC 90-42209. (Illus.). 192p. (Orig.). 1990. pap. 21.95 (0-913327-21-2) Quilt Digest Pr.

— Quilts, Quilts, & More Quilts! Nadel, Harold, ed. LC 93-28345. (Illus.). 176p. (Orig.). 1993. pap. 23.95 (0-914881-67-1) C & T Pub.

— Quilts! Quilts!! Quilts!!! The Complete Guide to Quiltmaking. LC 88-18563. (Illus.). 160p. (Orig.). 1989. pap. 21.95 (0-913327-16-6) Quilt Digest Pr.

McClune, Barry, jt. auth. see Sanders, Roger.

McCluney, Ross. Introduction to Radiometry & Photometry. LC 94-7674. 1994. 85.00 (0-89006-678-7) Artech Hse.

McCluney, William R., ed. Environmental Destruction of South Florida: A Handbook for Citizens. LC 78-154554. 1971. pap. 13.95 (0-87024-202-4) U of Miami Pr.

McClung, Cooky. Plugly, the Horse That Could Do Everything. (Illus.). 48p. (J). 1993. 16.95 (0-939481-32-4) Half Halt Pr.

McClung, David & Schaerer, Peter. The Avalanche Handbook. 2nd ed. LC 93-2027. (Illus.). 256p. 1993. pap. 19.95 (0-89886-364-3) Mountaineers.

McClung, Floyd. Basic Discipleship. LC 92-14863. 192p. 1992. reprint ed. pap. 9.99 (0-8308-1319-5) InterVarsity.

McClung, Floyd, Jr. El Corazon Paternal de Dios. Guerra, Francisco B., tr. 96p. 1988. reprint ed. pap. 3.50 (0-88113-027-3) Edit Betania.

— The Father Heart of God with Study Guide. LC 85-61075. (Orig.). 1985. pap. 7.99 (0-89081-491-0) Harvest Hse.

McClung, Floyd. Finding Friendship with God: An Invitation to Intimacy with the Most Important Person in the Universe. 208p. (Orig.). 1993. pap. 8.99 (0-89283-679-2, Vine Bks) Servant.

— Friendship Evangelism. 22p. (Orig.). 1988. reprint ed. pap. 0.45 (0-910796-15-7) Intl Students Inc.

— God's Man in the Family: Caring for the Ones You Love - The Nine Essentials. 1994. pap. 9.99 (1-56507-881-0) Harvest Hse.

— The Healing Power of Love. (Orig.). 1995. pap. 8.99 (1-56507-339-8) Harvest Hse.

— Learning to Love People You Don't Like: Love & Unity in Relationships. 120p. 1992. pap. 7.99 (0-927545-19-5) YWAM Pub.

— Living on the Devil's Doorstep: True Mission Story Set in Afghanistan & Amsterdam. 243p. 1988. pap. 8.99 (0-927545-45-4) YWAM Pub.

— O Imensuravel Amor De Deus. 96p. (POR.). 1991. 5.95 (0-8297-1649-1) Life Pubs Intl.

— Padre Que Seamos Uno. (SPA.). Date not set. pap. 5.99 (0-88113-109-1) Edit Betania.

McClung, Gavin. Astrology Plus Insight. LC 83-72571. 136p. 1984. 12.00 (0-86690-259-7, M2427-014) Am Fed Astrologers.

McClung, Jean. Effects of High Altitude on Human Birth: Observations on Mothers, Placentas, & the Newborn in Two Peruvian Populations. LC 72-91629. 168p. 1969. 17.95 (0-674-24065-0) HUP.

— Mischief & Mercy: Tales of the Saints. LC 93-2487. (Illus.). 224p. (YA). (gr. 7 up). 1993. pap. 10.95 (1-883672-02-3) Tricycle Pr.

McClung, Karen S., ed. GFWC Centennial Cookbook. (Illus.). 384p. 1988. write for info. (0-318-64786-9) Bright America.

McClung, L. Grant, Jr., ed. Azusa Street & Beyond. LC 86-70742. 245p. 1986. pap. 7.95 (0-88270-607-1) Bridge Pub.

McClung, Leland S. The Anaerobic Bacteria: Their Activities in Nature & Disease. LC 82-10085. 865p. reprint ed. Pt. 1 - Vol. 5: The Subject Listings for 1940-1969. pap. 180.00 (0-8357-5418-9, 2027072); reprint ed. Pt. 2 - Vol. 1: The Literature for 1970-1975. pap. 180.00 (0-8357-5419-7); reprint ed. Pt. 2 - Vol. 2: The Subject Listings for 1970-1975. pap. 99.50 (0-8357-5420-0) Bks Demand.

— The Anaerobic Bacteria: Their Activities in Nature & Disease, 4 vols., 1. LC 82-10085. 760p. reprint ed. pap. 180.00 (0-8357-5421-9, 2027072) Bks Demand.

— The Anaerobic Bacteria: Their Activities in Nature & Disease, 4 vols., 2. LC 82-10085. 757p. reprint ed. pap. 180.00 (0-8357-6274-2) Bks Demand.

— The Anaerobic Bacteria: Their Activities in Nature & Disease, 4 vols., 3. LC 82-10085. 792p. reprint ed. pap. 180.00 (0-8357-6275-0) Bks Demand.

— The Anaerobic Bacteria: Their Activities in Nature & Disease, 4 vols., 4. LC 82-10085. 732p. reprint ed. pap. 180.00 (0-8357-6276-9) Bks Demand.

— The Anaerobic Bacteria: Their Activities in Nature & Disease, 4 vols., Pt. 1. reprint ed. pap. write for info. (0-318-65438-5) Bks Demand.

McClung, Liz, ed. see Unknown Critic Staff.

McClung, Nellie. In Times Like These. LC 70-163829. (Social History of Canada Ser.). 160p. 1972. pap. 12.95 (0-8020-6125-7) U of Toronto Pr.

McClung, Nellie L. Purple Springs. 2nd ed. (Illus.). 400p. 1992. 40.00 (0-8020-5924-4); pap. 19.95 (0-8020-6864-2) U of Toronto Pr.

McClung, Patricia A., ed. Selection of Library Materials in the Humanities, Social Sciences, & Sciences. LC 85-20084. 1985. 20.00 (0-8389-3305-X) ALA.

McClung, Paul. Papa Jack: Cowman from the Wichitas. LC 76-19071. 249p. reprint ed. 71.00 (0-8357-9738-4, 2016238) Bks Demand.

McClung, Robert. Hugh Glass, Mountain Man. LC 90-37814. (Illus.). 224p. (YA). (gr. 5 up). 1990. 15.00 (0-688-08092-8) Morrow Jr Bks.

— Old Bet & the Start of the American Circus. LC 92-11020. 32p. (J). (gr. k up). 1993. 15.00 (0-688-10642-0); lib. bdg. 14.93 (0-688-10643-9) Morrow Jr Bks.

— Snakes: Their Place in the Sun. (Illus.). 64p. (J). (gr. 2-4). 1991. 14.95 (0-8050-1718-6, Bks Young Read) H Holt & Co.

McClung, Robert M. America's First Elephant. LC 89-13764. (Illus.). 40p. (J). (gr. k up). 1991. lib. bdg. 14.88 (0-688-08359-5) Morrow Jr Bks.

— Gorilla. LC 84-718. (Illus.). 96p. (J). (gr. 3-7). 1984. 11.00 (0-688-03875-1) Morrow Jr Bks.

— Hugh Glass: Mountain Man. LC 92-43790. 176p. (YA). (gr. 7 up). 1993. pap. 3.95 (0-688-04595-2, Pub. by Beech Tree Bks) Morrow.

— Lili: A Giant Panda of Sichuan. LC 87-28271. (Illus.). 96p. (J). (gr. 3-7). 1988. 15.00 (0-688-06942-8); lib. bdg. 14.93 (0-688-06943-6) Morrow Jr Bks.

— Snakes: Their Place in the Sun. LC 91-692. (Illus.). 64p. (J). (gr. 2-4). 1993. pap. 5.95 (0-8050-2893-5, Bks Young Read) H Holt & Co.

— The True Adventures of Grizzly Adams. LC 85-8886. (Illus.). 208p. (J). (gr. 5 up). 1985. 11.95 (0-688-05794-2) Morrow Jr Bks.

— Whitetail. LC 86-18183. (Illus.). 96p. (J). (gr. 3-7). 1987. 12.95 (0-688-06126-5); lib. bdg. 12.88 (0-688-06127-3) Morrow Jr Bks.

McClung, Siegel. Sales: The Fast Track for Women. 1982. 12.95 (0-02-610640-X) Macmillan.

McClung, William A. The Country House in English Renaissance Poetry. 1977. 45.00 (0-520-03137-7) U CA Pr.

***McClure, ed.** Vegetarian ALT, Vol. 1. 1995. pap. 30.00 (0-945934-16-5) New Wrld Lib.

McClure, A. K. Our Presidents & How We Make Them. LC 79-130559. (Select Bibliographies Reprint Ser.). 1977. reprint ed. 28.95 (0-8369-5532-3) Ayer.

McClure, Abbot, jt. auth. see Eberlein, Harold D.

McClure, Alexander K. Colonel Alexander K. McClure's Recollections of Half a Century. LC 76-172762. reprint ed. 34.75 (0-404-00086-X) AMS Pr.

McClure, Alexander K., ed. The Annals of the Civil War. LC 94-11563. (Illus.). 808p. 1994. reprint ed. pap. 19.95 (0-306-80606-1) Da Capo.

McClure, Amy A. Sunrises & Songs: Reading & Writing Poetry in an Elementary Classroom. LC 89-19919. (Illus.). 274p. (Orig.). 1990. pap. text ed. 19.00 (0-435-08507-7) Heinemann.

McClure, Amy A. & Kristo, Janice V., eds. Inviting Children's Responses to Literature: Guides to 57 Notable Books. 145p. (Orig.). 1994. pap. 12.95 (0-8141-2379-1) NCTE.

McClure, Arthur F. Memories of Splendor: The Midwestern World of William Inge. LC 89-62833. (Illus.). 85p. 1989. pap. 10.95 (0-87726-038-9) Kansas St Hist.

— The Truman Administration & the Problems of Postwar Labor 1945-1948. LC 68-57718. 267p. 1975. 35.00 (0-8386-6999-9) Fairleigh Dickinson.

McClure, Arthur F. & Rice, C. David, eds. A Bibliographical Guide to the Works of William Inge 1913-1973. LC 91-30669. (Studies in American Literature: Vol. 14). 180p. 1991. lib. bdg. 79.95 (0-7734-9688-2) E Mellen.

McClure, Arthur F., jt. auth. see Lynn, Naomi B.

McClure, Arthur F., et al. Education for Work: The Historical Evolution of Vocational & Distributive Education in America. LC 83-49203. 168p. 1985. 29.50 (0-8386-3205-X) Fairleigh Dickinson.

McClure, Arthur f., et al. More Character People. (Illus.). 256p. 1983. 19.95 (0-8065-0876-0, Citadel Pr); pap. 12.95 (0-8065-1026-9, Citadel Pr) Carol Pub Group.

An Asterisk (*) at the beginning of an entry indicates that the title is appearing in BIP for the first time.

McClure, Arthur F., et al, eds. Ronald Reagan: His First Career, a Bibliography of the Movie Years. LC 88-7198. (Studies in American History: Vol. 1). 240p. 1988. lib. bdg. 89.95 (*0-685-20058-2*) E Mellen.

McClure, Carma L. CASE I-S Software Automation. 304p. 1988. text ed. 77.00 (*0-13-119330-9*) P-H.

— The Three R's of Automation: Re-engineering, Repository, Reusability. 320p. 1991. text ed. 59.00 (*0-13-915240-7*) P-H.

McClure, Carma L., jt. auth. see Martin, James.

McClure, Charles, ed. see Eisenberg, Michael & Berkowitz, Robert.

McClure, Charles, ed. see Harman, Keith.

McClure, Charles, ed. see Harris, Roma.

McClure, Charles, jt. auth. see Hernon, Peter.

McClure, Charles, ed. see Hernon, Peter, et al.

McClure, Charles, ed. see Hernon, Peter.

McClure, Charles, ed. see Johnson, Debra W.

McClure, Charles, ed. see Powell, Ronald.

McClure, Charles E., Jr. Vertical Fiscal Imbalance & the Assignment of Taxing Powers in Australia. LC 93-2405. (Essays in Public Policy Ser.: No. 40). 1993. 5.00 (*0-8179-5452-X*) Hoover Inst Pr.

McClure, Charles M., jt. auth. see Harman, Keith.

McClure, Charles R. Information for Academic Library Decision Making: The Case for Organizational Information Management. LC 79-8412. (Contributions in Librarianship & Information Science Ser.: No. 31). (Illus.). xvi, 227p. 1980. text ed. 55.00 (*0-313-21398-4*, MCA/) Greenwood.

— Libraries & the Internet. 500p. 1994. pap. 35.00 (*0-88736-824-7*) Mecklermedia.

— State Library Services & Issues. LC 85-2287. 320p. 1986. text ed. 49.50 (*0-89391-317-0*) Ablex Pub.

McClure, Charles R., ed. Planning for Library Services: A Guide to Utilizing Planning Methods for Library Management. LC 82-896. (Journal of Library Administration: Vol. 2, Nos. 2-4). 250p. 1982. 39.95 (*0-917724-84-4*) Haworth Pr.

McClure, Charles R. & Hernon, Peter. Academic Library Use of NTIS: Suggestions for Services & Core Collections. LC 86-228871. 72p. (Orig.). 1986. pap. 12. 00 (*0-934213-04-6*) Natl Tech Info.

— Library & Information Science Research: Perspectives & Strategies for Improvement. LC 90-25018. (Information Management, Policies, & Services Ser.: Vol. 18). 416p. (C). 1991. text ed. 69.50 (*0-89391-731-1*); pap. text ed. 32.50 (*0-89391-732-X*) Ablex Pub.

— United States Scientific & Technical Information Policies: Views & Perspectives. LC 89-278. (Information Management, Policies & Services Ser.: Vol. 8). 336p. (C). 1989. text ed. 49.50 (*0-89391-571-8*) Ablex Pub.

McClure, Charles R., ed. see Eisenberg, Michael B. & Berkowitz, Robert E.

McClure, Charles R., jt. auth. see Hernon, Peter.

McClure, Charles R., et al. Linking the U. S. National Technical Information Service with Academic & Public Libaries. LC 86-8067. 320p. 1986. text ed. 47.50 (*0-89391-377-4*) Ablex Pub.

— The National Research & Education Network (NREN) Research & Policy Perspectives. Hernon, Peter, ed. (Information Management, Policies & Services Ser.). 760p. (C). 1991. text ed. 95.00 (*0-89391-813-X*) Ablex Pub.

— Planning & Role Setting for Public Libraries: A Manual of Options & Procedures. LC 87-11445. 140p. 1987. pap. text ed. 20.00 (*0-8389-3341-6*) ALA.

— Public Libraries & the Internet: Study Results, Poicy Issues, & Recommendations. (Illus.). 62p. (Orig.). (C). 1994. pap. text ed. 30.00 (*0-7881-1391-7*) Diane Pub.

— United States Government Information Policies: Views & Perspectives. LC 88-35081. (Information Management, Policies & Services Ser.: Vol. 5). 352p. (C). 1989. text ed. 57.50 (*0-89391-563-7*) Ablex Pub.

McClure, Charlotte S. Gertrude Atherton. LC 76-45133. (Western Writers Ser.: No. 23). 47p. 1976. pap. 3.95 (*0-88430-022-6*) Boise St U W Writ Ser.

McClure, Charlotte S., jt. auth. see Fowlkes, Diane L.

McClure, Cole R., Jr., jt. ed. see Hatheway, Allen W.

McClure, Cynthia R. The Courage to Go On: Life after Addiction. 192p. (Orig.). 1990. pap. 8.99 (*0-8010-6263-2*) Baker Bk.

McClure, Diane K., ed. Probate Court Records, Cook County, Illinois, 1872-1873. 92p. 1992. pap. 12.00 (*1-881125-13-0*) Chi Geneal Soc.

McClure, Elliot. Whistling Wings: Dove Chronicles. 1991. 9.95 (*0-940168-19-7*) Boxwood.

McClure, Elliott. Bird Banding. (Illus.). 340p. (Orig.). 1984. pap. 15.00 (*0-910286-65-5*) Boxwood.

McClure, F. A. The Bamboos. (Illus.). 368p. (C). 1993. reprint ed. pap. text ed. 16.95 (*1-56098-323-X*) Smithsonian.

McClure, Floyd A. The Bamboos, a Fresh Perspective. (Illus.). 365p. reprint ed. pap. 104.10 (*0-8357-4130-3*, 2057065) Bks Demand.

McClure, George W. Sorrow & Consolation in Italian Humanism. 309p. (C). 1990. text ed. 45.00 (*0-691-05598-X*) Princeton U Pr.

***McClure, Gillian.** The Christmas Donkey. (Illus.). 32p. Date not set. 4.95 (*0-374-41191-3*) FS&G.

— Christmas Donkey: A New Version of the Nativity Story. (J). (ps-3). 1993. 15.00 (*0-374-31261-3*) FS&G.

McClure, Grace. The Bassett Women. LC 85-7143. (Illus.). 270p. 1985. text ed. 25.00 (*0-8040-0876-0*); pap. 9.95 (*0-8040-0877-9*) Swallow.

McClure, Gregory L., ed. Computerized Quantitative Infrared Analysis. LC 86-26534. (Special Technical Publication Ser.: No. 934). (Illus.). viii, 186p. 1987. text ed. 37.00 (*0-8031-0929-6*, 04-939000-39) ASTM.

McClure, H. Elliott. Ihago - Children of Rice. LC 92-74250. 1993. pap. 17.95 (*0-87212-259-X*) Libra.

McClure, Holly S. Island Magic. 1993. 13.95 (*0-8034-9001-1*) Bouregy.

McClure, J. D., ed. Scotland & the Lowland Tongue: Studies in the Language & Literature of Lowland Scotland in Honour of David Donald Murison. 248p. 1983. text ed. 38.00 (*0-08-028482-5*, Pergamon Pr) Elsevier.

McClure, J. Derrick. Why Scots Matters. 1989. 40.00 (*0-685-31783-8*, Pub. by Saltire Soc) St Mut.

McClure, James. The Blood of an Englishman. large type ed. 498p. 1982. 15.95 (*0-7089-0744-X*) Ulverscroft.

— Cop World: Policing the Streets of San Diego. LC 85-217205. 1984. write for info. (*0-333-30688-0*) Macmillan.

— Song Dog. 1991. 17.95 (*0-89296-274-7*) Mysterious Pr.

McClure, James, jt. ed. see Silber, Bettina.

***McClure, Janet.** Evolution. (Orig.). 1995. pap. 14.95 (*0-929385-54-3*) Light Tech Comns Servs.

— Light Techniques That Trigger Transformation. Harben, Lillian, ed. 147p. (Orig.). 1989. pap. 11.95 (*0-929385-00-4*) Light Tech Comns Servs.

— Sanat Kumara. 179p. (Orig.). 1990. pap. 11.95 (*0-929385-17-9*) Light Tech Comns Servs.

— Scopes of Dimensions. 159p. (Orig.). 1989. pap. 11.95 (*0-929385-09-8*) Light Tech Comns Servs.

— The Source Adventure. Harben, Lillian, ed. 157p. (Orig.). 1988. pap. 11.95 (*0-929385-06-3*) Light Tech Comns Servs.

McClure, Janet & Harben, Lillian. Aha! The Realization Book. 120p. (Orig.). 1990. pap. 11.95 (*0-929385-14-4*) Light Tech Comns Servs.

McClure, Joanna. Hard Edge. (Morning Coffee Chapbook Ser.). 15p. (Orig.). 1987. pap. 7.50 (*0-918273-35-8*) Coffee Hse.

McClure, John. Explanations, Accounts, & Illusions: A Critical Analysis. (European Monographs in Social Psychology). 216p. (C). 1991. 54.95 (*0-521-38532-6*) Cambridge U Pr.

McClure, John A. Kipling & Conrad: The Colonial Fiction. LC 81-4117. 195p. (C). 1981. 25.00 (*0-674-50529-8*) HUP.

— Late Imperial Romance. LC 93-42312. (Haymarket Ser.). 1994. 59.95 (*0-86091-447-X*, Pub. by Verso UK); pap. 18.95 (*0-86091-612-X*, Pub. by Verso UK) Routledge Chapman & Hall.

McClure, John C., jt. ed. see Singh, Vijay P.

McClure, John R. God's Plan of Redemption. Cagle, J. C., ed. 138p. (Orig.). 1990. pap. 3.95 (*0-934942-84-6*, 149) White Wing Pub.

— God's Plan of Redemption Leader's Guide. Cagle, J. C., ed. (Orig.). 1990. teacher ed 2.95 (*0-934942-85-4*, 231) White Wing Pub.

***McClure, John S.** Proclamation Five: Pentecost 1: Interpreting the Lessons of the Church Year, Ser. C. LC 92-22973. 1994. pap. 4.50 (*0-8006-4198-1*, Fortress Pr) Augsburg Fortress.

— The Roundtable Pulpit: Where Leadership & Preaching Meet. LC 95-3956. 144p. 1996. pap. 14.95 (*0-687-01142-6*) Abingdon.

McClure, Joy & Layne, Kendall. Cooking for Consciousness: Whole Food Recipes for the Vegetarian Kitchen. McClure, Vimala, ed. LC 93-18069. (Illus.). 272p. (Orig.). 1993. reprint ed. pap. 14.00 (*0-945934-12-2*) New Wrld Lib.

McClure, Judith, ed. see Bede.

McClure, Lynne, jt. auth. see Arnold, Bill.

McClure, Lynne, jt. auth. see Arnold, William E.

McClure, Margaret L., et al. Magnet Hospitals: Attraction & Retention of Professional Nurses. 150p. (Orig.). (C). 1983. pap. 21.65 (*1-55810-070-9*, G-160, Am Acad Nursing) Am Nurses Pub.

McClure, Mark S., jt. auth. see Denno, Robert F.

McClure, Mary B. Reclaiming the Heart: A Handbook of Help & Hope for Survivors of Incest. 1990. pap. 9.95 (*0-446-39141-7*) Warner Bks.

McClure, Michael. Acorn Alone. Robertson, Jon, ed. LC 94-6638. (Illus.). (J). 1994. 14.95 (*0-87604-326-0*) ARE Pr.

— Antechamber & Other Poems. LC 77-25300. 1978. pap. 2.95 (*0-8112-0682-3*, NDP455) New Directions.

— Fragments of Perseus. LC 83-2134. 1983. pap. 6.25 (*0-8112-0867-2*, NDP554) New Directions.

— Francesco Clemente: Testa Coda. Foye, Raymond, ed. (Gagosian Gallery Ser.). (Illus.). 112p. (Orig.). 1992. pap. 29.95 (*0-8478-1469-6*) Rizzoli Intl.

— General Gorgeous. 1982. pap. 4.75 (*0-8222-0436-3*) Dramatists Play.

— Gorf. LC 76-14932. (Illus.). 1976. pap. 1.95 (*0-8112-0612-2*, NDP416) New Directions.

— Lighting the Corners: On Nature, Art, & the Visionary: Essays & Interviews. LC 93-7610. (American Poetry Ser.). 352p. 1994. reprint ed. pap. 19.95 (*0-8263-1534-8*) U of NM Pr.

— The Mad Cub. 1995. 10.95 (*1-56201-087-5*) Blue Moon Bks.

— Rebel Lions. LC 90-48705. 128p. (Orig.). 1991. pap. 10. 95 (*0-8112-1164-9*, NDP712) New Directions.

— Scratching the Beat Surface: Essays on New Vision from Blake to Kerouac. 192p. 1994. 10.95 (*0-14-023252-4*, Penguin Bks) Viking Penguin.

— Selected Poems. LC 85-21477. 128p. 1986. 8.95 (*0-8112-0950-4*) New Directions.

— September Blackberries. LC 73-89482. 160p. 1974. pap. 3.25 (*0-8112-0524-X*, NDP370) New Directions.

— Simple Eyes & Other Poems. LC 93-46673. 144p. (Orig.). 1994. pap. 10.95 (*0-8112-1265-3*, NDP780) New Directions.

— Three Poems: Dolphin Skull, Rare Angel & Dark Brown. LC 94-47326. 256p. 1995. pap. 12.95 (*0-14-058709-8*, Penguin Bks) Viking Penguin.

McClure, Michael, jt. auth. see Logan, Ron.

McClure, Nancee. Clip & Copy Art: Creative Curriculum Cutouts. (Illus.). (J). (gr. k-8). 1989. 12.95 (*0-86653-487-3*, GA1086) Good Apple.

— Clip & Copy Art: Holidays, Seasons & Events. (Illus.). (J). (gr. k-8). 1989. 12.95 (*0-86653-486-5*, GA1085) Good Apple.

— Creative Egg Carton Crafts. (Early Childhood Paper Craft Ser.). (Illus.). 64p. (J). (ps-2). 1989. student ed 8.95 (*0-86653-471-7*, GA1077) Good Apple.

— The Good Apple Book of Reproducible Patterns. 352p. (J). (gr. 1-6). 1991. 24.95 (*0-86653-622-1*, GA1341) Good Apple.

McClure, Nancee & Rhodes, Janis. Free & Inexpensive Arts & Crafts to Make & Use. 112p. (J). (gr. 2-6). 1987. student ed 10.95 (*0-86653-387-7*, GA 1003) Good Apple.

McClure, Nancee, jt. auth. see Orange, Tom.

McClure, Norman E., ed. Sixteenth-Century English Poetry. LC 73-139767. (Granger Index Reprint Ser.). 1977. 36. 95 (*0-8369-6221-4*) Ayer.

McClure, Pat. Country Lovin' (Illus.). 40p. 1985. pap. 7.50 (*0-941284-29-8*) J Shaw Studio.

— Sweet, Soft, & Country. (Illus.). 32p. 1984. pap. 6.50 (*0-941284-25-5*) J Shaw Studio.

McClure, Patricia. And You Think You Have Problems: Teen Dilemmas. Bird, Tate, ed. LC 90-70582. (Illus.). 150p. (J). (gr. 8-9). 1990. 14.27 (*0-914127-73-X*) Univ Class.

— Getting to the Heart of It: Stories about My Friends & Me. 3rd ed. Bard, Tate, ed. (Illus.). 110p. (J). (gr. 4-6). 1985. 14.27 (*0-914127-99-3*) Univ Class.

McClure, Patricia, jt. auth. see West Virginia Writers, Inc., Staff.

McClure, Paul. Early Marriages in Bath Co., KY: Bonds 1811-1850 & Returns 1811-1852. 209p. 1994. pap. text ed. 31.00 (*1-55613-952-7*) Heritage Bk.

McClure, Paul, jt. auth. see Philpott-Jones, Pamela.

McClure, Peggy J. & Boyd, Arrie F. Basic Chemistry: An Introductory Approach - a Self-Teaching Textbook - Workbook. 640p. (C). 1994. per., pap. text ed. 61.95 (*0-8403-8849-7*) Kendall-Hunt.

McClure, Rhyder. Fast Access: Microsoft Word 5.0. 320p. 1989. pap. 18.95 (*0-13-307604-0*) P-H.

Mcclure, Rhyder. Fast Access Desktop Publishing with WordPerfect (5.0 and 5.1) (Illus.). (Orig.). 1990. pap. 14. 95 (*0-13-306952-4*) Brady Compu Bks.

McClure, Rhyder. Fast Access-Wordperfect Library. 320p. 1989. disk, pap. 39.95 (*0-685-28296-1*) P-H.

— Fast Access WordPerfect 5.1. (Illus.). 320p. 1990. pap. 14.95 (*0-13-307646-6*) Brady Compu Bks.

— Rhyder McClure's Short Course in Lotus 1-2-3. Date not set. pap. 22.67 (*0-13-780875-5*) P-H.

— Rhyder McClure's Short Course in Paradox. Date not set. pap. 22.67 (*0-13-780883-6*) P-H.

— Rhyder McClure's Short Course in Quattro Pro. Date not set. pap. 22.67 (*0-13-780891-7*) P-H.

McClure, Robert C., et al. Cat Anatomy: An Atlas, Text, & Dissection Guide. LC 73-3094. 248p. reprint ed. pap. 70. 70 (*0-685-15877-2*, 2056190) Bks Demand.

McClure, Robert D., jt. auth. see Fowler, Linda L.

McClure, Robert J. The Discovery of the North-West Passage by H.M.S. Investigator: 1850-54. Osborn, Sherard, ed. LC 74-5853. reprint ed. 26.50 (*0-404-11660-4*) AMS Pr.

McClure, Roger J., jt. auth. see Solem, Richard R.

McClure, Ronale, et al. Quick Spanish Phrases for Employers: Easy Communication with Employees & Domestic Help. LC 92-50861. 30p. (Orig.). 1993. pap. 3.95 (*0-88247-973-3*) R & E Pubs.

McClure, Ronale, ed. see Thomas, D.

McClure, Ruth K. Coram's Children: The London Foundling Hospital in the Eighteenth Century. LC 80-21375. (Illus.). 322p. (C). 1981. text ed. 42.00 (*0-300-02465-7*) Yale U Pr.

McClure, Samuel S. My Autobiography. (American Biography Ser.). 266p. 1991. reprint ed. lib. bdg. 69.00 (*0-7812-8281-0*) Rprt Serv.

***McClure, Sandy.** Christie Whitman for the People: A Political Biography. 270p. 1996. 24.95 (*1-57392-014-2*) Prometheus Bks.

McClure, Stanley W. Ford's Theatre: National Historic Site. (National Park Service Historical Handbook: No. 3). (Illus.). 43p. 1984. pap. 1.50 (*0-16-003416-7*, S/N 024-005-00226-0) USGPO.

McClure, Susan. Companion Planting. LC 93-44918. (Rodale's Successful Organic Gardening Ser.). 1994. 24. 95 (*0-87596-615-2*); pap. 14.95 (*0-87596-616-0*) Rodale Pr Inc.

— The Greater Cleveland Garden Guide. 280p. (Orig.). 1993. pap. 14.95 (*0-9631738-3-9*) Gray & Co Pubs.

— The Harvest Gardener: Growing for Maximum Yield, Prime Flavor, & Garden-Fresh Storage. Steege, Gwen, ed. LC 92-53951. (Illus.). 288p. 1993. 24.95 (*0-88266-798-X*, Garden Way Pub); pap. 17.95 (*0-88266-797-1*, Garden Way Pub) Storey Comm Inc.

***McClure, Susan, ed.** Preserving Summer's Bounty: A Quick & Easy Guide to Freezing, Canning, Preserving & Drying What You Grow. (Illus.). 384p. 1995. 26.95 (*0-87596-648-9*) Rodale Pr Inc.

McClure, Susan, text. Perennials. LC 92-45809. (Rodale's Successful Organic Gardening Ser.). (Illus.). 1993. 24.95 (*0-87596-559-8*); pap. 14.95 (*0-87596-560-1*) Rodale Pr Inc.

McClure, Susan, jt. auth. see Hynes, Erin.

***McClure, Susan, et al.** Cleveland Garden Handbook: Expert Local Advice on Growing a Beautiful Lawn & Garden in Northeast Ohio. 2nd rev. ed. (Illus.). 256p. 1995. pap. 12.95 (*1-886228-00-0*) Gray & Co Pubs.

McClure, T. J. Nutritional & Metabolic Infertility in the Cow. 145p. 1994. 42.50 (*0-85198-892-X*) CAB Intl.

McClure, Thomas A., ed. see Lipinsky, Edward S.

McClure, Vimala. Bangladesh: Rivers in a Crowded Land. LC 88-35911. (Discovering Our Heritage Ser.). (Illus.). 128p. (J). (gr. 5 up). 1989. lib. bdg. 14.95 (*0-87518-404-9*, Dillon Silver Burdett) Silver Burdett Pr.

— The Ethics of Love: Using Yoga's Timeless Wisdom to Heal Yourself, Others & the Earth. (Illus.). 128p. (Orig.). 1992. pap. 9.00 (*0-945934-08-4*) New Wrld Lib.

— The Ethics of Love: Using Yoga's Timeless Wisdom to Heal Yourself, Others & the Earth. 2nd ed. xx, 176p. (Orig.). 1994. pap. 10.00 (*0-945934-15-7*) New Wrld Lib.

— Some Still Want the Moon: A Woman's Introduction to Tantra Yoga. LC 88-15181. (Illus.). 128p. (Orig.). 1989. pap. 9.95 (*0-945934-00-9*) New Wrld Lib.

— The Tao of Motherhood. LC 91-14290. (Illus.). 176p. (Orig.). 1991. pap. 10.95 (*0-945934-05-X*) New Wrld Lib.

McClure, Vimala, ed. The Vegetarian Alternative: How & Why to Stop Eating Meat with 19 Delicious Meatless Recipes. 64p. (Orig.). 1994. pap. 2.00 (*0-945934-14-9*) New Wrld Lib.

McClure, Vimala, ed. see DePeyer, Katia.

McClure, Vimala, ed. see Friedman, Mark.

McClure, Vimala, ed. see Lake, Gina.

McClure, Vimala, ed. see McClure, Joy & Layne, Kendall.

McClure, Vimala, ed. see Perkins, Annabel.

McClure, W., jt. auth. see Wildermuth, K.

McClure, W. K. Italy in North Africa. 434p. 1986. 350.00 (*0-685-18879-5*, Darf Pubs Ltd) St Mut.

— Italy in North Africa. 434p. (C). 1989. 115.00 (*1-85077-092-1*, Darf Pubs Ltd) St Mut.

McClure, Wallace. International Executive Agreements: Democratic Procedure Under the Constitution of the United States. LC 41-10428. reprint ed. 19.50 (*0-404-04106-X*) AMS Pr.

McClure, Wallace M. New American Commercial Policy As Evidenced by Section 317 of the Tariff Act of 1922. LC 70-82240. (Columbia University. Studies in the Social Sciences: No. 255). reprint ed. 27.50 (*0-404-51255-0*) AMS Pr.

***McClurg, Bob.** Mustang, the Next Generation. LC 94-70071. (Illus.). 208p. 1994. 39.95 (*0-9640895-0-5*) Bolder Ventures.

McClurg, C. L. Yes I Can. 1971. 2.99 (*3-901170-29-4*) CEF Press.

McClurg, Cynthia. No Longer Lost. (J). (gr. k-6). 1985. 2.99 (*3-901170-31-6*) CEF Press.

— Work on Your Attitudes. (Illus.). 1985. 4.99 (*3-901170-30-8*) CEF Press.

McClurg, Kathy, ed. see Schermerhorn, Candy.

McClurg, Mike. Ford Mustang. (Classics in Color Ser.). (Illus.). 96p. 1993. pap. 17.95 (*1-872004-92-X*, Pub. by Windrow & Green UK) Motorbooks Intl.

***McClurg, R. S.** The Rummager's Handbook: Finding, Buying, Cleaning, Fixing, Using & Selling Secondhand Treasures. LC 94-47930. 160p. 1995. pap. 12.95 (*0-88266-894-3*, Storey Pub) Storey Comm Inc.

***McClurken, James M.** Gah-Baeh-Jhagwah-Buk, the Way It Happened: A Visual Culture History of the Little Traverse Bay Bands of Odawa. Caltrider, Suzanne, ed. (Illus.). 130p. (Orig.). 1991. 22.95 (*0-944311-06-7*); pap. 16.95 (*0-944311-05-9*) MSU Museum.

McCluskey. Criminal Appeals 1991. 1992. pap. 50.00 (*0-406-10529-4*) Butterworth Legal Pubs.

McCluskey, ed. Antigen Processing - Recognition. 248p. 1991. 167.00 (*0-8493-6932-0*, RB52) CRC Pr.

McCluskey, Edward J. Logic Design Principles. (Illus.). 512p. 1986. text ed. 79.00 (*0-13-539784-7*) P-H.

McCluskey, Jim. Road Form & Townscape. 2nd ed. (Illus.). 344p. 1992. pap. text ed. 90.00 (*0-7506-1245-2*, Butterwrth Archit) Buttrwrth-Heinemann.

McCluskey, John, Jr. Mr. America's Last Season Blues. LC 83-7968. 243p. 1983. 18.95 (*0-8071-1120-1*) La State U Pr.

McCluskey, John, Jr., ed. The City of Refuge: The Collected Stories of Rudolph Fisher. 240p. 1991. pap. 15.95 (*0-8262-0786-3*) U of Mo Pr.

McCluskey, John, ed. see Ceasor, Ebraska, et al.

McCluskey, John A., ed. see Ceasor, Frank, Sr. & Gaines, Edith.

McCluskey, John A., ed. see Johnston, Brenda A., et al.

McCluskey, John A., ed. see Johnston, Brenda A. & Pruitt, Pamela.

McCluskey, John A., ed. see Pruitt, Pamela, et al.

McCluskey, John A., ed. see Shepard, Mary L. & Gaines, Edith.

McCluskey, Kathleen. Reverberations: Sound & Structure in the Novels of Virginia Woolf. LC 85-21015. (Studies in Modern Literature: No. 54). (Illus.). 156p. reprint ed. pap. 44.50 (*0-8357-1710-0*, 2070508) Bks Demand.

McCluskey, Kathleen A. & Reese, Hayne W., eds. Life-Span Development Psychology: Historical & Generational Effects. 1984. text ed. 73.00 (*0-12-482420-X*) Acad Pr.

McCluskey, Kathleen A., jt. ed. see Callahan, Edward J.

McCluskey, Lord. Appeals in Scottish Criminal Cases. 1991. U.K. pap. 47.00 (*0-406-12135-4*) Butterworth Legal Pubs.

McCluskey, Robert T. & Andres, Giuseppe A., eds. Immunologically Mediated Renal Diseases: Criteria for Diagnosis & Treatment. LC 78-10283. (Immunology Ser.: No. 10). 123p. reprint ed. pap. 35.10 (*0-7837-0792-4*, 2041106) Bks Demand.

McCluskey, William J. Comparative Property Tax Systems. 206p. 1991. text ed. 68.95 (*1-85628-133-7*, Pub. by Avebury Pub UK) Ashgate Pub Co.

McClusky, Pamela. African Art: From Crocodiles to Convertibles in the Collection of the Seattle Art Museum. LC 87-61752. (Illus.). 32p. 1987. pap. 4.95 (*0-932216-24-2*) Seattle Art.

— Praise Poems: The Katherine White Collection. LC 83-51840. (Illus.). 122p. 1984. 40.00 (*0-932216-16-1*); pap. 22.95 (*0-932216-15-3*) Seattle Art.
— Praise Poems: The Katherine White Collection. LC 83-51840. (Illus.). xiv, 122p. 1985. lib. bdg. 45.00 (*0-226-73445-5*, 73445-5); pap. 20.00 (*0-226-73446-3*, 73446-3) U Ch Pr.
McClusky, William & Moss, Peter. The Uniform Business Rate: A Practical Guide. 180p. 1992. 66.00 (*1-85190-149-3*, Pub. by Tolley Pubng UK) St Mut.
***McClyer, Eric, ed.** Your Property Taxes: 1995 Appraised Values in Sedgwick County. 124p. 1995. 5.00 (*1-880652-44-7*) Wichita Eagle.
McClymer, John F. War & Welfare: Social Engineering in America, 1890-1925. LC 79-54060. (Contributions in American History Ser.: No. 84). xvi, 248p. 1980. text ed. 55.00 (*0-313-21129-9*, MWW/, Greenwood Pr) Greenwood.
McClymer, John F., jt. auth. see Estus, Charles W., Sr.
McClymonds, Marita P., jt. ed. see Bauman, Thomas.
McClymonds, Martha. A Chain of Love. 288p. (Orig.). 1981. pap. 2.75 (*0-8439-1002-X*) Dorchester Pub Co.
McClymont, Diane. Books. Young, Richard, ed. LC 91-20532. (First Technology Library). (Illus.). 32p. (J). (gr. 3-5). 1991. lib. bdg. 15.93 (*1-56074-010-8*) Garrett Ed Corp.
— Water. Young, Richard, ed. LC 91-20536. (First Technology Library). (Illus.). 32p. (J). (gr. 3-5). 1991. lib. bdg. 15.93 (*1-56074-006-X*) Garrett Ed Corp.
McClymont, Mary, et al. Health Visiting & the Elderly People. 2nd ed. (Illus.). 340p. 1991. pap. text ed. 40.00 (*0-443-04228-4*) Churchill.
McClynomt, W. G. The Exploration of New Zealand. LC 86-318. (Illus.). 139p. 1986. reprint ed. text ed. 49.75 (*0-313-25167-3*, MCEX, Greenwood Pr) Greenwood.
McCoard, R. W. English Perfect: Tense-Choice & Pragmatic Inferences. (North-Holland Linguistic Ser.: Vol. 38). 1978. 64.00 (*0-444-85154-2*, North Holland) Elsevier.
McCoid, Catherine H. Carrying Capacities of Nation-States. LC 84-152784. (Cross-Cultural Research Ser.). 1984. 22.00 (*0-317-07533-0*) HRAFP.
McCoin, John M. Adult Foster Homes: Their Managers & Residents. LC 82-6083. 232p. 1983. 35.95 (*0-89885-087-8*) Human Sci Pr.
McCole, C. J. Lucifer at Large. LC 68-57457. (Studies in Fiction: No. 34). 1969. reprint ed. lib. bdg. 75.00 (*0-8383-0595-4*) M S G Haskell Hse.
McCole, C. John. Lucifer at Large. LC 68-16949. (Essay Index Reprint Ser.). 1977. reprint ed. 19.95 (*0-8369-0643-8*) Ayer.
McCole, Connie. Breakfast in Bed: Morning Menus for Sensational Beginnings. (Illus.). 64p. 1992. 13.00 (*0-688-10724-9*) Morrow.
— Picnics in the Park: Moveable Feasts for Dining Alfresco. LC 92-36352. (Illus.). 1993. 12.95 (*0-688-11823-2*) Hearst Bks.
McCole, John. Walter Benjamin & the Antinomies of Tradition. LC 92-21431. 352p. 1993. 45.00 (*0-8014-2465-8*); pap. 18.95 (*0-8014-9711-6*) Cornell U Pr.
McColgan, Kristin P., jt. ed. see Durham, Charles W.
McColl, Arch, III & McColloch, Mike. Erisman's Reversible Errors in Texas Criminal Cases, 2 vols., Vols. 1 & 2. 3rd ed. 1981. Vol. 1, 400 pp., Vol. 2, 150 pp. ring bd. 185.00 (*1-878337-16-5*) Knowles Law.
McColl, Arch, III & McCormack, David R. Extraneous Offenses & Uncharged Conduct. 295p. 1986. ring bd. 135.00 (*1-878337-17-3*) Knowles Law.
McColl, Duncan. The Magic of Mind Power: Awareness Techniques for the Creative Mind. 184p. (Orig.). 1986. pap. 11.95 (*0-946551-43-X*, Pub. by Gateway Bks UK) Atrium Pubs.
McColl, Mary Ann, et al. Theoretical Basis of Occupational Therapy: An Annotated Bibliography of Applied Theory in the Professional Literature. LC 93-24422. (Illus.). 344p. (C). 1993. pap. text ed. 23.00 (*1-55642-151-6*) SLACK Inc.
McCollam, jt. auth. see Brownstead.
McCollam, C. Harold. The Brick & Tile Industry in Stark County, 1809-1976: A History. LC 76-17281. 351p. reprint ed. pap. 100.10 (*0-8357-7400-7*, 2024925) Bks Demand.
McCollam, Dan, jt. auth. see Betts, Keith.
***McColley.** Winners & Losers. (J). 1996. 15.00 (*0-689-80270-6*, Aladdin Paperbacks) S&S Childrens.
McColley, Diane K. A Gust for Paradise: Milton's Eden & the Visual Arts. LC 92-13654. (Illus.). 356p. 1993. 49.95 (*0-252-01828-1*) U of Ill Pr.
— Milton's Eve. LC 83-1313. (Illus.). 247p. 1983. 24.95 (*0-252-00980-0*) U of Ill Pr.
McColley, Grant. Milton's Technique of Source Adaptation. 50p. (C). 1938. reprint ed. pap. 39.95 (*0-8383-0053-7*) M S G Haskell Hse.
McColley, Grant, tr. see Campanella, Tommasso.
McColley, Kevin. Pecking Order. LC 93-17768. 224p. (YA). (gr. 7 up). 1994. 16.00 (*0-06-023554-3*); lib. bdg. 15.89 (*0-06-023555-1*) HarpC Child Bks.
— Sun Dance. LC 94-33162. (J). 1995. 15.00 (*0-689-80008-8*) Macmillan.
McColley, Robert, jt. ed. see Posadas, Barbara.
McCollister, Betty, ed. Voices for Evolution. 141p. 1989. pap. 5.00 (*0-939873-51-6*) Natl Ctr Sci Educ.
McCollister, John. So Help Me God: The Faith of America's Presidents. 208p. (Orig.). 1992. pap. 11.99 (*0-664-25210-9*) Westminster John Knox.
— So Help Me God: The Faith of America's Presidents, Set. 208p. (Orig.). 1992. pap. 107.99 (*0-664-25448-9*) Westminster John Knox.
***McCollister, John, comp.** Writing for Dollars. LC 94-43195. 1995. write for info. (*0-8246-0372-9*) Jonathan David.
McCollister, John C. The Christian Book of Why. 340p. 1983. 12.95 (*0-8246-0297-8*) Jonathan David.
— The Christian Book of Why. 360p. 1986. pap. 12.95 (*0-8246-0317-6*) Jonathan David.
McCollister, Tom. Golf in Georgia: A Comprehensive Guide to All Public & Private Courses. LC 92-84009. (Illus.). 180p. 1993. pap. 9.95 (*1-56352-075-3*) Longstreet Pr Inc.
McColloch, Mark. White Collar Workers in Transition: The Boom Years, 1940-1970. LC 83-5546. (Contributions in Labor History Ser.: No. 15). xii, 193p. 1983. text ed. 42.95 (*0-313-23785-9*, MCW/, Greenwood Pr) Greenwood.
McColloch, Mark D., jt. auth. see Filippelli, Ronald L.
McColloch, Mike, jt. auth. see McColl, Arch, III.
McCollom, Marion, jt. ed. see Gillette, Jonathon.
McCollough, Albert W. The New Book of Buddy "L" Toys, Vol. I. (Illus.). 192p. 1991. text ed. 49.95 (*0-89778-127-9*, 10-7240) Greenberg Bks.
— New Book of Buddy "L" Toys, Vol. II. (Illus.). 192p. 1991. text ed. 49.95 (*0-89778-128-7*, 10-7245) Greenberg Bks.
McCollough, C. R., jt. ed. see Faulkner, Charles H.
McCollough, Charles. Heads of Heaven, Feet of Clay: Ideas & Stories for Adult Faith Education. LC 83-19379. 144p. (Orig.). 1983. pap. 11.95 (*0-8298-0693-8*) Pilgrim OH.
McCollough, Charles R. Resolving Conflict with Justice & Peace. LC 90-7869. 228p. (Orig.). 1991. pap. 14.95 (*0-8298-0870-1*) Pilgrim OH.
McCollough, E. Gaylon. Before & after. 496p. 1994. 19.95 (*0-9637600-0-9*); pap. 14.95 (*0-9637600-1-7*) McCollough Pub.
— Shoulders of Giants. (Illus.). 224p. 1986. 15.95 (*0-932919-04-9*) Albright & Co.
McCollough, Gaylon. Nasal Plastic Surgery. LC 93-26436. (Illus.). 400p. 1994. text ed. 132.50 (*0-7216-4067-2*) Saunders.
McCollough, Thomas E. Moral Imagination & Public Life: Raising the Ethical Question. LC 91-6821. (Chatham House Studies in Political Thinking). 192p. (Orig.). (C). 1991. pap. text ed. 17.95 (*0-934540-85-3*) Chatham Hse Pubs.
McCollum, jt. auth. see Schneider.
McCollum, Allan. Allan McCollum. (Illus.). 68p. 1988. 35.00 (*3-88375-100-6*, Pub. by Walther Konig GW) Dist Art Pubs.
McCollum, Allan & Lawson, Thomas. Allan McCollum. (Illus.). 64p. 1993. pap. 25.00 (*0-932183-14-X*) ART Pr CA.
McCollum, Audrey T. The Trauma of Moving: Psychological Issues for Women. (Library of Social Research: Vol. 182). 312p. (C). 1990. text ed. 49.95 (*0-8039-3699-0*); pap. text ed. 24.00 (*0-8039-3700-8*) Sage.
McCollum, Dee. The Summer Mountain. 36p. 1986. write for info. (*0-933959-03-6*) Merton Pr.
McCollum, Harriet L. What Makes a Master. 114p. 1975. reprint ed. spiral bd. 8.80 (*0-7873-0596-0*) Mokelumne.
McCollum, John H., jt. ed. see Holsoe, Svend E.
McCollum, Michele D., et al, eds. Proceedings of the Third International Workshop on Transducers for Sonics & Ultrasonics. LC 92-62615. 420p. 1992. text ed. 165.00 (*0-87762-993-5*) Technomic.
McCollum, Rocky. The Prime Mover, Opus III: The String Model Universe Where Strings Are Everything. 2nd ed. (Illus.). 500p. 1988. reprint ed. pap. 10.00 (*0-317-91063-9*) KIVA Pub.
— The Prime Mover, Opus Three: The String Model Universe, Where Strings Are Everything. 3rd ed. (Illus.). 500p. (C). 1988. reprint ed. pap. 10.00 (*0-317-91116-3*) KIVA Pub.
McCollum, Rocky & Slick, Gandalf. The Higher Self. (Illus.). 170p. (Orig.). 1988. pap. 8.95 (*0-317-91064-7*) KIVA Pub.
***McCollum, Susan & Risley, Teena.** Plant Basics: A Manual for the Care of Indoor Plants. 86p. 1994. pap. 14.95 (*0-9644264-0-4*) McCollum Risley.
***McCollum, Thomas C., 3rd.** Tainted Blood: A Frightening Possibility. 368p. 1995. 25.00 (*0-88040-411-6*, Shoji Bks) Bkwrights.
McColm, Bruce, ed. Freedom in the World: Political Rights & Civil Liberties, 1989-1990. (Illus.). 336p. (C). 1990. pap. text ed. 23.25 (*0-932088-56-2*) Freedom Hse.
McColm, I. J. Ceramic Hardness. (Illus.). 336p. 1989. 85.00 (*0-306-43287-0*, Plenum Pr) Plenum.
— Dictionary of Ceramic Science & Engineering. 2nd ed. 1994. 75.00 (*0-306-44542-5*, Plenum Pr) Plenum.
McColm, I. J. & Clark, N. J. The Forming, Shaping & Working of High-Performance Ceramics. 320p. 1988. text ed. 115.00 (*0-412-01271-5*, Chap & Hall NY) Chapman & Hall.
McColm, Michelle. Adoption Reunions: A Book for Adoptees, Birthparents & Adoptive Families. 175p. (Orig.). 1993. pap. 15.95 (*0-929005-41-4*, Pub. by Second Story Pr CN) InBook.
McColm, R. Bruce. El Salvador: Peaceful Revolution or Armed Struggle? (Perspectives on Freedom Ser.: No. 1). (Illus.). 47p. 1982. pap. 9.50 (*0-932088-03-1*) Freedom Hse.
— To License a Journalist? A Landmark Decision in the Schmidt Case. LC 86-18407. 1986. 13.50 (*0-932088-09-0*) Freedom Hse.
McColm, R. Bruce, ed. see Chalidze, Valery & Schifter, Richard.
McColman, John, ed. Scanner Master Metro D. C.-Virginia Guide. 3rd ed. (Frequency Guide Ser.: No. 6). (Illus.). 350p. 1991. 29.95 (*0-685-51888-4*) Scanner Master.
***Mccomas.** Talk of the Town. (Loveswept Ser.: No. 738). 1995. mass mkt. 3.50 (*0-553-44486-7*, Loveswept) Bantam.
***McComas, Annette P.** Kansas & Me: Memories of a Jewish Childhood. Kravetz, Nathan, ed. LC 94-40787. (Studies in Judaica & the Holocaust: No. 10). 144p. 1995. lib. bdg. 27.00 (*0-8095-0408-1*); pap. 17.00 (*0-8095-1408-7*) Borgo Pr.
McComas, Dan, jt. auth. see Sanow, Arnold.
McComas, Henry C. Psychology of Religious Sects. LC 70-172763. reprint ed. 20.00 (*0-404-04107-8*) AMS Pr.
McComas, J. Francis. Graveside Companion. 1962. 12.95 (*0-8392-1040-X*) Astor-Honor.
***McComas, Mary K.** Passing Through Midnight. (Loveswept Ser.: No. 722). 1995. pap. 3.50 (*0-553-44485-9*, Loveswept) Bantam.
McComas, Mary Kay. Wait for Me. (Loveswept Ser.: No. 702). 1994. pap. 3.50 (*0-553-44213-9*) Bantam.
McComas, Stuart T., ed. Thermodynamics Exam File. LC 84-24688. (Exam File Ser.). 250p. (Orig.). (C). 1985. pap. 13.50 (*0-910554-49-8*) Engineering.
McComas, Terence. Pearl Harbor Fact & Reference Book: Everything to Know about Dec. 7, 1941. 132p. 1991. pap. 9.95 (*0-935180-02-8*) Mutual Pub HI.
McComas, Tom. Lionel: a Collector's Guide & History, Vol. 1: Prewar O Gauge. 144p. 1993. pap. 19.95 (*0-8019-8507-2*) Chilton.
— Lionel: a Collector's Guide & History, Vol. 2: Prewar O Gauge. 192p. 1993. pap. 19.95 (*0-8019-8508-0*) Chilton.
— Lionel: a Collector's Guide & History, Vol. 3: Standard Gauge. 144p. 1993. pap. 19.95 (*0-8019-8509-9*) Chilton.
— Lionel: a Collector's Guide & History, Vol. 4: 1970-1980 Gauge. 192p. 1993. pap. 19.95 (*0-8019-8510-2*) Chilton.
— Lionel: a Collector's Guide & History, Vol. 5: The Archives. 128p. 1993. pap. 19.95 (*0-8019-8511-0*) Chilton.
— Lionel: a Collector's Guide & History, Vol. 6: Advertising & Art. 176p. 1993. pap. 19.95 (*0-8019-8512-9*) Chilton.
McComas, Tom & Tuohy, James. Great Tox Train Layouts of America. (Illus.). 143p. 1987. pap. 29.95 (*0-937522-04-X*) TM Bks.
— Lionel: A Collector's Guide & History: Postwar. 2nd ed. (Lionel Collector's Ser.: Vol. II). (Illus.). 30.00 (*0-317-40984-0*) TM Bks.
— Lionel: A Collector's Guide & History: Prewar O Gauge. (Lionel Collector's Ser.: Vol. I). (Illus.). 30.00 (*0-317-40968-9*) TM Bks.
— Lionel: A Collector's Guide & History: The Archives, Vol. V. (Lionel Collector's Ser.). (Illus.). 144p. 1981. 35.00 (*0-937522-01-5*) TM Bks.
— Lionel: A Collector's Guide & History: 1970-1980, Vol. IV. (Lionel Collector's Ser.). 138p. 1980. 24.95 (*0-937522-00-7*) TM Bks.
— Lionel Postwar Price & Rarity Guide. (Illus.). 102p. pap. 15.00 (*0-937522-03-1*) TM Bks.
***McComb, et al.** Using WordPerfect Version 6.1 for Windows. (Illus.). 1200p. (Orig.). 1995. pap. 29.99 (*0-7897-0083-2*) Que.
McComb, A. J. & Lake, P. S., eds. The Conservation of Australian Wetlands. (Illus.). 200p. (C). 1988. text ed. 175.00 (*0-949324-13-2*, Pub. by Surrey Beatty & Sons AT) St Mut.
***McComb, Arthur J., ed.** Eutropic Shallow Estuaries & Lagoons. LC 94-37997. 1995. write for info. (*0-8493-6839-1*) CRC Pr.
McComb, Carol. Country Blues Guitar for the Musically Hopeless. (Illus.). 96p. (Orig.). 1986. audio, pap. 12.95i (*0-932592-12-0*) Klutz Pr.
McComb, Colin. Complete Book of Elves. (Advanced Dungeons & Dragons, Second Edition; Al-Qadim Ser.). (Illus.). 1992. 18.00 (*1-56076-376-0*) TSR Inc.
— Complete Gladiators Handbook. (Advanced Dungeons & Dragons, Second Edition; Al-Qadim Ser.). (Illus.). 1993. pap. 15.00 (*1-56076-616-6*) TSR Inc.
— Howls in the Night: Ravenloft Adventure. (Advanced Dungeons & Dungeons 2nd Ed. Ser.). 1995. pap. 6.95 (*1-56076-927-0*) TSR Inc.
— Islands of Terror. (Advanced Dungeons & Dragons, Second Edition; Al-Qadim Ser.). (Illus.). 1992. pap. 10.95 (*1-56076-349-3*) TSR Inc.
— Knight's Sword. (Advanced Dungeons & Dragons, Second Edition; Al-Qadim Ser.). (Illus.). 1992. pap. 6.95 (*1-56076-421-X*) TSR Inc.
— Thunder Rift. (Dungeons & Dragons Ser.). (Illus.). 1992. pap. 6.95 (*1-56076-381-7*) TSR Inc.
— Well of Worlds: Planetscape Adventure. 1994. 15.00 (*1-56076-893-2*) TSR Inc.
McComb, David. Annual Editions: World History, Vol. 1. 3rd ed. LC 90-656260. (Illus.). 256p. 1993. pap. text ed. 12.95 (*1-56134-134-7*) Dushkin Pub.
— Annual Editions: World History, Vol. 2. 3rd ed. LC 90-656260. (Illus.). 256p. 1992. pap. text ed. 12.95 (*1-56134-135-5*) Dushkin Pub.
McComb, David G. Galveston: A History. LC 85-20956. (Illus.). 293p. 1986. 28.50 (*0-292-72049-1*); pap. 13.95 (*0-292-72053-X*) U of Tex Pr.
— Texas: A Modern History. LC 89-31666. (Illus.). 208p. 1989. 24.95 (*0-292-73048-9*); pap. 13.95 (*0-292-74665-2*) U of Tex Pr.
— The Young Oxford Illustrated History of Texas. (Oxford Illustrated Histories Ser.). (Illus.). 144p. (J). 1995. lib. bdg. 23.95 (*0-19-509247-3*); pap. 21.95 (*0-19-509246-5*) OUP.
McComb, Gordon. Fantastic Lost Inventions You Can Build. (Illus.). 320p. 1992. 27.95 (*0-8306-7421-7*, 3421); pap. 17.95 (*0-8306-3421-5*, 3421) TAB Bks.
— First Book of PC Tools 8. Flynn, Jennifer, ed. (First Bks.). (Illus.). (Orig.). 1992. pap. 18.95 (*1-56761-003-X*) Alpha Bks IN.
— First Book of Quicken. 1990. pap. 14.95 (*0-672-27306-3*, Bobbs) Macmillan.
— Gordon McComb's Gadgeteers Gold. (Illus.). 400p. 1990. 29.95 (*0-8306-8360-7*, 3360); pap. 19.95 (*0-8306-3360-X*) TAB Bks.
— Gordon McComb's Gadgeteer's Goldmine! Fifty-Five Space-Age Projects. 1990. pap. text ed. 21.95 (*0-07-155983-3*) McGraw.
— Gordon McComb's Tips & Techniques for the Electronics Hobbyist. (Illus.). 300p. 1991. 27.95 (*0-8306-7485-3*, 3485, TAB/TPR) TAB Bks.
— I Hate Chicago. 1994. pap. 18.99 (*1-56529-922-1*) Que.
— The Laser Cookbook: Eighty-Eight Practical Projects. 1988. pap. text ed. 19.95 (*0-07-155335-5*) McGraw.
— The Laser Cookbook: Ninety-Nine Practical Projects. (Illus.). 304p. 1988. 25.95 (*0-8306-9090-5*, 3090); pap. 19.95 (*0-8306-9390-4*, 3090) TAB Bks.
— Model Building & Finishing Guide. (Illus.). 128p. (Orig.). 1989. pap. write for info. (*0-938545-05-1*) Jennings & Keefe.
— Robot Builder's Bonanza: Ninety-Nine Inexpensive Robotics Projects. 1987. pap. 16.95 (*0-8306-2800-2*) TAB Bks.
— Robot Builders Bonanza: 99 Inexpensive Robotics Projects. 1987. pap. text ed. 17.95 (*0-07-157146-9*) McGraw.
— Security Systems for Your Home & Automobile. (Illus.). 130p. 1994. pap. 16.95 (*0-7906-1054-X*) H W Sams.
— Speakers for Your Home & Automobile: How to Build & Enjoy a Quality Audio System. 1992. pap. 14.95 (*0-7906-1025-6*, Prompt Pubns) H W Sams.
— Troubleshooting & Repairing Fax Machines. (Illus.). 224p. 1991. 26.95 (*0-8306-7778-X*, 3778); pap. 16.95 (*0-8306-3778-8*) TAB Bks.
— Troubleshooting & Repairing VCRs. 1988. text ed. 27.95 (*0-07-156452-7*) McGraw.
— Troubleshooting & Repairing VCRs. (Illus.). 432p. 1988. 26.95 (*0-8306-0060-4*, 2960) TAB Bks.
— Troubleshooting & Repairing VCRs. 2nd ed. 1991. text ed. 32.95 (*0-07-157737-8*); pap. text ed. 19.95 (*0-07-157736-X*) McGraw.
— Troubleshooting & Repairing VCRs. 2nd ed. (Illus.). 352p. 1991. 29.95 (*0-8306-7777-1*, 3777); pap. 19.95 (*0-8306-3777-X*) TAB Bks.
— Troubleshooting & Repairing VCRs. 3rd ed. LC 95-3221. 1995. text ed. 34.95 (*0-07-155016-X*); pap. text ed. 22.95 (*0-07-155017-8*) TAB Bks.
— The Video Book. 1992. pap. 16.95 (*0-7906-1030-2*, Prompt Pubns) H W Sams.
— WordPerfect 5.1 Macros & Templ. 1990. pap. 44.95 (*0-679-79023-3*) Random.
— WordPerfect 6.0 for Windows Power Tool with Disk. 1994. pap. 40.00 (*0-679-75319-2*) Random.
— WordPerfect 6.0 Power Tools: Macros, Templates & More. 1994. 40.00 (*0-679-75156-4*) Random.
McComb, Gordon & Cook, J. Compact Disc Player Maintenance & Repair Service Manual. 1987. pap. text ed. 17.95 (*0-07-157051-9*) McGraw.
McComb, Gordon & Cook, John. Compact Disc Player Maintenance & Repair Manual. 256p. 1987. 19.95 (*0-8306-0190-2*, 2790H); pap. 15.95 (*0-8306-2790-1*) TAB Bks.
***McComb, Gordon & Que Staff.** Special Edition Using WordPerfect 5.1 & 5.1 Plus for DOS. (Illus.). 1264p. (Orig.). 1995. pap. 29.99 (*0-7897-0239-8*) Que.
McComb, Gordon, jt. auth. see Alperson, Jay R.
McComb, H. G., Jr., jt. auth. see Noor, A. K.
McComb, Henry G., ed. The National Municipal Gazeteer, 1994. 5th rev. ed. (Illus.). 500p. (C). 1994. pap. 95.00 (*1-878684-04-3*) Target Exchange.
— The National Municipal Gazetteer: New York 1991. (Illus.). 600p. (Orig.). 1990. pap. 95.00 (*1-878684-01-9*) Target Exchange.
— The National Municipal Gazetteer: New York, 1992. 3rd ed. (Illus.). 529p. 1992. pap. write for info. (*1-878684-02-7*) Target Exchange.
— The National Municipal Gazetteer, New York 1993 Volume. 4th ed. (Illus.). 525p. 1993. pap. write for info. (*1-878684-03-5*) Target Exchange.
— The National Municipal Gazetteer, New York 1995 Volume. (Illus.). 525p. (C). 1995. pap. 95.00 (*0-614-06029-X*) Target Exchange.
McComb, John P., Jr. Governing Community Hospitals: A Primer for Trustees & Health Care Executives. LC 92-2939. (Health-Management Ser.). 200p. 1992. 32.95 (*1-55542-440-6*) Jossey-Bass.
McComb, S. The Making of the English Bible. 1973. 59.95 (*0-8490-0578-7*) Gordon Pr.
— The Power of Self-Suggestion. 1991. lib. bdg. 69.95 (*0-8490-4542-8*) Gordon Pr.
McComb, Samuel. The Power of Self-Suggestion. 53p. 1971. reprint ed. spiral bd. 4.40 (*0-7873-1241-X*) Mokelumne.
McComb, Thomas L. Scar. (Illus.). 138p. 1993. pap. text ed. write for info. (*1-883517-00-1*) Alef Bet Comns.
McComb, W. D. The Physics of Fluid Turbulence. (Oxford Engineering Science Ser.: No. 25). (Illus.). 608p. 1992. reprint ed. pap. 55.00 (*0-19-856256-X*) OUP.
McCombe, Pamela A., jt. auth. see Pender, Michael P.
McCombe, R. S. & Haney, Sharon. Alaska on the Cover. LC 83-90140. (Illus.). (Orig.). 1983. pap. 4.75 (*0-9611326-0-4*) Windsong Pr.
McCombie, Sharon L., ed. The Rape Crisis Intervention Handbook: A Guide to Victim Care. LC 80-14191. (Illus.). 250p. 1980. 39.50 (*0-306-40401-X*, Plenum Pr) Plenum.
McCombs, Barbara L. & Brannan, Linda. Accepting Criticism - Role Playing. (Skills for Job Success Ser.). (Illus.). 52p. (Orig.). 1990. pap. 39.95 (*1-56119-055-1*) Educ Pr MD.
— Adjusting to a New Boss. (Skills for Job Success Ser.). (Illus.). 32p. (Orig.). 1990. student ed. pap. 4.95 (*1-56119-025-X*) Educ Pr MD.
— Adjusting to a New Boss. (Skills for Job Success Ser.). (Illus.). 32p. (Orig.). (YA). (gr. 7-12). 1990. teacher ed 1.95 (*1-56119-026-8*); disk 39.95 (*1-56119-113-2*) Educ Pr MD.

An Asterisk (*) at the beginning of an entry indicates that the title is appearing in BIP for the first time.

— Adjusting to a New Boss, Set. (Skills for Job Success Ser.). (Illus.). 32p. (Orig.). (YA). (gr. 7-12). 1990. 44.95 (*1-56119-071-3*) Educ Pr MD.

— Asking for Help - Role Playing. (Skills for Job Success Ser.). (Illus.). 52p. (Orig.). 1990. teacher ed, pap. 39.95 (*1-56119-056-X*) Educ Pr MD.

— Consideration for Co-Worker Rights. (Skills for Job Success Ser.). (Illus.). 32p. (Orig.). 1990. student ed, pap. 4.95 (*1-56119-009-8*) Educ Pr MD.

— Consideration for Co-Worker Rights. (Skills for Job Success Ser.). (Illus.). 32p. (Orig.). (YA). (gr. 7-12). 1990. teacher ed 1.95 (*1-56119-010-1*); disk 39.95 (*1-56119-105-1*) Educ Pr MD.

— Consideration for Co-Worker Rights, Set. (Skills for Job Success Ser.). (Illus.). 32p. (Orig.). (YA). (gr. 7-12). 1990. student ed, teacher ed 44.95 (*1-56119-063-2*) Educ Pr MD.

— Do. (Skills for Job Success Ser.). (Illus.). 32p. (Orig.). 1990. student ed, pap. 4.95 (*1-56119-005-5*) Educ Pr MD.

— Do. (Skills for Job Success Ser.). (Illus.). 32p. (Orig.). 1990. teacher ed 1.95 (*1-56119-006-3*); disk 39.95 (*1-56119-103-5*) Educ Pr MD.

— Do, Set. (Skills for Job Success Ser.). (Illus.). 32p. (Orig.). 1990. 44.95 (*1-56119-061-6*) Educ Pr MD.

— Done on Time. (Skills for Job Success Ser.). (Illus.). 32p. (Orig.). 1990. student ed, pap. 4.95 (*1-56119-047-0*) Educ Pr MD.

— Done on Time. (Skills for Job Success Ser.). (Illus.). 32p. (Orig.). 1990. teacher ed 1.95 (*1-56119-048-9*); disk 39.95 (*1-56119-124-8*) Educ Pr MD.

— Done on Time, Set. (Skills for Job Success Ser.). (Illus.). 32p. (Orig.). 1990. 44.95 (*1-56119-082-9*) Educ Pr MD.

— Good Grooming Habits. (Skills for Job Success Ser.). (Illus.). 32p. (Orig.). 1990. student ed, pap. 4.95 (*1-56119-043-8*) Educ Pr MD.

— Good Grooming Habits. (Skills for Job Success Ser.). (Illus.). 32p. (Orig.). (YA). (gr. 7-12). 1990. teacher ed 1.95 (*1-56119-044-6*); disk 39.95 (*1-56119-122-1*) Educ Pr MD.

— Good Grooming Habits, Set. (Skills for Job Success Ser.). (Illus.). 32p. (Orig.). (YA). (gr. 7-12). 1990. student ed, teacher ed 44.95 (*1-56119-080-2*) Educ Pr MD.

— Help, Please! (Skills for Job Success Ser.). (Illus.). 32p. (Orig.). 1990. student ed, pap. 4.95 (*1-56119-037-3*) Educ Pr MD.

— Help, Please! (Skills for Job Success Ser.). (Illus.). 32p. (Orig.). (YA). (gr. 7-12). 1990. teacher ed 1.95 (*1-56119-038-1*); disk 39.95 (*1-56119-119-1*) Educ Pr MD.

— Help, Please!, Set. (Skills for Job Success Ser.). (Illus.). 32p. (Orig.). (YA). (gr. 7-12). 1990. 44.95 (*1-56119-077-2*) Educ Pr MD.

— How Does It Work? (Skills for Job Success Ser.). (Illus.). 32p. (Orig.). 1990. student ed, pap. 4.95 (*1-56119-033-0*) Educ Pr MD.

— How Does It Work? (Skills for Job Success Ser.). (Illus.). 32p. (Orig.). (YA). (gr. 7-12). 1990. teacher ed 1.95 (*1-56119-034-9*); disk 39.95 (*1-56119-117-5*) Educ Pr MD.

— How Does It Work?, Set. (Skills for Job Success Ser.). (Illus.). 32p. (Orig.). (YA). (gr. 7-12). 1990. 44.95 (*1-56119-075-6*) Educ Pr MD.

— How Should I Do It? (Skills for Job Success Ser.). (Illus.). 32p. (Orig.). 1990. student ed, pap. 4.95 (*1-56119-021-7*) Educ Pr MD.

— How Should I Do It? (Skills for Job Success Ser.). (Illus.). 32p. (Orig.). (YA). (gr. 7-12). 1990. teacher ed 1.95 (*1-56119-022-5*); disk 39.95 (*1-56119-111-6*) Educ Pr MD.

— How Should I Do It?, Set. (Skills for Job Success Ser.). (Illus.). 32p. (Orig.). (YA). (gr. 7-12). 1990. 44.95 (*1-56119-069-1*) Educ Pr MD.

— Keep Calm! (Skills for Job Success Ser.). (Illus.). 32p. (Orig.). 1990. student ed, pap. 4.95 (*1-56119-023-3*) Educ Pr MD.

— Keep Calm! (Skills for Job Success Ser.). (Illus.). 32p. (Orig.). (YA). (gr. 7-12). 1990. teacher ed 1.95 (*1-56119-024-1*); disk 39.95 (*1-56119-112-4*) Educ Pr MD.

— Keep Calm!, Set. (Skills for Job Success Ser.). (Illus.). 32p. (Orig.). (YA). (gr. 7-12). 1990. teacher ed 44.95 (*1-56119-070-5*) Educ Pr MD.

— Late for Work. (Skills for Job Success Ser.). (Illus.). 32p. (Orig.). 1990. student ed, pap. 4.95 (*1-56119-013-6*) Educ Pr MD.

— Late Work. (Skills for Job Success Ser.). (Illus.). 32p. (Orig.). (YA). (gr. 7-12). 1990. teacher ed 1.95 (*1-56119-014-4*); disk 39.95 (*1-56119-107-8*) Educ Pr MD.

— Late Work, Set. (Skills for Job Success Ser.). (Illus.). 32p. (Orig.). (YA). (gr. 7-12). 1990. teacher ed 44.95 (*1-56119-065-9*) Educ Pr MD.

— Leaving Early. (Skills for Job Success Ser.). (Illus.). 32p. (Orig.). 1990. student ed, pap. 4.95 (*1-56119-039-X*) Educ Pr MD.

— Leaving Early. (Skills for Job Success Ser.). (Illus.). 32p. (Orig.). (YA). (gr. 7-12). 1990. teacher ed 1.95 (*1-56119-040-3*); disk 39.95 (*1-56119-120-5*) Educ Pr MD.

— Leaving Early, Set. (Skills for Job Success Ser.). (Illus.). 32p. (Orig.). (YA). (gr. 7-12). 1990. teacher ed 44.95 (*1-56119-078-0*) Educ Pr MD.

— Making the Best Use of Time. (Skills for Job Success Ser.). (Illus.). 32p. (Orig.). 1990. student ed, pap. 4.95 (*0-685-30372-1*) Educ Pr MD.

— Making the Best Use of Time. (Skills for Job Success Ser.). (Illus.). 32p. (Orig.). 1990. teacher ed 1.95 (*1-56119-030-6*); disk 39.95 (*1-56119-115-9*) Educ Pr MD.

— Making the Best Use of Time, Set. (Skills for Job Success Ser.). (Illus.). 32p. (Orig.). 1990. student ed, teacher ed 44.95 (*1-56119-073-X*) Educ Pr MD.

— May I Try It? (Skills for Job Success Ser.). (Illus.). 32p. (Orig.). 1990. student ed, pap. 4.95 (*1-56119-053-5*) Educ Pr MD.

— May I Try It? (Skills for Job Success Ser.). (Illus.). 32p. (Orig.). (YA). (gr. 7-12). 1990. teacher ed 1.95 (*1-56119-054-3*); disk 39.95 (*1-56119-127-2*) Educ Pr MD.

— May I Try It?, Set. (Skills for Job Success Ser.). (Illus.). 32p. (Orig.). (YA). (gr. 7-12). 1990. 44.95 (*1-56119-085-3*) Educ Pr MD.

— Neatness Counts. (Skills for Job Success Ser.). (Illus.). 32p. (Orig.). 1990. student ed, pap. 4.95 (*1-56119-045-4*) Educ Pr MD.

— Neatness Counts. (Skills for Job Success Ser.). (Illus.). 32p. (Orig.). (YA). (gr. 7-12). 1990. teacher ed 1.95 (*1-56119-046-2*); disk 39.95 (*1-56119-123-X*) Educ Pr MD.

— Neatness Counts, Set. (Skills for Job Success Ser.). (Illus.). 32p. (Orig.). (YA). (gr. 7-12). 1990. 44.95 (*1-56119-081-0*) Educ Pr MD.

— Notice & Think. (Skills for Job Success Ser.). (Illus.). 32p. (Orig.). 1990. student ed, pap. 4.95 (*1-56119-001-2*) Educ Pr MD.

— Notice & Think. (Skills for Job Success Ser.). (Illus.). 32p. (Orig.). (YA). (gr. 7-12). 1990. teacher ed 1.95 (*1-56119-002-0*); disk 39.95 (*1-56119-101-9*) Educ Pr MD.

— Notice & Think, Set. (Skills for Job Success Ser.). (Illus.). 32p. (Orig.). (YA). (gr. 7-12). 1990. 44.95 (*1-56119-059-4*) Educ Pr MD.

— On the Job Training. (Skills for Job Success Ser.). (Illus.). (Orig.). 1990. pap. 49.95 (*1-56119-057-8*) Educ Pr MD.

— Respect for Property. (Skills for Job Success Ser.). (Illus.). 32p. (Orig.). 1990. student ed, pap. 4.95 (*1-56119-027-6*) Educ Pr MD.

— Respect for Property. (Skills for Job Success Ser.). (Illus.). 32p. (Orig.). (YA). (gr. 7-12). 1990. teacher ed 1.95 (*1-56119-028-4*); disk 39.95 (*1-56119-114-0*) Educ Pr MD.

— Respect for Property, Set. (Skills for Job Success Ser.). (Illus.). 32p. (Orig.). (YA). (gr. 7-12). 1990. student ed, teacher ed 44.95 (*1-56119-072-1*) Educ Pr MD.

— Say. (Skills for Job Success Ser.). (Illus.). 32p. (Orig.). 1990. student ed, pap. 4.95 (*1-56119-003-9*) Educ Pr MD.

— Say. (Skills for Job Success Ser.). (Illus.). 32p. (Orig.). (YA). (gr. 7-12). 1990. teacher ed 1.95 (*1-56119-004-7*); disk 39.95 (*1-56119-102-7*) Educ Pr MD.

— Say, Set. (Skills for Job Success Ser.). (Illus.). 32p. (Orig.). (YA). (gr. 7-12). 1990. student ed, teacher ed 44.95 (*1-56119-060-8*) Educ Pr MD.

— Social Skills for Job Success: Teacher's Guide. (Skills for Job Success Ser.). 150p. (Orig.). 1990. ring bd. 16.95 (*1-56119-058-6*) Educ Pr MD.

— Taking Breaks. (Skills for Job Success Ser.). (Illus.). 32p. (Orig.). 1990. student ed, pap. 4.95 (*1-56119-041-1*) Educ Pr MD.

— Taking Breaks. (Skills for Job Success Ser.). (Illus.). 32p. (Orig.). (YA). (gr. 7-12). 1990. teacher ed 1.95 (*1-56119-042-X*); disk 39.95 (*1-56119-121-3*) Educ Pr MD.

— Taking Breaks, Set. (Skills for Job Success Ser.). (Illus.). 32p. (Orig.). (YA). (gr. 7-12). 1990. student ed, teacher ed 44.95 (*1-56119-079-9*) Educ Pr MD.

— Too Much Talking. (Skills for Job Success Ser.). (Illus.). 32p. (Orig.). 1990. student ed, pap. 4.95 (*1-56119-011-X*) Educ Pr MD.

— Too Much Talking. (Skills for Job Success Ser.). (Illus.). 32p. (Orig.). (YA). (gr. 7-12). 1990. teacher ed 1.95 (*1-56119-012-8*); disk 39.95 (*1-56119-106-X*) Educ Pr MD.

— Too Much Talking, Set. (Skills for Job Success Ser.). (Illus.). 32p. (Orig.). (YA). (gr. 7-12). 1990. student ed, teacher ed 44.95 (*1-56119-064-0*) Educ Pr MD.

— What Should I Do? (Skills for Job Success Ser.). (Illus.). 32p. (Orig.). 1990. student ed, pap. 4.95 (*1-56119-031-4*) Educ Pr MD.

— What Should I Do? (Skills for Job Success Ser.). (Illus.). 32p. (Orig.). (YA). (gr. 7-12). 1990. teacher ed 1.95 (*1-56119-032-2*); disk 39.95 (*1-56119-116-7*) Educ Pr MD.

— What Should I Do?, Set. (Skills for Job Success Ser.). (Illus.). 32p. (Orig.). (YA). (gr. 7-12). 1990. 44.95 (*1-56119-074-8*) Educ Pr MD.

— What's Next? (Skills for Job Success Ser.). (Illus.). 32p. (Orig.). 1990. student ed, pap. 4.95 (*1-56119-019-5*) Educ Pr MD.

— What's Next? (Skills for Job Success Ser.). (Illus.). 32p. (Orig.). (YA). (gr. 7-12). 1990. teacher ed 1.95 (*1-56119-020-9*); disk 39.95 (*1-56119-110-8*) Educ Pr MD.

— What's Next?, Set. (Skills for Job Success Ser.). (Illus.). 32p. (Orig.). (YA). (gr. 7-12). 1990. 44.95 (*1-56119-068-3*) Educ Pr MD.

— What's the Proper Way? (Skills for Job Success Ser.). (Illus.). 32p. (Orig.). 1990. student ed, pap. 4.95 (*1-56119-017-9*) Educ Pr MD.

— What's the Proper Way? (Skills for Job Success Ser.). (Illus.). 32p. (Orig.). (YA). (gr. 7-12). 1990. teacher ed 1.95 (*1-56119-018-7*); disk 39.95 (*1-56119-109-4*) Educ Pr MD.

— What's the Proper Way?, Set. (Skills for Job Success Ser.). (Illus.). 32p. (Orig.). (YA). (gr. 7-12). 1990. 44.95 (*1-56119-067-5*) Educ Pr MD.

— Which Tools to Use. (Skills for Job Success Ser.). (Illus.). 32p. (Orig.). 1990. student ed, pap. 4.95 (*1-56119-049-7*) Educ Pr MD.

— Which Tools to Use? (Skills for Job Success Ser.). (Illus.). 32p. (Orig.). (YA). (gr. 7-12). 1990. teacher ed 1.95 (*1-56119-050-0*); disk 39.95 (*1-56119-125-6*) Educ Pr MD.

— Which Tools to Use?, Set. (Skills for Job Success Ser.). (Illus.). 32p. (Orig.). (YA). (gr. 7-12). 1990. 44.95 (*1-56119-083-7*) Educ Pr MD.

— Which Way Is Right? (Skills for Job Success Ser.). (Illus.). 32p. (Orig.). 1990. student ed, pap. 4.95 (*1-56119-051-9*) Educ Pr MD.

— Which Way Is Right? (Skills for Job Success Ser.). (Illus.). 32p. (Orig.). (YA). (gr. 7-12). 1990. teacher ed 1.95 (*1-56119-052-7*); disk 39.95 (*1-56119-126-4*) Educ Pr MD.

— Which Way Is Right?, Set. (Skills for Job Success Ser.). (Illus.). 32p. (Orig.). (YA). (gr. 7-12). 1990. 44.95 (*1-56119-084-5*) Educ Pr MD.

— Who Can Help. (Skills for Job Success Ser.). (Illus.). 32p. (Orig.). 1990. student ed, pap. 4.95 (*1-56119-035-7*) Educ Pr MD.

— Who Can Help? (Skills for Job Success Ser.). (Illus.). 32p. (Orig.). (YA). (gr. 7-12). 1990. teacher ed 1.95 (*1-56119-036-5*); disk 39.95 (*1-56119-118-3*) Educ Pr MD.

— Who Can Help?, Set. (Skills for Job Success Ser.). (Illus.). 32p. (Orig.). (YA). (gr. 7-12). 1990. 44.95 (*1-56119-076-4*) Educ Pr MD.

— Will You Do Me a Favor? (Skills for Job Success Ser.). (Illus.). 32p. (Orig.). 1990. student ed, pap. 4.95 (*1-56119-015-2*) Educ Pr MD.

— Will You Do Me a Favor? (Skills for Job Success Ser.). (Illus.). 32p. (Orig.). (YA). (gr. 7-12). 1990. teacher ed 1.95 (*1-56119-016-0*); disk 39.95 (*1-56119-108-6*) Educ Pr MD.

— Will You Do Me a Favor?, Set. (Skills for Job Success Ser.). (Illus.). 32p. (Orig.). (YA). (gr. 7-12). 1990. 44.95 (*1-56119-066-7*) Educ Pr MD.

— Working Too Slowly! (Skills for Job Success Ser.). (Illus.). 32p. (Orig.). 1990. student ed, pap. 4.95 (*1-56119-007-1*) Educ Pr MD.

— Working Too Slowly. (Skills for Job Success Ser.). (Illus.). 32p. (Orig.). (YA). (gr. 7-12). 1990. teacher ed 1.95 (*1-56119-008-X*); disk 39.95 (*1-56119-104-3*) Educ Pr MD.

— Working Too Slowly, Set. (Skills for Job Success Ser.). (Illus.). 32p. (Orig.). (YA). (gr. 7-12). 1990. 44.95 (*1-56119-062-4*) Educ Pr MD.

McCombs, Barbara L. & Pope, James E. Motivating Hard to Reach Students. LC 94-8336. (Psychology in the Classroom Ser.). 130p. (Orig.). 1994. pap. text ed. 17.95 (*1-55798-220-1*) Am Psychol.

McCombs, Betsy, jt. ed. see Wayne, Ellen.

McCombs, Gillian M., ed. Access Services: The Convergence of Reference & Technical Services. LC 91-35637. (Reference Librarian Ser.). 190p. 1991. lib. bdg. 39.95 (*1-56024-170-5*) Haworth Pr.

McCombs, Judith. Against Nature: Wilderness Poems. (American Dust Ser.: No. 9). 1979. 7.95 (*0-913218-83-9*); pap. 2.95 (*0-913218-84-7*) Dustbooks.

McCombs, Judith, ed. Critical Essays on Margaret Atwood. (Critical Essays on World Literature Ser.). 312p. 1988. text ed. 45.00 (*0-8161-8840-8*) G K Hall.

McCombs, Judith & Palmer, Carole L. Margaret Atwood: A Reference Guide. (Reference Guides to Literature Ser.). 300p. 1991. text ed. 60.00 (*0-8161-8940-4*, Hall Reference) Macmillan.

McCombs, M., jt. ed. see Protess, D.

McCombs, Maryglenn, ed. see Chapman, Lisa M.

McCombs, Maryglenn, ed. see Cohn, Robin.

McCombs, Maryglenn, ed. see Collins, Nancy & Sedoris, Jan.

McCombs, Maryglenn, ed. see Davis, Dee & Price, Annie.

McCombs, Maryglenn, ed. see Grant, Lee.

McCombs, Maryglenn, ed. see Hulan, Leah.

McCombs, Maryglenn, ed. see King, Thom & Peterson, Debora.

McCombs, Maryglenn, ed. see Mathews, Alice & Sprintz, Alyse.

McCombs, Maryglenn, ed. see Meeker, Frances & Berryhill, Judy.

McCombs, Maryglenn, ed. see Queener, Elizabeth.

McCombs, Maryglenn, ed. see Resta, Bart & Harvill, Kitty.

McCombs, Maryglenn, ed. see Womack, Tommy.

McCombs, Maryglenn, ed. see Young, Buck.

McCombs, Maxwell, et al. Contemporary Public Opinion: Issues & the News. (Communication Textbook Series, Journalism Subseries). 128p. 1991. text ed. 29.95 (*0-8058-0537-0*); pap. 14.95 (*0-8058-1102-8*) L Erlbaum Assocs.

McCombs, Nancy K. Earth Spirit, Victim, or Whore: The Prostitute in German Literature, 1880-1925. (American University Studies: Germanic Languages & Literature: Ser. I, Vol. 34). 287p. 1986. text ed. 36.00 (*0-8204-0306-7*) P Lang Pubs.

McCombs, Philip A., jt. auth. see Klose, Kevin.

McCombs, Robert P. Fundamentals of Internal Medicine: A Physiologic & Clinical Approach to Disease. 4th ed. LC 74-115098. (Illus.). 939p. reprint ed. pap. 180.00 (*0-317-58144-9*, 2029738) Bks Demand.

McComish, Charles D. & Lambert, Rebecca T. History of Colusa & Glenn Counties, California. (Illus.). 1074p. 1993. reprint ed. lib. bdg. 105.00 (*0-8328-3233-2*) Higginson Bk Co.

McComish, William A. The Epigones: A Study of the Theology of the Synod of Dort, with Special Reference to Giovanni Diodati. LC 87-11073. (Princeton Theological Monograph Ser.: No. 13). (Orig.). 1989. pap. 20.00 (*0-915138-62-X*) Pickwick.

McComiskey, Thomas E. The Minor Prophets: An Exegetical & Expository Commentary, Vol. 1, Hosea, Joel & Amos. LC 91-38388. 400p. 1992. text ed. 34.99 (*0-8010-6285-3*) Baker Bk.

— Reading Scripture in Public: A Guide for Preachers & Lay Readers. LC 91-6908. (Orig.). 1991. pap. 9.99 (*0-8010-6278-0*) Baker Bk.

McComiskey, Thomas E., ed. The Minor Prophets: An Exegetical & Expository Commentary, Vol. 2: Obadiah-Habakkuk. LC 91-38388. 416p. 1993. text ed. 34.99 (*0-8010-6307-8*) Baker Bk.

McComiskey, Thomas E., jt. ed. see Woodbridge, John D.

***McCommachie.** Elmer & Chick vs. Big L. 1994. 4.99 (*0-517-13543-4*) Random Hse Value.

McConachie, Bruce A. Melodramatic Formations: American Theatre & Society, 1820-1870. LC 91-44085. (Studies in Theatre History & Culture). (Illus.). 334p. 1992. text ed. 42.95 (*0-87745-359-4*); pap. 16.95 (*0-87745-360-8*) U of Iowa Pr.

McConachie, Bruce A. & Friedman, Daniel P., eds. Theatre for Working-Class Audiences in the United States, 1830-1980. LC 84-19773. (Contributions in Drama & Theatre Studies: No. 14). (Illus.). viii, 264p. 1985. text ed. 59.95 (*0-313-24629-7*, MTU/) Greenwood.

McConachie, Bruce A., jt. ed. see Postlewait, Thomas.

McConachie, Helen. Parents & Young Mentally Handicapped Children: A Review of Research Issues. 276p. 1986. text ed. 29.95 (*0-914797-28-X*) Brookline Bks.

McConachie, Helen, jt. ed. see Mittler, Peter.

McConagha, Glenn L. Blackburn College 1837-1987: An Anecdotal & Analytical History of the Private College. (Illus.). 533p. (C). 1988. 20.00 (*0-9621555-0-0*) Blackburn Univ.

McConaghy, June. Children Learning Through Literature: A Teacher Researcher Study. LC 89-71089. (Illus.). 80p. (Orig.). 1990. pap. text ed. 13.50 (*0-435-08515-8*) Heinemann.

McConaghy, N. Sexual Behavior: Management & Problems. (Applied Clinical Psychology Ser.). (Illus.). 400p. (C). 1993. 60.00 (*0-306-44177-2*, Plenum Pr) Plenum.

McConaughey, J. Who Rules America? 1980. lib. bdg. 150.00 (*0-8490-3205-9*) Gordon Pr.

McConaughty, Stephanie H., jt. auth. see Achenbach, Thomas M.

McConaughty, Stephanie M. & Achenbach, Thomas M. Guide for the Semistructured Clinical Interview for Children Aged 6 to 11. (Illus.). 80p. 1990. pap. 11.00 (*0-938565-05-2*) U of VT Psych.

McConaughy, Mark A., ed. Rench: A Stratified Site in the Central Illinois River Valley. (Reports of Investigations Ser.: No. 50). (Illus.). 430p. 1993. pap. 20.00 (*0-89792-143-7*) Ill St Museum.

***McConaughy, Stephanie H. & Achenbach, Thomas M.** Manual for the Semistructured Clinical Interview for Children & Adolescents. 228p. (Orig.). 1994. pap. 25.00 (*0-938565-32-X*) U of VT Psych.

McConaughy, Stephanie H., jt. auth. see Achenbach, Thomas M.

McConchie, David M., jt. auth. see Lewis, D. W.

McConchie, Lyn, jt. auth. see Norton, Andre.

McConcohie, Jean, ed. see Christie, Mary.

***McConduit, Denise W.** D.J. & the Zulu Parade. LC 94-12210. (Illus.). 32p. (J). (gr. 4-8). 1994. 14.95 (*1-56554-063-8*) Pelican.

McConica, Carol M., jt. ed. see Blewer, Robert S.

McConica, James K. Erasmus. (Past Masters Ser.). 112p. 1991. pap. 7.95 (*0-19-287599-X*) OUP.

— The History of the University of Oxford Vol. III: The Collegiate University. (Illus.). 780p. 1986. 125.00 (*0-19-951013-X*) OUP.

McConkey, A., jt. auth. see Eastop, Thomas D.

McConkey, Dale D. No-Nonsense Delegation. rev. ed. 288p. 1986. 17.95 (*0-8144-5853-X*) AMACOM.

McConkey, Dale S. How Staff Managers Make Things Happen: Productivity Through MBO. LC 83-60030. 1983. 15.95 (*0-912164-09-3*) Masterco Pr.

McConkey, David J. Programmed Cell Death (Apoptosis) 1995. write for info. (*0-8493-5113-8*) CRC Pr.

McConkey, Edwin H. Human Genetics: Molecular Revolution. 336p. (C). 1993. boxed 48.75 (*0-86720-854-6*) Jones & Bartlett.

McConkey, Edwin H., ed. Protein Synthesis, Vol. 1. LC 74-155743. 314p. reprint ed. pap. 89.50 (*0-7837-0017-2*, 2027112) Bks Demand.

— Protein Synthesis, Vol. 2. LC 75-155743. 400p. reprint ed. pap. 114.00 (*0-685-16250-8*, 2027112) Bks Demand.

McConkey, Gladys, ed. Plasma Studies at Cornell University. 64p. 1988. write for info. (*0-918531-01-2*) Cornell Coll Eng.

McConkey, James. La Consumacion Del Siglo: The End of the Age. (SPA.). 3.25 (*84-7645-039-7*, 223111, Pub. by Edit Clie SP) TSELF.

— Court of Memory. 1993. pap. 13.95 (*0-87923-983-2*) Godine.

— Stories from My Life with Other Animals. 160p. 1993. 19.95 (*0-87923-967-0*) Godine.

McConkey, James, ed. Chekhov & Our Age. 237p. 1985. 24.95 (*0-86731-078-2*); pap. 8.95 (*0-86731-081-2*) Cornell CIS RDC.

McConkey, James H. Oracion: Prayer. (SPA.). 3.95 (*84-7645-034-6*, 223113, Pub. by Edit Clie SP) TSELF.

— El Triple Secreto Del Espiritu Santo. Agostini, Beatrice, tr. Orig. Title: The Three Fold Secret of the Holy Spirit. 112p. (SPA.). 1987. pap. 2.50 (*0-311-09090-7*) Casa Bautista.

— Triple Secreto del Espiritu Santo: Three Fold Secret of the Holy Spirit. (SPA.). 3.25 (*84-7645-150-4*, 223201, Pub. by Edit Clie SP) TSELF.

McConkey, K. M., jt. ed. see Bennett, A. F.

An Asterisk (*) at the beginning of an entry indicates that the title is appearing in BIP for the first time.

McConkey, Kenneth. British Impressionism. (Illus.). 160p. 1989. 49.50 (*0-8109-1236-8*) Abrams.

— Edwardian Portraits: Images of an Age of Opulence. (Illus.). 264p. 1987. 49.50 (*1-85149-060-4*) Antique Collect.

— A Free Spirit, Irish Art, 1860-1960. (Illus.). 228p. 1990. 59.50 (*1-85149-127-9*) Antique Collect.

— Impressionism in Britain. LC 94-41771. 1995. write for info. (*0-300-06334-2*) Yale U Pr.

— Impressionism in Britain. LC 94-41771. 1995. 55.00 (*0-300-06335-0*) Yale U Pr.

McConkey, Kevin M., jt. auth. see Sheehan, Peter W.

McConkey, Lois. Sea & Cedar: How the Northwest Coast Indians Lived. (Illus.). 32p. (J). (gr. 3-7). 1991. pap. 8.95 (*0-88894-371-7*, Pub. by Groundwood-Douglas & McIntyre CN) Firefly Bks Ltd.

McConkey, Roy. Working with Parents: A Practical Guide for Teachers & Therapists. 325p. 1985. pap. text ed. 21.95 (*0-914797-14-X*) Brookline Bks.

McConkey, Wilfred J. Haute As in Oat: A Pronunciation Guide to European Wines & Cuisines. 184p. 1989. 17.95 (*0-8191-6823-8*); pap. 7.95 (*0-8191-6824-6*) Madison Bks UPA.

McConkie & Millet. Doctrinal Commentary on the Book of Mormon, 2 vols., 1. 13.95 (*0-88494-632-0*) Bookcraft Inc.

— Doctrinal Commentary on the Book of Mormon, 2 vols., 2. 13.95 (*0-88494-655-X*) Bookcraft Inc.

— The Holy Ghost. 10.95 (*0-88494-707-6*) Bookcraft Inc.

— In His Holy Name. 8.95 (*0-88494-677-0*) Bookcraft Inc.

— The Life Beyond. 10.95 (*0-88494-601-0*) Bookcraft Inc.

McConkie & Parry. A Guide to Scriptural Symbols. 10.95 (*0-88494-726-2*) Bookcraft Inc.

McConkie, Bruce R. Doctrinal New Testament Commentary, 1. 17.95 (*0-88494-137-X*) Bookcraft Inc.

— Doctrinal New Testament Commentary, 2. 15.95 (*0-88494-216-3*) Bookcraft Inc.

— Doctrinal New Testament Commentary, 3. 15.95 (*0-88494-250-3*) Bookcraft Inc.

— The Messiah Series, 6 titles, Set. 3234p. 1990. pap. 37.95 (*0-87579-401-7*) Deseret Bk.

— Mormon Doctrine. 17.95 (*0-88494-062-4*); pap. 8.95 (*0-88494-446-8*) Bookcraft Inc.

— The Mortal Messiah: From Bethlehem to Calvary, Bk. 3. LC 79-19606. 486p. 1980. 16.95 (*0-87747-825-2*) Deseret Bk.

— The Mortal Messiah: From Bethlehem to Calvary, Bk. 4. LC 79-19606. 447p. 1981. 16.95 (*0-87747-856-2*) Deseret Bk.

— The Mortal Messiah, Bk. 2: From Bethlehem to Calvary. LC 79-19606. (Messiah Ser.). 424p. 1990. reprint ed. pap. 9.95 (*0-87579-404-1*) Deseret Bk.

— The Mortal Messiah, Bk. 3: From Bethlehem to Calvary. LC 79-19606. (Messiah Ser.). 486p. 1990. reprint ed. pap. 10.95 (*0-87579-405-X*) Deseret Bk.

— The Promised Messiah: The First Coming of Christ. LC 78-3478. (Messiah Ser.). 636p. 1990. reprint ed. pap. 11.95 (*0-87579-402-5*) Deseret Bk.

***McConkie, Clay.** The Gathering of the Waters. 100p. (Orig.). Date not set. pap. 7.95 (*0-7610-0276-6*) NW Pub.

McConkie, Joseph F. Gospel Symbolism. 11.95 (*0-88494-568-5*) Bookcraft Inc.

— Here We Stand. 1995. 14.95 (*1-57345-045-6*) Deseret Bk.

— Prophets & Prophecy. 10.95 (*0-88494-667-3*) Bookcraft Inc.

— Sons & Daughters of God. 1994. 14.95 (*0-88494-936-2*) Bookcraft Inc.

— Teach & Reach. 5.95 (*0-88494-289-9*) Bookcraft Inc.

McConkie, Joseph F. & Millet, Robert L. Doctrinal Commentary on the Book of Mormon, Vol. 3. 1991. 14.95 (*0-88494-807-2*) Bookcraft Inc.

McConkie, Joseph F., jt. auth. see Millet, Robert L.

McConkie, Joseph F., et al. Doctrinal Commentary on the Book of Mormon, No. 4. 14.95 (*0-88494-818-8*) Bookcraft Inc.

McConkie, Mark L. Doctrines of the Restoration: The Sermons & Writings of Bruce R. McConkie. 15.95 (*0-88494-644-4*) Bookcraft Inc.

— The Father of the Prophet. 1993. 12.95 (*0-88494-887-0*) Bookcraft Inc.

— Joseph Smith & the First Vision. 1993. pap. 2.95 (*0-88494-897-8*) Bookcraft Inc.

McConn, Rita, ed. The Role of Chemical Mediators in the Pathophysiology of Acute Illness & Injury. 408p. 1982. text ed. 134.00 (*0-89004-682-4*) Raven.

McConnachie, Brian. Elmer & Chickens vs. Big Bird. (J). 1993. pap. 3.99 (*0-517-11135-7*) Random Hse Value.

— Elmer & the Chickens vs. the Big League. LC 91-2914. (Illus.). 32p. (J). (ps-2). 1992. 14.00 (*0-517-57616-3*) Crown Bks Yng Read.

McConnachie, John. Barthian Theology. LC 72-2493. (Select Bibliographies Reprint Ser.). 1977. reprint ed. 21.95 (*0-8369-6861-1*) Ayer.

McConnaughey, Bayard & McConnaughey, Evelyn. Pacific Coast. Elliott, Charles, ed. LC 84-48673. (Audubon Society Nature Guides Ser.). (Illus.). 633p. 1985. pap. 19.00 (*0-394-73130-1*) Knopf.

McConnaughey, Bayard H. & Zottoli, Robert. Introduction to Marine Biology. 4th ed. (Illus.). 638p. (C). 1989. reprint ed. pap. text ed. 33.95 (*0-88133-446-4*) Waveland Pr.

McConnaughey, Evelyn. Sea Vegetables: Harvesting Guide & Cookbook. (Illus.). 244p. 1985. 16.95 (*0-87961-150-2*); pap. 9.95 (*0-87961-151-0*) Naturegraph.

McConnaughey, Evelyn, jt. auth. see McConnaughey, Bayard.

McConnaughy, James, jt. ed. see Langstaff, Bard.

McConnel, Charles R. The Health Care Supervisor on Professional Nursing Management. (Health Care Supervisor Ser.). 236p. 1993. pap. 36.00 (*0-8342-0369-3*) Aspen Pub.

McConnel, Frances, ed. One Step Closer: New Poetry by Women of the West Coast. 1976. pap. 3.95 (*0-915242-09-5*) Pygmalion Pr.

McConnel, John L. Western Characters: Or, Types of Border Life in the Western States. LC 75-110. (Mid-American Frontier Ser.). (Illus.). 1975. reprint ed. 33.95 (*0-405-06877-8*) Ayer.

***McConnel, Patricia.** Eye of the Beholder. (Chapbook Ser.). 32p. 1994. pap. 5.95 (*1-884106-02-1*) Jumping Cholla.

— Sing Soft, Sing Loud. 272p. 1995. pap. 12.00 (*0-9643253-0-6*) Logoria.

McConnel, Stephen, jt. auth. see Kew, Jonathan.

Mcconnell. Computerizing the Corporation: The Intimate Link Between People & Machines. 1990. text ed. 39.95 (*0-442-31877-4*) Van Nos Reinhold.

***McConnell.** Vibration Testing: Theory & Practice. Date not set. text ed. 84.95 (*0-471-30435-2*) Wiley.

McConnell, A. J. Applications of Tensor Analysis. pap. 7.50 (*0-486-60373-3*) Dover.

***McConnell, Allan.** State Policy Formation & the Origin of the Poll Tax. 250p. 1995. text ed. 59.95 (*1-85521-488-1*, Pub. by Dartmth Pub UK) Ashgate Pub Co.

McConnell, Allen. A Russian Philosophe, Alexander Radischev, Seventeen Forty-Nine to Eighteen Hundred Two. LC 79-2911. 228p. 1981. reprint ed. 23.00 (*0-8305-0080-4*) Hyperion Conn.

— Tsar Alexander I: Paternalistic Reformer. LC 70-101949. (Europe since 1500 Ser.). 240p. (C). 1970. pap. text ed. write for info. (*0-88295-745-7*) Harlan Davidson.

McConnell, Anita, ed. see Abrams, Lesley.

McConnell, Anita, jt. auth. see Lambert, David.

McConnell, Anita, ed. see Wallis, Helen.

McConnell, Anita, jt. ed. see Wallis, Helen.

***McConnell, Ashley.** The Fountains of Mirlacca. 208p. (Orig.). Date not set. pap. text ed. 6.50 (*0-441-00206-4*) Ace Bks.

— Quantum Leap: Random Measures. 240p. (Orig.). 1995. pap. text ed. 4.99 (*0-441-00182-3*) Ace Bks.

— Quantum Leap: The Novel. 304p. (Orig.). 1992. mass mkt. 4.99 (*0-441-69322-9*) Ace Bks.

— Quantum Leap: The Wall. 256p. (Orig.). 1994. mass mkt. 4.99 (*0-441-00015-0*) Ace Bks.

— Quantum Leap: Too Close for Comfort. 272p. (Orig.). 1993. mass mkt. 4.99 (*0-441-69323-7*) Ace Bks.

— Quantum Leap Number Four: Prelude. 256p. (Orig.). 1994. mass mkt. 4.99 (*0-441-00076-2*) Ace Bks.

McConnell, B. D., ed. see Spring Lubrication Symposium (1972, Boston).

***McConnell, Brian.** Holy Killers: True Stories of Murderous Clerics, Priests & Religious Leaders. (Illus.). 288p. 1995. pap. 9.95 (*0-7472-4440-5*, Pub. by Headline UK) Trafalgar.

McConnell, C. R. & Brue, S. L. Contemporary Labor Economics. 4th ed. 688p. 1994. text ed. write for info. (*0-07-045657-7*) McGraw.

McConnell, Campbell R. Economics. 12th ed. 1993. text ed. write for info. (*0-07-045559-7*) McGraw.

— Economics: Principles, Practices & Policies. 8th rev. ed. (Illus.). 992p. 1981. text ed. write for info. (*0-07-044930-9*) McGraw.

— Economics: Principles, Problems & Practices. 9th ed. LC 83-13349. (Illus.). 928p. (C). 1984. text ed. write for info. (*0-07-044944-9*) McGraw.

— Economics Concepts: A Programmed Approach. 7th ed. 1984. pap. text ed. write for info. (*0-07-044937-6*) McGraw.

— Macroeconomics Course Package. 11th ed. (C). 1990. Course package. text ed. 200.00 (*0-07-909781-2*); Instr's. resource manual. teacher ed 34.95 (*0-07-045549-X*); Instr's. resource manual. teacher ed 34.95 (*0-07-045546-5*); Test Bank II. 34.95 (*0-07-074438-6*); Test Bank II. 34.95 (*0-07-074436-X*) McGraw.

McConnell, Campbell R. & Brue, Stanley L. Contemporary Labor Economics. 3rd ed. 1992. text ed. write for info. (*0-07-045555-4*); pap. text ed. write for info. (*0-07-045556-2*) McGraw.

— Economics: Principles, Problems & Policies Course Package. 11th ed. 1990. teacher ed 19.95 (*0-685-28469-7*); text ed. 200.00 (*0-07-909780-4*); trans. 20.00 (*0-07-045516-3*); 50.00 (*0-07-045517-1*); 49.95 (*0-07-045518-X*) McGraw.

— Economics Principles, Problems, & Policies. 13th ed. LC 95-13487. 1995. write for info. (*0-07-046814-1*) McGraw.

— Macroeconomics: Principles, Problems, & Policies. 12th ed. LC 92-20050. 1993. text ed. write for info. (*0-07-045603-8*) McGraw.

— Microeconomics: Principles, Problems, & Policies. 12th ed. LC 92-17817. 1993. text ed. write for info. (*0-07-045617-8*) McGraw.

— Microeconomics Course Package. 11th ed. (C). 1990. Incl. instr's. manual & study guide. student ed, teacher ed 200.00 (*0-07-909782-0*) McGraw.

McConnell, Cecil. Comentario Sobre los Himnos Que Cantamos. 368p. (SPA.). 1985. pap. 8.95 (*0-311-32433-9*) Casa Bautista.

McConnell, Cecil & McConnell, Mary. Objetos Que Ensenan de Dios. 96p. (SPA.). 1986. pap. 3.50 (*0-311-44007-X*) Casa Bautista.

McConnell, Cecilio. A Que Dedicare Me Vida. (SPA.). Date not set. pap. 5.99 (*0-89922-174-2*) Edit Caribe.

McConnell, Cecilio, jt. auth. see Crane, James D.

***McConnell-Celi, Sue.** Jane Fixes Cars. 10p. (J). (gr. k-2). 1995. 6.50 (*0-614-07062-7*) Lavender Crystal.

— Making Friends with Nature. (J). (ps). 1993. pap. 7.95 (*0-9636909-1-4*) Lavender Crystal.

McConnell-Celi, Sue, ed. Torch to the Heart: Anthology of Lesbian Art & Drama. (Illus.). 250p. (Orig.). 1994. pap. 18.25 (*1-884541-00-3*) Lavender Crystal.

— Twenty First Century Challenge: Lesbians & Gays in Education: Bridging the Gap. LC 93-78393. (Illus.). 200p. (Orig.). 1993. pap. text ed. 17.95 (*0-9636909-0-6*) Lavender Crystal.

McConnell, Charles. Home Plumbing Handbook. 3rd rev. ed. 1985. pap. 15.95 (*0-672-23413-0*, Audel) Macmillan.

McConnell, Charles N. Home Plumbing Handbook. 4th ed. 224p. 1993. pap. 17.00 (*0-02-079651-X*) Macmillan.

McConnell, Charles R. The Effective Health Care Supervisor. 3rd ed. LC 93-10915. 470p. 1993. 49.00 (*0-8342-0377-4*, 20377) Aspen Pub.

— The Health Care Manager's Guide to Performance Appraisal. LC 92-17876. 240p. 1992. 55.00 (*0-8342-0348-0*, 20348) Aspen Pub.

McConnell, Charles R., ed. The Health Care Supervisor on Career Development. LC 93-195. (Health Care Supervisor Ser.). 238p. 1993. pap. 36.00 (*0-8342-0364-2*) Aspen Pub.

— The Health Care Supervisor on Effective Communication. (Health Care Supervisor Ser.). 228p. 1993. pap. 36.00 (*0-8342-0365-0*) Aspen Pub.

— The Health Care Supervisor on Effective Employee Relations. (Health Care Supervisor Ser.). 240p. 1993. pap. 36.00 (*0-8342-0366-9*) Aspen Pub.

— The Health Care Supervisor on Law. (Health Care Supervisor Ser.). 238p. 1993. pap. 36.00 (*0-8342-0367-7*) Aspen Pub.

— The Health Care Supervisor on Productivity. LC 93-9324. (Health Care Supervisor Ser.). 240p. 1993. pap. 36.00 (*0-8342-0368-5*) Aspen Pub.

— Health Care Supervisor Series. 1993. pap. 165.00 (*0-8342-0370-7*) Aspen Pub.

McConnell, Chris. A Nation of Amor. LC 93-36291. 187p. 1994. 22.00 (*1-877946-40-0*) Permanent Pr.

McConnell, Curt. Great Cars of the Great Plains. LC 94-3860. (Illus.). 1995. 40.00 (*0-8032-3163-6*) U of Nebr Pr.

McConnell, Dan R. A Different Gospel: A Historical & Biblical Analysis of the Modern Faith Movement. 208p. 1988. pap. 7.95 (*0-913573-78-7*) Hendrickson MA.

— A Different Gospel: Biblical & Historical Insights into the Word of Faith Movement. rev. ed. 224p. 1995. pap. 12.95 (*1-56563-132-3*) Hendrickson MA.

McConnell, David. Computer-Supported Collaborative Learning. 220p. 1994. text ed. 54.95 (*0-7494-1237-2*, Pub. by Kogan Page UK) Nichols Pub.

McConnell, David, jt. auth. see Parker, Lois.

McConnell, David, jt. auth. see Thomas, Steven.

McConnell, David B. Discover Michigan. LC 81-6722. (Illus.). 144p. (J). (gr. 4). 1989. teacher ed 7.45 (*0-910726-33-7*); text ed. 19.95x (*0-910726-07-8*) Hillsdale Educ.

— Explore Michigan A to Z. McConnell, Stella M., ed. LC 93-17430. (Illus.). 48p. (Orig.). (J). (gr. 3-4). 1993. pap. 7.95 (*0-910726-55-8*) Hillsdale Educ.

— Forging the Peninsulas. 410p. 1995. 28.70x (*0-910726-83-3*) Hillsdale Educ.

— A Puzzle Book for Young Michiganians. (Illus.). 24p. (Orig.). (J). (gr. 3-6). 1982. pap. 5.50 (*0-910726-17-5*) Hillsdale Educ.

McConnell, Deb, ed. see Allred, Michael.

McConnell, Donald. Economic Virtues in the United States. LC 73-2520. (Big Business; Economic Power in a Free Society Ser.). 1973. reprint ed. 12.95 (*0-405-05100-X*) Ayer.

McConnell, Donald K., Jr. Public Company Auditor Changes & Big Eight Firms: Disagreements & Other Issues. Farmer, Richard, ed. LC 83-5953. (Research for Business Decisions Ser.: No. 62). 330p. reprint ed. 94.10 (*0-8357-1425-X*, 2070406) Bks Demand.

McConnell, Donna. Lively Little Logs. Reikes, Ursula, ed. LC 93-8014. (Illus.). 72p. (Orig.). 1993. pap. 17.95 (*1-56477-027-3*, B157) That Patchwork.

McConnell, Edwina A. Clinical Considerations in Perioperative Nursing. LC 64-4347. 1987. text ed. 24.95 (*0-397-54494-4*, Lippincott Nursing) Lippincott.

McConnell, Edwina A. & Lewis, LuVerne W. Lippincott's State Board Review for NCLEX-RN. 4th ed. 1989. text ed. 24.50 (*0-397-54722-6*, Lippincott Nursing) Lippincott.

McConnell, Edwina A. & Zimmerman, Mary F. Care of Patients with Urologic Problems. (Illus.). 309p. 1982. text ed. 22.50 (*0-397-54402-2*, 64-03430, Lippincott Nursing) Lippincott.

McConnell, Eleanor S., jt. auth. see Matteson, Mary A.

McConnell, Em. The Great Farm Adventure. (Learn-a-Lot Ser.). (J). (gr. k-3). 4.95 (*0-932715-07-9*) Evans FL.

— Strange Sounds. (Learn-a-Lot Ser.). (J). (gr. k-3). audio 4.95 (*0-932715-09-5*) Evans FL.

McConnell-Falk, Judith, jt. ed. see Bolin, Francis S.

McConnell, Francis J. Borden Parker Bowne, His Life & Philosophy. LC 75-3077. reprint ed. 20.50 (*0-404-59078-0*) AMS Pr.

McConnell, Francis J., ed. A Basis for the Peace to Come: Proceedings of the National Study Conference of the Churches on a Just & Durable Peace, 1st, Ohio Wesleyan University, 1942. 1977. 12.95 (*0-8369-7277-5*, 8076) Ayer.

McConnell, Frank. Blood Lake. 256p. 1987. 16.95 (*0-8027-5673-5*) Walker & Co.

— The Frog King. 192p. 1990. 18.95 (*0-8027-5748-0*) Walker & Co.

— The Frog King. large type ed. 1992. pap. 19.95 (*0-7927-1175-0*, Curley Lrg Print) Chivers N Amer.

— Liar's Poker: A Harry Garnish Mystery. LC 92-43525. 234p. 1993. 19.95 (*0-8027-3229-1*) Walker & Co.

McConnell, Frank, ed. The Bible & the Narrative Tradition. 160p. 1991. reprint ed. pap. 14.95 (*0-19-507002-X*) OUP.

McConnell, Frank D. The Confessional Imagination: A Reading of Wordsworth's Prelude. LC 73-19333. 224p. 1974. 30.00 (*0-8018-1574-6*) Johns Hopkins.

— The Spoken Seen: Film & the Romantic Imagination. LC 75-11342. 214p. reprint ed. pap. 61.00 (*0-317-42067-4*, 2025886) Bks Demand.

McConnell, Frank D., ed. see Byron, George G.

McConnell, Freeman, ed. see National Symposium on Deafness in Childhood Staff.

***McConnell, Gail A.** Saskatoon: Hub City of the West. 128p. 1983. 27.95 (*0-89781-070-8*) Preferred Mktg.

McConnell, Gerald. Assemblage: Three Dimensional Picture Making. (Illus.). 96p. 1976. pap. 15.95 (*0-442-25264-1*) Madison Square.

McConnell-Ginet, Sally, jt. auth. see Chierchia, Gennaro.

McConnell-Ginet, Sally, jt. ed. see Kramsch, Claire.

McConnell-Ginet, Sally, et al, eds. Women & Language in Literature & Society. LC 80-20816. 358p. 1980. text ed. 75.00 (*0-275-90520-9*, C0520, Praeger Pubs) Greenwood.

McConnell, Grant. Private Power & American Democracy. LC 65-18761. 1970. pap. text ed. 4.95 (*0-07-553716-8*) McGraw.

— The Spirit of Private Government. (Reprint Series in Social Sciences). (C). 1993. reprint ed. pap. text ed. 1.00 (*0-8290-2738-6*, PS-196) Irvington.

— Stehekin: A Valley in Time. LC 88-9095. 200p. 1988. 14.95 (*0-89886-181-0*) Mountaineers.

McConnell, H. H. Five Years a Cavalryman. LC 75-133525. (Select Bibliographies Reprint Ser.). 1977. reprint ed. 20.95 (*0-8369-5557-9*) Ayer.

McConnell, Harold & Yaseen, David W., eds. Models of Spatial Variation. LC 75-149933. (Perspectives in Geography Ser.: Vol. 1). (Illus.). 131p. 1971. 18.50 (*0-87580-024-6*) N Ill U Pr.

McConnell, Imogene, jt. auth. see McLane, Bobbie J.

***McConnell, Inez B.** The Taming of the Wilderness in Northern New York: Wm. C. Pierrepont's 1826 Journal. (The/Piereepont Journals). 86p. 1993. pap. 10.00 (*1-886303-03-7*) Write to Print.

McConnell, J. C. & Robson, J. C. Noncommutative Noetherian Rings. LC 87-8153. (Pure & Applied Mathematics Ser.). 650p. 1988. text ed. 325.00 (*0-471-91550-5*) Wiley.

McConnell, J. D., jt. auth. see Putnis, Andrew.

McConnell, J. R. The Theory of Nuclear Magnetic Relaxation in Liquids. (Illus.). 200p. 1987. 74.95 (*0-521-32112-3*) Cambridge U Pr.

McConnell, J. R., jt. auth. see Gaiduk, V. I.

McConnell, James. Guide to Safe Stairways, Walkways, & Railings. (Illus.). 20p. 1978. pap. text ed. 8.00 (*0-88698-153-0*, 1.50010) PETEX.

— Rotational Brownian Motion & Dielectric Theory. 1980. text ed. 150.00 (*0-12-481850-1*) Acad Pr.

McConnell, James, illus. Ambrose Bierce: Great American Short Stories II. LC 94-75024. (Classic Short Stories Ser.). 80p. 1994. pap. 4.50 (*1-56103-016-3*) Lake Pub Co.

— Anton Chekhov: Great Short Stories from Around the World I. LC 94-75341. (Classic Short Stories Ser.). 80p. 1994. pap. 4.50 (*1-56103-040-6*) Lake Pub Co.

— Arthur Conan Doyle: Great British & Irish Short Stories I. LC 94-75351. (Classic Short Stories Ser.). 80p. 1994. pap. 4.50 (*1-56103-026-0*) Lake Pub Co.

— E. M. Forster: Great British & Irish Short Stories I. LC 94-75356. (Classic Short Stories Ser.). 80p. 1994. pap. 4.50 (*1-56103-031-7*) Lake Pub Co.

— Edgar Allan Poe: Great American Short Stories I. LC 94-75016. (Classic Short Stories Ser.). 80p. 1994. pap. 4.50 (*1-56103-006-6*) Lake Pub Co.

— Edith Wharton: Great American Short Stories II. LC 94-75026. (Classic Short Stories Ser.). 80p. 1994. pap. 4.50 (*1-56103-018-X*) Lake Pub Co.

— Frank R. Stockton: Great American Short Stories II. LC 94-75028. (Classic Short Stories Ser.). 80p. 1994. pap. 4.50 (*1-56103-020-1*) Lake Pub Co.

— Guy de Maupassant: Great Short Stories from Around the World I. LC 94-75350. (Classic Short Stories Ser.). 80p. 1994. pap. 4.50 (*1-56103-039-2*) Lake Pub Co.

— H. G. Wells: Great British & Irish Short Stories I. LC 94-75358. (Classic Short Stories Ser.). 80p. 1994. pap. 4.50 (*1-56103-033-3*) Lake Pub Co.

— James Joyce: Great British & Irish Short Stories I. LC 94-75360. (Classic Short Stories Ser.). 80p. 1994. pap. 4.50 (*1-56103-035-X*) Lake Pub Co.

— John Galsworthy: Great British & Irish Short Stories I. LC 94-75359. (Classic Short Stories Ser.). 80p. 1994. pap. 4.50 (*1-56103-034-1*) Lake Pub Co.

— Katherine Mansfield: Great British & Irish Short Stories I. LC 94-75354. (Classic Short Stories Ser.). 80p. 1994. pap. 4.50 (*1-56103-029-5*) Lake Pub Co.

— Leo Tolstoy: Great Short Stories from Around the World I. LC 94-75342. (Classic Short Stories Ser.). 80p. 1994. pap. 4.50 (*1-56103-041-4*) Lake Pub Co.

— Nathaniel Hawthorne: Great American Short Stories I. LC 94-75013. (Classic Short Stories Ser.). 80p. 1994. pap. 4.50 (*1-56103-003-1*) Lake Pub Co.

— Robert Louis Stevenson: Great British & Irish Short Stories I. LC 94-75357. (Classic Short Stories Ser.). 80p. 1994. pap. 4.50 (*1-56103-032-5*) Lake Pub Co.

— Rudyard Kipling: Great British & Irish Short Stories I. LC 94-75353. (Classic Short Stories Ser.). 80p. 1994. pap. 4.50 (*1-56103-028-7*) Lake Pub Co.

— Saki: Great British & Irish Short Stories I. LC 94-75352. (Classic Short Stories Ser.). 80p. 1994. pap. 4.50 (*1-56103-027-9*) Lake Pub Co.

An Asterisk (*) at the beginning of an entry indicates that the title is appearing in BIP for the first time.

— Selma Lagerlof: Great Short Stories from Around the World I. LC 94-75343. (Classic Short Stories Ser.). 80p. 1994. pap. 4.50 (*1-56103-042-2*) Lake Pub Co.

— Thomas Hardy: Great British & Irish Short Stories I. LC 94-75355. (Classic Short Stories Ser.). 80p. 1994. pap. 4.50 (*1-56103-030-9*) Lake Pub Co.

McConnell, James V. Understanding Human Behavior: An Introduction to Psychology. 6th ed. 768p. (C). 1989. 12.95 (*0-318-43181-5*); text ed. 29.95 (*0-318-43180-7*) HB Coll Pubs.

McConnell, James V. & Gorenflo, Daniel. Classic Readings in Psychology. 288p. (C). 1989. pap. text ed. 16.00 (*0-03-025463-9*) HB Coll Pubs.

McConnell, James V. & Gorenflo, Daniel W., eds. Classic Readings in Psychology. LC 89-7620. (C). 1989. 13.00 (*0-03-027614-4*) HB Coll Pubs.

McConnell, James V. & Philipchalk, Ronald P. Understanding Human Behavior. 7th ed. 750p. (C). 1991. text ed. write for info. (*0-318-69127-2*) HB Coll Pubs.

McConnell, James V., jt. auth. see Philipchalk, Ronald P.

McConnell, Jean S. A Farm At Shwando. (Illus.). 1993. 10.95 (*0-9627860-7-1*) Lone Oak MN.

McConnell, Jennifer, jt. auth. see Crosbie, Jack.

McConnell, Joan. A Vocabulary Analysis of Gadda's "Pasticciaccio" LC 73-81570. (Romance Monographs: No. 2). 1973. 24.00 (*84-399-0685-4*); pap. 19.00 (*0-686-31729-7*) Romance.

McConnell, John. Network Management. 1995. text ed. 33.00 (*0-13-127176-8*) P-H.

McConnell, John H. How to Audit the Human Resources Department. 256p. 1986. 75.00 (*0-8144-1143-6*) AMACOM.

McConnell, John S. Analysis & Control of Variation: Control Chart Techniques for TQC Practitioners. 4th rev. ed. (Illus.). 144p. 1987. pap. 20.00 (*0-9588324-2-0*, Pub. by Delaware Grp AT) Am Overseas Bk Co.

— Safer Than a Known Way. 2nd rev. ed. (Illus.). 266p. 1988. 40.00 (*0-9588324-3-9*, Pub. by Delaware Grp AT) Am Overseas Bk Co.

— The Seven Tools of TQC. 4th ed. (Illus.). 176p. 1986. pap. 25.00 (*0-9588324-0-4*, Pub. by Delaware Grp AT) Am Overseas Bk Co.

McConnell, Kathleen. Salvation: A Comparative Analysis of Differing Theological Traditions. LC 94-17139. (Catholic Scholars Press Ser.). 264p. 1995. text ed. 64.95 (*1-883255-67-8*, Cath Scholar Pr) Intl Scholars.

— Salvation: A Comparative Analysis of Differing Theological Traditions. LC 94-17139. (Catholic Scholars Press Ser.). 264p. 1995. pap. text ed. 44.95 (*1-883255-66-X*) Intl Scholars.

McConnell, Keith. The AnimAlphabet Encyclopedia. (NaturEncyclopedia Library). (Illus.). 48p. (J). (gr. 4 up). 1982. pap. 5.95 (*0-916144-97-6*) Stemmer Hse.

— Dinosaurs from A to Z. (NaturEncyclopedia Library). (Illus.). 40p. (Orig.). (J). (gr. 2 up). 1988. pap. 5.95 (*0-88045-095-9*) Stemmer Hse.

— The ReptAlphabet Encyclopedia. (NaturEncyclopedia Ser.). (Illus.). 48p. (Orig.). (J). (gr. 4 up). 1984. pap. 5.95 (*0-88045-045-2*) Stemmer Hse.

— The SeAlphabet Encyclopedia. (NaturEncyclopedia Library). (Illus.). 48p. (J). (gr. 4 up). 1982. pap. 5.95 (*0-88045-016-9*) Stemmer Hse.

McConnell, Kenneth, et al. FAX: Facsimile Technology & Applications Handbook. 2nd ed. (Telecommunications Library). 400p. 1992. text ed. 78.00 (*0-89006-495-4*) Artech Hse.

McConnell, Kevin. Collecting Art Deco. LC 90-62902. (Illus.). 144p. 1990. 49.95 (*0-88740-279-8*) Schiffer.

— Heintz Art Metal. LC 90-64023. (Illus.). 128p. 1991. pap. 19.95 (*0-88740-298-4*) Schiffer.

— More Roycroft Art Metal. (Illus.). 160p. (Orig.). 1995. pap. 19.95 (*0-88740-848-6*) Schiffer.

— Redware, America's Folk Art Pottery. LC 88-64156. (Illus.). 96p. 1989. pap. 12.95 (*0-88740-159-7*) Schiffer.

— Roycroft Art Metal. LC 89-63420. (Illus.). 144p. 1989. pap. 14.95 (*0-88740-217-8*) Schiffer.

— Roycroft Art Metal. rev. ed. (Illus.). 144p. 1994. pap. 16.95 (*0-88740-694-7*) Schiffer.

— Spongeware & Spatterware. LC 90-60599. (Illus.). 128p. 1990. pap. 14.95 (*0-88740-253-4*) Schiffer.

***McConnell, Malcolm.** Inside Hanoi's Secret Archives. 1995. 25.00 (*0-671-87118-8*) S&S Trade.

— Into the Mouth of the Cat: The Story of Lance Sijan, a Hero of Vietnam. LC 84-14901. 253p. 1984. 13.95 (*0-393-01899-7*) Norton.

McConnell, Malcolm, jt. auth. see Ballard, Robert D.

McConnell, Malcolm, jt. auth. see Singlaub, John K.

McConnell, Malcolm, jt. auth. see Zuyev, Alexander.

McConnell, Marie-Antoinette, tr. see Rougeyron, Andre.

McConnell, Mark K. Risk a Thousand, Make a Million? How to Trade Stock Index Futures. (Illus.). 34p. (Orig.). 1989. pap. 6.95 (*0-9622816-0-3*) Capital Growth.

McConnell, Mary, jt. auth. see McConnell, Cecil.

McConnell, Mary M. Outdoor Adventures with Kids. 200p. 1994. pap. 12.95 (*0-87833-849-7*) Taylor Pub.

McConnell, Michael, jt. auth. see Golden, Renny.

McConnell, Michael N. A Country Between: The Upper Ohio Valley & Its Peoples, 1724-1774. LC 91-42867. (Illus.). xiv, 357p. 1992. 40.00 (*0-8032-3142-3*) U of Nebr Pr.

Mcconnell, Mick. Lax: The Los Angeles Experiment: Architecture Design. 1994. pap. 25.00 (*0-930829-36-0*) Lumen Inc.

McConnell, Missy. Plain Jane Vanilla. (Illus.). 48p. 1980. 22.00 (*0-88014-018-6*) Mosaic Pr OH.

McConnell, Molly. Advent: Prepare Ye the Way of the Lord. large type ed. (Illus.). 1987. pap. 9.95 (*0-8027-2598-8*) Walker & Co.

McConnell, Molly C. A Lenten Companion. LC 90-47610. (Illus.). 136p. (Orig.). 1990. pap. 9.95 (*0-8192-1543-0*) Morehouse Pub.

McConnell, Nancy P. Different & Alike. 3rd ed. Cliff, Donna, ed. LC 93-70957. (Illus.). 40p. (J). (gr. 1-6). 1993. pap. 7.20 (*0-944943-32-2*, CODE 22164-6) Current Inc.

— Dusty D. Dawg Has Feelings, Too! Gress, Jonna, ed. (Illus.). 16p. (J). (ps-3). 1992. pap. text ed. 14.25 (*0-944943-15-2*, CODE 20018-8) Current Inc.

— Please Touch the Animals! Gress, Jonna, ed. (Illus.). 12p. (J). (ps-00). 1992. reprint ed. pap. text ed. 16.20 (*0-944943-16-0*, CODE 20017-9) Current Inc.

McConnell, Nancy P., jt. auth. see Brummett, Nancy P.

McConnell, Nelie D. At the Miranda. 1981. 30.00 (*0-7223-1436-1*, Pub. by A H S Ltd UK) St Mut.

McConnell, P. S., et al. Adaptive Capabilities of the Nervous System. (Progress in Brain Research Ser.: Vol. 53). 107p. 1980. pap. 132.50 (*0-444-80207-X*) Elsevier.

McConnell, Patty. Adult Children of Alcoholics: A Workbook for Healing. 150p. (Orig.). 1986. pap. 11.95 (*0-86683-526-1*) Harper SF.

McConnell, Paul. Thing at the Threshold. Herber, Keith, ed. (Call of Cthulhu System Ser.). (Illus.). 98p. (Orig.). 1992. pap. text ed. 16.95 (*0-933635-90-7*, 2339) Chaosium.

McConnell, R., et al, eds. The Genetics & Epidemiology of Inflammatory Bowel Disease. (Frontiers of Gastrointestinal Research Ser.: Vol. 11). (Illus.). viii, 180p. 1986. 113.75 (*3-8055-4265-8*) S Karger.

McConnell, R. A. Introduction to Parapsychology in the Context of Science. LC 82-99945. (Illus.). xiv, 337p. 1983. pap. 12.00 (*0-9610232-3-6*) McConnell.

— Parapsychology in Retrospect: My Search for the Unicorn. LC 86-90590. (Illus.). 240p. (Orig.). 1987. pap. 15.00 (*0-9610232-4-4*) McConnell.

McConnell, R. A., ed. Encounters with Parapsychology. LC 81-90032. (Illus.). ix, 235p. 1982. pap. 9.00 (*0-9610232-1-X*) McConnell.

— Parapsychology & Self-Deception in Science. LC 81-90464. (Illus.). vii, 150p. 1983. pap. 7.00 (*0-9610232-2-8*) McConnell.

McConnell, R. A., jt. auth. see Schmeidler, Gertrude R.

McConnell, R. D. & Noufi, R., eds. Science & Technology of Thin Film Superconductors 2. (Illus.). 650p. 1990. 125.00 (*0-306-43803-8*, Plenum Pr) Plenum.

McConnell, R. D. & Wolf, Stuart A., eds. Science & Technology of Thin Film Superconductors. (Illus.). 572p. 1989. 115.00 (*0-306-43215-3*, Plenum Pr) Plenum.

McConnell, Rachel, jt. ed. see Brodie, David.

McConnell, Richard E. The Debt Penalty. LC 91-91155. 120p. 1991. 24.95 (*0-9630852-0-4*) R E McConnell.

***McConnell, Robert.** Far Out in the New Age: The Subversion of Science by Cultural Communism. LC 94-76288. (Illus.). iv, 200p. (Orig.). 1995. pap. 24.00 (*0-9610232-6-0*) McConnell.

McConnell, Robert L., et al. Electrical Engineering Design Compendium. (Illus.). 200p. (C). 1993. text ed. 25.75 (*0-201-56612-5*) Addison-Wesley.

McConnell, Robert R., ed. see Technical Association of the Pulp & Paper Industry Staff.

McConnell, Roland C. Negro Troops of Antebellum Louisiana: A History of the Battalion of Free Men of Color. LC 68-15430. (Louisiana State University Studies, Social Science Ser.: No. 13). 158p. reprint ed. pap. 45.10 (*0-317-08286-8*, 2007164) Bks Demand.

McConnell, Scott. Leftward Journey: The Education of Vietnamese Students in France, 1919-1939. 220p. 1988. 39.95 (*0-88738-238-X*) Transaction Pubs.

McConnell, Scott R., jt. auth. see Walker, Hill M.

McConnell, Sophie. Metropolitan Jewelry. (Illus.). 112p. 1991. 15.50 (*0-8212-1877-8*) Bulfinch Pr.

McConnell, Stella M., ed. see McConnell, David B.

McConnell, Steve. Code Complete: A Practical Handbook of Software Construction. LC 92-41059. 1993. 35.00 (*1-55615-484-4*) Microsoft.

McConnell, Stuart. Glorious Contentment: The Grand Army of the Republic, 1865-1900. LC 91-50793. (Illus.). xx, 312p. (C). 1992. 32.50 (*0-8078-2025-3*) U of NC Pr.

McConnell, T. R., jt. auth. see Mortimer, Kenneth P.

McConnell, Terrance. Gratitude. LC 92-25292. 288p. (C). 1993. 39.95 (*1-56639-038-9*) Temple U Pr.

McConnell, Thomas G. Conversations with General Grant: An Informal Biography. LC 89-29620. (Illus.). 248p. (Orig.). 1990. 19.95 (*1-878332-11-2*); pap. 9.95 (*1-878332-10-4*) Walnut VA.

McConnell, Vicki P. The Burnton Widows: A Nyla Wade Mystery. LC 94-42465. (Orig.). 1994. pap. 10.95 (*0-9630822-7-2*) Madwoman Pr.

— Double Daughter. 1994. pap. 9.95 (*0-9630822-5-6*) Madwoman Pr.

— Mrs. Porter's Letter. (Orig.). 1994. pap. 9.95 (*0-9630822-6-4*) Madwoman Pr.

McConnell, Weston J. Social Cleavages in Texas. LC 79-82237. (Columbia University. Studies in the Social Sciences: No. 265). reprint ed. 17.50 (*0-404-51265-8*) AMS Pr.

McConnell, William J. Frontier Law: A Story of Vigilante Days. LC 78-156027. (Illus.). reprint ed. 19.50 (*0-404-09177-6*) AMS Pr.

McConnell, Winder, tr. Kudrun. LC 92-16058. (Studies in German Literature, Linguistics & Culture: Vol. 73). 206p. 1992. 59.95 (*1-879751-12-7*) Camden Hse.

— The Lament of the Nibelungen. 248p. 1994. 55.95 (*1-879751-73-9*) Camden Hse.

McConnen, Harold L. Destruction. 128p. 1988. pap. write for info. (*0-318-64421-5*) Talking Leaf Pubs.

McConoch. Twentieth Century American Short Stories. 1986. 9.95 (*0-02-971270-X*) Macmillan.

McConochie. Twentieth Century American Short Stories. 1975. pap. 17.95 (*0-8384-3233-6*) Heinle & Heinle.

McConochie, Jean. Secret among the Ruins. (Readers Ser.). 1984. pap. text ed. 2.25 (*0-88345-575-7*) Prentice ESL.

— Twentieth-Century American Short Stories Vol. 1. 2nd rev. ed. 160p. 1995. pap. 16.95 (*0-8384-4851-8*) Heinle & Heinle.

McConochie, Jean & Therriault, Ginny W., eds. As Long as the Rivers Shall Run. (Readers Ser.). 1987. pap. text ed. 3.50 (*0-13-049297-3*) Prentice ESL.

McConochie, Jean, ed. see Agor, Barbara J. & Agor, Stewart C.

McConochie, Jean, ed. see Barkman, Bruce.

McConochie, Jean, ed. see Bernkopf, Michael.

McConochie, Jean, ed. see Brown, James W.

McConochie, Jean, ed. see Emanuel, James A.

McConochie, Jean, ed. see Gabriel, Gary.

McConochie, Jean, ed. see Gogan, Robert.

McConochie, Jean, ed. see Hale, Edward E.

McConochie, Jean, ed. see Kearney, Mary A. & Kearney, Edward.

McConochie, Jean, ed. see Messec, Jerry.

McConochie, Jean, jt. auth. see Osman, Alice H.

McConochie, Jean, ed. see Winer, Lise.

***McConochie, Jean A., comp.** An Anthology of Twentieth Century American Short Stories. LC 94-43027. 1995. pap. 20.95 (*0-8384-6146-8*) Heinle & Heinle.

McConoughey, Jana. Bald Eagle. LC 83-5162. (Wildlife Habits & Habitats Ser.). (Illus.). 48p. (J). (gr. 5). 1983. text ed. 12.95 (*0-89686-218-6*, Crstwood Hse) Silver Burdett Pr.

— Squirrels. LC 83-2085. (Wildlife Habits & Habitats Ser.). (Illus.). 48p. (J). (gr. 5). 1983. text ed. 12.95 (*0-89686-223-2*, Crstwood Hse) Silver Burdett Pr.

— The Wolves. LC 83-2086. (Wildlife Habits & Habitats Ser.). (Illus.). 48p. (J). (gr. 5). 1983. text ed. 12.95 (*0-89686-225-9*, Crstwood Hse) Silver Burdett Pr.

McConville, Chris. St. Kevin's College, 1918-1993. 336p. 44.95 (*0-522-84532-0*) Intl Spec Bk.

McConville, J. G. Chronicles. 288p. 1993. pap. 25.00 (*0-7152-0527-7*) St Mut.

— Judgment & Promise: An Interpretation of the Book of Jeremiah. 208p. 1993. pap. 14.95 (*0-931464-81-1*) Eisenbrauns.

McConville, J. Gordon. Grace in the End: A Study of Deuteronomic Theology. 176p. 1993. pap. 16.99 (*0-310-51421-5*) Zondervan.

***McConville, James & Rickaby, Glenys.** Shipping Business & Maritime Economics: An Annotated International Bibliography. annot. ed. LC 94-23314. 512p. 1995. 120.00 (*0-7201-2180-9*, Mansell Pub) Cassell.

***McConville, James & Sheldracke, John, eds.** Transport in Transition: Aspects of British & European Experience. 211p. (C). 1995. boxed, pap. text ed. 60.95 (*1-85628-664-9*, Pub. by Avebury Pub UK) Ashgate Pub Co.

McConville, John. Managing Construction Purchasing. 300p. 1993. 59.95 (*0-87629-316-X*, 67302) R S Means.

***McConville, Mark.** Adolescence: Psychotherapy & the Emergent Self. LC 95-16964. (Social & Behavioral Studies). 1995. 32.95 (*0-7879-0124-5*) Jossey-Bass.

McConville, Michael & Bridges, Lee, eds. Criminal Justice in Crisis. LC 94-5165. (Law in Its Social Setting Ser.). 1994. 59.95 (*1-85898-003-8*, Pub. by E Elgar Pub UK) Ashgate Pub Co.

McConville, Mike, et al. The Case for the Prosecution: Police Suspects & the Construction of Criminality. 256p. 1991. 74.50 (*0-415-05577-6*, A5673) Routledge.

— The Case for the Prosecution: Police Suspects & the Construction of Criminality. LC 93-14811. 240p. 1993. reprint ed. pap. 17.95 (*0-415-10103-4*, B0892) Routledge.

— Standing Accused: The Organization & Practices of Criminal Defence Lawyers in Britain. (Oxford Monographs on Criminal Law & Justice). 328p. 1994. 55.00 (*0-19-825868-2*) OUP.

McConville, Sean. English Local Prisons 1860-1900: Next Only to Death. LC 94-1389. (Illus.). 688p. 1995. 99.00x (*0-415-03295-4*, B2324) Routledge.

McConville, Sean, jt. ed. see Gottfredson, Stephen D.

McConway, Kevin, ed. Studying Health & Disease. LC 93-43194. (Health & Disease Ser.: Bk. 2). 132p. 1994. pap. 26.00 (*0-335-19252-1*, Open Univ Pr) Taylor & Francis.

McCoog, Thomas M., ed. see Bangert, William V.

McCook, Henry C. The Latimers. 1993. reprint ed. lib. bdg. 89.00 (*0-7812-5486-8*) Rprt Serv.

McCook, Kathleen de la Pena, et al, eds. Developing Readers' Advisory Services: Concepts & Commitments. LC 93-22853. 120p. 1993. pap. 29.95 (*1-55570-163-9*) Neal-Schuman.

McCool, A. Dimensions of Non-Commerical Foodservice Management. 392p. 1994. text ed. 44.95 (*0-442-01358-2*) Van Nos Reinhold.

***McCool, Audrey C.** Inflight Catering Management. LC 94-42490. 1995. text ed. 44.95 (*0-471-04253-6*) Wiley.

McCool, Daniel. Command of the Waters: Iron Triangles, Federal Water Development, & Indian Water. 321p. 1994. reprint ed. pap. 16.95 (*0-8165-1502-6*) U of Ariz Pr.

***McCool, Daniel, ed.** Public Policy Theories, Models & Concepts: An Anthology. LC 94-22744. 352p. 1994. pap. text ed. write for info. (*0-13-737867-X*) P-H.

— Waters of Zion: The Law, Policy, & Politics of Water in Utah. 256p. (Orig.). 1995. pap. text ed. 24.95 (*0-87480-473-6*) U of Utah Pr.

McCool, Daniel, jt. auth. see Clarke, Jeanne N.

McCool, Gerald. The Neo-Thomists. (Orig.). (C). 1994. pap. 20.00 (*0-87462-601-3*) Marquette.

McCool, Gerald A. From Unity to Pluralism: The Internal Evolution of Thomism. LC 89-80460. 250p. 1992. reprint ed. pap. 19.95 (*0-8232-1242-4*) Fordham.

— Nineteenth Century Scholasticism: The Quest for a Unitary Method. LC 89-85007. 301p. 1989. pap. 14.95 (*0-8232-1257-2*) Fordham.

McCool, Gerald A., ed. The Universe As Journey: Conversations with W. Norris Clarke, S.J. LC 88-80357. viii, 183p. (C). 1988. text ed. 60.00 (*0-8232-1208-4*) Fordham.

***McCool, Kenneth B.** Aviation Meteorology Unscrambled: For VFR & IFR Operations - Certificates & Ratings. 6th ed. LC 95-79659. (Illus.). 625p. (C). Date not set. pap. text ed. write for info. (*0-9621387-9-7*) K B McCool.

— Aviation Meteorology Unscrambled: For VFR & IFR Operations/Certificated & Ratings. rev. ed. (Illus.). 580p. (C). 1995. pap. text ed. 40.00 (*0-9621387-5-4*) K B McCool.

McCool, Samuel A., jt. auth. see Cornesky, Robert A.

McCord. Dinosaurs. (Picture History Ser.). (Illus.). (J). (gr. 4-6). 1977. lib. bdg. 13.96 (*0-88110-680-1*, Usborne); pap. 6.95 (*0-7460-1469-4*, Usborne) EDC.

— Prehistoric Mammals. (Picture History Ser.). (Illus.). (J). (gr. 4-6). 1977. pap. 13.96 (*0-88110-120-6*, Usborne); pap. 6.95 (*0-86020-128-7*, Usborne) EDC.

McCord, A. Prehistoric Life (B - U) (Picture History Ser.). (Illus.). 96p. (J). (gr. 2-7). 1993. pap. 12.95 (*0-86020-490-1*) EDC.

McCord Adams, Marilyn. William Ockham, 2 vols. LC 86-40337. (Mediaeval Studies: No. 26). 1216p. 1989. text ed. 90.00 (*0-268-01940-1*); pap. text ed. 42.95 (*0-268-01945-2*) U of Notre Dame Pr.

McCord, Arline, jt. auth. see McCord, William.

McCord, Bruce E. Designing Pneumatic Control Circuits: Efficient Techniques for Practical Application. LC 82-2103. (Fluid Power & Control Ser.: No. 2). (Illus.). 176p. reprint ed. pap. 50.20 (*0-7837-0940-4*, 2041245) Bks Demand.

McCord, Charles H. The American Negro As Dependent, Defective & Delinquent. 1973. 59.95 (*0-87968-609-X*) Gordon Pr.

McCord, Charles L., jt. auth. see Kneer, Marian E.

McCord, Christian. Across the Shining Mountains: The Odyssey Nathaniel Wyeth. LC 86-7238. (Frontier Library). 450p. 1987. 18.95 (*0-915463-31-8*) Green Hill.

McCord, Christopher K., ed. Nielsen Theory & Dynamical Systems: AMS-IMS-SIAM Joint Summer Research Conference on Nielsen Theory & Dynamical Systems. LC 93-26685. (Contemporary Mathematics Ser.: No. 152). 350p. 1993. pap. 52.00 (*0-8218-5181-0*) Am Math.

McCord, Cindy. Animal Rhythms Alphabet. (Illus.). 64p. (J). (ps-2). 1986. teacher ed, pap. 6.95 (*0-912107-69-3*, MM 976) Monday Morning Bks.

McCord, Cindy & Ross, Shirley. Animal Rhythms Consonants. 64p. (J). (ps-2). 1988. 6.95 (*0-912107-70-7*, MM977) Monday Morning Bks.

— Animal Rhythms Vowels. 64p. (J). (ps-2). 1988. 6.95 (*0-912107-71-5*, MM978) Monday Morning Bks.

McCord, Clinton D., Jr., et al, eds. Oculoplastic Surgery. 3rd ed. LC 94-11199. (Illus.). 6772p. 1995. text ed. 125.00 (*0-7817-0192-9*) Raven.

McCord, David. All Day Long: Fifty Rhymes of the Never Was & Always Is. (J). (gr. 4-7). 1992. mass mkt. 6.95 (*0-316-55532-0*) Little.

— All Small. (Illus.). (J). (gr. 6-8). 1986. lib. bdg. 12.95 (*0-316-55519-3*); mass mkt. 4.95 (*0-316-55520-7*) Little.

— As Built with Second Thoughts, Reforming What Was Old. pap. 2.00 (*0-686-70266-2*) Boston Public Lib.

— Harvard: A Living Portrait. Patrick, James B., ed. (College Ser.). 144p. 1982. 35.00 (*0-940078-02-3*) Foremost Pubs.

— One at a Time. (Illus.). (J). (gr. 4 up). 1986. 18.95 (*0-316-55516-9*) Little.

— Speak Up: More Rhymes of the Never Was & Always Is. (Illus.). 80p. (J). (gr. 5 up). 1980. 13.95 (*0-316-55517-7*) Little.

— Take Sky. (Illus.). (J). (gr. 4 up). 1962. 12.95 (*0-316-55509-6*) Little.

McCord, David & Cleveland, William. The Armstrongs of South Carolina: African American Magicians. (Illus.). 40p. 1989. pap. 16.95 (*0-685-26487-4*) Dreamkeeper Pr.

— Black & Red: The Historical Meeting of Africans & Native Americans. (Illus.). (Orig.). 1989. pap. 16.95 (*0-685-26486-6*) Dreamkeeper Pr.

McCord, David, et al. Art & Education. 1966. 5.00 (*0-89073-024-5*) Boston Public Lib.

McCord, David T. In Sight of Sever, Essays from Harvard. LC 63-19143. 298p. reprint ed. pap. 85.00 (*0-7837-2298-2*, 2057386) Bks Demand.

McCord, Edward A. The Power of the Gun: The Emergence of Modern Chinese Warlordism. LC 92-31375. 384p. 1993. 45.00 (*0-520-08128-5*) U CA Pr.

McCord, Grace D., jt. auth. see Long, John.

McCord, Howard. Fire Visions. (Orig.). 1970. pap. 6.00 (*0-686-66340-3*) Twowindows Pr.

— Friend. 1974. pap. 1.25 (*0-912284-54-4*) New Rivers Pr.

— Mirrors. (Illus.). 1973. 5.00 (*0-685-37097-6*) Stone-Marrow Pr.

McCord, Hugo. From Heaven or from Men. 1970. pap. 2.75 (*0-88027-033-0*) Firm Foun Pub.

— Hobbih Zabet - New Testament: Bilingual New Testament. 590p. (ENG & RUS.). 1992. pap. 4.75 (*1-56794-043-9*, A300R) Star Bible.

McCord, James. Borland C Plus Plus Programmer's Guide to Graphics. 800p. (Orig.). 1991. pap. 29.95 (*0-672-30201-2*) Sams.

— Borland C Plus Plus 3.1 Programmers Reference. 2nd ed. 1000p. 1992. pap. 29.95 (*1-56529-082-8*) Que.

— Developing Windows Applications with Borland C Plus Plus 3.1. 2nd ed. 1992. pap. 39.95 (*0-672-30060-5*) Sams.

— Developing Windows Three Applications with Borland C Plus Plus 3.1. 2nd ed. (Illus.). 4000p. 1991. pap. 39.95 (*0-672-30231-4*) Sams.

— Uninstalling Windows Applications. (Illus.). 208p. (Orig.). 1995. pap. 19.99 (*0-7897-0358-0*) Que.
— Windows NT Developers Treasure Chest. 1993. pap. 49.95 (*0-672-30294-2*) Sams.
— Windows Programmer's Guide to Borland C Plus Plus Tools. (Illus.). (Orig.). 1992. pap. 39.95 (*0-672-30177-6*) Sams.
— Windows 3.1 Programmer's Reference. 1100p. (Orig.). 1992. pap. 39.95 (*0-88022-787-7*) Que.
— Win32 API Desktop Reference. 1568p. 1993. 49.95 (*0-672-30364-7*) Sams.
McCord, James W. The Litigation Paralegal: A Systems Approach. 2nd ed. Hannan, ed. 510p. (C). 1992. text ed. 56.75 (*0-314-93370-0*) West Pub.
McCord, James W. H. & McCord, Sandra L. Criminal Law & Procedure for the Paralegal: A Systems Approach. LC 94-13488. 600p. 1994. text ed. 45.25 (*0-314-03917-1*) West Pub.
***McCord, Joan, ed.** Coercion & Punishment in Long-Term Perspectives. (Illus.). 400p. (C). 1995. 59.95 (*0-521-45069-1*) Cambridge U Pr.
— Facts, Frameworks, & Forecasts. (Advances in Criminological Theory Ser.: Vol. 3). 224p. (C). 1991. text ed. 39.95 (*0-88738-363-7*) Transaction Pubs.
***McCord, Joan & Laub, John H., eds.** Contemporary Masters in Criminology. (Plenum Series in Crime & Justice). 410p. 1995. 65.00 (*0-306-44960-9*) Plenum.
McCord, Joan & McCord, William. Origins of Crime: A New Evaluation of the Cambridge-Sommerville Youth Study. LC 69-14939. (Criminology, Law Enforcement, & Social Problems Ser.: No. 49). (C). 1969. reprint ed. 26.00 (*0-87585-049-9*); reprint ed. pap. 12.00 (*0-87585-908-9*) Patterson Smith.
McCord, Joan & Tremblay, Richard E., eds. Preventing Antisocial Behavior: Interventions from Birth Through Adolescence. LC 92-1444. 391p. 1992. lib. bdg. 40.00 (*0-89862-882-2*) Guilford Pr.
McCord, Joan, jt. auth. see McCord, William.
McCord, John H., et al. Course Materials on Buying, Selling, & Merging Businesses. 351p. 1975. Supplement 1978. 3.00 (*0-317-30795-9*, B145) Am Law Inst.
— Course Materials on Buying, Selling, & Merging Businesses, Incl. 1978 suppl. 351p. 1975. Incl. 1978 supplement. 51.00 (*0-317-30793-2*, B145/B146) Am Law Inst.
***McCord, John S.** The Baynes Clan No. 1: Montana Horseman. 256p. (Orig.). 1995. pap. text ed. 4.99 (*0-515-11532-0*) Jove Pubns.
— The Baynes Clan No. 2: Texas Comebacker. 256p. (Orig.). 1995. pap. text ed. 4.99 (*0-515-11585-1*) Jove Pubns.
— The Baynes Clan No. 3: Wyoming Giant. 256p. 1995. pap. text ed. 6.50 (*0-515-11651-3*) Jove Pubns.
McCord, Monty. Police Cars: A Photographic History. LC 91-61302. 304p. 1991. pap. 14.95 (*0-87341-171-4*) Krause Pubns.
McCord, Nancy. Please Don't Eat My Garden! Expert Strategies & Old. LC 91-39100. 160p. 1992. pap. 9.95 (*0-8069-8522-4*) Sterling.
McCord, Norman. The Anti-Corn League. (Modern Revivals in History Ser.). 224p. 1993. 59.95 (*0-7512-0147-2*, Pub. by Gregg Pub UK) Ashgate Pub Co.
— English History, 1815-1906. (Short Oxford History of the Modern World Ser.). 420p. 1991. 95.00 (*0-19-822857-0*, 10276); pap. 19.95 (*0-19-822858-9*) OUP.
— Strikes. 1980. text ed. 29.95 (*0-312-76640-8*) St Martin.
McCord, Robert. The Four Hundred Fifty-Nine Best Public Golf Courses in the United States, Canada, Mexico, & the Caribbean. LC 92-56832. 720p. 1993. pap. 20.00 (*0-679-73975-0*) Random.
— The Golf Book of Days: Fascinating Golf Facts & Stories for Every Day of the Year. LC 94-44302. 1995. 18.95 (*1-55972-292-4*, Birch Ln Pr) Carol Pub Group.
McCord, Sandra L., jt. auth. see McCord, James W. H.
***McCord, Shirley.** Travel Accounts of Indiana, 1679-1961. 331p. 1970. 10.00 (*1-885323-24-7*) IN Hist Bureau.
***McCord, Sue.** The Storybook Journey: Pathways to Literature Through Story & Play. LC 95-1304. 1995. write for info. (*0-13-183997-7*, Merrill Pub Co) Macmillan.
McCord, William. The Dawn of the Pacific Century: Implications for Three Worlds of Development. 224p. 1990. 34.95 (*0-88738-367-X*) Transaction Pubs.
McCord, William & McCord, Arline. Paths to Progress: Bread & Freedom in Developing Societies. LC 85-29809. 1986. 17.95 (*0-393-02307-9*) Norton.
McCord, William & McCord, Joan. Origins of Alcoholism. xi, 193p. 1960. 27.50 (*0-8047-0033-8*) Stanford U Pr.
McCord, William, jt. auth. see McCord, Joan.
McCordick, David, ed. The Civil War Letters of Private Henry Kauffman (1862-1865) The Harmony Boys Are All Well. LC 91-34380. (Illus.). 124p. 1991. lib. bdg. 59.95 (*0-7734-9684-X*) E Mellen.
McCorduck, Pamela. Aaron's Code: Meta-Art, Artificial Intelligence & the Work of Harold Cohen. LC 90-36940. (Illus.). 224p. (C). 1995. text ed. write for info. (*0-7167-2173-2*) W H Freeman.
McCorduck, Pamela, jt. auth. see Feigenbaum, Edward A.
McCorison. Additions & Corrections to Vermont Imprints. 1985. 3.50 (*0-912296-72-0*, Am Antiquarian) Am Antiquarian.
McCorison, Marcus A., comp. Additions & Corrections to Vermont Imprints, 1778-1820, 1. (Orig.). 1968. pap. 5.00 (*0-912296-35-6*, Am Antiquarian) Am Antiquarian.
— Additions & Corrections to Vermont Imprints, 1778-1820, 2. (Orig.). 1968. pap. 3.00 (*0-912296-36-4*, Am Antiquarian) Am Antiquarian.
McCorison, Marcus A., ed. see Thomas, Isaiah.
McCorkle, Beth. The Gurdjieff Years: 1929-1949: Recollections of Louise March. 106p. (Orig.). 1990. pap. write for info. (*0-9626729-0-4*) Work Study Assn.
— The Kramurg. (Illus.). 32p. (Orig.). (J). (gr. 1-8). 1991. pap. write for info. (*0-9626729-1-2*) Work Study Assn.
McCorkle, Chester O., Jr., ed. Economics of Food Processing in the United States. (Food Science & Technology Ser.). 449p. 1987. text ed. 92.00 (*0-12-482185-5*) Acad Pr.
McCorkle, Chester O. & Archibald, Sandra O. Management & Leadership in Higher Education. LC 82-48073. (Jossey-Bass Series in Higher Education). (Illus.). 264p. reprint ed. pap. 75.30 (*0-8357-4908-8*, 2037838) Bks Demand.
McCorkle, Constance M. Farmer Innovation in Niger. (Studies in Technology & Social Change: No. 21). 52p. (Orig.). (C). 1994. pap. 7.00 (*0-945271-33-6*) ISU-TSCP.
McCorkle, Constance M., ed. Plants, Animals, & People: Agropastoral Systems Research. 196p. (C). 1992. pap. text ed. 54.50 (*0-8133-8097-9*) Westview.
— The Social Sciences & International Agricultural Research: Lessons from the CRSPs. LC 89-32083. 300p. 1989. lib. bdg. 42.00 (*1-55587-133-X*) Lynne Rienner.
McCorkle, Constance M., jt. auth. see Mathias-Mundy, Evelyn.
McCorkle, Denny E. & Diriker, Mehmet F. The Self-Marketing Advantage for Business Careers: A Workbook & Resource Guide to Developing Self-Marketing Skills & Strategies for Student Career Planning & Job Search Success. 317p. (Orig.). (C). 1993. 30.00 (*0-9634230-0-2*) Self-Mktg Inst.
McCorkle, James. The Still Performance: Writing, Self, & Interconnection in Five Postmodern American Poets. LC 88-35305. 225p. 1989. text ed. 29.50 (*0-8139-1196-6*) U Pr of Va.
McCorkle, James, ed. Conversant Essays: Contemporary Poets & Poetry. LC 89-32152. 597p. (C). 1990. 45.00 (*0-8143-2099-6*); pap. text ed. 23.95 (*0-8143-2100-3*) Wayne St U Pr.
McCorkle, Jill. The Cheer Leader. 288p. 1984. 15.95 (*0-912697-11-3*) Algonquin Bks.
— The Cheer Leader. 288p. 1992. pap. 8.95 (*1-56512-001-9*, 72001, Frnt Porch PB) Algonquin Bks.
— Crash Diet. 1993. mass mkt. 4.99 (*0-449-22222-5*, Crest) Fawcett.
— Crash Diet: Stories by Jill McCorkle. Ravenel, Shannon, ed. 256p. 1992. 16.95 (*0-945575-75-0*) Algonquin Bks.
— Ferris Beach. 380p. 1990. 18.95 (*0-945575-39-4*) Algonquin Bks.
— Ferris Beach. 1991. mass mkt. 4.99 (*0-449-21996-8*) Fawcett.
— July Seventh. 368p. 1984. 17.95 (*0-912697-12-1*) Algonquin Bks.
— July Seventh. 400p. 1992. pap. 8.95 (*1-56512-002-7*, 72002, Frnt Porch PB) Algonquin Bks.
— Tending to Virginia. 328p. 1987. 15.95 (*0-912697-65-2*) Algonquin Bks.
— Tending to Virginia. 1988. mass mkt. 4.95 (*0-449-21624-1*, Crest) Fawcett.
— Tending to Virginia. large type ed. (General Ser.). 464p. 1989. lib. bdg. 19.95 (*0-8161-4698-5*, Large Print Bks) Hall.
McCorkle, John. Three Years with Quantrell. Barton, D. S., ed. LC 67-6851. (American Biography Ser.: No. 32). 1970. lib. bdg. 75.00 (*0-8383-1107-5*) M S G Haskell Hse.
McCorkle, John & Barton, O. S. Three Years with Quantrill: A True Story Told by His Scout. LC 92-54158. (Western Frontier Library: Vol. 60). (Illus.). 240p. 1992. 18.95 (*0-8061-2451-2*) U of Okla Pr.
McCorkle, Llyod, jt. auth. see MacNamara, Donal E.
McCorkle, Ruth & Grant, Marcia, eds. Pocket Companion for Cancer Nursing. LC 94-6847. (Illus.). 544p. 1994. pap. text ed. 34.50 (*0-7216-5410-X*) Saunders.
McCormac. Ohio Civil Rules Practice with Forms. 494p. 1970. 50.00 (*0-685-07349-1*) Anderson Pub Co.
— Ohio Civil Rules Practice with Forms. suppl. ed. 494p. 1991. 32.50 (*0-685-07350-5*) Anderson Pub Co.
McCormac, B. M. Radiation Trapped in the Earth's Magnetic Field. 908p. 1966. text ed. 251.00 (*0-677-01210-1*) Gordon & Breach.
McCormac, Billy M., ed. Atmospheres of Earth & the Planets. LC 75-4954. (Astrophysics & Space Science Library: No. 51). 430p. 1975. lib. bdg. 172.50 (*90-277-0575-5*) Kluwer Ac.
— Introduction to the Scientific Study of Atmospheric Pollution. LC 70-170340. 169p. 1971. lib. bdg. 69.00 (*90-277-0215-2*); pap. text ed. 36.50 (*90-277-0243-8*) Kluwer Ac.
— Magnetospheric Particles & Fields. (Astrophysics & Space Science Library: No. 58). 1976. lib. bdg. 112.50 (*90-277-0702-2*) Kluwer Ac.
— Weather & Climate Responses to Solar Variations. LC 82-73247. 636p. reprint ed. pap. 180.00 (*0-685-16387-3*, 2027297) Bks Demand.
McCormac, Billy M., ed. see Advanced Study Institute Staff.
McCormac, Billy M., ed. see Advanced Study Institute Symposium Staff & ESRO Symposium Staff.
McCormac, Billy M., ed. see Advanced Summer Institute Staff.
McCormac, Billy M., ed. see Summer Advanced Study Institute Staff.
***McCormac, E. I.** James K. Polk: A Political Biography Vol. 2: To the End of a Career 1845-1849. Speirs, Katherine E., ed. (Signature Ser.). (Illus.). 384p. 1995. reprint ed. 32.50 (*0-945707-10-X*) Amer Political.
— James K. Polk: A Political Biography Vol. I: To the Prelude to War 1795-1845. Speirs, Katherine E., ed. (Signature Ser.). (Illus.). 384p. 1995. reprint ed. 32.50 (*0-945707-09-6*) Amer Political.
McCormac, Eugene I. White Servitude in Maryland, 1634-1820. LC 78-63901. (Johns Hopkins University. Studies in the Social Sciences. Thirtieth Ser. 1912: 3-4). reprint ed. 15.00 (*0-404-61154-0*) AMS Pr.
McCormac, Jack C. Design of Reinforced Concrete. 2nd ed. 624p. (C). 1989. text ed. 51.25 (*0-06-044345-6*); write for info. (*0-318-59890-6*) HarpCollege.
— Reinforced Concrete. 3rd ed. (C). 1992. 82.00 (*0-06-500491-4*) HarpCollege.
— Structural Analysis. 4th ed. 640p. (C). 1989. text ed. 82.00 (*0-06-044342-1*) HarpCollege.
— Structural Steel Design. 4th ed. (C). 1992. text ed. 79.00 (*0-06-500060-9*) HarpCollege.
— Structural Steel Design: LRFD Method. 2nd ed. LC 94-29972. (C). 1995. 48.00 (*0-06-501627-0*) HarpC.
— Surveying. 3rd ed. LC 94-6281. 400p. 1994. pap. text ed. 45.00 (*0-13-031162-6*) P-H.
— Surveying Fundamentals. 2nd ed. 608p. 1990. text ed. 71.00 (*0-13-878026-9*) P-H.
McCormac, Jack C. & Elling, Rudolph E. Structural Analysis: A Classical & Matrix Approach. 5th ed. 608p. (C). 1989. text ed. 87.50 (*0-06-044341-3*) HarpCollege.
McCormac, John W. Ohio Civil Rules Practice with Forms. 494p. 1970. 50.00 (*0-87084-596-9*) Anderson Pub Co.
— Wrongful Death in Ohio, with Forms. LC 82-244891. (Illus.). 209p. 1982. 37.50 (*0-685-06820-X*) Anderson Pub Co.
— Wrongful Death in Ohio with Forms. 194p. 1982. 37.50 (*0-87084-560-8*) Anderson Pub Co.
— Wrongful Death in Ohio, with Forms. suppl. ed. LC 82-244891. (Illus.). 209p. 1989. 12.00 (*0-685-06821-8*) Anderson Pub Co.
McCormac, John W., et al. Anderson's Ohio Civil Practice with Forms, 7 vols., 8 bks., Set. 1991. ring bd. 475.00 (*0-87084-594-2*) Anderson Pub Co.
McCormac, Richard. Explorations in Macroeconomics. 1993. pap. text ed. 34.60 (*1-56226-153-3*) CT Pub.
— Explorations in Microeconomics. 3rd ed. 1993. pap. text ed. 36.70 (*1-56226-152-5*) CT Pub.
McCormack, jt. auth. see Chromcek.
McCormack, A. Ross. Reformers, Rebels, & Revolutionaries: The Western Canadian Radical Movement, 1899-1919. (Reprints in Canadian History Ser.). 256p. 1992. pap. 18.95 (*0-8020-7682-3*) U of Toronto Pr.
McCormack, Alan. Inventors Workshop. LC 80-84185. (Crafts Workshop Ser.). (J). (gr. 3-8). 1981. pap. 10.99 (*0-8224-9783-2*) Fearon Teach Aids.
***McCormack, Alan J.** The Great Bone Mysteries. (Illus.). 198p. (Orig.). 1990. pap. text ed. 19.95 (*1-885041-05-5*) Idea Factory.
McCormack, Alfred. History of Special Branch, M.I.S., in World War II. 84p. 1994. pap. 20.80 (*0-89412-231-2*) Aegean Park Pr.
McCormack, Allen E., ed. see Dance Magazine Inc. Staff.
McCormack, Allison, jt. auth. see Davis, William S.
McCormack, Andrew R. Reformers, Rebels, & Revolutionaries: The Western Canadian Radical Movement, 1899-1919. LC 78-4338. 246p. reprint ed. pap. 70.20 (*0-317-27019-2*, 2023646) Bks Demand.
McCormack, Barbara, jt. auth. see Borland, Deedee.
***McCormack, Bruce L.** Karl Barth's Critically Realistic Dialectical Theology: Its Genesis & Development 1909-1936. 500p. 1995. text ed. 65.00 (*0-19-826337-6*) OUP.
McCormack, Carol. The Joy of Backyard Boat Building. LC 84-2320. (Illus.). 207p. 1984. pap. 12.00 (*0-918024-32-3*) Ox Bow.
***McCormack, Colette.** Mary-Anne's Famine. (Bright Sparks Ser.). 116p. (Orig.). (YA). 1995. pap. 9.99 (*1-85594-185-6*, Pub. by Attic IE) InBook.
McCormack, Curt, jt. auth. see Rowland, Barbara.
McCormack, David R. RICO, 2 vols., Vols. 1 & 2. 1988. Vol. 1, 350 pp., Vol. 2, 350 pp. ring bd. 185.00 (*1-878337-18-1*) Knowles Law.
McCormack, David R., jt. auth. see McColl, Arch, III.
McCormack, Don & Kanda, Allen. McCormack's Contra Costa & Solano, 1993. (Illus.). 240p. (Orig.). 1993. pap. 6.95 (*0-931299-34-9*) McCormacks Guides.
— McCormack's Marin - Napa - Sonoma, 1993. (Annual Relocation Guides Ser.). (Illus.). 208p. (Orig.). 1993. pap. 6.95 (*0-931299-33-0*) McCormacks Guides.
— McCormack's Sacramento County, 1993. (Illus.). 176p. (Orig.). 1993. pap. 6.95 (*0-931299-32-2*) McCormacks Guides.
— McCormack's San Francisco & San Mateo, 1993. (Illus.). 224p. 1993. pap. 6.95 (*0-931299-37-3*) McCormacks Guides.
— McCormack's Santa Clara County, 1993. (Illus.). 192p. (Orig.). 1993. pap. 6.95 (*0-931299-36-5*) McCormacks Guides.
McCormack, Don, jt. auth. see Kanda, Allen.
***McCormack, Edward.** Now the Days Are Getting Shorter: Poems for Those in a Captured Audience. 1994. 12.95 (*0-533-10847-0*) Vantage.
McCormack, Eric. The Mysterium: A Novel of Deconstructionism. 272p. 1994. 20.95 (*0-312-11320-X*) St Martin.
McCormack, Erliss. Cairn Terriers. (Illus.). 160p. 1989. lib. bdg. 11.95 (*0-86622-871-3*, KW169) TFH Pubns.
McCormack, Frank. Never Lose: A Decade of Sports & Politics in Sacramento. LC 89-80370. 200p. (Orig.). 1989. pap. 16.95 (*0-9622140-9-4*) First Ink Pub Hse.
McCormack, Gavan. Chang Tso-lin in Northeast China, 1911-1928: China, Japan, & the Manchurian Idea. LC 76-48028. (Illus.). x, 334p. 1977. 42.50 (*0-8047-0945-9*) Stanford U Pr.
McCormack, Gavan, ed. Democracy in Contemporary Japan. LC 86-17744. 272p. 1986. pap. text ed. 25.95 (*0-87332-398-X*) M E Sharpe.
McCormack, Gavan & Gittings, John, eds. The Crisis in Korea. 190p. 1977. pap. 22.50 (*0-85124-187-5*, Pub. by Spokesman Bks UK) Coronet Bks.
McCormack, Gavan, jt. auth. see Halliday, Jon.
McCormack, Gavan, jt. auth. see Lone, Stewart.
McCormack, Gavan, jt. auth. see Nelson, Hank.
McCormack, J., et al. X Tool Kit: Intrinsics & Athena Widgets. 300p. (Orig.). 1990. pap. 29.95 (*0-929306-04-X*) Silicon Pr.
McCormack, Jack. Structural Steel Design Using the LRFD Method. 432p. (C). 1990. 82.00 (*0-06-044346-4*) HarpCollege.
***McCormack, James, et al.** Drug Therapy Decision Making Guide. 992p. 1995. pap. text ed. write for info. (*0-7216-4215-2*) Saunders.
McCormack, James G. & Cobbold, Peter H., eds. Cellular Calcium: A Practical Approach. (Practical Approach Ser.). (Illus.). 400p. 1991. 79.00 (*0-19-963131-X*, IRL Pr); pap. 44.00 (*0-19-963130-1*, IRL Pr) OUP.
McCormack, Jerusha H. John Gray: Poet, Dandy, & Priest. LC 90-50906. (Illus.). 334p. 1991. text ed. 45.00 (*0-87451-533-5*) U Pr of New Eng.
McCormack, Jerusha H., intro. The Selected Prose of John Gray. LC 92-81206. (British Authors, 1880-1920 Ser.). 316p. 1992. lib. bdg. 30.00 (*0-944318-06-1*) ELT Pr.
***McCormack, Joe.** Conqueror. 1995. 14.95 (*0-8062-5289-8*) Carlton.
***McCormack, John.** Fields & Pastures New: My First Year As a Country Vet. 1995. 23.00 (*0-517-59686-5*, Crown) Crown Pub Group.
Mccormack, John. Self Made in America: Plain Talk for Plain People about Extraordinary Success. 1990. 19.18 (*0-201-55099-7*) Addison-Wesley.
McCormack, John & Legge, David R. Self-Made in America: Plain Talk for Plain People about the Meaning of Success. (Illus.). 240p. 1992. pap. 9.57 (*0-201-60823-5*) Addison-Wesley.
McCormack, John A. Deathblow. LC 87-91069. 1988. 18.95 (*0-87212-207-7*) Libra.
— Murder at the Arma Homecoming. 153p. (Orig.). 1989. pap. 4.95 (*0-685-29964-3*) Lester Allen & Sherrill.
McCormack, John E. Watch for a Cloud of Dust: Memories of a Dixie Veterinarian. LC 85-81587. 193p. (Orig.). 1985. pap. 4.95 (*0-932147-01-1*) Hoard & Sons Co.
— Watch for a Cloud of Dust II: More Memories of a Dixie Veterinarian. LC 85-81587. 192p. (Orig.). 1990. pap. 4.95 (*0-932147-09-7*) Hoard & Sons Co.
McCormack, Kathleen. Definitive Book of Tarot. (Illus.). 177p. 1989. 10.95 (*0-88079-468-2*) US Games Syst.
McCormack, Kelli, ed. see Stone, Scott C.
McCormack, Kenneth A. Broken Promise. 99p. (C). 1989. text ed. 45.00 (*1-872795-65-X*, Pub. by Pentland Pr UK) St Mut.
McCormack, M. D., jt. auth. see Tatham, Robert H.
McCormack, Maida, jt. auth. see Coker, Sharon.
McCormack, Mark. World of Professional Golf, 1994. 1993. 29.95 (*0-87884-306-X*) Unicorn Ent.
McCormack, Mark H. Hit the Ground Running: The Insider's Guide to Executive Travel. 268p. Date not set. pap. 14.00 (*1-878843-09-5*) Intl Merc OH.
— McCormack: On Negotiating. 288p. 1995. 19.95 (*0-7871-0295-4*) Dovebks.
— One Hundred & Ten Percent Solution: Using Good Old American Know-How to Manage Your Time. 1991. 19.50 (*0-394-57256-4*, Villard Bks) Random.
— The Terrible Truth about Lawyers: What I Should Have Learned at Yale Law School. 1988. mass mkt. 4.95 (*0-380-70652-0*) Avon.
— What They Don't Teach You at Harvard Business School: Notes from a Street-Smart Executive. 1986. pap. 13.95 (*0-553-34583-4*) Bantam.
— What They Still Don't Teach You at Harvard Business School: Selling More, Managing Better, & Getting the Job Done in the '90s. 1990. pap. 13.95 (*0-553-34961-9*) Bantam.
— The World of Professional Golf, Nineteen Ninety-One. (Illus.). 596p. 1991. 24.95 (*1-878843-01-X*) Intl Merc OH.
— The World of Professional Golf 1989: Presented by ICI. (Illus.). 556p. 1989. 24.95 (*0-9615344-5-1*) Intl Merc OH.
— The World of Professional Golf, 1990. (Illus.). 1990. 24.95 (*0-9615344-8-6*) Intl Merc OH.
— The World of Professional Golf, 1992. 1992. 24.95 (*0-685-57141-6*) Contemp Bks.
— The World of Professional Golf, 1994. (Illus.). 640p. 1994. 29.95 (*1-878843-06-0*) Intl Merc OH.
— The World of Professional Golf, 1995. (Illus.). 640p. 1995. 29.95 (*1-878843-12-5*) Intl Merc OH.
— World of Professional Golf '92. 1992. 24.95 (*0-87884-303-5*) Unicorn Ent.
McCormack, Michael, ed. see Cox, Arthur B., Jr.
McCormack, Michael K., ed. Prevention of Mental Retardation & Other Developmental Disabilities. LC 80-24771. (Pediatric Habilitation Ser.: No. 1). (Illus.). 680p. reprint ed. pap. 180.00 (*0-7837-0831-9*, 2041145) Bks Demand.
McCormack, Nancy. Death: Words of Comfort. 82p. 1986. 35.00 (*0-7223-2029-9*, Pub. by A H S Ltd UK) St Mut.
McCormack, Nancy, ed. see Kirby, Jackie M.
McCormack, Nell J. Creative Quantity Cooking. LC 89-186. 369p. 1989. 101.00 (*0-8342-0058-9*) Aspen Pub.
McCormack, P. D., et al, eds. Terrestrial Space Radiation & Its Biological Effects. (NATO ASI Series A, Life Sciences: Vol. 154). (Illus.). 850p. 1988. 165.00 (*0-306-43020-7*, Plenum Pr) Plenum.
McCormack, Peggy. The Rule of Money: Gender, Class, & Exchange Economics in the Fiction of Henry James. LC 89-20489. (Studies in Modern Literature: No. 116). 132p. (C). reprint ed. 37.40 (*0-8357-2059-4*, 2070743) Bks Demand.
McCormack, Pete. Shelby. LC 93-27527. 267p. 1994. 22.00 (*1-877946-47-8*) Permanent Pr.

An Asterisk (*) at the beginning of an entry indicates that the title is appearing in BIP for the first time.

McCormack Publishing Co. Staff, ed. InnViews: The Traveler's Guide to Unique Accommodations. (Illus.). 470p. 1992. ring bd. 72.50 (*1-880956-00-4*) McCormack Pub.

McCormack, T. J., tr. see Mach, Ernst.

McCormack, Thelma, ed. The Decade of Dissent: Impact of the Sixties. (Studies in Communications Ser.: Vol. 1). 200p. 1980. lib. bdg. 73.25 (*0-89232-146-6*) Jai Pr.

McCormack, Thelma, jt. auth. see Crum, Gary.

McCormack, Thomas. The Fiction Editor. 1988. 12.95 (*0-312-02209-3*) St Martin.

— The Fiction Editor, the Novel & the Novelist. 224p. 1994. pap. 6.95 (*0-312-11467-2*) St Martin.

— The Financial Health of the American Furniture Industry. LC 94-8697. 1994. 280.00 (*0-921577-42-7*) AKTRIN.

McCormack, Thomas J., tr. see Cumont, Franz.

McCormack, Thomas P. The AIDS Benefits Handbook: Everything You Need to Know to Get Social Security, Welfare, Medicaid, Medicare, Food Stamps, Housing, Drugs, & Other Benefits. 240p. (C). 1990. text ed. 32.00 (*0-300-04736-3*); pap. 12.00 (*0-300-04721-5*) Yale U Pr.

***McCormack, Thomas W.** American Demand for Household Furniture & Anticipated Trends. 2nd ed. 70p. (Orig.). 1994. pap. 280.00 (*0-921577-46-X*) AKTRIN.

— The American Demand for Office Furniture & Anticipated Trends. 2nd ed. LC 94-20733. 72p. 1994. pap. text ed. 280.00 (*0-921577-44-3*) AKTRIN.

— The Canadian Demand for Household Furniture & Anticipated Trends: Handbook of Furniture Manufacturing & Retailing. 3rd ed. LC 93-43951. (Illus.). 60p. 1993. pap. 280.00 (*0-921577-39-7*) AKTRIN.

— The Canadian Demand for Office Furniture & Anticipated Trends. 3rd ed. LC 94-45282. 76p. (Orig.). 1995. pap. text ed. 280.00 (*0-921577-48-6*) AKTRIN.

— Employment & Wages in Furniture Manufacturing & Retailing in the U. S. A. LC 93-33188. (Handbook of Furniture Manufacturing & Retailing Ser.: Vol. 8, Ch. 2). (Illus.). 68p. (Orig.). 1993. pap. 280.00 (*0-921577-35-4*, HD5718.F92U65) AKTRIN.

— Employment & Wages in Furniture Manufacturing & Trading in Canada. 2nd ed. LC 95-11576. 65p. 1995. 280.00 (*0-921577-51-6*) AKTRIN.

McCormack, Tom. American Roulette. 1969. pap. 2.75 (*0-8222-0036-8*) Dramatists Play.

McCormack, Vincent & O'Hara, Joe. Enduring Inequality: Religious Discrimination in Employment in Northern Ireland. 79p. (C). 1990. pap. text ed. 35.00 (*0-946088-37-3*, Pub. by NCCL UK) St Mut.

McCormack, Vincent F. Developing Microcomputer Models for Cost Analysis & Decision Making. 1994. pap. text ed. write for info. (*0-07-044772-1*) McGraw.

McCormack, W. J. Ascendancy & Tradition in Anglo-Irish Literary History from 1789 to 1939. LC 84-27182. 384p. 1985. 55.00 (*0-19-812806-1*) OUP.

— Dissolute Characters: Irish Literary History Through Balzac, Sheridan Le Fanu, Yeats, & Bowen. LC 92-37200. 1993. text ed. 69.95 (*0-7190-3962-2*, Pub. by Manchester Univ Pr UK) St Martin.

— The Dublin Paper War of 1786-88. 176p. 1993. text ed. 39.50 (*0-7165-2505-4*, Pub. by Irish Acad Pr IE) Intl Spec Bk.

McCormack, W. J. & Stead, Alistair, eds. James Joyce & Modern Literature. 224p. 1982. 29.50 (*0-7100-9058-7*, RKP) Routledge.

McCormack, W. J., ed. see Edgeworth, Maria.

McCormack, W. J., ed. see Le Fanu, Joseph S.

McCormack, W. J., ed. see Trollope, Anthony.

McCormack, William & Krishnamurthi, M. G. Kannada: A Cultural Introduction to the Spoken Styles of the Language. 216p. 1966. text ed. 22.75 (*0-299-03840-8*) U of Wis Pr.

McCormack, William C. & Wurm, Stephen A. Approaches to Language: Anthropological Issues. (World Anthropology Ser.). xiv, 674p. 1978. 93.50 (*90-279-7660-0*) Mouton.

McCormack, William C. & Wurm, Stephen A., eds. Language & Society. (World Anthropology Ser.). 771p. 1979. text ed. 90.00 (*90-279-7800-X*) Mouton.

***McCormally, Kevin.** Kiplinger's New-Ways to Save On Your Taxes. 1995. pap. 15.00 (*0-8129-2643-9*, Times Bks) Random.

— Kiplinger's Sure Way to Cut Your Taxes 1995. 1995. pap. 13.95 (*0-938721-36-4*) Kiplinger Bks.

— Kiplinger's Sure Ways to Cut Your Taxes. 1994. pap. 13.95 (*0-938721-29-1*) Kiplinger Bks.

— New Ways to Save on Your Taxes. 1995. 13.95 (*0-938721-40-2*) Kiplinger Bks.

McCormally, Timothy J., ed. see Tax Executives Institute, Inc. Staff.

McCormich, Colin, jt. auth. see Sabbionet, Anna M.

***McCormick.** The Global Environmental Movement. 2nd ed. Date not set. pap. text ed. 34.95 (*0-471-94940-X*) Wiley.

McCormick & Fritz. Damages. 2nd ed. 1952. text ed. 27.00 (*0-88277-356-9*) Foundation Pr.

McCormick & Rushman. Deductive Interpretation of Progressed Horoscopes. LC 77-10369. 120p. 1977. 8.00 (*0-86690-127-2*, M1306-014) Am Fed Astrologers.

McCormick, jt. auth. see Pressley.

***McCormick & Co. Staff.** McCormick/Schilling New Spice Cookbook. LC 94-33284. 1994. write for info. (*0-87502-251-0*) Benjamin Co.

McCormick, A. Science Now: Health Physics. (C). 1989. 50.00 (*0-7487-0205-9*, Pub. by S Thornes Pubs UK) St Mut.

McCormick, Allen, ed. Germans in America: Aspects of German-American Relations in the Nineteenth Century. LC 82-61910. (Studies on Society in Change: No. 27). 1983. text ed. 48.00 (*0-88033-025-2*) Col U Pr.

McCormick, Anita L. Shortwave Listener's Q & A Book. 1994. pap. text ed. 12.95 (*0-07-044774-8*) McGraw.

— Shortwave Radio Listening for Beginners. 1993. pap. 10.95 (*0-07-044991-0*); pap. text ed. 19.95 (*0-07-044990-2*) McGraw.

— Shortwave Radio Listening for Beginners. LC 92-41603. 1993. 18.95 (*0-8306-4136-X*); pap. 10.60 (*0-8306-4135-1*) TAB Bks.

— Space Exploration. LC 93-1830. (Overview Ser.). (J). (gr. 4 up). 1994. 16.95 (*1-56006-149-9*) Lucent Bks.

— Vanishing Wetlands. (Lucent Overview Ser.). (Illus.). (J). (gr. 5-8). 1995. 16.95 (*1-56006-162-6*) Lucent Bks.

McCormick, Anne. World at Home. LC 70-121486. (Essay Index Reprint Ser.). 1977. 23.95 (*0-8369-1985-8*) Ayer.

McCormick, B. J. Hayek & the Keynesian Avalanche. LC 92-8903. 304p. 1992. text ed. 65.00 (*0-312-08359-9*) St Martin.

— The World Economy: Patterns of Growth & Change. LC 88-14639. 256p. (Orig.). (C). 1988. lib. bdg. 75.50 (*0-389-20800-0*, N8358); pap. text ed. 38.50 (*0-389-20801-9*, N8359) B&N Imports.

McCormick, Barbara. Outreach Teaching. 110p. 1979. 6.00 (*0-934024-06-5*) Intl Childbirth.

***McCormick, Barnes W.** Aerodynamics, Aeronautics & Fight Mechanics. 2nd ed. LC 94-222312. 1994. text ed. write for info. (*0-471-57506-2*) Wiley.

McCormick, Barnes W., Jr. Aerodynamics, Aeronautics & Flight Mechanics. LC 79-11073. 652p. 1979. Net. text ed. write for info. (*0-471-03032-5*) Wiley.

McCormick, Barnes W., Jr., ed. Aerodynamics of V-STOL Flight. 1967. text ed. 66.00 (*0-12-482350-5*) Acad Pr.

***McCormick, Barnes W. & Papadakis, Myron P.** Aviation Accident Reconstruction & Litigation. (Illus.). 800p. 1995. text ed. 99.00 (*0-913875-15-5*, 5155) Lawyers & Judges.

***McCormick, Barrett & Unger, Jonathan, eds.** China after Socialism: In the Footsteps of Eastern Europe or East Asia? (Socialism & Social Movements Ser.). (Illus.). 262p. 1995. 55.00 (*1-56324-666-X*); pap. 25.00 (*1-56324-667-8*) M E Sharpe.

McCormick, Barrett L. Political Reform in Post-Mao China: Democracy & Bureaucracy in a Leninist State. LC 89-20440. 256p. 1990. 42.00 (*0-520-06765-7*) U CA Pr.

McCormick, Barry. Paediatric Audiology: Zero to Five Years. 280p. 1988. 80.00 (*0-85066-462-4*); pap. 36.00 (*0-85066-463-2*) Singular Publishing.

***McCormick, Barry, ed.** The Medical Practitioners' Guide to Paediatric Audiology. (Illus.). 100p. (C). 1995. pap. write for info. (*0-521-45988-5*) Cambridge U Pr.

McCormick, Barry, et al. Cochlear Implants for Young Children: The Nottingham Approach to Assessment & Habilitation. (Illus.). 300p. (Orig.). (C). 1994. pap. text ed. 52.50 (*1-56593-372-9*, 0720) Singular Publishing.

McCormick, Betty L., ed. Quality & Education: Critical Linkages. (Illus.). 325p. 1993. 35.95x (*1-883001-04-8*) Eye On Educ.

McCormick, Bob. The Story of Tahoe Tessie: The Original Lake Tahoe Monster. 5th rev. ed. (Illus.). (J). (gr. 1-4). 1990. pap. 5.95 (*0-9626792-6-7*) Tahoe Tourist.

McCormick, Bret, jt. auth. see Steinfeld, Adam.

McCormick, C. A., ed. see Pirandello, Luigi.

McCormick, C. B., et al, eds. Cognitive Strategy Research. (Illus.). 345p. 1989. 68.00 (*0-387-96869-5*) Spr-Verlag.

McCormick, C. P., Jr. Pepper People. LC 92-75558. 1993. write for info. (*0-87502-246-4*) Benjamin Co.

McCormick, Carlo. Anton Van Dalen - "The Memory Cabinet" (Illus.). 32p. (Orig.). 1988. pap. 15.00 (*0-913263-24-9*) Exit Art.

— The Strange Case of T.L. Art by Tony Labat & Fiction by Carlo McCormick. 56p. 1995. 15.00 (*0-9631095-4-5*) Artspace Bks.

McCormick, Carlo, et al. Joshua Neustein. (Illus.). 47p. (Orig.). 1987. pap. 15.00 (*0-913263-18-4*) Exit Art.

McCormick, Carlynn L. & Chamberlin, J. Allen. Psychiatry: Help or Betrayal? An Authoritative Text on the History & Development of Psychiatry. 1991. pap. 12.95 (*0-9631117-0-1*) Gavilan Hills.

McCormick, Charles H. Leisler's Rebellion. (Outstanding Studies in Early American History). 417p. 1989. reprint ed. 25.00 (*0-8240-6190-X*) Garland.

— This Nest of Vipers: McCarthyism & Higher Education in the Mundel Affair, 1951-52. LC 88-29592. (Illus.). 248p. 1989. 24.95 (*0-252-01614-9*) U of Ill Pr.

McCormick, Charles T. & Aaron, Richard I. Evidence: Adaptable to Courses Utilizing Materials by McCormick. LC 87-114969. (Legalines Ser.). 318p. 12.95 (*0-685-18530-3*) HarBrace.

McCormick, Charles T., et al. Author's Suggestions for the Use of Cases & Materials on Federal Courts. 9th ed. (University Casebook Ser.). 44p. (C). 1992. pap. text ed. write for info. (*1-56662-054-6*) Foundation Pr.

— Cases & Materials on Federal Courts. 9th ed. LC 92-5649. (University Casebook Ser.). 1992. text ed. 42.95 (*0-88277-991-5*) Foundation Pr.

— Evidence, Cases & Materials. 7th ed. LC 92-5652. (American Casebook Ser.). 932p. 1992. text ed. 47.50 (*0-314-00426-2*) West Pub.

McCormick, Christine, jt. auth. see Pressley, Michael.

McCormick, Christine E. & Mason, Jana M. Little Books, Ages Four-Six. 80p. 1989. pap. 8.95 (*0-673-38878-6*) GdYrBks.

McCormick, Claire. Murder in Cowboy Bronze. 192p. 1985. 14.95 (*0-8027-5623-9*) Walker & Co.

McCormick, Colin. An Italian Vocabulary. Sabbione, Anna M., ed. 112p. (C). 1988. 65.00 (*0-86787-064-8*, Pub. by S Thornes Pubs UK) St Mut.

McCormick, Curtis & Steele, Valerie, eds. Washington Representatives 1992: Sixteenth Annual Edition. 825p. (Orig.). 1992. pap. 60.00 (*0-910416-97-4*) Columbia Bks.

McCormick, D. B., jt. ed. see Edmondson, D. E.

McCormick, David, jt. auth. see Huguenard, John.

McCormick, David A., jt. auth. see Huguenard, John.

McCormick, Dell J. Paul Bunyan Swings His Axe. LC 36-33409. (Illus.). (J). (gr. 4-6). 1936. 11.95 (*0-87004-093-6*) Caxton.

— Tall Timber Tales: More Paul Bunyan Stories. LC 39-20778. (Illus.). (J). (gr. 4-6). 1939. 11.95 (*0-87004-094-4*) Caxton.

McCormick, Donald. Erotic Literature: A Connoisseur's Guide. LC 92-6970. 288p. 1992. 24.95 (*0-8264-0574-6*) Continuum.

— Seventeen F the Life of Ian Fleming. 232p. 1994. 35.00 (*0-7206-0888-0*, Pub. by P Owen Ltd UK) Dufour.

***McCormick, Donald B., ed.** Annual Review of Nutrition, Vol. 15. 1995. lib. bdg. 48.00 (*0-8243-2815-9*) Annual Reviews.

— Vitamins & Hormones, Vol. 42. 372p. 1985. text ed. 134.00 (*0-12-709842-9*) Acad Pr.

McCormick, Donald B., jt. ed. see Aurbach, Gerald D.

McCormick, Donald D., ed. Vitamins & Hormones, Vol. 40. (Serial Publication Ser.). 1983. text ed. 134.00 (*0-12-709840-2*) Acad Pr.

McCormick, Donald M., jt. ed. see Aurbach, Gerald D.

McCormick, Donald W., jt. auth. see Hemphill, Phyllis D.

McCormick, E. Allen. Theodor Storm's Novellen: Essays on Literary Technique. LC 64-64253. (North Carolina. University. Studies in the Germanic Languages & Literatures: No. 47). reprint ed. 27.00 (*0-404-50947-9*) AMS Pr.

McCormick, E. Allen, jt. auth. see Ryder, Frank G.

McCormick, Edgar L. They Also Served: Citizen Soldiers in the Air Force Training & Service Commands. LC 93-32304. (Illus.). 200p. (C). 1994. 19.95 (*0-942597-60-5*, Burd St Pr) White Mane Pub.

McCormick, Edward A., tr. see Lessing, Gotthold E.

McCormick, Elizabeth W. The Heart Attack Recovery Book: A Look at the Emotional & Practical Problems Encountered During Rehabilitation, for Patients & Their Families. 1991. pap. 9.95 (*0-904575-37-3*, Coventure Ltd) Sigo Pr.

***McCormick, Ellen.** Our Good Teachers: What the Real Experts Are Saying about Education. 96p. 1995. pap. 8.95 (*0-9629972-5-0*) Meredith VA.

McCormick, Ellen R., jt. auth. see Oliver, Carolyn C.

McCormick, Ernest J. & IlGen, Daniel. Industrial & Organizational Psychology. 8th ed. (Illus.). 480p. (C). 1984. text ed. write for info. (*0-13-463092-0*) P-H.

McCormick, Ernest J., jt. auth. see Sanders, Mark S.

McCormick, Floyd G. The Power of Positive Thinking. LC 92-42276. 336p. 1994. 39.50 (*0-89464-831-4*) Krieger.

McCormick, Frank. Sir John Vanbrugh: A Reference Guide. LC 92-13099. (Reference Bks.). 200p. 1992. text ed. 45.00 (*0-8161-8990-0*, Hall Reference) Macmillan.

McCormick, Frank G. Sir John Vanbrugh: The Playwright as Architect. (Illus.). 224p. 1991. 32.50 (*0-271-00723-0*) Pa St U Pr.

McCormick, G. P., jt. auth. see Fiacco, A. V.

McCormick, Gail J. Our Proud Past, Vol. I. rev. ed. 186p. 1993. 18.95 (*0-9635889-1-5*) G McCormick Pub.

McCormick, Gary E. One of the Many Roses. 80p. (Orig.). 1991. pap. 9.50 (*0-9630037-0-4*) GEM MI.

McCormick, Gene. Uncompromising Chess: The Games of Viktor Kupreichik. 66p. (Orig.). 1986. pap. 6.00 (*0-931462-58-4*) Chess Ent Inc.

McCormick, Gordon H. & Bissell, Michael E., eds. Strategic Dimensions of Economic Behavior. LC 84-13292. 288p. 1984. text ed. 45.00 (*0-275-91225-6*, C1225, Praeger Pubs) Greenwood.

McCormick, Harold J. Two Years Behind the Mast: An American Landlubber at Sea in World War Two. (Illus.). 147p. (Orig.). 1991. pap. 16.00 (*0-89745-138-4*) Sunflower U Pr.

McCormick, Harvey L. Medicare & Medicaid Claims & Procedures, 2 vols. LC 86-9150. 1440p. 1986. text ed. write for info. (*0-314-97401-6*) West Pub.

— Social Security Claims & Procedure, Vols. 1 & 2. 4th ed. 1991. text ed. write for info. (*0-314-77340-1*); Vol. 1, 549p. write for info. (*0-318-67297-9*); Vol. 2, 706 p. write for info. (*0-318-67298-7*) West Pub.

McCormick, Hugh D. Confederate Son. 260p. 1993. 17.95 (*0-9636351-0-7*) Shenandoah Univ.

McCormick, J. Life of the Forest. (Our Living World of Nature Ser.). 1966. 18.95 (*0-07-044875-2*) McGraw.

McCormick, J. Frank, jt. ed. see Kormondy, Edward J.

McCormick, J. Michael & Thiruvathukal, John V. Elements of Oceanography. 464p. 1993. per. 46.95 (*0-8403-8625-7*) Kendall-Hunt.

— Elements of Oceanography. 2nd ed. 448p. (C). 1981. text ed. 47.00 (*0-03-057806-X*) SCP.

McCormick, Jack, jt. comp. see Leonard, Larry.

McCormick, James, jt. auth. see Skrabanek, Petr.

McCormick, James B. Eighteenth Century Microscopes: Synopsis of History & Workbook. (History of Microscopy Ser.). 88p. 1987. 52.00 (*0-940095-01-7*) Sci Heritage Ltd.

McCormick, James C. The Stone Bruise. LC 93-70998. 386p. 1993. 23.00 (*1-880909-11-1*) Baskerville.

McCormick, James M. American Foreign Policy & Process. 2nd ed. LC 91-67848. 584p. 1992. pap. 35.00 (*0-87581-360-7*) Peacock Pubs.

McCormick, James R., jt. auth. see Choy, Penelope.

McCormick, Janice, jt. ed. see Frommer, Judith G.

McCormick, Jennie, jt. auth. see McCormick, Robert.

McCormick, Jim. Light up & Live: An Intelligent Guide to Safer Smoking. LC 89-91979. (Illus.). 75p. (Orig.). 1989. pap. 6.95 (*0-9623895-0-1*) Brighton Pr Chi.

McCormick, Joe & McKenney, Tom. Holy Spirit Baptism. (Illus.). 23p. (Orig.). 1982. pap. 3.95 (*0-934527-02-4*) Words Living Minis.

***McCormick, John.** British Politics & Environment. 1990. 15.95 (*1-85383-090-9*, Pub. by Erthscan Pubns UK) Island Pr.

— Careers in Conservation. 112p. (Orig.). 1989. pap. 17.95 (*0-8464-1402-3*) Beekman Pubs.

— Comparative Politics in Transition. LC 94-23386. (Illus.). 476p. 1995. text ed. 32.95 (*0-534-18900-8*) Intl Thomson.

— Computer & the Americans: A Manager's Guide to Adaptive Office Technology. 1993. text ed. 34.95 (*0-07-045013-7*); pap. text ed. 22.95 (*0-07-045014-5*) McGraw.

— Computers & the Americans with Disabilities Act: A Manager's Guide. 1993. text ed. 34.95 (*0-8306-4444-X*, Windcrest); pap. text ed. 22.95 (*0-8306-4445-8*, Windcrest) TAB Bks.

— Deductive Interpretation of Natal Horoscope. 76p. 1976. 6.50 (*0-86690-126-4*, M1305-014) Am Fed Astrologers.

— Dion Bocicault (1820-1890) (Theatre in Focus Ser.). 1987. sl., pap. 105.00 (*0-85964-194-5*) Chadwyck-Healey.

— Melodrama Theatres of the French Boulevard. (Theatre in Focus Ser.). (Illus.). 120p. 1982. sl., pap. 105.00 (*0-85964-117-1*) Chadwyck-Healey.

— Popular Theatres of Nineteenth Century France. LC 92-9964. (Illus.). 272p. 1993. 62.50 (*0-415-08854-2*, A9885) Routledge.

— Reclaiming Paradise: The Global Environmental Movement. LC 87-46408. (Illus.). 278p. (Orig.). 1989. 35.00 (*0-253-34952-4*); pap. 12.50 (*0-253-20660-X*, MB-660) Ind U Pr.

— The Right Kind of War. 384p. 1994. pap. 4.99 (*0-451-40450-5*, Onyx) NAL-Dutton.

— The Right Kind of War. large type ed. LC 92-44777. (General Ser.). 548p. 1993. reprint ed. lib. bdg. 18.95 (*1-56054-663-8*) Thorndike Pr.

— The Right Kind of War: A Novel. LC 92-19546. 333p. 1992. 21.95 (*1-55750-574-8*) Naval Inst Pr.

McCormick, John, ed. see Hanson, F. E.

McCormick, John, ed. see Trollope, Anthony.

McCormick, John A. Create Your Own Multimedia System. 1994. disk, pap. 32.95 (*0-07-046034-5*) McGraw.

— Fantastic Fax Machines: Communicate with Your PC, Mac, or LAN. LC 93-39901. 1994. pap. text ed. 21.95 (*0-07-046028-0*, P A Stroock) TAB Bks.

— New Optical Storage Technology: Including Multimedia, CD-ROM, & Optical Drives. 2nd ed. 368p. 1993. pap. 30.00 (*1-55623-907-6*) Irwin Prof Pubng.

McCormick, John F. St. Thomas & the Life of Learning. (Aquinas Lectures). 1937. 10.00 (*0-87462-101-1*) Marquette.

***McCormick, John J. & Vaughn, John C.** Special Education: A Biblical Approach. Sutton, Joe P., ed. & pref. by. (Illus.). 408p. (Orig.). (C). 1993. pap. text ed. 14.95 (*0-9634315-0-1*) Hidden Treas.

McCormick, John O., ed. see Livingston College, Faculty of Comparative Literature.

***McCormick, John S. & Sillito, John R., eds.** A World We Thought We Knew: New Readings in Utah History. (Illus.). 540p. 1995. text ed. 65.00x (*0-87480-483-3*); pap. 24.95x (*0-87480-484-1*) U of Utah Pr.

McCormick, John S., jt. auth. see McCormick, Nancy D.

McCormick, John W. Project Factors & Influences Integral to the Development of Fire Protection Solutions. 1984. 4.35 (*0-318-03821-8*, TR84-4) Society Fire Protect.

McCormick, Jon. The Automobile Sales Manager's Complete Success Formula: A Current Guide to Managing a Profitable Car Dealership. 330p. (Orig.). 1994. 39.95 (*1-57002-003-5*); pap. 29.95 (*1-57002-004-3*) Univ Publng Hse.

McCormick, Katherine. Britain. (Language & Travel Guides Ser.). (Illus.). 266p. (Orig.). 1994. pap. 14.95 (*0-7818-0290-3*) Hippocrene Bks.

McCormick, Kathleen. Reducing the Risk, Vol. 2: A School Leader's Guide to AIDS Education. 2nd ed. 43p. (Orig.). 1990. pap. text ed. 5.00 (*0-88364-170-4*) Natl Sch Boards.

— Ulysses, "Wandering Rocks," & the Reader: Multiple Pleasures in Reading. LC 90-21975. (Studies in British Literature: Vol. 12). 196p. 1991. lib. bdg. 79.95 (*0-88946-493-6*) E Mellen.

McCormick, Kathleen & Steinberg, Erwin R. Approaches to Teaching Joyce's "Ulysses" LC 93-736. (Approaches to World Literature Ser.). 220p. 1993. text ed. 37.50 (*0-87352-711-9*); pap. 18.00x (*0-87352-712-7*) Modern Lang.

McCormick, Kathleen, jt. auth. see Flatter, Charles H.

McCormick, Kathleen A. The Culture of Reading & the Teaching of English. LC 93-28179. 1994. text ed. 19.95 (*0-7190-3245-8*, Pub. by Manchester Univ Pr UK) St Martin.

McCormick, Kathleen A., et al. Reading Texts: Reading, Responding, Writing. LC 86-82150. 320p. (C). 1987. pap. text ed. 14.00 (*0-669-09564-8*) Heath.

McCormick, L. J. McCormick Family Record & Biography. (Illus.). 490p. 1989. reprint ed. lib. bdg. 81.50 (*0-8328-0860-1*); reprint ed. pap. 73.50 (*0-8328-0861-X*) Higginson Bk Co.

McCormick, Larry, et al. Living with Long Island's South Shore. LC 83-20670. (Living with the Shore Ser.). (Illus.). xiii, 167p. (C). 1984. text ed. 31.95 (*0-8223-0501-1*); pap. 14.95 (*0-8223-0502-X*) Duke.

McCormick, Linda, jt. auth. see Noonan, Mary J.

McCormick, Linda, jt. auth. see Stodden, Norma J.

McCormick, M. P. & Lovill, J. E., eds. Space Observations of Aerosols & Ozone: Proceedings of the Topical Meeting of the COSPAR Interdisciplinary Scientific Commission A (Meetings A1 & A2) of the COSPAR 24th Plenary Meeting held in Ottawa, Canada, 16 May-2 June, 1982, Vol. 2/5. (Illus.). 120p. 1983. pap. 50.00 (*0-08-030427-3*, Pergamon Pr) Elsevier.

McCormick, M. Patrick, jt. ed. see Hobbs, Peter V.

M

McCormick, Malachi. Cat Tales: Folktales Collected & Retold. 1989. 14.00 (*0-517-57256-7*, C P Pubs) Crown Pub Group.

— A Collection of English Proverbs. (Proverbs of the World Ser.). (Illus.). 60p. (Orig.). 1981. pap. text ed. 15.00 (*0-943984-03-3*) Stone St Pr.

— A Collection of Irish Proverbs. (Proverbs of the World Ser.). (Illus.). 60p. 1981. pap. text ed. 15.00 (*0-943984-00-9*) Stone St Pr.

— A Collection of Yiddish Proverbs. (Proverbs of the World Ser.). (Illus.). 60p. (Orig.). 1982. pap. text ed. 15.00 (*0-943984-02-5*) Stone St Pr.

— Dark Secrets: Cooking with Stout - Porter. 40p. 1988. 8.00 (*0-943984-34-3*) Stone St Pr.

— A Decent Cup of Tea. 80p. 1991. 12.00 (*0-517-58462-X*, C P Pubs) Crown Pub Group.

— Early Irish Nature Poetry, Bk. 1. 96p. 1992. write for info. (*0-943984-50-5*) Stone St Pr.

— Early Irish Nature Poetry, Bk. 2. 96p. 1992. write for info. (*0-943984-51-3*) Stone St Pr.

— Early Irish Nature Poetry, Bk. 3. 96p. 1992. write for info. (*0-943984-52-1*) Stone St Pr.

— Early Irish Nature Poetry, 3 vols., Set. 96p. 1992. boxed 27.00 (*0-943984-49-1*) Stone St Pr.

— Herself Long Ago, Bk. 1. 96p. 1990. write for info. (*0-943984-38-6*) Stone St Pr.

— Herself Long Ago, Bk. 2. 96p. 1990. write for info. (*0-943984-39-4*) Stone St Pr.

— Herself Long Ago, Bk. 3. 96p. 1990. write for info. (*0-943984-40-8*) Stone St Pr.

— Herself Long Ago, 3 vols., Set. 96p. 1990. boxed 27.00 (*0-943984-37-8*) Stone St Pr.

— How to Make a Decent Cup of Tea. 24p. 1986. 4.00 (*0-943984-27-0*) Stone St Pr.

— How to Make a Perfect Cup of Coffee. 24p. 1992. 4.00 (*0-943984-55-6*) Stone St Pr.

— In Praise of Irish Breakfasts. 42p. 1991. 13.00 (*0-943984-42-4*) Stone St Pr.

— Irish Bread & Cake: Classic Recipes. 28p. (Orig.). 1981. pap. text ed. 7.00 (*0-943984-01-7*) Stone St Pr.

— Irish Festive Fare. (Irish Traditional Cooking Ser.). 32p. 1984. 8.00 (*0-943984-14-9*) Stone St Pr.

— Irish Traditional Cooking, 3 Vols., Set. 92p. (Orig.). 1984. boxed 22.00 (*0-943984-20-3*) Stone St Pr.

— Irish Traditional Soups. (Irish Traditional Cooking Ser.). 32p. 1984. 8.00 (*0-943984-19-X*) Stone St Pr.

— Listening to the River: Family Biography. 60p. 1989. 22.00 (*0-943984-35-1*) Stone St Pr.

— Love of Frog, 3 vols., 3. 96p. 1993. write for info. (*0-318-70248-7*) Stone St Pr.

— Love of Frog, 3 vols., Vol. 1. (Special Paste Paper Miniature Collections Ser.). 84p. 1993. write for info. (*0-943984-57-2*) Stone St Pr.

— Love of Frog, 3 vols., Vol. 2. (Special Paste Paper Miniature Collections Ser.). 84p. 1993. write for info. (*0-943984-58-0*) Stone St Pr.

— Love of Frog, 3 vols., Vol. 3. (Special Paste Paper Miniature Collections Ser.). 84p. 1993. write for info. (*0-943984-59-9*) Stone St Pr.

McCormick, Malachi, ed. Cat Folk Tales, 5 vols., 1. 120p. 1987. write for info. (*0-943984-29-7*) Stone St Pr.

— Cat Folk Tales, 5 vols., 2. 120p. 1987. write for info. (*0-943984-30-0*) Stone St Pr.

— Cat Folk Tales, 5 vols., 3. 120p. 1987. write for info. (*0-943984-31-9*) Stone St Pr.

— Cat Folk Tales, 5 vols., 4. 120p. 1987. write for info. (*0-943984-32-7*) Stone St Pr.

— Cat Folk Tales, 5 vols., 5. 120p. 1987. write for info. (*0-943984-33-5*) Stone St Pr.

— Cat Folk Tales, 5 vols., Set. 120p. 1987. boxed 20.00 (*0-943984-28-9*) Stone St Pr.

— Collected Nursery Rhymes: Four Verses. 80p. (J). 1985. boxed 20.00 (*0-943984-21-1*) Stone St Pr.

— A Collection of African Proverbs. 60p. 1992. 15.00 (*0-943984-53-X*) Stone St Pr.

McCormick, Malachi, ed. & tr. Cutting down an Ancient Tree: Seventeenth Century. (Miniatures Ser.). 24p. Date not set. pap. 7.00 (*0-943984-47-5*) Stone St Pr.

— Cutting Down an Ancient Tree: Seventeenth Century. 24p. 1989. 7.00 (*0-943984-36-X*) Stone St Pr.

McCormick, Malachi, ed. Deer's Cry: St. Patrick's Breast Plate. (Illus.). 24p. (Orig.). (ENG & IRI.). 1982. pap. text ed. 7.00 (*0-943984-05-X*) Stone St Pr.

McCormick, Malachi, ed. & tr. Hail to the Herring: Sixteenth Century Poem. 20p. 1984. 4.00 (*0-943984-16-5*) Stone St Pr.

— Irish Poetry Set, 3 vols., Set. 96p. 1986. 22.00 (*0-943984-24-6*) Stone St Pr.

McCormick, Malachi, ed. Letter from Koln, Christmas 1935. 32p. 1987. 7.00 (*0-943984-25-4*) Stone St Pr.

— The Love of Irish Women. 32p. 1984. 7.00 (*0-943984-15-7*) Stone St Pr.

— Maxims Concerning Patriotism (Berkeley) 24p. 1985. 6.00 (*0-943984-22-X*) Stone St Pr.

McCormick, Malachi, ed. & tr. Not Sweet (The Snoring Poem) 24p. 1986. 7.00 (*0-943984-26-2*) Stone St Pr.

— Old Irish Monastic Prayer-Poetry. (Irish Poetry Ser.). 32p. 1986. 8.00 (*0-943984-23-8*) Stone St Pr.

McCormick, Malachi, ed. Other Cats: Six Handmade Books of Poems about Cats. (Illus.). 120p. (Orig.). 1983. Six Paperbound in hardcover slipcase. boxed, pap. 20.00 (*0-943984-06-8*) Stone St Pr.

McCormick, Malachi, ed. & tr. Pangur Bawn the Cat: Ninth Century. (Miniatures Ser.). 24p. 1991. pap. 7.00 (*0-943984-48-3*) Stone St Pr.

— Pangur Bawn the Cat: Ninth Century Poem. 20p. 1983. 4.00 (*0-943984-07-6*) Stone St Pr.

McCormick, Malachi, ed. The Pleasures of Irish Nature Poetry. 32p. 1984. 8.00 (*0-943984-18-1*) Stone St Pr.

— We Three Cats, 3 vols., 1. 84p. 1991. write for info. (*0-943984-44-0*) Stone St Pr.

— We Three Cats, 3 vols., 2. 84p. 1991. write for info. (*0-943984-45-9*) Stone St Pr.

— We Three Cats, 3 vols., 3. 84p. 1991. write for info. (*0-943984-46-7*) Stone St Pr.

— We Three Cats, 3 vols., Set. 84p. 1991. boxed 20.00 (*0-943984-43-2*) Stone St Pr.

McCormick, Malachi, ed. & tr. Who Will Buy a Poem? Seventeenth Century. (Miniatures Ser.). 24p. 1991. 7.00 (*0-943984-41-6*); 7.00 (*0-685-65461-3*) Stone St Pr.

McCormick, Malachi, ed. see Provisional Government of Ireland Staff.

McCormick, Margaret. World Evolution: Our Future in the Twenty-First Century. LC 91-91572. 240p. 1991. pap. 12.95 (*0-9631930-3-1*) Channel CA.

McCormick, Marjorie J. Mothers in the English Novel: From Stereotype & Archetype. LC 91-249241. (Gender & Genre in Literature Ser.: Vol. 1). 265p. 1991. 30.00 (*0-8240-7131-X*, H1302) Garland.

McCormick, Mark, ed. see Cook, J. Sue & Fontaine, Karen L.

McCormick, Mark, ed. see Eliopoulos, Charlotte.

McCormick, Mark, ed. see Maas, Meridean, et al.

McCormick, Mark, ed. see Prendergast, Alice.

McCormick, Mark, jt. auth. see Starr, V. Hale.

McCormick, Mark, ed. see Wilson, Holly S.

McCormick, Mary J. Enduring Values in a Changing Society. LC 75-18288. 208p. reprint ed. pap. 59.30 (*0-685-24014-2*, 2031603) Bks Demand.

McCormick, Maxine. Chimpanzee. LC 89-28272. (Wildlife Ser.). (Illus.). 48p. (J). (gr. 5). 1990. text ed. 12.95 (*0-89686-514-2*, Crstwood Hse) Silver Burdett Pr.

— Pretty As You Please. LC 92-39310. (J). 1994. 15.95 (*0-399-22536-6*, Philomel Bks) Putnam Pub Group.

— Sequoia & Kings Canyon. LC 88-20214. (National Parks Ser.). (Illus.). 48p. (J). (gr. 4-5). 1988. text ed. 13.95 (*0-89686-409-X*, Crstwood Hse) Silver Burdett Pr.

McCormick, Maxine, jt. auth. see Root, Phyllis.

McCormick, Michael. Across the Pond. 1993. 10.95 (*0-533-10579-X*) Vantage.

— Eternal Victory: Triumphal Rulership in Late Antiquity, Byzantium & the Early Medieval West. (Past & Present Publications). (Illus.). 470p. (C). 1990. pap. 24.95 (*0-521-38659-4*) Cambridge U Pr.

McCormick, Michael E., ed. Anchoring Systems. 1979. 36.00 (*0-08-022694-9*, Pergamon Pr) Elsevier.

— Port & Ocean Engineering under Arctic Conditions: Selected Papers from the 3rd International Conference. 1977. pap. 29.00 (*0-08-021421-5*, Pergamon Pr) Elsevier.

McCormick, Michael E. & Kim, Young C., eds. Utilization of Ocean Waves - Wave to Energy Conversion. 212p. 1987. 24.00 (*0-87262-624-5*) Am Soc Civil Eng.

McCormick, Mike, jt. auth. see Schwartz, Bill.

McCormick, Nancy D. & McCormick, John S. Saltair. LC 85-665. (Bonneville Bks.). (Illus.). 117p. (Orig.). reprint ed. pap. 33.40 (*0-8357-4375-6*, 2037205) Bks Demand.

McCormick, Naomi B. Sexual Salvation: Affirming Women's Sexual Rights & Pleasures. LC 94-6378. 304p. 1994. text ed. 22.95 (*0-275-94359-3*, Praeger Pubs) Greenwood.

McCormick, Norman J. Reliability & Risk Analysis: Methods & Nuclear Power Applications. LC 81-2758. 1981. text ed. 85.00 (*0-12-482360-2*) Acad Pr.

McCormick, Norman J., jt. ed. see Williams, M. M.

McCormick, Norman J., jt. ed. see Williams, M. R.

McCormick, P., ed. Developing & Applying End of Arm Tooling. 264p. 1986. 42.00 (*0-87263-211-3*) SME.

McCormick, Patrick T. Sin As Addiction. 1989. pap. 7.95 (*0-8091-3064-5*) Paulist Pr.

McCormick, Peggy. Making a Home in Stillwater. LC 88-83680. (Illus.). 96p. 1989. pap. 14.95 (*0-934188-28-9*) Evans Pubns.

McCormick, Peggy, jt. auth. see Gardiner, Joanna.

McCormick, Penny, jt. ed. see McCormick, Tom.

McCormick, Peter & Elliston, Frederick A., eds. Husserl: Shorter Works. LC 80-53178. 440p. (C). 1982. text ed. 30.00 (*0-268-01703-4*); pap. text ed. 18.95 (*0-268-01077-3*) U of Notre Dame Pr.

McCormick, Peter, jt. ed. see Dziemidok, Bohdan.

McCormick, Peter, jt. ed. see Elliston, Frederick.

McCormick, Peter, tr. see Marcel, Gabriel.

McCormick, Peter J. Fictions, Philosophies, & the Problems of Poetics. LC 88-47783. 384p. 1988. 46.50 (*0-8014-2204-3*); pap. 16.95 (*0-8014-9519-9*) Cornell U Pr.

— Modernity, Aesthetics, & the Bounds of Art. LC 89-71309. (Illus.). 368p. 1990. 46.50 (*0-8014-2452-6*); pap. 16.95 (*0-8014-9740-X*) Cornell U Pr.

McCormick, R. J., et al. Costs for Hazardous Waste Incineration: Capital, Operation & Maintenance, Retrofit. LC 85-16839. (Pollution Technology Review Ser.: No. 123). (Illus.). 274p. 1986. 39.00 (*0-8155-1047-0*) Noyes.

McCormick, Richard A. Ambiguity in Moral Choice. (Pere Marquette Lectures). 1977. pap. 10.00 (*0-87462-505-X*) Marquette.

— Corrective Vision: Explorations in Moral Theology. LC 93-21332. 256p. (Orig.). 1994. pap. 15.95 (*1-55612-601-8*) Sheed & Ward MO.

— The Critical Calling: Reflections on Moral Dilemmas since Vatican II. LC 89-7622. 401p. (Orig.). 1989. pap. 16.95 (*0-87840-464-3*) Georgetown U Pr.

— Health & Medicine in the Roman Catholic Tradition: Tradition in Transition. (Health & Medicine in Faith Tradition Ser.). 176p. 1984. 19.95 (*0-8245-0661-8*) Crossroad NY.

McCormick, Richard A. & Curran, Charles E. Readings in Moral Theology, No. 6: Dissent in the Church. 560p. 1988. pap. 14.95 (*0-8091-2930-2*) Paulist Pr.

McCormick, Richard A. & Ramsey, Paul, eds. Doing Evil to Achieve Good: Moral Choice in Conflict Situations. LC 78-11316. 1978. 10.35 (*0-8294-0285-3*) Loyola Univ Pr.

McCormick, Richard A., jt. ed. see Curran, Charles E.

McCormick, Richard J. Notes on Moral Theology: 1981-1984. 242p. 1985. lib. bdg. 44.00 (*0-8191-4351-0*); pap. text ed. 20.00 (*0-8191-4352-9*) U Pr of Amer.

McCormick, Richard L. From Realignment to Reform: Political Change in New York State 1893-1910. (Illus.). 368p. 1981. 42.50 (*0-8014-1326-5*) Cornell U Pr.

— The Party Period & Public Policy: American Politics from the Age of Jackson to the Progressive Era. 384p. (C). 1988. reprint ed. pap. text ed. 18.95 (*0-19-504784-2*) OUP.

— Public Life in Industrial America, 1877-1917. (New American History Ser.). 30p. (C). 1991. reprint ed. 5.00 (*0-87229-055-7*) Am Hist Assn.

McCormick, Richard L., jt. auth. see Link, Arthur S.

McCormick, Richard P. New Jersey from Colony to State, 1609-1789. (Classics Ser.). (Illus.). 191p. pap. 12.95 (*0-911020-02-0*) NJ Hist Soc.

— The Presidential Game: The Origins of American Presidential Politics. 1984. pap. 16.95 (*0-19-503455-4*) OUP.

McCormick, Richard P. & Schlatter, Richard, eds. The Selected Speeches of Mason Gross. 160p. 1980. 32.95 (*0-87855-388-6*) Transaction Pubs.

McCormick, Richard S., jt. ed. see Curran, Charles E.

McCormick, Richard W. Politics of the Self: Feminism & the Postmodern in West German Literature & Film. (Illus.). 283p. 1991. text ed. 49.50 (*0-691-06851-8*); pap. text ed. 15.95 (*0-691-01483-3*) Princeton U Pr.

McCormick, Robert. The Concept of Happiness in the Spanish Poetry of the Eighteenth Century. LC 80-68000. (Coleccion de Estudios Hispanicos - Hispanic Studies Collection). 206p. (Orig.). 1980. pap. 19.95 (*0-89729-264-2*) Ediciones.

— Freedom of the Press. LC 77-125705. (American Journalists Ser.). 1976. reprint ed. 14.95 (*0-405-01686-7*) Ayer.

McCormick, Robert & McCormick, Jennie. Probing Worthington's Heritage. (Illus.). 123p. (Orig.). 1990. pap. 6.50 (*0-918887-04-6*) Cottonwood Pubns.

— Worthington Landmarks: Photo-Essays of Historic Worthington Properties. LC 92-16116. (Illus.). 128p. (Orig.). 1992. pap. 17.95 (*0-918887-05-4*) Cottonwood Pubns.

McCormick, Robert & McKinnon, Matthew. Sports Law. 358p. (C). 1992. ring bd. 45.50 (*1-879581-02-7*) Lupus Pubns.

McCormick, Robert, jt. ed. see Cross, Anita.

McCormick, Robert, et al, eds. Teaching & Learning Technology. LC 92-37018. 1992. 32.00 (*0-201-63169-5*) Addison-Wesley.

— Technology for Technology Education. LC 92-36800. 1992. write for info. (*0-201-63168-7*) Addison-Wesley.

McCormick, Robert E. Managerial Economics. 544p. 1992. text ed. write for info. (*0-13-544750-X*) P-H.

McCormick, Robert E. & Tollison, Robert D. Politicians, Legislation, & the Economy: An Inquiry into the Interest-Group Theory of Government. (Rochester Studies in Economics & Policy Issues). 160p. 1981. lib. bdg. 40.50 (*0-89838-058-8*) Kluwer Ac.

McCormick, Roger, jt. auth. see Neate, Francis.

McCormick, Ross. For Sale by Owner - A Practical Guide for Selling Your Home. 110p. 1991. lib. bdg. write for info. (*0-9630593-1-9*); pap. 18.95 (*0-9630593-0-0*) Gt Falls North.

McCormick, Roy. Coverages Applicable. 144p. 1992. 39.00 (*0-942326-28-8*, 30040) Rough Notes.

McCormick, Sandra. Remedial & Clinical Reading Instruction. 544p. (C). 1987. write for info. (*0-675-20284-1*, Merrill Pub Co) Macmillan.

— Remedial & Clinical Reading Instruction. 2nd ed. (Illus.). 608p. (C). 1994. text ed. write for info. (*0-02-379271-X*) Macmillan.

McCormick, Sandra & Schiefelbusch. Early Language Intervention. 2nd ed. 480p. (C). 1990. pap. write for info. (*0-675-21194-8*, Merrill Pub Co) Macmillan.

McCormick, Sandra, jt. ed. see Neuman, Susan B.

McCormick, Scott, Jr. Behold the Man: Re-Reading Gospels, Re-Humanizing Jesus. 180p. (C). 1994. 19.95 (*0-8264-0680-7*) Continuum.

McCormick, Shawn H. The Angolan Economy: Prospects for Growth in a Postwar Economy. LC 94-11211. (Significant Issues Ser.). 88p. (Orig.). (C). (gr. 13). 1994. pap. 8.95 (*0-89206-187-1*) CSI Studies.

McCormick, Stephen. Multigrid Methods. (Lecture Notes in Pure & Applied Mathematics Ser.: Vol. 110). 672p. 1988. 165.00 (*0-8247-7979-7*) Dekker.

— Multilevel Adaptive Methods for Partial Differential Equations. (Frontiers in Applied Mathematics Ser.: No. 6). ix, 162p. 1989. pap. 26.50 (*0-89871-247-5*) Soc Indus-Appl Math.

McCormick, Stephen, ed. Multigrid Methods. LC 87-60444. (Frontiers in Applied Mathematics Ser.: No. 3). xvii, 282p. 1987. text ed. 40.75 (*0-89871-214-9*) Soc Indus-Appl Math.

McCormick, Stephen F. Multilevel Projection Methods for Partial Differential Equations. (CBMS-NSF Regional Conference Series in Applied Mathematics: No. 62). vi, 114p. (Orig.). (C). 1992. pap. text ed. 20.50 (*0-89871-292-0*) Soc Indus-Appl Math.

McCormick, Susan, ed. Administration & Finance Report. (ASTC Science Center Survey Report Ser.). (Illus.). 78p. 1989. pap. 15.00 (*0-685-29593-1*) AST Ctrs.

— Education Report & Directory. (ASTC Science Center Survey Report Ser.). (Illus.). 100p. 1988. pap. 20.00 (*0-685-29592-3*) AST Ctrs.

McCormick, Susan, jt. ed. see Bridal, Tessa.

McCormick, Susan, jt. ed. see Pollock, Wendy.

McCormick, Susan P., jt. ed. see Petroski, Richard J.

McCormick, Thelma. Studies in Communications: News & Knowledge, Vol. 3. 1986. 73.25 (*0-89232-363-9*) Jai Pr.

McCormick, Theresa. Creating the Nonsexist Classroom. 224p. (C). 1994. text ed. 37.00 (*0-8077-3348-2*); pap. text ed. 16.95 (*0-8077-3347-4*) Tchrs Coll.

McCormick, Thomas. Charles-Louis Clerisseau & the Genesis of Neoclassicism: The Birth of Neoclassicism. (Illus.). 272p. 1990. 40.00 (*0-262-13262-1*) MIT Pr.

McCormick, Thomas & LaFeber, Walter, eds. Behind the Throne: Servants of Power to Imperial Presidents, 1898-1968. LC 93-18754. 288p. (C). 1993. text ed. 45.50 (*0-299-13740-6*) U of Wis Pr.

McCormick, Thomas C. Comparative Study of Rural Relief & Non-Relief Households. LC 70-165684. (Research Monograph Ser.: Vol. 2). 1971. reprint ed. lib. bdg. 22.50 (*0-306-70334-3*) Da Capo.

McCormick, Thomas J. America's Half-Century: U. S. Foreign Policy in the Cold War. LC 89-45488. (American Moment Ser.). 304p. 1989. text ed. 42.50 (*0-8018-3876-2*); pap. text ed. 12.95 (*0-8018-3877-0*) Johns Hopkins.

— America's Half-Century: United States Foreign Policy in the Cold War & After. 2nd rev. ed. LC 94-34698. (American Moment Ser.). 312p. 1994. text ed. 38.95x (*0-8018-5010-X*); pap. text ed. 13.95x (*0-8018-5011-8*) Johns Hopkins.

— China Market: America's Quest for Informal Empire, 1893-1901. 252p. 1990. pap. 9.95 (*0-929587-24-3*, Elephant Paperbacks) I R Dee.

***McCormick, Thomas J., Jr.** A Partial Edition of les Fais Des Rommains with a Study of its Style & Syntax. LC 94-48863. 264p. 1995. text ed. 89.95 (*0-7734-2918-2*) E Mellen.

McCormick, Thomas W. Theories of Reading in Dialogue: An Interdisciplinary Study. LC 88-20821. 410p. (Orig.). (C). 1988. lib. bdg. 62.00 (*0-8191-7168-9*); pap. text ed. 33.00 (*0-8191-7169-7*) U Pr of Amer.

McCormick, Tim, jt. auth. see Rumsey, Francis.

McCormick, Tom & McCormick, Penny, eds. Nursing Home Ministry: A Manual. (Orig.). 1982. pap. text ed. 6.95 (*0-934688-08-7*) Great Comm Pubns.

***McCormick, Virginia E.** Scioto Company Descendants. 310p. (Orig.). 1995. pap. 28.00 (*0-918887-06-2*) Cottonwood Pubns.

McCormik, David, et al. Measurement Statistics & Computation. (Analytical Chemistry by Open Learning Ser.). 1988. pap. text ed. 79.95 (*0-471-91367-7*) Wiley.

McCormley, Jane H. Celebrate with Soup. (Illus.). 80p. pap. 3.95 (*0-936369-27-2*) Son-Rise Pubns.

McCormmach, Russell. Historical Studies in the Physical Sciences, Vol. 5. LC 77-75220. (Illus.). 197p. pap. 56.20 (*0-8357-8899-7*, 2033394) Bks Demand.

— Night Thoughts of a Classical Physicist. LC 81-6674. (Illus.). 225p. 1982. 25.00 (*0-674-62460-2*) HUP.

— Night Thoughts of a Classical Physicist. (Illus.). 232p. 1991. pap. text ed. 9.95 (*0-674-62461-0*, MCCNIX) HUP.

McCormmach, Russell, ed. Historical Studies in the Physical Sciences, 6. LC 73-8263. (Illus.). 1975. 85.00 (*0-691-08166-2*) Princeton U Pr.

— Historical Studies in the Physical Sciences, Vol. 6. LC 77-75220. Date not set. reprint ed. pap. 160.80 (*0-7837-9387-1*, 2060131) Bks Demand.

— Historical Studies in the Physical Sciences, Vol. 7. LC 77-75220. 526p. pap. 150.00 (*0-7837-0043-1*, 2040278) Bks Demand.

McCormmach, Russell & Pyenson, Lewis, eds. Historical Studies in the Physical Sciences, Vol. 9. LC 77-75220. 374p. reprint ed. pap. 106.60 (*0-685-15525-0*, 2026328) Bks Demand.

McCormmach, Russell, jt. auth. see Jungnickel, Christa.

McCormmach, Russell, et al, eds. Historical Studies in the Physical Sciences, Vol. 10. LC 77-75220. 344p. reprint ed. pap. 98.10 (*0-8357-8166-6*, 2034144) Bks Demand.

McCornack & Jarett. Advanced Programming Tips for the HP-41. (Illus.). 340p. (Orig.). 1987. pap. text ed. 9.95 (*0-9612174-6-4*, 491) EduCALC Pubns.

***McCorquodale, Robert & Orosz, Nicholas, eds.** Tibet: The Position of International Law. (Illus.). 238p. 1995. pap. 25.00 (*0-906026-34-2*, Pub. by Serindia UK) Weatherhill.

McCorquodale, Robert, jt. ed. see Dixon, Martin.

McCorquodale, Robin. Stella Landry. 1992. 20.00 (*0-688-11528-4*) Morrow.

— Stella Landry. 320p. 1993. reprint ed. pap. 8.00 (*0-380-71882-0*) Avon.

McCorristine, Laurence. Revolt of Silken Thomas: A Challenge to Henry VIII. (Illus.). 176p. 1987. 29.95 (*0-86327-120-0*, Pub. by Wolfhound Pr IE); pap. 17.95 (*0-86327-126-X*, Pub. by Wolfhound Pr IE) Dufour.

McCorry, Frank. Preventing Substance Abuse: A Comprehensive Program for Catholic Education. 111p. (Orig.). 1990. pap. 8.70 (*1-55833-040-2*) Natl Cath Educ.

McCort, Dennis. States of Unconsciousness in Three Tales by C. F. Meyer. LC 87-47786. 136p. 1988. 28.50 (*0-8387-5130-X*) Bucknell U Pr.

McCort, James J., ed. Trauma Radiology. (Illus.). 483p. 1990. text ed. 135.00 (*0-443-08645-1*) Churchill.

McCorvey, Norma. I Am Roe: My Life, Roe v. Wade, & Freedom of Choice. LC 92-56216. 256p. 1994. 23.00 (*0-06-017010-7*, HarpT) HarpC.

***McCorvey, Norma & Meisler, Andy.** I Am Roe. 1995. pap. 11.00 (*0-06-092638-4*, PL) HarpC.

McCorvie, Mary R. The Davis, Baldridge, & Huggins Sites: Three 19th Century Upland South Farmsteads in Perry County, Illinois. (Preservation Ser.: No. 4). (Illus.). 323p. 1987. 10.00 (*0-913415-03-0*) Am Resources.

McCorvie, Mary R., jt. auth. see Wagner, Mark J.

McCorvie, Mary R., jt. ed. see Wagner, Mark J.

An Asterisk (*) at the beginning of an entry indicates that the title is appearing in BIP for the first time.

McCory, David L. Technology Education: Industrial Arts in Transition, A Review & Synthesis of the Research. 4th ed. 69p. 1987. 7.00 (*0-318-35275-3*, IN 325) Ctr Educ Trng Employ.

McCory, J. R., jt. auth. see Jacobs, G.

McCory, Moy. The Fading Shrine. 289p. 1992. 22.95 (*0-224-02796-4*, Pub. by Jonathan Cape UK) Trafalgar.

McCosh, A. M., jt. ed. see Lee, R. M.

McCosh, F. W. Boussingault. 1984. lib. bdg. 119.00 (*90-277-1682-X*) Kluwer Ac.

McCosh, James. Development: What It Can Do & What It Cannot Do. LC 75-3252. reprint ed. 19.00 (*0-404-59240-6*) AMS Pr.

— The Development Hypothesis: Is It Sufficient. LC 75-3251. reprint ed. 19.00 (*0-404-59239-2*) AMS Pr.

— First & Fundamental Truths: Being a Treatise on Metaphysics. LC 75-3255. reprint ed. 25.50 (*0-404-59242-2*) AMS Pr.

— Ideas in Nature Overlooked by Dr. Tyndall. LC 75-3256. reprint ed. 18.50 (*0-404-59243-0*) AMS Pr.

— The Intuitions of the Mind Inductively Investigated. 3rd ed. LC 75-3257. reprint ed. 31.50 (*0-404-59244-9*) AMS Pr.

— Our Moral Nature. LC 75-3260. reprint ed. 18.00 (*0-404-59247-3*) AMS Pr.

— The Prevailing Types of Philosophy: Can They Logically Reach Reality? LC 75-3262. reprint ed. 18.00 (*0-404-59248-1*) AMS Pr.

— Psychology: The Cognitive Powers. LC 75-3263. reprint ed. 17.00 (*0-404-59249-X*) AMS Pr.

— Psychology: The Motive Powers-Emotions, Conscience, Will. LC 75-3264. reprint ed. 18.00 (*0-404-59250-3*) AMS Pr.

— Realistic Philosophy Defended in a Philosophic Series, 2 vols. LC 75-3265. reprint ed. 49.50 (*0-404-59251-1*) AMS Pr.

— The Scottish Philosophy, Bibliographical, Expository, Critical, from Hutcheson to Hamilton. ix, 481p. 1966. reprint ed. 89.70 (*0-685-66492-9*, 05101276, Pub. by Georg Olms GW); reprint ed. write for info. (*0-318-71927-4*, Pub. by Georg Olms GW) Lubrecht & Cramer.

— The Scottish Philosophy, Biographical, Expository, Critical, from Hutcheson to Hamilton. LC 75-3266. (Philosophy in America Ser.). 496p. 1980. reprint ed. 69.50 (*0-404-59254-6*) AMS Pr.

— The Supernatural in Relation to the Natural. LC 75-3267. reprint ed. 38.00 (*0-404-59255-4*) AMS Pr.

McCoshan, Andrew, jt. auth. see Bennett, Robert J.

McCosker, John E., jt. auth. see Ellis, Richard.

McCoubrey, H. The Development of Naturalist Legal Theory. 224p. 1987. 59.95 (*0-7099-4669-4*, Pub. by Croom Helm UK) Routledge Chapman & Hall.

— International Humanitarian Law. 240p. 1990. text ed. 51.95 (*1-85521-040-1*, Pub. by Dartmth Pub UK) Ashgate Pub Co.

McCoubrey, Hilaire & White, N. D. International Law & Armed Conflict. 350p. 1992. 69.95 (*1-85521-229-3*, Pub. by Dartmth Pub UK) Ashgate Pub Co.

***McCoubrey, Hilaire & White, Nigel D.** International Organizations & Civil Wars. LC 94-21208. 250p. 1995. 63.95 (*1-85521-468-7*, Pub. by Dartmth Pub UK) Ashgate Pub Co.

— Textbook on Jurisprudence. 259p. 1993. pap. 36.00 (*1-85431-265-0*, Pub. by Blackstone Pr UK) W W Gaunt.

McCoubrey, J., jt. auth. see Mazo, R.

McCoubrey, John W., ed. American Art, 1700-1960: Sources & Documents. (Orig.). 1965. pap. text ed. 37.80 (*0-13-024521-6*) P-H.

McCourt, Frederick R., et al. Nonequilibrium Phenomena in Polyatomic Gases, Vol. 1: Dilute Gases. (International Series of Monographs on Chemistry: No. 18). (Illus.). 600p. 1990. 110.00 (*0-19-855631-4*) OUP.

McCourt, James. Time Remaining: Stories. LC 92-54798. (Borzoi Reader Ser.). 1993. 21.00 (*0-679-41266-2*) Knopf.

— Victoria de L A-Bio-Voi. Date not set. pap. write for info. (*0-679-44150-6*) Random.

McCourt, Kathleen. Working-Class Women & Grass-Roots Politics. LC 76-26340. 262p. reprint ed. pap. 74.70 (*0-317-09718-0*, 2017628) Bks Demand.

McCourt-Perring, C., jt. auth. see Youll, P. J.

McCourt, Rick, jt. ed. see Anton, Ted.

McCourtney, Lorena. Shadows of the Heart. large type ed. 1992. pap. 16.95 (*0-7927-1237-4*, Curley Lrg Print) Chivers N Amer.

McCowan, Alexandra. Chicken. LC 93-49627. (Cooking with Style Ser.). (Illus.). 96p. 1994. 13.95 (*1-57145-002-5*) Thunder Bay CA.

McCowen, Jake. Cowboy Crafts: Projects with a Western Flair. LC 94-16837. (Illus.). 144p. (Orig.). 1994. 24.95 (*0-8069-0816-5*, Chapelle) Sterling.

— Cowboy Crafts: Projects with a Western Flair. (Illus.). 144p. (Orig.). 1995. pap. 14.95 (*0-8069-0817-3*, Chapelle) Sterling.

***McCowen, Michael W.** Rio Oro. LC 94-69824. 208p. (Orig.). 1995. pap. 11.95 (*0-9644823-0-4*) Capitan Pub.

McCown, Ada C. Congressional Conference Committee. LC 76-181952. (Columbia University. Studies in the Social Sciences: No. 290). reprint ed. 16.50 (*0-404-51290-9*) AMS Pr.

McCown, Clint. Sidetracks. LC 77-3475. (Bree Bks.: No. 1). (Orig.). 1977. pap. 3.95 (*0-917492-06-4*) Jackpine Pr.

McCown, Donald E. & Haines, Richard C. Nippur One: Temple of Enlil, Scribal Quarter & Soundings, Set. LC 66-17104. (Illus.). 1967. fiche, lib. bdg. 10.00 (*0-226-55688-3*, OIP78) U Ch Pr.

McCown, Donald E., et al. Nippur II: The North Temple & Sounding E: Excavations of the Joint Expedition to Nippur of the American Schools of Oriental Research & the Oriental Institute of the University of Chicago. LC 77-74719. (Oriental Institute Publications: No. 97). (Illus.). 1978. lib. bdg. 60.00 (*0-918986-04-4*) Orientl Inst Pr IT.

McCown, Edna, tr. see Hackl, Erich.

McCown, Edna, tr. see Hasler, Eveline.

McCown, Edna, tr. see Hurlimann, Thomas.

McCown, Edna, tr. see Mettler, Felix.

McCown, Jack. Patterns in Mathematics. (Mathematics Ser.). 1994. text ed. 53.95 (*0-534-18786-2*) PWS Pubs.

McCown, Joe. Availability: Gabriel Marcel & the Phenomenology of Human Openness. LC 77-22358. (American Academy of Religion. Studies in Religion: No. 14). 94p. reprint ed. pap. 26.80 (*0-7837-5481-7*, 2045246) Bks Demand.

McCown, Rick R. & Roop, Peter G. Educational Psychology & Classroom Practice: A Partnership. 656p. (C). 1992. pap. 47.00 (*0-205-13144-1*) Allyn.

McCown, Wayne & Massey, James, eds. God's Word for Today. (Wesleyan Theological Perspectives Ser.: Vol. II). 1989. 14.95 (*0-87162-257-2*, D4851) Warner Pr.

McCown, Wayne, jt. ed. see Carpenter, Eugene C.

McCown, William G., et al. Therapy with Treatment Resistant Families: A Consultation-Crisis Intervention Model. LC 93-35618. 328p. 1993. 59.95 (*1-56024-244-2*); pap. 19.95 (*1-56024-245-0*) Haworth Pr.

McCown, William G., et al, eds. The Impulsive Client: Theory, Research, & Treatment. (Illus.). 465p. 1993. text ed. 49.95 (*1-55798-208-2*) Am Psychol.

McCoy. Boy of Kanawha. 1984. pap. 3.50 (*0-941092-12-7*) Mtn St Pr.

— Indiana Jones & the Philosopher's Stone. 1995. mass mkt. (*0-553-56196-0*) Bantam.

— Wild Rider. 1995. mass mkt. (*0-553-56444-7*) Bantam.

McCoy, Adam D. Holy Cross: A Century of Anglican Monasticism. LC 87-5513. 285p. 1987. 29.95 (*0-8192-1403-5*) Morehouse Pub.

McCoy, Alexandra. Political Affiliations of American Economic Elites: Wayne County, Michigan, 1844-1860 As a Test Case. (Nineteenth Century American Political & Social History Ser.). 291p. 1989. reprint ed. 20.00 (*0-8240-4069-4*) Garland.

McCoy, Alfred W. The Politics of Heroin: CIA Complicity in the Global Drug Trade. LC 90-47398. 640p. 1991. 29.00 (*1-55652-126-X*); pap. 19.95 (*1-55652-125-1*) L Hill Bks.

McCoy, Alfred W., ed. An Anarchy of Families: State & Family in the Philippines. LC 93-71487. 541p. 1993. 45.00 (*1-881261-08-5*); pap. 24.95 (*1-881261-09-3*) U Wisc Ctr SE Asian.

— Southeast Asia Under Japanese Occupation: Transition & Transformation. LC 80-610. (Monograph Ser.: No. 22). (Illus.). 250p. 1980. pap. 14.00 (*0-938692-08-9*) Yale U SE Asia.

McCoy, Alfred W. & Block, Alan A., eds. The War on Drugs: Studies in the Failure of U. S. Narcotics Policy. 359p. (C). 1992. text ed. 57.50 (*0-8133-8551-2*) Westview.

McCoy, Artie N. Green Fields. 84p. 1987. pap. write for info. (*0-943461-01-4*) Hill & Valley Pub.

McCoy, Barbara. A Christmas Death. 1979. pap. 2.00 (*0-913719-39-0*) High-Coo Pr.

McCoy, Barry & Wu, Tai T. The Two-Dimensional Ising Model. LC 72-188972. (Illus.). 438p. 1973. 38.50 (*0-674-91440-6*) HUP.

McCoy, Betsy. Cosmetic Plastic Surgery. Osborn, John M., ed. LC 92-62104. (Illus.). 176p. 1993. 24.95 (*0-9633816-0-1*) Paradise Sacramento.

McCoy, Betty S. Miracles & Other Happenings. (Illus.). 80p. 1993. pap. write for info. (*0-935648-42-9*) Halldin Pub.

***McCoy, Beverly A.** Threads of Silver, Cords of Gold. 458p. Date not set. pap. 9.95 (*1-56901-604-6*) NW Pub.

***McCoy, Bill W., III.** Listing & Selling Small Commercial Properties. LC 94-41135. 1995. write for info. (*0-7931-1407-1*, Real Estate Ed) Dearborn Finan.

McCoy, C. T. Sturgeon: A Genealogical History of the Sturgeons of North America. (Illus.). 239p. 1991. reprint ed. lib. bdg. 48.00 (*0-8328-1791-0*); reprint ed. pap. 38.00 (*0-8328-1792-9*) Higginson Bk Co.

McCoy, Candace. Politics & Plea Bargaining: Victims' Rights in California. LC 92-46518. (Law in Social Context Ser.). 248p. (Orig.). (C). 1993. text ed. 36.95 (*0-8122-3190-2*); pap. text ed. 18.95 (*0-8122-1433-1*) U of Pa Pr.

— Teacher's Manual to Accompany Criminal Justice: Introductory Cases & Materials. 5th ed. 300p. 1993. pap. text ed. write for info. (*1-56662-127-5*) Foundation Pr.

McCoy, Carol P. Managing a Small HRD Department: You Can Do More Than You Think. LC 92-43607. (Management Ser.). 302p. 1993. 35.95 (*1-55542-529-1*) Jossey-Bass.

McCoy, Charles A. Polk & the Presidency. LC 72-10451. (American Biography Ser.: No. 32). 1973. reprint ed. lib. bdg. 75.00 (*0-8383-1686-7*) M S G Haskell Hse.

***McCoy, Charles N.** On the Intelligibility of Political Philosophy: Essays of Charles N. R. McCoy. Schall, James V. & Schrems, John J., eds. LC 88-31601. reprint ed. pap. 90.70 (*0-7837-9109-7*, 2049911) Bks Demand.

— The Structure of Political Thought: A Study in the History of Political Ideas. LC 74-25996. 323p. 1978. reprint ed. text ed. 52.50 (*0-8371-7880-0*, MCPT, Greenwood Pr) Greenwood.

McCoy, Charles S. & McCoy, Marjorie C. The Transforming Cross. LC 77-10884. reprint ed. 27.80 (*0-8357-9030-4*, 2016417) Bks Demand.

McCoy, Charles S., jt. auth. see Baker, J. Wayne.

McCoy, Charles S., ed. see Pomeroy, Richard M.

McCoy, Clyde B. & Inciardi, James A. Sex, Drugs, & the Continuing Spread of AIDS. (Illus.). 181p. (Orig.). (C). 1994. pap. text ed. 18.95 (*0-935732-64-0*) Roxbury Pub Co.

***McCoy, David B.** The Geometry of Blue. 112p. 1995. pap. 12.00 (*0-945568-17-7*) Spare Change Pr.

McCoy, Deborah. For the Bride. (Illus.). 368p. 1994. 34.95 (*0-9638939-0-4*) JE Hse Pubng.

McCoy, Dell & Collman, Russ. The R.G.S. Story, Vol. 1: Over the Bridges - Ridgway to Telluride. (Illus.). 416p. 1990. 65.00 (*0-913582-48-4*) Sundance.

McCoy, Diana L. The Secret: A Child's Story of Sex Abuse, Ages 7-10. 32p. (Orig.). (J). (gr. 2-5). 1986. pap. text ed. 6.00 (*0-9619250-1-9*) Magic Lantrn.

— A Special Place: A Child's Story about Entering Counseling for Children Ages 4 Through 6. (Illus.). 32p. (Orig.). (J). (gr. 2-5). 1988. pap. text ed. 5.50 (*0-9619250-3-5*) Magic Lantrn.

— A Special Place: A Child's Story about Entering Counseling for Children Ages 4 Through 6. (Illus.). 24p. (Orig.). (J). (ps-1). 1988. pap. 5.50 (*0-9619250-2-7*) Magic Lantrn.

McCoy, Donald R. Calvin Coolidge: The Quiet President. LC 67-11629. xvi, 472p. 1988. reprint ed. pap. 14.95 (*0-7006-0351-4*) U Pr of KS.

— Landon of Kansas. LC 65-16190. (Illus.). 631p. reprint ed. pap. 179.90 (*0-8357-3807-8*, 2036535) Bks Demand.

— The National Archives: America's Ministry of Documents, 1934-1968. LC 78-2314. (Illus.). xi, 437p. 1978. 34.95 (*0-8078-1327-3*) U of NC Pr.

— The National Archives: America's Ministry of Documents, 1934-1968. LC 78-2314. 447p. reprint ed. pap. 127.40 (*0-7837-3757-2*, 2043574) Bks Demand.

— The Presidency of Harry S. Truman. LC 84-3624. (American Presidency Ser.). xii, 356p. 1984. 25.00 (*0-7006-0252-6*); pap. 14.95 (*0-7006-0255-0*) U Pr of KS.

McCoy, Doyle. Oklahoma Wildflowers. (Illus.). 206p. 1987. 19.95 (*0-9619985-0-4*); pap. 16.95 (*0-9619985-1-2*) McCoy Pub Co.

— Roadside Flowers of Oklahoma, Vol. 1. (Illus.). 116p. 1976. reprint ed. pap. 10.00 (*0-9619985-2-0*) McCoy Pub Co.

— Roadside Flowers of Oklahoma, Vol. 2. (Illus.). 60p. 1978. reprint ed. pap. 5.00 (*0-9619985-3-9*) McCoy Pub Co.

— Roadside Trees & Shrubs of Oklahoma. LC 80-5944. (Illus.). 180p. (Orig.). 1981. pap. 16.95 (*0-8061-1556-4*) U of Okla Pr.

— Roadside Wild Fruits of Oklahoma. LC 79-6705. (Illus.). 96p. (Orig.). 1980. pap. 14.95 (*0-8061-1626-9*) U of Okla Pr.

McCoy, Drew R. The Elusive Rebublic: Political Economy in Jeffersonian America. 288p. (C). 1983. pap. text ed. 9.95 (*0-393-95239-8*) Norton.

— The Elusive Republic: Political Economy in Jeffersonian America. LC 79-20952. 278p. reprint ed. pap. 79.30 (*0-7837-6859-1*, 2046688) Bks Demand.

— The Last of the Fathers: James Madison & the Republican Legacy. (Illus.). 384p. (C). 1989. 44.95 (*0-521-36407-8*) Cambridge U Pr.

— The Last of the Fathers: James Madison & the Republican Legacy. (Illus.). 416p. (C). 1991. pap. 17.95 (*0-521-40772-9*) Cambridge U Pr.

Mccoy, Duff. Cutter: Panhandle Payback. 1990. pap. 3.50 (*1-55817-378-1*, Pinnacle NY) Windsor NY.

— Gut Shot. (Cutter Ser.: No. 2). 1990. pap. 3.50 (*1-55817-416-8*, Pinnacle NY) Windsor NY.

McCoy, Duff. Savage Blood. (Cutter Ser.: No. 3). 1991. pap. 3.50 (*1-55817-482-6*, Pinnacle NY) Windsor NY.

McCoy, E. Sue, jt. auth. see Grinder, Alison L.

McCoy, Earl D., jt. auth. see Shrader-Frechette, Kristin S.

***McCoy, Edain.** Celtic Myth & Magick: Harness the Power of the Gods & Goddesses. LC 95-1369. (World Religion & Magic Ser.). 1995. 19.95 (*1-56718-661-0*) Llewellyn Pubns.

— How to Do Automatic Writing. LC 94-35157. (How to Ser.). (Illus.). 240p. 1994. pap. 3.99 (*1-56718-662-9*) Llewellyn Pubns.

— In a Graveyard at Midnight: Folk Magic & Wisdom from the Heart of Appalacia. 240p. 1995. pap. 14.95 (*1-56718-664-5*) Llewellyn Pubns.

— Lady of the Night: A Handbook of Moon Magick & Ritual. (Llewellyn's Modern Witchcraft Ser.). (Illus.). 240p. 1995. pap. 14.95 (*1-56718-660-2*) Llewellyn Pubns.

— The Sabbats: A New Approach to Living the Old Ways. LC 94-29602. (Illus.). 320p. 1994. pap. 14.95 (*1-56718-663-7*) Llewellyn Pubns.

— A Witch's Guide to Faery Folk: Reclaiming Our Working Relationship with Invisible Helpers. LC 93-50837. (Illus.). 336p. 1994. pap. 12.95 (*0-87542-733-2*) Llewellyn Pubns.

— Witta: An Irish Pagan Tradition. LC 93-26366. (Llewellyn's New World Magic Ser.). (Illus.). 272p. 1993. pap. 12.95 (*0-87542-732-4*) Llewellyn Pubns.

McCoy, Edward, ed. Commercial Cockle Farming in Southern Thailand. (ICLARM Translations Ser.: No. 7). 13p. 1986. pap. 2.00 (*971-10-2220-6*, Pub. by ICLARM PH) Intl Spec Bk.

McCoy, Elin. Cards for Kids: Games, Tricks & Amazing Facts. LC 91-11373. (Illus.). 160p. (J). (gr. 1-7). 1991. text ed. 13.95 (*0-02-765461-3*, Mac Bks Young Read) S&S Childrens.

McCoy, Ernest, jt. auth. see Lott, Ira.

McCoy, Esther. Case Study Houses, 1945-1962. 2nd ed. LC 77-14499. (Illus.). 1977. reprint ed. pap. 24.50 (*0-912158-71-9*) Hennessey.

— The Second Generation. LC 83-14898. (Illus.). 200p. 1984. 27.50 (*0-317-65616-3*) Hennessey.

— Vienna to Los Angeles: Two Journeys. LC 78-54270. (Illus.). 1979. 17.50 (*0-931228-01-8*); pap. 10.95 (*0-931228-02-6*) Arts & Arch.

McCoy, Esther & Goldstein, Barbara. Guide to U. S. Architecture: Nineteen Forty to Nineteen Eighty. LC 80-67534. (Illus.). (Orig.). 1982. pap. 9.95 (*0-931228-06-9*) Arts & Arch.

McCoy, Esther & Makinson, Randell L. Five California Architects. 2nd ed. LC 74-19818. (Illus.). 200p. 1987. reprint ed. pap. 22.50 (*0-685-18517-6*) Hennessey.

***McCoy, Eugene B.** Climbing Up the Mountain: The Musical Life & Times of Dr. Mattie Moss Clark. LC 94-35097. 1994. write for info. (*0-917143-32-9*) Sparrow TN.

McCoy, F. N. Researching & Writing in History: A Practical Handbook for Student. 1974. pap. 11.00 (*0-520-02621-7*) U CA Pr.

— Robert Baillie & the Second Scots Reformation. LC 73-76110. 256p. reprint ed. pap. 73.00 (*0-318-34900-0*, 2031307) Bks Demand.

McCoy, Garnett, intro. The Card Catalog of the Oral History Collections of the Archives of American Art. LC 83-27098. 343p. 1984. lib. bdg. 75.00 (*0-8420-2216-3*) Scholarly Res Inc.

McCoy, George F., jt. auth. see Clarizio, Harvey F.

***McCoy, Gerard.** Hong Kong Cases 1993, Vol. 2. 672p. 1994. write for info. (*0-409-99710-2*) Butterworth Legal Pubs.

— Hong Kong Cases 1993, Vol. 2. 742p. 1994. write for info. (*0-409-99727-7*) Butterworth Legal Pubs.

McCoy, Gerard, jt. auth. see Bruce, Andrew.

McCoy, Glen. Doctor Who: Time Lash. 12.00 (*0-491-03851-8*) Carol Pub Group.

***McCoy, Gray.** The Charge of the Dwarf Brigade. 1994. 15.95 (*0-533-11034-3*) Vantage.

***McCoy Hatfield Staff.** Philistine Prophecy: A Parody. 1994. pap. 7.95 (*0-452-27474-5*, Plume) NAL-Dutton.

McCoy, Henry B. The Carpenter-Wier Family of Upper South Carolina & Other Ancestors, Including Benson, Beryy, Blassingame, Caldwell, Maxwell, Richey, Sloan, Stewart, Wilson. (Illus.). 326p. 1993. reprint ed. lib. bdg. 61.00 (*0-8328-3109-3*); reprint ed. pap. 51.00 (*0-8328-3110-7*) Higginson Bk Co.

McCoy, Horace. Adieu la Vie, Adieu l'Amour (Demian II Fera Nuit) 306p. (FRE.). 1987. pap. 11.95 (*0-7859-4513-X*, 207037887X) Fr & Eur.

— J'Aurais du Rester Chez Nous. (FRE.). 1982. pap. 10.95 (*0-7859-4173-8*) Fr & Eur.

— On Acheve Bien les Chevaux. (FRE.). 1977. pap. 10.95 (*0-7859-4086-3*) Fr & Eur.

— Le Scalpel. (FRE.). 1984. pap. 11.95 (*0-7859-4203-3*) Fr & Eur.

— They Shoot Horses, Don't They? 2nd ed. (Midnight Classics Ser.). 132p. 1995. pap. 9.99 (*1-85242-401-X*) Serpents Tail.

— They Shoot Horses Don't They? 1993. reprint ed. lib. bdg. 19.95 (*1-56849-241-3*) Buccaneer Bks.

McCoy, J. H. & Sarhan, M. E. Livestock & Meat Marketing. 3rd ed. (Illus.). 688p. 1988. text ed. 94.95 (*0-442-20488-4*) Van Nos Reinhold.

McCoy, J. J. Animals in Research: Issues & Conflicts. LC 92-21117. (Impact Bks.). (Illus.). 128p. (YA). (gr. 9-12). 1993. lib. bdg. 14.98 (*0-531-13023-1*) Watts.

— How Safe Is Our Food Supply? LC 90-35043. (Impact Bks.). (Illus.). 144p. (YA). (gr. 7-12). 1990. lib. bdg. 14.98 (*0-531-10935-6*) Watts.

McCoy, James C. Darby's Rainbow. LC 88-70551. (Illus.). 32p. (J). (gr. k-3). 1990. pap. 3.50 (*0-943864-52-6*) Davenport.

McCoy, James C., et al. Comic Tales Anthology, No. 2. 2nd ed. LC 88-70551. (Illus.). 100p. (Orig.). (YA). (gr. 7-12). 1988. pap. 6.95 (*0-943864-53-4*) Davenport.

McCoy, James W. Chemical Analysis of Industrial Water. (Illus.). 1969. 65.00 (*0-8206-0017-2*) Chem Pub.

— Chemical Treatment of Boiler Water. (Illus.). 1981. 58.50 (*0-8206-0284-1*) Chem Pub.

— Chemical Treatment of Cooling Water. 2nd ed. (Illus.). 1983. 58.50 (*0-8206-0298-1*) Chem Pub.

— Industrial Chemical Cleaning. (Illus.). 1984. 58.50 (*0-8206-0305-8*) Chem Pub.

***McCoy, Jennifer, et al, eds.** Venezuelan Democracy under Stress. 300p. (C). 1994. pap. 21.95 (*1-56000-770-2*) Transaction Pubs.

McCoy, Joann. The Fifties: The Age, the Era & the Attitudes. 48p. 1994. pap. 6.95 (*0-8059-3490-1*) Dorrance.

McCoy, John & Light, Timothy. Contributions to Sino-Tibetan Studies. (Cornell Linguistic Contributions Ser.: Vol. 5). 477p. 1986. 103.00 (*90-04-07850-9*) E J Brill.

McCoy, John B., et al. Bottomline Banking: A Strategic Vision. 1993. 32.50 (*1-55738-389-8*) Probus Pub Co.

McCoy, Joseph G. Historic Sketches of the Cattle Trade of the West & Southwest. Bieber, Ralph P., ed. & intro. by. LC 85-27348. (Illus.). 460p. 1986. reprint ed. pap. 9.95 (*0-8032-8134-X*) U of Nebr Pr.

McCoy, Judy. Rap Music in the Nineteen Eighties: A Reference Guide. 275p. 1992. 32.50 (*0-8108-2649-6*) Scarecrow.

McCoy, K. Landscape Planning for a New Australian Town. (Developments in Landscape Management & Urban Planning Ser.: Vol. 3). 1976. 46.25 (*0-444-41340-5*) Elsevier.

McCoy, K. Byron. Roberta White v. Reliable Realtors, Inc. 128p. 1989. 10.00 (*1-55681-192-6*, FBA0192); teacher ed 5.00 (*1-55681-193-4*, FBA0193) Natl Inst Trial Ad.

McCoy, K. Byron, jt. auth. see Lucas, Richard H.

McCoy, Karen, jt. ed. see Brill, Steven.

McCoy, Karen, jt. auth. see Spiller, Jan.

McCoy, Karen K. A Tale of Two Tengu. LC 93-2. (Illus.). (J). (gr. 1-3). 1993. 14.95 (*0-8075-7748-0*) A Whitman.

McCoy, Kathleen. Solo Parenting: Your Essential Guide. 1987. pap. 7.95 (*0-317-56843-4*, Plume) NAL-Dutton.

— Understanding Your Teenager's Depression: Issues & Insights for Every Parent. 352p. (Orig.). 1994. pap. 13.00 (*0-399-51856-8*, Perigree Bks) Berkley Pub.

McCoy, Kathleen & Harlan, Judith. English Literature from Seventeen Eighty-Five. LC 91-58271. (Outline Ser.). 288p. (Orig.). (C). 1992. pap. 12.00 (*0-06-467150-X*, Harper Ref) HarpC.

— Introduction to English Literature to Seventeen Eighty-Five. LC 91-55401. (College Outline Ser.). 288p. (Orig.). (C). 1992. pap. 12.00 (*0-06-467114-3*, Harper Ref) HarpC.

***McCoy, Kathleen M.** Teaching Special Learners in the General Education Classroom: Methods & Techniques. 2nd rev. ed. Orig. Title: Teaching Mainstreamed Students. 496p. 1995. text ed. write for info. (*0-89108-238-7*) Love Pub Co.

McCoy, Kathy & Wibbelsman, Charles. Growing & Changing: A Handbook for Preteens. LC 86-17059. (Illus.). 192p. 1987. pap. 13.00 (*0-399-51280-2*, Perigree Bks) Berkley Pub.

— The New Teenage Body Book. rev. ed. (Illus.). 288p. (YA). (gr. 9-12). 1992. pap. 15.00 (*0-399-51725-1*, Body Pr-Perigree) Berkley Pub.

McCoy, Katie, jt. auth. see Haines, Stephen.

McCoy, Keith. The Mount Adams Country: Forgotten Corner of the Columbia River Gorge. James, David, ed. (Illus.). 196p. 1987. 24.95 (*0-9618402-0-X*); pap. 18.95 (*0-9618402-1-8*) Pahto Pubns.

McCoy, Kim. Economics & Contemporary Issues: Instructor's Manual, Test Bank, & Transparency Masters to Accompany Edgmand-Moomaw-Olson. 2nd ed. 675p. (C). 1993. teacher ed, pap. text ed. 69.25 (*0-03-098000-3*) Dryden Pr.

— Economics & Contemporary Issues: Study Guide to Accompany Edgmand-Moomaw-Olson. 2nd ed. 427p. (C). 1993. pap. text ed. 18.75 (*0-03-098001-1*) Dryden Pr.

McCoy, Kirby. VMS Files Systems Internals. (VAX-VMS Ser.). (Illus.). 460p. (Orig.). 1990. pap. 49.95 (*1-55558-056-4*, Digital DEC) Buttrwrth-Heinemann.

McCoy, Leah P. Elementary Math Flipper, No. 1. 39p. (YA). (gr. 4 up). 1989. 6.25 (*1-878383-13-2*) C Lee Pubns.

***McCoy, Leighann.** The Incredible Journey of Gina GA: Member Book for Older Girls in Action. McClain, Cindy, ed. 40p. (Orig.). (J). (gr. 5-6). 1995. pap. text ed. 1.95 (*1-56309-126-7*) Womans Mission Union.

***McCoy, Lew.** Lew McCoy on Antennas. (Illus.). 128p. (Orig.). 1995. pap. 15.95 (*0-943016-08-8*) CQ Commns Inc.

McCoy, Lewistine, tr. see Kirkpatrick, Dow, ed.

***McCoy, Linda P.** Twenty Something & Breast Cancer: Images in Healing. Keitlen, Tomi & Swearenger, Marsha, eds. LC 95-76050. (Illus.). 160p. (Orig.). 1995. pap. 13.95 (*1-886966-02-8*) In Print.

McCoy, Lois, et al. The Byte Brothers Input an Investigation. (Illus.). (J). 1983. pap. 2.25 (*0-380-85571-2*, 85571, Camelot) Avon.

McCoy, Lowell E., jt. ed. see Walz, Daniel A.

McCoy, Marjorie C., jt. auth. see McCoy, Charles S.

McCoy, Mary V., et al. Cross-Cultural Orientation: A Guide for Leaders & Educators. rev. ed. Fantini, Alvino F., ed. (International Exchange Ser.). 230p. 1984. pap. text ed. 10.00 (*0-936141-01-8*) Experiment Pr.

McCoy, Maureen. Walking after Midnight. pap. 5.95 (*0-685-18036-0*) PB.

Mccoy, Max. Sixth Rider. 1994. pap. 3.99 (*0-553-56438-2*) Bantam.

***McCoy, Max.** Sons of Fire. 1995. mass mkt. 3.99 (*0-553-56439-0*) Bantam.

McCoy, Michael. Montana: Off the Beaten Path: A Guide to Unique Places. LC 93-16428. (Voyager Book Ser.). (Illus.). 160p. 1993. pap. 9.95 (*1-56440-171-5*) Globe Pequot.

— Mountain Bike Adventures in the Four Corners Region. LC 90-40743. (Illus.). 240p. (Orig.). 1990. pap. 12.95 (*0-89886-251-5*) Mountaineers.

— Mountain Bike Adventures in the Northern Rockies. LC 89-3007. (Illus.). 224p. (Orig.). 1989. pap. 10.95 (*0-89886-190-X*) Mountaineers.

— The Wild West: A Traveler's Guide. LC 94-30768. (Discover Historic America Ser.). (Illus.). 384p. 1995. pap. 15.95 (*1-56440-521-4*) Globe Pequot.

McCoy, Ozzie. Making Moonshine Fuel. LC 80-82732. (Illus.). 96p. (Orig.). 1981. lib. bdg. 12.95 (*0-915216-91-4*) Marathon Intl Bk.

McCoy, Patricia, jt. ed. see Votroubek, Wendy L.

McCoy, R. A. & Ntantu, I. Topological Properties of Spaces of Continuous Functions. (Lecture Notes in Mathematics Ser.: Vol. 1315). 124p. 1988. pap. 28.10 (*0-387-19302-2*) Spr-Verlag.

McCoy, R. D. & Tanenhaus, M. E., eds. Synthetic Aperture Radar. 1992. 53.00 (*0-8194-0776-3*, 1630) SPIE.

McCoy, R. L. PETROCALC (R) 3: Reservoir Economics & Evaluation. LC 84-558. (PETROCALC (R) Software for Petroleum Engineers Ser.). 1984. disk 95.00 (*0-87201-729-X*) Gulf Pub.

— PETROCALC (R) 7: Applied Well Log Analysis. LC 85-12564. (PETROCALC (R) Software for Petroleum Engineers Ser.). 80p. 1985. disk 95.00 (*0-87201-734-6*) Gulf Pub.

***McCoy, Ralph.** Children's Puzzle Packet. rev. ed. Sladkey, Sandra, ed. (H. I. S. Songs for Children Ser.). (Illus.). 18p. (J). (gr. 1-5). 1994. pap. 1.95 (*1-885819-06-4*) His Songs.

— Halloween Harvest Handbook: A Positive Alternative. rev. ed. Gruszewski, Ellen & Sladkey, Sandra, eds. (Illus.). 20p. 1994. pap. 3.00 (*1-885819-00-5*) His Songs.

— Poster Song Book. rev. ed. Sladkey, Sandra, ed. (Illus.). 60p. (J). (gr. 1-5). 1994. pap. 23.95 (*1-885819-05-6*) His Songs.

— Teacher's Resource Manual. rev. ed. Gruszewski, Ellen & Sladkey, Sandra, eds. (H. I. S. Songs for Children Ser.). (Illus.). 45p. 1994. teacher ed, pap. 7.95 (*1-885819-04-8*) His Songs.

McCoy, Ralph E. Freedom of the Press: A Bibliocyclopedia. Ten Year Supplement (1967-1977) LC 78-16573. 544p. 1979. 42.50 (*0-8093-0844-4*) S Ill U Pr.

— Freedom of the Press: An Annotated Bibliography. LC 67-10032. 576p. 1968. 32.50 (*0-8093-0335-3*) S Ill U Pr.

— Freedom of the Press: An Annotated Bibliography: Second Supplement, 1978-1992. LC 92-8395. 576p. (C). 1994. 100.00 (*0-8093-1583-1*) S Ill U Pr.

McCoy, Ramelle & Morand, Martin J., eds. Short-Time Compensation: A Formula for Work Sharing. LC 83-13265. 223p. 1984. 31.00 (*0-08-030148-7*, 29/59/4) Work in Amer.

McCoy, Robert, jt. comp. see Hinkle, James C.

McCoy, Robert, jt. auth. see Hinkle, James.

McCoy, Ron. Kiowa Memories: Images from Indian Territory, 1880. (Illus.). 67p. 1987. 35.00 (*0-317-67928-7*) Morning Star Gal.

— People of the Plateau. (Plateau Ser.). 32p. 1993. pap. 6.95 (*0-89734-117-1*) Mus Northern Ariz.

McCoy, Ron, ed. The Best of Deming. 175p. reprint ed. pap. 6.00 (*0-945320-37-X*) SPC Pr.

McCoy, Ronald. The Fine Young Chief. 32p. 1990. 4.95 (*0-89734-099-X*, PL61-1) Mus Northern Ariz.

— Summoning the Gods: Sandpainting of the Native American Southwest. (Plateau Ser.: PL 59: 1). (Illus.). 32p. 1988. pap. 5.95 (*0-89734-059-0*) Mus Northern Ariz.

McCoy, Ronald, jt. auth. see McCoy, Tim.

***McCoy, Rosemarie.** Inspirations: Poetry & Artwork. (Illus.). 171p. (Orig.). 1994. pap. 11.95 (*0-9641925-0-0*) L McCoy.

McCoy, Sandy. Something Happened to Me: Helping a Child to Become a Sexual Abuse Survivor. 18p. (J). (ps-2). 1993. 4.95 (*1-882811-01-1*) Skyline Pubns.

***McCoy, Sharon.** The Best Friends Book. LC 94-35076. (J). 1995. write for info. (*1-56565-204-5*) Lowell Hse Juvenile.

— Fifty Nifty Friendship Bracelets, Rings & Other Things. 64p. (J). (gr. 3-7). 1994. pap. 4.95 (*1-56565-130-8*) Lowell Hse.

— Fifty Nifty Ways to Jazz up Your Jeans. (Illus.). 64p. (J). 1994. pap. 4.95 (*1-56565-168-5*) Lowell Hse Juvenile.

McCoy, Sharon, jt. auth. see Scarborough, Sheryl.

McCoy, Theresa. Getting Ready for Adoption. 26p. (J). (gr. 1-7). 1993. student ed 7.95 (*0-9639685-0-5*) Adoption Wrld.

McCoy, Thomas J. Compensation & Motivation: Maximizing Employee Performance with Behavior-Based Incentive Plans. 320p. 1992. 65.00 (*0-8144-5029-6*) AMACOM.

McCoy, Thomas S. Voices of Difference: Studies in Critical Philosophy & Mass Communication. Good, Leslie T., ed. LC 93-357. (Communication Series: Critical Studies in Communication). 288p. (C). 1993. text ed. 52.50 (*1-881303-55-1*); pap. text ed. 22.95 (*1-881303-56-X*) Hampton Pr NJ.

McCoy-Thompson, Steven, jt. ed. see Pu, S. C.

McCoy, Tim & McCoy, Ronald. Tim McCoy Remembers the West. LC 87-30091. xxiv, 306p. 1988. pap. 8.95 (*0-8032-8155-2*) U of Nebr Pr.

McCoy, W. U. Performing & Visual Arts Writing & Reviewing. 182p. (Orig.). (C). 1992. pap. text ed. 18.50 (*0-8191-8774-7*) U Pr of Amer.

***McCoy, William.** Father's Day: Notes from a New Dad in the Real World. 1995. 22.00 (*0-8129-2405-3*, Times Bks) Random.

McCoy, William & McGeary, Mitchell. Every Little Thing: The Definitive Guide to Beatles Recording Variations, Rare Mixes & Other Musical Oddities, 1958-1986. Schultheiss, Tom, ed. LC 89-92321. (Rock & Roll Reference Ser.: No. 20). (Illus.). 380p. 1990. 37.50 (*1-56075-004-9*) Popular Culture.

McCoy, William R., jt. auth. see Warren, James R.

McCrachen, Betsy. Farm Journal's Homemade Pickles & Relishes. LC 76-14048. 128p. (Orig.). 1976. pap. 3.95 (*0-89795-018-6*) Farm Journal.

McCrackan, William D. The New Palestine: An Authoritative Account of Palestine Since the Great War; the Problems, Political, Economic & Racial, That Confront the British Administration. Davis, Moshe, ed. LC 77-70722. (America & the Holy Land Ser.). (Illus.). 1977. reprint ed. lib. bdg. 47.95 (*0-405-10266-6*) Ayer.

McCracken & Sutherland. Deaf Ability, Not Disability. 1991. 19.95 (*1-85359-080-0*, Pub. by Multilingual Matters UK); pap. 59.00 (*1-85359-081-9*, Pub. by Multilingual Matters UK) Taylor & Francis.

McCracken, jt. auth. see Orten.

***McCracken, Catherine.** Status, Management & Commercialization of the American Black Bear (Ursus Americanus) LC 95-6971. 1995. pap. write for info. (*0-89164-143-2*) World Wildlife Fund.

McCracken County Genelogical-Historical Society, Inc., Staff. History & Families McCracken Co., Kentucky. LC 89-50044. 376p. 1989. 49.95 (*0-938021-36-2*) Turner Pub KY.

McCracken, Daniel D. A Guide to NOMAD for Applications Development. pap. text ed. write for info. (*0-318-50142-2*) Addison-Wesley.

— Guide to PL-M Programming for Microcomputer Applications. 1978. pap. text ed. 20.76 (*0-201-04575-3*) Addison-Wesley.

— Public Policy & the Expert: Ethical Problems of the Witness. LC 76-171075. 1971. pap. 2.00 (*0-87641-212-6*) Carnegie Ethics & Intl Affairs.

— A Second Course in Computer Science with Pascal. LC 86-32586. (Illus.). 432p. (C). 1987. Net. text ed. write for info. (*0-471-01062-6*) Wiley.

McCracken, Daniel D. & Golden, Donald G. A Simplified Guide to Structured COBOL Programming. 2nd ed. LC 87-34608. 630p. 1988. Net. pap. text ed. write for info. (*0-471-88658-0*) Wiley.

— Simplified Structured COBOL with Microsoft-Microfocus COBOL. 1990. pap. text ed. 50.00 (*0-471-51407-1*) Wiley.

McCracken, Daniel D. & Salmon, William I. Computering for Engineers & Scientists with FORTRAN 77. 2nd ed. 730p. 1988. Net. pap. text ed. write for info. (*0-471-62552-3*) Wiley.

— A Second Course on Computer Science with MODULA 2. LC 87-14230. 496p. (C). 1987. Net. text ed. write for info. (*0-471-63111-6*) Wiley.

McCracken, Daniel D., jt. auth. see Dorn, William S.

McCracken, Dave. Advanced Dredging Techniques, Vol. 2, Pt. 1: Finding & Recovering Paystreaks. (Illus.). 176p. (Orig.). (C). 1983. pap. 7.95 (*0-685-75274-7*) New Era CA.

— Advanced Dredging Techniques, Vol. 2, Pt. 2: Succeeding at a Gold Dredging Venture. (Illus.). 164p. (Orig.). (C). 1983. pap. 7.95 (*0-685-75273-9*) New Era CA.

— Gold Mining in the Nineteen-Eighties. rev. ed. (Illus.). 260p. (Orig.). (C). 1988. reprint ed. pap. text ed. 15.95 (*0-317-90481-7*) Keene Engr Co Inc.

— Gold Mining in the 1990's: The Complete Book of Modern Gold Mining Procedures. (Illus.). 279p. (Orig.). 1993. pap. 19.95 (*0-9636015-0-4*) New Era CA.

McCracken, David. The Scandal of the Gospels: Jesus, Story, & Offense. 240p. 1994. 29.95 (*0-19-508428-4*) OUP.

McCracken, Donald L. A Production System Version of the Hearsay-Two Speech Understanding System. LC 81-7459. (Computer Science: Artificial Intelligence Ser.: No. 2). 151p. reprint ed. pap. 43.10 (*0-685-20828-1*, 2070044) Bks Demand.

McCracken, Donna. No More Litter: How to Train Your Cat to Use the Toilet. (Illus.). 64p. (Orig.). 1991. pap. 7.95 (*0-9629301-0-5*) Purr Pubns.

McCracken, Elizabeth, ed. To Mother: An Anthology of Mother Verse. LC 17-13752. (Granger Poetry Library). (Illus.). (J). (gr. 7-12). 1976. reprint ed. 17.50 (*0-89609-051-5*) Roth Pub Inc.

McCracken, Ellen. Decoding Women's Magazines: From Mademoiselle to Ms. LC 92-102. 288p. 1992. text ed. 45.00 (*0-312-07972-9*); pap. 18.95 (*0-312-07971-0*) St Martin.

McCracken-Flesher, Caroline, jt. ed. see Spilka, Mark.

McCracken Flesher, Paul V. Targum Studies, Vol. 1: Textual & Contextual Studies in the Pentateuchal Targums. (USF Studies in the History of Judaism). 155p. 1992. 59.95 (*1-55540-754-4*, 240055) Scholars Pr GA.

McCracken, Floyd. Southwest Corner Stories: Seventy-Five Years of Memories. LC 98-85273. (Illus.). 176p. (Orig.). 1993. pap. 8.95 (*0-9637445-7-7*) Shasta Valley.

McCracken, George H. & Nelson, John D., eds. Antimicrobial Therapy for Newborns: Practical Application. 2nd ed. 234p. 1983. text ed. 43.00 (*0-8089-1565-7*, 792831, Grune) Saunders.

McCracken, Grant. Culture & Consumption: New Approaches to the Symbolic Character of Consumer Goods & Activities. LC 87-45394. (Illus.). 190p. (Orig.). 1988. 27.95 (*0-253-31526-3*); pap. 10.95 (*0-253-20628-6*, MB-628) Ind U Pr.

— The Long Interview. (Qualitative Research Methods Ser.: Vol. 13). 96p. (C). 1988. text ed. 21.50 (*0-8039-3352-5*); pap. text ed. 9.50 (*0-8039-3353-3*) Sage.

McCracken, Harold. Great Painters & Illustrators of the West. 240p. 1988. pap. 8.95 (*0-486-25731-2*) Dover.

McCracken, J. L., ed. see Irish Conference of Historians Staff.

McCracken, Janet, ed. see Brown, Audrey & Gross, Toby.

McCracken, Janet B. Valuing Diversity: The Primary Years. LC 93-84576. (Illus.). 104p. 1993. pap. text ed. 5.00 (*0-935989-55-2*, 238) Natl Assn Child Ed.

McCracken, Janet B., ed. Reducing Stress in Young Children's Lives. LC 86-62564. (Illus.). 170p. 1986. pap. 7.00 (*0-935989-03-X*, NAEYC 216) Natl Assn Child Ed.

***McCracken, Jim.** Fish & Seafood. 93p. 1994. write for info. (*1-57215-004-1*) World Pubns.

McCracken, Karen H. Connie Hagar: The Life History of a Texas Birdwatcher. LC 85-40748. 312p. 1986. pap. 11.95 (*0-89096-406-8*) Tex A&M Univ Pr.

McCracken, Kathleen. The Constancy of Objects. 96p. 1988. 9.95 (*0-920806-98-8*, Pub. by Penumbra Pr CN) U of Toronto Pr.

McCracken, Kevin, jt. auth. see Curson, Peter.

McCracken, Lisa. The Lilies' Edge. LC 86-40282. (Illus.). 48p. (J). (gr. 1-3). 1987. 5.95 (*1-55523-036-9*) Winston-Derek.

McCracken, Marlene J. & McCracken, Robert A. Animals. rev. ed. (Themes Ser.). (Illus.). 83p. (J). (gr. k-4). 1985. pap. 11.95 (*0-920541-12-7*) Peguis Pubs Ltd.

— Celebrations. rev. ed. (Themes Ser.). (Illus.). 67p. (J). (gr. k-4). 1986. pap. 11.95 (*0-920541-72-0*) Peguis Pubs Ltd.

— Fall. (Themes Ser.). (Illus.). 88p. (J). (gr. k-4). 1987. pap. 11.95 (*0-920541-16-X*) Peguis Pubs Ltd.

— Fantasy. 4th ed. (Themes Ser.). (Illus.). 39p. (Orig.). (J). (gr. k-4). 1992. pap. 11.95 (*0-920541-02-X*) Peguis Pubs Ltd.

— Halloween. rev. ed. (Themes Ser.). 74p. (J). (gr. k-4). 1984. pap. 11.95 (*0-920541-76-3*) Peguis Pubs Ltd.

— Myself. rev. ed. (Themes Ser.). (Illus.). 84p. (J). (gr. k-4). 1984. pap. 11.95 (*0-920541-78-X*) Peguis Pubs Ltd.

— Reading Is Only the Tiger's Tail. 12th ed. 224p. (gr. k-4). 1987. teacher ed 14.95 (*0-920541-13-5*) Peguis Pubs Ltd.

— Reading, Writing & Language: A Practical Guide for Primary Teachers - Grades K-3. 2nd rev. ed. 136p. 1994. 14.95 (*1-895411-70-X*) Peguis Pubs Ltd.

— The Sea & Other Water. rev. ed. (Themes Ser.). (Illus.). 71p. (J). (gr. k-4). 1985. pap. 11.95 (*0-920541-80-1*) Peguis Pubs Ltd.

— Spelling Through Phonics: A Practical Guide for K-3. rev. ed. 102p. 1982. teacher ed 13.95 (*0-920541-00-3*) Peguis Pubs Ltd.

— Spring. rev. ed. (Themes Ser.). (Illus.). 83p. (J). (gr. k-4). 1987. pap. 11.95 (*0-920541-14-3*) Peguis Pubs Ltd.

— Stories, Songs & Poetry to Teach Reading & Writing. rev. ed. (Illus.). 157p. (J). (gr. k-4). 1987. teacher ed 14.95 (*0-920541-35-6*) Peguis Pubs Ltd.

— Tiger Cub Chants & Poems, 8 bks., Set. rev. ed. (Tiger Cub Bks.). (Illus.). 128p. (J). (gr. k-3). 1988. 19.95 (*0-920541-66-6*) Peguis Pubs Ltd.

— Tiger Cub Readers, 8 bks., Set. rev. ed. (Tiger Cub Bks.). (Illus.). 128p. (J). (gr. k-1). 1988. 19.95 (*0-920541-62-3*) Peguis Pubs Ltd.

— Tiger Cub Songs, 8 bks., Set. rev. ed. (Tiger Cub Bks.). (Illus.). 16p. (J). (gr. k-2). 1988. 19.95 (*0-920541-68-2*) Peguis Pubs Ltd.

— Tiger Cub Stories, 8 bks., Set. rev. ed. (Tiger Cub Bks.). (Illus.). 128p. (J). (gr. k-2). 1988. 19.95 (*0-920541-64-X*) Peguis Pubs Ltd.

— Winter. rev. ed. (Themes Ser.). (Illus.). 67p. (J). (gr. k-4). 1987. pap. 11.95 (*0-920541-10-0*) Peguis Pubs Ltd.

McCracken, Marlene J., jt. auth. see McCracken, Robert A.

McCracken, Nancy M. & Appleby, Bruce C., eds. Gender Issues in the Teaching of English. LC 92-11979. 220p. 1992. pap. text ed. 21.50 (*0-86709-310-2*) Boynton Cook Pubs.

McCracken, Paul W., et al. Consumer Installment Credit & Public Policy. LC 65-4634. (Michigan Business Studies: Vol. 17, No. 1). 260p. reprint ed. pap. 74.10 (*0-317-28350-2*, 2022083) Bks Demand.

— On Key Economic Issues. LC 84-70039. (AEI Studies: No. 399). 56p. reprint ed. pap. 25.00 (*0-8357-4518-X*, 2037377) Bks Demand.

McCracken, Philip. Philip McCracken. Tacoma Art Museum Staff, ed. LC 80-51071. (Illus.). 136p. 1980. 20.00 (*0-295-95771-9*) U of Wash Pr.

McCracken, Philip G. Your Retirement Money: How to Make It Last. 263p. (Orig.). 1992. pap. 17.95 (*0-9633349-0-5*) B&G Pub.

McCracken, Raven C. The World of Synnibarr. 514p. 1991. 29.95 (*0-9630336-0-3*) Real Dream.

McCracken, Robert A. & McCracken, Marlene J. Stories, Songs, & Poetry for Teaching Reading & Writing: Literacy Through Language. 176p. (C). 1986. pap. text ed. 16.95 (*0-8077-2856-X*) Tchrs Coll.

— Stories, Songs & Poetry to Teach Reading & Writing: Langauge Through Literacy. LC 86-1150. 160p. 1987. pap. text ed. 20.00 (*0-8389-0450-5*) ALA.

McCracken, Robert A., jt. auth. see McCracken, Marlene J.

McCracken, Robert D. The Fallacies of Women's Liberation. LC 72-89863. (Illus.). 150p. (C). 1972. pap. 5.95 (*0-88310-000-2*) Publishers Consult.

McCracken, Scott, ed. see Kee Yong Lim & Long, John.

McCracken, Scott, jt. ed. see Ledger, Sally.

***McCracken, Susan.** For the Love of a Friend. LC 94-7130. 157p. 1994. 9.95 (*0-944350-29-1*) Friends United.

***McCracken, Theresa, et al, illus.** 1995 Daily Job Log. 352p. (Orig.). 1994. pap. 24.50 (*1-57218-009-9*) Craftsman.

McCracken, Thomas O., jt. auth. see Kainer, Robert A.

McCracken, Thomas O., jt. auth. see Twietmeyer, T. Alan.

McCracken, Ursula E., ed. see Zeri, Federico & Packard, Elisabeth.

McCracken, William D. Rise of the Swiss Republic. 2nd ed. LC 75-130235. reprint ed. 29.45 (*0-404-04109-4*) AMS Pr.

McCrady, Barbara S. & Miller, William R. Research on Alcoholics Anonymous: Opportunities & Alternatives. LC 92-63233. 440p. (Orig.). (C). 1993. pap. 25.95 (*0-911290-24-9*, BBK-139) Rutgers Ctr Alcohol.

McCrady, Barbara S., jt. ed. see Paolino, Thomas J.

McCrady, Edward. History of South Carolina, Sixteen Seventy to Seventeen Eighty-Three, 4 Vols, 1. LC 69-18185. reprint ed. write for info. (*0-404-04121-3*) AMS Pr.

— History of South Carolina, Sixteen Seventy to Seventeen Eighty-Three, 4 Vols, 2. LC 69-18185. reprint ed. write for info. (*0-404-04122-1*) AMS Pr.

— History of South Carolina, Sixteen Seventy to Seventeen Eighty-Three, 4 Vols, 3. LC 69-18185. reprint ed. write for info. (*0-404-04123-X*) AMS Pr.

— History of South Carolina, Sixteen Seventy to Seventeen Eighty-Three, 4 Vols, 4. LC 69-18185. reprint ed. write for info. (*0-404-04124-8*) AMS Pr.

— History of South Carolina, Sixteen Seventy to Seventeen Eighty-Three, 4 Vols, Set. LC 69-18185. reprint ed. 195.00 (*0-404-04120-5*) AMS Pr.

McCrady, Edward, III, ed. Seen & Unseen: A Biologist Views the Universe. 1990. pap. 14.95 (*0-918769-16-7*) Univ South Pr.

McCrady, Edward, jt. auth. see Feduccia, Alan.

McCrady, Ellen R. North American Permanent Papers. 46p. (Orig.). 1994. pap. 7.00 (*0-9622071-2-8*) Abbey Pubns.

McCrady, Ellen R., ed. see Laursen, Per M.

McCrae, et al, eds. Specialist Mathematical: Core. 260p. (C). 1993. text ed. 24.95 (*0-522-84578-9*) Intl Spec Bk.

McCrae, Alister. Scots in Burma: Golden Times in a Golden Land. (Illus.). 120p. (C). 1995. pap. 25.00 (*1-870838-50-5*, Pub. by Kiscadale UK) Weatherhill.

McCrae, Ian. Global Economics: Seeking a Christian Ethic, a Workbook for Beginners. LC 92-42908. 1993. pap. 7.95 (*0-377-00253-4*) Friendship Pr.

An Asterisk (*) at the beginning of an entry indicates that the title is appearing in BIP for the first time.

McCrae, Jody. Lake of Dreams. large type ed. 244p. 1992. reprint ed. lib. bdg. 13.95 (*1-56054-409-0*) Thorndike Pr.
McCrae, Robert R. & Costa, Paul T., Jr. Personality in Adulthood. LC 89-78494. 198p. 1990. pap. text ed. 17. 95 (*0-89862-528-9*) Guilford Pr.
McCrae, William. Basic Organic Reactions. LC 72-75486. (Illus.). 230p. reprint ed. pap. 65.60 (*0-8357-8814-8*, 2033341) Bks Demand.
McCraig, Linda F. & McLemorel, Thomas. Plan & Operation of the National Hospital Ambulatory Medical Care Survey. LC 94-12448. (Vital & Health Statistics, Series 1, Programs & Collection Procedures: No. 34). 1994. 6.00 (*0-8406-0493-9*) Natl Ctr Health Stats.
McCraig, William, tr. see Rosselli, Carlo.
McCraken, Elizabeth. Here's Your Hat What's Your Hurry. 1993. 20.00 (*0-679-40026-5*) Random.
McCraken, Sheelagh. Bankers Remedy of Set Off. 300p. 1993. 180.00 (*0-406-00909-0*, UK) Butterworth Legal Pubs.
McCraney, Leah, jt. auth. see Barnwell, Thomas.
McCraney, Leah, jt. auth. see Barnwell, Tom.
McCranie, James & Wilson, Larry. The Biogeography of the Herpetofauna of the Pine-Oak Woodlands of the Sierra Madre Occidental of Mexico. (Contributions in Biology & Geology Ser.: No. 72). 30p. 1987. pap. text ed. 5.95 (*0-89326-153-X*) Milwaukee Pub Mus.
McCranie, James R. & Wilson, Larry D. A New Hylid Frog of the Genus Plectrohyla from a Cloud Forest in Honduras. (Occasional Papers: No. 92). 7p. 1981. 1.00 (*0-317-04882-1*) U of KS Mus Nat Hist.
McCrank, Lawrence J. Education for Rare Book Librarianship: A Reexamination of Trends & Problems. LC 80-622854. (University of Illinois, Graduate School of Library Science Occasional Papers: No. 144). (Illus.). 98p. reprint ed. pap. 28.00 (*0-7837-1175-1*, 2041703) Bks Demand.
McCrank, Lawrence J., comp. Mt. Angel Abbey: A Centennial History of the Benedictine Community & Its Library, 1882-1982. LC 83-10536. 224p. 1983. pap. 20. 00 (*0-8420-2212-0*) Scholarly Res Inc.
McCrank, Lawrence J., ed. Archives & Library Administration: Divergent Tradition & Common Concerns. LC 86-19405. 184p. 1986. text ed. 39.95 (*0-86656-590-6*) Haworth Pr.
— Bibliographical Foundations of French Historical Studies. LC 91-25540. (Primary Sources & Original Works). (Illus.). 245p. 1991. lib. bdg. 39.95 (*1-56024-150-0*) Haworth Pr.
McCrank, Lawrence J., intro. Discovery in the Archives of Spain & Portugal: Quincentenary Essays, 1492-1992. LC 93-50115. (Primary Sources & Original Works). (Illus.). 347p. 1994. 119.95 (*1-56024-643-X*) Haworth Pr.
McCraren, Joseph P., ed. The Aquaculture of Striped Bass. 6.50 (*0-943676-16-9*) MD Sea Grant Col.
McCrary, J. C. Good Morning, Sun! A Novel of Transformation. 154p. (Orig.). 1989. pap. 8.95 (*0-9623541-0-4*) Redite Pr.
McCrary, Jim. Coon Creek. 20p. (Orig.). 1972. ring bd. 1.00 (*0-685-30031-5*) Cottonwood KS.
— West of Mass. Moritz, John & Dillon, Curtis, eds. (Illus.). 76p. (Orig.). 1992. pap. 8.00 (*1-881175-01-4*) Tansy Pr.
McCrary, Larry F., jt. auth. see Edmonds, Thomas P.
McCrary, Peyton. Abraham Lincoln & Reconstruction: The Louisiana Experiment. LC 78-51181. 1978. 69.50 (*0-691-04660-3*) Princeton U Pr.
— Abraham Lincoln & Reconstruction: The Louisiana Experiment. LC 78-51181. 441p. reprint ed. pap. 125.70 (*0-7837-1404-1*, 2041758) Bks Demand.
McCrary, Sharie. Love, Lust, & Handcuffs: Understanding the Sex Abuser. LC 92-45167. 166p. (Orig.). 1993. pap. 8.95 (*1-880489-03-1*) Hoopuka Pr.
McCrary, Susan N. El Ultimo Godo' & the Dynamics of the Urdrama. 116p. 1990. 27.50 (*0-916379-36-1*) Scripta.
McCrary, William C. & Madrigal, Jose A. Studies in Honor of Everett W. Hesse. LC 80-53824. 208p. (Orig.). reprint ed. pap. 59.30 (*0-685-15879-9*, 2027062) Bks Demand.
McCraw, John B. & Arnold, Phillip G. Head & Neck Reconstruction. LC 87-82109. (McGraw & Arnold's Atlas of Muscle & Musculocutaneous Flaps Ser.). (Illus.). 262p. 1988. 163.50 (*0-939789-02-7*) Raven.
— McCraw & Arnold's Atlas of Muscle & Musculocutaneour Flaps. LC 86-82307. (Illus.). 748p. 1986. 291.50 (*0-939789-00-0*) Raven.
McCraw, Thomas K. America Versus Japan: A Comparative Study. 1988. text ed. 35.00 (*0-07-103255-X*); pap. text ed. 19.95 (*0-07-103254-1*) McGraw.
— Prophets of Regulation. (Illus.). 416p. 1986. pap. text ed. 14.95 (*0-674-71608-6*) Belknap Pr.
— Prophets of Regulation: Charles Francis Adams, Louis D. Brandeis, James M. Landis, Alfred E. Kahn. LC 84-296. 416p. 1984. 32.00 (*0-674-71607-8*) Belknap Pr.
— Regulation in Perspective: Historical Essays. 1982. text ed. 18.50 (*0-07-103281-9*); pap. text ed. 10.95 (*0-07-103282-7*) McGraw.
McCraw, Thomas K., ed. The Essential Alfred Chandler: Essays Toward a Historical Theory of Big Business. 1992. pap. text ed. 19.95 (*0-07-103317-3*) McGraw.
McCraw, Thomas K., intro. The Essential Alfred Chandler: Essays Toward a Historical Theory of Big Business. 538p. 1991. pap. 19.95 (*0-87584-306-9*) Harvard Busn.
McCray, Alexa T., jt. ed. see Van Bemmel, Jan H.
McCray, Carrie A. Piece of Time. 36p. (Orig.). 1993. 7.95 (*0-9619111-4-X*) Chicory Blue.
McCray, James A. & Cahill, Thomas A. Electronic Circuit Analysis for Scientists. LC 72-8986. (Illus.). 308p. reprint ed. pap. 87.80 (*0-317-08897-1*, 2012462) Bks Demand.
McCray, K., ed. Criteria, Guidelines, Practices, Procedures & Standards of the Ground Water Industry. 40p. 1988. 6.25 (*1-56034-065-7*, K454) Natl Water Well.
McCray, Marilyn. Electroworks. LC 79-67569. (Illus.). 1979. pap. text ed. 10.00 (*0-935398-01-5*) G Eastman Hse.
McCray, Philip R. The McCrays of America. 2nd ed. (Illus.). xiv, 441p. (Orig.). 1993. pap. 43.00 (*1-55613-829-6*) Heritage Bk.
McCray, Richard, ed. Supernovae & Supernova Remnants: IAU Colloquium 145. (Illus.). 400p. (C). 1994. write for info. (*0-521-46080-8*) Cambridge U Pr.
McCray, Ronald E. The First Manager. Van Treese, James B., ed. 200p. 1994. pap. 7.95 (*1-56901-077-3*) NW Pub.
***McCray, Walter A.** The American Young Adult Test: A Self-Help Adult Maturity Workbook. 48p. (Orig.). 1995. pap. 2.99 (*0-933176-18-X*) Black Light Fellow.
— Black Folks & Christian Liberty: Be Christian, Be Black, Be Culturally & Socially Free. 2nd ed. (Black Light Fellowship Ser.). 210p. (Orig.). 1987. pap. 10.00 (*0-933176-08-2*) Black Light Fellow.
— The Black Presence in the Bible & the Table of Nations (Genesis 10: 1-32), Vol. 2: With Emphasis on the Hamitic Genealogical Line from a Black Perspective. LC 90-83436. (Illus.). 210p. (Orig.). (C). 1991. pap. 19.95 (*0-933176-13-9*) Black Light Fellow.
— The Black Presence in the Bible, Vol. 1: Discovering the Black & African Identity of Biblical Persons & Nations. LC 90-80108. (Illus.). 208p. (Orig.). (C). 1991. pap. 19. 95 (*0-933176-12-0*) Black Light Fellow.
— The Black Young Adult Test (Christian Version) How Mature Are You? LC 94-96612. 48p. (Orig.). (YA). (gr. 11 up). 1995. pap. 2.99 (*0-933176-15-5*) Black Light Fellow.
— The Black Young Adult Test (General Version) How Mature Are You? LC 94-96611. 48p. (Orig.). 1995. pap. 2.99 (*0-933176-16-3*) Black Light Fellow.
— Black Young Adults - How to Reach Them, What to Teach Them: Strengthening the Black Church & Community by Educating Black Young Adults. 2nd ed. LC 92-72415. 144p. (gr. 12 up). 1992. reprint ed. pap. 8.95 (*0-933176-09-0*) Black Light Fellow.
— God's Righteousness for People. 1988. pap. text ed. 4.95 (*0-940955-02-4*); teacher ed. pap. text ed. 3.95 (*0-940955-03-2*) Urban Ministries.
— How to Stick Together During Times of Tension: Directives for Christian Black Unity. LC 83-70288. 170p. (Orig.). (C). 1983. pap. 7.50 (*0-933176-03-1*); boxed 11.95 (*0-933176-04-X*) Black Light Fellow.
— A Rationale for Black Christian Literature. 2nd ed. LC 92-72557. 56p. (C). 1992. reprint ed. pap. 4.95 (*0-933176-14-7*) Black Light Fellow.
McCrea, Barbara, jt. auth. see Rossi, Ernest E.
McCrea, Brian. Addison & Steele Are Dead: The English Department, Its Canon, & the Professionalization of Literary Criticism. LC 88-40600. 280p. 1990. 40.00 (*0-87413-366-1*) U Delaware Pr.
McCrea, Frances B. Minutes to Midnight: Nuclear Weapons Protest in America. (Violence, Cooperation, & Peace Ser.). 240p. (C). 1989. text ed. 52.00 (*0-8039-3417-3*); pap. text ed. 24.00 (*0-8039-3418-1*) Sage.
***McCrea, Henry V.** Red Dirt & Isinglass: A Wartime Biography of a Confederate Soldier. 578p. 1992. 31.95 (*0-9646766-0-5*) Chipola Pr.
McCrea, Joan. Texas Labor Laws. 3rd ed. LC 77-90788. 90p. (Orig.). 1978. pap. 9.95 (*0-87201-414-2*) Gulf Pub.
McCrea, John D. Pediatric Orthopedics of the Lower Extremity: An Instructional Handbook. (Illus.). 360p. 1985. 42.50 (*0-87993-230-9*) Futura Pub.
McCrea, Nancy. Developing High Impact Projects Downtown: Managing the Development Process to Minimize Risk. Murphy, Jenny, ed. 48p. (Orig.). 1988. pap. 18.00 (*0-317-04837-6*) Natl Coun Econ Dev.
— Incubator Resource Kit. 130p. (Orig.). 1988. pap. 35.00 (*0-317-04899-6*) Natl Coun Econ Dev.
— Minority Enterprise Development. Murphy, Jenny, ed. 46p. (Orig.). 1989. pap. 21.50 (*0-317-04808-2*) Natl Coun Econ Dev.
McCrea, Nancy, ed. see Gillen, Lori.
McCrea, S., ed. see Deming, W. Edwards.
***McCrea, Steve.** The NGV (Natural Gas Vehicle) Activity Book. (Illus.). 20p. (J). 1995. pap. text ed. 4.00 (*1-57074-246-4*) Greyden Pr.
— A Speculative Investor's Guide to the Electric Vehicle Industry. (Illus.). 40p. 1995. pap. text ed. 13.00 (*1-57074-263-4*) Greyden Pr.
— Where's My AFV (Alternative Fuel Vehicle)? (Illus.). 1995. pap. text ed. write for info. (*1-57074-251-0*) Greyden Pr.
***McCrea, Steve & Minner, R.** Why Wait for Detroit? Drive an Electric Car Today! (Illus.). 170p. 1995. pap. text ed. 20.00 (*1-57074-236-7*) Greyden Pr.
McCreadie, Marsha. The Casting Couch & Other Front Row Seats: Women in Films of the 1970s & 1980s. LC 89-72131. 208p. 1990. text ed. 49.95 (*0-275-92912-4*, C2912, Praeger Pubs) Greenwood.
— Women on Film: The Critical Eye. LC 82-13221. 176p. 1983. text ed. 49.95 (*0-275-91042-3*, C1042, Praeger Pubs) Greenwood.
— The Women Who Write the Movies: From Frances Marion to Nora Ephron. LC 94-18113. (Illus.). 256p. 1995. 19.95 (*1-55972-251-7*, Birch Ln Pr) Carol Pub Group.
McCready. Canadian Microeconomics. (C). Date not set. 32. 50 (*0-06-044348-0*, HarpT) HarpC.
— Canadian Public Sector Case. 1985. 50.00 (*0-409-84816-6*, Pub. by Buttrwrth Can Acad CN) Buttrwrth-Heinemann.
McCready, Benjamin W. On the Influence of Trades, Professions & Occupations in the United States in the Production of Disease. LC 78-180583. (Medicine & Society in America Ser.). 144p. 1980. reprint ed. 19.95 (*0-405-03960-3*) Ayer.
McCready, Douglas. Jesus Christ for the Modern World: The Christology of the Catholic Tubingen School. LC 90-33275. (American University Studies: Theology & Religion: Ser. VII, Vol. 77). 353p. (C). 1990. text ed. 52. 95 (*0-8204-1337-2*) P Lang Pubs.
McCready, Jack. Furred & Feathered Wild Game: From Bullet to Table. LC 93-60865. (Illus.). 141p. 1993. reprint ed. pap. 9.95 (*1-56664-031-8*) WorldComm.
***McCready, Karen.** Art Deco & Modernist Ceramics. LC 94-61467. (Illus.). 192p. 1995. 45.00 (*0-500-01669-0*) Thames Hudson.
McCready, Pauline I., jt. auth. see Strebeigh, Barbara.
McCready, R. R. Chess. LC 81-83687. 64p. 1981. 24.00 (*0-88014-035-6*) Mosaic Pr OH.
McCready, Richard R. Business Mathematics. 6th ed. 311p. (C). 1990. pap. 49.95 (*0-534-91993-6*) PWS Pubs.
McCready, Sam. Lucille Lortel: A Bio-Bibliography. LC 93-23892. (Bio-Bibliographies in the Performing Arts Ser.: No. 42). 304p. 1993. text ed. 59.95 (*0-313-27605-6*, MUC/, Greenwood Pr) Greenwood.
McCready, V. Ralph, jt. auth. see Cosgrove, David O.
McCready, William C., ed. Culture, Ethnicity, & Identity: Current Issues in Research. LC 82-22651. 1983. text ed. 72.00 (*0-12-482920-1*) Acad Pr.
McCreaner, A., jt. auth. see Green, J.
***McCreary, Alf.** Spirit of the Age: The Story of "Old Bushmills" 232p. 1983. 25.00 (*0-8159-6837-X*) Devin.
McCreary, C., jt. auth. see Foumeny, E.
McCreary, David. Rolling Around Puget Sound: Thirty-Six Places You Can Skate in Snohomish, King & Pierce Counties. 96p. 1994. pap. write for info. (*0-9642001-0-4*) McCreary Direct.
McCreary, Don R. Japanese-U. S. Business Negotiations: A Cross-Cultural Study. LC 86-554. 130p. 1986. text ed. 55.00 (*0-275-92006-2*, C2006, Praeger Pubs) Greenwood.
McCreary, Edward, jt. auth. see Zeckendorf, William.
McCreary, Jane. Story of Christmas: A Trim a Tree Story Six Wonderful Ornaments Tell the Christmas Story. (J). (ps-3). 1992. 10.99 (*0-87403-866-9*, 24-03556) Standard Pub.
McCreary, Lew. The Minus Man. (Contemporary American Fiction Ser.). 256p. 1994. pap. 9.95 (*0-14-013450-6*, Penguin Bks) Viking Penguin.
McCreary, Mallory, ed. see McCreary, Susan A.
***McCreary, Michael.** Havens: Celebrities' Favorite Rooms. Allerton, Colby & Hoffman, Peter, eds. (Illus.). 144p. 1995. 40.00 (*1-881649-30-X*) Genl Pub Grp.
McCreary, Paul. The Maze Book. (Ann Arbor Educational Ser.). (Illus.). (J). (gr. 2-4). 1979. pap. 8.00 (*0-87879-712-2*, Ann Arbor Div) Acad Therapy.
— Perceptual Activities: A Multitude of Perceptual Actitivies, Level 2-Advanced, Consumerable (Coloring) Edition. 1972. student ed. 10.00 (*0-87879-711-4*, Ann Arbor Div) Acad Therapy.
— Perceptual Activities: A Multitude of Reusable Perceptual Activities, Level 1-Primary. 1972. 10.00 (*0-87879-708-4*, Ann Arbor Div) Acad Therapy.
— Perceptual Activities: Level 2 - Elementary. 9.00 (*0-87879-709-2*) Acad Therapy.
— Perceptual Activities Level 1 Primary: A Multitude of Perceptual Activities. rev. ed. 62p. (gr. 2-4). 1976. 10.00 (*0-87879-710-6*, Ann Arbor Div) Acad Therapy.
McCreary, Scott T., jt. auth. see Sorensen, Jens C.
McCreary, Susan A. Cupid's Cuisine, the Foods of Love. LC 85-22279. (Illus.). 160p. 1985. pap. 6.00 (*0-9608428-4-5*) Straw Patchwork.
— Parsley, Sage, Rosemary & Mine: An Herbal Faire. LC 91-37719. (Illus.). 160p. (Orig.). 1991. pap. 8.00x (*0-9608428-5-3*) Straw Patchwork.
— Strawberry Patchwork. (Illus.). 104p. 1977. reprint ed. pap. 5.00x (*0-9608428-1-0*) Straw Patchwork.
— A Strawberry Serendipity: Unexpected Discoveries. McCreary, Mallory, ed. LC 95-68715. (Illus.). 160p. (Orig.). 1995. pap. 8.00x (*0-9608428-6-1*) Straw Patchwork.
— Sugarplum Visions: Old Christmases Made New. LC 83-18300. (Illus.). 160p. 1983. pap. 6.00 (*0-9608428-3-7*) Straw Patchwork.
McCreary, W. Burgess. One Thousand Bible Drill Questions. 1980. pap. 3.95 (*0-87162-263-7*, WP#D5899) Warner Pr.
McCreath, D., jt. ed. see Kaiser, P. K.
McCreath, Douglas. St. Andrew's College of Education. (C). 1989. 40.00 (*1-85098-144-2*, Pub. by Jordanhill College UK) St Mut.
McCreddan, Lyn. James McAuley. (Australian Writers Ser.). 128p. 1993. pap. 15.95 (*0-19-553349-6*) OUP.
McCredie, L. Wills, Probate & the Administration of the Estates of Deceased Persons in Victoria. 2nd ed. 280p. 1989. Australia. 76.00 (*0-409-49474-7*); Australia. pap. 60.00 (*0-409-49475-5*) Butterworth Legal Pubs.
McCree. John Sjolander: Poet of Cedar Bayou. (Illus.). 200p. 1988. 10.95 (*0-89015-569-0*) Sunbelt Media.
McCree, Charlene S. Art Japanese Style. LC 92-62005. (Illus.). 64p. (Orig.). 1994. pap. 8.00 (*1-56002-239-6*, Univ Edtns) Aegina Pr.
***McCree, Suesetta T.** Leisure & Play in Therapy: Theory, Goals & Activities. 140p. 1993. pap. text ed. 35.00 (*0-88450-656-8*, 4281) Commun Skill.
McCreede, Jess. Big Horn Massacre. 1991. mass mkt. 3.99 (*1-55817-569-5*, Pinnacle NY) Windsor NY.
— Blue Sky, Night Thunder: The Utes of Colorado. 416p. Date not set. 19.95 (*1-879915-08-1*) Affil Writers America.
— Colorado Ambush. 1989. pap. 2.95 (*1-55817-186-X*, Pinnacle NY) Windsor NY.
— Gold Rush Revenge. 352p. 1992. mass mkt. 3.99 (*1-55817-643-8*, Pinnacle NY) Windsor NY.
— High Mountain Ambush. 1990. pap. 2.95 (*0-8217-3127-0*) Zebra.
— Mountain Man's Blood. 1990. pap. 2.95 (*1-55817-326-9*, Pinnacle NY) Windsor NY.
— Mountain Men on the Santa Fe Trail. 1992. mass mkt. 3.99 (*1-55817-594-6*, Pinnacle NY) Windsor NY.
McCreery, Charles, jt. auth. see Green, Celia.
McCreery, David. Desarrollo Economico y Politica Nacional: El Ministerio de Fomento de Guatemala, 1871-1885. LC 82-230313. (CIRMA Serie Monografica: No.1). (Illus.). 177p. (Orig.). (SPA.). 1981. pap. 9.00 (*0-910443-00-9*) CIRMA.
— Development & the State in Reforma Guatemala, 1871-1885. LC 81-22545. (Papers in International Studies: Latin America Ser.: No. 10). 128p. (Orig.). reprint ed. pap. 36.50 (*0-7837-6472-3*, 2046476) Bks Demand.
— Rural Guatemala, 1760-1940. LC 93-27405. 1994. 47.50 (*0-8047-2318-4*) Stanford U Pr.
McCreery, Elaine. Worship in the Primary School. (Roehampton Teaching Studies Ser.). 144p. 1993. pap. 29.00 (*1-85346-233-0*, Pub. by D Fulton UK) Taylor & Francis.
McCreery, Henry F. The Recovery of Religious Roots. (Illus.). 192p. 1993. 13.50 (*0-9637435-0-3*) Sea Stack Pr.
McCreery, Kathleen, jt. auth. see Stourac, Richard.
McCreery, Ruth S., jt. auth. see Ekiguchi, Kunio.
McCreesh, Thomas P. Biblical Sound & Sense: Poetic Sound Patterns in Proverbs 10-29. (JSOT Supplement Ser.: No. 128). 175p. (C). 1991. 22.50 (*1-85075-326-1*, Pub. by Sheffield Acad UK) CUP Services.
McCreight, John L. Making Membership Meaningful. 1994. pap. 6.95 (*1-55673-582-0*, 7981) CSS OH.
McCreight, Robert G. A Promise Kept at Christmas: Christmas Eve Service. (Orig.). 1994. pap. write for info. (*0-7880-0096-9*) CSS OH.
McCreight, Tim. The Complete Metalsmith: An Illustrated Handbook. rev. ed. LC 81-66573. (Illus.). 189p. (Orig.). 1991. pap. 18.95 (*0-87192-240-1*) Davis Mass.
— Custom Knifemaking: Ten Projects from a Master Craftsman. LC 85-2844. (Illus.). 224p. (Orig.). 1985. pap. 14.95 (*0-8117-2175-2*) Stackpole.
— Practical Jewelry Rendering. (Illus.). 96p. (C). 1993. pap. text ed. 24.95 (*0-9615984-4-1*) Brynmorgen.
McCreight, Tim, ed. & illus. Metals Technic: A Collection of Techniques for Metalsmiths. 160p. (C). 1992. 24.95 (*0-9615984-3-3*) Brynmorgen.
McCrickard, Eleanor, jt. auth. see Gianturco, Carolyn.
McCrickard, Francis. The Boy & the Book: A Story of Early Christian Ireland. 104p. 1989. pap. 30.00 (*1-85390-018-4*, Pub. by Veritas IE) St Mut.
— Faith Questions: Helping Young Adults Develop Their Faith. 126p. 1989. pap. 30.00 (*1-85390-097-4*, Pub. by Veritas IE) St Mut.
McCrie, Robert D., ed. Security Letter Source Book 1987-1988. 416p. 1987. pap. 75.00 (*0-317-62323-0*) Security Let.
— Security Letter Source Book, 1990-91. 416p. 1990. pap. 75.00 (*0-9609820-3-5*) Security Let.
— Security Letter Source Book, 1993. 450p. 1992. pap. 75. 00 (*0-9609820-4-3*) Buttrwrth-Heinemann.
McCrie, Thomas. The Early Years of John Calvin: A Fragment, 1509-1536. LC 83-45622. reprint ed. 28.00 (*0-404-19840-6*) AMS Pr.
— History of the Progress & Suppression of the Reformation in Italy. LC 72-1006. reprint ed. 22.45 (*0-404-04118-3*) AMS Pr.
— Life of John Knox. LC 83-45584. (Illus.). reprint ed. 57. 50 (*0-404-19902-X*) AMS Pr.
McCright, Grady E. & Powell, James H. Jessie Evans: Lincoln Country Badman. LC 83-20902. (Early West Ser.). (Illus.). 239p. 1983. 18.95 (*0-932702-28-7*); pap. 8.95 (*0-932702-30-9*) Creative Texas.
— Jessie Evans: Lincoln Country Badman. deluxe ed. LC 83-20902. (Early West Ser.). (Illus.). 239p. 1983. 75.00 (*0-932702-29-5*) Creative Texas.
McCrillis, Philip, jt. auth. see Simons, George.
McCrimmin, Barbara. Richard Garnett: The Scholar & Librarian. (Publications in Librarianship: No. 46). 211p. 1989. 30.00 (*0-685-72689-4*) Assn Coll & Res Libs.
McCrimmon, Ian. Big Bang Theory - or Rotating Universe? (C). 1992. text ed. 25.00 (*0-9514698-7-8*, Pub. by Cosmatom UK) St Mut.
— The Body & the Spirit. (C). 1992. text ed. 30.00 (*0-9514698-6-X*, Pub. by Cosmatom UK) St Mut.
— Flying Saucers: The Alternation of Space & Time. (C). 1992. text ed. 25.00 (*1-874686-02-5*, Pub. by Cosmatom UK) St Mut.
— Imaginary Time: Journeys in Space Faster Than Light. (C). 1992. text ed. 19.00 (*1-874686-03-3*, Pub. by Cosmatom UK) St Mut.
— Mass & Antimass (Positive & Negative Mass) in Five Dimensions. (C). 1992. text ed. 19.00 (*1-874686-01-7*, Pub. by Cosmatom UK) St Mut.
— The Nature of the Fifth Dimension: De Revolutionibus Orbium Rotantium. 512p. (C). 1990. text ed. 195.00 (*0-9514698-0-0*, Pub. by Cosmatom UK) St Mut.
— Proof of God. (C). 1992. text ed. 19.00 (*0-9514698-5-1*, Pub. by Cosmatom UK) St Mut.
— The Strange Case of the Disapparing Antiproton. (C). 1992. text ed. 19.00 (*0-9514698-9-4*, Pub. by Cosmatom UK) St Mut.
— TCP Invariance & Charge Quantization: Anti-Hydrogen & the Fifth Dimension. (C). 1992. pap. 25.00 (*0-9514698-8-6*, Pub. by Cosmatom UK) St Mut.
— Twelve Questions for Theologians. (C). 1992. text ed. 59. 95 (*0-9514698-1-9*, Pub. by Cosmatom UK) St Mut.
— Twenty Questions for Scientists. (C). 1992. text ed. 30.00 (*0-9514698-2-7*, Pub. by Cosmatom UK) St Mut.
— The Unity in the Trinity. (C). 1992. text ed. 30.00 (*0-9514698-4-3*, Pub. by Cosmatom UK) St Mut.
— A Whirling Mass of Space - Time. (C). 1992. text ed. 25. 00 (*1-874686-00-9*, Pub. by Cosmatom UK) St Mut.

McCrimmon, James M. Writing with a Purpose. 6th ed. 1976. text ed. 10.95 (0-685-42615-7) HM.

***McCrimmon, Mitch.** Unleash the Entrepreneur Within: How to Make Everyone an Enterpreneur & Stay Effecient. 240p. 1995. 29.95 (0-273-61456-8) Natl Bk Netwk.

McCrindle, J. W. Ancient India: As Described by in Classical Literature Being a Collection of Greek & Latin. 246p. 1974. 25.00 (1-55528-085-4, Pub. by Today & Tomorrows P & P II) Scholarly Pubns.

— Ancient India: As Described by Ktesias the Knidian. reprint ed. 25.00 (1-55528-062-5, Pub. by Today & Tomorrows P & P II) Scholarly Pubns.

— Ancient India: As Described by Megasthenes & Arriyan. 315p. 1972. reprint ed. 30.00 (0-88065-158-X, Messers Today & Tomorrow) Scholarly Pubns.

— Ancient India: As Described by Ptolemy. Jain, Ramachandra, ed. 450p. 1985. 25.00 (1-55528-034-X, Pub. by Today & Tomorrows P & P II) Scholarly Pubns.

— Ancient India: As Desribed by Arrian Q. Curtius, Diodorus, Plutarch & Justin in "Invasion of India by Alexander the Great" 470p. 1973. reprint ed. 25.00 (0-88065-159-8, Messers Today & Tomorrow) Scholarly Pubns.

McCrindle, John W. Ancient India As Described in Classical Literature. 247p. reprint ed. text ed. 28.50 (0-685-13414-8) Coronet Bks.

McCrohan, Donna. Archie & Edith, Mike & Gloria: The Tumultuous History of "All in the Family" LC 87-42743. 280p. 1988. pap. 7.95 (0-89480-527-4, 1527) Workman Pub.

— Get What You Pay for - Or Don't Pay at All. LC 93-23498. 1994. pap. 12.00 (0-517-88048-2, Crown) Crown Pub Group.

— The Honeymooners' Companion. LC 77-93033. (Illus.). 244p. 1978. pap. 7.95 (0-89480-022-1, 175) Workman Pub.

— The Life & Times of Maxwell Smart. (Illus.). 224p. 1988. pap. 12.95 (0-312-00030-8) St Martin.

McCrohan, Donna & Crescenti, Peter. The Honeymooners' Lost Episodes. LC 86-40203. (Illus.). 224p. (Orig.). 1986. pap. 8.95 (0-89480-157-0, 1157) Workman Pub.

McCrone, Carole N. & Rose-Hancock, Marga, eds. Fresh, Fast, & Fabulous. 190p. 1982. pap. 8.95 (0-89716-122-X) P B Pubng.

McCrone, David. Understanding Scotland. LC 91-34756. 256p. 1993. 65.00 (0-415-06747-2, A7315) Routledge.

McCrone, David, jt. ed. see Brown, Alice.

Mccrone, David, jt. ed. see Kendrick, Stephen.

McCrone, Gavin. Scotland's Future: An Essay on the Economics of Nationalism. LC 71-92501. 1969. 22.95 (0-678-06252-8) Kelley.

McCrone, John. The Ape That Spoke. 288p. 1992. pap. 10.00 (0-380-71399-3) Avon.

— The Myth of Irrationality. 352p. 1994. 24.00 (0-7867-0067-X) Carroll & Graf.

McCrone, Kathleen E. Playing the Game: Sport & the Physical Emancipation of English Women, 1870-1914. LC 87-32038. (Illus.). 336p. 1988. 35.00 (0-8131-1641-4) U Pr of Ky.

***McCrone, R. G. & Stephens, Mark.** Housing Policy in Britain & Europe. 256p. 1995. 79.00x (1-85728-410-0, Pub. by UCL Pr UK); pap. 29.95x (1-85728-411-9, Pub. by UCL Pr UK) Taylor & Francis.

McCrone, William P., et al, eds. Networking & Deafness. (Readings in Deafness Ser.: No. 9). (Illus.). 247p. 1983. pap. text ed. 7.95 (0-914494-10-4) Am Deaf & Rehab.

McCrorey, Dolores, jt. auth. see McCrorey, Helen.

McCrorey, Helen & McCrorey, Dolores. The Business of Family Day Care. LC 87-61785. 128p. (Orig.). 1988. pap. 12.95 (0-915677-35-0) Roundtable Pub.

McCrorie, Edward. After a Cremation. 1974. pap. 3.00 (0-914476-32-7) Thorp Springs.

***McCrorie, Edward, tr.** The Aeneid of Virgil. 1994. 39.50 (0-472-09595-1) U of Mich Pr.

— The Aeneid of Virgil. 1995. pap. 14.95 (0-472-06595-5) U of Mich Pr.

McCrory & Shifrin. Geometry & Topology: Manifold, Varieties & Knots. (Lecture Notes in Pure & Applied Mathematics Ser.: Vol. 105). 368p. 1987. 125.00 (0-8247-7621-6) Dekker.

McCrory, ed. see Cervantes.

McCrory, David E. Liquor Licenses: A Guide to California Retail Alcoholic Beverage Licensing. LC 86-83036. (Illus.). 186p. (Orig.). 1987. pap. 29.95 (0-9617755-0-5) Full Ct Pr CA.

McCrory, Elliot S., ed. Accelerator Instrumentation: Second Annual Workshop. 220p. 1991. 75.00 (0-685-60542-6) Am Inst Physics.

McCrory, Elliott S., ed. Accelerator Instrumentation. LC 91-55347. (AIP Conference Proceedings Ser., Subseries: Particle & Fields: No. 229, 44). 304p. 1991. lib. bdg. 85.00 (0-88318-832-5) Am Inst Physics.

McCrory, G. Jacobs. Softball Rules in Pictures. rev. ed. (Sports Rules in Pictures Ser.). (Illus.). 80p. (J). 1992. pap. 7.95 (0-399-51728-6, Perigree Bks) Berkley Pub.

McCrory, Martin & Moulder, Robert. French Revolution for Beginners. 12.95 (0-318-00805-X); pap. 7.95 (0-86316-015-8) Writers & Readers.

McCrory, Moy. Those Sailing Ships of His Boyhood Dreams. 153p. 1992. 22.95 (0-224-03160-0, Pub. by Jonathan Cape UK) Trafalgar.

McCrory, R. H. Lock, Stock & Barrel. 1966. 6.00 (0-913150-68-1) Pioneer Pr.

— Make Muzzleloader Accessories. 1971. 4.50 (0-913150-67-3) Pioneer Pr.

— The Modern Kentucky Rifle. 1968. 6.00 (0-913150-66-5) Pioneer Pr.

McCrory, Wallace W. Developmental Nephrology. LC 72-75399. (Commonwealth Fund Publications). (Illus.). 230p. 1972. 29.95 (0-674-20275-9) HUP.

McCroskey. Introduction Interpersonal Communication. pap. 27.95 (0-8087-7646-0) Burgess MN Intl.

McCroskey & Richmond. Communication in Educational Organizations. pap. 29.95 (0-8087-7641-X) Burgess MN Intl.

McCroskey, ed. see Daniels, Jerry & Mara, Mary J.

McCroskey, J. Introduction to Communication in the Classroom. pap. 29.95 (0-8087-7638-X) Burgess MN Intl.

McCroskey, James C. An Introduction to Rhetorical Communication. 6th ed. LC 92-25120. 320p. (C). 1992. pap. text ed. 24.00 (0-13-474578-7) P-H.

McCroskey, James C. & Daly, John A., eds. Personality & Interpersonal Communication. (Series in Interpersonal Communication: Vol. 6). 288p. 1987. text ed. 49.95 (0-8039-2645-6); pap. text ed. 24.00 (0-8039-2646-4) Sage.

— Personality & Interpersonal Communication. LC 86-6651. (Sage Series in Interpersonal Communication: No. 6). 351p. reprint ed. pap. 100.10 (0-7837-6722-6, 2046349) Bks Demand.

McCroskey, James C., jt. ed. see Daly, John A.

McCroskey, James C., jt. auth. see Richmond, Virginia P.

McCroskey, James C., jt. ed. see Richmond, Virginia P.

McCrossan, T. J. Bodily Healing & the Atonement. 1982. pap. 3.95 (0-89276-505-4) Hagin Ministries.

***McCrudden, Christopher.** Equality of Treatment Between Men & Women in Social Security. 1994. pap. text ed. 193.00 (0-406-03767-1, UK) Butterworth Legal Pubs.

McCrudden, Christopher, ed. Anti-Discrimination Law. (International Library of Essays in Law & Legal Theory). 484p. 1991. text ed. 150.00 (0-8147-5466-X) NYU Pr.

McCrudden, Christopher & Chambers, Gerald, eds. Individual Rights & the Law in Britain. 72800p. 1994. 89.00 (0-19-825741-4) OUP.

— Individual Rights & the Law in Britain. 728p. 1995. pap. 35.00 (0-19-826022-9) OUP.

McCrudden, John & Avenoso, Ellen, eds. The Long Island Job Source. 80p. (Orig.). 1989. pap. 4.95 (0-9623212-0-6) LIU SC.

— The Long Island Job Source. rev. ed. 125p. (Orig.). 1990. pap. text ed. 4.95 (0-9623212-1-4) LIU SC.

McCrudder, Christopher, jt. ed. see Baldwin, Robert.

McCrum, I., jt. auth. see Cahill, S. J.

McCrum, Michael. Thomas Arnold, Head Master: A Reassessment. (Illus.). 168p. 1990. 39.95 (0-19-211798-X) OUP.

McCrum, N. G. Anelastic & Dielectric Effects in Polymeric Solids. 1991. pap. 15.95 (0-486-66752-9) Dover.

McCrum, N. G., et al. Principles of Polymer Engineering. (Illus.). 408p. 1988. pap. text ed. 32.50 (0-19-856152-0) OUP.

— Solutions Manual to Accompany Principles of Polymer Engineering. (Illus.). 190p. (C). 1989. pap. text ed. 24.95 (0-19-856201-2) OUP.

***McCrum, R. C.** Dear Mom: World War II Remembered in a Sailor's Letters. LC 94-61069. (Illus.). 210p. 1994. pap. 19.95 (0-89101-083-1) U Maine Pr.

McCrum, Robert. The Psychological Moment. LC 93-34830. 1994. 22.00 (0-679-42987-5) Knopf.

— The World Is a Banana. large type ed. 171p. (J). 1992. 16.95 (0-7451-1611-6, Galaxy Child Lrg Print) Chivers N Amer.

McCrum, Robert, et al. The Story of English. rev. ed. (Illus.). 400p. 1993. pap. 17.50 (0-14-015405-1, Penguin Bks) Viking Penguin.

McCrumb, Bernadette. When Time Stands Still. 1992. 16.95 (0-533-09663-4) Vantage.

***McCrumb, Sharon.** She Walks These Hills. 448p. 1995. pap. 6.50 (0-451-18472-6, Sig) NAL-Dutton.

Mccrumb, Sharyn. Bimbos of the Death Sun. LC 86-1267. 1987. pap. 3.95 (0-88038-455-7) TSR Inc.

McCrumb, Sharyn. The Hangman's Beautiful Daughter. 384p. 1993. pap. 5.50 (0-451-40370-3, Onyx) NAL-Dutton.

— The Hangman's Beautiful Daughter: A Novel of Suspense. 288p. 1992. text ed. 19.00 (0-684-19407-4, Scribners) S&S Trade.

— Highland Laddie Gone. 1991. mass mkt. 4.99 (0-345-36036-2) Ballantine.

— If Ever I Return, Pretty Peggy-O. 324p. 1990. text ed. 17.95 (0-684-19104-0, Scribners) S&S Trade.

— If Ever I Return, Pretty Peggy O. 1991. mass mkt. 4.99 (0-345-36906-8) Ballantine.

***Mccrumb, Sharyn.** If I'd Killed Him When I Met Him: An Elizabeth MacPherson Novel. LC 94-23701. 1995. 20.00 (0-345-38229-3) Ballantine.

McCrumb, Sharyn. Lovely in Her Bones. 224p. 1990. reprint ed. mass mkt. 4.99 (0-345-36035-4) Ballantine.

Mccrumb, Sharyn. MacPherson's Lament. (Southern Mysteries Ser.). 1993. mass mkt. 5.99 (0-345-38474-1) Ballantine.

McCrumb, Sharyn. Missing Susan. 1992. reprint ed. mass mkt. 4.99 (0-345-37945-4) Ballantine.

Mccrumb, Sharyn. Missing Susan: An Elizabeth MacPherson Mystery. large type ed. LC 92-46703. (General Ser.). 408p. 1993. pap. 17.95 (0-8161-5566-6, Large Print Bks) Hall.

McCrumb, Sharyn. Paying the Piper. 1988. mass mkt. 4.99 (0-345-34518-5) Ballantine.

— She Walks These Hills: A Novel of Suspense. 320p. 1994. text ed. 20.00 (0-684-19556-9, Scribners) S&S Trade.

— Sick of Shadows. 240p. 1989. pap. 3.95 (0-345-35653-5) Ballantine.

— The Windsor Knot. 1991. mass mkt. 4.99 (0-345-36427-9) Ballantine.

— Zombies of the Gene Pool. 1993. mass mkt. 4.99 (0-345-37914-4) Ballantine.

— Zombies of the Gene Pool: A Jay Omega Mystery. 192p. 1992. 18.00 (0-671-70526-1) S&S Trade.

McCrumb, Sharyn & Helper, Mona W. Our Separate Days. LC 89-10584. (Illus.). 114p. (Orig.). 1989. pap. 9.95 (0-926487-01-9) Rowan Mtn Pr.

McCrumb, Sharyn, et al. Partners in Crime: Mysteries That Take Two to Untangle. Chase, Elaine R., ed. 272p. (Orig.). 1994. pap. 4.99 (0-451-40504-8, Sig) NAL-Dutton.

McCuaig, William. Carlo Sigonio: The Changing World of the Late Renaissance. 316p. (C). 1989. text ed. 55.00 (0-691-05558-0) Princeton U Pr.

McCuaig, William, tr. see Frugoni, Chiara.

McCuan, Walter R., jt. ed. see Markley, Oliver W.

McCubbin, Bob. The Gay Question: A Marxist Appraisal. 84p. 4.00 (0-89567-023-2) World View Forum.

***McCubbin, Bob.** Roots of Lesbian & Gay Oppression: A Marxist View. 1993. pap. 7.95 (0-89567-116-6) World View Forum.

McCubbin, Hamilton I. & Dahl, Barbara. Marriage & Family: Individuals & Life Cycles. LC 84-11810. 450p. (C). 1985. write for info. (0-02-379000-8) Macmillan.

McCubbin, Hamilton I. & Figley, Charles R., eds. Stress & the Family Vol. I: Coping with Normative Transitions. LC 83-6048. (Psychosocial Stress Ser.: No. 2). 296p. 1983. 29.95 (0-87630-321-1) Brunner-Mazel.

McCubbin, Hamilton I. & Thompson, Anne I. Balancing Work & Family Life on Wall Street. 224p. (Orig.). 1989. write for info. (0-8087-7617-7) Burgess MN Intl.

McCubbin, Hamilton I., jt. ed. see Figley, Charles R.

***McCubbin, Hamilton I., et al.** Family Stress, Coping, & Social Support. (Illus.). 294p. 1982. pap. 24.95 (0-398-06275-7) C C Thomas.

— Family Stress, Coping, & Social Support. (Illus.). 294p. (C). 1982. 38.95 (0-398-04692-1) C C Thomas.

— Family Types & Strengths. 228p. (Orig.). 1988. pap. text ed. write for info. (0-8087-7607-X) Burgess MN Intl.

***McCubbin, Hamilton I., et al, eds.** Resiliency in Ethnic Minority Families: African American Families, Vol. 2. LC 94-61816. 350p. (Orig.). (C). 1995. pap. text ed. 30.00 (0-9639334-3-4) U of Wis CEFM.

— Resiliency in Ethnic Minority Families: Native & Immigrant American Families, Vol. 1. 453p. (Orig.). 1994. pap. text ed. 30.00 (0-9639334-2-6) U of Wis CEFM.

— Sense of Coherence & Resiliency: Stress, Coping, & Health. (Resiliency & Families Ser.). 300p. (Orig.). (C). 1994. pap. write for info. (0-9639334-0-X) U of Wis CEFM.

— Social Stress & the Family: Advances & Developments in Family Stress Therapy & Research. LC 83-190. (Marriage & Family Review Ser.: Vol. 6, Nos. 1-2). 231p. 1983. text ed. 49.95 (0-86656-163-3) Haworth Pr.

McCubbin, Jack H. & Fuqua, Marjorie V. The Unborn Baby Book. (Illus.). 128p. (Orig.). 1985. pap. 7.95 (0-9615085-7-4) Tex Med Pr.

McCubbin, Jack H. & McCubbin, Marjorie F. The Unborn Baby Book. 2nd ed. LC 85-51698. (Illus.). 144p. (Orig.). 1986. pap. 7.95 (0-9615085-8-2) Tex Med Pr.

McCubbin, James A., et al, eds. Stress, Neuropeptides, & Systemic Disease. (Illus.). 485p. 1990. 89.95 (0-685-39111-6) Acad Pr.

McCubbin, Jeffrey A., jt. auth. see Adams, Ronald C.

McCubbin, Marjorie F., jt. auth. see McCubbin, Jack H.

McCubbin, Virginia. Oklahoma City Secrets: A Resource Guide for the Home & Garden. (Illus.). 224p. (Orig.). 1993. pap. 12.95 (1-883554-02-0) City Secrets.

McCubbins, Mathew, jt. ed. see Cowhey, Peter F.

McCubbins, Mathew D., ed. Under the Watchful Eye: Managing Presidential Campaigns in the Television Era. LC 92-24570. 193p. 1992. 20.95 (0-87187-752-X) Congr Quarterly.

McCubbins, Mathew D. & Sullivan, Terry, eds. Congress: Structure & Policy. (Political Economy of Institutions & Decisions Ser.). (Illus.). 540p. 1987. 69.95 (0-521-33169-2); pap. 22.95 (0-521-33750-X) Cambridge U Pr.

McCubbins, Mathew D., jt. auth. see Kiewiet, D. Roderick.

McCubbins, Matthew D., jt. auth. see Cox, Gary W.

***McCue.** Kitty's Carrier. (J). 3.50 (0-679-86016-9) Random.

— Little Fuzzytail. (J). 3.50 (0-679-86007-X) Random.

— Private Practice. 1991. 30.00 (0-316-55531-2) Little.

McCue, C. F., et al, eds. Performance Testing of Lubricants for Automotive Engines & Transmissions. (Illus.). 811p. 1974. 99.00 (0-85334-468-X, Pub. by Elsevier Applied Sci UK) Elsevier.

McCue, Dick. Baby Elephant's Bedtime. (Animal Shape Board Bks.). (Illus.). 24p. (J). (ps). 1985. pap. 2.95 (0-671-55853-6, Litl Simon S&S) S&S Childrens.

— Bunny's Numbers. (Animal Shape Board Bks.). (Illus.). 24p. (J). (ps). 1984. pap. 2.95 (0-671-50944-6, Litl Simon S&S) S&S Childrens.

— Panda's Playtime. (Animal Shape Board Bks.). (Illus.). 12p. (J). (ps). 1985. 2.95 (0-671-55850-1, Litl Simon S&S) S&S Childrens.

— Raccoon's Hide & Seek. (Animal Shape Board Bks.). (Illus.). 12p. (J). (ps). 1985. 2.95 (0-671-55854-4, Litl Simon S&S) S&S Childrens.

McCue, Dick & McCue, Lisa. Puppy's Day. (Animal Shape Board Bks.). (J). (ps). 1984. pap. 2.95 (0-671-50945-4, Litl Simon S&S) S&S Childrens.

McCue, Edward R. & Talaske, Richard H., eds. Acoustical Design of Music Education Facilities. LC 90-83693. 236p. 1990. pap. 20.00 (0-88318-810-4) Am Inst Physics.

McCue, Francis. The Stenographer's Breakfast. LC 91-41839. (Bernard New Women Poets Ser.). 96p. 1992. pap. 12.00 (0-8070-6817-9) Beacon Pr.

McCue, Gary. Trekking in Tibet: A Traveler's Guide. LC 91-24874. (Illus.). 240p. 1991. pap. 16.95 (0-89886-239-6) Mountaineers.

McCue, George, ed. Music in American Society 1776-1976. LC 76-24527. (Illus.). 201p. 1976. text ed. 34.95 (0-87855-209-X); pap. text ed. 18.95 (0-87855-634-6) Transaction Pubs.

McCue, George & Peters, Frank. A Guide to the Architecture of St. Louis. LC 88-9998. (Illus.). 248p. 1989. pap. 14.95 (0-8262-0679-4) U of Mo Pr.

McCue, Greg S. & Bloom, Clive. Dark Knights: The New Comics in Context. LC 92-36707. 154p. (C). 1993. pap. text ed. 18.95 (0-7453-0663-2) Westview.

— Dark Knights: The New Comics in Context. LC 92-36707. 154p. (C). 1993. text ed. 55.50 (0-7453-0662-4) Westview.

McCue, Helga P., jt. ed. see Garret, Agnes.

McCue, Helga P., jt. auth. see Garrett, Agnes.

McCue, Helga P., jt. ed. see Garrett, Agnes.

McCue, Jack D., et al. Geriatric Drug Handbook for Long-Term Care. LC 92-23440. (Illus.). 216p. 1993. pap. 29.00 (0-683-05793-6) Williams & Wilkins.

McCue, Jack D., ed. Medical Cost-Containment Crisis: Fears, Opinions & Facts. LC 88-34784. 310p. 1989. pap. 33.00 (0-910701-43-1, 0893) Health Admin Pr.

McCue, Jack D., jt. ed. see Rogers, C. Stewart.

McCue, Janice H. Online Searching in Public Libraries: A Comparative Study of Performance. LC 88-18482. 288p. 1988. 27.50 (0-8108-2171-0) Scarecrow.

McCue, Jim, ed. see Clough, Arthur H.

McCue, Kathleen & Bonn, Ron. How to Help Children Through a Parent's Serious Illness. (Illus.). 192p. 1994. 18.95 (0-312-11350-1) St Martin.

***McCue, Lisa.** Christmas Stories & Poems. LC 94-18344. (Illus.). 32p. (J). (gr. k-3). 1994. lib. bdg. 11.89 (0-8167-3597-2); pap. text ed. 2.25 (0-8167-3514-X) Troll Assocs.

— Corduroy Goes to the Doctor. (Illus.). (J). (ps). 1987. pap. 3.99 (0-670-81495-4) Viking Child Bks.

— Corduroy on the Go. (Illus.). (J). (ps). 1987. pap. 3.50 (0-670-81497-0) Viking Child Bks.

— Corduroy's Busy Street. (Illus.). (J). (ps). 1987. pap. 3.99 (0-670-81496-2) Viking Child Bks.

— Fuzzytail Bunny. (Chunky Shape Bks.). (Illus.). 22p. (J). (ps). 1992. bds. 3.25 (0-679-81721-2) Random Bks Yng Read.

— Fuzzytail Farm & the Great Gift Hunt. (J). Date not set. 3.99 (0-679-87201-9) Random.

— Fuzzytail Lamb. (Chunky Shape Bks.). (Illus.). 22p. (J). (ps). 1992. bds. 3.25 (0-679-81720-4) Random Bks Yng Read.

— Fuzzytall Bunny Book & Bunny Set. (Chunky Shape Bks.). (Illus.). 22p. (J). (ps). 1994. 10.00 (0-679-85103-8) Random Bks Yng Read.

— Kittens Love. LC 89-61137. (Illus.). 24p. (J). (ps-1). 1990. 4.95 (0-394-82876-3) Random Bks Yng Read.

— The Little Chick. LC 85-63658. (Board Bks.). (Illus.). 7p. (J). (ps). 1993. bds. 3.95 (0-394-88017-X) Random Bks Yng Read.

— Nighty-Night, Little One. LC 87-42786. (Chunky Bks.). (Illus.). 28p. (J). (ps). 1988. bds. 2.95 (0-394-89476-6) Random Bks Yng Read.

— Puppies Love. LC 89-61140. (Illus.). 24p. (J). (ps-1). 1990. 4.95 (0-394-82875-5) Random Bks Yng Read.

McCue, Lisa, illus. The Animals' Advent. (Lift-&-Peek-a-Board Bks.). 14p. (J). (ps-00). 1994. bds. 4.50 (0-679-86015-0) Random Bks Yng Read.

— Bunnies Love. LC 90-61307. 24p. (J). (ps-1). 1991. 4.95 (0-679-80385-8) Random Bks Yng Read.

— Corduroy's Christmas. 16p. (J). (ps-1). 1992. 10.99 (0-670-84477-2) Viking Child Bks.

— Corduroy's Halloween: A Lift-the-Flap Book. 16p. (J). 1995. 10.99 (0-670-86193-6) Viking Child Bks.

— Ducky's Seasons. (Animal Shape Board Bks.). (J). (ps-2). 1983. pap. 2.95 (0-671-45491-9, Litl Simon S&S) S&S Childrens.

— Froggie's Treasure. (Animal Shape Board Bks.). (J). (ps-2). 1983. 2.95 (0-671-45488-9, Litl Simon S&S) S&S Childrens.

— Kitten's Christmas. (Animal Shape Board Bks.). (J). 1985. pap. 2.95 (0-671-55851-X, Litl Simon S&S) S&S Childrens.

— Kitty's Colors. (Animal Shape Board Bks.). (J). (ps-2). 1983. pap. 2.95 (0-671-45489-7, Litl Simon S&S) S&S Childrens.

— Puppy Peek-a-Boo. LC 88-60759. (Peek-a-Boo Board Bks.). 14p. (J). (ps). 1989. bds. 3.99 (0-394-81950-0) Random Bks Yng Read.

— Teddy Dresses. (Animal Shape Board Bks.). (J). 1983. 2.95 (0-671-45490-0, Litl Simon S&S) S&S Childrens.

— Ten Little Puppy Dogs. LC 86-63577. (Chunky Bks.). 28p. (J). (ps). 1987. 2.95 (0-394-89149-X) Random Bks Yng Read.

McCue, Lisa, intro. Corduroy's Day. (J). (ps-k). 1987. Incl. cass. audio 12.95 (0-87499-041-6) Live Oak Media.

McCue, Lisa, jt. auth. see McCue, Dick.

McCue, Lois. Learning Letters Through All Five Senses: A Language Development Activity Book. (Illus.). (Orig.). (ps-00). 1983. pap. 9.95 (0-87659-106-3) Gryphon Hse.

McCue, Margaret. Domestic Violence: A Reference Handbook. (Contemporary World Issues Ser.). 200p. 1995. lib. bdg. 39.50 (0-87436-762-X) ABC-CLIO.

McCue, Noelle B. Forever Eden. 192p. 1994. reprint ed. pap. 3.99 (0-8439-3585-5) Dorchester Pub Co.

— Forever Eden-Only the Present, 2 vols. in 1. 368p. 1990. reprint ed. pap. 3.95 (0-8439-2891-3) Dorchester Pub Co.

— Moonlight Dream. (Silhouette Desire Ser.). 1993. mass mkt. 2.99 (0-373-05815-2, 5-05815-1) Silhouette.

— Ocean of Regrets-Once More with Passion, 2 vols. in 1. 384p. 1990. pap. 3.95 (0-8439-2924-3) Dorchester Pub Co.

— Once More with Passion. 192p. (Orig.). 1994. reprint ed. pap. 3.99 (0-8439-3609-6) Dorchester Pub Co.

An Asterisk (*) at the beginning of an entry indicates that the title is appearing in BIP for the first time.

McCue, Noelle B. & Reisser, Anne N. A Valentine Sampler: Only the Present; The Face of Love, 2 bks. in 1. 368p. 1994. pap. 4.99 (*0-8439-3571-5*) Dorchester Pub Co.
McCue, Noelle B., jt. auth. see Delton, Judy.
***McCue, Sarah & Clowes, Julie.** Trade Secrets: Answers to the Most Commonly Asked Exporting Questions. 200p. 1994. pap. 14.95 (*1-886641-00-5*) MI Small Busn.
***McCue, Sarah S. & Clowes, Julie A.** Trade Secrets: The Export Answer Book. LC 94-37338. 1994. write for info. (*0-615-00376-1*) MI Small Busn.
McCuen, Anne K. Abstracts of Some Greenville, South Carolina, Records Concerning Black People, Free & Slave, 1791-1861, Vol. 1. LC 89-24121. 240p. 1991. 25.00 (*0-87152-440-6*) Reprint.
McCuen, Gary, ed. Children Having Children: Global Perspectives on Teenage Pregnancy. LC 87-91954. (Ideas in Conflict Ser.). (Illus.). 210p. 1988. lib. bdg. 12.95 (*0-86596-064-X*) G E M.
— Illiteracy in America. LC 87-9151. (Ideas in Conflict Ser.). (Illus.). 152p. 1988. lib. bdg. 12.95 (*0-86596-067-4*) G E M.
— Poor & Minority Health Care. LC 87-91953. (Ideas in Conflict Ser.). (Illus.). 202p. 1988. lib. bdg. 12.95 (*0-86596-065-8*) G E M.
— Treating the Mentally Disabled. (Ideas in Conflict Ser.). (Illus.). 140p. 1988. lib. bdg. 12.95 (*0-86596-066-6*) G E M.
McCuen, Gary E. Ecocide & Genocide in the Vanishing Forest: The Rainforest & Native People. (Ideas in Conflict Ser.). (Illus.). 133p. (C). 1993. lib. bdg. 12.95 (*0-86596-087-9*) G E M.
— Militarism & Global Ecology. (Ideas in Conflict Ser.). (Illus.). 134p. (C). 1993. lib. bdg. 12.95 (*0-86596-086-0*) G E M.
— Toxic Nightmare: Ecocide in the USSR & Eastern Europe. Swanson, Ronald P., ed. (Ideas in Conflict Ser.). (Illus.). 134p. 1993. lib. bdg. 12.95 (*0-86596-090-9*) G E M.
McCuen, Gary E., ed. The AIDS Crisis: Conflicting Social Values. (Ideas in Conflict Ser.). (Illus.). 176p. 1987. lib. bdg. 12.95 (*0-86596-061-5*) G E M.
— Apartheid Reader. (Ideas in Conflict Ser.). (Illus.). 173p. 1986. lib. bdg. 12.95 (*0-86596-057-7*) G E M.
— Born Hooked: Poisoned in the Womb. rev. ed. (Ideas in Conflict Ser.). (Illus.). 159p. 1994. lib. bdg. 12.95 (*0-86596-091-7*) G E M.
— Children of Violence in America. (Ideas in Conflict Ser.). (Illus.). 164p. (YA). (gr. 7-12). 1995. lib. bdg. 12.95 (*0-86596-095-X*) G E M.
— Crimes of Gender: Violence Against Women. (Ideas in Conflict Ser.). (Illus.). 156p. 1994. lib. bdg. 12.95 (*0-86596-092-5*) G E M.
— Doctor Assisted Suicide: And the Euthanasia Movement. (Ideas in Conflict Ser.). (Illus.). 172p. 1994. lib. bdg. 12.95 (*0-86596-093-3*) G E M.
— Ending War Against the Earth. (Ideas in Conflict Ser.). (Illus.). 176p. 1991. 12.95 (*0-86596-081-X*) G E M.
— Foreign Intervention & Global Security. (Ideas in Conflict Ser.). 155p. (YA). (gr. 7-12). 1995. lib. bdg. 12.95 (*0-86596-097-6*) G E M.
— The Global Arms Trade. (Ideas in Conflict Ser.). (Illus.). 128p. 1992. lib. bdg. 12.95 (*0-86596-082-8*) G E M.
— Health Care & Human Values. (Ideas in Conflict Ser.). (Illus.). 180p. (C). 1993. lib. bdg. 12.95 (*0-86596-088-7*) G E M.
— Homosexuality & Gay Rights. (Ideas in Conflict Ser.). (Illus.). 165p. 1994. lib. bdg. 12.95 (*0-86596-094-1*) G E M.
— Human Rights & the Politics of Terror. (Ideas in Conflict Ser.). (Illus.). 178p. (YA). (gr. 7-12). 1995. lib. bdg. 12.95 (*0-86596-098-4*) G E M.
— Inner-City Violence. (Ideas in Conflict Ser.). (Illus.). 165p. 1990. lib. bdg. 12.95 (*0-86596-073-9*) G E M.
— The International Drug Trade. LC 88-62174. (Ideas in Conflict Ser.). (Illus.). 160p. 1989. lib. bdg. 12.95 (*0-86596-071-2*) G E M.
— Manipulating Life: Debating the Genetic Revolution. (Ideas in Conflict Ser.). (Illus.). 136p. 1985. lib. bdg. 12.95 (*0-86596-054-2*) G E M.
— A New World Order & Military Intervention. (Ideas in Conflict Ser.). (Illus.). 146p. 1992. lib. bdg. 12.95 (*0-86596-085-2*) G E M.
— The Nicaraguan Revolution. (Ideas in Conflict Ser.). (Illus.). 184p. 1986. lib. bdg. 12.95 (*0-86596-058-5*) G E M.
— Nuclear Winter. (Ideas in Conflict Ser.). (Illus.). 140p. 1987. lib. bdg. 12.95 (*0-86596-062-3*) G E M.
— Political Murder in Central America: Death Squads & U. S. Policies. (Ideas in Conflict Ser.). (Illus.). 136p. 1985. lib. bdg. 12.95 (*0-86596-050-X*) G E M.
— Population & Human Survival. (Ideas in Conflict Ser.). (Illus.). 158p. (C). 1993. lib. bdg. 12.95 (*0-86596-089-5*) G E M.
— Protecting Water Quality. (Ideas in Conflict Ser.). 180p. 1986. lib. bdg. 12.95 (*0-86596-056-9*) G E M.
— Religion & Politics: Issues in Religious Liberty. LC 88-42848. (Ideas in Conflict Ser.). (Illus.). 172p. 1989. lib. bdg. 12.95 (*0-86596-069-0*) G E M.
— The Religious Right. LC 87-43346. (Ideas in Conflict Ser.). (Illus.). 205p. 1989. lib. bdg. 12.95 (*0-86596-068-2*) G E M.
— Secret Democracy: Civil Liberties vs. the National Security State. (Ideas in Conflict Ser.). (Illus.). 167p. 1990. 12.95 (*0-86596-074-7*) G E M.
— Transforming the Warfare State: Global Militarism & Economic Conversion. (Ideas in Conflict Ser.). (Illus.). 155p. 1992. lib. bdg. 12.95 (*0-86596-083-6*) G E M.
— Workfare vs. Welfare. LC 88-43117. (Ideas in Conflict Ser.). (Illus.). 151p. 1989. lib. bdg. 12.95 (*0-86596-072-0*) G E M.
McCuen, Gary E., ed. see Lyon, Victor L.
McCuen, Jo R. & Winkler, Anthony C. From Idea to Essay: A Rhetoric Reader & Handbook. 6th ed. (Illus.). 608p. (C). 1992. pap. write for info. (*0-02-379016-4*) Macmillan.
— From Idea to Essay: A Rhetoric Reader & Handbook. 7th ed. (Illus.). 640p. (C). 1995. pap. write for info. (*0-02-379001-6*) Macmillan.
— Reading, Writing, & the Humanities. 750p. (C). 1991. pap. text ed. 21.50 (*0-15-575512-9*) HB Coll Pubs.
— Readings for Writers. 6th ed. 1008p. (C). 1989. pap. text ed. 21.50 (*0-15-575835-7*) HB Coll Pubs.
— Readings for Writers. 7th ed. 850p. (C). 1992. pap. text ed. 22.75 (*0-15-575837-3*); pap. text ed. 3.50 (*0-15-575838-1*) HB Coll Pubs.
— Rewriting Writing: A Rhetoric & Reader. 2nd ed. 733p. (C). 1990. teacher ed write for info. (*0-318-67028-3*); pap. text ed. 22.75 (*0-15-576719-4*) HB Coll Pubs.
— Rewriting Writing: A Rhetoric, Reader & Handbook. 2nd ed. 835p. (C). 1990. teacher ed write for info. (*0-318-67021-6*); text ed. 25.50 (*0-15-576721-6*) HB Coll Pubs.
McCuen, Jo R., jt. auth. see Winkler, Anthony C.
McCuen, Jo R., jt. auth. see Winkler, Anthony.
McCuen, JoRay, jt. auth. see Winkler, Anthony.
McCuen, R. H. & Hromadka, T. V., eds. Computational Hydrology '87: Proceedings of the First International Conference, Anaheim, CA, U.S.A., July 1987. LC 87-81446. (Illus.). 268p. (Orig.). 1987. pap. text ed. 24.00 (*0-914055-06-2*) Lighthouse Pubns.
McCuen, Richard H. FORTRAN Programming for Civil Engineers. 1975. pap. write for info. (*0-13-329417-X*) P-H.
— Hydrologic Analysis & Design. 950p. 1988. text ed. 76.00 (*0-13-447954-8*) P-H.
— Microcomputer Applications in Statistical Hydrology. 320p. 1992. text ed. 94.00 (*0-13-585290-0*) P-H.
McCuen, Richard H., et al. Dynamic Communication for Engineers. LC 93-9395. 192p. 1993. 29.00 (*0-87262-856-6*) Am Soc Civil Eng.
McCuistion, Dennis & McCuistion, Niki N. Selling Strategies for Today's Banker: A Survival Guide for Tomorrow. LC 91-26941. 175p. 1991. 32.95 (*0-7931-0212-X*, 5609-0101) Dearborn Trade.
McCuistion, Niki N. & Senne, Jeffrey N. The Quality Sales Leadership System for Today's Financial Executive. LC 93-16074. 192p. 1993. 32.95 (*0-7931-0444-0*, 5609-03) Dearborn Finan.
McCuistion, Niki N., jt. auth. see McCuistion, Dennis.
McCulla, Patricia E. Bahamas. (Places & Peoples of the World Ser.). (Illus.). 104p. (J). (gr. 5 up). 1988. lib. bdg. 14.95 (*1-55546-191-3*) Chelsea Hse.
— Tanzania. (Places & Peoples of the World Ser.). (Illus.). 112p. (J). (gr. 5 up). 1989. lib. bdg. 14.95 (*1-55546-784-9*) Chelsea Hse.
***McCullagh, James C.** Cycling for Health, Fitness & Well-Being. LC 94-36392. 1995. write for info. (*0-440-50601-8*) Dell.
McCullagh, P. S., jt. auth. see Hammond, R.
McCullagh, Peter. Brain Dead, Brain Absent, Brain Donors: Human Subjects or Human Objects? LC 92-49197. 200p. 1993. text ed. 95.00 (*0-471-93736-3*) Wiley.
— The Foetus As Transplant Donor: Scientific, Social & Ethical Perspectives. 1987. text ed. 95.00 (*0-471-91223-9*) Wiley.
McCullagh, Peter & Nelder, J. A. Generalized Linear Model. 2nd ed. 400p. 1989. 49.95 (*0-412-31760-5*, A3827) Chapman & Hall.
McCullagh, Suzanne F., jt. auth. see Joachim, Harold.
McCullar, Michael. Restoring Texas: Raiford Stripling's Life & Architecture. LC 85-40052. (Illus.). 1985. 29.95 (*0-89096-254-5*) Tex A&M Univ Pr.
***McCullen, Geoffrey & Miller, Ryle.** Hip & Knee Replacement: A Patient's Guide. (Illus.). 256p. 1995. 23.00 (*0-393-03834-3*) Norton.
***McCullen, Richard.** Deep Down Things: Selected Writing. LC 95-2255. 1995. pap. write for info. (*1-56548-033-3*) New City.
McCullers, Carson. Ballad of the Sad Cafe. 1976. 16.95 (*0-8488-0573-9*) Amereon Ltd.
— The Ballad of the Sad Cafe & Other Stories. 160p. 1983. mass mkt. 4.99 (*0-553-27254-3*, Bantam Classics) Bantam.
— Collected Stories. 1987. pap. 12.95 (*0-395-44243-5*) HM.
— The Heart Is a Lonely Hunter. 320p. 1983. mass mkt. 5.50 (*0-553-26963-1*, Bantam Classics) Bantam.
— The Heart Is a Lonely Hunter. 1994. lib. bdg. 19.95x (*1-56849-462-9*) Buccaneer Bks.
— The Heart is a Lonely Hunter. 1993. 15.50 (*0-679-42474-1*, Modern Lib) Random.
— Member of the Wedding. (YA). (gr. 9-12). 1985. mass mkt. 4.50 (*0-553-25051-5*) Bantam.
— The Member of the Wedding. LC 51-10532. 1963. pap. 7.95 (*0-8112-0093-0*, NDP153) New Directions.
— Reflections in a Golden Eye. 1991. mass mkt. 4.99 (*0-553-56968-6*) Bantam.
— The Square Root of Wonderful. 159p. 1958. 16.95 (*0-910278-60-1*) Boulevard.
— The Square Root of Wonderful. LC 90-47728. 169p. 1990. reprint ed. 24.95 (*0-87797-188-9*) Cherokee.
— Sucker. LC 85-29114. (Creative's Classic Short Stories Ser.). 40p. (J). (gr. 4 up). 1986. lib. bdg. 13.95 (*0-88682-053-7*) Creative Ed.
— A Tree, a Rock, a Cloud. (Creative Short Stories Ser.). (YA). (gr. 4-12). 1989. 13.95 (*0-88682-349-8*, 97225-098) Creative Ed.
McCullers, Carson, jt. adapt. see Albee, Edward.
McCullers, Jamey, jt. auth. see Robinson, Bryan.
McCullers, Jamie, jt. auth. see Robinson, Bryan.
McCulley, Denny. Denny McCulley's Guide to Moving: For Senior Citizens & Anyone Making a Major Move. 112p. 1994. write for info. (*0-9639628-0-9*) Sr Concerns.
McCulley, Johnston. Black Star. reprint ed. lib. bdg. 20.95 (*0-89190-995-8*, Rivercity Pr) Amereon Ltd.
— Black Star's Campaign. reprint ed. lib. bdg. 20.95 (*0-89190-996-6*, Rivercity Pr) Amereon Ltd.
— Black Star's Return. reprint ed. lib. bdg. 20.95 (*0-89190-997-4*, Rivercity Pr) Amereon Ltd.
— The Mark of Zorro. 1976. reprint ed. lib. bdg. 22.95 (*0-89190-999-0*, Rivercity Pr) Amereon Ltd.
— The Mark of Zorro. 1990. reprint ed. lib. bdg. 25.95x (*0-89968-541-2*) Buccaneer Bks.
McCulley, Richard T. Banks & Politics During the Progressive Era: The Origins of the Federal Reserve System, 1897-1913. LC 92-27522. (Financial Sector of the American Economy Ser.). 352p. 1992. 81.00 (*0-8153-0958-9*) Garland.
— The Social Safety Net Reexamined: FDR to Reagan. (Policy Research Project Report Ser.: No. 86). 240p. 1992. reprint ed. 10.00 (*0-89940-693-9*) LBJ Sch Pub Aff.
McCulley, Richard T., jt. auth. see Redford, Emmette S.
McCulloch. Focus on Coronary Care. (Illus.). 203p. 1985. pap. text ed. 39.95 (*0-433-32630-1*) Buttrwrth-Heinemann.
McCulloch, A., jt. auth. see Abrams, P.
McCulloch, Alan. The Encyclopedia of Australian Art. rev. ed. (Illus.). 880p. (C). 1994. text ed. 115.00 (*0-8248-1688-9*, Kolowalu Bk) UH Pr.
McCulloch, Bruce C. One Hundred & One Ways to Beat the Blues. (Celebrate Life Bks.: No. 1). (Illus.). 112p. (Orig.). 1984. pap. 2.95 (*0-9614507-0-3*) Celebrate Life Ent.
McCulloch, Edith. The Prints of Don Freeman: A Catalogue Raisonne. LC 87-8141. (Illus.). 192p. 1988. 45.00 (*0-8139-1135-4*) U Pr of Va.
McCulloch, Frank, ed. Drawing the Line. LC 84-70269. 98p. 1984. pap. 4.95 (*0-943086-03-5*) Am Soc News.
McCulloch, Gary. Educational Reconstruction: The 1944 Education Act & the Twenty-First Century. LC 94-21265. (Woburn Education Ser.). 230p. 1994. 35.00 (*0-7130-0191-7*, Pub. by Woburn Pr); pap. 19.50 (*0-7130-4019-X*, Pub. by Woburn Pr) Intl Spec Bk.
— Philosophers & Kings: Education for Leadership in Twentieth-Century England. 180p. (C). 1991. 54.95 (*0-521-39175-X*) Cambridge U Pr.
— The Secondary Technical School: A Usable Past? (Studies in Curriculum History Ser.). 230p. 1989. 70.00 (*1-85000-496-X*, Falmer Pr); pap. 35.00 (*1-85000-497-8*, Falmer Pr) Taylor & Francis.
McCulloch, Graham. Ingenious Shop Aids & Jigs: Professional Shortcuts for the Home Workshop. LC 92-45041. (Illus.). 224p. 1993. pap. 14.95 (*0-8069-0300-7*) Sterling.
— Workshop Shortcuts: Tips, Tricks, Jigs & Aids for Woodworkers. LC 93-44539. (Illus.). 1994. pap. 17.95 (*0-8069-0650-2*) Sterling.
McCulloch, Gregory. The Game of the Name: Introducing Logic, Language & Mind. 336p. 1989. 62.00 (*0-19-875087-0*) OUP.
— The Mind & Its World. LC 94-33896. (Problems of Philosophy Ser.). 264p. 1995. 55.00x (*0-415-09330-9*, C0418); pap. 17.95 (*0-415-12205-8*, C0419) Routledge.
— Using Sartre: An Analytical Introduction to Early Sartrean Themes. LC 93-33903. 160p. 1994. 49.95x (*0-415-10953-1*, B3951); pap. 15.95 (*0-415-10954-X*, B3955) Routledge.
McCulloch, Hugh. Men & Measures of Half a Century. LC 77-87404. (American Scene Ser.). 1969. reprint ed. lib. bdg. 65.00 (*0-306-71548-1*) Da Capo.
McCulloch, Ian. The Efficiency of Killers. 72p. 1988. 9.95 (*0-920806-97-X*, Pub. by Penumbra Pr CN) U of Toronto Pr.
— Moon of Hunger. 48p. 1982. 5.95 (*0-920806-33-3*, Pub. by Penumbra Pr CN) U of Toronto Pr.
McCulloch, J. W. & Philip, A. E. Suicidal Behavior. LC 72-188140. 133p. (C). 1972. 63.00 (*0-08-016855-8*, Pub. by Pergamon Repr UK) Franklin.
McCulloch, J. W., et al. Social Work Research & the Analysis of Social Data. LC 74-32369. 252p. (C). 1975. 106.00 (*0-08-018213-5*, Pub. by Pergamon Repr UK) Franklin.
McCulloch, James & Edvinsson, Lars, eds. Peptidergic Mechanisms in the Cerebral Circulation. LC 87-3039. (Ellis Horwood Series in Biomedicine). (Illus.). 240p. 1987. lib. bdg. 155.00 (*0-89573-576-8*) VCH Pubs.
McCulloch, James A. A Medical Greek & Latin Workbook. 2nd ed. 212p. 1984. spiral bd., pap. 28.95 (*0-398-04905-X*) C C Thomas.
McCulloch, James A., ed. Arctic & Global Change: Proceedings of the Symposium on the Arctic & Global Change. (Illus.). 156p. (Orig.). 1990. pap. 25.00 (*0-9623610-1-1*) Climate Inst.
McCulloch, Janis. Performance Teams: Completing the Feedback Loop - Leaders. (Illus.). 171p. 1982. 15.00 (*0-937100-02-1*) Perf Manage.
— Performance Teams: Completing the Feedback Loop - Members. (Illus.). 1982. pap. 9.95 (*0-937100-03-X*) Perf Manage.
McCulloch, Jay, ed. see Stern, Daniel.
McCulloch, Jock. Black Soul White Artifact: Fanon's Clinical Psychology & Social Theory. LC 82-14605. 240p. 1983. 54.95 (*0-521-24700-4*) Cambridge U Pr.
— Colonial Psychiatry & 'The African Mind' 192p. (C). 1995. 54.95 (*0-521-45330-5*) Cambridge U Pr.
McCulloch, John A. Principles of Microsurgery for Lumbar Disc Disease. 317p. 1989. 126.00 (*0-88167-487-7*) Raven.
McCulloch, John A., jt. auth. see Macnab, Ian.
McCulloch, John R. The Literature of Political Economy: A Classified Catalogue of Select Publications in the Different Departments of the Science, with Historical, Critical & Biographical Notices. LC 86-7486. (Reprints of Economic Classics Ser.). xiii, 407p. 1991. reprint ed. lib. bdg. 49.50 (*0-678-01457-4*) Kelley.
— Principles of Political Economy: With Some Inquiries Respecting Their Application. 5th ed. LC 65-19651. (Reprints of Economic Classics Ser.). 1965. reprint ed. 49.50 (*0-678-00097-2*) Kelley.
— Treatise on the Circumstances Which Determine the Rate of Wages & the Conditions of the Labouring Classes. LC 64-56231. (Reprints of Economic Classics Ser.). 1967. reprint ed. 25.00 (*0-678-00005-0*) Kelley.
— Treatise on the Principles & Practical Influence of Taxation & the Funding System. 2nd ed. LC 67-28411. (Reprints of Economic Classics Ser.). xvi, 552p. 1986. reprint ed. 49.50 (*0-678-00331-9*) Kelley.
— Treatises & Essays on Subjects Connected with Economical Policy: With Biographical Sketches of Quesnay, Adam Smith & Ricardo. LC 67-20088. (Reprints of Economic Classics Ser.). vii, 487p. 1968. reprint ed. 49.50 (*0-678-00255-X*) Kelley.
McCulloch, John R., et al. Letters of John Ramsay McCulloch to David Ricardo. 1979. 17.95 (*0-405-10625-4*) Ayer.
***McCulloch, Joseph M., et al, eds.** Wound Healing: Alternatives in Management. LC 94-1175. (Contemporary Perspectives in Rehabilitation Ser.). 442p. 1994. 36.00 (*0-8036-5966-0*) Davis Co.
McCulloch, Lou W. Card Photographs, a Guide to Their History & Value. LC 81-51444. (Illus.). 235p. 1981. 30.00 (*0-916838-56-0*) Schiffer.
McCulloch, Margery. Edwin Muir: Poet, Critic & Novelist. (Modern Scottish Writers Ser.). 144p. 1993. pap. 25.00 (*0-7486-0406-5*, Pub. by Edinburgh U Pr UK) Col U Pr.
McCulloch, Merran. Peoples of Sierra Leone. LC 67-4643. (Ethnographic Survey of Africa: Western Africa Ser.: Pt. 2). 121p. reprint ed. pap. 34.50 (*0-8357-6961-5*, 2039021) Bks Demand.
McCulloch, Myrna & Madsen, Sharon, eds. Spelling & Usage Vocabulary Builder. large type ed. (Illus.). 478p. (J). (gr. k-2). 1993. reprint ed. 26.50 (*0-924277-04-1*) K & M Pub.
McCulloch, Myrna T. America's Spelling & Reading with Riggs Series: Supplements to The Writing Road to Reading. Huneger, R. J., ed. (Illus.). 1993. write for info. (*0-318-66814-9*); Self-study course with audio cass. 17.50 (*0-924277-08-4*); Orton phonogram cards with handwriting instructions, boxed set of 70. 20.00 (*0-924277-06-8*); Orton phonogram tape with visual aids & spelling rules. 6.50 (*0-924277-07-6*); Spelling & Usage Vocabulary Builder, 478p. 26.50 (*0-685-74194-X*); Tchr.'s ed. teacher ed. pap. 43.50 (*0-924277-02-5*); Lesson plans, study guide, syllabus, 25p. pap. 12.95 (*0-924277-09-2*) K & M Pub.
McCulloch, Rachel. Research & Development As a Determinant of U. S. International Competitiveness. LC 78-63432. (Committee on Changing International Realities Ser.). 60p. 1978. 3.00 (*0-89068-044-2*) Natl Planning.
— Unexpected Real Consequences of Floating Exchange Rates. LC 83-10857. (Essays in International Finance Ser.: No. 153). 1983. pap. text ed. 8.00 (*0-88165-060-9*) Princeton U Int Finan Econ.
McCulloch, Richard. Destiny of Angels. (Illus.). 314p. 1986. 20.00 (*0-9608928-1-8*) Towncourt Ent.
— The Ideal & Destiny. LC 82-82103. 534p. 1982. 20.00 (*0-9608928-0-X*) Towncourt Ent.
— The Nordish Quest. 108p. 1989. pap. 5.00 (*0-9608928-2-6*) Towncourt Ent.
— The Racial Compact: A Call for Racial Rights, Preservation & Independence. 135p. (Orig.). 1994. pap. 7.95 (*0-9608928-3-4*) Towncourt Ent.
***McCulloch, Ron.** How Baseball Began: The Long Overdue Truth about the Birth of Baseball. (Illus.). 160p. (Orig.). 1995. pap. 18.95 (*1-895629-44-6*, Pub. by Warwick Pub CN) Firefly Bks Ltd.
McCulloch, Rook, ed. W. S. McCulloch, 4 vols., Set. 1392p. 1989. pap. text ed. 84.00 (*0-685-25893-9*) Intersystems Pubns.
McCulloch, Ros & Mathieson, Margaret. English 16-19: Entitlement at "A" Level. 160p. 1993. pap. 32.00 (*1-85346-214-4*, Pub. by D Fulton UK) Taylor & Francis.
— Moral Education Through English 11-16. 144p. 1995. pap. 24.95x (*1-85346-276-4*, Pub. by D Fulton UK) Taylor & Francis.
McCulloch, W. Bengali Household Tales. LC 78-63211. (Folktale Ser.). reprint ed. 28.00 (*0-404-16146-4*) AMS Pr.
McCulloch, W. F. Forester on the Job. 2nd ed. 1981. write for info. (*0-318-68343-1*) Oreg St U Bkstrs.
McCulloch, Warren S. Embodiments of Mind. 440p. 1988. pap. 15.95 (*0-262-63114-8*, Bradford Bks) MIT Pr.
McCulloch, Wendell H., Jr., jt. auth. see Ball, Donald A.
McCulloch-Williams, Martha. Dishes & Beverages of the Old South. LC 88-2981. 344p. 1988. reprint ed. 14.95 (*0-87049-580-1*) U of Tenn Pr.
McCulloch, Winifred. A Short History of the American Teilhard Association. 1979. pap. 3.00 (*0-89012-013-7*) Anima Pubns.
McCullogh, Jeffrey F. Two Handed Tennis: How to Play a Winner's Game. LC 83-20759. (Illus.). 192p. 1983. pap. 7.95 (*0-87131-491-6*) M Evans.
McCullogh, T. H., jt. ed. see Naeser, N. D.

McCulloh, Gerald O. Ministerial Education in the American Methodist Movement. LC 80-69028. (Informed Ministry Series, Two Hundred Years of American Methodist Thought: 200 Years of American Methodist Thought). 342p. (Orig.). 1980. pap. 3.95 (*0-938162-00-4*) United Meth Educ.

McCulloh, Gerald W. Christ's Person & Life-Work in the Theology of Albrecht Ritschi: With Special Attention to Munus Triplex. 234p. (Orig.). (C). 1990. lib. bdg. 49.00 (*0-8191-7885-3*) U Pr of Amer.

McCulloh, Judith, jt. ed. see Malone, Bill C.

McCulloh, William E. Longus. LC 77-99541. (Twayne's World Authors Ser.). 1970. lib. bdg. 17.95 (*0-8057-2540-7*) Irvington.

McCullough & Baker. Slices. 1980. pap. 8.95 (*0-937816-08-6*) Tech Data.

McCullough, Alastair E. Oracle PL-SQL for SQL Forms: An Introduction for Those Using SQL Forms Version 3.0. LC 93-48263. 1994. 22.50 (*0-07-707925-6*) McGraw.

McCullough, Anne R. Letters from the Far Side of the Shining Sea. LC 92-61998. 152p. (Orig.). 1994. pap. text ed. 9.00 (*1-56002-218-3*, Univ Edtns) Aegina Pr.

McCullough, Ashley M. A Critical Analysis of the Fuel Management Program for Schools: Selected New Jersey Cities Compared with Nation-Wide Practice. LC 72-177019. (Columbia University. Teachers College. Contributions to Education Ser.: No. 713). reprint ed. 22.50 (*0-404-55713-9*) AMS Pr.

McCullough, Bonnie R. Bonnie's Household Budget Book. 2nd rev. ed. 64p. 1987. pap. 8.95 (*0-312-00992-5*) St Martin.

— Bonnie's Household Budget Book: The Essential Guide for Getting Control of Your Money. 3rd rev. ed. LC 92-34393. 1992. pap. 8.95 (*0-312-08708-X*) St Martin.

— Bonnie's Household Organizer: The Essential Guide for Getting Control of Your Home. rev. ed. (Illus.). 192p. 1983. pap. 6.95 (*0-312-08795-0*) St Martin.

— Seventy-Six Ways to Get Organized for Christmas. 1992. mass mkt. 3.99 (*0-312-92940-4*) St Martin.

— Totally Organized the Bonnie McCullough Way. (Illus.). 400p. 1986. pap. 12.95 (*0-312-80747-3*) St Martin.

McCullough, Bonnie R. & Mon, Susan. Four Hundred-One Ways to Get Your Kids to Work at Home. (Illus.). 224p. 1981. pap. 9.95 (*0-312-30147-2*) St Martin.

McCullough, Bruce. Representative English Novelists: Defoe to Conrad. LC 72-5807. (Essay Index Reprint Ser.). 1977. reprint ed. 27.95 (*0-8369-7298-8*) Ayer.

McCullough, Burton V. Letters of Credit. 1987. ring bd. write for info. (*0-8205-1387-3*) Bender.

***McCullough, Christopher.** Nobody's Victim. 224p. 1995. 22.00 (*0-517-59801-9*) Random.

McCullough, Christopher J. Always at Ease. 272p. (Orig.). 1993. mass mkt. 5.50 (*0-425-14012-1*) Berkley Pub.

— Managing Your Anxiety: Regaining Control When You Feel Stressed, Helpless & Alone. Mann, Robert W., ed. 320p. 1994. reprint ed. pap. text ed. 5.99 (*0-425-14295-7*) Berkley Pub.

McCullough, Christopher J. & Mann, Robert W. Managing Your Anxiety: Regaining Control When You Feel Stressed, Helpless & Alone. LC 85-9783. 314p. 1986. pap. 12.95 (*0-87477-400-4*) J P Tarcher.

McCullough, Clint. Nevada. 736p. 1986. 19.95 (*0-8184-0350-0*) Carol Pub Group.

McCullough, Colleen. A Creed for the Third Millennium. 464p. 1986. mass mkt. 5.99 (*0-380-70134-0*) Avon.

— The First Man in Rome. 1104p. 1991. mass mkt. 6.95 (*0-380-71081-1*) Avon.

— The First Man in Rome: Augustus. LC 90-37080. (Illus.). 700p. Date not set. write for info. (*0-688-09372-8*) Morrow.

— The First Man in Rome: Caesar. LC 90-37080. (Illus.). Date not set. write for info. (*0-688-09371-X*) Morrow.

— Fortune's Favorites. 1072p. 1994. mass mkt. 6.99 (*0-380-71083-8*) Avon.

— Fortune's Favorites. LC 93-534. 1993. 25.00 (*0-688-09370-1*) Morrow.

— The Grass Crown. 1104p. 1992. mass mkt. 6.99 (*0-380-71082-X*) Avon.

— An Indecent Obsession. 336p. 1982. mass mkt. 5.99 (*0-380-60376-4*) Avon.

— The Ladies of Missalonghi. 192p. 1988. mass mkt. 4.99 (*0-380-70458-7*) Avon.

— Una Obsesion Indecente. 320p. (SPA.). 1992. pap. 4.95 (*1-56780-235-4*) La Costa Pr.

Mccullough, Colleen. Thorn Birds. 704p. 1978. mass mkt. 5.99 (*0-380-01817-9*) Avon.

McCullough, Colleen. Tim. 1990. mass mkt. 4.99 (*0-380-71196-6*) Avon.

— Tim. large type ed. 362p. 1992. 22.95 (*1-85089-362-4*, Pub. by ISIS UK) Transaction Pubs.

— Tovismadarak. Goncz, Arpad & Borbas, Margit, trs. 568p. (HUN.). 1984. 20.00 (*0-935484-11-6*) Universe Pub Co.

McCullough, D. & Miller, A. Homeomorphisms of 3-Manifolds with Compressible Boundary. LC 86-3387. (Memoirs of the AMS Ser.: Vol. 61/344). 100p. 1986. pap. text ed. 21.00 (*0-8218-2346-9*, MEMO 61/344) Am Math.

McCullough, Dale R. The George Reserve Deer Herd: Population Ecology of a K-Selected Species. (Illus.). 1979. lib. bdg. 34.50 (*0-472-08611-1*, 08611) U of Mich Pr.

— The Tule Elk: Its History, Behavior, & Ecology. LC 75-626287. (University of California Publications in Social Welfare: No. 88). (Illus.). 219p. reprint ed. pap. 62.50 (*0-685-23671-4*, 2029053) Bks Demand.

McCullough, Dale R. & Barrett, Reginald H., eds. Wildlife Two Thousand One: Populations. LC 92-11248. 1992. write for info. (*1-85166-876-4*, Pub. by Elsevier Applied Sci UK) Elsevier.

McCullough, David. Brave Companions: Portraits in History. 256p. 1992. pap. 12.00 (*0-671-79276-8*, Touchstone Bks) S&S Trade.

— The Great Bridge. 1983. pap. 16.00 (*0-671-45711-X*, Touchstone Bks) S&S Trade.

— The Johnstown Flood. 21.50 (*0-8446-6292-5*) Peter Smith.

— The Johnstown Flood. 304p. 1987. pap. 11.00 (*0-671-20714-8*, Touchstone Bks) S&S Trade.

— Mornings on Horseback. 1994. 23.75 (*0-8446-6732-3*) Peter Smith.

— Mornings on Horseback. 1982. pap. 14.95 (*0-671-44754-8*, Touchstone Bks) S&S Trade.

— The Path Between the Seas: The Creation of the Panama Canal 1870-1914. 700p. 1977. 14.95 (*0-685-75146-5*, SS09-4) Am Soc Civil Eng.

— The Path Between the Seas: The Creation of the Panama Canal 1870-1914. (Illus.). 1978. pap. 14.95 (*0-671-24409-4*, Touchstone Bks) S&S Trade.

— Truman. (Illus.). 896p. 1992. 30.00 (*0-671-45654-7*) S&S Trade.

— Truman. (Illus.). 1120p. 1993. pap. 15.00 (*0-671-86920-5*, Touchstone Bks) S&S Trade.

McCullough, David, ed. see Shapiro, Michael E. & Hassrick, Peter H.

McCullough, David G., ed. see Sulzberger, C. L.

McCullough, David L. State of the Art Extracorporeal Shock Wave Lithotripsy. Kandel, Lawrence B. & Harrison, Lloyd H., eds. (Illus.). 400p. 1987. 55.00 (*0-87993-309-7*) Futura Pub.

McCullough, David W. Point No-Point: A Ziza Todd Mystery. large type ed. LC 92-17644. 439p. 1992. reprint ed. lib. bdg. 17.95 (*1-56054-469-4*) Thorndike Pr.

McCullough, Dennis J., tr. Kids Coping with War: How Young People React to Military Conflict. (Illus.). 112p. (J). 1991. pap. 6.95 (*0-933879-37-7*); audio 9.95 (*0-933879-39-3*) Alegra Hse Pubs.

McCullough, Donald W. Finding Happiness in the Most Unlikely Places. LC 90-39841. 175p. 1991. reprint ed. pap. 8.99 (*0-8308-1295-4*, 1295, Saltshaker Bk) InterVarsity.

— The Trivialization of God: The Dangerous Illusion of a Manageable Deity. LC 95-14409. 176p. 1995. 16.00 (*0-89109-909-3*, NavPr) NavPress.

McCullough, Duane K. Spirit of Atlantis Version 2: The Treasure Adventure. rev. ed. LC 88-92585. 128p. (C). 1994. reprint ed. pap. 20.00 (*0-9621605-3-9*) D K McCullough.

— Spirit of Atlantis, Version 1-E: The Treasure Adventure, 4 vols. LC 88-92585. (Illus.). 100p. (Orig.). 1989. pap. text ed. write for info. (*0-9621605-2-0*) D K McCullough.

McCullough, E. J. & Calder, R., eds. Time As a Human Resource. 354p. (Orig.). 1992. pap. text ed. 25.95 (*1-895176-04-2*, Pub. by Univ Calgary CN) Paul & Co Pubs.

McCullough, Edo. World's Fair Midways: An Affectionate Account of American Amusement Areas from the Crystal Palace to the Crystal Ball. LC 75-22828. (America in Two Centuries Ser.). (Illus.). 1976. reprint ed. 18.95 (*0-405-07700-9*) Ayer.

McCullough, Fran & Witt, Barbara. Great Food Without Fuss: Simple Recipes from the Best Cooks. LC 92-8473. 352p. 1992. 25.00 (*0-8050-2230-9*) H Holt & Co.

McCullough, Frances. Great Food Without Fuss: Simple Recipes from the Best Cooks. 288p. 1993. pap. 14.95 (*0-8050-3001-8*) H Holt & Co.

***McCullough, Frances & Witt, Barbara.** Great Entertaining Food Without Fuss. LC 95-11615. 1995. write for info. (*0-679-43139-X*, Villard Bks) Random.

McCullough, Frances, jt. ed. see Hughes, Ted.

McCullough, Grace A. Speech Improvement Work & Practice Book. text ed. 3.50 (*0-686-00149-4*) Expression.

***McCullough, Harrell.** The Mystery of Bill Dalton. (Illus.). 100p. 1995. pap. 5.95 (*0-9625915-2-1*) Paragon Pubs.

— Selden Lindsey, U. S. Deputy Marshall. 2nd ed. LC 89-92792. (Illus.). 350p. (Orig.). 1992. pap. 14.95 (*0-9625915-1-3*) Paragon Pubs.

McCullough, Helen C. Brocade by Night: 'Kokin Wakashu' & the Court Style in Japanese Classical Poetry. LC 84-50637. 608p. 1985. 62.50 (*0-8047-1246-8*) Stanford U Pr.

— Bungo Manual: Selected Reference Materials for Students of Classical Japanese. (Cornell East Asia Ser.: No. 48). 104p. 1993. reprint ed. 10.00 (*0-939657-03-1*) Cornell East Asia Pgm.

McCullough, Helen C., ed. Classical Japanese Prose: An Anthology. LC 89-78331. (Illus.). 596p. 1990. 65.00 (*0-8047-1628-5*); pap. 19.95 (*0-8047-1960-8*) Stanford U Pr.

McCullough, Helen C., tr. & intro. Genji & Heike: Selections from the 'Tale of Genji' & 'The Tale of Heike' LC 93-20623. 1994. 69.50 (*0-8047-2257-9*); pap. 18.95 (*0-8047-2258-7*) Stanford U Pr.

McCullough, Helen C., tr. Kokin Wakashu: The First Imperial Anthology of Japanese Poetry: With "Tosa Nikki" & "Shinsen Waka" LC 84-50756. 400p. 1985. 52.50 (*0-8047-1258-1*) Stanford U Pr.

— Okagami, the Great Mirror: Fujiwara Michinaga 966-1027 & His Times. LC 79-3222. (Library of Asian Translations). 1980. 55.00 (*0-691-06419-9*) Princeton U Pr.

McCullough, Helen C., tr. & intro. Okagami, the Great Mirror: Fujiwara Michinaga (966-1027) & His Times. LC 90-21410. (Michigan Classics in Japanese Studies: No. 4). x, 381p. 1991. reprint ed. pap. 12.95 (*0-939512-50-5*) U MI Japan.

McCullough, Helen C., tr. The Tale of the Heike. LC 87-18001. (Illus.). 504p. 1988. 69.50 (*0-8047-1418-5*); pap. 16.95 (*0-8047-1803-2*) Stanford U Pr.

— Tales of Ise: Lyrical Episodes from Tenth-Century Japan. 277p. 1968. 35.00 (*0-8047-0653-0*) Stanford U Pr.

— Yoshitsune: A Fifteenth-Century Japanese Chronicle. viii, 367p. 1966. 35.00 (*0-8047-0270-5*) Stanford U Pr.

McCullough, Helen C., jt. tr. see McCullough, William H.

McCullough, Herb, jt. auth. see Whitten, Wendy.

McCullough, Ian, illus. Little Irish Songbook: Words & Music to 27 Classic Irish Songs. 60p. 1992. 7.95 (*0-8118-0187-X*) Chronicle Bks.

McCullough, Ian, jt. auth. see Wallace, Martin.

McCullough, J. & Scott, D. Experimental Thermodynamics, Vol. 1: Calorimetry of Non-Reacting Systems. 1968. 253.00 (*0-08-020831-2*, Pub. by Pergamon Repr UK) Franklin.

McCullough, Jack W. Living Pictures of the New York Stage. LC 83-16754. (Theater & Dramatic Studies: No. 13). (Illus.). 212p. reprint ed. pap. 60.50 (*0-8357-1479-9*, 2070561) Bks Demand.

McCullough, Jeffrey, et al. Granulocyte Serology: A Clinical & Laboratory Guide. LC 87-19264. (Illus.). 275p. 1988. pap. text ed. 35.00 (*0-89189-254-0*, 45-6-015-00) Am Soc Clinical.

McCullough, Joseph, ed. see Garland, Hamlin.

McCullough, Joseph, jt. auth. see Harp, Richard.

McCullough, Joseph B., ed. see Twain, Mark, pseud.

McCullough, Kae. Skin Deep. 288p. (Orig.). 1993. mass mkt. 4.99 (*0-425-14009-1*) Berkley Pub.

McCullough, Karen M. The Ruin Islanders: Early Thule Culture Pioneers in the Eastern High Arctic. (Illus.). xviii, 348p. 1990. pap. 24.95 (*0-660-10793-7*) U Ch Pr.

McCullough, Kathleen. Concrete Poetry: An Annotated International Bibliography, with an Index of Poets & Poems. LC 87-50085. 1100p. 1989. 90.00 (*0-87875-332-X*) Whitston Pub.

McCullough, Ken. Sycamore - Oriole. Boyer, Dale K., ed. LC 91-71532. (Ahsahta Press Modern & Contemporary Poets of the West Ser.). 60p. (Orig.). 1991. pap. 6.95 (*0-916272-50-8*) Ahsahta Pr.

McCullough, Kenneth C. Monoclonal Antibodies in Biotechnology: Theoretical & Practical Aspects. Spier, Raymond E., ed. (Cambridge Studies in Biotechnology: No. 8). (Illus.). (C). 1990. 115.00 (*0-521-25890-1*) Cambridge U Pr.

McCullough, L. E. The Complete Irish Tin Whistle Tutor. (Illus.). 80p. 1987. pap. 8.95 (*0-8256-0311-0*, OK64923, Oak) Music Sales.

— Ice Babies in Oz: Character Monologues for Actors. LC 95-2289. (Monologue Audition Ser.). 1995. write for info. (*1-880399-82-2*) Smith & Kraus.

McCullough, Laura, jt. auth. see Phillips, Vicki.

McCullough, Laurence B. & Chervenak, Frank A. Ethics in Obstetrics & Gynecology. LC 93-6426. 296p. 1994. 39.95 (*0-19-506005-9*) OUP.

***McCullough, Laurence B. & Wilson, Nancy L., eds.** Long-Term Care Decisions: Ethical & Conceptual Dimensions. 280p. 1995. text ed. 40.00x (*0-614-02690-3*) Johns Hopkins.

***McCullough, Lawrence B. & Wilson, Nancy L., eds.** Long-Term Care Decisions: Ethical & Conceptual Dimensions. LC 94-37416. (Illus.). 304p. 1994. text ed. 42.50x (*0-8018-4993-4*) Johns Hopkins.

McCullough, Malcolm, jt. auth. see Mitchell, William J.

McCullough, Malcolm, et al, eds. The Electronic Design Studio: Architectural Knowledge & the Media in Computer Era. (Illus.). 300p. 1990. 60.00 (*0-262-13254-0*) MIT Pr.

McCullough, Marshall E. Roughage for Dairy Cows. Kau, Elvira B., ed. (Illus.). 40p. (C). 1989. pap. text ed. 3.00 (*0-932147-08-9*) Hoard & Sons Co.

— Total Mixed Rations & Supercows. (Illus.). 56p. (C). 1991. pap. text ed. 3.50 (*0-932147-12-7*) Hoard & Sons Co.

— Total Mixed Rations & Supercows. rev. ed. (Illus.). 63p. (C). 1994. pap. text ed. 4.00 (*0-932147-22-4*, Hoards Dairyman) Hoard & Sons Co.

McCullough, Mary F. Brown Eyes, Blue Eyes. (Illus.). 32p. (Orig.). (J). (ps). 1986. pap. text ed. 3.95 (*0-936625-04-X*, New Hope AL) Womans Mission Union.

— The City: Sights, Sounds, & Smells. McClain, Cindy, ed. (Illus.). 32p. (Orig.). (J). (ps). 1991. pap. text ed. 3.95 (*0-936625-96-1*, New Hope AL) Womans Mission Union.

***McCullough, Myrna.** America's Spelling & Reading with Riggs Series. (Illus.). 1993. pap. write for info. (*0-924277-10-6*) K & M Pub.

McCullough, Nance. Equal vs. Unequal. (Illus.). 23p. 1980. pap. 3.50 (*0-936916-00-1*) NAMAC.

— Love Formulas: The Works. (Illus.). 85p. 1980. pap. 4.40 (*0-936916-01-X*) NAMAC.

— Love Formulas: The Works. rev. ed. (Illus.). 85p. 1981. pap. 6.65 (*0-936916-02-8*) NAMAC.

McCullough, R. L. Concepts of Fiber-Resin Composites. LC 76-150245. (Monographs & Textbooks in Material Science: No. 2). (Illus.). 126p. reprint ed. pap. 36.00 (*0-8357-6071-5*, 2034551) Bks Demand.

McCullough, Ralph C. Civil Trial Manual. 2nd ed. 908p. 1980. Suppl., 1987, 419p. & Rev. Contents Table, 34p. ring bd., pap. 95.00 (*0-685-00157-1*, B544/B603) Am Law Inst.

— Civil Trial Manual. 2nd suppl. ed. 908p. 1980. ring bd. 189.00 (*0-686-31970-2*, B108/B544/B603) Am Law Inst.

McCullough, Ralph C. & Underwood, James L. Civil Trial Manual II: 1987 Supplement. 385p. 1987. pap. 86.00 (*0-8318-0544-7*, B544) Am Law Inst.

McCullough, Rita I., ed. Sources: An Annotated Bibliography of Women's Issues. 320p. (Orig.). 1991. pap. 24.95 (*1-879198-28-2*) Knwldg Ideas & Trnds.

McCullough, Robert. The Landscape of Community: A History of Communal Forests in New England. LC 94-35541. (Illus.). 472p. 1994. text ed. 55.00x (*0-87451-696-X*) U Pr of New Eng.

McCullough, Robert J. & Everard, Kenneth. Bank Reconciliation Projects. 3rd ed. 1987. 7.08 (*0-02-830530-2*) Glencoe.

McCullough, Robert N. Math for Data Processing. 448p. (C). 1988. pap. write for info. (*0-697-06766-1*) Wm C Brown Pubs.

McCullough, Rose. ABCs of Agency Evaluation, Acquisition & Merger. 1991. 18.00 (*0-942326-37-7*, 30181) Rough Notes.

McCullough, Rose V. Handbook of Agency Procedures. 1991. 18.00 (*0-942326-59-8*, 30183) Rough Notes.

— Suitproofing Your Agency Against Errors & Omissions. 1987. 22.00 (*0-942326-62-8*, 30187) Rough Notes.

McCullough, Roy L., jt. auth. see Whitney, James M.

McCullough, Sally, jt. auth. see Lindsay, Jeanne W.

McCullough, Sandra, ed. Older Residents' Legal Rights: Supported Accommodation in New South Wales. 546p. 1992. pap. 64.00 (*1-86287-090-X*, Pub. by Federation Pr AU) W W Gaunt.

McCullough, Stacy. Your Special Baby: Real Lamaze Prepared Childbirth. (Illus.). 90p. Date not set. 10.95 (*0-9643837-0-5*) Luckenbooth. YOUR SPECIAL BABY "...imparts the best knowledge & training possible for coping with labor & childbirth. Very attractively illustrated & easy to understand, this workbook is ideal..." - Childbirth Graphics 1994. YOUR SPECIAL BABY: REAL LAMAZE PREPARED CHILDBIRTH relates everything a pregnant woman wants to know about Lamaze & childbirth but is too busy to ask. Written by a labor & delivery RN, a certified Lamaze childbirth educator, a college educator, & a Fellow of the American College of Childbirth Educators (FACCE), Ms. McCullough brings a wealth of information on pregnancy & childbirth to the reader in a reader-friendly format. Topics include a thorough & comprehensive explanation with ample illustrations of the anatomy & physiology of pregnancy, all labor coping strategies, routine hospital/ medical procedures & interventions presented in a balanced risk-benefit format, the emotional & behavioral changes of the woman in the 4 stages of labor, a comprehensive labor partners guide, interactive charts, & more. A MUST HAVE BOOK for every pregnant woman who plans to go through labor. Distributed by Luckenbooth Press. Individual orders call: 912-987-8222.** ***Publisher Provided Annotation.

McCullough, Steven. Becoming Responsible. (Active Bible Curriculum Ser.). (Illus.). 48p. 1991. pap. 9.99 (*1-55945-109-2*) Group Pub.

McCullough, Virginia, ed. see Benton, John T.

McCullough, Virginia, jt. auth. see Cukier, Daniel.

McCullough, Virginia E., jt. auth. see Cukier, Daniel.

McCullough, W. S., ed. The Seed of Wisdom: Essays in Honour of T. J. Meek. 212p. reprint ed. pap. 60.50 (*0-317-11296-1*, 2014302) Bks Demand.

McCullough, W. Stewart. A Short History of Syriac Christianity to the Rise of Islam. LC 80-29297. (Scholars Press Polebridge Bks.). 1982. 24.95 (*0-89130-454-1*, 00-03-04) Scholars Pr GA.

McCullough, W. W. Sticky Fingers: A Close Look at America's Fastest-growing Crime. LC 80-69696. 158p. reprint ed. pap. 45.10 (*0-317-26942-9*, 2023591) Bks Demand.

***McCullough, William E.** Listen to the Howl of the Wolf. LC 95-4128. (J). 1995. write for info. (*1-57168-026-8*, Eakin Pr) Sunbelt Media.

McCullough, William H. & McCullough, Helen C., trs. A Tale of Flowering Fortunes: Annals of Japanese Aristocratic Life in the Heian Period, 2 vols., Set. LC 78-66183. (Illus.). 930p. 1980. 89.50 (*0-8047-1039-2*) Stanford U Pr.

McCullough, William S. The History & Literature of the Palestinian Jews from Cyrus to Herod, 550 B. C. to 4 B. C. LC 74-80889. 266p. reprint ed. pap. 75.90 (*0-318-34722-9*, 2031933) Bks Demand.

McCullum, Emily, jt. ed. see Harding, Lee E.

McCully, Bruce T. English Education & the Origins of Indian Nationalism. 1966. 11.75 (*0-8446-1308-8*) Peter Smith.

McCully, C. B. A Dictionary of Fly-Fishing. LC 92-32413. (Oxford Paperback Reference Ser.). (Illus.). 288p. (C). 1993. pap. 11.95 (*0-19-283126-7*) OUP.

McCully, C. B., jt. auth. see Hogg, Richard M.

McCully, Emily A. The Amazing Felix. LC 92-10929. 32p. (J). (ps-3). 1993. 14.95 (*0-399-22428-9*, Putnam) Putnam Pub Group.

An Asterisk (*) at the beginning of an entry indicates that the title is appearing in BIP for the first time.

— The Bobbin Girl. LC 95-6997. (J). 1996. write for info. (0-8037-1827-6); lib. bdg. write for info. (0-8037-1828-4) Dial Bks Young.
— The Christmas Gift. LC 87-45758. (Illus.). 32p. (J). (ps-1). 1988. lib. bdg. 12.89 (0-06-024212-4) HarpC Child Bks.
— Crossing the New Bridge. LC 93-16047. (Illus.). 32p. (J). (ps-3). 1994. lib. bdg. 15.95 (0-399-22618-4, Putnam) Putnam Pub Group.
— The Evil Spell. LC 89-24536. (Illus.). 32p. (J). (gr. k-3). 1990. lib. bdg. 14.89 (0-06-024154-3) HarpC Child Bks.
— First Snow. LC 84-43244. (Illus.). 32p. (J). (ps-1). 1985. lib. bdg. 14.89 (0-06-024129-2) HarpC Child Bks.
— First Snow. LC 84-43244. (Trophy Picture Bk.). (Illus.). 32p. (J). (ps-1). 1988. pap. 4.95 (0-06-443181-9, Trophy) HarpC Child Bks.
— The Grandma Mix-Up. LC 87-29378. (Harper I Can Read Bk.). (Illus.). 64p. (J). (gr. k-3). 1988. lib. bdg. 14.89 (0-06-024202-7) HarpC Child Bks.
— The Grandma Mix-Up. LC 87-29378. (Trophy I Can Read Bk.). (Illus.). 64p. (J). (gr. k-3). 1991. pap. 3.50 (0-06-444150-4, Trophy) HarpC Child Bks.
— Grandmas at Bat. LC 92-8318. (I Can Read Bk.). (Illus.). 64p. (J). (gr. k-3). 1993. lib. bdg. 13.89 (0-06-021032-X) HarpC Child Bks.
— Grandmas at Bat. LC 92-8318. (I Can Read Bk.). (Illus.). 64p. (J). (gr. k-3). 1993. 14.00 (0-06-021031-1) HarpC Child Bks.
— Grandmas at Bat. LC 92-8318. (I Can Read Bks.). (Illus.). 64p. (J). (gr. k-3). 1995. pap. 3.50 (0-06-444193-8, Trophy) HarpC Child Bks.
— Grandmas at the Lake. LC 89-26590. (I Can Read Bk.). (Illus.). 64p. (J). (gr. k-3). 1990. lib. bdg. 14.89 (0-06-024127-6) HarpC Child Bks.
— Grandmas at the Lake. LC 89-36590. (I Can Read Bk.). (Illus.). 64p. (J). (gr. k-3). 1994. pap. 3.50 (0-06-444177-6, Trophy) HarpC Child Bks.
— Little Kit, or, the Industrious Flea Circus Girl. LC 93-40658. (J). 1995. 14.99 (0-8037-1671-0); lib. bdg. 14.89 (0-8037-1674-5) Dial Bks Young.
— Mirette on the Highwire. (Illus.). 32p. (J). (ps-3). 1992. 14.95 (0-399-22130-1, Putnam) Putnam Pub Group.
— My Real Family. LC 92-46290. (J). 1994. 14.00 (0-15-277698-2, Browndeer Pr) HarBrace.
— Picnic. LC 83-47913. (Illus.). 32p. (J). (ps-1). 1984. lib. bdg. 14.89 (0-06-024100-4) HarpC Child Bks.
— Picnic. LC 83-47913. (Trophy Picture Bk.). (Illus.). 32p. (J). (ps-1). 1989. pap. 3.95 (0-06-443199-1, Trophy) HarpC Child Bks.
— The Pirate Queen. LC 94-5389. (Illus.). (J). 1995. write for info. (0-399-22657-5) Putnam Pub Group.
— School. LC 87-156. (Illus.). 32p. (J). (ps-2). 1987. lib. bdg. 14.89 (0-06-024133-0) HarpC Child Bks.
— School. LC 87-156. (Trophy Picture Bk.). (Illus.). 32p. (J). (ps-1). 1990. pap. 4.95 (0-06-443233-5, Trophy) HarpC Child Bks.
— Speak up, Blanche! LC 90-36945. (Illus.). 32p. (J). (gr. k-3). 1991. 15.00 (0-06-024227-2); lib. bdg. 14.89 (0-06-024228-0) HarpC Child Bks.
McCully, Johnston. The Scarlet Scourge. reprint ed. lib. bdg. 20.95 (0-89190-998-2, Rivercity Pr) Amereon Ltd.
McCully, Marilyn, jt. auth. see Richardson, John.
McCully, Robert S. The Enigma of Symbols in Fairy Tales: Zimmer's Dialogue Renewed. LC 90-22128. (Studies in Comparative Literature: Vol. 14). 102p. 1991. lib. bdg. 59.95 (0-88946-498-7) E Mellen.
McCully, Ron. Testing Program: Up with Math. Jacobs, Helen J., ed. 120p. (Orig.). (gr. 5-12). 1979. teacher ed 1.75 (0-918272-06-8); pap. 2.95 (0-918272-05-X) Jacobs.
— Up with Math: Basic Skills Step by Step. Jacobs, Russell F., ed. (Illus.). (J). (gr. 5-12). 1979. teacher ed 6.25 (0-918272-04-1); pap. text ed. 6.95 (0-918272-03-3) Jacobs.
***McCumber, David.** Playing Off the Rail: A Pool Hustler's Journey. 1995. 24.00 (0-679-42374-5) Random.
— X-Rated. 544p. 1994. mass mkt. 4.99 (1-55817-780-9, Pinnacle NY) Windsor NY.
— X-Rated: The Mitchell Brothers - A True Story of Sex, Money & Death. (Illus.). 320p. 1992. 23.00 (0-671-75156-5) S&S Trade.
McCumber, John. The Company of Words: Hegel, Language, & Systematic Philosophy. (Studies in Phenomenology & Existential Philosophy). 400p. (Orig.). 1993. 59.95 (0-8101-1055-5); pap. 22.50 (0-8101-1082-2) Northwestern U Pr.
— Poetic Interaction: Language, Freedom, Reason. LC 88-19831. 504p. 1988. pap. text ed. 24.95 (0-226-55704-9) U Ch Pr.
— Poetic Interaction: Language, Freedom, Reason. LC 88-19831. 504p. 1989. lib. bdg. 60.00 (0-226-55703-0) U Ch Pr.
McCumber, W. E. All Our Days. 1989. pap. 2.95 (0-8341-1320-1) Beacon Hill.
— The God of New Beginnings: Brief Messages from Genesis & Exodus. 144p. 1991. pap. 7.95 (0-8341-1365-1) Beacon Hill.
— Love Conquers All: Essays on Holy Living. 99p. (Orig.). 1993. per. 5.95 (0-8341-1455-0, 14993) Beacon Hill.
— Was It Not I? And Other Questions God Asks. 194p. 1994. pap. 9.95 (0-8341-1485-2) Beacon Hill.
— The Widening Circle: Sermons in Acts. 80p. (Orig.). 1983. pap. 4.95 (0-8341-0838-0) Beacon Hill.
McCumber, W. E., ed. Great Holiness Classics, Vol. 5: Holiness Preachers & Preaching. 408p. 1989. 21.95 (0-8341-1289-2) Beacon Hill.
McCumber, William. Take a Bible Break. 115p. 1986. pap. 5.95 (0-8341-1080-6) Beacon Hill.
McCumber, William E., et al. Beacon Bible Expositions, Vol. 1: Matthew. (Beacon Bible Exposition Ser.). 223p. 1975. 12.50 (0-8341-0312-5) Beacon Hill.
McCune, Allison & Spears, Tomye. Rationalizations for Women Who Do Too Much: While Running with the Wolves. 1994. pap. 5.95 (1-55850-380-3) Adams Pubng.
McCune, Bob. Gambling Times Guide to Football Handicapping. (Illus.). (Orig.). 1984. pap. text ed. 5.95 (0-89746-022-7) Gambling Times.
McCune, D. L., ed. IFDC Annual Report, 1978. (Circular Ser.: No. S-2). (Illus.). 22p. (Orig.). 1979. pap. 4.00 (0-88090-028-8) Intl Fertilizer.
— IFDC Annual Report, 1979. (Circular Ser.: No. S-3). (Illus.). 64p. (Orig.). 1980. pap. 4.00 (0-88090-029-6) Intl Fertilizer.
McCune, Dan. Michael Jordan. LC 87-29021. (Sports Close-Ups 2 Ser.). (Illus.). 48p. (J). (gr. 5-6). 1988. text ed. 11.95 (0-89686-364-6, Crstwood Hse) Silver Burdett Pr.
McCune, David, tr. see Vedung, Evert.
McCune, Dianne, et al. The Welcome Back to School Book. (Illus.). 112p. (J). (gr. k-4). 1987. pap. 10.95 (0-86653-383-4, GA1001) Good Apple.
McCune, Donald L. Fertilizers for Tropical & Subtropical Agriculture. Thompson, Marie K., ed. LC 82-11908. (Special Publications: No. SP-2). (Illus.). 30p. (Orig.). 1982. pap. text ed. 4.00 (0-88090-040-7) Intl Fertilizer.
McCune, Evelyn. Empress: A Novel. 512p. (Orig.). 1994. pap. 12.00 (0-449-90749-X, ExPress) Fawcett.
McCune, George M. Korea Today. LC 82-20290. xxi, 372p. 1982. reprint ed. text ed. 69.50 (0-313-23446-9, MCKT, Greenwood Pr) Greenwood.
McCune, Kelly. The Art of Grilling: A Menu Cookbook. LC 89-45792. (Illus.). 108p. 1990. pap. 17.00 (0-06-096462-6, PL) HarpC.
— The Grill Book: A Menu Cookbook. LC 85-45213. (Illus.). 108p. 1986. pap. 17.00 (0-06-096006-X, PL) HarpC.
McCune, Kelly & Ingalls, Thomas. The Fish Book. LC 87-45639. (Illus.). 108p. (Orig.). 1988. pap. 14.95 (0-06-096201-1, PL-6201, PL) HarpC.
McCune, Marjorie W., ed. see Colloquium on Myth in Literature Staff, et al.
McCune, Nancy & Putnam, Cindy. Ortho's Plant Selector. LC 90-86162. 112p. 1991. pap. 9.95 (0-89721-234-7) Ortho Info.
McCune, Sandra K., et al. How to Prepare for the TASP: Texas Academic Skills Program. 2nd ed. 520p. 1994. pap. 12.95 (0-8120-1979-2) Barron.
McCune, Shannon. Intelligence on the Economic Collapse of Japan in 1945. LC 89-16677. 124p. (C). 1989. lib. bdg. 44.50 (0-8191-7560-9) U Pr of Amer.
McCune, Shannon, et al. The American Society for Professional Geographers: Papers Presented on the Occasion of the Fiftieth Anniversary of Its Founding. LC 93-18849. (Occasional Publications of the Association of American Geographers: No. 3). 1993. 5.00 (0-89291-211-1) Assn Am Geographers.
McCune, Shannon B. Geographical Aspects of Agricultural Changes in the Ryukyu Islands. LC 75-11729. (University of Florida Monographs: Social Sciences: No. 54). 94p. reprint ed. pap. 26.80 (0-7837-5090-0, 2044789) Bks Demand.
McCune, Shirley, jt. auth. see Milanovich, Norma J.
McCune, Shirley D. & Brandt, Ronald. Guide to Strategic Planning for Educators. LC 86-71841. 86p. (Orig.). 1986. pap. text ed. 6.00 (0-87120-140-2, 611-86044) Assn Supervision.
McCune, Shirley D., et al. Growing Free: Ways to Help Children Overcome Sex-Role Stereotypes. Cohen, Monroe D. & Martin, Lucy P., eds. 34p. (C). 1976. pap. 2.00 (0-87173-002-2) ACEI.
McCune, Wesley. Who's Behind Our Farm Policy. LC 75-14699. 374p. 1975. reprint ed. text ed. 65.00 (0-8371-8238-7, MCWB, Greenwood Pr) Greenwood.
McCunn, Donald H. Computer Programming for the Compleat Idiot: IBM-PC Edition. 2nd ed. (Illus.). 192p. 1984. 18.95 (0-932538-13-4); pap. 10.95 (0-932538-14-2) Design Ent SF.
— Computer Programming for the Compleat Idiot: Microsoft BASIC Edition. 2nd ed. (Illus.). 224p. 1984. 18.95 (0-932538-11-8); pap. 10.95 (0-932538-12-6) Design Ent SF.
— How to Make Sewing Patterns. LC 77-85078. (Illus.). 192p. (C). 1977. pap. 7.95 (0-932538-00-2) Design Ent SF.
— Write, Edit, & Print: Word Processing with Personal Computers. LC 80-67880. (Illus.). 527p. 1983. pap. 24.95 (0-932538-06-1); The Word Worker Disk I for IBM-PC with 64k. disk 29.95 (0-932538-50-9); Commodore 64 with VIC 1541 & PET-CBM 32k with a CBM 4040 drive. disk 29.95 (0-932538-51-7); TRS-80 I-III with 48k & 2 Disk Drives. disk 29.95 (0-932538-52-5); Apple II & IIe with 48k. disk 29.95 (0-932538-53-3) Design Ent SF.
McCunn, J. C., ed. see Stubbs, George.
McCunn, Ruthanne L. Chinese Proverbs. (Little Book Ser.). (Illus.). 60p. 1992. 6.95 (0-8118-0083-0) Chronicle Bks.
— An Illustrated History of the Chinese in America. LC 79-50114. (Illus.). 136p. (J). (gr. 5 up). 1979. pap. 7.95 (0-932538-02-9) Design Ent SF.
— Pie-Biter. (Illus.). 32p. (CHI & ENG.). (J). (gr. k up). 1983. 11.95 (0-932538-09-6); 11.95 (0-932538-10-X) Design Ent SF.
— Sole Survivor. LC 85-71877. (Illus.). 240p. 1985. 14.95 (0-932538-61-4); pap. 6.95 (0-932538-62-2) Design Ent SF.
— Thousand Pieces of Gold. LC 88-47881. (Asian Voices Ser.). 312p. 1989. pap. 12.00 (0-8070-8317-8, BP812) Beacon Pr.
— Thousand Pieces of Gold: A Biographical Novel. LC 81-68270. (Illus.). 308p. 1981. 10.95 (0-932538-07-X); pap. 5.95 (0-932538-08-8) Design Ent SF.
— Wooden Fish Songs. LC 94-42797. 1995. 22.95 (0-525-93927-X, Dutton) NAL-Dutton.
McCunnall, J., et al. Field Drainage. (Illus.). 224p. 1984. 75.00 (0-7134-3833-9, Pub. by Batsford UK) Trafalgar.
McCunney, Robert J. & Brandt-Rauf, Paul W., eds. A Practical Approach to Occupational & Environmental Medicine. 2nd rev. ed. LC 94-11269. Orig. Title: Handbook of Occupational Medicine. 1994. reprint ed. 59.95 (0-316-55534-7) Little.
McCurchin, Isaac. Life - Its Purpose: Religion, Prayer, & Success, & AIDS Awareness & Coping. 1993. 10.95 (0-533-10498-X) Vantage.
McCurdy. Public Administration: A Bibliographic Guide to the Literature. (Public Administration & Public Policy Ser.: Vol. 29). 328p. 1986. 79.75 (0-8247-7518-X) Dekker.
McCurdy, A. K., jt. auth. see Every, A. G.
McCurdy, Catherine. Book of Irish School Jokes. 1990. pap. 4.95 (0-85342-778-X) Dufour.
McCurdy, Dave, et al. Conventional Combat Priorities: An Approach for the New Strategic Era. (CSIS Panel Report). 100p. (Orig.). 1990. pap. text ed. 14.95 (0-89206-160-X) CSI Studies.
McCurdy, David, jt. auth. see Spradley, James.
McCurdy, David W. & Spradley, James P., eds. Issues in Cultural Anthropology: Selected Readings. 390p. 1987. reprint ed. pap. text ed. 16.95 (0-88133-298-4) Waveland Pr.
McCurdy, David W., jt. auth. see Spradley, James P.
McCurdy, Dwight R. Park Management. LC 84-27653. 272p. 1985. 32.50 (0-8093-1226-3); pap. 29.95 (0-8093-1202-6) S Ill U Pr.
McCurdy, Dwight R., et al. How to Choose Your Tree: A Guide to Parklike Landscaping in Illinois, Indiana, & Ohio. LC 74-156791. (Illus.). 255p. 1972. 10.00 (0-8093-0514-3) S Ill U Pr.
McCurdy, Garvin. Salt on the Windowpane: Doggered, Counterpoint & Main Theme from the New England Seacoast. rev. ed. (Illus.). 90p. 1994. 11.00 (0-9641979-0-1) Info Age Handyman.
McCurdy, Howard E. Inside NASA: High Technology & Organizational Change in the American Space Program. (New Series in NASA History). (Illus.). 240p. 1993. text ed. 32.95 (0-8018-4452-5) Johns Hopkins.
— Inside NASA: High Technology & Organizational Change in the American Space Program. (New Series in NASA History). 232p. 1994. reprint ed. pap. text ed. 13.95x (0-8018-4975-6) Johns Hopkins.
— The Space Station Decision: Incremental Politics & Technological Choice. LC 90-30831. (New Series in NASA History). (Illus.). 320p. 1990. text ed. 45.00x (0-8018-4004-X) Johns Hopkins.
McCurdy, J. Facial Plastic Surgery of the Asian Face. (American Academy of Facial Plastic & Reconstructive Surgery Monograph). (Illus.). 160p. 1990. text ed. 75.00 (0-86577-329-7) Thieme Med Pubs.
McCurdy, Jack. Building Better Board-Administrator Relations. Hymes, Don, ed. (Critical Issues Report Ser.). 126p. 1992. pap. 14.95 (0-87652-180-4) Am Assn Sch Admin.
McCurdy, James G. Indian Days at Neah Bay. Newell, Gordon, ed. (Northwest Historical Classics Ser.). (Illus.). 123p. 1981. reprint ed. pap. text ed. 7.95 (0-939806-03-7) Hist Soc Seattle.
McCurdy, John A. A Complete Guide to Cosmetic Facial Surgery. rev. ed. (Illus.). 288p. 1993. 17.95 (0-8119-0740-6); pap. 12.95 (0-8119-0681-7) LIFETIME.
McCurdy, Michael. The Devils Who Learned to Be Good. (Illus.). 32p. (J). (gr. 2-5). 1987. 13.95 (0-316-55527-4, Joy St Bks) Little.
— Hannah's Farm: Seasons on an Early American Homestead. LC 87-29631. (Illus.). 32p. (J). (ps-4). 1988. lib. bdg. 12.95 (0-8234-0700-4) Holiday.
— McCurdy's World: Postcard Book. (Illus.). 30p. (Orig.). 1992. pap. 7.95 (0-88496-354-3) Capra Pr.
McCurdy, Michael, illus. Earth Apples: The Poetry of Edward Abbey. 112p. 1994. 14.95 (0-312-11265-3) St Martin.
McCurdy, Michael & Peich, Michael. The First Ten: A Penmaen Press Bibliography. LC 78-52650. (Illus.). 1978. 22.50 (0-915778-20-3) Penmaen Pr.
McCurdy, Michael, ed. see Douglass, Frederick.
McCurdy, Wendy, ed. A June Wedding. 1992. mass mkt. 3.99 (0-8217-3781-3) Zebra.
— A Mother's Heart. 1992. mass mkt. 3.99 (0-8217-3756-2) Zebra.
***McCurley, Foster R. & Weitzman, Alan.** Making Sense Out of Sorrow: A Journey of Faith. LC 95-6281. 60p. (Orig.). 1995. pap. 7.00 (1-56338-113-3) TPI PA.
McCurley, Robert L. Handbook for Alabama Probate Judges. write for info. (0-318-61031-0) AL Law Inst.
McCurley, Robert L., Jr. & Davis, Penny A. Real Estate Handbook: Land Laws of Alabama. 5th suppl. ed. 685p. 1990. 80.00 (0-87473-508-4) Michie Butterworth.
McCurley, Steve. Recruiting Volunteers for Difficult or Long-Term Positions. 1991. pap. 7.00 (0-911029-30-3) Heritage Arts.
— Volunteer Management Forms. (Volunteer Management Ser.). (Orig.). 1988. pap. 7.00 (0-911029-08-7) Heritage Arts.
— Volunteer Management Policies. (Volunteer Management Ser.). 1990. pap. 7.00 (0-911029-23-0) Heritage Arts.
McCurley, Steve & Lynch, Rick. Essential Volunteer Management. (Volunteer Management Ser.). 136p. 1989. 11.95 (0-911029-14-1) Heritage Arts.
— Volunteer Management. 1995. 12.95 (0-911029-45-1) Heritage Arts.
McCurley, Steve & Vineyard, Sue. One Hundred & One Ideas for Volunteer Programs. (Brainstorm Ser.). (Illus.). 72p. (Orig.). 1986. pap. text ed. 9.95 (0-911029-04-4) Heritage Arts.
McCurley, Steve, jt. auth. see Vineyard, Sue.
McCurley, Steve, jt. ed. see Vineyard, Sue.
McCurnin, Dennis M. Veterinary Practice Management. LC 65-9467. 1988. text ed. 57.50 (0-397-50782-8, Lippincott Medical) Lippincott.
McCurnin, Dennis M., ed. Clinical Textbook for Veterinary Technicians. 3rd ed. LC 93-10417. (Illus.). 816p. 1993. text ed. 57.95 (0-7216-3792-2) Saunders.
McCurnin, Dennis M. & Poffenbarger. Small Animal Physical Diagnosis & Clinical Procedures. (Illus.). 244p. 1990. text ed. 46.50 (0-7216-5931-4) Saunders.
McCurrie, R. A., ed. The Structure & Properties of Ferromagnetic Materials. (Illus.). 320p. 1994. text ed. 69.95 (0-12-482495-1) Acad Pr.
McCurry, Dan C., et al, eds. The Labor of Women in the Production of Cotton. LC 74-30616. (American Farmers & the Rise of Agribusiness Ser.). (Illus.). 1975. reprint ed. 28.95 (0-405-06761-5) Ayer.
McCurry, Dan C. & Rubenstein, Richard E., eds. American Farmers & the Rise of Agribusiness: Seeds of Struggle, 46 bks., Set. 1975. 1,674.00 (0-405-06760-7) Ayer.
— Bankers & Beef: An Original Press Anthology. LC 74-30618. (American Farmers & the Rise of Agribusiness Ser.). (Illus.). 1975. reprint ed. 33.95 (0-405-06763-1) Ayer.
— Cannery Captives: Women Workers in the Produce Processing Industry (an Original Press Anthology) LC 74-30623. (American Farmers & the Rise of Agribusiness Ser.). (Illus.). 1975. 46.95 (0-405-06770-4) Ayer.
— Children in the Fields: An Original Anthology. LC 74-30624. (American Farmers & the Rise of Agribusiness Ser.). (Illus.). 1975. 29.95 (0-405-06775-5) Ayer.
— The Farmer-Labor Party-History, Platform & Programs: An Original Press Anthology. LC 74-30628. (American Farmers & the Rise of Agribusiness Ser.). 1975. 19.95 (0-405-06790-9) Ayer.
— Grange Melodies. LC 74-30647. (American Farmers & the Rise of Agribusiness Ser.). 1975. reprint ed. 26.95 (0-405-06819-0) Ayer.
— Land Speculation - New England's Old Problem: An Original Arno Press Anthology. LC 74-30640. (American Farmers & the Rise of Agribusiness Ser.). 1975. 19.95 (0-405-06808-5) Ayer.
— The National Nonpartisan League Debate: An Original Anthology. LC 74-30645. (American Farmers & the Rise of Agribusiness Ser.). (Illus.). 1975. 29.95 (0-405-06815-8) Ayer.
McCurry, Dan C., ed. see Bivins, Frank J.
McCurry, Dan C., ed. see Brinton, J. W.
McCurry, Dan C., ed. see Caldwell, Erskine & Bourke-White, Margaret.
McCurry, Dan C., ed. see Commission on Country Life, Jr.
McCurry, Dan C., ed. see Cooperative Central Exchange Staff.
McCurry, Dan C., ed. see Dies, Edward J.
McCurry, Dan C., ed. see Education & Labor Committee.
McCurry, Dan C., ed. see Federal Trade Commission.
McCurry, Dan C., ed. see Hill, John, Jr.
McCurry, Dan C., ed. see Howe, Frederic C.
McCurry, Dan C., ed. see Kerr, William H.
McCurry, Dan C., ed. see Kinney, J. P.
McCurry, Dan C., ed. see Lord, Russell.
McCurry, Dan C., ed. see Loucks, Henry L.
McCurry, Dan C., ed. see Murphy, Jerre C.
McCurry, Dan C., ed. see Rochester, Anne.
McCurry, Dan C., ed. see Russell, Charles E.
McCurry, Dan C., ed. see Simonsen, Sigurd J.
McCurry, Dan C., ed. see Todes, Charlotte.
McCurry, Dan C., ed. see U. S. Department of Labor, Bureau of Statistics Staff.
McCurry, Dan C., ed. see Wallace, Henry C.
McCurry, Dan C., ed. see Watson, Thomas E.
McCurry, Dan C., ed. see White, Roland A.
McCurry, Dan C., ed. see Whitney, Caspar.
McCurry, Jim. CTA. 1976. pap. 1.50 (0-686-20607-X) Ghost Dance.
McCurry, Leta. Commercial Real Estate: An Intro to Marketing Investment Properties. 304p. 1990. text ed. 51.00 (0-13-151465-2) P-H.
***McCurry, Stephanie.** Masters of Small Worlds: Yeoman Households, Gender Relations, & the Political Culture of the Antebellum South Carolina Low Country. 352p. 1995. text ed. 39.95 (0-19-507236-7) OUP.
McCurry, Tom, ed. see Rued, Tim.
McCurtain, Margaret & Moy, Juellen. From Dublin to New Orleans: The Journey of Alice & Nora. (Illus.). 144p. (Orig.). 1994. pap. 19.99 (1-85594-089-2, Pub. by Attic IE) InBook.
McCurtie, Francis E. Jane's Fighting Ships of World War Two. 1989. 24.99 (0-517-67963-9) Random Hse Value.
McCurtin, Peter. Buffalo War. (Sundance Ser.: No. 39). 192p. (Orig.). 1981. pap. 1.95 (0-8439-0990-0) Dorchester Pub Co.
— The Cage. (Sundance Ser.: No. 41). 208p. 1982. pap. 2.25 (0-8439-1077-1) Dorchester Pub Co.
— Choctaw County War. (Sundance Ser.). 208p. 1982. pap. 2.25 (0-8439-1101-8) Dorchester Pub Co.
— Day of the Halfbreeds. (Sundance Ser.: No. 29). 1979. pap. 1.75 (0-8439-0693-6) Dorchester Pub Co.
— Death Dance. (Sundance Ser.). 224p. 1984. pap. 2.50 (0-8439-2159-5) Dorchester Pub Co.
— Death Dance. large type ed. 416p. 1983. 21.95 (0-7089-1055-6) Ulverscroft.
— Death Squad. (Soldier of Fortune Ser.). 224p. 1985. pap. 2.50 (0-8439-2190-0) Dorchester Pub Co.
— Double-Barrel Carmody: Tough Bullet & The Killers. 304p. 1989. pap. 3.95 (0-8439-2847-6) Dorchester Pub Co.
— Double-Barrel Sundance: The Savage - Gold Strike. 384p. 1988. pap. 3.95 (0-8439-2651-1) Dorchester Pub Co.

— Double Barrel Western--Sundance: The Marauders & Day of the Halfbreed. 368p. pap. 3.95 (0-8439-2689-9) Dorchester Pub Co.
— Drumfire. (Sundance Ser.: No. 38). 192p. 1982. pap. 1.95 (0-8439-0976-5) Dorchester Pub Co.
— Drumfire - Buffalo War. (Double Barrel Sundance Ser.). 384p. 1989. reprint ed. pap. 3.95 (0-8439-2742-9) Dorchester Pub Co.
— Gold Strike. (Sundance Ser.). 192p. 1984. pap. 2.25 (0-8439-2181-1) Dorchester Pub Co.
— Golden Triangle. (Soldier of Fortune Ser.). 224p. (Orig.). 1984. pap. 2.50 (0-8439-2169-2) Dorchester Pub Co.
— Green Hell. (Soldier of Fortune Ser.). 224p. 1984. pap. 2.50 (0-8439-2107-2) Dorchester Pub Co.
— Gunbelt. (Sundance Ser.: No. 23). 176p. 1982. pap. 2.25 (0-8439-1105-0) Dorchester Pub Co.
— Hangman's Knot - Apache War. (Double Barrel Sundance Ser.). 368p. 1988. pap. 3.95 (0-8439-2716-X) Dorchester Pub Co.
— The Hunters. (Sundance Ser.: No. 40). 208p. (Orig.). 1981. pap. 1.95 (0-8439-1010-0) Dorchester Pub Co.
— Iron Men. (Sundance Ser.: No. 37). 192p. 1981. pap. 1.95 (0-8439-0977-3) Dorchester Pub Co.
— Kalahari. (Soldier of Fortune Ser.). 224p. (Orig.). 1984. pap. 2.50 (0-8439-2144-7) Dorchester Pub Co.
— Marauders. (Sundance Ser.: No. 31). 1980. pap. 1.75 (0-8439-0740-1) Dorchester Pub Co.
— Moro. (Soldier of Fortune Ser.). 224p. (Orig.). 1984. pap. 2.50 (0-8439-2124-2) Dorchester Pub Co.
— Nightriders. (Sundance Ser.: No. 26). 1979. reprint ed. pap. 1.75 (0-8439-0653-7, LB346NK) Dorchester Pub Co.
— Los Olvidados. (Sundance Ser.). 1985. pap. 1.75 (0-8439-2203-6) Dorchester Pub Co.
— Los Olvidados. large type ed. (Linford Western Library). 1989. pap. 11.95 (0-7089-6763-9, Linford) Ulverscroft.
— The Pleasure Principle. 1974. pap. 1.25 (0-8439-0213-2) Dorchester Pub Co.
— Rockwell. large type ed. 448p. 1984. 21.95 (0-7089-1215-X) Ulverscroft.
— The Savage. (Sundance Ser.: No. 28). 1979. pap. 1.75 (0-8439-0678-2) Dorchester Pub Co.
— Soldier of Fortune: Blood Island, No. 9. (Soldier of Fortune Ser.). 224p. (Orig.). 1985. pap. 2.50 (0-8439-2261-3) Dorchester Pub Co.
— Soldier of Fortune: Bloodbath, No. 7. (Soldier of Fortune Ser.). 224p. (Orig.). 1985. pap. 2.50 (0-8439-2212-5) Dorchester Pub Co.
— Soldier of Fortune: Somali Smashout, No. 8. (Soldier of Fortune Ser.). 224p. (Orig.). 1985. pap. 2.50 (0-8439-2240-0) Dorchester Pub Co.
— Summer Friends. 400p. (Orig.). 1983. pap. 3.50 (0-8439-1167-0) Dorchester Pub Co.
— Sundance: Apache War. (Sundance Ser.: No. 34). 192p. 1985. reprint ed. pap. 2.25 (0-8439-2285-0) Dorchester Pub Co.
— Sundance: Hangman's Knot. large type ed. (Linford Western Library). 256p. 1989. pap. 11.95 (0-7089-6718-3, Linford) Ulverscroft.
— Sundance: Iron Men. large type ed. (Linford Western Library). 272p. 1988. pap. 11.95 (0-7089-6530-X, Linford) Ulverscroft.
— Sundance: Scorpion. (Sundance Ser.). 208p. 1985. reprint ed. pap. 2.25 (0-8439-2223-0) Dorchester Pub Co.
— Sundance: The Cage. large type ed. (Linford Western Library). 368p. 1992. pap. 14.95 (0-7089-7299-3, Trailtree Bookshop) Ulverscroft.
— Sundance: Trail Drive. 192p. 1986. reprint ed. pap. 2.50 (0-8439-2384-9) Dorchester Pub Co.
— Texas Empire. (Sundance Ser.: No. 43). 208p. (Orig.). 1982. pap. 2.25 (0-8439-1124-7) Dorchester Pub Co.
— Trail Drive. (Sundance Ser.: No. 36). 1981. pap. 1.95 (0-8439-0878-5) Dorchester Pub Co.
— Trail Drive. large type ed. Bd. with Hunters. 544p. 1984. 21.95 (0-7089-1075-0) Ulverscroft.
— Yellow Rain. (Soldier of Fortune Ser.). 224p. 1984. pap. 2.50 (0-8439-2089-0) Dorchester Pub Co.

McCurty, Darlene M. I'm Special Too. 6.95 (0-913543-27-6) African Am Imag.

McCusker, Brian. The Quest for Quarks. LC 83-7459. (Illus.). 160p. 1984. 18.95 (0-521-24850-7) Cambridge U Pr.

McCusker, Ginny. Dance, Daphne, Dance. rev. ed. 1995. 7.95 (0-8062-4916-1) Carlton.

McCusker, Honor. Fifty Years of Music in Boston. 3.00 (0-686-70271-9) Boston Public Lib.

McCusker, Honor C. John Bale: Dramatist & Antiquary. LC 79-148890. (Select Bibliographies Reprint Ser.). 1977. reprint ed. 19.95 (0-8369-5678-8) Ayer.

McCusker, John J. How Much Is That in Real Money? A Historical Price Index. 78p. (C). 1992. pap. text ed. 10.95 (0-944026-33-8) Am Antiquarian.
— Money & Exchange in Europe & America, 1600-1775: A Handbook. (Institute of Early American History & Culture Ser.). xiii, 367p. 1992. pap. 29.95 (0-8078-4367-9) U of NC Pr.
— Rum & the American Revolution, 2 vols., Set. (Outstanding Studies in Early American History). 1396p. 1989. reprint ed. 75.00 (0-8240-6191-8) Garland.

McCusker, John J. & Menard, Russell R. The Economy of British America, 1607-1789. rev. ed. LC 91-50283. (Institute of Early American History & Culture Ser.). xxiv, 513p. (C). 1991. reprint ed. pap. 19.95 (0-8078-4351-2) U of NC Pr.

McCusker, Paul. Behind the Locked Door. (Adventures in Odyssey Ser.: No. 4). (J). (gr. 3-7). 1993. pap. 4.99 (1-56179-133-4) Focus Family.
— Catacombs. 1985. 6.50 (0-685-68721-X, MP-630); 25.00 (0-685-68722-8) Lillenas.
— Danger Lies Ahead. LC 95-7714. (Adventures in Odyssey Ser.: No. 7). (J). 1995. write for info. (1-56179-369-8) Focus Family.
— Family Outings. 1988. 8.50 (0-8341-9080-X, MP-643); 25.00 (0-685-68711-2) Lillenas.
— High Flyer with a Flat Tire. (Adventures in Odyssey Ser.: No. 2). (J). (gr. 4-7). 1991. pap. 4.99 (1-56179-100-8) Focus Family.
— The King's Quest. (Adventures in Odyssey Ser.: No. 6). 150p. 1994. pap. 4.99 (1-56179-167-9) Focus Family.
— Lights Out at Camp What-a-Nut. (Adventures in Odyssey Ser.: No. 5). 150p. (J). (gr. 3-7). 1993. pap. 4.99 (1-56179-134-2) Focus Family.
— Pap's Place: A Two-Act Play about Family & Change. 1993. 8.50 (0-685-72852-8, MP-688) Lillenas.
— The Secret Cave of Robinwood. (Adventures in Odyssey Ser.: No. 3). (J). (gr. 4-7). 1991. pap. 4.99 (1-56179-102-4) Focus Family.
— Snapshots & Portraits: A Two-Act Play about the Family. 1989. 8.50 (0-8341-9298-5, MP-652) Lillenas.
— A Strange Journey Back. (Adventures in Odyssey Ser.). (J). (gr. 4-7). 1991. pap. 4.99 (1-56179-101-6) Focus Family.
— Vantage Points. 1987. 8.50 (0-685-68718-X, MP-636) Lillenas.
— A Work in Progress: Christian-to-Christian Satire. 1991. 8.50 (0-685-68685-X, MP-669); 25.00 (0-685-68686-8) Lillenas.

McCusker, Paul, jt. auth. see Bolte, Chuck.

McCuskey, Dorothy. Bronson Alcott, Teacher. LC 71-89201. (American Education: Its Men, Institutions & Ideas, Ser.). 1977. reprint ed. 21.95 (0-405-01440-6) Ayer.

McCutchan, Ann. Marcel Moyse: Voice of the Flute. LC 93-33357. (Illus.). 344p. 1994. 29.95 (0-931340-68-3, Amadeus Pr) Timber.

McCutchan, Betty. Rachel's Star. LC 91-75205. 97p. (YA). (gr. 6 up). 1992. 8.95 (1-55523-464-X) Winston-Derek.

McCutchan, J. Wilson. Macbeth Complete Study Guide. 1963. pap. 4.95 (0-8220-1427-0) Cliffs.

McCutchan, Kenneth P. Evansville: At the Bend in the River. LC 82-50191. 144p. 1982. 22.95 (0-89781-060-0) Preferred Mktg.

McCutchan, Nell. Focus on Reading. (English As a Second Language Ser.). (Illus.). 1980. pap. text ed. write for info. (0-13-322776-6) P-H.

McCutchan, Philip. The Abbot of Stockbridge. 192p. 1992. 23.95 (0-340-51340-3, Pub. by H & S UK) Trafalgar.
— Apprentice to the Sea. 1995. 17.95 (0-312-11743-4) St Martin.
— Assignment Andalusia. large type ed. (Dales Mystery Ser.). 297p. 1993. pap. 16.95 (1-85389-388-9, Dales) Ulverscroft.
— Assignment Fenland. large type ed. (Dales Large Print Ser.). 1994. pap. 16.95 (1-85389-509-1, Pub. by Magna Print Bks) Ulverscroft.
— Assignment Gaolbreak. 240p. 1994. pap. 16.95 (1-85389-474-5, Dales) Ulverscroft.
— Assignment London. large type ed. (Dales Ser.). 325p. 1994. pap. 16.95 (1-85389-432-X, Dales) Ulverscroft.
— Burn-Out: A Commander Shaw Novel. 224p. 1995. 27.00 (0-340-60096-9, Pub. by H & S UK) Trafalgar.
— Call for Simon Shard. large type ed. 1976. 21.95 (0-85456-499-3) Ulverscroft.
— Cameron's Crossing. 176p. 1993. 17.95 (0-312-09762-X) St Martin.
— Coach North. large type ed. 1977. 21.95 (0-85456-535-3) Ulverscroft.
— Halfhyde's Island. large type ed. 1978. 21.95 (0-7089-0159-X) Ulverscroft.
— Hartinger's Mouse. large type ed. 1978. 21.95 (0-7089-0143-3) Ulverscroft.
— Lieutenant Cameron RNVR. large type ed. LC 95-11465. 256p. 1995. pap. 19.95 (0-7862-0474-5) Thorndike Pr.
— Polecat Brennan. (Commander Shaw Novel Ser.). 224p. 1994. 26.95 (0-340-60025-X, Pub. by H & S UK) Trafalgar.
— Shard at Bay. large type ed. (Magna Adventure Suspense Ser.). 364p. 1992. 21.95 (0-7505-0429-3) Ulverscroft.
— Shard Calls the Tune. large type ed. 320p. 1994. 18.95 (0-7505-0537-0, Pub. by Magna Print Bks) Ulverscroft.

McCutchen, Ann, ed. The NESFA Index to the Science-Fiction Magazines & Original Anthologies: 1977-1978. 74p. 1983. pap. 7.00 (0-915368-17-X) New Eng SF Assoc.
— The NESFA Index to the Science-Fiction Magazines & Original Anthologies: 1982. 64p. 1983. pap. 5.00 (0-915368-21-8) New Eng SF Assoc.

McCutchen, Ann A., ed. The NESFA Index to the Science Fiction Magazines & Original Anthologies, 1979-80. (Index Ser.). 90p. 1982. pap. 7.00 (0-915368-09-9) New Eng SF Assoc.
— The NESFA Index to the Science Fiction Magazines & Original Anthologies, 1981. (Index Ser.). (Illus.). 60p. 1982. pap. 5.00 (0-915368-10-2) New Eng SF Assoc.

McCutchen, David. The Red Record: The Wallam Olum, the Oldest Native American History. LC 92-23247. 240p. 1993. pap. 14.95 (0-89529-525-3) Avery Pub.

McCutchen, G. Calvin, Sr. & Chappelle, T. Oscar, Sr. Guidebook for Church Workers: Pointers for Pastors, Officers, Boards, Auxiliaries & Special Committees. rev. ed. Smith, Marvin L., ed. LC 90-81708. 50p. 1990. pap. text ed. 5.00 (0-9625115-3-6) Campbell Rd Pr.

***McCutchen, Heather.** Alabama Rain. Date not set. 5.00 (0-87129-566-0, A62) Dramatic Pub.

McCutchen, Lynn, jt. auth. see Williams, Richard.

McCutcheon. Water Quality Modeling Vol. 2: Biochem - Geochem Cycles - Rivers. 1995. 195.00 (0-8493-6972-X) CRC Pr.

McCutcheon, Allan L. Latent Class Analysis. (Quantitative Applications in the Social Sciences Ser.: Vol. 64). 88p. 1987. pap. 9.95 (0-8039-2752-5) Sage.

McCutcheon, Elsie. The Rat War. LC 85-4593. 111p. (J). (gr. 4 up). 1986. 10.95 (0-374-36182-7) FS&G.

Mccutcheon, Gail. Developing the Curriculum: Solo & Group Deliberation. LC 94-8965. 256p. (C). 1995. pap. text ed. 27.50 (0-8013-0949-2) Longman.

McCutcheon, George B. Beverly of Graustark. 1976. lib. bdg. 16.25 (0-89968-057-7, Lghtyr Pr) Buccaneer Bks.
— Brewster's Millions. 1976. lib. bdg. 19.95 (0-89968-058-5, Lghtyr Pr) Buccaneer Bks.
— Castle Craneycrow. 1976. lib. bdg. 17.25 (0-89968-059-3, Lghtyr Pr) Buccaneer Bks.
— The Daughter of Anderson Crow. 1976. lib. bdg. 15.75 (0-89968-060-7, Lghtyr Pr) Buccaneer Bks.
— Graustark. 1976. lib. bdg. 19.95 (0-89968-061-5, Lghtyr Pr) Buccaneer Bks.
— Graustark: The Story of a Love Behind a Throne. LC 72-145159. 1971. reprint ed. 18.00 (0-403-01087-X) Scholarly.
— Jane Cable. 1976. lib. bdg. 15.25 (0-89968-062-3, Lghtyr Pr) Buccaneer Bks.
— Nedra. 1976. lib. bdg. 15.75 (0-89968-063-1, Lghtyr Pr) Buccaneer Bks.
— Prince of Graustark. 1976. 21.95 (0-8488-0289-6) Amereon Ltd.

McCutcheon, Hildreth. Recipes & Rhymes of Late Victorian Times: An Authentic & Endearing Collection. LC 90-86106. 167p. 1991. pap. 15.95 (0-9629644-0-9) Buckle Pub.

***McCutcheon, Hildreth V.** Secrets of a Victorian Childhood: How Gentle Tales & Simple Toys Fostered Good Little Girls & Boys. Lubeck, Mary B., ed. (Illus.). 145p. (Orig.). 1995. pap. 9.95 (0-9629644-2-5) Buckle Pub.

McCutcheon, James M. China & America: A Bibliography of Interactions, Foreign & Domestic. LC 74-190449. 85p. (Orig.). reprint ed. pap. 25.00 (0-8357-8678-1, 2056835) Bks Demand.

McCutcheon, John T., et al. John McCutcheon's Book. LC 83-46027. (Classics of Modern American Humor Ser.). reprint ed. 64.50 (0-404-19937-2) AMS Pr.

McCutcheon, Lynn. Getting Something out of Applied Psychology. 238p. (C). 1990. pap. text ed. 26.70 (0-929655-79-6) CT Pub.
— Getting Something Out of Applied Psychology Test Bank. (C). 1990. pap. text ed. write for info. (1-56226-005-7) CT Pub.

McCutcheon, Lynn E. Rhythm & Blues. (Illus.). 1971. 10.95 (0-87948-028-9); pap. 7.95 (0-686-96672-4) Beatty.

McCutcheon, Marc. The Compass in Your Nose & Other Astonishing Facts about Humans. (Illus.). 208p. (Orig.). 1989. pap. 8.95 (0-87477-544-2) J P Tarcher.
— Descriptionary. 356p. 1992. lib. bdg. 40.00 (0-8160-2487-1) Facts on File.
— Descriptionary: A Thematic Dictionary. 496p. 1993. pap. 12.00 (0-345-38256-0, Ballantine Trade) Ballantine.
— Roget's Superthesaurus. LC 94-34221. 624p. 1995. 22.99 (0-89879-658-X) Writers Digest.
— Writer's Guide to Everyday Life: Prohibition to World War II. 272p. 1995. 18.99 (0-89879-697-0) Writers Digest.
— The Writer's Guide to Everyday Life in the 1800's. (Illus.). 320p. 1993. 18.99 (0-89879-541-9) Writers Digest.

McCutcheon, Maureen. Exploring Health Careers. LC 92-14924. 317p. 1993. text ed. 25.95 (0-8273-4897-5) Delmar.
— Exploring Health Careers: Instructor's Guide. 133p. 1993. 14.00 (0-8273-4898-3) Delmar.
— Exploring Health Careers Workbook. 350p. 1993. 14.95 (0-8273-4899-1) Delmar.

McCutcheon, Meredith A. Guitar & Vihuela: An Annotated Bibliography of the Literature on Their History. LC 85-17437. (Illus.). 1985. lib. bdg. 83.00 (0-918728-28-2) Pendragon NY.

McCutcheon, Mike. Rebuilding God's People: Strategies for Revitalizing Declining Churches. LC 92-74654. 200p. (Orig.). 1993. pap. text ed. 9.99 (0-87509-505-4) Chr Pubns.

***McCutcheon, Pam.** Golden Prophecies. 400p. (Orig.). 1995. mass mkt. 4.99 (0-505-52005-2, Love Spell) Dorchester Pub Co.

McCutcheon, Paul, jt. auth. see Byrne, Raymond.

McCutcheon, Priscilla & Tecott, Karen. Developing Older Audiences: Guidelines for Performing Arts Groups. 12p. 1985. 2.00 (0-910883-18-1, 126) Natl Coun Aging.

McCutcheon, Priscilla, jt. ed. see Fowler, M. W.

McCutcheon, Randall. Can You Find It? 25 Library Scavenger Hunts to Sharpen Your Research Skills. rev. ed. LC 91-30105. (Illus.). 208p. (YA). (gr. 9 up). 1991. pap. 10.95 (0-915793-38-5) Free Spirit Pub.

McCutcheon, Randall, et al. Communication Matters. LC 93-10452. (J). 1993. text ed. 46.50 (0-314-01390-3) West Pub.

McCutcheon, Randall J. Get off My Brain: A Survival Guide for Lazy Students. LC 84-82166. (Illus.). 120p. (YA). (gr. 9 up). 1985. reprint ed. pap. 8.95 (0-915793-02-4) Free Spirit Pub.

McCutcheon, Steve C. Water Quality Modeling, Vol. 1: River Transport & Surface Exchange. (Illus.). 553p. 1990. 228.00 (0-8493-6971-1, TD370) CRC Pr.

McCutcheon, W. A. The Industrial Archaeology of Northern Ireland. LC 81-72046. (Illus.). 640p. 1984. 90.00 (0-8386-3125-8) Fairleigh Dickinson.

McCutchion, David. The Epistles of David-Kaka to Plalm'n. (Writers Workshop Greybird Ser.). 94p. 1975. 12.00 (0-88253-536-6); pap. text ed. 4.80 (0-88253-535-8) Ind-US Inc.
— The Temples of Bankura District. 12.00 (0-89253-673-X); 6.75 (0-89253-674-8) Ind-US Inc.

McDade. Eight Seconds to Glory. 1994. mass mkt. 4.99 (0-06-100752-8, Harp PBks) HarpC.
— Gray Knight. 1994. mass mkt. 4.99 (0-06-100678-5, Harp PBks) HarpC.
— Sitting Bull. (War Chiefs Ser.). 1994. mass mkt. 4.99 (0-06-100660-2, Harp PBks) HarpC.

McDade, Charlie. Black Mamba. 1993. mass mkt. 4.99 (0-06-100477-4, Harp PBks) HarpC.

Mcdade, Charlie. Red Spider. 1991. mass mkt. 4.50 (0-06-100141-4, PL) HarpC.

McDade, Christina. Apples in the Sky. LC 89-84590. 108p. (Orig.). 1989. pap. 3.95 (0-939810-12-3) Jordan Valley.

McDade, Jim. More of the Stuff I Wrote Before I Got Famous. 56p. (Orig.). 1988. pap. text ed. 4.95 (0-932837-02-6) Sandspur Pr.
— My Lawn Mower Died & Other Stories. (Illus.). 52p. (Orig.). 1984. pap. 3.95 (0-932837-01-8) Sandspur Pr.

McDade, Lucinda A., et al. La Selva: Ecology & Natural History of a Neotropical Rainforest. LC 93-1776. (Illus.). 486p. 1994. lib. bdg. 90.00 (0-226-03950-1); pap. text ed. 28.95 (0-226-03952-8) U Ch Pr.

McDade, Paul, ed. see Wines, E. C.

McDade, Sharon A. Higher Education Leadership: Enhancing Skills through Professional Development Programs. Fife, Jonathan D., ed. LC 88-70150. (ASHE-ERIC Higher Education Report Ser.: No. 5, 1987). 145p. (Orig.). 1988. pap. 10.00 (0-913317-40-3) GWU Schl E&HD.

***McDade, Sharon A. & Lewis, Phyllis H., eds.** Developing Administrative Excellence: Creating a Culture of Leadership. LC 85-644752. (New Directions for Higher Education Ser.: No. 87). 110p. (Orig.). 1994. pap. 16.95 (0-7879-9986-5) Jossey-Bass.

McDade, Sharon A., jt. auth. see Green, Madeleine F.

McDanel, Ralph C. The Virginia Constitutional Convention of 1901-1902. LC 75-146556. (American Constitutional & Legal History Ser). 1972. reprint ed. lib. bdg. 24.50 (0-306-70204-5) Da Capo.

McDaniel. Aging & Social Policy in Canada. 1993. pap. write for info. (0-409-89345-5, Pub. by Buttrwrth Can Acad CN) Buttrwrth-Heinemann.
— Don't Die, My Love. 1995. mass mkt. 3.99 (0-553-56715-2) Bantam.

McDaniel & Pearce. Images of Brookland: The History & Architecture of a Washington Suburb. 1982. 7.00 (0-318-21780-5) G Washington Univ.

McDaniel, Antonio. Swing Low, Sweet chariot: The Mortality Cost of Colonizing Liberia in the Nineteenth Century. (Illus.). 208p. 1995. 34.00 (0-226-55724-3) U Ch Pr.

McDaniel, Audrey. Greatest of These Is Love. LC 64-23538. (Illus.). 1972. 9.50 (0-8378-1713-7) Gibson.
— Hope for Every Heart. large type ed. (Large Print Inspirational Ser.). 1987. pap. 5.95 (0-8027-2584-8) Walker & Co.

McDaniel, Becky B. Fue Carmelita (Katie Did It) LC 83-7260. (Rookie Reader Ser.). (Illus.). 32p. (SPA.). (J). (ps-2). 1988. lib. bdg. 10.35 (0-516-32043-2); pap. 2.95 (0-516-52043-1) Childrens.
— Fue Carmelita-Libro Grande: Katie Did It-Big Book. (Rookie Reader Big Bks.). (Illus.). 32p. (J). (ps-2). 1988. lib. bdg. 22.95 (0-516-59512-1) Childrens.
— Katie Can. LC 87-5190. (Rookie Reader Ser.). (Illus.). 32p. (J). (ps-2). 1987. lib. bdg. 10.35 (0-516-02082-X); pap. 2.95 (0-516-42082-8) Childrens.
— Katie Couldn't. LC 85-11666. (Rookie Reader Ser.). (Illus.). 30p. (J). (gr. 1-2). 1985. lib. bdg. 10.35 (0-516-02069-2); pap. 2.95 (0-516-42069-0) Childrens.
— Katie Did It. LC 83-7260. (Rookie Reader Ser.). (Illus.). 32p. (J). (ps-2). 1983. lib. bdg. 10.35 (0-516-02043-9); pap. 2.95 (0-516-42043-7) Childrens.
— Katie Did It Big Book. (Rookie Reader Ser.). (Illus.). 32p. (J). (gr. 5-9). 1988. lib. bdg. 22.95 (0-516-49512-7) Childrens.
— Larry & the Cookie. LC 92-37871. (Rookie Reader Ser.). (Illus.). 32p. (J). (ps-2). 1993. lib. bdg. 10.35 (0-516-02014-5); pap. 2.95 (0-516-42014-3) Childrens.

McDaniel, Burruss. How to Know the Mites & Ticks. (Pictured Key Nature Ser.). 350p. (C). 1979. spiral bd. write for info. (0-697-04757-1) Wm C Brown Pubs.

McDaniel, Carl, Jr. & Darden. Marketing. 768p. 1986. teacher ed write for info. (0-318-61505-3, H0517-6); trans. write for info. (0-318-61507-X, H05192); write for info. (0-318-61506-1, H0518-4); write for info. (0-318-61508-8, H1313-9) Allyn.

McDaniel, Carl, Jr. & Gates, Roger. Marketing Research Essentials. LC 94-20227. 550p. 1994. pap. text ed. 46.00 (0-314-04283-0) West Pub.

McDaniel, Carl, Jr. & Gates, Roger H. Contemporary Marketing Research. 2nd ed. Leyh, ed. LC 92-17896. 750p. (C). 1993. text ed. 64.00 (0-314-01026-2) West Pub.

McDaniel, Carl, Jr., jt. auth. see Gitman, Lawrence J.

McDaniel, Carl

McDaniel, Charlotte. Health Care Benefits Problem Solver for Human Resource Professionals & Managers. LC 93-36894. 1994. text ed. 59.95 (0-471-00658-0) Wiley.

McDaniel, Colleen, jt. auth. see McDaniel, Jack.

McDaniel, David. The Bride of Film Book Reference Guide. (Illus.). 56p. (Orig.). 1991. pap. 8.00 (0-88734-901-3) Players Pr.
— The Final Affair: A "Man from U.N.C.L.E" Novel. 176p. 1984. 14.00 (0-935892-03-6) Exteguer.

***McDaniel, David B.** Paradox 5.0 for Windows at a Glance. (At a Glance Ser.). 136p. (Orig.). 1995. pap. 15.95 (1-55622-456-7) Wordware Pub.

McDaniel, Deborah. Foster Care in the 1980s. 174p. 1981. pap. 16.75 (0-08-028096-X, Pergamon Pr) Elsevier.

McDaniel, Don. Body Fat: A Loser's Manual. (Illus.). 185p. (Orig.). 1992. pap. 12.95 (0-9624378-2-4) Life Fitness.

An Asterisk (*) at the beginning of an entry indicates that the title is appearing in BIP for the first time.

— Weightshaping: Body Sculpting & Body Performance: An Instruction Manual. (Illus.). 130p. (Orig.). 1994. pap. text ed. 14.95 (*0-9624378-0-8*) Life Fitness.

McDaniel, Don M., jt. auth. see Wyskida, Richard M.

McDaniel, Dorothy. After the Hero's Welcome: A POW Wife's Story of the Battle Against a New Enemy. 240p. 1991. 17.95 (*0-929387-52-X*) Bonus Books.

McDaniel, Douglas E. United States Technology Export Control: An Assessment. LC 91-45608. 304p. 1993. text ed. 55.00 (*0-275-94164-7*, C4164, Praeger Pubs) Greenwood.

***McDaniel, Drew.** Fundamental Communication Electronic. 192p. (C). 1995. pap. text ed., spiral bd. 19.95 (*0-7872-0594-X*) Kendall-Hunt.

— Fundamentals of Communication Electronics. 168p. 1992. spiral bd. 14.95 (*0-8403-8030-5*) Kendall-Hunt.

McDaniel, Drew O. Broadcasting in the Malay World: Radio, Television, & Video in Brunei, Indonesia, Malaysia, & Singapore. LC 93-46297. (Communication & Information Science Ser.). 352p. 1994. 49.50 (*1-56750-070-6*); pap. 22.50 (*1-56750-071-4*) Ablex Pub.

McDaniel, Dwight. Understanding the Dispensation. 125p. 1993. pap. text ed. 9.95 (*1-883866-00-6*) Clarion Pub.

McDaniel, E. & Lawrence, C. Levels of Cognitive Complexity: An Approach to the Measurement of Thinking. (Recent Research in Psychology Ser.). (Illus.). xii, 97p. 1990. pap. 48.00 (*0-387-97301-X*) Spr-Verlag.

McDaniel, Earl W. Atomic Collisions - Electron & Photon Projectiles. 1989. text ed. 146.00 (*0-471-85307-0*) Wiley.

McDaniel, Earl W., jt. auth. see Mason, Edward A.

McDaniel, Earl W., et al. Atomic Collisions: Heavy Particle Projectiles. 648p. 1993. text ed. 149.00 (*0-471-85308-9*) Wiley.

McDaniel, Edwin B., ed. Second Asian Regional Workshop on Injectable Contraceptives. (Illus.). 93p. 1982. pap. 5.00 (*0-942716-04-3*) World Neigh.

McDaniel, Effie. Taste of Louisiana: Cajun - Creole Recipes. 2nd ed. Millang, Theresa, ed. 163p. 1989. write for info. (*0-318-65739-2*) id Pub.

***McDaniel, Ellen.** Guide to the EOS Computing Environment at North Carolina State University. 208p. (C). 1994. pap. text ed., spiral bd. 9.50 (*0-8403-9815-8*) Kendall-Hunt.

McDaniel, Ernest. Understanding Educational Measurement. 384p. 1994. boxed write for info. (*0-697-13208-0*) Brown & Benchmark.

McDaniel, Gary M. Floral Design & Arrangement. 2nd ed. 288p. 1988. text ed. 66.00 (*0-13-322264-0*) P-H.

— Ornamental Horticulture. 2nd ed. (C). 1982. text ed. 81.00 (*0-8359-5348-3*, Reston) P-H.

McDaniel, George, comp. IBM Dictionary of Computing. 10th ed. LC 93-20948. 1993. text ed. 39.50 (*0-07-031488-8*); pap. text ed. 24.95 (*0-07-031489-6*) McGraw.

***McDaniel, George W.** Smith Wildman Brookhart: Iowa's Renegade Republican. (Illus.). 320p. 1995. 29.95 (*0-8138-2107-X*) Iowa St U Pr.

McDaniel, George W. & Pearce, John N., eds. Images of Brookland: The History & Architecture of a Washington Suburb, Vol. M10. 1982. 7.00 (*0-317-01776-4*) GWU CWAS.

McDaniel, Ivan G. Realizing Eternal Selfhood. Ricchio, Paul P., ed. 297p. 1981. 12.95 (*0-932785-41-7*) Philos Pub.

McDaniel, Ivan G. & Clymer, R. Swinburne. Lamp of the Soul. 268p. 1943. 16.95 (*0-932785-29-8*) Philos Pub.

McDaniel, J. Lesbian Couples Guide. 1995. pap. 13.00 (*0-06-095021-8*) HarpC.

McDaniel, J. R. Making Automation Work: Successful Strategies for Managing New Technology. rev. ed. LC 92-27799. (Series in Entrepreneurship). 232p. 1992. 59.00 (*0-8153-0997-X*) Garland.

McDaniel, Jack & McDaniel, Colleen. Pooches & Small Fry: Parenting Skills for Dogs (& Kids!) Luther, Luana, ed. LC 94-69540. (Parenting Skills for Dogs & Kids Ser.). (Illus.). 174p. 1995. pap. 14.95 (*0-944875-37-8*) Doral Pub.

McDaniel, James W. Physical Disability & Human Behavior. 2nd ed. 232p. 1976. 79.00 (*0-08-019722-1*, Pub. by Pergamon Repr UK) Franklin.

McDaniel, Jan. Heart's Holiday. 1993. 13.95 (*0-8034-9005-4*) Bouregy.

— Just Like Heaven. 1993. 13.95 (*0-8034-9022-4*) Bouregy.

— An Old-Fashioned Love Song. 1994. 17.95 (*0-8034-9085-2*, 094523) Bouregy.

— Once & Forever. 192p. 1992. 13.95 (*0-8034-8974-9*, Avalon Bks) Bouregy.

— One Golden Summer. 1993. 13.95 (*0-8034-8991-9*) Bouregy.

— Sand Castles. 192p. 1994. 17.95 (*0-8034-9042-9*, Avalon Bks) Bouregy.

— Yesterday's Love Song. 192p. 1994. 17.95 (*0-8034-9044-5*, Avalon Bks) Bouregy.

McDaniel, Jay B. Earth, Sky, Gods, & Mortals: Developing an Ecological Spirituality. LC 89-51581. 224p. (Orig.). (C). 1990. pap. 14.95 (*0-89622-412-0*) Twenty-Third.

— Of God & Pelicans: A Theology of Reverance for Living. 192p. (Orig.). 1989. pap. 12.99 (*0-664-25076-9*) Westminster John Knox.

— With Roots & Wings: Christianity in an Age of Ecology & Dialogue. LC 95-500359. (Ecology & Justice Ser.). 280p. (Orig.). 1995. pap. 16.95 (*1-57075-001-7*) Orbis Bks.

McDaniel, Jay B., jt. auth. see Pinches, Charles.

***McDaniel, Jeffrey.** Alibi School. LC 95-2002. 80p. (Orig.). 1995. pap. 8.95 (*0-916397-38-6*) Manic D Pr.

McDaniel, John M. Spring Turkey Hunting: The Serious Hunter's Guide. LC 85-27723. (Illus.). 224p. 1986. 21.95 (*0-8117-1688-0*) Stackpole.

McDaniel, Judith. Just Say Yes: A Novel. LC 91-310. 176p. (Orig.). 1991. lib. bdg. 20.95 (*0-932379-97-4*); pap. 9.95 (*0-932379-96-6*) Firebrand Bks.

— Metamorphosis: Reflections on Recovery. LC 89-80611. 80p. 1989. lib. bdg. 16.95 (*0-932379-62-1*); pap. 7.95 (*0-932379-61-3*) Firebrand Bks.

— Sanctuary, A Journey. LC 87-7398. 176p. (Orig.). 1987. lib. bdg. 16.95 (*0-932379-24-9*); pap. 7.95 (*0-932379-23-0*) Firebrand Bks.

McDaniel, Julie A., jt. auth. see Ohles, Judith K.

McDaniel, June. The Madness of the Saints: Ecstatic Religion in Bengal. LC 88-35657. (Illus.). 352p. 1989. lib. bdg. 45.00 (*0-226-55722-7*); pap. text ed. 16.95 (*0-226-55723-5*) U Ch Pr.

McDaniel, Kenneth L. Introduction to FORTRAN. (Illus.). 138p. reprint ed. pap. 6.50 (*0-16-002070-0*, S/N 008-047-00306-4) USGPO.

McDaniel, L. L., et al, eds. American Type Culture Collection Catalogue of Plant Viruses & Antisera. 7th ed. 84p. 1993. pap. text ed. write for info. (*0-930009-48-7*) ATCC.

McDaniel, Laraine. Within the Law. (Intrigue Ser.). 1994. mass mkt. 2.99 (*0-373-22272-6*, 1-22272-8) Harlequin Bks.

McDaniel, Loraine. One Foot in Heaven. (American Romance Ser.). 1993. mass mkt. 3.50 (*0-373-16499-8*, 1-16499-5) Harlequin Bks.

McDaniel, Lurlene. All the Days of Her Life. (One Last Wish Ser.: No. 10). (YA). 1994. pap. 3.50 (*0-553-56264-9*) Bantam.

— Baby Alicia Is Dying. (YA). 1993. pap. 3.50 (*0-553-29605-1*) Bantam.

— Goodbye Doesn't Mean Forever. (YA). (gr. 7 up). 1989. pap. 3.50 (*0-553-28007-4*, Starfire) Bantam.

— Happily Ever after. (YA). 1992. pap. 3.50 (*0-553-29056-8*) Bantam.

— I Want to Live. 128p. (J). (gr. 5-8). 1987. 2.99 (*0-87406-237-3*) Willowisp Pr.

— If I Should Die Before I Wake. 128p. (J). (gr. 5-8). 1992. pap. 2.99 (*0-87406-486-4*) Willowisp Pr.

— The Legacy: Making Wishes Come True. (One Last Wish Ser.: No. 7). (YA). 1993. pap. 3.50 (*0-553-56134-0*) Bantam.

— Let Him Live. (One Last Wish Ser.: No. 6). (YA). 1993. pap. 3.50 (*0-553-56067-0*) Bantam.

— Mother, Help Me Live: One Last Wish. (YA). 1992. pap. 3.50 (*0-553-29811-9*) Bantam.

— No Time to Cry. 160p. (J). (gr. 5-8). pap. 2.99 (*0-87406-637-9*) Willowisp Pr.

— Now I Lay Me down to Sleep. (YA). 1991. pap. 3.50 (*0-553-28897-0*) Bantam.

— One Last Wish, No. 1. 1992. pap. 3.50 (*0-553-29809-7*) Bantam.

— One Last Wish, No. 2. 1992. pap. 3.50 (*0-553-29810-0*) Bantam.

— Please Don't Die. (J). (gr. 10 up). 1993. pap. 3.50 (*0-553-56262-2*) Bantam.

— A Season for Goodbye. (One Last Wish Ser.: No. 11). (YA). 1995. pap. 3.50 (*0-553-56265-7*) Bantam.

— She Died Too Young. (One Last Wish Ser.: No. 9). (YA). 1994. pap. 3.50 (*0-553-56263-0*) Bantam.

— Sixteen & Dying. (One Last Wish Ser.: No. 5). (YA). 1992. pap. 3.50 (*0-553-29932-8*) Bantam.

— So Much to Live For. 160p. (J). (gr. 5-8). 1991. pap. 2.99 (*0-685-57448-2*) Willowisp Pr.

— Someone Dies, Someone Lives. (One Last Wish Ser.: No. 4). (YA). 1992. pap. 3.50 (*0-553-29842-9*) Bantam.

— Somewhere Between Life & Death. (J). (gr. 5 up). 1991. pap. 3.50 (*0-553-28349-9*, Starfire) Bantam.

— Time to Let Go. (J). (gr. 5 up). 1991. pap. 3.50 (*0-553-28350-2*, Starfire) Bantam.

— Too Young to Die. (YA). (gr. 7 up). 1989. pap. 3.50 (*0-553-28008-2*, Starfire) Bantam.

McDaniel, M. A. & Pressley, M., eds. Imagery & Related Mnemonic Processes. (Illus.). 440p. 1987. 115.00 (*0-387-96427-4*) Spr-Verlag.

McDaniel, M. A., jt. ed. see Cornoldi, C.

***McDaniel, Melissa.** Andy Warhol. (Pop Culture Legends Ser.). (J). 1995. 18.95 (*0-7910-2347-8*) Chelsea Hse.

— The Powhatan Indians. LC 95-2497. (Junior Library of American Indians). (J). 1995. write for info. (*0-7910-2494-6*); pap. write for info. (*0-7910-2495-4*) Chelsea Hse.

— The Sac & Fox Indians. LC 94-44785. (Junior Library of American Indians). (Illus.). 80p. (J). (gr. 3-7). 1995. lib. bdg. 14.95 (*0-7910-1670-6*) Chelsea Hse.

— The Sac & Fox Indians. LC 94-44785. (Junior Library of American Indians). 1995. pap. write for info. (*0-7910-2034-7*) Chelsea Hse.

— Stephen Hawking: Physicist. (Great Achievers: Lives of the Physically Challenged Ser.). (Illus.). (J). 1994. 18.95 (*0-7910-2078-9*, Am Art Analog) Chelsea Hse.

***McDaniel, Nello.** Artists' Projects. Conger, Shelley, ed. 64p. (Orig.). (C). 1994. pap. text ed. write for info. (*1-884345-02-6*) ARTS Action.

***McDaniel, Nello & Thorn, George.** Arts Boards: Creating a New Community Equation. rev. ed. Carlisle, Barbara & Conger, Shelley, eds. 104p. (C). 1994. pap. text ed. 12.00 (*1-884345-03-4*) ARTS Action.

— The Quiet Crisis in the Arts. rev. ed. Rockwell, Mark & McBride, Donna, eds. 48p. (C). 1993. pap. text ed. 6.00 (*1-884345-01-8*) ARTS Action.

— Toward a New Arts Order: Process, Power, Change. Block, Sharon, ed. 88p. (Orig.). (C). 1993. pap. text ed. 10.00 (*1-884345-00-X*) ARTS Action.

McDaniel, Norman. Yet Another Voice. 1978. reprint ed. pap. 1.50 (*0-8439-0516-6*) Dorchester Pub Co.

McDaniel, Patricia. Drugstore Collectibles. LC 94-1495. 144p. 1994. 17.95 (*0-87069-691-2*, Wallace-Hmestead) Chilton.

McDaniel, Paul R. & Ault, Hugh J. Introduction to United States International Taxation. 3rd rev. ed. (Series on International Taxation). 226p. 1989. 80.00 (*90-6544-423-8*) Kluwer Law Tax Pubs.

McDaniel, Paul R. & Surrey, Stanley S. International Aspects of Tax Expenditures: A Comparative Study. LC 84-12575. (Series on International Taxation: No. 5). 1985. 214.00 (*90-6544-163-8*) Kluwer Law Tax Pubs.

McDaniel, Paul R., jt. auth. see Surrey, Stanley S.

McDaniel, Paul R., et al. Federal Income Taxation: Cases & Materials. 3rd ed. Simmons, Daniel L., ed. (University Casebook Ser.). 1291p. 1994. text ed. 47.00 (*1-56662-170-4*) Foundation Pr.

— Federal Income Taxation of Business Organizations. (University Casebook Ser.). 1102p. 1990. text ed. 41.75 (*0-88277-843-9*) Foundation Pr.

— Federal Income Taxation of Business Organizations: 1993 Supplement. (University Casebook Ser.). 124p. 1993. pap. text ed. 8.95 (*1-56662-085-6*) Foundation Pr.

— Federal Income Taxation of Business Organizations: 1994 Supplement. (University Casebook Ser.). 140p. 1994. pap. text ed. 8.95 (*1-56662-179-8*) Foundation Pr.

— Federal Income Taxation of Partnerships & S Corporations. (University Casebook Ser.). 326p. 1990. text ed. 28.75 (*0-88277-825-0*) Foundation Pr.

— Federal Income Taxation of Partnerships & S Corporations: 1994 Supplement. (University Casebook Ser.). 82p. 1994. pap. text ed. 5.95 (*1-56662-178-X*) Foundation Pr.

— Supplement to Federal Income Taxation of Partnerships & S Corporations, 1993. (University Casebook Ser.). 67p. 1993. pap. text ed. 5.95 (*1-56662-087-2*) Foundation Pr.

McDaniel, Rebecca. Scared Speechless: Public Speaking Step by Step. (C). 1994. text ed. 39.95 (*0-8039-5173-6*); pap. text ed. 16.95 (*0-8039-5174-4*) Sage.

McDaniel, Rebecca, jt. auth. see Hansen, Barbara.

McDaniel, Richard. Richard McDaniel: Catskill Mountain Drawings. (Illus.). 112p. 1990. pap. 10.00 (*0-935796-17-7*) Purple Mnt Pr.

— Richard McDaniel: Hudson River Drawings. LC 94-7378. (Illus.). 111p. 1994. pap. 12.50 (*0-935796-48-7*) Purple Mnt Pr.

McDaniel, Robert A. The Shuster Mission & the Persian Constitutional Revolution. LC 72-96696. (Studies in Middle Eastern History: No. 1). 1974. 30.00 (*0-88297-004-6*) Bibliotheca.

McDaniel, Robert E. Eternal Success Through Internal Assurance, 1 Vol., Vol. 1. (Illus.). 12p. (Orig.). 1989. pap. 3.95 (*0-685-31086-8*) Zanni Pubs.

— Fourth Estate. (Orig.). 1992. pap. 9.95 (*0-9623475-6-6*) Zanni Pubs.

— Jud Troy Syndrome: How to Build a Barn or Succeed at Anything. (Illus.). 6p. (Orig.). (C). 1989. pap. 3.95 (*0-9623475-2-3*) Zanni Pubs.

— Syndromic Living. 153p. (Orig.). 1989. pap. 9.95 (*0-9623475-0-7*) Zanni Pubs.

— Vending Machine Syndrome: Side-Step One on the Road to Success. 12p. (Orig.). 1989. pap. 4.95 (*0-9623475-1-5*) Zanni Pubs.

McDaniel, Robert W. & Dethloff, Henry C. Pattillo Higgins & the Search for Texas Oil. LC 88-32638. (Montague History of Oil Ser.: No. 5). (Illus.). 192p. 1989. 19.95 (*0-89096-379-7*) Tex A&M Univ Pr.

McDaniel, S., et al. Family-Oriented Primary Care. (Illus.). 400p. 1989. pap. 49.00 (*0-387-97056-8*) Spr-Verlag.

McDaniel, S. T., jt. auth. see Lee, D.

McDaniel, Sandy & Bielen, Peggy. Project Self-Esteem: A Parent-Involvement Program for Children Grades K-6. rev. ed. Lovelady, Janet, ed. LC 89-84056. (Creative Teaching & Parenting Ser.). (Illus.). 408p. 1990. reprint ed. pap. 39.95 (*0-915190-59-1*, JP9059-1) Jalmar Pr.

McDaniel, Sandy S. Recipes from Parenting. (Orig.). 1990. pap. 12.50 (*0-9626359-0-1*) S McDaniel Enter.

***McDaniel, Stanley V.** The McDaniel Report: On the Failure of Executive, Congressional, & Scientific Responsibility in Investigating Possible Evidence of Artificial Structures on the Surface of Mars & in Setting Mission Priorities for NASA's Mars Exploration Program. (Illus.). 174p. (Orig.). (C). 1994. pap. 20.00 (*1-55643-088-4*) North Atlantic.

— The Philosophical Etymology of Hobbit. 24p. (Orig.). 1995. pap. 3.50 (*1-881799-10-7*) Am Tolkien Soc.

McDaniel, Stephen, jt. auth. see Hise, Richard.

***McDaniel, Susan.** Counseling Families with Chronic Illness. 1995. 17.95 (*1-55620-144-3*) Am Coun Assn.

McDaniel, Susan H., et al. Medical Family Therapy: Psychosocial Treatment of Families with Health Problems. LC 92-11151. 1992. text ed. 35.00 (*0-465-04437-9*) Basic.

McDaniel, Susan L., jt. ed. see Pederson, Lee.

McDaniel, Thomas. At Home in South Carolina. (J). (gr. 3). 1991. 29.95 (*0-87844-099-2*) Sandlapper Pub Co.

McDaniel, Thomas R. Improving Student Behavior: Essays on Classroom Management & Motivation. LC 86-28228. 148p. (Orig.). 1987. lib. bdg. 40.50 (*0-8191-6064-4*); pap. text ed. 18.00 (*0-8191-6065-2*) U Pr of Amer.

McDaniel, Tim. Autocracy, Capitalism, & Revolution in Russia. LC 86-30790. 510p. 1987. pap. 17.00 (*0-520-06071-7*) U CA Pr.

— Autocracy, Modernization & Revolution in Russia & Iran. 256p. 1991. text ed. 49.50 (*0-691-03147-9*) Princeton U Pr.

— Autocracy, Modernization, & Revolution in Russia & Iran. 256p. 1993. pap. text ed. 15.95 (*0-691-02482-0*) Princeton U Pr.

McDaniel, William D., jt. auth. see McGrew, P. C.

McDaniel, William D., jt. auth. see Mcgrew, Patricia C.

McDaniel, William H. The History of Beech: Fifty Years of Excellence. rev. ed. LC 32-1640. (Illus.). 604p. reprint ed. write for info. (*0-911978-00-3*) McCormick-Armstrong.

McDaniel, Wilma E. Flowers in a Tin Can. 36p. (Orig.). 1982. pap. 4.00 (*0-935390-07-3*) Wormwood Bks & Mag.

— A Girl from Buttonwillow. 48p. (Orig.). 1990. pap. 4.00 (*0-935390-15-4*) Wormwood Bks & Mag.

— Junkyard Sculpture. Meyer, Maggi H., ed. 28p. 1984. pap. 3.00 (*0-915727-09-9*) im-Press.

— The Last Dust Storm. LC 95-9865. 104p. 1995. 20.00 (*1-882413-17-2*); pap. 12.00 (*1-882413-16-4*) Hanging Loose.

— A Primer for Buford. 1990. pap. 9.00 (*0-914610-87-2*); boxed 15.00 (*0-914610-88-0*) Hanging Loose.

— A Prince Albert Wind. 1994. 10.95 (*0-9636829-1-1*); pap. 7.95 (*0-9636829-2-X*) Mother Road.

— Sister Vayda's Song. 1982. pap. 6.00 (*0-914610-27-9*) Hanging Loose.

— Tollbridge. 32p. 1980. 3.00 (*0-936556-01-3*) Contact Two.

— Vito & Zona. (Dog River Review Poetry Ser.). 40p. (Orig.). 1993. pap. 4.00 (*0-916155-21-8*) Trout Creek.

McDaniels, Abigail. Dead Voices. 256p. 1994. mass mkt. 4.50 (*0-8217-4695-2*) Zebra.

— House of Four Seasons. 256p. (Orig.). 1992. pap. 3.99 (*0-8439-3244-9*) Dorchester Pub Co.

— House of Four Seasons. 256p. (Orig.). 1995. mass mkt., pap. 4.99 (*0-505-52061-3*) Dorchester Pub Co.

— Playmates. 256p. 1993. mass mkt. 4.50 (*0-8217-4296-5*) Zebra.

— The Uprising. 320p. 1994. mass mkt. 4.50 (*0-8217-4501-8*) Zebra.

McDaniels, Carl. The Changing Workplace: Career Counseling Strategies for the 1990s & Beyond. LC 88-46081. (Management Ser.). 280p. 1989. 28.95 (*1-55542-146-6*) Jossey-Bass.

— Developing a Professional Vita or Resume. rev. ed. LC 90-3029. (Illus.). 108p. 1990. pap. 10.95 (*0-912048-81-6*) Garrett Pk.

McDaniels, Carl & Gysbers, Norman C. Counseling for Career Development: Theories, Resources, & Practice. LC 91-25851. (Management Ser.). 485p. 1992. 36.95 (*1-55542-399-X*) Jossey-Bass.

McDaniels, Carl, jt. intro. see Parsons, Frank.

McDaniels, Carl, et al. A Career Success Formula: Career Equals Work Plus Leisure. LC 91-27707. (Illus.). 114p. (Orig.). (C). 1991. pap. 10.95 (*0-912048-91-3*) Garrett Pk.

McDaniels, David K. The Sun: Our Future Energy Source. 360p. (C). 1991. reprint ed. lib. bdg. 37.50 (*0-89464-594-3*) Krieger.

McDaniels, Mike. The Pro 3-4: Winning Football with a Multipurpose Defense. 264p. 1986. 19.95 (*0-13-711433-8*) P-H.

McDaniels, William. Abdul & the Designer Tennis Shoes. (YA). 1990. pap. 6.95 (*0-913543-15-2*) African Am Imag.

McDannel, Kathleen H., et al. Advanced Series. (Hedman Stenotype System Ser.). (Illus.). 153p. (C). 1980. text ed. 17.00 (*0-939056-02-X*) Hedman Steno.

McDannell, Colleen. The Christian Home in Victorian America, 1840-1900. LC 85-42947. (Religion in North America Ser.). (Illus.). 216p. 1986. 25.00 (*0-253-31376-7*); pap. 12.95 (*0-253-20882-3*) Ind U Pr.

McDannold, Thomas A., jt. auth. see Matley, Ben G.

McDargh, Eileen. How to Work for a Living & Still Be Free to Live. write for info. (*0-318-59592-3*) S&S Trade.

— How to Work for a Living & Still Be Free to Live. (Illus.). 192p. 1989. reprint ed. pap. 14.95 (*0-9623190-0-7*) Loch Lomond Pr.

McDargh, John. Psychoanalytic Object Relations Theory & the Study of Religion: On Faith & the Imaging of God. 296p. (C). 1983. lib. bdg. 53.00 (*0-8191-3510-0*); pap. text ed. 25.00 (*0-8191-3511-9*) U Pr of Amer.

McDarrah, Fred. The Artist's World in Pictures: The Photo Classic That Documents the New York School Action Painters. LC 88-42845. (Illus.). 1989. 14.95 (*0-944007-28-7*); pap. 9.95 (*0-944007-20-1*) Sure Sellers.

Mcdarrah, Fred W. Gay Pride: Photographs from Stonewall to Today. LC 94-4994. 1994. pap. 20.00 (*1-55652-214-2*) Chicago Review.

McDarrah, Fred W. & Mcdarrah, Fred W. Museums in New York. 1990. pap. 13.95 (*0-312-04356-2*) St Martin.

— Museums in New York. (Illus.). pap. 7.95 (*0-686-45239-9*) S&S Trade.

McDarrah, Fred W. & McDarrah, Patrick J. The Greenwich Village Guide. LC 92-27916. (Illus.). 144p. (Orig.). 1992. pap. 11.95 (*1-55652-151-0*) A cappella Bks.

Mcdarrah, Fred W., jt. auth. see McDarrah, Fred W.

McDarrah, Patrick J., jt. auth. see McDarrah, Fred W.

McDavid, Edmund R., III. Let God Speak: Let Us Listen. 382p. 1991. 14.95 (*0-9630447-0-2*); pap. 10.95 (*0-9630447-1-0*) Hope AL.

McDavid, Mary C., jt. ed. see Krogh, Peter F.

McDavid, Raven I., Jr. Varieties of American English: Essays by Raven I. McDavid, Jr. Dil, Anwar S., ed. LC 78-59374. (Language Science & National Development Ser.). 400p. 1980. 47.50 (*0-8047-0982-3*) Stanford U Pr.

McDavid, Raven I., Jr. & O'Cain, Raymond K. Linguistic Atlas of the Middle & South Atlantic States: Fascicles 1 & 2, 2. LC 79-24748. (Illus.). 1980. pap. text ed. 15.00 (*0-226-55744-8*) U Ch Pr.

McDavid, Raven I., Jr., jt. ed. see Blair, Walter.

McDavid, Raven I., jt. auth. see Kurath, Hans.

McDavid, Raven I., Jr., ed. see Mencken, H. L.

McDavid, Raven Ioor & Green, Donald C. The Structure of American English: Workbook. 147p. reprint ed. pap. 41.90 (*0-317-09501-3*, 2012513) Bks Demand.

McDavid, Virginia, ed. see Jaffe, Hilda.

McDavitt, Kathryn, jt. auth. see McDavitt, Richard.

McDavitt, Richard & McDavitt, Kathryn. Preserve Your Memories in This Lifetime Diary: From Birth to Death. 450p. 1994. reprint ed. boxed 24.00 (*1-885591-04-7*) Morris Pubng.

An Asterisk (*) at the beginning of an entry indicates that the title is appearing in BIP for the first time.

McDeritt, Anne. Your Good Health: A Womans A-Z. 144p. (Orig.). 1994. pap. 19.99 (*1-85594-094-9*, Pub. by Attic IE) InBook.

McDermed, Ann A., jt. auth. see Clark, Robert L.

***McDermid.** Clean Break. 1995. 20.00 (*0-684-80461-1*, Scribners) S&S Trade.

McDermid, J. A., jt. ed. see Ghezzi, C.

McDermid, J. A., et al, eds. Integrated Project Support Environments. (Computing Ser.). 216p. 1985. boxed 72.00 (*0-86341-050-2*, CM005) Inst Elect Eng.

McDermid, John, jt. ed. see Tooley, Mike.

Mcdermid, John A., ed. Software Engineer's Reference Book. 1032p. 1991. text ed. 199.00 (*0-7506-1040-9*) Buttrwrth-Heinemann.

McDermid, John A., ed. Software Engineer's Reference Book. 1993. 79.95 (*0-8493-7766-8*, QA76) CRC Pr.

McDermid, John A. & Whysall, Peter. Formal Specification & Implementation Using Z. 300p. 1992. pap. text ed. 40.00 (*0-13-326380-0*) P-H.

McDermid, Patt. Instructor's Manual to Accompany Steppngstones: Ways to Better Reading. LC 92-33024. (C). 1993. teacher ed, pap. text ed. write for info. (*1-55934-164-5*) Mayfield Pub.

— Steppingstones: Ways to Better Reading. LC 92-33024. 379p. (C). 1993. pap. text ed. 28.95 (*1-55934-163-7*) Mayfield Pub.

McDermid, Patt C. Mountainhouse: A Novella. LC 81-83724. 137p. (Orig.). pap. 9.95 (*0-912288-17-5*) Perivale Pr.

McDermid, Terry Z. A Tapestry of Reading: Introducing Literary Genres, Grades 4-6. (Illus.). 130p. (Orig.). 1994. pap. 10.95 (*0-673-36090-3*) GdYrBks.

McDermid, Val. Crack Down. 1994. text ed. 20.00 (*0-684-19756-1*, Scribners) S&S Trade.

— Kickback. 192p. 1993. 17.95 (*0-312-09836-7*) St Martin.

— Kickback. 1994. write for info. (*0-7862-0360-9*) Thorndike Pr.

***McDermitt, Carl B.** A Soft Day in Paradise. 380p. Date not set. pap. 9.95 (*0-7610-0237-5*) NW Pub.

McDermott. Legal Aspects of Corporate Finance. 1986. write for info. (*0-8205-0221-9*, 405); teacher ed write for info. (*0-8205-0222-7*) Bender.

— Reducing Drug Related Harm. 1993. 59.50 (*1-56593-575-6*, 0321) Singular Publishing.

McDermott, A., jt. ed. see Cos-Gayon, C. S.

McDermott, A. C., ed. An Eleventh-Century Buddhist Logic of 'Exists' Ratnakirti's Ksanabhangasiddih Vyatirekatmika. (Foundations of Language Supplementary Ser.: No. 11). 88p. 1969. lib. bdg. 43.00 (*90-277-0081-8*) Kluwer Ac.

McDermott, A. Charlene. Godfrey of Fontaine's Abridgement of Boethius of Dacia's Modi Significandi Sive Quaestiones Super Priscianum Maiorem. (Studies in History of Linguistics: No. 22). ix, 237p. 1980. 59.00x (*90-272-4503-7*, SIHOL 22) Benjamins North Am.

McDermott, Alice. At Weddings & Wakes. 1993. mass mkt. 5.99 (*0-440-21523-4*) Dell.

— At Weddings & Wakes. 1992. 19.00 (*0-374-10674-6*) FS&G.

— At Weddings & Wakes. large type ed. LC 92-31035. (General Ser.). 320p. 1993. 20.95 (*0-8161-5570-4*); pap. 16.95 (*0-8161-5571-2*) G K Hall.

— That Night. LC 87-45641. 192p. 1988. reprint ed. pap. 10.00 (*0-06-097141-X*, PL-7141, PL) HarpC.

McDermott, Annella, tr. see Abeles, Marc.

McDermott, Annella, tr. see Xitu, Uanhenga.

McDermott, Anthony. Egypt from Nasser to Mubarak: A Flawed Revolution. 320p. 1988. text ed. 39.50 (*0-7099-1736-8*) Routledge Chapman & Hall.

McDermott, Anthony, et al, eds. The Multinational Force in Beirut, 1982-1984. (Illus.). 293p. 1991. lib. bdg. 32.95 (*0-8130-1051-9*) U Press Fla.

McDermott, Betty. Violin Pieces Country Style. (Illus.). 72p. 1977. pap. 9.95 (*0-8256-2164-X*, AM32426) Music Sales.

McDermott, Bobbye, jt. auth. see McDermott, John W.

McDermott, Bobbye, ed. see McDermott, John W.

McDermott, Bobbye, jt. auth. see McDermott, John.

McDermott, Bobbye, ed. see McDermott, John.

McDermott, Bobbye, jt. auth. see McDermott, John.

McDermott, Bobbye, jt. ed. see McDermott, John.

McDermott, Bobbye L., ed. How to Get Lost & Found in Fiji. 4th rev. ed. (Australia, California, Cook Islands, Fiji, Hawaii, Japan, London, New Zealand, & Tahiti Ser.). (Illus.). 208p. 1984. pap. 9.95 (*0-912273-08-9*) Orafa Pub Co.

McDermott, Bobbye L., ed. see McDermott, John W.

McDermott, Brian C. Word Become Flesh: Dimensions & Christology. (New Theology Studies: No. 9). 302p. (Orig.). 1993. 17.95 (*0-8146-5015-5*, M Glazier) Liturgical Pr.

McDermott, Brian O. What Are They Saying about the Grace of Christ? (What Are They Saying about...Ser.). 1984. pap. 4.95 (*0-8091-2584-6*) Paulist Pr.

McDermott, Catherine. Design. LC 90-10000. (Arts Ser.). (Illus.). 48p. (YA). (gr. 6-11). 1990. lib. bdg. 11.95 (*0-8114-2364-6*) Raintree Steck-V.

— English Eccentrics: The Textile Designs of Helen Littman. (Illus.). 120p. (C). 1993. pap. 16.95 (*0-7148-2915-3*, Pub. by Phaidon Press UK) Chronicle Bks.

— Essential Design. 215p. 1994. pap. 15.95 (*0-7475-1458-5*, Pub. by Bloomsbury Pub Ltd UK) Trafalgar.

— Essential Design. 216p. 1995. pap. 9.95 (*0-7475-1936-6*, Pub. by Bloomsbury Pub Ltd UK) Trafalgar.

— Street Style: British Design in the 1980s. (Illus.). 144p. (C). 1987. pap. 22.95x (*0-85072-173-3*, Pub. by Design Council Bks UK) Ashgate Pub Co.

McDermott, Charlene, intro. Comparative Philosophy: Selected Essays. 566p. (Orig.). (C). 1983. pap. text ed. 34.00 (*0-8191-3487-2*) U Pr of Amer.

McDermott, David, jt. auth. see Davies, Rex.

McDermott, Drew, jt. auth. see Charniak, Eugene.

McDermott, Drew, jt. auth. see Hendler, James.

McDermott, Edwim J. Distinctive Qualities of the Catholic School. 78p. 1986. 6.60 (*0-318-20560-2*) Natl Cath Educ.

McDermott, Emily A. Euripides' Medea: The Incarnation of Disorder. LC 88-17905. 166p. 1989. lib. bdg. 27.50 (*0-271-00647-1*) Pa St U Pr.

McDermott, Gerald. Arrow to the Sun: A Pueblo Indian Tale. (Picture Puffins Ser.). (Illus.). (J). (gr. 1 up). 1977. pap. 4.99 (*0-14-050211-4*, Puffin) Puffin Bks.

— Arrow to the Sun: A Pueblo Indian Tale. LC 73-16172. (Illus.). 48p. (J). (gr. 1 up). 1974. pap. 15.99 (*0-670-13369-8*) Viking Child Bks.

— Daniel O'Rourke. LC 85-20188. (Viking Kestrel Picture Bks.). (Illus.). 32p. (J). (ps-3). 1986. pap. 12.95 (*0-670-80924-1*) Viking Child Bks.

— Daniel O'Rourke: An Irish Tale. (J). 1988. pap. 4.99 (*0-14-050673-X*, Puffin) Puffin Bks.

Mcdermott, Gerald. Flecha al Sol. (SPA.). (J). (ps-3). 1991. 15.95 (*0-670-83748-2*) Viking Child Bks.

McDermott, Gerald. Flecha al Sol: Un Cuento do Los Indios Pueblo. (Illus.). 48p. (SPA.). (J). (ps-3). 1991. pap. 4.99 (*0-14-054364-3*, Puffin) Puffin Bks.

— The Magic Tree. (J). 1994. 15.95 (*0-8050-3080-8*) H Holt & Co.

— Musicians of the Sun. LC 93-44050. (J). 1994. 14.95 (*0-590-47337-9*, Blue Sky Press) Scholastic Inc.

— Papagayo: The Mischief Maker. LC 91-4036. (J). (ps-3). 1992. pap. 6.95 (*0-15-259464-7*, HB Juv Bks) HarBrace.

— Papagayo: The Mischief Maker. LC 91-4036. (J). (ps-3). 1992. 16.95 (*0-15-259465-5*, HB Juv Bks) HarBrace.

— Raven: A Trickster Tale from the Pacific Northwest. LC 91-14563. (J). (ps-3). 1993. 14.95 (*0-15-265661-8*, HB Juv Bks) HarBrace.

— The Stonecutter. (Illus.). (J). (gr. 1-3). 1978. pap. 4.99 (*0-14-050289-0*, Puffin) Puffin Bks.

— Tim O'Toole & the Little People. (Viking Kestrel Picture Bks.). (J). (ps-3). 1990. pap. 13.95 (*0-670-80393-6*) Viking Child Bks.

— Tim O'Toole & the Wee Folk. (Illus.). 32p. (J). (ps-3). 1992. pap. 4.99 (*0-14-050675-6*) Puffin Bks.

— Zomo the Rabbit. (J). 1992. 14.95 (*0-15-299967-1*, HB Juv Bks) HarBrace.

McDermott, Gerald, illus. & ret. Anansi the Spider: A Tale from the Ashanti. LC 76-150028. 48p. (J). (ps-2). 1972. 15.95 (*0-8050-0310-X*, Bks Young Read) H Holt & Co.

— Anansi the Spider: A Tale from the Ashanti. LC 76-150028. 48p. (J). (ps-2). 1987. pap. 5.95 (*0-8050-0311-8*, Bks Young Read) H Holt & Co.

McDermott, Gerald, illus. & teller. Coyote: A Trickster Tale from the Southwest. LC 92-32979. (J). (ps-3). 1994. 14.95 (*0-15-220724-4*) HarBrace.

— Jabuti the Tortoise: A Trickster Tale from the Amazon. LC 94-23290. 1995. lib. bdg. 14.95 (*0-15-292874-X*) HarBrace.

***McDermott, Gerald, illus. & adapt.** The Stonecutter: A Japanese Folk Tale. LC 94-23302. (J). 1995. write for info. (*0-15-200400-9*); pap. write for info. (*0-15-200399-1*) HarBrace.

McDermott, Gerald, illus. & teller. The Voyage of Osiris: A Myth of Ancient Egypt. LC 94-7067. (J). 1995. pap. write for info. (*0-15-294446-X*) HarBrace.

McDermott, Gerald, teller. The Voyage of Osiris: A Myth of Ancient Egypt. LC 94-7067. (Illus.). (J). 1995. write for info. (*0-15-200216-2*) HarBrace.

McDermott, Gerald, jt. auth. see Mayer, Marianna.

McDermott, Gerald R. One Holy & Happy Society: The Public Theology of Jonathan Edwards. 256p. 1992. 29.95 (*0-271-00850-4*) Pa St U Pr.

McDermott, Gerald R., jt. auth. see Fintel, William A.

McDermott, Henry J. Handbook of Ventilation for Contaminant Control. 2nd ed. (Illus.). 256p. 1985. text ed. 52.95 (*0-250-40641-1*) Buttrwrth-Heinemann.

***McDermott, Hubert, ed.** Vertue Rewarded: or The Irish Princess: A New Novel. 107p. 1994. lib. bdg. 42.00 (*0-86140-305-3*, Pub. by C Smythe Ltd UK) B&N Imports.

McDermott, J. How to Get Lost & Found in the New Japan. 288p. (Orig.). 1987. pap. 9.95 (*1-55650-016-5*) Hunter NJ.

McDermott, J., jt. auth. see Dougherty, J.

McDermott, James. Maker, Lover & Keeper. 112p. (C). 1988. 35.00 (*0-85597-454-0*, Pub. by McCrimmon Pub) St Mut.

McDermott, James P. Development in the Early Buddhist Concept of Kamma-Karma. 1984. 14.50 (*0-8364-2542-1*, Pub. by Munshiram Manoharial II) S Asia.

McDermott, Jeanne. The Killing Winds: The Menace of Biological Warfare. LC 73-82181. 230p. 1987. 19.95 (*0-87795-896-3*) Morrow.

McDermott, John. Corporate Society: Class, Property, & Contemporary Capitalism. (Interventions: Theory & Contemporary Politics Ser.). 208p. 1991. text ed. 65.00 (*0-8133-0707-4*) Westview.

— Corporate Society: Class, Property, & Contemporary Capitalism. (Interventions: Theory & Contemporary Politics Ser.). 208p. (C). 1991. pap. text ed. 20.95 (*0-8133-0708-2*) Westview.

— Crisis in the Working Class: Some Arguments for Creating a New Labor Movement. LC 80-51437. 255p. (Orig.). 1980. pap. 6.00 (*0-89608-014-5*) South End Pr.

— An Historical & Cultural Introduction to Philosophy. (C). 1985. text ed. write for info. (*0-07-554360-5*) McGraw.

— How to Get Lost & Found in Tahiti. 2nd ed. McDermott, Bobbye, ed. LC 86-62292. (Australia, California, Cook Islands, Fiji, Hawaii, Japan, London, New Zealand, & Tahiti Ser.). (Illus.). 272p. 1986. reprint ed. pap. 9.95 (*0-912273-13-5*) Orafa Pub Co.

— Kingsley Amis: An English Moralist. 240p. 1989. text ed. 29.95 (*0-312-02103-8*) St Martin.

McDermott, John & McDermott, Bobbye. How to Get Lost & Found in Our Hawaii. LC 85-61324. (Australia, California, Cook Islands, Fiji, Hawaii, Japan, London, New Zealand, & Tahiti Ser.). Orig. Title: Our Hawaii: What We Tell Friends To Do In Our Islands. (Illus.). 296p. (Orig.). 1986. pap. 9.95 (*0-912273-12-7*) Orafa Pub Co.

— How to Get Lost & Found in Upgraded New Zealand. LC 86-62291. (Australia, California, Cook Islands, Fiji, Hawaii, Japan, London, New Zealand, & Tahiti Ser.). (Illus.). 320p. 1987. reprint ed. pap. 9.95 (*0-912273-11-9*) Orafa Pub Co.

McDermott, John & McDermott, Bobbye, eds. How to Get Lost & Found in London. (Australia, California, Cook Islands, Fiji, Hawaii, Japan, London, New Zealand, & Tahiti Ser.). (Illus.). 336p. 1988. pap. 9.95 (*0-912273-17-8*) Orafa Pub Co.

McDermott, John, jt. ed. see Connolly, Michael B.

McDermott, John, jt. ed. see Steels, Luc.

McDermott, John, et al. Hendrix: Setting the Record Straight. (Orig.). 1992. pap. 13.99 (*0-446-39431-9*) Warner Bks.

McDermott, John D. Forlorn Hope: The Battle of White Bird Canyon & the Beginning of the Nez Perce War. LC 78-2706. (Illus.). 245p. 1978. 14.95 (*0-931406-00-5*) U of Idaho Pr.

***McDermott, John E.** The Diabetic Foot. 1995. 30.00 (*0-89203-119-0*) Amer Acad Ortho Surg.

McDermott, John F. Seth Eastman, Pictorial Historian of the Indian. LC 61-15145. (Illus.). 302p. reprint ed. pap. 86.10 (*0-685-09010-8*, 2005846) Bks Demand.

McDermott, John F., ed. The French in the Mississippi Valley. LC 65-11736. (Illus.). 299p. reprint ed. pap. 85.30 (*0-317-09969-8*, 2020213) Bks Demand.

— Frenchmen & French Ways in the Mississippi Valley. LC 68-24622. (Illus.). 320p. reprint ed. 91.20 (*0-8357-9677-9*, 2014941) Bks Demand.

— Research Opportunities in American Cultural History. LC 77-22111. 205p. 1977. reprint ed. text ed. 55.00 (*0-8371-9754-6*, MCRO, Greenwood Pr) Greenwood.

— The Spanish in the Mississippi Valley: 1762-1804. LC 72-75490. (Illus.). 434p. 1974. 39.95 (*0-252-00269-5*) U of Ill Pr.

— Travelers on the Western Frontier. LC 77-100375. (Illus.). 363p. reprint ed. 103.50 (*0-8357-9700-7*, 2014920) Bks Demand.

McDermott, John F. & Harrison, Saul I., eds. Psychiatric Treatment of the Child. LC 76-45569. 839p. 1977. 40.00 (*0-87668-289-1*) Aronson.

McDermott, John F., jt. ed. see Harrison, Saul I.

McDermott, John F., Jr.

McDermott, John F., Jr., et al, eds. People & Cultures of Hawaii: A Psychocultural Profile. LC 80-11959. 252p. 1980. pap. 8.95 (*0-8248-0706-5*) UH Pr.

Mcdermott, John J. A Cultural Introduction to Philosophy, Vol. 2. 1000p. (C). 1988. text ed. write for info. (*0-394-34727-7*) Knopf.

McDermott, John J. Streams of Experience: Reflections on the History & Philosophy of American Culture. LC 85-16494. 296p. 1986. pap. 16.95 (*0-87023-597-4*) U of Mass Pr.

McDermott, John J., ed. see Dewey, John.

McDermott, John J., ed. see James, William.

McDermott, John J., et al, eds. The Correspondence of William James: William & Henry, 1897-1910, Vol. 3. 608p. (C). 1994. text ed. 45.00 (*0-8139-1510-4*) U Pr of Va.

— The Correspondence of William James Vol. 4: 1856-1877, Vol. 4. 600p. (C). 1995. text ed. 55.00 (*0-8139-1616-X*) U Pr of Va.

McDermott, John M. The Bible on Human Suffering. 155p. (C). 1990. 49.00 (*0-85439-363-3*, Pub. by St Paul Pubns UK) St Mut.

McDermott, John M., tr. see Rousselot, Pierre.

McDermott, John T., ed. Legal Aspects of Investment & Trade with the Republic of China, No. 1. 94p. 1991. 6.00 (*0-925153-13-3*, 102) Occasional Papers.

McDermott, John W. How to Get Lost & Found in Australia. 2nd ed. McDermott, Bobbye L. & Suga, Roger, eds. (Australia, California, Cook Islands, Fiji, Hawaii, Japan, London, New Zealand, & Tahiti Ser.). (Illus.). 304p. 1984. pap. 9.95 (*0-912273-07-0*) Orafa Pub Co.

— How to Get Lost & Found in California & Other Lovely Places. McDermott, Bobbye L., ed. (Australia, California, Cook Islands, Fiji, Hawaii, Japan, London, New Zealand, & Tahiti Ser.). (Illus.). 308p. 1982. pap. 9.95 (*0-912273-05-4*) Orafa Pub Co.

— How to Get Lost & Found in New Japan. McDermott, Bobbye L., ed. (Australia, California, Cook Islands, Fiji, Hawaii, Japan, London, New Zealand, & Tahiti Ser.). (Illus.). 286p. 1984. pap. 9.95 (*0-912273-06-2*) Orafa Pub Co.

— How to Get Lost & Found in the Cook Islands. McDermott, Bobbye L., ed. (New Zealand, Fiji, Tahiti, Australia, the Cook Islands, Hawaii, Japan Ser.). (Illus.). 236p. 1979. pap. 9.95 (*0-912273-03-8*) Hunter NJ.

— Kelleys of the Outrigger. McDermott, Bobbye, ed. (Illus.). 304p. 1990. 19.95 (*0-912273-18-6*); write for info. (*0-912273-20-8*); pap. 10.95 (*0-912273-19-4*) Orafa Pub Co.

McDermott, John W. & McDermott, Bobbye. How to Get Lost & Found in the Cook Islands. 2nd ed. LC 86-62293. (Australia, California, Cook Islands, Fiji, Hawaii, Japan, London, New Zealand, & Tahiti Ser.). (Illus.). 236p. 1987. reprint ed. pap. 9.95 (*0-912273-15-1*) Orafa Pub Co.

McDermott, Kathleen. Peter the Great. (World Leaders - Past & Present Ser.). (Illus.). 112p. (YA). (gr. 5 up). 1991. 17.95 (*1-55546-821-7*) Chelsea Hse.

McDermott, Kathleen, jt. auth. see Allen, David G.

McDermott, Kevin. The Czech Red Unions, Nineteen Eighteen to Nineteen Twenty-Nine. (East European Monographs: No. 239). 384p. 1988. text ed. 54.00 (*0-88033-136-4*) East Eur Quarterly.

McDermott, LeeAnne, jt. auth. see Sandler, Corey.

McDermott, LeeAnne, jt. auth. see Sandler, Cory.

McDermott, Lynda C. Caught in the Middle: How to Survive & Thrive in Today's Management Squeeze. LC 92-20791. 1992. text ed. 21.95 (*0-13-121229-X*) P-H.

— Caught in the Middle: How to Survive & Thrive in Today's Management Squeeze. 1994. pap. 12.95 (*0-13-311424-4*) P-H.

***McDermott, M. Hubert.** Novel & Romance: The Odyssey to Tom Jones. 192p. 1989. text ed. 53.50 (*0-389-29869-7*, N8427) B&N Imports.

McDermott, Margaret H., jt. auth. see Reams, Bernard D., Jr.

McDermott, Margaret H., jt. ed. see Reams, Bernard D., Jr.

***McDermott, Marianne.** 1995-96 Directory of Greeting Card Sales Representatives. 3rd ed. Albertson, Mila, ed. 124p. 1995. pap. 95.00 (*0-938369-24-5*) Greeting Card Assn.

— 1995-96 Greeting Card Industry Directory: A Comprehensive Guide to the Products & Services of the Greeting Card Industry. 8th ed. Albertson, Mila, ed. 276p. (Orig.). 1995. pap. 75.00 (*0-938369-25-3*) Greeting Card Assn.

McDermott, Mark N., ed. Physics for the 1990s: AAPT Conference of Department Chairs in Physics. (AAPT Topical Conference Ser.: No. 4). (Illus.). 110p. (Orig.). (C). 1989. pap. text ed. 12.00 (*0-917853-35-0*, TC-4) Am Assn Physics.

***McDermott, Michael.** Stories of the Fire: Personal Growth Through Firewalking. 179p. (Orig.). (C). 1994. write for info. (*0-9640871-0-3*) Frog & Latte.

McDermott, Michael, jt. auth. see Bisyak, Steven.

McDermott, Michael C. & Tagart, James H. The Essence of International Business. LC 92-45582. 1993. 17.00 (*0-13-288077-6*) P-H.

McDermott, Michael T., ed. Endocrinology Secrets: Questions You Will Be Asked on Rounds, in the Clinic, on Oral Exams. (Secrets Ser.). (Illus.). 300p. (Orig.). 1994. pap. text ed. 30.95 (*1-56053-116-9*) Hanley & Belfus.

McDermott, Nancie. Five in Ten Pasta & Noodle Cookbook: Five Ingredients in 10 Minutes or Less. LC 94-8504. 1994. 15.00 (*0-688-13475-0*) Hearst Bks.

— Real Thai: The Best of Thailand's Regional Cooking. 224p. 1992. pap. 9.95 (*0-8118-0017-2*) Chronicle Bks.

***McDermott, Pamela.** Green Acres School's Going Places with Children in Washington, D. C. 14th ed. LC 95-966. (Illus.). 1995. 11.95 (*0-9608998-4-7*) Green Acres Schl.

McDermott, Patrice. Politics & Scholarship: Feminist Academic Journals & the Production of Knowledge. LC 93-31206. 208p. (C). 1994. 36.95 (*0-252-02078-2*); pap. 13.95 (*0-252-06369-4*) U of Ill Pr.

McDermott, Patricia, jt. ed. see Briskin, Linda.

McDermott, Patricia, jt. ed. see Fudge, Judy.

McDermott, Patti. How to Talk to Your Husband - How to Talk to Your Wife. 192p. 1994. pap. 9.95 (*0-8092-3682-6*) Contemp Bks.

— Sisters & Brothers: Resolving Your Adult Sibling Relationships. 1992. 21.95 (*0-929923-56-1*) Lowell Hse.

— Sisters & Brothers: Resolving Your Adult Sibling Relationships. 240p. 1993. pap. 14.95 (*1-56565-083-2*, Legcy) Lowell Hse.

***McDermott, Paul A.** ASCA: National Profiles in Youth Psychopathology. 64p. 1993. 34.95 (*0-9638072-3-4*) Ed & Psych.

McDermott, Paul D., jt. auth. see Rabenhorst, Thomas.

McDermott, Richard J., ed. see Laura, Ronald S. & Dutton, Kenneth R.

McDermott, Richard J., ed. see Magee, John.

McDermott, Robert A., ed. The Essential Rudolf Steiner. LC 82-48934. 320p. 1984. pap. 18.00 (*0-06-065345-0*, RD-399) Harper SF.

— Focus on Buddhism. LC 81-8084. 160p. (C). 1981. text ed. 4.95 (*0-89012-020-X*); pap. 2.50 (*0-89012-021-8*) Anima Pubns.

McDermott, Robert A., ed. see Morgan, Kenneth W. & Smith, Daniel.

McDermott, Robert J., jt. auth. see Sarvela, Paul.

***McDermott, Robin E.** Leadership in a Total Quality Environment. (Massachusetts Dept. of Employment & Training TQS Ser.). (Illus.). 81p. (C). 1994. teacher ed 275.00 (*1-882307-04-6*); student ed 35.00 (*1-882307-10-0*) Res Engineering.

— Making Sense of TQS. (Massachusetts Department of Employment & Training TQS Ser.). (Illus.). 58p. (C). 1994. teacher ed 225.00 (*1-882307-03-8*); student ed 25.00 (*1-882307-11-9*) Res Engineering.

— Process Redesign. (Illus.). 80p. (C). 1995. teacher ed 275.00 (*1-882307-08-9*); student ed 35.00 (*1-882307-09-7*) Res Engineering.

— Seven Step Improvement Process. (Massachusetts Dept. of Employment & Training TQS Ser.). (Illus.). 109p. (C). 1994. teacher ed 275.00 (*1-882307-06-2*); student ed 35.00 (*1-882307-15-1*) Res Engineering.

— Working on a Process Improvement Team. (Massachusetts Dept. of Employment & Training TQS Ser.). (Illus.). (C). 1995. teacher ed 275.00 (*1-882307-07-0*); student ed 35.00 (*1-882307-16-X*) Res Engineering.

An Asterisk (*) at the beginning of an entry indicates that the title is appearing in BIP for the first time.

McDermott, Robin E., et al. Employee-Driven Quality: Releasing the Creative Spirit of Your Organization Through Suggestion Systems. LC 93-11078. 256p. 1993. 26.95 (*0-527-91670-6*) Qual Resc.
— Making Sense of TQM. (Illus.). 24p. (C). 1995. teacher ed 50.00 (*1-882307-00-3*); student ed 8.88 (*1-882307-14-3*); pap. text ed. 8.99 (*0-614-04150-3*) Res Engineering.
— That Stuff Will Never Work Here. (Illus.). 17p. (C). 1995. teacher ed 5.00 (*1-882307-05-4*) Res Engineering.
— Tools of Continuous Improvement. (Illus.). 40p. (C). 1993. teacher ed 50.00 (*1-882307-01-1*); student ed 8.99 (*1-882307-13-5*) Res Engineering.
McDermott, Rosalie, jt. auth. see Modugno, Carolyn.
***McDermott, Sean & Woulfe, Richard.** Compulsory Purchase & Compensation in Ireland: Law & Practice. 1992. boxed 104.00 (*1-85475-102-6*, IE) Butterworth Legal Pubs.
McDermott, Sean, ed. see Bongay, Amie.
McDermott, Shirley F., ed. see Kirkham, Lester D.
McDermott, Stella. Metaphysics of Raw Foods. 78p. 1963. reprint ed. spiral bd. 3.85 (*0-7873-0597-9*) Mokelumne.
***McDermott, Thomas J.** McDermott's Handbook of Ohio Real Estate Law. 2nd ed. 304p. 1980. 15.00 (*0-614-05898-8*) Michie Butterworth.
McDermott, Timothy, tr. see St. Thomas Aquinas.
McDermott, Timothy, ed. see St. Thomas Aquinas.
McDermott, Vern A. & Bonawitz, Jack, Jr. Learning Appleworks Step by Step: Fundamentals. LC 87-37502. (Personal Computing Ser.). 304p. (C). 1995. pap. text ed. write for info. (*0-7167-8157-3*, Computer Sci Pr) W H Freeman.
McDermott, William C., ed. see Gregory Of Tours.
McDermut, W. E. & Trautmann, William E., eds. Founding Convention of the IWW: Proceedings. 2nd ed. LC 70-85538. Orig. Title: Proceedings of the First Convention of the Industrial Workers of the World: Officially Approved, Stenographically Reported. 1969. 27.00 (*0-87348-013-9*) Pathfinder NY.
McDevitt, ARthur S. Inscriptions from Thessaly. 159p. 1970. write for info. (*0-318-70972-4*, Pub. by Georg Olms GW) Lubrecht & Cramer.
McDevitt, Arthur S. Inscriptions from Thessaly. 159p. (GER.). 1970. write for info. (*0-318-70444-7*, Pub. by Georg Olms GW); write for info. (*0-318-72104-X*, Pub. by Georg Olms GW) Lubrecht & Cramer.
— Inscriptions from Thessaly: An Analytical Handlist & Bibliography. 159p. 1970. 37.70 (*0-685-66493-7*, 05102705, Pub. by Georg Olms GW) Lubrecht & Cramer.
McDevitt, Howard. Howie Houses. 20p. 1993. pap. 5.95 (*1-883612-00-4*) Bks Unltd.
McDevitt, J., jt. auth. see Levin, J.
McDevitt, Jack. The Engines of God. LC 94-7131. 432p. 1994. text ed. 21.95 (*0-441-00077-0*) Ace Bks.
McDevitt, John B. & Settlage, Calvin F., eds. Separation-Individuation: Essays in Honor of Margaret S. Mahler. LC 78-143378. 520p. 1971. text ed. 67.50x (*0-8236-6065-6*) Intl Univs Pr.
McDevitt, Mary. Fascinating Foods. (Illus.). 157p. 1979. teacher ed 12.95 (*0-8134-2059-8*, 2059); teacher ed 5.00 (*0-8134-2061-X*, 2061); pap. text ed. 9.95 (*0-8134-2060-1*, 2060) Interstate.
McDevitt, Matthew. Joseph McKenna. LC 73-21874. (American Constitutional & Legal History Ser). 250p. 1974. reprint ed. lib. bdg. 32.50 (*0-306-70632-6*) Da Capo.
McDevitt, S. C., jt. ed. see Carey, W. B.
McDevitt, Sean C., jt. auth. see Carey, William B.
McDevitt, Sean C., jt. ed. see Carey, William B.
***McDevitt, Tom.** Health America. 615p. 1992. teacher ed, pap. 37.56 (*0-933046-06-5*) Little Red Hen.
— Health America, Chapter 26 Supplement. 1995. pap. 8.95 (*0-614-05285-8*) Little Red Hen.
— Mike O'Garry's Pocket: Selected Short Stories. 1986. pap. 2.00 (*0-933046-04-9*) Little Red Hen.
— No Slouch. LC 78-70914. 1979. 8.95 (*0-933046-00-6*) Little Red Hen.
— Smoking-Is It a Sin? 80p. (Orig.). 1981. pap. 1.00 (*0-933046-03-0*) Little Red Hen.
McDevitt, W. E. Functional Anatomy Masticatory System. 122p. 1989. pap. text ed. 39.95 (*0-7236-1523-3*, Pub. by John Wright UK) Buttrwrth-Heinemann.
McDiarmid, D. R. & Gattinger, R., eds. Instruments & Analysis Techniques for Space Physics: Proceedings of Workshop VI of the COSPAR 24th plenary meeting held in Ottawa, Canada, 16 May-2 June, 1982, Vol. 2/7. (Illus.). 200p. 1983. pap. 55.00 (*0-08-030431-1*, Pergamon Pr) Elsevier.
McDiarmid, G. Williamson. Getting It Together in Chevak: A Case Study of a Youth Organization in a Rural Alaskan Village. (Romance Ser.: No. 4). 53p. 1981. 3.00 (*0-685-52899-5*, Silhouette Lrg Print) Univ AK Ctr CCS.
— Kathy: A Case of Innovative Mathematics Teaching in a Multicultural Classroom. Kleinfeld, Judith, ed. (Teaching Cases in Cross-Cultural Education Ser.: No. 9). (Orig.). (C). 1992. pap. text ed. 7.50 (*1-877962-24-4*) Univ AK Ctr CCS.
McDiarmid, G. Williamson, et al. The Inventive Mind: Portraits of Rural Alaska Teachers. (Illus.). 179p. (C). 1988. pap. text ed. 10.00 (*1-877962-04-X*) Univ AK Ctr CCS.
McDiarmid, Lucy. Auden's Apologies for Poetry. 200p. 1990. text ed. 27.50 (*0-691-06784-8*) Princeton U Pr.
McDiarmid, Orville J. Unskilled Labor for Development: Its Economic Cost. LC 76-47398. 219p. reprint ed. pap. 62.50 (*0-7837-4276-2*, 2043968) Bks Demand.
McDiarmid, T. Making Money. (I Can Do Ser.). (Illus.). 48p. (J). (gr. 2-6). 1988. pap. 5.95 (*0-88625-152-4*) Durkin Hayes Pub.
McDicken, W. N. Diagnostic Ultrasonics: Principles & Use of Instruments. 3rd ed. (Illus.). 367p. 1991. text ed. 85.00 (*0-443-04132-6*) Churchill.
McDill, Edward L. & Rigsby, Leo C. Structure & Process in Secondary Schools: The Academic Impact of Educational Climates. LC 73-8123. 224p. reprint ed. pap. 63.90 (*0-317-41751-7*, 2025861) Bks Demand.
McDill, S. Rutherford. Shattered & Broken: Wife Abuse in the Christian Community; Guidelines for Hope & Healing. LC 90-46455. 1991. pap. 8.99 (*0-8007-5382-8*) Revell.
McDill, Wayne. The Twelve Essential Skills for Great Preaching. LC 93-38953. 1994. 17.99 (*0-8054-2012-6*) Broadman.
McDirmit, Evan & McDirmit, Marilynn. Milk, Meat & Strong Meat of the Bible: Deep Spiritual Nutrition. (Illus.). 416p. (Orig.). (C). 1995. pap. 19.95 (*0-9623953-2-3*) Eagle Pubn Co.
McDirmit, Marilynn. Devotional Diary: An Inspiring Journey Through the Psalms. (Illus.). 136p. (Orig.). 1986. pap. 5.00 (*0-9623953-0-7*) Eagle Pubn Co.
— Reincarnation - A Biblical Doctrine? Whose Time Has Come for the Evangelical Christian. 118p. (Orig.). (C). 1990. pap. 9.95 (*0-9623953-1-5*) Eagle Pubn Co.
McDirmit, Marilynn, jt. auth. see McDirmit, Evan.
McDivitt, James M. & Manners, Gerald. Minerals & Men: An Exploration of the World of Minerals & Metals, Including Some of the Major Problems That Are Posed. 2nd ed. LC 73-8138. xiii, 175p. 1974. pap. 15.95 (*0-8018-1827-3*) Resources Future.
McDivitt, Robert W. Atlas of Tumor Pathology: Tumors of the Breast, Fascicle 2. (Second Ser.). (Illus.). 158p. 1990. reprint ed. per., pap. 8.50 (*0-16-001829-3*, S/N 008-023-000) USGPO.
McDivitt, Robert W., jt. ed. see Hoogstraten, Barth.
***McDole, Carol.** In the Starlight. (Illus.). (Orig.). 1995. pap. 10.95 (*0-8062-5276-6*) Carlton.
***McDonagh, Barbara S.** Makana Aloha: Gift of Love. 24p. (J). (gr. k-8). 1994. 12.95 (*0-9643781-0-8*) Liko Pubng.
McDonagh, Bernard. Belgium & Luxembourg. 8th ed. (Blue Guides Ser.). (Illus.). 448p. 1993. pap. 24.95 (*0-393-30989-4*) Norton.
— Blue Guide to Turkey. 2nd rev. ed. (Blue Guide Ser.). (Illus.). 736p. 1995. pap. 27.50 (*0-393-31195-3*, Norton Paperbks) Norton.
McDonagh, Don. The Rise & Fall & Rise of Modern Dance. rev. ed. LC 90-37637. (Illus.). 240p. 1990. reprint ed. pap. 14.95 (*1-55652-089-1*) A cappella Bks.
McDonagh, Edward W. Chelation Can Cure: How to Reverse Heart Disease, Diabetes, Stroke, High Blood Pressure & Poor Circulation Without Drugs or Surgery. 225p. (Orig.). 1983. pap. 9.95 (*0-912815-00-0*) Platinum Pen Pubs.
McDonagh, Francis, tr. see Amin, Samir.
McDonagh, Francis, tr. see Casaldaliga, Pedro & Vigil, Jose M.
McDonagh, Francis, tr. see Mesters, Carlos.
McDonagh, Francis, tr. see Sobrino, Jon.
McDonagh, Francis, et al. Prophets Two. LC 71-173033. (Scripture Discussion Commentary Ser.: Vol. 4). 184p. 1972. pap. text ed. 4.95 (*0-87946-003-2*, 214) ACTA Pubns.
McDonagh, Jan, et al. Factor Thirteen. 280p. 1993. pap. text ed. 57.00 (*0-471-30786-6*) Wiley.
McDonagh, Josephine. De Quincey's Disciplines. LC 93-39460. 250p. 1994. 42.00 (*0-19-811285-8*, Clarendon Pr) OUP.
McDonagh, Kathryn J., ed. Patient-Centered Hospital Care: Reform from Within. LC 93-14569. 222p. 1993. text ed. 42.00 (*1-56793-002-6*, 0936) Health Admin Pr.
***McDonagh, Maitland.** Broken Mirrors - Broken Minds. (Illus.). 293p. (Orig.). Date not set. pap. 19.95 (*0-9517012-4-X*, Pub. by Sun Tavern Flds UK) AK Pr Dist.
— Broken Mirrors - Broken Minds: The Dark Dreams of Dario Angento. LC 93-45770. 1994. 18.95 (*0-8065-1514-7*, Citadel Pr) Carol Pub Group.
— Filmmaking on the Fringe: The Good, the Bad & the Deviant Directors. LC 94-20342. 1994. pap. 18.95 (*0-8065-1557-0*, Citadel Pr) Carol Pub Group.
McDonagh, P. F., ed. Microvascular Perfusion & Transport in Health & Disease. (Illus.). x, 254p. 1987. 193.00 (*3-8055-4394-8*) S Karger.
McDonagh, Sean. The Greening of the Church. LC 90-33049. 1990. pap. 16.95 (*0-88344-694-4*) Orbis Bks.
— Passion for the Earth: The Christian Vocation to Promote Justice, Peace, & the Integrity of Creation. (Ecology & Justice Ser.). 173p. (Orig.). 1995. pap. 13.95 (*1-57075-021-1*) Orbis Bks.
***McDonal.** How to Meditate. 1994. pap. 8.95 (*0-8356-1903-6*, Quest) Theos Pub Hse.
McDonald. German Proverbs. 1988. pap. 8.95 (*0-941016-41-2*) Penfield.
— The Hummingbird Tree. 2nd ed. (Caribbean Writers Ser.). 182p. (C). 1992. pap. 9.95 (*0-435-98934-0*) Heinemann.
— Linear Algebra over Commutative Rings. (Pure & Applied Mathematics Ser.: Vol. 87). 568p. 1984. 145.00 (*0-8247-7122-2*) Dekker.
— Modern Chess Miniatures. 1995. pap. 17.95 (*1-85744-166-4*, Scribners) S&S Trade.
— Reciprocity Among Private Multiemployer Pension Plans. (C). 1975. 12.95 (*0-256-01736-0*) Irwin.
— Retail Marketing Plans. 1993. 39.95 (*0-7506-0154-X*) Buttrwrth-Heinemann.
— Winning with the Kalashnikov. (Batsford Chess Library). 1995. pap. 20.00 (*0-8050-3907-4*) H Holt & Co.
McDonald, ed. The Radio Broadcaster's Big Book, Set, Vols. I, II, III, IV. (The Broadcaster's Big Book Ser.). (Illus.). 140p. (C). 1990. student ed 349.00 (*0-938023-07-1*) Wind River Inst Pr.
Mcdonald & Avery. Dentistry for the Child & Adolescent. 5th ed. 960p. 1987. 54.95 (*0-8016-3272-2*) Mosby Yr Bk.
McDonald, jt. auth. see Turner.
***McDonald, et al.** Animal Nutrition. 5th ed. Date not set. pap. text ed. 49.95 (*0-470-23488-1*) Wiley.
McDonald, A. G., ed. Selective Studies in Health & Social Services. (OMEGA Special Issue Ser.: Vol. 9, No. 5). 104p. 1981. pap. 35.00 (*0-08-023620-0*, Pergamon Pr) Elsevier.
McDonald, Adrian & Kay, David. Water Resources: Issues & Strategies. 1989. pap. text ed. 53.95 (*0-470-21150-4*) Wiley.
McDonald, Agnes, ed. Journey Proud: Southern Women's Personal Writings. 156p. 1994. pap. 10.95 (*0-932112-36-6*) Carolina Wren.
McDonald, Alan T., jt. auth. see Fox, Robert W.
McDonald, Alice, ed. & pref. To Touch the Future: The Educators' Book of Quotations. LC 86-82570. 179p. (Orig.). 1986. pap. 8.95 (*0-935680-31-4*) Kentucke Imprints.
McDonald, Alvis E. A Multiplicity-Independent, Global Iteration for Meromorphic Functions. LC 73-130610. 116p. 1969. 19.00 (*0-403-04516-9*) Scholarly.
McDonald, Ann L. Communicating with Legal Databases: Terms & Abbreviations for the Legal Researcher. 206p. 1987. pap. 75.00 (*0-918212-95-2*) Neal-Schuman.
McDonald, Anthony C. Robot Technology: Theory, Design & Applications. (Illus.). 384p. 1986. text ed. 32.95 (*0-685-12427-4*, Reston) P-H.
— Robotics Design & Maintenance. (C). 1986. teacher ed write for info. (*0-8359-6689-5*, Reston) P-H.
McDonald, Anthony C. & Lowe, Harold. Feedback & Control Systems. 1981. text ed. 51.00 (*0-8359-1898-X*, Reston); write for info. (*0-8359-1899-8*, Reston) P-H.
***McDonald, Archie.** The Japanese Experience in Butte County, California. 176p. 1993. 12.50 (*0-614-05680-2*) Assn NC Records.
McDonald, Archie, jt. auth. see McGlone, John.
McDonald, Archie, ed. see McGlone, John.
McDonald, Archie P. Helpful Cooking Hints for HouseHusbands of Uppity Women. 256p. 1988. 12.95 (*0-935014-11-X*) E-Heart Pr.
— The Old Stone Fort. 1981. pap. 2.95 (*0-87611-057-X*) Tex St Hist Assn.
— Republic of Texas. (Texas History Ser.). (Illus.). 40p. (C). 1981. pap. text ed. 3.95 (*0-89641-073-0*) American Pr.
— Texas: All Hail the Mighty State. 288p. 1983. pap. 12.95 (*0-89015-389-2*) Sunbelt Media.
— Texas? What Do You Know about the Lone Star State? LC 93-14665. (Illus.). 190p. (C). 1993. pap. 12.95 (*0-87565-120-8*) Tex Christian.
— The Trail to San Jacinto. (Texas History Ser.). (Illus.). 45p. 1982. pap. text ed. 3.95x (*0-89641-074-9*) American Pr.
— William Barrett Travis: A Biography. Eakin, Edwin M., ed. (Illus.). 216p. 1989. 15.95 (*0-89015-656-5*, Eakin Pr) Sunbelt Media.
McDonald, Archie P., comp. The Texas Experience. LC 85-40755. (Texas Committee for the Humanities Ser.). (Illus.). 192p. 1986. 19.95 (*0-89096-281-2*) Tex A&M Univ Pr.
McDonald, Archie P., ed. Hurrah for Texas: The Diary of Adolphus Sterne, 1838-1851. 222p. 1986. 15.95 (*0-89015-558-5*) Sunbelt Media.
— Shooting Stars: Heroes & Heroines of Western Film. LC 85-45988. (Illus.). 287p. reprint ed. pap. 81.80 (*0-8357-3957-0*, 2057053) Bks Demand.
McDonald, Archie P. & Spiller, Ronald L. Notable East Texans. 216p. 1986. 19.95 (*0-89015-564-X*) Sunbelt Media.
McDonald, Archie P., ed. see Hotchkiss, Jedediah.
McDonald, Archie P., jt. ed. see Procter, Ben.
McDonald, Arlys L. & Hixon, Donald L. Ned Rorem: A Bio-Bibliography. LC 89-2139. (Bio-Bibliographies in Music Ser.: No. 23). 294p. 1989. text ed. 49.95 (*0-313-25565-2*, MNR/, Greenwood Pr) Greenwood.
McDonald, Arthur W., jt. ed. see Fitzsimmons, Linda.
McDonald, B., jt. ed. see Przbylski, R.
McDonald, Barbara A. The Intergenerational Transfer of Cognitive Skills, Vol. 1: Programs, Policies & Research Issues. Sticht, Thomas G. et al, eds. (Cognition & Literacy Ser.). 224p. 1992. text ed. 45.00 (*0-89391-736-2*) Ablex Pub.
McDonald, Barbara A., jt. auth. see Sticht, Thomas G.
McDonald, Barrie C., jt. ed. see Jopling, Alan V.
McDonald, Ben. The Vietnam Book List. 2nd ed. LC 89-81201. 180p. 1990. ring bd. 29.95 (*0-685-37770-9*) Biblio Unlimited.
McDonald, Ben, comp. The Vietnam Book List. 164p. 1990. 34.95 (*0-685-35161-0*); ring bd. 19.95 (*0-9626437-0-X*) Biblio Unlimited.
McDonald, Ben, ed. see DeBraak, LaRonna.
McDonald, Ben, ed. see Hubalek, Linda K.
McDonald, Ben, ed. see Johnson, George G., Jr.
McDonald, Benjamin R. The Vietnam Book List. 3rd ed. 1991. pap. 23.95 (*0-9626437-3-4*) Biblio Unlimited.
McDonald, Bernard. Geometric Algebra & Local Rings. (Pure & Applied Mathematics Ser.: Vol. 36). 440p. 1976. 140.00 (*0-8247-6528-1*) Dekker.
McDonald, Bernard, ed. Ring Theory & Algebra III. (Lecture Notes in Pure & Applied Mathematics Ser.: Vol. 55). (Illus.). 448p. 1980. 140.00 (*0-8247-1158-0*) Dekker.
McDonald, Bernard R. Finite Rings with Identity. (Pure & Applied Mathematics Ser.: Vol. 28). 448p. 1974. 140.00 (*0-8247-6161-8*) Dekker.
— R-Linear Endomorphisms of R(n) Preserving Invariants. LC 83-15648. (Memoirs Ser.: No. 46/287). 67p. 1983. pap. 17.00 (*0-8218-2287-X*, MEMO 46/287) Am Math.
McDonald, Bernard R., ed. see Ring Theory Conference Staff.
McDonald, Bettye, jt. auth. see McClelland, Donna.
McDonald, Bill. The Nunda Irish: A Story of Irish Immigrants: the Joys & Sorrows of Their Life in America & Dakota. (Illus.). 275p. (Orig.). 1991. pap. 10.00 (*0-9629033-0-2*) Farmstead MN.
McDonald, Boyd. Cruising the Movies. 175p. (Orig.). 1985. pap. 10.95 (*0-685-65204-1*) Gay Pr NY.
— Filth. 198p. (Orig.). 1985. pap. 12.00 (*0-914017-09-8*) Gay Pr NY.
***McDonald, Boyd, ed.** Cream: True Homosexual Experiences, Vol. 7. 2nd ed. (STH Ser.). (Illus.). 176p. 1994. pap. 14.95 (*0-943595-55-X*) Leyland Pubns.
— Cum: True Homosexual Experiences from S. T. H. Writers, Vol. 4. (Illus.). 192p. (Orig.). 1983. pap. 12.00 (*0-917342-30-5*) Gay Sunshine.
— Juice: True Homosexual Experiences from STH Writers, Vol. 5. (Illus.). 208p. (Orig.). 1984. pap. 12.00 (*0-917342-36-4*) Gay Sunshine.
— Meat: True Homosexual Experiences from S. T. H., Vol. 1. (STH Ser.). (Illus.). 192p. 1994. reprint ed. pap. 14.95 (*0-917342-78-X*) Gay Sunshine.
— Wads: True Homosexual Experiences from STH Writers, Vol. 6. (Illus.). 192p. (Orig.). 1985. pap. 12.00 (*0-917342-11-9*) Leyland Pubns.
McDonald, Bridget, tr. see Nancy, Jean-Luc.
***McDonald, C. J.** Enzymes in Molecular Biology: Essential Data. (Bios Essential Data Series). pap. text ed. 19.95 (*0-471-94842-X*) Wiley.
McDonald, C. J., ed. Buying Equipment & Programs for Home or Office. (M.D. Computing: Benchmark Papers). (Illus.). 205p. 1987. 54.00 (*0-387-96455-X*) Spr-Verlag.
— Tutorials. (M.D. Computing: Benchmark Papers). 1987. 49.00 (*0-387-96505-X*) Spr-Verlag.
McDonald, Camille. R-r-rhubarb: From Soup to Nuts. 34p. (Orig.). 1988. pap. 3.35 (*0-9625416-0-5*) Cynthia Promos.
McDonald, Caroline, ed. see Steele, Sandy.
McDonald, Charles W. Diesel Locomotive Rosters: United States, Canada & Mexico. 3rd ed. Drury, George, ed. (Illus.). 240p. (Orig.). 1992. pap. 16.95 (*0-89024-112-0*) Kalmbach.
McDonald, Cherokee P. Blue Truth. 1992. mass mkt. 4.99 (*0-312-92773-8*) St Martin.
— Blue Truth: Walking the Thin Blue Line - One Cop's Story of Life in the Streets. 1991. 18.95 (*1-55611-246-7*) D I Fine.
— Summer's Reason. LC 94-71110. 240p. 1994. 19.95 (*1-55611-409-5*) D I Fine.
— Under Contract: The True Account of a Cop Hired to Kill. 1992. 21.00 (*1-55611-322-6*) D I Fine.
McDonald, Cherokee P. & Smith, Allen E. Under Contract: The True Account of a Cop Hired to Kill. 288p. 1993. mass mkt. 4.50 (*1-55817-716-7*, Pinnacle NY) Windsor NY.
McDonald, Christie. The Proustian Fabric: Associations of Memory. LC 90-21940. xiv, 247p. 1991. 35.00 (*0-8032-3150-4*) U of Nebr Pr.
McDonald, Christie & Wihl, Gary, eds. Transformations in Personhood & Culture: The Languages of History, Aesthetics, & Ethics. LC 93-23859. (Literature & Philosophy Ser.). (Illus.). 224p. (C). 1994. 35.00 (*0-271-01010-X*); pap. 16.95 (*0-271-01011-8*) Pa St U Pr.
McDonald, Claudette M., jt. auth. see McDonald, Patrick J.
McDonald, Clement J. Action-Oriented Decisions in Ambulatory Medicine. LC 80-20451. (Illus.). 394p. reprint ed. pap. 112.30 (*0-8357-5086-8*, 2033003) Bks Demand.
McDonald, Cleveland. Creating a Successful Christian Marriage. LC 74-20202. 1975. 19.99 (*0-8010-5957-7*) Baker Bk.
McDonald, Cleveland & McDonald, Philip M. Creating a Successful Christian Marriage. 4th ed. LC 93-29180. 1994. 29.99 (*0-8010-6310-8*) Baker Bk.
***McDonald, Colin.** Advertising Reach & Frequency: Maximizing Advertising Results Through Effective Frequency. Date not set. 39.95 (*0-614-06754-5*) Assn Natl Advertisers.
McDonald, Collin. The Chilling Hour. (Trophy Chiller Bk.). 160p. (J). (gr. 3-7). 1994. pap. 3.95 (*0-06-440493-5*, Trophy) HarpC Child Bks.
— The Chilling Hour: Tales of the Real & Unreal. (Illus.). 128p. (J). (gr. 4 up). 1992. 14.99 (*0-525-65101-2*, Cobblehill Bks) Dutton Child Bks.
— Nightwaves: Scary Tales for after Dark. LC 90-35234. (J). (gr. 4-7). 1990. 13.00 (*0-525-65043-1*, Cobblehill Bks) Dutton Child Bks.
— Shadows & Whispers: Tales from the Other Side. LC 94-2143. 160p. (J). (gr. 4 up). 1994. 13.99 (*0-525-65184-5*, Cobblehill Bks) Dutton Child Bks.
McDonald, Cornelia P. A Woman's Civil War: A Diary with Reminiscences of the War, from March 1862. Gwin, Minrose C., ed. LC 91-32345. (Studies in American Autobiography). (Illus.). 314p. (Orig.). (C). 1992. lib. bdg. 49.50 (*0-299-13260-9*); pap. 14.95 (*0-299-13264-1*) U of Wis Pr.
McDonald, Corry. The Dilemma of Wilderness. LC 86-5839. 120p. (Orig.). 1987. pap. 10.95 (*0-86534-088-9*) Sunstone Pr.
— Wilderness: A New Mexico Legacy. LC 84-26691. (Illus.). 128p. (Orig.). 1985. pap. 15.95 (*0-86534-056-0*) Sunstone Pr.
McDonald, Craig, ed. Johannes de Irlandia's Meroure of Wyssdome III. 250p. 1991. pap. text ed. 50.00 (*0-08-037001-2*, Pub. by Aberdeen U Pr) Macmillan.
McDonald, D. Perspective Primer for Architects & Designers. 1993. pap. write for info. (*0-442-01433-3*) Van Nos Reinhold.

M

McDonald, D. D. & Bolc, Leonard, eds. Natural Language Generation Systems. (Symbolic Computation - Artificial Intelligence Ser.). (Illus.). 389p. 1988. 51.00 (*0-387-96691-9*) Spr-Verlag.

McDonald, D. G. & Hodgdon, J. A. Psychological Effects of Aerobic Fitness Training: Research & Theory. xi, 224p. 1991. pap. 39.00 (*0-387-97603-5*) Spr-Verlag.

***McDonald, Daniel & Burton, Larry.** The Language of Argument. 8th ed. LC 94-48481. (C). 1995. write for info. (*0-673-99507-0*) HarpCollege.

McDonald, Daniel L. The Language of Argument. 6th ed. 320p. (C). 1990. pap. text ed. 17.25 (*0-06-044352-9*) HarpCollege.

— The Language of Argument. 7th ed. LC 92-23334. (C). 1992. teacher ed 10.00 (*0-06-500584-8*); pap. 26.00 (*0-06-500583-X*) HarpCollege.

McDonald, Daniel L., ed. see Addison, Joseph & Steele, Richard.

***McDonald, Daniel W.** Negotiating the Great American Dream. 470p. 1995. pap. 12.95 (*1-56901-773-5*) NW Pub.

McDonald, David M. United Government & Foreign Policy in Russia, 1900-1914. 276p. (C). 1992. 45.00 (*0-674-92239-5*) HUP.

McDonald, David R. Masters' Theses in Anthropology: A Bibliography of Theses from United States Colleges & Universities. LC 77-7867. (Bibliographies Ser.). 460p. 1977. 25.00 (*0-87536-217-6*) HRAFP.

McDonald, David R., jt. auth. see Mail, Patricia D.

McDonald, Deirdre, ed. see Hyatt, James.

McDonald, Deirdre, ed. see National Association of College & University Business Officers Staff.

McDonald, Don. Icebreaker. LC 85-90322. (Illus.). 52p. (Orig.). 1985. pap. 6.00 (*0-933829-01-9*) Ponce Pr.

McDonald, Donald F., Jr., ed. Advanced Skills & Knowledge of Cost Engineering, Vol. 1. 102p. 1989. pap. 32.50 (*0-930284-39-9*) AACE Intl.

— Skills & Knowledge of Cost Engineering. 3rd rev. ed. 164p. 1992. pap. 32.50 (*0-930284-50-X*) AACE Intl.

McDonald, Donogh, jt. ed. see Lipchitz, Leslie.

McDonald, Dorothy C. & Simons, Gene M. Musical Growth & Development: Birth Through Six. 304p. 1988. text ed. 30.00 (*0-02-873070-4*) Schirmer Bks.

— Musical Growth & Development: Birth Through Six. 304p. 1989. audio 10.00 (*0-02-871347-8*) Schirmer Bks.

McDonald, Dorothy T. Music in Our Lives: The Early Years. LC 79-51509. 68p. 1979. pap. text ed. 4.00 (*0-912674-65-2*, NAEYC #107) Natl Assn Child Ed.

McDonald, Doug, jt. ed. see Brislin, Joann.

McDonald, Douglas. The Camels in Nevada. (Illus.). 32p. 1983. pap. 3.95 (*0-913814-56-3*) Nevada Pubns.

— A Catalogue of Nevada Checks, 1860-1933. (Illus.). 128p. 1993. 19.50 (*1-879767-02-3*) Castenholz Sons.

— Julia Bulette & the Red Light Ladies of Nevada. (Illus.). 32p. 1980. 3.95 (*0-913814-55-5*) Nevada Pubns.

— Nevada Lost Mines & Buried Treasure. (Illus.). 128p. 1981. 6.95 (*0-913814-37-7*) Nevada Pubns.

— Virginia City & the Silver Region of the Comstock Lode. (Illus.). 1982. 24.95 (*0-913814-50-4*); pap. 12.95 (*0-913814-47-4*) Nevada Pubns.

McDonald, Douglas & Goldtown. Bodie Boomtown of California. (Illus.). 48p. 1988. pap. 4.95 (*0-913814-88-1*) Nevada Pubns.

McDonald, Douglas & McDonald, Gina. History of the Weaverville Joss House & the Chinese of Trinity County, California. (Illus.). 32p. 1986. pap. 2.95 (*0-932151-02-7*) Gypsyfoot Ent.

McDonald, Douglas C. Punishment Without Walls: Community Service Sentences in New York City. 278p. 1989. pap. text ed. 15.00 (*0-8135-1469-X*) Rutgers U Pr.

— Punishment Without Walls: Community Service Sentences in New York City. LC 85-26185. (Crime, Law, & Deviance Ser.). 297p. reprint ed. pap. 84.70 (*0-7837-5676-3*, 2059103) Bks Demand.

McDonald, Douglas C., ed. Private Prisons & the Public Interest. LC 90-30616. (Crime, Law & Deviance Ser.). 235p. (C). 1990. text ed. 40.00 (*0-8135-1574-2*) Rutgers U Pr.

***McDonald, Douglas C. & Carlson, Kenneth E.** Sentencing in the Federal Courts: Does Race Matter? The Transition to Sentencing Guidelines, 1986-90. (Illus.). 229p. (Orig.). (C). 1994. pap. text ed. 50.00x (*0-7881-1472-7*) Diane Pub.

McDonald, Dugan. Who Is Jesus? 163p. (Orig.). 1989. pap. 6.95 (*0-685-27181-1*) Bible Key Pubns.

McDonald, Duncan, jt. auth. see Kessler, Lauren.

McDonald, E. L. Stories for Speakers & Writers. LC 72-126559. (Speakers & Toastmasters Library). 112p. 1991. reprint ed. pap. 6.99 (*0-8010-5853-8*) Baker Bk.

McDonald, Eileen M., jt. auth. see Adger, Hoover, Jr.

***McDonald, Elizabeth.** Am I the Only One Who's Crazy? 208p. (Orig.). 1995. pap. text ed. 6.50 (*1-879331-53-5*, Classc Pub) Marciel Pub & Print.

— Wildflowers of the Wallum. 71p. (C). 1990. 33.00 (*0-908175-16-7*, Pub. by Boolarong Pubns AT) St Mut.

McDonald, Ellen S., jt. auth. see McDonald, Forrest.

***McDonald, Elvin.** The Color Garden (White) Single Color Plantings for Dramatic Landscapes. 1995. 15.00 (*0-00-225090-X*) Collins SF.

— Easy Gardens. LC 77-89551. (Illus.). 144p. 1981. 9.95 (*0-318-33062-8*) Dorison Hse.

— The Four Hundred Best: An Encyclopedia for the Beginning Gardener. LC 94-35385. 1995. 40.00 (*0-679-43943-9*) Random.

— The New Houseplant: Bringing the Garden Indoors. LC 92-22292. 270p. 1993. text ed. 40.00 (*0-02-583126-7*) Macmillan.

— Northeast Gardening: The Diverse Art & Special Considerations of Gardening in the Northeast. 160p. 1990. text ed. 35.00 (*0-02-583125-9*) Macmillan.

— Successful Rose Gardening. (Better Homes & Gardens Bks.). (Illus.). 224p. 1993. 29.95 (*0-696-00059-8*) Meredith Bks.

***McDonald, Elvin, photos & text.** The Color Garden (Blue) Single Color Plantings for Dramatic Landscapes. LC 94-37702. (Illus.). 1995. 15.00 (*0-00-225085-3*) Collins SF.

— The Color Garden (Red) Single Color Plantings for Dramatic Landscapes. LC 94-37918. 1995. 15.00 (*0-00-225075-6*) Collins SF.

— The Color Garden (Yellow) Single Color Plantings for Dramatic Landscapes. LC 94-378910. (Illus.). 1995. 15. 00 (*0-00-225080-2*) Collins SF.

McDonald, Elvin, jt. ed. see Hobhouse, Penelope.

McDonald, Eugene T., ed. Treating Cerebral Palsy: For Clinicians by Clinicians. LC 86-22568. (For Clinicians by Clinicians Ser.). (Illus.). 312p. 1987. pap. text ed. 29. 00 (*0-89079-141-4*, 1412) PRO-ED.

McDonald, Eugene T. & Chance, B., Jr. Cerebral Palsy. 1964. pap. text ed. 25.67 (*0-13-122812-9*) P-H.

McDonald, Eugene T. & Gallagher, Diane L., eds. Facilitating Social-Emotional Development in Multiply Handicapped Children. 285p. (Orig.). (C). 1985. pap. text ed. write for info. (*0-9613558-0-8*) Home Merciful SFCC.

McDonald, Eva. The Lady from Yorktown. large type ed. 1977. 12.00 (*0-7089-0002-X*) Ulverscroft.

***McDonald, Ewen & Engsberg, Juliana.** Binocular: In Stillness & Motion. (Illus.). 112p. Date not set. pap. 14. 95 (*0-646-22593-6*) Dist Art Pubs.

McDonald, Forrest. Alexander Hamilton: A Biography. (Illus.). 480p. 1982. pap. 14.95 (*0-393-30048-X*) Norton.

— The American Presidency: An Intellectual History. LC 93-30235. 624p. (Orig.). (C). 1995. 29.95 (*0-7006-0652-1*) U Pr of KS.

— The American Presidency: An Intellectual History. LC 93-30235. (Orig.). (C). 1995. pap. 17.95 (*0-7006-0749-8*) U Pr of KS.

— E Pluribus Unum. LC 79-4130. 1979. reprint ed. 12.00 (*0-913966-58-4*); reprint ed. pap. 5.00 (*0-913966-59-2*) Liberty Fund.

— Liberty's Five Flags. Cahill, George F., ed. (Flag Plaza Standard Ser.: Special Edition: Vol. 4). (Illus.). 12p. (Orig.). 1988. pap. 2.50 (*0-934021-06-6*) Natl Flag Foun.

— Novus Ordo Seclorum: The Intellectual Origins of the Constitution. LC 85-13544. xiv, 362p. 1985. 29.95 (*0-7006-0284-4*); pap. 9.95 (*0-7006-0311-5*) U Pr of KS.

— The Presidency of George Washington. LC 73-11344. (American Presidency Ser.). xiv, 210p. 1974. 25.00 (*0-7006-0110-4*); pap. 9.95 (*0-7006-0359-X*) U Pr of KS.

— The Presidency of Thomas Jefferson. LC 76-803. (American Presidency Ser.). xii, 204p. 1976. 25.00 (*0-7006-0147-3*); pap. 9.95 (*0-7006-0330-1*) U Pr of KS.

— We the People: The Economic Origins of the Constitution. 455p. (C). 1992. pap. text ed. 21.95 (*1-56000-574-2*) Transaction Pubs.

McDonald, Forrest & McDonald, Ellen S. Requiem: Variations on Eighteenth-Century Themes. LC 88-14033. xii, 220p. 1988. 25.00 (*0-7006-0370-0*) U Pr of KS.

McDonald, Frances B. Censorship & Intellectual Freedom: A Survey of School Librarians' Attitudes & Moral Reasoning. LC 93-29500. 237p. 1993. 29.50 (*0-8108-2680-1*) Scarecrow.

McDonald, Frank. Provenance. large type ed. 656p. 1983. 23.95 (*0-7089-8158-5*, Charnwood) Ulverscroft.

McDonald, Frank & Dearden, Stephen. European Economic Integration. 2nd ed. 320p. (C). 1995. pap. text ed. 25.95 (*0-582-25141-9*, 76763, Pub. by Longman UK) Longman.

***McDonald, Fred & Marshall, Jeremy, eds.** Questions of English. (Illus.). 224p. 1995. 16.95 (*0-19-869230-7*) OUP.

McDonald, G. J., jt. auth. see White, J. J.

McDonald, Gail. Learning to Be Modern: Pound, Eliot, & the American University. 256p. 1993. 49.95 (*0-19-811980-1*) OUP.

McDonald, Garland. If Your Broker's So Smart, Why Aren't You Rich. 128p. (C). 1990. per. 16.95 (*0-8403-5903-9*) Kendall-Hunt.

***McDonald, George.** The Curate's Awakening & The Ladies Confession, 2 vols. in 1. Phillips, Michael R., ed. 480p. 1992. 9.95 (*1-56865-062-0*, GuildAmerica) Dblday Bk Music.

McDonald, George, jt. ed. see Peterson, Steve.

McDonald, George, jt. auth. see Wood, Katie.

McDonald, George A., et al. Atlas of Haematology. 5th ed. (Illus.). 296p. 1989. text ed. 110.00 (*0-443-02560-6*) Churchill.

McDonald, Gerald. Training & Careers for the Professional Musician. 112p. 1979. 21.00 (*0-905418-03-4*, Pub. by Gresham Bks UK) St Mut.

McDonald, Gerald D., et al. A Checklist of American Newspaper Carriers' Addresses, 1720-1820. (Illus.). 248p. 1990. 30.00 (*0-944026-16-8*) Am Antiquarian.

— The Complete Films of Charlie Chaplin. rev. ed. (Illus.). 224p. 1988. reprint ed. pap. 15.95 (*0-8065-1095-1*, Citadel Pr) Carol Pub Group.

McDonald, Giles N., jt. ed. see Jordan, Darryl F.

McDonald, Gina, jt. auth. see McDonald, Douglas.

McDonald, Glen & Kirkwood, John. How Come I'm Dead? (Illus.). 288p. (Orig.). 1985. pap. 12.95 (*0-88839-187-0*) Hancock House.

McDonald, Gordon. El Padre Eficaz: The Effective Father. (SPA.). 5.50 (*84-7228-695-9*, 220656, Pub. by Edit Clie SP) TSELF.

McDonald, Grace. History of the Irish in Wisconsin in the Nineteenth Century. LC 76-6355. (Irish Americans Ser.). (Illus.). 1976. reprint ed. 29.95 (*0-405-09348-9*) Ayer.

Mcdonald, Gregory. The Brave. LC 91-19312. 1991. 15.95 (*0-942637-34-8*) Barricade Bks.

McDonald, Gregory. Carioca Fletch. LC 85-16378. 288p. (Orig.). 1988. mass mkt. 4.99 (*0-446-34899-6*) Warner Bks.

— Confess, Fletch. 272p. 1976. mass mkt. 4.99 (*0-380-00814-9*) Avon.

— The Education of Gregory McDonald. 256p. (Orig.). 1985. mass mkt. 7.95 (*0-446-38214-0*) Warner Bks.

— Fletch. 256p. 1976. mass mkt. 4.99 (*0-380-00645-6*) Avon.

— Fletch & the Man Who. 288p. (Orig.). 1988. mass mkt. 4.99 (*0-446-35560-7*) Warner Bks.

— Fletch & the Widow Bradley. 1989. mass mkt. 4.99 (*0-446-35997-1*) Warner Bks.

Mcdonald, Gregory. Fletch Reflected. LC 94-16640. 1994. write for info. (*0-399-13983-4*, Putnam) Putnam Pub Group.

— Fletch Reflected. 288p. Date not set. pap. text ed. 5.99 (*0-515-11676-9*) Jove Pubns.

McDonald, Gregory. Fletch, Too. LC 85-41001. 1987. mass mkt. 4.99 (*0-446-34614-4*) Warner Bks.

— Fletch, Too. large type ed. LC 86-23181. (Basic Ser.). 327p. 1993. reprint ed. lib. bdg. 21.95 (*0-89621-769-8*) Thorndike Pr.

— Fletch Won. 272p. 1986. mass mkt. 4.99 (*0-446-34095-2*) Warner Bks.

— Fletch Won. large type ed. LC 85-24497. 383p. 1993. reprint ed. lib. bdg. 21.95 (*0-89621-677-2*) Thorndike Pr.

— Fletch's Fortune. 1988. mass mkt. 4.99 (*0-380-37978-3*) Avon.

— Fletch's Moxie. 288p. 1989. mass mkt. 4.99 (*0-446-35976-9*) Warner Bks.

— Flynn. 1977p. 1977. pap. 3.95 (*0-380-01764-4*) Avon.

— Running Scared. 1964. 12.95 (*0-8392-1095-7*) Astor-Honor.

***Mcdonald, Gregory.** Skylar. 1995. write for info. (*0-688-14163-3*) Morrow.

— Son of Fletch. LC 93-684. 240p. 1993. 19.95 (*0-399-13831-5*, Putnam) Putnam Pub Group.

— Son of Fletch. 272p. (Orig.). 1994. pap. text ed. 5.99 (*0-515-11470-7*) Jove Pubns.

— Son of Fletch. large type ed. LC 93-33295. 1993. 21.95 (*0-7862-0079-0*) Thorndike Pr.

McDonald, Gregory, ed. Last Laughs: The Mystery Writers of America Anthology, 1986. (Illus.). 208p. 1986. 16.95 (*0-89296-246-1*) Mysterious Pr.

McDonald, H. D. The New Testament Concept of the Atonement: The Gospel of the Calvary Event. LC 93-16802. 144p. (Orig.). 1994. pap. 9.99 (*0-8010-6309-4*) Baker Bk.

McDonald, Helen B. & Steinhorn, Audrey I. Understanding Homosexuality: A Guide for Those Who Know, Love, or Counsel Gay & Lesbian Individuals. Orig. Title: Homosexuality. 186p. 1993. reprint ed. pap. 11.95 (*0-8245-1215-4*) Crossroad NY.

McDonald, Helen B., jt. auth. see Steinhorn, Audrey I.

***McDonald, Helen P.** The Park Bench. (Illus.). 40p. (Orig.). (J). 1994. pap. write for info. (*1-56167-169-X*) Am Literary Pr.

McDonald, Henry. Normative Basis of Culture: A Philosophical Inquiry. LC 85-23795. xii, 241p. 1986. text ed. 35.00 (*0-8071-1280-1*) La State U Pr.

McDonald, Hope. Descubramos Como Orar. Coleman, F. G., tr. 128p. (SPA.). 1987. reprint ed. pap. 3.95 (*0-311-40040-X*) Casa Bautista.

McDonald, Hugh C. Appointment in Dallas: The Final Solution to the Assassination of JFK. (Illus.). 210p. (Orig.). 1992. mass mkt. 3.99 (*0-8217-3893-3*) Zebra.

McDonald, Hugh J. & Lappe, Robert J. Ionography: Electrophoresis in Stabilized Media. 278p. reprint ed. pap. 79.30 (*0-317-08649-9*, 2011928) Bks Demand.

McDonald, I. A., ed. see Kruger, F. J. & Ferrar, A. A.

McDonald, Ian. The Boer War in Postcards. (Illus.). 192p. 1991. 30.00 (*0-86299-737-2*) A Sutton Pub.

— The Broken Land. 1992. 22.50 (*0-553-08983-8*, Spectra); pap. 11.00 (*0-553-37054-5*, Spectra) Bantam.

— Broken Land. 1993. mass mkt. 5.99 (*0-553-56324-6*, Spectra) Bantam.

— Essequibo. (C). 1992. pap. 10.95 (*0-934257-90-6*) Story Line.

— King of Morning, Queen of Day. 1991. mass mkt. 4.99 (*0-553-29049-5*) Bantam.

— Scissors Cut Paper. 1994. mass mkt. 3.99 (*0-553-56116-2*, Spectra) Bantam.

— Terminal Care. LC 94-21958. 277p. 1994. pap. 12.95 (*0-553-37416-8*) Bantam.

McDonald, Ian & Brown, Stewart, eds. The Heinemann Book of Caribbean Poetry. (Caribbean Writers Ser.). 236p. 1992. pap. 9.95 (*0-435-98817-4*, 98817) Heinemann.

McDonald, Ian & Lyttleton, David. Kling Klang Klatch. (VG Graphics Ser.). (Illus.). 80p. (Orig.). 1992. pap. 11. 95 (*1-878574-41-8*) Dark Horse Comics.

McDonald, Ian M. Inflation & Unemployment: Macroeconomics with a Range of Equilibria. (Illus.). 208p. 1990. text ed. 44.95 (*0-631-17301-3*) Blackwell Pubs.

McDonald, Ian R., jt. auth. see Hansen, J. P.

McDonald, Ian R., jt. auth. see Hansen, Jean P.

***McDonald, Irene.** For the Least of My Brethren: A Centenary History of St. Michael's Hospital. (Illus.). 350p. Date not set. 29.99 (*0-614-06790-1*); pap. 22.99 (*0-614-06791-X*) Dun.

McDonald, Irene M., ed. see Whitty, Mike.

McDonald, Irene M., jt. auth. see Whitty, Mike.

McDonald, J. The Magic Story. 1984. pap. 3.95 (*0-912576-09-X*) R Collier.

McDonald, J. C., ed. Fundamentals of Digital Switching. 2nd ed. LC 89-72201. (Illus.). 508p. 1990. 69.50 (*0-306-43347-8*, Plenum Insight) Plenum.

McDonald, J. I. Biblical Interpretation & Christian Ethics. LC 93-16555. (New Studies in Christian Ethics: No. 2). 260p. (C). 1994. 59.95 (*0-521-43059-3*) Cambridge U Pr.

McDonald, J. I. & Shaw, W. A. Gospel of Matthew. (C). 1988. 45.00 (*0-7157-2154-2*) St Mut.

McDonald, J. I., jt. auth. see Chilton, Bruce.

McDonald, J. K., ed. see Barrett, Alan J.

McDonald, J. Ken, jt. auth. see Barrett, Alan J.

McDonald, J. Michael, jt. ed. see Woodruff, Jean L.

***McDonald, J. R., et al.** The Professional Security Manager's Handbook: Personal, Vehicle & Premises Security. (Illus.). 100p. 1995. student ed 79.00 (*0-938023-13-6*) Wind River Inst Pr.

McDonald, Jack. Something to Cheer About: Legends from the Golden Age of Sports. 240p. (Orig.). 1986. pap. 6.95 (*0-15-683804-4*, Harvest Bks) HarBrace.

McDonald, Jack, jt. auth. see Holsopple, Curtis R.

McDonald, James, ed. see Hester, William.

McDonald, James, jt. auth. see Wang, Ixfan.

McDonald, James H., jt. ed. see Dubinskas, Franks A.

McDonald, James J., Jr. Mental & Emotional Injuries in Employment Litigation. Kulick, Francine B., ed. LC 94-15827. 500p. 1994. text ed. 125.00 (*0-87179-832-8*) BNA.

McDonald, James O. Management Without Tears. LC 81-68516. 160p. 1981. pap. 9.95 (*0-8442-3068-5*, Crain Bks) NTC Pub Grp.

McDonald, James P. John Demjanjuk. (Illus.). 200p. (Orig.). (C). 1990. pap. 8.95 (*0-915597-79-9*) Amana Bks.

McDonald, James R. The European Scene: A Geographic Appreciation. 400p. 1991. text ed. 58.00 (*0-13-290941-3*) P-H.

McDonald, Jason, jt. auth. see Becskehazi, Attila.

McDonald, Jean, jt. auth. see Clarke, Marianne.

McDonald, Jerry N. The North American Bison: Their Classification & Evolution. LC 79-65765. 1981. 55.00 (*0-520-04002-3*) U CA Pr.

— Old Bones & Serpent Stones: A Guide to Interpreted Fossil Localities in Canada & the United States, Vol. 1: Eastern Sites. (Guides to the American Landscape Ser.). (Illus.). 225p. (Orig.). 1995. pap. 14.95 (*0-939923-08-4*) M & W Pub Co.

McDonald, Jerry N. & Woodward, Susan L. Indian Mounds of the Atlantic Coast: A Guide to Sites from Maine to Florida. LC 87-90428. (Illus.). ix, 162p. (Orig.). 1987. pap. 12.95 (*0-939923-03-3*) M & W Pub Co.

McDonald, Jerry N., jt. auth. see Woodward, Susan L.

McDonald, Jesse. Michelangelo. (Illus.). 112p. 1995. 14.98 (*0-8317-5789-2*) Smithmark.

— Toulouse-Lautrec. 1994. 5.98 (*0-7858-0209-6*) Bk Sales Inc.

***McDonald, Jim, comp.** The Radio Broadcaster's Big Book Vol. II: FCC Rules & Dictionary. (The Broadcaster's Big Book Ser.). (Illus.). 1500p. (C). 1994. student ed 99.00 (*0-938023-10-1*) Wind River Inst Pr.

***McDonald, Jim, ed. & intro.** The Radio Broadcaster's Big Book - 1995 Revision Vol. I: Operations & FCC Compliance. (The Broadcaster's Big Book Ser.). (Illus.). 100p. (C). 1995. student ed 99.00 (*0-938023-14-4*) Wind River Inst Pr.

McDonald, Jim, jt. auth. see Wang, Xifan.

***McDonald, Jim, et al.** The Radio Broadcaster's Big Book Vol. III: Public File. (The Broadcaster's Big Book Ser.). 100p. (C). 1995. student ed 99.00 (*0-938023-15-2*) Wind River Inst Pr.

— The Radio Broadcaster's Big Book Vol. IV: Encyclopedia. (The Broadcaster's Big Book Ser.). (Illus.). (C). 1994. student ed 99.00 (*0-938023-11-X*) Wind River Inst Pr.

— The Translator Big Book: Licensee Manual & Site Book, Set. (Illus.). 200p. 1995. student ed 129.00 (*0-938023-18-7*) Wind River Inst Pr.

— The Translator Big Book: Licensee Manual, TV & FM Translators. (The Broadcaster's Big Book Project Ser.). (Illus.). 100p. Date not set. student ed 99.00 (*0-614-04925-3*) Wind River Inst Pr.

— The Translator Big Book No. 1: Site Book, TV & FM Translators. (The Broadcaster's Big Book Project Ser.). (Illus.). 100p. Date not set. student ed 39.00 (*0-938023-17-9*) Wind River Inst Pr.

McDonald, Joe. The Complete Guide to Wildlife Photography. (Illus.). 160p. 1992. pap. 24.95 (*0-8174-3718-5*, Amphoto) Watsn-Guptill.

— Designing Wildlife Photographs: Professional Field Techniques for Composing Great Pictures. LC 94-16283. 144p. 1994. pap. 24.95 (*0-8174-3781-9*) Watsn-Guptill.

McDonald, John. The Message of a Master: A Classic Tale of Wealth, Wisdom, & the Secret of Success. Dieter, Katherine & Allen, Marc, eds. LC 91-38486. 96p. 1993. reprint ed. pap. 8.95 (*0-931432-95-2*) New Wrld Lib.

— The Sacraments in the Christian Life. (C). 1988. 39.00 (*0-85439-226-2*, Pub. by St Paul Pubns UK) St Mut.

— Soft Touch. 1982. pap. 2.25 (*0-449-12353-7*) Fawcett.

McDonald, John A. Handbook of Three Dimension Seismic Data Acquisition. 200p. 1993. text ed. 40.00 (*0-13-381955-8*) P-H.

McDonald, John A. & Mecham, Robert P., eds. Receptors for Extracellular Matrix. (Biology of Extracellular Matrix Ser.). (Illus.). 330p. 1991. text ed. 83.00 (*0-12-483365-9*) Acad Pr.

McDonald, John A., et al, eds. Seismic Studies in Physical Modeling. LC 82-81374. (Illus.). 284p. 1983. text ed. 54. 00 (*0-934634-39-4*) Intl Human Res.

McDonald, John F. Employment Location & Industrial Land Use in Metropolitan Chicago. 224p. (Orig.). 1984. pap. text ed. 7.80 (*0-87563-242-4*) Stipes.

McDonald, John F., ed. Transposable Elements & Evolution. LC 93-17743. (Contemporary Issues in Genetics & Evolution Ser.: Vol. 1). 350p. (C). 1993. lib. bdg. 165.00 (*0-7923-2338-6*) Kluwer Ac.

McDonald, John F., jt. ed. see Mills, Edwin S.

An Asterisk (*) at the beginning of an entry indicates that the title is appearing in BIP for the first time.

McDonald, John S., jt. auth. see Bonica, John J.

McDonald, John W., Jr. The North-South Dialogue & the United Nations. LC 82-1039. 24p. (Orig.). 1982. pap. 4.00 (*0-934742-16-2*) Geo U Inst Dplmcy.

— The North-South Dialogue & the United Nations. 26p. (Orig.). (C). 1985. reprint ed. pap. text ed. 11.50 (*0-8191-5058-4*, Inst Study Diplomacy) U Pr of Amer.

McDonald, John W., Jr. & Bendahmane, Diane B., eds. United States-Soviet Summitry: Roosevelt Through Carter. LC 87-619871. (Study of Foreign Affairs Ser.). 170p. (Orig.). 1987. pap. 9.00 (*0-16-004473-1*, S/N 044-000-02206-1) USGPO.

McDonald, John W., jt. ed. see Bendamane, Diane.

McDonald, Joseph. The Wildlife Photographer's Field Manual. (Illus.). 192p. 1991. pap. 14.95 (*0-936262-07-9*) Amherst Media.

McDonald, Joseph & Micikas, Basney. Academic Libraries: The Dimensions of Their Effectiveness. LC 93-14464. (New Directions in Information Management Ser.). 208p. 1994. text ed. 49.95 (*0-313-27269-7*, Greenwood Pr) Greenwood.

McDonald, Joseph P. Teaching: Making Sense of an Uncertain Craft. (Professional Development & Practice Ser.). 160p. (C). 1992. text ed. 38.00 (*0-8077-3168-4*); pap. text ed. 15.95 (*0-8077-3167-6*) Tchrs Coll.

McDonald, Joseph P., et al. Graduation by Exhibition: Assessing Genuine Achievement. LC 92-46613. 1993. 11.95 (*0-87120-204-2*) Assn Supervision.

McDonald, Julie. Amalie's Story. rev. ed. LC 71-128605. 256p. 1985. 7.95 (*0-930942-08-6*) Sutherland MA.

— The Ballad of Bishop Hill. LC 85-90372. 1986. 7.95 (*0-930942-02-7*) Sutherland MA.

— The Heather & the Rose. LC 86-90362. 1987. 7.95 (*0-930942-07-8*) Sutherland MA.

— Nils Discovers America Adventures with Eric. 96p. (J). (gr. 2-6). pap. 7.95 (*0-941016-74-9*) Penfield.

— Reaching. LC 88-61287. 202p. (Orig.). 1988. pap. 7.95 (*0-930942-12-4*) Sutherland MA.

— Scottish Proverbs. Zug, John & Liffring-Zug, Joan, eds. (Illus.). 30p. (Orig.). 1987. pap. 8.95 (*0-941016-42-0*) Penfield.

— Young Rakes. Bergren, Anne B. & Joy, Melissa M., eds. 140p. (Orig.). 1991. pap. 9.95 (*1-878326-01-5*) East Hall Pr.

McDonald, Julie J. Delectably Danish: Recipes & Reflections. LC 82-81568. (Illus.). 64p. 1982. pap. 7.95 (*0-941016-04-8*) Penfield.

McDonald, Julie J., ed. Scandinavian Proverbs. 30p. 1993. pap. 8.95 (*0-941016-27-7*) Penfield.

McDonald, Kathleen. How to Meditate: A Practical Guide. rev. ed. Courtin, Robina, ed. LC 88-51646. 221p. 1994. pap. 12.95 (*0-86171-009-6*) Wisdom MA.

McDonald, Kathy, ed. BASIC Programming One: Course Code 303-2. rev. ed. (Illus.). 78p. (gr. 5). 1989. reprint ed. pap. text ed. 9.95 (*0-917531-90-6*) CES Compu-Tech.

McDonald, Kathy, ed. see Broadie, Kim, et al.

McDonald, Keiko, ed. Ugetsu. LC 92-8419. (Films in Print Ser.: Vol. 17). (Illus.). 200p. (C). 1992. 37.00 (*0-8135-1861-X*); pap. 15.00 (*0-8135-1862-8*) Rutgers U Pr.

McDonald, Keiko I. Cinema East: A Critical Study of Major Japanese Films. LC 81-65870. (Illus.). 280p. 1983. 45.00 (*0-8386-3094-4*) Fairleigh Dickinson.

***McDonald, Keiko J.** Japanese Classical Theater in Films. LC 92-54669. (Illus.). 360p. 1994. 48.50 (*0-8386-3502-4*) Fairleigh Dickinson.

McDonald, Kendall. Divers. Stefoff, Rebecca, ed. LC 91-46577. (Living Dangerously Ser.). (Illus.). 32p. (J). (gr. 5-9). 1992. lib. bdg. 17.26 (*1-56074-043-4*) Garrett Ed Corp.

McDonald, Kyle C. & Ulaby, Fawaaz T. Modeling Microwave Backscatter from Discontinuous Tree Canopies. (Technical Report Ser.: No. 026511-2-T). 377p. reprint ed. pap. 107.50 (*0-7837-1390-8*, 2041571) Bks Demand.

McDonald, L. Racial Equality. Haiman, Franklyn S., ed. (To Protect These Rights Ser.). 168p. 1983. pap. 12.95 (*0-8442-6004-5*, Natl Textbk) NTC Pub Grp.

McDonald, L. E., ed. Veterinary Endocrinology & Reproduction. 4th ed. LC 88-9015. (Illus.). 571p. 1989. text ed. 57.00 (*0-8121-1134-6*) Williams & Wilkins.

McDonald, Laughlin & Powell, John A. The Rights of Racial Minorities: The Basic ACLU Guide to Racial Minority Rights. rev. ed. LC 93-15756. (American Civil Liberties Union Handbook Ser.). 344p. (C). 1993. pap. text ed. 7.95 (*0-8093-1888-1*) S Ill U Pr.

— The Rights of Racial Minorities: The Basic ACLU Guide to Racial Minority Rights. 2nd rev. ed. LC 93-15756. (American Civil Liberties Union Handbook Ser.). 344p. (C). 1993. 34.95 (*0-8093-1899-7*) S Ill U Pr.

McDonald, Laurie A. From Lydia B's Galley. LC 91-91299. (Illus.). 125p. (Orig.). 1991. pap. 9.95 (*0-9630977-0-9*) Mtn View Ent.

McDonald, Lawrence P. We Hold These Truths: A Reverent Review of the U. S. Constitution. 1992. 16.95 (*0-9632809-0-2*); pap. 9.95 (*0-9632809-1-0*); ring bd. 59.95 (*0-9632809-2-9*) L McDonald Mem.

McDonald, Lee C. Western Political Theory: From Its Origins to the Present, 3 vols. Incl. Vol. 1. Ancient & Medieval. 228p. (C). 1970. pap. text ed. 18.00 (*0-15-595297-8*); Vol. 2. From Machiavelli to Burke. 297p. (C). 1970. pap. text ed. 18.00 (*0-15-595298-6*); Vol. 3. Nineteenth & Twentieth Centuries. 239p. (C). 1970. pap. text ed. 18.00 (*0-15-595299-4*); (C). 1970. Set pap. text ed. write for info. (*0-318-52978-5*) HB Coll Pubs.

***McDonald, Lee M.** Formation of the Christian Biblical Canon. expanded rev. ed. 250p. 1995. pap. 14.95 (*1-56563-052-1*) Hendrickson MA.

McDonald, Leslie E., jt. auth. see Booth, Nicholas H.

McDonald, Leslie S., jt. auth. see Hillgren, Susan H.

McDonald, Linda. Bones to Biscuits. LC 77-1236. 1977. pap. 6.95 (*0-916198-03-0*) Oaklawn Pr.

— Everything You Need to Know about Babies. LC 77-21017. (Illus.). 1978. pap. 12.95 (*0-916198-04-9*) Oaklawn Pr.

— Instant Baby Food. LC 75-27760. (Illus.). 113p. 1975. 8.95 (*0-916198-02-2*); pap. 6.95 (*0-916198-01-4*) Oaklawn Pr.

— The Joy of Breastfeeding. LC 77-18536. (Illus.). 1978. pap. 8.95 (*0-916198-07-3*) Oaklawn Pr.

McDonald, Linda, jt. auth. see Criswell, Ann.

McDonald, Linda, jt. auth. see Steves, Renie.

McDonald, Lois, jt. auth. see White, Thelma B.

McDonald, Lois, ed. see White, Thelma B. & McDonald, Lois.

McDonald, Lois H. Elsie Hamburger: I Never Look Back. LC 88-92825. (Illus.). 212p. 1989. pap. 11.75 (*0-9621992-1-4*) Paradise Fact & Folklore.

McDonald, Lorna. Cattle Country. 250p. (C). 1990. 90.00 (*0-685-67404-5*, Pub. by Boolarong Pubns AT) St Mut.

— Gladstone: The City That Waited. 464p. (C). 1990. 90.00 (*0-9599124-1-X*, Pub. by Boolarong Pubns AT) St Mut.

McDonald, Lucile. Alaska Steam: A Pictorial of the Alaska Steamship Company. Chapman, Jean & Rennick, Penny, eds. LC 84-216730. (Alaska Geographic Ser.: Vol. 11, No. 4). (Illus.). 160p. (Orig.). 1984. pap. 15.95 (*0-88240-268-4*) Alaska Geog Soc.

— Search for the Northwest Passage. LC 58-11860. (Illus.). 142p. (gr. 4-9). 1958. 8.95 (*0-8323-0029-2*); pap. 6.95 (*0-8323-0253-8*) Binford Mort.

— Swan Among the Indians: Life of James Swan, 1818-1900. LC 72-85230. (Illus.). 280p. 1972. 14.95 (*0-8323-0066-7*) Binford Mort.

McDonald, Lucille. Early Gig Harbor Steamboats. 72p. 1984. pap. write for info. (*0-939116-13-8*) Frontier OR.

McDonald, Lyman L., et al, eds. Estimation & Analysis of Insect Populations. (Lecture Notes in Statistics Ser.: Vol. 55). (Illus.). xiv, 492p. 1989. pap. 65.00 (*0-387-96998-5*) Spr-Verlag.

McDonald, Lynn. The Early Origins of the Social Sciences. 448p. 1994. 49.95 (*0-7735-1124-5*, Pub. by McGill CN) U of Toronto Pr.

McDonald, M., jt. auth. see Butterworth, C.

McDonald, M., tr. see Ichikawa, T.

McDonald, M. B. & Copeland, L. O. Seed Science & Technology Laboratory Manual. LC 88-83562. (Illus.). 240p. (C). 1989. pap. text ed. 23.95 (*0-8138-0190-7*) Iowa St U Pr.

— Seed Science & Technology Laboratory Manual. (C). 1992. text ed. 225.00 (*81-7233-038-3*, Pub. by Scientific Pubs II) St Mut.

McDonald, M. B., Jr. & Nelson, C. J., eds. Physiology of Seed Deterioration. 123p. 1986. 18.00 (*0-89118-522-4*) Crop Sci Soc Am.

McDonald, M. B., Jr. & Pardee, W. D., eds. The Role of Seed Certification in the Seed Industry. 46p. 1985. 12.00 (*0-89118-521-6*) Crop Sci Soc Am.

McDonald, M. B., jt. auth. see Stanwood, P. C.

McDonald, M. V., tr. The History of al-Tabari, Vol. 7: The Foundation of the Community - Muhammad at al-Madina, A. D. 622-626. LC 87-12940. (SUNY Series in Near Eastern Studies). 182p. 1987. 57.50 (*0-88706-344-6*); pap. 18.95 (*0-88706-345-4*) State U NY Pr.

McDonald, M. V., jt. ed. see Watt, W. Montgomery.

McDonald, Malcolm. Strategic Marketing Planning. (Cranfield Management Research Ser.). pap. text ed. write for info. (*0-7494-0767-0*, Pub. by Kogan Page Educ UK) Taylor & Francis.

***McDonald, Malcolm, ed.** Marketing Strategies: New Approaches New Techniques. (Best of Long Range Planning Ser.: Vol. 2). 250p. 1995. text ed. 56.00 (*0-08-042572-0*, Pergamon Pr) Elsevier.

McDonald, Malcolm & Leppard, John. Marketing by Matrix: One Hundred One Practical Ways to Improve Your Strategic & Tactical marketing. 176p. 1993. pap. 24.95 (*0-8442-3455-9*, NTC Busn Bks) NTC Pub Grp.

McDonald, Malcolm & Morris, Peter. Selling: Services & Products: A Pictorial Guide. (Illus.). 96p. 1991. text ed. 22.95 (*0-7506-0069-1*) Buttrwrth-Heinemann.

McDonald, Malcolm H. The Marketing Audit. 176p. 1991. 39.95 (*0-7506-0089-6*) Buttrwrth-Heinemann.

— The Marketing Planner. (Marketing Practitioner Ser.). 156p. 1993. pap. 19.95 (*0-7506-1709-8*) Buttrwrth-Heinemann.

— Marketing Plans: How to Prepare Them, How to Use Them. 3rd ed. (Professional Development Ser.). 485p. 1995. pap. 34.95 (*0-7506-2213-X*, Focal) Buttrwrth-Heinemann.

McDonald, Malcolm H. & Leppard, John. The Marketing Audit: Translating Marketing Theory into Practice. (Marketing Practitioner Ser.). 285p. 1993. pap. 19.95 (*0-7506-1706-3*) Buttrwrth-Heinemann.

McDonald, Malcolm H., jt. auth. see De Chernatony, Leslie.

McDonald, Mandi. Babes in Toyland. (Heirloom Collection Ser.). (Illus.). 72p. (J). (gr. 3-7). 1990. 11.95 (*0-88101-100-2*) Unicorn Pub.

***McDonald, Marc.** Hotel, Restaurant & Public House Law: Registrations, Licenses & Names. 1992. pap. text ed. 92.00 (*0-85475-105-X*, IE) Butterworth Legal Pubs.

***McDonald, Marci.** Yankee Doodle Dandy: Brian Mulroney & the American Agenda. 320p. 1995. 24.95 (*0-7737-2880-5*, Pub. by Stoddart Publng CN) Pubs Dist MI.

McDonald, Margaret M., ed. Towards Excellence: Case Studies of Good School Libraries. LC 85-44387. (Illus.). 104p. reprint ed. pap. 29.70 (*0-7837-5328-4*, 2045068) Bks Demand.

McDonald, Marge, ed. see Pfeifer, Diane.

McDonald, Marge, jt. auth. see Schneider, Jane.

McDonald, Marge, et al. A Marmac Guide to Atlanta. 8th ed. (Marmac Guide Ser.). (Illus.). 288p. 1989. pap. 9.95 (*0-88289-735-7*) Pelican.

McDonald, Marianne. Ancient Sun, Modern Light. (Illus.). 288p. 1991. text ed. 35.00 (*0-231-07654-1*) Col U Pr.

McDonald, Marie. Ka Lei. (Illus.). 1985. pap. text ed. 19.95 (*0-914916-32-7*) Ku Paa.

— Marie's Moments: A Collection of Columns by Marie McDonald. Mah, Julie, ed. (Illus.). 160p. (Orig.). 1994. pap. 9.95 (*1-880652-36-6*) Wichita Eagle.

McDonald, Marilyn. Inspired by a Child of God Called Marilyn. LC 90-71950. 44p. (YA). (gr. 9-12). 1991. 5.95 (*1-55523-416-X*) Winston-Derek.

McDonald, Marilyn, ed. BookNotes: The Booklover's Organizer. 178p. (Orig.). 1994. pap. 12.95 (*0-943097-02-9*) Jackson Creek Pr.

McDonald, Marjorie. Not by the Color of Their Skin: The Impact of Racial Differences on the Child's Development. LC 73-134334. Orig. Title: Integration & Skin Color. 242p. 1971. text ed. 35.00 (*0-8236-3690-9*); pap. text ed. 24.95 (*0-8236-8166-1*, 23690) Intl Univs Pr.

McDonald, Mark, jt. auth. see Farquhar, Bobby.

McDonald, Mary, jt. auth. see Pollard, Neil.

McDonald, Mary A. Flying Squirrels. LC 93-9118. (Naturebook Ser.). (J). (gr. 2-6). 1993. lib. bdg. 22.79 (*1-56766-058-4*) Childs World.

— Jupiter. LC 93-3595. (Visionbooks Ser.). (Illus.). 32p. (ENG & SPA.). (J). 1993. lib. bdg. 22.79 (*1-56766-022-3*) Childs World.

— Jupiter. LC 93-3595. (Vision Bks.). (Illus.). (ENG & SPA.). (J). 1993. pap. 22.79 (*1-56766-041-X*) Childs World.

***McDonald, Mary L.** The Christian's Guide to Money Matters for Women. 240p. 1995. pap. 14.99 (*0-310-50160-1*) Zondervan.

Mcdonald, Maryon. Gender, Drink & Drugs. 1994. 49.95 (*0-85496-719-2*); pap. 17.50 (*0-85496-867-9*) Berg Pubs.

McDonald, Maryon. We Are Not French! Language, Culture, & Identity in Brittany. (Illus.). 272p. 1990. 62.50 (*0-415-00632-5*, A4070) Routledge.

McDonald, Maurice. Milkshine-Curry Easy Buzzard Reader. (Orig.). 1970. pap. 8.00 (*0-912136-18-9*) Twowindows Pr.

McDonald, Maurice E., jt. auth. see Gaunt, Larry D.

McDonald, Megan. The Bridge to Nowhere. LC 92-50844. 160p. (YA). (gr. 6 up). 1993. 15.95 (*0-531-05478-0*); lib. bdg. 15.99 (*0-531-08628-3*) Orchard Bks Watts.

— The Great Pumpkin Switch. LC 91-39660. (Illus.). 32p. (J). (ps-2). 1992. 15.95 (*0-531-05450-0*); lib. bdg. 15.99 (*0-531-08600-3*) Orchard Bks Watts.

— The Great Pumpkin Switch. LC 91-39660. (Illus.). 32p. (J). (ps-2). 1995. pap. 5.95 (*0-531-07065-4*) Orchard Bks Watts.

— Insects Are My Life. LC 94-21960. (Illus.). 32p. (J). (ps-2). 1995. 14.95 (*0-531-06874-9*); lib. bdg. 14.99 (*0-531-08724-7*) Orchard Bks Watts.

— Is This a House for Hermit Crab? LC 89-35653. (Illus.). 32p. (J). (ps-1). 1990. 15.95 (*0-531-05855-7*); lib. bdg. 15.99 (*0-531-08455-8*) Orchard Bks Watts.

— Is This a House for Hermit Crab? LC 89-35653. (Illus.). 32p. (J). (ps-1). 1993. pap. 5.95 (*0-531-07041-7*) Orchard Bks Watts.

— The Potato Man. LC 90-7758. (Illus.). 32p. (J). (ps-2). 1991. 15.95 (*0-531-05914-6*); lib. bdg. 15.99 (*0-531-08514-7*) Orchard Bks Watts.

— The Potato Man. LC 90-7758. (Illus.). 32p. (J). (ps-2). 1994. pap. 5.95 (*0-531-07053-0*) Orchard Bks Watts.

— Whoo-oo Is It? LC 91-18494. (Illus.). 32p. (J). (ps-1). 1992. 14.95 (*0-531-05974-X*); lib. bdg. 14.99 (*0-531-08574-0*) Orchard Bks Watts.

McDonald, Michael. The Quiz of Enchantment. Vigil, Arnold, ed. LC 91-67865. (Illus.). 136p. (Orig.). 1992. pap. 6.95 (*0-937206-23-7*) New Mexico Mag.

McDonald, Michael, jt. auth. see Adkison, Peter.

McDonald, Michael, jt. auth. see Golvan, Colin.

McDonald, Michael, ed. see Sym, John.

McDonald, Michael J. & Muldowny, John. TVA & the Dispossessed: The Resettlement of Population in the Norris Dam Area. LC 81-16333. (Illus.). 352p. 1982. 38.00x (*0-87049-345-0*) U of Tenn Pr.

McDonald, Michael J. & Wheeler, Bruce. Knoxville, Tennessee: Continuity & Change in an Appalachian City. LC 83-1402. (Illus.). 200p. 1983. 35.00x (*0-87049-393-0*) U of Tenn Pr.

McDonald, Michael J. & Wheeler, William B. Knoxville, Tennessee: Continuity & Change in an Appalachian City. LC 83-1402. (Illus.). 200p. 1983. pap. 16.00x (*0-87049-648-4*) U of Tenn Pr.

McDonald, Michael J., jt. auth. see Wheeler, William B.

McDonald, Mike, ed. see Gonzales, Rod & Faurot, Chip.

McDonald, Mildred, jt. auth. see Held, Colbert C.

McDonald, Miller B., jt. auth. see Copeland, Lawrence O.

McDonald, Mort. The Panty Junkyard. (Illus.). 1975. 6.00 (*0-685-79061-4*) Twowindows Pr.

— Trouble in the Men's Room. 1975. 5.00 (*0-685-79060-6*) Twowindows Pr.

McDonald, Nancy, ed. see Volden, Jon.

***McDonald, Neil.** Positional Sacrifices. 128p. 1994. pap. 15.95 (*1-85744-110-9*, Pub. by Cadogan Books UK) Macmillan.

— War Cameraman: The Story of Damien Parer. (Illus.). 258p. (Orig.). 1995. pap. 29.95 (*0-85091-341-1*, Pub. by Lothian Pub AT) Seven Hills Bk.

***McDonald, Neil R., intro.** Pacific Basin Nuclear Conference, Ninth, 1994: Nuclear Energy, Science & Technology, Pacific Partnership, 2 vols., Set. (National Conference Publication Ser.: No. 94-6). (Illus.). 1087p. (Orig.). 1994. pap. 105.50x (*0-85825-602-9*, Pub. by Inst Engrs Aust-EA Bks AT) Accents Pubns.

McDonald, Nicholas. Fatigue, Safety & the Truck Driver. (Illus.). 213p. 1984. 75.00 (*0-85066-207-9*) Taylor & Francis.

McDonald, Nora M. & Weibel, Ruth E. Principles of Flat Pattern Design. (Illus.). 320p. 1988. pap. text ed. write for info. (*0-318-62257-2*) P-H.

***McDonald, P.** Animal Nutrition. 5th rev. ed. LC 95-53. 1995. write for info. (*0-470-23988-3*) Wiley.

— Directory of Low Temperature Research in Europe. (Illus.). 408p. 1992. 102.00 (*0-7503-0176-7*) IOP Pub.

— Tire Imprint Identification: Practical Aspects of Criminal Forensic Investigation Ser. 448p. 1989. 45.00 (*0-444-01456-X*, CRC Reprint) Franklin.

McDonald, P., et al. Animal Nutrition. 4th ed. LC 86-28723. 543p. 1988. pap. text ed. 58.95 (*0-470-20791-4*) Halsted Pr.

— The Biochemistry of Silage. 2nd ed. (Illus.). 340p. (C). 1991. text ed. 110.00 (*0-948617-22-5*, Pub. by Chalcombe Pubns UK) Scholium Intl.

McDonald, P. W., jt. auth. see Tisdell, Clement A.

McDonald, Patricia, ed. see Beach, Lynn.

McDonald, Patricia, ed. see Pevsner, Stella.

McDonald, Patricia, ed. see Stine, R. L.

McDonald, Patricia A. & Haney, Margaret. Counseling the Older Adult: A Training Manual for Paraprofessionals & Beginning Counselors. 2nd ed. 224p. (Orig.). 1988. pap. 27.95 (*0-669-16970-6*) Free Pr.

McDonald, Patrick. Make 'Em Talk: Principles of Military Interrogation. 80p. 1993. pap. 14.00 (*0-87364-728-9*) Paladin Pr.

***McDonald, Patrick D. & Bouvier, Edouard S., eds.** Solid Phase Extraction Applications Guide & Bibliography: A Resource for Sample Preparation Methods Development. 6th ed. LC 95-60173. (Illus.). 646p. (Orig.). (C). 1995. pap. text ed. 75.00 (*1-879732-06-8*) Waters MA.

***McDonald, Patrick H.** Continuum Mechanics. LC 94-23728. 1996. text ed. 68.95 (*0-534-93984-8*) PWS Pubs.

***McDonald, Patrick J. & McDonald, Claudette M.** The Soul of a Marriage. LC 94-44929. 160p. (Orig.). 1995. pap. 9.95 (*0-8091-3555-8*) Paulist Pr.

— Soul Work: A Workbook for Couples. 88p. (Orig.). 1995. pap. 10.95 (*0-8091-3558-2*) Paulist Pr.

McDonald, Paul R. Forty-One Years in the D.C. & H. LC 83-90109. (Illus.). 81p. (Orig.). 1987. pap. 14.95 (*0-9611258-0-2*) McDonald P R.

McDonald, Paula, et al. Crossing the Border Fast & Easy: How to Get in - & Out! - of Baja, Mexico, Without the Hassle. LC 92-90310. (Illus.). 208p. (Orig.). 1992. pap. 6.95 (*0-9633517-0-2*) Borderline Assocs.

McDonald-Pavelka, Mary. Monkeys of the Mesquite: The Social Life of the American Snow Monkey. 112p. (C). 1993. per., pap. text ed. 12.95 (*0-8403-8986-8*) Kendall-Hunt.

McDonald, Penny, jt. auth. see Marcus, Susan A.

McDonald, Peter. Biting the Wax. LC 89-82484. 64p. 1990. pap. 11.95 (*1-85224-077-6*, Pub. by Bloodaxe Bks UK) Dufour.

— Louis MacNeice: The Poet in His Contexts. 256p. 1991. 55.00 (*0-19-811766-3*) OUP.

— Tire Imprint Evidence. (Practical Aspects of Criminal & Forensic Investigations Ser.). 1992. 50.00 (*0-8493-9515-1*, HV8097) CRC Pr.

— Tire Imprint Evidence. 220p. 1989. 39.50 (*0-685-29755-1*) Elsevier.

McDonald, Peter, ed. The Literature of Soil Science. LC 93-27394. (Literature of the Agricultural Sciences Ser.). (Illus.). 456p. 1994. 67.50 (*0-8014-2921-8*) Cornell U Pr.

McDonald, Peter, ed. see MacNeice, Louis.

McDonald, Peter C. Grieving: A Healing Process. 24p. (Orig.). 1985. pap. 1.55 (*0-89486-318-5*, 5350B) Hazelden.

McDonald, Philip M., jt. auth. see McDonald, Cleveland.

McDonald, Philip R. Factors Influencing Fuel Oil Growth. Bruchey, Stuart, ed. LC 78-22700. (Energy in the American Economy Ser.). (Illus.). 1979. lib. bdg. 35.95 (*0-405-12002-8*) Ayer.

McDonald, Philip R. & Baldwin, George C. Builder's & Contractor's Handbook of Construction Claims. 350p. 1989. text ed. 60.00 (*0-13-085796-3*) P-H.

McDonald, Phyllis P. Cloning & Genetic Engineering: Social & Legal Implications. 82p. 1978. student ed 18.90 (*1-877960-02-0*, 2-505) Kemtec Educ.

McDonald, R. C., et al. Australian Soil & Land Survey Field Handbook, Vol. 1. 172p. 1984. pap. 30.00 (*0-909605-32-7*, Pub. by Inkata Pr AT) Intl Spec Bk.

McDonald, R. Robin. Black Widow: The True Story of the Hilley Poisonings. LC 85-12676. 409p. 1986. 18.95 (*0-88282-020-6*) New Horizon NJ.

McDonald, Ralph E. & Avery, David R., eds. Dentistry for the Child & Adolescent. 6th ed. LC 93-20508. 784p. 1993. 54.95 (*0-8016-6705-4*) Mosby Yr Bk.

McDonald, Ralph J. A Down-Home Gallery of American Wildlife. (Illus.). 101p. 1980. 39.95 (*0-9605428-1-7*) Countryside Studio.

— A Down-Home Gallery of American Wildlife. deluxe limited ed. (Illus.). 101p. 1980. 95.00 (*0-9605428-0-9*) Countryside Studio.

McDonald, Robert. Art of the States: Works from a Santa Barbara Collection. LC 84-51013. (Illus.). 76p. (Orig.). 1984. pap. 15.00 (*0-89951-053-1*) Santa Barb Mus Art.

— The Carolyn & Jack Farris Collection: Selected Contemporary Works. LC 82-81520. (Illus.). 68p. 1982. 13.50 (*0-934418-13-6*) Mus Contemp Art.

— A Contemporary Collection on Loan from the Rothschild Bank AG, Zurich. LC 82-84588. (Illus.). 72p. 1983. 13.50 (*0-934418-16-0*) Mus Contemp Art.

— Craig Kauffman. 1989. pap. 15.00 (*0-932499-35-X*) Lapis Pr.

— Craig Kauffman: A Comprehensive Survey 1957-1980. LC 80-70807. (Illus.). 95p. 1980. pap. 12.00 (*0-934418-09-8*) Mus Contemp Art.

An Asterisk (*) at the beginning of an entry indicates that the title is appearing in BIP for the first time.

— D. J. Hall: Selected Works 1974-1985. De Alcuaz, Marie & Ianco-Starrels, Josine, eds. LC 85-82100. (Illus.). 32p. (Orig.). 1986. pap. 12.00 (*0-936429-00-3*) LA Municipal Art.

McDonald, Robert, ed. Sense of Place. 24p. (Orig.). 1987. 15.00 (*0-9602974-8-0*) USC Fisher Gallery.

McDonald, Robert, text. Craig Kauffman: A Comprehensive Survey, 1957-1980. LC 80-70807. (Illus.). 96p. (Orig.). 1981. pap. 15.00 (*0-911291-06-7*) Fellows Cont Art.

McDonald, Robert & Rabkin, Leo. Leo Rabkin Works. LC 81-83642. (Illus.). 73p. (Orig.). 1981. pap. 15.00 (*0-934418-11-X*) Mus Contemp Art.

McDonald, Robert, jt. auth. see Adler, Sebastian.

McDonald, Robert, ed. see Buelteman, Robert.

McDonald, Robert, jt. auth. see Stilwill, Clarence.

McDonald, Robert A. Adjustment of School Organization to Various Population Groups. LC 70-177021. (Columbia University. Teachers College. Contributions to Education Ser.: No. 75). reprint ed. 22.50 (*0-404-55075-4*) AMS Pr.

McDonald, Robert C. Introducton to General Chemistry: Laboratory Manual. 112p. (C). 1994. spiral bd. 13.95 (*0-8403-9350-4*) Kendall-Hunt.

McDonald, Robin R. Black Widow. 1989. mass mkt. 4.95 (*0-312-92068-7*) St Martin.

McDonald, Rochelle L. How to Pinch a Penny Till It Screams: How to Stretch Your Dollar in the Nineties. LC 93-8827. 284p. 1994. pap. 8.95 (*0-89529-529-6*) Avery Pub.

McDonald, Roderick A. Economy & Material Culture of Slaves: Goods & Chattels on the Sugar Plantations of Jamaica & Louisiana. LC 93-392. (Illus.). 400p. (C). 1993. text ed. 39.95 (*0-8071-1794-3*) La State U Pr.

— Successful Object Sermons. (Object Lesson Ser.). 112p. (Orig.). 1990. pap. 5.99 (*0-8010-6270-5*) Baker Bk.

McDonald, Roderick P. Factor Analysis & Related Methods. 272p. (C). 1985. text ed. 39.95 (*0-89859-388-3*) L Erlbaum Assocs.

McDonald, Roger. Nineteen Fifteen. (Paperbacks Ser.). 434p. (YA). (gr. 10 up). 1989. reprint ed. pap. 16.95 (*0-7022-2134-1*, Pub. by Univ Queensland Pr AT) Intl Spec Bk.

McDonald, Ronald, jt. auth. see Hallwood, Paul.

McDonald, Roy W. McDonald Texas Civil Practice, 1981-1990, 5 vols. Elliott, Frank W., ed. LC 80-28736. 337.00 (*0-8321-0051-X*) Bancroft Whitney Co.

***McDonald, Russ.** Shakespeare & Jonson, Jonson & Shakespeare. LC 87-19158. 249p. 1988. reprint ed. pap. 71.00 (*0-7837-8894-0*, 2049605) Bks Demand.

— Shakespeare in Context: A Documentary Companion. 320p. 1995. pap. text ed. 10.64 (*0-312-10075-2*) St Martin.

McDonald, Russ, ed. Shakespeare Reread: The Texts in New Contexts. (Illus.). 296p. 1994. 39.95 (*0-8014-2917-X*); pap. 15.95 (*0-8014-8144-9*) Cornell U Pr.

McDonald, S., tr. see Ichikawa, T.

McDonald, S. Ramelle. Fast Spiritual Food. 16p. 1994. pap. 4.95 (*0-8059-3472-3*) Dorrance.

McDonald, Scott, jt. auth. see Hellweg, Paul.

McDonald, Shel. Living Paradox Dying. xii, 52p. 1975. 6.50 (*0-87881-027-7*) Mojave Bks.

McDonald, Sherry, jt. auth. see Ferrara, Matthew L.

McDonald, Solon W. Age One - Part One: For Parents or Teachers of Children One Year of Age or Older. 1993. pap. 7.95 (*0-533-10361-4*) Vantage.

McDonald, Stephen L. The Leasing of Federal Lands for Fossil Fuels Production. LC 78-23437. 184p. 1979. 21.95 (*0-8018-2194-0*) Resources Future.

— Petroleum Conservation in the United States: An Economic Analysis. LC 71-149242. (Resources for the Future Ser.). (Illus.). 288p. 1971. 22.50 (*0-8018-1261-5*) Johns Hopkins.

McDonald, Stephen L. & Mohammadioun, Mina, eds. The Role of Natural Gas in Environmental Policy. (Illus.). 63p. (Orig.). (C). 1994. pap. text ed. 40.00 (*0-7881-0274-5*) Diane Pub.

McDonald, Steven, et al. The Steven McDonald Story. (Illus.). 356p. 1989. 17.95 (*1-55611-133-9*) D I Fine.

McDonald, Susan. Kissing Games: A Study in Fokelore. 1978. 3.00 (*0-916750-32-9*) Dayton Labs.

McDonald, Susan & Gerrick, David J. Folklore of Kissing Games. 84p. (Orig.). 1981. pap. 3.00 (*0-685-01374-X*) Dayton Labs.

McDonald, Susan, ed. see Blair, Laurence R. & Blair, Mary E.

McDonald, Susan, ed. see Wallace, William G.

McDonald, T. David. Technological Transformation of China. (Illus.). 221p. 1990. per. 5.50 (*0-16-001720-3*, S/N 008-020-01172-0) USGPO.

McDonald, T. F. Connective Tissues in Arterial & Pulmonary Disease. Chandler, A. B., ed. (Illus.). 355p. 1981. pap. 79.00 (*0-387-90623-1*) Spr-Verlag.

McDonald, T. Liam. The 11th Hour 7th Guest Companion. 300p. 1995. 14.99 (*0-7821-1558-6*) Sybex.

— Tom McDonald's PC Games Extravaganza! 200p. 1995. 19.99 (*0-7821-1654-X*) Sybex.

McDonald-Taylor, Margaret. Dictionary of Marks N - E: Ceramics, Metalwork, Furniture, Tapestry. (Illus.). 336p. 1993. pap. 22.95 (*0-7126-5303-1*, Pub. by Barrie & Jenkins) Trafalgar.

McDonald, Terrence J., ed. see Riordan, William L.

McDonald, Thomas F. Target: Tomorrow, Quality of Life for Residential Elders. 60p. 6.50 (*0-318-17114-7*, 110060) Am Health Care Assn.

McDonald, Timothy. Illustrated Novell NetWare 2.X-3.X Software. (Illustrated Ser.). (Illus.). 352p. 1992. pap. 23.95 (*1-55622-235-1*) Wordware Pub.

McDonald, Vincent R., ed. The Caribbean Economies. LC 72-8622. 196p. 1972. pap. text ed. 8.95 (*0-8422-0258-7*) Irvington.

McDonald, Vincent R., jt. ed. see Hogan, Lloyd.

McDonald, W. Ian & Silberberg, Donald H., eds. Multiple Sclerosis. (Butterworth International Medical Reviews Rheumatology Ser.: Vol. 6). 208p. 1986. text ed. 65.00 (*0-407-00411-4*) Buttrwrth-Heinemann.

McDonald, W. N. History of the Laurel Brigade. reprint ed. 49.95 (*0-87948-018-1*) Beatty.

McDonald, W. W., ed. see Parks, Anthony D.

McDonald, Walter. After the Noise of Saigon. LC 87-20582. 80p. (Orig.). (C). 1988. lib. bdg. 17.50 (*0-87023-600-8*); pap. 9.95 (*0-87023-601-6*) U of Mass Pr.

— Anything, Anything. LC 79-26383. 54p. (Orig.). 1980. pap. 4.25 (*0-934332-22-3*) LEpervier Pr.

— A Band of Brothers. LC 89-36088. xvi, 144p. (C). 1989. 16.50 (*0-89672-208-2*); pap. 9.00 (*0-89672-209-0*) Tex Tech Univ Pr.

— Burning the Fence. LC 80-54792. 58p. (Orig.). 1981. 7.95 (*0-89672-088-8*); pap. 4.95 (*0-89672-087-X*) Tex Tech Univ Pr.

— Counting Survivors. LC 94-43044. 1995. write for info. (*0-8229-3874-X*); pap. write for info. (*0-8229-5555-5*) U of Pittsburgh Pr.

— The Digs in Escondido Canyon. xii, 52p. 1991. 16.95 (*0-89672-258-9*) Tex Tech Univ Pr.

— The Flying Dutchman: The George Elliston Poetry Prize, 1987. LC 86-31169. 70p. 1987. 18.95 (*0-8142-0434-1*); pap. 12.50 (*0-8142-0441-4*) Ohio St U Pr.

— Rafting the Brazos. LC 88-28073. (Texas Poetry Ser.: No. 1). 112p. 1988. pap. 9.95 (*0-929398-00-9*) UNTX Pr.

— Where Skies Are Not Cloudy. LC 93-14496. (Texas Poets Ser.: Vol. 4). 65p. 1993. pap. 10.95 (*0-929398-60-2*) UNTX Pr.

— Where Skies Are Not Cloudy. (Texas Poets Ser.: Vol.4). 1993. 14.95 (*0-929398-61-0*) UNTX Pr.

McDonald, Walter & Williams, Miller. Caliban in Blue. 51p. (Orig.). 1976. 4.50 (*0-89672-054-3*); pap. 2.25 (*0-89672-053-5*) Tex Tech Univ Pr.

McDonald, Ward. Johnny Reb: Confederate Spy. Willis, Mary M., ed. 288p. 1993. 25.00 (*0-89896-187-4*); pap. 14.95 (*0-89896-186-6*) Larksdale.

McDonald, Wil, jt. auth. see Duren, Lista.

McDonald, William. Letters to the Thessalonians. rev. ed. 1982. pap. 5.00 (*0-937396-43-5*) Walterick Pubs.

McDonald, William, jt. ed. see Carson, Chris.

McDonald, William, tr. see Kierkegaard, Soren.

McDonald, William A. Bill McDonald's Poems of Life. 1991. 12.95 (*0-533-09162-4*) Vantage.

McDonald, William A. & Rapp, George R., Jr., eds. The Minnesota Messenia Expedition: Reconstructing a Bronze Age Regional Environment. LC 75-187168. (Illus.). 356p. 1972. spiral bd. 49.95 (*0-8166-0636-6*) U of Minn Pr.

McDonald, William A. & Thomas, Carol G. Progress into the Past: The Rediscovery of Mycenaean Civilization. 2nd ed. LC 89-45196. (Illus.). 558p. 1990. 29.95 (*0-253-33627-9*); pap. 14.95 (*0-253-20553-0*, MB-553) Ind U Pr.

McDonald, William A. & Wilkie, Nancy C., eds. Excavations at Nichoria in Southwest Greece Vol. The Bronze Age Occupation, Vol. 2. (Illus.). 1000p. (C). 1991. text ed. 155.95 (*0-8166-1935-2*) U of Minn Pr.

McDonald, William A., et al, eds. Excavations at Nichoria in Southwest Greece Vol. III: Dark Age & Byzantine Occupation. LC 78-3198. (Illus.). 559p. 1983. text ed. 49.95 (*0-8166-1144-0*) U of Minn Pr.

McDonald, William C. Arthur & Tristan: On the Intersection of Legends in German Medieval Literature. LC 91-40230. 308p. 1992. lib. bdg. 99.95 (*0-7734-9448-0*) E Mellen.

— Ritual Illumination: Poems. Schultz, Patricia, ed. LC 90-41266. (Mellen Poetry Ser.: Vol. 12). 72p. 1990. lib. bdg. 24.95 (*0-88946-836-2*); pap. 12.95 (*0-685-35739-2*) E Mellen.

— The Tristan Story in German Literature of the Late Middle Ages & Early Renaissance: Tradition & Innovation. LC 90-41478. (Studies in German Language & Literature: Vol. 5). 250p. 1990. lib. bdg. 89.95 (*0-88946-075-2*) E Mellen.

McDonald, William C., jt. ed. see Classen, Albrecht.

McDonald, William C., jt. ed. see DuBruck, Edelgard E.

McDonald, William F., ed. Criminal Justice & the Victim. LC 75-42754. (Sage Criminal Justice System Annuals Ser.: No. 6). 288p. reprint ed. pap. 82.10 (*0-8357-8496-7*, 2034771) Bks Demand.

McDonald, William J. The General Council: Special Studies in Doctrinal & Historical Background. LC 62-20329. 192p. reprint ed. pap. 54.80 (*0-317-07854-2*, 2005223) Bks Demand.

— The Social Value of Property According to St. Thomas Aquinas: A Study in Social Philosophy. 1972. 59.95 (*0-8490-1068-3*) Gordon Pr.

McDonald, William L. Dallas Rediscovered. 1988. 14.95 (*0-932018-01-7*) Dallas His Soc.

McDonald, William N. History of the Laurel Brigade. 449p. 1988. reprint ed. 30.00 (*0-942211-59-6*) Olde Soldier Bks.

McDonald, Winnie P. & Peters, Bonnie H. Our Union County Families. (Illus.). 420p. 1993. lib. bdg. 50.00 (*0-9636662-0-7*) McDonald Peters.

McDonalld, Hugh J. & Sapone, Frances M. Nutrition for the Prime of Life: The Adult's Guide to Healthier Living. 355p. 1993. 26.95 (*0-306-44503-4*, Plenum Insight) Plenum.

McDonell, Edwin D. Document Imaging Technology: How Automated Solutions Are Revolutionizing the Way Organizations & People Work. 300p. 1992. 47.50 (*1-55738-336-7*) Probus Pub Co.

***McDonell, J. M.** Half Crazy: A Novel, Vol. 1. LC 94-33348. 1995. 19.95 (*0-316-55560-6*) Little.

McDonell, James. Stained Glass Craft Made Simple: Step-by-Step Instructions Using the Modern Copper-Foil Method. 32p. 1985. pap. 2.95 (*0-486-24963-8*) Dover.

McDonell, James & Sibbett, Ed, Jr. Getting Started in Stained Glass: Instructions & Patterns, 2 bks. 96p. 1986. pap. 7.90 (*0-486-25268-X*) Dover.

McDonell, Katherine M. Medicine in Antebellum Indiana. (Illus.). 58p. 1984. pap. 3.00 (*0-87195-096-0*) Ind Hist Soc.

McDonell, Katherine M., intro. The Journals of William A. Lindsay: An Ordinary Nineteenth-Century Physician's Surgical Cases. LC 88-32003. No. 2. (Illus.). 216p. 1989. 27.50 (*0-87195-029-4*) Ind Hist Soc.

McDonnel, Anna. Bill Mack. (Illus.). 166p. (C). 1989. write for info. (*0-318-65799-6*) Maresa Editions.

McDonnell. Kidculture: Children, Adults & Popular Culture. (NFS Canada Ser.). 1994. pap. 14.95 (*0-929005-64-3*, Pub. by Second Story Pr CN) InBook.

McDonnell, Andy. Ready Or Not It's Barndoor Bones. (Illus.). 64p. 1995. pap. 3.95 (*0-8059-3576-2*) Dorrance.

McDonnell, Betty & Riley, Jo Ann. The Newfoundland. LC 85-14211. (Breed Bks.). (Illus.). 1985. 29.95 (*0-87714-110-X*) Denlingers.

— The Newfoundland Handbook. LC 84-13524. (Breed Bks.). (Illus.). 1985. pap. 6.95 (*0-87714-108-8*) Denlingers.

McDonnell, Christine. Friends First. LC 92-20290. 176p. (J). (gr. 5 up). 1992. pap. 3.99 (*0-14-032477-1*) Puffin Bks.

— Toad Food & Measle Soup. 1995. 17.25 (*0-8446-6800-1*) Peter Smith.

— Toad Food & Measle Soup. (Storybooks Ser.). (Illus.). 112p. (J). 1984. pap. 3.99 (*0-14-031724-4*, Puffin) Puffin Bks.

McDonnell, Denis L. & Monroe, John G. Kerr on the Law of Fraud & Mistake: Including Misrepresentation Generally, Undue Influence, Fiduciary Relationship, Constructive & Imputed Notice, etc. 7th ed. (Legal Reprint Ser.). (Illus.). liv, 738p. 1986. reprint ed. lib. bdg. 60.00 (*0-421-35540-9*) Rothman.

McDonnell, Eugene E., ed. A Source Book in APL: Papers by Adin D. Falkoff & Kenneth E. Iverson. 144p. (Orig.). 1981. pap. 15.00 (*0-917326-10-5*) APL Pr.

***McDonnell, Evelyn & Powers, Ann, comps.** Rock She Wrote. LC 95-5835. 1995. write for info. (*0-385-31250-4*, Delta) Dell.

McDonnell, Flora. I Love Animals. LC 93-2463. 32p. (J). (ps up). 1994. 14.95 (*1-56402-387-7*) Candlewick Pr.

— I Love Boats. LC 94-4861. (Illus.). 32p. 1995. 15.95 (*1-56402-539-X*) Candlewick Pr.

McDonnell, Frances. Emigrants from Ireland to America, 1735-1743: A Transcription of the Report of the Irish House of Commons into Enforced Emigration to America. 142p. 1992. 18.50 (*0-8063-1331-5*, 3510) Genealog Pub.

McDonnell, Ginny, jt. auth. see Mogard, Sue.

McDonnell, Greg. Signatures in Steel. Hudson, Noel, ed. (Illus.). 208p. 1991. 50.00 (*0-7737-2554-7*, Pub. by Boston Mills Pr CN) Genl Dist Srvs.

McDonnell, Jacqueline. Evelyn Waugh. LC 87-26102. (Modern Novelists Ser.). 192p. 1988. text ed. 24.95 (*0-312-01618-2*) St Martin.

McDonnell, James & Trampiets, Frances. Communicating Faith in a Technological Age. 256p. (C). 1990. 75.00 (*0-85439-314-5*, Pub. by St Paul Pubns UK) St Mut.

McDonnell, James, ed. see DeGiacomo, F. P.

McDonnell, James A., ed. Cosmic Dust. LC 77-2895. (Illus.). 713p. reprint ed. pap. 180.00 (*0-685-20665-3*, 2030453) Bks Demand.

McDonnell, Jane T. News from the Border: A Mother's Memoir of Her Autistic Son. LC 93-15711. 384p. 1993. 21.95 (*0-395-60574-1*) Ticknor & Fields.

McDonnell, Janet. Animal Camouflage: Hide & Seek Animals. LC 89-28083. (Discovery World Ser.). (Illus.). 32p. (J). (ps-2). 1990. lib. bdg. 21.36 (*0-89565-562-4*) Childs World.

— Animal Talk: Barks, Growls, Hisses, Howls. LC 89-23990. (Discovery World Ser.). (Illus.). 32p. (J). (ps-2). 1990. lib. bdg. 21.36 (*0-89565-558-6*) Childs World.

— Baby Animals: Safe & Sound. LC 89-23978. (Discovery World Ser.). (Illus.). 32p. (J). (ps-2). 1990. lib. bdg. 21.36 (*0-89565-554-3*) Childs World.

— Bear's Adventure in Alphabet Town. LC 91-20543. (Read Around Alphabet Town Ser.). (Illus.). 32p. (J). (ps-2). 1992. lib. bdg. 11.85 (*0-516-05402-3*) Childrens.

— Celebrating Earth Day. LC 93-37714. (Circle the Year with Holidays Ser.). (Illus.). 32p. (J). (ps-2). 1994. lib. bdg. 12.30 (*0-516-00689-4*) Childrens.

— Celebrating Earth Day. (J). (ps-2). 1994. pap. 3.95 (*0-516-40689-2*) Childrens.

— Christmas in Other Lands. LC 93-7632. (Circle the Year with Holidays Ser.). (Illus.). 32p. (J). (ps-2). 1993. lib. bdg. 12.30 (*0-516-00682-7*); pap. 3.95 (*0-516-40682-5*) Childrens.

— The Easter Surprise. LC 93-11004. (Circle the Year with Holidays Ser.). (Illus.). 32p. (J). (ps-2). 1993. lib. bdg. 12.30 (*0-516-00683-5*); pap. 3.95 (*0-516-40683-3*) Childrens.

— Fall: A Tale of What's to Come. LC 93-20171. (Four Seasons Ser.). (Illus.). 32p. (J). (gr. 2 up). 1993. lib. bdg. 12.30 (*0-516-00676-2*) Childrens.

— Fall: A Tale of What's to Come. (J). (ps-2). 1994. pap. 3.95 (*0-516-40676-0*) Childrens.

— The Fourth of July. LC 94-4827. (Circle the Year with Holidays Ser.). (Illus.). 32p. (J). (ps-2). 1994. lib. bdg. 12.30 (*0-516-00694-0*); pap. 3.95 (*0-516-40694-9*) Childrens.

— Fox's Adventure in Alphabet Town. LC 91-20546. (Read Around Alphabet Town Ser.). (Illus.). 32p. (J). (ps-2). 1992. lib. bdg. 11.85 (*0-516-05406-6*) Childrens.

— Goat's Adventure in Alphabet Town. LC 91-20548. (Read Around Alphabet Town Ser.). (Illus.). 32p. (J). (ps-2). 1992. lib. bdg. 11.85 (*0-516-05407-4*) Childrens.

— Good Health: A Visit from Droopy. LC 90-1871. (Discovery World Ser.). (Illus.). 32p. (J). (ps-2). 1990. lib. bdg. 21.36 (*0-89565-582-9*) Childs World.

— Hippo's Adventure in Alphabet Town. LC 91-20549. (Read Around Alphabet Town Ser.). (Illus.). 32p. (J). (ps-2). 1992. lib. bdg. 11.85 (*0-516-05408-2*) Childrens.

— Ichabod's Adventure in Alphabet Town. LC 91-20547. (Read Around Alphabet Town Ser.). (Illus.). 32p. (J). (ps-2). 1992. lib. bdg. 11.85 (*0-516-05409-0*) Childrens.

— Kangaroo's Adventure in Alphabet Town. LC 91-20540. (Read Around Alphabet Town Ser.). (Illus.). 32p. (J). (ps-2). 1992. lib. bdg. 11.85 (*0-516-05411-2*) Childrens.

— Martin Luther King Day. LC 93-13251. (Circle the Year with Holidays Ser.). (Illus.). 32p. (J). (ps-2). 1993. lib. bdg. 12.30 (*0-516-00687-8*); pap. 3.95 (*0-516-40687-6*) Childrens.

— Mouse's Adventure in Alphabet Town. LC 91-47717. (Read Around Alphabet Town Ser.). (Illus.). 32p. (J). (ps-2). 1992. lib. bdg. 11.85 (*0-516-05413-9*) Childrens.

— Quarterback's Adventure in Alphabet Town. LC 92-1067. (Read Around Alphabet Town Ser.). (Illus.). 32p. (J). (ps-2). 1992. lib. bdg. 11.85 (*0-516-05417-1*) Childrens.

— Raccoon's Adventure in Alphabet Town. LC 92-1066. (Read Around Alphabet Town Ser.). (Illus.). 32p. (J). (ps-2). 1992. lib. bdg. 11.85 (*0-516-05418-X*) Childrens.

— Sharing Hanukkah. LC 93-13250. (Circle the Year with Holidays Ser.). (Illus.). 32p. (J). (ps-2). 1993. lib. bdg. 12.30 (*0-516-00685-1*); pap. 3.95 (*0-516-40685-X*) Childrens.

— Space Travel: Blast-Off Day. LC 89-23999. (Discovery World Ser.). (Illus.). 32p. (J). (ps-2). 1990. lib. bdg. 21.36 (*0-89565-556-X*) Childs World.

— Spring: New Life Everywhere. LC 93-10309. (Four Seasons Ser.). (Illus.). 32p. (J). (gr. 2 up). 1993. lib. bdg. 12.30 (*0-516-00677-0*) Childrens.

— Spring: New Life Everywhere. (J). (ps-2). 1994. pap. 3.95 (*0-516-40677-9*) Childrens.

— Success. LC 88-4348. (Values to Live By Ser.). (Illus.). 32p. (ENG & SPA.). (J). (ps-2). 1988. lib. bdg. 21.36 (*0-89565-376-1*) Childs World.

— Success. LC 88-4348. (Values to Live By Ser.). (Illus.). 32p. (ENG & SPA.). (J). (ps-2). 1988. lib. bdg. 21.36 (*0-89565-955-7*) Childs World.

— Summer, a Growing Time. LC 93-1182. (Four Seasons Ser.). (Illus.). 32p. (J). (gr. 2 up). 1993. pap. 3.95 (*0-516-40678-7*) Childrens.

— Summer, a Growing Time. LC 93-1182. (Four Seasons Ser.). (Illus.). 32p. (J). (gr. 2 up). 1993. lib. bdg. 12.30 (*0-516-00678-9*) Childrens.

— Thankfulness. LC 88-2657. (Values to Live By Ser.). (Illus.). 32p. (ENG & SPA.). (J). (ps-2). 1988. lib. bdg. 21.36 (*0-89565-375-3*) Childs World.

— Thankfulness. LC 88-2657. (Values to Live By Ser.). (Illus.). 32p. (ENG & SPA.). (J). (ps-2). 1988. lib. bdg. 21.36 (*0-89565-956-5*) Childs World.

— Turtle's Adventure in Alphabet Town. LC 92-2984. (Read Around Alphabet Town Ser.). (Illus.). 32p. (J). (ps-2). 1992. lib. bdg. 11.85 (*0-516-05420-1*) Childrens.

— Two Special Valentines. LC 93-37097. (Circle the Year with Holidays Ser.). (Illus.). 32p. (J). (ps-2). 1994. lib. bdg. 12.30 (*0-516-00692-4*) Childrens.

— Two Special Valentines. 1994. pap. 3.95 (*0-516-40692-2*) Childrens.

— Victor's Adventure in Alphabet Town. LC 92-4036. (Read Around Alphabet Town Ser.). (Illus.). 32p. (J). (ps-2). 1992. lib. bdg. 11.85 (*0-516-05422-8*) Childrens.

— Wind: What Can It Do? LC 89-24011. (Discovery World Ser.). (Illus.). 32p. (J). (ps-2). 1990. lib. bdg. 21.36 (*0-89565-555-1*) Childs World.

— Winter. (Tracks in the Snow Ser.). (J). (ps-2). 1994. pap. 3.95 (*0-516-40679-5*) Childrens.

— Winter: Tracks in the Snow. LC 93-20172. (Four Season Ser.). (Illus.). 32p. (J). (gr. 2 up). 1993. lib. bdg. 12.30 (*0-516-00679-7*) Childrens.

— An XYZ Adventure in Alphabet Town. LC 92-2985. (Read Around Alphabet Town Ser.). (Illus.). 32p. (J). (ps-2). 1992. lib. bdg. 11.85 (*0-516-05424-4*) Childrens.

McDonnell, Janet, tr. Goldilocks & the Three Bears. LC 88-36870. (Classic Tale Ser.). (Illus.). 32p. (J). (gr. 1-4). 1988. lib. bdg. 13.95 (*0-89565-465-2*) Childs World.

— Snow White & the Seven Dwarfs: A Classic Tale. LC 88-35210. (Illus.). 32p. (J). (gr. k-3). 1988. lib. bdg. 19.93 (*0-89565-479-2*) Childs World.

— The Three Little Pigs: A Classic Tale. LC 88-35314. (Illus.). 32p. (J). (gr. k-3). 1988. lib. bdg. 19.95 (*0-89565-459-8*) Childs World.

McDonnell, Janet & Ziegler, Sandra. What's So Special about Me? I'm One of a Kind. LC 88-2872. (What's So Special Ser.). (Illus.). 32p. (J). (ps-2). 1988. lib. bdg. 21.36 (*0-89565-419-9*) Childs World.

McDonnell, Janet, tr. see Andersen, Hans Christian.

McDonnell, Janet A. The Dispossession of the American Indian, 1887-1934. LC 90-44508. (Illus.). 176p. 1991. 20.00 (*0-253-33628-7*) Ind U Pr.

***McDonnell, Jean-Marie, et al.** Mobile: A Gulf Coast Treasure. Gilreath, Lenita & Turner, James, eds. LC 94-30172. (Illus.). 240p. 1994. 45.00 (*1-885352-00-X*); pap. 24.95 (*1-885352-01-8*) Community Comm.

McDonnell, Jim. Public Service Broadcasting: A Reader. 128p. 1991. 74.50 (*0-415-03707-7*, A5553) Routledge.

McDonnell, John, jt. ed. see McGwire, Michael.

McDonnell, John, et al. Secondary Programs for Students with Developmental Disabilities. 315p. 1991. text ed. 58.00 (*0-205-12862-9*, H28624) Allyn.

McDonnell, John J. The Concept of an Atom from Democritus to John Dalton. LC 91-40434. 144p. 1992. lib. bdg. 69.95 (*0-7734-9649-1*) E Mellen.

An Asterisk (*) at the beginning of an entry indicates that the title is appearing in BIP for the first time.

— An Introduction to Persons with Severe Disabilities: Educational & Social Issues. LC 94-32871. 1995. text ed. write for info. (*0-205-15090-X*) Allyn.
— The World Council of Churches & the Catholic Church. (Toronto Studies in Theology: Vol. 21). 479p. 1985. lib. bdg. 109.95 (*0-88946-765-X*) E Mellen.
***McDonnell, John R., et al, eds.** Evolutionary Programming IV: Proceedings of the Fourth Annual Conference on Evolutionary Programming March 1-3, 1995 San Diego, CA. 1995. 65.00x (*0-262-13317-2*, Bradford Bks) MIT Pr.
McDonnell, Judith, jt. ed. see Litoff, Judy B.
McDonnell, Jullian B. & Coleman, Elizabeth. Commercial & Consumer Warranties: Drafting, Performing & Litigating, 3 vols. 1987. Updates. ring bd. write for info. (*0-8205-1824-7*) Bender.
McDonnell, Kevin, jt. auth. see Freeman, John M.
McDonnell, Kilian. John Calvin, the Church, & the Eucharist. LC 65-17149. 420p. reprint ed. pap. 119.70 (*0-317-08461-5*, 2010572) Bks Demand.
McDonnell, Kilian, ed. Open the Windows: The Popes & Charismatic Renewal. LC 88-83044. xxvii, 67p. (Orig.). 1989. pap. 5.95 (*0-937779-06-7*) Greenlawn Pr.
— Toward a New Pentecost: For a New Evangelization: Malines Document I. 2nd ed. LC 92-46910. 80p. 1993. pap. text ed. 5.95 (*0-8146-5846-6*, M Glazier) Liturgical Pr.
McDonnell, Kilian & Montague, George T. Christian Initiation & Baptism in the Holy Spirit. 368p. (C). 1991. pap. 14.95 (*0-8146-5009-0*) Liturgical Pr.
— Fanning the Flame: What Does Baptism in the Holy Spirit Have to Do with Christian Initiation? 30p. (Orig.). 1991. pap. text ed. 1.95 (*0-8146-5013-9*) Liturgical Pr.
McDonnell, L. M., et al. Federal Support for Training Foreign Language & Area Specialists: The Education & Careers of FLAS Fellowship Recipients. LC 83-17761. 1983. 15.00 (*0-8330-0524-3*, R-3070-ED) Rand Corp.
McDonnell, L. P. & Kaumeheiwa, A. I. The Use of Hand Woodworking Tools. 2nd ed. LC 76-48504. 301p. (C). 1978. teacher ed 10.00 (*0-8273-1099-4*); pap. 21.95 (*0-8273-1098-6*) Delmar.
McDonnell, Leo & Ball, John. Blueprint Reading & Sketching for Carpenters: Residential. LC 80-66027. (Blueprint Reading Ser.). (Illus.). 151p. (C). 1981. teacher ed 12.00 (*0-8273-1355-1*); pap. text ed. 22.50 (*0-8273-1354-3*) Delmar.
McDonnell, Lorraine M. & Hill, Paul T. Newcomers in American Schools: Meeting the Educational Needs of Immigrant Youths. LC 93-19883. 1993. write for info. (*0-8330-1392-0*, MR-103-AWM) Rand Corp.
McDonnell, Mark J. & Pickett, Steward T., eds. Humans as Components of Ecosystems: The Ecology of Subtle Human Effects & Populated Areas. LC 93-10444. 1993. 49.00 (*0-387-94062-6*) Spr-Verlag.
McDonnell, Mary A. Village Streets. 64p. 1991. pap. 10.00 (*0-9632201-0-1*) Zeugpress.
***McDonnell, Patricia & Plante, Michael.** Dictated by Life: Marsden Hartley's German Paintings & Robert Indiana's Hartley Elegies. (Illus.). 112p. Date not set. pap. 32.95 (*1-885116-01-2*) Dist Art Pubs.
Mcdonnell, Patrick. They Said It. 1990. pap. 5.95 (*0-8487-1028-2*) Oxmoor Hse.
McDonnell, Patrick, et al. Krazy Kat: The Art of George Herriman. (Illus.). 224p. 1986. 35.00 (*0-8109-1211-2*); pap. 14.95 (*0-8109-2313-0*) Abrams.
McDonnell, Peter J., jt. auth. see Thompson, Frank B.
McDonnell, Porter. Introduction to Map Projections. 2nd ed. 198p. 1991. pap. 38.00 (*0-910845-39-5*, 462) Landmark Ent.
McDonnell, Rea. Catholic Epistles & Hebrews. (Message of Biblical Spirituality Ser.: Vol. 14). 150p. 1986. 12.95 (*0-8146-5564-5*); pap. 7.95 (*0-8146-5580-7*) Liturgical Pr.
— When God Comes Close: A Journey Through Scripture. rev. ed. LC 94-1614. 208p. 1994. pap. 5.25 (*0-8198-8271-2*) Pauline Bks.
McDonnell, Rea & Callahan, Rachel. Hope for Healing: Good News for Adult Children of Alcoholics. 1988. pap. 4.95 (*0-8091-2929-9*) Paulist Pr.
McDonnell, Robert, ed. see Kleeman, Mary.
McDonnell, Robert W., jt. auth. see Partington, Paul G.
McDonnell, Sharon, jt. auth. see Wallman, Lester.
McDonnell, Thomas. Pinpointing Student Behavioral Problems. (Orig.). 1988. pap. 9.95 (*1-55804-950-9*) Info Res Cons.
— RATS: (Rapid Assessment & Treatment Strategies for Human Resource Personnel) (Orig.). 1989. pap. 9.95 (*0-931821-97-5*) Info Res Cons.
McDonnell, Thomas P., ed. Classic Catholic Poetry. LC 88-60924. 144p. 1988. 13.95 (*0-87973-494-9*, 494) Our Sunday Visitor.
— A Thomas Merton Reader. LC 74-29. 600p. 1974. pap. 12.95 (*0-385-03292-7*, Image Bks) Doubleday.
McDonnell, Unity, jt. ed. see Edwardss, Marcia.
McDonnell-Wieczorek, Colleen. Go to College but Don't Go to Class: The Guide to Alternate Methods of Earning College Credits. 200p. (Orig.). 1994. pap. 19.95 (*1-885097-02-6*) NAOACS.
— The Guide for Adults Thinking about Going to College. 120p. (Orig.). 1994. pap. 12.95 (*1-885097-01-8*) NAOACS.
McDonogh, Gary, ed. Conflict in Catalonia: Images of an Urban Society. LC 86-956. (University of Florida Social Sciences Monographs: No. 71). 112p. (Orig.). 1985. pap. 19.95 (*0-8130-0821-2*) U Press Fla.
McDonogh, Gary, jt. auth. see Rotenberg, Robert.
McDonogh, Gary W. Black & Catholic in Savannah, Georgia. LC 93-15389. (Illus.). 360p. (Orig.). (C). 1993. 42.95x (*0-87049-810-X*); pap. 18.95 (*0-87049-811-8*) U of Tenn Pr.
McDonogh, Gary W., ed. The Florida Negro: A Federal Writers' Project Legacy. LC 92-28493. 184p. 1993. 30.00 (*0-87805-588-6*) U Pr of Miss.
McDonough, Adrian M. & Garrett, Leonard J. Management Systems: Working Concepts & Practices. LC 65-17698. (Irwin Series in Management). 315p. reprint ed. pap. 89.80 (*0-317-26677-2*, 2055961) Bks Demand.
McDonough, Alex. Scorpio Six: Dragon Claw. 176p. (Orig.). 1993. mass mkt. 4.99 (*0-441-75514-3*) Ace Bks.
***McDonough, Ann.** The Golden State: Dramatic Activities for Older Adults. 304p. 1994. per., pap. text ed. 18.95 (*0-8403-9762-3*) Kendall-Hunt.
McDonough, Barbara. Meet Me at the Fair: A "Choose Your Own Adventure" that lets You Explore the Exciting Treasures of the 1904 St. Louis World's Fair. (Illus.). 64p. (Orig.). (J). (gr. 4-6). 1988. pap. 4.50 (*0-931821-43-6*) Info Res Cons.
***McDonough, Brian, ed.** Talking Health with Dr. Brian McDonough. LC 94-6020. (Health, Society, & Policy Ser.). 288p. (C). 1994. pap. 16.95 (*0-614-03075-7*) Temple U Pr.
McDonough, Brian P., ed. Talking Health with Dr. Brian McDonough. LC 94-6020. (Health, Society, & Policy Ser.). 288p. (C). 1994. 27.95 (*1-56639-207-1*) Temple U Pr.
***McDonough, Chris.** White Wolf MEAT Magazine No. 52. Cliffe, Ken, ed. 96p. 1995. 4.25 (*1-56504-952-7*, 04952) White Wolf.
McDonough, Chris, illus. Mother Goose Monsters ABC's Sticker Book. (Mother Goose Monsters Ser.). 24p. (J). (ps-2). 1992. pap. 2.95 (*1-56293-246-2*) McClanahan Bk.
— Mother Goose Monsters Counting Sticker Book. (Mother Goose Monsters Ser.). 24p. (J). (ps-2). 1992. pap. 2.95 (*1-56293-247-0*) McClanahan Bk.
McDonough, Connie. Am I on the Right Plane? Transcendental Airlines Puts You on a Different Plane. Chandler, Patricia M., ed. (Illus.). 201p. (Orig.). 1991. pap. 7.95 (*0-9630660-0-5*) Hagall.
McDonough, D. Annotated Mergers & Acquisitions Law of Australia. 3rd ed. 470p. 1993. pap. 70.00 (*0-455-21182-5*, Pub. by Law Bk Co) W W Gaunt.
McDonough, Gary W. Good Families of Barcelona: A Social History of Power in the Industrial Era. 288p. 1986. pap. 45.00 (*0-691-09426-8*) Princeton U Pr.
McDonough, Gerald M. The Hogles. 539p. 1988. 22.50 (*0-914740-33-4*) Western Epics.
McDonough, Irene R. History of the Public Library in Vigo County, 1816-1975. LC 77-18403. (Illus.). 203p. 1977. 6.00 (*0-9601522-1-0*) Vigo Cnty Pub Lib.
McDonough, James. Limits of Glory. 1991. 19.95 (*0-89141-384-7*) Presidio Pr.
— Platoon Leader. 1986. mass mkt. 4.99 (*0-553-27582-8*) Bantam.
McDonough, James L. Chattanooga: A Death Grip on the Confederacy. LC 83-23582. 318p. 1984. 31.95 (*0-87049-425-2*); pap. 16.95 (*0-87049-630-1*) U of Tenn Pr.
— Shiloh-in Hell Before Night. LC 76-18864. (Illus.). 272p. 1977. 31.95 (*0-87049-199-7*); pap. 16.95 (*0-87049-232-2*) U of Tenn Pr.
— Stones River: Bloody Winter in Tennessee. LC 80-11580. 286p. 1980. 31.95 (*0-87049-301-9*); pap. 16.95 (*0-87049-373-6*) U of Tenn Pr.
— War in Kentucky: From Shiloh to Perryville. LC 94-4508. (Illus.). 408p. (C). 1994. 32.00 (*0-87049-847-9*) U of Tenn Pr.
McDonough, James L. & Connelly, Thomas L. Five Tragic Hours: The Battle of Franklin. LC 83-3449. (Illus.). 232p. 1983. 31.95 (*0-87049-396-5*); pap. 16.95 (*0-87049-397-3*) U of Tenn Pr.
McDonough, James L. & Gardner, Richard S. The Skyriders: History of the 327-401 Glider Infantry. LC 80-67956. (Airborne Ser.: No. 11). (Illus.). 176p. 1980. 25.00 (*0-89839-034-6*) Battery Pr.
McDonough, James R. Defense of Hill Seven Eighty-One: An Allegory of Modern Mechanized Combat. 224p. 1993. pap. 12.95 (*0-89141-475-4*) Presidio Pr.
— Platoon Leader. (Illus.). 208p. 1985. 18.95 (*0-89141-235-2*) Presidio Pr.
McDonough, Jerome. Addict. (Illus.). 47p. (Orig.). (YA). (gr. 7-12). 1985. pap. 3.50 (*0-88680-241-5*) I E Clark.
— Alky. 40p. (Orig.). (YA). (gr. 7-12). 1991. pap. 3.00 (*0-88680-354-3*) I E Clark.
— Asylum. (Illus.). 40p. 1975. pap. 10.00 (*0-88680-009-9*); pap. 3.00 (*0-88680-008-0*) I E Clark.
— B. A. T. S. (Illus.). 56p. (Orig.). 1988. pap. 4.00 (*0-88680-289-X*) I E Clark.
— Blues: An Ensemble Play in One Act. 28p. (Orig.). 1990. pap. 3.50 (*0-88680-323-3*) I E Clark.
— Butterfly. (Illus.). 22p. (Orig.). 1993. pap. 3.00 (*0-88680-390-X*) I E Clark.
— Carol-A Christmas. (Orig.). 1989. pap. 3.00 (*0-88680-312-8*) I E Clark.
— Carriers. 34p. (Orig.). (YA). (gr. 7-12). 1992. pap. 3.00 (*0-88680-370-5*) I E Clark.
— A Christmas Carol. (Illus.). 34p. (Orig.). 1976. pap. 2.00 (*0-88680-024-2*) I E Clark.
— Dolls. 28p. (Orig.). 1988. pap. 3.00 (*0-88680-298-9*) I E Clark.
— Eden. 38p. 1978. pap. 3.50 (*0-88680-044-7*) I E Clark.
— Fables. (Illus.). 40p. 1974. pap. 10.00 (*0-88680-048-X*); pap. 3.00 (*0-88680-047-1*) I E Clark.
— F.A.U.G.H. Fine Arts Under-Graduate Housing. (Illus.). 36p. (Orig.). 1986. pap. 4.00 (*0-88680-281-4*) I E Clark.
— Hoods. 22p. (Orig.). (YA). (gr. 7-12). 1992. pap. 3.00 (*0-88680-369-1*) I E Clark.
— It's Sad, So Sad When an Elf Goes Bad. (Illus.). 24p. (Orig.). (J). (gr. k-6). 1979. pap. 2.50 (*0-88680-100-1*) I E Clark.
— Juvie. (Illus.). 32p. (Orig.). (YA). (gr. 7-12). 1982. pap. 3.50 (*0-88680-103-6*) I E Clark.
— Limbo. 28p. (Orig.). (YA). (gr. 7 up). 1984. pap. 3.00 (*0-88680-219-9*) I E Clark.
— Mirrors. (Illus.). 32p. (YA). (gr. 7 up). 1987. pap. 3.00 (*0-88680-278-4*) I E Clark.
— The Nearest Star. 28p. 1981. pap. 3.00 (*0-88680-137-0*) I E Clark.
— Not Even A. Mouse: A Chris-Mouse Tale. (Illus.). 20p. (Orig.). (J). (gr. k-9). 1984. pap. 2.00 (*0-88680-220-2*) I E Clark.
— O, Little Town. (Illus.). 27p. (Orig.). 1978. pap. 3.00 (*0-88680-144-3*) I E Clark.
— Plots. 24p. (Orig.). 1981. pap. 3.00 (*0-88680-154-0*) I E Clark.
— Posadas. Alderete, Betty, tr. (Illus.). 26p. 1994. pap. 3.00 (*0-88680-398-5*) I E Clark.
— Requiem. (Illus.). 41p. 1977. pap. 10.00 (*0-88680-164-8*); pap. 3.00 (*0-88680-163-X*) I E Clark.
— Roomers: A One-Act Comedy. 36p. 1983. pap. 3.00 (*0-88680-165-6*) I E Clark.
— Stages. (Illus.). 52p. 1979. pap. 10.00 (*0-88680-184-2*); pap. 3.00 (*0-88680-183-4*) I E Clark.
— Stations. (Illus.). 32p. (Orig.). 1988. pap. 3.00 (*0-88680-291-1*) I E Clark.
— Turners. 40p. (Orig.). (YA). (gr. 7-12). 1989. pap. 4.00 (*0-88680-320-9*) I E Clark.
McDonough, Jerome, adapt. Alice: A One-Act Play. (Illus.). 36p. (Orig.). (J). (gr. 4-12). 1990. pap. 3.00 (*0-88680-336-5*) I E Clark.
McDonough, Jerome, jt. auth. see Brinsley, Richard.
McDonough, Jo & Shaw, Christopher. Materials & Methods in ELT: A Teachers Guide. (Applied Language Studies). 288p. 1993. 49.95 (*0-631-18002-8*); pap. 16.95 (*0-631-18003-6*) Blackwell Pubs.
McDonough, John J., jt. auth. see Culbert, Samuel A.
McDonough, John J., ed. see French, Benjamin B.
McDonough, Kathleen, jt. auth. see Fox, Micheal.
McDonough, Kathleen L. School Survival Skills: Student Syllabus. (Illus.). 64p. (YA). (gr. 8 up). 1985. pap. 7.95 (*0-89420-246-4*, 340025) Natl Book.
McDonough, Kristin & Langstaff, Eleanor. Access Information: Research in Social Sciences & Humanities. 300p. 1991. pap. text ed. 25.95 (*0-8403-6739-2*) Kendall-Hunt.
McDonough, Larry, et al. MapView User's Guide. LC 93-10349. 1993. write for info. (*0-8330-1363-7*, MR-160-AF) Rand Corp.
McDonough, Mark G., jt. auth. see Harrison, Michael M.
McDonough, Mark G., jt. auth. see Spector, Leonard S.
McDonough, Peter. Men Astutely Trained: A History of the Jesuits in the American Century. 600p. 1991. text ed. 27.95 (*0-02-920527-1*) Free Pr.
— Men Astutely Trained: A History of the Jesuits in the American Century. 1994. pap. 14.95 (*0-02-920528-X*) Free Pr.
— Power & Ideology in Brazil. LC 81-47147. 356p. 1981. 55.00x (*0-691-07628-6*); pap. 17.95x (*0-691-02203-8*) Princeton U Pr.
McDonough, R. P., jt. auth. see Brallier, Jess M.
McDonough, Richard. The Argument of the "Tractatus" Its Relevance to Contemporary Theories of Logic, Language, Mind, & Philosophical Truth. LC 85-9916. (Logic & Language Ser.). 311p. (C). 1986. 64.50 (*0-88706-152-4*); pap. 21.95 (*0-88706-153-2*) State U NY Pr.
McDonough, Robert. Mixing for the Process Industries. (Illus.). 400p. 1991. text ed. 52.95 (*0-442-23434-1*) Chapman & Hall.
McDonough, Robert E. No Other World. 64p. (Orig.). 1988. pap. 6.00 (*0-914946-72-2*) Cleveland St Univ Poetry Ctr.
***McDonough, Robert N. & Whalen, A. D.** Detection of Signals in Noise. 2nd ed. (Illus.). 495p. 1995. boxed 74.95 (*0-12-744852-7*) Acad Pr.
McDonough, Robert N., jt. auth. see Curlander, John C.
***McDonough, Sheila.** Gandhi's Responses to Islam. (C). 1994. 14.00 (*81-246-0035-X*, Pub. by DK Pubs Dist II) S Asia.
***McDonough, Steven.** Strategy & Skill in Learning a Foreign Language. LC 95-5125. 1995. text ed. write for info. (*0-340-59109-9*) St Martin.
McDonough, Steven H. Psychology in Foreign Language Teaching. 2nd ed. (Illus.). 192p. 1987. pap. text ed. 16.95 (*0-04-418006-3*) Routledge Chapman & Hall.
***McDonough, Steven M.** Strategy & Skill in Learning a Foreign Language. LC 95-5125. 1995. text ed. write for info. (*0-340-62532-5*) St Martin.
McDonough, Sue, jt. ed. see Angers, Trent.
McDonough, Sue, ed. see Angers, W. Thomas.
McDonough, Thomas R. The Architects of Hyperspace. 272p. 1987. pap. 2.95 (*0-380-75144-5*) Avon.
***McDonough, Will, et al, eds.** Seventy-Five Seasons: The Complete Story of the National Football League, 1920-1995. LC 94-3580. 1994. 39.95 (*1-57036-056-1*) Turner Pub GA.
McDonough, Yona Z. Eve & Her Sisters: Women of the Old Testament. LC 93-9378. (Illus.). 32p. (J). (gr. k up). 1994. 15.00 (*0-688-12512-3*); lib. bdg. 14.93 (*0-688-12513-1*) Greenwillow.
— Frank Lloyd Wright. (Library of Biography). (Illus.). 112p. (YA). (gr. 5 up). 1992. lib. bdg. 17.95 (*0-7910-1626-9*) Chelsea Hse.
— Frank Lloyd Wright. (J). (gr. 4-7). 1992. pap. 7.95 (*0-7910-1633-1*) Chelsea Hse.
McDorman, Kathryne S. Ngaio Marsh. (Twayne's English Authors Ser.: No. 481). 190p. (C). 1991. text ed. 21.95 (*0-8057-6999-4*, Twayne) Macmillan.
McDoudal, W. Scott, ed. Operative Surgery: Urology. 4th ed. (Rob & Smith's Operative Surgery Ser.). (Illus.). 804p. 1986. text ed. 180.00 (*0-407-00658-3*) Buttrwrth-Heinemann.
McDougal. World's Greatest Golf Jokes. 1983. pap. 4.95 (*0-8065-0831-0*, Citadel Pr) Carol Pub Group.
McDougal, Charles. The Kulunga Rai: A Study in Kinship & Marriage Exchange. 1979. 60.00 (*0-7855-0315-3*, Pub. by Ratna Pustak Bhandar) St Mut.
— The Kulunge RAI: A Study in Kinship & Marriage Exchange. 170p. (C). 1989. 90.00 (*0-89771-125-4*, Pub. by Ratna Pustak Bhandar) St Mut.
— The Kulunge Rai: A Study in Kinship & Marriage Exchange. 1979. 60.00 (*0-7855-0229-7*, Pub. by Ratna Pustak Bhandar) St Mut.
McDougal, Dennis. Angel of Darkness. 1991. 19.95 (*0-446-51538-8*) Warner Bks.
— Angel of Darkness. (Illus.). 416p. 1992. mass mkt. 6.99 (*0-446-36302-2*) Warner Bks.
— In the Best of Families: The Anatomy of a True Tragedy. (Illus.). 352p. 1994. 21.95 (*0-446-51672-4*) Warner Bks.
— Mother's Day. 1995. pap. 5.99 (*0-449-14930-7*) Fawcett.
***McDougal, Gwynn.** The Last Camilles: Taking the TB Cure: The Rutland Years, 1949-1953. LC 94-24918. 1995. write for info. (*0-08-749986-X*) Acropolis.
— The Last Camilles: The Rutland Years, 1949-1953. Gordon, Esther, ed. LC 94-24918. 266p. 1995. 14.95 (*0-87491-986-X*) Acropolis.
McDougal, Harold. Laying Biblical Foundations. 154p. 1994. pap. 5.95 (*1-884369-03-0*) McDougal Pubng.
***McDougal, Luther L., III.** Louisiana Oil & Gas Law. suppl. ed. 1994. write for info. (*0-614-03738-7*) Butterworth Legal Pubs.
McDougal, Luther L., 3rd. Louisiana Oil & Gas Law. 430p. 1988. ring bd. 120.00 (*0-409-25095-3*) Michie Butterworth.
McDougal, Luther L., III & Felix, Robert L. Casenote Law Outlines Conflicts of Law. Goldenberg, Norman et al, eds. (Law Outlines Ser.). (Orig.). (C). 1992. pap. text ed. write for info. (*0-87457-186-3*, 5070) Casenotes Pub.
McDougal, Myers S., & Associates Staff, et al. Studies in World Public Order. 1986. lib. bdg. 257.50 (*0-89838-900-3*) Kluwer Ac.
McDougal, Myres S. & Burke, William T. The Public Order of the Oceans: A Contemporary International Law of the Sea. LC 86-14171. (New Haven Studies in International Law & World Public Order: No. 5). 1987. lib. bdg. 294.50 (*0-89838-901-1*) Kluwer Ac.
McDougal, Myres S. & Reisman, W. Michael. International Law Essays: A Supplement to International Law in Contemporary Perspective. (University Casebook Ser.). reprint ed. pap. text ed. 20.50 (*0-88277-484-0*) Foundation Pr.
— International Law in Contemporary Perspective: Public Order of the World Community. LC 81-5584. (University Casebook Ser.). 1584p. (C). 1981. text ed. 39.95 (*0-88277-035-7*) Foundation Pr.
McDougal, Myres S., et al. The Interpretation of Agreements & World Public Order: Principles of Content & Procedure. LC 93-39683. (New Haven Studies in International Law & World Public Order). 536p. 1994. lib. bdg. 190.00 (*0-7923-2569-9*) Kluwer Ac.
McDougal, Russel W. Mirror of Mind. LC 76-17152. 1977. pap. 8.95 (*0-917694-01-5*) Open Window.
McDougal, Stan. World's Greatest Golf Jokes. 1990. 4.98 (*0-89009-600-7*) Bk Sales Inc.
McDougal, Stan, ed. World's Greatest Golf Jokes. (Illus.). 180p. 1991. pap. 4.95 (*0-8216-2502-0*, Carol Paperbacks) Carol Pub Group.
McDougal, Stuart Y. Made into Movies: From Literature to Films. 528p. (C). 1985. pap. text ed. 28.00 (*0-03-063804-6*) HB Coll Pubs.
McDougal, Stuart Y., ed. Dante among the Moderns. LC 85-4804. xiv, 176p. 1985. 27.50 (*0-8078-1662-0*) U of NC Pr.
McDougal, W. S., et al. Manual of Burns. LC 78-18210. (Comprehensive Manuals of Surgical Specialties Ser.). (Illus.). 1978. 107.00 (*0-387-90319-4*) Spr-Verlag.
***McDougal, W. Scott & Skerrett, Pat.** The Massachusetts Guide to Prostate Disease: The Most Comprehensive, up to Date Information Available to Help You Understand Your Condition, Make the Right Treatment Choices & Cope Effectively. LC 95-15175. 1995. 14.00 (*0-8129-2319-7*, Times Bks) Random.
McDougald, Larry R. Handbook of Poultry Parasitology. Long, Peter L., ed. LC 83-2141. 250p. 1985. 29.50 (*0-03-062489-4*, Praeger Pubs) Greenwood.
McDougall, A. & Dowling, C., eds. Computers in Education: Proceedings of the IFIP TC3 Fifth World Conference, Sydney, Australia 9-13 July, 1990, 2 vols., Set. 1140p. 1990. 151.50 (*0-444-88750-4*, North Holland) Elsevier.
McDougall, Allan K. John P. Robarts: His Life & Government. (Ontario Economic Council Research Studies). 352p. 1986. 30.00 (*0-8020-3426-8*) U of Toronto Pr.
McDougall, Angus & Hampton, Veita J. Picture Editing & Layout: A Guide to Better Visual Communication. LC 89-51942. (Illus.). 300p. 1990. text ed. 37.50 (*0-9625137-0-9*) Viscom Pr.
McDougall, Anne, jt. auth. see Squires, David.
McDougall, Betsey, ed. see Burke, Marcus.
McDougall, Bonnie S. Mao Zedong's "Talks at the Yan'an Conference on Literature & Art": A Translation of the 1943 Text with Commentary. LC 80-18443. (Michigan Monographs in Chinese Studies: No. 39). 112p. 1980. pap. 6.00 (*0-89264-039-1*) Ctr Chinese Studies.
— The Yellow Earth: A Film by Chen Kaige with a Complete Translation of the Filmscript. 275p. (Orig.). 1991. pap. 27.50 (*962-201-499-2*, Pub. by Chinese Univ HK) Coronet Bks.
McDougall, Bonnie S., ed. Popular Chinese Literature & Performing Arts in the People's Republic of China, 1949-1979. LC 82-21942. (Studies on China: Vol. 2). 450p. (C). 1984. 58.00 (*0-520-04852-0*) U CA Pr.
McDougall, Bonnie S., tr. see Bei Dao.
McDougall, Bonnie S., tr. see Wang, Anyi.
McDougall, Colette, jt. auth. see Gold, Michael I.

An Asterisk (*) at the beginning of an entry indicates that the title is appearing in BIP for the first time.

McDougall, Colin. Execution. 233p. 1988. pap. 5.95 (0-7715-9280-9, Pub. by Stoddart Pubng CN) Genl Dist Srvs.

McDougall, Dorothy. Madeleine De Scudery: Her Romantic Life & Death. LC 72-80149. (Illus.). 1972. reprint ed. 26.95 (0-405-08764-0, Pub. by Blom Pubns UK) Ayer.

McDougall, E. Ann, ed. Sustainable Agriculture in Africa. LC 89-81235. (Comparative Studies in African-Caribbean Literature Ser.). 345p. (C). 1990. 45.00 (0-86543-147-7); pap. 14.95 (0-86543-148-5) Africa World.

McDougall, Elizabeth, ed. see Sullivan, Edward.

McDougall, Elspeth M., jt. ed. see Clayman, Ralph V.

McDougall, Frances H. Shahmah in Pursuit of Freedom. LC 71-154082. (Black Heritage Library Collection). 1977. 34.95 (0-8369-8793-4) Ayer.

McDougall, Garry. Heritage Walks in New South Wales. (Illus.). 160p. (Orig.). 1993. pap. 9.95 (0-86417-383-0, Pub. by Kangaroo Pr AT) Seven Hills Bk.

McDougall, Harold A. Black Baltimore: A New Theory of Community. LC 92-32548. 288p. 1993. 39.95 (1-56639-037-0); pap. 18.95 (1-56639-193-8) Temple U Pr.

McDougall, Harriette. Sketches of Our Life at Sarawak. (Illus.). 260p. 1992. reprint ed. 39.00 (0-19-588583-X) OUP.

McDougall, I. Ross. Thyroid Disease in Clinical Practice. (Illus.). 344p. 1992. 85.00 (0-19-520936-2) OUP.

McDougall, Ian & Harrison, T. Mark. Geochronology & Thermochronology by the 40Ar-39Ar Method. (Oxford Monographs on Geology & Geophysics: No. 9). (Illus.). 224p. 1988. 59.95 (0-19-504302-2) OUP.

McDougall, Jain, ed. Diodorus Siculus - Lexicon in Diodorum Siculum, 2 vols., Set. (Alpha-Omega, Reihe A Ser.: Bd. LXIV). 1780p. 1983. write for info. (3-487-07324-2, Pub. by Georg Olms GW) Lubrecht & Cramer.

McDougall, Jo. Towns Facing Railroads. 64p. 1991. 16.95 (1-55728-181-5); pap. 8.95 (1-55728-199-8) U of Ark Pr.

McDougall, John. Canadian Pacific: A Brief History. LC 68-23392. 212p. reprint ed. pap. 60.50 (0-317-26031-6, 2023833) Bks Demand.

McDougall, John A. The McDougall Program: Twelve Days to Dynamic Health. 496p. 1990. 19.95 (0-453-00659-0) NAL-Dutton.

— The McDougall Program: Twelve Days to Dynamic Health. 448p. 1991. reprint ed. pap. 12.00 (0-452-26639-4, Plume) NAL-Dutton.

— The McDougall Program for Maximum Weight Loss. 336p. 1995. pap. 11.95 (0-452-27380-3, Plume) NAL-Dutton.

— McDougall's Medicine: A Challenging Second Opinion. LC 85-21686. 298p. 1986. pap. 11.95 (0-8329-0448-1) New Win Pub.

McDougall, John A. & McDougall, Mary. The McDougall Program for Maximum Weight Loss. 416p. 1994. 23.95 (0-525-93678-5, Dutton) NAL-Dutton.

— The New McDougall Cookbook. 480p. 1993. 24.00 (0-525-93610-6, Dutton) NAL-Dutton.

McDougall, John A. & McDougall, Mary A. The McDougall Plan. LC 83-19412. (Illus.). 352p. 1985. pap. 10.95 (0-8329-0392-2) New Win Pub.

McDougall, John N. The Politics & Economics of Eric Kierans: A Man for All Canadas. 320p. 1993. 34.95 (0-7735-1122-9, Pub. by McGill CN) U of Toronto Pr.

***McDougall, Joyce.** The Many Faces of Eros: A Psychoanalytic Exploration of Human Sexuality. 256p. 1995. 30.00 (0-393-70215-4) Norton.

— Plea for a Measure of Abnormality. LC 92-29739. 493p. 1992. reprint ed. pap. 38.95 (0-87630-701-2) Brunner-Mazel.

— Theaters of the Body: A Psychoanalytic View of Psychosomatic Illness. (C). 1989. 22.95 (0-393-70082-8) Norton.

— Theaters of the Mind: Illusion & Truth on the Psychoanalytic Stage. LC 91-20628. 320p. 1991. pap. 27.95 (0-87630-648-2) Brunner-Mazel.

McDougall, Joyce & Lebovici, Serge. Dialogue with Sammy: A Psychoanalytic Contribution to the Understanding of Child Psychosis. 296p. 1989. pap. 20.00 (1-85343-109-5) Col U Pr.

McDougall, Kay. Simple Task-Centered Exercises as an Aid to Social Work Training. 1977. 25.00 (0-317-42899-3, Pub. by Natl Inst Soc Work) St Mut.

McDougall, Kay, jt. ed. see McCaughan, Nano.

McDougall, Kristin, jt. ed. see Howell, David G.

McDougall, Kristin A., jt. auth. see Dunne, George C.

***McDougall, Len.** Made for the Outdoors. (Illus.). 160p. 1995. pap. 12.95 (1-55821-329-5) Lyons & Burford.

— Practical Outdoor Survival. (Illus.). 176p. 1993. pap. 11.95 (1-55821-228-0) Lyons & Burford.

McDougall, Marion G. Fugitive Slaves 1619-1865. LC 75-154083. (Black Heritage Library Collection). 1977. 17.95 (0-8369-8794-2) Ayer.

McDougall, Mark, jt. ed. see Matson, Ted.

McDougall, Mary, jt. auth. see McDougall, John A.

McDougall, Mary A. The McDougall Health-Supporting Cookbook, Vol. 1. LC 85-5056. 122p. (Orig.). 1985. pap. 9.95 (0-8329-0393-0) New Win Pub.

— McDougall Health-Supporting Cookbook, Vol. II. LC 86-5606. 1986. pap. 9.95 (0-8329-0422-8) New Win Pub.

McDougall, Mary A., jt. auth. see DeRoche, Frederick W.

McDougall, Mary A., jt. auth. see McDougall, John A.

McDougall, Mary Lynn. The Working Class in Modern Europe. (Problems in European Civilization Ser.). 176p. (C). 1975. pap. text ed. 8.50 (0-669-92833-X) Heath.

McDougall, Richard, tr. Herculine Barbin: Being the Recently Discovered Memoirs of a Nineteenth-Century French Hermaphodite. 1980. 8.95 (0-394-50821-1); pap. 10.36 (0-394-73862-4) Pantheon.

McDougall, Ruth B. Tell Me a Story. LC 85-17214. (Illus.). 152p. (Orig.). 1985. pap. 7.95 (0-89407-070-3) Strawberry Hill.

McDougall, Suzee, jt. auth. see Thornton, Elizabeth.

***McDougall, Walter A.** Let the Sea Make a Noise. 816p. 1994. pap. 17.50 (0-380-72467-7) Avon.

— Let the Sea Make a Noise: A History of the North Pacific from Magellan to MacArthur. LC 92-56175. (Illus.). 848p. 1993. 30.00 (0-465-05152-9) Basic.

McDougall, William. The Group Mind. 2nd ed. LC 73-2976. (Classics in Psychology Ser.). 1976. reprint ed. 29.95 (0-405-05148-4) Ayer.

— Is America Safe for Democracy? Grob, Gerald, ed. LC 76-46088. (Anti-Movements in America Ser.). 1977. lib. bdg. 19.95 (0-405-09961-4) Ayer.

— Religion & the Sciences of Life: With Other Essays on Allied Topics. LC 70-39108. (Essay Index Reprint Ser.). 1977. reprint ed. 23.95 (0-8369-2700-1) Ayer.

McDougall, William, jt. auth. see Hose, Charles.

McDouglas, Myres S. & Feliciano, Florentino P. The International Law of War: Transnational Coercion & World Public Order. LC 93-41147. (New Haven Studies in International Law & World Public Order: Vol. 9). 1994. lib. bdg. 300.00 (0-7923-2584-2) Kluwer Ac.

McDow, George, Jr. Booms & Mushrooms: The Saga of Susanvile & the McDow Boys from 1910 to 1930. (Illus.). 171p. 1988. pap. 12.95 (0-938373-05-6) Lahontan Images.

— Maggie Greeno: The Life of Margaret Ann Wallace Greeno. (Illus.). (Orig.). 1995. pap. write for info. (0-938373-15-3) Lahontan Images.

McDowall. Thomas Hardy. 1972. 59.95 (0-8490-1197-3) Gordon Pr.

McDowall, Arthur S. Ruminations. LC 68-22925. (Essay Index Reprint Ser.). 1977. 17.95 (0-8369-0646-2) Ayer.

McDowall, David. Britain in Close-Up. LC 92-18031. 1993. write for info. (0-582-06461-9) Longman.

— The Kurds: A Nation Denied. (Illus.). 200p. 1992. text ed. 49.95 (1-873194-30-7, Pub. by Minority Rts Pubns UK); pap. text ed. 17.95 (1-873194-15-3, Pub. by Minority Rts Pubns UK) Paul & Co Pubs.

— Palestine & Israel: The Uprising & Beyond. (Illus.). 335p. 1991. reprint ed. pap. 15.00 (0-520-07653-2) U CA Pr.

— The Palestinians: The Road to Nationhood. (Illus.). 224p. 1995. 24.95 (1-873194-70-6, Pub. by Minority Rts Pubns UK) Paul & Co Pubs.

McDowall, David, et al. Interrupted Time Series Analysis. (Quantitative Applications in the Social Sciences Ser.: Vol. 21). (Illus.). 96p. 1980. pap. 9.95 (0-8039-1493-8) Sage.

McDowall, Duncan. Steel at the Sault: Francis H. Clergue, Sir James Dunn, & the Algoma Steel Corporation, 1901-1956. 352p. 1988. pap. text ed. 18.95 (0-8020-6736-0) U of Toronto Pr.

— Steel at the Sault: Francis H. Clergue, Sir James Dunn, & the Algoma Steel Corporation, 1901-1956. LC 85-115719. (Illus.). 348p. reprint ed. pap. 99.20 (0-8357-3768-3, 2036497) Bks Demand.

McDowall, Duncan, jt. ed. see Marchildon, Gregory P.

McDowall, R. D., ed. Laboratory Information Management Systems: Concepts & Applications. 400p. (Orig.). 1988. pap. 77.50 (1-85058-083-9, Pub. by Sigma Press UK) Coronet Bks.

— Laboratory Information Management Systems: Concepts, Integration & Implementation. 383p. 1988. text ed. 78.95 (0-470-20947-X) Wiley.

McDowall, R. J. The Whiskies of Scotland. rev. ed. LC 87-21962. (Illus.). 192p. 1987. pap. 11.95 (0-941533-06-9) New Amsterdam Bks.

McDowall, Roddy, comp. Double Exposure, Take Four. LC 92-43984. 1993. 65.00 (0-688-11309-5) Morrow.

McDowall, Roddy, photos & comp. Double Exposure, Take Three. (Illus.). 256p. 1992. 65.00 (0-688-10063-5) Morrow.

McDowall, William. Burns in Dumfriesshire. 3rd ed. LC 74-144516. reprint ed. 14.50 (0-404-08518-0) AMS Pr.

McDowell. Choosing Using Four Bit Micro-Controllers. 1994. pap. 34.95 (0-7506-1916-3) Buttrwrth-Heinemann.

McDowell & Hollingworth, eds. Seventeenth International Congress on High Speed Photography & Photonics. 600p. 1986. 79.00 (0-89252-709-9, 674) SPIE.

McDowell, jt. auth. see Martin.

McDowell, Banks. The Crisis in Insurance Regulation. LC 93-11891. 192p. 1994. text ed. 55.00 (0-89930-853-8, Quorum Bks) Greenwood.

— Deregulation & Competition in the Insurance Industry. LC 88-32391. 158p. 1989. text ed. 59.95 (0-89930-381-1, MDT/, Quorum Bks) Greenwood.

— Ethical Conduct & the Professional's Dilemma: Choosing Between Service & Success. LC 91-18. 208p. 1991. text ed. 42.95 (0-89930-596-2, MTJ, Quorum Bks) Greenwood.

McDowell, Bart. Inside the Vatican. Kogod, Charles M. & Newhouse, Elizabeth L., eds. (Illus.). 1991. 29.95 (0-87044-857-9); 41.95 (0-87044-858-7) Natl Geog.

McDowell, Bert, Jr. From Pilot to Poet. (Illus.). 160p. (Orig.). 1990. pap. 14.95 (0-89745-137-6) Sunflower U Pr.

McDowell, Betty L., jt. auth. see McDowell, W. Jack.

McDowell, Bonney, ed. see Marais, Marin.

McDowell, Bruce D. & Lemers, Andrew C., eds. Uses of Risk Analysis to Achieve Balanced Safety in Building Design an Operations. (Studies in Management of Building Technicians). 84p. (C). 1992. pap. text ed. 19.00 (0-309-04680-7) Natl Acad Pr.

McDowell, C. Forrest. Leisure Wellness Series. Incl. Introduction. 1983. 2.25 (0-942064-01-1); Concepts & Principles. 1.50 (0-942064-02-X); Intimate Relationships. 1983. 1.00 (0-942064-03-8); Identity & Social Roles. 1983. 1.75 (0-942064-04-6); Strategies for Fitness. 1983. 1.50 (0-942064-05-4); Assessing Your Leisurestyle & Formulating Strategies. 1983. 2.25 (0-942064-06-2); Coping Strategies & Managing Stress. 1983. 1.75 (0-942064-07-0); Managing Attitudes, Affirmation & Assertion. 1983. 2.00 (0-942064-08-9); Managing Economics, Time & Cultural Forces. 1983. 1.75 (0-942064-09-7); 1983. Set. 12.95 (0-942064-00-3); 1983. write for info. (0-318-57603-1) SunMoon Pr.

McDowell, Charles P. Criminal Justice: A Community Relations Approach. 462p. 1984. pap. 18.95 (0-685-42744-7) Pilgrimage Inc.

— Criminal Justice in the Community. 2nd ed. LC 92-70235. (Illus.). 482p. (C). 1993. pap. text ed. write for info. (0-87084-559-4) Anderson Pub Co.

McDowell, Charles P., ed. see Andrews, Paul M.

***McDowell, Colin.** The Designer Scam. (Illus.). 232p. 1995. 29.95 (0-09-177612-0, Pub. by Hutchnson UK) Trafalgar.

— Dressed to Kill: Sex, Power & Clothes. (Illus.). 192p. 1993. 29.95 (0-09-174464-4, Pub. by Hutchnson UK) Trafalgar.

— Hats: Five Centuries of Status, Style, & Glamour. (Illus.). 224p. 1992. 50.00 (0-8478-1572-2) Rizzoli Intl.

— Shoes: Fashion & Fantasy. LC 93-61542. (Illus.). 224p. 1994. pap. 24.95 (0-500-27755-9) Thames Hudson.

McDowell, D. & Weinkove, C. Multiple Choice Questions & Case Histories in Clinical Chemistry. LC 88-39149. 160p. 1989. text ed. 12.95 (0-7190-2241-X, Pub. by Manchester Univ Pr UK) St Martin.

McDowell, Daniele, tr. see Greimas, A. J.

McDowell, Danny B., jt. auth. see Mills, Larry W.

McDowell, David. Palestine & Israel: The Uprising & Beyond. 1990. 30.00 (0-520-06902-1) U CA Pr.

McDowell, David L. & Ellis, Rod, eds. Advances in Multiaxial Fatigue STP 1191. LC 93-11048. (Special Technical Publication Ser.). (Illus.). 465p. 1993. text ed. 108.00 (0-8031-1862-7, 04-011910-30) ASTM.

McDowell, Deborah, ed. see Larson, Nella.

McDowell, Deborah E. The Changing Same: Studies in Fiction by Black Women. LC 94-10663. Date not set. 29.95 (0-253-33629-5); pap. 12.95 (0-253-20926-9) Ind U Pr.

McDowell, Deborah E. & Rampersad, Arnold, eds. Slavery & the Literary Imagination. LC 88-45405. (Selected Papers from the English Institute; 1982-83, New Ser.: No. 13). 184p. 1989. reprint ed. pap. text ed. 12.95x (0-8018-3948-3) Johns Hopkins.

McDowell, Don. The Beat of the Drum: The History, People, & Events of Drum Barracks Wilmington, California. LC 92-75536. 320p. 1993. 29.95 (1-882824-02-4); pap. 19.95 (1-882824-03-2) Graphic Pubs.

***McDowell, Donald.** Dreams & Fantasy-Forever. 50p. 1995. pap. 6.95 (0-7610-0140-9) NW Pub.

***McDowell, Dottie.** Mom's Check-Up. 104p. 1994. student ed 14.95 (1-57326-019-3) Core Ministries.

McDowell, Dottie, jt. auth. see McDowell, Josh.

McDowell, Douglas S. Affirmative Action After the Johnson Decision: Practical Guidance for Planning & Compliance. 166p. 1988. 25.00 (0-916559-14-9) EPF.

— Alternative Dispute Resolution Techniques: Options & Guidelines to Meet Your Company's Needs. (Orig.). 1993. pap. 25.00 (0-916559-43-2) EPF.

— Can an Educated Workforce Be a "Business Necessity"? 33p. 1991. pap. 10.00 (0-614-06155-5, 2025-PP-4040) EPF.

— "Disparate Impact" & "Business Necessity" - an Assessment & Guidelines for the Civil Rights Debate. 68p. 1991. pap. 10.00 (0-614-06158-X, 2029-PP-4040) EPF.

McDowell, Douglas S., ed. The Civil Rights Act of 1991: Legislative History, 2 vols., Set. 1467p. (Orig.). 1992. pap. 120.00 (0-916559-40-8) EPF.

McDowell, Duncan. The Light: Brazilian Traction, Light & Power Co. Ltd., 1899-1945. (Illus.). 495p. (C). 1988. text ed. 39.95 (0-8020-5783-7) U of Toronto Pr.

McDowell, Earl E. Interviewing Practices for Technical Writers. (Technical Communications Ser.). 251p. 1991. text ed. 28.95 (0-89503-073-X); pap. text ed. 21.75 (0-89503-072-1) Baywood Pub.

McDowell, Elizabeth M., ed. Lung Carcinomas. LC 86-33361. (Current Problems in Tumor Pathology Ser.). (Illus.). 410p. 1987. text ed. 72.00 (0-443-03165-7) Churchill.

McDowell, Elizabeth M. & Beals, Theodore F. Biopsy Pathology of the Bronchi. (Illus.). 410p. 1987. text ed. 98.95 (0-03-012119-1) Saunders.

McDowell, Elizabeth V. Educational & Emotional Adjustments of Stuttering Children. LC 74-177022. (Columbia University. Teachers College. Contributions to Education Ser.: No. 314). reprint ed. 22.50 (0-404-55314-1) AMS Pr.

McDowell, Ernest. P-39 in Action. (Aircraft in Action Ser.). (Illus.). 50p. 1980. pap. 8.95 (0-89747-102-4) Squad Sig Pubns.

***McDowell, Ernest R.** Checkertails: The 325th Fighter Group in WW II. (Groups - Squadrons Ser.). (Illus.). 80p. 1994. pap. 10.95 (0-89747-316-7) Squad Sig Pubns.

— Flying Scoreboards: Aircraft Mission & Kill Markings. (Aircraft Specials Ser.). (Illus.). 64p. 1993. pap. 9.95 (0-89747-305-1) Squad Sig Pubns.

McDowell, Ernie. Forty-Ninth Fighter Group. (Fighter Groups - Squadrons Ser.). (Illus.). 64p. 1989. pap. 9.95 (0-89747-221-7, 6171) Squad Sig Pubns.

— FR-1 Fireball "Mini" in Action. (Mini in Action Ser.). (Illus.). 50p. 1995. pap. 5.95 (0-89747-344-2) Squad Sig Pubns.

McDowell, Ernie & Bowers, Peter. Triplanes. (MBI Ser.). (Illus.). 160p. 1992. pap. 19.95 (0-87938-614-2) Motorbooks Intl.

McDowell, Ernie & Greer, Don. B-25 Mitchell in Action. (Aircraft in Action Ser.). (Illus.). 50p. 1984. pap. 8.95 (0-89747-033-8, 1034) Squad Sig Pubns.

McDowell, Frederick P. Caroline Gordon. LC 66-64592. (University of Minnesota Pamphlets on American Writers Ser.: No. 59). 48p. (Orig.). reprint ed. pap. 25.00 (0-7837-2874-3, 2057581) Bks Demand.

— E. M. Forster. rev. ed. (English Authors Ser.). 192p. (C). 1982. text ed. 21.95 (0-8057-6817-3, Pub. by Royal Botanic Garden UK) Macmillan.

— Elizabeth Madox Roberts. (Twayne's United States Authors Ser.). 1963. pap. 13.95 (0-8084-0119-X, T38) NCUP.

— Ellen Glasgow & the Ironic Art of Fiction. 304p. 1962. pap. 6.95 (0-299-02114-9) U of Wis Pr.

— Ellen Glasgow & the Ironic Art of Fiction. LC 60-9551. 304p. reprint ed. pap. 86.70 (0-7837-7026-X, 2046841) Bks Demand.

McDowell, Frederick P., ed. E. M. Forster: An Annotated Bibliography of Writings about Him. LC 73-18797. (Annotated Secondary Bibliography Series on English Literature in Transition, 1880-1920). 924p. 1976. 30.00 (0-87580-046-7) N Ill U Pr.

— Poet As Critic. LC 67-12675. 127p. reprint ed. 36.20 (0-8357-9466-0, 2014767) Bks Demand.

McDowell, Gary L. Equity & the Constitution: The Supreme Court, Equitable Relief, & Public Policy. LC 81-16006. 168p. 1982. 20.00 (0-226-55814-2) U Ch Pr.

McDowell, Gary L. & Hickok, Eugene W., Jr. Justice vs. Law: The Courts in America. 300p. 1993. text ed. 24.95 (0-02-920529-8) Free Pr.

McDowell, George L. & Sokolik, Merle, trs. The Data of Euclid: Translated from the Text of Menge. LC 93-60045. (Illus.). 228p. (C). 1993. 40.00 (0-9635924-1-6); pap. 25.00 (0-9635924-0-8) Union Square.

McDowell, Gerald E. A Tail Gunner's Tale. 1991. 13.95 (0-533-09100-4) Vantage.

McDowell, Ian. The Reuters Handbook for Journalists. LC 92-5673. 1992. 39.95 (0-7506-0551-0) Buttrwrth-Heinemann.

Mcdowell, Ian & Newell, Claire. Measuring Health: Guide to Rating Scales & Questionnaires. (Illus.). 359p. 1987. 49.95 (0-19-504101-1) OUP.

McDowell, J. Como Preparar-Su Hijo-Decir No-Presiones Sexuale (How to Help Your Kids Say No to Sexual Pressure) (SPA.). Date not set. 4.99 (0-945792-39-5, 498403) Editorial Unilit.

— Cristianismo (Christianity) Historia O Farsa (Hoax Or History?) (SPA.). Date not set. 2.49 (0-685-74923-1, 498056) Editorial Unilit.

— La Mejor Forma De Resolver-Conflicto (Resolving Conflict) (SPA.). Date not set. 1.79 (1-56063-131-7, 497408) Editorial Unilit.

***McDowell, Jack.** Sports Illustrated Backpacking. 1989. pap. 9.95 (1-56800-064-2, Pub. by Sports Illus Bks) Natl Bk Netwk.

McDowell, Jack C. Power of Purpose: Your Pathway to Dynamic Living, Wealth, & Personal Success. 1993. pap. 14.95 (0-9625485-1-0) Epiphany GA.

***McDowell, James K. & Melsher, Kenneth J., eds.** Knowledge-Based Applications in Materials Science & Engineering: Proceedings of the Symposium of the ASM-MSD Computer Simulation Committee. LC 94-77799. 115p. 1994. pap. 36.00 (0-87339-238-8) Minerals Metals.

McDowell, Jennifer, ed. Black Politics: A Study & Annotated Bibliography of the Mississippi Freedom Democratic Party. LC 68-58320. 1971. pap. 6.95 (0-930142-02-0) Merlin Pr.

McDowell, Jennifer, jt. auth. see Loventhal, Milton.

McDowell, Jim. Peace Conspiracy: Yishiro Fujimura: Warrior-Businessman. 264p. (Orig.). 1993. pap. write for info. (0-9635944-0-0) McBo Corp Pubs.

McDowell, John. Mind & World. LC 93-44418. 201p. (C). 1994. text ed. 27.50 (0-674-57609-8, MCDMIN) HUP.

McDowell, John & Hostetler, Bob. The Love Killer. LC 93-25122. (J). (gr. 6 up). 1993. 8.99 (0-8499-3509-1) Word Pub.

McDowell, John, ed. see Evans, Gareth.

McDowell, John, tr. see Plato.

McDowell, John H. Sayings of the Ancestors: The Spiritual Life of the Sibundoy Indians. LC 89-5435. 216p. 1989. 24.00 (0-8131-1671-6) U Pr of Ky.

— So Wise Were Our Elders: Mythic Narratives from the Kamsa. LC 93-5083. 296p. 1994. text ed. 45.00 (0-8131-1826-3) U Pr of Ky.

McDowell, John P. Social Gospel in the South: The Woman's Home Mission Movement in the Methodist Episcopal Church, South, 1886-1939. LC 82-15292. x, 167p. (C). 1982. text ed. 27.50 (0-8071-1022-1) La State U Pr.

McDowell, Josh. Building Your Self-Image. 220p. 1986. 4.99 (0-8423-1395-8) Tyndale.

— Christianity: Hoax or History. 96p. 1989. pap. 2.99 (0-8423-0367-7) Tyndale.

— Con Todo Mi Amor, Papa (Love, Dad) (SPA.). 1992. 4.50 (1-56063-020-5, 490225) Editorial Unilit.

— Evidence That Demands a Verdict. Han, Paul et al, trs. 544p. (CHI.). 1993. pap. 13.00 (1-56582-011-8) Christ Renew Min.

— Evidencia Que Exige un Veredicto II: Evidence That Demands a Verdict II. (SPA.). 18.95 (84-7645-301-9, 223348, Pub. by Edit Clie SP) TSELF.

An Asterisk (*) at the beginning of an entry indicates that the title is appearing in BIP for the first time.

— El Factor De la Resurreccion: The Resurrection Factor. (SPA.). 6.50 (*84-7645-299-3*, 223369, Pub. by Edit Clie SP) TSELF.

— Guia Para Entender la Biblia: Guide to Understand the Bible. (SPA.). 6.95 (*84-7645-312-4*, 223450, Pub. by Edit Clie SP) TSELF.

— How to Be a Hero to Your Kids. 1993. pap. 10.99 (*0-8499-3826-0*) Word Inc.

— How To Help Your Child Say "No" to Sexual Pressure. 160p. 1987. pap. 8.99 (*0-8499-3093-6*) Word Inc.

— Influencia Paterna: Su Papel en la Educacion Sexual de los Hijos (The Dad Difference: Creating an Environment for Your Child's Sexual Wholeness) 202p. (Orig.). (SPA.). 1992. pap. 5.95 (*84-7645-559-3*, 223621, Pub. by Edit Clie SP) TSELF.

— Jesus: Una Defensa De la Deidad De: Jesus: A Defense of His Deity. (SPA.). 4.95 (*84-7645-277-2*, 223363, Pub. by Edit Clie SP) TSELF.

— Josh McDowell Answers Five Tough Questions. 1991. 16. 99 (*0-8423-7909-6*) Tyndale.

— Lo Que Deseo Que Mis Padres Sepan Acerca de Mi Sexualidad: Los Jovenes Hablan. Bruchez, Dardo, tr. 210p. (Orig.). (SPA.). 1988. pap. 4.95 (*0-945792-03-4*) Editorial Unilit.

— Love Dad. 1991. pap. 7.99 (*0-8499-3350-1*) Word Inc.

— Mas Que un Carpintero. 137p. 1978. 3.50 (*0-88113-203-9*) Edit Betania.

— More Than a Carpenter. 128p. 1980. pap. 3.99 (*0-8423-4552-3*) Tyndale.

— Motivo de Gozo y Alegria. 192p. (Orig.). (SPA.). 1990. pap. 4.95 (*0-88113-089-3*) Edit Betania.

— Por Que Esperar? Lo Que Deseo Padres... (Why Wait? What I Wish Parents Knew About...) (SPA.). Date not set. 5.99 (*0-8423-6523-0*, 498401) Editorial Unilit.

— Profecia: Hechos O Ficcion? Prophecy: Fact or Fiction? (SPA.). 5.50 (*84-7645-257-8*, 223290, Pub. by Edit Clie SP) TSELF.

— The Secret of Loving. (Living Bks.). 240p. reprint ed. 5.99 (*0-8423-5845-5*) Tyndale.

— El Secreto de Amar & de Ser Amado. Araujo, Juan S., tr. 272p. (SPA.). (C). 1988. pap. 5.95 (*0-88113-271-3*) Edit Betania.

— Sex, Guilt & Forgiveness. 1990. 2.99 (*0-8423-5908-7*, 725908-7) Tyndale.

— Skeptics Who Demanded a Verdict. 96p. 2.99 (*0-8423-5925-7*) Tyndale.

— Thirteen Things You Gotta Know to Keep Your Love Life Alive & Well. 1994. pap. 5.99 (*0-8499-3534-2*) Word Inc.

— Under Siege. 192p. (J). 1992. pap. 8.99 (*0-8499-3363-3*) Word Inc.

McDowell, Josh & Hostetler, Bob. Don't Check Your Brains at the Door. (YA). (gr. 7 up). 1992. pap. write for info. (*0-8499-3234-3*) Word Inc.

— Right from Wrong: What You Need to Know to Help Youth Make the Right Choices. LC 94-27539. 1994. 19. 99 (*0-8499-1079-X*); pap. 14.99 (*0-8499-3604-7*) Word Inc.

— Thirteen Things You Gotta Know: To Make It As a Christian. LC 92-33490. (YA). 1992. 4.99 (*0-8499-3413-3*) Word Pub.

— The Truth Slayers: A Battle of Right from Wrong. LC 94-47961. (J). 1995. write for info. (*0-8499-3662-4*) Word Pub.

McDowell, Josh & Jones, Bill. Teenage Q & A Book. 160p. 1990. pap. write for info. (*0-8499-3232-7*) Word Inc.

McDowell, Josh & Lewis, Paul. Givers, Takers & Other Kinds of Lovers. 1981. pap. 3.99 (*0-8423-1031-2*) Tyndale.

— Las Tres Caras Del Amor. 96p. 1983. 3.50 (*0-88113-289-6*) Edit Betania.

McDowell, Josh & McDowell, Dottie. Katie's Adventure at Blueberry Pond. LC 88-14039. (Illus.). 32p. (J). (ps-2). 1988. 8.99 (*1-55513-598-6*, Chariot Bks) Chariot Family.

— Pizza for Everyone. LC 88-14041. (Illus.). 32p. (J). (ps-2). 1988. 8.99 (*1-55513-596-X*, Chariot Bks) Chariot Family.

McDowell, Josh & Stewart, Don. Answers. 256p. (Orig.). 1986. 4.99 (*0-8423-0021-X*) Tyndale.

— Demons, Witches & the Occult. abr. ed. (Pocket Guides Ser.). 96p. 1986. 2.99 (*0-8423-0541-6*) Tyndale.

— Ocultismo: Fraude o Realidad? 178p. (SPA.). 1988. pap. write for info. (*0-318-63980-7*) Life Pubs Intl.

— Reasons. (Living Bks.). 256p. 1986. 4.99 (*0-8423-5287-2*) Tyndale.

— Respuestas a Preguntas Dificles. 216p. (SPA.). 1986. 5.95 (*0-8297-0689-5*) Life Pubs Intl.

McDowell, Josh & Wakefield, Norm. Friend of the Lonely Heart. 1991. pap. write for info. (*0-8499-3233-5*) Word Inc.

McDowell, Judith A. & Lyon, Jim. British Columbia: Land of Rich Diversity. (Canadian Enterprise Ser.). 144p. 1991. 32.95 (*0-89781-371-5*) Preferred Mktg.

McDowell, Judith H., tr. see Rousseau, Jean-Jacques.

McDowell, Lee R. Minerals in Animal & Human Nutrition: Comparative Aspects to Human Nutrition. Cunha, Tony J., ed. (Animal Feeding & Nutrition Ser.). (Illus.). 524p. (C). 1992. text ed. 99.00 (*0-12-483369-1*) Acad Pr.

— Vitamins in Animal Nutrition: Comparative Aspects to Human Nutrition. Cunha, Tony J., ed. (Animal Feeding & Nutrition Ser.). 486p. 1989. text ed. 88.00 (*0-12-483372-1*) Acad Pr.

McDowell, Lee R., ed. Nutrition of Grazing Ruminants in Warm Climates. (Animal Feeding & Nutrition Ser.). 1985. text ed. 115.00 (*0-12-483370-5*) Acad Pr.

McDowell, Linda, jt. auth. see Allen, John.

McDowell, Margaret & Trottier, Maxine. The Big Heart. (Illus.). 32p. (J). (ps-2). 1991. pap. 29.50 (*1-55037-186-X*, Pub. by Annick CN) Firefly Bks Ltd.

McDowell, Margaret B. Carson McCullers. (United States Authors Ser.: No. 354). 160p. 1980. text ed. 20.95 (*0-8057-7297-9*, Twayne) Macmillan.

— Edith Wharton. rev. ed. (Twayne's United States Authors Ser.). 168p. 1990. text ed. 20.95 (*0-8057-7618-4*, TUSAS 265, Pub. by Royal Botanic Garden UK) Macmillan.

McDowell, Martin R., jt. auth. see Bransden, Brian H.

McDowell, Michael. Clue. 1986. pap. 2.95 (*0-449-13049-5*) Fawcett.

— Toplin. (Illus.). 186p. 1985. lib. bdg. 22.50 (*0-910489-11-4*) Scream Pr.

McDowell, Mildred. The Little People. LC 72-133255. (Story & Its Verse Ser.). (Illus.). 44p. (J). (gr. 1-2). 1971. 2.50 (*0-87884-002-8*) Unicorn Ent.

— The Squirrel & the Frog. LC 76-133256. (Story & Its Verse Ser.). (Illus.). 44p. (J). (gr. 1-2). 1971. 2.50 (*0-87884-007-9*) Unicorn Ent.

McDowell, N. Hemingway. (Life & Works). (Illus.). (J). (gr. 7 up). 1989. 14.95 (*0-685-58634-0*); lib. bdg. 19.94 (*0-86592-298-5*) Rourke Corp.

McDowell, Nancy. The Mundugumor: From the Field Notes of Margaret Mead & Reo Fortune. LC 90-24915. (Ethnographic Inquiry Ser.). (Illus.). 352p. (C). 1991. text ed. 45.00 (*1-56098-062-1*) Smithsonian.

McDowell, Patricia. Daughter of the Boyne. 221p. 1993. pap. 13.95 (*0-86327-349-1*, Pub. by Wolfhound Pr IE) Dufour.

McDowell, Peggy & Meyer, Richard. The Revival Styles in American Memorial Art. LC 93-72851. (Illus.). 1994. 49.95 (*0-87972-633-4*); pap. 22.95 (*0-87972-634-2*) Bowling Green Univ.

McDowell, Philip. Choosing & Using Four Bit Microcontrollers. LC 93-15660. 246p. 1993. 75.00 (*0-8247-9153-3*) Dekker.

McDowell, R. Bruce. Evolution of the Winchester. Suydam, Charles R. & Hoyem, George A., eds. LC 85-72662. (Illus.). 200p. 1985. 37.95 (*0-9604982-4-9*) Armory Pubns.

McDowell, R. E. Dairying with Improved Breeds in Warm Climates. LC 93-81317. (Illus.). 10p. (C). 1994. pap. text ed. 19.00 (*1-880762-05-6*) Kinnic Pubs.

— A Partnership for Humans & Animals. vii, 95p. 1991. pap. text ed. 10.00 (*1-880762-03-X*) Kinnic Pubs.

McDowell, Ray. Por Que Esperar? Lo Que Usted Necesita Saber... (Why Wait? What You Need to Know about Teen Sex) (SPA.). 1990. 12.99 (*0-945792-48-4*, 498402) Editorial Unilit.

***McDowell, Robert.** The Diviners: A Book Length Poem. 108p. 1995. 18.00 (*1-885266-19-7*, Pub. by Peterloo Poets UK); pap. 10.00 (*1-885266-10-3*, Pub. by Peterloo Poets UK) Story Line.

— Quiet Money. 90p. 1987. pap. 9.95 (*0-685-70162-X*) Story Line.

McDowell, Robert, ed. Poetry after Modernism. (New Criticism Ser.). 376p. 1991. 24.95 (*0-934257-36-1*); pap. 15.95 (*0-934257-35-3*) Story Line.

McDowell, Robert, jt. auth. see Lavitt, Edward.

McDowell, Robert, tr. see Pavel, Ota.

McDowell, Robert, ed. see Valvano, James T.

McDowell, Robert B. Ireland in the Age of Imperialism & Revolution, 1760-1801. 750p. 1991. reprint ed. pap. 39. 95 (*0-19-822167-3*) OUP.

— The Irish Administration, 1801-1914. LC 75-35336. 328p. 1976. reprint ed. text ed. 65.00 (*0-8371-8561-0*, MCIA, Greenwood Pr) Greenwood.

McDowell, Robert B., ed. see Burke, Edmund E.

McDowell, Robert E. & Lavitt, Edward, eds. Third World Voices for Children. LC 71-169091. (Odarkai Book Ser.). (Illus.). 156p. (J). (gr. 5-9). 1981. 7.95 (*0-89388-020-5*, Odakai) Okpaku Communications.

McDowell, Robert E., et al. Asia-Pacific Literatures in English: Bibliographies. LC 78-62030. (Illus.). (Orig.). 1978. 26.00 (*0-89410-072-6*); pap. 15.00 (*0-89410-073-4*) Three Continents.

McDowell, Robert H., jt. auth. see Gillman, Leonard.

McDowell, Roddy. Double Exposure: A Gallery of the Celebrated with Commentary by the Equally Celebrated. (Illus.). 272p. 1991. 49.50 (*0-688-10062-7*) Morrow.

— Double Exposure, Take Two: A Gallery of the Celebrated with Commentary by the Equally Celebrated. (Illus.). 272p. 1989. 64.50 (*0-688-08464-8*) Morrow.

McDowell, Ruth, jt. auth. see Engelhardt, Carolyn H.

McDowell, Ruth B. Pattern on Pattern: Stunning Quilts from Simple Traditional Blocks. LC 90-29178. (Illus.). 160p. (Orig.). 1991. pap. 21.95 (*0-913327-31-X*) Quilt Digest Pr.

— Symmetry: A Design System for Quiltmakers. Nadel, Harold & Kuhn, Barbara K., eds. LC 93-40036. (Illus.). 114p. (Orig.). 1994. pap. 21.95 (*0-914881-78-7*) C & T Pub.

***McDowell, Stephen K.** In God We Trust: A Tour Guide for America's Christian Landmarks of Liberty. 108p. 1988. pap. 6.95 (*1-887456-03-1*) Providence Found.

***McDowell, Stephen K. & Beliles, Mark A.** Liberating the Nations: Biblical Principles of Government, Education, Economics, & Politics. 215p. 1993. pap. 11.95 (*1-887456-01-5*) Providence Found.

McDowell, Stephen K., jt. auth. see Beliles, Mark A.

McDowell, Steve, jt. auth. see Brewer, Bob.

McDowell, Stewar. Demonios, Brujeria, Ocultismo (Demons, Witches & the Occult) (SPA.). Date not set. 2.49 (*0-945792-72-7*, 498045) Editorial Unilit.

McDowell, W. H. The History of BBC Broadcasting in Scotland, 1923-1983. 376p. 1992. text ed. 79.00 (*0-7486-0376-X*, Pub. by Edinburgh U Pr UK) Col U Pr.

***McDowell, W. J.** The Incomparable Book. 13p. 1988. pap. 1.00 (*0-85151-543-6*) Banner of Truth.

McDowell, W. Jack & McDowell, Betty L. Liquid Scintillation Alpha Spectrometry. LC 93-8546. 160p. 1993. 69.95 (*0-8493-5288-6*) CRC Pr.

McDowell, William L., Jr., ed. Documents Relating to Indian Affairs 1750-1754. 592p. 1992. pap. text ed. write for info. (*1-880067-08-0*) SC Dept of Arch & Hist.

— Documents Relating to Indian Affairs 1754-1765. 657p. 1992. pap. text ed. write for info. (*1-880067-09-9*) SC Dept of Arch & Hist.

— Journals of the Commissioners of the Indian Trade 1710-1718. 368p. 1992. pap. text ed. write for info. (*1-880067-10-2*) SC Dept of Arch & Hist.

McDowelle, James O., jt. auth. see Miller, Patricia S.

McDuell, B. Examining GCSE Chemistry. (C). 1989. text ed. 80.00 (*0-09-164631-6*, Pub. by S Thornes Pubs UK) St Mut.

— Science Now: Chemicals on the Farm. (C). 1990. 40.00 (*0-7487-0212-1*, Pub. by S Thornes Pubs UK) St Mut.

— Science Now: Metals & Corrosion. (C). 1985. 30.00 (*0-7487-0211-3*, Pub. by S Thornes Pubs UK) St Mut.

— Science Now: Plastics a Plenty. (C). 1990. 30.00 (*0-7487-0210-5*, Pub. by S Thornes Pubs UK) St Mut.

McDuff, David, ed. Ice Around Our Lips. LC 88-51313. 208p. 1988. pap. 19.95 (*1-85224-011-3*, Pub. by Bloodaxe Bks UK) Dufour.

McDuff, David, tr. see Agren, Gosta.

McDuff, David, ed. see Babel, Isaac.

McDuff, David, tr. see Dostoyevsky, Fyodor.

McDuff, David, tr. see Forsstrom, Tua.

McDuff, David, tr. see Lonn, Oystein.

McDuff, David, tr. see Ratushinkaya, Irina.

McDuff, David, tr. see Ratushinskaya, Irina.

McDuff, David, tr. see Sodergran, Edith.

McDuff, David, tr. see Tolstoy, Leo.

McDuff, David, tr. see Tsvetayeva, Marina.

***McDuff, Dusa & Salamon, Dietmar.** J-Holomorphic Curves & Quantum Cohomology. LC 94-25414. (University Lectures: Vol. 6). 207p. 1994. pap. 42.00 (*0-8218-0332-8*) Am Math.

McDuff, G., jt. ed. see Burkes, T. R.

McDuff, G. G. Pulse Power for Lasers Three, Vol. 1411. 1991. 53.00 (*0-8194-0501-9*) SPIE.

McDuff, Judith, tr. see Yeh, Ning.

McDuff, Wilbur S., jt. auth. see Maloy, Richard H.

McDuffee, Franklin. Church Records of Rochester, New Hampshire. 52p. 1984. pap. 6.50 (*0-912606-21-5*) Hunterdon Hse.

— Church Records of Rochester, NH. 1986. reprint ed. pap. 6.50 (*0-935207-61-9*) Danbury Hse Bks.

— History of Rochester from 1722 to 1890, Vol. One. Hayward, Silvanus, ed. (Illus.). 378p. 1988. reprint ed. lib. bdg. 39.50 (*0-8328-0069-4*, NH0051) Higginson Bk Co.

— History of Rochester, New Hampshire, from 1722 to 1890, Vol. Two. Hayward, Silvanus, ed. (Illus.). 327p. 1988. reprint ed. lib. bdg. 33.50 (*0-8328-0070-8*, NH0052) Higginson Bk Co.

— History of the Town of Rochester, New Hampshire 1722-1890. Hayward, Silvanus, ed. LC 88-61833. (Illus.). 758p. 1989. reprint ed. 60.00 (*0-89725-071-0*) Picton Pr.

McDuffee, Mary A., jt. ed. see Soreff, Stephen M.

McDuffie, et al. Deathlok, No. 3. 48p. 1990. 3.95 (*0-87135-678-3*) Marvel Entmnt.

— Deathlok, No. 1. 48p. 1990. 3.95 (*0-87135-668-6*) Marvel Entmnt.

— Deathlok, No. 2. 48p. 1990. 3.95 (*0-87135-677-5*) Marvel Entmnt.

— Deathlok, No. 4. 48p. 1990. 3.95 (*0-87135-679-1*) Marvel Entmnt.

— She Hulk Ceremony, Pt. I. 48p. 1990. 3.95 (*0-87135-632-5*) Marvel Entmnt.

— She Hulk Ceremony, Pt. II. 48p. 1990. 3.95 (*0-87135-633-3*) Marvel Entmnt.

McDuffie, Dwayne. Prince: Alter Ego. Clark, Margaret, ed. 32p. 1991. pap. 2.00 (*1-56389-058-5*, Piranha Pr) DC Comics.

McDuffie, Harriet E., et al. Transitions. 416p. 1994. per. 34. 95 (*0-8403-9019-X*) Kendall-Hunt.

McDuffie, Helen H., et al, eds. Human Sustainability in Agriculture: Health, Safety, Environment. LC 93-33021. 1994. write for info. (*0-87371-617-5*, RC965) Lewis Pubs.

McDuffie, Merrilee T. QuickCalc: Med Dose Calculations. LC 93-39298. (C). 1994. pap. text ed. 24.75 (*0-8053-1366-4*) Benjamin-Cummings.

McDuffie, Norton G. Bioreactor Design Fundamentals. 137p. 1991. text ed. 42.95 (*0-7506-9107-7*) Buttrwrth-Heinemann.

McDunn, Mark, jt. auth. see Severson, Paul.

McDyer, James. The Island of the Setting Sun. 1989. pap. 15.00 (*0-86217-227-6*, Pub. by Veritas IE) St Mut.

McDysan, David, jt. auth. see Spohn, Darren L.

McEachern, A. W. Organizational Illusions. LC 84-51382. (Illus.). 200p. 1984. 25.00 (*0-930237-00-5*); pap. 12.50 (*0-930237-01-3*) Shale Bks.

McEachern, Alton H. Layman's Bible Book Commentary: Psalms, Vol. 8. LC 79-56593. 1991. 8.99 (*0-8054-1178-X*) Broadman.

McEachern, Doug. A Class Against Itself: Power & the Nationalisation of the British Steel Industry. LC 79-41766. 239p. reprint ed. pap. 68.20 (*0-318-34822-5*, 2031689) Bks Demand.

McEachern, Douglas. Economics: A Contemporary Introduction. 3rd ed. (C). 1994. text ed. 57.95 (*0-538-82849-8*, HB83CA) S-W Pub.

— The Expanding State: Class & Economy in Europe since 1945. LC 90-31758. 241p. 1990. text ed. 45.00 (*0-312-04652-9*) St Martin.

McEachern, George R. Growing Fruits, Berries, & Nuts in the South. 2nd ed. (Illus.). 100p. 1989. pap. 12.95 (*0-88415-040-2*) Gulf Pub.

McEachern, John & Towle, Edward. Ecological Guidelines for Island Development. 65p. 1974. 7.50 (*0-318-14613-4*) Isl Resources.

McEachern, Michael. A Color Guide to Corn Snakes Captive-Bred in the U. S. 48p. 1992. pap. text ed. 8.50 (*1-882770-15-3*) Adv Vivarium.

— The Keeping & Breeding of Corn Snakes. 60p. 1991. pap. text ed. 8.50 (*1-882770-16-1*) Adv Vivarium.

McEachern, Robert. Human & Machine Intelligence: An Evolutionary View. Parker, Diane, ed. LC 92-56391. 260p. 1993. pap. 17.95 (*0-88247-956-3*, 956) R & E Pubs.

McEachrane, Helen, jt. auth. see Idone, Christopher.

McEachron, D. L., ed. Functional Mapping in Biology & Medicine: Computer Assisted Autoradiography. (Experimental Biology & Medicine Ser.: Vol. 11). (Illus.). viii, 280p. 1987. 207.25 (*3-8055-4325-5*) S Karger.

McEachron-Hirsch, Gail, ed. Student Self-Esteem: Integrating the Self. LC 93-60638. 440p. 1993. text ed. 39.00 (*1-56676-031-3*) Technomic.

McEathron, Margaret & Holmes, Fenwicke. I Am Two Men. LC 80-15442. 1983. pap. 14.95 (*0-87949-190-6*) Ashley Bks.

McEdward, Larry R., ed. Ecology of Marine Invertebrate Larvae. 480p. 1995. 99.95 (*0-8493-8046-4*, 8046) CRC Pr.

McElderry, Bruce R., Jr. Thomas Wolfe. (United States Authors Ser.: No. 50). 208p. 1965. text ed. 20.95 (*0-8057-0833-2*, Pub. by Royal Botanic Garden UK) Macmillan.

McElderry, Bruce R., Jr., ed. see Shelley, Percy Bysshe.

Mcelderry, Hilary. Multiplication Tables & Coloring Book. 1993. pap. 7.95 (*0-906212-85-5*, Pub. by Tarquin UK) Parkwest Pubns.

***McElderry, Mona.** Out of the Bulrushes: A Tale of Romanian Adoptions. (Orig.). 1995. pap. 16.95 (*0-9641573-1-4*) Sisu Pr.

— To Seek His Fortune. LC 96-66997. (Illus.). 64p. 1994. 10.00 (*0-9641573-0-6*) Sisu Pr.

McEldowney, B. A., jt. ed. see Hench, Larry L.

McEldowney, Eugene. A Kind of Homecoming. 256p. 1994. 20.95 (*0-312-11016-2*) St Martin.

McEldowney, J. & O'Higgins, R., eds. The Common Law Tradition: Essays in Legal History Irish. 220p. 1989. 39. 50 (*0-7165-2397-3*, Pub. by Irish Acad Pr IE) Intl Spec Bk.

McEldowney, John & Hancher, Leigh. Electricity Industry Handbook: Law & Practice. 454p. 1993. text ed. 150.00 (*0-471-93668-5*, Pub. by Wiley Chancery Law UK) Wiley.

McEldowney, John, jt. auth. see Lomas, Owen.

McEldowney, Sharron, et al. Pollution: Ecology & Biotreatment. LC 92-36776. 1993. write for info. (*0-582-08655-8*) Longman.

McElfish, James M., Jr. & Beier, Ann E. Environmental Regulation of Coal Mining: SMCRA's Second Decade. 282p. 1990. pap. 28.00 (*0-911937-35-8*) Environ Law Inst.

McElfresh, Adeline. Jill Nolan, R.N. (Inflation Fighter Ser.). 160p. 1982. pap. 1.25 (*0-8439-1069-0*) Dorchester Pub Co.

***McElfresh, Andrew J., et al.** Romac Report: Restaurant Guide to Philadelphia. 256p. (Orig.). 1994. pap. 9.95 (*0-9644383-0-5*) Romac Report.

McElfresh, Beth. Chuck Wagon Cookbook. LC 60-8068. 75p. 1960. pap. 6.95 (*0-8040-0042-5*) Swallow.

McElfresh, Patricia M. Scottsdale: Jewel in the Desert. LC 84-19605. (Illus.). 136p. 1988. 22.95 (*0-89781-105-4*) Preferred Mktg.

McElhaney, James W., intro. Classics of the Courtroom, Vol. XIV: Highlights from the Direct & Cross-Examination of Richard Hauptmann in the State of New Jersey vs. Hauptmann. 326p. 1988. pap. 20.00 (*0-943380-20-0*) PEG MN.

— Classics of the Courtroom Vol. XXIV: Pennzoil vs. Texaco, Inc. 55p. 1992. pap. 12.00 (*0-943380-30-8*) PEG MN.

— Classics of the Courtroom, Vol. XII: Vincent Fuller's Summation in U. S. vs. Hinckley. 54p. 1988. pap. 12.00 (*0-943380-18-9*) PEG MN.

— Classics of the Courtroom, Vol. XIX: Daniel K. Webb's Direct Examination of Oliver North & Summation in U. S. vs. John M. Poindexter. 348p. 1991. pap. 20.00 (*0-943380-25-1*) PEG MN.

— Classics of the Courtroom, Vol. XVI: Ulysses in Court: the Litigation Surrounding the First Publication of James Joyce's Novel in the United States. 68p. 1988. pap. 12. 00 (*0-943380-22-7*) PEG MN.

— Classics of the Courtroom, Vol. XXII: Clarence Darrow's Summation in People vs. Henry Sweet (1926) 42p. 1992. pap. 12.00 (*0-943380-28-6*) PEG MN.

McElhaney, Judy. Ghost Stories of Woodlawn Plantation. LC 92-12007. (Illus.). 1992. pap. 8.95 (*0-939009-64-1*) EPM Pubns.

McElheny, Kenneth R., jt. ed. see Moffett, James.

McElheny, Victor K. & Abrahamson, Seymour, eds. Assessing Chemical Mutagens: The Risk to Humans. LC 79-998. (Banbury Report Ser.: No. 1). (Illus.). 367p. 1979. 44.00 (*0-87969-200-6*) Cold Spring Harbor.

McElheran, Brock. Conducting Technique for Beginners & Professionals. rev. ed. 148p. 1989. pap. 8.95 (*0-19-385830-4*) OUP.

McElherton, Paul, jt. auth. see Mirams, Mike.

***McElhiney, Annette, et al.** Women's Studies: Thinking Women. 608p. (C). 1994. per., pap. text ed. 38.95 (*0-8403-9583-3*) Kendall-Hunt.

McElhiney, Paul T. Transportation for Marketing & Business Students. (Quality Paperback Ser.: No. 290). 232p. (Orig.). 1975. pap. 9.95 (*0-8226-0290-3*) Littlefield.

McElhinney, Thomas K. Human Values Teaching Programs for Health Professionals. LC 81-11599. 200p. 1981. 12. 95 (*0-87426-051-5*) Whitmore.

M

McElhinny, M. W. & Valencio, D. A. Paleoreconstruction of the Continents. (Geodynamics Ser.: Vol. 2). 194p. 1981. 20.00 (*0-87590-511-0*) Am Geophysical.

McElhinny, Michael W., jt. ed. see Lock, J.

McElhinny, Michael W., et al. Global Reconstruction & the Geomagnetic Field During the Palaeozoic. 1981. lib. bdg. 77.50 (*90-277-1231-X*) Kluwer Ac.

McElhoes, Patrick W. Little Things. Scurlock-Koole, Joan, ed. 128p. 1994. per. 15.95 (*1-882188-07-1*) Magnolia Mktg.

***McElhone, Alice P. & Butler, Edward B. Mail It! High Impact Business Mail: From Input to In-Basket. (Illus.). 250p. (Orig.). 1995. pap. write for info. (*0-9647121-0-5*) Benchmark CT. MAIL IT! HIGH-IMPACT BUSINESS MAIL is a guide for small businesses, non-profit organizations & corporate departments that describes in easy-to-understand language how to use a desktop computer to generate revenue through the mail. These five sections of the book cover most forms of business correspondence from the formal letter to a beginner's desktop marketing kit. DESIGN: simple guidelines for designing more effective business communications. These easy tips will point you in the right direction for improving your organization's professional image. DESKTOP MARKETING: tips for developing a beginner's marketing kit; expert advice & examples of marketing communications from some well-known corporations. PRODUCTION: concepts about the PC as a business mail production machine & producing P.C. (Postally Correct) business mail. DELIVERY: accurate information on how you can meet the U.S. Postal Service half way to give your mail the swiftest, surest route through the system. REFERENCE: a brief refresher course on personal computing; step-by-step examples of a personal mailing list manager in action, & useful facts related to each of the four major topics. The book is sponsored by Pitney Bowes, the recognized leader in the business mail field. For ordering information, call Benchmark Publications, Inc., at 203-966-6653 or FAX to: 203-972-7129.**

Publisher Provided Annotation.

McEliece, Robert J. Finite Fields for Computer Scientists & Engineers. 1986. lib. bdg. 72.00 (*0-89838-191-6*) Kluwer Ac.

— Introduction to Discrete Math. 1989. text ed. write for info. (*0-07-557015-7*) McGraw.

McEliece, Robert J. & Ash, Robert B. Introduction to Discrete Mathematics. 500p. (C). 1988. text ed. 27.50 (*0-317-58264-X*) Random.

McEligot, D. M., ed. Gas Turbine Heat Transfer - 1993. (HTD Ser.: Vol. 242). 68p. 1993. 30.00 (*0-7918-1155-7*, G00799) ASME.

McEllhenney, John G., et al, eds. United Methodism in America: A Compact History. 160p. (Orig.). 1992. pap. 8.95 (*0-687-43170-0*) Abingdon.

McElligott, Arlene F. & McElligott, Joseph P. The Catholic Elementary School Extension Program. 33p. 1986. 5.30 (*0-318-20576-9*) Natl Cath Educ.

McElligott, David, jt. auth. see Cofer, Rebecca.

McElligott, Joseph P., jt. auth. see McElligott, Arlene F.

***McElligott, Ken.** Bartending & Cocktail Serving: A Complete Course. (Illus.). 120p. 1994. ring bd. 29.95 (*0-9618067-0-2*) McElligott Ent.

McElligott, Mary E., ed. Transactions of the Illinois State Historical Society: Selected Papers from the Seventh Annual History Symposium & the Eighth Annual History Symposium. LC 89-28563. 90p. 1989. pap. 12.50 (*0-912226-25-0*) Ill St Hist Soc.

McElligott, Mary E. & O'Neal, Patrick H., eds. Transactions of the Illinois State Historical Society: Selected Papers from the Fifth & Sixth Illinois History Symposium of the Illinois State Historical Society. LC 89-28563. 132p. (Orig.). 1988. pap. text ed. 12.50 (*0-912226-21-8*) Ill St Hist Soc.

McElliott, Kim, jt. auth. see Teel, Rhonda.

McElliott, Kimberly, jt. auth. see Teel, Rhonda.

McElmeel, Sharron L. ABCs of an Author-Illustrator Visit. (Professional Growth Ser.). 100p. 1994. 29.95 (*0-938865-33-1*) Linworth Pub.

— Adventures with Social Studies (Through Literature) 275p. 1991. pap. text ed. 23.50 (*0-87287-828-7*) Teacher Ideas Pr.

— An Author a Month (for Dimes) (Illus.). 175p. (Orig.). 1993. pap. text ed. 23.50 (*0-87287-952-6*) Teacher Ideas Pr.

— An Author a Month (for Nickels) (Illus.). 172p. 1990. pap. text ed. 24.00 (*0-87287-827-9*) Libs Unl.

— An Author a Month (for Pennies) (Illus.). 224p. 1988. pap. text ed. 24.50 (*0-87287-661-6*) Libs Unl.

— Authors for Children: A Calendar. 1992. 10.00 (*0-931510-43-0*) Hi Willow.

— Book People: A First Album. (Illus.). 176p. 1990. pap. text ed. 19.00 (*0-87287-720-5*) Teacher Ideas Pr.

— Book People: A Second Album. (Illus.). 200p. 1990. pap. text ed. 20.00 (*0-87287-721-3*) Teacher Ideas Pr.

— Bookpeople: A Multicultural Album. LC 92-13252. (Illus.). 1992. pap. text ed. 23.50 (*0-87287-953-4*) Teacher Ideas Pr.

— Educator's Companion to Children's Literature Vol. 1: Mysteries, Animal Tales, Books of Humor, Adventure Stories, & Historical Fiction. LC 95-11608. (Illus.). 200p. 1995. pap. text ed. 23.50 (*1-56308-329-9*) Teacher Ideas Pr.

— Educator's Companion to Children's Literature Vol. 2: Folklore, Contemporary Realistic Fiction, Fantasy, Biographies, & Tales from Here & There. (Illus.). 200p. 1996. pap. text ed. 24.00 (*1-56308-330-2*) Teacher Ideas Pr.

— Great New Nonfiction Reads. (Illus.). 200p. 1995. pap. text ed. 21.00 (*1-56308-228-4*) Teacher Ideas Pr.

— The Latest & Greatest Read-Alouds. (Illus.). 200p. 1994. pap. text ed. 18.50 (*1-56308-140-7*) Libs Unl.

— McElmeel Booknotes: Literature Across the Curriculum. (Illus.). 200p. (Orig.). 1993. pap. 21.00 (*0-87287-951-8*) Teacher Ideas Pr.

— My Bag of Book Tricks. 200p. 1989. pap. text ed. 24.50 (*0-87287-722-1*) Libs Unl.

Mcelmeel, Sharron L. The Poet Tree. LC 93-20268. (Illus.). 180p. 1993. pap. text ed. 23.50 (*1-56308-102-4*) Teacher Ideas Pr.

McElmurray, Mary A. Trivial Pursuit - Language Arts (Jr. High) (Illus.). 64p. (J). (gr. 7-9). 1992. 12.95 (*0-86653-650-7*, GA1384) Good Apple.

***McElmurry, Beverly J. & Parker, Randy S., eds.** Annual Review of Women's Health, Vol. I. 1993. pap. 37.95 (*0-88737-598-7*) Natl League Nurse.

— Annual Review of Women's Health, Vol. II. 1995. pap. 37.95 (*0-88737-636-3*) Natl League Nurse.

McElmurry, Beverly J., et al, eds. Women's Health & Development: Global Perspective. 400p. 1993. boxed 46.25 (*0-86720-799-X*) Jones & Bartlett.

McElmurry, Mary A. Appreciating. (Illus.). 64p. (J). (gr. 2-8). 1983. student ed 8.95 (*0-9607366-1-1*, GA 493) Good Apple.

— Belonging. (Illus.). 64p. (J). (gr. 2-8). 1983. student ed 8.95 (*0-9607366-0-3*, GA 492) Good Apple.

— Caring. 64p. (J). (gr. 4-8). 1981. 8.95 (*0-86653-052-5*, GA275) Good Apple.

— Cooperating. 64p. (J). (gr. 3-8). 1985. student ed 8.95 (*0-86653-334-6*, GA 680) Good Apple.

McElmurry, Mary Anne. Feelings. 80p. (J). (gr. 3-8). 1981. 9.95 (*0-86653-027-4*, GA 276) Good Apple.

McElrath, Clifford. On Santa Cruz Island. 128p. (Orig.). 1993. pap. 12.95 (*0-9634635-3-5*) Caractacus.

McElrath, Dale & Finney, Fred A. The McLean Site. (American Bottom Archaeology Ser.: Selected FAI-270 Site Reports: Vol. 14). (Illus.). 152p. 1986. pap. 15.95 (*0-252-01076-0*) U of Ill Pr.

McElrath, Dale L. & Finney, Fred A. The George Reeves (11-S-650) Site: Late Archaic, Late Woodland, Emergent Mississippian, & Mississippian Components. (American Bottom Archaeology Ser.: Selected FAI-270 Site Reports: Vol. 15). (Illus.). 464p. 1987. pap. 25.95 (*0-252-01077-9*) U of Ill Pr.

McElrath, Dale L. & Fortier, Andrew C. The Missouri Pacific Number 2 (11-S-46) Site: A Late Archaic Occupation. LC 83-8156. (American Bottom Archaeology Ser.: Selected FAI-270 Site Reports: Vol. 3). (Illus.). 272p. 1983. pap. 14.95 (*0-252-01065-5*) U of Ill Pr.

McElrath, J. Frank Norris Revisited. (Twayne's United States Authors Ser.). 150p. 1992. text ed. 21.95 (*0-8057-3965-3*, Pub. by Royal Botanic Garden UK) Macmillan.

McElrath, Joseph R., Jr. Frank Norris: A Descriptive Bibliography. LC 92-7198. (Series in Bibliography). (Illus.). 376p. (C). 1992. text ed. 120.00 (*0-8229-3712-3*) U of Pittsburgh Pr.

— Walden Notes. 1971. pap. 3.95 (*0-8220-1358-4*) Cliffs.

McElrath, Karen, jt. ed. see Inciardi, James A.

McElrath, Roger G. Trade Unions & the Industrial Relations Climate in Spain. LC 88-83384. (Multinational Industrial Relations Ser.: No. 10). 192p. 1989. pap. 25.00 (*0-89546-074-2*) U PA Wharton Ctr Human Resc.

McElrath, Ruth G., tr. see McElrath, William N.

McElrath, William N. Bible Dictionary for Young Readers. LC 65-15604. (Illus.). (J). (gr. 4-6). 1965. 12.99 (*0-8054-4404-1*, 4244-04) Broadman.

— Bible Guidebook. LC 72-79174. 144p. (J). (gr. 3-6). 1972. 12.99 (*0-8054-4410-6*) Broadman.

— Mi Primer Diccionario Biblico. McElrath, Ruth G., tr. (Illus.). 128p. (SPA.). (J). (gr. 4-6). 1991. reprint ed. pap. 4.50 (*0-311-03656-2*) Casa Bautista.

— Mi Primer Diccionario Biblico: My First Bible Dictionary. 122p. (SPA.). 1978. pap. 7.95 (*0-8288-5252-9*, S37577) Fr & Eur.

McElreath, Mark. Managing Systematic & Ethical Public Relations. 496p. (C). 1992. boxed write for info. (*0-697-10534-2*) Brown & Benchmark.

— Managing Systematic & Ethical Public Relations. 496p. (C). 1994. pap. text ed. write for info. (*0-697-28321-6*) Brown & Benchmark.

McElreath, T. Jack. IMS Design & Implementation Techniques. 2nd ed. Ward, Janet B., ed. LC 90-38715. 252p. 1990. 39.95 (*0-89435-282-2*) Wiley.

— IMS Design & Implementation Techniques. 2nd rev. ed. Ward, Janet, ed. 238p. 1990. 39.95 (*0-471-58370-7*) Wiley.

McElroy. Eyes of the Hawk. (Gunsmoke Western Ser.). 12.95 (*0-85997-828-1*, C1008, Gunsmoke) Chivers N Amer.

— Jesus Forgives Peter. (Arch Bks.). 24p. (Orig.). (J). (gr. k-4). 1985. pap. 1.99 (*0-570-06192-X*, 59-1293) Concordia.

McElroy & Tye, eds. Thermal Insulation Performance - STP 718. 566p. 1980. 43.00 (*0-8031-0794-3*, 04-718000-10) ASTM.

McElroy, Ann & Townsend, Patricia K. Medical Anthropology in Ecological Perspective. 2nd ed. 453p. (C). 1989. pap. text ed. 25.95 (*0-8133-0742-2*) Westview.

McElroy, Bernard. Fiction of the Modern Grotesque. LC 87-27866. 224p. 1989. text ed. 35.00 (*0-312-01340-X*) St Martin.

— Shakespeare's Mature Tragedies. LC 72-5389. 266p. reprint ed. pap. 75.90 (*0-7837-4326-2*, 2044030) Bks Demand.

McElroy, Charles H. & Lienhart, David A., eds. Rock for Erosion Control. LC 92-44625. (ASTM Special Technical Publication Ser.: No. 1177). (Illus.). 150p. 1993. 46.00 (*0-8031-1489-3*, 04-011770-38) ASTM.

McElroy, Colleen. Jesus & Fat Tuesday & Other Stories. LC 87-70508. 216p. 1987. pap. 8.95 (*0-88739-023-4*) Creat Arts Bk.

— Looking for a Country under Its Original Name. (Illus.). 1984. pap. 8.00 (*0-911287-05-1*) Blue Begonia.

— Winters Without Snow. LC 79-92501. 81p. 1980. pap. 5.95 (*0-918408-17-2*) Reed & Cannon.

McElroy, Colleen, jt. intro. see Cady, Jack.

McElroy, Colleen J. Bone Flames. LC 86-32463. (Wesleyan Poetry Ser.). 80p. 1987. 22.50 (*0-8195-2148-5*, Wesleyan Univ Pr); pap. 10.95 (*0-8195-1149-8*, Wesleyan Univ Pr) U Pr of New Eng.

— Driving under the Cardboard Pines: And Other Stories. 224p. (Orig.). 1989. pap. 10.95 (*0-88739-073-0*) Creat Arts Bk.

— Queen of the Ebony Isles. LC 84-7494. (Wesleyan Poetry Ser.). (Illus.). 100p. 1984. pap. 10.95 (*0-8195-6101-0*, Wesleyan Univ Pr) U Pr of New Eng.

— What Madness Brought Me Here: New & Selected Poems, 1968-1988. LC 89-37803. (Wesleyan Poetry Ser.). 118p. 1990. 27.50 (*0-8195-2186-8*, Wesleyan Univ Pr); pap. 12.95 (*0-8195-1188-9*, Wesleyan Univ Pr) U Pr of New Eng.

McElroy, D. L. & Kimpflen, J. F., eds. Insulation Materials, Testing & Applications STP 1030. LC 89-17743. (Special Technical Publication (STP) Ser.). (Illus.). 800p. 1990. text ed. 95.00 (*0-8031-1278-5*, 04-010300-61) ASTM.

McElroy, Davis. Existentialism & Modern Literature. 1.95 (*0-8065-0158-8*, Citadel Pr) Carol Pub Group.

McElroy, Davis D. Existentialism & Modern Literature: An Essay in Existential Criticism. LC 68-8087. (Illus.). 58p. 1969. reprint ed. text ed. 45.00 (*0-8371-0179-4*, MCEL, Greenwood Pr) Greenwood.

— Scotland's Age of Improvement: A Survey of Eighteenth-Century Literary Clubs & Societies. LC 73-9172. 183p. reprint ed. pap. 52.20 (*0-8357-4567-8*, 2037477) Bks Demand.

McElroy, Dorothy P. Fundamentals of Petroleum Maps. LC 86-22920. (Illus.). 138p. 1986. 36.00 (*0-87201-494-0*) Gulf Pub.

McElroy, Elam E. Applied Business Statistics: An Elementary Approach. 2nd ed. 1979. student ed 9.95 (*0-8162-5536-9*); text ed. 26.95 (*0-8162-5535-0*); teacher ed 6.00 (*0-8162-5537-7*) Holden-Day.

McElroy, Eugene J. Needle-Nosed Ned. LC 89-50144. (J). (gr. 4-8). 1989. pap. 3.95 (*0-932433-54-5*) Windswept Hse.

McElroy, Frank E., jt. auth. see Konikow, Robert B.

McElroy, Frank E., ed. see National Safety Council Staff.

McElroy, Guy C. & Gates, Henry L., Jr. Facing History: The Black Image in American Art, 1710-1940. (Illus.). 190p. 1990. 50.00 (*0-938491-39-3*); pap. 24.95 (*0-938491-38-5*) Chronicle Bks.

McElroy, J. & McNeal, R. J. Remote Sensing of Atmospheric Chemistry, Vol. 1491. 1991. 70.00 (*0-8194-0600-7*) SPIE.

McElroy, J. M. McElroy: The Scotch-Irish McElroys in America, 1717-1900 A.D. 183p. 1992. reprint ed. lib. bdg. 38.00 (*0-8328-2686-3*); reprint ed. pap. 28.00 (*0-8328-2687-1*) Higginson Bk Co.

McElroy, Janice H., ed. Our Hidden Heritage: Pennsylvania Women in History. LC 83-71272. (Illus.). 440p. (J). (gr. 7-8). 1983. pap. 12.00 (*0-9611476-0-1*) Am Assoc U Women.

McElroy, Jerome E., et al. Community Policing in New York: The CPOP Research. (Illus.). 216p. (C). 1992. 44.00 (*0-8039-4789-5*); pap. 19.95 (*0-8039-4790-9*) Sage.

McElroy, Jerome L. & Caines, Joseph E. Consumer Expenditure Patterns: A Survey of St. Thomas, U. S. V. I., 1975-1976. LC 79-22424. 118p. reprint ed. pap. 33.70 (*0-7837-5062-5*, 2044752) Bks Demand.

McElroy, Jerome L. & De Albuquerque, Klaus. An Integrated Sustainable Ecotourism for Small Caribbean Islands. Conway, Dennis, ed. (Series on Environment & Development). 49p. (Orig.). 1992. pap. 2.00 (*1-881157-09-1*) In Ctr Global.

McElroy, John. Andersonville: A Story of Rebel Military Prisons. (Illus.). 664p. 1993. reprint ed. pap. text ed. 38.00 (*1-55613-851-2*) Heritage Bk.

— This Was Andersonville. (Illus.). 1957. 29.95 (*0-8392-1117-1*) Astor-Honor.

McElroy, John H. Finding Freedom: America's Distinctive Cultural Formation. LC 88-26547. (Illus.). 208p. (C). 1989. 24.95 (*0-8093-1515-7*) S Ill U Pr.

McElroy, John H. & Heacock, Larry E., eds. Space Applications of the Crossroads. (Science & Technology Ser.: Vol. 55). (Illus.). 308p. 1983. 35.00 (*0-87703-187-8*, Pub. by Am Astro Soc); lib. bdg. 45.00 (*0-87703-186-X*, Pub. by Am Astro Soc) Univelt Inc.

McElroy, John H., et al, eds. Space Science & Applications. LC 85-23817. 260p. 1986. 49.95 (*0-87942-195-9*, PC01909) Inst Electrical.

McElroy, Joseph. Plus. 224p. 1987. pap. 8.95 (*0-88184-289-3*) Carroll & Graf.

— Women & Men. 1987. 27.50 (*0-394-50344-9*) Knopf.

— Women & Men. LC 92-29481. 1192p. 1993. reprint ed. pap. 15.95 (*1-56478-023-6*) Dalkey Arch.

McElroy, Keith. Early Peruvian Photography: A Critical Case Study. LC 84-16119. (Studies in Photography: No. 7). (Illus.). 216p. reprint ed. pap. 61.60 (*0-8357-1583-3*, 2070562) Bks Demand.

McElroy, M. B., jt. auth. see Brandt, J. C.

McElroy, Margaret D., jt. ed. see Rassi, Judith A.

McElroy, Mark W. The Corporate Cabling Guide. LC 92-32245. (Telecommunications Ser.). 110p. (C). 1992. text ed. 60.00 (*0-89006-663-9*) Artech Hse.

McElroy, Martin P., jt. ed. see Meyer, Katharine M.

McElroy, Mary L., et al. Business Application Software: An IBM PC Lab Manual. (Orig.). (C). 1986. pap. text ed. 12.95 (*0-938188-34-8*); disk write for info. (*0-318-61046-9*) Mitchell Pub.

McElroy, Nan. Acting in Atlanta: An Introductory Guide to the Atlanta & Regional Film & Television Market. 3rd ed. 95p. 1994. pap. 16.95 (*1-885436-21-1*) Twoworkingactors.

— Acting in Atlanta: An Introductory Guide to the Atlanta Film & Television Market. 2nd ed. 80p. 1994. pap. 15.95 (*1-885436-20-3*) Twoworkingactors.

— Acting in Atlanta Directory, Jan. 1994. 1994. pap. 10.95 (*1-885436-50-5*) Twoworkingactors.

McElroy, Paul S. Holiday Toasts & Graces. Kohn, Barbara, ed. (Christmas Keepsakes Ser.). (Illus.). 56p. 1993. 7.99 (*0-88088-853-9*) Peter Pauper.

— New Beginnings. (Petites Ser.). 80p. 1992. 4.95 (*0-88088-737-0*) Peter Pauper.

McElroy, Robert C. Automotive Engine Electronics. (Illus.). 112p. 1990. 13.95 (*0-929603-37-0*) Accuracy Pub Co.

McElroy, Robert M. Jefferson Davis; the Unreal & the Real, 2 vols., Set. (History - United States Ser.). 1993. reprint ed. lib. bdg. 150.00 (*0-7812-4900-7*) Rprt Serv.

— Levi Parsons Morton: Banker, Diplomat & Statesman. LC 75-2646. (Wall Street & the Security Market Ser.). (Illus.). 1975. reprint ed. 33.95 (*0-405-06971-5*) Ayer.

McElroy, Robert W. Morality & American Foreign Policy: The Role of Ethics in International Affairs. (Illus.). 244p. 1993. text ed. 29.95 (*0-691-08621-4*); pap. text ed. 12.95 (*0-691-00078-6*) Princeton U Pr.

— The Search for an American Public Theology: The Contribution of John Courtney Murray. 1989. pap. 10.95 (*0-8091-3051-3*) Paulist Pr.

McElroy, Thomas P., Jr. The New Handbook of Attracting Birds. (Illus.). 258p. 1985. pap. 9.95 (*0-393-30280-6*) Norton.

McElroy, Walter, tr. see Corbiere, Tristan.

McElroy, Wendy, comp. Liberty: Eighteen Eighty-One to Nineteen Hundred Eight-A Comprehensive Index. LC 82-1383. 162p. 1982. 30.00 (*0-9602574-2-X*) M E Coughlin.

McElroy, Wendy, ed. Freedom, Feminism & the State: An Overview of Individualist Feminism. 2nd ed. LC 82-22010. (Independent Institute Ser.). 264p. 1991. 39.95 (*0-8419-1227-0*); pap. 19.95 (*0-8419-1225-4*) Holmes & Meier.

McElroy, William. Fences & Retaining Walls. 400p. (Orig.). 1990. pap. 23.25 (*0-934041-53-9*) Craftsman.

— Painter's Handbook. 320p. (Orig.). 1987. pap. 21.25 (*0-934041-28-8*) Craftsman.

McElroy, William C. Forms Library for the Professional Construction Contractor. 288p. 1993. text ed. 40.00 (*0-13-174558-1*) P-H.

— Roof Builder's Handbook. 528p. 1992. text ed. 45.00 (*0-13-781816-5*) P-H.

McElroy, William D., ed. see Light & Life Symposium Staff.

McElroy, William D., ed. see Symposium on the Chemical Basis of Heredity Staff.

McElvaine, Robert S. The Great Depression: America, 1929-1941. 1993. pap. 14.00 (*0-8129-2327-8*) Random.

McElvaine, Robert S., ed. Down & Out in the Great Depression: Letters from the Forgotten Man. LC 82-7022. (Illus.). xvii, 251p. 1983. pap. 10.95 (*0-8078-4099-8*) U of NC Pr.

McElvaney, Leigh F., ed. Proceedings of the Sixth Southeastern Safety & Health Conference & Exhibition, 1992. 227p. 1993. 40.00 (*0-9624647-7-5*) GA Tech Rsch Inst.

— Proceedings of the Southeastern Safety & Health Conference & Exhibition, 1993. 318p. 1993. 40.00 (*0-9624647-8-3*) GA Tech Rsch Inst.

McElvaney, William K. Good News Is Bad News Is Good News. LC 79-22032. 144p. (Orig.). reprint ed. pap. 41.10 (*0-8357-2685-1*, 2040221) Bks Demand.

— Preaching from Camelot to Covenant. LC 89-14948. 144p. 1989. pap. 10.95 (*0-687-33842-5*) Abingdon.

— Winds of Grace, Ways of Faith: Expanding the Horizons of Christian Spirituality. 144p. (Orig.). 1992. pap. 11.99 (*0-664-25120-X*) Westminster John Knox.

McElveen, Floyd. Mormones, Sus Doctrinas y Sus Errores: Will the Saints Go Marching in? (SPA.). 5.50 (*84-7228-519-7*, 220608, Pub. by Edit Clie SP) TSELF.

McElveen, Floyd C. The Beautiful Side of Death. (Orig.). 1988. 3.95 (*0-9620963-0-X*) Inst Rel Rsch.

— The Compelling Christ: Why We Can Be Sure of the Bible, Christ, & Salvation. (Illus.). 56p. (Orig.). 1989. pap. 0.95 (*0-9620963-1-8*) Inst Rel Rsch.

An Asterisk (*) at the beginning of an entry indicates that the title is appearing in BIP for the first time.

— God's Word: Final, Infallible & Forever. 2nd ed. 386p. (Orig.). 1985. pap. 4.95 (*0-9620963-4-2*) Inst Rel Rsch.

McElvoy, Anne. The Saddled Cow: East Germany's Life & Legacy. 288p. 1992. 22.95 (*0-571-16591-5*) Faber & Faber.

McElwain, Dean. The Gavel & the Gun - The Last Gunfight. (Double Preacher's Law Ser.). 448p. 1990. pap. 3.95 (*0-8439-3012-8*) Dorchester Pub Co.

— Preacher's Law No. 5: Slaughter at Ten Sleep. (Preacher's Law Ser.). 192p. (Orig.). pap. 2.75 (*0-8439-2588-4*) Dorchester Pub Co.

— Trail of Death. (Preacher's Law Ser.: No. 2). 224p. (Orig.). 1987. pap. 2.75 (*0-8439-2528-0*) Dorchester Pub Co.

— Widow Maker. (Preacher's Law Ser.: No. 1). 224p. (Orig.). 1987. pap. 2.50 (*0-8439-2508-6*) Dorchester Pub Co.

— Widow Maker - Trail of Death. (Double Preacher's Law Ser.). 448p. 1990. pap. 3.95 (*0-8439-3002-0*) Dorchester Pub Co.

McElwain, T., tr. see Laato, Timo.

***McElwain, Wilbur J.** Cumberland County, PA, Cemetery Records Collected by Jeremiah Zeamer. 266p. (Orig.). 1994. pap. text ed. 36.00 (*0-7884-0075-4*) Heritage Bk.

— Genealogical Data Abstracted from History of Middle Spring Presbyterian Church, Middle Spring, Pennsylvania, 1738-1900. vi, 180p. (Orig.). 1992. pap. text ed. 27.50 (*1-55613-722-2*) Heritage Bk.

— United States Direct Tax of 1798: Tax Lists for Cumberland Co., PA. (Illus.). 231p. (Orig.). 1995. pap. text ed. 33.00 (*0-7884-0118-1*) Heritage Bk.

McElwain, Wilbur J., ed. Genealogical Data Abstracted from History of the Big Spring Presbyterian Church. 130p. (Orig.). 1992. pap. 27.50 (*1-55613-707-9*) Heritage Bk.

***McElwee, Bob.** St. Charles: Missouri. (Illus.). 64p. 1994. 29.95 (*1-886154-00-7*) Phoenix IL.

***McElwee, Cheryl A.** Only You. 382p. 1994. pap. 9.95 (*1-56901-359-4*) NW Pub.

McElwee, David A., et al, eds. Media Resource Guide. 5th ed. (Illus.). 108p. 1987. pap. 10.00 (*0-910755-05-1*) Foun Am Comm.

McElwee, William L. The Art of War: Waterloo to Mons. LC 74-17459. 352p. 1975. pap. 10.95 (*0-253-20214-0*, MB-214) Ind U Pr.

— Britain's Locust Years: Nineteen Eighteen to Nineteen Forty. LC 78-25900. 292p. 1979. reprint ed. text ed. 59.75 (*0-313-21162-0*, MCBL, Greenwood Pr) Greenwood.

— The Reign of Charles V, 1516-1558. LC 83-45657. reprint ed. 36.00 (*0-404-19807-4*) AMS Pr.

— The Wisest Fool in Christendom. LC 74-7449. (Illus.). 296p. 1974. reprint ed. text ed. 35.00 (*0-8371-7522-4*, MCWF, Greenwood Pr) Greenwood.

McElya, Lisa C. Dallas Party & Event Planners Sourcebook: To Throw an Unforgettable Party or Special Event, Here's What You Need, & Where To Find It! McElya, Shirley, ed. (Orig.). 1988. 19.95 (*0-929708-02-4*) Applause TX.

McElya, Shirley, ed. see McElya, Lisa C.

Mcelyea, Louann, jt. auth. see Kowlakowski, Frank.

McEnaney, Frank, jt. auth. see Hemstock, Gillian.

McEneaney, Terry. The Birder's Guide to Montana. LC 92-55084. (Falcon Guidebook Ser.). (Illus.). 316p. (Orig.). 1993. pap. 14.95 (*1-56044-189-5*) Falcon Pr MT.

McEnerney, Barbara, ed. see Arroyo, Stephen.

McEnerney, John, tr. see Cyril of Alexandria, St.

McEnerney, John I., tr. see Cyril.

McEnery, A. M. Computational Linguistics: A Handbook & Toolbox for Natural Language Processing. 270p. (Orig.). 1992. pap. 52.50 (*1-85058-177-0*, Pub. by Sigma Press UK) Coronet Bks.

McEnery, John H. Epilogue in Burma, 1945-48. 200p. (C). 1991. 85.00 (*0-946771-84-7*, Pub. by Spellmount UK) St Mut.

McEnery, Thomas. California Cavalier: The Journal of Captain Thomas Fallon. Muller, Kathleen, ed. (American Travel Ser.). (Illus.). 112p. 1986. reprint ed. lib. bdg. 24.25 (*0-914139-05-3*) San Jose His Mus Assn.

McEnery, Tom. The New City State: Change & Renewal in America's Cities. LC 94-66090. 300p. 1994. 24.95 (*1-879373-40-8*) R Rinehart.

McEnery, Tony & Paice, Chris, eds. IRSG '92: Proceedings of the BCS 14th Information Retrieval Colloquium, University of Lancaster, 13-14 April 1992. LC 93-7747. (Workshops in Computing Ser.). 1993. 69.00 (*0-387-19808-3*) Spr-Verlag.

McEniry, Joan, jt. ed. see Hidalgo, Hilda.

McEniry, John H., Jr. A Marine Dive-Bomber Pilot at Guadacanal. LC 86-16053. (Illus.). 200p. 1987. 26.50 (*0-8173-0330-8*) U of Ala Pr.

McEnroe, Robert E. The Silver Whistle. 1950. pap. 4.75 (*0-8222-1028-2*) Dramatists Play.

***McEntarfer, Dave.** Greenberg's Guide to Lionel Trains, 1901-1942 Vol. 4, Vol. 4. 176p. 1995. 44.95 (*0-89778-394-8*, 10-7800) Greenberg Bks.

McEntee, Art, et al. Computerized Accounting: Tutorial & Applications. LC 92-33453. 1992. write for info. (*0-07-017739-2*) Glencoe.

McEntee, Grace H. The Island, the Ox, You & Me. (Illus.). 27p. (Orig.). 1986. pap. 3.95 (*0-917012-82-8*) RI Pubns Soc.

McEntee, Kenneth. Reproductive Pathology of Domestic Mammals. 401p. 1990. text ed. 116.00 (*0-12-483375-6*) Acad Pr.

***McEntee, Margaret, ed.** Resources for Catechists & Chaplains. 216p. (Orig.). 1994. pap. 12.95 (*1-85607-108-1*, Pub. by Columba Pr IE) Twenty-Third.

McEntee, Phil, jt. auth. see Francey, David.

McEntee, Sean. Lectionary for Masses with Children: Cycle C. 192p. (Orig.). (J). (gr. 2-8). 1988. pap. text ed. 19.95 (*0-89622-385-X*) Twenty-Third.

— Preaching & Teaching the Gospels to Children: Year A. LC 92-81720. 176p. (Orig.). 1992. pap. 9.95 (*0-89622-524-0*) Twenty-Third.

— Preaching & Teaching the Gospels to Children (Year B) LC 93-60368. 168p. (Orig.). 1993. pap. 9.95 (*0-89622-569-0*) Twenty-Third.

— Preaching & Teaching the Gospels to Children-Year C. LC 91-90950. 152p. (Orig.). (gr. 4-8). 1991. pap. 9.95 (*0-89622-491-0*, C60) Twenty-Third.

McEntee, Sean & Breen, Michael. Lectionary for Masses with Children: Cycle A. vi, 216p. (Orig.). (J). (gr. 1-6). 1989. pap. 19.95 (*0-89622-411-2*) Twenty-Third.

— Lectionary for Masses with Children Year B. 216p. (Orig.). 1990. pap. 19.95 (*0-89622-435-X*) Twenty-Third.

McEnteer, James. Fighting Words: Independent Journalists in Texas. LC 91-32797. (Illus.). 238p. 1992. 24.95 (*0-292-72474-8*) U of Tex Pr.

McEnteer, Jim, ed. Tilted Planet Tales Number Three: Easy Orbit Fiction from Central Texas. (Illus.). 212p. (Orig.). 1986. lib. bdg. 21.00 (*0-912973-06-4*); pap. text ed. 8.00 (*0-912973-07-2*) Tilted Planet.

McEntire, Frank. Dreams & Shields: Spiritual Dimensions in Contemporary Art. (Illus.). 130p. (Orig.). 1992. pap. 17.95 (*0-942291-01-8*) Salt Lake Art Ctr.

McEntire, Mark H. The Function of Sacrifice in Chronicles, Ezra, & Nehemiah. LC 93-2688. 140p. 1993. text ed. 69.95 (*0-7734-2362-1*) E Mellen.

McEntire, P. L., et al, eds. Distributed Computing: Concepts & Implementations. LC 84-6648. 460p. 1984. 59.95 (*0-87942-175-4*, PC01693) Inst Electrical.

McEntire, Patricia. Mommy I'm Hungry: How to Feed Your Child Nutritiously. LC 81-68292. 168p. 1982. pap. 7.95 (*0-917982-11-8*) Cougar Bks.

McEntire, Reba & Carter, Tom. Reba: My Story. LC 94-1466. 1994. 22.95 (*0-553-09607-9*) Bantam.

McEntire, Sandra. The Doctrine of Compunction in Medieval England: Holy Tears. LC 90-22127. (Studies in Mediaeval Literature: Vol. 8). 200p. 1991. lib. bdg. 79.95 (*0-88946-225-9*) E Mellen.

McEntire, Sandra J., ed. Margery Kempe: A Book of Essays. LC 92-6437. (Reference Library of the Humanities: Vol. 1468). 280p. 1992. 41.00 (*0-8153-0378-5*) Garland.

McEntire, Walter F. Was Christopher Columbus a Jew? 1976. lib. bdg. 59.95 (*0-8490-1278-3*) Gordon Pr.

McEntyre. Practical Guide to the Care of the Surgical Patient. 3rd ed. 368p. 1989. spiral bd. 25.95 (*0-8016-3330-3*) Mosby Yr Bk.

McEntyre, John G. Land Survey Systems. (Illus.). 537p. 1986. reprint ed. 55.00 (*0-910845-27-1*, 511) Landmark Ent.

— Workbook for Land Survey Systems. (Illus.). 186p. 1990. pap. 38.00 (*0-910845-41-7*) Landmark Ent.

McEuen, Caroline K., ed. see Gittinger, Mattiebelle.

McEuen, James. Snake Country. 60p. (Orig.). 1990. pap. 8.00 (*0-915380-26-9*) Word Works.

McEuen, Vivi S., jt. auth. see Keaveney, Madeline M.

McEvedy, Colin. Atlas of African History. 1980. pap. 10.00 (*0-14-051083-4*, Penguin Bks) Viking Penguin.

— The New Penguin Atlas of Medieval History. enl. rev. ed. (Illus.). 128p. 1992. pap. 12.00 (*0-14-051249-7*, Penguin Bks) Viking Penguin.

— The Penguin Atlas of Ancient History. 1986. pap. 12.00 (*0-14-051151-2*, Penguin Bks) Viking Penguin.

— The Penguin Atlas of Medieval History. 1986. pap. 9.95 (*0-14-051152-0*, Penguin Bks) Viking Penguin.

— The Penguin Atlas of Modern History. 1986. pap. 10.00 (*0-14-051153-9*, Penguin Bks) Viking Penguin.

— The Penguin Atlas of North American History to 1870. 112p. 1988. pap. 11.00 (*0-14-051128-8*, Penguin Bks) Viking Penguin.

— The Penguin Atlas of Recent History. 1986. pap. 10.00 (*0-14-051154-7*, Penguin Bks) Viking Penguin.

McEvenne, Sean E. Narrative Style of the Priestly Writer. (Analecta Biblica Ser.: Vol. 50). 1971. pap. 17.00 (*88-7653-050-9*) Loyola Univ Pr.

McEvenue, Sean. Interpretation & Bible: Essays on Truth in Literature. 208p. (Orig.). 1994. pap. text ed. 12.95 (*0-8146-5036-8*, M Glazier) Liturgical Pr.

— Interpreting the Pentateuch. (Old Testament Studies: No. 4). 194p. (Orig.). 1990. pap. 14.95 (*0-8146-5654-4*) Liturgical Pr.

McEvenue, Sean E. & Meyer, Ben F., eds. Lonergan's Hermeneutics: Its Development & Application. LC 88-28383. 313p. 1989. 44.95 (*0-8132-0670-7*) Cath U Pr.

McEvers, Joan, ed. Astrological Counseling: The Path to Self-Actualization. LC 90-46437. (New World Astrology Ser.). 304p. (Orig.). 1990. pap. 14.95 (*0-87542-385-X*) Llewellyn Pubns.

— The Astrology of the Macrocosm: New Directions in Mundane Astrology. LC 90-35088. (New World Astrology Ser.). 420p. (Orig.). 1990. pap. 14.95 (*0-87542-384-1*) Llewellyn Pubns.

— The Houses: Power Places of the Horoscope. LC 89-28295. (New World Astrology Ser.). 400p. 1990. pap. 12.95 (*0-87542-383-3*) Llewellyn Pubns.

— Intimate Relationships: The Astrology of Attraction. LC 91-10207. (New World Astrology Ser.). 256p. (Orig.). 1991. pap. 14.95 (*0-87542-386-8*) Llewellyn Pubns.

— Planets: The Astrological Tools. LC 88-38614. (Llewellyn's New World Astrology Ser.). 384p. (Orig.). 1989. pap. 12.95 (*0-87542-381-7*) Llewellyn Pubns.

— Spiritual, Metaphysical & New Trends in Modern Astrology. LC 88-6760. (New World Astrology Ser.). 264p. 1988. pap. 9.95 (*0-87542-380-9*) Llewellyn Pubns.

— Web of Relationships: Spiritual, Karmic & Psychological Bonds. LC 91-41814. (New World Astrology Ser.). 248p. 1992. pap. 14.95 (*0-87542-388-4*) Llewellyn Pubns.

McEvers, Joan, jt. auth. see March, Marion D.

McEvey, Shane F., ed. see Paterson, Hugh E.

McEvilley, Thomas. Art & Discontent: Theory at the Millennium. LC 90-48316. 1993. pap. 12.00 (*0-929701-31-3*) McPherson & Co.

— Art & Otherness: Crisis in Cultural Identity. LC 92-7120. 176p. 1992. 20.00 (*0-929701-21-6*) McPherson & Co.

— Art & Otherness: Crisis in Cultural Identity. LC 92-7120. 174p. 1995. reprint ed. pap. 12.00 (*0-929701-48-8*) McPherson & Co.

— The Exile's Return: Toward a Redefinition of Painting for the Postmodern Era. LC 93-20213. (Contemporary Artists & Their Critics Ser.). (Illus.). 240p. (C). 1994. 65.00 (*0-521-41672-8*); pap. 19.95 (*0-521-45615-0*) Cambridge U Pr.

— The Lost Book. 224p. Date not set. 20.00 (*0-929701-47-X*); pap. 12.00 (*0-929701-46-1*) McPherson & Co.

— North of Yesterday. LC 86-33250. 288p. 1987. 20.00 (*0-914232-86-X*); pap. 10.00 (*0-914232-85-1*) McPherson & Co.

— Pat Steir. LC 94-30546. (Illus.). 1995. write for info. (*0-8109-4459-6*) Abrams.

— Soil & Sky: Mel Chin at the Fabric Workshop. (Illus.). 32p. 1993. pap. write for info. (*0-9619760-3-9*) Fabric Workshop Inc.

McEvilley, Thomas, contrib. Julian Schnabel Fox Farm Paintings. (Illus.). 38p. 1989. pap. write for info. (*1-878283-02-2*) PaceWildenstein.

McEvilley, Thomas, ed. Fusion: African Artists. (Focus on African Art Ser.). (Illus.). 96p. 1993. pap. 19.95 (*3-7913-1327-4*, Pub. by Prestel) TeNeues.

McEvilley, Thomas, jt. auth. see Baraka, Amiri.

McEvilley, Thomas, jt. auth. see Howard, Richard.

McEvilley, Thomas, jt. auth. see Jacob, Mary J.

McEvilley, Thomas, et al. Allocations: Art for a Natural & Artificial Environment. (Illus.). 1992. 55.00 (*90-800914-2-1*) Dist Art Pubs.

— Lucas Samaras: Objects & Subjects 1969-1986. (Illus.). 224p. 1988. 65.00 (*0-89659-803-9*) Abbeville Pr.

McEvily, A. J., Jr., ed. Atlas of Stress - Corrosion & Corrosion Fatigue Curves: Corrosion & Corrosion Fatigue Curves. 541p. 1990. 156.00 (*0-87170-374-2*) ASM.

McEvily, A. J., jt. ed. see Iida, K.

McEvily, A. J., jt. auth. see Tetelman, A. S.

McEvoy, Alan. When Disaster Strikes. 1992. 6.95 (*1-55691-053-3*, 533) Learning Pubns.

McEvoy, Alan & Erickson, Edsel. Youth & Exploitation: A Process Leading to Running Away, Violence, Substance Abuse & Suicide. 1990. pap. 12.95 (*1-55691-042-8*) Learning Pubns.

McEvoy, Alan & McEvoy, Marcia. Preventing Youth Suicide. 1994. write for info. (*1-55691-056-8*) Learning Pubns.

McEvoy, Alan W. & Brookings, Jeff B. Helping Battered Women: A Volunteer's Handbook. 2nd ed. 1990. pap. write for info. (*1-55691-067-3*, 673) Learning Pubns.

— If She Is Raped: A Book for Husbands, Fathers & Male Friends. 2nd ed. 1990. pap. 12.95 (*1-55691-062-2*) Learning Pubns.

McEvoy, Alan W. & Brookings, Jeff D. If She Is Raped: A Book for Husbands, Fathers & Male Friends, 4 vols., Set. 2nd unabridged ed. 176p. 1990. pap. 11.95 (*1-55691-061-4*) Learning Pubns.

McEvoy, Alan W. & Erickson, Edsel. Abused Children: The Educator's Guide to Prevention & Intervention. 1994. 22.95 (*1-55691-052-5*, 525) Learning Pubns.

McEvoy, Arthur F. The Fisherman's Problem: Ecology & Law in California Fisheries, 1850-1980. (Illus.). 392p. (C). 1990. pap. 19.95 (*0-521-38586-5*) Cambridge U Pr.

— The Fisherman's Problem: Ecology & Law in the California Fisheries, 1850-1980. (Studies in Environment & History). (Illus.). 512p. 1986. 64.95 (*0-521-32427-0*) Cambridge U Pr.

McEvoy, Colleen A. Career Focus: One Day at a Time. 369p. 1992. pap. text ed. 8.95 (*0-9633810-0-8*) C A McEvoy.

McEvoy, Donald W. The Police & Their Many Publics. LC 76-6851. 154p. reprint ed. pap. 43.90 (*0-317-52035-0*, 2027494) Bks Demand.

McEvoy, Emma, ed. see Lewis, Matthew.

***McEvoy, Gerald K.** AHFS Drug Information, 1995. rev. ed. 2500p. 1995. per., pap. text ed. 115.00 (*1-879907-53-4*) Am Soc Hlth-Syst.

McEvoy, Gerald K., ed. AHFS Drug Information, 1994. rev. ed. 2500p. 1994. pap. text ed. 115.00 (*1-879907-35-6*) Am Soc Hlth-Syst.

McEvoy, H. K. Knife-Throwing. 7.95 (*0-685-63762-X*) Wehman.

McEvoy, Harry. Knife & Tomahawk Throwing. (Illus.). 28p. 1985. 3.00 (*0-940362-10-4*) Knife World.

— Scagel: The Man & his Knives. (Illus.). 28p. 1985. 3.00 (*0-940362-09-0*) Knife World.

McEvoy, Harry K. Knife & Tomahawk Throwing: The Art of the Experts. LC 88-50409. (Illus.). 152p. 1988. pap. 8.95 (*0-8048-1542-9*) C E Tuttle.

— Knife Throwing: A Practical Guide. LC 72-91550. (Illus.). 112p. 1973. pap. 6.95 (*0-8048-1099-0*) C E Tuttle.

McEvoy, J. D. Winning Secrets of a Poker Master. 32p. 1986. pap. 6.95 (*0-934650-11-X*) Sunnyside.

McEvoy, James. Robert Grosseteste, Exegete & Philosopher. LC 94-5847. (Collected Studies: No. CS 446). 205p. 1994. 82.50 (*0-86078-433-9*, Pub. by Variorum UK) Ashgate Pub Co.

McEvoy, James E., ed. Catalysts for the Control of Automotive Pollutants. LC 75-20298. (Advances in Chemistry Ser.: No. 143). 199p. 1975. 27.95 (*0-8412-0219-2*) Am Chemical.

— Partnerships in Chemical Research & Education. LC 91-32420. (ACS Symposium Ser.: No. 478). (Illus.). 250p. 1991. 49.95 (*0-8412-2173-1*) Am Chemical.

McEvoy, John G. & Schwartz, Truman, eds. Motion Toward Perfection: The Achievement of Joseph Priestley, 1733-1804. (Orig.). 1989. 7.00 (*1-55896-010-4*, Skinner Hse Bks) Unitarian Univ.

McEvoy, Joseph E. Swim Your Way to Fitness: A Lifetime of Exercise Programs. (Illus.). 192p. 1993. pap. 14.95 (*0-8117-3090-5*) Stackpole.

McEvoy, Joseph P. Reading the Building Code: A Short Hermeneutic. 89p. (C). 1991. pap. text ed. 20.00 (*0-89801-020-9*) NE Univ Pub.

McEvoy, K. & Tucker, J. V., eds. Theoretical Foundations of VLSI Design. (Tracts in Theoretical Computer Science Ser.: No. 10). (Illus.). 250p. (C). 1991. 59.95 (*0-521-36631-3*) Cambridge U Pr.

McEvoy, Kathleen, jt. ed. see Resnick, Robert J.

McEvoy, Ken, jt. auth. see Frantzen, Trond.

McEvoy, Marcia, jt. auth. see McEvoy, Alan.

McEvoy, Marjorie. Dusky Cactus. large type ed. 272p. 1980. 12.00 (*0-7089-0525-0*) Ulverscroft.

McEvoy, Nion, ed. see Blumer, Bob.

McEvoy, Nion, ed. see Jung, Betty.

McEvoy, Nion, ed. see Saeks, Diane D.

McEvoy, Nion, ed. see Sansweet, Stephen J.

McEvoy, Nion, ed. see Welsh, Pat.

McEvoy, Nion, ed. see Zwaerepoel, Jean-Pierre.

McEvoy, R. C., jt. ed. see Ginsberg-Fellner, F.

McEvoy, Seth & Wartik, Nancy. Albert's Riddle. (Illus.). 224p. (J). (gr. 6-8). 1989. 9.95 (*0-318-37482-X*) Kipling Pr.

***McEvoy, Tom.** Tournament Poker. 312p. (Orig.). 1995. 59.95 (*1-884466-06-0*); pap. 39.95 (*1-884466-05-2*) Poker & Plus.

McEwan, Angela, tr. see Miranda, Veronica.

McEwan, Barbara. Agricultural Crisis in America. (Contemporary World Issues Ser.). 260p. 1995. lib. bdg. 39.50 (*0-87436-737-9*) ABC-CLIO.

— Thomas Jefferson: Farmer. LC 91-52748. 232p. 1991. lib. bdg. 28.50 (*0-89950-633-X*) McFarland & Co.

— White House Landscapes: Horticultural Achievements of American Presidents. 224p. 1992. 24.95 (*0-8027-1192-8*) Walker & Co.

McEwan, Barbara, ed. Practicing Judicious Discipline: An Educator's Guide to a Democratic Classroom. 92p. 1990. pap. text ed. 11.95 (*0-9625945-5-5*) Caddo Gap Pr.

— Practicing Judicious Discipline: An Educator's Guide to a Democratic Classroom. 2nd ed. 128p. (C). 1994. pap. text ed. 14.95 (*1-880192-09-8*) Caddo Gap Pr.

McEwan, Bonnie G., ed. The Spanish Missions of la Florida. LC 93-7937. (Illus.). 488p. 1993. lib. bdg. 49.95 (*0-8130-1231-7*); pap. text ed. 24.95 (*0-8130-1232-5*) U Press Fla.

McEwan, Calvin W., et al. Soundings at Tell Fakhariyah. LC 57-11216. (Oriental Institute Publications: No. 79). (Illus.). 1958. lib. bdg. 40.00 (*0-226-62180-4*, OIP79) U Ch Pr.

McEwan, Chris. Pinocchio. (J). 1990. pap. 13.95 (*0-385-41327-0*) Doubleday.

McEwan, Dorothea, jt. auth. see Isherwood, Lisa.

McEwan, Elaine. How to Raise a Reader. LC 87-3973. 176p. 1987. pap. 8.99 (*1-55513-211-1*, LifeJourney) Chariot Family.

***McEwan, Elaine K.** Attention Deficit Disorder. (Guides for Parents & Educators Ser.). 180p. 1995. pap. 11.99 (*0-87788-056-5*) Shaw Pubs.

— Murphy's Mansion. Norton, LoraBeth, ed. 96p. (J). (gr. 3-6). Date not set. pap. 4.99 (*0-7814-0160-7*, Chariot Bks) Chariot Family.

— My Mother, My Daughter: Women Speak Out. 208p. (Orig.). 1992. per., pap. 8.99 (*0-87788-570-2*) Shaw Pubs.

— Operation Garbage: A Josh McIntire Book. LC 92-43761. (J). 1993. pap. 4.99 (*0-7814-0121-6*, Chariot Bks) Chariot Family.

— The Parent's Guide to Solving School Problems: Kindergarten Through Middle School. 336p. (Orig.). 1992. pap. 9.99 (*0-87788-640-7*) Shaw Pubs.

— Quality Decision Making: Leading Your Team to Excellence. (Illus.). 192p. 1995. 24.95x (*0-590-49466-X*) Scholastic Inc.

— School Success: Preparing Your Young Child. (Guides for Parents & Educators Ser.). 160p. 1995. pap. 8.99 (*0-87788-635-0*) Shaw Pubs.

— Schooling Options: Choosing the Best for You & Your Child. 192p. (Orig.). 1991. pap. 8.99 (*0-87788-753-5*) Shaw Pubs.

— Seven Steps to Effective Instructional Leadership. LC 93-31780. 1995. 24.95 (*0-590-49467-8*, 2831.66m38 1994) Scholastic Inc.

— Underground Hero. LC 92-27104. (J). (gr. 3-6). 1993. pap. 4.99 (*0-7814-0113-5*, Chariot Bks) Chariot Family.

McEwan, Glenn H. Introduction to Computer Systems. 2nd ed. 1993. text ed. write for info. (*0-07-044351-3*); write for info. (*0-07-044352-1*) McGraw.

McEwan, Gordon F., jt. ed. see Isbell, William H.

***McEwan, Hunter & Egan, Kieran, eds.** Narrative in Teaching, Learning & Research. (Critical Issues in Curriculum Ser.). 256p. (C). 1995. pap. text ed. 21.95x (*0-8077-3399-7*) Tchrs Coll.

— Narrative in Teaching, Learning & Research. (Critical Issues in Curriculum Ser.). 256p. (C). 1995. text ed. 44.00x (*0-8077-3400-4*) Tchrs Coll.

McEwan, Ian. Black Dogs. LC 93-20992. 1994. pap. 7.95 (*0-553-37367-6*) Bantam.

— The Cement Garden. 1994. pap. 10.00 (*0-679-75018-5*, Villard Bks) Random.

— The Child in Time. 272p. 1988. pap. 10.95 (*0-14-011246-4*, Penguin Bks) Viking Penguin.

— Comfort of Strangers. 1994. pap. 9.00 (*0-679-74984-5*, Vin) Random.

M

An Asterisk (*) at the beginning of an entry indicates that the title is appearing in BIP for the first time.

M

— The Daydreamer. LC 93-44476. (Illus.). 208p. (J). (gr. 3 up). 1994. 14.00 (*0-06-024426-7*); lib. bdg. 13.89 (*0-06-024427-5*) HarpC Child Bks.

— First Love, Last Rites. 1994. pap. 10.00 (*0-679-75019-3*, Publishers Consult) Random.

— In Between the Sheets. 1994. pap. 10.00 (*0-679-74983-7*, Vin) Random.

— Innocent. 1991. mass mkt. 6.99 (*0-553-55000-4*) Bantam.

— The Innocent. large type ed. LC 90-44880. 452p. 1990. reprint ed. bds. 20.95 (*1-56054-064-8*) Thorndike Pr.

McEwan, J. R., ed. Condition Monitoring, Vol. 3. 284p. 1992. 79.00 (*0-87201-224-7*) Gulf Pub.

***McEwan, Janet M., ed.** Writing for Our Lives Vol. 2, No. 1: Creative Expressions in Writing by Women. 80p. 1993. per. 6.00 (*0-9633743-2-X*) Running Deer.

— Writing for Our Lives Vol. 2, No. 2: Creative Expressions in Writing by Women. 80p. 1993. per. 6.00 (*0-9633743-3-8*) Running Deer.

— Writing for Our Lives Vol. 3, No. 1: Creative Expressions in Writing by Women. 80p. 1994. per. 6.00 (*0-9633743-4-6*) Running Deer.

— Writing for Our Lives Vol. 3, No. 2: Creative Expressions in Writing by Women. 80p. 1994. per. 6.00 (*0-9633743-5-4*) Running Deer.

— Writing for Our Lives Vol. 4, No. 1: Creative Expressions in Writing by Women. 80p. 1995. per. 6.00 (*0-9633743-6-2*) Running Deer.

— Writing for Our Lives Vol. 4, No. 2: Creative Expressions in Writing by Women. 80p. 1995. per. 6.00 (*0-9633743-7-0*) Running Deer.

— Writing for Our Lives, Vol. 1, No. 1: Creative Expressions in Writing by Women. 64p. 1992. per. 4.00 (*0-9633743-0-3*) Running Deer.

— Writing for Our Lives, Vol. 1, No. 1: Creative Expressions in Writing by Women, Vol. 1, No. 2. 80p. 1992. per. 4.00 (*0-9633743-1-1*) Running Deer.

McEwan, Neil. Anthony Powell. Page, Norman, ed. LC 90-43271. (Modern Novelists Ser.). 160p. 1991. text ed. 35.00 (*0-312-05571-4*) St Martin.

— Perspectives in British Historical Fiction Today. LC 86-7200. 200p. 1987. 25.00 (*0-89341-547-2*, Longwood Academic) Hollowbrook.

McEwan, Neil, ed. The Twentieth Century (Nineteen Hundred to Present) LC 89-70174. (St. Martin's Anthologies of English Literature Ser.: Vol. No. 5). 646p. 1990. text ed. 20.00 (*0-312-04475-5*) St Martin.

McEwan, Peter J. Dictionary of Scottish Art & Architecture. (Illus.). 626p. 1995. 99.50 (*1-85149-134-1*) Antique Collect.

McEwan, Peter J., ed. International Conference on Social Science & Medicine, 6th, Amsterdam, 1979: Second Special Conference Issue. 80p. 1981. pap. 17.25 (*0-08-026763-7*, Pergamon Pr) Elsevier.

— Second Special Conference Issue. 144p. 1983. pap. 22.00 (*0-08-027937-6*, Pergamon Pr) Elsevier.

— Social Science & Medicine: Seventh International Conference Background Papers. (Journal of Social Science & Medicine Ser.: Vol. 15A, No. 3). 100p. 1981. pap. 18.00 (*0-08-028130-3*, Pergamon Pr) Elsevier.

— Some Case Studies in Latin America. 88p. 1983. pap. 25.00 (*0-08-030843-0*, 27, Pergamon Pr) Elsevier.

McEwan, S. & Pickard, G. Decollage. Smith, M., ed. (C). 1989. student ed 50.00 (*0-7487-0058-7*, Pub. by S Thornes Pubs UK); teacher ed 175.00 (*0-7487-0059-5*, Pub. by S Thornes Pubs UK); audio 125.00 (*0-7487-0060-9*, Pub. by S Thornes Pubs UK) St Mut.

McEwen & Larsen. Mass Spectrometry of Biological Materials. (Practical Spectroscopy Ser.: Vol. 8). 536p. 1990. 175.00 (*0-8247-8182-1*) Dekker.

McEwen, jt. auth. see Merritt.

McEwen, Bruce S. & Schmeck, Harold M., Jr. The Hostage Brain. LC 94-67849. (Illus.). 323p. 1994. pap. text ed. 19.95 (*0-87470-056-6*) Rockefeller.

— The Hostage Brain. LC 94-67849. (Illus.). 323p. 1994. text ed. 39.95 (*0-87470-054-X*) Rockefeller.

McEwen, Charles N., jt. ed. see Merritt, Charles, Jr.

McEwen, Colleen M., ed. see Cox, Bobbi & Flanagan, Beth.

McEwen, Craig A., jt. auth. see Rogers, Nancy H.

McEwen, Currier. The Japanese Iris. LC 89-24974. (Illus.). 167p. 1990. 29.95 (*0-87451-512-2*) U Pr of New Eng.

— The Siberian Iris. LC 95-14643. (Illus.). 1996. write for info. (*0-88192-329-X*) Timber.

McEwen, Douglas & Mitchell, Claire. Fundamentals of Recreation Programming for Campgrounds & RV Parks. LC 91-60387. 212p. 1991. pap. 13.95 (*0-915611-37-6*) Sagamore Pub.

McEwen, Evelyn, ed. Age: The Unrecognised Discrimination. (C). 1989. 49.00 (*0-86242-094-6*, Pub. by Age Concern Eng UK) St Mut.

McEwen, F. L. The Use & Significance of Pesticides. LC 78-23368. 554p. 1989. 55.50 (*0-471-03903-9*) Krieger.

McEwen, Gerald N., ed. see CTFA Staff.

McEwen, Gilbert D. The Oracle of the Coffee House: John Dunton's Athenian Mercury. LC 78-171109. 243p. 1972. 18.00 (*0-87328-056-3*) Huntington Lib.

McEwen, Indra K. Socrates' Ancestor: An Essay on Architectural Beginnings. LC 93-21863. (Illus.). 208p. 1993. pap. 16.50 (*0-262-63148-2*) MIT Pr.

McEwen, Indra K., tr. see Perrault, Claude.

McEwen, James, jt. auth. see Finlayson, Angela.

***McEwen, John.** John Bellany. (Illus.). 232p. 1995. 55.00 (*1-85158-632-6*, Pub. by Mnstream UK) Trafalgar.

— Paula Rego. rev. ed. (Illus.). 240p. (C). 1995. pap. 29.95 (*0-7148-2958-7*, Pub. by Phaidon Press UK) Chronicle Bks.

McEwen, Patricia, jt. auth. see Treffinger, Donald.

McEwen, W. E. & Berlin, K. D., eds. Organophosphorous Stereochemistry, 2 pts. Incl. Pt. 1. Origins of P(3&4) Compounds. 387p. 1975. 77.00 (*0-12-787031-8*); Pt. 2. P(5) Compounds. 1975. 70.00 (*0-12-787032-6*); (Benchmark Papers in Organic Chemistry: Vols. 3 & 4). 1975. write for info. (*0-318-50321-2*) Acad Pr.

McEwen, William J., jt. auth. see Tompson, James D.

McEwin, C. Kenneth. Focus on Interscholastic Sports & the Middle School. Romano, Louis G., ed. (Illus.). 18p. 1981. pap. text ed. 3.00 (*0-918449-03-0*) MI Middle Educ.

McEwin, C. Kenneth, jt. auth. see Scales, Peter S.

McFadden, Alneer A. & Burk, Janelle M. The Fritter Tree & the Honey Pond. (Illus.). 168p. 1985. 13.95 (*0-9615736-0-0*) Milestone Pr.

McFadden, Billie. The New Boxer. (Illus.). 256p. 1989. 25.95 (*0-87605-062-3*) Howell Bk.

***McFadden, Carol H. & Keeton, William T.** Biology: An Exploration of Life. (Illus.). (C). 1995. text ed. 75.95 (*0-393-96692-5*); student ed, pap. text ed. 19.95 (*0-393-95718-7*); student ed, pap. text ed. write for info. (*0-393-95947-3*) Norton.

— Biology: An Exploration of Life. 4th ed. LC 93-1530. (Illus.). 700p. (C). 1995. text ed. 63.95 (*0-393-95716-0*) Norton.

McFadden, Carol H., jt. auth. see Keeton, William T.

McFadden, Charles. Christianity Confronts Communism. 1983. 6.95 (*0-8199-0841-X*, Frncscn Herld) Franciscan Pr.

McFadden, Christine. New Vegetarian Food. LC 93-33435. (Illus.). 112p. 1994. pap. 15.00 (*0-02-034623-9*, Collier S&S) S&S Trade.

McFadden, Corey. Deception at Midnight. 368p. (Orig.). 1993. pap. 4.50 (*0-8439-3520-0*) Dorchester Pub Co.

McFadden, D., ed. Neural Mechanisms in Behavior: A Texas Symposium. (Illus.). 350p. 1980. 69.00 (*0-387-90468-9*) Spr-Verlag.

McFadden, D. L., jt. ed. see Engle, R. F.

McFadden, Daniel & Richter, Marcel K. Preferences, Uncertainty, & Optimality: Essays in Honor of Leonid Hurwicz. Chipman, John S. et al, eds. 307p. 1990. text ed. 93.50 (*0-8133-0723-6*) Westview.

McFadden, David. My Body Was Eaten by Dogs: Selected Poems. Bowering, George, ed. & intro. by. 120p. 1981. 12.95 (*0-916696-19-7*); pap. 6.95 (*0-916696-18-9*) Cross Country.

— A New Romance. 1979. pap. 3.00 (*0-916696-10-3*) Cross Country.

— The Saladmaker. rev. ed. 1977. reprint ed. pap. 2.00 (*0-916696-03-0*) Cross Country.

McFadden, David, jt. auth. see Phillips, Calvin.

McFadden, David A., jt. auth. see Phillipps, Calvin C.

McFadden, David R. & Adams, Brooks. Hair. LC 80-67094. (Exhibition Catalogue Ser.). (Illus.). 32p. (Orig.). 1980. pap. 6.95 (*0-910503-31-1*) Cooper-Hewitt Museum.

McFadden, David R., et al. L' Art de Vivre: Decorative Arts & Design in France, 1789-1989. Aakre, Nancy, ed. LC 88-63278. (Illus.). 256p. 1989. text ed. 60.00 (*0-86565-976-1*) Vendome.

McFadden, David W. Alternative Paths: Soviet-American Relations, 1917-1920. LC 92-17949. 464p. 1993. 60.00 (*0-19-507187-5*) OUP.

McFadden, Dorothy L. Drama in the Garden: Extraordinary Stories of the Creators of Twelve Unique Old Gardens in Seven Countries of Europe. LC 92-97120. 128p. 1992. pap. 19.95 (*0-9634140-0-3*) Little Owl Pr.

McFadden, E. & Rogers, Dawn, eds. Thoughts of Christmas: Childrens Christmas Party. (Illus.). 56p. (Orig.). (J). (gr. 3-6). 1994. pap. 4.99 (*0-9640168-1-8*) Pirate Writings.

McFadden, Emily J., ed. Child Welfare Around the World. 303p. 1991. pap. 7.50 (*0-87868-424-7*) Child Welfare.

***McFadden, Faith A.** Acts of Faith: A Memoir. 274p. (Orig.). 1994. pap. 14.95 (*0-89870-527-4*) Ignatius Pr.

Mcfadden, Fred R. Database Management. 3rd ed. 1991. text ed. 51.75 (*0-8053-6040-9*) Benjamin-Cummings.

McFadden, Fred R. & Hoffer, Jeffery A. Database Management. 2nd ed. (Illus.). 650p. (C). 1988. teacher ed 10.75 (*0-8053-6784-5*); text ed. 47.50 (*0-8053-6783-7*); trans. 10.75 (*0-8053-6787-X*); boxed 10.75 (*0-8053-6785-3*); 10.75 (*0-8053-6786-1*) Benjamin-Cummings.

McFadden, Fred R. & Hoffer, Jeffrey A. Modern Database Management. 4th ed. LC 93-31795. (C). 1994. text ed. 56.95 (*0-8053-6047-6*) Benjamin-Cummings.

McFadden, George. Discovering the Comic. LC 81-15825. 288p. 1982. 37.00 (*0-691-06496-2*) Princeton U Pr.

— Dryden, the Public Writer, 1660-1685. LC 77-85551. 319p. reprint ed. pap. 91.00 (*0-8357-3422-6*, 2039679) Bks Demand.

McFadden, Gerald. Federal Sentencing Manual, 2 vols. 1990. ring bd. write for info. (*0-8205-1471-3*) Bender.

McFadden, Grant, ed. Viroceptors, Virokines & Related Immune Modulators Encoded by DNA Viruses. (Molecular Biology Intelligence Unit Ser.). 214p. 1995. 89.00 (*1-57059-167-9*) R G Landes.

McFadden, Hugh, ed. see Jordan, John.

McFadden, Jenny, jt. auth. see McFadden, Judith.

McFadden, John, ed. Transcultural Counseling: Bilateral & International Perspectives. LC 93-7970. 347p. 1993. 35.95 (*1-55620-121-4*) Am Coun Assn.

McFadden, John, tr. see Erdozain, Placido.

McFadden, John J., ed. Financial Services Professional's Guide to the State of the Art. 3rd ed. LC 92-83888. 350p. (C). 1993. pap. text ed. 35.00 (*0-943590-44-2*) Amer College.

McFadden, John J., jt. auth. see Beam, Burton T., Jr.

McFadden, John J., jt. auth. see Beam, Burton.

McFadden, Johnjoe, ed. Molecular Biology of the Mycobacteria. (Surrey Seminars in Molecular Microbiology Ser.). 233p. 1990. text ed. 94.00 (*0-12-483378-0*) Acad Pr.

***McFadden, Judith & McFadden, Jenny.** Find Your Natural Weight the NECTAR Way. LC 94-68732. (Illus.). 192p. (Orig.). 1994. pap. 12.00 (*0-944337-24-4*) New View Pubns.

McFadden, L. D., jt. ed. see Knuepfer, P. L.

McFadden, Louis T. Federal Reserve Corporation. 1973. 59.95 (*0-8490-0157-9*) Gordon Pr.

McFadden, Margaret, jt. auth. see Gerber, Leslie E.

McFadden, Maria, ed. see Canavan, Francis.

***McFadden, Marlene E.** When Shannon Came Home. (Rainbow Romances Ser.). 160p. 1994. 14.95 (*0-7090-5432-7*, 919, Hale-Parkwest) Parkwest Pubns.

Mcfadden, Patrick. Electing Justice: The Law & Ethics of Judicial Election Campaigns. LC 90-82507. (Studies of the Justice System). 224p. (Orig.). 1990. pap. 6.00 (*0-938870-44-0*) Am Judicature.

McFadden, Roy. After Seymour's Funeral. 61p. 1990. pap. 13.95 (*0-85640-434-9*, Pub. by Blackstaff Pr IE) Dufour.

— Letters to the Hinterland. (C). 1986. pap. 15.00 (*0-948268-15-8*, Pub. by Dedalus Pr IE) St Mut.

McFadden, S. Little Book of Native American Wisdom. 1994. 5.95 (*1-85230-566-5*) Element MA.

McFadden, S. Michele, ed. see Abraham, Samuel V.

McFadden, S. Michele, ed. see Bonito, Grace.

McFadden, S. Michele, ed. see Gilliland, Ken.

McFadden, S. Michele, ed. see Grice, Charles P., Jr.

McFadden, S. Michele, ed. see Grones, Freda.

McFadden, S. Michele, ed. see Rowe, Leah.

McFadden, S. Michele, ed. see Stockton, Elizabeth.

McFadden, S. Michele, et al, eds. Trucking: A Truck Driver's Training Handbook. LC 79-90760. (Illus.). 434p. (Orig.). (C). 1986. pap. text ed. 24.95 (*0-89262-025-0*) Career Pub.

McFadden, Sarah & Ratcliff, Carter. Art Materialized: Selections from the Fabric Workshop. LC 81-84586. (Illus.). 60p. 1982. 10.00 (*0-916365-04-2*) Ind Curators.

***McFadden, Sarah & Simon, Joan, eds.** Carnegie International, 1988. LC 88-30021. (Illus.). 202p. 1988. pap. 22.95 (*0-88039-019-0*) Mus Art Carnegie.

McFadden, Stephen, jt. auth. see Groh, Trauger.

McFadden, Steven. Ancient Voices, Current Affairs: The Legend of the Rainbow Warriors. (Illus.). 176p. (Orig.). 1992. pap. 14.95 (*1-879181-00-2*) Bear & Co.

McFadden, Steven S. Profiles in Wisdom: Native Elders Speak about the Earth. LC 90-49873. (Illus.). 256p. (Orig.). 1991. pap. 14.95 (*0-939680-71-8*) Bear & Co.

McFadden, Susan H., jt. auth. see Magai, Carol.

McFadden, Terry T. & Bennett, F. Lawrence. Construction in Cold Regions: A Guide for Planners, Engineers, Contractors & Managers. LC 09-110317. (Series of Practical Construction Guides: No. 1344). 640p. 1991. text ed. 89.95 (*0-471-52503-0*) Wiley.

McFadden, Thomas M., ed. Does Jesus Make a Difference? 240p. reprint ed. pap. 22.50 (*0-8191-4155-0*) U Pr of Amer.

McFadden, William. Techniques of Combined Gas Chromatography-Mass Spectrometry: Applications in Organic Analysis. LC 87-35344. 482p. (C). 1988. reprint ed. lib. bdg. 70.00 (*0-89464-280-4*) Krieger.

McFadden, William C., ed. Georgetown at Two Hundred: Faculty Reflections on the University's Future. LC 90-32745. 353p. (Orig.). 1990. 24.95 (*0-87840-502-X*); pap. 14.95 (*0-87840-503-8*) Georgetown U Pr.

McFaden, H., tr. see Aizenberg, L A. & Yuzhakov, A P.

McFaden, H., tr. see Akhiezer.

McFaden, H., tr. see Egorychev, G P.

McFaden, H., tr. see Reshtenyak, Y.

McFaden, H. H., tr. see Berezanskii, Yu.

McFaden, H. H., tr. see Monakhov, V. N.

McFaden, H. H., tr. see Skorokhod, A. V.

McFaden, Michael. The Love Knot. (Illus.). 32p. (Orig.). 1975. pap. 3.00 (*0-88680-118-4*) I E Clark.

***McFaden, Tex.** Sketches in Poetry. 1995. 10.95 (*0-8062-5193-X*) Carlton.

McFadyen, Alistair I. The Call to Personhood: A Christian Theory of the Individual in Social Relationships. 336p. (C). 1990. 74.95 (*0-521-38471-0*); pap. 19.95 (*0-521-40929-2*) Cambridge U Pr.

McFadyen, Anne. Special Care Babies & Their Developing Relationships. LC 94-8491. 208p. 1994. 59.95x (*0-415-10613-3*, B4305); pap. 17.95 (*0-415-10614-1*, B4309) Routledge.

McFadyen, Deidre, jt. ed. see Rosen, Fred.

***McFadyen, Stuart, et al, eds.** Cultural Development in an Open Economy. (C). 1995. pap. 24.95 (*0-9698983-0-4*, Pub. by Wilfrid Laurier CN) Humanities.

McFadzean, Anita. One Special Star. LC 90-21485. (Illus.). 32p. (J). (ps-1). 1991. pap. 11.95 (*0-671-74023-7*, S&S Bks Young Read); pap. 3.95 (*0-671-74024-5*, S&S Bks Young Read) S&S Childrens.

McFadzean, Frank, ed. Towards an Open World Economy. LC 72-91277. 264p. 1973. text ed. 29.95 (*0-312-81060-1*) St Martin.

McFadzean, J. A. Flagyl: The Story of a Pharmaceutical Discovery. (History of Medicine Ser.). (Illus.). 117p. 1986. 38.00 (*1-85070-125-3*) Prthnon Pub.

McFague, Sallie. The Body of God: An Ecological Theology. LC 93-6584. 208p. 1993. pap. 15.00 (*0-8006-2735-0*, 1-2735) Augsburg Fortress.

— Metaphorical Theology: Models of God in Religious Language. LC 82-7246. 240p. (C). 1982. pap. 15.00 (*0-8006-1687-1*, 1-1687, Fortress Pr) Augsburg Fortress.

— Models of God: Theology for an Ecological, Nuclear Age. LC 86-46435. 240p. 1987. pap. 15.00 (*0-8006-2051-8*, 1-2051, Fortress Pr) Augsburg Fortress.

— Speaking in Parables: A Study in Metaphor & Theology. LC 74-26338. 192p. 1975. pap. 12.00 (*0-8006-1097-0*, 1-1097, Fortress Pr) Augsburg Fortress.

McFall, Gardner. Naming the Animals. LC 93-14532. (Illus.). (J). (ps-3). 1994. lib. bdg. 13.99 (*0-670-84814-X*) Viking Child Bks.

McFall, Lynne. Dancer with Bruised Knees. 224p. 1994. 18.95 (*0-8118-0787-8*) Chronicle Bks.

— Happiness. (Studies in Moral Philosophy: Vol. 1). 129p. (C). 1989. text ed. 27.50 (*0-8204-0711-9*) P Lang Pubs.

McFall, Mary L. Passports to Change. LC 93-17723. 241p. 1993. pap. 12.95 (*0-87604-307-4*, 389) ARE Pr.

McFall, Nancy, ed. see Brady, John C., II.

McFall, Pat. Index to Conway County, Arkansas, Deed Books A & B, 1825-1843. 50p. 1989. pap. 14.00 (*0-941765-48-2*) Arkansas Res.

McFall, Patricia. Night Butterfly. 304p. 1992. 18.95 (*0-312-07750-5*, Pub. by Thomas Dunne Bks) St Martin.

McFall, Robert J. Railway Monopoly & Rate Regulation. LC 79-76704. (Columbia University. Studies in the Social Sciences: No. 164). reprint ed. 16.50 (*0-404-51164-3*) AMS Pr.

McFalls, Joseph A., Jr. & McFalls, Marguerite H. Disease & Fertility: Monograph. (Studies in Population). 1984. text ed. 91.00 (*0-12-483380-2*) Acad Pr.

McFalls, Laurence H. Communism's Collapse, Democracy's Demise? The Cultural Context & Consequences of the East German Revolution. LC 94-20535. 1995. 40.00 (*0-8147-5521-6*) NYU Pr.

McFalls, Marguerite H., jt. auth. see McFalls, Joseph A., Jr.

McFann, Cathy. Nuclear Meditations. (Fastbook 1985 Ser.). 20p. 1985. 6.00 (*0-911051-16-3*) Plain View.

McFann, Jane. Be Mine. (J). (gr. 12 up). 1994. pap. 3.25 (*0-590-46690-9*) Scholastic Inc.

— Deathtrap & Dinosaur. 224p. (Orig.). 1989. pap. 2.75 (*0-380-75624-2*, Flare) Avon.

— Free the Conroy Seven. 160p. (Orig.). 1993. pap. 3.50 (*0-380-76401-6*, Flare) Avon.

— Maybe by Then I'll Understand. 192p. (Orig.). 1987. pap. 2.50 (*0-380-75221-2*, Flare) Avon.

— No Time for Rabbits. 176p. 1991. pap. 2.95 (*0-380-76085-1*, Flare) Avon.

— Nothing More, Nothing Less. 176p. (Orig.). (J). (gr. 5). 1993. pap. 3.50 (*0-380-76636-1*, Flare) Avon.

— One More Chance. 192p. (YA). (gr. 6 up). 1988. pap. 2.50 (*0-380-75466-5*, Flare) Avon.

Mcfann, Jane. One Step Short. 1990. pap. 2.95 (*0-380-75805-9*, Flare) Avon.

McFann, Julia B. We Can Play. (Illus.). 13p. (Orig.). (J). (gr. 1). 1993. pap. text ed. write for info. (*1-882225-15-5*) Tott Pubns.

McFarlan, Donald. Wizard of the Great Lakes. (Stories of Faith & Fame Ser.). (J). (gr. 5-9). 1979. pap. 3.95 (*0-87508-631-4*) Chr Lit.

McFarlan, Donald, ed. see Stevenson, Robert Louis.

McFarlan, Donald, et al, eds. The Guinness Book of Records 1992. 320p. 1991. 22.95 (*0-8160-2643-2*) Facts on File.

McFarlan, F. Warren. The Information Systems Research Challenge. 1984. pap. text ed. 35.00 (*0-07-103257-6*) McGraw.

McFarland. Hearing Aids. 256p. 1990. 49.95 (*0-8151-6045-3*, Yr Bk Med Pubs) Mosby Yr Bk.

— Nursing Diagnosis & Intervention: Planning for Patient Care. (Illus.). 1040p. 1989. pap. text ed. 32.95 (*0-8016-3222-6*) Mosby Yr Bk.

— Nursing Diagnosis & Intervention: Planning for Patient Care. 2nd ed. 832p. 1993. pap. 32.95 (*0-8016-6703-8*) Mosby Yr Bk.

McFarland, Alan R. & Bishop, Wayne S. Union Authorization Cards & the NLRB: A Study of Congressional Intent, Administrative Policy, & Judicial Review. LC 70-78136. (Labor Relations & Public Policy Ser.: No. 2). 112p. reprint ed. pap. 32.00 (*0-8357-3160-X*, 2039423) Bks Demand.

McFarland, Andrew S. Common Cause: Lobbying in the Public Interest. LC 84-7732. (Chatham House Series on Change in American Politics). (Illus.). 224p. 1984. pap. text ed. 14.95 (*0-934540-28-4*) Chatham Hse Pubs.

— Cooperative Pluralism: The National Coal Policy Experiment. LC 93-8156. (Studies in Government & Public Policy). 192p. 1993. 29.95 (*0-7006-0617-3*); pap. 14.95 (*0-7006-0618-1*) U Pr of KS.

— Power & Leadership in Pluralist Systems. LC 68-26781. xii, 273p. 1969. 37.50 (*0-8047-0677-8*) Stanford U Pr.

***McFarland, Barbara.** Brief Therapy & Eating Disorders: A Practical Guide to Solution-Focused Work with Clients. LC 94-38947. (Social & Behavioral Sciences-Health Ser.). 288p. 1995. 29.95 (*0-7879-0053-2*) Jossey-Bass.

— Sexuality & Recovery. 20p. (Orig.). (C). 1984. pap. 1.55 (*0-89486-246-4*, 1398B) Hazelden.

McFarland, Barbara & Baker-Baumann, Tyeis. Feeding the Empty Heart: Adult Children of Alcoholics & Compulsive Fasting. 112p. 1989. pap. 9.00 (*0-89486-501-3*, 5038A) Hazelden.

— Shame & Body Image: Culture & the Compulsive Eater. 1990. pap. 9.95 (*1-55874-064-3*) Health Comm.

McFarland, Barbara & Baumann, Tyeis B. Feeding the Empty Heart: Adult Children & Compulsive Eating. LC 87-46216. 128p. (Orig.). 1988. pap. 9.00 (*0-06-255483-2*, Hazelden SF) Harper SF.

McFarland, Barbara & Erb, Ann M. Abstinence in Action: Food Planning for Compulsive Eaters. 140p. 1989. pap. 16.95 (*0-89486-538-2*, 5045A) Hazelden.

McFarland, Carl, jt. auth. see Cummings, Homer.

McFarland, Claxel. One Cool Evening. LC 90-70670. 159p. (Orig.). 1990. pap. 8.00 (*1-56002-011-3*) Aegina Pr.

McFarland, Cynthia. Hoofbeats: The Story of a Thoroughbred. LC 92-14255. (Illus.). 32p. (J). (gr. 1-3). 1993. text ed. 14.95 (*0-689-31757-3*, Atheneum Bks Young) S&S Childrens.

McFarland, Dalton E. Managerial Innovation Change in the Metropolitan Hospital. LC 79-14551. (Praeger Special Studies). 336p. 1979. text ed. 65.00 (*0-275-90390-7*, C0390, Praeger Pubs) Greenwood.

An Asterisk (*) at the beginning of an entry indicates that the title is appearing in BIP for the first time.

McFarland, Dalton E. & Kitterman. Secretarial Procedures for the Automated Office. (C). 1985. teacher ed write for info. (*0-8359-6598-8*, Reston) P-H.

McFarland, Dalton E., jt. ed. see Wickert, Frederic R.

McFarland, Daniel M. Historical Dictionary of Upper Volta. LC 77-14987. (African Historical Dictionaries Ser.: No. 14). (Illus.). 239p. 1978. 27.50 (*0-8108-1088-3*) Scarecrow.

McFarland, Daniel M., jt. auth. see Owusu-Ansah, David.

***McFarland, David.** Dictionnaire du Comportement Animal. 1013p. (FRE.). 1990. pap. 55.00 (*0-7859-7802-X*, 2221052811) Fr & Eur.

McFarland, David J. Animal Behavior: Psychobiology, Ethology & Evolution. 576p. 1985. text ed. 43.25 (*0-8053-6790-X*) Benjamin-Cummings.

— Animal Behaviour. 2nd ed. 585p. 1993. pap. text ed. 52. 95 (*0-470-22047-3*) Halsted Pr.

— Animal Behaviour: Psychobiology, Ethology, & Evolution. 2nd ed. LC 92-16276. 1993. write for info. (*0-582-06721-9*) Longman.

McFarland, David J., ed. The Oxford Companion to Animal Behavior. (Illus.). 657p. 1982. 49.95 (*0-19-866120-7*) OUP.

McFarland, David J. & Bosser, Thomas. Intelligent Behavior in Animals & Robots. LC 92-40583. (Bradford Series in Complex Adaptive Systems). (Illus.). 328p. (C). 1993. 42.50x (*0-262-13293-1*, Bradford Bks) MIT Pr.

McFarland, Dennis. The Music Room. 288p. 1991. reprint ed. pap. 8.95 (*0-380-71456-6*) Avon.

— School for the Blind. 1994. 21.95 (*0-395-64497-6*) HM.

— School for the Blind. 1995. mass mkt. 6.99 (*0-8041-1350-5*) Ivy Books.

McFarland, Dorothy, ed. see Weil, Simone.

McFarland, Dorothy T. Simone Weil. LC 82-25609. (Literature & Life Ser.). 207p. (C). 1983. 19.95 (*0-8044-2604-X*, F Ungar Bks) Continuum.

***McFarland, Douglas & Keppel, William J.** Minnesota Civil Practice. suppl. ed. 1994. ring bd. 65.00 (*0-614-03153-2*) Butterworth Legal Pubs.

McFarland, Douglas D. & Keppel, William J. Minnesota Civil Practice, 4 vols., Set. 2nd ed. 2560p. 1994. boxed 295.00 (*0-86678-858-1*) Michie Butterworth.

McFarland, Douglas D., jt. auth. see Park, Roger C.

McFarland, Douglas D., jt. auth. see Park, Roger.

McFarland, Elaine. Protestants First: Orangeism in 19th Century Scotland. (Illus.). 224p. 1992. pap. 25.00 (*0-7486-0216-X*, Pub. by Edinburgh U Pr UK) Col U Pr.

McFarland, Elizabeth F. Forever Frontier: The Gila Cliff Dwellings. LC 67-63242. (Illus.). 68p. 1967. pap. 2.50 (*0-9615359-0-3*) Crest Pr Inc.

— Wilderness of the Gila. LC 74-78494. (Illus.). 74p. 1974. pap. 2.50 (*0-9615359-2-X*) Crest Pr Inc.

McFarland, Floyd B. Economic Philosophy & American Problems: Classical Mechanism, Marxist Dialectic, & Cultural Evolution. 256p. (C). 1991. text ed. 49.00 (*0-8476-7670-6*) Rowman.

McFarland, George B. Thai-English Dictionary. xxi, 1060p. 1944. 42.50 (*0-8047-0383-3*) Stanford U Pr.

McFarland, Gerald. The Counterfeit Man: The True Story of the Boorn-Colvin Murder Case. LC 90-52524. (Illus.). 256p. 1991. 22.95 (*0-394-58009-5*) Pantheon.

McFarland, Gerald W. The Counterfeit Man: The True Story of the Boorn-Colvin Murder Case. LC 92-43533. (Illus.). 264p. (C). 1993. reprint ed. pap. 15.95 (*0-87023-837-X*) U of Mass Pr.

— A Scattered People: An American Family Moves West. LC 91-16751. (Illus.). 304p. (C). 1991. reprint ed. pap. 15.95 (*0-87023-765-9*) U of Mass Pr.

McFarland, Gerald W., ed. Mugwumps, Morals, & Politics, 1884-1920. LC 74-21242. 292p. 1975. 32.50x (*0-87023-175-8*) U of Mass Pr.

McFarland, Gertrude K., et al. Nursing Diagnosis & Process Psychiatric Mental Health. 2nd ed. (Illus.). 336p. 1992. text ed. 23.95 (*0-397-54758-7*) Lippincott.

McFarland, Gertrude K. & Thomas, Mary D. Psychiatric Mental Health Nursing: Application of the Nursing Process. (Illus.). 1029p. 1990. text ed. 47.95 (*0-397-54678-5*) Lippincott.

McFarland, Gertrude K. & Wasli, Evelyn L. Nursing Diagnoses & Process in Psychiatric-Mental Health Nursing. LC 64-5161. 308p. 1986. text ed. 17.95 (*0-397-54598-3*, Lippincott Nursing) Lippincott.

McFarland, Gertrude K., et al. Nursing Leadership & Management: Contemporary Strategies. LC 83-16724. 349p. (C). 1984. text ed. 32.95 (*0-8273-4309-4*) Delmar.

McFarland, J. W. Sulfonyl Isocyanates & Sulfonyl Isothiocyanates. (Sulfur Report Ser.). 54p. 1981. pap. text ed. 53.00 (*3-7186-0255-5*) Gordon & Breach.

McFarland, Jeannie. Advanced Pattern Book: For Pine Needle Raffia Basketry. rev. ed. (Illus.). 64p. (C). 1993. reprint ed. pap. 11.00 (*0-9618828-1-6*) Baskets & Bullets.

— Pine Needle Raffia Basketry. rev. ed. (Illus.). 48p. 1993. reprint ed. pap. 9.00 (*0-9618828-0-8*) Baskets & Bullets.

McFarland, Jeffery, jt. auth. see Tolman, Ruth.

McFarland, Joe S. Coaching Pitchers. 2nd ed. LC 89-37721. (Illus.). 152p. 1990. pap. text ed. 20.95 (*0-88011-368-5*, PMCF0368) Human Kinetics.

McFarland, John. The Exploding Frog: & Other Fables from Aesop. (Illus.). (J). (gr. 3 up). 1981. write for info. (*0-316-55577-0*) Little.

McFarland, John R. Now That I Have Cancer...I Am Whole: Meditations for Cancer Patients & Those Who Love Them. 220p. (Orig.). 1993. 14.95 (*0-8362-2424-8*); pap. 8.95 (*0-8362-2426-4*) Andrews & McMeel.

McFarland, Joseph F. Twentieth Century History of the City of Washington & Washington County, Pennsylvania. (Illus.). 1369p. 1993. reprint ed. lib. bdg. 139.00 (*0-8328-3113-1*) Higginson Bk Co.

***McFarland, June & Gieselman, Mary E.** Comprehensive Index of the Publications of the American Association of Petroleum Geologists 1956-1965. 792p. 1967. 27.00 (*0-89181-498-1*) AAPG.

***McFarland, June & Hart, Ronald L.** Comprehensive Index of Publications of the American Association of Petroleum Geologists 1976-1980. 334p. 1984. 36.00 (*0-89181-502-3*) AAPG.

***McFarland, June & Rice, Peggy.** Comprehensive Index of Publications of the American Association of Petroleum Geologists 1971-1975. 906p. 1979. 33.00 (*0-89181-501-5*) AAPG.

***McFarland, June & Van Beuren, Victor V.** Comprehensive Index of Publications of the American Association of Petroleum Geologists 1981-1985. 360p. 1986. 42.00 (*0-89181-503-1*) AAPG.

McFarland, K. T. Allegheny County Archives, Vol. 4. 157p. 1991. text ed. 19.95 (*1-55856-068-8*) Closson Pr.

— Allegheny County, PA Archives, Vol. 1. 185p. 1991. text ed. 19.95 (*1-55856-052-1*) Closson Pr.

— Allegheny County, PA Archives, Vol. 2. 136p. 1990. text ed. 19.95 (*1-55856-065-3*) Closson Pr.

— Allegheny County, PA Archives, Vol. 3. 174p. 1991. text ed. 19.95 (*1-55856-067-X*) Closson Pr.

— Allegheny County, PA Archives, Vol. 5. 117p. 1991. text ed. 19.95 (*1-55856-069-6*) Closson Pr.

— Allegheny County, PA Archives, Vol. 6. 167p. 1991. text ed. 19.95 (*1-55856-060-2*) Closson Pr.

— Allegheny County, PA Archives, Vol. 8: Partition Dockets 4-7, 1873-1884. 127p. 1994. text ed. 19.95 (*1-55856-166-8*) Closson Pr.

— Early West Virginia Wills. 167p. 1993. pap. text ed. 14.95 (*1-55856-156-0*) Closson Pr.

— Hollidaysburg Records: Marriages, Deaths, & Petitions from Weekly Newspapers of Hollidaysburg, Huntingdon-Blair Counties, PA, 1836-1852. 129p. 1994. pap. text ed. 12.95 (*1-55856-167-6*) Closson Pr.

— Inscriptions from Two German Protestant Cemeteries: Allegheny (Now Pittsburgh) PA, St. John's Lutheran Cemetery (Springhill), & Boegtly Cemetery (Troy Hill) 132p. 1988. per., pap. text ed. 11.95 (*0-933227-70-1*) Closson Pr.

— Will Abstracts of Brooke County, (West) Virginia 1797-1850. 88p. per. 9.50 (*0-933227-26-4*) Closson Pr.

McFarland, K. T., comp. Inscriptions from Chartiers Cemetery, Pittsburgh, PA, Vol. II. 248p. 1988. pap. text ed. 16.95 (*0-933227-78-7*) Closson Pr.

— Inscriptions from Highwood Cemetery, Allegheny (Now Pittsburgh), PA, Vol. I. 138p. 1988. pap. text ed. 11.95 (*0-933227-74-4*) Closson Pr.

McFarland, K. T., ed. Inscriptions from Chartiers Cemetery, Pittsburgh, PA, Vol. I. 118p. 1988. pap. text ed. 11.95 (*0-933227-76-0*) Closson Pr.

— Inscriptions from Highwood Cemetery, Allegheny (Now Pittsburgh), PA, Vol. II. 229p. pap. text ed. 16.95 (*0-933227-75-2*) Closson Pr.

McFarland, Kathleen & Larkin, Judy. Colleen Marie. (Illus.). 56p. (Orig.). (J). (ps). 1985. pap. write for info. (*0-9621691-1-0*, TX 1-705-162) B Bumpers Inc.

— Meet Colleen Marie. (Illus.). 22p. (Orig.). (J). (ps). 1985. pap. write for info. (*0-9621691-0-2*, TX 1-650-724) B Bumpers Inc.

***McFarland, Kathy, ed.** Real-Life Beauty. (Illus.). 150p. 1995. text ed. 40.00 (*0-929870-29-8*) Advanstar Commns.

McFarland, Kay F. Love Grows When Shared. LC 90-71472. 51p. 1991. 5.95 (*1-55523-401-1*) Winston-Derek.

McFarland, Ken. Let's Get Acquainted. (Outreach Ser.). 32p. 1987. pap. 0.79 (*0-8163-0691-5*) Pacific Pr Pub Assn.

McFarland, Ken, ed. Union Dale Cemeteries, Vol. 2. 112p. per. 11.95 (*0-933227-25-6*) Closson Pr.

— Union Dale Cemetery, Vol. I. 109p. pap. text ed. 11.95 (*0-933227-24-8*) Closson Pr.

McFarland, Ken, jt. auth. see Holland, Kenneth J.

McFarland, Ken, ed. see Vandeman, George.

McFarland, Kenneth T. Bedford County, PA Archives, Vol. 6: Bedford Records, Births, Marriages, & Partitions 1850-1870. 227p. 1994. pap. 16.00 (*1-55856-158-7*) Closson Pr.

McFarland, Lee J. SimPleat. 41p. 1988. pap. 6.00 (*1-883763-03-7*) Kideko Hse.

— Swimsuits: Drafting & Design. 80p. 1989. pap. 12.00 (*1-883763-00-2*) Kideko Hse.

McFarland, Lynne J., et al. Twenty-First Century Leadership: Dialogues with One-Hundred Top Leaders. 336p. 1993. 21.95 (*0-9636018-0-6*); pap. 15.95 (*0-9636018-1-4*) Ldrship Pr.

McFarland, Marvin W., ed. Papers of Wilbur & Orville Wright, 2 Vols, 1. LC 79-169428. (Literature & History of Aviation Ser.). 1979. reprint ed. 54.95 (*0-405-03814-3*) Ayer.

— Papers of Wilbur & Orville Wright, 2 Vols, 2. LC 79-169428. (Literature & History of Aviation Ser.). 1979. reprint ed. 54.95 (*0-405-03815-1*) Ayer.

— Papers of Wilbur & Orville Wright, 2 Vols, Set. LC 79-169428. (Literature & History of Aviation Ser.). 1979. reprint ed. 104.95 (*0-405-03771-6*) Ayer.

McFarland, Mary B. Nursing Implications of Laboratory Tests. 3rd ed. 1994. pap. 28.95 (*0-8273-5135-6*) Delmar.

Mcfarland, Mike. Never Walk When You Can Ride. LC 89-42666. (Illus.). 142p. (Orig.). 1989. pap. 9.95 (*0-87358-493-7*) Northland AZ.

***McFarland, Minnie B.** A Young & Ardent Eye: The Story of Minnie Bullack McFarland. Olsen, Afton S., ed. & intro. by. 106p. (Orig.). Date not set. pap. text ed. 25.00 (*0-9629578-6-0*) Intl Long WA.

McFarland, Norman. Delivered from Death Unto Life. 70p. 1974. pap. write for info. (*1-881909-06-9*) Advent Christ Gen Conf.

***McFarland, Peggy A. & Carter, Cheryl J.** Becoming Women of Strength. LC 94-28283. 1994. pap. 9.95 (*1-55503-708-9*) Covenant Comms.

McFarland, Philip J., et al. Themes in World Literature. (Literature Ser.). (Illus.). 1975. teacher ed. pap. 25.64 (*0-395-20157-8*) HM.

McFarland, Randy, ed. see Chevchuc, Carol L.

McFarland, Rhoda. Coping Through Assertiveness. rev. ed. (Coping Ser.). (Illus.). 140p. (YA). (gr. 7-12). 1992. lib. bdg. 15.95 (*0-8239-1374-0*) Rosen Group.

— Coping Through Self-Esteem. rev. ed. Rosen, Ruth, ed. (Coping Ser.). (YA). (gr. 7 up). 1993. lib. bdg. 15.95 (*0-8239-1654-5*) Rosen Group.

— Coping with Stigma. Rosen, Ruth, ed. (Coping Ser.). (YA). (gr. 7-12). 1989. lib. bdg. 15.95 (*0-8239-0998-0*) Rosen Group.

— Coping with Substance Abuse. rev. ed. Rosen, Ruth, ed. (Coping Ser.). 144p. (YA). (gr. 7 up). 1990. lib. bdg. 15. 95 (*0-8239-1135-7*) Rosen Group.

— Drugs & Your Brothers & Sisters. rev. ed. (Drug Abuse Prevention Library). (YA). (gr. 7-12). 1993. lib. bdg. 15. 95 (*0-8239-1754-1*) Rosen Group.

— The World of Work. Rosen, Ruth, ed. (Life Skills Library). (YA). (gr. 7-12). 1993. 13.95 (*0-8239-1467-4*) Rosen Group.

McFarland, Ron. David Wagoner. LC 89-60062. (Western Writers Ser.: No. 88). (Illus.). 55p. (Orig.). 1989. pap. 3.95 (*0-88430-087-0*) Boise St U W Writ Ser.

— The Haunting Familiarity of Things. Wilson, Don D., ed. 56p. (Orig.). 1993. pap. 7.50 (*1-880286-12-2*) Singular Speech Pr.

— Norman Maclean. LC 93-70135. (Western Writers Ser.: No. 107). (Illus.). 55p. 1993. pap. 3.95 (*0-88430-106-0*) Boise St U W Writ Ser.

— Tess Gallagher. LC 95-75727. (Western Writers Ser.: No. 120). (Illus.). 55p. (C). 1995. pap. 3.95x (*0-88430-119-2*) Boise St U W Writ Ser.

McFarland, Ron, ed. see Maclean, Norman.

McFarland, Ron, et al, eds. Deep Down Things: Poems of the Inland Pacific Northwest. LC 90-24601. 220p. 1991. 20.00 (*0-87422-081-5*); pap. 14.95 (*0-87422-078-5*) Wash St U Pr.

McFarland, Ronald E. The Villanelle: The Evolution of a Poetic Form. LC 87-24136. 183p. 1987. pap. 14.95 (*0-89301-121-5*) U of Idaho Pr.

McFarland, Ronald E., ed. Idaho's Poetry: A Centennial Anthology. LC 88-27660. 288p. 1989. pap. 16.95 (*0-89301-128-2*) U of Idaho Pr.

***McFarland, Stephen L.** America's Pursuit of Precision Bombing. LC 94-21955. (History of Aviation Ser.). 368p. 1995. 29.95 (*1-56098-407-4*) Smithsonian.

McFarland, Stephen L. & Newton, Wesley P. To Command the Sky: The Battle for Air Superiority over Germany, 1942-1944. LC 91-9712. (History of Aviation Ser.). (Illus.). 344p. (C). 1991. text ed. 35.00 (*1-56098-069-9*) Smithsonian.

McFarland, Thomas. Originality & Imagination. LC 84-47949. 248p. (C). 1985. text ed. 36.00x (*0-8018-2517-2*) Johns Hopkins.

— Romantic Cruxes: The English Essayists & the Spirit of the Age. 150p. 1988. 36.00 (*0-19-812895-9*) OUP.

— Romanticism & the Forms of Ruin: Wordsworth, Coleridge & Modalities of Fragmentation. LC 80-7546. 432p. 1981. 67.50x (*0-691-06437-7*) Princeton U Pr.

— Romanticism & the Heritage of Rousseau. 320p. 1995. 55. 00 (*0-19-818287-2*) OUP.

— Shakespeare's Pastoral Comedy. LC 72-81325. 228p. reprint ed. pap. 65.00 (*0-7837-3752-1*, 2043569) Bks Demand.

— Shapes of Culture. LC 86-14670. 201p. 1987. text ed. 27. 95 (*0-87745-162-1*) U of Iowa Pr.

— William Wordsworth: Intensity & Achievement. 185p. 1992. 45.00 (*0-19-811253-X*) OUP.

McFarland, Thomas D. & Parker, Reese. Expert Systems in Education & Training. LC 89-38713. (Illus.). 280p. 1990. 34.95 (*0-87778-210-5*) Educ Tech Pubns.

McFarland, Tom, ed. see Mitrione, Dan.

McFarlane, jt. auth. see Anderson.

McFarlane, A. G., jt. auth. see Pang, G. K.

McFarlane, Anthony. The British in the Americas, 1480-1815. LC 94-6450. (Studies in Modern History). (C). 1994. text ed. 63.95 (*0-582-20950-1*, 76702, Pub. by Longman UK) Longman.

— The British in the Americas, 1480-1815. LC 94-6450. (Studies in Modern History). (C). 1995. pap. text ed. 22. 95 (*0-582-20949-8*, 76701, Pub. by Longman UK) Longman.

— Colombia Before Independence: Economy, Society, & Politics under Bourbon Rule. LC 92-42299. (Cambridge Latin American Studies: No. 75). (Illus.). 400p. (C). 1993. 59.95 (*0-521-41641-8*) Cambridge U Pr.

***McFarlane, Brian.** Hockey for Kids: Heroes, Tips & Facts. (Illus.). (J). (gr. 3-7). 1995. pap. 9.95 (*1-55074-215-9*) IPG Chicago.

— Stanley Cup Fever: One Hundred Years of Hockey Greatness. 256p. 1992. pap. 15.95 (*0-7737-5554-3*, Pub. by Stoddart Pubng CN) Genl Dist Srvs.

McFarlane, Brian, ed. Sixty Voices: Celebrities Recall the Golden Age of British Cinema. (Illus.). 272p. (C). 1993. 60.00 (*0-85170-353-4*, Pub. by British Film Inst UK); pap. 29.95 (*0-85170-349-6*, Pub. by British Film Inst UK) Ind U Pr.

McFarlane, Brian & Mayer, Geoff. New Australian Cinema: Sources & Parallels in British & American Film. (Illus.). 280p. (C). 1992. 54.95 (*0-521-38363-3*); pap. 19.95 (*0-521-38768-X*) Cambridge U Pr.

McFarlane, Bruce. Yugoslavia. (Marxist Regimes Ser.). 220p. 1988. text ed. 49.00 (*0-86187-452-8*, Pub. by Pinter Pubs UK); text ed. 17.50 (*0-86187-453-6*, Pub. by Pinter Pubs UK) St Martin.

McFarlane, Bruce, jt. auth. see Groenewegen, Peter D.

McFarlane, Bruce, jt. auth. see Wheelwright, E. L.

McFarlane, Bruce, jt. auth. see Wheelwright, Edward.

McFarlane, C., jt. auth. see Hayward, Arthur L.

McFarlane-Castledine. A Guide to the Practice of Nursing. 176p. 1982. pap. 10.00 (*0-8016-3278-1*) Mosby Yr Bk.

McFarlane, Craig, jt. ed. see Trapp, Stefan.

McFarlane, G. Copyright Through Cases. 352p. 1986. pap. 30.00 (*0-08-039208-3*, Pergamon Pr) Elsevier.

— Customs & Excise Cases. (Criminal Law Library). 384p. 1988. 100.00 (*0-08-039245-8*, Pergamon Pr) Elsevier.

— A Practical Introduction to Copyright. 2nd ed. (Waterlow Practitioner's Library). 448p. 1990. reprint ed. pap. 59.95 (*0-08-033074-6*, Pergamon Pr) Elsevier.

McFarlane, Gavin. McFarlane's Customs Law Handbook, 1989-90. 320p. (C). 1990. 275.00 (*1-85431-057-7*, Pub. by Blackstone Pr UK) St Mut.

— McFarlane's Customs Law Handbook, 1990-1991. 494p. (C). 1991. 64.00 (*1-85431-147-6*, Pub. by Blackstone Pr UK) W W Gaunt.

— VAT. (C). 1991. text ed. 22.00 (*1-85431-134-4*, Pub. by Blackstone Pr UK) W W Gaunt.

McFarlane, Graham, jt. auth. see Donnan, Hastings.

McFarlane, I. D., ed. Acta Conventus Neo-Latini Sanctandreani: Papers from the Fifth International Congress, 1982, at St. Andrews. (Medieval & Renaissance Texts & Studies: Vol. 38). (Illus.). 656p. 1986. 60.00 (*0-86698-070-9*) MRTS.

— The Entry of Henri II into Paris, 1549: 16 June 1549. LC 81-18925. (Renaissance Triumphs & Magnificences, Medieval & Renaissance Texts & Studies: Vol. 7). 208p. 1982. 26.00 (*0-86698-013-X*) MRTS.

McFarlane, I. D., ed. see D'Aubigne, Agrippa.

McFarlane, I D., jt. ed. see Smith, Pauline M.

McFarlane, James. Ibsen & Meaning: Studies, Essays & Prefaces, 1953-87. 396p. 1988. pap. 25.00 (*1-870041-07-0*, Pub. by Norvik Pr UK) Dufour.

McFarlane, James, ed. The Cambridge Companion to Ibsen. (Companions to Literature Ser.). (Illus.). 304p. (C). 1994. 59.95 (*0-521-41166-1*); pap. 16.95 (*0-521-42321-X*) Cambridge U Pr.

McFarlane, James, jt. auth. see Bradbury, Malcolm.

McFarlane, James, tr. see Hamsun, Knut.

McFarlane, James, ed. see Ibsen, Henrik.

McFarlane, James, tr. see Ibsen, Henrik.

McFarlane, James, jt. ed. see Naess, Harald.

McFarlane, James, tr. see Obstfelder, Sigbjorn.

McFarlane, James R. Traction in Franklin County Vermont - St. Albans Street Railway St. Albans & Swanton Traction Company: St. Albans Street Railway, St. Albans & Swanton Traction Company. Harris, Marion, ed. LC 94-14087. (Illus.). 48p. 1994. pap. 16.50 (*0-933449-21-6*) Transport Trails.

McFarlane, James R., jt. auth. see Benedict, Roy G.

McFarlane, James W., tr. see Hamsun, Knut.

McFarlane, John E., ed. A Treasury of Jamaican Poetry. 1977. lib. bdg. 59.95 (*0-8490-2760-8*) Gordon Pr.

— Voices from Summerland: An Anthology of Jamaican Poetry. 1977. lib. bdg. 59.95 (*0-8490-2802-7*) Gordon Pr.

***McFarlane, Judith & Parker, Barbara.** Abuse During Pregnancy: A Protocol for Prevention & Intervention. Damus, Karla & Freda, Margaret C., eds. LC 94-34250. 1994. write for info. (*0-86525-059-6*) March of Dimes.

McFarlane, Judith, jt. auth. see Whitson, Betty J.

McFarlane, Judith M. The Clinical Handbook of Family Nursing. LC 85-31446. 562p. 1986. pap. text ed. 32.95 (*0-8273-4304-3*) Delmar.

McFarlane, K. B. England in the Fifteenth Century: Collected Essays. 307p. (C). 1982. text ed. 50.00 (*0-9506882-5-8*); pap. 20.00 (*0-907628-01-X*) Hambledon Press.

McFarlane, Kee, jt. auth. see Cunningham, Carolyn.

McFarlane, M. J., ed. Laterites - Some Aspects of Current Research: Proceedings of the Laterite Workshop, 1st International Geomorphological Conference, 1985. (Annals of Geomorphology Ser.: Suppl. 64). (Illus.). 180p. 1987. pap. text ed. 68.60 (*3-443-21064-3*, Pub. by Gebrueder Borntraeger GW) Lubrecht & Cramer.

McFarlane, Marilyn. Best Places to Stay in California. 3rd ed. 1994. pap. 16.95 (*0-395-65569-2*) HM.

— Best Places to Stay in the Pacific Northwest. 3rd ed. (Best Places to Stay Ser.). (Illus.). 512p. 1993. pap. 14.95 (*0-395-62229-8*) HM.

— Best Places to Stay in the Pacific Northwest. 4th ed. (Best Places to Stay Ser.). 1995. pap. 16.95 (*0-395-70008-6*) HM.

— Northwest Discoveries: 100 Great Vacation Getaways. (Illus.). 213p. (Orig.). 1993. pap. 12.95 (*0-9634970-3-0*) Far Corner.

— The Older Americans Cookbook. 201p. 1988. 16.95 (*0-936389-04-4*); pap. 8.95 (*0-936389-05-2*) Tudor Pubs.

— Quick Escapes in the Pacific Northwest: Forty Weekend Trips from Portland, Seattle & Vancouver, B.C. 2nd ed. LC 93-29768. (Voyager Book Ser.). (Illus.). 336p. 1994. pap. 13.95 (*1-56440-283-5*) Globe Pequot.

McFarlane, Marilyn, jt. auth. see Osmont, Kelly.

McFarlane, Marilyn, ed. see Osmont, Kelly.

McFarlane, R. M., et al, eds. Dupuytren's Disease: Biology & Treatment. (Hand & Upper Limb Ser.: Vol. 5). (Illus.). 451p. 1990. text ed. 110.00 (*0-443-03818-X*) Churchill.

***McFarlane, Robert C. & Smardz, Zofia.** Special Trust: Pride, Principle & Politics Inside the White House. LC 94-32882. 1994. 25.00 (*1-56977-880-9*) Cadell & Davies.

McFarlane, Robert W. Stillness in the Pines: The Ecology of the Red-Cockaded Woodpecker. 1994. pap. 10.95 (*0-393-31167-8*) Norton.

McFarlane, Robert W., jt. ed. see Esch, Gerald W.

***McFarlane, Sheryl.** Jessie's Island. (Illus.). 32p. (Orig.). (J). (gr. 1-4). 1992. pap. 7.95 (*0-920501-76-1*) Orca Bk Pubs.

— Moonsnail Song. (Illus.). 32p. (J). (gr. 1-4). 1994. lib. bdg. 14.95 (*1-55143-008-8*) Orca Bk Pubs.

M

An Asterisk (*) at the beginning of an entry indicates that the title is appearing in BIP for the first time.

— Waiting for the Whales. LC 92-25117. (Illus.). 32p. (J). (ps-3). 1993. lib. bdg. 14.95 (*0-399-22515-3*, Philomel Bks) Putnam Pub Group.

McFarlane, Stephen C., jt. auth. see Boone, Daniel R.

***McFarlane, Todd.** Spawn. (Illus.). 116p. (YA). Date not set. pap. 9.95 (*1-887279-01-6*) Image Comics.

— Torment. (Spiderman Ser.). (Illus.). 128p. 1992. pap. 12.95 (*0-87135-805-0*) Marvel Entmnt.

McFarlane, Todd, jt. auth. see Michelinie, David.

McFarlane, William, ed. see Green, John L., Jr.

McFarlane, William R., ed. Family Therapy in Schizophrenia. LC 82-11742. (Guilford Family Therapy Ser.). 355p. 1983. lib. bdg. 40.00 (*0-89862-042-2*) Guilford Pr.

McFarquhar, A. M., ed. Europe's Future Food & Agriculture. (Asepelt Ser.: Vol. 3). 1971. 46.25 (*0-444-10052-0*, North Holland) Elsevier.

McFate, K. L., ed. Electrical Energy in Agriculture. (Energy in World Agriculture Ser.: No. 3). 352p. 1990. 143.75 (*0-444-43026-1*) Elsevier.

McFate, Katherine, ed. The Metropolitan Area Fact Book. 118p. 1988. pap. 18.25 (*0-941410-65-X*) Jt Ctr Pol Studies.

McFate, Katherine, et al, eds. Poverty, Inequality, & the Future of Social Policy: Western States in the New World Order. 704p. 1995. 70.00 (*0-87154-510-1*) Russell Sage.

McFate, Patricia. The Writings of James Stephens: Variations on a Theme of Love. LC 78-13287. 1979. text ed. 29.95 (*0-312-89509-7*) St Martin.

McFate, Patricia, ed. The Uncollected Prose of James Stephens, 1907-1948, I. LC 82-10560. 170p. 1983. text ed. 29.95 (*0-312-82859-4*) St Martin.

McFather, Nelle. Ecstasy's Captive. 416p. 1983. pap. 3.50 (*0-8439-2006-8*) Dorchester Pub Co.

— Entangled. 480p. 1988. mass mkt. 4.50 (*1-55817-059-6*, Pinnacle NY) Windsor NY.

— Moonspell. 448p. (Orig.). 1994. mass mkt., pap. text ed. 4.99 (*0-505-51964-X*) Dorchester Pub Co.

— Southern Secrets. 1993. mass mkt. 4.99 (*0-312-95023-3*) St Martin.

— Tears of Fire. 448p. (Orig.). 1994. pap. 4.99 (*0-505-51932-1*, Love Spell) Dorchester Pub Co.

— Woman Alive! 304p. 1984. pap. 3.25 (*0-8439-2146-3*) Dorchester Pub Co.

McFather, Nellie. Lovespell. 400p. (Orig.). 1992. pap. 4.50 (*0-8439-3203-1*) Dorchester Pub Co.

McFaul, John M. The Politics of Jacksonian Finance. LC 72-4635. 245p. 1972. 35.00 (*0-8014-0738-9*) Cornell U Pr.

McFaul, Michael. Post-Communist Party Politics. LC 93-7396. (Significant Issues Series - Creating the Post-Communist Order: Vol. 15, No. 3). 132p. (gr. 13). 1993. pap. text ed. 17.00 (*0-89206-208-8*) CSI Studies.

— Understanding Russia's 1993 Parlimentary Elections: Implications for U. S. Foreign Policy. LC 94-10757. (Essays in Public Policy Ser.: No. 49). 1994. 5.00 (*0-8179-5542-9*) Hoover Inst Pr.

***McFaul, Michael, ed.** Can the Russian Military-Industrial Complex Be Privatized? 60p. (Orig.). 1993. pap. 6.00 (*0-935371-29-X*) CFISAC.

McFaul, Michael & Markov, Sergei. The Troubled Birth of Russian Democracy: Parties, Personalities, & Programs. (Hoover Press Publications: Vol. 415). 384p. (C). 1993. 39.95 (*0-8179-9231-6*); pap. 24.95 (*0-8179-9232-4*) Hoover Inst Pr.

McFaul, Michael, ed. see Perlmutter, Tova.

McFeat, Tom. Small-Group Cultures. 1974. 96.00 (*0-08-017073-0*, Pub. by Pergamon Repr UK) Franklin.

McFeat, Tom, ed. Indians of the North Pacific Coast. LC 88-20675. 286p. 1967. pap. 8.95 (*0-295-74095-7*) U of Wash Pr.

***McFedries, Paul.** The Complete Idiot's Guide to Internet E-Mail. (Illus.). 325p. (Orig.). 1995. pap. 16.99 (*1-56761-596-1*) Alpha Bks IN.

— The Complete Idiot's Guide to Windows. 2nd ed. (Illus.). 350p. 1995. pap. text ed. 16.95 (*1-56761-546-5*) Alpha Bks IN.

— The Complete Idiot's Guide to Windows 95. 375p. 1995. 16.99 (*1-56761-495-7*) Alpha Bks IN.

— Complete Idiot's Guide to WordPerfect. 2nd ed. 375p. 1994. 16.95 (*1-56761-499-X*) Alpha Bks IN.

— The Complete Idiot's Guide to WordPerfect for Windows 6.1. 2nd ed. (Illus.). 350p. (Orig.). 1994. pap. text ed. 16.95 (*1-56761-543-0*) Alpha Bks IN.

— The Complete Idiot's Next Step with Windows. 400p. 1994. 19.95 (*1-56761-525-2*) Alpha Bks IN.

— The Complete Idiot's Next Step with Windows 95. 400p. 1995. 19.99 (*1-56761-614-3*) Alpha Bks IN.

— DOS 6 for the Guru Wanna-Be. 384p. 1993. pap. 18.95 (*0-672-30349-3*) Sams.

— First Book of Quattro Pro for Windows. (Illus.). (Orig.). 1992. pap. 18.95 (*0-672-27404-3*) Alpha Bks IN.

— First Book of Quicken 6. rev. ed. (First Bks.). (Illus.). (Orig.). 1992. pap. 19.95 (*1-56761-020-X*) Alpha Bks IN.

— Ten Minute Guide to the Norton Utilities 6.0. (Ten Minute Guides Ser.). (Illus.). 160p. (Orig.). 1991. pap. 9.95 (*0-672-30183-0*) Alpha Bks IN.

— Windows Woes. 1992. 12.95 (*1-56761-122-2*) Alpha Bks IN.

McFee, Graham. The Concept of Dance Education. LC 93-9997. 1994. write for info. (*0-415-08376-1*) Routledge.

McFee, June K. & Degge, Rogena M. Art, Culture, & Environment: A Catalyst for Teaching. 416p. (C). 1992. per. 29.95 (*0-8403-7418-6*) Kendall-Hunt.

McFee, Malcolm. Modern Blackfeet: Montanans on a Reservation. (Illus.). 134p. 1984. reprint ed. pap. text ed. 8.95 (*0-88133-043-4*) Waveland Pr.

McFee, Michael. Plain Air. LC 83-9109. (University of Central Florida Contemporary Poetry Ser.). 65p. 1983. 14.95 (*0-8130-0774-7*) U Press Fla.

— Sad Girl Sitting on a Running Board. LC 91-72899. 80p. (Orig.). 1991. pap. 10.50 (*0-917788-49-4*) Gnomon Pr.

— Vanishing Acts. LC 89-80713. 64p. (Orig.). 1989. pap. 10.50 (*0-917788-38-9*) Gnomon Pr.

McFee, Michael, ed. The Language They Speak Is Things to Eat: Fourteen Contemporary North Carolina Poets. LC 94-4239. (Illus.). 270p. 1994. 24.95 (*0-8078-2172-1*); pap. 12.95 (*0-8078-4483-7*) U of NC Pr.

McFee, Michael, ed. & intro. The Spectator Reader. LC 85-61379. (Illus.). 224p. (Orig.). 1985. pap. 7.95 (*0-9614785-1-9*) Spectator Publ.

McFee, Michael, jt. auth. see Matheson, Elizabeth.

McFee, William. Swallowing the Anchor. LC 70-128275. (Essay Index Reprint Ser.). 1977. 21.95 (*0-8369-1986-6*) Ayer.

McFeeley, Daniel, jt. auth. see Hamilton, Eugene.

McFeeley, Neil D. Appointment of Judges: The Johnson Presidency. 2nd ed. (Administrative History of the Johnson Presidency Ser.). 213p. 1986. text ed. 28.50 (*0-292-70377-5*) U of Tex Pr.

McFeely, Mary D. Lady Inspectors: The Campaign for a Better Workplace, 1893-1921. LC 91-4006. 216p. 1991. pap. 15.00 (*0-8203-1391-2*) U of Ga Pr.

McFeely, Mary D., ed. The Women's Annual: 1984-1985, No. 5. (Reference Publications, Women's Studies Annual). 184p. (C). 1985. text ed. 45.00 (*0-8161-8717-7*, Hall Reference); pap. 20.00 (*0-8161-8741-X*, Hall Reference) Macmillan.

McFeely, Mary D. & McFeely, William S., eds. Memoirs & Selected Letters: Ulysses S. Grant. 1199p. 1990. 35.00 (*0-940450-58-5*) Library of America.

McFeely, Richard A., ed. Advances in Veterinary Science & Comparative Medicine, Vol. 34: Animal Cytogenetics. 322p. 1990. text ed. 96.00 (*0-12-039234-8*) Acad Pr.

McFeely, William S. Frederick Douglass. (Illus.). 480p. 1992. pap. 14.00 (*0-671-75971-X*, Touchstone Bks) S&S Trade.

— Frederick Douglass. (Illus.). 1991. 24.95 (*0-393-02823-2*) Norton.

— Frederick Douglass. (Illus.). 480p. 1995. pap. 12.95 (*0-393-31376-X*, Norton Paperbks) Norton.

— Grant: A Biography. (Illus.). 608p. 1982. pap. 16.95 (*0-393-30046-3*) Norton.

— Sapelo's People. LC 93-45968. 1994. 18.95 (*0-393-03643-X*) Norton.

— Sapelo's People: A Long Walk into Freedom. 208p. 1995. pap. 11.00 (*0-393-31377-8*, Norton Paperbks) Norton.

— Yankee Stepfather: General O. O. Howard & the Freedmen. 1994. pap. 10.95 (*0-393-31178-3*) Norton.

McFeely, William S., jt. ed. see McFeely, Mary D.

McFeely, William S., jt. auth. see Sherman, William T.

McFerran, Douglass D. Logic in Writing: A Critical Reasoning Workbook. 124p. 1993. per. 24.95 (*0-8403-8487-4*) Kendall-Hunt.

— Symbolic Logic: A Conceptual Approach. 2nd ed. 68p. 1993. per. 19.95 (*0-8403-8354-1*) Kendall-Hunt.

— Thinking Clearly. 124p. 1993. per. 24.95 (*0-8403-9015-7*) Kendall-Hunt.

McFerran, J. B. & McNulty, M. S., eds. Acute Virus Infections of Poultry. (Current Topics in Veterinary Medicine & Animal Science Ser.). 1986. lib. bdg. 115.50 (*0-89838-809-0*) Kluwer Ac.

— Virus Infections of Birds. (Virus Infections of Vertebrates Ser.: Vol. 4). 640p. 1993. 242.75 (*0-444-89899-9*) Elsevier.

McFerran, J. B., jt. ed. see McNulty, M. S.

McFerren, Martha. Contours for Ritual. Poems. LC 87-12486. 64p. 1987. text ed. 13.95 (*0-8071-1421-9*); pap. 6.95 (*0-8071-1422-7*) La State U Pr.

— Delusions of a Popular Mind. Cassin, Maxine, ed. (Journal Press Books: Louisiana Legacy). (Illus.). 80p. 1983. pap. 7.00 (*0-938498-04-5*) New Orleans Poetry.

— Get Me out of Here. 72p. 1984. 7.95 (*0-931694-29-9*) Wampeter Pr.

— Women in Cars: Poems. 72p. (Orig.). 1992. pap. 9.95 (*0-9627460-6-1*) Helicon Nine Eds.

McFerrin, John B. Caldwell & Company: A Southern Financial Empire. LC 75-100905. 312p. 1985. reprint ed. 19.95 (*0-8265-1148-1*) Vanderbilt U Pr.

McFerrin, Linda W. The Impossibility of Redemption Was Something We Hadn't Figured on. 64p. 1990. pap. 6.95 (*0-917658-27-2*) BPW & P.

McFerron, Martha. Animals & Babies. (Science Ser.). 24p. (gr. 2-3). 1980. student ed 5.00 (*0-8209-0160-1*, S-22) ESP.

— Basic Skills Outline & Organize Workbook. (Basic Skills Workbooks). 32p. (gr. 4-7). 1983. 1.98 (*0-8209-0581-X*, OW-1) ESP.

— Learning to Outline & Organize: Grades 4-7. (Language Arts Ser.). 24p. 1979. student ed 5.00 (*0-8209-0327-2*, LA-13) ESP.

— Mammals. (Science Ser.). 24p. (gr. 3-6). 1982. student ed 5.00 (*0-8209-0161-X*, S-23) ESP.

— Plants. (Science Ser.). 24p. (gr. 3-6). 1982. student ed 5.00 (*0-8209-0162-8*, S-24) ESP.

McFeters, G. A., ed. Drinking Water Microbiology. (Contemporary Bioscience Ser.). (Illus.). 528p. 1990. 69.00 (*0-387-97162-9*, 3531) Spr-Verlag.

***McFetridge Britt, Stephanie, illus.** My Little Psalms. LC 95-1446. (J). 1995. write for info. (*0-8499-1193-1*) Word Pub.

McFetridge, D. Word Processing Six Intermediate Test Papers. (C). 1988. 70.00 (*0-85950-829-3*, Pub. by S Thornes Pubs UK) St Mut.

McFetridge, D. G. Government Support of Scientific Research & Development: An Economic Analysis. LC 77-371187. (Ontario Economic Council Research Studies: No. 8). (Illus.). 104p. reprint ed. pap. 29.70 (*0-8357-3995-3*, 2036695) Bks Demand.

McFetridge, Donald, ed. Foreign Investment Technology & Economic Growth. 392p. (Orig.). 1992. pap. text ed. 39.95 (*1-895176-10-7*, Pub. by Univ Calgary CN) Paul & Co Pubs.

McField, R. C. The Missles at Jarmah. Costa, Gwen, ed. LC 90-43990. 1991. pap. 14.95 (*0-87949-310-0*) Ashley Bks.

McForan, Desmond. The World Held Hostage: The War Waged by International Terrorism. LC 87-4776. 278p. 1987. text ed. 39.95 (*0-312-00835-X*) St Martin.

***McFredies, Paul.** The Complete Idiot's Guide to USENET. (Illus.). 325p. (Orig.). 1995. pap. text ed. 16.95 (*1-56761-592-9*) Alpha Bks IN.

McFredries, Paul. Complete Idiot's Guide to Access. 1994. pap. 14.95 (*1-56761-457-4*) Alpha Bks IN.

***McGaa Eagle Man, Ed.** Native Wisdom: Perceptions of the Natural Way. (Illus.). 260p. (Orig.). 1995. pap. 15.00 (*0-9645173-1-0*) Four Dir Pub.

McGaa, Ed & Eagle Man. Mother Earth Spirituality: Native American Paths to Healing Ourselves & Our World. LC 89-46149. (Illus.). 304p. (Orig.). 1990. pap. 15.00 (*0-06-250596-3*) Harper SF.

McGaa, Ed & Man, Eagle. Rainbow Tribe: Ordinary People Journeying on the Red Road. LC 91-55325. 1992. pap. 15.00 (*0-06-250611-0*) Harper SF.

McGaffey, David C. & Chasek, Pamela S. Bread & Politics: Multilateral Negotiations at the FAO Governing Conference. LC 93-2865. (FPI Case Studies: No. 23). 1993. write for info. (*0-941700-83-6*) JH FPI SAIS.

McGaffey, G. W. McGaffey. Genealogical History of the McGaffey Family, Including Also the Fellows, Ethridge & Sherman Families. (Illus.). 145p. 1991. lib. bdg. 33.50 (*0-8328-1965-4*) Higginson Bk Co.

— McGaffey. Genealogical History of the McGaffey Family, Including Also the Fellows, Ethridge & Sherman Families. (Illus.). 145p. 1991. reprint ed. pap. 23.50 (*0-8328-1966-2*) Higginson Bk Co.

McGaffey, Jere. McGaffey Legal Forms with Tax Analysis: 1977-1990, 6 vols. LC 77-12085. 495.00 (*0-317-11955-9*) Clark Boardman Callaghan.

McGaffey, Jere D. Buying, Selling & Merging Businesses. 2nd ed. LC 89-84075. 579p. 1989. text ed. 99.00 (*0-8318-0519-6*, B519) Am Law Inst.

McGaha, Agnes. Stair-Step Wit. McGaha, Michael, ed. (Took Modern Poetry in English Ser.: No. 10). (Illus.). 28p. (Orig.). 1991. pap. 5.00 (*1-879457-18-0*) Norton Coker Pr.

McGaha, Michael. Cervantes & the Renaissance. Lathrop, Thomas et al, eds. 246p. Date not set. 16.50 (*0-936388-00-5*) Juan de la Cuesta.

McGaha, Michael, jt. ed. see Casa, Frank.

McGaha, Michael, ed. see Gomez, Antonio E.

McGaha, Michael, ed. see McGaha, Agnes.

McGaha, Michael D., tr. Antonio Mira de Amescua: The Devil's Slave (El esclavo del demonio) 114p. 1985. reprint ed. pap. 8.00 (*0-919473-46-6*, DH55, Pub. by Dovehouse CN) MRTS.

McGaha, Michael D. & Casa, Frank P., eds. Editing the Comedia. LC 81-50963. (Michigan Romance Studies: Vol. 11). 162p. (Orig.). 1991. pap. 10.00 (*0-939730-10-3*) Mich Romance.

McGaha, Michael D., tr. see De Vega, Lope.

McGahan, Andrew. Praise. LC 92-46446. 288p. 1993. 19.95 (*0-88184-938-3*) Carroll & Graf.

McGahan, John P., ed. Controversies in Ultrasound. (Clinics in Diagnostic Ultrasound Ser.: Vol. 20). (Illus.). 371p. 1987. text ed. 51.00 (*0-443-08492-0*) Churchill.

McGahan, John P. & Porto, Manuel. Diagnostic Obstetrical Ultrasound. (Illus.). 640p. 1994. 99.00 (*0-397-51320-8*) Lippincott.

McGahern, John. Amongst Women. 192p. 1991. reprint ed. pap. 10.00 (*0-14-009255-2*, Penguin Bks) Viking Penguin.

— Collected Stories. 1993. 24.00 (*0-679-41913-6*) Knopf.

— Collected Stories. LC 93-43483. 1994. pap. 12.00 (*0-679-74401-0*, Vin) Random.

— High Ground. 156p. 1993. pap. 10.00 (*0-14-017708-6*, Penguin Bks) Viking Penguin.

***McGahey, Jeanne.** Homecoming with Reflections. (QRL Poetry Book Ser.: Vols. XXVIII-XXIX). 20.00 (*0-614-06426-0*); pap. 10.00 (*0-614-06427-9*) Quarterly Rev.

McGahey, Richard & Jeffries, John. Minorities & the Labor Market: Twenty Years of Misguided Policy. (Orig.). 1985. pap. 12.25 (*0-941410-53-6*) Jt Ctr Pol Studies.

McGahey, Robert. The Orphic Moment: Shaman to Poet-Thinker in Plato, Nietzsche, & Mallarme. (SUNY Series, The Margins of Literature). 209p. (C). 1994. 59.50x (*0-7914-1941-X*); pap. 19.95x (*0-7914-1942-8*) State U NY Pr.

McGahran, Kathleen, jt. auth. see Shillinglaw, Gordon.

McGann, Dairmuid. Journey Within Transcendence: A Jungian Perspective on the Gospel of John. 224p. 1988. pap. 8.95 (*0-8091-2952-3*) Paulist Pr.

McGann, Daniel M. & Robinson, L. R. The Doctor's Sore Foot Book: 1994 Edition. LC 93-46818. 1994. 6.99 (*0-517-10128-9*, Pub. by Wings Bks) Random Hse Value.

***McGann, James G.** The Competition for Dollars, Scholars & Influence in the Public Policy Research Industry. 216p. (C). 1995. lib. bdg. 48.00 (*0-8191-9750-5*); pap. text ed. 26.50 (*0-8191-9751-3*) U Pr of Amer.

McGann, Jerome. Black Riders: The Visible Language of Modernism. LC 92-29109. (Illus.). 192p. (C). 1993. 35.00 (*0-691-06985-9*); pap. 12.95 (*0-691-01544-9*) Princeton U Pr.

McGann, Jerome, ed. Historical Studies & Literary Criticism. LC 85-40374. 312p. 1985. text ed. 30.00 (*0-299-10280-7*) U of Wis Pr.

— Historical Studies & Literary Criticism. LC 85-40374. 312p. 1986. pap. 10.95 (*0-299-10284-X*) U of Wis Pr.

McGann, Jerome J. Byron. (Oxford Authors Ser.). 800p. 1986. pap. 19.95 (*0-19-281349-8*) OUP.

— A Critique of Modern Textual Criticism. LC 92-14702. 160p. (C). 1992. reprint ed. pap. text ed. 12.95 (*0-8139-1418-3*) U Pr of Va.

— The Romantic Ideology: A Critical Investigation. LC 82-17494. 184p. (C). 1985. pap. text ed. 10.95 (*0-226-55850-9*) U Ch Pr.

— Social Values & Poetic Acts: The Historical Judgment of Literary Work. LC 87-14649. 296p. 1988. 37.00 (*0-674-81495-9*) HUP.

— The Textual Condition. (Illus.). 210p. 1991. text ed. 32.50 (*0-691-06931-X*); pap. text ed. 11.95 (*0-691-01518-X*) Princeton U Pr.

— Textual Criticism & Literary Interpretation. LC 84-16174. (Illus.). 240p. 1985. lib. bdg. 22.00 (*0-226-55842-8*) U Ch Pr.

— Towards a Literature of Knowledge. 150p. 1989. 24.95 (*0-226-55839-8*) U Ch Pr.

McGann, Jerome J., ed. The New Oxford Book of Romantic Period Verse. LC 93-32333. (Illus.). 864p. 1994. reprint ed. pap. 16.95 (*0-19-282329-9*) OUP.

— The New Oxford Book of Romantic Verse. (Illus.). 864p. 1993. 35.00 (*0-19-214158-9*) OUP.

— Victorian Connections. LC 89-30993. (Virginia Victorian Studies). 214p. 1989. text ed. 29.50 (*0-8139-1218-0*) U Pr of Va.

McGann, Jerome J., ed. see Byron, George G.

McGann, Jerome J., ed. see Byron, George Gordon.

McGann, Jerome J., ed. see Byron.

McGann, John, jt. auth. see Breslin, Jud.

McGann, Leonard D. Out of the Angel's Hand. LC 93-90560. 204p. 1993. pap. 14.99 (*0-9636783-0-2*) Bell Pub NC.

McGann, Mary, jt. auth. see Foley, Edward.

McGann, Terry, jt. auth. see Silva, Michael.

McGann, Thomas F., tr. see Romero, Jose L.

McGann, Thomas F., jt. ed. see Ross, Stanley R.

McGannon, A., jt. auth. see Rost, M.

***McGannon, Michael.** The Urban Book of Solutions: Staying Healthy, Fit & Sane in the Business Jungle. 240p. 1995. 22.00 (*0-273-61307-3*, Pub. by Pitman Pub UK) Natl Bk Netwk.

McGarey, William A. Edgar Cayce & the Palma Christi: A Study of the Use of Castor Oil Packs As Suggested Through the Unconscious Mind of Edgar Cayce, Followed in the Practice of General Medicine. 132p. 1970. 9.95 (*0-87604-045-8*) ARE Pr.

— Edgar Cayce Remedies. 1983. mass mkt. 5.99 (*0-553-27427-9*) Bantam.

McGarigle, Bob. Nantasket Beach Branch, NY, NH & HRR. (Illus.). 76p. 1981. 12.00 (*0-910506-21-3*) De Vito.

McGarity, Thomas, jt. contrib. see Hadden, Susan.

McGarity, Thomas O. Reinventing Rationality: The Role of Regulatory Analysis in the Federal Bureaucracy. (Illus.). 375p. (C). 1991. 69.95 (*0-521-40256-5*) Cambridge U Pr.

McGarity, Thomas O. & Shapiro, Sidney A. Workers at Risk: The Failed Promise of the Occupational Safety & Health Administration. LC 92-1753. 376p. 1993. text ed. 59.95 (*0-275-94281-3*, C4281, Praeger Pubs) Greenwood.

McGarity, Thomas O., jt. auth. see Bonine, John E.

McGarr, Arthur, ed. Induced Seismicity. LC 93-30034. 1993. 34.50 (*0-8176-2918-1*) Birkhauser.

McGarr, Nancy S., jt. auth. see Hargrove, Patricia M.

McGarrah, Meg. Help Yourself: A Guide to Organizing a Phobia Self-Help Group. 100p. 1990. pap. write for info. (*0-935943-01-3*) Anxiety Disorders.

McGarrah, Robert E. Manufacturing for the Security of the United States: Reviving Competitiveness & Reducing Deficits. LC 89-28942. 208p. 1990. text ed. 55.00 (*0-89930-427-3*, MDG/, Quorum Bks) Greenwood.

McGarrahan, Peggy. Transcending AIDS: Nurses & HIV Patients in New York City. LC 93-26279. (Studies in Health, Illness, & Caregiving). 200p. (Orig.). (C). 1994. text ed. 29.95 (*0-8122-3203-8*); pap. text ed. 13.95 (*0-8122-1418-8*) U of Pa Pr.

McGarrell, Edmund F. Juvenile Correctional Reform: Two Decades of Policy & Procedural Change. LC 87-24499. (SUNY Series in Critical Issues in Criminal Justice). (Illus.). 219p. 1988. 64.50 (*0-88706-759-X*); pap. 21.95 (*0-88706-760-3*) State U NY Pr.

McGarrell, Edmund F., jt. auth. see Duffee, David E.

McGarrity, Mark. A Guide to Mental Retardation: A Comprehensive Resource for Parents, Teachers, & Helpers Who Know, Love, & Care for People with Mental Retardation at Every Stage of Their Lives. 256p. 1993. 29.95 (*0-8245-1274-X*) Crossroad NY.

— White Rush - Green Fire. 464p. 1992. mass mkt. 4.99 (*0-380-71097-8*) Avon.

McGarry, Annie. Lucy! (Illus.). 80p. 1993. 9.98 (*0-8317-5401-X*) Smithmark.

McGarry, Betty. Practical Guide to Florida Retirement. 2nd ed. LC 88-31220. 250p. 1989. pap. 9.95 (*0-910923-61-2*) Pineapple Pr.

McGarry, Daniel, tr. see John of Salisbury.

McGarry, Daniel D., ed. Educational Freedom. 56p. 1981. 5.00 (*0-318-14007-1*) Ed Freedom.

McGarry, Daniel D., tr. see John of Salisbury.

McGarry, Dorothy. Directory of Catalogers in the Special Libraries Association. LC 89-111094. (Illus.). 96p. reprint ed. pap. 27.40 (*0-7837-1182-4*, 2041711) Bks Demand.

An Asterisk (*) at the beginning of an entry indicates that the title is appearing in BIP for the first time.

McGarry, Jean. Airs of Providence. LC 85-8905. (Poetry & Fiction Ser.). 144p. 1985. 16.95 (*0-8018-2909-7*) Johns Hopkins.
— The Courage of Girls. LC 91-23149. (Fiction Ser.). 250p. 1992. 22.95 (*0-8135-1771-0*) Rutgers U Pr.
— Home at Last. LC 93-45676. (Poetry & Fiction Ser.). 1994. 32.50 (*0-8018-4852-0*); pap. 19.95 (*0-8018-4853-9*) Johns Hopkins.
— The Red Coat. limited ed. (Illus.). 24p. 1990. 35.00 (*0-9623585-0-9*) Flockophobic Pr.
— The Very Rich Hours. LC 86-46290. (Johns Hopkins Poetry & Fiction Ser.). 144p. 1987. 16.95 (*0-8018-3504-6*) Johns Hopkins.
McGarry, Jean, et al. Mogana Inc. limited ed. (Illus.). 40p. 1992. 38.00 (*1-880392-01-1*) Flockophobic Pr.
***McGarry, John & O'Leary, Brendan.** Explaining Northern Ireland: Broken Images. (Illus.). 544p. (C). 1995. write for info. (*0-631-18348-5*); pap. write for info. (*0-631-18349-3*) Blackwell Pubs.
McGarry, John & O'Leary, Brendan, eds. The Politics of Ethnic Conflict Regulation: Case Studies of Protracted Ethnic Conflicts. LC 92-45848. 224p. 1993. 49.95 (*0-415-07522-X*, A7686, Routledge NY); pap. 18.95 (*0-415-09931-5*, B2390, Routledge NY) Routledge.
McGarry, John, jt. auth. see O'Leary, Brendan.
McGarry, M. Frances. Allegorical & Metaphorical Language in the Autos Sacramentales of Calderon. LC 79-94165. (Catholic University of America. Studies in Romance Languages & Literatures: No. 16). reprint ed. 23.00 (*0-404-50316-0*) AMS Pr.
McGarry, Megan. A Hundred Dead Roses. LC 93-71166. 256p. (Orig.). 1993. pap. 12.95 (*0-9636057-0-4*) Eros Bks.
McGarry, Michael J. & Schmitz, Andrew, eds. The World Grain Trade: Grain Marketing, Institutions, & Policies. (C). 1992. text ed. 77.50 (*0-8133-8336-6*) Westview.
McGarry, Patricia A., ed. Managing the Prosecutor's Office: With Appendix of Sample Forms. 324p. (Orig.). 1987. pap. 25.00 (*0-910397-12-0*) Natl Coll DA.
McGarry, Richard G. The Subtle Slant: A Cross-Linguistic Discourse Analysis Model for Evaluating Interethnic Conflict in the Press. (Illus.). 196p. 1994. 35.00 (*0-9635752-1-X*) Pkway Pubs.
McGarry, Richard M. Marker Magic. 1993. text ed. 39.95 (*0-442-00769-8*) Van Nos Reinhold.
— Tracing File for Interior & Architectural Rendering. (Illus.). 280p. 1988. pap. 39.95 (*0-442-20530-9*) Van Nos Reinhold.
McGarry, Richard M. & Madsen, Greg. Scale Elements for Design Elevations. (Illus.). 160p. 1991. pap. 29.95 (*0-442-00694-2*) Van Nos Reinhold.
McGartland, Grace. Thunderbolt Thinking: Transform Your Insights & Options into Powerful Business Results. 1993. 26.95 (*0-9632785-1-7*); pap. 16.95 (*0-9632785-0-9*) Bernard-Davis.
McGarty, Raymond. Impasse: Resistance & Addiction Treatment: Combining Brief, Strategic & Twelve Step Approaches. 110p. (Orig.). (C). 1993. pap. text ed. 10.00 (*0-9638389-0-3*) Addiction Therap.
McGarty, Terrence B. Business Plans That Win Venture Capital. 1989. text ed. 94.95 (*0-471-50180-8*) Wiley.
McGarvey, Brian & Swallow, Derek. Microteaching in Teacher Education & Training. (New Patterns of Learning Ser.). 320p. 1986. 37.50 (*0-7099-4613-9*, Pub. by Croom Helm UK) Routledge Chapman & Hall.
McGarvey, Carol. Family Reunion Potluck: For When the Whole Gang Gets Together. (Wooden Spoon Cookbook Ser.). 117p. (Orig.). 1992. spiral bd. 8.50 (*1-882835-23-9*) STA-Kris.
— Fruits of the Season. (Wooden Spoon Cookbook Ser.). 108p. (Orig.). 1992. spiral bd. 8.50 (*1-882835-25-5*) STA-Kris.
— Hand-Picked Apple Recipes. 113p. (Orig.). 1992. spiral bd. 8.50 (*1-882835-20-4*) STA-Kris.
***McGarvey, Carol & McCartan, Marie.** The Des Moines Register Cookbook. Mitchell, C. R., ed. LC 95-13459. (Bur Oak Original Ser.). (Illus.). 272p. (Orig.). 1995. pap. 14.95 (*0-87745-515-5*) U of Iowa Pr.
***McGarvey, Charles L., III.** Physical Therapy for the Cancer Patient. LC 90-32270. (Clinics in Physical Therapy Ser.). (Illus.). reprint ed. pap. 57.60 (*0-7837-9592-0*, 2060348) Bks Demand.
McGarvey, Charles L., III, ed. Physical Therapy for the Cancer Patient. (Clinics in Physical Therapy Ser.). (Illus.). 188p. 1990. text ed. 44.00 (*0-443-08667-2*) Churchill.
McGarvey, Glenn J. Advances in Asymmetric Induction, Vol. 1. 1991. 90.25 (*1-55938-156-6*) Jai Pr.
McGarvey, Judith T. My Grandmother's Family: The Strocks from Andrew County, Missouri. (Illus.). 174p. 1986. 16.00 (*0-932619-00-2*) JD McG Pubns.
McGarvey, Tracy. You Don't Dance to the Juke Box: The Bar Book. Richardson, Francis, ed. (Illus.). 300p. (Orig.). 1990. pap. 10.00 (*0-9627146-0-7*) Trac Pub Serv.
McGary, Howard, Jr. & Lawson, Bill E. Between Slavery & Freedom: Philosophy & American Slavery. LC 92-7738. (Blacks in the Diaspora Ser.). 176p. 1992. 29.95 (*0-253-33272-9*); pap. 10.95 (*0-253-20745-2*, MB-745) Ind U Pr.
McGary, Jane, ed. see Herbert, Belle.
McGary, Jane M., jt. ed. see Peter, Katherine.
McGary, Ruth W. Healthy Homestyle Cookbook. LC 93-1898. 1993. pap. 12.50 (*0-945448-29-5*) Am Diabetes.
***McGaskill, Dan.** Contingency Planning for Industrial Hazardous Spills & Releases. (Environmental Management Guides Ser.). 17p. 1994. pap. text ed. 17.50 (*0-86587-433-6*) Gov Insts.
McGaugh, J. L., jt. ed. see Fredericksen, R. C.
McGaugh, J. L., et al. Brain & Memory: Modulation & Mediation of Neuroplasticity. (Illus.). 416p. 1995. 75.00 (*0-19-508294-X*) OUP.
McGaugh, James L., jt. auth. see Cotman, Carl W.
McGaugh, James L., et al, eds. Brain Organization & Memory: Cells, Systems, & Circuits. (Illus.). 432p. 1990. 75.00 (*0-19-505496-2*) OUP.
— Brain Organization & Memory: Cells, Systems, & Circuits. (Illus.). 448p. 1992. pap. 39.95 (*0-19-507712-1*) OUP.
— Plasticity in the Central Nervous System: Learning & Memory. 232p. 1995. text ed. 45.00 (*0-8058-1573-2*) L Erlbaum Assocs.
McGaugh, Lawrence. Vacuum Cantos. 1969. pap. 1.50 (*0-685-04679-6*) Oyez.
McGaughey, Janet M. Practical Ear Training Workbook. 1977. pap. 7.95 (*0-8008-6473-5*, Crescendo) Taplinger.
***McGaughey, Neil.** And Then There Were Ten: A Stokes Moran Mystery. LC 94-44395. 1995. 20.00 (*0-684-19760-X*, Scribners) S&S Trade.
— Otherwise Known As Murder: A Mystery Introducing Stokes Moran. LC 94-1527. 224p. 1994. text ed. 20.00 (*0-684-19674-3*, Scribners) S&S Trade.
McGaughey, Stephen E. & Gregersen, Hans M. Investment Policies & Financing Mechanisms for Sustainable Forestry Development. 126p. 1988. write for info. (*0-940602-26-1*) IADB.
McGaughey, Stephen E. & Gregersen, Hans M., eds. El Desarrollo Forestal en America Latina. 236p. 1983. write for info. (*0-940602-08-3*) IADB.
— Forest-Based Development in Latin America. 216p. 1983. write for info. (*0-940602-07-5*) IADB.
McGaughey, William, Jr. A Shorter Workweek in the 1980's. LC 80-54666. 320p. (Orig.). 1981. pap. 6.95 (*0-9605630-0-8*) Thistlerose.
— A U. S. - Mexico - Canada Free-Trade Agreement: Do We Just Say No? 230p. (Orig.). 1992. pap. 11.95 (*0-9605630-2-4*) Thistlerose.
McGaughey, William, jt. auth. see McCarthy, Eugene.
McGauley, Nancy, jt. auth. see Heiman, Barbara.
McGauran, Joanna. Love so Fierce. 1993. mass mkt. 4.99 (*0-440-21365-7*) Dell.
McGauvran, Mary, ed. see Blewett, Mary H. & McKenna, Christine.
McGavic, Adrian D. From McGuffock to McGaffick to McGavock, McGavic & McGavick: A Scotch-Irish American Genealogy. LC 88-90779. (Illus.). 585p. (C). 1988. 39.60 (*0-9620628-0-4*) McGavic Geneal Pubns.
McGavin, jt. auth. see Carlton.
McGavin, George C. Bugs of the World. (Of the World Ser.). (Illus.). 192p. 1993. 25.95 (*0-8160-2737-4*) Facts on File.
— Insects. LC 94-27459. (Science Nature Guides Ser.). (J). (gr. 1-8). 1995. 12.95 (*1-57145-017-3*) Thunder Bay CA.
— Insects of the Northern Hemisphere. (American Nature Guide Ser.). 1992. 9.98 (*0-8317-6951-3*) Smithmark.
McGavin, M. Donald & Thompson, Samuel W. Specimen Dissection & Photography: For the Pathologist, Anatomist & Biologist. (Illus.). 300p. (C). 1988. text ed. 68.95 (*0-398-05451-7*) C C Thomas.
McGavin, P. A. Economic Security in Melanesia: Key Issues for Managing Contract Stability & Mineral Resources Development in Papua New Guinea, Solomon Islands, & Vanuatu. LC 93-23306. (Research Report Ser.: No. 16). 112p. (C). 1994. pap. text ed. 8.00 (*0-86638-159-7*) EW Ctr HI.
McGavin, P. A. & Millett, John. Industrialization in Papua New Guinea: Unrealized Potential? (Economic Report Ser.: No. 5). 45p. 1994. pap. 10.00 (*0-86638-156-2*) EW Ctr HI.
McGavin, Patrick Z., ed. Facets Gay & Lesbian Video Guide. (Illus.). 230p. 1993. pap. 10.95 (*0-89733-401-9*) Academy Chi Pubs.
McGavran, Donald. The Satnami Story: A Thrilling Drama of Religious Change. LC 89-39652. 192p. (Orig.). 1990. pap. 8.95 (*0-87808-225-5*, WCL225-5) William Carey Lib.
McGavran, Donald & Hunter, George G., III. Church Growth: Strategies That Work. LC 79-26962. (Creative Leadership Ser.). (Orig.). 1980. pap. 8.95 (*0-687-08160-2*) Abingdon.
McGavran, Donald A. The Bridges of God: A Study in the Strategy of Missions. LC 55-3682. 194p. reprint ed. pap. 55.30 (*0-7837-1951-5*, 2042168) Bks Demand.
— Ethnic Realities & the Church: Lessons from India. LC 78-11517. (Illus.). 202p. 1979. pap. 9.95 (*0-87808-168-2*) William Carey Lib.
— Understanding Church Growth. 3rd ed. (Orig.). 1990. pap. 16.99 (*0-8028-0463-2*) Eerdmans.
McGavran, Donald A., ed. Church Growth Bulletin: Second Consolidated Volume (Sept. 1969 -July 1975) LC 77-5192. 1977. pap. 8.95 (*0-87808-702-8*) William Carey Lib.
McGavran, Donald A., jt. auth. see Montgomery, James H.
McGavran, James H., Jr., ed. Romanticism & Children's Literature in Nineteenth-Century England. LC 90-36157. 256p. 1991. 35.00 (*0-8203-1289-4*) U of Ga Pr.
McGaw, Barry. Making Schools More Effective. (C). 1992. 70.00 (*0-86431-135-4*, Pub. by Aust Council Educ Res AT) St Mut.
McGaw, Charles & Clark, Larry D. Acting Is Believing: A Basic Method. 6th ed. 288p. (C). 1992. text ed. 36.00 (*0-03-055334-2*) HB Coll Pubs.
McGaw, Charles J. & Blake, Gary. Acting Is Believing: A Basic Method. 5th ed. 272p. (C). 1986. text ed. 34.75 (*0-03-007169-0*) HB Coll Pubs.
McGaw, David. Environmental Auditing & Compliance Manual. LC 93-13466. 1993. text ed. 69.95 (*0-442-01646-8*) Van Nos Reinhold.
McGaw, Francis. John Hyde. LC 86-70507. (Men of Faith Ser.). 64p. 1986. reprint ed. pap. 4.99 (*0-87123-909-4*) Bethany Hse.
McGaw, Francis, et al. Juan Hyde: Apostol de Oracion. Ward, Rhode F., tr. 144p. (SPA.). (C). 1988. pap. text ed. 3.50 (*0-88113-158-X*) Edit Betania.
McGaw, Francis A., et al. Praying Hyde. pap. 4.99 (*1-56632-009-7*) Revival Lit.
McGaw, Judith A. Most Wonderful Machine: Mechanization & Social Change in Berkshire Paper Making, 1801-1885. (Illus.). 457p. 1992. text ed. 59.50 (*0-691-04740-5*); pap. text ed. 17.95 (*0-691-00625-3*) Princeton U Pr.
McGaw, Judith A., ed. Early American Technology: Making & Doing Things from the Colonial Era to 1850. LC 94-4913. (Institute of Early American History & Culture Ser.). (Illus.). 500p. 1994. text ed. 49.95 (*0-8078-2173-X*); pap. text ed. 19.95 (*0-8078-4484-5*) U of NC Pr.
McGaw, Martha M. Stevenson in Hawaii. LC 77-13757. (Illus.). 182p. 1978. reprint ed. text ed. 49.75 (*0-8371-9864-X*, MCSH, Greenwood Pr) Greenwood.
McGaw, Nancy, ed. see Wray, Vicki.
McGaw, Robert A. The Vanderbilt Campus: A Pictorial History. LC 78-9913. (Illus.). 1978. 24.95 (*0-8265-1210-0*) Vanderbilt U Pr.
McGaw, William C. Savage Scene: The Life & Times of Mountain Man Jim Kirker. LC 76-38962. (Illus.). 242p. 1989. reprint ed. pap. 9.95 (*0-944383-04-1*) High-Lonesome.
— Southwest Saga: The Way It Really Was. LC 88-6078. (Illus.). 160p. (Orig.). (C). 1988. pap. 5.95 (*0-914846-35-3*) Golden West Pub.
McGeachie, J. Smooth Muscle Regeneration: A Review & Experimental Study. (Monographs in Developmental Biology: Vol. 9). (Illus.). vii, 90p. 1975. 44.00 (*3-8055-2058-1*) S Karger.
McGeagh, Robert. Juan de Onate's Colony in the Wilderness: An Early History of the American Southwest. Smith, James C., Jr., ed. LC 90-49998. (Illus.). 64p. (Orig.). 1990. pap. 8.95 (*0-86534-153-2*) Sunstone Pr.
McGear, Reba & Simms, Jo. Telephone Triage & Management: A Nursing Process Approach. (Illus.). 256p. 1988. Book & Tape. audio 44.00 (*0-7216-2406-5*) Saunders.
***McGeary, David & Plummer, Charles C.** Physical Geology: Earth Revealed. 2nd ed. 540p. (C). 1994. pap. 40.00 (*0-697-24675-2*) Wm C Brown Pubs.
McGeary, David, jt. auth. see Plummer, Charles C.
***McGeary, Golzen & McGeary, Laura, eds.** The Association of MBAs Guide to Business Schools, 1995-96 Edition. 350p. 1995. pap. 49.50 (*0-273-61306-5*, Pub. by Pitman Pub Ltd UK) Trans-Atl Phila.
McGeary, Laura, jt. ed. see Golzen, Godfrey.
McGeary, Laura, jt. ed. see McGeary, Golzen.
McGeary, Mitchell, jt. auth. see McCoy, William.
McGeary, Thomas. The Music of Harry Partch: A Descriptive Catalog. LC 91-70674. (I.S.A.M. Monographs: No. 31). (Illus.). xiv, 186p. (Orig.). 1991. pap. 20.00 (*0-914678-34-5*) Inst Am Music.
McGeary, Thomas, ed. see Partch, Harry.
***McGechan, Justice.** The Principles of the Law of Evidence. 7th ed. 445p. 1984. pap. 63.00 (*0-409-70174-2*, NZ) Butterworth Legal Pubs.
McGee, Adolph P. How to Correct Your Own Credit, Vol. 1. (Illus.). 50p. (Orig.). 1984. student ed. 24.95 (*0-685-25238-8*) A&J Consult.
— How to Correct Your Own Credit: A Workbook to Correct Your Credit. rev. ed. 1990. write for info. (*0-9621957-0-7*) A&J Consult.
McGee, Andrew. Company Law. 180p. (C). 1990. pap. 40.00 (*1-85352-762-9*, Pub. by HLT Pubns UK) St Mut.
— The Financial Services Ombudsmen. 69p. 1992. 33.00 (*1-85190-169-8*, Pub. by Tolley Pubng UK) St Mut.
— Limitation Periods Vol. 1. 2nd ed. 1994. 176.00 (*0-421-48560-4*, Pub. by Sweet & Maxwll) W W Gaunt.
McGee, Arthus. The Elizabethan Hamlet. LC 87-13271. 208p. 1987. text ed. 28.00 (*0-300-03988-3*) Yale U Pr.
McGee, Barbara. Counting Sheep. (Illus.). 24p. (J). (gr. k-3). 1991. 12.95 (*1-55037-157-6*, Pub. by Annick CN); pap. 4.95 (*1-55037-160-6*, Pub. by Annick CN) Firefly Bks Ltd.
McGee, Brenda. Felita: A Study Guide. Friedland, Joyce & Kessler, Rikki, eds. (Novel-Ties Ser.). (J). (gr. 1-4). 1991. pap. text ed. 14.95 (*0-88122-567-3*) Lrn Links.
McGee, Brenda H. Global Geography: Research Activities for All Seasons. (Illus.). 48p. (J). (gr. 3-7). 1994. 6.95 (*0-86653-793-7*, GA1487) Good Apple.
— Old Yeller: A Study Guide. Friedland, Joyce & Kessler, Rikki, eds. (Novel-Ties Ser.). 21p. (YA). (gr. 9-12). 1990. pap. text ed. 15.95 (*0-88122-415-4*) Lrn Links.
— Rascal: A Study Guide. Friedland, Joyce & Kessler, Rikki, eds. (Novel-Ties Ser.). 26p. (YA). (gr. 9-12). 1990. pap. text ed. 15.95 (*0-88122-416-2*) Lrn Links.
— Robin Hood of Sherwood Forest. Friedland, J. & Kessler, R., eds. (Novel-Ties Ser.). (J). (gr. 3-5). 1993. student ed. pap. text ed. 15.95 (*0-88122-909-1*) Lrn Links.
McGee, C. E., ed. The Elizabethan Theatre XII: Papers Given at the Twelfth International Conference on Elizabethan Theatre Held at the University of Waterloo in July 1987. (Illus.). 1993. 48.00 (*0-88835-036-8*) P D Meany.
McGee, Charles M., Jr., jt. auth. see Lander, Ernest M., Jr.
McGee, Charles T. Heart Frauds: The Misapplication of High Technology in Heart Disease. Zirschky, Martha, ed. (Illus.). 263p. (Orig.). 1993. pap. 11.95 (*0-9636979-4-3*) MediPress.
— How to Survive Modern Technology. LC 80-82327. 256p. (Orig.). 1981. pap. 2.95 (*0-87983-230-4*) Keats.
McGee, Charlie. Winning Secrets of a Master Sports Bettor - Baseball. 32p. 1992. pap. 6.95 (*0-934650-21-7*) Sunnyside.
McGee, Charmayne. So Sings the Blue Deer. LC 93-26580. 160p. (J). (gr. 3-7). 1994. text ed. 14.95 (*0-689-31888-X*, Atheneum Bks Young) S&S Childrens.
McGee-Cooper, Ann & Trammell, Duane. Time Management for Unmanageable People. LC 93-47683. 1994. pap. 10.95 (*0-553-37071-5*) Bantam.
McGee-Cooper, Ann, et al. You Don't Have to Go Home from Work Exhausted! 288p. 1992. pap. 10.95 (*0-553-37061-8*) Bantam.
— You Don't Have to Go Home from Work Exhausted! The Energy Engineering Approach. Tartt, Alison, ed. (Illus.). 376p. 1990. 29.95 (*0-9625617-0-3*) Bowen & Rogers Pub.
— You Don't Have to Go Home from Work Exhausted! The Energy Engineering Approach. Tartt, Alison, ed. (Illus.). 376p. 1990. pap. 19.95 (*0-9625617-1-1*) Bowen & Rogers Pub.
McGee, D. C. Soybean Diseases: A Reference Source for Seed Technologists. 1993. 28.00 (*0-89054-141-8*) Am Phytopathol Soc.
McGee, Denis C. Maize Diseases: A Reference Source for Seed Technologists. LC 88-70647. (Illus.). 150p. (Orig.). 1988. pap. text ed. 28.00 (*0-89054-090-X*) Am Phytopathol Soc.
McGee, Donald, ed. see Thayer, Lucien H.
McGee, Eddie. The Emergency Handbook. Arico, Diane, ed. (Corgi Bks.). (Illus.). 176p. (J). (gr. 8-12). 1985. reprint ed. lib. bdg. 9.79 (*0-671-60484-8*); reprint ed. pap. 4.95 (*0-671-60483-X*) S&S Trade.
McGee, Edward J. & Cox, G. Robert. The Ad Game: Playing to Win. 160p. 1990. pap. 15.95 (*0-13-004490-3*) P-H.
McGee, Elizabeth A. & Blank, Susan. A Stitch in Time: Helping Young Mothers Complete High School. 70p. 1989. pap. 8.00 (*0-89492-068-5*) Acad Educ Dev.
McGee, Frank. UCI: The First Twenty-Five Years. Cronin, Barbara, ed. (Illus.). 155p. 1992. text ed. 24.95 (*0-9634697-0-3*) U CA Alumni.
McGee, Fred H. Introduction to Programming in BASIC. (Rate Training Manual & Officer-Enlisted Correspondence Course Ser.: NAVEDTRA 10079-2). (Illus.). 169p. 1985. pap. 7.00 (*0-16-002080-8*, S/N 008-047-00382-0) USGPO.
McGee, G. Kay, jt. auth. see McGee, Norman T.
McGee, Gary. Systematic Theology: A Pentecostal Perspective. Horton, Stanley M. et al, eds. LC 93-23568. (Logion Press Ser.). 704p. 1994. text ed. 32.95 (*0-88243-319-9*, 02-0319) Gospel Pub.
McGee, Gary B. This Gospel...Shall Be Preached: A History & Theology of Assemblies of God Foreign Missions Since 1959, 2 vols., Vol. 2. LC 86-80015. (Illus.). 368p. (Orig.). (C). 1989. pap. 12.95 (*0-88243-673-2*, 02-0673) Gospel Pub.
McGee, Gary B., ed. How Sweet the Sound: God's Grace for Suffering Christians. 112p. (Orig.). 1994. pap. 7.95 (*0-88243-315-6*, 02-0315) Gospel Pub.
— Initial Evidence: Historical & Biblical Perspectives on the Pentecostal Doctrine of Spirit Baptism. LC 91-32847. 256p. 1991. pap. 11.95 (*0-943575-41-9*) Hendrickson MA.
McGee, Gary B., jt. auth. see Burgess, Stanley M.
McGee, Gloria, et al. Black, Beautiful & Recovering. (Orig.). 1985. pap. 1.30 (*0-89486-280-4*, 1219B) Hazelden.
McGee, Harold. The Curious Cook: More Kitchen Science & Lore. LC 90-7087. (Illus.). 352p. 1990. 21.00 (*0-86547-452-4*, North Pt Pr) FS&G.
McGee, Harold, illus. Six MicMac Stories. 51p. 1992. pap. 5.95 (*0-919680-35-6*, Pub. by Nimbus Publishing Ltd CN) Chelsea Green Pub.
McGee, Harold, jt. auth. see Whitehead, Ruth H.
McGee, Harold J. The Curious Cook. (Illus.). 336p. 1992. reprint ed. pap. 13.00 (*0-02-009801-4*, Collier S&S) S&S Trade.
— On Food & Cooking. 704p. 1988. pap. 21.00 (*0-02-034621-2*, Collier S&S) S&S Trade.
— On Food & Cooking: The Science & Lore of the Kitchen. (Illus.). 672p. 1984. text ed. 45.00 (*0-684-18132-0*, Scribners) S&S Trade.
McGee, Howard, jt. auth. see Richards, Lynne.
McGee, J. J. & Menolascino, Frank J. Beyond Gentle Teaching: A Nonaversive Approach to Helping Those in Need. (Illus.). 260p. 1991. 32.50 (*0-306-43856-9*, Plenum Pr) Plenum.
McGee, J. Sears, ed. see Bunyan, John.
McGee, James & Prusak, Laurence. Managing Information Strategically: Increase Your Company's Competitiveness & Efficiency by Using Information As a Strategic Tool. (Ernst & Young Information Management Ser.). 272p. 1993. text ed. 34.95 (*0-471-57544-5*) Wiley.
McGee, James, et al. Kings, Saints & Parliament: A Sourcebook for Western Civilization, 1050-1715. 2nd ed. 208p. (C). 1994. spiral bd. 18.36 (*0-8403-9070-X*) Kendall-Hunt.
McGee, James O., jt. ed. see Herrington, C. S.
McGee, James O., jt. ed. see Lewis, C. E.
McGee, James O., jt. ed. see Lewis, Claire E.
McGee, James O., jt. auth. see Polak, Julia M.
McGee, James O., et al, eds. The Oxford Textbook of Pathology, 3 bks., Set, Vols. 1 & 2. 1 & 2. 1992. Set. 295.00 (*0-19-261976-4*) OUP.
— The Oxford Textbook of Pathology, Vol. 1: General Principles of Pathology. 900p. 1992. pap. 85.00 (*0-19-261972-1*) OUP.
— The Oxford Textbook of Pathology, Vol. 2: Pathology of Systems, 2 bks. 1300p. 1992. pap. 160.00 (*0-19-261974-8*) OUP.
McGee, James S. The Godly Man in Stuart England: Anglicans, Puritans, & the Two Tables, 1620-1670. LC 75-43325. (Yale Historical Publications: Miscellany: No. 110). 319p. reprint ed. pap. 91.00 (*0-8357-8147-X*, 2033820) Bks Demand.

M

McGee, Jeffrey E. Cooperative Strategy & New Venture Performance: The Role of Managerial Experience. rev. ed. LC 93-39453. (Studies in Entrepreneurship). 240p. 1994. 49.00 (*0-8153-1673-9*) Garland.

***McGee, Jerry.** Whiskey Wiley & the Other Tales of Mount St. Helens. 320p. (Orig.). Date not set. pap. 9.95 (*0-7610-0279-0*) NW Pub.

McGee, John S. The Robinson-Patman Act & Effective Competition. Bruchey, Stuart & Carosso, Vincent P., eds. LC 78-18968. (Small Business Enterprise in America Ser.). (Illus.). 1979. lib. bdg. 56.95 (*0-405-11472-9*) Ayer.

McGee, Kate & Matthews, Catherine, eds. The Design of Interactive Computer Displays: A Guide to the Select Literature. LC 85-60627. 647p. 1985. pap. 84.50 (*0-916313-08-5*) Ergosyst Assocs.

McGee, Kate, et al, eds. The Design of Interactive Computer Displays II: A Guide to Selected Periodicals. LC 85-28169. (Orig.). 1986. pap. 15.00 (*0-916313-10-7*) Ergosyst Assocs.

McGee, Lea, jt. auth. see Jones, Candy.

McGee, Lea M. & Richgeis, Donald J. Literacy's Beginnings: Supporting Young Readers & Writers. 480p. 1989. pap. text ed. write for info. (*0-205-12045-8*, H20456) Allyn.

***McGee, Lea M. & Richgels, Donald J.** Literacy's Beginnings: Supporting Young Readers & Writers. 2nd ed. LC 95-7783. 1995. pap. text ed. write for info. (*0-205-16732-2*) Allyn.

McGee, Lea M., jt. auth. see Tompkins, Gail E.

McGee, Lee, jt. auth. see Jones, Candy.

McGee, Leo & Boone, Robert, eds. The Black Rural Landowner - Endangered Species: Social, Political, & Economic Implications. LC 78-69538. (Contributions in Afro-American & African Studies: No. 44). (Illus.). 200p. 1979. text ed. 47.95 (*0-313-20609-0*, MCB/) Greenwood.

McGee, Leo & Neufeldt, Harvey G., comps. Education of the Black Adult in the United States: An Annotated Bibliography. LC 84-19785. (Bibliographies & Indexes in Afro-American & African Studies: No. 4). xiii, 108p. 1985. text ed. 45.00 (*0-313-23473-6*, MBA/) Greenwood.

McGee, Leo, jt. ed. see Neufeldt, Harvey G.

McGee, M. W. Ambosia Dancing at Mary's. Lomax, Joseph F. & Whitebird, J., eds. (Illus.). 1977. pap. 15.00 (*0-930324-02-1*) Wings Pr.

***McGee, Marie.** Millersburg Glass. Measell, James, ed. (Illus.). 160p. (Orig.). 1995. 37.95 (*1-57080-006-5*); pap. 29.95 (*1-57080-005-7*) Antique Pubns.

McGee, Mark. Human Spatial Abilities: Sources of Sex Difference. 145p. 1979. text ed. 49.95 (*0-275-90391-5*, C0391, Praeger Pubs) Greenwood.

— Roger Corman: The Best of the Cheap Acts. LC 87-46389. 261p. 1988. lib. bdg. 32.50x (*0-89950-330-6*) McFarland & Co.

McGee, Mark G. & Wilson, David W. Psychology: Science & Application. (Illus.). 666p. (C). 1984. text ed. 58.75 (*0-314-77927-2*) West Pub.

McGee, Mark T. Beyond Ballyhoo: Motion Picture Promotion & Gimmicks. LC 89-42731. 253p. 1989. lib. bdg. 32.50 (*0-89950-435-3*) McFarland & Co.

— Faster & Furiouser: The Revised & Fattened Fable of American International Pictures. 304p. 1995. lib. bdg. 40.00 (*0-7864-0137-0*) McFarland & Co.

— The Rock & Roll Movie Encyclopedia of the 1950s. LC 89-43657. (Illus.). 224p. 1990. lib. bdg. 28.50x (*0-89950-500-7*) McFarland & Co.

McGee, Marni. The Alphabet Between. LC 91-25489. (Illus.). 32p. (J). (ps-1). 1995. text ed. 14.95 (*0-689-31753-0*, Atheneum Bks Young) S&S Childrens.

— Diego Columbus: Adventures on the High Seas. (Illus.). 128p. (J). (gr. 3-7). 1992. pap. 6.99 (*0-8007-5433-6*) Revell.

— The Forest Child. LC 92-37148. (Illus.). (J). 1994. 15.00 (*0-671-86608-7*, Green Tiger S&S) S&S Childrens.

— The Quiet Farmer. LC 90-37930. (Illus.). 32p. (J). (ps-1). 1991. text ed. 13.95 (*0-689-31678-X*, Atheneum Bks Young) S&S Childrens.

McGee, Marsha G., jt. ed. see Johnson, Christopher J.

McGee, Marty & Tellington-Jones, Linda. Llama Handling & Training: The Team Approach. LC 92-60582. (Illus.). 200p. (Orig.). 1992. pap. text ed. 24.75 (*0-9633002-0-2*) Zephyr Farm.

McGee, Mary P., jt. auth. see Pace, Ruth.

McGee, May L., tr. see Bustamante, Cecilia.

McGee, Michael V. Stark Drama. (Illus.). 20p. (Orig.). 1992. pap. 3.00 (*0-88680-375-6*) I E Clark.

McGee, Norman T. & McGee, G. Kay. United States Census of Putnam County Tennessee, 1870. LC 89-80386. (Illus.). 170p. (Orig.). 1989. pap. 25.00 (*0-9622403-1-1*) Lilac Hill Pubns.

McGee, O. D., jt. ed. see Herrington, C. S.

McGee, P. Tristan. Development of the Regional Policy of the European Communities. (C). 1982. 40.00 (*0-685-30279-2*, Pub. by Oxford Polytechnic UK) St Mut.

— Local Government & the Regional Policy of the European Communities: Overview. (C). 1982. 29.00 (*0-685-30278-4*, Pub. by Oxford Polytechnic UK) St Mut.

McGee, Patrick. Paperspace: Style As Ideology in Joyce's "Ulysses" LC 87-19074. x, 243p. 1988. 30.00 (*0-8032-3115-6*) U of Nebr Pr.

— Telling the Other: The Question of Value in Modern & Postcolonial Writing. LC 91-48247. 232p. 1992. 36.50 (*0-8014-2749-5*); pap. 13.95 (*0-8014-8027-2*) Cornell U Pr.

McGee, Paula. Teaching Transcultural Care: A Guide for Teachers of Nursing & Health Care. LC 92-22885. 1992. write for info. (*1-56593-065-7*) Singular Publishing.

McGee, R. Harley. Getting It Right: Regional Development in Canada. 384p. 1992. 42.95 (*0-7735-0921-6*, Pub. by McGill CN) U of Toronto Pr.

McGee, R. Jon. Life, Ritual, & Religion among the Lacandon Maya. 158p. (C). 1990. pap. 17.95 (*0-534-12186-1*) Intl Thomson.

McGee, Reece. Academic Janus: The Private College & Its Faculty. LC 70-149913. (Jossey-Bass Higher Education Ser.). 288p. reprint ed. 82.10 (*0-8357-9293-5*, 2013819) Bks Demand.

McGee, Robert. Chemical Dependency. 68p. 1991. pap. 2.99 (*0-945276-27-3*) Rapha Pub.

McGee, Robert S. La Busqueda de Significado - The Search for Significance. Duffer, Hiran & De Duffer, Beatriz L., trs. 174p. (Orig.). (SPA.). 1992. pap. 7.99 (*0-311-46129-8*) Casa Bautista.

— Discipline with Love. 122p. 1991. pap. 7.99 (*0-945276-02-8*) Rapha Pub.

— Discipline with Love. 122p. 1991. write for info. (*0-945276-06-0*) Word Inc.

— Father Hunger. 250p. 1993. pap. 12.99 (*0-89283-818-3*, Vine Bks) Servant.

— The Search for Freedom: Demolishing the Strongholds That Diminish Your Faith, Hope, & Confidence in God. 220p. 1995. 10.99 (*0-89283-862-0*, Vine Bks) Servant.

— Search for Significance. 189p. 1990. pap. write for info. (*0-945276-11-7*) Word Inc.

— Search for Significance. rev. ed. 200p. 1990. pap. 9.99 (*0-685-62305-X*) Rapha Pub.

— Search for Significance Devotional. 1993. pap. 10.99 (*0-945276-41-9*) Rapha Pub.

— The Search for Significance Small Group Leader's Guide. 58p. 1990. pap. 5.00 (*0-945276-09-5*) Rapha Pub.

— The Search for Significance, Workbook. rev. ed. 502p. 1990. pap. 12.99 (*0-945276-07-9*) Rapha Pub.

McGee, Robert S. & Mountcastle, William D. Rapha's Twelve-Step Program for Overcoming Eating Disorders. 1990. pap. 14.95 (*0-945276-19-2*) Rapha Pub.

McGee, Robert S. & Springle, Pat. Bitterness. 56p. 1991. pap. 2.99 (*0-945276-38-9*) Rapha Pub.

— Getting Unstuck. 1992. pap. 12.99 (*0-945276-32-X*) Rapha Pub.

McGee, Robert S., jt. auth. see McAllister, Dawson.

McGee, Robert S., et al. Rapha's Twelve Step Program for Overcoming Chemical Dependency. 302p. 1990. pap. 12.99 (*0-945276-10-9*) Rapha Pub.

— Your Parents & You Small Group Leader's Guide. 85p. 1990. pap. 5.00 (*0-945276-15-X*) Rapha Pub.

McGee, Robert W. Accounting & Tax Aspects for Computer Software Manufactures. LC 87-15140. 176p. 1987. text ed. 55.00 (*0-275-92273-1*, C2273, Praeger Pubs) Greenwood.

— Accounting for Data Processing Costs. LC 87-24933. 208p. 1988. text ed. 55.00 (*0-89930-214-9*, MGA/, Quorum Bks) Greenwood.

— Accounting for Income Taxes. 250p. 12.95 (*0-86641-102-X*, 84155) Inst Mgmt Account.

— Accounting for Software Costs. 200p. 12.95 (*0-86641-104-6*, 84153) Inst Mgmt Account.

— Fundamentals of Accounting & Finance: Making Intelligent Decisions in an Unpredictable Economy. 216p. (C). 1987. reprint ed. pap. text ed. 24.00 (*0-8191-6289-2*) U Pr of Amer.

— A Model Program for Schools of Professional Accountancy. LC 86-28226. 206p. (Orig.). 1987. pap. text ed. 22.50 (*0-8191-6095-4*) U Pr of Amer.

— Tax Planning in Divorce Settlements. LC 86-133322. 64p. write for info. (*0-13-778846-0*) P-H.

— A Trade Policy for Free Societies: The Case Against Protectionism. LC 93-42760. 216p. 1994. text ed. 55.00 (*0-89930-898-8*, Quorum Bks) Greenwood.

McGee, Robert W., ed. Business Ethics & Common Sense. LC 92-9568. 320p. 1992. text ed. 49.95 (*0-89930-728-0*, MNN, Quorum Bks) Greenwood.

— The Market Solution to Economic Development in Eastern Europe. LC 92-16214. 332p. 1992. lib. bdg. 99.95 (*0-7734-9545-2*) E Mellen.

McGee, Robert W., jt. auth. see Georges, Walter.

McGee, Robert W., jt. ed. see Greaves, Bettina B.

McGee, Rose, jt. ed. see Clark, Jane C.

McGee, Rosemary & Farrow, Andrea. Test Questions for Physical Education Activities. LC 86-21093. 1987. pap. text ed. 23.00x (*0-87322-412-4*, BMCG0412) Human Kinetics.

— Test Questions for Physical Education Activities. LC 86-21093. (Illus.). 440p. (C). 1987. text ed. 42.00 (*0-87322-088-9*, BMCG0088) Human Kinetics.

McGee, S. W., jt. ed. see Bewley, J. G.

McGee, Sherwood W., ed. see National Powder Metallurgy Conference Staff.

McGee, Steven R., jt. auth. see Fihn, Stephan D.

McGee, Terence, jt. auth. see Armstrong, Warwick.

McGee, Terry G. Doubts about Dualism: Implications for Development Planning. (Working Papers Ser.: No. 78-3). 25p. 1978. pap. 5.00 (*0-686-78219-4*, CRD013) UNIPUB.

McGee, Therese. Real Grandmas Don't Bake Cookies Anymore. Conn, Carmelita J., ed. LC 88-23949. (Illus.). 96p. (Orig.). 1988. pap. text ed. 8.00 (*0-943663-00-8*) San Joaquin Eagle.

McGee, Thomas D. A History of the Irish Settlers in North America. 240p. 1989. reprint ed. 18.95 (*0-685-60528-0*, 3520) Clearfield Co.

— A History of the Irish Settlers in North America. 187p. 1989. reprint ed. pap. 12.50 (*1-55613-212-3*) Heritage Bk.

— Principles & Methods of Temperature Measurement. LC 87-22926. 525p. 1988. text ed. 89.95 (*0-471-62767-4*) Wiley.

***McGee, Timothy, ed.** Taking a Stand: Essays in Honour of John Beckwith. 320p. 1995. 65.00 (*0-8020-0583-7*) U of Toronto Pr.

McGee, Timothy J. Medieval & Renaissance Music: A Performer's Guide. LC 86-149637. (Illus.). 303p. reprint ed. pap. 86.40 (*0-8357-6363-3*, 2035717) Bks Demand.

— Medieval & Renaissance Music: A Performer's Guide. (Illus.). 304p. 1988. reprint ed. pap. 18.95 (*0-8020-6729-8*) U of Toronto Pr.

— Medieval Instrumental Dances. LC 88-45498. (Music: Scholarship & Performance Ser.). (Illus.). 192p. 1990. spiral bd. 27.95 (*0-253-33353-9*) Ind U Pr.

— The Music of Canada. (C). 1985. pap. text ed. 11.95 (*0-393-95376-9*) Norton.

***McGee, Tom.** Betty Grable: The Girl with the Million Dollar Legs. LC 94-31145. 1994. 29.95 (*1-879511-15-0*); pap. 19.95 (*1-879511-18-5*) Vestal.

McGee, Tomothy J., jt. auth. see Eastman, Sheila J.

McGee, Vann. Truth, Vagueness, & Paradox: An Essay on the Logic of Truth. LC 89-27742. 280p. (C). 1990. 34.95 (*0-87220-087-6*) Hackett Pub.

McGee, Vern, tr. see Schmidt, Paul, ed.

McGee, Vern W., tr. see Bakhtin, M. M.

McGee, W. J. & Governors in the White House Conference Staff, eds. Proceedings of the Governors in the White House Conference, Washington, D.C., May 13-15, 1908. LC 72-2855. (Use & Abuse of America's Natural Resources Ser.). 1972. 35.95 (*0-405-04519-0*) Ayer.

McGeehan, Charles, tr. see Schierbeek, Bert.

McGeehan, John. Barron's Regents Exams & Answers, U. S. History & Government. 1992. pap. 5.95 (*0-8120-3344-2*) Barron.

— U. S. History & Government Power Pack: Let's Review: U. S. History & Government. 2nd ed. 1995. student ed, pap. 14.95 (*0-8120-8274-5*) Barron.

McGeehan, John & Gall, Morris. Let's Review: U. S. History & Government. 704p. 1990. pap. 11.95 (*0-8120-4048-1*) Barron.

— Let's Review: U. S. History & Government. 2nd ed. LC 94-29829. (Review Course Ser.). 1995. write for info. (*0-8120-1962-8*) Barron.

McGeehan, Jude J. Ministry to the Sick & Dying. (Synthesis Ser.). 1981. 1.95 (*0-8199-0836-3*, Frncscn Herld) Franciscan Pr.

McGeehan, P. J., ed. Advances in Powder Metallurgy, 3 vols., Set. LC 90-42924. (Illus.). 1712p. 1990. text ed. 150.00 (*1-878954-00-8*) Metal Powder.

— Advances in Powder Metallurgy, 1990, Vol. 1. LC 90-42924. (Illus.). 624p. 1990. text ed. 57.50 (*1-878954-01-6*) Metal Powder.

— Advances in Powder Metallurgy, 1990, Vol. 2. LC 90-42924. (Illus.). 576p. 1990. text ed. 57.50 (*1-878954-02-4*) Metal Powder.

— Advances in Powder Metallurgy, 1990, Vol. 3. LC 90-42924. (Illus.). 512p. 1990. text ed. 57.50 (*1-878954-03-2*) Metal Powder.

McGeehan, Robert. The German Rearmament Question: American Diplomacy & European Defense after World War II. LC 79-146009. 296p. reprint ed. pap. 84.40 (*0-317-09264-2*, 2020237) Bks Demand.

McGeehee, Ralph W. Deadly Deceits: My Twenty-Five Years in the CIA. 1990. pap. 9.95 (*0-941781-06-2*) IMA NYC.

McGeehin, P., ed. Fibre Optics '89. 355p. 1989. 70.00 (*0-8194-0156-0*, VOL. 1120) SPIE.

McGeer, Edith G., et al, eds. Kainic Acid As a Tool in Neurobiology. LC 78-55812. 283p. 1978. 74.50 (*0-89004-279-9*) Raven.

***McGeer, Eric.** Sowing the Dragon's Teeth: Byzantine Warfare in the Tenth Century. LC 94-29133. Vol. 33. 1995. write for info. (*0-88402-224-2*, Dumbarton Rsch Lib) Dumbarton Oaks.

McGeer, Gerald G. Conquest of Poverty: A Challenge to the Money Power Bankers. 1979. lib. bdg. 59.95 (*0-8490-2901-5*) Gordon Pr.

McGeer, Patrick C. & Brayton, Robert K. Integrating Functional & Temporal Domains in Logic Design: The False Path Problem & Its Implications. 1991. lib. bdg. 63.50 (*0-7923-9163-2*) Kluwer Ac.

McGeer, Patrick L., et al. Molecular Neurobiology of the Mammalian Brain. 2nd ed. LC 86-25333. 800p. 1987. 85.00 (*0-306-42329-4*, Plenum Pr); pap. 42.50 (*0-306-42511-4*, Plenum Pr) Plenum.

McGeever, Patrick J. Reverend Charles Owen Rice: Apostle of Contradiction. LC 88-19766. (Illus.). 320p. 1989. 28.95 (*0-8207-0209-9*); pap. 18.00 (*0-8207-0210-2*) Duquesne.

***McGehee.** Beyond Happiness: Intimate Memoirs Of Billy Lee Belle. 1993. per. 9.95 (*1-55050-050-3*, Pub. by Coteau Bks CN) InBook.

— The I. Q. Zoo. Date not set. per. 10.95 (*1-55050-026-0*, Pub. by Coteau Bks CN) InBook.

McGehee, Elise. Small Voice. 76p. 1982. 12.50 (*0-88289-375-0*) Pelican.

McGehee, Fielding M., III, jt. ed. see Moore, Rebecca.

McGehee, Jean, ed. see Marsh, Howard C.

***McGehee, Linda F.** A Companion Project Book: For Texture with Textiles. (Illus.). 40p. 1994. pap. text ed. 14.95 (*0-9637160-1-8*) Ghees.

— More Texture with Textiles. 52p. 1993. pap. text ed. 14.95 (*0-9637160-0-X*) Ghees.

McGehee, Liz, ed. Folded Fabric Fun. LC 90-34192. (Illus.). 32p. (Orig.). (C). 1990. pap. 7.95 (*0-943574-69-2*) That Patchwork.

— Your Hot Button. LC 90-34193. (Illus.). 24p. (Orig.). (C). 1990. pap. 4.95 (*0-943574-71-4*) That Patchwork.

McGehee, Liz, ed. see Dietrich, Mimi.

McGehee, Liz, ed. see Hanson, Joan.

McGehee, Liz, ed. see Hickey, Mary.

McGehee, Liz, ed. see Hughes, Trudie.

McGehee, Liz, ed. see Kimball, Jeana.

McGehee, Liz, ed. see Kime, Janet.

McGehee, Liz, ed. see Martin, Nancy J.

McGehee, Liz, ed. see McCloskey, Marsha.

McGehee, Liz, ed. see Miller, Margaret J.

McGehee, Liz, ed. see Palmer, Carolann M.

McGehee, Liz, ed. see Schneider, Sally.

McGehee, Liz, ed. see Smith, Nancy & Milligan, Lynda.

McGehee, Liz, ed. see Thomas, Donna L.

McGehee, Lucius P. Due Process of Law Under the Federal Constitution. (Studies in Constitutional Law). x, 452p. 1981. reprint ed. lib. bdg. 37.50 (*0-8377-0837-0*) Rothman.

McGehee, Michael. God's Word Expressed in Human Words: The Bible's Literary Forms. 104p. (Orig.). 1991. pap. text ed. 7.95 (*0-8146-2009-4*) Liturgical Pr.

***McGehee, Nicole.** No More Lonely Nights: A Novel. LC 94-37442. 1995. 21.95 (*0-316-55854-0*) Little.

— Regret Not a Moment. 528p. 1994. mass mkt. 5.99 (*0-446-60071-7*) Warner Bks.

— Regret Not a Moment: A Novel. LC 92-41732. 1993. 19.95 (*0-316-55853-2*) Little.

McGehee, O. C., jt. auth. see Graham, C. C.

McGehee, Peggy L., jt. auth. see Horton, Andrew M.

McGehee, Peter. Boys Like Us. (Stonewall Inn Editions Ser.). 176p. 1992. pap. 8.95 (*0-312-06913-8*) St Martin.

— Sweetheart. (Stonewall Inn Editions Ser.). 224p. 1993. pap. 8.95 (*0-312-09399-3*) St Martin.

— Sweetheart: A Novel. 208p. 1992. 17.95 (*0-312-07863-3*) St Martin.

McGehee, Richard, et al, eds. Twist Mappings & Their Applications. LC 92-14149. (IMA Volumes in Mathematics & Its Applications Ser.: Vol. 44). (Illus.). xiii, 199p. 1992. 44.00 (*0-387-97858-5*) Spr-Verlag.

McGehee, Robin A., jt. auth. see Taylor, Robert A.

McGeoch, A. J. Collected Poems. 125p. 1986. 30.00 (*0-905075-22-6*, Pub. by Wilfion Bks UK) Dufour.

McGeoch, Catherine C., jt. ed. see Johnson, David S.

McGeoch, Lyle A. & Sleator, Daniel D., eds. On-Line Algorithms. LC 91-43417. (DIMACS Series in Descrete Mathematics & Theoretical Computer Science: Vol. 7). 179p. 1992. 32.00 (*0-8218-6596-X*, DIMACS/7C) Am Math.

McGeorge, Bundy & Kissinger, Henry A. The Dimensions of Diplomacy. Johnson, E. A., ed. LC 64-25072. 150p. reprint ed. pap. 42.80 (*0-317-41745-2*, 2025858) Bks Demand.

McGeorge, Constance W. Boomer's Big Day. LC 93-27273. (Illus.). (J). 1994. 12.95 (*0-8118-0526-3*) Chronicle Bks.

— The Snow Riders. LC 94-47214. (Illus.). (J). 1995. 13.95 (*0-8118-0873-4*) Chronicle Bks.

McGeorge, H. D. Marine Electrical Equipment & Practice. 2nd ed. 158p. 1993. pap. 85.00 (*0-7506-1647-4*) Buttrwrth-Heinemann.

McGeorge, H. D., ed. General Engineering Knowledge. 3rd ed. 160p. 1991. pap. text ed. 32.95 (*0-7506-0006-3*) Buttrwrth-Heinemann.

***McGeorge, W. D.** Marine Auxiliary Machinery. 7th ed. LC 95-3360. 1995. write for info. (*0-7506-1843-4*, Focal) Buttrwrth-Heinemann.

McGeough, J. A. Advanced Methods of Machining. 300p. 1988. text ed. 52.50 (*0-412-31970-5*) Chapman & Hall.

McGeough, J. A., jt. auth. see Venkatesh, V. C.

McGeown, Mary G. Clinical Management of Electrolyte Disorders. 1983. lib. bdg. 89.00 (*0-89838-559-8*) Kluwer Ac.

McGeown, Mary G., ed. Clinical Management of Renal Transplantation. (Developments in Nephrology Ser.). 400p. (C). 1992. lib. bdg. 169.00 (*0-7923-1604-5*) Kluwer Ac.

McGerr. Death in a Million Living Rooms. (Black Dagger Crime Ser.). 16.50 (*0-86220-788-6*, C1028, Black Dagger) Chivers N Amer.

— The Seven Deadly Sisters. (Black Dagger Crime Ser.). 16.50 (*0-86220-818-1*, BD017, Black Dagger) Chivers N Amer.

McGerr, Michael E. The Decline of Popular Politics: The American North, 1865-1928. 1986. 22.00 (*0-19-503682-4*) OUP.

McGerr, Rosemarie P., ed. The Pilgrimage of the Soul: A Critical Edition of the Middle English Dream Vision, Vol. I. (Medieval Texts Ser.: Vol. 16). 250p. 1990. 36.00 (*0-8240-6617-0*) Garland.

McGervey, John D. Introduction to Modern Physics. 2nd ed. 756p. 1983. text ed. 59.00 (*0-12-483560-0*) Acad Pr.

— Probabilities in Everyday Life. 288p. 1989. mass mkt. 4.99 (*0-8041-0532-4*) Ivy Books.

— Probabilities in Everyday Life. LC 86-2406. 269p. 1986. 28.95 (*0-8304-1045-7*) Nelson-Hall.

— Quantum Mechanics: Concepts & Applications. (Illus.). 456p. 1995. text ed., disk 54.95 (*0-12-483545-7*) Acad Pr.

***McGettigan, Barbara & Henderson, Frances.** Managing Your Career in Nursing. 1994. 28.95 (*0-88737-629-0*) Natl League Nurse.

McGettigan, Barbara O., jt. auth. see Henderson, Frances C.

McGettigan, James P. Soccer Drills for Individual & Team Play. 276p. 1986. 21.95 (*0-13-815309-4*, Parker Publishing Co) P-H.

— Soccer Drills for Individual & Team Play. 240p. 1989. 9.95 (*0-13-815366-3*) P-H.

— Winning Soccer Drills. LC 80-15783. 1983. pap. 5.95 (*0-13-961086-3*, Reward) P-H.

McGettrick, Andrew D., jt. auth. see Gehani, Narain.

McGettrick, Andrew D., jt. auth. see Thayer, Richard H.

McGhee, George. At the Creation of a New Germany. LC 88-18029. 256p. (C). 1989. 32.00 (*0-300-04250-7*) Yale U Pr.

An Asterisk (*) at the beginning of an entry indicates that the title is appearing in BIP for the first time.

— The U. S. Turkish NATO Middle East Connection: How the Truman Doctrine & Turkey's NATO Entry Contained the Soviets in the Middle East. 1990. text ed. 39.95 (*0-312-03540-3*) St Martin.

McGhee, George C. International Community: A Goal for a New World Order. LC 92-10570. (Miller Center Series on a New World Order: Vol. 1). 1992. 39.50 (*0-8191-8538-8*); pap. 19.50 (*0-8191-8539-6*) U Pr of Amer.

McGhee, George C., ed. Diplomacy for the Future. LC 87-3455. 116p. (Orig.). 1987. pap. text ed. 13.00 (*0-934742-41-3*) Geo U Inst Dplmcy.

— Diplomacy for the Future. LC 87-3455. 118p. (Orig.). 1987. lib. bdg. 35.50 (*0-8191-6487-9*, Inst Study Diplomacy); pap. text ed. 13.00 (*0-8191-6488-7*, Inst Study Diplomacy) U Pr of Amer.

McGhee, George C., et al, eds. National Interest & Global Goals. LC 89-36331. (Exxon Education Foundation Series on Rhetoric & Political Discourse: Vol. 16). 224p. 1989. lib. bdg. 46.00 (*0-8191-7542-0*, Pub. by White Miller Center); pap. text ed. 24.00 (*0-8191-7543-9*, Pub. by White Miller Center) U Pr of Amer.

McGhee, Jerry R. & Mestecky, Jiri, eds. Secretory Immune System. 1983. 175.00 (*0-89766-210-5*); pap. 175.00 (*0-89766-211-3*, VOL. 409) NY Acad Sci.

McGhee, Jery R., jt. ed. see Kiyono, Hiroshi.

McGhee, Jim. True Lies: The Architecture of the Fantastic in the Plays of Sam Shepard. LC 93-9537. (American University Studies: Theatre Arts: Ser. XXVI, Vol. 18). 224p. (C). 1993. text ed. 42.95 (*0-8204-2052-2*) P Lang Pubs.

McGhee, John. Introductory Statistics. 619p. (C). 1985. text ed. 58.25 (*0-314-85277-8*) West Pub.

McGhee, Laura, et al. Three Novellas. Miller, Philip, ed. 178p. (Orig.). 1993. pap. 10.00 (*0-939391-17-1*) B Woodley Pr.

McGhee, Michael. The Gospel According to Deborah. 192p. (Orig.). 1993. 9.95 (*0-8146-2105-8*) Liturgical Pr.

McGhee, Michael, ed. Philosophy, Religion, & the Spiritual Life. LC 92-5707. (Royal Institute of Philosophy Supplements Ser.: Vol. 32). 176p. (C). 1992. pap. 21.95 (*0-521-42196-9*) Cambridge U Pr.

***McGhee, Paul.** How to Develop Your Sense of Humor: An 8-Step Training Program for Learning to Use Humor to Cope with Stress. 224p. 1994. per., pap. text ed. 20.00 (*0-8403-9734-8*) Kendall-Hunt.

— Humor Log. 128p. 1994. per., pap. text ed. 12.00 (*0-8403-9645-7*) Kendall-Hunt.

McGhee, Paul E. Humor & Children's Development: A Guide to Practical Applications. LC 88-37931. (Journal of Children in Contemporary Society Ser.: Vol. 20, Nos. 1-2). 280p. 1989. text ed. 39.95 (*0-86656-681-3*) Haworth Pr.

— Punchline: How to Think Like a Humorist If You're Humor Impaired. 144p. 1993. pap. text ed. 10.00 (*0-8403-8482-3*) Kendall-Hunt.

McGhee, Paul E. & Chapman, Antony J., eds. Children's Humour. LC 79-40648. 336p. reprint ed. pap. 95.80 (*0-318-35027-0*, 2030927) Bks Demand.

McGhee, Paul E. & Goldstein, J. H., eds. Handbook of Humor Research: Applied Studies, Vol. 2. (Illus.). 215p. 1983. 63.00 (*0-387-90853-6*) Spr-Verlag.

McGhee, Paul E., jt. ed. see Goldstein, Jeffrey H.

McGhee, Richard D. Guilty Pleasures: William Wordsworth's Poetry of Psychoanalysis. LC 92-81065. 351p. 1992. 35.00 (*0-87875-431-8*) Whitston Pub.

— John Wayne: Actor, Artist, Hero. LC 89-43658. (Illus.). 399p. 1990. lib. bdg. 38.50x (*0-89950-501-5*) McFarland & Co.

— Marriage, Duty, & Desire in Victorian Poetry & Drama. LC 80-11962. x, 318p. (C). 1980. 35.00 (*0-7006-0203-8*) U Pr of KS.

McGhee, Robert. Ancient Canada. (Canadian Museum of Civilization Mercury Ser.). (Illus.). 175p. 1992. 29.95 (*0-660-10795-3*) U Ch Pr.

McGhee, Scott, tr. see Barakat, Halim I.

McGhee, Terrence. Water Supply & Sewerage. 6th ed. (Water Resources & Environmental Engineering Ser.). 665p. 1991. text ed. write for info. (*0-07-060938-1*); 14. 95 (*0-07-060939-X*) McGraw.

McGhee, Valerie L., jt. auth. see Teague, Michael L.

McGhehey, M. A., jt. auth. see Moran, K. D.

McGhie, Andrew R., jt. auth. see Sloan, Gilbert J.

McGhie, Anna E. The Miracle Hand Around the World. 1989. pap. 8.99 (*0-88019-251-8*) Schmul Pub Co.

McGibbon, Ian. New Zealand & the Korean War, Vol. 1: Politics & Diplomacy. (Illus.). 530p. 1993. 59.00 (*0-19-558253-5*) OUP.

McGibbon, Ian, ed. Undiplomatic Dialogue: Letters Between Carl Berendsen & Alister McIntosh, 1943-1952. (Auckland University Press Book Ser.). 336p. 1994. 28. 00 (*1-86940-095-X*) OUP.

McGibbon, Rob, jt. auth. see McGibbon, Robin.

McGibbon, Robin. New Kids on the Block: The Whole Story by Their Friends. 1990. pap. 6.95 (*0-380-76344-3*) Avon.

McGibbon, Robin & McGibbon, Rob. Simply Mick: Mick Hucknall of Simply Red - The Inside Story. (Illus.). 224p. 1994. pap. 15.95 (*1-85797-211-2*) Trafalgar.

***McGiffen-Newkirk, Dawn.** Homeowners' Planner: Decorating-Remodeling-Building. (Illus.). 73p. 1995. pap. write for info. (*0-9646730-1-0*) L D L Pubng.

McGiffert, A. C. Protestant Thought Before Kant. 11.25 (*0-8446-0204-3*) Peter Smith.

McGiffert, Arthur C. Jonathan Edwards. LC 75-3134. (Philosophy in America Ser.). reprint ed. 28.00 (*0-404-59143-4*) AMS Pr.

McGiffert, Arthur C., Jr. Public Prayers. LC 83-83269. (Studies in Ministry & Parish Life). 44p. 1984. pap. 3.95 (*0-913552-24-0*) Exploration Pr.

McGiffert, Michael, ed. God's Plot: Puritan Spirituality in Thomas Shepard's Cambridge. rev. ed. LC 94-2899. 256p. 1994. lib. bdg. 40.00 (*0-87023-926-0*); pap. text ed. 15.95x (*0-87023-915-5*) U of Mass Pr.

McGiffin, Heather & Brownley, Nancie, eds. Animals in Education. 160p. (Orig.). (gr. 9-12). 1980. pap. 9.95 (*0-937712-00-0*) Inst Study Animal.

***McGiffin, Janet.** Elective Murder. 1995. mass mkt. 5.50 (*0-449-14925-0*, GM) Fawcett.

McGiffin, Robert F. Furniture Care & Conservation. 2nd rev. ed. LC 89-6610. (Illus.). 256p. 1989. 19.95 (*0-942063-02-3*) AASLH.

McGill. Computers in the Office. 1989. pap. 15.95 (*0-8384-3325-1*) Heinle & Heinle.

McGill, A. The McGills: Celts, Ulstermen, & American Pioneers: History, Heraldry, & Tradition. (Illus.). 345p. 1989. reprint ed. lib. bdg. 60.00 (*0-8328-0862-8*); reprint ed. pap. 52.00 (*0-8328-0863-6*) Higginson Bk Co.

McGill, Allyson. The Swedish Americans. (Peoples of North America Ser.). (Illus.). 112p. (J). (gr. 5 up). 1988. lib. bdg. 17.95 (*1-55546-135-2*) Chelsea Hse.

***McGill, Angus.** Evening Standard London Pub Guide 1995. (Illus.). 224p. 1995. pap. 16.95 (*1-85793-326-5*, Pub. by Pavilion UK) Trafalgar.

***McGill, Ann & Wilson, Glynis.** Mending Your Broken Heart: A Survival Kit. (Life Line Ser.). 128p. (Orig.). 1994. pap. 14.95 (*1-55059-091-X*) Temeron Bks.

McGill, Ann M. Hiring the Best. LC 93-4. 112p. 1993. pap. 10.00 (*1-55623-865-7*) Irwin Prof Pubng.

— Supervising the Difficult Employee. LC 94-2845. (Business Skills Express Ser.). 120p. 1994. pap. 10.00 (*0-7863-0219-4*) Irwin Prof Pubng.

McGill, Arthur C. Suffering: A Test of Theological Method. LC 82-6934. 130p. 1982. pap. 10.99 (*0-664-24448-3*, Westminster) Westminster John Knox.

***McGill, Dan.** Employer Guarantee of Pension Benefits. (C). 1974. 6.50 (*0-256-01704-2*) Irwin.

— Financing the Civil Service Retirement System. (C). 1979. 13.50 (*0-256-02250-X*) Irwin.

— Guaranty Fund for Private Pension Obligations. (C). 1970. 9.95 (*0-256-00659-8*) Irwin.

— No Supplies Required Crowdbreakers & Games. Parolini, Stephen, ed. LC 95-16195. 96p. 1995. pap. 11.99 (*1-55945-700-7*) Group Pub.

McGill, Dan M., ed. Social Investing. LC 83-82624. (Pension Research Council Publications). 184p. (C). 1984. text ed. 33.95 (*0-256-03170-3*) U of Pa Pr.

— Social Security & Private Pension Plans: Competitive or Complementary? 200p. (C). 1977. text ed. 20.95 (*0-256-01968-1*, U of Pa Pr) Irwin.

McGill, Dan M. & Grubbs, Donald S. Fundamentals of Private Pensions. 6th rev. ed. LC 88-10341. (Pension Research Council Publications). 816p. (C). 1988. text ed. 45.95 (*0-256-06041-X*) U of Pa Pr.

McGill, David, illus. The Kid from Matata: Memories of a Postwar Pakeha Childhood. 112p. (C). 1988. 60.00 (*1-86934-011-6*, Pub. by Grantham Hse NZ) St Mut.

McGill, David J. & King, Wilton W. Engineering Mechanics: An Introduction to Dynamics. 2nd ed. 608p. (C). 1989. text ed. 60.95 (*0-534-91786-0*) PWS Pubs.

— Engineering Mechanics: An Introduction to Dynamics. 3rd ed. LC 94-33846. 608p. 1995. text ed. 64.95 (*0-534-93399-8*) PWS Pubs.

— Engineering Mechanics: An Introduction to Statics. 3rd ed. LC 94-37333. 1216p. 1995. text ed. 80.95 (*0-534-93405-6*) PWS Pubs.

— Engineering Mechanics: Statics. 2nd ed. 600p. (C). 1989. text ed. 63.95 (*0-534-91788-7*) PWS Pubs.

— Engineering Mechanics: Statics. 3rd ed. LC 94-33845. 600p. 1995. text ed. 64.95 (*0-534-93393-9*) PWS Pubs.

McGill, Dott. The Ol' Cookbook. (Illus.). 240p. (Orig.). 1992. pap. 13.95 (*0-935069-13-5*) White Oak Pr.

McGill, Douglas C. Michael Heizer: Effigy Tumuli. 1990. 39.95 (*0-8109-1166-3*) Abrams.

McGill, Frances. Go Not Gently: Letters from a Patient with Amyotrophic Lateral Sclerosis. Kutscher, Lillian G., ed. LC 79-48047. (Foundation of Thanatology Ser.). 1980. lib. bdg. 20.95 (*0-405-12643-3*) Ayer.

McGill-Franzen, Anne. Shaping the Preschool Agenda: Early Literacy, Public Policy, & Professional Beliefs. LC 91-34722. (SUNY Series, Literacy, Culture, & Learning: Theory & Practice). (Illus.). 227p. (C). 1992. 59.50 (*0-7914-1195-8*); pap. 19.95 (*0-7914-1196-6*) State U NY Pr.

McGill, Gordon. Little Buddha. 208p. (Orig.). 1994. pap. text ed. 4.99 (*0-425-14157-8*) Berkley Pub.

Mcgill, Gordon. Stallion. 1991. pap. 3.95 (*1-55773-449-6*, Charter Bks) Michie Butterworth.

McGill, Graham. Arctic Rendezvous. 293p. 1993. pap. 13.95 (*0-87604-305-8*, 388) ARE Pr.

McGill, H. G. Telecommunications - Physics Now! (C). 1988. text ed. 50.00 (*0-09-182277-7*, Pub. by S Thornes Pubs UK) St Mut.

McGill, Ian & Beaty, Liz, eds. Action Learning: A Practitioners Guide. 180p. 1992. pap. 48.00 (*0-7494-0580-5*, Pub. by Kogan Page Educ UK) Taylor & Francis.

McGill, Ian, jt. ed. see Weil, Susan W.

McGill, John K., jt. auth. see Blair, W. Charles.

McGill, L. Jerome, jt. auth. see Norheim, Carol.

McGill, Lyndon. Mating Game: What Every Woman Should Know. LC 91-91486. (Illus.). 208p. 1992. pap. 12.95 (*0-9631771-0-9*) Sundial Pr.

McGill, M., ed. Bibliotheca Susanna: A Used Book Sales Record. 3rd ed. 322p. 1993. 49.95 (*0-9623826-0-4*) Chinook OR.

Mcgill, Marcy. Louisa May Alcott. (Orig.). (J). (gr. k-6). 1988. pap. 2.95 (*0-440-40022-8*, YB) Dell.

McGill, Mary M. Stories to Invite Faith-Sharing: Experiencing the Lord Through the Seasons. LC 92-37. (Illus.). 144p. (Orig.). 1992. pap. 8.95 (*0-89390-230-6*) Resource Pubns.

McGill, Marylyn E., jt. auth. see Cleveland, William C.

McGill, Meredith, ed. see Blair, W. Charles & McGill, John K.

McGill, Michael & Slocum, John W. The Smarter Organization: How to Build a Business That Learns & Adapts to Marketplace Needs. LC 94-10732. 1994. text ed. 29.95 (*0-471-59846-1*) Wiley.

McGill, Michael, jt. auth. see Van Houweling, Douglas.

McGill, Michael E. Organization Development for Operating Managers. LC 76-50051. 189p. reprint ed. pap. 53.90 (*0-317-26243-2*, 2052139) Bks Demand.

McGill, Michael L. & Ammond, Lorna L. How to Get the Most out of Atlanta Libraries: A Comprehensive Guidebook. 100p. (Orig.). 1990. pap. 9.95 (*0-9618236-0-7*) McGill Rsch.

***McGill, Ormond.** Chalk Talks! The Magical Art of Drawing with Chalk. LC 95-1952. (Illus.). 80p. (J). (gr. 3-6). 1995. 19.90 (*1-56294-669-2*) Millbrook Pr.

— Hypnotism & Meditation. England, Diane L. & Mignosa, Charles, eds. 99p. (Orig.). (C). 1981. audio 12.95 (*0-930298-08-X*) Westwood Pub Co.

— Hypnotism & Mysticism of India. 2nd ed. (Illus.). 208p. (C). 1979. reprint ed. text ed. 19.95 (*0-930298-01-2*) Westwood Pub Co.

— Mind Magic: Tricks for Reading Minds. LC 94-20324. (Illus.). 64p. (J). (gr. 3-6). 1995. lib. bdg. 14.40 (*1-56294-465-7*) Millbrook Pr.

— Paper Magic: Creating Fantasies & Performing Tricks with Paper. LC 91-20996. (Illus.). 64p. (J). (gr. 4-6). 1992. lib. bdg. 13.40 (*1-56294-136-4*) Millbrook Pr.

— Professional Stage Hypnotism. (Illus.). 203p. 1994. reprint ed. pap. 14.95 (*0-930298-03-9*) Westwood Pub Co.

— Voice Magic: Secrets of Ventriloquism & Voice Conjuring. LC 91-21000. (Illus.). 64p. (J). (gr. 4-6). 1992. lib. bdg. 13.90 (*1-56294-137-2*) Millbrook Pr.

McGill, Ralph. The South & the Southerner. LC 92-6038. (Brown Thrasher Bks.). 328p. 1992. reprint ed. pap. 14. 95 (*0-8203-1443-9*) U of Ga Pr.

— Southern Encounters: Southerners of Note in Ralph McGill's South. Logue, Calvin M, ed. LC 83-953. 344p. 1982. 23.50 (*0-86554-050-0*, MUP-H48) Mercer Univ Pr.

McGill, Robert. Moving to the Country. LC 86-50758. (Illus.). 187p. (Orig.). (C). 1987. 14.95 (*0-935069-27-5*); pap. 8.95 (*0-935069-17-8*) White Oak Pr.

McGill, T. C., et al, eds. Growth & Optical Properties of Wide-Gap II - VI Low-Dimensional Semoconductors. (NATO ASI Series B, Physics: Vol. 200). (Illus.). 372p. 1989. 79.50 (*0-306-43221-8*, Plenum Pr) Plenum.

McGill University, Blacker - Wood Library of Zoology & Ornithology Staff. A Dictionary Catalogue of the Blacker - Wood Library of Zoology & Ornithology, 9 vols., Set. 6300p. 1970. lib. bdg. 930.00 (*0-8161-0719-X*, Hall Library) G K Hall.

McGill University, Graduate Studies & Research Staff. McGill University Thesis Directory, Vol. 1: 1881-1959. Spitzer, Frank & Silvester, Elizabeth, eds. LC 78-317433. reprint ed. pap. 180.00 (*0-7837-1166-2*, 2041695) Bks Demand.

McGill University, Graduate Studies & Research Faculty. McGill University Thesis Directory, Vol. 2: 1960-1973. rev. ed. Spitzer, Frank & Silvester, Elizabeth, eds. LC 78-317433. 871p. reprint ed. pap. 180.00 (*0-7837-4724-1*, 2041695) Bks Demand.

McGill, Vivian J. Schopenhauer. LC 77-159487. (Studies in Philosophy: No. 40). 1971. lib. bdg. 75.00 (*0-8383-1258-6*) M S G Haskell Hse.

McGill, William A., ed. see Wilcox, Frank N.

McGill, William J., Jr. Maria Theresa. LC 85-17856. (Twayne's Rulers & Statesmen of the World Ser.). 169p. (C). 1972. lib. bdg. 17.95 (*0-8290-1738-0*) Irvington.

McGillem, C. D., jt. auth. see Cooper, G. R.

McGillem, Clare D. & Cooper, George R. Continuous & Discrete Signal & System Analysis. 3rd ed. 494p. (C). 1991. text ed. 65.25 (*0-03-051019-8*); Solutions manual. write for info. (*0-03-051022-8*) SCP.

McGillem, Clare D. & McLauchlan, William P. Hermes Bound: The Policy & Technology of Telecommunications. LC 77-86267. (Science & Society: Series in Science, Technology, & Human Values: Vol. 2). (Illus.). 304p. 1978. pap. 7.95 (*0-931682-03-7*) Purdue U Pubns.

McGillem, Clare D., jt. auth. see Cooper, George R.

McGilligan, Pat, ed. Ed Elson: I Told You I Was Serious. 1985. pap. 2.00 (*0-685-10176-2*) Quixote.

McGilligan, Patrick. Backstory Two: Interviews with Screenwriters of the 1940s & 1950s. LC 85-28949. (Illus.). 356p. 1991. 30.00 (*0-520-07169-7*) U CA Pr.

— Cagney: The Actor As Auteur. (Quality Paperbacks Ser.). (Illus.). 1980. reprint ed. pap. 6.95 (*0-306-80120-5*) Da Capo.

— Jack's Life: A Biography of Jack Nicholson. 320p. 1994. 25.00 (*0-393-03482-8*) Norton.

— Jack's Life: A Biography of Jack Nicholson. 512p. 1995. pap. 14.00 (*0-393-31378-6*, Norton Paperbks) Norton.

— Robert Altman: Jumping Off the Cliff. 1991. pap. 14.95 (*0-312-05505-6*) St Martin.

McGilligan, Patrick, ed. Backstory: Interviews with Screenwriters of Hollywood's Golden Age. (Illus.). 1986. 40.00 (*0-520-05666-3*); pap. 15.00 (*0-520-05689-2*) U CA Pr.

— White Heat. LC 83-40257. (Warner Bros. Screenplay Ser.). 1984. 19.95 (*0-299-09670-X*); pap. 9.95 (*0-299-09674-2*) U of Wis Pr.

— Yankee Doodle Dandy. LC 80-52293. (Warner Bros. Screenplay Ser.). (Illus.). 192p. (Orig.). 1981. 19.95 (*0-299-08470-1*); pap. 9.95 (*0-299-08474-4*) U of Wis Pr.

McGillion, Frank. The Opening Eye. 1991. pap. 8.95 (*0-904575-03-9*, Coventure Ltd) Sigo Pr.

***McGillis.** A Little Princess. 1994. 23.95 (*0-8057-8818-2*, Twayne); pap. 12.95 (*0-8057-8819-0*, Twayne) Macmillan.

McGillis, K. A., jt. auth. see Presley, M. W.

McGillis, Roderick. For the Childlike: George MacDonald's Fantasies for Children. LC 92-8991. (Children's Literature Association Ser.). 244p. 1992. 29.50 (*0-8108-2459-0*) Scarecrow.

McGillivary, Alice, jt. auth. see Scammon, Richard.

McGillivray, Alice V. Congressional & Gubernatorial Primaries, 1991-1992: A Handbook of Election Statistics. 265p. 1993. 129.00 (*0-87187-906-9*) Congr Quarterly.

— Congressional & Gubernatorial Primaries 1993-1994: A Handbook of Election Statistics. LC 93-11872. 450p. 1995. 134.00 (*0-87187-899-2*) Congr Quarterly.

— Presidential Primaries & Caucuses, 1992: A Handbook of Election Statistics. LC 92-33506. 294p. 1992. 135.00 (*0-87187-890-9*) Congr Quarterly.

***McGillivray, Alice V. & Scammon, Richard M.** America at the Polls, 2 vols. LC 94-30937. 1905p. 1994. 295.00 (*1-56802-051-1*) Congr Quarterly.

***McGillivray, Alice V. & Scammon, Richard M., eds.** America at the Polls: A Handbook of American Presidential Election Statistics Vol. 2: Kennedy to Clinton, 1960-1992. LC 94-30937. 1994. 295.00 (*1-56802-058-9*); 295.00 (*1-56802-059-7*) Congr Quarterly.

McGillivray, Alice V., jt. auth. see Scammon, Richard A.

McGillivray, Alice V., jt. auth. see Scammon, Richard M.

McGillivray, Alice V., jt. auth. see Scammon, Richard.

***McGillivray, David.** Doing Rude Things: History of the British Sex Film. (Illus.). 141p. Date not set. pap. 19.95 (*0-9517012-2-3*, Pub. by Sun Tavern Flds UK) AK Pr Dist.

McGillivray, Donald J. Grevillea: A Taxonomic Revision. 1992. text ed. 225.00 (*0-522-84439-1*) Intl Spec Bk.

McGillivray, E. J. & Parkington, M. Insurance Law. (C). 1988. 1,110.00 (*0-685-32776-0*, Pub. by Witherby & Co UK) St Mut.

McGillivray, Murray. Memorization in the Transmission of the Middle English Romances. LC 90-3313. (Albert Bates Lord Studies in Oral Tradition: Vol. 5). 152p. 1990. 20.00 (*0-8240-3423-6*, 1275) Garland.

McGillivray, R., jt. tr. see Lieblein, L.

McGilloway, Olly. Greyhood. 148p. 1988. pap. 9.95 (*0-85640-401-2*, Pub. by Blackstaff Pr IE) Dufour.

McGilly, Kate, ed. Classroom Lessons: Integrating Cognitive Theory & Classroom Practice. (Illus.). 450p. 1994. 45.00 (*0-262-13300-8*, Bradford Bks) MIT Pr.

McGillycuddy, Julia B. Blood on the Moon: Valentine McGillycuddy & the Sioux. LC 90-35176. (Illus.). xx, 291p. 1990. reprint ed. pap. 10.95 (*0-8032-8170-6*, Bison Books) U of Nebr Pr.

McGilp & Michael. The Home-School Connection: Guidelines for Working with Parents. 86p. 1994. pap. text ed. 15.00 (*0-435-08820-3*) Heinemann.

McGilton, Henry & Compione, Mary. PostScript by Example. LC 92-19743. 1992. pap. 34.95 (*0-201-63228-4*) Addison-Wesley.

McGilton, Henry & Morgan, Rachel. Introducing the UNIX System. (Illus.). 480p. 1983. pap. text ed. 29.95 (*0-07-045001-3*, BYTE Bks) McGraw.

McGilton, Henry, jt. auth. see Morgan, Rachel.

McGilvary, Daniel. A Half Century Among the Siamese & the Lao: An Autobiography. LC 77-87044. reprint ed. 33.00 (*0-404-16838-8*) AMS Pr.

McGilvary, Tony, jt. auth. see Webber, Marlene.

***McGilvery, Carole.** Encyclopedia of Aromatherapy, Massage & Yoga. 1994. 19.98 (*0-8317-2741-1*) Smithmark.

— Essential Aromatherapy. 1994. 12.98 (*0-8317-6506-2*) Smithmark.

— Step-by-Step Massage: A Guide to Massage Techniques for Health, Relaxation & Vitality. 1994. 10.98 (*0-8317-6514-3*) Smithmark.

McGilvery, Laurence, ed. Artforum, 1962-1968: A Cumulative Index to the First Six Volumes. LC 65-8747. 1970. lib. bdg. 12.00 (*0-910938-19-9*); pap. 10.00 (*0-910938-18-0*) McGilvery.

McGilvery, Lynette, ed. An Index to the Paperback Little Magazines. 1980. pap. 7.95 (*0-910938-64-4*) McGilvery.

McGilvery, R. W. & Pogell, B. M., eds. Fructose-One, Six-Diphosphates & Its Role in Gluconeogenesis. 1964. 12. 50 (*0-934454-40-X*) Lubrecht & Cramer.

McGilvray, Barbara, tr. see Verri, Pietro.

McGilvray, Ian, tr. see Ingaro, Bruna & Israel, Giorgio.

McGilvray, Ian, tr. see Petruccioli, Sandro.

McGilvray, James A. Tense, Reference, & Worldmaking. 1991. 55.00 (*0-7735-0871-6*, Pub. by McGill CN) U of Toronto Pr.

McGilvray, Richard. Don't Climb out of the Window Tonight. LC 92-28136. (Illus.). (J). (ps-2). 1993. 13.99 (*0-8037-1373-8*) Dial Bks Young.

***McGilvrey, Carole & Reed, Jimi.** The Essential Aromatherapy Book: A Full-Color Guide to Using Essential Oils for Health, Relaxation & Pleasure. (Illus.). 96p. 1995. 25.00 (*1-85967-151-9*) Stewart Tabori & Chang.

McGimsey, Charles R., jt. ed. see Wiant, Michael D.

McGimsey, Robert H. Sweet Little Jesus Boy: A Soliloquy. 32p. 1973. pap. 2.95 (*0-911336-53-2*) Sci of Mind.

McGing, B. C. The Foreign Policy of Mithridates VI Eupator, King of Pontus. (Mnemosyne Ser.: Supplement 89). ix, 204p. 1986. pap. 45.75 (*90-04-07591-7*) E J Brill.

McGing, Brian C., ed. see Parke, H. W.

McGinity. Aqueous Polymeric Coatings for Pharmaceutical Dosage Forms. (Drugs & the Pharmaceutical Sciences Ser.: Vol. 36). 424p. 1989. 170.00 (*0-8247-7907-X*) Dekker.

MCGinley, Bernard, ed. see Joyce, James, et al.

McGinley, Carol. Stepping Into Fantasy & Other Places. LC 90-70320. 1990. 5.95 (*1-55523-340-6*) Winston-Derek.

***McGinley, Gerald & Waye, Vicki.** Evidence Handbook. 270p. 1994. pap. 29.00 (*0-455-21264-3*, Pub. by Law Bk Co) W W Gaunt.

McGinley, Jerry. Waupaca County: Seven A. M. 46p. 1986. 20.00 (*0-9616222-0-2*); pap. 5.50 (*0-9616222-1-0*) Indian Crossing Bks.

McGinley, John W. Shame! An Other Guide for the Perplexed. LC 93-18431. 310p. (Orig.). (C). 1993. lib. bdg. 46.50 (*0-8191-9093-4*); pap. text ed. 24.50 (*0-8191-9094-2*) U Pr of Amer.

McGinley, Ken & O'Neill, Eamonn P. No Risk Involved: The Ken McGinley Story Survivor of a Nuclear Experiment. (Illus.). 192p. 1992. 29.95 (*1-85158-337-8*, Pub. by Mnstream UK) Trafalgar.

McGinley, Phyllis. Most Wonderful Doll in the World. (J). 1990. 10.95 (*0-590-43476-4*) Scholastic Inc.

— The Most Wonderful Doll in the World. (J). 1992. 3.95 (*0-590-43477-2*, Blue Ribbon Bks) Scholastic Inc.

— Saint-Watching. (Crossroad Paperback Ser.). 256p. 1982. pap. 11.95 (*0-8245-0450-X*) Crossroad NY.

McGinley, Ronald J. Systematics of the Colletidae Based on Mature Larvae with Phenetic Analysis of Apoid Larvae (Hymenoptera, Apoidea) LC 80-15362. (University of California Publications in Social Welfare: No. 91). (Illus.). 333p. reprint ed. pap. 95.00 (*0-685-24002-9*, 2031587) Bks Demand.

***McGinn.** Visions of the End: Apocalypt. 1979. pap. text ed. write for info. (*0-231-04594-8*) Col U Pr.

McGinn, Bernard. Antichrist: Two Thousand Years of the Human Fascination with Evil. LC 94-14396. (Illus.). 416p. 1994. 32.50 (*0-06-065543-7*) Harper SF.

— Antichrist: Two Thousand Years of the Human Fascination with Evil. LC 94-14396. (Illus.). 416p. 1994. pap. 18.00 (*0-06-065282-9*) Harper SF.

— Apolcalypticism in the Western Tradition. (Collected Studies). 336p. 1994. 89.95 (*0-86078-396-0*, Pub. by Variorum UK) Ashgate Pub Co.

— The Foundations of Mysticism: Origins to the Fifth Century. 518p. 1994. reprint ed. pap. 19.95 (*0-8245-1404-1*) Crossroad NY.

— The Golden Chain: A Study in the Theological Anthropology of Isaac of Stella. LC 70-152487. (Cistercian Studies: No. 15). 280p. 1972. 7.50 (*0-87907-815-4*) Cistercian Pubns.

— The Growth of Mysticism: From Gregory the Great Through the Twelfth Century. 600p. 1994. 49.50 (*0-8245-1450-5*) Crossroad NY.

McGinn, Bernard, ed. The Foundations of Mysticism: Origins to the Fifth Century. (Presence of God: A History of Christian Mysticism Ser.: Vol. 1). (Illus.). 448p. 1991. 39.50 (*0-8245-1121-2*) Crossroad NY.

— Meister Eckhart & the Beguine Mystics: Hadewijch of Brabant, Mechthild of Magdeburg, & Marguerite Porete. 160p. (C). 1994. 19.95 (*0-8264-0681-5*) Continuum.

— Three Treatises on Man: A Cistercian Anthropology. LC 77-184906. (Cistercian Fathers Ser.: No. 24). 1977. 13.95 (*0-87907-024-2*) Cistercian Pubns.

McGinn, Bernard, tr. Apocalyptic Spirituality. LC 79-90834. (Classics of Western Spirituality Ser.). 352p. 1979. pap. 18.95 (*0-8091-2242-1*) Paulist Pr.

McGinn, Bernard & Eliade, Mircea. The Galabrian Abbot: Joachim of Flora in the History of Western Thought. 1985. write for info. (*0-317-18119-X*) Macmillan.

McGinn, Bernard & Meyendorff, John, eds. Christian Spirituality, Vol. I: Origins to the Twelfth Century. (World Spirituality Ser.: Vol. 16). (Illus.). 600p. 1987. pap. 22.95x (*0-8245-0847-5*) Crossroad NY.

McGinn, Bernard & Otten, Willemien, eds. Eriugena: East & West. LC 93-42514. (Conferences in Medieval Studies: Vol. 5). (C). 1994. text ed. 39.95 (*0-268-00929-5*) U of Notre Dame Pr.

McGinn, Bernard, jt. ed. see Burrell, David B.

McGinn, Bernard, jt. tr. see Colledge, Edmund.

McGinn, Bernard, jt. ed. see Emmerson, Richard K.

McGinn, Bernard, et al. Meister Eckhart: Teacher & Preacher. (Classics of Western Spirituality Ser.: Vol. 52). 448p. 1986. 15.95 (*0-8091-0377-X*); pap. 12.95 (*0-8091-2827-6*) Paulist Pr.

McGinn, Colin. The Character of Mind. 1982. pap. 15.95 (*0-19-289159-6*) OUP.

— Mental Content. 1991. pap. 21.95 (*0-631-18029-X*) Blackwell Pubs.

— Moral Literacy: Or How to Do the Right Thing. 110p. (Orig.). (C). 1993. lib. bdg. 29.95 (*0-87220-197-X*); pap. text ed. 7.95 (*0-87220-196-1*) Hackett Pub.

— The Problem of Consciousness: Essays Towards a Resolution. 216p. 1993. pap. 19.95 (*0-631-18803-7*) Blackwell Pubs.

— Problems in Philosophy: The Limits of Inquiry. LC 93-14752. 208p. 1994. 44.95 (*1-55786-474-8*); pap. 17.95 (*1-55786-475-6*) Blackwell Pubs.

— The Subjective View: Secondary Qualities & Indexical Thoughts. 1983. pap. 19.95 (*0-19-824695-1*) OUP.

McGinn, Daniel F. Actuarial Fundamentals for Multiemployer Plans. 2nd ed. Brzezinski, Mary J., ed. LC 92-72176. 187p. (Orig.). 1992. pap. 39.00 (*0-89154-439-9*) Intl Found Employ.

— Corporate Retirement Plans: An Actuarial Perspective. Lehman, June M., ed. LC 88-81842. 270p. (Orig.). 1988. pap. 10.00 (*0-89154-351-1*) Intl Found Employ.

— Joint Trust Pension Plans: Understanding & Administering Collectively Bargained Multiemployer Plans under ERISA. 368p. (C). 1978. text ed. 20.95 (*0-256-02105-8*, U of Pa Pr) Irwin.

McGinn, Elinor M. At Hard Labor: Inmate Labor at the Colorado State Penitentiary, 1871-1940. LC 92-34581. (American University Studies: History: Ser. IX, Vol. 137). 171p. (C). 1994. text ed. 39.95 (*0-8204-2097-2*) P Lang Pubs.

McGinn, Joseph C. Lawyers: A Client's Manual. 1977. 11.95 (*0-13-526814-1*); pap. 5.95 (*0-13-526806-0*); Fourteen set tapes. 215.00 (*0-13-530444-X*) P-H.

McGinn, Kerry A. The Informed Woman's Guide to Breast Health: Breast Changes That Are Not Cancer. rev. ed. Bull, David C., ed. (Illus.). 200p. (Orig.). 1992. pap. 12.95 (*0-923521-24-0*) Bull Pub.

McGinn, Kerry A. & Haylock, Pamela J. Women's Cancers: How to Prevent Them, How to Treat Them, How to Beat Them. LC 92-41408. (Illus.). 448p. 1993. 26.95 (*0-89793-103-3*); pap. 16.95 (*0-89793-102-5*) Hunter Hse.

McGinn, Kerry A., jt. auth. see Mullen, Barbara D.

***McGinn, Linda.** Leader's Guide to Saying Yes to God: Esther. (Women in the Word Ser.). 128p. (Orig.). 1995. teacher ed, pap. 7.99 (*0-8010-5246-7*) Baker Bk.

— Leader's Guide to Walking with Jesus: Luke. (Women in the Word Ser.). 128p. (Orig.). 1995. teacher ed, pap. 7.99 (*0-8010-5247-5*) Baker Bk.

— Resource Guide for Women's Ministries. LC 89-71084. (Orig.). 1990. pap. 7.99 (*0-8054-3005-9*) Broadman.

McGinn, Linda R. The Bible Answers Questions Children Ask. (Orig.). 1992. pap. 7.99 (*0-8054-5092-0*) Broadman.

— Equipped for Life: Ephesians, Philippians, Colossians. 1994. pap. 3.99 (*0-8010-3876-6*) Baker Bk.

— Saying Yes to God: Esther. (Women in the Word Ser.). 64p. (Orig.). 1995. pap. 3.99 (*0-8010-5044-8*) Baker Bk.

— Seeing Jesus: 1 Peter to 3 John. 1994. pap. 3.99 (*0-8010-3877-4*) Baker Bk.

— Walking with Jesus: Luke. (Women in the Word Ser.). 64p. (Orig.). 1995. pap. 3.99 (*0-8010-5009-X*) Baker Bk.

McGinn, Linda R., ed. The Strength of a Woman. LC 92-35746. (Orig.). 1993. pap. 9.99 (*0-8054-5353-9*) Broadman.

McGinn, Linda R. & Hollingsworth, T. R. Investing Your Life in Things that Matter. LC 94-21476. 1995. 16.99 (*0-8054-6147-7*) Broadman.

McGinn, Mary, jt. auth. see Moody, Kim.

McGinn, Matt. Fry the Little Fishes. 1994. pap. 9.95 (*0-7145-0992-2*) Riverrun NY.

***McGinn, Noel F. & Borden, Allison M.** Framing Questions, Constructing Answers: Linking Research with Education Policy for Developing Countries. LC 94-21886. (Harvard Studies in International Development: Harvard Institute for International Development: Vol. 8). 1994. pap. text ed. 15.00 (*0-674-31715-7*, MCGFRA) HUP.

McGinn, Noel F., et al. Education & Development in Korea. (East Asian Monographs: No. 90). 311p. 1980. 16.50 (*0-674-23810-9*) HUP.

McGinn, Richard. Studies in Austronesian Linguistics. LC 87-11242. (Monographs in International Studies, Southeast Asia Ser.: No. 76). 650p. 1986. pap. text ed. 20.00 (*0-89680-137-3*, Ohio U Ctr Intl) Ohio U Pr.

McGinn, Robert E. Science, Technology & Society. 304p. (C). 1990. pap. text ed. write for info. (*0-13-794736-4*) P-H.

McGinn, Thomas A., jt. auth. see McCann, Nancy D.

***McGinness, Frederick J.** Right Thinking & Sacred Oratory in Counter-Reformation Rome. LC 95-3104. 1995. write for info. (*0-691-03426-5*) Princeton U Pr.

McGinness, Joe. Son of Alyandabu. 1991. pap. 16.95 (*0-7022-2335-2*, Pub. by Univ Queensland Pr AT) Intl Spec Bk.

McGinnies, Elliott. Social Psychology A to Z. 356p. 1993. pap. text ed. 32.50 (*0-89876-210-3*) Gardner Pr.

McGinnies, W. G., jt. ed. see Bishay, A.

McGinnies, William G. Discovering the Desert: The Legacy of the Carnegie Desert Botanical Laboratory. LC 81-1554. 276p. (C). 1981. pap. 13.95 (*0-8165-0728-7*) U of Ariz Pr.

McGinnies, William G., et al, eds. Deserts of the World: An Appraisal of Research into Their Physical & Biological Environments. LC 68-9338. 816p. reprint ed. pap. 180.00 (*0-318-34747-4*, 2031483) Bks Demand.

— Food, Fiber & the Arid Land. LC 75-152038. 447p. reprint ed. pap. 127.40 (*0-317-51986-7*, 2027384) Bks Demand.

***McGinnis.** Power of Optimism. 1994. pap. 3.99 (*0-517-13252-4*) Random Hse Value.

McGinnis, et al, eds. Texas Employment Laws & Regulations: How to Comply. 148p. 1993. pap. 65.00 (*0-685-67824-5*) Amer CC Pubs.

McGinnis, Alan L. La Amistad Factor Decisivo. Orig. Title: The Friendship Factor. 204p. (SPA.). 1986. reprint ed. pap. 5.95 (*0-311-46093-3*, Edit Mundo) Casa Bautista.

— Bringing Out the Best in People: How to Enjoy Helping Others Excel. LC 84-28400. 192p. 1985. pap. 5.99 (*0-8066-2151-6*, 10-0922, Augsburg) Augsburg Fortress.

— Confidence: How to Succeed at Being Yourself. LC 87-1470. 192p. (Orig.). 1987. pap. 5.99 (*0-8066-2262-8*, 10-1639, Augsburg) Augsburg Fortress.

— The Power of Optimism. 1993. pap. 5.50 (*0-685-67757-5*, Harp PBks) HarpC.

— Power of Optimism. 1994. mass mkt. 5.50 (*0-06-104088-6*, Harp PBks) HarpC.

— The Romance Factor. LC 81-47839. 224p. 1982. 11.45 (*0-06-065360-4*) Harper SF.

— The Romance Factor. LC 90-55150. 240p. 1990. reprint ed. pap. 11.00 (*0-06-065366-3*) Harper SF.

— Sea Alguien! Como Lograr lo Mejor de Uno Mismo. Canclini, Arnoldo, tr. 176p. (Orig.). (SPA.). 1988. pap. 5.95 (*0-311-46115-8*) Casa Bautista.

— La Superacion: Como Se Logra en Otros y en Nosotros. Canclini, Arnoldo, tr. 169p. (Orig.). (SPA.). 1987. pap. 4.95 (*0-311-46107-7*) Casa Bautista.

McGinnis, Allen R. The Rest of Your Life. Thompson, Nancy V., ed. LC 85-23731. 175p. 1986. 10.00 (*0-9616042-0-4*) J & N Pubs.

McGinnis, Anthony. Counting Coup & Cutting Horses: Intertribal Warfare on the Northern Plains, 1738-1889. LC 90-45306. (Illus.). 250p. 1990. pap. 14.95 (*0-917895-29-0*) Cordillera CO.

McGinnis, Carol. Virginia Genealogy: Sources & Resources. 505p. 1993. 35.00 (*0-8063-1379-X*, 3526) Genealog Pub.

McGinnis, Christopher J. Two Hundred Two Tips Even the Best Business Travelers May Not Know. LC 94-2846. 160p. 1994. pap. 10.00 (*1-55623-966-1*) Irwin Prof Pubng.

McGinnis, Claude. Pocket Guide to Good Cheap Wines, 1992. 72p. (Orig.). 1992. pap. 7.95 (*0-9628530-4-6*) Bookmark GA.

McGinnis, Claude, comp. Expert's Guide to Excellent Wines: More Than 600 Highly-Rated Wines for 10 Dollars or Under. (Illus.). 200p. (Orig.). 1993. pap. 9.95 (*0-8128-8554-6*, Scrbrough Hse) Madison Bks UPA.

McGinnis, Ellen & Goldstein, Arnold P. Skillstreaming in Early Childhood: Teaching Prosocial Skills to the Preschool & Kindergarten Child. LC 90-60925. (Illus.). 200p. (Orig.). 1990. pap. text ed. 14.95 (*0-87822-320-7*, 4423); Program forms. pap. text ed. 13.95 (*0-87822-321-5*, 4424) Res Press.

McGinnis, Ellen, et al. Skillstreaming the Elementary School Child: A Guide for Teaching Prosocial Skills. LC 84-61282. 256p. (Orig.). (C). 1984. pap. text ed. 14.95 (*0-87822-235-9*, 2359); 12.95 (*0-87822-236-7*, 2360) Res Press.

McGinnis, Esther, jt. auth. see Davis, Edith.

***McGinnis, Eva.** Wings to My Breath. 112p. (Orig.). (C). 1992. pap. 9.95 (*1-878555-03-0*) Oakbridge Univ Pr.

McGinnis, Gary D., jt. ed. see Biermann, Christopher J.

McGinnis, Grant, ed. Let's Travel Pathways Through Minnesota: A Compilation of the Best in Minnesota Travel. 2nd ed. (Let's Travel Pathways Through America Ser.). Orig. Title: Pathways Through Minnesota. (Illus.). 640p. (Orig.). 1995. reprint ed. pap. 16.95 (*0-9626647-1-5*) Clark & Miles.

McGinnis, Helen. Hiking Mississippi: A Trail Guide. (Illus.). 256p. 1994. 35.00 (*0-87805-704-8*); pap. 15.95 (*0-87805-664-5*) U Pr of Miss.

McGinnis, Helen J. Carnegie's Dinosaurs. LC 82-70212. (Illus.). 120p. (Orig.). 1982. pap. 15.95 (*0-911239-00-6*) Carnegie Mus.

McGinnis, James. Journey into Compassion: A Spirituality for the Long Haul. 148p. (Orig.). 1993. reprint ed. pap. 10.95 (*0-88344-926-9*) Orbis Bks.

McGinnis, James & McGinnis, Kathleen. Parenting for Peace & Justice: Ten Years Later. rev. ed. LC 89-77688. 1990. pap. 11.95 (*0-685-47516-6*) Orbis Bks.

McGinnis, James, et al. Educating for Peace & Justice: A Manual for Teachers, 3 vols., Set. rev. ed. LC 83-145843. (Illus.). 1985. pap. text ed. 37.00 (*0-912765-09-7*) Inst Peace.

— Educating for Peace & Justice: Global Dimensions, Vol. II. rev. ed. LC 83-145843. (Illus.). 324p. 1984. pap. text ed. 14.25 (*0-912765-11-9*) Inst Peace.

— Educating for Peace & Justice: National Dimensions, Vol. I. rev. ed. LC 85-160342. (Illus.). 300p. 1985. pap. text ed. 14.25 (*0-912765-12-7*) Inst Peace.

— Educating for Peace & Justice: Religious Dimensions, Vol. III. rev. ed. LC 83-145843. (Illus.). 243p. 1984. pap. text ed. 14.25 (*0-912765-10-0*) Inst Peace.

— Global Family Puppets. LC 85-159827. (Illus.). 28p. 1984. pap. text ed. 4.00 (*0-912765-14-3*) Inst Peace.

— Puppets for Peace. LC 85-159843. (Illus.). 44p. 1984. pap. text ed. 5.00 (*0-912765-13-5*) Inst Peace.

McGinnis, James, et al, eds. Partners in Peacemaking: Family Workshop Models Guidebook for Leaders. LC 85-159853. 170p. 1984. pap. text ed. 10.75 (*0-912765-08-9*) Inst Peace.

McGinnis, James B. Solidarity with the People of Nicaragua. LC 84-27202. (Illus.). 176p. (Orig.). reprint ed. pap. 50.20 (*0-8357-8547-5*, 2034886) Bks Demand.

McGinnis, Janice D., ed. see Jackson, Mary P.

McGinnis, Jeanne, jt. auth. see Eagen, Jane.

McGinnis, Joe. Blind Faith. 1990. pap. 5.99 (*0-451-16806-2*, Sig) NAL-Dutton.

— Heroes. 1990. pap. 8.95 (*0-671-69511-8*) S&S Trade.

McGinnis, John, ed. Changing Times - Changing Styles: The Ruth Stoever Fleming Collection of Southern California Art. LC 85-5011. (Illus.). 80p. 1985. pap. 10.00 (*0-9614891-1-1*) Newport Mesa Sch.

McGinnis, K. C. Eleventh Annual BACUS Symposium on Photomask Technology. 1991. 62.00 (*0-8194-0733-X*) SPIE.

McGinnis, Kathleen. Family Activities Guide. 1989. pap. 7.95 (*0-685-28773-4*) Baptist Peace.

McGinnis, Kathleen, jt. auth. see McGinnis, James.

McGinnis, Ken, jt. auth. see Berdan, David.

McGinnis, L., ed. Dry Valley Drilling Project. (Antarctic Research Ser.: Vol. 33). (Illus.). 480p. 1981. 39.00 (*0-87590-152-2*) Am Geophysical.

***McGinnis, Lila S.** If Daddy Only Knew Me. LC 95-3135. (Illus.). (J). 1995. write for info. (*0-8075-3537-0*) A Whitman.

— The Twenty-Four Hour Genie. LC 89-77786. (Illus.). 80p. (J). (gr. 2-4). 1990. 12.95 (*0-8050-1303-2*, Redfeather BYR) H Holt & Co.

— The Twenty-Four Hour Genie. LC 89-77786. (Redfeather Paperback Ser.). (Illus.). 80p. (J). (gr. 2-4). 1991. pap. 4.95 (*0-8050-1845-X*, Redfeather BYR) H Holt & Co.

***McGinnis, Linda.** The Art of Hairdressing Success. 208p. 1995. pap. text ed. 18.95 (*1-886203-64-4*) Paradime Pubng.

McGinnis, Mark W. Lakota & Dakota Animal Wisdom Stories. (Illus.). 24p. (J). 1994. pap. 11.98 (*1-877976-14-8*, 406-0016) Tipi Pr.

McGinnis, Mary, jt. auth. see Sanders, Jo.

McGinnis, Michael R. Current Topics in Medical Mycology. Vol. 2. (Illus.). 385p. 1987. 146.00 (*0-387-96543-2*) Spr-Verlag.

— Laboratory Handbook of Medical Mycology. 1980. text ed. 99.00 (*0-12-482850-7*) Acad Pr.

McGinnis, Michael R., ed. Current Topics in Medical Mycology, Vol. 1. (Illus.). 360p. 1985. 132.00 (*0-387-96095-3*) Spr-Verlag.

McGinnis, Michael R. & Borgers, M., eds. Current Topics in Medical Mycology. (Illus.). 448p. 1989. 173.00 (*0-387-96941-1*, 2540) Spr-Verlag.

McGinnis, Patrick E. Oklahoma's Depression Radicals: Ira M. Finley & the Veterans of Industry of America. LC 90-19401. (Recent American History Ser.: Vol. 3). 196p. (C). 1991. text ed. 36.95 (*0-8204-1295-3*) P Lang Pubs.

McGinnis, Ralph & Smith, Calvin. Abraham Lincoln & the Western Territories. 1993. text ed. 28.95 (*0-8304-1247-6*); pap. text ed. 18.95 (*0-8304-1375-8*) Nelson-Hall.

McGinnis, Ralph Y. Quotations from Abraham Lincoln. LC 77-24595. (Illus.). 144p. 1978. 34.95 (*0-88229-316-8*) Nelson-Hall.

McGinnis, Richard G. Learning CADKey. 1991. pap. text ed. write for info. (*0-07-044791-8*) McGraw.

McGinnis, Samuel M. Freshwater Fishes of California. LC 83-5113. (California Natural History Guides Ser.: No. 49). (Illus.). 350p. 1984. 35.00 (*0-520-04881-4*); pap. 13.00 (*0-520-04891-1*) U CA Pr.

McGinnis, Terri. The Well Cat Book: The Classic Comprehensive Handbook of Cat Care. rev. ed. LC 92-56834. 292p. 1993. 23.00 (*0-394-58769-3*) Random.

— The Well Dog Book: The Classic, Comprehensive Handbook of Dog Care. LC 91-52680. (Illus.). 272p. 1992. 23.00 (*0-394-58768-5*) Random.

McGinnis, William. Whitewater Rafting. LC 74-24280. (Illus.). 1978. pap. 12.95 (*0-8129-6301-6*, Times Bks) Random.

McGinnis, William N. School Administrative & Supervisory Organizations in Cities of 20,000 to 50,000 Population. LC 71-177024. (Columbia University. Teachers College. Contributions to Education Ser.: No. 392). reprint ed. 22.50 (*0-404-55392-3*) AMS Pr.

McGinniss, Alan L. The Friendship Factor: How to Get Closer to the People You Care for. LC 79-50076. 192p. 1979. pap. 5.99 (*0-8066-1711-X*, 10-2411, Augsburg) Augsburg Fortress.

McGinniss, Joe. Cruel Doubt. Rubenstein, Julie, ed. 512p. 1992. reprint ed. mass mkt. 5.99 (*0-671-77539-1*) PB.

— Fatal Vision. 1984. pap. 4.95 (*0-451-16050-9*, Sig); pap. 6.99 (*0-451-16566-7*, Sig) NAL-Dutton.

— Going to Extremes. 228p. 1989. pap. 10.95 (*0-452-26301-8*, Plume) NAL-Dutton.

— The Last Brother. 1994. pap. 6.99 (*0-671-89452-8*) PB.

— The Last Brother. 640p. 1993. pap. 25.00 (*0-671-67945-7*) S&S Trade.

— The Selling of the President. 288p. 1988. pap. 12.00 (*0-14-011240-5*, Penguin Bks) Viking Penguin.

McGinniss, Michael J., ed. see Christian Brothers Staff.

McGinnity, Gerard. Celebrating with Mary: Reflections for Personal Prayer & Parish Devotions. 92p. (Orig.). 1987. pap. 7.95 (*0-86217-289-6*, Pub. by Veritas Publns IE) Ignatius Pr.

McGinty. Prelude & Fugue in C Major: Bach Flute Choir. 1990. 10.00 (*0-685-32130-4*, 77193) Hansen Ed Mus.

McGinty & Jackson. Current Therapy in Orthopaedics. 1991. write for info. (*1-55664-040-4*) Mosby Yr Bk.

McGinty, jt. auth. see Bach.

McGinty, Gerald P. Videocassette Recorders: Theory & Servicing. (Illus.). 1979. pap. text ed. 20.35 (*0-07-044988-0*) McGraw.

McGinty, Jean & Fish, John. Further Education in the Market-Place: Equity, Opportunity, & Individual Learning. LC 93-7346. 1994. write for info. (*0-415-10040-2*); pap. write for info. (*0-415-10041-0*) Routledge.

— Learning Support for Young People in Transition: Leaving School for Further Education & Work. 112p. 1992. 90.00 (*0-335-09766-9*, Open Univ Pr); pap. 32.00 (*0-335-09765-0*, Open Univ Pr) Taylor & Francis.

McGinty, John B., et al, eds. Operative Arthroscopy. 816p. 1991. 262.50 (*0-88167-633-0*) Raven.

— Operative Arthroscopy. 2nd ed. LC 95-15899. 1996. write for info. (*0-7817-0294-1*) Raven.

McGinty, Kevin J. The Fundamentals of Capital Markets Products. Behr, Joan H., ed. LC 88-32944. (Illus.). 48p. (Orig.). 1988. pap. text ed. 17.00 (*0-936742-61-5*, 31071) Robt Morris Assocs.

McGinty, Martha E., tr. see Foucher De Chartres.

McGinty, Mary P. The Sacrament of Christian Life. 1992. pap. 12.95 (*0-88347-270-8*) Thomas More.

***McGinty, Michael J.** Medicare Reimbursement & the Quality of Hospital Care. 137p. (Orig.). (C). 1994. pap. text ed. 40.00x (*0-7881-1053-5*) Diane Pub.

McGinty, Park. Interpretation & Dionysos: Method in the Study of a God. (Religion & Reason Ser.: No. 16). 1978. 62.70 (*90-279-7844-1*) Mouton.

McGinty, Patricia. Dirges to Dance by. Galvin, Suzanne & LaRue, James, eds. (Chapbook Ser.: No. 9). 23p. 1982. pap. 3.00 (*0-932884-08-3*) Red Herring.

McGinty, Sarah M. Writing Your College Application Essay. rev. ed. 131p. (Orig.). 1991. pap. 9.95 (*0-87447-429-9*) College Bd.

McGinty, Sarah M., jt. auth. see MacGowan, Sandra F.

McGirk, Jan S. Exploring Rural Spain. (Exploring Rural Europe Ser.). 178p. 1988. pap. 12.95 (*0-8442-9462-4*, Passport Bks) NTC Pub Grp.

McGirr, Nancy, jt. ed. see Franklin, Kristine L.

McGirr, Randall D. Learning How to Read New Testament Greek: With People Just Like You. 420p. (Orig.). 1992. pap. 24.95 (*0-9631877-0-8*) Context Script.

An Asterisk (*) at the beginning of an entry indicates that the title is appearing in BIP for the first time.

— Learning How to Use New Testament Reference Books with People Just Like You. (Illus.). 290p. Date not set. pap. 24.95 (*0-9631877-1-6*) Context Script.

McGirt, Dan. Dirty Work. (Jason Cosmo Ser.). 288p. (Orig.). 1993. pap. 4.50 (*0-451-45215-1*, ROC) NAL-Dutton.

— Jason Cosmo. 240p. 1989. pap. 3.95 (*0-451-16288-9*, Sig) NAL-Dutton.

— Royal Chaos. 240p. 1990. pap. 3.95 (*0-451-45014-0*) NAL-Dutton.

McGirt, James E. Avenging the Maine, a Drunken A. B. & Other Poems. LC 73-133160. (Black Heritage Library Collection). 1977. 13.95 (*0-8369-8715-2*) Ayer.

— The Triumphs of Ephraim. LC 79-39093. (Black Heritage Library Collection). 1977. reprint ed. 22.95 (*0-8369-9031-5*) Ayer.

McGiverin, Rolland H. Educational & Psychological Tests in the Academic Library. LC 90-4052. (Behavioral & Social Sciences Librarian Ser.: Vol. 8, Nos. 3 - 4). 95p. 1990. text ed. 29.95 (*0-86656-915-4*) Haworth Pr.

McGivern. Fast & Fancy Revolver Shooting. LC 84-62402. 1975. 17.95 (*0-8329-0557-7*) New Win Pub.

McGivern, Diane O., jt. ed. see Mezey, Mathy D.

McGivern, Gene. Here's Johnny Orr. LC 92-24569. (Illus.). 312p. 1992. pap. 15.95 (*0-8138-1291-7*) Iowa St U Pr.

McGivern, Maureen D., jt. auth. see McGivern, William P.

McGivern, William P. & McGivern, Maureen D. The Seeing. 288p. (Orig.). 1984. reprint ed. pap. 3.50 (*0-8439-2161-7*) Dorchester Pub Co.

McGivney & Castleberry. McCracken's Removable Partial Prosthodontics, No. 9. 550p. 1994. 61.95 (*0-8016-7964-8*) Mosby Yr Bk.

McGivney, et al. McCracken's Removable Partial Prosthodontics. 8th ed. (Illus.). 544p. 1989. 63.95 (*0-8016-2155-0*) Mosby Yr Bk.

McGivney, Joseph H., jt. auth. see McGivney, Shawn A.

McGivney, Shawn A. & McGivney, Joseph H. Eternally Young: A Guide to Aging Well. LC 89-85373. (Illus.). (Orig.). 1989. pap. text ed. 9.95 (*0-9623941-0-6*) Ageless Pub.

McGlade, Shirley. Daddy, Where Are You? large type ed. (Illus.). 400p. 1993. 23.95 (*0-7089-8701-X*, Trail West Pubs) Ulverscroft.

McGlade, William G. Oil & Gas Geology of the Amity & Claysville Quadrangles, Pennsylvania. (Mineral Resource Report: No. 54). (Illus.). 131p. 1984. reprint ed. pap. 29.90 (*0-8182-0022-7*) Commonweal PA.

McGladrey & Pullan. The Americans with Disabilities Act: A Practical Guide to Cost-Effective Compliance. 160p. 69.00 (*1-878375-92-X*) Panel Pubs.

***McGladrey & Pullen.** The Americans with Disabilities Act: A Practical Guide to Cost-Effective Compliance. 200p. 1993. 79.00 (*1-56706-052-8*) Aspen Pub.

McGlamry, E. Dalton, et al. Comprehensive Textbook of Foot Surgery, Set, Vols. 1 & 2. 2nd ed. (Illus.). 1840p. 1992. Set. text ed. 325.00 (*0-683-05857-6*) Williams & Wilkins.

***McGlashan, C. F.** History of the Donner Party: A Tragedy of the Sierra. 1995. pap. text ed. 18.00 (*0-7884-0115-7*) Heritage Bk.

McGlashan, Charles F. History of the Donner Party: A Tragedy of the Sierra. rev. ed. Hinkle, George H. & Hinkle, Bliss M., eds. (Illus.). lvii, 261p. 1947. 19.95 (*0-8047-0366-3*); pap. 10.95 (*0-8047-0367-1*) Stanford U Pr.

McGlashan, J. E., ed. Modern Trends in Sludge Management, No. 115. (Water Science & Technology Ser.: Vol. 15). (Illus.). 254p. 1983. pap. 44.00 (*0-08-030416-8*, Pergamon Pr) Elsevier.

McGlashan, M. L. Chemical Thermodynamics. LC 79-40919. 1980. text ed. 88.00 (*0-12-482650-4*) Acad Pr.

McGlashan, M. L., jt. ed. see Beynon, J. H.

McGlashan, N. D., ed. Health Problems in Australia & New Zealand. 180p. 1980. pap. 24.00 (*0-08-026103-5*, Pergamon Pr) Elsevier.

McGlashan, Neil & Blunden, John R., eds. Geographic Aspects of Health. 1983. text ed. 113.00 (*0-12-483780-8*) Acad Pr.

McGlashan, Robert & Singleton, Timothy M. Strategic Management: Text & Cases. 800p. (C). 1987. write for info. (*0-675-20100-4*, Merrill Pub Co) Macmillan.

McGlashan, Thomas H. The Borderline: Current Empirical Research. LC 85-6102. (Progress in Psychiatry Ser.). 128p. 1985. boxed, pap. 22.00 (*0-88048-068-8*, 8068) Am Psychiatric.

McGlashan, Thomas H. & Keats, Christopher J. Schizophrenia: Treatment Process & Outcome. LC 88-24228. 207p. 1989. text ed. 32.00 (*0-88048-281-8*) Am Psychiatric.

McGlashen, Don, jt. auth. see Dadson, Philip.

McGlasson, Paul. God the Redeemer: A Theology of the Gospel. LC 92-13034. 192p. (Orig.). 1992. pap. 11.99 (*0-664-25377-6*) Westminster John Knox.

— Jesus & Judas: Biblical Exegesis in Barth. 168p. 1991. 24.95 (*1-55540-567-3*); pap. 14.95 (*1-55540-568-1*) Scholars Pr GA.

McGlathery, Glenn & Livo, Norma J. Who's Endangered on Noah's Ark? Literary & Scientific Activities for Teachers & Parents. LC 92-19570. (Illus.). 1992. pap. text ed. 22.00 (*0-87287-949-6*) Teacher Ideas Pr.

McGlathery, Glenn & Malone, Larry. Tons of Scientifically Provocative & Socially Acceptable Things to Do with Balloons under the Guise of Teaching Science. 140p. 1991. pap. text ed. 18.00 (*0-87287-783-3*) Teacher Ideas Pr.

McGlathery, James, ed. Music & German Literature: Studies on Their Relationship Since the Middle Ages. (Studies in German Literature, Linguistics & Culture: Vol. 66). (Illus.). 400p. 1992. 59.00 (*1-879751-03-8*) Camden Hse.

McGlathery, James M. Fairy Tale Romance: The Grimms, Basile, & Perault. 240p. 1991. 29.95 (*0-252-01741-2*) U of Ill Pr.

— Grimm's Fairy Tales: A History of Criticism on a Popular Classic. LC 93-37093. (Studies in German Literature, Linguistics & Culture). 1993. 49.95 (*1-879751-90-9*) Camden Hse.

McGlathery, James M., et al, eds. The Brothers Grimm & Folktale. (Illus.). 280p. 1991. pap. 12.95 (*0-252-06191-8*) U of Ill Pr.

McGlathrey, James, ed. German Source Readings in the Arts & Sciences. 1974. 16.80 (*0-87563-083-9*) Stipes.

McGlen, Nancy E. & O'Connor, Karen. Women, Politics & American Society. LC 94-20216. 336p. 1994. pap. text ed. write for info. (*0-13-962192-X*) P-H.

McGlen, Nancy E. & Sarkees, Meredith R. Women in Foreign Policy: The Insiders. 368p. 1993. Acid free. 49.95 (*0-415-90511-7*, A6484, Routledge NY); pap. 15.95 (*0-415-90512-5*, A6488, Routledge NY) Routledge.

McGlew, James F. Tyranny & Political Culture in Ancient Greece. LC 93-15653. 232p. 1993. 31.50 (*0-8014-2787-8*) Cornell U Pr.

***McGlew, Polly.** Young Lawyer's Handbook - Legal Administration Office: What They Don't Teach You in Law School. 154p. (C). 1990. pap. text ed. 15.95 (*1-885477-06-6*) Fut Educ.

***McGlew, Polly A., ed.** International Conference Proceedings, 1993: Autism - A World of Options. 2nd ed. 276p. 1993. pap. text ed. 34.95 (*1-885477-03-1*) Fut Educ.

McGlew, Polly A., jt. auth. see Bilz, Reed K.

McGlew, Polly A., ed. see Future Education Inc. Staff.

McGlinchee, Claire. James Russell Lowell. (Twayne's United States Authors Ser.). 1967. pap. 13.95 (*0-8084-0173-4*, T120) NCUP.

McGlinchey, Charles. Last of the Name. LC 86-1161. (Illus.). 144p. 1993. reprint ed. pap. 12.95 (*0-85640-361-X*, Pub. by Blackstaff Pr IE) Dufour.

McGlinn, Judith, comp. Mrs. Boone's Wild Game Cookbook. (Illus.). 176p. (Orig.). 1991. pap. 12.95 (*1-879094-08-8*) Momentum Bks.

McGlohan, Loonis, jt. auth. see Kuralt, Charles.

McGloin, Joe. Graduating into Happiness: Goals & Guidelines for High School Grads. 160p. (Orig.). 1990. pap. 8.99 (*0-8010-6262-4*) Baker Bk.

— Graduating into Life. (Illus.). 144p. 1988. 8.99 (*0-8010-6226-8*) Baker Bk.

McGloin, Joseph. Listen, Lord: Prayer for Plodders. (Illus.). (Orig.). pap. 2.95 (*0-8199-0915-7*, Frncscn Herld) Franciscan Pr.

***McGloin, Joseph T.** How to Get More Out of the Mass. LC 74-80938. 143p. (C). 1974. pap. 4.95 (*0-8294-0626-3*, Campion Bks) Loyola Univ Pr.

McGlone, et al, eds. A Nation of Sovereign States: Secession & War in the Confederacy. LC 94-8654. (Journal of Confederate History Ser.: Vol. 10). 175p. (Orig.). 1994. pap. 12.00 (*0-9631963-5-9*) So Herit Pr.

McGlone, Bill, et al. The Petroglyphs of Southeast Colorado & the Oklahoma Panhandle. (Illus.). 128p. (Orig.). 1994. pap. write for info. (*0-9641333-0-X*) Mithras.

McGlone, John. Journal of Confederate History Book Series. McDonald, Archie, ed. (Illus.). 200p. (Orig.). 1992. pap. 12.00 (*0-9631963-1-6*) So Herit Pr.

McGlone, John & McDonald, Archie. Confederate Nation Series. 1992. 23.00 (*0-9631963-9-1*) So Herit Pr.

McGlone, Randall K. Guts & Glory. Tobias, Eric, ed. 224p. (Orig.). 1992. pap. 4.99 (*0-671-76062-9*) PB.

McGlone, William R., et al. Ancient American Inscriptions: Plowmarks or History? (Illus.). 415p. (Orig.). (C). 1993. pap. 19.95 (*1-884810-00-4*) Early Sites.

McGlothin, Bruce. Great Grooming for Guys. Rosen, Ruth, ed. (Life Skills Library). (YA). (gr. 7-12). 1993. 13.95 (*0-8239-1468-2*) Rosen Group.

McGlothlen, Ronald L. Controlling the Waves: Dean Acheson & U. S. Foreign Policy in Asia. LC 92-38848. 352p. 1993. 27.95 (*0-393-03520-4*) Norton.

***McGlothlin, Bruce.** Careers Inside the World of Sports & Entertainment. (Careers & Opportunities Ser.). (Illus.). 64p. (YA). (gr. 7-12). 1995. 14.95 (*0-8239-1899-8*) Rosen Group.

— Search & Succeed: A Guide to Using the Classifieds. LC 93-47545. (Life Skills Library). (YA). 1994. 13.95 (*0-8239-1695-2*) Rosen Group.

McGlothlin, Chris A. World's Fair Spoons, Vol. I: The World's Columbian Exposition. LC 85-70480. (Illus.). 1985. 35.00 (*0-9614824-0-0*) Fla Rare Coin.

McGlothlin, Christopher. Atarron. 360p. 1994. pap. 5.95 (*0-9639383-0-4*) Delacroix Pubng.

McGlown, D. Developmental Reflexive Rehabilitation. 264p. 1991. 59.95 (*0-86377-189-0*) L Erlbaum Assocs.

McGlynn, Anita. United Arts Fundraising 1991. (Illus.). 58p. (Orig.). 1992. spiral bd. 100.00 (*1-879903-08-3*) Am Council Arts.

McGlynn, Elizabeth A., jt. auth. see Haaga, John G.

McGlynn, Frank & Drescher, Seymour, eds. The Meaning of Freedom: Economics, Politics, & Culture after Slavery. LC 91-26606. (Latin American Ser.). (Illus.). 352p. 1992. 49.95 (*0-8229-3695-X*); pap. 19.95 (*0-8229-5479-6*) U of Pittsburgh Pr.

McGlynn, Frank & Tuden, Arthur. Anthropological Approaches to Political Behavior: Contributions from Ethnology. LC 90-50916. 352p. (C). 1991. 49.95 (*0-8229-1162-0*); pap. 19.95 (*0-8229-6094-X*) U of Pittsburgh Pr.

McGlynn Gaffney, Edward, Jr. & Sorensen, Philip C. Ascending Liability in Religious & Other Nonprofit Organizations. Griffin, Howard R., ed. LC 84-22823. (Studies in Law & Religion: No. 2). xvi, 147p. 1984. 14.95 (*0-86554-153-1*, MUP H143, Baylor U J M Dawson) Mercer Univ Pr.

McGlynn, George. Dynamics of Fitness: A Practical Approach. 2nd ed. 304p. 1990. pap. write for info. (*0-697-07637-7*) Brown & Benchmark.

— Dynamics of Fitness: A Practical Approach. 3rd ed. 336p. (C). 1993. pap. text ed. write for info. (*0-697-12647-1*) Brown & Benchmark.

McGlynn, George, jt. auth. see Moran, Gary T.

***McGlynn, Hud.** Aruba Digest. 100p. Date not set. pap. 7.95 (*0-7610-0352-5*) NW Pub.

McGlynn, John H., tr. see Marahimin, Ismail.

McGlynn, John H., tr. see Pane, Armijn.

McGlynn, R. P., ed. see Harvey, J. H., et al.

McGlynn, Sue, jt. auth. see Hayward, Richard.

McGlynn, Terrence D. Montana Tech: Eighteen Ninety-Three to Nineteen Eighty-Four. (Illus.). 112p. 1984. 19.95 (*0-318-03525-1*) Montana Tech.

McGlynn, Thomas J. & Metcalf, Harry L., eds. Diagnosis & Treatment of Anxiety Disorders: A Physician's Handbook. 2nd ed. 118p. Date not set. spiral bd. 28.50 (*0-88048-523-X*) Am Psychiatric.

McGoey, Chris E. Security: Adequate or Not? The Complete Guide to Premises Liability Litigation. Fouteck, Lou-Anne, ed. (Illus.). (C). 1989. pap. 29.95 (*0-9623543-0-9*) Aegis Bks.

***McGoldrich, Gerry.** Quality Solution. 160p. (C). 1994. ring bd. 450.00x (*0-273-61080-5*, Pub. by Pitman Pubng UK) St Mut.

***McGoldrick.** Video Technology for Personal Computers. 1995. 50.00 (*0-07-045018-8*) McGraw.

McGoldrick, Ann & Copper, Cary. Early Retirement. 1989. text ed. 68.95 (*0-566-05244-X*, Pub. by Gower UK) Ashgate Pub Co.

McGoldrick, Dominic. The Human Rights Committee: Its Role in the Development of the International Covenant on Civil & Political Rights. (Oxford Monographs in International Law). 648p. 1994. reprint ed. pap. 29.95 (*0-19-825894-1*) OUP.

McGoldrick, Gerry. The Complete Quality Manual: A Blueprint for Producing Your Own Quality System. (Financial Times Management Ser.). 224p. 1994. 62.50x (*0-273-60558-5*, Pub. by Pitman Pub Ltd UK) Trans-Atl Phila.

McGoldrick, J. E. Luther's English Connection. 1979. pap. 7.50 (*0-8100-0070-9*, 15-0368) Northwest Pub.

McGoldrick, James E. Baptist Successionism: A Crucial Question in Baptist History. LC 93-5931. (American Theological Library Association Monograph: No. 32). 190p. 1994. 27.50 (*0-8108-2726-3*) Scarecrow.

— Luther's Scottish Connection. LC 88-46054. 128p. 1989. 28.50 (*0-8386-3357-9*) Fairleigh Dickinson.

McGoldrick, Joseph D. Law & Practice of Municipal Home Rule, 1916-1930. LC 33-22314. reprint ed. 22.45 (*0-404-04128-0*) AMS Pr.

***McGoldrick, Kathryn E., ed.** Ambulatory Anesthesiology: A Problem-Oriented Approach. LC 94-1854. 808p. 1994. 89.00 (*0-683-05875-4*) Williams & Wilkins.

McGoldrick, Linda C. Nora Unwin: Artist & Wood Engraver. (Illus.). 1990. 35.00 (*0-87233-096-6*) Bauhan.

***McGoldrick, May.** The Thistle & the Rose. 384p. 1995. pap. 4.99 (*0-451-40626-5*) NAL-Dutton.

McGoldrick, Monica. Women in Families: A Framework for Family Therapy. 1991. pap. 18.95 (*0-393-30776-X*) Norton.

— You Can Go Home Again: Reconnecting with Your Family. LC 93-48812. 1994. 27.50 (*0-393-03494-1*) Norton.

McGoldrick, Monica & Gerson, Randy. Genograms in Family Assessment. LC 85-15269. (Illus.). 1985. pap. 12.95 (*0-393-70002-X*) Norton.

McGoldrick, Monica, jt. auth. see Carter.

McGoldrick, Monica, jt. ed. see Walsh, Froma.

McGoldrick, Monica, et al, eds. Ethnicity & Family Therapy. LC 81-20198. (Guilford Family Therapy Ser.). 600p. 1982. lib. bdg. 39.95 (*0-89862-040-6*) Guilford Pr.

— Women in Families: A Framework for Family Therapy. 1989. 34.95 (*0-393-70067-4*) Norton.

***McGoldrick, Peter & Davies, Gary, eds.** International Retailing: Trends & Strategies. 208p. 1995. pap. 52.50 (*0-273-61183-6*, Pub. by Pitman Pub Ltd UK) Trans-Atl Phila.

McGoldrick, Peter, jt. auth. see Thompson, Mark.

McGoldrick, Peter J. Retailing of Financial Services. LC 94-7269. 1994. write for info. (*0-07-707613-3*) McGraw.

McGonagall, William. The World's Worst Poet. (Orig.). 1979. pap. 6.95 (*0-87243-088-X*) Templegate.

McGonagill, Grady. Overcoming Barriers to Education Restructuring: A Call for System Literacy. 40p. 1993. pap. 2.50 (*0-87652-194-4*) Am Assn Sch Admin.

McGonagle, Cindy. Garden Notes: From the Nature Devas. (Illus.). 94p. 1993. pap. 10.00 (*0-9640243-0-6*) Botanic Reprod.

— Queen D's Fairy Recipe Book. Alder, Debora, ed. (Illus.). 92p. 1994. pap. 13.25 (*0-9640243-1-4*) Botanic Reprod.

McGonagle, Jack. To Touch the Sun: A Portrait of Muhammed Ali. LC 93-85308. 94p. 1995. 8.95 (*1-55523-639-1*) Winston-Derek.

McGonagle, John C., Jr., jt. auth. see Vella, Carolyn M.

McGonagle, John J., Jr. & Vella, Carolyn M. Outsmarting the Competition: Practical Approaches to Finding & Using Competitive Information. LC 92-46122. 1993. 25.00 (*0-07-707755-5*) McGraw.

— Outsmarting the Competition: Practical Approaches to Finding & Using Competitive Information. LC 90-31866. 388p. 1990. 29.95 (*0-942061-06-3*, Sourcebooks Trade); pap. 17.95 (*0-942061-04-7*, Sourcebooks Trade) Sourcebks.

McGonagle, John J., Jr., jt. auth. see Vella, Carolyn M.

McGonagle, John J., Jr., et al. Master Guide to Control of Corporations with Checklists, Forms & Agreements. LC 85-8651. 281p. 1985. 59.50 (*0-87624-365-0*) P-H.

McGonagle, Sara R. Mid-Level Practitioners: Their Role in Providing Quality Health Care. (Working Paper Ser.: No. 64). 42p. 1992. 5.00 (*0-685-66566-6*) LBJ Sch Pub Aff.

McGonigel, Mary J., et al, eds. Guidelines & Recommended Practices for the Individualized Family Service Plan. 2nd ed. 208p. 1991. pap. 15.00 (*0-937821-77-2*, R-3097-1) Assn Care Child.

McGonigle, Thomas. The Corpse Dream of N. Petkov. LC 86-72661. 134p. 1987. 20.00 (*0-916583-19-8*) Dalkey Arch.

— Going to Patchogue. LC 91-13068. (Illus.). 220p. 1992. 19.95 (*0-916583-87-2*) Dalkey Arch.

— In Patchogue. 32p. (Orig.). 1985. pap. 5.00 (*0-916351-00-9*) Adrift Edns.

McGonigle, Thomas D. & Quigley, James F. A History of the Christian Tradition: From Its Jewish Origins to the Reformation. 224p. 1988. pap. 12.95 (*0-8091-2964-7*) Paulist Pr.

McGonnagle, W., ed. International Advances in Nondestructive Testing, Vol. 7. 450p. 1981. text ed. 227.00 (*0-677-15700-2*) Gordon & Breach.

McGonnagle, W. J., ed. Internation Advances in Nondestructive Testing, Vol. 17. 1994. text ed. 150.00 (*2-88124-582-X*) Gordon & Breach.

— International Advances in Nondestructive Testing, Vol. 10. 349p. 1984. text ed. 176.00 (*2-88124-101-8*) Gordon & Breach.

— International Advances in Nondestructive Testing, Vol. 15. 1990. text ed. 103.00 (*2-88124-445-9*) Gordon & Breach.

McGonnagle, Warren J. International Advances in Nondestructive Testing, Vol. 5. 414p. 1977. text ed. 201.00 (*0-677-12000-1*) Gordon & Breach.

— International Advances in Nondestructive Testing, Vol. 8. 361p. 1981. text ed. 176.00 (*0-677-16240-5*) Gordon & Breach.

— Nondestructive Testing. 2nd ed. (Illus.). 468p. 1971. text ed. 156.00 (*0-677-00500-8*) Gordon & Breach.

McGonnagle, Warren J., ed. Automated Nondestructive Testing: Proceedings of a Topical Seminar. (Nondestructive Testing Monographs & Tracts: Vol. 4). 296p. 1986. pap. text ed. 154.00 (*2-88124-056-9*) Gordon & Breach.

— International Advances in Nondestructive Testing, Vol. 6. 380p. 1979. text ed. 198.00 (*0-677-12470-8*) Gordon & Breach.

— International Advances in Nondestructive Testing, Vol. 9. LC 77-2536. (Illus.). 371p. 1983. text ed. 173.00 (*0-677-16440-8*) Gordon & Breach.

— International Advances in Nondestructive Testing, Vol. 11. 384p. 1985. text ed. 123.00 (*2-88124-034-8*) Gordon & Breach.

— International Advances in Nondestructive Testing, Vol. 14. 371p. 1989. text ed. 113.00 (*2-88124-327-4*) Gordon & Breach.

— Physics & Nondestructive Testing, Vol. 1. 578p. 1967. text ed. 254.00 (*0-677-10580-0*) Gordon & Breach.

— Physics & Nondestructive Testing, Vol. 2. LC 65-27852. (Illus.). 302p. (C). 1971. text ed. 207.00 (*0-677-15250-7*) Gordon & Breach.

— Physics & Nondestructive Testing, Vol. 3. LC 65-27852. (Illus.). 338p. (C). 1971. text ed. 207.00 (*0-677-15260-4*) Gordon & Breach.

McGoodwin, Henry. Architectural Shades & Shadows. (Illus.). 120p. (Orig.). (C). 1991. 29.95 (*1-55835-053-5*) AIA Press.

McGoodwin, James R. Crisis in the World's Fisheries: People, Problems, & Policies. LC 90-37484. 247p. 1991. 39.50 (*0-8047-1790-7*) Stanford U Pr.

— Crisis in the World's Fisheries: People, Problems, & Policies. 1994. pap. 13.95 (*0-8047-2371-0*) Stanford U Pr.

McGoodwin, James R., jt. ed. see Dyer, Christopher L.

***McGoogan.** Visions of Kerouac. 1993. per. 16.95 (*0-919001-75-0*, Pub. by Pottersfield Pr CN) InBook.

***McGoogan, Kenneth.** Canada's Undeclared War: Fighting Words from the Literary Trenches. 277p. (Orig.). 1991. pap. 18.95 (*1-55059-032-4*) Temeron Bks.

McGoon, Cliff, ed. see International Association of Business Communicators Staff.

McGoon, Dwight C. Parkinson's Handbook. 1994. pap. 10.95 (*0-393-31143-0*) Norton.

McGoon, Dwight C., ed. Cardiac Surgery. 2nd ed. LC 70-6558. (Cardiovascular Clinics Ser.: Vol. 14, No. 1). (Illus.). 446p. 1987. text ed. 79.00 (*0-8036-5984-9*) Davis Co.

McGorian, Gladys. The Prince Regent's Silver Bell. 256p. 1987. 16.95 (*0-8027-0954-0*) Walker & Co.

McGough, Barry M. Georgia Divorce. LC 79-91143. (Practice Systems Library Manual). 1134p. ring bd. 120.00 (*0-317-00582-0*) Lawyers Cooperative.

— Georgia Divorce. suppl. ed. LC 79-91143. (Practice Systems Library Manual). 1134p. 1993. Suppl. 1993. 60.00 (*0-317-03208-9*) Lawyers Cooperative.

McGough, Edward M. Beyond the Far Ridge: Pioneering in the Rocky Mountain High Country. LC 91-32596. (Illus.). 192p. (Orig.). 1992. pap. 10.95 (*0-931271-15-0*) Hi Plains Pr.

— Young Rider of the High Country. 3rd ed. LC 93-81214. (Illus.). 180p. (YA). (gr. 5-12). 1994. pap. 9.95 (*1-882420-13-6*, 1-882420-13-6) Hearth KS.

McGough, Lucy S. Child Witnesses: Fragile Voices in the American Legal System. LC 93-49769. 1994. 30.00 (*0-300-05748-2*) Yale U Pr.

McGough, Michael R. Gettysburg Battlefield Tour Book. (Illus.). 32p. 1987. pap. 3.50 (*0-939631-06-7*) Thomas Publications.

— Hey, Mr. McRay! 100p. (Orig.). (YA). (gr. 7-12). 1995. pap. 6.00 (*0-9639450-3-3*) Joy Ent.

— Pennsylvania from Wilderness Colony to National Leader. (Illus.). 44p. (J). (gr. 4-6). 1989. pap. text ed. 5.95 (*0-939631-15-6*) Thomas Publications.

McGough, Michael R., see Dr. Mike, pseud..

McGough, Robert, jt. auth. see Finch, Curtis.

McGough, Roger. The Lighthouse That Ran Away. (Illus.). 32p. (J). (ps-2). 1992. 16.95 (*0-370-31471-9*, Pub. by Bodley Head UK) Trafalgar.

***McGough, Wallace D.** The Adventures of Walter Ant Bk. 1: The Unknown. (Illus.). 56p. (J). 1995. 11.95 (*0-9645180-1-5*) Fam Val Pub.

— The Adventures of Walter Ant Bk. I: The Unknown. 56p. (J). Date not set. pap. 9.95 (*0-9645180-0-7*) Fam Val Pub.

McGouldrick, Paul F. New England Textiles in the Nineteenth Century: Profits & Investment. LC 68-14267. (Economic Studies: No. 131). (Illus.). 1990. 20.00 (*0-674-61400-3*) HUP.

McGoun, William E. Prehistoric Peoples of South Florida. LC 92-40833. 176p. 1993. pap. 19.95 (*0-8173-0686-2*) U of Ala Pr.

McGourty, Fred, ed. see Ferguson, Nicola.

McGourty, Frederick. The Perennial Gardener. (Illus.). 256p. 1991. pap. 16.95 (*0-395-57229-0*) HM.

McGourty, Frederick, ed. Perennials & Their Uses. (Plants & Gardens Ser.). (Illus.). 1989. per. 5.95 (*0-945352-24-7*, Sterling) Bklyn Botanic.

McGoveran, D. & Date, C. J. A Guide to Sybase & SQL Server. (Illus.). (C). 1992. text ed. 49.50 (*0-201-55710-X*) Addison-Wesley.

McGovern. Bonsai: The Art of Growing & Keeping Miniature Trees. 1987. 12.98 (*0-89009-946-4*) Bk Sales Inc.

McGovern & Lawrence. Contracts & Sales: Cases & Problems. 1986. write for info. (*0-8205-0106-9*, 206); teacher ed write for info. (*0-8205-0107-7*) Bender.

***McGovern, et al.** Rhode Island Environmental Law Handbook. 2nd ed. 231p. 1994. pap. text ed. 85.00 (*0-86587-424-7*) Gov Insts.

McGovern, Ann. Christopher Columbus. (J). 1992. 4.95 (*0-590-45765-9*, 051) Scholastic Inc.

— The Defenders. 128p. (Orig.). (J). (gr. 3-7). 1987. pap. 2.95 (*0-590-43866-2*) Scholastic Inc.

— Down Under, Down Under: Diving Adventures on the Great Barrier Reef. LC 88-30530. (Illus.). 50p. (J). (gr. 2-6). 1989. text ed. 14.95 (*0-02-765770-1*, Mac Bks Young Read) S&S Childrens.

— Drop Everything, It's D. E. A. R. Time! (J). (ps-3). 1993. pap. 3.95 (*0-590-45802-7*) Scholastic Inc.

— Happy Silly Birthday to Me. (Read with Me Paperbacks Ser.). (Illus.). 32p. (J). (gr. k-3). 1994. pap. 2.50 (*0-590-46365-9*, Cartwheel) Scholastic Inc.

— If You Grew up with Abraham Lincoln. (Illus.). 64p. (J). 1992. pap. 4.95 (*0-590-45154-5*) Scholastic Inc.

— If You Sailed on the May Flower. (Illus.). 80p. (J). 1991. pap. 4.95 (*0-590-45161-8*) Scholastic Inc.

— Nicholas Bentley Stoningpot III. (Illus.). 32p. (J). (ps-3). 1992. lib. bdg. 14.95 (*1-56397-104-6*) Boyds Mills Pr.

— Night Dive. LC 84-7163. (Illus.). 64p. (J). (gr. 2-5). 1984. lib. bdg. 14.95 (*0-02-765710-8*, Mac Bks Young Read) S&S Childrens.

— The Pilgrim's First Thanksgiving. 48p. (J). (gr. k-5). 1984. pap. 2.50 (*0-590-40617-5*) Scholastic Inc.

— Pilgrims' First Thanksgiving. (J). 1993. pap. 3.95 (*0-590-46188-5*) Scholastic Inc.

— Playing with Penguins & Other Adventures in Antarctica. (J). (gr. 4-7). 1995. pap. 4.95 (*0-590-44175-2*) Scholastic Inc.

— Robin Hood of Sherwood Forest. 128p. (J). (gr. 3-7). 1991. pap. 2.95 (*0-590-45441-2*) Scholastic Inc.

— The Secret Soldier: The Story of Deborah Sampson. 64p. (J). (gr. 3-7). 1990. pap. 2.99 (*0-590-43052-1*) Scholastic Inc.

— The Secret Soldier: The Story of Deborah Sampson. LC 75-15819. (Illus.). 64p. (J). (gr. 1-5). 1987. text ed. 13.95 (*0-02-765780-9*, Four Winds Pr) S&S Childrens.

— Shark Lady. (Illus.). 96p. (J). (gr. k-3). 1991. pap. 2.50 (*0-590-44771-8*) Scholastic Inc.

— Shark Lady: True Adventures of Eugenie Clark. LC 78-22126. (Illus.). 96p. (J). (gr. 3-7). 1984. text ed. 13.95 (*0-02-767060-0*, Four Winds Pr) S&S Childrens.

— Sharks. 48p. (J). (gr. k-3). 1995. pap. 4.95 (*0-590-41360-0*) Scholastic Inc.

— Stone Soup. (Illus.). 32p. (J). (gr. k-2). 1986. pap. 2.50 (*0-590-41602-2*) Scholastic Inc.

— Swimming with Sea Lions. 48p. (J). 1992. 13.95 (*0-590-45282-7*, Scholastic Hardcover) Scholastic Inc.

— Too Much Noise. (J). (gr. k-3). 1967. 14.95 (*0-395-18110-0*) HM.

— Too Much Noise. (Illus.). 48p. (J). (gr. k-3). 1992. pap. 5.95 (*0-395-62985-3*, Sandpiper) HM.

— Too Much Noise. (Illus.). 48p. (J). (gr. k-3). pap. 1.95 (*0-590-02435-3*) Scholastic Inc.

— Wanted Dead Or Alive: The True Story of Harriet Tubman. 64p. (J). (gr. 2-4). 1991. 3.95 (*0-590-44212-0*) Scholastic Inc.

McGovern, Ann, ret. Aesop's Fables. 80p. (J). (gr. 4-7). 1990. pap. 2.75 (*0-590-43880-8*) Scholastic Inc.

McGovern, Arthur. Liberation Theology & Its Critics: Toward an Assessment. 250p. 1989. pap. 16.95 (*0-88344-595-6*) Orbis Bks.

— Marxism: An American Christian Perspective. LC 79-27257. 352p. (Orig.). 1980. pap. 16.95 (*0-88344-301-5*) Orbis Bks.

McGovern, Arthur F., jt. auth. see Cavanagh, Gerald F.

McGovern, Barbara. Anne Finch & Her Poetry: A Critical Biography. LC 91-23862. 264p. 1992. 40.00 (*0-8203-1410-2*) U of Ga Pr.

McGovern, Carolyn, ed. The Changing Landscape of Indexing: Proceedings of the 26th Annual Meeting of the American Society of Indexers. 59p. 1994. pap. text ed. 25.00 (*0-936547-23-5*) Am Soc Index.

McGovern, Constance M. Masters of Madness: Social Origins of the American Psychiatric Profession. LC 85-40491. (Illus.). 278p. 1985. text ed. 35.00 (*0-87451-352-9*) U Pr of New Eng.

***McGovern, Dan.** The Campo Indian Landfill War: The Fight for Gold in California's Garbage. LC 95-5857. 1995. write for info. (*0-8061-2755-4*) U of Okla Pr.

McGovern, Dennis & Winer, Deborah. I Remember Too Much: Eighty-Nine Opera Stars Speak Candidly about Their Work, Their Lives, & Their Colleagues. LC 89-13876. (Illus.). 388p. 1990. 27.95 (*0-688-08447-8*) Morrow.

McGovern, Dennis & Winer, Deborah G. Sing Out Louise! 150 Stars of the Musical Theatre Remember 50 Years on Broadway. (Illus.). 256p. 1993. text ed. 28.00 (*0-02-871394-X*) Schirmer Bks.

McGovern, Don, jt. auth. see White, Ron.

***McGovern, Don, et al.** Reading: Student's Book. LC 94-19762. (Series English for Academic Study). 1994. 9.75 (*0-01-397872-1*) P-H Intl.

McGovern, Edythe M. They're Never Too Young for Books: Literature for Pre-Schoolers. LC 80-80216. 294p. (Orig.). 1980. pap. 10.00 (*0-9604064-0-9*) Mar Vista.

McGovern, Edythe M. & Muller, Helen D. They're Never Too Young for Books: A Guide to Children's Books Ages 1-8. 342p. 1994. pap. 14.95 (*0-87975-858-9*) Prometheus Bks.

McGovern, G. S., et al. Vietnam: Four American Perspectives - Lectures by George S. McGovern, William C. Westmoreland, Edward N. Luttwak, & Thomas J. McCormick. Hearden, Patrick J., ed. LC 89-24267. 128p. 1990. 17.50 (*1-55753-002-5*); pap. 9.95 (*1-55753-003-3*) Purdue U Pr.

McGovern, Gail, jt. auth. see Rubin, Rhea J.

McGovern, George S. Food & Popuation: The World in Crises. 1976. 27.95 (*0-405-06663-5*, 1752) Ayer.

McGovern, James. The Child Abuse Man. LC 88-50592. 215p. (Orig.). 1989. pap. 10.00 (*0-916383-70-9*, Univ Edtns) Aegina Pr.

McGovern, James I. Spring of Second Comings. LC 92-91048. 152p. (Orig.). 1994. pap. 9.00 (*1-56002-226-4*, Univ Edtns) Aegina Pr.

McGovern, James R. Anatomy of a Lynching: The Killing of Claude Neal. LC 81-17140. (Illus.). 170p. (C). 1992. pap. 9.95 (*0-8071-1766-8*) La State U Pr.

— Black Eagle: General Daniel "Chappie" James, Jr. LC 84-8. (Illus.). 216p. 1985. 24.50 (*0-8173-0179-8*) U of Ala Pr.

— Yankee Family. LC 75-4470. 191p. 1978. pap. text ed. 19.95 (*0-87855-674-5*) Transaction Pubs.

McGovern, James R., ed. World of Columbus. 160p. 1992. 24.95 (*0-86554-414-X*, MUP/H336) Mercer Univ Pr.

McGovern, Jim. Hubbard: The Electric Barnum. 1995. 12.95 (*0-9627860-9-8*) Lone Oak MN.

McGovern, John, jt. ed. see Starck, Patricia.

McGovern, John P., jt. auth. see DuPont, Robert L.

McGovern, John T. Diogenes Discovers Us. LC 67-26758. (Essay Index Reprint Ser.). 1977. 21.95 (*0-8369-0647-0*) Ayer.

McGovern, Patrick E., jt. auth. see James, Frances W.

McGovern, Patrick E., et al. The Late Bronze Age & Early Iron Ages of Central Jordan: The Baq'ah Valley Project, 1977-1981. (University Museum Monographs: No. 65). (Illus.). 365p. 1987. text ed. 95.00 (*0-685-67660-9*) U PA Mus Pubns.

McGovern, Peter J., jt. auth. see Sannito, Thomas.

McGovern, Robert. A Feast of Flesh & Other Occasions. 63p. 1971. pap. 6.00 (*0-912592-08-7*) Ashland Poetry.

— A Poetry Ritual for Grammar Schools. 42p. 1974. pap. 2.50 (*0-912592-23-0*) Ashland Poetry.

McGovern, Robert & Haven, Stephen, eds. Scarecrow Poetry: The Muse in Post-Middle Age. 178p. (Orig.). 1994. pap. 19.00 (*0-912592-36-2*) Ashland Poetry.

McGovern, Robert & Snyder, Richard, eds. Our Only Hope Is Humor: Some Public Poems. 88p. (C). 1972. pap. 5.00 (*0-912592-13-3*) Ashland Poetry.

— Seventy on the Seventies: A Decade's History in Verse. 100p. 1981. pap. 7.00 (*0-912592-24-9*) Ashland Poetry.

McGovern, Robert, jt. auth. see McNamee, John P.

McGovern, Robert, ed. see Snyder, Richard.

McGovern, Robert, et al, eds. Eighty on the Eighties: A Decade's History in Verse. LC 90-83622. 131p. 1990. pap. 8.00 (*0-912592-28-1*) Ashland Poetry.

McGovern, Terrence J., jt. ed. see Coffey, Thomas F.

McGovern, Thomas V., ed. Handbook for Enhancing Undergraduate Education in Psychology. 283p. (Orig.). 1993. pap. text ed. 29.95 (*1-55798-196-5*) Am Psychol.

McGovern, V. J., ed. see International Pigment Cell Conference Staff.

McGovern, Vincent J. Malignant Melanoma: Clinical & Histological Diagnosis. LC 76-3793. (Wiley Medical Publication). 192p. reprint ed. pap. 54.80 (*0-317-28936-5*, 2055988) Bks Demand.

McGovern, William M. Completely Prime Maximal Ideals & Quantization. LC 93-48292. (Memoirs of the American Mathematical Society Ser.: Vol. 519). 1994. pap. 29.00 (*0-8218-2580-1*) Am Math.

McGovern, William M. From Luther to Hitler: The History of Fascist-Nazi Political Philosophy. LC 75-180412. reprint ed. 58.50 (*0-404-56137-3*) AMS Pr.

— Introduction to Mahayana Buddhism. LC 70-149665. reprint ed. 17.00 (*0-404-04129-9*) AMS Pr.

— A Manual of Buddhist Philosophy. LC 78-70097. reprint ed. 27.50 (*0-404-17346-2*) AMS Pr.

McGovern, William M., Jr. Wills, Trusts & Estates. Switzer, Robert J., ed. (Law Outlines Ser.). 210p. (Orig.). 1991. pap. text ed. 16.95 (*0-87457-183-9*, 5220) Casenotes Pub.

McGovern, William M., jt. auth. see Collingwood, David H.

McGovern, William M., Jr., et al. Wills, Trusts & Estates, Including Taxation & Future Interests: Student Edition. (Hornbook Ser.). 996p. 1993. reprint ed. text ed. 39.00 (*0-314-36114-6*) West Pub.

***McGowan.** Irishman. 1995. mass mkt. 4.99 (*0-7860-0120-8*, Pinnacle NY) Windsor NY.

McGowan, Bob & Farren, Richard. Fishing the Big Bend: Freshwater. LC 91-68574. (Big Bend Ser.: Vol. I). 88p. (Orig.). 1992. pap. text ed. 8.95 (*0-9632059-0-0*) Woodland Prods.

— Fishing the Big Bend: Inshore Saltwater. LC 93-60545. (Big Bend Ser.: Vol. II). (Illus.). 117p. (Orig.). 1993. pap. 11.95 (*0-9632059-1-9*) Woodland Prods.

McGowan, Brenda. Trends in Employee Counseling Programs. (Studies in Productivity: Highlights of the Literature Ser.: No. 37). 55p. 1984. pap. 55.00 (*0-08-032361-8*, PS37) Work in Amer.

McGowan, Brenda G. & Blumenthal, Karen L. Why Punish the Children? A Study of Children of Women Prisoners. 124p. 1978. 6.50 (*0-318-15376-9*) Natl Coun Crime.

***McGowan, Chris.** Entertainment in the Cyber Zone: A Behind the Scenes Look. 1995. pap. 19.00 (*0-679-75804-6*) Random.

— In the Beginning: A Scientist Shows Why the Creationists Are Wrong. LC 83-62997. (Illus.). 208p. 1984. pap. 19.95 (*0-87975-240-8*) Prometheus Bks.

McGowan, Chris & Pessanha, Ricardo. The Brazilian Sound. (Illus.). 208p. 1991. pap. 18.95 (*0-8230-7673-3*, Billboard Bks) Watsn-Guptill.

McGowan, Christopher. Diatoms to Dinosaurs: The Size & Scale of Living Things. (Illus.). 272p. 1994. 24.95 (*1-55963-304-2*) Island Pr.

— Dinosaurs, Spitfires, & Sea Dragons. LC 90-41552. (Illus.). 384p. 1991. text ed. 29.95 (*0-674-20769-6*, MCGDIN) HUP.

— Dinosaurs, Spitfires, & Seadragons. (Illus.). 384p. (Orig.). 1992. pap. text ed. 14.95 (*0-674-20770-X*) HUP.

— Discover Dinosaurs: A Royal Ontario Museum Book. (Illus.). (J). (gr. 3-7). 1993. pap. 10.95 (*1-55074-048-2*) Addison-Wesley.

— Discover Dinosaurs: Become a Dinosaur Detective. LC 92-42627. (Illus.). 96p. (J). (gr. 4-7). 1993. pap. 9.57 (*0-201-62267-X*) Addison-Wesley.

McGowan, Clement L., jt. auth. see Marca, David A.

McGowan, Cynthia. Robinson Crusoe Notes. (Orig.). 1976. pap. text ed. 3.50 (*0-8220-1150-6*) Cliffs.

— Who's Afraid of Virginia Woolf? Notes. (Orig.). 1979. pap. text ed. 4.50 (*0-8220-1383-5*) Cliffs.

McGowan, Cynthia C. Walden Two Notes. (gr. 10-12). 1979. pap. 3.95 (*0-8220-1361-4*) Cliffs.

McGowan, D. A., et al. Maxillary Sinus & Its Dental Implications. (Illus.). 150p. 1993. 70.00 (*0-7236-0813-X*, Pub. by John Wright UK) Buttrwrth-Heinemann.

McGowan, Don. What Is Wrong with Jung. 217p. 1994. 26.95 (*0-87975-859-7*) Prometheus Bks.

McGowan, E. M. Horses & Ponies, A Photo-Fact Book. (Illus.). (Orig.). (J). 1988. pap. 1.95 (*0-942025-26-1*) Kidsbks.

McGowan, Helene. James Stewart. 1992. 9.99 (*0-517-06708-0*) Random Hse Value.

McGowan, Hugh. Leprechauns, Legends & Irish Tales. (Illus.). 128p. 1994. 13.95 (*0-575-05765-3*, Pub. by V Gollancz UK) Trafalgar.

McGowan, Ian, ed. The Restoration & Eighteenth Century (Sixteen Sixty to Seventeen Ninety-Eight) LC 89-70174. (St. Martin's Anthologies of English Literature Ser.: Vol. No. 3). 612p. 1990. text ed. 20.00 (*0-312-04477-1*) St Martin.

McGowan, J. W. & John, P. K., eds. Gaseous Electronics. 132p. 1975. pap. 25.75 (*0-444-10777-0*, North Holland) Elsevier.

McGowan, James. Station Master on the Underground Railroad: The Life & Letters of Thomas Garrett. LC 77-84816. (Illus.). 181p. 1977. 7.95 (*0-916178-00-5*) Whimsie Pr.

McGowan, James & DeVore, Lynn, eds. Benchmark: Anthology of Contemporary Illinois Poetry. LC 88-60183. 331p. 1988. pap. 11.95 (*0-935153-09-8*) Stormline Pr.

McGowan, James, tr. see Baudelaire, Charles.

McGowan, James A. Hear Today! Here to Stay! A Personal History of Rhythm & Blues. LC 83-61178. (Illus.). 196p. (Orig.). 1983. pap. 7.95 (*0-913911-00-3*) Akashic Pr.

McGowan, James W., ed. The Excited State in Chemical Physics, Vol. 1. LC 74-6240. (Advances in Chemical Physics Ser.: No. 28). 502p. reprint ed. pap. 143.10 (*0-7837-3455-7*, 2057781) Bks Demand.

McGowan, Jill. Murder...Now & Then. 304p. 1993. 20.95 (*0-312-10006-X*, Pub. by Thomas Dunne Bks) St Martin.

— The Murders of Mrs. Austin & Mrs. Beale. 1993. reprint ed. mass mkt. 4.99 (*0-449-22162-8*, Crest) Fawcett.

McGowan, John. Postmodernism & Its Critics. LC 90-55758. 320p. 1991. 45.00 (*0-8014-2494-1*); pap. 14.95 (*0-8014-9738-8*) Cornell U Pr.

McGowan, John & DuBern, Roger. Do-It-Yourself Decorating. LC 90-23100. (Home Handbooks Ser.). (Illus.). 240p. (Orig.). 1991. pap. 16.00 (*0-89577-381-3*, Random) RD Assn.

McGowan, John & Dubern, Roger. The Good Housekeeping Illustrated Book of Home Maintenance. LC 85-80003. 240p. 1985. 22.95 (*0-688-04315-1*) Hearst Bks.

***McGowan, John J.** Direct Digital Control: A Guide to Distributed Building Automation. LC 94-32120. 1994. write for info. (*0-88173-166-8*) Fairmont Pr.

McGowan, John J., jt. auth. see Fairmont Press Staff.

McGowan, John J., jt. auth. see Payne, F. William.

McGowan, Kate, jt. ed. see Easthope, Anthony.

McGowan, Kathleen, jt. auth. see McGuire, Terrance P.

McGowan, Kimberly. Bearings: Plain, Ball & Roller - U. S. Manufacturers & Selected Distributors: 1992 Competitive Analysis. 1993. pap. text ed. 2,400.00 (*1-878218-38-7*) World Info Tech.

— A Competitive Analysis of Electronic Wire & Cable End-Use Markets - Copper Vs. Fiber: 1993-1998 Analysis & Forecasts. 74p. 1994. pap. text ed. 1,900.00 (*1-878218-46-8*) World Info Tech.

— Electronic Filters: U. S. Markets, Applications & Competitors, 1991-1997 Analysis. (Illus.). 162p. 1992. pap. text ed. 1,595.00 (*1-878218-33-6*) World Info Tech.

— Electronic Wire & Cable - U.S. Markets & Opportunities: 1993-1998 Analysis & Forecasts. 76p. 1994. pap. text ed. 2,400.00 (*1-878218-43-3*) World Info Tech.

— Gaskets, Packings & Mechanical Seals: U. S. Markets, Competitors, & Opportunities: 1994-1999 Analysis & Forecasts. 100p. 1995. pap. text ed. 1,900.00 (*1-878218-53-0*) World Info Tech.

— Gaskets, Packings & Mechanical Seals - U. S. Markets, Competitors & Opportunities: 1991-1997 Analysis. (Illus.). 110p. 1992. pap. text ed. 1,295.00 (*1-878218-29-8*) World Info Tech.

— Telecommunications Outside Plant - U.S. Markets, Customers, & Competitors: 1994-1999 Analysis & Forecasts. 258p. 1994. pap. text ed. 2,400.00 (*1-878218-49-2*) World Info Tech.

— U. S. & Canadian Electrical & Electronic Wire & Cable Manufacturers, 1993: Competitive Analysis. 600p. 1993. pap. text ed. 2,400.00 (*1-878218-39-5*) World Info Tech.

McGowan, Linda B., jt. ed. see Warner, Isiah M.

McGowan, Margaret, jt. ed. see Craig, George.

McGowan, Margaret M. Ideal Forms in the Age of Ronsard. LC 82-23839. (Una's Lectures: No. 5). 1985. 50.00 (*0-520-04864-4*) U CA Pr.

***McGowan, Mark G. & Clarke, Brian P., eds.** Catholics at the "Gathering Place" Historical Essays on the Archidiocese of Toronto 1841-1991. (Illus.). 352p. Date not set. pap. 18.99 (*0-614-06787-1*) Dun.

McGowan, Martha. Literature: Experience & Meaning. 1105p. (C). 1988. pap. text ed. 2.00 (*0-15-551085-1*) HB Coll Pubs.

— Literature: Experience & Meaning. 1105p. (C). 1989. pap. text ed. 26.75 (*0-15-551084-3*) HB Coll Pubs.

McGowan, Mary. The Girl Without a Country. 197p. 1985. 9.95 (*0-930061-03-9*) Interspace Bks.

— Mollie O'Leary. 117p. 1990. pap. 9.95 (*0-930061-51-9*) Interspace Bks.

McGowan, Mary, ed. see Slappey, Mary M.

McGowan, Meredith, jt. auth. see McGowan, Thomas.

McGowan, Meredith, jt. auth. see McGowan, Tom.

McGowan, Meredith, et al. Appreciating Diversity Through Children's Literature: Teaching Activities for the Primary Grades. LC 94-4543. 150p. 1994. pap. text ed. 23.00 (*1-56308-117-2*) Teacher Ideas Pr.

McGowan, Pat, jt. ed. see Kegley, Charles W., Jr.

McGowan, Phillip, jt. comp. see Dekker, Rene W.

***McGowan, Richard.** Business, Politics, & Cigarettes: Multiple Levels, Multiple Agendas. LC 95-7279. 184p. 1995. text ed. 55.00 (*0-89930-964-X*, Quorum Bks) Greenwood.

McGowan, Richard A. Italian Baroque Solo Sonatas for the Recorder & the Flute. LC 77-92345. (Detroit Studies in Music Bibliography: No. 37). 70p. 1978. 14.00 (*0-911772-90-1*) Info Coord.

McGowan, Richard S. J. Painless Revenue or Painful Mirage? States & Legalized Gambling. LC 94-15884. 192p. 1994. text ed. 49.95 (*0-89930-859-7*, Quorum Bks) Greenwood.

McGowan, Robert & Ottensmeyer, Ed, eds. Technology & Economic Development. 192p. (Orig.). 1987. pap. 12.00 (*0-918592-91-7*) Pol Studies.

McGowan, Robert & Ottensmeyer, Edward, eds. Differing Perspectives on Economic Development. (Orig.). 1989. pap. 12.00 (*0-944285-10-4*) Pol Studies.

McGowan, Robert P. & Ottensmeyer, Edward J., eds. Economic Development Strategies for State & Local Governments. LC 92-38093. (Illus.). 1993. text ed. 28.95 (*0-8304-1298-0*) Nelson-Hall.

McGowan, Robert P., jt. auth. see Stevens, John M.

***McGowan, Spencer.** Investor's Information Sourcebook: A Quick Reference to Investment Information & Advice. 1994. pap. 21.95 (*0-13-125162-7*) P-H.

McGowan, Thomas & McGowan, Meredith. Telling America's Story: Teaching American History Through Children's Literature. (Illus.). 116p. (Orig.). 1989. pap. text ed. 17.95 (*0-931205-41-7*) Jenson Pubns.

McGowan, Tom & McGowan, Meredith. Children, Literature & Social Studies: Activities for the Intermediate Grades. (Illus.). 218p. (J). (gr. 4-6). 1986. spiral bd. 18.95 (*0-938594-06-0*) Spec Lit Pr.

— Integrating the Primary Curriculum: Social Studies & Children's Literature. Champlin, John, ed. (Library & Literature Ser.). (Illus.). 86p. 1988. pap. 18.95 (*0-938594-11-7*) Spec Lit Pr.

McGowan, Whitman. Contents May Have Shifted. (Illus.). 52p. (Orig.). 1994. pap. 6.00 (*1-880298-07-4*) Viridiana.

***McGowan, Wynema.** The Irishman. 400p. 1995. pap. 4.99 (*0-8217-0120-7*) Zebra.

McGowen, Al. Extraction of Free Gold: Virgin Placer Gold. (Illus.). 64p. (Orig.). 1973. pap. 6.95 (*0-941620-26-3*) Carson Ent.

McGowen, Carolyn S. Teaching Literature by Women Authors. Lewis, Warren, ed. LC 93-34695. 224p. (Orig.). 1993. pap. 16.95 (*0-927516-38-1*, EDINFO Pr) ERIC-REC.

McGowen, Charles H. In Six Days. 108p. 1986. reprint ed. pap. 3.95 (*0-936369-03-5*) Son-Rise Pubns.

An Asterisk (*) at the beginning of an entry indicates that the title is appearing in BIP for the first time.

***McGowen, Darrell.** Recovery of Damages for Crimes & Intentional Wrongs. LC 92-75760. 500p. 1993. 95.00 (0-915544-24-5) Lawpress CA.

McGowen, Darrell, et al. Criminal & Civil Tax Fraud: Law, Practice, Procedure, with 1992 Cumulative Supplements, 2 vols. 1986. Volume 1. write for info. (0-930273-20-6); Volume 2. write for info. (0-930273-21-4) Michie Butterworth.

— Criminal & Civil Tax Fraud: Law, Practice, Procedure, with 1992 Cumulative Supplements, 2 vols. suppl. ed. 1992. 65.00 (0-87473-964-0) Michie Butterworth.

— Criminal & Civil Tax Fraud: Law, Practice, Procedure, with 1992 Cumulative Supplements, 2 vols., Set. 1986. 160.00 (0-930273-22-2) Michie Butterworth.

— Criminal Tax Fraud, 3 vols., Set. 1994. 240.00 (1-55834-133-1) Michie Butterworth.

McGowen, Drusilla. Traveling the Way. 1977. 6.55 (0-686-20047-0) Rod & Staff.

McGowen, J. H. Gum Hollow Fan Delta, Nueces Bay, Texas. (Report of Investigations Ser.: RI 69). (Illus.). 91p. 1984. reprint ed. 5.50 (0-318-03627-4) Bur Econ Geology.

McGowen, J. H. & Groat, C. G. Van Horn Sandstone, West Texas: An Alluvial Fan Model for Mineral Exploration. (Report of Investigations Ser.: RI 72). (Illus.). 57p. 1982. reprint ed. 2.50 (0-318-03173-6) Bur Econ Geology.

McGowen, J. H., jt. auth. see Morton, R. A.

McGowen, J. H., et al. Depositional Framework of the Lower Dockum Group (Triassic), Texas Panhandle. (Report of Investigations Ser.: RI 97). (Illus.). 60p. 1979. 2.00 (0-318-03233-3) Bur Econ Geology.

— Geochemistry of Bottom Sediments, Matagorda Bay System, Texas. (Geological Circular Ser.: GC 79-2). (Illus.). 64p. 1979. 1.50 (0-686-29329-0) Bur Econ Geology.

McGowen, M. K. & Lopez, C. M. Depositional Systems in the Nacatoch Formation (Upper Cretaceous), Northeast Texas & Southwest Arkansas. (Report of Investigations Ser.: RI 137). (Illus.). 59p. 1983. 2.00 (0-318-03297-X) Bur Econ Geology.

McGowen, Mary K., jt. ed. see Keller, Margaret A.

McGowen, Mercedes, jt. auth. see Garrison, Catherine.

***McGowen, Tom.** The Black Death. LC 95-2122. (First Bks.). (J). 1995. lib. bdg. 13.93 (0-531-20199-6) Watts.

— The Korean War. LC 91-14747. (First Bks.). (Illus.). 64p. (J). (gr. 5-8). 1992. lib. bdg. 13.93 (0-531-20040-X) Watts.

— The Korean War. (First Bks.). (Illus.). 64p. (J). (gr. 5-8). 1993. pap. 5.95 (0-531-15655-9) Watts.

— 1900-1919. (Yearbooks in Science Ser.). (Illus.). 80p. (J). (gr. 5-8). 1995. lib. bdg. 16.98 (0-8050-3431-5) TFC Bks NY.

— 1960-1969. (Yearbooks in Science Ser.). (Illus.). 80p. (J). (gr. 5-8). 1995. lib. bdg. 16.98 (0-8050-3436-6) TFC Bks NY.

— A Question of Magic. (Age of Magic Trilogy Ser.: Bk. 3). 160p. (J). (gr. 5-9). 1993. 14.99 (0-525-67380-6, Lodestar Bks) Dutton Child Bks.

— A Trial of Magic. (Age of Magic Trilogy Ser.: Bk. 2). 144p. (J). (gr. 5-9). 1992. 15.00 (0-525-67376-8, Lodestar Bks) Dutton Child Bks.

— World War I. LC 92-28329. (First Book Ser.). (J). 1993. 13.93 (0-531-20149-X); pap. 5.95 (0-531-15660-5) Watts.

— World War II. LC 92-28328. (First Book Ser.). (J). 1993. 13.93 (0-531-20150-3) Watts.

— World War II. (First Bks.). (Illus.). 64p. (J). (gr. 5-8). 1993. pap. 5.95 (0-531-15661-3) Watts.

***McGowin, Diana F.** Living in the Labyrinth: A Personal Journey Through the Maze of Alzheimer's. 1994. pap. 8.95 (0-385-31318-7, Delta) Dell.

— Living in the Labyrinth: A Personal Journey through the Maze of Alzheimer's. large type ed. LC 93-33820. Date not set. pap. 12.95 (0-7862-0067-7); bds. 19.95 (0-7862-0066-9) Thorndike Pr.

McGowin, Diane F. Living in the Labyrinth: A Personal Journey Through the Maze of Alzheimer's Disease. 133p. 1993. pap. 10.95 (0-943873-18-5) Elder Bks.

McGown, A., et al, eds. Performance of Reinforced Soil Structures. 484p. 1991. text ed. 200.00 (0-7277-1637-9, Pub. by T Telford UK) Am Soc Civil Eng.

McGown, Alan, jt. ed. see Jarrett, Peter M.

McGown, Carl. Science of Coaching Volleyball. LC 93-24319. (Science of Coaching Ser.). (Illus.). 200p. 1993. pap. 19.95 (0-87322-572-4, PMCG0572) Human Kinetics.

McGown, Carl, ed. Science of Coaching Volleyball. 1993. write for info. (0-318-71686-0) Human Kinetics.

***McGown, Clint.** The Member-Guest: A Novel in Stories. LC 94-28218. 1995. 20.00 (0-385-47655-8) Doubleday.

McGown, Jill. Gone to Her Death. 1991. mass mkt. 4.99 (0-449-21966-6, Crest) Fawcett.

— Gone to Her Death. large type ed. (General Ser.). 330p. 1991. text ed. 22.95 (0-8161-5094-X, Large Print Bks) Hall.

— Murder at the Old Vicarage. 1991. mass mkt. 4.99 (0-449-21819-8) Fawcett.

— Murder at the Old Vicarage. large type ed. (General Ser.). 348p. 1990. lib. bdg. 18.95 (0-8161-4838-4) G K Hall.

— Murder Movie. 1992. mass mkt. 3.99 (0-449-22070-2) Fawcett.

— Murder...Now & Then. 1995. mass mkt. 5.99 (0-449-22311-6, Crest) Fawcett.

— The Other Woman. LC 92-41160. 1993. 17.95 (0-312-08868-X, Pub. by Thomas Dunne Bks) St Martin.

— The Other Woman. 1994. mass mkt. 4.99 (0-449-22272-1, Crest) Fawcett.

Mcgown, Jill. A Perfect Match. 192p. 1990. mass mkt. 4.95 (0-449-21820-1, Crest) Fawcett.

McGown, Linda B. & Bockris, John O. How to Obtain Abundant Clean Energy. LC 79-24468. 276p. 1980. 39.50 (0-306-40399-4, Plenum Pr) Plenum.

McGrade, A. S., ed. see William of Ockham.

McGrade, Arthur S., ed. see Ockham, William.

McGrady. A Guide to Organizing Unions. 160p. 1989. pap. 40.00 (0-409-80953-5) Butterworth Legal Pubs.

McGrady, Donald. Mateo Aleman. LC 67-25196. (Twayne World Authors Ser.). 1968. lib. bdg. 17.95 (0-8057-2028-6) Irvington.

McGrady, Donald, ed. see De Vega, Lope.

McGrady, Donald, ed. see Tamariz, Cristobal de.

McGrady, L. J. How to Publish Your Genealogy. 3rd ed. LC 83-91302. (Illus.). 80p. 1984. pap. 6.75 (0-318-00804-1) L J McGrady.

McGrady, Mike. The Best Restaurants on Long Island. (Illus.). 192p. 1986. pap. 6.95 (0-8065-0989-9, Citadel Pr) Carol Pub Group.

McGrady, Mike, jt. auth. see Lovelace, Linda.

McGrady, Patrick, jt. auth. see Pritikin, Nathan.

McGrady, Sean. Dead Letter. Chelius, Jane, ed. 240p. (Orig.). 1992. mass mkt. 4.99 (0-671-74267-1) PB.

— Gloom of Night. Chelius, Jane, ed. 256p. (Orig.). 1993. mass mkt. 4.99 (0-671-74268-X) PB.

— Sealed with a Kiss. Chelius, Jane, ed. 256p. (Orig.). 1995. mass mkt. 5.50 (0-671-86941-8) PB.

McGrady, Thomas. Beyond the Black Ocean: A Story of Social Revolution. LC 75-154450. (Utopian Literature Ser.). 1976. reprint ed. 25.95 (0-405-03532-2) Ayer.

McGrail, Janet, jt. auth. see Wilson, Bruce L.

McGrail, Janet, et al. Looking at Schools: Instruments & Processes for School Analysis. 140p. 1991. reprint ed. pap. 23.95 (1-56602-038-7) Research Better.

McGrail, Sean, ed. see Johnstone, Paul.

McGrain, Eleanore, jt. auth. see Bronstein, Leona B.

McGrain, John W. From Pig Iron to Cotton Duck: A History of Manufacturing Villages in Baltimore County, Vol. 1. (Baltimore County Heritage Publications). (Illus.). 350p. 1985. 25.00 (0-937076-01-5) Baltimore Co Pub Lib.

McGrain, Mark. Music Notation. 207p. 1991. pap. 16.95 (0-7935-0847-9, 50449399, Berklee Pr) H Leonard.

McGranaghan, Edmund. The Life's Work of a Minor Poet: Collected Fiction, Journalism, & Poetry of Edmund McGranaghan. McKinley, Sarah, ed. & intro. by. LC 83-80303. (Illus.). 254p. (Orig.). 1983. pap. 12.50 (0-912681-00-4) Fidelio Pr.

McGranahan, Carole, jt. auth. see Forbes, Ann.

McGrane, Bernard. Beyond Anthropology: Society & the Other. 176p. 1989. text ed. 31.00 (0-231-06684-8) Col U Pr.

— Beyond Anthropology: Society & the Other. 176p. (C). 1992. pap. 15.00 (0-231-06685-6) Col U Pr.

— The Un-TV & the Ten MPH Car: Experiments in Personal Freedom & Everyday Life. LC 93-87106. (Illus.). 350p. (Orig.). 1994. pap. 17.50 (1-878020-05-6) Small Pr CA.

McGrane, Helen F., jt. auth. see Cochrane, Barbara T.

McGrane, Reginald C., ed. see Biddle, Nicholas.

***Mcgrata, Jinks.** Enameling - First Steps. 1994. 12.98 (0-7858-0033-6) Bk Sales Inc.

McGrath. History of One Hundred Twenty-Seventh New York Volunteers. 1976. 25.95 (0-8488-1558-0) Amereon Ltd.

McGrath, Alice, ed. see Tegner, Bruce.

McGrath, Alice, jt. auth. see Tegner, Bruce.

***McGrath, Alister.** Evangelicalism & the Future of Christianity. 1995. 16.99 (0-8308-1694-1) InterVarsity.

— A Life of John Calvin: A Study in the Shaping of Western Culture. (Illus.). 320p. 1993. reprint ed. pap. 19.95 (0-631-18947-5) Blackwell Pubs.

— The Renewal of Anglicanism. LC 93-35681. 144p. (Orig.). 1993. pap. 9.95 (0-8192-1603-8) Morehouse Pub.

— Suffering with God: Looking for Hope When Life Falls Apart. 128p. 1994. pap. 12.99 (0-310-40691-9) Zondervan.

McGrath, Alister, intro. The Blackwell Encyclopedia of Modern Christian Thought. 700p. 1993. 94.95 (0-631-16896-6) Blackwell Pubs.

McGrath, Alister E. Christian Theology: An Introduction. LC 93-18797. (Illus.). 528p. 1993. 59.95 (0-631-16078-7); pap. 20.95 (0-631-16079-5) Blackwell Pubs.

— A Cloud of Witnesses. 1991. pap. 9.99 (0-310-29671-4) Zondervan.

— The Genesis of Doctrine: A Study in the Foundations of Doctrinal Criticism. 272p. 1990. text ed. 54.95 (0-631-16658-0) Blackwell Pubs.

— I Believe. 160p. 1991. pap. 9.99 (0-310-30041-X) Zondervan.

— The Intellectual Origins of the European Reformation. 232p. 1993. pap. 19.95 (0-631-18688-3) Blackwell Pubs.

— Intellectuals Don't Need God & Other Modern Myths: Christian Apologetics for Today. 228p. 1993. pap. 14.99 (0-310-59091-4) Zondervan.

— Iustitia Dei: A History of the Christian Doctrine of Justification, Vol. 1: Beginnings to the Reformation. 252p. (C). 1989. pap. 22.95 (0-521-37973-3) Cambridge U Pr.

— Iustitia Dei: a History of the Christian Doctrine of Justification, Vol. 2: From 1500 to the Present Day. 272p. (C). 1993. pap. 18.95 (0-521-44846-8) Cambridge U Pr.

— A Life of John Calvin: A Study in the Shaping of Western Culture. 320p. 1990. text ed. 49.95 (0-631-16398-0) Blackwell Pubs.

— A Life of John Calvin: A Study in the Shaping of Western Culture. 348p. 1995. reprint ed. pap. 19.99 (0-8010-2010-7) Baker Bk.

— Luther's Theology of the Cross. 208p. 1990. pap. 21.95 (0-631-17549-0) Blackwell Pubs.

— Luther's Theology of the Cross: Martin Luther's Theological Breakthrough. 200p. 1995. reprint ed. pap. 19.99 (0-8010-2011-5) Baker Bk.

— The Making of Modern German Christology. 256p. 1994. pap. 24.99 (0-310-40481-9) Zondervan.

— Reformation Thought: An Introduction. 2nd ed. LC 92-12336. 272p. 1993. 19.95 (0-631-18651-4) Blackwell Pubs.

— Spirituality in an Age of Change: Rediscovering the Spirit of the Reformers. 240p. 1994. pap. 16.99 (0-310-42921-8) Zondervan.

— The Sunnier Side of Doubt: What It Is & How to Handle It. 160p. 1990. pap. 9.99 (0-310-29661-7) Zondervan.

— Understanding Doctrine: What It Is & Why It Matters. 192p. 1992. pap. 12.99 (0-310-47951-7) Zondervan.

— Understanding Jesus. 1990. pap. 14.99 (0-310-29811-3) Zondervan.

— Understanding the Trinity. 1990. pap. 10.99 (0-310-29681-1) Zondervan.

— What Was God Doing on the Cross? 112p. 1993. pap. 9.99 (0-310-59451-0) Zondervan.

***McGrath, Alister E., ed. & intro.** The Christian Theology Reader. 544p. 1995. write for info. (0-631-19584-X) Blackwell Pubs.

— The Christian Theology Reader. 544p. 1995. pap. write for info. (0-631-19585-8) Blackwell Pubs.

***McGrath, Ann E.** Feathers & Fur. LC 95-75083. 192p. (YA). 1995. 16.95 (0-8338-0220-8) M Jones.

McGrath, Anne. Wildflowers of the Adirondacks. 3rd ed. (Illus.). 128p. 1981. pap. 14.95 (0-932052-27-4) North Country.

McGrath, Anne, ed. Bookman's Price Index: CUM Index, Vol. 537-46. 1000p. 1993. 245.00 (0-8103-9554-1) Gale.

***McGrath, Anne F.** Bookman's Price Index, Vol. 50. 930p. 1995. pap. 245.00 (0-8103-9147-3) Gale.

McGrath, Brian. Transparent Cities. 1994. pap. 29.00 (0-930829-17-4) Lumen Inc.

McGrath, Brian J. Duck Calls & Other Game Calls. LC 88-90614. (Illus.). 1988. 40.00 (0-9620155-0-4) T B Reel.

McGrath, Brian J., jt. auth. see Gard, Ronald J.

McGrath, Brian J., ed. see Kelly, Mary K.

McGrath, Brian J., ed. see Vernon, Steven K. & Stewart, Frank M., III.

McGrath, Campbell. American Noise. LC 93-20698. 1994. 23.00 (0-88001-335-4) Ecco Pr.

— American Noise: Poems. 1994. pap. 11.00 (0-88001-374-5) Ecco Pr.

— Capitalism. LC 89-24962. (Wesleyan New Poets Ser.). 64p. 1990. 22.50 (0-8195-2193-0, Wesleyan Univ Pr); pap. 10.95 (0-8195-1195-1, Wesleyan Univ Pr) U Pr of New Eng.

McGrath, Carol R., et al. Road Trip. 80p. 1993. pap. text ed. 12.95 (0-944459-71-4) ECS Lrn Systs.

McGrath, Cindy. Rejoice in Remembering. 8.00 (0-945905-20-3) Family Hstory Pubns.

McGrath, Connell. With Words. 32p. 1991. pap. 4.00 (1-879645-04-1) Garlic MA.

McGrath, Cynthia, jt. ed. see Boyd, Susan.

McGrath, Daniel F. Bookman's Price Index, Vol. 30. 944p. 1985. 245.00 (0-8103-0643-3) Gale.

— Bookman's Price Index, Vol. 35. 1250p. 1987. 245.00 (0-8103-1806-7) Gale.

— Bookman's Price Index, Vol. 38. 1989. 245.00 (0-8103-1811-3) Gale.

— Bookman's Price Index, Vol. 42. 1991. 245.00 (0-8103-1815-6) Gale.

— Bookman's Price Index, Vol. 43. 1991. 245.00 (0-8103-1816-4) Gale.

— Bookman's Price Index, Vol. 44. 1992. 245.00 (0-8103-7493-5) Gale.

— Bookman's Price Index, Vol. 45. 1992. 245.00 (0-8103-7494-3) Gale.

— Bookman's Price Index, Vol. 48. 1994. 245.00 (0-8103-5602-3, 004148) Gale.

— Bookman's Price Index, Vol. 49. 1994. 245.00 (0-8103-5603-1, 004149) Gale.

— Bookman's Price Index, Vol. 39, Vol. 39. 1000p. 1989. 245.00 (0-8103-1812-1) Gale.

McGrath, Daniel F., ed. Bookman's Price Index, Vol. 26. 896p. 1984. 245.00 (0-8103-0639-5) Gale.

— Bookman's Price Index, Vol. 27. 920p. 1984. 245.00 (0-8103-0640-9) Gale.

— Bookman's Price Index, Vol. 28. 880p. 1984. 245.00 (0-8103-0641-7) Gale.

— Bookman's Price Index, Vol. 29. 992p. 1985. 245.00 (0-8103-0642-5) Gale.

— Bookman's Price Index, Vol. 31. 1020p. 1985. 245.00 (0-8103-0636-0) Gale.

— Bookman's Price Index, Vol. 33. 1000p. 1986. 245.00 (0-8103-1804-0) Gale.

— Bookman's Price Index, Vol. 34. 1232p. 1987. 245.00 (0-8103-1805-9) Gale.

— Bookman's Price Index, Vol. 37. 1000p. 1988. 245.00 (0-8103-1808-3) Gale.

— Bookman's Price Index, Vol. 40. 1000p. 1990. 245.00 (0-8103-1813-X) Gale.

— Bookman's Price Index, Vol. 41. 1990. 245.00 (0-8103-1814-8) Gale.

— Bookman's Price Index: A Guide to the Values of Rare & Other Out-of-Print Books, 25 vols. Incl. Vol. 1. LC 64-8723. 2008p. 1964. 245.00 (0-8103-0601-8); Vol. 2. LC 64-8723. 1314p. 1967. 245.00 (0-8103-0602-6); Vol. 3. LC 64-8723. 1098p. 1968. 245.00 (0-8103-0603-4); Vol. 5. LC 64-8723. 1032p. 1971. 245.00 (0-8103-0605-0); Vol. 6. LC 64-8723. 706p. 1973. 245.00 (0-8103-0606-9); Vol. 7. LC 64-8723. 678p. 1973. 245.00 (0-8103-0607-7); Vol. 8. LC 64-8723. 676p. 1974. 245.00 (0-8103-0608-5); Vol. 9. LC 64-8723. 730p. 1974. 245.00 (0-8103-0609-3); Vol. 10. LC 64-8723. 750p. 1975. 245.00 (0-8103-0635-2); Vol. 11. LC 64-8723. 804p. 1976. 245.00 (0-8103-0611-5); Vol. 12. LC 64-8723. 808p. 1977. 245.00 (0-8103-0612-3); Vol. 13. LC 64-8723. 768p. 1978. 245.00 (0-8103-0613-1); Vol. 14. LC 64-8723. 768p. 1978. 245.00 (0-8103-0614-X); Vol. 15. LC 64-8723. 760p. 1979. 245.00 (0-8103-0615-8); Vol. 16. LC 64-8723. 736p. 1979. 245.00 (0-8103-0616-6); Vol. 17. LC 64-8723. 768p. 1979. 245.00 (0-8103-0617-4); Vol. 18. LC 64-8723. 792p. 1980. 245.00 (0-8103-0618-2); Vol. 19. LC 64-8723. 808p. 1980. 245.00 (0-8103-0619-0); Vol. 21. LC 64-8723. 792p. 1981. 245.00 (0-8103-0621-2); Vol. 22. LC 64-8723. 880p. 1981. 245.00 (0-8103-0622-0); Vol. 23. LC 64-8723. 792p. 1983. 245.00 (0-8103-0623-9); Vol. 24. LC 64-8723. 792p. 1983. 245.00 (0-8103-0624-7); Vol. 25. LC 64-8723. 776p. 1983. 245.00 (0-8103-0638-7); LC 64-8723. 218.00 (0-318-52353-1) Gale.

— Bookman's Price Index: Modern First Edition, Vol. 1. 1000p. 1987. 216.00 (0-8103-2535-7, 004340-99584) Gale.

— Bookman's Price Index, Vol. 36, Vol. 36. 1000p. 1988. 245.00 (0-8103-1807-5) Gale.

McGrath, Delia M. Rainbows ... & Roses. (Illus.). 200p. (Orig.). 1986. pap. 10.00 (0-9617794-0-3) Laurel Pub TX.

McGrath, Dennis & Spear, Martin B. The Academic Crisis of the Community College. LC 90-34599. (SUNY Series, Literacy, Culture, & Learning: Theory & Practice). 195p. 1991. 59.50 (0-7914-0562-1); pap. 19.95x (0-7914-0563-X) State U NY Pr.

***McGrath, Dennis J. & Smith, Dane.** Professor Wellstone Goes to Washington: The Inside Story of a Grassroots U. S. Senate Campaign. LC 94-41361. (Illus.). 328p. 1995. 24.95 (0-8166-2662-6) U of Minn Pr.

— Professor Wellstone Goes to Washington: The Inside Story of a Grassroots U. S. Senate Campaign. (Illus.). 328p. 1995. pap. 17.95 (0-8166-2663-4) U of Minn Pr.

McGrath, Donald, tr. see Kolbowski, Silvia, et al.

McGrath, Eamonn. Charnel House. 240p. 1990. pap. 14.95 (0-85640-447-0, Pub. by Blackstaff Pr IE) Dufour.

— The Fish in the Stone. 236p. 1994. pap. 13.95 (0-85640-524-8, Pub. by Blackstaff Pr IE) Dufour.

— Honour Thy Father. 256p. 1990. pap. 11.95 (0-85640-433-0, Pub. by Blackstaff Pr IE) Dufour.

McGrath, Earl J. & Webber, Robert S. Effective Functioning: A Study of Fifteen Successful Independent Institutions of Higher Education. (Illus.). 140p. (Orig.). 1985. pap. text ed. 3.95 (0-933939-00-0) Inst Christ Leadership.

McGrath, Ed. The Superinsulated House: A Working Guide for Owner-Builders & Architects. (Illus.). 128p. 1982. pap. 11.95 (0-918270-12-X) That New Pub.

***McGrath, Elizabeth Z.** The Art of Ethics. LC 93-36798. (Values & Ethics Ser.: Vol. VII). 163p. 1993. 13.95 (0-8294-0804-5, Campion Bks) Loyola.

McGrath, Ellen. When Feeling Bad Is Good: An Innovative Self-Help Program for Women to Convert Healthy Depression into New Sources of Growth & Power. 1994. mass mkt. 5.99 (0-553-56513-3) Bantam.

McGrath, Ellen, et al, eds. Women & Depression: Risk Factors & Treatment Issues. 137p. (Orig.). 1990. pap. text ed. 19.95 (1-55798-104-3) Am Psychol.

McGrath, Elsie, jt. auth. see Craghan, John.

***McGrath, Elsie H., ed.** Journey of Faith Participant's Booklet Cycle A: Participant Book. (Cycle A Ser.). 64p. 1995. pap. 1.95 (0-89243-559-3) Liguori Pubns.

McGrath, Elsie H., ed. see Krings, James, et al.

***McGrath, Elsie H., et al.** Advent Magazine 1994: Season of Wonder. (Illus.). 24p. 1995. pap. 1.95 (0-89243-806-1) Liguori Pubns.

McGrath, Fergal. The Consecration of Learning: Lectures on Newman's Idea of a University. LC 62-22015. 351p. reprint ed. pap. 100.10 (0-7837-0454-2, 2040777) Bks Demand.

McGrath, Gail. Workbook for Voice & Articulation for the Electronic Media. 141p. (C). 1993. student ed 15.98 (1-56870-070-9) RonJon Pub.

McGrath, H. G. & Charles, M. E., eds. Origin & Refining of Petroleum. LC 73-164409. (Advances in Chemistry Ser.: No. 103). 1971. 24.95 (0-8412-0120-X) Am Chemical.

McGrath-Heiss, Arleen. Barbara Bush. (Library of Biography). (Illus.). 128p. (YA). (gr. 5 up). 1992. lib. bdg. 17.95 (0-7910-1627-7) Chelsea Hse.

McGrath, I. & Sidall, R. Advances in Magnetohydrodynamics: Proceedings of Colloquium Department of Fuel Technology & Chemical Engineering. LC 62-22054. 1963. 68.00 (0-08-009815-0, Pub. by Pergamon Repr UK) Franklin.

McGrath, Ian, jt. ed. see Howard, Ron.

McGrath, J. E., et al. New Elastomer Synthesis for High Performance Applications. LC 87-31549. (Illus.). 118p. 1988. 36.00 (0-8155-1156-6) Noyes.

McGrath, J. J., ed. Advances in Biological Heat & Mass Transfer - 1992. (HTD Ser.: Vol. 231). 152p. 1992. 45.00 (0-7918-1111-5, G00755) ASME.

McGrath, Jack. Using the 1-2-3 Solver. (Illus.). (Orig.). 1992. pap. 44.95 (0-13-635335-5) Brady Compu Bks.

M

McGrath, James. Behind My Eyes: A Visit, Vol. 1. Benny, Louis M., ed. (Illus.). 65p. (Orig.). 1989. pap. 11.95 (*1-877608-00-9*) Rinky Inc.

McGrath, James, tr. see Gottfried.

McGrath, James, tr. see Hoffsummer, Willi.

McGrath, James E., ed. Anionic Polymerization. LC 81-14911. (Symposium Ser.: No. 166). 594p. 1981. 63.95 (*0-8412-0643-0*) Am Chemical.

McGrath, James E., et al, eds. Polyimides: Synthesis, Characterization, & Adhesion. (CASS Review Ser.: Vol. I). x, 212p. 1992. pap. write for info. (*0-936015-37-3*) Pocahontas Pr.

***McGrath, Jane L.** Building Strategies for College Reading: A Text with Thematic Reader. LC 94-32425. 448p. (C). 1994. pap. text ed. write for info. (*0-13-043894-4*) P-H.

***McGrath, Jill.** The Rune of Salt Air. Warren, Shirley, ed. (Illus.). 36p. 1991. pap. 5.00 (*1-877801-16-X*) Still Waters.

McGrath, Jim, jt. auth. see Doughty, Carolyn.

McGrath, John. A Good Night Out. 144p. 1988. pap. 11.95 (*0-413-48700-8*, A0116, Pub. by Methuen UK) Heinemann.

— The Official Chicago Bar Guide: An Up-to-the-Minute Guide to over 300 Chicago Nightspots. 152p. (Orig.). 1994. pap. text ed. 9.95 (*0-9638893-2-X*) Buckingham Bks.

— Yobbo Nowt. 72p. (Orig.). 1981. pap. 6.95 (*0-904383-76-8*, NO. 4135) Routledge Chapman & Hall.

McGrath, John A. Baron Friedrich von Hugel & the Debate on Historical Christianity 1902-1905. LC 93-396. 380p. 1993. 99.95 (*0-7734-9817-6*) E Mellen.

McGrath, John M. Prisoner of War: Six Years in Hanoi. LC 75-11400. (Illus.). 114p. 1975. 17.95 (*0-87021-527-2*) Naval Inst Pr.

McGrath, Joseph E., ed. Social Psychology of Time: New Perspectives. (Focus Editions Ser.: Vol. 91). 320p. (C). 1988. text ed. 49.95 (*0-8039-2766-5*); pap. text ed. 24.95 (*0-8039-2767-3*) Sage.

McGrath, Joseph E. & Hollingshead, Andrea B. Groups Interacting with Technology: Ideas, Evidence, Issues & an Agenda. LC 93-34627. (Library of Social Research: Vol. 194). (C). 1993. text ed. 49.95 (*0-8039-4897-2*); pap. text ed. 24.00 (*0-8039-4898-0*) Sage.

McGrath, Joseph E. & Kelly, Janice R. Time & Human Interaction: Toward a Social Psychology of Time. LC 86-396. (Guilford Social Psychology Ser.). 183p. 1986. lib. bdg. 30.00 (*0-89862-111-9*) Guilford Pr.

McGrath, Joseph E., jt. auth. see Brinberg, David.

McGrath, Joseph E., jt. auth. see Kelly, Janice R.

McGrath, Kate & Elias, Stephen. Patent, Copyright & Trademark: A Desk Reference to Intellectual Property Law. LC 94-352. 256p. 1994. pap. 24.95 (*0-87337-236-0*) Nolo Pr.

McGrath, Kate, jt. auth. see Elias, Stephen.

McGrath, Kristina. House Work: A Novel. LC 94-13257. 192p. 1994. 19.95 (*1-882593-07-3*) Bridge Wrks.

***McGrath, Laura.** I Am...by Mac! 18p. 1994. pap. 7.95 (*0-9645696-0-4*) Mac & Co.

McGrath, Leueen, jt. auth. see Kaufman, George S.

McGrath, Linda. Set Free: A Woman's Victory over Eating Disorders. 112p. (Orig.). 1992. pap. 12.95 (*0-87040-795-3*) Japan Pubns USA.

McGrath, Madeleine S. These Women? Women Religious in the History of Australia: The Sisters of Mercy, Parramatta 1888-1988. 312p. 1990. 34.95 (*0-86840-299-0*, Pub. by New South Wales Univ Pr AT) Intl Spec Bk.

McGrath, Mary. Trespassing Stoplights & Attitudes. (Illus.). 44p. (Orig.). 1980. pap. 5.00 (*0-930012-43-7*) J Mudfoot.

McGrath, Mary, jt. auth. see Pridmore, Saxby.

***McGrath, Mary Z.** Teachers Today: A Guide to Surviving Creatively. (Illus.). 144p. 1995. 42.95 (*0-8039-6336-X*); pap. 18.95 (*0-8039-6229-0*) Corwin Pr.

McGrath, Meggan. My Grapes. LC 93-24057. (Illus.). 48p. (Orig.). (J). 1993. pap. 16.95 (*0-938586-99-8*) Pfeifer-Hamilton.

***McGrath, Michael E.** Product Strategy for High-Technology Companies: How to Achieve Growth, Competitive Advantage, & Increased Profits. LC 94-27340. 284p. 1994. 40.00 (*0-7863-0146-5*) Irwin Prof Pubng.

McGrath, Michael E., jt. auth. see Pittiglio, Rabin, Todd.

McGrath, Michael J., ed. Liberalism & the Modern Polity: Essays in Contemporary Political Theory. LC 78-2583. (Political Science Ser.: No. 5). 319p. reprint ed. pap. 91.00 (*0-8357-6190-8*, 2034550) Bks Demand.

McGrath, Michael J., jt. ed. see Barber, Benjamin.

McGrath, Michael R., ed. see Quinn, Robert E., et al.

McGrath, Morag. Multi-Disciplinary Teamwork: Community Mental Handicap Teams. (Care in the Community Studies). 217p. 1991. text ed. 52.95 (*1-85628-152-3*, Pub. by Avebury Pub UK) Ashgate Pub Co.

McGrath, Morag, jt. auth. see Hadley, Roger.

McGrath, Norman. Photographing Buildings Inside & Out. enl. rev. ed. LC 92-42306. (Illus.). 208p. 1993. pap. 24.95 (*0-8230-4016-X*, Whitney Lib) Watsn-Guptill.

— Photographing Buildings Inside & Out. 2nd enl. rev. ed. LC 92-42306. (Illus.). 208p. 1993. 32.50 (*0-8230-4017-8*, Whitney Lib) Watsn-Guptill.

McGrath, P. J. & Unruh, A. M. Pain in Children & Adolescents. Vol. 1. 351p. 1987. write for info. (*0-318-63282-9*, Excerpta Medica) Elsevier.

McGrath, P. J., jt. ed. see Anand, K. J.

McGrath, P. J., et al. Help Yourself: A Treatment for Migraine Headaches. 120p. 1990. 10.00 (*0-7766-0249-7*, Pub. by Univ Ottawa Pr CN); 20.00 (*0-7766-0248-9*, Pub. by Univ Ottawa Pr CN) Paul & Co Pubs.

McGrath, Patricia A. Pain in Children: Nature, Assessment & Treatment. LC 89-11009. 466p. 1989. lib. bdg. 46.95 (*0-89862-390-1*) Guilford Pr.

McGrath, Patricia L. The Unfinished Assignment: Equal Education for Women. 1976. pap. write for info. (*0-916468-06-2*) Worldwatch Inst.

McGrath, Patrick. Dr. Haggard's Disease. 1994. pap. 10.00 (*0-679-75261-7*) Random.

— Dr. Haggard's Disease. 192p. 1993. 20.00 (*0-671-72733-8*) S&S Trade.

— The Lewis & Clark Expedition. LC 84-40381. (Turning Points in American History Ser.). (Illus.). 64p. (J). (gr. 5 up). 1984. lib. bdg. 14.95 (*0-382-06828-9*); pap. 7.95 (*0-382-09899-4*) Silver Burdett Pr.

— Spider. LC 91-50095. (Vintage Contemporaries Ser.). 224p. 1991. pap. 10.00 (*0-679-73630-1*, Vin) Random.

McGrath, Patrick, ed. see Browne, John.

McGrath, Patrick, jt. ed. see Morrow, Bradford.

McGrath, Patrick J. John Garfield: The Illustrated Career in Films & on Stage. LC 92-56666. (Illus.). 286p. 1993. lib. bdg. 29.95 (*0-89950-867-7*) McFarland & Co.

McGrath, Patrick J. & Firestone, Philip, eds. Pediatric & Adolescent Behavioral Medicine: Treatment Issues. (Behavior Therapy & Behavioral Medicine Ser.: Vol. 10). (Illus.). 256p. 1983. 26.95 (*0-8261-4010-6*) Springer Pub.

***McGrath, Paul & Dervan, Cathal.** Ooh Aah Paul McGrath: The Black Pearl of Inchicore. 237p. 1995. 29.95 (*1-85158-647-4*, Pub. by Mnstream UK) Trafalgar.

McGrath, Philomena & Mills, P. Atlas of Sectional Anatomy. 2nd ed. (Illus.). viii, 238p. 1985. 65.75 (*3-8055-4060-4*) S Karger.

Mcgrath, Richard. Where's the Manual. 1991. pap. 39.95 (*0-442-00425-7*) Van Nos Reinhold.

McGrath, Robert L. A Wild Sort of Beauty: Public Places & Private Visions. Gilborn, Alice W., ed. (Illus.). 48p. 1992. pap. 10.00 (*0-910020-43-4*) Adirondack Mus.

McGrath, Robert L. & Glick, Paula F. Paul Sample: Painter of the American Scene. LC 87-28943. (Illus.). 112p. 1988. pap. 19.95 (*0-944722-01-6*) U Pr of New Eng.

McGrath, Roger D. Gunfighters, Highwaymen, & Vigilantes: Violence on the Frontier. LC 83-6886. (Illus.). 288p. (C). 1984. pap. 14.00 (*0-520-06026-1*) U CA Pr.

McGrath, Roland. GNU C Library Reference Manual. 698p. 1993. pap. 50.00 (*1-882114-22-1*) Free Software.

McGrath, Roland, jt. auth. see Stallman, Richard M.

McGrath, Sally V., ed. see Martin, Christopher.

McGrath, Scott, jt. auth. see Wissolik, Richard D.

McGrath, Susan. Your World of Pets. Crump, Donald J., ed. LC 85-7288. (Books for World Explorers Series 6: No. 4). (Illus.). 104p. (J). (gr. 3-8). 1985. lib. bdg. 12.50 (*0-87044-522-7*) Natl Geog.

McGrath, Susan & National Geographic Society Staff. How Animals Talk, 4 vols., Set. Crump, Donald J., ed. (Books for Young Explorers Ser.: Set 14, No. 3). (Illus.). 32p. (J). (ps-3). 1993. pap. 8.00 (*0-87044-679-7*) Natl Geog.

McGrath, Susan & National Geographic Staff. Your World of Pets. Crump, Donald J., ed. LC 85-7288. (Books for World Explorers Series 6: No. 4). (Illus.). 104p. (J). (gr. 3-8). 1994. 12.50 (*0-87044-517-0*) Natl Geog.

McGrath, Sylvia W. Charles Kenneth Leith, Scientific Adviser. 278p. 1971. 10.00 (*0-299-05970-7*) U of Wis Pr.

McGrath, Thomas. Death Song. Hamill, Sam, ed. LC 90-85091. 128p. (Orig.). 1991. 19.00 (*1-55659-035-0*); pap. 10.00 (*1-55659-036-9*) Copper Canyon.

— The Gates of Ivory, the Gates of Horn. rev. ed. LC 87-72336. 128p. 1987. reprint ed. pap. 7.95 (*0-9614644-2-9*) Another Chicago Pr.

— Letter to an Imaginary Friend, Pts. 3 & 4. LC 84-73335. 128p. 1985. 16.00 (*0-914742-85-X*); pap. 9.00 (*0-914742-86-8*) Copper Canyon.

— Letters to Tomasito. Perlman, James, ed. (Orig.). 1977. pap. 2.00 (*0-930100-01-8*) Holy Cow.

— The Movie at the End of the World: Collected Poems. LC 72-91918. 188p. 1980. reprint ed. pap. 11.95 (*0-8040-0606-7*) Swallow.

— Passages Toward the Dark. 150p. (Orig.). 1982. pap. 10.00 (*0-914742-63-9*) Copper Canyon.

— Selected Poems Nineteen Thirty-Eight to Nineteen Eighty-Eight. Hamill, Sam, ed. LC 87-172648. 208p. 1988. pap. 10.00 (*1-55659-012-1*) Copper Canyon.

McGrath, Thomas, et al. Voyages to the Inland Sea, Vol 3. Judson, John, ed. LC 73-78705. 83p. 1973. 10.00 (*0-917540-03-4*); pap. 7.00 (*0-917540-12-3*) Ctr Cont Poetry.

***McGrath, Thomas B., ed.** Architectural Sketches of the Spanish Era Forts of Guam: From the Holdings of the Servicio Historico Militar, Madrid. Driver, Marjorie G. & Brunal-Perry, Omaira, trs. (MARC Educational Ser.: No. 17). 62p. 1994. 20.00 (*1-878453-18-1*); pap. 10.00 (*0-614-07000-7*) Univ Guam MAR Ctr.

McGrath, Tom. Longshot O'Leary Counsels Direct Action. Whitehead, Fred, ed. 32p. (Orig.). 1983. pap. 2.00 (*0-931122-28-7*) West End.

— Video Killed the Radio Star: How MTV Rocked the World. LC 94-26874. 1995. write for info. (*0-679-42219-6*, Villard Bks) Random.

McGrath, William. A Devotional Study of the Sermon on the Mount. 1991. pap. 3.00 (*0-935409-00-9*) Amish Mennonite.

— Separation Throughout Church History. 4th rev. ed. 72p. 1990. pap. 2.00 (*0-935409-01-7*) Amish Mennonite.

— Why We Are Conscientious Objectors to War. 1991. pap. 1.50 (*0-935409-02-5*) Amish Mennonite.

McGrath, William C. Stride & Glide: A Guide to Wisconsin's Best Cross-Country Ski Trails. LC 94-71147. (Illus.). 112p. 1994. pap. 12.95 (*0-9640613-0-9*) Amherst Pr.

McGrath, William J. Dionysian Art & Populist Politics in Austria. LC 73-86908. 279p. reprint ed. pap. 79.60 (*0-8357-8096-1*, 2033821) Bks Demand.

— Freud's Discovery of Psychoanalysis: The Politics of Hysteria. LC 85-47704. (Illus.). 336p. (C). 1987. pap. 16.95 (*0-8014-9411-7*) Cornell U Pr.

McGrath, William R., ed. Amish Folk Remedies for Plain & Fancy Ailments. 104p. 1988. pap. 6.99 (*0-9617405-8-2*) S Schupp.

— God Given Herbs. 97p. 1988. 6.99 (*0-9617405-9-0*) S Schupp.

***McGraw.** The Moorchild. (J). 1996. 15.00 (*0-689-80654-X*, McElderry) S&S Childrens.

McGraw, Betty R., jt. ed. see Ungar, Steven.

McGraw, Cameron. Piano Duet Repertoire: Music Originally Written for One Piano, Four Hands. LC 80-8097. 384p. 1981. 25.00 (*0-253-14766-2*) Ind U Pr.

McGraw, Charles C., jt. auth. see Garland, Mark.

McGraw, Charles G., jt. auth. see Garland, Mark A.

McGraw, Daniel H. The Amazing Karate Workbook. (Illus.). 136p. (Orig.). 1988. pap. text ed. 10.95 (*0-911929-49-5*) Onami Pubns.

— Basic Karate for College. (Illus.). 76p. (C). 1983. pap. text ed. 7.98 (*0-911929-00-2*) Onami Pubns.

— Kyusho: Vital Striking Points of the Human Body. (Illus.). 153p. (Orig.). 1983. pap. text ed. 19.95 (*0-911929-03-7*) Onami Pubns.

McGraw, Eloise. Hideaway. LC 83-2786. 224p. (YA). (gr. 7 up). 1990. pap. 3.95 (*0-02-044482-6*, Collier Bks Young) S&S Childrens.

— The Seventeenth Swap. 160p. (J). (gr. 4-8). 1987. reprint ed. pap. 2.95 (*0-8167-1050-3*) Troll Assocs.

— The Striped Ships. LC 91-7729. 240p. (YA). (gr. 7 up). 1991. lib. bdg. 15.95 (*0-689-50532-9*, McElderry) S&S Childrens.

— Tangled Webb. LC 92-27911. 160p. (YA). (gr. 5 up). 1993. lib. bdg. 13.95 (*0-689-50573-6*, McElderry) S&S Childrens.

— The Trouble with Jacob. LC 87-22719. 288p. (J). (gr. 4-7). 1988. lib. bdg. 14.95 (*0-689-50447-0*, McElderry) S&S Childrens.

McGraw, Eloise J. The Golden Goblet. (Newbery Library). 248p. (J). (gr. 5-9). 1986. pap. 4.99 (*0-14-030335-9*, Puffin) Puffin Bks.

— Mara, Daughter of the Nile. LC 85-567. 280p. (J). (gr. 5-9). 1985. pap. 4.99 (*0-14-031929-8*, Puffin) Puffin Bks.

— Moccasin Trail. (Newbery Library). 256p. (J). (gr. 5-9). 1986. pap. 4.99 (*0-14-032170-5*, Puffin) Puffin Bks.

— A Really Weird Summer. LC 90-31542. 224p. (YA). (gr. 7 up). 1990. reprint ed. pap. 3.95 (*0-02-044483-4*, Collier Bks Young) S&S Childrens.

— Sawdust in His Shoes. 1994. reprint ed. lib. bdg. 27.95 (*1-56849-310-X*) Buccaneer Bks.

— The Seventeenth Swap. LC 86-8791. 160p. (J). (gr. 4-7). 1986. text ed. 13.95 (*0-689-50398-9*, McElderry) S&S Childrens.

McGraw, Eric. Population: The Human Race. 145p. 1990. pap. 14.95 (*1-85219-032-9*, Pub. by Bishopsgte Pr UK) Intl Spec Bk.

— Population Growth. (World Issues Ser.). (Illus.). 48p. (J). (gr. 5 up). 1987. 13.95 (*0-86592-276-4*) Rourke Corp.

— Population Growth, Set. (World Issues Ser.). (Illus.). 48p. (J). (gr. 5 up). 1987. lib. bdg. 18.60 (*0-317-60380-9*) Rourke Corp.

McGraw, Erin. Bodies at Sea: Stories. (Illinois Short Fiction Ser.). 168p. 1989. 14.95 (*0-252-01631-9*) U of Ill Pr.

McGraw-Hill, College Division Staff. Author's Guide to Manuscript Preparation. 1992. pap. text ed. write for info. (*0-07-046733-1*) McGraw.

McGraw-Hill Continuing Education Center Staff. Contemporary Electronic Communication. 368p. 1989. pap. text ed. 29.95 (*0-07-045078-1*) McGraw.

McGraw-Hill Editors. Communications Source Book. (Science Reference Ser.). 352p. 1989. text ed. 49.50 (*0-07-045510-4*) McGraw.

— Dictionary of Chemical Terms. LC 85-11696. 464p. 1986. pap. text ed. 27.95 (*0-07-045417-5*) McGraw.

— Dictionary of Electronics & Computer Science. 582p. 1985. text ed. 49.50 (*0-07-045416-7*) McGraw.

— Dictionary of Engineering. Parker, Sybil P., ed. 659p. 1985. text ed. 49.50 (*0-07-045412-4*) McGraw.

— Dictionary of Science & Engineering. 942p. 1984. text ed. 54.50 (*0-07-045483-3*) McGraw.

— Guidelines for Bias-Free Publishing. 1983. text ed. write for info. (*0-07-045033-1*) McGraw.

— McGraw-Hill Concise Encyclopedia of Science & Technology. 2nd ed. 1989. text ed. 119.50 (*0-07-045512-0*) McGraw.

— McGraw-Hill Encyclopedia of Electronics & Computers. 2nd ed. (Illus.). 992p. 1988. text ed. 90.50 (*0-07-045499-X*) McGraw.

— McGraw-Hill Encyclopedia of World Biography, 12 vols., Set. 1975. text ed. 550.00 (*0-07-079633-5*) McGraw.

— McGraw-Hill Encyclopedia of World Drama, 5 vols. 2nd ed. LC 83-9919. (Illus.). 2828p. 1983. text ed. 425.00 (*0-07-079169-4*) McGraw.

— Meteorology Source Book: Meteorology. (Science Reference Ser.). (Illus.). 304p. 1989. text ed. 49.50 (*0-07-045511-2*) McGraw.

— Nuclear & Practice Physics Source Book. (Science Reference Ser.). 550p. 1989. text ed. 49.50 (*0-07-045509-0*) McGraw.

— Spectroscopy Source Book. (Science Reference Ser.). (Illus.). 300p. 1988. text ed. 49.50 (*0-07-045505-8*) McGraw.

McGraw-Hill Editors, et al, eds. McGraw-Hill Nursing Dictionary. (Illus.). 1200p. 1979. text ed. 23.95 (*0-07-045019-6*) Hlth Prof Div.

***McGraw-Hill Encyclopedia Staff.** McGraw-Hill 1995 Yearbook of Science & Technology. 1994. 116.75 (*0-07-051545-X*) McGraw.

McGraw-Hill Publishing Co. Staff. McGraw-Hill Yearbook of Science & Technology, 1992. 500p. 1992. text ed. 80.00 (*0-07-046707-2*) McGraw.

McGraw Hill Staff. Diccionario de las Ciencias de la Vida. 940p. 1990. 125.00 (*0-7859-6236-0*, 8476006195) Fr & Eur.

— Diccionario de Terminos Cientificos, Vol. 1. 336p. 1987. 39.95 (*0-7859-6013-9*, 8439506651) Fr & Eur.

— Diccionario de Terminos Cientificos, Vol. 2. 312p. 1988. 39.95 (*0-7859-6470-3*) Fr & Eur.

— Diccionario de Terminos Cientificos, Vol. 3. 312p. 1988. 39.95 (*0-7859-6014-7*, 8439506678) Fr & Eur.

— Diccionario de Terminos Cientificos, Vol. 4. 320p. 1988. 39.95 (*0-7859-6015-5*, 8439506686) Fr & Eur.

— Diccionario de Terminos Cientificos, Vol. 5. 320p. 1988. 39.95 (*0-7859-6016-3*, 8439506694) Fr & Eur.

— Diccionario de Terminos Cientificos, Vol. 6. 320p. 1988. 39.95 (*0-7859-6017-1*, 8439506708) Fr & Eur.

McGraw-Hill Staff. Encyclopedia of Science & Technology. 7th ed. 1992. 1,900.00 (*0-685-49345-8*); 1,700.00 (*0-685-49346-6*) McGraw.

— Legal Briefs for the Construction Industry. 1980. 147.00 (*0-07-045308-X*) McGraw.

McGraw Hill Staff. McGraw Hill Dictionary of Scientific & Technical Terms: English-Arabic, 4 vols., Set. 1985. 295.00 (*0-86685-562-9*) Intl Bk Ctr.

McGraw-Hill Staff. McGraw-Hill Encyclopedia of Science & Technology, Vol. 1. 5th ed. 1982. 105.00 (*0-07-045461-2*) McGraw.

— McGraw-Hill Encyclopedia of World Biography, 12 vols., Vol. 1. 1975. 55.00 (*0-07-045271-7*) McGraw.

— McGraw-Hill Encyclopedia of World Biography, 12 Assocs., Vol. 2. 1975. 55.00 (*0-07-045272-5*) McGraw.

— McGraw-Hill Encyclopedia of World Biography, 12 vols., Vol. 3. 1975. 55.00 (*0-07-045273-3*) McGraw.

— McGraw-Hill Encyclopedia of World Biography, 12 Vols., Vol. 4. 1975. 55.00 (*0-07-045274-1*) McGraw.

— McGraw-Hill Encyclopedia of World Biography, 12 vols., Vol. 5. 1975. 55.00 (*0-07-045275-X*) McGraw.

— McGraw-Hill Encyclopedia of World Biography, 12 vols., Vol. 6. 1975. 55.00 (*0-07-045276-8*) McGraw.

— McGraw-Hill Encyclopedia of World Biography, 12 vols., Vol. 7. 1975. 55.00 (*0-07-045277-6*) McGraw.

— McGraw-Hill Encyclopedia of World Biography, 12 vols., Vol. 8. 1975. 55.00 (*0-07-045278-4*) McGraw.

— McGraw-Hill Encyclopedia of World Biography, 12 vols., Vol. 9. 1975. 55.00 (*0-07-045279-2*) McGraw.

— McGraw-Hill Encyclopedia of World Biography, 12 vols., Vol. 10. 1975. 55.00 (*0-07-045280-6*) McGraw.

— Mcgraw-Hill Encyclopedia of World Biography, 12 vols., Vol. 11. 1975. 55.00 (*0-07-045281-4*) McGraw.

— McGraw-Hill Encyclopedia of World Biography, 12 vols., Vol. 12. 1975. 55.00 (*0-07-045282-2*) McGraw.

— McGraw-Hill Encyclopedia of World Drama, 5 Vols., 1. 2nd ed. 1984. 72.00 (*0-07-045181-8*) McGraw.

— McGraw-Hill Encyclopedia of World Drama, 5 Vols., 2. 1984. 72.00 (*0-07-045182-6*) McGraw.

— McGraw-Hill Encyclopedia of World Drama, 5 Vols., 3. 1984. 72.00 (*0-07-045183-4*) McGraw.

— McGraw-Hill Encyclopedia of World Drama, 5 Vols., 4. 1984. 72.00 (*0-07-045184-2*) McGraw.

— McGraw-Hill Encyclopedia of World Drama, 5 Vols., 5. 1984. 72.00 (*0-07-045185-0*) McGraw.

— McGraw-Hill Multimedia Encyclopedia of Science & Technology. 1994. 1,300.00 (*0-07-046759-5*) McGraw.

— Standard & Poor's Stock & Bond Game 1994 Edition. 1994. pap. text ed. 19.95 (*0-07-052097-6*) McGraw.

McGraw, James R., ed. see Gregory, Dick.

***McGraw, John J.** My Thirty Years in Baseball. 265p. (C). 1995. pap. 12.95 (*0-8032-8139-0*, Bison Books) U of Nebr Pr.

— My Thirty Years in Baseball. LC 74-15746. (Popular Culture in America Ser.). (Illus.). 314p. 1975. reprint ed. 28.95 (*0-405-06381-4*) Ayer.

McGraw, Karen L. Creating Desktop Presentations That Work. 288p. 1991. pap. text ed. write for info. (*0-13-189390-4*) P-H.

— User Interfaces for Knowledge-Base Systems. 300p. 1992. text ed. 45.00 (*0-13-932674-X*) P-H.

McGraw, Kathleen M., jt. ed. see Lodge, Milton.

McGraw, Kenneth. Developmental Psychology. 840p. (C). 1987. text ed. 46.75 (*0-15-517623-4*) HB Coll Pubs.

McGraw, Lauren, jt. auth. see Jarvis McGraw, Eloise.

McGraw, Lora G. Guiding Strabismus Therapy. Corngold, Sally M., ed. (Illus.). 90p. (C). 1991. lib. bdg. 9.95 (*0-929780-02-7*) VisionExtension.

McGraw, M. Loretta, jt. auth. see Lydon, William T.

McGraw, Myrtle B. Growth: A Study of Johnny & Jimmie. LC 74-21422. (Classics in Child Development Ser.). 372p. 1975. reprint ed. 35.95 (*0-405-06471-3*) Ayer.

— The Neuromuscular Maturation of the Human Infant. (Classics in Developmental Medicine Ser.: No. 4). (Illus.). 117p. (C). 1991. 15.95 (*0-521-41329-X*, Pub. by Mc Keith Pr UK) Cambridge U Pr.

McGraw, Robert. The Rogue & the Horse. (Illus.). 32p. (Orig.). (J). (ps-3). 1993. pap. 5.95 (*0-9633385-0-1*) Imagin Pr.

McGraw, S. This Old New House. (Illus.). 32p. (J). (ps-8). 1989. 12.95 (*1-55037-035-9*, Pub. by Annick CN); pap. 4.95 (*1-55037-034-0*, Pub. by Annick CN) Firefly Bks Ltd.

***McGraw, Sheila.** Gifts Kids Can Make. (Illus.). 96p. (J). 1994. lib. bdg. 19.95 (*1-895565-36-7*); pap. 9.95 (*1-895565-35-9*) Firefly Bks Ltd.

— Je t'Aimera Toujours. (J). (ps-3). 1988. pap. 4.95 (*0-920668-49-6*) Firefly Bks Ltd.

— Papier Mache for Kids. (Illus.). 72p. (J). 1991. pap. 9.95 (*0-920668-93-3*) Firefly Bks Ltd.

— Papier Mache for Kids. (Illus.). 72p. (YA). 1991. 17.95 (*0-920668-92-5*) Firefly Bks Ltd.

— Papier-Mache Today. (Illus.). 144p. (Orig.). 1990. pap. 19.95 (*0-920668-85-2*) Firefly Bks Ltd.

— Soft Toys to Sew. (Illus.). 160p. (Orig.). 1992. pap. 19.95 (*1-895565-11-1*) Firefly Bks Ltd.

McGraw, Sheila & Cline, Paul. My Father's Hands. (Illus.). 32p. (J). 1992. 6.95 (*0-9625261-6-9*, Green Tiger S&S) S&S Childrens.

An Asterisk (*) at the beginning of an entry indicates that the title is appearing in BIP for the first time.

*McGray, Brian E. Handling Trophy Game: A How-to Field Guide for Hunters & Anglers. 72p. 1995. pap. 9.95 (1-886975-00-0) Goose Hse Pubns.
— How to Carve a Duck Decoy: A Step-by-Step Guide for Beginners. 1991. pap. 2.95 (0-486-26735-0) Dover.
McGray, K., ed. Understanding Heat Pumps, Ground Water, & Wells. 39p. 1983. 10.00 (1-56034-048-7, T040) Natl Water Well.
McGrayne, Sharon B. Nobel Prize Women in Science: Their Lives, Struggles & Momentous Discoveries. (Illus.). 368p. 1992. 24.00 (1-55972-146-4, Birch Ln Pr) Carol Pub Group.
Mcgreal, Ian. Great Thinkers of the Eastern World. 1995. 45.00 (0-06-270085-5, Harper Ref) HarpC.
McGreal, Ian P. Great Thinkers of the Western World: The Major Ideas & Classic Works of More than 100 Outstanding Western Philosophers, Physical & Social Scientists, Psychologists, Religious Writers & Theologians. LC 91-38362. 592p. 1992. 45.00 (0-06-270026-X, Harper Ref) HarpC.
McGreal, T., et al. Teacher Evaluation: Six Prescriptions for Success. LC 88-19308. 173p. (Orig.). 1988. pap. 11.95 (0-87120-153-4, 611-88048) Assn Supervision.
McGreal, Thomas L. Successful Teacher Evaluation. LC 83-71704. 176p. 1983. 8.75 (0-87120-120-8, 611-83300) Assn Supervision.
*McGreal, Wilfred. Guilt & Healing. 112p. (Orig.). 1994. reprint ed. pap. 12.95 (0-87061-206-9, 6901) Chr Classics.
McGreavy, C., ed. Computer Integrated Process Engineering. 314p. 1990. 105.00 (0-89116-973-3) Hemisp Pub.
— Polymer Reactor Engineering. LC 93-21352. 1993. write for info. (0-7514-0083-1, Pub. by Blackie Acad & Prof UK) Routledge Chapman & Hall.
— Polymer Reactor Engineering. LC 93-21352. 1993. 95.00 (1-56081-595-7) VCH Pubs.
McGreavy, C., tr. see Naka, Y., et al, eds.
McGreevey, Carla & Kelinson, Roberta. Blooming Health: Fun Health Activities for Language Enrichment Based on Bloom's Taxonomy. 80p. (J). (ps-3). 1991. pap. 15.95 (1-55999-204-2) LinguiSystems.
McGreevey, Carla & Kelinson, Roberta M. Blooming Math: Fun Activities for Beginning Math Based on Benjamin Bloom's Taxonomy. (J). (ps-3). 1988. pap. 15.95 (1-55999-027-9) LinguiSystems.
McGreevey, John. Seeds of Suspicion. 1952. pap. 2.50 (0-87129-195-9, S23) Dramatic Pub.
McGreevey, Thomas. Richard Aldington. LC 74-1231. (Twayne's English Authors Ser.). (C). 1974. lib. bdg. 17.95 (0-8290-2404-2) Irvington.
— Richard Aldington. LC 74-1231. (English Biography Ser.: No. 31). 1974. lib. bdg. 43.95 (0-8383-1785-5) M S G Haskell Hse.
— Thomas Stearns Eliot: A Study. LC 74-164026. (Studies in T. S. Eliot: No. 11). 1971. reprint ed. lib. bdg. 75.00 (0-8383-1327-2) M S G Haskell Hse.
McGreevey, Tom, jt. auth. see Yeck, Joanne L.
McGreevey, William. Social Security in Latin America: Issues & Options for the World Bank. (Discussion Paper Ser.: No. 110). 120p. 1990. pap. 7.95 (0-8213-1701-6, 11701) World Bank.
McGreevy, Ann. My Book of Things & Stuff: An Interest Questionnaire for Young Children. 1982. pap. 14.95 (0-936386-17-7) Creative Learning.
McGreevy, Joyce. The Wind Eagle. (Wonders! Ser.: Level 2). (Illus.). 16p. (Orig.). (J). (gr. 2-4). 1992. pap. text ed. 29.95 (1-56334-178-6); pap. text ed. 6.00 (1-56334-179-4) Hampton-Brown.
— The Wind Eagle: Level 2, 6-pack. (Wonders! Ser.). (Illus.). 16p. (Orig.). 1992. pap. 36.00 (1-56334-225-1) Hampton-Brown.
McGreevy, Linda F. The Life & Works of Otto Dix: German Critical Realist. LC 81-1895. (Studies in the Fine Arts: The Avant-Garde: No. 12). (Illus.). 164p. reprint ed. pap. 46.80 (0-8357-1165-X, 2070235) Bks Demand.
McGreevy, Mary. Dreams & Illusions. 20p. Date not set. write for info. (1-883331-02-1) Anderie Poetry.
McGreevy, Mary & Rosenbaum, Dora. To a Sailor: Poems. (Illus.). 58p. (Orig.). 1989. pap. 10.00 (0-685-28888-9) M McGreevy.
McGreevy, Michael. Death Is Only a Horizon: Thoughts in Time of Bereavement. (Illus.). 16p. 1990. reprint ed. pap. text ed. 1.95 (0-89243-446-5) Liguori Pubns.
*McGreevy-Nichols, Susan & Scheff, Helene. Building Dances: A Guide to Putting Movements Together. LC 95-8141. 128p. 1995. pap. write for info. (0-87322-573-2, BMCG 0573) Human Kinetics.
McGreevy, Patrick. Imagining Niagara: The Meaning & Making of Niagara Falls. LC 93-35720. (Illus.). 208p. 1994. lib. bdg. 25.00 (0-87023-916-3) U of Mass Pr.
— The Wall of Mirrors: Nationalism & Perceptions of the Border at Niagara Falls. (Borderlands Monograph Ser.: No. 5). 1-18p. (C). 1991. pap. text ed. 5.00 (0-9625055-4-4) Canadian-Amer Ctr.
McGreevy, Susan B. & Gorman, R. C. Maria: The Legend, the Legacy. LC 81-14512. (Illus.). 32p. (Orig.). 1982. 4.50 (0-86534-005-6) Sunstone Pr.
McGreevy, William J., jt. auth. see Brown, Sandra.
McGregor. Environmental Law & Enforcement. 1993. 59.95 (0-87371-745-7, KF3775) Lewis Pubs.
— Membrane Separation in Biotechnology. (Bioprocess Technology Ser.: Vol. 1). 408p. 1986. 145.00 (0-8247-7465-5) Dekker.
McGregor & Gulacy. Sabre. (Illus.). 1990. pap. 5.95 (0-913035-65-3) Eclipse Bks.
McGregor, A. M., ed. Immunology of Endocrine Diseases. (Immunology & Medicine Ser.). 1986. lib. bdg. 84.50 (0-85200-963-1) Kluwer Ac.
McGregor, Adrian. Greg Chappell. 1991. pap. 16.95 (0-7022-2342-5, Pub. by Univ Queensland Pr AT) Intl Spec Bk.
— King Wally: The Story of Wally Lewis. (Illus.). 247p. 1988. pap. 14.95 (0-7022-2037-X, Pub. by Univ Queensland Pr AT) Intl Spec Bk.
— Wally Lewis: The Last Emperor. pap. 18.95 (0-7022-2493-6, Pub. by Univ Queensland Pr AT) Intl Spec Bk.
McGregor, Alan, ed. & intro. Evolution, Creative Intelligence & Intergroup Competition. (Mankind Quarterly Monographs: No. 3). 96p. (Orig.). (C). 1986. pap. text ed. 12.00 (0-941694-30-5) Inst Study Man.
McGregor, Alan D., tr. see Nigst, H., et al.
McGregor, Alexander C. Counting Sheep: From Open Range to Agribusiness on the Columbia Plateau. LC 82-15903. (Illus.). 516p. 1989. pap. 14.95 (0-295-96814-1) U of Wash Pr.
McGregor, Andrew. The Fiji Fresh Ginger Industry: A Case Study in Non-Traditional Export Development. (Research Report Ser.: No. 10). 56p. 1989. pap. 6.00 (0-86638-109-0, Eastwest Ctr Pr) UH Pr.
McGregor, Andrew, jt. auth. see Sturton, Mark.
McGregor, Andrew, et al. Commercial Management Companies in the Agricultural Development of the Pacific Islands. LC 92-16884. (Research Report Ser.: No. 15). 56p. 1993. pap. text ed. 6.00 (0-86638-151-1) EW Ctr HI.
— Private Sector Development: Policies & Programs for the Pacific Islands. LC 92-40076. (Illus.). 264p. (C). 1993. pap. text ed. 12.95 (0-86638-155-4) EW Ctr HI.
*McGregor, Bede & Norris, Thomas, eds. The Beauty of Christ: An Introduction to the Theology of Hans Urs Von Balthasar. 296p. 1994. text ed. 39.95 (0-567-09697-1, Pub. by T & T Clark UK) Bks Intl VA.
*McGregor, Colin, et al. Fundamentals of University Mathematics. 250p. 1995. 29.95 (1-898563-09-8, Pub. by Albion Pubng UK) Paul & Co Pubs.
McGregor, Craig. Headliners: 14 Social Portraits. 1991. pap. 14.95 (0-7022-2344-1, Pub. by Univ Queensland Pr AT) Intl Spec Bk.
— Real Lies. LC 87-10770. 126p. (Orig.). 1987. pap. 14.95 (0-7022-2088-4, Pub. by Univ Queensland Pr AT) Intl Spec Bk.
McGregor, Craig, ed. Bob Dylan: The Early Years: A Retrospective. (Quality Paperbacks Ser.). (Illus.). 424p. 1990. reprint ed. pap. 13.95 (0-306-80416-6) Da Capo.
McGregor, D. The Human Side of Enterprise: 25th Anniversary Printing. 256p. 1985. text ed. write for info. (0-07-045098-6) McGraw.
McGregor, D. I., jt. ed. see Kimber, D.
McGregor, Diana, et al. Fizzle, Bubble, Pop & WOW! Simple Science Experiments for Young Children. 63p. (J). (ps-4). 1992. pap. 12.00 (0-9638539-0-2) Exper First Pr.
McGregor, Don. Dragonflame & Other Bedtime Nightmares. LC 77-17761. (Illus.). 1978. pap. 7.00 (0-934882-02-9) Fictioneer Bks.
— The Variable Syndrome: A Science Fiction Story. 144p. 1981. pap. 10.00 (0-934882-05-3) Fictioneer Bks.
McGregor, Don & Russell, P. Craig. Killraven. 64p. 1983. 5.95 (0-939766-59-0) Marvel Entmnt.
McGregor, Don & Turner, Dwayne. Black Panther "Panther's Prey", No. 1. 48p. 1991. 3.95 (0-87135-723-2) Marvel Entmnt.
— Black Panther "Panther's Prey", No. 2. 48p. 1991. 3.95 (0-87135-724-0) Marvel Entmnt.
— Black Panther "Panther's Prey", No. 3. 48p. 1991. 3.95 (0-87135-725-9) Marvel Entmnt.
— Black Panther "Panther's Prey", No. 4. 48p. 1991. 3.95 (0-87135-726-7) Marvel Entmnt.
McGregor, Donald. Louisiana Lil. (Orig.). 1980. pap. 1.75 (0-8439-0737-1) Dorchester Pub Co.
*McGregor, Duncan F.M. & Thompson, Donald A., eds. Geomorphology & Land Management in a Changing Environment. LC 94-24604. (British Geomorphological Research Group Symposia Ser.). 1995. text ed. 119.95 (0-471-95511-6) Wiley.
McGregor, Eugene B., Jr. Strategic Management of Human Knowledge, Skills, & Abilities: Workforce Decision Making in the Postindustrial Era. LC 90-20738. (Public Administration - Management Ser.). 376p. 1991. 37.95 (1-55542-307-8) Jossey-Bass.
McGregor, Frances M., jt. auth. see McGregor, Ian A.
McGregor, Francis C. After Plastic Surgery: Adaptation & Adjustment. 160p. (C). 1979. 39.95 (0-03-052131-9) Phoenix Soc.
McGregor, Gaile. Eccentric Visions: Reconstructing Australia. 360p. (C). 1994. pap. 35.00 (0-88920-229-X, Pub. by Wilfrid Laurier CN) Humanities.
— The Noble Savage in the New World Garden: Notes Toward a Syntactics of Place. LC 87-72549. 357p. (C). 1988. 34.95 (0-87972-416-1); pap. 17.95 (0-87972-417-X) Bowling Green Univ.
— The Wacousta Syndrome: Explorations in the Canadian Langscape. 488p. 1985. 47.50 (0-8020-2554-4); pap. 20.95 (0-8020-6570-8) U of Toronto Pr.
McGregor, Gordon. A Church College in the Twenty-First Century. (C). 1989. 59.00 (1-85072-080-0, Pub. by W Sessions UK); pap. 39.00 (1-85072-079-7, Pub. by W Sessions UK) St Mut.
McGregor, Gordon D. The Broken Pot Restored: Le Jeu de la Feuillee of Adam de la Halle. LC 90-84433. (Edward C. Armstrong Monographs on Medieval Literature: No. 6). 185p. (Orig.). 1991. pap. 14.95 (0-917058-76-3) French Forum.
McGregor, Graham & White, R. S. Reception & Response: Hearer Creativity & the Analysis of Spoken & Written Texts. 272p. 1990. 59.95 (0-415-01075-6, A4184) Routledge.
McGregor, Gregor I., et al. Massachusetts Environmental Law. LC 90-63090. 938p. 1991. ring bd. 125.00 (0-944490-34-4) Mass CLE.
McGregor, H. McGregor on Damages. (C). 1988. 1,125.00 (0-685-32718-3, Pub. by Witherby & Co UK) St Mut.
McGregor, Heather. A Guide to Glenwood Canyon. (Illus.). (Orig.). 1992. pap. 7.50 (0-9634382-0-4) Pika Pub.
— A Guide to Glenwood Canyon. 2nd rev. ed. (Illus.). 32p. (Orig.). 1993. pap. 7.50 (0-9634382-1-2) Pika Pub.
McGregor, Horace C., tr. see Cicero, Marcus T.
McGregor, Ian A. Fundamental Techniques of Plastic Surgery & Their Surgical Applications. 8th ed. (Illus.). 235p. 1989. pap. text ed. 49.95 (0-443-03353-6) Churchill.
McGregor, Ian A. & Howard, David J. Rob & Smith's Operative Surgery: Head & Neck, 2 vols., 1. 4th ed. (Illus.). 1991. 297.50 (0-7506-0296-1) Buttrwrth-Heinemann.
— Rob & Smith's Operative Surgery: Head & Neck, 2 vols., 2. 4th ed. (Illus.). 1991. write for info. (0-7506-0297-X) Buttrwrth-Heinemann.
— Rob & Smith's Operative Surgery: Head & Neck, 2 vols., Set. 4th ed. (Illus.). 1991. 595.00 (0-7506-0298-8) Buttrwrth-Heinemann.
McGregor, Ian A. & McGregor, Frances M. Cancer of the Face & Mouth: Pathology & Management for Surgeons. (Illus.). 624p. 1986. text ed. 215.00 (0-443-02455-3) Churchill.
*McGregor, Iona & Kidd, Dorothy. Bairns: Scottish Children in Photographs. (Illus.). 152p. 1995. 29.95 (0-948636-61-0, 610, Pub. by Natl Mus Scotland UK) A Schwartz & Co.
— Barins-Scottish Children in Photographs. (Illus.). 152p. (Orig.). 1995. pap. 22.50 (0-948636-65-3, Pub. by Natl Mus Scotland UK) A Schwartz & Co.
McGregor, J. & Watt, A. The Art of Graphics for the IBM PC. 448p. (C). 1986. pap. text ed. 31.25 (0-201-18089-8) Addison-Wesley.
McGregor, J. F. Radical Religion in the English Revolution. Reay, B., ed. 219p. 1986. pap. 24.95 (0-19-873045-4) OUP.
McGregor, J. L., ed. Monoclonal Antibodies & Human Blood Platelets. 328p. 1986. 112.00 (0-444-80780-2) Elsevier.
McGregor, James H. The Image of Antiquity in Boccaccio's Filocolo, Filostrato & Teseida. LC 89-32667. (Studies in Italian Culture: Literature in History: Vol. 1). 202p. (C). 1990. text ed. 44.95 (0-8204-0985-5) P Lang Pubs.
— The Shades of Aeneas: The Imitation of Vergil & the History of Paganism in Boccaccio's Filostrato, Filocolo, & Teseida. LC 90-42488. 144p. 1991. 30.00 (0-8203-1301-7) U of Ga Pr.
McGregor, James H., tr. see Guicciardini, Luigi.
McGregor, James J. & Watt, Alan H. Pascal for Science & Engineering. 350p. (C). 1983. pap. text ed. 120.00 (0-273-01889-2, Pub. by Pitman Pubng UK) St Mut.
— Simple Pascal. 190p. (C). 1981. pap. text ed. 80.00 (0-273-01704-7, Pub. by Pitman Pubng UK) St Mut.
McGregor, James L., jt. auth. see Berg, Paul.
McGregor, James P., ed. Alternative Careers for Political Scientists. 114p. (C). 1984. pap. text ed. 5.00x (0-915654-63-6) Am Political.
McGregor, Jeffrey P., jt. auth. see Barnett, Donald L.
McGregor, Jim. I Love Me Enough to Let Me Go. 2nd ed. 69p. reprint ed. pap. text ed. 7.95 (0-9633662-0-3) Willeo Pub.
— Tao of Discovery. 1994. pap. 4.99 (0-517-11561-1) Random.
McGregor, John C. The Pool & Irving Villages: A Study of Hopewell Occupation in the Illinois River Valley. LC 58-5605. (Illus.). 244p. reprint ed. 69.60 (0-8357-9694-9, 2015864) Bks Demand.
— Southwestern Archaeology. 2nd ed. LC 65-10079. (Illus.). 518p. 1982. pap. 19.95 (0-252-00989-4) U of Ill Pr.
McGregor, Joy & Nydell, Margaret. Update - Saudi Arabia. rev. ed. LC 90-83788. (Country Orientation Ser.). 192p. 1990. pap. text ed. 19.95 (0-933662-90-4) Intercult Pr.
McGregor, L., jt. ed. see Wochert, G.
McGregor, Leslie J. The Greek Text of Ezekiel: An Examination of Its Homogeneity. (Society of Biblical Literature & SCS Ser.). (C). 1985. 25.95 (0-89130-902-0, 06-0418); pap. 16.95 (0-89130-903-9) Scholars Pr GA.
McGregor, Lynn, et al. Learning Through Drama: Schools Council Drama Teaching Project. 1977. pap. text ed. 15.00 (0-435-18565-9) Heinemann.
McGregor, M. E. Making Sense of Algebra: Cognitive Processes: Influencing Comprehension. 139p. (C). 1991. pap. 71.00x (0-7300-1282-4, ECT403, Pub. by Deakin Univ AT) St Mut.
McGregor, M. J., jt. ed. see Dent, J. B.
*McGregor, Malcolm F. The Athenians & Their Empire. 244p. 1987. pap. 19.95 (0-7748-0269-3) U of Wash Pr.
McGregor, Malcolm F., jt. auth. see Bradeen, Donald W.
*McGregor, Maxine. Chris McGregor & the Brotherhood of Breath. (Illus.). 260p. 1995. lib. bdg. 43.00 (0-8095-6508-0) Borgo Pr.
— Chris McGregor & the Brotherhood of Breath: My Life with a South African Jazz Pioneer. (Illus.). (Orig.). 1995. pap. write for info. (0-318-72938-5) Bamberger.
McGregor, Merideth. Cowgirl. 32p. (J). 1992. 14.95 (0-8027-8170-5); lib. bdg. 15.85 (0-8027-8171-3) Walker & Co.
McGregor, P. K., ed. Playback & Studies of Animal Communication. (NATO ASI Series A, Life Sciences: Vol. 228). (Illus.). 224p. (C). 1992. 75.00 (0-306-44205-1, Plenum Pr) Plenum.
*McGregor, Pat, et al. Mastering the Internet. LC 94-69309. 825p. 1995. 39.99 (0-7821-1645-0) Sybex.
McGregor, Philip. The Rigger Black Book: A Shadowrun Sourcebook. Ippolito, Donna & Mulvihill, Sharon T., eds. (Shadowrun Ser.). 136p. (Orig.). 1991. pap. 15.00 (1-55560-169-3) FASA Corp.
McGregor, R., ed. McGregor's Who Owns Whom, 1993: The Southern African Edition. 1100p. (C). 1993. lib. bdg. 480.00 (1-85333-908-3) Kluwer Ac.
McGregor, R. C. An Outline of Hindi Grammar. (ENG & HIN.). 1991. 29.95 (0-8288-8467-6, F29977) Fr & Eur.
McGregor, R. M., jt. auth. see Corlett, M.
McGregor, R. R. Herbal Birth Control: A Brief History with Ancient & Modern Herbal Recipes. (Illus.). 64p. (Orig.). 1993. pap. 10.00 (0-9636602-0-9) Cloud Chief.
McGregor, R. S. Exercises in Spoken Hindi. (Illus.). 1971. audio 49.50 (0-521-07488-6) Cambridge U Pr.
— An Outline of Hindi Grammar. 2nd ed. 1977. 19.95 (0-19-560797-X) OUP.
— Outline of Hindi Grammar: With Exercises. 3rd ed. (Illus.). 336p. 1995. 56.00 (0-19-870007-5); audio, pap. 45.00 (0-19-870009-1); pap. 24.00 (0-19-870008-3) OUP.
McGregor, R. S., ed. Devotional Literature in South Asia: Current Research, 1985-1988. (University of Cambridge Oriental Publications: No. 46). 328p. (C). 1992. 105.00 (0-521-41311-7) Cambridge U Pr.
— The Oxford Hindi-English Dictionary. 1104p. 1994. 75.00 (0-19-864317-9) OUP.
McGregor, Rob R. Audition & Performance Preparation for Trumpet. (Orchestral Literature Studies: Vol. III). 160p. 1993. pap. 18.95 (0-9630856-2-X) Balquhidder.
— Audition & Performance Preparation for Trumpet, Vol. 1: Orchestral Literature Studies. 128p. 1992. pap. text ed. 17.95 (0-9630856-0-3) Balquhidder.
— Audition & Performance Preparation for Trumpet, Vol. 2: Orchestral Literature Studies. 112p. 1992. pap. text ed. 17.95 (0-9630856-1-1) Balquhidder.
McGregor, Rob R., jt. auth. see Stewart, Harry E.
McGregor, Robert & Meiers, Marion. Telling the Whole Story. (C). 1990. 75.00 (0-86431-082-X, Pub. by Aust Council Educ Res AT) St Mut.
McGregor, Roberta. Prehistoric Basketry of the Lower Pecos, Texas. LC 91-42880. (Monographs in World Archaeology: No. 6). 192p. (C). 1992. pap. text ed. 15.00 (0-9629110-4-6) Prehistory Pr.
McGregor, Ronald J. Buying a Business. Gerould, Philip, ed. LC 92-82770. (Small Business & Entrepreneurship Ser.). 200p. (Orig.). 1993. pap. 15.95 (1-56052-166-X) Crisp Pubns.
McGregor, Ronald L., jt. auth. see Fitch, Henry S.
McGregor, William. A Functional Grammar of Gooniyandi. LC 89-17877. (Studies in Language Companion: No. 22). xx, 618p. 1990. 133.00x (90-272-3025-0) Benjamins North Am.
McGrew, Annette, ed. see McGrew, Chuck.
McGrew, Anthony & Lewis, Paul. Global Politics: Globalization & the Nation State. (Illus.). (C). 1992. pap. text ed. 24.95 (0-7456-0756-X) Blackwell Pubs.
McGrew, Anthony G., jt. auth. see Maidment, Richard A.
*McGrew, Chuck. Don't Look Back: Terror Is Never Far Behind. McGrew, Annette, ed. (Illus.). 160p. (Orig.). 1995. pap. 19.00 (0-9641674-0-9) Mind Ventures.
McGrew, D. R. Traffic Accident Investigation & Physical Evidence. (Illus.). 132p. 1976. spiral bd. 27.95x (0-398-03503-2) C C Thomas.
McGrew, J. R., et al. The American Wine Society Presents "Growing Wine Grapes" Reichwage, Randall J., ed. (Illus.). 96p. (Orig.). 1993. pap. 10.95 (0-9619072-0-7) G W Kent.
McGrew, Julia H. & Thomas, George, eds. Sturlunga Saga, Vol. 2: Shorter Sagas of the Icelanders. LC 71-120536. (Library of Scandinavian Literature). (Illus.). 1974. lib. bdg. 49.00 (0-8057-3365-5); pap. text ed. 11.75 (0-8290-2035-7) Irvington.
McGrew, Julia H. & Thomas, George R., eds. Sturlunga Saga, Vol. 1: The Saga of Hvamm-Sturla & the Sage of the Icelanders. LC 71-120536. (Library of Scandinavian Literature). (Illus.). 1970. lib. bdg. 49.00 (0-8057-3364-7); pap. text ed. 9.75 (0-8290-2036-5) Irvington.
McGrew, Kevin S. Clinical Interpretation of the Woodcock-Johnson Tests of Cognitive Ability. rev. ed. LC 93-31670. 1994. write for info. (0-205-14701-1) Allyn.
— Clinical Interpretation of the Woodcock-Johnson Tests of Cognitive Ability. rev. ed. LC 93-31670. 269p. 1994. 43.95 (0-205-14801-8, Longwood Div) Allyn.
McGrew, Mac. American Metal Typefaces of the Twentieth Century. 2nd ed. (Illus.). 384p. 1993. 75.00 (0-938768-34-4); pap. 49.95 (0-938768-39-5) Oak Knoll.
*McGrew, Milt. Exploring the Power of AutoCAD. 1990. pap. 29.95 (0-8273-3694-2) Delmar.
McGrew, Myrtle W. Sweet Aroma, Falling in Love: Inspirational Thoughts from a Country Girl's Diary. LC 91-77500. (Illus.). 192p. (Orig.). 1992. pap. 8.95 (0-9624398-8-6) Abel II Pub.
McGrew, P. C. & McDaniel, William D. On-Line Text Management: Hyertext & Other Techniques. 242p. 1989. text ed. 51.00 (0-07-046263-1) McGraw.
Mcgrew, Patricia C. & McDaniel, William D. In-House Publishing in a Mainframe Environment. 2nd ed. 384p. 1991. text ed. 40.00 (0-07-046271-2) McGraw.
McGrew, Patrick. Landmarks of San Francisco. 1991. 49.50 (0-8109-3557-0) Abrams.
McGrew, Patrick & Julian, Robert, photos. Landmarks of Los Angeles. LC 93-21192. 1994. 49.50 (0-8109-3572-4) Abrams.
McGrew, R. Brownell. R. Brownell McGrew. LC 78-53113. (Illus.). 148p. 1978. 25.00 (0-913504-43-2) Lowell Pr.
McGrew, Roderick E. Paul I of Russia, 1754-1801. (Illus.). 424p. 1992. 79.00 (0-19-822567-9) OUP.

— Russia & the Cholera, Eighteen Twenty-Three to Eighteen Thirty-Two. (Illus.). 240p. 1965. 27.50 (0-299-03710-X) U of Wis Pr.

*McGrew, Timothy. The Foundations of Knowledge. 174p. (Orig.). (C). 1995. lib. bdg. 48.50 (0-8226-3042-7); pap. text ed. 22.95 (0-8226-3043-5) Rowman.

McGrew, Tony, jt. ed. see Simpson, John.

McGrew, W. C. Chimpanzee Material Culture: Implications for Human Evolution. (Illus.). 350p. (C). 1992. 79.95 (0-521-41303-6); pap. 27.95 (0-521-42371-6) Cambridge U Pr.

McGrew, William W. Land & Revolution in Modern Greece, 1800-1881: The Transition in the Tenure & Exploitation of Land from Ottoman Rule to Independence. LC 84-27789. (Illus.). 355p. 1986. 35.00 (0-87338-316-8) Kent St U Pr.

McGriff, Duane, et al. A Beginner's Guide to List Processing: The Other Side of Logo. (Illus.). 128p. 1986. pap. text ed. 15.00 (0-13-071705-3) P-H.

McGriffin, Craig R., jt. auth. see Davis, Peter T.

McGrindell, Andrew L. A Guide to Insurance Accounting. 293p. 1981. 230.00 (0-948691-02-6, Pub. by Witherby & Co UK) St Mut.

McGrinder, Michael. Heathen Piper. LC 78-59774. (Scene Award Ser.). 104p. (Orig.). 1979. pap. 5.00 (0-912292-56-3) The Smith.

McGroarty & Faltis, eds. Languages in School & Society: Policy & Pedagogy. (Contributions to the Sociology of Language Ser.: No. 58). x, 570p. (C). 1991. lib. bdg. 163.00 (0-89925-716-X) Mouton.

McGroarty, Mary E. & Faltis, Christian J., eds. Languages in School & Society: Policy & Pedagogy. 1991. 163.00 (3-11-012576-5) Mouton.

McGrory, David. Coventry: History & Guide. (History & Guide Ser.). (Illus.). 128p. 1992. pap. 16.00 (0-7509-0194-2) A Sutton Pub.

McGrotha, Bill. Seminoles! The First Forty Years. LC 87-51238. (Illus.). 256p. 1987. 20.95 (0-9613040-1-4) Talla Dem.

McGuane, et al. Fiction, Flyfishing & the Search for Innocence: Short Stories on Fly Fishing. (Sporting Life Ser.). (Illus.). 196p. 1994. 30.00 (0-913559-20-2) Birch Brook Pr.

— Fiction, Flyfishing & the Search for Innocence: Short Stories on Fly Fishing, Signal Edition. deluxe ed. (Sporting Life Ser.). (Illus.). 200p. 1994. 175.00 (0-614-03158-3) Birch Brook Pr.

McGuane, Thomas. The Bushwacked Piano. 1994. pap. 11.00 (0-394-25886-X) Random.

— The Bushwhacked Piano. LC 84-40014. (Vintage Contemporaries Ser.). 224p. 1984. pap. 11.00 (0-394-72642-1, Vin) Random.

— In the Crazies: Book & Portfolio. deluxe limited ed. (Illus.). 112p. 1984. 1,500.00 (0-916947-02-5) Winn Bks.

— Keep the Change. LC 90-50155. (Vintage Contemporaries Ser.). 240p. 1990. pap. 11.00 (0-679-73033-8, Vin) Random.

— Keep the Change. 1994. pap. 11.00 (0-394-25889-4) Random.

— Ninety-Two in the Shade. 1995. pap. 10.00 (0-679-75289-7) Random.

— Nobody's Angel. 1982. 14.50 (0-394-52264-8); pap. 6.95 (0-394-70565-3) Random.

— Nobody's Angel. (Vintage Contemporaries Ser.). 1986. pap. 11.00 (0-394-74738-0, Vin) Random.

— Nobody's Angel. 1994. pap. write for info. (0-394-25885-1) Random.

— Nothing But Blue Skies. 320p. 1992. 21.95 (0-395-54540-4) HM.

— Nothing but Blue Skies. 1994. pap. 12.00 (0-679-74778-8) Random.

— Outside Chance: Classic & New Essays on Sport. 1992. pap. 9.95 (0-395-60575-X) HM.

— Panama. 1995. pap. 10.00 (0-679-75291-9) Random.

— Panama. 176p. 1987. mass mkt. 10.00 (0-14-009908-5, Penguin Bks) Viking Penguin.

— Something to Be Desired. (Vintage Contemporaries Ser.). 1985. pap. 10.00 (0-394-73156-5, Vin) Random.

— Something to Be Desired. 1994. pap. 10.00 (0-394-25887-8) Random.

— Sons. deluxe ed. 1993. 75.00 (0-935716-58-0) Lord John.

— The Sporting Club. 1994. lib. bdg. 24.95x (1-56849-401-7) Buccaneer Bks.

— The Sporting Club. Date not set. pap. write for info. (0-679-75290-0) Random.

— Thomas McGuane: Three Complete Novels. LC 93-34511. 1994. 12.99 (0-517-10019-3, Pub. by Wings Bks) Random Hse Value.

— To Skin a Cat. LC 87-40093. (Vintage Contemporaries Ser.). 224p. 1987. pap. 10.00 (0-394-75521-9, Vin) Random.

— To Skin a Cat. 1994. pap. 10.00 (0-394-25888-6) Random.

McGuane, Tom. Cutting Horse. 1991. 29.95 (0-9627181-7-3) NCHA.

McGuaran, Joanna. By My Lady's Honor. 1994. mass mkt. 4.99 (0-440-21368-1) Dell.

McGucken, William. Biodegradable: Detergents & the Environment. LC 90-29035. (Environmental History Ser.: No. 12). (Illus.). 160p. 1991. 38.50 (0-89096-479-3) Tex A&M Univ Pr.

— Nineteenth-Century Spectroscopy: Development of the Understanding of Spectra, 1802-1897. LC 74-94886. 249p. reprint ed. pap. 71.00 (0-317-08471-2, 2011868) Bks Demand.

— Scientists, Society & State: The Social Relations of Science Movement in Great Britain, 1931-1947. LC 83-8320. 395p. 1984. 46.50 (0-8142-0351-5) Ohio St U Pr.

McGuckian, M. & Archer, Nuala. Two Women, Two Shores. (New Poets Ser.: Vol. 16). 64p. 1989. pap. 5.95 (0-932616-19-4) New Poets Chestnut Hills.

*McGuckian, Medbh. Captain Lavender. LC 94-61972. 83p. 1994. 15.95 (0-916390-67-5); pap. 9.95 (0-916390-66-7) Wake Forest.

— Marconi's Cottage. LC 91-67446. 112p. 1992. pap. 8.95 (0-916390-51-9) Wake Forest.

— On Ballycastle Beach. LC 87-40624. 59p. 1988. pap. 6.95 (0-916390-30-6) Wake Forest.

McGuckin, Henry E. Memoirs of a Wobbly. LC 87-80042. (First Person Ser.: No. 2). (Illus.). 96p. (Orig.). 1987. pap. 8.00 (0-88286-157-3) C H Kerr.

McGuckin, J. Patrick. New ASTM Standard: Tools for Complying with Phase 1. 1994. text ed., disk 75.00 (0-07-045174-5) McGraw.

McGuckin, John A. St. Cyril of Alexandria: The Christological Controversy: Its History, Theology, & Texts. LC 94-11851. (Supplements to Vigilae Christianae: Vol. 23). 1994. 145.75 (90-04-09990-5) E J Brill.

— The Transfiguration of Christ in Scripture & Tradition. LC 86-23892. (Studies in Bible & Early Christianity: Vol. 9). 352p. 1986. lib. bdg. 99.95 (0-88946-609-2) E Mellen.

McGuckin, Paul, tr. see St. Symeon.

McGuerty, David L. & Lester, Kent. The Complete Guide to Contracting Your Home: A Step-by-Step Method for Managing Home Construction. 2nd rev. ed. (Illus.). 288p. (Orig.). 1992. pap. 18.99 (1-55870-229-6) Betterway Bks.

McGuffey, Allan, jt. auth. see Cobb, Gena.

McGuffey, Verne. Differences in the Activities of Teachers in Rural One-Teacher Schools & of Grade Teachers in Cities. LC 79-177026. (Columbia University. Teachers College. Contributions to Education Ser.: No. 346). reprint ed. 22.50 (0-404-55346-X) AMS Pr.

McGuffey, W. H. McGuffey's New High School Reader. 1974. 250.00 (0-87968-147-0) Gordon Pr.

McGuffey, William H. McGuffey Readers, 9 vols., Set. 1973. lib. bdg. 2,500.00 (0-8490-0571-X) Gordon Pr.

— McGuffey's Eclectic Readers: Primer Through the Sixth Revised Editions, Set. 1920. Boxed set. boxed 49.95 (0-442-23989-0) Van Nos Reinhold.

— McGuffeys Eclectic Spelling Book. 7.95 (0-317-64211-1) Van Nos Reinhold.

— McGuffey's Illustrated Address Book. 1980. text ed. 12.95 (0-442-21257-7) Van Nos Reinhold.

— The Original McGuffey's Eclectic Series, 7 Vols. (J). (gr. k-12). 1982. reprint ed. 89.95 (0-88062-014-5) Mott Media.

— Original McGuffey's Eclectic Series, 8 vols., Set. 1982. Boxed set, incl. tchr's. guide. teacher ed, boxed 99.95 (0-88062-029-3) Mott Media.

McGuffie, Chris. Working in Metal Management & Labour in the Metal Industries of Europe & the U. S. A., 1890-1914. (C). 1985. text ed. 29.95 (0-85036-312-8, Pub. by Merlin Pr UK) Humanities.

McGuffie, K., jt. auth. see Henderson-Sellers, A.

McGuffie, T. H. The Siege of Gibraltar, Seventeen Seventy-Nine to Seventeen Eighty-Three. LC 64-25508. (Illus.). 1965. 15.95 (0-8023-1074-5) Dufour.

*McGuffin, Gary & McGuffin, Joan. Superior: Journeys on an Inland Sea. (Illus.). 160p. 1995. write for info. (1-55971-483-2) NorthWord.

McGuffin, Gary & McGuffin, Joanie. Where Rivers Run: A Six Thousand Mile Exploration of Canada by Canoe. (Illus.). 272p. 1989. 23.95 (0-913276-54-5) Stone Wall Pr.

McGuffin, Joan, jt. auth. see McGuffin, Gary.

McGuffin, Joanie, jt. auth. see McGuffin, Gary.

McGuffin, John. In Praise of Poteen. 2nd ed. (Irish Life & Lore Ser.). (Illus.). 112p. 1989. pap. 12.95 (0-86281-213-5, Pub. by Appletree Pr IE) Irish Bks Media.

McGuffin, Peter & Murray, Robin M., eds. New Genetics of Mental Illness. 288p. 1991. text ed. 95.00 (0-7506-0029-2) Buttrwrth-Heinemann.

McGugan, Jim. Josepha. LC 94-6603. (J). 1994. 13.95 (0-8118-0802-5) Chronicle Bks.

Mcgugan, Peter M. Beating Burnout: The Survival Guide for the 90s. 2nd ed. Hickman, Irene, ed. (Illus.). 224p. 1991. pap. write for info. (0-9694312-0-1) Potentls Pr.

McGugan, Peter M. When Something Changes Everything: How to Recover from the Zero Zone of Loss & Change. (Illus.). 200p. (Orig.). 1991. pap. text ed. 12.95 (0-9694312-1-X) Potentls Pr.

McGuigan, F. J. Biological Psychology: A Cybernetic Science. LC 93-35572. 1993. text ed. write for info. (0-13-146655-0) P-H.

McGuigan, F. J. & Ban, Thomas A., eds. Critical Issues in Psychology, Psychiatry & Physiology: A Memorial to W. Horsley Gantt. (Monographs in Psychobiology: Vol. 2). 392p. 1987. text ed. 67.00 (2-88124-137-9) Gordon & Breach.

McGuigan, Frank J. Calm Down: Stress Control. 256p. 1992. per. 32.00 (0-8403-7172-1) Kendall-Hunt.

— Cognitive Psychophysiology: Principles of Covert Behavior. LC 78-18542. (Century Psychology Ser.). 1978. 34.95 (0-13-139519-X) P-H.

— Cognitive Psychophysiology: Principles of Covert Behavior. LC 78-18542. (Century Psychology Ser.). 544p. reprint ed. pap. 155.10 (0-8357-3403-X, 2039660) Bks Demand.

— Experimental Psychology. 5th ed. 400p. (C). 1990. Casebound. boxed write for info. (0-13-295023-5) P-H.

— Experimental Psychology: Methods of Research. 6th ed. LC 92-33356. 1992. text ed. 39.95 (0-13-291014-4) P-H.

— Psychophysiological Measurement of Covert Behavior: A Guide for the Laboratory. LC 79-18482. (Illus.). 143p. reprint ed. pap. 40.80 (0-8357-4208-3, 2036985) Bks Demand.

McGuigan, Frank J., ed. Thinking: Studies of Covert Language Processes. LC 66-15745. (Century Psychology Ser.). (Illus.). 1966. pap. text ed. 16.95 (0-89197-450-4) Irvington.

McGuigan, Frank J., et al, eds. Stress & Tension Control, Vol. 2. 420p. 1985. 85.00 (0-306-41815-0, Plenum Pr) Plenum.

— Stress & Tension Control, Vol. 3: Stress Management. (Illus.). 298p. 1989. 85.00 (0-306-43327-3, Plenum Pr) Plenum.

McGuigan, James R. & Moyer, R. Charles. Managerial Economics. 6th ed. Schiller, ed. LC 92-18132. 650p. (C). 1993. text ed. 61.50 (0-314-01220-6) West Pub.

McGuigan, Jim. Cultural Populism. LC 92-248. 240p. 1992. 79.95 (0-415-06294-2, A7750); pap. 15.95 (0-415-06295-0, A7754) Routledge.

McGuigan, Jim & Gray, Ann, eds. Studying Culture: An Introductory Reader. LC 93-7215. 256p. 1993. 60.00 (0-340-58793-8, B2562, Pub. by E Arnold UK); pap. 16.95 (0-340-55628-5, Pub. by E Arnold UK) Routledge Chapman & Hall.

McGuigan, K., ed. Flexible Manufacturing for Small to Medium Enterprises. 200p. 1988. 119.00 (0-387-50077-4) Spr-Verlag.

McGuigan, Mary A. Cloud Dancer. LC 93-5562. 128p. (J). (gr. 6-8). 1994. text ed. 14.95 (0-684-19632-8, C Scribner Sons Young) S&S Childrens.

McGuigan, Patrick B. & Pascale, Jon S., eds. Crime & Punishment in Modern America. LC 86-82505. (Illus.). 430p. 1986. 26.25 (0-942522-00-1) Free Congr Res.

McGuigan, Patrick B. & Rader, Randall R., eds. A Blueprint for Judicial Reform. LC 81-70375. (Orig.). 1981. pap. text ed. 27.25 (0-942522-08-7) Free Congr Res.

McGuigan, Patrick B. & Weyrich, Dawn M. Ninth Justice: The Fight for Bork. LC 89-23661. 340p. (C). 1990. 21.95 (0-942522-15-X) Free Congr Res.

McGuiggan, Jim. The Book of Ezekiel (Commentary) (Looking into the Bible Ser.). 366p. 1979. text ed. 13.95 (1-56794-009-9, C2232); pap. 9.95 (1-56794-008-0, C2231) Star Bible.

— The Book of Revelation (Commentary) (Looking into the Bible Ser.). 332p. 1976. text ed. 13.95 (1-56794-010-2, C2238) Star Bible.

— The Irish Papers: Lessons from Life. 45p. (Orig.). 1992. pap. 2.95 (0-940999-92-7, C2251) Star Bible.

— The Reign of God. 120p. (Orig.). 1992. pap. 6.95 (0-940999-88-9, C2226) Star Bible.

McGuineas, Anne, ed. see Thiel, Michael F.

*McGuiness & Dapper. Fifty State Construction Lien & Bond Law Vol. 3, Vol. 3. (Construction Law Library). Date not set. text ed. 39.95 (0-471-11039-6) Wiley.

McGuiness, John. Teachers, Pupils & Behavior: A Managerial Approach. Lang, Peter & Best, Ron, eds. (Studies in Pastoral Care, Personal & Social Education). (Illus.). 176p. 1994. text ed. 70.00 (0-304-32784-0); pap. text ed. 24.95 (0-304-32785-9) Cassell.

McGuiness, Kenneth C., jt. auth. see Potter, Edward E.

McGuiness, Mary, ed. Myers-Briggs Type Indi-cator: Australian Perspectives. (C). 1992. 75.00 (0-86431-128-1, Pub. by Aust Council Educ Res AT) St Mut.

McGuinn, Dana. Bargain Hunters Guide - Atlanta-Athens Area, 1992. (Illus.). 224p. 1992. pap. 8.95 (1-880163-03-9) Firefly Pub.

— Bargain Hunters Guide - Georgia & Atlanta: Descriptive Reviews of over 350 Consignment Shops, Outlets, Food, Fleas & Antiques & Entertainment. (Illus.). 245p. 1993. pap. 10.95 (1-880163-04-7) Firefly Pub.

— Six Cups! Six Bowls! Six Spoons! Humorous Hints from a Formerly Frazzled Mom on How to Get Your House in Order & Keep It That Way. (Illus.). 48p. 1993. pap. 6.95 (1-880163-06-3); vhs 18.95 (1-880163-07-1) Firefly Pub.

McGuinn, Dana, jt. auth. see Johnson, Joe A.

*McGuinn, Doug. Cold Toes & Busted TVs. 128p. (Orig.). 1994. pap. 8.95 (0-614-01954-0) Dan River Pr.

— Just Plain Heroes. LC 90-70454. 256p. (Orig.). 1993. pap. 9.00 (1-56002-111-X, Univ Edtns) Aegina Pr.

McGuinn, Nicholas, ed. see Stevenson, Robert L.

McGuinn, Rex. Landing in Minneapolis. 72p. (Orig.). 1993. pap. 8.95 (1-879934-19-1) St Andrews NC.

McGuinn, Y., jt. auth. see Theodore, L.

McGuinn, Young C., jt. auth. see Theodore, Louis.

McGuinne, Dermot. Irish Type Design: A History of Printing Types in the Irish Character. (Illus.). 224p. 1992. text ed. 47.50 (0-7165-2463-5, Pub. by Irish Acad Pr IE) Intl Spec Bk.

McGuinnes, Celia & Whelan, Leo. Report on the Australian Royal Commission on Aboriginal & Torres Strait Islander Deaths in Custody. Minnesota Lawyers International Human Rights Committee Staff, ed. 32p. (Orig.). 1988. pap. 3.00 (0-929293-18-5) MN Advocates.

McGuinness, Arthur E. George Fitzmaurice. (Irish Writers Ser.). 96p. 1975. 8.50 (0-8387-7870-4); pap. 1.95 (0-8387-7980-8) Bucknell U Pr.

— Seamus Heaney: Poet & Critic. LC 92-43156. (Irish Studies: Vol. 3). 199p. (C). 1994. text ed. 39.95 (0-8204-2065-4) P Lang Pubs.

McGuinness, B. F., ed. see Wittgenstein, Ludwig.

McGuinness, Brian & Oliveri, Gianluigi, eds. The Philosophy of Michael Dummett. LC 94-9709. (Synthese Library: Vol. 239). 402p. (C). 1994. lib. bdg. 113.00 (0-7923-2804-3) Kluwer Ac.

*McGuinness, Brian & Von Wright, G. H., eds. Ludwig Wittgenstein: Cambridge Letters: Correspondence with Russell, Keynes, Moore, Ramsey & Sraffa. 200p. (C). 1995. write for info. (0-631-19015-5) Blackwell Pubs.

McGuinness, Brian F. Wittgenstein: A Life: Young Ludwig, 1889-1921. 321p. (C). 1988. 30.00 (0-520-06451-8) U CA Pr.

McGuinness, Brian F., ed. Ernst Mach: Knowledge & Error. Foulkes, Paul, tr. LC 73-75641. (Vienna Circle Collection: Vol. 3). 432p. 1975. lib. bdg. 140.00 (90-277-0281-0); pap. text ed. 84.00 (90-277-0282-9) Kluwer Ac.

— Friedrich Waismann: Philosophical Papers. Kaal, Hans, tr. (Vienna Circle Collection Ser.: No. 8). 1977. lib. bdg. 84.00 (90-277-0712-X); pap. text ed. 50.00 (90-277-0713-8) Kluwer Ac.

— Hans Hahn Empiricism, Logic & Mathematics: Philosophical Papers. Kaal, Hans, tr. (Vienna Circle Collection Ser.: No. 13). 164p. 1980. lib. bdg. 64.00 (90-277-1065-1) Kluwer Ac.

— Hans Hahn Empiricism, Logic & Mathematics: Philosophical Papers. Kaal, Hans, tr. (Vienna Circle Collection Ser.: No. 13). 164p. 1980. pap. text ed. 36.50 (90-277-1066-X) Kluwer Ac.

— The Infinite in Mathematics. (Vienna Circle Collection: No. 9). 1978. lib. bdg. 94.00 (90-277-0847-9) Kluwer Ac.

— Moritz Schlick. 1985. lib. bdg. 61.50 (90-277-2096-7) Kluwer Ac.

— Unified Science. (C). 1987. lib. bdg. 154.50 (90-277-2484-9) Kluwer Ac.

— Wittgenstein & His Times. LC 81-52670. (C). 1982. 15.00 (0-226-55881-9) U Ch Pr.

McGuinness, Brian F., ed. see Boltzmann, Ludwig.

McGuinness, Dee. How to Make Money with Desktop Publishing: Guide for a Small Business Owner. (Illus.). 112p. (Orig.). 1989. pap. 11.95 (0-317-93980-7) Adare Pub.

McGuinness, Diane, ed. Dominance, Aggression & War. LC 86-8191. 328p. (C). 1987. text ed. 24.95 (0-89226-035-1, ICUS) Paragon Hse.

McGuinness, Elizabeth A. People Waging Peace: Stories of Americans Striving for Peace & Justice in the World Today. LC 87-73030. (Illus.). 416p. 1988. 19.95 (0-944758-10-X); pap. 13.95 (0-944758-11-8) Alberti Pr.

McGuinness, Frank. Observe the Sons of Ulster Marching Towards the Somme. 72p. (Orig.). 1986. pap. 8.95 (0-571-14611-2) Faber & Faber.

— Someone Who'll Watch over Me. 96p. (Orig.). 1993. pap. 8.95 (0-571-16804-3) Faber & Faber.

McGuinness, Jamie. Trekking in the Everest Region. (Nepal Trekking Guides Ser.). (Illus.). 240p. (Orig.). 1994. pap. 12.95 (1-873756-02-X, Pub. by Trlblazer Pubn UK) Seven Hills Bk.

*McGuinness, Keith P. Charting the Mexican Labyrinth: A Practical Guide to Success in Mexico. (Illus.). (Orig.). 1995. pap. 48.00 (0-9623014-9-3) HPH Partners.

McGuinness, Kenneth C. How to Take a Case Before the National Labor Relations Board. 4th rev. ed. LC 74-32565. 557p. reprint ed. pap. 158.80 (0-685-15903-5, 2026797) Bks Demand.

McGuinness, Nora A. The Literary Universe of Jack B. Yeats. LC 90-2536. 288p. 1992. text ed. 45.95 (0-8132-0737-1) Cath U Pr.

McGuinness, Peter J., jt. auth. see Shapiro, Irving.

McGuinness, Tony, jt. ed. see Clarke, Roger.

McGuinness, William J. & Stein, Benjamin J. Building Technology: Mechanical & Electrical Systems. LC 76-14961. 596p. 1977. teacher ed 5.00 (0-471-01601-2); text ed. 79.95 (0-471-58433-9) Wiley.

*McGuinnis, Alan L. The Friendship Factor - Confidence, 2 vols. in 1. 384p. 1995. 11.95 (1-56865-145-7, GuildAmerica) Dblday Bk Music.

McGuire. American Garden Design. 1994. 22.00 (0-671-79921-5, P-H Gardening) P-H Gen Ref & Trav.

— Pumps for Chemical Processing. 304p. 1990. 110.00 (0-8247-8324-7) Dekker.

McGuire, jt. auth. see Campbell.

McGuire, jt. auth. see Harvey.

McGuire, Alistair, et al, eds. Providing Health Care: The Economics of Alternative Systems of Finance & Delivery. (Illus.). 300p. 1994. reprint ed. pap. 19.95 (0-19-828872-7) OUP.

*McGuire, Anna R. Twelve Months. (Illus.). 32p. (Orig.). (J). (ps-2). 1995. pap. 6.95 (0-9646240-0-1) Phoenix WI.

McGuire, Bill & Wheeler, Leslie. American Cultural Leaders: From Colonial Times to Present. Ludwig, Richard et al, eds. 550p. 1993. lib. bdg. 65.00 (0-87436-673-9) ABC-CLIO.

— American Social Leaders: From Colonial Times to Present. Gerstle, Gary & MacPherson, James, eds. 500p. 1993. lib. bdg. 65.00 (0-87436-633-X) ABC-CLIO.

McGuire, Brian P. Brother & Lover: Aelred of Rievaulx. LC 93-49884. 256p. 1994. 22.95 (0-8245-1405-X) Crossroad NY.

— The Cistercians in Denmark: Their Attitudes, Roles, & Functions in Medieval Society. (Cistercian Studies: No. 35). 1982. 35.00 (0-87907-835-9) Cistercian Pubns.

— The Difficult Saint: Bernard of Clairvaux & His Tradition. (Cistercian Studies: No. 126). 302p. 1991. write for info. (0-87907-626-7) Cistercian Pubns.

— Friendship & Community: The Monastic Experience, 350-1250. 1988. 26.95 (0-317-68106-0); pap. 11.95 (0-317-68107-9) Cistercian Pubns.

McGuire, C. B. Rational Investment Behavior in the Face of Floods. LC 79-135090. 151p. 1969. 29.00 (0-403-04517-7) Scholarly.

McGuire, C. B. & Radner, Roy, eds. Decision & Organization. 2nd ed. LC 86-11407. 400p. 1987. pap. text ed. 15.95 (0-8166-1365-6) U of Minn Pr.

McGuire, Carl, jt. auth. see El Mallakh, Ragaei.

McGuire, Charles. The Legal Environment of Business. 2nd ed. 672p. (C). 1989. write for info. (0-675-21067-4, Merrill Pub Co); pap. write for info. (0-675-21171-9, Merrill Pub Co) Macmillan.

*McGuire, Christine. Until Proven Guilty. Rubenstein, Julie, ed. 384p. 1995. mass mkt. 5.99 (0-671-75012-7) PB.

An Asterisk (*) at the beginning of an entry indicates that the title is appearing in BIP for the first time.

McGuire, Christine & Norton, Carla. Perfect Victim. 1989. mass mkt. 5.50 (0-440-20442-9) Dell.

McGuire, Christine H., et al. Handbook of Health Professions Education. LC 83-48160. (Jossey-Bass Higher Education Ser.). (Illus.). 571p. reprint ed. pap. 162.80 (0-8357-4910-X, 2037840) Bks Demand.

***McGuire, David D.** Lori Longhorn. 180p. (J). Date not set. pap. 7.95 (0-7610-0343-6) NW Pub.

***McGuire, Deborah, et al.** Cancer Pain Management. 2nd ed. (Nursing Ser.). 500p. 1995. 64.95 (0-86720-725-6) Jones & Bartlett.

McGuire, Dennis J. Healing the Wounds of Childhood: A Recovery Guide for Adult Children of Dysfunctional Families. 192p. (Orig.). 1990. pap. 9.95 (0-399-51615-8, Perigree Bks) Berkley Pub.

McGuire, Diane K. Gardens of America: Three Centuries of Design. LC 89-50584. (Illus.). 144p. 1989. 19.98 (0-934738-53-X) Thomasson-Grant.

McGuire, Diane K., ed. Beatrix Farrand's Plant Book for Dumbarton Oaks. LC 80-12169. (Illus.). 1980. pap. 15.00 (0-88402-102-5) Dumbarton Oaks.

McGuire, Diane K. & Fern, Lois, eds. Beatrix Jones Farrand, Fifty Years of American Landscape Architecture: Colloquium on the History of Landscape Architecture, Vol. 8. LC 82-2439. (Illus.). 232p. 1982. 24.00 (0-88402-106-8) Dumbarton Oaks.

McGuire, Donald D. The Country Kids' Encounter with Buttsy. (J). 1992. 7.95 (0-533-10346-0) Vantage.

McGuire, Ed. Guitar Fingerboard Harmony. 1993. 9.95 (1-56222-042-X, 93398) Mel Bay.

McGuire, Edward, jt. ed. see Kursh, Elroy D.

McGuire, Francis A., ed. Computer Technology & the Aged: Implications & Applications for Activity Programs. LC 85-21999. (Activities, Adaptation & Aging Ser.: Vol. 8, No. 1). 119p. 1986. text ed. 29.95 (0-86656-481-0) Haworth Pr.

McGuire, Francis A., et al, eds. Therapeutic Humor with the Elderly. LC 92-43465. (Activities, Adaptation & Aging Ser.: No. 17(1)). (Illus.). 116p. 1993. lib. bdg. 24.95 (1-56024-310-4) Haworth Pr.

McGuire, Francis G. Security Intelligence Sourcebook. large type ed. (Illus.). 304p. (Orig.). (C). 1990. pap. 169.95 (0-929457-02-1) Intrsts Ltd.

McGuire, Frank G., ed. Security Intelligence Incident Log, 1990-91. 84p. (Orig.). 1992. pap. 39.95 (0-929457-03-X) Intrsts Ltd.

McGuire, Frederick L. Psychology Aweigh! A History of Clinical Psychology in the United States Navy, 1900-1988. LC 90-279. 266p. 1990. 40.00 (1-55798-086-1) Am Psychol.

McGuire, G, jt. auth. see Miller, H.

McGuire, Gary E., ed. Characterization of Semiconductor Materials: Principles & Methods, Vol. 1. LC 89-30273. (Illus.). 330p. 1989. 64.00 (0-8155-1200-7) Noyes.

— Semiconductor Materials & Process Technology Handbook: For Very Large Scale Integration (VLSI) & Ultra Large Scale Integration (ULSI) LC 87-31529. (Illus.). 675p. 1988. 92.00 (0-8155-1150-7) Noyes.

McGuire, George T. A Gentle Wind Came with Us. LC 88-51485. 314p. 1989. 12.95 (1-55523-203-5) Winston-Derek.

McGuire, J. E. & Tamny, Martin. Certain Philosophical Questions: Newton's Trinity Notebook. LC 82-22200. 512p. 1983. 125.00 (0-521-23164-7) Cambridge U Pr.

McGuire, J. J., jt. ed. see Rustum, Y.

***McGuire, J. V., et al.** Bridges: A Self-Esteem Activity Book for Students in Grades 4-6. LC 94-30011. (Illus.). (J). (gr. 4-6). 1994. 29.95 (0-205-16504-4, Longwood Div) Allyn.

McGuire, Jack. My Pop: Poems of Praise. LC 88-35619. (Illus.). (Orig.). 1989. pap. 4.00 (0-915541-20-3) Star Bks Inc.

McGuire, Jacqueline & Richman, Naomi. Pre-School Behavior Checklist (PBCL) 1988. teacher ed, ring bd. 45.00 (0-87879-638-X); lp 12.00 (0-87879-639-8); 4.00 (0-685-44973-4); 12.00 (0-685-44974-2) Acad Therapy.

***McGuire, James.** What Works: Reducing Reoffending : Guidelines from Research & Practice. LC 94-44567. (Offender Rehabilitation Ser.). 1995. text ed. 32.95 (0-471-95053-X) Wiley.

***McGuire, James, ed.** What Works: Reducing Reoffending : Guidelines from Research & Practice. LC 94-44564. (Offender Rehabilitation Ser.). 1995. pap. 26.00 (0-471-95686-4) Wiley.

McGuire, James & Priestley, Philip. Life after School: A Social Skills Curriculum. (Illus.). 230p. 1981. text ed. 59.00 (0-08-025192-7, Pergamon Pr) Elsevier.

— Offending Behavior: Skills & Stratagems for Going Straight. LC 84-18395. 256p. 1985. text ed. 32.50 (0-312-58208-0) St Martin.

McGuire, James B., jt. auth. see Clark, David R.

McGuire, James E. & Lee, Jasper S. Advertising & Display: Promotion in Agribusiness. (Career Preparation for Agriculture-Agribusiness Ser.). (Illus.). 1979. text ed. 16.96 (0-07-045129-X) McGraw.

McGuire, James E., jt. auth. see Bogen, James.

McGuire, James L., jt. auth. see Schlotzhauer, Tammi L.

McGuire, James L., jt. auth. see Sholtzhauer, Tammi L.

McGuire, James P. Hermann Lungkwitz: Romantic Landscapist on the Texas Frontier. (Illus.). 245p. 1983. 35.00 (0-292-73026-8) U of Tex Pr.

***McGuire, James R.** The Sumerian Roots of the American Preamble. pap. 19.95 (0-685-72080-2) Lough Erne.

McGuire, James T. The Sumerian Roots of the American Preamble. LC 93-81291. (Illus.). 285p. (Orig.). Date not set. pap. 19.95 (0-9640880-0-2) Lough Erne.

McGuire, Jerry. Flagpole Dance. LC 90-6487. (Contemporary Poets Ser.). 80p. (Orig.). 1990. 15.00 (0-89924-033-X); pap. 8.00 (0-89924-070-4) Lynx Hse.

— Write Like a Pro! A Guide for Freelance Writers. (Illus.). 224p. (Orig.). (C). 1992. pap. 22.95 (0-9632004-0-2) J L McGuire.

McGuire, Jerry, jt. ed. see Myrsiades, Kostas.

McGuire, John. Basketry: The Nantucket Tradition. LC 89-83931. (Illus.). 144p. 1990. 24.95 (0-937274-50-X) Lark Books.

— Basketry: The Shaker Tradition. LC 87-83653. (Illus.). 128p. (Orig.). 1989. 24.95 (0-937274-46-1) Lark Books.

McGuire, John E. Old New England Splint Baskets & How to Make Them. LC 85-61526. (Illus.). 100p. (Orig.). 1985. pap. 12.95 (0-88740-045-0) Schiffer.

McGuire, John E., jt. auth. see Freeman, Chester D.

McGuire, John M., Jr. An Architect's Rome. LC 94-1268. (Architecture-Travel Ser.). (Illus.). 176p. 1994. pap. 18.95 (0-8212-1954-5) Bulfinch Pr.

McGuire, Joseph, jt. ed. see Ohkawara, Akira.

McGuire, Judith S. & Popkin, Barry M. Helping Women Improve Nutrition in the Developing World: Beating the Zero Sum Game. (Technical Paper Ser.: No. 114). 102p. 1990. 7.95 (0-8213-1415-7, 11415) World Bank.

***McGuire, Judith W.** Diary of a Southern Refugee During the War. 368p. 1995. pap. 12.00 (0-8032-8223-0, Bison Books) U of Nebr Pr.

— Diary of a Southern Refugee, During the War. LC 72-2614. (American Women Ser.: Images & Realities). 364p. 1974. reprint ed. 32.95 (0-405-04468-2) Ayer.

***McGuire, Kathryn S. & Lee, James W., eds.** New Texas '94: Poetry & Fiction. 171p. (Orig.). 1994. pap. 14.95 (1-885196-04-0) Ctr Tex Studies.

McGuire, Kenneth B. State of the Art in Community-Based Education in the American Community College. Harlacher, Ervin L., ed. LC 88-151056. 83p. reprint ed. pap. 25.00 (0-7837-2482-9, 2042638) Bks Demand.

McGuire, Kenneth J. Impressions from Our Most Worthy Competitor. LC 84-72770. 88p. 1984. 14.00 (0-935406-59-X) Am Prod & Inventory.

McGuire, Kevin. Building Outdoor Play Structures. LC 94-13704. (Illus.). 144p. 1994. 24.95 (0-8069-0808-4) Sterling.

— Wood on Wheels: Making Toys That Rock & Roll, Wiggle & Shake. LC 94-37136. (Illus.). 144p. 1995. pap. 16.95 (0-8069-1286-3) Sterling.

— Woodworking for Kids: Forty Fabulous, Fun, & Useful Things for Kids to Make. LC 93-20489. (Illus.). 160p. (J). (gr. 4 up). 1993. 21.95 (0-8069-0429-1) Sterling.

— Woodworking for Kids: Forty Fabulous, Fun & Useful Things for Kids to Me. (Illus.). 144p. 1994. pap. 13.95 (0-8069-0430-5) Sterling.

McGuire, Kevin T. The Supreme Court Bar: Legal Elites in the Washington Community. LC 93-3074. (Constitutionalism & Democracy Ser.). 320p. (C). 1993. 40.00 (0-8139-1449-3) U Pr of Va.

***Mcguire, Kim.** The Irish Wedding Book: Everything You Need to Plan a Wedding. 192p. 1995. pap. 18.95 (0-86327-376-9) Dufour.

***McGuire, Kristen W.** The Glory to Be Revealed in You: A Spiritual Companion to Pregnancy. LC 94-40880. (Orig.). 1994. pap. 8.95 (0-8189-0721-5) Alba.

McGuire, Leo. Intelligizer: Prime Fitness, Intellect, & Aesthetic Development. 176p. (Orig.). 1988. pap. text ed. 15.00 (0-9621698-0-3) Earthtrek Intl.

McGuire, Leslie. Anastasia: Czarina or Fake? Opposing Viewpoints. LC 89-35584. (Great Mysteries Ser.). (Illus.). 112p. (J). (gr. 5-8). 1989. 16.95 (0-89908-074-X) Greenhaven.

— Big Dan's Moving Van. LC 90-4417. (Pictureback Ser.). (Illus.). 32p. (Orig.). (J). (ps-1). 1993. pap. 2.25 (0-679-80565-6) Random Bks Yng Read.

— The Bouncing-Quitely Lessons: Winnie the Pooh. (Comes to Life Bks.). 16p. (J). (ps-2). 1995. write for info. (1-57234-053-3) YES Ent.

— Brush Your Teeth Please. LC 92-85152. (Illus.). 10p. (J). (ps-k). 1993. 9.95 (0-89577-474-7) RD Assn.

— Busy Firefighter. LC 94-1402. (Random House Pictureback Ser.). (Illus.). (J). (gr. 4 up). 1995. 2.99 (0-679-85438-X) Random.

— Casper: The Movie Storybook. LC 94-24860. (J). (gr. 1-8). 1995. 8.95 (0-8431-3856-4) Price Stern.

— Catherine the Great. (World Leaders - Past & Present Ser.). (Illus.). 112p. (YA). (gr. 5 up). 1986. lib. bdg. 17.95 (0-87754-577-4) Chelsea Hse.

— Comes to Life Storyplayer (Phase 2) & Micky Mouse: The Eagle's Treasure. (Comes to Life Bks.). 16p. (J). (ps-2). 1995. write for info. (1-57234-054-1) YES Ent.

— Death & Illness. (Family Ser.). (Illus.). 64p. (YA). (gr. 7 up). 1990. lib. bdg. 17.27 (0-86593-079-1); lib. bdg. 12.95 (0-685-46439-3) Rourke Corp.

— The Eagle's Treasure: Mickey Mouse. (Comes to Life Bks.). 16p. (J). (ps-2). 1995. write for info. (1-57234-052-5) YES Ent.

— Eureeka's Castle: Magellan Saves the Day. (Golden Little Look-Look Book Ser.). (Illus.). (J). (ps-00). 1991. pap. 1.25 (0-307-11512-7, Golden Pr) Western Pub.

Mcguire, Leslie. Fred & the Pet Show. 1991. pap. 2.95 (0-449-90503-9) Fawcett.

— Fred in Charge. 1991. pap. 2.95 (0-449-90502-0) Fawcett.

— Fred Saves the Day. 1991. pap. 2.95 (0-449-90504-7) Fawcett.

McGuire, Leslie. Is There Life after Sixth Grade? LC 89-20615. (Making the Grade Ser.). (Illus.). 96p. (J). (gr. 4-6). 1990. lib. bdg. 9.89 (0-8167-1706-0); pap. text ed. 2.95 (0-8167-1707-9) Troll Assocs.

— Miss Mopp's Lucky Day. LC 94-11309. (Illus.). 1994. lib. bdg. 14.60 (0-8368-0992-0) Gareth Stevens Inc.

— Miss Mopp's Lucky Day. LC 81-4879. (Illus.). 48p. (J). (ps-3). 1982. 5.95 (0-8193-1061-1); lib. bdg. 5.95 (0-8193-1062-X) Parents.

— Napoleon Bonaparte. (World Leaders - Past & Present Ser.). (Illus.). 112p. (YA). (gr. 5 up). 1986. lib. bdg. 17.95 (0-87754-554-5) Chelsea Hse.

— Sammy Saves the Day. (Play Along Ser.). 16p. (J). (ps-2). 1995. write for info. (1-57234-060-6) YES Ent.

— Suicide. (Troubled Society Ser.). (Illus.). 64p. (YA). (gr. 7 up). 1990. lib. bdg. 17.27 (0-86593-069-4); lib. bdg. 12.95 (0-685-46444-X) Rourke Corp.

— The Terrible Truth about Third Grade. LC 90-26788. (Making the Grade Ser.). (Illus.). 96p. (J). (gr. 2-4). 1992. lib. bdg. 9.89 (0-8167-2382-6); pap. text ed. 2.95 (0-8167-2383-4) Troll Assocs.

— This Farm Is a Mess. LC 80-25811. (Illus.). 48p. (J). (ps-3). 1981. 5.95 (0-8193-1045-X); lib. bdg. 5.95 (0-8193-1046-8) Parents.

— This Farm Is a Mess. LC 94-11354. (Read Aloud Original Ser.). (J). 1994. write for info. (0-8368-0983-1) Parents.

— Time for Bed? LC 93-85491. (J). (ps-3). 1994. 11.95 (0-89577-572-7, Readers Digest Kids) RD Assn.

— Victims. LC 91-11041. (Women Today Ser.). 64p. (J). (gr. 5-7). 1991. 12.95 (0-86593-120-8) Rourke Corp.

McGuire, Leslie, jt. auth. see Farrington, Liz.

***McGuire, M. & Townsend, C., eds.** Periodontal Disease Management. (Illus.). 100p. (Orig.). 1994. pap. 65.00 (0-9624699-5-5) Amer Acad Periodontology.

McGuire, M. T., ed. The St. Kitts Vervet. (Contributions to Primatology Ser.: Vol. 1). 202p. 1974. 45.00 (3-8055-1692-4) S Karger.

McGuire, Marion. Dictionary of Essential English. (Illus.). 464p. 1987. teacher ed 12.99 (0-86601-625-2); student ed 4.99 (0-86601-626-0); text ed. 18.49 (0-86601-624-4) Media Materials.

McGuire, Martin C. Secrecy & the Arms Race: A Theory of the Accumulation of Strategic Weapons & How Secrecy Affects It. LC 65-22062. (Economic Studies: No. 125). (Illus.). 1990. 16.50 (0-674-79665-9) HUP.

McGuire, Martin R. The Political & Cultural History of the Ancient World: A Syllabus with Suggested Readings. 218p. reprint ed. pap. 62.20 (0-317-09243-X, 2005215) Bks Demand.

McGuire, Mary, ed. see Eckhart, Frank.

McGuire, Melvin W. & Hadley, Robert. Bloody Skies. LC 92-61289. (Illus.). 448p. (Orig.). 1993. pap. 22.95 (1-881325-07-5) Yucca Tree Pr.

McGuire, Meredith B. Religion: The Social Context. 3rd ed. 340p. (C). 1992. pap. 25.95 (0-534-16968-6) Intl Thomson.

Mcguire, Meredith B. & Kantor, Debra. Ritual Healing in Suburban America. 335p. (C). 1988. text ed. 45.00 (0-8135-1312-X); pap. text ed. 15.00 (0-8135-1313-8) Rutgers U Pr.

McGuire, Meredith B., jt. auth. see Freund, Peter E. S.

McGuire, Michael. An Eye for Fractals: A Graphic-Photographic Essay. (Illus.). 160p. (C). 1990. text ed. 29.95 (0-201-55440-2, Adv Bk Prog) Addison-Wesley.

Mcguire, Michael. The Ice Forest. LC 90-60883. 96p. (Orig.). 1990. pap. 9.95 (0-910395-59-4) Marlboro Pr.

McGuire, Michael J. & Suffet, Irwin H., eds. Treatment of Water by Granular Activated Carbon. LC 82-22662. (Advances in Chemistry Ser.: No. 202). 600p. 1983. lib. bdg. 68.95 (0-8412-0665-1) Am Chemical.

McGuire, Michael T. The Neurotransmitter Revolution: Serotonin, Social Behavior, & the Law. Masters, Roger D., ed. LC 92-49968. 272p. (C). 1993. 39.95 (0-8093-1792-3); pap. 19.95 (0-8093-1801-6) S Ill U Pr.

McGuire, Michael T., ed. Human Nature & the New Europe. LC 93-22945. 207p. (C). 1993. text ed. 52.50 (0-8133-8719-1) Westview.

McGuire, Mike, jt. auth. see Hartman, Bob.

McGuire, Molly. My Prince Charming. (American Romance Ser.). 1993. mass mkt. 3.39 (0-373-16484-X, 1-16484-7) Harlequin Bks.

McGuire, Nina. An Uncommon Guide to Florida: A Resident's Guide to the Real Florida. LC 91-66907. 224p. 1991. pap. 12.95 (0-9631241-0-2) Tail Tours.

McGuire, O. R., ed. see Beck, James M.

McGuire, Pat, jt. auth. see Johnson, Dora B.

McGuire, Patricia D. Lullaby of Broadway: A Biography of Al Dubin. (Illus.). 256p. 1983. 14.95 (0-8065-0871-X, Citadel Pr) Carol Pub Group.

McGuire, Patricia J., ed. see Martin, Christopher.

McGuire, Patrick. French Texans. 2nd rev. ed. 1991. 4.95 (0-86701-046-0) U of Tex Inst Tex Culture.

— Hungarian Texans. 312p. 1993. 23.95 (0-86701-041-X); pap. 14.95 (0-86701-048-7) U of Tex Inst Tex Culture.

McGuire, Patrick L. Red Stars: Political Aspects of Soviet Science Fiction. LC 84-28099. (Studies in Speculative Fiction: No. 7). 170p. reprint ed. pap. 48.50 (0-8357-1579-5, 2070509) Bks Demand.

McGuire, Paul. Breakthrough Manual. 320p. (Orig.). 1992. pap. 9.95 (0-88270-658-6) Bridge Pub.

— Who Will Rule the Future? LC 91-55197. 208p. 1991. pap. 8.99 (0-910311-94-3) Huntington Hse.

McGuire, Paula, ed. Nobel Prize Winners: Supplement, 1987-1991. LC 92-12197. 35.00 (0-8242-0834-X) Wilson.

McGuire, Peter. Multimedia Everywhere: Designing Practical Applications. (Illus.). 320p. 1995. cd-rom, pap. text ed. 39.95 (0-12-484060-4, AP Prof) Acad Pr.

McGuire, Peter J. & Putzell, Sara M. A Guide to Technical Writing. 415p. (C). 1988. pap. text ed. 20.00 (0-15-530327-9); pap. text ed. 1.50 (0-15-530328-7) HB Coll Pubs.

McGuire, Philip. He, Too, Spoke for Democracy: Judge Hastie, World War II, & the Black Soldier. LC 87-24943. (Contributions in Afro-American & African Studies: No. 110). 176p. 1988. text ed. 49.95 (0-313-26115-6, MHD/, Greenwood Pr) Greenwood.

McGuire, Philip C. Shakespeare: The Jacobean Plays. LC 93-42847. (English Dramatists Ser.). 1994. text ed. 35.00 (0-312-10628-9) St Martin.

McGuire, Philip C. & Samuelson, David A., eds. Shakespeare: The Theatrical Dimension. LC 77-78320. (Studies in the Renaissance: No. 3). 1979. lib. bdg. 34.50 (0-404-16002-6) AMS Pr.

McGuire, Phillip, comp. Taps for a Jim Crow Army: Letters from Black Soldiers in World War II. LC 93-1718. 320p. 1993. reprint ed. 35.00 (0-8131-1851-4); reprint ed. pap. 19.00 (0-8131-0822-5) U Pr of Ky.

McGuire, Randall H. Death, Society, & Ideology in a Hohokam Community. 209p. (C). 1992. pap. text ed. 42.50 (0-8133-8350-1) Westview.

— A Marxist Archaeology. (Illus.). 326p. 1992. text ed. 49.95 (0-12-484078-7) Acad Pr.

McGuire, Randall H., ed. Ethnology of the Indians of Northwest Mexico. LC 91-33940. (Spanish Borderlands Sourcebooks Ser.: Vol. 6). 474p. 1992. 72.00 (0-8240-0833-2) Garland.

McGuire, Randall H. & Paynter, Robert, eds. The Archaeology of Inequality. (Social Archaeology Ser.). 256p. 1991. pap. 21.95 (0-631-17959-3) Blackwell Pubs.

McGuire, Randall H. & Schiffer, Michael B., eds. Hohokam & Patayan: Prehistory of Southwestern Arizona. LC 82-3942. 1982. text ed. 79.00 (0-12-484080-9) Acad Pr.

McGuire, Randall H., jt. ed. see Mathien, Frances J.

McGuire, Richard. Night Becomes Day. LC 94-9923. 32p. (J). (ps up). 1994. lib. bdg. 13.99 (0-670-85547-2) Viking Child Bks.

— Orange Book. 1992. 14.95 (0-8478-1465-3) Rizzoli Intl.

— The Orange Book. (Illus.). 40p. (J). (ps-3). 1994. pap. 4.99 (0-14-055342-8) Puffin Bks.

— What Comes Around Goes Around. LC 95-12337. (Illus.). 32p. (J). 1995. 13.99 (0-670-86396-3, Viking) Viking Penguin.

McGuire, Richard K., jt. auth. see Tunkel, Jay A.

McGuire, Richard L. Passionate Attention: An Introduction to Literary Study. (C). 1973. pap. text ed. 6.95 (0-393-09324-7) Norton.

Mcguire, Rick, jt. auth. see Fox, James.

***McGuire, Rik.** Angel Whispers. 1995. 11.95 (0-8062-5245-6) Carlton.

McGuire, Sean, ed. see Woelfl, Genevieve.

McGuire, Simon. The Handbook of Convertibles. 220p. 1991. 34.95 (0-13-376062-6) NY Inst Finance.

McGuire, Steven, jt. ed. see Ackland, Len.

McGuire, Sumiye O. & Davis, Lester A. Foreign Direct Investment in the United States: An Update: Review & Analysis of Current Developments. (Illus.). 232p. (Orig.). (C). 1994. pap. text ed. 75.00 (0-7881-0610-4) Diane Pub.

McGuire, Terrance P. & McGowan, Kathleen. Care for the Caregiver: A Guide for Staff in the Helping Professions. LC 90-62085. 64p. (Orig.). (C). 1991. pap. 8.95 (1-55612-400-7) Sheed & Ward MO.

McGuire, Therese J. & Naimark, Dana W., eds. State & Local Government Finance for the 1990's: A Case Study of Arizona. 500p. (C). 1991. pap. text ed. write for info. (1-879286-01-7) AZ Bd Regents.

McGuire, Thomas. Tooth Fitness: Your Guide to Healthy Teeth. Klein, Alice, ed. LC 93-85744. (Illus.). 336p. (J). (ps up). 1993. 24.95 (0-9638321-3-1); pap. 16.95 (0-9638321-2-3) Saint Michaels.

McGuire, Thomas & Grant, Faye. Understanding Child Sexual Abuse: Therapeutic Guidelines for Professionals Working with Children. 60p. 1990. pap. 12.00 (0-409-89771-X) Butterworth Legal Pubs.

McGuire, Thomas, et al, eds. Indian Water in the New West. LC 93-15609. 237p. 1993. 35.00 (0-8165-1392-9) U of Ariz Pr.

McGuire, Thomas R. Politics & Ethnicity on the Rio Yaqui: Potam Revisited. LC 86-11445. (PROFMEX Ser.). 186p. 1986. 24.95 (0-8165-0893-3) U of Ariz Pr.

McGuire-Turcotte, Casey A. How Honu the Turtle Got His Shell. (Publish-a-Book Contest Ser.). (Illus.). 32p. (J). (gr. 2-4). 1990. lib. bdg. 29.28 (0-8172-2788-1) Raintree Steck-V.

— How Honu the Turtle Got His Shell. (Publish-a-Book Ser.). (Illus.). 30p. (J). (gr. k up). 1991. lib. bdg. 19.97 (0-8172-2783-0); pap. 3.95 (0-8114-4304-3) Raintree Steck-V.

McGuire, W. J., et al, eds. Monitoring Active Volcanoes: Strategies, Procedure & Techniques. 352p. 1994. 99.00 (1-85728-036-9, Pub. by UCL Pr UK) Taylor & Francis.

McGuire, William. Bollingen: An Adventure in Collecting the Past. LC 82-47625. (Bollingen Ser.). (Illus.). 340p. (C). 1989. 47.50 (0-691-09951-0); pap. text ed. 15.95 (0-691-01885-5) Princeton U Pr.

— The Final Four (NCAA Basketball) (Great Moments in Sports Ser.). 32p. (J). (gr. 4). 1990. lib. bdg. 14.95 (0-88682-310-2) Creative Ed.

Mcguire, William. Poetry's Catbird Seat: The Consultantship in Poetry in the English Language at the Library of Congress, 1937-1987. LC 87-33876. 512p. 1988. 21.00 (0-685-48152-2, 030-000-00204-1) Lib Congress.

McGuire, William. Southeast Asians. LC 90-12996. (Recent American Immigrants Ser.). (Illus.). (J). (gr. 5-10). 1991. lib. bdg. 13.68 (0-531-11108-3) Watts.

— The Stanley Cup. (Great Moments in Sports Ser.). 32p. (J). (gr. 4). 1990. lib. bdg. 14.95 (0-88682-316-1) Creative Ed.

— The Summer Olympics. (Great Moments in Sports Ser.). 32p. (J). (gr. 4). 1990. lib. bdg. 14.95 (0-88682-318-8) Creative Ed.

— The World Series. (Great Moments in Sports Ser.). 32p. (J). (gr. 4). 1990. lib. bdg. 14.95 (0-88682-313-7) Creative Ed.

McGuire, William & Gallagher, Richard H. Matrix Structural Analysis. LC 78-8471. 460p. 1979. Net. text ed. write for info. (0-471-03059-7) Wiley.

McGuire, William, ed. see Burnham, John C.

McGuire, William, ed. see Freud, Sigmund & Jung, Carl G.

McGuire, William, ed. see Freud, Sigmund.

M

McGuire, William, ed. see Jung, C. G.

McGuire, William, ed. see Jung, Carl G.

McGuire, William J., jt. ed. see Iyengar, Shanto.

McGuire, William L., ed. Breast Cancer: Advances in Research & Treatment, Vol. 4. LC 79-646815. 246p. 1981. 75.00 (*0-306-40667-5*, Plenum Med Bk) Plenum.

— Hormones, Receptors, & Breast Cancer. LC 77-90595. (Progress in Cancer Research & Therapy Ser.: Vol. 10). 383p. 1978. 82.50 (*0-89004-261-6*) Raven.

— Hormones, Receptors, & Breast Cancer. fac. ed. LC 77-90595. (Progress in Cancer Research & Therapy Ser.: No. 10). (Illus.). 383p. Date not set. pap. 109.20 (*0-7837-7170-3*, 2047127) Bks Demand.

McGuire, William L., jt. ed. see Hansen, Heine H.

McGuire, William L., jt. ed. see Henderson, I. Craig.

McGuire, William L., jt. ed. see Lepor, Herbert.

***McGuire, William L., et al, eds.** Progesterone Receptors in Normal & Neoplastic Tissues. fac. ed. LC 77-72065. (Progress in Cancer Research & Therapy Ser.: No. 4). (Illus.). 357p. Date not set. pap. 101.80 (*0-7837-7353-6*, 2047162) Bks Demand.

***McGuire, William P. & Rowinsky, Erick K., eds.** Paclitaxel in Cancer Treatment. LC 95-2352. (Basic & Clinical Oncology Ser.: Vol. 8). 1995. write for info. (*0-8247-9307-2*) Dekker.

McGuirk, Bernard, ed. & intro. Redirections in Critical Theory: Truth, Self, Action, History. LC 93-14031. 1994. write for info. (*0-415-07756-7*) Routledge.

McGuirk, Bernard & Cardwell, Richard, eds. Gabriel Garcia Marquez: New Readings. (Cambridge Iberian & Latin American Studies). 240p. 1987. 54.95 (*0-521-32836-5*) Cambridge U Pr.

McGuirk, Bernard & Millington, Mark, eds. Inequality & Difference in Hispanic & Latin American Cultures: Critical Theoretical Approaches. LC 94-47533. 184p. 1995. text ed. 79.95 (*0-7734-9476-6*) E Mellen.

McGuirk, Bernard, jt. ed. see Cardwell, Richard A.

McGuirk, Carol. Robert Burns & the Sentimental Era. LC 84-12378. 224p. 1985. 30.00 (*0-8203-0739-4*) U of Ga Pr.

McGuirk, Carol, ed. see Burns, Robert.

McGuirk, Dal. Rommel's Army in Africa. (Illus.). 192p. 1993. 29.95 (*0-87938-835-8*) Motorbooks Intl.

McGuirk, James & McGuirk, Mary E. For Want of a Child: A Psychologist & His Wife Explore the Emotional Effects & Challenges of Infertility. 160p. 1991. 17.95 (*0-8245-1310-X*) Crossroad NY.

McGuirk, James F., jt. auth. see Hall, Betty L.

McGuirk, Mary E., jt. auth. see McGuirk, James.

McGuirk, Russell. Colloquial Arabic of Egypt. 320p. 1986. audio 29.95 (*0-415-00072-6*, RKP); pap. 14.95 (*0-7100-9936-3*, A2559, RKP) Routledge.

— Colloquial Arabic of Egypt: Hermeneutics As Method, Philosophy, & Critique. 1986. pap. 14.95 (*0-415-05172-X*, Pub. by Tavistock UK) Routledge Chapman & Hall.

McGuirk, Stephanie, ed. see Allbritton, Cliff.

McGuirl, Thomas, jt. auth. see Feist, Uwe.

McGuirt, Curtis R., ed. see Caron, D. Phillip.

McGullion, Bart. Rite of Survivorship. (Illus.). 66p. (Orig.). 1994. pap. 4.00 (*0-88680-221-0*) I E Clark.

McGurk, H., ed. Ecological Factors in Human Development. LC 76-30321. (Illus.). 296p. 1977. 59.00 (*0-7204-0488-6*, North Holland) Elsevier.

McGurk, Harry, jt. ed. see Dickerson, John W. T.

McGurk, Jeanette. You Can Too: A Guide to Homestyle Cajun Cooking. 2nd ed. (Illus.). 170p. (C). 1989. reprint ed. pap. 9.95 (*0-9624251-0-9*) Cajun Pantry.

McGurk, Patrick, jt. ed. see Darlington, R. R.

McGurk, Russell & Nierenberg, Claudia. U. S. Economic Policy & Sustainable Growth in Latin America. (Critical Issues Ser.: No. 92.5). 42p. Date not set. pap. 4.95 (*0-87609-133-8*) Coun Foreign.

McGurn, Jim. Comparing Languages: English & Its European Relatives. (Awareness of Language Ser.). (Illus.). 48p. (C). 1991. pap. 10.95 (*0-521-33638-4*) Cambridge U Pr.

McGurn, Larry. The Printer. 68p. 1981. pap. 3.50 (*0-939391-00-7*) B Woodley Pr.

***McGurn, Pat.** The IRRC Handbook on Proxy Voting Duties & Guideline Development. Carroll, Margaret, ed. 32p. (Orig.). Date not set. pap. 75.00 (*1-879775-20-4*) IRRC Inc DC.

McGurn, Patrick & Misenheimer, Barry. Reforming the Proxy System. 1991. pap. 95.00 (*0-931035-79-1*) IRRC Inc DC.

McGurn, Patrick, et al. State Takeover Laws. 150p. 1989. 200.00 (*0-931035-34-1*) IRRC Inc DC.

McGurn, Patrick S. Confidential Proxy Voting. 118p. 1989. pap. 50.00 (*0-931035-73-2*) IRRC Inc DC.

McGurn, Sheelagh. Under One Roof: Caring for an Aging Parent. 174p. (Orig.). 1992. pap. 12.00 (*0-942421-38-8*) Hazelden.

McGurn, William, ed. Terrorist or Freedom Fighter? The Cost of Confusion. (C). 1990. 35.00 (*0-907967-83-3*, Pub. by Inst Euro Def & Strat UK) St Mut.

McGurrin, James. Bourke Cockran: A Free Lance in American Politics. LC 74-172219. (Right Wing Individualist Tradition in America Ser.). 1972. reprint ed. 28.95 (*0-405-00428-1*) Ayer.

McGurrin, Joseph, et al. Interstate Fisheries of the Atlantic Coast. Hamer, Paul, ed. LC 91-71535. (Illus.). 120p. (Orig.). 1991. pap. 9.95 (*0-9630072-0-3*) Atlan States MFC.

McGurrin, Martin C. Pathological Gambling: Conceptual, Diagnostic, & Treatment Issues. Smith, Harold H., Jr., ed. LC 91-50928. (Practitioner's Resource Ser.). 96p. 1992. pap. 14.70 (*0-943158-69-9*, PGCBP, Prof Resc Pr) Pro Resource.

McGushin. Sallust: The Conspiracy of Catiline: A Companion to the Penguin Translation. 124p. 1987. 12.50 (*0-86292-267-4*, Pub. by Brstl Class Pr UK) Focus Info Gr.

McGushin, Patrick. The Transmission of the Punica of Silius Italicus. iv, 165p. 1985. 27.00 (*90-256-0895-7*, Pub. by A M Hakkert NE) Benjamins North Am.

McGushin, Patrick, ed. see Sallust.

McGushin, Patrick, tr. see Sallust.

***McGuy, Bruce.** Even Santa Cries Sometimes. 64p. 1994. pap. 7.95 (*0-9642311-0-7*) Home Run Pub.

McGwire, Michael & McDonnell, John, eds. Soviet Naval Influence: Domestic & Foreign Dimensions. LC 75-23982. (Special Studies). 698p. 1977. text ed. 95.00 (*0-275-90271-4*, C0271, Praeger Pubs) Greenwood.

McHaffie, jt. auth. see Cline.

***McHale.** The Intimate Alphabet. 1994. per. 10.95 (*0-920953-49-2*, Pub. by Cormorant Bks CN) InBook.

McHale, A. E., ed. Phase Equilibria Diagrams Annual '92. 182p. 1992. pap. 60.00 (*0-944904-51-3*, PHAN92) Am Ceramic.

McHale, Anna E., ed. Phase Equilibria Diagrams Annual 1991. (Illus.). 312p. 1991. pap. 60.00 (*0-944904-42-4*, PHAN91) Am Ceramic.

— Phase Equilibria Diagrams Annual '93. 227p. 1993. pap. 60.00 (*0-944904-62-9*, PHAN93) Am Ceramic.

***McHale, Anna E., et al, eds.** Phase Equilibria Diagrams: Phase Diagrams for Ceramists Vol. X: Borides, Carbides & Nitrides. 475p. 1994. 150.00 (*0-944904-74-2*, 3BCP1ON) Am Ceramic.

McHale, B., tr. see Sok-yong, Hwang, et al.

McHale, Barbara, jt. auth. see Bartlett, Janet.

McHale, Brian. Constructing Postmodernism. 256p. 1992. 49.95 (*0-415-06013-3*, A6014); pap. 15.95 (*0-415-06014-1*, A6018) Routledge.

— Post Modernist Fiction. 300p. 1987. 42.50 (*0-416-36390-3*, A0751); pap. 14.95 (*0-415-04513-4*, A0755) Routledge Chapman & Hall.

McHale, D., tr. see Azencott, R. & Dacunha-Castelle, D.

McHale, D., tr. see Dacunha-Castelle, D. & Duflo, M.

McHale, Frank, comp. Pieces That Have Won Prizes: Also Many Encore Pieces; Enlarged Edition. LC 79-39381. (Granger Index Reprint Ser.). 1977. reprint ed. 21.95 (*0-8369-6346-6*) Ayer.

***McHale, Hank.** Actual Experience of a CEO: How to Make Continuous Improvement in Manufacturing Succeed for Your Company. 1995. 24.00 (*0-87389-329-8*) ASQC Qual Pr.

McHale, Jean V. Medical Confidentiality & Legal Privilege. LC 92-26235. (Social Ethics & Policy Ser.). (Illus.). 240p. 1993. 67.00 (*0-415-04695-5*, A6026) Routledge.

McHale, John. The Expendable Ikon. 67p. 1984. 13.95 (*0-914782-54-1*) Buffalo Acad.

McHale, John & McHale, Magda C. Basic Human Needs: A Framework for Action. LC 77-17100. (Illus.). 249p. 1978. 32.95 (*0-87855-272-3*) Transaction Pubs.

***McHale, John E., Jr.** Dr. Samuel A. Mudd & the Lincoln Assassination. LC 94-24551. (People in Focus Bks.). (Illus.). (YA). (gr. 5 up). 1995. 13.95 (*0-87518-629-7*, Dillon Silver Burdett); pap. 7.95 (*0-382-24963-1*, Dillon Silver Burdett) Silver Burdett Pr.

McHale, Kathryn. Comparative Psychology & Hygiene of the Overweight Child. LC 72-177027. (Columbia University. Teachers College. Contributions to Education Ser.: No. 221). reprint ed. 22.50 (*0-404-55221-8*) AMS Pr.

McHale, Magda C., jt. auth. see McHale, John.

McHale, Magda C., et al. Children in the World. LC 78-24731. (Illus.). 1979. pap. 3.00 (*0-917136-03-9*) Population Ref.

McHale, Mary C., jt. auth. see McHale, Thomas R.

McHale, Michael J., jt. auth. see Romano, John F.

Mchale, Thomas. Basic Mathematics: Programmed. 1992. pap. text ed. write for info. (*0-201-05696-8*) Addison-Wesley.

McHale, Thomas J. & Witzke, Paul T. Advanced Algebra. (Milwaukee Area Technical College Mathematics Ser.). 1972. pap. text ed. 32.76 (*0-201-04633-4*) Addison-Wesley.

— Applied Algebra I. (C). 1979. pap. text ed. 46.25 (*0-201-04767-5*) Addison-Wesley.

— Applied Algebra II. (C). 1980. pap. text ed. 50.50 (*0-201-04775-6*) Addison-Wesley.

— Arithmetic Module Series: One Volume Non-Programmed Edition. 400p. (C). 1976. pap. text ed. write for info. (*0-201-04757-8*); write for info. (*0-318-50126-0*) Addison-Wesley.

— Arithmetic Modules. 125p. (C). 1975. Module 1, whole nos. pap. text ed. 18.25 (*0-201-04751-9*); Module 2, fractions. pap. text ed. 20.50 (*0-201-04752-7*); Module 3, decimals. pap. text ed. 20.50 (*0-201-04753-5*); Module 4, perfect ratio. pap. text ed. 20.50 (*0-201-04754-3*); Module 5. pap. text ed. 15.16 (*0-201-04756-X*) Addison-Wesley.

— Basic Algebra. (Milwaukee Area Technical College Mathematics Ser.). 1971. pap. text ed. 41.95 (*0-201-04625-3*) Addison-Wesley.

— Calculation & Calculators. 1977. write for info. (*0-201-04772-1*) Addison-Wesley.

— Calculation & Calculators. (C). 1977. pap. text ed. 45.25 (*0-201-04771-3*) Addison-Wesley.

— Technical Mathematics I. 704p. (C). 1988. pap. text ed. 49.50 (*0-201-15408-0*) Addison-Wesley.

McHaLe, Thomas J. & Witzke, Paul T. Technical Mathematics II. (Illus.). 704p. (C). 1988. pap. text ed. 49.50 (*0-201-15409-9*) Addison-Wesley.

McHale, Thomas J., et al. Intermediate Algebra: Programmed. LC 86-10918. 400p. 1987. text ed. write for info. (*0-201-15880-9*) Addison-Wesley.

— Introductory Algebra: Programmed. 544p. (C). 1977. text ed. write for info. (*0-201-04747-0*) Addison-Wesley.

— Introductory Algebra: Programmed. 2nd ed. LC 85-11848. 528p. (C). 1986. pap. text ed. 45.25 (*0-201-15887-6*); write for info. (*0-201-15888-4*) Addison-Wesley.

McHale, Thomas R. Pacific Rim Energy Demand & Capital Requirements in the 1990s. 20p. 1992. pap. 10.00 (*0-918714-32-X*) Intl Res Ctr Energy.

— Saudi Oil Policy & the Changing World Energy Balance. 20p. 1986. pap. 10.00 (*0-918714-09-5*) Intl Res Ctr Energy.

McHale, Thomas R. & McHale, Mary C. Early American-Philippine Trade: The Journal of Nathaniel Bowditch in Manila, 1796. (Monograph Ser.: No. 2). viii, 63p. 1962. 4.75 (*0-938692-16-X*) Yale U SE Asia.

McHale, Vincent & Skowronski, Sharon, eds. Political Parties of Europe, 2 vols., Set. LC 82-15408. (Greenwood Encyclopedia of the World's Political Parties Ser.). (Illus.). 1400p. 1983. text ed. 195.00 (*0-313-21405-0*, MPP/) Greenwood.

— Political Parties of Europe, 2 vols., Vol. I. LC 82-15408. (Greenwood Encyclopedia of the World's Political Parties Ser.). (Illus.). xix, 700p. 1983. text ed. 125.00 (*0-313-23804-9*, MPP/01) Greenwood.

— Political Parties of Europe, 2 vols., Vol. 2. LC 82-15408. (Greenwood Encyclopedia of the World's Political Parties Ser.). (Illus.). 1297p. 1983. Vol. II: 1297p. text ed. 100.00 (*0-313-23805-7*, MPP/02) Greenwood.

Mchallam, Andrew, jt. ed. see Frost, Gerald.

McHam, Sarah B. The Chapel of St. Anthony at the Santo & the Development of Venetian Renaissance Sculpture. LC 92-43078. (Illus.). 608p. (C). 1994. 125.00 (*0-521-41853-4*) Cambridge U Pr.

McHaney, Pearl A., jt. auth. see Burger, Nash K.

McHaney, Pearl A., ed. see Welty, Eudora.

McHaney, Roger. Computer Simulation: A Practical Perspective. (Illus.). 276p. 1991. text ed. 49.95 (*0-12-484140-6*) Acad Pr.

McHaney, T., ed. see Faulkner, William, et al.

McHaney, Thomas, ed. see Faulkner, William.

McHann, Marjorie, ed. What Every Home Health Nurse Needs to Know: A Book of Readings. 200p. 1994. pap. 40.00 (*0-9640767-0-5*) Cnslts in Care.

McHardy, A. K., intro. Clerical Poll-Taxes of the Diocese of Lincoln, 1377-81. (Publications of the Lincoln Record Society: No. 81). (Illus.). 296p. (C). 1992. text ed. 35.00 (*0-901503-54-1*, Lincoln Record Soc) Boydell & Brewer.

McHardy, John & Ludwig, Frank, eds. Electrochemistry of Semiconductors & Electronics: Processes & Devices. LC 91-46659. (Illus.). 359p. 1992. 64.00 (*0-8155-1301-1*) Noyes.

McHardy, K. C., et al. Illustrated Cases in Acute Clinical Medicine. LC 93-14398. 1994. pap. text ed. 22.00 (*0-443-04697-2*) Churchill.

McHarg, Ian L. Design with Nature. 208p. 1991. text ed. 69.95 (*0-471-55797-8*) Wiley.

— Design with Nature. (Series in Sustainable Design). 1995. pap. text ed. 39.95 (*0-471-11460-X*) Wiley.

— Design with Nature. LC 76-77344. 1971. pap. 15.95 (*0-385-05509-9*) Natural Hist.

McHargue, Carl J., et al, eds. Structure-Property Relationships in Surface-Modified Ceramics. (C). 1989. lib. bdg. 169.00 (*0-7923-0310-5*) Kluwer Ac.

McHarris, W., ed. Exotic Nuclear Spectroscopy. (Illus.). 668p. 1991. 135.00 (*0-306-43882-8*, Plenum Pr) Plenum.

McHarry, Hugh, comp. General & Everyname Index to the History of Hancock Co., IL (1880) 60p. (Orig.). 1989. pap. 6.50 (*0-9623531-0-8*) H McHarry.

***McHarry, Jan.** The Great Recycling Adventure: Lift-A-Flap Look at Old Things Made New. LC 94-13070. (Illus.). (J). (gr. 1 up). 1994. 12.95 (*1-57036-063-4*) Turner Pub GA.

***McHattie.** Investor's Guide to Trading in Warrants: A Step-by-Step Guide to Successful Dealing. 1995. 55.00 (*0-273-61242-5*, Pub. by Pitman Publishing UK) Krieger.

— Investor's Guide to Warrants: Capitalize on the Fastest Growing Sector of the Markets. 2nd ed. 1995. 55.00 (*0-273-61241-7*, Pub. by Pitman Publishing UK) Krieger.

***McHattie, Andrew.** The Investor's Guide to Warrants. 256p. 1992. 135.00 (*0-273-03751-X*, Pub. by Pitman Pubng UK) St Mut.

McHattie, Grace. The Cat Lover's Dictionary: The Easy Reference Guide to Cats & Cat Care. (Illus.). 160p. (Orig.). 1994. pap. 12.95 (*0-7867-0093-9*) Carroll & Graf.

— Cat Tales: The Life & Times of Cats of This Century. (Illus.). 128p. 1992. 9.95 (*0-681-41570-3*) Longmeadow Pr.

— Going Live! Cat Book. (Illus.). 94p. (YA). 1992. pap. 3.95 (*0-563-20880-5*, BBC-Parkwest) Parkwest Pubns.

— My Cat Is Driving Me Crazy! An Owner's Guide to Cat Care with Natural Remedies. (Illus.). 160p. 1995. pap. 10.95 (*0-7867-0160-9*) Carroll & Graf.

— That's Cats: A Guide to Understanding Your Cat's Behavior. (Illus.). 192p. 1993. pap. 19.95 (*0-7153-0126-8*, Pub. by D & C Pub UK) Sterling.

McHatton, Robert J. Total Telemarketing: Complete Guide to Increasing Sales & Profits. LC 87-21547. 246p. 1988. text ed. 42.50 (*0-471-62754-2*); pap. text ed. 16.95 (*0-471-62755-0*) Wiley.

McHearin, George S. American Glass. 1989. 22.99 (*0-517-68237-0*) Random Hse Value.

McHedlidze, G. A. Fossil Cetacea of the Caucasus. Rao, P. M., tr. (Russian Translation Ser.: No. 68). (Illus.). 150p. (C). 1989. text ed. 70.00 (*90-6191-933-9*, Pub. by A A Balkema NE) Ashgate Pub Co.

— General Features of the Paleobiological Evolution of Cetacea. Chakravarty, R., tr. 180p. (ENG.). (C). 1984. text ed. 75.00 (*90-6191-438-8*, Pub. by A A Balkema NE) Ashgate Pub Co.

***Mchedlishvili, G. I., et al.** Brain Blood Supply. 320p. (C). 1977. 54.00x (*963-05-1130-4*, Pub. by Akad Kiado HU) St Mut.

— Brain Edema: A Pathogenetic Analysts. 365p. (C). 1986. 120.00x (*963-05-4378-8*, Pub. by Akad Kiado HU) St Mut.

— Regulation of Cerebral Circulation. 268p. 1979. 89.00 (*0-569-08589-6*, Pub. by Collets UK) Pro-Am Music.

— Regulation of Cerebral Circulation: Proceedings of the Fourth Tbilisi Symposium on Cerebral Circulation, Tbilist, 19-21 April, 1978. 266p. (C). 1979. 60.00x (*963-05-2209-8*, Pub. by Akad Kiado HU) St Mut.

Mchedlishvili, George I. Arterial Behavior & Blood Circulation of the Brain. Bevan, John A., tr. 354p. 1986. 89.50 (*0-306-10985-9*, Consultants) Plenum.

Mchedlishvili, Georgii I. Vascular Mechanisms of the Brain. LC 70-141241. 127p. reprint ed. pap. 36.20 (*0-317-07810-0*, 2020684) Bks Demand.

Mchedlishvili, G., et al, eds. Microcirculation of the Brain: A Synoptic View by World Experts. 282p. (C). 1992. text ed. 105.00 (*1-56072-014-X*) Nova Sci Pubs.

Mchels, Greg, ed. Governments of Missouri, 1985. (Governments of Your State Ser.). 1984. 120.00 (*1-55507-059-0*); text ed. 150.00 (*0-317-38121-0*) Municipal Analysis.

McHenry, Dean E., Jr. Limited Choices: The Political Struggle for Socialism in Tanzania. LC 94-14623. 288p. 1994. lib. bdg. 49.95 (*1-55587-429-0*) Lynne Rienner.

— Limited Choices: The Political Struggle for Socialism in Tanzania. LC 94-14623. 288p. 1994. pap. text ed. 18.95 (*1-55587-556-4*) Lynne Rienner.

McHenry, Dean E. The Third Force in Canada: The Cooperative Commonwealth Federation,1932-1948. LC 76-2061. 351p. 1976. reprint ed. text ed. 69.50 (*0-8371-8767-2*, MCTF, Greenwood Pr) Greenwood.

McHenry, Dean E., jt. auth. see Ferguson, John H.

McHenry, Deni M. Donald Baechler. (Illus.). 12p. (Orig.). 1993. pap. 5.00 (*0-914489-12-7*) Univ Miss-KS Art.

McHenry, Donald. United States Firms in South Africa. (African Humanities Ser.). 74p. (Orig.). 1975. pap. text ed. 4.00 (*0-941934-15-2*) Indiana Africa.

McHenry, Donald F. Micronesia: Trust Betrayed. LC 75-42570. 276p. 1975. text ed. 10.00 (*0-87003-000-0*) Carnegie Endow.

McHenry, E. W., jt. ed. see Beaton, G. H.

McHenry, Ellen J. Inside a Freight Train. LC 92-23225. (Lift-the-Flap Book Ser.). (Illus.). (J). (ps-3). 1993. 9.99 (*0-525-65099-7*, Cobblehill Bks) Dutton Child Bks.

— Little Tropical Fish Coloring Book. (Illus.). (J). (gr. k-3). 1994. pap. 1.00 (*0-486-27951-0*) Dover.

McHenry, Harry I. & Potter, John M., eds. Fatigue & Fracture Testing of Weldments, STP 1058. LC 90-251. (Special Technical Publication (STP) Ser.). (Illus.). 299p. 1990. text ed. 69.00 (*0-8031-1277-7*) ASTM.

***McHenry, Hugh.** Manual for Computer Literacy. 200p. (C). 1995. pap. text ed., ring bd. 13.69 (*0-7872-1048-X*) Kendall-Hunt.

McHenry, Hugh L. A Laboratory Manual for Computer Literacy. 288p. (C). 1993. spiral bd. 15.95 (*0-8403-8890-X*) Kendall-Hunt.

— A Quiz Manual for Computer Literacy, 1994-1995 Edition. 212p. (C). 1994. spiral bd. 10.95 (*0-8403-9500-0*) Kendall-Hunt.

McHenry, James. Sidelight on History. LC 75-140875. (Eyewitness Accounts of the American Revolution Ser., No. 1). 1971. reprint ed. 15.95 (*0-405-01225-X*) Ayer.

— The Wilderness; or Braddock's Times: A Tale of the West, 2 vols., Set. LC 78-64078. reprint ed. 75.00 (*0-404-17270-9*) AMS Pr.

McHenry, Janet H. And the Winner Is.... Reck, Sue, ed. LC 94-6636. (Golden Rule Duo Ser.). 48p. (J). (gr. 2-4). 1994. pap. 2.99 (*0-7814-0170-4*, Chariot Bks) Chariot Family.

— Time Out! (Golden Rule Duo Ser.). (Illus.). 48p. (Orig.). (J). (gr. 2-5). 1995. pap. 2.99 (*0-7814-0173-9*) Chariot Family.

— Trick 'n' Trouble. Reck, Sue, ed. LC 94-6635. (Golden Rule Duo Ser.). 48p. (J). (gr. 2-4). 1994. pap. 2.99 (*0-7814-0171-2*, Chariot Bks) Chariot Family.

McHenry, Keith, jt. auth. see Butler, C. T.

McHenry, Lawrence C., Jr., ed. Garrison's History of Neurology. (Illus.). 568p. 1969. 87.95x (*0-398-01261-X*) C C Thomas.

— Garrison's History of Neurology. (Illus.). 586p. 1969. pap. 45.95 (*0-398-06276-5*) C C Thomas.

McHenry, Leemon & Adams, Frederick. Reflections on Philosophy: Introductory Essays. LC 92-50010. 227p. (C). 1992. pap. text ed. 14.00 (*0-312-06777-1*) St Martin.

McHenry, Leemon B. Whitehead & Bradley: A Comparative Analysis. LC 91-12725. (SUNY Series in Philosophy). 213p. (C). 1991. 59.50 (*0-7914-0915-5*); pap. 19.95 (*0-7914-0916-3*) State U NY Pr.

McHenry, Paul G., Jr. Adobe: Build It Yourself. 2nd rev. ed. LC 85-8432. (Illus.). 158p. 1985. pap. 22.95 (*0-8165-0948-4*) U of Ariz Pr.

— Adobe & Rammed Earth Buildings: Design & Construction. LC 89-5053. (Illus.). 217p. 1989. reprint ed. pap. 24.95 (*0-8165-1124-1*) U of Ariz Pr.

McHenry, Poke, pseud. & Smith, Vic. Early Poke: A Great Southern Humorist looks at Life's Pitfalls & Pinnacles. (Illus.). 352p. 1994. 23.95 (*0-9630463-4-9*) S & D.

EARLY POKE is a collection of human interest newspaper columns that appeared in the daily Florida Times-Union of Jacksonville, Florida & were written by Vic Smith, veteran of more

An Asterisk (*) at the beginning of an entry indicates that the title is appearing in BIP for the first time.

than 50 years in the business, under the pen name Poke McHenry. The anthology runs the gamut of human activities & emotions & is written with the consummate skills of an exceptional wordsmith. The stories are laced liberally with clean & original humor, wit, amazing insight, provocative thinking, & common sense that go even beyond the uncommon level & often roam the realms of the unique. The author dips generously into his long lifetime of marvelous memories of magic moments for much of his warmly entertaining prose. He covers the field from baseball to bass fishing & from the cotton mill spinning room to the peregrinations of presidents with countless wayside stops between. He's been there & he tells you about it in superb word pictures that entwine the reader in a warm web of pure reading pleasure. Whatever your age or station in life, you'll find this book a comforting companion & you'll adopt Poke as a true friend. To order call 1-800-330-1325. ***Publisher Provided Annotation.***

McHenry, Robert, ed. Famous American Women: A Biographical Dictionary from Colonial Times to the Present. 1984. 22.00 (*0-8446-6096-5*) Peter Smith.
— Famous American Women: A Biographical Dictionary from Colonial Times to the Present. (Americana Ser.). 482p. 1983. reprint ed. pap. 11.95 (*0-486-24523-3*) Dover.
— Webster's American Military Biographies. 22.50 (*0-8446-6143-0*) Peter Smith.
— Webster's American Military Biographies. LC 84-8004. 548p. 1984. reprint ed. pap. 13.95 (*0-486-24758-9*) Dover.
McHenry, Robert, ed. see Fujimura, Thomas H.
McHenry, Roy C. & Roper, Walter F. Smith & Wesson Hand Guns. 1994. 32.00 (*1-879356-35-X*) Wolfe Pub Co.
McHenry, Ruth W., ed. Ends & Means: The National Conference on Continuing Education in Nursing, 1970. LC 70-157408. (Notes & Essays Ser.: No. 69). 1971. pap. 2.50 (*0-87060-041-9*, NES 69) Syracuse U Cont Ed.
McHenry, Sherry, jt. auth. see L'Abate, Luciano.
M'Cheyne, R. M. Sermons of R. M. M'Cheyne. 1985. reprint ed. pap. 7.50 (*0-85151-165-1*) Banner of Truth.
McHoes, Ann, jt. auth. see Flynn, Ida M.
Mchombo, Sam A., ed. Theoretical Aspects of Bantu Grammar. LC 93-29496. (CSLI Lecture Notes Ser.: No. 38). 1993. 45.00 (*0-937073-73-3*); pap. 22.95 (*0-937073-72-5*) Ctr Study Language.
McHone, Jeff. Creation of Wealth: No Money Down. 176p. 1985. per. 13.95 (*0-8403-3515-6*) Kendall-Hunt.
McHose, Allen I. Teachers Dictation Manual. (Eastman School of Music Ser.). 26.95 (*0-89197-437-7*); pap. text ed. 12.95 (*0-89197-960-3*) Irvington.
McHose, Andre. Manufacturing Development Applications: Guidelines for Attaining Quality & Productivity. 275p. 1992. 45.00 (*1-55623-572-0*) Irwin Prof Pubng.
McHoul, Alec & Wills, David. Writing Pynchon: Strategies in Fictional Analysis. 256p. 1990. 29.95 (*0-252-01700-5*); pap. 12.95 (*0-252-06115-2*) U of Ill Pr.
McHoul, Lilian. Wild Flowers of Marin: A Layman's Handbook. LC 79-51455. (Illus.). 1979. pap. 4.95 (*0-912908-08-4*) Tamal Land.
Mchoy, Peter. Cats. 1988. 6.98 (*1-55521-218-2*) Bk Sales Inc.
***McHoy, Peter.** Complete Houseplant Book. 256p. 1995. 19.98 (*0-8317-1175-2*) Smithmark.
— Containers & Baskets for Year Round Colour. (Illus.). 128p. 1994. pap. 14.95 (*0-7063-7237-9*, Pub. by Ward Lock UK) Sterling.
— Garden Ornaments & Statuary. (Gardening by Design Ser.). (Illus.). 80p. 1990. pap. 8.95 (*0-7063-6921-1*, Pub. by Ward Lock UK) Sterling.
— Gardening Through the Year. (Illus.). 160p. 1995. 15.98 (*0-8317-3869-3*) Smithmark.
— Houseplant Care Manual. 1994. 14.98 (*0-8317-4661-0*) Smithmark.
— Pruning: A Practical Guide. 1993. 30.00 (*1-55859-634-8*) Abbeville Pr.
— Small Garden Book. 160p. 1995. 15.98 (*0-8317-7995-0*) Smithmark.
— Step by Step: Low Maintenance Gardening. (Illus.). 96p. 1995. 9.98 (*0-8317-6547-X*) Smithmark.
McHoy, Peter, et al. The Complete Book of Container Gardening. Toogood, Alan, ed. (Illus.). 192p. 1993. 29.95 (*0-943955-66-1*) Trafalgar.
***McHugh.** Calamitous Courting of Hetty King. 1995. pap. 3.99 (*0-553-48127-4*) Bantam.
McHugh, Andrew. The Cultivation of Ferns. (Illus.). 168p. 1992. 55.00 (*0-7134-6492-5*, Pub. by Batsford UK) Trafalgar.
McHugh, Bryan. An Exchange of Quivers. 32p. 1990. pap. 9.00 (*0-916258-21-1*) Left Hand Bks.
McHugh, Cathy L. Mill Family: The Labor System in the Southern Cotton Textile Industry. 160p. 1988. 37.50 (*0-19-504299-9*) OUP.
McHugh, Christopher. Animals. LC 93-43265. (Discovering Art Ser.). (Illus.). 32p. (J). (gr. 4-6). 1993. 14.95 (*1-56847-025-8*) Thomson Lrning.
— Faces. LC 93-20400. (Discovering Art Ser.). (Illus.). 32p. (J). (gr. 4-6). 1993. 14.95 (*1-56847-071-1*) Thomson Lrning.
— Food. LC 93-20399. (Discovering Art Ser.). (Illus.). 32p. (J). (gr. 4-6). 1993. 14.95 (*1-56847-070-3*) Thomson Lrning.
— People at Work. LC 93-20405. (Discovering Art Ser.). 32p. (J). (gr. 4-6). 1993. 14.95 (*1-56847-111-4*) Thomson Lrning.
— Town & Country. LC 93-20401. (Discovering Art Ser.). (Illus.). 32p. (J). (gr. 4-6). 1993. 14.95 (*1-56847-110-6*) Thomson Lrning.
— Water. LC 92-43266. (Discovering Art Ser.). (Illus.). 32p. (J). (gr. 4-6). 1993. 14.95 (*1-56847-024-X*) Thomson Lrning.
— Western Art 1600-1800. (Art & Artists Ser.). (Illus.). 48p. (J). (gr. 6-10). 1994. 16.95 (*1-56847-218-8*) Thomson Lrning.
McHugh, Christopher, ed. The Bankruptcy Yearbook & Almanac, 1991. 270p. (Orig.). 1991. pap. 195.00 (*0-9628991-0-0*) New Gen Research.
McHugh, Christopher M., ed. The Bankruptcy Yearbook & Almanac, 1993. 3rd ed. 600p. 1993. 145.00 (*0-9628991-2-7*) New Gen Research.
— The 1995 Bankruptcy Yearbook & Almanac. 5th ed. 622p. 1995. pap. 175.00 (*0-9628991-4-3*) New Gen Research.
— The Nineteen Ninety-Four Bankruptcy Yearbook & Almanac. 4th ed. 610p. 1994. pap. 175.00 (*0-9628991-3-5*) New Gen Research.
— The Nineteen Ninety Two Bankruptcy Yearbook & Almanac. 2nd ed. 499p. 1992. pap. 125.00 (*0-9628991-1-9*) New Gen Research.
McHugh, David, jt. auth. see Thompson, Paul.
McHugh, Denise. Discover George Mason: Home, State, & Country: A Sampler of Lesson Plans, Activities, & Resources for Teachers of Students in Grades 3 Through 6. rev. ed. (Illus.). vi, 101p. 1993. pap. 9.50 (*1-884085-02-4*) Bd Regents.
— George Mason, Planter & Patriot: A Sampler of Lesson Plans Exploring Primary Sources for Teachers of Students in Grades 7 Through 12. (Illus.). viii, 200p. (Orig.). 1992. pap. 14.00 (*1-884085-00-8*) Bd Regents.
McHugh, Donald. Table Attendant Training. LC 83-720057. (Series 925). (Orig.). 1983. student ed 8.00 (*0-8064-0401-9*); audio 169.00 (*0-8064-0402-7*) Bergwall.
McHugh, Dorothea H. A Personal Pathway to Prayer. LC 85-51408. 104p. 1985. 6.95 (*0-938232-90-8*, Baker & Taylor) Winston-Derek.
McHugh, Fiona. Of Corsets & Secrets & True, True Love. (Road to Avonlea Ser.: No. 14). (J). (gr. 4-7). 1993. mass mkt. 3.99 (*0-553-48040-5*) Bantam.
— Song of the Night, No. 3. (Road to Avonlea Ser.). (J). (gr. 3-7). 1992. pap. 3.99 (*0-553-48029-4*, Skylark) Bantam.
McHugh, Florence, tr. see Ts'Ao, Chan.
McHugh, Frances Y. The Ghost Wore Black. large type ed. (Linford Mystery Library). 1991. pap. 13.95 (*0-7089-7031-1*) Ulverscroft.
— Vow of Love. large type ed. (Dales Romance Ser.). 211p. 1992. pap. 16.95 (*1-85389-331-5*, Medcom-Trainex) Ulverscroft.
McHugh, Francis P., jt. ed. see Frowen, Stephen F.
McHugh, Francis P., et al, eds. Things Old & New: Catholic Social Teaching Revisited. LC 92-27123. 436p. (Orig.). (C). lib. bdg. 71.50 (*0-8191-8901-4*); pap. text ed. 33.00 (*0-8191-8902-2*) U Pr of Amer.
McHugh, Gretchen. The Hungry Hiker's Book of Good Cooking. (Illus.). 288p. 1982. pap. 19.00 (*0-394-70774-5*) Knopf.
McHugh, Heather. Broken English: Poetry & Partiality. LC 93-13612. (Illus.). 158p. 1993. text ed. 35.00 (*0-8195-5268-2*, Wesleyan Univ Pr); pap. 14.95 (*0-8195-6272-6*, Wesleyan Univ Pr) U Pr of New Eng.
— Dangers. 1977. 5.95 (*0-685-53924-5*) HM.
— Hinge & Sign: Poems, 1968-1993. LC 93-35917. (Wesleyan Poetry Ser.). 237p. (C). 1994. 35.00x (*0-8195-2213-9*, Wesleyan Univ Pr); pap. 14.95 (*0-8195-1216-8*, Wesleyan Univ Pr) U Pr of New Eng.
— Shades. LC 87-21179. (Wesleyan Poetry Ser.). 83p. 1988. pap. 10.95 (*0-8195-1137-4*, Wesleyan Univ Pr) U Pr of New Eng.
— To the Quick. LC 85-29504. (Wesleyan Poetry Ser.). 69p. 1987. 22.50 (*0-8195-5156-2*, Wesleyan Univ Pr); pap. 10.95 (*0-8195-6162-2*, Wesleyan Univ Pr) U Pr of New Eng.
McHugh, Heather, tr. see Dimitrova, Blaga.
McHugh, Heather, tr. see Follain, Jean.
McHugh, Isabel, tr. see Ts'Ao, Chan.
McHugh, James F. Damages in Massachusetts Litigation. LC 93-77116. 404p. 1993. ring bd. 95.00 (*0-944490-37-9*) Mass CLE.
McHugh, James N. Hantu Hantu: An Account of Ghost Belief in Modern Malaya. 2nd ed. LC 77-87031. (Illus.). reprint ed. 14.50 (*0-404-16839-6*) AMS Pr.
McHugh, Jeanne. Alexander Holley & the Makers of Steel. LC 79-27414. (Johns Hopkins Studies in the History of Technology; New Ser.: No. 4). 416p. reprint ed. pap. 118.60 (*0-7837-2199-4*, 2042537) Bks Demand.
***McHugh, Joan C.** Feast of Faith: Confessions of a Eucharistic Pilgrim. Romb, Anselm W., ed. & pref. by. (Illus.). 256p. (Orig.). 1994. pap. 12.00 (*0-9640417-0-7*) Witness Min.
McHugh, Joe. Better Than Money: Tales to Treasure for a Lifetime. LC 91-70909. (Illus.). 125p. (J). (gr. 1-8). 1991. 11.95 (*0-9619943-1-2*) Catalpa Pr.
— Ruff Tales: High Octane Stories from the Ruff Creek General Store. LC 87-92243. (Illus.). 144p. 1988. 11.95 (*0-9619943-0-4*) Catalpa Pr.
— Visitor from the Past: An Audio Adventure in Ten Thrilling Episodes, 5 cass., Set. (Illus.). 40p. (YA). (gr. 6-11). 1993. teacher ed, audio 55.00 (*0-9619943-2-0*) Catalpa Pr.
McHugh, John, jt. auth. see Ripley, Brian J.
McHugh, Madeline & Balzert, Birgit. Guide to Germany. LC 93-39021. (Little Library). (Illus.). 32p. (J). (gr. 1-4). 1994. 3.95 (*1-85697-959-8*, Kingfisher LKC) LKC.
McHugh, Mark & Krukonis, Val. Supercritical Fluid Extraction. 2nd ed. (Chemical Engineering Technical Ser.). (Illus.). 608p. 1994. 94.95 (*0-7506-9244-8*) Buttrwrth-Heinemann.
Mchugh, Maureen E. Shaking Your Family Tree Workbook: A Basic Guide to Tracing Your Family's Genealogy. 64p. (Orig.). 1990. pap. 9.95 (*0-89909-309-4*, 80-551-7) Yankee Bks.
McHugh, Maureen F. China Mountain Zhang. 320p. 1992. 19.95 (*0-312-85271-1*) Tor Bks.
— China Mountain Zhang. 320p. 1993. mass mkt. 3.99 (*0-8125-0892-0*) Tor Bks.
— Half the Day Is Night. 320p. 1994. 21.95 (*0-312-85479-X*) Tor Bks.
— Half the Day Is Night. 320p. 1996. pap. 5.99 (*0-614-05512-1*) Tor Bks.
McHugh, Michael P., tr. see Ambrose.
McHugh, Neil. Holymen of the Blue Nile: The Making of an Arab Islamic Community in the Nilotic Sudan, 1500-1850. (Islam & Society in Africa Ser.). 240p. 1993. 54.95 (*0-8101-1069-5*) Northwestern U Pr.
***McHugh, Patrick, et al.** Beyond Business Process Reengineering: Towards the Holonic Enterprise. LC 94-30745. 1995. text ed. 29.95 (*0-471-95087-4*) Wiley.
McHugh, Paul R. & McKusick, Victor A. Genes, Brain, & Behavior. (Association for Research in Nervous & Mental Disease Research Publications: Vol. 69). 256p. 1991. 116.50 (*0-88167-725-6*, 2192) Raven.
McHugh, Paul R. & Slavney, Phillip R. The Perspectives of Psychiatry. LC 83-6157. (Contemporary Medicine & Public Health Ser.). 176p. 1983. text ed. 26.50 (*0-8018-3039-7*) Johns Hopkins.
— The Perspectives of Psychiatry. LC 83-6157. 176p. 1986. reprint ed. pap. text ed. 12.95 (*0-8018-3302-7*) Johns Hopkins.
McHugh, Paul R., jt. auth. see Slavney, Phillip R.
McHugh, Peter, jt. ed. see Blum, Alan.
McHugh, Roger, ed. Jack B. Yeats: A Centenary Gathering. 1971. 8.95 (*0-685-20029-9*, Pub. by Colin Smythe Ltd UK) Dufour.
— Jack B. Yeats, a Centenary Gathering. 1971. pap. 9.95 (*0-85105-205-3*, Pub. by Dolmen Pr IE) Dufour.
McHugh, Roland. Annotations to Finnegans Wake. rev. ed. LC 90-23512. 640p. 1991. pap. text ed. 26.50 (*0-8018-4190-9*) Johns Hopkins.
— Annotations to Finnegans Wake. 2nd rev. ed. LC 90-23512. 640p. 1991. 75.00 (*0-8018-4226-3*) Johns Hopkins.
— Annotations to Finnegans Wake. LC 79-18419. 640p. reprint ed. pap. 180.00 (*0-8357-7881-9*, 2036299) Bks Demand.
— The Finnegans Wake Experience. (Quantum Bks.: No. 19). 130p. 1981. 38.00 (*0-520-04298-0*) U CA Pr.
McHugh, Roy, et al. Pittsburgh Characters: Told by Pittsburgh Characters. LC 90-61417. 417p. (Orig.). 1991. pap. text ed. 5.95 (*1-878783-00-9*) Iconoclast Pr.
McHugh, Sean, ed. Illness Behavior: A Multidisciplinary Model. LC 87-2530. 442p. 1987. 85.00 (*0-306-42486-X*, Plenum Pr) Plenum.
McHugh, Thomas K., jt. auth. see Greenwald, Martin L.
McHugh, Thomas P., et al. Human Performance Workbook. 224p. 1991. spiral bd. 20.95 (*0-8403-6823-2*) Kendall-Hunt.
— The Wellness Workbook: An Interactive Test. 224p. (C). 1994. spiral bd. 20.95 (*0-8403-9451-9*) Kendall-Hunt.
***McHugh, Tom.** Flying Saucers Are Everywhere. (Illus.). 150p. 1995. pap. 12.95 (*0-87975-982-8*) Prometheus Bks.
McHugh, Tom & Hobson, Victoria. The Time of the Buffalo. LC 78-24261. (Illus.). xxiv, 383p. 1979. reprint ed. pap. 14.95 (*0-8032-8105-6*, Bison Books) U of Nebr Pr.
McHugh, Vincent. I Am Thinking of My Darling. LC 90-25933. 308p. 1991. reprint ed. pap. 9.95 (*1-878274-05-8*) Yarrow Pr.
— I Am Thinking of My Darling: An Adventure Story. Reginald, R. & Melville, Douglas, eds. LC 77-84254. (Lost Race & Adult Fantasy Ser.). 1978. reprint ed. lib. bdg. 28.95 (*0-405-10998-9*) Ayer.
McHugh, William D., jt. auth. see Granath, Lars.
Mcian, R. R. Clans & Tartans Library Style. 1989. pap. 0.99 (*0-517-67590-0*) Random Hse Value.
Mciiroy, M. D. Readings. 2nd ed. (Unix Programmer's Ser.: Vol. II). 630p. (C). 1990. pap. text ed. 35.75 (*0-03-047529-5*) SCP.
— Unix Research System Vol. 1: Programmer's Manual. 2nd ed. (Unix Programmer's Ser.: Vol. I). 702p. (C). 1990. pap. text ed. 34.75 (*0-03-047532-5*) SCP.
McIlhaney, Joe S., Jr. Safe Sex: A Doctor Explains the Risks & Realities of AIDS & Other STDs. 176p. 1992. pap. 8.99 (*0-8010-6294-2*) Baker Bk.
— Sexuality & Sexually Transmitted Diseases: A Doctor Confronts the Myth of "Safe" Sex. LC 90-649. 176p. (Orig.). (J). 1990. pap. 8.99 (*0-8010-6274-8*) Baker Bk.
McIlhaney, Joe S. & Nethery, Susan. Twelve Hundred Fifty Health-Care Questions Women Ask: With Straightforward Answers by an Obstetrician-Gynecologist. 2nd ed. LC 85-71179. 832p. 1992. 34.99 (*0-8010-6289-6*) Baker Bk.
McIlhaney, Joe S., Jr., jt. auth. see Sneed, Sharon M.
McIlhenny. Alligator's Life History. LC 76-6228. 1976. write for info. (*0-916984-01-X*); pap. write for info. (*0-916984-00-1*) SSAR.
McIlhenny, Chuck, et al. When the Wicked Seize a City. LC 91-78342. 240p. 1992. pap. 9.99 (*1-56384-024-3*) Huntington Hse.
McIlhenny, E. A. The Alligator's Life History. 128p. 1987. pap. 7.95 (*0-89815-230-5*) Ten Speed Pr.
McIlhenny, Edward A. The Wild Turkey & Its Hunting. (Illus.). 245p. 1984. 24.95 (*0-685-62740-3*) Real Turkeys Pubs.
McIlhenny, Edward A., ed. Befo' de War Spirituals: Words & Melodies. LC 72-1724. reprint ed. 37.50 (*0-404-08325-0*) AMS Pr.
McIlhenny, Paul & Hunter, Barbara. The Tabasco Cookbook: 125 Years of America's Favorite Pepper Sauce. LC 92-5520. 144p. 1993. 14.00 (*0-517-58965-6*, C P Pubs) Crown Pub Group.
McIlhenny, Robyn. Our Baby. LC 92-27268. (Voyages Ser.). (Illus.). (J). 1993. 3.75 (*0-383-03646-1*) SRA Schl Grp.
McIlhiney, David B. A Gentleman in Every Slum: Church or England Missions in East London, 1837-1914. (Princeton Theological Monograph Ser.: No. 16). x, 141p. (Orig.). 1988. pap. 10.00 (*0-915138-95-6*) Pickwick.
McIlhon, John J. Fifty Days Plus Forever: Daily Meditations for Easter. 163p. 1990. pap. 5.95 (*0-8146-1958-4*) Liturgical Pr.
— Forty Days Plus Three: Daily Reflections for Lent & Holy Week. 135p. 1989. pap. 5.95 (*0-8146-1769-7*) Liturgical Pr.
— God Is with Us: Daily Reflections for Advent. 96p. 1989. pap. 5.95 (*0-8146-1898-7*) Liturgical Pr.
— A Little Out of the Ordinary: Daily Readings for Ordinary Time. LC 93-40564. 216p. (Orig.). 1994. pap. text ed. 11.95 (*0-8146-2274-7*) Liturgical Pr.
— O Marvellous Exchange: Daily Reflections on Christmas & Epiphany. 88p. (Orig.). 1992. pap. text ed. 5.95 (*0-8146-2013-2*) Liturgical Pr.
McIlhone, James. The Word Made Clear. 1991. pap. 16.95 (*0-88347-268-6*) Thomas More.
McIllhaney, Joe S. 1,250 Health-Care Questions Women Ask. 1992. pap. 24.99 (*1-56179-089-3*) Focus Family.
McIllwaine, Cathy, jt. auth. see Chant, Sylvia.
McIlnay, Annabelle. Making Wine at Home. (Illus.). 192p. 1976. pap. 3.95 (*0-8065-0520-6*, Citadel Pr) Carol Pub Group.
McIlnay, Dennis P. Foundations & Higher Education: Dollars, Donors & Scholars. 206p. 1991. 29.50 (*0-914746-28-6*) G Kurian.
McIlquham, John, ed. Gallup 1985 Annual Report on Book Buying. 313p. 1986. spiral bd. 75.00 (*0-318-20071-6*) Gallup NJ.
McIlrath, T. J., ed. see American Institute of Physics.
McIlroy, Brian, jt. ed. see Loiselle, Andre.
McIlroy, Christopher. All My Relations. LC 93-23006. (Flannery O'Connor Award for Short Fiction Ser.). 200p. 1994. 19.95 (*0-8203-1602-4*) U of Ga Pr.
***McIlroy, John.** Trade Unions in Britain Today. 2nd ed. (Illus.). 304p. 1995. text ed. 59.95 (*0-7190-3982-7*, Pub. by Manchester Univ Pr UK); text ed. 19.95 (*0-7190-3983-5*, Pub. by Manchester Univ Pr UK) St Martin.
McIlroy, John & Jones, Bill. Going to University: The Student Guide. (Illus.). 300p. 1993. text ed. 12.95 (*0-7190-3182-6*, Pub. by Manchester Univ Pr UK) St Martin.
McIlroy, Kenneth, jt. ed. see Stoltzfus, Joel M.
McIlroy, Lydia L. Jenny's Journals. 1993. 14.95 (*0-533-10504-8*) Vantage.
McIlvain, Myra H. Texas Auto Trails: The Northeast. (Illus.). 277p. 1984. pap. 9.95 (*0-292-78055-9*) U of Tex Pr.
— Texas Auto Trails: The South & the Rio Grande Valley. (Illus.). 256p. 1985. pap. 9.95 (*0-292-78064-8*) U of Tex Pr.
— Texas Auto Trails: The Southeast. (Illus.). 293p. 1982. pap. 8.95 (*0-292-78050-8*) U of Tex Pr.
McIlvaine, Betsy. A Consumer's, Researcher's, & Student's Guide to Government Publications. LC 83-3621. 115p. 1983. pap. 18.00 (*0-8242-0690-8*) Wilson.
McIlvaine, Charles & MacAdam, Robert. One Thousand American Fungi. (Illus.). 729p. 1973. pap. 12.95 (*0-486-22782-0*) Dover.
McIlvaine, Charles & MacAdam, Robert K. One Thousand American Fungi. LC 72-91857. (Illus.). 1973. reprint ed. pap. 10.00 (*0-87110-094-0*) Ultramarine Pub.
McIlvaine, Eileen, et al. P. G. Wodehouse: A Comprehensive Bibliography & Checklist. (Wodehouse Monograph: No. 2). (Illus.). 544p. (Orig.). 1995. 135.00 (*0-87008-101-2*) JAS Heineman.
McIlvaine, Eileen, et al, eds. P. G. Wodehouse: A Comprehensive Bibliography & Checklist. (Illus.). 489p. 1991. lib. bdg. 135.00 (*0-87008-125-X*) JAS Heineman.
McIlvaine, Paul. Dead Towns of Sunbury & Dorchester. 3rd ed. LC 75-26008. 1976. 5.95 (*0-9600410-3-6*) P McIlvaine.
***McIlvanney, Hugh.** McIlvanney on Football. 283p. 1995. 34.95 (*1-85158-661-X*, Pub. by Mnstream UK) Trafalgar.
McIlvanney, William. Laidlaw. 1993. pap. 9.95 (*0-15-648109-X*) HarBrace.
— Papers of Tony Veitch. 1993. pap. 9.95 (*0-15-670828-0*) HarBrace.
— Shades of Grey: Glasgow 1956-1987. (Illus.). 224p. 1993. 34.95 (*1-85158-047-6*, Pub. by Mnstream UK) Trafalgar.
— Strange Loyalties. 1993. pap. 9.95 (*0-15-685644-1*) HarBrace.
McIlveen, J. F. Fundamentals of Weather & Climate. 544p. 1991. pap. write for info. (*0-412-41160-1*) Chapman & Hall.
— Fundamentals of Weather & Climate. (J). (gr. 5 up). 1991. pap. 39.95 (*0-442-31476-0*) Chapman & Hall.

McIlvenna, Ted. Complete Guide to Safer Sex: The Institute for Advanced Study of Human Sexuality. 1992. pap. 6.95 (0-942637-58-5) Barricade Bks.
— Meditations on the Gift of Sexuality. 77p. 1977. 12.95 (0-317-34148-0) Specific Pr.
— The "Yes" Book of Sex for Men. (Illus.). 128p. 1986. 20.00 (0-8184-0367-5) Carol Pub Group.
McIlvenna, Ted, ed. Safe Sex in the Age of AIDS. 96p. 1986. pap. 3.95 (0-8065-0996-1, Citadel Pr) Carol Pub Group.
McIlvenna, Ted, et al. The Complete Guide to Safe Sex. 200p. (Orig.). 1987. pap. text ed. 6.95 (0-930846-05-2) Specific Pr.
McIlvoy, Kevin. The Fifth Station. 224p. 1988. 12.95 (0-912697-76-8) Algonquin Bks.
— A Waltz. LC 80-26883. (Illus.). 105p. 1981. pap. 7.00 (0-89924-032-1) Lynx Hse.
McIlwain, et al. The Fifty-Plus Wellness Program. large type ed. 300p. 1991. reprint ed. lib. bdg. 19.95 (1-56054-216-0) Thorndike Pr.
— Fifty-Plus Wellness Program. large type ed. 300p. 1992. pap. 13.95 (1-56054-975-0) Thorndike Pr.
McIlwain, Charles H. The American Revolution: A Constitutional Interpretation. LC 74-166335. (Era of the American Revolution Ser.). 198p. 1973. reprint ed. lib. bdg. 27.50 (0-306-70249-5) Da Capo.
— Constitutionalism & the Changing World: Collected Papers. LC 75-103801. (Cambridge University Press Library Editions). 320p. reprint ed. pap. 91.20 (0-685-16092-0, 2027246) Bks Demand.
— The High Court of Parliament. Mayer, J. P., ed. LC 78-67368. (European Political Thought Ser.). 1980. reprint ed. lib. bdg. 33.95 (0-405-11719-1) Ayer.
*McIlwain, Harris H. & Bruce, Debra F. My Parent, My Turn. LC 94-45744. 1995. 12.99 (0-8054-6179-5) Broadman.
McIlwain, Harris H., et al. The Fifty Plus Wellness Program. 1990. pap. text ed. 12.95 (0-471-50686-9) Wiley.
— Winning with Arthritis. (Science Editions Ser.). 1991. pap. text ed. 14.95 (0-471-52847-1) Wiley.
— Winning with Back Pain. LC 93-8379. 1994. pap. text ed. 12.95 (0-471-30328-3) Wiley.
— Winning with Chronic Pain: A Complete Program for Health & Well-Being. 222p. (C). 1994. 24.95x (0-87975-900-3); pap. 16.95 (0-87975-878-3) Prometheus Bks.
— Winning with Heart Attack: A Complete Program for Health & Well-Being. (Illus.). 189p. (C). 1994. 27.95 (0-87975-914-3) Prometheus Bks.
— Winning with Heart Attack: A Complete Program for Health & Well-Being. (Illus.). 189p. (C). 1994. pap. 16.95 (0-87975-915-1) Prometheus Bks.
— Winning with Osteoporosis. 2nd ed. 160p. 1993. pap. text ed. 12.95 (0-471-30489-1) Wiley.
McIlwain, John. The Dorling Kindersley Children's Illustrated Dictionary. LC 94-9561. (Illus.). 256p. (J). (gr. 3-6). 1994. 19.95 (1-56458-625-1) Dorling Kindersley.
*McIlwaine, H. R., ed. Journals of the House of Burgesses of Virginia: 1742-1747, 1748-1749. 427p. 1995. reprint ed. pap. text ed. 52.00 (0-7884-0199-8) Heritage Bk.
— The Letters of Patrick Henry. LC 27-2700. (Official Letters of the Governors of the State of Virginia Ser.: Vol. 1). vii, 410p. 1926. 19.95 (0-88490-018-5) VA State Lib.
— The Letters of Thomas Nelson & Benjamin Harrison. LC 27-2700. (Official Letters of the Governors of Virginia Ser. Vol. 3). xii, 510p. 1929. 19.95 (0-88490-020-7) VA State Lib.
— Proceedings of the Committees of Safety of Cumberland & Isle of Wight Counties, Virginia, 1775-1776. 54p. 1919. text ed. 5.00 (0-685-52452-3) VA State Lib.
McIlwaine, H. R., ed. see House of Burgesses of Virginia Staff.
McIlwaine, Henry R. The Struggle of Protestant Dissenters for Religious Toleration in Virginia. LC 78-63830. (Johns Hopkins University. Studies in the Social Sciences. Thirtieth Ser. 1912: 4). reprint ed. 11.50 (0-404-61090-0) AMS Pr.
McIlwaine, Henry R., ed. Legislative Journals of the Council of Colonial Virginia. 2nd ed. LC 79-13108. xii, 1646p. 1979. reprint ed. 50.00 (0-88490-078-9) VA State Lib.
— Minutes of the Council & General Court of Colonial Virginia. 2nd ed. LC 79-13080. xviii, 668p. 1979. reprint ed. 29.95 (0-88490-077-0) VA State Lib.
McIlwaine, Ia, et al, eds. Bibliography & Reading: A Festschrift in Honour of Ronald Staveley. LC 82-21489. 180p. 1983. 25.00 (0-8108-1601-6) Scarecrow.
*McIlwaine, John. Maps & Mapping of Africa. 1996. write for info. (1-873836-76-7) Bowker-Saur.
— Writings on African Archives. 200p. 1995. 75.00 (1-873836-66-X) Bowker-Saur.
McIlwaine, John, ed. Africa: A Guide to Reference Material. (Regional Reference Guides Ser.: No. 1). 592p. 1993. 125.00 (0-905450-43-4, Pub. by H Zell Pubs UK) Bowker-Saur.
McIlwee, Judith S. & Robinson, J. Gregg. Women in Engineering: Gender, Power, & Workplace Culture. LC 91-2050. (SUNY Series in Science, Technology, & Society). (Illus.). 248p. (C). 1992. 74.50x (0-7914-0869-8); pap. 24.95x (0-7914-0870-1) State U NY Pr.
McIlwee, Terry. Personnel Management in Context: The Late 1980s. 335p. (C). 1986. 85.00 (0-946139-35-0, Pub. by Elm Pubns UK) St Mut.
McIlwraith, Archibald K., ed. Five Elizabethan Tragedies. LC 81-6574. xx, 399p. 1981. reprint ed. text ed. 75.00 (0-313-22528-1, MCFE, Greenwood Pr) Greenwood.
McIlwraith, C. Wayne. Diagnostic & Surgical Arthroscopy in the Horse. 2nd ed. LC 89-2463. (Illus.). 227p. 1990. text ed. 98.50 (0-8121-1186-9) Williams & Wilkins.
McIlwraith, Michael. Arthritis Diet Cookbook: A Personal Recipe for Total Fitness. 1992. pap. 11.95 (0-575-04265-6, Pub. by V Gollancz UK) Trafalgar.
McIlwraith, T. F. The Bella Coola Indians, Vols. 1 & 2. 2nd ed. 1536p. 1992. 125.00 (0-8020-2820-9); pap. 60.00 (0-8020-7692-0) U of Toronto Pr.
McIlwraith, W. Map of Oregon Trail: Wall. 1986. 5.95 (0-8323-0052-7) Binford Mort.
McIlwraith, Wayne, jt. auth. see Turner, A. Simon.
McIndoo, Ethel. Discover Girls in Action. 22p. (Orig.). (SPA.). (J). (gr. 4-6). 1988. pap. text ed. 1.50 (0-936625-74-0); pap. text ed. 1.50 (0-936625-41-4) Womans Mission Union.
— Missions Adventures 1. Massey, Barbara, ed. 32p. (Orig.). (J). (gr. 1-6). 1991. pap. text ed. 1.50 (1-56309-026-0) Womans Mission Union.
— Missions Adventures 2. Massey, Barbara, ed. 32p. (Orig.). (J). (gr. 1-6). 1991. pap. text ed. 1.50 (1-56309-027-9) Womans Mission Union.
— Missions Adventures 3. Massey, Barbara, ed. 32p. (J). (gr. 1-6). 1991. pap. text ed. 1.50 (1-56309-028-7) Womans Mission Union.
— Missions Adventures 4. Massey, Barbara, ed. 32p. (Orig.). (J). (gr. 1-6). 1991. pap. text ed. 1.50 (1-56309-029-5) Womans Mission Union.
— Missions Adventures 5. Massey, Barbara, ed. 32p. (Orig.). (J). (gr. 1-6). 1991. pap. text ed. 1.50 (1-56309-030-9) Womans Mission Union.
— Missions Adventures 6. Massey, Barbara, ed. 32p. (Orig.). (J). (gr. 1-6). 1991. pap. text ed. 1.50 (1-56309-031-7) Womans Mission Union.
— Too Late to Say Good-Bye: My Experience with Aging Parents. 64p. (Orig.). 1988. pap. 2.95 (0-936625-28-7, New Hope AL) Womans Mission Union.
McIndoo, Ethel & Massey, Barbara. Girls in Action Leader Manual. rev. ed. (Illus.). 96p. 1988. pap. text ed. 2.95 (0-936625-40-6) Womans Mission Union.
McIndoo, Ethel, jt. auth. see Kizer, Kathryn.
*McInerney. Brightness Falls. 1994. 3.99 (0-517-13614-7) Random Hse Value.
McInerney, ed. see Chekhov, Anton.
McInerney, Audrey. The Rebirth of Chilean Democracy. (Critical Issues Ser.: No. 1). 28p. 1992. pap. 4.95 (0-87609-125-7) Coun Foreign.
McInerney, Claire. Find It! The Inside Story at Your Library. (Study Skills Ser.). (Illus.). 56p. (J). (gr. 4 up). 1989. lib. bdg. 14.95 (0-8225-2425-2, Lerner Publctns) Lerner Group.
— Tracking the Facts: How to Develop Research Skills. (Study Skills Ser.). (Illus.). 64p. (J). (gr. 4 up). 1990. lib. bdg. 14.95 (0-8225-2426-0, Lerner Publctns) Lerner Group.
McInerney, Daniel J. The Fortunate Heirs of Freedom: Abolition & Republican Thought. LC 93-37454. xii, 232p. 1994. text ed. 37.50 (0-8032-3172-5) U of Nebr Pr.
McInerney, Francis & White, Sean. Beating Japan: How Hundreds of American Companies Are Beating Japan Now - & What Your Company Can Learn from Their Strategies & Successes. 352p. 1994. pap. 12.95 (0-452-27223-8, Plume-Truman Talley Bks) NAL-Dutton.
— The Total Quality Corporation: How 10 Major Companies Turned Quality & Environmental Challenges to Competitive Advantage in the 1990s. 320p. 1995. 24.95 (0-525-93928-8, Dutton-Truman Talley) NAL-Dutton.
McInerney, Jay. Bright Lights, Big City. LC 84-40074. (Vintage Contemporaries Ser.). 208p. (Orig.). 1984. pap. 9.00 (0-394-72641-3, Vin) Random.
— Brightness Falls. 1992. pap. 22.50 (0-679-40219-5) McKay.
— Brightness Falls. LC 92-50604. 1993. pap. 12.00 (0-679-74532-7, Vin) Random.
— Ransom. 280p. 1985. pap. 11.00 (0-394-74118-8, Vin) Random.
— Story of My Life. (Contemporaries Ser.). 1989. pap. 9.00 (0-679-72257-2, Vin) Random.
McInerney, Judith W. Judge Benjamin: The Superdog Gift. (Illus.). 128p. (J). (gr. 2-4). 1987. reprint ed. pap. 2.95 (0-8167-1043-0) Troll Assocs.
— Judge Benjamin: The Superdog Rescue. (Illus.). (J). (gr. 4-6). pap. 2.75 (0-317-66178-7, Minstrel Bks) PB.
McInerney, Kathleen H., jt. auth. see Courts, Patrick L.
McInerney, Merry. Burning down the House. 256p. 1994. 17.95 (0-312-85698-9) Forge NYC.
— Burning down the House. 320p. 1995. mass mkt. 5.99 (0-8125-3651-7) Forge NYC.
— Burning Point. 1996. 20.95 (0-312-85699-7) Forge NYC.
McInerney, Peter, jt. auth. see Maitland, Terrence.
McInerney, Peter K. Introduction to Philosophy. LC 91-58272. (Outline Ser.). (Illus.). 304p. (Orig.). (C). 1992. pap. 12.00 (0-06-467124-0, Harper Ref) HarpC.
— Time & Experience. 224p. 1991. 44.95 (0-87722-752-7) Temple U Pr.
— Time & Experience. 296p. 1993. pap. 22.95 (1-56639-010-9) Temple U Pr.
McInerney, Peter K. & Rainbolt, George W. Ethics. LC 93-50930. (College Outline Ser.). (Illus.). 224p. (Orig.). 1994. pap. 12.00 (0-06-467166-6, Hacker) HarpC.
McInerney, Ralph. Savings & Loam. large type ed. LC 90-47661. 257p. 1990. reprint ed. lib. bdg. 19.95 (1-56054-072-9) Thorndike Pr.
McInerny, Ralph. Abracadaver. large type ed. (Nightingale Ser.). 1990. pap. 12.95 (0-8161-4904-6) G K Hall.
— Aquinas Against the Averroists: On There Being Only One Intellect. LC 92-16179. (Series in the History of Philosophy). 240p. 1993. 32.00 (1-55753-028-9); pap. 14.95 (1-55753-029-7) Purdue U Pr.
— Aquinas on Human Action: A Theory of Practice. LC 90-27754. 244p. 1992. pap. text ed. 19.95 (0-8132-0761-4) Cath U Pr.
— Art & Prudence: Studies in the Thought of Jacques Maritain. LC 88-18826. (C). 1988. text ed. 21.95 (0-268-00619-9); pap. text ed. 9.95 (0-268-00620-2) U of Notre Dame Pr.
— The Basket Case. large type ed. LC 92-18387. (Nightingale Ser.). 280p. 1992. pap. 14.95 (0-8161-5569-0, Nightingale) Hall.
— Boethius & Aquinas. LC 89-15705. 268p. 1990. 34.95 (0-8132-0709-6) Cath U Pr.
— A Cardinal Offense. large type ed. LC 94-47945. 694p. 1995. 22.95 (0-7862-0402-8) Thorndike Pr.
— Cardinal Offense: A Father Dowling Mystery. 384p. 1994. 21.95 (0-312-11283-1) St Martin.
— The Case of the Constant Caller. LC 95-14716. (J). 1995. 16.95 (0-312-13037-6, Griffin) St Martin.
— The Case of the Dead Winner. LC 95-14727. (J). 1995. 16.95 (0-312-13038-4, Griffin) St Martin.
— Desert Sinner. (WWL Mystery Ser.). 1994. mass mkt. 3.99 (0-373-26158-6, 1-26158-5) Harlequin Bks.
— Desert Sinner. (Father Dowling Mystery Ser.). 192p. 1992. 16.95 (0-312-08177-4) St Martin.
— Desert Sinner. large type ed. (Popular Ser.). 320p. 1993. reprint ed. pap. 17.95 (1-56054-631-X) Thorndike Pr.
— Easeful Death. 256p. 1991. text ed. 19.95 (0-689-12131-8, Atheneum S&S) S&S Trade.
— Easeful Death. large type ed. 393p. 1992. reprint ed. lib. bdg. 19.95 (1-56054-351-5) Thorndike Pr.
— A First Glance at St. Thomas Aquinas: A Handbook for Peeping Thomists. LC 89-40392. (C). 1990. text ed. 19.95 (0-268-00976-7); pap. text ed. 9.95 (0-268-00975-9) U of Notre Dame Pr.
— Four on the Floor. 1994. mass mkt. 3.99 (0-373-26154-3) Harlequin Bks.
— Four on the Floor. braille ed. 295p. 1990. vinyl bd. 23.60 (1-56956-232-6, BR8248) W A T Braille.
— Infra Dig. 218p. 1992. text ed. 19.00 (0-689-12132-6, Pub. by Ctrl Bur voor Schimmel NE) Macmillan.
— Judas Priest. 1994. mass mkt. 3.99 (0-373-26156-X, 1-26156-9) Harlequin Bks.
— Judas Priest. large type ed. LC 92-814. 331p. 1992. reprint ed. lib. bdg. 17.95 (1-56054-376-0) Thorndike Pr.
— Judas Priest: A Father Dowling Mystery. 208p. 1991. 17.95 (0-312-06375-X) St Martin.
— Law & Ardor: An Andrew Broom Mystery. 256p. 1995. 20.00 (0-684-80462-X, Scribners) S&S Trade.
— Mom & Dead. 256p. 1994. text ed. 20.00 (0-689-12181-4, Atheneum S&S) S&S Trade.
— Mom & Dead: An Andrew Broom Mystery. large type ed. LC 94-6062. 302p. 1994. reprint ed. bds. 20.95 (0-7862-0211-4) Thorndike Pr.
— The Question of Christian Ethics. LC 92-25511. (Michael J. McGivney Lectures of the John Paul II Institutes for Studies on Marriage & Family: Vol. 1990). 74p. 1993. 21.95 (0-8132-0770-3); pap. 9.95 (0-8132-0771-1) Cath U Pr.
— Rest in Pieces. large type ed. (Nightingale Ser.). 280p. 1991. pap. 13.95 (0-8161-5107-5, Nightingale) Hall.
— Rhyme & Reason: St. Thomas & Modes of Discourse. LC 81-80234. (Aquinas Lectures). 84p. (C). 1981. 10.00 (0-87462-148-8) Marquette.
— The Search Committee. large type ed. 1991. 23.95 (0-7089-8613-7, Trail West Pubs) Ulverscroft.
— Seed of Doubt: A Father Dowling Mystery. 352p. 1993. 19.95 (0-312-09381-0) St Martin.
— St. Thomas Aquinas. LC 81-16293. 197p. (C). 1982. reprint ed. pap. text ed. 9.95 (0-268-01707-7) U of Notre Dame Pr.
McInerny, Ralph, ed. The Catholic Woman: Papers Presented at a Conference Sponsored by the Wethersfield Institute, 1990. LC 91-71498. (Westhersfield Institute Proceedings: No. III). 131p. (Orig.). 1991. pap. 10.95 (0-89870-369-7) Ignatius Pr.
— Modernity & Religion. LC 93-8804. (C). 1994. text ed. 21.95 (0-268-01408-6) U of Notre Dame Pr.
McInerny, Ralph, ed. see Maritain, Jacques.
McInerny, Ralph, ed. see Peters, Ellis, et al.
McInerny, Ralph, jt. pref. see St. Thomas Aquinas.
McInerny, Ralph, ed. see Wethersfield Institute Staff.
McInerny, Ralph M. A History of Western Philosophy, Vol. 3. LC 63-20526. 604p. reprint ed. pap. 172.20 (0-317-55787-4, 2029310) Bks Demand.
McInerny, Ralph M., ed. New Themes in Christian Philosophy. LC 68-20439. 1968. 37.95 (0-8290-1654-6); pap. text ed. 9.50 (0-8290-1606-6) Irvington.
— New Themes in Christian Philosophy. LC 68-20439. 1968. 24.95 (0-268-00192-8) U of Notre Dame Pr.
McInery, Timothy A. Private Man. 1962. 12.95 (0-8392-1087-6) Astor-Honor.
McInish, Thomas H., jt. auth. see Kudla, Ronald J.
McInnes, Adrian. Handbook on Damages. 133p. 1992. pap. 37.00 (0-455-21088-8, Pub. by Law Bk Co) W W Gaunt.
McInnes, Celia. Projects for Summer & Holiday Activities. Young, Richard G., ed. LC 89-11791. (Seasonal Projects Ser.). (Illus.). 32p. (J). (gr. 3-5). 1989. lib. bdg. 15.93 (0-944483-39-9) Garrett Ed Corp.
*McInnes, Colin & Rolls, Mark G., eds. Post-Cold War Security Issues in the Asia-Pacific Region. LC 94-3570. 1994. pap. write for info. (0-7146-4574-5, Pub. by F Cass Pubs UK) Intl Spec Bk.
McInnes, Colin J. NATO's Changing Strategic Agenda. 208p. (C). 1990. text ed. 49.95 (0-04-445211-X) Routledge Chapman & Hall.
McInnes, Colin J., ed. Security & Strategy in the New Europe. LC 92-9285. 256p. 1992. 69.95 (0-415-07120-8, A7655); pap. 17.95 (0-415-08303-6, A7659) Routledge.
McInnes, Colin J. & Sheffield, Gary D., eds. Warfare in the Twentieth Century: Theory & Practice. 256p. 1988. text ed. 55.00 (0-04-355034-7); pap. text ed. 19.95 (0-04-355035-5) Routledge Chapman & Hall.
McInnes, D. Keith, jt. auth. see Bitran, Ricardo A.
McInnes, Edward. Woyzeck, Cuchner: Critical Monographs in English. 1993. pap. 32.00 (0-85261-341-5, Pub. by Univ of Glasgow UK) St Mut.
McInnes, Ian. The Meritorious Service Medal to Aerial Forces. 63p. (C). 1987. 50.00 (0-902633-92-9, Pub. by Picton UK) St Mut.
— The Meritorious Service Medal to Naval Forces. 63p. (C). 1987. 50.00 (0-317-90380-2, Pub. by Picton UK) St Mut.
McInnes, Ian & Fraser, Mark. Ashanti, Eighteen Ninety-Five. (Illus.). 156p. (C). 1987. 126.00 (0-948251-12-3, Pub. by Picton UK) St Mut.
McInnes, J. M. & Treffry, J. A. Deaf-Blind Infants & Children: A Developmental Guide. 1994. pap. 17.95 (0-8020-7787-0) U of Toronto Pr.
McInnes, John C. Divorce Law & Practice in Scotland. 1990. 63.00 (0-406-13210-0, U.K.) Butterworth Legal Pubs.
McInnes, John M. & Treffry, J. A. Deaf-Blind Infants & Children: A Development Guide. LC 82-190483. 302p. reprint ed. pap. 86.10 (0-7837-2049-1, 2042324) Bks Demand.
McInnes, Mary D., jt. auth. see Sichel, Kim.
*McInnes, Mary D., et al. Alumni Drawings: Celebrating Forty Years of the Visual Arts at Boston University School for the Arts. (Illus.). 29p. (Orig.). (C). 1995. pap. text ed. 5.00 (1-881450-05-8) Boston U Art.
McInnes, Ron. Landlord-Tenant Rights in Ontario: Canadian Edition. 9th ed. (Legal Ser.). 232p. 1993. 8.95 (0-88908-396-7) Self-Counsel Pr.
McInnes, Val A., ed. New Visions: Historical & Theological Perspectives on the Jewish-Christian Dialogue. 252p. 1993. 18.95x (0-8245-1246-4) Crossroad NY.
— Renewing the Judeo-Christian Wellsprings. LC 86-24909. 160p. 1987. 16.95 (0-8245-0832-7) Crossroad NY.
McInnis-Dittrich, Kathleen. Integrating Social Welfare Policy & Social Work Practice. LC 93-4781. 1994. text ed. 29.95 (0-534-17430-2) Brooks-Cole.
McInnis, Edgar, jt. auth. see Soward, Frederic H.
McInnis, Marina. Running Your Business with Quattro Pro for Windows. 300p. 1993. pap. 34.95 (1-883327-42-3) TitleWave Pr.
McInnis, Noel & Albrecht, Don, eds. What Makes Education Environmental? 470p. 1984. pap. 11.95 (0-914604-01-5) Plexus Pub.
McInnis, Noel, ed. see Hubbard, Barbara M.
McInnis, Noel, jt. auth. see Yeaman, Douglas.
McInnis, Raymond G. New Perspectives for Reference Service in Academic Libraries. LC 77-94742. (Contributions in Librarianship & Information Science Ser.: No. 23). (Illus.). 351p. 1979. text ed. 55.00 (0-313-20311-3, MNP/, Greenwood Pr) Greenwood.
— Research Guide for Psychology. LC 81-1377. (Reference Sources for the Social Sciences & Humanities Ser.: No. 1). (Illus.). xxvi, 604p. 1982. text ed. 105.00 (0-313-21399-2, MCR/, Greenwood Pr) Greenwood.
McIntire, Alexander H., Jr. Political & Electoral Confrontation in Revolutionary Nicaragua. 65p. (C). 1985. 12.95 (0-685-63341-1, LA204) U Miami N-S Ctr.
McIntire, C. T., ed. The Legacy of Herman Dooyeweerd: Reflections on Critical Philosophy in the Christian Tradition. (Illus.). 198p. (Orig.). 1986. lib. bdg. 48.00 (0-8191-5033-9, Inst Christ Stud) U Pr of Amer.
McIntire, C. T. & Perry, Marvin, eds. Toynbee: A Reappraisal. 40.00 (0-8020-5785-3) U of Toronto Pr.
McIntire, C. T., jt. auth. see Moir, John S.
McIntire, Carol, jt. auth. see McIntire, Roger.
McIntire, Cecil L. Lab Manual & Supplement for Human Anatomy. 1990. spiral bd. 18.50 (0-88252-165-9) Paladin Hse.
*McIntire, Deborah & Windham, Robert. Home Schooling. (Home Education Ser.). 144p. 1995. 15.98 (0-916119-84-X) Creat Teach Pr.
McIntire, Dennis, jt. ed. see Cummings, David.
McIntire, Donald. The Pemaquid Loon from Temple. (Illus.). (J). 1988. pap. 5.99 (0-317-92307-2) Herit Print Co.
McIntire, Donald, ed. see Chetkowski, Emily.
McIntire, Eileen, ed. see Slacker, Calvin A.
McIntire, H. G. The Theatre of Jean Anouilh. 166p. 1981. bds. 36.00 (0-389-20182-0, 06958) B&N Imports.
McIntire, Jamie. Santa's Christmas Surprise. LC 93-24843. (Glow-in-the-Dark Book Ser.). (Illus.). (J). (gr. k-3). 1993. pap. text ed. 2.95 (0-8167-3257-4) Troll Assocs.
McIntire, Jim. Early Days in Texas: A Trip to Hell & Heaven. LC 91-30547. (Illus.). 192p. (C). 1992. 22.95 (0-8061-2407-5) U of Okla Pr.
McIntire, John, et al. Crop-Livestock Interaction in Sub-Saharan Africa. LC 92-23012. (Regional & Sectoral Studies). 260p. 1992. 14.95 (0-8213-2166-8, 12166) World Bank.
McIntire, John J. As I Saw It. 1977. 18.95 (0-8369-9189-3, 9058) Ayer.
McIntire, Marina L. CIT Fourth National Conference Proceedings: "New Dimensions in Interpreter Education" LC 84-60332. 337p. 1984. pap. text ed. 10.95 (0-317-06558-0) RID Pubns.
McIntire, Marina L., ed. New Dimensions in Interpreter Education: Curriculum & Instruction: Proceedings of the Sixth National Convention, Conference of Interpreter Trainers. 147p. (Orig.). (C). 1987. pap. 10.95 (0-916883-04-3) RID Pubns.

An Asterisk (*) at the beginning of an entry indicates that the title is appearing in BIP for the first time.

— New Dimensions in Interpreter Education: Task Analysis -- Theory & Application: Proceedings of the Fifth National Convention, Conference of Interpreter Trainers. 173p. (Orig.). (C). 1986. pap. 9.95 (0-916883-02-7) RID Pubns.

— Proceedings of the Ninth RID National Convention, 1985: Interpreting: The Art of Cross-Cultural Mediation. 192p. (C). 1990. reprint ed. pap. 10.95 (0-916883-05-1) RID Pubns.

McIntire, Paul & Mester, Michael, eds. ASNT Nondestructive Testing Handbook, Vol. 4: Electromagnetic Testing. 2nd ed. (Illus.). 701p. 1986. 121.25 (0-931403-01-4, 129) Am Soc Nondestructive.

McIntire, Paul, jt. ed. see Bryant, Lawrence E.

McIntire, Paul, jt. ed. see Miller, Ronnie K.

McIntire, Paul, ed. see Wenk, Samuel A. & McMaster, Robert C.

McIntire, Robert, jt. comp. see Dodge, Steve.

McIntire, Robert C., ed. Daily Gleaner Index. 210p. 1990. lib. bdg. 150.00 (0-932265-18-9); disk 150.00 (0-932265-20-0) White Sound.

McIntire, Robert C., et al. The Bahamas Index, 1988. 400p. 1989. lib. bdg. 150.00 (0-932265-10-3); disk 150.00 (0-932265-11-1) White Sound.

***McIntire, Roger & McIntire, Carol.** Teenagers & Parents: Ten Steps for a Better Relationship. 161p. 1995. pap. 9.95 (0-9640558-4-8) Summit Crossrds.

McIntire, Roger, ed. see Slacker, Calvin A.

***McIntire, Roger W.** Enjoy Successful Parenting: Practical Strategies You Can Use Today. 200p. (Orig.). 1995. pap. 14.95 (0-9640558-1-3) Summit Crossrds.

McIntire, Ronald G. & Fessenden, John T. The Self-Directed School: Empowering the Stakeholders. LC 93-34345. 1995. 29.95x (0-590-49267-5, 28063m35 1994) Scholastic Inc.

McIntire, Russell. Live Your Faith! LC 78-25579. 167p. 1979. 7.95 (0-88289-217-7) Pelican.

McIntire, Tim, jt. auth. see Friedman, Robert D.

McIntire, Virginia A. Affirmative Word Power: Interpretations on a Metaphysical Vocabulary. 64p. 1992. pap. 7.50 (0-9634894-1-0) V A McIntire.

— Color Energy: For Mind - Body - Spirit. 102p. 1992. reprint ed. pap. 7.50 (0-9634894-0-2) V A McIntire.

McIntoch & Twyman, trs. The Archko Volume: Archeological Writings of the Sanhedrim & Talmuds of the Jews. 248p. 1976. spiral bd. 9.90 (0-7873-0598-7) Mokelumne.

McIntosh, A., jt. auth. see Newman, Michael C.

McIntosh, A., et al. Guide to a Linguistic Atlas of Late Mediaeval English. (Aberdeen University Press Bks.). 24p. 1987. pap. 6.00 (0-08-035076-3, Pub. by Aberdeen U Pr) Macmillan.

— A Linguistic Atlas of Late Mediaeval English, 4 vols., Set. 2400p. 1987. 670.00 (0-08-032437-1, Pub. by Aberdeen U Pr) Macmillan.

McIntosh, Alison, jt. ed. see Finkle, Jason L.

McIntosh, Allen A. Fitting Linear Models: An Application of Conjugate Gradient Algorithms. (Lecture Notes in Statistics Ser.: Vol. 10). (Illus.). 200p. 1982. pap. 32.00 (0-387-90746-7) Spr-Verlag.

McIntosh, Andrew, ed. Employment Policy in the United Kingdom & the United States: A Comparison of Efficiency & Equity. 188p. 1984. reprint ed. pap. text ed. 45.00 (0-8191-4104-6) U Pr of Amer.

McIntosh, Arthur H. & Maramorosch, Karl, eds. Arthropod Cell Culture Systems. LC 93-38285. 1994. 169.95 (0-8493-7642-4) CRC Pr.

McIntosh, Arthur H., jt. ed. see Maramorosch, Karl.

McIntosh, Barbara. Mississippi Kiss. 432p. 1994. mass mkt. 4.50 (0-8217-4779-7) Zebra.

McIntosh, Bruce A., jt. ed. see Halliday, Ian.

McIntosh, Burr. The Little I Saw of Cuba. 1976. lib. bdg. 59.95 (0-8490-2174-X) Gordon Pr.

McIntosh, C. Alison. Population Policy in Western Europe: Responses to Low Fertility in France, Sweden, & West Germany. LC 82-5840. 292p. reprint ed. pap. 83.30 (0-8357-2616-9, 2040103) Bks Demand.

McIntosh, C. Alison, jt. ed. see Finkle, Jason L.

McIntosh, Carey. The Choice of Life: Samuel Johnson & the World of Fiction. LC 73-77160. 243p. reprint ed. pap. 69.30 (0-8357-8073-2, 2033822) Bks Demand.

— Common & Courtly Language: The Stylistics of Social Class in Eighteenth-Century British Literature. LC 85-17857. 168p. 1986. text ed. 29.95 (0-8122-7998-0) U of Pa Pr.

***McIntosh, Charles.** The Nebraska Sand Hills. 677p. 1995. text ed. 50.00 (0-8032-3184-9) U of Nebr Pr.

McIntosh, Charles F. Brief Abstract of Lower Norfolk County & Norfolk County Wills. 223p. 1994. reprint ed. pap. 25.50 (0-8328-4019-X) Higginson Bk Co.

— Brief Abstracts of Norfolk County Wills, 1710-1753. 344p. 1982. reprint ed. pap. 30.00 (0-89308-324-0) Southern Hist Pr.

McIntosh, Christopher. The Rose Cross & the Age of Reason: Eighteenth-Century Rosicrucianism in Central Europe & Its Relationship to the Enlightenment. LC 91-44752. (Brill's Studies in Intellectual History: Vol. 29). (Illus.). 200p. 1992. 63.00 (90-04-09502-0) E J Brill.

McIntosh, Clarence F., jt. auth. see Hutchinson, W. H.

McIntosh, Crumbum, jt. auth. see O'Shea, Catherine Q.

McIntosh, D. M. Statistics for the Teacher. 2nd ed. 1967. 65.00 (0-08-012254-X, Pub. by Pergamon Repr UK) Franklin.

McIntosh, Dave. High Blue Battle: The War Diary of No. 1 (401) Fighter Squadron, RCAF. (Illus.). 192p. 1990. 24.95 (0-7737-2338-2, Pub. by Stoddart Pubng CN) Genl Dist Srvs.

— High Blue Battle: The War Diary of No. 1 (401) Fighter Squadron, RCAF. (Illus.). 192p. 1991. pap. 14.95 (0-7737-5441-5, Pub. by Stoddart Pubng CN) Genl Dist Srvs.

— Visits: On the Road to Things Past. 240p. 1990. 24.95 (0-7737-2428-1, Pub. by Stoddart Pubng CN) Genl Dist Srvs.

— When the Work's All Done This Fall: Voices of Early Canada the Opening of the Land. (Illus.). 320p. 1989. 29.95 (0-7737-2323-4, Pub. by Stoddart Pubng CN) Genl Dist Srvs.

— Who's Running This Country Anyhow? Ottawa Unbuttoned. 256p. 1987. 21.95 (0-7737-2115-0, Pub. by Stoddart Pubng CN) Genl Dist Srvs.

McIntosh, David & Holmes, Majorie. Personal Injury Awards in EC Countries: An Industry Report. 199p. 1990. pap. 265.00 (1-85044-349-1) Lloyds London Pr.

McIntosh, David C. How to Build a Wooden Boat. (Illus.). 264p. 1988. 36.00 (0-937822-10-8) WoodenBoat Pubns.

McIntosh, David C. & Manning, Samuel F. How to Build a Wooden Boat. 1987. text ed. 36.00 (0-07-156792-5) McGraw.

McIntosh, DeCourcy E., ed. see Brachlianoff, Dominique.

McIntosh, Dianne, jt. auth. see Tompkins, Iverna.

***McIntosh, Don G.** Gold of the Hebrew God. 260p. 1995. pap. 8.95 (1-56901-728-X) NW Pub.

***McIntosh, Donald.** Self, Person, World: The Interplay of Conscious & Unconscious in Human Life. LC 94-47481. (Psychosocial Issues Ser.). 1995. write for info. (0-8101-1233-7); pap. write for info. (0-8101-1217-5) Northwestern U Pr.

McIntosh, Duncan. The Everyday Evangelist. 64p. 1984. pap. 5.00 (0-8170-1042-4) Judson.

McIntosh, Duncan & Rusbuldt, Richard E. Planning Growth in Your Church. 224p. 1983. pap. 19.00 (0-8170-1007-6) Judson.

McIntosh, Edith. Theory & Musicianship: Lessons with Worksheets & Supplements, Bk. 2, Pt. 2. 62p. 1957. pap. 6.50 (0-8258-0160-5, 04012) Fischer Inc NY.

McIntosh, Elaine. Internal Auditing in a Total Quality Environment. Campbell, Lee A., ed. 87p. 1992. 20.00 (0-89413-266-0) Inst Inter Aud.

***McIntosh, Elaine N.** American Food Habits in Historical Perspective. LC 95-7550. 1995. pap. text ed. write for info. (0-275-95331-9, Praeger Pubs) Greenwood.

— American Food Habits in Historical Perspective. LC 95-7550. 1995. text ed. write for info. (0-275-94601-0, Praeger Pubs) Greenwood.

McIntosh, Frank S., ed. How I Got My Piece of the Rock & Vital Life Insurance Information. 1979. pap. 19.95 (0-686-26460-6) Ins Res Svc.

McIntosh, G. L. How to Develop a Pastoral Compensation Plan: A Biblical Approach to Meeting the Needs of the Pastor & His Staff. Spear, Cindy G. & Johnson, Tamara, eds. 100p. 1991. ring bd. 39.95 (0-941005-43-7) Chrch Grwth VA.

— How to Develop a Policy Manual: To Insure a Consistent & Orderly Ministry. 141p. 1992. ring bd. 49.95 (0-941005-65-8) Chrch Grwth VA.

McIntosh, Gary & Martin, Glen. Finding Them, Keeping Them. (Orig.). 1992. pap. 6.99 (0-8054-6051-9) Broadman.

***McIntosh, Gary L.** The Exodus Principle: A 5-Part Strategy to Free Your People for Ministry. LC 95-6528. 1995. write for info. (0-8054-6187-6) Broadman.

— Three Generations: Riding the Waves of Change in Your Church. 224p. (Orig.). 1995. pap. 9.99 (0-8007-5544-8) Revell.

McIntosh, Gary L. & Martin, Glen S. Finding Them, Keeping Them: The Seminar, 3 cass., Set. 37p. 1994. student ed, audio 69.95 (1-57052-003-8) Chrch Grwth VA.

— Issachar Factor. LC 93-31202. 1994. 15.99 (0-8054-3014-8) Broadman.

McIntosh, Gary L., jt. auth. see Dean, Rodney J.

McIntosh, Gary L., jt. auth. see Martin, Glen S.

McIntosh, Gregory B., ed. Thermal Infrared Sensing for Diagnostics & Control: Thermosense XI. 209p. 1989. 70.00 (0-8194-0129-3, VOL. 1094) SPIE.

***McIntosh, Harriet P.** Yoo Hoo: I'm Over Here. (Illus.). 100p. (Orig.). 1995. pap. 9.95 (0-614-07235-2) Jokake Pr.

McIntosh, Hugh. Is Christ Infallible & the Bible True? 724p. lib. bdg. 27.99 (0-8254-5180-9) Kregel.

McIntosh, I. G. & Marshall, C. B. The Face of Scotland. 3rd ed. 1977. text ed. 104.00 (0-08-021321-9, Pub. by Pergamon Repr UK) Franklin.

McIntosh, J. D. Concrete & Statistics. (Illus.). 139p. 1963. 36.00 (0-85334-038-2, Pub. by Elsevier Applied Sci UK) Elsevier.

McIntosh, James, ed. Nathaniel Hawthorne's Tales. (Critical Editions Ser.). 480p. (Orig.). (C). 1987. pap. text ed. 11.95 (0-393-95426-9) Norton.

McIntosh, James C. & McIntosh, Marie, trs. The Committed Observer: Raymond Aron Interviews with Jean-Louis Missika & Dominque Wolton. LC 82-42902. 1983. 17.00 (0-89526-624-5) Regnery Pub.

McIntosh, James F. We're All Pink on the Inside: A Doctor's Irreverent View of Health Care in America. Balousek, Marv, ed. 200p. 1993. pap. 12.95 (1-878569-14-7) Waubesa Pr.

McIntosh, James T., ed. see Davis, Jefferson.

McIntosh, Jane. Archeology. LC 94-9378. (Eyewitness Books). (J). 1994. 16.00 (0-679-86572-1); pap. 17.99 (0-679-96572-6) Knopf.

— Native American. (Eyewitness Bks.). (Illus.). 64p. (YA). (gr. 5 up). 1995. 17.00 (0-679-86169-6); lib. bdg. 18.99 (0-679-96169-0) Knopf Bks Yng Read.

— The Practical Archaeologist. (Illus.). 192p. 1986. 24.95 (0-8160-1400-0) Facts on File.

— The Practical Archaeologist. (Illus.). 192p. 1988. pap. 14.95 (0-8160-1814-6) Facts on File.

McIntosh, Jennifer W. Airplane Activities: A Coloring Book with Games & Projects That Kids Can Do Again & Again. Gavin, Kathleen & Gavin, Marshall, eds. (Kids on the Go Ser.). (Illus.). 56p. (Orig.). (J). (ps-8). 1994. pap. 3.95 (1-885437-00-5) B dazzle.

— Car Activities: A Coloring Book with Games & Projects That Kids Can Do Again & Again. Gavin, Kathleen & Gavin, Marshall, eds. (Kids on the Go Ser.). (Illus.). 56p. (Orig.). (J). (ps-8). 1994. pap. 3.95 (1-885437-01-3) B dazzle.

— Cold Weather Activities: A Coloring Book with Games & Projects That Kids Can Do Again & Again. Gavin, Kathleen & Gavin, Marshall, eds. (Kids on the Go Ser.). (Illus.). 56p. (J). (ps-8). 1994. pap. 3.95 (1-885437-02-1) B dazzle.

— Indoor Activities: A Coloring Book with Games & Projects That Kids Can Do Again & Again. Gavin, Kathleen & Gavin, Marshall, eds. (Kids on the Go Ser.). (Illus.). 56p. (Orig.). (J). (ps-8). 1994. pap. 3.95 (1-885437-03-X) B dazzle.

— Kids' Box-O'-Fun. (J). 1993. 16.95 (0-8431-3564-6) Price Stern.

— Kids on the Go Box Set: Five Unique Books with Games & Projects That Kids Can Do Again & Again!, 5 bks. Gavin, Kathleen & Gavin, Marshall, eds. (Illus.). 280p. (J). (ps-8). 1994. boxed 19.75 (1-885437-05-6) B dazzle.

— Warm Weather Activities: A Coloring Book with Games & Projects That Kids Can Do Again & Again. Gavin, Kathleen & Gavin, Marshall, eds. (Kids on the Go Ser.). (Illus.). 56p. (Orig.). (J). (ps-8). 1994. pap. 3.95 (1-885437-04-8) B dazzle.

McIntosh, Jim. Communication & Awareness in a Cancer Ward. LC 76-30331. 1977. 22.50 (0-88202-109-5, Prodist) Watson Pub Intl.

McIntosh, Joan. Branch & Shadow Branch. 32p. 1982. pap. 3.00 (1-880649-11-X) Writ Ctr Pr.

McIntosh, Joel, ed. The Prufrock Anthology: A Collection of the Best Articles from the First Two Years of the Prufrock Journal. 132p. 1991. pap. 19.95 (1-882664-05-1) Prufrock Pr.

— Twenty More Ideas for Teaching Gifted Kids in the Middle School & High School. 115p. 1994. pap. 19.95 (1-882664-15-9) Prufrock Pr.

McIntosh, Joel & Meacham, April. Creative Problem Solving for Teens. 84p. 1993. pap. 19.95 (1-882664-07-8) Prufrock Pr.

— Creative Problem Solving in the Classroom: The Educator's Handbook for Teaching Effective Problem Solving Skills. 123p. 1991. pap. 19.95 (1-882664-00-0) Prufrock Pr.

McIntosh, John L., ed. Research on Suicide: A Bibliography. LC 84-15706. (Bibliographies & Indexes in Psychology Ser.: No. 2). xiii, 323p. 1985. text ed. 75.00 (0-313-23992-4, MLR/, Greenwood Pr) Greenwood.

McIntosh, John L., jt. comp. see Osgood, Nancy J.

McIntosh, John L., et al. Elder Suicide: Research, Theory, & Treatment. (Illus.). 272p. 1994. text ed. 39.95 (1-55798-240-6); pap. text ed. 19.95 (1-55798-242-2) Am Psychol.

McIntosh, John L., et al, eds. Suicide & Its Aftermath: Understanding & Counseling the Survivors. (Professional Bks.). (Illus.). 1987. 32.95 (0-393-70039-9) Norton.

***McIntosh, John W. & McIntosh, Margaret S.** The Reader's Companion, with Black Cover. 68p. 1994. ring bd. 19.95 (0-9644092-0-8) Creekside CO.

— The Reader's Companion, with Burgundy Cover. 68p. 1994. ring bd. 19.95 (0-9644092-1-6) Creekside CO.

McIntosh, Jon. Hooked on Golf. (Hooked on...Sports Ser.). (Illus.). 102p. (Orig.). 1982. pap. 4.95 (0-938864-04-1) Ipswich Pr.

***McIntosh, Ken.** Engineering Data Management: A Guide to Successful Implementation. LC 94-31154. 1995. text ed. 46.00 (0-07-707621-4) McGraw.

McIntosh, Malcolm. Arms Across the Pacific: Security & Trade Issues Across the Pacific. LC 87-32120. 189p. 1988. text ed. 45.00 (0-312-01868-1) St Martin.

— Japan Re-Armed. LC 86-3999. 200p. 1986. text ed. 35.00 (0-312-44055-3) St Martin.

McIntosh, Margaret E., jt. auth. see Greenlaw, M. Jean.

McIntosh, Margaret S., jt. auth. see McIntosh, John W.

McIntosh, Maria J. Conquest & Self-Conquest. LC 74-76928. (American Fiction Reprint Ser.). 1977. 16.95 (0-8369-7007-1) Ayer.

— Two Pictures. LC 72-39094. (Black Heritage Library Collection). 1977. reprint ed. 28.95 (0-8369-9032-3) Ayer.

McIntosh, Marie, jt. tr. see McIntosh, James C.

McIntosh, Marjorie K. Autonomy & Community: The Royal Manor of Havering, 1200-1500. (Cambridge Studies in Medieval Life & Thought: No. 5). (Illus.). 320p. 1986. 79.95 (0-521-32018-6) Cambridge U Pr.

— A Community Transformed: The Manor & Liberty of Havering-atte-Bower, 1500-1620. (Studies in Population, Economy & Society in Past Time: No. 16). (Illus.). 496p. (C). 1991. 79.95 (0-521-38142-8) Cambridge U Pr.

McIntosh, Mary. Fulfulde Syntax & Morphology. 200p. (Orig.). 1984. pap. 29.95 (0-7103-0074-3, Pub. by Kegan Paul Intl UK) Routledge Chapman & Hall.

McIntosh, Mary, jt. auth. see Barrett, Michele.

McIntosh, Mary, jt. ed. see Segal, Lynne.

McIntosh, Mathew. Lifetime Aerobics. 256p. (C). 1990. pap. write for info. (0-697-10562-8) Brown & Benchmark.

McIntosh, Michael. A. H. Fox: The Finest Gun in the World. deluxe limited ed. LC 92-74003. (Illus.). 408p. 1994. 95.00 (0-924357-25-8, 21100-B) Countrysport Pr.

— A. H. Fox: The Finest Gun in the World. enl. rev. ed. LC 92-74003. (Illus.). 408p. 1994. 49.00 (0-924357-24-X, 21100-A) Countrysport Pr.

— Best Guns. LC 89-60723. (Illus.). 292p. 1989. 39.00 (0-924357-02-9, 21200-A) Countrysport Pr.

— The Big-Bore Rifle: The Book of Fine Magazine & Double Rifles, .375 - .700 Calibers. LC 89-81948. (Illus.). 240p. 1990. 39.00 (0-924357-09-6) Countrysport Pr.

— The Big-Bore Rifle: The Book of Fine Magazine & Double Rifles, .375 - .700 Calibers. deluxe limited ed. LC 89-81948. (Illus.). 240p. 1990. 95.00 (0-924357-12-6) Countrysport Pr.

— In the Sporting Tradition: The Art of Herb Booth. LC 93-4144. (Joe & Betty Moore Texas Art Ser.: No. 8). (Illus.). 160p. (C). 1993. 49.50 (0-89096-571-4); write for info. (0-89096-577-3) Tex A&M Univ Pr.

Mcintosh, Michael. Masters of the Wild: Maass. 1990. 29.95 (0-87201-495-9) Gulf Pub.

***McIntosh, Michael.** Shotguns & Shooting. (Illus.). 272p. 1995. 30.00 (0-924357-48-7, 21150-A) Countrysport Pr.

— Shotguns & Shooting. deluxe limited ed. (Illus.). 272p. 1995. 95.00 (0-924357-49-5, 21150-B) Countrysport Pr.

McIntosh, Michael, ed. see Ruark, Robert C.

McIntosh, Michael, ed. see Tryon, Chuck & Tryon, Sharon.

McIntosh, Ned. Little League Drills & Strategies. (Illus.). 128p. (Orig.). 1987. pap. 7.95 (0-8092-4789-5) Contemp Bks.

— The Little League Guide to Tee Ball. LC 92-45097. 128p. 1993. pap. 6.95 (0-8092-3791-1) Contemp Bks.

— Managing Little League Baseball. (Illus.). 160p. (Orig.). 1985. pap. 11.95 (0-8092-5322-4) Contemp Bks.

McIntosh, Neil, jt. ed. see Campbell, Alex G.

McIntosh, Neil, jt. auth. see Daniel, W. W.

McIntosh, Noel, jt. auth. see Blumenthal, Paul D.

McIntosh, Noel, et al, eds. DIU Guide a l'Intention des Programmes de Planification Familiale. rev. ed. (Illus.). 160p. (FRE.). 1993. pap. text ed. 6.00 (0-929817-03-6) JHPIEGO.

— IUD Guidelines for Family Planning Service Programs: A Problem-Solving Reference Manual. 2nd ed. (Illus.). 190p. 1993. pap. text ed. 6.00 (0-929817-07-9) JHPIEGO.

— Norplant Guide Pratique a l'Intention des Programmes de Planification Familiale. rev. ed. (Illus.). 141p. (FRE.). 1993. pap. text ed. 6.00 (0-929817-05-2) JHPIEGO.

— Norplant Guidelines for Family Planning Service Programs: A Problem-Solving Reference Manual. rev. ed. (Illus.). 130p. 1993. pap. text ed. 6.00 (0-929817-04-4) JHPIEGO.

— Norplant Implants for Family Planning Service Programs: A Problem-Solving Reference Manual. 2nd ed. (Illus.). 1995. pap. text ed. 6.00 (0-929817-09-5) JHPIEGO.

McIntosh, Patrick S. & Dryer, Murray, eds. Solar Activity Observations & Predictions. LC 72-5953. (PAAS Ser.: Vol. 30). (Illus.). 444p. 1972. 54.95 (0-262-13086-6) AIAA.

***McIntosh, R. A., et al, eds.** Wheat Rusts. LC 95-7869. 1995. lib. bdg. write for info. (0-7923-3430-2) Kluwer Ac.

McIntosh, R. P., jt. ed. see Barclay, Wm. R.

McIntosh, Rawle M., et al, eds. Kidney Disease: Hematologic & Vascular Problems. LC 77-7529. (Perspectives in Nephrology & Hypertension Ser.). (Illus.). 188p. reprint ed. pap. 53.60 (0-317-09218-9, 2015196) Bks Demand.

McIntosh, Robert K. Is Franchising for You? 20p. 1985. 5.00 (0-317-66117-5) Intl Franchise Assn.

McIntosh, Robert L. Dielectric Behavior of Physically Absorbed Gases. LC 67-82258. 174p. reprint ed. pap. 49.60 (0-317-08353-8, 2055411) Bks Demand.

McIntosh, Robert P. The Background of Ecology: Concept & Theory. (Studies in Ecology). 400p. 1986. pap. 29.95 (0-521-27087-1) Cambridge U Pr.

— The Forests of the Catskill Mountains. 1977. pap. 5.00 (0-910746-07-9, FOT01) Hope Farm.

***McIntosh, Robert W., et al.** Tourism: Principles, Practices, Philosophies. 7th ed. LC 94-26244. 1994. text ed. write for info. (0-471-01557-1) Wiley.

McIntosh, Sandy. Endless Staircase. 72p. 1991. 5.75 (0-935252-48-7) Street Pr.

McIntosh, Sandy, ed. see Wok Talk Editors.

McIntosh, Scott. How to Be an Angel: The Book the Devil Did Not Want Published. (Illus.). 80p. (Orig.). (YA). 1993. pap. 9.95 (0-9632879-1-5) McIntosh Pubns.

McIntosh, Scott A. Love Letters That Work: Create Some Excitement in Your Life. (Illus.). 80p. (Orig.). 1992. pap. 7.95 (0-9632879-0-7) McIntosh Pubns.

McIntosh, Sheila, tr. see Margenat, Assumpta.

McIntosh, Stephen I. The Multimedia Producer's Legal Survival Guide. 215p. 1990. text ed. 250.00 (1-878955-00-4) Multimedia Computing.

***McIntosh, Susan K., ed.** Excavations at Jenne-Jeno, Hambarketolo, and Kaniana (Inland Niger Delta, Mali), the 1981 Season. LC 94-35017. (Publications in Anthropology: Vol. 20). 1995. pap. 78.00 (0-520-09785-8) U CA Pr.

McIntosh, Toby. Federal Information in the Electronic Age: Policy Issues for the 1990s. LC 90-2404. 1990. 75.00 (1-55871-170-8, BSP 184) BNA.

McIntosh, W. E. & Shell, Harvey. Indiancraft. (Illus.). 144p. 1987. 17.95 (0-87961-170-7); pap. 9.95 (0-87961-171-5) Naturegraph.

McIntosh, W. H. History of Wayne County New York. LC 75-37578. (Illus.). 1975. reprint ed. 60.00 (0-918426-01-4) Yankee Ped Bkshop.

McIntosh, Wayne V. The Appeal of Civil Law: A Political-Economic Analysis of Litigation. LC 88-29592. 240p. 1990. 26.95 (0-252-01628-9) U of Ill Pr.

McIntosh, William A. Guide to Effective Military Writing. 2nd ed. 256p. 1994. pap. 14.95 (0-8117-2541-3) Stackpole.

McIntosh, William D., jt. auth. see Mealey, Donna L.

McIntosk & Twyman, trs. The Archko Volume. LC 74-33199. 248p. 1975. 14.95 (0-87983-067-0) Keats.

*Mcintre, David A. Sanctuary. (Dr. Who Ser.). (Illus.). Date not set. pap. 5.95 (0-426-20439-5, London Bridge) Genl Dist Srvs.

*McIntyre. Expense of Glory. 1995. pap. 15.00 (0-00-638351-3) Basic.

— Herbal for Mother & Child. 1992. pap. 14.95 (1-85230-244-5) Element MA.

McIntyre, jt. auth. see Emery.

McIntyre, jt. auth. see Neil.

McIntyre, A. Contemporary Australian Collage & Its Origins. (Illus.). 224p. 1990. text ed. 65.00 (0-947131-31-0) Gordon & Breach.

McIntyre, A. D., jt. auth. see Holme, N. A.

*McIntyre, A. Dan. Individual Responsibility & the National Interest: The Willingness to Go to War. LC 95-10493. 1995. text ed. write for info. (0-312-07558-8) St Martin.

McIntyre, A. P. Bible Seven, History Zero. LC 88-51390. 154p. 1989. 9.95 (1-55523-201-9) Winston-Derek.

McIntyre, Albert A. The Last Grand Roundup. LC 89-90976. (Illus.). 104p. 1989. reprint ed. 12.95 (0-9622654-0-3) Chief Rsch.

McIntyre, Alice. Role Playing: A Real Estate Training Tool. Gerth, Dawn M., ed. LC 82-83133. (Illus.). 151p. (Orig.). 1982. pap. text ed. 16.00 (0-913652-43-1, BK 152) Realtors Natl.

McIntyre, Angus, ed. Aging & Political Leadership. LC 87-33614. 316p. (C). 1988. 59.50 (0-88706-823-5); pap. 19.95 (0-88706-824-3) State U NY Pr.

*McIntyre, Anne. The Complete Woman's Herbal: A Manual of Healing Herbs & Nutrition for Personal Well-Being & Family Care. LC 94-29291. (Reference Bks.). 1995. pap. 25.00 (0-8050-3537-0) H Holt & Co.

— Herbal Medicine. (Alternative Health Ser.). (Illus.). 128p. 1993. pap. 12.95 (0-8048-1837-1) C E Tuttle.

— Herbs for Common Ailments. (Illus.). 96p. (Orig.). 1992. pap. 12.00 (0-671-74632-4, Fireside) S&S Trade.

McIntyre, Anne, jt. auth. see Daniels, Brian.

McIntyre, Anne, jt. ed. see Shearer, William.

*McIntyre, Arnold M. Trade & Economic Development in Small Open Economies: The Case of the Caribbean Countries. LC 94-32931. 200p. 1995. text ed. 55.00 (0-275-94745-9, Praeger Pubs) Greenwood.

McIntyre, Bill. Grambling: Cradle of the Pros. Woolfolk, Doug, ed. (Illus.). 110p. 1980. 12.50 (0-86518-015-6) Moran Pub Corp.

McIntyre, Bryce T. Advanced Newsgathering. LC 90-38842. 304p. 1991. text ed. 65.00 (0-275-93521-3, C3521, Praeger Pubs); pap. text ed. 17.95 (0-275-93522-1, B3522, Praeger Pubs) Greenwood.

McIntyre, C. T., ed. see Butterfield, Herbert.

McIntyre, Catherine V. Writing Effective News Releases: How to Get Free Publicity for Yourself, Your Business, or Your Organization. LC 91-45516. (Illus.). 176p. (Orig.). 1992. pap. 16.95 (0-941599-19-1) Piccadilly Bks.

McIntyre, Charles, jt. auth. see Knoell, Dorothy M.

*McIntyre, Chris & Atkins, Simon. Guide to Namibia & Botswana. 2nd ed. (Bradt Guides Ser.). (Illus.). 304p. 1994. 16.95 (1-56440-541-9) Globe Pequot.

McIntyre, Cindy. Seattle, Tacoma & Puget Sound Region. (Illus.). 120p. 1993. 24.95 (0-942381-10-6) Sammamish Pr.

— Seattle, Tacoma & the Puget Sound Region. (Illus.). 128p. 1988. write for info. (0-942381-00-9) Sammamish Pr.

*McIntyre, Cindy & Callery, Terence. The Great Eastern Mussel Cookbook. (Illus.). 128p. 1995. pap. 14.95 (0-8397-2392-X) Eriksson.

McIntyre, Cordelia, ed. see Drexel, Paul.

McIntyre, D. A. Indoor Climate. (Illus.). xix, 422p. 1991. 132.00 (0-85334-868-5, Pub. by Elsevier Applied Sci UK) Elsevier.

McIntyre, David M. Al Pie de la Gloria: The Starting Place of Glory. (SPA.). 3.25 (84-7228-931-1, 220997, Pub. by Edit Clie SP) TSELF.

— Cristo el Camino: Christ the Way. (SPA.). 4.95 (84-7645-141-5, 223182, Pub. by Edit Clie SP) TSELF.

— Por la Senda de la Fe: Rest of Faith. (SPA.). 4.25 (84-7645-102-4, 223155, Pub. by Edit Clie SP) TSELF.

— La Vida de Oracion a Solas: The Hidden Life of Prayer. (SPA.). 3.25 (84-7228-700-9, 220948, Pub. by Edit Clie SP) TSELF.

McIntyre, Deborah, jt. auth. see Donovan, Denis M.

McIntyre, Donald & Gornick, F., eds. Light-Scattering from Dilute Polymer Solutions. (International Science Review Ser.). (Illus.). 332p. 1964. text ed. 191.00 (0-677-00510-5) Gordon & Breach.

McIntyre, Donald, jt. auth. see Brown, Sally.

*McIntyre, Donald, et al, eds. Mentoring: Perspectives on School-Based Teacher Education. 236p. 1994. pap. 24.95 (0-7494-1533-9, Pub. by Kogan Page Educ UK) Taylor & Francis.

McIntyre, Douglas A. & Hull, Karen S., eds. The Harvard Advocate One Hundred Twentieth Anniversary Anthology. (Illus.). 460p. 1987. 29.95 (0-87047-029-9) Schenkman Bks Inc.

McIntyre, Hugh C. Uranium, Nuclear Power, & Canada-U. S. Energy Relations. LC 78-54112. (Canadian-American Committee Ser.). 80p. 1978. 4.00 (0-88806-035-1) Natl Planning.

McIntyre, Ian. Dogfight: The Transatlantic Battle over Airbus. LC 92-168. 336p. 1992. text ed. 45.00 (0-275-94278-3, C4278, Praeger Pubs) Greenwood.

McIntyre, J. B. How to Survive in a World Out of Control. 2nd ed. LC 85-50698. 160p. (Orig.). 1987. pap. 8.95 (0-9614865-0-3) Sunburst Pub.

McIntyre, J. D., ed. see Symposium on the Chemistry & Physics of Electrocatalysis Staff.

McIntyre, J. Lewis. Giordano Bruno. 365p. 1992. pap. 24.95 (1-56459-141-7) Kessinger Pub.

McIntyre, J. W., ed. see Webster, Daniel.

McIntyre, Joan. All's Well. (Illus.). 48p. 1981. 24.00 (0-88014-040-2) Mosaic Pr OH.

McIntyre, Joan, ed. see Yagan, Murat.

McIntyre, John. Blowing Weather. 1993. reprint ed. lib. bdg. 89.00 (0-7812-5487-6) Rprt Serv.

McIntyre, John, Jr. The Boycott of the Milner Mission: A Study in Egyptian Nationalism. (American University Studies: History: Ser. IX, Vol. 9). 222p. 1985. text ed. 28.00 (0-8204-0162-5) P Lang Pubs.

McIntyre, John. The Shape of Soteriology. 144p. 1993. text ed. 29.95 (0-567-09615-7, Pub. by T & T Clark UK) Bks Intl VA.

— Steps Going Down. 1993. reprint ed. lib. bdg. 89.00 (0-685-62347-5) Rprt Serv.

McIntyre, John P. Customary Law in the "Corpus Iuris Canonici" LC 90-26653. (Distinguished Dissertations Ser.: Vol. 12). 260p. 1991. 89.95 (0-7734-9960-1) E Mellen.

McIntyre, John R. & Papp, Daniel S., eds. The Political Economy of International Technology Transfer. LC 85-28128. (Illus.). 280p. 1986. text ed. 69.50 (0-89930-128-2, MYP/, Quorum Bks) Greenwood.

*McIntyre, John S. DSM-IV Desk Reference to the Diagnostic Criteria from DSM-IV. 1994. spiral bd. 24.95 (0-89042-064-5) Am Psychiatric.

— DSM-IV Quick Reference to the Diagnostic Criteria from DSM-IV. 1994. pap. text ed. 20.75 (0-89042-063-7) Am Psychiatric.

McIntyre, John T. Ferment. LC 74-26117. (Labor Movement in Fiction & Non-Fiction Ser.). reprint ed. 33.75 (0-404-58448-9) AMS Pr.

McIntyre, Judith W. The Common Loon: Spirit of Northern Lakes. LC 88-4206. (Illus.). xii, 228p. 1988. 19.99 (0-8166-1651-5) U of Minn Pr.

McIntyre, Kellen K. Rio Grande Blankets: Late Nineteenth-Century Textiles in Transition. LC 92-19989. (Illus.). 88p. 1992. pap. 22.50 (0-9633710-0-2) Adobe Gallery.

McIntyre, Kenneth G. The Rebello Transcripts: Governor Phillip's Portugese Prelude. 257p. (C). 1984. 24.95 (0-285-62603-5, Pub. by Souvnir Pr UK) Intl Spec Bk.

McIntyre, Lawrence. Designated Landmarks of the Niagara Frontier. 1985. pap. 13.95 (0-9620314-2-9) Meyer Enter.

— Symbol & Show: Pan-American Exposition of 1901. 1986. pap. 13.95 (0-681-64104-5) Meyer Enter.

McIntyre, Lee C., jt. ed. see Martin, Michael.

McIntyre, Lisa J. Law in the Sociological Enterprise: A Reconstruction. LC 93-6418. 236p. (C). 1994. pap. text ed. 18.95 (0-8133-1949-8) Westview.

— Law in the Sociological Enterprise: A Reconstruction. LC 93-6418. 236p. (C). 1994. text ed. 52.50 (0-8133-1948-X) Westview.

*McIntyre, Lisa J. & Sussman, Marvin B., eds. Families & Law. LC 94-45052. (Marriage & Family Review Ser.). (Illus.). 318p. 1995. lib. bdg. 39.95 (1-56024-708-8) Haworth Pr.

McIntyre, Loren. Amazonia. LC 91-6573. (Illus.). 184p. 1991. 40.00 (0-87156-641-9) Sierra.

McIntyre, Loren, photos & text. Exploring South America. (Illus.). 1990. 40.00 (0-517-56134-4, C P Pubs) Crown Pub Group.

McIntyre, Margaret, comp. Early Childhood & Science. (Illus.). 136p. 1984. pap. text ed. 12.95 (0-87355-029-3) Natl Sci Tchrs.

McIntyre, Marie. Ears to Hear: Hearts to Praise. (Greeting Book Line Ser.). (Illus.). 32p. (Orig.). 1985. pap. 1.95 (0-89622-210-1) Twenty-Third.

— Female & Catholic: A Journal of Mind & Heart. LC 86-50658. 80p. (Orig.). 1986. pap. 3.95 (0-89622-307-8) Twenty-Third.

— Little Things Mean a Lot: Minute Meditations. (Greeting Book Line Ser.). (Illus.). 32p. 1982. pap. 1.95 (0-89622-155-5) Twenty-Third.

— Meditations on the Mass. (Greeting Book Line Ser.). 32p. 1983. pap. 1.95 (0-89622-201-2) Twenty-Third.

McIntyre, Michael. Herbal Medicine for Everyone. 176p. 1988. mass mkt. 5.95 (0-14-009900-X, Penguin Bks) Viking Penguin.

McIntyre, Michael, jt. auth. see Mabey, Richard.

McIntyre, Michael, et al. Peaceworld. LC 76-12410. (Illus.). 152p. (Orig.). reprint ed. pap. 43.40 (0-7837-1955-8, 2042172) Bks Demand.

McIntyre, Michael J. International Income Tax Rules of the United States, 2 vols. 1994. ring bd. 195.00 (0-88063-153-8) Butterworth Legal Pubs.

— International Income Tax Rules of the United States. suppl. ed. 1994. ring bd. write for info. (0-614-03610-0) Butterworth Legal Pubs.

McIntyre, Michael J., et al. Readings in Federal Taxation. 2nd ed. LC 83-16356. 625p. 1983. pap. text ed. 21.50 (0-88277-145-0) Foundation Pr.

McIntyre, Michael P., et al. Physical Geography. 5th ed. 1991. Net. pap. text ed. write for info. (0-471-62017-3); Net. student ed write for info. (0-471-53493-5) Wiley.

McIntyre, Mildred C., ed. see Wenger, Nanette K., et al.

McIntyre, Moni. Social Ethics & the Return to Cosmology: A Study of Gibson Winter. LC 92-10251. (American University Studies: Theology & Religion: Ser. VII, Vol. 131). 191p. (C). 1993. 38.95 (0-8204-1846-3) P Lang Pubs.

McIntyre, Moni, jt. auth. see MacKinnon, Mary H.

McIntyre, N., et al, eds. Oxford Textbook of Clinical Hepatology, 2 vols., Set. 1700p. 1992. 275.00 (0-19-261968-3) OUP.

McIntyre, Nancy. Four & Twenty Blackbirds: Cooking in Crust. rev. ed. (Illus.). 100p. 1990. pap. 7.95 (0-9616524-6-2) Cobble Mickle Bks.

— Magnificent Molds: Recipes for Make-Ahead Magic. rev. ed. (Illus.). 100p. 1990. pap. 7.95 (0-9616524-7-0) Cobble Mickle Bks.

— Terra Cotta Cuisine: Distinctive Recipes for Pottery Cookware. rev. ed. (Illus.). 100p. 1990. pap. 7.95 (0-9616524-8-9) Cobble Mickle Bks.

McIntyre, O. Ross, ed. see Leucocyte Culture Conference Staff.

McIntyre, P. & Mercer, A. D., eds. Corrosion & Related Aspects of Materials for Potable Water Supplies. (Illus.). 285p. 1994. 160.00 (0-901716-47-2, Pub. by Inst Materials UK) Ashgate Pub Co.

— Corrosion Standards: European & International Developments. 108p. 1991. 70.00 (0-901716-09-X, Pub. by Inst Materials UK) Ashgate Pub Co.

McIntyre, P., jt. auth. see George, W. O.

McIntyre, Pat. Teaching Structured Programming in Secondary Schools. LC 88-37600. 232p. 1991. lib. bdg. 29.50 (0-89464-360-6) Krieger.

McIntyre, Patrick. Intimacy with God. LC 92-91171. (Illus.). 128p. (Orig.). 1993. pap. 5.95 (0-9635050-0-9) White Harvest.

*McIntyre, Phillip. Don't Ask-Don't Tell. 100p. 1995. pap. 7.95 (1-56901-763-8) NW Pub.

McIntyre, Rick. Devali NAtional Park: An Island in Time. (Illus.). 80p. 1989. pap. 10.95 (0-917859-06-5) Sunrise SBCA.

— Grizzly Cub: Five Years in the Life of a Bear. LC 90-35587. (Illus.). 104p. (Orig.). (J). (gr. 4 up). 1990. pap. 14.95 (0-88240-373-7) Alaska Northwest.

— A Society of Wolves: National Parks & the Battle Over the Wolf. LC 93-15918. (Illus.). 128p. 1993. 29.95 (0-89658-194-2) Voyageur Pr.

*McIntyre, Rick, ed. War Against the Wolf: America's Campaign to Exterminate the Wolf. LC 94-28038. 1995. 24.95 (0-89658-264-7) Voyageur Pr.

McIntyre, Robert J. Bulgaria: Politics, Economics & Society. (Marxist Regimes Ser.). 225p. 1988. text ed. 49.00 (0-86187-398-X, Pub. by Pinter Pubs UK); text ed. 17.50 (0-86187-399-8, Pub. by Pinter Pubs UK) St Martin.

McIntyre, Robert L. Electric Motor Control Fundamentals. 3rd ed. (Illus.). 448p. (C). 1974. text ed. 44.95 (0-07-045103-6) McGraw.

McIntyre, Robert L. & Losee, Rex. Industrial Motor Control Fundamentals. 4th ed. 432p. 1989. text ed. 48.95 (0-07-045110-9); Answer key. teacher ed 6.95 (0-07-045111-7) McGraw.

McIntyre, Ron L. The Jelly Bean Principle: CyberIconics. LC 81-69380. (Illus.). 268p. 1981. 14.95 (0-685-01342-1) CyberIconics.

McIntyre, Ronald, jt. auth. see Smith, David W.

*McIntyre, Sally & Goltsman, Susan M. Safety First Checklist: Inspection & Maintenance Program for Children's Play Areas. 2nd ed. (Illus.). 208p. 1995. pap. text ed. 39.95 (0-944661-19-X) MIG Comns.

McIntyre, Sally, et al. Safety First Checklist: The Site Inspection System for Play Equipment. LC 89-91774. (Illus.). 125p. (Orig.). 1989. pap. 39.95 (0-944661-02-5) MIG Comns.

McIntyre, Stuart. A Colonial Liberalism: Lost Word of Three Victorian Visionaries. 264p. 1991. 29.95 (0-19-554760-8) OUP.

— Wilson Creek & the Big Bend Country, 1902-1907: An Index of the Big Bend Chief Newspaper. (Illus.). 225p. (C). 1991. 25.00 (0-9622654-1-1) Chief Rsch.

*McIntyre, Tami. Wait for Me: The Americanization of Tamara. 1995. 21.50 (0-533-11329-6) Vantage.

McIntyre, Thomas. Dreaming the Lion: Reflections on Hunting, Fishing, & a Search for the Wild. LC 93-73422. (Illus.). 318p. 1993. 35.00 (0-924357-34-7, 61120-A) Countrysport Pr.

— Dreaming the Lion: Reflections on Hunting, Fishing, & a Search for the Wild. deluxe limited ed. LC 93-73422. (Illus.). 318p. 1993. ring bd. 95.00 (0-924357-35-5, 61120-B) Countrysport Pr.

McIntyre, Tommy. Wolf in Sheep's Clothing: The Search for a Child Killer. LC 88-5738. (Great Lakes Bks.). 232p. 1988. 34.95 (0-8143-1966-1); pap. 15.95 (0-8143-1989-0) Wayne St U Pr.

McIntyre, Vergie. Split Level Christians. Jones, M. L., ed. 305p. (Orig.). 1994. pap. 9.95 (1-882270-16-9) Old Rugged Cross.

*McIntyre, Vonda N. The Crystal Star. LC 94-28939. (Star Wars Ser.). 1994. pap. 21.95 (0-553-08929-3) Bantam.

— Dreamsnake. 1994. mass mkt. 5.99 (0-553-29659-0, Spectra) Bantam.

Mcintyre, Vonda N. Entropy Effect. 1990. pap. 5.50 (0-671-72416-9) S&S Trade.

McIntyre, Vonda N. The Exile Waiting. 255p. 1976. 30.00 (0-575-02189-6) Ultramarine Pub.

— Fireflood & Other Stories. LC 79-17774. 281p. 1979. 25.00 (0-395-28422-8) Ultramarine Pub.

— Metaphase. 1992. mass mkt. 5.99 (0-553-29223-4) Bantam.

— Nautilus. 1994. mass mkt. 5.99 (0-553-56026-3, Spectra) Bantam.

— Star Trek II: The Wrath of Khan. 1991. mass mkt. 5.50 (0-671-74149-7) PB.

— Star Trek III: The Search for Spock. (Star Trek Ser.: No. 17). 1990. mass mkt. 5.50 (0-671-73133-5) PB.

— Starfarers. 1994. mass mkt. 5.99 (0-553-56341-6, Spectra) Bantam.

— Superluminal. LC 83-8568. 298p. 1983. 25.00 (0-89366-189-9) Ultramarine Pub.

— Transition. 1991. mass mkt. 5.99 (0-553-28850-4, Spectra) Bantam.

McIntyre, W. A. Practical Wills Drafting. 272p. 1992. text ed. 65.00 (0-409-89762-0) Butterworth Legal Pubs.

*McIntyre, W. David. Background into the Anzus Pact: Strategy & Diplomacy, 1945-55. LC 94-31762. 464p. 1995. 65.00 (0-312-12439-2) St Martin.

*McIntyre, W. John. Children of Peace. (McGill-Queen's Studies in the History of Religion: No. 14). 260p. 1994. 39.95 (0-7735-1195-4, Pub. by McGill CN) U of Toronto Pr.

McIntyre, Wally. Electronic Fundamentals, Study Guide. 2nd ed. 208p. (C). 1990. pap. write for info. (0-675-21406-8, Merrill Pub Co) Macmillan.

McIntyre, William. Christ's Cabinet. rev. ed. 143p. 1982. reprint ed. 4.95 (0-86544-017-4) Salv Army Suppl South.

***McIntyre, William S., IV & Gibson, Jack P. 101 Ways to Cut Business Insurance Costs Without Sacrificing Protection. 170p. 1995. pap. 24.95 (0-615-00775-9) Intl Risk Mgt.**

101 WAYS TO CUT BUSINESS INSURANCE COSTS WITHOUT SACRIFICING PROTECTION, is a "how-to" guide providing cost-cutting strategies for every major line of coverage. The book is designed to help insurance buyers & their agents/brokers do a better & quicker job of auditing their insurance program to reduce insurance costs without giving up necessary coverage. 101 WAYS TO CUT INSURANCE COSTS WITHOUT SACRIFICING PROTECTION is organized by line of coverage, to help you find information easily. Following are just a few samples of the cost-saving topics: AUTOMOBILE - Determine proper use classifications, avoid distance surcharges; COMMERCIAL GENERAL LIABILITY - Use lessor's risk only classification, delete overtime surcharges, use experience rating; WORKERS COMPENSATION - Use of "first-aid-folder," allocate claim costs to profit centers, use medical bill review services; PROPERTY INSURANCE - Report proper builders risk values, obtain coinsurance credits; CLAIMS - Request advance payment of property claims, use public adjusters on large property losses. 101 WAYS TO CUT BUSINESS INSURANCE COSTS WITHOUT SACRIFICING PROTECTION is published by International Risk Management Institute, Inc. & costs $24.95. To order or receive more information, write to IRMI, 12222 Merit Dr., Suite 1660, Dallas, TX 75251-2217; FAX 214-960-6037 or call 800-827-4242. ***Publisher Provided Annotation.***

McIrwin, Michael. The Lessons of Radical Infinitude. 72p. 1993. pap. 8.00 (0-944550-29-0) Pygmy Forest Pr.

McIsaac, Gregory & Edwards, William R., eds. Sustainable Agriculture in the American Midwest: Lessons from Natural & Human History, Prospects for the Future. LC 93-45671. (Environment & the Human Condition Ser.). 312p. 1994. 32.95 (0-252-02100-2) U of Ill Pr.

Mcisaac, Joseph. Hands on CPlus-Plus Programming. 1989. pap. 22.95 (0-201-51816-3) Addison-Wesley.

McIsaac, Paul, jt. ed. see Meyers, Ellen.

*McIver, Bruce. Just as long as I'm Riding Up Front: More Stories I Couldn't Tell While I Was a Pastor. LC 94-44566. 1995. write for info. (0-8499-3597-0) Word Pub.

— Stories I Couldn't Tell While I Was a Pastor. 1991. pap. 9.99 (0-8499-3418-4) Word Inc.

McIver, Bruce & Stevenson, Ruth, eds. Teaching with Shakespeare: Critics in the Classroom. LC 92-59966. 1994. write for info. (0-87413-491-9) U Delaware Pr.

McIver, Carole R., jt. auth. see Greenberg, Alan M.

McIver, Colin & Naylor, Geoffrey. Marketing Financial Services. 292p. 1981. 75.00 (0-85297-054-4, Pub. by Inst Bankers UK); pap. 39.00 (0-85297-055-2, Pub. by Inst Bankers UK) St Mut.

McIver, D. W., jt. auth. see Robbins, Marc L.

McIver, John P. & Carmines, Edward G. Unidimensional Scaling. (Quantitative Applications in the Social Sciences Ser.: Vol. 24). (Illus.). (C). 1981. pap. 9.95 (0-8039-1736-8) Sage.

McIver, M. & Naylor, N., eds. Marketing Financial Services. (C). 1989. 110.00 (0-85297-145-1, Pub. by Inst Bankers UK) St Mut.

McIver, Peter B., jt. auth. see Bedessem, Anne.

McIver, Stuart. Glimpses of South Florida History. (Illus.). 192p. 1988. pap. 19.95 (0-9613236-9-8) Florida Flair Bks.

— True Tales of the Everglades. (Illus.). 64p. 1989. pap. 3.95 (0-9613236-3-9) Florida Flair Bks.

McIver, Stuart B. Dreamers, Schemers, & Scalawags Vol. 1: The Florida Chronicles, Vol. I. (Illus.). 200p. 1994. 17.95 (1-56164-034-4) Pineapple Pr.

— Fort Lauderdale & Broward County. 1983. 24.95 (0-89781-081-3) Preferred Mktg.

— Hemingway's Key West. LC 93-14668. (Illus.). 1993. pap. 10.95 (1-56164-035-2) Pineapple Pr.

— Murder in the Tropics: The Florida Chronicles, Vol. II. (Illus.). 260p. 1995. 17.95 (1-56164-079-4) Pineapple Pr.

An Asterisk (*) at the beginning of an entry indicates that the title is appearing in BIP for the first time.

McIver, Tom. Anti-Evolution: A Reader's Guide to Writings Before & after Darwin. LC 92-16755. 408p. 1992. reprint ed. 15.95 (*0-8018-4520-3*) Johns Hopkins.
— Anti-Evolution: An Annotated Bibliography. LC 88-42683. 400p. 1988. lib. bdg. 43.50x (*0-89950-313-6*) McFarland & Co.
McIvor, A. J. & Jowitt, J. A., eds. Employers & Labour in the English Textile Industry, 1850-1939. 256p. 1988. lib. bdg. 55.00 (*0-415-00354-7*) Routledge.
McIvor, Aidan. A History of the Irish Naval Service. (Illus.). 240p. 1994. boxed 39.50 (*0-7165-2523-2*, Pub. by Irish Acad Pr IE) Intl Spec Bk.
***McIvor, Eloise E.** Child of the Homesteads. Date not set. 21.95 (*0-943099-10-2*) M&M Pr.
McIvor, Gill. Sentenced to Serve: The Operation & Impact of Community Service by Offenders. 211p. 1992. 59.95 (*1-85628-329-1*, Pub. by Avebury Pub UK) Ashgate Pub Co.
McIvor, J. G., ed. see Bray, R. A.
McIvor, J. S., jt. auth. see Beattie, D. R.
McIvor, Kirsten, tr. see Gibo, Aiko.
McJimsey, George. Harry Hopkins: Ally of the Poor & Defender of Democracy. LC 86-22764. (Illus.). 304p. 1990. 35.00 (*0-674-37287-5*) HUP.
McJimsey, George T. The Dividing & Reuniting of America, 1848-1877. 2nd ed. DeSantis, Vincent P., ed. (Forums American History Ser.). 1990. pap. text ed. write for info. (*0-88273-170-X*) Forum Pr IL.
McJoynt, Albert D., ed. see Prescott, William H.
McKae, Shirley, ed. see Ciccone, Diane.
MckAgnew, Neil, jt. auth. see Pyke, Sandra W.
***McKague, Thomas R.** Stormlight: Poems. LC 95-512. 64p. 1995. pap. 12.95 (*0-7734-2739-2*, Mellen Poetry Pr) E Mellen.
McKaig, Kathleen, et al. Beyond the Threshold: Families Caring for Their Children Who Have Significant Developmental Disabilities. LC 89-105211. 62p. (Orig.). 1986. pap. text ed. 6.00 (*0-88156-044-8*) Comm Serv Soc NY.
— Comprehensive Support for Families: Final Report of the Family Partnership Program. A Demonstration to Assist Families with Developmentally Disabled Children. LC 90-197879. 140p. (Orig.). 1989. pap. 15.00 (*0-88156-102-9*) Comm Serv Soc NY.
McKain, David. The Common Life. LC 82-71818. 72p. 1982. 15.95 (*0-914086-41-3*); pap. 9.95 (*0-914086-38-3*) Alicejamesbooks.
— Spellbound: Growing up in God's Country. LC 92-37590. 272p. 1993. reprint ed. pap. 14.95 (*0-8229-5507-5*) U of Pittsburgh Pr.
— Spirit Bodies: Poems by David McKain. LC 90-83510. (Ithaca House Poetry Ser.). 64p. (Orig.). (C). 1990. pap. 9.95 (*0-87886-133-5*) Greenfld Rev Lit.
McKain, Robert J. How to Get to the Top & Stay There. LC 80-67964. 193p. reprint ed. pap. 55.10 (*0-317-26694-2*, 2023507) Bks Demand.
McKale, Donald M. Curt Prufer: German Diplomat from the Kaiser to Hitler. LC 87-4114. 290p. 1987. 25.00 (*0-87338-345-1*) Kent St U Pr.
— The Swastika Outside Germany. LC 77-22304. 304p. reprint ed. pap. 86.70 (*0-8357-7043-5*, 2033316) Bks Demand.
McKale, Donald M., ed. Rewriting History: The Original & Revised World War II Diaries of Curt Prufer, Nazi Diplomat. LC 88-12034. 277p. 1988. 24.00 (*0-87338-364-8*) Kent St U Pr.
McKallip, Curtis. Visualizing Economics: The Art of Investing Without Statistics. (Illus.). 146p. 1991. pap. write for info. (*1-878353-22-5*) Silent Partners.
McKallip, Jonathan, ed. see Price, Margaret, et al.
McKallip, Jonathan, jt. auth. see Trabert, Judith A.
McKamey, Lynn. Secret of the Orient: Dwarf Rhapis Excelsa. LC 85-50589. (Illus.). 52p. (Orig.). 1983. pap. 6.00 (*0-9612130-0-0*) Rhapis Gardens.
McKane, A. J., jt. ed. see Bowler, K. C.
***McKane, Alan.** Scale Invariance, Interfaces, & Non-Equilibrium Dynamics. Droz, Michel et al, eds. (NATO ASI Series B, Physics: Vol. 344). 350p. 1995. 105.00 (*0-306-45005-4*) Plenum.
McKane, Elizabeth, tr. see Mandelstam, Osip.
***McKane, Janet A.** Help Wanted: All the Help You'll Ever Need for Resume & Interview Preparation. 2nd ed. 75p. (Orig.). 1995. pap. 12.00 (*0-9647084-0-X*) Exec Type.
McKane, John G. Ducks of the Mississippi Flyway. LC 79-105937. (Illus.). 1969. pap. 5.00 (*0-87839-003-0*) North Star.
***McKane, Larry & Kandel, Judy.** Microbiology: Essentials & Applications. 2nd ed. LC 94-25301. 1995. write for info. (*0-07-045154-0*) McGraw.
McKane, Larry K. & Kandel, J. Microbiology: Essentials & Applications. 800p. 1985. text ed. write for info. (*0-07-045125-7*) McGraw.
McKane, Larry K., jt. auth. see Brum, Gil D.
McKane, Richard. Amphora for Metaphors. LC 92-42540. 198p. (Orig.). 1993. pap. 12.00 (*0-922792-56-9*) Gnosis Pr.
McKane, Richard, tr. see Akhmatova, Anna.
McKane, Richard, tr. see Andreyeva, Victoria.
McKane, Richard, tr. see Mandelstam, Osip.
McKane, William. Jeremiah: Chapters 1-25, Vol. 1. Cranfield, Charles E. & Emerton, John A., eds. (International Critical Commentary Ser.). 784p. 1986. 54.95 (*0-567-05042-4*, Pub. by T & T Clark UK) Bks Intl VA.
— Selected Christian Hebraists. 256p. (C). 1989. 74.95 (*0-521-35507-9*) Cambridge U Pr.
McKarns, James. Give Us This Day, 3 vols., Set. Incl. Vol. 1. Year One. LC 91-7181. 145p. 1991. pap. 7.50 (*0-8189-0611-1*); Vol. 2. Year Two. LC 91-7181. 143p. 1991. pap. 7.50 (*0-8189-0612-X*); Vol. 3. Seasons & Saints. LC 91-7181. 159p. 1991. pap. 7.50 (*0-8189-0613-8*); LC 91-7181. 1991. Set pap. 19.95 (*0-8189-0614-6*) Alba.
— Go Tell Everyone: A Commentary on the Sunday Readings - Cycles A-B & C. LC 85-20036. 279p. 1985. pap. 9.95 (*0-8189-0488-7*) Alba.
— Lean Against the Wind: How to Face the Future. LC 93-41498. 150p. (Orig.). 1994. pap. 5.95 (*0-8189-0690-1*) Alba.
— Seldom-Told Bible Tales. 1985. 5.20 (*0-89536-738-6*, 5821) CSS OH.
McKaughan, Howard, ed. The Languages of the Eastern Family of the East New Guinea Highland Stock. LC 72-13131. (Anthropological Studies in the Eastern Highlands of New Guinea: No. 1). (Illus.). 848p. 1973. 40.00 (*0-295-95132-X*) U of Wash Pr.
McKaughan, Howard P. & Macaraya, Batua A. Maranao Dictionary. LC 67-13668. 878p. reprint ed. pap. 180.00 (*0-8357-9825-9*, 2016113) Bks Demand.
McKaughan, Howard P., ed. see Benton, Richard A.
McKaughan, Howard P., ed. see Bernabe, Emma, et al.
McKaughan, Howard P., ed. see Constantino, Ernesto.
McKaughan, Howard P., ed. see Forman, Michael L.
McKaughan, Howard P., ed. see Mirikitani, Leatrice T.
McKaughan, Howard P., ed. see Wolfenden, E. P.
McKaughan, Larry. Why Are Your Fingers Cold? LC 92-16549. (Illus.). 32p. (Orig.). (J). (ps-1). 1992. 14.95 (*0-8361-3604-7*) Herald Pr.
McKay. A Bibliography of Robert Bridges. 1972. 59.95 (*0-87968-740-1*) Gordon Pr.
— Cardiac Valvuloplasty. 1991. 90.00 (*1-55664-126-5*) Mosby Yr Bk.
— Technological Applications of Dispersions. LC 93-50099. (Surfactant Science Ser.: Vol. 52). 560p. 1994. 195.00 (*0-8247-9180-0*) Dekker.
— Use of Adsorbents for Removal of Pollutants from Wastewaters. 1994. write for info. (*0-8493-6920-7*) CRC Pr.
— WEESKA Electronic Communications Systems. (What Every Engineer Should Know Ser.: Vol. 25). 264p. 1989. 49.75 (*0-8247-8008-6*) Dekker.
Mckay. Word Processing Applications for Office Professionals. 1989. pap. text ed. 13.95 (*0-471-61249-9*) P-H.
McKay & Fanning. Self-Esteem. 1987. mass mkt. 5.99 (*0-312-90443-6*) St Martin.
McKay & Wong. Language Diversity. 1988. pap. 23.95 (*0-8384-2706-5*) Heinle & Heinle.
McKay, jt. auth. see Labrash.
McKay, jt. auth. see Tom.
McKay, ed. see Virgil.
McKay, jt. auth. see Virgil.
McKay, A. G. & Shepherd, D. M., eds. Roman Lyric Poetry. 1970. pap. text ed. 19.50 (*0-312-69055-X*) St Martin.
McKay, Alan B., et al. How to Evaluate Progressive Pharmaceutical Services. 159p. (Orig.). 1987. pap. text ed. 31.00 (*0-930530-81-0*) Am Soc Hlth-Syst.
McKay, Alexander G., jt. auth. see Hall, Jane H.
McKay, Anne. Computers in the Schools: The New Frontier. LC 85-106180. 66p. (Orig.). 1984. pap. 6.00 (*0-88156-027-8*) Comm Serv Soc NY.
McKay, Anne, ed. Wolf Girls at Vassar: Lesbian & Gay Experiences, 1930-1990. LC 92-42022. 1993. pap. 9.95 (*0-312-08923-6*) St Martin.
McKay, Barry, ed. Marbling Methods & Receipts from Four Centuries with Other Instructions Useful to Bookbinders. 104p. 1990. text ed. 125.00 (*0-938768-21-2*, 30757) Oak Knoll.
McKay, Bev. Ants & More Ants: An Integrated Activity Unit. (Illus.). 32p. 1993. pap. text ed. 4.95 (*0-86530-225-1*) Incentive Pubns.
— Bird Watch: An Integrated Activity Unit. (Illus.). 32p. 1993. pap. text ed. 4.95 (*0-86530-226-X*) Incentive Pubns.
— Dragons: An Integrated Activity Unit. (Illus.). 32p. (J). (gr. 4-7). 1992. pap. text ed. 4.95 (*0-86530-227-8*, IP NO. 140-2) Incentive Pubns.
— Dropping in on Gravity: An Integrated Activity Unit. (Illus.). 32p. 1993. pap. text ed. 4.95 (*0-86530-228-6*) Incentive Pubns.
— Footworks: An Integrated Activity Unit. (Illus.). 32p. (J). (gr. 4-7). 1992. pap. text ed. 4.95 (*0-86530-229-4*, IP NO. 140-4) Incentive Pubns.
— Our Prehistoric Ancestors: An Integrated Activity Unit. (Illus.). 32p. 1993. pap. text ed. 4.95 (*0-86530-230-8*) Incentive Pubns.
— Owls Great & Small: An Integrated Activity Unit. (Illus.). 32p. 1993. pap. text ed. 4.95 (*0-86530-231-6*) Incentive Pubns.
— Pirates of Old: An Integrated Activity Unit. (Illus.). 32p. 1993. pap. text ed. 4.95 (*0-86530-232-4*) Incentive Pubns.
— Time on the Line: An Integrated Activity Unit. (Illus.). 32p. 1993. pap. text ed. 4.95 (*0-86530-235-9*) Incentive Pubns.
— Trash Unlimited: Linking Environmental Studies with Everyday Life. (Illus.). 64p. (Orig.). 1993. teacher ed 7.95 (*0-86530-276-6*) Incentive Pubns.
— Whale Alert: An Integrated Activity Unit. (Illus.). 32p. 1993. pap. text ed. 4.95 (*0-86530-238-3*) Incentive Pubns.
McKay, Bev, jt. auth. see Catherall, Ed.
McKay, Bob. How to Draw Funny People. LC 81-69658. (Illus.). 32p. (J). (gr. 2-6). 1981. lib. bdg. 10.65 (*0-89375-688-1*); pap. text ed. 1.95 (*0-89375-408-0*) Troll Assocs.
McKay, Bobbie. What Ever Happened to the Family? A Psychologist Looks at Sixty Years of Change. LC 91-34114. 160p. (Orig.). 1991. pap. 10.95 (*0-8298-0915-5*) Pilgrim OH.
McKay, C. E. Stories of Hospital & Camp. LC 70-37312. (Black Heritage Library Collection). 1977. reprint ed. 25.95 (*0-8369-8949-X*) Ayer.
McKay, C. G. From Information to Intrigue: Studies in Secret Service: Based on the Swedish Experience, 1939-45. LC 92-35249. (Cass Series, Studies in Intelligence). 306p. 1993. 35.00 (*0-7146-3470-0*, Pub. by F Cass Pubs UK) Intl Spec Bk.
McKay, Carolyn, ed. see Smith, Leroy, Jr.
McKay, Charles W. Digital Circuits: A Preparation for Microprocessors. LC 77-13058. (Illus.). 1978. 32.95 (*0-685-03835-1*) P-H.
McKay, Christine, jt. ed. see Babcock, Marguerite.
McKay, Christopher P. The Case for Mars II. (Science & Technology Ser.: Vol. 62). (Illus.). 730p. (Orig.). 1985. lib. bdg. 30.00 (*0-87703-219-X*); pap. text ed. 20.00 (*0-87703-220-3*) Univelt Inc.
Mckay, Claire, jt. auth. see Little, Jean.
McKay, Claude. Banana Bottom. 317p. 1971. reprint ed. 15.95 (*0-911860-03-7*) Chatham Bkseller.
— Banana Bottom. LC 73-14676. 317p. 1974. reprint ed. pap. 9.00 (*0-15-610650-7*, Harvest Bks) HarBrace.
— Banjo. LC 79-17798. 327p. 1970. reprint ed. pap. 9.95 (*0-15-610675-2*, Harvest Bks) HarBrace.
— Constab Ballads. 1977. lib. bdg. 59.95 (*0-8490-1666-5*) Gordon Pr.
— The Dialect Poetry of Claude McKay, 2 vols in one. Incl. Vol. 1, Songs of Jamaica. LC 73-3801. (*0-318-50805-2*); Vol. 2, Constab Ballads. LC 73-3801. (*0-318-50806-0*); LC 73-3801. (Black Heritage Library Collection). 1977. reprint ed. 23.95 (*0-8369-8982-1*) Ayer.
— Gingertown. LC 72-37554. (Short Story Index Reprint Ser.). 1977. reprint ed. 28.95 (*0-8369-4113-6*) Ayer.
— Harlem Glory. 175p. 1990. lib. bdg. 24.95 (*0-88286-162-X*); pap. 9.95 (*0-88286-163-8*) C H Kerr.
— Home to Harlem. 360p. 1987. reprint ed. pap. text ed. 14.95 (*1-55553-024-9*) NE U Pr.
— A Long Way from Home. LC 74-77507. (American Negro: His History & Literature, Second Ser.). 1980. reprint ed. 29.95 (*0-405-01880-0*) Ayer.
— Long Way from Home. LC 76-11560. 354p. 1970. reprint ed. pap. 7.95 (*0-15-653145-3*, HB172, Harvest Bks) HarBrace.
— A Long Way from Home: An Autobiography. (American Biography Ser.). 354p. 1991. reprint ed. lib. bdg. 79.00 (*0-7812-8282-9*) Rprt Serv.
— Selected Poems of Claude McKay. LC 70-78698. 110p. 1969. reprint ed. pap. 5.95 (*0-15-680649-5*, Harvest Bks) HarBrace.
McKay, Claudia. The Kali Connection. LC 93-42942. 190p. (Orig.). 1994. pap. 9.95 (*0-934678-54-5*) New Victoria Pubs.
— Promise of the Rose Stone. LC 86-62343. 238p. 1986. pap. 7.95 (*0-934678-09-X*) New Victoria Pubs.
McKay, Craig G., tr. see Lindgren, Michael.
McKay, D. Jay & Combs, Robert M. Ren & Stimpy's Oh Joy of Cooking! (Illus.). 64p. (J). (gr. 3-7). 1994. pap. 5.95 (*0-448-40548-2*, G&D) Putnam Pub Group.
***McKay, Dave.** The Beginner's Guide: Microsoft Dos 5.0-6.2 - Microsoft Windows 3.1. 1995. write for info. (*1-881023-89-3*) Inst Publishing.
— The Beginner's Guide: Quicken-QuickBook-TurboTax. 1995. write for info. (*1-881023-91-5*) Inst Publishing.
— The Beginner's Guide: Windows '95. 1995. write for info. (*1-881023-90-7*) Inst Publishing.
McKay, David. American Politics & Society. 3rd ed. LC 93-7211. (Illus.). 340p. (YA). (gr. 10 up). 1993. pap. 19.95 (*0-631-18814-2*) Blackwell Pubs.
— Domestic Policy & Ideology: Presidents & the American State, 1964-1987. (Illus.). (C). 1989. 54.95 (*0-521-32033-X*) Cambridge U Pr.
McKay, David, et al, eds. Data Analysis & the Social Sciences. LC 83-42529. 291p. 1983. text ed. 35.00 (*0-312-18300-3*) St Martin.
McKay, David & Crawford, Richard. William Billings of Boston: Eighteenth-Century Composer. LC 74-2971. (Illus.). 320p. 1975. 55.00x (*0-691-09118-8*) Princeton U Pr.
McKay, David, jt. auth. see Budge, Ian.
McKay, David, jt. ed. see Budge, Ian.
McKay, David L. My Father: David O. McKay. LC 89-38108. (Illus.). 275p. 1989. 13.95 (*0-87579-278-2*) Deseret Bk.
McKay, David W. Space Science Projects for Young Scientists. (J). 1989. pap. 6.95 (*0-531-15134-4*) Watts.
McKay, David W. & Smith, Bruce G. Space Science Projects for Young Scientists. LC 86-7745. (Projects for Young Scientists Ser.). (Illus.). 128p. (YA). (gr. 7-12). 1986. lib. bdg. 14.77 (*0-531-10244-0*) Watts.
McKay, David W., jt. auth. see Smith, Bruce.
McKay, Deborah. Eve's Longing: The Infinite Possibilities in All Things. 139p. 1992. pap. 8.95 (*0-932511-65-1*) Fiction Coll.
Mckay, Derek & Scott, H. M. The Rise of the Great Powers: The Great Powers & European States Systems, 1648-1815. (C). 1983. text ed. write for info. (*0-318-56830-6*); pap. text ed. 25.50 (*0-582-48554-1*, 73299) Longman.
McKay, Donald C. The United States & France. LC 83-1558. xvii, 334p. (C). 1983. reprint ed. text ed. 65.00 (*0-313-23885-5*, MCUW, Greenwood Pr) Greenwood.
McKay, Donald C., ed. Essays in the History of Modern Europe. LC 68-14908. (Essay Index Reprint Ser.). 1977. 21.95 (*0-8369-0652-7*) Ayer.
McKay, Edward S. Marketing Mystique. rev. ed. 192p. 1993. pap. 17.95 (*0-8144-7808-5*) AMACOM.
McKay, Eleanor, ed. Papers of John L. Lewis, 1879-1969: Guide to a Microfilm Edition. 12p. 1970. pap. 55.00 (*0-685-48791-1*) Chadwyck-Healey.
McKay, Ernest. The Civil War & New York City. LC 90-32799. (New York State Bks.). (Illus.). 380p. 1991. text ed. 39.95x (*0-8156-0246-4*); pap. text ed. 15.95 (*0-8156-2545-6*) Syracuse U Pr.
***Mckay, Fodors.** Fodor Affordable France. 4th ed. Date not set. 16.50 (*0-679-02966-4*) Random Hse Value.
— Fodor's Affordable. Date not set. 19.00 (*0-679-02964-8*) Random Hse Value.
— Fodor's Affordable Britain. 4th ed. Date not set. 17.00 (*0-679-02967-2*) Random Hse Value.
— Fodor's Affordable Florida. 2nd ed. 1995. write for info. (*0-679-02965-6*) Random Hse Value.
— Fodor's Affordable London. 2nd ed. Date not set. pap. text ed. 12.00 (*0-679-02968-0*) Random Hse Value.
— Fodor's Alaska 1996. Date not set. 16.00 (*0-679-02969-9*) Random Hse Value.
— Fodor's Arizona 1996. Date not set. 15.95 (*0-679-02970-2*) Random Hse Value.
— Fodor's Arizona 1996. 1995. write for info. (*0-679-02971-0*) Random Hse Value.
— Fodor's New England 1996. 1995. write for info. (*0-679-02952-4*) Random Hse Value.
— Fodor's New England 1996. 1995. write for info. (*0-679-02953-2*) Random Hse Value.
— Fodor's NYC 1996. 1995. write for info. (*0-679-02954-0*) Random Hse Value.
McKay, Frances P. Let's Go Shelling. LC 68-3449. (Illus.). (Orig.). 1967. pap. 2.95 (*0-8200-0203-8*) Great Outdoors.
McKay, Frank W. A Workable Plan for Sensible Government. 116p. (Orig.). 1984. pap. 2.95 (*0-930333-00-4*) Switz Pr.
McKay, G. An English Gaelic Key to Dwelly. 1991. pap. 7.95 (*0-8288-3343-5*, F129235) Fr & Eur.
McKay, Gary & Dinkmeyer, Don. How You Feel Is up to You: The Power of Emotional Choice. 256p. 1994. pap. 10.95 (*0-915166-81-X*) Impact Pubs CA.
McKay, Gary, jt. auth. see Dinkmeyer, Don.
McKay, Gary, jt. auth. see Dinkmeyer, Don, Sr.
McKay, Gary D. & Dinkmeyer, Don, Sr. Systematic Training for Effective Parenting Parent's Handbook. rev. ed. 1989. pap. text ed. 13.95 (*0-88671-298-X*, 6202) Am Guidance.
McKay, Gary D., jt. auth. see Dinkmeyer, Don.
McKay, Gary D., jt. auth. see Dinkmeyer, Don, Sr.
McKay, Gary D., et al. Systematic Training for Effective Teaching (STET) Teacher's Resource Book: Activities for Teachers & Students. (Illus.). 161p. (Orig.). (C). 1980. pap. 15.95 (*0-913476-76-5*, 5007) Am Guidance.
McKay, George, jt. auth. see McKay, Louise.
McKay, George L. Bibliography of Robert Bridges. LC 33-31729. reprint ed. 9.00 (*0-404-04132-9*) AMS Pr.
McKay, Girvan. An English-Gaelic Key to Dwelly. (C). 1989. pap. 25.00 (*0-901771-47-3*, Pub. by Gairm Pubns UK) St Mut.
***McKay, Glynn.** Mask Making. 1994. 12.98 (*0-7858-0176-6*) Bk Sales Inc.
McKay, Harvey J. St. Paul, Oregon, Eighteen Thirty to Eighteen Ninety. LC 80-69228. (Illus.). 340p. 1980. 15.00 (*0-8323-0384-4*) Binford Mort.
McKay, Heather & Abigail, Tom. Write After. Date not set. pap. write for info. (*0-13-042763-2*) P-H.
McKay, Heather, jt. auth. see Tom, Abigail.
***McKay, Heather A.** Sabbath & Synagogue: The Question of Sabbath in Ancient Judaism. Vol. 122. 1994. 71.50 (*90-04-10060-1*) E J Brill.
***McKay, Hilary.** Dog Friday. LC 95-4446. (J). 1995. write for info. (*0-689-80383-4*, McElderry) S&S Childrens.
— The Exiles. LC 91-38220. 224p. (J). (gr. 4-7). 1992. text ed. 14.95 (*0-689-50555-8*, McElderry) S&S Childrens.
— The Exiles at Home. LC 94-14225. (J). 1994. text ed. 15.95 (*0-689-50610-4*, McElderry) S&S Childrens.
McKay, Ian. The Challenge of Modernity: A Reader on Post-Confederation Canada. 1991. pap. text ed. write for info. (*0-07-551150-9*) McGraw.
— The Quest of the Folk: Antimodernism & Cultural Selection in Twentieth-Century Nova Scotia. (Illus.). 392p. 1994. 55.00 (*0-7735-1179-2*, Pub. by McGill CN); pap. 19.95 (*0-7735-1248-9*, Pub. by McGill CN) U of Toronto Pr.
McKay, Ian & Leigh, Irene, eds. Growth Factors: A Practical Approach. LC 92-27317. (Practical Approach Ser.). (C). 1993. 70.00 (*0-19-963360-6*, IRL Pr); pap. 39.00 (*0-19-963359-2*, IRL Pr) OUP.
McKay, Irene. Beginning Interactive Grammar: Activities & Exercises. LC 92-29933. 1993. pap. 18.95 (*0-8384-3926-8*) Heinle & Heinle.
— Intermediate Interactive Grammar: Activities & Exercises. LC 94-25621. 1995. pap. 18.95 (*0-8384-5864-5*) Heinle & Heinle.
McKay, J. W. Sneap '92: Proceedings of the Symposium of North Eastern Accelerator Personnel, 1992. 232p. 1995. text ed. 78.00 (*981-02-1885-0*) World Scientific Pub.
***McKay, Jack A.** Schools in the Middle: Developing a Middle-Level Orientation. Herman, Jerry J. & Herman, Janice L., eds. (Roadmaps to Success). (Illus.). 72p. 1995. pap. 15.00 (*0-8039-6232-0*) Corwin Pr.
McKay, James. The Ferret & Ferreting Handbook. (Illus.). 144p. 1994. 34.95 (*1-85223-772-4*, Pub. by Crowood Pr UK) Trafalgar.
***McKay, John.** Anatomy of the Ship the 24-Gun Ship Pandora. (Illus.). 128p. (C). 1992. 32.95 (*0-9615021-9-3*) Phoen Pubns.
— Armed Transport Bounty. LC 88-62459. (Anatomy of the Ship Ser.). (Illus.). 120p. 1989. 36.95 (*0-87021-280-X*) Naval Inst Pr.

M

McKay, John, ed. Finite Groups--Coming of Age. LC 85-15049. (Contemporary Mathematics Ser.: Vol. 45). 350p. 1985. pap. 42.00 (*0-8218-5047-4*, CONM-45) Am Math.

McKay, John & Harland, John. The Flower Class Corvette Agassiz. (Anatomy of the Ship Ser.). (Illus.). 160p. 1994. 36.95 (*1-55068-084-6*) Naval Inst Pr.

McKay, John, ed. see Locke, Robert R.

McKay, John C. A Guide to Germanic Reference Grammars: The Modern Standard Languages. LC 84-14597. (Library & Information Sources in Linguistics: Vol. 15). xviii, 239p. 1984. 55.00x (*90-272-3736-0*) Benjamins North Am.

— A Guide to Romance Reference Grammars: The Modern Standard Languages. (Library & Information Sources in Linguistics: No. 6). xviii, 126p. 1979. 39.00x (*90-272-0997-9*) Benjamins North Am.

McKay, John F., jt. ed. see Miknis, Francis P.

McKay, John G., tr. see Campbell, John F.

McKay, John P. Pioneers for Profit: Foreign Entrepreneurship & Russian Industrialization, 1885-1913. LC 79-103932. 1970. lib. bdg. 30.00 (*0-226-55990-4*) U Ch Pr.

— Tramways & Trolleys: The Rise of Urban Mass Transport in Europe. LC 76-3261. (Illus.). 280p. 1976. 45.00x (*0-691-05240-9*) Princeton U Pr.

McKay, John P., tr. see Michelet, Jules.

McKay, John P., et al. A History of Western Society. 3rd ed. LC 86-81468. 1088p. (C). 1986. student ed 8.95 (*0-685-17244-9*) HM.

— A History of Western Society: From Antiquity to the Enlightenment, Vol. I; From Absolutism to the Present, Vol. II, 2 vols., 1. 4th ed. (C). 1991. write for info. (*0-395-43342-8*); student ed write for info. (*0-395-55873-5*) HM Soft Schl Col Div.

— A History of Western Society: From Antiquity to the Enlightenment, Vol. I; From Absolutism to the Present, Vol. II, 2 vols., 2. 4th ed. (C). 1991. write for info. (*0-395-43343-6*); student ed write for info. (*0-395-55874-3*) HM Soft Schl Col Div.

— A History of Western Society: From Antiquity to the Reformation, Vol. A; From the Renaissance to 1815, Vol. B; From the Revolutionary Era to the Present, Vol. C, 3 vols., A. 4th ed. (C). 1991. write for info. (*0-395-43344-4*) HM Soft Schl Col Div.

— A History of Western Society: From Antiquity to the Reformation, Vol. A; From the Renaissance to 1815, Vol. B; From the Revolutionary Era to the Present, Vol. C, 3 vols., B. 4th ed. (C). 1991. write for info. (*0-395-43345-2*) HM Soft Schl Col Div.

— A History of Western Society: From Antiquity to the Reformation, Vol. A; From the Renaissance to 1815, Vol. B; From the Revolutionary Era to the Present, Vol. C, 3 vols., C. 4th ed. (C). 1991. write for info. (*0-395-43346-0*) HM Soft Schl Col Div.

— A History of Western Society, Complete. 4th ed. (C). 1991. write for info. (*0-395-43341-X*) HM Soft Schl Col Div.

— A History of Western Society since 1400. 4th ed. (C). 1991. write for info. (*0-395-55875-1*) HM Soft Schl Col Div.

— A History of World Societies. 2nd ed. 1987. pap. 22.36 (*0-318-36898-6*) HM.

— A History of World Societies, 3 Vols. 3rd ed. (C). 1991. text ed. 57.16 (*0-395-47293-8*) HM.

— A History of World Societies, Vol. A: From Antiquity Through the Middle Ages, 3 Vols. 3rd ed. (C). 1991. pap. 35.56 (*0-395-47296-2*) HM.

— A History of World Societies, Vol. B: From 1300 Through the French Revolution, 3 Vols. 3rd ed. (C). 1991. pap. 35.56 (*0-395-47297-0*) HM.

— A History of World Societies, Vol. C: From the French Revolution to the Present, 3 Vols. 3rd ed. (C). 1991. pap. 35.56 (*0-395-47298-9*) HM.

— A History of World Societies, Vol. One: To 1715, 3 Vols. 3rd ed. (C). 1991. pap. 41.16 (*0-395-47294-6*) HM.

— A History of World Societies, Vol. Two: Since 1500, 3 Vols. 3rd ed. (C). 1991. pap. 41.16 (*0-395-47295-4*) HM.

McKay, Joyce, et al. Drug Free Parent Booklet. (Drug Free Ser.). 1989. pap. text ed. 13.95 (*0-88671-296-3*, 5110) Am Guidance.

McKay, Joyce L., et al. Drug Free Teachers Guide. (Drug Free Ser.). 1989. 28.95 (*0-88671-295-5*, 5101) Am Guidance.

McKay, Judith. Chemotherapy Survival Guide: Information, Suggestions, & Support to Help You Get Through. 1993. 24.95 (*1-879237-58-X*); pap. 11.95 (*1-879237-57-1*) New Harbinger.

McKay, Julie, ed. see Radha, Sivananda.

McKay, K. L. A New Syntax of the Verb in New Testament Greek: An Aspectual Approach. LC 92-44671. (Studies in Biblical Greek: Vol. 5). 203p. (Orig.). (C). 1994. pap. text ed. 29.95 (*0-8204-2123-5*) P Lang Pubs.

McKay, Kenneth M. Many Glancing Colours: An Essay in Reading Tennyson, 1809-1850. 301p. 1988. 40.00 (*0-8020-2658-3*) U of Toronto Pr.

McKay, Larry. The Personal Home Inspection Guide. LC 91-14522. 96p. 1991. pap. 14.95 (*0-942963-11-3*) Distinctive Pub.

***McKay, Lawrence, Jr.** Caravan. LC 95-2037. (Illus.). 32p. (J). (gr. k-4). 1995. 14.95 (*1-880000-23-7*) Lee & Low Bks.

McKay, Louise & McKay, George. Marny's Ride with the Wind. (Illus.). (J). (gr. k-3). 1979. 6.95 (*0-934986-00-2*) New Harbinger.

McKay, Lyn J., jt. auth. see Radencich, Marguerite C.

McKay, Malcolm, intro. Agricultural Engineering Conference, 1990. (Illus.). 533p. (Orig.). 1990. pap. 96.00 (*0-85825-509-X*) Accents Pubns.

McKay, Margaret. Peacock's Progress: Aspects of Artistic Development in the Novels of Thomas Love Peacock. (Studia Anglistica Upsaliensia Ser.: No. 78). 170p. (Orig.). 1992. pap. 41.00x (*91-554-2914-9*, Pub. by Almqv & Wiksell SW) Coronet Bks.

McKay, Maria E., tr. see Sand, George.

McKay, Marion & McKay, Neil. Fundamentals of Western Music. 211p. (C). 1986. pap. 30.95 (*0-534-05106-5*) Intl Thomson.

McKay, Matthew. Self-Esteem: A Proven Program of Cognitive Techniques for Assessing & Improving. 2nd ed. 1993. 24.95 (*1-879237-45-8*); pap. 12.95 (*1-879237-44-X*) New Harbinger.

McKay, Matthew & Fanning, Patrick. Being a Man: A Guide to the New Masculinity. 260p. (Orig.). 1992. text ed. 29.95 (*1-879237-41-5*); pap. text ed. 12.95 (*1-879237-40-7*) New Harbinger.

— Prisoners of Belief. 160p. (Orig.). 1991. 24.95 (*1-879237-05-9*); pap. 10.95 (*1-879237-04-0*) New Harbinger.

— Self-Esteem. 272p. 1987. 24.95 (*0-934986-42-8*); pap. 12.95 (*0-934986-41-X*) New Harbinger.

— Self Esteem. 1994. 7.98 (*1-56731-003-6*, MJF Bks) Fine Comms.

McKay, Matthew, et al. Couple Skills: Making Your Relationship Work. 224p. (Orig.). 1994. 24.95 (*1-879237-67-9*); pap. 12.95 (*1-879237-66-0*) New Harbinger.

— The Divorce Book. 264p. 1984. 24.95 (*0-934986-11-8*); pap. 11.95 (*0-934986-06-1*) New Harbinger.

— How to Communicate. 1994. 7.98 (*1-56731-031-1*, MJF Bks) Fine Comms.

— Messages: The Communication Skills Book. 1983. 24.95 (*0-934986-10-X*); pap. 12.95 (*0-934986-05-3*) New Harbinger.

— Messages: The Communication Skills Book. 1995. pap. 13.95 (*1-57224-022-9*) New Harbinger.

— Messages: The Communication Skills Book. 2nd ed. 300p. 1995. text ed. 24.95 (*1-57224-023-7*) New Harbinger.

— Thoughts & Feelings: The Art of Cognitive Stress Intervention. 224p. 1981. 24.95 (*0-934986-09-6*); pap. 13.95 (*0-934986-03-7*) New Harbinger.

— When Anger Hurts. 1994. 7.98 (*1-56731-028-1*, MJF Bks) Fine Comms.

— When Anger Hurts: Quieting the Storm Within. 208p. (Orig.). (C). 1992. 24.95 (*0-934986-77-0*); pap. 12.95 (*0-934986-76-2*) New Harbinger.

McKay, Neil, jt. auth. see McKay, Marion.

McKay, Nellie Y. Critical Essays on Toni Morrison. (Critical Essays Ser.). 216p. 1988. text ed. 45.00 (*0-8161-8884-X*) G K Hall.

— Jean Toomer, Artist: A Study of His Literary Life & Work, 1894-1936. LC 83-21570. xiv, 262p. 1984. 32.50 (*0-8078-1583-7*) U of NC Pr.

— Jean Toomer, Artist: A Study of His Literary Life & Work, 1894-1936. LC 83-21570. viv, 262p. 1987. pap. 14.95 (*0-8078-4171-4*) U of NC Pr.

McKay, Ogese T. Now It Can Be Told. 60p. 1991. pap. text ed. 10.00 (*0-9629807-0-6*) Ogese T McKay.

McKay, Pat. The Professional Programmers Guide to C. 202p. (C). 1989. pap. text ed. 100.00 (*0-273-02958-4*, Pub. by Pitman Pubng UK) St Mut.

McKay, Patricia L., et al. Microcomputers & Economic Analysis: Spreadsheet Templates for Local Government. rev. ed. (Bureau of Economic & Business Research Monographs). 182p. 1987. pap. text ed. 15.00 (*0-930885-03-1*) Bur Econ & Bus Res.

***McKay, Ray & Putnam, Russell.** Divorce Tax Practice & Planning Guide. 50p. 1994. ring bd. 145.00 (*1-886035-05-9*) Pro Tax & Business.

McKay, Raymond E., Jr., jt. auth. see Duncan, Andrew J.

McKay, Rena. Romancing Cody. (Silhouette Romance Ser.). 1994. pap. 2.75 (*0-373-19004-2*) Harlequin Bks.

— Romancing Cody. (Silhouette Romance Ser.). 1994. pap. 2.75 (*0-373-91004-5*, 5-91004-7) Silhouette.

McKay, Richard, jt. auth. see Hill, Malcolm R.

McKay, Richard C. South Street. LC 76-160128. (American History & Americana Ser.: No. 47). 1971. lib. bdg. 75.00 (*0-8383-1280-2*) M S G Haskell Hse.

McKay, Robert. Opportunities in Your Own Service Business. (Illus.). 160p. 1987. 10.95 (*0-8442-6232-3*, VGM Career Bks); pap. 13.95 (*0-8442-6231-5*, VGM Career Bks) NTC Pub Grp.

— Planning Your Military Career. 160p. 1984. pap. 6.95 (*0-8442-6672-8*, NTC Busn Bks) NTC Pub Grp.

McKay, Robert B. Human Dignity: The Internationalization of Human Rights. Cleveland, Harlan, ed. LC 78-11817. 203p. 1979. lib. bdg. 20.00 (*0-379-20650-1*) Oceana.

— Long Island: Between Ocean & Empire: An Illustrated History. LC 85-26605. 304p. 1985. 24.95 (*0-89781-143-7*) Preferred Mktg.

McKay, Robert B., jt. ed. see David, Jack.

McKay, Robert F. Under the Trapeze: Being the True & Unembellished Account of the Last Original Old-Fashioned All-American Independently Owned & Operated Family Circus. 500p. 1989. 20.00 (*0-317-93517-8*) Brass Ring.

McKay, Robert S. Modern American Knives & Self-Defense Skills. LC 86-51211. 200p. (Orig.). 1986. pap. 8.95 (*0-86568-086-8*, 330) Unique Pubns.

McKay, Ronald, et al, eds. Monoclonal Antibodies to Neural Antigens. LC 81-10185. (Cold Spring Harbor Reports in the Neurosciences: No. 2). 300p. reprint ed. pap. 85.50 (*0-7837-2085-8*, 2042359) Bks Demand.

McKay, Ronald D. The Role of Psychiatric Reports in the Crown Court Trial Process. 21p. 1986. pap. 5.00 (*0-948997-30-3*, Pub. by Leicester Poly Law Schl) Pickering Pubns.

McKay, Ronald D. & Russell, Kenneth V., eds. Psychiatry & the Criminal Process. (Leicester Polytechnic Law School Monograph Ser.). 48p. 1986. pap. 5.00 (*0-948997-28-1*) Milltak Ltd.

McKay, Sandra L. Agendas for Second Language Literacy. (Cambridge Language Education Ser.). 176p. (C). 1993. pap. 15.95 (*0-521-44664-3*) Cambridge U Pr.

— Agendas for Second Language Literacy. (Cambridge Language Education Ser.). 176p. (C). 1993. 39.95 (*0-521-44118-8*) Cambridge U Pr.

***McKay, Sandra L. & Hornberger, Nancy F., eds.** Sociolinguistics & Language Teaching. (Applied Linguistics Ser.). (Illus.). 400p. (C). 1995. write for info. (*0-521-48205-4*); pap. write for info. (*0-521-48434-0*) Cambridge U Pr.

McKay, Seth S. W. Lee O'Daniel & Texas Politics, 1938-1942. LC 83-45450. reprint ed. 58.00 (*0-404-20164-4*) AMS Pr.

McKay, Sharon & MacLeod, David. Chalk Around the Block: A Somerville House Book. LC 92-41495. (Illus.). 48p. (J). 1993. 9.95 (*0-8362-4502-4*) Andrews & McMeel.

— The Halloween Book & Pumpkin Carver Kit. 1994. pap. 9.95 (*0-8362-4225-4*) Andrews & McMeel.

— The Official Kick the Can. (Illus.). 64p. (J). 1995. pap. 10.95 (*0-8362-4515-6*) Andrews & McMeel.

McKay, Sharon E. The Picky Eater. 166p. (Orig.). 1994. pap. 12.00 (*0-00-637898-6*, Pub. by HarpC CN) HarpC.

McKay, Sindy. Color Crazy. (Muppet Magic Ser.). (Illus.). 26p. (J). (ps up). 1987. 12.95 (*1-55578-609-X*) Worlds Wonder.

— Something's Fishy. (Muppet Magic Ser.). (Illus.). 26p. (J). (ps up). 1986. 12.95 (*1-55578-610-3*) Worlds Wonder.

McKay, Sindy & Swerdlove, Larry. Radio Station K-E-R-M. (Muppet Magic Ser.). (Illus.). 26p. (J). (ps up). 1987. 12.95 (*1-55578-607-3*) Worlds Wonder.

***McKay, Stephen & Marsh, Alan.** Lone Parents & Work. (DSS Research Report Ser.: No. 25). 82p. 1994. pap. 25.00 (*0-11-762148-X*, HM2148X, Pub. by HMSO UK) UNIPUB.

McKay, Susan. The Assertive Approach to Childbirth. 44p. 1986. 1.50 (*0-934024-10-3*) Intl Childbirth.

— Humanizing Maternity Services Through Family-Centered Care. 52p. 1982. 2.00 (*0-934024-07-3*) Intl Childbirth.

McKay, Thomas J. Modern Symbolic Logic. 826p. (C). 1989. write for info. (*0-02-379286-8*) Macmillan.

McKay, Tom & Kmetz, Deborah. Agricultural Diversity in Wisconsin. LC 87-6482. (Illus.). 93p. 1987. pap. 4.00 (*0-87020-250-2*) State Hist Soc Wis.

Mckay, Valerie M., jt. ed. see Conzen, Michael P.

McKay, Virginia L. Moving Abroad: A Guide to International Living. rev. ed. LC 89-90449. 226p. 1990. pap. 14.95 (*962-7060-01-1*) VLM Enter.

McKay, W. D. Church Government in the Writings of George Gillespie: An Ecclesiastical Republic. LC 94-21822. (Rutherford Studies in Historical Theology: Vol. 6). 372p. 1994. text ed. 99.95 (*0-7734-1631-5*) E Mellen.

McKay, W. G. & Patera, J. Tables of Dimensions, Indices, & Branching Rules for Representations of Simple Lie Algebras. (Lecture Notes in Pure & Applied Mathematics Ser.: Vol. 69). (Illus.). 336p. 1981. 135.00 (*0-8247-1227-7*) Dekker.

McKay, William J. Me, An Evangelist? Every Christian's Guide to Caring Evangelism. 1992. pap. text ed. 11.95 (*0-9633831-0-8*) Stephen Minist.

— Nuts & Bolts Issues for ChristCare Group Leaders. 76p. (Orig.). Date not set. pap. text ed. 4.95 (*0-9633831-3-2*) Stephen Minist.

McKay, William J., jt. auth. see Haugk, Kenneth C.

McKay, Winsor. Windsor McKay's Dream Days: An Original Compilation. First Collection of Comic Strip Features by the Creator of Little Nemo from the Years 1903 to 1914. Blackbeard, Bill, ed. LC 76-53048. (Classic American Comic Strips Ser.). (Illus.). 1990. 33.50 (*0-88355-651-0*) Hyperion Conn.

***McKaye, Bessa.** The Crossroads of Destiny. 80p. Date not set. 12.95 (*1-56167-193-2*) Noble Hse MD.

McKaye-Ege, Arvia. The Secret Iron of the Heart. 192p. 1982. 15.00 (*0-932776-05-1*); pap. 9.50 (*0-932776-06-X*) Adonis Pr.

McKeachie, W. J., jt. ed. see Hartley, J.

McKeachie, Wilbert J. Teaching Tips: A Guidebook for the Beginning College Teacher. 8th ed. LC 85-60982. 353p. (C). 1990. pap. text ed. 16.00 (*0-669-06752-0*) Heath.

McKeachie, Wilbert J., jt. auth. see Eble, Kenneth E.

McKeag, Douglas B. & Hough, David. Primary Care Sports Medicine. 632p. 1993. boxed write for info. (*0-697-14841-6*) Brown & Benchmark.

McKeag, Edwin C. Mistake in Contract: A Study in Comparative Jurisprudence. LC 75-76675. (Columbia University. Studies in the Social Sciences: No. 59). reprint ed. 16.50 (*0-404-51059-0*) AMS Pr.

McKeag, Malcolm. Cruising Crew: How to Be Welcome on Board. 96p. (C). 1990. text ed. 59.00 (*0-906754-63-1*, Pub. by Fernhurst Bks UK) St Mut.

— Racing Crew. 96p. (C). 1990. text ed. 59.00 (*0-906754-68-2*, Pub. by Fernhurst Bks UK) St Mut.

McKeag, R. M. & Wilson, R. Studies in Operating Systems. (APIC Ser.). 1976. text ed. 134.00 (*0-12-484350-6*) Acad Pr.

McKeage, Jeff. Hillmen of the Trollshaws. (Illus.). 36p. (YA). (gr. 10-12). 1984. pap. 7.00 (*0-915795-24-8*, 8040) Iron Crown Ent Inc.

— The Lost Realm of Cardolan. Fenlon, Peter C., Jr., ed. (Middle-Earth Campaign Module Ser.). 64p. (Orig.). (YA). (gr. 10-12). 1987. pap. 12.00 (*0-915795-95-7*, 3700) Iron Crown Ent Inc.

— Raiders of Cardolan. Charlton, Coleman, ed. (Middle-Earth Ready-to-Run Adventure Ser.). (Illus.). 32p. (Orig.). (YA). (gr. 10-12). 1988. pap. 6.00 (*1-55806-005-7*, 8108) Iron Crown Ent Inc.

McKeage, Jeff & Fenlon, Peter C., Jr. Woses of the Black Wood. (Middle-Earth Read-to-Run Adventure Ser.). 32p. (YA). (gr. 10-12). 1987. pap. 6.00 (*0-915795-99-X*, 8107) Iron Crown Ent Inc.

McKeage, Jeffrey. Dark Mage of Rhudaur. Ney, Jessica, ed. (Middle Earth Ser.). (Illus.). 40p. (Orig.). (YA). (gr. 12). 1989. pap. 7.00 (*1-55806-072-3*, 8013) Iron Crown Ent Inc.

McKeague, Charles P. Algebra with Trigonometry for College Students. 2nd ed. 714p. (C). 1988. text ed. 42.75 (*0-15-502120-6*) SCP.

— Basic Mathematics. 3rd ed. 484p. (C). 1992. pap. 47.95 (*0-534-14460-8*) PWS Pubs.

— Beginning Algebra: A Text - Workbook. 542p. (C). 1989. student ed, teacher ed write for info. (*0-318-66683-9*) SCP.

— Beginning Algebra: A Text - Workbook. 3rd ed. 542p. (C). 1989. teacher ed 5.25 (*0-15-505235-7*); teacher ed 3.00 (*0-15-505236-5*); pap. text ed. 43.00 (*0-15-505234-9*); disk write for info. (*0-318-66681-2*); disk write for info. (*0-318-66682-0*); 22.75 (*0-15-555254-6*) SCP.

— Elementary Algebra. 4th ed. 484p. (C). 1989. pap. text ed. 47.00 (*0-15-520961-2*) SCP.

— Intermediate Algebra. 4th ed. 605p. (C). 1990. text ed. 47.00 (*0-15-541392-9*); vhs write for info. (*0-318-67022-4*); disk write for info. (*0-318-67023-2*); disk write for info. (*0-318-67024-0*); disk write for info. (*0-318-67025-9*); disk write for info. (*0-318-67026-7*); disk write for info. (*0-318-67027-5*) SCP.

— Intermediate Algebra. 4th ed. 605p. (C). 1990. student ed, pap. text ed. 18.50 (*0-15-541394-5*) SCP.

— Intermediate Algebra. 4th ed. 605p. (C). 1990. pap. text ed. 4.00 (*0-15-541393-7*) SCP.

— Intermediate Algebra: A Text-Workbook. 3rd ed. 635p. (C). 1989. pap. text ed. 42.75 (*0-15-541405-4*) SCP.

— Prealgebra. 2nd ed. 550p. (C). 1992. pap. 45.95 (*0-534-14466-7*) PWS Pubs.

— Prerequisite Algebra. 640p. (C). 1988. text ed. 48.00 (*0-15-571093-1*) SCP.

— Trigonometry. 2nd ed. 256p. (C). 1988. Student manual, 256. student ed, pap. text ed. 18.50 (*0-15-592364-1*) SCP.

— Trigonometry. 2nd ed. 413p. (C). 1988. text ed. 47.00 (*0-15-592362-5*) SCP.

McKean, Barb. Birds. (Discover Nature Ser.). (Illus.). 32p. (J). (gr. 3-7). 1985. pap. 3.50 (*0-88625-116-8*) Durkin Hayes Pub.

— Wild Animals. (Discover Nature Ser.). (Illus.). 32p. (J). (gr. 3-7). 1985. pap. 3.50 (*0-88625-117-6*) Durkin Hayes Pub.

McKean, Charles. Banff & Buchan: An Illustrated Architectural Guide. (Illus.). 176p. (C). 1990. pap. 35.00x (*1-85158-231-2*, Pub. by Rutland Pr UK) St Mut.

— The District of Moray: An Illustrated Architectural Guide. (Illus.). 172p. (C). 1987. pap. 35.00x (*0-7073-0528-4*, Pub. by Rutland Pr UK) St Mut.

— Edinburgh: An Illustrated Architectural Guide. (Illus.). 240p. (C). 1992. pap. 35.00x (*0-9501462-4-2*, Pub. by Rutland Pr UK) St Mut.

— The Scottish Thirties. 200p. (C). 1987. pap. 35.00x (*0-7073-0493-8*, Pub. by Rutland Pr UK) St Mut.

— Stirling & the Trossachs. 152p. (C). 1994. pap. 35.00x (*1-873190-21-2*, Pub. by Rutland Pr UK) St Mut.

***McKean, Charles & Walker, David.** Dundee: An Illustrated Architectural Guide. (Illus.). 184p. (C). 1993. pap. 35.00x (*1-873190-09-3*, Pub. by Rutland Pr UK) St Mut.

McKean, Charles, jt. auth. see Jaques, Richard.

***McKean, Charles, et al.** Central Glasgow: An Illustrated Architectural Guide. (Illus.). 208p. (C). 1993. pap. 35.00x (*1-873190-22-0*, Pub. by Rutland Pr UK) St Mut.

McKean, Dave. Cages. (Illus.). 48p. (Orig.). 1991. pap. 3.50 (*1-879450-17-8*) Tundra MA.

— Cages. (Illus.). 48p. (Orig.). 1991. pap. 3.50 (*1-879450-18-6*) Tundra MA.

McKean, David, jt. auth. see Frantz, Douglas.

***McKean, Gary O.** Through It All. 8p. 1994. pap. text ed. 3.00 (*0-944561-25-X*) Chr Legal.

McKean, H. P., Jr., jt. auth. see Ito, K.

McKean, H. P., jt. ed. see Keller, J. B.

McKean, Henry P., jt. auth. see Dym, Harry.

McKean, James. Headlong. LC 86-28200. (University of Utah Press Poetry Ser.). 78p. (Orig.). reprint ed. pap. 25.00 (*0-7837-6866-4*, 2046696) Bks Demand.

— Tree of Heaven. LC 94-49018. (Iowa Poetry Prize). 89p. (Orig.). 1995. pap. 10.95 (*0-87745-505-8*) U of Iowa Pr.

McKean, Jean. Learning from Segal: Walter Segal's Life, Work & Influence. 221p. 1988. 74.00 (*0-8176-1999-2*) Birkhauser.

McKean, Jerome B., jt. auth. see Hendricks, James E.

McKean, John. Crystal Palace: London 1851 Sir Joseph Paxton. (Illus.). 60p. (C). 1994. pap. 29.95 (*0-7148-2925-0*, Pub. by Phaidon Press UK) Chronicle Bks.

— Leicester Engineering Department Building: Leicester University 1959-1963, Sirling & Gowan. (Architecture in Detail Ser.). (Illus.). 60p. (Orig.). (C). 1994. pap. 29.95 (*0-7148-3154-9*, Pub. by Phaidon Press UK) Chronicle Bks.

McKean, Kay, jt. ed. see McKean, Randy.

McKean, Kay, jt. auth. see Orr, Nancy.

***McKean, Keith.** Understanding Social Science. 304p. (C). 1995. per., pap. text ed. 36.00 (*0-7872-0250-9*) Kendall-Hunt.

McKean, Keith F. The Moral Measure of Literature. LC 73-2339. 137p. 1973. reprint ed. text ed. 49.75 (*0-8371-6842-2*, MCMM, Greenwood Pr) Greenwood.

An Asterisk (*) at the beginning of an entry indicates that the title is appearing in BIP for the first time.

*McKean, Kip. First Principles. 40p. 1993. pap. 3.99 (*1-884553-25-7*) Discipleshp.

*McKean, Lise. Divine Enterprise: Gurus & the Hindu Nationalist Movement. (Illus.). 376p. 1996. 60.00x (*0-226-56009-0*); pap. 21.95x (*0-226-56010-4*) U Ch Pr.

McKean, M. Faith. Interplay of Realistic & Flamboyant Art Elements in the French Mysteres. LC 74-94196. (Catholic University of America. Studies in Romance Languages & Literatures: No. 60). reprint ed. 23.00 (*0-404-50360-8*) AMS Pr.

McKean, Margaret K. The Stop Smoking Book. LC 76-26302. 128p. 1987. reprint ed. pap. 6.95 (*0-915166-59-3*) Impact Pubs CA.

McKean, Randy, ed. Faire Des Disciples. 54p. (FRE.). 1991. 4.99 (*1-884553-03-6*) Discipleshp.

— Heart Convictions on Personal Finances. 22p. 1991. pap. 3.99 (*1-884553-26-5*) Discipleshp.

— Making Disciples. 51p. 1992. 4.99 (*1-884553-04-4*) Discipleshp.

*McKean, Randy & McKean, Kay, eds. The Mission. 1994. pap. 5.99 (*1-884553-29-X*) Discipleshp.

McKean, Robert B. St. Petersburg Between the Revolutions: Workers & Revolutionaries, June 1907-February 1917. 600p. (C). 1990. text ed. 50.00 (*0-300-04791-6*) Yale U Pr.

McKean, Robert B., ed. New Perspectives on Modern Russian History: Selected Papers from the Fourth World Congress of Soviet & East European Studies, Harrogate, 1990. 300p. 1992. text ed. 55.00 (*0-312-07594-4*) St Martin.

McKean, Robert N., ed. Issues in Defense Economics. (Universities National Bureau Conference Ser.: No. 20). 298p. 1967. 77.50 (*0-87014-490-1*) Natl Bur Econ Res.

McKean, Roland N., ed. Issues in Defense Economics. LC 67-19156. (Universities-National Burear Conference Ser.: No. 20). 298p. reprint ed. pap. 85.00 (*0-8357-3243-6*, 2057137) Bks Demand.

McKean, S., jt. ed. see Robinson, Dan.

McKean, Thomas. The Haunted Circus. LC 92-32713. 176p. (J). (gr. 4-7). 1993. pap. 13.00 (*0-671-72998-5*, S&S Bks Young Read) S&S Childrens.

— Hooray for Grandma Jo! LC 93-16376. (Illus.). (J). (ps-6). 1994. 14.00 (*0-517-57842-5*); lib. bdg. 14.99 (*0-517-57843-3*) Crown Bks Yng Read.

— The Search for Sara Sanderson. 160p. (J). (gr. 3-7). 1987. pap. 2.50 (*0-380-75295-6*, Camelot) Avon.

— Secret of the Seven Willows. LC 91-4447. 160p. (J). (gr. 4-7). 1993. pap. 2.95 (*0-671-86690-7*, Half Moon Paper) S&S Childrens.

— Secret of the Seven Willows. LC 91-4447. 160p. (J). 1991. pap. 12.95 (*0-671-72997-7*) S&S Trade.

— Vampire Vacation. LC 85-48073. 1986. pap. 2.50 (*0-380-89808-X*, Camelot) Avon.

***McKean, Thomas A. Soon Will Come the Light: A View from Inside the Autism Puzzle. Gilpin, R. Wayne, ed. (Illus.). 172p. (C). 1994. pap. 19.95 (*1-885477-11-2*) Fut Educ.**
Sure to be compared with his friend Donna William's best seller, NOBODY, NOWHERE, Mr. McKean's offering takes you inside the mind of a person with autism. He describes the sensory stimulations & challenges in a sensitive manner rarely seen in the autistic community. Mr. McKean even offers poems that offer the reader a unique perspective. Thomas takes you through his early childhood, the pain of misdiagnosis, being institutionalized for three & one-half years, the difficulty of relationships, & the fears & apprehensions of a person with autism. He also discusses different treatment options. This book is excellent for a family with a autistic member, anyone working with that community or students studying autism. To order: Future Education, Inc., 422 E. Lamar Suite 106, Arlington, TX 76011 or 1-800-489-0727. ***Publisher Provided Annotation.***

McKean, Warwick A. Equality & Discrimination under International Law. 1985. pap. 21.00 (*0-19-825519-5*) OUP.

McKeaney, Grace. Last Looks. 1984. pap. 4.75 (*0-8222-0636-6*) Dramatists Play.

McKeany, Maurine. The Absent Father & Public Policy in the Program of Aid to Dependent Children. LC 60-64080. (University of California Publications in Social Welfare: Vol. 1). 140p. reprint ed. pap. 39.90 (*0-8357-5020-5*, 2021396) Bks Demand.

McKearin, George S., jt. auth. see McKearin, Helen.

McKearin, Helen & McKearin, George S. American Glass. (Illus.). 1979. 22.50 (*0-517-00111-X*) Random Hse Value.

McKeating, Colm. Eschatology in the Anglican Sermons of John Henry Newman. LC 92-44666. 376p. 1993. text ed. 99.95 (*0-7734-9231-3*) E Mellen.

McKeating, H., tr. see Simon, Marcel.

McKechnie & Kern, eds. Hellenica Oxyrhynchia. (Classical Texts Ser.). 1988. 49.95 (*0-85668-357-4*, Pub. by Aris & Phillips UK); pap. 19.95 (*0-85668-358-2*, Pub. by Aris & Phillips UK) David Brown.

*McKechnie, Christine. Paper Collage: Painted Pictures. 80p. 1995. pap. 19.95 (*0-85532-784-7*, Pub. by Search Pr UK) A Schwartz & Co.

McKechnie, George E., jt. ed. see Craik, Kenneth H.

McKechnie, Paul. Outsiders in the Greek Cities of the Fourth Century. 320p. 1989. 45.00 (*0-415-00340-7*) Routledge.

McKechnie, Samuel. Popular Entertainments Through the Ages. LC 78-79998. (Illus.). 1972. reprint ed. 23.95 (*0-405-08768-3*) Ayer.

McKechnie, Sue. British Silhouette Artists & Their Work: 1760-1860. (Illus.). 798p. 1978. 85.00 (*0-85667-036-7*) Sothebys Pubns.

McKee. Cascadia. (Illus.). 394p. (C). reprint ed. 45.00 (*1-878907-51-4*) TechBooks.

*McKee, et al. Federal Taxation of Partners. 1992. 300.00 (*0-7913-0507-4*) Warren Gorham & Lamont.

McKee. Federal Taxation of Partnerships & Partners, Student Edition, No. 2918: 1991 Cumulative Supplement. 1991. per. 48.00 (*0-7913-0993-2*); Supplemented annually; write for info. write for info. (*0-318-67195-6*) Warren Gorham & Lamont.

McKee, jt. auth. see Tijunelis.

McKee, Alexander. Against the Odds: Battles at Sea, 1591-1949. (Illus.). 288p. 1991. 25.95 (*1-55750-025-8*) Naval Inst Pr.

— The Golden Wreck: The Tragedy of the 'Royal Charter' 224p. 1987. 29.95 (*0-285-62745-7*, Pub. by Souvnir Pr UK) Intl Spec Bk.

— The Queen's Corsair: Drake's Journey of Circumnavigation 1577-1580. 320p. (C). 1978. 16.95 (*0-285-62339-7*, Pub. by Souvnir Pr UK) Intl Spec Bk.

— The Race for the Rhine. (World at War Ser.: No. 12). 1979. pap. 2.50 (*0-89083-460-1*) Zebra.

— Strike from the Sky: The Story of the Battle of Britain. LC 72-169429. (Literature & History of Aviation Ser.). 1972. reprint ed. 29.95 (*0-405-03772-4*) Ayer.

McKee Anderson Group Staff, illus. Retirement. 78p. (Orig.). 1989. pap. 7.95 (*0-931089-82-4*) Great Quotations.

McKee-Anderson Group Staff, illus. Things You'll Learn If You Live Long Enough So You Might As Well Know Now. 78p. (Orig.). 1989. pap. 7.95 (*0-931089-81-6*) Great Quotations.

McKee, Barbara W. Stained Glass Alphabet Pattern Book, No. 2. (Illus.). 64p. 1988. pap. text ed. 10.95 (*0-935133-18-6*) CKE Pubns.

McKee, Bill. Social Security & SSI. 65p. pap. 6.25 (*0-685-23169-0*, 41,575S) NCLS Inc.

— The What-You-Need-to-Know-About Money Manual. (Illus.). 192p. (Orig.). 1989. pap. 7.95 (*0-89815-338-7*) Ten Speed Pr.

McKee, Brian R., jt. ed. see Sheets, Payson D.

McKee, Charles. Ceramics Handbook: A Guide to Glaze Calculation, Materials & Processes. (Illus.). 176p. (C). 1984. pap. text ed. 24.95 (*0-89863-072-X*) Star Pub CA.

McKee, Christian H. The Clan Mackay Society. 54p. 1989. pap. 5.00 (*0-9611046-1-9*) C H McKee.

— Scottish Legends, Folklore & Superstitiion. LC 83-80904. (Illus.). 56p. (Orig.). 1983. pap. 4.75 (*0-9611046-0-0*) C H McKee.

McKee, Christopher. Edward Preble. LC 79-6044. (Navies & Men Ser.). (Illus.). 1980. reprint ed. lib. bdg. 40.95 (*0-405-13080-5*) Ayer.

— A Gentlemanly & Honorable Profession: The Creation of the U. S. Naval Officer Corps, 1794-1815. LC 90-6232. (Illus.). 608p. 1991. 49.95 (*0-87021-283-4*) Naval Inst Pr.

McKee, Chuck & McKee, David. The Mystery of the Blue Arrows. (Illus.). 32p. (J). (ps-1). 1991. 15.95 (*0-86264-267-1*, Pub. by Andersen Pr UK) Trafalgar.

Mckee, Cynthia R. Dinero para la Universidad: Una Guia para Padres: Companero para Cash for College. 1994. pap. 9.00 (*0-688-13611-7*) Hearst Bks.

McKee, Cynthia R. & McKee, Phillip C., Jr. Cash for College. LC 92-42410. 1993. 16.95 (*0-688-12179-9*) Hearst Bks.

McKee, Daphne C., jt. ed. see Blumenthal, James A.

McKee, David. Elmer. (SPA.). (J). 13.95 (*84-372-6614-9*) Santillana.

— Elmer. LC 89-2285. (Illus.). 32p. (J). (ps-2). 1989. reprint ed. 14.00 (*0-688-09171-7*); reprint ed. lib. bdg. 13.93 (*0-688-09172-5*) Lothrop.

— Elmer Again. LC 91-38901. (Illus.). 32p. (J). (ps up). 1992. 14.00 (*0-688-11596-9*) Lothrop.

— Elmer on Stilts. (Illus.). 32p. (J). (ps-1). 1995. bds. 12.95 (*0-86264-427-5*, Pub. by Andersen Pr UK) Trafalgar.

— Elmer's Colors. LC 94-75212. (J). 1994. 4.95 (*0-688-13762-8*) Lothrop.

— Elmer's Day. LC 94-75215. (J). 1994. 4.95 (*0-688-13759-8*) Lothrop.

— Elmer's Friends. LC 94-75213. (J). 1994. 4.95 (*0-688-13761-X*) Lothrop.

— Elmer's Weather. LC 94-75214. (J). 1994. 4.95 (*0-688-13760-1*) Lothrop.

— The Sad Story of Veronica Who Played the Violin. (Illus.). 32p. (J). (gr. k-4). 1991. 10.95 (*0-916291-37-5*) Kane-Miller Bk.

— The School Bus Comes at Eight O'Clock. LC 93-79583. (Illus.). 32p. (J). (ps-3). 1994. 14.95 (*1-56282-662-X*); lib. bdg. 14.89 (*1-56282-663-8*) Hyprn Child.

— Tusk Tusk. (Illus.). 32p. (J). (ps-3). 1990. reprint ed. pap. 6.95 (*0-916291-28-6*) Kane-Miller Bk.

— Two Can Toucan. (Illus.). 32p. (J). (gr. k-3). 1987. 15.95 (*0-86264-094-6*, Pub. by Andersen Pr UK) Trafalgar.

— Who's a Clever Baby? Briley, D., ed. LC 88-22966. (Illus.). 32p. (J). (gr. 1-3). 1989. lib. bdg. 12.88 (*0-688-08596-2*) Lothrop.

— Zebra's Hiccups. LC 92-14453. (J). 1993. pap. 14.00 (*0-671-79440-X*, S&S Bks Young Read) S&S Childrens.

McKee, David, jt. auth. see McKee, Chuck.

McKee, David J. Tropospheric Ozone: Human Health & Agricultural Impacts. 368p. 1993. 79.95 (*0-87371-475-X*, RA577) Lewis Pubs.

McKee, David L. External Linkages & Growth in Small Economies. LC 93-25059. 176p. 1993. text ed. 49.95 (*0-275-94655-X*, C4655, Praeger Pubs) Greenwood.

— Growth, Development, & the Service Economy in the Third World. LC 88-14107. (Illus.). 152p. 1988. text ed. 49.95 (*0-275-92897-7*, C2897, Praeger Pubs) Greenwood.

— Schumpeter & the Political Economy of Change. LC 90-44404. 164p. 1991. text ed. 45.00 (*0-275-93679-1*, C3679, Praeger Pubs) Greenwood.

— Urban Environments in Emerging Economies. LC 94-7430. 192p. 1994. text ed. 49.95 (*0-275-94938-9*, Praeger Pubs) Greenwood.

McKee, David L., ed. Canadian-American Economic Relations: Conflict & Cooperation on a Continental Scale. LC 88-6610. 245p. 1988. text ed. 55.00 (*0-275-92836-5*, C2836, Praeger Pubs) Greenwood.

— Energy, the Environment, & Public Policy: Issues for the 1990s. LC 90-20000. 232p. 1991. text ed. 55.00 (*0-275-93719-4*, C3719, Praeger Pubs) Greenwood.

— Hostile Takeovers: Issues in Public & Corporate Policy. LC 89-30900. 200p. 1989. text ed. 55.00 (*0-275-93181-1*, C3181, Praeger Pubs) Greenwood.

McKee, David L. & Bennett, Richard E., eds. Structural Change in an Urban Industrial Region: The Northeastern Ohio Case. LC 86-30652. 268p. 1987. text ed. 55.00 (*0-275-92353-3*, C2353, Praeger Pubs) Greenwood.

McKee, David L. & Garner, Don E. Accounting Services, the International Economy, & Third World Development. LC 92-16548. 176p. 1992. text ed. 47.95 (*0-275-94115-9*, C4115, Praeger Pubs) Greenwood.

McKee, David L. & Tisdell, Clement A. Developmental Issues in Small Island Economies. LC 90-31967. 208p. 1990. text ed. 55.00 (*0-275-93393-8*, C3393, Praeger Pubs) Greenwood.

McKee, Delber L. Chinese Exclusion vs. the Open Door Policy, 1900-1906: Clashes Over China Policy in the Roosevelt Era. LC 76-47024. (Illus.). 293p. reprint ed. pap. 83.60 (*0-318-39774-9*, 2033176) Bks Demand.

McKee, Edwin D. Sedimentary Structures in Dunes of the Namib Desert, South West Africa. LC 81-20155. (Geological Society of America, Special Paper Ser.: No. 188). (Illus.). 68p. reprint ed. pap. 25.00 (*0-8357-6842-2*, 2035530) Bks Demand.

McKee, Elaine, jt. auth. see Townsend, Charles E.

McKee, Eliane & Gruzs, Melissa. A Votre Portee. Duggan, Vincent et al, eds. (Illus.). 208p. (Orig.). (FRE.). (C). 1988. pap. text ed. 23.50 (*0-03-006643-3*) HB Coll Pubs.

*McKee, Elsie A. Diakonia in the Classical Reformed Tradition & Today. fac. ed. LC 89-39372. 151p. (Orig.). 1989. reprint ed. pap. 43.10 (*0-7837-7963-1*, 2047719) Bks Demand.

McKee, George D., jt. ed. see Stein, Susan A.

McKee, Gerald, ed. see Coleman, Ellen.

McKee, Glenn. The Man from Maple Grove. Zarucchi, Roy & Page, Carolyn, eds. (Chapbook Ser.). (Illus.). 24p. (Orig.). 1990. pap. 5.00 (*0-9623862-4-3*) Nightshade Pr.

— Picking Time. (Illus.). 26p. 1994. 5.00 (*0-9636689-1-9*) White Wave ME.

McKee, Glenn, ed. see Wixson, Jennifer.

McKee, Gwen. The Little Gumbo Book: Twenty-Seven Carefully Created Recipes That Will Enable Everyone to Enjoy the Special Experience of Gumbo. (Illus.). 64p. (Orig.). 1986. 8.95 (*0-937552-17-8*) Quail Ridge.

— The Little New Orleans Cookbook: Fifty-Seven Classic Creole Recipes That Will Enable Everyone to Enjoy the Special Cuisine of New Orleans. (Illus.). 80p. (Orig.). 1991. 8.95 (*0-937552-42-9*) Quail Ridge.

McKee, Gwen & Moseley, Barbara, eds. Best of the Best from Alabama: Selected Recipes from Alabama's Favorite Cookbooks. LC 89-60781. (Illus.). 288p. (Orig.). 1989. pap. 14.95 (*0-937552-28-3*) Quail Ridge.

— Best of the Best from Arkansas: Selected Recipes from Arkansas' Favorite Cookbooks. LC 92-12155. (Best of the Best State Cookbook Ser.). (Illus.). 288p. (Orig.). 1992. pap. 14.95 (*0-937552-43-7*) Quail Ridge.

— Best of the Best from Florida: Selected Recipes from Florida's Favorite Cookbooks. (Illus.). 288p. (Orig.). 1986. pap. 14.95 (*0-937552-16-X*) Quail Ridge.

— Best of the Best from Georgia: Selected Recipes from Georgia's Favorite Cookbooks. LC 89-10205. (Illus.). 336p. (Orig.). 1989. pap. 14.95 (*0-937552-30-5*) Quail Ridge.

— Best of the Best from Illinois: Selected Recipes from Illinois' Favorite Cookbooks. (Best of the Best Ser.). (Illus.). 288p. (Orig.). 1995. pap. 14.95 (*0-937552-58-5*) Quail Ridge.

— Best of the Best from Indiana: Selected Recipes from Indiana's Favorite Cookbooks. (Best of the Best Ser.). (Illus.). 288p. (Orig.). 1995. pap. 14.95 (*0-937552-57-7*) Quail Ridge.

— The Best of the Best from Kentucky: Selected Recipes from Kentucky's Favorite Cookbooks. LC 88-90826. (Illus.). 288p. (Orig.). 1988. pap. 14.95 (*0-937552-27-5*) Quail Ridge.

— Best of the Best from Louisiana: Selected Recipes from Louisiana's Favorite Cookbooks. (Best of the Best Ser.). (Illus.). 288p. (Orig.). 1984. pap. 14.95 (*0-937552-13-5*) Quail Ridge.

— Best of the Best from Missouri: Selected Recipes from Missouri's Favorite Cookbooks. LC 92-25259. (Best of the Best State Cookbook Ser.). (Illus.). 288p. (Orig.). 1992. pap. 14.95 (*0-937552-44-5*) Quail Ridge.

— Best of the Best from New England: Selected Recipes from the Favorite Cookbooks of Rhode Island, Massachusetts, Connecticut, Vermont, New Hampshire & Maine. LC 94-5778. (Illus.). 368p. (Orig.). 1994. pap. 16.95 (*0-937552-50-X*) Quail Ridge.

— Best of the Best from North Carolina: Selected Recipes from North Carolina's Favorite Cookbooks. LC 90-45535. (Illus.). 536p. (Orig.). 1990. pap. 14.95 (*0-937552-38-0*) Quail Ridge.

— Best of the Best from Pennsylvania: Selected Recipes from Pennsylvania's Favorite Cookbooks. (Best of the Best State Cookbook Ser.). (Illus.). 320p. 1993. ring bd. 14.95 (*0-937552-47-X*) Quail Ridge.

— Best of the Best from South Carolina: Selected Recipes from South Carolina's Favorite Cookbooks. LC 90-42214. (Illus.). 288p. (Orig.). 1990. pap. 14.95 (*0-937552-39-9*) Quail Ridge.

— Best of the Best from Texas: Selected Recipes from Texas' Favorite Cookbooks. (Illus.). 352p. (Orig.). 1985. pap. 14.95 (*0-937552-14-3*) Quail Ridge.

— Best of the Best from Texas: Selected Recipes from Texas' Favorite Cookbooks. (Best of the Best Ser.). (Illus.). 352p. (Orig.). 1989. 16.95 (*0-937552-34-8*) Quail Ridge.

— Best of the Best from Virginia: Selected Recipes from Virginia's Favorite Cookbooks. LC 91-23169. (Best of the Best State Cookbook Ser.). (Illus.). 320p. 1991. pap. 14.95 (*0-937552-41-0*) Quail Ridge.

McKee, Gwen, ed. see Fellowship Church, Baton Rouge, La, Members.

McKee, Henry S. Journeys in Understanding. LC 68-58802. (Essay Index Reprint Ser.). 1977. 18.95 (*0-8369-0122-3*) Ayer.

*McKee, Jack. How to Build a Take Apart Playhouse. expanded rev. ed. 36p. 1993. 11.95 (*1-884894-00-3*) Hands on Bks.

McKee, James, jt. auth. see Tidwell, Gary.

McKee, James B. Sociology & The Race Problem: The Failure of a Perspective. LC 92-42293. 400p. 1993. 39.95 (*0-252-02022-7*); pap. 16.95 (*0-252-06328-7*) U of Ill Pr.

*McKee, James H. Civil War Record of the 144th Regiment NY Volunteer Infantry: Back "in War Times" (Illus.). 378p. 1994. pap. 28.00 (*0-7884-0007-X*) Heritage Bk.

McKee, James L. Lincoln: The Prairie Capital. LC 84-20796. (Illus.). 123p. 1989. reprint ed. pap. 16.95 (*0-934904-07-3*) J & L Lee.

— Lincoln, the Prairie Capital: An Illustrated History. rev. ed. 124p. 1988. pap. write for info. (*0-89781-311-1*) Preferred Mktg.

McKee, James L. & Zimmer, Edward. Havelock, Nebraska. (Illus.). 96p. (Orig.). 1993. pap. 12.95 (*0-934904-33-2*) J & L Lee.

McKee, James R. Kit Carson: Man of Fact & Fiction. 1981. 27.95 (*0-405-14097-5*) Ayer.

McKee, Jesse O. The Choctaw. (Indians of North America Ser.). (Illus.). 104p. (J). (gr. 5 up). 1989. 17.95 (*1-55546-699-0*) Chelsea Hse.

— Choctaw. 1994. pap. 7.95 (*0-7910-0375-2*) Chelsea Hse.

McKee, Jesse O., jt. auth. see Hepner, George F.

McKee, Jesse O., jt. ed. see Prenshaw, Peggy W.

McKee, John. A Martyr Bishop: The Life of St. Oliver Plunkett. 181p. 1975. 8.95 (*0-912414-21-9*) Lumen Christi.

Mckee, John. Photographs Nineteen Seventy-Three to Nineteen Eighty-Three. (Illus.). 1984. pap. 7.50 (*0-916606-06-6*) Bowdoin Coll.

McKee, John. William Allen White: Maverick on Main Street. LC 74-5991. (Contributions in American Studies: No. 17). (Illus.). 264p. 1975. text ed. 55.00 (*0-8371-7533-X*, MAW/, Greenwood Pr) Greenwood.

McKee, Judy. Sales Survival Guide. Caton, Sandra, ed. (Sales Ser.). 135p. (Orig.). 1989. pap. 12.95 (*0-685-44400-7*) Motivations Pub.

— Scriptwriting for Effective Telemarketing. Telemarketing Magazine Editorial Staff, ed. 100p. (Orig.). Date not set. pap. write for info. (*0-936840-12-9*) Tech Marketing.

McKee, Judy S., ed. The Developing Kindergarten: Programs, Children, & Teachers. 439p. (C). 1990. pap. text ed. 24.95 (*0-9629154-0-8*) Mich AEYC.

— Play: Working Partner of Growth. LC 86-22245. 88p. 1986. pap. 11.00 (*0-87173-112-6*) ACEI.

McKee, Karen A., illus. How to Draw Airplanes. 32p. (Orig.). (J). 1990. pap. 2.95 (*0-942025-73-3*) Kidsbks.

— How to Draw Airplanes. (How to Draw Ser.). 32p. (Orig.). (J). 1991. 3.98 (*1-56156-021-9*) Kidsbks.

— How to Draw Cars. (How to Draw Ser.). 32p. (J). 1991. pap. 2.95 (*1-56156-026-X*) Kidsbks.

— How to Draw Cars. (How to Draw Ser.). 32p. (J). 1991. 3.98 (*1-56156-017-0*) Kidsbks.

— How to Draw Trucks. (How to Draw Ser.). 48p. (J). 1992. pap. 2.95 (*1-56156-145-2*) Kidsbks.

McKee, Kathryn. Bible Puzzles for the Whole Year: Puzzles Based on the International Sunday School Lessons. Hayes, Theresa, ed. (Illus.). 96p. (Orig.). 1994. student ed 9.99 (*0-7847-0118-0*) Standard Pub.

McKee, Kathryn, ed. see Schrier, Martha S.

McKee, LaVonne. Get Ready to Say Goodbye: A Mother's Story of Senseless Violence, Tragedy, & Triumph. 1993. 22.95 (*0-88282-079-6*) New Horizon NJ.

McKee, Lewis W. & Bond, Lydia K. A History of Anderson County (Kentucky) 1780-1936. 288p. 1993. reprint ed. pap. 25.00 (*0-685-69952-8*, 3580) Clearfield Co.

McKee, Louis. The True Speed of Things. Zarucchi, Roy & Page, Carolyn, eds. (Chapbook Ser.). (Illus.). 24p. 1991. reprint ed. pap. 5.00 (*1-879205-06-8*) Nightshade Pr.

McKee, Lyn, et al. An Easy Guide to Loving Carefully for Men & Women. rev. ed. (Illus.). 65p. (Orig.). 1987. pap. text ed. 5.95 (*0-941816-40-0*) ETR Assocs.

McKee, Lynn A. Keeper of Dreams. 352p. (Orig.). 1993. mass mkt. 5.50 (*1-55773-921-8*) Diamond.

— Touches the Stars. 352p. (Orig.). 1992. mass mkt. 5.50 (*1-55773-752-5*) Diamond.

— Walks in Stardust. 352p. (Orig.). 1994. pap. 5.50 (*0-7865-0021-2*) Diamond.

— Woman of the Mists. 1991. pap. 5.50 (*1-55773-520-4*) Diamond.

*__McKee, Mac.__ Wolfer. LC 94-47095. (Novel of the West Ser.). 1995. 19.95 (0-87131-778-8) M Evans.

McKee, Margaret & Chisenhall, Fred. Beale Black & Blue: Life & Music on Black America's Main Street. LC 81-4995. (Illus.). 265p. 1993. pap. 11.95 (0-8071-1886-9) La State U Pr.

McKee, Mark & Boppart, Pat. Cap'n Happy's Shot Guide: Recipes for "Shots" Slammed Around the World. (Illus.). 128p. (Orig.). 1994. pap. 9.95 (1-882907-02-7) Old Market.

McKee, Martha. Circles. 72p. 1976. pap. 4.95 (0-913428-26-4) Landfall Pr.

— Single Circles. 132p. 1982. 8.95 (0-913428-42-6); pap. 5.95 (0-913428-43-4) Landfall Pr.

McKee, Mary M. Thirty-Two Elephant Reminders: A Book of Healthy Rules. (Illus.). 72p. (Orig.). 1987. pap. 3.95 (0-932194-59-1) Health Comm.

McKee, Michael, jt. auth. see Robertson, Ian.

McKee, P. H., jt. auth. see Fletcher, C. D.

McKee, Pam, et al. Afternoon Teas: Recipes, History, Menus. (Between Friends Cookbook Ser.). (Illus.). 64p. (Orig.). 1995. pap. 7.95 (1-56523-040-X) Fox Chapel Pub.

McKee, Patricia. Heroic Commitment in Richardson, Eliot, & James. LC 85-17018. 376p. 1986. text ed. 55.00 (0-691-06666-3) Princeton U Pr.

McKee, Patrick & Kauppinen, Heta. The Art of Aging: A Celebration of Old Age in Western Art. (Illus.). 208p. 1986. 29.95 (0-89885-304-4) Human Sci Pr.

McKee, Patrick, jt. auth. see McLerran, Jennifer.

McKee, Patrick L., ed. Philosophical Foundations of Gerontology. LC 81-2922. 352p. 1982. 43.95 (0-89885-040-1); pap. 24.95 (0-89885-041-X) Human Sci Pr.

McKee, Patrick L. & Thiem, Jon, eds. Real Life: Ten Stories of Aging. 192p. 1994. 24.95 (0-87081-354-4); pap. 14.95 (0-87081-355-2) Univ Pr Colo.

McKee, Patrick W. & Barbe, Richard H. The Special Educator Desk Book, 1994. 350p. 1992. pap. 55.00 (0-934753-73-3) LRP Pubns.

McKee, Patrick W., et al. Suicide & the School: A Practical Guide to Suicide Prevention. LC 93-12083. (Crisis Intervention Ser.). (Illus.). 160p. (Orig.). 1993. pap. 24.95 (0-934753-78-4) LRP Pubns.

McKee, Phillip C., Jr., jt. auth. see McKee, Cynthia R.

McKee, Rachel K., jt. auth. see Blake, Robert R.

*__McKee, Robert D.__ One Fortunate Fellow. LC 95-94340. 130p. Date not set. write for info. (0-9647019-0-1) R D McKee.

McKee, Russell, ed. Mackinac, the Gathering Place. LC 81-620009. 176p. 1981. 27.95 (0-941912-02-7) Mich Nat Res.

McKee, Samuel. Labor in Colonial New York, 1664-1776. 193p. 1993. reprint ed. lib. bdg. 69.00 (0-7812-5250-4) Rprt Serv.

McKee, Saundra J. American Government: The U. S. A. & West Virginia, Teacher's Manual. Buckalew, Marshall, ed. (Illus.). 353p. 1990. ring bd. 25.00 (0-914498-12-6) WV Hist Ed Found.

McKee, Sean & Elliott, Charles M. Industrial Numerical Analysis. (Illus.). 274p. 1986. text ed. 32.50 (0-19-853190-7) OUP.

McKee, Sharon, jt. tr. see Carlile, Cynthia.

McKee, Steve. Coach. LC 93-27901. 304p. 1994. 17.95 (0-8117-2537-5) Stackpole.

McKee, Suzanne P., ed. Optics, Physiology & Vision. (Vision Research Ser.: No. VR 263). 400p. 1990. 45.00 (0-08-040692-0, Pub. by PPI UK) Elsevier.

McKee, Thomas E. Modern Analytical Auditing: Practical Guidance for Auditors & Accountants. LC 88-23965. 174p. 1989. text ed. 55.00 (0-89930-354-4, MKA/, Quorum Bks) Greenwood.

McKee, Thomas H. National Conventions & Platforms of All Political Parties, 1789-1900. LC 77-107183. 1971. reprint ed. 15.00 (0-403-00356-3) Scholarly.

— National Conventions & Platforms of All Political Parties, 1789-1905. 6th enl. rev. ed. LC 70-130239. 1970. reprint ed. 16.00 (0-404-04133-7) AMS Pr.

*__McKee, Victoria.__ Working It Out: The Workaholics' Survival Book. 208p. 1995. 22.95 (0-86051-721-7, Robson-Parkwest) Parkwest Pubns.

McKee, William. How to Reach Out to Inactive Catholics: A Practical Parish Program. 40p. 1982. pap. 7.95 (0-89243-155-5) Liguori Pubns.

McKee, William, ed. Lectures for Bankers & Business Executives. LC 76-107724. (Essay Index Reprint Ser.). 1977. 39.95 (0-8369-1580-1) Ayer.

*__McKee, William J.__ Gould Farm: A Life of Sharing. (Illus.). 306p. (Orig.). 1994. pap. 11.00 (0-9642500-2-0) Wm J Gould.

McKee, William L. & Froeschle, Richard C. Where the Jobs Are: Identification & Analysis of Local Employment Opportunities. LC 85-10570. 175p. 1985. pap. text ed. 12.00 (0-88099-029-5) W E Upjohn.

McKee, William S., et al. Federal Taxation of Partnerships & Partners. 1990. Supplemented tri-annually; write for info. 205.00 (0-7913-0509-0) Warren Gorham & Lamont.

*__McKee, Wilma.__ Heritage Celebrations. LC 93-73915. 100p. 1993. pap. 10.95 (0-87303-219-5) Faith & Life.

McKeegan, Michelle. Abortion Politics: Mutiny in the Ranks of the Right. 320p. 1992. text ed. 24.95 (0-02-920533-6) Free Pr.

McKeehan, Julie & Rhodes, Neil. Programming for the Newton: Software Development with NewtonScript. (Illus.). 393p. 1994. disk 29.95 (0-12-484800-1, AP Prof) Acad Pr.

— Programming for the Newton Using Macintosh. 2nd ed. (Illus.). 400p. 1995. disk, pap. write for info. (0-12-484832-X) Acad Pr.

— Programming for the Newton Using Windows. (Illus.). 400p. 1995. pap. write for info. (0-12-484790-0) Acad Pr.

— Wireless for the Newton: Software Development for Mobile Communications. (Illus.). 352p. 1995. pap. text ed. 34.95 (0-12-484801-X, AP Prof) Acad Pr.

*__McKeehan, Louis W.__ Yale Science: The First Hundred Years, 1701-1801. 1947. 59.50 (0-614-00148-X) Elliots Bks.

McKeen, Gregory B., jt. auth. see Bield, Andrew R.

McKeen, W. E., ed. Blue Mold of Tobacco. LC 88-83539. (Illus.). 288p. 1989. 39.00 (0-89054-097-7) Am Phytopathol Soc.

McKeen, William. The Beatles: A Bio-Bibliography. LC 89-2219. (Popular Culture Bio-Bibliographies Ser.). 200p. 1989. text ed. 42.95 (0-313-25993-3, MBE/, Greenwood Pr) Greenwood.

— Bob Dylan: A Bio-Bibliography. LC 92-32212. (Popular Culture Bio-Bibliographies Ser.). 320p. 1993. text ed. 49.95 (0-313-27998-5, MKY, Greenwood Pr) Greenwood.

— Hunter S. Thompson. (Twayne's United States Authors Ser.: No. 574). 144p. (C). 1991. text ed. 20.95 (0-8057-7624-9, Pub. by Royal Botanic Garden UK) Macmillan.

— Tom Wolfe. (Twayne's United States Author Ser.). 1995. lib. bdg. 22.95x (0-8057-4004-X, Twayne) Macmillan.

McKeeside, Vincent, et al. A Rising Sun: Maine Commemorates the Bicentennial of the United States Constitution. 74p. (Orig.). 1988. pap. 5.00 (0-9621238-0-3) Maine Commn.

*__McKeever.__ Butterflies: Science Nature Guides. 1995. 12.95 (1-57145-018-1) Thunder Bay CA.

— Freshwater Life: Science Nature Guides. 1995. 12.95 (1-57145-019-X) Thunder Bay CA.

McKeever, Bill. Answering Mormons' Questions. 128p. 1991. pap. 7.99 (1-55661-201-X) Bethany Hse.

— Questions to Ask Your Mormon Friend: Effective Ways to Challenge a Mormon's Arguments Without. 1994. pap. 7.99 (1-55661-455-1) Bethany Hse.

McKeever, Catherine. A Place for Owls. (True Animal Stories Ser.). (Illus.). 96p. (J). (gr. 3 up). 1992. pap. 7.95 (0-920775-24-1, Pub. by Greey dePencier CN) Firefly Bks Ltd.

*__McKeever, Eric.__ Tales of the Mine Country. (Illus.). 124p. (Orig.). 1995. pap. 9.95 (0-9643905-0-7) E McKeever.

McKeever, Harry P. Hell above Water. 1981. pap. 2.25 (0-8439-0856-4) Dorchester Pub Co.

McKeever, Helen C., jt. auth. see Greenberg, Judith E.

McKeever, J. Ross, ed. see Urban Land Institute, Community Builders' Council Staff.

McKeever, J. Ross, ed. see Wittausch, William K.

McKeever, James. The Aids Plague. 180p. 1986. write for info. (0-86694-104-5) Omega Pubns OR.

— Become Like Jesus. 408p. 1984. write for info. (0-86694-101-0); pap. 6.95 (0-86694-100-2) Omega Pubns OR.

— Claim Your Birthright. 1989. pap. 7.95 (0-86694-112-6) Omega Pubns OR.

— El Plan Victorioso Para Leer la Biblia-Victory Bible Reading Plan. (SPA.). 1984. 1.00 (0-86694-118-5) Omega Pubns OR.

— The Rapture Book. 240p. (Orig.). 1987. pap. 6.95 (0-86694-106-1) Omega Pubns OR.

— Supernatural Power. 396p. 1990. pap. 9.95 (0-86694-120-7) Omega Pubns OR.

— Victory Bible Reading Plan. 1984. 1.25 (0-86694-102-9) Omega Pubns OR.

— Victory in Prayer. 32p. (Orig.). 1985. pap. 1.00 (0-86694-103-7) Omega Pubns OR.

— Where Will You Be in 300 Years? 1990. pap. 2.50 (0-86694-119-3) Omega Pubns OR.

— Why Were You Created? 1980. 1.95 (0-86694-083-9) Omega Pubns OR.

— Your Key to His Kingdom. 1991. pap. 10.95 (0-86694-124-X) Omega Pubns OR.

McKeever, James & McKeever, Jeani. Preparing for Emergencies: Disaster Can Strike Suddenly. (Preparation Ser.). (Illus.). 216p. (Orig.). 1993. pap. 11.99 (0-86694-125-8) Omega Pubns OR.

— Self-Reliant Living. 420p. 1994. 49.00 (0-86694-126-6) Omega Pubns OR.

McKeever, James, ed. see Conus, Leon & Conus, Olga.

McKeever, James M. It's in the Bible. 300p. 1988. 19.95 (0-86694-109-6); pap. 7.95 (0-86694-108-8) Omega Pubns OR.

McKeever, James R. Apartment Development: A Strategy for Successful Decision Making. LC 74-79436. (Urban Land Institute Special Report Ser.). 64p. reprint ed. pap. 25.00 (0-8357-5654-8, 2023493) Bks Demand.

— Business Parks, Office Parks, Plazas & Centers: A Study of Development Practices & Procedures. LC 72-127217. (Urban Land Institute Series Technical Bulletin: No. 65). (Illus.). 128p. reprint ed. pap. 36.50 (0-8357-7500-3, 2011369) Bks Demand.

McKeever, Jane, jt. ed. see Whitely, Sandy.

McKeever, Jeani. Fit as a Fiddle. 2nd ed. 1988. pap. 5.95 (0-86694-110-X) Omega Pubns OR.

McKeever, Jeani, jt. auth. see McKeever, James.

McKeever, Jim. Almighty & the Dollar Workbook. 1980. 23.95 (0-685-07327-0) Omega Pubns OR.

— Christians Will Go Through the Tribulation. LC 78-55091. (Illus.). 1978. 10.95 (0-931608-01-5); pap. 5.95 (0-931608-02-3) Omega Pubns OR.

— The Coming Climax of History. 324p. 1983. 15.95 (0-86694-098-7) Omega Pubns OR.

— Financial Guidance. rev. ed. 400p. 1987. pap. 7.95 (0-931608-10-4) Omega Pubns OR.

— The Future Revealed. Orig. Title: The Coming Climax of History. 1983. 6.95 (0-86694-099-5) Omega Pubns OR.

— How You Can Know the Will of God. 24p. 1982. 1.95 (0-86694-095-2) Omega Pubns OR.

— Knowledge of Good & Evil. 1981. 1.95 (0-86694-084-7) Omega Pubns OR.

— Only One Word. 1979. 1.95 (0-86694-011-1) Omega Pubns OR.

— Revelation for Layman. 1980. 10.95 (0-931608-07-4); pap. 5.95 (0-931608-08-2) Omega Pubns OR.

— You Can Overcome. 1981. 10.95 (0-86694-091-X); pap. 6.95 (0-86694-092-8) Omega Pubns OR.

McKeever, Joe & Knight, George W., eds. Clip-Art Announcement Panels: For Church Bulletins & Newsletters. 1989. pap. 5.99 (0-8010-6246-2) Baker Bk.

McKeever, Joe, et al, illus. Instant Cartoons for Church Newsletters, No. 2. 112p. 1984. pap. 5.99 (0-8010-5457-5) Baker Bk.

McKeever, Michael. A Short History of San Diego. (Short History Ser.). (Illus.). 144p. (Orig.). 1985. pap. 12.95 (0-938530-32-1) Lexikos.

McKeever, Michael & Irvine, Georgeanne. A Day in the Life of a Test Pilot. LC 90-37439. (Day in the Life of... Ser.). (Illus.). 32p. (J). (gr. 4-8). 1991. lib. bdg. 11.79 (0-8167-2224-2); pap. text ed. 2.95 (0-8167-2225-0) Troll Assocs.

McKeever, Michael, jt. auth. see Kaye, Allan.

McKeever, Michael C., jt. auth. see Green, Joel B.

McKeever, Mike. How to Write a Business Plan. 4th rev. ed. 1992. pap. 21.95 (0-87337-184-4) Nolo Pr.

McKeever, Paul E., jt. auth. see Nelson, James S.

McKeever, Robert J. Raw Judicial Power? The Supreme Court & American Society. LC 92-21097. 1993. text ed. 69.95 (0-7190-3424-8, Pub. by Manchester Univ Pr UK) St Martin.

McKeever, S. W. Thermoluminescence of Solids. (Cambridge Solid State Science Ser.). (Illus.). 400p. 1985. 105.00 (0-521-24520-6) Cambridge U Pr.

— Thermoluminescence of Solids. (Cambridge Solid State Science Ser.). (Illus.). 400p. 1988. pap. 44.95 (0-521-36811-1) Cambridge U Pr.

*__McKeever, Sujantra G.__ Learn to Meditate: Journey of Self Discovery. 84p. 1993. pap. 9.95 (1-885479-03-4) McKeever Pubng.

— Paths Are Many, Truth Is One: A Journey into the Essence of Spirituality & Religion. 150p. 1995. pap. text ed. 9.95 (1-885479-01-8) McKeever Pubng.

— Strategy for Success: An Outline for Personal Growth. 104p. 1994. pap. text ed. 10.00 (1-885479-00-X) McKeever Pubng.

*__McKeever, Susan.__ Ancient Rome. LC 94-24677. (DK Pockets Ser.). (Illus.). 160p. (YA). (gr. 7 up). 1995. pap. 5.95 (1-56458-888-2) Dorling Kindersley.

McKeganey, Neil & Barnard, Marina U. AIDS, Drugs & Sexual Risk: Lives in the Balance. 160p. 1992. 85.00 (0-335-09971-8, Open Univ Pr); pap. 32.00 (0-335-09970-X, Open Univ Pr) Taylor & Francis.

Mckeganey, Neil P., jt. ed. see Cunningham-Burley, Sarah.

McKeigue, Emily, ed. see Ford, Norman.

McKeigue, Emily, ed. see Thornhill, Annette.

McKeigue, Emily, ed. see Whitney, Charlotte.

McKeithan, Daniel M. Debt to Shakespeare in Beaumont & Fletcher Plays. LC 73-128189. 240p. (C). 1970. reprint ed. 50.00 (0-87752-070-4) Gordian.

— Debt to Shakespeare in the Beaumont & Fletcher Plays. LC 70-126691. reprint ed. 9.50 (0-404-04134-5) AMS Pr.

— A Mark Twain Notebook for 1892. (Essays & Studies on American Language & Literature: Vol. 17). (Orig.). 1965. pap. 18.00 (0-8115-0197-3) Periodicals Srv.

— The Morgan Manuscript of Mark Twain's "Pudd'nhead Wilson" (Essays & Studies on American Language & Literature: Vol. 12). (Orig.). 1969. pap. 18.00 (0-8115-0192-2) Periodicals Srv.

— Whitman's "Song of Myself" Thirty-Four & Its Background. (Essays & Studies on American Language & Literature: Vol. 18). (Orig.). 1969. pap. 18.00 (0-8115-0198-1) Periodicals Srv.

McKeithen, Daniel M., ed. see Hayne, Paul H.

McKeldin, Caroline. Japanese Jive: Wacky & Wonderful Products from Japan. (Illus.). 80p. (Orig.). 1993. pap. 9.95 (0-8348-0278-3, Tengu Bks) Weatherhill.

McKell, jt. auth. see Goldstein.

McKell, Cyrus M., ed. The Biology & Utilization of Shrubs. 850p. 1988. text ed. 202.00 (0-12-484810-9) Acad Pr.

McKell, Cyrus M., jt. ed. see Zeveloff, Samuel L.

McKell, Douglas C., jt. auth. see Goldstein, Douglas E.

McKell, Mimi, ed. see Barrell, Kay.

McKellar. Enzymes of Psychrotrophs in Raw Food. 1989. 228.00 (0-8493-6103-6, QR121) CRC Pr.

McKellar, A. R., et al, eds. Laser Spectroscopy Five: Proceedings. (Optical Sciences Ser.: Vol. 30). (Illus.). 495p. 1981. 52.00 (0-387-10914-5) Spr-Verlag.

McKellar, Angus D. Turmoil to Triumph: The Odyssey of Captain Harris O. Machus Through Six War Devastated Countries in Search of Survival. LC 86-72281. (Illus.). 257p. 1987. 18.95 (0-939528-00-2) Brookside Pub.

McKellar, H. S. A Practical Guide to French Pronunciation. 157p. reprint ed. pap. 44.80 (0-685-15383-5, 2026531) Bks Demand.

McKellar, J. F. & Allen, N. S. Photochemistry of Man Made Polymers. (Illus.). 306p. 1975. 84.75 (0-85334-799-9, Pub. by Elsevier Applied Sci UK) Elsevier.

McKellar, J. F., jt. ed. see Allen, N. S.

McKellar, Margaret M. Life on a Mexican Ranche. Latorre, Dolores L., ed. LC 93-42774. 1994. write for info. (0-934223-31-9) Lehigh Univ Pr.

McKellar, Peter. Abnormal Psychology: Its Experience & Behavior. 352p. 1989. 49.95 (0-415-02812-4, A3869); pap. 14.95 (0-415-03132-X, A3873) Routledge.

McKellar, Robert F. An Accident of Birth: A Chronicle of My Times, 1926-1990. LC 93-60913. (Illus.). 508p. 1994. pap. 11.95 (1-55523-654-5) Winston-Derek.

McKellar, Shona, sel. Counting Rhymes. LC 93-12383. (Illus.). 32p. (J). (ps-3). 1993. 12.95 (1-56458-309-0) Dorling Kindersley.

McKellips, Ann B., ed. see Youmans, J. Llewellyn.

McKellips, Art. A Practical Pattern Manual for Woodcarving & Other Crafts. LC 81-21254. 120p. (Orig.). 1981. pap. 12.95 (0-917304-67-5) Timber.

McKelvey & Hollingshead. Small Animal Anesthesia. (Fundamentals Ser.: Vol. II). 1994. write for info. (0-8016-7961-3) Mosby Yr Bk.

McKelvey, et al. Hosking's Pension Schemes & Retirement Benefits. (C). 1985. 240.00 (0-685-32803-1, Pub. by Witherby & Co UK) St Mut.

McKelvey, Blake. American Prisons: A History of Good Intentions. 2nd rev. ed. LC 75-14556. (Criminology, Law Enforcement, & Social Problems Ser.: No. 17). (Illus.). (C). 1977. 25.00 (0-87585-704-3) Patterson Smith.

— Rochester: A Brief History. 110p. 1984. lib. bdg. 59.95 (0-88946-026-4) E Mellen.

— Rochester, NY: Panoramic History. Date not set. 24.95 (0-89781-003-1) Preferred Mktg.

— Rochester on the Genesee: The Growth of a City. 2nd ed. LC 93-12303. (New York Classics Ser.). (Illus.). 330p. (C). 1993. pap. text ed. 17.95 (0-8156-2596-0) Syracuse U Pr.

— Snow in the Cities: A History of America's Urban Response. 256p. (C). 1995. text ed. 39.00 (1-878822-54-3) Univ Rochester Pr.

McKelvey, Carole A. & Stevens, JoEllen. Adoption Crisis: The Truth Behind Adoption & Foster Care. (Illus.). 420p. 1994. 22.95 (1-55591-172-2) Fulcrum Pub.

McKelvey, Carole A., jt. auth. see Magid, Ken.

McKelvey, Charles. Beyond Ethnocentrism: A Reconstruction of Marx's Concept of Science. LC 90-45602. (Contributions in Sociology Ser.: No. 94). 232p. 1991. text ed. 59.95 (0-313-27420-7, MBD, Greenwood Pr) Greenwood.

McKelvey, David. Bobby the Mostly Silky. LC 83-73327. (Illus.). 32p. (J). (gr. 1-3). 1984. lib. bdg. 10.95 (0-931722-28-4); pap. 3.95 (0-931722-27-6) Corona Pub.

— Commander the Gander. LC 84-72455. (Illus.). 48p. (J). (gr. 4-6). 1984. lib. bdg. 10.95 (0-931722-31-4); pap. 3.95 (0-931722-30-6) Corona Pub.

— Maverick the Lucky Longhorn. (Illus.). 32p. (J). (gr. k-3). 1986. lib. bdg. 10.95 (0-931722-48-9); pap. 3.95 (0-931722-47-0) Corona Pub.

McKelvey, Dennis, tr. see Guthrie, Kari H.

McKelvey, Doug. Cattail, Fishscale, & Snakeskin. 32p. 1994. pap. 5.00 (0-940895-24-2) Cornerstone IL.

McKelvey, Francis X., jt. auth. see Horonjeff, Robert.

McKelvey, James L. George III & Lord Bute: The Leicester House Years. LC 72-96682. 161p. reprint ed. pap. 45.90 (0-317-20453-X, 2023423) Bks Demand.

McKelvey, Jean T. AFL Attitudes Toward Production, 1900-1932. LC 73-22503. (Cornell Studies in Industrial & Labor Relations: No. Vol. 2-2). 148p. 1974. text ed. 49.75 (0-8371-6375-7, MCAP, Greenwood Pr) Greenwood.

McKelvey, Jean T., ed. The Changing Law of Fair Representation. LC 84-27831. 304p. 1985. 28.00 (0-87546-110-7); pap. 14.95 (0-87546-111-5) ILR Pr.

— Cleared for Takeoff: Airline Labor Relations since Deregulation. 400p. 1988. pap. 18.95 (0-87546-140-9) ILR Pr.

McKelvey, Jean T., ed. see National Academy of Arbitrators Staff.

McKelvey, John J., Jr., jt. ed. see Maramorosch, Karl.

McKelvey, John J., Jr., et al, eds. Vectors of Disease Agents: Interactions with Plants, Animals, & Men. LC 80-18676. 256p. 1980. text ed. 75.00 (0-275-90521-7, C0521, Praeger Pubs) Greenwood.

McKelvey, John P. Solid-State Physics for Engineering & Materials Science. LC 93-4226. 514p. (C). 1993. lib. bdg. 49.50 (0-89464-436-X) Krieger.

McKelvey, R., ed. Environmental & Natural Resources Mathematics. LC 85-3917. (Proceedings of Symposia in Applied Mathematics Ser.: Vol. 32). 143p. 1985. pap. text ed. 40.00 (0-8218-0087-6, PSAPM-32) Am Math.

McKelvey, Robbie. A Frog on a Log. (Illus.). 22p. (Orig.). (J). (gr. k-4). 1993. spiral bd. 3.95 (1-884525-00-8) Whimsical Pubns.

McKelvey, Susan. Color for Quilters, Vol. II. (Illus.). 80p. (Orig.). 1994. 17.95 (0-9639963-0-4) Wallflower Designs.

— Friendship's Offering: Techniques & Inspiration for Writing on Quilts. Hartley, Nadene, ed. LC 90-80501. (Illus.). 96p. 1990. 17.95 (0-914881-30-2) C & T Pub.

— A Treasury of Quilt Labels. LC 92-46212. (Illus.). 80p. (Orig.). 1993. pap. 17.95 (0-914881-60-4) C & T Pub.

McKelvey, Susan D. Botanical Exploration of the Trans-Mississippi West, 1790-1850. LC 91-24466. (Northwest Reprints Ser.). 1200p. 1991. 99.95 (0-87071-513-5) Oreg St U Pr.

McKelvey, William C. Through the Eyes & Mind of a Storyteller. LC 92-81942. (Illus.). 110p. (Orig.). 1992. pap. 10.95 (0-9633719-0-8) Eclipse Pub.

McKelvey, William J., Jr. Lehigh Valley Transit Company's Liberty Bell Route: A Photograhic History with Chronology, Historical Recollections, & Bibliography. LC 88-92760. (Illus.). 98p. 1989. 20.00 (0-9613675-1-2) Canal Captains.

McKelvie, Colin. Country Naturalist's Year. 1994. 34.95 (1-85310-446-9, Pub. by Airlife Pub Ltd UK) Voyageur Pr.

McKelvie, Colin L. The Woodcock. (Illus.). 208p. 1992. 35.95 (1-85310-113-3, Pub. by Airlife Pub Ltd UK) Voyageur Pr.

McKelvy, Charles. Billy & Other Stories. McKelvy, Natalie, ed. LC 90-82283. 417p. (Orig.). 1992. pap. 9.95 (0-944771-06-8) Dunery Pr.

An Asterisk (*) at the beginning of an entry indicates that the title is appearing in BIP for the first time.

— Clarke Street. McKelvy, Natalie, ed. LC 92-97496. 452p. (Orig.). 1993. pap. 5.00 (*0-944771-11-4*) Dunery Pr.
— Clarke Theatre: Act I. McKelvy, Natalie, ed. (James Clarke Novels Ser.). 430p. (Orig.). 1995. pap. 5.00 (*0-944771-15-7*) Dunery Pr.
— Holy Orders. LC 89-50230. 272p. (Orig.). 1989. pap. 8.95 (*0-944771-02-5*) Dunery Pr.
— James the Second. McKelvy, Natalie, ed. 188p. (Orig.). 1991. pap. 9.95 (*0-944771-09-2*) Dunery Pr.
McKelvy, Charles, ed. see McKelvy, Natalie.
McKelvy, David. Instant Harmonica Pak. (Illus.). (Orig.). 1989. pap. 15.95 (*0-88188-848-6*, 08720676) H Leonard.
McKelvy, James. Music for Conducting Class. 2nd ed. LC 88-82200. (Illus.). xi, 143p. 1988. pap. text ed. 18.95 (*0-916656-26-8*, MFBK 10) Mark Foster Mus.
McKelvy, Jeffrey F., jt. ed. see Barker, Jeffery L.
McKelvy, John E., Jr. Broad Reach. 223p. 1991. 27.95 (*0-9635668-0-6*) Pilot Press.
— Cruising Guide to the Nova Scotia Coast. 172p. (C). 1989. pap. 35.00 (*0-9635668-1-4*) Pilot Press.
McKelvy, Natalie. Cream Tortes & Other Works. McKelvy, Charles, ed. LC 90-82208. 394p. (Orig.). 1992. pap. 9.95 (*0-944771-07-6*) Dunery Pr.
— Dead Babies & Other Works. McKelvy, Charles, ed. LC 94-94129. 411p. (Orig.). 1994. pap. 5.00 (*0-944771-14-9*) Dunery Pr.
— Eddie & Mike & Other Works. McKelvy, Charles, ed. 430p. (Orig.). 1995. pap. 5.00 (*0-944771-16-5*) Dunery Pr.
— The Golden Book of Child Abuse & Other Works. McKelvy, Charles, ed. LC 92-97497. 414p. (Orig.). 1993. pap. 5.00 (*0-944771-12-2*) Dunery Pr.
— Mona & the Arabs & Other Works. McKelvy, Charles, ed. 439p. (Orig.). 1991. pap. 9.95 (*0-944771-10-6*) Dunery Pr.
— My California Friends & Other Stories: Fiction. 279p. (Orig.). 1988. pap. 8.95 (*0-944771-01-7*) Dunery Pr.
— Where's Ours? 200p. 1987. pap. 9.00 (*0-89733-277-6*) Academy Chi Pubs.
McKelvy, Natalie, ed. see McKelvy, Charles.
McKelway, Alexander J. The Freedom of God & Human Liberation. LC 90-44867. 112p. (Orig.). (C). 1991. pap. 10.95 (*0-334-02466-8*) TPI PA.
McKelway, Margaret. A World of Things to Do. Crump, Donald J., ed. (Books for World Explorers Series 8: No. 2). (Illus.). 104p. (J). 1987. lib. bdg. 12.50 (*0-87044-615-0*) Natl Geog.
McKelway, Margaret & National Geographic Society Staff. A World of Things to Do. Crump, Donald J., ed. (Books for World Explorers Series 8: No. 2). (Illus.). 104p. (J). 1994. 12.50 (*0-87044-610-X*) Natl Geog.
McKemmish, Jan. Only Lawyers Dancing. 192p. 1993. reprint ed. lib. bdg. 24.95 (*0-939416-70-0*); reprint ed. pap. 9.95 (*0-939416-69-7*) Cleis Pr.
McKend, H. Moving Gives Me a Stomach Ache. (Illus.). 32p. (J). (ps-8). 1988. pap. 4.95 (*0-88753-178-4*, Pub. by Black Moss Pr CN) Firefly Bks Ltd.
McKendall & Stroop, eds. Handbook of Neurovirology. (Neurological Disease & Therapy Ser.: Vol. 27). 832p. 1994. 195.00 (*0-8247-8870-2*) Dekker.
McKendrick, Brian & Hoffmann, Wilma, eds. People & Violence in South Africa. (Contemporary South African Debates Ser.). (Illus.). 504p. 1991. pap. 29.95 (*0-19-570581-5*) OUP.
McKendrick, Brian, jt. auth. see Issacs, Gordon.
McKendrick, Eddie. Sega Genesis Complete Sonic Play Guide. 1994. pap. 14.95 (*1-55958-536-6*) Prima Pub.
McKendrick, Ewan. Force Majeure & Frustration of Contract. 272p. 1991. 115.00 (*1-85044-370-X*) Lloyds London Pr.
— Tort. 270p. (C). 1991. 60.00 (*1-85352-799-8*, Pub. by HLT Pubns UK); 60.00 (*1-85352-378-X*, Pub. by HLT Pubns UK); pap. 60.00 (*1-85352-863-3*, Pub. by HLT Pubns UK) St Mut.
McKendrick, Ewan, ed. Commercial Aspects of Trusts & Fiduciary Obligations. LC 92-15521. 336p. 1992. 79.00 (*0-19-825765-1*, Clarendon Pr) OUP.
McKendrick, Jamie. The Kiosk on the Brink. LC 92-34890. 64p. 1993. pap. 10.95 (*0-19-283118-6*) OUP.
— The Sirocco Room. 64p. 1991. pap. 10.95 (*0-19-282820-7*) OUP.
McKendrick, Joseph. Executive Excellence: Your Success Plan for Managing Tomorrow. (Illus.). 132p. 1984. pap. 13.95 (*0-916323-00-5*) Admin Mgmt.
McKendrick, Melveena. Theatre in Spain, 1490-1700. (Illus.). 312p. (C). 1992. pap. 21.95 (*0-521-42901-3*) Cambridge U Pr.
McKendrick, Neil & Outhwaite, R. B., eds. Business Life & Public Policy: Essays in Honour of D. C. Coleman. 256p. 1986. 74.95 (*0-521-26275-5*) Cambridge U Pr.
***McKendry, Jennifer.** With Our Past Before Us: Nineteenth-Century Architecture in the Kingston Area. (Illus.). 250p. (C). 1995. pap. 29.95 (*0-8020-7474-X*) U of Toronto Pr.
McKendry, Maryann, jt. auth. see Double, Mary E.
McKenize, Janet. Education As a Political Issue. LC 93-3855. 314p. 1993. 59.95 (*1-85628-445-X*, Pub. by Avebury Pub UK) Ashgate Pub Co.
***McKenley, Yvonne.** A Taste of the Caribbean. (Food Around the World Ser.). (Illus.). 48p. (J). (gr. 3-5). 1995. 14.95 (*1-56847-187-4*) Thomson Lrning.
McKenna. Clover. (Illus.). 40p. 1994. pap. 10.95 (*0-8059-3532-0*) Dorrance.
McKenna & Murphy. Cancer Surgery. 1993. text ed. 145.00 (*0-397-51249-X*) Lippincott.
***McKenna & Technology Staff.** Pesticide Regulation Handbook. 3rd ed. 1994. text ed. 75.00 (*0-471-12596-2*); pap. text ed. 49.95 (*0-471-12595-4*) Wiley.
McKenna, jt. auth. see O'Shaughnessy.
McKenna, jt. auth. see Riskin.
McKenna, et al. Pesticide Regulation Handbook. rev. ed. 1991. pap. 75.00 (*1-55840-464-3*) Exec Ent Pubns.
— TSCA Handbook. 2nd ed. 490p. 1989. pap. 89.00 (*0-86587-791-2*) Gov Insts.
McKenna & Cuneo Incorporated Staff. Pesticide Regulation Handbook. 3rd ed. 1992. text ed. 69.50 (*0-07-045357-8*) McGraw.
McKenna, Allen J., jt. auth. see Garwood, Thomas C., Jr.
McKenna, Allen J., ed. see Garwood, et al.
***McKenna, Andrew & Thompson, Joanna.** Family Bushwalks in & Around Melbourne. (Family Bushwalks Ser.). (Illus.). 285p. (Orig.). 1995. pap. 14.95 (*0-85091-467-1*, Pub. by Lothian Pub AT) Seven Hills Bk.
— Family Bushwalks in & Around Sydney. (Family Bushwalks Ser.). (Illus.). 285p. (Orig.). 1995. pap. 14.95 (*0-85091-509-0*, Pub. by Lothian Pub AT) Seven Hills Bk.
McKenna, Andrew J. Violence & Difference: Girard, Derrida, & Deconstruction. 256p. 1992. 39.95 (*0-252-01837-0*); pap. 15.95 (*0-252-06202-7*) U of Ill Pr.
McKenna, Barbara, comp. Surveying Your Alumni: Guidelines & 22 Sample Questionnaires. 184p. 1983. 27.00 (*0-89964-212-8*) Coun Adv & Supp Ed.
McKenna, Breige. Miracles Do Happen Spanish: Los Milagros Si Ocurren. 180p. 1991. reprint ed. pap. 7.99 (*0-89283-739-X*) Servant.
McKenna, Brian, jt. auth. see Maltby, Arthur.
McKenna, Brian M., ed. Advances in Food Science, Vol. 1. 1991. 90.25 (*1-55938-354-2*) Jai Pr.
— Engineering & Food, 2 vols., Vol. 1, Engineering Sciences in the Food Industry. 1984. 156.75 (*0-85334-280-6*, I-320-84, Pub. by Elsevier Applied Sci UK) Elsevier.
— Engineering & Food, 2 vols., Vol. 2, Processing Applications. 1984. 156.75 (*0-85334-281-4*, I-321-84, Pub. by Elsevier Applied Sci UK) Elsevier.
***McKenna, Bridget.** Caught Dead. 240p. (Orig.). 1995. pap. text ed. 4.99 (*0-425-14493-3*, Prime Crime) Berkley Pub.
— Dead Ahead. 208p. (Orig.). 1994. pap. text ed. 4.50 (*0-425-14300-7*, Prime Crime) Berkley Pub.
— Murder Beach. 208p. (Orig.). 1991. pap. 4.50 (*1-55773-967-6*) Diamond.
McKenna, Briege. Miracles Do Happen. (Orig.). 1992. mass mkt. 4.99 (*0-312-92972-2*) St Martin.
McKenna, Briege & Libersat, Henry. Miracles Do Happen. 168p. (Orig.). 1987. pap. 8.99 (*0-89283-316-5*) Servant.
— Miracles Do Happen: The Best-Selling Account of One Woman's Ministry in the Church Today. 142p. 1989. pap. 22.00 (*0-86217-253-5*, Pub. by Veritas IE) St Mut.
McKenna, Bruce. Undercover Justice. 1990. 21.95 (*0-88282-067-2*) New Horizon NJ.
McKenna, C. J. & Rees, Ray. Economics: A Mathematical Introduction. (Illus.). 512p. 1993. 85.00 (*0-19-877292-0*); pap. 29.95 (*0-19-877291-2*) OUP.
McKenna, Catherine A. The Medieval Welsh Religious Lyric: Poems of the Gogynfeirdd, 1137-1282. 241p. 1991. 37.50 (*0-926689-02-9*) Ford & Bailie Pubs.
McKenna, Chris, jt. auth. see McNabb, Robert.
McKenna, Christine, jt. auth. see Blewett, Mary H.
McKenna, Christine A. Love, Infidelity, & Sexual Addiction: A Codependents Perspective. LC 91-76678. pap. 6.95 (*0-87029-241-2*) Abbey.
McKenna, Cilla, ed. Feel It: Detached Youth Work in Action. (C). 1990. 20.00 (*0-947988-32-7*, Pub. by Wild Goose Pubns UK) St Mut.
McKenna, Colleen. Good Grief... Third Grade. (J). (gr. 4-7). 1994. pap. 2.75 (*0-590-45124-3*) Scholastic Inc.
McKenna, Colleen O. The Brightest Light. (YA). 1992. 13.95 (*0-590-45347-5*, Scholastic Hardcover) Scholastic Inc.
— The Brightest Light. (YA). 1994. pap. 3.50 (*0-590-45348-3*) Scholastic Inc.
— Camp Murphy. LC 92-12691. 160p. (J). (gr. 3-7). 1993. 13.95 (*0-590-45807-8*) Scholastic Inc.
— Camp Murphy. (J). (gr. 4-7). 1994. pap. 3.25 (*0-590-45808-6*) Scholastic Inc.
— Cousins: Not Quite Sisters. (J). (gr. 4-7). 1993. pap. 2.95 (*0-590-49428-7*) Scholastic Inc.
— Cousins: Stuck in the Middle. (J). (gr. 4-7). 1993. pap. 2.95 (*0-590-49429-5*) Scholastic Inc.
— Fifth Grade: Here Comes Trouble. 128p. (J). (gr. 3-7). 1991. pap. 3.25 (*0-590-41734-7*, Apple Paperbacks) Scholastic Inc.
— Fourth Grade Is a Jinx. (J). (ps-3). 1990. pap. 2.95 (*0-590-41736-3*, Apple Paperbacks) Scholastic Inc.
— Good Grief, Third Grade. LC 92-33457. (J). 1993. 13.95 (*0-590-45123-5*) Scholastic Inc.
— Merry Christmas Miss McConnell. (J). (ps-3). 1990. 12.95 (*0-590-43554-X*, Scholastic Hardcover) Scholastic Inc.
— Merry Christmas, Miss McConnell. 160p. (J). 1991. pap. 2.95 (*0-590-43555-8*, Apple Paperbacks) Scholastic Inc.
— Mother Murphy. 160p. (J). (gr. 4-7). 1992. 13.95 (*0-590-44820-X*, Scholastic Hardcover) Scholastic Inc.
— Mother Murphy. 160p. (J). (gr. 4-7). 1993. pap. 2.95 (*0-590-44856-0*, Scholastic Hardcover) Scholastic Inc.
— Murphy's Island. (J). (gr. 4-7). 1990. 12.95 (*0-590-43552-3*) Scholastic Inc.
— Murphy's Island. 208p. (J). 1991. pap. 2.95 (*0-590-43553-1*, Apple Paperbacks) Scholastic Inc.
— Roger Friday: Live from the Fifth Grade. LC 93-13706. (YA). (gr. 5 up). 1994. 13.95 (*0-590-46684-4*) Scholastic Inc.
— Too Many Murphys. (J). (gr. 5-7). 1989. pap. 3.50 (*0-590-41732-0*) Scholastic Inc.
— The Truth about Sixth Grade. (J). 1991. pap. 12.95 (*0-590-44388-7*) Scholastic Inc.
— The Truth about Sixth Grade. 192p. (J). (gr. 3-7). 1992. pap. 3.25 (*0-590-44392-5*, Apple Paperbacks) Scholastic Inc.
McKenna, Constance, ed. see Hurst, Jane.
McKenna, D. Douglas. Positive Politics at Work. LC 93-24062. 144p. 1993. pap. 10.00 (*1-55623-879-7*) Irwin Prof Pubng.
McKenna, D. L. Farewell Dublin, But Never Goodbye. 91p. (C). 1989. text ed. 65.00 (*1-85821-011-9*, Pub. by Pentland Pr UK) St Mut.
McKenna, David. Communicator's Commentary, Vol. 2: Mark. 332p. 1991. reprint ed. pap. 10.99 (*0-8499-3275-0*) Word Inc.
— East Germany. (Let's Visit Places & Peoples of the World Ser.). (Illus.). 96p. (J). (gr. 5 up). 1988. 14.95 (*1-55546-197-2*) Chelsea Hse.
McKenna, David L. CC, NT, Vol. 2: Mark. 332p. 1982. write for info. (*0-8499-0155-3*) Word Inc.
— CC, OT, Vol. 12: Job. 331p. 1986. write for info. (*0-8499-0418-8*) Word Inc.
— The Coming Great Awakening: New Hope for the Nineties. LC 90-48722. 140p. (Orig.). 1990. pap. 9.99 (*0-8308-1735-2*, 1735) InterVarsity.
— Power to Follow, Grace to Lead. 199p. 1989. 12.99 (*0-8499-0674-1*) Word Inc.
— When Our Parents Need Us Most: Loving Care for the Aging Years. LC 93-42150. 144p. 1994. pap. 8.99 (*0-87788-902-3*) Shaw Pubs.
McKenna, Dennis, jt. auth. see McKenna, Terence.
McKenna, Edward, ed. The Collegeville Hymnal. 768p. 1990. text ed. 11.95 (*0-8146-1569-4*) Liturgical Pr.
McKenna, Edward J. The Ministry of Musicians. 40p. (Orig.). 1983. pap. 1.95 (*0-8146-1295-4*) Liturgical Pr.
***McKenna, Eugene & Beech, Nic.** The Essence of Human Resource Management. LC 95-10434. (Essence of Management Ser.). 1995. pap. 19.95 (*0-13-076357-8*) P-H.
McKenna, Eugene F. & Glendon, Ian. The Human Side of Safety. (Illus.). 304p. 1993. 99.95 (*0-412-40250-5*) Chapman & Hall.
McKenna, Frank. Schooling in America. 248p. (C). 1993. per. 25.95 (*0-8403-8699-0*) Kendall-Hunt.
McKenna, Gail T. Three Hundred Questions DREs Are Asking about People & Programs. 1990. pap. 8.95 (*0-8091-3185-4*) Paulist Pr.
— Through the Year with the DRE: A Seasonal Guide for Christian Educators. 128p. (Orig.). 1987. pap. 7.95 (*0-8091-2860-8*) Paulist Pr.
McKenna, George. The Drama of Democracy: American Government & Politics. 2nd ed. 744p. 1994. 37.95 (*1-56134-236-X*) Dushkin Pub.
— Reader & Study Guide for That Delicate Balance. 320p. (C). 1984. pap. text ed. write for info. (*0-07-554649-3*) McGraw.
— Rites. 240p. 1981. pap. 2.25 (*0-8439-0979-X*) Dorchester Pub Co.
McKenna, George & Feingold, Stanley, eds. Taking Sides: Clashing Views on Controversial Political Issues. 9th ed. LC 94-34809. (Illus.). 416p. 1995. pap. text ed. 13.95 (*1-56134-322-6*) Dushkin Pub.
McKenna, George, jt. ed. see Finsterbusch, Kurt.
McKenna, George L. Art by Chance: Fortuitous Impressions. LC 89-30073. (Illus.). 96p. 1989. pap. 14.95 (*0-942614-13-5*) Nelson-Atkins.
McKenna, George L., ed. see Sickman, Laurence, et al.
McKenna-Harmon, Kathleen & Harmon, Laurence C. Contemporary Apartment Marketing: New & Innovative Methods That Work! 236p. 1993. pap. 35.95 (*0-685-71690-2*, 919) Inst Real Estate.
— Contemporary Apartment Marketing: Strategies & Applications. LC 92-24419. (Illus.). 236p. (Orig.). 1992. pap. text ed. 34.95 (*0-944298-77-X*, 919) Inst Real Estate.
McKenna-Harmon, Kathleen M., jt. auth. see Harmon, Laurence C.
McKenna, Helen. Young Hickory. (J). (gr. 1-7). 1940. 5.00 (*0-87602-225-5*) Anchorage.
McKenna, Hugh. Secrets of Winning at Video Poker. 32p. (Orig.). 1990. pap. 6.95 (*0-934650-18-7*) Sunnyside.
McKenna, Hugh J. Humanity. 1993. pap. 13.95 (*0-533-10563-3*) Vantage.
McKenna, Hugh P. Nursing Theories & Quality of Care. LC 94-6399. (Developments in Nursing & Health Care Ser.: Vol. 23). 264p. 1994. 59.95 (*1-85628-670-3*, Pub. by Avebury Pub UK) Ashgate Pub Co.
McKenna, James & Teman, Roger, eds. ICIAM '87: Proceedings of the First International Conference on Industrial & Applied Mathematics. LC 88-61320. (Proceedings in Applied Mathematics Ser.: No. 34). xx, 380p. (C). 1988. text ed. 63.00 (*0-89871-224-6*) Soc Indus-Appl Math.
McKenna, James A. Black Range Tales. 1984. pap. 12.00 (*0-87380-142-3*) Rio Grande.
— Permission Not Granted: How People Raised in Crisis-Oriented Families Carry Their Childhood Don'ts into Adulthood. LC 90-82212. (Illus.). 180p. (Orig.). 1990. pap. 10.95 (*1-878953-00-1*) Emily Pubns.
McKenna, James B., ed. see Fernandez De Figueroa, Martin.
McKenna, Jamie, jt. auth. see Helfrich, Banks.
McKenna, John & McKenna, Sally. The Bridgestone One Hundred Best Places to Stay in Ireland. (Bridgestone Guides Ser.). (Illus.). 140p. (Orig.). 1993. pap. 9.95 (*1-874076-06-5*, Pub. by Estragon Pr Ltd IE) Irish Bks Media.
— The Bridgestone One Hundred Best Restaurants in Ireland 1993. 2nd ed. (Bridgestone Guides Ser.). (Illus.). 144p. 1993. pap. 9.95 (*1-874076-05-7*, Pub. by Estragon Pr Ltd IE) Irish Bks Media.
McKenna, John D. & Turner, James H. Fabric Filter Baghouse I: (A Reference Text) 476p. 1993. text ed. 85.00 (*1-882767-01-2*) ETS.
McKenna, John F., jt. auth. see Sikula, Andrew F.
***McKenna, Judith A., ed.** Structural & Other Alternatives for the Federal Courts of Appeals: Report to the U. S. Congress & the Judicial Conference of the U. S. (Illus.). 179p. (Orig.). (C). 1994. pap. text ed. 45.00x (*0-7881-1575-8*) Diane Pub.
McKenna, K. C. Survival: A Novel of the Donner Party. 320p. (Orig.). 1994. pap. text ed. 4.99 (*0-515-11405-7*) Jove Pubns.
McKenna, Katherine M. A Life of Propriety: Anne Murray Powell & Her Family, 1755-1849. 344p. 1994. 34.95 (*0-7735-1175-X*, Pub. by McGill CN) U of Toronto Pr.
McKenna, Lambert. The Social Teachings of James Connolly. 104p. 1989. pap. 22.00 (*1-85390-133-4*, Pub. by Veritas IE) St Mut.
McKenna, Lindsay. Brave Heart. (Historical Ser.). 1993. mass mkt. 3.99 (*0-373-28771-2*, 1-28771-3) Harlequin Bks.
— Commando: Morgan's Mercenaries. (Silhouette Special Edition Ser.). 1993. mass mkt. 3.50 (*0-373-09830-8*, 5-09830-6) Silhouette.
— Countdown. 1994. mass mkt. 3.50 (*0-373-09890-1*, 5-09890-0) Harlequin Bks.
— Dangerous Alliance. 1994. 3.50 (*0-373-09884-7*) Silhouette.
— Hangar 13. (Shadows Ser.). 1994. mass mkt. 3.50 (*0-373-27027-5*, 5-27027-7) Silhouette.
— Heart of the Eagle. (Western Lovers Ser.). 1995. mass mkt. 3.99 (*0-373-88542-3*, 1-88542-5) Harlequin Bks.
— Heart of the Wolf. (Special Edition Ser.). 1993. mass mkt. 3.50 (*0-373-09818-9*, 5-09818-1) Silhouette.
— Morgan's Rescue. 1995. pap. 3.75 (*0-373-23998-X*, 1-23998-7) Silhouette.
— Morgan's Son (Morgan's Mercenaries: Love & Danger) 1995. mass mkt. 3.75 (*0-373-09992-4*, 1-09992-8) Silhouette.
— Morgan's Wife. 1995. mass mkt. 3.75 (*0-373-09986-X*, 1-09986-0) Silhouette.
— No Quarter Given. (Silhouette Special Ser.: No. 667). 1991. mass mkt. 3.25 (*0-373-09667-4*) Silhouette.
— Point of Departure: Women of Glory, That Special Woman. (Silhouette Special Edition Ser.). 1993. mass mkt. 3.50 (*0-373-09853-7*, 5-09853-8) Silhouette.
— The Rogue. (Silhouette Special Edition Ser.). 1993. mass mkt. 3.50 (*0-373-09824-3*, 5-09824-9) Silhouette.
— Shadows & Light. (Silhouette Special Edition Ser.). 1994. mass mkt. 3.50 (*0-373-09878-2*, 5-09878-5) Silhouette.
— Too Near the Fire. (Men Made in America Ser.). 1995. mass mkt. 3.99 (*0-373-45185-7*, 1-45185-5) Harlequin Bks.
McKenna, Lindsay, et al. Lovers Dark & Dangerous. 1994. mass mkt. 4.99 (*0-373-48310-4*, 1-48310-6) Harlequin Bks.
McKenna, Margaret, jt. auth. see Wood, Merle W.
McKenna, Marian C. The Canadian & American Constitutions in Comparative Perspective. LC 93-91361. 250p. (Orig.). 1993. pap. text ed. 18.95 (*1-895176-26-3*, Pub. by Univ Calgary CN) Paul & Co Pubs.
McKenna, Maureen A. Julia Thecla. (Illus.). 62p. 1986. pap. 15.00 (*0-89792-108-9*) Ill St Museum.
***McKenna, Megan.** Angels Unawares. 176p. (Orig.). 1995. pap. 10.95 (*1-57075-030-0*) Orbis Bks.
— Mary: Shadow of Grace. LC 94-46242. 176p. (Orig.). 1995. pap. 10.95 (*0-88344-996-X*) Orbis Bks.
— Meditations for Lent. 176p. (Orig.). 1995. pap. 10.95 (*1-57075-045-9*) Orbis Bks.
— Not Counting Women & Children: Some Forgotten Stories from the Bible. LC 93-36627. 146p. (Orig.). 1994. pap. 10.95 (*0-88344-946-3*) Orbis Bks.
— Parables: The Arrows of God. LC 93-36627. 176p. (Orig.). 1994. pap. 10.95 (*0-88344-975-7*) Orbis Bks.
McKenna, Michael, jt. auth. see Miller, John W.
McKenna, Michael C. & Robinson, Richard D. Teaching Through Text: A Content Literacy Approach to Content Area Reading. LC 92-27870. 366p. (C). 1993. pap. text ed. 47.95 (*0-8013-0584-5*, 79560) Longman.
***McKenna, Mike.** Beyond Abstraction: Knowledge, Universality & the Dialectical Method. 1996. pap. 19.50 (*1-899438-19-X*, Pub. by Porcupine Bks UK) Humanities.
McKenna, Nancy D. A Family in Hong Kong. (Families the World Over Ser.). (Illus.). 32p. (J). (gr. 2-5). 1987. 14.95 (*0-8225-1676-4*, Lerner Publctns) Lerner Group.
Mckenna, Nancy D. A Zulu Family. (Families the World Over Ser.). (Illus.). 32p. (J). (gr. 2-5). 1986. lib. bdg. 13.50 (*0-8225-1666-7*, Lerner Publctns) Lerner Group.
McKenna, P. J. Schizophrenia & Related Syndromes. (Illus.). 352p. 1994. bds. 85.00 (*0-19-261780-X*) OUP.
McKenna, Patricia, jt. ed. see Walsh, Sharon.
McKenna, Paul. A History & Bibliography of a Roycroft Printing Shop. 2nd ed. LC 81-86148. (Illus.). 200p. 1995. 30.00 (*0-939892-00-6*) Tona Graphics.
— The Hypnotic World of Paul McKenna. 224p. (Orig.). 1993. pap. 8.95 (*0-571-16802-7*) Faber & Faber.
***McKenna, Ralph J.** The Undergraduate Researcher's Handbook: Creative Experimentation in Social Psychology. LC 94-32870. 1995. pap. text ed. write for info. (*0-205-15537-5*) Allyn.
McKenna, Regis. The Regis Touch: Million-Dollar Advice from America's Top Marketing Consultant. LC 84-28374. (Illus.). 256p. 1985. 15.34 (*0-201-13981-2*) Addison-Wesley.
— The Regis Touch: Million-Dollar Advice from America's Top Marketing Consultant. LC 84-28374. (Illus.). 256p. 1986. pap. 10.53 (*0-201-13964-2*) Addison-Wesley.
Mckenna, Regis. Relationship Marketing. 288p. 1991. 19.18 (*0-201-56769-5*) Addison-Wesley.
McKenna, Regis. Relationship Marketing: Successful Strategies for the Age of the Customer. 256p. 1993. pap. 13.46 (*0-201-62240-8*) Addison-Wesley.

An Asterisk (*) at the beginning of an entry indicates that the title is appearing in BIP for the first time.

— Who's Afraid of Big Blue? How Companies Are Challenging IBM - & Winning. (Illus.). 192p. 1988. 17. 26 (0-201-15574-5) Addison-Wesley.

McKenna, Richard. The Left-Handed Monkey Wrench: Stories & Essays. Shenk, Robert, ed. LC 86-2342. (Illus.). 335p. 1986. 19.95 (0-87021-345-8) Naval Inst Pr.

— New Eyes for the Old: The Quest for Education. 1963. 2.50 (0-87060-019-2, OCP 7) Syracuse U Cont Ed.

— Sand Pebbles. 1962. write for info. (0-318-66791-6) HarpC.

— The Sand Pebbles. 300p. 1991. reprint ed. lib. bdg. 37.95x (0-89966-857-7) Buccaneer Bks.

— The Sand Pebbles. LC 83-27007. (Classics of Naval Literature Ser.). 597p. 1984. reprint ed. 32.95 (0-87021-592-2) Naval Inst Pr.

McKenna, Richard P., jt. auth. see Ayres, Robert U.

McKenna, Robert G., jt. ed. see Moore, Thomas M.

McKenna, Robert P., jt. auth. see Ayres, Robert U.

McKenna, Rollie. A Life in Photography. LC 90-24632. (Illus.). 279p. 1991. 50.00 (0-394-57394-3) Knopf.

McKenna, Sally, jt. auth. see McKenna, John.

McKenna, Stephen. Tales of Intrigue & Revenge. LC 72-128738. (Short Story Index Reprint Ser.). 1977. 19.95 (0-8369-3629-9) Ayer.

McKenna, Stephen, tr. see Augustine.

McKenna, Steven R. Robert Henryson's Tragic Vision. LC 93-18358. (American University Studies, IV, English Language & Literature: Vol. 171). 221p. (C). 1994. text ed. 39.95 (0-8204-2265-7) P Lang Pubs.

McKenna, Steven R., ed. Selected Essays on Scottish Language & Literature: A Festschrift in Honor of Allan H. MacLaine. LC 92-24194. (Illus.). 284p. 1992. text ed. 89.95 (0-7734-9597-5) E Mellen.

McKenna, Tate. Legacy of Love - Captive Desire, 2 vols. in 1. 368p. 1992. pap. 4.50 (0-8439-3326-7) Dorchester Pub Co.

McKenna, Terence. The Archaic Revival: Speculations on Psychedelic Mushrooms, the Amazon, Virtual Reality, UFOs, Evolution, Shamanism, the Rebirth of the Goddess, & the End of History. LC 91-55290. (Illus.). 288p. 1992. pap. 14.00 (0-06-250613-7) Harper SF.

— Food of the Gods. 1993. pap. 14.95 (0-553-37130-4) Bantam.

— Synthesthesia. limited ed. (Illus.). 40p. 1992. 1,500.00x (1-887123-04-0) Granary Bks.

— True Hallucinations: Being an Account of the Author's Extraordinary Adventures in the Devil's Paradise. LC 91-58904. 256p. 1994. pap. 12.00 (0-06-250652-8) Harper SF.

McKenna, Terence & McKenna, Dennis. The Invisible Landscape: Mind, Hallucinogens, & the I Ching. LC 93-5195. 256p. 1994. pap. 14.00 (0-06-250635-8) Harper SF.

McKenna, Teresa & Ortiz, Flora I., eds. The Broken Web: The Educational Experience of Hispanic American Women. (Mujer Latina Ser.). 262p. 1989. pap. 23.95 (0-942177-00-2) Floricanto Pr.

McKenna, Terrence. Archaic Revival: Collected Essays & Conversations. 1991. pap. 14.95 (0-8065-1240-7, Citadel Pr) Carol Pub Group.

McKenna, Thomas. Praying with Vincent de Paul. Koch, Carl, ed. (Companions for the Journey Ser.). (Illus.). 116p. (Orig.). 1994. pap. 6.95 (0-88489-316-2) St Marys.

McKenna, Thomas, et al, eds. Single Neuron Computation. (Neural Networks: Foundations to Applications Ser.). (Illus.). 644p. 1992. text ed. 59.95 (0-12-484815-X) Acad Pr.

McKenna, Thomas N., jt. ed. see Stenger, David A.

McKenna, Virginia, et al, eds. Beyond the Bars: The Zoo Dilemma. 208p. (C). 1988. reprint ed. lib. bdg. 31.00x (0-8095-7076-9) Borgo Pr.

McKenna, Wendy, jt. auth. see Kessler, Suzanne J.

McKenna, William. Husserl's Introduction to Phenomenology. 1982. lib. bdg. 89.00 (90-247-2665-4) Kluwer Ac.

McKenna, William, et al, eds. A Priori & World: European Contributions to Husserlian Phenomenology. (Martinus Nijhoff Philosophy Texts Ser.: No. 2). 280p. 1981. lib. bdg. 84.00 (90-247-2375-2) Kluwer Ac.

McKenna, William R., jt. ed. see Mohanty, J. N.

McKenney. North American Indian Portfolios. 1993. pap. 10.95 (1-55859-601-1) Abbeville Pr.

McKenney & Hall. Indian Tribes of North America with Biographical Sketches & Anecdotes of the Principal Chiefs, 3 vols., Set. 1974. 275.00 (0-685-38426-8) Scholarly.

McKenney, Charles E. & Long, George F., III. Federal Unfair Competition: Lanham Act s43(a) LC 89-32831. (IP Ser.). 1989. ring bd. 140.00 (0-87632-640-8) Clark Boardman Callaghan.

Mckenney, Gerald P., ed. see Sande, Jonathan R.

McKenney, James B. Standard of Care: California Edition. Chaffee, Paul et al, eds. (Illus.). 165p. 1994. per. 19.50 (1-885104-00-6) Prof Pubng.

***McKenney, James L., et al.** Waves of Change: Business Revolution Through Information Technology. LC 94-3471. 1995. 29.95 (0-87584-564-9) Harvard Busn.

McKenney, Janice E. Air Defense Artillery. LC 84-14538. (Army Lineage Series, Center for Military History Publication: No. 60-5). 438p. 1985. 27.00 (0-16-001937-0, S/N 008-029-00130-6) USGPO.

McKenney, Joe, jt. auth. see Hirshberg, Al.

McKenney, Kenneth. Changeling. 272p. 1985. pap. 3.50 (0-380-89686-9) Avon.

McKenney, Ruth. Industrial Valley. (Literature of American Labor Ser.). 408p. 1992. reprint ed. pap. 16.95 (0-87546-183-2) ILR Pr.

— Industrial Valley. 1993. reprint ed. lib. bdg. 89.00 (0-7812-5389-6) Rprt Serv.

— My Sister Eileen. 1993. reprint ed. lib. bdg. 89.00 (0-7812-5388-8) Rprt Serv.

McKenney, Thomas L. Memoirs, Official & Personal. LC 72-94789. (Bison Book Ser.: BB565). (Illus.). 368p. reprint ed. pap. 104.90 (0-7837-6023-X, 2045835) Bks Demand.

— Sketches of a Tour to the Lakes. (Illus.). 1959. reprint ed. 25.00 (0-87018-042-8) Ross.

McKenney, Tom. The Deadly Deception: Freemasonry Exposed by One of Its Top Leaders. LC 88-81728. 159p. (Orig.). 1988. pap. 8.99 (0-910311-54-4) Huntington Hse.

— Please Tell Me: Questions People Ask about Free Masonry - & the Answers. LC 94-75443. 224p. 1994. 9.99 (1-56384-013-8) Huntington Hse.

McKenney, Tom, jt. auth. see McCormick, Joe.

McKenney, Tom C. Come & Live. LC 84-242781. (Illus.). 167p. 1981. pap. 4.95 (0-934527-00-8) Words Living Minis.

— Come & Live. LC 84-242781. (Illus.). 167p. 1982. 7.95 (0-934527-01-6) Words Living Minis.

— Holidays & Holy Days. (Illus.). 32p. (Orig.). 1987. pap. 2.50 (0-934527-07-5) Words Living Minis.

— Live Free. LC 84-91415. (Illus.). 317p. 1985. 12.95 (0-934527-04-0); pap. 8.95 (0-934527-06-7) Words Living Minis.

— So You're Going to Haiti? LC 88-50163. (Illus.). 56p. (Orig.). 1990. pap. 3.00 (0-934527-08-3) Words Living Minis.

— Trouble at the Glory Barn. LC 85-51173. (Illus.). 127p. (Orig.). 1985. pap. 6.95 (0-934527-05-9) Words Living Minis.

McKennon, Kelly. Multipliers, Positive Functionals, Positive-Definite Functions & Fourier-Stieltjes Transforms. LC 52-42839. (Memoirs Ser.: No. 1/111). 67p. 1971. pap. 16.00 (0-8218-1811-2, MEMO 1/111) Am Math.

McKenny, Janice E., ed. Field Artillery: Regular Army & Army Reserve. LC 85-3900. (Army Lineage Ser.: No. 60-11). 769p. 1985. 34.00 (0-16-001941-9, S/N 008-029-00136-5) USGPO.

McKenny, Margaret & Stuntz, Daniel E. The New Savory Wild Mushroom. enl. rev. ed. (Illus.). 264p. 1987. pap. 18.95 (0-295-96480-4) U of Wash Pr.

McKenny, Margaret, jt. auth. see Peterson, Roger T.

McKenrick, Robert, ed. Criminal Justice Ethics: Annotated Bibliography & Guide to Sources. LC 90-29186. (Research & Bibliographical Guides in Criminal Justice Ser.: No. 2). 136p. 1991. text ed. 47.95 (0-313-26791-X, SCK, Greenwood Pr) Greenwood.

McKenry. Mosby's Pharmacology in Nursing, No. 19. 1300p. 1994. 47.95 (0-8016-7896-X) Mosby Yr Bk.

— Text & Study Guide Package to Accompany Mosby's Pharmacology. 18th ed. 360p. 1991. pap. 53.95 (0-8016-6639-2) Mosby Yr Bk.

McKenry, Leda M. Mosby's Pharmacology in Nursing. 18th ed. 1248p. 1991. 48.95 (0-8016-3199-8) Mosby Yr Bk.

McKenry, Patrick C. & Price, Sharon J. Families & Change: Coping with Stressful Events. 336p. (C). 1994. text ed. 52.00 (0-8039-4925-1); pap. text ed. 24.95 (0-8039-4926-X) Sage.

Mckenry, Patrick C., jt. auth. see Price, Sharon J.

***McKenty, Bob.** Fallout from the Nuclear Family. 63p. (Orig.). 1994. pap. text ed. write for info. (1-880764-02-4) Northwind NJ.

McKenzie. ABC House. (J). 1994. 14.95 (0-8050-1946-4) H Holt & Co.

— Understand Your Health, No. 2: Study Guide & Activities. 1992. 18.95 (0-8016-7190-6) Mosby Yr Bk.

McKenzie, ed. see Kreutzer, Wolfgang.

McKenzie, et al. Daredevil: Marked for Death. (Illus.). 96p. 1990. pap. 9.95 (0-87135-634-1) Marvel Entmnt.

— Understanding Your Health Study Guide. 288p. 1991. pap. 14.95 (0-8016-6654-6) Mosby Yr Bk.

McKenzie, A., jt. auth. see Carruth, J. A.

McKenzie, A. Dean. Russian Icons in the Santa Barbara Museum of Art. LC 82-62426. (Illus.). 54p. (Orig.). 1982. pap. 8.25 (0-89951-049-3) Santa Barb Mus Art.

McKenzie, A. L., tr. The Letters of George Sand & Gustave Flaubert. 382p. 1979. 20.00 (0-915864-64-9); pap. 9.00 (0-915864-52-5) Academy Chi Pubs.

McKenzie, Alan. How to Draw & Sell Comic Strips. (Illus.). 144p. 1987. 19.95 (0-89134-214-1, 30009) North Light Bks.

McKenzie, Alan T. Certain, Lively Episodes: The Articulation of Passion in Eighteenth-Century Prose. LC 89-4826. (Illus.). 280p. 1990. 35.00 (0-8203-1167-7) U of Ga Pr.

McKenzie, Alan T., ed. A Grin on the Interface: Word Processing for the Academic Humanist. LC 84-2032. (Technology & the Humanities Ser.: No. 1). xi, 82p. 1984. 32.00 (0-87352-550-7); pap. 10.00 (0-87352-551-5) Modern Lang.

— Sent As a Gift: Eight Correspondences from the Eighteenth Century. LC 92-6568. 256p. 1993. 40.00 (0-8203-1466-8) U of Ga Pr.

McKenzie, Alexander A. World Record Wind: Measuring Gusts of 231 Miles an Hour. (Illus.). 36p. (Orig.). 1984. pap. 2.00 (0-9613227-0-5) A A McKenzie.

***McKenzie, Arthur.** Poems of a Biblical Nature. 1995. 12.95 (0-533-11136-6) Vantage.

McKenzie, Barbara. Mary McCarthy. (Twayne's United States Authors Ser.). 1966. pap. 13.95 (0-8084-0215-3, T108) NCUP.

— The Process of Fiction: Contemporary Stories & Criticism. 2nd ed. 611p. (C). 1974. pap. text ed. 18.75 (0-15-571986-6) HB Coll Pubs.

McKenzie, Barbara, ed. Fiction's Journey: 50 Stories. 559p. (C). 1978. pap. text ed. 18.75 (0-15-527320-5) HB Coll Pubs.

***McKenzie, Bert.** Fringe Benefits. (Orig.). 1995. pap. text ed. 5.95 (1-56333-354-6) Masquerade.

McKenzie, Beryl & Day, R. H., eds. Perceptual Developement in Early Infancy: Problems & Issues. (Child Psychology Ser.). 312p. 1987. text ed. 59.95 (0-89859-943-1) L Erlbaum Assocs.

***McKenzie-Brown, Peter, et al.** The Great Oil Age: The Petroleum Industry in Canada. (Illus.). 192p. 1993. 27.95 (1-55059-072-3) Temeron Bks.

McKenzie, Bruce. Employment Discrimination Redress. LC 87-92036. (Illus.). 200p. (Orig.). 1988. pap. 28.00 (0-9619802-0-6) Starvalley Ltd Pubs.

McKenzie, Bruce A. & Zachariah, Gerald. Understanding & Using Electricity. 2nd ed. 1982. 9.25 (0-8134-2204-3); text ed. 6.95 (0-685-02563-2) Interstate.

McKenzie, Bruce G. The Hammermill Guide to Desktop Publishing in Business. 248p. (Orig.). 1990. pap. 24.95 (0-9615651-1-X, Hammermill Paper) Slawson Comm.

McKenzie, C., ed. see Dickens, Charles.

***McKenzie, Carole.** Quotable Sex Vol. 1. 1994. pap. 4.99 (0-312-95405-0) St Martin.

McKenzie, Carole, comp. Quotable Sex. 208p. 1994. 15.95 (0-312-10529-0) St Martin.

***McKenzie, Cecile F., et al.** A Parent's Guide to Houston Private Schools. 3rd ed. 200p. 1994. 14.95 (0-9642974-0-X) McKenzie-Kurio.

McKenzie, Charles W. Minimum Distributions from Retirement Plans. 311p. 1993. ring bd. 49.95 (0-9638660-0-1) Actuarial Assocs.

McKenzie, Colin & Stutchbury, Michael, eds. Japanese Financial Markets & the Role of the Yen. 200p. pap. text ed. 24.95 (1-86373-240-3, Pub. by Allen Unwin AT) Paul & Co Pubs.

McKenzie, D. G. How to Make Marriage Work. (C). 1990. pap. 30.00 (0-86439-088-2, Pub. by Boolarong Pubns AT) St Mut.

— The Mango Tree Church. 84p. (C). 1990. pap. text ed. 30. 00 (0-86439-039-4, Pub. by Boolarong Pubns AT) St Mut.

McKenzie, Dan. The Infancy of Medicine: Influence of Folklore Upon Scientific Medicine. 1977. lib. bdg. 50.00 (0-8490-2057-3) Gordon Pr.

***McKenzie, Daniel H., et al, eds.** Ecological Indicators, 2 vols., Set. LC 91-26210. (Illus.). 1992. write for info. (1-85166-722-9) Elsevier.

— Ecological Indicators: Proceedings of the International Symposium on Ecological Indicators, Held Oct. 16-18, 1990, in Fort Lauderdale, Fla., Vol. 2. LC 91-26210. (Illus.). 1992. write for info. (1-85166-721-0) Elsevier.

— Ecological Indicators: Proceedings of the International Symposium on Ecological Indicators, Held Oct. 16-19, 1990, in Fort Lauderdale, Fla., Vol. 1. LC 91-26210. (Illus.). 1992. write for info. (1-85166-711-3) Elsevier.

McKenzie, Dennis J. & Betts, Richard M. Essentials of Real Estate Economics. 3rd ed. 352p. 1991. pap. text ed. 50.00 (0-13-287723-6, 160301) P-H.

McKenzie, Dennis J., et al. California Real Estate Principles. 3rd rev. ed. LC 88-17172. 388p. 1988. text ed. 38.95 (0-471-62140-4) P-H.

— California Real Estate Principles. 4th ed. LC 93-25065. (California Real Estate Ser.). 1993. text ed. 49.00 (0-13-117979-9) P-H.

McKenzie, Donald A. Death Notices from the Canada Christian Advocate, 1858-1872. 384p. 1992. lib. bdg. 27. 50 (0-912606-35-5) Hunterdon Hse.

— Death Notices from The Christian Guardian, 1836-1850. 368p. 1982. lib. bdg. 25.00 (0-912606-10-X) Hunterdon Hse.

— Death Notices from the Christian Guardian, 1851-1860. 365p. 1984. lib. bdg. 25.00 (0-912606-25-8) Hunterdon Hse.

— More Notices from Methodist Papers 1830-1857. 424p. 1986. lib. bdg. 25.00 (0-912606-29-0) Hunterdon Hse.

— Obituaries from Ontario's Christian Guardian, 1861-1870. 405p. 1988. lib. bdg. 25.00 (0-912606-33-9) Hunterdon Hse.

McKenzie, Donald A., tr. see Toletana, Luisa S.

McKenzie, Donald F. The Cambridge University Press, 1696-1712: A Bibliographical Study, 2 vols., 1. LC 66-10016. (Illus.). 466p. reprint ed. pap. 132.90 (0-8357-7982-3, 2030610) Bks Demand.

— The Cambridge University Press, 1696-1712: A Bibliographical Study, 2 vols., 2. LC 66-10016. (Illus.). 466p. reprint ed. pap. 111.50 (0-8357-7983-1, 2030610) Bks Demand.

McKenzie, Douglas, jt. auth. see Opie, Brenda.

McKenzie, Douglas H., jt. ed. see Prufer, Olaf H.

McKenzie, E. C. Fourteen Thousand Quips & Quotes: For Speakers, Writers, Editors, Preachers, & Teachers. 2nd ed. Orig. Title: Mac's Giant Book of Quips & Quotes. 600p. 1990. pap. 19.99 (0-8010-6266-7) Baker Bk.

— Fourteen Thousand Quips & Quotes for Writers & Speakers. 592p. 1988. pap. 12.99 (0-517-42712-5) Random Hse Value.

— Mac's Church Publication Quotebook, No. 2. 2nd ed. 224p. (Orig.). 1990. pap. 7.99 (0-8010-6264-0) Baker Bk.

— Quips & Quotes for Church Bulletins. (Direction Bks.). 1978. pap. 4.99 (0-8010-6221-7) Baker Bk.

McKenzie, Earl. A Boy Named Ossie: A Jamaican Childhood. (Caribbean Writers Ser.). (Illus.). 104p. (Orig.). (YA). 1991. pap. 8.95 (0-435-98816-6, 98816) Heinemann.

McKenzie, Edna C. Freedom in the Midst of a Slave Society. (YA). 1990. 12.50 (0-87498-003-8) Assoc Pubs DC.

McKenzie, Edward D. The Hills of Plaiston: Family Diaries Tell of Early Years in Small N. H. Town. 100p. 1994. pap. 12.50 (0-9617909-1-1) E D McKenzie.

— Surly Bonds of Earth. (Illus.). 160p. 1987. 20.00 (0-9617909-0-3) E D McKenzie.

McKenzie, Ellen K. A Bowl of Mischief. LC 92-24246. 144p. (J). (gr. 4-7). 1992. 14.95 (0-8050-2090-X, Bks Young Read) H Holt & Co.

— The King, the Princess, & the Tinker. LC 91-31316. (Illus.). 64p. (J). (gr. 2-4). 1993. 14.95 (0-8050-1773-9, Redfeather BYR); pap. 4.95 (0-8050-2951-6, Bks Young Read) H Holt & Co.

— Stargone John. LC 90-34119. (Illus.). 80p. (J). (gr. 2-4). 1990. 13.95 (0-8050-1451-9, Redfeather BYR) H Holt & Co.

— Stargone John. LC 90-34119. (Illus.). 64p. (J). (gr. 2-4). 1992. pap. 4.95 (0-8050-2069-1, Redfeather BYR) H Holt & Co.

— Taash & the Jesters. LC 92-12378. 256p. (YA). (gr. 5 up). 1992. 15.95 (0-8050-2381-X, Bks Young Read) H Holt & Co.

— Under the Bridge. (J). (gr. 4-7). 1995. 14.95 (0-8050-3398-X, Bks Young Read) H Holt & Co.

McKenzie, Evan. Privatopia: Homeowner Associations & the Rise of Residential Private Government. LC 93-37340. 248p. 1994. pap. 30.00 (0-300-05876-4) Yale U Pr.

McKenzie, Evan & Roos, Robert A. The Kids Nobody Wants: Treating the Seriously Delinquent Youth. 84p. 1982. 7.50 (0-318-21313-3) Natl Juv & Family Ct Judges.

McKenzie, Evan, jt. ed. see Barker, Jeffrey H.

McKenzie, Fred A. The American Invaders. Bruchey, Stuart & Bruchey, Eleanor, eds. LC 76-5016. (American Business Abroad Ser.). 1976. reprint ed. 24.95 (0-405-09284-9) Ayer.

McKenzie, Frederick A. Korea's Fight for Freedom. LC 76-111784. reprint ed. 19.45 (0-404-04137-X) AMS Pr.

McKenzie, Garry D. Gondwana Six: Stratigraphy, Sedimentology, & Paleontology. (Geophysical Monograph Ser.: Vol. 41). 260p. 26.00 (0-87590-067-4) Am Geophysical.

— Gondwana Six: Structure, Tectonics, & Geophysics. (Geophysical Monograph Ser.: Vol. 40). 338p. 33.00 (0-87590-064-X) Am Geophysical.

McKenzie, Garry D. & Utgard, Russell O., eds. Man & His Physical Environment: Readings in Environmental Geology. LC 79-187012. 350p. reprint ed. pap. 99.80 (0-317-11230-9, 2015870) Bks Demand.

McKenzie, George. Measuring Economic Welfare: New Methods. LC 82-4422. 208p. 1983. 59.95 (0-521-24862-0) Cambridge U Pr.

McKenzie, George & Thomas, Stephen B. Financial Instability & the International Debt Problem. LC 91-27767. 221p. 1992. text ed. 69.95 (0-312-07197-3) St Martin.

McKenzie, George J., tr. see Calvez, Jean Y.

McKenzie, Gordon. Organic Unity in Coleridge. LC 75-30008. reprint ed. 20.00 (0-404-14014-9) AMS Pr.

McKenzie, H. A. & Smythe, L. E., eds. Quantitative Trace Analysis of Biological Materials: Principles & Mehtods for Determination of Trace Elements & Trace Amounts of Some Macro Elements. 794p. 1988. 282.00 (0-444-80958-9) Elsevier.

McKenzie, H. S. The Law of Building & Engineering Contracts & Arbitration. 4th ed. 349p. 1988. 86.00 (0-7021-2066-9, Pub. by Juta SA) W W Gaunt.

— Law of Building & Engineering Contracts & Arbitration. 5th ed. 380p. 1994. 104.00 (0-7021-3272-1) W W Gaunt.

McKenzie, Harry, jt. auth. see Adoboyde, Olagoke F.

McKenzie, Harry, jt. auth. see Jaytu, Adeolu.

McKenzie, Hilda. Rosie Edwards. large type ed. (General Ser.). 544p. 1993. 21.95 (0-7089-2863-3) Ulverscroft.

— The Sisters. 384p. 1994. pap. 11.95 (0-7472-4116-3, Pub. by Headline UK) Trafalgar.

— The Sisters. large type ed. 1994. 22.95 (0-7089-3170-7) Ulverscroft.

McKenzie, Ian. Squash Workshop: A Complete Game Guide. (Illus.). 272p. 1993. 39.95 (1-85223-115-7, Pub. by Crowood Pr UK) Trafalgar.

— The Squash Workshop: A Complete Game Guide. (Illus.). 272p. 1993. pap. 29.95 (1-85223-728-7, Pub. by Crowood Pr UK) Trafalgar.

McKenzie, J. J. I Will Love Unloved: A Linguistic Analysis of Woman's Biblical Importance. 386p. (Orig.). (C). 1993. lib. bdg. 49.50 (0-8191-9229-5); pap. text ed. 32. 50 (0-8191-9230-9) U Pr of Amer.

McKenzie, J. L. Bible Dictionary: Dizionario Biblico. 1062p. (ITA.). 1981. 75.00 (0-8288-2315-4, M7640) Fr & Eur.

McKenzie, J. Steven, jt. auth. see Traynor, William J.

***McKenzie, James.** Troop Seventeen: The Making of Mounties. (Illus.). 184p. 1992. 49.95 (1-55059-039-1) Temeron Bks.

McKenzie, James & Pinger, Robert. An Introduction to Community Health. LC 94-20883. (C). 1995. 47.50 (0-06-500797-2) HarpC.

— An Introduction to Community Health. LC 94-20883. (C). 1995. Instr.'s ed. teacher ed 10.00 (0-06-500798-0) HarpC.

McKenzie, James E., jt. ed. see Sperling, Gerald B.

McKenzie, James F. & Jurs, Jan. Planning, Implementing, & Evaluating Health Education Programs: A Primer. LC 92-11604. (Illus.). 336p. (Orig.). (C). 1993. pap. write for info. (0-675-22162-5) Macmillan.

McKenzie, Jamieson. Administrators at Risk: Tools & Technologies for Securing Your Future. 170p. 1993. 19. 95 (1-879639-27-0) Natl Educ Serv.

McKenzie, Jamieson A. Making Change in Education: Preparing Schools for the Future. LC 86-40485. 150p. 1987. 22.95 (0-915253-11-9) Wilkerson Pub Co.

— Power Learning in the Classroom. Herman, Jerry J. & Herman, Janice L., eds. (Road Maps to Success Ser.). 72p. 1993. pap. 15.00 (0-8039-6056-5) Corwin Pr.

An Asterisk (*) at the beginning of an entry indicates that the title is appearing in BIP for the first time.

— Selecting, Managing & Marketing Technologies. Herman, Jerry J. & Herman, Janice L., eds. (Road Maps to Success Ser.). 72p. 1993. pap. 15.00 (*0-8039-6054-9*) Corwin Pr.

McKenzie, Janet. Arthur Boyd at Bundanon. (Illus.). 144p. 1994. 50.00 (*1-85490-337-3*, Academy Edits) St Martin.

— Arthur Boyd at Bundanon. (Illus.). 144p. 1994. pap. 38.00 (*1-85490-338-1*, Academy Edits) St Martin.

McKenzie, Jimmy C. & Hughes, Robert J. Office Machines: A Practical Approach. 3rd ed. 352p. 1989. pap. text ed. write for info. (*0-205-11873-9*, H18732) P-H.

McKenzie, Joanna, jt. auth. see Gonshack, Sol.

McKenzie, John. The Student Edition of MINITAB for Windows. 624p. 1994. pap. write for info. (*0-201-59157-X*) Addison-Wesley.

McKenzie, John G. Nervous Disorders & Religion: A Study of Souls in the Making. LC 79-8719. 183p. 1981. reprint ed. text ed. 35.00 (*0-313-22192-8*, MCND, Greenwood Pr) Greenwood.

McKenzie, John L. A Theology of the Old Testament. LC 86-9230. 336p. 1986. reprint ed. pap. text ed. 28.50 (*0-8191-5354-0*) U Pr of Amer.

McKenzie-Johnstone, Henry. Mission to Mexico: A Tale of British Diplomacy in the 1820s. 300p. 1992. text ed. 59.50 (*1-85043-555-3*, Pub. by I B Tauris UK) St Martin.

McKenzie, Joy. Solving Bible Mysteries. 96p. (J). 1994. pap. 9.99 (*0-310-59761-7*) Zondervan.

McKenzie, Judith. The Architecture of Petra. (British Academy Monographs in Archaeology: No. 1). (Illus.). 494p. 1991. 145.00 (*0-19-727000-X*) OUP.

— Two Mothers Speak. LC 90-71367. 138p. 1990. pap. 7.95 (*1-55523-390-2*) Winston-Derek.

McKenzie, K., ed. Antonio Pucci: Le Noie. (Elliott Monographs: Vol. 26). 1931. 30.00 (*0-527-02629-8*) Periodicals Srv.

McKenzie, K. G., ed. Shallow Tethys Two: Proceedings of the International Symposium on Shallow Tethys 2, Wagga Wagga, 15-17 September 1986. (Illus.). 587p. (C). 1987. text ed. 130.00 (*90-6191-647-X*, Pub. by A A Balkema NE) Ashgate Pub Co.

McKenzie, K. G. & Jones, P. J. Ostracoda in the Earth & Life Sciences: Proceedings of the Eleventh International Symposium, Warrnambool, July 1991. (Illus.). 600p. (C). 1994. 130.00 (*90-5410-306-X*, Pub. by A A Balkema NE) Ashgate Pub Co.

McKenzie, Laura. A Guide to London. 225p. 1988. pap. 10.95 (*0-89865-544-7*) Donning Co.

— A Guide to San Francisco. 225p. 1988. pap. 10.95 (*0-89865-547-1*) Donning Co.

McKenzie, Leon. Adult Education & Worldview Construction. 160p. (C). 1991. lib. bdg. 19.50 (*0-89464-488-2*) Krieger.

McKenzie, Leonard. In Pictures Yosemite: The Continuing Story. LC 91-60042. 48p. 1991. 6.95 (*0-88714-057-2*) KC Pubns.

McKenzie, Linda, jt. auth. see Childress, Casey.

McKenzie, Lorna. Pictures in Provence. large type ed. (Linford Romance Library). 240p. 1994. pap. 14.95 (*0-7089-7513-5*, Linford) Ulverscroft.

— Storm Damage. (Rainbow Romances Ser.: No. 907). 160p. 1994. 14.95 (*0-7090-4994-3*, Hale-Parkwest) Parkwest Pubns.

— To Sara - With Love. large type ed. (Romance Ser.). 1994. pap. 14.95 (*0-7089-7616-6*, Linford) Ulverscroft.

— Twentieth-Century Pirate. large type ed. (Linford Romance Library). 272p. 1994. pap. 14.95 (*0-7089-7545-3*, Linford) Ulverscroft.

McKenzie, M. Elizabeth, jt. auth. see Conway, Donal P.

McKenzie, Maisie. Fred McKay. 200p. (C). 1990. 90.00 (*0-86439-109-9*, Pub. by Boolarong Pubns AT) St Mut.

McKenzie, Marian. Choices in Your Life. (Literacy Volunteers of America Readers Ser.). 32p. (Orig.). 1988. pap. text ed. 3.00 (*0-8428-9620-1*) Cambridge Bk.

McKenzie, Marni S. Alphabet of Bible Creatures. (Illus.). 56p. (J). (ps-8). 1993. 14.95 (*1-882630-00-9*) Mercy Pr.

— The Creed & the Christian: A Twelve-Part Study of the Apostles' Creed. 56p. 1993. student ed 2.95 (*1-882630-02-5*); audio 24.95 (*1-882630-01-7*) Mercy Pr.

McKenzie, Melissa, jt. auth. see Edwards, Sally.

McKenzie, Michael. Madonna: Her Story. (Illus.). 1987. pap. 9.95 (*0-7119-1181-9*, BO10088, Pub. by Bobcat UK) Music Sales.

— Madonna: The Early Days. 96p. 1993. pap. text ed. 19.95 (*0-9638519-3-4*) Wrldwide Televid.

McKenzie, Michael, jt. auth. see Frank, Peter.

***McKenzie, Mike.** Faces of Victory: Europe: Liberating a Continent. (Illus.). 240p. 1995. 39.95 (*1-886110-00-X*) Addax Pubng.

— Faces of Victory: Europe: Liberating a Continent. limited ed. (Illus.). 240p. 1995. 75.00 (*1-886110-02-6*) Addax Pubng.

— Faces of Victory: Europe: Liberating a Continent; Pacific: The Fall of the Rising Sun, 2 vols. in 1, Set. deluxe ed. (Illus.). 480p. (C). 1995. 500.00 (*1-886110-05-0*) Addax Pubng.

— Faces of Victory: Europe: Liberating a Continent, Pacific: The Fall of the Rising Sun, 2 vols., Set. limited ed. (Illus.). 480p. 1995. 149.00 (*1-886110-04-2*) Addax Pubng.

— Faces of Victory: Pacific: The Fall of the Rising Sun. (Illus.). 240p. 1995. 39.95 (*1-886110-01-8*) Addax Pubng.

— Faces of Victory: Pacific: The Fall of the Rising Sun. limited ed. (Illus.). 240p. 1995. 75.00 (*1-886110-03-4*) Addax Pubng.

— Oklahoma State University: History-Making Basketball. Missouri Editing Group Staff & Anderson, Kelly, eds. (Illus.). 1992. write for info. (*1-56166-049-3*) Walsworth Pub.

McKenzie, N. L., jt. auth. see Kenneally, M. K.

McKenzie, N. L., et al, eds. Kimberley Rainforests Australia. 490p. (C). 1991. text ed. 190.00 (*0-949324-37-X*, Pub. by Surrey Beatty & Sons AT) St Mut.

McKenzie, Nancy. The Child Queen. 1994. mass mkt. 4.99 (*0-345-38244-7*, Del Rey) Ballantine.

— The High Queen. (Orig.). 1995. mass mkt., pap. 5.99 (*0-345-38245-5*, Del Rey) Ballantine.

McKenzie, Nancy F., ed. The AIDS Reader: Privacy, Poverty, Community. 1990. pap. 9.95 (*0-452-01048-9*, Mer) NAL-Dutton.

— The AIDS Reader: Social, Political, & Ethical Issues. 484p. 1991. pap. 15.00 (*0-452-01072-1*, Mer) NAL-Dutton.

— Beyond Crisis: Our National Health in the 1990s. 608p. (Orig.). 1994. pap. 19.95 (*0-452-01108-6*, Mer) NAL-Dutton.

— The Crisis in Health Care. 400p. 1990. pap. 15.00 (*0-452-01028-4*, Mer) NAL-Dutton.

McKenzie, Neil. Guests of the Nation: Manuscript Edition. 1960. pap. 13.00 (*0-8222-0488-6*) Dramatists Play.

McKenzie, Pamela, ed. see Spectra Publishing Co. Inc. Staff.

McKenzie, Paul L. How to Win at Shuffleboard. (Illus.). 40p. (Orig.). 1989. pap. 4.95 (*1-877633-03-8*) Luthers.

***McKenzie, Peter, et al, eds.** Competence & Accountability in Education. 165p. 1995. text ed. 42.95 (*1-85742-279-1*, Pub. by Arena UK) Ashgate Pub Co.

McKenzie, Phillip, jt. auth. see Lokan, Jan.

McKenzie, Phillip, jt. auth. see Maclean, Rupert.

McKenzie, R. & Valeriote, M. The Structure of Decidable Locally Finite Varieties. (Progress in Mathematics Ser.: No. 79). 224p. 1989. 42.00 (*0-8176-3439-8*) Birkhauser.

McKenzie, R., jt. auth. see Hobby, D.

McKenzie, R. A. Successful Business Plans for Architects. 1992. text ed. 42.00 (*0-07-045654-2*) McGraw.

McKenzie, Ralph & Givant, Steven, eds. Collected Works: Tarski, 4 vols., Set. 1986. 650.00 (*0-8176-3284-0*) Birkhauser.

— Collected Works: Tarski, 4 vols., Vol. 1: 1921-1934. 1987. 190.00 (*0-8176-3280-8*) Birkhauser.

— Collected Works: Tarski, 4 vols., Vol. 2: 1935-1944. 1987. 190.00 (*0-8176-3281-6*) Birkhauser.

— Collected Works: Tarski, 4 vols., Vol. 3: 1945-1957. 1987. 190.00 (*0-8176-3282-4*) Birkhauser.

— Collected Works: Tarski, 4 vols., Vol. 4: 1958-1979. 1987. 190.00 (*0-8176-3283-2*) Birkhauser.

McKenzie, Ralph, jt. auth. see Burris, Stanley.

McKenzie, Ralph, jt. auth. see Freese, Ralph.

McKenzie, Ralph N., et al. Algebras, Lattices, Varieties. LC 86-23239. (Mathematics Ser.: Vol. I). 361p. (C). 1987. boxed 63.00 (*0-534-07651-3*) Chapman & Hall.

McKenzie, Ray, jt. ed. see Lawson, Julie.

McKenzie, Richard. Economic Issues in Public Policy. (Illus.). 1980. text ed. write for info. (*0-07-045650-X*) McGraw.

— Economics. 704p. (C). 1986. disk write for info. (*0-318-60189-3*) HM.

— The Secret Place. 4.95 (*0-913343-21-8*) Inst Psych Inc.

McKenzie, Richard, ed. Plant Closings: Public or Private Choices? LC 84-14957. 326p. 1984. pap. 3.00 (*0-932790-42-9*) Cato Inst.

McKenzie, Richard & Lee, Dwight. Quicksilver Capital: How the Rapid Movement of Wealth Has Changed the World. 280p. 1991. text ed. 29.95 (*0-02-920535-2*) Free Pr.

McKenzie, Richard, jt. auth. see Lee, Dwight.

McKenzie, Richard.B. Bound to Be Free. (Publication Ser.: No. 255). 210p. 1982. 15.95 (*0-8179-7551-9*) Hoover Inst Pr.

— Competing Visions: The Political Conflict over America's Economic Future. LC 85-11305. 216p. 1985. 5.00 (*0-932790-51-8*); pap. 3.00 (*0-932790-52-6*) Cato Inst.

— The Fairness of Markets. 256p. 1987. text ed. 35.00 (*0-669-14801-6*) Free Pr.

— Fugitive Industry: The Economics & Politics of Deindustrialization. LC 83-22413. (Illus.). 281p. (C). 1984. 29.95 (*0-936488-66-2*); pap. 14.95 (*0-936488-67-0*) PRIPP.

— The Limits of Economic Science. 1982. lib. bdg. 37.50 (*0-89838-116-9*) Kluwer Ac.

— Times Change: The Minimum Wage & the New York Times. LC 94-15800. 1994. 19.95 (*0-936488-76-X*) PRIPP.

— What Went Right in the Nineteen Eighties. LC 93-7236. (Illus.). 250p. (Orig.). 1993. pap. 21.95 (*0-936488-71-9*) PRIPP.

McKenzie, Richard B. & Lee, Dwight R. Government in Retreat. 1991. pap. 10.00 (*0-943802-67-9*, 164) Natl Ctr Pol.

McKenzie, Richard B. & Tullock, Gordon. The Best of the New World of Economics. 5th ed. (C). 1988. pap. text ed. 28.95 (*0-256-06798-8*) Irwin.

McKenzie, Richard B., jt. auth. see Lee, Dwight R.

McKenzie, Robert. British Political Parties: The Distribution of Power Within the Conservation & Labour Parties. (Modern Revivals in History Ser.). 638p. 1992. 69.95 (*0-7512-0067-0*, Pub. by Gregg Pub UK) Ashgate Pub Co.

McKenzie, Robert & Silver, Allan. Angels in Marble: Working Class Conservatives in Urban England. LC 67-30555. (Studies in Contemporary Sociology). 307p. reprint ed. pap. 87.50 (*0-8357-5477-4*, 2024057) Bks Demand.

McKenzie, Robert, jt. auth. see Houk, Carolyn.

Mckenzie, Robert E. Representation Before the Collection Division of the IRS. 1990. 95.00 (*0-318-41449-X*) Clark Boardman Callaghan.

McKenzie, Robert E., et al. Representing the Audited Taxpayer. 1990. 69.95 (*0-685-31933-4*) Clark Boardman Callaghan.

McKenzie, Robert G., jt. auth. see Houk, Carolyn S.

McKenzie, Robert H. Degree Planning & Prior Learning. 2nd ed. 176p. 1991. per., pap. text ed. 17.95 (*0-8403-7145-4*) Kendall-Hunt.

McKenzie, Robert T. One South or Many? Plantation Belt & Upcountry in Civil War-Era Tennessee. (Illus.). 216p. (C). 1994. 39.95 (*0-521-46270-3*) Cambridge U Pr.

McKenzie, Robin A. The Cervical & Thoracic Spine: Mechanical Diagnosis & Therapy. (Illus.). 320p. (C). 1990. text ed. 75.00 (*0-9597746-7-X*, Pub. by Spinal Pubns Ltd NZ) Orthopedic Phys.

— The Lumbar Spine: Mechanical Diagnosis & Therapy. (Illus.). 164p. 1989. reprint ed. text ed. 54.00 (*0-473-00064-4*, Pub. by Spinal Pubns Ltd NZ) Orthopedic Phys.

— Treat Your Own Back. 6th ed. (Illus.). 73p. 1989. reprint ed. pap. text ed. 10.00 (*0-9597746-6-1*, Pub. by Spinal Pubns Ltd NZ); reprint ed. Spanish ed. pap. text ed. 10.00 (*0-473-00065-2*, Pub. by Spinal Pubns Ltd NZ) Orthopedic Phys.

— Treat Your Own Neck. 2nd ed. (Illus.). 61p. 1989. reprint ed. pap. text ed. 10.00 (*0-473-00209-4*, Pub. by Spinal Pubns Ltd NZ) Orthopedic Phys.

McKenzie, Roderick D. Neighborhood: A Study of Local Life in the City of Columbus, Ohio. LC 71-112560. (Rise of Urban America Ser.). (Illus.). 1974. reprint ed. 19.95 (*0-405-02465-7*) Ayer.

McKenzie, Sally. Performance Measurements: An Easy & Effective Method to Measure Dental Employee Performance. 1992. 192.95 (*0-318-72985-7*, D7069) PennWell Bks.

McKenzie, Shirlyn B. Textbook of Hematology. LC 87-3834. (Illus.). 507p. 1988. text ed. 48.50 (*0-8121-1096-X*) Williams & Wilkins.

McKenzie-Smith, I., jt. auth. see Browning, David R.

McKenzie, Steven L. The Chronicler's Use of the Deuteronomistic History. (Harvard Semitic Monographs: No. 33). (C). 1985. 19.50 (*0-89130-828-8*, 04 00 33) Scholars Pr GA.

McKenzie, Steven L. & Haynes, Stephen R., eds. To Each Its Own Meaning: An Introduction to Biblical Criticisms & Their Applications. LC 92-26563. 256p. (Orig.). 1993. pap. 12.99 (*0-664-25236-2*) Westminster John Knox.

***McKenzie, V. Michael.** Domestic Violence in America. LC 95-14147. 1995. write for info. (*1-55618-151-5*) Brunswick Pub.

McKenzie, Venetia. Creative Self-Communication. 1978. pap. 1.25 (*0-87516-254-1*) DeVorss.

McKenzie, Wendy. The Financial Times Guide to Using & Interpreting Company Accounts. (Financial Times Management Ser.). 224p. 1994. 90.00x (*0-273-60728-6*, Pub. by Pitman Pub Ltd UK) Trans-Atl Phila.

— The Financial Times Guide to Using & Interpreting Company Accounts. (Financial Times Management Ser.). 224p. 1995. pap. 45.00x (*0-273-60727-8*, Pub. by Pitman Pub Ltd UK) Trans-Atl Phila.

McKenzie, Wesley M., ed. see Douglas, Charles H.

McKenzie, William A. Dining Car Line to the Pacific: An Illustrated History of the NP Railway's "Famously Good" Food, with 150 Authentic Recipes. LC 89-27960. (Illus.). 164p. 1990. 39.95 (*0-87351-253-7*); pap. 19.95 (*0-87351-254-5*) Minn Hist.

McKenzie, William P., jt. ed. see Leach, James.

McKeogh, J. P. Butterworths Student Companion Series: Intellectual Property. 144p. 1988. Australia. pap. 19.00 (*0-409-49289-2*) Butterworth Legal Pubs.

McKeon, David, jt. auth. see Morrison, Grant.

Mckeon, Denise, jt. ed. see Samway, Katharine D.

Mckeon, Donald W., jt. auth. see Wilson, Clifford A.

***McKeon, Elizabeth.** From Hollywood: The Elvis Presley Cookbook: Recipes Fit for a King. LC 94-26883. (Illus.). 256p. 1994. 12.95 (*1-55853-301-X*) Rutledge Hill Pr.

McKeon, Elizabeth, et al. Fit for a King: The Elvis Presley Cookbook. LC 92-25266. (Illus.). 256p. 1992. spiral bd. 12.95 (*1-55853-196-3*) Rutledge Hill Pr.

McKeon, John. The Serpent's Crown. 208p. 1991. 19.95 (*0-8027-1146-4*) Walker & Co.

McKeon, Joseph, ed. Managing Logistics Change Through Innovative Information Technology. 220p. 1987. pap. write for info. (*0-318-61853-2*) Leaseway Trans Corp.

McKeon, Joseph E., ed. Partnerships: A Natural Evolution in Logistics. LC 88-81504. (Logistics Resource Forum Ser.: No. 7). 126p. (Orig.). 1988. pap. text ed. 19.95 (*0-9610146-5-2*) Leaseway Trans Corp.

***McKeon, Judith C.** The Encyclopedia of Roses: How to Grow & Enjoy America's Favorite Flower. LC 95-2174. 1995. 29.95 (*0-87596-656-X*) Rodale Pr Inc.

McKeon, Mary. Wasting Time in School: An Experiential Account of Chaplaincy in Secondary Schools. 128p. 1993. 25.00 (*0-85439-461-3*, Pub. by St Paul Pubns UK) St Mut.

McKeon, Michael. Origins of the English Novel, 1600-1740. LC 86-18495. 544p. 1988. reprint ed. pap. text ed. 18.95 (*0-8018-3746-4*) Johns Hopkins.

— Politics & Poetry in Restoration England: The Case of Dryden's Annus Mirabilis. LC 75-4508. (Illus.). 350p. reprint ed. pap. 99.80 (*0-7837-3867-6*, 2043689) Bks Demand.

McKeon, Patrick. Coping with Depression & Elation. large type ed. (Illus.). 160p. 1991. 18.95 (*1-85089-155-9*, Pub. by ISIS UK) Transaction Pubs.

McKeon, Richard. Freedom & History & Other Essays: The Thought of Richard McKeon. McKeon, Zahava K., ed. (Illus.). 304p. 1990. lib. bdg. 39.95 (*0-226-56028-7*); pap. text ed. 15.95 (*0-226-56029-5*) U Ch Pr.

— On Knowing: The Natural Sciences. McKeon, Zahava K., ed. LC 94-8953. (Illus.). 400p. 1994. pap. text ed. 17.95 (*0-226-56027-9*) U Ch Pr.

— On Knowing: The Natural Sciences. McKeon, Zahava K., ed. LC 94-8953. (Illus.). 400p. 1994. lib. bdg. 65.00 (*0-226-56026-0*) U Ch Pr.

— The Philosophy of Spinoza: The Unity of His Thought. LC 86-28563. 345p. 1987. reprint ed. 35.00 (*0-918024-47-1*); reprint ed. pap. 17.50 (*0-918024-48-X*) Ox Bow.

— Rhetoric: Essays in Invention & Discovery. LC 86-28574. xxxiv, 220p. (C). 1987. 30.00 (*0-918024-49-8*); pap. 14.95 (*0-918024-00-5*) Ox Bow.

McKeon, Richard, ed. Introduction to Aristotle. LC 92-50208. 1992. 18.50 (*0-679-60027-2*, Modern Lib) Random.

McKeon, Richard, jt. ed. see Nikam, N. A.

McKeon, Richard P., ed. Introduction to Aristotle. 2nd enl. rev. ed. (C). 1974. reprint ed. lib. bdg. 17.00 (*0-226-56032-5*) U Ch Pr.

McKeon, Richard P., ed. see Aristotle.

McKeon, Zahava K. Novels & Arguments: Inventing Rhetorical Criticism. LC 82-2677. 1982. lib. bdg. 22.50 (*0-226-56034-1*) U Ch Pr.

McKeon, Zahava K., ed. see McKeon, Richard.

***McKeone, Dermot.** Measuring Your Media Profile. 200p. 1995. 59.95 (*0-566-07578-4*) Ashgate Pub Co.

***McKeone, Dixie.** Son of Dawn. (First Quest Ser.). (Illus.). 320p. (Orig.). 1995. pap. 3.95 (*1-56076-884-3*) TSR Inc.

McKeone, Lee. The Clone Crisis. 224p. (Orig.). 1992. mass mkt. 4.99 (*0-446-36321-9*, Aspect) Warner Bks.

— Starfire Down. 1991. mass mkt. 4.95 (*0-446-36137-2*) Warner Bks.

McKeough, A. & Lupart, eds. Toward the Practice of Theory-Based Instruction: Current Cognitive Theories & Their Educational Promise. 208p. (C). 1991. text ed. 32.50 (*0-8058-0773-X*) L Erlbaum Assocs.

***McKeough, Anne, et al, eds.** Teaching for Transfer: Fostering Generalization in Learning. 256p. 1995. text ed. 49.95 (*0-8058-1309-8*) L Erlbaum Assocs.

***McKeough, D. Michael.** The Coloring Review of Neuroscience. 2nd ed. LC 94-45666. 1995. 22.95 (*0-316-56209-2*) Little.

***McKeough, J. & Stewart, A.** Intellectual Property in Australia. 481p. 1991. pap. 78.00 (*0-409-49581-6*, Austral) Butterworth Legal Pubs.

McKeough, J., jt. auth. see Blakeney, M. L.

McKeown, Anthony F. & Novak-Jandrey, Mary L., eds. Human Resources Management in the Health Care Setting. LC 91-17200. 320p. (Orig.). 1991. pap. 65.95 (*1-55648-070-9*, 088168) AHPI.

McKeown, Bonni. Peaceful Patriot: The Story of Tom Bennett. 224p. 1987. pap. 7.00 (*0-9621483-0-X*) Peaceful Patriot Pr.

McKeown, Bruce & Thomas, Dan. Q Methodology. (Quantitative Applications in the Social Sciences Ser.: Vol. 66). 93p. (C). 1988. pap. text ed. 9.95 (*0-8039-2753-3*) Sage.

McKeown, Charles & Gilliam, Terry. Adventures of Baron Munchausen: The Screenplay. (Illus.). 256p. (Orig.). 1989. pap. 8.95 (*1-55783-041-X*) Applause Theatre Bk Pubs.

McKeown, Charles, jt. auth. see Gilliam, Terry.

McKeown, Ciaran. Passion of Peace. 320p. 1990. pap. 11.95 (*0-85640-325-3*, Pub. by Blackstaff Pr IE) Dufour.

McKeown, Denny. Denny McKeown's Complete Guide to Midwest Gardening. LC 84-23996. (Illus.). 408p. 1985. 24.95 (*0-87833-382-7*) Taylor Pub.

McKeown, J. J., jt. auth. see Jennings, A.

McKeown, J. J., et al. An Introduction to Unconstrained Optimisation. (Illus.). 132p. (C). 1990. pap. 39.00 (*0-7503-0025-6*); 270.00 (*0-7503-0029-9*) IOP Pub.

***McKeown, James & McKeown, Joan C.** Price Guide to Antique & Classic Cameras 1995-1996. 9th ed. 608p. 1994. pap. 59.95 (*0-931838-21-5*) Centennial Photo Serv.

McKeown, James C., jt. auth. see Hopwood, Wm S.

McKeown, James M. & McKeown, Joan, eds. Price Guide to Antique & Classic Cameras, 1992-1993. 8th ed. LC 87-654177. (Illus.). 512p. 1992. 59.95 (*0-931838-19-3*, CP8193, Amphoto); pap. 49.95 (*0-931838-18-5*, CP8185, Amphoto) Watsn-Guptill.

McKeown, James M. & McKeown, Joan C. Collector's Guide to Kodak Cameras. (Illus.). 176p. (Orig.). 1981. pap. 16.95 (*0-931838-02-9*, CP3802, Amphoto) Watsn-Guptill.

— Price Guide to Antique & Classic Cameras 1995-1996. 9th ed. (Illus.). 608p. 1994. 69.95 (*0-931838-22-3*) Centennial Photo Serv.

McKeown, Joan, jt. ed. see McKeown, James M.

McKeown, Joan C. Sharing More Than a Pastor. (Illus.). 128p. (Orig.). 1993. pap. 9.95 (*0-9636183-0-X*) Arc Res.

McKeown, Joan C., jt. auth. see McKeown, James M.

McKeown, Joan C., jt. auth. see McKeown, James.

***McKeown, K. C.** Pasta Shmasta. 1995. 16.95 (*0-385-47581-0*) Doubleday.

McKeown, Karen C. Hog Wild! 224p. (Orig.). 1992. pap. 9.99 (*0-446-39250-2*) Warner Bks.

McKeown, Kate, jt. auth. see Mobley, Lou.

McKeown, Kathleen R. Text Generation: Using Discourse Strategies & Focus Constraints to Generate Natural Language Text. (Studies in Natural Language Processing). (Illus.). 256p. (C). 1992. pap. 19.95 (*0-521-43802-0*) Cambridge U Pr.

McKeown, Kieran. Marxist Political Economy & Marxist Urban Sociology: A Review & Elaboration of Recent Developments. 256p. 1987. text ed. 39.95 (*0-312-51794-7*) St Martin.

McKeown, Margaret G. & Curtis, Mary E., eds. The Nature of Vocabulary Acquisition. 208p. 1987. 39.95 (*0-89859-548-7*) L Erlbaum Assocs.

McKeown, Martha F. Come to Our Salmon Feast. LC 59-9823. (Illus.). 80p. (J). (gr. 4-9). 1959. 7.95 (*0-8323-0157-4*) Binford Mort.

— Linda's Indian Home. LC 56-8826. (Illus.). 80p. (J). (gr. 3-7). 1969. 7.95 (*0-8323-0151-5*) Binford Mort.

An Asterisk (*) at the beginning of an entry indicates that the title is appearing in BIP for the first time.

— Them Was the Days: An American Saga of the 70's. 298p. reprint ed. pap. 85.00 (0-7837-1641-9, 2041935) Bks Demand.

McKeown, P. A., ed. Automated Inspection & Product Control: Proceedings of the International Conference, 7th, Birmingham, U. K., March 26-28, 1985. 400p. 1985. 107.75 (0-444-87734-7, North Holland) Elsevier.

McKeown, Pat, jt. auth. see Gilbert, Edith.

McKeown, Patrick G. Computerized Test Bank (IBM 3.5) to Accompany Working with Computers. (C). 1992. teacher ed, disk 208.50 (0-15-500274-0) Dryden Pr.

— Living with Computers. 4th ed. LC 92-71698. 661p. (C). 1993. student ed, pap. text ed. 8.50 (0-03-097926-9) Dryden Pr.

— Living with Computers. 4th ed. LC 92-71698. 661p. (C). 1993. teacher ed 69.25 (0-03-097308-2); disk 14.75 (0-03-097310-4) Dryden Pr.

— Living with Computers. 4th ed. LC 92-71698. 661p. (C). 1993. disk 14.75 (0-03-097780-0); disk 14.75 (0-03-097309-0) Dryden Pr.

— Living with Computers: Commercial Software Version. 672p. (C). 1987. pap. text ed. 37.25 (0-15-551144-0); teacher ed, trans. write for info. (0-318-61978-4); write for info. (0-318-61977-6) Dryden Pr.

— Living with Computers: With BASIC. 3rd ed. 697p. (C). 1990. pap. text ed. 41.25 (0-15-551158-0) Dryden Pr.

— Living with Computers, with BASIC. 4th ed. LC 92-71695. 800p. (C). 1993. pap. text ed. 41.75 (0-03-096630-2) Dryden Pr.

— Living with Computers, with BASIC. 4th ed. LC 92-71695. 800p. (C). 1993. student ed, pap. text ed. 20.00 (0-03-097306-6) Dryden Pr.

— A Personal Computer Toolbox: Software Applications for the IBM PC. 304p. (C). 1987. Incl. diskette. pap. text ed. 39.00 (0-15-569380-8) Dryden Pr.

— Structured Programming Using FORTRAN 77. 482p. (C). 1985. pap. text ed. 35.00 (0-15-584411-3) Dryden Pr.

— Structured Programming Using WATFIV. 405p. (C). 1985. pap. text ed. 33.25 (0-15-584414-8) Dryden Pr.

— Working with Computers. 350p. (C). 1992. student ed, pap. text ed. 18.75 (0-15-596726-6) Dryden Pr.

— Working with Computers. 350p. (C). 1992. text ed. 32.00 (0-15-596723-1); pap. text ed. 10.50 (0-15-596727-4) Dryden Pr.

— Working with Computers. 2nd ed. LC 93-72076. 346p. (C). 1994. pap. text ed. 34.75 (0-03-098203-0) Dryden Pr.

— Working with Computers. 2nd ed. LC 93-72076. 285p. (C). 1994. teacher ed, pap. text ed. 70.00 (0-03-098205-7); pap. text ed. 28.50 (0-03-098207-3); 21.50 (0-03-098209-X); 21.50 (0-03-094843-6) Dryden Pr.

— Working with Computers: With Software Tutorials. 2nd ed. LC 93-72075. 747p. (C). 1993. pap. text ed. 43.00 (0-03-098204-9) Dryden Pr.

— Working with Computers with Software Tutorials. 560p. (C). 1991. pap. text ed. 44.75 (0-15-596724-X) Dryden Pr.

McKeown, Patrick G. & Badarinathi, Ravija. Applications Software Tutorials: A Computer Lab Manual Using WordPerfect 5.1, Lotus 1-2-3, dBase III PLUS & dBase IV. 300p. (C). 1993. pap. text ed. 21.00 (0-03-097504-2) Dryden Pr.

McKeown, Patrick G. & Leitch, Robert A. Computerized Test Bank (Macintosh) to Accompany Management Information Systems: Managing with Computers. (C). 1993. teacher ed, disk 21.50 (0-15-501112-X) Dryden Pr.

— Management Information Systems: Managing With Computers. LC 92-72917. 611p. (C). 1993. text ed. 51.00 (0-15-500112-4) Dryden Pr.

— Management Information Systems: Managing With Computers. LC 92-72917. 611p. (C). 1993. disk 14.75 (0-15-500817-X) Dryden Pr.

— Management Information Systems, Managing with Computers: Instructor's Manual. 384p. (C). 1993. pap. text ed., trans. 10.50 (0-15-500813-7) Dryden Pr.

McKeown, Patrick G., jt. auth. see Brown, Robert D.

McKeown, Ross. Learning Mathematics: A Program for Classroom Teachers. LC 89-19961. (Illus.). 139p. (Orig.). 1990. pap. text ed. 15.00 (0-435-08304-X) Heinemann.

McKeown, Roy B. Desperate Street. 68p. (Orig.). 1989. pap. 5.95 (0-939497-19-0) Promise Pub.

***McKeown, Sean.** The General Care & Maintenance of Day Geckos. 143p. 1993. pap. text ed. 18.00 (1-882770-22-6) Adv Vivarium.

McKeown, Shirley M. The Blocking Board: How to Make & Use the Sewing Tool You'll Never Want to Be Without. 52p. 1991. pap. text ed. 11.95 (0-9629970-0-5) S M McKeown.

McKeown, Thomas. The Origins of Human Disease. 1991. pap. 21.95 (0-631-17938-0) Blackwell Pubs.

— The Role of Medicine. LC 79-84025. 180p. 1980. 37.50x (0-691-08235-9); pap. 12.95 (0-691-02362-X) Princeton U Pr.

McKeown, Timothy J. Diplomacy, Force, & Leadership: Essays in Honor of Alexder L. George. Caldwell, Dan, ed. LC 93-19811. 322p. 1993. text ed. 65.00 (0-8133-1745-2) Westview.

McKeown, Timothy J., jt. auth. see Lynn, Leonard H.

McKeown, Tom. Powerful Business Writing: Say What You Mean, Get What You Want. 128p. 1992. pap. 12.95 (0-89879-528-1) Writers Digest.

— Write to Win. (Illus.). 120p. (Orig.). 1991. pap. 12.95 (0-9693134-0-3) Gordon Soules Bk.

McKeown, Tom & Cram, Carol. Better Business Writing: Write to the Point. (Illus.). 276p. (Orig.). 1991. pap. 24.95 (0-9693134-1-1) Gordon Soules Bk.

McKerchar, M. Paper Money Bibliography. 1979. 15.00 (0-686-51600-1) S J Durst.

McKerchar, Marit, jt. auth. see Spellerberg, Ian.

McKercher, B. J. Esme Howard: A Diplomatic Biography. 448p. (C). 1989. 79.95 (0-521-32257-X) Cambridge U Pr.

— The Second Baldwin Government & the United States, 1924-1929: Attitudes & Diplomacy. (International Studies). 272p. 1984. 59.95 (0-521-25802-2) Cambridge U Pr.

McKercher, B. J., ed. Arms Limitation & Disarmament: Restraints on War, 1899-1939. LC 92-1193. 272p. 1992. text ed. 59.95 (0-275-94059-4, C4059, Praeger Pubs) Greenwood.

***McKercher, B. J. & Aronsen, Lawrence, eds.** The North Atlantic Triangle in a Changing World: Anglo-American-Canadian Relations, 1902-1956. 304p. (C). 1995. 55.00 (0-8020-0520-9); pap. 19.95 (0-8020-6957-6) U of Toronto Pr.

McKercher, B. J. & Ion, A. Hamish, eds. Military Heretics: The Unorthodox in Policy & Strategy. LC 93-14116. 256p. 1993. text ed. 57.95 (0-275-94554-5, C4554, Praeger Pubs) Greenwood.

McKercher, B. J., jt. ed. see Errington, Elizabeth J.

McKercher, B. J., jt. ed. see Neilson, Keith.

***McKercher, Beriveth N.** Home Is Where the Heart Is. 88p. (Orig.). Date not set. pap. 8.95 (0-9645488-0-1) B N McKercher.

McKern & Koomsup. Mineral Processing in ASEAN. 1988. pap. text ed. 34.95 (0-04-330384-6, Pub. by Allen Unwin AT) Paul & Co Pubs.

— Minerals Industry of ASEAN. 1988. pap. text ed. 37.95 (0-04-301284-1, Pub. by Allen Unwin AT) Paul & Co Pubs.

McKern, Bruce, ed. The Transnational Corporations & the Exploitation of Natural Resources. LC 93-18760. (United Nations Library on Transnational Corporations: Vol. 10). 1993. write for info. (0-415-08543-8) Routledge.

McKern, Debra & Byrne, Sherry. ALA Target Packet for Preservation Microfilming. LC 91-8677. (Illus.). (C). 1991. pap. text ed. 32.00 (0-8389-7492-9) ALA.

McKern, W. C. Archaeology of Tonga. (BMB Ser.: No. 60). 1972. reprint ed. 25.00 (0-527-02166-0) Periodicals Srv.

McKernan, Brian, ed. see Wiese, Michael.

***McKernan-Cramer, Inc. Staff.** Tim McKernan Barrelman. 144p. 1995. pap. text ed. 15.95 (0-614-06605-0) Kendall-Hunt.

McKernan, James. Curriculum Action Research: A Handbook of Methods & Resources for the Reflective Practitioner. LC 91-21321. 288p. 1991. text ed. 49.95 (0-312-06761-5) St Martin.

McKernan, John. Walking Along the Missouri River. LC 77-8920. (Lost Roads Poetry Ser.: No. 5). 1978. pap. 3.00 (0-918786-09-6) Lost Roads.

— The Writer's Handbook. LC 87-4096. (Illus.). 800p. (C). 1988. pap. text ed. 16.00 (0-03-001582-0) HB Coll Pubs.

— The Writer's Handbook. 2nd ed. 544p. (C). 1991. pap. text ed. 18.75 (0-03-053453-4) HB Coll Pubs.

Mckernan, John R. Making the Grade: Why America Needs a Youth Apprenticeship System to Prepare Students for the... 1994. 19.95 (0-316-56224-6) Little.

McKernan, Llewellyn. Many Water:: Poems from West Virginia. LC 93-27131. (Poetry Ser.: Vol. 7). 1993. pap. 12.95 (0-88946-568-1, Mellen Poetry Pr) E Mellen.

— More Songs of Gladness (Suppl.) (Arch Bks.). (Illus.). 24p. (J). (gr. k-4). 1987. pap. 1.99 (0-570-09004-0, 59-1432) Concordia.

— This Is the Day. (Stardust Ser.). (Illus.). 24p. 1994. 4.50 (0-8378-7690-7) Gibson.

— This Is the Night. (Stardust Ser.). (Illus.). 24p. 1994. 4.50 (0-8378-7691-5) Gibson.

McKernan, Luke. Topical Budget: The Great British Newsfilm. (Illus.). 128p. 1992. 39.95 (0-253-33615-5, Pub. by British Film Inst UK); pap. 16.95 (0-85170-305-4, Pub. by British Film Inst UK) Ind U Pr.

***McKernan, Luke & Terris, Olwen, eds.** Walking Shadows: Shakespeare in the National Film & Television Archive. (Archive Monographs). (Illus.). 280p. 1994. text ed. 45.00 (0-85170-414-X) Ind U Pr.

— Walking Shadows: Shakespeare in the National Film & Television Archive. (Archive Monographs). (Illus.). 280p. 1994. pap. 21.95 (0-85170-486-7) Ind U Pr.

McKernan, Michael, intro. Makers of Australia's Sporting Traditions. (Illus.). 289p. 1993. 39.95 (0-522-84517-7) Intl Spec Bk.

McKernan, Susan, ed. see Vidal, Mary T.

McKernan, Tom, ed. see Jones, Larry K.

McKernan, Victoria. Crooked Island. 288p. 1994. 18.95 (0-88184-998-7) Carroll & Graf.

McKernie, Grant, jt. auth. see Watson, Jack.

McKerns, Joseph P. News Media & Public Policy: An Annotated Bibliography, Vol. 2. Bowman, James, ed. LC 83-49290. (Public Affairs & Administration Ser.). 192p. 1985. lib. bdg. 47.00 (0-8240-9004-7) Garland.

McKerns, Joseph P., ed. Biographical Dictionary of American Journalism. LC 88-25098. 834p. 1989. text ed. 59.95 (0-313-23818-9, MJO, Greenwood Pr) Greenwood.

McKerns, Kenneth W., ed. Regulation of Gene Expression by Hormones. LC 83-6310. (Biochemical Endocrinology Ser.). 278p. 1983. 85.00 (0-306-41204-7, Plenum Pr) Plenum.

— Reproductive Processes & Contraception. LC 80-20744. (Biochemical Endocrinology Ser.). 752p. 1981. 120.00 (0-306-40534-2, Plenum Pr) Plenum.

McKerns, Kenneth W. & Pantic, Vladimir, eds. Hormonally Active Brain Peptides: Stucture & Function. LC 82-9147. (Biochemical Endocrinology Ser.). 652p. 1982. 110.00 (0-306-40865-1, Plenum Pr) Plenum.

McKerns, Kenneth W., jt. ed. see Chretien, M.

McKerns, Kenneth W., ed. see International Foundation for Biochemical Endocrinology Staff.

McKerral, Andrew. The Clan Campbell. 2nd ed. (Johnston & Bacon Clan Histories Ser.). (Illus.). 32p. 1993. reprint ed. pap. 8.95 (0-685-69975-7, 9617) Clearfield Co.

McKerron, Wilhelmina. The Wheel of Destiny. 1981. 20.00 (0-7223-1408-6, Pub. by A H S Ltd UK) St Mut.

McKerrow, jt. auth. see Gronbeck.

McKerrow, Margaret, et al. The Cleverest Lawyer or Pierre Pathlin. (Orig.). 1986. pap. 10.00 (0-88734-506-9) Players Pr.

McKerrow, Paul, ed. see Sumeria Staff.

McKerrow, Phillip. Performance Measurement of Computer Systems. (Illus.). 256p. (C). 1988. text ed. 35.50 (0-201-17436-7) Addison-Wesley.

McKerrow, R. B., ed. A Newe Interlude of Impacyente Pouerte, 1560. (Material for the Study of the Old English Drama Ser.: No. 1, Vol. 33). 1974. reprint ed. 14.00 (0-8115-0282-1) Periodicals Srv.

McKerrow, R. B., jt. ed. see Bang, W.

McKerrow, R. M., ed. see Dekker, Thomas.

McKerrow, Raymie E., jt. auth. see Benjamin, James.

McKerrow, Ronald B. An Introduction to Bibliography for Literary Students. LC 94-7048. (Illus.). 400p. 1994. pap. 29.95 (1-884718-01-9) Oak Knoll.

— Printers' & Publishers' Devices in England & Scotland, 1485-1640. (Bibliographical Society, Illustrated Monographs: Vol. 16). (Illus.). 309p. reprint ed. pap. 88.10 (0-317-28612-9, 2055408) Bks Demand.

— Treatment of Shakespeare's Text by His Earlier Editors, 1709-1768. LC 79-109656. (Select Bibliographies Reprint Ser.). 1977. 15.95 (0-8369-5265-0) Ayer.

***Mckersie, Bryan D.** Stress & Stress Coping in Cultivated Plants. 260p. (C). 1994. lib. bdg. 132.00 (0-7923-2827-2) Kluwer Ac.

McKersie, Robert, jt. ed. see Abraham, Katherine.

McKersie, Robert B., jt. auth. see Walton, Richard E.

McKesney, Thomas L. Indian Tribes of North America: With Biographical Sketches & Anecdotes of the Principal Chiefs, 3 vols. reprint ed. lib. bdg. write for info. (0-7812-0302-3) Rprt Serv.

McKetta. Chemical Processing Handbook. LC 93-20256. 992p. 1993. 225.00 (0-8247-8701-3) Dekker.

— ECPD, Vol. 42. 528p. 1993. 175.00 (0-8247-2492-5) Dekker.

— ECPD, Vol. 43. 552p. 1993. 175.00 (0-8247-2493-3) Dekker.

— ECPD, Vol. 45. 568p. 1993. 175.00 (0-8247-2495-X) Dekker.

— ECPD, Vol. 46. 552p. 1993. 175.00 (0-8247-2496-8) Dekker.

— ECPD, Vol. 48. 496p. 1994. 175.00 (0-8247-2498-4) Dekker.

— ECPD, Vol. 49. 536p. 1994. 175.00 (0-8247-2499-2) Dekker.

— Encyclopedia of Chemical Processes, Vol. 31. 512p. 1989. 175.00 (0-8247-2481-X) Dekker.

— Encyclopedia of Chemical Processes, Vol. 32. 504p. 1989. 175.00 (0-8247-2482-8) Dekker.

— Encyclopedia of Chemical Processes, Vol. 33. 528p. 1990. 175.00 (0-8247-2483-6) Dekker.

— Encyclopedia of Chemical Processing & Design, Vol. 1. 496p. 1976. 175.00 (0-8247-2451-8) Dekker.

— Encyclopedia of Chemical Processing & Design, Vol. 2. 512p. 1977. 175.00 (0-8247-2452-6) Dekker.

— Encyclopedia of Chemical Processing & Design, Vol. 3. 512p. 1977. 175.00 (0-8247-2453-4) Dekker.

— Encyclopedia of Chemical Processing & Design, Vol. 4. 512p. 1977. 175.00 (0-8247-2454-2) Dekker.

— Encyclopedia of Chemical Processing & Design, Vol. 6. 504p. 1978. 175.00 (0-8247-2456-9) Dekker.

— Encyclopedia of Chemical Processing & Design, Vol. 7. 1978. 175.00 (0-8247-2457-7) Dekker.

— Encyclopedia of Chemical Processing & Design, Vol. 8. 526p. 1979. 175.00 (0-8247-2458-5) Dekker.

— Encyclopedia of Chemical Processing & Design, Vol. 9. 496p. 1979. 175.00 (0-8247-2459-3) Dekker.

— Encyclopedia of Chemical Processing & Design, Vol. 10. 464p. 1979. 175.00 (0-8247-2460-7) Dekker.

— Encyclopedia of Chemical Processing & Design, Vol. 11. 518p. 1980. 175.00 (0-8247-2461-5) Dekker.

— Encyclopedia of Chemical Processing & Design, Vol. 12. 408p. 1981. 175.00 (0-8247-2462-3) Dekker.

— Encyclopedia of Chemical Processing & Design, Vol. 13. 408p. 1981. 175.00 (0-8247-2463-1) Dekker.

— Encyclopedia of Chemical Processing & Design, Vol. 14. 504p. 1982. 175.00 (0-8247-2464-X) Dekker.

— Encyclopedia of Chemical Processing & Design, Vol. 15. 488p. 1982. 175.00 (0-8247-2465-8) Dekker.

— Encyclopedia of Chemical Processing & Design, Vol. 16. 456p. 1982. 175.00 (0-8247-2466-6) Dekker.

— Encyclopedia of Chemical Processing & Design, Vol. 17. 488p. 1983. 175.00 (0-8247-2467-4) Dekker.

— Encyclopedia of Chemical Processing & Design, Vol. 18. 512p. 1983. 175.00 (0-8247-2468-2) Dekker.

— Encyclopedia of Chemical Processing & Design, Vol. 19. 480p. 1983. 175.00 (0-8247-2469-0) Dekker.

— Encyclopedia of Chemical Processing & Design, Vol. 20. 520p. 1984. 175.00 (0-8247-2470-4) Dekker.

— Encyclopedia of Chemical Processing & Design, Vol. 23. 528p. 1985. 175.00 (0-8247-2473-9) Dekker.

— Encyclopedia of Chemical Processing & Design, Vol. 24. 520p. 1986. 175.00 (0-8247-2474-7) Dekker.

— Encyclopedia of Chemical Processing & Design, Vol. 25. 504p. 1986. 175.00 (0-8247-2475-5) Dekker.

— Encyclopedia of Chemical Processing & Design, Vol. 26. 520p. 1987. 175.00 (0-8247-2476-3) Dekker.

— Encyclopedia of Chemical Processing & Design, Vol. 28. 520p. 1988. 175.00 (0-8247-2478-X) Dekker.

— Encyclopedia of Chemical Processing & Design, Vol. 29. 528p. 1988. 175.00 (0-8247-2479-8) Dekker.

— Encyclopedia of Chemical Processing & Design, Vol. 30. 528p. 1989. 175.00 (0-8247-2480-1) Dekker.

— Encyclopedia of Chemical Processing & Design, Vol. 35. 520p. 1990. 175.00 (0-8247-2485-2) Dekker.

— Encyclopedia of Chemical Processing & Design, Vol. 36. 568p. 1990. 175.00 (0-8247-2486-0) Dekker.

— Encyclopedia of Chemical Processing & Design, Vol. 37. 520p. 1991. 175.00 (0-8247-2487-9) Dekker.

— Encyclopedia of Chemical Processing & Design, Vol. 38. 544p. 1991. 175.00 (0-8247-2488-7) Dekker.

— Encyclopedia of Chemical Processing & Design, Vol. 39. 528p. 1992. 175.00 (0-8247-2489-5) Dekker.

— Encyclopedia of Chemical Processing & Design, Vol. 41. 536p. 1992. 175.00 (0-8247-2491-7) Dekker.

— Encyclopedia of Chemical Processing & Design, Vol. 47. 528p. 1994. 175.00 (0-8247-2497-6) Dekker.

— Encyclopedia of Chemical Processing & Design, Vol. 52. 500p. 1995. write for info. (0-8247-2603-0) Dekker.

— Encyclopedia of Chemical Processing & Design, Vol.5. 512p. 1978. 175.00 (0-8247-2455-0) Dekker.

— Encyclopedia of Computer Processing & Design, Vol. 34. 420p. 1990. 175.00 (0-8247-2484-4) Dekker.

— Industrial Products Handbook, Vol. 1. 1760p. 1993. 330.00 (0-8247-8709-9) Dekker.

— Industrial Products Handbook, Vol. 2. 1760p. 1993. 330.00 (0-8247-8706-4) Dekker.

— Petroleum Processing Handbook. 792p. 1992. 250.00 (0-8247-8681-5) Dekker.

— Piping Design Handbook. 1280p. 1992. 250.00 (0-8247-8570-3) Dekker.

***McKetta, ed.** ECPD, Vol. 54. 500p. 1995. write for info. (0-8247-2605-7) Dekker.

— Encyclopedia of Chemical Processing & Design, Vol. 40. 528p. 1992. 175.00 (0-8247-2490-9) Dekker.

— Encyclopedia of Computer Processing & Design, Vol. 53. 500p. 1995. write for info. (0-8247-2604-9) Dekker.

McKetta, John, ed. Heat Transfer Design Methods. 640p. 1991. 199.00 (0-8247-8518-5) Dekker.

McKetta, John J. Inorganic Chemicals Handbook, Vol. 1. 1456p. 1993. 370.00 (0-8247-8686-6) Dekker.

— Inorganic Chemicals Handbook, Vol. 2. 1456p. 1993. 370.00 (0-8247-8687-4) Dekker.

McKetta, John J., ed. Unit Operations Handbook, Vol. 1. LC 92-25562. 1017p. 1992. 350.00 (0-8247-8669-6) Dekker.

— Unit Operations Handbook, Vol. 2. LC 92-25562. 742p. 1992. 350.00 (0-8247-8670-X) Dekker.

McKetta, John J., Jr., intro. Chemical Technology: An Encyclopedic Treatment, 8 vols. Incl. Vol. 4. Petroleum & Organic Chemicals. (Illus.). 792p. 1972. Pgs. 792. 68.50 (0-06-491105-5, 06298); Vol. 5. Natural Organic Materials & Related Synthetic Products. (Illus.). 898p. 1972. Pgs. 898. 68.50 (0-06-491106-3, 06299); Vol. 6. Wood, Paper, Textiles, Plastics & Photographic Materials. (Illus.). 686p. 1973. 68.50 (0-06-491107-1, 06300); Vol. 8. Edible Oils & Fats & Animal Food Products: Material Resources. (Illus.). 600p. 1975. Pgs. 600. 68.50 (0-06-491109-8, 06302); (Illus.). write for info. (0-318-51000-6) B&N Imports.

***McKevett, G. A.** Just Desserts. 1995. text ed. 16.95 (0-8217-4924-2) Windsor NY.

McKevitt, David & Lawton, Alan, eds. Public Sector Management: Theory, Critique & Practice. 320p. 1994. 75.00 (0-8039-7712-3); pap. 26.95 (0-8039-7713-1) Sage.

McKevitt, David, jt. ed. see Lawton, Alan.

McKevitt, Gerald. The University of Santa Clara: A History, 1851-1977. LC 78-65396. (Illus.). xii, 385p. 1979. 42.50 (0-8047-1024-4) Stanford U Pr.

***McKevitt, Paul, ed.** Integration of Natural Language & Vision Processing: Computational Models & Systems. LC 95-12. 1995. lib. bdg. write for info. (0-7923-3379-9) Kluwer Ac.

***McKew, Howard J.** Managing People in the HVAC-R Industry. Turpin, Joanna, ed. LC 94-33085. 120p. (Orig.). 1995. pap. 21.95 (0-912524-97-9) Busn News.

***McKew, Robert E., et al.** A Guide to the Consumer Bankruptcy Code. 1994. pap. text ed. 49.95 (0-471-11234-8) Wiley.

McKewin, Robert. Behold the Man. pap. 9.95 (0-910924-95-3) Macalester.

McKey, Eleanor F. Pathways to Yesterday. LC 92-53422. (Illus.). 80p. 1992. 11.00 (0-8233-0481-7) Golden Quill.

McKibben, Alan & McKibben, Susan. Cruising Guide to Lake Champlain. (Illus.). 1986. pap. 16.95 (0-9616412-0-7) Lke Champlain Pub.

— Cruising Guide to Lake Champlain. 2nd ed. (Illus.). 1988. pap. 18.95 (0-9616412-1-5) Lke Champlain Pub.

— Cruising Guide to Lake Champlain. 3rd ed. (Illus.). 1990. text ed. 19.95 (0-9616412-2-3) Lke Champlain Pub.

— Cruising Guide to Lake Champlain. 4th ed. (Illus.). 176p. 1993. pap. write for info. (0-9616412-3-1) Lke Champlain Pub.

McKibben, Bill. The Age of Missing Information. 272p. 1993. pap. 10.95 (0-452-26980-6, Plume) NAL-Dutton.

— The Comforting Whirlwind. 112p. (Orig.). (C). 1994. pap. 8.99 (0-8028-0499-3) Eerdmans.

— The End of Nature. 1990. pap. 10.95 (0-385-41604-0, Anchor Bks) Doubleday.

— The End of Nature. 230p. 1989. 19.95 (0-394-57601-2) Random.

***McKibben, Bill, et al.** Twenty Five Bicycle Tours in the Adirondacks: Road Adventures in the East's Largest Wilderness. (Bicycle Tour Ser.). (Illus.). 160p. (Orig.). 1995. pap. 13.00 (0-88150-318-5, Backcountry) Countryman.

McKibben, Jorge F., tr. see Davis, Guillermo H.

McKibben, Michael T., jt. auth. see Williams, Benjamin D.

McKibben-Stockwell. Nuevo Lexico Griego Espanol. 316p. (SPA.). 1985. reprint ed. pap. 7.95 (0-311-42072-9, Edit Mundo) Casa Bautista.

McKibben, Susan, jt. auth. see McKibben, Alan.

An Asterisk (*) at the beginning of an entry indicates that the title is appearing in BIP for the first time.

McKibbens, Thomas R., Jr. The Forgotten Heritage: A Lineage of Great Baptist Preaching. LC 86-705. (Orig.). 1986. pap. 18.95 (*0-86554-186-8*, MUP-P18) Mercer Univ Pr.

McKibbens, Thomas R., Jr. & Smith, Kenneth. The Life & Work of Morgan Edwards: First Baptist Historian in the United States. Gaustad, Edwin S., ed. LC 79-5269. (Baptist Tradition Ser.). 1980. lib. bdg. 25.95 (*0-405-12438-4*) Ayer.

McKibbin, Brian, et al. Saving Lives. (C). 1991. text ed. 59.95 (*0-255-36269-2*, Pub. by Inst Economic Affairs UK) St Mut.

McKibbin, Carroll R. In Pursuit of National Interests. 2nd ed. 256p. 1993. per. 20.76 (*0-8403-8453-X*) Kendall-Hunt.

McKibbin, Frank, jt. auth. see McKibbin, Jean.

McKibbin, Jean & McKibbin, Frank. Cookbook of Foods from Bible Days. 128p. 1993. pap. 4.99 (*0-88368-319-9*) Whitaker Hse.

— Cookbook of Foods from Bible Days. enl. rev. ed. LC 72-88527. (Illus.). 1972. reprint ed. 15.95 (*0-9601078-1-9*) Franje CA.

McKibbin, L. S. Vadecum del Cuidador de Caballos. pap. write for info. (*0-8288-7896-X*) Fr & Eur.

McKibbin, Lawrence, jt. auth. see Porter, Lyman W.

***McKibbin, Martin H., ed.** What If? Exploring the Paths Not Taken in American History. (Illus.). 1995. 20.00 (*0-9641651-1-2*) Sparrowhwk Pr.

McKibbin, Nonie. The Sea in the Desert: Explorer's Guide to the Gulf of California Seaside. Thomson, Jenean et al, eds. (Illus.). 130p. (Orig.). 1989. 10.00 (*0-685-34742-7*) Golden Puffer.

McKibbin, Nonie, jt. auth. see Thomson, Donald A.

McKibbin, Ross. The Ideologies of Class: Social Relations in Britain 1880-1950. 320p. 1994. reprint ed. pap. 23.00 (*0-19-820511-2*) OUP.

McKibbin, Warwick J. & Sachs, Jeffrey D. Global Linkages: Macroeconomic Interdependence & Cooperation in the World Economy. 277p. 1991. 34.95 (*0-8157-5600-3*); pap. 14.95 (*0-8157-5601-1*) Brookings.

***McKibbon, W. Stan.** The Anointed One: Messiah. 215p. (Orig.). 1994. pap. write for info. (*0-9642975-0-7*) S McKibbon Min.

***McKie.** Noah's Ark. 1995. 4.99 (*0-679-86654-X*) Random.

McKie, C., jt. auth. see McKie, D.

McKie, D. & McKie, C. Chemistry & Physics of Crystalline Solids. 1994. pap. write for info. (*0-632-01661-2*) Blackwell Sci.

— Essentials of Crystallography. 1986. pap. 46.95 (*0-632-01574-8*) Blackwell Sci.

McKie, David & Cook, Christopher. The Decade of Disillusion: Britain in the Sixties. LC 72-83416. 1972. text ed. 29.95 (*0-312-18900-1*) St Martin.

McKie, David, jt. auth. see McKie, Jyoti.

McKie, Douglas. Antoine Lavoisier. (Series in Science). (Illus.). 448p. 1990. reprint ed. pap. 14.95 (*0-306-80408-5*) Da Capo.

McKie, Douglas & De Heathcote, Niels. The Discovery of Specific & Latent Heats. LC 74-26274. (History, Philosophy & Sociology of Science Ser.). 1975. reprint ed. 21.95 (*0-405-06602-3*) Ayer.

McKie, Douglas, jt. auth. see Partington, James R.

McKie, James D., ed. Social Responsibility & the Business Predicament. LC 74-23967. (Studies in the Regulation of Economic Activity). 361p. 1975. 38.95 (*0-8157-5608-9*); pap. 16.95 (*0-8157-5607-0*) Brookings.

McKie, Jyoti & McKie, David. The Healing Earth Tarot: A Journey in Self-Discovery, Empowerment & Planetary Healing. LC 94-26218. (Illus.). 232p. 1994. pap. 34.95 (*1-56718-454-5*) Llewellyn Pubns.

McKie, Ronald. The Emergence of Malaysia. LC 72-13868. (Illus.). 310p. 1973. reprint ed. text ed. 65.00 (*0-8371-6763-9*, MCEM, Greenwood Pr) Greenwood.

McKie, Roy. The Joke Book. LC 78-62699. (Pictureback Ser.). (Illus.). (J). (ps-2). 1979. pap. 2.25 (*0-394-84077-1*) Random Bks Yng Read.

— The Riddle Book. LC 77-85237. (Pictureback Ser.). (J). (ps-2). 1978. lib. bdg. 5.99 (*0-394-93732-5*); pap. 2.50 (*0-394-83732-0*) Random Bks Yng Read.

McKie, Roy & Eastman, Philip D. Snow. LC 62-15114. (Illus.). 72p. (J). (gr. 1-2). 1962. 7.99 (*0-394-80027-3*); lib. bdg. 7.99 (*0-394-90027-8*) Beginner.

McKie, Roy, jt. auth. see Beard, Henry.

***Mckie, Simon.** Roll-Over Relief on Reinvestment. 140p. 1993. pap. text ed. 48.00 (*0-406-02800-1*, UK) Butterworth Legal Pubs.

McKie, William L. Scientific Hydrotherapy. 134p. 1993. reprint ed. spiral bd. 8.80 (*0-7873-0599-5*) Mokelumne.

McKiernan, Dennis. The Brega Path. 1987. pap. 4.99 (*0-451-45241-0*, ROC) NAL-Dutton.

Mckiernan, Dennis. Dragondoom. 1990. mass mkt. 5.99 (*0-553-28337-5*, Spectra) Bantam.

McKiernan, Dennis, et al. Citybook 4: On the Road. Jaquays, Paul, ed. & illus. by. 96p. 1990. pap. 11.95 (*0-940244-73-X*) Flying Buffalo.

McKiernan, Dennis L. The Brega Path. 272p. 1987. pap. 3.95 (*0-451-16645-0*, Sig) NAL-Dutton.

— Caverns of Socrates. LC 95-9856. 1995. pap. 24.95 (*0-451-45455-3*, ROC) NAL-Dutton.

— The Dark Tide. (Iron Tower Trilogy Ser.: No. 1). 304p. 1985. pap. 4.50 (*0-451-45102-3*, Sig) NAL-Dutton.

— The Darkest Day. (Iron Tower Trilogy Ser.: Bk. 3). 304p. 1985. pap. 4.50 (*0-451-45083-3*, ROC) NAL-Dutton.

— The Eye of the Hunter. LC 92-8544. 624p. 1992. 15.00 (*0-451-45179-1*, ROC); pap. 25.00 (*0-451-45229-1*, ROC) NAL-Dutton.

— The Eye of the Hunter. 592p. 1993. pap. 5.99 (*0-451-45268-2*, ROC) NAL-Dutton.

— Shadows of Doom. (Iron Tower Trilogy Ser.: Bk. 2). 304p. 1987. pap. 4.50 (*0-451-45103-1*, Sig) NAL-Dutton.

— Tales of Mithgar. LC 93-49356. 240p. 1994. 19.95 (*0-451-45410-3*, ROC); pap. 8.95 (*0-451-45430-8*, ROC) NAL-Dutton.

— Trek to Kraagen-Cor. (Silver Call Duolog Ser.: No. 1). 1987. pap. 2.95 (*0-451-14787-1*, Sig) NAL-Dutton.

— Trek to Kraagen-Cor. (Silver Call Duology Ser.: No. 1). (YA). (gr. 9-12). 1989. pap. 3.95 (*0-451-15563-7*, Sig) NAL-Dutton.

— Trek to Kraggen-Cor. (Silver Call Duology Ser.: No. 1). 256p. 1987. pap. 4.99 (*0-451-45165-1*, ROC) NAL-Dutton.

— Voyage of the Fox Rider. LC 93-3797. (Orig.). 1993. 25.00 (*0-451-45279-8*, ROC); pap. 15.00 (*0-451-45284-4*, ROC) NAL-Dutton.

— Voyage of the Fox Rider. 592p. (Orig.). 1994. pap. 5.99 (*0-451-45411-1*, ROC) NAL-Dutton.

McKiernan, Dennis L., et al. The Magic of Christmas: Holiday Stories of Fantasy & Science Fiction. 224p. (Orig.). 1992. pap. 4.99 (*0-451-45190-2*, ROC) NAL-Dutton.

McKiernan, Ethna. Caravan. LC 89-71292. (Illus.). 80p. (Orig.). 1989. pap. 5.95 (*0-935697-04-7*) Midwest Villages.

— Caravan. (Orig.). (C). 1990. pap. 15.00 (*0-948268-55-7*, Pub. by Dedalus Pr IE) St Mut.

McKiernan, F. Mark & Launius, Roger D., eds. Missouri Folk Heroes of the Nineteenth Century. (Illus.). 1989. pap. 15.00 (*0-8309-0547-2*) Herald Hse.

McKiernan, Peter. Strategies of Growth: Maturity, Recovery & Internationalization. 1992. pap. 16.95 (*0-415-05677-2*, Pub. by Tavistock UK) Routledge Chapman & Hall.

***McKillen, Elizabeth.** Chicago Labor & the Quest for a Democratic Diplomacy, 1914-1924. 256p. 1995. 35.00x (*0-8014-2905-6*) Cornell U Pr.

McKillip, Jack. Need Analysis: Tools for the Human Services & Education. (Applied Social Research Methods Ser.: Vol. 10). 160p. 1987. text ed. 37.00 (*0-8039-2647-2*); pap. text ed. 16.95 (*0-8039-2648-0*) Sage.

McKillip, Patricia. The House on Parchment Street. LC 90-27119. (Illus.). 192p. (J). (gr. 3-7). 1991. reprint ed. pap. 3.95 (*0-689-71471-8*, Aladdin Paperbacks) S&S Childrens.

***McKillip, Patricia A.** The Book of Atrix Wolfe. LC 94-33999. 256p. 1995. text ed. 24.50 (*0-441-00211-0*) Ace Bks.

— The Changeling Sea. 160p. 1989. mass mkt. 4.99 (*0-345-36040-0*, Del Rey) Ballantine.

— The Cygnet & the Firebird. LC 92-21149. 240p. (Orig.). 1993. pap. 17.95 (*0-441-12628-6*) Ace Bks.

— Harpist in the Wind, No. 3. 1985. mass mkt. 4.99 (*0-345-32440-4*) Ballantine.

— Heir of Sea & Fire, No. 2. 1987. mass mkt. 4.99 (*0-345-35184-3*, Del Rey) Ballantine.

— Riddlemaster of Hed, No. 1. 1985. mass mkt. 5.99 (*0-345-33104-4*) Ballantine.

— Something Rich & Strange. LC 94-11546. 1994. pap. 19.95 (*0-553-09674-5*) Bantam.

— Sorceress & the Cygnet. 1992. mass mkt. 4.99 (*0-441-77567-5*) Ace Bks.

Mckillip, Rebecca. Art Nouveau Abstract Designs. (International Design Library). (Illus.). 48p. (Orig.). 1983. pap. 5.95 (*0-88045-023-1*) Stemmer Hse.

McKillip, Rebecca. The Celtic Design Book. (International Design Library). (Illus.). 48p. (Orig.). 1981. pap. 5.95 (*0-916144-75-5*) Stemmer Hse.

— Pennsylvania Dutch Designs. (International Design Library). (Illus.). 48p. (Orig.). 1983. pap. 5.95 (*0-88045-032-0*) Stemmer Hse.

McKillip, William D., ed. see Pyshkalo, A. M.

McKillop, A. Aliphatic Chemistry, Vol. 2. 1972. 41.00 (*0-85186-512-7*, Pub. by Royal Soc Chem UK) Am Chemical.

— Aliphatic Chemistry, Vol. 3. 1973. 43.00 (*0-85186-542-9*, Pub. by Royal Soc Chem UK) Am Chemical.

— Aliphatic Chemistry, Vol. 4. 1974. 45.00 (*0-85186-572-0*, Pub. by Royal Soc Chem UK) Am Chemical.

— Aliphatic Chemistry, Vol. 5. 1975. 61.00 (*0-85186-602-6*, Pub. by Royal Soc Chem UK) Am Chemical.

McKillop, A. B. Contours of Canadian Thought. 163p. 1987. 14.95 (*0-8020-6652-6*); 30.00 (*0-8020-5740-3*) U of Toronto Pr.

— A Disciplined Intelligence: Critical Inquiry & Canadian Thought in the Victorian Era. 1979. 44.95 (*0-7735-0343-9*, Pub. by McGill CN) U of Toronto Pr.

— Matters of Mind: The University in Ontario 1791-1951. (Ontario Historical Studies). 776p. (C). 1994. 75.00 (*0-8020-0424-5*); pap. 35.00 (*0-8020-7216-X*) U of Toronto Pr.

McKillop, Alan D. The Early Masters of English Fiction. LC 79-16753. (Illus.). 233p. 1980. reprint ed. text ed. 35.00 (*0-313-21291-0*, MCEE, Greenwood Pr) Greenwood.

— English Literature from Dryden to Burns. (Illus.). 1948. 76.50 (*0-89197-145-9*) Irvington.

— English Literature from Dryden to Burns. 1988. reprint ed. lib. bdg. 69.00 (*0-7812-0054-7*) Rprt Serv.

— English Literature from Dryden to Burns. reprint ed. 69.00 (*0-403-04048-5*) Somerset Pub.

McKillop, Beth, jt. auth. see Ellis, David.

***McKillop, Debra.** Whodunnit. Date not set. pap. write for info. (*0-679-44143-3*) Random.

McKillop, Donal. Building Societies: Structure, Performance & Change. 272p. (C). 1993. lib. bdg. 69.00 (*1-85333-880-X*, Pub. by Graham & Trotman UK) Kluwer Ac.

McKillop, Donal G. & Hutchinson, Robert W. 68.95nal Financial Sectors in the British Isles. 188p. 1990. text ed. 68.95 (*1-85628-091-8*, Pub. by Avebury Pub UK) Ashgate Pub Co.

McKillop, J. H. & Fogelman, I., eds. Benign & Malignant Bone Disease. (Illus.). 160p. 1991. text ed. 30.00 (*0-443-04436-8*) Churchill.

McKillop, Laurene T., ed. see Shapiro, Susan.

***McKillp, Patricia A.** The Cygnet & the Firebird. 320p. Date not set. pap. text ed. 5.99 (*0-441-00237-4*) Ace Bks.

Mckim. Architecture of McKim Mead & White in Photographs Plans & Elevations. 1990. pap. 21.95 (*0-486-26556-0*) Dover.

McKim, et al. Monograph of the Work of McKim, Mead & White: 1879-1915. LC 75-152624. 1972. 55.95 (*0-405-08770-5*, Pub. by Blom Pubns UK) Ayer.

McKim, C. Lee, jt. auth. see Herrick, Clyde N.

McKim, Donald & Wright, David F. Encyclopedia of the Reformed Faith. 384p. (C). 1992. 90.00 (*0-685-60712-7*, Pub. by St Andrew UK) St Mut.

— Encyclopedia of the Reformed Faith. 384p. 1993. 85.00 (*0-7152-0660-5*) St Mut.

McKim, Donald K. The Bible in Theology & Preaching. LC 93-30549. 224p. (Orig.). 1994. pap. 12.95 (*0-687-44611-2*) Abingdon.

— Ramism in William Perkins' Theology. (American University Studies: Theology & Religion: Ser. VII, Vol. 15). 249p. (C). 1987. text ed. 38.90 (*0-8204-0285-0*) P Lang Pubs.

— Theological Turning Points: Major Issues in Christian Thought. LC 88-45432. 240p. 1988. pap. 15.99 (*0-8042-0702-X*) Westminster John Knox.

McKim, Donald K., ed. Encyclopedia of the Reformed Faith. 414p. 1992. 37.00 (*0-664-21882-2*) Westminster John Knox.

— How Karl Barth Changed My Mind. LC 86-19655. 196p. (Orig.). reprint ed. pap. 55.90 (*0-8357-4365-9*, 2037194) Bks Demand.

— Major Themes in the Reformed Tradition. fac. ed. LC 91-36867. 467p. 1992. reprint ed. per., pap. 133.10 (*0-7837-7964-X*, 204772000008) Bks Demand.

McKim, Elizabeth. Boat of the Dream. (Illus.). 108p. (Orig.). 1988. pap. 9.95 (*0-944941-01-X*) Talking Stone Pr.

— Body India. (Illus.). 56p. 1981. 12.95 (*0-938756-04-4*); pap. 6.95 (*0-938756-03-6*) Yellow Moon.

McKim, Elizabeth & Steinbergh, Judith W. Beyond Words, Writing Poems with Children: A Guide for Parents & Teachers. rev. ed. LC 82-70442. 152p. 1992. reprint ed. pap. text ed. 14.95 (*0-944941-03-6*) Talking Stone Pr.

McKim, Elizabeth, jt. auth. see Steinbergh, Judith.

McKim, John. Fly Tying: Adventures in Fur, Feathers, & Fun. LC 82-2077. (Illus.). 158p. (Orig.). 1986. reprint ed. pap. 15.00 (*0-87842-140-8*) Mountain Pr.

McKim, LindaJo. Presbyterian Hymnal Companion. LC 92-17830. 368p. (Orig.). 1993. pap. 22.99 (*0-664-25180-3*) Westminster John Knox.

McKim, Margaret G. The Reading of Verbal Material in Ninth Grade Algebra. LC 71-177032. (Columbia University. Teachers College. Contributions to Education Ser.: No. 850). reprint ed. 22.50 (*0-404-55850-X*) AMS Pr.

McKim, Musa. Alone with the Moon. 1994. per. 12.00 (*0-935724-67-2*) Figures.

McKim, Priscilla, ed. Let Your Light Shine: Pioneer Women Educators of Wyoming. 2nd ed. LC 84-63062. (Illus.). 182p. 1985. write for info. (*0-930535-01-4*) Rustler Print & Pub.

McKim, Randolph. Soldier's Recollections: Leaves from the Diary of a Confederate. 1983. reprint ed. 21.95 (*0-89201-104-1*) Zenger Pub.

McKim, Richard, tr. see Dragesco, Jean.

McKim, Robert H. Experiences in Visual Thinking. 2nd ed. LC 80-437. (C). 1980. pap. 30.95 (*0-8185-0411-0*) PWS Pubs.

McKim, Ruby S. One Hundred & One Patchwork Patterns. (Illus.). 15.75 (*0-8446-1711-3*) Peter Smith.

— One Hundred & One Patchwork Patterns. rev. ed. (Illus.). 1962. pap. 3.95 (*0-486-20773-0*) Dover.

McKim-Smith, Gridley. Examining Velazquez. LC 87-31872. (C). 1988. text ed. 45.00 (*0-300-03615-9*) Yale U Pr.

McKim, William A. Drugs & Behavior. 2nd ed. 352p. 1990. pap. text ed. 38.80 (*0-13-221532-2*) P-H.

McKinght, Bob. How to Pick Winning Horses. 1980. pap. 5.00 (*0-87980-266-9*) Wilshire.

McKinion, J. M., jt. ed. see Goodenough, J. L.

McKinlay, A. F. Thermoluminescence Dosimetry. (Medical Physics Handbooks Ser.: No. 5). (Illus.). 170p. 1981. 49.00 (*0-85274-520-6*) IOP Pub.

McKinlay, A. F., et al. Hazards of Optical Radiation: A Guide to Sources, Uses & Safety. (Illus.). 136p. 1988. 49.00 (*0-85274-265-7*) IOP Pub.

McKinlay, Alan & Morris, R. J., eds. The I. L. P. on Clydeside, Eighteen Ninety-Three to Nineteen Thirty-Two: From Foundation to Disintegration. LC 90-6291. 256p. 1991. text ed. 59.95 (*0-7190-2706-3*, Pub. by Manchester Univ Pr UK) St Martin.

McKinlay, Alan, jt. auth. see Starkey, Ken.

McKinlay, John, ed. Issues in the Political Economy of Health Care. 275p. 1984. 29.95 (*0-422-78040-5*, NO. 9330); pap. 14.95 (*0-422-78050-2*, NO. 9184) Routledge Chapman & Hall.

McKinlay, John B., jt. ed. see Hafferty, Fredric W.

Mckinlay, Robert. Third World Military Expenditure: A Political Economy Approach. 250p. 1992. 49.00 (*0-86187-721-7*, Pub. by Pinter Pubs UK) St Martin.

McKinlay, Robert D. & Little, Richard. Global Problems & World Order. LC 86-40489. 292p. 1987. pap. text ed. 15.50 (*0-299-11384-1*) U of Wis Pr.

McKinlay, Robert D. & Mughan, A. Aid & Arms to the Third World: The Distribution & Impact of U. S. Official Transfers. LC 83-40612. 280p. 1984. text ed. 39.95 (*0-312-01481-3*) St Martin.

McKinlay, S. L. Scottish Golf & Golfers. 203p. 1992. lib. bdg. 28.00 (*0-940889-37-4*) Classics Golf.

McKinley. Vegetable Crop Pests. 1992. 93.95 (*0-8493-7729-3*, SB608) CRC Pr.

McKinley, Ann. Two Quartets: Party of Four & Melodie for Recorders. (Contemporary Consort Ser.: No. 14). i, 18p. 1991. 8.00 (*1-56571-032-0*) PRB Prods.

McKinley, Archibald C. The Journal of Archibald C. McKinley. Humphries, Robert L., ed. LC 90-39090. 304p. 1991. 30.00 (*0-8203-1187-1*) U of Ga Pr.

McKinley, Bonam. Digital Concepts, Experiments for Troubleshooting. (C). 1993. 15.00 (*1-56870-105-5*) RonJon Pub.

McKinley, Brett, jt. auth. see Denver, Shad.

***McKinley, Catherine E. & DeLaney, L. Joyce, eds.** Afrekete: An Anthology of Contemporary Black Lesbian Writings. 1995. 27.95 (*0-385-47354-0*, Anchor NY); pap. 14.00 (*0-385-47355-9*, Anchor NY) Doubleday.

McKinley, Charles & Frase, Robert W. Launching Social Security: A Capture-&-Record Account, 1935-1937. LC 70-121771. 543p. reprint ed. pap. 154.80 (*0-8357-6782-5*, 2035459) Bks Demand.

***McKinley, Douglas.** The Open Road. LC 95-60356. 320p. 1995. 22.00 (*0-9619380-1-3*) Balboa Bks.

McKinley, E. H. Somebody's Brother: A History of the Salvation Army Men's Social Service Department 1891-1985. LC 86-8604. (Studies in American Religion: Vol. 21). 275p. 1986. lib. bdg. 89.95 (*0-88946-665-3*) E Mellen.

McKinley, Edward H. Marching to Glory. 290p. reprint ed. pap. 8.95 (*0-86544-039-5*) Salv Army Suppl South.

— Marching to Glory: The History of the Salvation Army in the United States, 1880-1992. 2nd ed. 440p. 1995. 24.99 (*0-8028-3761-1*) Eerdmans.

McKinley, James. Acts of Love. LC 87-708. 160p. 1987. 17.95 (*0-932576-47-8*); pap. 8.95 (*0-932576-67-2*) Breitenbush Bks.

— The Fickleman Suite & Other Stories. LC 92-4515. 184p. (Orig.). 1993. 22.95 (*1-55728-238-2*); pap. 16.95 (*1-55728-239-0*) U of Ark Pr.

— New Letters, Vol. 53, No. 3. (Illus.). 128p. 1987. pap. 4.00 (*0-317-64815-2*) New Letters MO.

— New Letters, Fall 1986, Vol. 53, No. 1. (Illus.). 119p. 1986. pap. 4.00 (*0-317-62345-1*) New Letters MO.

— New Letters, Winter 1986, Vol. 53, No. 2. (Illus.). 126p. 1986. pap. 4.00 (*0-317-62347-8*) New Letters MO.

McKinley, James, et al, eds. New Letters, Fall 1987, Vol. 54, No. 1. (Illus.). 126p. 1987. write for info. (*0-318-62726-4*) New Letters MO.

McKinley, James L., jt. auth. see Bent, Ralph D.

McKinley, Joe W. Fundamentals of Stress Analysis. (Illus.). 580p. 1979. 62.95 (*0-916460-24-X*, Matrix Pubs Inc) Weber Systems.

McKinley, John & Barrickman, John. Strategic Credit Risk Management. LC 93-35888. (Illus.). 120p. (Orig.). 1994. pap. text ed. 50.00 (*0-936742-98-4*, 31176) Robt Morris Assocs.

McKinley, John E. How to Analyze Your Bank's Credit Culture. Burke, Sarah A., ed. 60p. (Orig.). 1990. pap. text ed. 81.00 (*0-936742-75-5*, 31171) Robt Morris Assocs.

McKinley, John E., III, et al. Problem Loan Strategies. LC 84-27222. (Illus.). 168p. (Orig.). 1985. pap. text ed. 53.00 (*0-936742-20-8*) Robt Morris Assocs.

McKinley, Kenneth F. Saisir le Plan - Scanning the Plan: Old Testament Survey. (Illus.). 210p. (FRE.). 1991. reprint ed. pap. 10.00 (*0-9630161-0-5*) Bible Study Min.

— Scanning the Plan Vol. 1: Old Testament Survey. (Illus.). 210p. 1995. reprint ed. pap. 10.00 (*0-9630161-1-3*) Bible Study Min.

McKinley, Marvin. Wheels of Farm Progress. LC 80-68925. (Illus.). 160p. 1980. pap. 13.95 (*0-916150-24-0*, HO680) Am Soc Ag Eng.

McKinley, Mary B. Words in a Corner: Studies in Montaigne's Latin Quotations. LC 80-70810. (French Forum Monographs: No. 26). 129p. (Orig.). 1981. pap. 10.95 (*0-917058-25-9*) French Forum.

McKinley, Mary B., jt. ed. see Frame, Donald M.

McKinley, Mary B., jt. ed. see Lyons, John D.

McKinley, Mary B., jt. ed. see Rubin, David L.

McKinley, Michael. How to Attract Birds. Burke, Ken, ed. LC 82-63125. (Illus.). 96p. (Orig.). 1983. pap. 9.95 (*0-89721-011-5*) Ortho Info.

***Mckinley, Michael, ed.** The Gulf War: Critical Perspectives. 224p. 1995. pap. 24.95 (*1-86373-606-9*) Paul & Co Pubs.

***Mckinley, Michael & Dennis, John.** How to Attract Birds. rev. ed. Smith, Michael D. & Wood, Jessie, eds. LC 94-67709. (Illus.). 96p. (Orig.). 1995. pap. 9.95 (*0-89721-275-4*, UPC05400A) Ortho Info.

Mckinley, Michael, jt. auth. see Sinnes, A. Cort.

McKinley, Michael P. Keeping Alive. 1984. pap. 6.00 (*0-9610370-7-5*) Thinking Pubns.

McKinley, Mike, jt. auth. see Sinnes, A. Cort.

McKinley, Nancy, jt. auth. see Larson, Vicki L.

McKinley, Nancy L. Signs of Survival. (SOS Ser.: No. I). (Illus.). (YA). (gr. 5-12). 1986. Box 30 4x6 cards. 15.00 (*0-930599-10-1*) Thinking Pubns.

— Signs of Survival. (SOS Ser.: No. II). (Illus.). (YA). (gr. 5-12). 1987. Box 30 4x6 cards. 15.00 (*0-930599-15-2*) Thinking Pubns.

— Signs of Survival. (SOS Ser.: No. III). (Illus.). (YA). (gr. 5-12). 1991. 15.00 (*0-930599-69-1*) Thinking Pubns.

McKinley, Nancy L. & Schwartz, Linda. Make-It-Yourself Barrier Activities. 210p. (J). (gr. k-12). 1987. pap. 33.00 (*0-930599-16-0*) Thinking Pubns.

— Referential Communication: Barrier Activities for Speakers & Listeners, 2 pts., Pt. I. 100p. (Orig.). (J). (gr. k-8). 1985. pap. text ed. 85.00 (*0-930599-00-4*) Thinking Pubns.

M

— Referential Communication: Barrier Activities for Speakers & Listeners, 2 pts., Pt. II. 100p. (Orig.). (YA). (gr. 5 up). 1985. 89.00 (*0-930599-01-2*) Thinking Pubns.
McKinley, Nancy L., jt. auth. see **Larson, Vicki L.**
McKinley, Nancy L., jt. auth. see **Schwartz, Linda.**
McKinley, Olive, tr. see **Garst, Hitjo.**
McKinley, P. Michael. Pre-Revolutionary Caracas: Politics, Economy & Society 1777-1811. (Cambridge Latin American Studies: No. 56). (Illus.). 232p. 1986. 69.95 (*0-521-30450-4*) Cambridge U Pr.
McKinley, Robert. Personal Peace: Transcending Your Interpersonal Limits. 1989. 24.95 (*0-934986-58-4*); pap. 11.95 (*0-934986-57-6*) New Harbinger.
— Sculpting Dolls in Paperclay. Campbell, Barbara, ed. LC 94-66878. 76p. (Orig.). 1994. pap. text ed. 24.95 (*0-916809-78-1*) Scott Pubns MI.
McKinley, Robert B. Bankcard Barometer 91. 200p. (Orig.). (C). 1991. pap. text ed. 385.00 (*0-943329-72-8*) RAM Res Pub.
— Bankcard Barometer 91, No. 1: Cumulative Supplement. rev. ed. 50p. (C). 1991. pap. text ed. 120.00 (*0-943329-73-6*) RAM Res Pub.
— Bankcard Barometer 91, No. 2: Cumulative Supplement. rev. ed. 50p. (C). 1991. pap. text ed. 120.00 (*0-943329-74-4*) RAM Res Pub.
— Bankcard Barometer 91, No. 3: Cumulative Supplement. rev. ed. 50p. (C). 1991. pap. text ed. 120.00 (*0-943329-75-2*) RAM Res Pub.
— Bankcard Barometer 91, No. 4: Cumulative Supplement. rev. ed. 50p. (C). 1991. pap. text ed. 120.00 (*0-943329-76-0*) RAM Res Pub.
— Bankcard Barometer 93. 1000p. (C). 1993. pap. text ed. 995.00 (*0-943329-80-9*) RAM Res Pub.
— Cardsearch 91. 32p. (Orig.). (gr. 12). 1991. pap. text ed. 25.00 (*0-943329-77-9*) RAM Res Pub.
— Cardsearch 91. rev. ed. 32p. (Orig.). 1991. pap. text ed. 25.00 (*0-943329-78-7*) RAM Res Pub.
— Cardsearch 92. 1991. pap. text ed. 39.95 (*0-943329-79-5*) RAM Res Pub.
— Cardsearch 93. 100p. 1993. pap. text ed. 50.00 (*0-943329-81-7*) RAM Res Pub.
McKinley, Robert K. Dollmaking - One Artist's Approach. Nelson, Linda, ed. 166p. (Orig.). 1991. teacher ed write for info. (*0-9628821-0-0*) McKinley Bk.
McKinley, Robert L. The Complete Neuroticist. 125p. 1969. 12.50 (*0-9609644-1-X*) Candle Bks.
— The Neurotic's Handbook. 131p. (C). 1977. pap. 10.00 (*0-9609644-0-1*) Candle Bks.
McKinley, Robin. Beauty: A Retelling of the Story of Beauty & the Beast. LC 77-25636. 256p. (YA). (gr. 7-9). 1978. 16.00 (*0-06-024149-7*); lib. bdg. 15.89 (*0-06-024150-0*) HarpC Child Bks.
— Beauty: A Retelling of the Story of Beauty & the Beast. LC 77-25636. (Trophy Bk.). 256p. (J). (gr. 5 up). 1993. pap. 4.95 (*0-06-440477-3*, Trophy) HarpC Child Bks.
— Blue Sword. mass mkt. 4.99 (*0-441-06880-4*) Ace Bks.
— The Blue Sword. LC 82-2895. 288p. (YA). (gr. 7 up). 1982. 16.00 (*0-688-00938-7*) Greenwillow.
— Deerskin. LC 92-18460. 1993. 17.95 (*0-441-14226-5*) Ace Bks.
— Deerskin. 320p. 1994. pap. text ed. 4.99 (*0-441-00069-X*) Ace Bks.
— The Door in the Hedge. 1984. mass mkt. 4.99 (*0-441-15315-1*) Ace Bks.
— The Door in the Hedge. LC 80-21903. 224p. (J). (gr. 7 up). 1981. 11.75 (*0-688-00312-5*) Greenwillow.
— The Hero & the Crown. (J). 1987. mass mkt. 4.99 (*0-441-32809-1*) Ace Bks.
— The Hero & the Crown. LC 84-4074. 256p. (J). (gr. 7 up). 1984. 16.00 (*0-688-02593-5*) Greenwillow.
— Imaginary Lands. LC 85-21867. 160p. (J). (gr. 7 up). 1986. 11.75 (*0-688-05213-4*) Greenwillow.
— A Knot in the Grain & Other Stories. LC 93-17557. 208p. (J). (gr. 6 up). 1994. 14.00 (*0-688-09201-2*) Greenwillow.
— My Father Is in the Navy. LC 91-12566. 24p. (J). (ps up). 1992. 14.00 (*0-688-10639-0*); lib. bdg. 13.93 (*0-688-10640-4*) Greenwillow.
— Outlaws of Sherwood. LC 88-45227. 256p. (J). (gr. 7 up). 1988. 12.95 (*0-688-07178-3*) Greenwillow.
— The Outlaws of Sherwood. 1989. mass mkt. 4.99 (*0-441-64451-1*) Ace Bks.
— Rowan. LC 91-31809. (Illus.). 24p. (J). (ps-4). 1992. 14.00 (*0-688-10682-X*); lib. bdg. 13.93 (*0-688-10683-8*) Greenwillow.
— The Stone Fey. LC 95-3915. (Illus.). 1996. write for info. (*0-15-200017-8*) HarBrace.
McKinley, Rusty. The Complete Partner Stunt Book. (Illus.). 208p. (Orig.). 1982. pap. 14.95 (*0-914338-05-6*) Regmar Pub.
McKinley, Sarah, ed. see **McGranaghan, Edmund.**
***McKinley, Terry.** The Distribution of Wealth in Rural China. (Socialism & Social Movements Ser.). 256p. 1995. 65.00 (*1-56324-614-7*); pap. 27.50 (*1-56324-615-5*) M E Sharpe.
McKinley, Terry, jt. auth. see **Griffin, Keith.**
McKinnell, F. H., et al, eds. Forest Management in Australia. 386p. (C). 1991. text ed. 160.00 (*0-949324-36-1*, Pub. by Surrey Beatty & Sons AT) St Mut.
McKinnell, Robert G. Cloning: Of Frogs, Mice & Other Animals. rev. ed. LC 84-7514. (Illus.). 158p. (C). 1985. text ed. 15.95 (*0-8166-1360-5*) U of Minn Pr.
McKinney. Endosteal Dental Implants. (SPA.). 1993. 75.70 (*84-8086-062-6*) Mosby Yr Bk.
— Exercises in Invertebrate Paleontology. 1991. pap. 32.95 (*0-86542-074-2*) Blackwell Sci.
— Ground She Walks Upon. 1995. mass mkt. (*0-440-21579-X*) Dell.
— Walking Death Valley. Date not set. pap. 11.00 (*0-06-258515-0*, PL) HarpC.
McKinney, ed. see **Dirksen & Reves.**
McKinney, ed. see **Dirksen.**
McKinney, et al. Mediator Communication Competencies. 1993. pap. 19.95 (*0-685-65895-3*) Burgess MN Intl.
McKinney & McKinney Staff. The Texas Big Debt Survival Guide. 1988. 1988. pap. 19.95 (*0-9620366-0-9*) Marshall TX.
***McKinney, Anne.** Resumes & Cover Letters That Have Worked! A Book about Changing Careers & Jobs. 336p. 1996. pap. 35.00 (*1-885288-04-2*) PREP Pubng.
McKinney, Anne & Berteau, John T. Estate Planning in Tennessee. 1994. 24.95 (*1-56164-059-X*) Pineapple Pr.
McKinney, Antonio, jt. ed. see **Fraser, George C.**
McKinney, Aubrey R. Back Through the Looking Glass. LC 85-80422. (Flip Side Science Ser.). (Illus.). 177p. 1986. 24.95 (*0-914587-02-1*) Helix Pr.
— The Slender Thread. LC 84-80635. (Illus.). 384p. 1985. 24.95 (*0-914587-00-5*) Helix Pr.
McKinney, Aubrey R., ed. see **Barnes, Verle.**
McKinney, Aubrey R., ed. see **Lotring, Alfred H.**
McKinney, Aubrey R., ed. see **Morris, Edwin L.**
McKinney, B. B. Wherever He Leads: Por Donde Me Guie Ire. 72p. (SPA.). 1990. pap. 4.25 (*0-311-32084-8*) Casa Bautista.
McKinney, Barbara, jt. auth. see **Ross, John.**
McKinney, Beth & Romanski, Kate D. The English Cocker Spaniel: Jubilee Book of the English Cocker Spaniel Club of America, Inc., 2 vols., 1. LC 85-82051. (Illus.). 1986. write for info. (*0-9613761-2-0*) Eng Cocker Spaniel.
— The English Cocker Spaniel: Jubilee Book of the English Cocker Spaniel Club of America, Inc., 2 vols., 2. LC 85-82051. (Illus.). 1987. write for info. (*0-9613761-3-9*) Eng Cocker Spaniel.
— The English Cocker Spaniel: Jubilee Book of the English Cocker Spaniel Club of America, Inc., 2 vols., Set. LC 85-82051. (Illus.). 1987. 40.00 (*0-9613761-1-2*) Eng Cocker Spaniel.
McKinney, Beth C. & Romanski, Kate D., eds. The English Cocker Spaniel Handbook. 3rd ed. (Illus.). 152p. 1989. pap. 10.00 (*0-9613761-4-7*) Eng Cocker Spaniel.
McKinney, Betty J. Sheltie Talk. 2nd ed. LC 75-45831. (Illus.). 320p. 1985. 29.95 (*0-931866-17-0*) Alpine Pubns.
McKinney, Betty J., ed. see **Handler, Barbara S.**
***McKinney, Bobby J.** Confederates on the Caney: An Illustrated Account of the Civil War on the Texas Gulf Coast. LC 94-79109. (Illus.). 145p. (Orig.). (C). 1994. pap. write for info. (*0-9643351-0-7*) B J McKinney.
***McKinney, Bruce.** Hardcore Visual Basic. 1994. disk, pap. 39.95 (*1-55615-667-7*) Microsoft.
McKinney, Bruce C., jt. ed. see **Miller, Christine M.**
McKinney, Bruce C., et al. Mediation: Dispute Resolution Through Communication. 2nd ed. 208p. 1990. per. 22.95 (*0-8403-5770-2*) Kendall-Hunt.
***McKinney, Carolyn.** Gentle Giant of the Twenty-Sixth Division. 1994. 19.95 (*0-929915-11-9*) Headline Bks.
McKinney, Charles, jt. auth. see **Carter, Stephen.**
McKinney, D. T., jt. auth. see **McKinney, Lee.**
McKinney, David W., Jr. Endangered, Threatened, & Rare Fauna of North Carolina, Pt. 3: An Inquiry into the Failure of Social Science Research to Produce Demonstrable Knowledge. LC 72-173383. (Studies in the Social Sciences: No. 8). 304p. 1973. pap. text ed. 54.70 (*90-279-2487-2*) Mouton.
McKinney, Don. Magazine Writing That Sells. 1994. 16.95 (*0-89879-642-3*) Writers Digest.
McKinney, Donald. Living with Joy. LC 76-8203. reprint ed. 24.00 (*0-8357-9014-2*, 2016375) Bks Demand.
McKinney, E. Doris. Motor Learning: An Experiential Guide for Teachers. 1985p. pap. 14.95 (*0-932392-25-3*) Mouvement Pubns.
McKinney, Elizabeth, jt. auth. see **MacNair, Ray.**
McKinney, F. K. & Jackson, Jeremy B. Bryozoan Evolution. (Illus.). 256p. 1987. text ed. 55.00 (*0-04-560012-0*) Routledge Chapman & Hall.
McKinney, Floyd L., comp. Strengthening Computer Technology Programs: Examples from Developing Institutions. 120p. 1984. 10.50 (*0-318-22204-3*, SN49) Ctr Educ Trng Employ.
McKinney, Floyd L., et al. Increasing Job Placement Rates in Vocational Programs: Secondary & Postsecondary. 24p. 1984. 4.25 (*0-318-22131-4*, RD245) Ctr Educ Trng Employ.
McKinney, Frank K. & Jackson, Jeremy B. Bryozoan Evolution. (Illus.). 252p. 1991. pap. text ed. 15.95 (*0-226-56047-3*) U Ch Pr.
McKinney, H. Lewis. Wallace & Natural Selection. LC 72-75203. (Studies in the History of Science & Medicine Ser.: No. 8). (Illus.). 116p. reprint ed. 33.10 (*0-8357-9597-7*, 2013373) Bks Demand.
McKinney, H. Lewis, ed. Lamarck to Darwin: Contributions to Evolutionary Biology, 1809-1859. 124p. 1971. 7.50 (*0-87291-019-9*) Coronado Pr.
***McKinney, Hannah J.** The Development of Local Public Services, 1650-1860: Lessons from Middletown, Connecticut. LC 95-5269. (Contributions in Economics & Economic History Ser.: Vol. 166). 224p. 1995. text ed. 59.95 (*0-313-29590-5*, Greenwood Pr) Greenwood.
McKinney, Irene. Quick Fire & Slow Fire. 64p. 1989. pap. 7.95 (*1-55643-046-9*) North Atlantic.
— Six O'Clock Mine Report. LC 88-29084. (Poetry Ser.). 64p. 1989. 19.95 (*0-8229-3611-9*); pap. 10.95 (*0-8229-5415-X*) U of Pittsburgh Pr.
McKinney, Jack. Battle Cry, No. 2. 1987. mass mkt. 4.95 (*0-345-34134-1*, Del Rey) Ballantine.
— Battlehymn. (Robotech Ser.: No. 4). (Orig.). 1987. mass mkt. 4.95 (*0-345-34137-6*, Del Rey) Ballantine.
— Dark Powers. 1988. mass mkt. 4.99 (*0-345-35301-3*, Del Rey) Ballantine.
— Death Dance. (Sentinels Ser.). (YA). (gr. 10 up). 1988. mass mkt. 4.95 (*0-345-35302-1*, Del Rey) Ballantine.
— The Devil's Hand. 1988. mass mkt. 4.95 (*0-345-35300-5*, Del Rey) Ballantine.
— Doomsday. (Robotech Ser.: No.6). 224p. (Orig.). 1987. mass mkt. 4.95 (*0-345-34139-2*, Del Rey) Ballantine.
Mckinney, Jack. The End of the Circle: Robotech, No. 18. 352p. 1989. mass mkt. 4.95 (*0-345-36311-6*, Del Rey) Ballantine.
McKinney, Jack. Event Horizon. (Orig.). 1991. mass mkt. 4.95 (*0-345-37053-8*, Del Rey) Ballantine.
— The Final Nightmare. (Robotech Ser.: No. 9). 224p. (Orig.). 1987. pap. text ed. 5.99 (*0-345-34142-2*, Del Rey) Ballantine.
— Force of Arms. (Robotech Ser.: No. 5). 224p. (Orig.). 1987. mass mkt. 4.95 (*0-345-34138-4*, Del Rey) Ballantine.
— Homecoming. (Robotech Ser.: No. 3). (Orig.). 1987. mass mkt. 5.99 (*0-345-34136-8*, Del Rey) Ballantine.
— Hostile Takeover. (Black Hole Travel Agency Ser.: Bk. 4). (Orig.). 1993. mass mkt. 5.50 (*0-345-37079-1*, Del Rey) Ballantine.
Mckinney, Jack. Invid Invasion. (Robotech Ser.: No. 10). (Orig.). 1987. mass mkt. 4.95 (*0-345-34143-0*, Del Rey) Ballantine.
***McKinney, Jack.** The Masters' Gambit. (Robotech Ser.). (Orig.). 1995. mass mkt., pap. 5.99 (*0-345-38775-9*, Del Rey) Ballantine.
— Metal Fire. (Robotech Ser.: No. 8). 224p. 1987. mass mkt. 4.95 (*0-345-34141-4*, Del Rey) Ballantine.
— Metamorphosis. (Robotech Ser.: No. 11). 1987. mass mkt. 4.95 (*0-345-34144-9*, Del Rey) Ballantine.
— Robotech Genesis, No. 1. 1987. mass mkt. 4.95 (*0-345-34133-3*, Del Rey) Ballantine.
— Robotech Three-in-One: Battlehymn; Force of Arms; Doomsday. 1994. reprint ed. mass mkt. 5.99 (*0-345-39145-4*, Del Rey) Ballantine.
— RoboTech 3-in-1: Genesis; Battle Cry; Homecoming. (Orig.). 1994. mass mkt. 5.99 (*0-345-38900-X*) Ballantine.
— Robotech 3-in-1: Southern Cross; Metal Fire; The Final Nightmare. 1995. mass mkt. 5.99 (*0-345-39184-5*, Del Rey) Ballantine.
— Sentinels, No. 4: World Killers. 1988. mass mkt. 4.95 (*0-345-35304-8*, Del Rey) Ballantine.
Mckinney, Jack. Sentinels, No. 5: Rubicon. 1988. mass mkt. 4.95 (*0-345-35305-6*, Del Rey) Ballantine.
McKinney, Jack. Sentinels 3-in-1: The Devil's Hand; Dark Powers; Death Dance. 1995. mass mkt. 5.99 (*0-345-38901-8*) Ballantine.
— Southern Cross. (Robotech Ser.: No. 7). 224p. (Orig.). 1987. mass mkt. 4.95 (*0-345-34140-6*, Del Rey) Ballantine.
— Symphony of Light. (Robotech Ser.: No. 12). 224p. 1987. mass mkt. 4.95 (*0-345-34145-7*, Del Rey) Ballantine.
— The Zentraedi Rebellion. (Robotech, Lost Generation Ser.: No. 19). (Orig.). 1994. mass mkt. 5.99 (*0-345-38774-0*, Del Rey Discovery) Ballantine.
McKinney, James C. Lecciones Practicas Para el Canto (Practical Lessons in Singing) Herrington, Annette H., ed. Muskrat, Bruce, tr. (Illus.). 96p. (Orig.). (SPA.). 1991. pap. 3.40 (*0-311-32405-3*) Casa Bautista.
McKinney, James D. & Feagans, Lynne, eds. Current Topics in Learning Disabilities, Vol. 1. (Current Topics in Learning Disabilities Ser.). 384p. 1984. text ed. 75.00 (*0-89391-089-9*) Ablex Pub.
McKinney, Jeana. Making Workshops Work. 33p. 1994. 9.00 (*0-912207-29-9*) NAFSA Washington.
McKinney, Jerome B. Effective Financial Management in Public & Nonprofit Agencies: A Practical & Integrative Approach. LC 86-624. 543p. 1995. text ed. 59.95 (*0-89930-925-9*, Quorum Bks) Greenwood.
McKinney, John. Coast Walks: One Hundred Adventures along the California Coast. (Illus.). 264p. (Orig.). 1988. pap. 10.95 (*0-934161-03-8*) Olympus Pr.
— Day Hiker's Guide to Southern California, Vol. I. (Illus.). 264p. (Orig.). 1987. pap. 10.95 (*0-934161-02-X*) Olympus Pr.
— Day Hiker's Guide to Southern California, Vol. II. (Illus.). (Orig.). 1989. pap. 10.95 (*0-934161-05-4*) Olympus Pr.
— Great Southern California Outdoors Guide. Rae, Cheri, ed. (Illus.). 300p. (Orig.). 1991. pap. 12.95 (*0-934161-07-0*) Olympus Pr.
— Los Angeles Golf Courses. 1990. pap. 14.95 (*0-943798-13-2*) Recreation Sales Pub.
— A Walk Along Land's End. 1995. 20.00 (*0-06-258530-4*, HarpT) HarpC.
— Walk Los Angeles: Adventures on the Urban Edge. (Illus.). 310p. (Orig.). 1992. pap. 12.95 (*0-685-49237-0*) Olympus Pr.
Mckinney, John. Walking California's State Parks: Guide to over 100 Historic Parks, Preserves & Wilderness Areas. 1994. write for info. (*0-318-72331-X*) HarpC West.
McKinney, John. Walking California's State Parks: Recreational Trips to over 100 State Historic Parks, Preserves, & Wilderness Areas. LC 93-41518. (Illus.). 228p. (Orig.). 1994. pap. 12.00 (*0-06-258535-5*) HarpC West.
— Walking Los Angeles: Adventures on the Urban Edge. LC 93-14606. (Walking the West Ser.). (Illus.). 320p. 1994. 12.00 (*0-06-258510-X*) Harper SF.
— Walking Santa Barbara: City Strolls & Country Hikes. LC 93-14605. (Walking the West Ser.). (Illus.). 176p. 1994. pap. 12.00 (*0-06-258509-6*) Harper SF.
— Walking Southern California: A Day Hiker's Guide. rev. ed. LC 93-24210. (Walking the West Ser.). (Illus.). 384p. 1994. pap. 12.00 (*0-06-258511-8*) Harper SF.
— Walking the California Coast: One Hundred Adventures along the West Coast. LC 93-14604. (Walking the West Ser.). (Illus.). 272p. 1994. pap. 13.00 (*0-06-258513-4*) Harper SF.
McKinney, John & Rae, Cheri. Walking the East Mojave: A Visitor's Guide to Mojave National Park. LC 93-26564. (Illus.). 224p. 1994. pap. 12.00 (*0-06-258512-6*) Harper SF.
McKinney, John, jt. auth. see **Rae, Cheri.**
McKinney, John C. Constructive Typology & Social Theory. LC 66-25454. (Century Sociology Ser.). 1966. 27.50 (*0-89197-105-X*) Irvington.
— Dayhiker's Guide to Southern California. Rae, Cheri, ed. (Illus.). 400p. (Orig.). 1992. pap. 14.95 (*0-934161-12-7*) Olympus Pr.
McKinney, John C. & DeVyver, Frank T., eds. Aging & Social Policy. LC 66-25014. (Century Sociology Ser.). (C). 1980. reprint ed. 34.00 (*0-89197-003-7*); reprint ed. pap. text ed. 12.95 (*0-8290-2230-9*) Irvington.
McKinney, John W., III, jt. auth. see **Slack, Gary D.**
McKinney, Joseph A. & Rowley, Keith, eds. Readings in International Economic Relations. 299p. (C). 1989. pap. text ed. 17.80 (*0-87563-341-2*) Stipes.
McKinney, Joseph A. & Sharpless, M. Rebecca, eds. Implications of a North American Free Trade Region: Multidisciplinary Perspectives. (C). 1992. 25.00 (*1-878804-05-7*) Baylor U Reg Studies.
McKinney, Judy, et al. I Need Help Quick! Cookbook: Low-Cholesterol, Low-Fat, Low-Sodium Family Favorite Recipes. 144p. 1989. spiral bd. 11.95 (*0-9624485-0-8*) Health Saver.
McKinney, K. & Specher, S., eds. Sexuality in Close Relationships. 240p. (C). 1991. text ed. 45.00 (*0-8058-0719-5*) L Erlbaum Assocs.
McKinney, Kathleen & Sprecher, Susan, eds. Human Sexuality: The Societal & Interpersonal Context. LC 89-6854. 528p. 1989. text ed. 72.50 (*0-89391-544-0*); pap. 34.50 (*0-89391-613-7*) Ablex Pub.
McKinney, Kathleen, jt. auth. see **Sprecher, Susan.**
McKinney, Ken, tr. see **Bovon, Francois.**
***McKinney, Kevin.** Everyday Geography. (Illus.). 176p. 1993. 10.95 (*1-56865-032-9*, GuildAmerica) Dblday Bk Music.
— Everyday Geography: A Concise, Entertaining Review of Essential Information about the World We Live In. (Illus.). 176p. 1994. pap. 8.95 (*0-8092-3550-1*) Contemp Bks.
***McKinney, Laurence O.** Neurotheology: Virtual Religion in the 21st Century. 172p. (Orig.). 1994. pap. 10.95 (*0-945724-01-2*) Am Inst Mindfulness.
McKinney, Lee & McKinney, D. T. Colorado Traveler - Gems & Minerals: A Guide to Colorado's Native Gemstones. (American Traveler Ser.). (Illus.). 48p. (Orig.). 1987. pap. 4.95 (*1-55838-072-8*) R H Pub.
McKinney, Liz. You're Not Alone: A Planning Guide for Families. 63p. (Orig.). 1990. pap. 5.00 (*1-877592-17-X*) GSH&MC.
McKinney, M. L., ed. Heterochrony in Evolution: A Multidisciplinary Approach. LC 88-22573. (Topics in Geobiology Ser.: Vol. 7). (Illus.). 366p. 1988. 89.50 (*0-306-42947-0*, Plenum Pr) Plenum.
McKinney, Margaret. Footloose & Duty Free. (Illus.). 148p. (Orig.). 1985. text ed. 9.95 (*0-930982-07-X*) U of Evansville Pr.
McKinney, Mary. Soul to Soul: A Vegetarian Soul Food Cook Book. 2nd ed. 181p. 1992. reprint ed. pap. 19.95 (*0-9635395-0-7*) Soul to Soul.
McKinney, Mary B. Sharing Wisdom. 192p. 1987. pap. 9.95 (*0-89505-449-3*, 21101) Tabor Pub.
McKinney, Mary J., jt. ed. see **Altman, Edward I.**
***McKinney, Meagan.** Fair Is the Rose. LC 93-27046. 1993. 23.95 (*1-56895-031-4*) Wheeler Pub.
— Gentle from the Night. 384p. 1995. 18.95 (*0-8217-4825-4*) Kensington MI.
— The Ground She Walks Upon. large type ed. LC 93-32601. 620p. 1994. pap. 19.95 (*0-385-31020-X*) Delacorte.
— The Ground She Walks Upon. large type ed. LC 94-14260. 620p. 1994. 22.95 (*0-8161-7442-3*) Hall.
— Lions & Lace. 1992. mass mkt. 4.99 (*0-440-21230-8*) Dell.
— My Wicked Enchantress. (Orig.). 1988. mass mkt. 5.50 (*0-440-20301-5*) Dell.
— No Choice but Surrender. (Orig.). 1987. mass mkt. 4.99 (*0-440-16412-5*) Dell.
— Till Dawn Tames the Night. 1991. mass mkt. 4.99 (*0-440-20870-X*) Dell.
— When Angels Fall. 1990. mass mkt. 4.99 (*0-440-20521-2*) Dell.
McKinney, Meagan, jt. auth. see **Goodman.**
McKinney, Michael. Current Issues in Geology. Westby, ed. 254p. (C). Date not set. pap. text ed. 12.25 (*0-314-03726-8*) West Pub.
— A Thousand Bridges: A Novel. LC 92-15737. 153p. 1992. 19.95 (*0-8027-1223-1*) Walker & Co.
McKinney, Michael L. Evolution of Life: Processes, Patterns & Prospects. 400p. 1993. pap. text ed. 54.00 (*0-13-292939-2*) P-H.
McKinney, Mitchell S., jt. auth. see **Carlin, Diana B.**
McKinney, Nadine. Eyes in the Attic. LC 93-74952. 141p. (J). (gr. 3-5). 1994. pap. 7.95 (*0-943864-73-9*) Davenport.
McKinney, Peter & Cunningham, Bruce. Rhinoplasty. (Illus.). 190p. 1988. text ed. 134.00 (*0-443-08531-5*) Churchill.
McKinney, Peter & Cunningham, Bruce L. Aesthetic Facial Surgery. (Illus.). 234p. 1992. text ed. 134.00 (*0-443-08703-2*) Churchill.
McKinney, Phyliss. Revelations. 20p. (Orig.). (YA). (gr. 5 up). 1992. pap. text ed. 4.95 (*1-877860-09-3*) Eula Intl Pub.
McKinney, Ralph V., Jr. Endosteal Dental Implants: An Illustrated Handbook. (Illus.). 512p. 1989. 85.00 (*0-8151-6044-5*, Yr Bk Med Pubs) Mosby Yr Bk.

An Asterisk (*) at the beginning of an entry indicates that the title is appearing in BIP for the first time.

McKinney, Richard I. Religion in Higher Education among Negroes. LC 75-38785. (Religion in America, Ser. 2). 186p. 1975. reprint ed. 20.95 (*0-405-04075-X*) Ayer.

McKinney, Richard W., ed. Creation, Christ & Culture. 336p. 39.95 (*0-567-01019-8*, Pub. by T & T Clark UK) Bks Intl VA.

***McKinney, Rick.** Catcher in the Sky. Ingram, tr. 250p. 1996. pap. 8.95 (*0-7610-0445-9*) NW Pub.

McKinney, Robert. Out of This World: Handbook of Ghosts, Spirits, Alien Sightings & Psychic Phenomena. (Illus.). 1985. pap. 4.95 (*0-913290-67-X*) Camaro Pub.

McKinney, Robert L. Death in a Small Southern Town. Chirich, Nancy, ed. LC 87-21005. 218p. (Orig.). 1987. pap. 7.95 (*0-912761-10-5*) Cliffhanger Pr.

McKinney, Robert W., jt. ed. see Richmond, Jonathan Y.

McKinney, Roberta, ed. Songs for Children of the World. 16p. (Orig.). (J). (gr. 1-8). 1984. pap. 12.95 (*0-87487-740-7*, Suzuki Method) Summy-Birchard.

McKinney, Rozanne M., jt. auth. see McKinney, Samuel, III.

McKinney, Sally. Country Roads of Indiana. LC 92-81830. (Country Roads Ser.). (Illus.). 120p. (Orig.). 1993. pap. 9.95 (*1-56626-010-8*) Country Rds.

— Indiana, Illinois & Ohio Fairs & Festivals. (Fairs & Festivals Ser.). (Illus.). 180p. (Orig.). 1995. pap. 12.95 (*1-56626-134-1*) Country Rds.

McKinney, Sam. Bligh: A Chronicle of Mutiny Aboard His Majesty's Ship The Bounty. 1989. 22.95 (*0-318-41504-6*) TAB Bks.

— Bligh: A True Account of Mutiny Aboard His Majesty's Ship The Bounty. (Illus.). 208p. 1992. pap. 12.95 (*0-87742-355-5*, 60132) Intl Marine.

— Bligh: A True Account of the Mutiny Aboard His Majesty's Ship Bounty. 1992. pap. 12.95 (*0-07-045186-9*) McGraw.

— Bligh: History's Most Famous Mutiny. 1989. text ed. 22.95 (*0-07-157331-3*) McGraw.

— The Reach of Tide, Ring of History: A Coulmbia River Voyage. (Illus.). 176p. 1987. 19.95 (*0-87595-196-1*) Oregon Hist.

McKinney, Samuel, III & McKinney, Rozanne M. Big Debt Survival Guide: A Practical Legal Reference for Protecting Yourself, Family, & Business from All Types of Liability Exposure in or Out of Bankruptcy. 304p. (Orig.). 1992. pap. 24.95 (*0-9620366-1-7*) Marshall TX.

McKinney, Samuel B., jt. auth. see Massey, Floyd, Jr.

McKinney, Shawn, et al. Sesquicentennial Park: The Design Competition. (Illus.). 70p. (Orig.). (C). 1987. pap. 35.00 (*0-9618107-0-X*) Cent Houst Civic.

McKinney, Thomas H. & Davis, Dale A. Distribution of Federal Funds for Vocational Education to Community, Technical, & Junior Colleges. LC 88-170893. (AACJC-ACCT Keeping America Working Task Force Ser.: No. 6). 70p. reprint ed. pap. 25.00 (*0-7837-2480-2*, 2042636) Bks Demand.

McKinney, Thurman D., ed. Renal Complications of Neoplasia. 288p. 1985. text ed. 69.50 (*0-275-92031-3*, C2031, Praeger Pubs) Greenwood.

McKinney, Tim. Robert E. Lee & the Thirty Fifth Star. LC 93-84769. (Illus.). 152p. 1993. pap. 11.95 (*0-929521-75-7*) Pictorial Hist.

McKinney, Virginia. Sudden Ripples. Fischer, Barbara, ed. 1974. 2.95 (*0-912658-28-2*) J Mark Pr.

McKinney, W. R., jt. auth. see Lerner, J. M.

McKinney, W. Troy, jt. auth. see Trichter, Gary J.

McKinney, W. Troy, jt. auth. see Trichter, J. Gary.

***McKinney, William, ed.** The Responsibility People: Eighteen Senior Leaders of Protestant Churches & National Ecumenical Agencies Reflect on Church Leadership. LC 94-21600. 376p. 1994. pap. 24.99 (*0-8028-0744-5*) Eerdmans.

McKinney, William, jt. auth. see Roof, Wade C.

McKinney, William T. Models of Mental Disorders: A New Comparative Psychiatry. LC 88-2335. (Illus.). 212p. 1988. 45.00 (*0-306-42746-X*, Plenum Med Bk) Plenum.

McKinnis, Candace B. & Natella, Arthur A., Jr. Business in Mexico: Managerial Behavior, Protocol, & Etiquette. LC 93-23222. (Illus.). 159p. 1994. lib. bdg. 39.95 (*1-56024-406-2*) Haworth Pr.

McKinnis, James A. Handcoloring Photographs. LC 93-41704. 1994. 22.50 (*0-8174-3972-2*, Amphoto) Watsn-Guptill.

McKinnon, A., ed. Kierkegaard in Translation. LC 77-855336. (Kierkegaard Indices to Kierkegaard's Samlede Vaerker Ser.: Vol. I). 155p. 1979. 19.95 (*0-691-07248-5*) Princeton U Pr.

McKinnon, Alan. Physical Distribution Systems. 256p. 1989. 67.50 (*0-415-00438-1*) Routledge.

McKinnon, Alastair. Falsification & Belief. 106p. (C). 1979. reprint ed. lib. bdg. 27.00 (*0-917930-33-9*); reprint ed. pap. text ed. 11.00 (*0-917930-13-4*) Ridgeview.

McKinnon, Alastair, ed. Konkordans Til Kierkegaard's Samlede Vaerker. LC 72-181002. (Kierkegaard Indices to Kierkegaard's Samlede Vaerker Ser.: Vol. II). 1153p. 1979. 225.00 (*0-691-07249-3*) Princeton U Pr.

McKinnon, Angus & Voss, James. Equine Reproduction. LC 91-29283. (Illus.). 700p. 1992. text ed. 99.50 (*0-8121-1427-2*) Williams & Wilkins.

McKinnon, Dan. Bullseye - One Reactor. 208p. 1987. 14.95 (*0-941437-07-8*) House Hits.

— Everything You Need to Know Before You're Hijacked. 139p. (Orig.). 1987. pap. 4.95 (*0-941437-01-9*) House Hits.

Mckinnon, Dan. The Good Life. 173p. 1973. 8.95 (*0-941437-02-7*) House Hits.

***McKinnon, Dan.** The Ten Second Message. 130p. 1994. pap. 9.95 (*0-941437-04-3*) House Hits.

Mckinnon, Dan. Tombstones. 106p. 1995. pap. 14.95 (*0-941437-03-5*) House Hits.

***McKinnon, Dan.** Words of Honor. 352p. 1995. pap. 12.95 (*0-941437-00-0*) House Hits.

***McKinnon, Elizabeth.** Busy Bees Spring: Fun for Two's & Three's. Cubley, Kathleen & Warren, Jean, eds. LC 94-61016. (Busy Bee Ser.). (Illus.). 144p. (Orig.). 1995. pap. text ed. 14.95 (*1-57029-026-1*) Warren Pub Hse.

— Great Big Holiday Celebrations: Activities for Celebrating Major Holidays with Young Children. Bittinger, Gayle, ed. LC 91-65045. (Celebration Ser.). (Illus.). 224p. (Orig.). 1991. pap. text ed. 16.95 (*0-911019-43-X*) Warren Pub Hse.

— Play & Learn with Rubber Stamps. Warren, Jean, ed. LC 93-61083. (Play & Learn with Ser.). (Illus.). 64p. (Orig.). (J). 1994. pap. text ed. 7.95 (*0-911019-93-6*) Warren Pub Hse.

— Special Day Celebrations: Nontraditional Units. (Celebrations Ser.). (Illus.). 128p. (J). 1995. 14.95 (*0-614-06846-0*, WPH 0702) Totline Bks.

— Special Day Celebrations: Seasonal Mini Celebrations to Enjoy with Young Children. Bittinger, Gayle, ed. LC 89-50765. (Celebration Ser.). (Illus.). 128p. (Orig.). (J). (ps-1). 1989. pap. text ed. 14.95 (*0-911019-24-3*) Warren Pub Hse.

— The Teaching House. Cubley, Kathleen & Warren, Jean, eds. LC 95-60511. (Teaching House Ser.). (Illus.). 160p. (Orig.). 1995. pap. text ed. 7.95 (*1-57029-068-7*) Warren Pub Hse.

— The Teaching Town. Cubley, Kathleen & Warren, Jean, eds. LC 95-60512. (Teaching House Ser.). (Illus.). 160p. (Orig.). 1996. pap. text ed. 7.95 (*1-57029-069-5*) Warren Pub Hse.

— Teaching Trips. Cubley, Kathleen & Warren, Jean, eds. LC 95-60513. (Teaching House Ser.). (Illus.). 160p. (Orig.). 1996. pap. 7.95 (*1-57029-070-9*) Warren Pub Hse.

— Yankee Doodle Birthday Celebrations: All-American Birthdays to Celebrate with Young Children. Bittinger, Gayle, ed. LC 90-70414. (Celebration Ser.). (Illus.). 128p. (Orig.). (J). (ps-1). 1990. pap. text ed. 12.95 (*0-911019-32-4*) Warren Pub Hse.

— Yankee Doodle Birthday Celebrations: Antibias Units. (Celebrations Ser.). (Illus.). 128p. (J). 1995. 14.95 (*0-614-06847-9*, WPH 0703) Totline Bks.

***McKinnon, Elizabeth, ed.** More Piggyback Songs for School. LC 95-60006. (Piggyback Song Ser.). (Illus.). 80p. (Orig.). 1995. pap. 8.95 (*1-57029-067-9*) Warren Pub Hse.

***McKinnon, Elizabeth & Bittinger, Gayle.** Busy Bees for Fall: Fun for Two's & Three's. LC 93-61897. (Busy Bees Ser.). (Illus.). 136p. (J). (ps). 1994. pap. 14.95 (*1-57029-008-3*, WPH 2405) Warren Pub Hse.

— Busy Bees Summer: Fun for Two's & Three's. Cubley, Kathleen & Warren, Jean, eds. LC 94-61734. (Busy Bees Ser.). (Illus.). 144p. 1995. pap. text ed. 14.95 (*1-57029-066-0*) Warren Pub Hse.

McKinnon, Elizabeth & Bittinger, Gayle, eds. Alphabet Theme-a-Saurus: The Great Big Book of Letter Recognition. LC 90-71272. (Theme-A-Saurus Ser.). (Illus.). 280p. (J). (ps-1). 1991. pap. text ed. 19.95 (*0-911019-38-3*) Warren Pub Hse.

McKinnon, Elizabeth, ed. see Bittinger, Gayle.

McKinnon, Elizabeth, ed. see Warren, Jean.

McKinnon, Elizabeth, jt. auth. see Warren, Jean.

McKinnon, Elizabeth S., ed. One-Two-Three Colors: Activities for Introducing Color to Young Children. LC 87-51241. (Totline 1-2-3 Ser.). (Illus.). 160p. (Orig.). (J). (ps-1). 1988. pap. 14.95 (*0-911019-17-0*) Warren Pub Hse.

McKinnon, Elizabeth S., ed. see Warren, Jean.

McKinnon, Elizabeth S., jt. auth. see Warren, Jean.

McKinnon-Evans, Stuart, tr. see Frevert, Ute.

McKinnon, Gordon P., ed. see Brannigan, Francis L.

McKinnon, Helen D. Every Woman: Adopting to Mid-Life Change. 96p. 1987. pap. 9.95 (*0-7737-5079-7*, Pub. by Stoddart Pubng CN) Genl Dist Srvs.

McKinnon, James. Antiquity & the Middle Ages: From Ancient Greece to the Middle Ages. 400p. (C). 1990. pap. text ed. write for info. (*0-13-036161-5*) P-H.

McKinnon, John D. Guidebook to Florida Legislators 1993-1994. 540p. 1993. pap. 177.00 (*0-9635376-0-1*) Legis Guidebks.

McKinnon, Lawrence W. & Lawson, Lynne N. Instant Lotus 1-2-3. 60p. (Orig.). 1986. pap. 11.95 (*0-938862-80-4*) Weber Systems.

McKinnon, Lucille V. Grandma's Treasure Chest: Moral & Spiritual Values for Grandparents to share with Grandchildren. (Illus.). 124p. (Orig.). 1991. 24.95 (*0-941437-05-1*) House Hits.

McKinnon, Malcolm. Independence & Foreign Policy: New Zealand since 1935. (Auckland University Press Book). 352p. 1993. 29.95 (*1-86940-070-4*) OUP.

McKinnon, Matthew. The Law of Contracts. 1993. 464p. Date not set. ring bd. 64.00 (*1-879581-08-6*) Lupus Pubns.

McKinnon, Matthew, jt. auth. see McCormick, Robert.

McKinnon, Michael. Arabia: Sand, Sea & Sky. 224p. (C). 1990. 100.00 (*0-907151-63-9*, Pub. by IMMEL Pubng UK) St Mut.

— Arabia: Sand, Sea, Sky. (Illus.). 224p. 1992. 29.95 (*0-563-36106-9*, BBC-Parkwest) Parkwest Pubns.

McKinnon, Michal, jt. auth. see Vine, Peter.

***McKinnon, Patrick.** Out Past the Chain Links of Time. 2418p. (Orig.). 1994. pap. 3.95 (*0-9641986-5-7*) Poetry Harbor.

McKinnon, Patrick, ed. see Backen, Bud.

McKinnon, Patrick, ed. see Chmielarz, Sharon.

McKinnon, Patrick, ed. see Fitzgerald, Nancy.

McKinnon, Ronald I. Financial Liberalization & Economic Development: A Reassessment of Interest-Rate Policies in Asia & Latin America. 48p. 1988. pap. 6.95 (*1-55815-020-X*) ICS Pr.

— Gradual Versus Rapid Liberalization in Socialist Economies: Financial Policies in China & Russia Compared. LC 93-50170. (Sector Studies: Vol. 10). 1994. pap. write for info. (*1-55815-314-4*) ICS Pr.

— An International Standard for Monetary Stabilization. LC 83-22572. (Policy Analyses in International Economics Ser.: No. 8). 112p. (Orig.). reprint ed. pap. 32.00 (*0-8357-2825-0*, 2039061) Bks Demand.

— Money & Capital in Economic Development. LC 72-9928. 184p. 1973. pap. 11.95 (*0-8157-5613-5*) Brookings.

— The Order of Economic Liberalization: Financial Control in the Transition to a Market Economy. 2nd ed. (Johns Hopkins Studies in Development). 224p. (C). 1993. text ed. 45.00 (*0-8018-4742-7*); pap. text ed. 15.95 (*0-8018-4743-5*) Johns Hopkins.

McKinnon, Ronald I., ed. Money & Finance in Economic Growth & Development: Essays in Honor of Edward S. Shaw: Proceedings of the Conference Held at Stanford University. LC 75-21191. (Business Economics & Finance Ser.: No. 8). 351p. reprint ed. pap. 100.10 (*0-7837-0963-3*, 2041268) Bks Demand.

McKinnon, Sharon M. & Bruns, William J., Jr. The Information Mosaic. LC 91-46758. 288p. 1992. 27.95 (*0-87584-317-4*) Harvard Busn.

— The Information Mosaic. 1992. text ed. 27.95 (*0-07-103368-8*) McGraw.

McKinnon, Sharon M., jt. auth. see Edmonds, Thomas P.

McKinnon, Susan. From a Shattered Sun: Hierarchy, Gender & Alliance in the Tanimbar Islands. LC 91-50325. (Illus.). 342p. (Orig.). 1992. lib. bdg. 37.00 (*0-299-13150-5*); pap. 16.50 (*0-299-13154-8*) U of Wis Pr.

McKinsey, Elizabeth. Niagara Falls: Icon of the American Sublime. (Cambridge Studies in American Literature & Culture: No. 10). (Illus.). 350p. 1985. 54.95 (*0-521-25901-0*) Cambridge U Pr.

McKinsey, Elizabeth R. The Western Experiment: New England Transcendentalists in the Ohio Valley. LC 72-83467. (Essays in History & Literature Ser.). 78p. 1978. pap. 6.50 (*0-674-95040-2*) HUP.

McKinsey, Folger, jt. auth. see Williams, Thomas J.

McKinsey, James O., Jr. Managerial Accounting. Chandler, Alfred D., ed. LC 79-7551. (History of Management Thought & Practice Ser.). 1980. reprint ed. lib. bdg. 61.95 (*0-405-12335-3*) Ayer.

***McKinsey, Lauren & Konrad, Victor.** Borderlands Reflections: The Untied States & Canada. (Borderlands Monograph Ser.: No. 1). 37p. (C). 1989. pap. text ed. 5.00 (*0-614-04705-6*) Canadian-Amer Ctr.

***McKinsey, Martin, tr. & intro.** Late into the Night: The Last Poems of Yannis Ritsos. (Field Translation Ser.: No. 21). (Orig.). 1995. pap. 12.95 (*0-932440-71-1*) Oberlin Coll Pr.

McKinstry, Anne P. Can You Come with Me? (Illus.). 44p. (J). (gr. 4-8). 1986. 5.95 (*1-55523-034-2*) Winston-Derek.

McKinstry, Asako N., jt. auth. see McKinstry, John.

McKinstry, E. Richard, comp. Trade Catalogues at Winterthur: A Guide to Literature of Merchandising, 1750 to 1980. LC 93-13919. (Winterthur Book). 1993. reprint ed. 90.00 (*1-55655-480-X*) U Pubns Amer.

McKinstry, John & McKinstry, Asako N. Jinsei Annai: "Life's Guide" "Life's Guide": Glimpses of Japan Through a Popular Advice Column. LC 90-24303. 224p. 1991. 30.95 (*0-87332-762-4*) M E Sharpe.

McKinstry, John A., jt. auth. see Kerbo, Harold R.

McKinstry, Pamela. Adventure Travel in Africa. 224p. (C). 1990. 140.00 (*0-907151-98-1*, Pub. by IMMEL Pubng UK) St Mut.

— Discovery Guide to Central Africa. 224p. (C). 1990. 95.00 (*0-907151-96-5*, Pub. by IMMEL Pubng UK) St Mut.

— Discovery Guide to Game Parks of Southern Africa. 232p. (C). 1990. 79.00 (*0-907151-97-3*, Pub. by IMMEL Pubng UK) St Mut.

McKinstry, Pamela, ed. Discovery Guide to Southern Africa: Namibia, Botswana & South Africa. 256p. (C). 1990. 79.00 (*0-907151-73-6*, Pub. by IMMEL Pubng UK) St Mut.

McKinstry, Sam. Rowand Anderson. 1991. text ed. 50.00 (*0-7486-0252-6*, Pub. by Edinburgh U Pr UK) Col U Pr.

McKinstry, Steve. The Attic Treasure. (Illus.). 32p. 1982. 6.95 (*0-317-62219-6*) Lucy & Co.

— A Special Gift. (Illus.). 32p. 1981. 6.95 (*0-910079-01-3*) Lucy & Co.

McKinstry, Susan J., jt. ed. see Bauer, Dale M.

***McKinven, John A.** Stage Flying: 431 B. C. to Modern Times. LC 95-5936. 1995. 35.00 (*0-916638-81-2*) Meyerbooks.

McKinzie, Bruce W. Objectivity, Communication, & the Foundation of Understanding. 168p. (Orig.). (C). 1994. lib. bdg. 46.50 (*0-8191-9536-7*); pap. text ed. 24.50 (*0-8191-9537-5*) U Pr of Amer.

McKinzie, Harry. Family Reunions: How to Plan Yours. LC 87-19615. (Reunions Ser.). 305p. (Orig.). 1994. pap. 16.95 (*0-86626-013-7*) McKinzie Pub.

— High School Reunions: How to Plan Yours. (Reunions Ser.). 305p. (Orig.). 1994. pap. 16.95 (*0-86626-001-3*) McKinzie Pub.

— A Message from Elvis Presley. Date not set. pap. 16.95 (*0-86626-004-8*) McKinzie Pub.

— Reunions: How to Plan Yours. 305p. Date not set. pap. text ed. 16.95 (*0-86626-002-1*) McKinzie Pub.

— Women in Boxing. 1994. pap. 16.95 (*0-86626-012-9*) McKinzie Pub.

— Zthorg - God's Computer. 170p. (Orig.). pap. 20.00 (*0-86626-017-X*) McKinzie Pub.

McKinzie, Harry & Tindimwebwa, Issy. Names from East Africa. Campbell, Elisabeth, ed. 42p. (Orig.). (J). 1980. pap. 4.95 (*0-86626-007-2*) McKinzie Pub.

McKinzie, R. The New Deal for Artists. 1973. pap. 15.95 (*0-691-00584-2*) Princeton U Pr.

McKirahan, Richard, Jr. Philosophy Before Socrates: An Introduction with Texts & Commentary. LC 93-46837. 448p. (Orig.). (C). 1994. lib. bdg. 37.95 (*0-87220-176-7*); pap. text ed. 14.95 (*0-87220-175-9*) Hackett Pub.

McKirahan, Richard. Plato's Meno. (Greek Commentaries Ser.). 109p. (Orig.). (C). 1986. pap. text ed. 7.00 (*0-929524-30-6*) Bryn Mawr Commentaries.

McKirahan, Richard D., Jr. Principles & Proofs: Aristotle's Theory of Demonstrative Science. 356p. 1992. text ed. 49.50 (*0-691-07363-5*) Princeton U Pr.

McKisack, May. Fourteenth Century, Thirteen Seven to Thirteen Ninety-Nine. (Oxford History of England Ser.). 1959. 59.00 (*0-19-821712-9*) OUP.

— The Fourteenth Century, 1307-1399. (Oxford History of England Ser.: Vol. 5). 624p. 1991. reprint ed. pap. 18.95 (*0-19-285250-7*) OUP.

McKisack, May, ed. see Clarke, Maude V.

McKissack. One Family's Story. (J). 1997. 19.95 (*0-8050-1671-6*) H Holt & Co.

McKissack, Frederick, jt. auth. see McKissack, Patricia C.

McKissack, Frederick, jt. auth. see McKissack, Patricia.

McKissack, Frederick, Jr. & McKissack, Patricia C. Sojourner Truth: Ain't I a Woman? (YA). (gr. 8-12). 1994. pap. 3.50 (*0-590-44691-6*) Scholastic Inc.

McKissack, Fredrick, ed. see Duyff, Roberta L.

McKissack, Fredrick, Jr., jt. auth. see McKissack, Patricia C.

McKissack, Fredrick

McKissack, Fredrick, Jr.

McKissack, Fredrick

McKissack, Fredrick, Jr.

McKissack, Fredrick, jt. auth. see McKissack, Patricia.

Mckissack, Fredrick

McKissack, Fredrick

McKissack, Patricia. The Apache. LC 84-7803. (New True Bks.). (Illus.). 48p. (J). (gr. k-4). 1984. lib. bdg. 12.90 (*0-516-01925-2*); pap. 4.95 (*0-516-41925-0*) Childrens.

— The Aztec. LC 84-23142. (New True Bks.). (Illus.). 48p. (J). (gr. k-4). 1985. lib. bdg. 12.90 (*0-516-01936-8*); pap. 4.95 (*0-516-41936-6*) Childrens.

— The Dark-Thirty: Southern Tales of the Supernatural. LC 92-3021. (Illus.). 128p. (J). (gr. 3-7). 1992. 15.00 (*0-679-81863-4*); lib. bdg. 15.99 (*0-679-91863-9*) Knopf Bks Yng Read.

— The Inca. LC 85-6712. (New True Bks.). (Illus.). 45p. (J). (gr. 2-3). 1985. lib. bdg. 12.90 (*0-516-01268-1*); pap. 4.95 (*0-516-41268-X*) Childrens.

— Los Incas (The Inca) LC 85-6712. (Spanish New True Bks.). 48p. (SPA.). (J). (gr. k-4). 1987. lib. bdg. 12.90 (*0-516-31268-5*); pap. 4.95 (*0-516-51268-4*) Childrens.

— Long Hard Journey: The Story of the Pullman Porter. (YA). 1995. pap. 9.95 (*0-8027-7437-7*) Walker & Co.

— Martin Luther King, Jr. A Man to Remember. LC 83-23933. (People of Distinction Ser.). (Illus.). 128p. (J). (gr. 4 up). 1984. lib. bdg. 14.40 (*0-516-03206-2*); pap. 5.95 (*0-516-43206-0*) Childrens.

— The Maya. LC 85-9927. (New True Bks.). (Illus.). 45p. (J). (gr. 2-3). 1985. lib. bdg. 12.90 (*0-516-01270-3*); pap. 4.95 (*0-516-41270-1*) Childrens.

— Los Mayas (The Maya) LC 85-9927. (Spanish New True Bks.). (Illus.). 48p. (J). (gr. k-4). 1987. lib. bdg. 12.90 (*0-516-31270-7*); pap. 4.95 (*0-516-51270-6*) Childrens.

— Monkey-Monkey's Trick. LC 88-3072. (Step into Reading Bks.). (Illus.). 48p. (Orig.). (J). (gr. 1-3). 1988. lib. bdg. 7.99 (*0-394-99173-7*); pap. 3.50 (*0-394-89173-2*) Random Bks Yng Read.

— Paul Laurence Dunbar: A Poet to Remember. LC 84-7625. (People of Distinction Ser.). (Illus.). 112p. (J). (gr. 4 up). 1984. lib. bdg. 14.40 (*0-516-03209-7*); pap. 5.95 (*0-516-43209-5*) Childrens.

— Quien Viene? (Who Is Coming?) LC 86-11805. (Rookie Reader Ser.). (Illus.). 32p. (ENG & SPA.). (J). (ps-2). 1989. pap. 2.95 (*0-516-52073-3*) Childrens.

— Royal Kingdoms of Ghana, Mali, & Soghay: Life in Medieval Africa. (Illus.). 160p. (J). (gr. 5-9). 1994. 15.95 (*0-8050-1670-8*, Bks Young Read) H Holt & Co.

— Who Is Coming? LC 86-11805. (Rookie Readers Big Bks.). (Illus.). 32p. (J). (ps-3). 1990. lib. bdg. 10.35 (*0-516-02073-0*); pap. 2.95 (*0-516-42073-9*); pap. 22.95 (*0-516-49458-9*) Childrens.

— Who Is Who? LC 83-7361. (Rookie Reader Ser.). (Illus.). 32p. (J). (ps-2). 1983. lib. bdg. 10.35 (*0-516-02042-0*); pap. 2.95 (*0-516-42042-9*) Childrens.

McKissack, Patricia & McKissack, Frederick. All Paths Lead to Bethlehem. LC 87-70472. (Illus.). 32p. (Orig.). (J). (ps-3). 1987. pap. 5.99 (*0-8066-2265-2*, 10-0220, Augsburg) Augsburg Fortress.

— The Children's ABC Christmas. LC 87-73525. (Illus.). 32p. (J). (ps-6). 1988. pap. 5.99 (*0-8066-2356-X*, 10-1046, Augsburg) Augsburg Fortress.

— A Long Hard Journey. (American History Series for Young People). 144p. (J). (gr. 7-9). 1990. 17.95 (*0-8027-6884-9*); lib. bdg. 18.85 (*0-8027-6885-7*) Walker & Co.

— My Bible ABC Book. LC 87-70473. (Illus.). 32p. (Orig.). (J). (ps-3). 1987. pap. 5.99 (*0-8066-2271-7*, 10-4588, Augsburg) Augsburg Fortress.

— Oh, Happy, Happy Day! A Child's Easter in Story, Song, & Prayer. LC 88-83017. (Illus.). 32p. (J). 1989. pap. 5.99 (*0-8066-2394-2*, 10-4733, Augsburg) Augsburg Fortress.

— Red-Tail Angels: The Story of the Tuskegee Airmen of World War II. (Illus.). 144p. (YA). (gr. 5 up). 1995. 19.95 (*0-8027-8292-2*); lib. bdg. 20.85 (*0-8027-8293-0*) Walker & Co.

— Taking a Stand Against Racism & Racial Discrimination. LC 89-28627. (J). 1990. lib. bdg. 15.33 (*0-531-10924-0*) Watts.

McKissack, Patricia & McKissack, Fredrick. Ada, la Desordenada - Libro Grande: Messey Bessey-Big Book. (Rookie Reader Big Bks.). 32p. (J). (ps-2). 1988. lib. bdg. 22.95 (*0-516-59508-3*) Childrens.

— Ada, la Desordenada (Messy Bessey) LC 87-15079. (Rookie Readers - Spanish Ser.). (Illus.). 32p. (SPA.). (J). (ps-2). 1988. lib. bdg. 10.35 (*0-516-32083-1*); pap. 2.95 (*0-516-52083-0*) Childrens.

— African-American Inventors. LC 93-42625. (Proud Heritage Ser.). (Illus.). 96p. (J). (gr. 4-6). 1994. lib. bdg. 17.90 (*1-56294-468-1*) Millbrook Pr.

— African-American Scientists. LC 93-11226. (Proud Heritage Ser.). (Illus.). 96p. (J). (gr. 4-6). 1994. lib. bdg. 17.90 (*1-56294-372-3*) Millbrook Pr.

— Big Bug Book of Counting. LC 87-61655. (Big Bug Bks.). (Illus.). 24p. (Orig.). (J). (gr. k-1). 1987. pap. text ed. 4.95 (*0-88335-772-0*); spiral bd. 14.95 (*0-88335-762-3*) Milliken Pub Co.

McKissack, Patricia & Mckissack, Fredrick. Big Bug Book of Opposites. LC 87-61654. (Big Bug Bks.). (Illus.). 24p. (Orig.). (J). (gr. k-1). 1987. pap. text ed. 4.95 (*0-88335-773-9*); spiral bd. 14.95 (*0-88335-763-1*) Milliken Pub Co.

McKissack, Patricia & McKissack, Fredrick. Big Bug Book of Places to Go. LC 87-61652. (Big Bug Bks.). (Illus.). 24p. (Orig.). (J). (gr. k-1). 1987. pap. text ed. 4.95 (*0-88335-775-5*); spiral bd. 14.95 (*0-88335-765-8*) Milliken Pub Co.

— Big Bug Book of the Alphabet. LC 87-61653. (Big Bug Bks.). (Illus.). 24p. (Orig.). (J). (gr. k-1). 1987. pap. text ed. 4.95 (*0-88335-774-7*); spiral bd. 14.95 (*0-88335-764-X*) Milliken Pub Co.

— Big Bug Book of Things to Do. LC 87-61651. (Big Bug Bks.). (Illus.). 24p. (Orig.). (J). (gr. k-1). 1987. pap. text ed. 4.95 (*0-88335-776-3*); spiral bd. 14.95 (*0-88335-766-6*) Milliken Pub Co.

— Booker T. Washington: Leader & Educator. LC 92-5356. (Great African Americans Ser.). (Illus.). 32p. (J). (gr. 1-4). 1992. lib. bdg. 12.95 (*0-89490-314-4*) Enslow Pubs.

— Bugs! LC 88-22875. (Rookie Reader Ser.). (Illus.). 32p. (J). (ps-2). 1988. lib. bdg. 10.35 (*0-516-02088-9*); pap. 2.95 (*0-516-42088-7*) Childrens.

— Carter G. Woodson: The Father of Black History. LC 91-8813. (Great African Americans Ser.). (Illus.). 32p. (J). (gr. 1-4). 1991. lib. bdg. 12.95 (*0-89490-309-8*) Enslow Pubs.

— Cinderella. LC 85-12764. (Start-Off Stories Ser.). (Illus.). (J). (gr. 1-2). 1985. lib. bdg. 10.35 (*0-516-02361-6*); pap. 3.95 (*0-516-42361-4*) Childrens.

— The Civil Rights Movement in America from 1865 to the Present. 2nd ed. LC 86-9636. (Civil Rights Ser.). (Illus.). 352p. (J). (gr. 4 up). 1991. 30.90 (*0-516-00579-0*) Childrens.

— Constance Stumbles. (Rookie Reader Ser.). (Illus.). 32p. (J). (ps-2). 1988. lib. bdg. 10.35 (*0-516-02086-2*); pap. 2.95 (*0-516-42086-0*) Childrens.

— Country Mouse & City Mouse. LC 85-12759. (Start-Off Stories Ser.). (Illus.). (J). (ps-2). 1985. lib. bdg. 10.35 (*0-516-02362-4*); pap. 3.95 (*0-516-42362-2*) Childrens.

— Frederick Douglass: Leader Against Slavery. LC 91-3084. (Great African Americans Ser.). (Illus.). 32p. (J). (gr. 1-4). 1991. lib. bdg. 12.95 (*0-89490-306-3*) Enslow Pubs.

— Frederick Douglass: The Black Lion. LC 86-32695. (People of Distinction Ser.). (Illus.). 136p. (J). (gr. 4 up). 1987. lib. bdg. 14.40 (*0-516-03221-6*); pap. 5.95 (*0-516-43221-4*) Childrens.

— From Heaven Above: The Story of Christmas Proclaimed by the Angels. LC 92-70385. (Illus.). 32p. (J). (ps-2). 1992. pap. 4.99 (*0-8066-2609-7*, 9-2609, Augsburg) Augsburg Fortress.

— La Gallinita Roja: The Little Red Hen. LC 86-20801. (Spanish Start-Off Stories Ser.). (Illus.). 32p. (J). (ps-2). 1986. lib. bdg. 10.35 (*0-516-32363-6*); pap. 3.95 (*0-516-52363-5*) Childrens.

— George Washington Carver: The Peanut Scientist. LC 91-8814. (Great African Americans Ser.). (Illus.). 32p. (J). (gr. 1-4). 1991. lib. bdg. 12.95 (*0-89490-308-X*) Enslow Pubs.

— God Made Something Wonderful. LC 89-84938. (Illus.). 32p. (Orig.). (J). (gr. 3-5). 1989. pap. 5.99 (*0-8066-2434-5*, 9-2434) Augsburg Fortress.

— Great African Americans Series, 18 bks., Set. (Illus.). (J). (gr. 1-4). 1991. lib. bdg. 233.10 (*0-89490-376-4*) Enslow Pubs.

— Ida B. Wells-Barnett: A Voice Against Violence. LC 90-49848. (Great African Americans Ser.). (Illus.). 32p. (J). (gr. 1-4). 1991. lib. bdg. 12.95 (*0-89490-301-2*) Enslow Pubs.

— Insectos! Bugs! LC 88-22875. (Rookie Reader Ser.). (Illus.). 32p. (SPA.). (J). (ps-2). 1991. lib. bdg. 10.35 (*0-516-32088-2*); pap. 2.95 (*0-516-52088-1*) Childrens.

— James Weldon Johnson: Lift Every Voice & Sing. LC 89-77273. (Picture-Story Biographies Ser.). (Illus.). 32p. (J). (gr. 2-5). 1990. pap. text ed. 3.95 (*0-516-44174-4*) Childrens.

— Jesse Owens: Olympic Star. LC 92-3584. (Great African Americans Ser.). (Illus.). 32p. (J). (gr. 1-4). 1992. lib. bdg. 12.95 (*0-89490-312-8*) Enslow Pubs.

— King Midas & His Gold. LC 86-11744. (Start-Off Stories Ser.). (Illus.). 32p. (J). (ps-2). 1986. lib. bdg. 10.35 (*0-516-03984-9*); pap. 3.95 (*0-516-43984-7*) Childrens.

— The King's New Clothes. LC 86-33422. (Start-Off Stories Ser.). (Illus.). 32p. (J). (ps-3). 1987. pap. 3.95 (*0-516-42365-7*) Childrens.

— Langston Hughes: Great American Poet. LC 92-2583. (Great African Americans Ser.). (Illus.). 32p. (J). (gr. 1-4). 1992. lib. bdg. 12.95 (*0-89490-315-2*) Enslow Pubs.

— The Little Red Hen. LC 85-12760. (Start-Off Stories Ser.). (Illus.). (J). (ps-2). 1985. lib. bdg. 10.35 (*0-516-02363-2*); pap. 3.95 (*0-516-42363-0*) Childrens.

— Louis Armstrong: Jazz Musician. LC 91-12420. (Great African Americans Ser.). (Illus.). 32p. (J). (gr. 1-4). 1991. lib. bdg. 12.95 (*0-89490-307-1*) Enslow Pubs.

— Madam C. J. Walker: Self-Made Millionaire. LC 92-6189. (Great African Americans Ser.). (Illus.). 32p. (J). (gr. 1-4). 1992. lib. bdg. 12.95 (*0-89490-311-X*) Enslow Pubs.

— Marian Anderson: A Great Singer. LC 90-19163. (Great African Americans Ser.). (Illus.). 32p. (J). (gr. 1-4). 1991. lib. bdg. 12.95 (*0-89490-303-9*) Enslow Pubs.

— Martin Luther King, Jr. Man of Peace. LC 90-19156. (Great African Americans Ser.). (Illus.). 32p. (J). (gr. 1-4). 1991. lib. bdg. 12.95 (*0-89490-302-0*) Enslow Pubs.

— Mary Church Terrell: Leader for Equality. LC 91-3083. (Great African Americans Ser.). (Illus.). 32p. (J). (gr. 1-4). 1991. lib. bdg. 12.95 (*0-89490-305-5*) Enslow Pubs.

— Mary McLeod Bethune. LC 92-12098. (Cornerstones of Freedom Ser.). (Illus.). 32p. (J). (gr. 3-6). 1992. lib. bdg. 12.30 (*0-516-06658-7*) Childrens.

— Mary McLeod Bethune. LC 92-12098. (Cornerstones of Freedom Ser.). (Illus.). 32p. (J). (gr. 3-6). 1993. pap. 3.95 (*0-516-46658-5*) Childrens.

— Mary McLeod Bethune: A Great Teacher. LC 91-8818. (Great African Americans Ser.). (Illus.). 32p. (J). (gr. 1-4). 1991. lib. bdg. 12.95 (*0-89490-304-7*) Enslow Pubs.

— Messey Bessey Big Book. (Rookie Readers Big Bks.). (Illus.). 32p. (J). (ps-2). 1988. lib. bdg. 22.95 (*0-516-49508-9*) Childrens.

— Messy Bessey. LC 87-15079. (Rookie Reader Ser.). (Illus.). (J). (ps-2). 1987. lib. bdg. 10.35 (*0-516-02083-8*); pap. 2.95 (*0-516-42083-6*) Childrens.

— Messy Bessey's Garden. LC 91-15333. (Rookie Reader Ser.). (Illus.). 32p. (J). (ps-2). 1991. lib. bdg. 10.35 (*0-516-02008-0*); pap. 2.95 (*0-516-42008-9*) Childrens.

— Paul Robeson: A Voice to Remember. LC 92-2582. (Great African Americans Ser.). (Illus.). 32p. (J). (gr. 1-4). 1992. lib. bdg. 12.95 (*0-89490-310-1*) Enslow Pubs.

— Ralph J. Bunche: Peacemaker. LC 90-49849. (Great African Americans Ser.). (Illus.). 32p. (J). (gr. 1-4). 1991. lib. bdg. 12.95 (*0-89490-300-4*) Enslow Pubs.

— El Ratoncito del Campo y el Ratoncito de la Ciudad: Country Mouse & City Mouse. LC 86-21565. (Spanish Start-Off Stories Ser.). 32p. (J). (ps-2). 1986. pap. 3.95 (*0-516-52362-7*) Childrens.

— Satchel Paige: The Best Arm in Baseball. LC 92-3583. (Great African Americans Ser.). (Illus.). 32p. (J). (gr. 1-4). 1992. lib. bdg. 12.95 (*0-89490-317-9*) Enslow Pubs.

— Sojourner Truth: A Voice for Freedom. LC 92-6190. (Great African Americans Ser.). (Illus.). 32p. (J). (gr. 1-4). 1992. lib. bdg. 12.95 (*0-89490-313-6*) Enslow Pubs.

— The Story of Booker T. Washington. LC 91-15895. (Cornerstones of Freedom Ser.). (Illus.). 32p. (J). (gr. 3-6). 1991. lib. bdg. 12.30 (*0-516-04758-2*); pap. 3.95 (*0-516-44758-0*) Childrens.

— Tennessee Trailblazers. 96p. (J). (gr. 4-7). 1993. 13.95 (*0-9634824-0-8*) March Media.

— The Three Bears. LC 85-12765. (Start-Off Stories Ser.). (Illus.). 32p. (J). (ps-2). 1985. lib. bdg. 10.35 (*0-516-02364-0*); pap. 3.95 (*0-516-42364-9*) Childrens.

— Three Billy Goats Gruff. LC 86-33450. (Start-Off Stories Ser.). (Illus.). 32p. (J). (ps-2). 1987. lib. bdg. 10.35 (*0-516-02366-7*); pap. 3.95 (*0-516-42366-5*) Childrens.

— El Traje Nuevo del Emperador: (The King's New Clothes) LC 86-33422. (Start-Off Stories Ser.). (Illus.). 32p. (ENG & SPA.). (J). (ps-2). 1989. lib. bdg. 10.35 (*0-516-32365-2*); pap. 3.95 (*0-516-52365-1*) Childrens.

— Los Tres Chivitos. LC 86-33450. (Start-off Stories - Spanish Ser.). (Illus.). 32p. (SPA.). (J). (ps-2). 1988. lib. bdg. 10.35 (*0-516-32366-0*); pap. 3.95 (*0-516-52366-X*) Childrens.

— The Ugly Little Duck. LC 85-31428. (Start-Off Stories Ser.). (Illus.). 32p. (J). (ps-2). 1986. pap. 3.95 (*0-516-43982-0*) Childrens.

— When Do You Talk to God? Prayers for Small Children. LC 86-71903. (Illus.). 32p. (Orig.). (J). (gr. 3-8). 1986. pap. 5.99 (*0-8066-2239-3*, 10-7078, Augsburg) Augsburg Fortress.

— Zora Neale Hurston: Writer & Storyteller. LC 92-2588. (Great African Americans Ser.). (Illus.). 32p. (J). (gr. 1-4). 1992. lib. bdg. 12.95 (*0-89490-316-0*) Enslow Pubs.

McKissack, Patricia, ed. see Duyff, Roberta L.

McKissack, Patricia C. Flossie & the Fox. LC 86-2024. (Illus.). 32p. (J). (ps-3). 1986. 14.00 (*0-8037-0250-7*); lib. bdg. 13.89 (*0-8037-0251-5*) Dial Bks Young.

— Jesse Jackson: A Biography. 112p. (J). (gr. 3-7). 1990. 3.25 (*0-590-42395-9*) Scholastic Inc.

— Ma Dear's Aprons. LC 94-48450. 1997. 16.99 (*0-679-95099-0*, Apple Soup Bks) Knopf Bks Yng Read.

— Ma Dear's Aprons. LC 94-48450. (Illus.). (J). 1997. 16.00 (*0-679-85099-6*, Apple Soup Bks) Knopf Bks Yng Read.

— Mary McLeod Bethune: A Great American Educator. LC 85-12843. (People of Distinction Ser.). (Illus.). 111p. (J). (gr. 4 up). 1985. lib. bdg. 14.40 (*0-516-03218-6*); pap. 5.95 (*0-516-43218-4*) Childrens.

— A Million Fish...More or Less. LC 90-34322. (Illus.). 40p. (J). (ps-3). 1992. 14.00 (*0-679-80692-X*) Knopf Bks Yng Read.

— A Million Fish...More or Less. LC 90-34322. (Illus.). 40p. (J). (ps-3). 1992. lib. bdg. 14.99 (*0-679-90692-4*) Knopf Bks Yng Read.

— Mirandy & Brother Wind. LC 87-349. 32p. (J). (ps-3). 1988. 15.00 (*0-394-88765-4*) Knopf Bks Yng Read.

— Mirandy & Brother Wind. LC 87-349. 32p. (J). (ps-3). 1988. lib. bdg. 16.99 (*0-394-98765-9*) Knopf Bks Yng Read.

— Nettie Jo's Friends. LC 87-14080. (Illus.). 40p. (J). (ps-4). 1989. 16.00 (*0-394-89158-9*); lib. bdg. 15.99 (*0-394-99158-3*) Knopf Bks Yng Read.

— Nettie Jo's Friends. (Dragonfly Bks.). (Illus.). 40p. (J). (ps-3). 1994. pap. 5.99 (*0-679-86573-X*) Knopf Bks Yng Read.

— Quien Es Quien? (Who Is Who?) LC 83-7361. (Rookie Reader Ser.). (Illus.). 32p. (SPA.). (J). (ps-2). 1989. pap. 2.95 (*0-516-52042-3*) Childrens.

***McKissack, Patricia C. & Duyff, Roberta L.** So, Who's Dr. Rabbit? (Illus.). 32p. (J). (gr. 2-4). 1994. pap. text ed. write for info. (*0-9642684-0-X*) JMH Communs.

McKissack, Patricia C. & McKissack, Frederick. Christmas in the Big House, Christmas in the Quarters. LC 92-33831. (Illus.). (J). (gr. 2 up). 1994. 15.95 (*0-590-43027-0*) Scholastic Inc.

— Rebels Against Slavery. LC 94-41089. (J). 1996. write for info. (*0-590-45735-7*) Scholastic Inc.

McKissack, Patricia C. & McKissack, Fredrick, Jr. Black Diamond: The Story of the Negro Baseball Leagues. LC 93-22691. (Illus.). 192p. (J). (gr. 3-9). 1994. 13.95 (*0-590-45809-4*) Scholastic Inc.

McKissack, Patricia C. & McKissack, Fredrick. Messy Bessey's Closet. LC 89-34667. (Rookie Reader Ser.). (Illus.). 32p. (J). (ps-2). 1989. lib. bdg. 10.35 (*0-516-02091-9*); pap. 2.95 (*0-516-42091-7*) Childrens.

McKissack, Patricia C. & McKissack, Fredrick, Jr. Sojourner Truth: Ain't I a Woman. (J). 1992. 13.95 (*0-590-44690-8*, Scholastic Hardcover) Scholastic Inc.

McKissack, Patricia C. & McKissack, Fredrick. Los Tres Osos: (The Three Bears) LC 85-12765. (Start-Off Stories Ser.). (Illus.). 32p. (SPA.). (J). (ps-2). 1989. lib. bdg. 10.35 (*0-516-32364-4*); pap. 3.95 (*0-516-52364-3*) Childrens.

McKissack, Patricia C. & McKissack, Fredrick, Jr. W. E. B. Dubois. LC 90-37823. (Impact Biographies Ser.). (Illus.). 128p. (YA). (gr. 7-12). 1990. lib. bdg. 15.47 (*0-531-10939-9*) Watts.

McKissack, Patricia C., jt. auth. see McKissack, Fredrick, Jr.

McKissick, John & Baker, Billy G. John McKissick: Called to Coach. (Illus.). 409p. 1994. 23.95 (*0-915611-88-0*) Sagamore Pub.

***McKissick Museum Staff.** Crossroads in Clay: The Southern Alkaline-Glazed Stoneware Tradition. Date not set. pap. 14.95 (*0-87249-951-0*) U of SC Pr.

McKissock, P. Color Atlas of Mammaplasty. Goin, J. M., ed. (Operative Techniques in Plastic Surgery Ser.). (Illus.). 144p. 1991. text ed. 99.00 (*0-86577-385-8*) Thieme Med Pubs.

McKisson, Micki. Chrysalis: Nurturing Creative & Independent Thought in Children. (Illus.). 225p. (Orig.). (J). (gr. 4-12). 1983. pap. text ed. 29.95 (*0-913705-19-5*) Zephyr Pr AZ.

McKisson, Micki & MacRae-Campbell, Linda. Our Divided World: Poverty, Hunger & Overpopulation. (Our Only Earth Ser.). 104p. (J). (gr. 4-12). 1990. 19.95 (*0-913705-52-7*) Zephyr Pr AZ.

McKisson, Micki, jt. auth. see MacRae-Campbell, Linda.

McKisson, Micki, jt. auth. see Macrae-Campbell, Linda.

McKisson, Micki, jt. auth. see MacRae-Campbell, Linda.

McKitrick, Eric, jt. auth. see Elkins, Stanley.

McKitrick, Eric L. Andrew Johnson & Reconstruction. 544p. (C). 1988. pap. text ed. 17.95 (*0-19-505707-4*) OUP.

McKitrick, Eric L., jt. auth. see Elkins, Stanley.

McKitrick, M. D. A Genealogical Record of One Branch of the Donaldson Family in America; Descendants of Moses Donaldson, Huntington, Co., Penn., 1770. (Illus.). 332p. 1993. reprint ed. lib. bdg. 64.00 (*0-8328-3029-1*); reprint ed. pap. 54.00 (*0-8328-3030-5*) Higginson Bk Co.

McKitrick, Reuben. Public Land System of Texas, Eighteen Twenty-Three to Nineteen Ten. Bruchey, Stuart, ed. LC 78-56659. (Management of Public Lands in the U. S. Ser.). (Illus.). 1979. reprint ed. lib. bdg. 17.95 (*0-405-11342-0*) Ayer.

McKitterick, David. Cambridge University Library; A History: The Eighteenth & Nineteenth Centuries. (Illus.). 600p. 1986. 145.00 (*0-521-30655-8*) Cambridge U Pr.

— Four Hundred Years of University Printing & Publishing in Cambridge: 1584-1984. (Illus.). 150p. 1985. 59.95 (*0-521-25821-9*) Cambridge U Pr.

— A History of Cambridge University Press, Vol. 1: Printing & the Book Trade in Cambridge, 1534-1698. (Illus.). 512p. (C). 1992. 125.00 (*0-521-30801-1*) Cambridge U Pr.

***McKitterick, David, ed.** The Making of the Wren Library, Trinity College, Cambridge: From the Seventeenth to the Nineteenth Century. (Illus.). 275p. (C). Date not set. write for info. (*0-521-44305-9*) Cambridge U Pr.

McKitterick, David, ed. see Morison, Stanley.

McKitterick, David J., ed. Stanley Morison & D. B. Updike: Selected Correspondence. LC 79-87761. (Illus.). 1979. 25.00 (*0-89679-001-0*) Moretus Pr.

McKitterick, Molly. Murder in a Mayonnaise Jar. 224p. 1993. 17.95 (*0-312-09346-2*) St Martin.

McKitterick, Rosamond. Books, Scribes & Learning in the Frankish Kingdoms, 6th-9th Centuries. LC 94-7578. (Collected Studies: No. CS 452). (Illus.). 352p. 1994. 89.95 (*0-86078-406-1*, Pub. by Variorum UK) Ashgate Pub Co.

— The Carolingians & the Written Word. (Illus.). 296p. (C). 1989. 69.95 (*0-521-30539-X*); pap. 24.95 (*0-521-31565-4*) Cambridge U Pr.

— The Frankish Kingdoms under the Carolingians: 751-987. LC 82-8944. (Illus.). (Orig.). (C). 1985. pap. text ed. 17.95 (*0-582-49005-7*, 73441) Longman.

McKitterick, Rosamond, ed. Carolingian Culture: Emulation & Innovation. LC 92-36984. (Illus.). 352p. (C). 1993. 69.95 (*0-521-40524-6*); pap. 22.95 (*0-521-40586-6*) Cambridge U Pr.

— The New Cambridge Medieval History Vol. 2: c.700-c. 900. (Illus.). 1056p. (C). 1995. 95.00 (*0-521-36292-X*) Cambridge U Pr.

— The Uses of Literacy in Early Medieval Europe. (Illus.). 361p. (C). 1992. pap. 22.95 (*0-521-42896-3*) Cambridge U Pr.

***McKitterick, Rosamund.** Frankish Kings & Culture in the Early Middle Ages. (Collected Studies: Vol. CS477). 350p. 1995. 84.95 (*0-86078-458-4*, Pub. by Variorum UK) Ashgate Pub Co.

McKitterick, Thomas E. & Younger, Kenneth G., eds. Fabian International Essays. LC 75-80408. (Essay Index Reprint Ser.). 1977. 18.95 (*0-8369-1057-5*) Ayer.

McKittrick, Harold V., jt. ed. see Del Re, Robert.

McKittrick, Michael, jt. auth. see McKittrick, Rosemary.

McKittrick, Rosemary & McKittrick, Michael. The Official Price Guide to Fine Art. 2nd ed. 896p. 1993. pap. 20.00 (*0-87637-909-9*, House of Collect) Ballantine.

McKittrick, Sandra M., jt. auth. see Ayllon, Teodoro.

***McKiven, Henry M., Jr.** Iron & Steel: Class, Race, & Community in Birmingham, Alabama, 1875-1920. LC 94-27198. (Illus.). 290p. 1995. lib. bdg. 37.50 (*0-8078-2188-8*); pap. text ed. 14.95 (*0-8078-4524-8*) U of NC Pr.

McKivigan, John R. The War Against Proslavery Religion: Abolitionism & the Northern Churches, 1830-1865. LC 83-45933. 328p. 1984. 37.95 (*0-8014-1589-6*) Cornell U Pr.

McKivigan, John R., ed. see Douglass, Frederick.

McKivigan, John R., jt. ed. see Miller, Randall M.

McKlown, Patrick & Brown, Robert D. Business Analysis with Spreadsheets Using VP Planner Plus. 464p. (Orig.). (C). 1988. pap. text ed. 34.95 (*0-8162-5543-1*) Holden-Day.

McKnew, Donald H., Jr., jt. auth. see Cytryn, Leon.

McKnew, Donald H., Jr., et al. Why Isn't Johnny Crying? Coping with Depression in Children. 1985. pap. 5.95 (*0-393-30240-7*) Norton.

McKnew, Ed. Family & Express Cruisers: A McKnew & Parker Powerboat Guide, 1995 Edition. 1994. pap. text ed. 19.95 (*0-07-045196-6*) McGraw.

— Motor Yachts & Trawlers: A McKnew & Parker Powerboat Guide, 1995 Edition. 1994. pap. text ed. 19.95 (*0-07-045172-9*) McGraw.

— Sportsfishing: A McKnew & Parker Powerboat Guide, 1995. 1994. pap. text ed. 19.95 (*0-07-045171-0*) McGraw.

McKnew, Ed & Parker, Mark. Powerboat Guide. 3rd ed. (Illus.). 912p. 1992. pap. 29.95 (*0-87742-360-1*, 60348) Intl Marine.

McKnight, Bill N., ed. Biological Pollution: The Control & Impact of Invasive Exotic Species: Proceedings of a Symposium Held at the University Place Conference Center, Indiana University-Purdue University at Indianapolis on October 25 & 26, 1991. LC 93-3889. (Illus.). 270p. 1993. 30.00 (*1-883362-00-8*) IN Acad Sci.

McKnight, Bob. Eliminate the Losers. 1976. reprint ed. pap. 5.00 (*0-87980-319-3*) Wilshire.

— How to Beat the Claimers. 1979. 10.00 (*0-8065-0614-8*, Citadel Pr) Carol Pub Group.

McKnight, Brenda, ed. Peaches 'n Cream. 192p. 1988. 12.95 (*0-89015-650-6*) Sunbelt Media.

McKnight, Brian E. Law & Order in Sung China. (Studies in Chinese History, Literature & Institutions). (Illus.). 592p. (C). 1992. 79.95 (*0-521-41121-1*) Cambridge U Pr.

— Village & Bureaucracy in Southern Sung China. LC 72-159834. xii, 220p. 1983. pap. text ed. 6.95 (*0-226-56060-0*) U Ch Pr.

McKnight, Brian E., ed. Law & the State in Traditional East Asia: Six Studies on the Sources of East Asian Law. LC 86-25123. (Asian Studies at Hawaii: No. 33). 190p. 1987. pap. text ed. 20.00 (*0-8248-0838-X*) UH Pr.

McKnight, Brian E., tr. see Sung Tz'u.

McKnight, C., et al. Hypertext: A Psychological Perspective. 200p. 1993. 29.95 (*0-13-441643-0*); 42.50 (*0-13-441650-3*) P-H.

— Hypertext in Context. (Series on Electronic Publishing: No. 4). (Illus.). 200p. (C). 1991. 37.95 (*0-521-37488-X*) Cambridge U Pr.

McKnight, C. J. Little Wisdoms: Alchemy. LC 93-27406. 1994. 9.95 (*0-8118-0473-9*) Chronicle Bks.

McKnight, Catherine, ed. see Tillich, Paul.

McKnight, Charles. Our Western Border in Early Pioneer Days. (Illus.). 800p. 1993. reprint ed. pap. text ed. 42.00 (*1-55613-843-1*) Heritage Bk.

McKnight, Cynthia. Life Without Roe: Making Predictions about Illegal Abortions. 36p. 1992. 5.00 (*1-882192-00-1*) H R Storer Fnd.

McKnight, Darren S., jt. auth. see Dueber, Ross E.

McKnight, Darren S., jt. auth. see Johnson, Nicholas L.

McKnight, David. Australia's Spies & Their Secrets. 400p. 1994. pap. 24.95 (*1-86373-661-1*, Pub. by Allen Unwin AT) Paul & Co Pubs.

— The Lardil of Aboriginal Australia: Keepers of the Dreamtime. LC 94-40058. 1995. write for info. (*0-8118-0834-3*) Chronicle Bks.

McKnight, David A. The Electoral System of the United States... xii, 433p. 1993. reprint ed. lib. bdg. 45.00 (*0-8377-2446-5*) Rothman.

McKnight, Diane M., jt. ed. see Averett, Robert C.

Mcknight, Edgar V. Meaning in Texts: The Historical Shaping of a Narrative. LC 77-15238. 344p. reprint ed. pap. 98.10 (*0-685-15430-0*, 2026885) Bks Demand.

McKnight, Edgar V. What Is Form Criticism? Via, Dan O., Jr., ed. LC 71-81526. (Guides to Biblical Scholarship: New Testament Ser.). 96p. (Orig.). 1969. pap. 8.00 (*0-8006-0180-7*, 1-180, Fortress Pr) Augsburg Fortress.

McKnight, Edgar V., ed. Perspectives on Contemporary New Testament Questions: Essays in Honor of T. C. Smith. LC 92-41327. 136p. 1992. text ed. 69.95 (*0-7734-2852-6*) E Mellen.

***McKnight, Edgar V. & Malbon, Elizabeth S.** New Literary Criticism & the New Testament. LC 94-41734. 1994. pap. 20.00 (*1-56338-107-9*) TPI PA.

An Asterisk (*) at the beginning of an entry indicates that the title is appearing in BIP for the first time.

McKnight, Felicia B. Parish Alive! Making Every Parish a Spiritual Life Center. 144p. (Orig.). 1992. pap. 10.95 (0-8245-1187-5) Crossroad NY.

McKnight, Floyd, tr. see Steiner, Rudolf.

McKnight, G. H., jt. ed. see Lumby, J. R.

McKnight, George, ed. Middle English Humorous Tales in Verse. LC 77-144435. (Belles Lettres Ser. Section II: No. 1). reprint ed. 31.50 (0-404-53611-5) AMS Pr.

McKnight, George H. English Words & Their Background. LC 69-20052. 459p. (C). 1968. reprint ed. 75.00 (0-87752-071-2) Gordian.

— Middle English Humorous Tales in Verse. LC 78-128190. 211p. (C). 1971. reprint ed. 45.00 (0-87752-131-X) Gordian.

— St. Nicholas: His Legend & His Role in the Christmas Celebration & Other Popular Customs. (Illus.). 153p. 1974. reprint ed. 20.00 (0-87928-051-4) Corner Hse.

McKnight, Gerald. Gucci: A House Divided. LC 86-46390. 384p. 1987. 18.95 (1-55611-037-5) D I Fine.

McKnight, Harry F. Silva Mind Control Through Psychorientology. 5.95 (0-913343-40-4) Inst Psych Inc.

***McKnight, Hugh.** Cruising French Waterways. 2nd ed. (Illus.). 318p. Date not set. 50.00 (0-7136-3282-8) Sheridan.

— Slow Boat Through Germany. (Illus.). 228p. Date not set. 37.50 (0-7136-3778-1) Sheridan.

McKnight, Ivy. Holiday Hostess. large type ed. (Linford Romance Library). 304p. 1988. pap. 11.95 (0-7089-6473-7, Trailtree Bookshop) Ulverscroft.

McKnight, Jenna. Alligator Alley. (American Romance Ser.). 1993. mass mkt. 3.50 (0-373-16512-9, 1-16512-5) Harlequin Bks.

— The Bride, the Bachelor & the Baby. 1994. mass mkt. 3.50 (0-373-16539-0, 1-16539-8) Harlequin Bks.

— The Cowboy Hires a Wife (1-800-HUSBAND) 1995. mass mkt. 3.50 (0-373-16605-2) Harlequin Bks.

***McKnight, John.** The Careless Society: Community & Its Counterfeits. LC 95-1111. 208p. 1995. 21.00 (0-465-09125-3) Basic.

McKnight, John L., jt. auth. see Kretzmann, John P.

McKnight, Juilene, ed. see Fischer, William L.

McKnight, Kent H. & McKnight, Vera B. Field Guide to Mushrooms: North America. (Peterson Field Guide Ser.). (Illus.). 448p. 1987. 21.95 (0-395-42101-2); pap. 16.95 (0-395-42102-0) HM.

McKnight, Natalie. Idiots, Madmen & Other Prisoners in Dickens. LC 92-36304. 160p. 1993. text ed. 35.00 (0-312-08596-6) St Martin.

McKnight, Nigel. Nasa Wings. (Osprey Colour Library). (Illus.). 128p. 1992. pap. 15.95 (1-85532-216-1, Pub. by Osprey Pubng Ltd UK) Motorbooks Intl.

McKnight-Osborne, Juilene, ed. see Fischer, William L.

McKnight-Osborne, Juilene, ed. see Hass-Unger, Joan.

***McKnight, Phillip S.** Understanding Christoph Hein. LC 94-18721. (Understanding Modern European & Latin American Literature Ser.). 1994. write for info. (1-57003-015-4) U of SC Pr.

McKnight, Reed. Measurement Error & Banks' Reported Earnings. LC 83-1393. (Research for Business Decisions Ser.: No. 61). 128p. reprint ed. pap. 36.50 (0-685-44823-1, 2070407) Bks Demand.

McKnight, Reginald. African American Wisdom. LC 93-33729. (Classic Wisdom Collection). 96p. 1994. 12.95 (1-880032-34-1) New Wrld Lib.

— I Get on the Bus. 1992. pap. 9.95 (0-316-56058-8) Little.

— Kind of Light That Shines on Texas. 1993. pap. 9.95 (0-316-56059-6) Little.

— Moustapha's Eclipse. LC 88-6408. (Drue Heinz Literature Prize Ser.). 160p. 1988. 22.50 (0-8229-3589-9) U of Pittsburgh Pr.

— Moustapha's Eclipse. 144p. 1989. reprint ed. pap. 8.95 (0-88001-179-3) Ecco Pr.

***McKnight, Reginald, ed.** The Wisdom of Africa & the Carribean. (The Classic Wisdom Ser.). 128p. 1996. 12.95 (1-880032-56-2); 12.95 (1-880032-80-5) New Wrld Lib.

McKnight, Roger. Moberg's Emigrant Novels & the Journals of Andrew Peterson. Scott, Franklyn D., ed. LC 78-15196. (Scandinavians in America Ser.). 1979. lib. bdg. 23.95 (0-405-11649-7) Ayer.

McKnight, Roger, ed. see Moberg, Vilhelm.

McKnight, Rosemary. Those Who Wait: Learning How to Wait on the Lord in an Impatient World. 140p. 1990. pap. 6.99 (0-89225-365-7) Gospel Advocate.

McKnight, Scot. Interpreting the Synoptic Gospels: Guides to New Testament Exegesis. LC 88-10502. 135p. (Orig.). 1988. pap. 6.99 (0-8010-6235-7) Baker Bk.

— The NIV Application Commentary: Galatians. LC 94-18276. 352p. 1995. 21.99 (0-310-48470-7) Zondervan.

McKnight, Scot, ed. Introducing New Testament Interpretation. LC 89-28390. (Guides to New Testament Exegesis Ser.). 208p. (Orig.). 1990. pap. 11.99 (0-8010-6260-8) Baker Bk.

McKnight Staff & Miller, Wilbur R. Power Mechanics. LC 78-53394. (Basic Industrial Arts Ser.). (Illus.). 1978. pap. 7.72 (0-02-672870-2) Glencoe.

— Woodworking. LC 78-53386. (Basic Industrial Arts Ser.). (Illus.). 1978. pap. 7.72 (0-02-672800-1) Glencoe.

McKnight, Stephen A. Eric Voegelin's Search for Order in History. exp. ed. 252p. 1988. reprint ed. pap. text ed. 23.00 (0-8191-6557-3) U Pr of Amer.

— The Modern Age & the Recovery of Ancient Wisdom: A Reconsideration of Historical Consciousness, 1450-1650. (Illus.). 176p. 1991. text ed. 29.95 (0-8262-0781-2) U of Mo Pr.

McKnight, Stephen A., ed. Science, Pseudo-Science, & Utopianism in Early Modern Thought. (Illus.). 240p. (C). 1992. text ed. 37.95 (0-8262-0835-5) U of Mo Pr.

McKnight, Steven L. & Yamamoto, Keith R., eds. Transcriptional Regulation. LC 92-31461. (Monograph Ser.: Vol. 22). 1335p. 1993. 160.00 (0-87969-410-6); pap. 95.00 (0-87969-425-4) Cold Spring Harbor.

McKnight, T. S., jt. ed. see Mullins, E. J.

McKnight, Thomas. Friendly Vermin: A Survey of Feral Livestock in Australia. LC 73-62778. (University of California Publications in Social Welfare: Vol. 21). 112p. reprint ed. pap. 32.00 (0-317-29137-8, 2021276) Bks Demand.

— Thomas McKnight: Windows on Paradise. (Illus.). 200p. 1990. 75.00 (1-55859-126-5) Abbeville Pr.

McKnight, Thomas L. Feral Livestock in Anglo-America. LC 64-64237. (University of California Publications in Social Welfare: Vol. 16). 92p. reprint ed. pap. 26.30 (0-317-29511-X, 2021273) Bks Demand.

McKnight, Thomas W. Love-Tactics: Strategic Psychology to Win the One You Want. (Illus.). 76p. 1985. pap. 4.95 (0-9615050-0-1) Wisdom Pr.

— Voyage to Paradise: A Visual Odyssey. LC 92-42295. 1993. 65.00 (0-06-250977-2); pap. 25.00 (0-06-250807-5) Harper SF.

McKnight, Thomas W. & Phillips, Robert H. Love Tactics: How to Win the One You Want. LC 87-31935. 144p. 1988. pap. 7.95 (0-89529-367-6) Avery Pub.

— More Love Tactics: How to Win That Special Someone. LC 92-2729. 192p. 1993. pap. 8.95 (0-89529-531-8) Avery Pub.

McKnight, Tom. Oceania: The Geography of Australia, New Zealand & the Pacific Islands. 1994. text ed. 45.00 (0-13-123639-3) P-H.

McKnight, Tom L. Essentials of Physical Geography. 448p. 1991. pap. text ed. 43.00 (0-13-284910-0) P-H.

— Physical Geography: A Landscape Appreciation. 4th ed. 624p. 1993. text ed. write for info. (0-13-667130-6) P-H.

— Regional Geography of United States & Canada. 608p. 1991. text ed. 57.00 (0-13-352956-8) P-H.

McKnight, Tom L., jt. auth. see Bergman, Edward F.

McKnight, Vera B., jt. auth. see McKnight, Kent H.

McKnight, W. J. A Pioneer History of Jefferson County, Pennsylvania, 1755-1844. (Illus.). 670p. 1992. reprint ed. lib. bdg. 69.50 (0-8328-1415-6) Higginson Bk Co.

McKnight, William J. Jefferson County, Pennsylvania: Her Pioneers & People, 1800-1915, Vol. II: Genealogy-Biography. (Illus.). 701p. 1992. reprint ed. lib. bdg. 77.00 (0-8328-1410-5) Higginson Bk Co.

McKoin, Florence S. Between the Rivers: A West Carroll Chronicle. 1971. 12.50 (0-87511-082-7) Claitors.

***McKone, Harold T.** Separating & Identifying Some Food & Drug Dyes by Thin-Layer Chromatography. Neidig, H. A., ed. (Modular Laboratory Program in Chemistry Ser.). 7p. (C). 1994. pap. text ed. 1.25x (0-87540-445-6) Chem Educ Res.

McKoski, Martin M. & Hahn, Lynne C. Developing Sentence Sense. (C). 1993. text ed. 14.75 (0-673-46973-5) HarpCollege.

— Developing Writer. 4th ed. (C). 1991. text ed. 32.50 (0-673-46441-5) HarpCollege.

— Developing Writer Basic Skills. 3rd ed. (C). 1988. pap. text ed. 17.00 (0-673-38611-2) HarpCollege.

— Developing Writers at Work: Prize-Winning Essays. (C). 1988. pap. text ed. 16.00 (0-673-18399-8) HarpCollege.

McKowen, Clark. Get Your "A" out of College. 188p. 1988. 10.95 (0-931961-37-8) Crisp Pubns.

McKowen, K. D. Wildlife Activity & Coloring Book. (Illus.). 32p. (J). (gr. 2-6). 1987. student ed 1.50 (0-913635-02-2) Aspen Prods.

***McKowen, Ken.** California's Great Outdoor Events: One-Thousand Wild & Wonderful Things to Do in California's Parks & Public Lands. (Illus.). 576p. (Orig.). 1995. pap. 16.95 (0-935701-50-8) Foghorn Pr.

McKown, David. Engineer's Guide to Business-Writing for Career Growth. (Illus.). 19.95 (0-7803-0304-0, HL0452-3) Inst Electrical.

McKown, Delos. The Mythmaker's Magic: Behind the Illusion of "Creation Science" 180p. (C). 1992. 23.95 (0-87975-770-1) Prometheus Bks.

McKown, Delos B. With Faith & Fury. LC 84-43180. 440p. 1985. 26.95 (0-87975-280-7) Prometheus Bks.

***McKown, June R.** Marion: A Pictorial History. (Indiana Pictorial History Ser.). 1990. write for info. (0-614-04651-3) G Bradley.

McKown, Martha. Palm Sunday Parade. (Orig.). 1994. pap. write for info. (0-318-72857-5) CSS OH.

— Palm Sunday Parade. 20p. (Orig.). 1995. pap. 3.95 (0-7880-0322-4) CSS OH.

McKray, George, jt. ed. see Roemer, Ruth.

McKuen, Rod. And Autumn Came. 1969. 50.00 (0-318-00971-4) Cheval Bks.

— Beyond the Boardwalk. 1976. 5.95 (0-910368-01-5); 12.50 (0-686-14426-0); pap. 3.95 (0-686-14427-9) Cheval Bks.

— The Carols of Christmas. 1971. 3.95 (0-394-47420-1) Random.

— Listen to the Warm. 1969. 7.95 (0-394-40378-9) Random.

— The Lovers. (Orig.). 1982. pap. 2.95 (0-671-43615-5) PB.

— Moment to Moment. 1972. pap. 5.95 (0-318-00970-6) Cheval Bks.

— The Songs of Rod McKuen. 1960. 5.95 (0-318-00972-2) Cheval Bks.

— Stanyan Street & Other Sorrows. 1994. lib. bdg. 16.95x (1-56849-474-2) Buccaneer Bks.

McKune, Amy. To Love & to Cherish: The Great American Wedding. (Illus.). 21p. 1991. pap. 4.65 (0-943924-16-2) Mus Stony Brook.

McKusick, James C. Coleridge's Philosophy of Language. LC 86-7731. (Yale Studies in English: No. 195). 189p. reprint ed. pap. 53.90 (0-8357-3752-7, 2036478) Bks Demand.

McKusick, Leon, ed. What to Do about AIDS: Physicians & Mental Health Professionals Discuss the Issues. 224p. (C). 1986. 30.00 (0-520-05935-2); pap. 13.00 (0-520-05936-0) U CA Pr.

McKusick, Marjorie. Borderland. 252p. (Orig.). 1993. pap. 9.99 (1-56043-653-0) Destiny Image.

McKusick, Marshall. The Davenport Conspiracy Revisited. (Illus.). 206p. 1991. 24.95 (0-8138-0344-6) Iowa St U Pr.

McKusick, Victor, jt. ed. see Temtamy, Samia.

McKusick, Victor A. Medical Genetics: A Self-Instruction Guide & Workbook Based on Mendelian Inheritance in Man (MIM) LC 93-31306. 128p. 1994. pap. 30.00 (0-8018-4796-6) Johns Hopkins.

— Medical Genetics 1961-1963: Annotated Review. LC 61-18351. (Symposium Publications Division Ser.). 1966. 204.00 (0-08-011374-5, Pub. by Pergamon Repr UK) Franklin.

— Mendelian Inheritance in Man: Catalogs of Autosomal Dominant, Autosomal Recessive, & X-Linked Phenotypes. 2nd ed. LC 68-19441. 541p. reprint ed. pap. 154.20 (0-685-20378-6, 2029844) Bks Demand.

— Mendelian Inheritance in Man: Catalogs of Autosomal Dominant, Autosomal Recessive, & X-Linked Phenotypes. 8th ed. LC 88-9328. 1742p. reprint ed. pap. 180.00 (0-8357-6907-0, 2037965) Bks Demand.

McKusick, Victor A., ed. Medical Genetic Studies of the Amish: Selected Papers. LC 76-47386. (Illus.). 528p. 1978. 65.00 (0-8018-1934-2) Johns Hopkins.

McKusick, Victor A. & Osler, William. Mendelian Inheritance in Man: Catalogs of Autosomal Dominant, Autosomal Recessive, & X-Linked Phenotypes. 6th ed. LC 82-47975. 1448p. reprint ed. pap. 180.00 (0-317-58177-5, 2029706) Bks Demand.

McKusick, Victor A., jt. auth. see McHugh, Paul R.

McKusick, Victor A., jt. auth. see Temtamy, Samia A.

McKusick, Victor A., et al. Mendelian Inheritance in Man: A Catalog of Human Genes & Genetic Disorders. 11th ed. 1994. text ed. 165.00x (0-8018-4933-0) Johns Hopkins.

McKyes, E. Agricultural Engineering Soil Mechanics. (Developments in Agricultural Engineering Ser.: Vol. 10). 292p. 1989. 57.50 (0-444-88080-1) Elsevier.

— Soil Cutting & Tillage: Developments in Agricultural Engineering, No. 7. 218p. 1985. 84.75 (0-444-42548-9) Elsevier.

***McLachlan.** Off the Beaten Track: Poland. 1995. pap. text ed. 14.95 (1-56440-743-8) Globe Pequot.

McLachlan & Basford. Mixture Models: Inference & Applications to Clustering. (Statistics: Textbooks & Monographs: Vol. 84). 272p. 1988. 110.00 (0-8247-7691-7) Dekker.

McLachlan, Alan. Molecular Biology of the Hepatitis B Virus. (Illus.). 312p. 1991. 213.00 (0-8493-5516-8, QR749) CRC Pr.

Mclachlan, Anne. North African Handbook, 1994. 800p. 1993. 24.95 (0-8442-9978-2, Passport Bks) NTC Pub Grp.

***McLachlan, Campbell & Nygh, Peter, eds.** Transnational Tort Litigation: Jurisdictional Principles. 300p. 1995. 80.00 (0-19-825919-0) OUP.

***McLachlan, D. L.** Canada-U. S. Free Trade: The Faltering Impetus for a Historic Reversal. 62p. (Orig.). (C). 1987. pap. text ed. 7.95x (0-920490-74-3) Temeron Bks.

McLachlan, Dan, et al, eds. Crystallography in North America. LC 81-71539. 479p. 1985. reprint ed. 25.00 (0-937140-07-4) Polycrystal Bk Serv.

McLachlan, Dan H. & Ayres, Jak. The Fieldbook of Pacific Northwest Sea Creatures. LC 79-9769. (Illus.). 208p. (C). 1979. 20.95 (0-87961-069-7); pap. 12.95 (0-87961-068-9) Naturegraph.

McLachlan, Geoffrey. Discriminant Analysis & Statistical Pattern Recognition. (Probability & Mathematical Statistics: Applied Probability & Statistics Section Ser.: No. 1346). 1992. text ed. 89.95 (0-471-61531-5) Wiley.

McLachlan, Gordon. Improving the Common Weal: Aspects of Scottish Health Services, 1900-1984. 653p. 1988. 57.50 (0-85224-551-3, Pub. by Edinburgh U Pr UK) Col U Pr.

— Poland: Off the Beaten Track. (Off the Beaten Track Ser.). (Illus.). 320p. (Orig.). 1995. pap. 14.95 (1-56440-718-7, Pub. by Moorland Pubng UK) Globe Pequot.

McLachlan, Gordon, jt. auth. see Salter, Mark.

McLachlan, Gordon M. Berlin: Capital of the New Germany. 1994. pap. 16.95 (0-8442-9674-0, Passport Bks) NTC Pub Grp.

McLachlan, Ian. Eighth Air Force Bomber Stories. (Illus.). 208p. 1992. 34.95 (1-85260-367-4) Haynes Pubns.

McLachlan, J., ed. Princetonians, 1748-1768: A Biographical Dictionary. 1976. 110.00 (0-691-04639-5) Princeton U Pr.

McLachlan, J., jt. auth. see Young, E.

McLachlan, Jack L., jt. auth. see Bird, Carolyn J.

McLachlan, James M. The Desire to Be God: Freedom & the Other in Sartre & Berdyaev. LC 91-31770. (Studies in Phenomenological Theology: Vol. 1). 215p. (C). 1992. pap. text ed. 39.95 (0-8204-1711-4) P Lang Pubs.

Mclachlan, Jan. Night of the Intruders. (Illus.). 224p. 1994. 37.95 (1-85260-450-6, Pub. by J H Haynes & Co UK) Motorbooks Intl.

McLachlan, John M., et al, eds. Developmental Toxicology: Mechanisms & Risk. (Banbury Report Ser.: No. 26). (Illus.). 362p. (C). 1987. text ed. 70.00 (0-87969-226-X) Cold Spring Harbor.

McLachlan, Keith, ed. The Boundaries of Modern Iran. LC 93-40359. (SOAS-GRC Geopolitics Ser.). 1994. text ed. 49.95 (0-312-12062-1) St Martin.

McLachlan, Keith, jt. ed. see Beaumont, Peter.

McLachlan, N. A., jt. ed. see Brown, A. C.

McLachlin & Wallace. The Canadian Law of Architecture & Engineering. 512p. 1987. 115.00 (0-409-80481-9) Butterworth Legal Pubs.

McLachlin, John. Medical Embryology. LC 93-48171. (C). 1994. pap. text ed. 36.75 (0-201-54420-2) Addison-Wesley.

McLackhlan, K. S., ed. Developing Agriculture of the Middle East: Opportunities & Prospects. 74p. 1976. 43.00 (0-86010-046-4) G & T Inc.

***McLaehlan, Ian.** Final Flights: Dramatic Wartime Incidents Revealed by Archaeology. (Illus.). 256p. 1995. 29.95 (1-85260-122-1, Pub. by J H Haynes & Co UK) Motorbooks Intl.

McLafferty, Fred W. Mass Spectral Correlations. 2nd ed. LC 81-205644. (Advances in Chemistry Ser.: No. 40). 1982. 32.95 (0-8412-0702-X) Am Chemical.

— Registry of Mass Spectral Data. 5th ed. 1989. pap. text ed. 6,000.00 (0-471-51593-0) Wiley.

— Registry of Mass Spectral Data with Structures, CD-ROM. 5th ed. 1989. pap. text ed. 3,995.00 (0-471-51297-4) Wiley.

McLafferty, Fred W., ed. Tandem Mass Spectrometry. LC 83-10528. (Wiley-Interscience Publication Ser.). 526p. reprint ed. pap. 150.00 (0-7837-2401-2, 2040086) Bks Demand.

McLafferty, Fred W. & Stauffer, Douglas B. The Important Peak Index of the Registry of Mass Spectral Data, 3 vols., Set. 4080p. 1991. 825.00 (0-471-55270-4) Wiley.

— Registry of Mass Spectral Data. 2nd ed. LC 87-31645. 1000p. 1989. text ed. 995.00 (0-471-62886-7) Wiley.

McLafferty, Fred W. & Turecek, Frantisek. Interpretation of Mass Spectra. 4th ed. LC 92-82536. (Illus.). 400p. (C). 1993. text ed. 27.00 (0-935702-25-3) Univ Sci Bks.

McLafferty, Gerry. Elvis Presley in Hollywood: Celluloid Sell-Out. (Illus.). 240p. 1989. 29.50 (0-7090-3727-9) Trans-Atl Phila.

McLagan, Clinton R., jt. auth. see Shumaker, Gordon W.

McLagan, Elizabeth. A Peculiar Paradise: A History of Blacks in Oregon, 1788-1940. LC 80-52573. (Illus.). 1980. pap. 7.50 (0-9603408-2-3) Georgian Pr.

McLagan International, Inc. Staff, ed. see McLagan, Patricia A.

***McLagan, Patricia & Krembs, Peter.** On-the-Level: Performance Communication That Works. rev. ed. (Illus.). 140p. 1995. pap. 19.95 (1-881052-76-1) Berrett-Koehler.

***McLagan, Patricia & Nel, Christo.** The Age of Participation: A New Governance for the Workplace & the World. 312p. 1995. 27.95 (1-881052-56-7) Berrett-Koehler.

McLagan, Patricia & O'Brien, Michael. Designshop: Customer-Focused Instructional Design. 150p. 1992. ring bd. 79.95 (0-88390-308-3) Pfeiffer & Co.

McLagan, Patricia A. Getting Results Through Learning. rev. ed. McLagan International, Inc. Staff, ed. (Illus.). 69p. (C). reprint ed. pap. text ed. 12.95 (0-913147-20-6) McLagan Intl.

McLagan, Patricia A. & Krembs, Peter. On-the-Level: Performance Communication That Works. rev. ed. (Illus.). 124p. (C). reprint ed. 24.95 (0-913147-03-6) McLagan Intl.

McLaglen, John. Herne the Hunter: Cross-Draw. large type ed. (Linford Western Library). 272p. 1986. pap. 11.95 (0-7089-6196-7, Linford) Ulverscroft.

— Herne the Hunter: Vigilante! large type ed. (Linford Western Library). 272p. 1986. pap. 11.95 (0-7089-6203-3, Linford) Ulverscroft.

McLaglen, John J. Herne the Hunter: Billy the Kid. large type ed. (Linford Western Library). 240p. 1986. pap. 11.95 (0-7089-6219-X, Linford) Ulverscroft.

— Herne the Hunter: Death in Gold. large type ed. (Linford Western Library). 256p. 1985. pap. 11.95 (0-7089-6190-8, Trailtree Bookshop) Ulverscroft.

McLain, Christeen. Musings. 200p. (Orig.). 1995. pap. write for info. (0-9631750-4-1) Muse Pubns.

***McLain, Denson K.** Genetics, Diversity, & the Biosphere. LC 94-72454. (Illus.). 112p. (Orig.). (C). 1995. pap. 12.99 (1-884612-03-2) AudioText.

— Understanding the Cell. LC 94-72550. (Illus.). 126p. (Orig.). (C). 1994. pap. 12.99 (1-884612-01-6) AudioText.

McLain, Gary. The Indian Way: Learning to Communicate with Mother Earth. (Kids' Environment Ser.). (Illus.). 114p. (Orig.). (J). (gr. 3 up). 1990. pap. 9.95 (0-945465-73-4) John Muir.

— The Indian Way: Learning to Communicate with Mother Earth. (Orig.). 1994. 21.25 (0-8446-6781-1) Peter Smith.

McLain, James J. The Economic Writings of Du Pont de Nemours. LC 76-14769. 244p. 1977. 35.00 (0-87413-114-6) U Delaware Pr.

McLain, Kay, jt. auth. see Roggli, Linda S.

McLain, Margaret S. Class Piano. LC 73-19659. 304p. 1974. pap. 8.95 (0-253-31357-0) Ind U Pr.

McLain, Marjorie W. Peter C. Tamony: Word Man of San Francisco's Mission. LC 87-50071. 135p. (Orig.). 1986. pap. 10.50 (0-931703-01-8) Wellman Pub.

McLain, Michael, jt. ed. see Loades, Ann.

McLain, Rose, ed. see Crawford, William R. & Crawford, Lela A.

***McLain, Tim & Giagnocavo, Gregory.** Getting Connected to the Internet. Dmitzak, Lee, ed. (Illus.). 20p. 1995. 9.95 (0-932577-09-1) Wentworth Worldwide.

McLain, Timothy, jt. auth. see Giagnocavo, Gregory.

McLain, Wayne, et al. A Heavenly View: The Best of Rufus Moseley. 1993. pap. 8.95 (0-910924-96-1) Macalester.

McLaine, Patricia. Love Is Contagious. 1961. pap. 4.75 (0-8222-0693-5) Dramatists Play.

Mclaine, Patricia. The Wheel of Destiny. LC 90-28371. (Illus.). 480p. 1991. pap. 17.95 (0-87542-490-2) Llewellyn Pubns.

***McLamb, Jess R. & Ranz, Charlotte A.** Roper's 1994 Triangle Business Resource Guide. 80p. 1994. pap. 18.95 (0-9645096-0-1) Roper Grp.

— Roper's 1995-96 Triangle Business Resource Guide. 80p. 1995. pap. write for info. (0-9645096-1-X) Roper Grp.

McLamb, John W., Jr. & Shiba, Wendy C. Pennsylvania Corporation Law & Practice. (National Corporation Law Ser.). 1992. ring bd. 126.00 (*0-13-110462-4*) Aspen Law.
*__McLan, Peter.__ Musician's Guide to Home Recording: How to Make Great Recordings At Home. rev. ed. 1994. pap. 24.95 (*0-8256-1378-7*) Music Sales.
McLanahan, Connie, jt. auth. see McLanahan, Jack.
McLanahan, Jack & McLanahan, Connie. Cooperative-Credit Union Dictionary & Reference. LC 90-80911. 416p. (Orig.). 1990. 23.50 (*0-9625894-0-3*); pap. 14.50 (*0-9625894-1-1*) Coop Alumni Assn.
McLanahan, Sara & Sandefur, Gary. Growing Up with a Single Parent: What Hurts, What Helps. LC 94-19995. (Illus.). 208p. 1994. text ed. 19.95 (*0-674-36407-4*, MCLGRO) HUP.
McLanahan, Sara S., jt. auth. see Garfinkel, Irwin.
McLanathan, Richard. Art in America: A Brief History. (Illus.). 216p. (C). 1973. pap. text ed. 18.75 (*0-15-503466-9*) HB Coll Pubs.
— Peter Paul Rubens. LC 94-33330. (First Impressions Ser.). (J). 1995. text ed. write for info. (*0-8109-3780-8*) Abrams.
McLanathan, Richard B. Gilbert Stuart: The Father of American Portraiture. (Library of American Art). (Illus.). 160p. 1986. 39.95 (*0-8109-1501-4*) Abrams.
— Leonardo da Vinci. (First Impressions Ser.). (Illus.). 72p. (YA). (gr. 7 up). 1990. 19.95 (*0-8109-1256-2*) Abrams.
— Michelangelo. LC 92-27688. (First Impressions Ser.). (Illus.). 92p. (J). 1993. 19.95 (*0-8109-3634-8*) Abrams.
McLanathan, Richard B. & Brown, Gene. The Arts. (Great Contemporary Issues Ser.). 1978. 27.95 (*0-405-11153-3*) Ayer.
McLanathan, Richard B. K. Ship Models. 2nd ed. (Illus.). 48p. (Orig.). 1957. reprint ed. pap. 3.95 (*0-87846-220-1*) Mus Fine Arts Boston.
McLane, Alvin. An Archaeological Survey of Three Geothermal Drill Pads Near Borax Lake, Pueblo Valley, Harney County, Oregon. (Illus.). 14p. 1981. 2.00 (*0-945920-23-7*) Desert Rsch Inst.
— Cultural Resources Inventory in Spanish Spring Valley, Washoe County, Nevada. (Illus.). 23p. 1980. 4.00 (*0-945920-16-4*) Desert Rsch Inst.
— Report of a BLM Class III Cultural Resources Inventory of Two Seismic Lines in Big Smoky Valley, Lander County, Nevada. (Illus.). 25p. 1979. 4.00 (*0-945920-10-5*) Desert Rsch Inst.
McLane, Alvin, jt. auth. see Budy, Elizabeth.
McLane, Alvin, jt. auth. see Hattori, Eugene.
McLane, Alvin R., jt. auth. see Reno, Ronald L.
McLane, Bernard W., ed. The Royal Inquest in Lincolnshire, Thirteen Forty-One. (Lincoln Record Society Ser.: No. 78). 224p. 1989. 39.00 (*0-901503-51-7*) Boydell & Brewer.
McLane, Bobbie J. City of Hot Springs, Arkansas Death Records, 1896-1917. 270p. (Orig.). 1987. pap. 25.00 (*0-929604-59-8*) Arkansas Ancestors.
— Clark County, Arkansas Census, 1850. annot. ed. 53p. (Orig.). 1985. pap. 15.00 (*0-929604-37-7*) Arkansas Ancestors.
— Clark County, Arkansas Census, 1860. 104p. (Orig.). 1988. pap. 15.00 (*0-929604-44-X*) Arkansas Ancestors.
— Clark County, Arkansas Census, 1870. 408p. (Orig.). 1985. pap. 25.00 (*0-929604-61-X*) Arkansas Ancestors.
— Clark County, Arkansas Marriage Records 1821-1879. 266p. (Orig.). 1974. pap. 22.00 (*0-929604-26-1*) Arkansas Ancestors.
— Franklin County, Arkansas Census, 1860. 89p. (Orig.). 1986. pap. 12.00 (*0-929604-39-3*) Arkansas Ancestors.
— Fulton County, Arkansas Census, 1860. 61p. (Orig.). 1988. pap. 12.00 (*0-929604-40-7*) Arkansas Ancestors.
— Hempstead County, Arkansas Census with Notes Concerning 110 Families, 1850. 93p. (Orig.). 1967. pap. 15.00 (*0-929604-08-3*) Arkansas Ancestors.
— Hot Spring County, Arkansas Census, 1850, Including Marriage, Bk. A. 69p. (Orig.). 1965. pap. 12.00 (*0-929604-02-4*) Arkansas Ancestors.
— Hot Spring County, Arkansas Census, 1860. 81p. (Orig.). 1985. pap. 12.00 (*0-929604-38-5*) Arkansas Ancestors.
— Hot Springs County, Arkansas Marriage Records, 1825-1880. 155p. (Orig.). 1970. pap. 18.00 (*0-929604-21-0*) Arkansas Ancestors.
— Index to Census of Confederate Veterans - Arkansas, 1911. 280p. (Orig.). 1988. pap. 28.00 (*0-929604-57-1*) Arkansas Ancestors.
— Johnson County, Arkansas Census, 1860. 157p. (Orig.). 1988. pap. 15.00 (*0-929604-58-X*) Arkansas Ancestors.
— Lafayette County, Arkansas Census, 1860. 66p. (Orig.). 1985. pap. 12.00 (*0-929604-35-0*) Arkansas Ancestors.
— Ouachita County, Arkansas Census, 1860. annot. ed. 130p. (Orig.). 1987. pap. 18.00 (*0-929604-43-1*) Arkansas Ancestors.
— Pike County, Arkansas Census, 1860. 59p. (Orig.). 1985. pap. 12.00 (*0-929604-36-9*) Arkansas Ancestors.
— Saline County, Arkansas Census, 1860. 92p. (Orig.). 1986. pap. 15.00 (*0-929604-41-5*) Arkansas Ancestors.
*__McLane, Bobbie J. & Allen, Desmond W.__ Arkansas 1850 Census Every-Name Index. 480p. 1995. 49.50 (*1-56546-063-4*) Arkansas Res.
— 1850 Census of Central Arkansas: Hot Spring, Jefferson, Montgomery, Perry, Prairie, Pulaski, Saline, Scott & Yell Counties. 119p. 1995. pap. write for info. (*1-56546-065-0*) Arkansas Res.
— 1850 Census of Eastern Arkansas: Arkansas, Chicot, Crittenden, Desha, Greene, Mississippi, Monroe, Phillips, Poinsett & St. Francis Counties. 112p. 1995. pap. write for info. (*1-56546-068-5*) Arkansas Res.
— 1850 Census of North Central Arkansas: Conway, Fulton, Independence, Izard, Jackson, Lawrence, Marion, Randolph, Searcy, Van Buren & White Counties. 153p. 1995. pap. write for info. (*1-56546-067-7*) Arkansas Res.
— 1850 Census of Northwest Arkansas: Benton, Carroll, Crawford, Franklin, Johnson, Madison, Newton, Pope & Washington Counties. 170p. 1995. pap. write for info. (*1-56546-064-2*) Arkansas Res.
— 1850 Census of Southern Arkansas: Ashley, Bradley, Clark, Dallas, Drew, Hempstead, Lafayette, Ouachita, Pike, Polk, Sevier & Union Counties. 182p. 1995. pap. write for info. (*1-56546-066-9*) Arkansas Res.
McLane, Bobbie J. & Cline, Inez E. Garland County, Arkansas Tombstone Records, Vol. 1: Eastern Area. 202p. (Orig.). 1970. pap. 18.00 (*0-929604-17-2*) Arkansas Ancestors.
— Garland County, Arkansas Tombstone Records, Vol. 2: Western Area. 228p. (Orig.). 1969. pap. 18.00 (*0-929604-18-0*) Arkansas Ancestors.
— Garland County, Arkansas Tombstone Records, Vol. 3: City of Hot Springs. 311p. (Orig.). 1973. pap. 28.00 (*0-929604-19-9*) Arkansas Ancestors.
— Index to Eighteen Forty Arkansas Census. 127p. (Orig.). 1967. pap. 15.00 (*0-929604-09-1*) Arkansas Ancestors.
McLane, Bobbie J. & Gandrud, Pauline J. Alabama Soldiers (Revolution, War of 1812 & Indian Wars) Vol. 16: Surnames Lacey Thru Lewis. 89p. (Orig.). 1995. pap. 15.00 (*0-929604-74-1*) Arkansas Ancestors.
— Alabama Soldiers (Revolution, War of 1812 & Indian Wars) Vol. 17: Surnames Lightfoot Thru Lynn. 89p. (Orig.). 1995. 15.00 (*0-614-04067-1*) Arkansas Ancestors.
— Alabama Soldiers (Revolution, War of 1812 & Indian Wars), Vol. 1: Surnames A through Ba. 107p. (Orig.). 1975. pap. 15.00 (*0-929604-46-6*) Arkansas Ancestors.
— Alabama Soldiers (Revolution, War of 1812 & Indian Wars), Vol. 10: Surnames Grace through Hamner. 109p. (Orig.). 1986. pap. 15.00 (*0-929604-55-5*) Arkansas Ancestors.
— Alabama Soldiers (Revolution, War of 1812 & Indian Wars), Vol. 11: Surnames Hanby through Henderson. 100p. (Orig.). 1988. pap. 15.00 (*0-929604-56-3*) Arkansas Ancestors.
— Alabama Soldiers (Revolution, War of 1812 & Indian Wars), Vol. 12: Surnames Hendon through Holland. 104p. (Orig.). 1989. pap. 15.00 (*0-929604-60-1*) Arkansas Ancestors.
— Alabama Soldiers (Revolution, War of 1812 & Indian Wars), Vol. 13: Surnames Holley through End Hs. 100p. (Orig.). 1990. pap. 15.00 (*0-929604-66-0*) Arkansas Ancestors.
— Alabama Soldiers (Revolution, War of 1812 & Indian Wars), Vol. 14: Surnames I through Jones, James. 102p. (Orig.). 1991. pap. 15.00 (*0-929604-71-7*) Arkansas Ancestors.
— Alabama Soldiers (Revolution, War of 1812 & Indian Wars), Vol. 15: Surnames Jones, John Through K. 108p. (Orig.). 1992. pap. 15.00 (*0-929604-73-3*) Arkansas Ancestors.
— Alabama Soldiers (Revolution, War of 1812 & Indian Wars), Vol. 2: Surnames Be through Bond. 100p. (Orig.). 1977. pap. 15.00 (*0-929604-47-4*) Arkansas Ancestors.
— Alabama Soldiers (Revolution, War of 1812 & Indian Wars), Vol. 3: Surnames Bonner through Brynes. 152p. (Orig.). 1977. pap. 15.00 (*0-929604-48-2*) Arkansas Ancestors.
— Alabama Soldiers (Revolution, War of 1812 & Indian Wars), Vol. 4: Surnames Ca through Coker. 102p. (Orig.). 1978. pap. 15.00 (*0-929604-49-0*) Arkansas Ancestors.
— Alabama Soldiers (Revolution, War of 1812 & Indian Wars), Vol. 5: Surnames Cole through End Cs. 90p. (Orig.). 1978. pap. 15.00 (*0-929604-50-4*) Arkansas Ancestors.
— Alabama Soldiers (Revolution, War of 1812 & Indian Wars), Vol. 6: Surnames D. 128p. (Orig.). 1979. pap. 15.00 (*0-929604-51-2*) Arkansas Ancestors.
— Alabama Soldiers (Revolution, War of 1812 & Indian Wars), Vol. 7: Surnames E through Fl. 115p. (Orig.). 1983. pap. 15.00 (*0-929604-52-0*) Arkansas Ancestors.
— Alabama Soldiers (Revolution, War of 1812 & Indian Wars), Vol. 8: Surnames Forbes through Gary. 103p. (Orig.). 1983. pap. 15.00 (*0-929604-53-9*) Arkansas Ancestors.
— Alabama Soldiers (Revolution, War of 1812 & Indian Wars), Vol. 9: Surnames Gassaway through Gower. 98p. (Orig.). 1984. pap. 15.00 (*0-929604-54-7*) Arkansas Ancestors.
McLane, Bobbie J. & Glazner, Capitola. Arkansas CSA Soldiers, Vol. 1: Surnames A-D. 160p. (Orig.). 1977. pap. 20.00 (*0-929604-28-8*) Arkansas Ancestors.
— Arkansas CSA Soldiers, Vol. 2: Surnames E-Mc. 171p. (Orig.). 1978. pap. 20.00 (*0-929604-29-6*) Arkansas Ancestors.
— Arkansas CSA Soldiers, Vol. 3: Surnames M-Z. 200p. (Orig.). 1979. pap. 25.00 (*0-929604-30-X*) Arkansas Ancestors.
— Hempstead County, Arkansas Census, 1860. 129p. (Orig.). 1969. pap. 15.00 (*0-929604-20-2*) Arkansas Ancestors.
— Jefferson County, Arkansas Census & Marriage, 1850, Bks. A & B. 115p. (Orig.). 1967. pap. 15.00 (*0-929604-07-5*) Arkansas Ancestors.
— Lafayette County, Arkansas Marriage Records, 1828-1907. 266p. (Orig.). 1982. pap. 25.00 (*0-929604-33-4*) Arkansas Ancestors.
— Marriage Records of Hempstead County, Arkansas, 1817-1875. 182p. (Orig.). 1969. pap. 22.00 (*0-929604-15-6*) Arkansas Ancestors.
— Missouri, an Index to the Eighteen Thirty Census. 191p. (Orig.). 1966. pap. 25.00 (*0-929604-05-9*) Arkansas Ancestors.
— Mortality Schedules for Arkansas, 1850. 64p. (Orig.). 1968. pap. 15.00 (*0-929604-10-5*) Arkansas Ancestors.
— Mortality Schedules for Arkansas, 1860. 108p. (Orig.). 1969. pap. 15.00 (*0-929604-12-1*) Arkansas Ancestors.
— Mortality Schedules for Arkansas, 1870. 93p. (Orig.). 1971. pap. 15.00 (*0-929604-13-X*) Arkansas Ancestors.
— Mortality Schedules for Arkansas, 1880. 261p. (Orig.). 1975. pap. 28.00 (*0-929604-14-8*) Arkansas Ancestors.
— Pope County, Arkansas Census & Marriage, 1850, Bk. 1. 95p. (Orig.). 1966. pap. 15.00 (*0-929604-03-2*) Arkansas Ancestors.
— Pope County, Arkansas Census, 1860. 139p. (Orig.). 1967. pap. 15.00 (*0-929604-04-0*) Arkansas Ancestors.
— Pope County Arkansas Marriages, 1860-1892. 307p. (Orig.). 1972. pap. 25.00 (*0-929604-24-5*) Arkansas Ancestors.
— Sevier County, Arkansas Census, 1850 & Marriage Records Through 1852. 72p. (Orig.). 1964. pap. text ed. 12.00 (*0-929604-00-8*) Arkansas Ancestors.
— Sevier County, Arkansas Census, 1860 & Marriage Records, Bk. 2. 145p. (Orig.). 1967. pap. 15.00 (*0-929604-06-7*) Arkansas Ancestors.
McLane, Bobbie J. & Hanks, Bill. Johnson County, Arkansas Census, 1870. 133p. (Orig.). 1989. pap. 18.00 (*0-929604-64-4*) Arkansas Ancestors.
— Logan County, Arkansas Marriage Records, the First Fifty Years. 219p. (Orig.). 1991. pap. 28.00 (*0-929604-68-7*) Arkansas Ancestors.
— Logan County Tax Book, 1890: (Reconstructed 1890 Census) 118p. (Orig.). 1987. pap. 15.00 (*0-929604-42-3*) Arkansas Ancestors.
— Scott County, Arkansas Census, 1860. 147p. (Orig.). 1989. pap. 16.00 (*0-929604-62-8*) Arkansas Ancestors.
— Scott County, Arkansas Census, 1870. 221p. (Orig.). 1989. pap. 22.00 (*0-929604-63-6*) Arkansas Ancestors.
McLane, Bobbie J. & Harris, Mary S. Marriage Records of Independence County, Arkansas. 350p. (Orig.). 1970. pap. 28.00 (*0-929604-22-9*) Arkansas Ancestors.
McLane, Bobbie J. & Hubbard, Margaret. Saline County, Arkansas Marriage Records, 1836-1877. 105p. (Orig.). 1978. pap. 15.00 (*0-929604-32-6*) Arkansas Ancestors.
McLane, Bobbie J. & McConnell, Imogene. Johnson County, Arkansas Marriages, 1890-1908. 89p. (Orig.). 1990. pap. 15.00 (*0-929604-65-2*) Arkansas Ancestors.
McLane, Bobbie J. & Steele, Richard. Descendants of Hugh Jones of Orange County, VA. 239p. (Orig.). 1991. 35.00 (*0-929604-69-5*); pap. 25.00 (*0-929604-77-6*) Arkansas Ancestors.
McLane, Bobbie J. & Syler, Allen. Clark County, Arkansas Obituaries & Death Notices, 1869-1900, Vol. 1. 157p. (Orig.). 1991. pap. 20.00 (*0-929604-67-9*) Arkansas Ancestors.
McLane, Bobbie J. & Syler, Allen B. Clark County, Arkansas-Obituaries & Death Notices, 1901-1913, Vol. 2: Southern Standard Newspaper. 162p. (Orig.). 1992. pap. 22.00 (*0-929604-72-5*) Arkansas Ancestors.
McLane, Bobbie J., jt. auth. see Allen, Desmond W.
McLane, Bobbie J., jt. auth. see Gandrud, Pauline J.
McLane, Bobbie J., et al. Census Reconstruction Garland & Montgomery Counties, Arkansas, 1890. 175p. (Orig.). 1985. pap. 18.00 (*0-929604-34-2*) Arkansas Ancestors.
McLane, Carole, jt. auth. see McLane, Charles.
McLane, Charles & McLane, Carole. Islands of the Mid-Maine Coast: Muscongus Bay to Monhegan, Vol. III. LC 91-67939. (Illus.). 304p. 1992. 55.00 (*0-88448-127-1*); pap. 29.95 (*0-88448-128-X*) Tilbury Hse.
*__McLane, Charles B.__ Islands of the Mid-Maine Coast Vol. IV: Pemaquid Point to the Kennebec. (Illus.). 288p. 1995. 55.00 (*0-88448-145-X*); pap. text ed. 35.00 (*0-88448-146-8*) Tilbury Hse.
— Islands of the Mid-Maine Coast, Vol. Ia: Blue Hill Bay. rev. ed. LC 83-82922. (Illus.). 160p. 1990. pap. 15.95 (*0-685-59446-7*) Tilbury Hse.
— Soviet Policy & the Chinese Communists, 1931-1946. LC 73-37861. (Select Bibliographies Reprint Ser.). 1977. reprint ed. 18.95 (*0-8369-9964-9*) Ayer.
— Soviet-Third World Relations: Vol. 2: Soviet-Asian Relations. 1974. text ed. 43.00 (*0-903424-07-X*) Col U Pr.
— Soviet-Third World Relations, Vol. 3: Soviet-African Relations. 190p. 1975. pap. text ed. 38.50 (*0-903424-08-8*) Col U Pr.
McLane, Diasann. Terence Trent D'Arby. (Illus.). 144p. 1991. 24.95 (*0-7475-0321-4*, Pub. by Bloomsbury Pub Ltd UK) Trafalgar.
McLane, Graf, Raulerson & Middleton Staff. New Hampshire Environmental Law Handbook. (State Environmental Law Ser.). 330p. 1990. pap. text ed. 74.00 (*0-86587-308-9*) Gov Insts.
*__McLane, Gretel B.__ Kalia & the King's Horse. (Illus.). 88p. (J). (gr. 3-7). 1994. pap. 8.95 (*0-916630-70-6*) Pr Pacifica.
McLane, Joan B. & McNamee, Gillian D. Early Literacy. (Developing Child Ser.). (Illus.). 160p. 1990. 23.00 (*0-674-22164-8*); pap. text ed. 7.95 (*0-674-22165-6*) HUP.
McLane, John R. Indian Nationalism & the Early Congress. LC 77-72127. 417p. reprint ed. pap. 118.90 (*0-8357-8920-9*, 2033397) Bks Demand.
— Land & Local Kingship in Eighteenth-Century Bengal. (South Asian Studies: No. 53). (Illus.). 380p. (C). 1993. 64.95 (*0-521-41074-6*) Cambridge U Pr.
McLane, Kathleen, jt. auth. see Smarte, Lynn.
McLane, Larry L. First There Was Twogood: Pictorial History of Northern Josephine County. (Illus.). 285p. (Orig.). 1988. write for info. (*0-318-64390-1*) Sexton Enter.
McLane, Louis, ed. see U. S. Treasury Department Staff.
McLane, Lucy N. In Tune with Beauty. LC 58-59534. (Illus.). 1959. 12.95 (*0-87015-083-9*) Pacific Bks.
McLane, Merrill F. The Adventure of Blueberrying: On Cape Ann Massachusetts. (Illus.). (Orig.). 1994. pap. 12.95 (*0-938813-06-4*) Carderock Pr.
— East of Granada: Hidden Andalusia & its People. (Illus.). 250p. (Orig.). 1996. pap. write for info. (*0-938813-07-2*) Carderock Pr.
— Proud Outcasts: The Gypsies of Spain. LC 86-70790. (Illus.). 192p. (Orig.). 1987. pap. 10.95 (*0-938813-03-X*) Carderock Pr.
*__McLane, Michael.__ Sedimentology. (Illus.). 512p. (C). 1995. text ed. 59.95 (*0-19-507868-3*) OUP.
McLane, Robert M. Reminiscences, Eighteen Twenty-Seven to Eighteen Ninety-Seven. LC 72-79831. (China Library Ser.). 1972. reprint ed. lib. bdg. 21.00 (*0-8420-1375-X*) Scholarly Res Inc.
McLaney, jt. auth. see Harvey, H.
McLaney, Eddie, jt. auth. see Atrill, Peter.
McLannon, Tessa. Klinefelter Syndrome: Parent & Professional Resource Guide. 100p. Date not set. pap. 9.95 (*0-932970-97-4*) Prinit Pr.
McLaren. The DBase Management with dBase IV & & 3Plus. (C). 1991. text ed. 16.50 (*0-06-500529-5*) HarpCollege.
— Looking at dBASE III Plus. (C). 1992. text ed. 5.50 (*0-06-501130-9*) HarpCollege.
— Looking at dBASE IV. (C). 1992. text ed. 9.50 (*0-06-501129-5*) HarpCollege.
— Looking at Lotus 1-2-3. (C). 1992. text ed. 9.00 (*0-06-501131-7*) HarpCollege.
— Looking at WordPerfect. (C). 1992. text ed. 9.50 (*0-06-501132-5*) HarpCollege.
— Microcomputer Applications in Business. (C). 1991. pap. text ed. 42.50 (*0-673-46383-4*) HarpCollege.
— Spreadsheets with Lotus One-Two-Three. (C). 1991. text ed. 18.00 (*0-06-500530-9*) HarpCollege.
— Word Processing with Word Perfect 5.1. (C). 1991. text ed. 17.00 (*0-06-500531-7*) HarpCollege.
McLaren & Paul. Soil Biochemistry. (Books in Soils, Plants, & the Environment: Vol. 8). 296p. 1975. pap. 99.75 (*0-8247-7023-4*) Dekker.
McLaren, A. D. & Shugar, D. Photochemistry of Proteins & Nucleic Acids. 1964. 201.00 (*0-08-010139-9*, Pub. by Pergamon Repr UK) Franklin.
McLaren, A. Douglas & Peterson, George H., eds. Soil Biochemistry, Vol. 1. LC 66-27705. 523p. reprint ed. pap. 149.10 (*0-8357-3538-9*, 2027117) Bks Demand.
McLaren, A. Douglas, jt. ed. see Paul, Eldor A.
McLaren, Alan, jt. auth. see Indianapolis Community Hospital Staff.
McLaren, Alex C. Transmission Electron Microscopy of Minerals & Rocks. (Topics in Mineral Physics & Chemistry Ser.: No. 2). (Illus.). 350p. (C). 1991. 79.95 (*0-521-35098-0*) Cambridge U Pr.
McLaren, Angus. History of Contraception: From Antiquity to the Present Day. 1992. pap. 19.95 (*0-631-18729-4*) Blackwell Pubs.
— A Prescription for Murder: The Victorian Serial Killings of Dr. Thomas Neill Cream. LC 92-20219. (Chicago Series on Sexuality, History, & Society). (Illus.). 240p. (C). 1993. 22.50 (*0-226-56067-8*) U Ch Pr.
— A Prescription for Murder: The Victorian Serial Killings of Dr. Thomas Neill Cream. 218p. 1995. pap. 12.95 (*0-226-56068-6*) U Ch Pr.
— Reproductive Rituals: Perceptions of Fertility in Britain from the Sixteenth Century to the Nineteenth Century. 208p. (Orig.). 1985. pap. 13.95 (*0-416-37460-3*, NO. 9340) Routledge Chapman & Hall.
— Sexuality & Social Order: The Debate over the Fertility of Women & Workers in France, 1770-1920. LC 81-13299. 240p. 1983. 44.50 (*0-8419-0744-7*) Holmes & Meier.
McLaren, Anne. The Chinese Femme Fatale: Stories from the Ming Period. (University of Sydney East Asian Ser.: No. 8). 176p. (C). 1994. pap. text ed. 16.95 (*0-646-14924-5*, Pub. by Wild Peony Pty AT) UH Pr.
— Germ Cells & Soma: A New Look at an Old Problem. LC 81-2971. (Mrs. Hepsa Ely Silliman Memorial Lectures: No. 45). 128p. reprint ed. pap. 36.50 (*0-7837-2784-4*, 2043176) Bks Demand.
— Mammalian Chimaeras. LC 75-40988. (Developmental & Cell Biology Monographs: No. 4). (Illus.). 160p. 1977. 47.95 (*0-521-21183-2*) Cambridge U Pr.
McLaren, Anne & Wylie, C. C., eds. Current Problems in Germ Cell Differentiation. LC 83-1845. (British Society for Developmental Biology Symposium Ser.: No. 7). 350p. 1983. 100.00 (*0-521-25329-2*) Cambridge U Pr.
McLaren, Anne, jt. ed. see Le Douarin, Nicole.
McLaren, Arlene, jt. ed. see Gaskell, Jane.
McLaren, Arthur D. & Peterson, George H., eds. Soil Biochemistry, Vol. 2. LC 66-27705. (Books in Soil Science: Nos. 1 & 2). 547p. reprint ed. pap. 155.90 (*0-8357-3539-7*, 2027117) Bks Demand.
McLaren, Bruce J. Understanding & Using Microsoft Access. Leyh, ed. LC 93-38814. 450p. (C). 1993. pap. text ed. 26.75 (*0-314-02586-3*) West Pub.
— Understanding & Using Microsoft Access 2.0. LC 94-31178. (Microcomputing Ser.). 450p. 1994. pap. text ed. 26.75 (*0-314-04653-4*) West Pub.
McLaren, Clemence. Women of Destiny: A Story of the Trojan War. LC 93-8127. 192p. (YA). (gr. 7 up). 1996. text ed. 14.95 (*0-689-31820-0*, Atheneum Bks Young) S&S Childrens.
McLaren, David R. & Isham, Marty. Lockheed F-94 Starfire: A Photo Chronicle. LC 92-62387. (Illus.). 112p. (Orig.). 1993. pap. 19.95 (*0-88740-451-0*) Schiffer.
McLaren, Dell. The Seduction of Lucy Mattson. (Inflation Fighter Ser.). 192p. 1982. pap. write for info. (*0-8439-1137-9*) Dorchester Pub Co.
McLaren, Diane J. Schistosoma Mansoni: The Parasite Surface in Relation to Host Immunity. LC 80-40955. (Tropical Medicine Research Studies: No. 1). (Illus.). 245p. reprint ed. pap. 69.90 (*0-8357-3527-3*, 2034247) Bks Demand.
McLaren, Digby, jt. ed. see Mungall, Constance.

An Asterisk (*) at the beginning of an entry indicates that the title is appearing in BIP for the first time.

McLaren, Donald S. A Colour Atlas & Text of Diet-Related Disorders. LC 92-8481. 336p. 1992. 75.00 (*0-8151-5847-5*, Yr Bk Med Pubs) Mosby Yr Bk.

McLaren, Donald S., ed. Nutrition in the Community: A Critical Look at Nutrition. 2nd ed. LC 82-6992. (Wiley-Interscience Publication Ser.). 480p. reprint ed. pap. 136. 80 (*0-7837-4517-6*, 2044296) Bks Demand.

McLaren, Donald S., et al, eds. Textbook of Paediatric Nutrition. 3rd ed. (Illus.). 616p. 1991. text ed. 149.95 (*0-443-04090-7*) Churchill.

***McLaren, J.** A New Concise Xhosa - English Dictionary. 193p. 1994. pap. 35.00 (*0-7859-8718-5*) Fr & Eur.

— New Concise Xhosa English Dictionary. rev. ed. 194p. (ENG & XHO.). 1994. pap. 14.95 (*0-7818-0251-2*) Hippocrene Bks.

— Xhosa-English Dictionary. Bennie, W. G. & Jolobe, J. J., eds. (ENG & XHO.). 27.50 (*0-87559-069-1*) Shalom.

McLaren, J. D., jt. auth. see Treyvaud, E. R.

McLaren, J. S. Chemical Manipulation of Crop Growth. 1982. text ed. 125.00 (*0-408-10767-7*) Buttrwrth-Heinemann.

McLaren, James S. Power & Politics in Palestine: The Jews & the Governing of Judaea 100BC-AD70. (JSNT Supplement Ser.: No. 63). 250p. (C). 25.00 (*1-85075-319-9*, Pub. by Sheffield Acad UK) CUP Services.

McLaren, Jean & Brown, Heide, eds. Raging Grannies Songbook. 1993. lib. bdg. 39.95 (*0-86571-254-9*); spiral bd. 14.95 (*0-86571-255-7*) New Soc Pubs.

McLaren, John. New Pacific Literatures: Culture & Environment in the European Pacific. LC 92-1672. 416p. 1993. 62.00 (*0-8153-0496-X*, H1054) Garland.

***McLaren, John & Foster, Hamar, eds.** The Legal History of British Columbia & the Yukon: Essays in the History of Canadian Law. (C). 1995. pap. 45.00 (*0-8020-7151-1*) U of Toronto Pr.

— The Legal History of British Columbia & the Yukon: Essays in the History of Canadian Law, Vol. 6. 680p. (C). 1995. 70.00 (*0-8020-0789-9*) U of Toronto Pr.

***McLaren, John, et al, eds.** Law for the Elephant, Law for the Beaver: Essays in the Legal History of the North American West. 336p. 1992. pap. 19.95 (*0-88977-072-7*) Ninth Judicial CHS.

McLaren, Ken. Yes, with Variations. 72p. (Orig.). 1983. pap. 6.00 (*0-939196-00-X*) The Smith.

McLaren, Linie L., comp. High Living: Recipes from Southern Climes. LC 72-9798. (Cookery Americana Ser.). 1973. reprint ed. pap. 13.95 (*0-405-05051-8*) Ayer.

McLaren, Lynda H., ed. see DOE Technical Information Center Staff.

***McLaren, Lynn.** Ebb Tide - Flood Tide: Beaufort County... Jewel of the Low Country. rev. ed. (Illus.). 118p. 1995. 39.95 (*1-881576-47-7*) Providence Hse.

— Ebb Tide--Flood Tide: Beaufort County...Jewel of the Low Country. (Illus.). 116p. 1991. 40.00 (*0-87249-773-9*) U of SC Pr.

McLaren, M. Stevenson & Edinburgh. LC 73-21775. (English Biography Ser.: No. 31). 1974. lib. bdg. 48.95 (*0-8383-1831-2*) M S G Haskell Hse.

***McLaren, Maria.** Seven with One Blow. LC 94-32722. 24p. (J). (gr. 1-6). 1994. pap. 6.00 (*0-88734-517-4*) Players Pr.

McLaren, Mike. The Book of Crests of Scottish-American Clans. (Illus.). 273p. (Orig.). 1991. pap. 20.00 (*1-55613-401-0*) Heritage Bk.

McLaren, Moray. Bonnie Prince Charlie. (Dorset Reprints Ser.). 224p. 1990. 19.95 (*0-88029-508-2*) Marboro Bks.

McLaren-Owens, Iain. Astro-Degree Tables: Zodiacal Data. LC 94-96299. (Astro-Degrees Ser.). 200p. 1994. pap. text ed. 24.00 (*1-885500-00-9*, AD2) Astro-Cards.

— Spreads Set & Card Titles. LC 94-96298. (Astro-Cards System Ser.). 138p. 1994. pap. text ed. 15.00 (*1-885500-01-7*, AC2) Astro-Cards.

McLaren-Owens, Iain, ed. see Whitehead, Willis F.

McLaren-Owens, Lain, ed. see Richmond, Olney H.

McLaren, Paul & Ladd. Soil Biochemistry. (Books in Soils, Plants, & the Environment: Vol. 9). 504p. 1981. 199.00 (*0-8247-1131-9*) Dekker.

McLaren, Peter. Critical Pedagogy & Predatory Culture: Oppositional Politics in a Postmodern Era. LC 94-12153. 1994. pap. 17.95 (*0-415-11756-9*, B4721) Routledge.

— Critical Pedagogy & Predatory Culture: Oppositional Politics in a Postmodern Era. LC 94-12153. 288p. 1995. 55.00x (*0-415-06424-4*, B4717) Routledge.

— Life in Schools: An Introduction to Critical Pedagogy in the Foundations of Education. 2nd ed. LC 93-17627. 272p. (C). 1994. pap. text ed. 24.95 (*0-8013-0638-8*, 78573) Longman.

— Schooling As a Ritual Performance: Towards a Political Economy of Symbols & Gestures. 2nd rev. ed. LC 92-45839. 280p. 1993. pap. 17.95 (*0-415-08265-X*, B2392) Routledge.

McLaren, Peter & Lankshear, Colin, eds. Politics of Liberation: Paths from Freire. LC 93-825. 280p. 1994. 62.50 (*0-415-09126-8*, B0840); pap. 17.95 (*0-415-09127-6*, B0844) Routledge.

McLaren, Peter & Leonard, Peter, eds. Paulo Freire: A Critical Encounter. LC 92-9965. 208p. 1993. 49.95 (*0-415-03895-2*, A9842); pap. 16.95 (*0-415-08792-9*, A9846) Routledge.

McLaren, Peter, jt. ed. see Giroux, Henry A.

McLaren, Peter, jt. ed. see Kanpol, Barry.

***McLaren, Peter, et al.** Rethinking Media Literacy: A Critical Pedagogy of Representations. LC 94-40539. (Counterpoints Ser.: Vol. 4). 280p. (C). 1995. pap. text ed. 29.95 (*0-8204-1802-1*) P Lang Pubs.

McLaren, Peter L. & Giarelli, James M., eds. Critical Theory & Educational Research. LC 94-11201. (SUNY Series, Teacher Empowerment & School Reform). 384p. (C). 1995. text ed. 74.50 (*0-7914-2367-0*); pap. text ed. 24.95 (*0-7914-2368-9*) State U NY Pr.

McLaren, Peter L., jt. ed. see Lankshear, Colin.

McLaren, Peter L., jt. ed. see Sleeter, Christine E.

McLaren, Philip. Sweet Water-Stolen Land. pap. 14.95 (*0-7022-2551-7*, Pub. by Univ Queensland Pr AT) Intl Spec Bk.

McLaren, R. G. & Cameron, K. C. Soil Science: An Introduction to the Properties & Management of New Zealand Soils. (Illus.). 312p. 1990. pap. 55.00 (*0-19-558186-5*) OUP.

McLaren, Robert B. Christian Ethics: Foundations & Practice. 304p. (C). 1993. pap. text ed. write for info. (*0-13-132804-2*) P-H.

McLaren, Robert I. Organizational Dilemmas. LC 81-19745. (Illus.). 140p. reprint ed. pap. 39.90 (*0-8357-4601-1*, 2037534) Bks Demand.

McLaren, Ronald. Solving Moral Problems: A Strategy for Practical Inquiry. LC 88-31730. 84p. (C). 1989. pap. text ed. 13.95 (*0-87484-885-7*) Mayfield Pub.

McLaren, Ronald, et al. Aesthetic & Ethical Values in Japanese Culture. (Occasional Papers, Institute for Education on Japan: Vol. 1, No. 4). 48p. (C). 1990. reprint ed. pap. 5.00 (*0-9619977-6-1*) Earlham College Pr.

McLaren, Rory S. Troubleshooting Hydraulic Components Using Leakage Path Analysis Methods. 450p. (C). 1993. pap. text ed. 49.95 (*0-9639619-1-8*) R McLaren FPT.

***McLaren, Roy.** Consensus: A Liberal Looks at His Party. 128p. 1995. lib. bdg. 20.00 (*0-8095-4927-1*) Borgo Pr.

McLaren, Roy C., jt. auth. see Wilson, O. W.

McLaren, S. B. & Braun, J. K., eds. GIS Applications in Mammalogy. (Illus.). 41p. (Orig.). 1993. pap. 10.00 (*1-883090-06-7*) OK Museum.

McLaren, Walter W. Japanese Government Documents: Of the Meiji Era, 2 vols., I. LC 79-65472. (Studies in Japanese History & Civilization). 249p. 1979. reprint ed. text ed. 65.00 (*0-313-26912-2*, U6912) Greenwood.

— Japanese Government Documents: Of the Meiji Era, 2 vols., Vol. 2. LC 79-65472. (Studies in Japanese History & Civilization). 681p. 1979. reprint ed. text ed. 75.00 (*0-313-26913-0*, U6913) Greenwood.

— Political History of Japan During the Meiji Era, 1867-1912. 379p. 1966. 35.00 (*0-7146-2018-1*, Pub. by F Cass Pubs UK) Intl Spec Bk.

***McLarey, Myra.** Water from the Well. LC 95-14042. 1995. write for info. (*0-87113-610-4*, Atlntc Mnthly) Grove-Atltic.

McLarnan, Timothy, tr. see Vorobyov, N. N.

McLarney, James J. The Theism of Edgar Sheffied Brightman. LC 75-3089. reprint ed. 11.50 (*0-404-59087-X*) AMS Pr.

McLarney, V. James & Chaff, Linda F., eds. Effective Health Care Facilities Management. LC 91-17196. 186p. (Orig.). 1991. 59.95 (*1-55648-073-3*, 055975) AHPI.

McLarney, William. The Freshwater Aquaculture Book: A Handbook for Small Scale Fish Culture in North America. rev. ed. LC 84-80961. (Illus.). 600p. (C). 1988. pap. text ed. 24.95 (*0-88179-018-4*) Hartley & Marks.

McLarty, Colin. Elementary Categories, Elementary Toposes. (Oxford Logic Guide Ser.: Vol. 21). (Illus.). 280p. 1992. 95.00 (*0-19-853392-6*) OUP.

— Elementary Categories, Elementary Toposes. (Oxford Logic Guides Ser.: No. 21). (Illus.). 280p. (C). 1995. pap. text ed. 40.00 (*0-19-851473-5*) OUP.

McLarty, Donald. The Deep Blue Seize. large type ed. 384p. 1992. pap. 14.95 (*0-7089-7157-1*, Traiitree Bookshop) Ulverscroft.

McLarty, John, jt. auth. see Melashenko, E. Lonnie.

McLary, Kathleen. Amish Style: Clothing, Home Furnishing, Toys, Dolls, & Quilts. LC 92-43967. (C). 1993. 39.95 (*0-253-33622-8*); pap. 24.95 (*0-253-20820-3*) Ind U Pr.

McLatchie, G. R. & Lennox, C. M. Soft Tissues - Trauma & Sports Injury. 485p. 1993. 95.00 (*0-7506-0170-1*) Buttrwrth-Heinemann.

McLatchie, G. R., et al. The Essentials of Sports Medicine. 2nd ed. (Illus.). 272p. (Orig.). 1993. pap. text ed. 39.95 (*0-443-04541-0*) Churchill.

McLatchie, Gregor R. Oxford Handbook of Clinical & Operative Surgery. (Illus.). 800p. 1990. 29.95 (*0-19-261710-9*) OUP.

McLauchlan, Ian, ed. The Scottish Rugby Book. (Illus.). 208p. 1994. 29.95 (*1-85158-578-8*, Pub. by Mnstream UK) Trafalgar.

McLauchlan, William P. American Legal Processes. LC 76-26579. (Viewpoints on American Politics Ser.). 233p. reprint ed. pap. 66.50 (*0-7837-3497-2*, 2057830) Bks Demand.

— Federal Court Caseloads. LC 83-21270. 236p. 1984. text ed. 49.95 (*0-275-91226-4*, C1226, Praeger Pubs) Greenwood.

McLauchlan, William P., jt. auth. see McGillem, Clare D.

McLaufhlin, W. L., et al. Dosimetry for Radiation Processing. 260p. 1989. 90.00 (*0-85066-740-2*) Taylor & Francis.

McLaughin, Robert & Sasser, Susan B. Fix Your Own LAN. 2nd ed. LC 94-21851. 326p. 1994. pap. 27.95 (*1-55828-354-4*) MIS Press.

McLaughlin. Advanced Nursing & Health Care Research. (Illus.). 512p. 1990. text ed. 58.50 (*0-7216-3098-7*) Saunders.

— Applications of Lasers in Gynecology. (Illus.). 368p. 1990. text ed. 62.50 (*0-397-50986-3*) Lippincott.

— Powers of Their Own. Date not set. 19.95 (*0-06-016781-5*, HarpT) HarpC.

McLaughlin & Hart, eds. Cyclopedia of American Government, 3 vols. 24.00 (*0-8446-1142-5*) Peter Smith.

McLaughlin & Associates, ed. see Noel, Thomas J.

McLaughlin, A. C. Report on the Diplomatic Archives of the Department of State, 1789-1840. rev. ed. (CI Ser.). 1906. reprint ed. pap. 10.00 (*0-527-00682-3*) Periodicals Srv.

McLaughlin, Andrew. Regarding Nature: Industrialism & Deep Ecology. LC 92-14076. (SUNY Series in Radical, Social & Political Theory). 280p. 1993. 57.50 (*0-7914-1383-7*); pap. 18.95 (*0-7914-1384-5*) State U NY Pr.

McLaughlin, Andrew C. Constitutional History of the United States. 1989. reprint ed. 56.50 (*0-89197-103-3*); reprint ed. pap. text ed. 29.95 (*0-89197-104-1*) Irvington.

— The Courts, the Constitution & Parties. LC 70-87405. (American Scene Ser.). 312p. 1972. reprint ed. lib. bdg. 39.50 (*0-306-71549-X*) Da Capo.

— Lewis Cass. Morse, John T., Jr., ed. LC 70-128957. (American Statesmen Ser.: No. 24). reprint ed. 32.50 (*0-404-50874-X*) AMS Pr.

McLaughlin, Ann. Report of the President's Commission on Aviation Security & Terrorism. 188p. 1990. per. 13.00 (*0-16-022114-5*, S/N 050-000-00533-0) USGPO.

***McLaughlin, Ann, ed.** Word & Worship Desk Calendar 1996. (Illus.). 128p. (Orig.). 1995. pap. 10.95 (*0-8091-3517-5*) Paulist Pr.

— Word & Worship Pocket Calendar 1996. (Illus.). 128p. (Orig.). 1995. pap. 4.95 (*0-8091-3518-3*) Paulist Pr.

McLaughlin, Ann L. The Balancing Pole: A Novel. LC 91-10307. 192p. (Orig.). 1991. pap. 9.95 (*0-936784-90-3*) J Daniel.

— Lightning in July. LC 88-37410. 176p. (Orig.). 1989. pap. 9.95 (*0-936784-72-5*) J Daniel.

McLaughlin, Arthur J. Manual of Infection Control in Respiratory Care. (Little, Brown Spiral Manual Ser.). 179p. 1983. spiral bd. 27.50 (*0-316-56096-0*) Little.

McLaughlin, Arthur L. The Black Friar: Champion of the Poor. LC 82-51216. 54p. 1983. 6.95 (*0-938232-21-5*) Winston-Derek.

McLaughlin, Barry. Second Language Acquisition in Childhood, 2 vols., Set. 2nd ed. (C). 1987. pap. text ed. 65.00 (*0-8058-0097-2*) L Erlbaum Assocs.

— Second Language Acquisition in Childhood, 2 vols., Vol. 1. 2nd ed. 256p. (C). 1987. pap. text ed. 32.50 (*0-8058-0095-6*) L Erlbaum Assocs.

— Second Language Acquisition in Childhood, 2 vols., Vol. 2. 2nd ed. 304p. (C). 1987. pap. text ed. 32.50 (*0-8058-0096-4*) L Erlbaum Assocs.

— Theories. 1987. pap. 16.95 (*0-7131-6513-8*, Pub. by E Arnld UK) St Martin.

***McLaughlin, Barry, ed.** Second Language Acquisition in Childhood: School-Age Children, Vol. 1. 280p. 1985. 59. 95 (*0-89859-378-6*) L Erlbaum Assocs.

— Second Language Acquisition in Childhood: School-Age Children, Vol. 2. (Child Psychology Ser.). 304p. 1985. 59.95 (*0-89859-565-7*) L Erlbaum Assocs.

McLaughlin, Barry, jt. auth. see Weiss, Jacqueline B.

McLaughlin, Ben, jt. ed. see Kovacs, Ruth.

McLaughlin, Brian. Dretske & His Critics. 356p. 1991. 47. 95 (*1-55786-198-6*) Blackwell Pubs.

McLaughlin, Brian P. & Rorty, Amelia O., eds. Perspectives on Self Deception. (Topics on Philosophy Ser.: Vol. VI). (C). 1988. pap. 19.00 (*0-520-06123-3*) U CA Pr.

McLaughlin, Catherine K. The Do's & Don'ts of Parent Involvement: How to Build a Positive School-Home Partnership. Schilling, Dianne, ed. 192p. 1993. teacher ed 16.95 (*1-56499-015-X*) Innerchoice Pub.

McLaughlin, Cecil. Let Go of Your Baggage & Travel Light: A Manual for Changing Your Life. 64p. 1991. pap. 5.95 (*1-879838-00-1*) Travel Light.

McLaughlin, Charles & Chiasson, Robert B. Laboratory Anatomy of the Rabbit. 3rd ed. 124p. (C). 1990. spiral bd. write for info. (*0-697-04931-0*) Wm C Brown Pubs.

McLaughlin, Charles A. Mammals of Los Angeles County, California. (Science Ser.: No. 21). (Illus.). 34p. 1959. pap. 8.00 (*0-938644-02-5*) Nat Hist Mus.

McLaughlin, Charles B. Charlie the Bunny. LC 82-73040. 169p. 1982. pap. 4.25 (*0-686-40531-5*) Dnomro Pubns.

McLaughlin, Charles C., ed. The Papers of Frederick Law Olmsted, Vol. 1: The Formative Years, 1822-1852. LC 76-47378. (Papers of Frederick Law Olmsted). (Illus.). 448p. 1977. 55.00x (*0-8018-1798-6*) Johns Hopkins.

McLaughlin, Charles C., jt. ed. see Beveridge, Charles E.

McLaughlin, Charles H., jt. auth. see Devenish, Robert J.

McLaughlin, Chris, jt. auth. see Simmons, Michele.

McLaughlin, Christian. Glamourpuss. 240p. 1994. 19.95 (*0-525-93866-4*) NAL-Dutton.

— Glamourpuss. 256p. 1995. 10.95 (*0-452-27265-3*, Plume) NAL-Dutton.

McLaughlin, Colleen, jt. ed. see Bovair, Keith.

McLaughlin, Corinne. How to Evaluate Psychic Guidance & Channeling. (Orig.). 1987. pap. write for info. (*0-9617783-0-X*) Sirius Pub.

McLaughlin, Corinne & Davidson, Gordon. Spiritual Politics: Changing the World from the Inside Out. 464p. (Orig.). 1994. pap. 12.95 (*0-345-36983-1*) Ballantine.

McLaughlin, Corrine & Davidson, Gordon. Builders of the Dawn. LC 89-29638. (Illus.). 372p. (Orig.). 1990. pap. 17.95 (*0-913990-68-X*) Book Pub Co.

McLaughlin, Curtis P. & Kaluzny, Arnold D., eds. Continuous Quality Improvement in Health Care: Theory, Implementation & Applications. LC 93-48062. 480p. 1994. 59.00 (*0-8342-0536-X*, 20536) Aspen Pub.

McLaughlin, Curtis P., jt. auth. see Wilson, Marjorie P.

McLaughlin, D. W., ed. Inverse Problems: SIAM-AMS Proceedings. LC 84-392. (S I A M-A M S Proceedings Ser.: Vol. 14). 189p. 1984. 45.00 (*0-8218-1334-X*, SIAMS/14) Am Math.

McLaughlin, Dan J. The Complete Career Handbook. Parker, Diane, ed. LC 91-50988. 60p. 1992. pap. 4.95 (*0-88247-914-8*, 914) R & E Pubs.

McLaughlin, Daniel. Sketch of a Trip from Omaha to Salmon River. 23p. 1976. pap. 3.00 (*0-87770-159-8*) Ye Galleon.

— When Literacy Empowers: Navajo Language in Print. LC 92-377. 224p. 1992. 32.50x (*0-8263-1366-3*) U of NM Pr.

McLaughlin, Daniel & Tierney, William G., eds. Naming Silenced Lives: Personal Narratives & the Process of Educational Change. LC 93-20361. 1993. 49.95 (*0-415-90516-8*, A6577, Routledge NY); pap. 15.95 (*0-415-90517-6*, A6581, Routledge NY) Routledge.

McLaughlin, Dave. Take the High Ground: An Executive's Guide to Total Quality Management. LC 90-6469. (Illus.). viii, 187p. 1990. 19.95 (*0-931541-17-4*) Mancorp Pub.

McLaughlin, David J., ed. Executive Compensation & Performance. 208p. 1982. 100.00 (*0-685-51556-7*) Pentacle Pr.

— Executive Compensation in the 1980s. 229p. 1980. 100. 00 (*0-9604760-0-8*) Pentacle Pr.

McLaughlin, Dean B., jt. ed. see Aller, Lawrence H.

McLaughlin, Donal. Die Verlorene Ehre der Katharina Blum, Boll: Critical Monographs in English. 64p. 1993. pap. 32.00 (*0-85261-257-5*, Pub. by Univ of Glasgow UK) St Mut.

McLaughlin, Doris. Cooking on a Wood Stove. 200p. 1983. pap. 9.95 (*0-89015-396-5*) Sunbelt Media.

McLaughlin, Doris B. Michigan Labor: A Brief History from 1818 to the Present. LC 73-633304. (Orig.). 1970. 10.00 (*0-87736-312-9*); pap. 5.00 (*0-87736-333-1*) U of Mich Inst Labor.

McLaughlin, Doris B. & Schoomaker, Anita L. The Landrum-Griffin Act & Union Democracy. LC 78-12592. 294p. reprint ed. pap. 83.80 (*0-7837-4718-7*, 2059070) Bks Demand.

McLaughlin, Edward T. Studies in Medieval Life & Literature. LC 74-39101. (Essay Index Reprint Ser.). 1977. reprint ed. 18.95 (*0-8369-2701-X*) Ayer.

McLaughlin, Edward W. & Rao, Vithala R. Decision Criteria for New Product Acceptance & Success: The Role of Trade Buyers. LC 90-26408. 208p. 1991. text ed. 55.00 (*0-89930-525-3*, MDQ/, Quorum Bks) Greenwood.

McLaughlin, Eithne. Social Security & Community Care: The Case of the Invalid Care Allowance. 80p. 1991. pap. 25.00 (*0-11-761820-9*, HM2862) UNIPUB.

McLaughlin, Eithne, ed. Understanding Unemployment: New Perspectives on Active Labour Market Policies. 224p. 1992. 67.50 (*0-415-07805-9*, A9693) Routledge.

McLaughlin, Eithne, et al. Work & Welfare Benefits. 157p. 1989. text ed. 58.95 (*0-566-07028-6*, Pub. by Avebury Pub UK) Ashgate Pub Co.

McLaughlin, Enda. Memoir for the Wasp. 208p. (Orig.). 1989. pap. 11.95 (*0-907606-55-5*) Irish Bks Media.

McLaughlin, Eugene. Community, Policing & Accountability: The Politics of Policing in Manchester in the 1980s. 206p. 1994. 51.95 (*1-85628-488-3*, Pub. by Avebury Pub UK) Ashgate Pub Co.

McLaughlin, Eugene, jt. ed. see Cashmore, E. Ellis.

McLaughlin, Eugene, jt. ed. see Dallos, Rudi.

McLaughlin, Evelyn G. Critical Care of the Burn Patient: A Case Study Approach. 240p. 1989. 65.00 (*0-8342-0111-9*) Aspen Pub.

McLaughlin, G. A. A Clean Heart. 1986. pap. 2.99 (*0-88019-208-9*) Schmul Pub Co.

— Commentary on Romans. 1985. pap. 9.99 (*0-88019-167-8*) Schmul Pub Co.

— Commentary on Saint Luke. 1974. pap. 9.99 (*0-88019-012-4*) Schmul Pub Co.

— Commentary on Saint Mark974. pap. 9.99 (*0-88019-011-6*) Schmul Pub Co.

— Commentary on Saint Matthew. pap. 9.99 (*0-88019-010-8*) Schmul Pub Co.

McLaughlin, G. L., jt. auth. see Freedman, G.

McLaughlin, Garland. Black Americans on Postage Stamps. (Illus.). 1982. 20.00 (*0-933184-39-5*); pap. 10.00 (*0-933184-44-1*) Flame Intl.

***McLaughlin, Gene.** Bone Hill. 290p. Date not set. pap. 8.95 (*0-7610-0258-8*) NW Pub.

McLaughlin, Gerald & Freedman, George. Color Atlas of Tooth Whitening. Hacke, Gregory, ed. (Illus.). 112p. 1991. text ed. 50.00 (*0-912791-85-3*) Ishiyaku Euro.

McLaughlin, Ginger. Our Search for Yesterday. 180p. 1984. pap. 8.95 (*0-89697-154-6*) Intl Univ Pr.

McLaughlin, Gordon, ed. New Zealand Encyclopedia. 2nd ed. (Illus.). 640p. 1988. text ed. 56.00 (*0-8161-8986-2*, Hall Reference) Macmillan.

McLaughlin, Gregory. Total Quality in Research & Development. 300p. 1995. 39.95 (*1-884015-02-6*) St Lucie Pr.

McLaughlin, Harold J. Building Your Business Plan: A Step-by-Step Approach. LC 84-11938. (Small Business Management Ser.: No. 1-471). 297p. 1985. text ed. 29. 95 (*0-471-88358-1*, Ronald Pr) Wiley.

— The Entrepreneur's Guide to Building a Better Business Plan. 1992. pap. text ed. 19.95 (*0-471-55213-5*) Wiley.

— The Entrepreneur's Guide to Building a Better Business Plan: A Step-by-Step Approach. 304p. 1992. text ed. 64. 95 (*0-471-55212-7*) Wiley.

***McLaughlin, Helen E.** Footsteps in the Sky: An Informal Review of U. S. Airlines Inflight Service, 1920-Present. (Illus.). 352p. 1994. pap. 24.95 (*0-930161-02-5*) St of the Art Bk.

Mclaughlin, Herb. Good Eats. (Orig.). 1987. pap. 8.95 (*0-89716-188-2*) P B Pubng.

McLaughlin, Hugh S. & Boulding, J. Russell. Financial Management with Lotus 1-2-3. LC 85-12143. (Illus.). 224p. 1986. pap. 33.95 (*0-13-315409-2*, Busn) P-H.

McLaughlin, J. Michael, jt. auth. see Rhett, Anne.

Mclaughlin, Jack. Jefferson & Monticello: The Biography of a Builder. LC 87-23664. (Illus.). 496p. 1990. pap. 14.95 (*0-8050-1463-2*, Owl) H Holt & Co.

McLaughlin, Jack. People Piece Puzzles. (Illus.). (J). (gr. 2-8). 1973. pap. 7.95 (*0-918932-38-6*) Activity Resources.

— To His Excellency Thomas Jefferson: Letters to a President. (Illus.). 384p. 1993. reprint ed. pap. 12.00 (*0-380-71964-9*) Avon.

McLaughlin, James. My Friend the Indian. LC 89-4902. (Illus.). xxii, 475p. 1989. pap. 11.50 (*0-8032-8160-9*, Bison Books) U of Nebr Pr.

McLaughlin, James B., Jr., jt. auth. see Hetrick, Patrick K.

McLaughlin, James B.

McLaughlin, Jan & Weber, Bruce. These Poems Are Not Pretty. 124p. 1992. pap. 7.95 (*0-9615619-9-8*) Palmetto.

*McLaughlin, Jane P. Metamorphosis: An Educational Design. (Illus.). 32p. 1995. pap. 8.00 (*0-8059-3732-3*) Dorrance.

McLaughlin, Janet, jt. auth. see Fuller, Rose.

McLaughlin, Janie, ed. see Cleveland Ballet Council, Cookbook Committee Staff.

McLaughlin, John, ed. A Guide to National & State Arts Education Services. LC 87-18712. 84p. (Orig.). 1987. pap. 10.00 (*0-915400-60-X*, ACA Bks) Am Council Arts.

— Toward a New Era in Arts Education: The Interlochen Symposium. LC 88-16649. 138p. (Orig.). 1988. pap. 12.95 (*0-915400-69-3*, ACA Bks) Am Council Arts.

McLaughlin, John, ed. see Allard, C. Kenneth, et al.

McLaughlin, John, jt. auth. see Mertens, Donna M.

McLaughlin, John A., et al, eds. Evaluation Utilization. LC 85-644749. (New Directions for Program Evaluation Ser.: No. PE 39). 1988. 17.95 (*1-55542-894-0*) Jossey-Bass.

McLaughlin, John D. & Niemann, Bernard J., Jr., eds. Developments in Land Information Management. (Illus.). 184p. (C). 1989. 36.00 (*0-685-27199-4*) Inst Land Info.

McLaughlin, John D., jt. auth. see Dale, Peter F.

*McLaughlin, John F. Horseheaven Runners. 1995. 11.95 (*0-8062-5177-8*) Carlton.

*McLaughlin, John F. & McManus, Thomas E. Competitive Uses of Regulation in the Financial Services Arena. (Illus.). 83p. (Orig.). 1994. pap. text ed. write for info. (*1-879716-10-0*, I94-1) Ctr Info Policy.

*McLaughlin, Joseph. Memory, in Your Country. 40p. (Orig.). 1995. pap. 4.00 (*0-914720-10-4*) Pale Horse.

— An Outline & Manual of Logic. rev. ed. 165p. (C). 1994. pap. 15.00 (*0-87462-401-0*) Marquette.

— Zen in the Art of Golf. rev. ed. 80p. 1993. pap. 5.95 (*0-914720-09-0*) Pale Horse.

McLaughlin, Joseph, ed. Review Seventy-Six. 48p. 1976. pap. text ed. 2.00 (*0-914720-05-8*) Pale Horse.

McLaughlin, Joseph M. Federal Evidence Practice Guide, 3 vols. 1989. Updates. ring bd. write for info. (*0-8205-1473-X*) Bender.

McLaughlin, Joseph M., jt. auth. see Peterfreund, Herbert.

McLaughlin, Judith A., comp. Bibliography of the Works of Jean Piaget in the Social Sciences. LC 87-26136. 156p. (C). 1988. lib. bdg. 39.00 (*0-8191-6730-4*) U Pr of Amer.

McLaughlin, Judith B. & Riesman, David. Choosing a College President: Opportunities & Constraints. LC 90-47689. 377p. (Orig.). 1991. pap. 8.00 (*0-931050-40-5*) Carnegie Fnd Advan Teach.

*McLaughlin, Kate. My Son, Beloved Stranger. LC 95-3295. 1995. pap. 8.95 (*0-8163-1257-5*) Pacific Pr Pub Assn.

McLaughlin, Kathleen, tr. see Ricoeur, Paul.

McLaughlin, Kenneth, Jr. Texas Probate, 3 vols., Set. 1992. write for info. (*0-8205-1708-9*) Bender.

*McLaughlin, Kenneth. Waterloo: Life Portrait of Ontario. 1990. 29.95 (*0-89781-416-9*) Preferred Mktg.

McLaughlin, Kenneth, Jr. & Robinson, Lisa S. Texas Estate Planning, 3 vols., Set. 1992. write for info. (*0-8205-1238-9*) Bender.

McLaughlin, Kenneth F. Color Me Justice, 2 vols., Set. 1987. 30.00 (*0-685-19455-8*) Equity Pubng NH.

*McLaughlin, Kevin. Writing in Parts: Imitation & Exchange in Nineteenth-Century Literature. (Illus.). 200p. 1995. 32.50x (*0-8047-2411-3*) Stanford U Pr.

*McLaughlin, Kimberly S. Please Blow Me North. 20p. (J). 1995. pap. 9.95 (*0-7610-0138-7*) NW Pub.

McLaughlin, Linda M. Signs of His Coming. Hall, Kathryn, ed. (Illus.). 64p. 1994. pap. text ed. 9.95 (*1-56664-068-7*) WorldComm.

McLaughlin, Lissa. Approached by Fur. deluxe limited ed. (Burning Deck Poetry Ser.). (Illus.). 1976. 20.00 (*0-930900-25-1*) Burning Deck.

— Seeing the Multitudes Delayed. (Burning Deck Fiction Ser.). (Illus.). 1979. 15.00 (*0-930900-75-8*); pap. 4.00 (*0-930900-76-6*) Burning Deck.

— Troubled by His Complexion. (Prose Ser.). 120p. 1988. pap. 8.00 (*0-930901-52-5*) Burning Deck.

— Troubled by His Complexion. deluxe ed. (Prose Ser.). 120p. 1988. pap. 15.00 (*0-930901-53-3*) Burning Deck.

*McLaughlin, Margaret J. & Warren, Sandra H. Performance Assessment & Students with Disabilities: Usage in Outcomes-Based Accountability Systems. LC 94-26214. (CEC Mini-Library Performance Assessment). 1994. write for info. (*0-86586-250-8*, P5061) Coun Exc Child.

McLaughlin, Margaret L., et al, eds. Explaining One's Self to Others: Reason-Giving in a Social Context. (Communication Ser.). 320p. 1992. text ed. 59.95 (*0-8058-0799-3*) L Erlbaum Assocs.

McLaughlin, Maria. Gymnastics. (Competitive Sports Ser.). (Illus.). 64p. (J). (gr. 7-12). 1984. 24.95 (*0-7134-4283-2*, Pub. by Batsford UK) Trafalgar.

McLaughlin, Marie L. Myths & Legends of the Sioux. LC 90-33804. (Illus.). 200p. 1990. reprint ed. pap. 8.00 (*0-8032-8171-4*) U of Nebr Pr.

*McLaughlin, Marilyn. Ann Arbor: A Pictorial History. (Michigan History Ser.). (Illus.). 1995. write for info. (*0-943963-41-9*) G Bradley.

McLaughlin, Mark, jt. auth. see Johnson, Curt.

McLaughlin, Martin. The Mark Curtis Hoax: How the Socialist Workers Party Tried to Dupe the Labor Movement. (Illus.). 253p. (Orig.). (C). 1990. pap. 11.95 (*0-929087-46-1*) Labor Pubns Inc.

— Vietnam & the World Revolution: A Trotskyist Analysis. 151p. (Orig.). (C). 1985. pap. 9.95 (*0-929087-01-1*) Labor Pubns Inc.

McLaughlin, Martin, ed. Desert Slaughter: The Imperialist War Against Iraq. (Illus.). 508p. (Orig.). (C). 1991. pap. 18.95 (*0-929087-54-2*) Labor Pubns Inc.

*McLaughlin, Martin L. Literary Imitation in the Italian Renaissance: From Dante to Bembo. (Oxford Modern Languages & Literature Monographs). 280p. 1995. 49.95 (*0-19-815899-8*) OUP.

McLaughlin, Martin M., jt. auth. see Overseas Development Council Staff.

McLaughlin, Mary A. & Webb, Patricia K. Study Guide To Accompany the Emerging Child: Development Through Age Twelve. 156p. (C). 1988. pap. write for info. (*0-02-424921-1*) Macmillan.

McLaughlin, Mary M. Intellectual Freedom & Its Limitations in the University of Paris in the Thirteenth & Fourteenth Centuries. Metzger, Walter P., ed. LC 76-55187. (Academic Profession Ser.). 1977. reprint ed. lib. bdg. 37.95 (*0-405-10018-3*) Ayer.

McLaughlin, Mary M., jt. ed. see Ross, James B.

McLaughlin, Mary M., tr. see Weston, Jessie L.

McLaughlin, Megan. Consorting with Saints: Prayer for the Dead in Early Medieval France. LC 93-34803. (Illus.). 300p. 1994. 32.50 (*0-8014-2648-0*) Cornell U Pr.

McLaughlin, Mercedes & McSpiritt, Marian. The Irish Heritage Cookbook. (Illus.). 100p. (Orig.). 1984. pap. 7.95 (*0-906121-11-6*, Pub. by Careers & Educ Pub IE) Irish Bks Media.

McLaughlin, Michael. The Back of the Box Gourmet. (Illus.). 144p. 1991. 14.95 (*0-671-72356-1*) S&S Trade.

— Cooking for the Weekend: Food for the Fun of It. LC 92-38950. 1993. 25.00 (*0-671-72578-5*) S&S Trade.

— Fifty-Two Meat Loaves. LC 92-26921. (Illus.). 144p. 1993. 15.00 (*0-671-78539-7*) S&S Trade.

— For Those Who Cannot Speak. 1986. pap. 4.00 (*0-911038-93-0*) Noontide.

— The Little Book of Big Sandwiches. LC 95-12944. (Illus.). 1996. write for info. (*0-8118-0719-3*) Chronicle Bks.

— The Manhattan Chili Co. Southwest-American Cookbook: A Spicy Pot of Chiles, Fixins', & Other Regional Favorites with 65 Recipes & Other Essentials. 128p. 1988. 14.00 (*0-517-56317-7*, Harmony) Crown Pub Group.

— More Back of the Box Gourmet. LC 93-25840. 1994. 15.00 (*0-671-86721-0*) S&S Trade.

— The Mushroom Book: Recipes for Earthly Delights. LC 93-31693. (Illus.). 144p. 1994. 12.95 (*0-8118-0383-X*) Chronicle Bks.

*McLaughlin, Michael, photos. In Julia's Kitchen with Master Chefs. LC 94-39380. (Illus.). 1995. pap. 20.00 (*0-679-76005-9*) Knopf.

McLaughlin, Michael, ed. see Howard, Lori, et al.

McLaughlin, Michael, et al. Screw. LC 89-61207. 300p. 1989. 22.95 (*0-88282-048-6*) New Horizon NJ.

McLaughlin, Milbrey & Pfeiffer, R. Scott. Teacher Evaluation: Improvement, Accountability, & Effective Learning. 176p. (C). 1988. pap. text ed. 17.95 (*0-8077-2890-X*) Tchrs Coll.

McLaughlin, Milbrey, jt. ed. see Heath, Shirley B.

McLaughlin, Milbrey W., et al. Urban Sanctuaries: Neighborhood Organizations in the Lives & Futures of Inner-City Youth. LC 93-40706. (social & Behavioral Science Ser.). 272p. 1994. 25.00 (*1-55542-599-2*) Jossey-Bass.

McLaughlin, Milbrey W. & Phillips, D. C. Evaluation & Education: At Quarter Century. (National Society for the Study of Education Publication Ser.: No. 90, Pt. 2). 315p. 1991. 29.00 (*0-226-60155-2*) U Ch Pr.

McLaughlin, Milbrey W. & Phillips, D. C., eds. Evaluation & Education: At Quarter Century. (National Society for the Study of Education Publication Ser.). 315p. 1993. pap. 14.95 (*0-226-60162-5*, Natl Soc Stud Educ) U Ch Pr.

McLaughlin, Milbrey W., jt. ed. see Lieberman, Ann.

McLaughlin, Milbrey W., jt. ed. see Little, Judith W.

McLaughlin, Milbrey W., et al, eds. The Contexts of Teaching in Secondary Schools: Teachers' Realities. (Series on School Reform). 296p. (C). 1990. text ed. 42.95 (*0-8077-3027-0*); pap. text ed. 22.95 (*0-8077-3026-2*) Tchrs Coll.

McLaughlin, Miriam S. & Hazouri, Sandra P. The Race for Safe Schools: A Staff Development Curriculum. Sorenson, Don L., ed. LC 94-70339. (Illus.). 144p. 1994. teacher ed 49.95 (*0-932796-59-1*) Ed Media Corp.

McLaughlin, Molly. Dragonflies. (J). (gr. 1-5). 1989. 14.95 (*0-8027-6846-6*); lib. bdg. 15.85 (*0-8027-6847-4*) Walker & Co.

— Earthworms, Dirt, & Rotten Leaves. (Illus.). 96p. (J). 1990. pap. 3.50 (*0-380-71074-9*, Camelot) Avon.

— Earthworms, Dirt & Rotten Leaves: An Exploration in Ecology. LC 86-3318. (Illus.). 96p. (J). (gr. 3-7). 1986. text ed. 13.95 (*0-689-31215-6*, Atheneum Bks Young) S&S Childrens.

*McLaughlin, Nadine B. Young Voices of the Adirondacks. (Illus.). 100p. (Orig.). (J). 1994. pap. 10.95 (*0-9643452-0-X*) Graphic Express.

McLaughlin, Nancy. Guide to Self-Published Papers in Graphology, 1979. 15p. (C). 1979. pap. text ed. 5.95 (*1-877772-08-9*) AHAF.

McLaughlin, Pamela. Computer Applications in Education: The Best of ERIC, 1990. 112p. 1991. 10.00 (*0-937597-33-3*, IR-92) ERIC Clear.

— Computer-Based Education: The Best of ERIC, 1983-1985. 102p. 1986. 10.00 (*0-937597-10-4*, IR-69) ERIC Clear.

— Computer Based Education: The Best of ERIC, 1987. 119p. 1988. 10.00 (*0-937597-22-8*) ERIC Clear.

— Computer-Based Education: The Best of ERIC, 1989. 144p. 1990. 10.00 (*0-937597-29-5*) ERIC Clear.

— Computer Based Education: The Best Or ERIC, 1986. 89p. 1987. 10.00 (*0-937597-13-9*, IR 72) ERIC Clear.

McLaughlin, Patricia, jt. ed. see Geiger, Virginia.

McLaughlin, Patricia J., jt. ed. see Zagon, Ian S.

McLaughlin, Patrick F. The Practical Musical Instrument Owner's Guide Series, 4 bks. (Illus.). 40p. (J). (gr. 7 up). 1992. A Practical Owner's Guide to the B flat Clarinet. pap. text ed. 5.95 (*1-881158-00-4*); A Practical Owner's Guide to the Saxophone. pap. text ed. 5.95 (*1-881158-02-0*); A Practical Owner's Guide to the Flute. pap. text ed. 5.95 (*1-881158-01-2*); A Practical Owner's Guide to the Brasswinds. pap. text ed. 5.95 (*1-881158-03-9*) Instrument Pr.

— The Practical Musical Instrument Owner's Guide Series, 4 bks., Set. (Illus.). 40p. (J). (gr. 7 up). 1992. pap. text ed. write for info. (*1-881158-04-7*) Instrument Pr.

McLaughlin, Patrick J. AIDS: A Cause for Concern. (Orig.). pap. text ed. write for info. (*0-938279-01-7*) W P Smedley.

McLaughlin, Patti, ed. see Hoepke, Katie W.

McLaughlin, Paul. Family Remembers: How to Create a Family Memoir Using Video & Tape Recorders. (Reference Ser.). 1993. pap. 11.95 (*0-88908-293-6*) Self-Counsel Pr.

— Ford Pickup Trucks: Development History & Restoration Guide 1948-56. (Illus.). 128p. 1986. pap. 15.95 (*0-87938-213-9*) Motorbooks Intl.

— How to Interview: The Art of the Media Interview. 2nd ed. (Reference Ser.). 256p. 1990. pap. text ed. 9.95 (*0-88908-872-1*) Self-Counsel Pr.

— Illustrated Thunderbird Buyer's Guide. (Illus.). 160p. 1994. pap. text ed. 16.95 (*0-87938-870-6*) Motorbooks Intl.

— Love at Second Sight. 224p. 1995. 20.00 (*0-7867-0188-9*) Carroll & Graf.

McLaughlin, Paul G. Illustrated Ford Model T & A Buyer's Guide. (Illustrated Buyer's Guide Ser.). (Illus.). 160p. 1994. pap. 16.95 (*0-87938-950-8*) Motorbooks Intl.

— Illustrated Ford Pickup Buyer's Guide. (Illus.). 160p. 1991. pap. 16.95 (*0-87938-526-X*) Motorbooks Intl.

McLaughlin, Peter. Kant's Critique of Teleology in Biological Explanation: Antinomy & Teleology. LC 90-6202. (Studies in the History of Philosophy: Vol. 16). 212p. 1990. lib. bdg. 89.95 (*0-88946-275-5*) E Mellen.

McLaughlin, Peter J., jt. auth. see Loehr, James E.

McLaughlin, Philip J., jt. auth. see Wehman, Paul.

McLaughlin, Phillip J. & Wehman, Paul. Developmental Disabilities: A Handbook for Best Practices. 328p. 1992. 45.00 (*1-56372-023-X*) PRO-ED.

*McLaughlin, Phillip J. & Wehman, Paul, eds. Developmental Disabilities: A Handbook for Best Practices. 1995. write for info. (*0-89079-657-2*) PRO-ED.

McLaughlin, Phillip J., jt. auth. see Bender, William N.

McLaughlin, Phillip J., jt. ed. see Eaves, Ronald C.

McLaughlin, R., jt. ed. see Olsson, C.

McLaughlin, R. B. & Stone, J. L. Some Late Pleistocene Diatoms of the Kenai Peninsula, Alaska. (Nova Hedwigia Beiheft Ser.: No. 82). (Illus.). 150p. 1986. pap. 63.00 (*3-443-51002-7*) Lubrecht & Cramer.

McLaughlin, R. K. & Bronthon, W. John. Heating Service Design. 336p. 1981. text ed. 66.95 (*0-408-00380-4*) Buttrwrth-Heinemann.

McLaughlin, Robert. Fix Your Own PC. 1990. pap. 24.95 (*1-55828-031-6*) MIS Press.

Mclaughlin, Robert. Fix Your Own PC. 1990. pap. 24.95 (*1-55828-066-9*) MIS Press.

McLaughlin, Robert. Fix Your Own PC. 2nd ed. 1993. pap. 27.95 (*1-55828-232-7*) MIS Press.

— A Short Wait Between Trains. 1976. 19.95 (*0-8488-0829-0*) Amereon Ltd.

*Mclaughlin, Robert, et al. Fix Your Own PC. 3rd ed. 544p. 1995. pap. 29.95 (*1-55828-422-2*) MIS Press.

McLaughlin, Robert B. Accessories for the Light Microscope, Vol. 16. LC 74-79374. (Illus.). 1975. 30.00 (*0-904962-00-8*) Microscope Pubns.

— Special Methods in Light Microscopy, Vol. 17. LC 77-86749. (Illus.). 1977. 35.00 (*0-904962-06-7*) Microscope Pubns.

McLaughlin, Robert N. On the Logic of Ordinary Conditionals. LC 89-21611. (SUNY Series in Logic & Language). 202p. 1990. 64.50x (*0-7914-0293-2*); pap. 21.95x (*0-7914-0294-0*) State U NY Pr.

McLaughlin, Robert W. Broadway & Hollywood: A History of Economic Interaction. LC 73-21606. (Dissertations on Film Ser.: Vol. 3). 322p. 1977. 23.95 (*0-405-04873-4*) Ayer.

— Fishing for Fish Not in the Pond: Fifty-Two Essays. LC 68-20315. (Essay Index Reprint Ser.). 1977. 17.95 (*0-8369-0655-1*) Ayer.

McLaughlin, Sara P. Meeting God in Silence. LC 93-10371. 1993. 8.99 (*0-8423-4038-6*) Tyndale.

McLaughlin, Sara P. & Webb, Mark O. A Word Index to the Poetry of C.S. Lewis. LC 88-17562. 232p. (C). 1988. lib. bdg. 30.00 (*0-933951-21-3*) Locust Hill Pr.

McLaughlin, Sigrid, ed. & tr. The Image of Women in Contemporary Soviet Fiction: Selected Short Stories from the U. S. S. R. LC 88-33335. 256p. 1989. 49.95 (*0-312-02823-7*); text ed. 19.95 (*0-312-02824-5*) St Martin.

McLaughlin, Stephen, jt. auth. see Anzalone, Stephen.

McLaughlin, Stephen, jt. auth. see Layman, R. D.

McLaughlin, Stephen D. The Wayside Mechanic: An Analysis of Skills Acquisition in Ghana. 329p. (Orig.). 1980. pap. 6.00 (*0-932288-58-8*) Ctr Intl Ed U of MA.

McLaughlin, Steven D., et al. The Changing Lives of American Women. LC 88-9699. (Illus.). xix, 250p. (C). 1988. 27.50 (*0-8078-1813-5*); pap. 14.95 (*0-8078-4237-0*) U of NC Pr.

McLaughlin, Terence H., jt. ed. see Bridges, David.

McLaughlin, Terrence. Catholic School Finance & Church-State Relations. 81p. 1986. 6.60 (*0-318-20564-5*) Natl Cath Educ.

McLaughlin, Thomas. How to Find Peace in the Mexican Alps-Lake Chapala. (Illus.). 185p. (Orig.). 1986. pap. 11.95 (*0-317-38625-5*) Bookman Hse.

— How to Find Peace in the Mexican Alps-Lake Chapala. (Illus.). 185p. (Orig.). 1986. pap. 11.95 (*0-318-18533-4*) T R & C Pubs.

McLaughlin, Thomas & Lentricchia, Frank. Literature: The Power of Language. 1488p. (C). 1989. text ed. 32.00 (*0-15-551092-4*); 7.00 (*0-15-551093-2*) HB Coll Pubs.

McLaughlin, Thomas, jt. ed. see Lentricchia, Frank.

McLaughlin, Thomas A. The Entrepreneurial Nonprofit Executive: the Myths, the Money, the People: A Guide to Prudent Risk Taking in the Service of a Larger Mission. LC 91-71517. 264p. 1991. text ed. 40.00 (*0-930807-22-7*, 600209) Fund Raising.

— Streetsmart Financial Basic for Nonprofit Managers. (Nonprofit Law, Finance & Management Set). 1995. text ed. 49.95 (*0-471-04226-9*) Wiley.

— Streetsmart Financial Basics for Nonprofit Managers. (Nonprofit Law, Finance & Management Ser.). 1995. pap. text ed. 24.95 (*0-471-11457-X*) Wiley.

McLaughlin, Thomas G. Regressive Sets & the Theory of Isols. LC 82-5115. (Lecture Notes in Pure & Applied Mathematics Ser.: No. 66). 383p. reprint ed. pap. 109.20 (*0-7837-5172-9*, 2044902) Bks Demand.

*McLaughlin, Tim, ed. Ideas Number Fifty-Four. (Illus.). 55p. (Orig.). 1994. pap. 9.95 (*0-910125-39-2*) Youth Special.

— Ideas Number Fifty-Three. (Illus.). 57p. (Orig.). 1994. pap. 9.95 (*0-910125-38-4*) Youth Special.

McLaughlin, Tim, jt. ed. see Rice, Wayne.

McLaughlin, Tom. The Greatest Escape, or How to Live in Paradise, in Luxury, for 250 Dollars per Month. (Illus.). 200p. 1985. pap. 11.95 (*0-918464-52-8*) Bookman Hse.

McLaughlin, Vance. Police & the Use of Force: The Savannah Study. LC 92-10154. 176p. 1992. text ed. 45.00 (*0-275-94344-5*, C4344, Praeger Pubs) Greenwood.

McLaughlin, W. Research Methods in Law & Business Studies. 1987. 60.00 (*0-946706-39-5*, Pub. by Royston Ltd) St Mut.

McLaughlin, W. L., ed. Trends in Radiation Dosimetry. (Illus.). 320p. 1983. pap. 28.00 (*0-08-029143-0*, Pergamon Pr) Elsevier.

McLaughlin, Walt. Pagan Fishing & Other Poems. 48p. (Orig.). 1993. pap. 6.00 (*0-944550-26-6*) Pygmy Forest Pr.

McLaughlin, William. At Rest in the Midwest: Poems. (Cleveland Poets Ser.: No. 28). 48p. 1980. pap. 4.50 (*0-914946-26-9*) Cleveland St Univ Poetry Ctr.

McLaughlin, William F. The Relaxation Principle: Freedom Through a Change in Viewpoint. LC 87-82451. 208p. 1988. pap. 9.95 (*0-9619540-0-0*) Joy Pub NM.

McLaughlin, William J. Thoughts of an Ordinary Man. 1993. 10.95 (*0-533-10293-6*) Vantage.

McLauglin, Charles B. Donna's Hell. 50p. 1971. pap. 2.00 (*0-686-01900-8*) Dnomro Pubns.

McLaulin, Bryce, jt. auth. see Duffy, John C.

McLauren, Donald S. Nutritional Ophthalmology. 1980. text ed. 203.00 (*0-12-484240-2*) Acad Pr.

McLaurin, Allen, jt. ed. see Majumader, Robin.

McLaurin, Ann M., jt. ed. see Pederson, William O.

McLaurin, John J. Sketches in Crude-Oil. LC 75-6479. (History & Politics of Oil Ser.). (Illus.). xii, 470p. 1976. reprint ed. 32.40 (*0-88355-297-3*) Hyperion Conn.

McLaurin, Katie E., et al. Health System's Role in Abortion Care: The Need for a Pro-Active Approach. (Issues in Abortion Care Ser.). 34p. 1991. pap. 7.50 (*1-882220-00-5*) IPAS.

McLaurin, Melton A. Celia, A Slave. LC 90-23045. 160p. 1991. 19.95 (*0-8203-1352-1*) U of Ga Pr.

— Celia, a Slave. 192p. 1993. reprint ed. pap. 10.00 (*0-380-71935-5*) Avon.

— The Knights of Labor in the South. LC 77-87916. (Contributions in Labor History Ser.: No. 4). (Illus.). 232p. 1978. text ed. 55.00 (*0-313-20033-5*, MCK/, Greenwood Pr) Greenwood.

— Paternalism & Protest: Southern Mill Workers & Organized Labor, 1875-1905. LC 70-111261. (Contributions in Economics & Economic History Ser.: No. 3). 265p. 1971. text ed. 55.00 (*0-8371-4662-3*, MPP&, Greenwood Pr) Greenwood.

— Separate Pasts: Growing up White in the Segregated South. LC 86-27283. (Brown Thrasher Bks.). 164p. 1987. 19.95 (*0-8203-0943-5*); pap. 9.95 (*0-8203-1044-1*) U of Ga Pr.

McLaurin, Melton A. & Thomason, Michael V. The Image of Progress: Alabama Photographs, 1872-1917. LC 80-11441. (Illus.). 240p. (Orig.). 1980. pap. 24.80 (*0-8173-0043-0*) U of Ala Pr.

McLaurin, R. D., jt. auth. see Jureidini, Paul.

McLaurin, Robert L., ed. Extracerebral Collections. (Advances in Neurotraumatology Ser.: Vol. 1). (Illus.). 270p. 1986. 85.00 (*0-387-81876-6*) Spr-Verlag.

McLaurin, Robert L., et al, eds. Spina Bifida: A Multidisciplinary Approach. LC 86-8184. 509p. 1986. text ed. 95.00 (*0-275-92100-X*, C2100, Praeger Pubs) Greenwood.

An Asterisk (*) at the beginning of an entry indicates that the title is appearing in BIP for the first time.

McLaurin, Ron D. Middle East Foreign Policy: Issues & Processes. LC 82-13137. 336p. 1982. text ed. 45.00 (0-275-90858-5, C0858, Praeger Pubs) Greenwood.

McLaurin, Ron D., ed. Military Propaganda: Psychological Warfare & Operations. LC 81-22638. 400p. 1982. text ed. 59.95 (0-275-90859-3, C0859, Praeger Pubs) Greenwood.

McLaurin, Tim. The Acorn Plan. 1989. pap. 9.95 (0-393-30616-X) Norton.

— Cured by Fire. 240p. 1995. 21.95 (0-399-14003-4) Putnam Pub Group.

— Keeper of the Moon. LC 92-19733. 1992. 11.00 (0-385-42600-3) Doubleday.

— Woodrow's Trumpet: A Novel. LC 93-71404. 250p. 1993. reprint ed. pap. 11.95 (1-878086-25-1) Down Home NC.

McLaverty, Michael. Brightening Day. 278p. 1987. pap. 10.95 (0-905169-87-5, Pub. by Poolbeg Pr IE) Dufour.

— Call My Brother Back. 184p. 1979. pap. 8.95 (0-905169-21-2, Pub. by Poolbeg Pr IE) Dufour.

— The Choice. 240p. 1991. pap. 12.95 (1-85371-110-1, Pub. by Poolbeg Pr IE) Dufour.

— Collected Short Stories. 278p. 1978. pap. 10.95 (0-905169-14-X, Pub. by Poolbeg Pr IE) Dufour.

— Game Cock & Other Stories. (Illus.). 1947. 10.00 (0-8159-5600-2) Devin.

— In Quiet Places: Uncollected Prose, Letters & Criticism. Hillan-King, Sophia, ed. LC 89-82485. 256p. 1990. pap. 12.95 (1-85371-040-7, Pub. by Poolbeg Pr IE) Dufour.

— School for Hope. 256p. 1993. reprint ed. pap. 11.95 (1-85371-172-1, Pub. by Poolbeg Pr IE) Dufour.

— Truth in the Night. 255p. 1986. pap. 8.95 (0-905169-72-7, Pub. by Poolbeg Pr IE) Dufour.

McLay, A. L. & Toner, Peter G., eds. Subcelluar Taxonomy: An Ultrastructural Classification System with Diagnostic Applications. LC 83-10856. (Ultrastructural Pathology Publication). 86p. 1985. 67.00 (0-89116-293-3) Hemisp Pub.

McLay, Geoff & Holmes, D. Student Companion: Torts. 2nd ed. 124p. 1994. Australia. pap. 14.00 (0-409-30246-5, Austral) Butterworth Legal Pubs.

McLay, W. D., ed. Clinical Forensic Medicine. 376p. 1991. pap. text ed. 39.50 (0-86187-155-3, Pub. by Pinter Pubs UK) St Martin.

McLean. Astroelectronics. 1992. text ed. 45.00 (0-86187-662-8, Pub. by Pinter Pubs UK) St Martin.

McLean & Keok. Manufacturing U.S.A. Industry Analysis, Statistics, and Leading Companies 3, 2 vols., Set. 1994. 175.00 (0-8103-7576-1) Gale.

McLean & Koek, Karin. Consultants & Consulting Organizations Directory Supplement 15. 15th ed. 1995. 410.00 (0-8103-8064-1) Gale.

— Consultants & Consulting Organizations Directory, Vol. 1: List. 14th ed. 1993. write for info. (0-8103-8046-3) Gale.

— Manufacturing U.S.A. Industry Analysis, Statistics, and Leading Companies 3, 2 vols., Set. 1992. 175.00 (0-8103-7575-3) Gale.

McLean, jt. auth. see Wilson.

McLean, Adam. The Alchemical Mandala: A Survey of the Mandala in the Western Esoteric Traditions. LC 89-34803. (Hermetic Research Ser.: No. 3). (Illus.). 145p. (Orig.). 1989. 25.00 (0-933999-79-8); pap. 14.95 (0-933999-80-1) Phanes Pr.

— A Commentary on the Mutus Liber. LC 90-47419. (Magnum Opus Hermetic Sourceworks Ser.: No. 11). (Illus.). 82p. (Orig.). 1991. 27.00 (0-933999-89-5); pap. 15.00 (0-933999-90-9) Phanes Pr.

— The Triple Goddess: An Exploration of the Archetypal Feminine. LC 89-34802. (Hermetic Research Ser.: No. 1). (Illus.). 125p. 1989. 21.95 (0-933999-77-1); pap. 10.95 (0-933999-78-X) Phanes Pr.

— Whatever Next. (Illus.). 193p. (Orig.). 1992. pap. 9.95 (0-948747-09-9) Grosvenor USA.

McLean, Adam, comment. The Crowning of Nature. (Magnum Opus Hermetic Sourceworks Ser.: No. 3). (Illus.). 135p. (Orig.). Date not set. 30.00 (0-933999-20-8); pap. 17.00 (0-933999-21-6) Phanes Pr.

McLean, Adam, ed. The Magical Calendar: A Synthesis of Magical Symbolism from the Seventeenth Centry Renaissance of Medieval Occultism. (Magnum Opus Hermetic Sourceworks Ser.: No. 1). (Illus.). 135p. (Orig.). 1993. 35.00 (0-933999-32-1); pap. 18.00 (0-933999-33-X) Phanes Pr.

— The Rosary of the Philosophers. (Magnum Opus Hermetic Sourceworks Ser.: No. 6). (Illus.). 155p. (Orig.). Date not set. 30.00 (0-933999-30-5); pap. 17.00 (0-933999-31-3) Phanes Pr.

McLean, Adam C. & Gribble, Colin D. Geology for Civil Engineers. 2nd ed. (Illus.). 1985. text ed. 49.95 (0-04-624005-5); pap. text ed. 24.95 (0-04-624006-3) Routledge Chapman & Hall.

McLean, Alastair. Western European Military Space Policy. 200p. 1992. 59.95 (1-85521-115-7, Pub. by Dartmth Pub UK) Ashgate Pub Co.

McLean, Albert, Jr. William Cullen Bryant. (Twayne's United States Authors Ser.). 1964. pap. 13.95 (0-8084-0323-0, T59) NCUP.

McLean, Albert F. Point Park College: The First 25 Years; An Oral History. 1985. write for info. (0-318-60297-0) Point Park.

— William Cullen Bryant. (United States Authors Ser.: No. 59). 184p. 1989. text ed. 22.95 (0-8057-7528-5, TUSAS 59, Pub. by Royal Botanic Garden UK) Macmillan.

Mclean, Alex, jt. auth. see Wilson, William G.

McLean, Andrew. Home Equity Kit. 1989. pap. text ed. 12.95 (0-471-50642-7) Wiley.

McLean, Andrew J. Buying & Managing Residential Real Estate. 208p. (Orig.). 1989. pap. 12.95 (0-8092-4412-8) Contemp Bks.

— Investing in Real Estate. 222p. 1988. pap. text ed. 19.95 (0-471-60115-2) Wiley.

— Making a Fortune Quickly in Fix-up Properties. 1986. pap. 6.95 (0-8092-4839-5) Contemp Bks.

McLean, Antonia, jt. auth. see McLean, Ruari.

McLean, Austin, ed. RadiOutlook II: New Forces Shaping the Industry. 143p. 1991. 40.00 (0-89324-112-1) Natl Assn Broadcasters.

McLean, Bill. The Best Peanut Butter Sandwich in the Whole World. (Illus.). 28p. (J). (ps-2). 1990. pap. 4.95 (0-88753-207-1, Pub. by Black Moss Pr CN) Firefly Bks Ltd.

McLean, Bradley H. Citations & Allusions to Jewish Scripture in Early Christian & Jewish Writings Through 180 C. E. LC 91-38309. 144p. 1992. lib. bdg. 69.95 (0-7734-9430-8) E Mellen.

***McLean, C. C.** Singing on the Throne, Tales of a Country Vet in the South. 2nd ed. 150p. pap. 15.00 (0-614-01304-6) S P-Persephone Pr.

***McLean, Candi.** Surviving a Nuclear Powered Family. (Illus.). 119p. (Orig.). 1992. pap. 14.95 (1-55059-045-6) Temeron Bks.

McLean-Carr, Carol A., jt. auth. see Winer, Yvonne.

***McLean, Celia.** Hiking the Rockies with Kids. 224p. (Orig.). 1992. pap. 14.95 (0-920501-72-9) Orca Bk Pubs.

***McLean, Cheryl.** Careers for Shutterbugs: And Other Candid Types. 1994. pap. 9.95 (0-8442-4114-8, VGM Career Bks) NTC Pub Grp.

— Family Adventure Guide: Oregon. (Illus.). 160p. (Orig.). 1995. pap. 9.95 (1-56440-647-4) Globe Pequot.

***McLean, Cheryl & Brown, Clint.** Oregon's Quiet Waters: A Guide to Lakes for Canoeists & Other Paddlers. 2nd ed. (Illus.). 144p. (Orig.). 1995. pap. 12.95 (0-943097-03-7) Jackson Creek Pr.

McLean, Cheryl, jt. auth. see Brown, Clint.

McLean, Claire. The Bouvier des Flandres. 2nd ed. LC 80-66115. (Breed Bks.). (Illus.). 1981. 29.95 (0-87714-077-4) Denlingers.

McLean, Claire D. Bouvier Records. (Breed Bks.). (Illus.). 1991. pap. 24.95 (0-87714-149-5) Denlingers.

McLean, Clifton C. Singing on the Throne: And Other Tales of a Country Vet in the South. Campbell, MaryBelle, ed. (Illus.). 160p. 1993. pap. 14.95 (1-879009-12-9) S P-Persephone Pr.

— Singing on the Throne: And Other Tales of a Country Vet in the South. Campbell, Mary B., ed. (Illus.). 160p. 1994. reprint ed. pap. 14.95 (1-879009-16-1) S P-Persephone Pr.

McLean, Dabney N. Henry Soane, Progenitor of Thomas Jefferson. (Illus.). 36p. (Orig.). 1985. pap. 4.95 (0-9614934-0-2) D N McLean.

— Mary Horsmanden Byrd of "Westover" (Illus.). 48p. (Orig.). 1989. pap. 20.00 (0-9614934-1-0) D N McLean.

McLean, Daniel W. Minnesota Legal Forms: Family Law. 240p. disk, ring bd. 69.95 (0-917126-85-8) Butterworth Legal Pubs.

— Minnesota Legal Forms: Family Law. 240p. 1994. digital audio, ring bd. 69.95 (0-614-05903-8) Michie Butterworth.

— Minnesota Legal Forms: Family Law. suppl. ed. 1994. ring bd. 40.00 (0-614-03157-5) Butterworth Legal Pubs.

McLean, David. Timothy Pickering & the Age of the American Revolution. 1981. 60.95 (0-405-14098-3) Ayer.

— War, Diplomacy & Informal Empire Vol. 1: Britain, France & Latin America. 1995. text ed. 59.50 (1-85043-867-6, Pub. by I B Tauris UK) St Martin.

McLean, Diane, ed. see Roeder, Rick.

McLean, Don. The Do-It-Yourself Gunpowder Cookbook. (Illus.). 80p. 1992. pap. 12.00 (0-87364-675-4) Paladin Pr.

— The Spy's Workshop: America's Clandestine Weapons. (Illus.). 288p. 1989. pap. 30.00 (0-87364-512-X) Paladin Pr.

McLean, Don, jt. auth. see DeRemer, Dale.

McLean, Donald H. Recognition, Identification & Prevention of Acute Viral Infections. 389p. 1991. 42.50 (0-87527-480-3) Green.

McLean, Donald J., ed. see Labrun, N. R.

McLean, Donald M. & Smith, John A. Medical Microbiology Synopsis. LC 90-5597. (Illus.). 305p. 1991. pap. text ed. 34.50 (0-8121-1304-7) Williams & Wilkins.

McLean, Donald M. & Wong, Kathleen K. Same-Day Diagnosis of Human Virus Infections. 144p. 1984. 84.00 (0-8493-6590-2, QR387, CRC Reprint) Franklin.

McLean, Duncan. Bucket of Tongues. 256p. 1994. pap. 15.95 (0-436-27631-3, Pub. by W Heinemann Ltd) Trafalgar.

McLean, Duse, ed. see Ferguson, Robert.

McLean, Duse F. Pocket Guide to Seattle. 4th ed. (Illus.). 160p. 1994. pap. 8.95 (0-9621935-3-4) Thistle Pr.

McLean, E., ed. see IFIP WG8.3 Working Conference.

McLean, Edward B. Law & Civilization: The Legal Thought of Roscoe Pound. 342p. (C). 1992. lib. bdg. 47.50 (0-8191-8698-8) U Pr of Amer.

— Roman Catholicism & the Right to Work. 186p. (Orig.). (C). 1986. lib. bdg. 46.00 (0-8191-5009-6) U Pr of Amer.

McLean, Edwin, ed. see Faber, Nancy & Faber, Randall.

McLean, Elizabeth, ed. see Cloud, Enoch C.

McLean, Evalyn W. Father Struck it Rich. (American Biography Ser.). 316p. 1991. reprint ed. lib. bdg. 79.00 (0-7812-8283-7) Rprt Serv.

McLean, Evalyn W. & Sparkes, Boyden. Father Struck It Rich. rev. ed. Benham, Jack L., ed. (Illus.). 384p. 1981. reprint ed. text ed. 24.95 (0-941026-10-8); reprint ed. pap. 10.95 (0-941026-09-4) Bear Creek Pub.

— Father Struck It Rich. LC 75-1856. (Leisure Class in America Ser.). (Illus.). 1975. reprint ed. 26.95 (0-405-06922-7) Ayer.

McLean, Francis G., jt. ed. see Hansen, Kenneth D.

McLean, Francis G., jt. ed. see Ko, Hon-Yim.

McLean, Francis G., et al, eds. Geotechnical Engineering Congress, 1991, Set, Vols. I & II. LC 91-17797. 1385p. 1991. Set. pap. text ed. 98.00 (0-87262-806-X) Am Soc Civil Eng.

McLean, Franklin C. & Urist, Marshall R. Bone: Fundamentals of the Physiology of Skeletal Tissue. 3rd rev. ed. LC 68-16703. 336p. reprint ed. pap. 95.80 (0-8357-7339-6, 2024121) Bks Demand.

McLean, Gary & Davison, Leslie. Electronic Keyboarding. (Illus.). 175p. (C). 1992. pap. text ed. 28.75 (0-939693-24-0) Collegiate Pr.

McLean, Gary & Lyons, Art. Writing for Workplace Success. 299p. (C). 1991. pap. text ed. 15.95 (1-56118-228-1); teacher ed, pap. text ed. 8.00 (1-56118-229-X) Paradigm MN.

McLean, Gary, et al. Writing: Skill Enhancement. 1994. teacher ed 8.00 (0-318-70383-1); text ed. 9.95 (1-56118-232-X); disk 20.00 (1-56118-231-1); 3.5 hd 20.00 (1-56118-230-3) Paradigm MN.

***McLean, Gary N.** Teaching Keyboarding. rev. ed. 69p. (C). 1995. pap. text ed. 12.00 (1-881530-00-0) Delta Pi Epsilon.

***McLean, Gary N., et al, eds.** Performance Appraisal: Perspectives on a Quality Management Approach. LC 94-70393. 218p. 1994. reprint ed. pap. 19.00 (1-56286-004-6) Am Soc Train & Devel.

McLean, George, et al, eds. Plant Virus Epidemics: Monitoring, Modeling & Predicting Outbreaks. 1986. text ed. 128.00 (0-12-485060-X) Acad Pr.

McLean, George F. Tradition, Harmony, & Transcendence. LC 93-4607. (Cultural Heritage & Contemporary Life Series I. Culture & Values: Vol. 4). 1993. 45.00 (1-56518-030-5); pap. 17.50 (1-56518-031-3) Coun Res Values.

McLean, George F., ed. Ethical Wisdom East &-or West. LC 78-106891. (Proceedings of the American Catholic Philosophical Association Ser.: Vol. 51). 1977. pap. 20.00 (0-918090-11-3) Am Cath Philo.

— The Existence of God. LC 73-161203. (Proceedings of the American Catholic Philosophical Association Ser.: Vol. 46). 1972. pap. 20.00 (0-918090-06-7) Am Cath Philo.

— Freedom. LC 77-153528. (Proceedings of the American Catholic Philosophical Association Ser.: Vol. 50). 1976. pap. 20.00 (0-918090-10-5) Am Cath Philo.

— The Human Person. LC 80-66375. (Proceedings of the American Catholic Philosophical Association Ser.: Vol. 53). 1979. pap. 20.00 (0-918090-13-X) Am Cath Philo.

— Immateriality. LC 79-88689. (Proceedings of the American Catholic Philosophical Association Ser.: Vol. 52). 1978. pap. 20.00 (0-918090-12-1) Am Cath Philo.

— Myth & Philosophy. LC 72-184483. (Proceedings of the American Catholic Philosophical Association Ser.: Vol. 45). 1971. pap. 20.00 (0-918090-05-9) Am Cath Philo.

— The Philosopher As Teacher. LC 74-166186. (Proceedings of the American Catholic Philosophical Association Ser.: Vol. 47). 1973. pap. 20.00 (0-918090-07-5) Am Cath Philo.

— Philosophy & Civil Law. LC 76-150281. (Proceedings of the American Catholic Philosophical Association Ser.: Vol. 49). 1975. pap. 20.00 (0-918090-09-1) Am Cath Philo.

— Philosophy & the Future of Man. (Proceedings of the American Catholic Philosophical Association Ser.: Vol. 42). 1968. pap. 20.00 (0-918090-02-4) Am Cath Philo.

— Reading Philosophy for the Twenty-First Century. LC 89-30882. (Cultural Heritage & Contemporary Life Series I. Culture & Values: Vol. 3). 336p. (Orig.). 1989. 45.00 (0-8191-7414-9); pap. 15.00 (0-8191-7415-7) Coun Res Values.

— Research on Culture & Values: The Intersection of Universities, Churches & Nations. LC 88-33914. (Cultural Heritage & Contemporary Life Series I. Culture & Values: Vol. 1). 196p. (Orig.). 1989. 45.00 (0-8191-7352-5); pap. 14.00 (0-8191-7353-3) Coun Res Values.

— Scholasticism in the Modern World. (Proceedings of the American Catholic Philosophical Association Ser.: Vol. 40). 1966. pap. 20.00 (0-918090-00-8) Am Cath Philo.

— Thomas & Bonaventure: A Septicentenary Commemoration. LC 75-319639. (Proceedings of the American Catholic Philosophical Association Ser.: Vol. 48). 1974. pap. 20.00 (0-918090-08-3) Am Cath Philo.

— Truth & the Historicity of Man. (Proceedings of the American Catholic Philosophical Association Ser.: Vol. 43). 1969. pap. 20.00 (0-918090-03-2) Am Cath Philo.

McLean, George F. & Dougherty, Jude P., eds. Philosophy & Christian Theology. (Proceedings of the American Catholic Philosophical Association Ser.: Vol. 44). 1970. pap. 20.00 (0-918090-04-0) Am Cath Philo.

McLean, George F. & Ellrod, Frederick, eds. Philosophical Foundations for Moral Education & Character Development: Act & Agent. 2nd ed. LC 91-30829. (Cultural Heritage & Contemporary Change Series VI: Foundations of Moral Education,: Vol. I). 366p. (Orig.). 1992. 45.00 (1-56518-001-1, BJ1012.A26); pap. 17.50 (1-56518-000-3) Coun Res Values.

McLean, George F. & Kromkowski, John, eds. Relations Between Cultures. (Cultural Heritage & Contemporary Change Series VI: Foundations of Moral Education,: Vol. I, No. 4). 396p. (Orig.). 1991. 45.00 (1-56518-009-7, JC330.R45); pap. 17.50 (1-56518-008-9) Coun Res Values.

— Urbanization & Values. (Cultural Heritage & Contemporary Change Series VI: Foundations of Moral Education,: Vol. I, No. 5). 380p. (Orig.). 1991. 45.00 (1-56518-011-9, HT361.U725); pap. 17.50 (1-56518-010-0) Coun Res Values.

McLean, George F. & Meynell, Hugo, eds. The Nature of Metaphysical Knowledge. LC 88-164. (International Society for Metaphysics Studies in Metaphysics Ser.: Vol. IV). 180p. (Orig.). 1988. 45.00 (0-8191-6926-9); pap. 14.00 (0-8191-6927-7) Coun Res Values.

— Person & God. LC 88-161. (International Society for Metaphysics Studies in Metaphysics: Vol. III). 377p. (Orig.). 1988. 45.00 (0-8191-6937-4); pap. 17.50 (0-8191-6938-2) Coun Res Values.

— Person & Nature. LC 88-14368. (International Society for Metaphysics Studies in Metaphysics: Vol. I). 235p. (Orig.). 1988. 45.00 (0-8191-7025-9); pap. 15.00 (0-8191-7026-7) Coun Res Values.

— Person & Society. LC 88-128. (International Society for Metaphysics Studies in Metaphysics: Vol. II). 145p. (Orig.). 1988. 45.00 (0-8191-6924-2); pap. 15.00 (0-8191-6925-0) Coun Res Values.

McLean, George F. & Pegoraro, Olinto, eds. The Social Context & Values: Perspectives of the Americas. LC 88-37080. (Cultural Heritage & Contemporary Life Series I. Culture & Values). 215p. (Orig.). 1989. 45.00 (0-8191-7354-1); pap. 15.00 (0-8191-7355-X) Coun Res Values.

McLean, George F. & Voorhies, Valerie, eds. The Nature of Philosophical Inquiry. (Proceedings of the American Catholic Philosophical Association Ser.: Vol. 41). 1967. pap. 20.00 (0-918090-01-6) Am Cath Philo.

McLean, George F. & Wolak, Richard, eds. Normative Ethics & Objective Reason: Ethics at the Crossroads, Vol. 1. LC 92-13187. (Cultural Heritage & Contemporary Change Series VI: Foundations of Moral Education,: Vol. 7). 300p. 1994. 45.00 (1-56518-023-2); pap. 15.00 (1-56518-022-4) Coun Res Values.

— Personalist Ethics & Human Subjectivity: Ethics at the Crossroads, Vol. 2. LC 92-13188. (Cultural Heritage & Contemporary Change Series VI: Foundations of Moral Education,: Vol. 8). 300p. 1994. 45.00 (1-56518-025-9); pap. 15.00 (1-56518-024-0) Coun Res Values.

McLean, George F., jt. ed. see Knowles, Richard T.

McLean, George F., tr. see Said al-Ashmawy, Muhammad.

McLean, George F., et al, eds. Culture, Human Rights & Peace in Central America. LC 88-37136. (Cultural Heritage & Contemporary Change Series VI: Foundations of Moral Education,: Vol. 2). 220p. (Orig.). 1989. 45.00 (0-8191-7356-8); pap. 14.00 (0-8191-7357-6) Coun Res Values.

— The Place of the Person in Social Life. (Cultural Heritage & Contemporary Change Series VI: Foundations of Moral Education,: Vol. I, No. 6). 398p. (Orig.). 1991. 45.00 (1-56518-013-5, BD450.P5477); pap. 17.50 (1-56518-012-7) Coun Res Values.

McLean, George N. The Rise & Fall of Anarchy in America. LC 72-885. (American History & Americana Ser.: No. 47). 1973. reprint ed. lib. bdg. 75.00 (0-8383-1426-0) M S G Haskell Hse.

McLean, Gill. Time to Get Up. LC 93-18114. (Illus.). (J). 1993. 3.95 (1-870516-11-7) Childs Play.

McLean, Gill, et al. Abena & the Rock: A Story from Ghana. LC 93-12122. (BBC TV Science Challenge Ser.). (Illus.). (J). 1993. 7.95 (1-870516-08-7) Childs Play.

— Five Things to Find: A Story from Tunisia. LC 93-12121. (BBC TV Science Challenge Ser.). (Illus.). (J). 1993. 3.95 (1-870516-07-9) Childs Play.

— Just a Pile of Rice: A Story from China. LC 93-6645. (BBC TV Science Challenge Ser.). (Illus.). (J). 1993. 3.95 (1-870516-06-0) Childs Play.

— The Snowball Rent: A Story from Scotland. LC 93-16156. (BBC TV Science Challenge Ser.). (Illus.). (J). 1993. 3.95 (1-870516-09-5) Childs Play.

McLean, Gill L. Facing Death: Conversations with a Cancer Patient. LC 93-21524. (Illus.). 224p. (Orig.). 1993. pap. text ed. 22.00 (0-443-04667-0) Churchill.

McLean, Gordon. Cities of Lonesome Fear: God among the Gangs. 1991. pap. 8.99 (0-8024-1136-3) Moody.

McLean, H. L. The Last Trump. LC 90-82592. (Illus.). 245p. (Orig.). 1990. pap. 8.95 (0-9627225-0-2) Epiphany Pubns.

McLean, Hugh. Nikolai Leskov: The Man & His Art. 796p. 1977. 50.00 (0-674-62471-8) HUP.

McLean, Hugh, ed. In the Shade of the Giant: Essays on Tolstoy. (California Slavic Studies: No. 13). 1989. 35.00 (0-520-06405-4) U CA Pr.

McLean, Hugh, ed. see Zoshchenko, Mikhail.

McLean, Hugh, et al, eds. Harvard Slavic Studies, Vol. 4: Russian Thought & Politics. LC 72-167353. (Essay Index Reprint Ser.). 1977. reprint ed. 28.95 (0-8369-2454-1) Ayer.

McLean, Hulda H. Tide-Drift Shells of the Monterey Bay Region. LC 92-81082. (Illus.). 72p. (Orig.). 1992. pap. 9.95 (0-9632480-0-6) Santa Cruz Mus Assn.

McLean, Iain. Democracy & New Technology. (Illus.). 220p. 1989. text ed. 49.95 (0-7456-0447-1) Blackwell Pubs.

— Public Choice: An Introduction. 224p. 1987. pap. text ed. 24.95 (0-631-13839-0) Blackwell Pubs.

McLean, Iain & Hewitt, Fiona, eds. Condorcet: Foundations of Social Choice & Political Theory. Hewitt, Fiona, tr. LC 93-50634. 1994. 89.95 (1-85898-068-2, Pub. by E Elgar Pub UK) Ashgate Pub Co.

McLean, Iain & Urken, Arnold B., eds. Classics of Social Choice. 476p. (C). 1993. text ed. 49.50 (0-472-10450-0) U of Mich Pr.

McLean, Ian. The Timex TS 2000: Your Personal Computer. (Illus.). 240p. 1984. pap. text ed. 12.95 (0-13-921974-9) P-H.

McLean, Ian, jt. auth. see Gordon, John.

McLean, Ian, jt. auth. see Stone, Marcus.

McLean, Ian S., ed. Infrared Astronomy with Arrays: The Next Generation. LC 94-7722. 550p. (C). 1994. lib. bdg. 168.50 (0-7923-2778-0) Kluwer Ac.

McLean, J., jt. auth. see Smith, J. C.

M

*McLean, J. A. Dimensions in Spirituality: Reflections on the Meaning of Spiritual Life & Transformation in Light of the Baha'i Faith. 336p. (Orig.). 1994. pap. 21.95 (0-85398-376-3) G Ronald Pub.

McLean, J. A. & Tobin, G. Animal & Human Calorimetry. (Illus.). 352p. 1988. 94.95 (0-521-30905-0) Cambridge U Pr.

Mclean, J. W. So You Want to Be the Boss. 1990. pap. 15. 95 (0-13-815432-5) P-H.

McLean, J. W. & Weitzel, William. Leadership: Magic, Myth, or Method? 240p. 1992. 22.95 (0-8144-5054-7) AMACOM.

McLean, James & McLean, Judy, eds. Gettysburg Sources, Vol. 3. (Illus.). 223p. (C). 1991. 26.50 (0-935523-22-7) Butternut & Blue.

*McLean, James E. Improving Education Through Action Research: A Guide for Administrators & Teachers. Herman, Jerry J. & Herman, Janice L., eds. (Roadmaps to Success). (Illus.). 88p. 1995. pap. 15.00 (0-8039-6186-3) Corwin Pr.

McLean, James H., jt. auth. see Keen, A. Myra.

*McLean, James L., Jr. Cutler's Brigade at Gettysburg. 2nd rev. ed. (Illus.). 264p. (C). 1995. 35.00x (0-935523-42-1) Butternut & Blue.

McLean, James L., ed. & intro. Gettysburg Sources, Vol. 1. (Illus.). 149p. 1986. 20.00 (0-935523-04-9) Butternut & Blue.

McLean, James L. & McLean, Judy W., eds. Gettysburg Sources, Vol. 2. (Illus.). 187p. 1987. 23.50 (0-935523-06-5) Butternut & Blue.

*McLean, Janet. Dog Tales. LC 94-32221. (Illus.). (J). 1995. write for info. (0-395-72288-8) Ticknor & Flds Bks Yng Read.

— Fire-Engine Lil. (Illus.). 32p. (Orig.). (J). (gr. k-2). 1993. pap. 6.95 (0-04-928067-8, Pub. by Allen & Unwin Aust Pty AT) IPG Chicago.

— Hector & Maggie. (Illus.). 32p. (Orig.). (J). (gr. k-2). 1993. 16.95 (0-04-442162-1, Pub. by Allen & Unwin Aust Pty AT); pap. 6.95 (0-04-442245-8, Pub. by Allen & Unwin Aust Pty AT) IPG Chicago.

— Oh, Kipper! (Illus.). 32p. (Orig.). (J). (gr. k-2). 1993. 16. 95 (1-86373-013-3, Pub. by Allen & Unwin Aust Pty AT); pap. 6.95 (1-86373-080-X, Pub. by Allen & Unwin Aust Pty AT) IPG Chicago.

McLean, Janice, ed. Directory of Fund Raising & Nonprofit Management Consultants. 390p. 1992. pap. 50.00 (0-930807-25-1, 600313) Fund Raising.

McLean, Janice, jt. ed. see Wasserman, Paul.

McLean, Janice N. & Knights, Sheila A. Phobics & Other Panic Victims: A Practical Guide for Those Who Help Them. 240p. 1989. 17.95 (0-8245-1336-3) Crossroad NY.

McLean, Jim. The Eight Step Swing: A Revolutionary Golf Technique by a PGA Pro Coach. (Illus.). 224p. 1994. 25. 00 (0-06-017073-5, HarpT) HarpC.

— The Eight Step Swing: A Revolutionary Golf Technique by a Pro Coach. 224p. 1995. pap. 15.00 (0-06-092589-2, PL) HarpC.

*McLean, Jim & Andrisani, John. The Wedge-Game Pocket Campanion. 1995. 10.00 (0-06-270141-X, Harper Ref) HarpC.

McLean, Jim & Dennis, Larry. The Golf Digest Book of Drills. 1990. pap. 21.00 (0-671-72556-4) PB.

*McLean, Jim & Pirozzolo, Fran. The Putter's Pocket Companion. LC 94-18734. 1994. 10.00 (0-06-017189-8, HarpT) HarpC.

McLean, John. Arizona Puzzles. 64p. 1991. pap. 6.95 (0-9631657-0-4) AZ Puzzles.

— Notes of a Twenty-Five Years' Service in the Hudson's Bay Territory, Vol. 19. Wallace, W. S., ed. LC 68-28607. 402p. 1968. reprint ed. text ed. 65.00 (0-8371-5057-4, MCNS, Greenwood Pr) Greenwood.

— The Science & Art of Dental Ceramics, Vol. I. (Illus.). 334p. 1979. text ed. 68.00 (0-931386-04-7) Quint Pub Co.

— The Science & Art of Dental Ceramics, Vol. II. (Illus.). 496p. 1980. text ed. 156.00 (0-931386-11-X) Quint Pub Co.

*McLean, John L., ed. & intro. The Poems & Plays of Thomas Wade. 400p. 1995. write for info. (0-87875-463-6) Whitston Pub.

McLean, John S. & Johnson, A. Ivan, eds. Aquifers of the Western Mountain Area: Regional Aquifer Systems of the United States. (Monograph Ser.: No. 14). (Illus.). 229p. (Orig.). 1989. pap. 18.00 (1-882132-05-X) Am Water Resources.

McLean, John W., ed. Dental Ceramics: Proceedings of the First International Symposium on Ceramics. (Illus.). 400p. 1983. text ed. 156.00 (0-86715-112-9) Quint Pub Co.

McLean, Joyce. Scatter the Tempest. 368p. (Orig.). 1988. pap. 3.95 (0-8439-2568-X) Dorchester Pub Co.

— Shower of Stars. 480p. (Orig.). 1987. pap. 3.95 (0-8439-2491-8) Dorchester Pub Co.

McLean, Judy, jt. ed. see McLean, James.

McLean, Judy W., jt. ed. see McLean, James L.

McLean, K. A. Drying & Storing Combinable Crops. 2nd ed. (Illus.). 268p. 1989. 49.95 (0-85236-193-9, Pub. by Farming Pr UK) Diamond Farm Bk.

McLean, Kathleen. Planning for People in Museum Exhibitions. (Illus.). 196p. (C). 1993. text ed. 35.00 (0-944040-32-2, 67-0) AST Ctrs.

McLean, Kathleen, jt. ed. see Dorn, William J.

McLean, Kathleen, jt. auth. see McNamera, John.

McLean, Ken. Quest for a Classic Winner: Pedigree Patterns of the Racehorse. (Illus.). 280p. 1987. 60.00 (0-9619432-0-3) K A & C J McLean.

McLean, Lawrence E. Computer Models in Finance. (Illus.). 176p. (Orig.). (C). 1993. pap. write for info. (0-02-379391-0) Macmillan.

McLean, M., ed. Physical & Elastic Characterisation. (Characterisation of High-Temperature Materials Ser.: No. IV). vi, 226p. 1989. text ed. 52.50 (0-901462-66-7, Pub. by Inst Materials UK) Ashgate Pub Co.

McLean, M., jt. ed. see Curbishley, I.

McLean, Margaret. Make Your Own Musical Instruments. (Do It Yourself Bks.). (Illus.). 32p. (J). (gr. 4-7). 1988. lib. bdg. 14.95 (0-8225-0895-8, Lerner Publctns); pap. 4.95 (0-8225-9558-3, Lerner Publctns) Lerner Group.

McLean, Marianne. The People of Glengarry: Highlanders in Transition, 1745-1820. (Illus.). 1991. 49.95 (0-7735-0814-7, Pub. by McGill CN) U of Toronto Pr.

— The People of Glengarry: Highlanders in Transition, 1745-1820. (Illus.). 1993. pap. 18.95 (0-7735-1156-3, Pub. by McGill CN) U of Toronto Pr.

McLean, Martin, jt. auth. see Holmes, Brian.

McLean, Mary L. & Voytek, Kenneth P. Understanding Your Economy: Using Analysis to Guide Local Strategic Planning. rev. ed. LC 92-73812. (Illus.). 245p. 1993. 49. 95 (0-918286-82-4); pap. 36.95 (0-918286-81-6) Planners Pr.

*McLean, Mervyn. An Annotated Bibliography of Oceanic Music & Dance. 2nd enl. rev. ed. LC 95-9755. (Detroit Studies in Music Bibliography: No. 74). 1995. write for info. (0-89990-073-9) Info Coord.

— Supplement: An Annotated Bibliography of Oceanic Music & Dance. 74p. 1981. pap. text ed. 8.00 (0-8248-0862-2) UH Pr.

McLean, Mervyn, jt. auth. see Orbell, Margaret.

McLean, Michael. Distant Serenade. LC 93-73186. (Illus.). 44p. 1993. 9.99 (0-87579-777-6) Deseret Bk.

— The Forgotten Carols. LC 91-30686. (Illus.). 128p. 1991. 13.95 (0-87579-554-4) Deseret Bk.

— The Well-Tempered Violin. 52p. 1992. pap. text ed. 8.95 (0-87487-434-3) Summy-Birchard.

McLean, Mick, ed. The Information Explosion: The New Electronic Media in Japan & Europe. LC 85-12666. (Emerging Patterns of Work & Communications in an Information Age Ser.: No. 3). xiv, 130p. 1985. text ed. 47.95 (0-313-25091-X, MIX/) Greenwood.

— Mechatrônics: Developments in Japan & Europe. LC 83-22925. vii, 129p. 1983. text ed. 55.00 (0-89930-087-1, MMT/, Quorum Bks) Greenwood.

McLean, Mick & Rolland, Thomas. The INMOS Saga. LC 85-2441. vii, 199p. 1986. text ed. 49.95 (0-89930-165-7, MNI/, Quorum Bks) Greenwood.

McLean, Mina, illus. February Holidays Handbook. LC 84-15572. (Holiday Handbooks Ser.). 96p. 1985. lib. bdg. 25.64 (0-89565-270-6) Childs World.

McLean, Mollie. Adventures Greek Heroes. 1972. pap. 5.95 (0-395-13714-4) HM.

McLean, Mollie & Wiseman, Anne. The Adventures of Greek Heroes. LC 61-10628. (Merit Ser.). (Illus.). 192p. (J). (ps-3). 1973. 16.95 (0-395-06913-0, Sandpiper); pap. 5.95 (0-685-42189-9, Sandpiper) HM.

*McLean, Oakland. The Evidence for Creation: Examining the Origin of Planet Earth. 192p. 1995. pap. write for info. (0-9637797-1-0) Oakland Communs.

McLean, P., et al. Building Understanding (Primary) (J). (gr. 1-3). 1990. 7.95 (0-918932-96-3) Activity Resources.

McLean, Pamela D., jt. auth. see Hudson, Frederic M.

McLean, Paul D. A Triune Concept of the Brain & Behavior: Papers Presented at Queen's University, Ontario, 1969. LC 72-90742. 177p. reprint ed. pap. 50. 50 (0-317-27771-5, 2055959) Bks Demand.

McLean, Peggy. Mirror Explorations. (J). (gr. k-4). 1994. pap. text ed. 7.95 (1-882293-01-0) Activity Resources.

McLean, Peggy & Sternberg, Betty. People Piece Primer. (Orig.). (J). (gr. k-3). 1975. pap. 7.50 (0-918932-37-8) Activity Resources.

McLean, Peggy, jt. auth. see Jenkins, Lee.

McLean, Peggy, jt. auth. see Laycock, Mary.

McLean, Peggy, jt. auth. see Laycook, Mary.

McLean, Peggy, et al. Let's Pattern Block It. (Illus.). (Orig.). (J). (gr. k-8). 1973. pap. 12.50 (0-918932-26-2) Activity Resources.

— Multilink Explorations. (Illus.). 48p. (J). (gr. 1-6). 1986. pap. 7.95 (0-918932-88-2) Activity Resources.

*McLean, R. Hugh. Guys & Ghouls. 32p. (Orig.). 1994. pap. 4.00 (1-885857-08-X) Four Wnds Pubng.

— The Sellabration of Jesus. Eldredge, A., ed. 32p. (Orig.). 1995. pap. 4.00 (1-885857-10-1) Four Wnds Pubng.

McLean, Raymond W. Fiddle a Little. Forbes, John, ed. (Fiddle a Little Ser.). 107p. 1983. student ed 12.95 (0-685-14891-2) KET.

McLean, Robert A. & Anderson, Virgil L. Applied Factorial & Fractional Designs. LC 84-7015. (Statistics, Textbooks & Monographs: Vol. 55). 389p. reprint ed. pap. 110.90 (0-7837-0271-X, 2040580) Bks Demand.

McLean, Robert A., jt. auth. see Anderson, Virgil L.

McLean, Ruari. Edward Bawden: War Artist & Letters Home 1940-1945. (Illus.). 112p. 1989. text ed. 49.95 (0-85967-695-1, Pub. by Scolar Pr UK) Ashgate Pub Co.

Mclean, Ruari. Jan Tschichold: Typographer. 1990. pap. 25. 00 (0-87923-841-0) Godine.

McLean, Ruari. Joseph Cundall, a Victorian Publisher. 96p. 1976. 28.00 (0-900002-13-1, Pub. by Priv Lib Assn UK) Oak Knoll.

— Nicholas Bentley Drew the Pictures. (Illus.). 160p. 1990. text ed. 37.50 (0-85967-843-1, Pub. by Scolar Pr UK) Ashgate Pub Co.

— The Thames & Hudson Manual of Typography. LC 80-50803. (Illus.). 216p. 1992. pap. 14.95 (0-500-68022-1) Thames Hudson.

*McLean, Ruari, ed. Typographers on Type: An Illustrated Anthology. (Illus.). 180p. 1995. 27.00 (0-393-70201-4) Norton.

McLean, Ruari & McLean, Antonia. Benjamin Fawcett: Engraver & Colour Printer. 196p. 1988. text ed. 79.95 (0-85967-789-3, Pub. by Scolar Pr UK) Ashgate Pub Co.

McLean, Scott, ed. see Snyder, Gary.

McLean, Sheila. Compensation for Damage: An International Perspective. 200p. 1993. 59.95 (1-85521-169-6, Pub. by Dartmth Pub UK) Ashgate Pub Co.

— Legal Issues in Human Reproduction. (Medico-Legal Issues Ser.: Vol. 1). 1989. text ed. 59.95 (0-566-05393-4, Pub. by Dartmth Pub UK); pap. 24.95 (1-85521-008-8, Pub. by Dartmth Pub UK) Ashgate Pub Co.

McLean, Sheila, ed. Law Reform & Human Reproduction. (Medico-Legal Issues Ser.). 200p. 1992. 59.95 (1-85521-026-6, Pub. by Dartmth Pub UK) Ashgate Pub Co.

— Law Reform & Personal Injury Litigation. (Medico-Legal Ser.). (Illus.). 180p. 1995. text ed. 59.95 (1-85521-534-9, Pub. by Dartmth Pub UK) Ashgate Pub Co.

— Legal Issues in Medicine. 234p. 1981. text ed. 52.95 (0-566-00428-3) Ashgate Pub Co.

McLean, Sheila & Maher, Gerry. Medicine, Morals & the Law. 113p. 1983. text ed. 65.00 (0-566-00533-6) Ashgate Pub Co.

McLean, Sheila A. A Patient's Right to Know: Information Disclosure, the Doctor & the Law. 270p. 1989. text ed. 59.95 (1-85521-010-X, Pub. by Dartmth Pub UK) Ashgate Pub Co.

McLean, Sheila A. & Burrows, Noreen. The Legal Relevance of Gender: Some Aspects of Sex-Based Discrimination. LC 87-4067. 220p. (C). 1988. text ed. 45.00 (0-391-03536-3) Humanities.

McLean, Susan. Pennies for the Piper. (YA). 1993. pap. 4.50 (0-374-45754-9, Sunburst Bks) FS&G.

McLean, Vianne. The Human Encounter: Teachers & Children Living Together in Preschools. 250p. 1991. 65. 00 (1-85000-724-1, Falmer Pr); pap. 29.00 (1-85000-725-X, Falmer Pr) Taylor & Francis.

— The Human Encounter: Teachers & Children Living Together in the Pre-School. 224p. 1991. 50.00 (1-85000-926-0, Falmer Pr); pap. 22.00 (1-85000-927-9, Falmer Pr) Taylor & Francis.

McLean, Virginia O. Chasing the Moon to China. LC 87-60411. (Illus.). 40p. (J). (gr. k-6). 1987. 21.95 (0-9606046-1-8) Redbird.

— Pastatively Italy. LC 94-65440. (Illus.). 40p. (J). (gr. k-6). 1996. audio 21.95 (0-9606046-6-9) Redbird.

McLean, Virginia O. & Klyce, Katherine P. Kenya, Jambo! LC 88-63987. (Illus.). 36p. (J). (gr. k-6). 1989. 21.95 (0-9606046-4-2) Redbird.

McLean, Will, jt. auth. see Singman, Jeffrey L.

McLean, William G. & Nelson, E. W. Schaum's Outline of Engineering Mechanics. 4th ed. (Schaum's Outline Ser.). 448p. 1988. pap. text ed. 12.95 (0-07-044822-1) McGraw.

McLear, Michael F. & Conti-Ramsden, Gina, eds. Pragmatic Disability in Children. (Illus.). (Orig.). (C). 1992. pap. text ed. 39.95x (1-879105-56-X, 0237) Singular Publishing.

McLeary, Joseph W. Morality, Economic Justice, & Profits. 1991. 15.00 (0-533-09560-3) Vantage.

McLeary, Michael P., tr. see Akavia, Miriam.

McLeash, K. & McLeash, V. Long to Reign over Us. large type ed. (Charnwood Library). (Illus.). 336p. 1993. 23.95 (0-7089-8740-0, Charnwood) Ulverscroft.

McLeash, V., jt. auth. see McLeash, K.

McLeay, Alison. Passage Home. 656p. 1991. mass mkt. 5.99 (0-380-71532-5) Avon.

— Passage Home. 1990. write for info. (0-671-94490-8) S&S Trade.

McLeay, Elizabeth. The Cabinet & Political Power in New Zealand. (Readings in New Zealand Politics Ser.: No. 5). (Illus.). 192p. 1995. pap. 35.00 (0-19-558312-4) OUP.

McLeay, Stuart, jt. ed. see Garrod, Neil.

McLeeland, C. & Baird, I. Low Cost CAD in Building Services. (C). 1987. 105.00 (0-86022-114-8, Pub. by Build Servs Info Assn UK) St Mut.

McLees, Ainslie A. Baudelaire's "Argot Plastique" Poetic Caricature & Modernism. LC 88-35244. (Illus.). 208p. 1990. 27.50 (0-8203-1151-0) U of Ga Pr.

McLees, Mary H. A Study of the Elementary Teaching Personnel of Hunterdon, Morris, Sussex & Warren Counties, New Jersey, with Particular Reference to the State Program of Teacher Training. LC 79-177034. (Columbia University. Teachers College. Contributions to Education Ser.: No. 512). reprint ed. 22.50 (0-404-55512-8) AMS Pr.

McLees, Nectaria. A Gathered Radiance: The Life of Alexandra Romanov, Russia's Last Empress. Isenberg, Jean, ed. LC 92-64455. (Illus.). 140p. (Orig.). 1992. pap. 9.95 (0-938635-90-5) St Herman AK.

McLees, Nectaria, et al. A Cloud of Witnesses: Woman's Struggle for Sanctity: Talks from an Orthodox Women's Conference. 143p. (Orig.). 1992. pap. 9.95 (0-938635-91-3) St Herman AK.

McLeese, Don & Philbin, Marianne, eds. All We Are Saying: Popular Musicians & the Struggle for Peace. (Illus.). 1987. pap. write for info. (0-394-75626-6) Pantheon.

McLeester, Dick. Welcome to the Magic Theatre. 2nd ed. LC 76-29541. (Illus.). (Orig.). 1977. pap. 3.75 (0-686-23238-0) Health Journal.

McLeigh, Kenneth, tr. see Sophocles.

*McLeish, Andrew. Underwater Concreting & Repair. LC 94-36568. 1994. 49.95 (0-470-23403-2) Halsted Pr.

McLeish, Barry, jt. auth. see Rust, Brian.

*McLeish, Barry J. Marketing Strategies for Nonprofit Organizations. (Nonprofit Law, Finance & Management Ser.). Date not set. text ed. 45.00 (0-471-10568-6); pap. text ed. 19.95 (0-471-10567-8) Wiley.

McLeish, Barry L. The Donor Bond: How to Nurture Your Donors Using Strategic Marketing & Management Techniques. 173p. 1991. 27.95 (0-930807-16-2, 600224) Fund Raising.

McLeish, C. W., jt. auth. see Evans, G.

McLeish, D. L. & Small, C. S. The Theory & Applications of Statistical Inference Functions. (Lecture Notes in Statistics Ser.: Vol. 44). (Illus.). vi, 124p. 1988. pap. 39. 00 (0-387-96720-6) Spr-Verlag.

McLeish, D. L., jt. auth. see Small, Christopher G.

McLeish, Ewan. Spread of Deserts. LC 90-10018. (Conserving Our World Ser.). (Illus.). 48p. (J). (gr. 4-9). 1990. lib. bdg. 22.13 (0-8114-2390-5); pap. 5.95 (0-8114-3456-7) Raintree Steck-V.

*McLeish, John. Cosmology: Science & the Meanings of the Universe. (Illus.). 212p. 1995. 39.95 (0-7475-1145-4, Pub. by Bloomsbury Pub Ltd UK) Trafalgar.

— Development of Modern Behavioural Psychology. 228p. (Orig.). (C). 1981. pap. text ed. 14.95x (0-920490-20-4) Temeron Bks.

— Number: Prehistoric. 1992. 19.50 (0-449-90693-0) Fawcett.

— The Story of Numbers: How Mathematics Has Shaped Civilization. Orig. Title: Number. (Illus.). 272p. 1994. reprint ed. pap. 11.00 (0-449-90938-7, ExPress) Fawcett.

McLeish, John A. Creativity in the Later Years: An Annotated Bibliography. LC 91-32398. 155p. 1992. 23. 00 (0-8240-4645-5, SS552) Garland.

McLeish, John L. Highlights of the Mexican Revolution. 1976. lib. bdg. 5.95 (0-8490-1950-8) Gordon Pr.

McLeish, K. Roman Comedy. 80p. 1986. reprint ed. 12.50 (0-86292-186-4, Pub. by Brstl Class Pr UK) Focus Info Gr.

McLeish, Kenneth. The Seven Wonders of the World. 32p. (J). (gr. 4-7). 1986. 18.50 (0-521-26538-X) Cambridge U Pr.

— The Seven Wonders of the World. (Illus.). (J). 1989. pap. 10.95 (0-521-37911-3) Cambridge U Pr.

— Shakespeare's Characters: A Players Press Guide. 300p. 1992. 40.00 (0-88734-608-1) Players Pr.

McLeish, Kenneth, ed. Key Ideas in Human Thought. LC 93-24150. 789p. 1993. 45.00 (0-8160-2707-2) Facts on File.

— Key Ideas in Human Thought. LC 94-34096. 1995. write for info. (1-55958-650-8) Prima Pub.

McLeish, Kenneth & McLeish, Valerie. Famous People. LC 90-37910. (Illus.). 96p. (J). (gr. 3-6). 1991. lib. bdg. 14. 89 (0-8167-2238-2); pap. text ed. 6.95 (0-8167-2239-0) Troll Assocs.

— The Listener's Guide to Classical Music: An Introduction to the Great Classical Composers & their Works. 288p. 1991. text ed. 30.00 (0-8161-7369-9, Hall Reference) Macmillan.

— The Listener's Guide to Classical Music: An Introduction to the Great Classical Composers & their Works. 288p. 1992. pap. 15.95 (0-8161-7370-2, Hall Reference) Macmillan.

— Long to Reign over Us: Memories of Coronation Day & Life in the 1950s. (Illus.). 196p. 1993. 34.95 (0-7475-1126-8, Pub. by Bloomsbury Pub Ltd UK) Trafalgar.

— The Oxford First Companion to Composers & Their Music. (Illus.). 1982. pap. 16.95 (0-19-321438-5) OUP.

— The Oxford First Companion to Instruments & Orchestras. (Illus.). 1982. pap. 16.95 (0-19-321435-0) OUP.

— The Oxford First Companion to Music. (Illus.). 192p. 1982. 29.95 (0-19-314303-8) OUP.

— The Oxford First Companion to Music Round the World. (Illus.). 1982. pap. 16.95 (0-19-321434-2) OUP.

— The Oxford First Companion to the Story of Music. (Illus.). 1982. pap. 16.95 (0-19-321437-7) OUP.

McLeish, Kenneth, tr. see Aeschylus.

McLeish, Kenneth, ed. see Buchanan, David A.

McLeish, Kenneth, ed. see McLellan, Elizabeth.

McLeish, Kenneth, ed. see Nichols, Roger & Nichols, Sarah.

McLeish, Kenneth, jt. ed. see Nichols, Roger.

McLeish, Kenneth, tr. see Sophocles.

McLeish, Norman. The Nature of Religious Knowledge. 174p. 1938. 29.95 (0-567-02193-9, Pub. by T & T Clark UK) Bks Intl VA.

McLeish, Robert. Radio Production: A Manual for Broadcasters. 3rd ed. LC 94-1103. 272p. 1994. 34.95 (0-240-51366-5, Focal) Buttrwrth-Heinemann.

— The Technique of Radio Production. 2nd ed. 272p. 1988. 36.95 (0-240-51266-9, Focal) Buttrwrth-Heinemann.

McLeish, Valerie, ed. see Buchanan, David A.

McLeish, Valerie, jt. auth. see McLeish, Kenneth.

McLeish, Valerie, ed. see McLellan, Elizabeth.

McLeish, Valerie, ed. see Nichols, Roger & Nichols, Sarah.

McLellan, Betty. Overcoming Anxiety: A Positive Approach to Dealing with Severe Anxiety in Your Life. 160p. (Orig.). 1993. pap. 16.95 (1-86373-078-8, Pub. by Allen & Unwin Aust Pty AT) IPG Chicago.

McLellan, Dave & Warrick, Bill. The Lake Shore & Michigan Southern. Riehle, Ginger, ed. (Illus.). 200p. 1989. write for info. (0-318-64859-8) Transport Trails.

McLellan, David. Unto Caesar: The Political Relevance of Christianity. LC 92-53753. (Loyola Lecture Series in Political Analysis). (C). 1993. text ed. 19.95 (0-268-01900-2) U of Notre Dame Pr.

McLellan, David, ed. The Essential Left: Five Classic Texts on the Principles of Socialism. 2nd ed. (Counterpoint Ser.). 320p. (C). 1986. pap. text ed. 19.95 (0-04-335056-9) Routledge Chapman & Hall.

— Marxism: Essential Writings. 4327p. 1988. pap. 16.95 (0-19-827517-X) OUP.

McLellan, David & Sayers, Sean, eds. Socialism & Morality. 224p. 1990. text ed. 45.00 (0-312-03700-7); pap. 14.95 (0-312-03701-5) St Martin.

McLellan, David, jt. ed. see Cohn-Sherbok, Daniel.

McLellan, David, ed. see Marx, Karl & Engels, Friedrich.

McLellan, David, ed. see Marx, Karl.

An Asterisk (*) at the beginning of an entry indicates that the title is appearing in BIP for the first time.

McLellan, David P. & Warrick, Bill. The Lake Shore & Michigan Southern Railway. Riehle, Ginger, ed. LC 89-20230. (Illus.). 208p. 1989. text ed. 40.00 (*0-933449-09-7*) Transport Trails.

McLellan, David S. Cyrus Vance. LC 85-10785. (Cooper Square American Secretaries of State & Their Diplomacy Ser.: No. 20). (Illus.). 240p. 1985. text ed. 50.00 (*0-8476-7146-1*) Rowman.

McLellan, Dermot & Stocks, Barry. McLellan & Stocks: VAT: Input Tax Recovery. 300p. 1993. 130.00 (*0-406-01139-7*, U.K.) Butterworth Legal Pubs.

McLellan, Elizabeth. Minoan Crete. McLeish, Kenneth & McLeish, Valerie, eds. (Aspects of Greek Life Ser.). (Illus.). 64p. (Orig.). (gr. 7-12). 1976. pap. text ed. 9.00 (*0-582-20671-5*, 70818) Longman.

McLellan, Evelyn. The Winter's Tale Notes. 66p. (Orig.). (C). 1984. pap. text ed. 3.95 (*0-8220-0096-2*) Cliffs.

McLellan, Gerald D. Massachusetts Family Law Handbook. 2nd ed. 439p. (C). 1982. 37.50 (*0-318-03672-X*) Lawyers Weekly.

McLellan, Gerald D. & Zack, Ellen, eds. Massachusetts Family Law Handbook Supplement, 1985. 1985. 9.80 (*0-318-18707-8*) Lawyers Weekly.

McLellan, H. J. Elements of Physical Oceanography. 1965. 73.00 (*0-08-011320-6*, Pub. by Pergamon Repr UK) Franklin.

McLellan, Hilary. Virtual Reality: A Selected Bibliography. Milheim, William D., ed. LC 92-8488. (Educational Technology Selected Bibliography Ser.: Vol. 6). 60p. (Orig.). 1992. 19.95 (*0-87778-246-6*) Educ Tech Pubns.

— Virtual Reality: Case Studies in Design for Collaboration & Learning. 200p. 1994. pap. text ed. 35.00 (*0-88736-893-X*) Learned Info.

McLellan, Hugh D. History of Gorham, Maine. LC 92-62184. (Illus.). 1088p. 1992. reprint ed. 59.50 (*0-89725-094-X*) Picton Pr.

***McLellan, James.** The Great Spirits Finger. Ingram, tr. 130p. Date not set. pap. 7.95 (*0-7610-0454-8*) NW Pub.

McLellan, Mark R., jt. ed. see Day, John G.

McLellan, Robert. Hypocrite. (Orig.). 1988. pap. 10.95 (*0-7145-0280-4*) Riverrun NY.

— The Isle of Arran. (Pevensey Island Guides Ser.). (Illus.). 112p. 1995. pap. 14.95 (*0-907115-91-8*, Pub. by D & C Pub UK) Sterling.

— McLellan: Collected Plays, Vol. 1: Includes Torwatletie, Jamie the Saxt, The Flowers o' Edinburgh & The Carlin Moth. (Illus.). (Orig.). 1987. pap. 13.95 (*0-7145-3818-3*) Riverrun NY.

McLellan, Tom & Bragg, Alicia. Escape from Anxiety & Stress. (Encyclopedia of Psychoactive Drugs Ser.: No. 1). (Illus.). 1992. lib. bdg. 19.95 (*0-685-52241-5*) Chelsea Hse.

McLellan, Vern. Batter Up: Humorous Quotes on Baseball. 78p. (Orig.). 1993. pap. 7.95 (*1-56245-067-0*) Great Quotations.

— Double Dribble. (Illus.). 78p. (Orig.). 1992. pap. 7.95 (*1-56245-008-5*) Great Quotations.

— Happiness Walks on Busy Feet. 168p. (Orig.). 1992. pap. 5.95 (*1-56245-059-X*) Great Quotations.

— Hornet's Hoop Lines. (Illus.). 128p. 1991. write for info. (*0-926918-90-7*) Associates Pr.

— Krazy Quotes for Kids. 1993. pap. 3.99 (*1-56507-070-4*) Harvest Hse.

— Proverbs for People. LC 82-83841. (Illus.). 1983. mass mkt. 3.99 (*0-89081-326-4*) Harvest Hse.

— Wise & Wacky Wit. 160p. 1992. pap. text ed. 3.99 (*0-8423-8249-6*) Tyndale.

McLelland. Color Atlas of Avian Anatomy. 1991. text ed. 84.00 (*0-7216-3536-9*) Saunders.

McLelland, C., jt. ed. see Wix, J.

M'Clelland, J. The Calcutta Journal of Natural History, Set: Vols. 1-5. 5645p. 1985. reprint ed. Set. 2,500.00 (*81-7089-030-6*, Pub. by Intl Bk Distr II) St Mut.

McLelland, J., jt. auth. see Skerrit, G. C.

McLelland, John, jt. ed. see King, A. S.

McLellon, Waldron M. Leather & Soul: A Civil War Odyssey. LC 93-74230. 513p. (Orig.). 1995. pap. 16.95 (*1-884489-00-1*) Butternut.

***McLemee, Scott, ed.** C. L. R. James & the "Negro Question" 224p. 1996. lib. bdg. 40.00 (*0-87805-807-9*); pap. 16.95 (*0-87805-823-0*) U Pr of Miss.

McLemee, Scott & Le Blanc, Paul, eds. C. L. R. James & Revolutionary Marxism: Selected Writings 1939-1949. LC 92-20631. (Revolutionary Studies). 264p. (C). 1993. pap. 18.50 (*0-391-03824-9*) Humanities.

— C. L. R. James & Revolutionary Marxism: Selected Writings 1939-1949. LC 92-20631. (Revolutionary Studies). 264p. (C). 1993. text ed. 49.95 (*0-391-03786-2*) Humanities.

McLemore, Anna M. No Toads Allowed! 80p. 1992. pap. 8.95 (*0-9630120-0-2*) Relational Pr.

***McLemore, George, et al.** Pak: Presentational Speaking. 320p. (C). 1994. 26.25 (*0-7872-0024-7*) Kendall-Hunt.

McLemore, Henry, jt. auth. see Kahn, Ely J.

McLemore, Ivy. The Texas Highschool Basketball Scrapbook. Eakin, Edwin M., ed. (Illus.). 128p. (Orig.). 1989. pap. 12.95 (*0-89015-723-5*) Sunbelt Media.

McLemore, J. Quality Assurance in Diagnostic Radiology. (Illus.). 228p. 1981. 35.00 (*0-8151-5832-7*, BKL-1, Yr Bk Med Pubs) Mosby Yr Bk.

McLemore, Joy M. Quality Assurance in Diagnostic Radiology. LC 80-27154. (Illus.). 237p. reprint ed. pap. 67.60 (*0-685-23928-4*, 2033002) Bks Demand.

McLemore, Richard A., ed. A History of Mississippi, Vol. 1. LC 72-76857. (Illus.). 781p. reprint ed. pap. 180.00 (*0-7837-1068-2*, 2041591) Bks Demand.

— A History of Mississippi, Vol. 2. LC 72-76857. (Illus.). 743p. reprint ed. pap. 180.00 (*0-7837-1069-0*, 2041591) Bks Demand.

McLemore, S. Dale. Racial & Ethnic Relations in America. 4th ed. LC 93-2934. 1993. text ed. write for info. (*0-205-14346-6*) Allyn.

McLemore, William P., ed. Teach with Discipline. LC 93-5605. 148p. (Orig.). (C). 1993. pap. text ed. 22.50 (*0-8191-9265-1*) U Pr of Amer.

McLemorel, Thomas, jt. auth. see McCraig, Linda F.

McLenaghan, John B., et al. Currency Convertibility in the Economic Community of West African States. (Occasional Paper Ser.: No. 13). 46p. 1982. pap. 5.00 (*1-55775-059-9*) Intl Monetary.

Mclenaghan, R. G., jt. auth. see Mann, R. B.

***McLendon, Jacquelyn Y.** The Politics of Color in the Fiction of Jessie Fauset & Nella Larsen. 160p. (C). 1995. text ed. 29.50 (*0-8139-1553-8*) U Pr of Va.

McLendon, James. Papa: Hemingway in Key West. rev. ed. LC 88-81528. (Illus.). 240p. 1990. reprint ed. 24.95 (*0-911607-08-0*) Langley Pr Inc.

— Papa: Hemingway in Key West. rev. ed. LC 88-81528. (Illus.). 240p. 1995. reprint ed. pap. 13.95 (*0-911607-07-2*) Langley Pr Inc.

McLendon, Karen. A Challenge to Women. 22p. (Orig.). 1994. pap. 1.25 (*0-9629470-9-1*) FatherSon Pub.

McLendon, Winzola. Martha: The Biography of Martha Mitchell. LC 77-90289. (Illus.). 1979. 12.95 (*0-394-41124-2*) Random.

McLenighan, Valjean. China: A History to Nineteen Forty-Nine. LC 83-14260. (Enchantment of the World Ser.). (Illus.). 128p. (J). (gr. 5-9). 1983. lib. bdg. 20.55 (*0-516-02754-9*) Childrens.

— One Whole Doughnut...One Doughnut Hole. LC 82-12838. (Rookie Reader Ser.). (Illus.). 32p. (J). (ps-2). 1982. lib. bdg. 10.35 (*0-516-02031-5*); pap. 2.95 (*0-516-42031-3*) Childrens.

— People's Republic of China. LC 84-7025. (Enchantment of the World Ser.). (Illus.). 128p. (J). (gr. 5-9). 1984. lib. bdg. 20.55 (*0-516-02781-6*) Childrens.

— Stop-Go, Fast-Slow. LC 81-17080. (Rookie Reader Ser.). (Illus.). 32p. (J). (ps-2). 1982. lib. bdg. 10.35 (*0-516-03617-3*); pap. text ed. 2.95 (*0-516-43617-1*) Childrens.

McLennaghan, Bonnie G., ed. Originals. (Illus.). 266p. 1994. 19.95 (*0-9625396-2-7*) Lindal Cedar.

McLennan, Bardi. Dogs & Kids: A Guide for Parents. (Illus.). 240p. 1993. 18.95 (*0-87605-535-8*) Howell Bk.

— Welsh Terrier. (Illus.). 192p. 1993. 11.95 (*0-86622-585-4*, KW213) TFH Pubns.

McLennan, D. J. A Revised Transition State Spectrum for Concerted Bimolecular B - Eliminations. 1976. pap. 15.50 (*0-08-020472-4*, Pergamon Pr) Elsevier.

McLennan, Deborah A., jt. auth. see Brooks, Daniel R.

McLennan, Dermot, jt. auth. see Scott, Howard.

McLennan, G. Scots Gaelic: A Brief Introduction. 28p. (ENG & GAE.). 1987. 12.95 (*0-8288-3345-1*, F132982) Fr & Eur.

McLennan, Gregor. Marxism & the Methodologies of History. 272p. 1985. pap. text ed. 13.95 (*0-86091-743-6*, Pub. by Verso UK) Routledge Chapman & Hall.

— Marxism, Pluralism & Beyond: Classic Debates & New Departures. 320p. 1990. 59.95 (*0-7456-0350-5*); pap. 24.95 (*0-7456-0351-3*) Blackwell Pubs.

McLennan, Gregor, et al, eds. State & Society in Contemporary Britain: A Critical Introduction. 400p. 1985. pap. 17.95 (*0-7456-0009-3*) Blackwell Pubs.

***McLennan, Gregory.** Pluralism. (Concepts in Social Thought Ser.). 1995. text ed. 37.95 (*0-8166-2814-9*); pap. text ed. 14.95 (*0-8166-2815-7*) U of Minn Pr.

McLennan, H., et al, eds. Advances in Physiological Research. LC 81-14181. 516p. 1987. 115.00 (*0-306-42575-0*, Plenum Pr) Plenum.

McLennan, J. M., tr. see Beklemishev, V. N.

McLennan, Kenneth, jt. ed. see Baumol, William J.

McLennan, Rob. Growing Proteas. (Growing Ser.). (Illus.). 80p. (Orig.). 1994. pap. 13.95 (*0-86417-499-3*, Pub. by Kangaroo Pr AT) Seven Hills Bk.

McLennan, Roy. Managing Organizational Change. 576p. (C). 1989. pap. text ed. write for info. (*0-13-551508-4*) P-H.

McLennan, S., jt. auth. see Taylor, S.

McLennon, Gregor, et al, eds. The Idea of the Modern State. LC 84-19019. 256p. 1984. 85.00 (*0-335-15021-7*, Open Univ Pr); pap. 29.00 (*0-335-10597-1*, Open Univ Pr) Taylor & Francis.

McLeod. Composite Bows from Tomb of Tutankhamun. (Tutankhamuns Tomb Ser.: Vol. 3). 1970. 34.00 (*0-900416-00-9*, Pub. by Aris & Phillips UK) David Brown.

— Conference on Pioneers & Peers, 1988. 70p. 1988. pap. 20.00 (*0-911801-37-5*) Soc Computer Sim.

— Conference on Toward Understanding Our Environment 1991. 108p. 1991. pap. 40.00 (*0-911801-93-6*, MC91-3) Soc Computer Sim.

— The Fearsome Dilemma. 1994. per. 18.95 (*1-55128-010-8*) InBook.

— Introduction to Neurology. 2nd ed. 1989. pap. 29.95 (*0-86793-017-9*) Blackwell Sci.

— Principles of Good Practice: Computer Modeling & Simulation. (Simulations Series of Bks.). 178p. 1982. 36.00 (*0-685-66833-9*, SS10-2) Soc Computer Sim.

— Self Bows & Other Archery Tackle from Tomb of Tutankhamun. (Tutankhamuns Tomb Ser.: Vol. 4). 1982. 60.00 (*0-900416-33-5*, Pub. by Aris & Phillips UK) David Brown.

McLeod, A. I., jt. auth. see Hipel, K. W.

McLeod, A. L. Subjects Worthy of Fame: Essays on Commonwealth Literature in Honour of H. H. Anniah Gowda. 176p. 1989. text ed. 20.00 (*81-207-0949-7*, Pub. by Sterling Pubs II) Apt Bks.

McLeod, A. L., ed. Claude McKay: Centennial Studies. 200p. (C). 1992. 27.50 (*81-207-1403-2*) Apt Bks.

McLeod, A. L., ed. see Narayan, R. K.

McLeod, Alan L., ed. The Pattern of Australian Culture. (Illus.). 493p. 1963. 52.50 (*0-8014-0285-9*) Cornell U Pr.

McLeod, Alex N. The Practice of Economics: Economic Systems & Decision Making in Western Societies. 368p. (C). 1992. 39.95 (*1-56000-083-X*) Transaction Pubs.

McLeod, Beverly, ed. Language & Learning: Educating Linguistically Diverse Students. LC 93-11659. (SUNY Series, the Social Context of Education). 311p. (C). 1994. 64.50x (*0-7914-1891-X*); pap. 21.95x (*0-7914-1892-8*) State U NY Pr.

McLeod, Bob, jt. auth. see Claremont.

McLeod, Charles. All Change. 222p. 1970. 29.95 (*0-8464-1454-6*) Beekman Pubs.

McLeod, Charlotte, comp. Mistletoe Mysteries. 256p. 1989. 16.95 (*0-89296-400-6*) Mysterious Pr.

McLeod, Christian, pseud. The Heart of the Stranger: A Story of Little Italy. LC 74-17947. (Italian American Experience Ser.). (Illus.). 240p. 1975. reprint ed. 18.95 (*0-405-06417-9*) Ayer.

McLeod, D. B. & Adams, V. M., eds. Affect & Mathematical Problem Solving. (Illus.). 280p. 1989. 53.00 (*0-387-96924-1*) Spr-Verlag.

McLeod, Daniel R., jt. ed. see Hoehn-Saric, Rudolf.

McLeod, Deborah, ed. see Pumtree, Anne.

***McLeod, Deborah, jt. auth.** Ex Voto: Art As Invocation. 18p. 1995. pap., vhs 3.00 (*1-886845-00-X*) Penin Fine Arts.

McLeod, Dennis & King, Roger. Database System Design & Implementation. (Illus.). 400p. (C). 1987. text ed. 35.00 (*0-13-197195-6*) P-H.

McLeod, Donald C. & Miller, William A., eds. The Practice of Pharmacy: Institutional & Ambulatory Pharmaceutical Services. LC 81-51777. (Illus.). 502p. 1981. text ed. 15.95 (*0-9606488-0-1*) H W Bks.

McLeod, Donald W., ed. Canadian Writers & Their Works: Cumulated Index, Fiction Series. 102p. (C). 1993. pap. text ed. 20.00 (*1-55022-142-6*, Pub. by ECW Press CN) Genl Dist Srvs.

— Canadian Writers & Their Works: Cumulated Index, Poetry Series. 137p. (C). 1993. pap. text ed. 20.00 (*1-55022-143-4*, Pub. by ECW Press CN) Genl Dist Srvs.

McLeod, Douglas, jt. auth. see Lyle, Jack.

McLeod, Eileen. Women's Experience of Feminist Therapy & Counselling. LC 93-40802. 1994. pap. write for info. (*0-335-19222-X*, Open Univ Pr) Taylor & Francis.

McLeod, Emilie W. The Bear's Bicycle. (Illus.). 32p. (J). (gr. k-3). 1975. lib. bdg. 14.95 (*0-316-56203-3*, Joy St Bks) Little.

— The Bear's Bicycle. (Illus.). 32p. (J). (gr. k-3). 1986. mass mkt. 5.95 (*0-316-56206-8*, Joy St Bks) Little.

— The Bear's Bicycle. (Illus.). (J). (gr. 1-3). 1986. audio 22.95 (*0-87499-025-4*); audio, pap. 14.95 (*0-87499-023-8*) Live Oak Media.

— The Bear's Bicycle, 4 bks., Set. (Illus.). (J). (gr. 1-3). 1986. audio, pap. 33.95 (*0-87499-024-6*) Live Oak Media.

McLeod, Enid, tr. see Colette.

McLeod, Evelyn, jt. auth. see Ferguson, Marian.

McLeod, G. Goats: Homeopathic Remedies. 192p. (Orig.). Date not set. pap. 29.95 (*0-8464-4217-5*) Beekman Pubs.

McLeod, Gary, jt. auth. see Hura, Myron.

McLeod, Gary W., jt. auth. see Hura, Myron.

McLeod, Gerald E. Texas One Day Adventures & Weekend Getaways. 1994. pap. 8.95 (*1-56943-033-0*, Tribune) Contemp Bks.

McLeod, Glenda. Virtue & Venom: Catalogs of Women from Antiquity to the Renaissance. (Women & Culture Ser.). 184p. (C). 1991. text ed. 37.50 (*0-472-10206-0*) U of Mich Pr.

McLeod, Glenda, intro. Visitors to the City: Readers of Christine De Pizan. 225p. (Orig.). (C). 1989. pap. 20.00 (*0-941107-04-3*) MARC Pub Co.

McLeod, Glenda K., ed. The Reception of Christine De Pizan from the Fifteenth Through the Nineteenth Centuries: Visitors to the City. LC 91-44257. 184p. 1992. lib. bdg. 79.95 (*0-7734-9689-0*) E Mellen.

McLeod, Glenda K., tr. Christine de Pizan: Christine's Vision. LC 92-37726. (Library of Medieval Literature: Vol. 68B). 232p. 1993. 33.00 (*0-8240-6048-2*) Garland.

McLeod, Grant, tr. see Justinian.

McLeod, Grover S. The Bottom Stories. 194p. 1971. 19.95 (*1-884150-00-4*) Manchester AL.

— Civil Actions at Law in Alabama. 2nd ed. 686p. 1987. text ed. 75.00 (*1-884150-25-X*) Manchester AL.

— Civil Actions at Law in Alabama: Pocket Parts, 1993. 2nd ed. 285p. (C). 1993. 32.00 (*1-884150-26-8*) Manchester AL.

— Drake: Captain of the South Seas. (Illus.). 488p. 1994. 24.95 (*1-884150-10-1*) Manchester AL.

— Equitable Remedies & Extraordinary Writs in Alabama. 635p. (C). 1994. text ed. 89.00 (*1-884150-37-3*) Manchester AL.

— The Ghost of the Chimera. 143p. 1988. 19.95 (*0-87651-977-X*); pap. 16.95 (*0-685-46265-X*) Southern U Pr.

— The Ghost of the Chimera: And the Stowaway. 143p. 1988. 19.95 (*1-884150-03-9*); pap. 16.95 (*1-884150-02-0*) Manchester AL.

— The Legal Circus. 287p. 1992. 22.00 (*1-884150-06-3*) Manchester AL.

— Sub Duty. 580p. 1986. pap. 19.95 (*1-884150-01-2*) Manchester AL.

— Sub Duty. 581p. 1986. pap. 19.95 (*0-87651-975-3*) Southern U Pr.

— The Sultan's Gold. 138p. 1988. 19.95 (*0-87651-976-1*); pap. 16.95 (*0-685-35678-7*) Southern U Pr.

— The Sultan's Gold: And Other Fleet Type Submarine Stories. 138p. 1988. 19.95 (*1-884150-04-7*); pap. 16.95 (*1-884150-05-5*) Manchester AL.

— Trial Practice & Procedure in Alabama. 2nd ed. 786p. 1991. text ed. 79.00 (*1-884150-20-9*) Manchester AL.

— The Trials of FAT. 260p. 1989. 19.95 (*0-87651-949-4*) Southern U Pr.

— The Trials of FAT: An Illustrious Member of the Criminal Bar. 251p. 1989. 19.95 (*1-884150-07-1*) Manchester AL.

— Worker's Compensation in Alabama for On-the-Job Injuries. 349p. 1990. text ed. 69.00 (*1-884150-30-6*) Manchester AL.

***McLeod, Hugh.** Piety & Poverty: Working-Class Religion in Berlin, London, & New York, 1870-1914. (Europe Past & Present Ser.). 400p. (C). 1995. text ed. 40.00 (*0-8419-1356-0*) Holmes & Meier.

McLeod, Hugh, ed. European Religion in the Age of the Great Cities, 1830-1930. LC 94-9724. (Christianity & Society in the Modern World Ser.). 1995. write for info. (*0-415-09522-0*) Routledge.

McLeod, Hugh, ed. see Brown, Callum.

McLeod, Ian, tr. see Derrida, Jacques.

McLeod, Ian, tr. see Lyotard, Jean-Francois.

McLeod, James R. Theodore Roethke: A Manuscript Checklist. LC 70-121652. (Serif Series: Bibliographies & Checklists: No. 21). 315p. reprint ed. pap. 89.80 (*0-7837-0566-2*, 2040910) Bks Demand.

McLeod, Jenny, tr. see Schat, Peter.

***McLeod, John.** Doing Counselling Research. 224p. 1994. 45.00 (*0-8039-7803-0*); pap. 19.95 (*0-8039-7804-9*) Sage.

— An Introduction to Counselling. LC 92-40324. 1993. pap. 27.50 (*0-335-19018-9*, Open Univ Pr) Taylor & Francis.

McLeod, John, ed. Life Sciences Simulation: Then, Now & When. 66p. 1990. pap. 32.00 (*0-911801-70-7*, EMC90-2) Soc Computer Sim.

McLeod, John & McLeod, Rita. NewGAP. 40p. (Orig.). 1990. pap. text ed. 19.00 (*0-87879-892-7*); 22.00 (*0-87879-893-5*); 6.00 (*0-87879-894-3*) Acad Therapy.

— NewGAP, Set. 40p. (Orig.). 1990. teacher ed 50.00 (*0-685-46301-X*) Acad Therapy.

McLeod, John, jt. auth. see House, Peter W.

McLeod, Jonah. Winchester Disks in Microcomputer. 194p. 1983. 95.00 (*0-317-05224-1*) Elsevier.

McLeod, Jonathan W. Workers & Workplace Dynamics in Reconstruction-Era Atlanta: A Case Study. LC 89-963. (Afro-American Culture & Society Ser.). (Illus.). 138p. 1989. pap. 15.00 (*0-89215-155-2*) U Cal LA Indus Rel.

— Workers & Workplace Dynamics in Reconstruction-Era Atlanta: A Case Study. LC 89-963. (Afro-American Culture & Society Monograph Ser.: Vol. 10). (Illus.). 135p. 1989. pap. 15.95 (*0-934934-34-7*) UCLA CAAS.

McLeod, Joseph. Rim Poems. 72p. 1990. pap. 9.95 (*0-921254-22-9*, Pub. by Penumbra Pr CN) U of Toronto Pr.

McLeod, Judyth A. Lavender, Sweet Lavender. (Illus.). 120p. 1994. pap. 14.95 (*0-86417-601-5*, Pub. by Kangaroo Pr AT) Seven Hills Bk.

— A Posy of Violets. (Illus.). 104p. (Orig.). 1995. pap. 13.95 (*0-86417-643-0*) Seven Hills Bk.

McLeod, Karen. Henry Handel Richardson: A Critical Study. (Illus.). 270p. 1985. 69.95 (*0-521-30304-4*) Cambridge U Pr.

McLeod, Keith A., jt. ed. see Dansei, Marcel.

McLeod, Ken, tr. see Kongtrul, Jamgon & Erlewine, Michael.

McLeod, Ken, tr. see Kongtrul, Jamgon.

Mcleod, Laura, comp. Index to Canadian Historical Review: 1971-1990. 192p. 1994. 90.00 (*0-8020-2796-2*) U of Toronto Pr.

McLeod, Lloyd, jt. auth. see McAlister, George A.

McLeod, Lyons. Travels in Eastern Africa, 2 vols., Set. 1971. reprint ed. 95.00 (*0-7146-1832-2*, Pub. by F Cass Pubs UK) Intl Spec Bk.

McLeod, M. C., ed. see Lucian.

McLeod, Malcolm & Mack, John. Ethnic Sculpture. (British Museum Ser.). (Illus.). 72p. (Orig.). 1985. pap. 11.95 (*0-674-26854-7*) HUP.

McLeod, Marion & Manhire, Bill, eds. Some Other Country: New Zealand's Best Short Stories. 256p. 1985. pap. text ed. 14.95 (*0-86861-633-8*) Routledge Chapman & Hall.

McLeod, Mark S. Rationality & Theistic Belief: An Essay on Reformed Epistemology. LC 93-7544. (Cornell Studies in the Philosophy of Religion). 288p. 1993. 37.50 (*0-8014-2863-7*) Cornell U Pr.

McLeod, Mark S., jt. ed. see Craig, William L.

McLeod, Mark W. The Vietnamese Response to French Intervention, 1862-1874. LC 90-44389. 192p. 1991. text ed. 45.00 (*0-275-93562-0*, C3562, Praeger Pubs) Greenwood.

Mcleod, Mark W., tr. see Martin, Marie A.

McLeod, Mary Alice & Dudley, Cliff. I Almost Murdered This Child (by Abortion) LC 82-82017. 112p. 1983. pap. 4.95 (*0-89221-101-6*) New Leaf.

McLeod, Merikay. Betrayal: The Shattering Sex Discrimination Case of Silver vs. Pacific Press Publishing Association. LC 84-62638. 356p. (Orig.). 1985. pap. 10.00 (*0-9614230-0-5*) Mars Hill Pubns.

McLeod, Milt. Below the Surface. Sofranko, Michael, ed. (New Texas Poetry Sampler Ser.: No. 6). 28p. (Orig.). 1992. 10.00 (*0-930324-25-0*) Wings Pr.

McLeod, Neil, et al. Essential Tax Legislation. 302p. 1993. pap. 30.00 (*0-455-21185-X*, Pub. by Law Bk Co) W W Gaunt.

— Essential Tax Legislation 1995. 4th ed. 660p. 1995. pap. 35.00 (*0-455-21311-9*, Pub. by Law Bk Co) W W Gaunt.

McLeod, Nicole J., jt. auth. see Woods, Edward G.

McLeod, Norman. Distant Voices, Different Drums: An Anthology of True Stories Chosen from Annals of Northern California & the State of Nevada, Historically Dated from 1805 to 1915. (Illus.). 251p. (Orig.). 1990. pap. 10.95 (*0-9618678-1-7*) Goldridge Pr.

— Gold, Guns & Gallantry: True Tales of the Old Northern California Gold Rush Country. 165p. 1987. pap. 9.95 (*0-9618678-0-9*) Goldridge Pr.

McLeod, Norman, jt. auth. see Keller, Gerta.

McLeod, R., ed. Crisis in Editing: Texts of the English Renaissance. LC 89-17583. (Conference on Editorial Problems Ser.: No. 24). 1993. 29.50 (0-404-63674-8) AMS Pr.

McLeod, Ray. Vital Star. 1994. 12.95 (0-533-10715-6) Vantage.

McLeod, Raymond, Jr. Information Systems. 480p. (C). 1990. pap. write for info. (0-02-379545-X) Macmillan.

— Information Systems Concepts. (Illus.). 462p. (Orig.). (C). 1994. pap. write for info. (0-02-379473-9) Macmillan.

— Management Information Systems: A Study of Computer-Based Information Systems. (Illus.). 848p. (C). 1992. write for info. (0-318-69918-4) Macmillan.

— Management Information Systems: A Study of Computer-Based Information Systems. 5th ed. (Illus.). 848p. (C). 1993. text ed. write for info. (0-02-379481-X) Macmillan.

— Management Information Systems: A Study of Computer-Based Information Systems. 6th ed. LC 94-5017. 864p. (C). 1995. write for info. (0-02-379501-8) Macmillan.

— Systems Analysis & Design: An Organizational Approach. 804p. (C). 1993. text ed. 59.75 (0-03-055154-4) Dryden Pr.

— Systems Analysis & Design: An Organizational Approach. 804p. (C). 1994. disk 21.50 (0-03-003032-3); disk 21.50 (0-03-003028-5); disk 21.50 (0-03-003029-3) Dryden Pr.

— Systems Analysis & Design: An Organizational Approach. 498p. (C). 1994. teacher ed, pap. text ed. 70.00 (0-03-076682-6) Dryden Pr.

McLeod, Rita, jt. auth. see McLeod, John.

McLeod, Robert M. The Generalized Riemann Integral. (Carus Mathematical Monograph: No. 20). xiii, 275p. 12.00 (0-88385-021-4) Math Assn.

McLeod, Robin J. & Wachspress, Eugene L., eds. Frontiers of Applied Geometry: Proceedings of a Symposium, Las Cruces, New Mexico, 1980. 128p. 1981. pap. 29.00 (0-08-026487-5, Pergamon Pr) Elsevier.

McLeod, Russell. Feng Youlan, Jiang Qing, & the "Twenty-five Poems on History" LC 83-80351. (Current Chinese Language Project Ser.: No. 21). (Illus.). 108p. 1983. pap. 2.50x (0-912966-59-9) IEAS.

***McLeod, Stephen D.** Building Lotus Notes X.0 AP. Date not set. write for info. (0-679-76190-X) Random.

McLeod, Susan, ed. see Oberly, Jim.

McLeod, Susan, ed. see Pfaff, Tim.

McLeod, Susan, et al. Writing about the World. 608p. (C). 1990. pap. text ed. 21.50 (0-15-597754-7) HB Coll Pubs.

— Writing about the World. 2nd ed. (Illus.). 800p. (C). 1994. pap. text ed. 28.00 (0-15-501314-9) HB Coll Pubs.

McLeod, Susan H., ed. Strengthening Programs for Writing Across the Curriculum. LC 85-644763. (New Directions for Teaching & Learning Ser.: No. TL 36). 1988. 16.95 (1-55542-899-1) Jossey-Bass.

McLeod, Susan H. & Soven, Margot, eds. Writing across the Curriculum: A Guide to Developing Programs. (Illus.). 304p. 1992. 52.00 (0-8039-4599-X); pap. 24.95 (0-8039-4600-7) Sage.

McLeod, Susan H., jt. ed. see Frederick, Bonnie.

McLeod, T. H., ed. see Nuffield Canadian Seminar Staff.

McLeod, Thomas E. The Work of the Church Treasurer. rev. ed. LC 92-23564. 64p. 1992. pap. 10.00 (0-8170-1189-7) Judson.

McLeod, Thomas H., ed. Post-Secondary Education in a Technological Society: L'enseignement post-secondaire dans une societe technologique. 260p. (C). 1973. 29.95 (0-7735-0162-2, Pub. by McGill CN) U of Toronto Pr.

***McLeod, W. H.** Historical Dictionary of Sikhism. LC 95-15853. (Religion, Philosophies & Movements Ser.: Vol. 5). 1995. write for info. (0-8108-3035-3) Scarecrow.

— Popular Sikh Art. (Illus.). 152p. 1992. 24.95 (0-19-562791-1) OUP.

— Punjabis in New Zealand. 198p. 1986. 16.00 (0-8364-1907-3, Pub. by Nanak Dev Univ IA) S Asia.

— The Sikhs: History, Religion, & Society. 188p. 1989. text ed. 42.00 (0-231-06814-X) Col U Pr.

— Sikhs: History, Religion, & Society. 1991. pap. text ed. 12.50 (0-231-06815-8) Col U Pr.

— Way of the Sikh. (Way Ser.). (J). (gr. 4-8). 1986. pap. 7.95 (0-7175-0731-9) Dufour.

— Who Is a Sikh? The Problem of Sikh Identity. (Illus.). 152p. 1989. 39.95 (0-19-826548-4) OUP.

McLeod, W. H., ed. Sikhism. LC 84-410. (Textual Sources for the Study of Religion Ser.). 208p. 1984. 50.00 (0-389-20479-X, 08041) B&N Imports.

McLeod, W. H., ed. & tr. Textual Sources for the Study of Sikhism. (Textual Sources for the Study of Religion Ser.). (Illus.). x, 166p. 1990. pap. text ed. 12.95 (0-226-56085-6) U Ch Pr.

McLeod, W. H., jt. ed. see Schomer, Karine.

McLeon, Neil S., jt. auth. see Skipper, Ann.

McLeroth, Diane. The Briard. LC 83-138458. (Illus.). 240p. 1982. 20.00 (0-9639860-0-7) Aubry Assocs.

McLeroy, Jamie. Business Insurance Guide, 1993-1994: How to Purchase the Best & Most Affordable Coverage. Abromovitz, Les, ed. LC 93-39676. 416p. 1993. ring bd. 89.50 (1-56759-009-8) Summers Pr.

McLeroy, Jamie M. Indiana Employer's Guide, 1992-1994: A Handbook of Employment Laws & Regulations. LC 92-33984. 340p. 1994. 89.50 (1-56759-001-2) Summers Pr.

McLeRoy, Sherrie S. Black Land, Red River: A Pictorial History of Grayson County, Texas. LC 93-23092. 1993. write for info. (0-89865-868-3) Donning Co.

McLeRoy, Sherrie S. & McLeRoy, William R. Strangers in Their Midst: The Free Black Population of Amherst County, Virginia. iv, 237p. (Orig.). 1993. pap. text ed. 23.00 (1-55613-786-9) Heritage Bk.

McLeRoy, William R., jt. auth. see McLeRoy, Sherrie S.

McLerran, jt. auth. see Baym, Gordon.

***McLerran, A.** Dreamsong. Date not set. pap. 3.98 (0-8317-4357-3) Smithmark.

McLerran, Alice. Dreamsong. LC 91-32622. (Illus.). 32p. (J). (gr. k up). 1992. 14.00 (0-688-10105-4, Tambourine Bks); lib. bdg. 13.93 (0-688-10106-2, Tambourine Bks) Morrow.

— The Ghost Dance. LC 94-34231. (Illus.). (J). 1995. 15.95 (0-395-63168-8, Clarion Bks) HM.

— Hugs. (Illus.). 32p. (J). (ps-3). 1993. 4.95 (0-590-44637-1) Scholastic Inc.

— I Want to Go Home. LC 91-9599. (Illus.). 32p. (J). (ps-3). 1992. 15.00 (0-688-10144-5, Tambourine Bks); lib. bdg. 14.93 (0-688-10145-3, Tambourine Bks) Morrow.

— Kisses. (Illus.). 32p. (J). (ps-3). 1993. 4.95 (0-590-44711-4) Scholastic Inc.

— The Mountain That Loved a Bird. LC 85-9391. (Illus.). 32p. (J). (ps up). 1991. pap. 15.95 (0-88708-000-6, Picture Book Studio) S&S Childrens.

Mclerran, Alice. Roxaboxen. (J). (ps-3). 1991. 14.95 (0-688-07592-4); lib. bdg. 14.88 (0-688-07593-2) Lothrop.

McLerran, Alice. Roxaboxen. (Picture Puffins Ser.). (Illus.). 32p. (J). (ps-3). 1992. pap. 5.99 (0-14-054475-5, Puffin) Puffin Bks.

McLerran, Jennifer & McKee, Patrick. Old Age in Myth & Symbol: A Cultural Dictionary. LC 91-9163. 208p. 1991. text ed. 47.95 (0-313-27845-8, MGM, Greenwood Pr) Greenwood.

McLewin, Will. In Monte Viso's Horizon: Climbing All the Alpine 4000m Peaks. (Illus.). 255p. 1991. 29.95 (0-948153-09-1) Menasha Ridge.

— Linear Programming & Applications: A Course Text. (Illus.). xvi, 216p. 1990. text ed. 33.00 (0-904870-11-1, Pub. by Input-Output Pub UK) Kelley.

McLiam, John. The Sin of Pat Muldoon. 1957. pap. 4.75 (0-8222-1031-2) Dramatists Play.

McLiam Wilson, Robert. Ripley Bogle. 288p. 1991. 22.95 (0-233-98392-9, Pub. by A Deutsch UK) Trafalgar.

McLimore & Larwood. Strategies...Success...Senior Executives Speak Out. 416p. (C). 1991. pap. text ed. 24.76 (0-8403-7095-4) Kendall-Hunt.

McLin, Elva B. Athens State College: A Definitive History 1821-1991. 220p. 1991. 25.00 (0-9629883-0-8) Athens State.

McLin, Gwen F., jt. auth. see Greenwood, Lee.

McLin, Jon. Social & Economic Effects of Petroleum Development in Non-OPEC Developing Countries: Synthesis Report. xiii, 104p. (Orig.). 1986. pap. 16.00 (92-2-105505-1) Intl Labour Office.

McLin, Jon, jt. ed. see Huddleston, Barbara.

McLin, Lena. Pulse: A History of Music. LC 77-75478. (Illus.). (YA). (gr. 6-12). 1977. pap. 10.95 (0-8497-5600-6, WE 3) Kjos.

McLinn, Patricia. Grady's Wedding. (Special Edition Ser.). 1993. mass mkt. 3.39 (0-373-09813-8, 5-09813-2) Silhouette.

— Rodeo Nights. (Special Edition Ser.). 1994. mass mkt. 3.50 (0-373-09904-5, 1-09904-3) Harlequin Bks.

— A Stranger in the Family: (The Family Way) (Special Edition Ser.). 1995. pap. 3.75 (0-373-09959-2, 1-09959-7) Silhouette.

McLintock, David, tr. see Bernhard, Thomas.

McLintock, David, tr. see Boll, Heinrich.

McLintock, David, tr. see Meier, Christian.

McLintock, David, tr. see Warnke, Martin.

***McLintock, I. S., ed.** Bremsstrahlung from Radio-nuclides: Practical Guidance for Radiation Protection. (C). 1994. 120.00x (0-948237-23-6, Pub. by H&H Sci Cnslts UK) St Mut.

McLintock, I. S., jt. auth. see Connor, K. J.

McLintock, James D. Royal Cars. 1989. pap. 25.00 (0-7478-0167-3, Pub. by Shire UK) St Mut.

McLish, Rachel & Reynolds, Bill. Flex Appeal by Rachel. 1984. pap. 13.99 (0-446-38105-5) Warner Bks.

McLish, Rachel & Vedral, Joyce L. Perfect Parts. 256p. 1987. pap. 12.99 (0-446-38534-4) Warner Bks.

Mclleron, Geoff, et al, eds. The Complete Book of Southern African Birds. 752p. (C). 1989. 500.00 (1-85368-019-2, Pub. by New Holland Pubs UK) St Mut.

McLnnes, A. W., ed. Computational Mathematics. 300p. (C). 1995. text ed. 48.00 (981-02-0203-2) World Scientific Pub.

Mclntyre, John R., jt. ed. see Papp, Daniel S.

McLoone-Basta, Margo & Siegel, Alice. The Second Kids' World Almanac of Records & Facts. World Almanac Staff, ed. 288p. (J). (gr. 3-9). 1987. pap. 7.95 (0-88687-317-7) Wrld Almnc.

McLoone, Margo, jt. auth. see Siegel, Alice.

McLoud. Thoracic Radiology - the Requisites. 384p. 1994. 65.00 (0-8016-6354-7) Mosby Yr Bk.

McLoughland, Beverly. Hippo's a Heap: And Other Animal Poems. 32p. (J). (ps-3). 1993. 14.95 (1-56397-017-1, Wordsong) Boyds Mills Pr.

***McLoughlin, Barry J.** Communicate with Power: Encountering the Media Pocket Tips Booklet. 132p. (Orig.). (C). Date not set. pap. write for info. (1-886712-00-X) McLoughlin MultiMed.

McLoughlin Bros. Staff. Magic Mirror, an Antique Optical Toy. pap. 3.50 (0-486-23847-4) Dover.

McLoughlin, Caven S., jt. auth. see Holly, Mary L.

McLoughlin, Caven S., et al. Getting Employed, Staying Employed: Job Development & Training for Persons with Severe Handicaps. LC 87-13185. 256p. (Orig.). 1987. pap. text ed. 24.00 (0-933716-70-2) P H Brookes.

***McLoughlin, Chris.** Entree to Halkidiki: An Eat & Sleep Guide. 1995. pap. 11.95 (1-899163-02-6) Cimino Pub Grp.

McLoughlin, Daniel P. Principles of Real Estate. 1992. text ed. write for info. (0-07-045434-5) McGraw.

***McLoughlin, David, et al.** The Adult Dyslexic: Assessment, Counseling & Training. 150p. 1994. text ed. 34.95 (1-56593-241-2, 0561) Singular Publishing.

McLoughlin, Emmett. Famous Ex-Priests. LC 68-18759. 1968. 4.95 (0-8184-0030-7) Carol Pub Group.

— Letters to an Ex-Priest. 1965. 4.95 (0-8184-0050-1) Carol Pub Group.

McLoughlin, Ian & Clark, Jon. Technological Change at Work. 224p. 1988. 90.00 (0-335-15417-4, Open Univ Pr); pap. 32.00 (0-335-15416-6, Open Univ Pr) Taylor & Francis.

— Technological Change at Work. 2nd ed. LC 93-27839. 1994. pap. 13.99 (0-335-19009-X, Open Univ Pr) Taylor & Francis.

***McLoughlin, Ian & Gourlay, Stephen.** Enterprise Without Unions: Industrial Relations in a Non-Union Firm. LC 94-25725. (Managing Work & Organizations Ser.). 160p. 1994. 85.00x (0-335-19031-6, Open Univ Pr); pap. 29.00x (0-335-19030-8, Open Univ Pr) Taylor & Francis.

McLoughlin, J., ed. Environmental Pollution Control: An Introduction to Principles & Practice of Administration. (International Environmental Law & Policy Ser.). 288p. (C). 1993. lib. bdg. 110.00 (1-85333-577-0) Kluwer Ac.

***McLoughlin, J. & O'Boyle, F. J., eds.** Top Tips in Urology. LC 95-11624. 1995. write for info. (0-86542-610-4) Blackwell Sci.

McLoughlin, J. B., jt. auth. see Diamond, Donald R.

McLoughlin, J. B., jt. ed. see Diamond, Donald R.

McLoughlin, J. B., jt. auth. see Huxley, M.

McLoughlin, J. Brian. Shaping Melbourne's Future? Town Planning, the State & Civil Society. (Illus.). 320p. (C). 1993. 69.95 (0-521-41334-6) Cambridge U Pr.

McLoughlin, James A. & Lewis, Rena B. Assessing Special Students: Strategies & Procedures. 4th ed. 712p. (C). 1994. text ed. write for info. (0-02-379492-5, Merrill Pub Co) Macmillan.

McLoughlin, James A., jt. auth. see Wallace, Gerald.

McLoughlin, Jane. Coincidence. 256p. 1992. 24.95 (1-85381-478-4, Pub. by Virago Pr UK) Trafalgar.

— Coincidence. 240p. 1993. pap. 13.95 (1-85381-603-5, Pub. by Virago Pr UK) Trafalgar.

***McLoughlin, Jane, ed.** On the Death of a Parent. 256p. 1995. 16.95 (1-85381-803-8, Pub. by Virago Pr UK) Trafalgar.

***McLoughlin, John.** Letters of Dr. John McLoughlin. (American Autobiography Ser.). 376p. 1995. reprint ed. lib. bdg. 89.00 (0-7812-8587-9) Rprt Serv.

McLoughlin, Kate, jt. auth. see Northrop, Suzane.

McLoughlin, L. J. Learner's Dictionary of Classical Arabic Idioms: Arabic - English. 1988. 12.00 (0-86685-467-3) Intl Bk Ctr.

McLoughlin, Leslie. Colloquial Arabic of the Levant. (Colloquial Ser.). 152p. 1988. pap. 14.95 (0-7100-0668-3, RKP); audio 14.95 (0-415-01854-4, RKP) Routledge.

— Colloquial Arabic of the Levant. (Colloquial Ser.). 152p. 1988. audio 27.50 (0-415-00073-4, A2571, RKP); 14.95 (0-415-05107-X, RKP) Routledge.

— Course in Colloquial Arabic. (ARA.). 1982. 14.95x (0-86685-043-0) Intl Bk Ctr.

— A Further Course in Colloquial Arabic. 1979. 15.00 (0-86685-277-8) Intl Bk Ctr.

McLoughlin, Leslie, tr. see Awwad, Tawfiq Y.

McLoughlin, Leslie J. A Learner's Dictionary of Arabic Colloquial Idioms: Arabic - English. 1988. 12.00 (0-86685-468-1) Intl Bk Ctr.

***McLoughlin, Marlene.** The Road to Rome: An Artist's Year in Italy. LC 94-27239. 1995. 16.95 (0-8118-0577-8) Chronicle Bks.

McLoughlin, Michael. Electronics for You a Practical Course for GCSE. 256p. (C). 1994. pap. 30.00x (0-09-173044-9, Pub. by S Thornes Pubs UK) St Mut.

McLoughlin, Pat, ed. Woman's Hour Book of Short Stories 2. 282p. (Orig.). 1993. pap. 9.95 (0-563-36389-4, BBC-Parkwest) Parkwest Pubns.

McLoughlin, Pat, intro. Woman's Hour Book of Short Stories. 256p. 1991. pap. 7.95 (0-563-20905-4, BBC-Parkwest) Parkwest Pubns.

McLoughlin, Patrick. Commercial Leases & Insolvency. 200p. 1992. U.K. pap. 60.00 (0-406-00640-7) Butterworth Legal Pubs.

McLoughlin, Peter F. Language Switching As an Index of Socialization in the Republic of the Sudan. LC 64-64256. (University of California Publications in Social Welfare: Vol. 1). 78p. reprint ed. pap. 25.00 (0-317-29082-7, 2021418) Bks Demand.

McLoughlin, Quin. Relativistic Naturalism: A Cross-Cultural Approach to Human Science. LC 91-430. 280p. 1991. text ed. 59.95 (0-275-93870-0, C3870, Praeger Pubs) Greenwood.

McLoughlin, William G. After the Trail of Tears: The Cherokees' Struggle for Sovereignty, 1839-1880. LC 93-18532. xvi, 440p. (C). 1994. 39.95 (0-8078-2111-X); pap. 17.95 (0-8078-4433-0) U of NC Pr.

— American Evangelicals, 1800-1900: An Anthology. 12.00 (0-8446-0793-2) Peter Smith.

— Cherokee Renascence in the New Republic. (Illus.). 494p. 1992. text ed. 69.50 (0-691-04741-3); pap. text ed. 18.95 (0-691-00627-X) Princeton U Pr.

— The Cherokees & Christianity, 1794-1870: Essays on Acculturation & Cultural Persistence. Conser, Walter H., Jr., ed. LC 93-38460. 368p. 1994. 45.00 (0-8203-1639-3) U of Ga Pr.

— Cherokees & Missionaries, 1789-1839. 2nd ed. LC 94-36184. 400p. 1995. pap. 18.95 (0-8061-2723-6) U of Okla Pr.

— New England Dissent, 1630-1833: The Baptists & the Separation of Church & State, 2 vols. Set. LC 70-131464. (Center for the Study of the History of Liberty in America Ser.). (Illus.). 1346p. 1971. 125.00 (0-674-61175-6) HUP.

— Revivals, Awakening, & Reform: An Essay on Religion & Social Change in America, 1607 to 1977. LC 77-27830. xvi, 240p. 1980. pap. text ed. 10.95 (0-226-56092-9, P891) U Ch Pr.

— Soul Liberty: The Baptists' Struggle in New England, 1630-1833. LC 90-43369. 357p. 1991. text ed. 35.00 (0-87451-532-7) U Pr of New Eng.

McLoughlin, William G., ed. see Backus, Isaac.

McLoughlin, William G., jt. auth. see Clarke, John.

McLouth, Lawrence A., tr. see Zwingli, Ulrich.

McLoyd, Vonnie C. & Flanagan, Constance A., eds. Economic Stress: Effects on Family Life & Child Development. LC 85-644581. (New Directions for Child Development Ser.: No. CD 46). 1990. 17.95 (1-55542-845-2) Jossey-Bass.

McLucas, Anne D., ed. see Fechter, Charles.

McLucas, John L. Space Commerce. LC 90-43957. (Frontiers of Space Ser.: No. 3). (Illus.). 241p. 1991. 32.00 (0-674-83020-2, MCLSPA) HUP.

McLucas, John L. & Sheffield, Charles, eds. Commercial Operations in Space Nineteen Eighty to Two Thousand. (Science & Technology Ser.: Vol. 51). (Illus.). 214p. 1981. lib. bdg. 30.00 (0-87703-140-1, Pub. by Am Astro Soc); pap. text ed. 20.00 (0-87703-141-X, Pub. by Am Astro Soc) Univelt Inc.

— Commercial Operations in Space Nineteen Eighty to Two Thousand. suppl. ed. (Science & Technology Ser.: Vol. 51). (Illus.). 214p. 1981. fiche 10.00 (0-87703-165-7, Pub. by Am Astro Soc) Univelt Inc.

McLucas, Suzanne. A Provencal Kitchen: Healthy Cooking from the South of France. LC 92-891. 368p. 1992. reprint ed. pap. 12.95 (1-55566-093-2) Johnson Bks.

McLuckie, Craig M. & Colbert, Patrick J., eds. Critical Perspectives on Dennis Brutus. 224p. 1995. pap. 16.00 (0-89410-770-4) Three Continents.

— Critical Perspectives on Dennis Brutus. 224p. 1995. 28.00 (0-89410-769-0) Three Continents.

McLuckie, Craig W. Nigerian Civil War Literature: Seeking an "Imagined Community" LC 90-6689. (Studies in African Literature: Vol. 3). 172p. 1990. lib. bdg. 79.95 (0-88946-727-7) E Mellen.

***McLuen, Dennis.** Equipped to Serve Kit: Youth Specialties' Volunteer Youth Worker Training Course. 96p. 1995. One Leader's Guide. pap. 44.99 (0-310-48791-9) Zondervan.

McLuhan, Eric, jt. auth. see McLuhan, Marshall.

McLuhan, H. Marshall. Gutenberg Galaxy: The Making of Typographic Man. LC 62-4860. 294p. 1962. pap. 19.95 (0-8020-6041-2) U of Toronto Pr.

McLuhan, Marshall. Understanding Media: The Extensions of Man. 392p. 1994. pap. 14.95 (0-262-63159-8) MIT Pr.

— Understanding Media: The Extensions of Man. 320p. 1966. pap. 4.95 (0-451-62496-3, ME2170, Ment) NAL-Dutton.

McLuhan, Marshall & Fiore, Quentin. The Medium Is the Massage. 1989. pap. 10.00 (0-671-68997-5, Touchstone Bks) S&S Trade.

— War & Peace in the Global Village. 1989. pap. 8.95 (0-671-68996-7, Touchstone Bks) S&S Trade.

McLuhan, Marshall & McLuhan, Eric. Laws of Media: The New Science. 258p. 1988. 30.00 (0-8020-5782-9) U of Toronto Pr.

— Laws of Media: The New Science. 262p. 1992. pap. 18.95 (0-8020-7715-3) U of Toronto Pr.

McLuhan, Marshall & Powers, Bruce R. The Global Village: Transformations in World Life & Media in the 21st Century. (Illus.). 240p. 1992. pap. 10.95 (0-19-507910-8) OUP.

McLuhan, T. C. Touch the Earth. 1989. 7.98 (0-88394-000-0) Promntory Pr.

— Touch the Earth: A Self Portrait of Indian Existence. 1976. pap. 14.00 (0-671-22275-9, Touchstone Bks) S&S Trade.

— Way of the Earth. 1994. 30.00 (0-671-75939-6) S&S Trade.

Mcluman, M. G. Marriage & Divorce: God's Call, God's Compassion. 1991. pap. 8.99 (0-8423-4193-5) Tyndale.

McLung, James W., comp. Annual Report of the Librarian of Congress: For the Fiscal Year Ending September 30, 1991. 93p. 1992. 3.50 (0-16-037931-8) Lib Congress.

M'Clung, John A. Sketches of Western Adventure. LC 76-90184. (Mass Violence in America Ser.). 1969. reprint ed. 16.95 (0-405-01326-4) Ayer.

McLure, Charles, ed. State Corporation Income Tax. 550p. 1984. 59.95 (0-8179-7881-X) Hoover Inst Pr.

McLure, Charles E., Jr. Economic Perspectives on State Taxation of Multijurisdictional Corporations. 337p. (Orig.). 1987. pap. 34.95 (0-918255-04-X) Tax Analysts.

— Must Corporate Income Be Taxed Twice? LC 78-27905. (Studies of Government Finance). 262p. 1979. 32.95 (0-8157-5620-8); pap. 12.95 (0-8157-5619-4) Brookings.

— Tax Policy Lessons for LDCs & Eastern Europe. 1992. pap. 5.00 (1-55815-194-X) ICS Pr.

McLure, Charles E., Jr. & Mieszkowski, Peter, eds. Fiscal Federalism & the Taxation of Natural Resources. LC 82-48581. 269p. reprint ed. pap. 76.70 (0-7837-5761-1, 2045423) Bks Demand.

McLure, Charles E., Jr., jt. ed. see Boskin, Michael J.

McLure, Charles E., Jr., et al. The Taxation of Income from Business & Capital in Colombia: Fiscal Reform in the Developing World. LC 89-11832. 422p. 1990. lib. bdg. 68.00 (0-8223-0925-4) Duke.

M'Clure, David & Parish, Elijah. Memoirs of the Rev. Eleazar Wheelock, D. D. LC 75-38454. (Religion in America, Ser. 2). 338p. 1972. reprint ed. 24.95 (0-405-04074-1) Ayer.

McLure, James. The Day They Shot John Lennon. 1984. pap. 4.75 (0-8222-0279-4) Dramatists Play.

— Ghost World. 4.75 (0-8222-8433-2) Dramatists Play.

— Laundry & Bourbon. 1981. pap. 2.75 (*0-8222-0645-5*) Dramatists Play.

— Lone Star. 1980. pap. 2.75 (*0-8222-0685-4*) Dramatists Play.

— Max & Maxie. 1989. pap. 4.75 (*0-8222-0741-9*) Dramatists Play.

— Pvt. Wars (Full-Length) 1980. pap. 4.75 (*0-8222-0925-X*) Dramatists Play.

— Pvt. Wars (One-Act) 1980. pap. 2.75 (*0-8222-0924-1*) Dramatists Play.

— Wild Oats: A Romance of the Old West. 1985. pap. 4.75 (*0-8222-1257-9*) Dramatists Play.

McLure, John. Baba a Louis Bakery Bread Book: The Secret Book of the Bread. Gay, Olivia & Mueller, Kate, eds. LC 93-78237. (Illus.). 132p. (Orig.). 1993. pap. 13.95 (*0-9636892-0-7*) B A L Bakery.

McLure, John R. The Ventilation of School Buildings: A Study of Present Practices & Costs in the Light of Experimental Research. LC 72-177035. (Columbia University. Teachers College. Contributions to Education Ser.: No. 157). reprint ed. 22.50 (*0-404-55157-2*) AMS Pr.

McLure, Patricia, jt. auth. see Newkirk, Thomas.

Mclure, Rhyder. Fast Access WordPerfect. (Orig.). (C). 1987. pap. 16.95 (*0-13-307489-7*) P-H.

McLuskey, Fraser, tr. see Bornkamm, Gunther.

McLuskey, Irene, tr. see Bornkamm, Gunther.

McLuskie, Kathleen E. Dekker & Heywood: Professional Dramatists. LC 93-30472. 160p. 1994. text ed. 39.95 (*0-312-10629-7*) St Martin.

McLusky, Donald S. The Estuarine Ecosystem. 200p. 1989. 69.95 (*0-412-02091-2*, A3608, Chap & Hall NY); pap. 29.95 (*0-412-02101-3*, A3612, Chap & Hall NY) Chapman & Hall.

McLusky, Donald S., ed. see Twelfth European Symposium on Marine Biology Staff.

McLusky, Donald S., et al, eds. North Sea: Estuaries Interactions, Proceedings of the 18th EBSA Symposium. (Developments in Hydrobiology Ser.). (C). 1990. lib. bdg. 154.00 (*0-7923-0694-5*) Kluwer Ac.

McLyman. Transformer & Inductor Design Handbook. 2nd ed. (Electrical Engineering & Electronics Ser.: Vol. 49). 440p. 1988. 75.00 (*0-8247-7828-6*) Dekker.

McLyman, William T. Designing Magnetic Components for High Frequency DC-DC Converters. 435p. 1993. 80.00 (*1-883107-00-8*) KG Magnetics.

McLynn, Francis. France & the Jacobite Rising of Seventeen Forty-Five. 277p. 1981. 27.50 (*0-85224-404-5*, Pub. by Edinburgh U Pr UK) Col U Pr.

McLynn, Frank. Charles Edward Stuart: A Tragedy in Many Acts. 608p. 1988. text ed. 29.95 (*0-415-00272-9*, A2597) Routledge.

— Crime & Punishment in Eighteenth Century England. 368p. 1989. 45.00 (*0-415-01014-4*, A3792) Routledge.

— Fitzroy MacLean. (Illus.). 432p. 1994. pap. 29.95 (*0-7195-5611-2*, Pub. by John Murray UK) Trafalgar.

— Hearts of Darkness: The European Exploration of Africa. (Illus.). 400p. 1994. pap. 14.95 (*0-7867-0084-X*) Carroll & Graf.

— The Jacobites. (Illus.). 228p. 1988. pap. text ed. 14.95 (*0-415-00267-2*, RKP) Routledge.

— Robert Louis Stevenson: A Biography. 1994. 30.00 (*0-679-41284-0*) Random.

McLynn, Frank, ed. Famous Letters: Messages & Thoughts That Shaped Our World. LC 93-5848. (Illus.). 192p. 1993. 25.00 (*0-89577-521-2*, Random) RD Assn.

McLynn, Neil. Ambrose of Milan: Church & Court in a Christian Capital. LC 94-2261. (Transformation of the Classical Heritage Ser.: Vol. 22). 1994. 45.00 (*0-520-08461-6*) U CA Pr.

McLysaght, William & Clifford, Sigerson. The Tragic Story of the Colleen Bawn. (Illus.). 128p. 1982. reprint ed. pap. text ed. 6.95 (*0-900068-60-4*, Pub. by Anvil Bks Ltd IE) Irish Bks Media.

McMackin, Dorothy. Newspaper Gleanings from Andrew County, MO. LC 86-82190. 580p. 29.95 (*0-685-60290-7*) Jordan Valley.

McMackin, Dorothy J., comp. Newspaper Gleanings of Andrew County (MO.) & Surrounding Area. LC 86-82190. 584p. 1986. 29.95 (*0-939810-05-0*) Jordan Valley.

McMackin, Frank J., et al. Mathematics of the Shop. 4th ed. LC 76-6726. 628p. (C). 1978. 39.95 (*0-8273-1297-0*); teacher ed 10.00 (*0-8273-1298-9*) Delmar.

McMackin, Greg. Coaching the Defensive Backfield. LC 91-43957. (Illus.). 128p. (Orig.). 1992. 12.00 (*0-9624779-3-1*) Harding Pr.

McMackin, Lorin. Thoughts on Freedom: Two Essays. LC 81-23297. 111p. 1982. 12.50 (*0-8093-1076-7*) S Ill U Pr.

McMahan, Candace, ed. see Keffer, Lois.

McMahan, Dean. Ajuna's Star. LC 90-82569. (Illus.). 24p. (SPA.). (J). (ps-2). 1990. pap. 4.95 (*0-9626254-3-4*) Ajuna Unlimited.

McMahan, Dean & Rose, Willi. Ajuna's Star. 1990. English version. audio 8.95 (*0-9626254-5-0*); Spanish version. audio 8.95 (*0-9626254-6-9*) Ajuna Unlimited.

— Ajuna's Star. rev. ed. LC 90-80841. (Illus.). 24p. (J). (ps-2). 1990. reprint ed. pap. 4.95 (*0-9626254-1-8*); reprint ed. audio write for info. (*0-9626254-2-6*) Ajuna Unlimited.

McMahan, Elizabeth. Crash Course in Composition. 4th ed. 256p. 1989. pap. text ed. write for info. (*0-07-045478-7*); With Readings. pap. text ed. write for info. (*0-07-045479-5*) McGraw.

McMahan, Elizabeth & Day, Susan. The Writer's Handbook. 2nd ed. 1988. pap. text ed. write for info. (*0-07-045432-9*) McGraw.

— The Writer's Rhetoric & Handbook. 3rd rev. ed. 544p. (C). 1988. text ed. write for info. (*0-07-045426-4*) McGraw.

McMahan, Elizabeth, jt. auth. see Day, Susan.

McMahan, Elizabeth, jt. ed. see Day, Susan.

McMahan, Elizabeth, et al. Literature & the Writing Process. 3rd ed. (Illus.). 1120p. (C). 1993. pap. write for info. (*0-02-379705-3*) Macmillan.

McMahan, Ernest E. Needs: Of People & Their Communities & the Adult Educator. 55p. 1970. 3.00 (*0-88379-004-1*) A A A C E.

McMahan, Eva M. Elite Oral History Discourse: A Study of Cooperation & Coherence. LC 88-36913. (Studies in Rhetoric & Communication). 192p. (C). 1989. text ed. 24.50 (*0-8173-0437-1*) U of Ala Pr.

McMahan, Eva M. & Rogers, Kim L., eds. Interactive Oral History Interviewing. (Communication Ser.). 184p. 1994. text ed. 39.95 (*0-8058-0576-1*) L Erlbaum Assocs.

McMahan, Forrest R. Near Death. Cox, Mary K., ed. LC 85-72753. (Illus.). 130p. (Orig.). 1985. pap. 7.95 (*0-910217-07-6*) Synergetics WV.

***McMahan, Gary C. & Lawler, Edward E., 3rd.** Effects of Union Status on Employee Involvement: Diffusion & Effectiveness. 29p. 1994. pap. 15.00x (*0-614-06144-X*, 2052-PP-4040) EPF.

McMahan, Jacqueline H. California Rancho Cooking. LC 83-72309. (Illus.). 248p. 1983. 14.95 (*0-9612150-0-3*) Olive Pr.

— California Rancho Cooking. rev. ed. (Illus.). 1988. pap. 12.95 (*0-9612150-7-0*) Olive Pr.

— The Chipotle Chile Cookbook: Fire with Flavor. Hightower, Ruth, ed. (Illus.). 172p. (Orig.). 1994. pap. 14.95 (*1-881656-03-9*) Olive Pr.

— Healthy Fiesta: Low Fat & Low-Salt Versions of Classic Southwestern & Mexican Recipes. 187p. 1990. pap. 12.95 (*0-9612150-9-7*) Olive Pr.

— The Healthy Mexican: A Fresh Approach to Mexican Recipes. 2nd rev. ed. Hightower, Ruth, ed. 215p. 1994. pap. text ed. 16.95 (*1-881656-04-7*) Olive Pr.

— Mexican Breakfast Cookbook: Spicy & Sweet Morning Meals. 180p. 1992. pap. 14.95 (*1-881656-00-4*) Olive Pr.

— The Red & Green Chile Book: Southwestern & Mexican Recipes. 2nd ed. (Illus.). 220p. 1992. reprint ed. pap. 14.95 (*0-9612150-5-4*) Olive Pr.

— The Salsa Book. LC 85-63671. 160p. 1986. 12.95 (*0-9612150-2-X*); per. 9.95 (*0-9612150-3-8*) Olive Pr.

— The Salsa Book. rev. ed. (Illus.). 180p. 1989. 12.95 (*0-9612150-8-9*) Olive Pr.

McMahan, Jeff. Reagan & the World: Imperial Policy in the New Cold War. 320p. 1985. pap. 10.00 (*0-85345-678-X*) Monthly Rev.

McMahan, Jeffrey. Vampires Anonymous. 252p. (Orig.). 1991. pap. 8.95 (*1-55583-183-4*) Alyson Pubns.

McMahan, Jeffrey N. Somewhere in the Night. LC 89-85941. (Orig.). 1989. pap. 7.95 (*1-55583-157-5*) Alyson Pubns.

***McMahan, John M.** Farmer John Outdoors: A Hoosier's Guide to Country Living. 235p. 1995. pap. 11.95 (*1-887112-00-6*) CompuArt Designs.

McMahan, Richard H., Jr., ed. Cogeneration: Why, When & How to Assess & Implement a Project. LC 86-19795. (Series of Special Reports: No. 16). (Illus.). 367p. reprint ed. pap. 104.60 (*0-7837-0684-7*, 2041017) Bks Demand.

McMahan, Robert. McMahan Guide to Classroom Photography. (Illus.). 286p. 1985. 14.95 (*0-9612150-1-1*) Olive Pr.

— Pixel Photography. 235p. 1993. pap. 18.95 (*1-881656-01-2*) Olive Pr.

McMahan, U. J., ed. Steve: Remembrances of Stephen W. Kuffler. LC 90-10383. (Illus.). 142p. (Orig.). 1990. pap. 17.95x (*0-87893-516-9*) Sinauer Assocs.

***McMahon.** Nursing As Therapy. 234p. 1991. pap. 43.25 (*1-56593-012-6*, 0253) Singular Publishing.

McMahon, A. Michael & Morris, Stephanie A. Technology in Industrial America: Records of the Committee on Science & the Arts of the Franklin Institute, 1824-1900: A Guide. LC 77-77872. 1977. 40.00 (*0-8420-2123-X*) Scholarly Res Inc.

McMahon, Agnes, ed. Celtic Way of Life. 1988. pap. 8.95 (*0-86278-236-8*) Dufour.

— Celtic Way of Life. (Illus.). 72p. 1988. reprint ed. pap. 10.95 (*0-905140-16-8*, Pub. by OBrien Pr IE) Dufour.

— Heroic Tales from the Ulster Cycle. 64p. 1984. pap. 7.95 (*0-86278-020-9*, Pub. by OBrien Pr IE) Dufour.

McMahon, Agnes, jt. auth. see Wallace, Mike.

McMahon, Alexander R. The Karens of the Golden Chersonese. LC 77-87018. reprint ed. 29.00 (*0-404-16840-X*) AMS Pr.

***McMahon, Alice T.** All about Childbirth: A Manual for Prepared Childbirth. 4th ed. LC 94-27717. (Illus.). 208p. 1994. pap. 6.95 (*0-931128-04-8*) Family Pubns.

***McMahon, Ann P. & Brake, Kimberly A.** Catalyst's Adventure in Science: Simple Machines. (Illus.). 32p. (J). (gr. k-4). 1995. pap. 9.95 (*0-9642550-1-4*) Curiosity Unltd.

— Catalyst's Adventures in Science: Bubble Rainbows. rev. ed. LC 94-67847. (Illus.). 32p. (J). (gr. k-4). 1994. pap. 9.95 (*0-9642550-0-6*) Curiosity Unltd.

McMahon, Annette Flad. Petals: Change Your Perspective Change Your Life. (Illus.). 223p. (Orig.). 1987. 24.95 (*0-944005-21-7*); lib. bdg. write for info. (*0-944005-23-3*); pap. write for info. (*0-944005-22-5*) Columbia NY.

McMahon, April M. Understanding Language Change. 336p. (C). 1994. 64.95 (*0-521-44119-6*); pap. 17.95 (*0-521-44665-1*) Cambridge U Pr.

McMahon, Barbara. Island Paradise. large type ed. 1992. reprint ed. lib. bdg. 18.95 (*0-263-13099-1*, Pub. by Mills & Boon UK) Thorndike Pr.

— One Stubborn Cowboy. (Desire Ser.). 1995. pap. 3.25 (*0-373-05915-9*, 1-05915-3) Silhouette.

— Wanted: Wife & Mother. (Romance Ser.). 1995. mass mkt. 2.99 (*0-373-03369-9*, 1-03369-5) Harlequin Bks.

McMahon, Betsy M. The Days of My Life: A Journal for the Teen Years. (Illus.). 288p. (Orig.). 1987. 13.95 (*0-942257-05-7*) New Chapter Pr.

McMahon, Bob & Leopold, Jay. Who Are the Best? The Sports Survey Book. 2nd ed. (Illus.). 144p. 1984. pap. 11.95 (*0-88011-256-5*, PMCM0256) Human Kinetics.

McMahon, Brian, jt. ed. see Hablutzel, Nancy.

McMahon, Brian R., jt. ed. see Burggren, Warren W.

McMahon, Brian T. & Evans, Randall W., eds. The Shortest Distance: The Pursuit of Independence for Person with Acquired Brain Injury. LC 93-87363. 170p. 1994. pap. text ed. 29.95 (*1-878205-68-4*) GR Press.

McMahon, Brian T. & Shaw, Linda R., eds. Work Worth Doing: Advances in Brain Injury Rehabilitation. LC 91-71166. (Illus.). xxx, 412p. 1991. 40.00 (*1-878205-19-6*) GR Press.

McMahon, Bryan & Binchy, William. Casebook on the Irish Law of Torts. 2nd ed. U.K. pap. 64.00 (*1-85475-176-X*) Butterworth Legal Pubs.

McMahon, Bryan M. European Community Law in Ireland. 1989. boxed 143.00 (*1-85475-000-3*, IE) Butterworth Legal Pubs.

McMahon, Bryan M. & Binchy, William. McMahon & Binchy: Irish Law of Torts. 2nd ed. 1990. 136.00 (*1-85475-155-7*) Butterworth Legal Pubs.

McMahon, Charles J., Jr., ed. Microplasticity, Vol. 2. LC 68-4384. (Advances in Materials Research Ser.). 439p. reprint ed. pap. 125.20 (*0-317-11076-4*, 2007402) Bks Demand.

McMahon, Chris & Browne, James J. CAD - CAM: From Principles to Practice. LC 93-16384. 508p. (C). 1993. text ed. 69.95 (*0-201-56502-1*) Addison-Wesley.

McMahon, Christine A. & Harding, Joan, eds. Knowledge to Care: A Handbook for Care Assistants. LC 93-2082. 1993. write for info. (*0-632-03585-4*) Blackwell Sci.

McMahon, Christopher. Authority & Democracy: A General Theory of Government & Management. LC 94-1366. (Studies in Moral, Political, & Legal Philosophy). 1994. 35.00 (*0-691-03662-4*) Princeton U Pr.

McMahon, Christopher, photos. The Gardens at Filoli. LC 94-17778. (Illus.). 128p. 1994. pap. 19.95 (*1-56640-993-4*) Pomegranate Calif.

McMahon, Clara P. Education in Fifteenth-Century England. LC 68-54991. (Illus.). 181p. 1969. reprint ed. text ed. 49.75 (*0-8371-0586-2*, MCEC, Greenwood Pr) Greenwood.

McMahon, Dierdre, tr. see Tierou, Alphonse.

McMahon, Donald R., ed. Tiebacks for Bulkheads. (Sessions Proceedings, Geotechnical Special Publication Ser.: No. 4). 90p. 1986. 13.00 (*0-317-60383-3*, 525-1) Am Soc Civil Eng.

McMahon, E. J., jt. ed. see Bartnikas, R.

McMahon, Ed. Ed McMahon's Superselling. 1990. mass mkt. 4.95 (*0-312-92302-3*) St Martin.

McMahon, Edward T., jt. auth. see Furlong, Mary S.

McMahon, Edward T., et al. Street Law: A Course in Practical Law. 3rd ed. LC 85-26560. (Illus.). 446p. 1986. pap. text ed. 38.25 (*0-314-89283-4*) West Pub.

McMahon, Edwin. Beyond the Myth of Dominance: An Alternative to a Violent Society. LC 92-38036. 288p. (Orig.). 1993. pap. 16.95 (*1-55612-563-1*) Sheed & Ward MO.

McMahon, Edwin M., jt. auth. see Campbell, Peter A.

***McMahon, Eileen M.** What Parish Are You from? A Chicago Irish Community & Race Relations. 240p. 1995. text ed. 32.95 (*0-8131-1877-8*) U Pr of Ky.

McMahon, Elizabeth, et al, eds. Nine Short Novels by American Women. LC 92-61003. 715p. (C). 1993. pap. text ed. 17.00 (*0-312-07587-1*) St Martin.

McMahon, Ernest E. Needs - of the People & Their Communities - & the Adult Educator. 55p. 1988. 1.95 (*0-318-36408-5*, AEA1-5) A A A C E.

McMahon, F. Gilbert. Management of Essential Hypertension: The Once-a-Day Era. 3rd ed. (Illus.). 704p. 1990. 59.50 (*0-87993-390-9*) Futura Pub.

McMahon, Franci. Staying the Distance: A Novel. LC 93-49793. 200p. (Orig.). 1994. lib. bdg. 20.95 (*1-56341-047-8*); pap. 9.95 (*1-56341-046-X*) Firebrand Bks.

McMahon, Frank A. & Carter, Earl M. The Great Training Robbery: A Managers Guide to the Purchase of Quality Training. 224p. 1990. 55.00 (*1-85000-882-5*, Falmer Pr); pap. 28.00 (*1-85000-883-3*, Falmer Pr) Taylor & Francis.

McMahon, Frank B., et al. Psychology & You. 2nd ed. LC 93-41159. 1993. text ed. 52.00 (*0-314-02772-6*) West Pub.

***McMahon, Gary, ed.** Lessons in Economic Policy for Eastern Europe from Latin America. LC 95-2566. (International Political Economy Ser.). 1995. write for info. (*0-312-12647-6*) St Martin.

McMahon, Gary, jt. ed. see Morales, Juan A.

McMahon, Gregory. The Hittite State Cult of the Tutelary Deities. LC 91-60344. (Assyriological Studies: No. 25). xxi, 302p. 1991. pap. 30.00 (*0-918986-69-9*) Orientl Inst Pr IT.

McMahon, Helen. Criticism of Fiction: A Study of Trends in the Atlantic Monthly. LC 74-148278. reprint ed. 18.00 (*0-404-04144-2*) AMS Pr.

McMahon, J. T. Building Managerial Effectiveness. (Work in America Institute Studies in Productivity: No. 39). 56p. 1984. pap. 39.00 (*0-317-66816-1*, Pergamon Pr) Elsevier.

McMahon, J. Timothy. Building Managerial Effectiveness. LC 85-9352. (Studies in Productivity: Highlights of the Literature Ser.: Vol. 39). 1985. 55.00 (*0-08-029512-6*) Work in Amer.

McMahon, James. Deserts. Elliott, Charles, ed. LC 84-48674. (Audubon Society Nature Guides Ser.). (Illus.). 638p. 1985. pap. 19.00 (*0-394-73139-5*) Knopf.

— Forty-Seven Alligators. Little, Carl, ed. (Illus.). 48p. (Orig.). (J). (ps-3). 1993. pap. 8.95 (*0-932433-95-2*) Windswept Hse.

— The Music of Early Minnesang. LC 88-62941. (Studies in German Literature, Linguistics & Culture: Vol. 41). (Illus.). 230p. 1989. 43.00 (*0-938100-64-5*) Camden Hse.

McMahon, James P. The Walking Fish. Weinberger, Jane, ed. LC 90-70520. (Illus.). 54p. (Orig.). (J). (ps-3). 1990. pap. 7.95 (*0-932433-70-7*) Windswept Hse.

McMahon, Joan, jt. auth. see Zinner, Ellen.

McMahon, Joanne D., jt. auth. see Coly, Lisette.

McMahon, John P., jt. ed. see Healy, Nicholas J.

McMahon, John V. An Historical View of the Government of Maryland: From Its Colonization to the Present Day. LC 68-30882. (Illus.). 1968. reprint ed. 25.00 (*0-87152-046-X*) Reprint.

McMahon, Joseph. How to Select the Best Psychological Theory to Be an Effective Counselor to Your Clients. LC 88-12266. (Studies in Health & Human Services: Vol. 15). 150p. 1989. lib. bdg. 69.95 (*0-88946-004-3*) E Mellen.

McMahon, Joseph A. Agriculture Trade, Protectionism & the Problems of Development: A Legal Perspective. 240p. 1992. text ed. 55.00 (*0-312-07608-8*) St Martin.

— Education & Culture in European Community Law. (European Community Law Ser.: Vol. 8). 240p. (C). 1995. text ed. 90.00 (*0-485-70013-1*, Pub. by Athlone Pr UK) Humanities.

— European Trade Policy in Agricultural Products. (C). 1988. lib. bdg. 117.50 (*90-247-3780-X*) Kluwer Ac.

McMahon, Joseph H. The Imagination of Jean Genet. LC 80-16963. (Yale Romantic Studies Second Ser.: 2nd Ser., No. 10). viii, 273p. 1980. reprint ed. text ed. 35.00 (*0-313-22430-7*, MCIM, Greenwood Pr) Greenwood.

McMahon, Joseph J. Discovering the Spirit: Source of Personal Freedom. LC 93-6009. 192p. (Orig.). 1994. pap. 12.95 (*1-55612-669-7*) Sheed & Ward MO.

McMahon, June, ed. Organizing Asian Pacific Workers in Southern California. (Current Issues Ser.: No. 9). 42p. 1993. reprint ed. pap. 7.00 (*0-89215-149-8*) U Cal LA Indus Rel.

McMahon, Karen, jt. auth. see Levetin, Estelle.

McMahon, Kay. Bandit's Brazen Kiss. 1990. mass mkt. 4.50 (*0-8217-2863-6*) Zebra.

— Dara's Desire. 1985. pap. 3.95 (*0-8217-1642-5*) Zebra.

Mcmahon, Kay. Defiant Spitfire. 1988. pap. 3.95 (*0-8217-2326-X*) Zebra.

McMahon, Kay. Love's Desperate Deceit. 512p. 1988. pap. 3.95 (*0-8217-2480-0*) Zebra.

— Passion's Slave. 1983. pap. 3.50 (*0-685-07884-1*) Zebra.

— River Rapture. 496p. 1986. pap. 3.95 (*0-8217-1942-4*) Zebra.

— Tender Lies. 1990. mass mkt. 4.50 (*0-8217-2981-0*) Zebra.

Mcmahon, Kay. Virginia Vixen. 1989. pap. 3.95 (*0-8217-2648-X*) Zebra.

McMahon, Kay. Yankee's Lady. pap. 3.95 (*0-317-43142-0*) Zebra.

McMahon, Kay E., jt. auth. see Nance, Virginia L.

***McMahon, Keith.** Misers, Shrews & Polygamists: Sexuality and Male-Female Relations in Eighteenth-Century China. LC 94-33072. (Illus.). 384p. 1995. lib. bdg. 49.95 (*0-8223-1555-6*); pap. 19.95 (*0-8223-1566-1*) Duke.

McMahon, Kevin T. Sexuality: Theological Voices. 266p. (Orig.). 1987. pap. 14.95 (*0-935372-20-2*) Pope John Ctr.

***McMahon, Leonard A.** McMahon Heavy Construction Cost Guide. Strychaz, Stanley J., ed. 300p. 1995. pap. 69.95 (*0-931708-51-6*) Saylor.

McMahon, Linnet. The Handbook of Play Therapy. 304p. (Orig.). 1992. 79.95 (*0-415-07923-3*, A6909, Tavistock); pap. 25.00 (*0-415-05986-0*, A6913, Tavistock) Routledge.

McMahon, Luella E. Lovers in Midsummer. 46p. 1970. pap. 2.50 (*0-87129-148-7*, L35) Dramatic Pub.

McMahon, Lynne. Devolution of the Nude. 80p. 1993. pap. 12.95 (*0-87923-955-7*) Godine.

— Faith. LC 86-32440. (Wesleyan New Poets Ser.). 62p. 1988. 22.50 (*0-8195-2133-7*, Wesleyan Univ Pr); pap. 10.95 (*0-8195-1135-8*, Wesleyan Univ Pr) U Pr of New Eng.

— White Tablecloths. (International Poetry Chapbook Ser.). 11p. (Orig.). (C). 1984. pap. 4.00 (*0-936600-04-7*) Riverstone Foothills.

McMahon, M. The Making of a Profession: A Century of Electrical Engineering in America. LC 83-22325. 320p. 1984. 39.95 (*0-87942-173-8*, PC01677) Inst Electrical.

McMahon, M. Catharine. Aesthetics & Art in the Astree of Honore d'Urfe. LC 78-94197. (Catholic University of America. Studies in Romance Languages & Literatures: No. 1). reprint ed. 21.00 (*0-404-50301-2*) AMS Pr.

McMahon, Maeve W. The Persistent Prison? Rethinking Decarceration & Penal Reform. 320p. 1992. 45.00 (*0-8020-2817-9*); pap. 17.95 (*0-8020-7689-0*) U of Toronto Pr.

McMahon, Maria. The General Method of Social Work Practice: A Problem Solving Approach. 2nd ed. 368p. (C). 1989. text ed. write for info. (*0-13-350380-1*) P-H.

McMahon, Maria O'Neil. Advanced Generalist Practice: With an International Perspective. LC 93-39940. 1993. text ed. write for info. (*0-13-120635-4*) P-H.

McMahon, Marie P. The Radical Whigs, John Trenchard & Thomas Gordon: Libertarian Loyalists to the New House of Hanover. LC 89-22642. 226p. (C). 1990. lib. bdg. 41.00 (*0-8191-7627-3*) U Pr of Amer.

McMahon, Marilyn, et al. Report Writing in dBASE II. 15.95 (*0-317-06186-0*) P-H.

McMahon, Marshall E. Federal Reserve Behavior, 1923-1931. rev. ed. LC 92-35292. (Financial Sector of the American Economy Ser.). 216p. 1993. 50.00 (*0-8153-0965-1*) Garland.

An Asterisk (*) at the beginning of an entry indicates that the title is appearing in BIP for the first time.

*__McMahon, Martha.__ Engendering Motherhood: Identity & Self-Transformation in Women's Lives. LC 95-16209. (Perspectives on Marriage & the Family Ser.). 1995. write for info. (*1-57230-002-7*) Guilford Pr.

McMahon, Martin H., jt. auth. see Bittker, Boris I.

McMahon, Michael. A Day's Work. 1976. pap. 2.25 (*0-913006-08-4*) Puckerbrush.

— Dead of Winter. Hunting, Constance, ed. 27p. (Orig.). 1982. pap. 3.50 (*0-913006-25-4*) Puckerbrush.

McMahon, Mike, jt. auth. see Dixon, Chuck.

McMahon, Patricia. Chi-Hoon: A Korean Girl. LC 92-81331. (Illus.). 48p. (J). (gr. 4-7). 1993. 16.95 (*1-56397-026-0*) Boyds Mills Pr.

— Listen for the Bus: David's Story. LC 94-73316. (Illus.). 48p. (J). (gr. k-5). 1995. 15.95 (*1-56397-368-5*, Wordsong) Boyds Mills Pr.

McMahon, Patrick, jt. auth. see Baillie, Richard.

McMahon, R. J. & Peters, R. DeV., eds. Behavior Disorders of Adolescence: Research, Intervention, & Policy in Clinical & School Settings. LC 91-1957. (Illus.). 224p. 1991. 75.00 (*0-306-43813-5*, Plenum Pr) Plenum.

McMahon, Richard. Camping Hawai'i: A Complete Guide. LC 93-47502. (Illus.). 256p. (C). 1994. pap. 16.95 (*0-8248-1551-3*, Kolowalu Bk) UH Pr.

— A Practical Approach to Road Traffic Law. 300p. 1993. 40.00 (*1-85431-260-X*, Pub. by Blackstone Pr UK) W W Gaunt.

McMahon, Richard, jt. ed. see Buckeldee, Jill.

McMahon, Robert. Augustine's Prayerful Ascent: An Essay on the Literary Form of the Confessions. LC 88-27893. 200p. 1989. 27.50 (*0-8203-1126-X*) U of Ga Pr.

McMahon, Robert J. The Cold War on the Periphery: The United States, India, & Pakistan, 1947-1965. LC 93-38724. 431p. 1993. 30.00 (*0-231-08226-6*) Col U Pr.

— Colonialism & Cold War: The United States & the Struggle for Indonesian Independence, 1945-49. LC 81-66648. 338p. 1981. 39.95 (*0-8014-1388-5*) Cornell U Pr.

— Major Problems in the History of the Vietnam War. 2nd ed. (Major Problems in American History Ser.). 576p. (C). 1995. pap. text ed. write for info. (*0-669-35252-7*) Heath.

McMahon, Robert J., ed. Major Problems in the History of the Vietnam War: Documents & Essays. (Major Problems in American History Ser.). 635p. (C). 1990. pap. text ed. write for info. (*0-669-18013-0*) Heath.

McMahon, Robert J. & Peters, Ray D. Childhood Disorders: Behavioral-Developmental Approaches. LC 84-26341. 290p. 1985. pap. 30.95 (*0-87630-616-4*) Brunner-Mazel.

McMahon, Robert J., jt. auth. see Forehand, Rex L.

McMahon, Robert J., jt. ed. see Paterson, Thomas G.

McMahon, Robert J., jt. auth. see Peters, Ray D.

McMahon, Robert S. Federal Regulation of the Radio & Television Broadcast Industry in the United States: 1927-1959. Sterling, Christopher H., ed. LC 78-21727. (Dissertations in Broadcasting Ser.). 1980. lib. bdg. 30.95 (*0-405-11766-3*) Ayer.

McMahon, Robert W. Introduction to Greenhouse Production-SM. rev. ed. King, Muriel N., ed. (Illus.). 321p. 1992. 32.95 (*1-56502-002-2*, 9502M) Ohio Agri Educ.

*__McMahon, Sean.__ Carpe Diem: Seize the Day: A Little Book of Latin Phrases. (Illus.). 1995. text ed. 7.95 (*0-8118-0931-5*) Chronicle Bks.

— Light on Illancrone. 1990. pap. 7.95 (*1-85371-083-0*, Pub. by Poolbeg Pr IE) Dufour.

— A Little Book of Irish Quotations. (Little Irish Book Ser.). (Illus.). 60p. 1995. 7.95 (*0-86281-480-4*, Pub. by Appletree Pr IE) Irish Bks Media.

— The Poolbeg Book of Irish Ballads. 188p. (Orig.). 1991. pap. 9.95 (*1-85371-127-6*, Pub. by Poolbeg Pr IE) Dufour.

— The Poolbeg Book of Irish Placenames. 113p. (Orig.). (YA). (gr. 10-12). 1990. pap. 8.95 (*1-85371-087-3*, Pub. by Poolbeg Pr IE) Dufour.

— The Three Seals. 181p. (Orig.). (J). (gr. 7-9). 1992. pap. 7.95 (*1-85371-148-9*, Pub. by Poolbeg Pr IE) Dufour.

McMahon, Sean, ed. Best from "The Bell" Great Irish Writing. 186p. 1991. reprint ed. pap. 12.95 (*0-86278-046-2*, Pub. by OBrien Pr IE) Dufour.

— A Book of Irish Quotations. 240p. 1985. 16.95 (*0-87243-127-4*) Templegate.

— Fair City: A Thousand Years of Dublin. 200p. 1989. pap. 8.95 (*1-85371-005-9*, Pub. by Poolbeg Pr IE) Dufour.

— My Native Land: A Celebration of Britain. 360p. 1987. pap. 12.95 (*0-905169-97-2*, Pub. by Poolbeg Pr IE) Dufour.

— Poolbeg Book of Children's Verse. 240p. (J). 1987. pap. 9.95 (*0-905169-88-3*, Pub. by Poolbeg Pr IE) Dufour.

— Poolbeg Golden Treasury of Well Loved Poems. 1989. pap. 8.95 (*1-85371-008-3*, Pub. by Poolbeg Pr IE) Dufour.

— Rich & Rare. 380p. 1987. pap. 14.95 (*0-905169-86-7*, Pub. by Poolbeg Pr IE) Dufour.

McMahon, Sean, jt. auth. see Byrne, Art.

McMahon, Susanna. The Portable Therapist. LC 93-30957. 1994. 7.95 (*0-440-50603-4*) Dell.

McMahon, Suzanne, et al, eds. A Changing World: Proceedings of the North American Serials Interest Group, Inc. LC 91-39991. (Serials Librarian Ser.). 218p. 1992. lib. bdg. 24.95 (*1-56024-263-9*); pap. text ed. 19.95 (*1-56024-298-1*) Haworth Pr.

McMahon, T. A. & Mein, R. G. River & Reservoir Yield. 375p. 1987. text ed. 35.00 (*0-918334-61-6*) WRP.

McMahon, T. A., jt. auth. see Hunt, Dave.

McMahon, T. A., jt. auth. see Hunt, David.

McMahon, Thomas & Bonner, James. On Size & Life. (Scientific American Library). (Illus.). 255p. 1995. text ed. write for info. (*0-7167-5000-7*) W H Freeman.

McMahon, Thomas A. Muscles, Reflexes, & Locomotion. LC 82-61378. (Illus.). 331p. 1984. 70.00 (*0-691-08322-3*); pap. 22.95 (*0-691-02376-X*) Princeton U Pr.

*__McMahon, Timothy E.__ The McMahon Chronicles: The Story of an Irish-American Family in Rhode Island, 1870-1994. (Illus.). 115p. 1994. 35.00 (*0-9643509-9-8*) Taurus Hse Pubns.

McMahon, Tom. Big Meeting, Big Results. 1994. 19.95 (*0-8442-3192-4*, NTC Busn Bks) NTC Pub Grp.

— It Works for Us: Proven Child Care Tips from Experienced Parents Across the Country. Zion, Claire, ed. 272p. (Orig.). 1993. pap. 10.00 (*0-671-77733-5*) PB.

— Orient: Hero Guide Dog of the Appalachian Trail. (Illus.). 32p. (J). (ps-3). 1995. 14.95 (*1-56796-006-5*) WRS Group.

McMahon, W. E. Hans Reichenbach's Philosophy of Grammar. (Janua Linguarum, Ser.: No. 90). 284p. 1976. text ed. 68.00 (*90-279-3204-2*) Mouton.

McMahon, William. Pine Barrens Legends, Lore & Lies. (Illus.). 149p. (J). (gr. 6 up). 1986. pap. 8.95 (*0-912608-19-6*) Mid Atlantic.

— South Jersey Towns: History & Legend. LC 78-163961. (Illus.). 384p. 1990. reprint ed. pap. 12.95 (*0-8135-0718-9*) Rutgers U Pr.

McMahon, William E. Dreadnought Battleships & Battle Cruisers. LC 78-50769. (Illus.). 1978. lib. bdg. 27.00 (*0-8191-0465-5*) U Pr of Amer.

— The Higher Humanism of Wallace Stevens. LC 90-22574. (Studies in American Literature: Vol. 12). 180p. 1991. lib. bdg. 79.95 (*0-88946-792-7*) E Mellen.

McMains, Harvey J. & Wilcox, Lyle, eds. Alternatives for Growth: The Engineering & Economics of Natural Resources Development. LC 77-11870. 270p. reprint ed. pap. 77.00 (*0-8357-5333-6*, 2056366) Bks Demand.

McMains, Joel. Dog Logic - Companion Obedience: Rapport-Based Training. (Illus.). 224p. 1992. 21.95 (*0-87605-510-2*) Howell Bk.

— Dog Training Projects for Young People. (Illus.). 288p. 1995. pap. 14.95 (*0-87605-506-4*) Howell Bk.

McMains, Joel M. Advanced Obedience - Easier Than You Think. (Illus.). 256p. 1993. 25.95 (*0-87605-522-6*) Howell Bk.

— Kennels & Kenneling. LC 93-30076. (Illus.). 256p. 1994. 25.95 (*0-87605-661-3*) Howell Bk.

McMains, June. Fast Food: Thirty Minute Gourmet Meals Without Thinking. (Illus.). 128p. (Orig.). 1988. pap. 6.95 (*0-9620721-0-9*) P Jam Pubns.

McMaken, Sandra, jt. auth. see Erickson, Millard J.

McMakin, Jacqueline & Dyer, Sonya. Working from the Heart: A Guide to Recovering the Soul at Work. LC 92-54615. 240p. 1994. pap. 14.00 (*0-06-065381-7*) Harper SF.

McMakin, Jacqueline & Nar. Meeting Jesus in the New Testament. LC 92-53916. 128p. 1993. pap. 7.00 (*0-06-065378-7*) Harper SF.

McMakin, Jacqueline & Nary, Rhoda. The Doorways Series, 2. LC 92-53917. 1993. pap. 7.00 (*0-06-065377-9*) Harper SF.

— The Doorways Series, Vol. 1: Encountering God in Others. LC 92-53917. 1993. 7.00 (*0-685-61102-7*) Harper SF.

— The Doorways Series, Vol. 3: Journeying with the Spirit. LC 92-53917. 1993. pap. 7.00 (*0-06-065379-5*) Harper SF.

— The Doorways Series, Vol. 4: Discovering Gifts Vision Call. LC 92-53917. 1993. pap. 7.00 (*0-06-065380-9*) Harper SF.

— Doorways to Christian Growth. 300p. 1984. pap. 9.95 (*0-86683-818-X*) Harper SF.

McMakin, Patrick D. A Field Guide to the Flowering Plants of Thailand. 2nd ed. (Illus.). 343p. 1993. 39.50 (*1-879155-16-8*) Lotus WA.

McManamin, Francis G. The American Years of John Boyle O'Reilly. LC 76-6356. (Irish American Ser.). 1976. 29.95 (*0-405-09349-7*) Ayer.

McManamon, Francis P., jt. auth. see Stuart, George E.

McManamon, John M. Funeral Oratory & the Cultural Ideals of Italian Humanism. LC 88-19840. xiv, 344p. (C). 1989. 60.00 (*0-8078-1783-X*) U of NC Pr.

McManaway, James G. Authorship of Shakespeare. LC 62-4031. (Folger Guides to the Age of Shakespeare Ser.). 1962. pap. 4.95 (*0-918016-25-8*) Folger Bks.

— Studies in Shakespeare, Bibliography, & Theatre. Hosley, Richard et al, eds. (Illus.). 417p. 1990. 50.00 (*0-918016-48-7*) Folger Bks.

McManaway, James G. & Roberts, Jeanne A. Selective Bibliography of Shakespeare: Editions, Textual Studies, Commentary. (Special Publications Ser.). 1978. 30.00 (*0-918016-02-9*); pap. 12.95 (*0-918016-03-7*) Folger Bks.

McMane, Fred. My Hero. (J). (gr. 4-7). 1994. pap. 3.99 (*0-553-48164-9*) Bantam.

— Winning Women: Eight Great Athletes & Their Unbeatable Stories. (J). (gr. 4-7). 1995. 3.99 (*0-553-48290-4*) Bantam.

McMane, Fred & Wolf, Cathrine. The Worst Day I Ever Had. (Illus.). (J). (gr. 3-7). 1991. pap. 8.95 (*0-316-55354-9*, Spts Illus Kids) Little.

McManimie, Robert J. Relationships. 106p. (C). 1992. pap. text ed. 9.95 (*0-9631253-1-1*) Devsyn.

McManis, Charles R. Unfair Trade Practices in a Nutshell. 3rd ed. (Nutshell Ser.). 440p. 1992. pap. text ed. 17.00 (*0-314-01122-6*) West Pub.

McManis, Douglas R. European Impressions of the New England Coast, 1497-1620. LC 70-187026. (Research Papers Ser.: No. 139). (Illus.). 147p. 1972. pap. 12.00 (*0-89065-046-2*, 139) U Chicago Comm Geo.

McManis, Gerald L. & Stewart, Jerrie A. Personnel Management in Associations. 143p. (Orig.). 1988. reprint ed. pap. text ed. 30.00 (*0-88034-010-X*) Am Soc Assn Execs.

*__McManis, Kent.__ Fetishes & Carvings of the Zuni. (Illus.). 48p. (Orig.). 1995. pap. 7.95 (*0-918080-77-0*) Treas Chest Bks.

McManis, Philip & Schlabach, Gerald, eds. Relentless Persistence: Nonviolent Action in Latin America. 308p. (Orig.). 1990. lib. bdg. 39.95 (*0-86571-181-X*); pap. 16.95 (*0-86571-182-8*) New Soc Pubs.

McMann, Evelyn. Canadian Who's Who Index 1898-1984: Incorporating Men & Women of the Time. 528p. 1986. 125.00 (*0-8020-4633-9*) U of Toronto Pr.

McMann, Evelyn de R. Montreal Museum of Fine Arts, Formerly Art Association of Montreal: Spring Exhibitions 1880-1970. 418p. 1988. text ed. 125.00 (*0-8020-2650-8*) U of Toronto Pr.

*__McManners, Hugh.__ The Backpacker's Handbook. LC 94-32042. (Illus.). 160p. 1995. 14.95 (*1-56458-852-1*) Dorling Kindersley.

— The Complete Wilderness Training Book. LC 93-5686. (Illus.). 192p. 1994. 29.95 (*1-56458-488-7*) Dorling Kindersley.

McManners, John. Death & the Enlightenment: Changing Attitudes to Death among Christians & Unbelievers in Eighteenth-Century France. 640p. 1982. 39.95 (*0-19-826440-2*) OUP.

— The French Revolution & the Church. LC 82-15532. x, 161p. (C). 1982. reprint ed. text ed. 52.50 (*0-313-23074-9*, MCFR, Greenwood Pr) Greenwood.

McManners, John, ed. The Oxford History of Christianity. 784p. 1994. pap. 15.95 (*0-19-285291-4*) OUP.

— The Oxford Illustrated History of Christianity. (Oxford Illustrated Histories Ser.). (Illus.). 760p. 1990. 49.95 (*0-19-822928-3*) OUP.

— The Oxford Illustrated History of Christianity. (Oxford Illustrated Histories Ser.). (Illus.). 768p. 1992. pap. 25.00 (*0-19-285259-0*) OUP.

McMannis, William J., jt. auth. see Reid, Rolland R.

McMannon, Karen. Calligraphy Techniques. (Illus.). 192p. 1990. 8.99 (*0-517-69910-9*) Random Hse Value.

McMannus, Maggie, jt. auth. see Reilly, Ed.

*__McManus.__ Classics & Feminism. 1995. 26.95 (*0-8057-9757-2*, Twayne) Macmillan.

— Jiggs is Back. 1990. pap. 12.95 (*0-913666-82-3*) Turtle Isl Foun.

McManus, Anne. Terse Verse. 192p. 1994. pap. 19.95 (*1-85619-194-X*, Sinclair-Stevenson) Trafalgar.

— They Said I Was Dead: The Complete Alternative Cure for Addiction. 1993. pap. 15.50 (*1-85727-091-6*) InBook.

— They Said I Was Dead: The Complete Alternative Cure for Addiction. 128p. 1994. 45.00 (*1-85727-086-X*) InBook.

McManus, Barbara F., jt. auth. see Henderson, Katherine U.

*__McManus, Catherine O. & Arnold, Krystyn E.__ The Lazy Cook: Delicious Recipes Take 10 Minutes Or Less to Prepare. Hall, Kathryn, ed. (Illus.). 208p. Date not set. pap. text ed. 12.95 (*1-57090-012-4*) Alexander Bks.

McManus, Chris. Psychology in Medicine. (Illus.). 327p. 1992. pap. 39.95 (*0-7506-0496-4*) Buttrwrth-Heinemann.

McManus, Donald P., jt. auth. see Smyth, J. D.

McManus, Dorothy. Song of Sirius. Myhre, M., ed. 155p. (Orig.). (YA). 1990. pap. 8.00 (*0-929686-01-2*) Temple Golden Pubns.

McManus, Ed & Nicholas, Bill. We're Roasting Harry Tuesday Night: How to Plan, Write & Conduct the Business-Social Roast. 221p. 1984. 18.95 (*0-13-950163-0*, Busn) P-H.

McManus, Edgar J. Black Bondage in the North. LC 72-12425. (Illus.). 260p. reprint ed. pap. 74.10 (*0-8357-8045-7*, 2034098) Bks Demand.

— A History of Negro Slavery in New York. LC 66-15471. 235p. reprint ed. pap. 67.00 (*0-7837-3177-9*, 2042781) Bks Demand.

— Law & Liberty in Early New England: Criminal Justice & Due Process, 1620-1692. LC 92-18719. 296p. 1993. 32.50x (*0-87023-824-8*) U of Mass Pr.

McManus, Ethel. Grandpa, 1851-1947: A McManus Family Link with U. S. History. (Illus.). 116p. 1992. 14.95 (*0-910303-32-0*) Writers Pub Serv.

*__McManus, Francis.__ Environmental Health Law. 257p. 1994. pap. 44.00 (*1-85431-317-7*) W W Gaunt.

— Environmental Health Law in Scotland. 262p. 1990. text ed. 68.95 (*0-566-07036-7*, Pub. by Avebury Pub UK) Ashgate Pub Co.

McManus, Frederick R. Liturgical Participation: An Ongoing Assessment. 44p. 1988. pap. 3.00 (*0-8146-1936-3*) Liturgical Pr.

McManus, George. Bringing up Father: An Original Compilation - First Collection of the Complete First of the Daily Strip 1913-14. LC 76-53049. (Classic American Comic Strips Ser.). (Illus.). 1986. 32.00 (*0-88355-653-7*) Hyperion Conn.

McManus, Glenda, ed. Hungry Poets' Cookbook. 140p. (Orig.). 1987. pap. 12.95 (*0-930090-34-9*) Applezaba.

McManus, Howard R. The Battle of Cloyd's Mountain & the Virginia & Tennessee Railroad Raid. (Virginia Civil War Battles & Leaders Ser.). (Illus.). 107p. 1989. 19.95 (*0-930919-89-0*) H E Howard.

McManus, Irene. Dreamscapes: The Art of Juan Gonzalez. LC 94-13849. (Illus.). 200p. 1994. 50.00 (*1-55595-082-5*) Hudson Hills.

— The Watercolors of Carolyn Brady: Including a Catalogue Raisonne 1972-1990. LC 91-71548. (Illus.). 192p. 1991. 50.00 (*1-55595-048-5*) Hudson Hills.

McManus, J. & Duck, R. W., eds. Geomorphology & Sedimentology of Lakes & Reservoirs. LC 92-23465. (British Geomorphological Research Group Symposia Ser.). 278p. 1993. text ed. 165.00 (*0-471-93773-8*) Wiley.

McManus, J. Donald. Toodle-oo Taxahaw: One Hundred One Tales or a Small History of the World. (Illus.). 228p. (Orig.). 1991. pap. 10.00 (*0-939710-15-3*) Meridional Pubns.

McManus, James. Curtains. LC 85-72236. 130p. (Orig.). 1985. pap. 8.95 (*0-9614644-0-2*) Another Chicago Pr.

— Great America: Poems. LC 92-54851. 128p. 1993. pap. 11.00 (*0-06-096994-6*, HarpT) HarpC.

McManus, James I., jt. ed. see Schulmeyer, G. Gordon.

McManus, James L. Antonio Salazar Is Dead. (Illus.). 56p. (Orig.). 1980. pap. 3.00 (*0-9603794-0-1*) Syncline.

Mcmanus, Jane. Getting to Know Cuba. 1989. 14.95 (*0-312-02848-2*) St Martin.

McManus, Jane. Getting to Know Cuba: An Insider's Guide. (Illus.). 190p. (Orig.). 1988. pap. 12.95 (*0-685-24336-2*) Bedell Pubs.

McManus, Jane P., jt. auth. see Marler, Don C.

*__McManus, John.__ Keeping the Team in Shape. 116p. (C). 1994. pap. 18.00x (*0-85292-550-6*, Pub. by IPM Hse UK) St Mut.

McManus, John, ed. see Health Promotion Resource Center Staff.

*__McManus, John F.__ Changing Commands: The Betrayal of America's Military. Gow, Thomas G., ed. 240p. (Orig.). Date not set. pap. text ed. 8.95 (*1-881919-03-X*) John Birch.

— Financial Terrorism: Hyjacking America under the Threat of Bankruptcy. Gow, Tom G., ed. 256p. (Orig.). 1993. pap. text ed. 8.95 (*1-881919-02-1*) John Birch.

McManus, John H. Market Driven Journalism: Let the Citizen Beware? LC 93-49517. 302p. (C). 1994. text ed. 48.00 (*0-8039-5252-X*); pap. text ed. 21.50 (*0-8039-5253-8*) Sage.

*__McManus, Judith A. & Osborn, Edward.__ Creating an Effective Speech. (Illus.). 123p. (C). 1994. pap. text ed. 18.95 (*0-9642994-0-2*) Annies Pr.

McManus, Liz. Acts of Subversion. 236p. (Orig.). 1991. pap. 12.95 (*1-85371-124-1*, Pub. by Poolbeg Pr IE) Dufour.

McManus, Marianne L. Quake Stress: Preparation for the Psychological Effects of a Major Disaster. LC 88-71569. 44p. (Orig.). 1988. text ed. 12.95 (*0-922248-08-7*); pap. 6.95 (*0-922248-02-8*); audio 7.95 (*0-922248-06-0*) Calif Psychol Pubs.

*__McManus, Michael.__ From Fate to Choice: Private Bobbies, Public Beats. 165p. 1995. boxed, pap. 55.95 (*1-85972-099-4*, Pub. by Avebury Pub UK) Ashgate Pub Co.

McManus, Michael J. Fifty Practical ways to Take Our Kids Back from the World. LC 93-4596. 1993. pap. 8.99 (*0-8423-1242-0*) Tyndale.

— Marriage Savers: A Study Guide. 96p. 1994. pap. text ed. 4.00 (*1-885481-02-0*) Quadrus Media.

— Marriage Savers: Helping Your Friends & Family Stay Married. 272p. 1993. 15.99 (*0-310-48240-2*); audio 9.99 (*0-310-48248-8*) Zondervan.

— Marriage Savers: Helping Your Friends & Family Stay Married. 2nd rev. ed. 352p. 1995. pap. 14.99 (*0-310-38661-6*) Zondervan.

— Marriage Savers: How to Help Your Friends & Family Avoid Divorce. LC 92-39968. 1993. pap. 10.99 (*0-310-48241-0*) Zondervan.

McManus, Mick. Troublesome Behavior in the Classroom. 224p. 1989. pap. 27.95 (*0-89397-346-7*) Nichols Pub.

— Troublesome Behaviour in the Classroom: Meeting Individual Needs. 2nd ed. LC 94-34160. (Illus.). 224p. 1995. pap. 17.95 (*0-415-11360-1*, C0070) Routledge.

McManus, Pat. McManus Treasury 1 & 2 Special Offer. 1993. pap. 55.00 (*0-8050-3081-6*) H Holt & Co.

McManus, Patricia. The Babysitting Co-op Guidebook: Building a Community Support Network. (Illus.). 40p. (Orig.). (C). 1993. pap. 14.95x (*1-56806-365-2*) Diane Pub.

McManus, Patrick. Never Sniff a Gift Fish. LC 83-147. 228p. 1983. 17.95 (*0-8050-0527-7*) H Holt & Co.

— Never Sniff a Gift Fish. LC 83-147. 228p. 1984. pap. 6.95 (*0-8050-0031-3*, Owl) H Holt & Co.

McManus, Patrick E. A Fine & Pleasant Misery. LC 77-13452. 248p. 1978. 16.95 (*0-8050-0166-2*) H Holt & Co.

— A Fine & Pleasant Misery. LC 80-24733. 228p. 1981. pap. 6.95 (*0-8050-0032-1*, Owl) H Holt & Co.

— They Shoot Canoes, Don't They? LC 80-24131. 288p. 1981. 18.95 (*0-8050-0165-4*) H Holt & Co.

— They Shoot Canoes, Don't They? LC 80-24131. 288p. 1982. pap. 6.95 (*0-8050-0030-5*, Owl) H Holt & Co.

McManus, Patrick F. The Good Samaritan Strikes Again. LC 92-10633. 224p. 1992. 17.95 (*0-8050-2042-X*) H Holt & Co.

— Good Samaritan Strikes Again. 224p. 1993. pap. 7.95 (*0-8050-2922-2*) H Holt & Co.

Mcmanus, Patrick F. The Good Samaritan Strikes Again. large type ed. LC 92-38587. (General Ser.). 233p. 1993. 18.95 (*0-8161-5689-1*) G K Hall.

McManus, Patrick F. The Grasshopper Trap. LC 84-29768. 224p. 1985. 13.95 (*0-03-000738-0*) H Holt & Co.

— The Grasshopper Trap. 228p. 1986. pap. 6.95 (*0-8050-0111-5*, Owl) H Holt & Co.

— How I Got This Way. LC 94-16971. 1994. 19.95 (*0-8050-3481-1*) H Holt & Co.

— Kid Camping from Aaaaiii! to Zip. LC 79-13152. (Illus.). (J). (gr. 3-8). 1979. 12.95 (*0-688-41910-0*) Lothrop.

— Kid Camping from AAAAIII! to Zip. (Illus.). 144p. (J). (gr. 6-7). 1991. reprint ed. pap. 3.99 (*0-380-71311-X*, Camelot) Avon.

— The McManus Treasury I, 4 bks., Set. 1986. pap. 27.50 (*0-8050-0112-3*, Owl) H Holt & Co.

— McManus Treasury II, 4 bks., Set. 1993. pap. 27.50 (*0-8050-2970-2*) H Holt & Co.

— The Night the Bear Ate Goombaw. 1989. 19.95 (*0-8050-1033-5*) H Holt & Co.

— The Night the Bear Ate Goombaw. LC 88-34618. 192p. 1990. pap. 7.95 (*0-8050-1340-7*, Owl) H Holt & Co.

— The Night the Bear Ate Goombaw. large type ed. (General Ser.). 253p. 1990. 18.95 (*0-8161-4889-9*, Large Print Bks) Hall.

— Real Ponies Don't Go Oink! 224p. 1991. 16.95 (*0-8050-1651-1*) H Holt & Co.

— Real Ponies Don't Go Oink! 208p. 1992. pap. 6.95 (*0-8050-2107-8*, Owl) H Holt & Co.

— Rubber Legs & White Tail-Hairs. LC 87-8494. 216p. 1987. 14.95 (*0-8050-0544-7*) H Holt & Co.

— Rubber Legs & White Tail-Hairs. 216p. 1988. pap. 6.95 (*0-8050-0912-4*, Owl) H Holt & Co.

McManus, Patrick F. & Gass, Patricia M. Whatchagot Stew: A Memoir of an Idaho Childhood, with Recipes & Commentaries. 288p. 1992. pap. 7.95 (*0-8050-2377-1*, Owl) H Holt & Co.

— Whatchagot Stew & the Troll's Idaho Cookbook. 288p. 1989. 16.95 (*0-8050-0922-1*) H Holt & Co.

McManus, Roger E., jt. ed. see Escherich, Peter C.

McManus, Samuel P., jt. ed. see Harris, J. Milton.

McManus, Thomas E., jt. auth. see McLaughlin, John F.

Mcmarco, Peter. Matchbox Toys: A Collector's Guide. 1993. 17.98 (*1-55521-937-3*) Bk Sales Inc.

McMartin, Barbara. Adventures in Hiking. 110p. (J). 1993. pap. 12.50 (*0-925168-25-4*) North Country.

— Fifty Hikes in the Adirondacks: Short Walks, Day Trips & Extended Hikes Throughout the Park. 2nd ed. LC 88-7456. (Fifty Hikes Ser.). (Illus.). 256p. 1989. pap. 12.95 (*0-88150-124-7*, Backcountry) Countryman.

— Fun on Flatwater: An Introduction to Adirondack Canoeing. LC 95-15935. (Illus.). 1995. pap. 12.50 (*0-925168-40-8*) North Country.

— The Great Forest of the Adirondacks. 266p. 1994. 27.50 (*0-925168-29-7*) North Country.

— Hides, Hemlocks & Adirondack History. 332p. 1992. 30.00 (*0-932052-99-1*) North Country.

— Realizing the Recreational Potential of Adirondack Wild Forests. (Twenty Twenty Vision: Fulfilling the Promise of the Adirondack Park Ser: Vol. III). 52p. 1990. pap. 10.00 (*0-9621202-2-7*) Adirondack Council.

McMartin, Barbara & Kick, Peter. Fifty Hikes in the Hudson Valley: From the Catskills to the Taconics, & from the Ramapos to the Helderbergs. LC 85-1436. (Fifty Hikes Ser.). 224p. 1985. pap. 12.95 (*0-942440-23-4*, Backcountry) Countryman.

— Fifty Hikes in the Hudson Valley: From the Catskills to the Taconics, & from the Ramapos to the Helderbergs. 2nd ed. (Fifty Hikes Ser.). (Illus.). 232p. 1994. pap. 14.00 (*0-88150-292-8*, Backcountry) Countryman.

McMartin, Barbara, jt. auth. see Rosevear, Francis.

***McMartin, Jim.** Personality Psychology: A Student Centered Approach. 216p. 1995. text ed. 38.00 (*0-8039-5343-7*); pap. text ed. 17.95 (*0-8039-5344-5*) Sage.

McMaster, ALison A. Copycat. (Linford Romance Library). 256p. 1992. pap. 14.95 (*0-7089-7210-1*, Trailtree Bookshop) Ulverscroft.

McMaster, Carolyn. Malawi: Foreign Policy & Development. LC 74-80653. 288p. (C). 1974. text ed. 25.00 (*0-312-50925-1*) St Martin.

McMaster, Clara W. Sing a Happy Song: Beloved Children's Favorites. (J). 1992. 8.98 (*0-88290-451-5*, 2929) Horizon Utah.

McMaster, Dale. Vocabulary Development. (Language Arts Ser.). 24p. (gr. 6-9). 1976. student ed 5.00 (*0-8209-0312-4*, VD-4) ESP.

McMaster, Hamilton J. The Urban Principal's Handbook. (C). 1988. 21.25 (*0-932957-28-5*) Natl School.

McMaster, Helen N. Margaret Fuller As a Literary Critic. 1972. 59.95 (*0-8490-0585-X*) Gordon Pr.

McMaster, James. Urban Financial Management: A Training Manual. (EDI Technical Materials Ser.). 192p. 1991. 10.95 (*0-8213-1615-X*, 11615) World Bank.

McMaster, James H., ed. The ABCs of Sports Medicine. LC 80-20636. 400p. 1982. lib. bdg. 35.00 (*0-88275-890-X*) Krieger.

McMaster, James H., jt. ed. see Novak, Josef F.

McMaster, John. Sabotaging the Shogun: Western Diplomats Open Japan, 1859-69. 1992. 16.95 (*0-533-10250-2*) Vantage.

McMaster, John & Stone, Frederick B. Pennsylvania & the Federal Constitution 1787-1788, 2 vols, Set. LC 74-87406. (American Constitutional & Legal History Ser.). 1970. reprint ed. lib. bdg. 79.50 (*0-306-71550-3*) Da Capo.

McMaster, John B. Benjamin Franklin As a Man of Letters. LC 70-125706. (American Journalists Ser.). 1978. reprint ed. 28.95 (*0-405-01687-5*) Ayer.

— Benjamin Franklin As Man of Letters. 1972. 59.95 (*0-87968-722-3*) Gordon Pr.

— With the Fathers: Studies in the History of the United States. LC 75-173113. 1972. reprint ed. 20.95 (*0-405-08771-3*, Pub. by Blom Pubns UK) Ayer.

McMaster, John B., ed. The American Explorer Series, 10 titles in 17 vols., Set. reprint ed. 565.00 (*0-404-54900-4*) AMS Pr.

***McMaster, Juliet.** Jane Austen, the Novelist: Essays Past & Present. LC 95-14700. 1995. write for info. (*0-312-12753-7*) St Martin.

— Thackeray: The Major Novels. LC 76-151380. (Illus.). 246p. reprint ed. pap. 70.20 (*0-8357-8345-6*, 2034019) Bks Demand.

McMaster, Juliet, ed. see Armstrong, Frances.

McMaster, Juliet, ed. see Bradley, Alexander.

McMaster, Juliet, ed. see Comstock, Cathy.

McMaster, Juliet, ed. see Ellis, William.

McMaster, Juliet, ed. see Flaxman, Rhoda L.

McMaster, Juliet, ed. see Kalikoff, Beth.

McMaster, Juliet, ed. see Koppel, Gene.

McMaster, Juliet, ed. see Morse, Deborah D.

McMaster, Juliet, ed. see Thomas, Keith G.

McMaster, Marvin C. HPLC, a Practical User's Guide. LC 93-42139. 1994. 55.00 (*1-56081-636-8*) VCH Pubs.

McMaster, Michael. Performance Management: Creating the Conditions for Results. (Performance Management Ser.). 320p. (Orig.). (C). 1987. 21.95 (*0-943920-69-8*) Metamorphous Pr.

— Performance Management: Creating the Conditions for Results. rev. ed. 320p. (Orig.). 1993. pap. 18.95 (*1-55552-041-3*) Metamorphous Pr.

McMaster, Michael & Grinder, John. Precision: A New Approach to Communication. LC 93-28602. 304p. 1994. pap. 15.95 (*1-55552-049-9*) Grinder Delozier.

McMaster, Peter, jt. auth. see Jacob, Isaac.

McMaster, R. D. Thackeray's Cultural Frame of Reference: Allusion in The Newcomes. 234p. (C). 1991. text ed. 49.95 (*0-7735-0838-4*, Pub. by McGill CN) U of Toronto Pr.

McMaster, R. E. Christianity at a Glance. 1989. write for info. (*0-318-61880-X*) Reaper Pub.

McMaster, R. E., Jr. No Time for Slaves. 300p. 1986. write for info. (*0-9605316-8-8*) Reaper Pub.

— There Is a Better Way. 1989. write for info. (*0-318-61644-0*) Reaper Pub.

— The Way to God, Peace & Prosperity. 1989. write for info. (*0-318-61879-6*) Reaper Pub.

— Wealth for All: Economics, 2 Bks., Book 2. rev. ed. 280p. 1982. 14.95 (*0-9605316-2-9*) Reaper Pub.

— Win Win Win. 1989. pap. 2.25 (*0-9605316-6-1*) Reaper Pub.

McMaster, Raymond, jt. auth. see McAllister, Angus.

McMaster, Robert B. & Shea, K. Stuart. Generalization in Digital Cartography. Cromley, Ellen K. & Cromley, Robert G., eds. LC 92-25730. (Resource Publications for College Geography). (C). 1992. pap. 10.00 (*0-89291-209-X*) Assn Am Geographers.

McMaster, Robert B., jt. auth. see Buttenfield, Barbara P.

McMaster, Robert C., ed. ASNT Nondestructive Testing Handbook, Second Edition: Leak Testing, Vol. 1. (Illus.). 850p. 1982. 121.25 (*0-87170-125-1*, 125) Am Soc Nondestructive.

— ASNT Nondestructive Testing Handbook, Vol. 2: Liquid Penetrant Tests. (Illus.). 616p. 1982. 121.25 (*0-87170-126-X*, 126) Am Soc Nondestructive.

McMaster, Robert C., ed. see American Society for Nondestructive Testing Staff.

McMaster, Robert C., jt. auth. see Wenk, Samuel A.

***McMaster, Sandy & Baird, Teddi.** The Ultimate Educator's Handbook. DSMV Publishing Staff, ed. 378p. (Orig.). (C). 1994. pap. 49.95 (*0-9642852-0-7*) DSMV Pubng.

***McMaster, Sandy & Baird, Teddi L.** The Ultimate Educator's Handbook. DSMV Publishing Staff, ed. 378p. (Orig.). 1994. pap. 49.95 (*0-9642852-1-5*) DSMV Pubng.

***McMasters, Clyde V.** Witnessing Throughout the Twentieth Century: First Presbyterian Church of Sapula, Oklahoma, Celebrates One Hundred Years. 256p. 1995. 16.95 (*1-881576-58-2*) Providence Hse.

McMasters, Dale. Basic Skills Buying Skills Workbook. (Basic Skills Workbooks). 32p. (gr. 5-8). 1983. 1.98 (*0-8209-0570-4*, MW-3) ESP.

— Basic Skills Dictionary Workbook. (Basic Skills Workbooks). 32p. (gr. 4-7). 1983. 1.98 (*0-8209-0536-4*, DW-1) ESP.

— Basic Skills Holidays Workbook. (Basic Skills Workbooks). 32p. (gr. 4-7). 1983. 1.98 (*0-8209-0560-7*, SSW-8) ESP.

— Basic Skills How to Study Workbook. (Basic Skills Workbooks). 32p. (gr. 5-9). 1983. 1.98 (*0-8209-0534-8*, HSW-1) ESP.

— Basic Skills Library Workbook. (Basic Skills Workbooks). 32p. (gr. 4-7). 1983. 1.98 (*0-686-42990-7*, LW-1) ESP.

— Basic Skills Word Building Workbook. (Basic Skills Workbooks). 32p. (gr. 4-7). 1983. 1.98 (*0-8209-0568-2*, WBW-1) ESP.

— Basic Skills Written Problems in Math Workbook. (Basic Skills Workbooks). 32p. (gr. 3-4). 1983. 1.98 (*0-8209-0574-7*, MW-7) ESP.

— Basic Study & Research. (Language Arts Ser.). 24p. (gr. 5-9). 1979. student ed 5.00 (*0-8209-0304-3*, BSR-1) ESP.

— The Dictionary. (Language Arts Ser.). 24p. (gr. 6 up). 1980. student ed 5.00 (*0-8209-0308-6*, D-1) ESP.

— Everyday Vocabulary. (Language Arts Ser.). 24p. (gr. 4-6). 1976. student ed 5.00 (*0-8209-0310-8*, VD-2) ESP.

— Learning Buying Skills. (Math Ser.). 24p. (gr. 5-9). 1981. student ed 5.00 (*0-8209-0125-3*, A-35) ESP.

— Vocabulary Study. (Language Arts Ser.). 24p. (gr. 5-7). 1976. student ed 5.00 (*0-8209-0311-6*, VD-3) ESP.

— Word Building. (Language Arts Ser.). 24p. (gr. 4-7). 1976. student ed 5.00 (*0-8209-0305-1*, WB-1) ESP.

— Written Problems in Math: Grade 4. (Math Ser.). 24p. 1981. student ed 5.00 (*0-8209-0124-5*, A-34) ESP.

***McMasters, Don & Gillette, M. L.** Approximating Avogadro's Number Using Glass Beads & Monomolecular Film. (Modular Laboratory Program in Chemistry Ser.). 12p. (C). 1987. pap. text ed. 1.10x (*0-87540-354-9*) Chem Educ Res.

***McMasters, Jake.** Blood Bounty. (White Apache Ser.: No. 7). 176p. (Orig.). 1995. mass mkt., pap. text ed. 3.99 (*0-8439-3790-4*) Dorchester Pub Co.

— Blood on the Arrows. (Cheyenne Giant Edition Ser.). 368p. (Orig.). 1995. mass mkt. 4.99 (*0-8439-3839-0*) Dorchester Pub Co.

— Blood Treachery. (White Apache Ser.: No. 6). 176p. (Orig.). 1995. mass mkt. 3.99 (*0-8439-3739-4*) Dorchester Pub Co.

— Bloodbath. (White Apache Ser.: No. 5). 176p. (Orig.). 1994. mass mkt. 3.99 (*0-8439-3689-4*) Dorchester Pub Co.

— Desert Fury. (Whate Apache Ser.: No. 9). 176p. (Orig.). 1995. mass mkt., pap. 3.99 (*0-8439-3871-4*) Dorchester Pub Co.

— Hangman's Knot. (White Apache Ser.: No. 1). 176p. (Orig.). 1993. pap. 3.99 (*0-8439-3535-9*) Dorchester Pub Co.

— Quick Killer. (White Apache Ser.: No. 4). 176p. (Orig.). 1994. mass mkt., pap. text ed. 3.99 (*0-8439-3646-0*) Dorchester Pub Co.

— The Trackers. (White Apache Ser.: Vol. 8). 176p. (Orig.). 1995. mass mkt. 3.99 (*0-8439-3830-7*) Dorchester Pub Co.

— Warpath. (White Apache Ser.: No. 2). 176p. (Orig.). 1994. pap. 3.99 (*0-8439-3575-8*) Dorchester Pub Co.

— Warrior Born. (White Apache Ser.: No. 3). 176p. (Orig.). 1994. pap. 3.99 (*0-8439-3613-4*) Dorchester Pub Co.

McMasters, S. Y. A Biographical Index to the History of England. 1973. 59.95 (*0-87968-752-5*) Gordon Pr.

McMasters, William H. Originality, & Other Essays. LC 67-28759. (Essay Index Reprint Ser.). 1977. 16.95 (*0-8369-0656-X*) Ayer.

McMath, F. M. McMath: Collections for a History of the Ancient Family of McMath. (Illus.). 272p. 1992. reprint ed. lib. bdg. 53.00 (*0-8328-2323-6*); reprint ed. pap. 43.00 (*0-8328-2324-4*) Higginson Bk Co.

McMath, John M. The Now of Our Human Destiny. LC 88-71529. 1990. 12.95 (*0-8158-0453-9*) Chris Mass.

***McMath, Meredith B.** Annabelle Bk. 2: Celebrating the American Woman. 350p. 1995. pap. 10.99 (*0-89283-895-7*, Vine Bks) Servant.

— Theodosia Bk. 1: Celebrating the American Woman. 350p. 1995. pap. 10.99 (*0-89283-890-6*, Vine Bks) Servant.

McMath, Phillip H. Arrival Point. 238p. 1991. 16.95 (*0-943099-08-0*) M&M Pr.

McMath, Robert. American Populism. 1992. pap. 10.95 (*0-374-52264-2*, Noonday) FS&G.

Mcmath, Robert. American Populism. 1992. 30.00 (*0-8090-7796-5*) Hill & Wang.

McMath, Robert C. Populist Vanguard: A History of the Southern Farmers' Alliance. LC 75-9751. 235p. reprint ed. pap. 67.00 (*0-7837-0294-9*, 2040615) Bks Demand.

McMath, Robert C., Jr. William Henry Emerson: And the Scientific Discipline at Georgia Tech. 130p. 1993. write for info. (*0-9639968-9-4*) C L Emerson.

McMath, Robert C., Jr., jt. ed. see Burton, Orville V.

McMath, Robert C., Jr., et al. Engineering the New South: Georgia Tech, 1885-1985. LC 85-969. (Illus.). 576p. 1985. 45.00 (*0-8203-0784-X*) U of Ga Pr.

McMath, Sandy S. Africa Alone: Odyssey of an American Traveller. 2nd ed. (Illus.). 383p. 1989. reprint ed. 24.95 (*0-9622515-0-X*); reprint ed. pap. 9.95 (*0-9622515-1-8*) Columbus & Co.

— Southern Passage: Soundings Overland: Tijuana to Tierra del Fuego. (Illus.). 543p. (C). 1993. 34.95 (*0-9622515-2-6*) Columbus & Co.

***McMeans, Tracie.** Little Bitty Wittys: 501 Witticisms for Families with Little Bittys. (Illus.). 128p. (Orig.). 1994. pap. 7.95 (*1-880092-18-2*) Bright Bks TX.

— Little Bitty Wittys: 501 Witticisms for Families with Little Bittys, 6 Pk. 128p. (Orig.). Date not set. reprint ed. pap. 47.70 (*1-880092-27-1*) Bright Bks TX.

McMeeken, Joan, et al. Sports Physiotherapy: Applied Science & Practice. 1994. write for info. (*0-443-04804-5*) Churchill.

McMeekin, Dorothy. Diego Rivera: Science & Creativity in the Detroit Murals. Moon, Maria E., tr. (Illus.). 72p. 1986. reprint ed. 16.95 (*0-87013-239-3*) Mich St U Pr.

McMeekin, Ivan. Notes for Potters in Australia. (Illus.). 310p. 1985. pap. 24.95 (*0-86840-209-5*, Pub. by New South Wales Univ Pr AT) Intl Spec Bk.

McMeekin, T. A., et al. Predictive Microbiology: Theory & Application. LC 93-15673. (Innovation in Microbiology Ser.: Vol. 5). 1993. text ed. 99.95 (*0-471-93545-X*) Wiley.

McMeen, Albert, jt. auth. see Carlin, Tom.

McMeen, Albert R., III. Debt Repayment Capacity: Cash Flow Forecasting for Borrowers & Lenders. 336p. 1992. 59.95 (*0-8144-5956-0*) AMACOM.

— Equipment Leasing Guide for Lessees, 1990. 1990. text ed. 115.00 (*0-471-51608-2*) Wiley.

— Equipment Leasing Guide for Lessees, 1990. suppl. ed. 1990. 50.00 (*0-471-59210-2*) Wiley.

— Treasurer's & Controller's New Equipment Leasing Guide. LC 84-6994. 251p. 1984. 59.95 (*0-13-930876-8*, Busn) P-H.

McMenamin, Ann M., jt. auth. see McMenamin, Milton J.

McMenamin, Dianna L., jt. auth. see McMenamin, Mark A.

McMenamin, G. R. Forensic Stylistics. 268p. 1993. 160.00 (*0-444-81544-9*) Elsevier.

McMenamin, J. Michael. Applied Electronic Devices & Analog Integrated Circuits. LC 94-59. (Illus.). 800p. 1995. 59.95 (*0-8273-5416-9*) Delmar.

McMenamin, James F., ed. see Shaw, William T.

McMenamin, Mark, ed. see Khakhina, Liya N.

McMenamin, Mark A. & McMenamin, Dianna L. The Emergence of Animals: The Cambrian Breakthrough. (Illus.). 216p. 1990. text ed. 45.00 (*0-231-06646-5*); pap. text ed. 18.50 (*0-231-06647-3*) Col U Pr.

— Hypersea: Life on the Land. LC 94-15324. (Illus.). 262p. 1994. 29.95 (*0-231-07530-8*) Col U Pr.

McMenamin, Michael. Linear Integrated Circuits: Operation & Application. (Illus.). 400p. (C). 1985. text ed. 52.00 (*0-13-537333-6*) P-H.

McMenamin, Michael & McNamara, Walter. Milking the Public: Political Scandals of the Dairy Lobby from LBJ to Jimmy Carter. LC 80-11546. 312p. 1980. 31.95 (*0-88229-552-7*) Nelson-Hall.

McMenamin, Milton J. & McMenamin, Ann M. Designs in Drama. 188p. (C). 1991. lib. bdg. 34.50 (*0-89464-485-8*) Krieger.

McMenamin, Paul. Adventure World Sourcebook, Series I. (Illus.). 432p. 1991. pap. 24.95 (*0-685-48070-4*) Boken Commns.

— The Ultimate Adventure Sourcebook. Watrous, Susan, ed. (Illus.). 432p. 1992. text ed. 39.95 (*1-878685-19-8*); pap. 29.95 (*1-878685-18-X*) Turner Pub GA.

McMenamin, R. W. & Kralovec, William P. Clergy & Teacher Malpractice Recognition & Prevention. Lippert, JoAnn L., ed. 238p. 1987. 37.50 (*0-943279-00-3*); pap. 18.50 (*0-943279-01-1*) Jomac Pub.

McMenamin, Robert W. Clergy Malpractice. LC 86-81075. 150p. 1986. lib. bdg. 35.00 (*0-89941-483-4*, 304100); pap. 20.00 (*0-89941-513-X*) W S Hein.

— Volunteers & the Law, a Guidebook. Lippert, JoAnn L., ed. 182p. (Orig.). 1995. pap. write for info. (*0-943279-02-X*) Jomac Pub.

McMenamin, Stephen M. & Palmer, John F. Essential Systems Analysis. LC 84-11913. (Illus.). 408p. (Orig.). 1986. pap. text ed. 65.00 (*0-13-287905-0*, Yourdon) P-H.

McMenemin, Barbera, et al. An Investigation of Cursive vs. Printing Characteristics in Handwriting. (Illus.). (Orig.). 1982. pap. text ed. 10.00 (*1-877772-03-8*) AHAF.

***McMenemy, John.** The Language of Canadian Politics: A Guide to Important Terms & Concepts. rev. ed. 366p. (C). 1995. pap. 35.00 (*0-88920-230-3*, Pub. by Wilfrid Laurier CN) Humanities.

McMican, Ann, jt. ed. see Davey, Richard J.

McMichael, A. & Fabre, J., eds. O.S.I. 1982. text ed. 148.00 (*0-12-485580-6*) Acad Pr.

***McMichael, A. J.** Planetary Overload: Global Environmental Change & the Health of the Human Species. (Canto Bk.). (Illus.). 368p. (C). Date not set. pap. 11.95 (*0-521-55871-9*) Cambridge U Pr.

— Planetary Overload: Global Environmental Change & the Health of the Human Species. LC 92-38292. (Illus.). 360p. (C). 1993. 64.95 (*0-521-44138-2*) Cambridge U Pr.

— Planetary Overload: Global Environmental Change & the Health of the Human Species. LC 92-38292. (Illus.). 360p. (C). 1993. pap. 17.95 (*0-521-45759-9*) Cambridge U Pr.

McMichael, A. J. & Bodmer, W. F., eds. A New Look at Tumour Immunology. (Cancer Surveys Ser.: Vol. 13). (Illus.). 208p. (C). 1992. text ed. 66.00 (*0-87969-370-3*) Cold Spring Harbor.

McMichael, A. J., et al, eds. Leucocyte Typing III: White Cell Differentiation Antigens. (Illus.). 1088p. 1987. 175.00 (*0-19-261552-1*) OUP.

McMichael, Andrew, jt. ed. see Feldmann, Marc.

McMichael, B. L., jt. auth. see Persson, H.

McMichael, Barbara Lloyd, ed. Baby Dreams of Childless Women. LC 93-84754. (Illus.). 90p. (Orig.). 1993. pap. 5.95 (*0-9636683-0-7*) Pacific Cent.

McMichael, George, ed. Anthology of American Literature, Vol. 1: Colonial Through Romantic. 5th ed. 2384p. (C). 1993. pap. write for info. (*0-02-379601-4*) Macmillan.

McMichael, George, et al, eds. Anthology of American Literature, Vol. 2: Realism to the Present, Vol. 2. 5th ed. LC 92-11568. 2432p. (C). 1993. pap. write for info. (*0-02-379604-9*) Macmillan.

— Concise Anthology of American Literature. 2nd ed. 2080p. (C). 1985. pap. write for info. (*0-02-379510-7*) Macmillan.

— Concise Anthology of American Literature. 3rd ed. LC 93-12566. (Illus.). 2200p. (C). 1993. pap. write for info. (*0-02-379561-1*) Macmillan.

McMichael, Jack R. & Taft, Barbara, eds. The Writings of William Walwyn. LC 87-18162. 616p. 1989. 45.00 (*0-8203-1017-4*) U of Ga Pr.

McMichael, James. Each in a Place Apart. LC 93-31265. (Phoenix Poets Ser.). 1994. lib. bdg. 20.00 (*0-226-56106-2*); pap. 9.95 (*0-226-56107-0*) U Ch Pr.

— Ulysses & Justice. 198p. 1991. text ed. 37.50 (*0-691-06547-0*) Princeton U Pr.

McMichael, LaVeria, jt. ed. see Rice, Ferill J.

McMichael, Lois, comp. Butts County, Georgia, 1825-1976, the History Of. rev. ed. 792p. 1988. reprint ed. 37.50 (*0-89308-628-2*, BGA 85) Southern Hist Pr.

McMichael, Nancy. Snowdomes. (Illus.). 96p. 1990. 21.95 (*1-55859-036-6*) Abbeville Pr.

McMichael, Philip. Food & Agrarian Orders in the World Economy. LC 94-17977. (Studies in the Political Ecomony of the World-System: No. 160). 287p. 1995. text ed. 65.00 (*0-313-29399-6*, Greenwood Pr); pap. text ed. 19.95 (*0-275-94966-4*, Greenwood Pr) Greenwood.

McMichael, Philip D., ed. The Global Restructuring of Agro-Food Systems. (Food Systems & Agrarian Change Ser.). (Illus.). 320p. 1994. 42.50 (*0-8014-2940-4*); pap. 16.95 (*0-8014-8156-2*) Cornell U Pr.

McMichael, Ralph N., Jr., ed. Creation & Liturgy: Studies in Honor of H. Boone Porter. (Orig.). 1993. pap. text ed. 24.95 (*1-56929-001-6*) Pastoral Pr.

McMichael, Scott. Stumbling Bear: Soviet Military Performance in Afghanistan. (Illus.). 180p. 1991. 57.00 (*0-08-040982-2*, Pub. by Brasseys UK) Brasseys Inc.

***McMichael, Stephen J.** Was Jesus of Nazareth the Messiah? Alphonso de Espina's Argument Against the Jews in the "Fortalitium Fidei" (c. 1464) LC 93-39350. (South Florida Studies in the History of Judaism). 703p. 1994. 134.95 (*1-55540-930-X*, 240096) Scholars Pr GA.

McMichael, Steven. Alphonso de Espina & the Fortalitium Fidei. (USF Studies in the History of Judaism: Vol. 96). 1994. write for info. (*0-614-03783-2*) Scholars Pr GA.

***McMilen, Marilyn M., et al.** Dropout Rates in the U. S., 1992. (Illus.). 168p. (Orig.). (C). 1994. pap. text ed. 45.00x (*0-7881-0892-1*) Diane Pub.

***McMillan.** Baby Zoo. (J). 1995. pap. 3.95 (*0-590-44635-5*) Scholastic Inc.

— Day Late & a Dollar Short. 1995. (*0-670-86042-5*, Viking) Viking Penguin.

— Oppenheimer. Date not set. 22.00 (*0-06-016782-3*, HarpT) HarpC.

— Surgical Word Book. 1992. 16.95 (*0-87434-477-8*) Springhouse Pub.

— Waiting to Exhale. 1995. pap. 6.99 (*0-671-53745-8*) PB.

McMillan & Gardner. Mini-Map 'Ninety-Three: A Practical Application & Standards to Manufacturing Cell Networks. 300p. 1994. pap. 60.00 (*0-9639941-0-7*) Open I T.

Mcmillan, jt. auth. see Young.

McMillan, A. & Scott, G. Sexually Transmitted Diseases. (Colour Aids Ser.). (Illus.). 112p. (Orig.). 1991. pap. text ed. 19.95 (*0-443-04052-4*) Churchill.

McMillan, A. S. & Tucker, G. M., eds. International Conference on Millimeter Wave & Far-Infrared Technology: Proceedings of the International Conference on Millimeter Wave & Far-Infrared Technology, Beijing, China, 19-23 June 1989. (International Academic Publishers Ser.). 600p. 1990. 170.00 (*0-08-037880-3*, 1105, Pub. by IAP UK) Elsevier.

McMillan, Adell, ed. College Unions: Seventy-Five Years. 192p. 1989. 30.00 (*0-923276-00-9*) Assn Coll Unions Intl.

— College Unions: Seventy-Five Years. limited ed. 192p. 1989. 60.00 (*0-923276-01-7*) Assn Coll Unions Intl.

McMillan, Anita. Ready-to-Use Language Articulation & Development Activities for Special Children. 244p. 1992. spiral bd. 24.95 (*0-87628-807-7*) Ctr Appl Res.

McMillan, Beverly, jt. auth. see Starr, Cecie.

***McMillan, Bill.** The Border's Guide to Arizona. (Falcon Guide Ser.). (Illus.). 200p. 1995. pap. 14.95 (*1-56044-230-1*) Falcon Pr MT.

McMillan, Brett, jt. auth. see McMillan, Bruce.

McMillan, Bruce. The Alphabet Symphony. (Illus.). 32p. (J). (gr. k-2). 1977. 15.00 (*0-688-80112-9*) Apple Isl Bks.

— Apples, How They Grow. (Illus.). 48p. (J). (ps-3). 1979. 17.95 (*0-395-27806-6*) HM.

— The Baby Zoo. 32p. (J). 1992. 13.95 (*0-590-44634-7*, Scholastic Hardcover) Scholastic Inc.

— Beach Ball - Left, Right. LC 91-32802. (Illus.). 32p. (J). (ps-3). 1992. lib. bdg. 14.95 (*0-8234-0946-5*) Holiday.

— A Beach for the Birds. LC 92-10920. (Illus.). 32p. (J). (gr. 2-5). 1993. 15.95 (*0-395-64050-4*) HM.

— Becca Backward, Becca Frontward: A Book of Concept Pairs. LC 86-7221. (Illus.). 32p. (J). (ps-1). 1986. 16.00 (*0-688-06282-2*); lib. bdg. 15.93 (*0-688-06283-0*) Lothrop.

— Counting Wildflowers. LC 85-16607. (Illus.). 32p. (J). (ps-1). 1986. 16.00 (*0-688-02859-4*); lib. bdg. 15.93 (*0-688-02860-8*) Lothrop.

— Counting Wildflowers. Cohn, Amy, ed. LC 85-16607. (Illus.). 32p. (J). (ps up). 1995. reprint ed. pap. 4.95 (*0-688-14027-0*, Mulberry) Morrow.

— Dry or Wet? LC 86-27345. (Illus.). 32p. (J). (ps-2). 1988. 12.95 (*0-688-07100-7*); lib. bdg. 12.88 (*0-688-07101-5*) Lothrop.

— Eating Fractions. (J). (ps-3). 1991. 14.95 (*0-590-43770-4*, Scholastic Hardcover) Scholastic Inc.

— Eating Fractions. (J). 1992. pap. 19.95 (*0-590-72732-X*) Scholastic Inc.

— Fire Engine Shapes. LC 87-38145. (Illus.). 32p. (J). (ps-2). 1988. 12.95 (*0-688-07842-7*); lib. bdg. 12.88 (*0-688-07843-5*) Lothrop.

— Going on a Whale Watch. (Illus.). (J). (ps up). 1992. 14.95 (*0-590-45768-3*, 016, Scholastic Hardcover) Scholastic Inc.

— Grandfather's Trolley. LC 95-10637. (Illus.). (J). 1995. write for info. (*1-56402-633-7*) Candlewick Pr.

— Growing Colors. LC 88-2767. (Illus.). 40p. (J). (ps-2). 1988. 16.00 (*0-688-07844-3*); lib. bdg. 15.93 (*0-688-07845-1*) Lothrop.

— Growing Colors. LC 93-28804. (Illus.). 32p. (J). (ps up). 1994. reprint ed. pap. 4.95 (*0-688-13112-3*, Mulberry) Morrow.

— Mouse Views: What the Class Pet Saw. LC 92-25921. (Illus.). 32p. (J). (ps-3). 1993. lib. bdg. 15.95 (*0-8234-1008-0*); pap. 5.95 (*0-8234-1132-X*) Holiday.

— Nights of the Pufflings. LC 94-14808. (Illus.). (J). (ps-3). 1995. 14.95 (*0-395-70810-9*) HM.

Mcmillan, Bruce. One Sun: A Book of Terse Verse. LC 89-24625. (Illus.). 32p. (J). (ps-3). 1990. lib. bdg. 15.95 (*0-8234-0810-8*); pap. 5.95 (*0-8234-0951-1*) Holiday.

McMillan, Bruce. One Two One Pair. LC 90-37410. (J). (ps-3). 1991. 12.95 (*0-590-43767-4*, Scholastic Hardcover) Scholastic Inc.

— Penguins at Home: Gentoos of Antarctica. LC 92-34769. (Illus.). (J). 1993. 15.95 (*0-395-66560-4*) HM.

— Play Day: A Book of Terse Verse. LC 90-29077. (Illus.). 32p. (J). (ps-3). 1991. lib. bdg. 14.95 (*0-8234-0894-9*) Holiday.

— Puffins Climb, Penguins Rhyme. LC 94-27225. (Illus.). (J). (gr. k up). 1995. 14.00 (*0-15-200362-2*, Gulliver Bks) HarBrace.

— The Remarkable Riderless Runaway Tricycle. rev. ed. (Illus.). 48p. (J). (gr. k-4). 1985. reprint ed. pap. 10.00 (*0-934313-00-8*) Apple Isl Bks.

— Sense Suspense. LC 93-30272. (Illus.). (J). 1994. 15.95 (*0-590-47904-0*) Scholastic Inc.

— Step by Step. (Illus.). 28p. (J). (ps-2). 1990. lib. bdg. 15.00 (*0-685-35118-1*) Apple Isl Bks.

— Step by Step. LC 87-4195. (Illus.). 32p. (J). (ps-2). 1987. 13.95 (*0-688-07233-X*) Lothrop.

— Summer Ice, Antarctic Life. LC 93-38831. (Illus.). (J). 1994. 15.95 (*0-395-66561-2*) HM.

— Super, Super, Superwords. LC 88-9342. (Illus.). 32p. (J). (ps-2). 1989. 12.95 (*0-688-08098-7*) Lothrop.

— Super, Super, Superwords. LC 88-9342. (Illus.). 32p. (J). (ps-2). 1989. lib. bdg. 12.88 (*0-688-08099-5*) Lothrop.

— The Weather Sky. (Illus.). 40p. (J). (gr. 5 up). 1991. 16.95 (*0-374-38261-1*) FS&G.

McMillan, Bruce & McMillan, Brett. Puniddles. (Illus.). (J). (gr. 2 up). 1982. pap. 5.95 (*0-395-32076-3*) HM.

McMillan, C. J., jt. ed. see Hickson, D. J.

McMillan, C. Scott, jt. auth. see Rogers, Ronald L.

McMillan, Carl H. Multinationals from the Second World: Growth of Foreign Investment by Soviet & East European Enterprises. 256p. 1987. text ed. 45.00 (*0-312-55253-X*) St Martin.

McMillan, Carl H., jt. ed. see Hardt, John P.

McMillan, Catherine, ed. see Williams-Sam, Sheffra.

McMillan, Ceclily. Charleston, Savannah, & Coastal Islands Book: A Complete Guide. 1993. pap. 14.95 (*0-936399-39-2*) Berkshire Hse.

McMillan, Charles J. The Japanese Industrial System. rev. ed. LC 84-1742. (Studies in Organization: No. 1). (Illus.). xii, 356p. 1989. pap. 26.95 (*3-11-012033-X*) De Gruyter.

— The Japanese Industrial System. 2nd rev. ed. LC 84-1742. (Studies in Organization: No. 1). (Illus.). xii, 356p. 1989. 67.70 (*3-11-010410-5*) De Gruyter.

— The Japanese Industrial System. 2nd rev. ed. (Studies in Organization: No. 1). (Illus.). xii, 356p. 1989. pap. 26.95 (*0-89925-005-X*) De Gruyter.

McMillan, Clare, tr. see Gehlen, Arnold.

McMillan, Claude. Mathematical Programming. LC 74-23273. (Wiley Management & Administration Ser.). 664p. (C). reprint ed. 180.00 (*0-8357-9931-X*, 2017000) Bks Demand.

***McMillan, Dana.** Center Time: A Complete Guide to Learning Centers. 144p. 1994. teacher ed, pap. 11.95 (*1-57310-007-2*) Teachng & Lrning Co.

McMillan, Dana, jt. auth. see Martin, Sidney.

McMillan, Daniel. Winning the Battle Against Drugs: Rehabilitation Programs. LC 91-16344. (Non-Fiction Ser.). (Illus.). 160p. (YA). (gr. 9-12). 1991. lib. bdg. 15.33 (*0-531-11063-X*) Watts.

***McMillan, Della E.** Sahel Visions: Planned Settlement & River Blindness Control in Burkina Faso. LC 94-21940. (Studies in Human Ecology). 270p. 1995. lib. bdg. 35.00x (*0-8165-1487-9*); pap. text ed. 14.95x (*0-8165-1489-5*) U of Ariz Pr.

McMillan, Della E., ed. Anthropology & Food Policy: Human Dimensions of Food Policy in Africa & Latin America. LC 90-11000. (Southern Anthropological Society Proceedings Ser.: No. 24). (Illus.). 208p. 1991. 30.00 (*0-8203-1287-8*); pap. 15.00 (*0-8203-1288-6*) U of Ga Pr.

McMillan, Della E., et al. Settlement & Development in the River Blindness Control Zone. LC 92-39287. (Technical Paper Ser.: No. 192). 136p. 1993. 7.95 (*0-8213-2296-6*, 12296) World Bank.

— Settlement & Development in the River Blindness Control Zone: Case Study, Burkina Faso. LC 93-9380. (Technical Paper, Series on River Blindness Control in West Africa: No. 200). 178p. 1994. 10.95 (*0-8213-2381-4*, 12381) World Bank.

— Settlement & Development in the River Blindness Control Zone: Case Study-Burkina Faso. (Technical Paper Ser.: No. 200). 178p. (FRE.). 1994. 10.95 (*0-8213-2719-4*, 12719) World Bank.

— Settlement & Development in the River Blindness Control Zone - Installation de Populations et Developpement dans la Zone de Lutte Contre l'Onchocercose. (Technical Paper Ser.: No. 192). 136p. (FRE.). 1993. 7.95 (*0-8213-2629-5*, 12629) World Bank.

McMillan, Don, jt. auth. see Bhaerman, Steve.

***McMillan, Dorothy.** Vile Acts. 1995. pap. 4.99 (*0-7860-0100-3*, Pinnacle NY) Windsor NY.

— Vile Acts. 400p. 1995. pap. 4.99 (*0-8217-0100-2*) Zebra.

McMillan, Dougald & Fehsenfeld, Martha. Beckett in the Theatre: The Author As Practical Playwright & Director. LC 86-13813. (Illus.). 352p. 1989. pap. 19.95 (*0-7145-4151-6*) Riverrun NY.

McMillan, Douglas J. Approaches to Teaching Goethe's Faust. LC 86-33191. (Approaches to Teaching World Literature Ser.: No. 14). xiii, 170p. 1987. 37.50 (*0-87352-501-9*, AP14C); pap. 18.00x (*0-87352-502-7*, AP14P) Modern Lang.

McMillan, Duncan, jt. auth. see Lewison, Jeremy.

McMillan, E. Norman, tr. see Seleskovitch, Danica.

McMillan, Earle. The Gospel According to Mark. LC 72-86991. 1984. 12.95 (*0-915547-19-8*) Abilene Christ U.

McMillan, Edward J. Budgeting & Financial Management Handbook. LC 94-20960. 1994. 48.00 (*0-88034-089-4*) Am Soc Assn Execs.

— Essential Financial Considerations for Not-for-Profit Organizations. LC 94-20921. 1994. 59.95 (*0-88034-088-6*) Am Soc Assn Execs.

— Model Accounting & Financial Policies & Procedures Handbook for Not-for-Profit Organizations. LC 94-20961. 1994. 48.00 (*0-88034-087-8*) Am Soc Assn Execs.

McMillan, Elizabeth, jt. auth. see Bader, Diana.

***McMillan, Elsie B.** The Atom & Eve. 1995. 16.95 (*0-533-11131-5*) Vantage.

McMillan, F. R. & Tuthill, Lewis H. Concrete Primer. 4th ed. 28.25 (*0-685-72804-8*, SP-1) ACI.

McMillan, G. & Weiner, S. Logical Thoughts at Four O'Clock A. M. 118p. 1991. pap. 20.00 (*1-55617-332-6*) Instru Soc.

McMillan, G. K. Biochemical Measurement & Control. LC 87-2954. 150p. 1987. text ed. 50.00 (*0-87664-942-8*, 1942-8) Instru Soc.

— Centrifugal & Axial Compressor Control. LC 83-216995. (Instructional Resource Package Ser.). 1983. Slides (97 in set). sl. 410.00 (*0-685-08930-4*, 1746-8SL); Classroom Pkg. (10 stdt. texts, instr. gd., 1 set slides). 410.00 (*0-87664-746-8*, 1746-8) Instru Soc.

— Continuous Control Techniques for Distributed Control Systems. (Independent Learning Module Ser.). 240p. 1989. text ed. 50.00 (*1-55617-172-2*, A172-2) Instru Soc.

— A Funny Thing Happened on the Way to the Control Room. 130p. 1989. pap. text ed. 20.00 (*1-55617-215-X*, A215-X) Instru Soc.

— Tuning & Control Loop Performance: A Practitioners Guide. 3rd ed. 320p. text ed. 70.00 (*1-55617-492-6*, A492-6) Instru Soc.

McMillan, G. K. & Weiner, S. How to Become an Instrument Engineer: The Making of a Prima Donna. LC 88-134784. (Illus.). 148p. 1987. pap. text ed. 20.00 (*1-55617-007-6*, A007-6); 3.95 (*0-318-35521-3*) Instru Soc.

McMillan, G. R., et al. Applications of Human Performance Models to Systems Design. (Defense Research Ser.: Vol. 2). (Illus.). 568p. 1989. 125.00 (*0-306-43242-0*, Plenum Pr) Plenum.

McMillan, George. Old Breed: A History of the First Marine Division in World War II. LC 79-16880. reprint ed. 49.95 (*0-89201-052-5*) Zenger Pub.

McMillan, George, et al. Uncommon Valor: Marine Divisions in Action. (Elite Unit Ser.: 5th). (Illus.). 272p. 1986. reprint ed. 19.95 (*0-89839-094-X*) Battery Pr.

McMillan, Greg. PC Lab: Experiments in DC & AC Circuits. 1992. disk 29.95 (*0-8273-4821-5*) Delmar.

McMillan, Gregory, et al. How to Become an Instrument Engineer Part 1.52: New & Improved! 52 Per Cent More Entertaining Than Original. LC 94-16752. 1994. write for info. (*1-55617-520-5*) Instru Soc.

McMillan, Gregory K. PH Measurement & Control. 2nd ed. LC 84-29976. (Independent Learning Module Ser.). 300p. 1994. 60.00 (*1-55617-483-7*, A483-7) Instru Soc.

McMillan, Ian, intro. & sel. Six: The Versewagon Poetry Manual. 128p. (C). 1988. 50.00 (*0-947612-13-0*, Pub. by Rivelin Grapheme Pr); pap. 30.00 (*0-947612-14-9*, Pub. by Rivelin Grapheme Pr) St Mut.

McMillan, James. Napoleon III. 208p. (C). 1991. pap. text ed. 21.95 (*0-582-49483-4*, 78832) Longman.

McMillan, James B. Annotated Bibliography of Southern American English. LC 70-129666. 1971. 10.95 (*0-87024-183-4*) U of Miami Pr.

— James B. McMillan: Essays in Linguistics by His Friends & Colleagues. Raymond, James C. & Russell, I. Willis, eds. LC 77-7169. (Illus.). 203p. 1977. pap. 57.90 (*0-7837-8400-7*, 2059211) Bks Demand.

McMillan, James B. & Montgomery, Michael B. Annotated Bibliography of Southern American English. LC 88-36856. 464p. (C). 1989. 34.95 (*0-8173-0448-7*) U of Ala Pr.

McMillan, James F. Housewife or Harlot: The Place of Women in French Society, 1870-1940. LC 80-18675. 229p. 1984. pap. 11.95 (*0-312-39348-2*) St Martin.

— Twentieth-Century France: Politics & Society in France 1898-1991. 2nd ed. LC 91-30407. 256p. 1992. pap. 16.95 (*0-340-52239-9*, A6101, Pub. by E Arnold UK) Routledge Chapman & Hall.

McMillan, James H. Educational Research: Fundamentals for the Consumers. (C). 1991. text ed. 49.00 (*0-673-38449-7*) HarpCollege.

McMillan, James H., ed. Assessing Students' Learning. LC 85-644763. (New Directions for Teaching & Learning Ser.: No. TL 34). 1988. 16.95 (*1-55542-929-7*) Jossey-Bass.

McMillan, James H. & Schumacher. Research in Education. 2nd ed. (C). 1989. text ed. 37.50 (*0-673-39792-0*) HarpCollege.

— Research in Education. 3rd ed. (C). 1992. 59.50 (*0-673-52214-8*) HarpCollege.

— Research in Education. 3rd ed. (C). 1993. student ed 12.00 (*0-673-52316-0*) HarpCollege.

McMillan, Jerry, comp. George Herms: The Secret Archives. (Illus.). 64p. (Orig.). 1992. 25.00 (*1-882299-00-0*) Dirs Gallery BAP.

McMillan, Joe. High Green to Marceline. LC 89-92344. (Illus.). 1989. 49.50 (*0-934228-16-7*) McMillan Pubns.

— Wheat Lines & Super Freights. (Illus.). 1992. 64.95 (*0-934228-17-5*) McMillan Pubns.

McMillan, John. Game Theory in International Economics. (Fundamentals of Pure & Applied Economics Ser.: Vol.1, pt. 1). 111p. 1986. pap. text ed. 33.00 (*3-7186-0277-6*) Gordon & Breach.

— Games, Strategies, & Managers. (Illus.). 288p. 1992. 27.50 (*0-19-507430-0*) OUP.

McMillan, John, jt. ed. see McAfee, R. Preston.

McMillan, John C., et al. Economic Growth, Political & Civil Liberties. LC 94-6152. (Occasional Papers: No. 38). 1994. pap. 6.95 (*1-55815-355-1*) ICS Pr.

McMillan, Joseph P., jt. auth. see Egan, Michael E.

McMillan, Kenneth L. Symbolic Model Checking. LC 93-24859. 216p. (C). 1993. lib. bdg. 76.00 (*0-7923-9380-5*) Kluwer Ac.

McMillan, Kent. Hydroslide Kneeboarding: An Illustrated Guide to Learning & Mastering the Sport. Robertson, Jo, ed. LC 88-50672. (Illus.). 166p. (Orig.). (YA). 1988. pap. 12.95 (*0-944406-03-3*) World Pub FL.

McMillan, Lawrence G. Options As a Strategic Investment: A Comprehensive Analysis of Listed Option Strategies. LC 92-23160. 1992. 49.95 (*0-13-636002-5*) P-H.

McMillan, Len. Parentwise. LC 92-33309. 1992. pap. 8.95 (*0-8280-0687-3*) Review & Herald.

McMillan, Len & Wray, Marvin. First Class Male: A Christian Man's Role in Today's World. LC 94-2254. 1994. write for info. (*0-8280-0786-1*) Review & Herald.

McMillan, Len D. Parent - Teen: An Adventist Counselor on Living with Teens - & Loving It. LC 93-26952. 1993. pap. 8.95 (*0-8280-0732-2*) Review & Herald.

McMillan, Malcolm C. Constitutional Development in Alabama, 1798-1901: A Study in Politics, the Negro, & Sectionalism. LC 78-2258. 1978. reprint ed. 25.00 (*0-87152-258-6*) Reprint.

McMillan, Malcolm C., ed. The Alabama Confederate Reader. LC 92-8817. (Library of Alabama Classics). 512p. (C). 1992. reprint ed. pap. 24.95 (*0-8173-0595-5*) U of Ala Pr.

McMillan, Mary. Baby Jesus. (Color, Cut & Paste Ser.). 48p. (J). (ps-1). 1986. student ed 7.95 (*0-86653-369-9*, SS 1800, Shining Star Pubns) Good Apple.

— Bible Story Bulletin Boards. (Bulletin Board Ser.). 96p. (J). (ps-3). 1988. 10.95 (*0-86653-430-X*, SS1828, Shining Star Pubns) Good Apple.

— Christian Celebrations for Autumn & Winter. (Christian Parties & Celebrations Ser.). 96p. (J). (gr. 2-7). 1990. 10.95 (*0-86653-546-2*, SS1821, Shining Star Pubns) Good Apple.

— Christian Crafts from Hand-Shaped Art. (Christian Craft Ser.). 64p. (J). (ps-5). 1991. 8.95 (*0-86653-629-9*, SS1886, Shining Star Pubns) Good Apple.

— Christian Parties for Autumn & Winter. (Christian Parties & Celebrations Ser.). 96p. (J). (ps-3). 1989. 10.95 (*0-86653-497-0*, SS1815, Shining Star Pubns) Good Apple.

— Christian Parties for Spring & Summer. (Illus.). 96p. (J). (ps-3). 1989. 10.95 (*0-86653-473-3*, SS1814, Shining Star Pubns) Good Apple.

— Classroom Starters for Any Occasion. 144p. 1989. 12.95 (*0-86653-508-X*, GA1130) Good Apple.

— God's ABC Zoo. (Color, Cut & Paste Ser.). 48p. (J). (ps-1). 1987. pap. 7.95 (*0-86653-405-9*, SS1802, Shining Star Pubns) Good Apple.

— Lifesavers for Substitutes. (Illus.). 160p. 1992. student ed 12.95 (*0-86653-678-7*, 1412) Good Apple.

— The Story of Jesus. (Color, Cut & Paste Ser.). 48p. (J). (ps-1). 1988. 7.95 (*0-86653-454-7*, SS1804, Shining Star Pubns) Good Apple.

McMillan, May F. The Shortest Way to the Essay: Rhetorical Strategies. LC 84-20567. xxii, 274p. (C). 1984. 19.45 (*0-86554-132-9*, H123) Mercer Univ Pr.

McMillan, Merna M., jt. auth. see Gentile, Lance M.

McMillan, Michael, jt. auth. see Richstad, Jim.

McMillan, Moira. Scottish Business Law. 2nd ed. 480p. 1993. pap. 57.50 (*0-273-60105-9*, Pub. by Pitman Pub Ltd UK) Trans-Atl Phila.

***McMillan, Naomi.** Cinderella. (Storytime Ser.). (Illus.). 24p. (J). (ps-2). 1995. pap. 0.99 (*1-56293-539-9*) McClanahan Bk.

— Jack & the Beanstalk. (Storytime Ser.). (Illus.). 24p. (J). (ps-2). 1995. pap. 0.99 (*1-56293-538-0*) McClanahan Bk.

— Wish You Were Here. LC 90-85435. (Minnie 'n Me Ser.). (Illus.). 32p. (J). (gr. k-3). 1991. 5.95 (*1-56282-036-2*) Disney Pr.

McMillan, P. W. Glass Ceramics. 2nd ed. 1979. text ed. 137.00 (*0-12-485660-8*) Acad Pr.

McMillan, Patricia & Kennedy, James R., Jr. Library Research Guide to Sociology: Illustrated Search Strategy & Sources. LC 80-83513. (Library Research Guides Ser.: No. 5). 1981. 25.00 (*0-87650-121-8*); pap. 15.00 (*0-87650-122-6*) Pierian.

***McMillan, Peter, et al.** The Greatest Flight. (Illus.). 256p. 1995. 39.95 (*1-57036-238-6*) Turner Pub GA.

McMillan, R. Bruce. Gasconade Prehistory: A Survey & Evaluation of the Archaeological Resources. Bray, Robert T., ed. (Missouri Archaeologist Ser.: Vol. 27, No. 3-4). (Illus.). 114p. (Orig.). 1965. pap. 3.00 (*0-943414-45-8*) MO Arch Soc.

McMillan, Richard C. Religion in the Public Schools: An Introduction. LC 84-9147. x, 301p. 1984. 21.95 (*0-86554-093-4*, H85) Mercer Univ Pr.

McMillan, Richard C., et al. Euthanasia & the Newborn: Conflicts Regarding Saving Lives. LC 86-33835. (Philosophy & Medicine Ser.: Vol. 24). (C). 1987. pap. text ed. 44.50 (*1-55608-039-5*) Kluwer Ac.

McMillan, Robin. Three Hundred Sixty-Five One Minute Golf Lessons. 400p. 1994. 19.95 (*0-06-017087-5*, HarpT) HarpC.

McMillan, Robin, ed. Golfer's Home Companion. (Illus.). 288p. 1993. 35.00 (*0-671-70054-5*) S&S Trade.

McMillan, Robin & Andrisani, John. The Golf Doctor. (Illus.). 1990. 19.95 (*0-394-58529-1*, Villard Bks) Random.

McMillan, Ronald J. We Are Forever Voyageurs of Space. LC 92-59947. 550p. 1993. pap. 18.95 (*1-55523-572-7*) Winston-Derek.

***McMillan, Rosalyn.** Knowing. 1996. write for info. (*0-446-51866-2*) Warner Bks.

McMillan, Sally. The Crossroad at Bethany. LC 92-60292. 226p. 1992. pap. 7.95 (*1-55523-524-7*) Winston-Derek.

McMillan, Stephen, jt. auth. see Chaisson, Eric.

McMillan, Steve, jt. auth. see Chaisson, Eric J.

McMillan, Stuart. Neither Confirm nor Deny: The Nuclear Ships Dispute Between New Zealand & the United States. LC 87-15853. 185p. 1987. text ed. 55.00 (*0-275-92352-5*, C2352, Praeger Pubs) Greenwood.

McMillan, Susan C., ed. see Oncology Nursing Society Staff.

McMillan, Terry. Disappearing Acts. Rosenman, Jane, ed. 384p. 1993. pap. 6.99 (*0-671-87200-1*, Pocket Star Bks) PB.

— Disappearing Acts. LC 88-40412. 272p. 1989. 23.95 (*0-670-82461-5*) Viking Penguin.

— Disappearing Acts. large type ed. LC 93-30217. 1993. 24.95 (*1-56895-033-0*) Wheeler Pub.

— Mama. Rosenman, Jane, ed. 1991. pap. 10.00 (*0-671-74523-9*, WSP) PB.

— Mama. 1994. mass mkt. 6.50 (*0-671-88448-4*, Pocket Star Bks) PB.

— Mama. large type ed. LC 93-14585. 1994. pap. 21.95 (*0-7927-1776-7*, Curley Lrg Print) Chivers N Amer.

— Waiting to Exhale. 1993. pap. 6.50 (*0-671-86417-3*) PB.

— Waiting to Exhale. 416p. 1992. 22.00 (*0-670-83980-9*, Viking) Viking Penguin.

— Waiting to Exhale. large type ed. LC 92-27196. (General Ser.). 600p. 1993. 23.95 (*0-8161-5617-4*); pap. 16.95 (*0-8161-5618-2*) G K Hall.

— Waiting to Exhale. Rosenman, Jane, ed. 416p. 1994. reprint ed. pap. 12.00 (*0-671-50148-8*, WSP) PB.

An Asterisk (*) at the beginning of an entry indicates that the title is appearing in BIP for the first time.

McMillan, Terry, ed. Breaking Ice: An Anthology of Contemporary American Black Fiction. 400p. 1990. pap. 14.95 (*0-14-011697-4*, Penguin Bks) Viking Penguin.

McMillan, Thomas C., jt. auth. see Collins, William J.

McMillan, Victoria. Writing Papers in the Biological Sciences. 150p. (C). 1988. pap. text ed. 10.00 (*0-312-89489-9*) St Martin.

***McMillan, Victoria E.** Writing Papers in the Biological Sciences. 2nd ed. 176p. (C). 1995. pap. text ed. 13.30 (*0-312-11504-0*) St Martin.

***McMillan, W.** Exercise & Fitness: HP 628 Course Study Guide. rev. ed. 249p. 1994. spiral bd. write for info. (*0-933195-17-6*) Allied Hlth Pubns.

McMillan, William. Education of a Headmaster. LC 82-24372. 1986. 13.95 (*0-87949-232-5*) Ashley Bks.

— The Worship of the Scottish Reformed Church, 1550-1638: The Hastie Lectures in the University of Glasgow, 1930. LC 83-45585. reprint ed. 35.00 (*0-404-19903-8*) AMS Pr.

McMillan, William J. Let's Get America Moving Again. LC 81-85202. 101p. 1981. spiral bd. 12.95 (*0-918214-08-4*) F E Peters.

— Private School Management. 1977. 7.95 (*0-918214-00-9*, 76-51885) F E Peters.

— Private School Management. 2nd ed. LC 79-50904. 1979. 14.95 (*0-918214-03-3*) F E Peters.

— Private Schools: Boards & Heads. LC 80-81654. 88p. (Orig.). 1980. pap. 5.95 (*0-918214-06-8*) F E Peters.

— Private Schools of the Future. LC 81-66535. 117p. (C). 1981. spiral bd. 12.95 (*0-918214-07-6*) F E Peters.

McMillen Conger, Syndy, ed. Sensibility in Transformation: Creative Resistance to Sentiment from the Augustans to the Romantics; Essays in Honor of Jean H. Hagstrum. LC 88-46055. (Illus.). 240p. 1990. 36.50 (*0-8386-3352-8*) Fairleigh Dickinson.

McMillen, Donald H., ed. Asian Perspectives on International Security. LC 83-24576. 226p. 1984. text ed. 35.00 (*0-312-05643-5*) St Martin.

McMillen, Donald H. & DeGolyer, Michael E., eds. One Culture, Many Systems: Politics in the Reunification of China. 334p. (Orig.). 1993. pap. 48.50 (*962-201-577-8*, Pub. by Chinese Univ HK) Coronet Bks.

***McMillen, Donald H. & Man Si-wai, eds.** The Other Hong Kong Report, 1994. 600p. 1994. pap. 49.50x (*962-201-633-2*, Pub. by Chinese Univ HK) Coronet Bks.

McMillen, Lauretta, jt. auth. see Nelson, Eric.

McMillen, Loretta, jt. auth. see Fingado, Dorothy.

McMillen, Margot F. Paris, Tightwad, & Peculiar: Missouri Place Names. (Missouri Heritage Readers Ser.). (Illus.). 96p. 1994. pap. 7.95 (*0-8262-0972-6*) U of Mo Pr.

McMillen, Neil R. The Citizens' Council: Organized Resistance to the Second Reconstruction, 1954-64. LC 94-18858. 1994. write for info. (*0-252-06441-0*) U of Ill Pr.

— Dark Journey: Black Mississippians in the Age of Jim Crow. LC 88-17123. (Illus.). 464p. 1990. pap. 14.95 (*0-252-06156-X*) U of Ill Pr.

McMillen, Pat. The Working Woman's Cookbook & Entertainment Guide. LC 83-3814. 252p. 1983. write for info. (*0-672-52708-1*) Macmillan.

McMillen, Persis W. Currents of Malice: Mary Towne Esty & Her Family in Salem Witchcraft. (Illus.). 650p. 1990. 35.00 (*0-914339-31-1*) P E Randall Pub.

McMillen, Russell, jt. auth. see Jong, Elaine C.

McMillen, S. I. Nenhuma Enfermidade. Orig. Title: None of These Diseases. (POR.). 1987. 8.95 (*0-8297-0964-9*) Life Pubs Intl.

— Ninguna Enfermedad. Orig. Title: None of These Diseases. (SPA.). 1987. 6.95 (*0-8297-0965-7*) Life Pubs Intl.

— None of These Diseases. rev. ed. Stern, David E., ed. LC 84-6807. 192p. 1984. pap. 8.99 (*0-8007-5233-3*) Revell.

— None of These Diseases. 2nd ed. LC 63-13359. (Illus.). 160p. 1993. reprint ed. pap. 4.99 (*0-8007-8030-2*, Spire) Revell.

— Sante ou Maladie. rev. ed. Orig. Title: None of These Diseases. (FRE.). 1987. 6.95 (*0-8297-0963-0*) Life Pubs Intl.

McMillen, Sally G. Motherhood in the Old South: Pregnancy, Childbirth, & Infant Rearing. LC 89-34679. 272p. 1989. text ed. 30.00 (*0-8071-1517-7*) La State U Pr.

— Southern Women: Black & White in the Old South. Franklin, John H. & Wakelyn, Jon L., eds. (American History Ser.). 140p. 1992. pap. text ed. write for info. (*0-88295-881-X*) Harlan Davidson.

McMillen, Sheila, jt. ed. see Garrett, George.

McMillen, Wheeler. Farmer. LC 66-14227. (U. S. A. Survey Ser.). (Illus.). 126p. 1966. 4.95 (*0-87107-004-9*) Potomac.

— Feeding Multitudes. 491p. 1981. pap. 12.00 (*0-8134-2192-6*) Interstate.

McMiller, Kathy. Being a Medical Records Clerk. 224p. (C). 1991. 23.10 (*0-89303-807-5*, 740504) P-H.

McMillian & Andrisani, John. Golf Doctor: Premium Edition. 1991. write for info. (*0-679-74052-X*) McKay.

McMillian, Ben, ed. see Peebles, Joseph.

McMillian, Cecily. The Charleston, Savannah, & Coastal Islands Book: A Complete Guide. 1993. pap. 14.95 (*0-317-05523-2*) Natl Bk Netwk.

McMillian, Deborah. Science Boosters. (Illus.). 64p. (J). (gr. 2-6). 1988. teacher ed, pap. 6.95 (*0-912107-82-0*, MM 998) Monday Morning Bks.

McMillian, Elizabeth. Beach Houses from Malibu to Laguna. LC 93-38144. 208p. 1994. 50.00 (*0-8478-1802-0*) Rizzoli Intl.

McMillian, Joyce. Charter for the Arts in Scotland. 128p. 1993. pap. 25.00 (*0-11-494231-5*, HM42315, Pub. by HMSO UK) UNIPUB.

McMillian, Len D. Slaying Your Dragons. (Lifeline Ser.). 95p. 1989. pap. 2.99 (*0-8163-0865-9*) Pacific Pr Pub Assn.

McMillin, jt. auth. see Rogers.

McMillin, Arnold. Under Eastern Eyes: The West As Reflected in Recent Russian Emigre Writing. 1992. text ed. 55.00 (*0-312-06809-3*) St Martin.

McMillin, Arnold, ed. Aspects of Modern Russian & Czech Literature: Selected Papers from the Third World Congress for Soviet & East European Studies. 239p. (Orig.). 1989. pap. 19.95 (*0-89357-194-6*) Slavica.

— From Pushkin to Palisandriia: Essays on the Russian Novel in Honour of Richard Freeborn. LC 90-32157. 190p. 1990. text ed. 45.00 (*0-312-04639-1*) St Martin.

***McMillin, Bruce M.** Fault Tolerance for Multicomputers: The Application Oriented Paradigm. (Computer Engineering & Computer Science Ser.). (Illus.). 208p. 1995. 52.50 (*0-89391-884-9*) Ablex Pub.

McMillin, Chandler S., jt. auth. see Rogers, Ronald L.

McMillin, Laurence. The Schoolmaker: Sawney Webb & the Bell Buckle Story. LC 72-144336. 218p. reprint ed. pap. 62.20 (*0-7837-2065-3*, 2042340) Bks Demand.

McMillin, Lois P. Love, Faith & Onions. 44p. 1986. 5.95 (*1-55523-026-1*) Winston-Derek.

McMillin, Scott. The Elizabethan Theatre & "The Book of Sir Thomas More" LC 86-47996. 184p. 1987. 24.95 (*0-8014-2008-3*) Cornell U Pr.

— Henry Fourth, Pt. I. (Shakespeare in Performance Ser.). 176p. 1991. text ed. 14.95 (*0-7190-2730-6*, Pub. by Manchester Univ Pr UK) St Martin.

McMillin, Scott, ed. Restoration & Eighteenth Century Comedy. (Critical Editions Ser.). (C). 1973. pap. text ed. 12.95 (*0-393-09997-0*) Norton.

McMillion, Bill. Wilderness U: Opportunities for Outdoor Education in the U. S. & Abroad. LC 92-19616. (Illus.). 320p. 1992. pap. 12.95 (*1-55652-158-8*) Chicago Review.

McMillion, Mac. Who'll Sing For Me. LC 87-91267. 130p. (Orig.). (J). 1987. pap. 10.00 (*0-9619399-0-7*) M McMillion Pub.

McMillon, Bill. The Archaeology Handbook: A Field Manual & Resource Guide. 272p. 1991. text ed. 24.95 (*0-471-55015-9*); pap. text ed. 16.95 (*0-471-53051-4*) Wiley.

— Best Hikes with Children in San Francisco's North Bay. LC 91-45547. (Illus.). 230p. (Orig.). 1992. pap. 12.95 (*0-89886-276-0*) Mountaineers.

— Camping with Kids in California: The Complete Guide--Where to Go & What to Do for a Fun-Filled, Stress-Free Camping Vacation. LC 95-2141. 1995. write for info. (*0-7615-0003-0*) Prima Pub.

— Country Roads of Florida. LC 93-42114. (Country Roads Ser.). (Illus.). 148p. (Orig.). 1994. pap. 9.95 (*1-56626-039-6*) Country Rds.

— Great Outdoor Getaways of the Southwest. 420p. (Orig.). 1995. pap. 16.95 (*0-935701-42-7*) Foghorn Pr.

— Seasonal Guide to the Natural Year: A Month by Month Guide to Natural Events - Northern California. (Illus.). 360p. 1995. pap. 15.95 (*1-55591-157-9*) Fulcrum Pub.

— Volunteer Vacations: Short Term Adventures That Will Benefit You & Others. 5th expanded rev. ed. LC 94-48174. (Illus.). 480p. 1995. pap. 13.95 (*1-55652-235-5*) Chicago Review.

McMillon, Bill & McMillon, Kevin. Best Hikes with Children: San Francisco's South Bay. LC 92-18482. (Illus.). (Orig.). 1992. pap. 12.95 (*0-89886-277-9*) Mountaineers.

— Best Hikes with Children Around Sacramento. LC 93-2010. (Illus.). 224p. 1993. pap. 12.95 (*0-89886-278-7*) Mountaineers.

McMillon, Kevin, jt. auth. see McMillon, Bill.

McMinds, Donald, et al. Writing Motif Widgets. 448p. 1994. pap. text ed. 32.00 (*0-13-104191-6*) P-H.

McMinds, Donald L. Mastering OSF-Motif Widgets. (Illus.). 450p. 1991. pap. 39.95 (*0-201-56342-8*) Addison-Wesley.

McMinn. Color Atlas of Human Form & Function. Date not set. write for info. (*0-8151-5853-X*, Yr Bk Med Pubs) Mosby Yr Bk.

— The Human Skeleton. (C). 1986. 39.95 (*0-8151-5795-9*) Mosby Yr Bk.

McMinn & Hutchings, R. T. Color Atlas of Human Anatomy. 2nd ed. (Illus.). 352p. 1988. 53.95 (*0-8151-5854-8*, AJ-2, Yr Bk Med Pubs); pap. 37.95 (*0-8151-5855-6*, AJP-2, Yr Bk Med Pubs) Mosby Yr Bk.

McMinn, jt. auth. see Seeley.

McMinn, et al. Color Atlas of Applied Anatomy. (Illus.). 214p. 1984. pap. 64.95 (*0-8151-5827-0*, QMM-1, Yr Bk Med Pubs) Mosby Yr Bk.

McMinn, A. & Russell, G. J. Training of Medical Laboratory Technicians: A Handbook for Tutors. (Offset Publication Ser.: No. 21). 1975. pap. 6.00 (*92-4-170021-1*) World Health.

McMinn, Curtis J., ed. see Metallurgical Society of AIME Staff.

McMinn, D. G., jt. ed. see Hill, H. H.

McMinn, Don. Entering His Presence: Experiencing the Joy of True Worship. LC 86-70743. 257p. 1986. pap. 8.95 (*0-88270-608-X*) Bridge Pub.

McMinn, Don, ed. see Elliff, Thomas D.

McMinn, Howard E. An Illustrated Manual of California Shrubs. 1939. 48.00 (*0-520-00847-2*) U CA Pr.

McMinn, Howard E. & Maino, Evelyn. An Illustrated Manual of Pacific Coast Trees. 2nd ed. 1937. 37.00 (*0-520-00846-4*); pap. 15.00 (*0-520-04364-2*) U CA Pr.

McMinn, Joseph. Jonathan Swift: A Literary Life. LC 90-42058. 210p. 1991. text ed. 39.95 (*0-312-05275-8*) St Martin.

— Jonathan's Travels: Swift & Ireland. LC 94-3781. 1995. write for info. (*0-312-12354-X*) St Martin.

McMinn, Joseph, ed. Internationalism of Irish Literature & Drama. 300p. (C). 1991. text ed. 64.50 (*0-389-20962-7*) B&N Imports.

McMinn, Mark. RCC, Vol. 27: Cognitive Therapy. 1991. 13.99 (*0-8499-0876-0*) Word Inc.

McMinn, Mark R. Your Hidden Half: Blending Your Private & Public Self--A Quest for Personal Wholeness. LC 88-22267. (Orig.). 1988. pap. 8.99 (*0-8010-6243-8*) Baker Bk.

McMinn, Mark R. & Foster, James D. Christians in the Crossfire. LC 90-82741. 180p. (Orig.). 1990. pap. 9.95 (*0-913342-68-8*) Barclay Pr.

McMinn, R., ed. see Struns, William.

McMinn, R. M. Color Atlas of Head & Neck Anatomy. (Illus.). 240p. 1981. 69.95 (*0-8151-5826-2*, BKW-1, Yr Bk Med Pubs) Mosby Yr Bk.

McMinn, R. M. & Hobdell, M. H. The Functional Anatomy of the Digestive System. (Illus.). 282p. 1974. pap. text ed. 45.00 (*0-272-00123-6*) St Mut.

McMinn, R. M., et al. Color Atlas of Foot & Ankle Anatomy. (Illus.). 96p. 1982. 54.95 (*0-8151-5829-7*, GZF-1, Yr Bk Med Pubs) Mosby Yr Bk.

— A Colour Atlas of Head & Neck Anatomy. 2nd ed. LC 93-43540. (Illus.). 1994. reprint ed. boxed write for info. (*0-7234-1994-9*, Wolfe Pub) Mosby Yr Bk.

— Picture Tests in Anatomy. (Illus.). 128p. 1985. 14.95 (*0-8151-5836-X*, WFA-1, Yr Bk Med Pubs) Mosby Yr Bk.

McMinn, R. M. H., ed. Last's Anatomy, Regional & Applied. 9th ed. LC 94-5560. (Illus.). 1994. 55.00 (*0-443-04662-X*) Churchill.

McMinn, Robert M., et al. A Colour Atlas of Human Anatomy. 3rd ed. LC 92-48935. 359p. 1993. 54.95 (*0-8151-5851-3*, Yr Bk Med Pubs); pap. 37.95 (*0-8151-5858-0*, Yr Bk Med Pubs) Mosby Yr Bk.

McMinn, Russ, ed. see Struns, William.

McMinn, Suzanne. Never Say Goodbye. 224p. (Orig.). 1993. pap. 2.95 (*1-56597-065-9*) Meteor Pub.

McMinn, Tom. Los Caudill: Misioneros Audaces. (Meet the Missionary-Conoce al Misionero Ser.). Orig. Title: Caudills: Courageous Missionaries. 64p. 1987. pap. 2.75 (*0-311-01072-5*) Casa Bautista.

McMinn, W. G. George Reid. 1989. 49.95 (*0-522-84373-5*) Intl Spec Bk.

— Nationalism & Federalism in Australia. 346p. 1995. pap. 32.00 (*0-19-553667-3*) OUP.

McMinnies, William. Premier Hotels of Great Britain. 55th ed. (International Guide Ser.). (Illus.). 400p. (Orig.). 1994. pap. 17.95 (*1-56554-008-5*) Pelican.

— Premier Hotels of Great Britain. 56th ed. 400p. 1995. pap. 15.95 (*1-56554-120-0*) Pelican.

McMlelland, David C. Psychoanalysis & Religious Mysticism. (C). 1959. pap. 3.00 (*0-87574-104-5*) Pendle Hill.

McMonagle, Gary R. Instant Money: How to Use the Hidden Power of Your Mind to Attract Incredible Wealth. Darbey, Barbara R., ed. 197p. 1990. 19.95 (*0-9626363-0-4*) RMA Pub OH.

McMonagle, Pat. Michigan Mountain Biking: A Guide to Mountain Bike Trails in Michigan. 112p. 1994. pap. 13. 95 (*0-9641141-0-0*) Broken Spoke.

McMoneagle, Joe. Mind Trek. (Illus.). 300p. (Orig.) 1993. pap. 10.95 (*1-878901-72-9*) Hampton Roads Pub Co.

***McMonnies, Alistair & McSporran, W. S.** Developing Object Oriented Data Structures Using C++ LC 94-42779. (International Software Engineering Ser.). 1995. write for info. (*0-07-707982-5*) McGraw.

***McMorland, D. E.** Vendor & Purchaser. 163p. 1979. pap. 45.00 (*0-409-64522-2*, NZ) Butterworth Legal Pubs.

McMorland, D. E., jt. auth. see Hinde, G. E.

McMorries, Edward Y. History of the First Regiment Alabama Volunteer Infantry, C.S.A. LC 79-126243. (Select Bibliographies Reprint Ser.). 1977. reprint ed. 15. 95 (*0-8369-5470-X*) Ayer.

McMorris, Bill & McMorris, Jo. Camp Cooking: A Backpacker's Pocket Guide. (Illus.). 112p. 1989. pap. 7.95 (*1-55821-023-7*) Lyons & Burford.

McMorris, Jo, jt. auth. see McMorris, Bill.

McMorris, Mark. Palinurus Suite. 47p. (Orig.). 1992. pap. 5.00 (*0-945926-37-5*) Paradigm RI.

McMorris, Neville. The Natures of Science. LC 87-46376. 264p. 1989. 38.50 (*0-8386-3321-8*) Fairleigh Dickinson.

McMorris, Penny, intro. Nancy Crow: Work in Transition. LC 92-12986. 32p. 1992. pap. 12.95 (*0-89145-995-2*) Collector Bks.

***McMorrow.** Stonehenge. Date not set. pap. write for info. (*0-679-97499-7*) Random Hse Value.

***McMorrow, Catherine.** Gold Fever. (Step into Reading Ser.: No. 3). (J). Date not set. 9.99 (*0-679-96432-0*) Random.

— Gold Fever-Step Reading Three. Date not set. 3.99 (*0-679-86432-6*) Random.

McMorrow, George J., tr. see Simon, Yves R.

McMorrow, Martin J., jt. auth. see Foxx, Richard M.

McMorrow, Martin J., et al. Looking for the Words: Teaching Functional Language Strategies. LC 86-62486. 109p. (Orig.). 1986. pap. 12.95 (*0-87822-284-7*, 2847) Res Press.

McMullan, Audrey. Theatre on Trial: Samuel Beckett's Later Drama. LC 92-30605. 176p. 1993. 59.95 (*0-415-05202-5*, B0359) Routledge.

McMullan, Gordon. The Politics of Unease in the Plays of John Fletcher. LC 93-28554. (Massachusetts Studies in Early Modern Culture). 352p. 1994. lib. bdg. 37.50x (*0-87023-892-2*) U of Mass Pr.

McMullan, J. T. Physical Techniques In Medicine, 2 vols. Incl. Vol. 2. Physical Techniques in Medicine. 158p. 1980. text ed. 149.95 (*0-471-27695-2*); write for info. (*0-318-56433-5*, Wiley-Interscience) Wiley.

McMullan, J. T., ed. Innovation in Europe's Traditional Industries Proceedings of the Sprint Conf..., No. EUR 13173. 206p. 1991. pap. 25.00 (*92-826-2155-3*, CD-NA-13173-EN-C, Pub. by Europ Com) UNIPUB.

McMullan, James. High-Focus Drawing: A Revolutionary Approach to Drawing the Figure. (Illus.). 224p. 1995. 29.95 (*0-87951-536-8*) Overlook Pr.

— High-Focus Drawing: A Revolutionary Approach to Drawing the Figure. (Illus.). 160p. 1995. pap. 19.95 (*0-87951-604-6*) Overlook Pr.

McMullan, Jim. This Face You Got: The Art of the Illustrator. (Illus.). 192p. 1994. 60.00 (*1-885203-01-2*) Jrny Editions.

McMullan, Jim & Gautier, Dick. Actors As Artists. 1992. 40.00 (*0-8048-1783-9*) C E Tuttle.

— Actors As Artists. (Illus.). 176p. 1994. reprint ed. pap. 25. 00 (*1-885203-02-0*) Jrny Editions.

— Musicians As Artists. (Illus.). 144p. 1994. 30.00 (*1-885203-06-3*) Jrny Editions.

McMullan, Jim & Levin, Michael. Instant Zen: A Do-It-Yourself Guide to Awareness & Discovery. 112p. 1994. spiral bd. 8.95 (*0-8048-3016-9*) C E Tuttle.

***McMullan, Jim & McMullan, Kate.** Hey, Pipsqueak! (Michael di Capua Books). (Illus.). 32p. (J). (ps up). 1995. 14.95 (*0-06-205100-8*); lib. bdg. 14.89 (*0-06-205101-6*) HarpC Child Bks.

McMullan, Jim, jt. auth. see McMullan, Kate.

McMullan, Joan, tr. see Monition, Lucien, et al.

McMullan, John, ed. see Guindon, Hubert.

McMullan, John T., et al. Energy Resources & Supply. LC 75-6973. (Illus.). 520p. reprint ed. pap. 148.20 (*0-685-20704-8*, 2030488) Bks Demand.

McMullan, Kate. The Biggest Mouth in Baseball. LC 92-24467. (All Aboard Reading Ser.). (Illus.). 48p. (J). (gr. 2-4). 1993. lib. bdg. 7.99 (*0-448-40516-4*, G&D); pap. 3.50 (*0-448-40515-6*, G&D) Putnam Pub Group.

— Dinosaur Hunters. LC 88-30742. (Step into Reading Bks.). (Illus.). 48p. (Orig.). (J). (gr. 2-4). 1989. 3.50 (*0-394-81150-X*); lib. bdg. 7.99 (*0-394-91150-4*) Random Bks Yng Read.

— Goodnight, Stella. LC 93-876. (Illus.). 32p. (J). (ps up). 1994. 14.95 (*1-56402-065-7*) Candlewick Pr.

— The Great Eggspectations of Lila Fenwick. (Illus.). 148p. (J). (gr. 3-7). 1991. bds. 13.95 (*0-374-32774-2*) FS&G.

— Nutcracker Noel. LC 93-77115. (Michael di Capua Bks.). (Illus.). 32p. (J). (ps up). 1993. 15.00 (*0-06-205039-7*) HarpC Child Bks.

— Nutcracker Noel. LC 93-77115. (Michael di Capua Bks.). (Illus.). 32p. (J). (ps up). 1993. lib. bdg. 14.89 (*0-06-205040-0*) HarpC Child Bks.

— Under the Mummy's Spell. 176p. (J). (gr. 5 up). 1992. 16. 00 (*0-374-38033-3*) FS&G.

— Under the Mummy's Spell. (J). (gr. 4-7). 1994. pap. 3.25 (*0-590-47897-4*) Scholastic Inc.

McMullan, Kate & McMullan, Jim. The Noisy Giants' Tea Party. LC 92-52692. (Michael di Capua Bks.). (Illus.). 32p. (J). (ps-3). 1992. lib. bdg. 14.89 (*0-06-205018-4*) HarpC Child Bks.

McMullan, Kate, jt. auth. see McMullan, Jim.

McMullan, Margaret. When Warhol Was Still Alive: A Novel. LC 93-38634. 1994. 18.95 (*0-89594-651-3*) Crossing Pr.

McMullan, R. Environmental Science in Building. 2nd ed. (Macmillan Building & Surveying Ser.). (Illus.). 283p. (C). 1990. text ed. 80.00 (*0-333-49116-5*, Pub. by Macmill Press UK); pap. text ed. 29.00 (*0-333-49117-3*, Pub. by Macmill Press UK) Scholium Intl.

McMullan, Randall. Dictionary of Building. 256p. 1991. 59. 50 (*0-87683-601-5*) GP Pub.

— Illustrated Supercalc. (Illus.). 48p. (Orig.). 1990. pap. 29. 95 (*0-8464-4326-0*) Beekman Pubs.

— Illustrated Wordstar. (Illus.). 32p. (Orig.). 1988. pap. 32. 95 (*0-8464-4328-7*) Beekman Pubs.

***McMullen.** Enchanted Boy. Date not set. per. 10.95 (*0-85449-098-1*, Pub. by Gay Mens Pr UK) InBook.

McMullen, Ann & Handsman, Russell G., eds. A Key into the Language of Woodsplint Baskets. LC 86-70023. (Illus.). 196p. 1987. pap. 20.00 (*0-936322-04-7*) Am Indian Arch.

McMullen, Ann & Kopec, Diane, eds. An Island in Time: Three Thousand Years of Cultural Exchange on Mount Desert Island. (Robert Abbe Museum Bulletin Ser.: No. XII). 42p. 1994. reprint ed. pap. write for info. (*1-885410-01-8*) R Abbe Museum.

McMullen, Anne W., jt. auth. see McMullen, Cyd.

McMullen, B. Starr. Profits & the Cost of Capital to the U. S. Trunk Airline Industry under CAB Regulation. LC 92-38639. (Government & the Economy Ser.). 128p. 1993. 39.00 (*0-8153-1230-X*) Garland.

McMullen, Charles W. Real Estate Investments: A Step-by-Step Guide. LC 80-20704. (Real Estate For Professional Practitioners Ser.). 192p. reprint ed. pap. 54.80 (*0-317-41743-6*, 2023143) Bks Demand.

— Tax-Deferred Exchanges of Real Estate Investments. LC 81-3041. (Real Estate For Professional Practitioners Ser.). 98p. reprint ed. pap. 28.00 (*0-7837-3456-5*, 2057782) Bks Demand.

McMullen, Christopher J. Mediation of the West New Guinea Dispute, 1962: A Case Study. 86p. (C). 1985. reprint ed. pap. text ed. 12.00 (*0-8191-5052-5*, Inst Study Diplomacy) U Pr of Amer.

— Resolution of the Yemen Crisis, 1963: A Case Study in Mediation. LC 80-25944. 56p. (Orig.). 1980. pap. 5.00 (*0-934742-07-3*) Geo U Inst Dplmcy.

— Resolution of the Yemen Crisis, 1963: A Case Study in Mediation. 60p. (Orig.). (C). 1985. reprint ed. pap. text ed. 11.50 (*0-8191-5065-7*, Inst Study Diplomacy) U Pr of Amer.

An Asterisk (*) at the beginning of an entry indicates that the title is appearing in BIP for the first time.

McMullen, Christopher J., intro. Mediation of the West New Guinea Dispute 1962: A Case Study. LC 81-20006. 88p. (Orig.). 1981. pap. 5.00 (0-934742-14-6) Geo U Inst Dplmcy.

McMullen, Clarence O. Religious Beliefs & Practices of the Sikhs in Rural Punjab. (C). 1989. 18.50 (0-945921-09-8) S Asia.

***McMullen, Curtis T.** Complex Dynamics & Renormalization. LC 94-29390. (Annals of Mathematics Studies: 135). 1994. 49.50 (0-691-02982-2) Princeton U Pr.

McMullen, Cyd & McMullen, Anne W. Cowboy Poetry Cookbook: Menus & Verse for Western Celebrations. (Illus.). 96p. (Orig.). 1992. pap. 14.95 (0-87905-457-3, Peregrine Smith) Gibbs Smith Pub.

McMullen, D. L. State & Scholars in T'ang China. (Cambridge Studies in Chinese History, Literature & Institutions). 448p. 1988. 74.95 (0-521-32991-4) Cambridge U Pr.

McMullen, David. Atlantis: The Missing Continent. LC 77-22138. (Great Unsolved Mysteries Ser.). (Illus.). 48p. (J). (gr. 4 up). 1983. reprint ed. lib. bdg. 21.36 (0-8172-1047-4) Raintree Steck-V.

— Mystery in Peru: The Lines of Nazca. LC 77-10456. (Great Unsolved Mysteries Ser.). (Illus.). 48p. (J). (gr. 4 up). 1983. reprint ed. lib. bdg. 21.36 (0-8172-1058-X) Raintree Steck-V.

McMullen, E. Wallace, ed. Names in Various Aspects: Selected Papers of the Names Institute. (International Library of Names). 400p. text ed. write for info. (0-8290-1211-7) Irvington.

McMullen, Eunice & McMullen, Nigel. Dragon for Breakfast. (Illus.). 28p. (J). (ps-3). 1990. lib. bdg. 18.95 (0-87614-650-7, Carolrhoda) Lerner Group.

McMullen, George. Red Snake. 1993. 9.95 (1-878901-58-3) Hampton Roads Pub Co.

***McMullen, George & Schwartz, Stephan A.** One White Crow. 208p. (Orig.). 1995. pap. 8.95 (1-57174-007-4) Hampton Roads Pub Co.

McMullen, Helen. Assessment in the Primary School. Cullingford, Cedric, ed. (Children, Teachers & Learning Ser.). 192p. 1993. text ed. 70.00 (0-304-32595-3); pap. text ed. 22.50 (0-304-32586-4) Cassell.

McMullen, I. J. Genji Gaiden: The Origins of Kumazawa Banzan's Commentary on the Tale of Genji. (Oxford Oriental Institute Monographs: Vol. 13). 272p. 1991. text ed. 60.00 (0-86372-153-2, Pub. by Ithaca UK) Paul & Co Pubs.

McMullen, I. J., jt. ed. see Kornicki, P. F.

McMullen, James P. Cry of the Panther: Quest of a Species. LC 84-16684. 416p. 1984. 17.95 (0-910923-09-4) Pineapple Pr.

McMullen, Jeanine. My Small Country Living. (Illus.). 224p. 1985. pap. 8.95 (0-446-38305-8) Warner Bks.

— A Small Country Living Goes On. (Illus.). 272p. 1991. 19.95 (0-393-03039-3) Norton.

— A Small Country Living Goes On. large type ed. 467p. 1992. reprint ed. lib. bdg. 17.95 (1-56054-420-1) Thorndike Pr.

— Wind in the Ash Tree. (Illus.). 1989. pap. 8.95 (0-393-30627-5) Norton.

McMullen, John. The Basic Essentials of Snowboarding. LC 91-21207. (Basic Essentials Ser.). (Illus.). 72p. (Orig.). 1991. pap. 5.99 (0-934802-77-7) ICS Bks.

— Breach of Employment Contracts & Wrongful Dismissal. Date not set. U.K. pap. write for info. (0-406-11841-8) Butterworth Legal Pubs.

— Business Transfers & Employee Rights. 2nd ed. 1992. 90.00 (0-406-00084-0, U.K.) Butterworth Legal Pubs.

— The Canting Crew: London's Criminal Underworld, 1550-1700. 192p. 1984. text ed. 40.00 (0-8135-1022-8) Rutgers U Pr.

— The Complete Idiot's Guide to Unix. 400p. 1995. 19.99 (1-56761-511-2) Alpha Bks IN.

McMullen, John, jt. auth. see Skinner, Todd.

McMullen, John R. Extensions of Positive-Definite Functions. LC 52-42893. (Memoirs Ser.: No. 1/117). 71p. 1972. pap. 16.00 (0-8218-1817-1, MEMO 1/117) Am Math.

McMullen, Linda S. & Welch, Ron. Kansas: America, Center Stage. 1990. 29.95 (0-89781-296-4) Preferred Mktg.

McMullen, Lorraine. Ernest Thompson Seton & His Works. (Canadian Author Studies). 54p. (C). 1989. pap. text ed. 9.95 (1-55022-051-9, Pub. by ECW Press CN) Genl Dist Srvs.

— Frances Brooke & Her Works. (Canadian Author Studies). 38p. (C). 1983. pap. text ed. 9.95 (0-920763-38-3, Pub. by ECW Press CN) Genl Dist Srvs.

McMullen, Lorraine, ed. Rediscovering Our Foremothers: Nineteenth Century Canadian Women Writers. 210p. 1990. pap. 21.00 (0-7766-0197-0, Pub. by Univ Ottawa Pr CN) Paul & Co Pubs.

McMullen, Lorraine, jt. ed. see Campbell, Sandra.

McMullen, Lynn B. The Service Load in Teacher Training Institutions of the United States. LC 73-177038. (Columbia University. Teachers College. Contributions to Education Ser.: No. 244). reprint ed. 22.50 (0-404-55244-7) AMS Pr.

McMullen, M. Cooperative Learning: ESL Techniques. (Teacher Training Through Video Ser.). 1993. 375.00 (0-8013-1005-9, 79311) Longman.

McMullen, Melanie, ed. Network Remote Access & Mobile Computing: Implementing Effective Remote Access to Networks & E-Mail. (Illus.). 240p. (Orig.). 1994. pap. 29.95 (0-87930-334-4) Miller Freeman.

— Networks 2000: Internet, Information Highway Multimedia Networks, & Beyond. (Illus.). 320p. (Orig.). 1994. pap. 24.95 (0-87930-335-2) Miller Freeman.

McMullen, Neil. The Newly Industrializing Countries in the World Economy. (British-North American Committee Ser.). 1982. 7.00 (0-685-06045-4) Natl Planning.

McMullen, Nigel, jt. auth. see McMullen, Eunice.

McMullen, Phillip. Grassroots of America: Index to American State Papers, Land Grants & Claims, 1789-1837. (Illus.). 520p. 1990. reprint ed. text ed. 49.50 (0-941765-85-7) Arkansas Res.

McMullen, R. T. Down Channel. 328p. 1984. reprint ed. 18.95 (0-916025-01-2) Armchair Sail Pub.

McMullen, Richard E. Like Heaven. 18p. (Orig.). 1993. pap. 7.50 (1-884763-00-6) Ltd Mailing.

McMullen, Roy. Mona Lisa: The Picture & the Myth. LC 77-23574. (Quality Paperbacks Ser.). 1977. reprint ed. pap. 7.95 (0-306-80067-5) Da Capo.

McMullen, Shawn. A New Home. LC 91-43071. (Timely Tales Ser.). (Illus.). 32p. (J). (gr. 4-8). 1992. 5.99 (0-87403-976-2, 24-03866) Standard Pub.

McMullen, Shawn A. Justin Ordinary Squirrel. (Illus.). 32p. (J). (ps-2). 1991. pap. text ed. 3.99 (0-87403-807-3, 24-03897) Standard Pub.

McMullen, Stewart Y. Financial Statements: Form, Analysis, & Interpretation. 7th ed. LC 78-70981. (Willard J. Graham Series in Accounting). 598p. reprint ed. pap. 170.50 (0-317-27998-X, 2055809) Bks Demand.

McMullen, W. A. Posthumous Meditations: A Dialogue in Three Acts. LC 82-916. (HPC Dialogues Ser.). 79p. (C). 1982. pap. text ed. 3.95 (0-915145-35-9) Hackett Pub.

McMullen, W. Edward & Long, Wayne A. Developing Entrepreneurial Ventures. 516p. (C). 1990. teacher ed 2.00 (0-15-517592-0); text ed. 39.00 (0-15-517591-2) Dryden Pr.

McMullen, William W. Soloistic English Horn Literature (1736-1984) (Juilliard Performance Guides Ser.: No. 4). (Illus.). 1994. lib. bdg. 48.00 (0-918728-78-9) Pendragon NY.

McMullin, Ernan. The Concept of Matter in Greek & Medieval Philosophy. LC 65-23511. 333p. reprint ed. pap. 95.00 (0-318-34707-5, 2031907) Bks Demand.

— The Inference That Makes Science. LC 92-80351. (Aquinas Lectures). 1992. 10.00 (0-87462-159-3) Marquette.

McMullin, Ernan, ed. The Social Dimensions of Science. LC 91-50577. (Studies in Science & the Humanities from the Reilly Center for Science, Technology, & Values: Vol. III). (C). 1992. text ed. 37.95 (0-268-01741-7); pap. text ed. 19.95 (0-268-01742-5) U of Notre Dame Pr.

McMullin, Ernan, jt. ed. see Cushing, James T.

McMullin, Neil. Buddhism & the State in Sixteenth Century Japan. LC 84-42572. 452p. reprint ed. pap. 128.90 (0-8357-3390-4, 2039647) Bks Demand.

McMullin, Rian E. Handbook of Cognitive Therapy Techniques. (Professional Bks.). 1986. 34.95 (0-393-70035-6) Norton.

McMullin, Rian E. & Casey, Bill. Hablese con Sentido A Si Mismo: Una Guia de Terapia de Restructuracion Cognitiva. Navas R, Jose J., tr. Orig. Title: Talk Sense to Yourself: A Guide to Cognitive Restructuring Therapy. (Illus.). 45p. (Orig.). (SPA.). 1975. pap. 4.00 (0-935205-04-7) Counseling Res.

— Talk Sense to Yourself: A Guide to Cognitive Restructuring Therapy. (Illus.). 57p. (Orig.). 1975. pap. 4.00 (0-935205-02-0) Counseling Res.

McMullin, Rian E., et al. Straight Talk to Parents: Cognitive Restructuring Training for Families. (Illus.). 63p. (Orig.). 1978. pap. 4.00 (0-935205-03-9) Counseling Res.

McMullin, Stan. Thomas Chandler Haliburton & His Works. (Canadian Author Studies). 50p. (C). 1989. pap. text ed. 9.95 (1-55022-047-0, Pub. by ECW Press CN) Genl Dist Srvs.

McMullin, Thomas A. & Walker, David. Biographical Directory of American Territorial Governors. LC 84-9095. 350p. 1984. text ed. 79.50 (0-313-28101-7, MTN/, Greenwood Pr) Greenwood.

McMullins, Hilda L. Story Book Time. LC 92-45560. 64p. 1995. pap. 12.95 (0-7734-2772-4, Mellen Poetry Pr) E Mellen.

McMunn, Meradith T., jt. ed. see Clark, Willene B.

McMurchie, Susan. Understanding LD (Learning Differences) A Curriculum to Promote LD Awareness, Self Esteem & Coping Skills in Students Ages 8-13. 160p. 1994. pap. 21.95 (0-915793-75-X) Free Spirit Pub.

McMurdie, H. F., jt. ed. see Cook, L. P.

McMurdie, Howard F., jt. ed. see Levin, Ernest M.

McMurphy, John, et al. Speaking of Mother Earth: Myths, Rituals, Essays, & Verse. (Illus.). 219p. (Orig.). 1994. pap. 13.95 (0-9635487-7-8) Amaranth Pub.

McMurphy, John H. Living Deliberately: Experiments in Practical Spirituality. 180p. (Orig.). 1993. pap. 13.95 (0-9635487-8-6) Amaranth Pub.

— Secrets from Great Minds. 254p. (Orig.). 1993. reprint ed. pap. 13.95 (0-9635487-9-4) Amaranth Pub.

***McMurphy, R. P.** Tales from the Edge. LC 95-69085. (Illus.). 100p. (Orig.). 1996. pap. 7.95 (0-9646566-0-4) Southestrn Pr.

McMurrain, T. Thomas, jt. auth. see Wilson, Gary B.

McMurran, jt. auth. see Hodge.

McMurran, Mary. The Psychology of Addiction. LC 94-16356. (Contemporary Psychology Ser.). 1994. write for info. (0-7484-0187-3, Pub. by Tay Francis Ltd UK); pap. write for info. (0-7484-0188-1, Pub. by Tay Francis Ltd UK) Taylor & Francis.

— Young Offenders & Alcohol Related Crime: A Practitioner's Guidebook. 1993. text ed. 44.50 (0-471-93925-0) Wiley.

McMurran, Mary & Hodge, John, eds. The Assessment of Criminal Behaviour in Secure Settings. 200p. 1993. pap. 37.50 (1-85302-124-5, Pub. by J Kingsley Pubs UK) Taylor & Francis.

McMurrary, John, et al, eds. Annual Reports in Organic Synthesis, Vol. 12. (Serial Publication Ser.). 1982. pap. text ed. 106.00 (0-12-040812-0) Acad Pr.

McMurray. Contemporary Theatre Film & TV, Vol. 9. 1991. 128.00 (0-8103-2072-X) Gale.

McMurray, Becky, jt. auth. see Goodwin, Glena.

***McMurray, Emily J. & Olendorf, Donna, eds.** Notable Twentieth Century Scientists, Vol. 4. LC 94-5263. 2397p. 1994. 295.00 (0-8103-9181-3) Gale.

McMurray, G. R., ed. Gorda Ridge. (Illus.). 320p. 1989. 119.00 (0-387-97034-7) Spr-Verlag.

McMurray, George R., ed. Critical Essays on Gabriel Garcia Marquez. (Critical Essays Ser.). 224p. 1987. text ed. 45.00 (0-8161-8834-3, Hall Reference) Macmillan.

McMurray, Georgia L. Social Policy Issues Affecting the Poor. 37p. 1983. pap. text ed. 3.50 (0-88156-018-9) Comm Serv Soc NY.

McMurray, Georgia L. & Kazanjian, Dolores P. Day Care & the Working Poor: The Struggle for Self-Sufficiency. LC 82-199119. 140p. 1982. pap. 10.00 (0-88156-001-4) Comm Serv Soc NY.

McMurray, Janice, intro. Creative Arts with Older People. LC 89-20049. (Activities, Adaptation & Aging Ser.: Vol. 14, Nos. 1 & 2). (Illus.). 138p. 1989. text ed. 29.95 (0-86656-929-4) Haworth Pr.

McMurray, John & Miller, R. Bryan, eds. Annual Reports in Organic Synthesis, Vol. 14. (Serial Publication Ser.). 1984. pap. text ed. 92.00 (0-12-040814-7) Acad Pr.

***McMurray, Madeline.** Beyond Heroics: Living Our Myths. 240p. (Orig.). 1995. pap. 12.95 (0-89254-031-1) Nicolas-Hays.

— Illuminations: The Healing Image. LC 88-11467. (Illus.). 86p. (Orig.). 1988. pap. 12.95 (0-914728-63-6) Wingbow Pr.

McMurray, Mark. Type Specimens of Caliban Press. limited ed. (Illus.). 1991. 200.00 (0-936897-11-2) Caliban.

McMurray, Sara M. Quantum Mechanics. LC 93-43852. 374p. 1994. pap. 53.75 (0-685-71176-5) Addison-Wesley.

McMurray, William J., et al. History of the Twentieth Tennessee Regiment Volunteer Infantry, C.S.A. LC 08-19472. (Illus.). 1976. reprint ed. 75.00 (0-918450-12-8) C Elder.

***McMurren, Scott.** Umbrella Guide to Southcentral Alaska: Including Anchorage, Matanuska-Susitna Valleys, Kenai Peninsula, & Prince William Sound. Ummel, Christine, ed. (Illus.). 160p. 1995. pap. 12.95 (0-945397-40-2, Umbrella Bks) Epicenter Pr.

McMurrey, David A. Processes in Technical Writing. 1303p. (C). 1988. pap. write for info. (0-02-379700-2) Macmillan.

McMurrian, Howard P., et al. Guide to Physicians & Other Health Care Professionals, 2 vols., 1. 1993. write for info. (1-56433-311-6) Prctnrs Pub Co.

— Guide to Physicians & Other Health Care Professionals, 2 vols., 2. 1993. write for info. (1-56433-312-4) Prctnrs Pub Co.

— Guide to Physicians & Other Health Care Professionals, 2 vols., Set. 1993. ring bd. 115.00 (1-56433-310-8) Prctnrs Pub Co.

— Guide to Physicians & Other Health Care Professionals, 2 vols., Set. 1994. ring bd. 125.00 (1-56433-503-8) Prctnrs Pub Co.

— Guide to Physicians & Other Health Care Professionals Vol. 1. 1994. ring bd. write for info. (1-56433-504-6) Prctnrs Pub Co.

— Guide to Physicians & Other Health Care Professionals Vol. 2. 1994. ring bd. write for info. (1-56433-505-4) Prctnrs Pub Co.

— Guide to Physicians & Other Healthcare Professionals, 2 vols., Set. 857p. 1992. ring bd. 115.00 (1-56433-174-1) Prctnrs Pub Co.

— Guide to Physicians & Other Healthcare Professionals, 2 vols., Set. rev. ed. 900p. 1991. ring bd. 115.00 (1-56433-054-0) Prctnrs Pub Co.

— Guide to Physicians & Other Healthcare Professionals, Vol. 1. 447p. 1992. write for info. (1-56433-175-X) Prctnrs Pub Co.

— Guide to Physicians & Other Healthcare Professionals, Vol. 1. rev. ed. 450p. 1991. write for info. (1-56433-055-9) Prctnrs Pub Co.

— Guide to Physicians & Other Healthcare Professionals, Vol. 2. 410p. 1992. write for info. (1-56433-176-8) Prctnrs Pub Co.

— Guide to Physicians & Other Healthcare Professionals, Vol. 2. rev. ed. 450p. 1991. write for info. (1-56433-056-7) Prctnrs Pub Co.

— Guide to Quality Control. 1993. ring bd. 105.00 (1-56433-285-3) Prctnrs Pub Co.

— Guide to Quality Control. 1994. ring bd. 120.00 (1-56433-433-3) Prctnrs Pub Co.

— Guide to Quality Control. 1995. ring bd. 125.00 (1-56433-596-8) Prctnrs Pub Co.

McMurrin, Sterling M. The Philosophical Foundations of Mormon Theology. 1959. reprint ed. pap. 5.95 (0-87480-169-9) U of Utah Pr.

— Religion, Reason, & Truth: Historical Essays in the Philosophy of Religion. LC 82-4813. 302p. reprint ed. pap. 86.10 (0-685-20459-6, 2029852) Bks Demand.

— The Tanner Lectures on Human Values, Vol. I. LC 81-641369. 268p. reprint ed. pap. 76.40 (0-685-20458-8, 2029851) Bks Demand.

McMurrin, Sterling M., ed. The Tanner Lectures on Human Values, Vol. VIII. 333p. (C). 1988. text ed. 30.00 (0-87480-302-0) U of Utah Pr.

— The Tanner Lectures on Human Values, Vol. IV: 1983. 300p. 1983. 30.00 (0-87480-216-4) U of Utah Pr.

— The Tanner Lectures on Human Values, Vol. V: 1984. 220p. 1984. 30.00 (0-87480-234-2) U of Utah Pr.

— The Tanner Lectures on Human Values, Vol. VI: 1985. 300p. 1985. 30.00 (0-87480-243-1) U of Utah Pr.

— The Tanner Lectures on Human Values, Vol. VII: 1986. 288p. 1986. 30.00 (0-87480-259-8) U of Utah Pr.

McMurrin, Sterling M., ed. see Ashby, Eric, et al.

McMurrin, Sterling M., ed. see Coles, Robert, et al.

McMurrin, Sterling M., ed. see Dyson, Freeman J., et al.

McMurrin, Trudy, jt. ed. see Plenk, Henry P.

McMurry, Dean S., tr. see Maier, Klaus A., et al.

McMurry, Dean S., tr. see Schreiber, Gerhard, et al.

McMurry, Donald L. Coxey's Army: A Study of the Industrial Army Movement of 1894. LC 75-120222. reprint ed. 26.45 (0-404-04145-0) AMS Pr.

McMurry, Douglas & Worthington, Everett L., Jr. Value Your Mate: How to Strengthen Your Marriage. LC 93-36060. (Strategic Christian Living Ser.). 128p. (Orig.). 1994. pap. 7.99 (0-8010-9727-4) Baker Bk.

McMurry, Douglas, jt. auth. see Long, Zeb B.

McMurry, Douglas, jt. auth. see Worthington, Everett L., Jr.

McMurry, James. The Catskill Witch & Other Tales of the Hudson Valley. LC 74-17067. (York State Book Ser.). 168p. reprint ed. pap. 47.90 (0-317-51995-6, 2027391) Bks Demand.

McMurry, John. Essentials of General, Organic, & Biological Chemistry. 600p. (C). 1988. text ed. 63.00 (0-13-286261-1) P-H.

— Fundamentals of Organic Chemistry. 3rd ed. LC 93-25587. 1994. text ed. 62.95 (0-534-21210-7) Brooks-Cole.

— Organic Chemistry. 3rd ed. 1264p. (C). 1992. text ed. 74.95 (0-534-16218-5) Brooks-Cole.

McMurry, John & Castellion, Mary E. Fundamentals of General, Organic & Biological Chemistry. 800p. (C). 1992. text ed. write for info. (0-13-351867-1) P-H.

— Fundamentals of Organic & Biological Chemistry. LC 93-39094. 1994. text ed. 41.25 (0-13-293085-4) P-H.

***McMurry, John & Fay, Robert C.** Chemistry. 1994. text ed. 75.00 (0-13-350281-3) P-H.

McMurry, John & Miller, R. Bryan, eds. Annual Reports in Organic Synthesis, Vol. 3. (Serial Publication Ser.). 1973. pap. text ed. 106.00 (0-12-040803-1) Acad Pr.

McMurry, Linda O. George Washington Carver: Scientist & Symbol. (Illus.). 1982. pap. 12.95 (0-19-503205-5) OUP.

— Recorder of the Black Experience: A Biography of Monroe Nathan Work. LC 84-10008. (Southern Biography Ser.). (Illus.). 154p. 1985. text ed. 27.50 (0-8071-1171-6) La State U Pr.

McMurry, Richard M. John Bell Hood & the War for Southern Independence. LC 92-12987. (Illus.). xiv, 239p. 1992. reprint ed. pap. 9.95 (0-8032-8191-9, Bison Books) U of Nebr Pr.

— Two Great Rebel Armies: An Essay in Confederate Military History. LC 88-14374. (Illus.). xviii, 204p. (C). 1989. 22.50 (0-8078-1819-4) U of NC Pr.

McMurry, Robert N. The Maverick Executive. LC 73-85189. 205p. reprint ed. pap. 58.50 (0-317-19936-6, 2023571) Bks Demand.

McMurry, Sally. Transforming Rural Life: Dairying Families & Agricultural Change, 1820-1885. (Revisiting Rural America Ser.). 296p. 1995. text ed. 39.95x (0-8018-4889-X) Johns Hopkins.

McMurry, Sara. Quantum Mechanic. (C). 1993. pap. text ed. 53.75 (0-201-54439-3) Addison-Wesley.

McMurry, Sara M. Quantum Mechanics. LC 93-43852. 1993. 26.00 (0-685-70937-X) Addison-Wesley.

McMurtie, D. C., ed. see Schorbach, Karl.

McMurtray, Frances. Allied Health Reading Vocabulary Workbook. 122p. 1978. pap. text ed. 7.95x (0-89641-008-0) American Pr.

McMurtrey, Ernest L. High Performance Solid & Liquid Lubricants: An Industrial Guide. LC 87-12205. (Illus.). 438p. 1988. 54.00 (0-8155-1137-X) Noyes.

McMurtrey, Martin. Loose to the Wilds. 2nd ed. 162p. (YA). reprint ed. pap. 6.00 (0-9623961-0-9) M A McMurtrey.

— Mariachi Bishop: The Life of Patrick Flores, First Mexican-American Bishop in the U. S. LC 87-70378. (Illus.). 181p. (Orig.). 1987. pap. 6.95 (0-931722-56-X) Corona Pub.

McMurtrey, Martin, ed. see Von Le Fort, Gertrud.

McMurtrie, D. C. Check List of Kentucky Imprints, 1811-1820, with Notes in Supplement to the Check List of 1787-1810. Allen, A. H., ed. (Historical Records Survey Monographs). 1972. reprint ed. 20.00 (0-527-01903-8) Periodicals Srv.

McMurtrie, D. C. & Allen, A. H. American Imprints Inventory No. Five: Check List of Kentucky Imprints, 1787-1810. (Historical Records Survey Monographs). 1972. reprint ed. pap. 20.00 (0-527-01902-X) Periodicals Srv.

McMurtrie, Douglas C. The Book: Story of Printing & Bookmaking. (Dorset Press Reprints Ser.). (Illus.). 450p. 1990. 29.95 (0-88029-348-9) Dorset Pr.

— The Disabled Soldier. Phillips, William R. & Rosenberg, Janet, eds. LC 79-6921. (Physically Handicapped in Society Ser.). (Illus.). 1980. reprint ed. lib. bdg. 25.95 (0-405-13140-2) Ayer.

— The Evolution of National Systems of Vocational Reeducation for Disabled Soldiers & Sailors. Phillips, William R. & Rosenberg, Janet, eds. LC 79-6916. (Physically Handicapped in Society Ser.). 1980. reprint ed. lib. bdg. 31.95 (0-405-13127-5) Ayer.

— Historical Records Survey: Check List of the Imprints of Sag Harbor, L. I., 1791-1820, No. 12. (Historical Records Survey Monographs). 1939. pap. 16.00 (0-527-01909-7) Periodicals Srv.

— King Arthur: Hero & Legend. (Dorset Press Reprints Ser.). 500p. 1990. 29.95 (0-88029-347-0) Dorset Pr.

McMurtrie, Douglas C., jt. auth. see Axford, Wendy A.

McMurtrie-Perkins, Nancy, jt. auth. see Perkins, William M.

An Asterisk (*) at the beginning of an entry indicates that the title is appearing in BIP for the first time.

McMurtrie, W. Hogin & Rikel, James E. The Coloring Review Guide to Human Anatomy. 448p. (C). 1990. spiral bd. write for info. (0-697-03150-0) Wm C Brown Pubs.

***McMurtry.** Beware the Snake's Venom. (Choose Your Own Nightmare Ser.: No. 2). (J). 1995. pap. 3.50 (0-553-48230-0) Bantam.

— Buffalo Girls. 1995. pap. 6.99 (0-671-53615-X) Silhouette.

— Harmony. 1994. 22.00 (0-671-79283-0) S&S Trade.

— Streets of Loredo. 1995. pap. 7.99 (0-671-53746-6) PB.

McMurtry, John M. The Structure of Marx's World-View. LC 77-85552. 283p. reprint ed. pap. 80.70 (0-8357-4047-1, 2036737) Bks Demand.

McMurtry, Ken. A History Mystery: The Mystery of the Roswell UFO. 96p. (Orig.). (J). 1992. pap. 3.50 (0-380-76843-7, Camelot) Avon.

— Survival! in the Mountains. 112p. (Orig.). (J). 1993. pap. 3.50 (0-380-76602-7, Camelot) Avon.

McMurtry, Larry. All My Friends Are Going to Be Strangers. 1989. pap. 7.95 (0-671-68103-6, Touchstone Bks) S&S Trade.

— All My Friends Are Going to Be Strangers. Grose, Bill, ed. 288p. 1992. reprint ed. pap. 6.50 (0-671-75871-3) PB.

— Anything for Billy. Grose, Bill, ed. 416p. 1991. mass mkt. 5.99 (0-671-74605-7) PB.

— Buffalo Girls. 1990. 19.95 (0-685-38917-0) S&S Trade.

— Buffalo Girls. large type ed. (General Ser.). 436p. 1991. text ed. 14.95 (0-8161-5242-X, Large Print Bks) Hall.

Mcmurtry, Larry. Cadillac Jack. Grose, Bill, ed. 1990. pap. 6.50 (0-671-73902-6) PB.

McMurtry, Larry. Cadillac Jack. 1987. pap. 10.00 (0-671-63720-7, Fireside Bks) S&S Trade.

— Dead Man's Walk: A Novel. 1995. 26.00 (0-684-80753-X) S&S Trade.

— The Desert Rose. Grose, Bill, ed. 288p. 1990. mass mkt. 4.95 (0-671-72763-X) PB.

— Desert Rose. 1976. 20.95 (0-8488-0371-X) Amereon Ltd.

Mcmurtry, Larry. Desert Rose. 1987. pap. 7.95 (0-671-63721-5, Fireside) S&S Trade.

***McMurtry, Larry.** Evening Star. 1992. 6.99 (0-517-11176-4) Random Hse Value.

— The Evening Star. Rubenstein, ed. 624p. 1993. reprint ed. mass mkt. 5.99 (0-671-79904-5, Pocket Star Bks) PB.

— The Evening Star: A Novel. large type ed. LC 92-41444. (General Ser.). 765p. 1993. 24.95 (0-8161-5648-4, Large Print Bks) Hall.

— The Evening Star: A Novel. large type ed. LC 92-41444. (General Ser.). 765p. 1993. pap. 17.95 (0-8161-5649-2, Large Print Bks) Hall.

— Film Flam: Essays on Hollywood. 1988. pap. 6.95 (0-671-63322-8, Touchstone Bks) S&S Trade.

— Horseman, Pass By. 1976. 18.95 (0-8488-0372-8) Amereon Ltd.

— Horseman, Pass By. 192p. 1992. pap. 9.00 (0-671-75499-8, Touchstone Bks) S&S Trade.

— Horseman, Pass By. Grose, Bill, ed. 256p. 1992. reprint ed. mass mkt. 5.50 (0-671-75384-3) PB.

— In a Narrow Grave: Essays on Texas. 1989. pap. 7.95 (0-671-68102-8, Touchstone Bks) S&S Trade.

— Irving Paul Lazar: 1907-1993. 14p. (C). 1994. pap. 20.00x (0-614-01629-0) Flood Plain.

— Irving Paul Lazar: 1907-1993. deluxe limited ed. 14p. (C). 1994. 1,000.00 (0-614-01630-4) Flood Plain.

— The Last Picture Show. 1976. 20.95 (0-89190-889-7, Am Repr) Amereon Ltd.

— The Last Picture Show. Grose, Bill, ed. 1992. pap. 6.50 (0-671-75381-9) PB.

— The Last Picture Show. 224p. 1992. pap. 10.00 (0-671-75487-4, Touchstone Bks) S&S Trade.

— The Late Child: A Novel. LC 95-2419. 461p. 1995. 25.00 (0-684-80998-2) S&S Trade.

— Leaving Cheyenne. 1976. 20.95 (0-8488-0373-6) Amereon Ltd.

— Leaving Cheyenne. 256p. 1992. pap. 11.00 (0-671-75490-4, Touchstone Bks) S&S Trade.

— Leaving Cheyenne. Grose, Bill, ed. 320p. 1992. reprint ed. mass mkt. 5.99 (0-671-75380-0) PB.

— Lonesome Dove. 1988. pap. 6.99 (0-671-68390-X) PB.

— Lonesome Dove. 1993. pap. 6.99 (0-671-74471-2) PB.

— Lonesome Dove. Grose, Bill, ed. 960p. 1995. pap. 7.99 (0-671-79589-9) PB.

— Lonesome Dove. 1985. 25.00 (0-671-50420-7) S&S Trade.

— Moving On. Grose, Bill, ed. 1991. pap. 6.99 (0-671-74408-9) PB.

— Moving On. 800p. 1987. pap. 9.95 (0-671-63320-1, Touchstone Bks) S&S Trade.

— Selected from Lonesome Dove. abr. ed. Literacy Volunteers of New York City Staff & Margolis, Seth, eds. (Writers' Voices Ser.). 64p. (Orig.). 1992. pap. text ed. 3.50 (0-929631-58-7, Signal Hill) New Readers.

— Some Can Whistle. large type ed. (General Ser.). 399p. 1990. lib. bdg. 20.95 (0-8161-4987-9, Large Print Bks) Hall.

— Some Can Whistle. Grose, William, ed. 384p. 1990. reprint ed. mass mkt. 5.99 (0-671-72213-1) PB.

— Somebody's Darling. Grose, Bill, ed. 352p. 1991. mass mkt. 5.99 (0-671-74585-9) PB.

— Somebody's Darling. 1987. pap. 8.00 (0-671-63319-8, Fireside) S&S Trade.

— Streets of Laredo. 1994. pap. 6.99 (0-671-79282-2) PB.

— Streets of Laredo: A Novel. 864p. 1993. pap. 25.00 (0-671-79281-4) S&S Trade.

— Streets of Laredo: A Novel. large type ed. LC 93-47082. 1994. pap. 18.95 (0-8161-5956-4, Large Print Bks) Hall.

— Terms of Endearment. Grose, Bill, ed. 1992. pap. 6.50 (0-671-75872-1) PB.

— Terms of Endearment. 1989. pap. 8.95 (0-671-68208-3, Touchstone Bks) S&S Trade.

— Texasville. Grose, Bill, ed. 576p. 1990. pap. 6.99 (0-671-73517-9) PB.

McMurtry, Larry & Ossana, Diana. Pretty Boy Floyd. 1994. 24.00 (0-671-89165-0) S&S Trade.

McMurtry, Newell, jt. auth. see Magnani, David.

McMurtry, R. Gerald, jt. auth. see Harkness, David J.

McMurtry, R. Gerald, jt. auth. see Neely, Mark E., Jr.

McMurtry, Richard K. John McMurtry & the American Indian: A Frontiersman in the Struggle for the Ohio Valley. LC 80-7469. (Illus.). (Orig.). 1980. pap. 14.95 (0-936012-05-6) Current Issues.

McMurtry, Ruth, jt. auth. see Cohen, Uriel.

McMylor, Peter. Alasdair MacIntyre: Critic of Modernity. LC 93-3490. 1993. write for info. (0-415-04426-X); pap. write for info. (0-415-04427-8) Routledge.

McMylor, Peter, jt. ed. see Halfpenny, Peter.

McNab, Alan A. Manual of Orbital & Lacrimal Surgery. LC 93-36802. (Illus.). 1994. 63.00 (0-443-04791-X) Churchill.

McNab, Alexander. The Tennis Doctor. LC 92-56835. 1993. 19.95 (0-679-41993-4, Villard Bks) Random.

McNab, Alexander, jt. auth. see Ashe, Arthur.

Mcnab, Andy. Bravo Two Zero: The Harrowing True Story of a Special Forces Patrol Behind the Lines in Iraq. 1994. mass mkt. 5.99 (0-440-21880-2) Dell.

McNab, Beulah. Perceptions of Phobia & Phobics: The Quest for Control. (Illus.). 253p. 1993. text ed. 95.00 (0-12-485960-7) Acad Pr.

McNab, Claire. Body Guard: Sixth Carol Ashton Mystery. 224p. 1994. pap. 10.95 (1-56280-073-6) Naiad Pr.

— Cop Out. (Orig.). 1991. pap. 9.95 (0-941483-84-3) Naiad Pr.

— Dead Certain. (Carol Ashton Mystery Ser.: No. 5). 224p. 1992. pap. 9.95 (1-56280-027-2) Naiad Pr.

— Death Down Under. 240p. 1990. pap. 9.95 (0-941483-39-8) Naiad Pr.

— Double Bluff: A Carol Ashton Mystery. 192p. 1995. pap. 10.95 (1-56280-096-5) Naiad Pr.

— Fatal Reunion. 216p. 1989. pap. 8.95 (0-941483-40-1) Naiad Pr.

— Lessons in Murder. (Carol Ashton Mystery Ser.). 216p. 1988. pap. 9.95 (0-941483-14-2) Naiad Pr.

— The Silent Heart. 192p. 1993. pap. 9.95 (1-56280-036-1) Naiad Pr.

— Under the Southern Cross. 224p. 1992. pap. 9.95 (1-56280-011-6) Naiad Pr.

McNab, Gregory, tr. see De Melo, Dias.

McNab, J. Strathearn, tr. see Frey, Arthur.

***McNab, Nan.** Victoria's Market. (J). (ps-3). 1994. 14.95 (1-86373-235-7); pap. 6.95 (1-86373-383-3) IPG Chicago.

McNab, Nora S. The Beckoning: A Story of Love. 261p. 1990. pap. 11.95 (0-942323-09-2) N Amer Heritage Pr.

McNab, Rosi. Teach Yourself German, Beginner's. (Teach Yourself Ser.). 1992. 13.95 (0-8288-8340-8); 33.95 (0-8288-8341-6) Fr & Eur.

McNab, Tom. Flanagan's Run. large type ed. 704p. 1983. 23.95 (0-7089-8142-9, Trail West Pubs) Ulverscroft.

— Rings of Sand. large type ed. 432p. 1985. 23.95 (0-7089-8247-6, Trail West Pubs) Ulverscroft.

McNabb, Bill & Mabry, Steve. Teaching the Bible Creatively to Young People. 192p. 1990. pap. 9.99 (0-310-52921-2) Zondervan.

McNabb, F. M. Thyroid Hormones. 356p. 1992. text ed. 84.00 (0-13-921123-3) P-H.

McNabb, J. W., jt. auth. see Muvdi, B. B.

McNabb, Robert & McKenna, Chris. Inflation in Modern Economies. LC 90-37552. 156p. 1990. text ed. 49.95 (0-312-05219-7) St Martin.

McNabb, Robert & Whitfield, Keith, eds. The Market for Training: International Perspectives on Theory, Methodology & Policy. 406p. 1994. 76.95 (1-85628-599-5, Pub. by Avebury Pub UK) Ashgate Pub Co.

McNabb, Vincent J. Francis Thompson & Other Essays. LC 68-22117. (Essay Index Reprint Ser.). 1977. 17.95 (0-8369-0659-4) Ayer.

McNabb, William R. Tradition, Innovation, & Romantic Images: The Architecture of Historic Knoxville. 80p. 1991. 39.95 (1-880174-00-6) U TN F H McClung.

McNabney, Raymond. War Notes: From the Letters of Sgt. Raymond McNabney. Whitworth, E. Andra, ed. LC 94-71567. (Illus.). 224p. (Orig.). 1994. pap. 12.95 (0-9640706-0-X) Cock-a-Hoop.

McNack, Eddie C. A Study Guide for General Biology I. 156p. (C). 1989. pap. text ed. 15.95x (0-89641-179-6) American Pr.

McNail, Stanley. Something Breathing. LC 87-82454. (Illus.). 58p. (Orig.). reprint ed. pap. 6.00 (0-940945-01-0) Embassy Hall Edns.

McNail, Stanley, ed. Sorcerer's Samplecase: Selected Poems in a Jugular Vein. (Illus.). 26p. (Orig.). (YA). (gr. 7 up). 1986. pap. 3.00 (0-940945-00-2) Embassy Hall Edns.

McNair, Amy, tr. see Yu Fei-an.

McNair, Arnold D., jt. auth. see Buckland, W. W.

McNair, Brian. Glasnost, Perestroika & the Soviet Media. (Communication & Society Ser.). (Illus.). 224p. 1991. 49.95 (0-415-03551-1, A5678) Routledge.

— Images of the Enemy. 288p. 1988. text ed. 37.50 (0-415-00645-7); pap. text ed. 13.95 (0-415-00646-5) Routledge.

— An Introduction to Political Communication. LC 94-48753. (Communication & Society Ser.). 1995. text ed. write for info. (0-415-10853-5); pap. write for info. (0-415-10854-3) Routledge.

— News & Journalism in the UK: A Textbook. LC 93-12718. (Communication & Society Ser.). (C). 1993. write for info. (0-415-06022-2); pap. write for info. (0-415-06023-0) Routledge.

McNair, C. J. & Leibfried, Kathleen H. Benchmarking: A Tool for Continuous Improvement. LC 93-61001. 344p. (C). 1993. pap. 18.00 (0-939246-53-8) Oliver Wight.

McNair, Carol J. Benchmarking: Adding Distinctive Value to Every Aspect of Your Business. 1992. 29.00 (0-88730-548-2) Harper Busn.

— The Profit Potential: Taking High Performance to the Bottom Line. 224p. (C). 1994. 75.00x (0-939246-66-X) Oliver Wight.

— World-Class Accounting & Finance. (APICS Ser.). 372p. 1993. 45.00 (1-55623-550-X) Irwin Prof Pubng.

McNair, Carol J. & Mosconi, William. Beyond the Bottom Line: Measuring World Class Performance. (APICS Series in Production Management). 350p. 1989. text ed. 47.50 (1-55623-194-6) Irwin Prof Pubng.

McNair, Carol J., jt. auth. see Stasey, Robert.

McNair, Charles. Land O'Goshen. 288p. 1994. 20.95 (0-312-11296-3) St Martin.

McNair, Chris, ed. see McNair, George R.

McNair, Doug & McNair, Wallace Y. Black Organizations: A Directory & Community Events Planning Calendar. 96p. 1992. pap. 35.00 (0-9627600-4-8) Wstrn Images.

— Colorado Hispanic Leadership Profiles: "Who's Who among Colorado's Outstanding Leaders" 186p. 1991. 40.00 (0-9627600-1-3) Wstrn Images.

— Women Leaders of Colorado: "A Success Network of Outstanding Leaders" 78p. 1992. 60.00 (0-9627600-2-1) Wstrn Images.

***McNair, E. Clark, Jr., et al, eds.** Dredging 1994: Proceedings of the Second International Conference on Dredging & Dredged Material Placement, Walt Disney World, Lake Buena Vista, Florida, November 13-16, 1994. 1994. write for info. (0-7844-0010-5) Am Soc Civil Eng.

McNair, Frances M., jt. auth. see Causey, Denzil Y., Jr.

McNair, George R. Shrub It Up: A Guide for Pacific Northwest Landscaping. McNair, Chris, ed. (Illus.). 66p. 1986. pap. 7.96 (0-9619034-0-6) CGM Pub Co.

McNair, Georgia T. France, 1985. Fisher, Robert C., ed. (Fisher Annotated Travel Guides Ser.). 320p. 1984. 12.95 (0-8116-0071-8) NAL-Dutton.

McNair, Harold M. Cromatografia de Gases. Dominguez, Xorge A., tr. (Serie de Quimica: Monografia No. 23). 90p. (C). 1981. pap. 3.50 (0-8270-1360-4) OAS.

McNair, J. B. McNair, McNear & McNeir Genealogies: Second Supplement. (Illus.). 457p. 1991. reprint ed. lib. bdg. 81.00 (0-8328-1717-1); reprint ed. pap. 71.00 (0-8328-1718-X) Higginson Bk Co.

— McNair, McNear & McNeir Genealogies: Third Supplement. (Illus.). 314p. 1991. reprint ed. lib. bdg. 56.50 (0-8328-1719-8); reprint ed. pap. 46.50 (0-8328-1720-1) Higginson Bk Co.

McNair, James. Breakfast. LC 87-11561. 96p. 1987. pap. 14.95 (0-87795-928-5) Morrow.

— Chicken. LC 86-29880. (Illus.). 96p. 1987. 19.95 (0-87701-439-6); pap. 11.95 (0-87701-411-6) Chronicle Bks.

— Cold Pasta. LC 85-363. (Illus.). 96p. 1985. pap. 11.95 (0-87701-353-5) Chronicle Bks.

— James McNair Cooks Southeast Asian. LC 95-12942. (Illus.). 1995. write for info. (0-8118-0483-6); pap. write for info. (0-8118-0453-4) Chronicle Bks.

— James McNair's Beef Cookbook. (Illus.). 96p. 1989. 19.95 (0-87701-591-0); pap. 11.95 (0-87701-583-X) Chronicle Bks.

— James McNair's Cheese Cookbook. (Illus.). 96p. 1989. 19.95 (0-87701-705-0); pap. 11.95 (0-87701-653-4) Chronicle Bks.

— James McNair's Cold Cuisine. LC 88-2578. (Illus.). 1988. pap. 11.95 (0-87701-487-6) Chronicle Bks.

— James McNair's Corn Cookbook. LC 90-1776. (Illus.). 96p. 1990. 19.95 (0-87701-645-3); pap. 11.95 (0-87701-638-0) Chronicle Bks.

— James McNair's Custards, Mousses & Puddings. 19.95 (0-87701-823-5); pap. 11.95 (0-87701-829-4) Chronicle Bks.

— James McNair's Custards, Mousses & Puddings. (Illus.). 96p. 1992. 19.95 (0-8118-0098-9); pap. 11.95 (0-8118-0093-8) Chronicle Bks.

— James McNair's Fish Cookbook. (Illus.). 96p. (Orig.). 1991. 19.95 (0-8118-0002-4) Chronicle Bks.

— James McNair's Fish Cookbook. (Illus.). 96p. (Orig.). 1991. pap. 11.95 (0-87701-821-9) Chronicle Bks.

— James McNair's Grill Cookbook. (Illus.). 96p. 1990. 19.95 (0-87701-719-0); pap. 11.95 (0-87701-710-7) Chronicle Bks.

— James McNair's Pie Cookbook. LC 89-34354. (Illus.). 96p. 1989. 19.95 (0-87701-600-3); pap. 11.95 (0-87701-595-3) Chronicle Bks.

— James McNair's Potato Cookbook. LC 89-17380. (Illus.). 96p. 1989. 19.95 (0-87701-650-X); pap. 11.95 (0-87701-640-2) Chronicle Bks.

— James McNair's Rice Cookbook. (Illus.). 96p. 1988. 19.95 (0-87701-525-2); pap. 11.95 (0-87701-519-8) Chronicle Bks.

— James McNair's Salads. (Illus.). 96p. (Orig.). 1991. 19.95 (0-87701-825-1); pap. 11.95 (0-87701-819-7) Chronicle Bks.

— James McNair's Salmon Cookbook. LC 87-17382. (Illus.). 96p. 1987. 19.95 (0-87701-478-7); pap. 11.95 (0-87701-453-1) Chronicle Bks.

— James McNair's Soups. LC 90-2222. (Illus.). 96p. 1990. 19.95 (0-87701-761-1); pap. 11.95 (0-87701-753-0) Chronicle Bks.

— James McNair's Squash Cookbook. LC 88-36600. (C). 1989. 19.95 (0-87701-586-4); pap. 11.95 (0-87701-579-1) Chronicle Bks.

— James McNair's Stews & Casseroles. (James McNair Ser.). (Illus.). 96p. 1991. 19.95 (0-8118-0081-4); pap. 11.95 (0-8118-0077-6) Chronicle Bks.

— Pizza. LC 87-17381. (Illus.). 96p. 1987. 19.95 (0-87701-481-7); pap. 11.95 (0-87701-448-5) Chronicle Bks.

McNair, James, photos. James McNair's Vegetarian Pizza. LC 92-46362. (Illus.). 1993. 19.95 (0-8118-0109-8); pap. 11.95 (0-8118-0100-4) Chronicle Bks.

McNair, James, jt. auth. see Wolf, Rex.

McNair, James, jt. auth. see Wolfe, Rex.

McNair, John D. McNear: The William McNear Family, 1770-1990. 63p. 1993. reprint ed. pap. 13.00 (0-8328-3373-8) Higginson Bk Co.

McNair, John F. & Barlow, Thomas L. Oral Tradition from the Indus. rev. ed. Dorson, Richard M., ed. LC 77-70609. (International Folklore Ser.). (Illus.). 1977. reprint ed. lib. bdg. 17.95 (0-405-10108-2) Ayer.

McNair Law Firm. South Carolina Environmental Law Handbook. 224p. (Orig.). 1992. pap. text ed. 69.00 (0-86587-294-5) Gov Insts.

McNair, Mattie, jt. auth. see Landry, Paul.

McNair, Peter L. The Legacy. (Illus.). 194p. (Orig.). 1984. pap. 26.95 (0-295-96166-X) U of Wash Pr.

McNair, Raymond F. Ascent to Greatness: The Incredible Story of America's Rise to World Super-Power. LC 75-27253. (Illus.). 550p. 1976. 14.95 (0-685-68396-6) Triumph Pub.

McNair, S. New Hampshire. LC 91-540. (America the Beautiful Ser.). 144p. (J). (gr. 4 up). 1991. lib. bdg. 20.55 (0-516-00475-1) Childrens.

McNair, Sylvia. Alabama. LC 88-11744. (America the Beautiful Ser.). (Illus.). 144p. (J). (gr. 4 up). 1988. lib. bdg. 20.55 (0-516-00447-6) Childrens.

— Alabama. braille ed. 178p. (J). 1993. vinyl bd. 15.40 (1-56956-159-1, BR9022) W A T Braille.

— Hawaii. LC 89-35084. (America the Beautiful Ser.). 144p. (J). (gr. 4 up). 1989. lib. bdg. 20.55 (0-516-00457-3) Childrens.

— Hawaii. braille ed. 187p. (J). 1993. vinyl bd. 15.40 (1-56956-177-X, BR9050) W A T Braille.

— India. LC 89-25435. (Enchantment of the World Ser.). (Illus.). 128p. (J). (gr. 5-9). 1990. lib. bdg. 20.55 (0-516-02719-0) Childrens.

— Indonesia. LC 93-3401. (Enchantment of the World Ser.). (Illus.). 128p. (J). (gr. 5-9). 1993. lib. bdg. 20.55 (0-516-02618-6) Childrens.

— Kentucky. LC 87-34150. (America the Beautiful Ser.). (Illus.). 144p. (J). (gr. 4 up). 1988. lib. bdg. 20.55 (0-516-00463-8) Childrens.

— Kentucky. braille ed. 199p. (J). 1993. vinyl bd. 15.40 (1-56956-163-X, BR9015) W A T Braille.

— Korea. LC 85-23273. (Enchantment of the World Ser.). (Illus.). 127p. (J). (gr. 5-6). 1986. lib. bdg. 20.55 (0-516-02771-9) Childrens.

— New Hampshire. braille ed. 197p. (J). 1993. vinyl bd. 15.40 (1-56956-156-7, BR9009) W A T Braille.

— Tennessee. LC 89-25285. (America the Beautiful Ser.). (Illus.). 144p. (J). (gr. 4 up). 1990. lib. bdg. 20.55 (0-516-00488-3) Childrens.

— Tennessee. braille ed. 202p. (J). 1993. vinyl bd. 15.40 (1-56956-162-1, BR9016) W A T Braille.

— Thailand. LC 86-29933. (Enchantment of the World Ser.). (Illus.). 128p. (J). (gr. 5-9). 1987. lib. bdg. 20.55 (0-516-02792-1) Childrens.

— Vermont. LC 90-21117. (America the Beautiful Ser.). (Illus.). 144p. (J). (gr. 4 up). 1991. lib. bdg. 20.55 (0-516-00491-3) Childrens.

— Vermont. braille ed. 208p. (J). 1993. vinyl bd. 15.40 (1-56956-160-5, BR9014) W A T Braille.

— Virginia. LC 88-38203. (America the Beautiful Ser.). (Illus.). 144p. (J). (gr. 4 up). 1989. lib. bdg. 20.55 (0-516-00492-1) Childrens.

— Virginia. braille ed. 195p. (J). 1993. vinyl bd. 15.40 (1-56956-170-2, BR9010) W A T Braille.

McNair, Wallace Y. The African Connection: A Study of Black Behavior. 150p. (Orig.). (C). 1993. pap. text ed. write for info. (0-9627600-5-6) Wstrn Images.

— Black & Beautiful: A Self-Discovery Coloring Book. (Illus.). 26p. (Orig.). (J). (gr. 2 up). 1992. pap. 10.00 (0-9627600-3-X) Wstrn Images.

McNair, Wallace Y., jt. auth. see McNair, Doug.

McNair, Wesley. My Brother Running. 1994. 19.95 (0-87923-985-9) Godine.

— Twelve Journeys in Maine. (Illus.). 48p. 1992. 195.00 (0-913341-16-9); pap. 9.95 (0-913341-15-0) Coyote Love.

McNair, Wesley, ed. The Quotable Moose: A Contemporary Maine Reader. LC 93-38324. 269p. (C). 1994. pap. 16.95 (0-87451-673-0) U Pr of New Eng.

McNair, Will L. SCR & New Technology in Electric Rig Drilling: A Safety & Efficiency Handbook. 296p. 1991. 25.00 (0-87814-368-8, P4485) PennWell Bks.

McNair, William & Rumley, Hilary. Pioneer Aboriginal Mission. (Illus.). 162p. (Orig.). pap. 19.95 (0-85564-178-9, Pub. by Univ of West Aust Pr AT) Intl Spec Bk.

McNairn, Alan. The Young Van Dyck. (Illus.). 1980. pap. 19.95 (0-88884-468-9, 56578-5, Pub. by Natl Mus Sci Tech CN) U Ch Pr.

McNairn, Barbara. The Method & Theory of V. Gordon Childe. 184p. 1980. pap. 12.50 (0-85224-389-8, Pub. by Edinburgh U Pr UK) Col U Pr.

McNairn, Colin H. Governmental & Intergovernmental Immunity in Australia & Canada. LC 78-302669. 219p. reprint ed. pap. 62.50 (0-317-27014-1, 2023648) Bks Demand.

McNairn, Jack & MacMullen, Jerry. Ships of the Redwood Coast. (Illus.). x, 156p. 1945. 10.95 (0-8047-0386-8) Stanford U Pr.

— Ships of the Redwood Coast. 111p. reprint ed. pap. 30.00 (0-7837-2354-7, 2042570) Bks Demand.

M

An Asterisk (*) at the beginning of an entry indicates that the title is appearing in BIP for the first time.

*McNairn, Marie, ed. & intro. Death Records of Monroe County, MI Vol. 1: 1867-1878, with Index. 346p. 1994. 22.50 (0-614-03320-9) Monroe County Lib.

McNairn, Peggi & Shioleno, Cindy. Quick Tech Readable, Repeatable Stories & Activities. (Illus.). 223p. (Orig.). 1994. spiral bd. 24.00 (1-884135-08-0) Mayer-Johnson.

McNairn, William N. The Accountant's Guide to Computer-Age Accounting Manuals. (Illus.). 236p. (Orig.). 1985. student ed 34.95 (0-932621-00-7) Quotamus Pr.

— The Smart Attorney's Guide to Accounting Documents for Discovery & Evidence. (Illus.). 100p. 1987. pap. text ed. 14.95 (0-932621-02-3) Quotamus Pr.

McNair's, James. James McNair's Pasta Cookbook. (Illus.). 96p. 1990. 19.95 (0-87701-648-8); pap. 11.95 (0-87701-618-6) Chronicle Bks.

McNall, Neil A. An Agricultural History of the Genesee Valley, 1790-1860. LC 75-25260. (Illus.). 276p. 1976. reprint ed. text ed. 59.75 (0-8371-8396-0, MCGV, Greenwood Pr) Greenwood.

McNall, Sally A. Who Is in the House? A Psychological Study of Two Centuries of Women's Fiction in America, 1795 to the Present. LC 80-26601. 153p. 1981. text ed. 35.00 (0-444-99081-X, MWH/) Greenwood.

McNall, Sally A., jt. auth. see McNall, Scott G.

McNall, Scott G. Current Perspectives in Social Theory, Vol. 5. 1985. 73.25 (0-89232-511-9) Jai Pr.

— The Road to Rebellion: Class Formation & Kansas Populism 1865-1900. (Illus.). xviii, 354p. 1988. lib. bdg. 49.95 (0-226-56126-7) U Ch Pr.

— The Road to Rebellion: Class Formation & Kansas Populism 1865-1900. (Illus.). xviii, 354p. 1988. pap. text ed. 19.95 (0-226-56127-5) U Ch Pr.

McNall, Scott G., ed. Current Perspectives in Social Theory, Vol. 6. 1985. 73.25 (0-89232-531-3) Jai Pr.

McNall, Scott G. & Howe, Gary N. Current Perspectives in Social Theory, Vol. 2. 375p. 1981. 73.25 (0-89232-190-3) Jai Pr.

McNall, Scott G. & Howe, Gary N., eds. Current Perspectives in Social Theory, Vol. 1. 394p. 1980. 73.25 (0-89232-154-7) Jai Pr.

McNall, Scott G. & McNall, Sally A. Plains Families: Exploring Sociology Through Social History. 384p. 1983. teacher ed write for info. (0-318-56959-0) St Martin.

— Sociology. 624p. (C). 1991. text ed. 32.00 (0-13-497595-2, 610802) P-H.

McNall, Scott G. & Wilson, John, eds. Current Perspectives in Social Theory, Vol. 3. 295p. 1982. 73.25 (0-89232-297-7) Jai Pr.

— Current Perspectives in Social Theory, Vol. 4. 358p. 1983. 73.25 (0-89232-379-5) Jai Pr.

— Current Perspectives in Social Theory, Vol. 7. 196p. 1986. 73.25 (0-89232-713-8) Jai Pr.

McNall, Scott G., jt. ed. see Wilson, John.

McNall, Scott G., et al, eds. Bringing Class Back In: Contemporary & Historical Perspectives. 344p. (C). 1991. text ed. 64.00 (0-8133-1049-0, MCNBRIH); pap. text ed. 21.50 (0-8133-1050-4) Westview.

McNally, Andrew, jt. auth. see Cannon, Caroline C.

*McNally, Bob. Bass in Depth. (Bob McNally's Complete Bks.). (Illus.). 300p. (Orig.). 1995. pap. text ed. 16.95 (0-9646265-0-0) McNally Outdoor Prodns.

— Fishermen's Knots, Fishing Rigs, & How to Use Them. (Illus.). 304p. (Orig.). 1993. pap. text ed. 14.95 (0-937866-38-5) Atlantic Pub Co.

— Fishermen's Knots, Fishing Rigs & How to Use Them. 286p. (Orig.). 1993. pap. write for info. (0-923155-20-1) Fisherman Lib.

— Fishermen's Knots, Fishing Rigs & How to Use Them. rev. ed. (Bob McNally's Complete Bks.). (Illus.). 304p. 1995. pap. text ed. 16.95 (0-9646265-1-9) McNally Outdoor Prodns.

*McNally, Bruce J. Animals in Wild Life: Biology, Behavior & Vectorisms for Disease. 150p. 1995. 37.50 (0-7883-0638-3); pap. 34.50 (0-7883-0639-1) ABBE Pubs Assn.

McNally, Catherine, ed. see Mills, Selwyn & Weisser, Max.

McNally, Clare. Addison House. 304p. (Orig.). 1988. mass mkt. 4.50 (0-380-75587-4) Avon.

— Cries of the Children. 320p. (Orig.). 1992. pap. 4.99 (0-451-40320-7, Onyx) NAL-Dutton.

— Hear the Children Calling. 1990. pap. 4.95 (0-451-40200-6, Onyx) NAL-Dutton.

— Somebody Come & Play. 320p. 1987. pap. 4.99 (0-8125-2164-1) Tor Bks.

— Stage Fright. 256p. (Orig.). 1995. mass mkt. 5.99 (0-8125-4839-6) Tor Bks.

— There He Keeps Them Very Well. 368p. (Orig.). 1994. mass mkt. 4.99 (0-8125-3525-1) Tor Bks.

McNally, Clayton L., Jr. Micro Focus CICS Option 3.0: Developing CICS Applications on the PC. LC 93-3390. 1993. pap. 39.95 (0-89435-460-4) Wiley.

— Micro Focus CICS Option 3.0: Developing CICS Applications on the PC. 1993. pap. text ed. 44.95 (0-471-58406-1, GD4604) Wiley.

McNally, Clayton L. & Molchan, Peter. Micro Focus COBOL Workbench for the Application Developer. 1993. pap. text ed. 42.00 (0-471-58420-7) Wiley.

McNally, Clayton L., Jr. & Molchan, Peter. Micro Focus COBOL-2 Workbench for the Application Developer. (Orig.). 1992. pap. 34.95 (0-89435-437-X) Wiley.

McNally, David. Against the Market: Political Economy, Market Socialism & the Marxist Critique. 280p. 1993. 59.95 (0-86091-431-3, B2496, Pub. by Verso UK); pap. 18.95 (0-86091-606-5, B2500, Pub. by Verso UK) Routledge Chapman & Hall.

— Even Eagles Need a Push: Learning to Soar in a Changing World. 1991. 21.95 (0-385-30502-8) Delacorte.

— Even Eagles Need a Push: Learning to Soar in a Changing World. 1994. pap. 11.95 (0-440-50611-5) Dell.

— Even Eagles Need a Push: Learning to Soar in a Changing World. 170p. 1990. 19.95 (0-9626921-0-7) Trans-Form Pr.

— Political Economy & the Rise of Capitalism: A Reinterpretation. 345p. 1989. pap. 15.00 (0-520-07192-1) U CA Pr.

McNally, Dennis. Sacred Space: An Aesthetic for the Liturgical Environment. LC 85-51230. 215p. (Orig.). (C). 1990. text ed. 24.95 (1-55605-154-9); pap. 14.95 (0-932269-45-1) Wyndhall Pr.

McNally, Derek, ed. Highlights of Astronomy: As Presented at the XXth General Assembly of the IAU, 1988. (C). 1989. lib. bdg. 207.50 (0-7923-0280-X); pap. text ed. 91.50 (0-7923-0281-8) Kluwer Ac.

— Reports of Astronomy, Vol. 21A: Transactions of the International Astronomical Union. (C). 1991. lib. bdg. 164.00 (0-7923-1172-8) Kluwer Ac.

— Transactions of the International Astronomical Union, Vol. XXB: Proceedings of the Twentieth General Assembly, Baltimore, 1988. (C). 1990. lib. bdg. 253.50 (0-7923-0550-7) Kluwer Ac.

— The Vanishing Universe: Adverse Environmental Impacts on Astronomy: Proceedings of the Conference Sponsored by Unesco Held at Unesco, Paris, June 30-July 2, 1992. LC 93-41980. (Illus.). 450p. (C). 1994. 79.95 (0-521-45020-9) Cambridge U Pr.

McNally, Emily, jt. auth. see Finnegan, Dana.

McNally, Fiona. Women for Hire: A Study of the Female Office Worker. LC 79-12793. 1979. text ed. 29.95 (0-312-88735-3) St Martin.

McNally, Jeffrey A. The Adult Development of Career Army Officers. LC 91-8028. 296p. 1991. text ed. 65.00 (0-275-93698-8, C3698, Praeger Pubs) Greenwood.

McNally, Kenneth. Standing Stones & Other Monuments of Early Ireland. (Illus.). 128p. 1991. reprint ed. pap. 14.95 (0-86281-201-1, Pub. by Appletree Pr IE) Irish Bks Media.

McNally, Margaret. Hot Health-Care Careers. 1993. pap. 10.95 (0-942361-85-7) MasterMedia Ltd.

— Hot Health-Care Careers. 1993. 17.95 (0-942361-86-5) MasterMedia Ltd.

McNally, Mary E., jt. ed. see Bright, Frank V.

*McNally, Mary M. International Wheat Subsidies: Who Really Profits? rev. ed. LC 94-23662. (Foreign Economic Policy of the United States Ser.). 176p. 1995. 51.00 (0-8153-2018-3) Garland.

McNally, Michael J. Catholicism in South Florida, 1868-1968. LC 84-7389. 334p. (Orig.). 1984. pap. 19.95 (0-8130-0788-7) U Press Fla.

McNally, R. T., ed. Philosophical Works of Peter Chaadaev. 324p. (C). 1991. lib. bdg. 119.50 (0-7923-1285-6) Kluwer Ac.

McNally, Raymond, jt. auth. see Florescu, Radu.

McNally, Raymond T. & Florescu, Radu. In Search of Dracula: The History of Dracula & Vampires. LC 94-18233. (Illus.). 320p. 1994. pap. 14.95 (0-395-65783-0) HM.

McNally, Richard J. Panic Disorder: A Critical Analysis. 1994. lib. bdg. 30.00 (0-89862-263-8) Guilford Pr.

McNally, Robert. The Bible in the Early Middle Ages. (Reprints & Translations Ser.). (C). 1986. reprint ed. pap. 15.95 (0-89130-912-8, 00-07-14) Scholars Pr GA.

McNally, Robert, ed. Old Ireland. LC 65-20468. 264p. reprint ed. pap. 75.30 (0-7837-5583-X, 2045374) Bks Demand.

McNally, Ruth, jt. auth. see Wheale, P. R.

McNally, Ruth, jt. auth. see Wheale, Peter.

McNally, Stephen. Child in Amber. LC 92-33398. 80p. 1993. lib. bdg. 20.00 (0-87023-839-6); pap. 9.95 (0-87023-840-X) U of Mass Pr.

*McNally, Stephen M. Data Conversion Operator Exam 710-714 & Mark-up Clerk Automated: U. S. Postal Service - Postal Exam Study Guide. rev. ed. 120p. 1995. pap. 19.95 (0-614-04916-4) PETC.

— General Entrance Test Battery 470 & Rural Carrier Exam 460: U. S. Postal Service - Postal Exam Study Guide. 107p. 1993. pap. 19.95 (0-614-04915-6) PETC.

McNally, T. M. Low Flying Aircraft: Stories by T. M. McNally. LC 91-14100. (Flannery O'Connor Award for Short Fiction Ser.). 176p. 1991. 17.95 (0-8203-1378-5) U of Ga Pr.

— Until Your Heart Stops. 1994. mass mkt. 5.99 (0-8041-1243-6) Ivy Books.

McNally, Terrence. And Things That Go Bump in the Night. 1969. pap. 4.75 (0-8222-0046-5) Dramatists Play.

— Apple Pie: Three One Act Plays. 1968. pap. 4.75 (0-8222-0061-9) Dramatists Play.

— Bad Habits, Acting Ed. rev. ed. 1990. pap. 4.75 (0-8222-1435-0) Dramatists Play.

— Cuba Si! - Bringing It All Back Home - Last Gasps. 1970. pap. 4.75 (0-8222-0257-3) Dramatists Play.

— Frankie & Johnny in the Clair De Lune. 1988. pap. 4.75 (0-8222-0420-7) Dramatists Play.

— Hidden Agenda & Other Short Plays. 1995. pap. 4.75 (0-8222-1419-9) Dramatists Play.

— It's Only a Play. rev. ed. 1992. pap. 4.75 (0-8222-0582-3) Dramatists Play.

— Lips Together, Teeth Apart. (Illus.). 164p. (Orig.). 1991. 7.99 (1-56865-080-9, GuildAmerica) Dblday Bk Music.

— Lips Together, Teeth Apart. (Orig.). 1992. pap. 4.75 (0-8222-0670-6) Dramatists Play.

— Lips Together, Teeth Apart. 112p. (Orig.). 1992. pap. 8.95 (0-452-26807-9, Plume) NAL-Dutton.

— The Lisbon Traviata. rev. ed. 1992. pap. 4.75 (0-8222-0673-0) Dramatists Play.

— Love! Valour! Compassion! 1995. 4.75 (0-8222-1467-9) Dramatists Play.

— Love! Valour! Compassion! & a Perfect Ganesh: Two Plays. 224p. (Orig.). 1995. pap. 9.95 (0-452-27309-9, Plume) NAL-Dutton.

— A Perfect Ganesh. (Illus.). 144p. 1994. 8.99 (1-56865-075-2, GuildAmerica) Dblday Bk Music.

— A Perfect Ganesh. 1994. pap. 4.75 (0-8222-1379-6) Dramatists Play.

— Sweet Eros & Witness: Two One-Act Plays. 1969. pap. 4.75 (0-8222-1105-X) Dramatists Play.

— Terrence McNally: Fifteen Short Plays. (Plays for Actors Ser.). 256p. 1994. pap. 14.95 (1-880399-34-2) Smith & Kraus.

— Three Plays by Terrence McNally. 256p. 1990. pap. 11.00 (0-452-26425-1, Plume) NAL-Dutton.

— Where Has Tommy Flowers Gone? 1972. pap. 4.75 (0-8222-1241-2) Dramatists Play.

— Whiskey. 1973. pap. 2.75 (0-8222-1243-9) Dramatists Play.

McNally, Terry & Schiff, Peter. Contemporary Business Writing: A Problem-Solving Approach. 641p. (C). 1986. text ed. 44.95 (0-534-05784-5) Intl Thomson.

McNally, Thomas & Storey, William. Day by Day: The Notre Dame Prayerbook for Students. (Illus.). 208p. 1975. pap. 3.95 (0-87793-100-3) Ave Maria.

McNally, Thomas & Storey, William G., eds. Lord Hear Our Prayer. LC 78-67423. (Illus.). 368p. 1978. 8.95 (0-87793-163-1) Ave Maria.

McNally, Tom. The Complete Book of Fly Fishing. 2nd ed. LC 93-9152. 1993. 29.95 (0-87742-345-8, Ragged Mntn) Intl Marine.

— The Complete Book of Fly Fishing. 2nd ed. 1993. 29.95 (0-07-045672-0) McGraw.

— Mostly about Dogs. (Illus.). 254p. 1972. pap. 4.95 (0-87955-403-7) O'Hara.

*McNamara. Principles of Risk Management & Insurance. (C). 1994. student ed, text ed. 15.00 (0-673-99028-1) HarpCollege.

— Understanding Trade Unions. 1988. pap. 6.95 (0-86278-146-9, Pub. by OBrien Pr IE) Dufour.

*McNamara, et al. The Targum of Geofiti One: Leviticus: Targum Pseudo-Jonathan: Leviticus. (Aramaic Bible Ser.: No. 3). (Orig.). 1995. pap. text ed. 79.95 (0-8146-5478-9, M Glazier) Liturgical Pr.

McNamara, B., ed. Radiation in Plasmas: Proceedings of the Topical Conference on Radiation in Plasmas, Trieste, Italy, 1983, 2 vols., 1. 1000p. 1984. write for info. (9971-966-37-9) World Scientific Pub.

— Radiation in Plasmas: Proceedings of the Topical Conference on Radiation in Plasmas, Trieste, Italy, 1983, 2 vols., 2. 1000p. 1984. write for info. (0-318-57891-3) World Scientific Pub.

— Radiation in Plasmas: Proceedings of the Topical Conference on Radiation in Plasmas, Trieste, Italy, 1983, 2 vols., Set. 1000p. 1984. 159.00 (0-317-00845-5) World Scientific Pub.

— Twenty Years of Plasma Physics: Proceedings of the Workshop on Twenty Years of Plasma Physics (1964-1984), Trieste, Italy, September 1984. 376p. 1985. 70.00 (9971-978-31-8) World Scientific Pub.

McNamara, B. J., jt. auth. see Lerner, J. M.

McNamara, Barry E. The Resource Room: A Guide for Special Educators. LC 88-20086. 148p. (C). 1989. 74.50 (0-88706-983-5); pap. 24.95 (0-88706-984-3) State U NY Pr.

*McNamara, Barry E. & McNamara, Francine J. Keys to Parenting a Child with a Learning Disability. LC 95-112. (Parenting Keys Ser.). 1995. write for info. (0-8120-9033-0) Barron.

— Keys to Parenting Children with Attention Deficit Disorders. LC 92-16966. (Parenting Keys Ser.). 208p. 1993. pap. 5.95 (0-8120-1459-6) Barron.

McNamara, Bernard, jt. auth. see McNamara, Joan.

McNamara, Brooks. The Shuberts of Broadway: A History Drawn from the Collection of the Shubert Archive. (Illus.). 258p. 1990. 35.00 (0-19-506542-5) OUP.

— Step Right Up. (Illus.). 264p. 1995. reprint ed. text ed. 40.00 (0-87805-831-1); reprint ed. pap. 16.95 (0-87805-832-X) U Pr of Miss.

McNamara, Brooks, ed. American Popular Entertainments: A Collection of Jokes, Monologues & Comedy Routines. LC 83-61192. 1983. 28.50 (0-933826-36-2); pap. 12.95 (0-933826-37-0) PAJ Pubns.

— Plays from Contemporary American Theatre. 1988. pap. 6.99 (0-451-62753-9) NAL-Dutton.

— Plays from the Contemporary American Theater. 1988. pap. 4.95 (0-451-62580-3, Ment) NAL-Dutton.

McNamara, Brooks, et al, eds. The Drama Review: Thirty Years of Commentary on the Avant-Garde. LC 86-11316. (Theater & Dramatic Studies: No. 35). 372p. 1986. reprint ed. 109.80 (0-8357-1746-1, 2070469) Bks Demand.

McNamara, Brooks, intro. Plays from the Contemporary British Theater. 480p. (Orig.). 1992. pap. 6.99 (0-451-62851-9, Ment) NAL-Dutton.

McNamara, Carole & Siewert, John. Whistler: Prosaic Views, Poetic Vision. (Illus.). 230p. 1994. pap. 29.95 (0-685-72256-2) Michigan Mus.

— Whistler: Prosaic Views, Poetic Visions: Works on Paper from the University of Michigan Museum of Art. LC 93-61541. (Illus.). 208p. 1994. pap. 29.95 (0-500-27761-3) Thames Hudson.

McNamara, D. A., et al. Introduction to the Uniform Geometrical Theory of Diffraction. (Microwave Library). (Illus.). 585p. 1990. text ed. 92.00 (0-89006-301-X) Artech Hse.

McNamara, David. Classroom Pedagogy & Primary Practice. LC 93-17212. 1994. write for info. (0-415-08311-7); pap. write for info. (0-415-08312-5) Routledge.

McNamara, Dennis L. The Colonial Origins of Korean Enterprise. (Illus.). 240p. (C). 1990. 64.95 (0-521-38565-2) Cambridge U Pr.

— Textiles & Industrial Transition in Japan. LC 94-43122. 288p. 1995. 37.50x (0-8014-3100-X) Cornell U Pr.

McNamara, Dympna. Love Poems of W. B. Yeats. 77p. 1991. pap. 10.95 (0-946645-12-4, Pub. by Mercier Pr IE) Dufour.

McNamara, E. F., jt. auth. see Sheldon, D. R.

McNamara, Eileen. Breakdown: Sex, Suicide, and the Harvard Psychiatrist. 1994. 22.00 (0-671-79620-8) S&S Trade.

— Breakdown: Sex, Suicide, & the Harvard Psychiatrist. Miller, Tom, ed. 368p. 1995. pap. 6.50 (0-671-79621-6, Pocket Star Bks) PB.

McNamara, Ellen, ed. see McNamara, Tom.

McNamara, Ellen, ed. see Nuventures Consultants, Inc. Staff.

McNamara, Ernest, et al. Australia's Defence Resources: A Compendium of Data. 3rd ed. 192p. 1986. pap. 22.00 (0-08-029881-8, T110, T120, T130, K122, PPA) Elsevier.

McNamara, Eugene. Laura As Novel, Film, & Myth. LC 92-6560. 120p. 1992. 59.95 (0-7734-9506-1) E Mellen.

McNamara, Francine J., jt. auth. see McNamara, Barry E.

McNamara, Francis J. U. S. Counterintelligence Today. Nathan Hale Institute Staff, ed. 88p. (Orig.). 1985. 9.95 (0-935067-06-X) Nathan Hale Inst.

McNamara, Francis T. France in Black Africa. LC 89-12996. (Illus.). 315p. 1990. per. 8.00 (0-16-001715-7, S/N 008-020-01167-3) USGPO.

McNamara, George. George & the Pitching Machine. (Illus.). (J). (gr. k-4). 1994. pap. 4.99 (0-9625632-6-9) NUVENTURES Pub.

— George & the Tricky Fish. (Illus.). (J). (ps-4). 1995. pap. 4.99 (0-9625632-8-5) NUVENTURES Pub.

McNamara, Helen, et al. Individual Progression. LC 74-88052. (C). 1970. pap. write for info. (0-672-60633-X, Bobbs) Macmillan.

McNamara, J. A., ed. Control Mechanisms in Craniofacial Growth. (Craniofacial Growth Ser.: Vol. 3). (Illus.). 131p. 1975. 29.00 (0-929921-02-X) UM CHGD.

— Nasorespiratory Function & Craniofacial Growth. (Craniofacial Growth Ser.: Vol. 9). (Illus.). 332p. 1985. reprint ed. 49.00 (0-929921-06-2) UM CHGD.

McNamara, J. A., jt. ed. see Carlson, D. S.

McNamara, J. A., et al, eds. The Effect of Surgical Intervention on Craniofacial Growth. (Craniofacial Growth Ser.: Vol. 12). (Illus.). 382p. 1982. 48.00 (0-929921-09-7) UM CHGD.

McNamara, J. Regis, ed. Critical Issues, Developments & Trends in Professional Psychology, Vol. 2. LC 81-15863. 320p. 1984. text ed. 59.95 (0-275-91227-2, C12272, Praeger Pubs) Greenwood.

McNamara, J. Regis & Appel, Margaret A., eds. Critical Issues, Developments & Trends in Professional Psychology, Vol. 3. LC 81-15863. 262p. 1986. text ed. 55.00 (0-275-92250-2, C22503, Praeger Pubs) Greenwood.

McNamara, J. Regis, jt. auth. see Grossman, Kandee S.

McNamara, James. In the Presence of the Wise & Gentle Christ. LC 92-36141. 168p. 1993. pap. 9.95 (0-8091-3375-X) Paulist Pr.

McNamara, James, tr. see Fraenkel, R.

McNamara, James A. Neuromuscular & Skeletal Adaptations to Altered Orofacial Function. (Craniofacial Growth Monograph Ser.: Vol. 1). (Illus.). 194p. reprint ed. pap. 55.30 (0-318-39696-3, 2052264) Bks Demand.

McNamara, James A., ed. Esthetics & the Treatment of Facial Form. (Craniofacial Growth Ser.: Vol. 28). (Illus.). 216p. 1993. 55.00 (0-929921-24-0) UM CHGD.

McNamara, James A., Jr. & Ribbens, Katherine A., eds. Malocclusion & the Periodontium. (Craniofacial Growth Monograph Ser.: No. 15). (Illus.). 280p. reprint ed. pap. 79.80 (0-8357-8667-6, 2052310) Bks Demand.

McNamara, James A., Jr., ed. see Symposium on Craniofacial Growth (2nd: 1975: University of Michigan) Staff.

McNamara, James A., Jr., ed. see Symposium on Craniofacial Growth (3rd: 1976: University of Michigan) Staff.

McNamara, James A., Jr., ed. see Symposium on Craniofacial Growth Staff.

McNamara, James A., jt. ed. see Trotman, Carroll-Ann.

McNamara, James A., Jr., et al, eds. Clinical Alteration of the Growing Face: Proceedings of a Sponsored Symposium Honoring Professor Robert E. Moyers, Held February 26 & 27, 1982, in Ann Arbor, MI. LC 83-147016. (Craniofacial Growth Monograph Ser.: No. 14). (Illus.). 339p. reprint ed. pap. 96.70 (0-8357-7561-5, 2052325) Bks Demand.

McNamara, James F. Surveys & Experiments in Education Research. LC 94-60492. 220p. 1994. pap. text ed. 29.00 (1-56676-167-0) Technomic.

McNamara, James F., jt. ed. see Johnston, A. P.

McNamara, Jay. Advertising Agency Management. 225p. 1989. text ed. 35.00 (1-55623-230-6) Irwin Prof Pubng.

*McNamara, Jean. A Catalog of Types of Cleoptera in the Canadian National Collection of Insects Supplement No. III. 65p. (Orig.). 1993. pap. 32.45x (0-660-57939-1, Pub. by Canada Commun Grp CN) Accents Pubns.

*McNamara, Jill W. My Mom Is Dying: A Child's Diary. LC 94-78745. (J). (gr. 4-7). 1994. pap. 4.99 (0-8066-2697-6, Augsburg) Augsburg Fortress.

McNamara, Jo A., et al, eds. Sainted Women of the Dark Ages. LC 91-24544. 357p. 1992. lib. bdg. 45.00 (0-8223-1200-X); pap. text ed. 18.95 (0-8223-1216-6) Duke.

McNamara, Jo Ann. A New Song: Celibate Women in the First Three Christian Centuries. LC 83-10852. (Women & History Ser.: Nos. 6 & 7). 154p. 1983. text ed. 39.95 (0-86656-249-4) Haworth Pr.

— A New Song: Celibate Women in the First Three Christian Centuries. LC 85-8505. (Women & History Ser.: Nos. 6 & 7). 154p. 1985. reprint ed. pap. 11.95 (0-918393-17-5) Harrington Pk.

An Asterisk (*) at the beginning of an entry indicates that the title is appearing in BIP for the first time.

McNamara, Jo Ann, tr. see Riche, Pierre.

McNamara, Joan & McNamara, Bernard. Adoptions & the Sexually Abused Child. 1990. write for info. (*0-939561-06-9*) Univ South ME.

McNamara, JoAnn. Gilles Aycelin: The Servant of Two Masters. LC 73-6575. 232p. reprint ed. pap. 66.20 (*0-8357-3984-8*, 2036682) Bks Demand.

McNamara, JoAnn K., jt. ed. see Harris, Barbara J.

***McNamara, John.** Agency. 211p. 1995. 22.00 (*0-9646347-0-8*) Possiblts Pr.

— Extra: U. S. War Correspondents in Action. LC 72-10756. (Essay Index Reprint Ser.). (Illus.). 1977. reprint ed. 21.95 (*0-8369-7229-5*) Ayer.

— History in Asphalt: The Origin of Bronx Street & Place Names. 3rd ed. 1993. pap. 40.00 (*0-941980-16-2*) Bronx County.

— McNamara's Old Bronx. Ultan, Lloyd, ed. (Illus.). 254p. (Orig.). 1989. pap. 19.00 (*0-941980-25-1*) Bronx County.

— Present Tense & Personal Effects: A Pair of Comedies. 60p. 1986. pap. 4.75 (*0-8222-0910-1*) Dramatists Play.

McNamara, John E. Local Area Networks: Introduction to the Technology. 165p. (Orig.). 1985. pap. 29.00 (*0-932376-79-7*, EY-00051-DP, Digital DEC) Buttrwrth-Heinemann.

McNamara, John E., jt. auth. see Digital Press Staff.

McNamara, John N. Free Hand Figure Piping. rev. ed. (Illus.). 32p. 1983. pap. 8.00 (*0-932770-03-7*) McNamara Pubns.

— Lessons Learned. (Illus.). 32p. (Orig.). 1984. pap. 4.00 (*0-932770-05-3*) McNamara Pubns.

— Shaped & Cut-Out Cakes: The Easy Professional Way. (Illus.). 40p. (Orig.). (C). 1984. pap. 9.00 (*0-932770-04-5*) McNamara Pubns.

McNamara, John R. The Economics of Innovation in the Telecommunications Industry. LC 91-15932. 208p. 1991. text ed. 49.95 (*0-89930-558-X*, MEZ, Quorum Bks) Greenwood.

McNamara, Joseph D. The Blue Mirage. LC 90-30025. 324p. 1990. 19.95 (*0-688-09518-6*) Morrow.

McNamara, K., jt. ed. see Bradley, P. N.

McNamara, K. J., ed. Evolutionary Trends. (Illus.). 368p. (Orig.). (C). 1991. text ed. 50.00 (*0-8165-1233-7*); pap. text ed. 26.95 (*0-8165-1234-5*) U of Ariz Pr.

***McNamara, Kenneth J., ed.** Evolutionary Change & Heterochrony. LC 95-6588. 1995. write for info. (*0-471-95837-9*) Wiley.

McNamara, Kevin. Law & Morality. 1989. pap. 15.00 (*0-86217-290-X*, Pub. by Veritas IE) St Mut.

— Penance. 1989. pap. 15.00 (*0-86217-216-0*, Pub. by Veritas IE) St Mut.

— Pluralism: Unravelling a Riddle of Our Time. 1989. 15.00 (*0-86217-265-9*, Pub. by Veritas IE) St Mut.

— Sacrament of Salvation. 1981. 4.95 (*0-8199-0806-1*, Frncscn Herld) Franciscan Pr.

McNamara, Leo F. The Ionosphere: Communications, Surveillance, & Direction Finding. 248p. 1991. 74.50 (*0-89464-040-2*) Krieger.

— Radio Amateurs Guide to the Ionosphere. LC 92-32988. 176p. (Orig.). (C). 1994. pap. 39.50 (*0-89464-804-7*) Krieger.

McNamara, Linda. Drinker at the Spring of Kardaki. 151p. 1993. pap. 13.95 (*0-86327-333-5*, Pub. by Wolfhound Pr IE) Dufour.

McNamara, M. Frances, ed. Ragbag of Legal Quotations. LC 92-74141. xi, 334p. reprint ed. 50.00 (*0-9630106-3-8*) Lawbk Exchange.

McNamara, Martha J. Work in Progress: Writing in English As a Second Language. LC 93-38195. 1994. pap. 18.95 (*0-8384-4822-4*) Heinle & Heinle.

McNamara, Martin. Palestinian Judaism & the New Testament. LC 82-84410. (Good News Studies: Vol. 4). 279p. 1983. pap. 12.95 (*0-8146-5274-3*) Liturgical Pr.

— Studies on Tests of Early Irish Latin Gospels (a.d. 600-1200) (C). 1990. pap. text ed. 129.50 (*0-7923-0916-2*) Kluwer Ac.

— The Targum Neofiti to Genesis. (Aramaic Bible Ser.). 256p. (Orig.). 1992. pap. text ed. 65.00 (*0-8146-5476-2*) Liturgical Pr.

McNamara, Martin, tr. & intro. Targum Neofiti One: Targum Pseudo Jonathan: Exodus. LC 94-2487. (Aramaic Bible Ser.: Vol. 2). 344p. (Orig.). 1994. pap. text ed. 79.95 (*0-8146-5477-0*, M Glazier) Liturgical Pr.

***McNamara, Martin & Clarke, Ernst.** Targum of Numbers: Neofiti 1 & Pseudo-Jonathan. (Aramaic Bible Ser.: Vol. 4). (Orig.). 1995. pap. text ed. write for info. (*0-8146-5483-5*, M Glazier) Liturgical Pr.

McNamara, Martin, jt. ed. see Herbert, Maire.

McNamara, Mary C. & Doherty, Dorothy A. Out of the Skin into the Soul: The Art of Aging. Geiger, Lura J., ed. (Illus.). 192p. (Orig.). 1993. pap. 14.95 (*0-931055-81-4*) LuraMedia.

McNamara, Mike. Crashproof Your BBC: Software Tips for BBC & Electron Programs. LC 84-17343. 67p. reprint ed. pap. 25.00 (*0-685-44426-0*, 2032662) Bks Demand.

McNamara, P., et al. Appellants' Perceptions of the Planning Appeal System. (C). 1986. 45.00 (*0-685-30257-1*, Pub. by Oxford Polytechnic UK) St Mut.

McNamara, Pat, jt. ed. see Johnson, Frederick.

McNamara, Patrick H. Conscience First, Tradition Second: A Study of Young American Catholics. (SUNY Series in Religion, Culture, & Society). 221p. (C). 1992. 59.50 (*0-7914-0813-2*); pap. 19.95 (*0-7914-0814-0*) State U NY Pr.

McNamara, Patty, et al, eds. What Research Says about Learning in Science Museums, Vol. 2. 44p. (Orig.). 1993. pap. 14.00 (*0-944040-31-4*, 68-0) AST Ctrs.

McNamara, Paul. Land Release & Development in Areas of Restraint: Restraint Policy & Development Interests. Housing in Dacorum & North Hertfordshire. (C). 1984. 29.00 (*0-685-30270-9*, Pub. by Oxford Polytechnic UK) St Mut.

— Restraint Policy in Action: Housing in Dacorum & North Hertfordshire. (C). 1984. 29.00 (*0-685-30269-5*, Pub. by Oxford Polytechnic UK) St Mut.

McNamara, Paul, jt. auth. see Elson, Martin.

McNamara, Peggy, jt. ed. see Matson, Theodore A.

McNamara, Peter L. Loneliness of the Palm. 88p. (Orig.). 1993. pap. 8.95 (*1-879934-11-6*) St Andrews NC.

McNamara, Peter L., ed. Critics on Wallace Stevens. LC 78-173694. (Readings in Literary Criticism Ser.: No. 19). 1972. 10.95 (*0-87024-232-6*) U of Miami Pr.

McNamara, Regis & Barclay, Allan G., eds. Critical Issues, Developments, & Trends in Professional Psychology, Vol. 1. LC 81-15863. 336p. 1982. text ed. 65.00 (*0-275-90860-7*, C08601, Praeger Pubs) Greenwood.

McNamara, Richard B. Constitutional Limitations on Criminal Procedure. (Federal Publications). 419p. 1982. text ed. 95.00 (*0-07-045674-7*) Shepards-McGraw.

— Criminal Practice & Procedure, Vols. 1 & 2. (New Hampshire Practice Ser.). 1050p. 1987. Set. 72.00 (*0-685-19441-8*) Equity Pubng NH.

— Criminal Practice & Procedure, 3 vols., Vols. 1, 2 & 2A. 2nd ed. (New Hampshire Practice Ser.: Vols. 1-2A). 1530p. 1994. boxed 210.00 (*0-88063-485-5*) Michie Butterworth.

— New Hampshire Personal Injury: Tort & Insurance Practice, 1988-1993. suppl. ed. 1993. ring bd. 32.00 (*0-614-03166-4*) Butterworth Legal Pubs.

— New Hampshire Personal Injury: Tort & Insurance Practice, 1988-1993, Vols. 8 & 9. (New Hampshire Practice Ser.). 950p. 1988. 130.00 (*0-88063-489-8*) Butterworth Legal Pubs.

McNamara, Rita. Fourteen Basic Roots & the Key to 100, 000 English Words. 52p. (YA). (gr. 9-12). 1991. spiral bd. 3.95 (*0-939507-18-8*, B117) Amer Classical.

— Toward Balance: Psycho-Physical Integration & Vibrational Therapy. (Illus.). 144p. 1989. pap. 8.95 (*0-87728-693-0*) Weiser.

McNamara, Robert. Second Messengers. LC 89-32935. (Wesleyan New Poets Ser.). 64p. 1990. 22.50 (*0-8195-2182-5*, Wesleyan Univ Pr); pap. 10.95 (*0-8195-1184-6*, Wesleyan Univ Pr) U Pr of New Eng.

McNamara, Robert P. The Times Square Hustler: Male Prostitution in New York City. LC 94-21689. 168p. 1994. text ed. 49.95 (*0-275-95003-4*, Praeger Pubs) Greenwood.

— The Times Square Hustler: Male Prostitution in New York City. LC 94-21689. 149p. 1994. pap. text ed. 15.95 (*0-275-95186-3*, Praeger Pubs) Greenwood.

McNamara, Robert S. The McNamara Years at the World Bank: Major Policy Addresses of Robert S. NcNamara, 1968-1981. LC 81-3743. 691p. reprint ed. pap. 180.00 (*0-7837-4266-5*, 2043958) Bks Demand.

— The Military Role of Nuclear Weapons: Perceptions & Misperceptions. (CISA Working Paper Ser.: No. 45). 41p. (Orig.). Date not set. pap. 10.00 (*0-86682-058-2*) Ctr Intl Relations.

***McNamara, Robert S. & Vandemark, Brian.** In Retrospect: The Tragedy & Lessons of Vietnam. 1995. 27.50 (*0-8129-2523-8*, Times Bks) Random.

McNamara, Roderick, et al. Inland Marine Insurance, 2 vols., Set. LC 87-82150. (Orig.). (C). 1991. pap. 26.00 (*0-89462-042-8*) IIA.

McNamara, Sylvia & Moreton, Gill. Teaching Special Needs: Strategies & Activities for Children in the Primary Classroom. 96p. 1993. pap. 25.00 (*1-85346-247-0*, Pub. by D Fulton UK) Taylor & Francis.

***McNamara, Sylvie & Moreton, Gill.** Changing Behaviour: Teaching Children with Emotional & Behavioural Difficulties in Primary & Secondary Classrooms (Resource Materials for Teachers) 96p. 1995. pap. 19. 95x (*1-85346-350-7*, Pub. by D Fulton UK) Taylor & Francis.

McNamara, T. F., jt. auth. see Quinn, T. J.

McNamara, Tom. Henry Lunt & the Ranger. 1992. pap. 5.95 (*0-9625632-2-6*) NUVENTURES Pub.

— Henry Lunt & the Ranger: A Novel of Espionage & High Adventure During the American Revolution. McNamara, Ellen, ed. (Illus.). 352p. 1991. 18.95 (*0-9625632-3-4*) NUVENTURES Pub.

— Henry Lunt & the Spymaster. 1994. pap. 10.95 (*0-9625632-5-0*) NUVENTURES Pub.

— Skull & Cross Bones. 1995. pap. 10.95 (*0-9625632-7-7*) NUVENTURES Pub.

McNamara, Walter, jt. auth. see McMenamin, Michael.

McNamara, William. The Catholic Church on the Northern Indiana Frontier, 1789-1844. LC 73-3567. (Catholic University of America. Studies in Romance Languages & Literatures: No. 12). reprint ed. 19.00 (*0-404-57762-8*) AMS Pr.

— Christian Mysticism. (Wellspring Bks.). 176p. 1988. pap. 9.95 (*0-916349-29-2*) Amity Hse Inc.

— Christian Mysticism: Psychotheology. LC 80-13139. 173p. 1981. pap. 9.50 (*0-8199-0793-6*, Frncscn Herld) Franciscan Pr.

— Christian Mysticism: The Art of the Inner Way. 176p. 1994. reprint ed. pap. text ed. 12.95 (*0-8264-0763-3*) Continuum.

— The Human Adventure. (Wellspring Bks.). 192p. 1988. pap. 9.95 (*0-916349-28-4*) Amity Hse Inc.

— The Human Adventure: The Art of Contemplative Living. 192p. 1994. reprint ed. pap. text ed. 11.95 (*0-8264-0762-5*) Continuum.

— Mystical Passion. (Wellspring Bks.). 128p. 1988. pap. 8.95 (*0-916349-27-6*) Amity Hse Inc.

— Mystical Passion: The Art of Christian Loving. 140p. 1994. reprint ed. pap. text ed. 11.95 (*0-8264-0761-7*) Continuum.

McNamee, Abigail S., jt. ed. see Sunderlin, Sylvia.

McNamee, Brendan. Man Who Lived in Sorcy Wood. 62p. 1987. pap. 7.95 (*1-85186-026-6*) Dufour.

McNamee, D. Internal Audit of Purchasing. Campbell, Lee A., ed. (Practice Set Ser.). 102p. 1992. 130.00 (*0-89413-280-6*) Inst Inter Aud.

McNamee, Dan & Graft, Janine. TAAS Master Math, Exit Level: Teacher's Handbook for Texas Assessment of Academic Skills. Mammen, Lori, ed. (Illus.). 144p. (Orig.). 1990. pap. text ed. 17.95 (*0-944459-18-8*) ECS Lrn Systs.

McNamee, Dan, jt. auth. see Graft, Janine.

McNamee, Daniel, ed. TAAS Quick Review Mathematics: Grade 9. (Illus.). 112p. 1992. pap. text ed. 14.95 (*0-944459-34-X*) ECS Lrn Systs.

McNamee, Eoin. Last of Deeds. 96p. 1990. 19.95 (*1-85186-053-3*) Dufour.

McNamee, Fantan, ed. see Steeman, T.

McNamee, Fintan, ed. see O'Doherty, E. F.

McNamee, Gillian D., jt. auth. see McLane, Joan B.

McNamee, Gregory. Gila: The Life & Death of an American River. LC 93-32938. 1994. 24.00 (*0-517-59163-4*, Orion Bks) Crown Pub Group.

McNamee, Gregory, ed. Living in Words: Interviews from the Bloomsbury Review 1981-1988. LC 88-12132. 178p. 1988. 19.95 (*0-932576-62-1*); pap. 8.95 (*0-932576-63-X*) Breitenbush Bks.

— Named in Stone & Sky: An Arizona Anthology. LC 92-24494. 196p. (Orig.). (C). 1993. lib. bdg. 29.95 (*0-8165-1278-7*); pap. 15.95 (*0-8165-1348-1*) U of Ariz Pr.

— The Sierra Club Desert Reader: A Literary Companion. LC 95-5603. 384p. (Orig.). 1995. pap. 16.00 (*0-87156-426-2*) Sierra.

McNamee, Gregory, ed. see Chavez, Thomas.

McNamee, Gregory, ed. see Viele, Catherine.

McNamee, John. Diary of a City Priest. LC 93-11924. 270p. (Orig.). 1993. pap. 14.95 (*1-55612-662-X*) Sheed & Ward MO.

***McNamee, John P. & McGovern, Robert.** Clay Vessels & Other Poems. (Orig.). 1995. pap. write for info. (*1-55612-812-6*) Sheed & Ward MO.

McNamee, Kevin P. The Chiropractic College Admissions & Curriculum Directory: 1990-91. 2nd ed. 250p. 1990. pap. 23.95 (*0-945947-01-1*) KM Enterprises.

McNamee, Kevin P., et al. The Chiropractic College Directory: 1992-93. 3rd ed. 223p. 1992. pap. 9.95 (*0-945947-02-X*) KM Enterprises.

— The Chiropractic College Directory: 1994-95. 4th ed. 224p. (YA). (gr. 10 up). 1994. pap. 9.95 (*0-685-71256-7*) KM Enterprises.

— The Chiropractic College Directory: 1994-95. 4th ed. 224p. (YA). (gr. 10 up). 1994. pap. 9.95 (*0-945947-03-8*) KM Enterprises.

McNamee, Laurence & Biffle, Kent. A Few Words. LC 88-10184. 208p. (Orig.). 1988. pap. 8.95 (*0-87833-615-X*, F602H) Taylor Pub.

McNamee, Lawrence, ed. Dissertations in English & American Literature: Theses Accepted by American, British & German Universities, 1865-1964. LC 68-27446. 1136p. reprint ed. pap. 180.00 (*0-8357-9041-X*, 2013297) Bks Demand.

McNamee, Maurice B., ed. Essays by the Masters. LC 67-28299. (Composition & Rhetoric Ser.: No. 10). 1968. pap. 2.50 (*0-672-60896-0*, CR10, Bobbs) Macmillan.

McNamee, Patrick. Management Accounting: Strategic Planning & Marketing. 416p. 1988. pap. 39.95 (*0-7506-0339-9*) Buttrwrth-Heinemann.

McNamee, Patrick B. Strategic Management: A PC Based Approach. 224p. 1993. pap. 39.95 (*0-7506-0505-7*) Buttrwrth-Heinemann.

— Tools & Techniques for Strategic Management. (Illus.). 350p. 1985. text ed. 74.00 (*0-08-031810-X*, Pergamon Pr); pap. text ed. 29.00 (*0-08-031809-6*, Pergamon Pr) Elsevier.

McNamee, Peter & Celona, John. Decision Analysis with Supertree. 320p. 1991. teacher ed (*0-89426-190-8*); 5.25 hd, pap. 57.50 (*0-89426-187-8*); disk, pap. 57.50 (*0-89426-188-6*); mac hd, pap. 57.50 (*0-89426-189-4*) Boyd & Fraser.

McNamee, Sheila & Gergen, Kenneth J. Therapy As Social Construction. (Inquiries in Social Construction Ser.). 224p. (C). 1992. 59.95 (*0-8039-8302-6*); pap. 21.95 (*0-8039-8303-4*) Sage.

McNamee, Stephen. And We're Off! LC 86-42963. 165p. 1987. 13.75 (*0-930950-01-1*); pap. 8.75 (*0-930950-02-X*) Nopoly Pr.

— The Devil's Disaster. LC 87-5576. 287p. 1987. 17.75 (*0-930950-07-0*); pap. 10.75 (*0-930950-09-7*) Nopoly Pr.

— A Gift of Faith. LC 87-15245. 171p. 1987. 12.75 (*0-930950-10-0*); pap. 8.75 (*0-930950-08-9*) Nopoly Pr.

— Ten Thousand Days Has Our Youth, Vol. 1. LC 86-42964. 328p. 1987. 17.75 (*0-930950-03-8*); pap. 10.75 (*0-930950-04-6*) Nopoly Pr.

McNamee, Thomas. The Grizzly Bear. LC 84-47640. (Illus.). 281p. 1984. 24.95 (*0-394-52998-7*) Knopf.

— The Grizzly Bear. 320p. 1990. pap. 9.95 (*0-14-012812-3*, Penguin Bks) Viking Penguin.

— Nature First: Keeping our Wild Places & Wild Creatures Wild. 54p. 1987. 12.95 (*0-911797-33-5*); pap. 5.95 (*0-911797-45-9*) R Rinehart.

McNamee, Tom. Return Yellow Wolf. 1996. 27.50 (*0-8050-3101-4*) H Holt & Co.

***McNamee, Tom & Cahan, Rich. The Towery Report on Lake County, IL. (Towery Report on New American Communities Ser.). (Illus.). 192p. (Orig.). 1994. pap. 9.50 (*1-881096-12-2*) Towery Pub.**

THE TOWERY REPORT ON LAKE COUNTY, ILLINOIS is a photojournal on the area complete with an affectionate essay of the area as well as company profiles of those organizations which have contributed to the success of the Lake County area. The Lake County volume is the first in Towery's New American Communities series. Each book is distributed as a series to individuals & organizations with a variety of interests in successful, growing areas. The series is received by Fortune 500 & Fortune 1000 companies; by corporations, individuals, & families intending to relocate; by national & international site selection committees; by real estate firms which specialize in relocation; by all participating businesses; by business schools, & college & university population, demographics, & business programs. Areas profiled in the series are designated through research conducted by Towery Publishing & Jeffrey Hallett. A chief researcher for 1982's MEGATRENDS, Hallett now heads the consulting firm PresentFutures. Research conducted for the NEW AMERICAN COMMUNITIES books identifies those communities that are places of rapid, recent growth & development. Each book in the series is prepared & presented in a way that allows for meaningful comparisons between communities. 1995 volumes in the series will include Fairfield, CT; Mesa, AZ, Bergen County, NJ; DuPage County, IL; & Northern Kentucky. To order: Towery Publishing Inc., 1-800-685-2001. ***Publisher Provided Annotation.***

McNamee, Tom, jt. auth. see Hayner, Don.

McNamee, William L., jt. auth. see Schuler, Charles A.

McNamer, Deirdre. One Sweet Quarrel: A Novel. 320p. 1994. 22.00 (*0-06-016868-4*, HarpT) HarpC.

— One Sweet Quarrel: A Novel. 288p. 1995. pap. 11.00 (*0-06-092605-8*, PL) HarpC.

— Rima in the Weeds: A Novel. LC 90-39207. 320p. 1992. reprint ed. pap. 11.00 (*0-06-092262-1*, PL) HarpC.

McNamer, Elizabeth & Smith, Virginia. Scripture from Scratch: A Basic Bible Study Program - Participant's Manual. 130p. 1991. spiral bd. 11.95 (*0-86716-146-9*) St Anthony Mess Pr.

McNamer, Elizabeth, jt. auth. see Smith, Virginia.

McNamer, Elizabeth M. The Education of Heloise: Methods, Content, & Purpose of Learning in the Twelfth Century. LC 91-40386. (Mediaeval Studies: Vol. 8). 196p. 1991. lib. bdg. 79.95 (*0-7734-9657-2*) E Mellen.

***McNamera, John & McLean, Kathleen.** Academic Success in Middle School. 94p. (C). 1994. pap. text ed. 10.00 (*1-57074-234-0*) Greyden Pr.

McNanny, Dorie, jt. auth. see McNanny, Keith.

McNanny, Dorie, ed. see McNanny, Keith & McNanny, Dorie.

***McNanny, Keith & McNanny, Dorie.** McNanny's Price Guide for Collectible Soundtrack Records. McNanny, Dorie, ed. LC 94-96474. (Illus.). 240p. (Orig.). 1995. pap. 29.95 (*0-9643539-1-1*) W Pt Recs.

McNarie, Alan D. Yeshua: The Gospel of St. Thomas. 1993. 21.00 (*0-916366-83-9*) Pushcart Pr.

McNarney, Betty J. The Glider Pilot Training Program, 1941-1943. (USAF Historical Studies: No. 1). 99p. 1943. pap. text ed. 21.95 (*0-89126-147-8*) MA-AH Pub.

McNaron, T., ed. The Sister Bond: A Feminist View of a Timeless Connection. (Athene Ser.: No. 6). (Illus.). 142p. 1985. text ed. 35.00 (*0-08-032367-7*, Pergamon Pr); pap. text ed. 14.95 (*0-08-032366-9*, Pergamon Pr) Elsevier.

McNaron, Toni. I Dwell in Possibility. 216p. 1992. 35.00 (*1-55861-049-9*); pap. 12.95 (*1-55861-050-2*) Feminist Pr.

***McNaron, Toni, et al, eds.** Lesbian Studies: Present & Future. 2nd ed. 300p. (C). 1996. text ed. write for info. (*1-55861-135-5*); pap. write for info. (*1-55861-136-3*) Feminist Pr.

McNaron, Toni A., ed. The Sister Bond: A Feminist View of a Timeless Connection. (Athene Ser.). 146p. (C). pap. text ed. 14.95 (*0-8077-6232-6*) Tchrs Coll.

McNaron, Toni A. & Morgan, Yarrow, eds. Voices in the Night: Women Speaking about Incest. LC 82-71369. 187p. (Orig.). (C). 1982. pap. 9.95 (*0-939416-02-6*) Cleis Pr.

McNaron, Toni A. & Olano, Pamela J. Multicultural Nests: Finding a Writing Voice about Literature by Women of Color. Bridwell-Bowles, Lillian & Batchelder, Susan, eds. (Technical Report Ser.: No. 4). 28p. (Orig.). 1993. pap. 3.00 (*1-881221-08-3*) U Minn Ctr Interdis.

***McNary, Kyle.** Ted "Double Duty" Radcliffe: 36 Years of Pitching & Catching in Baseball's Negro Leagues. (Illus.). 288p. (Orig.). (C). 1994. pap. 14.95 (*0-9642002-0-1*) K McNary.

M

McNaspy, C. J. Conquistador Without Sword: The Life of Roque Gonzalez S.J. 1984. 12.95 (*0-8294-0455-4*) Loyola Univ Pr.

— A Guide to Christian Europe. (Request Reprint Ser.). 255p. 1984. 9.95 (*0-8294-0204-7*) Loyola Univ Pr.

McNaspy, C. J., tr. see De Montoya, Antonio R.

McNatt, Jo Ann. The Novels of Roger Vailland: The Amateur & the Professional. (American University Studies: Romance Languages & Literature: Ser. II, Vol. 48). 205p. 1986. text ed. 25.00 (*0-8204-0336-9*) P Lang Pubs.

McNaugher, Thomas L. Arms & Oil: U. S. Military Strategy & the Persian Gulf. LC 84-45850. 226p. 1985. 31.95 (*0-8157-5624-0*); pap. 12.95 (*0-8157-5623-2*) Brookings.

— The M-16 Controversies: Military Organizations & Weapons Acquisition. LC 83-24574. 220p. 1984. text ed. 55.00 (*0-275-91741-X*, C1741, Praeger Pubs) Greenwood.

— New Weapons, Old Politics: America's Military Procurement Muddle. 252p. 1989. 34.95 (*0-8157-5626-7*); pap. 14.95 (*0-8157-5625-9*) Brookings.

McNaught, Allan. Race & Health Policy. 160p. 1987. lib. bdg. 45.00 (*0-7099-4673-2*, Pub. by Croom Helm UK) Routledge Chapman & Hall.

McNaught, Allan, ed. Managing Community Health Services. 200p. 1990. pap. 27.50 (*0-412-31900-4*, A5043) Chapman & Hall.

McNaught, Ann B. & Callander, Robin. Nurses' Illustrated Physiology. 4th rev. ed. (Illus.). 158p. 1983. pap. text ed. 14.95 (*0-443-02703-X*) Churchill.

McNaught, Brian. Gay Issues in the Workplace. 160p. 1993. 17.95 (*0-312-09808-1*) St Martin.

— Gay Issues in the Workplace. 1994. pap. 10.95 (*0-312-11798-1*) St Martin.

Mcnaught, Brian. On Being Gay. (Stonewall Inn Editions Ser.). 1989. pap. 8.95 (*0-312-02959-4*) St Martin.

McNaught, Chriss. The Beef Lover's Guide to Weight Control & Lower Cholesterol. (Illus.). 258p. 1989. spiral bd. 15.00 (*0-943255-27-9*) Portfolio Pub.

— What's This Green Stuff, Flo? (Flo's Cooking Ser.). (Illus.). 64p. (Orig.). 1993. pap. 6.95 (*1-879894-05-X*) Laffing Cow.

McNaught, Harry. Animal Babies. LC 76-24175. (Pictureback Bks.). (Illus.). (J). (ps-1). 1977. 2.25 (*0-394-83570-0*) Random Bks Yng Read.

— Baby Animals. LC 75-36462. (Board Bks.). (Illus.). 14p. (J). (ps-1). 1976. reprint ed. bds. 3.95 (*0-394-83241-8*) Random Bks Yng Read.

— Los Camiones. (Spanish Translations Picturebacks Ser.). (Illus.). 32p. (SPA.). (J). (ps-3). 1993. 2.25 (*0-394-85220-6*) Random Bks Yng Read.

— Five Hundred Words to Grow on. LC 73-2442. (Pictureback Ser.). (Illus.). (J). (ps-1). 1973. pap. 2.50 (*0-394-82668-X*) Random Bks Yng Read.

— Muppets in My Neighborhood. LC 77-74472. (Illus.). (J). (ps-00). 1977. bds. 3.95 (*0-394-83593-X*) Random Bks Yng Read.

— The Truck Book. LC 77-79851. (Pictureback Ser.). (J). (ps-2). 1978. pap. 2.50 (*0-394-83703-7*) Random Bks Yng Read.

— Trucks. LC 75-36463. (Board Bks.). (Illus.). 14p. (J). (ps-1). 1976. reprint ed. bds. 3.95 (*0-394-83240-X*) Random Bks Yng Read.

McNaught, John J. Massachusetts Evidence: A Courtroom Evidence. LC 87-62743. 391p. 1988. ring bd. 75.00 (*0-944490-03-4*) Mass CLE.

McNaught, John J. & Flannery, J. Harold. Massachusetts Evidence: A Courtroom Reference, 1990 Supplement. LC 87-62743. 350p. 1990. ring bd. 24.50 (*0-944490-21-2*) Mass CLE.

McNaught, Judith. Almost Heaven. Marrow, Linda, ed. 528p. 1991. pap. 6.50 (*0-671-74255-8*) PB.

— Almost Heaven. large type ed. LC 91-18384. 882p. 1991. reprint ed. lib. bdg. 20.95 (*1-56054-209-8*) Thorndike Pr.

— Double Standards. Marrow, Linda, ed. 1991. pap. 6.50 (*0-671-73760-0*) PB.

— Double Standards. large type ed. (General Ser.). 306p. 1992. text ed. 20.95 (*0-8161-5261-6*) G K Hall.

— A Kingdom of Dreams. Marrow, Linda, ed. (Orig.). 1991. pap. 6.50 (*0-671-73761-9*) PB.

— Once & Always. Marrow, Linda, ed. 1990. pap. 6.50 (*0-671-73762-7*) PB.

— Once & Always. large type ed. 1993. 22.95 (*1-56895-041-1*) Wheeler Pub.

— Paradise. Marrow, Linda, ed. 720p. 1992. pap. 6.50 (*0-671-77680-0*) PB.

— Paradise. large type ed. LC 91-26432. 995p. 1992. reprint ed. lib. bdg. 20.95 (*1-56054-247-0*) Thorndike Pr.

— Paradise. large type ed. LC 91-26432. 995p. 1992. pap. 14.95 (*1-56054-955-6*) Thorndike Pr.

— Perfect. large type ed. LC 93-10503. 1993. bds. 22.95 (*1-56054-731-6*) Thorndike Pr.

— Perfect. large type ed. 1008p. 1994. pap. 14.95 (*1-56054-876-2*) Thorndike Pr.

— Perfect. Marrow, Linda, ed. 688p. 1994. reprint ed. pap. 6.50 (*0-671-79553-8*) PB.

— Something Wonderful. Marrow, Linda, ed. 432p. 1991. pap. 6.50 (*0-671-73763-5*) PB.

— Something Wonderful. 1990. reprint ed. 19.95 (*0-7278-4017-7*) Severn Hse.

— Tender Triumph. Marrow, Linda, ed. 1991. pap. 6.50 (*0-671-74256-6*) PB.

— Tender Triumph. 493p. 1991. text ed. 39.44 (*1-56956-321-7*, BR8501) W A T Braille.

— Tender Triumph. large type ed. 1993. 21.95 (*1-56895-013-6*) Wheeler Pub.

— Until You. Marrow, Linda, ed. 464p. 1995. mass mkt. 6.50 (*0-671-88060-8*, Pocket Star Bks) PB.

— Until You. large type ed. LC 94-40738. 1994. 26.95 (*1-56895-160-4*) Wheeler Pub.

— Whitney My Love. Marrow, Linda, ed. 1991. pap. 6.50 (*0-671-73764-3*) PB.

— Whitney, My Love. large type ed. LC 94-17376. 1994. 25.95 (*1-56895-107-8*) Wheeler Pub.

McNaught, Judith, et al. A Holiday of Love. Marrow, Linda & Tolley, Caroline, eds. 352p. (Orig.). 1994. mass mkt. 5.99 (*0-671-50252-2*) PB.

— A Holiday of Love. large type ed. LC 94-47588. 1995. write for info. (*0-7862-0409-5*) Thorndike Pr.

McNaught, Kenneth. Pelican History of Canada. rev. ed. 350p. 1975. mass mkt. 6.95 (*0-14-021083-0*, Penguin Bks) Viking Penguin.

— The Penguin History of Canada. 416p. 1988. pap. 8.95 (*0-14-011033-X*, Penguin Bks) Viking Penguin.

McNaught, L. W. Nuclear, Biological & Chemical Warfare. (Brassey's Battlefield Weapons Systems & Technology Ser.: Vol. 4). 60p. 1984. text ed. 35.95 (*0-08-028328-4*, Pergamon Pr); pap. text ed. 19.95 (*0-08-028329-2*, Pergamon Pr) Elsevier.

McNaught, Rosemond L., comp. Christmas Selections: For Readings & Recitations. LC 74-38601. (Granger Index Reprint Ser.). 1977. reprint ed. 15.95 (*0-8369-6333-4*) Ayer.

McNaughton. Wigmore, Vol. 8. 4th ed. 1961. 145.00 (*0-316-93978-1*) Little.

McNaughton, Colin. Captain Abdul's Pirate School. LC 93-21293. (Illus.). 40p. (J). (ps up). 1994. 16.95 (*1-56402-429-6*) Candlewick Pr.

— Here Come the Aliens! LC 94-48912. 1995. 15.95 (*1-56402-642-6*) Candlewick Pr.

— If Dinosaurs Were Cats & Dogs. rev. ed. LC 90-22870. (Illus.). 32p. (J). (ps-3). 1991. text ed. 13.95 (*0-02-765785-X*, Four Winds Pr) S&S Childrens.

— Making Friends with Frankenstein: A Book of Monstrous Poems & Pictures. LC 93-20027. (Illus.). 96p. (J). (ps up). 1994. 19.95 (*1-56402-308-7*) Candlewick Pr.

— Suddenly! LC 94-12995. (Illus.). (J). 1995. 13.95 (*0-15-200308-8*) HarBrace.

— Walk Rabbit Walk. LC 91-32608. (Illus.). 32p. (J). (ps-3). 1992. reprint ed. 13.00 (*0-688-11410-5*, Tambourine Bks) Morrow.

— Who's That Banging on the Ceiling? LC 91-58768. (Illus.). 32p. (J). (ps up). 1994. pap. 5.99 (*1-56402-384-2*) Candlewick Pr.

McNaughton, David. Moral Vision: An Introduction to Ethics. 288p. 1988. pap. text ed. 21.95x (*0-631-15945-2*) Blackwell Pubs.

— A Science Miscellany. 1991. 14.95 (*0-533-09464-X*) Vantage.

McNaughton, Deborah, jt. auth. see Avanzini, John.

McNaughton, Diana, et al. Banking Institutions in Developing Markets, 2 vols., Vol. 1: Building Strong Management & Responding to. LC 92-27893. 1992. Vol. 1, Building Strong Management & Responding to Change. 15.95 (*0-8213-2217-6*, 12217) World Bank.

— Banking Institutions in Developing Markets, 2 vols., Vol. 2: Interpreting Financial Statements. LC 92-27893. 1992. Vol. 2, Interpreting Financial Statements. 15.95 (*0-8213-2218-4*, 12218) World Bank.

McNaughton, Duncan. The Pilot. 64p. 1991. pap. 7.00 (*0-9631462-0-3*) Blue Millennium.

— Valparaiso. (Poetry Ser.: No. 2). 144p. 1995. pap. text ed. 10.00 (*0-9639321-2-8*) Listening Chamber.

McNaughton, Kenneth J., jt. ed. see Chemical Engineering Magazine Editors.

***McNaughton, Marimar & Yocum, Tom.** Insiders' Guide to North Carolina's Outer Banks. 16th ed. 1995. 14.95 (*0-912367-76-8*) Insiders Guide.

***McNaughton, Maureen.** Maureen McNaughton's Potpourri. (Illus.). 54p. 1991. pap. 8.95 (*0-941284-85-9*) J Shaw Studio.

McNaughton, Neil. Biology & Emotion. (Problems in the Behavioral Sciences Ser.). (Illus.). 175p. (C). 1989. pap. 21.95 (*0-521-31938-2*) Cambridge U Pr.

McNaughton, Patrick R. The Mande Blacksmiths: Knowledge, Power, & Art in West Africa. LC 86-46347. (Traditional Arts of Africa Ser.). (Illus.). 270p. 1988. 37.95 (*0-253-33683-X*); pap. 14.95 (*0-253-20798-3*) Ind U Pr.

McNaughton, Robert. Elementary Computability, Formal Languages, & Automata. LC 93-32105. 1993. 56.00 (*0-9623885-6-4*) ZB Pub Indus.

McNaughton, Stuart. Being Skilled. 220p. (C). 1988. lib. bdg. 59.95 (*0-416-01622-7*, A2450) Routledge Chapman & Hall.

***McNaughton-Stuart, Candace.** The Chicken & Other Stories. (Illus.). 48p. 1995. lib. bdg. 20.00 (*0-8095-4809-7*) Borgo Pr.

McNaughton, Wayne L. Business Basics: An Outline of Business Theory & Practice. (Quality Paperback Ser.: No. 317). 344p. (Orig.). 1976. pap. 13.00 (*0-8226-0317-9*) Littlefield.

McNaughton, William. Reading & Writing Chinese: A Guide to the Chinese Writing System. LC 77-77699. (Illus.). 368p. 1989. reprint ed. pap. 14.95 (*0-8048-1583-6*) C E Tuttle.

McNaughton, William, ed. Taoist Vision. LC 70-143183. (Illus.). 1971. 18.95 (*0-472-09174-3*) U of Mich Pr.

McNaughton, William, jt. auth. see Mayhew, Lenore.

McNay, Ian. Visions of Post-Compulsory Education. 176p. 1992. 85.00 (*0-335-09779-0*, Open Univ Pr); pap. 32.00 (*0-335-09778-2*, Open Univ Pr) Taylor & Francis.

McNay, Lois. Foucault: A Critical Introduction. 250p. (C). 1994. 27.95 (*0-8264-0778-1*) Continuum.

— Foucault & Feminism: Power, Gender, & the Self. LC 92-27536. 1993. reprint ed. 37.50 (*1-55553-152-0*); reprint ed. pap. 14.95 (*1-55553-153-9*) NE U Pr.

McNay, Roxi I. Close Encounters: A Journey of Spiritual Discovery & Adventure. (Illus.). 320p. (Orig.). 1991. pap. 14.95 (*0-9517206-1-9*) Roximillion Pubns.

McNeal, Alvin R., jt. ed. see Protopappas, John J.

McNeal, Barbara. Electronic Mail among University Training Centers: A Demonstration in National Network Building. 38p. 1980. 6.00 (*0-318-19194-6*, R-49) Inst Future.

McNeal, Brenda. Springboards for Writing. (gr. 8-12). 1979. pap. text ed. 15.00 (*0-87879-222-8*) Acad Therapy.

McNeal, Catherine J., ed. Analysis of Peptides & Proteins by Mass Spectrometry: Proceedings of the Fourth Texas Symposium on Mass Spectrometry. 322p. 1988. text ed. 270.00 (*0-471-92062-2*) Wiley.

— Mass Spectrometry in the Analysis of Large Molecules: Proceedings of the Texas Symposium of Mass Spectrometry. LC 86-18927. 221p. 1986. text ed. 260.00 (*0-471-91262-X*) Wiley.

McNeal, E. H., jt. auth. see Thatcher, Oliver J.

McNeal, James U. Children As Consumers: Insights & Implications. LC 86-45052. (Illus.). 240p. 1986. text ed. 35.00 (*0-669-13087-7*) Free Pr.

— Kids As Customers: A Handbook of Marketing to Children. 224p. 1992. text ed. 35.00 (*0-669-27627-8*) Free Pr.

McNeal, Kathleen, jt. auth. see Prater, Bayliss.

McNeal, Patricia. Harder Than War: Catholic Peacemaking in Twentieth-Century America. LC 91-16814. 310p. (C). 1992. text ed. 40.00 (*0-8135-1739-7*); pap. text ed. 15.00 (*0-8135-1740-0*) Rutgers U Pr.

McNeal, Patricia F. The American Catholic Peace Movement, 1928-1972. (Classic Quilt Ser.). 20p. 1978. 35.95 (*0-405-10840-0*, 11820) Ayer.

McNeal, R. A., ed. Nicholas Biddle in Greece: The Journals & Letters of 1806. LC 92-35459. (Illus.). 240p. 1993. 35.00 (*0-271-00914-4*) Pa St U Pr.

McNeal, R. J., jt. auth. see McElroy, J.

McNeal, Robert H. Guide to the Decisions of the Communist Party of the Soviet Union, 1917-1967. LC 75-185723. 379p. reprint ed. pap. 108.10 (*0-317-29885-2*, 2019429) Bks Demand.

— Stalin: Man & Ruler. LC 88-15525. (Illus.). 400p. 1988. 45.00x (*0-8147-5443-0*); pap. 18.50 (*0-8147-5455-4*) NYU Pr.

— Tsar & Cossack, Eighteen Fifty-Five to Nineteen Fourteen. LC 85-1942. 288p. 1987. text ed. 39.95 (*0-312-82188-3*) St Martin.

McNeal, Roxane L. Aquatic Therapy: Various Uses & Techniques. (Illus.). 134p. 1988. pap. 39.95 (*0-685-27210-9*) Aquatic Therapy.

— Aquatic Therapy; Various Uses & Techniques: Patient Manual. (Illus.). 56p. 1988. pap. text ed. 11.95 (*0-685-27211-7*) Aquatic Therapy.

McNeal, William W. The Life & Times of Our Family. 65p. 1993. ring bd., vinyl bd. 34.50 (*0-9636747-0-6*) Wrthngton Hse.

***McNealy, Roderick M.** Making Customer Satisfaction Happen. 1994. 29.95 (*0-412-58920-6*, Blackie & Son-Chapman NY) Routledge Chapman & Hall.

McNear, Robert & Glassman, Bruce. The Marathon Race Mystery. LC 84-16395. (Solve-It-Yourself Ser.). (Illus.). 128p. (J). (gr. 3-7). 1985. lib. bdg. 9.49 (*0-8167-0444-9*) Troll Assocs.

McNease, Cathy, jt. auth. see Ni, Maoshing.

McNee, Gerry. In the Footsteps of the Quiet Man. (Illus.). 168p. 1992. 24.95 (*1-85158-321-1*, Pub. by Mnstream UK); pap. 15.95 (*1-85158-490-0*, Pub. by Mnstream UK) Trafalgar.

McNeece, C. Aaron & DiNitto, Diana M. Chemical Dependency: A Systems Approach. LC 93-31569. 1993. text ed. write for info. (*0-13-859299-3*) P-H.

McNeece, C. Aaron, jt. auth. see Dinitto, Diana M.

McNeel, R. W. Beating the Stock Market. LC 63-22594. 1963. reprint ed. 12.00 (*0-87034-008-5*) Fraser Pub Co.

McNeel, Timothy G., see Tyrone Throb, pseud..

***McNeely.** Animus Aeternus. 1995. pap. 18.00 (*0-919123-50-3*) Atrium Pubs.

— Touching. 1995. pap. 15.00 (*0-919123-29-5*) Atrium Pubs.

***McNeely, Connie L.** Constructing the Nation-State: International Organization & Prescriptive Action. LC 95-5270. (Contributions in Sociology Ser.: Vol. 113). 1995. text ed. write for info. (*0-313-29398-8*, Greenwood Pr) Greenwood.

***McNeely, Del.** Women & the Trickster. 160p. 1996. pap. 17.00 (*0-88214-366-2*) Spring Jrnl.

— Women & the Trickster. (Dunquin Ser.). 120p. 1996. pap. 17.00 (*0-88214-224-0*) Spring Pubns.

McNeely, Jeffery, ed. Protecting Nature: Regional Reviews of Protected Areas. 376p. (C). 1994. pap. text ed. 50.00 (*2-8317-0119-8*, Pub. by IUCN SZ) Island Pr.

McNeely, Jeffrey A. Economics & Biological Diversity: Developing & Using Economic Incentives to Conserve Biological Resources. 256p. 1988. pap. 20.00 (*2-88032-964-7*, Pub. by IUCN SZ) Island Pr.

McNeely, Jeffrey A., ed. Expanding Partnerships in Conservation. 368p. (C). 1995. pap. text ed. 34.95 (*1-55963-351-4*) Island Pr.

— Parks for Life: Report of the Fourth World Congress on National Parks & Protected Areas, Caracas, Venzuela, 10-21 February 1992. 260p. (C). 1993. pap. text ed. 20.00 (*2-8317-0162-7*, Pub. by IUCN SZ) Island Pr.

McNeely, Jeffrey A. & Miller, Kenton R., eds. National Parks, Conservation, & Development: The Role of Protected Areas in Sustaining Society. LC 84-600007. (Illus.). 848p. 1984. pap. 29.95 (*0-87474-663-9*, MCNPP) Smithsonian.

***McNeely, Jeffrey A. & Sochaczewski, Paul S.** Soul of the Tiger: Searching for Nature's Answers in Southeast Asia. LC 94-45557. (Illus.). 432p. 1995. pap. 18.95 (*0-8248-1669-2*, Kolowalu Bk) UH Pr.

McNeely, Jeffrey A., jt. auth. see Munasinghe, Mohan.

McNeely, Jeffrey A., et al. Conserving the World's Biological Diversity. 193p. (Orig.). 1989. pap. 25.00 (*0-915825-42-2*, Pub. by IUCN SZ) Island Pr.

— Conserving the World's Biological Diversity. 204p. (Orig.). 1990. 14.95 (*0-8213-1384-3*, 11384) World Bank.

McNeely, Jerry. The Staring Match. 1957. pap. 2.75 (*0-8222-1072-X*) Dramatists Play.

McNeely, Kenneth. What Do We Really Know about God? LC 86-91364. 1987. 12.00 (*0-87212-201-8*) Libra.

McNeely, L., jt. auth. see Harrison, M.

McNeely, Marian G. Symphonies, Shamrocks & Songs: Poems. Myers, M., ed. LC 91-77716. 75p. (Orig.). 1991. pap. text ed. 7.95 (*1-879183-15-3*) Bristol Banner.

McNeely, Michael D. Microcomputer Applications in the Clinical Laboratory. LC 87-967. (Illus.). 375p. 1987. pap. text ed. 36.00 (*0-89189-218-4*) Am Soc Clinical.

McNeely, Richard. Judicial Jeopardy: When Business Collides with the Courts. LC 86-7945. 288p. 1986. 19.18 (*0-201-05736-0*) Addison-Wesley.

— Primero y Segundo de Reyes: (Comentario Biblico Portavoz) Orig. Title: First & Second Kings (Everyman's Bible Commentary). 160p. (SPA.). 1993. pap. 6.99 (*0-8254-1476-8*) Kregel.

McNeely, Richard A., ed. see Dunton, Sabina M. & Fanning, Melody S.

McNeely, Richard A., ed. see Dunton, Sabina & Miller, Kathy A.

McNeer, May. America's Abraham Lincoln. LC 90-48982. (American Cavalcade Ser.). (Illus.). 128p. (J). (gr. 6-10). 1991. lib. bdg. 9.95 (*1-55905-090-X*) Marshall Cavendish.

— The California Gold Rush. LC 87-4685. (Landmark Bks.: No. 6). 160p. (J). (gr. 5-9). 1987. reprint ed. pap. 4.99 (*0-394-89177-5*) Random Bks Yng Read.

McNees, Eleanor J. Eucharistic Poetry: The Search for Presence in the Writings of John Donne, Gerard Manley Hopkins, Dylan Thomas, & Geoffrey Hill. LC 90-56215. 248p. 1992. 38.50 (*0-8387-5205-5*) Bucknell U Pr.

McNees, Pat. An American Biography: An Industrialist Remembers the Twentieth Century. LC 94-37891. (Illus.). 342p. 1995. 19.95 (*0-918535-20-4*) Farragut Pub.

Mcnees, Pat. Contemporary Latin American Short Stories. 1988. mass mkt. 4.95 (*0-449-30060-9*) Fawcett.

McNeese State University Faculty, Alumni, Students & Friends. McNeese Hospitality: A Golden Treasury of College Cooking, 1939-1989. Cookbook Committee Staff, ed. 288p. 1989. 14.95 (*0-685-28893-5*) McNeese St Univ.

McNeese, Tim. America's Early Canals. LC 91-41353. (Americans on the Move Ser.). (Illus.). 48p. (J). (gr. 5). 1993. text ed. 11.95 (*0-89686-730-7*, Crstwood Hse) Silver Burdett Pr.

— America's First Railroads. LC 91-738. (Americans on the Move Ser.). (Illus.). 48p. (J). (gr. 5). 1993. text ed. 11.95 (*0-89686-729-3*, Crstwood Hse) Silver Burdett Pr.

— Clippers & Whaling Ships. LC 91-27187. (Americans on the Move Ser.). (Illus.). 48p. (J). (gr. 5). 1993. text ed. 11.95 (*0-89686-735-8*, Crstwood Hse) Silver Burdett Pr.

— Conestogas & Stagecoaches. LC 91-24064. (Americans on the Move Ser.). (Illus.). 48p. (J). (gr. 5). 1993. text ed. 11.95 (*0-89686-732-3*, Crstwood Hse) Silver Burdett Pr.

— Early River Travel. LC 91-42302. (Americans on the Move Ser.). (Illus.). 48p. (J). (gr. 5). 1993. text ed. 11.95 (*0-89686-733-1*, Crstwood Hse) Silver Burdett Pr.

— From Trails to Turnpikes. LC 91-41352. (Americans on the Move Ser.). (Illus.). 48p. (J). (gr. 5). 1993. text ed. 11.95 (*0-89686-731-5*, Crstwood Hse) Silver Burdett Pr.

— West by Steamboat. LC 91-22822. (Americans on the Move Ser.). (Illus.). 48p. (J). (gr. 5). 1993. text ed. 11.95 (*0-89686-728-5*, Crstwood Hse) Silver Burdett Pr.

— Western Wagon Trains. LC 91-42076. (Americans-Discover-America Ser.). (Illus.). 48p. (J). (gr. 5). 1993. text ed. 11.95 (*0-89686-734-X*, Crstwood Hse) Silver Burdett Pr.

McNeese, William & Klein, R. A. Statistical Methods for the Process Industries. (Quality & Reliability Ser.: Vol. 28). 528p. 1991. 59.75 (*0-8247-8524-X*) Dekker.

McNeil. How Things Began. (Children's World Ser.). (J). (gr. 2-5). 1975. lib. bdg. 14.96 (*0-88110-114-1*, Usborne); pap. 7.95 (*0-86020-199-6*, Usborne) EDC.

— Reading Comprehension: New Directions for Classroom Practice. (C). 1991. text ed. 26.00 (*0-673-46425-3*) HarpCollege.

McNeil, Alex. Total Television: A Comprehensive Guide to Programming from 1948 to the Present. 3rd ed. (Illus.). 1991. pap. 19.95 (*0-14-015736-0*, Penguin Bks) Viking Penguin.

McNeil, B. M. & Harvey, L. M., eds. Fermentation: A Practical Approach. (Practical Approach Ser.). (Illus.). 240p. 1990. 44.00 (*0-19-963044-5*, IRL Pr) OUP.

McNeil, Barbara. Biography & Genealogy Master Index, 1990. 1100p. 1989. 305.00 (*0-8103-4800-4*) Gale.

— Biography & Genealogy Master Index, 1992. 1991. 305.00 (*0-8103-4802-0*) Gale.

— Biography & Genealogy Master Index, 1993. 1992. 305.00 (*0-8103-7605-9*) Gale.

— Biography & Genealogy Master Index, 1994. 1993. 305.00 (*0-8103-8002-1*) Gale.

McNeil, Barbara, ed. Author Biography Master Index. 3rd ed. 409p. 1988. 250.00 (*0-8103-2770-8*) Gale.

— BGMI CD-ROM 95 IBM Single User Version. (Global Access: BGMI Ser.). 1994. 1,250.00 (*0-8103-6197-3*) Gale.

— Biography & Genealogy Master Index, 1981-85, 5 vols., Set. 4423p. 1985. 925.00 (*0-8103-1506-8*) Gale.

— Biography & Genealogy Master Index 1984. 936p. 1984. 305.00 (*0-8103-1508-4*) Gale.

— Biography & Genealogy Master Index 1985. 664p. 1985. 305.00 (*0-8103-1507-6*) Gale.

— Biography & Genealogy Master Index, 1986. 650p. 1986. 305.00 (*0-8103-1511-4*) Gale.

An Asterisk (*) at the beginning of an entry indicates that the title is appearing in BIP for the first time.

— Biography & Genealogy Master Index, 1986-1990: Cumulation of Supplements, 3 vols., Set. 3600p. 1990. 925.00 (*0-8103-4803-9*) Gale.
— Biography & Genealogy Master Index, 1987. 823p. 1986. 305.00 (*0-8103-1513-0*) Gale.
— Biography & Genealogy Master Index, 1988. 1080p. 1987. 305.00 (*0-8103-1514-9*) Gale.
— Biography & Genealogy Master Index, 1989. 1988. 305. 00 (*0-8103-2794-5*) Gale.
— Biography & Genealogy Master Index, 1991. 1200p. 1990. 305.00 (*0-8103-4801-2*) Gale.
— Business Biography Master Index. 652p. 1987. 189.00 (*0-8103-1499-1*) Gale.
— Twentieth-Century Author Biographies Master Index. 539p. 1984. 69.00 (*0-8103-2095-9*); pap. 39.00 (*0-8103-2096-7*) Gale.
McNeil, Barbara & Herbert, Miranda C., eds. Historical Biographical Dictionaries Master Index. LC 80-10719. (Biographical Index Ser.: No. 7). 1016p. 1980. 250.00 (*0-8103-1089-9*) Gale.
— Performing Arts Biography Master Index: A Consolidated Guide to over 270,000 Biographical Sketches of Persons Living & Dead, As They Appear in over 100 of the Principal Biographical Dictionaries Devoted to the Performing Arts. 2nd ed. (Biographical Index Ser.: No. 5). 728p. 1982. 175.00 (*0-8103-1097-X*) Gale.
McNeil, Barbara, jt. ed. see Herbert, Miranda C.
McNeil, Barbara J. & Abrams, Herbert L. Brigham & Women's Hospital Handbook of Diagnostic Imaging. 342p. 1985. 21.00 (*0-316-56322-6*) Little.
McNeil, Barbara J., ed. see Cravalho, Ernest G.
***McNeil, Beth & Johnson, Denise J., eds.** Patron Behavior in Libraries: A Handbook of Positive Approaches to Negative Situations. 200p. (Orig.). 1995. pap. text ed. 25.00x (*0-8389-0662-1*) ALA.
McNeil, Brian. Christ in the Psalms. 104p. (Orig.). 1980. pap. 4.95 (*0-905092-87-2*, Pub. by Veritas Publns IE) Ignatius Pr.
McNeil, Brian, tr. see Fuchs, Josef.
McNeil, Brian, tr. see Urs Von Balthasar, Hans.
McNeil, Brian, tr. see Von Balthasar, Hans U.
McNeil, Brian, ed. see Von Balthasar, Hans U.
McNeil, Brian, tr. see Von Balthasar, Hans U.
McNeil, Brian, tr. see Von Speyr, Adrienne.
McNeil, Bruce J. Nonqualified Deferred Compensation Plans. 210p. 1994. pap. text ed. write for info. (*0-314-04029-3*) West Pub.
— Pension Answer Book: Nonqualified Deferred Compensation. Persons, Mark D., ed. 277p. 1991. 89.00 (*1-878375-40-7*) Panel Pubs.
McNeil, Bruce J. & Lloyd, Michael E. Four-O-One (K) Plans: A Comprehensive Guide. LC 92-21471. (Employee Benefits - Human Resources Library). 424p. 1993. text ed. 128.00 (*0-471-58578-5*) Wiley.
McNeil, Bruce J. & Persons, Mark D. The Pension Answer Book: Non-qualfied Deferred Compensation. 169p. 1990. pap. text ed. 49.00 (*1-878375-17-2*) Panel Pubs.
McNeil, Charles, ed. see American Academy of Orofacial Pain Staff.
McNeil, Cheryl B., jt. auth. see Hembree-Kigin, Toni L.
McNeil, Christine. Kissing the Night. 64p. 1994. pap. 12.95 (*1-85224-220-5*, Pub. by Bloodaxe Bks UK) Dufour.
McNeil, Christopher B. Kansas Statute of Limitations & Time Standards. rev. ed. 1990. 125.00 (*0-942357-33-7*) KS Bar CLE.
McNeil, D. Coal Carbonization Products. LC 66-6880. 1966. 76.00 (*0-08-011446-6*, Pub. by Pergamon Repr UK) Franklin.
McNeil, D., ed. Interactive Statistics: Proceedings of the Applied Statistics Conference. 254p. 1980. 102.75 (*0-444-85412-6*, North Holland) Elsevier.
McNeil, D., jt. auth. see Lunn, A. D.
McNeil, Dani, jt. auth. see Owen, Sandy.
McNeil, Daniel. Fuzzy Logic: The Revolutionary Computer Technology That Is Changing Our World. 1994. pap. 12. 00 (*0-671-87535-3*, Touchstone Bks) S&S Trade.
McNeil, David. The Grotesque Depiction of War & the Military in Eighteenth-Century English Fiction. LC 88-50584. (Illus.). 232p. 1990. 39.50 (*0-87413-369-6*) U Delaware Pr.
McNeil, Don. Moving Through Here. 1990. pap. 9.95 (*0-8065-1165-6*, Citadel Pr) Carol Pub Group.
McNeil, Donald E., jt. ed. see Childs, William M.
McNeil, Donald R. Wiring the Ivory Tower: A Round Table on Technology in Higher Education. 36p. 1990. pap. 7.00 (*0-685-59937-X*) Acad Educ Dev.
McNeil, Donald S., ed. Jewelers' Dictionary. 3rd ed. LC 76-26012. 268p. 1979. 39.95 (*0-931744-01-6*, CR-002) Jewelers Bk Club.
— Who's Who in the Jewelry Industry. LC 79-27501. 231p. 1980. 24.95 (*0-931744-02-4*) Jewelers Bk Club.
McNeil, Edna. Poems, Quotes, Mini Stories & True Life Experiences in God Power. Moore, Denise, ed. (Orig.). 1989. pap. text ed. 24.94 (*0-9613082-3-0*, TX369163) Bootstrap.
McNeil, Elton B. Quiet Furies: Man & Disorder. 1968. pap. text ed. 20.00 (*0-13-749770-9*) P-H.
McNeil, Elton B., jt. auth. see Rubin, Zick.
***McNeil, Florence.** Breathing Each Other's Air. 176p. (Orig.). 1995. pap. 11.95 (*0-919591-87-6*, Pub. by Polestar Bk Pubs CN) Orca Bk Pubs.
McNeil, Francis & Sato, Seizaburo. The Future of U. S.-Japan Relations - A Conference Report. 32p. 1988. pap. 8.95 (*0-87609-053-6*) Coun Foreign.
McNeil, Frank. Democracy in Japan: The Emerging Global Concern. 1994. 25.00 (*0-517-59014-X*, Crown) Crown Pub Group.
McNeil, Freed H. McNeil's Mount Hood: Wyeast THE Mountain Revisited. rev. ed. (Illus.). 224p. 1990. reprint ed. pap. write for info. (*0-9614498-7-X*) Zig Zag Paper.
McNeil, Genna R. Groundwork: Charles Hamilton Houston & the Struggle for Civil Rights. LC 82-40483. (Illus.). 320p. 1983. pap. 19.95 (*0-8122-1179-0*) U of Pa Pr.
McNeil, Genna R., jt. auth. see Franklin, John H.
McNeil, Genna R., jt. ed. see Franklin, John H.
McNeil, Genna Rae & Winston, Michael, eds. Historical Judgments Reconsidered: Selected Howard University Lectures in Honor of Rayford W. Logan. 270p. 1988. 21. 95 (*0-88258-173-2*) Howard U Pr.
McNeil, George. Tales of Pocahontas County. 1958. pap. 5.00 (*0-685-61019-5*) McClain.
McNeil, Gil, ed. Soul Providers: Writings by Single Parents. 240p. 1994. pap. 13.95 (*1-85381-710-4*, Pub. by Virago Pr UK) Trafalgar.
McNeil, Heather. Hyena & the Moon: Stories to Tell from Kenya. (World Folklore Ser.). (Illus.). 158p. 1994. lib. bdg. 23.00 (*1-56308-169-5*) Libs Unl.
***McNeil, Ian & Day, Lance, eds.** Biographical Dictionary of the History of Technology. 800p. 1995. 125.00 (*0-415-06042-7*, B0378) Routledge.
McNeil, J. A. & Price, C. E. From Fundamental Fields to Nuclear Phenomena. 296p. 1991. text ed. 93.00 (*981-02-0513-9*); pap. 36.00 (*981-02-0514-7*) World Scientific Pub.
McNeil, Jame. Hsing - I. LC 91-67318. 1991. 12.95 (*0-86568-155-4*) Unique Pubns.
McNeil, Jean, tr. see Deleuze, Gilles & Von Sacher-Masoch, Leopold.
McNeil, Jesse J., Sr. The Preacher-Prophet in Mass Society. rev. ed. Jones, Amos, Jr., ed. LC 93-40626. 1994. text ed. 7.95 (*0-910683-12-3*) Townsnd-Pr.
McNeil, Jesse Jai. Minister's Service Book. 212p. 1961. 12. 99 (*0-8028-0650-3*) Eerdmans.
McNeil, Joan, jt. auth. see Corr, Charles A.
McNeil, John. The Art of Jazz Trumpet, Vol. 1. (Illus.). 64p. 1993. pap. 10.00 (*0-9628467-2-4*) Gerard Sarzin Pub.
— Curriculum: The Teacher's Initiative. LC 94-6194. 288p. (C). 1994. pap. write for info. (*0-02-379761-4*, Merrill Pub Co) Macmillan.
— Forjadores Del Cristianismo - Tomo II: Makers of Christianity - II. (SPA.). 6.95 (*84-7645-228-4*, 223316, Pub. by Edit Clie SP) TSELF.
— Spy Game. 1982. pap. 2.95 (*0-686-97470-0*) Zebra.
— Vida Llena del Espiritu: Spirit Filled Life. (SPA.). 4.95 (*84-7645-108-3*, 223162, Pub. by Edit Clie SP) TSELF.
McNeil, John, jt. auth. see Sprang, Ginny.
McNeil, John D. Curriculum: A Comprehensive Introduction. 4th ed. (C). 1990. text ed. 61.00 (*0-673-52021-8*) HarpCollege.
— Curriculum: A Comprehensive Introduction. 5th ed. LC 95-14586. 1995. write for info. (*0-673-52352-7*) HarpCollege.
— Reading Comprehension: New Directions for Classroom Practice. 2nd ed. (C). 1987. pap. text ed. 15.25 (*0-673-18406-4*) HarpCollege.
McNeil, John D. & Schave, Barbara. Issues in School Reform: A View from the Bottom-Up. LC 84-20627. (Illus.). 192p. (Orig.). 1985. pap. text ed. 29.95 (*0-911575-50-2*) Optimization Soft.
McNeil, John D. & Wiles, Jon. Essentials of Teaching: Decisions, Plans, Methods. 459p. (C). 1989. pap. write for info. (*0-02-389410-5*) Macmillan.
McNeil, John M., jt. auth. see Bennefield, Robert L.
McNeil, John S., ed. see Health-Mental Health Conference Staff.
McNeil, John S., et al. Military Retirement: Social, Economic & Mental Health Dilemmas. (Illus.). 156p. 1983. text ed. 50.00 (*0-86598-078-0*) Rowman.
McNeil, John T. On God & Political Duty: Calvin. 128p. (C). 1956. pap. write for info. (*0-02-379760-6*) Macmillan.
McNeil, Judy & McNeil, Keith. Manual of Program DPLINEAR: For Use with McNeil, Kelly, McNeil "Testing Research Hypotheses Using Multiple Linear Regression" LC 74-25176. 53p. 1975. pap. text ed. 1.95 (*0-8093-0729-4*) S Ill U Pr.
McNeil, Katherine, jt. auth. see Langworthy, J. Lamont.
McNeil, Keith & Reese, Terence. Bid Against the Masters: The Best of Bidding Forum. 128p. 1993. pap. 15.95 (*0-575-05450-6*, Pub. by V Gollancz UK) Trafalgar.
McNeil, Keith, jt. auth. see McNeil, Judy.
McNeil, Keith, et al. Testing Research Hypotheses Using Multiple Linear Regression. LC 75-6639. 600p. 1975. pap. text ed. 7.95 (*0-8093-0755-3*) S Ill U Pr.
McNeil, Kent. Common Law Aboriginal Title. (Illus.). 408p. 1989. 84.00 (*0-19-825223-4*) OUP.
McNeil, Linda M. Contradictions of Control: School Structure & School Knowledge. (Critical Social Thought Ser.). 234p. 1988. pap. text ed. 12.95 (*0-415-90075-1*, Routledge NY) Routledge.
McNeil, Lynda D. Recreating the World - Word: The Mythic Mode as Symbolic Discourse. LC 91-17324. (SUNY Series, The Margins of Literature). 326p. 1992. 59.50 (*0-7914-1007-2*); pap. 19.95 (*0-7914-1008-0*) State U NY Pr.
McNeil, M. Abby Aldrich Rockefeller Folk Art Center Address Book. (Museum Gift Bks.). (Illus.). 160p. 1984. 14.95 (*0-939456-10-9*) Galison.
McNeil, M. E. The Magic Storysinger: From the Finnish Epic Kalevala. (Illus.). 96p. (J). (gr. 4-8). 1993. 16.95 (*0-88045-128-9*) Stemmer Hse.
McNeil, M. J. Flying Models. (KnowHow Bks.). (Illus.). 32p. (J). (gr. 3-6). 1977. pap. 6.95 (*0-86020-007-8*) EDC.
McNeil, Malcolm R., et al, eds. The Dysarthrias: Physiology, Acoustics, Perception & Management. LC 83-14394. (Illus.). 272p. 1983. 36.00 (*0-316-56299-8*) Singular Publishing.
McNeil, Marcia D., jt. ed. see Filion, Roy C.
McNeil, Mark A. An Analysis of the "Oneness Pentecostal" Movement. 1993. pap. 1.95 (*1-56186-520-6*) Pilgrim Pubns.
McNeil, Mary. Earth Sciences Reference. 709p. (YA). (gr. 6 up). 1991. 55.00 (*0-938905-00-7*); pap. 49.00 (*0-938905-01-5*) Flamingo Pr.
McNeil, Mary E. Say a Fast Goodbye to Fat Forever! (Illus.). 272p. (Orig.). 1987. pap. 9.95 (*0-915451-08-5*) New Start Pubns.
McNeil, Maureen. Under the Banner of Science: Erasmus Darwin & His Age. (History of Science Ser.). 340p. 1988. text ed. 59.95 (*0-7190-1492-1*, Pub. by Manchester Univ Pr UK) St Martin.
McNeil, Maureen, ed. National Gallery Book of Days. (Museum Gift Bks.). (Illus.). 160p. (Orig.). 1982. 10.00 (*0-939456-05-2*) Galison.
— The National Gallery of Art Heritage Address Book. (Illus.). 208p. 1982. 10.95 (*0-939456-02-8*) Galison.
McNeil, Maureen, et al, eds. The New Reproductive Technologies. LC 89-10640. 384p. 1990. text ed. 45.00 (*0-312-03599-3*) St Martin.
McNeil, Mellicent. A Comparative Study of Entrance to Teacher-Training Institutions. LC 79-177042. (Columbia University. Teachers College. Contributions to Education Ser.: No. 443). reprint ed. 22.50 (*0-404-55443-1*) AMS Pr.
McNeil, Nellie, ed. see Wolfe, Thomas, et al.
McNeil, Robert A. & Valk, Barbara G., eds. Latin American Studies: A Basic Guide to Sources. 2nd ed. LC 89-34133. 470p. 1990. 42.50 (*0-8108-2236-9*) Scarecrow.
McNeil, Robert D. Valiant for Truth: Clarence True Wilson & Prohibition. LC 91-68406. (Illus.). 172p. (Orig.). 1992. pap. 9.95 (*0-9632048-0-7*) Rockwood UMC.
McNeil, Samuel. McNeil's Travels. 57p. 1989. 14.95 (*0-87770-467-8*) Ye Galleon.
***McNeil, Tony D.** How to Max Your PT Test & Improve Your Physical Fitness. (Illus.). 150p. (Orig.). (YA). (gr. 9 up). 1994. pap. 7.95 (*0-9644690-0-6*) TDM Pub.
Mcneil, W. K. Ozark Country. (Folklife in the South Ser.). (Illus.). 180p. 1995. text ed. 40.00 (*0-87805-728-5*); pap. 16.95 (*0-87805-729-3*) U Pr of Miss.
McNeil, W. K. Ozark Mountain Humor. 240p. 1989. 18.95 (*0-87483-085-0*); pap. 8.95 (*0-87483-086-9*) August Hse.
— Southern Folk Ballads, Vol. I. LC 87-751904. (American Folklore Ser.). 220p. 1987. 24.95 (*0-87483-038-9*); pap. 11.95 (*0-87483-039-7*) August Hse.
— Southern Folk Ballads, Vol. II. (American Folklore Ser.). 1988. pap. 11.95 (*0-87483-046-X*) August Hse.
— Southern Mountain Folksongs: Traditional Folksongs for Worshiping, for Wooing, for Socializing, for Cradeling, for Working, & Comic Relief. (American Folklore Ser.). 240p. 1992. 24.95 (*0-87483-284-5*); pap. 12.95 (*0-87483-285-3*) August Hse.
Mcneil, W. K., ed. Appalachian Images in Folk & Popular Culture. 2nd ed. LC 94-18229. 368p. (C). 1995. pap. text ed. 23.00x (*0-87049-866-5*) U of Tenn Pr.
McNeil, W. K. & Clements, William M., eds. An Arkansas Folklore Sourcebook. LC 92-5544. (Illus.). 288p. 1992. 30.00 (*1-55728-254-4*) U of Ark Pr.
McNeil, W. K., ed. see Jackson, Thomas W.
McNeil, W. K., ed. see Rattlehead, David.
McNeil, William C. American Money & the Weimar Republic: Economics & Politics on the Eve of the Great Depression. 320p. 1988. text ed. 50.50 (*0-231-06236-2*); pap. text ed. 16.00 (*0-231-06237-0*) Col U Pr.
— Renegotiating International Debt: The "Young Plan" Conference of 1929. (Pew Case Studies in International Affairs). 50p. (C). 1993. pap. text ed. 2.50 (*1-56927-208-5*) Geo U Inst Dplmcy.
McNeil, William J., ed. Salmon Production, Management, & Allocation: Biological, Economic, & Policy Issues. LC 87-22135. (Illus.). 208p. 1988. 35.95x (*0-87071-354-X*) Oreg St U Pr.
McNeil, William J. & Himsworth, Daniel C., eds. Salmonid Ecosystems of the North Pacific. LC 80-17800. (Illus.). 348p. 1980. pap. 26.95 (*0-87071-335-3*) Oreg St U Pr.
McNeilan, Ray A. & Ronningen, Micheline. Pacific Northwest Guide to Home Gardening. LC 82-5039. (Illus.). 302p. 1989. 24.95 (*0-88192-154-8*) Timber.
McNeile, H. C. Bulldog Drummond. 1976. 18.95 (*0-8488-1151-8*) Amereon Ltd.
— Bulldog Drummond Returns. 1976. reprint ed. lib. bdg. 18.95 (*0-89190-841-2*, Rivercity Pr) Amereon Ltd.
— Bulldog Drummond Strikes Back. 1976. reprint ed. lib. bdg. 22.95 (*0-89190-842-0*, Rivercity Pr) Amereon Ltd.
McNeill, jt. auth. see Andersson.
McNeill, Barbara, ed. see Underwood, Paula.
McNeill, Carol. Orienteering. (Skills of the Game Ser.). (Illus.). 128p. 1991. pap. 16.95 (*1-85223-558-6*, Pub. by Crowood Pr UK) Trafalgar.
McNeill, Charles, ed. Current Controversies in Temporomandibular Disorders: Proceedings of the 10th Annual Squaw Valley Winter Seminar, Squaw Valley, California, January 23-27, 1991. LC 92-49813. 1992. text ed. 58.00 (*0-86715-252-4*) Quint Pub Co.
McNeill, Charles, ed. see American Academy of Craniomandibular Disorders Staff.
McNeill, D. B., jt. auth. see Jerrard, H. G.
McNeill, D. H., tr. see Tsytovich, V. N. & Oiringel, I. M., eds.
McNeill, Daniel & Freiberger, Paul. Fuzzy Logic. (Illus.). 320p. 1993. 22.00 (*0-671-73843-7*) S&S Trade.
McNeill, David. Hand & Mind: What Gestures Reveal about Thought. LC 91-32575. (Illus.). 424p. 1992. 34.95 (*0-226-56132-1*) U Ch Pr.
— Hand & Mind: What Gestures Reveal about Thought. (Illus.). xii, 416p. 1995. pap. 17.95x (*0-226-56134-8*) U Ch Pr.
McNeill, Don, et al. Compassion: A Reflection on the Christian Life. LC 83-45045. (Illus.). 160p. (C). 1983. mass mkt. 8.00 (*0-385-18957-5*, Image Bks) Doubleday.
McNeill, Donald H., tr. see Gabovich, M. D., et al.
McNeill, Donald H., tr. see Golant, V. E. & Fedorov, V. I.
McNeill, Earldene, et al. Cultural Awareness for Young Children. rev. ed. (Illus.). 160p. 1981. pap. 14.95 (*0-317-56977-5*) CAYC Learning Tree.
McNeill, Elisabeth. A Bridge in Time. 448p. 1994. pap. 8.95 (*1-85797-406-9*) Trafalgar.
— St. James' Fair. large type ed. 682p. 1993. 21.95 (*0-7505-0491-9*) Ulverscroft.
— Wild Heritage. 448p. 1995. 27.00 (*1-85797-666-5*, Pub. by Orion) Trafalgar.
McNeill, Elizabeth. Nine & a Half Weeks. 160p. 1987. pap. 3.95 (*0-425-10384-6*) Berkley Pub.
— Nine & a Half Weeks. 1993. reprint ed. lib. bdg. 18.95 (*1-56849-171-9*) Buccaneer Bks.
— Perseverance Place. large type ed. 590p. 1992. 21.95 (*0-7505-0339-4*, Pub. by Magna Print Bks) Ulverscroft.
Mcneill, F. Marian. The Silver Bough, 4 vols. 1982. 127.00 (*0-686-45783-8*, Pub. by Stuart Titles Ltd UK) St Mut.
McNeill, F. Marian. The Silver Bough, Vol. II: A Calendar of Scottish National Festivals, Candlemas to Harvest Home. 163p. (C). 1988. 40.00 (*0-317-93231-4*, Pub. by Stuart Titles Ltd UK) St Mut.
— The Silver Bough, Vol. III: A Calendar of Scottish National Festivals Hallowe'en to Yule. 180p. (C). 1988. 40.00 (*0-85335-162-7*, Pub. by Stuart Titles Ltd UK) St Mut.
— The Silver Bough, Vol. IV: The Local Festivals of Scotland. 272p. (C). 1988. 40.00 (*0-85335-002-7*, Pub. by Stuart Titles Ltd UK) St Mut.
— The Silver Bough, Vol. 1: Scottish Folklore & Folk Belief. 220p. (C). 1988. 40.00 (*0-85335-161-9*, Pub. by Stuart Titles Ltd UK) St Mut.
McNeill, F. Martin & Thro, Ellen. Fuzzy Logic: A Practical Approach. (Illus.). 350p. 1994. disk, pap. 39.95 (*0-12-485965-8*, AP Prof) Acad Pr.
McNeill, G. D. The Last Forest. 2nd ed. 1990. reprint ed. pap. 9.95 (*0-685-52308-X*) McClain.
McNeill, George. Mysterious Places. (Illus.). 128p. 1993. 14. 95 (*0-914427-59-8*) W S Konecky Assocs.
McNeill, George E., ed. Labor Movement: The Problem of To-Day: The History, Purpose & Possibilities of Labor Organizations in Europe & America. LC 66-21683. (Library of American Labor History). (Illus.). x, 639p. 1971. reprint ed. 57.50 (*0-678-00713-6*) Kelley.
McNeill, Geraldine, jt. auth. see Gillespie, Stuart.
McNeill, Ian. To Long Tan: The Second in the Official History Series of Australia's Operations in Vietnam. (Illus.). 552p. 1993. 49.00 (*1-86373-282-9*, Pub. by Allen Unwin AT) Paul & Co Pubs.
McNeill, J. Lyrics from Cotton Land. 1972. 59.95 (*0-8490-0567-1*) Gordon Pr.
McNeill, J. C., III. The McNeills' SR Ranch: 100 Years in Blanco Canyon. LC 88-2204. (Centennial Series of the Association of Former Students: No. 28). (Illus.). 224p. 1988. 18.95 (*0-89096-340-1*) Tex A&M Univ Pr.
McNeill, J. R. The Mountains of the Mediterranean World: An Environmental History. (Studies in Environment & History). (Illus.). 432p. (C). 1992. 69.95 (*0-521-33248-6*) Cambridge U Pr.
***McNeill, John.** The Loire Valley. (Blue Guide Ser.). (Illus.). 256p. 1995. pap. 15.95 (*0-393-31414-6*, Norton Paperbks) Norton.
— Normandy. (Blue Guides Ser.). (Illus.). 256p. 1993. pap. 18.95 (*0-393-30971-1*) Norton.
McNeill, John & Williams, Bryan, eds. Containing Crime: Community Based Approaches. (Aberdeen University Press Bks.). 200p. 1991. pap. text ed. 29.00 (*0-08-040911-3*, Pub. by Aberdeen U Pr) Macmillan.
McNeill, John, jt. ed. see Karras, Alan L.
McNeill, John C. The Pocket: Selected Poems. Gibson, Grace E., ed. (Scottish Heritage Ser.). 74p. (Orig.). 1990. pap. 7.50 (*0-932662-82-X*) St Andrews NC.
McNeill, John J. The Church & the Homosexual. 4th ed. LC 93-7088. 288p. 1993. pap. 14.00 (*0-8070-7931-6*) Beacon Pr.
— Freedom, Glorious Freedom: The Spiritual Journey to the Fullness of Life for Gays, Lesbians, & Everybody Else. LC 94-15723. 256p. 1994. 24.00 (*0-8070-7936-7*) Beacon Pr.
— Taking a Chance on God: Liberating Theology for Gays, Lesbians & Their Lovers, Families & Friends. LC 87-47875. 240p. 1989. pap. 13.00 (*0-8070-7903-0*, BP830) Beacon Pr.
McNeill, John R. Atlantic Empires of France & Spain: Louisburg & Havana, 1700-1763. LC 85-1105. xvii, 329p. 1985. 45.00 (*0-8078-1669-8*) U of NC Pr.
McNeill, John S., jt. ed. see Lecca, Pedro J.
McNeill, John T. Books of Faith & Power. LC 75-134112. (Essay Index Reprint Ser.). 1977. 20.95 (*0-8369-1996-3*) Ayer.
— The History & Character of Calvinism. 1967. pap. 14.95 (*0-19-500743-3*) OUP.
McNeill, John T. & Garner, Helena M. Medieval Handbooks of Penance: A Translation of the Principal Libri Poenitentiales. 476p. 1990. text ed. 58.00 (*0-231-00889-9*); pap. text ed. 12.50 (*0-231-09629-1*) Col U Pr.
McNeill, John T., ed. see Calvin, John.
McNeill, Louise. Fermi Buffalo. 104p. (Orig.). 1994. 29.95 (*0-8229-3795-6*); pap. 12.95 (*0-8229-5528-8*) U of Pittsburgh Pr.
— Gauley Mountain. 3rd ed. 1989. reprint ed. pap. 9.95 (*0-87012-489-7*) McClain.
— Hill Daughter: New & Selected Poems. Anderson, Maggie, ed. LC 91-8429. 168p. 1991. 29.95 (*0-8229-3685-2*); pap. 12.95 (*0-8229-5456-7*) U of Pittsburgh Pr.
— The Milkweed Ladies. LC 88-1334. 136p. (Orig.). 1988. 29.95 (*0-8229-3587-2*); pap. 10.95 (*0-8229-5406-0*) U of Pittsburgh Pr.

M

McNeill, Mary. Life & Times of Mary Ann McCracken, 1770-1866: A Belfast Panorama. 328p. 1988. pap. 11.95 (*0-85640-403-9*, Pub. by Blackstaff Pr IE) Dufour.

McNeill, Moyra. Pulled Thread Embroidery. (Illus.). 208p. 1994. reprint ed. pap. text ed. 6.95 (*0-486-27857-3*) Dover.

McNeill, Moyra, jt. auth. see Geddes, Elisabeth.

McNeill, Particia. Landlording in Canada: Canadian Edition. 5th ed. (Legal Ser.). 152p. 1993. 14.95 (*0-88908-290-1*) Self-Counsel Pr.

McNeill, Patricia, jt. auth. see Geever, Jane C.

McNeill, Patrick & Townley, Charles, eds. Fundamentals of Sociology. 2nd ed. 464p. 1986. pap. 36.50 (*0-7487-0269-5*, Pub. by Stanley Thornes UK) Trans-Atl Phila.

McNeill, Paul M. The Ethics & Politics of Human Experimentation. LC 92-32322. (Illus.). 328p. (C). 1993. 59.95 (*0-521-41627-2*) Cambridge U Pr.

McNeill, Pearlie. Because You Want to Write: A Workbook for Women. 238p. 1992. pap. 17.95 (*1-85727-030-4*, Pub. by Scarlet Pr UK) InBook.

— Because You Want to Write: A Workbook for Women. 238p. 1993. 49.95 (*1-85727-035-5*) InBook.

McNeill, Pearlie, et al, eds. Women Talk Sex: Autobiographical Writing on Sex, Sexuality & Sexual Identity. 233p. 1992. pap. 15.50 (*1-85727-000-2*, Pub. by Scarlet Pr UK) InBook.

— Women Talk Sex: Autobiographical Writing on Sex, Sexuality & Sexual Identity. 233p. 1993. 45.00 (*1-85727-010-X*) InBook.

McNeill, Philip, jt. auth. see Howarth, Sarah.

McNeill, Robert C. Understanding the Weather. rev. ed. (Illus.). 250p. (C). 1991. pap. text ed. write for info. (*0-9623781-8-6*) Arbor Pubs.

— Understanding the Weather. 2nd rev. ed. (Illus.). 250p. (C). 1991. pap. write for info. (*0-9623781-7-8*) Arbor Pubs.

McNeill, T. W., jt. auth. see Andersson, G. B.

McNeill, Tom. English Heritage Book of Castles. (Illus.). 152p. 1993. pap. 29.95 (*0-7134-7025-9*, Pub. by Batsford UK) Trafalgar.

McNeill, Walter G., jt. auth. see Green, Edward F.

McNeill, William, jt. auth. see Atkin, Nicholas.

McNeill, William, tr. see Haar, Michel.

McNeill, William, tr. see Heidegger, Martin.

McNeill, William H. The Age of Gunpowder Empires, 1450-1800. Adas, Michael, ed. LC 89-84997. (Essays on Global & Comparative History Ser.). 49p. 1989. pap. 6.00 (*0-87229-043-3*) Am Hist Assn.

— Arnold J. Toynbee: A Life. (Illus.). 368p. 1989. 30.00 (*0-19-505863-1*) OUP.

— Arnold J. Toynbee: A Life. (Illus.). 368p. 1990. reprint ed. pap. 10.95 (*0-19-506335-X*) OUP.

— La Civilizacion de Occidente: Manual de Historia. 6th ed. 586p. (C). 1986. pap. 11.25 (*0-8477-0833-0*) U of PR Pr.

— Europe's Steppe Frontier, Fifteen Hundred to Eighteen Hundred: A Study of the Eastward Movement in Europe. LC 64-22248. (Midway Reprint Ser.). 252p. 1975. 10.50 (*0-226-56151-8*) U Ch Pr.

— Historia del Mundo. Millares Vazquez, Manuel et al, trs. (Illus.). 523p. 1969. reprint ed. 6.50 (*0-8477-0834-9*) U of PR Pr.

— A History of the Human Community: Prehistory to the Present. 4th ed. 720p. 1992. text ed. write for info. (*0-13-388273-X*) P-H.

— History of the Human Community, Vol. 1: Prehistory to 1500. 4th ed. 384p. 1992. pap. text ed. write for info. (*0-13-389701-X*) P-H.

— History of the Human Community, Vol. 2: 1500 to the Present. 4th ed. 368p. 1992. pap. text ed. write for info. (*0-13-389719-2*) P-H.

— History of Western Civilization: A Handbook. 6th ed. LC 85-24545. (Illus.). xviii, 672p. 1986. lib. bdg. 40.00 (*0-226-56159-3*); pap. text ed. 17.95 (*0-226-56160-7*) U Ch Pr.

— The Human Condition & Other Essays. 168p. 1993. text ed. 35.00 (*0-691-08648-6*); pap. text ed. 12.95 (*0-691-02559-2*) Princeton U Pr.

— Hutchins' University: A Memoir of the University of Chicago, 1929-1950. LC 91-9322. (Centennial Publication Ser.). (Illus.). 208p. 1991. 24.95 (*0-226-56170-4*) U Ch Pr.

— Keeping Together in Time: Dance & Drill in Human History. LC 95-8794. (Illus.). 184p. (C). 1995. 22.00 (*0-674-50229-9*) HUP.

— The Metamorphosis of Greece since World War II. LC 77-26105. (Illus.). 1978. 12.95 (*0-226-56156-9*) U Ch Pr.

— Mythistory & Other Essays. LC 85-8584. x, 226p. 1985. 19.95 (*0-226-56135-6*) U Ch Pr.

— Plagues & People. 1992. 20.50 (*0-8446-6492-8*) Peter Smith.

— Plagues & People. LC 76-2798. (Illus.). 1977. mass mkt. 9.95 (*0-385-12122-9*, Anchor NY) Doubleday.

— Polyethnicity & National Unity in World History. pap. 10.95 (*0-8020-6643-7*) U of Toronto Pr.

— Polyethnicity & National Unity in World History. LC 88-128714. (Donald G. Creighton Lectures: No. 1985). 97p. reprint ed. pap. 27.70 (*0-7837-1791-1*, 2041992) Bks Demand.

— Population & Politics since 1750. LC 89-28772. (Richard Lectures). 96p. 1990. text ed. 18.50x (*0-8139-1257-1*) U Pr of Va.

— The Pursuit of Power: Technology, Armed Force & Society since A. D. 1000. LC 81-24095. (Illus.). x, 406p. 1984. pap. text ed. 13.95 (*0-226-56158-5*) U Ch Pr.

— The Rise of the West: A History of the Human Community. 844p. 1991. pap. 22.95 (*0-226-56141-0*) U Ch Pr.

— The Shape of European History. 1974. pap. 12.95 (*0-19-501807-9*) OUP.

— A World History. (Illus.). 1979. pap. text ed. 25.00 (*0-19-502555-5*) OUP.

McNeill, William H. & Adams, Ruth S., eds. Human Migration: Patterns & Policies. LC 77-23685. 460p. reprint ed. pap. 131.10 (*0-317-27837-1*, 2056047) Bks Demand.

McNeill, William H. & Waldman, Marilyn R., eds. The Islamic World. LC 83-18246. xviii, 468p. 1984. pap. text ed. 16.95 (*0-226-56155-0*) U Ch Pr.

McNeill, William H., ed. see Acton, John E.

McNeill, William H., ed. see Aronowicz, Annette.

McNeill, William H., ed. see Brooks, Charles W.

McNeill, William H., ed. see Bundy, Frank J.

McNeill, William H., ed. see Burney, John M.

McNeill, William H., ed. see Callender, Ann B.

McNeill, William H., ed. see Carden, Ron M.

McNeill, William H., ed. see Conrad, Stephen A.

McNeill, William H., ed. see Donovan, Robert K.

McNeill, William H., ed. see Edmonson, James M.

McNeill, William H., ed. see Epstein, Irene R.

McNeill, William H., ed. see Epstein, Klaus W.

McNeill, William H., ed. see Farr, Barbara S.

McNeill, William H., ed. see Franklin, R. W.

McNeill, William H., ed. see Godfrey, Christopher.

McNeill, William H., ed. see Greenburg, Reva P.

McNeill, William H., ed. see Greenlee, James G.

McNeill, William H., ed. see Griffiths, A. R.

McNeill, William H., ed. see Hamlin, Christopher.

McNeill, William H., ed. see Hasiotis, Arthur C.

McNeill, William H., ed. see Haury, David A.

McNeill, William H., ed. see Heath, Roy E.

McNeill, William H., ed. see Hein, Virginia H.

McNeill, William H., ed. see Hiemstra, Paul A.

McNeill, William H., ed. see Hildreth, Martha.

McNeill, William H., ed. see Holland, Mary G.

McNeill, William H., ed. see Hutcheson, John A., Jr.

McNeill, William H., ed. see Karchmar, Lucien.

McNeill, William H., ed. see King, Richard D.

McNeill, William H., ed. see Knudsen, Erik L.

McNeill, William H., ed. see Krukones, James H.

McNeill, William H., ed. see Krumpe, Elizabeth C.

McNeill, William H., ed. see Meininger, Thomas A.

McNeill, William H., ed. see Michelson, Paul E.

McNeill, William H., ed. see Millard, A. J.

McNeill, William H., ed. see Miller, John T.

McNeill, William H., ed. see Morrison, Daniel.

McNeill, William H., ed. see Mueller, Christine L.

McNeill, William H., ed. see Nelms, Brenda.

McNeill, William H., ed. see Rapp, Dean.

McNeill, William H., ed. see Rowley, David G.

McNeill, William H., ed. see Ryan, W. Michael.

McNeill, William H., ed. see Sanders, Joseph L.

McNeill, William H., ed. see Segal, Paul H.

McNeill, William H., ed. see Seid, Roberta P.

McNeill, William H., ed. see Share, Michael.

McNeill, William H., ed. see Stein, Margot B.

McNeill, William H., ed. see Thompson, Thomas W.

McNeill, William H., ed. see Travers, Tim.

McNeill, William H., ed. see Urness, Carol.

McNeill, William H., ed. see Wilgus, Mary H.

McNeill, William H., ed. see Williams, Virginia P.

McNeillie, Andrew. The Essays of Virginia Woolf, Vol. I: 1904-1912. 1987. 19.95 (*0-318-42591-2*, Harvest Bks) HarBrace.

McNeillie, Andrew, ed. Essays of Virginia Woolf, Vol. I. 1989. pap. 12.95 (*0-15-629054-5*, Harvest Bks) HarBrace.

— The Essays of Virginia Woolf, Vol. II, 1912-1918. 416p. 1990. pap. 14.95 (*0-15-629055-3*, Harvest Bks) HarBrace.

— The Essays of Virginia Woolf, Vol. III: 1919-1924. 544p. 1989. 22.95 (*0-15-129057-1*) HarBrace.

— Essays of Virginia Woolf, Vol. III, 1919-1924. 1991. pap. 18.95 (*0-15-629056-1*, Harvest Bks) HarBrace.

McNeillie, Andrew, intro. The Essays of Virginia Woolf, Vol. II: 1912-1918. 448p. 1988. 22.95 (*0-15-129056-3*) HarBrace.

McNeillie, Andrew, ed. see Woolf, Virginia.

***McNeilly, Rob & Brown, Jenny.** Healing with Words. 108p. (Orig.). 1994. pap. 14.95 (*0-85572-246-0*) Seven Hills Bk.

McNeilly, Steve. How to Read Weather Statements & Charts. LC 93-31899. (Illus.). 160p. (Orig.). (C). 1993. pap. 12.95 (*0-8138-2238-6*) Iowa St U Pr.

McNeils, E. B. & Sayigh, S. Solar Electricity for Development. (C). 1989. 130.00 (*0-685-33096-6*, Pub. by Interntl Solar Energy Soc UK) St Mut.

McNeilus, James. The Three Legged Chair. 476p. 1988. reprint ed. 16.75 (*0-9620256-0-7*) J McNeilus.

McNeily, Curtlan R., jt. auth. see Moriarty, John P.

McNeir, Leo. Cassell Multilingual Dictionary of Local Government & Business. 288p. (ENG, FRE & GER.). 1993. text ed. 74.95 (*0-304-32715-8*) Cassell.

McNeir, Waldo F. Merchant of Venice Notes. 1981. pap. 3.50 (*0-8220-0052-0*) Cliffs.

— Studies in English Renaissance Literature. (Essay Index Reprint Ser.). 1977. reprint ed. 22.95 (*0-518-10153-3*) Ayer.

McNeir, Waldo F. & Levy, Leo B., eds. Studies in American Literature. (Essay Index Reprint Ser.). 1977. reprint ed. 17.95 (*0-518-10152-5*) Ayer.

McNeish, A. S., jt. auth. see Walker-Smith, J. A.

McNeley, James K. Holy Wind in Navajo Philosophy. LC 80-27435. 115p. 1981. pap. 12.95 (*0-8165-0724-4*) U of Ariz Pr.

McNelis, B. & Morton, J. Solar Energy for Developing Countries Power for Villages (C44) 83p. (C). 1986. 95.00 (*0-685-30228-8*, Pub. by Interntl Solar Energy Soc UK) St Mut.

McNelis, B. & Morton, J., eds. Solar Energy for Developing Countries...Power for the Villages. (C). 1986. 100.00 (*0-685-33087-7*, Pub. by Interntl Solar Energy Soc UK) St Mut.

McNelley, T. R. & Heikkenen, H. C., eds. Superplasticity in Aerospace. LC 88-43025. (Illus.). 385p. 1988. 95.00 (*0-87339-048-2*, 339) Minerals Metals.

— Superplasticity in Aerospace, No. II. (Illus.). 383p. 1990. 115.00 (*0-87339-157-8*, 383) Minerals Metals.

McNellis, D., jt. ed. see Maulik, D.

McNellis, D., et al, eds. The Onset of Labor: Cellular & Integrative Mechanisms. LC 88-9848. (Reproductive & Perinatal Medicine Ser.: No. IX). (Illus.). 1988. 77.50 (*0-916859-40-1*) Perinatology.

McNellis, Jerry & Nettles, Jack. Compression Planning. (Illus.). (Orig.). 1990. write for info. (*0-318-66540-9*) Braintrain.

— Exploding the Meeting Myth: Compression Planning...a Proven System for Better, Faster, Sharper Solutions. 240p. 1992. pap. 24.95 (*0-9625078-4-9*) Braintrain.

McNelly, Theodore. Politics & Government in Japan. 3rd ed. (Illus.). 284p. (Orig.). 1985. reprint ed. pap. text ed. 18.50 (*0-8191-4359-6*) U Pr of Amer.

McNelly, Willis E., jt. ed. see Magill, Frank N.

***McNergney, Robert F. & Herbert, Joann.** Foundations of Education. LC 94-29562. 1994. text ed. 39.00 (*0-205-13962-0*) Allyn.

***McNerney, Gerald.** Enter the Third Level. rev. ed. Orig. Title: Terrorism & Fear. 256p. 1994. reprint ed. pap. 10.95 (*0-9642956-0-1*) Contemporary Pr.

— Terrorism & Fear: Enter the Third Level. LC 93-86071. 210p. (Orig.). 1994. pap. 10.95 (*0-9637293-5-7*) Storm Pub.

McNerney, Joan. Noah's Daughters. (Kestrel Ser.: No. 10). 24p. (Orig.). 1984. pap. 3.00 (*0-914974-42-4*) Holmgangers.

McNerney, Kathleen. Tirant lo Blanc Revisited: A Critical Study. LC 83-62143. (Medieval & Renaissance Monograph Ser.: Vol. 4). 139p. reprint ed. pap. 39.70 (*0-685-17117-5*, 2027025) Bks Demand.

— Understanding Gabriel Garcia Marquez. Hardin, James N., ed. (Understanding Contemporary European & Latin Literature Ser.). 176p. (C). 1989. text ed. 34.95 (*0-87249-563-9*); pap. 14.95 (*0-87249-564-7*) U of SC Pr.

McNerney, Kathleen, ed. On Our Own Behalf: Women's Tales from Catalonia. LC 87-12465. (European Women Writers Ser.). viii, 234p. 1988. 30.00 (*0-8032-3122-9*) U of Nebr Pr.

***McNerney, Kathleen & Enriques De Salamanca, Cristina, eds.** Double Minorities of Spain: A Bio-Bibliographic Guide to Women Writers of the Catalan, Galician, & Basque Countries. LC 94-27639. 432p. 1995. lib. bdg. 50.00 (*0-87352-397-0*) Modern Lang.

McNerney, Kathleen & Vosburg, Nancy, eds. The Garden Across the Border: Merce Rodoreda's Fiction. LC 93-44028. (C). 1993. write for info. (*0-945636-63-6*) Susquehanna U Pr.

McNerney, Kathleen, jt. ed. see Galerstein, Carolyn L.

McNerney, Kathleen, tr. see Oliver, Maria-Antonia.

McNerney, Kathryn. American Oak Furniture. (Illus.). 176p. 1990. pap. 9.95 (*0-89145-250-8*, 1457) Collector Bks.

— American Oak Furniture, Bk. II. 1993. pap. 12.95 (*0-89145-557-4*) Collector Bks.

— Antique Iron. (Illus.). 224p. 1989. pap. 9.95 (*0-89145-238-9*) Collector Bks.

— Antique Tools: Our American Heritage. (Illus.). 153p. 1991. pap. 9.95 (*0-89145-125-0*) Collector Bks.

— Blue & White Stoneware. (Illus.). 160p. 1991. pap. 9.95 (*0-89145-179-X*) Collector Bks.

— Kitchen Antiques, 1750-1940. 1991. pap. 14.95 (*0-89145-447-0*) Collector Bks.

— Pine Furniture Our American Heritage. 1989. pap. 14.95 (*0-89145-398-9*) Collector Bks.

— Primitives: Our American Heritage, Second Series. (Illus.). 160p. 1991. pap. 14.95 (*0-89145-331-8*, 1759) Collector Bks.

— Victorian Furniture: Our American Heritage. (Illus.). 252p. 1991. pap. 9.95 (*0-89145-164-1*) Collector Bks.

— Victorian Furniture: Our American Heritage. 1994. pap. 12.95 (*0-89145-598-1*) Collector Bks.

***McNerney, Michael J. & Meyer, Herb.** Pioneer Gravestones of Pope County, Illinois. LC 94-72149. (Illus.). 48p. (Orig.). 1994. pap. 10.00x (*0-913415-07-3*) Am Resources.

McNerney, Michael J., jt. auth. see Haas, Daniel R.

McNerney, Patricia A. Follow Your Own Yellow Brick Road. 40p. 1989. 6.00 (*0-910347-11-5*) Chatham Comm Inc.

McNerney, Terry, jt. auth. see Delaney, Richard J.

McNerney, Therese, jt. auth. see Lewis, Carole B.

McNerney, Therese, ed. see Lewis, Carole B.

McNett, Ian. Charting a Course: A Guide to the Excellence Movement in Education. 55p. (C). 1984. pap. 8.95 (*0-931989-06-X*) Coun Basic Educ.

McNett, Ian, ed. Early Alert: The Impact of Federal Education Cutbacks on the States. 64p. (Orig.). 1983. pap. 6.95 (*0-937846-99-6*) Inst Educ Lead.

— Let's Not Reinvent the Wheel: Profiles of School-Business Collaboration. 72p. (Orig.). 1983. pap. 6.95 (*0-937846-97-X*) Inst Educ Lead.

McNew, Delbert A., jt. auth. see Seacrest, Betty R.

McNew, Ed & Parker, Mark. Powerboat Guide. 3rd ed. 1992. pap. 29.95 (*0-07-048576-3*) McGraw.

McNichol, Andrea & Nelson, Jeffrey A. Handwriting Analysis: Putting It to Work for You. (Illus.). 368p. (Orig.). 1994. pap. 16.95 (*0-8092-3566-8*) Contemp Bks.

McNichol, Stella. The Early Twentieth Century British Novel: A Modern Introduction. 224p. 1992. pap. 16.95 (*0-7131-6540-5*, A5372, Pub. by E Arnold UK) Routledge Chapman & Hall.

— Virginia Woolf & the Poetry of Fiction. 208p. (C). 1988. lib. bdg. 47.50 (*0-415-00329-6*) Routledge.

McNicholas, Dick. Amusement Machines: Your Route to Success. 48p. (Orig.). 1981. pap. 6.95 (*0-943592-00-3*, TX 773-174) Publishers Pr.

— Bulk Vending Machines: Your Route to Success. (Illus.). 35p. 1985. pap. 6.95 (*0-943592-01-1*) Publishers Pr.

McNicholas, T. A. & Tinker, J., eds. Lasers in Urology: Principles & Practice. (Bloomsbury Series in Clinical Science). (Illus.). xii, 168p. 1990. 115.00 (*0-387-19615-3*) Spr-Verlag.

McNicholl, Geoffrey & Cain, Mead, eds. Rural Development & Population: Institutions & Policy - A Supplement to Population & Development Review, Vol. 15, 1989. (Population & Development Review Supplements Ser.: No. 1). 376p. 1991. 29.95 (*0-19-506847-5*); pap. 12.00 (*0-19-506849-1*) OUP.

McNichols, Charles L. Crazy Weather. LC 38-32977. viii, 195p. 1967. reprint ed. pap. 7.95 (*0-8032-8219-2*, Bison Books) U of Nebr Pr.

McNichols, Charles W. Data Base Management System Design Using dBASE II. (C). 1984. text ed. 40.60 (*0-8359-1222-1*, Reston) P-H.

— IBM-PC Statistics: BASIC Programs & Applications. 1984. write for info. (*0-318-57662-7*) P-H.

— IBM-PC Statistics: BASIC Programs & Applications. (C). 1984. pap. 20.50 (*0-8359-3014-9*, Reston) P-H.

— Microcomputer Based Data Analysis for the IBM Personal Computer. (C). 1984. teacher ed write for info. (*0-8359-4350-X*, Reston); pap. text ed. 34.00 (*0-8359-4349-6*, Reston) P-H.

McNichols, Charles W. & Clark, Thomas. Microcomputer-Based Information & Decision Support Systems. (C). 1983. text ed. 38.00 (*0-8359-4359-3*, Reston); pap. text ed. 32.00 (*0-8359-4358-5*, Reston) P-H.

McNichols, Charles W. & Rushinek, Sara F. Database Management: A Microcomputer Approach. (Illus.). 480p. (C). 1987. text ed. 63.00 (*0-13-195901-8*) P-H.

McNichols, Donald. Portrait of a Quaker. LC 80-66654. (Illus.). 180p. 1980. 12.50 (*0-913342-24-6*) Barclay Pr.

— Seattle Pacific University: A Growing Vision. LC 89-10574. (Illus.). 288p. 1989. lib. bdg. 19.95 (*0-9602642-2-1*); pap. text ed. 19.95 (*0-9602642-3-X*) Seattle Pac Univ.

McNichols, William H., jt. auth. see Pennington, M. Basil.

McNichols, William H., jt. auth. see Stevens, Clifford.

***McNickle.** To Be Mayor of New York: Ethnic Politics in the City. 1995. pap. text ed. 17.50 (*0-231-07637-1*) Col U Pr.

McNickle, Chris. To Be Mayor of New York: Ethnic Politics in the City. Jackson, Kenneth T., ed. LC 92-32583. (Columbia History of Urban Life Ser.). (Illus.). 300p. (C). 1993. 30.00 (*0-231-07636-3*) Col U Pr.

McNickle, D'Arcy. The Hawk Is Hungry & Other Stories. Hans, Birgit, ed. LC 92-8623. (Sun Tracks Ser.: Vol. 22). 180p. (Orig.). 1992. lib. bdg. 29.95 (*0-8165-1326-0*); pap. 14.95 (*0-8165-1331-7*) U of Ariz Pr.

— Native American Tribalism: Indian Survivals & Renewals. Iverson, Peter, ed. (Illus.). 208p. 1993. pap. 10.95 (*0-19-508422-5*) OUP.

— Runner in the Sun. LC 87-5986. (Zia Books Ser.). (Illus.). 260p. (J). 1987. reprint ed. pap. 12.95 (*0-8263-0974-7*) U of NM Pr.

— The Surrounded. LC 77-91886. (Zia Books Ser.). 311p. 1978. pap. 12.95 (*0-8263-0469-9*) U of NM Pr.

— Wind from an Enemy Sky. LC 87-17575. 268p. 1988. reprint ed. pap. 12.95 (*0-8263-1100-8*) U of NM Pr.

McNickle, R. G. Crosstraining. 256p. 1994. pap. 12.95 (*0-681-41686-6*) Longmeadow Pr.

McNicol, jt. auth. see Jones.

McNicol, B. D. & Rand, D. A., eds. Power Sources for Electric Vehicles. (Studies in Electrical & Electronic Engineering: No. 11). 1066p. 1984. 310.25 (*0-444-42315-X*, I-134-84) Elsevier.

McNicol, Donald. Radio's Conquest of Space: The Experimental Rise in Radio Communication. LC 74-4689. (Telecommunications Ser.). (Illus.). 388p. 1974. reprint ed. 31.95 (*0-405-06052-1*) Ayer.

McNicol, Jane. Your Child's Food Allergies: Detecting & Treating Hyperactivity, Congestion, Irritability & Other Symptoms Caused by Common Food Allergies. 176p. 1992. pap. text ed. 9.95 (*0-471-55801-X*) Wiley.

McNicol, M. W., jt. auth. see Tattersfield, A. E.

McNicol, Pamela. Flowers for Weddings. (Illus.). 128p. 1992. 34.95 (*0-7134-6061-X*, Pub. by Batsford UK) Trafalgar.

McNicol, Pamela & Cooke, Dorothy, eds. A History of Flower Arranging. (Illus.). 1989. 34.95 (*0-434-90252-7*) Buttrwrth-Heinemann.

McNicol, Suzanne B. The Law of Privilege. 562p. 1992. 120.00 (*0-455-21149-3*, Pub. by Law Bk Co) W W Gaunt.

McNicoll, Andre, ed. see Awang, Kamis, et al.

McNicoll, Andre, jt. auth. see Croes, Martin.

***McNicoll, Geoffrey & Cain, Mead, eds.** Rural Development & Population: Institutions & Policy - Supplement to Population & Development Review, Vol. 15. 366p. 1989. pap. text ed. 12.00 (*0-614-00626-0*) Population Coun.

McNicoll, Geoffrey, jt. auth. see Hicks, George L.

McNicoll, R. E., ed. see Miami University, Hispanic American Institute Staff.

McNiece, Gerald. The Knowledge That Endures: Coleridge, German Philosophy & the Logic of Romantic Thought. LC 91-24838. 244p. 1991. text ed. 59.95 (*0-312-06799-2*) St Martin.

— Shelley & the Revolutionary Idea. LC 75-88808. 317p. reprint ed. 90.40 (*0-8357-9178-5*, 2011601) Bks Demand.

An Asterisk (*) at the beginning of an entry indicates that the title is appearing in BIP for the first time.

McNiece, Ray. The Bone-Orchard Conga. 2nd rev. ed. (Illus.). 70p. 1994. pap. 6.95 (1-883731-08-9) Poetry Alive.

McNiel, N. A. & Magill, C. W. Genetics. 2nd ed. (Illus.). 225p. 1977. pap. text ed. 9.95x (0-89641-004-8) American Pr.

McNiff, Jean. Teaching As Learning: An Action Research Approach. LC 92-32095. 128p. 1993. 59.95 (0-415-08980-8, B0175); pap. 16.95 (0-415-08390-7, B0179) Routledge.

McNiff, Philip J., ed. Switzerland: A View from Boston. 1984. pap. 10.00 (0-89073-077-6) Boston Public Lib.

— Twelve Mayors of Boston: 1900-1970. (Illus.). 1970. 2.00 (0-89073-033-4) Boston Public Lib.

McNiff, Shaun. Art As Medicine: Creating a Therapy of the Imagination. LC 92-50117. (Illus.). 224p. (Orig.). 1992. pap. 16.00 (0-87773-658-8) Shambhala Pubns.

— The Arts & Psychotherapy. (Illus.). 258p. 1981. pap. 18.95 (0-398-06277-3) C C Thomas.

— The Arts & Psychotherapy. (Illus.). 258p. 1981. 32.95 (0-398-04112-1) C C Thomas.

— Depth Psychology of Art. (Illus.). 258p. 1989. pap. 29.95 (0-398-06278-1) C C Thomas.

— Depth Psychology of Art. (Illus.). 258p. (C). 1989. text ed. 48.95x (0-398-05535-1) C C Thomas.

— Earth Angels: Engaging the Sacred in Everyday Things. LC 95-3900. 240p. 1995. 20.00 (1-57062-048-2) Shambhala Pubns.

— Educating the Creative Arts Therapist: A Profile of the Profession. 296p. 1986. pap. 29.95 (0-398-06279-X) C C Thomas.

— Educating the Creative Arts Therapist: A Profile of the Profession. 296p. (C). 1986. 46.95x (0-398-05172-0) C C Thomas.

— Fundamentals of Art Therapy. (Illus.). 262p. 1988. pap. 29.95 (0-398-06280-3) C C Thomas.

— Fundamentals of Art Therapy. (Illus.). 262p. (C). 1988. text ed. 48.95x (0-398-05388-X) C C Thomas.

McNiff, Veronica, jt. auth. see Niles, Bo.

McNiff, William J. Heaven on Earth: A Planned Mormon Society. LC 72-8632. reprint ed. 23.00 (0-404-11007-X) AMS Pr.

— Heaven on Earth: A Planned Mormon Society. LC 72-187474. (American Utopian Adventure Ser.). 262p. 1973. reprint ed. lib. bdg. 37.50 (0-87991-001-1) Porcupine Pr.

McNight, C. The Underachieving Curriculum: Assessing U. S. School Mathematics from an International Perspective. Travers, Ken, ed. 140p. 1987. pap. text ed. 8.00 (0-87563-298-X) Stipes.

McNight, Thomas. Book of Days & Nights. (Illus.). 128p. 1993. 14.95 (0-8212-2021-7) Bulfinch Pr.

McNinch, Thomas W., jt. auth. see Everett, John O.

McNitt, Franck. Navajo Wars: Military Campaign, Slave Raids, & Reprisals. LC 90-12610. 492p. 1990. reprint ed. pap. 19.95 (0-8263-1226-8) U of NM Pr.

McNitt, Frank. The Indian Traders. LC 62-16469. (Illus.). 432p. 1989. pap. 16.95 (0-8061-2213-7) U of Okla Pr.

— Richard Wetherill: Anasazi. rev. ed. LC 65-29102. (Illus.). 380p. 1974. reprint ed. pap. 14.95 (0-8263-0329-3) U of NM Pr.

McNitt, Lawrence. Productivity Software Applications for Management Information Systems. 320p. 1994. pap. write for info. (0-697-22529-1) Bus & Educ Tech.

McNitt, Lawrence L. The Handbook of APL for the IBM PC. (Illus.). 350p. 1988. text ed. 34.95 (0-89433-268-6, NO. 8227) Petrocelli.

— Invitation to APL for the IBM Personal Computer. 1988. pap. 24.95 (0-07-156162-5) McGraw.

— Invitation to APL for the IBM Personal Computer. (Illus.). 250p. 1988. pap. text ed. 24.95 (0-89433-267-8, NO. 8221) Petrocelli.

— Invitation to "C" Programming Language. (Illus.). 300p. 1987. 29.95 (0-89433-280-5, NO. 8143); pap. text ed. 24.95 (0-89433-300-3) Petrocelli.

— Invitaton to Turbo Pascal. (Illus.). 280p. 1988. pap. 24.95 (0-89433-282-1, NO. 8231) Petrocelli.

McNitt, Virgil B., ed. A Tale of Two Conventions: An Account of the Republican & Democratic National Conventions of June, 1912. LC 73-19136. (Politics & People Ser.). (Illus.). 336p. 1974. reprint ed. 25.95 (0-405-05860-8) Ayer.

McNiven, Helen & McNiven, Peter. Making Masks. (First Arts & Crafts Ser.). (Illus.). 32p. (J). (gr. 1-4). 1994. 14.95 (1-56847-212-9) Thomson Lrning.

— Models. LC 94-22442. (First Arts & Crafts Ser.). (Illus.). 32p. (J). (gr. 1-4). 1994. 14.95 (1-56847-214-5) Thomson Lrning.

— Puppets. (First Arts & Crafts Ser.). (Illus.). 32p. (J). (gr. 1-4). 1994. 14.95 (1-56847-215-3) Thomson Lrning.

— Toys & Games. (First Arts & Crafts Ser.). (Illus.). 32p. (J). (gr. 1-4). 1994. 14.95 (1-56847-213-7) Thomson Lrning.

McNiven, Peter. Heresy & Politics in the Reign of Henry IV: The Burning of John Badby. 250p. 1987. 79.00 (0-85115-467-0) Boydell & Brewer.

McNiven, Peter, jt. auth. see Clayton, Dorothy.

McNiven, Peter, jt. auth. see McNiven, Helen.

McNulty Development Incorporated Staff. UNIX Reference Guide. (Illus.). 100p. 1986. 33.95 (0-13-938952-0) P-H.

McNulty, Edward. Hazardous to Your Health: AIDS, Steroids & Eating Disorders. (Active Bible Curriculum Ser.). 48p. (Orig.). 1990. pap. 9.99 (1-55945-200-5) Group Pub.

McNulty, Elizabeth G. & Holderby, Robert A. Hospice: A Caring Challenge. (Illus.). 192p. 1983. 28.95x (0-398-04798-7) C C Thomas.

— Hospice: A Caring Challenge. (Illus.). 192p. 1983. pap. 15.95 (0-398-06281-1) C C Thomas.

***McNulty, Elizabeth W.** Planted in Love: The Enneagram-Reasoning & Conversation. 142p. 1994. pap. 35.00 (0-85439-502-4, Pub. by St Paul Pubns UK) St Mut.

McNulty, Faith. The Burning Bed. 288p. 1981. pap. 3.95 (0-05-024747-6) Bantam.

— The Burning Bed: The True Story of an Abused Wife. 320p. 1989. mass mkt. 4.50 (0-380-70771-3) Avon.

— Dancing with Manatees. LC 93-7593. (Hello Reader! Ser.: Level 4). (Illus.). 48p. (J). (ps-4). 1994. pap. 2.95 (0-590-46401-9) Scholastic Inc.

— The Elephant Who Couldn't Forget. LC 79-2741. (Harper I Can Read Bk.). (Illus.). 64p. (J). (gr. k-3). 1980. lib. bdg. 14.89 (0-06-024146-2) HarpC Child Bks.

— Endangered Animals. LC 95-13236. (Hello Reader! Ser.: Level 3). (Illus.). (J). 1996. write for info. (0-590-22859-5, Cartwheel) Scholastic Inc.

— How to Dig a Hole to the Other Side of the World. LC 78-22479. (Illus.). 32p. (J). (ps-3). 1979. lib. bdg. 14.89 (0-06-024148-9) HarpC Child Bks.

— How to Dig a Hole to the Other Side of the World. LC 78-22479. (Trophy Picture Bk.). (Illus.). 32p. (J). (gr. k-3). 1990. pap. 4.95 (0-06-443218-1, Trophy) HarpC Child Bks.

— How to Dig a Hole to the Other Side of the World. (Illus.). (J). (gr. 2-4). 1991. audio 22.95 (0-87499-234-6); audio, pap. 14.95 (0-87499-233-8) Live Oak Media.

— How to Dig a Hole to the Other Side of the World, 4 bks., Set. (Illus.). (J). (gr. 2-4). 1991. audio, pap. 31.95 (0-87499-235-4) Live Oak Media.

— The Lady & the Spider. LC 85-5427. (Illus.). 48p. (J). (gr. 1-4). 1986. lib. bdg. 14.89 (0-06-024192-6) HarpC Child Bks.

— The Lady & the Spider. LC 85-5427. (Trophy Picture Bk.). (Illus.). 48p. (J). (gr. 1-4). 1987. pap. 4.95 (0-06-443152-5, Trophy) HarpC Child Bks.

— Listening to Whales Sing. LC 94-40993. (Hello Reader! Ser.). (Illus.). (J). 1995. write for info. (0-590-47871-0) Scholastic Inc.

— The Orphan. 48p. (J). 1992. 11.95 (0-590-43838-7, Scholastic Hardcover) Scholastic Inc.

— A Snake in the House. LC 92-27939. (Illus.). 32p. (J). (ps-3). 1994. 14.95 (0-590-44758-0) Scholastic Inc.

Mcnulty, Faith. With Love from Koko. (J). (gr. k up). 1990. pap. 12.95 (0-590-42774-1) Scholastic Inc.

***McNulty, Francis R.** Black Cats & Blue Birds. 220p. 1995. pap. 8.95 (1-56901-825-1) NW Pub.

McNulty, Henry. Vogue Cocktails, Vol. 1. (Illus.). 80p. 1993. 9.95 (0-8212-2013-6) Bulfinch Pr.

McNulty, J. Bard. The Narrative Art of the Bayeux Tapestry Master. LC 86-47841. (Studies in the Middle Ages: No. 13). 47.50 (0-404-61443-4) AMS Pr.

McNulty, J. Bard, ed. The Correspondence of Thomas Cole & Daniel Wadsworth. (Illus.). 96p. (Orig.). 1983. pap. 14.75 (0-940748-88-6) Conn Hist Soc.

McNulty, J. Bard, jt. ed. see Bickford, Christopher P.

McNulty, J. G. Interventional Radiology of the Gallbladder: Percutaneous Cholecystostomy. (Illus.). xiii, 65p. 1990. pap. 64.00 (0-387-52905-5) Spr-Verlag.

— Minimally Invasive Therapy of the Liver & Biliary System. LC 93-42224. (Illus.). 205p. 1994. 99.00 (0-86577-514-1) Thieme Med Pubs.

McNulty, James F. Words of Power. LC 83-2514. 226p. (Orig.). 1983. pap. 8.95 (0-8189-0442-9) Alba.

McNulty, John K. Federal Estate & Gift Taxation in a Nutshell. 4th ed. (Nutshell Ser.). 496p. 1991. pap. text ed. 17.00 (0-314-48842-1) West Pub.

— Federal Estate & Gift Taxation in a Nutshell. 5th ed. (Nutshell Ser.). 486p. Date not set. pap. text ed. 18.00 (0-314-04247-4) West Pub.

— Federal Income Taxation of Individuals in a Nutshell. 4th ed. (Nutshell Ser.). 503p. 1992. reprint ed. pap. text ed. 17.00 (0-314-42967-0) West Pub.

— Federal Income Taxation of Individuals in a Nutshell. 5th ed. (Nutshell Ser.). 489p. 1995. pap. text ed. write for info. (0-314-06580-6) West Pub.

— Federal Income Taxation of S Corporations. (University Textbook Ser.). 216p. 1991. pap. text ed. 13.75 (0-88277-972-9) Foundation Pr.

McNulty, K. K., Sr. Is It I? rev. ed. (One of the Answers Ser.). (Illus.). 280p. 1989. 21.95 (0-935025-03-0) Data & Res Tech.

— Is It I? The Witness of Monsignor Charles Owen Rice. (One of the Answers Ser.). (Illus.). 247p. (Orig.). (C). 1989. pap. text ed. 19.95 (0-935025-01-4) Data & Res Tech.

McNulty, M. S. & McFerran, J. B., eds. Recent Advances in Virus Diagnosis. (Current Topics in Veterinary Medicine & Animal Science Ser.). 1984. lib. bdg. 94.00 (0-89838-674-8) Kluwer Ac.

McNulty, M. S., jt. ed. see McFerran, J. B.

McNulty, Marjorie G. Glastonbury: from Settlement to Suburb: A History of the 300-Year-Old Town. rev. ed. (Illus.). 163p. 1983. 10.00 (0-9610676-0-8) Hist Soc Glastonbury.

McNulty, Maureen, jt. auth. see Johansen, Robert.

McNulty, P. A., tr. see Cabasilas, Nicholas.

McNulty, Paul J. The Origins & Development of Labor Economics. 1980. reprint ed. pap. 12.95 (0-262-63097-4) MIT Pr.

McNulty, Robert H. & Weare, Carol S., eds. Issues in Urban Archaeology, Vol. 2. (Livability Digest Ser.: No. 3). 71p. 1983. pap. 6.00 (0-317-44282-1) Partners Livable.

***McNulty, Tim.** Art of Nature: Reflections of the Grand Design. (Illus.). 1994. pap. 24.95 (0-930861-07-8) Prior Pub Co.

— As a Heron Unsettles a Quiet Pool: Nine Poems for Mary. 16p. 1988. 5.00 (1-882623-05-3) Exiled-Am Pr.

— In Blue Mountain Dusk. LC 92-70011. 128p. (Orig.). 1992. pap. 12.95 (0-913089-32-X) Broken Moon.

— Washington's Wild Rivers: The Unfinished Work. LC 89-13562. (Illus.). 144p. 1990. 14.95 (0-89886-170-5) Mountaineers.

McNulty, Tom & Suvino, Dawn M. Access to Information: Materials, Technologies, & Services for Print-Impaired Readers. 161p. 1993. pap. 28.00 (0-8389-7641-7) ALA.

McNurlin, Barbara, jt. auth. see Stockwell, Shelley.

McNurlin, Barbara C., jt. auth. see Sprague, Ralph H., Jr.

McNurney, John M., jt. ed. see Dowden, Lisa G.

***McNutt, et al.** System Administrator Tools. (Illus.). (Orig.). 1995. pap. write for info. (1-56592-118-6) OReilly & Assocs.

McNutt, Charles H. Early Puebloan Occupations of Tesuque By-Pass & in the Upper Rio Grande Valley. LC 79-631330. (University of Michigan, Museum of Anthropology, Anthropological Papers: No. 40). (Illus.). 158p. reprint ed. pap. 45.10 (0-8357-8601-3, 2034997) Bks Demand.

McNutt, Charles H., ed. The Archaic Period in the Mid-South: Proceedings of the 1989 Mid-South Archaeological Conference. LC 91-620836. (Mississippi Department of Archives & History Archaeological Reports: No. 24). (Illus.). 95p. 1991. 8.00 (0-938896-60-1) Mississippi Archives.

McNutt, Gladys, see Andeya, pseud..

McNutt, James A., Jr. Exploring the West Indies. (Nautilus Explorer Ser.). 112p. 1993. pap. 19.00 (1-884104-01-0) Hydrodyne Marine.

— Quest for Shipwrecks, 2 vols., Set, Vols. 1 & 2. (Nautilus Explorer Ser.). 1991. Set, Vol. 1, 202p. Vol. 2, 231p. pap. 18.00 (1-884104-00-2) Hydrodyne Marine.

McNutt, James S., Jr. Business & Careers in Marine Sciences. 332p. 1993. pap. text ed. 24.00 (1-884104-02-9) Hydrodyne Marine.

McNutt, Jean-Isabel. Echoes of Eden: Being a Commonplace Book about Animals, Lovers, Food, Eccentrics, Artists, & Me. LC 93-3386. 1993. 15.00 (0-374-14637-3) FS&G.

McNutt, Jim, ed. see Whipple, Melvin.

McNutt, John. Counting Money. 1992. 149.00 (1-56304-032-8) J Stanfield.

McNutt, John G., jt. ed. see Hoff, Marie D.

***McNutt, Joni.** In Praise of Wine: An Offering of Hearty Toasts, Quotations, Witticisms, Proverbs & Poetry Throughout History. 236p. 1993. lib. bdg. 33.00x (0-8095-4122-X) Borgo Pr.

— In Praise of Wine: An Offering of Hearty Toasts, Quotations, Witticisms, Proverbs & Poetry Throughout History. LC 93-1886. (Illus.). 236p. 1993. pap. 12.95 (0-88496-372-1) Capra Pr.

McNutt, Nan. The Artifact, Unit One: Field Notebook. (Project Archeology Series: Saving Traditions). (J). (gr. 5-8). 1987. student ed 1.25 (0-944584-01-2) Sopris.

— The Bentwood Box. 3rd ed. (Northwest Coast Indian Art Ser.). (Illus.). 36p. (Orig.). (J). (gr. 3-8). 1989. pap. text ed. 9.95 (0-9614534-0-0) N McNutt Assocs.

— The Button Blanket. 2nd ed. (Northwest Coast Indian Art Ser.). (Illus.). 44p. (J). (gr. k-3). 1989. pap. 7.95 (0-9614534-1-9) N McNutt Assocs.

— The Button Blanket. 2nd ed. (Northwest Coast Indian Art Ser.). (Illus.). 44p. (J). (gr. k-3). 1989. pap. 7.95 (0-9614534-3-5) Workshop Pubns.

— The Cedar Plank Mask. (Illus.). 34p. (J). (gr. 3-6). 1991. pap. 9.95 (0-9614534-2-7) N McNutt Assocs.

— The Culture, Unit Three: Field Notebook. (Project Archeology Series: Saving Traditions). (J). (gr. 5-8). 1987. student ed 1.25 (0-944584-03-9) Sopris.

— Northwest Coast Indian Art Series, 3 bks., Set. rev. ed. (Illus.). 118p. (J). (gr. k-8). 1992. pap. text ed. 29.95 (0-9614534-5-1) N McNutt Assocs.

— Project Archeology: Saving Traditions: Archeology for the Classroom. (Illus.). 202p. 1992. teacher ed 14.50 (0-944584-56-X) Sopris.

— The Site, Unit Two: Field Notebook. (Project Archeology Series: Saving Traditions). (J). (gr. 5-8). 1987. student ed 1.25 (0-944584-02-0) Sopris.

McNutt, Paula M., ed. see Lind, Michael.

McNutt, Paula M., ed. see Weeks, John M.

***McNutt, Randy.** Ghosts: Lost Arts & Forgotten Places. (Illus.). 220p. 1995. text ed. 25.00 (1-882203-05-4) Orange Frazer.

— We Wanna Boogie: An Illustrated History of the American Rockabilly Movement. 2nd ed. (Illus.). 288p. 1989. pap. 22.95 (0-940152-05-3) Hamilton Hobby.

McNutt, Randy, comp. No Left Turns, a Handbook for Conservatives: Based on the Writings of John M. Ashbrook. LC 85-80376. (Illus.). 128p. 1986. 12.95 (0-940152-03-7) Hamilton Hobby.

McNutt, Randy & Bauer, Cheryl. Talking Machine Madness: The Story of America's Early Phonograph Shows. (Illus.). 30p. 1985. pap. 6.00 (0-940152-02-9) Hamilton Hobby.

***McNutt, Timothy E., Sr.** Alley Alligator's Awesome Smile. (Illus.). (J). (ps). 1994. pap. text ed. 3.95 (0-9642475-0-X) T E McNutt.

McOmber, Howard J., II. With Love As Our Weapon. Holt, Pamela, ed. (Illus.). 104p. (Orig.). (C). 1990. pap. 9.95 (0-9626734-0-4) Plowshare Prodns.

McOmber, Rachel B., ed. McOmber Phonics Storybooks: A Box. rev. ed. (Illus.). (J). write for info. (0-944991-13-0) Swift Lrn Res.

— McOmber Phonics Storybooks: A Game for Champions. rev. ed. (Illus.). (J). write for info. (0-944991-68-8) Swift Lrn Res.

— McOmber Phonics Storybooks: A Hum-Bug. rev. ed. (Illus.). (J). write for info. (0-944991-20-3) Swift Lrn Res.

— McOmber Phonics Storybooks: A Nifty Ball of String. rev. ed. (Illus.). (J). write for info. (0-944991-50-5) Swift Lrn Res.

— McOmber Phonics Storybooks: A Night to Celebrate. rev. ed. (Illus.). (J). write for info. (0-944991-71-8) Swift Lrn Res.

— McOmber Phonics Storybooks: A Package from Hong Kong. rev. ed. (Illus.). (J). write for info. (0-944991-61-0) Swift Lrn Res.

— McOmber Phonics Storybooks: A Red Hen. rev. ed. (Illus.). (J). write for info. (0-944991-25-4) Swift Lrn Res.

— McOmber Phonics Storybooks: A Trip to China. rev. ed. (Illus.). (J). write for info. (0-944991-70-X) Swift Lrn Res.

— McOmber Phonics Storybooks: At the Fair. rev. ed. (Illus.). (J). write for info. (0-944991-60-2) Swift Lrn Res.

— McOmber Phonics Storybooks: Bags . . . Bags (Animals) rev. ed. (Illus.). (J). write for info. (0-944991-97-1) Swift Lrn Res.

— McOmber Phonics Storybooks: Bags . . . Bags (Holidays) rev. ed. (Illus.). (J). write for info. (0-944991-98-X) Swift Lrn Res.

— McOmber Phonics Storybooks: Ben Has a Pet. rev. ed. (Illus.). (J). write for info. (0-944991-26-2) Swift Lrn Res.

— McOmber Phonics Storybooks: Ben in Bed. rev. ed. (Illus.). (J). write for info. (0-944991-29-7) Swift Lrn Res.

— McOmber Phonics Storybooks: Ben Will Get Well. rev. ed. (Illus.). (J). write for info. (0-944991-30-0) Swift Lrn Res.

— McOmber Phonics Storybooks: Boe E. Toad. rev. ed. (Illus.). (J). write for info. (0-944991-54-8) Swift Lrn Res.

— McOmber Phonics Storybooks: Boyer's Toy Store. rev. ed. (Illus.). (J). write for info. (0-944991-69-6) Swift Lrn Res.

— McOmber Phonics Storybooks: Bug. rev. ed. (Illus.). (J). write for info. (0-944991-19-X) Swift Lrn Res.

— McOmber Phonics Storybooks: Chatsworth. rev. ed. (Illus.). (J). write for info. (0-944991-74-2) Swift Lrn Res.

— McOmber Phonics Storybooks: Choose Which One - 1. rev. ed. (Illus.). (J). write for info. (0-944991-67-X) Swift Lrn Res.

— McOmber Phonics Storybooks: Everyone Knows a Pitcher. rev. ed. (Illus.). (J). write for info. (0-944991-79-3) Swift Lrn Res.

— McOmber Phonics Storybooks: Fizz in the Pit. rev. ed. (Illus.). (J). write for info. (0-944991-12-2) Swift Lrn Res.

— McOmber Phonics Storybooks: Fizz Mix. rev. ed. (Illus.). (J). write for info. (0-944991-11-4) Swift Lrn Res.

— McOmber Phonics Storybooks: Fizz Mud. rev. ed. (Illus.). (J). write for info. (0-944991-21-1) Swift Lrn Res.

— McOmber Phonics Storybooks: Hello Again. rev. ed. (Illus.). (J). write for info. (0-944991-84-X) Swift Lrn Res.

— McOmber Phonics Storybooks: Hen Pox. rev. ed. (Illus.). (J). write for info. (0-944991-28-9) Swift Lrn Res.

— McOmber Phonics Storybooks: Humps & Lumps. rev. ed. (Illus.). (J). write for info. (0-944991-62-9) Swift Lrn Res.

— McOmber Phonics Storybooks: In the Dell. rev. ed. (Illus.). (J). write for info. (0-944991-32-7) Swift Lrn Res.

— McOmber Phonics Storybooks: Jud & Nell. rev. ed. (Illus.). (J). write for info. (0-944991-33-5) Swift Lrn Res.

— McOmber Phonics Storybooks: Kim. rev. ed. (Illus.). (J). write for info. (0-944991-07-6) Swift Lrn Res.

— McOmber Phonics Storybooks: Max. rev. ed. (Illus.). (J). write for info. (0-944991-01-7) Swift Lrn Res.

— McOmber Phonics Storybooks: Max is Six. rev. ed. (Illus.). (J). write for info. (0-944991-43-2) Swift Lrn Res.

— McOmber Phonics Storybooks: Max Ran. rev. ed. (Illus.). (J). write for info. (0-944991-02-5) Swift Lrn Res.

— McOmber Phonics Storybooks: Max the Grand. rev. ed. (Illus.). (J). write for info. (0-944991-57-2) Swift Lrn Res.

— McOmber Phonics Storybooks: Me & the Bee. rev. ed. (Illus.). (J). write for info. (0-944991-46-7) Swift Lrn Res.

— McOmber Phonics Storybooks: Miss Vie. rev. ed. (Illus.). (J). write for info. (0-944991-48-3) Swift Lrn Res.

— McOmber Phonics Storybooks: Mom & Dad Hop-Jig. rev. ed. (Illus.). (J). write for info. (0-944991-16-5) Swift Lrn Res.

— McOmber Phonics Storybooks: Number Fun. rev. ed. (Illus.). (J). write for info. (0-944991-58-0) Swift Lrn Res.

— McOmber Phonics Storybooks: On TV. rev. ed. (Illus.). (J). write for info. (0-944991-17-3) Swift Lrn Res.

— McOmber Phonics Storybooks: Pete's Bike Ride. rev. ed. (Illus.). (J). write for info. (0-944991-40-8) Swift Lrn Res.

— McOmber Phonics Storybooks: Razz. rev. ed. (Illus.). (J). write for info. (0-944991-06-8) Swift Lrn Res.

— McOmber Phonics Storybooks: Razz Visits Raz in Israel. rev. ed. (Illus.). (J). write for info. (0-944991-75-0) Swift Lrn Res.

— McOmber Phonics Storybooks: Robin Hood's Cook. rev. ed. (Illus.). (J). write for info. (0-944991-64-5) Swift Lrn Res.

— McOmber Phonics Storybooks: Snores & More. rev. ed. (Illus.). (J). write for info. (0-944991-59-9) Swift Lrn Res.

— McOmber Phonics Storybooks: Starfish of Norway. rev. ed. (Illus.). (J). write for info. (0-944991-72-6) Swift Lrn Res.

M

— McOmber Phonics Storybooks: String Art, Vol. 1. rev. ed. (Illus.). (J). write for info. (*0-944991-96-3*) Swift Lrn Res.

— McOmber Phonics Storybooks: String Art, Vol. 2. rev. ed. (Illus.). (J). write for info. (*0-944991-95-5*) Swift Lrn Res.

— McOmber Phonics Storybooks: Tale of the Green Glob. rev. ed. (Illus.). (J). write for info. (*0-944991-65-3*) Swift Lrn Res.

— McOmber Phonics Storybooks: Teacher's Manual. rev. ed. (Illus.). write for info. (*0-944991-00-9*) Swift Lrn Res.

— McOmber Phonics Storybooks: Ten in the Hut. rev. ed. (Illus.). (J). write for info. (*0-944991-27-0*) Swift Lrn Res.

— McOmber Phonics Storybooks: The Bag. rev. ed. (Illus.). (J). write for info. (*0-944991-03-3*) Swift Lrn Res.

— McOmber Phonics Storybooks: The Big Deal. rev. ed. (Illus.). (J). write for info. (*0-944991-47-5*) Swift Lrn Res.

— McOmber Phonics Storybooks: The Big Hole. rev. ed. (Illus.). (J). write for info. (*0-944991-38-6*) Swift Lrn Res.

— McOmber Phonics Storybooks: The Bon-Bon Box. rev. ed. (Illus.). (J). write for info. (*0-944991-14-9*) Swift Lrn Res.

— McOmber Phonics Storybooks: The Box Mix. rev. ed. (Illus.). (J). write for info. (*0-944991-15-7*) Swift Lrn Res.

— McOmber Phonics Storybooks: The Cake. rev. ed. (Illus.). (J). write for info. (*0-944991-44-0*) Swift Lrn Res.

— McOmber Phonics Storybooks: The Confection Connection. rev. ed. (Illus.). (J). write for info. (*0-944991-73-4*) Swift Lrn Res.

— McOmber Phonics Storybooks: The Cove of Gloom. rev. ed. (Illus.). (J). write for info. (*0-944991-83-1*) Swift Lrn Res.

— McOmber Phonics Storybooks: The Fumes. rev. ed. (Illus.). (J). write for info. (*0-944991-39-4*) Swift Lrn Res.

— McOmber Phonics Storybooks: The Gal Pals. rev. ed. (Illus.). (J). write for info. (*0-944991-42-4*) Swift Lrn Res.

— McOmber Phonics Storybooks: The Haircut. rev. ed. (Illus.). (J). write for info. (*0-944991-53-X*) Swift Lrn Res.

— McOmber Phonics Storybooks: The Hum-Bug Hop. rev. ed. (Illus.). (J). write for info. (*0-944991-31-9*) Swift Lrn Res.

— McOmber Phonics Storybooks: The Invisible Crocodiles. rev. ed. (Illus.). (J). write for info. (*0-944991-80-7*) Swift Lrn Res.

— McOmber Phonics Storybooks: The Kit. rev. ed. (Illus.). (J). write for info. (*0-944991-08-4*) Swift Lrn Res.

— McOmber Phonics Storybooks: The Land of Morning. rev. ed. (Illus.). (J). write for info. (*0-944991-82-3*) Swift Lrn Res.

— McOmber Phonics Storybooks: The Lemonade Sale. rev. ed. (Illus.). (J). write for info. (*0-944991-41-6*) Swift Lrn Res.

— McOmber Phonics Storybooks: The Magic "E" rev. ed. (Illus.). (J). write for info. (*0-944991-37-8*) Swift Lrn Res.

— McOmber Phonics Storybooks: The Map. rev. ed. (Illus.). (J). write for info. (*0-944991-05-X*) Swift Lrn Res.

— McOmber Phonics Storybooks: The Neat Trick. rev. ed. (Illus.). (J). write for info. (*0-944991-55-6*) Swift Lrn Res.

— McOmber Phonics Storybooks: The Pit Kit. rev. ed. (Illus.). (J). write for info. (*0-944991-09-2*) Swift Lrn Res.

— McOmber Phonics Storybooks: The Prime Time Trick. rev. ed. (Illus.). (J). write for info. (*0-944991-56-4*) Swift Lrn Res.

— McOmber Phonics Storybooks: The Prize. rev. ed. (Illus.). (J). write for info. (*0-944991-49-1*) Swift Lrn Res.

— McOmber Phonics Storybooks: The Quiz Is (1) rev. ed. (Illus.). (J). write for info. (*0-944991-34-3*) Swift Lrn Res.

— McOmber Phonics Storybooks: The Quiz Is (2) rev. ed. (Illus.). (J). write for info. (*0-944991-35-1*) Swift Lrn Res.

— McOmber Phonics Storybooks: The Rope. rev. ed. (Illus.). (J). write for info. (*0-944991-45-9*) Swift Lrn Res.

— McOmber Phonics Storybooks: The Sub. rev. ed. (Illus.). (J). write for info. (*0-944991-22-X*) Swift Lrn Res.

— McOmber Phonics Storybooks: The Tan Cab. rev. ed. (Illus.). (J). write for info. (*0-944991-04-1*) Swift Lrn Res.

— McOmber Phonics Storybooks: The Time Box. rev. ed. (Illus.). (J). write for info. (*0-944991-52-1*) Swift Lrn Res.

— McOmber Phonics Storybooks: The Tin Lid. rev. ed. (Illus.). (J). write for info. (*0-944991-10-6*) Swift Lrn Res.

— McOmber Phonics Storybooks: The Tub. rev. ed. (Illus.). (J). write for info. (*0-944991-24-6*) Swift Lrn Res.

— McOmber Phonics Storybooks: The TV Box. rev. ed. (Illus.). (J). write for info. (*0-944991-18-1*) Swift Lrn Res.

— McOmber Phonics Storybooks: The Video Show. rev. ed. (Illus.). (J). write for info. (*0-944991-63-7*) Swift Lrn Res.

— McOmber Phonics Storybooks: The Wizz Kid. rev. ed. (Illus.). (J). write for info. (*0-944991-23-8*) Swift Lrn Res.

— McOmber Phonics Storybooks: Tid Bits. rev. ed. (Illus.). (J). write for info. (*0-944991-36-X*) Swift Lrn Res.

— McOmber Phonics Storybooks: Under the Rainbow. rev. ed. (Illus.). (J). write for info. (*0-944991-81-5*) Swift Lrn Res.

— McOmber Phonics Storybooks: Writing Book No. 1. rev. ed. (Illus.). (J). write for info. (*0-944991-93-9*) Swift Lrn Res.

— McOmber Phonics Storybooks: Writing Book No. 2. rev. ed. (Illus.). (J). write for info. (*0-944991-94-7*) Swift Lrn Res.

— McOmber Phonics Storybooks: Yellow Crocodile. rev. ed. (Illus.). (J). write for info. (*0-944991-76-9*) Swift Lrn Res.

— McOmber Phonics Storybooks: You Can Make It. rev. ed. (Illus.). (J). write for info. (*0-944991-51-3*) Swift Lrn Res.

M'Conechy, James, ed. Papers Illustrative of the Political Condition of the Highlands of Scotland. LC 75-175587. (Maitland Club, Glasgow. Publications: No. 64). reprint ed. 17.50 (*0-404-53071-0*) AMS Pr.

McOntyre, A. M. Australian Contemporary Drawings. 162p. (C). 1990. 120.00 (*0-86439-037-8*, Pub. by Boolarong Pubns AT) St Mut.

McOscar, Diane L., ed. see Gross, Andrew C., et al.

McOustra, Christopher. Love in the Economy. 122p. (C). 1989. 39.00 (*0-85439-324-2*, Pub. by St Paul Pubns UK) St Mut.

McOwan, Rennie. Light on Dumyat. 152p. (C). 1992. pap. 32.00 (*0-685-66161-X*, Pub. by St Andrew UK) St Mut.

— Light on Dumyat. 152p. 1993. pap. 22.00 (*0-7152-0544-7*, Pub. by St Andrew UK) St Mut.

— Walks in the Trossachs & Rob Roy Country. 184p. (C). 1991. pap. text ed. 39.00 (*86-15-30563-3*, Pub. by St Andrew UK) St Mut.

— Walks in the Trossachs & Rob Roy Country. 192p. (C). 1992. pap. 35.00 (*0-685-66160-1*, Pub. by St Andrew UK) St Mut.

— Walks in the Trossachs & Rob Roy Country. 192p. 1993. pap. 35.00 (*0-7152-0563-3*, Pub. by St Andrew UK) St Mut.

— The White Stag Adventure. 160p. (C). 1992. pap. 32.00 (*0-685-60702-X*, Pub. by St Andrew UK) St Mut.

— The White Stag Adventure. 160p. 1993. pap. 22.00 (*0-7152-0665-6*, Pub. by St Andrew UK) St Mut.

McParland, Stephen, jt. auth. see Blair, John.

McParland, Stephen J. It's Party Time: A Musical Appreciation of the Beach Party Film Genre. (Illus.). 204p. (Orig.). 1992. pap. 25.00 (*0-9601880-2-9*) J Blair.

McParr, Nigel. The Story of a Victorian Maid. (Orig.). 1995. pap. text ed. 5.95 (*1-56333-241-8*) Masquerade.

McPartian, Paul. One in Two Thousand? Towards Catholic-Orthodox Unity. 192p. 1993. 30.00 (*0-85439-439-7*, Pub. by St Paul Pubns UK) St Mut.

McPartlan, Paul. The Eucharist Makes the Church: Henri de Lubac & John Zizioulas in Dialogue. 368p. 1993. text ed. 49.95 (*0-567-09640-8*, Pub. by T & T Clark UK) Bks Intl VA.

— The Eucharist Makes the Church: Henri De Lubac & John Zizioulas in Dialogue. 368p. 1994. pap. text ed. 24. 95 (*0-567-29263-0*, Pub. by T & T Clark UK) Bks Intl VA.

McPartland, jt. auth. see ABC Staff.

McPartland, Joe, ed. Ulster Reciter. 1984. pap. 8.95 (*0-85640-321-0*) Dufour.

— Ulster Reciter: Ballads, Poems & Recitations for Every Occasion. 90p. 1984. pap. 7.95 (*0-685-25949-8*, Pub. by Blackstaff Pr IE) Dufour.

McPartland, John. Danger for Breakfast. large type ed. (Linford Mystery Library). 288p. 1992. pap. 14.95 (*0-7089-7304-3*, Trailtree Bookshop) Ulverscroft.

— The Face of Evil. large type ed. (Linford Mystery Library). 1991. pap. 13.95 (*0-7089-7076-1*) Ulverscroft.

— Love Me Now. large type ed. (Linford Mystery Library). 400p. 1994. pap. 14.95 (*0-7089-7475-9*, Linford) Ulverscroft.

***McPartland, Joseph A.** Nineteen Ninety-Five Yearbook Supplement to McGraw-Hill's National Electrical Code Handbook. 1995. text ed. 29.95 (*0-07-045982-7*) McGraw.

Mcpartland, Joseph F. McGraw-Hill National Electrical Code Handbook: 1994 Supplement. 21th ed. 1994. text ed. 29.50 (*0-07-045978-9*) McGraw.

McPartland, Joseph F. McGraw Hill's National Electrical Code Handbook. 21th ed. 1993. text ed. 54.50 (*0-07-045901-0*) McGraw.

McPartland, Joseph F. & Novak, William J. Electrical Design Details. LC 82-94. 240p. 1983. reprint ed. 21.50 (*0-89874-412-1*) Krieger.

McPartland, Joseph F., et al. McGraw-Hill's Handbook of Electrical Construction Calculations. LC 93-3994. (Illus.). 454p. 1993. text ed. 49.50 (*0-07-045682-8*) McGraw.

McPartland, Marian. All in Good Time. (Illus.). 192p. 1987. 18.95 (*0-19-504871-7*) OUP.

— The Artistry of Marian McPartland. 1985. pap. 10.95 (*0-89898-415-7*) CPP Belwin.

McPartland, Pamela. Americana: A Basic Reader. 171p. (C). 1983. pap. text ed. 14.75 (*0-15-502597-X*) HB Coll Pubs.

— Take It Easy: American Idioms & Two Word Verbs for Students of English As a Foreign Language. (English As a Second Language Ser.). 176p. 1981. pap. text ed. 15.95 (*0-13-882902-0*) P-H.

— Take It Easy: American Idioms & Two Word Verbs for Students of English As a Foreign Language. (English As a Second Language Ser.). 176p. 1981. 17.50 (*0-13-882910-1*) P-H.

McPartland, Patricia A. Promoting Health in the Workplace. 288p. (C). 1991. text ed. 35.00 (*3-7186-0528-7*) Gordon & Breach.

McPartland, Scott. Edwin Land. LC 93-22077. (Masters of Invention Ser.). (J). (gr. 7-8). 1993. 15.93 (*0-86592-150-4*); 11.95 (*0-685-66592-5*) Rourke Enter.

— Gordon Gould. LC 93-2819. (Masters of Invention Ser.). (J). 1993. 15.93 (*0-86592-079-6*); 11.95 (*0-685-66585-2*) Rourke Enter.

McPartland, Suzy. Good Morning, Sun. (Pee Wee Pops Ser.). (Illus.). 12p. (J). (ps-00). 1994. bds. 4.95 (*0-689-71747-4*, Aladdin Paperbacks) S&S Childrens.

— Sleepy-Time Moon. (Pee Wee Pops Ser.). (Illus.). 12p. (J). (ps-00). 1994. bds. 4.95 (*0-689-71748-2*, Aladdin Paperbacks) S&S Childrens.

— Toy-Shop Surprise. (Pee Wee Pops Ser.). (Illus.). 12p. (J). (ps-00). 1994. bds. 4.95 (*0-689-71749-0*, Aladdin Paperbacks) S&S Childrens.

— Zoom, Car, Zoom. (Pee Wee Pops Ser.). (Illus.). 12p. (J). (ps-00). 1994. bds. 4.95 (*0-689-71750-4*, Aladdin Paperbacks) S&S Childrens.

***McPeak-Bailey, Bobbi.** Chicken Pox Christmas. (Illus.). 64p. (Orig.). (J). (gr. k-4). 1994. pap. 9.95 (*0-9625005-2-6*) Wee Pr.

— The Christmas Tree That Cried. (Illus.). 36p. (J). (gr. k-6). 1982. 11.95 (*0-9625005-0-X*) Wee Pr.

— Emma's Happy Birthday Piano. (Illus.). 36p. (J). (gr. k-4). 1991. pap. 7.95 (*0-9625005-1-8*) Wee Pr.

McPeak, Fay. Time's Masquerade. abr. ed. 170p. 1995. pap. 7.95 (*1-56901-296-2*) NW Pub.

McPeak, Ronald H., et al. The Amber Forest: Beauty & Biology of California's Submarine Forests. Brunton, Jolee & Loyst, Ken, eds. LC 88-51680. (Illus.). 160p. (Orig.). 1988. 39.95 (*0-685-23081-3*); pap. 24.95 (*0-922769-00-1*) Watersport Pub.

McPeake, Francis. Pocket Tin Whistle Tutor. (Appletree Pocket Guides Ser.). 72p. 1983. pap. 7.95 (*0-86281-112-0*, Pub. by Appletree Pr IE) Irish Bks Media.

McPeck, John E., et al. Teaching Critical Thinking. (Philosophy of Education Research Library). 176p. 1990. 32.50 (*0-415-90225-8*, A4032, Routledge NY) Routledge.

McPeek, James A., jt. auth. see Baldwin, Robert.

McPhail. Introduction to Santhali. 1983. 19.95 (*0-8288-8468-4*) Fr & Eur.

***McPhail, Bob.** The Tijuana Handbook & Souvenir Guide. 48p. 1995. pap. text ed. 3.00 (*0-9646406-0-0*) CF Pub CA.

***McPhail, Brenda M., ed.** NAFTA Now! The Changing Political Economy of North America. 145p. (C). 1994. lib. bdg. 48.00 (*0-8191-9701-7*) U Pr of Amer.

— NAFTA Now! The Changing Political Economy of North America. 145p. (Orig.). (C). 1994. pap. text ed. 18.50 (*0-8191-9702-5*) U Pr of Amer.

McPhail, Clark. Myth of the Madding Crowd. (Social Institutions & Social Change Ser.). 295p. (Orig.). 1991. lib. bdg. 49.95 (*0-202-30424-8*); pap. text ed. 25.95 (*0-202-30375-6*) Aldine de Gruyter.

McPhail, David. Annie & Co. LC 90-34119. 40p. (J). (gr. 2-4). 1991. 13.95 (*0-8050-1596-5*, Bks Young Read) H Holt & Co.

— Annie & Company II. 40p. (J). 1997. 13.95 (*0-8050-2819-6*) H Holt & Co.

— The Bear's Toothache. (Illus.). 32p. (J). (gr. k-3). 1972. lib. bdg. 14.95 (*0-316-56312-9*, Joy St Bks) Little.

— The Bear's Toothache. (Illus.). (J). (ps-3). 1988. mass mkt. 5.95 (*0-316-56325-0*, Joy St Bks) Little.

— The Bear's Toothache. (Illus.). (J). (gr. k-2). 1986. reprint ed. audio 22.95 (*0-87499-081-5*); reprint ed. audio, pap. 14.95 (*0-87499-080-7*) Live Oak Media.

— The Bear's Toothache, 4 bks., Set. (Illus.). (J). (gr. k-2). 1986. reprint ed. audio, pap. 33.95 (*0-87499-082-3*) Live Oak Media.

— David McPhail's Animals A to Z. (Illus.). 32p. (J). (ps-1). 1993. 2.50 (*0-590-46462-0*, Cartwheel) Scholastic Inc.

Mcphail, David. David Mcphail's Animals A to Z. (J). 1989. pap. 2.50 (*0-590-40347-8*) Scholastic Inc.

McPhail, David. The Dream Child. LC 84-18755. (Unicorn Paperbacks Ser.). (Illus.). 32p. (J). (ps-3). 1988. pap. 4.95 (*0-525-44366-5*, 0383-120, DCB) Dutton Child Bks.

— Ed & Me. LC 86-3175. (Illus.). 32p. (J). (ps-3). 1990. 13. 95 (*0-15-224888-9*) HarBrace.

— Emma's Pet. LC 85-4414. (Illus.). 24p. (J). (ps-00). 1985. 9.95 (*0-525-44210-3*, DCB) Dutton Child Bks.

— Emma's Pet. LC 85-4414. (Unicorn Paperbacks Ser.). (Illus.). 24p. (J). (ps-00). 1988. pap. 3.95 (*0-525-44430-0*, DCB) Dutton Child Bks.

— Emma's Pet. (J). (ps-2). 1988. audio 19.95 (*0-87499-107-2*); audio 12.95 (*0-87499-106-4*); audio 27. 95 (*0-87499-108-0*) Live Oak Media.

— Emma's Vacation. LC 86-24066. (Illus.). 24p. (J). (ps-00). 1987. 7.95 (*0-525-44315-0*, DCB) Dutton Child Bks.

— Emma's Vacation. LC 86-24066. (Unicorn Paperback Ser.). (Illus.). 24p. (J). (ps-00). 1991. pap. 3.95 (*0-525-44737-7*, Puffin) Puffin Bks.

— Farm Boy's Year. LC 91-4982. (Illus.). 32p. (J). (gr. k-3). 1992. text ed. 13.95 (*0-689-31679-8*, Atheneum Bks Young) S&S Childrens.

— Farm Morning. D'Andrade, Diane, ed. (Illus.). 32p. (J). (ps-3). 1991. pap. 3.95 (*0-15-227300-X*, HB Juv Bks) HarBrace.

— First Flight. LC 86-28804. (Illus.). (J). (ps-3). 1987. 14.95i (*0-316-56323-4*, Joy St Bks) Little.

— First Flight. (Illus.). (J). (ps-3). 1991. reprint ed. 4.95 (*0-316-56332-3*, Joy St Bks) Little.

— Fix-It. LC 83-16459. (Illus.). 24p. (J). (ps-00). 1984. 11.00 (*0-525-44093-3*, DCB) Dutton Child Bks.

— Fix-It. LC 83-16459. (Unicorn Paperbacks Ser.). (Illus.). 24p. (J). (ps-00). 1987. pap. 3.95 (*0-525-44323-1*, 0383-120, DCB) Dutton Child Bks.

— Fix-It. (J). (gr. k-3). 1988. audio 19.95 (*0-87499-084-X*); audio 12.95 (*0-87499-083-1*) Live Oak Media.

— Fix-It. (Giant Bk. Ser.). (Illus.). 24p. (J). (ps-00). 1993. pap. 17.99 (*0-14-054931-5*, Puff Unicorn) Puffin Bks.

— Fix-It, 4 cass., Set. (J). (gr. k-3). 1988. student ed, audio 27.95 (*0-87499-085-8*) Live Oak Media.

— Fix It All. (J). (ps). 1992. pap. 4.99 (*0-14-054752-5*) Puffin Bks.

— Goldilocks & the Three Bears. LC 93-43992. (J). 1995. 4.95 (*0-590-48117-7*) Scholastic Inc.

— Great Cat. LC 81-12654. (Unicorn Paperbacks Ser.). (Illus.). 32p. (J). (gr. k up). 1986. pap. 4.95 (*0-525-44273-1*, DCB) Dutton Child Bks.

— Henry Bear's Park. (Illus.). 48p. (J). (gr. 1-3). 1976. lib. bdg. 14.95 (*0-316-56315-3*, Joy St Bks) Little.

— Little Red Riding Hood. LC 93-43990. (J). 1995. 4.95 (*0-590-48116-9*) Scholastic Inc.

— Lost. 1990. 13.95 (*0-316-88841-9*) Little.

— Lost! (J). (gr. 4-8). 1993. mass mkt. 5.95 (*0-316-56336-6*, Joy St Bks) Little.

— Lost, Vol. 1. (J). (ps-3). 1990. 14.95 (*0-316-56329-3*, Joy St Bks) Little.

— Moony B. Finch, the Fastest Draw in the West. LC 93-37408. (Illus.). 32p. (J). 1994. 12.95 (*0-307-17554-5*, Artsts Writrs) Western Pub.

— The Party. 1990. 14.95 (*0-316-88860-5*) Little.

— The Party. (J). (ps-4). 1990. 14.95 (*0-316-56330-7*, Joy St Bks) Little.

— Pig Pig & the Magic Photo Album. LC 85-20459. (Illus.). 24p. (J). (ps-3). 1986. 10.95 (*0-525-44238-3*, DCB) Dutton Child Bks.

Mcphail, David. Pig Pig Gets a Job. LC 89-25606. (Illus.). 24p. (J). (ps-3). 1990. 12.95 (*0-525-44619-2*, DCB) Dutton Child Bks.

McPhail, David. Pig Pig Goes to Camp. LC 83-1412. (Illus.). 24p. (J). (ps-3). 1983. 12.95 (*0-525-44064-X*, 0966-290, DCB) Dutton Child Bks.

— Pig Pig Goes to Camp. LC 83-1412. (Unicorn Paperbacks Ser.). (Illus.). 24p. (J). (ps-3). 1987. pap. 3.95 (*0-525-44302-9*, DCB) Dutton Child Bks.

— Pig Pig Goes to Camp. (J). (ps-3). 1993. pap. 4.99 (*0-14-054778-9*) Dutton Child Bks.

— Pig Pig Grows Up. LC 80-377. (Illus.). 32p. (J). (ps-2). 1980. pap. 3.95 (*0-525-44195-6*, DCB) Dutton Child Bks.

— Pig Pig Grows Up. (J). (ps-2). 1985. audio 22.95 (*0-941078-96-5*); audio, pap. 14.95 (*0-941078-94-9*) Live Oak Media.

— Pig Pig Grows Up, 4 bks., Set. (J). (ps-2). 1985. student ed, audio 31.95 (*0-941078-95-7*) Live Oak Media.

— Pig Pig Rides. LC 82-9777. (Unicorn Paperbacks Ser.). (Illus.). 24p. (J). (ps-3). 1985. pap. 3.95 (*0-525-44222-7*, DCB) Dutton Child Bks.

— Pig Pig Rides. (J). (gr. 1-3). 1988. audio 22.95 (*0-87499-090-4*); audio, pap. 14.95 (*0-87499-089-0*) Live Oak Media.

— Pig Pig Rides, 4 bks., Set. (J). (gr. 1-3). 1988. student ed, audio 31.95 (*0-87499-091-2*) Live Oak Media.

— Pig Pig Rides Again. (J). (ps-3). 1992. pap. 4.99 (*0-14-054781-9*) Puffin Bks.

— Pigs Aplenty, Pigs Galore. LC 92-27986. (J). (ps-2). 1993. 13.99 (*0-525-45079-3*, DCB) Dutton Child Bks.

— Santa's Book of Names. LC 92-37279. (J). 1993. 14.95 (*0-316-56335-8*, Joy St Bks) Little.

— Sisters. LC 84-3775. (Illus.). 32p. (J). (ps-3). 1984. 12.95 (*0-15-275319-2*, HB Juv Bks) HarBrace.

Mcphail, David. Sisters. 32p. (J). (ps-3). 1990. pap. 3.95 (*0-15-275320-6*, Voyager Bks) HarBrace.

McPhail, David. Snow Lion. LC 82-8119. (Illus.). 48p. (J). (ps-3). 1987. 5.95 (*0-8193-1097-2*); lib. bdg. 5.95 (*0-8193-1098-0*) Parents.

— Snow Lion. (Gold Banner Bks.). (Illus.). 48p. (J). (gr. 3-7). 1990. pap. 2.95 (*0-448-04335-1*, G&D) Putnam Pub Group.

— Something Special. (J). (ps-3). 1992. mass mkt. 4.95 (*0-316-56333-1*, Joy St Bks) Little.

— Those Terrible Toy-Breakers. LC 80-10450. (Illus.). 48p. (J). (ps-3). 1980. 5.95 (*0-8193-1019-0*); lib. bdg. 5.95 (*0-8193-1020-4*) Parents.

— Those Terrible Toy Breakers. (Gold Banner Bks.). (Illus.). 48p. (J). (ps-2). 1990. pap. 2.95 (*0-448-04343-2*, G&D) Putnam Pub Group.

— The Three Little Pigs. LC 93-43991. (J). 1995. 4.95 (*0-590-48118-5*) Scholastic Inc.

— The Train. (J). (gr. 3-6). 1977. lib. bdg. 15.95 (*0-316-56316-1*, Joy St Bks) Little.

— Train. (J). (ps-3). 1990. write for info. (*0-318-66965-X*, Joy St Bks); mass mkt. 5.95 (*0-316-56331-5*, Joy St Bks) Little.

— Train. 1990. 4.95 (*0-316-88847-8*) Little.

— The Train. (Illus.). (J). (gr. k-3). 1991. audio, pap. 14.95 (*0-87499-207-9*) Live Oak Media.

— The Train. (Illus.). (J). (gr. k-3). 1991. audio 22.95 (*0-87499-208-7*) Live Oak Media.

— The Train, 4 bks., Set. (Illus.). (J). (gr. k-3). 1991. audio, pap. 33.95 (*0-87499-209-5*) Live Oak Media.

McPhail, David M. The Glerp. LC 94-20298. (Illus.). (J). 1994. 14.95 (*0-382-24669-1*); lib. bdg. 16.95 (*0-382-24668-3*); pap. 6.95 (*0-382-24670-5*) Silver Burdett Pr.

— Yesterday I Lost a Sneaker (And Found the Great Goob Sick) LC 94-22862. (Illus.). (J). 1995. 16.95 (*0-382-24905-4*); 14.95 (*0-382-24906-2*); pap. text ed. 4.95 (*0-382-24907-0*) Silver Burdett Pr.

McPhail, Helen, tr. see French Ramblers Association Staff.

McPhail, Helen, tr. see Gimpel, Jean.

McPhail, Helen, tr. see Laidi, Zaki, ed.

McPhail, Helen, tr. see Noiriel, Gerard.

McPhail, Helen, tr. see Prost, Antoine.

McPhail, Ian. How to Avoid California Probate & Estate Taxes: Preserving Your Estate for Your Heirs. 175p. (Orig.). 1992. pap. 16.95 (*1-55958-178-6*) Prima Pub.

— Planning Your Will With Your Family In Mind: How Your Estate Planning Decisions Will Affect the Ones You Love. LC 93-17734. 1993. pap. 14.95 (*1-55958-364-9*) Prima Pub.

An Asterisk (*) at the beginning of an entry indicates that the title is appearing in BIP for the first time.

McPhail, Mac. Emma's Pet. (J). (ps). 1993. pap. 4.99 (0-14-054749-5, DCB) Dutton Child Bks.

McPhail, Mark L. The Rhetoric of Racism. LC 93-8188. 170p. (C). 1994. lib. bdg. 36.50 (0-8191-9180-9) U Pr of Amer.

— Zen in the Art of Rhetoric: An Inquiry into Coherence. (SUNY Series in Speech Communication). 192p. (C). 1996. text ed. 57.50x (0-7914-2803-6); pap. text ed. 18.95x (0-7914-2804-4) State U NY Pr.

McPhail, Robyn & Ward, David E. Morality & Agency. LC 88-10336. 186p. (Orig.). (C). 1988. pap. text ed. 20.00 (0-8191-6981-1) U Pr of Amer.

McPhail, Roger. Fishing Season: An Artist's Fishing Year. (Illus.). 164p. 1992. boxed 37.95 (1-85310-145-1) Voyageur Pr.

— Open Season: An Artist's Sporting Year. (Illus.). 156p. 1992. 35.95 (0-906393-68-X, Pub. by Airlife Pub Ltd UK) Voyageur Pr.

McPhail, Thomas L. Electronic Colonialism. rev. ed. (Library of Social Research: Vol. 126). 256p. (Orig.). 1987. pap. text ed. 24.00 (0-8039-2731-2) Sage.

— Electronic Colonialism. 2nd rev. ed. (Library of Social Research: Vol. 126). 256p. (Orig.). 1987. text ed. 49.95 (0-8039-2730-4) Sage.

— Electronic Colonialism: The Future of International Broadcasting & Communication. 2nd rev. ed. LC 86-6635. (Sage Library of Social Research: No. 126). 311p. reprint ed. pap. 88.70 (0-8357-4777-8, 2037714) Bks Demand.

McPhail, Virginia, ed. see James, Earl.

McPharlin, Michalene, jt. ed. see Rumwell, Claudia.

McPhatter, Thomas H. Caught in the Middle: A Dichotomy of an African American Man (They Called Him Troublemaker) (Illus.). (Orig.). (C). 1993. write for info. (0-9634658-0-5); pap. 24.95 (0-9634658-1-3) Audacity Pubns.

McPhedran, R. C., jt. auth. see Melrose, Donald B.

McPhee, Alan. Automania: The Complete Book of Automobile Trivia. (Illus.). 240p. 1990. pap. 12.95 (0-929091-11-6) Firefly Bks Ltd.

McPhee, Allan. Economic Revolution in British West Africa. 322p. 1971. reprint ed. 40.00 (0-7146-2766-6, Pub. by F Cass Pubs UK) Intl Spec Bk.

***McPhee, Brian.** Thailand, Malaysia, & Singapore by Rail. (Bradt Guides Ser.). (Illus.). 214p. 1994. 14.95 (1-56440-560-5) Globe Pequot.

McPhee, Carl, ed. ASHRAE Pocket Guide for Air-Conditioning, Heating, Ventilation & Refrigeration. rev. ed. 138p. (C). 1994. pap. 18.00 (1-883413-01-X) Am Heat Ref & Air Eng.

McPhee, Charles. Stop, Sleep, Dream. 1995. pap. 12.95 (0-8050-2515-4) H Holt & Co.

— Stop Sleeping Through Your Dreams: A Guide to Awakening Consciousness During Dream Sleep. 304p. 1995. 22.50 (0-8050-2500-6) H Holt & Co.

McPhee, Colin. The Balinese Wajang Koelit & Its Music. LC 77-86983. 56p. reprint ed. 29.00 (0-404-16765-9) AMS Pr.

— A House in Bali. (Oxford in Asia Paperbacks Ser.). (Illus.). 214p. 1987. pap. 12.95 (0-19-580448-1) OUP.

— A House in Bali. LC 77-86965. (Illus.). reprint ed. 26.50 (0-404-16766-7) AMS Pr.

— Music in Bali. LC 76-4979. (Music Reprint Ser.). 1976. reprint ed. lib. bdg. 79.50 (0-306-70778-0) Da Capo.

McPhee, J. Control of Nature. Date not set. write for info. (0-7126-5030-X) Random.

McPhee, John. Alaska: Images of the Country. 1992. 19.98 (0-88394-060-4) Promntory Pr.

— Annals of the Former World, 2 bks. limited ed. 1983. Set incls. Basin & Range & In Suspect Terrain. 75.00 (0-374-10519-7) FS&G.

— Assembling California. 1993. 21.00 (0-374-10645-2) FS&G.

— Assembling California. 1994. pap. 9.00 (0-374-52393-2) FS&G.

— Basin & Range. (Illus.). 216p. (C). 1981. 19.95 (0-374-10914-1) FS&G.

— Basin & Range. (Illus.). 216p. (C). 1982. pap. 9.00 (0-374-51690-1) FS&G.

— Coming into the Country. LC 77-12249. 438p. 1977. 22.95 (0-374-12645-3) FS&G.

— Coming into the Country. 1991. pap. 9.95 (0-374-52287-1, Noonday) FS&G.

— The Control of Nature. (Illus.). 288p. 1989. 17.95 (0-374-12890-1) FS&G.

— Control of Nature. 1990. pap. 10.00 (0-374-52259-6, Noonday) FS&G.

— The Crofter & the Laird. LC 77-113774. (Illus.). 160p. 1970. 18.95 (0-374-13192-9) FS&G.

— The Crofter & the Laird. LC 77-113774. (Illus.). 160p. 1992. pap. 10.00 (0-374-51465-8) FS&G.

— The Curve of Binding Energy. 224p. 1974. 19.95 (0-374-13373-5) FS&G.

— The Curve of Binding Energy. 224p. 1980. pap. 10.00 (0-374-51598-0) FS&G.

— The Curve of Binding Energy: A Journey into the Awesome & Alarming World of Theodore B. Taylor. 160p. 1979. pap. 2.25 (0-345-28000-8) Ballantine.

— The Deltoid Pumpkin Seed. 192p. 1973. 18.95 (0-374-13781-1) FS&G.

— The Deltoid Pumpkin Seed. 192p. 1992. pap. 9.00 (0-374-51635-9) FS&G.

— Encounters with the Archdruid. 256p. 1971. 19.95 (0-374-14822-8) FS&G.

— Encounters with the Archdruid. 256p. 1977. pap. 9.00 (0-374-51431-3) FS&G.

— Giving Good Weight. (Illus.). 261p. 1979. 19.95 (0-374-16306-5) FS&G.

— Giving Good Weight. (Illus.). 261p. 1980. pap. 12.00 (0-374-51600-6) FS&G.

— The Headmaster: Frank L. Boyden of Deerfield. 149p. 1966. 16.95 (0-374-16860-1) FS&G.

— The Headmaster: Frank L. Boyden of Deerfield. 149p. 1992. pap. 9.00 (0-374-51496-8) FS&G.

— Heirs of General Practice. 1986. pap. 8.00 (0-374-51974-9) FS&G.

— Heirs of General Practice. 1994. 19.00 (0-8446-6733-1) Peter Smith.

— In Suspect Terrain. LC 82-21031. (Illus.). 210p. 1983. 19.95 (0-374-17650-7) FS&G.

— In Suspect Terrain. LC 82-21031. (Illus.). 210p. 1984. pap. 11.00 (0-374-51794-0) FS&G.

— The John McPhee Reader. Howarth, William L., ed. 385p. 1976. 25.00 (0-374-17992-1) FS&G.

— The John McPhee Reader. Howarth, William L., ed. 385p. 1982. pap. 12.00 (0-374-51719-3) FS&G.

— Levels of the Game. 160p. 1969. 18.95 (0-374-18568-9) FS&G.

— Levels of the Game. 160p. 1979. pap. 9.00 (0-374-51526-3) FS&G.

— Looking for a Ship. 242p. 1990. 18.95 (0-374-19077-1) FS&G.

— Looking for a Ship. 242p. 1991. pap. 9.95 (0-374-52319-3, Noonday) FS&G.

— Looking for a Ship. large type ed. 294p. 1991. reprint ed. bds. 19.95 (1-56054-102-4) Thorndike Pr.

— Oranges. LC 66-20125. 149p. 1967. 16.95 (0-374-22688-1) FS&G.

— Oranges. LC 66-20125. 149p. 1975. pap. 8.00 (0-374-51297-3) FS&G.

— Pieces of the Frame. 320p. 1975. 19.95 (0-374-23281-4) FS&G.

— Pieces of the Frame. 320p. 1979. pap. 10.00 (0-374-51498-4) FS&G.

— The Pine Barrens. LC 67-22439. (Illus.). 157p. 1978. 17.95 (0-374-23360-8); pap. 9.00 (0-374-51442-9) FS&G.

— La Place de la Concorde Suisse. LC 83-27466. 160p. 1985. 18.95 (0-374-18241-8); pap. 10.00 (0-374-51932-3) FS&G.

— The Ransom of Russian Art. LC 94-14723. 1994. 20.00 (0-374-24682-3) FS&G.

— The Ransom of Russian Art. 192p. Date not set. pap. 10.00 (0-374-52450-5) FS&G.

— Rising from the Plains. 224p. 1986. 19.95 (0-374-25082-0) FS&G.

— Rising from the Plains. 224p. 1987. pap. 9.00 (0-374-52065-8) FS&G.

— A Roomful of Hovings & Other Profiles. LC 68-23746. 250p. 1969. 19.95 (0-374-25208-4) FS&G.

— A Roomful of Hovings & Other Profiles. LC 68-23746. 250p. 1979. pap. 11.00 (0-374-51501-8) FS&G.

— The Second John McPhee Reader. 388p. Date not set. 14.00 (0-374-52463-7) FS&G.

— A Sense of Where You Are: A Profile of William Warren Bradley. (Illus.). 206p. 1978. pap. 10.00 (0-374-51485-2) FS&G.

— A Sense of Where You Are: A Profile of William Warren Bradley. 2nd ed. (Illus.). 206p. 1978. 19.95 (0-374-26093-1) FS&G.

— The Survival of the Bark Canoe. (Illus.). 146p. 1975. 18.95 (0-374-27207-7) FS&G.

— The Survival of the Bark Canoe. (Illus.). 146p. 1982. pap. 9.00 (0-374-51693-6) FS&G.

— Table of Contents. 293p. 1985. 19.95 (0-374-27241-7) FS&G.

— Table of Contents. 1986. pap. 10.95 (0-374-52008-9) FS&G.

McPhee, John, ed. Manual para la Familia Catolica Hispana de Hoy. Diaz, Olimpia, tr. (SPA.). 1979. pap. 3.95 (0-89243-123-7) Liguori Pubns.

— Tu Fe. Diaz, Olimpia, tr. (SPA.). (YA). (gr. 9-12). 1979. pap. 3.95 (0-89243-124-5) Liguori Pubns.

McPhee, John, ed. see Norquist, Marilyn.

McPhee, John, jt. auth. see Rowell, Galen.

McPhee, Mark S., et al. Key References in Gastroenterology: An Annotated Guide. LC 82-14661. (Key References in Internal Medicine Ser.). 127p. reprint ed. pap. 36.20 (0-7837-2563-9, 2042722) Bks Demand.

McPhee, Marnie. Western Oregon: Portrait of the Land & Its People. (Oregon Geographic Ser.: No. 2). (Illus.). 104p. (Orig.). 1987. pap. 14.95 (0-938314-34-3) Am Wrld Geog.

McPhee, Norma H. Sensitivity & Awareness: A Guide for Developing Understanding among Children. (Illus.). 56p. 1994. pap. 9.95 (0-944727-28-X) Jason & Nordic Pubs.

McPhee, Penelope & McPhee, Raymond. Your Future in Space: The U. S. Space Camp Training Program. LC 86-9003. (Illus.). 128p. (YA). (gr. 7 up). 1986. pap. 14.95 (0-517-56418-1) Crown Bks Yng Read.

McPhee, Penelope O., jt. auth. see Schulke, Flip.

McPhee, Peter. The Politics of Rural Life: Political Mobilization in the French Countryside 1846-1852. (Illus.). 318p. 1992. 69.00 (0-19-820225-3) OUP.

— The Social History of France, 1780-1880. (Social History of the Modern World Ser.). 384p. 1992. 49.95 (0-415-01615-0, A1634) Routledge.

— A Social History of France, 1780-1880. (Social History of the Modern World Ser.). 360p. 1993. pap. 15.95 (0-415-01616-9, B2473) Routledge.

McPhee, Raymond, jt. auth. see McPhee, Penelope.

McPhee, Robert D., jt. ed. see Cushman, Donald P.

***McPhee, Stephen J.** Pathophysiology of Disease: An Introduction to Clinical Medicine. (C). 1995. pap. text ed. 29.95 (0-8385-7815-2) Appleton & Lange.

McPhee, William N. & Glaser, William A., eds. Public Opinion & Congressional Elections. LC 80-29534. (Illus.). x, 326p. 1981. reprint ed. text ed. 59.75 (0-313-22779-9, MCOP, Greenwood Pr) Greenwood.

McPheeters, Annie L. Library Service in Black & White: Some Personal Recollections, 1921-1980. LC 88-1979. (Illus.). 184p. 1988. 22.50 (0-8108-2104-4) Scarecrow.

— Negro Progress in Atlanta, Georgia, 1961-1970: A Selective Bibliography on Race & Human Relations from Four Atlanta Newspapers, Vol. 2. 225p. 1972. 15.00 (0-9618498-0-0) A L McPheeters.

McPheeters, D. W. Camilo Jose Cela. LC 74-75876. (Twayne's World Authors Ser.). 1969. lib. bdg. 17.95 (0-8057-2204-1) Irvington.

— Estudios Humanisticos Sobre La "Celestina" 110p. 1984. 20.00 (0-916379-09-4) Scripta.

McPheeters, D. W., ed. Guia De Nuevos Temas De Literatura Espanola. 415p. 1972. 12.00 (0-685-42187-2); pap. 9.00 (0-87535-118-2) Hispanic Soc.

McPheron, Bruce A., jt. auth. see Chung Kim.

McPheron, Judith. This Leaving We Cannot Live Without. LC 84-46169. (Poets Ser.). 64p. 1985. pap. 6.95 (0-931722-34-9) Corona Pub.

McPheron, William. Bibliography of Contemporary American Fiction, 1945-1988: An Annotated Checklist. 190p. 1989. text ed. 42.95 (0-313-27702-8) Greenwood.

— Bibliography of Contemporary American Poetry, 1945-1985. 72p. 1986. text ed. 42.95 (0-313-27703-6) Greenwood.

— Edward Dorn. LC 87-73498. (Western Writers Ser.: No. 85). (Illus.). 53p. (Orig.). 1988. pap. 3.95 (0-88430-084-6) Boise St U W Writ Ser.

— Gilbert Sorrentino: A Descriptive Bibliography. LC 90-3674. (Bibliography Ser.: No. 2). (Illus.). 240p. 1991. 49.95 (0-916583-67-8) Dalkey Arch.

McPherren, Charlotte. Love & Fortune. 368p. (Orig.). 1994. pap. 4.50 (0-8439-3560-X) Dorchester Pub Co.

— Song of the Willow. 368p. (Orig.). 1993. pap. 4.50 (0-8439-3483-2) Dorchester Pub Co.

McPherrin, Irene T., ed. see American Allergy Association Staff.

McPherron, Alan & Srejovic, Dragoslav, eds. Divostin & the Neolithic of Central Serbia. LC 87-83523. (Ethnology Monographs: No. 10). (Illus.). xiv, 492p. 1988. ring bd. 56.00 (0-945428-00-6) Ethnology Monographs.

***McPherson.** Refiners Fire. 1995. pap. 18.00 (0-919123-54-6) Atrium Pubs.

— Respiratory Therapy Equipment, No. 5. 1994. write for info. (0-8016-7989-3) Mosby Yr Bk.

McPherson & Miller. Respiratory Care. 848p. Date not set. 51.95 (0-8016-5855-1) Mosby Yr Bk.

McPherson & Spearman. Respiratory Therapy Equipment. 4th ed. (Illus.). 512p. 1990. 52.95 (0-8016-3341-9); student ed 15.95 (0-8016-3378-8) Mosby Yr Bk.

McPherson, A., et al, eds. Are You a Born Survivor? (C). 1984. 30.00 (0-86158-692-1, Pub. by S Thornes Pubs UK) St Mut.

— Going Anywhere This Summer? (C). 1984. 35.00 (0-86158-691-3, Pub. by S Thornes Pubs UK) St Mut.

McPherson, A. S. & Wissotzky, N. Passages for Russian Translation & Comprehension. 95p. (C). 1972. 60.00 (0-569-07481-9, Pub. by Collets UK) Pro-Am Music.

***McPherson, Alan.** Fifty Nature Walks in Southern Illinois. (Illus.). 300p. 1993. pap. text ed. 13.95 (0-9627422-3-6) Cache River Pr.

— Indian Names in Indiana. 1993. pap. 12.50 (0-9636978-0-3) A McPherson.

— Nature Walks in Orange County. (Illus.). 200p. (Orig.). 1990. pap. 9.95 (0-939919-09-5) Bear Flag Bks.

— Nature Walks in Southern Indiana. (Illus.). 416p. (Orig.). 1991. pap. 13.95 (0-9628469-0-2) Hoosier Chap-Sierra Club.

McPherson, Alexander. The History of Faulkner Co., Arkansas 1873-1927. Sperry, Phillip A. & Goss, Joe R., eds. (Illus.). 133p. 1993. reprint ed. 24.95 (1-56869-010-X); reprint ed. pap. 17.95 (1-56869-011-8) Oldbuck Pr.

— History of the Greenbrier Baptist Association. Sperry, Phillip A., ed. (Illus.). 93p. 1994. reprint ed. 22.95 (1-56869-008-8); reprint ed. pap. 14.95 (1-56869-009-6) Oldbuck Pr.

— Preparation & Analysis of Protein Crystals. LC 88-32577. 384p. (C). 1989. reprint ed. lib. bdg. 54.50 (0-89464-355-X) Krieger.

McPherson, Alfred H. A Creative Strategy for Assuring Success. 1991. 18.95 (0-533-09443-7) Vantage.

McPherson, Andrew & Raab, Charles. The Making of Scottish Educational Policy: Government & Secondary Schooling Since 1945. 352p. 1986. 60.00 (0-85224-515-7, Pub. by Edinburgh U Pr UK) Col U Pr.

McPherson, Andrew, jt. auth. see Gow, Lesley.

McPherson, Ann, ed. Women's Problems in General Practice. LC 92-48910. (Oxford General Practice Ser.: No. 22). 1993. pap. 37.00 (0-19-262065-7) OUP.

McPherson, Ann, jt. auth. see Austoker, Joan.

***McPherson, B. H.** The Supreme Court of Queensland: History, Jurisdiction, Procedure. 464p. 1989. boxed 120.00 (0-409-49444-5, Austral) Butterworth Legal Pubs.

McPherson, Barry, jt. ed. see Marshall, Victor.

McPherson, Barry D., ed. Sport & Aging. LC 85-18124. 296p. (C). 1986. text ed. 36.00x (0-87322-012-9, BMCP0012) Human Kinetics.

McPherson, Barry D., et al. The Social Significance of Sport: An Introduction to the Sociology of Sport. LC 89-1975. (Illus.). 352p. (C). 1989. text ed. 36.00 (0-87322-235-0, BMCPO235) Human Kinetics.

McPherson, Betty. A Mayflower Adventure. (Pocket Tales Ser.: Bk. 1). (Illus.). 32p. (J). (ps-1). 1985. 6.00 (0-918823-00-5) Boyce-Pubns.

— A Picnic at Bull Run. (Pocket Tales Ser.: Bk. 3). (Illus.). 40p. (J). (ps-1). 1991. 6.00 (0-918823-05-6) Boyce-Pubns.

— The Small Patriot. (Pocket Tales Ser.: Bk. 2). (Illus.). 32p. (J). (ps-1). 1987. 6.00 (0-918823-01-3) Boyce-Pubns.

McPherson, Bruce, jt. auth. see Lusk, Diane.

McPherson, Bruce A. & Steck, Gary A., eds. Proceedings of the Fourth International Congress on Fruit Flies of Economic Importance. (Illus.). 672p. 1995. lib. bdg. 100.00 (1-877743-25-9) Sandhill Crane.

McPherson, Bruce R., ed. see DeGrazia, Emilio, et al.

McPherson, Bruce R., ed. see Schneemann, Carolee.

McPherson, Carole, jt. auth. see Post, Jory.

McPherson, Charles W., jt. ed. see Van Hoosier, G. L., Jr.

McPherson Co, History Book Committee. Families-Fiction-Facts, McPherson Co. 784p. text ed. 40.00 (0-9615586-8-7) Loup Valley.

McPherson, D. Jayne. Afterbeats. Mycue, Edward, ed. (Took Modern Poetry in English Ser.: No. 20). (Illus.). 28p. (Orig.). 1991. pap. 3.00 (1-879457-19-9) Norton Coker Pr.

McPherson, David. Shakespeare, Jonson, & the Myth of Venice. LC 89-40722. (Illus.). 160p. 1991. 33.50 (0-87413-397-1) U Delaware Pr.

McPherson, Dolly A. Order Out of Chaos: The Autobiographical Works of Maya Angelou. 1992. pap. 13.95 (1-85381-213-7, Pub. by Virago Pr UK) Trafalgar.

McPherson, Don. Leading Ladies. 1989. 14.99 (0-517-67654-0) Random Hse Value.

McPherson, Donald. Resolving Relievances: A Practical Approach. (C). 1983. teacher ed write for info. (0-8359-6664-X, Reston); pap. text ed. 21.00 (0-8359-6663-1, Reston) P-H.

McPherson, E. & Ashton, D. L. Metric Engineering Drawing Examples. (Illus.). 69p. (Orig.). reprint ed. pap. 25.00 (0-685-23762-1, 2032837) Bks Demand.

McPherson, E. W. Holcombe. The Holcombes: Nation Builders. (Illus.). 1346p. 1991. reprint ed. lib. bdg. 152.50 (0-8328-1989-1); reprint ed. pap. 142.50 (0-8328-1990-5) Higginson Bk Co.

McPherson, Edward. Handbook of Politics, 12 vols. in 4, Set. LC 72-146558. (Law, Politics & History Ser.). 1973. reprint ed. lib. bdg. 225.00 (0-306-70030-1) Da Capo.

— The Political History of the U. S. A. During the Period of Reconstruction. Hyman, Harold & Trefousse, Hans, eds. LC 77-127288. (Studies in American History & Government). 648p. 1973. reprint ed. lib. bdg. 85.00 (0-306-71206-7) Da Capo.

— Political History of the United States of America During the Great Rebellion. LC 73-127287. (American Constitutional & Legal History Ser). 1972. reprint ed. lib. bdg. 75.00 (0-306-71207-5) Da Capo.

McPherson, Edwin M., ed. Apparel Manufacturing Management Systems: A Computer-Oriented Approach. LC 87-12239. (Illus.). 392p. 1988. 48.00 (0-8155-1141-8) Noyes.

McPherson, Elizabeth & Cowan, Gregory. Plain English Please. 5th ed. 512p. (C). 1987. pap. text ed. write for info. (0-07-554227-7) McGraw.

McPherson, Elizabeth, jt. auth. see Cowan, Gregory.

McPherson, Emma S. Reveries of Raleigh. 286p. 1987. 75.00 (0-942179-02-1); pap. 35.00 (0-685-19192-3) Shelby Hse.

McPherson, Gene. When I Am Dictator of the U. S. A. A Plan to Save America. 231p. 1994. pap. 9.95 (0-9640797-0-4) Mt Adams Media.

McPherson, George & Laramore, Robert D. An Introduction to Electrical Machines & Transformers. 2nd ed. 216p. 1990. teacher ed 20.75 (0-471-51929-4); Net. text ed. write for info. (0-471-63529-4) Wiley.

McPherson, Geri, jt. auth. see McPherson, John.

McPherson, Gertrude H. Small Town Teacher. LC 71-188349. 259p. 1972. reprint ed. pap. 73.90 (0-7837-4170-7, 2059019) Bks Demand.

***McPherson, Harry.** A Political Education: A Washington Memoir. LC 94-32805. (Illus.). 520p. 1995. pap. 19.95 (0-292-75181-8) U of Tex Pr.

McPherson, Hugo. Hawthorne As Myth-Maker: A Study in Imagination. LC 76-430856. (University of Toronto, Department of English Studies & Texts: No. 16). 274p. reprint ed. pap. 78.10 (0-685-16026-2, 2026409) Bks Demand.

McPherson, J. B. Holey Bible. 276p. 1992. pap. 14.95 (0-9633589-7-9) Splendor Pub.

McPherson, J. C., jt. auth. see Eckert, W. J.

McPherson, J. E. The Pentatomoidea (Hemiptera) of Northeastern North America With Emphasis on the Fauna of Illinois. LC 81-9167. (Illus.). 253p. 1982. 30.00 (0-8093-1040-6) S Ill U Pr.

McPherson, J. G. Fun with Electronics. (Pocket Scientist Ser.). 64p. (J). (gr. 3-6). 1983. lib. bdg. 11.96 (0-88110-160-5); pap. 4.95 (0-86020-525-8) EDC.

McPherson, James. Gettysburg. (Illus.). 128p. 1993. 24.95 (1-878685-79-1) Turner Pub GA.

— Gettysburg. (Illus.). 1994. 250.00 (1-57036-052-9) Turner Pub GA.

McPherson, James A. Elbow Room. (Black History Titles Ser.). 1986. mass mkt. 5.99 (0-449-21357-9, Crest) Fawcett.

— Elbow Room: Short Stories. (Scribner Signature Edition Ser.). 256p. 1987. pap. 10.00 (0-684-18822-8, Scribners) S&S Trade.

— Hue & Cry. 1979. pap. 2.25 (0-449-24192-0, Crest) Fawcett.

McPherson, James M. The Abolitionist Legacy: From Reconstruction to the NAACP. LC 75-22101. 450p. reprint ed. pap. 128.30 (0-7837-3876-5, 2043718) Bks Demand.

— Abraham Lincoln & the Second American Revolution. 192p. 1991. 20.00 (0-19-505542-X) OUP.

— Abraham Lincoln & the Second American Revolution. (Illus.). 192p. 1992. pap. 9.95 (0-19-507606-0) OUP.

— Battle Cry of Freedom. 1989. pap. 17.50 (0-345-35942-9, Ballantine Trade) Ballantine.

M

An Asterisk (*) at the beginning of an entry indicates that the title is appearing in BIP for the first time.

— Battle Cry of Freedom: The Era of the Civil War. (History of U.S. Ser.: Vol. VI). (Illus.). 928p. (C). 1988. 39.95 (0-19-503863-0) OUP.

— Marching Toward Freedom: Blacks in the Civil War, 1861-1865. (Library of American History). (Illus.). 128p. (YA). (gr. 7-12). 1990. 16.95 (0-8160-2337-9) Facts on File.

— Marching Toward Freedom: Blacks in the Civil War 1861-1865. Scott, John A., ed. (Library of American History). (Illus.). 128p. 1994. reprint ed. pap. 8.95 (0-8160-3092-8) Facts on File.

— Negro's Civil War: How American Blacks Felt & Acted During the War for the Union. 1991. pap. 12.00 (0-345-37120-8, Ballantine Trade) Ballantine.

— Ordeal by Fire, Vol. 1. 2nd ed. LC 92-23635. 1992. pap. text ed. write for info. (0-07-045837-5) McGraw.

— Ordeal by Fire, Vol. 2. 2nd ed. LC 92-23635. 1992. pap. text ed. write for info. (0-07-045838-3) McGraw.

— Ordeal by Fire: The Civil War & Reconstruction. LC 81-11832. (Illus.). 1981. 29.95 (0-685-02839-9) McGraw.

— Ordeal by Fire: The Civil War & Reconstruction. 2nd ed. 1992. text ed. write for info. (0-07-045842-1) McGraw.

— What They Fought for, 1861-1865. LC 93-36934. (Walter Lynwood Fleming Lectures in Southern History). 96p. (C). 1994. 16.95 (0-8071-1904-0) La State U Pr.

— What They Fought for 1861-1865. LC 94-38423. 1995. 10.00 (0-385-47634-5, Anchor NY) Doubleday.

McPherson, James M., ed. The Atlas of the Civil War. LC 94-16962. 1994. text ed. 40.00 (0-02-579050-1) Macmillan.

— Battle Chronicles of the Civil War, 6 vols. (Illus.). 1989. text ed. 150.00 (0-02-920661-8) Macmillan.

— We Cannot Escape History: Lincoln & the Last Best Hope of Earth. LC 95-2279. 1995. write for info. (0-252-02190-8) U of Ill Pr.

McPherson, James M. & Katz, William L., eds. Anti-Slavery Crusade in America, 70 vols., Set. 1970. 1,102.00 (0-405-00600-4) Ayer.

McPherson, Jan. The Dog School. LC 90-10085. (Highgate Collection). (Illus.). 24p. (J). (gr. 1-4). 1990. lib. bdg. 15.96 (0-8114-2697-1) Raintree Steck-V.

— In the Cold, Cold Dawn. LC 92-31918. (Voyages Ser.). (J). 1993. 4.25 (0-383-03578-3) SRA Schl Grp.

McPherson, Jean. Collection of Short Stories. 56p. 1993. pap. 10.95 (0-8059-3363-8) Dorrance.

***McPherson, John.** The Adventures of Buck Felner. LC 94-43860. 1995. pap. 7.99 (0-310-48681-5) Zondervan.

— Close to Home. 1994. pap. 6.95 (0-8362-1750-0) Andrews & McMeel.

— Close to Home Revisited. (Illus.). 1995. pap. 12.95 (0-8362-0427-1) Andrews & McMeel.

— Dangerously Close To Home: A Close to Home Collection. (Illus.). 128p. 1995. pap. 6.95 (0-8362-1782-9) Andrews & McMeel.

— High School Isn't Pretty. (Illus.). 104p. (Orig.). 1993. pap. 6.95 (0-8362-1728-4) Andrews & McMeel.

— Life at McPherson High. 144p. 1991. pap. 6.99 (0-310-71161-4) Zondervan.

— Life at McPherson High. 160p. 1995. pap. text ed. 3.99 (0-06-100909-1) Zondervan.

— McPherson Goes to Church. (Illus.). 128p. 1994. pap. 6.99 (0-310-48181-3) Zondervan.

— McPherson Goes to Work. 128p. 1992. pap. 6.99 (0-310-58611-9) Zondervan.

— McPherson Goes to Work. (Illus.). 128p. 1994. mass mkt. 3.99 (0-06-100863-X) Zondervan.

— McPherson on Parenting. 128p. 1992. pap. 6.99 (0-310-58071-4) Zondervan.

— McPherson's Marriage Album. 112p. 1991. pap. 6.99 (0-310-53901-3) Zondervan.

— McPherson's Marriage Album. 1994. pap. text ed. 3.99 (0-06-100865-6) Zondervan.

— McPherson's Sports & Fitness Manual. 128p. 1993. pap. 6.99 (0-310-61431-7) Zondervan.

— One Step Closer to Home. 1994. pap. 6.95 (0-8362-1764-0) Andrews & McMeel.

McPherson, John & McPherson, Geri. Primitive Wilderness Living & Survival Skills. (Illus.). 408p. 1993. pap. 24.95 (0-89745-997-0) Sunflower U Pr.

McPherson, John C., ed. see Reid, Thomas.

McPherson, John H. History of Liberia. LC 78-63806. (Johns Hopkins University. Studies in the Social Sciences. Thirtieth Ser. 1912: No. 9). reprint ed. 11.50 (0-404-61069-2) AMS Pr.

***McPherson, John R.** Build Your Own Mobile Power Tool Centers. (Illus.). 144p. (Orig.). 1995. pap. 19.99 (1-55870-380-2) Betterway Bks.

McPherson, Joseph M. Primitive Beliefs in the North-East of Scotland. Dorson, Richard M., ed. LC 77-70605. (International Folklore Ser.). 1977. reprint ed. lib. bdg. 26.95 (0-405-10109-0) Ayer.

McPherson, Joseph W. The Moulids of Egypt: Egyptian Saints-Days. LC 77-87654. reprint ed. 28.50 (0-404-16408-0) AMS Pr.

***McPherson, Joyce.** Blaise Pascal: Seeker of Truth. 130p. (J). (gr. 4-8). 1996. pap. 7.95 (1-882514-17-3) Greenleaf TN.

McPherson, Karen S. Incriminations: Guilty Women - Telling Stories. LC 93-39520. 1994. 29.95 (0-691-03252-1) Princeton U Pr.

McPherson, Kate, jt. ed. see Kinsley, Carol W.

McPherson, Kenneth. The Indian Ocean: A History of Peoples & the Sea. (Illus.). 328p. 1994. 26.00 (0-19-563374-1) OUP.

— Muslim Microcosm: Calcutta, 1918-1935. 174p. (Orig.). 1974. pap. text ed. 39.50 (3-515-01992-8) Coronet Bks.

McPherson Library - Reference Division - University of Victoria Staff. Creative Canada: A Biographical Dictionary of Twentieth-Century Creative & Performing Artists, 2 vols., 2. LC 73-80898. 1972. 35.00 (0-8020-3285-0) U of Toronto Pr.

McPherson, M., jt. auth. see Feldman, Ron.

McPherson, M. B. Prospects for Metropolitan Water Management. 240p. 1970. pap. 7.00 (0-87262-026-3) Am Soc Civil Eng.

McPherson, M. J., ed. Directed Mutagenesis: A Practical Approach. (Practical Approach Ser.). (Illus.). 282p. 1991. pap. 44.00 (0-19-963140-9, IRL Pr) OUP.

McPherson, M. J., et al, eds. PCR: A Practical Approach. (Practical Approach Ser.). (Illus.). 280p. 1991. pap. 39.00 (0-19-963196-4, IRL Pr) OUP.

— PCR Vol. 2: A Practical Approach. (The Practical Approach Ser.: No. 150). (Illus.). 352p. 1995. pap. text ed. 45.00 (0-19-963424-6, IRL Pr) OUP.

— PCR Vol. 2: A Practical Approach. (The Practical Approach Ser.: No. 150). (Illus.). 352p. 1995. text ed. 79.00 (0-19-963425-4, IRL Pr) OUP.

McPherson, Malcolm J., intro. Proceedings of the 4th US Mine Ventilation Symposium. LC 89-60828. (Illus.). 611p. 1989. 83.50 (0-87335-082-0, 082-0) SMM&E Inc.

McPherson, Marion W., jt. auth. see Popplestone, John A.

McPherson, Marion W., jt. auth. see Popplestone, John.

McPherson, Mark. Caring for Your Cat. LC 84-223. (Pet Library Ser.). (Illus.). 48p. (J). (gr. 3-7). 1985. lib. bdg. 9.89 (0-8167-0115-6); pap. text ed. 2.95 (0-8167-0116-4) Troll Assocs.

— Caring for Your Dog. LC 84-222. (Pet Library Ser.). (Illus.). 48p. (J). (gr. 3-7). 1985. lib. bdg. 9.89 (0-8167-0113-X); pap. 2.95 (0-8167-0114-8) Troll Assocs.

— Caring for Your Fish. LC 84-8563. (Pet Library Ser.). (Illus.). 48p. (J). (gr. 3-7). 1985. lib. bdg. 9.89 (0-8167-0109-1); pap. text ed. 2.95 (0-8167-0110-5) Troll Assocs.

— Choosing Your Pet. LC 84-226. (Pet Library Ser.). (Illus.). 48p. (J). (gr. 3-7). 1985. lib. bdg. 9.89 (0-8167-0111-3) Troll Assocs.

McPherson, Michael. Singing with the Owls. 58p. 1983. pap. 5.95 (0-932136-05-2) Petronium HI.

McPherson, Michael S. & Schapiro, Morton O. Keeping College Affordable: Government & Educational Opportunity. 262p. 1991. 34.95 (0-8157-5642-9); pap. 14.95 (0-8157-5641-0) Brookings.

McPherson, Michael S., ed. see Pechman, Joseph.

McPherson, Michael S., et al, eds. Paying the Piper: Productivity, Incentives, & Financing in U. S. Higher Education. (Economics of Education Ser.). 300p. (C). 1993. text ed. 59.50 (0-472-10404-7) U of Mich Pr.

McPherson, Murray B. Regional Earth Science Information in Local Water Management. 185p. 1975. pap. 14.00 (0-87262-151-0) Am Soc Civil Eng.

McPherson, Natalie. Machines & Economic Growth: The Implications for Growth Theory. LC 93-44509. (Contributions in Economics & Economic History Ser.). 280p. 1994. text ed. 59.95 (0-313-29255-8, Greenwood Pr) Greenwood.

McPherson, Richard A., jt. auth. see Sacher, Ronald.

McPherson, Robert G., jt. auth. see Sinnema, William.

McPherson, Robert S. Sacred Land, Sacred View: Navajo Perceptions of the Four Corners Region. LC 91-33322. (Illus.). 160p. 1992. pap. 8.95 (1-56085-008-6) Signature Bks.

McPherson, Sandra. Elegies for the Hot Season. LC 81-5455. (American Poetry Ser.: Vol. 23). 71p. 1982. reprint ed. pap. 5.95 (0-912946-92-X) Ecco Pr.

— Floralia. (Poetry Ser.). (Illus.). 24p. (Orig.). 1985. pap. 9.95 (0-317-39884-9) Seluzicki Fine Bks.

— Floralia. deluxe ed. (Poetry Ser.). (Illus.). 24p. (Orig.). 1985. 50.00 (0-317-39885-7) Seluzicki Fine Bks.

— The God of Indeterminacy: Poems. LC 92-14714. (Illus.). 104p. (C). 1993. pap. 11.95 (0-252-06271-X) U of Ill Pr.

— Patron Happiness. LC 82-11490. (American Poetry Ser.). 70p. 1984. pap. 6.50 (0-88001-022-3) Ecco Pr.

— Pheasant Flower. (Poetry Chapbook Ser.). 32p. (Orig.). 1985. pap. 4.00 (0-937669-18-0) Owl Creek Pr.

— Radiation. LC 73-81356. (American Poetry Ser.: Vol. 1). 80p. 1973. pap. 6.95 (0-912946-05-9) Ecco Pr.

— Streamers. 175p. (C). 1988. 13.95 (0-88001-213-7) Ecco Pr.

— Streamers. LC 88-4253. 1989. pap. 7.95 (0-88001-214-5) Ecco Pr.

— The Year of Our Birth. LC 77-85295. (American Poetry Ser.: No. 15). 1978. 12.95 (0-912946-48-2) Ecco Pr.

— The Year of Our Birth. LC 77-85295. (American Poetry Ser.: No. 15). 1979. pap. 6.95 (0-912946-49-0) Ecco Pr.

McPherson, Scott. Marvin's Room. (Orig.). 1992. pap. 4.75 (0-8222-1312-5) Dramatists Play.

— Marvin's Room. LC 92-53545. 128p. (Orig.). 1992. pap. 9.00 (0-452-26922-9, Plume) NAL-Dutton.

McPherson, Stephanie. Rooftop Astronomer: A Story about Maria Mitchell. (Illus.). 32p. (J). (gr. 3-6). 1990. lib. bdg. 15.95 (0-87614-410-5, Carolrhoda) Lerner Group.

McPherson, Stephanie S. I Speak for the Women: A Story about Lucy Stone. LC 92-13786. (Creative Minds Ser.). (Illus.). (J). 1992. 15.95 (0-87614-740-6, Carolrhoda) Lerner Group.

— Ordinary Genius: The Story of Albert Einstein. LC 93-1408. (Trailblazers Ser.). 96p. (J). (gr. 3-7). 1995. lib. bdg. 17.50 (0-87614-788-0, Carolrhoda) Lerner Group.

— Peace & Bread: The Story of Jane Addams. LC 93-6736. (J). (gr. 4-7). 1993. 17.50 (0-87614-792-9, Carolrhoda) Lerner Group.

— Workers' Detective: A Story about Alice Hamilton. (J). (gr. 3-6). 1992. 15.95 (0-87614-699-X, Carolrhoda) Lerner Group.

McPherson, Thomas. The Dodge Story. LC 92-26168. (Motorbooks International Crestline Ser.). (Illus.). 320p. 1992. 29.95 (0-87938-697-5) Motorbooks Intl.

McPherson, William H. Public Employee Relations in West Germany. LC 77-634396. (Comparative Studies in Public Employment Labor Relations Ser.). 1971. 10.95 (0-87736-009-X); pap. 5.95 (0-87736-010-3) U of Mich Inst Labor.

McPherson, Woodrow W., ed. Economic Development of Tropical Agriculture: Theory, Policy, Strategy, & Organization. LC 68-24368. (Illus.). 344p. reprint ed. pap. 98.10 (0-7837-5102-8, 2044801) Bks Demand.

McPherson, Yaffa. Yaffa, God's Prickly Pear. LC 92-97176. 208p. (Orig.). 1992. pap. 10.95 (0-9634792-0-2) Intimate Awe.

McPhetres, Sam. The Practical User's Guide to the Trust Territory Archives. (Educational Ser.: No. 14). 45p. 1992. pap. 7.50 (1-878453-12-2) Univ Guam MAR Ctr.

McPhillips, Martin. The Constitutional Convention. LC 85-40169. (Turning Points in American History Ser.). (Illus.). 64p. (J). (gr. 5 up). 1985. lib. bdg. 14.95 (0-382-06827-0) Silver Burdett Pr.

— Hiroshima. LC 85-40170. (Turning Points in American History Ser.). (Illus.). 64p. (J). (gr. 5 up). 1985. lib. bdg. 14.95 (0-382-06829-7) Silver Burdett Pr.

***McPoil, Thomas G.** Physical Therapy of the Foot & Ankle. 2nd ed. Hunt, Gary C., ed. LC 95-7870. (Clinics in Physical Therapy Ser.). 1995. write for info. (0-443-08925-6) Churchill.

McPolin, James. John. LC 79-64670. (New Testament Message Ser.: Vol. 6). 273p. 1979. pap. 12.95 (0-8146-5129-1) Liturgical Pr.

McPolin, M. John. 1989. pap. 21.00 (0-86217-013-3, Pub. by Veritas IE) St Mut.

***McProud, C. G., ed.** Audio Anthology Vol. 1: When Audio Was Young. LC 87-62118. (Illus.). 124p. 1987. pap. text ed. 16.95 (0-8338-0195-3) Audio Amateur.

— Audio Anthology Vol. 2: When Audio Was Young. (Illus.). 124p. 1989. pap. text ed. 16.95 (0-8338-0197-X) Audio Amateur.

— Audio Anthology Vol. 3: When Audio Was Young. LC 90-80999. (Illus.). 124p. 1990. pap. text ed. 16.95 (0-9624191-1-7) Audio Amateur.

— Audio Anthology Vol. 4: When Audio Was Young. LC 91-72106. (Illus.). 144p. 1991. pap. text ed. 16.95 (0-9624191-9-2) Audio Amateur.

McQ, Joe. The Steps We Took. (Illus.). 180p. (Orig.). 1990. pap. 10.00 (0-87483-151-2) August Hse.

McQain, Jeff, jt. auth. see Malless, Stan.

***McQoron, Ted.** Computers & What You Absolutely Need to Know about Them. 61p. (YA). (gr. 7-12). 1995. pap. write for info. (1-57515-047-6) PPI Pubng.

McQuade, Donald. Harper American Literature Complete with Huck Finn. (C). 1990. text ed. 38.50 (0-06-044353-7) HarpCollege.

McQuade, Donald & Atwan, Robert. HarperCollins' American Literature, 2 vols. (C). 1994. text ed. 38.50 (0-06-500965-7) HarpCollege.

— HarperCollins' American Literature, 2 vols., 1. (C). 1994. text ed. 38.50 (0-06-500964-9) HarpCollege.

— The Winchester Reader. LC 89-63916. 1000p. (Orig.). (C). 1991. pap. text ed. 18.50 (0-312-04880-7, Bedford Bks); pap. text ed. 1.27 (0-312-04879-3, Bedford Bks) St Martin.

— The Writer's Presence: A Pool of Essays. 704p. 1994. pap. text ed. 18.00 (0-312-08480-3) St Martin.

McQuade, Donald & Turner, Michael. Student Writers at Work & in the Company of Others: The Bedford Prizes. 3rd ed. Sommers, Nancy et al, eds. LC 88-70420. 704p. (C). 1989. pap. text ed. 18.50 (0-312-00247-5) St Martin.

McQuade, Donald, jt. auth. see Atwan, Robert.

McQuade, Donald, ed. see Emerson, Ralph Waldo.

McQuade, Donald A., ed. The Territory of Language: Linguistics, Stylistics, & the Teaching of Composition. LC 85-2080. 376p. (Orig.). (C). 1986. text ed. 29.95 (0-8093-1217-4); pap. text ed. 19.95 (0-8093-1215-8) S Ill U Pr.

McQuade, Finlay & Champagne, David W. How to Make a Better School. LC 94-2066. 1994. 34.95 (0-205-14120-X) Allyn.

McQuade, Joseph M., jt. auth. see Glick, Robert R.

McQuade, Lawerence C. East-West Trade: Managing Encounter & Accommodation. 194p. 1977. 15.00 (0-317-33691-6); pap. 5.95 (0-317-33692-4) Atl Coun US.

***McQuade, Molly.** An Unsentimental Education: Writers & Chicago. LC 94-43441. 1995. 18.95 (0-226-56210-7) U Ch Pr.

McQuade, Ralph J. Cases in Financial Accounting & Reporting. LC 92-20563. 1992. pap. text ed. write for info. (0-07-045655-0) McGraw.

McQuade, Stanley. Medical Information Systems for Lawyers, 2 vols. 2nd ed. LC 93-73676. 1993. ring bd. 225.00 (0-685-59889-6) Clark Boardman Callaghan.

McQuade, Susan. Great-Grandpa. LC 92-27235. (Voyages Ser.). (Illus.). (J). 1993. 3.75 (0-383-03622-4) SRA Schl Grp.

McQuade, Walter & Aikman, Ann. Stress: What It Is, What It Can Do to Your Health, How to Handle It. rev. ed. 288p. 1993. pap. 5.99 (0-451-17651-0, Sig) NAL-Dutton.

McQuaid. Outlaw Territory. (Gunsmoke Western Ser.). 12.95 (0-86220-916-1, C0993, Gunsmoke) Chivers N Amer.

McQuaid, E. Patrick & Stahl, Barbara J. How to Get into an Ivy League School. write for info. (0-318-59705-5) S&S Trade.

McQuaid, Elwood. Come, Walk with Me. LC 89-82580. 1990. pap. 5.95 (0-915540-47-9) Frnds Israel.

— It Is No Dream. LC 78-51766. 1978. pap. 5.95 (0-915540-21-5) Frnds Israel.

— Not to the Strong. LC 91-71438. 1991. pap. 5.95 (0-915540-45-2) Frnds Israel.

— The Outpouring. LC 85-29866. 1990. pap. 5.95 (0-915540-49-5) Frnds Israel.

— ZVI. LC 78-56149. 1978. pap. 4.95 (0-915540-23-1) Frnds Israel.

— Zvi & the Next Generation. LC 88-80875. 1988. pap. 5.95 (0-915540-43-6) Frnds Israel.

McQuaid, Gary. Limiting Concept of Phase-Lock Hypnotherapy. Kaufmann, Ron, ed. LC 89-71746. 236p. (Orig.). 1991. pap. 16.95 (0-940539-08-X) Heridonius.

McQuaid, J., ed. Heavy Gas Dispersion Trails at Thorney Islands: Proceedings of a Symposium Held at the University of Sheffield, Great Britain, 3-5 April, 1984. (Chemical Engineering Monographs 1984: 22). 436p. 1985. 172.00 (0-444-42507-1) Elsevier.

McQuaid, Jameste P., ed. Index to American Photographic Collections. 1982. lib. bdg. 85.00 (0-8161-0400-X, Hall Library) G K Hall.

McQuaid, Kim. The Anxious Years: America in the Vietnam-Watergate Era. LC 88-47907. 368p. 1989. 19.95 (0-685-54178-9) Basic.

— Uneasy Partners: Big Business in American Politics, 1945-1990. LC 93-17520. (American Moment Ser.). 272p. (C). 1993. text ed. 38.95 (0-8018-4651-X); pap. text ed. 12.95 (0-8018-4652-8) Johns Hopkins.

McQuaid, Kim, jt. auth. see Berkowitz, Edward D.

McQuaid, Matilda. Santiago Calatrava: Structure & Expression. (Illus.). 40p. 1993. pap. 9.95 (0-685-65844-9); pap. 9.95 (0-8109-6128-8) Abrams.

McQuaid, Matilda, jt. ed. see Berkeley, Ellen P.

McQuaid, Robert W. The Craft of Writing Technical Manuals. LC 82-91154. (Illus.). 54p. 1983. 15.00 (0-912259-00-0) R W McQuaid.

— The Craft of Writing Technical Manuals. 2nd ed. LC 82-91154. (Handbook Edition Ser.). (Illus.). 107p. (C). 1990. student ed 20.00 (0-912259-01-9) R W McQuaid.

McQuaid, Ronald, jt. ed. see Breheny, Michael.

McQuaig, Douglas J. College Accounting. 4th ed. 1989. teacher ed write for info. (0-318-63321-3) HM.

— CW Hale Medical Practice Set. 2nd ed. (College Accounting Fundamentals). 12.95 (0-685-42419-7) HM.

McQuaig, Jack, et al. How to Interview & Hire Productive People. LC 80-70952. 320p. 1981. 17.95 (0-8119-0332-X) LIFETIME.

McQuaig, Jack H. Your Business, Your Son & You. 192p. 20.00 (0-686-62444-0) B Klein Pubns.

McQuail, Denis. Communication. LC 75-11683. (A.O.M.S. Social Processes Ser.). (Illus.). 240p. 1975. pap. text ed. 14.95 (0-582-29578-5) Longman.

— Mass Communication Theory: An Introduction. 3rd ed. 448p. 1994. 65.00 (0-8039-7784-0); pap. 22.95 (0-8039-7785-9) Sage.

— Media Performance: Mass Communication & the Public Interest. 352p. (C). 1992. text ed. 65.00 (0-8039-8294-1); pap. text ed. 21.95 (0-8039-8295-X) Sage.

— Towards a Sociology of Mass Communications. 1969. pap. text ed. write for info. (0-686-66487-6, 97480) Macmillan.

McQuail, Denis & Windahl, Sven. Communication Models for the Study of Mass Communications. 2nd ed. LC 92-28665. (C). 1994. pap. text ed. 21.95 (0-582-03650-X, 79758) Longman.

McQuain, Jeff, jt. auth. see Malless, Stan.

McQuain, Jeffrey, jt. ed. see Manser, Martin.

McQuaker, R. J. Computer Choice: A Manual for the Practitioner. 178p. 1979. 59.00 (0-444-85250-6, North Holland) Elsevier.

McQuany, Joe. Big Book Study Guide. 145p. 1986. pap. text ed. 8.95 (1-883094-00-3) Kelly Fnd.

— Recovery Dynamics: Client Guide Book. 104p. 1989. pap. text ed. 15.00 (1-883094-02-X) Kelly Fnd.

— Recovery Dynamics: Counselors Manual. 400p. 1989. text ed. 60.00 (1-883094-01-1) Kelly Fnd.

— Recovery Dynamics: Individual Evaluation Packet. 96p. 1989. pap. text ed. 14.00 (1-883094-03-8) Kelly Fnd.

McQuarie, Donald. Marx: Sociology-Social Change-Capitalism. 15.95 (0-7043-3221-3, Pub. by Quartet UK); pap. 6.95 (0-686-82876-3, Pub. by Quartet UK) Charles River Bks.

Mcquarie, Donald & Denisoff, R. Serge, eds. Readings in Contemporary Sociological Theory: From Modernity to Post-Modernity. LC 94-3991. 440p. 1994. pap. text ed. write for info. (0-13-104266-1) P-H.

McQuarrie. General Chemistry. 2nd ed. (C). 1995. pap. text ed. write for info. (0-7167-1913-4) W H Freeman.

— General Chemistry Package. (C). 1995. pap. text ed. write for info. (0-7167-2305-0) W H Freeman.

— Re-Operative General Surgery: Timing Tactics & Techniques. 856p. 1991. 135.00 (0-8151-5860-2, Yr Bk Med Pubs) Mosby Yr Bk.

— Study Guide-Solutions Manual to Accompany General CChemistry. 3rd ed. (C). 1995. pap. text ed. write for info. (0-7167-2179-1) W H Freeman.

McQuarrie, Donald A. Quantum Chemistry. LC 82-51234. (Physical Chemistry Ser.). (Illus.). 517p. (C). 1983. text ed. 48.50 (0-935702-13-X) Univ Sci Bks.

— Quantum Chemistry Solutions Manual. (Physical Chemistry Ser.). 241p. (C). 1985. student ed 22.00 (0-935702-16-4) Univ Sci Bks.

— Statistical Mechanics. (Chemistry Ser.). 640p. (C). 1990. text ed. 92.50 (0-06-044366-9) HarpCollege.

— Statistical Thermodynamics. 343p. (C). 1985. pap. text ed. 39.00 (0-935702-18-0) Univ Sci Bks.

McQuarrie, Donald A., ed. see Rock, Peter A.

McQuarrie, Donald G., et al. Head & Neck Cancer: Clinical Decisions & Management Principles. (Illus.). 540p. 1986. 165.00 (0-8151-5848-3, ACZ-1, Yr Bk Med Pubs) Mosby Yr Bk.

McQuarrie, Edward F. Customer Visits: Tools to Build Market Focus. (Illus.). 176p. (C). 1993. text ed. 46.00 (0-8039-4669-4); pap. text ed. 21.50 (0-8039-4670-8) Sage.

An Asterisk (*) at the beginning of an entry indicates that the title is appearing in BIP for the first time.

McQuarrie, John. Canadian Fighter Pilot. 1992. 34.95 (*0-07-551480-X*, Pub. by McGrw-Hill Ryerson CN) Howell Pr VA.
— Til We Meet Again. 1992. 34.95 (*0-07-551301-3*, Pub. by McGrw-Hill Ryerson CN) Howell Pr VA.
***McQuarrie, Ralph, illus.** The Illustrated Star Wars Universe. LC 95-14854. 1995. write for info. (*0-553-09302-9*) Bantam.
McQuarrie, Rock. General Chemistry. 3rd ed. LC 90-3706. (Illus.). 1184p. (C). 1995. teacher ed 16.95 (*0-7167-2185-6*); text ed. write for info. (*0-7167-2132-5*); trans. 295.00 (*0-7167-2186-4*); 69.95 (*0-7167-2187-2*) W H Freeman.
McQuattie, Shiela, jt. auth. see Dale, Catherine.
McQuay, Chris. Behold, Thy Handmaid. 208p. (Orig.). (C). 1992. pap. 7.95 (*0-9619761-1-X*) Chris Life Ctr.
McQuay, Earl P. Joseph: Seeing God in the Worst of Times. 1990. 3.95 (*0-89636-257-4*, AC 193); teacher ed 5.95 (*0-685-38715-1*, ATRM 193) Accent CO.
— Keys to Interpreting the Bible. (Orig.). 1993. pap. 8.99 (*0-8054-8158-3*) Broadman.
— Learning to Study the Bible. (Orig.). 1992. pap. 9.99 (*0-8054-8159-1*) Broadman.
McQuay, Mike. State of Siege. 1994. mass mkt. 5.99 (*0-553-56292-4*) Bantam.
McQueary, Carl, jt. auth. see Paulissen, Maisie.
***McQueary, Rod & Wallis, Sue, eds.** Whole Cowboy Catalog: An Entertaining Guide to Everything Western. LC 95-13702. (Illus.). 1995. pap. 14.95 (*0-87905-689-4*) Gibbs Smith Pub.
McQueen. Essentials of Classroom Management & Discipline. (C). 1991. text ed. 28.50 (*0-673-46354-0*) HarpCollege.
— What Does Sunny Bunny Love? (Wee Pudgy Board Bks.). (J). (gr. 2 up). 1988. 2.50 (*0-448-09252-2*, G&D) Putnam Pub Group.
McQueen, ed. see Herodotus.
***McQueen, Alex. S.** History of Charlton County. LC 78-12909. (Illus.). 295p. 1988. reprint ed. 25.00 (*0-87152-286-1*) Reprint.
McQueen, Alex S. History of Charlton County, Georgia. (Illus.). 269p. 1993. reprint ed. lib. bdg. 32.50 (*0-8328-2933-1*) Higginson Bk Co.
McQueen, Barbara, jt. auth. see McQueen, Jim.
McQueen, C. Richard & Crestol, Jack. Federal Tax Aspects of Bankruptcy. LC 84-11. (Tax & Estate Planning Ser.). 776p. 1984. 110.00 (*0-685-42684-X*) Shepards-McGraw.
McQueen, Charlene A. In Vitro Toxicology. 450p. 1989. 81.95 (*0-936923-23-7*, RA1199) CRC Pr.
McQueen, Cyrus B. Field Guide to the Peat Mosses of Boreal North America. LC 89-40615. (Illus.). 154p. 1990. 22.95 (*0-87451-522-X*) U Pr of New Eng.
McQueen, David V., jt. ed. see Martin, Claudia J.
McQueen, H. J., ed. see Metallurgical Society of AIME Staff.
***McQueen, Ian.** Japan: A Budget Travel Guide. (Illus.). 663p. 1995. pap. 20.00 (*4-7700-1645-X*) Kodansha.
McQueen, Iris. Sexual Harassment in the Workplace: The Management View. Levers, Joan et al, eds. LC 82-99921. (Illus.). 138p. (Orig.). 1983. text ed. 24.95 (*0-9609354-1-X*); pap. 14.95 (*0-9609354-0-1*) McQueen & Son.
McQueen, Jeff A. Gently, with a Dead Steven. 136p. (Orig.). 1994. pap. 4.95 (*0-940096-02-1*) Fine Line Bks.
McQueen, Jim & McQueen, Barbara. Orchids of Thailand. (Illus.). 208p. Date not set. pap. write for info. (*0-88192-301-X*) Timber.
McQueen, John & McQueen, Winifred, eds. Walter Bower's Scotichronicon, Bks. III & IV. (Scotichronicon Ser.). 400p. 1989. Books III & IV. text ed. 70.00 (*0-08-036410-1*, Pub. by Aberdeen U Pr) Macmillan.
McQueen, Judy, ed. IOLS '92: Proceedings of the 7th Integrated Online Library Systems Meeting, May 6-7, 1992. 200p. 1992. pap. 30.00 (*0-938734-62-8*) Learned Info.
McQueen, Judy, jt. auth. see Basch, N. Bernard.
McQueen, Kelly & Fassler, David. Let's Talk Trash: The Kids' Book about Recycling. LC 90-21400. (Illus.). 168p. (J). (ps-6). 1991. pap. 14.95 (*0-914525-19-0*); 18.95 (*0-914525-20-4*) Waterfront Bks.
McQueen, Kelly, jt. auth. see Fassler, David.
McQueen, Lucinda. Counting Bears. (Wee Pudgy Board Bks.). (Illus.). 24p. (J). (gr. 1-3). 1990. bds. 2.50 (*0-448-02263-X*, G&D) Putnam Pub Group.
— La Gallinita Roja. (SPA.). (J). 1989. pap. 19.95 (*0-590-71879-7*) Scholastic Inc.
Mcqueen, Lucinda. La Gallinita Roja. (J). (ps). 1991. pap. 2.95 (*0-590-44927-3*) Scholastic Inc.
McQueen, Lucinda. Little Lamb's Easter Surprise. (Illus.). 10p. (J). (ps). 1994. bds. 4.95 (*0-590-47803-6*, Cartwheel) Scholastic Inc.
— Pet the Baby Farm Animals: Their Fur Feels Real! (Illus.). 16p. (J). (ps). 1994. 8.95 (*0-590-47687-4*, Cartwheel) Scholastic Inc.
— Santa's Christmas Surprise. (Sparkling Christmas Tree Books Ser.). (Illus.). 10p. (J). (ps). 1994. bds. 4.95 (*0-590-48041-3*, Cartwheel) Scholastic Inc.
— Snowman's Christmas Surprise. (Sparkling Christmas Tree Books Ser.). (Illus.). 10p. (J). (ps). 1994. bds. 4.95 (*0-590-48042-1*, Cartwheel) Scholastic Inc.
McQueen, Lucinda, illus. Coloring Bears. LC 90-83242. (Wee Pudgy Board Bks.). 24p. (J). (ps). 1991. 2.50 (*0-448-40126-6*, G&D) Putnam Pub Group.
— The Little Red Hen. (Easy to Read Folktales Ser.). 32p. (Orig.). (J). (gr. k-2). 1985. Big book. 19.95 (*0-590-71718-9*); pap. 2.50 (*0-590-41145-4*) Scholastic Inc.
— Pudgy Zoo Babies. (Pudgy Board Bks.). 16p. (J). 1989. bds. 2.95 (*0-448-02256-7*, G&D) Putnam Pub Group.
McQueen, Marcia, jt. auth. see Faughn, Jackie.
McQueen, Matthew. SI Unit Pocket Guide. LC 89-18044. 144p. 1990. 22.50 (*0-89189-282-6*) Am Soc Clinical.
McQueen, Melvin E. The Spoon Fed Christian. 144p. 1993. 14.95 (*0-926099-01-9*) Netcom.
McQueen, Priscilla L. Around the World in Twenty Legends. (Basic Readers Ser.). 1970. teacher ed 3.25 (*0-685-36208-6*); student ed 2.30 (*0-685-36209-4*) McQueen.
— Carousel of Stories. (Basic Readers Ser.). 1970. 10.98 (*0-917186-13-3*); student ed 7.53 (*0-917186-14-1*) McQueen.
— Getting Ready for Reading, Writing & Arithmetic. (Illus.). teacher ed 3.42 (*0-685-16724-0*) McQueen.
— How Many. (Illus.). (J). (gr. k). 1968. pap. 2.54 (*0-685-16725-9*) McQueen.
— Imagine That. (Basic Readers Ser.). 1970. teacher ed 3.25 (*0-685-36210-8*); teacher ed 2.30 (*0-685-36211-6*) McQueen.
— Our Own Country. (Basic Readers Ser.). 1970. teacher ed 3.25 (*0-685-36212-4*); student ed 2.30 (*0-685-36213-2*) McQueen.
— We Can Read: Story Pack-54 Little Stories. (J). 1973. pap. 18.66 (*0-685-47089-X*) McQueen.
— What Kind. (Illus.). (J). (gr. k). 1968. pap. 2.07 (*0-685-16726-7*) McQueen.
— Which One. (Illus.). (J). (gr. k). 1968. pap. 6.15 (*0-685-16727-5*) McQueen.
***McQueen, Richard & Williams, Jack.** Tax Aspects of Bankruptcy Law & Practice. 2nd ed. LC 94-44017. (Tax & Estate Planning Ser.). 1994. write for info. (*0-07-172646-2*) Shepards-McGraw.
McQueen, Shawna, jt. auth. see Eisenhauer, Jack.
***McQueen, Steffani S.** Dr. Mom's Low-Fat, No-Fat Fix It Fast Cookbook. 180p. 1994. pap. 11.95 (*0-9643854-0-6*) Sterling Texas.
McQueen, Tiffany, jt. auth. see Grubbs, Tabitha.
McQueen, Tom. Passing the FAA Written Exam: Commercial. 1991. pap. text ed. 9.95 (*0-07-155964-7*) McGraw.
Mcqueen, Tom. Passing the FAA Written Exam: Commercial. 1991. pap. 9.95 (*0-8306-3579-3*, TAB-Aero) TAB Bks.
McQueen, Tom. Passing the FAA Written Exam: Instrument. 1991. pap. text ed. 11.95 (*0-07-155977-9*) McGraw.
— Passing the FAA Written Exam: Instrument. (Illus.). 210p. 1990. pap. 11.95 (*0-8306-3580-7*, 3580, TAB-Aero) TAB Bks.
— Passing the FAA Written Exam: Private Pilot. (Illus.). 130p. 1991. pap. 9.95 (*0-8306-3581-5*, 3581, TAB-Aero) TAB Bks.
McQueen, William A., intro. A Selection of Emblems. LC 92-22032. (Augustan Reprints Ser.: No. 155-156 (1972)). reprint ed. 18.50 (*0-404-70155-8*, PR1209) AMS Pr.
McQueen, William A., jt. auth. see Hanford, James H.
McQueen-Williams, Morvyth & Apisson, Barbara. A Diet for One Hundred Healthy Happy Years: Health Secrets from the Caucasus. Ober, Norman, ed. LC 76-30710. 1977. 9.95 (*0-685-03832-7*) P-H.
McQueen, Winifred, jt. ed. see McQueen, John.
McQueeney, Robert M. & Vacon, Bob. Unpardonable Sins: A Father's Fight for Justice. LC 91-68140. 1992. 21.95 (*0-88282-068-0*) New Horizon NJ.
McQuere, Gordon D. Russian Theoretical Thought in Music. LC 83-9097. (Russian Music Studies: No. 10). (Illus.). 404p. reprint ed. pap. 115.20 (*0-8357-1457-8*, 2070510) Bks Demand.
McQuerry, James P., jt. ed. see Culp, Robert D.
McQuilkin. Runner's Outdoor Sports Photography. (Illus.). 1982. 9.95 (*0-02-499580-0*) Macmillan.
McQuilkin, Eleanor A. Mornings. 80p. (Orig.). 1986. 13.95 (*0-9608824-2-1*); pap. 8.95 (*0-9608824-3-X*) Stereopticon Pr.
McQuilkin, Frank. Forgottenville: The Town That Arrested Santa Claus. (Illus.). 48p. (J). (gr. k-7). 1982. 11.95 (*0-941316-00-9*) TSM Books.
McQuilkin, Rennie. North Northeast: New England Poems. LC 85-13343. (Illus.). 96p. (Orig.). 1985. 12.95 (*0-87233-080-X*); pap. 8.95 (*0-87233-081-8*) Bauhan.
— We All Fall Down. LC 87-60219. (Illus.). 76p. (C). 1986. 15.95 (*0-930501-14-4*); pap. 7.95 (*0-930501-15-2*) Livingston U Pr.
McQuilkin, Robert. Comfort Below Freezing. LC 79-28741. (Illus.). 176p. (Orig.). 1980. pap. 5.95 (*0-89037-184-9*) Anderson World.
— How to Cut Photo Costs. rev. ed. Campbell, Susan, ed. LC 85-117511. (Illus.). 206p. 1985. pap. 14.95 (*0-911445-02-1*) M C I Pub.
— Runner's World Outdoor Sports Photography Book. 200p. 1982. pap. 9.95 (*0-89037-243-8*) Anderson World.
McQuilkin, Robertson. The Great Omission. 96p. 1984. pap. 4.99 (*0-8010-6167-9*) Baker Bk.
— Introduction to Biblical Ethics. 576p. 1989. pap. 15.99 (*0-8423-1619-1*) Tyndale.
— Understanding & Applying the Bible. rev. ed. (Orig.). 1992. pap. 12.99 (*0-8024-9091-3*) Moody.
***McQuilkin, Robertson J.** An Introduction to Biblical Ethics. rev. ed. LC 94-42397. 1995. 19.99 (*0-8423-1731-7*) Tyndale.
McQuilkin, Susan, ed. see Campbell, Siri.
McQuillan, Alan D. & McQuillan, M. K. Titanium. LC 56-4724. (Metallurgy of the Rarer Metals Ser.: No. 4). 486p. reprint ed. pap. 138.60 (*0-317-42137-9*, 2025759) Bks Demand.
McQuillan, D. Aidan. Prevailing Over Time: Ethnic Adjustment on the Kansas Prairies, 1875-1925. LC 89-28957. (Illus.). xx, 292p. 1990. 40.00 (*0-8032-3143-1*) U of Nebr Pr.
***McQuillan, Deirdre.** Irish Country House Cooking. 1994. 15.99 (*0-517-10245-5*) Random Hse Value.
— Perfectly Simple Fish. (Perfectly Simple Cookbooks Ser.). (Illus.). 60p. 1992. 6.95 (*0-399-13784-X*, Putnam) Putnam Pub Group.
***McQuillan, Karin.** The Cheetah Chase. 1995. pap. 5.99 (*0-345-39780-0*) Ballantine.
— Deadly Safari. (Boston Mysteries Ser.). 1991. mass mkt. 4.99 (*0-345-37057-0*) Ballantine.
— Deadly Safari. large type ed. 1994. 23.95 (*0-7089-3189-8*) Ulverscroft.
— Elephants' Graveyard. LC 92-54391. 304p. 1993. 19.00 (*0-345-38182-3*) Ballantine.
— Elephants' Graveyard. (Boston Mysteries Ser.). 1994. mass mkt. 4.99 (*0-345-38862-3*) Ballantine.
McQuillan, M. K., jt. auth. see McQuillan, Alan D.
McQuillan, Melissa. Van Gogh. (Illus.). 1989. pap. 14.95 (*0-500-20232-X*) Thames Hudson.
McQuillan, Robert & Ardus, D. A. Exploring the Geology of Shelf Seas. (Illus.). 246p. reprint ed. pap. 70.20 (*0-685-20379-4*, 2030140) Bks Demand.
McQuillan, Susan, jt. auth. see Ricketts, David.
McQuillan, Thomas, tr. see Norberg-Schulz, Christian.
McQuillen, Connie, ed. & tr. Robert Burton: Philosophaster. (Medieval & Renaissance Texts & Studies: Vol. 103). 240p. 1992. 25.00 (*0-86698-123-3*) MRTS.
McQuillen, Connie, tr. see Schleiner, Louise.
McQuillen, Kevin & Prince, Anne. DOS - VSE Assembler Language. LC 86-60203. 242p. 1986. teacher ed, ring bd. 75.00 (*0-911625-32-1*) M Murach & Assoc.
— DOS-VSE Assembler Language. rev. ed. LC 85-63465. 492p. 1986. pap. 36.50 (*0-911625-31-3*) M Murach & Assoc.
— MVS Assembler Language. rev. ed. LC 86-63830. 528p. (C). 1987. pap. 36.50 (*0-911625-34-8*); teacher ed, ring bd. 75.00 (*0-911625-35-6*) M Murach & Assoc.
***McQuillen-Martensen, Kathy.** Radiograhic Critique. (Illus.). 320p. 1995. text ed. write for info. (*0-7216-4978-5*) Saunders.
McQuillen, Michael J. Eriez Magnetics: From Pioneer to World Leader. LC 91-75933. 120p. 1991. 15.00 (*0-9630652-0-3*) Eriez Mfg.
McQuillin, F. J., ed. Homogeneous Hydrogenation in Organic Chemistry. LC 75-37874. (Homogeneous Catalysis in Organic & Inorganic Chemistry: No. 1). vi, 146p. 1975. lib. bdg. 62.00 (*90-277-0646-8*) Kluwer Ac.
McQuillin, F. J., et al. Transition Metal Organometallics for Organic Synthesis. (Illus.). 672p. (C). 1992. 200.00 (*0-521-33353-9*) Cambridge U Pr.
McQuillin, R., et al. An Introduction to Seismic Interpretation. 2nd ed. LC 84-80958. (Illus.). 288p. 1985. 49.00 (*0-87201-774-5*); pap. text ed. 29.00 (*0-87201-773-7*) Gulf Pub.
***McQuinn.** Gail Hamilton. 1996. text ed. 21.95 (*0-8057-4021-X*) Macmillan.
— Witch. pap. write for info. (*0-345-39737-1*) Ballantine.
McQuinn, Anna. Kingdom of Giants. LC 93-85640. (Illus.). 16p. (J). (gr. 3-7). 1994. 9.95 (*0-89577-571-9*) RD Assn.
McQuinn, Cann, jt. auth. see Colombo, Luann.
***McQuinn, Conn.** Fun with Electronics. (J). 1994. pap. 19.95 (*0-8362-4231-9*) Andrews & McMeel.
McQuinn, Donald E. Wanderer. 608p. 1993. pap. 10.00 (*0-345-37840-7*, Del Rey) Ballantine.
— Wanderer. 1994. mass mkt. 6.99 (*0-345-39018-0*, Del Rey) Ballantine.
— Warrior. 1990. pap. 8.95 (*0-345-36504-6*, Ballantine Trade) Ballantine.
— Warrior. 672p. 1991. mass mkt. 5.99 (*0-345-37348-0*, Del Rey) Ballantine.
— Witch. 512p. (Orig.). 1994. pap. 10.00 (*0-345-37841-5*, Del Rey) Ballantine.
McQuire, Martin C. Coping with Foreign Dependence: The Simple Analytics of Stockpiling versus Protection. 21p. 1990. pap. text ed. 12.50 (*981-3035-53-6*, Pub. by Inst SE Asian Studies SI) Ashgate Pub Co.
McQuirk, Dal. Afrikakorps: Self Portrait. LC 92-35384. (Illus.). 196p. 1992. 34.95 (*0-87938-719-X*) Motorbooks Intl.
***McQuiston, Chris M. & Webb, Adele A.** Foundations of Nursing Theory: Contributions of 12 Key Theorists. 650p. 1995. text ed. 65.00 (*0-8039-7136-2*); pap. text ed. 29.95 (*0-8039-7137-0*) Sage.
McQuiston, Debra, jt. auth. see McQuiston, Don.
***McQuiston, Don & McQuiston, Debra.** Dolls & Toys of Native America: A Journey Through Childhood. LC 94-34678. 1995. 35.00 (*0-8118-0572-7*); 19.95 (*0-8118-0570-0*) Chronicle Bks.
— The Woven Spirit of the Southwest. LC 95-7347. (Illus.). 1995. write for info. (*0-8118-0864-5*); pap. write for info. (*0-8118-0880-7*) Chronicle Bks.
McQuiston, F. & Spitler, J. Cooling & Heating Load Calculation Manual. 2nd ed. Forman, C. & Parsons, B., eds. (Illus.). 209p. (C). 1992. text ed. 80.00 (*0-910110-85-9*) Am Heat Ref & Air Eng.
McQuiston, F. W., Jr. Gold: The Saga of the Empire Mine 1850-1956. Steinfeld, Charles, ed. (Illus.). 96p. (Orig.). 1986. pap. 7.95 (*0-931892-07-4*) B Dolphin Pub.
***McQuiston, F. W. & Shoemaker, R. S.** Gold & Silver Cyanidation Plant Practice Vol. 1. fac. ed. LC 75-309162. (Illus.). 245p. 1975. reprint ed. pap. 69.90 (*0-7837-7862-7*, 2047621) Bks Demand.
— Gold & Silver Cyanidation Plant Practice Vol. 2. fac. ed. LC 75-309162. (Illus.). 323p. 1981. reprint ed. pap. 92.10 (*0-7837-7863-5*, 2047621) Bks Demand.
McQuiston, F. W. & Shoemaker, Roberts. Primary Crushing Plant Design. LC 77-94869. (Illus.). 297p. reprint ed. pap. 84.70 (*0-685-24006-1*, 2031591) Bks Demand.
McQuiston, Faye C. & Parker, Jerald D. Heating, Ventilating, & Air Conditioning. 3rd ed. LC 87-34604. 746p. 1988. Net. text ed. write for info. (*0-471-63757-2*); 7.50 (*0-471-61224-3*) Wiley.
— Heating, Ventilating & Air Conditioning Analysis & Design. 4th ed. 768p. 1993. text ed. write for info. (*0-471-58107-0*) Wiley.
McQuiston, L., jt. ed. see Bicknell, J.
McQuiston, L. B. McQuiston-McCuiston-McQuesten Families 1620-1937. 750p. 1991. reprint ed. lib. bdg. 119.00 (*0-8328-1929-8*); reprint ed. pap. 109.00 (*0-685-48713-X*) Higginson Bk Co.
***McQuiston, Liz.** Graphic Agitation: Social & Political Graphics since The Sixties. (Illus.). 240p. 1995. pap. 35.00 (*0-7148-3458-0*, Pub. by Phaidon Press UK) Chronicle Bks.
— Graphic Agitation: Social & Political Graphics since the Sixties. (Illus.). 240p. (C). 1993. reprint ed. 49.95 (*0-7148-2878-5*, Pub. by Phaidon Press UK) Chronicle Bks.
McQuiston, Mary G., jt. auth. see Jones, David P.
McQuiston, Susan, jt. auth. see Garrison, William T.
McQuitty, Louis L. Pattern-Analytical Clustering: Theory, Method, Research & Configural Findings. LC 87-13346. (Illus.). 816p. 1987. lib. bdg. 102.00 (*0-8191-6449-6*) U Pr of Amer.
McQuitty, Robert. Fresh English. 4th ed. 352p. (C). 1993. spiral bd. 29.95 (*0-8403-9178-1*) Kendall-Hunt.
McQuoid-Mason, D. J., et al. Allemansreg - Street Law, Bk. 1: Inleiding Tot Suid-Afrikaanse Reg en die Regstelsel. 99p. 1987. teacher ed write for info. (*0-318-72248-8*, Pub. by Juta SA); student ed, pap. write for info. (*0-7021-2463-X*, Pub. by Juta SA) W W Gaunt.
— Consumer Law. (Human Rights for All Ser.: Bk. 3). 108p. 1988. student ed, pap. write for info. (*0-7021-2469-9*, Pub. by Juta SA) W W Gaunt.
— Consumer Law. (Human Rights for All Ser.: Bk. 3). 91p. 1991. teacher ed, pap. write for info. (*0-7021-2470-2*, Pub. by Juta SA) W W Gaunt.
— Criminal Law & Juvenile Justice. (Human Rights for All Ser.: Bk. 2). 104p. 1987. student ed, pap. write for info. (*0-7021-2465-6*, Pub. by Juta SA); teacher ed, pap. write for info. (*0-7021-2466-4*, Pub. by Juta SA) W W Gaunt.
— Family Law. (Human Rights for All Ser.: Bk. 4). 108p. 1990. student ed, pap. write for info. (*0-7021-2410-9*, Pub. by Juta SA); teacher ed, pap. write for info. (*0-7021-2411-7*, Pub. by Juta SA) W W Gaunt.
— Strafreg en Jeugregspleging. Bk. 2. 1993. student ed write for info. (*0-318-72249-6*, Pub. by Juta SA); teacher ed write for info. (*0-318-72250-X*, Pub. by Juta SA) W W Gaunt.
— Street Law - Allemansreg, Bk. 1: Introduction to South African Law & the Legal System. (Human Rights for All Ser.). 70p. 1987. student ed, pap. write for info. (*0-7021-2461-3*, Pub. by Juta SA) W W Gaunt.
— Street Law - Allemansreg, Bk. 1: Introduction to South African Law & the Legal System. (Human Rights for All Ser.). 93p. 1990. teacher ed, pap. write for info. (*0-7021-2462-1*, Pub. by Juta SA) W W Gaunt.
McQuown, Judith H. Incorporate Yourself. LC 91-58366. (Illus.). 288p. 1993. reprint ed. pap. 13.00 (*0-88730-611-X*) Harper Busn.
McQuown, Norman A. Language, Culture, & Education: Essays by Norman A. McQuown. Dil, Anwar S., ed. LC 81-50705. (Language Science & National Development Ser.). 256p. 1982. 35.00 (*0-8047-1122-4*) Stanford U Pr.
— Spoken Turkish. LC 74-152747. (Spoken Language Ser.). 378p. (gr. 9-12). 1971. audio 70.00 (*0-87950-245-2*) Spoken Lang Serv.
— Spoken Turkish, Bk. 1. LC 74-152747. (Spoken Language Ser.). 378p. (gr. 9-12). 1971. audio 80.00 (*0-87950-246-0*) Spoken Lang Serv.
— Spoken Turkish, Bk. 1, Units 1-12. LC 74-152747. (Spoken Language Ser.). 378p. (gr. 9-12). 1971. pap. 15.00 (*0-87950-240-1*) Spoken Lang Serv.
— Spoken Turkish, Bk. 2, Units 13-30. LC 74-152747. (Spoken Language Ser.). 378p. (gr. 9-12). 1971. pap. 15.00 (*0-87950-241-X*) Spoken Lang Serv.
McQuown, Richard C., jt. auth. see Henning, Harry L.
McRae, Barbara S. Franklin's Ancient Mound: Myth & History of Old Nikwasi, Franklin, N.C. (Illus.). 56p. (Orig.). 1993. pap. 6.95 (*0-9638930-0-9*) Teresita Pr.
— Records of Old Macon County, North Carolina, 1829-1850. 212p. 1991. 25.00 (*0-685-60423-3*, 9235) Clearfield Co.
***McRae, Barbara S., ed.** Atahita Journal: A Collection of Prose & Poetry from the Southern Mountains. 78p. (Orig.). Date not set. pap. 8.00 (*0-9638930-1-7*) Teresita Pr.
McRae, Barry. Dizzy Gillespie. (Illus.). 136p. pap. 11.95 (*0-7119-1441-9*, OP44635) Omnibus NY.
— The Jazz Cataclysm. LC 84-1827. (Roots of Jazz Ser.). 198p. 1985. reprint ed. lib. bdg. 25.00 (*0-306-76240-4*) Da Capo.
— The Jazz Handbook. (Monograph Ser.). 272p. 1990. text ed. 25.00 (*0-8161-9096-8*, Hall Reference); pap. 15.95 (*0-8161-1828-0*, Hall Reference) Macmillan.
***McRae, Bill & Jewell, Judy.** Pacific Northwest: U. S. A. Guide. (Illus.). 856p. 1995. pap. 19.95 (*0-86442-240-7*) Lonely Planet.
McRae, Bobbi. Colors from Nature: Growing, Collecting, & Using Natural Dyes. Steege, Gwen, ed. LC 92-53808. (Illus.). 168p. 1993. 26.95 (*0-88266-806-4*, Storey Pub); pap. 17.95 (*0-88266-799-8*, Storey Pub) Storey Comm Inc.
McRae, Bobbi A. The Frugal Gardener - More Than 200 Ways to Save Resources (& Money) by Recycling in Your Garden. (Illus.). 96p. (Orig.). 1992. pap. 8.95 (*0-944577-04-0*) Fiberworks Pubns.
— The Herb Companion Wish Book & Resource Guide. LC 92-2942. (Illus.). 304p. (Orig.). 1992. pap. 16.95 (*0-934026-74-2*) Interweave.
— Nature's Dyepot: A Resource Guide for Spinners, Weavers & Dyers. (Illus.). 65p. (Orig.). 1991. pap. 8.95 (*0-944577-02-4*) Fiberworks Pubns.

M

— The New Fiberworks Sourcebook: Being an Essential Mail-Order Guide to Supplies & Services for the Fiber Arts. LC 93-12584. (Illus.). 320p. (Orig.). 1993. pap. 15.95 (*0-944577-06-7*) Fiberworks Pubns.

McRae, Bradley C. Practical Time Management: How to Get More Things Done in Less Time. 1992. pap. 7.95 (*0-88908-281-2*) Self-Counsel Pr.

***McRae, David.** Developing the VCE. 95p. 1992. pap. 45.00 (*0-7300-1388-X*, ECT436, Pub. by Deakin Univ AT) St Mut.

***McRae, David & Frenkel, Dean.** The Essential Meditation Guide. (Illus.). 64p. (Orig.). 1995. pap. 7.95 (*0-85572-253-3*, Pub. by Hill Content Pubng AT) Seven Hills Bk.

McRae, Diana. All the Muscle You Need. LC 88-23954. 288p. (Orig.). 1988. pap. 8.95 (*0-933216-59-9*) Spinsters Ink.

McRae, Donald, jt. ed. see Kaplan, William.

McRae, Donald M. & Steger, Debra P., eds. Understanding the Free Trade Agreement. 254p. 1989. pap. text ed. 23.95 (*0-88645-079-9*, Pub. by Inst Res Pub CN) Ashgate Pub Co.

McRae, Floyd W., Jr., ed. see Dickey, Thomas S. & George, Peter C.

McRae, Gail C. Borzois. (Illus.). 192p. 1989. lib. bdg. 11.95 (*0-86622-676-1*, KW-167) TFH Pubns.

McRae, Glen, et al. An Ounce of Prevention: Waste Reduction Strategies for Health Care Facilities. (Illus.). 222p. (Orig.). 1993. pap. 50.00 (*0-87258-637-5*, 057007) Am Hospital.

***McRae, Hamish.** The World in 2020: Power, Culture & Prosperity. LC 94-24545. 1995. 24.95 (*0-87584-604-1*) Harvard Busn.

McRae, Heather, et al. Aboriginal Legal Issues: Commentary & Materials. 350p. 1991. pap. 69.00 (*0-455-21017-9*, Pub. by Law Bk Co) W W Gaunt.

McRae, I. I. The Geodetic World Map. 126p. 1988. 13.00 (*0-86690-349-6*, M2822-014) Am Fed Astrologers.

McRae, James J., ed. see Ali, Ansara.

McRae, James J., jt. auth. see Coffey, William J.

***McRae, Jenna.** Renderings. (Rose Cottage Papers). (Illus.). 34p. (Orig.). Date not set. pap. 7.00 (*1-887106-00-6*) McRae Banker.

***McRae, John.** Blood of the Lion. 240p. 1994. 16.98 (*0-88290-509-0*, 1981) Horizon Utah.

— Eagle Red. Van Treese, James B., ed. 294p. 1994. pap. 9.95 (*1-56901-099-4*) NW Pub.

— Fire in the Snow. LC 93-27311. 239p. 1993. pap. 10.95 (*0-87579-752-0*) Deseret Bk.

McRae, John & Boardman, Roy. Reading Between the Lines. 120p. 1984. pap. 11.95 (*0-521-27789-2*); pap. 12.95 (*0-521-27790-6*) Cambridge U Pr.

— Reading Between the Lines, 2 cass., Set. 120p. 1984. pap. 29.95 (*0-521-25992-4*) Cambridge U Pr.

McRae, John M. Elderly in the Environment: Northern Europe. LC 76-352614. 121p. (Orig.). reprint ed. pap. 34.50 (*0-7837-4912-0*, 2044577) Bks Demand.

McRae, John M., ed. see Southern Conference on Gerontology Staff.

McRae, John R. The Northern School of & the Formation of Early Ch'an Buddhism. LC 86-4062. (Studies in East Asian Buddhism: No. 3). 354p. 1987. 40.00 (*0-8248-1056-2*) UH Pr.

McRae, K. Conflict & Compromise in Multilingual Societies, Vol. 2: Belgium. (Politics of Cultural Diversity Ser.: No. V. 1-2). 384p. (C). 1986. pap. 19.95 (*0-88920-195-1*, Pub. by Wilfrid Laurier CN) Humanities.

— Conflict & Compromise in Multilingual Societies, Vol. 2: Belgium. 3rd ed. (Politics of Cultural Diversity Ser.: No. V. 1-2). 384p. (C). 1986. text ed. 49.95 (*0-88920-163-3*, Pub. by Wilfrid Laurier CN) Humanities.

***McRae, Lee.** Handbook of the Renaissance: Europe: 1400-1600. 3rd ed. (Illus.). 56p. 1995. reprint ed. pap. 12.00 (*0-9626075-2-5*) L McRae.

McRae-McMahon, Dorothy. Being Clergy, Staying Human: Taking Our Stand in the River. LC 92-72457. (Orig.). 1992. pap. 10.95 (*1-56699-061-0*, AL135) Alban Inst.

McRae, Melinda. The Highland Lord. (Signet Regency Romance Ser.). (Orig.). 1992. pap. 3.99 (*0-451-17469-0*, Sig) NAL-Dutton.

— Lady Leprechaun. (Regency Romance Ser.). 224p. 1993. pap. 3.99 (*0-451-17524-7*, Sig) NAL-Dutton.

— Prince of Thieves. 384p. (Orig.). 1994. pap. 4.99 (*0-451-40489-0*, Topaz) NAL-Dutton.

— Stolen Hearts. (Historical Romance Ser.). 384p. 1995. pap. 5.50 (*0-451-40611-7*, Topaz) NAL-Dutton.

— An Unlikely Attraction. (Regency Romance Ser.). 224p. (Orig.). 1991. pap. 3.99 (*0-451-17063-6*, Sig) NAL-Dutton.

McRae, Michael J. Continental Drifter: Dispatches from the Uttermost Parts of the Earth. 256p. 1993. 21.95 (*1-55821-243-4*) Lyons & Burford.

McRae, Murdo W., ed. The Literature of Science: Perspectives on Popular Scientific Writing. LC 92-22013. 320p. 1993. 45.00 (*0-8203-1506-0*) U of Ga Pr.

McRae, Ocee. Romance in the Oil Fields of Texas. 182p. 1990. 6.95 (*0-911724-01-X*, 962) Lunan-Ferguson.

McRae, Patricia B., tr. see Mandel, Richard D.

McRae, Patrick, illus. Here Comes Peter Cottontail. 24p. (Orig.). (J). (ps-3). 1986. pap. 3.95 (*0-8249-8106-5*, Ideals Child) Hambleton-Hill.

— Here Comes Peter Cottontail. 2nd ed. 24p. (J). (ps-3). 1986. pap. 3.95 (*0-8249-8663-6*) Ideals.

McRae, Robert. The Problem of the Unity of the Sciences: Bacon to Kant. LC 62-2304. 160p. reprint ed. pap. 45.60 (*0-8357-8905-5*, 2014318) Bks Demand.

McRae, Robert F. Leibniz: Perception, Apperception, & Thought. LC 76-6084. 158p. reprint ed. pap. 45.10 (*0-8357-3647-4*, 2036374) Bks Demand.

McRae, Robert Grant. Philosophy & the Absolute: The Modes of Hegel's Speculation. 1985. lib. bdg. 77.50 (*90-247-3151-8*) Kluwer Ac.

McRae, Ronald. Clinical Orthopaedic Examination. 3rd ed. (Illus.). 288p. 1990. pap. text ed. 32.95 (*0-443-04038-9*) Churchill.

— Practical Fracture Treatment. 3rd ed. LC 93-7651. 384p. 1994. pap. text ed. 46.95 (*0-443-04809-6*) Churchill.

***McRae, Shirley.** High Praise! 45 Descants on Familiar Hymns. 64p. (Orig.). 1995. pap. 4.95 (*0-687-01148-5*) Abingdon.

McRae, Shirley W. Chatter with the Angels: Folk Songs from the American Black Tradition for Voices & Orff Instruments. 44p. 1980. pap. 8.95 (*0-918812-09-7*, SE 0239) MMB Music.

— Directing the Children's Choir: A Comprehensive Resource. (Illus.). 232p. 1991. text ed. 26.00 (*0-02-871785-6*) Schirmer Bks.

McRae, Thomas W. Computers & Accounting. LC 75-6793. 179p. reprint ed. pap. 51.10 (*0-8357-2590-1*, 2052370) Bks Demand.

— Statistical Sampling for Audit & Control. LC 73-19329. (Wiley-Interscience Publication Ser.). 299p. reprint ed. pap. 85.30 (*0-7837-4518-4*, 2044297) Bks Demand.

McRae, Thomas W., jt. auth. see Fothergill, Kenneth R.

McRae, W. C. & Jewell, Judy. Montana Handbook. 2nd ed. LC 94-6877. 400p. (Orig.). 1994. pap. 15.95 (*1-56691-054-4*) Moon Pubns CA.

McRae, Wallace. Cowboy Curmudgeon & Other Poems. (Illus.). 144p. (Orig.). 1992. pap. 11.95 (*0-87905-463-8*, Peregrine Smith) Gibbs Smith Pub.

McRae, Wallace D. & Walton, Jeri D. Up North Is down the Crick. LC 85-60892. (Illus.). 70p. (Orig.). 1985. pap. 6.95 (*0-933819-00-5*) Museum Rockies.

McRae, William J. The Dynamics of Spiritual Gifts. 144p. 1983. reprint ed. pap. 8.99 (*0-310-29091-0*, 9976P) Zondervan.

— Preparing for Your Marriage. 160p. (Orig.). 1980. pap. 8.99 (*0-310-42761-4*, 9366P) Zondervan.

McRandle, James H. The Antique Drums of War. LC 93-41325. (Military History Ser.: No. 33). (Illus.). 256p. 1994. 39.50 (*0-89096-591-9*); pap. 15.95 (*0-89096-611-7*) Tex A&M Univ Pr.

McRaven, Charles. Building & Restoring the Hewn Log House. 176p. (Orig.). 1994. pap. 18.95 (*1-55870-325-X*) Betterway Bks.

— Building with Stone. LC 88-62875. (Illus.). 192p. 1989. reprint ed. pap. 14.95 (*0-88266-550-2*, Garden Way Pub) Storey Comm Inc.

***McRaven, William H.** Spec Ops: Case Studies in Special Operations Warfare: Theory & Practice. LC 94-46452. 432p. 1995. 27.95 (*0-89141-544-0*) Presidio Pr.

McRay, John. Archaeology & the New Testament. LC 91-11663. 480p. (Orig.). 1990. text ed. 39.99 (*0-8010-6267-5*) Baker Bk.

McRay, Ron. The Last Days. 150p. (Orig.). (YA). (gr. 9-12). 1990. pap. 5.95 (*0-9621311-3-X*) E E Stevens Pub.

— Through the Water, Through the Fire. 64p. 1992. per. 3.95 (*0-9631167-0-3*) R McRay.

McReady, William, jt. ed. see Cafferty, Pastora.

McRedmond, Louis. Thrown among Strangers: John Henry Newman in Ireland. 223p. (Orig.). 1990. pap. 16.95 (*1-85390-180-6*, Pub. by Veritas Publns IE) Ignatius Pr.

McRee, Duncan E. Practical Protein Crystallography. (Illus.). 386p. 1993. text ed. 69.00 (*0-12-486050-8*) Acad Pr.

McReynolds, Edwin C. Oklahoma: History of the Sooner State. rev. ed. LC 54-10052. (Illus.). 477p. 1962. 24.95 (*0-8061-0302-7*) U of Okla Pr.

— Seminoles. LC 57-11198. (Civilization of the American Indian Ser.: No. 47). (Illus.). 1975. reprint ed. pap. 15.95 (*0-8061-1255-7*) U of Okla Pr.

McReynolds, Edwin C., et al. Oklahoma: The Story of Its Past & Present. rev. ed. LC 61-17309. (Illus.). 500p. 1985. reprint ed. 22.95 (*0-8061-0509-7*) U of Okla Pr.

McReynolds, Elaine, jt. auth. see McReynolds, Ray.

McReynolds, George E., jt. auth. see Tupper, Eleanor.

***McReynolds, Glenna.** Dragon's Eden. (Loveswept Ser.: No. 726). 1995. pap. 3.50 (*0-553-44487-5*, Loveswept) Bantam.

McReynolds, Janet. Something Supernatural. 103p. 1986. pap. 3.95 (*0-88144-038-8*) Christian Pub.

McReynolds, Kathy, jt. auth. see Luter, Boyd.

McReynolds, Louise. The News under Russia's Old Regime: The Development of a Mass-Circulation Press. (Illus.). 326p. 1991. text ed. 49.50 (*0-691-03180-0*) Princeton U Pr.

McReynolds, P., jt. ed. see Rosen, J. C.

McReynolds, P., et al, eds. Advances in Psychological Assessment, Vol. 7. LC 78-647160. (Illus.). 330p. 1990. 55.00 (*0-306-43399-0*, Plenum Pr) Plenum.

McReynolds, Paul, ed. Advances in Psychological Assessment, Vol. 3. LC 73-21077. (Jossey-Bass Behavioral Science Ser.). 572p. reprint ed. pap. 163.10 (*0-8357-5181-3*, 2021088) Bks Demand.

— Advances in Psychological Assessment, 3 vols., Vol. 4. LC 78-647160. (Jossey-Bass Social & Behavioral Science Ser.). (Illus.). 611p. reprint ed. pap. 174.20 (*0-8357-4714-X*, 2021088) Bks Demand.

— Advances in Psychological Assessment, 3 vols., Vol. 5. LC 78-647160. (Jossey-Bass Social & Behavioral Science Ser.). (Illus.). 582p. reprint ed. pap. 165.90 (*0-8357-4715-8*, 2021088) Bks Demand.

— Advances in Psychological Assessment, 3 vols., Vol. 6. LC 78-647160. (Jossey-Bass Social & Behavioral Science Ser.). (Illus.). 399p. reprint ed. pap. 113.80 (*0-8357-4716-6*, 2021088) Bks Demand.

McReynolds, Paul R. Mark. (Bible Studies). 192p. 1989. pap. text ed. 11.99 (*0-87403-162-1*, 40102) Standard Pub.

McReynolds, Peter. Process Control Charting with Quattro Pro for Windows. 250p. 1993. pap. 39.95 (*1-883327-41-5*) TitleWave Pr.

McReynolds, Ray. Room Finishing: A Step by Step Guide. (How-to Ser.). 48p. (Orig.). 1991. Canadian Edition. pap. 4.95 (*0-88908-957-4*) Self-Counsel Pr.

— Step by Step Guide Book on Home Plumbing. (Illus.). 56p. 1975. pap. text ed. write for info. (*0-9619201-1-4*) S by S Guide.

— Step by Step Guide Book on Home Wiring. (Illus.). 48p. 1982. pap. text ed. write for info. (*0-9619201-0-6*) S by S Guide.

— Step by Step Guide Book on Sprinkling Systems. (Illus.). 38p. (Orig.). (C). 1974. pap. text ed. write for info. (*0-9619201-2-2*) S by S Guide.

— Step by Step Guide Books on Home Wiring Diagrams. (Illus.). 48p. 1982. pap. text ed. write for info. (*0-9619201-4-9*) S by S Guide.

McReynolds, Ray & McReynolds, Elaine. Basic Home Wiring Diagrams: A Step-by-Step Guide. (How-to Ser.). (Illus.). 48p. (Orig.). 1990. Canadian ed. pap. 2.95 (*0-88908-869-1*) Self-Counsel Pr.

— Home Plumbing: A Step-by-Step Guide. (How-to Ser.). (Illus.). 56p. (Orig.). 1989. Canadian Edition. pap. 4.95 (*0-88908-870-5*) Self-Counsel Pr.

— Home Wiring: A Step-by-Step Guide, Canadian Ed. 2nd ed. (How-to Ser.). (Illus.). 48p. (Orig.). 1994. pap. 4.95 (*0-88908-791-1*) Self-Counsel Pr.

McReynolds, Rebecca A., jt. auth. see Morris, Richard J.

McReynolds, W. O. Gas Chromatographic Retention Data. 1966. 45.00 (*0-912474-01-7*) Preston Pubns.

M'Crindle, John. Invasion of India by Alexander the Great. LC 74-155621. reprint ed. 12.50 (*0-404-04119-1*) AMS Pr.

McRitchie, Margaret. Structured BASIC & Program Design. 416p. (C). 1989. pap. text ed. 40.00 (*0-03-921892-9*) SCP.

Mcroan, Fred J., photos. Jean-Louis: Cooking with the Seasons. LC 88-51106. 216p. 1989. 49.95 (*0-934738-49-1*) Thomasson-Grant.

McRobb. Purchasing & Quality. (Quality & Reliability Ser.: Vol. 19). 400p. 1989. 89.75 (*0-8247-8075-2*) Dekker.

— Specification Writing & Management. (Quality & Reliability Ser.: Vol. 20). 240p. 1989. 89.75 (*0-8247-8082-5*) Dekker.

McRobbie, Angela. Feminism & Youth Culture: From Jackie to Just Seventeen. 252p. (C). 1990. text ed. 49.95 (*0-04-445910-6*); pap. text ed. 16.95 (*0-04-445911-4*) Routledge Chapman & Hall.

— Postmodernism & Popular Culture. LC 93-41812. (Illus.). 232p. 1994. 59.95x (*0-415-07712-5*, B4291); pap. 16.95 (*0-415-07713-3*, B4295) Routledge.

McRobbie, Angela, ed. Zootsuits & Second-Hand Dresses: An Anthology of Fashion & Music. 288p. 1989. text ed. 49.00 (*0-04-445236-5*); pap. text ed. 17.95 (*0-04-445237-3*) Routledge Chapman & Hall.

McRobbie, James. What the Bible Teaches. pap. 8.99 (*0-88019-122-8*) Schmul Pub Co.

McRobert, Iain. Windows Black Pentecostalism in Britain: Origins, Functions & Theology. 352p. 1993. pap. 40.00 (*0-86153-154-X*, Pub. by St Andrew UK) St Mut.

McRoberts, Colin J. Laughter, Tears, & Bullet Wounds. 48p. (Orig.). 1989. pap. text ed. write for info. (*0-318-65574-8*) Quest Pr.

— Seventy-Three Haiku of a Candle. 48p. (Orig.). 1989. pap. text ed. write for info. (*0-318-65573-X*) Quest Pr.

***McRoberts, Kenneth, ed.** Beyond Quebec: Taking Stock of Canada. 464p. 1995. 44.95 (*0-7735-1301-9*) U of Toronto Pr.

— Beyond Quebec: Taking Stock of Canada. 464p. 1995. pap. 22.95 (*0-7735-1314-0*) U of Toronto Pr.

McRoberts, Kenneth & Monahan, Patrick, eds. The Charlottetown Accord: The Referendum, & the Future of Canada. LC 93-94681. 361p. 1993. 55.00 (*0-8020-2989-2*) U of Toronto Pr.

McRoberts, Kerry. New Age or Old Lie? LC 89-12831. 192p. 1989. pap. 7.95 (*0-943575-30-3*) Hendrickson MA.

McRoberts, Robert. Lip Service. LC 76-55803. 59p. 1976. 3.50 (*0-87886-078-9*, Greenfld Rev Pr) Greenfld Rev Lit.

McRobie, George. Tools for Organic Farming: A Manual of Appropriate Equipment & Treatments. 80p. (Orig.). 1990. pap. 11.50 (*0-942850-19-X*) Intermediate Tech.

McRovie, Louise, ed. see Klein, John.

McRoy, C. Peter & Helfferich, Carla, eds. Seagrass Ecosystems: A Scientific Perspective. LC 76-9466. (Marine Science Ser.: No. 4). 328p. reprint ed. pap. 93.50 (*0-318-35008-4*, 2030868) Bks Demand.

McRoy, Ruth G. & Zurcher, Louis A., Jr. Transracial & Inracial Adoptees: The Adolescent Years. 168p. 1983. 31.95x (*0-398-04840-1*) C C Thomas.

— Transracial & Inracial Adoptees: The Adolescent Years. 168p. 1983. pap. 16.95 (*0-398-06282-X*) C C Thomas.

McRoy, Ruth G., et al. Emotional Disturbance in Adopted Adolescents: Origins & Development. LC 87-1053. 226p. 1988. text ed. 55.00 (*0-275-92913-2*, C2913, Praeger Pubs) Greenwood.

— Openness in Adoption: New Practices, New Issues. LC 88-2471. 171p. 1988. text ed. 49.95 (*0-275-92933-7*, C2933, Praeger Pubs) Greenwood.

McRuer, Duane, et al. Aircraft Dynamics & Automatic Control. LC 73-134350. 624p. (Orig.). 1990. 135.00x (*0-691-08083-6*); pap. text ed. 42.50 (*0-691-02440-5*) Princeton U Pr.

McSean, Tony, ed. Library Association Directory of Supplies & Services. 103p. 1994. pap. 30.00 (*1-85604-112-3*, LAP1123, Pub. by Lib Assn Pub UK) UNIPUB.

McSeveney, Margaret, jt. auth. see Richardson, Ros.

McShane, Barbara, tr. see Rodgers, Mary.

McShane, Claudette. Warning! Dating May Be Hazardous to Your Health! LC 88-60718. 192p. (Orig.). 1988. pap. 9.95 (*0-941300-08-0*) Mother Courage.

McShane, Clay. Down the Asphalt Path: The Automobile & the American City. LC 93-17219. (History of Urban Life Ser.). 288p. 1994. 37.50 (*0-231-08390-4*) Col U Pr.

McShane, E. J. Order-Preserving Maps & Integration Processes. (Annals of Mathematics Studies: No. 31). 1974. reprint ed. 15.00 (*0-527-02747-2*) Periodicals Srv.

— A Riemann-Type Integral That Includes Lebesgue-Stieltjes, Bochner & Stochastic Integrals. LC 52-42839. (Memoirs Ser.: No. 1/88). 54p. 1983. reprint ed. pap. 17.00 (*0-8218-1288-2*, MEMO 1/88) Am Math.

— Unified Integration. LC 82-16266. (Pure & Applied Mathematics Ser.). 1983. text ed. 121.00 (*0-12-486260-8*) Acad Pr.

McShane, Hazel M. A Nurse's Journey. 1995. 9.95 (*0-8062-5015-1*) Carlton.

McShane, Ivan, pref. An Anthology of Mentor Poetry for the Sixties. pap. 7.50 (*0-87423-015-2*) Westburg.

McShane, Ivan & Westburg, Martial. The First Selected Poems of Ivan McShane. Westburg, John E., ed. (Illus.). 80p. 1965. 10.00 (*0-87423-001-2*) Westburg.

McShane, John. Cognitive Development: An Information Processing Approach. (Illus.). 288p. (Orig.). (C). 1991. pap. text ed. 24.95 (*0-631-17019-7*) Blackwell Pubs.

McShane, John, jt. auth. see Dockrell, Julie.

McShane, Joseph M. Sufficiently Radical: Catholicism, Progressivism, & the Bishops Program of 1919. LC 86-9735. 308p. 1986. 38.95 (*0-8132-0631-6*) Cath U Pr.

— Sufficiently Radical: Catholicism, Progressivism, & the Bishops' Program of 1919. LC 86-9735. 319p. Date not set. reprint ed. pap. 91.00 (*0-7837-9117-8*, 2049918) Bks Demand.

McShane, Marilyn D. & Krause, Wesley. Community Corrections. (Illus.). 530p. (C). 1993. text ed. write for info. (*0-02-379765-7*) Macmillan.

McShane, Marilyn D. & Williams, Frank P., III. The Management of Correctional Institutions. LC 92-27791. (Current Issues in Criminal Justice Ser.: Vol. 5). 352p. 1993. 53.00 (*0-8153-1082-X*, SS869) Garland.

McShane, Marilyn D. & Williams, Franklin P., III. Criminological Theory. 2nd ed. LC 93-35798. 288p. 1994. pap. text ed. 25.33 (*0-13-030289-9*) P-H.

McShane, Marilyn D., jt. auth. see Williams, Frank P., III.

McShane, Mark. The Hostage Game. (Orig.). 1979. pap. 2.25 (*0-89083-458-X*) Zebra.

— Seance on a Wet Afternoon. 15.95 (*0-89190-628-2*, Am Repr) Amereon Ltd.

— Seance on a Wet Afternoon. 189p. 1990. pap. 3.95 (*0-88184-615-5*) Carroll & Graf.

McShane, Philip. The Shaping of the Foundations: Being at Home in the Transcendental Method. 24.00 (*0-8191-0209-1*) U Pr of Amer.

McShane, Roger. Exploring Applesoft. 170p. 1983. pap. 18.95 (*0-13-295916-X*) P-H.

McShane, Roger B. The Foreign Policy of the Attalids of Pergamun. LC 63-7251. (Illinois Studies in the Social Sciences: Vol.53). 253p. reprint ed. pap. 72.20 (*0-317-11215-5*, 2015038) Bks Demand.

McShane, Rudolph, jt. tr. see Cutler, Ann.

McShane, Terry. Working Well...? How to Correct the Unhealthy Workplace: The Ergonomic Approach, Vol. 1. (Illus.). (Orig.). 1993. pap. 14.95 (*0-9636940-0-6*) T&M Assocs.

McShane, William R. & Roess, Roger P. Traffic Engineering. 704p. 1990. text ed. 77.00 (*0-13-926148-6*) P-H.

McSharry, Patra & Rosen, Roger, eds. Apartheid: Calibrations of Color. (World Issues Ser.: Vol. 2). (Illus.). 176p. (YA). (gr. 7-12). 1991. lib. bdg. 16.95 (*0-8239-1330-9*); pap. 8.95 (*0-8239-1331-7*) Rosen Group.

— Coca Cola Culture: Icons of Pop. (Icarus World Issues Ser.). (YA). (gr. 7-12). 1993. 16.95 (*0-8239-1593-X*); pap. 8.95 (*0-8239-1594-8*) Rosen Group.

— On Heroes & the Heroic: In Search of Good Deeds. (Icarus World Issues Ser.). (YA). (gr. 7-12). 1993. 16.95 (*0-8239-1384-8*); pap. 8.95 (*0-8239-1385-6*) Rosen Group.

— The People of This Place: Natural & Unnatural Habitats. (Icarus World Issues Ser.). (YA). (gr. 7-12). 1993. 16.95 (*0-8239-1381-3*); pap. 8.95 (*0-8239-1382-1*) Rosen Group.

— Urbanities: Visions of the Metropolis. (Icarus World Issues Ser.). (YA). (gr. 7-12). 1993. 16.95 (*0-8239-1387-2*); pap. 8.95 (*0-8239-1388-0*) Rosen Group.

McSharry, Patra, ed. see Epshtein, Yaacov.

McSharry, Patra, ed. see Gindin, Irina.

McSharry, Patra, ed. see Kilov, Haim, et al.

McSharry, Patra, ed. see Kokoshvili, Simon, et al.

McSharry, Patra, ed. see Litvin, Valentin.

McShea, Robert J. Morality & Human Nature: A New Route to Ethical Theory. 240p. 1990. 39.95 (*0-87722-735-7*) Temple U Pr.

— The Political Philosophy of Spinoza. LC 68-17553. 224p. reprint ed. pap. 63.90 (*0-317-07751-1*, 2007204) Bks Demand.

McShea, Susanna H. Hometown Heroes. 320p. 1992. mass mkt. 4.99 (*0-380-71675-5*) Avon.

— Ladybug, Ladybug. 3352p. 1994. 21.95 (*0-312-11017-0*, Pub. by Thomas Dunne Bks) St Martin.

— Ladybug, Ladybug. (Hometown Heroes Mystery Ser.). 352p. 1995. reprint ed. mass mkt. 5.50 (*0-380-71981-9*) Avon.

— The Pumpkin-Shell Wife. 352p. 1993. mass mkt. 4.99 (*0-380-71980-0*) Avon.

McSheehy, William R. Skid Row: An Institutional Analysis. 160p. 1975. pap. 11.95 (*0-87073-181-5*) Schenkman Bks Inc.

An Asterisk (*) at the beginning of an entry indicates that the title is appearing in BIP for the first time.

*__McSheffrey, Shannon.__ Gender & Heresy: Women & Men in Lollard Communities, 1420-1530. (Middle Ages Ser.). (Illus.). 264p. 1995. text ed. 38.95 (0-8122-3310-7); pap. text ed. 18.95 (0-8122-1549-4) U of Pa Pr.

*__McSheffrey, Shannon, tr. & intro.__ Love & Marriage in Late Medieval London. LC 94-47339. (Documents of Practice Ser.). 1995. pap. write for info. (1-879288-53-2) Medieval Inst.

Mcsherry, Frank. Civil War Women. 1990. pap. 10.00 (0-671-70248-3) S&S Trade.

McSherry, Frank, et al, eds. Eastern Ghosts. LC 90-44724. (American Ghost Ser.). 208p. (Orig.). 1990. pap. 9.95 (1-55853-091-6) Rutledge Hill Pr.

McSherry, Frank, Jr., et al, eds. Great American Ghost Stories. LC 91-24148. 496p. 1991. 21.95 (1-55853-146-7) Rutledge Hill Pr.

McSherry, Frank, et al, eds. New England Ghosts. LC 90-43189. (American Ghost Ser.). 214p. (Orig.). 1990. pap. 9.95 (1-55853-090-8) Rutledge Hill Pr.

McSherry, Frank D., Jr. The Blink of an Eye: The Invisibility Theme in Modern Fantastic Literature. (I. O. Evans Studies in the Philosophy & Criticism of Literature: No. 12). 128p. Date not set. lib. bdg. write for info. (0-89370-311-7); pap. write for info. (0-89370-411-3) Borgo Pr.

McSherry, Frank D. More Dixie Ghosts: More Spine-Chilling Stories from the American South. LC 94-7992. 1994. pap. 9.95 (1-55853-299-4) Rutledge Hill Pr.

McSherry, Frank D. & Waugh, C. Treasury of American Horror Stories. 1988. 9.99 (0-517-48075-1) Random Hse Value.

McSherry, Frank D. & Waugh, Charles G. The Best Horror Stories of Arthur Conan Doyle. Greenberg, Martin H. et al, eds. LC 88-3436. 294p. 1989. pap. 8.00 (0-89733-265-2) Academy Chi Pubs.

McSherry, Frank D., Jr., ed. see Waugh, Charles G. & Greenberg, Martin H.

McSherry, Frank D., Jr., jt. ed. see Waugh, Charles G.

McSherry, Frank D., et al. Ghosts of the Heartland: Haunting, Spine Chilling Stories from the American Midwest. LC 90-30532. 224p. (Orig.). 1990. pap. 9.95 (1-55853-068-1) Rutledge Hill Pr.

McSherry, Frank D., Jr., et al, eds. Dixie Ghosts. LC 88-1991. (American Ghost Ser.). 1990. pap. 9.95 (0-934395-73-X) Rutledge Hill Pr.

— Great American Ghost Stories, Vol. II. 272p. 1993. mass mkt. 4.99 (0-425-13623-X) Berkley Pub.

— Western Ghosts. LC 90-8072. (American Ghost Ser.). 224p. (Orig.). 1990. pap. 9.95 (1-55853-069-X) Rutledge Hill Pr.

McSherry, James. History of Maryland. James, Bartlett B., ed. LC 68-30881. (Illus.). 1968. reprint ed. 20.00 (0-87152-047-8) Reprint.

McSherry, Richard M. The National Medals of the United States. LC 72-14409. (Maryland Historical Society. Fund-Publications: No. 25). reprint ed. 10.00 (0-404-57625-7) AMS Pr.

McShine, Kynaston, ed. Andy Warhol: A Retrospective. (Illus.). 480p. 1991. pap. 35.00 (0-87070-681-0, 0-8109-6082-6) Mus of Modern Art.

— Joseph Cornell. (Illus.). 296p. 1990. 65.00 (3-7913-1063-1, Pub. by Prestel) TeNeues.

McShine, Kynaston, jt. ed. see D'Harnoncourt, Anne.

McSmith, Andy. John Smith: Playing the Long Game. LC 93-17532. 1993. 28.95 (0-86091-475-5, Pub. by Verso UK) Routledge Chapman & Hall.

— Kenneth Clarke: A Political Biography. LC 94-25664. 1994. write for info. (0-86091-443-7, Pub. by Verso UK) Routledge Chapman & Hall.

McSorley, Edward. Our Own Kind. LC 76-6357. (Irish Americans Ser.). 1976. reprint ed. 26.95 (0-405-09350-0) Ayer.

McSorley, Joseph. Isaac Hecker & His Friends. 314p. 1972. pap. 1.45 (0-8091-1605-7) Paulist Pr.

McSorley, Richard. It's a Sin to Build a Nuclear Weapon: The Collected Works on War & Christian Peacemaking. 348p. (Orig.). 1991. 22.95 (1-879175-07-X); pap. 16.95 (1-879175-06-1) Fortkamp.

— Kill? For Peace. 2nd rev. ed. LC 70-135455. 140p. (C). 1982. reprint ed. pap. 3.75 (0-912239-06-9) Ctr Peace Studies.

— Peace Eyes. LC 77-9240. 219p. 1978. pap. 3.75 (0-912239-03-4) Ctr Peace Studies.

McSorley, Richard T. New Testament Basis of Peacemaking. 3rd enl. rev. ed. LC 84-25121. 165p. reprint ed. pap. 47.10 (0-7837-5116-8, 2044815) Bks Demand.

McSorley, Richard T., jt. auth. see Durland, William R.

McSpadden, Barbara. Bargain Hunting along the Coast of Maine, 1987-88. rev. ed. (Illus.). 104p. pap. 4.95 (0-9617533-0-7) Thrifty Yankee.

McSpadden, J. Walker. Robin Hood. (Heirloom Classic Ser.). (Illus.). 160p. (J). 1991. 14.95 (0-88101-272-6) Unicorn Pub.

McSpadden, Joseph W. Famous Sculptors of America. LC 68-57331. (Essay Index Reprint Ser.). 1977. 27.95 (0-8369-0086-3) Ayer.

McSpadden, Joseph W., ed. Famous Dogs in Fiction, Vol. 1. rev. ed. LC 72-4373. (Short Story Index Reprint Ser.). 1977. reprint ed. 25.95 (0-8369-4184-5) Ayer.

— Famous Ghost Stories. LC 70-152949. (Short Story Index Reprint Ser.). 1977. reprint ed. 18.95 (0-8369-3808-9) Ayer.

— Famous Psychic & Ghost Stories, 2 vols. in 1. LC 73-77. (Short Story Index Reprint Ser.). 1977. reprint ed. 44.95 (0-8369-4248-5) Ayer.

McSpadden, Lynn. Four & Twenty: Songs for the Mountain Dulcimer. (Illus.). 44p. 1977. pap. 6.95 (0-8256-2635-8, AM41229) Music Sales.

McSpadden, Mary C. Merrily Strum: Mountain Dulcimer for Children. (Illus.). 24p. 1975. pap. 5.95 (0-8256-2636-6, AM41237) Music Sales.

McSpirit, Marian, jt. auth. see McLaughlin, Mercedes.

McSporran, W. S., jt. auth. see McMonnies, Alistair.

McSquare, Eddie. Metallica: Whiplash. (Illus.). 1990. pap. 12.95 (0-8256-1282-9, AM79799) Music Sales.

— Motley Crue. (Illus.). 1990. pap. 12.95 (0-8256-1301-9, 46374) Music Sales.

McSquare, Eddy. Bon Jovi: An Illustrated Biography. (Illus.). 64p. 1990. pap. 15.95 (0-7119-2104-0, OP45731) Omnibus NY.

— Guns 'n Roses: Lowlife in the Fast Lane. (Illus.). 80p. 1991. pap. 17.95 (0-7119-2793-6, OP45616) Omnibus NY.

— Led Zeppelin: Good Times, Bad Times. (Illus.). 64p. 1991. pap. 12.95 (0-7119-2737-5, BO10138, Pub. by Bobcat UK) Music Sales.

McStay, Kyran P. The Efficiency of New Issue Markets. rev. ed. LC 92-34079. (Financial Sector of the American Economy Ser.). 144p. 1992. 42.00 (0-8153-0966-X) Garland.

McSwain, Harold W. A Relational Aesthetic. LC 93-22887. (New Studies in Aesthetics: Vol. 18). 307p. (C). 1994. text ed. 58.95 (0-8204-2185-5) P Lang Pubs.

*__McSwain, Kate.__ Art-Istry for Children: Color. 212p. (Orig.). (J). (gr. 1-6). 1992. pap. 29.95 (1-878347-39-X) NL Assocs.

McSwain, Mary E. & Morihara, Bonnie V. VIA-U. S. A.'s Living & Working in America, Vol. I. Higuchi, Yuko & Ikeda, Kazuko, trs. (Illus.). ix, 178p. (Orig.). (ENG & JPN.). (C). 1988. pap. 15.95 (0-317-91317-4); vhs 200.00 (0-685-21729-9) VIA Pr.

— VIA-U. S. A.'s Living & Working in America, Vol. I. 80p. (Orig.). (C). 1989. student ed 9.95 (0-317-91313-1); teacher ed 22.95 (0-317-91314-X); audio 19.95 (0-685-21726-4) VIA Pr.

— VIA-U. S. A.'s Living & Working in America, Vol. II. (Illus.). 120p. (Orig.). (C). 1988. pap. 15.95 (0-317-91309-3) VIA Pr.

— VIA-U. S. A.'s Living & Working in America, Vol. II. (Illus.). 150p. (Orig.). (C). 1989. teacher ed 22.95 (0-317-91322-0); student ed 9.95 (0-317-91323-9); audio 19.95 (0-317-91324-7); vhs 250.00 (0-685-21730-2) VIA Pr.

— VIA-U. S. A.'s Living & Working in America, Vol. II. Higuchi, Yuko & Toyoshima, Morio, trs. 75p. (Orig.). (JPN.). (C). 1989. pap. text ed. 6.95 (0-317-91311-5) VIA Pr.

— VIA-U. S. A.'s Living & Working in America, Vol. III. (Illus.). 120p. (Orig.). (C). 1988. pap. 15.95 (0-317-91310-7) VIA Pr.

— VIA-U. S. A.'s Living & Working in America, Vol. III. Higuchi, Yuko & Toyoshima, Morio, trs. 75p. (Orig.). (JPN.). (C). 1989. pap. text ed. 6.95 (0-317-91312-3) VIA Pr.

— VIA-U. S. A.'s Living & Working in America, Vol. III. (Illus.). (Orig.). (C). 1989. Two audio cassettes & transcript. 19.95 (0-317-91315-8); teacher ed 22.95 (0-685-21727-2); student ed. pap. 9.95 (0-317-91316-6); vhs 250.00 (0-685-21728-0) VIA Pr.

McSwain, Norman & Ware, Drue N. Atlas of Emergency Trauma Surgical Procedures. LC 90-4546. (Illus.). 184p. 1994. 98.50 (0-89640-179-0) Igaku-Shoin.

McSwain, Norman E., Jr. & Kerstein, Morris D. Evaluation & Management of Trauma. (Illus.). 470p. 1987. boxed 90.00 (0-8385-2472-9, A2472-7) Appleton & Lange.

McSwain, Norman E., Jr., jt. ed. see Frame, Scott B.

McSwain, Norman E., Jr., ed. see Pre-Hospital Trauma Life Support Committee of the National Association of Emergency Medical Technicians.

McSwain, Norman E., et al. EMT & Paramedic Quick Reference. (Illus.). 336p. (C). 1994. pap. text ed. write for info. (1-884225-02-0) Communs Skills.

McSwain, Ross. Another Look Out Yonder, Vol. 2. 190p. Date not set. write for info. (0-943639-15-8) Anchor Pub Co.

McSwain, Stephen B. Basic Bible Sermons on Spiritual Living. 1992. pap. 5.99 (0-8054-2274-9) Broadman.

McSween, H. Y., Jr., et al. An Introduction to the Petrographic Microscope: A Programmed Text. (Illus.). iii, 53p. (C). 1982. student ed 5.00 (0-910249-04-0) U of Tenn Geo.

McSween, Harry Y., Jr. Stardust to Planets: A Geological Tour of the Solar System. 256p. 1993. 22.95 (0-312-09394-2) St Martin.

McSween, Terry E. A Behavioral Approach to Occupational Safety: A Values Based Approach. (Illus.). 250p. 1995. text ed. 39.95 (0-442-01945-9) Van Nos Reinhold.

McSweeney, Dean & Zvesper, John. American Political Parties: The Formation, Decline & Reform of the American Party System. 288p. 1991. 75.00 (0-415-01169-8, A5500); pap. 17.95 (0-415-01170-1, A5504) Routledge.

McSweeney, Edward A., jt. auth. see Beverly, David P.

McSweeney, Jeanne & Leocha, Charles. Getting to Know Kids in Your Life: Activities, Questions & Ways to Get to Know Kids Better. 160p. (Orig.). 1995. pap. 6.95 (0-915009-27-7) World Leis Corp.

— Getting to Know Kids in Your Life: Activities, Questions & Ways to Get to Know Kids Better. 160p. (Orig.). 1995. 83.40 (0-915009-39-0) World Leis Corp.

— Getting to Know You: Three Hundred Sixty-Five Questions, Activities, & Ways to Get to Know Another Person Better. 160p. (Orig.). 1993. pap. 6.95 (0-915009-23-4) World Leis Corp.

— Getting to Know You: Three Hundred Sixty-Five Questions & Activities to Enhance Relationships. rev. ed. 160p. 1994. 83.40 (0-915009-31-5); pap. 6.95 (0-915009-30-7) World Leis Corp.

McSweeney, Kerry. Four Contemporary Novelists: Angus Wilson, Brian Moore, John Fowles, V. S. Naipaul. 232p. 1983. 39.95 (0-7735-0399-4, Pub. by McGill CN) U of Toronto Pr.

— George Eliot (Marian Evans) A Literary Life. 1991. text ed. 39.95 (0-312-06574-4) St Martin.

— Invisible Man: Race & Identity. (Masterwork Studies: No. 17). 168p. 1988. text ed. 21.95 (0-8057-7977-9, Pub. by Royal Botanic Garden UK); pap. 7.95 (0-8057-8027-0, Twayne) Macmillan.

— Middlemarch. (Unwin Critical Library). 176p. 1984. text ed. 39.95 (0-04-800031-0); pap. text ed. 19.95 (0-04-800032-9) Routledge Chapman & Hall.

— Moby Dick: Ishmael's Mighty Book. (Twayne's Masterwork Studies: No. 3). 120p. (C). 1986. text ed. 22.95 (0-8057-7954-X, Twayne); pap. 12.95 (0-8057-8002-5, Twayne) Macmillan.

— Mordecai Richler & His Works. (Canadian Author Studies). 49p. (C). 1985. pap. text ed. 9.95 (0-920802-67-2, Pub. by ECW Press CN) Genl Dist Srvs.

— Tennyson & Swinburne As Romantic Naturalists. 240p. 1981. 30.00 (0-8020-2381-9) U of Toronto Pr.

McSweeney, Kerry, ed. see Carlyle, Thomas.

McSweeney, Sean & Bunnett, Chris. Gymnastics. (Sportscene Ser.). (Illus.). 64p. (YA). (gr. 7-10). 1993. 24.95 (0-7134-7129-8, Pub. by Batsford UK) Trafalgar.

McSweeney, Sean & Sampson, Rebecca. Swimming. (Sportscene Ser.). (Illus.). 64p. (YA). (gr. 7-10). 1993. 24.95 (0-7134-7128-X, Pub. by Batsford UK) Trafalgar.

McSweeney, Terry, illus. Great Gift & the Wish-Fulfilling Gem. LC 86-19767. (Jataka Tales Ser.). 32p. (J). (gr. k-5). 1987. lib. bdg. 15.95 (0-89800-157-9); pap. 7.95 (0-89800-143-9) Dharma Pub.

McSweeney, William. Roman Catholicism: The Search for Relevance. 1980. text ed. 26.00 (0-312-68969-1) St Martin.

McSweeny & Grant. Chronic Obstructive Pulmonary Disease: A Behavioral Perspective. (Lung Biology in Health & Disease Ser.: Vol. 36). 336p. 1988. 140.00 (0-8247-7693-3) Dekker.

McSwigan, Marie. Snow Treasure. 160p. (J). (gr. 3-7). 1986. pap. 2.95 (0-590-42537-4) Scholastic Inc.

McSwiney, R., jt. auth. see Prunty, F.

McTaggart, Debra, jt. auth. see McTaggart, Stephen.

McTaggart, Douglas. Bigwin Inn. Hudson, Noel, ed. (Illus.). 144p. 35.00 (1-55046-035-8, Pub. by Boston Mills Pr CN) Genl Dist Srvs.

McTaggart, Fred. Kalamazoo County: Where Quality Is a Way of Life. 1989. 29.95 (0-89781-268-9) Preferred Mktg.

— Wolf That I Am: In Search of the Red Earth People. LC 84-7352. 216p. 1984. reprint ed. pap. 12.95 (0-8061-1905-5) U of Okla Pr.

McTaggart, J. E. The Nature of Existence, 1. 1988. pap. 27.95 (0-521-35768-3) Cambridge U Pr.

— The Nature of Existence, 2. 1988. pap. 29.95 (0-521-35769-1) Cambridge U Pr.

McTaggart, James M., et al. The Value Imperative: Managing for Superior Shareholder Returns. 288p. 1994. text ed. 35.00 (0-02-920670-7) Free Pr.

McTaggart, John. Human Immortality & Pre-Existence. 1969. reprint ed. 28.00 (0-527-59950-6) Periodicals Srv.

McTaggart, John M. Nature of Existence, 2 vols., Set. 1968. 69.00 (0-403-00129-3) Scholarly.

— Philosophical Studies. Keeling, S. V., ed. LC 67-22104. (Essay Index Reprint Ser.). 1977. 20.95 (0-8369-0660-8) Ayer.

— Studies in Hegelian Cosmology. 2nd ed. (C). 1986. reprint ed. lib. bdg. 21.95 (0-935005-59-5); reprint ed. pap. text ed. 11.95 (0-935005-60-9) Lincoln-Rembrandt.

McTaggart, M. Horse & His Schooling. (Illus.). 98p. 1984. reprint ed. pap. text ed. 15.00 (0-87556-385-6) Saifer.

McTaggart, Robin. Action Research: A Short Modern History. 134p. (C). 1991. pap. 68.00 (0-7300-1217-4, EED402, Pub. by Deakin Univ AT) St Mut.

— Getting Started in Arts Education Research: Monograph, No. 1. 1991. pap. 29.00 (0-646-06270-0, Pub. by Deakin Univ AT) St Mut.

*__McTaggart, Stephen & McTaggart, Debra.__ ABC Talking Book Adventures. (Talking Book Adventures Ser.). (Illus.). 12p. (J). 1995. text ed. 19.95 (0-9627001-2-6) Futech Educ Prods.

— Bookee's Sounds Around. (Talking Book Adventures Ser.). (Illus.). 12p. (J). 1995. 19.95 (0-9627001-0-X) Futech Educ Prods.

McTaggart, T. The Big Box. (C). 1989. pap. 60.00 (0-907526-27-6, Alloway Pub) St Mut.

— Pioneers of Heavy Haulage. (C). 1988. pap. 60.00 (0-907526-17-9, Alloway Pub) St Mut.

McTaggart, Timothy, ed. Jardin Musiqual, Contenant Plusieurs Belles Fleurs De Chansons...Le Premier Livre (Antwerp, c. 1556) And Jardin Musical Contenant Plusieurs Belles Fleurs De Chansons Spirituelles a Quatre Parties..Livre Second (Antwerp, c. 1556) LC 92-23321. (Sixteenth Century Chanson Ser.: Vol. 1). 272p. 1992. 80.00 (0-8240-3100-8) Garland.

McTaggart, Timoty, ed. Jardin Musical, Contenant Plusieurs Belles Fleurs de Chansons a Quatre Parties, Le Tiers Livre, Antwerp, c.1556. LC 92-23321. (Sixteenth-Century Chanson Ser.: Vol. 2). (Illus.). 216p. 1992. 71.00 (0-8240-3101-6) Garland.

McTaggart, W. Donald. Industrial Development in West Malaysia, 1968. 65p. 1972. pap. 6.00 (0-939252-00-7) ASU Ctr Asian.

McTaggert, J. M. A Commentary on Hegel's Logic. (C). 1986. reprint ed. pap. text ed. 14.00 (0-935005-50-1) Lincoln-Rembrandt.

McTaggert, T. The Iron Men of the Road. (C). 1988. pap. 68.00 (0-907526-41-1, Alloway Pub) St Mut.

McTague, Dan & Smith, Doug. The Alarm Book: A Guide to Burglar & Fire Alarms. 192p. 1991. pap. 24.95 (0-7506-9316-9) Buttrwrth-Heinemann.

*__McTague, Fiona.__ Nursery Needlepoint: 30 Delightful Needlework Projects. (Illus.). 120p. 1995. 19.95 (0-09-178446-8, Pub. by Ebury Pr UK) Trafalgar.

McTavish, Donald G. Descriptive & Inferential Statistics: An Introduction. 4th ed. LC 92-10348. 1992. text ed. write for info. (0-205-14019-X) Allyn.

McTavish, Donald G., jt. auth. see Loether, Herman.

McTavish, Hugh. Ending War in Our Lifetime: A Concrete, Realistic Plan. 320p. (Orig.). 1993. 24.95 (0-9636865-0-X); pap. 17.95 (0-9636865-1-8) West Fork Pr.

Mctavish, John. Tomorrow We Go to Bethlehem. 1986. pap. 4.25 (0-687-42330-9) Abingdon.

McTavish, John B., ed. see Barth, Karl.

McTavish, Ronald, jt. ed. see Concordia University Staff.

McTeague, Frank. Shared Reading in the Middle & High School Years. LC 92-39116. 93p. 1992. pap. text ed. 14.00 (0-435-08735-5, 08735) Heinemann.

McTeague, James H. Before Stanislavsky: American Professional Acting Schools & Acting Theory, 1875-1925. LC 93-26669. 1993. 39.50 (0-8108-2657-7) Scarecrow.

— Playwrights & Acting: Acting Methodologies of Brecht, Ionesco, Pinter & Shepard. LC 94-17979. (Contributions in Drama & Theatre Studies). 216p. 1994. text ed. 49.95 (0-313-28975-1, Greenwood Pr) Greenwood.

McTear, M. & Creaney, N., eds. AI & Cognitive Science '90: Proceedings of the Third Irish Conference on Artificial Intelligence & Cognitive Science 20-22 September 1990, Ulster. (Workshops in Computing Ser.). xv, 392p. 1991. pap. 59.00 (0-387-19653-6) Spr-Verlag.

McTee, Cindy. A Music Calligrapher's Handbook: Tools, Materials, & Techniques. 44p. (Orig.). 1987. pap. 3.95 (0-918812-55-0, SB 0006) MMB Music.

McTernan, Oliver. A Call to Witness: Reflections on the Gospel of Matthew. 120p. 1989. pap. 4.95 (0-8146-1838-3) Liturgical Pr.

McTernan, William F. & Kaplan, Edward, eds. Risk Assessment for Groundwater Pollution Control. LC 90-20924. 368p. 1990. pap. text ed. 33.00 (0-87262-784-5) Am Soc Civil Eng.

McTevia, James V. Bankrupt! A Society Living in the Future. LC 92-27533. 227p. 1992. 21.95 (1-879094-18-5) Momentum Bks.

— Financial Reality: How Individuals, Companies, & Our Government Can Avoid Debt. 224p. 1992. pap. 12.95 (1-57101-020-3) MasterMedia Ltd.

*__McThenia, Andrew W., Jr., ed.__ Radical Christian & Exemplary Lawyer: Honoring William Stringfellow. LC 95-1892. 161p. (Orig.). 1995. pap. 14.99 (0-8028-0133-1) Eerdmans.

McThenia, Andrew W., jt. auth. see Epstein, David J.

McTighe, Esme, ed. Autonomation - Automation. Kelsey, Michael, tr. (Factory Management Notebook Ser.). (Illus.). 191p. 1991. 125.00 (1-56327-002-1) Prod Press.

— Kanban Card System & Stockless Production. Kelsey, Michael, tr. (Factory Management Notebook Ser.). (Illus.). 181p. 1992. 125.00 (1-56327-023-4) Prod Press.

— Mixed-Model Production: Mixed-Model Production. Kelsey, Michael, tr. LC 90-23555. (Factory Management Notebook Ser.). 180p. 1991. 125.00 (0-915299-97-6) Prod Press.

McTighe, James. Roadside History of Colorado. rev. ed. LC 89-84757. (Illus.). (Orig.). 1989. pap. 13.95 (1-55566-054-1) Johnson Bks.

McTighe, Michael J. A Measure of Success: Protestants & Public Culture in Antebellum Cleveland. LC 93-26789. 283p. (C). 1994. 74.50 (0-7914-1825-1); pap. 24.95 (0-7914-1826-X) State U NY Pr.

McTighe Musil, Caryn, ed. Executive Summary of the Courage to Question. 12p. 1992. pap. 7.00 (0-911696-59-8) Assn Am Coll.

McTigue, G. Gaynor. Life's Little Frustration Book. 1994. mass mkt. 5.99 (0-312-95215-5) St Martin.

— You Know You're Middle-Aged When... 96p. 1994. pap. 4.50 (0-7860-0066-X) Windsor NY.

McTigue, Geraldine, ed. see Washington, Booker T.

McTigue, James. A Survival Manual for Consumers: Get Mad then Get Even. (Self Confidence - Self Competence Ser.). 200p. (Orig.). 1987. pap. 11.95 (0-932123-03-1) Stone Trail Pr.

McTigue, Mary. Acting Like a Pro: Who's Who, What's What, & the Way Things Really Work in the Theatre. (Illus.). 288p. (Orig.). 1992. pap. 14.95 (1-55870-223-7) Betterway Bks.

McTigue, Mickey. Mountain Biking the Coast Range, Guide 4: Ventura County & the Sespe. 3rd ed. 1993. 9.95 (0-938665-18-9) Fine Edge Prods.

McTigue, William R., Jr., jt. auth. see Phifer, Russell W.

McTurk, Rory, tr. see Hallberg, Peter.

McTwigan, Michael. Ron Nagle: A Survey Exhibition. LC 93-79949. 84p. 1993. pap. 25.00 (0-9638030-0-X) Mills Art Gal.

— Ron Nagle: A Survey Exhibition 1958-1993. (Illus.). 84p. 1994. pap. 30.00 (0-295-97370-6) U of Wash Pr.

McTyeire, Holland N., et al. Duties of Masters to Servants. LC 79-154084. (Black Heritage Library Collection). 1977. 18.95 (0-8369-8795-0) Ayer.

McVan, Alice J. Antonio Machado. (Illus.). 1959. 10.00 (0-87535-095-X) Hispanic Soc.

— Antonio Machado. (Illus.). 256p. 1959. 6.00 (0-685-07664-4) Interbk Inc.

McVan, Barbara, jt. auth. see Cahill, Matthew.

McVan, Barbara, jt. auth. see Robinson, Jean.

McVan, Barbara, jt. ed. see Williams, Susan R.

McVan, Barbara, jt. ed. see Williams, Susan.

McVarish, Emily, tr. see Lichtenstein, Jacqueline.

McVaugh, Julia A., ed. see Swalin, Benjamin.

M

McVaugh, Michael, et al. Medical Licensing & Learning in 14th-Century Valencia. LC 89-84935. (Transactions Ser.: Vol. 79, Pt. 6). (Illus.). 130p. (C). 1990. pap. 15.00 (*0-87169-796-3*, T796-MCM) Am Philos.

McVaugh, Michael R. Medicine Before the Plague: Practitioners & Their Patients in the Crown of Aragon, 1285-1345. LC 92-49626. (History of Medicine Ser.). 350p. (C). 1993. 59.95 (*0-521-41235-8*) Cambridge U Pr.

McVaugh, Michael R., jt. auth. see Mauskopf, Seymour H.

McVaugh, Rogers. Edward Palmer, Plant Explorer of the American West. LC 56-11234. (Illus.). 1977. reprint ed. 15.00 (*0-913728-26-8*) Theophrastus.

McVay, Barry L. Buying Surplus Property from the U. S. Government. 20p. (Orig.). 1987. pap. 12.50 (*0-912481-04-8*) Panoptic Ent.

— The Federal Procurement Process. 31p. (Orig.). 1989. pap. 12.50 (*0-912481-10-2*) Panoptic Ent.

— Federal Profit Policy. 24p. (Orig.). 1989. pap. 12.50 (*0-912481-11-0*) Panoptic Ent.

— Getting Started in Federal Contracting. LC 86-60100. 318p. 1987. pap. 21.95 (*0-912481-03-X*) Panoptic Ent.

— Getting Started in Federal Contracting: A Guide Through the Federal Procurement Maze. 3rd ed. LC 94-69891. (Federal Contracting Ser.). 396p. 1995. pap. 29.95 (*0-912481-21-8*) Panoptic Ent.

— The Panoptic Federal Protest Package: How to Challenge Improprieties & Errors in the Procurement Process. (Federal Contracting Ser.). 150p. 1993. ring bd. 35.95 (*0-912481-17-X*) Panoptic Ent.

— Proposals That Win Federal Contracts: How to Plan, Price, Write & Negotiate to Get Your Fair Share of Government Business. LC 88-62678. (Federal Contracting Ser.). 334p. (Orig.). 1989. pap. 24.95 (*0-912481-08-0*) Panoptic Ent.

McVay, Barry L. & McVay, Vivina H. Public Law 99-661: The Department of Defense 5 percent Minority Contracting Goal. rev. ed. 26p. 1990. pap. 12.50 (*0-912481-09-9*) Panoptic Ent.

McVay, Freda & Thornhill, Ashton. Lubbock: City of Land & Sky. (Urban Tapestry Ser.). (Illus.). 300p. 1994. 39.50 (*1-881096-09-2*) Towery Pub.

McVay, Jo, jt. auth. see Flint, Patricia.

McVay, Martha, ed. see Herman, Sonya J.

McVay, Robert, ed. see Herman, Sonya J.

McVay, Vivina H., jt. auth. see McVay, Barry L.

McVea, Harry. Financial Conglomerates & the Chinese Wall: Regulating Conflicts of Interest. LC 92-47415. 1993. 55.00 (*0-19-825713-9*, Clarendon Pr) OUP.

McVea, Mildred L. Sugar Petite. (Illus.). 184p. 1990. pap. 9.95 (*0-8071-1622-X*) La State U Pr.

McVeagh, Diana, et al. The New Grove Twentieth Century English Masters: Elgar, Delius, Vaughan, Tippett, Holst, Williams, Walton & Britten. 1986. 25.00 (*0-393-02285-4*); pap. 16.95 (*0-393-30351-9*) Norton.

McVeagh, Diana M. Edward Elgar, His Life & Music. LC 78-62332. (Encore Music Editions Ser.). (Illus.). 1984. reprint ed. 24.25 (*0-88355-750-9*) Hyperion Conn.

***McVeagh, J. P.** Land Valuation Law. 7th ed. 1979. boxed 58.00 (*0-409-64584-2*, NZ) Butterworth Legal Pubs.

McVeagh, John. All Before Them: 1660-1780, Vol. 1. LC 88-7489. (English Literature & the Wider World Ser.). (Illus.). 320p. (C). 1990. text ed. 55.00 (*0-948660-08-2*, Pub. by Ashfield Pr UK) Humanities.

McVeagh, John, jt. ed. see Hadfield, Andrew.

***McVeigh, Alice.** While the Music Lasts. 234p. 1995. 24.95 (*1-85797-939-7*, Pub. by Orion) Trafalgar.

McVeigh, Amy. Mackinac Connection: An Insider's Guide. LC 89-12356. 176p. (Orig.). (C). 1989. pap. 8.95 (*0-9623213-0-3*) Mackinac Pub.

— Mackinac Connection: An Insider's Guide. rev. ed. LC 92-23695. (Orig.). 1992. pap. 8.95 (*0-9623213-1-1*) Mackinac Pub.

McVeigh, Amy, jt. auth. see Jolliffe, Susan D.

***McVeigh, C. A.** A Dictionary of the High Court Rules. 216p. 1989. pap. 63.00 (*0-409-78793-0*, NZ) Butterworth Legal Pubs.

McVeigh, J. C. Energy Around the World: An Introduction to Energy Studies: Global Resources, Needs, Utilization. (Illus.). 253p. 1984. text ed. 114.00 (*0-08-031649-2*, Pub. by Pergamon Repr UK) Franklin.

— Sun Power Supplement. 2nd ed. 1983. 34.00 (*0-08-031134-2*, Pub. by Pergamon Repr UK) Franklin.

McVeigh, J. C., jt. ed. see Sayigh, A. A.

McVeigh, Joe. Renewing the Irish Church: Towards an Irish Liberation Theology. 144p. 1994. pap. 13.95 (*1-85635-039-8*, Pub. by Mercier Pr IE) Dufour.

McVeigh, Joseph, jt. ed. see Trommler, Frank.

McVeigh, Malcolm. God in Africa. 1982. 25.95 (*0-8283-0003-8*) Branden Pub Co.

McVeigh, Ruth M. & Turner, Trudy. Fogswamp. (Illus.). 255p. pap. 11.95 (*0-88839-104-8*) Hancock House.

McVeigh, Shaun & Wheeler, Sally. Law, Health & Medical Regulation. (Contemporary Legal Issues Ser.). 250p. 1993. 59.95 (*1-85521-283-8*, Pub. by Dartmth Pub UK) Ashgate Pub Co.

McVeigh, Simon. Concert Life in London from Mozart to Hadyn. LC 92-565. (Illus.). 280p. (C). 1993. 59.95 (*0-521-41353-2*) Cambridge U Pr.

McVeigh, Simon W. The Violinist in London's Concert Life, 1750-1784: Felice Giardini & His Contemporaries. LC 89-11872. (British Music Theses Ser.). 440p. 1989. 40.00 (*0-8240-2018-9*) Garland.

McVeigh, Terrence A., tr. Wyclif on Simony. LC 92-9844. ix, 179p. 1992. 27.00 (*0-8232-1349-8*) Fordham.

McVety, Paul J. Fundamentals of Menu Planning. 1989. pap. 39.95 (*0-442-26492-5*) Van Nos Reinhold.

McVey & Associates Staff. Job Interviews. (Follet Coping Skills Ser.). 64p. 1988. pap. text ed. write for info. (*0-8428-2329-8*) Cambridge Bk.

— Using Transportation. (Follet Coping Skills Ser.). 64p. 1988. pap. text ed. 5.50 (*0-8428-2330-1*) Cambridge Bk.

McVey, Frances J. & Jewell, Robert. Uncle Will of Wildwood: Nineteenth-Century Life in the Bluegrass. LC 74-7877. (Kentucky Bicentennial Bookshelf Ser.). (Illus.). 128p. 1974. 10.00 (*0-8131-0206-5*) U Pr of Ky.

McVey, James P., ed. Handbook of Mariculture: Crustacean Aquaculture, Vol. I. 456p. 1983. 212.95 (*0-8493-0220-X*, SH138) CRC Pr.

McVey, Kathleen, ed. see St. Ephrem the Syrian.

McVey, Kathleen E., intro. Ephrem the Syrian. (Classics of Western Spirituality Ser.). 1989. 24.95 (*0-8091-0429-6*); pap. 17.95 (*0-8091-3093-9*) Paulist Pr.

McVey, Mary A. Bridge Basics: An Introduction to the Game. 2nd ed. 120p. 1982. pap. 5.50 (*0-910475-01-6*) KET.

— Play Bridge! 1983. pap. 6.50 (*0-910475-22-9*) KET.

McVey, Mary A. & Lehtcmaa, Linda R. Play More Bridge. (Bridge Ser.). 228p. 1985. pap. text ed. 7.00 (*0-910475-32-6*) KET.

McVey, Pamela W., ed. Will Book Two: 1772-1778. LC 87-405383. (Wills of Norfolk County, Virginia, 1755-1802 Ser.: 1755-1802). (Illus.). 245p. (Orig.). 1986. pap. 23.50 (*1-878515-85-3*) W S Dawson.

McVey, R. Parker. The Missing Rock Star Caper. LC 84-8721. (Solve-It-Yourself Ser.). (Illus.). 128p. (J). (gr. 3-7). 1985. lib. bdg. 9.49 (*0-8167-0398-1*); pap. text ed. 2.95 (*0-8167-0399-X*) Troll Assocs.

— Mystery at the Ball Game. LC 84-8486. (Solve-It-Yourself Ser.). (Illus.). 128p. (J). (gr. 3-7). 1985. lib. bdg. 9.49 (*0-8167-0336-1*); pap. text ed. 2.95 (*0-8167-0337-X*) Troll Assocs.

McVey, Ruth, ed. Southeast Asian Capitalists. (Studies on Southeast Asia: No. 9). 220p. (Orig.). (C). 1992. pap. text ed. 16.00 (*0-87727-708-7*) Cornell SE Asia.

McVey, Ruth T. Soviet View of the Indonesian Revolution. (Interim Reports: No. 7). 1969. reprint ed. pap. 2.50 (*0-87763-018-6*) Cornell Mod Indo.

McVey, Ruth T. & Suddard, Adrienne, eds. Southeast Asian Transitions: Approaches Through Social History. LC 78-4171. (Yale Southeast Asia Studies: No. 8). 252p. reprint ed. pap. 71.90 (*0-7837-2989-8*, 2043194) Bks Demand.

McVey, Ruth T., jt. auth. see Anderson, Benedict R.

McVey, Ruth T., jt. ed. see Benda, Harry J.

McVey, Sharel. Excel Four for Windows Quickstart. (QuickStart Ser.). (Illus.). 400p. (Orig.). 1992. pap. 21.95 (*0-88022-925-X*) Que.

— Excel Version 5 for Windows: The Original Step-by-Step Approach Corporate Edition. 1994. pap. 21.95 (*1-56529-730-X*) Que.

— Excel Version 5.0 for Windows Quickstart. 2nd ed. (Illus.). 608p. 1993. pap. 21.95 (*1-56529-531-5*) Que.

***McVey, Steve.** Grace Walk. LC 94-47485. (Orig.). 1995. pap. 7.99 (*1-56507-321-5*) Harvest Hse.

McVey, Vicki. Sierra Club Book of Weatherwisdom. 112p. (J). (gr. 4-7). 1991. 15.95 (*0-316-56341-2*) Little.

— The Sierra Club Kid's Guide to Planet Care & Repair. LC 91-38307. (Illus.). 96p. (J). (gr. 4-7). 1993. 16.95 (*0-87156-567-6*) Sierra.

— The Sierra Club Wayfinding Book. (Illus.). 96p. (J). (gr. 4-7). 1989. 14.95 (*0-316-56340-4*) Little.

McVicar, Clyde, ed. see Fotiades, John M.

McVicar, George, jt. ed. see Davie, Cedric T.

***McVicar, Jekka.** Herbs for the Home. (Herb Gardening Ser.). 1995. 27.95 (*0-670-86352-1*, Penguin Bks) Viking Penguin.

McVicar, M., jt. auth. see Midwinter, A.

McVicar, Wes. Clown Act Omnibus. LC 87-42958. (Illus.). 192p. 1986. reprint ed. pap. 10.95 (*0-916260-41-0*, B-118) Meriwether Pub.

McVickar, John. Outlines of Political Economy. LC 64-22240. (Reprints of Economic Classics Ser.). 1965. reprint ed. 39.50 (*0-678-00118-9*) Kelley.

McVickar, M. H. & Walker, W. M. Using Commercial Fertilizers. 4th ed. (Illus.). 363p. 1978. 26.60 (*0-8134-1894-1*); text ed. 19.95 (*0-685-38491-8*) Interstate.

McVicker, Dee. Easy Recycling Handbook: What to Recycle & How to Buy Recycled...Without All the Garbage. LC 93-79984. (Illus.). 128p. (Orig.). 1994. pap. 8.95 (*0-9638428-5-4*) Grassroots Bks.

McVicker, Donald & Southard, Edna C., eds. Testimony of Images: Pre-Columbian Art. LC 92-85435. (Illus.). 200p. (Orig.). (C). Date not set. pap. write for info. (*0-940784-15-7*) Miami Univ Art.

McVicker, Galina. Citizen, Turn Back! A Russian-American Odyssey. (Illus.). 128p. (Orig.). 1993. 16.95 (*1-56474-076-5*); pap. 8.95 (*1-56474-070-6*) Fithian Pr.

McVicker, Mary F. Small Business Matters: Topics, Procedures & Strategies. LC 87-47977. 320p. 1988. pap. 14.95 (*0-8019-7813-0*) Chilton.

McVicker, Mary L. The Writings of J. Frank Dobie: A Bibliography. LC 68-23421. 1968. 13.95 (*0-685-85505-8*) Mus Great Plains.

— The Writings of J. Frank Dobie: A Bibliography. deluxe limited ed. LC 68-23421. 1968. boxed 25.00 (*0-685-85504-X*) Mus Great Plains.

McVie, J. G., et al, eds. Clinical & Experimental Pathology of Lung Cancer. (Developments in Oncology Ser.). 1985. lib. bdg. 105.50 (*0-89838-764-7*) Kluwer Ac.

***McVie, J. Gordon, et al, eds.** Autologous Bone Marrow Transplantation & Solid Tumors. LC 84-13380. (Monograph Series of the European Organization for Research on Treatment of Cancer: No. 14). (Illus.). Date not set. reprint ed. pap. 59.30 (*0-7837-9561-0*, 2060310) Bks Demand.

McVinney, L. Donald, ed. Picasso Linoleum Cuts: The Mr. & Mrs. Charles Kramer Collection in the Metropolitan Museum of Art. 1985. 60.00 (*0-394-54692-X*) Random.

McVittie, Donald R. Describing Nonstandard Gears: An Alternative to the Rack Shift Coefficient. (Fall Technical Meeting Papers). (Illus.). 23p. 1986. pap. 30.00 (*1-55589-465-8*, 86-FTM1) AGMA.

McVittie, Donald R. & Errichello, Robert L. Application of Miner's Rule to Industrial Gear Drives. (Fall Technical Meeting Papers 99FTM9). (Illus.). 22p. 1988. pap. text ed. 30.00 (*1-55589-514-X*) AGMA.

McVitty, Walter, ed. Children & Learning. (Illus.). 120p. (Orig.). (C). 1985. pap. text ed. 14.00 (*0-909955-53-0*, 00586, Pub. by PETA AT) Heinemann.

— Getting It Together: Organising the Reading-Writing Classroom. (Illus.). vi, 122p. (Orig.). 1987. pap. text ed. 15.00 (*0-909955-63-8*, 00590, Pub. by PETA AT) Heinemann.

McVoy, D. Stevens, jt. auth. see Baldwin, Thomas F.

McVoy, L. C. Louisiana in the Short Story. LC 73-130264. (American History & Americana Ser.: No. 47). 1970. reprint ed. lib. bdg. 59.95 (*0-8383-1171-7*) M S G Haskell Hse.

McWade, Patricia. Financing Graduate School: How to Get the Money You Need for Your Graduate School Education. LC 93-33244. 208p. 1992. pap. 14.95 (*1-56079-147-0*) Petersons Guides.

McWaid, Helen & Machac, Kathy. Home Stuff: Teach-away with Toss-away. (Home-School-Education Ser.). (Illus.). 159p. (Orig.). (J). (gr. 1-6). 1982. pap. text ed. 8.95 (*0-9611480-0-4*) Custom Curriculum.

McWalter, jt. auth. see Hayes, Peter L.

***McWalters, Edward, et al.** Heroes of the Faith. 54p. 1994. pap. 9.95 (*1-57326-022-3*) Core Ministries.

McWane, John W., jt. auth. see Smith, Malcolm K.

McWane, John W., et al. Photodetectors. 75p. 1976. 15.00 (*0-318-41567-4*, PT22) Am Assn Physics.

McWaters, J. F., jt. ed. see Crestin, J. P.

McWaters, J. F., jt. ed. see Storr, A.

McWaters, J. Glenn. Deep Water Exercise for Health & Fitness. LC 87-35861. (Illus.). 192p. (Orig.). 1988. 16.95 (*0-913581-07-0*); pap. 11.95 (*0-913581-08-9*) Publitec.

McWaters, Marcus M. & Lin, You-Feng. Intermediate Algebra. LC 84-80462. 517p. (C). 1985. text ed. 29.00 (*0-669-05123-3*); Student study guide. student ed 4.50 (*0-669-05122-5*); Student soln. guide. student ed 7.50 (*0-669-05126-8*); Instr.'s guide. teacher ed 2.00 (*0-669-05125-X*); Solns. to even-numbered exercises. teacher ed 6.50 (*0-669-09198-7*) Heath.

McWeeney, Tom, jt. auth. see Hedden, Rich.

McWeeny, R. Methods of Molecular Quantum Mechanics. 2nd ed. (Theoretical Chemistry Ser.). 592p. 1992. reprint ed. pap. text ed. 64.95 (*0-12-486552-6*) Acad Pr.

Mcweeny, R. & Jones, H. Symmetry: Introduction to Group Theory & Its Applications. LC 63-10017. (International Encyclopedia of Physical Chemistry & Chemical Physics Ser.: Vol. 3, Pt. 1). 1963. 107.00 (*0-08-010141-0*, Pub. by Pergamon Repr UK) Franklin.

McWeeny, R. & Sutcliffe, B. J., eds. Methods of Molecular Quantum Mechanics. 2nd ed. (Theoretical Chemistry Ser.). 573p. 1989. text ed. 170.00 (*0-12-486551-8*) Acad Pr.

McWeeny, R., ed. see Farina, John E.

McWeeny, Roy, ed. see Coulson, Charles A.

McWhan, D. B., ed. Crystal Structure at High Pressure. (Transactions of the American Crystallographic Association Ser.: Vol. 5). 162p. 1969. pap. 25.00 (*0-686-60376-1*) Polycrystal Bk Serv.

***McWhiney, Grady.** Battle in the Wilderness: Grant Meets Lee. (Civil War Campaigns & Commanders Ser.). (Illus.). 132p. (Orig.). 1995. pap. write for info. (*1-886661-00-6*) Ryan Place Pub.

— Braxton Bragg & Confederate Defeat, Vol. I. 1991. 22.50 (*0-8173-0545-9*) U of Ala Pr.

— Cracker Culture: Celtic Ways in the Old South. LC 86-16052. (Illus.). 336p. 1989. pap. 19.50 (*0-8173-0458-4*) U of Ala Pr.

McWhiney, Grady & Jamieson, Perry D. Attack & Die: Civil War Military Tactics & the Southern Heritage. LC 81-902. (Illus.). xvii, 232p. 1982. pap. 14.50 (*0-8173-0229-8*) U of Ala Pr.

McWhiney, Grady, jt. ed. see Freeman, Douglas S.

McWhinney, Edward. Conflict & Compromise: International Law & World Order in a Revolutionary Age. LC 80-29045. 152p. (C). 1981. 29.50 (*0-8419-0694-7*); pap. 16.95 (*0-8419-0696-3*) Holmes & Meier.

— Constitution-Making: Principles, Process, Practices. 240p. 1981. 30.00 (*0-8020-5553-2*) U of Toronto Pr.

— Quebec & the Constitution, Nineteen Sixty to Nineteen Seventy-Eight. LC 79-316335. 186p. reprint ed. pap. 53.10 (*0-8357-4159-1*, 2036933) Bks Demand.

— United Nations Law Making: Cultural & Ideological Relativism & International Law for an Era of Transition. 310p. (C). 1984. 34.50 (*0-8419-0948-2*); pap. 24.50 (*0-8419-1008-1*) Holmes & Meier.

McWhinney, Edward, ed. Law, Foreign Policy, & the East-West Detente. LC 65-899. 131p. reprint ed. pap. 37.40 (*0-317-09595-1*, 2014321) Bks Demand.

McWhinney, Edward J. The International Law of Detente. 260p. 1978. lib. bdg. 80.50 (*90-286-0338-7*) Kluwer Ac.

— Judge Shigeru Oda & the Progressive Development of International Law: Opinions, Declarations, Separate Opinions, Dissents, on the International Court of Justice, 1976-1992. LC 93-884. (Judges Ser.). 1993. lib. bdg. 175.00 (*0-7923-2257-6*) Kluwer Ac.

— Judicial Settlement of International Disputes: Jurisdiction Justiciability & Judicial Law-Making of the Contemporary International Court. (C). 1991. lib. bdg. 89.00 (*0-7923-0991-X*) Kluwer Ac.

— Supreme Courts & Judicial Law-Making: Constitutional Tribunals & Constitutional Review. 1986. lib. bdg. 127.00 (*90-247-3203-4*) Kluwer Ac.

— The World Court & the Contemporary International Law-Making Process. 227p. 1979. lib. bdg. 74.50 (*90-286-0908-3*) Kluwer Ac.

McWhinney, Edward J., ed. From Coexistence to Cooperation: International Law & Organization in the Post-Cold War Era. 312p. (C). 1991. lib. bdg. 112.50 (*0-7923-1401-8*) Kluwer Ac.

McWhinney, Edward J., jt. auth. see Singh, Nagendra.

McWhinney, Edward J., et al, eds. Federalism in the Making: Contemporary Canadian & German Constitutionalism, National & Transnational. LC 92-31199. 1992. lib. bdg. 89.00 (*0-7923-1975-3*) Kluwer Ac.

McWhinney, Ian R. A Textbook of Family Medicine. (Illus.). 400p. 1989. pap. 32.50 (*0-19-505037-1*) OUP.

McWhinney, Will. Paths of Change: Stragetic Choices for Organizations & Society. (Illus.). 280p. 1992. 49.95 (*0-8039-3930-2*); pap. 22.95 (*0-8039-3931-0*) Sage.

McWhirr, Alan. Roman Crafts & Industries. 1989. pap. 25.00 (*0-85263-594-X*, Pub. by Shire UK) St Mut.

— Roman Gloucestershire. (Illus.). 192p. 1993. pap. text ed. 15.00 (*0-904387-60-7*) A Sutton Pub.

***McWhirter.** Guinness Book of Womens Sports. 1979. (*0-8069-0162-4*) Sterling.

***McWhirter, Darien.** Managing People: Creating the Team-Based Organization. (Business Advisor Ser.). 300p. (Orig.). 1995. pap. 12.95 (*1-55850-485-0*) Adams Pubng.

— The Personnel Policy Handbook for Growing Companies: How to Create Comprehensive Guidelines, Procedures, & Checklist. (An Adams Business Advisor Ser.). 1994. pap. 10.95 (*1-55850-430-3*) Adams Pubng.

McWhirter, Darien A. Equal Protection. LC 94-37866. (Exploring the Constitution Ser.). 216p. 1994. 29.95 (*0-89774-855-7*) Oryx Pr.

— Freedom of Speech, Press, & Assembly. LC 94-4842. (Exploring the Constitution Ser.). 168p. 1994. 29.95 (*0-89774-853-0*) Oryx Pr.

— Search Seizure & Privacy. LC 94-27882. (Exploring the Constitution Ser.). 192p. 1994. 29.95 (*0-89774-854-9*) Oryx Pr.

— Separation of Church & State. (Exploring the Constitution Ser.). 184p. 1994. 29.95 (*0-89774-852-2*) Oryx Pr.

— Sharing Ownership: The Business Manager's Guide to ESOP's & Other Ownership Incentive Plans. 288p. 1993. text ed. 34.95 (*0-471-57733-2*) Wiley.

— Your Rights at Work. 2nd ed. 320p. 1992. pap. text ed. 19.95 (*0-471-57692-1*) Wiley.

McWhirter, Darien A. & Bible, Jon D. Privacy As a Constitutional Right: Sex, Drugs, & the Right to Life. LC 91-47986. 224p. 1992. text ed. 49.95 (*0-89930-638-1*, MWV, Quorum Bks) Greenwood.

McWhirter, Darien A., jt. auth. see Bible, Jon D.

McWhirter, David. Desire & Love in Henry James: A Study of the Late Novels. (Illus.). (C). 1989. 64.95 (*0-521-35328-9*) Cambridge U Pr.

— Millennial Harbinger - Index. LC 81-65031. (Millennial Harbinger Ser.). 776p. (C). 1981. 19.95 (*0-89900-228-5*) College Pr Pub.

***McWhirter, David & Rowe, John C., eds.** Henry James's New York Edition: The Construction of Authorship. LC 95-1325. (Illus.). 334p. 1995. 37.50x (*0-8047-2564-0*) Stanford U Pr.

McWhirter, David P. & Mattison, Andrew M. The Male Couple: How Relationships Develop. 334p. 1985. 18.95 (*0-13-547661-5*, Busn); pap. 9.95 (*0-13-547563-5*, Busn) P-H.

McWhirter, Ellen H. Counseling for Empowerment. LC 94-3945. 270p. 1994. 33.95 (*1-55620-135-4*) Am Coun Assn.

McWhirter, George, ed. see Pacheco, Jose E.

McWhirter, J. G. Mathematics in Signal Processing III. (Institute of Mathematics & Its Applications Conference Series, New Ser.: No. 49). (Illus.). 256p. 1994. 98.00 (*0-19-853480-9*) OUP.

McWhirter, J. R., ed. Use of High Purity Oxygen in the Activated Sludge Process, 2 vols., Vol. 1. (Uniscience Ser.). 296p. 1978. 89.00 (*0-8493-5101-4*, TD756, CRC Reprint) Franklin.

— Use of High Purity Oxygen in the Activated Sludge Process, 2 vols., Vol. 2. (Uniscience Ser.). 292p. 1978. 89.00 (*0-8493-5102-2*, CRC Reprint) Franklin.

McWhirter, Jay D., jt. auth. see Rawnsley, L. Scott.

McWhirter, Jeffries, et al. At-Risk Youth: A Comprehensive Response. LC 92-26966. 1993. pap. 25.95 (*0-534-19842-2*) Brooks-Cole.

McWhirter, Louis. Astrology & Stock Market Forecasting. Weingarten, H., ed. 1977. reprint ed. 35.00 (*0-88231-034-8*) ASI Pubs Inc.

McWhirter, Norris. Guinness Book of World Records, 1987. 1987. pap. 4.95 (*0-685-57360-5*) Bantam.

— Guinness...1987. 1987. pap. 4.95 (*0-685-52275-X*) Bantam.

McWhorter. The Electricity Book. 1992. pap. 14.95 (*0-7906-1023-X*, Prompt Pubns) H W Sams.

McWhorter & Harden, O. Elizabeth. Maria Edgeworth's Art of Prose Fiction. 258p. 1971. text ed. 35.40 (*3-10-800307-0*) Mouton.

***McWhorter, Abner.** An Introduction to Business for African-American Youth. Adams, Debra, ed. (Illus.). 162p. (Orig.). (YA). (gr. 6-12). 1995. pap. 10.95 (*0-9645840-1-8*) Xpression Pub.

McWhorter, C. G. & Gebhardt, M. R., eds. Methods of Applying Herbicides. 358p. 1988. text ed. 35.00 (*0-911733-08-6*) Weed Sci Soc.

McWhorter, Celane M., jt. ed. see Kaiser, Ann P.

McWhorter, David B. & Sunada, Daniel K. Ground Water Hydrology & Hydraulics. LC 77-74259. 1981. reprint ed. 40.00 (*0-918334-18-7*) WRP.

McWhorter, Don & McWhorter, Jane. Living Together in Knowledge: What Husbands & Wives Can Learn about Marriage from Each Other. 172p. 1988. pap. text ed. 5.95 (*0-317-90952-5*) Pub Designs.

***McWhorter, Eugene W.** The Club & the Town: The Rotary Club & the City of Longview, Texas, Year by Year from 1920-1995. LC 95-75960. (Illus.). 112p. 1995. 35.00 (0-9646100-9-4) Longview Rotary Endow Fund.
— Traditions of the Land: The History of Gregg County, Texas. LC 89-80785. (Illus.). 128p. (C). 1989. 29.95 (0-9623844-0-2) Gregg Cty Hist Found.
McWhorter, Frankie. Cowboy Fiddler. (Illus.). viii, 112p. 1992. 17.50 (0-89672-248-1) Tex Tech Univ Pr.
— Play It Lazy: The Bob Wills Fiddle Legacy. Fiel, Lanny, tr. (Illus.). 62p. 1992. pap. 9.95 (0-685-59077-1); audio 18.95 (0-89672-307-0); digital audio 9.98 (0-89672-308-9) Tex Tech Univ Pr.
McWhorter, George T. Burroughs Dictionary: An Alphabetical List of Proper Names, Word, Phrases & Concepts Contained in the Published Works of Edgar Rice Burroughs. LC 87-14266. (Illus.). 462p. 1987. lib. bdg. 65.00 (0-8191-6512-3) U Pr of Amer.
— Edgar Rice Burroughs Memorial Collection. (Bibliographies & Indexes in Science Fiction, Fantasy, & Horror Ser.: No. 4). 1990. 79.95 (0-313-27696-X, MWB, Greenwood Pr) Greenwood.
McWhorter, Jane. Caterpillars or Butterflies. (Illus.). 1977. pap. 6.50 (0-89137-410-8) Quality Pubns.
— Let This Cup Pass. (Illus.). 1979. pap. 6.50 (0-89137-414-0) Quality Pubns.
— Meet My Friend David. 1982. 6.50 (0-89137-420-5) Quality Pubns.
— Now I Can Fly! 1987. pap. 6.50 (0-89137-437-X) Quality Pubns.
— She Hath Done What She Could. 1973. 6.50 (0-89137-405-1) Quality Pubns.
McWhorter, Jane, jt. auth. see McWhorter, Don.
McWhorter, Kathleen T. Academic Reading. 2nd ed. (C). 1993. text ed. 20.50 (0-673-52283-0) HarpCollege.
— College Reading & Study Skills. 4th ed. (C). 1989. pap. text ed. 19.75 (0-673-39664-9) HarpCollege.
— College Reading & Study Skills. 5th ed. (C). 1991. text ed. 31.50 (0-673-46442-3) HarpCollege.
— College Reading & Study Skills. 6th ed. LC 94-18645. (C). 1995. 24.00 (0-673-99373-6) HarpC.
— Efficient & Flexible Reading. 3rd ed. (C). 1991. text ed. 32.00 (0-673-46032-0) HarpCollege.
— Efficient & Flexible Reading. 4th ed. LC 95-2677. (C). 1995. student ed, pap. write for info. (0-673-99495-3, Harp PBks); teacher ed, pap. write for info. (0-673-99504-6, Harp PBks) HarpC.
— Guide to College Reading. 2nd ed. (C). 1988. pap. text ed. 17.00 (0-673-39665-7) HarpCollege.
— Guide to College Reading. 3rd ed. LC 92-19573. (C). 1992. 22.50 (0-673-52235-0) HarpCollege.
— Study & Critical Thinking Skills in College. 3rd ed. LC 95-3935. (C). 1995. student ed write for info. (0-673-99496-1, HarpT); teacher ed write for info. (0-673-99503-8, HarpT) HarpC.
— Study & Thinking Skills. 2nd ed. (C). 1991. text ed. 31.50 (0-673-46443-1) HarpCollege.
McWhorter, LaDelle. Heidegger & the Earth: Issues in Environmental Philosophy. 160p. (C). 1992. 35.25 (0-943549-08-6) TJU Pr.
McWhorter, Lucullus V. Hear Me, My Chiefs: Nez Perce Legend & History. LC 52-5209. (Illus.). 640p. 1984. reprint ed. 27.95 (0-87004-316-1); reprint ed. pap. 19.95 (0-87004-310-2) Caxton.
— Yellow Wolf: His Own Story. LC 85-16659. (Illus.). 324p. 1984. reprint ed. 19.95 (0-87004-317-X); reprint ed. pap. 15.95 (0-87004-315-3) Caxton.
***McWhorter, Lucullus Virgil.** Tragedy of the Wahk-Shum: The Death of Andrew J. Bolon, Yakima Indian Agent As Told by Sue-el-lil, Eyewitness; Also, The Suicide of Gen. Geo. A. Custer As Told by Owl Child, Eyewitness. Hines, Donald M., ed. LC 94-79277. (Illus.). 105p. 1995. pap. text ed. 10.95 (0-9629539-4-6) Great Eagle Pub.
McWhorter, Margaret L. Autumn Leaves. LC 81-51943. (Illus.). 60p. (Orig.). 1981. pap. 4.95 (0-9604342-1-6) Ransom Hill.
— Poems That Tell Me Who I Am. LC 80-51481. (Illus.). 57p. 1978. reprint ed. pap. 4.95 (0-9604342-0-8) Ransom Hill.
— Tea Cup Tales: Tales of Tea & How to Read the Tea Leaves. LC 83-62916. (Illus.). 42p. (Orig.). 1993. reprint ed. pap. 5.95 (0-9604342-3-2) Ransom Hill.
***McWhorter, Margarmet L.** San Diego County Writers & Publishers Resource Guide: The Writer's Red Book. 2nd ed. 336p. (C). 1995. pap. write for info. (0-941903-14-1) Ransom Hill.
McWhorter, Mitzi, jt. ed. see Randle, Mike.
McWhorter, R. Clayton, jt. auth. see Hardy, Owen B.
***McWilliam, Candia.** Debatable Land. LC 94-26104. 1995. 23.50 (0-385-26310-4) Doubleday.
***McWilliam, Erica.** In Broken Images: Feminist Tales for a Different Teacher Education. 208p. (C). 1995. text ed. 40.00x (0-8077-3387-3); pap. text ed. 19.95x (0-8077-3386-5) Tchrs Coll.
McWilliam, G. H., tr. see Boccaccio, Giovanni.
McWilliam, J. Book of Freezing. 1977. reprint ed. 20.00 (0-85941-010-2) St Mut.
McWilliam, Joanne, et al. Augustine: From Rhetor to Theologian. 200p. (C). 1992. text ed. 35.00 (0-88920-203-6, Pub. by Wilfrid Laurier CN) Humanities.
McWilliam, N., jt. ed. see Winser, S.
McWilliam, Neil. Dreams of Happiness: Social Art & the French Left, 1830-1850. LC 92-38222. (Illus.). 424p. 1993. text ed. 49.50 (0-691-03155-X) Princeton U Pr.
McWilliam, Neil, ed. A Bibliography of Salon Criticism from the July Monarchy to the Second Republic, 1831-1851, Vol. 2. (Studies in the History of Art). 300p. (C). 1991. 15.00 (0-521-40091-0) Cambridge U Pr.
— A Bibliography of Salon Criticism in Paris from the Ancien Regime to the Restoration, 1699-1827, Vol. 1. (Studies in the History of Art). 275p. (C). 1991. 15.00 (0-521-34634-7) Cambridge U Pr.
McWilliam, P. J. & Bailey, Donald B., Jr., eds. Working Together with Children & Families: Case Studies in Early Intervention. LC 92-42852. 288p. 1993. 25.00 (1-55766-123-5) P H Brookes.
McWilliams, et al. Cleft Palate Speech. 2nd ed. (Illus.). 400p. (C). 1990. 58.95 (1-55664-238-5) Mosby Yr Bk.
McWilliams, Anne W. Cuando Triunfa la Fe. Martinez, Jose L., tr. Orig. Title: Champion of Faith: David Gomez. 152p. 1983. pap. 3.10 (0-311-01071-7) Casa Bautista.
McWilliams, Barry. This Ain't Hell, but You Can See It from Here: A Desert Storm Sketchbook. 256p. 1992. pap. 9.95 (0-89141-443-6) Presidio Pr.
McWilliams, Bernard F., tr. see Dussel, Enrique D.
McWilliams, Bernard F., tr. see Paoli, Arturo.
***McWilliams, Brendan.** Weather Eye. (Illus.). 160p. (Orig.). 1994. pap. 11.95 (1-874675-38-4, Pub. by Lilliput Pr Ltd IE) Irish Bks Media.
McWilliams, Carey. Ambrose Bierce, a Biography. (BCL1-PS American Literature Ser.). 358p. 1992. reprint ed. lib. bdg. 89.00 (0-7812-6677-7) Rprt Serv.
— California, the Great Exception. LC 75-138398. xiii, 377p. 1971. reprint ed. text ed. 35.00 (0-8371-5926-1, MCCA, Greenwood Pr) Greenwood.
— Ill Fares the Land: Migrants & Migratory Labor in the United States. Cortes, Carlos E., ed. LC 76-1255. (Chicano Heritage Ser.). 1977. reprint ed. 35.95 (0-405-09514-7) Ayer.
— A Mask for Privilege: Anti-Semitism in America. LC 78-26197. 299p. 1979. reprint ed. text ed. 59.75 (0-313-20880-8, MCMP, Greenwood Pr) Greenwood.
— North from Mexico: The Spanish-Speaking People of the United States. Meier, Matt S., ed. LC 89-17031. 376p. 1990. text ed. 59.95 (0-313-26631-X, MNX/, Greenwood Pr); pap. text ed. 14.95 (0-275-93224-9, B3224, Greenwood Pr) Greenwood.
— Southern California: An Island on the Land. LC 73-77787. 415p. 1973. pap. 12.95 (0-87905-007-1, Peregrine Smith) Gibbs Smith Pub.
— Southern California Country: An Island on the Land. LC 76-111847. (Essay Index Reprint Ser.). 1977. 29.95 (0-8369-1674-3) Ayer.
McWilliams, D., jt. auth. see Congdon, Tim.
***McWilliams, D. G.** Never Too Old to Cry. 484p. 1994. pap. 12.95 (1-56901-586-4) NW Pub.
McWilliams, Dean. John Gardner. (Twayne's United States Authors Ser.). 152p. 1990. text ed. 21.95 (0-8057-7602-8, TUSAS 561, Twayne) Macmillan.
— The Narratives of Michel Butor: The Writer As Janus. LC 77-92254. x, 150p. 1978. 17.95 (0-8214-0389-3) Ohio U Pr.
McWilliams, Dee-Dee. Yesterday's Lifestyle-Today's Survival: The Life of a Real Ozark Mountain Hillbilly. (Illus.). 80p. (Orig.). 1983. pap. 7.95 (0-943962-01-3) Viewpoint Pr.
McWilliams, Donald B, jt. auth. see Pinney, William E.
McWilliams, Donald B.
McWilliams, J., jt ed. see Herring, J.
McWilliams, James P. Armscor: South Africa's Arms Merchant. 197p. 1989. 48.00 (0-08-036709-7, Pub. by Brasseys UK) Brasseys Inc.
***McWilliams, Jimmie.** Corn Pone: Half-Baked, Half-Fried Staple Corn Bread Patties. (Illus.). 216p. (Orig.). 1992. pap. 19.95 (0-9633194-1-8) D R Virtue Pr.
McWilliams, John. John McWilliams: Land of Deepest Shade. (Illus.). 95p. 1989. 15.00 (0-939802-58-9) High Mus Art.
— Last of the Mohicans: Civil Savagery & Savage Civility. LC 94-14564. (Twayne's Masterwork Studies: No. 143). (Illus.). 128p. 1994. text ed. 22.95x (0-8057-8389-X, Twayne) Macmillan.
— Last of the Mohicans: Civil Savagery & Savage Civility. (Twayne's Masterwork Studies Ser.: No. 143). (Illus.). 128p. 1994. pap. 12.95 (0-8057-4457-6, Twayne) Macmillan.
McWilliams, John, photos. Land of the Deepest Shade. (Illus.). 108p. 1989. 35.00 (0-89381-392-3) Aperture.
McWilliams, John C. The Protectors: Harry J. Anslinger & the Federal Bureau of Narcotics, 1930-1962. LC 88-40328. 256p. 1990. 40.00 (0-87413-352-1) U Delaware Pr.
McWilliams, John P., Jr. The American Epic: Transformations of a Genre 1770-1860. (Cambridge Studies in American Literature & Culture: No. 36). 304p. (C). 1989. 54.95 (0-521-37322-0) Cambridge U Pr.
McWilliams, John P., Jr., ed. see Cooper, James Fenimore.
McWilliams, John P., Jr., jt. ed. see Dekker, George.
McWilliams, Joyce. Roses Are Dead: Divorce Means Never Having to Say I Love You. (Illus.). 110p. (Orig.). 1991. pap. 6.95 (0-9630605-0-3) PrimRose CA.
***McWilliams, Judith.** Anything's Possible! (Desire Ser.). 1995. mass mkt. 3.25 (0-373-05911-6, 1-05911-2) Silhouette.
— Betrayed: Northpoint. (Historical Ser.). 1994. mass mkt. 3.99 (0-373-28849-2, 1-28849-7) Harlequin Bks.
— In Good Faith. (Men Made in America Ser.). 1995. mass mkt. 3.59 (0-373-45182-2, 1-45182-2) Harlequin Bks.
— Not My Baby! (Temptation Ser.). 1993. mass mkt. 2.99 (0-373-25540-3, 1-25540-5) Harlequin Bks.
— Suspicion. (Historical Ser.). 1994. mass mkt. 3.99 (0-373-28815-8, 1-28815-8) Harlequin Bks.
— That's My Baby. large type ed. (Silhouette Desire Ser.). 1993. 17.95 (0-373-58830-5, Silhouette Lrg Print); pap. 16.95 (0-373-58922-0, Silhouette Lrg Print) Chivers N Amer.
McWilliams, K. Richard, jt. auth. see El-Najjar, Mahmoud Y.
McWilliams, Keith E., jt. auth. see Sullivan, Jim.
McWilliams, Lois R., ed. So Blow Ye Winds: A Diary of Oscar Rice. (Illus.). 85p. (Orig.). 1990. pap. 9.95 (0-9625505-1-5) SOS Pubns NJ.
McWilliams, Margaret. Experimental Foods Laboratory Manual. 3rd ed. (Illus.). 348p. (C). 1989. 18.95 (0-916434-14-1) Plycon Pr.
— Experimental Foods Laboratory Manual. 4th ed. (Illus.). 356p. 1994. 19.95 (0-916434-13-3) Plycon Pr.
— Food Fundamentals. 5th ed. (Illus.). 608p. 1992. pap. text ed. 42.95 (0-916434-03-6) Plycon Pr.
— Food Fundamentals. 6th ed. (Illus.). 1995. pap. write for info. (0-916434-06-0) Plycon Pr.
— Foods: Experimental Perspectives. 2nd ed. LC 92-31289. (Illus.). 608p. (C). 1993. write for info. (0-02-379811-4) Macmillan.
— Fundamentals of Meal Management. 2nd ed. (Illus.). 350p. (C). 1993. pap. text ed. 34.95 (0-916434-31-1) Plycon Pr.
— Illustrated Guide to Food Preparation. 5th ed. (Illus.). 1986. 15.95 (0-916434-23-0) Plycon Pr.
— Illustrated Guide to Food Preparation. 6th rev. ed. (Illus.). 284p. (C). 1990. pap. text ed. 19.95 (0-916434-24-9) Plycon Pr.
— Meatless Cookbook. (Illus.). 1973. pap. 1.30 (0-916434-10-9) Plycon Pr.
— Nutrition for the Growing Years. 5th ed. (Illus.). 1993. pap. text ed. 39.95 (0-916434-04-4) Plycon Pr.
McWilliams, Nancy. Psychoanalytic Diagnosis: Understanding Personality Structure in the Clinical Process. 398p. 1994. lib. bdg. 35.00 (0-89862-199-2) Guilford Pubns.
***McWilliams, Peter.** Ain't Nobody's Business If You Do. 1995. pap. 5.95 (0-931580-58-7) Prelude Press.
— Ain't Nobody's Business If You Do: The Absurdity of Consensual Crimes in a Free Society. 818p. 1993. 11.47 (0-931580-53-6) Prelude Press.
— Come Love with Me & Be My Life: The Complete Romantic Poetry of Peter McWilliams. 250p. 1991. 12.95 (0-931580-03-X) Prelude Press.
— Come Love with Me & Be My Life: The Complete Romantic Poetry of Peter McWilliams, 2 audiotapes, Set. 250p. 1991. audio 12.95 (0-931580-74-9) Prelude Press.
— Do It! Let's Get off Our Buts. 1995. audio 24.95 (0-931580-15-3) Prelude Press.
— I Marry You Because. 192p. 1993. pap. 5.95 (0-931580-85-4) Prelude Press.
— Life 101: Everything We Wish We Had Learned about Life in School - but Didn't. 1995. audio 22.95 (0-931580-16-1) Prelude Press.
— Life 101: Everything We Wish We Had Learned about Life in School - but Didn't. rev. ed. 400p. 1994. pap. 5.95 (0-931580-78-1) Prelude Press.
— Life 102: What to Do When Your Guru Sues You. 423p. 1994. 19.95 (0-931580-34-X) Prelude Press.
— Love 101: To Love Oneself Is the Beginning of a Lifelong Romance. (Life 101 Ser.). 432p. (Orig.). 1995. pap. 11.95 (0-931580-70-6) Prelude Press.
— Peter McWilliam's Personal Electronics Book, 1988. 1989. pap. 10.95 (0-318-32500-4) P-H.
— Portraits: A Book of Photographs by Peter McWilliams. (Illus.). 252p. 1992. 34.95 (0-931580-77-3) Prelude Press.
— That Book about Drugs. 384p. Date not set. pap. 5.95 (0-931580-60-9) Prelude Press.
— What Jesus & the Bible Really Said about Drugs, Sex, Gays, Gambling, Prostitution, Alternative Healing, Assisted Suicide, & Other Consensual "Sins" Date not set. pap. 5.95 (0-931580-59-5) Prelude Press.
— You Can't Afford the Luxury of a Negative Thought: A Book for People with Any Life-Threatening Illness - Including Life. 1995. audio 24.95 (0-931580-13-7) Prelude Press.
— You Can't Afford the Luxury of a Negative Thought: A Book for People with Any Life-Threatening Illness - Including Life. rev. ed. 622p. 1995. pap. 5.95 (0-931580-24-2) Prelude Press.
McWilliams, Peter, jt. auth. see Bloomfield, Harold H.
McWilliams, Peter, jt. auth. see John-Roger.
McWilliams, Phil. The Solution Strategy: Your Handbook for Solving Life's Problems. Parker, Diane, ed. LC 91-61309. (Illus.). 1991. pap. 9.95 (0-88247-875-3) R & E Pubs.
McWilliams, Richebourg. Iberville's Gulf Journals. 208p. 1991. pap. 16.50 (0-8173-0539-4) U of Ala Pr.
McWilliams, Richebourg G., ed. & tr. Fleur de Lys & Calumet: Being the Penicaut Narrative of French Adventure in Louisiana. LC 88-14203. (Library of Alabama Classics). xx, 352p. 1988. reprint ed. pap. 16.95 (0-8173-0414-2) U of Ala Pr.
McWilliams, Roger, ed. Radio-Frequency Power in Plasmas. LC 89-45805. (AIP Conference Proceedings Ser.: No. 190). 520p. 1990. lib. bdg. 70.00 (0-88318-397-8) Am Inst Physics.
McWilliams, Tennant S. New South Faces the World: Foreign Affairs & the Southern Sense of Self, 1877-1950. LC 87-32485. viii, 165p. 1988. 27.50 (0-8071-1402-2) La State U Pr.
McWilliams, Warren. Christ & Narcissus: Prayer in a Self-Centered World. 160p. (Orig.). 1992. pap. 11.95 (0-8361-3569-5) Herald Pr.
McWilliams, Wayne C. & Piotrowski, Harry. The World since 1945: A History of International Relations. 3rd ed. LC 93-16357. 558p. (C). 1993. pap. text ed. 19.95 (1-55587-319-7) Lynne Rienner.
McWilliams, Wilson C. The Idea of Fraternity in America. LC 73-101339. 1973. 47.50 (0-520-01650-5); pap. 10.00 (0-520-02772-8) U CA Pr.
— Military Honor After Mylai. LC 72-90523. (Special Studies Ser.). 1972. pap. 2.00 (0-87641-213-4) Carnegie Ethics & Intl Affairs.
— The Politics of Disappointment: American Elections, 1976-94. LC 95-18753. (Studies in Political Thinking). 224p. (Orig.). (C). 1995. pap. text ed. 17.95x (1-56643-028-3) Chatham Hse Pubs.
McWilliams, Wilson C. & Gibbons, Michael T., eds. The Federalists, the Antifederalists, & the American Political Tradition. LC 91-25724. (Contributions in Political Science Ser.: No. 287). 152p. 1992. text ed. 45.00 (0-313-27724-9, GFI, Greenwood Pr) Greenwood.
***McWillliams, Peter.** Do It! Let's Get off Our Buts. rev. ed. 494p. 1994. pap. 5.95 (0-931580-79-X) Prelude Press.
McWorkman, Lee G. From Two to Seventy-Two. (Illus.). 284p. (Orig.). pap. 9.95 (0-9624492-0-2) McWorkman.
McWright, G. M. & Wojtunik, Henry J., eds. Optoelectronic Materials, Devices, Packaging & Interconnects Two, Vol. 994. 1988. 51.00 (0-8194-0029-7) SPIE.
Mda, Zakes. The Plays of Zakes Mda. 256p. (Orig.). 1989. pap. 24.95 (0-86975-389-4, Pub. by Ravan Pr ZA) Ohio U Pr.
— Ways of Dying. (Southern African Writing Ser.). 192p. 1995. pap. 9.95 (0-19-571106-8) OUP.
— When People Play People: Development Communications Through Theatre. LC 93-18987. 288p. (C). 1993. text ed. 55.00 (1-85649-199-4, Pub. by Zed Books UK); pap. 25.00 (1-85649-200-1, Pub. by Zed Books UK) Humanities.
M'Duffee, John. Oregon Crisis. 25p. 1970. reprint ed. pap. 4.95 (0-87770-063-X) Ye Galleon.
***Mdurvwa, Hajara E.** Down in Africa. (Illus.). 16p. (J). 1995. pap. 5.95 (0-8059-3689-0) Dorrance.
Mea, Giuseppe. Italian-Portuguese Dictionary. 2256p. (ITA & POR.). Date not set. 95.00 (0-8288-9427-2) Fr & Eur.
— Portuguese - Italian Dictionary. 2256p. (ITA & POR.). Date not set. 95.00 (0-8288-9426-4) Fr & Eur.
Meaburn, J. Detection & Spectrometry of Faint Light. (Astrophysics & Space Science Library: No. 56). 1976. lib. bdg. 99.00 (90-277-0678-6) Kluwer Ac.
— Detection & Spectrometry of Faint Light. (Astrophysics & Space Science Library: No. 56). 1980. pap. text ed. 33.00 (90-277-1198-4) Kluwer Ac.
Meacham, Alfred B. Wi-Ne-Ma the Woman-Chief & Her People. LC 76-43773. reprint ed. 27.50 (0-404-15628-2) AMS Pr.
Meacham, April, jt. auth. see McIntosh, Joel.
Meacham, Beth, ed. Terry's Universe. 288p. 1989. pap. 3.95 (0-8125-4592-3) Tor Bks.
Meacham, Carla M. Haliotis Ornaments of the Windmiller Culture, Central California. (Illus.). iv, 233p. 1979. reprint ed. pap. text ed. 18.75 (1-55567-028-8) Coyote Press.
Meacham, Charles M. History of Christian County, Kentucky. (Illus.). 695p. 1993. reprint ed. lib. bdg. write for info. (0-8328-2927-7) Higginson Bk Co.
Meacham, Daniel. The Magic of Self-Confidence. 1985. pap. 5.95 (0-317-06937-3, Fireside) S&S Trade.
Meacham, Esther A. & Sarbaugh, Mabel M., eds. Professional Development. 113p. (Orig.). (C). 1979. pap. text ed. 9.00 (0-89894-022-2) Advocate Pub Group.
Meacham, J. A., ed. Family & Individual Development. (Contributions to Human Development Ser.: Vol. 14). (Illus.). x, 114p. 1985. 58.50 (3-8055-4037-X) S Karger.
— Interpersonal Relations: Family, Peers, Friends. (Contributions to Human Development Ser.: Vol. 18). (Illus.). x, 134p. 1987. 72.00 (3-8055-4515-0) S Karger.
Meacham, J. A., jt. ed. see Kuhn, D.
Meacham, John A., ed. Action Theory. (Journal: Human Development: Vol. 27, No. 3-4). (Illus.). 112p. 1984. 31.25 (3-8055-3895-2) S Karger.
***Meacham, Kenneth S.** The MRI Study Guide for Technologists. LC 95-10164. 1995. write for info. (0-387-94489-3) Spr-Verlag.
Meacham, Margaret. Boy on the Beach. (Illus.). 144p. (Orig.). (J). (gr. 4-8). 1992. pap. 8.95 (0-87033-441-7, Tidewtr Pubs) Cornell Maritime.
— Call Me Cathy. Clancy, Lisa, ed. (Real Life Ser.). 160p. (Orig.). (J). 1995. pap. 3.50 (0-671-87272-9) PB.
— The Secret of Heron Creek. LC 90-50373. 136p. (Orig.). (J). (gr. 5-8). 1991. pap. 7.95 (0-87033-414-X, Tidewtr Pubs) Cornell Maritime.
Meacham, Mary, jt. auth. see Carroll, Frances L.
Meacham, Mary, jt. ed. see Carroll, Frances L.
Meacham, Standish. Lord Bishop: The Life of Samuel Wilberforce, 1805-1873. LC 70-102669. 338p. 1970. 29.00 (0-674-53913-3) HUP.
— Toynbee Hall & Social Reform, 1880-1914: The Search for Community. LC 86-28269. (Illus.). 233p. reprint ed. pap. 66.50 (0-7837-4536-2, 2080263) Bks Demand.
Meacham, Standish, ed. see Bulwer-Lytton, Edward G.
Meachem, Mary, jt. auth. see Lenz, Millicent.
Meachen, George N. A Short History of Tuberculosis. LC 75-23738. reprint ed. 31.50 (0-404-13295-2) AMS Pr.
Meachen, Marie. Tune In! Music Listening Discovery Kit: Ready-to-Use Activities & Audiocassettes for Teaching Children How & Why to Listen. LC 93-44848. 1994. write for info. (0-13-609009-5, Parker Publishing Co) P-H.
Meacher, M., ed. New Methods of Mental Health Care. LC 78-40285. (Illus.). 246p. 1979. 106.00 (0-08-022264-1, Pub. by Pergamon Repr UK) Franklin.
Meacher, Michael. Diffusing the Power. (C). 1992. pap. text ed. 23.00 (0-7453-0693-4) Westview.
— Diffusing the Power. (C). 1992. text ed. 55.50 (0-7453-0692-6, Pub. by Pluto Pr UK) Westview.
Meacher, Michael & Beckett, Margaret. Making the Poor Poorer: The Welfare State after the Fowler Reviews. 1986. 40.00 (0-85124-425-4, Bertrand Russell Soc); pap. 29.00 (0-85124-435-1, Bertrand Russell Soc) St Mut.
Meachim, Helen, ed. see Edgar, Herbert.

M

***Meachum, Virginia.** Janet Reno: United States Attorney General. LC 94-27995. (People to Know Ser.). (Illus.). 128p. (YA). (gr. 6 up). 1995. lib. bdg. 17.95 (0-89490-549-X) Enslow Pubs.

Meacock, M. H. Refrigeration Processes: A Practical Handbook on the Physical Properties of Refrigerants & Their Applications. (International Series in Heating, Ventilation & Refrigeration: Vol. 12). 1979. text ed. 100.00 (0-08-024211-1, Pub. by Pergamon Repr UK) Franklin.

Mead. Brown's Signal Reminder. (C). 1987. 22.00 (0-85174-127-4, Pub. by Brwn Son Ferg) St Mut.

— Principles of Passive Vibration Control. Date not set. text ed. 54.95 (0-471-95065-3) Wiley.

Mead, jt. auth. see Smith.

Mead, Alice. Crossing the Starlight Bridge. 128p. (J). (gr. 4-6). 1994. text ed. 14.95 (0-02-765950-X, Bradbury S&S) S&S Childrens.

— Junebug. LC 95-5421. 112p. (J). 1995. 14.00 (0-374-33964-3) FS&G.

— Walking the Edge. (J). (gr. 4-7). 1995. 13.95 (0-8075-8649-8) A Whitman.

Mead, Andrew. An Introduction to the Music of Milton Babbit. LC 92-37178. (Illus.). 264p. (C). 1993. text ed. 29.95 (0-691-03314-5) Princeton U Pr.

Mead Art Museum Staff. Collegial Collectors: American Art from the Class of 1967. (Illus.). 12p. (Orig.). 1992. pap. 5.00 (0-914337-15-7) Mead Art Mus.

Mead, B. A. Apollonius of Tyana, the Philosopher-Reformer of the First Century A.D. 159p. 1964. spiral bd. 8.25 (0-7873-0600-2) Mokelumne.

— The Gospels & the Gospel. 215p. 1972. reprint ed. spiral bd. 9.45 (0-7873-0602-9) Mokelumne.

— Plotinus: The Theosophy of the Greeks. 48p. 1966. reprint ed. spiral bd. 4.40 (0-7873-0601-0) Mokelumne.

Mead, C., jt. auth. see Tolley, E.

Mead, Carver. Analog VLSI & Neural Systems. (Computation & Neural Systems Ser.). (Illus.). 384p. (C). 1989. text ed. 49.50 (0-201-05992-4, Adv Bk Prog) Addison-Wesley.

Mead, Carver & Ismail, Mohammed I., eds. Analog VLSI Implementation of Neural Systems. (C). 1989. lib. bdg. 67.00 (0-7923-9040-7) Kluwer Ac.

***Mead, Charles.** The Gingerbread Man. LC 95-7140. (HandClaps & FingerSnaps Ser.: Bk. 1). (Illus.). 32p. (J). 1995. audio 17.95 (0-918812-84-4) MMB Music.

Mead, Charles, jt. auth. see Rychner, Lorenz M.

Mead, Charles R. Application for Employment: A Campaign Document. (Orig.). 1988. pap. 9.50 (0-317-91373-5) Mead Comm.

Mead, Cheryl. The Matt Dillon Scrap Book. (Illus.). 96p. 1984. pap. 7.95 (0-312-52301-7) St Martin.

***Mead, Chris.** Champion Joe Louis: A Biography. (Illus.). 330p. 1995. pap. 12.95 (0-86051-848-5, Robson-Parkwest) Parkwest Pubns.

***Mead, Chris & Tolley, Emelie.** Gardening with Herbs. LC 94-23825. (J). 1995. 45.00 (0-517-58332-1, Clarkson Potter) Crown Bks Yng Read.

Mead, Chris, jt. auth. see Emmerling, Mary E.

Mead, Chris, jt. auth. see Tolley, Emilie.

Mead, Chris, Inc. Staff. Herbal Pantry. 1992. 18.00 (0-517-58331-3, C P Pubs) Crown Pub Group.

Mead, Christopher. Charles Garnier's Paris Opera: Architectural Empathy & the Renaissance of French Classicism. (Illus.). 496p. 1991. 75.00x (0-262-13275-3) MIT Pr.

— Space for the Continuous Present in the Residential Architecture of Bart Prince. (Illus.). 49p. (Orig.). 1989. pap. 9.95 (0-944282-03-2) UNM Art Mus.

Mead, Clifford. Thomas Pynchon: A Bibliography of Primary & Secondary Materials. LC 88-30415. (Illus.). 176p. 1989. 39.95 (0-916583-37-6) Dalkey Arch.

Mead, D. & Silbert, J. The Injured Child: An Action Plan for Nurses. (Illus.). 199p. 1991. pap. 28.00 (1-871364-33-7) Ishiyaku Euro.

Mead, D. Eugene. Effective Supervision: A Task-Oriented Model for the Mental Health Professions. LC 90-2257. 200p. 1990. 24.95 (0-87630-600-8) Brunner-Mazel.

Mead, D. J., jt. ed. see Richards, E. J.

Mead, Daniel M. A History of the Town of Greenwich, Connecticut. 340p. 1993. reprint ed. pap. 25.00 (1-55613-728-1) Heritage Bk.

— A History of the Town of Greenwich, Fairfield County, CT. 318p. 1993. reprint ed. lib. bdg. 35.00 (0-8328-3200-6) Higginson Bk Co.

Mead, Daniel R. Encyclopedia of Slot Machines. (Illus.). 300p. 1997. write for info. (0-934422-17-6) Mead Pub Corp.

Mead, Daniel R., jt. auth. see Geddes, Robert N.

Mead, Daniel R., ed. see Geddes, Robert N.

Mead, Daniel R., jt. auth. see Geddes, Robert N.

Mead, Daniel R., jt. auth. see Mead, Deborah L.

Mead, Daniel R., ed. see Schulte, Richard F.

Mead, Daniel R., ed. see Vinson, Barney.

Mead, Deborah L. & Mead, Daniel R. Owner's Pictorial Guide for the Care & Understanding of the Pace Bell Slot Machine. LC 82-73747. (Owner's Pictorial Guide Ser.). (Illus.). 142p. 1983. pap. 29.95 (0-934422-03-6, 100285) Mead Pub Corp.

Mead, Douglas S. Literary Comparison in Jacobean Prose. (English Literature Ser.: No. 33). 1970. reprint ed. pap. 24.95 (0-8383-0054-5) M S G Haskell Hse.

Mead, Edna. The Bronx Triangle: A Portrait of Norwood. Hermalyn, Gary & Ultan, Lloyd, eds. (Illus.). 141p. 1982. 12.00 (0-941980-09-X) Bronx County.

Mead, Elwood. Irrigation Institutions: A Discussion of the Economic & Legal Questions Created by the Growth of Irrigated Agriculture in the West. LC 72-2856. (Use & Abuse of America's Natural Resources Ser.). 406p. 1972. reprint ed. 28.95 (0-405-04520-4) Ayer.

Mead, Frank S. Handbook of Denominations. 9th rev. ed. LC 90-32830. 336p. 1990. 13.95 (0-687-16572-5) Abingdon.

— The Handbook of Denominations in the United States. 320p. 1995. 15.95 (0-687-01478-6) Abingdon.

— Saints & Sinners in the Bible. 256p. 1995. 7.98 (0-8317-6513-5) Smithmark.

— Ten Decisive Battles of Christianity. LC 72-117823. (Essay Index Reprint Ser.). 1977. 18.95 (0-8369-1812-6) Ayer.

— Who's Who in the Bible. (Christian Library). 250p. 1986. reprint ed. 7.99 (0-916441-56-3) Barbour & Co.

Mead, Frank S., comp. Twelve Thousand Religious Quotations. 534p. (Orig.). 1989. pap. 19.99 (0-8010-6253-5) Baker Bk.

Mead, G., jt. ed. see Hess, W.

Mead, G. C., ed. Processing of Poultry. 422p. 1989. 117.00 (1-85166-305-3) Elsevier.

Mead, G. M. Current Issues in Cancer. (Illus.). 147p. 1992. pap. text ed. 25.00 (0-7279-0775-1, BMJ Pubng Grp) Amer Coll Phys.

Mead, G. P., jt. ed. see Barquin, R. C.

Mead, G. R. Apollonius of Tyana. 196p. 1980. 15.00 (0-89005-350-2) Ares.

— Apollonius of Tyana. 170p. 1992. pap. 13.95 (1-56459-131-X) Kessinger Pub.

— The Chaldaean Oracles, Set, Vols. 1 & 2. 190p. 1992. Set. pap. 18.00 (1-56459-250-2) Kessinger Pub.

— Concerning H. P. Blavatsky. 1992. pap. 9.00 (1-56459-252-9) Kessinger Pub.

— Did Jesus Live One Hundred B. C.? 440p. 1992. pap. 29.95 (1-56459-130-1) Kessinger Pub.

— Did Jesus Live One Hundred B.C.? 440p. 1993. spiral bd. 16.50 (0-7873-0603-7) Mokelumne.

— Did Jesus Live One Hundred Years B. C. An Inquiry into the Talmud Jesus Stories, the Toldoth, Jeschu, a Study of Christian Origins. 1991. lib. bdg. 79.95 (0-8490-4304-2) Gordon Pr.

— The Divine Pymander of Hermes Trismegistus. 1990. pap. 5.95 (1-55818-152-0, Pub. by Alexandrian Pr) Holmes Pub.

— The Doctrine of the Subtle Body in Western Tradition. 109p. 1993. pap. 12.95 (1-56459-312-6) Kessinger Pub.

— The Doctrine of the Subtle Body in Western Tradition. 164p. 1974. reprint ed. spiral bd. 5.50 (0-7873-0607-X) Mokelumne.

— Five Years of Theosophy: Mystical, Philosophical, Theosophical, Historical & Scientific Essay. LC 75-36850. (Occult Ser.). 1976. reprint ed. 33.95 (0-405-07966-4) Ayer.

— Fragments of a Faith Forgotten. 2nd ed. 633p. 1976. reprint ed. spiral bd. 27.50 (0-7873-0605-3) Mokelumne.

— Fragments of a Faith Forgotten. 633p. 1992. reprint ed. pap. text ed. 29.95 (0-922802-22-X) Kessinger Pub.

— Fragments of a Faith Forgotten: Gnostics & Christian Origins. 1991. lib. bdg. 79.95 (0-8490-4285-2) Gordon Pr.

— The Gnostic Crucifixion. 83p. 1992. pap. 5.95 (1-56459-129-8) Kessinger Pub.

— The Gnostic Crucifixion. reprint ed. pap. 6.95 (1-55818-176-8, Pub. by Alexandrian Pr) Holmes Pub.

— Gnostic John the Baptizer: Selections from the Mandaean John-Book Together with Studies on John & Christian Origins, the Slavonic Josephus' Account of John & Jesus, & John & the Fourth Gospel Proem. 137p. 1993. pap. 14.95 (1-56459-375-4) Kessinger Pub.

— The Gospels & the Gospel. 215p. 1992. reprint ed. pap. 18.95 (0-922802-78-5) Kessinger Pub.

— The Hymn of Jesus. 76p. 1992. pap. 9.95 (1-56459-158-1) Kessinger Pub.

— The Hymn of the Robe of Glory. 99p. 1993. pap. 14.95 (1-56459-360-6) Kessinger Pub.

— The Hymns of Hermes. LC 91-27216. 85p. 1991. pap. 7.00 (0-933999-17-8) Phanes Pr.

— The Hymns of Hermes. 1991. reprint ed. pap. 6.95 (1-55818-144-X, Pub. by Alexandrian Pr) Holmes Pub.

— A Mithraic Ritual. 1994. pap. 5.95 (1-55818-288-8) Holmes Pub.

— Mithriac Ritual. 77p. (Orig.). 1992. pap. text ed. 9.95 (1-56459-117-4) Kessinger Pub.

— Mysteries of Mithra. 90p. 1992. pap. 6.95 (1-56459-249-9) Kessinger Pub.

— Mysteries of Mithra. 1993. reprint ed. pap. 7.95 (1-55818-209-8, Pub. by Alexandrian Pr) Holmes Pub.

— Orphic Pantheon. 1984. pap. 6.95 (0-916411-18-4, Pub. by Alexandrian Pr) Holmes Pub.

— Pistis Sophia. 325p. 1992. reprint ed. pap. 24.95 (0-922802-87-4) Kessinger Pub.

— Pistis Sophia: A Gnostic Gospel. 1991. lib. bdg. 88.75 (0-8490-5036-7) Gordon Pr.

— Pistis Sophia: A Gnostic Gospel. 394p. reprint ed. spiral bd. 27.50 (0-7873-1104-9) Mokelumne.

— Pistis Sophia: A Gnostic Gospel, Vol. 21. 3rd ed. LC 83-83170. 408p. 1984. reprint ed. lib. bdg. 30.00 (0-89345-041-3, Spir Sci Lib) Garber Comm.

— Plotinus. 1983. reprint ed. pap. 6.95 (0-916411-01-X, Pub. by Alexandrian Pr) Holmes Pub.

— Plotinus: The Theosophy of the Greeks. 1991. lib. bdg. 75.00 (0-8490-4543-6) Gordon Pr.

— Quests Old & New. 338p. 1992. reprint ed. pap. 29.95 (0-922802-79-3) Kessinger Pub.

— Simon Magus: An Essay on the Founder of Simonianism Based on the Ancient Sources with a Re-Evaluation of His Philosophy & Teachings. 1991. pap. 8.95 (1-55818-177-6) Holmes Pub.

— Simon Magus: An Essay on the Founder of Simonianism Based on the Ancient Sources with a Re-Evaluation of His Philosophy & Teachings. 91p. 1994. pap. 7.95 (1-56459-439-4) Kessinger Pub.

— Some Mystical Adventures. 303p. 1993. pap. 19.95 (1-56459-359-2) Kessinger Pub.

— Thrice Greatest Hermes, 3 vols., Set. 1986. reprint ed. spiral bd. 55.00 (0-7873-0604-5) Mokelumne.

— Thrice Greatest Hermes: Studies in Hellenistic Theosophy & Gnosis. LC 91-47189. 864p. 1992. reprint ed. 49.95 (0-87728-751-1) Weiser.

— Thrice Greatest Hermes: Studies in Hellenistic Theosophy & Gnosis Being a Translation of the Extant Sermons & Fragments of the Trismegistic Literature with Prolegomena, Commentaries, & Notes. 864p. 1992. pap. 39.95 (1-56459-186-7) Kessinger Pub.

— The Upanishads, Set, Vols. 1 & 2. 237p. 1992. reprint ed. Set. pap. 14.95 (0-922802-77-7) Kessinger Pub.

— The Virgin of the World, or Apple of the Eye of the World. 1990. reprint ed. pap. text ed. 7.95 (1-55818-129-6, Pub. by Alexandrian Pr) Holmes Pub.

— The Wedding Song of Wisdom. 107p. 1992. pap. 12.95 (1-56459-155-7) Kessinger Pub.

— The World Mystery. 2nd ed. 200p. 1974. reprint ed. spiral bd. 9.35 (0-7873-0606-1) Mokelumne.

— The World Mystery. 200p. 1992. reprint ed. pap. 17.95 (0-922802-91-2) Kessinger Pub.

Mead, G. R., ed. Select Works of Plotinus. Taylor, Thomas, tr. 421p. 1994. pap. 37.00 (1-56459-429-7) Kessinger Pub.

Mead, G. R., ed. see Blavatsky, Helena P.

Mead, G. R. S. Simon Magus. 1978. reprint ed. 12.50 (0-89005-258-1) Ares.

Mead, George C., jt. auth. see Miller, Herbert E.

Mead, George F., Jr., et al, eds. Introductory Algebra. 2nd ed. LC 92-18690. 396p. 1992. 29.50 (0-931541-41-7) Mancorp Pub.

Mead, George H. George Herbert Mead on Social Psychology. Strauss, Anselm L., ed. LC 64-23419. 1964. pap. text ed. 17.95 (0-226-51665-2, P170) U Ch Pr.

— The Individual & the Social Self: Unpublished Work of George Herbert Mead. Miller, David L., ed. LC 82-4885. (Chicago Original Paperback Ser.). 232p. (C). 1982. pap. text ed. 12.95 (0-226-51674-1) U Ch Pr.

— Mind, Self, & Society: From the Standpoint of a Social Behaviorist. Morris, Charles W., ed. 1967. pap. text ed. 12.95 (0-226-51668-7) U Ch Pr.

— The Philosophy of the Present. Murphy, Arthur E., ed. LC 80-16334. 240p. 1980. pap. text ed. 8.95 (0-226-51670-9, P909) U Ch Pr.

— Selected Writings, George Herbert Mead. Reck, Andrew J., ed. LC 80-27048. lxxii, 416p. (C). 1981. pap. text ed. 12.95 (0-226-51671-7) U Ch Pr.

— The Social Self. (Reprint Series in Sociology). (C). 1993. reprint ed. pap. text ed. 1.00 (0-8290-2918-4, S-187) Irvington.

Mead, George R. The Hymn of Jesus. 78p. 1973. reprint ed. pap. 2.95 (0-8356-0432-2, Quest) Theos Pub Hse.

Mead, Gretchen, jt. auth. see Chioffi, Nancy.

Mead, Helen. Wyving & Thryving: The Making of the English Gementwoman 1550-1750. (C). 1988. 45.00 (0-9515798-3-5, Pub. by H Copeman UK) St Mut.

Mead, Hunter. Types & Problems of Philosophy. 3rd ed. LC 59-6277. 1959. text ed. 37.95 (0-03-006240-3) Irvington.

Mead, Irene K., tr. see Pexton, Patricia D.

Mead, James, et al. Investigating Child Abuse. 2nd ed. (Illus.). 145p. reprint ed. 100.00 (0-317-62651-5); reprint ed. pap. 25.00 (0-317-62650-7) R C Law & Co.

— Investigating Child Abuse. (Illus.). 145p. (C). 1987. reprint ed. pap. 25.00 (0-939925-17-6); reprint ed. ring bd. 100.00 (0-939925-18-4) R C Law & Co.

Mead, James F., et al. Lipids: Chemistry, Biochemistry, & Nutrition. LC 85-19304. 494p. 1986. 110.00 (0-306-41990-4, Plenum Pr) Plenum.

Mead, James R. Hunting & Trading on the Great Plains, 1859-1875. Jones, Schuyler, ed. LC 86-4343. (American Exploration & Travel Ser.: Vol. 69). (Illus.). 296p. 1986. 27.95 (0-8061-1894-6) U of Okla Pr.

Mead, Jane, ed. Many & More: A Celebration of Love in Later Life. LC 94-5303. 246p. 1994. 22.00 (0-943221-21-8) Timken Pubs.

***Mead, Jane & Sherline, Reid, eds.** Acts of Faith: Stories. 180p. 1995. 18.95 (0-943221-25-0) Timken Pubs.

Mead, Jere. Handbook of Physiology: Section 3, The Respiratory System, Vol. III, Pts. 1 & 2: Mechanics of Breathing. Macklem, Peter T., ed. (American Physiological Society Book). (Illus.). 834p. 1988. 245.00 (0-19-520669-X) OUP.

Mead, Jim I. & Meltzer, David J., eds. Environments & Extinctions: Man in Late Glacial North America. 209p. 1985. pap. 25.00 (0-912933-02-X) Ctr Study First Am.

Mead, Joan T., jt. auth. see Gilliland, Joan F.

Mead, John S. Haynes Peugeot 504 (Diesel) Owners Workshop Manual, No. 663: '74-'83. 16.95 (1-85010-376-3) Haynes Pubns.

— Haynes VW Vanagon (Air-cooled) Owners Workshop Manual, No. 1029: 1980-1983. 16.95 (1-85010-029-2) Haynes Pubns.

Mead, John S. & Hawse, Mara L., eds. Proceedings Coal, Energy & Environment. (Illus.). 632p. 1994. lib. bdg. write for info. (1-885189-02-8) Coal Res Ctr.

Mead, Jude. The Servant of God Mother Mary Angeline Teresa, O. Carm: Daughter of Carmel, Mother to the Aged. LC 90-32360. (Illus.). 256p. 1990. 12.95 (0-932506-81-X); pap. 9.95 (0-932506-79-8) St Bedes Pubns.

Mead, Judson. Walls, Floors & Ceilings. Roundtable Press Editors, ed. LC 84-17052. (Illus.). 160p. (Orig.). 1984. pap. 9.95 (0-932944-72-8) Creative Homeowner.

Mead, Julie F., jt. auth. see Underwood, Julie K.

Mead, Kate C. A History of Women in Medicine from the Earliest Times to the Beginning of the 19th Century. LC 75-23739. (Illus.). reprint ed. 57.50 (0-404-13296-0) AMS Pr.

Mead, Katherine H., ed. The Preston Morton Collection of American Art. LC 81-52029. (Illus.). 272p. (Orig.). 1981. pap. 12.00 (0-89951-043-4) Santa Barb Mus Art.

***Mead, Kenneth E.** Highway Contracting: Disadvantaged Business Program Meets Contract Goal, But Refinements Are Needed. (Illus.). 67p. (Orig.). (C). 1994. pap. text ed. 35.00x (0-7881-1328-3) Diane Pub.

***Mead, Kenneth M.** Information Superhighway: Issues Affecting Development. (Illus.). 76p. (Orig.). (C). 1994. pap. text ed. 40.00 (0-7881-1421-2) Diane Pub.

— Railroad Safety: Continued Emphasis Needed for an Effective Track Safety Inspection Program. (Illus.). 60p. (Orig.). (C). 1994. pap. text ed. 35.00x (0-7881-1466-2) Diane Pub.

Mead, Lawrence M. Beyond Entitlement: The Social Obligations of Citizenship. 336p. (C). 1985. 29.95 (0-02-920890-4) Free Pr.

— The New Politics of Poverty: The Non-Working Poor in America. LC 91-55458. 368p. 1993. pap. 15.00 (0-465-05069-7) Basic.

Mead, Loren B. Critical Moment of Ministry: A Change of Pastors. LC 86-72582. 78p. (Orig.). 1986. pap. 8.95 (1-56699-017-3, AL94) Alban Inst.

— More Than Numbers: The Ways Churches Grow. LC 92-75724. 1993. pap. 10.95 (1-56699-109-9, AL141) Alban Inst.

— The Once & Future Church: Reinventing the Congregation for a New Missions Frontier. LC 91-72968. 100p. (Orig.). 1991. pap. 9.95 (1-56699-050-5, AL129) Alban Inst.

— Transforming Congregations for the Future. (Once & Future Church Ser.: Vol. 3). Date not set. 11.95 (1-56699-126-9, AL152) Alban Inst.

Mead, Lucia A. Swords & Ploughshares; Or, the Supplanting of the System of War by the System of Law. LC 71-143431. (Peace Movement in America Ser.). xiv, 249p. 1972. reprint ed. lib. bdg. 28.95 (0-89198-079-2) Ozer.

Mead, Lynda. The Female Nude: Art, Obscenity, & Sexuality. LC 92-10516. (Illus.). 240p. 1993. 49.95 (0-415-02677-6, A9655); pap. 15.95 (0-415-02678-4, A9659) Routledge.

Mead, Margaret. And Keep Your Powder Dry: An Anthropologist Looks at America. LC 77-156694. (Essay Index Reprint Ser.). 1977. reprint ed. 20.95 (0-8369-2416-9) Ayer.

— Blackberry Winter. 24.75 (0-614-03203-2) Peter Smith.

— Changing Culture of an Indian Tribe. LC 72-84468. (Columbia University. Contributions to Anthropology Ser.: No. 15). reprint ed. 32.50 (0-404-50565-1) AMS Pr.

— Coming of Age in Samoa. 22.75 (0-8446-2571-X) Peter Smith.

— Coming of Age in Samoa. 1971. pap. 12.50 (0-688-30974-7, Quill) Morrow.

— Cooperation & Competition among Primitive Peoples. enl. ed. 13.25 (0-8446-2570-1) Peter Smith.

— Culture & Commitment. 1978. text ed. 35.50 (0-231-04632-4) Col U Pr.

— Growing up in New Guinea. 21.50 (0-8446-2569-8) Peter Smith.

— Growing up in New Guinea. LC 75-21740. 400p. 1975. pap. 13.45 (0-688-07989-X, Quill) Morrow.

— Inquiry into the Question of Cultural Stability in Polynesia. LC 70-82354. (Columbia Univ. Contributions to Anthropology Ser.: Vol. 9). reprint ed. 18.00 (0-404-50559-7) AMS Pr.

— Kinship in the Admiralty Islands. LC 91-41796. 175p. 1992. reprint ed. lib. bdg. 35.00 (0-86527-403-7) Fertig.

— Ruth Benedict. LC 74-6400. (Leaders of Modern Anthropology Ser.). (Illus.). 1978. text ed. 40.00 (0-231-03519-5); pap. text ed. 15.50 (0-231-03520-9) Col U Pr.

— Science & the Concept of Race. 1968. text ed. 43.00 (0-231-03101-7) Col U Pr.

— Science & the Concept of Race. 1969. pap. text ed. 16.50 (0-231-08594-X) Col U Pr.

— Sex & Temperament in Three Primitive Societies. 1971. pap. 10.45 (0-688-06016-1, Quill) Morrow.

— Soviet Attitudes Toward Authority: An Interdisciplinary Approach to Problems of Soviet Character. LC 78-10846. 148p. 1979. reprint ed. text ed. 49.75 (0-313-21081-0, MESO, Greenwood Pr) Greenwood.

— To Grandmother with Love: A Special Tribute. (Illus.). 96p. 1992. 15.00 (0-8362-8001-6) Andrews & McMeel.

Mead, Margaret, ed. Cultural Patterns & Technical Change. LC 85-14839. 348p. 1985. reprint ed. text ed. 55.50 (0-313-24839-7, MEPA, Greenwood Pr) Greenwood.

Mead, Margaret & Byers, Paul. The Small Conference. 1968. text ed. 18.70 (90-279-6049-6) Mouton.

***Mead, Margaret & Lutkehaus, Nancy.** Blackberry Winter: My Earlier Years. Turner, Philip, ed. (Globe Trade Paperback Ser.). (Illus.). 320p. 1995. pap. 14.00 (1-56836-069-X, Kodansha Globe) Kodansha.

Mead, Margaret, jt. auth. see Baldwin, James.

Mead, Margaret, ed. see Benedict, Ruth.

Mead, Marian. Four Studies in Wordsworth. LC 65-15890. (Studies in Wordsworth: No. 29). 1969. reprint ed. lib. bdg. 61.95 (0-8383-0596-2) M S G Haskell Hse.

Mead, Marica S. The Virginia County Supervisors' Manual. 5th rev. ed. 360p. 1988. 25.00 (0-318-04157-X) U VA Ctr Pub Serv.

Mead, Marjorie L., jt. auth. see Dorsett, Lyle W.

Mead, Mary A. Michigan Tax Handbook. 328p. 1988. pap. 17.00 (0-13-580457-4) P-H.

— Michigan Tax Handbook. 1,987th ed. 1986. pap. 17.00 (0-13-579913-9) P-H.

— Michigan Tax Handbook 1985. write for info. (0-318-58206-6) P-H.

Mead, Mary A., jt. auth. see George, Peter.

Mead, Matthew. The Almost Christian Discovered: The False Professor Tried & Cast. Kistler, Don, ed. 172p. 1994. 16.95 (1-877611-72-7) Soli Deo Gloria.

An Asterisk (*) at the beginning of an entry indicates that the title is appearing in BIP for the first time.

— The Sermons of Matthew Mead: Original Sermons on the Jews & Falling into the Hands of the Living God. 440p. 1991. reprint ed. 21.95 (*1-877611-29-8*) Soli Deo Gloria.

Mead, Matthew, tr. see Bobrowski, Johannes.

Mead, Melissa. Shadowcaster Clue Book: Illuminations. (Illus.). 80p. (Orig.). 1993. pap. 14.95 (*0-929373-15-4*) Origin Syst.

— Ultima VIII Clue Book: Pentology. (Illus.). 96p. (Orig.). 1994. pap. 14.95 (*0-929373-18-9*) Origin Syst.

— Wings of Glory Playtesters' Guide. (Illus.). 64p. (Orig.). Date not set. pap. 9.95 (*0-929373-20-0*) Origin Syst.

Mead, Michael. Aids to General Practice. 2nd ed. (Illus.). 170p. 1991. pap. text ed. 22.00 (*0-443-04589-5*) Churchill.

— Aids to General Practice. 3rd ed. LC 94-43949. 1995. write for info. (*0-443-05277-8*) Churchill.

Mead, Michael & Patterson, Henry. Tutorials in General Practice. 2nd ed. (Illus.). 206p. (Orig.). 1992. pap. text ed. 36.00 (*0-443-04332-9*) Churchill.

***Mead, Murray.** The Secrets to Staying Happily Married. (Illus.). 60p. (Orig.). 1994. pap. text ed. 19.95 (*0-9642629-9-1*) Murray Pubng.

Mead, P. J. Census of India, 1911 Bombay, 2 vols., Set. 923p. (C). 1987. 135.00 (*0-8364-2166-3*, Pub. by Usha II) S Asia.

Mead, Petr. Orde Wingate & the Historians. (C). 1989. 50.00 (*0-86303-318-0*, Pub. by Merlin Bks UK) St Mut.

Mead, Philip. European Community Company Law. LC 91-66804. 1992. Annual release. ring bd. 150.00 (*0-379-01035-6*) Oceana.

Mead, R., et al. Statistical Methods in Agriculture & Experimental Biology. 2nd ed. (Statistical Textbooks Ser.). 352p. 1993. 99.95 (*0-412-35470-5*, A9669); pap. 35.00 (*0-412-35480-2*, A9673) Chapman & Hall.

Mead, Richard. Cross-Cultural Management Communication. 273p. 1992. text ed. 65.95 (*0-471-92660-4*); pap. text ed. 48.95 (*0-471-93718-5*) Wiley.

— A Discourse on the Plague. 9th enl. rev. ed. LC 75-23742. reprint ed. 45.00 (*0-404-13297-9*) AMS Pr.

— International Management: Cross Cultural Dimensions. 488p. 1994. 69.95 (*0-631-18369-8*); pap. 34.95 (*0-631-18368-X*) Blackwell Pubs.

— Malaysia's National Language Policy & the Legal System. LC 87-50360. (Monograph Ser.: No. 30). ix, 118p. 1988. pap. 13.00 (*0-938692-30-5*) Yale U SE Asia.

— The Medical Works of Richard Mead. LC 75-23740. reprint ed. 94.50 (*0-404-13550-1*) AMS Pr.

Mead, Rita H. Doctoral Dissertations in American Music: A Classified Bibliography. LC 74-18893. (I.S.A.M. Monographs: No. 3). 155p. (Orig.). 1974. pap. 8.00 (*0-914678-02-7*) Inst Am Music.

— Henry Cowell's New Music, 1925-1936: The Society, the Music Editions, & the Recordings. LC 81-1510. (Studies in Musicology: No. 40). (Illus.). 636p. reprint ed. pap. 180.00 (*0-685-20810-9*, 2070024) Bks Demand.

Mead, Robert D. The Canoer's Bible. rev. ed. LC 74-33610. 1989. pap. 12.00 (*0-385-24578-5*) Doubleday.

Mead, Robert G., ed. Foreign Languages: Key Links in the Chain of Learning. (Reports of the Northeast Conference on the Teaching of Foreign Languages). 169p. 1983. pap. 10.95 (*0-915432-83-8*) NE Conf Teach Foreign.

***Mead, Robin.** Haunted Hotels: A Guide to American & Canadian Inns & Their Ghosts. 224p. (Orig.). 1995. pap. 9.95 (*1-55853-369-9*) Rutledge Hill Pr.

Mead, Roger. The Design of Experiments: Statistical Principles for Practical Applications. (Illus.). 640p. (C). 1990. pap. 42.95 (*0-521-28762-6*) Cambridge U Pr.

Mead, Ruth, tr. see Bienek, Horst.

Mead, Ruth, tr. see Bobrowski, Johannes.

Mead, S. Jean. Maverick Writers. LC 88-39272. (Illus.). 271p. (Orig.). 1989. pap. 14.95 (*0-87004-331-5*) Caxton.

Mead, S. P. History & Genealogy of the Mead Family of Fairfield County, Connecticut, Eastern New York, Western Vermont, & Western Pennsylvania from 1180-1900. (Illus.). 480p. 1989. reprint ed. lib. bdg. 80.00 (*0-8328-0864-4*); reprint ed. pap. 72.00 (*0-8328-0865-2*) Higginson Bk Co.

***Mead, Shepherd.** How to Succeed in Business Without Really Trying: The Dastard's Guide to Fame & Fortune. 160p. 1995. pap. 9.00 (*0-684-80020-9*, Fireside) S&S Trade.

Mead, Sidney E. History & Identity. LC 78-26543. (American Academy of Religion. Studies in Religion: No. 19). 71p. reprint ed. pap. 25.00 (*0-7837-5477-9*, 2045242) Bks Demand.

— Love & Learning. Doyle, Mary L., ed. 1978. lib. bdg. 12.95 (*0-914914-13-8*); pap. 5.00 (*0-914914-12-X*) New Horizons.

***Mead, Spencer P.** Ye Historie of Ye Town of Greenwich, Co. of Fairfield & State of Conn., with Genealogical Notes on (Many) Families. (Illus.). 768p. 1995. reprint ed. lib. bdg. 77.50 (*0-8328-4605-8*) Higginson Bk Co.

— Ye Historie of Ye Town of Greenwich, Connecticut. LC 92-60184. (Illus.). 862p. 1992. reprint ed. 49.50 (*0-89725-079-6*) Picton Pr.

***Mead, Stephen.** Grandpa, Tell Me More! A Colorful Portrait of a Country Lad. VanStratt, Teresa & Urbaniak, Christine, eds. (Illus.). 124p. (J). (gr. 3-12). Date not set. 15.00 (*0-9644211-0-0*) T VanStratt.

Mead, Sydney J. Studio Image 1. (Portfolio Ser.). (Illus.). (Orig.). 1988. 17.00 (*0-929463-00-5*) Oblagon.

— Studio Image 2. (Portfolio Ser.). (Illus.). (Orig.). 1989. 19.00 (*0-929463-01-3*) Oblagon.

—Studio Image 3. Servick, Roger, ed. (Portfolio Ser.). (Illus.). 36p. (Orig.). 1994. 21.00 (*0-929463-02-1*) Oblagon. This long awaited third edition of the STUDIO IMAGE series completes the "RGB" collection & brings together some of the finest full color illustrations of SYD MEAD'S illustrious career. Never before seen concept drawings for theme park attractions & television shows such as JOURNEY TO THE CENTER OF THE EARTH along with movies, such as, PRINCESS OF MARS, ALIENS & SOLAR CRISIS take the viewer on a visual fantasy excursion to a place in time not yet seen by anyone but Syd Mead. Its 36 pages are bound to delight & fascinate everyone with an interest in the future. Available as a single copy or as part of the set with STUDIO IMAGE I & STUDIO IMAGE II, for $50.00, a savings of $7.00. To order write: Oblagon Inc., 1716 N. Gardener St., Hollywood, CA 90046. Phone (213) 850-5225 or FAX (213) 850-5225. SRP $21.00 plus $3.00 S&H & CA Tax if applicable. Wholesale discounts available on orders of 5 or more. MasterCard & Visa orders accepted.

Publisher Provided Annotation.

Mead, Taylor. On Amphetamine & in Europe: Excerpts from the Anonymous Diary of a New York Youth, Vol. 3. 1968. pap. 12.00 (*0-932430-01-5*) Boss Bks.

Mead, Tray C. & Price, Robert C. Mesa: In the Shadow of the Superstitions. 144p. 1988. 29.95 (*0-89781-254-9*, 5274) Preferred Mktg.

Mead, Virginia H., jt. auth. see Cutietta, Robert A.

Mead, W. The English Medieval Feast. 1972. 59.95 (*0-8490-0114-5*) Gordon Pr.

Mead, W. L., ed. Advances in Mass Spectrometry: Proceedings of a Conference Held in Paris, September, 1964, Vol. 3. 1098p. reprint ed. pap. 180.00 (*0-8357-5171-6*, 2023993) Bks Demand.

Mead, W. L., jt. ed. see Institute of Petroleum Staff.

Mead, W. R. An Historical Geography of Scandinavia. LC 81-66377. 1981. text ed. 107.00 (*0-12-487420-7*) Acad Pr.

Mead, Walter B. The United States Constitution: Personalities, Principles, & Issues. LC 87-16162. 236p. (C). 1987. pap. text ed. 14.95 (*0-87249-523-X*) U of SC Pr.

Mead, Walter J., jt. auth. see Yousuf Hasan Mohammad.

Mead, Walter J., et al. Offshore Lands: Oil & Gas Leasing & Conservation on the Outer Continental Shelf. LC 85-63548. (Illus.). 172p. (Orig.). (C). 1985. 29.95 (*0-936488-10-7*); pap. 10.95 (*0-936488-01-8*) PRIPP.

Mead, Walter R. The Low-Wage Challenge to Global Growth: The Labor Cost-Productivity Imbalance in Newly Industrialized Countries. 48p. 1990. 12.00 (*0-944826-21-0*) Economic Policy Inst.

Mead, William B. Baseball Goes to War. LC 84-45528. Orig. Title: Even the Browns. (Illus.). 255p. 1985. reprint ed. pap. 7.95 (*0-918535-02-6*) Farragut Pub.

— The Explosive Sixties. LC 89-3548. (World of Baseball Ser.). (Illus.). 192p. 1989. 14.95 (*0-924588-01-2*) Redefinition Inc.

— The Inside Game: Baseball's Master Strategists. (World of Baseball Ser.). (Illus.). 192p. 1990. 14.95 (*0-924588-10-1*) Redefinition Inc.

Mead, William B. & Dickson, Paul. Baseball: The Presidents' Game. LC 92-45077. (Illus.). 225p. 1993. 24.95 (*0-918535-16-6*) Farragut Pub.

Mead, William B., jt. auth. see Strassels, Paul N.

Mead, William E. The Grand Tour in the Eighteenth Century. LC 72-83604. (Illus.). 1972. reprint ed. 30.95 (*0-405-08784-5*) Ayer.

Mead, William E., ed. Squyr of Lowe Degre: A Middle English Metrical Romance Edited in All Extant Forms, with Introduction, Notes & Glossary. LC 76-178506. reprint ed. 21.00 (*0-404-56676-6*) AMS Pr.

Meade. Aquaculture Management. 1989. text ed. 60.95 (*0-442-20570-8*) Chapman & Hall.

— Eleanor of Aquitaine. 1980. pap. 11.95 (*0-8015-2232-3*, Dutton) NAL-Dutton.

Meade, Bishop. Old Churches, Ministers, & Families of Virginia, 2 vols., Set. (Illus.). 1067p. (Orig.). 1993. reprint ed. pap. text ed. 58.00 (*1-55613-691-9*) Heritage Bk.

Meade, C. Wade. Egyptology & Rome: A Handbook for Students of Egyptian Archaeology in Rome. 97p. (Orig.). 1987. pap. text ed. 16.95 (*0-936638-02-8*) Palatine Pubns.

— Ruins of Rome: A Guide to the Classical Antiquities. LC 80-81128. (Illus.). 1980. 21.95 (*0-936638-00-1*); pap. 16.95 (*0-936638-01-X*) Palatine Pubns.

Meade, Catherine M. My Nature Is Fire: Saint Catherine of Siena. LC 91-9224. 1991. pap. 12.50 (*0-8189-0615-4*) Alba.

Meade, Dorothy C. Heart Bags & Hand Shakes: The Story of the Cook Collection. LC 94-66130. (Illus.). xii, 60p. (Orig.). 1994. pap. 10.95 (*0-9628075-4-0*) Natl Woodlands Pub.

***Meade, Erica H.** Tell It by Heart: Women & the Healing Power of Story. 224p. 1995. 38.95 (*0-8126-9301-9*); pap. 16.95 (*0-8126-9302-7*) Open Court.

Meade, Everard. The Dignity of Danger. LC 92-75973. 168p. 1993. 14.95 (*1-878179-09-8*) Burning Gate Pr.

— The Dragonfly. 174p. 1987. 14.95 (*0-933905-00-9*) Claycomb Pr.

— Dragonfly. (YA). 1992. pap. 7.95 (*0-933905-20-3*) Claycomb Pr.

Meade, F. H., et al. Religions of the World. rev. ed. (Illus.). (C). 1988. 90.00 (*0-7157-2355-3*) St Mut.

Meade, G. R. The Doctrine of the Subtle Body in Western Tradition. 128p. 1995. pap. 8.95 (*1-873616-01-5*, Pub. by Solos UK) Atrium Pubs.

Meade, Gary, ed. see Ehrlichman, John & Dunnington, Jacqueline.

***Meade, George.** The Life & Letters of George Gordon Meade, Major-General United States Army. Meade, George G., ed. (Army of the Potomac Ser.). (Illus.). 965p. (C). 1994. text ed. 100.00 (*0-935523-38-3*) Butternut & Blue.

Meade, George G., ed. see Meade, George.

Meade, J. E. Agathotopia: The Economics of Partnership. (David Hume Papers: No. 16). 150p. 1989. pap. text ed. 14.00 (*0-08-037967-2*, Pub. by Aberdeen U Pr) Macmillan.

— Full-Employment Regained? (Cambridge Department of Applied Economics Occasional Papers: No. 61). 106p. (C). 1995. write for info. (*0-521-55327-X*); pap. write for info. (*0-521-55697-X*) Cambridge U Pr.

— Liberty, Equality, & Efficiency: Apologia Pro Agathotopia Mea. LC 92-34923. 1993. 65.00 (*0-8147-5491-0*) NYU Pr.

Meade, James. Excel 3 for Windows Bible. (Bible Ser.). 1000p. (Orig.). 1991. pap. 29.95 (*0-672-30092-3*) Sams.

Meade, James E. The Intelligent Radical's Guide to Economic Policy: The Mixed Economy. 1975. pap. text ed. 10.95 (*0-04-330257-2*) Routledge Chapman & Hall.

— The Just Economy. (Principles of Political Economy Ser.: Vol. 4). 1977. reprint ed. pap. text ed. 21.95 (*0-04-330279-3*) Routledge Chapman & Hall.

— A Neo-Classical Theory of Economic Growth. LC 83-1748. xiii, 185p. (C). 1983. reprint ed. text ed. 49.75 (*0-313-23965-7*, MENE, Greenwood Pr) Greenwood.

Meade, James E., et al. Economic & Social Structure of Mauritius. 246p. 1968. reprint ed. 32.00 (*0-7146-1233-2*, Pub. by F Cass Pubs UK) Intl Spec Bk.

Meade, Jeff. Home Sweet Office: The Ultimate Out-of-Office Experience: Working Your Company Job from Home. Colton, Kitty & Hupping, Carol, eds. LC 93-8563. 208p. (Orig.). 1993. pap. 12.95 (*1-56079-240-X*) Petersons Guides.

Meade, Jim. Ami Pro for Dummies. 356p. 1993. pap. 19.95 (*1-56884-049-7*) IDG Bks.

— Ami Pro X for Dummies. 2nd ed. 1995. pap. 19.99 (*1-56884-232-5*) IDG Bks.

— Using Ami Pro. 2nd ed. 1994. pap. 29.95 (*1-56529-653-2*) Que.

Meade, Jim & Walkowski, Debbie. Using PowerPoint 3. 1992. pap. 29.95 (*1-56529-102-6*) Que.

Meade, Jim, jt. auth. see Wolverton, Van.

Meade, John S. Split Decision. 90p. 1990. 10.95 (*0-533-08644-2*) Vantage.

Meade, Judith D. Something Olde, Something New, Something Borrowed - Ever True. 48p. (Orig.). 1988. pap. 4.95 (*0-945785-01-1*) LFL Creations.

Meade, L. Manual of Forensic Quotations. 1972. 175.00 (*0-8490-0582-5*) Gordon Pr.

Meade, L. T. Stories from the Diary of a Doctor. LC 75-32767. (Literature of Mystery & Detection Ser.). (Illus.). 1976. reprint ed. 31.95 (*0-405-07886-2*) Ayer.

Meade, M. L. & Dillon, C. R. Signals & Systems. 2nd ed. (Tutorial Guides in Electronic Engineering Ser.: No. 8). 160p. 1991. pap. 27.95 (*0-412-40110-X*) Chapman & Hall.

Meade, Marion. Dorothy Parker: What Fresh Hell Is This? LC 87-40189. 480p. 1987. 22.50 (*0-394-54440-4*, Villard Bks) Random.

— Dorothy Parker: What Fresh Hell Is This? (Illus.). 480p. 1989. pap. 15.95 (*0-14-011616-8*, Penguin Bks) Viking Penguin.

— Eleanor of Aquitaine. 1991. pap. 15.00 (*0-14-015338-1*, Penguin Bks) Viking Penguin.

— Eleanor of Aquitaine: A Biography. (Illus.). (C). 1980. pap. 12.95 (*0-8015-9017-5*, Dutton) NAL-Dutton.

— Stealing Heaven. LC 79-1182. (Hera Ser.). 415p. 1994. pap. 15.00 (*1-56947-011-1*) Soho Press.

Meade, Melinda, et al. Medical Geography. LC 87-19673. 340p. 1988. lib. bdg. 36.95 (*0-89862-781-8*) Guilford Pr.

Meade, Michael J. Men & the Water of Life: Initiation & the Tempering of Men. LC 92-56405. 464p. 1994. reprint ed. pap. 12.00 (*0-06-250726-5*) Harper SF.

Meade, Robert C., Jr. The Red Brigades: The Story of Italian Terrorism. 313p. 1989. text ed. 29.95 (*0-312-03593-4*) St Martin.

Meade, Robert D. Judah P. Benjamin: Confederate Statesman. LC 74-29506. (Modern Jewish Experience Ser.). (Illus.). 1975. reprint ed. 38.95 (*0-405-06733-X*) Ayer.

Meade, Russell. Foundations of Electronics. 345p. 1994. teacher ed 25.00 (*0-8273-6466-0*) Delmar.

— Foundations of Electronics: PC Lab Sampler. 1991. teacher ed 12.00 (*0-8273-4822-3*) Delmar.

Meade, Russell L. Computer Test Bank for Foundations of Electronics. 1991. 69.95 (*0-8273-4588-7*) Delmar.

— Foundations of Electronics. 2nd ed. LC 93-38058. 1994. text ed. 56.95 (*0-8273-5971-3*) Delmar.

— Foundations of Electronics: Circuits & Devices. LC 93-38059. 1137p. 1994. text ed. 62.95 (*0-8273-5970-5*) Delmar.

— Foundations of Electronics & Circuits & Devices: Lab Manual. 2nd ed. 401p. 1994. pap. text ed. 24.95 (*0-8273-6467-9*) Delmar.

— Foundations of Electronics Instructors Guide. 1991. 20.00 (*0-8273-2994-6*) Delmar.

— Foundations of Electronics Printed Test Bank. 1991. 40.00 (*0-8273-4587-9*) Delmar.

Meade, Russell L. & Wilson, Edward A. Foundations of Electronics: Flashcards. 186p. 1994. 17.95 (*0-8273-6461-X*) Delmar.

Meade, T. W., ed. Anticoagulants & Myocardial Infarction: A Reappraisal. LC 84-5053. (Wiley-Medical Publication Ser.). (Illus.). 284p. reprint ed. pap. 81.00 (*0-8357-4620-8*, 2037552) Bks Demand.

Meade, Teresa & Walker, Mark, eds. Science, Medicine & Cultural Imperialism. LC 90-45331. 190p. 1991. text ed. 45.00 (*0-312-04779-7*) St Martin.

Meade, Tom. Essential Fly Fishing. (Illus.). 160p. 1994. pap. 15.95 (*1-55821-334-1*) Lyons & Burford.

Meade, Vicki, ed. see American Pharmaceutical Association Staff.

Meade, Vicki L., ed. Pharmacy Education & Careers: The APhA Resource Book. 88p. 1988. pap. 17.00 (*0-917330-59-5*) Am Pharm Assn.

Meade, Walter F. In the Catskill Mountains: A Personal Approach to Nature. LC 91-12887. (Illus.). 128p. 1991. 25.00 (*0-935796-20-7*) Purple Mnt Pr.

Meaden, George T. The Circles Effect & Its Mysteries. 116p. (C). 1989. text ed. 80.00 (*0-9510590-3-3*, Pub. by Artetech Pub Co UK) St Mut.

— The Stonehenge Solution: Sacred Marriage & the Goddess. 224p. 1995. 24.95 (*0-285-63057-1*, Pub. by Souvenir UK) Atrium Pubs.

Meaden, Nicola & Fox Andrews, Mark. Futures Fund Management. LC 92-19934. 1992. 29.95 (*0-13-345729-X*) P-H.

Meaden, Pat A. Anakah: Little Ferret of Galilee. 1993. 9.95 (*0-8062-4077-6*) Carlton.

Meader, James L. Normal School Education in Connecticut. LC 74-177065. (Columbia University. Teachers College. Contributions to Education Ser.: No. 307). reprint ed. 37.50 (*0-404-55307-9*) AMS Pr.

Meader, John T. Dell Turner: The Stories of His Life. Ives, Edward D., ed. (Illus.). 150p. (Orig.). 1988. pap. 10.00 (*0-943197-19-8*) ME Folklife Ctr.

***Meader, Jonathan. The Wordless Travel Book: Point at These Pictures to Communicate with Anyone. (Illus.). 14p. 1995. ring bd. 8.95 (*0-9645616-0-3*) J Meader. COMMUNICATE WITH ANYONE, in any country. SIMPLY POINT out one of the 300+ BEAUTIFULLY PAINTED PICTURES that fill this EXCITING BOOK. Travel is difficult if you don't speak the language. NOW, with THIS BOOK IN HAND, TRAVEL ANYWHERE, CONFIDENT KNOWING YOU WILL ALWAYS BE ABLE TO COMMUNICATE. RICHLY COLORED pictures include: FOODS, DRINKS, TRANSPORTATION, HOTEL ROOM ITEMS, SHOPS, CHURCHES, EMERGENCY NEEDS, TOILETS, & much more. These pictures were created to make communicating FUN as well as HELPFUL. The author, whose art is in major MUSEUM COLLECTIONS, has spent years living & traveling abroad. This book makes a DELIGHTFUL, INEXPENSIVE, & extremely USEFUL GIFT for the traveler, student, & anyone who can't speak. CUSTOMIZE your book with additional 'special interest' pages. MIDDLE EASTERN FOODS, INDIAN FOODS, MAGIC MARKING PAGE, COOKING IMPLEMENTS, HOME REPAIR TOOLS, & others soon. 'Special' pages are laminated, snap easily into your book, & are available by mail for $2 each. Separate sheet TRANSLATIONS are available in 13 languages for $2 each. Book $8.95. Min. $10 order. Flat $2 shipping. Contact: CONNECTIONS PUBLISHING, P.O. Box 97-B, Mill Valley, CA, 94942. FAX (415) 383-0425.**

Publisher Provided Annotation.

Meader, Robert F. Illustrated Guide to Shaker Furniture. pap. 8.95 (*0-486-22819-3*) Dover.

Meaders, Daniel, comp. Eighteenth-Century White Slaves: Fugitive Notices, Pennsylvania, 1729-1760, Vol. 1. LC 93-8973. (Documentary Reference Collections). 608p. 1993. text ed. 99.50 (*0-313-27987-X*, Greenwood Pr) Greenwood.

Meaders, Daniel E., comp. Kidnappers in Philadelphia: Isaac Hopper's Tales of Oppression, 1780-1843. LC 94-10190. 408p. 1994. 74.00 (*0-8153-1776-X*) Garland.

Meaders, Donald O. Putting Relevancy into Extension Worker Pre-Service Education in Nepal. 7p. 1981. pap. 1.00 (*0-318-23183-2*) Am-Nepal Ed.

Meades, P. Modern Russian Reader. 156p. (C). 1985. 28.00 (*0-569-08486-5*, Pub. by Collets UK) Pro-Am Music.

Meador, Betty D. Uncursing the Dark: Treasures from the Underworld. 184p. (Orig.). 1992. pap. 15.95 (*0-933029-65-9*) Chiron Pubns.

M

An Asterisk (*) at the beginning of an entry indicates that the title is appearing in BIP for the first time.

Meador, C., tr. see Andreyev, Leonid.
Meador, C., jt. auth. see Davidson, P.
Meador, Clifton K. A Little Book of Doctors' Rules. 128p. (Orig.). 1992. pap. text ed. 9.95 (*1-56053-061-8*) Hanley & Belfus.
Meador, Clifton K., jt. ed. see Hammerschmidt, Rosalie.
Meador, D. J. His Father's House. LC 93-37982. 384p. 1994. 21.95 (*1-56554-032-8*) Pelican.
Meador, Daniel J. American Courts. 113p. 1992. reprint ed. pap. text ed. 9.50 (*0-314-86717-1*) West Pub.
— Habeas Corpus & Magna Carta: Dualism of Power & Liberty. LC 65-28634. (Magna Carta Essays Ser.). 94p. reprint ed. pap. 26.80 (*0-8357-9801-1*, 2010036) Bks Demand.
— Impressions of Law in East Germany: Legal Education & Legal Systems in the German Democratic Republic. LC 86-7756. (Illus.). 350p. 1986. text ed. 40.00 (*0-8139-1110-9*) U Pr of Va.
Meador, Daniel J. & Bernstein, Jordana. Appellate Courts in the United States. 160p. 1994. pap. text ed. 10.00 (*0-314-03748-9*) West Pub.
Meador, Debbie. Top Producers - Siberian Huskies. (Other Dog Bks.). (Illus.). 1985. pap. 24.95 (*0-87714-104-5*) Denlingers.
Meador, Don. Laplace Circuit Analysis & Active Filters. 384p. 1990. text ed. 77.00 (*0-13-523481-6*) P-H.
Meador, Mary, ed. see Workman, Joe.
Meador, Nancy, jt. auth. see Harman, Betty.
Meador, Nancy, jt. ed. see Harman, Betty.
Meador, Prentice. Genesis: "The Great Story" 130p. 1993. pap. write for info. (*0-945441-17-7*) Res Pubns AR.
Meador, Prentice A. & Chisholm, Bob G. Walk with Me: Meditations on Mark. Roe, Earl O., ed. LC 90-41245. 125p. 1990. pap. 7.99 (*0-8307-1436-7*, 5421407) Regal.
Meador, Roy. Guidelines for Preparing Proposals. 2nd ed. (Illus.). 195p. 1991. 34.95 (*0-87371-588-8*, HF5718) Lewis Pubs.
***Meadors, Edward P.** Jesus, the Herald of Salvation. A Study of Q & Mark. (WissUNT Zum Neuen Testament Ser.). 360p. (Orig.). 1994. pap. text ed. 88.50 (*3-16-146251-3*, Pub. by J C B Mohr GW) Coronet Bks.
Meadors, Gary. New Testament Essays. 1991. 17.50 (*0-88469-231-0*) BMH Bks.
Meadow. Lecture Notes on Paediatrics. 5th ed. 1986. 17.95 (*0-8016-3372-9*) Mosby Yr Bk.
Meadow, Anthony. System 7 Revealed. 1991. pap. 22.95 (*0-201-55040-7*) Addison-Wesley.
Meadow, Barry. Money Secrets at the Racetrack. LC 87-51583. 160p. (Orig.). 1990. pap. 24.95 (*0-945322-02-X*) TR Pub.
— Success at the Harness Races. 1970. 4.95 (*0-685-08136-2*, Citadel Pr) Carol Pub Group.
— Success at the Harness Races. 1976. reprint ed. pap. 7.00 (*0-87980-320-7*) Wilshire.
Meadow, Charles T. Text Information Retrieval Systems. (Library & Information Science Ser.). (Illus.). 302p. 1992. text ed. 47.50 (*0-12-487410-X*) Acad Pr.
Meadow, Kathryn P. Deafness & Child Development. LC 74-81435. 1980. 32.00 (*0-520-02819-8*) U CA Pr.
Meadow, Mary J. Gentling the Heart: Buddhist Loving-Kindness Practice for Christians. 160p. (Orig.). 1994. pap. 13.95 (*0-8245-1434-3*) Crossroad NY.
***Meadow, Mary Jo.** Through a Glass Darkly: A Spiritual Psychology of Faith. LC 95-13753. 1995. pap. write for info. (*0-8245-1510-2*) Crossroad NY.
Meadow-Orlans, Kathryn, jt. ed. see Moores, Donald.
Meadow Orlans, Kathryn P. & Wallace, Ruth A., eds. Gender & the Academic Experience: Berkeley Women Sociologists. LC 93-27763. (C). 1994. 14.95x (*0-8032-3558-5*); pap. 35.00 (*0-8032-8606-6*) U of Nebr Pr.
Meadow, Pauline M., jt. ed. see Bull, Alan T.
Meadow, Phyllis W., jt. auth. see Spotnitz, Hyman.
Meadow, Richard H., ed. Harappa Excavations 1986-1990: A Multidisciplinary Approach to Third Millennium Urbanism. LC 91-39504. (Monographs in World Archaeology: No. 3). 1992. 33.00 (*0-9629110-1-1*) Prehistory Pr.
Meadow, Robert G. & Jackson-Beeck, Marilyn. The Presidential Debates: Media, Electoral & Policy Perspective. Bishop, George F. et al, eds. LC 78-70323. 324p. 1978. text ed. 65.00 (*0-275-90285-4*, C0285, Praeger Pubs) Greenwood.
Meadow, Rosalyn M. Women's Conflicts about Eating & Sexuality: The Relationship Between Food & Sex. LC 91-19205. 1993. pap. 10.95 (*0-918393-98-1*) Harrington Pk.
Meadow, Rosalyn M. & Weiss, Lillie. Women's Conflicts about Eating & Sexuality: The Relationship Between Food & Sex. LC 91-4120. 212p. 1992. lib. bdg. 29.95 (*1-56024-131-4*) Haworth Pr.
Meadow, Roy, ed. ABC of Child Abuse. 2nd ed. (Illus.). 75p. 1989. pap. text ed. 27.00 (*0-7279-0764-6*, BMJ Pubng Grp) Amer Coll Phys.
Meadow, S. R. & Smithells, R. W. Lecture Notes on Paediatrics. 6th ed. (Lecture Notes Ser.). (Illus.). 259p. 1991. pap. 32.95 (*0-632-03113-1*) Blackwell Sci.
***Meadow, Tony.** Inside Ole 2.0 for Macintosh. 1994. cd-rom, pap. 44.95 (*1-55851-421-X*) M&T Bks.
Meadowbrook Creations Staff. My First Years Calendar. 17p. 1983. pap. 10.00 (*0-88166-021-3*) Meadowbrook.
— My First Years Photo Album. 20p. 1984. 10.00 (*0-88166-022-1*) Meadowbrook.
— My First Years Record Book. 32p. 1983. 15.00 (*0-915658-98-4*) Meadowbrook.
— Our Baby's First Year: A Baby Record Calendar. 30p. 1983. pap. 10.00 (*0-88166-003-5*) Meadowbrook.
***Meadowbrook Press Staff.** Do They Ever Grow Up? 1984. mass mkt. 6.00 (*0-671-54478-0*) Meadowbrook.
Meadowcourt, Richard. Milton's Paradise Regained: Two Eighteenth-Century Critiques, 2 vols. in 1. Wittreich, Joseph A., Jr., ed. LC 76-161937. 1971. reprint ed. 50.00 (*0-8201-1087-6*) Schol Facsimiles.
Meadowcraft, Stan, jt. auth. see Hardy, Ron.
Meadowcroft, Cedric. The Homeowner's Guide to the Law. 152p. 1987. 95.00 (*1-85190-023-3*, Pub. by Fourmat Pub UK) St Mut.
Meadowcroft, D. B. & Manning, M. I., eds. Corrosion Resistant Materials for Coal Conversion Systems. 612p. 1983. 156.75 (*0-85334-198-2*, I-208-83, Pub. by Elsevier Applied Sci UK) Elsevier.
***Meadowcroft, James.** Conceptualizing the State: Innovation & Dispute in British Political Thought, 1880-1914. (Oxford Historical Monographs). 310p. 1995. 55.00 (*0-19-820601-1*) OUP.
Meadowcroft, James, ed. see Hobhouse, Leonard T.
Meadowcroft, P., tr. see Reinken, Gunter.
Meadowcroft, Pamela & Trout, Barbara A. Troubled Youth in Treatment Homes: A Handbook of Therapeutic Foster Care. (Trilogy Ser.: Bk. 2). 1990. pap. 22.95 (*0-87868-354-2*) Child Welfare.
Meadowcroft, Sam, jt. auth. see Brown, Dave.
***Meadows.** Earth Medicine. 1995. pap. 9.95 (*1-85230-668-8*) Element MA.
Meadows, jt. auth. see Meadows, S.
Meadows, A. J. Early Solar Physics. LC 74-103021. (C). 1970. 137.00 (*0-08-006653-4*, Pub. by Pergamon Repr UK) Franklin.
— Stellar Evolution. 2nd ed. 1978. text ed. 81.00 (*0-08-021668-4*, Pub. by Pergamon Repr UK) Franklin.
Meadows, A. J., ed. Development of Science Publishing in Europe. 272p. 1981. 51.50 (*0-444-41915-2*) Elsevier.
Meadows, A. J., jt. auth. see Brock, W. H.
Meadows, A. J., et al. Dictionary of Computing & Information Technology. 3rd ed. 282p. 1987. 39.50 (*0-89397-273-8*) Nichols Pub.
Meadows, Anne. Digging Up Butch & Sundance. (Illus.). 416p. 1994. 24.95 (*0-312-10968-7*, Pub. by Thomas Dunne Bks) St Martin.
Meadows, Audrey. Love, Alice: My Life as a Honeymooner. large type ed. 1994. pap. 21.00 (*0-679-75647-7*) Random.
Meadows, Audrey & Daley, Joseph A. Love, Alice: My Life As a Honeymooner. LC 94-5870. 1994. 22.00 (*0-517-59881-7*, Crown) Crown Pub Group.
Meadows, Carolyn, ed. see Meadows, Iris C.
Meadows, Carolyn J., ed. see Meadows, Iris C.
Meadows, Cecil A. The Victorian Ironmonger. 1989. pap. 25.00 (*0-85263-704-7*, Pub. by Shire UK) St Mut.
Meadows, Daniel. Set Pieces: Being about Film Stills, Mostly. (Illus.). 116p. (C). 1993. 52.95 (*0-85170-389-5*, Pub. by British Film Inst UK); pap. 22.95 (*0-85170-390-9*, Pub. by British Film Inst UK) Ind U Pr.
***Meadows, David.** Worldbits! Calendar: Country-a-Day Calendar. 384p. 1994. pap. 9.95 (*0-9644055-0-4*) Worldbits.
***Meadows, David H.** Worldbits! Calendar 1996: Country-a-Day Calendar. (Illus.). 384p. 1995. pap. 9.95 (*0-9644055-1-2*) Worldbits.
Meadows, Denis. Five Remarkable Englishmen. (Illus.). 1961. 10.00 (*0-8159-5506-5*) Devin.
— A Saint & a Half. 220p. 1963. 10.00 (*0-8159-6803-5*) Devin.
— A Short History of the Catholic Church. 246p. 1959. 14.95 (*0-8159-6813-2*) Devin.
Meadows, Dennis, et al. Dynamics of Growth in a Finite World. LC 74-84400. (Illus.). 637p. (C). 1974. text ed. 60.00 (*0-262-13142-0*) Prod Press.
Meadows, Dennis L. Dynamics of Commodity Production Cycles. LC 70-125415. (Illus.). 104p. (C). 1970. text ed. 35.00 (*0-262-13141-2*) Prod Press.
Meadows, Dennis L. & Meadows, Donella, eds. Toward Global Equilibrium: Collected Papers. LC 72-81804. (Illus.). 358p. 1973. text ed. 45.00 (*0-262-13143-9*) Prod Press.
Meadows, Don. Califonia Paisano: The Life of William McPherson. 1972. 10.00 (*0-87093-163-6*) Dawsons.
***Meadows, Donela H., et al.** Beyond the Limits. 300p. 1992. 19.95 (*0-614-02997-X*) Amer Forum.
Meadows, Donella, jt. ed. see Meadows, Dennis L.
Meadows, Donella H. The Electronic Oracle Computer Models & Social Decisions. LC 84-13060. 445p. 1985. text ed. 180.00 (*0-471-90558-5*) Wiley.
— The Global Citizen. LC 90-20899. 297p. (Orig.). 1991. 24.95 (*1-55963-059-0*); pap. 14.95 (*1-55963-058-2*) Island Pr.
Meadows, Donella H., et al. Beyond the Limits: Confronting Global Collapse, Envisioning a Sustainable Future. (Illus.). 320p. 1993. reprint ed. pap. 16.95 (*0-930031-62-8*) Chelsea Green Pub.
— Groping in the Dark: The First Decade of Global Modelling. fac. ed. LC 81-14713. (Illus.). 339p. 1994. pap. 96.70 (*0-7837-7660-8*, 2047413) Bks Demand.
Meadows, Donella H., et al, eds. Groping in the Dark: The First Decade of Global Modelling. LC 81-14713. 340p. 1982. pap. text ed. 71.50 (*0-471-10027-7*, Wiley-Interscience) Wiley.
Meadows, Douglas S., jt. auth. see Paliouras, John D.
Meadows, Eddie S. Jazz Reference & Research Materials: A Bibliography. LC 80-8521. (Critical Studies in Black Life & Culture: Vol. 22). 312p. 1981. lib. bdg. 56.00 (*0-8240-9463-8*) Garland.
— Theses & Dissertations on Black American Music. LC 80-128580. (Front Music Publications: No. 1). ii, 19p. (Orig.). 1980. pap. 5.00 (*0-934082-01-4*) Theodore Front.
Meadows, Edward S. U. S. Military Holsters & Pistol Cartridge Boxes. (Illus.). 432p. 1987. 45.00 (*0-9618191-0-3*) Ordnance Pubns.
Meadows, F. L. & Ames, J. M. Reed, Descendants of Reade or Reed: William Reade & Mabel (Kendall), His Wife; Supply Reed & Susannah (Byam), His Wife; John Reed & Rebecca (Bearce), His Wife. 285p. 1993. reprint ed. lib. bdg. 54.00 (*0-8328-3239-1*); reprint ed. pap. 44.00 (*0-8328-3240-5*) Higginson Bk Co.
***Meadows, Ferguson B., Jr., et al.** Using Guidance Skills in the Classroom. (Illus.). 314p. 1982. pap. 29.95 (*0-398-06283-8*) C C Thomas.
— Using Guidance Skills in the Classroom. (Illus.). 314p. (C). 1982. 46.95x (*0-398-04597-6*) C C Thomas.
Meadows, Iris C. Jenny of the Ozark Mountains: Growing up in Rural South Missouri in the 1920's & '30's. Meadows, Carolyn, ed. (Illus.). 219p. (Orig.). 1989. pap. 5.95 (*0-9624710-0-3*) Culver-Meadows.
— Jenny of the Ozark Mountains: Growing up in Rural South Missouri in the '20s & '30s. 2nd ed. Meadows, Carolyn J., ed. (Illus.). 203p. 1993. 5.95 (*0-9624710-1-1*) Culver-Meadows.
Meadows, Iris C., jt. auth. see Hatch, Aileen M.
Meadows, Jack. The Great Scientists. (Illus.). 256p. 1987. 40.00 (*0-19-520620-7*) OUP.
— The Great Scientists. (Illus.). 256p. 1989. pap. 23.95 (*0-19-520815-3*) OUP.
— Innovation in Information: Twenty Years of the British Library Research & Development Department. LC 94-9975. (British Library Research). 175p. 1994. 40.00 (*1-85739-100-4*) Bowker-Saur.
— Project Elvyn: An Experiment in Electronic Journal Delivery. (British Library Research). 200p. 1995. 45.00 (*1-85739-161-6*) Bowker-Saur.
Meadows, Jack, ed. Information Technology & the Individual. 1992. text ed. 57.50 (*0-86187-877-9*, Pub. by Pinter Pubs UK) St Martin.
***Meadows, James D.** Geometric Dimensioning & Tolerancing: Applications & Techniques for Use in Design, Manufacturing, & Inspection. LC 95-12153. (Mechanical Engineering Ser.: Vol. 96). 1995. write for info. (*0-8247-9309-9*) Dekker.
Meadows, Janice. The Antarctic. (World Bibliographical Ser.). 1994. lib. bdg. 87.50 (*1-85109-121-1*) ABC-CLIO.
Meadows, Jayne, jt. auth. see Allen, Steve.
Meadows, Kenneth. Earth Medicine. 1989. pap. 16.95 (*1-85230-117-1*) Element MA.
— Medicine Way: A Shamanic Path to Self-Mastery. 1990. pap. 15.95 (*1-85230-151-1*) Element MA.
— Rune Power. 1995. pap. 14.95 (*1-85230-706-4*) Element MA.
— The Shamanic Experience: A Practical Guide to Contemporary Shamanism. (Illus.). 256p. 1991. pap. 14.95 (*1-85230-226-7*) Element MA.
— Where Eagles Fly: A Shamanic Way to Inner Wisdom. LC 94-25152. (Earth Quest Ser.). 1995. pap. write for info. (*1-85230-585-1*, Pub. by Element Bks UK) Element MA.
— Where Eagles Fly: The Shamanic Way to Inner Wisdom. 1995. pap. text ed. 14.95 (*1-85230-620-3*) Element MA.
Meadows, Leon R. A Study of the Teaching of English Composition in Teachers Colleges of the United States, with a Suggested Course of Procedure. LC 78-177066. (Columbia University. Teachers College. Contributions to Education Ser.: No. 311). reprint ed. 37.50 (*0-404-55311-7*) AMS Pr.
Meadows, M. Communication Systems. (C). 1990. 120.00 (*0-09-175791-6*, Pub. by S Thornes Pubs UK) St Mut.
— Science: A First Course. (C). 1989. 120.00 (*0-09-182361-7*, Pub. by S Thornes Pubs UK) St Mut.
Meadows, M. E., jt. auth. see Stephenson, D.
Meadows, R. & Parsons, A. J., eds. Microprocessors: Essentials, Components & Systems. 256p. (C). 1983. pap. text ed. 130.00 (*0-273-01904-X*, Pub. by Pitman Pubng UK) St Mut.
Meadows, R. G. & Parsons, A. J. Satellite Communications. (C). 1989. 130.00 (*0-09-175903-X*, Pub. by S Thornes Pubs UK) St Mut.
Meadows, Richard. Pascal for Electronics & Communications. 160p. (C). 1985. pap. text ed. 120.00 (*0-273-02155-9*, Pub. by Pitman Pubng UK) St Mut.
***Meadows, Robert J.** Fundamentals of Protection & Safety for the Private Protection Officer. LC 94-22259. 240p. 1994. pap. text ed. 34.00 (*0-13-720509-0*) PH School.
Meadows, Roy W., ed. see Hatch, Aileen M. & Meadows, Iris C.
Meadows, S. & Meadows. The Environmental Impact of Burrowing Animals & Animal Burrows. (Symposia of the Zoological Society of London Ser.: No. 63). (Illus.). 384p. 1992. 95.00 (*0-19-854680-7*) OUP.
Meadows, Sara. The Child As Thinker: The Development & Acquisition of Cognition in Childhood. LC 92-40457. 416p. 1993. 62.50 (*0-415-01142-6*, B0773); pap. 22.50 (*0-415-01143-4*, B0777) Routledge.
Meadows, Sara & Cashdan, Asher. Helping Children Learn: Contribution to a Cognitive Curriculum. 144p. (Orig.). 1990. pap. 32.95 (*0-8464-1448-1*) Beekman Pubs.
Meadows, Taylor. The Confessions of a Thug. 1986. 22.00 (*0-8364-1737-2*, Pub. by Manohar II) S Asia.
— The Confessions of a Thug. 1988. reprint ed. 17.50 (*81-206-0330-3*, Pub. by Asian Educ Servs II) S Asia.
— A Noble Queen: A Romance of Indian History. 486p. 1986. reprint ed. 22.00 (*0-685-14349-X*, Pub. by Usha II) S Asia.
— Tippoo Sultan: A Tale of Mysore War. 460p. 1986. reprint ed. 22.00 (*0-8364-1734-8*, Pub. by Usha II) S Asia.
Meadows, Wayne. Fugitive: Wanted. 285p. 1993. 19.95 (*0-9636522-0-6*); pap. text ed. 9.95 (*0-9636522-1-4*) M&M Pub FL.
Meads, Al. Captain Al's Inboard Boat Manual: A Complete Guide to Electric & Mechanical Systems. 1993. pap. 24.95 (*1-883177-51-0*) Phoenix Florida.
Meadwell, Kenneth W. L' Avalee des Avales, l'Hiver De Force et les Enfantomes De Rejean Ducharme: Une Fiction Mot a Mot et Sa Litterarite. LC 90-20062. (Canadian Studies: Vol. 11). 284p. (FRE.). 1990. lib. bdg. 89.95 (*0-88946-382-4*) E Mellen.
***Meagher.** Helen: Myth, Legend & the Culture of Misogyny. 224p. 1995. 29.50 (*0-8264-0850-8*) Continuum.
Meagher, et al. Doctors & Hospitals: Legal Duties. 464p. 1991. 79.00 (*0-409-89767-1*) Butterworth Legal Pubs.
Meagher, Christine A. Satellite Regulatory Compendium. LC 85-206066. 1985. 197.00 (*0-934960-26-7*) Phillips Pub Inc.
Meagher, Ellen, jt. auth. see Kahn, Renee.
Meagher, F. Robert. Law & Social Change (Indo-American Reflection) (C). 1988. 110.00 (*0-685-27896-4*) St Mut.
Meagher, Jack. Sportsmassage: A Complete Program for Increasing Performance in Fifteen Popular Exercises. 1990. pap. 14.95 (*0-685-34812-1*) Station Hill Pr.
Meagher, Jack & Boughton, Pat. Sportsmassage: A Complete Program for Increasing Performance in Fifteen Popular Exercises. rev. ed. (Illus.). 224p. 1990. pap. 14.95 (*0-88268-096-X*) Station Hill Pr.
Meagher, James L. How Christ Said the First Mass or the Lord's Last Supper. LC 82-74246. 438p. 1985. reprint ed. pap. 16.50 (*0-89555-207-8*) TAN Bks Pubs.
Meagher, John C. Clumsy Construction in Mark's Gospel: A Critique of Form & Redaktionsgeschichte. LC 79-66373. (Toronto Studies in Theology: Vol. 3). 178p. 1979. lib. bdg. 79.95 (*0-88946-876-1*) E Mellen.
***Meagher, Justice.** Equity: Doctrines & Remedies. 1992. boxed 162.00 (*0-614-05470-2*, Austral) Butterworth Legal Pubs.
— Equity: Doctrines & Remedies. 3rd ed. 1992. pap. 119.00 (*0-409-30187-6*, Austral) Butterworth Legal Pubs.
Meagher, Laura. Teaching Children about Global Awareness. (Illus.). 144p. (Orig.). 1991. pap. 9.95 (*0-8245-1085-2*) Crossroad NY.
Meagher, Linda D. & Devine, Thomas G. Handbook of College Teaching. LC 91-14532. 300p. (C). 1993. text ed. 35.00 (*0-89341-637-1*, Longwood Academic); pap. text ed. 18.50 (*0-89341-638-X*, Longwood Academic) Hollowbrook.
Meagher, Linda D., jt. auth. see Devine, Thomas G.
Meagher, Paul K., et al. The Encyclopedic Dictionary of Religion, 3 vols., Set. LC 78-62029. 3815p. (C). 1979. 69.95 (*0-9602572-3-3*) Cath U Pr.
Meagher, R. P. & Gummow, Justice. Jacobs' Law of Trusts in Australia. 5th ed. 1986. Australia. 158.00 (*0-409-49076-8*); Australia. pap. 94.00 (*0-409-49079-2*) Butterworth Legal Pubs.
***Meagher, R. P., et al.** Equity Doctrines & Remedies. 3rd ed. 1992. pap. text ed. 119.00 (*0-614-05551-2*, Austral); boxed 162.00 (*0-409-30186-8*, Austral) Butterworth Legal Pubs.
Meagher, Robert. Mortal Vision: The Wisdom of Euripides. 160p. 1989. text ed. 35.00 (*0-312-02720-6*) St Martin.
Meagher, Robert E., tr. see Euripides.
Meagher, Robert F. Law & Social Change Indo-American Reflections. (C). 1988. 75.00 (*0-89771-287-0*) St Mut.
***Meagher, Shelah.** Storytelling Gardens. 96p. 1995. 28.00 (*1-55046-108-7*, Pub. by Stoddart Publng CN) Pubs Dist MI.
Meagher, Sylvia. Accessories after the Fact: The Warren Commission, the Authorities & the Report. 1992. pap. 15.00 (*0-679-74315-4*, Vin) Random.
Meagher, Timothy J., ed. From Paddy to Studs: Irish American Communities in the Turn of the Century Era, 1880-1920. LC 85-27304. (Contributions in Ethnic Studies: No. 13). 216p. 1986. text ed. 55.00 (*0-313-24670-X*, MPD/, Greenwood Pr) Greenwood.
Meagher, Timothy J., jt. ed. see Bayor, Ronald H.
Meah, M, jt. auth. see Watson, D.
***Meahan, Ronald.** Meahan on Leadership. 1995. 10.95 (*0-8062-5069-0*) Carlton.
Meaker, Gerald H. The Revolutionary Left in Spain: 1914-1923. LC 73-80622. xii, 564p. 1974. 62.50 (*0-8047-0845-2*) Stanford U Pr.
Meakin, Annette M. Ribbon of Iron. LC 70-115540. (Russia Observed, Series I). 1970. reprint ed. 20.95 (*0-405-03050-9*) Ayer.
— Russia: Travels & Studies. LC 72-115565. (Russia Observed Ser.). (Illus.). 1971. reprint ed. 35.95 (*0-405-03086-X*) Ayer.
Meakin, B. The Land of the Moors. 490p. 1986. 350.00 (*1-85077-100-6*, Darf Pubs Ltd) St Mut.
Meakin, David. Man & Work: Literature & Culture in Industrial Society. LC 75-45269. 215p. 1976. 21.50 (*0-8419-0259-3*) Holmes & Meier.
Meakin, David, ed. see Robbe-Grillet, Alain.
Meakin, Greg. The Car Shopping Workbook: For Insiders Only. 70p. (Orig.). 1992. pap. write for info. (*0-9631181-1-0*) US Pub.
— Secrets from the Inside: How to Buy a New Car below Dealer Cost. 141p. 1991. pap. 12.95 (*0-9631181-0-2*) US Pub.
Meakin, J. O., jt. ed. see Coutts, T. J.
Meakin, W. The New Industrial Revolution. Wilkins, Mira, ed. LC 76-29998. (European Business Ser.). 1977. reprint ed. lib. bdg. 25.95 (*0-405-09756-5*) Ayer.
Meakins, Jonathan L., ed. Surgical Infections: Diagnosis & Treatment. LC 93-29195. (Illus.). 500p. (C). 1993. text ed. 89.00 (*0-89454-016-5*) Sci Am Medicine.
Meale, Carol M., ed. Readings in Medieval English Romance. LC 93-47652. 256p. (C). 1994. text ed. 53.00 (*0-85991-404-6*, DS Brewer) Boydell & Brewer.
— Women & Literature in Britain, 1150-1500. LC 92-11691. (Cambridge Studies in Medieval Literature: Vol. 17). (Illus.). 220p. (C). 1993. 49.95 (*0-521-40018-X*) Cambridge U Pr.

An Asterisk (*) at the beginning of an entry indicates that the title is appearing in BIP for the first time.

Mealer, Tamara. My World in French Coloring Book. (Illus.). 64p. (FRE.). (J). 1991. pap. 4.95 (*0-8442-1393-4*, Natl Textbk) NTC Pub Grp.
— My World in German Coloring Book. (Illus.). 96p. (GER.). (J). 1991. pap. 4.95 (*0-8442-2169-4*, Natl Textbk) NTC Pub Grp.
— My World in Italian Coloring Book. (Illus.). 96p. (ITA.). (J). 1991. pap. 4.95 (*0-8442-8067-4*, Natl Textbk) NTC Pub Grp.
— My World in Spanish Coloring Book. (Illus.). 64p. (SPA.). (J). 1991. pap. 4.95 (*0-8442-7552-2*, Natl Textbk) NTC Pub Grp.
Mealey, Catherine E. Best of Wyoming. xvi, 203p. 1990. pap. 12.95 (*0-9627054-0-3*) Meadowlark Wy.
Mealey, Donna L. & McIntosh, William D. Studying for Psychology. LC 94-12577. (C). 1995. 14.00 (*0-06-500648-8*) HarpCollege.
Mealey, Oretta N. Elusive Butterflies. 1994. 8.95 (*0-8062-4835-1*) Carlton.
Mealiea, Laird. Skills for Managers in Organizations. LC 94-1347. (C). 1994. pap. text ed. 19.95 (*0-256-15948-3*) Irwin.
***Mealiea, Laird W. & Latham, Gary P.** A. S. K. Attitudes, Skills & Knowledge Necessary for Managerial Success. LC 95-12121. 544p. (C). 1995. 37.95 (*0-256-12454-X*) Irwin.
Mealing, Stuart. The Art & Science of Computer Animation. 320p. (Orig.). 1992. pap. text ed. 37.95 (*1-871516-16-1*, Pub. by Intellect Bks UK) Cromland.
— Mac3D: Modelling & Rendering. 320p. (Orig.). 1994. pap. text ed. 29.95 (*1-871516-46-3*, Pub. by Intellect Bks UK) Cromland.
Meals, Dianna, ed. Christmas Carols. 30p. (Orig.). 1985. pap. 2.95 (*0-940844-57-5*) Wellspring.
Meals, Jim. The Price of Sparrows. 1995. pap. 15.95 (*0-934468-50-8*) Gaslight.
Meals, R. A. Hand Surgery Review. 2nd ed. 364p. 1986. pap. 28.00 (*0-88416-492-6*, Yr Bk Med Pubs) Mosby Yr Bk.
***Meals, Roy A.** Hand Surgery Review. 4th ed. 1995. 22.95 (*0-942219-82-1*) Quality Med Pub.
Meals, Roy A. & Lesavoy, Malcolm A. Hand Surgery Review. 2nd ed. LC 85-3677. 364p. pap. 103.80 (*0-8357-7860-6*, 2036277) Bks Demand.
Meals, Roy A. & Seeger, Leanne L. Atlas of Forearm & Hand Cross-Sectional Anatomy with Computed Tomography & Magnetic Resonance Imaging Correlation. (Illus.). 199p. 1991. text ed. 59.95 (*0-443-08805-5*) Churchill.
Mealy, Doug. Put Yourself on the Fast Track: A Guide for Supervisors & Managers Who Want to Get Promoted. LC 84-28648. (Illus.). 104p. 1986. pap. 12.95 (*0-88280-110-4*) ETC Pubns.
Mealy, Norman & Rock, Judith. Music, Dance & Religion: The Performing Arts in Worship. (Illus.). 192p. 1985. 15.95 (*0-13-607219-4*); pap. 8.95 (*0-13-607201-1*) P-H.
***Mealy, Rosemari.** Fidel & Malcolm X: Memories of a Meeting. (Illus.). 89p. 1994. pap. 9.95 (*1-875284-67-2*, Pub. by Ocean Pr AT) Talman.
Mealy, Virginia, jt. auth. see Polette, Nancy.
Mealy, Virginia T. Happy Birthday Author. (Illus.). 128p. (J). (gr. k-4). 1986. pap. 12.95 (*0-913839-50-7*) Bk Lures.
— Newbery Book. rev. ed. (Illus.). 128p. 1991. pap. 12.95 (*1-879287-02-1*) Bk Lures.
Mealy, Webb J. After the Thousand Years: Resurrection & Judgment in Revelation 20. (JSNT Supplement Ser.: No. 70). 275p. (C). 1992. 35.00 (*1-85075-363-6*, Pub. by Sheffield Acad UK) CUP Services.
Meandzja, B. & Westcott, J., eds. Integrated Network Management: Proceedings of the IFIP TCG WG6.6 Symposium, Boston , MA, 16-17 May, 1989, Vol. 1. 666p. 1989. 100.00 (*0-444-87398-8*, North Holland) Elsevier.
Meaney, Constance S. Stability & the Industrial Elite in China & the Soviet Union. LC 87-83158. (China Research Monographs: No. 34). 160p. (Orig.). 1988. pap. 15.00 (*0-912966-98-X*) IEAS.
Meaney, Gerardine. Sex & Nation: Women in Irish Culture & Politics. (C). 1989. 45.00 (*1-85594-015-9*, Pub. by Attic Pr IE) St Mut.
— Unlike Subjects: Women, Theory, Fiction. LC 92-36699. (Gender, Culture, Difference Ser.). 264p. 1993. 55.00 (*0-415-07098-8*, B0705, Routledge NY); pap. 17.95 (*0-415-07099-6*, B0709, Routledge NY) Routledge.
Meaney, James. Evaluating & Buying a Franchise. LC 87-2523. 48p. (Orig.). 1987. pap. 3.95 (*0-87576-136-4*) Pilot Bks.
Meaney, John W. O'Malley of Notre Dame. LC 90-50968. (Orig.). 1991. pap. text ed. 10.95 (*0-268-01505-8*) U of Notre Dame Pr.
Meaning of Working International Team Staff & Drenth, P. J., eds. The Meaning of Work: An International View. (Organizational & Occupational Psychology Ser.). 1987. text ed. 119.00 (*0-12-509360-8*) Acad Pr.
Meanley, Brooke. Birdlife at Chincoteague & the Virginia Barrier Islands. LC 79-27187. (Illus.). 128p. 1981. pap. 7.95 (*0-87033-257-0*, Tidewtr Pubs) Cornell Maritime.
— Birds & Marshes of the Chesapeake Bay Country. LC 75-17558. (Illus.). 172p. 1975. pap. 8.95 (*0-87033-207-4*, Tidewtr Pubs) Cornell Maritime.
— Great Dismal Swamp. (Illus.). 39p. 1973. 1.50 (*0-318-20251-4*) Audubon Naturalist.
— The Marsh Hen: A Natural History of the Clapper Rail of the Atlantic Coast Salt Marsh. LC 84-40825. (Illus.). reprint ed. pap. 38.80 (*0-7837-9081-3*, 2049831) Bks Demand.
***Meanley, John A., ed.** Maritime Services Directory, 1995. 960p. 1995. pap. 89.00 (*0-9623031-2-7*) Aegis Pubns.
Meanor, Patrick. John Cheever Revisited. LC 94-11347. (Twayne's United States Author Ser.: No. 647). 232p. 1994. text ed. 21.95x (*0-8057-3999-8*, Twayne) Macmillan.
Means. How to Estimate with Metric Units. 190p. 1993. pap. 46.95 (*0-87629-317-8*, 67304) R S Means.
— Means Unit Price Estimating. 2nd ed. 432p. 1993. 59.95 (*0-87629-315-1*, 67303) R S Means.
Means, et al. Activities for the New Physical Education: A Resource Book for the Middle School Teacher. 240p. 1988. pap. text ed. 16.95 (*0-88725-097-1*) Hunter Textbks.
— The New Physical Education & Me. 82p. 1988. student ed, pap. text ed. 4.95 (*0-88725-096-3*) Hunter Textbks.
***Means, Alexander.** Diary for 1861. (American Autobiography Ser.). 46p. 1995. reprint ed. lib. bdg. 69.00 (*0-7812-8588-7*) Rprt Serv.
***Means, Anthony R.** Calcium Regulation of Cellular Function. (Advances in Second Messenger & Phosphoprotein Research Ser.: Vol. 30). 416p. 1995. 99.00 (*0-7817-0233-X*) Raven.
Means, Anthony R. & O'Malley, Bert W. Methods in Enzymology: Hormone Action: Calmodulin & Calcium-Binding Proteins, Vol. 102, Pt. G. 1983. text ed. 125.00 (*0-12-182002-5*) Acad Pr.
Means, Anthony R., jt. ed. see Conn, P. Michael.
Means, Barbara, ed. Technology & Education Reform: The Reality Behind the Promise. LC 93-45336. (Education Ser.). 256p. 1994. 29.95 (*1-55542-625-5*) Jossey-Bass.
Means, Barbara, jt. auth. see Cole, Michael.
Means, Barbara, et al, eds. Teaching Advanced Skills to At-Risk Students: Views from Research & Practice. LC 91-21683. (Education-Higher Education Ser.). 317p. 1991. 32.95 (*1-55542-393-0*) Jossey-Bass.
Means, Beth & Lindner, Lindy. Everything You Needed to Learn about Writing in High School - But: A. You Were in Love - B. You Have Forgotten - C. You Fell Asleep - D. They Didn't Tell You - E. All of the Above. 180p. 1989. pap. text ed. 14.50 (*0-87287-711-6*) Libs Unl.
Means, David. A Quick Kiss of Redemption & Other Stories. LC 90-19559. 224p. 1991. 18.00 (*0-688-09459-7*) Morrow.
Means, Eldred K. Black Fortune. LC 72-4739. (Black Heritage Library Collection). 1977. reprint ed. 27.95 (*0-8369-9110-9*) Ayer.
— E. K. Means: Negro Stories. 1977. 20.95 (*0-8369-9190-7*, 9059) Ayer.
— Further E. K. Means. LC 72-4648. (Black Heritage Library Collection). (Illus.). 1977. reprint ed. 31.95 (*0-8369-9111-7*) Ayer.
— More E. K. Means. LC 72-4738. (Black Heritage Library Collection). (Illus.). 1977. reprint ed. 32.95 (*0-8369-9112-5*) Ayer.
Means, Evan. Hiking Tennessee Trails: Hikes along the Appalachian Trail, Trail of the Lonesome Pine, Cherokee National Forest Trail & many others. 4th ed. Brown, Robert, ed. LC 93-39425. (Illus.). 160p. 1994. pap. 9.95 (*1-56440-377-7*) Globe Pequot.
Means, Florence. Carvers' George. LC 90-59179. (American Cavalcade Ser.). (Illus.). 160p. (J). (gr. 6-10). 1991. lib. bdg. 9.95 (*1-55905-075-6*) Marshall Cavendish.
Means, Florence C. The Moved-Outers. LC 92-13706. 156p. (J). 1993. pap. 6.95 (*0-8027-7386-9*) Walker & Co.
Means, Florence G. But What, My Dear, Do You Know about Hotels? And Other Stories about Old Times in Colorado. Mason, Lorna C., ed. (Illus.). 144p. (Orig.). 1992. pap. 8.95 (*0-944720-02-1*) Greenridge Pr.
Means, Gardiner C. A Monetary Theory of Employment. Smith, Warren J. & Lee, Frederic S., eds. (Studies in Institutional Economics). 292p. 1994. pap. text ed. 25.95 (*1-56324-478-0*) M E Sharpe.
— Pricing Power & the Public Interest: A Study Based on Steel. LC 75-39260. (Getting & Spending: the Consumer's Dilemma Ser.). (Illus.). 1976. reprint ed. 31.95 (*0-405-08033-6*) Ayer.
Means, Gardiner C., jt. auth. see Berle, Adolf A., Jr.
Means, Gardiner C., jt. auth. see Berle, Adolph A.
Means, Gay G. The Guy Mannering Letters of Henry Watkins Allen: A Journey Through the South in 1953. 1985. 10.00 (*0-940984-25-3*) U of SW LA Ctr LA Studies.
Means, Gordon P. Malaysian Politics: The Second Generation. (South-East Asian Social Science Monographs). (Illus.). 388p. 1991. 59.00 (*0-19-588983-5*) OUP.
Means, Howard. Colin Powell. 1993. mass mkt. 5.99 (*0-345-38381-8*) Ballantine.
— Colin Powell: A Biography. 1993. mass mkt. 5.99 (*0-345-90236-X*) Ballantine.
— Colin Powell: Soldier-Statesman - Statesman-Soldier. LC 92-53079. (Illus.). 368p. 1992. 23.00 (*1-55611-335-8*) D I Fine.
Means, James, Jr. Schaum's Three Thousand Solved Problems in Electronics. 1989. pap. 19.95 (*0-07-041190-5*) McGraw.
Means, James E. Effective Pastors for a New Century: Helping Leaders Strategize for Success. LC 93-2853. 256p. (Orig.). 1993. pap. 13.99 (*0-8010-6302-7*) Baker Bk.
— Leadership in Christian Ministry. LC 89-7024. 224p. (Orig.). 1989. pap. text ed. 13.99 (*0-8010-6250-0*) Baker Bk.
Means, Jeffery L. & Hinchee, Robert E., eds. Emerging Technology for Bioremediation of Metals. LC 94-2906. 1994. write for info. (*1-56670-085-X*) Lewis Pubs.
Means, Jeffrey, jt. auth. see Smith, Lawrence.
Means, Jeffrey L., et al. The Application of Solidification-Stabilization to Waste Materials. 200p. 1994. 69.95 (*1-56670-080-9*, L1080) Lewis Pubs.
***Means, John.** Maryland's Catoctin Mountain Parks: An Interpretive Guide to Catoctin Mountain Park & Cunningham Falls State Park. (Illus.). 250p. (Orig.). 1995. pap. text ed. 14.95 (*0-939923-38-6*) M & W Pub Co.
Means, Laurel, ed. Medieval Lunar Astrology: A Collection of Representative Middle English Texts. LC 93-22743. 372p. 1993. text ed. 99.95 (*0-7734-9299-2*) E Mellen.
Means, Marie H.
Means, Michael H. The Consolatio Genre in Medieval English Literature. LC 73-178985. (University of Florida Humanities Monographs: No. 36). 114p. reprint ed. pap. 32.50 (*0-7837-4966-X*, 2044632) Bks Demand.
Means, Philip A. Ancient Civilization of the Andes. LC 64-8175. 586p. 1964. reprint ed. 75.00 (*0-87752-072-0*) Gordian.
— Biblioteca Andina, Pt. One: The Chroniclers, or, the Writers of the Sixteenth & Seventeenth Centuries Who Treated of the Pre-Hispanic History & Culture of the Andean Countries. (Connecticut Academy of Arts & Sciences Ser., Trans.: Vol. 29). 1928. pap. 100.00 (*0-685-22806-1*) Elliots Bks.
— Fall of the Inca Empire & the Spanish Rule in Peru, 1530-1780. LC 64-8176. (Illus.). 351p. 1964. reprint ed. 75.00 (*0-87752-073-9*) Gordian.
— History of the Spanish Conquest of Yucatan & of the Itzas. (HU PMP Ser.). (Illus.). 1917. 26.00 (*0-527-01210-6*) Periodicals Srv.
— Spanish Main: Focus of Envy, 1492-1700. LC 65-24994. (Illus.). 278p. 1965. reprint ed. 75.00 (*0-87752-074-7*) Gordian.
— A Study of Andean Social Institutions. (Connecticut Academy of Arts & Sciences Ser., Trans.: Vol. 27). 1925. pap. 69.50 (*0-685-22815-0*) Elliots Bks.
— A Survey of Ancient Peruvian Art. (Connecticut Academy of Arts & Sciences Ser., Trans.: Vol. 21). 1917. pap. 75.00 (*0-685-44363-9*) Elliots Bks.
Means, Philip A., ed. see Montesinos, L. Fernando.
Means, Philip A., tr. see Pizarro, P.
***Means, R. S.** Builders' Costs for Hundred Best-Selling Home Plans. 1994. pap. 34.95 (*0-87629-356-9*) R S Means.
— Building Spec Homes Profitably. 1994. pap. 29.95 (*0-87629-357-7*) R S Means.
— Means Forms for Contractors. 1990. 74.95 (*0-87629-214-7*, 67288) R S Means.
— Means Illustrated Construction Dictionary. (Illus.). 1991. pap. 54.95 (*0-87629-219-8*, 67282) R S Means.
— Means Illustrated Construction Dictionary. unabridged ed. (Illus.). 1991. 99.95 (*0-87629-218-X*, 67292) R S Means.
Means, R. S. & Moylan, John. Means Mechanical Estimating. 2nd ed. 1992. 59.95 (*0-87629-213-9*, 67294) R S Means.
Means, R. S., Company, Inc. Staff. Means Graphic Construction Standards. (Illus.). 500p. 1986. 119.95 (*0-911950-79-6*, 67210) R S Means.
Means, R. S., Company, Inc. Staff & Grant, Roger J. Means Forms for Building Construction Professionals. 2nd ed. 325p. 1986. 89.95 (*0-911950-87-7*, 67231) R S Means.
Means, Robert C. Underdevelopment & the Development of Law: Corporations & Corporation Law in Nineteenth Century Colombia. LC 79-23936. (Studies in Legal History). 350p. reprint ed. pap. 99.80 (*0-8357-3894-9*, 2036626) Bks Demand.
Means, Robin, jt. ed. see Malpass, Peter.
Means, Spencer, jt. auth. see Weiner, Alan R.
Means, Sterling. Ethiopia: The Missing Link in African History. pap. 6.95 (*0-686-00436-1*) Hakims Pubs.
Means, Thomas L., jt. auth. see Henson, Carol.
Means, W. D. Stress & Strain: Basic Concepts of Continuum Mechanics for Geologists. (Illus.). 336p. (C). 1991. pap. text ed. 36.00 (*0-387-07556-9*) Spr-Verlag.
***Meanwell, Ernest & Rockne, Knute.** Training, Conditioning, & the Care of Injuries. (Illus.). 200p. Date not set. 75.00 (*0-930405-68-4*) Norman SF.
Meany, Janet & Pfaff, Paula. Rag Rug Handbook. 3rd ed. 1992. pap. 19.95 (*0-932394-21-3*) Dos Tejedoras.
Meara, Anne. After Play, Acting Ed. 1995. pap. 4.75 (*0-8222-0459-2*) Dramatists Play.
Meara, David. A. W. N. Pugin & the Revival of Memorial Brasses. (Illus.). 192p. 1991. text ed. 80.00 (*0-7201-2070-5*, Mansell Pub) Cassell.
Meara, Jane C., jt. auth. see Cavolina, Ellen.
Meara, Naomi M., jt. auth. see Patton, Michael J.
Meardon, S. L. The Elements of Fiber Optics. 256p. 1992. text ed. 52.00 (*0-13-249699-2*) P-H.
Meares, Ainslie. Ainslie Meares Compendium: Dialogue on Meditation, from the Quiet Place & a Kind of Believing. 156p. (Orig.). 1994. pap. 10.95 (*0-85572-195-2*, Pub. by Hill Content Pubng AT) Seven Hills Bk.
— The Introvert. 150p. (Orig.). 1994. pap. 10.95 (*0-85572-076-X*) Seven Hills Bk.
— Thoughts. 62p. (Orig.). 1994. pap. 6.95 (*0-85572-116-2*, Pub. by Hill Content Pubng AT) Seven Hills Bk.
— A Way of Doctoring. 180p. (Orig.). 1994. pap. 9.95 (*0-85572-150-2*, Pub. by Hill Content Pubng AT) Seven Hills Bk.
— Wealth Within. 170p. (Orig.). 1994. pap. 11.95 (*0-85572-086-7*, Pub. by Hill Content Pubng AT) Seven Hills Bk.
Meares, Alison, jt. auth. see Loudiyi, Dounia.
Meares, Bernard, tr. see Mandelstam, Osip.
Meares, Charlotte, jt. auth. see Caron, George.
Meares, Claude F., ed. Perspectives in Bioconjugate Chemistry. LC 93-15385. (Illus.). 210p. 1993. 34.95 (*0-8412-2672-5*) Am Chemical.
Meares, John. The Memorial of John Meares. 97p. 1985. reprint ed. 12.00 (*0-87770-341-8*) Ye Galleon.
Meares, L. G. & Hymowitz, C. E. Simulating with Spice. Marks, S. N. & Robson, J. T., eds. (Spice Ser.). (Illus.). 283p. (Orig.). 1988. pap. 65.00 (*0-923345-00-0*) INTUSOFT.
— Spice Applications Handbook, Vol. 1. (Illus.). 200p. (Orig.). (C). 1990. pap. 29.95 (*0-923345-01-9*) INTUSOFT.
Meares, P., ed. Membrane Separation Processes. 1976. 179.50 (*0-444-41446-0*) Elsevier.
Meares, Russell. The Metaphor of Play: Disruption & Restoration in the Borderline Experience. LC 92-49186. 232p. 1993. 30.00 (*0-87668-275-1*) Aronson.
Mearing, Judith S. Working for Children. LC 78-1148. (Jossey-Bass Social & Behavioral Science Ser.). 368p. reprint ed. pap. 104.90 (*0-317-09508-0*, 2021731) Bks Demand.
Mearns, Barbara & Mearns, Richard. Audubon to Xantus: The Lives of Those Commemorated in North American Bird Names. (Illus.). 588p. 1992. text ed. 39.95 (*0-12-487423-1*) Acad Pr.
— Biographies for Birdwatchers: The Lives of Those Commemorated in Western Palearctic Bird Names. (Books about Birds). 490p. 1988. text ed. 39.95 (*0-12-487422-3*) Acad Pr.
Mearns, Dan, jt. ed. see Paulick, Raymond S.
Mearns, Dave & Dryden, Windy, eds. Experiences of Counselling in Action. (Counselling in Action Ser.). 160p. (C). 1989. text ed. 44.00 (*0-8039-8192-9*); pap. text ed. 19.95 (*0-8039-8193-7*) Sage.
***Mearns, Dave & Thorne, Brian.** Developing Person-Centered Counselling. 192p. 1994. 39.95 (*0-8039-8981-4*); pap. 18.95 (*0-8039-8982-2*) Sage.
— Person Centered Counselling in Action. (Counselling in Action Ser.). 160p. (C). 1988. text ed. 44.00 (*0-8039-8049-3*); pap. text ed. 19.95 (*0-8039-8050-7*) Sage.
Mearns, David J., jt. ed. see Gray, John N.
Mearns, Edgar A. Mammals of the Mexican Boundary of the United States: Catalogue of the Species of Mammals Occuring in That Region, Part 1, Families Didelphiidae to Muridae. LC 73-18787. (Natural Sciences in America Ser.). 576p. 1974. reprint ed. 44.95 (*0-405-05777-6*) Ayer.
Mearns, Hughes. Creative Power: The Education of Youth in Creative Arts. (Illus.). 288p. 1958. pap. 6.50 (*0-486-20490-1*) Dover.
Mearns, James. Early Latin Hymnaries. 127p. reprint ed. lib. bdg. 31.07 (*0-685-13869-0*, 05102527, Pub. by Georg Olms GW) Lubrecht & Cramer.
— Early Latin Hymnaries. xx, 107p. 1970. reprint ed. write for info. (*0-318-71173-7*, Pub. by Georg Olms GW) Lubrecht & Cramer.
Mearns, Richard, jt. auth. see Mearns, Barbara.
Mears. Surgery of the Pelvis & Acetabulum. 800p. 1995. 150.00 (*0-8016-7852-8*) Mosby Yr Bk.
Mears, Arthur I. Colorado Avalanche Area Studies & Guidelines for Avalanche-Hazard Planning. (Special Publication Ser.: No. 7). (Illus.). 124p. (Orig.). 1979. pap. 8.00 (*1-884216-36-6*) Colo Geol Survey.
— Snow-Avalanche Hazard Analysis for Land-Use Planning & Engineering. (Bulletin Ser.: No. 49). (Illus.). 55p. (Orig.). 1992. pap. 12.00 (*1-884216-10-2*) Colo Geol Survey.
Mears, Eileen. What's Cooking "Down Home" (Illus.). 494p. (Orig.). 1994. spiral bd. 16.50 (*0-9641341-0-1*) E Mears.
***Mears, Eileen, ed.** A Treasury of Farm Women's Humor. 300p. 1994. pap. 12.95 (*0-942936-25-6*) Lincoln-Herndon Pr.
Mears, Eliot G. Resident Orientals on the American Pacific Coast. Daniels, Roger, ed. LC 78-54827. (Asian Experience in North America Ser.). 1979. reprint ed. lib. bdg. 40.95 (*0-405-11284-X*) Ayer.
Mears, Gillian, ed. Ride a Cock Horse. 164p. (C). 1990. 30.00 (*0-947087-12-5*, Pub. by Pascoe Pub AT) St Mut.
Mears, Gillian, et al. Sisters. Modjeska, Drusilla, ed. 183p. (Orig.). 1994. pap. 12.00 (*0-207-17790-2*, Pub. by Angus & Robertson AT) HarpC.
Mears, H. De Que Trata la Biblia (What the Bible Is All About) (SPA.). Date not set. 14.99 (*1-56063-164-3*, 498490) Editorial Unilit.
Mears, Helen. Year of the Wild Boar. LC 73-7457. 346p. 1973. reprint ed. text ed. 65.00 (*0-8371-6936-4*, MEWB, Greenwood Pr) Greenwood.
Mears, Henrietta. De Que Trata la Biblia (What the Bible Is All About) Jovenes Exploradores (Young Explorers) (SPA.). 1992. 12.99 (*1-56063-325-5*, 498491) Editorial Unilit.
— What the Bible Is All about Quick Reference Edition. Durham, Ron, ed. LC 89-36325. 365p. 1989. 12.99 (*0-8307-1390-5*, 5111887) Regal.
Mears, Henrietta C. What the Bible Is All About. rev. ed. 642p. 1987. pap. 12.99 (*0-8423-7902-9*) Tyndale.
— What the Book Is All About. 540p. 1987. pap. 4.95 (*0-8423-7906-1*) Tyndale.
Mears, Henrietta C., et al. What the Bible Is All About. rev. ed. LC 83-4333. 1982. 13.99 (*0-8307-1608-4*, 5112327); pap. 9.99 (*0-8307-1607-6*, 5422238) Regal.
Mears, Isabella, tr. Tao Teh King. 1983. pap. 7.25 (*0-7229-0300-6*) Theos Pub Hse.
Mears, James A., comp. Plant Taxonomic Literature: Bibliographic Guide. 177p. 1989. 189.00 (*0-85964-217-8*) Chadwyck-Healey.
— Types & Special Collections (Flowering Plants & Ferns) of the Herbarium of the Academy of Natural Sciences of Philadelphia: Indices to the Microfiche. 274p. 1984. 370.00 (*0-930466-87-X*) Chadwyck-Healey.
— Vascular Plant Type Collection of the United States National Arboretum Index. 78p. 1985. 100.00 (*0-930466-94-2*) Chadwyck-Healey.
Mears, Lisa, ed. see Sullo, Robert A.

M

Mears, Patrick E. Bankruptcy Law & Practice in Michigan. LC 87-80722. 552p. 1987. Incl. 1992 cumulative suppl. ring bd. 110.00 (*0-685-22684-0*, 87-007) U MI Law CLE.

— Bankruptcy Law & Practice in Michigan. suppl. ed. LC 87-80722. 552p. 1992. Nineteen Eighty-Eight supp. 60.00 (*0-685-22685-9*, 92-028) U MI Law CLE.

Mears, Peter. Hands on Quality. 400p. 1994. 39.95 (*1-884015-23-9*) St Lucie Pr.

— Healthcare Teams: Building Continuous Quality Improvement. (Illus.). 200p. 1994. student ed 19.95 (*1-884015-41-7*) St Lucie Pr.

— Healthcare Teams: Building Continuous Quality Improvement Facilitator's Guide. (Illus.). 120p. 1994. teacher ed 49.95 (*1-884015-43-3*) St Lucie Pr.

— The Keyboard Instructor for the Apple IIe. 158p. 1987. pap. text ed. 32.75 (*0-314-58913-9*) West Pub.

— The Keyboard Instructor for the IBM PC. 174p. 1987. Avail. software disk. pap. text ed. 32.75 (*0-314-58914-7*) West Pub.

— Organization Teams: Building Continuous Quality Improvement. (Illus.). 200p. 1994. student ed 19.95 (*1-884015-42-5*) St Lucie Pr.

— Organization Teams: Building Continuous Quality Improvement Facilitator's Guide. (Illus.). 120p. 1994. teacher ed 49.95 (*1-884015-44-1*) St Lucie Pr.

— Quality Improvement Tools & Techniques. LC 94-34752. 1994. 29.95 (*0-07-041219-7*) McGraw.

— Quality Improvement Tools & Techniques. LC 94-34752. 1994. disk write for info. (*0-07-852726-0*) McGraw.

— Quality Improvement Tools & Techniques. LC 94-34752. 1994. text ed. 49.95 (*0-07-041229-4*) McGraw.

— Teach Yourself Apple BASIC. 192p. 1983. spiral bd. write for info. (*0-318-57868-9*) Addison-Wesley.

— The Team Building Facilitators' Guide. (Illus.). 120p. (C). 1994. spiral bd. 39.95 (*0-614-07077-5*) St Lucie Pr.

***Mears, Peter & Voehl, Frank.** The Executive Guide to Implementing Quality Systems. 200p. 1995. text ed. 39.95 (*1-884015-53-0*) St Lucie Pr.

— Team Building Manual: A Structural Learning Approach. (Illus.). 192p. (C). 1994. 19.95x (*1-884015-15-8*) St Lucie Pr.

Mears, Peter M. BASIC Programming with the IBM PC. 2nd ed. LC 89-30443. 480p. (C). 1990. pap. 47.95 (*0-534-12156-X*) PWS Pubs.

Mears, Raymond. The Outdoor Survival Handbook: A Guide to the Resources & Material Available in the Wild & How to Use Them for Food, Shelter, Warmth, & Navigation. LC 93-9683. (Illus.). 240p. (Orig.). 1993. pap. 13.95 (*0-312-09359-4*) St Martin.

Mears, Richard C. Ebb of the River. LC 86-19545. 208p. 1986. pap. 8.95 (*0-88191-044-9*) Freundlich.

Mears, Rona R., jt. ed. see Gitlin, Richard A.

Mears, T. Lambert. The Institutes of Gaius & Justinian: The Twelve Tables & the CXVIIIth & CXVIIth Novels, with Introduction & Translations. LC 93-79703. 686p. 1994. reprint ed. 135.00 (*1-56169-061-9*) W W Gaunt.

Mears, Walter, jt. auth. see Chancellor, John.

Mearsheimer, John J. Conventional Deterrence. LC 83-5317. (Cornell Studies in Security Affairs). 296p. (C). 1983. 39.95 (*0-8014-1569-1*); pap. 14.95 (*0-8014-9346-3*) Cornell U Pr.

— Liddell Hart & the Weight of History. LC 88-47748. (Cornell Studies in Security Affairs). 264p. 1988. 28.50 (*0-8014-2089-X*) Cornell U Pr.

Mearsheimer, John J., ed. Liddell Hart & the Weight of History. 264p. 1989. 28.00 (*0-08-036701-1*, Pub. by Brasseys UK) Brasseys Inc.

Measday, Ellen & Knight, Lisa F. Speak Out! Authentic Communication Activities for the Intermediate & Advanced ESL Student. 160p. (C). 1994. per. 16.95 (*0-8403-9536-1*) Kendall-Hunt.

***Measday, Stephen.** The News They Didn't Use. (YA). 1995. 11.95 (*0-7022-2711-0*, Pub. by Univ Queensland Pr AT) Intl Spec Bk.

Mease, James. Picture of Philadelphia. LC 75-112561. (Rise of Urban America Ser.). (Illus.). 1970. reprint ed. 23.95 (*0-405-02466-5*) Ayer.

Measell, James. D. C. Jenkins Glass Company Catalog. 32p. 1984. reprint ed. 5.25 (*0-317-44747-5*) Ferguson Comns Pubs.

— Dugan Diamond: The Story of Indiana, Pennsylvania Glass. (Illus.). 205p. (Orig.). 1993. 42.95 (*0-915410-92-3*); pap. 34.95 (*0-915410-91-5*) Antique Pubns.

— New Martinsville Glass, 1900-1944. 1994. 42.95 (*0-915410-00-1*) Antique Pubns.

— New Martinsville Glass, 1900-1944. (Illus.). 234p. 1994. pap. 34.95 (*0-915410-85-0*) Antique Pubns.

— P. R. the Right Stuff. 208p. (C). 1995. pap. text ed. 32.95 (*0-7872-1073-0*) Kendall-Hunt.

Measell, James & Smith, Don E. Findlay Glass. (Illus.). 146p. (Orig.). 1986. 27.95 (*0-915410-26-5*); pap. 19.95 (*0-915410-25-7*) Antique Pubns.

Measell, James, ed. see McGee, Marie.

***Measell, James S.** Teaching the Introductory Public Relations Course: Communication Perspective. Lewis, Warren, ed. LC 90-14056. (Illus.). 79p. (C). 1990. pap. 8.95 (*0-927516-20-9*) ERIC-REC.

***Measell, Jim, et al.** Wheeling Glass 1829-1939 Collection of the Oglebay Institute Glass Museum. (Illus.). 177p. 1994. pap. 34.95 (*1-57080-002-2*) Antique Pubns.

Measham, Anthony R., jt. auth. see Herz, Barbara.

Measom, George. The Illustrated Guide to the Great Western Railway 1852. 64p. 1987. 30.00 (*0-905392-47-7*) St Mut.

Meason, George & Cubbison, Greg. Pocket Guide to Speckled Trout & Redfish: South Texas Coast Edition. 96p. 1989. 5.95 (*0-88415-639-7*) Gulf Pub.

— Pocket Guide to Speckled Trout & Redfish: Upper Texas Coast Edition. 96p. 1990. 5.95 (*0-88415-627-3*) Gulf Pub.

Measor, Lynda & Sikes, Patricia J. Gender & Schools. 192p. 1992. text ed. 50.00 (*0-685-63589-9*); pap. text ed. 16.95 (*0-685-63590-2*) Cassell.

— Gender & Schools. 192p. 1992. text ed. 65.00 (*0-304-32401-9*, Tycooly Pub); pap. text ed. 25.00 (*0-304-32397-7*, Tycooly Pub) Weidner & Sons.

Measor, Lynda, jt. auth. see Woods, Peter.

Meastro, Betsy. Snow Day. (J). (ps-3). 1992. pap. 4.95 (*0-590-46083-8*) Scholastic Inc.

Measurements Group, Inc. Technical Staff. Strain Gage Based Transducers: Their Design & Construction. (Illus.). 74p. (Orig.). (C). 1988. pap. 10.00 (*0-9619057-0-0*) Measure Grp.

Measures, John. Wildlife Travelling Companion: Spain. (Illus.). 240p. 1993. pap. 29.95 (*1-85223-610-8*, Pub. by Crowood Pr UK) Trafalgar.

Measures, Raymond M. Laser Remote Sensing: Fundamentals & Applications. LC 91-20352. 524p. (C). 1992. reprint ed. lib. bdg. 74.50 (*0-89464-619-2*) Krieger.

Measures, Raymond M., ed. Laser Remote Chemical Analysis. LC 87-13380. (Chemical Analysis Ser.). 546p. 1988. text ed. 140.00 (*0-471-81640-X*) Wiley.

Meates, G. W. The Roman Villa at Lullingstone, Kent: The Site, Vol. 1. (Illus.). 222p. 1993. text ed. 40.00 (*0-85033-341-5*) A Sutton Pub.

— The Roman Villa at Lullingstone, Kent: The Wall Paintings & Finds, Vol. 2. (Illus.). 368p. 1993. text ed. 86.00 (*0-906746-09-4*) A Sutton Pub.

Meath-Lang, Bonnie, jt. auth. see Lang, Harry G.

Meats, Stephen. Looking for the Pale Eagle. 62p. (Orig.). 1993. pap. 8.00 (*0-939391-18-X*) B Woodley Pr.

Meatyard, Ralph E. The Family Album of Lucybelle Crater. Williams, Jonathan, ed. LC 74-76773. (Illus.). 88p. 1974. 12.50 (*0-912330-02-3*); pap. 10.00 (*0-912330-03-1*) Jargon Soc.

Meaus. Basic Medical Terminology Instructors Guide. 1987. 5.84 (*0-02-685470-8*) Macmillan.

Meban, Cowan. Cytochemistry of the Gas-Exchange Area in Vertebrate Lungs. (Progress in Histochemistry & Cytochemistry Ser.: Vol. 17, No. 1). 70p. 1987. pap. 45.90 (*0-89574-237-3*, Pub. by Gustav Fischer Verlag) VCH Pubs.

Mebane, Dorothy M., ed. see Fulton, Alvenia M.

Mebane, John C. The April of Her Age: The Buried Treasure of Robert Louis Stevenson & Princess Victoria Kaiulani. (Illus.). 248p. (Orig.). 1994. pap. 14.95 (*0-9641844-1-9*) Windward HI.

Mebane, John S. Renaissance Magic & the Return of the Golden Age: The Occult Tradition & Marlowe, Jonson & Shakespeare. LC 88-22068. xviii, 317p. 1989. reprint ed. pap. 12.95 (*0-8032-8179-X*) U of Nebr Pr.

Mebane, Robert & Rybolt, Thomas. Air & Other Gases. (Everyday Material Science Experiments Ser.). (Illus.). 64p. (J). (gr. 5-8). 1995. lib. bdg. 15.98 (*0-8050-2839-0*) TFC Bks NY.

— Metals. (Everyday Material Science Experiments Ser.). (Illus.). 64p. (J). (gr. 5-8). 1995. lib. bdg. 15.98 (*0-8050-2842-0*) TFC Bks NY.

— Plastics & Polymers. (Everyday Material Science Experiments Ser.). (Illus.). 64p. (J). (gr. 5-8). 1995. lib. bdg. 15.98 (*0-8050-2843-9*) TFC Bks NY.

— Salts & Solids. (Everyday Material Science Experiments Ser.). (Illus.). 64p. (J). (gr. 5-8). 1995. lib. bdg. 15.98 (*0-8050-2841-2*) TFC Bks NY.

— Water Liquids. (Everyday Material Science Experiments Ser.). (Illus.). 64p. (J). (gr. 5-8). 1995. lib. bdg. 15.98 (*0-8050-2840-4*) TFC Bks NY.

***Mebane, Robert C. & Rybolt, Thomas R.** Adventures with Atoms & Molecules Bk. V: Chemistry Experiments for Young People. (Adventures with Science Ser.). (Illus.). 96p. (J). (gr. 4-9). 1995. lib. bdg. 16.95 (*0-89490-606-2*) Enslow Pubs.

— Adventures with Atoms & Molecules, Bk. I: Chemistry Experiments for Young People. LC 85-10177. (Adventures with Science Ser.). (Illus.). 82p. (J). (gr. 4-9). 1985. lib. bdg. 16.95 (*0-89490-120-6*) Enslow Pubs.

— Adventures with Atoms & Molecules, Bk. II: Chemistry Experiments for Young People. LC 85-10177. (Adventures with Science Ser.). (Illus.). 96p. (J). (gr. 4-9). 1987. lib. bdg. 16.95 (*0-89490-164-8*) Enslow Pubs.

— Adventures with Atoms & Molecules, Bk. III: Chemistry Experiments for Young People. LC 85-10177. (Adventures with Science Ser.). (Illus.). 96p. (J). (gr. 4-9). 1991. lib. bdg. 16.95 (*0-89490-254-7*) Enslow Pubs.

— Adventures with Atoms & Molecules, Bk. IV: Chemistry Experiments for Young People. LC 85-10177. (Adventures with Science Ser.). (Illus.). 96p. (J). (gr. 4-9). 1992. lib. bdg. 16.95 (*0-89490-336-5*) Enslow Pubs.

Mebane, Robert C., jt. auth. see Rybolt, Thomas R.

Mebane, Rodney, jt. auth. see Calderon-Young, Estelita.

Mebrate, Assefa, jt. auth. see Kalb, Jon E.

Mebrathu, Mewail, et al. Time Table for California Courts: Deadlines for Filing & Serving Documents in Civil Litigation in California Courts. iii, 55p. (Orig.). 1990. pap. text ed. 8.50 (*1-878943-00-6*) SD Cnty Law Lib.

Mebs, jt. auth. see Shier.

Mebust, Larry E. Gray Whales, a Bird's-Eye View: A Fieldguide for Boat Skippers & Whalewatchers. 37p. 1992. pap. 7.95 (*0-9635485-0-6*) Offshore Pub.

***Mecartea, Bruce.** Quest for a Tomorrow. 407p. (Orig.). 1995. pap. 6.95 (*0-9646744-0-8*) Dawn Pub CA.

***Mecca, Andrew M., ed.** Prevention Action Plan for Alcohol-Related Problems. (Illus.). 90p. (Orig.). (C). 1994. pap. text ed. 40.00x (*0-7881-1430-1*) Diane Pub.

— Prevention 2000 - a Public-Private Partnership. (Illus.). 126p. 1994. reprint ed. pap. text ed. 40.00x (*0-7881-1429-8*) Diane Pub.

Mecca, Andrew M., et al. Toward a State of Esteem: The Final Report of the California Task Force to Promote Self-Esteem & Personal & Social Responsibility. (Illus.). 160p. 1990. pap. 6.00 (*0-8011-0846-2*) Calif Education.

— Toward a State of Esteem: The Final Report of the California Task Force to Promote Self-Esteem & Personal & Social Responsibility. Blockley, Rain, ed. (Illus.). 160p. (SPA.). 1992. pap. 6.00 (*0-8011-1028-9*) Calif Education.

Mecca, Judy T. Plays That Teach: Plays, Activities, & Songs with a Message. Keeling, Jan, ed. (Illus.). 96p. (Orig.). 1992. pap. text ed. 9.95 (*0-86530-153-0*, 195-2) Incentive Pubns.

— Special Plays for Special Days: 30 Minute Holiday & Seasonal Plays. (Illus.). 96p. (Orig.). 1991. pap. text ed. 8.95 (*0-86530-203-0*, IP 194-4) Incentive Pubns.

Mecca, Stephen J. & Robertshaw, Joseph E. Home Energy Management: Principles & Practices. (Illus.). 160p. 1981. 12.95 (*0-89433-146-9*) Petrocelli.

Mecca, Stephen J., jt. auth. see Robertshaw, Joseph E.

Mecca, Tommi A. Between Little Rock & a Hard Place. 1993. pap. 9.95 (*0-9635289-3-9*) Williams OR.

Mecchi, Irene, ed. see Caen, Herb.

***Mech, Doris.** Joy with Honey. LC 94-47239. 1995. pap. 12.95 (*0-312-11836-8*) St Martin.

Mech, Edmund V., ed. Independent-Living Services for At-Risk Adolescents. 138p. 1988. pap. 14.95 (*0-87868-359-3*) Child Welfare.

Mech, L. David. The Arctic Wolf: Living with the Pack. (Illus.). 128p. 1992. pap. 19.95 (*0-89658-211-6*) Voyageur Pr.

— Handbook of Animal Radio-Tracking. LC 83-6733. (Illus.). 120p. (C). 1983. pap. 9.95 (*0-8166-1221-8*) U of Minn Pr.

— The Way of the Wolf. (Illus.). 120p. 1991. 29.95 (*0-89658-163-2*) Voyageur Pr.

— The Wolf: The Ecology & Behavior of an Endangered Species. LC 80-27364. (Illus.). 385p. (C). 1981. reprint ed. pap. 15.95 (*0-8166-1026-6*) U of Minn Pr.

Mech, Terrence F., jt. ed. see Farmer, D. W.

Mecham, John L. Church & State in Latin America: A History of Politico Ecclesiastical Relations. rev. ed. LC 66-15511. 477p. reprint ed. pap. 136.00 (*0-7837-0315-5*, 2040637) Bks Demand.

Mecham, Merlin J. Cerebral Palsy. Halpern, Harvey, ed. LC 86-3271. (PRO-ED Studies in Communicative Disorders). (Illus.). 64p. (Orig.). 1986. pap. text ed. 9.00 (*0-89079-087-6*, 1376) PRO-ED.

Mecham, Milo R., jt. auth. see Antieau, Chester J.

Mecham, Robert, ed. see Arri.

Mecham, Robert P., ed. Regulation of Matrix Accumulation. (Biology of Extracellular Matrix Ser.: Vol. 1). 1986. text ed. 125.00 (*0-12-487425-8*) Acad Pr.

Mecham, Robert P., jt. ed. see Church, David A.

Mecham, Robert P., jt. ed. see McDonald, John A.

Mecham, Robert P., jt. ed. see Roberts, David D.

Mecham, Robert P., jt. ed. see Schwartz, Stephan M.

Mecham, Robert P., jt. ed. see Wight, Thomas N.

Mechan, D., jt. auth. see Dalgleish, G.

Mechan, Derek J., jt. auth. see Hubbard, Judy L.

Mechanic, David. From Advocacy to Allocation: The Evolving American Health Care System. 256p. 1986. text ed. 27.95 (*0-02-920830-0*); pap. 15.95 (*0-02-920860-2*) Free Pr.

— Future Issues in Health Care: Notes on Illness, Behavior & Social Policy. LC 78-63413. 1979. pap. 27.95 (*0-02-920710-X*) Free Pr.

— Inescapable Decisions: The Imperatives of Health Reform. LC 93-13425. 256p. (C). 1993. text ed. 34.95 (*1-56000-121-6*) Transaction Pubs.

— Medical Sociology. 2nd ed. LC 77-3850. 1978. text ed. 29.95 (*0-02-920720-7*) Free Pr.

— Mental Health & Social Policy. 3rd ed. 256p. (C). 1988. pap. text ed. write for info. (*0-13-576034-8*) P-H.

— Painful Choices: Research & Essays on Health Care. 320p. 1989. 34.95 (*0-88738-258-4*) Transaction Pubs.

— Students under Stress: A Study in the Social Psychology of Adaptation. LC 77-91058. 268p. 1978. reprint ed. 20.00 (*0-299-07470-6*); reprint ed. pap. text ed. 10.95 (*0-299-07474-9*) U of Wis Pr.

Mechanic, David, ed. Handbook of Health, Health Care & the Health Professions. (Illus.). 832p. 1983. text ed. 75.00 (*0-02-920690-1*) Free Pr.

— Improving Mental Health Services: What the Social Sciences Can Tell Us. LC 87-646993. (New Directions for Mental Health Services Ser.: No. MHS 36). 1987. 17.95 (*1-55542-944-0*) Jossey-Bass.

— Readings in Medical Sociology. LC 79-7578. (Illus.). 1980. pap. 16.95 (*0-02-920700-2*) Free Pr.

Mechanic, David & Aiken, Laura H., eds. Paying for Services: Promises & Pitfalls of Capitation. LC 87-646993. (New Directions for Mental Health Services Ser.: No. MHS 43). 1989. 17.95 (*1-55542-852-5*) Jossey-Bass.

Mechanic, David, jt. ed. see Aiken, Linda H.

Mechanic, Janevive J. The Logic of Decision Making: An Introduction to Critical Thinking. (American University Studies: Philosophy: Ser. V, Vol. 39). 210p. 1988. text ed. 35.50 (*0-8204-0484-5*) P Lang Pubs.

Mechanical Failures Prevention Group, Meeting (35th: 1982: National Bureau of Standards) Staff. Time-Dependent Failure Mechanisms & Assessment Methodologies: Proceedings of the 35th Meeting of the Mechanical Failures Prevention Group, National Bureau of Standards, Gaithersburg, MD, April 20-22, 1982. Early, James G. et al, eds. LC 82-19892. 331p. reprint ed. pap. 94.40 (*0-318-34782-2*, 2031643) Bks Demand.

Mechanisms of Vasodilatation Symposium Staff. Mechanisms of Vasodilation Symposium, Abstracts. Vanhoutte, P. M., ed. (Journal: Blood Vessels: Vol. 17, No. 3). 56p. 1980. pap. 29.75 (*3-8055-1252-X*) S Karger.

Mechem & Atkinson. Wills & Administration. 5th ed. 1961. text ed. 27.00 (*0-88277-392-5*) Foundation Pr.

Mechem, Floyd R. Elements of the Law of Partnership. LC 12-36583. (Business Enterprises Reprint Ser.). xxxviii, 277p. 1982. reprint ed. text ed. 44.00 (*0-89941-180-0*, 302300) W S Hein.

Mechem, Kirke, ed. see Owen, Jennie S.

Mechery, F. A. & Tikekar, Maneesha, eds. Indian Socialism: Past & Present. xii, 231p. 1985. 16.00 (*0-685-67627-7*, Pub. by Himalaya Pub Hse II) Nataraj Bks.

Mechie, Stewart. The Church & Scottish Social Development, 1780-1870. LC 75-3740. 181p. 1975. reprint ed. text ed. 49.75 (*0-8371-8060-0*, MECS, Greenwood Pr) Greenwood.

Mechikoff, Robert A. & Estes, Steven. History & Philosophy of Sport & Physical Education: From the Ancient Greeks to the Present. 416p. (C). 1993. pap. text ed. write for info. (*0-697-12159-3*) Brown & Benchmark.

Mechlenburg, Roy, jt. auth. see Davidson, Harold.

***Mechler, Gary.** Constellations of the Northern Skies. LC 94-34032. (National Audubon Society Pocket Guides Ser.). 1995. 7.99 (*0-679-77998-1*) Knopf.

***Mechler, Gary, et al.** The Sun & the Moon. LC 94-42421. (National Audubon Society Pocket Guide Ser.). 1995. pap. 7.99 (*0-679-76056-3*) Knopf.

Mechlin, K. H. Lecture Notes for P & B 301-501. 448p. 1992. spiral bd. 19.95 (*0-8403-8471-8*) Kendall-Hunt.

Mechling, Jay. Church, State, & Public Policy: The New Shape of the Church - State Debate. LC 79-17711. (AEI Symposia Ser.: No. 79F). (Illus.). 136p. reprint ed. pap. 38.80 (*0-8357-4449-3*, 2037286) Bks Demand.

Mechling, Jay, jt. ed. see Gillespie, Angus K.

Mechnikov, et al. Founders of Modern Medicine. Berger, D., tr. LC 78-142669. (Essay Index Reprint Ser.). 1977. 23.95 (*0-8369-2111-9*) Ayer.

Mecholsky, J. J. & Powell, S. R., Jr., eds. Fractography of Ceramic & Metal Failures - STP 827. LC 83-71813. 272p. 1984. text ed. 42.00 (*0-8031-0215-1*, 04-827000-30) ASTM.

Mechoulam, Raphael. Cannabinoids As Therapeutic Agents. 200p. 1986. 168.00 (*0-8493-5772-1*, RM666, CRC Reprint) Franklin.

Mechoulan, Henry, ed. see Ben-Israel, Menasseh.

Mechthild, Leutner, jt. ed. see Kuo, Heng-yo.

Mechtly, E. H. The International System of Units. 1977. pap. 2.80 (*0-87563-139-8*) Stipes.

Meck, Charles. Fishing Small Streams with a Fly Rod. (Illus.). 224p. 1991. pap. 15.00 (*0-88150-202-2*, Backcountry) Countryman.

— Pennsylvania Trout Streams & Their Hatches. 2nd rev. ed. (Illus.). 384p. (Orig.). 1993. pap. 17.00 (*0-88150-272-3*, Backcountry) Countryman.

Meck, Charles & Hoover, Greg. Great Rivers - Great Hatches. LC 92-3957. (Illus.). 392p. 1992. 24.95 (*0-8117-1282-6*) Stackpole.

***Meck, Charles R.** Patterns, Hatches, Tactics & Trout. LC 95-12008. 1995. write for info. (*1-55629-050-0*) Vivid Pub.

Mecke, Gunter. Hair, or, the Ligurinus Shock: On a Narcissistic Crisis in Puberty & Its Recurrence in the Man of Fifty. LC 74-82753. 1975. 10.00 (*0-87212-044-9*) Libra.

Meckel, Adrienne M., jt. auth. see Duke, Daniel L.

Meckel, Christoph. Snow Creatures & Other Stories. Bedwell, Carol, tr. LC 90-37811. (Studies in German Language & Literature: Vol. 3). (Illus.). 104p. 1991. lib. bdg. 59.95 (*0-88946-581-9*) E Mellen.

— Zund & Other Stories. Bedwell, Carol, tr. LC 90-37947. (Studies in German Language & Literature: Vol. 2). (Illus.). 120p. 1991. lib. bdg. 59.95 (*0-88946-580-0*) E Mellen.

Meckel, Daniel J., ed. see Hall, James A.

Meckel, Daniel J., ed. see Moore, Robert L.

***Meckel, Mary V.** A Sociological Analysis of the California Taxi-Dancer: The Hidden Halls. LC 94-38355. 168p. 1995. text ed. 79.95 (*0-7734-9039-6*) E Mellen.

Meckel, Richard A. Save the Babies: American Public Health Reform & the Prevention of Infant Mortality, 1850-1929. LC 89-15389. (Henry E. Sigerist Series in the History of Medicine). (Illus.). 360p. 1990. text ed. 48.00x (*0-8018-3879-7*) Johns Hopkins.

Meckenstock, Guenter, ed. Schleiermachers Bibliothek: Bearbeitung des Faksimilierten Rauchschen Auktionskatalogs & der Hauptbuecher des Verlages G. Reimer. (Schleiermacher-Archiv Ser.: Bd 10). vii, 349p. (GER.). (C). 1993. lib. bdg. 152.35 (*3-11-013619-8*) De Gruyter.

Meckenstock, Guenter, ed. see Schleiermacher, Friedrich D.

Meckenstock, Gunter & Ringleben, Joachim, eds. Schleiermacher & die Wissenschaftliche Kultur des Christentums. (Theologische Bibliothek Toepelmann Ser.: Vol. 51). xvi, 521p. (GER.). (C). 1991. lib. bdg. 152.35 (*3-11-012857-8*) De Gruyter.

Meckert, U. Russian for Restaurant & Hotels: Russisch fuer das Gaststaetten-und Hotelwesen. 3rd ed. 184p. (GER & RUS.). 1982. 29.95 (*0-8288-1476-7*, M15241) Fr & Eur.

Meckier, Jerome. Hidden Rivalries in Victorian Fiction: Dickens, Realism, & Revaluation. LC 87-6177. 320p. 1987. 35.00 (*0-8131-1622-8*) U Pr of Ky.

— Innocent Abroad: Charles Dickens' American Engagements. LC 89-16530. 288p. 1990. text ed. 34.00 (*0-8131-1707-0*) U Pr of Ky.

***Meckier, Jerome, ed.** Critical Essays on Aldous Huxley. LC 95-12209. (Critical Essays on British Literature Ser.). 1995. write for info. (*0-8161-8873-4*) G K Hall.

Meckier, Jerome, jt. ed. see Clubbe, John.

Mecklenburg, Frank, tr. see Bloch, Ernst.

Mecklenburg, Frank, tr. see Degenhart, Bernhard & Schmitt, Annegrit.

An Asterisk (*) at the beginning of an entry indicates that the title is appearing in BIP for the first time.

Mecklenburg, Virginia & Ausfeld, Margaret L. Advancing American Art: Politics & Aesthetics in the U. S. State Department Exhibition, 1946-48. LC 83-19301. (Illus.). 120p. (Orig.). (ps-12). 1984. pap. 12.00 (*0-89280-021-6*) Montgomery Mus.

Mecklenburg, Virginia M. The Patricia & Phillip Frost Collection: American Abstraction, 1930-45. LC 89-43055. (Illus.). 192p. (C). 1989. pap. 24.95 (*0-87474-717-1*) Smithsonian.

Mecklenburger, James A. & Hostrop, Richard W., eds. Education Vouchers: From Theory to Alum Rock. LC 72-8872. 410p. 1972. pap. 23.95 (*0-88280-002-7*) ETC Pubns.

Mecklenburgh, J. C. Plant Layout: A Guide to the Layout of Process Plant & Sites. LC 74-181804. 160p. reprint ed. pap. 45.60 (*0-317-27761-8*, 2025234) Bks Demand.

Mecklenburgh, J. C. & Hartland, S. The Theory of Backmixing: The Design of Continuous Flow Chemical Plant with Backmixing. LC 74-32190. 529p. reprint ed. pap. 150.80 (*0-317-41980-3*, 2025977) Bks Demand.

Meckler, Alan M. Micropublishing: A History of Scholarly Micropublishing in America, 1938-1980. LC 81-6955. (Contributions in Librarianship & Information Science Ser.: No. 40). (Illus.). xiv, 179p. 1982. text ed. 49.95 (*0-313-23096-X*, MMP/) Greenwood.

Meckler, Alan M., jt. auth. see Shenton, James.

Meckler, Brenda W. Papa Was a Farmer: The Story of an Immigrant Jewish Family's Life in America's Heartland. LC 88-3463. (American Places of the Heart Ser.: Vol. IV). (Illus.). 318p. 1988. 15.95 (*0-912697-95-4*) Algonquin Bks.

***Meckler, Jack M. & Treasury Management Association Staff.** The Corporate Guide to Payments System Risk: Assessing & Controlling Payments Risk. (Illus.). 186p. 1995. 60.00 (*1-55738-885-7*) Probus Pub Co.

Meckler, Milton, ed. Indoor Air Quality - Design Guidebook. 1991. 62.00 (*0-88173-088-2*) Fairmont Pr.

— Retrofitting of Buildings for Energy Conservation. LC 94-4801. 1994. write for info. (*0-88173-183-8*) Fairmont Pr.

Meckler, Milton, jt. auth. see Fairmont Press Staff.

Meckler, R. Wippo, jt. auth. see Koren, Leonard.

***Mecklermedia Staff.** Virtual Reality Market Place 1995. 250p. 1995. pap. 39.95 (*0-88736-990-1*) Mecklermedia.

Mecklin, John M. Democracy & Race Friction. LC 70-124244. (Select Bibliographies Reprint Ser.). 1977. reprint ed. 20.95 (*0-8369-5432-7*) Ayer.

— Democracy & Race Friction: A Study in Social Ethics. LC 78-172717. reprint ed. 24.50 (*0-404-00090-8*) AMS Pr.

Meckna, Michael. Twentieth-Century Brass Soloists: Bio-Critical Source Books on Musical Performance. LC 93-23943. 291p. 1994. text ed. 75.00 (*0-313-26468-6*, MTC/, Greenwood Pr) Greenwood.

— Virgil Thomson: A Bio-Bibliography. LC 86-14229. (Bio-Bibliographies in Music Ser.: No. 4). 217p. 1986. text ed. 49.95 (*0-313-25010-3*, MVN/, Greenwood Pr) Greenwood.

Meckna, Michael, ed. The Collected Works of Alfred B. Sedgwick. LC 94-707. (Nineteenth-Century American Musical Theater Ser.: No. 7). 488p. 1994. reprint ed. 130.00 (*0-8153-1369-1*) Garland.

Med-Facts, Inc. Staff. Injury & Illness Prevention Program. rev. ed. 122p. 1992. 199.95 (*1-884006-26-4*) Med-Facts.

— OSHA's Bloodborne Pathogen Procedures Made Cost Effective: or FED-OSHA Mandated Exposure Control for Occupational Exposure Control to Bloodborne Pathogens. 118p. 1993. student ed 495.00 (*1-884006-25-6*) Med-Facts.

Meda, L., jt. auth. see Cerofolini, G. F.

Medalia, Jonathan, et al, eds. Nuclear Weapons & Security: The Effects of Alternative Test Ban Treaties. 275p. (C). 1991. pap. text ed. 48.00 (*0-8133-8261-0*) Westview.

Medalia, Leon S., Jr. My First Ninety Years. 300p. 1974. 12.00 (*0-685-41734-4*) Fountainhead.

Medalia, Nahum Z. & Larsen, Otto N. Diffusion & Belief in a Collective Delusion: The Seattle Windshield Pitting Epidemic. (Reprint Series in Social Sciences). (C). 1993. reprint ed. pap. text ed. 1.90 (*0-8290-2718-1*, S-602) Irvington.

Medalie, David. The Shooting of the Christmas Cows. 144p. (Orig.). 1990. pap. 9.95 (*0-86486-146-X*, Pub. by D Philip SA) Interlink Pub.

Medard, L. Gas Encyclopedia. 1150p. 1976. 277.00 (*0-444-41492-4*) Elsevier.

Medaris, Gene. Ted McRoberts: North Country Marshal. (Illus.). 224p. 1986. 29.95 (*0-937708-04-6*) Great Northwest.

— Ted McRoberts: North Country Marshal. 224p. 1987. pap. 19.95 (*0-937708-06-2*) Great Northwest.

Medaris, L. G., Jr., ed. Early Proterozoic Geology of the Great Lakes Region. (Memoir Ser.: No. 160). (Illus.). 148p. 1983. 8.50 (*0-8137-1160-6*) Geol Soc.

Medaris, L. G., Jr., et al, eds. Proterozoic Geology: Selected Papers from an International Proterozoic Symposium. (Memoir Ser.: No. 161). (Illus.). 324p. 1984. 10.00 (*0-8137-1161-4*) Geol Soc.

Medawar, J. S., jt. auth. see Medawar, P. B.

Medawar, Mardi O. People of the Whistling Waters. 442p. 1993. 19.95 (*1-879915-05-7*) Affil Writers America.

Medawar, P. B. Advice to a Young Scientist. 128p. 1981. reprint ed. pap. 13.00 (*0-465-00092-4*) Basic.

Medawar, P. B. & Medawar, J. S. Aristotle to Zoos: A Philosophical Dictionary of Biology. (Illus.). 319p. 1983. 34.50 (*0-674-04535-1*) HUP.

— Aristotle to Zoos: A Philosophical Dictionary of Biology. LC 84-16529. 319p. 1985. pap. text ed. 12.50 (*0-674-04537-8*) HUP.

Medawar, Peter. Memoir of a Thinking Radish. large type ed. 272p. 1989. reprint ed. lib. bdg. 9.97 (*1-85089-301-2*, Pub. by ISIS UK) Transaction Pubs.

— Memoir of a Thinking Radish: An Autobiography. (Illus.). 224p. 1986. 19.95 (*0-19-217737-0*) OUP.

— Pluto's Republic: Incorporating "The Art of the Soluble" & "Induction & Intuition in Scientific Thought" (Illus.). 1982. 29.95 (*0-19-217726-5*) OUP.

— Pluto's Republic: Incorporating "The Art of the Soluble" & "Induction & Intuition in Scientific Thought" (Illus.). 1984. pap. 10.95 (*0-19-283039-2*) OUP.

— The Threat & the Glory: Reflections on Science & Scientists. Pyke, David, ed. 320p. 1991. pap. 9.95 (*0-19-286128-X*) OUP.

Medawar, Peter B. Induction & Intuition in Scientific Thought. LC 69-17272. (Memoirs Ser.: Vol. 75). 1980. pap. 10.00 (*0-87169-075-6*, M075-MEP) Am Philos.

— The Limits of Science. 128p. 1988. pap. 9.95 (*0-19-505212-9*) OUP.

— The Uniqueness of the Individual. 192p. 1981. reprint ed. pap. 6.95 (*0-486-24042-8*) Dover.

Medbh, Maighread. The Making of a Pagan. 66p. (Orig.). 1990. pap. 11.95 (*0-85640-455-1*, Pub. by Blackstaff Pr IE) Dufour.

Medbury, James K. Men & Mysteries of Wall Street. LC 67-30971. 1968. reprint ed. 18.00 (*0-87034-035-2*) Fraser Pub Co.

Medcalf, Bill. Retrieve: A New, Gentle Approach to Retriever Training. (Illus.). 200p. 1990. 19.95 (*0-9620226-0-8*) Medcalf Pub Co.

Medcalf, Donald, jt. auth. see Russell, Ronald.

Medcalf, G. Marketing & the Brand Manager. 1967. 120.00 (*0-08-012602-2*, Pub. by Pergamon Repr UK) Franklin.

Medcalf, John. A Parish at War: Letters from Nicaragua. 1989. pap. 7.95 (*0-87243-182-7*) Templegate.

Medcalf, Linda. Law & Identity: Lawyers, Native Americans & Legal Practice. LC 78-588. (Sage Library of Social Research: Vol. 62). 148p. reprint ed. pap. 42.20 (*0-317-08812-2*, 2021931) Bks Demand.

Medcalf, Linda J., jt. auth. see Dolbeare, Kenneth M.

Medcalf, Stephen, ed. The Later Middle Ages. LC 81-6509. (Context of English Literature Ser.). 300p. 1981. 39.50 (*0-8419-0725-0*); pap. 21.50 (*0-8419-0726-9*) Holmes & Meier.

— Poems for All Purposes: Selected Poems of G. K. Chesterton. (Illus.). 208p. 1994. pap. 17.95 (*0-7126-5881-5*, Pub. by Pimlico) Trafalgar.

***Medcraft, Rosalie & Gee, Valda.** The Sausage Tree. 200p. 1995. pap. 16.95 (*0-7022-2783-8*, Pub. by Univ Queensland Pr AT) Intl Spec Bk.

Medd, R. W., jt. auth. see Auld, B. A.

Meddaugh, Susan. Beast. (Illus.). 32p. (J). (gr. k-3). 1985. pap. 3.95 (*0-317-18511-X*) HM.

— Beast Pa. (J). (ps-3). 1985. pap. 5.95 (*0-395-38366-8*) HM.

— Hog Eye. LC 95-3951. (Illus.). 1995. 14.95 (*0-395-74276-5*) HM.

— Martha Calling. (Illus.). (J). 1994. 14.95 (*0-395-69825-1*) HM.

— Martha Speaks. LC 91-48455. (Illus.). 32p. (J). (ps-3). 1992. 14.95 (*0-395-63313-3*) HM.

— Martha Speaks. LC 91-48455. (J). (ps-3). 1995. pap. 4.95 (*0-395-72024-9*) HM.

— Martha Speaks. (Illus.). 1995. pap. 4.95 (*0-395-72952-1*, Sandpiper) HM.

— Tree of Birds. (Illus.). 32p. (J). (gr. k-3). 1990. 13.95 (*0-395-53147-0*) HM.

— Tree of Birds. (J). (ps-3). 1994. pap. 4.95 (*0-395-68978-3*) HM.

— The Witches' Supermarket. (Illus.). 32p. (J). (gr. k-3). 1991. 13.95 (*0-395-57034-4*, Sandpiper) HM.

— The Witches' Supermarket. (Illus.). (J). 1994. pap. 4.95 (*0-395-70092-2*) HM.

Meddaugh, Susan, illus. Two Ways to Count to Ten. LC 86-33513. 32p. (J). (ps-2). 1988. 14.95 (*0-8050-0407-6*, Bks Young Read) H Holt & Co.

Meddemmen, John, tr. see Segre, Cesare.

Medding, Peter Y. The Founding of Israeli Democracy, 1948-1967. 264p. 1990. 42.00 (*0-19-505648-5*) OUP.

— Mapai in Israel: Political Organisation & Government in a New Society. LC 75-184900. 338p. reprint ed. pap. 96.40 (*0-685-16065-3*, 2027240) Bks Demand.

Medding, Peter Y., ed. Israel: State & Society, 1948-1988. (Studies in Contemporary Jewry: Vol. V). 448p. 1989. 29.95 (*0-685-27143-9*) OUP.

— Studies in Contemporary Jewry: A New Jewry? America since the Second World War, Vol. VIII. (Illus.). 448p. 1992. 45.00 (*0-19-507449-1*) OUP.

— Studies in Contemporary Jewry, Vol. V: Israel: State & Society, 1948-1988. 448p. 1989. 38.00 (*0-19-505827-5*) OUP.

Medding, Peter Y., ed. see Institute of Contemporary Jewry of the Hebrew University of Jerusalem Staff.

Meddock, Sally. Super Soups. Winquist, Jeannine, ed. 64p. (Orig.). 1986. pap. 3.49 (*0-942320-23-9*) Am Cooking.

***Medearis, Angela.** Bye-bye, Babies! LC 94-41791. (Illus.). (J). 1995. bds. write for info. (*1-56402-258-7*) Candlewick Pr.

— Eat, Babies, Eat! LC 94-41790. (Illus.). (J). 1995. bds. write for info. (*1-56402-257-9*) Candlewick Pr.

***Medearis, Angela S.** The Adventures of Sugar & Junior. LC 94-42368. (Illus.). 32p. (J). 1995. lib. bdg. 15.95 (*0-8234-1182-6*) Holiday.

— Annie's Gifts. LC 92-71998. (Feeling Good Ser.). (Illus.). 32p. (J). (gr. 1-4). 1994. 14.95 (*0-940975-30-0*); pap. 6.95 (*0-940975-31-9*) Just Us Bks.

— Come This Far to Freedom: A History of African Americans. LC 92-31251. (Illus.). 160p. (J). (gr. 3-7). 1993. text ed. 14.95 (*0-689-31522-8*, Atheneum Bks Young) S&S Childrens.

— Dancing with the Indians. LC 90-28666. (Illus.). 32p. (J). (ps-3). 1991. lib. bdg. 15.95 (*0-8234-0893-0*) Holiday.

— Dancing with the Indians. (Illus.). (J). (gr. k-3). 1994. audio 22.95 (*0-87499-333-4*); audio, pap. 14.95 (*0-87499-332-6*) Live Oak Media.

— Dancing with the Indians, 4 bks., Set. (Illus.). (J). (gr. k-3). 1994. audio, pap. 33.95 (*0-87499-334-2*) Live Oak Media.

— Dancing with the Indians: A Reading Rainbow Review Book. (Illus.). (J). (ps-3). 1993. reprint ed. pap. 5.95 (*0-8234-1023-4*) Holiday.

— Dare to Dream: Coretta Scott King & the Civil Rights Movement. LC 93-33573. (Rainbow Biography Ser.). (Illus.). 64p. (J). (gr. 3-6). 1994. 13.99 (*0-525-67426-8*, Lodestar Bks) Dutton Child Bks.

— The Kwanzaa Celebration Cookbook. (Illus.). 188p. 1995. 17.95 (*0-525-94070-7*, Dutton) NAL-Dutton.

— Little Louis & the Jazz Band: The Story of Louis "Satchmo" Armstrong. LC 93-23596. (Rainbow Biography Ser.). (Illus.). (J). 1994. 13.99 (*0-525-67424-1*, Lodestar Bks) Dutton Child Bks.

— Nannie. LC 95-10360. (Illus.). (J). 1996. write for info. (*0-689-31858-8*, Atheneum Bks Young) S&S Childrens.

— Our People. LC 92-44499. (Illus.). 32p. (J). (gr. k-3). 1994. text ed. 14.95 (*0-689-31826-X*, Atheneum Bks Young) S&S Childrens.

— Picking Peas for a Penny. (Illus.). 40p. (J). (gr. 1-4). 1993. pap. 4.95 (*0-590-45942-2*) Scholastic Inc.

— Picking Peas for a Penny. LC 89-49754. (Illus.). 36p. (J). (gr. 1-4). 1990. 11.95 (*0-938349-54-6*) State House Pr.

— Poppa's New Pants. LC 94-20489. (Illus.). (J). (ps-3). 1995. lib. bdg. 15.95 (*0-8234-1155-9*) Holiday.

— Rum-A-Tum-Tum. LC 94-9929. (Illus.). (J). Date not set. write for info. (*0-8234-1143-5*) Holiday.

— Seven Days of Kwanzaa. (J). (gr. 4-7). 1994. pap. 2.95 (*0-590-46360-8*) Scholastic Inc.

— The Singing Man. (Illus.). 1995. pap. 6.95 (*0-8234-1208-3*) Holiday.

— Skin Deep: And Other Teenage Reflections. (Illus.). (YA). (gr. 5 up). 1995. 15.00 (*0-02-765980-1*, Atheneum Bks Young) S&S Childrens.

— 100th Day of School. LC 95-13214. (Hello Reader Ser.: Level 2). (Illus.). (J). 1996. write for info. (*0-590-25944-X*, Cartwheel) Scholastic Inc.

— Treemonisha. (Illus.). (J). 1995. 15.95 (*0-8050-1748-8*) H Holt & Co.

***Medearis, Angela Shelf.** We Play on a Rainy Day. (Hello Reader Ser.). 1995. write for info. (*0-590-26265-3*, Cartwheel) Scholastic Inc.

Medearis, Kenneth. Report on an Investigation of the Feasibility of Establishing a National Civil Engineering Software Center to the American Society of Civil Engineers for the Research Council on Computer Practices. LC 79-302366. 128p. reprint ed. pap. 36.50 (*0-317-20732-6*, 2023822) Bks Demand.

Medearis, Mary. Big Doc's Girl. LC 84-45641. 142p. (YA). (gr. 7-12). 1985. reprint ed. pap. 9.95 (*0-87483-105-9*) August Hse.

Medee, jt. auth. see Eurydice.

***Medeiros.** Fairest of Them All. 1995. mass mkt. (*0-553-56333-5*) Bantam.

***Medeiros, Arthur C. & Loope, Lloyd L.** Rare Plants & Animals of Haleakala National Park. (Illus.). 58p. (Orig.). 1995. pap. text ed. 7.95 (*0-940295-13-X*) HI Natural Hist.

Medeiros, Benjamin A. Surplus Values Revisited. 1993. 14.95 (*0-533-10394-0*) Vantage.

Medeiros, Mark D., jt. auth. see Zingg, Paul J.

Medeiros-Neto, Geraldo A., jt. ed. see Gaitan, Eduardo.

Medeiros, Richard, ed. see Roeper, Annemarie.

Medeiros, Teresa. Heather & Velvet. 1992. pap. 5.99 (*0-553-29407-5*) Bantam.

— Once an Angel. 1993. mass mkt. 5.50 (*0-553-29409-1*) Bantam.

— Thief of Hearts. 1994. mass mkt. 5.50 (*0-553-56332-7*) Bantam.

— Thief of Hearts. large type ed. LC 94-40173. 623p. 1995. 19.95 (*0-7862-0372-2*) Thorndike Pr.

— Whisper of Roses. 1993. mass mkt. 5.50 (*0-553-29408-3*) Bantam.

— A Whisper of Roses. large type ed. LC 93-33801. 1994. 20.95 (*0-7862-0070-7*) Thorndike Pr.

***Medem, R.** Argalis. deluxe limited ed. (Illus.). 304p. 1994. boxed 150.00 (*1-57157-027-6*) Safari Pr.

Medema, K. Gorgles. Vreeman, J., ed. (Orig.). (J). 1985. pap. 3.95 (*0-918789-05-2*) FreeMan Prods.

— Rennis the Nam. Vreeman, J., ed. (Illus.). 16p. (Orig.). (J). 1985. pap. 3.95 (*0-918789-04-4*) FreeMan Prods.

Medema, Steven G. Ronald H. Coase. LC 93-37501. 1994. text ed. 59.95 (*0-312-12039-7*, Pub. by Macm UK) St Martin.

***Medema, Steven G., ed.** The Legacy of Ronald Coase in Economic Analysis, 2 vols., Set. LC 94-32261. 1000p. 1995. 589.95 (*1-85898-010-0*, Pub. by E Elgar Pub UK) Ashgate Pub Co.

Medema, Steven G., jt. auth. see Samuels, Warren J.

Medenbach, O. & Wilk, H. The Magic of Minerals. White, J. S., tr. (Illus.). 204p. 1989. 72.00 (*0-387-15730-1*) Spr-Verlag.

Medenica, W. V. The M. I. C. Archipelago & Two Plays. LC 88-50589. 182p. (Orig.). 1989. pap. 9.00 (*0-916383-62-8*, Univ Edtns) Aegina Pr.

***Meder, Heinz.** Karibische Geschichten: Dominikanische Republik von und fur "Insider" (Illus.). 216p. (GER.). 1993. pap. 14.00 (*1-886254-00-1*) Edic Nue Mun.

— Tales of a Caribbean Isle: The Dominican Republic by & for an Insider. (Illus.). 197p. 1994. pap. 14.00 (*1-886254-06-0*) Edic Nue Mun.

Meder, J. & Handbuck, Ein. Durer-Katalog. LC 75-87642. (Graphic Art Ser.: Vol. 12). (Illus.). 358p. 1971. reprint ed. lib. bdg. 85.00 (*0-306-71788-3*) Da Capo.

Meder, Joseph. The Mastery of Drawing, 2 vols., Set. Ames, Winslow, tr. LC 76-22300. (Illus.). 720p. 98.00 (*0-913870-16-1*) Abaris Bks.

Meder, Marylouise D., ed. Library School Review, Vol. 16. 1976. pap. 2.00 (*0-941044-00-9*) Sch Lib Sci.

— Library School Review, Vol. 18. 1979. pap. 2.00 (*0-686-26897-0*) Emporia State.

— Library School Review, Vol. 18. 1979. pap. 2.00 (*0-941044-02-5*) Sch Lib Sci.

— Library School Review, Vol. 19. 1980. pap. 2.00 (*0-941044-03-3*) Sch Lib Sci.

Mederis, Angela S. The African-American Kitchen: Cooking from Our Heritage. LC 94-1323. 1994. 23.95 (*0-525-93834-6*) NAL-Dutton.

Medewitz, Jeanette. Reilly's Investments. 3rd ed. 448p. (C). 1992. student ed, pap. text ed. 18.75 (*0-03-032667-2*) Dryden Pr.

Medford, Bernard R. The Fall of Christian Standards in America. 1992. 10.95 (*0-533-09523-9*) Vantage.

Medford, Connie, jt. auth. see Medford, Robert.

Medford Historical Society Staff. Landscape of War: Recently Discovered Civil War Photographs. Pohanka, Brian, ed. (Illus.). 224p. 1999. 35.00 (*0-395-47692-5*) HM.

Medford, Robert & Medford, Connie. The Families of Haywood & Jackson Counties, North Carolina: Based on the 1850 Census Records. 144p. 1994. pap. 23.00 (*1-56664-070-9*) WorldComm.

— The Families of Haywood County: Based on the 1860 Census Records. 136p. Date not set. pap. text ed. 23.00 (*1-56664-071-7*) WorldComm.

Medford, Roberta, ed. Statistical Sources on the California Hispanic Population. 210p. 1990. 14.95 (*0-685-47549-2*) Floricanto Pr.

Medford, Roberta & Loh, Eudora. Online Information on Hispanics & Other Ethnic Groups. 324p. 1988. pap. 29.95 (*0-915745-07-0*) Floricanto Pr.

Medford, Roberta, jt. comp. see Loh, Eudora.

Medgyessy, Pal. Decomposition of Superpositions of Distribution Functions. LC 59-14874. 228p. reprint ed. pap. 65.00 (*0-685-15698-2*, 2026292) Bks Demand.

***Medhanie, Tesfatsion.** Eritrea & Neighbours. (Bremen African Studies). (C). 1995. pap. text ed. 22.95 (*3-8258-2193-5*) Westview.

Medhi, J. Recent Development in Bulk Queueing Models. (C). 1986. 18.00 (*0-85226-549-2*, Pub. by Wiley Eastern II) S Asia.

Medhi, Jyoti P. Statistics: Theory & Methods. 438p. 1993. text ed. 63.95 (*0-470-22085-6*) Halsted Pr.

— Stochastic Models in Queueing Theory. 444p. 1991. text ed. 79.95 (*0-12-487550-5*) Acad Pr.

— Stochastic Processes. 2nd ed. LC 92-36071. 598p. 1994. text ed. 44.95 (*0-470-22053-8*) Halsted Pr.

Medhurst, David. A Brief & Practical Guide to EC Law. 2nd ed. LC 93-46402. 256p. 1994. pap. write for info. (*0-632-03432-7*, Pub. by Blckwell Sci Pubns UK) Blackwell Sci.

Medhurst, Kenneth H. & Moyser, George H. Church & Politics in a Secular Age. (Illus.). 410p. 1988. 79.00 (*0-19-826454-2*) OUP.

Medhurst, Kenneth M. Government in Spain: The Executive at Work. (C). 1973. pap. 108.00 (*0-08-016940-6*, Pub. by Pergamon Repr UK) Franklin.

Medhurst, Kenneth N. The Church & Labour in Colombia. LC 82-62254. 320p. (C). 1988. text ed. 75.00 (*0-7190-0969-3*, Pub. by Manchester Univ Pr UK) St Martin.

Medhurst, Martin, ed. Landmark Essays on American Public Address. (Landmark Essays Ser.: Vol. 1). xliii, 227p. (C). 1993. pap. text ed. 15.95 (*1-880393-04-2*) Hermagoras Pr.

Medhurst, Martin J. Dwight D. Eisenhower: Strategic Communicator. LC 92-36608. (Great American Orators Ser.: No. 19). 280p. 1993. text ed. 59.95 (*0-313-26140-7*, MDW, Greenwood Pr) Greenwood.

— Eisenhower's War of Words: Rhetoric & Leadership. 1993. 39.95 (*0-87013-340-3*) Mich St U Pr.

Medhurst, Martin J., et al. Cold War Rhetoric: Strategy, Metaphor & Ideology. LC 89-25906. (Contributions to the Study of Mass Media & Communications Ser.: No. 19). 248p. 1990. text ed. 49.95 (*0-313-26766-9*, MCX/, Greenwood Pr) Greenwood.

Medhurst, Martin J., et al, eds. Communication & the Culture of Technology. LC 90-12257. xviii, 330p. 1990. pap. 30.00 (*0-87422-068-8*) Wash St U Pr.

Medhurst, W. H. China: Its State & Prospects with Special Reference to the Spread of the Gospel. LC 72-79833. (China Library Ser.). 1972. reprint ed. 42.00 (*0-8420-1379-2*) Scholarly Res Inc.

Media Inc. Staff. Media Incorporated Master List Northwest. 1992. pap. 9.95 (*0-940317-10-9*) Media Index Pub.

Media Institute Staff. Energy Coverage-Media Panic: An International Perspective. Smith, Nelson & Theberge, Leonard, eds. LC 82-14810. (Public Communication Ser.). (Illus.). 316p. 1983. 33.95 (*0-582-29018-X*) Longman.

— Using New Communications Technologies: A Guide for Organizations. LC 85-63320. 70p. (Orig.). 1986. pap. 12.95 (*0-937790-30-3*, 4250) Media Institute.

Media Institute Staff, ed. see Prato, Lou.

Media Institute Staff, ed. see Smith, Ted J., III.

Media International Promotions, Inc. Research Staff, comp. Japanese Electronics Companies & Their Foreign Allies, 1985-1989: The Source Book. 126p. 1990. 135.00 (*0-317-03784-6*) Media Intl Promo.

Media Referral Service Staff. The Film File 1982-83. 2nd ed. 314p. (Orig.). 1982. pap. 30.00 (*0-911125-01-9*) Media Ref.

— The Film File 1983-84. 3rd ed. 425p. 1983. pap. 35.00 (*0-911125-02-7*) Media Ref.

M

— The Film File 1984-85. 4th ed. 450p. (Orig.). 1984. pap. 39.95 (*0-911125-03-5*) Media Ref.

Media-Siegel Graphics, tr. see Richards, Denise.

***Media Terra Staff.** Explore the Grand Canyon. 1995. 49.99 (*1-883577-48-9*) Coriolis Grp.

***Mediansky, F., ed.** Strategic Cooperation & Competition in the Pacific Islands. 391p. (Orig.). 1995. pap. write for info. (*1-884296-02-5*) Austlia-NZ Studies.

Mediansky, Fedor & Palfreeman, Anthony C. In Pursuit of National Interests: Australian Foreign Policy in the 1990s. (Illus.). 320p. 1988. pap. text ed. 24.00 (*0-08-034428-3*, Pergamon Pr) Elsevier.

***Medic, Kris.** Pruning. LC 94-26692. (Rodale's Successful Organic Gardening Ser.). (Illus.). 1995. pap. text ed. 24. 95 (*0-87596-661-6*); pap. text ed. 14.95 (*0-87596-662-4*) Rodale Pr Inc.

Medical Association of Georgia Auxiliary Staff. Georgia Land: A Collection of Georgia Recipes, Historic Landmarks & Scenic Attractions. (Illus.). 288p. 1992. write for info. (*0-9632174-1-0*) Aux Med Assn GA.

Medical Care Costs Committee. Medical Care for the American People: Proceedings of the Committee on the Costs of Medical Care, October, 1932. LC 75-180569. (Medicine & Society in America Ser.). 242p. 1977. reprint ed. 19.95 (*0-405-03944-1*) Ayer.

Medical Cyclotron Users Conference Staff. Medical Cyclotrons in Nuclear Medicine: Proceedings of the Medical Cyclotron Users Conference, 4th, Miami, 1976. Roesler, H. et al, eds. (Progress in Nuclear Medicine Ser.: Vol. 4). 1977. 79.25 (*3-8055-2670-9*) S Karger.

Medical Economics Company Staff. Accounting & Record System for the Retail Pharmacy. 1977. pap. 49.95 (*0-87489-990-7*) Med Economics.

***Medical Economics Data Staff.** Physician's Desk Reference Generics: The New Information Standard for Prescription Drugs. 1995. pap. 69.95 (*1-56363-118-0*) Med Econ Data.

Medical Economics Inc., Staff. Physicians Desk Reference for Nonprescription Drugs. 1,989th ed. 1989. 28.95 (*0-87489-701-7*) Med Economics.

Medical Economics Staff. PDR Family Guide to Women's Health & Prescription Drugs. 1994. pap. 24.95 (*1-56363-086-9*) Med Econ Data.

— Physician's Desk Reference Supplement A & B. 1994. pap. 18.95 (*1-56363-076-1*) Med Econ Data.

— Physicians Desk Reference-1995. 49th ed. 1994. 61.95 (*1-56363-088-5*) Med Econ Data.

— Veterinary Pharmaceutical & Biologicals. 1995. 59.00 (*0-935078-46-0*) Veterinary Med.

Medical Education Board & Waintrub, Mauricio W. Preparation for the United States Medical Licensing Examinations, Step 1, Bklt. C. 76p. (C). Date not set. student ed 0.30 (*0-685-72383-6*); lib. bdg. 0.20 (*1-884083-04-8*); pap. 0.40 (*0-685-72381-X*); pap. text ed. 0.20 (*0-685-72382-8*) Maval USA.

— Preparation for the United States Medical Licensing Examinations, Step 1, Bklt. D. 60p. (C). Date not set. student ed 0.20 (*0-685-72386-0*); lib. bdg. 0.20 (*1-884083-06-4*); pap. 0.30 (*0-685-72384-4*); pap. text ed. 0.20 (*0-685-72385-2*) Maval USA.

— Preparation for the United States Medical Licensing Examinations, Step 1, Bklt. A. 76p. (C). Date not set. student ed 0.30 (*0-685-72377-1*); lib. bdg. 0.20 (*1-884083-01-3*); pap. 0.40 (*0-685-72375-5*); pap. text ed. 0.20 (*0-685-72376-3*) Maval USA.

— Preparation for the United States Medical Licensing Examinations, Step 1, Bklt. B. 76p. (C). Date not set. student ed 0.30 (*0-685-72380-1*); lib. bdg. 0.20 (*1-884083-02-1*); pap. 0.40 (*0-685-72378-X*); pap. text ed. 0.20 (*0-685-72379-8*) Maval USA.

— Preparation for the United States Medical Licensing Examinations, Step 1, Bklt. E. 60p. (C). Date not set. student ed 0.20 (*0-685-72389-5*); lib. bdg. 0.20 (*1-884083-07-2*); pap. 0.30 (*0-685-72387-9*); pap. text ed. 0.20 (*0-685-72388-7*) Maval USA.

— Preparation for the United States Medical Licensing Examinations, Step 2, Bklt. 1. 76p. (C). Date not set. student ed 0.30 (*0-685-72392-5*); lib. bdg. 0.20 (*1-884083-50-1*); pap. 0.40 (*0-685-72390-9*); pap. text ed. 0.20 (*0-685-72391-7*) Maval USA.

— Preparation for the United States Medical Licensing Examinations, Step 2, Bklt. 2. 76p. (C). Date not set. student ed 0.30 (*0-685-72395-X*); lib. bdg. 0.20 (*1-884083-52-8*); pap. 0.40 (*0-685-72393-3*); pap. text ed. 0.20 (*0-685-72394-1*) Maval USA.

— Preparation for the United States Medical Licensing Examinations, Step 2, Bklt. 3. 76p. (C). Date not set. student ed 0.30 (*0-685-72398-4*); lib. bdg. 0.20 (*1-884083-53-6*); pap. 0.40 (*0-685-72396-8*); pap. text ed. 0.20 (*0-685-72397-6*) Maval USA.

— Preparation for the United States Medical Licensing Examinations, Step 2, Bklt. 4. 60p. (C). Date not set. student ed 0.20 (*0-685-72401-8*); lib. bdg. 0.20 (*1-884083-54-4*); pap. 0.30 (*0-685-72399-2*); pap. text ed. 0.20 (*0-685-72400-X*) Maval USA.

— Preparation for the United States Medical Licensing Examinations, Step 2, Bklt. 5. 60p. (C). Date not set. student ed 0.20 (*0-685-72404-2*); lib. bdg. 0.20 (*1-884083-55-2*); pap. 0.30 (*0-685-72402-6*); pap. text ed. 0.20 (*0-685-72403-4*) Maval USA.

— Preparation for the United States Medical Licensing Examinations, Step 3, Bklt. B. 76p. (C). Date not set. student ed 0.30 (*0-685-72411-5*); lib. bdg. 0.20 (*0-685-72408-5*); pap. 0.40 (*0-685-72409-3*); pap. text ed. 0.20 (*0-685-72410-7*) Maval USA.

***Medical Index Division, contrib.** Coding Illustrated Bladder & Urethra. LC 94-19658. (Coding Illustrated Ser.). (Illus.). (Orig.). 1994. 39.95 (*1-56337-110-3*) Medicode Pubns.

Medical Information Technology & Training Limited Staff, ed. Information Technology & Health Care. 1988. text ed. 45.00 (*0-566-05190-7*, Pub. by Gower UK) Ashgate Pub Co.

Medical Library Association Staff. Directory of the Medical Library Association, 1989-90. 151p. 1989. pap. 43.75 (*0-912176-27-X*) Med Lib Assn.

— Directory of the Medical Library Association, 1990-91. 168p. 1990. pap. 43.75 (*0-912176-31-8*) Med Lib Assn.

— Directory of the Medical Library Association, 1991-92. 175p. 1991. pap. 95.00 (*0-912176-32-6*) Med Lib Assn.

— Directory of the Medical Library Association, 1993-94. 200p. 1993. pap. 150.00 (*0-912176-35-0*) Med Lib Assn.

— Directory of the Medical Library Association 1993-94. (ISSN: 0543-2772). 196p. 1993. pap. 150.00 (*0-614-01349-6*) Med Lib Assn.

— Directory of the Medical Library Association 1994-95. (ISSN: 0543-2772 (Annual)). 221p. 1994. pap. 150.00 (*0-614-01350-X*) Med Lib Assn.

— Salary Survey, 1992. 39p. 1992. pap. 52.00 (*0-912176-33-4*) Med Lib Assn.

Medical Management Institute Staff. Negotiating Managed Care Contracts. 200p. 1994. pap. 39.95 (*0-07-600705-7*) Hlthcare Mgmt Grp.

Medical Publishers Ltd. Staff. HCPCS Level Two Code Book. 100p. 1993. pap. text ed. 49.00 (*1-881072-07-X*) Y W Omd Med.

— National Dental Advisory Service: Comprehensive Fee Report. 11th ed. 75p. 1993. pap. text ed. 49.00 (*1-881072-06-1*) Y W Omd Med.

— Physicians' Fee Reference. 10th ed. 200p. 1993. pap. text ed. 129.00 (*1-881072-02-9*) Y W Omd Med.

— Physicians' Form Letter Reference. 120p. 1993. pap. text ed. 69.00 (*1-881072-05-3*) Y W Omd Med.

— Physicians' Insurance Reference, 1993. 4th ed. 211p. 1992. pap. text ed. 69.00 (*1-881072-03-7*); spiral bd. 69. 00 (*1-881072-04-5*) Y W Omd Med.

— Physicians' Lab Reference, 1992-1993. 220p. pap. text ed. 59.00 (*1-881072-00-2*); spiral bd. 59.00 (*1-881072-01-0*) Y W Omd Med.

***Medical Records Briefing Staff.** Health Information Management: Challenges & Solutions. 241p. 1994. pap. text ed. 62.00 (*1-885829-10-8*) Opus Communs.

***Medical Support Systems Staff, ed.** Complications of Laparoscopy & Flexible Endoscopy: Postgraduate Course of the Annual Meeting of the Society of American Gastrointenstinal Endoscopic Surgeons (SAGES) 1994. 1994. 125.00 (*0-387-14219-3*) Spr-Verlag.

Medical Tribune, Inc. Staff. Medicine: The Year in Review, 1992. 320p. 1992. 49.95 (*0-931861-81-0*) Med Tribune.

Medical View Staff. Stedman's English-Japanese-English Medical Dictionary. 2nd ed. 1973p. 1984. 250.00 (*0-8288-1850-9*) Fr & Eur.

Medici, Angelo, ed. see Warren, Bert.

***Medici, Constantine.** Win at Jai-Alai. 64p. 1995. pap. 5.95 (*0-9646951-0-3*) CCM Prods.

Medici, Geraldine A. Drug Dosage Calculation. 2nd ed. 373p. 1988. pap. text ed. 26.95 (*0-8385-1775-7*, A1775-4) Appleton & Lange.

Medici, Marina. Love Magic. LC 93-3847. 1994. 16.00 (*0-671-79684-4*, Fireside) S&S Trade.

Medici, Mario, jt. ed. see Conati, Marcello.

Medicine, Beatrice, jt. auth. see Albers, Patricia.

Medicine Crow, Joseph. From the Heart of the Crow Country: The Crow Indians' Own Stories. LC 94-9656. (Library of the American Indian). 1994. pap. 9.00 (*0-517-88220-5*) Crown Pub Group.

Medicine Eagle, Brooke. Buffalo Woman Comes Singing: The Spirit Song of a Rainbow Medicine Woman. 480p. (Orig.). 1991. pap. 12.50 (*0-345-36143-1*, Ballantine Trade) Ballantine.

Medicine Grizzlybear Lake. Native Healer. 1993. pap. 5.50 (*0-685-66342-6*, Harp PBks) HarpC.

— Native Healer: Initiation into an Ancient Art. 1991. pap. 10.95 (*0-8356-0667-8*, Quest) Theos Pub Hse.

Medicine Hawk & Grey Cat. American Indian Ceremonies: A Practical Workbook & Study Guide to the Medicine Path. (Illus.). 144p. 1992. reprint ed. 12.95 (*0-938294-72-5*) Glob Comm-Inner Lght.

Medicine, Story. Children of the Morning Light: Wampanoag Tales As Told by Manitonquat. LC 92-32328. (Illus.). 72p. (J). (gr. 1 up). 1994. text ed. 16.95 (*0-02-765905-4*, Mac Bks Young Read) S&S Childrens.

Medicine Story, pseud. Return to Creation: A Survival Manual for Native & Natural People. (Illus.). 210p. 1991. pap. 9.95 (*0-943404-20-7*) Bear Tribe.

Medick, Hans & Sabean, David W., eds. Interest & Emotion: Essays on the Study of Family & Kinship. 428p. 1988. pap. 29.95 (*0-521-35763-2*) Cambridge U Pr.

***Medicode, Med-Index Division Staff.** Coding Illustrated Lower Face: Skeletal Structures & Dentition. 3rd ed. LC 95-1220. (Coding Illustrated Ser.). (Illus.). 198p. 1995. 39.95 (*1-56337-153-7*) Medicode Pubns.

— Coding Illustrated Midface: Maxillary Soft Tissue. 2nd ed. LC 95-1221. (Coding Illustrated Ser.). (Illus.). 232p. 1995. 39.95 (*1-56337-154-5*) Medicode Pubns.

***Medicode Staff.** Coding Illustrated the Kidney. 2nd ed. LC 95-1219. (Coding Illustrated Ser.). (Illus.). 200p. 1995. 39.95 (*1-56337-152-9*) Medicode Pubns.

Medicus, F. Johann Gottlieb Fichte: Thirteen Vorlesungen, Gehalten An der Universitat Halle. 240p. reprint ed. write for info. (*0-318-71928-2*, Pub. by Georg Olms GW) Lubrecht & Cramer.

Medicus, Heinrich A, jt. auth. see Bitter, Francis.

Medicus Staff & Hubbard, L. Ron. All about Radiation. 1989. 20.00 (*0-88404-446-7*) Bridge Pubns Inc.

Medieros, Wendy A. Marbling Techniques: How to Create Traditional & Contemporary Designs on Paper & Fabric. LC 94-19095. (Illus.). 144p. 1994. pap. 24.95 (*0-8230-3005-9*) Watsn-Guptill.

Medieval Hebrew Masters Staff. Hiddushe Haramah We-Shitot Kadmonim Al Massekheth Gittin, 2 vols., Set. 779p. (HEB.). (C). 1989. 32.00 (*1-881255-02-6*) OFEQ Inst.

— Hiddushe Haramah We-Shitot Kadmonim Al Massekheth Gittin, Vol. I. 347p. (HEB.). (C). 1989. 16.00 (*1-881255-00-X*) OFEQ Inst.

— Hiddushe Haramah We-Shitot Kadmonim Al Massekheth Gittin, Vol. II. 432p. (HEB.). (C). 1989. 16.00 (*1-881255-01-8*) OFEQ Inst.

— Sifra on Leviticus: Vayiqra Dibura DeHobah, Vol. 3. 550p. (HEB.). (C). 1992. 24.00 (*1-881255-10-7*) OFEQ Inst.

— Sifra on Leviticus, Vol. I: Baraita de-R. Ishmael (The 13 Hermeneutic Rules of R. Ishmael) LC 91-60934. 142p. (HEB.). (C). 1991. 14.00 (*1-881255-09-3*) OFEQ Inst.

***Medill, Robert.** Klondike Diary. (American Autobiography Ser.). 188p. 1995. reprint ed. lib. bdg. 69.00 (*0-7812-8589-5*) Rprt Serv.

Medin, Doug, ed. The Psychology of Learning & Motivation, Vol. 28: Advances in Research & Theory. (Illus.). 296p. 1992. text ed. 65.00 (*0-12-543328-X*) Acad Pr.

Medin, Douglas L., ed. The Psychology of Learning & Motivation, Vol. 31. (Illus.). 366p. 1994. text ed. 79.95 (*0-12-543331-X*) Acad Pr.

— Psychology of Learning & Motivation, Vol. 33. (Illus.). 334p. 1995. text ed. write for info. (*0-12-543333-6*) Acad Pr.

Medin, Douglas L. & Ross, Brian H. Cognitive Psychology. 450p. (C). 1992. text ed. 46.75 (*0-15-507872-0*) HB Coll Pubs.

Medin, Douglas L., jt. auth. see Smith, Edward E.

Medin, Douglas L., et al. Processes of Animal Memory. LC 76-22197. 267p. 1976. 18.50 (*0-470-15189-7*, Wiley) Krieger.

Medin, Tzvi. Cuba: The Shaping of Revolutionary Consciousness. LC 89-39433. 192p. 1990. lib. bdg. 37.00 (*1-55587-187-9*) Lynne Rienner.

Medina. Neck Dissection: An Atlas of Surgical Technique. (Illus.). 256p. 1993. 135.00 (*0-8016-3340-0*) Mosby Yr Bk.

Medina, Amelia C. A Comparative Analysis of Evaluation Theory & Practice for the Instructional Component of Bilingual Programs. Cordasco, Francesco, ed. LC 77-90549. (Bilingual-Bicultural Education in the U. S. Ser.). 1978. lib. bdg. 33.95 (*0-405-11089-8*) Ayer.

Medina, Angel. Diccionario de Musica Sevilla 1818. 107p. 1991. write for info. (*0-7859-6225-5*, 8474682924) Fr & Eur.

Medina, Augusto G., jt. ed. see Singh, R. Paul.

Medina, Barbara F. Structured System Analysis: A New Technique. 96p. 1981. text ed. 99.00 (*0-677-05570-6*) Gordon & Breach.

Medina, Belen T. The Filipino Family: A Text with Selected Readings. 292p. (C). 1992. text ed. 22.00 (*971-10-5060-9*, Pub. by U of Philippines Pr) UH Pr.

Medina, Cecila. The Legal Status of Indians in Brazil. 10.00 (*0-944253-64-4*) Inst Dev Indian Law.

Medina, Cecilia. The Legal Status of Indians in Bolivia. 10. 00 (*0-944253-63-6*) Inst Dev Indian Law.

— The Legal Status of Indians in Chile. 10.00 (*0-944253-65-2*) Inst Dev Indian Law.

— The Legal Status of Indians in Columbia. 10.00 (*0-944253-66-0*) Inst Dev Indian Law.

— The Legal Status of Indians in Guatemala. 15.00 (*0-944253-67-9*) Inst Dev Indian Law.

— The Legal Status of Indians in Paraguay. 10.00 (*0-944253-68-7*) Inst Dev Indian Law.

Medina County Historical Society Staff, ed. History of Medina County, Ohio. 419p. 1993. reprint ed. lib. bdg. 43.50 (*0-8328-2833-5*) Higginson Bk Co.

Medina, D., et al, eds. Cellular & Molecular Biology of Mammary Cancer. LC 87-25756. (Illus.). 528p. 1988. 125.00 (*0-306-42761-3*, Plenum Pr) Plenum.

Medina, David. Elohim's Nursery. 158p. 1984. 30.00 (*0-7212-0626-3*, Pub. by Regency Press) St Mut.

Medina, Dennis, ed. We Like Ike: The Eisenhower Presidency & 1950s America. LC 90-70503. (Illus.). 114p. (Orig.). 1990. pap. 5.00 (*0-939324-42-3*) Wichita Art Mus.

***Medina, Elsie.** Through Rose-Colored Glasses. 240p. (Orig.). 1995. pap. 8.95 (*0-7610-0118-2*) NW Pub.

Medina, Enrique. Las Tumbas: The Tombs. LC 92-23401. (Library of World Literature in Translation: Vol. 4). 334p. 1992. 61.00 (*0-8240-7436-X*) Garland.

***Medina, Francis X. & Marra, Dorothy B.** Ciao, Francesco. 224p. 1995. 17.50 (*0-9645371-0-9*) F X Medina.

Medina-Gaud, Silverio, jt. auth. see Maldonado-Capriles, Jenaro.

Medina, Harold R. Corrected Opinion of Harold R. Medina, United States Circuit Judge in United States of America, Plaintiff, v. Henry S. Morgan, Harold Stanley et al... LC 75-2647. (Wall Street & the Security Market Ser.). 1975. reprint ed. 35.95 (*0-405-06972-3*) Ayer.

Medina, Hector & Porter, Phoebe A. Exploraciones Imaginativas: Quince Cuentos Hispanoamericanos. 230p. (ENG & SPA.). (C). 1989. pap. text ed. write for info. (*0-13-033762-5*) P-H.

Medina, Jeremy T. Introduction to Spanish Literature. LC 81-8293. 360p. 1982. reprint ed. 34.50 (*0-89874-365-6*) Krieger.

Medina, Jorge, jt. ed. see Izquierdo, Ivan.

Medina, Jose T., ed. The Discovery of the Amazon. 2nd ed. (Illus.). 480p. 1988. reprint ed. pap. 9.95 (*0-486-25589-1*) Dover.

Medina, Joyce. Cezanne & Modernism: The Poetics of Painting. (SUNY Series, The Margins of Literature). (Illus.). 320p. (C). 1995. text ed. 59.50 (*0-7914-2231-3*); pap. 19.95 (*0-7914-2232-1*) State U NY Pr.

Medina, Manuel, ed. see IFIP TC6-WG6.5 International Working Conference Staff.

Medina, Pablo. Arching into the Afterlife. LC 90-24943. 96p. 1991. pap. 9.00 (*0-927534-12-6*) Biling Rev-Pr.

— Exiled Memories: A Cuban Childhood. (Illus.). 139p. 1990. text ed. 14.95 (*0-292-77636-5*) U of Tex Pr.

— The Marks of Birth. LC 93-33609. 1994. 22.00 (*0-374-20296-6*) FS&G.

Medina, Pablo K., jt. auth. see Daners, Daniel.

Medina, Pat. Paralegal Discovery: Procedures & Forms. 2nd ed. 1994. text ed. 98.00 (*0-471-31076-X*) Wiley.

Medina, Pol, Jr. The Best of Pugad Baboy. (Tagalog Ser.). (Illus.). 78p. (Orig.). 1991. pap. 6.25 (*971-10-0440-2*, Pub. by New Day Pub PH) Cellar.

— Pugad Baboy Three. (Illus.). 80p. (Orig.). (TAG.). 1992. pap. text ed. 7.50 (*971-10-0518-2*, Pub. by New Day Pub PH) Cellar.

Medina-Quiroga, Cecilia. The Battle of Human Rights. (C). 1988. lib. bdg. 122.00 (*90-247-3687-0*) Kluwer Ac.

Medina, Robert C., ed. see Maze, Carol M.

Medina, Roberto. Fabian No Se Muere. LC 78-7307. (Orig.). (SPA.). 1978. pap. text ed. 4.95 (*0-933196-01-6*) Bilingue Pubns.

Medina, Ruben. Amor de Lejos: Fool's Love. Sternbach, Jennifer & Jones, Robert, trs. 128p. (Orig.). (ENG & SPA.). 1986. pap. 7.00 (*0-934770-67-0*) Arte Publico.

Medina, Vincente. Social Contract Theories. 150p. (C). 1990. lib. bdg. 43.50 (*0-8476-7624-2*) Rowman.

Medina, William A. Changing Bureaucracies. (Public Administration & Public Policy Ser.: Vol. 11). (Illus.). 160p. 1982. 65.00 (*0-8247-1672-8*) Dekker.

Medine, Allen & Anderson, Michael, eds. Environmental Engineering. LC 83-71587. 989p. 1983. pap. 82.00 (*0-87262-369-6*) Am Soc Civil Eng.

Medine, Peter E. Thomas Wilson. (Twayne's English Authors Ser.: No. 431). 216p. 1986. text ed. 25.95 (*0-8057-6929-3*, Pub. by Royal Botanic Garden UK) Macmillan.

Medinger, Ann, jt. ed. see Spagnolo, Samuel V.

Medinnis, Bernice & Parker, Robert. Developing Children's Reflective & Critical Thinking Abilities: A Video Based Inservice Training for the Elementary Classroom Teacher. (How to Ser.). 150p. (C). 1994. teacher ed, vhs 1,390.00 (*1-885178-03-4*) Superior Lrning.

— Developing Children's Reflective & Critical Thinking Abilities Vol. 1: A Video Based Inservice Training Program & Interactive Training Manual for the Elementary Classroom Teacher, 2 Vol. Set. (How to Ser.). 150p. 1994. teacher ed, vdisk 1,390.00 (*1-885178-06-9*) Superior Lrning.

— Developing Children's Reflective & Critical Thinking Abilities Vol. 2: A Video Based Inservice Training Program & Interactive Training Manual for the Elementary Classroom Teacher, 2 Vol. Set. (How to Ser.). 150p. 1994. teacher ed, vdisk 1,390.00 (*1-885178-07-7*) Superior Lrning.

Medinnus, Gene R., ed. Readings in the Psychology of Parent-Child Relations. LC 67-12565. 384p. reprint ed. 109.50 (*0-8357-9973-5*, 2055146) Bks Demand.

Medinnus, Gene R., jt. auth. see Johnson, Ronald C.

***Medio, Alfredo.** Chaotic Dynamics: Theory & Applications to Economics. (Illus.). 362p. (C). 1995. pap. 19.95 (*0-521-48461-8*) Cambridge U Pr.

Medio, Alfredo & Gallo, Giampaolo. Chaotic Dynamics: Theory & Applications to Economics. (Illus.). 250p. (C). 1993. 64.95 (*0-521-39488-0*) Cambridge U Pr.

— Chaotic Dynamics: Theory & Applications to Economics. (Illus.). 250p. (C). 1993. pap. 49.95 (*0-521-42107-1*) Cambridge U Pr.

Medish, Vadim. The Soviet Union. 4th rev. ed. 432p. (C). 1990. pap. text ed. write for info. (*0-13-818196-9*) P-H.

Mediterraneo Staff. Basic Illustrated Spanish-English Dictionary: Diccionario Basico Ilustrado Espanol-Ingles, 4 vols., Set. 1200p. (ENG & SPA.). 1982. 395.00 (*0-8288-2321-9*, S2567) Fr & Eur.

Mediterreneo Staff. Diccionario Basico Illustrado Espanol - Ingles - Gallego, 4 vols. 1200p. (ENG & SPA.). 1982. 395.00 (*0-7859-3445-6*) Fr & Eur.

— Diccionario Basico Ilustrado Espanol-Ingles-Euskera, 4 vols., Set. 1200p. (BAS, ENG & SPA.). 1982. 395.00 (*0-7859-3370-0*, M29970) Fr & Eur.

Medizinische Hochschule Meeting Staff. Transplacental Carcinogenesis: Proceedings of the Medizinische Hochschule Meeting, Hannover, Federal Republic of Germany, October 6-7, 1971. Tomatis, L. et al, eds. (IARC Scientific Pub.: No. 4). 1973. 16.00 (*0-686-16794-5*) World Health.

Medjati, Z. M. & Trice, J. E. English & Continental Systems of Adminstrative Law. 1978. pap. 59.00 (*0-444-85198-4*) Elsevier.

Medland, A. J. Computer-Based Design Process. 2nd ed. 224p. 1992. 49.95 (*0-442-31515-5*) Chapman & Hall.

***Medland, Mary.** Plays. Friedland, J. & Kessler, R., eds. (Novel-Ties Ser.). (YA). (gr. 6-10). 1990. student ed, pap. text ed. 15.95 (*0-88122-863-X*) Lrn Links.

— The Red Badge of Courage: A Study Guide. (Novel-Ties Ser.). (YA). (gr. 9-12). 1990. pap. text ed. 15.95 (*0-88122-414-6*) Lrn Links.

— Where the Lilies Bloom: A Study Guide. Friedland, Joyce & Kessler, Rikki, eds. (Novel-Ties Ser.). 30p. (YA). (gr. 9-12). 1990. pap. text ed. 15.95 (*0-88122-399-9*) Lrn Links.

Medland, Michael B. Happier Families: Raising Responsible, Self-Managed Children. 185p. (Orig.). 1992. pap. 11.95 (*0-9633009-6-2*) Barcroft Pub.

An Asterisk (*) at the beginning of an entry indicates that the title is appearing in BIP for the first time.

— Self-Management Strategies: Theory, Curriculum & Teaching Procedures. LC 90-31211. 320p. 1990. text ed. 65.00 (0-275-93519-1, C3519, Praeger Pubs) Greenwood.

Medland, William J. The Cuban Missile Crisis of Nineteen Sixty-Two: Needless or Necessary? LC 87-36025. 175p. 1988. text ed. 49.95 (0-275-92844-6, C2844, Praeger Pubs) Greenwood.

Medler, John T. Insects of Nigeria. (Memoir Ser.: No. 30). 919p. 1980. 75.00 (1-56665-028-3) Assoc Pubs FL.

Medley. A Proposito! 1992. pap. 12.95 (0-8384-2399-X) Heinle & Heinle.

— Sin Duda. 1992. pap. 9.95 (0-8384-2378-7) Heinle & Heinle.

Medley, Donald B. Computer Operations. 1988. pap. text ed. write for info. (0-07-555390-2) McGraw.

Medley, G., jt. ed. see Isham, V.

Medley, H. Anthony. Sweaty Palms: The Neglected Art of Being Interviewed. rev. ed. (Illus.). 194p. 1992. reprint ed. pap. 8.95 (0-89815-403-0) Ten Speed Pr.

Medley, J. Country Boys, City Boys. 448p. (Orig.). 1994. pap. 12.95 (1-877978-51-5) Woldt.

Medley, James. Huck & Billy. (Orig.). 1994. pap. text ed. 4.95 (1-56333-245-0) Masquerade.

Medley, M. W., jt. auth. see Allen, James L.

Medley, Max W., Jr. Microwave & RF Circuits: Analysis, Synthesis & Design. (Microwave Ser.). 480p. 1992. text ed. 88.00 (0-89006-546-2) Artech Hse.

Medley, Steven P. The Complete Guidebook to Yosemite National Park. (Illus.). 112p. 1991. 10.95 (0-939666-55-3) Yosemite Assn.

— The Complete Guidebook to Yosemite National Park. rev. ed. LC 94-10712. (Illus.). 112p. 1994. 9.95 (0-939666-74-X) Yosemite Assn.

— Map & Guide to Tuolumne Meadows. 1994. pap. 2.50 (0-939666-72-3) Yosemite Assn.

— Map & Guide to Wawona & Mariposa Grove. Reineck & Reineck Staff, tr. (Illus.). 1991. 2.50 (0-939666-29-4) Yosemite Assn.

— Der Vollstaendige Fuehrer des Yosemite National Parkes - Complete Guidebook to Yosemite National Park. (Illus.). 112p. (GER.). 1993. pap. 10.95 (0-939666-64-2) Yosemite Assn.

Medley, Steven P., jt. ed. see Bates, Craig D.

Medley, Steven P., ed. see Bunnell, Lafayette H.

Medley, Steven P., ed. see Ross, Michael E.

Medley, Tom. Hot Rod History Bk. 2, Bk. 2. (Illus.). 200p. 1994. pap. 19.95 (1-884089-08-9) CarTech.

— Hot Rod History, Bk. 1: The Beginnings. (Illus.). 202p. 1994. pap. 19.95 (1-884089-05-4) CarTech.

Medley, Wes. Original Arizona Cookin' Mohanna, Tim, ed. (Illus.). 1992. pap. write for info. (0-9633651-1-8) Orig Western.

— Original Cowboy Cookbook. (Illus.). 106p. pap. text ed. 12.95 (0-9633651-0-X) Orig Western.

Medlicott, Mary, ed. Tales for Children: From Around the World. LC 92-53095. (Illus.). 96p. (J). (gr. k-5). 1992. 16.95 (1-85697-824-9, Kingfisher LKC) LKC.

***Medlicott, Mary & Akintola, Ademola, comps.** The River That Went to the Sky. LC 94-44607. (J). 1995. 16.95 (1-85697-608-4, Kingfisher LKC) LKC.

Medlicott, William N. Congress of Berlin & After. 442p. 1963. 34.00 (0-7146-1501-3, Pub. by F Cass Pubs UK) Intl Spec Bk.

***Medlik.** Managing Tourism. 358p. 1995. pap. 32.95 (0-7506-2355-1, Focal) Buttrwrth-Heinemann.

Medlik, S. The Business of Hotels. 2nd ed. 200p. 1989. pap. 25.95 (0-434-91294-8) Buttrwrth-Heinemann.

— The Business of Hotels. 3rd ed. 206p. 1995. pap. 24.95 (0-7506-2080-3, Focal) Buttrwrth-Heinemann.

— Dictionary of Travel, Tourism & Hospitality. 240p. 1993. pap. 21.95 (0-7506-0953-2) Buttrwrth-Heinemann.

Medlik, S., ed. Managing Tourism. 344p. 1991. text ed. 59.95 (0-7506-0033-0) Buttrwrth-Heinemann.

Medlik, S., jt. auth. see Burkart, A. J.

Medlin, D. M. The Verbal Art of Jean Francois Regnard, Vol. 1. 156p. 1966. pap. 7.00 (0-912788-00-3) Tulane Romance Lang.

Medlin, Dorothy, jt. ed. see Merrick, Jeffrey W.

Medlin, Eugene & Doane, Colin. The French Modele Nineteen Thirty-Five Pistols: Thirty Twos with a French Accent. LC 90-82574. (Illus.). 288p. 1990. 40.00 (0-9627605-0-1) BFH.

Medlin, Eugene & Huon, Jean. Military Handguns of France, 1858-1958. (Illus.). 180p. 1993. pap. 24.95 (1-880677-02-4) Excalibur NY.

Medlin, V. D, ed. The Russian Revolution. LC 79-4332. (European Problem Studies). 218p. 1979. reprint ed. pap. 11.50 (0-88275-937-X) Krieger.

Medlin, Virgil D., ed. see Nabokov, Vladimir D.

Medlin, William K. Moscow & East Rome: A Political Study of the Relation of Church & State in Muscovite Russia. LC 79-2913. 252p. 1992. reprint ed. 26.00 (0-8305-0082-0) Hyperion Conn.

Medlock, Dudley. Hospital Business Office Policies & Procedures. 153p. 1990. boxed 60.00 (0-8403-5658-7) Hlthcare Fin Mgmt.

Medlock, Scott, illus. Extra Innings: Baseball Poems. LC 92-13013. (YA). (gr. 4 up). 1993. 14.95 (0-15-226833-2) HarBrace.

— Opening Days: Sports Poems. LC 94-43364. (J). 1996. write for info. (0-15-200270-7) HarBrace.

Medlycott, J., jt. auth. see Gibson, J.

Medlycott, Mervyn, jt. auth. see Gibson, J. S.

Mednick, Birgitte R., jt. auth. see Baker, Robert L.

***Mednick, Murray.** The Coyote Cycle: Seven Plays by Murray Mednick. (Illus.). 175p. (Orig.). 1993. pap. 15.95 (0-9630126-1-4) Padua Hills Play.

Mednick, Murray & Barsha, Tony. The Hawk: An Improvisational Play. LC 68-29295. (Illus.). 113p. 1968. 12.95 (0-910278-37-7) Boulevard.

***Mednick, Murray, et al, eds.** Best of the West: An Anthology of Plays from the 1989 & 1990 Padua Hills Playwrights Festivals. 2nd ed. 320p. (Orig.). 1994. pap. 14.95 (0-9630126-2-2) Padua Hills Play.

***Mednick, Sarnoff A. & Hollister, J. Meggin, eds.** Neural Development & Schizophrenia Theory & Research: Proceedings of a NATO ASI Held in Castelvecchio Pascoli, Italy, September 22-October 1, 1993. LC 95-3584. (NATO ASI Series A: Vol. 275). 250p. (C). 1995. 79.50 (0-306-44996-X, Plenum Pr) Plenum.

Mednick, Sarnoff A., jt. ed. see Goodwin, Donald W.

Mednick, Sarnoff A., jt. ed. see Moffitt, Terrie E.

Mednick, Sarnoff A., jt. auth. see Van Dusen, Katherine Teilmann.

Mednick, Sarnoff A., et al. Psychology: Explorations in Behavior & Experience. LC 74-22239. 606p. reprint ed. pap. 172.80 (0-7837-3457-3, 2057783) Bks Demand.

Mednick, Sarnoff A., et al, eds. Developmental Neuropathology of Schizophrenia. (NATO ASI Series A, Life Sciences: Vol. 217). (Illus.). 210p. 1992. 79.50 (0-306-44081-4, Plenum Pr) Plenum.

— Fetal Neural Development & Adult Schizophrenia. (Illus.). 240p. (C). 1992. 94.95 (0-521-39158-X) Cambridge U Pr.

— Handbook of Longitudinal Research, 2 Vols., Vol. 1: Birth & Childhood Cohorts. LC 83-24723. 740p. 1981. Vol. 1, Birth & Childhood Cohorts, 740 pp. text ed. 125.00 (0-275-90681-7, C06811, Praeger Pubs) Greenwood.

— Handbook of Longitudinal Research Vol. 2: Teenage & Adult Cohorts, 2 Vols., Vol. 2. LC 83-24723. 608p. 1984. text ed. 105.00 (0-275-91228-0, C12282, Praeger Pubs) Greenwood.

Mednikova, E. English-Russian Dictionary of Verbal Collocations. 636p. (C). 1986. 100.00 (0-685-54118-5, Pub. by Collets); 110.00 (0-685-39372-0, Pub. by Collets) St Mut.

— English-Russian Dictionary of Verbal Collocations. 668p. (C). 1990. 75.00 (0-89771-825-9, Pub. by Collets) St Mut.

Mednikova, E., jt. ed. see Gal'perin, L.

***Mednis.** How to Defeat a Superior Opponent. 1995. pap. text ed. 14.95 (0-945806-01-9) Summit CA.

Mednis, Edmar. From the Middlegame into the Endgame. (Chess Ser.). (Illus.). 185p. 1987. 29.95 (0-08-032037-6, Pergamon Pr); pap. 19.90 (0-08-032038-4, Pergamon Pr) Elsevier.

— From the Opening into the Endgame. (Chess Ser.). (Illus.). 176p. 1983. 25.90 (0-08-026917-6, Pergamon Pr); pap. 15.90 (0-08-026916-8, Pergamon Pr) Elsevier.

— Gewinne das Endspiel! (Praxis Schach Ser.: Bd. 7). 240p. (GER.). 1992. write for info. (3-283-00251-7, Pub. by Georg Olms GW) Lubrecht & Cramer.

— How Karpov Wins. 2nd enl. rev. ed. (Illus.). 400p. 1994. reprint ed. pap. text ed. 9.95 (0-486-27881-6) Dover.

— How to Be a Complete Tournament Player. (Chess Library). 160p. 1991. pap. 15.95 (0-08-037795-5, Pub. by CHES UK) Macmillan.

— How to Defeat a Superior Opponent. Darin, Dodd M., ed. (Illus.). 336p. (Orig.). 1989. pap. 16.95 (0-945806-00-0) Summit CA.

— How to Play Good Opening Moves. 1984. pap. 6.95 (0-679-14109-X) McKay.

— King Power in Chess. 1980. pap. 7.95 (0-679-14107-3) McKay.

— Practical Bishop Endings. 134p. (Orig.). 1990. pap. 7.95 (0-945470-04-5) Chess Ent Inc.

— Practical Endgame Lessons. pap. 7.95 (0-679-14102-2) McKay.

— Practical Knight Endings. 188p. (Orig.). 1993. pap. 12.95 (0-945470-35-5) Chess Ent Inc.

— Practical Rook Endings. (Illus.). 71p. (Orig.). 1982. pap. 5.50 (0-931462-16-9) Chess Ent Inc.

— Questions & Answers on Practical Endgame Play. 135p. (Orig.). 1987. pap. 7.95 (0-931462-69-X) Chess Ent Inc.

— Spiele Gute Eroffnungszuge! (Praxis Schach Ser.: Bd. 6). 120p. (GER.). 1992. write for info. (3-283-00250-9, Pub. by Georg Olms GW) Lubrecht & Cramer.

— Strategic Chess: Mastering the Closed Game. 1993. pap. 14.95 (0-945806-11-6) Summit CA.

— Strategic Themes in Endgames. 124p. (Orig.). 1990. pap. 7.95 (0-931462-94-0) Chess Ent Inc.

Mednis, Edmar & Crouch, Colin. Rate Your Endgame. (Chess Library). 200p. 1991. pap. 19.95 (0-08-037803-X, Pub. by CHES UK) Macmillan.

Medoff, Francine. The Mouse in the Matzah Factory. LC 82-23349. (Illus.). 40p. (J). (ps-3). 1983. pap. 4.95 (0-930494-19-9) Kar Ben.

Medoff, Jack. Puntoons. LC 92-53810. (Illus.). 96p. (Orig.). 1992. pap. 4.95 (1-56138-179-9) Running Pr.

Medoff, Mark. Big Mary. 1989. pap. 4.75 (0-8222-0117-8) Dramatists Play.

— Children of a Lesser God. 1980. pap. 4.75 (0-8222-0203-4) Dramatists Play.

— Dreams of Long Lasting. 560p. 1993. mass mkt. 5.99 (0-446-36460-6) Warner Bks.

— Four Short Plays by Mark Medoff. 1974. pap. 4.75 (0-8222-0744-3) Dramatists Play.

— The Hands of Its Enemy. 1987. pap. 4.75 (0-8222-0494-0) Dramatists Play.

— The Heart Outright. 1990. pap. 4.75 (0-8222-0506-8) Dramatists Play.

— The Homage That Follows. Date not set. 4.75 (0-8222-1469-5) Dramatists Play.

— The Kramer. 1976. pap. 4.75 (0-8222-0620-X) Dramatists Play.

— Kringle's Window. 1994. 4.75 (0-8222-1356-7) Dramatists Play.

— The Majestic Kid. 1986. pap. 4.75 (0-8222-0717-6) Dramatists Play.

— Stefanie Hero. 1994. 4.75 (0-8222-1370-2) Dramatists Play.

— Stumps, Acting Ed. Date not set. 4.75 (0-614-03319-5) Dramatists Play.

— The Wager. 1975. pap. 4.75 (0-8222-1214-5) Dramatists Play.

— When You Comin' Back, Red Ryder? 1974. pap. 4.75 (0-8222-1240-4) Dramatists Play.

Medoff, Mark & Johnson, Carleene. The Odyssey of Jeremy Jack. 1973. pap. 4.75 (0-8222-0835-0) Dramatists Play.

Medoff, Norman J. & Tanguary, Tom. Portable Video: ENG & EFP. 2nd ed. (Illus.). 230p. 1992. 45.00 (0-86729-294-6); student ed, pap. 29.95 (0-86729-320-9) Knowledge Indus.

Medoff, Norman J. & Tanquary, Tom. Portable Video: ENG & EFP. (Professional Librarian Ser.). (Illus.). 191p. (C). 1988. text ed. 45.00 (0-86729-147-8, Hall Reference); student ed, pap. 27.95 (0-86729-148-6, Hall Reference) Macmillan.

Medoff, Peter & Sklar, Holly. Streets of Hope: The Fall & Rise of an Urban Neighborhood. 320p. (Orig.). (C). 1994. lib. bdg. 40.00 (0-89608-483-3); pap. 16.00 (0-89608-482-5) South End Pr.

Medoff, Rafael. The Deafening Silence: American Jewish Leaders & the Holocaust, 1933-1945. 328p. 1987. 18.95 (0-933503-63-6) Sure Sellers.

***Medova, Marie-Laure.** Ballet for Beginners. LC 95-9224. (Illus.). 112p. 1995. 19.95 (0-8069-3876-5) Sterling.

Medovar, B. I., et al. Welding & Surfacing Reviews: Special Electrometallurgy (a Review) Paton, B. E., ed. (Soviet Technology Reviews Ser.: Vol. 1, Pt. 5). iv, 68p. 1989. pap. text ed. 46.00 (3-7186-4976-4) Gordon & Breach.

Medovar, B. I., et al, eds. Electroslag Technology. (Material Research & Engineering Ser.). (Illus.). xxii, 270p. 1991. 89.50 (0-387-97333-8) Spr-Verlag.

Medovoy, A. I. The Indian Economy. 206p. 1984. 35.00 (0-685-17087-X, Pub. by Collets UK) Pro-Am Music.

***Medrano, Fidel A.** Historia de los Hospitales Coloniales de Hispanoamerica: Historia de los Hospitales Coloniales de Venezuela, Vol. IX. Garcia, Lucia, ed. (Illus.). (C). 1994. text ed. 50.00 (0-9641506-1-1) Edit Interamerica.

Medrano, M. D., jt. auth. see Piper, D. Z.

Medrich, Alice. Chocolate & the Art of Low-Fat Desserts. (Illus.). 192p. 1994. 35.00 (0-446-51666-X) Warner Bks.

— Cocolat: Extraordinary Chocolate Desserts. (Illus.). 1990. 35.00 (0-446-51419-5) Warner Bks.

Medrich, Elliott A., et al. The Serious Business of Growing Up: A Study of Children's Lives Outside School. LC 81-7650. 412p. 1981. pap. 13.00 (0-520-05071-1) U CA Pr.

— The Serious Business of Growing Up: A Study of Children's Lives Outside School. LC 81-7630. 419p. reprint ed. pap. 119.50 (0-7837-4754-3, 2044501) Bks Demand.

Medsi-McGraw-Hill Staff. AIDS Eighty-Nine to Ninety News & Views on Research. 295p. 1990. pap. text ed. 45.00 (0-07-041308-8) McGraw.

Medsker, Larry & Liebowitz, Jay. Design & Development of Expert Systems & Neural Networks. LC 93-3185. 273p. (C). 1994. text ed. write for info. (0-02-380131-X) Macmillan.

***Medsker, Larry R.** Hybrid Intelligent Systems. 312p. (C). 1995. lib. bdg. 97.50 (0-7923-9588-3) Kluwer Ac.

— Hybrid Neural Network & Expert Systems. LC 93-38572. 256p. (C). 1993. lib. bdg. 87.50 (0-7923-9423-2) Kluwer Ac.

Meduci, Nerina, ed. see Novello, Vincent & Novello, Mary.

Meduna, Ladislas J. Oneirophrenia: The Confusional State. LC 50-6278. (Illus.). 112p. reprint ed. pap. 32.00 (0-317-07831-3, 2015023) Bks Demand.

Medunitsyn, N. V., et al. Mediators of the Immune Response. 320p. 1987. text ed. 134.00 (3-7186-0310-1) Gordon & Breach.

Meduno. Technical Diving. 288p. 1993. pap. 29.95 (0-8016-7478-6) Mosby Yr Bk.

***Meduri, P. J.** The Crib & the Cross: A Students Guide Through the Life of Christ. 162p. (Orig.). (YA). (gr. 6 up). 1994. pap. 8.95 (1-887002-18-9) Cross Trng.

Medve, Mary L., jt. auth. see Medve, Richard J.

Medve, Richard J. & Medve, Mary L. Edible Wild Plants of Pennsylvania & Neighboring States. LC 89-22830. (Illus.). 256p. 1990. lib. bdg. 35.00 (0-271-00690-0); pap. 16.95 (0-271-00697-8) Pa St U Pr.

Medve, William J., jt. auth. see Peto, Gloria J.

Medvec, Emily, ed. see Adams, Ansel.

Medved, Diane. The Case Against Divorce. 320p. 1989. 18.95 (1-55611-127-4) D I Fine.

— Case Against Divorce. 272p. 1990. mass mkt. 5.99 (0-8041-0633-9) Ivy Books.

Medved, Eva. Food: Preparation & Theory. (Illus.). 448p. 1985. text ed. write for info. (0-13-323064-3) P-H.

Medved, Harry & Medved, Michael. Son of Golden Turkey Awards. 1986. pap. 10.95 (0-394-74341-5, Villard Bks) Random.

Medved, M. Functions of Dynamical Systems & Bifurcation Theory. 308p. 1992. 69.00 (0-7503-0150-3) IOP Pub.

Medved, Michael. Hollywood vs. America. LC 92-52604. 400p. 1993. reprint ed. pap. 12.00 (0-06-092435-7, PL) HarpC.

Medved, Michael, jt. auth. see Medved, Harry.

***Medved, Robert.** Excel 5 NOW! (for Windows 3.1) A Simple Guide to Learning Excel Quickly & Easily! (Illus.). 240p. (Orig.). 1995. pap. 19.99x (0-9643450-2-1) Easel Pubng.

— Windows 3.1 Now! A Simple Guide to Learning Windows Quickly & Easily! 2nd ed. Murray, Katharine, ed. LC 95-60174. (Illus.). 216p. 1995. pap. 17.99x (0-9643450-0-5) Easel Pubng.

— Windows '95 NOW! A Simple Guide to Learning Windows '95 Quickly & Easily! (Illus.). 240p. (Orig.). 1995. pap. 19.99x (0-9643450-3-X) Easel Pubng.

***Medved, Robert & Ames, Jennifer.** Word 6 NOW! (for Windows 3.1) A Simple Guide to Learning Word Quickly & Easily. LC 95-60569. (Illus.). 208p. (Orig.). 1995. pap. 18.99 (0-9643450-1-3) Easel Pubng.

Medvedeff, Robert, ed. see Chantico Publishing Company Staff.

Medvedev, Anthony. The Young Elder: From Ambrose of Milkova. 70p. 1974. pap. 3.00 (0-317-30442-9) Holy Trinity.

Medvedev, E. S. & Osherov, V. I. Radiationless Transitions in Polyatomic Molecules. LC 94-19897. (Series in Chemical Physics: Vol. 57). 1994. 99.00 (0-387-57769-6) Spr-Verlag.

Medvedev, F. A. Scenes from the History of Real Functions. (Science Networks - Historical Studies: Vol. 7). 268p. 1992. 132.00 (0-8176-2572-0) Birkhauser.

Medvedev, G. S. Keys to the Insects of the European Part of the U. S. S. R., Vol. IV, Pt. II. (C). 1989. 75.00 (81-7087-047-X) S Asia.

Medvedev, G. S., ed. Keys to the Insects of the European Part of the U. S. S. R., Vol. 4: Lepidoptera, Pt. 2. (Illus.). x, 1092p. 1990. 160.00 (90-04-08926-8) E J Brill.

***Medvedev, G. V., ed.** Keys to the Insects of the European Part of the U. S. S. R. Pt. 4, Braconidae: Hymenoptera, Vol. III. Sharma, S. K. & Kothekar, V. S., trs. 900p. 1995. text ed. 147.50 (1-886106-23-1) Science Pubs.

— Keys to the Insects of the European Part of the U. S. S. R. Pt. 5, Braconidae: Hymenoptera, Vol. III. Kothekar, V. S., tr. 490p. 1995. text ed. 95.00 (1-886106-24-X) Science Pubs.

Medvedev, Grigori. No Breathing Room: The Aftermath of Chernobyl. 224p. 1994. reprint ed. pap. 11.00 (0-465-05115-4) Basic.

Medvedev, P. N., jt. auth. see Bakhtin, M. M.

Medvedev, Pavel N. & Bakhtin, M. M. The Formal Method in Literary Scholarship: A Critical Introduction to Sociological Poetics. LC 77-15529. (Goucher College Ser.). 218p. reprint ed. pap. 62.20 (0-317-29215-3, 2022226) Bks Demand.

Medvedev, Roi. Problems in the Literary Biography of Mikhail Sholokhov. Briggs, A. D., tr. LC 76-14032. 235p. reprint ed. pap. 67.00 (0-317-20597-8, 2024491) Bks Demand.

Medvedev, Roy A. An End to Silence: Uncensored Opinion in the Soviet Union. 376p. 1984. pap. 9.95 (0-393-30127-3) Norton.

Medvedev, Roy A., et al. Khrushchev: The Years in Power. LC 76-19104. 197p. 1976. text ed. 38.00 (0-231-03939-5) Col U Pr.

Medvedev, Roy A. Leninism & Western Socialism. Briggs, A. D., tr. 310p. 1985. pap. text ed. 14.95 (0-86091-739-8, Pub. by Verso UK) Routledge Chapman & Hall.

— Let History Judge: The Origins & Consequences of Stalinism. enl. rev. ed. Shriver, George, ed. & tr. by. 891p. 1989. text ed. 68.50 (0-231-06350-4) Col U Pr.

— Let History Judge: The Origins & Consequences of Stalinism. rev. ed. 1990. pap. text ed. 19.50 (0-231-06351-2) Col U Pr.

— The October Revolution. Saunders, George, tr. LC 79-9855. 232p. 1985. pap. text ed. 18.50 (0-231-04591-3) Col U Pr.

— On Soviet Dissent: Interviews with Piero Ostellino. Packer, William A., tr. LC 79-27877. 158p. 1985. text ed. 34.50 (0-231-04812-2); pap. text ed. 12.50 (0-231-04813-0) Col U Pr.

— Political Essays. (European Socialist Thought Ser.: No. 8). 151p. 1976. 33.50 (0-85124-151-4, Pub. by Spokesman Bks UK) Coronet Bks.

Medvedev, Roy A., ed. The Samizdat Register. 1977. pap. text ed. write for info. (0-393-09081-7) Norton.

— The Samizdat Register. (C). 1977. text ed. 10.95 (0-393-05652-X) Norton.

Medvedev, Roy A. & Medvedev, Zhores A. Khrushchev: The Years in Power. 1978. reprint ed. pap. 8.95 (0-393-00879-7) Norton.

Medvedev, V. A., jt. ed. see Glushko, V. P.

Medvedev, Zhores. The Rise & Fall of T. D. Lysenko. Lawrence, Lucy G., ed. Lerner, I. Michael, tr. LC 79-77519. 304p. reprint ed. pap. 86.70 (0-317-26082-0, 2023770) Bks Demand.

Medvedev, Zhores A. Gorbachev. 288p. 1987. pap. 8.95 (0-393-30408-6) Norton.

— Legacy of Chernobyl. 1990. 24.95 (0-393-02802-X) Norton.

— The Legacy of Chernobyl. (Illus.). 352p. 1990. 24.95 (0-685-46194-7) Norton.

— The Legacy of Chernobyl. (Illus.). 376p. 1992. pap. 10.95 (0-393-30814-6) Norton.

— National Frontiers & International Scientific Cooperation. (Medvedev Papers: Vol. One). 296p. (Orig.). 1975. pap. 28.50 (0-85124-127-1, Pub. by Spokesman Bks UK) Coronet Bks.

— Protein Biosynthesis & Problems of Heredity Development & Aging. LC 67-71423. 606p. reprint ed. pap. 172.80 (0-317-28826-1, 2020702) Bks Demand.

Medvedev, Zhores A., jt. auth. see Medvedev, Roy A.

Medvedeva, Natallia. Mama, Ia Zhulika Liubliu. 170p. (Orig.). (RUS.). 1988. pap. 15.00 (0-89830-114-9) Russica Pubs.

Medvedkov, Yuri, ed. Amelioration of the Human Environment: IGU Congress, Moscow, 1976, Proceedings, Pt. 1. 1977. pap. 23.00 (0-08-021322-7, Pergamon Pr) Elsevier.

— Regional Systems: IGU Congress, Moscow, 1976, Proceedings, Pt. 2. 1977. pap. 23.00 (0-08-021323-5, Pergamon Pr) Elsevier.

— Urbanization: IGU Congress, Moscow, Proceedings, Pt. 3. 1977. pap. 23.00 (0-08-021324-3, Pergamon Pr) Elsevier.

M

An Asterisk (*) at the beginning of an entry indicates that the title is appearing in BIP for the first time.

Medvedow, Jill & Phillpot, Clive. What Are You Waiting for? LC 84-9777. (Illus.). 32p. 1984. pap. 6.00 (*0-941104-11-7*) Real Comet.

Medvei, V. C. The History of Clinical Endocrinology. (History of Medicine Ser.). (Illus.). 650p. 1993. 128.00 (*1-85070-427-9*) Prthnon Pub.

— A History of Endocrinology. (Illus.). 900p. 1982. lib. bdg. 189.50 (*0-85200-245-9*) Kluwer Ac.

Medvekov, Olga. Soviet Urbanisation. 224p. 1990. 55.00 (*0-415-03869-3*, A3947) Routledge.

Medvene, Arnold, intro. Storms & Rainbows: The Many Faces of Death. 200p. (Orig.). 1992. pap. 9.95 (*0-9630598-0-7*) Lilith Pr.

Medvene, Mark. Foilrigami. (Illus.). (J). (gr. 4-7). 1968. 10.95 (*0-685-06619-3*) Astor-Honor.

Medvin, O'Brien, jt. auth. see Parvati, Jeannine.

Medwadowski, S. J., ed. see Symposium on Concrete Thin Shells (1970: New York) Staff.

Medwadowski, Stefan J., jt. ed. see Popov, Egor P.

Medwall, Henry. Nature One & Two. LC 71-133709. (Tudor Facsimile Texts. Old English Plays Ser.: No. 17). reprint ed. 49.50 (*0-404-53317-5*) AMS Pr.

— The Plays of Henry Medwall. Nelson, Alan H., ed. (Tudor Interludes Ser.: No. II). 245p. 1980. 71.00 (*0-85991-054-7*) Boydell & Brewer.

Medway, jt. ed. see Goodson, Ivor F.

Medway, Frederic & Cafferty, Thomas, eds. School Psychology: A Social Psychological Perspective. 496p. 1991. text ed. 89.95 (*0-8058-0536-2*) L Erlbaum Assocs.

Medway, Peter. Finding a Language: Autonomy & Learning in School. (Chameleon Education Ser.). 148p. (Orig.). 1981. pap. 4.95 (*0-906495-41-5*) Writers & Readers.

— Shifting Relations Science Technology & Technoscience. 110p. 1993. 60.00 (*0-7300-1606-4*, ESC810, Pub. by Deakin Univ AT) St Mut.

Medway, Peter, jt. ed. see Freedman, Aviva.

Medway, Peter, jt. auth. see Torbe, Mike.

Medwell, Jane, jt. auth. see Wray, David.

Medwell, Jane, jt. ed. see Wray, David.

Medwid, Daria, jt. auth. see Weston, Denise C.

Medwin, Herman, jt. auth. see Clay, Clarence S.

Medwin, Thomas. Life of Percy Bysshe Shelley. 1971. reprint ed. 59.00 (*0-403-01100-0*) Scholarly.

— Life of Percy Bysshe Shelly. 1988. reprint ed. lib. bdg. 59.00 (*0-7812-0194-2*) Rprt Serv.

Medyckyj-Scott, David & Hearnshaw, Hilary M., eds. Human Factors in Geographical Information Systems. LC 93-28508. 266p. 1994. text ed. 79.95 (*0-471-94725-3*) Wiley.

Medzerian, George. Crack: Treating Cocaine Addiction. 140p. 1991. pap. 12.95 (*0-8306-3622-6*, 3622, TAB-Human Servs Inst) TAB Bks.

Medzhitova, E. D. & Trofimov, A. A., eds. Chuvash Folk Art. (Illus.). 246p. (CHV & RUS.). 1981. 250.00 (*0-317-57298-9*, Pub. by Collets UK) St Mut.

Medzini, Meron. French Policy in Japan During the Closing Years of the Tokugawa Regime. (East Asian Monographs: No. 41). 257p. 1971. pap. 11.00 (*0-674-32230-4*) HUP.

Mee, C. Dennis. The Physics of Magnetic Recording. (North-Holland Personal Library). 286p. 1987. reprint ed. pap. 32.50 (*0-444-87043-1*, North Holland) Elsevier.

Mee, C. Dennis & Daniel, Eric D. Magnetic Recording, Vol. II: Computer Data Storage. 432p. 1988. text ed. 55.00 (*0-07-041272-3*) McGraw.

— Magnetic Recording, Vol. III: Video, Audio & Instrumentation Recording. 448p. 1989. text ed. 55.00 (*0-07-041273-1*) McGraw.

Mee, Charles L., Jr. Playing God: Seven Fateful Moments When Great Men Met to Change the World. LC 93-1599. 304p. 1993. 23.00 (*0-671-67888-4*) S&S Trade.

Mee, G. Miners, Adult Education & Community Service 1920-1984. (C). 1985. 40.00 (*1-85041-006-2*, Pub. by Univ Nottingham UK) St Mut.

Mee, G., jt. auth. see Wallis, J.

Mee, Graham. Miners, Adult Education & Community Service, 1920-1984. (C). 1983. 60.00 (*0-317-94044-9*, Pub. by Univ Nottingham UK) St Mut.

Mee, Graham & Wiltshire, Harold. Structure & Performance in Adult Education. LC 77-7051. 1978. pap. text ed. 9.50 (*0-582-48944-X*) Longman.

Mee, John M. Direct Mass Spectrometry of Body Metabolites: Quantitative Methodology & Clinical Appications. (Illus.). ix, 135p. 1984. pap. 15.00 (*0-318-04438-2*) Brandon-Lane-Pr.

Mee, Jon. Dangerous Enthusiasm: William Blake & the Culture of Radicalism in the 1790s. (Illus.). 280p. 1994. reprint ed. pap. 21.00 (*0-19-818329-1*) OUP.

***Mee, Michelle.** The Sky Is Blue with Clouds Like Fishbones. (Storybridge Ser.). 64p. (J). (gr. 1-4). 1995. pap. 9.95 (*0-7022-2707-2*, Pub. by Univ Queensland Pr AT) Intl Spec Bk.

Mee, Seet A. Open Universities: An Asian Perspective. 1992. pap. 10.00 (*981-3016-30-2*, Pub. by Inst SE Asian Studies SI) Ashgate Pub Co.

Mee, Susie. Girl Who Loved Elvis. 224p. 1993. 18.95 (*1-56145-080-4*) Peachtree Pubs.

— The Undertaker's Daughter. 80p. (Orig.). 1992. pap. 9.00 (*1-881523-01-2*) Junction CA.

Meece, Judith L., jt. ed. see Schunk, Dale H.

Meech, Julia. The Matsukata Collection of Ukiyo-E Prints: Masterpieces from the Tokyo National Museum. (Illus.). 126p. (Orig.). 1989. pap. 22.95 (*0-8135-1467-3*) Rutgers U Pr.

Meech-Pekarik, Julia. The Hogen & Heiji Battle Screens in the Metropolitan Museum of Art. Ruzicka, Molly B., ed. (Illus.). 1984. pap. 12.00 (*0-916235-00-9*) Jacksonville Art.

— The World of the Meiji Print: Impressions of a New Civilization. (Illus.). 299p. 1986. 60.00 (*0-8348-0209-0*) Weatherhill.

Meech-Pekarik, Julia, jt. auth. see Pal, Pratapaditya.

Meech, Sanford B. Design in Chaucer's Troilus. LC 76-88981. 529p. 1969. reprint ed. text ed. 38.50 (*0-8371-2118-3*, MECT, Greenwood Pr) Greenwood.

Meech, Sanford B., ed. see Kempe, Margery B.

Meech, Susan B. A Supplement to the Descendants of Peter Spicer Containing Additions & Corrections. (Illus.). 269p. reprint ed. lib. bdg. 52.00 (*0-8328-1652-3*); reprint ed. pap. 42.00 (*0-8328-1653-1*) Higginson Bk Co.

Meeck, Julia. Rain & Snow: The Umbrella in Japanese Art. (Illus.). 143p. 1993. pap. text ed. 32.00 (*0-913304-36-0*) Japan Soc.

Meed, Douglas V. Bloody Border: Riots, Battles & Adventures along the Turbulent U. S.-Mexican Borderlands. (Great West & Indian Ser.: Vol. 58). (Illus.). 1992. 26.95 (*0-87026-081-2*) Westernlore.

— They Never Surrendered: Bronco Apaches of the Sierra Madres, 1890-1935. (Great West & Indian Ser.: Vol. 59). (Illus.). 1993. 23.95 (*0-87026-086-3*) Westernlore.

Meed, Steven, tr. see Meed, Vladka.

Meed, Vladka. On Both Sides of the Wall. Meed, Steven, tr. LC 78-71300. (Illus.). 304p. 1979. pap. 16.95 (*0-89604-012-7*) Holocaust Pubns.

— On Both Sides of the Wall. Meed, Steven, tr. LC 78-71300. (Illus.). 304p. 1979. pap. 13.95 (*0-89604-013-5*) Holocaust Pubns.

— On Both Sides of the Wall. (Illus.). 304p. reprint ed. pap. 4.95 (*0-686-95078-X*) ADL.

***Meedk, Stephen.** Autobiography of a Mountain Man. (American Autobiography Ser.). 17p. 1995. reprint ed. lib. bdg. 69.00 (*0-7812-8590-9*) Rprt Serv.

Meegan, Mary. Climbing the Mountain: A Journey in Prayer. (Illus.). 107p. (Orig.). 1984. pap. 9.95 (*0-89505-132-X*, 21080) Tabor Pub.

— Climbing the Mountain, Teacher's Guide. (Illus.). 112p. 1984. pap. 9.95 (*0-317-60039-7*) Tabor Pub.

Meegan, Richard, jt. ed. see Massey, Doreen.

Meehan. Holy Women of Russia. LC 92-53919. 224p. 1993. 17.00 (*0-06-065472-4*) Harper SF.

— Life & Letters of G. Stratton-Porter. 1976. 21.95 (*0-8488-0833-9*) Amereon Ltd.

Meehan, Aidan. Celtic Design: A Beginner's Manual. LC 90-71434. (Illus.). 160p. (Orig.). 1991. pap. 14.95 (*0-500-27629-3*) Thames Hudson.

— Celtic Design: Animal Patterns. LC 91-67307. (Illus.). 160p. 1992. pap. 14.95 (*0-500-27662-5*) Thames Hudson.

— Celtic Design: Illuminated Letters. LC 92-80339. (Illus.). 160p. 1992. pap. 15.95 (*0-500-27685-4*) Thames Hudson.

— Celtic Design: Knotwork. LC 90-71465. (Illus.). 160p. (Orig.). 1991. pap. 15.95 (*0-500-27630-7*) Thames Hudson.

— Celtic Design: Maze Patterns. LC 93-61000. (Illus.). 160p. 1994. pap. 15.95 (*0-500-27747-8*) Thames Hudson.

— Celtic Design: Spirals. LC 92-62132. (Illus.). 160p. 1993. pap. 14.95 (*0-500-27705-2*) Thames Hudson.

— Celtic Design: The Dragon & the Griffin. LC 94-60346. (Illus.). 160p. (Orig.). 1995. pap. 15.95 (*0-500-27792-3*) Thames Hudson.

— Celtic Design: The Tree of Life. LC 94-61399. (Celtic Design Ser.). (Illus.). 160p. (Orig.). 1995. pap. 15.95 (*0-500-27827-X*) Thames Hudson.

Meehan, Bernard. The Book of Kells. rev. ed. LC 94-60268. (Illus.). 96p. 1994. pap. 19.95 (*0-500-27790-7*) Thames Hudson.

Meehan, Bill. Collector's Guide to Lu-ray Pastels: Ts&T Premier Potters of America. 1994. pap. 17.95 (*0-89145-608-2*) Collector Bks.

Meehan, Brian. Plain Song. 24p. 1982. pap. 10.00 (*0-936576-07-3*) Symposium Pr.

Meehan, Bridget. Nine Ways to Reach God: A Prayer Sampler. LC 89-63838. 128p. (Orig.). 1990. pap. 3.95 (*0-89243-312-4*) Liguori Pubns.

Meehan, Bridget M. Delighting in the Feminine Divine. 150p. (Orig.). 1994. pap. 9.95 (*1-55612-658-1*) Sheed & Ward MO.

— Exploring the Feminine Face of God. LC 91-60016. (Illus.). 100p. (Orig.). 1991. pap. 8.95 (*1-55612-454-6*, LL1454) Sheed & Ward MO.

— God Delights in You: A Four-Week Prayer Journal. LC 94-60352. (Orig.). 1994. pap. 7.95 (*0-89622-603-4*) Twenty-Third.

— Prayers, Activities, Celebrations (& More) for Catholic Families. LC 94-61850. 96p. (Orig.). 1995. pap. 9.95 (*0-89622-641-7*) Twenty-Third.

— Praying with Passionate Women: Mystics, Martyrs, & Mentors. 144p. (Orig.). 1995. pap. 10.95 (*0-8245-1477-7*) Crossroad NY.

— Your Prayerful Journal for Advent. 98p. (Orig.). 1993. spiral bd. 9.95 (*0-89243-524-0*) Liguori Pubns.

— Your Prayerful Journal for Lent. LC 93-79677. 180p. (Orig.). 1994. spiral bd. 13.95 (*0-89243-534-8*) Liguori Pubns.

***Meehan, Bridget M. & Oliver, Regina M.** Celebrating the Liturgy with Children Cycle A. 1995. pap. text ed. write for info. (*0-8146-2359-X*, Liturg Pr Bks) Liturgical Pr.

Meehan, Denis, tr. see Gregory of Nazianzus, St.

Meehan, Dennis. Takeover: Promises vs. Realities. rev. ed. (Illus.). 25p. 1986. pap. 1.00 (*0-317-59996-8*) Reddy Comm.

Meehan, Dennis B., illus. Is the Forecast Acid Rain? 12p. (Orig.). (gr. 7-12). 1982. Minimum order of 20. pap. 1.00 (*0-9603716-2-1*) Reddy Comm.

Meehan, Diane. An Introduction to Fourth Generation Languages. 168p. (Orig.). 1990. pap. 42.50 (*0-7487-0400-0*, Pub. by Stanley Thornes UK) Trans-Atl Phila.

Meehan, Elizabeth. Citizenship & the European Community. (Illus.). 224p. 1993. 45.00 (*0-8039-8428-6*); pap. 19.95 (*0-8039-8429-4*) Sage.

Meehan, Elizabeth & Sevenhuijsen, Selma, eds. Equality Politics & Gender. (Modern Politics Ser.: Vol. 29). 224p. (C). 1991. text ed. 55.00 (*0-8039-8482-0*); pap. text ed. 19.95 (*0-8039-8483-9*) Sage.

Meehan, Elizabeth, jt. ed. see Kahn, Peggy.

Meehan, Elizabeth M. Women's Rights at Work: Campaigns & Policy in Britain & the United States. LC 84-1597. 253p. 1985. text ed. 35.00 (*0-312-88793-0*) St Martin.

Meehan, Eugene J. Assessing Governmental Performance: An Analytical Framework. LC 92-25740. (Contributions in Political Science Ser.: No. 310). 216p. 1992. text ed. 49.95 (*0-313-28720-1*, GM8720, Greenwood Pr) Greenwood.

— Cognitive Education & Testing: A Methodological Approach. LC 91-3. (Contributions to the Study of Education Ser.: No. 47). 224p. 1991. text ed. 49.95 (*0-313-27889-X*, MGN, Greenwood Pr) Greenwood.

— Economics & Policymaking: The Tragic Illusion. LC 81-20311. (Contributions in Economics & Economic History Ser.: No. 47). (Illus.). 194p. 1982. text ed. 49.95 (*0-313-23313-6*, MEE/, Greenwood Pr) Greenwood.

— Ethics for Policymaking: A Methodological Analysis. LC 89-25763. (Contributions in Political Science Ser.: No. 257). 248p. 1990. text ed. 55.00 (*0-313-27342-1*, MEW/, Greenwood Pr) Greenwood.

— The Quality of Federal Policymaking: Programmed Failure in Public Housing. LC 78-27663. 256p. reprint ed. pap. 73.00 (*0-7837-3200-7*, AU00428) Bks Demand.

— Reasoned Argument in Social Science. LC 80-1198. (Linking Research to Policy Ser.). (Illus.). xvi, 218p. 1981. text ed. 55.00 (*0-313-22481-1*, MRE/, Greenwood Pr) Greenwood.

— Social Inquiry: Needs, Possibilities, Limits. LC 93-39678. 224p. (Orig.). (C). 1994. pap. text ed. 29.95x (*1-56643-006-2*) Chatham Hse Pubs.

— The Thinking Game: A Guide to Effective Study. LC 88-4335. (Chatham House Studies in Political Thinking). (Illus.). 256p. (Orig.). (C). 1988. pap. text ed. 19.95x (*0-934540-64-0*) Chatham Hse Pubs.

— The Thinking Game: A Guide to Effective Study. (Orig.). 1988. teacher ed write for info. (*0-934540-63-2*) Chatham Hse Pubs.

Meehan, Francis J. Contrast in Shakespeare's Historical Plays. LC 72-8981. (Studies in Shakespeare: No. 24). 1973. reprint ed. lib. bdg. 32.95 (*0-8383-1681-6*) M S G Haskell Hse.

Meehan, Francis X., ed. A Contemporary Social Spirituality. LC 82-2253. 133p. (Orig.). 1982. pap. 14.95 (*0-88344-022-9*) Orbis Bks.

Meehan, J. F., et al. Managua, Nicaragua Earthquake of December 23, 1972. 214p. 1973. 12.00 (*0-318-16321-7*, EP-12) Earthquake Eng.

Meehan, J. P. The Lady of the Limberlost: A Biography. 22.95 (*0-8488-0094-X*, Amereon Hse) Amereon Ltd.

Meehan, James, jt. auth. see Bruyn, Severyn T.

Meehan, James R., jt. auth. see Polisky, Mildred K.

Meehan, James W., Jr., jt. ed. see Larner, Robert J.

Meehan, Jeannette P. Freckles Comes Home. reprint ed. lib. bdg. 22.95 (*0-89190-931-1*, Rivercity Pr) Amereon Ltd.

Meehan, Joe. The Complete Book of Photographic Lenses: How to Select & Use Optics for Every Format. (Illus.). 144p. 1991. pap. 22.50 (*0-8174-3697-9*, Amphoto) Watsn-Guptill.

Meehan, Johanna, ed. Feminists Read Habermas: Gendering the Subject of Discourse. LC 94-20585. (Thinking Gender Ser.). 256p. 1995. pap. 16.95 (*0-415-90714-4*, A9798, Routledge NY) Routledge.

— Feminists Read Habermas: Gendering the Subject of Discourse. LC 94-20585. (Thinking Gender Ser.). 256p. 1995. 55.00 (*0-415-90713-6*, A9794, Routledge NY) Routledge.

Meehan, John, jt. auth. see Friedman, Jon.

***Meehan, Joseph.** Manual SLRs. (Magic Lantern Guides Ser.). (Illus.). 160p. (Orig.). 1994. pap. 19.95 (*1-883403-10-3*, H153, Silver Pixel Pr) Saunders Photo.

— Photographer's Guide to Using Filters. 1992. pap. 22.50 (*0-8174-5449-7*, Amphoto) Watsn-Guptill.

— Photography for Graphic Designers. LC 92-44351. (Illus.). 128p. 1993. pap. 19.95 (*0-8230-4012-7*, Watsn-Guptill) Watsn-Guptill.

Meehan, Joseph, jt. auth. see Huber, Michael.

Meehan, Kerry F., jt. auth. see Nowicki, Joseph.

Meehan, Maude. Before the Snow. 112p. (Orig.). 1991. pap. 10.95 (*0-939952-10-6*) Moving Parts.

Meehan, Michael. Liberty & Poetics in Eighteenth Century England. LC 85-22404. 1985. 37.50 (*0-7099-4623-6*, Pub. by Croom Helm UK) Routledge Chapman & Hall.

Meehan, Michael D. & Purviance, John. Yield & Reliability in Microwave Circuit & System Design. LC 92-27018. (Microwave Ser.). 243p. (C). 1992. text ed. 81.00 (*0-89006-527-6*) Artech Hse.

***Meehan, Norma.** Art Deco Paper Doll Wardrobe 1920-1939. (Illus.). 1994. 4.95 (*0-87588-422-9*, 4734) Hobby Hse.

— Edwarden Paper Doll Wardrobe. (Illus.). 32p. 1993. pap. 4.95 (*0-87588-405-9*, 4529) Hobby Hse.

— Nana's Trunk Paperdolls. 24p. 1995. 5.95 (*0-87588-438-5*) Hobby Hse.

— Victorian Paper Doll Wardrobe. 32p. 1992. spiral bd. 4.95 (*0-87588-387-7*) Hobby Hse.

***Meehan, Patricia.** Stencil Source Book, Vol. 2. (Illus.). 144p. 1995. 22.99 (*0-89134-695-3*) North Light Bks.

— Stencil Source Book: Over Two Hundred Designs to Make Stencils for All Around the House. (Illus.). 144p. 1994. 22.95 (*0-89134-586-8*) North Light Bks.

Meehan, Patrick J. Frank Lloyd Wright: A Research Guide to Archival Sources. LC 81-47448. 715p. 1983. lib. bdg. 141.00 (*0-8240-9342-9*) Garland.

— Frank Lloyd Wright Remembered. (Illus.). 256p. 1991. 29.95 (*0-89133-187-5*) Preservation Pr.

Meehan, Patrick J., ed. The Master Architect: Conversations with Frank Lloyd Wright. LC 84-11931. 330p. 1984. text ed. 54.95 (*0-471-80025-2*, Wiley-Interscience) Wiley.

Meehan, Patrick J., intro. Truth Against the World: Frank Lloyd Wright Speaks for an Organic Architecture. LC 92-14034. (Illus.). 496p. 1992. pap. 24.95 (*0-89133-174-3*) Preservation Pr.

***Meehan, Paula.** The Man Who Was Marked by Winter. 66p. 1995. 21.00 (*0-910055-13-0*); pap. 12.00 (*0-910055-14-9*) Paul & Co Pubs.

Meehan, Richard L. The Atom & the Fault: Experts, Earthquakes, & Nuclear Power. 184p. 1986. reprint ed. 19.95x (*0-262-13199-4*) MIT Pr.

— Getting Sued & Other Tales of the Engineering Life. 264p. 1981. reprint ed. pap. 11.95x (*0-262-63089-3*) MIT Pr.

Meehan, Sheila, jt. ed. see Dowdall, Mike.

Meehan, Suzi, ed. see Moreno, Richard.

Meehan, Thomas C., tr. see Sorrentino, Fernando.

Meehan, Tim. Great Photoshop Technique. 1994. pap. 39.95 (*1-55828-366-8*) MIS Press.

— Introducing Desktop Prepress. LC 94-47609. 1995. cd-rom, pap. text ed. 27.95 (*1-55828-364-1*) MIS Press.

***Meehan, Tom. When the Sacred Marriage Ends. LC 95-94377. 271p. (Orig.). 1995. pap. 14.40 (*0-9646166-0-2*) Dollar Spec Pubns.**

A Divorce Novel of selfish, greedy & cold people. THE STORY OF A MAN WHO IS DENIED HIS RIGHT TO BE HEARD IN COURT. The flagrant denial of a man's First Amendment rights. Details of the FLORIDA DIVORCE IN ABSENTIA & the APPEALS PROCESS are highlighted with quarrels, unscrupulous lawyers, inept judges, affidavits, arbitrations, depositions, trials, appeal & whim of the judges. The court does not notify Tim of the divorce & trial date. She gets a SOLO DIVORCE WITH ALL HIS ASSETS & INCOME. HE HAS TO LIVE IN POVERTY. HER LAWYER GOOFS. THE DIVORCE ORDER IS NOT A QUALIFYING GOVERNMENT DOMESTIC RELATIONS ORDER. THEY HAVE NO GOVERNMENT BENEFITS. THE INEPT APPEAL JUDGES DO NOT LISTEN TO ORAL ARGUMENTS & DO NOT CONSIDER THE COURT RECORD. THEY DO NOT CONSIDER THE STATEMENT OF TRIAL EVIDENCE. This story is based on true facts & occurrences, but fictional to protect the innocent. Only $14.40 plus $3.00 S&H. Send check or money order to: Dollar Specialty Publications, 1290 Hwy 70 West, Alamogordo, NM 88310. 505-434-1548. ***Publisher Provided Annotation.***

Meehan, Tony. Goodbye Maigida. 176p. (C). 1989. text ed. 45.00 (*1-872795-18-8*, Pub. by Pentland Pr UK) St Mut.

Meehan, Trudy, ed. see Davis, Lynn.

Meehan, Valerie C. Experiments for Medical Chemistry. 128p. (C). 1994. 10.95 (*0-8403-9219-2*) Kendall-Hunt.

Meehan, Virginia M. Christopher Marlowe Poet & Playwright Studies in Poetical Method. LC 74-79321. (De Proprietatibus Litterarum, Ser. Practica: No. 81). 100p. 1974. pap. text ed. 52.35 (*90-279-3382-0*) Mouton.

Meehan, W. R., ed. Influences of Forest & Rangeland Management on Salmonid Fishes & Their Habitat. LC 91-55216. (Special Publication Ser.: No. 19). 751p. (C). 1991. text ed. 68.50 (*0-913235-68-7*) Am Fisheries Soc.

***Meehl, Joanne H.** The Recovering Catholic: Personal Journeys of Women Who Left the Church. 272p. 1995. 24.95 (*0-87975-927-5*) Prometheus Bks.

Meehl, Paul E. Clinical Versus Statistical Prediction: A Theoretical Analysis & a Review of the Evidence. LC 54-11774. 159p. reprint ed. pap. 45.40 (*0-317-29449-0*, 2055890) Bks Demand.

— Selected Philosophical & Methodological Papers. 512p. (C). 1991. text ed. 39.95 (*0-8166-1855-0*) U of Minn Pr.

***Meeinig.** Shaping of America: A Geographical Prespective on 500 Years of History, Vol. 2: Continental. 1995. pap. text ed. 20.00 (*0-300-06290-7*) Yale U Pr.

Meek, A. J., jt. auth. see Gassan, Arnold.

Meek, Basil, ed. Twentieth Century History of Sandusky County, Ohio. (Illus.). 934p. 1993. reprint ed. lib. bdg. 95.00 (*0-8328-3448-3*) Higginson Bk Co.

Meek, Brian, et al, eds. User Needs in IT Standards. (Illus.). 320p. 1993. pap. 85.00 (*0-7506-1559-1*) Buttrwrth-Heinemann.

Meek, Carroll L., ed. Post-Traumatic Stress Disorder: Assessment, Differential Diagnosis, & Forensic Evaluation. LC 89-43413. 264p. 1990. 28.20 (*0-943158-35-4*, PTSDBP) Pro Resource.

An Asterisk (*) at the beginning of an entry indicates that the title is appearing in BIP for the first time.

Meek, Charles J. Conducting Made Easy for Directors of Amateur Musical Organizations. LC 88-18356. (Illus.). 150p. 1988. 20.00 (*0-8108-2167-2*); pap. 12.50 (*0-8108-2179-6*) Scarecrow.

Meek, Charles K. Colonial Law: A Bibliography with Special Reference to Native African Systems of Law & Land Tenure. LC 78-14383. xiii, 58p. 1979. text ed. 49.75 (*0-313-21011-X*, MECL, Greenwood Pr) Greenwood.

— Land Law & Custom in the Colonies. 2nd ed. 337p. 1968. reprint ed. 32.50 (*0-7146-1698-2*, Pub. by F Cass Pubs UK) Intl Spec Bk.

— Law & Authority in a Nigerian Tribe. LC 76-44756. reprint ed. 28.50 (*0-404-15951-6*) AMS Pr.

— Northern Tribes of Nigeria: Ethnographical Account of the Northern Provinces of Nigeria Together with a Report of the 1921 Decennial Census, 2 vols. (Illus.). 1971. reprint ed. 95.00 (*0-7146-2686-4*, Pub. by F Cass Pubs UK) Intl Spec Bk.

— Tribal Studies in Northern Nigeria, 2 vols., Set. LC 74-15066. reprint ed. 134.50 (*0-404-12107-1*) AMS Pr.

Meek, Charles S. Beyond the Crash: The Real World of Investing. (Illus.). 200p. 1988. 19.95 (*0-938619-41-1*) Live Oak TX.

— Money Matters: Financial Planning & Investment Ideas for the Non Finance Professional. 1990. 24.95 (*1-55738-136-4*) Probus Pub Co.

Meek, Christine E. The Commune of Lucca Under Pisan Rule, 1342-1369. LC 78-70245. 1980. 20.00 (*0-910956-69-3*, SAM6); pap. 12.00 (*0-910956-80-4*) Medieval Acad.

Meek, Christopher, et al. Managing by the Numbers: Absentee Owners & the Decline of American Industry. 208p. 1988. 19.18 (*0-201-16129-X*) Addison-Wesley.

Meek, Christopher B. & Woodworth, Werner P. Creating Labor-Management Partnerships. (Illus.). 208p. (C). 1995. pap. text ed. 26.95 (*0-201-58823-4*) Addison-Wesley.

Meek, Cindy. Catalog of Nonsmoking Hotel Rooms: A Consumer Service. rev. ed. 146p. (Orig.). 1986. pap. 43.50 (*0-938619-24-1*) Live Oak TX.

Meek, Devon W., jt. ed. see Alyea, Elmer C.

Meek, Ed. Flying: Poems. LC 92-15308. 64p. 1992. pap. 12.95 (*0-7734-0040-0*) E Mellen.

Meek, Forrest B. Lumbering in Eastern Canada: Lumbering in Eastern Canada During the 18th & 19th Centuries. Edgewood Press Staff, ed. (White Pine Lumbering Era Ser.). 111p. (Orig.). (C). 1991. pap. 24.95 (*0-9602472-4-6*) Edgewood.

— Michigan's Heartland. (Illus.). 449p. 1979. lib. bdg. 17.95 (*0-9602472-0-3*) Edgewood.

— Michigan's Timber Battleground. 2nd rev. ed. (Illus.). 483p. 1991. reprint ed. lib. bdg. 29.95 (*0-9602472-1-1*) Edgewood.

— One Year in China: An Account of the Academic Year in the People's Republic of China 1986-1987. Edgewood Press Staff, ed. Wuhan University English Department Staff, tr. 220p. (CHI & ENG.). 1991. pap. 24.95 (*0-9602472-2-X*) Edgewood.

Meek, Forrest B. & Bajema, Carl J. Michigan's Logging Trams & Railroads. (White Pine History Ser.). 100p. (C). 1992. student ed 39.95 (*0-9602472-3-8*) Edgewood.

Meek, Frank. Haynes Kawasaki 250, 350 & 400 (3-cyl) Models '72-'79, No. M134. 1979. 16.95 (*0-85696-134-5*) Haynes Pubns.

— Haynes Triumph Trident & BSA Rocket 3 Owners Workshop Manual, No. 136: '69-'75. 1979. 16.95 (*0-85696-136-1*) Haynes Pubns.

Meek, Gary E., et al. Business Statistics. 800p. 1986. write for info. (*0-685-17397-6*) Allyn.

Meek, Geoffrey A. Practical Electron Microscopy for Biologists. 2nd ed. LC 75-4955. 550p. reprint ed. pap. 156.80 (*0-685-20912-1*, 2052242) Bks Demand.

Meek, George W. After We Die, What Then? LC 79-90909. (Life's Energy Fields Ser.: Vol. 3). (Illus.). (Orig.). 1980. 8.95 (*0-935436-00-6*) Metascience.

— After We Die, What Then? rev. ed. LC 79-909. (Illus.). 216p. (Orig.). 1987. reprint ed. pap. 11.95 (*0-89804-099-X*, Metasci) Ariel GA.

Meek, H. A. Guarino Guarini & His Architecture. 256p. (C). 1990. reprint ed. 26.50 (*0-300-04748-7*) Yale U Pr.

Meek, Harold. Guarino Guarini. LC 87-24636. 256p. (C). 1988. text ed. 60.00 (*0-300-03989-1*) Yale U Pr.

— The Synagogue: The Complete History of the Art & Architecture of the Synagogue. (Illus.). 240p. (C). 1995. 59.95 (*0-7148-2932-3*, Pub. by Phaidon Press UK) Chronicle Bks.

Meek, J. L. Computer Methods in Structural Analysis. (Illus.). 512p. 1991. write for info. (*0-419-15440-X*, E & FN Spon) Routledge Chapman & Hall.

Meek, J. M. & Craggs, J. D. Electrical Breakdown of Gases. LC 77-2784. 888p. reprint ed. 180.00 (*0-8357-9879-8*, 2019472) Bks Demand.

Meek, James. The Land & People of Scotland. LC 88-27215. (Portraits of the Nations Ser.). (Illus.). 256p. (J). (gr. 6 up). 1990. 18.00 (*0-397-32332-8*, Lipp Jr Bks); lib. bdg. 14.89 (*0-397-32333-6*, Lipp Jr Bks) HarpC Child Bks.

***Meek, James A.** Steps to Success. (Discover Life Ser.). 1994. pap. 17.95 (*1-56212-091-3*) CRC Pubns.

Meek, Jay. Drawing on the Walls. LC 79-51607. (Poetry Ser.). 1980. 16.95 (*0-915604-31-0*); pap. 9.95 (*0-915604-32-9*) Carnegie-Mellon.

— Earthly Purposes. 1984. 16.95 (*0-915604-94-9*); pap. 9.95 (*0-915604-95-7*) Carnegie-Mellon.

— Stations. 80p. 1989. pap. 8.95 (*0-88748-081-0*) Carnegie-Mellon.

— Windows. LC 93-73472. (Poetry Ser.). 80p. (Orig.). 1994. 17.95 (*0-88748-170-1*); pap. 10.95 (*0-88748-171-X*) Carnegie-Mellon.

Meek, Jay, jt. ed. see Meek, Martha.

Meek, Jay, jt. ed. see Reeve, F. D.

Meek, Joseph. Big Gun Bushwhacker. (Mountain Jack Pike Ser.: No. 9). 1991. pap. 3.50 (*1-55817-530-X*, Pinnacle NY) Windsor NY.

— Crow Bait. (Mountain Jack Pike Ser.: No. 4). 1989. pap. 2.95 (*1-55817-282-3*, Pinnacle NY) Windsor NY.

— Fire in the Hole. (Mountain Jack Pike Ser.: No. 12). 256p. 1993. pap. 3.50 (*1-55817-679-9*, Pinnacle NY) Windsor NY.

— Green River Hunt. (Mountain Jack Pike Ser.: No. 5). 1990. pap. 2.95 (*1-55817-341-2*, Pinnacle NY) Windsor NY.

— Hard for Justice. (Mountain Jack Pike Ser.: No. 8). 1991. pap. 3.50 (*1-55817-502-4*, Pinnacle NY) Windsor NY.

— High Country Climax. (Mountain Jack Pike Ser.: No. 13). 256p. 1993. pap. 3.50 (*1-55817-706-X*, Pinnacle NY) Windsor NY.

— Mountain Jack Pike. (Mountain Jack Pike Ser.: No. 1). 224p. 1988. pap. 2.95 (*1-55817-092-8*, Pinnacle NY) Windsor NY.

— Mountain Jack Pike, No. 10: Bull's Eye Blood. 1992. pap. 3.50 (*1-55817-617-9*, Pinnacle NY) Windsor NY.

— Mountain Jack Pike, No. 11: Deep Canyon Kill. 256p. 1992. pap. 3.50 (*1-55817-657-8*, Pinnacle NY) Windsor NY.

— Mountain Jack Pike, No. 14: Trail Heat. 1993. pap. 3.50 (*1-55817-733-7*, Pinnacle NY) Windsor NY.

— Rough Trade. (Mountain Jack Pike Ser.: No. 15). 224p. 1993. pap. 3.50 (*1-55817-762-0*, Pinnacle NY) Windsor NY.

— The Russian Bear. (Mountain Jack Pike Ser.: No. 7). 1991. pap. 2.95 (*1-55817-467-2*, Pinnacle NY) Windsor NY.

— St. Louis Fire. (Mountain Jack Pike Ser.: No. 6). 1990. pap. 2.95 (*1-55817-380-3*, Pinnacle NY) Windsor NY.

Meek, M. R. A Loose Connection. 224p. 1991. mass mkt. 3.50 (*0-373-26070-9*) Harlequin Bks.

— This Blessed Plot. (Worldwide Library Mystery: No. 93). 1992. mass mkt. 3.99 (*0-373-26093-8*, 1-26093-4) Harlequin Bks.

— Touch & Go. 1994. mass mkt. 3.99 (*0-373-26146-2*, 1-26146-0) Harlequin Bks.

— Touch & Go: A Lennox Kemp Mystery. 224p. 1993. text ed. 20.00 (*0-684-19518-6*, Scribners) S&S Trade.

Meek, M. R. D. Touch & Go. large type ed. LC 92-47098. (General Ser.). 352p. 1993. reprint ed. lib. bdg. 17.95 (*1-56054-674-3*) Thorndike Pr.

Meek, Margaret. Achieving Literacy: Longitudinal Studies of Adolescents Learning to Read. (Language, Education & Society Ser.). 256p. (Orig.). 1983. pap. 15.95 (*0-7100-9463-9*, RKP) Routledge.

— On Being Literate. 266p. 1992. pap. 16.95 (*0-435-08726-6*, 08726) Heinemann.

Meek, Margaret, ed. Opening Moves: Work in Progress in the Study of Children's Language Development. 84p. (Orig.). 1985. pap. text ed. 10.00 (*0-435-08250-7*) Heinemann.

Meek, Margaret & Mills, Colin, eds. Language & Literacy in the Primary School. (Contemporary Analysis in Education Ser.). 275p. 1988. 65.00 (*1-85000-352-1*, Falmer Pr); pap. 33.00 (*1-85000-357-2*, Falmer Pr) Taylor & Francis.

Meek, Mark. Bible & the Nineties. LC 93-70206. 1995. 14.95 (*0-8158-0492-X*) Chris Mass.

***Meek, Martha.** Rude Noises. 1995. 3.00 (*0-941127-16-8*) Dacotah Terr Pr.

***Meek, Martha & Meek, Jay, eds.** Prairie Volcano: An Anthology of North Dakota Writing. 1995. per. 14.95 (*0-941127-15-X*) Dacotah Terr Pr.

Meek, Martyn. Haynes Suzuki GS1000 Fours Owners Workshop Manual, No. 484: '77 On. 16.95 (*0-85696-484-0*) Haynes Pubns.

— Haynes Suzuki GS850 Fours Owners Workbook Manual, No. 536: '78 On. pap. 16.95 (*1-85010-571-5*) Haynes Pubns.

— Haynes Suzuki Suzy Moped FZ50, 78-83. (Haynes Ser.). (Illus.). 100p. 1992. pap. 18.95 (*0-85696-575-8*) Motorbooks Intl.

Meek, Martyn & Choate, Curt. Haynes Honda ATC 70, 90, 110, 185 & 200 Owners Workshop Manual, No. M565: '71-'82. pap. 16.95 (*0-85696-855-2*) Haynes Pubns.

Meek, Mary E., jt. auth. see David, Alfred.

Meek, Michael K. The Australian Legal System. (LBC Nutshell Ser.). x, 134p. 1988. pap. 11.95 (*0-455-20824-7*, Pub. by Law Bk Co) W W Gaunt.

Meek, Ronald L. The Economics of Physiocracy: Essays & Translations. (Reprints of Economic Classics Ser.). 432p. 1993. reprint ed. lib. bdg. 45.00 (*0-678-01466-3*) Kelley.

— Studies in the Labor Theory of Value. LC 74-7792. 332p. 1978. pap. 10.00 (*0-85345-428-0*) Monthly Rev.

Meek, Ronald L., tr. see Quesnay, Francois.

Meek, Stephanie. Group Therapy: Thematic Activities for Language Impaired Adults & Adolescents. LC 92-38672. (Illus.). (C). 1993. spiral bd. 26.00 (*0-89079-577-0*, 6592) PRO-ED.

Meek, Theophile J. Hebrew Origins. 1960. 11.25 (*0-8446-2572-8*) Peter Smith.

Meeke, Mary. Count St. Blancard: Or, the Prejudiced Judge. Varma, Devendra P., ed. LC 77-2044. (Gothic Novels III Ser.). 1977. reprint ed. 72.95 (*0-405-10142-2*) Ayer.

Meeker. Alexander's Care of the Patient in Surgery. 9th ed. (Illus.). 1088p. 1990. 55.95 (*0-8016-3387-7*) Mosby Yr Bk.

— Alexander's Care of the Patient in Surgery, No. 10. 1248p. 1994. 56.95 (*0-8016-7924-9*) Mosby Yr Bk.

Meeker, Barbara, jt. auth. see Hage, Jerald.

Meeker, Barbara, ed. see Williams, Ruby.

Meeker, Belva, jt. auth. see Johnson, Elizabeth A.

Meeker, Clare H. The Tale of Two Rice Birds. (Illus.). 32p. (J). (ps up). 1994. 14.95 (*1-57061-008-8*) Sasquatch Bks.

Meeker, David. Jazz in the Movies. enl. ed. LC 81-17365. (Quality Paperbacks Ser.). (Illus.). 336p. 1982. pap. 13.50 (*0-306-80170-1*) Da Capo.

— Jazz in the Movies. rev. ed. LC 81-17364. (Roots of Jazz Ser.). (Illus.). 336p. 1982. lib. bdg. 35.00 (*0-306-76147-5*) Da Capo.

Meeker, E. Washington Territory. 56p. reprint ed. pap. 3.95 (*0-8466-0194-X*, S194) Shorey.

Meeker, Ezra. The Old Emigrant Trail: Story of the Lost Trail to Oregon, the Oregon Trail. LC 93-43227. 64p. 1994. 7.50 (*0-936738-78-2*) Webb Research.

— Pioneer Reminiscences of Puget Sound. 1991. 19.95 (*0-685-49162-5*); pap. 10.95 (*0-685-49163-3*) Hist Soc Seattle.

— Pioneer Reminiscenses of Puget Sound. (Northwest Historical Classics Ser.). (Illus.). 199p. 1980. reprint ed. pap. 10.95 (*0-939806-01-0*) Hist Soc Seattle.

— Story of the Lost Trail to Oregon. 32p. 1984. pap. 4.95 (*0-87770-321-3*) Ye Galleon.

— The Tragedy of Leschi. 1991. 19.95 (*0-939806-02-9*); pap. 10.95 (*0-685-49164-1*) Hist Soc Seattle.

— Uncle Ezra's Short Stories for Children. 100p. reprint ed. pap. 4.95 (*0-8466-0242-3*, S242) Shorey.

Meeker, Ezra, ed. see Bagley, Clarence B.

***Meeker, Frances & Berryhill, Judy.** Country Sunshine: The Dottie West Story. Courtney, Richard & McCombs, Maryglenn, eds. LC 94-62009. 128p. (Orig.). 1995. pap. text ed. 12.95 (*1-886371-08-3*) Eggman Pub.

Meeker, James E. Short Selling. LC 75-2648. (Wall Street & the Security Market Ser.). 1975. reprint ed. 25.95 (*0-405-06973-1*) Ayer.

— The Work of the Stock Exchange (Revised Edition) LC 75-2649. (Wall Street & the Security Market Ser.). (Illus.). 1975. reprint ed. 64.95 (*0-405-06974-X*) Ayer.

Meeker, Joseph W. Minding the Earth: Thinly Disguised Essays on Human Ecology. LC 87-83609. (Illus.). 110p. (Orig.). 1988. pap. 8.95 (*0-931735-01-7*) Latham Found Pubn.

Meeker, Judith, jt. auth. see Gronski, Claudette.

***Meeker, Larry, et al.** Experiential Activities for High Performance Leadership. 1994. ring bd. 79.95 (*0-87425-987-8*) Human Res Dev Pr.

Meeker-Lowry, Susan. Economics As If the Earth Really Mattered: A Catalyst Guide to Socially Conscious Investing. 294p. (Orig.). 1988. 34.95 (*0-86571-120-8*); pap. 12.95 (*0-86571-121-6*) New Soc Pubs.

— Invested in the Common Good: Economics As If the Earth Really Mattered. 272p. 1995. pap. 16.95 (*0-86571-292-1*) New Soc Pubs.

— Invested in the Common Good: Economics As If the Earth Really Mattered. 272p. 1995. lib. bdg. 39.95 (*0-86571-291-3*) New Soc Pubs.

Meeker, M. F., jt. auth. see Perrin, A. F.

Meeker, Michael E. The Pastoral Son & the Spirit of Patriarchy: Religion, Society, & Person among East African Stock Keepers. LC 88-40438. (New Directions in Anthropological Writing Ser.). 228p. (Orig.). (C). 1989. text ed. 37.50 (*0-299-11740-5*); pap. text ed. 18.25 (*0-299-11744-8*) U of Wis Pr.

Meeker, William Q., jt. auth. see Hahn, Gerald J.

Meeker, William Q., Jr., et al. Vol. 7. (Selected Tables in Mathematical Statistics). 256p. 1981. 34.00 (*0-8218-1907-0*, TABLES 7) Am Math.

Meekings, B. A., et al. A Book on C. 3rd ed. (Illus.). 194p. (C). 1993. pap. text ed. 35.00 (*0-333-56919-9*, Pub. by Macmill Educ UK) Scholium Intl.

Meekings, C. A. Studies in Thirteenth Century Justice & Administration. 342p. (C). 1982. text ed. 60.00 (*0-9506882-3-1*) Hambledon Press.

Meekins, Inez P. Meekins' Ceremonies. 40p. 1982. pap. 3.00 (*0-88053-326-9*, S-101) Macoy Pub.

Meeks, ed. Hepatoxicology. 1991. 103.95 (*0-8493-8810-4*, R) CRC Pr.

Meeks, Anna R. Guidance in Elementary Education. LC 68-13472. 247p. reprint ed. pap. 70.40 (*0-8357-4707-7*, 2012379) Bks Demand.

Meeks, Arone R. Enora & the Black Crane. LC 92-32123. (J). 1993. 14.95 (*0-590-46375-6*) Scholastic Inc.

***Meeks, Blair G., ed.** All Saints among the Churches. (Liturgy Ser.). (Illus.). 70p. (Orig.). 1995. pap. 10.95 (*0-918208-69-6*) Liturgical Conf.

— And at the Last. (Liturgy Ser.). (Illus.). 90p. (Orig.). 1992. pap. 10.95 (*0-918208-60-2*) Liturgical Conf.

— Jubilee. (Illus.). 96p. (Orig.). 1993. pap. 10.95 (*0-918208-61-0*) Liturgical Conf.

— No East or West: Discovering the Gifts of Diversity. (Liturgy Ser.). (Illus.). 80p. (Orig.). 1994. pap. 10.95 (*0-918208-67-X*) Liturgical Conf.

— Practicing Ecumenism. (Liturgy Ser.). 80p. (Orig.). 1992. pap. 10.95 (*0-918208-57-2*) Liturgical Conf.

— Ritual & Reconciliation: Advent, Christmas, Epiphany. (Liturgy Ser.). (Illus.). 120p. (Orig.). 1991. pap. 10.95 (*0-918208-55-6*) Liturgical Conf.

— We Proclaim. (Liturgy Ser.). 96p. (Orig.). 1993. pap. 10.95 (*0-918208-62-9*) Liturgical Conf.

— Worship That Forms Faith. (Liturgy Ser.). (Illus.). 80p. (Orig.). 1995. pap. 10.95 (*0-918208-68-8*) Liturgical Conf.

Meeks, Blair G. & Sloyan, Virginia, eds. The Christmas Cycle: Advent, Christmas, Epiphany. (Liturgy Ser.). (Illus.). 120p. (Orig.). 1991. pap. 10.95 (*0-918208-54-8*) Liturgical Conf.

— From Ashes to Fire, Year B: Planning for the Paschal Season. (Liturgy Ser.). (Illus.). 100p. (Orig.). 1993. pap. 10.95 (*0-918208-63-7*) Liturgical Conf.

— From Ashes to Fire, Year C: Planning for the Paschal Season. (Liturgy Ser.). 1994. pap. 10.95 (*0-918208-66-1*) Liturgical Conf.

Meeks, Blair G., jt. ed. see Sloyan, Virginia.

Meeks, Blair G., et al, eds. From Ashes to Fire - A. (Liturgy Ser.). (Illus.). 100p. (Orig.). 1992. pap. 10.95 (*0-918208-58-0*) Liturgical Conf.

Meeks, Carrier M. Satan's Fat Attack!!! Williams, Martha, ed. (Illus.). 168p. (Orig.). 1986. pap. 9.95 (*0-941513-00-9*) C & M Pubs & Distributors.

Meeks, Carroll L. Italian Architecture, Seventeen-Fifty to Nineteen-Fourteen. LC 65-22334. 574p. reprint ed. pap. 163.60 (*0-317-10128-5*, 2013375) Bks Demand.

— The Railroad Station: An Architectural History. LC 95-2517. (Illus.). 320p. 1995. pap. text ed. 12.95 (*0-486-28627-4*) Dover.

Meeks, Catherine. I Want Somebody to Know My Name. rev. ed. LC 94-13426. 128p. 1994. pap. 10.95 (*1-880837-78-1*) Smyth & Helwys.

Meeks, Christopher. Arnold Schwarzenegger: Hard Work Brought Success. LC 92-42288. (Reaching Your Goal Bks.). (J). 1993. 14.60 (*0-86593-260-3*); 10.95 (*0-685-66328-0*) Rourke Corp.

— Japan. (World Partners Ser.). (Illus.). 64p. (YA). (gr. 7 up). 1990. lib. bdg. 17.27 (*0-86593-089-9*); lib. bdg. 12.95 (*0-685-36366-X*) Rourke Corp.

— Roald Dahl. LC 92-42286. (J). (gr. 3-7). 1993. 14.60 (*0-86593-259-X*); 10.95 (*0-685-66357-4*) Rourke Corp.

— Skydiving. (Action Sports Ser.). 48p. (J). (gr. 3-4). 1991. lib. bdg. 11.95 (*1-56065-051-6*) Capstone Pr.

Meeks, Gordon, Jr. Pesticide Applications: States Move to Limit Farmer Liability for Groundwater Contamination. (State Legislative Reports: Vol. 15, No. 15). 7p. 1990. pap. text ed. 5.00 (*1-55516-271-1*, 7302-1515) Natl Conf State Legis.

Meeks, Harold A. Vermont's Land & Resources. LC 86-50973. (Illus.). 336p. (Orig.). 1986. pap. 16.95 (*0-933050-40-2*) New Eng Pr VT.

Meeks, J. Gay, ed. Thoughtful Economic Man: Essays on Rationality, Moral Rules & Benevolence. (Illus.). 160p. (C). 1991. 34.95 (*0-521-32574-9*) Cambridge U Pr.

Meeks, James E., jt. auth. see Christie, George C.

Meeks, John, tr. see Bockemuhl, Jochen.

Meeks, John, tr. see Bockemuhl, Jochen, et al.

Meeks, John E. High Times - Low Times: The Many Faces of Adolescent Depression. 144p. (Orig.). 1988. pap. 7.95 (*0-929162-05-6*) PIA Pr.

Meeks, John E. & Bernet, William. The Fragile Alliance: An Orientation to the Psychiatric Treatment of the Adolescent. 4th ed. LC 90-4107. 616p. (C). 1990. lib. bdg. 51.50 (*0-89464-375-4*) Krieger.

Meeks, Larry M., jt. auth. see Elkins, Randolph H.

Meeks, Linda & Heit, Philip. Comprehensive School Health Education: Totally Awesome Strategies for Teaching Health. 100p. (C). 1992. teacher ed, pap. text ed. write for info. (*0-9630009-1-8*) Meeks Heit.

— Violence Prevention: How to Be Hip, Cool, & Violence-Free. (Illus.). 125p. (YA). 1995. text ed. 14.00 (*0-9630009-6-9*) Meeks Heit.

— Violence Prevention: Totally Awesome Teaching Strategies for Safe & Drug-Free Schools. DeVillers, Julie & Turple, Ann, eds. (Illus.). 350p. (Orig.). (C). 1994. pap. text ed. 50.00 (*0-9630009-4-2*) Meeks Heit.

***Meeks, Linda, et al.** Comprehensive School Health Education: Totally Awesome Strategies for Teaching Health. 2nd ed. DeVillers, Julie & Turpie, Ann, eds. (Illus.). 650p. (C). Date not set. pap. text ed. 50.00 (*1-886693-09-9*) Meeks Heit.

— Comprehensive School Health Education: Totally Awesome Strategies for Teaching Health. 2nd ed. (Illus.). 600p. (C). 1992. pap. text ed. 50.00 (*0-9630009-0-X*) Meeks Heit.

— Drugs, Alcohol, & Tobacco: Totally Awesome Teaching Strategies. Baker, Mary, ed. LC 93-91774. (Illus.). 620p. (Orig.). (C). 1994. pap. text ed. 48.00 (*0-9630009-3-4*) Meeks Heit.

— Drugs, Alcohol, & Tobacco: Totally Awesome Teaching Strategies. rev. ed. Baker, Mary & Turpie, Ann, eds. (Illus.). 612p. (Orig.). (C). 1994. pap. text ed. 45.00 (*0-9630009-5-0*) Meeks Heit.

— Education for Sexuality & HIV - AIDS: Curriculum & Teaching Strategies. (Illus.). 650p. (C). 1993. pap. text ed. write for info. (*0-9630009-2-6*) Meeks Heit.

— Totally Awesome Health: Grade K. DeVillers, Julie, ed. (Illus.). 650p. 1995. teacher ed, ring bd. 95.00 (*1-886693-00-5*) Meeks Heit.

— Totally Awesome Health: Grade 1. DeVillers, Julie, ed. (Illus.). 650p. 1995. teacher ed, ring bd. 95.00 (*1-886693-01-3*) Meeks Heit.

— Totally Awesome Health: Grade 2. DeVillers, Julie, ed. (Illus.). 650p. 1995. teacher ed, ring bd. 95.00 (*1-886693-02-1*) Meeks Heit.

— Totally Awesome Health: Grade 3. DeVillers, Julie, ed. (Illus.). 650p. 1995. teacher ed, ring bd. 95.00 (*1-886693-03-X*) Meeks Heit.

— Totally Awesome Health: Grade 4. DeVillers, Julie, ed. (Illus.). 650p. 1995. teacher ed, ring bd. 95.00 (*1-886693-04-8*) Meeks Heit.

— Totally Awesome Health: Grade 5. DeVillers, Julie, ed. (Illus.). 650p. 1995. teacher ed, lib. bdg. 95.00 (*1-886693-05-6*) Meeks Heit.

— Totally Awesome Health: Grade 6. DeVillers, Julie, ed. (Illus.). 650p. 1995. teacher ed, ring bd. 95.00 (*1-886693-06-4*) Meeks Heit.

— Totally Awesome Health: Grade 7. DeVillers, Julie, ed. (Illus.). 650p. 1995. teacher ed, ring bd. 95.00 (*1-886693-07-2*) Meeks Heit.

— Totally Awesome Health: Grade 8. DeVillers, Julie, ed. (Illus.). 650p. 1995. teacher ed, ring bd. 95.00 (*1-886693-10-2*) Meeks Heit.

Meeks, M. Douglas. God the Economist: The Doctrine of God & Political Economy. LC 89-12013. 208p. 1989. pap. 15.00 (*0-8006-2329-0*, 1-2329, Fortress Pr) Augsburg Fortress.

Meeks, M. Douglas, ed. The Portion of the Poor: Good News to the Poor in the Wesleyan Tradition. (Kingswood Ser.). 160p. (Orig.). 1995. pap. 12.95 (*0-687-15529-0*) Abingdon.

Meeks, M. Littleton. Radar Propagation at Low Altitudes. (Artech Radar Library). (Illus.). 105p. (C). 1982. 29.00 (*0-89006-118-1*) Artech Hse.

Meeks, Martha F. Models for Teaching. (Bridges for Ideas Handbook Ser.). 1956. pap. text ed. 6.00 (*0-913648-11-6*) U Tex Austin Film Lib.

Meeks, Robert G. Hepatotoxicology. 500p. 1990. 59.50 (*0-936923-46-6*) Telford Pr.

Meeks, Ronald L., jt. auth. see Fratoe, Frank A.

***Meeks, Steve.** The Last Great Revival. 1994. 7.00 (*0-9630425-1-3*) Calvary TX.

— Relational Christianity: Experiencing Intimacy & Companionship with the Living God. (Orig.). 1991. pap. 5.00 (*0-9630425-0-5*) Calvary TX.

***Meeks, Trevor, photos.** The Hunting Year. (Illus.). 128p. 1995. 34.95 (*0-600-58506-9*, Pub. by Hamlyn UK) Trafalgar.

Meeks, Wayne, ed. see St. Paul.

Meeks, Wayne A. The First Urban Christians: The Social World of the Apostle Paul. LC 82-8447. 312p. 1984. reprint ed. pap. 15.00 (*0-300-03244-7*, Y-503) Yale U Pr.

— The Moral World of the First Christians. LC 86-5504. (Library of Early Christianity: Vol. 6). 180p. (C). 1986. reprint ed. pap. 12.99 (*0-664-25014-9*, Westminster) Westminster John Knox.

— The Origins of Christian Morality: The First Two Centuries. LC 93-10226. 304p. 1993. 30.00 (*0-300-05640-0*) Yale U Pr.

Meeks, Wayne A., ed. Library of Early Christianity, 8 vols., Set. 1987. 89.99 (*0-664-25103-X*) Westminster John Knox.

Meeks, Wayne A., jt. ed. see Malherbe, Abraham J.

Meeldijk, Victor. Electronic Components: Selection & Application Guidelines. LC 93-44638. 1994. 450.00 (*0-471-02287-X*, Wiley-Interscience) Wiley.

Meelis, Evert, jt. auth. see Haccou, Patsy.

Meem, J. L. Two Group Reactor Theory. 430p. 1964. text ed. 241.00 (*0-677-00520-2*) Gordon & Breach.

Meema, K. M., jt. auth. see Hutchinson, Thomas C.

Meema, K. M., jt. ed. see Hutchinson, Thomas C.

***Meena, James C.** The Very Best of X: Lifestyles in Christ Meditations on Orthodox Christian Living. 118p. (Orig.). 1995. pap. 8.95x (*0-9634940-5-8*) York Pub.

Meenach, Antoinette E., jt. auth. see Williamson, Doris M.

Meenaghan, Thomas & Kilty, Keith. Policy Analysis & Research Technology: Political & Ethical Considerations. LC 93-30524. 248p. 1994. pap. text ed. 24.95 (*0-925065-46-3*) Lyceum IL.

Meenaghan, Thomas M. & Washington, Robert O. Social Policy & Social Welfare: Structure & Applications. LC 79-54669. (Illus.). 1980. text ed. 29.95 (*0-02-920750-9*) Free Pr.

Meenaghan, Thomas M., et al. Macro-Level Practice in the Human Services: An Introduction to Planning, Administration & Evaluation. (Illus.). 288p. (C). 1982. text ed. 27.95 (*0-02-920850-5*) Free Pr.

Meenai, S. A. The Islamic Development Bank: A Case Study of Islamic Co-Operation. 200p. 1989. 69.50 (*0-7103-0329-7*) Routledge Chapman & Hall.

Meenakshi. Hindi-English Dictionary. 2nd ed. 802p. 1984. 49.95 (*0-8288-1743-X*) Fr & Eur.

Meenan, Daniel F., tr. see Iparraguirre, Ignacio.

Meenan, Robert F., et al. Epidemiology & Health Services Research; Orthopedic Conditions; Nonarticular Rheumatism. (Current Opinion in Rheumatology Ser.). (Illus.). 234p. (Orig.). 1994. pap. text ed. 39.95 (*1-85922-643-4*) Current Science.

Meer, Ameena. Bombay Talkie. Silverberg, Ira, ed. (Orig.). 1994. pap. 11.99 (*1-85242-325-0*) Serpents Tail.

Meer, Claudia G. Customer Education. LC 84-6938. 168p. 1985. lib. bdg. 34.95 (*0-8304-1049-X*) Nelson-Hall.

Meer, Claudia G., et al. Sex Role Stereotyping in Occupational Choices: A Career Counseling Manual. 62p. 1982. 6.00 (*0-941312-01-1*) Inst Mgmt & Labor.

Meer, Jeff. Drugs & Sports. (Encyclopedia of Psychoactive Drugs Ser.: No. 2). (Illus.). 136p. (YA). (gr. 5 up). 1988. lib. bdg. 19.95 (*1-55546-226-X*); pap. 9.95 (*0-7910-0794-4*) Chelsea Hse.

— Drugs & Sports. (Encyclopedia of Psychoactive Drugs - Compact Paperback Library). (Illus.). 32p. (YA). (gr. 5 up). 1991. pap. 4.49 (*1-55546-996-5*) Chelsea Hse.

Meer, Kathleen V., ed. see Cummins, Marjorie.

Meer, Nancy V., jt. auth. see Warmington, Judy.

Meera, Mother. Answers. (Illus.). 120p. (Orig.). 1991. pap. text ed. 9.95 (*0-9622973-3-X*) Meeramma Pubns.

Meerbaum, Samuel, ed. Myocardial Perfusion, Reperfusion, Coronary Venous Retroperfusion. 160p. 1990. pap. 101.00 (*0-387-91362-9*) Spr-Verlag.

Meerbaum, Samuel & Melzer, Richard, eds. Myocardial Contrast Two Dimensional Echocardiography. (Developments in Cardiovascular Medicine Ser.). (C). 1989. lib. bdg. 120.00 (*0-7923-0205-2*) Kluwer Ac.

Meerbote, R. & Hudson, H., eds. Kant's Aesthetics. (North American Kant Society Studies in Philosophy: Vol. 1). viii, 146p. (Orig.). 1991. lib. bdg. 36.00 (*0-924922-56-7*); pap. text ed. 18.00 (*0-924922-06-0*) Ridgeview.

Meerbote, Ralf, jt. ed. see Harper, William A.

Meerdink, Jan, ed. Directory of Broodmare Buyers. 200p. 1992. ring bd. 125.00 (*0-685-55024-9*) R Meerdink Co Ltd.

— Directory of Two-Year-Old Buyers. 1992. ring bd. 125.00 (*0-685-55023-0*) R Meerdink Co Ltd.

— Directory of Two Year Old Buyers, 1990. 255p. (Orig.). 1990. ring bd. 125.00 (*0-929346-08-4*) R Meerdink Co Ltd.

— Directory of Yearling Buyers, 1992. 200p. 1992. ring bd. 125.00 (*0-929346-16-5*) R Meerdink Co Ltd.

Meerdink, Jan, ed. see Research Staff of the Russell Meerdink Company.

Meerloo, Joost A. Patterns of Panic. LC 50-5823. 120p. reprint ed. pap. 34.20 (*0-317-10375-X*, 2010445) Bks Demand.

— The Two Faces of Man: Two Studies on the Sense of Time & on Ambivalence. LC 54-12141. 251p. reprint ed. pap. 71.60 (*0-317-10297-4*, 2010703) Bks Demand.

Meerman, Frans, jt. auth. see Kiss, Agnes.

Meerman, G. A Logic Programming Approach to Pedigree Analysis. 106p. 1992. pap. 67.00 (*90-5170-077-6*, Pub. by Thesis Pubs NE) IBD Ltd.

***Meerman, Michael V.** The Complete Credit & Collection Letters Kit. Donohue, Teresa, ed. 140p. 1994. pap. 32.00 (*0-934914-90-7*) NACM.

Meermann, Rolf, jt. auth. see Vandereycken, Walter.

Meeron, E., ed. The Physics of Many-Particle Systems. (Many-Body Problem: Current Research & Reviews Ser.). 698p. 1966. text ed. 405.00 (*0-677-10330-1*) Gordon & Breach.

Meeropol, Michael, ed. The Rosenberg Letters: A Complete Edition of the Prison Correspondence of Julius & Ethel Rosenberg. LC 93-40860. 792p. 1994. 75.00 (*0-8240-5948-4*, H1184) Garland.

Meeropol, Michael, jt. auth. see Meeropol, Robert.

Meeropol, Robert & Meeropol, Michael. We Are Your Sons: The Legacy of Ethel & Julius Rosenberg. 2nd ed. LC 85-30892. (Illus.). 508p. 1986. 34.95 (*0-252-01263-1*) U of Ill Pr.

Meerov, M. V. Multivariable Control Systems. 296p. 1968. text ed. 76.00 (*0-7065-0464-X*, Pub. by Keter Pub IS) Coronet Bks.

Meerovich, Boris, tr. see Vorobyev, Nicolai.

***Meers, P. & Sedgwick, J.** Microbiology & Epidemiology of Infection for Health Science Students. (Illus.). 320p. 1995. pap. text ed. 41.50 (*1-56593-350-8*, 0674) Singular Publishing.

Meers, Peter, et al. Hospital Infection Control for Nurses. LC 92-49510. 1992. write for info. (*1-56593-060-6*) Singular Publishing.

Meerschaert, Mark M. Mathematical Modeling. (Illus.). 287p. 1993. text ed. 49.95 (*0-12-487650-1*) Acad Pr.

Meerschaut, A., ed. Incommensurate Sandwiched Layered Compounds. 436p. 1992. text ed. 146.00 (*0-87849-643-2*, Pub. by Trans Tech GW) LPS Dist Ctr.

Meerschwam, David M. Breaking Financial Boundaries: Global Capital, National Deregulation, & Financial Services Firms. 320p. 1990. 35.00 (*0-87584-253-4*) Harvard Busn.

Meerschwam, David M., jt. auth. see Hayes, Samuel L., III.

Meerschwan, David M. Breaking Financial Boundaries: Global Capital, National Deregulation & Financial Services Firms. 1991. text ed. 35.00 (*0-07-103305-X*) McGraw.

Meersman, R. A. & Sernadas, A. C., eds. Data Knowledge (DS-2) Proceedings of 2nd IFIP TC2 WG2.6 Working Conf. on Database Semantics, Albufeira, Portugal, 3-7 Nov., 1986. 430p. 1988. 102.75 (*0-444-70528-7*, North Holland) Elsevier.

Meersman, R. A., jt. ed. see Flach, P. A.

Meersman, R. A., jt. ed. see Steel, T. B., Jr.

Meersman, R. A., et al. Object-Oriented Databases: Analysis, Design & Construction. 1991. 113.00 (*0-444-88929-9*, DS-4) Elsevier.

Meersman, R. A., et al, eds. Artificial Intelligence in Databases & Information Systems (DS-3) Proc. of the TC2WG2.6 - TC8WG8.1 Working Conf., Guangzhou, China 4-8 July, 1988. 584p. 1990. 110.25 (*0-444-88645-1*, North Holland) Elsevier.

Meerson, Felix Z. Adaptive Protection of the Heart: Protecting Against Stress & Ischemic Damage. (Illus.). 320p. 1990. 121.00 (*0-8493-5150-2*, QP114) CRC Pr.

— The Failing Heart: Adaptation & Deadaptation. Katz, Arnold M., ed. (Illus.). 342p. 1983. text ed. 104.00 (*0-89004-550-X*) Raven.

Meertens, L. G., ed. Program Specification & Transformation: Proceedings of the IFIP TC2-WG,1 Working Conference, Bad-Tolz, FRG, 15-17 April, 1986. 536p. 1987. 107.75 (*0-444-70223-7*, North Holland) Elsevier.

Meertens, Roel W., jt. auth. see Wilke, Henk A. M.

Meerwarth, Rudolf, et al. Die Einwirkung des Krieges Auf Bevolkerungsbewegung, Einkommen Und Lebenshaltung in Deutschland. (Wirtschafts-Und Sozialgeschichte des Weltkrieges (Osterreichische Und Ungarische Serie)). (GER.). 1932. 150.00 (*0-317-27461-9*) Elliots Bks.

Mees, A. I. Dynamics of Feedback Systems. LC 80-40501. (Illus.). 224p. reprint ed. pap. 63.90 (*0-8357-6651-9*, 2035320) Bks Demand.

Mees, Arthur. Choirs & Choral Music. LC 69-13995. 250p. 1970. reprint ed. text ed. 45.00 (*0-8371-1967-7*, MECM, Greenwood Pr) Greenwood.

— Choirs & Choral Music. LC 68-25296. (Studies in Music: No. 42). 1969. reprint ed. lib. bdg. 59.95 (*0-8383-0308-0*) M S G Haskell Hse.

Mees-Christeller, Eva. The Practice of Artistic Therapy. Vunderink, Margreet, tr. (Illus.). 78p. (Orig.). 1985. pap. 8.00 (*0-936132-77-9*) Merc Pr NY.

Mees, Inger, jt. auth. see Collins, Beverley.

Mees, L. F. Blessed by Illness. 248p. (Orig.). 1983. reprint ed. pap. 10.95 (*0-88010-054-0*) Anthroposophic.

— Secrets of the Skeleton: Form in Metamorphosis. Bohr, Ellen & Adams, David, eds. (Illus.). 108p. (Orig.). 1984. pap. 16.95 (*0-88010-087-7*) Anthroposophic.

Mees, Walter H., Jr. Who Is God? (Active Bible Curriculum Ser.). (Illus.). 48p. 1991. pap. 9.99 (*1-55945-218-8*) Group Pub.

Meese. Systematische Grammatikvermittlung und Spracharbeit. 224p. pap. 24.50 (*3-468-49431-9*) Langenscheidt.

Meese, Edwin, III. With Reagan: The Inside Story. LC 92-4222. (Illus.). 350p. 1992. 24.95 (*0-89526-522-2*) Regnery Pub.

Meese, Edwin, intro. Report to the Attorney General on the Admission of Criminal Histories at Trial. 59p. (Orig.). 1988. pap. 2.25 (*0-16-003628-3*, S/N 027-000-01306-6) USGPO.

Meese, Elizabeth. Sem, Erotics: Theorizing Lesbian: Writing. (Cutting Edge: Lesbian Life & Literature Ser.). 304p. 1992. text ed. 45.00 (*0-8147-5469-4*); pap. 14.95 (*0-8147-5470-8*) NYU Pr.

Meese, Elizabeth & Parker, Alice, eds. The Difference Within: Feminism & Critical Theory. LC 88-7916. (Critical Theory Ser.: Vol. 8). xi, 219p. (C). 1988. 65.00x (*1-55619-042-5*) Benjamins North Am.

Meese, Elizabeth A. Crossing the Double-Cross: The Practice of Feminist Criticism. LC 85-20920. xiii, 180p. 1986. 27.50 (*0-8078-1683-3*); pap. 11.95 (*0-8078-4149-8*) U of NC Pr.

— Ex-Tensions: Re-Figuring Feminist Criticism. 224p. 1990. 27.50 (*0-252-01682-3*); pap. 11.95 (*0-252-06105-5*) U of Ill Pr.

Meese, Elizabeth A., jt. ed. see Parker, Alice A.

Meese, R. Gregory, ed. see Technical Association of the Pulp & Paper Industry Staff.

Meese, Ruth L. Teaching Learners with Mild Disabilities: Integrating Research & Practice. LC 93-28274. 1994. pap. 40.95 (*0-534-21102-X*) Brooks-Cole.

Meeske, Milan D. & Norris, R. C. Copywriting for the Electronic Media: A Practical Guide. 2nd ed. 377p. (C). 1992. pap. 34.95 (*0-534-15624-X*) Intl Thomson.

Meeson, Brian. Shapings. 110p. 1981. pap. 4.95 (*0-7725-5006-9*, Pub. by Stoddart Pubng CN) Genl Dist Srvs.

Meeson, N. Ship & Aircraft Mortgages. 217p. 1988. 110.00 (*1-85044-104-9*) Lloyds London Pr.

Meessen, Karl M., ed. International Law of Export Control: Jurisdictional Issues. 208p. (C). 1992. lib. bdg. 90.00 (*1-85333-483-9*, Pub. by Graham & Trotman UK) Kluwer Ac.

Meester, Greert T. & Pinciroli, Francesco, eds. Databases for Cardiology. (Developments in Cardiovascular Medicine Ser.). (C). 1991. lib. bdg. 202.50 (*0-7923-0886-7*) Kluwer Ac.

Meester, Greert T., jt. ed. see Serruys, Patrick W.

Meester, J. & Setzer, H. W., eds. The Mammals of Africa: An Identification Manual. LC 70-169904. 505p. reprint ed. pap. 144.00 (*0-685-20923-7*, 2056496) Bks Demand.

***Meeta, Madhu.** Diseases of Ornamental Plants in India. (C). 1994. 42.50x (*81-7035-129-4*, Pub. by Daya Pub Hse II) S Asia.

Meeten, G. H., ed. Optical Properties of Polymers. 416p. 1986. 115.25 (*0-85334-434-5*) Elsevier.

Meeter, Daniel J. Meeting Each Other in Church Doctrine, Liturgy, & Government: The Bicentennial of the Celebration of the Constitution of the Reformed Church in America. LC 93-5093. (Historical Series of the Reformed Church in America: No. 24). 240p. (Orig.). 1993. pap. text ed. 12.99 (*0-8028-0717-8*) Eerdmans.

Meeter, Glenn. Letters to Barbara. LC 81-15235. 274p. reprint ed. pap. 78.10 (*0-317-30154-3*, 2025336) Bks Demand.

Meeter, Glenn, jt. ed. see Detweiler, Robert.

Meeter, Henry H. The Basic Ideas of Calvinism. 6th ed. LC 90-33204. 224p. 1990. pap. 12.99 (*0-8010-6269-1*) Baker Bk.

Meeter, Merle, ed. The Armor of Light. 208p. (Orig.). (C). 1979. pap. 6.95 (*0-932914-01-2*) Dordt Coll Pr.

Meeth, L. Richard, jt. ed. see Hodgkinson, Harold L.

Meeth, Louis R. Quality Education for Less Money. LC 73-18502. (Jossey-Bass Higher Education Ser.). 224p. reprint ed. pap. 63.90 (*0-317-41803-3*, 2025663) Bks Demand.

Meetham, A. R. Encyclopedia of Linguistics, Information & Control. 1969. 301.00 (*0-08-012337-6*, Pub. by Pergamon Repr UK) Franklin.

Meetham, A. R., et al. Atmospheric Pollution: Its History, Origins & Prevention. 4th ed. (Illus.). 288p. 1981. 105.00 (*0-08-024003-8*, Pub. by Pergamon Repr UK) Franklin.

Meeting on Critical Evaluation of Cardiac Rehabilitation Staff. Critical Evaluation of Cardiac Rehabilitation, Tel-Aviv, Nov.-Dec. 1975: Proceedings of the Meeting on Critical Evaluation of Cardiac Rehabilitation, Tel-Aviv, Nov.-Dec. 1975. Kellerman, J. J., ed. (Bibliotheca Cardiologica Ser.: No. 36). (Illus.). 1977. 49.75 (*3-8055-2373-4*) S Karger.

***Meeting on Physical Techniques in Cardiological Imaging Staff.** Physical Techniques in Cardiological Imaging: Proceedings of the Meeting on Physical Techniques in Cardiological Imaging Held at the Medical & Biological Sciences Building, University of Southampton, 8-9 July 1982. fac. ed. Short, M. D. et al, eds. LC 83-20768. (Illus.). 221p. 1983. reprint ed. pap. 63.00 (*0-7837-8014-1*, 2047770) Bks Demand.

Meeus. Astronomical Algorithms. 1991. 24.95 (*0-943396-35-2*) Willmann-Bell.

— Astronomical Formulae for Calculators. 4th ed. 1988. pap. 14.95 (*0-943396-22-0*) Willmann-Bell.

— Elements of Solar Eclipses, 1951-2200. 1989. 19.95 (*0-943396-21-2*) Willmann-Bell.

— Transits. 1990. 14.95 (*0-943396-26-3*) Willmann-Bell.

Meeus, J. & Grosjean, C. Canon of Solar Eclipses: 1966 Edition. LC 64-25676. 1966. 305.00 (*0-08-011015-0*, Pub. by Pergamon Repr UK) Franklin.

Meeus, Jean. Astronomical Tables of the Sun, Moon, & Planets. LC 83-5762. 400p. (Orig.). 1983. pap. text ed. 19.95 (*0-943396-02-6*) Willmann-Bell.

— Astronomical Tables of the Sun, Moon & Planets. 2nd ed. LC 95-3657. 1995. write for info. (*0-943396-45-X*) Willmann-Bell.

Meeus, Wim, et al, eds. Adolescence, Careers, & Cultures. LC 92-45751. (Prevention & Intervention in Childhood & Adolescence Ser.: No. 13). x, 428p. (C). 1993. lib. bdg. 98.95 (*3-11-013679-1*) De Gruyter.

Meeuse, B. J. D. Pollination. Head, John J., ed. LC 83-71165. (Carolina Biology Readers Ser.: No. 133). (Illus.). 16p. (C). (gr. 10 up). 1984. pap. 2.75 (*0-89278-333-8*, 45-9733) Carolina Biological.

Meeuwissen, Tony. The Key to the Kingdom: An Enchanted Deck. (Illus.). 120p. 1992. 19.95 (*1-56138-079-2*) Running Pr.

Meezan, William & Shireman, Joan F. Care & Commitment: Foster Parent Adoption Decisions. LC 85-2730. 247p. 1985. 64.50 (*0-88706-103-6*); pap. 21.95 (*0-88706-104-4*) State U NY Pr.

Meffe, Gary K. & Carroll, C. Ronald. Principles of Conservation Biology. LC 93-48913. (Illus.). 600p. (C). 1994. text ed. 48.95 (*0-87893-519-3*) Sinauer Assocs.

***Megahead, S., et al.** Rechargeable Lithium & Lithium Ion (RCT) Batteries. 510p. 1995. 70.00 (*1-56677-087-4*, PV 94-28) Electrochem Soc.

Megahed, S. Principles of Robot Modelling & Simulation. 312p. 1993. text ed. 79.95 (*0-471-93348-1*) Wiley.

Megakinetics Staff. Baby Loves... (CIS Ser.: No. 05004). (J). (gr. k-5). 1991. pap. text ed. 15.00 (*1-56495-007-7*) Megakinetics.

— What It Takes to Be a Millionaire. (ACS Ser.: No. 02005). 25p. 1991. 15.95 (*1-56495-014-X*) Megakinetics.

Megalli, Mary D. On the Road in Egypt: A Motorist's Guide. (Illus.). 78p. 1990. pap. 14.95 (*0-685-46361-3*, Pub. by Am Univ Cairo Pr UA) Col U Pr.

Megargee, E. I. & Spielberger, C. O., eds. Personality Assessment in America: A Retrospective on the Occasion of the Fiftieth Anniversary of the Society for Personality Assessment. 200p. (C). 1991. text ed. 39.95 (*0-8058-0928-7*) L Erlbaum Assocs.

Megargee, Edwin I. The California Psychological Inventory Handbook. LC 76-186581. (Jossey-Bass Behavioral Science Ser.). 324p. reprint ed. pap. 92.40 (*0-7837-2503-5*, 2042662) Bks Demand.

— Guide to Obtaining a Psychology Internship. 2nd ed. LC 90-82565. vi, 235p. (C). 1992. pap. text ed. 17.95 (*1-55959-043-2*) Accel Devel.

Megargee, Frank, jt. ed. see Megargee, Sue.

Megargee, Sue & Megargee, Frank, eds. Shore Writer's Sampler II: Stories & Poems by Eastern Shore Writers Selected with the Help of Cynthia Voigt & David Bergman. (Illus.). xii, 222p. (Orig.). 1988. pap. 9.50 (*0-9618993-1-X*) Friendly Harbor.

Megarry, J. Compact Discs & Computers: Converging Technologies. 1994. pap. 33.00 (*0-412-37880-9*, Blackie & Son-Chapman NY) Routledge Chapman & Hall.

Megas, George A. The Greek House: Its Evolution & Its Relation to the Houses of Other Balkan Peoples. LC 77-87522. (Ministry of Reconstruction Publications: 37). (GRE.). reprint ed. 15.00 (*0-404-16595-8*) AMS Pr.

Megateli, Abderrahmane. Investment Policies of National Oil Companies. LC 80-12841. 344p. 1980. text ed. 65.00 (*0-275-90522-5*, C0522, Praeger Pubs) Greenwood.

Megaw, E. D., ed. Contemporary Ergonomics 1988 - Ergonomics Giving Quality to Life: Proceedings of the 1988 Annual Conference of the Ergonomics Society, Manchester, UK April 1988. 350p. 1988. 85.00 (*0-85066-410-1*) Taylor & Francis.

— Contemporary Ergonomics 1989: Ergonomics - Design Progress. 550p. 1989. 69.00 (*0-85066-484-5*) Taylor & Francis.

Megaw, E. D., jt. ed. see Kumashiro, M.

Megaw, Helen D. Crystal Structures. (Illus.). 563p. (C). reprint ed. 60.00 (*1-878907-40-9*) TechBooks.

Megaw, J. V. & Simpson, D. D. Introduction to British Prehistory: From the Arrival of Homo Sapiens to the Claudian Invasion. (Illus.). 560p. (C). 1992. pap. text ed. 54.50 (*0-389-20982-1*) B&N Imports.

Megaw, Ruth & Megaw, Vincent. Celtic Art: From Its Beginnings to the Book of Kells. LC 88-50245. (Illus.). 288p. 1990. pap. 24.95 (*0-500-27585-8*) Thames Hudson.

Megaw, T. M. & Bartlett, John. Tunnels: Planning, Design, Construction, 2 vols., Set. LC 81-4111. (Engineering Science Ser.). 605p. 1982. text ed. 204.00 (*0-470-27217-1*) P-H.

Megaw, Vincent, jt. auth. see Megaw, Ruth.

***Megay-Nespoli, Karen.** The First Year for Elementary School Teachers: A Practical Plan for Dealing with the Short & Long-Term Management of Teaching Duties & Responsibilities. LC 92-42964. (Illus.). 204p. 1993. pap. 16.95 (*0-398-06284-6*) C C Thomas.

— The First Year for Elementary School Teachers: A Practical Plan for Dealing with the Short & Long-Term Management of Teaching Duties & Responsibilities. LC 92-42964. (Illus.). 204p. 1993. 31.95 (*0-398-05842-3*) C C Thomas.

Megedanz, Thomas C. Historical Perspectives on the Pick-Sloan Plan. 1988. pap. 1.00 (*1-55614-130-0*) U of SD Gov Res Bur.

Megens, Inc. America Aid to NATO Allies in the 1950s: The Dutch Case. 320p. 1994. pap. 30.00 (*90-5170-252-3*, Pub. by Thesis Pubs NE) IBD Ltd.

Megerian, Maureen, jt. auth. see Sandler, Irving.

***Megerssa, G.** The Booran. (Heritage Library of African Peoples Ser.). (Illus.). 64p. 1995. 15.95 (*0-8239-1769-X*) Rosen Group.

Megerssa, Gemetchu, jt. auth. see Kassam, Aneesa.

Meggaard, I., jt. auth. see Russell, C. H.

Megged, Eyal, tr. see Alkalay-Gut, Karen.

Megged, Matti. Animal That Never Was. 1992. 12.95 (*0-930829-20-4*) Lumen Inc.

An Asterisk (*) at the beginning of an entry indicates that the title is appearing in BIP for the first time.

*Meggers, Betty & Evans, Clifford. Archeological Investigations at the Mouth of the Amazon. (Bureau of American Ethnology Bulletins Ser.). 664p. 1995. lib. bdg. 149.00 (0-7812-4167-7) Rprt Serv.

Meggers, Betty, jt. auth. see Evans, Clifford.

Meggers, Betty J. Environmental Limitation on the Development of Culture. (Reprint Series in Social Sciences). (C). 1993. reprint ed. pap. text ed. 1.90 (0-8290-2692-4, S-189) Irvington.

— Prehistoric America: An Ecological Perspective. 2nd ed. LC 78-169504. 208p. 1979. lib. bdg. 36.95 (0-202-33078-8) Aldine de Gruyter.

— Prehistoric America: An Ecological Perspective. 2nd ed. LC 78-169504. 208p. 1979. pap. 19.95 (0-202-33079-6) Aldine de Gruyter.

Meggers, Betty J., ed. Prehistoria Sudamericana: Nuevas Perspectivas. LC 91-66122. (Illus.). 381p. (Orig.). (POR & SPA.). 1992. pap. 20.00 (0-9602822-6-2) Taraxacum.

Meggers, William, jt. auth. see Ehrhardt, Roy.

Meggett, Joan M. Music Periodical Literature: An Annotated Bibliography of Indexes & Bibliographies. LC 77-19120. 126p. 1978. 20.00 (0-8108-1109-X) Scarecrow.

Meggett, Joan M., comp. Keyboard Music by Women Composers: A Catalog & Bibliography. LC 81-4130. (Illus.). 232p. 1981. text ed. 47.95 (0-313-22833-7, MKM/, Greenwood Pr) Greenwood.

Megginson, David, et al. Human Resource Development. 160p. (Orig.). 1993. pap. text ed. 25.95 (0-7494-1062-0, Pub. by Kogan Page UK) Nichols Pub.

Megginson, Leon C. Management. (C). 1992. 23.50 (0-06-500695-X) HarpCollege.

— Management. 4th ed. (C). 1991. text ed. 70.00 (0-06-044475-4) HarpCollege.

— Personnel. 2nd ed. (C). 1972. 14.50 (0-256-00360-2) Irwin.

— Personnel & Human Resources Administration. 3rd ed. (C). 1977. 18.95 (0-256-01909-6) Irwin.

Megginson, Leon C. & Mosley, Donald C. Management: Concepts & Applications. 3rd ed. 640p. (C). 1990. text ed. 32.00 (0-06-044466-5) HarpCollege.

Megginson, Leon C., et al. Successful Small Business Management. 6th ed. 880p. (C). 1990. text ed. 56.95 (0-256-08635-4) Irwin.

Megginson, William L., et al. Small Business Management: An Entrepreneur's Guide to Success. LC 93-6704. 576p. (C). 1993. pap. text ed. 42.95 (0-256-14094-4) Irwin.

Meggison, Peter F., jt. auth. see Kaliski, Burton S.

Meggitt, Beverley, jt. auth. see Grattan, Ken.

Meggitt, Mervyn. Blood Is Their Argument: Warfare among the Mae Enga Tribesmen of the New Guinea Highlands. Edgerton, Robert B. & Langness, L. L., eds. LC 76-28116. (Illus.). 223p. (C). 1977. pap. text ed. 14.95 (0-87484-394-4) Mayfield Pub.

Meggitt, Mervyn J., jt. auth. see Gordon, Robert J.

Meggle, Georg & Wessels, Ulla, eds. Analyomen One: Proceedings of the First Conference Perspectives in Analytical Philosophy. (Perspektiven der Analytischen Philosophie Ser.: Vol. 1). xx, 989p. (C). 1994. lib. bdg. 364.65 (3-11-013581-7, 2-94) De Gruyter.

— Analyomen 1: Analyomen 1: Perspectives in Analytical Philosophy. 1993. write for info. (0-318-72342-5) De Gruyter.

Meggs, Philip & High, Steven. Tomas Gonda: A Life in Design. LC 93-74787. 92p. (Orig.). 1994. 15.00 (0-935519-17-3) Anderson Gal.

Meggs, Philip B. Type & Image: The Language of Graphic Design. (Illus.). 208p. 1992. pap. 34.95 (0-442-01165-2) Van Nos Reinhold.

Meggs, Philip B., ed. A History of Graphic Design. 2nd ed. (Illus.). 540p. 1992. text ed. 49.95 (0-442-31895-2) Van Nos Reinhold.

Meghdessian, Samira R. The Status of the Arab Woman: A Select Bibliography. LC 80-1028. 176p. 1980. text ed. 49.95 (0-313-22548-6, MEA/, Greenwood Pr) Greenwood.

Meghnagi, David. Freud & Judaism. 174p. 1993. pap. 35.95 (1-85575-002-3, Pub. by Karnac Bks UK) Brunner-Mazel.

Megiddo, N., ed. Progress in Mathematical Programming. (Illus.). x, 158p. 1988. 59.50 (0-387-96847-4) Spr-Verlag.

Megiddo, Nimrod. Essays in Game Theory: In Honor of Michael Maschler. LC 93-48255. (Illus.). 216p. 1994. 39.00 (0-387-94224-6) Spr-Verlag.

Megier, Jacques, jt. ed. see Hill, Joachim.

Megill, Allan. Prophets of Extremity: Nietzsche, Heidegger, Foucault, Derrida. 1985. pap. 15.00 (0-520-06028-8) U CA Pr.

Megill, Allan, ed. Rethinking Objectivity. (Post-Contemporary Interventions Ser.). 352p. 1994. lib. bdg. 45.95 (0-8223-1479-7); pap. text ed. 15.95 (0-8223-1494-0) Duke.

Megill, David W. & Tanner, Paul D. Jazz Issues: A Critical History. 416p. (C). 1995. pap. text ed. write for info. (0-697-12571-8) Brown & Benchmark.

Megill, Donald D. Music & Musicians: An Introduction. LC 92-38407. 1993. pap. text ed. 35.00 (0-13-034919-4) P-H.

Megill, Donald D. & Demory, Richard S. Introduction to Jazz History. 3rd ed. 320p. 1992. pap. text ed. 41.33 (0-13-481854-7) P-H.

Megill, Ken. Making the Information Revolution: A Handbook for Information Resources Management. 1994. write for info. (0-318-72176-7) Assn Inform & Image Mgmt.

*Megill, Kenneth A., et al. Making the Information Revolution: A Handbook on Federal Information Resources Management. 1995. pap. 36.00 (0-89258-293-6, R041) Assn Inform & Image Mgmt.

Megill, Robert E. The Business Side of Geology: A Collection of Articles Reprinted from the AAPG Explorer, 1987-1988. (Illus.). v, 48p. 1989. ring bd. 15.00 (0-89181-812-X) AAPG.

— Introduction to Exploration Economics. 3rd ed. 256p. 1988. 69.95 (0-87814-331-9, P4458) PennWell Bks.

— An Introduction to Risk Analysis. 2nd ed. 288p. 1984. 69.95 (0-87814-257-6, P4351) PennWell Bks.

— Long Range Exploration Planning: A Guide to Preparing Goals, Strategies, & Action Plans. 96p. 1985. 44.95 (0-87814-286-X, P4408) PennWell Bks.

Megill, Robert E., comp. Evaluating & Managing Risk. 160p. 1985. 34.95 (0-87814-283-5, P4412) PennWell Bks.

*Megill, Robert E., ed. Economics & the Explorer. (AAPG Studies in Geology: No. 19). (Illus.). viii, 95p. 1985. pap. 21.00 (0-89181-025-0) AAPG.

Meginess, et al. History of Tioga County. (Illus.). 1186p. 1989. reprint ed. lib. bdg. 109.00 (0-8328-0577-7) Higginson Bk Co.

Meginness, John F. Biography of Frances Slocum, the Lost Sister of Wyoming: A Complete Narrative of Her Captivity & Wanderings Among the Indians. LC 74-3963. (Women in America Ser.). 260p. 1977. reprint ed. 23.95 (0-405-06112-9) Ayer.

— Frances Slocum, Lost Daughter of Wyoming. 264p. 1991. lib. bdg. 24.00 (1-880484-02-1) Zebrowski Hist.

Meginnis, Margaret A. One - We All Worship One God: A Sharing of Five Major Religions. 1993. 13.95 (0-533-10568-4) Vantage.

Megiveron, Gene E. The Effective High School Principal. LC 91-14490. (Effective School Administration Ser.: No. 4). (Illus.). 528p. 1992. 28.95 (0-88280-096-5) ETC Pubns.

Megiveron, Gene E., jt. auth. see Herman, Jerry J.

Meglitsch, Paul A. & Schram, Frederick R. Invertebrate Zoology. 3rd ed. (Illus.). 640p. (C). 1991. text ed. 47.95 (0-19-504900-4) OUP.

Megna, Laura L., jt. auth. see Morici, Peter.

Megnik, Sarnoff A., jt. ed. see Buikhuisen, Wouter.

Megranahan, Mike. Counselling: A Practical Guide for Employers. 304p. (C). 1989. 94.00 (0-85292-397-X, Pub. by IPM Hse UK) St Mut.

Megraud, F. & Lamouliatte, H., eds. Gastroduodenal Pathology & Campylobacter Pylori: Proceedings of the 1st Meeting of the European Campylobacter Pylori Study Group, Bordeaux, France, 7-8 Oct., 1988. (International Congress Ser.: No. 847). 660p. 1989. 174.50 (0-444-81159-1, Excerpta Medica) Elsevier.

Megraw, Robert A. Wood Quality Factors in Loblolly Pine. 96p. 1985. 50.00 (0-89852-048-7, 0102B048) TAPPI.

Megret, M. Computed Tomography of the Cranial Skeleton: Face & Skull. Wackenheim, M. T., tr. (Exercises in Radiological Diagnosis Ser.). (Illus.). 190p. 1986. pap. 32.00 (0-387-15389-6) Spr-Verlag.

Megrey, B. A., jt. ed. see Edwards, E. F.

Megrian, Leon D., tr. see Isahakian, Avetik S.

Megroz, R. L. The Dream World, the History & Myth of Dreams. 1972. 59.95 (0-8490-0061-0) Gordon Pr.

— Francis Thompson: A Study in Poetic Mysticism. 1973. 250.00 (0-87968-075-X) Gordon Pr.

— Walter De La Mare: A Biography & Critical Study. 1988. reprint ed. lib. bdg. 69.00 (0-7812-0050-4) Rprt Serv.

— Walter De la Mare: A Biography & Critical Study. LC 72-145175. 305p. 1972. reprint ed. 39.00 (0-403-01103-5) Scholarly.

Megroz, Rodolphe. Dante Gabriel Rossetti: Painter, Poet of Heaven in Earth. LC 74-173851. (English Biography Ser.: No. 31). 1971. reprint ed. lib. bdg. 75.00 (0-8383-1336-1) M S G Haskell Hse.

Megroz, Rodolphe L. Dante Gabriel Rossetti, Painter Poet of Heaven in Earth. (BCL1-PR English Literature Ser.). 339p. 1992. reprint ed. lib. bdg. 89.00 (0-7812-7631-4) Rprt Serv.

— Dante Gabriel Rossetti, Painter Poet of Heaven in Earth. LC 75-145173. (Illus.). 1971. reprint ed. 39.00 (0-403-01101-9) Scholarly.

— Five Novelist Poets of Today. LC 71-84327. (Essay Index Reprint Ser.). 1977. 17.95 (0-8369-1097-4) Ayer.

— Francis Thompson: The Poet of Earth & Heaven. LC 77-131778. 1971. reprint ed. 39.00 (0-403-00665-1) Scholarly.

— Francis Thompson: The Poet of Earth in Heaven. (BCL1-PR English Literature Ser.). 288p. 1992. reprint ed. lib. bdg. 79.00 (0-685-54939-9) Rprt Serv.

— Three Sitwells: A Biographical & Critical Study. LC 79-145174. 1971. reprint ed. 29.00 (0-403-01102-7) Scholarly.

Megson, G. M. An Introduction to Systolic Algorithm Design. (Illus.). 360p. 1992. 76.95 (0-19-853813-8) OUP.

Megson, G. M., jt. auth. see Aleksandrov, V. N.

Megson, T. H. Aircraft: Structures for Engineering Students. 2nd ed. 1990. pap. text ed. 64.95 (0-470-21653-0) Halsted Pr.

Meguid, S. A. Engineering Fracture Mechanics. 392p. 1989. 113.50 (1-85166-282-0) Elsevier.

— Integrated Computer-Aided Design of Mechanical Systems. 200p. 1987. 72.00 (1-85166-021-6, Pub. by Elsevier Applied Sci UK) Elsevier.

Meguid, S. A., ed. Surface Engineering: Proceedings of the International Conference: Current Trends & Future Prospects, University of Toronto, Ontario, Canada, 25-27 June, 1990. 714p. 1990. 144.00 (1-85166-507-2) Elsevier.

Megura, Jim. The Official Identification & Price Guide to Bottles. 11th ed. (Illus.). 480p. 1992. pap. 14.00 (0-87637-843-2, House of Collect) Ballantine.

*Megyeri, J. Eisenbahn-Bewegungsgeometrie. 608p. (GER.). 1994. 80.00 (963-05-6505-6, Pub. by A K HU) Intl Spec Bk.

*Megyesy, Eugene F. Pressure Vessel Handbook. 10th ed. 490p. 1995. 118.00 (0-914458-18-3) Pressure.

Mehafdi, Messaoud, jt. auth. see Emmanuel, Clive R.

Mehaffey, J. R., ed. Mathematical Modeling of Fire, Vol. STP 983. 140p. 1988. pap. 26.00 (0-8031-0992-X, 04-983000-31) ASTM.

Mehaffey, Karen R. Victorian American Women, 1840-1880: An Annotated Bibliography. LC 91-22206. 192p. 1991. 25.00 (0-8240-7142-5) Garland.

Mehaffey, Robert H. You Can Win Your Florida Election: A Step-by-Step Guide. 239p. 1992. 29.95 (0-9634145-0-X) R H Mehaffey & Assocs.

Mehaffy, George L., jt. auth. see Lanman, Barry A.

Mehaffy, Irene, jt. auth. see Mehaffy, Robert E.

Mehaffy, Robert E. & Mehaffy, Irene. Writing on the Job. Orig. Title: Writing for the Real World. 380p. (C). 1987. pap. text ed. 20.95 (0-917962-89-3) T H Peek.

*Mehale, Alilali G. Deep Water Training & Aerobics: A New Approach to a Total Physical Fitness. Davis, Denise et al, eds. (Illus.). 80p. (Orig.). (C). 1994. pap. text ed. 9.00 (0-9642960-6-3) Scientific Sports.

*Mehallis, Emanuel. Der Crisscross. 340p. Date not set. pap. 9.95 (0-7610-0406-8) NW Pub.

Mehan, Hugh. Learning Lessons: Social Organization in the Classroom. LC 78-24298. (Illus.). 247p. reprint ed. pap. 70.40 (0-8357-8205-0, 2033937) Bks Demand.

Mehan, Hugh, et al. Handicapping the Handicapped: Decision Making in Students' Educational Careers. LC 85-22084. (Illus.). xvi, 193p. 1986. 32.50 (0-8047-1304-9) Stanford U Pr.

Mehan, Richard J. & Dierker. Missouri Causes of Action: Torts. 400p. 1993. ring bd. 95.00 (1-56257-326-8) Michie Butterworth.

Mehan, Vivek K., jt. auth. see Meier, Bernhard.

Meharg, Amy, jt. ed. see Griffin, Linda.

Mehary, Hagos. The Strained U. S. - Ethiopian Relations. 175p. (Orig.). 1989. pap. 41.00x (91-22-01321-0, Pub. by Almqv & Wiksell SW) Coronet Bks.

Mehay, Stephen L., jt. ed. see Eitelberg, Mark J.

Mehay, Stephen L., jt. auth. see Shoup, Donald C.

Mehdi, Istaqbal. The Role of the Public Sector in Developing Countries: Pakistan. (ICPE Country Studies: No. 4). 124p. 1987. 10.00 (92-9038-804-8, Pub. by Intl Ctr Pub Ent XV) Kumarian Pr.

Mehdi, M. T. Islam & Intolerance a Reply to Salman Rushdie. 1990. 7.95 (0-685-66741-3, 14) Tahrike Tarsile Quran.

— Peace in Palestine. LC 75-43266. 1976. pap. 10.00 (0-911026-08-8) New World Press NY.

— Terrorism: Why America Is the Target! LC 87-62974. 128p. 1988. pap. 10.00 (0-911119-10-8) New World Press NY.

Mehdi, Mohammad T. Kennedy & Sirhan, Why. LC 68-57262. (Illus.). (Orig.). pap. 10.00 (0-911026-04-5, KSW) New World Press NY.

— Nation of Lions...Chained. LC 62-17245. 1963. pap. 15.00 (0-911026-05-3) New World Press NY.

Mehdi, Mohammad T., ed. Palestine & the Bible. LC 71-114557. 1971. pap. 5.00 (0-911026-06-1) New World Press NY.

Mehdi, Rubya. The Islamization of Laws in Pakistan. (Scandinavian Institute of Asian Studies Monograph: No. 60). 340p. (C). 1993. pap. 35.00 (0-7007-0236-9, Pub. by Curzon Pr UK) Humanities.

Mehedinti, S. What Is Transylvania? 124p. 1986. write for info. (0-937019-02-X); pap. 15.00 (0-937019-03-8) Romanian Hist.

Mehegan, J. J. O'Higgins of Chile. 1976. lib. bdg. 59.95 (0-8490-2366-1) Gordon Pr.

Mehegan, John. Improvising Jazz Piano. (It's Easy to Play Ser.). (Illus.). 104p. 1985. pap. 12.95 (0-8256-2256-5, AM32483); pap. write for info. (0-318-70316-5, AM82844); audio write for info. (0-318-70317-3, AM72844) Music Sales.

Mehendiratta, Pradeep. University Administration in India & U. S. A. 1985. 28.50 (0-8364-1308-3, Pub. by Oxford IBH II) S Asia.

Mehetre, M. G. Energy Crisis in India. 1990. 40.00 (81-85076-89-8, Pub. by Chugh Pubns II) S Asia.

Meheus, A. & Spier, R. E. Vaccines for Sexually Transmitted Diseases. (Illus.). 315p. 1990. text ed. 120.00 (0-408-04755-0) Buttrwrth-Heinemann.

Mehew, Ernest, jt. ed. see Booth, Bradford A.

Mehew, Ernest, jt. ed. see Booth, Bradford E.

Mehew, Karen, jt. auth. see Mehew, Randall.

Mehew, Randall & Mehew, Karen. The Best Manners Book Ever. (Virtue & Values Ser.). (Illus.). 68p. (J). 1990. pap. text ed. 5.95 (0-929985-55-9) Jackman Pubng.

— Gospel Basic Busy Book, Vol. I. (Illus.). 100p. (J). 1989. reprint ed. pap. text ed. 6.95 (0-910613-13-3) Millenial Pr.

— Gospel Basic Busy Book, Vol. II. (Illus.). 100p. (J). 1990. pap. text ed. 6.95 (0-910613-08-7) Millenial Pr.

Mehew, Randall K. A Most Convincing Witness. (Personal Enrichment Ser.). 41p. (Orig.). 1991. pap. write for info. (0-929985-63-X) Jackman Pubng.

— Organizing Families & Reunions. (Personal Enrichment Ser.). 125p. (Orig.). 1991. pap. write for info. (0-929985-76-1) Jackman Pubng.

— Our Family History. (Personal Enrichment Ser.). 27p. (Orig.). 1991. write for info. (0-929985-74-5) Jackman Pubng.

— Personal Life History. (Personal Enrichment Ser.). 32p. (Orig.). 1991. pap. write for info. (0-929985-73-7) Jackman Pubng.

— Seeds of Faith. (Personal Enrichment Ser.). 132p. (Orig.). 1991. pap. write for info. (0-929985-75-3) Jackman Pubng.

Mehihan, Thomas J. John C. Menihan Lithographs & Watercolors. John C. Menihan Enterprises Staff, ed. (Illus.). 36p. (Orig.). Date not set. pap. text ed. 20.00 (0-9639675-0-9) J C Menihan.

Mehl, Bronislav R. Agnosticism & Anecdotes: With Some Personal Medical Experiences & Self-Help Ideas. 1991. 16.95 (0-533-08959-X) Vantage.

— Successes & Failures-Flowing Sweet Waters. 1993. 17.95 (0-533-10058-5) Vantage.

Mehl, Dieter. Shakespeare's Tragedies: An Introduction. 281p. 1987. pap. 19.95 (0-521-31690-1) Cambridge U Pr.

*Mehl, Dieter, ed. The Fox, the Captain's Doll, the Ladybird. 272p. 1995. 9.95 (0-14-018779-0, Penguin Classics) Viking Penguin.

Mehl, Dieter, ed. see Lawrence, D. H.

Mehl, Duane. The High Road. 208p. (Orig.). 1988. pap. 9.95 (0-942421-05-1) Hazelden.

— The High Road. 208p. (Orig.). 1988. pap. 9.95 (1-56838-097-6) Hazelden.

Mehl, Lewis & Peterson, Gayle. Art of Healing. 350p. text ed. write for info. (0-8290-1804-2); audio (0-318-61266-6) Irvington.

Mehl, Lewis E. Healing Ceremonies: Bridging Native American Medicine & Spirituality with the Modern World Frontiers & Consciousness. 250p. 1992. 19.95 (0-685-49013-0) Irvington.

Mehl, Lewis E. & Peterson, Gayle H. Mind Body Medicine: The Language of Healing, Vol. II. (Frontiers of Consciousness Ser.). 250p. 1992. 19.95 (0-8290-2469-7) Irvington.

— Mind Body Medicine, Vol. I: The Stages of Healing. (Frontiers of Consciousness Ser.). (Illus.). 250p. 1992. 19.95 (0-8290-2468-9) Irvington.

Mehl, Roger. Condition of the Christian Philosopher. Kushner, Eva, tr. 221p. 1963. 9.00 (0-227-67654-8) Attic Pr.

Mehl, Ron. God Works the Night Shift. 220p. 1994. 16.99 (0-88070-654-6, Multnomah Bks) Questar Pubs.

— Surprise Endings: Ten Good Things about Bad Things. 1993. 12.99 (0-88070-489-6, Multnomah Bks) Questar Pubs.

Mehl, Ron, Jr. & Gundersen, Sandy. The Littlest Shepherd. (Illus.). 40p. (J). (ps-3). 1991. pap. 4.99 (0-88070-449-7, Gold & Honey) Questar Pubs.

Mehler, Howard S. Lactic Acid Metabolism: A Monograph on Carbohydrate Metabolism in the Blood & Brain of the Suckling Rat. LC 88-90631. (Illus.). 115p. (C). 1988. 69.95 (0-9621181-0-9) Mehler Pub.

Mehler, Irving M., jt. auth. see Faulk, Martha.

Mehler, J. Amati, et al, eds. The Babel of the Unconscious: Mother Tongue & Foreign Languages in the Psychoanalytic Dimension. 322p. 1993. text ed. 50.00 (0-8236-0530-2) Intl Univs Pr.

Mehler, Jacques & Dupoux, Emmanuel. What Infants Know: The New Cognitive Science of Early Development. Southgate, Patsy, tr. LC 93-10147. 240p. 1993. 39.95 (1-55786-369-5); pap. 17.95 (1-55786-370-9) Blackwell Pubs.

Mehler, Jacques & Noizet, Georges, eds. Textes pour une Psycholinguistique. Noizet, Yvonne, tr. (Textes de Sciences Sociales Ser.: No. 10). 1974. pap. 41.55 (90-279-7285-0) Mouton.

Mehler, Jacques, jt. ed. see Pinker, Steven.

Mehler, Kelly. The Table Saw Book. 1993. pap. 25.95 (1-56158-011-2) Taunton.

Mehlhorn, H., ed. Parasitology in Focus. (Illus.). 1040p. 1988. 211.00 (0-387-17838-4) Spr-Verlag.

Mehlhorn, K. Data Structures & Algorithms One: Sorting & Searching. (EATCS Monographs on Theoretical Computer Science). (Illus.). xiv, 336p. 1987. 50.00 (0-387-13302-X) Spr-Verlag.

Mehling, Betty, jt. auth. see Pendleton, Bonnie.

*Mehling, Franz N. Knaurs Lexikon von A-Z. 1088p. (GER.). 1991. 65.00 (0-7859-6929-2) Fr & Eur.

*Mehling, Gunther. Naturstein-Lexikon: Fur Handwerk und Industrie. 4th ed. 668p. (GER.). 1993. 135.00 (0-7859-8458-5, 3766710540) Fr & Eur.

Mehling, Harold. Assumption of Guilt. 352p. 1994. reprint ed. pap. text ed. 5.99 (0-515-11450-2) Jove Pubns.

Mehling, M. B. Cowdrey - Cowdery - Cowdray Genealogy: William Cowdery of Lynn, Mass., 1630, & His Descendants. (Illus.). 451p. 1989. reprint ed. lib. bdg. 79.50 (0-8328-0430-4); reprint ed. pap. 69.50 (0-8328-0431-2) Higginson Bk Co.

Mehlinger, Howard & Davis, O. L., Jr., eds. The Social Studies. LC 80-83744. (National Society for the Study of Education Publication Ser.: No. 80, Pt II). 300p. (C). 1981. lib. bdg. 16.00 (0-226-60131-5) U Ch Pr.

Mehlinger, Howard D., ed. Teaching about the Constitution: In American Secondary Schools. (Project Ser.: No. 87). 161p. (Orig.). (C). 1981. text ed. 10.50 (0-915654-48-2); pap. text ed. 6.50 (0-685-46203-X) Am Political.

Mehlinger, Howard D., et al. Global Studies for American Schools. LC 79-13014. (Developments in Classroom Instruction Ser.). 88p. reprint ed. pap. 25.10 (0-317-42173-5, 2025923) Bks Demand.

Mehlman, Ira H., jt. auth. see Fox, Robert W.

Mehlman, Israel. Genozot Sefarim: Bibliographical Essays. 1979. 12.95 (0-405-12617-4) Ayer.

Mehlman, Jeffrey. Cataract: A Study in Diderot. LC 76-65332. 121p. reprint ed. pap. 34.50 (0-7837-0217-5, 2040525) Bks Demand.

— Genealogies of the Text Literature, Psychoanalysis, & Politics in Modern France. (Cambridge Studies in French: No. 54). 280p. (C). 1995. write for info. (0-521-47213-X) Cambridge U Pr.

— Legacies of Anti-Semitism in France. LC 83-3685. 155p. reprint ed. pap. 44.20 (0-7837-2934-0, 2057520) Bks Demand.

M

— Revolution & Repetition: Marx - Hugo - Balzac. LC 76-24589. (Quantum Bks.: No. 10). 1977. pap. 10.00 (*0-520-03531-3*) U CA Pr.

— Walter Benjamin for Children: An Essay on His Radio Years. LC 92-28496. 126p. (C). 1993. 17.50 (*0-226-51865-5*) U Ch Pr.

Mehlman, Jeffrey, tr. see Foucault, Michel & Blanchot, Maurice.

Mehlman, Jeffrey, tr. see Hollier, Denis.

Mehlman, Jeffrey, tr. see Laplanche, Jean.

Mehlman, Jeffrey, tr. see Sartre, Jean-Paul.

Mehlman, Jeffrey, tr. see Vidal-Naquet, Pierre.

Mehlman, M. A., ed. Benchmarks: Alternative Methods in Toxicology. LC 88-63539. 220p. 1989. 55.00 (*0-911131-19-1*) Princeton Sci Pubs.

— Environmental & Occupational Cancer: Scientific Update. LC 89-6864. 300p. 1990. 65.00 (*0-911131-17-5*) Princeton Sci Pubs.

— Health Hazards & Risks from Exposure to Complex Mixtures & Air Toxic Chemicals. (Illus.). 241p. 1991. 65.00 (*0-911131-24-8*) Princeton Sci Pubs.

— Safety Evaluation: Toxicology, Methods, Concepts & Risk Assessment. LC 87-609437. (Illus.). 278p. 1987. 65.00 (*0-911131-13-2*) Princeton Sci Pubs.

***Mehlman, M. A. & Lutkenhuff, Steven D., eds.** Management of Chemical Mixtures. (Illus.). 320p. 1990. 65.00 (*0-911131-98-1*) Princeton Sci Pubs.

***Mehlman, M. A. & Upton, A., eds.** Identification & Control of Environmental & Occupational Diseases Pt. 1. (Advances in Modern Environmental Toxicology Ser.). (Illus.). 518p. 1994. 135.00 (*0-911131-50-7*) Princeton Sci Pubs.

— Identification & Control of Environmental & Occupational Diseases Pt. 2. (Advances in Modern Environmental Toxicology Ser.). (Illus.). 700p. 1994. 135.00 (*0-911131-51-5*) Princeton Sci Pubs.

Mehlman, M. A., jt. ed. see Brunton, Jerry.

Mehlman, M. A., et al, eds. Recent Developments in Pesticide Toxicology & Registration. (Illus.). 250p. 1988. 58.00 (*0-911131-34-5*) Princeton Sci Pubs.

Mehlman, Maxwell J. & Youngner, Stuart J., eds. Delivering High Technology Home Care: Issues for Decisionmakers. LC 91-4741. 256p. 1991. 33.95 (*0-8261-7610-0*) Springer Pub.

Mehlman, Maxwell J., jt. ed. see Grubb, Andrew.

Mehlman, Myron A., jt. ed. see Tobin, Richard B.

Mehlman, Myron A., et al, eds. Phosgene Induced Edema: Diagnosis & Therapeutic Countermeasures. LC 85-61949. (Illus.). 160p. 1986. 48.00 (*0-911131-91-4*) Princeton Sci Pubs.

Mehlmann, A. Applied Differential Games. LC 88-15248. (Illus.). 208p. 1988. 55.00 (*0-306-42897-0*, Plenum Pr) Plenum.

Mehlmann, Jeffrey, tr. see Derrida, Jacques.

Mehlmann, Marybeth, jt. auth. see Waters, Michelle.

Mehlmann, Marybeth A., jt. auth. see Waters, Michelle.

Mehlmeister, jt. auth. see May.

Mehmert-Meland, Ralph J. ECU in Business: How to Prepare for the Single Currency in the European Union. 258p. (C). 1994. lib. bdg. 99.00 (*1-85966-082-7*, Pub. by Graham & Trotman UK) Kluwer Ac.

Mehmet, Ozay. Islamic Identity & Development: Studies of the Islamic Periphery. 244p. 1990. 49.95 (*0-415-04386-7*, A4346) Routledge.

— Westernizing the Third World: Eurocentricity of Economic Development Theories. LC 94-33805. (Illus.). 208p. 1995. pap. 18.95 (*0-415-11829-8*, C0090) Routledge.

— Westernizing the Third World: Eurocentricity of Economic Development Theories. LC 94-33805. (Illus.). 208p. 1995. 59.95x (*0-415-11828-X*, C0089) Routledge.

Mehner, A. & Hartfiel, W., eds. Handbuch der Gefluegelphysiologie, 2 Pts., Set. (Illus.). 1156p. 1984. 320.00 (*3-8055-3738-7*) S Karger.

Mehnert, H., jt. ed. see Bachmann, W.

Mehnert, Klaus. Peking & the New Left: At Home & Abroad. LC 70-627631. (China Research Monographs: No. 4). 156p. reprint ed. pap. 44.50 (*0-317-08396-1*, 2003419) Bks Demand.

— The Russians & Their Favorite Books. LC 83-6108. (Publication Ser.: No. 282). (Illus.). 296p. 1983. 19.95 (*0-8179-7821-6*) Hoover Inst Pr.

— Soviet Man & His World. Rosenbaum, Maurice, tr. LC 76-14778. 310p. 1976. reprint ed. text ed. 59.75 (*0-8371-8567-X*, MESOM, Greenwood Pr) Greenwood.

— Youth in Soviet Russia. Davidson, Michael, tr. LC 79-2914. 270p. 1981. reprint ed. 25.00 (*0-8305-0083-9*) Hyperion Conn.

Mehnert, Ralph J. User's Guide to the Ecu. 250p. (C). 1992. lib. bdg. 75.00 (*1-85333-742-0*, Pub. by Graham & Trotman UK) Kluwer Ac.

Mehok, E. & Weber, G., eds. Guia para Leer el Antiguo Testamento: Primera Parte: Dios Comienza. rev. ed. LC 85-70360. 96p. 1986. pap. 2.50 (*0-914070-37-1*, 206) ACTA Pubns.

— Guia para Leer el Antiguo Testamento: Segundo Parte: El Escenario Esta Puesto. rev. ed. LC 85-70360. 96p. 1986. pap. 2.50 (*0-914070-38-X*, 207) ACTA Pubns.

— Guia para Leer el Nuevo Testamento: Primera Parte: Misterio de Jesus. rev. ed. LC 85-70360. 96p. 1986. pap. 2.50 (*0-914070-39-8*, 208) ACTA Pubns.

— Guia para Leer el Nuevo Testamento: Segunda Parte: El Cristo Total. rev. ed. LC 85-70369. 96p. 1986. pap. 2.50 (*0-914070-40-1*, 209) ACTA Pubns.

— Guide to Reading the New Testament: Part 1: The Mystery of Jesus. rev. ed. LC 85-70359. 96p. 1986. pap. 2.50 (*0-914070-23-1*, 203) ACTA Pubns.

— Guide to Reading the New Testament: Part 2: The Whole Christ. rev. ed. LC 85-70359. 96p. 1985. pap. 2.50 (*0-914070-24-X*, 204) ACTA Pubns.

— Guide to Reading the Old Testament: Part 1: God Begins. rev. ed. LC 85-70360. 96p. 1985. pap. 2.50 (*0-914070-21-5*, 201) ACTA Pubns.

— Guide to Reading the Old Testament: Part 2: The Stage Is Set. rev. ed. LC 85-70360. 96p. 1986. pap. 2.50 (*0-914070-22-3*, 202) ACTA Pubns.

Mehoke, James S. Robert Graves: Peace-Weaver. (Studies in English Literature: No. 63). 168p. 1975. pap. text ed. 53.85 (*90-279-3194-1*) Mouton.

Mehr. Clinical Positron Emission Tomography. 1991. 74.95 (*0-8151-5875-0*, Yr Bk Med Pubs) Mosby Yr Bk.

Mehr, Farhang. The Zoroastrian Tradition: An Introduction to the Ancient Wisdoms of Zarathustra. 144p. 1991. pap. 14.95 (*1-85230-254-2*) Element MA.

***Mehr, Joseph.** Human Services: Concepts & Intervention Strategies. 6th rev. ed. LC 94-21884. 1994. text ed. 35.25 (*0-205-15634-7*) Allyn.

Mehr, Joseph J. Abnormal Psychology. 578p. (C). 1983. text ed. 50.75 (*0-03-056631-2*) HB Coll Pubs.

— Human Services: Concepts & Intervention Strategies. 4th ed. 384p. 1988. teacher ed write for info. (*0-318-63897-5*, H19045); text ed. 42.00 (*0-205-11899-2*, H18997) Allyn.

Mehr, Marilyn, jt. auth. see Walker, Betty A.

Mehr, Norman. Group Piano Teaching. LC 66-2085. 42p. reprint ed. pap. 25.00 (*0-317-10070-X*, 2003555) Bks Demand.

Mehr, Sheldon. Music Fundamentals. 140p. 1989. spiral bd. 14.95 (*0-8403-5014-7*) Kendall-Hunt.

Mehra, A. K., jt. auth. see Panandiker, Vapai.

Mehra, Achal. Free Flow of Information: A New Paradigm. LC 85-27157. (Contributions to the Study of Mass Media & Communications Ser.: No. 7). 238p. 1986. text ed. 55.00 (*0-313-25235-1*, MIF/, Greenwood Pr) Greenwood.

***Mehra, Ajay.** A Strategic Analysis of the United States Banking Industry. rev. ed. LC 95-16134. (Financial Sector of the American Economy Ser.). (Illus.). 160p. 1995. 44.00 (*0-8153-2007-8*) Garland.

Mehra, Ajay K. Police in Changing India. 1985. 18.00 (*0-8364-1414-4*, Pub. by Usha II) S Asia.

Mehra, Diane. Breakfast Is Served in the St. Croix Valley: A Bed & Breakfast Guide. 1993. pap. 14.95 (*0-9637143-0-9*) Im-Pr Ent.

***Mehra, J.** The Collected Works of Eugene Paul Wigner Vol. VI, Pt. B: Historical Reflections & Syntheses. 640p. 1994. 148.00 (*0-387-56986-3*) Spr-Verlag.

Mehra, Jagdish. The Beat of a Different Drum: The Life & Science of Richard P. Feynman. LC 93-28295. (Illus.). 600p. (C). 1994. 35.00 (*0-19-853948-7*, Clarendon Pr) OUP.

— The Quantum Principle. LC 74-77965. 150p. 1974. lib. bdg. 51.50 (*90-277-0469-4*) Kluwer Ac.

— The Solvay Conferences on Physics: Aspects of the Development of Physics Since 1911. LC 75-28332. 424p. 1975. lib. bdg. 164.00 (*90-277-0635-2*) Kluwer Ac.

Mehra, Jagdish, ed. The Physicist's Conception of Nature. LC 73-75765. 1973. lib. bdg. 239.00 (*90-277-0345-0*) Kluwer Ac.

Mehra, Jagdish & Rechenberg, H. The Historical Development of Quantum Theory. 640p. 1987. 119.00 (*0-387-96377-4*) Spr-Verlag.

— The Historical Development of Quantum Theory: Erwin Schrodinger & the Rise of Wave Mechanics, Pt. 1, Vol. 5. 385p. 1987. 79.00 (*0-387-96284-0*) Spr-Verlag.

— The Historical Development of Quantum Theory: Quantum Theory of Planck, Einstein, Bohr & Sommerfeld; Its Foundation & the Rise of Its Difficulties 1900-1925, Vol. I, Pt. 1. (Illus.). 400p. 1982. 79.00 (*0-387-90642-8*) Spr-Verlag.

— The Historical Development of Quantum Theory, Vol. I, Pt. 2: Quantum Theory of Planck, Einstein, Bohr, & Sommerfeld - Foundation & Rise of Difficulties 1900-1925. (Illus.). 506p. 1982. 79.00 (*0-387-90667-3*) Spr-Verlag.

— The Historical Development of Quantum Theory, Vol. II: The Discovery of Quantum Mechanics. (Illus.). 320p. 1982. 79.00 (*0-387-90674-6*) Spr-Verlag.

— Historical Development of Quantum Theory, Vol. IV: Fundamental Equations of Quantum Mechanics - Reception of the New Quantum Mechanics. 322p. 1982. 79.00 (*0-387-90680-0*) Spr-Verlag.

Mehra, Jagdish & Rechenberg, Helmut. The Formulation of Matrix Mechanics & Its Modifications, 1925-1926. LC 82-3253. 334p. 1982. 79.00 (*0-387-90675-4*) Spr-Verlag.

Mehra, Jagdish, jt. ed. see Enz, C. P.

Mehra, M. L., ed. Handbook of Drug Laws. (C). 1990. 235.00 (*0-89771-176-9*) St Mut.

Mehra, Pankaj & Wah, Ben. Artificial Neural Networks: Concepts & Theory. LC 91-46288. 680p. 1992. text ed. 70.00 (*0-8186-8997-8*, 1997) IEEE Comp Soc.

***Mehra, Pankaj & Wah, Benjamin W.** Load Balancing: An Automated Learning Approach. LC 94-46515. 152p. 1995. text ed. 28.00 (*981-02-2135-5*) World Scientific Pub.

Mehra, Parshotam. An Agreed Frontier: Ladakh & India's Northernmost Borders. (Illus.). 264p. 1993. 23.00 (*0-19-562758-X*) OUP.

— Negotiating with the Chinese, 1846-1987: Problems & Perspectives. xvi, 316p. 1990. text ed. 40.00 (*0-685-34692-7*, Pub. by Reliance Pub Hse II) Apt Bks.

Mehra, R. K., jt. auth. see Malik, S. B.

Mehra, V. Handbook of Drug Laws. (C). 1988. 200.00 (*0-685-25693-6*) St Mut.

Mehrabadi, M. M., ed. Mechanics of Granular Materials & Powder Systems. (MD Ser.: Vol. 37). 152p. 1992. 45.00 (*0-7918-1098-4*, G00742) ASME.

Mehrabian, A. Temperament & Eating Characteristics. (Illus.). 150p. 1987. 64.00 (*0-387-96510-6*) Spr-Verlag.

Mehrabian, Albert. The Name Game: The Decision That Lasts a Lifetime. 208p. (Orig.). 1992. pap. 4.50 (*0-451-17262-0*) NAL-Dutton.

— The Name Game: The Decision That Lasts a Lifetime. 160p. (Orig.). 1991. pap. 9.95 (*0-915765-75-6*) Natl Pr Bks.

— Silent Messages: Implicit Communication of Emotions & Attitudes. 2nd ed. 196p. (C). 1981. pap. 19.95 (*0-534-00910-7*) Intl Thomson.

— Your Inner Path to Investment Success: Insights into the Psychology of Investing. 225p. 1991. 22.95 (*1-55738-210-7*) Probus Pub Co.

Mehrabian, Albert, jt. auth. see Wiener, Morton.

Mehrabian, Robert, ed. see Conference on Modeling of Casting & Welding Processes Staff.

Mehrabkhani, Ruhu'llah. Mulla Husayn: Disciple at Dawn. 1987. 19.95 (*0-933770-37-5*) Kalimat.

Mehraj-Ud-Din, Mir. Crime & Criminal Justice System in India. 338p. 1984. 44.95 (*0-318-36848-X*) Asia Bk Corp.

— Crime & Criminal Justice System in India. (C). 1990. 110.00 (*0-89771-179-3*) St Mut.

Mehran, Hassanali, ed. External Debt Management. LC 85-23995. x, 322p. 1985. 17.50 (*0-939934-48-5*); pap. 11.50 (*0-939934-56-6*) Intl Monetary.

— External Debt Management. LC 85-23995. 332p. reprint ed. pap. 94.70 (*0-685-23534-3*, 2029094) Bks Demand.

Mehregan, Amir & Hashimoto, Ken. Pinkus'Guide to Dermatohistopathology. 5th ed. (Illus.). 784p. (C). 1991. text ed. 120.00 (*0-8385-7902-7*, A7902-8) Appleton & Lange.

***Mehregan, Amir H.** Pinkus' Guide to Dermatohistopathology. 6th ed. (C). 1995. text ed. 150.00 (*0-8385-8077-7*, A8077-8) Appleton & Lange.

Mehregan, Virginia, ed. Marriage Records of Monroe County, Michigan, Vol. IV. 368p. 1992. pap. 19.50 (*0-940696-35-5*) Monroe County Lib.

Mehregan, Virginia, intro. Marriage Records of Monroe County, Michigan, Vol. III. 387p. 1992. pap. 19.50 (*0-940696-31-2*) Monroe County Lib.

Mehregoan, Amir H., jt. auth. see Hashimoto, Ken.

Mehren, August F. Die Rhetorik der Araber, Nach Den Wichtigsten Quellen Dargestellt und Mit Angefugten Textauszugen. 144p. 1973. reprint ed. write for info. (*0-318-71532-5*, Pub. by Georg Olms GW) Lubrecht & Cramer.

Mehren, Elizabeth. Born Too Soon. 416p. 1993. mass mkt. 4.50 (*1-55817-751-5*, Pinnacle NY) Windsor NY.

***Mehren, Michael J.** Common Cents Livestock Feeding. (Illus.). 156p. (Orig.). (C). 1990. write for info. (*0-9626390-0-1*) Haywire Pub.

Mehrens, Gloria & Wick, Karen. Bagging It with Puppets. (J). (gr. k-2). 1988. pap. 16.99 (*0-8224-0677-2*) Fearon Teach Aids.

— It's All in the Bag. 1990. pap. 12.99 (*0-8224-6451-9*) Fearon Teach Aids.

Mehrens, William A. & Lehmann, Irvin J. Measurement & Evaluation in Education & Psychology. 3rd ed. (C). 1984. text ed. 46.75 (*0-03-062491-6*) HB Coll Pubs.

— Measurement & Evaluation in Education & Psychology. 4th ed. 672p. (C). 1991. text ed. 44.00 (*0-03-030407-5*) HB Coll Pubs.

***Mehrer, Mark W.** Cahokia's Countryside: Household Archaeology, Settlement Patterns, & Social Power. LC 94-45750. (Illus.). 225p. (Orig.). 1995. pap. 29.00 (*0-87580-565-5*) N Ill U Pr.

Mehretu, Assefa. Geographical Perspectives of Global Interdependence, a Thematical Course Outline. 2nd ed. 112p. 1993. spiral bd. 12.95 (*0-8403-8667-2*) Kendall-Hunt.

Mehrez, Samia. Arabic, Egyptian: Spoken. 250p. (Orig.). 1985. audio 175.00 (*0-88432-131-2*, AFA400); 15.95 (*0-88432-539-3*, AFA999) J Norton Pubs.

— Egyptian Arabic. 250p. audio, text ed. 15.00 (*0-88432-536-9*, AFA400); text ed. 185.00 (*0-685-76668-3*, AFA400) Audio-Forum.

***Mehrhoff, Charlie.** And I the Wind. 36p. 1994. pap. 4.00 (*0-9629902-2-1*) Hummngbrd WI.

— Medicine Bullet. Daniel, Darrin, ed. (Spike Ser.: No. 7). 110p. (Orig.). Date not set. pap. write for info. (*0-614-03558-9*) Cityful Pr.

Mehrhoff, Charlie, ed. see Chorlton, David, et al.

Mehrhoff, W. Arthur. The Gateway Arch: Fact & Symbol. LC 92-73687. 1993. 40.95 (*0-87972-567-2*); pap. 20.95 (*0-87972-568-0*) Bowling Green Univ.

Mehring, M., jt. auth. see Kanert, O.

Mehring, M., et al, eds. Congress Ampere on Magnetic Resonance & Related Phenomena, 25th: Extended Abstracts Stuttgart, 1990. xxx, 642p. 1991. pap. 89.00 (*0-387-53136-X*) Spr-Verlag.

Mehring, Margaret. The Screenplay: A Blend of Film Form & Content. (Illus.). 312p. 1990. pap. 29.95 (*0-240-80007-9*, Focal) Buttrwrth-Heinemann.

Mehringer, Hartmut. Waldemar von Knoeringen: Der Veg vom Revolutionaren Sozialismus zur Sozialen Demokratie. Eine Politische Biographie. Institut fur Zeitgeschichte - Friedrich-Ebert-Stiftung Staff, ed. (Schriftenreihe der Georg-von-Vollmar-Akademie Ser.). 529p. (GER.). 1989. lib. bdg. 38.00 (*3-598-22021-9*) K G Saur.

Mehrkam, Deborah, ed. see Conway, Martin.

Mehrl, C. & Bennett, John M. Pumped Gravel. 1980. 2.00 (*0-686-73431-9*) Luna Bisonte.

— Pumped Gravel. deluxe limited ed. 1980. 5.00 (*0-686-73432-7*) Luna Bisonte.

Mehrling, Perry G., jt. auth. see Hart, Albert G.

Mehrmann, V. L., et al, eds. The Autonomous Linear Quadratic Control Problem: Theory & Numerical Solution. (Lecture Notes in Control & Information Sciences Ser.: Vol. 163). (Illus.). 184p. 1991. pap. 33.00 (*0-387-54170-5*) Spr-Verlag.

Mehrotra, A. K., ed. The Absent Traveller: Prakrit Love Poetry from the Gathasaptasati of Satavahana Hala. xii, 92p. 1991. 15.95 (*0-685-50305-4*) Apt Bks.

Mehrotra, Arvind K. Absent Traveller: Prakrit Love Poetry from the Gashasaptasati of Satavahanan Hala. 1991. 10.00 (*0-86311-253-6*, Pub. by Ravi Dayal II) S Asia.

— Oxford India Anthology of Twelve Modern Indian Poets. 1993. pap. 10.95 (*0-19-562867-5*) OUP.

Mehrotra, Arvind K., jt. ed. see Weissbort, Daniel.

Mehrotra, Asha. Cellular Radio: Analog & Digital Systems. LC 94-5944. 1994. 89.00 (*0-89006-731-7*) Artech Hse.

— Cellular Radio Performance Engineering. LC 94-7673. 1994. 89.00 (*0-89006-748-1*) Artech Hse.

***Mehrotra, Chandra, et al.** Family Caregiving: A Manual for Caregivers of Older Adults. (Illus.). 102p. 1988. teacher ed write for info. (*0-9621122-0-8*) Coll St Scholastica Dept Psy.

Mehrotra, K. C. Culpable Homicide & Legal Defence. 438p. 1967. 60.00 (*0-317-54874-3*) St Mut.

— Law of Bails, Forfeiture of Bonds & Habeas Corpus. 391p. 1985. 225.00 (*0-317-54872-7*) St Mut.

— Law of Bails, Forfeiture of Bonds & Habeas Corpus, 1985: With Supplement. 2nd rev. ed. (C). 1990. 90.00 (*0-685-39689-4*) St Mut.

— Sessions Trial. 5th rev. ed. (C). 1991. 95.00 (*0-685-47800-9*) St Mut.

Mehrotra, K. C., ed. Culpable Homicide & Legal Defence. (C). 1967. 65.00 (*0-685-39680-0*) St Mut.

Mehrotra, N. C., jt. auth. see Sharma, Hari D.

Mehrotra, Piyush, et al, eds. Unstructured Scientific Computation on Scalable Multiprocessors. LC 91-48051. (Scientific & Engineering Computation Ser.). 405p. 1992. 39.95 (*0-262-13272-9*, Q183) MIT Pr.

Mehrotra, R. R. Nehru, Man among Men. 1990. 21.50 (*81-7099-196-X*, Pub. by Mittal II) S Asia.

Mehrotra, R. S. An Introduction to Mycology. (C). 1991. pap. 17.50 (*81-224-0089-2*, Pub. by Wiley Eastern II) S Asia.

Mehrotra, Raja R. Names of India. (International Library of Names). 250p. text ed. write for info. (*0-8290-1293-1*) Irvington.

— Sociolinguistics in Hindi Contexts. (Contributions to the Sociology of Language Ser.: No. 38). xii, 153p. 1985. 73.10 (*0-89925-139-0*) Mouton.

***Mehrotra, Raja R., ed.** Book of Indian Names. (C). 1994. 22.00 (*81-7167-149-7*, Pub. by Rupa II) S Asia.

Mehrotra, Rajiv & Varanasi, Murali R. Multirobot Systems. LC 89-46154. 138p. 1989. 28.00 (*0-8186-1977-5*, 1977) IEEE Comp Soc.

Mehrotra, Ram C. & Singh, Anirudh. Organometallic Chemistry: A Unified Approach. 634p. 1991. text ed. 68.95 (*0-470-21019-2*) Halsted Pr.

Mehrotra, S. R. Towards India's Freedom & Partition. 322p. 1979. 24.95 (*0-7069-0712-4*) Asia Bk Corp.

Mehrotra, Santosh K. India & the Soviet Union: Trade & Technology Transfer. (Cambridge Russian, Soviet & Post-Soviet Studies: No. 73). (Illus.). 240p. (C). 1991. 59.95 (*0-521-36202-4*) Cambridge U Pr.

Mehrtens, John M. Living Snakes of the World in Color. LC 87-9932. (Illus.). 480p. 1987. 60.00 (*0-8069-6460-X*) Sterling.

— Turtles. (Illus.). 80p. 1984. pap. text ed. 5.95 (*0-86622-235-9*, PB-129) TFH Pubns.

Mehrtens, Patricia A. One Hundred Years Ago in Burrillville (RI) Selected Stories from the Local Newspapers. viii, 231p. (Orig.). 1993. pap. 21.00 (*1-55613-716-8*) Heritage Bk.

Mehrtens, Susan E., jt. auth. see Maynard, Herman B., Jr.

Mehrtens, Susan E., jt. auth. see Nahser, F. Byron.

Mehta. An Introduction to Quality Control for the Apparel Industry. LC 92-19333. (Quality & Reliability Ser.: Vol. 36). 296p. 1992. 49.75 (*0-8247-8679-3*) Dekker.

Mehta, Anita J., ed. Estuarine Cohesive Sediment Dynamics. (Lecture Notes on Coastal & Estuarine Studies: Vol. 14). vi, 473p. 1986. pap. 65.00 (*0-387-96296-4*) Spr-Verlag.

— Granular Matter: An Interdisciplinary Approach. (Illus.). 300p. 1993. write for info. (*3-540-94065-0*) Spr-Verlag.

— Granular Matter: An Interdisciplinary Approach. LC 93-1503. (Illus.). 296p. 1993. 89.00 (*0-387-94065-0*) Spr-Verlag.

Mehta, Ashish J., ed. Nearshore & Estuarine Cohesive Sediment Transport. (Coastal & Estuarine Studies: Vol. 42). 1993. 54.00 (*0-87590-256-1*) Am Geophysical.

Mehta, Ashvin. Himalaya: Encounters with Eternity. LC 90-70358. (Illus.). 104p. 1991. pap. 19.95 (*0-500-27604-8*) Thames Hudson.

Mehta, Asoka. Perception of Asian Personality. 264p. 1978. 16.95 (*0-940500-63-9*) Asia Bk Corp.

Mehta, Atul, jt. ed. see Wang, Ko-Pen.

Mehta, B. C. Agrarian Relations & Rural Exploitation. 268p. (C). 1987. 31.50 (*81-7024-163-4*, Pub. by Ashish II) S Asia.

— Fertility Behaviour of Tribals in Rajasthan. 211p. (C). 1994. 60.00x (*81-85880-41-7*, Pub. by Print Hse II) St Mut.

— Rural Poverty in India. 1993. 23.00 (*81-7022-432-2*, Pub. by Concept II) S Asia.

Mehta, Brenda. Corps Infirme, Corps Infame: La Femme Dans le Roman Balzacien. LC 92-81520. 128p. (FRE.). 1992. lib. bdg. 29.95 (*0-917786-86-6*) Summa Pubns.

Mehta, Chetan S. Environmental Protection & the Law. (C). 1991. 28.00 (*81-7024-381-5*, Pub. by Ashish II) S Asia.

Mehta, D. Paul & Thumann, Albert. Handbook of Energy Engineering. 2nd ed. LC 89-34318. 429p. 1989. text ed. 67.00 (*0-88173-096-3*, 0287) Fairmont Pr.

Mehta, D. Paul, jt. auth. see Thumann, Albert.

Mehta, D. S. Handbook of Disabled in India. 392p. (C). 1983. 24.95 (*0-685-08979-7*, Pub. by Allied Pubs II) Asia Bk Corp.

An Asterisk (*) at the beginning of an entry indicates that the title is appearing in BIP for the first time.

— Mass Communication & Journalism in India. 313p. 1979. 20.95 (*0-318-37284-3*) Asia Bk Corp.

— Mass Communication & Journalism in India. (C). 1992. pap. 14.00 (*81-7023-353-4*, Pub. by Allied II) S Asia.

Mehta, Deepa & Vali, S. A. Speaking Of: Diabetics & Diet. 128p. 1991. text ed. 18.95 (*81-207-1047-9*, Pub. by Sterling Pubs II) Apt Bks.

Mehta, Dina. Brides Are Not for Burning: A Play in Two Acts. (C). 1993. pap. 9.00 (*81-7167-114-4*, Pub. by Rupa II) S Asia.

— The Other Woman & Other Stories. 121p. 1981. 16.95 (*0-685-21572-5*) Asia Bk Corp.

Mehta, Dinesh. Atlas of Endoscopic Sinonasal Surgery. (Illus.). 118p. 1992. text ed. 95.00 (*0-8121-1471-X*) Williams & Wilkins.

Mehta, Dinesh, jt. auth. see Mehta, Meera.

Mehta, G., jt. auth. see Bridges, D.

Mehta, G. S. Socio-Economic Aspects of Migration. (C). 1991. 20.00 (*81-7100-362-1*, Pub. by Deep) S Asia.

Mehta, Ghanshyam, jt. auth. see Bridges, Douglas.

Mehta, Gita. Karma Cola Marketing Mystic Earth. 1991. pap. 10.00 (*0-449-90604-3*) Fawcett.

— Raj. 1991. pap. 9.95 (*0-449-90566-7*) Fawcett.

— A River Sutra. LC 92-35779. 1993. 20.00 (*0-385-47007-X*, N A Talese) Doubleday.

— River Sutra. 1994. pap. 11.00 (*0-679-75247-1*, Vin) Random.

Mehta, Gurleena & Narang, Harish. Apartheid in Fiction. 1990. 33.00 (*81-7169-052-1*, Commonwealth) S Asia.

Mehta, H. S., ed. Fracture Mechanics - Applications & New Materials. (PVP Ser.: Vol. 260). 224p. 1993. 50.00 (*0-7918-0987-0*, H00819) ASME.

— Fracture Mechanics Applications: Proceedings of the Pressure Vessels & Piping Conference, Minneapolis, MN, 1994. LC 94-71666. (PVP Ser.: Vol. 287). 165p. 1994. pap. 50.00 (*0-7918-1360-6*) ASME.

Mehta, Hansa. Prince of Ayodhya. (Nehru Library for Children). (Illus.). (J). (gr. 1-9). 1979. pap. 2.50 (*0-89744-178-8*) Auromere.

Mehta, Haroobhai & Patel, H., eds. Dynamics of Reservation Policy. 315p. 1986. 31.00 (*0-8364-1818-2*, Pub. by Minerva II) S Asia.

Mehta, J. B. Presidential System: A Better Alternative. (Illus.). 79p. 1979. 7.95 (*0-318-36606-1*) Asia Bk Corp.

Mehta, J. K. Gandhian Thought: An Analytical Study. 243p. 1985. 37.95 (*0-318-36649-5*) Asia Bk Corp.

— Gandhian Thought: An Analytical Study. 1985. 26.00 (*0-8364-1388-1*, Pub. by Ashish II) S Asia.

Mehta, J. L. Advanced Study in the History of Medieval India, Vol. 1. 2nd rev. ed. 376p. 1987. text ed. 37.50 (*81-207-0573-4*, Pub. by Sterling Pubs II) Apt Bks.

Mehta, J L. India & the West: The Problem of Understanding-Selected Essays of J.L. Mehta. (Studies in World Religions: No. 4). (C). 1985. pap. 14.75 (*0-89130-827-X*, 03 00 04) Scholars Pr GA.

Mehta, J. L. Philosophy & Religion: Essays in Interpretation. 1990. 26.00 (*0-685-47342-2*, Pub. by Munshiram Manoharial II) S Asia.

Mehta, J. L. & Conti, C. Richard. Thrombosis & Platelets in Myocardial Ischemia. LC 70-6558. (Cardiovascular Clinics Ser.: Vol. 18, No. 1). (Illus.). 294p. 1987. text ed. 70.00 (*0-8036-6051-0*) Davis Co.

Mehta, Jagat S., ed. Third World Militarization: A Challenge to Third World Diplomacy. LC 85-50860. (Tom Slick World Peace Ser.). 295p. 1985. 8.00 (*0-89940-006-X*) LBJ Sch Pub Aff.

Mehta, Jashwant B. Electoral Reforms. (C). 1990. 40.00 (*0-89771-243-9*) St Mut.

— Quest for a Better Democratic Alternative. (C). 1995. 18.00x (*0-7069-8491-9*, Pub. by Vikas II) S Asia.

Mehta, Kishor C., et al, eds. Guide to the Use of the Wind Load Provisions of ASCE 7-88. LC 91-38210. 99p. 1991. pap. text ed. 20.00 (*0-87262-852-3*) Am Soc Civil Eng.

Mehta, Kumud, tr. see Tendulkar, Vijay.

Mehta, M. K. & Schmidt, J. J. Computation & Analysis of Nuclear Data: Relevant to Nuclear Energy & Safety. 1000p. 1993. text ed. 178.00 (*981-02-1224-0*) World Scientific Pub.

Mehta, M. L. Random Matrices. 2nd enl. rev. ed. 562p. 1990. text ed. 95.00 (*0-12-488051-7*) Acad Pr.

Mehta, Makrand, jt. auth. see Tripathi, Dwijendra.

Mehta, Markand, ed. Regional Roots of Indian Nationalism: Gunarat, Maharashtra & Rajasthan. (C). 1990. 42.00 (*0-8364-2485-9*, Pub. by Criterion II) S Asia.

Mehta, Mayur & Vieira, Gary. Small Business Computer Systems. 2nd ed. 144p. 1992. ring bd. 12.95 (*0-8403-7908-0*) Kendall-Hunt.

Mehta, Meera & Mehta, Dinesh. Metropolitan Housing Market: A Study of Ahmedabad. 192p. (C). 1990. text ed. 25.00 (*0-8039-9596-2*) Sage.

Mehta, Mira. How to Use Yoga. 96p. 1994. 12.98 (*0-8317-1757-2*) Smithmark.

— Yoga the Iyengar Way. 1990. pap. 20.00 (*0-679-72287-4*) Knopf.

Mehta, N. K., tr. see Petrukhin, V. P.

Mehta, N. K., tr. see Shvets, V. B.

Mehta, N. K., tr. see Ter-Martirosyan, Z. G.

Mehta, N. K., tr. see Tseitlin, A. I. & Kusainov, A. A.

Mehta, P. C., jt. auth. see Rampal, V. V.

Mehta, P. C., jt. auth. see Vyas, N. N.

Mehta, P. D. Buddhahood. 200p. 1990. pap. 15.95 (*1-85230-055-8*) Element MA.

— Holistic Consciousness. 1989. pap. 13.95 (*1-85230-108-2*) Element MA.

Mehta, P. K., ed. Cement Standards: Evolution & Trends - STP 663. 119p. 1979. pap. 20.00 (*0-8031-0298-4*, 04-663000-07) ASTM.

Mehta, P. Kumar. Concrete: Structure, Properties, & Materials. (Illus.). 416p. (C). 1986. text ed. 43.95 (*0-685-10931-3*) P-H.

Mehta, P. Kumar & Monteiro, Paulo. Concrete: Structure, Properties, & Materials. 2nd ed. LC 92-15278. 576p. 1993. text ed. 81.00 (*0-13-175621-4*) P-H.

Mehta, Parkash. Operations Research in Agriculture. 1986. 32.50 (*0-8364-1551-5*, Pub. by Ashish II) S Asia.

Mehta, Parkash & Kumari, Anjala. Poverty & Farm Size in India. 1990. 17.00 (*81-7099-199-4*, Pub. by Mittal II) S Asia.

***Mehta, Praful.** ISO 9000 Audit Questionnaire & Registration Guidelines. LC 94-26830. (Briefing Ser.). 1994. 13.00 (*0-87389-299-2*) ASQC Qual Pr.

Mehta, Prayag. Bureaucracy, Organisational Behaviour, & Development. 188p. (C). 1989. text ed. 24.00 (*0-8039-9614-4*) Sage.

Mehta, Priti. World of Rice. 1991. 45.00 (*1-869828-06-2*, Pub. by Moonstone Bks UK) St Mut.

Mehta, R. Divorced Hindu Women. 173p. 1975. 12.95 (*0-7069-0385-4*) Asia Bk Corp.

Mehta, R. J. Masterpieces of Indian Temples. (Illus.). 67p. (C). 1981. text ed. 30.00 (*0-86590-040-X*, Pub. by Taraporevala II) Apt Bks.

Mehta, Rama. Sociolegal Status of Women in India. 192p. 1987. 24.00 (*0-8364-2080-2*, Pub. by Mittal II) S Asia.

Mehta, Rohit. Creative Silence. 1986. 9.95 (*81-7059-017-5*) Theos Pub Hse.

— Eternal Light. 1961. 11.95 (*0-8356-7004-X*) Theos Pub Hse.

— The Fullness of the Void: The Yoga of Theosophy, the Transcendental Wisdom. (C). 1982. 15.00 (*0-8364-2506-5*, Pub. by Motilal Banarsidass II) S Asia.

— J. Krishnamurti & the Nameless Experience. (C). 1989. reprint ed. 22.50 (*81-208-0589-5*, Pub. by Motilal Banarsidass II); reprint ed. pap. 14.50 (*81-208-0590-9*, Pub. by Motilal Banarsidass II) S Asia.

— The Journey with Death. (C). 1987. reprint ed. 9.50 (*81-208-0295-0*, Pub. by Motilal Banarsidass II) S Asia.

— The Science of Meditation. 199p. 1978. 12.95 (*0-318-36390-9*) Asia Bk Corp.

— Science of Meditation. (C). 1991. reprint ed. 14.00 (*81-208-0297-7*, Pub. by Motilal Banarsidass II); reprint ed. pap. 6.00 (*81-208-0298-5*, Pub. by Motilal Banarsidass II) S Asia.

— The Secret of Self-Transformation: A Synthesis of Tantra & Yoga. (C). 1987. 21.00 (*81-208-0381-7*, Pub. by Motilal Banarsidass II); pap. text ed. 10.00 (*81-208-0402-3*, Pub. by Motilal Banarsidass II) S Asia.

Mehta, Rohit, ed. Dialogue with Death: Shri Aurobindo's Savitri: A Mystical Approach. (C). 1983. reprint ed. 17.50 (*0-8364-2507-3*, Pub. by Motilal Banarsidass II) S Asia.

Mehta, Rohit & Mehta, Shridevi. J. Krishnamurti & Sant Kabir: A Study in Depth. 1990. 21.00 (*81-208-0667-0*, Pub. by Motilal Banarsidass II) S Asia.

Mehta, Rustam J. Masterpieces of Female Form in Indian Art. (Illus.). 56p. 1981. text ed. 35.00 (*0-86590-054-X*, Pub. by Taraporevala II) Apt Bks.

— Masterpieces of Indian Bronzes & Metal Sculpture. 2nd ed. (Illus.). 48p. 1981. text ed. 40.00 (*0-86590-047-7*, Pub. by Taraporevala II) Apt Bks.

— Masterpieces of Indian Craftmanship in Marble & Sandstone. (Illus.). 110p. (C). 1981. text ed. 45.00 (*0-86590-030-2*, Pub. by Taraporevala II) Apt Bks.

— Masterpieces of Indian Textiles. (Illus.). 132p. 1979. 42.95 (*0-318-36266-X*) Asia Bk Corp.

— Masterpieces of Indian Textiles. 4th ed. (Illus.). 56p. (C). 1981. reprint ed. text ed. 30.00 (*0-686-32160-X*, Pub. by Taraporevala II) Apt Bks.

Mehta, Rustam J., intro. Konarak: The Sun Temple of Love. (Illus.). 46p. 1981. text ed. 15.00 (*0-86590-065-5*, Pub. by Taraporevala II) Apt Bks.

Mehta, S. M. Indian Constitutional Law. rev. ed. (C). 1990. 188.00 (*0-89771-202-1*) St Mut.

Mehta, S. S. Indian Textiles. (C). 1989. 22.00 (*81-204-0468-8*) S Asia.

Mehta, Satish C. Development Planning in an African Economy: The Experience of Nigeria, Vol. I: 1950-1980. 1990. 36.00 (*81-85163-14-6*, Pub. by Kalinga) S Asia.

— Development Planning in an African Economy, Vol. 1: 1950-1980: The Experience of Nigeria. (Illus.). vii, 244p. 1990. 22.00 (*0-685-63300-4*, Pub. by Kalinga Pubns) Nataraj Bks.

— Development Planning in an African Economy, 1950-1980, Vol. 1: The Experience of Nigeria. (Illus.). vii, 244p. 1990. 22.00 (*0-685-62647-4*, Pub. by Kalinga Pubns) Nataraj Bks.

Mehta, Shirin. The Peasantry & Nationalism. 16.00 (*0-8364-1222-2*, Pub. by Manohar II) S Asia.

Mehta, Shridevi, jt. auth. see Mehta, Rohit.

Mehta, Swarnjit. Migration: A Spatial Perspective. (C). 1990. 19.00 (*81-7033-096-3*, Pub. by Rawat II) S Asia.

Mehta, T. A Handbook of Forest Utilization. 208p. 1981. 100.00 (*0-685-21850-3*, Pub. by Intl Bk Distr II) St Mut.

— A Handbook of Forest Utilization. 208p. (C). 1981. text ed. 160.00 (*0-89771-585-3*, Pub. by Intl Bk Distr II) St Mut.

Mehta, Uday S. The Anxiety of Freedom: Imagination & Individuality in Locke's Political Thought. LC 92-8147. (Contestations Ser.). 192p. 1992. 25.95 (*0-8014-2756-8*) Cornell U Pr.

Mehta, Usha. Gandhi's Contribution to the Emancipation of Women. (C). 1991. 14.00 (*81-7154-536-X*, Pub. by Popular Prakashan II) S Asia.

Mehta, Usha, et al. Women & Men Voters: The 1977-80 Experiment. 120p. 1981. 120.00 (*0-317-61991-8*, Pub. by Archives Pubs II) St Mut.

Mehta, V. Attitudes of Educated Women Towards Social Issues. 126p. 1979. 15.95 (*0-318-37044-1*) Asia Bk Corp.

Mehta, V. R. Ideology Modernisation & Politics in India. (C). 1988. reprint ed. 24.00 (*0-317-90977-0*, Pub. by Manohar II) S Asia.

Mehta, Ved. A Family Affair: India under Three Prime Ministers. 1982. 25.00 (*0-19-503118-0*) OUP.

— Fly & the Fly-Bottle. LC 82-22024. (Morningside Bk.). (Illus.). 1983. reprint ed. text ed. 50.00 (*0-231-05618-4*); reprint ed. pap. text ed. 15.50 (*0-231-05619-2*) Col U Pr.

— The Ledge Between the Streams. (Illus.). 525p. 1984. reprint ed. 17.50 (*0-393-01828-8*) Norton.

— Mahatma Gandhi & His Apostles. 288p. (C). 1993. reprint ed. pap. text ed. 16.00 (*0-300-05539-0*) Yale U Pr.

— Portrait of India. 544p. (C). 1993. reprint ed. pap. 20.00 (*0-300-05538-2*) Yale U Pr.

— Rajiv Gandhi & Rama's Kingdom. 224p. 1994. 20.00 (*0-300-06038-6*) Yale U Pr.

— Sound-Shadows of the New World. LC 85-5045. 1987. pap. 8.95 (*0-393-30437-X*) Norton.

— Vedi. (Illus.). 272p. 1987. reprint ed. pap. 7.95 (*0-393-30417-5*) Norton.

Mehta, Vera, jt. ed. see Constable, Robert.

Mehta, Vinod. The Sanjay Story. 192p. 1978. 9.95 (*0-318-37220-7*) Asia Bk Corp.

— Soviet Economy: New Economic Strategy. 210p. 1987. text ed. 27.50 (*81-207-0670-6*, Pub. by Sterling Pubs II) Apt Bks.

Mehtabdin, Khalid R. Comparative Management: Business Styles in Japan & the United States. LC 86-16395. (Mellen Studies in Business: Vol. 1). 140p. 1986. pap. 69.95 (*0-88946-153-8*) E Mellen.

— Forecasting: The State of the Art, the State of the Science. LC 86-21657. (Edwin Mellen Texts Ser.). 1986. pap. 39.95 (*0-88946-203-8*) E Mellen.

— Reaganomics: Successes & Failures. LC 86-21674. 1986. pap. 59.95 (*0-88946-204-6*) E Mellen.

Mehtar, Shaheen. Hospital Infection Control: Setting Up a Cost-Effective Resources. LC 92-49489. (Illus.). 208p. (C). 1992. 45.00 (*0-19-262266-8*); 26.50 (*0-19-262033-9*) OUP.

Mehul, Etienne N. Melidore et Phrosine: Drame Lyrique. Bartlet, Elizabeth, ed. LC 85-75346. (French Opera in the 17th & 18th Centuries Ser.: No. 4,vol. LXXIII). (Illus.). 300p. 1990. lib. bdg. 82.00 (*0-918728-81-9*) Pendragon NY.

Mehuron, Kate & Percesepe, Gary. Free Spirits: Feminist Philosophers on Culture. LC 94-6867. 521p. (C). 1994. pap. 26.67 (*0-02-380135-2*) Macmillan.

Mehuron, Tamar A., ed. Points of Light: New Approaches to Ending Welfare Dependency. 154p. (C). 1991. lib. bdg. 38.50 (*0-89633-151-2*); pap. 12.95 (*0-89633-152-0*) Ethics & Public Policy.

Mei, C. C. The Applied Dynamics of Ocean Surface Waves. (Advanced Series in Ocean Engineering: Vol. 1). 764p. 1989. text ed. 76.00 (*9971-5-0773-0*, E-B752); pap. text ed. 38.00 (*9971-5-0789-7*) World Scientific Pub.

***Mei, Cheng.** Chinese Stories. 1995. pap. 16.00 (*0-89410-796-8*) Three Continents.

Mei Cherng & Wang Bor. Mei Cherng's Seven Stimuli & Wang Bor's Pavilion of King Terng. Mair, Victor H., tr. LC 87-23959. (Illus.). 154p. 1987. lib. bdg. 89.95 (*0-88946-020-5*) E Mellen.

***Mei, Chiang C.** Mathematical Analysis in Engineering: How to Use the Basic Tools. (Illus.). 470p. (C). 1995. 54.95 (*0-521-46053-0*) Cambridge U Pr.

Mei, David, jt. auth. see Turino, Jon.

***Mei, Jacqueline T.** The Yacht Chef's Guide to Freelancing. LC 95-68752. 80p. (Orig.). 1995. pap. text ed. 15.00 (*0-9646837-0-9*) Clouseau Pubns.

Mei, Jian-Ping. New Methods for the Arbitrage Pricing Theory & the Present Value Model. 100p. 1994. text ed. 30.00 (*981-02-1839-7*) World Scientific Pub.

Mei, V., jt. ed. see Herold, K. E.

Mei Xia, et al. The Re-Emerging Securities Market in China. LC 92-9824. 200p. 1992. text ed. 49.95 (*0-89930-755-8*, GEF, Quorum Bks) Greenwood.

Mei Xie, et al. Using Water Efficiently: Technological Options. LC 93-15614. (Technical Paper Ser.: Vol. 205). 61p. 1993. 6.95 (*0-8213-2455-1*, 12455) World Bank.

Mei, Yi-pao, tr. see Mo Ti.

Mei, Zu-yan, ed. Mechanical Design & Manufacturing of Hydraulic Machinery. (Hydraulic Machinery Book Ser.). 574p. 1991. 110.00 (*1-85628-820-X*, Pub. by Avebury Pub UK) Ashgate Pub Co.

Meibar, Basheer. Political Culture, Foreign Policy & Conflict: The Palestine Area Conflict System. LC 81-427. (Contributions in Political Science Ser.: No. 63). (Illus.). 352p. 1982. text ed. 55.00 (*0-313-22941-4*, MEP/, Greenwood Pr) Greenwood.

Meiberg, Charles, jt. auth. see Sihler, William W.

Meiburg, A. Stanley. Project & Enhance: "Juridical Democracy" & the Prevention of Significant Deterioration of Air Quality. LC 91-6852. (Environment: Problems & Solutions Ser.). 472p. 1991. 80.00 (*0-8240-4049-X*) Garland.

Meichenbaum, Donald & Jaremko, Matt, eds. Stress Reduction & Prevention. 512p. 1983. 47.50 (*0-306-41066-4*, Plenum Pr) Plenum.

Meichenbaum, Donald & Turk, Dennis C. Facilitating Treatment Adherence: A Practitioner's Handbook. LC 87-15397. (Illus.). 310p. 1987. 37.50 (*0-306-42638-2*, Plenum Pr) Plenum.

Meiczinger, John. How to Draw Indian Arts & Crafts. LC 88-50807. (How to Draw Ser.). (Illus.). 32p. (J). (gr. 2-6). 1989. lib. bdg. 10.65 (*0-8167-1537-8*); pap. text ed. 1.95 (*0-8167-1515-7*) Troll Assocs.

Meid & Yingling. U. S. Marine Operations in Korea, Vol. IV: Operations in West Korea. (Illus.). 656p. (C). 1992. reprint ed. lib. bdg. 25.00 (*0-944495-05-2*) R J Speights.

Meid, Wolfgang, jt. auth. see Krahe, Hans.

Meidan, Arthur. Insurance Marketing. 158p. 1984. pap. 75.00 (*0-907721-16-8*, Pub. by Graham Burn Prods UK) St Mut.

Meidan, Arthur, ed. Insurance Marketing. (C). 1984. 75.00 (*0-685-32775-2*, Pub. by Witherby & Co UK) St Mut.

Meiden, Walter, jt. auth. see Carlut, Charles.

Meiden, Walter, jt. auth. see Euwe, Max.

Meiden, Walter, jt. auth. see Iglesias, Mario.

Meidl, James H. Flammable Hazardous Materials. 2nd ed. 328p. (C). 1978. text ed. write for info. (*0-02-476570-8*) Macmillan.

Meidner, Hans, jt. auth. see Weyers, Jonathan.

Meiehnhofer, Johannes, jt. ed. see Gross, Erhard.

Meienberg, Otmar. Saccadic Eye Movements in Neurological & Ophthalmological Diagnosis. (Neurology Ser.: Vol. 29). (Illus.). xii, 115p. 1988. text ed. 79.00 (*0-387-18547-X*) Spr-Verlag.

Meienhofer, Johannes, jt. ed. see Gross, Erhard.

Meienhofer, Johannes, jt. ed. see Udenfriend, Sidney, Jr.

Meier. Black Experience: Transformation of Activism. LC 72-94820. 203p. 1970. pap. 17.95 (*0-87855-558-7*) Transaction Pubs.

— Coronary Angioplasty. 1987. text ed. 76.95 (*0-8089-1892-3*, Grune) Saunders.

Meier, jt. ed. see Newport.

Meier, Ann, ed. see Hirzy, Ellen C.

Meier-Arendt, W. Die Hinkelstein-Gruppe. Der Uebergang vom Frueh-zum Mittelneolithikum in Suedwestdeutschland: Text-Vol. & Vol. with Plates. (Roemisch-Germanische Forschungen Ser.: Vol. 35). (Illus.). x, 237p. (C). 1975. 200.00 (*3-11-004758-6*) De Gruyter.

Meier, Arnold R., et al. A Curriculum for Citizenship: A Total School Approach to Citizenship Education. LC 52-13495. 425p. reprint ed. pap. 121.20 (*0-7837-3673-8*, 2043547) Bks Demand.

Meier, Aryeh, jt. auth. see Rone, Jemera.

Meier, August. Negro Thought in America, 1880-1915: Racial Ideologies in the Age of Booker T. Washington. 1963. pap. 21.95 (*0-472-06118-6*, 118, Ann Arbor Bks) U of Mich Pr.

— A White Scholar & the Black Community, 1945-1965: Essays & Reflections. LC 92-3205. 1992. 40.00 (*0-87023-809-4*); pap. 16.95 (*0-87023-810-8*) U of Mass Pr.

Meier, August, ed. Black Protest Thought in the Twentieth Century. LC 79-119007. (American Heritage Ser.). (C). 1971. pap. write for info. (*0-02-380120-4*, AHS-56R) Macmillan.

Meier, August & Rudwick, Elliott. Black Detroit & the Rise of the UAW. (Illus.). 1981. pap. 9.95 (*0-19-502895-3*) OUP.

— Black History & the Historical Profession, 1915-1980. LC 85-16817. (Blacks in the New World Ser.). 400p. 1986. pap. 16.95 (*0-252-01274-7*) U of Ill Pr.

— CORE: A Study in the Civil Rights Movement, 1942-1968. LC 72-92294. 580p. 1975. reprint ed. pap. 15.95 (*0-252-00567-8*) U of Ill Pr.

— From Plantation to Ghetto. 3rd ed. (American Century Ser.). (Illus.). 406p. 1976. pap. 11.95 (*0-8090-0122-5*) Hill & Wang.

Meier, August, jt. ed. see Franklin, John Hope.

Meier, August, jt. ed. see Litwack, Leon F.

Meier, August, jt. auth. see Litwack, Leon.

Meier, August, et al, eds. Black Protest in the Sixties: Essays from the New York Times Magazine, 1990. 2nd ed. LC 90-13071. 396p. 1991. text ed. 34.95 (*1-55876-031-8*); pap. text ed. 14.95 (*1-55876-032-6*) Wiener Pubs Inc.

Meier, B., ed. Interventional Cardiology: Proceedings of the Sixth Course in International Cardiology. LC 89-15255. 352p. 1990. text ed. 58.00 (*0-920887-75-9*) Hogrefe & Huber Pubs.

Meier, Barbara, jt. auth. see Strauch, Inge.

Meier-Baumgartner, H., jt. auth. see Wunderli, J.

Meier, Bernadette, ed. see Fejer, Paul H.

***Meier, Bernhard & Mehan, Vivek K.** Atlas of Coronary Balloon Angioplasty. LC 94-30841. (Fundamental & Clinical Cardiology Ser.: 23). 1994. 99.75 (*0-8247-9407-9*) Dekker.

Meier, Bill. Autorental Europe: A Guide to Choosing & Driving a Rental Car in Europe. 192p. 1993. pap. text ed. 12.95 (*0-9634749-0-1*) Lansing Pubns.

Meier-Brugger, Michael. Griechische Sprachwissenschaft, 2 vols. (Sammlung Goschen Ser.: No. 2241, 2242). (GER.). (C). 1992. pap. 22.95 (*3-11-012550-1*, 54-92); pap. 20.65 (*3-11-013526-4*) De Gruyter.

Meier, C. A. Harvest Dream & Ritual. 210p. pap. 17.95 (*0-317-05123-7*, Pub. by Daimon Verlag SZ) Atrium Pubs.

— Healing Dream & Ritual. 210p. 1995. pap. 17.95 (*3-85630-510-6*, Pub. by Daimon Verlag SZ) Atrium Pubs.

— Personality, Vol. IV: The Individuation Process in the Light of C. G. Jung's Typology. 1991. 40.00 (*0-938434-13-6*); pap. 16.95 (*0-938434-71-3*) Sigo Pr.

— The Psychology of C. G. Jung. Rolfe, Eugene, tr. LC 85-13996. (Unconscious in Its Empirical Manifestations Ser.: Vol. I). (Illus.). 236p. (C). 1985. 35.00 (*0-938434-10-1*); pap. 16.95 (*0-938434-68-3*) Sigo Pr.

— The Psychology of C. G. Jung: The Meaning & Significance of Dreams, Vol. II. 163p. 1987. 40.00 (*0-938434-11-X*); pap. 16.95 (*0-938434-69-1*) Sigo Pr.

— Soul & Body. Butterfield, Julia et al, eds. LC 85-50669. 351p. (C). 1986. 29.95 (*0-932499-00-7*); pap. 15.95 (*0-932499-01-5*) Lapis Pr.

Meier, Carl A. The Psychology of C. G. Jung, Vol. III: Consciousness, Vol. III. Roscoe, David, tr. (Illus.). 128p. (C). 1989. 40.00 (*0-938434-12-8*); pap. 16.95 (*0-938434-70-5*) Sigo Pr.

Meier, Carl A., tr. see Steiner, Rudolf.

Meier, Christian. The Greek Discovery of Politics. McLintock, David, tr. 305p. 1990. 40.00 (*0-674-36232-2*) HUP.

M

An Asterisk (*) at the beginning of an entry indicates that the title is appearing in BIP for the first time.

— The Political Art of Greek Tragedy. 250p. (C). 1993. text ed. 36.50 (*0-8018-4727-3*) Johns Hopkins.

Meier, D., ed. Block Copolymers: Science & Technology. (MMI Press Symposium Ser.: Vol. 3). 210p. 1983. text ed. 174.00 (*3-7186-0144-3*) Gordon & Breach.

Meier, D. J. Molecular Basis of Transitions & Relaxations. (Midland Macromolecular Monographs). 442p. 1978. text ed. 266.00 (*0-677-11240-8*) Gordon & Breach.

Meier, Deborah. Becoming a Teacher. (DeGarmo Lecture Ser.: No. 16). 1991. 3.00 (*0-685-51004-2*) Soc Profs Ed.

— The Power of Their Ideas: Lessons for America from a Small School in Harlem. LC 94-40196. 224p. 1995. 15.00 (*0-8070-3110-0*) Beacon Pr.

Meier, Eduard, tr. see Stevens, Wendelle C.

Meier, F. & Zakharchenya, B. P., eds. Optical Orientation. (Modern Problems in Condensed Matter Sciences Ser.: Vol. 8). 540p. 1985. 159.00 (*0-444-86741-4*, North Holland) Elsevier.

Meier, Frieda E. Competency-Based Instruction for Teachers of Students with Special Learning Needs. 464p. (C). 1991. pap. text ed. 46.00 (*0-205-13210-3*) Allyn.

Meier, G. Francisco Goya. 70p. (GER.). 1982. 60.00 (*0-317-57215-6*, Pub. by Collets UK) St Mut.

Meier, G. E. & Thompson, P. A. Adiabatic Waves in Liquid-Vapor Systems. (International Union of Theoretical & Applied Mechanics Symposia Ser.). (Illus.). 456p. 1990. 96.00 (*0-387-50203-3*) Spr-Verlag.

Meier, Gary & Meier, Gloria. Brewed in the Pacific Northwest: A History of Beer Making in Oregon & Washington. LC 91-23402. (Western Writers Ser.: No. 3). 216p. (Orig.). 1991. 25.95 (*0-940242-54-0*) Fjord Pr.

— Naughty Ladies of the Old Northwest. (Illus.). 144p. 1990. pap. 12.95 (*0-89288-180-1*) Maverick.

Meier, Gerald M. Emerging from Poverty: The Economics that Really Matters. 268p. 1985. pap. 15.95 (*0-19-503714-6*) OUP.

— Financing Asian Development: Performance & Prospects. LC 86-23328. (Asian Agenda Report Ser.: No. 6). (Illus.). 88p. (Orig.). (C). 1987. lib. bdg. 25.50 (*0-8191-5681-7*, The Asia Society); pap. text ed. 10.50 (*0-8191-5682-5*, The Asia Society) U Pr of Amer.

— International Economics: The Theory of Policy. (Illus.). 1980. text ed. 25.00 (*0-19-502636-5*) OUP.

— Leading Issues in Economic Development. 6th ed. (Illus.). 576p. (C). 1995. pap. text ed. 35.00 (*0-19-507180-8*) OUP.

— Politics & Policy Making in Developing Countries. 369p. 1991. 34.95 (*1-55815-095-1*); pap. 14.95 (*1-55815-079-X*); 2.00 (*1-55815-135-4*) ICS Pr.

— Pricing Policy for Development Management. LC 81-48175. 480p. 1983. pap. 14.95 (*0-8018-2804-X*) Johns Hopkins.

Meier, Gerald M., ed. From Classical Economics to Development Economics. LC 93-37497. 1994. text ed. 59.95 (*0-312-12033-8*) St Martin.

Meier, Gerald M. & Seers, Dudley, eds. Pioneers in Development. 372p. (C). 1985. pap. 14.95 (*0-19-520479-4*) OUP.

— Pioneers in Development. 384p. 1984. 14.95 (*0-614-02826-4*, 60479) World Bank.

Meier, Gerald M. & Steel, William F., eds. Industrial Adjustment in Sub-Saharan Africa. (EDI Series in Economic Development). (Illus.). 312p. 1989. 29.95 (*0-19-520784-X*) OUP.

Meier, Gisela. Ghosts & Poltergeists. (Unexplained Ser.). 48p. (J). (gr. 3-4). 1991. lib. bdg. 11.95 (*1-56065-040-0*) Capstone Pr.

— Minorities. LC 91-11651. (Women Today Ser.). 64p. (J). (gr. 5-7). 1991. 12.95 (*0-86593-124-0*); lib. bdg. 17.27 (*0-685-59203-0*) Rourke Corp.

— Teenage Pregnancy. LC 93-14169. (Life Issues Ser.). (J). 1993. 14.95 (*1-85435-611-9*) Marshall Cavendish.

Meier, Gloria, jt. auth. see Meier, Gary.

Meier-Graefe, J. Dostoevsky, the Man & His Work. LC 77-38843. (Studies in European Literature: No. 56). 406p. 1972. reprint ed. lib. bdg. 75.00 (*0-8383-1390-6*) M S G Haskell Hse.

Meier-Graefe, Julius. Degas. (Fine Art Ser.). (Illus.). 128p. 1988. reprint ed. pap. 4.50 (*0-486-25702-9*) Dover.

— Modern Art, Being a Contribution to a New System of Aesthetics, 2 vols. LC 68-9239. (Contemporary Art Ser.). (Illus.). 1968. reprint ed. 96.95 (*0-405-00719-1*) Ayer.

— Modern Art, Being a Contribution to a New System of Aesthetics, 2 vols., 1. LC 68-9239. (Contemporary Art Ser.). (Illus.). 1968. reprint ed. 48.95 (*0-405-00826-0*) Ayer.

— Modern Art, Being a Contribution to a New System of Aesthetics, 2 vols., 2. LC 68-9239. (Contemporary Art Ser.). (Illus.). 1968. reprint ed. 48.95 (*0-405-00827-9*) Ayer.

— Vincent Van Gogh: A Biographical Study. Holroyd-Reece, John, tr. LC 76-109788. 239p. 1970. reprint ed. text ed. 35.00 (*0-8371-4278-4*, MEVG, Greenwood Pr) Greenwood.

— Vincent Van Gogh: A Biography. 160p. 1987. reprint ed. pap. 4.95 (*0-486-25253-1*) Dover.

Meier, Gretl S. Job Sharing: A New Pattern for Quality of Work & Life. LC 79-4145. 187p. 1979. pap. 8.00 (*0-911558-59-4*) W E Upjohn.

— Worker Learning & Worktime Flexibility: A Policy Discussion Paper. LC 83-1348. 64p. (Orig.). 1983. pap. text ed. 4.00 (*0-88099-007-4*) W E Upjohn.

Meier, Hans. Solange das Licht Brennt. 114p. 1990. pap. 4.50 (*0-87486-050-4*) Plough.

Meier, Hans W. Construction Specifications Handbook. 4th ed. 784p. 1989. ring bd. 89.95 (*0-13-168931-2*) P-H.

— Library of Specifications, 4 vols., Set. 3rd ed. 1994. 275.00 (*0-13-535675-X*) P-H.

— Library of Specifications Sections, 4 vols., A. LC 82-10149. 1983. write for info. (*0-13-535468-4*, Busn) P-H.

— Library of Specifications Sections, 4 vols., B. LC 82-10149. 1983. write for info. (*0-13-535476-5*, Busn) P-H.

— Library of Specifications Sections, 4 vols., C. LC 82-10149. 1983. write for info. (*0-13-535484-6*, Busn) P-H.

— Library of Specifications Sections, 4 vols., D. LC 82-10149. 1983. write for info. (*0-13-535492-7*, Busn) P-H.

— Library of Specifications Sections, 4 vols., Set. LC 82-10149. 1983. ring bd. 250.00 (*0-686-84600-1*, Busn) P-H.

— Library of Specifications Sections, 4 vols., Set. 2nd ed. 1568p. 1988. ring bd. 295.00 (*0-13-535352-1*, Busn) P-H.

***Meier, Heinrich.** Carl Schmitt & Leo Strauss: The Hidden Dialogue; Including Strauss's Notes on Schmitt's Concept of the Political & Three Letters from Strauss to Schmitt. Lomax, J. Harvey, tr. LC 95-8803. 1995. 18.95 (*0-226-51889-2*) U Ch Pr.

Meier, Heinz K. Observations on the Governance of Public Schools in Switzerland. (TWEC World Education Monographs). 11p. 1977. 2.00 (*0-685-05152-8*) I N Thut World Educ Ctr.

— Switzerland. (World Bibliographical Ser.). 1990. lib. bdg. 98.00 (*1-85109-107-6*) ABC-CLIO.

Meier, Helmt M. E. Enciclopedia Agropecuaria Sistematica: Plantas Cultivos y Cosechas, Ganderia, Tecnologia Agropecuaria y Forestal, 3 vols., Set. 1492p. (SPA.). 1978. 125.00 (*0-8288-5208-1*, S50556) Fr & Eur.

Meier, Henri B. The Swiss Equity Market. LC 85-12195. (Illus.). xiv, 210p. 1986. text ed. 49.95 (*0-89930-147-9*, MEQ/, Quorum Bks) Greenwood.

Meier, Joel. Backpacking. rev. ed. LC 91-68424. (Illus.). 150p. 1993. reprint ed. pap. 9.95 (*0-915611-53-8*) Sagamore Pub.

Meier, Joel F. & Mitchell, Viola. Camp Counseling: Leadership & Programming for the Organized Camp. 7th ed. 544p. (C). 1993. boxed write for info. (*0-697-10967-4*) Brown & Benchmark.

Meier, John. The Mission of Christ & His Church: Studies in Christology & Ecclesiology. (Good News Studies). 327p. (Orig.). 1990. pap. text ed. 17.95 (*0-8146-5795-8*) Liturgical Pr.

Meier, John, jt. auth. see Brown, Raymond E.

Meier, John P. Marginal Jew: Rethinking the Historical Jesus: Roots of the Problem & the Person. 1991. 30.00 (*0-385-26425-9*) Doubleday.

— Marginal Jew Vol. 2: Rethinking the Historical Jesus: Mentor, Message & Miracles. 1994. 35.00 (*0-385-46992-6*) Doubleday.

— Matthew. LC 79-55807. (New Testament Message Ser.: Vol. 3). 264p. 1980. pap. 14.95 (*0-8146-5126-7*) Liturgical Pr.

— The Vision of Matthew: Christ, Church & Morality in the First Gospel. 280p. 1991. pap. 16.95 (*0-8245-1092-5*) Crossroad NY.

Meier, Judith, comp. Advertisements & Notices of Interest from Norristown, Vol. II: 1822-1827. 187p. 1989. pap. text ed. 19.95 (*1-55856-031-9*) Closson Pr.

Meier, Judith A. Advertisements & Notices of Interest from Norristown, PA Newspapers, Vol. 6: 1844-1848. 324p. 1992. pap. 22.95 (*1-55856-108-0*) Closson Pr.

— Advertisements & Notices of Interest from Norristown, Pennsylvania Newspapers, 1799-1821. 1988. pap. text ed. 19.95 (*0-933227-89-2*) Closson Pr.

— Runaway Women Elopements & Other Miscreant Deeds As Advertised in the Pennsylvania Gazette, 1728-1789. 113p. 1993. pap. 10.95 (*1-55856-119-6*) Closson Pr.

Meier, Judith A., comp. Advertisements & Notices of Interest from Norristown, Pennsylvania Newspapers, Vol. 3. 199p. 1990. pap. text ed. 19.95 (*1-55856-057-2*) Closson Pr.

Meier, Judy. Making Beautiful Wax Dolls. LC 89-61679. (Orig.). 1989. pap. text ed. 15.95 (*0-916809-32-3*) Scott Pubns MI.

Meier, Jurg & White, Julian, eds. Handbook of Clinical Toxicology of Animal Venoms & Poisons. 768p. 1995. 99.95 (*0-8493-4489-1*, 4489) CRC Pr.

Meier, Kenneth J. The Political Economy of Regulation: The Case of Insurance. LC 87-33769. (SUNY Series in Public Administration). (Illus.). 230p. 1988. 74.50 (*0-88706-731-X*); pap. 24.95 (*0-88706-732-8*) State U NY Pr.

— Politics & the Bureaucracy: Policy Making in the Fourth Branch of Government. 2nd ed. LC 86-1437. 255p. (C). 1987. pap. text ed. write for info. (*0-534-06990-8*) Intl Thomson.

— The Politics of Sin: Drugs, Alcohol, & Public Policy. (Bureaucracies, Public Administration & Public Policy Ser.). (Illus.). 280p. 1994. text ed. 50.00 (*1-56324-298-2*); pap. text ed. 21.95 (*1-56324-299-0*) M E Sharpe.

Meier, Kenneth J. & Brudney, Jeffrey L. Applied Statistics for Public Administration. 3rd ed. LC 92-17744. 452p. (C). 1993. pap. 32.95 (*0-534-19590-3*) Intl Thomson.

Meier, Kenneth J. & Stewart, Joseph, Jr. The Politics of Hispanic Education: Un Paso Pa'Lante y Dos Pa'Tras. LC 90-33101. 275p. 1991. 64.50 (*0-7914-0507-9*); pap. 21.95 (*0-7914-0508-7*) State U NY Pr.

Meier, Kenneth J., jt. auth. see Smith, Kevin B.

Meier, Kenneth J., et al. Race, Class & Education: The Politics of Second Generation Discrimination. LC 89-40262. 240p. (Orig.). (C). 1990. pap. text ed. 15.95 (*0-299-12214-X*) U of Wis Pr.

Meier, Klaus V., jt. ed. see Morgan, William J.

Meier, Leo. Texas Wildflowers. 1990. 29.99 (*0-517-05059-5*) Random Hse Value.

Meier, Leslie. Tippy Toe Murder. LC 93-30615. 224p. 1994. 18.95 (*0-670-84791-7*, Viking) Viking Penguin.

***Meier, Levi.** Jacob. 132p. (C). 1994. lib. bdg. 36.00 (*0-8191-9667-3*) U Pr of Amer.

— Jacob. 132p. (Orig.). (C). 1994. pap. text ed. 19.95 (*0-8191-9668-1*) U Pr of Amer.

— Jewish Values in Health & Medicine. 220p. (Orig.). (C). 1991. lib. bdg. 47.50 (*0-8191-8173-0*); pap. text ed. 21.50 (*0-8191-8174-9*) U Pr of Amer.

— Jewish Values in Jungian Psychology. 198p. (Orig.). (C). 1991. lib. bdg. 46.50 (*0-8191-8323-7*); pap. text ed. 18.00 (*0-8191-8324-5*) U Pr of Amer.

Meier, Levi, ed. Jewish Values in Bioethics. 195p. 1986. 35.95 (*0-89885-299-4*) Human Sci Pr.

Meier, Lorraine, ed. see Howard, Eleanor M.

Meier, M. Matthew. 1989. pap. 30.00 (*0-685-65275-0*, Pub. by Veritas IE) St Mut.

Meier, Manfred, et al, eds. Neuropsychological Rehabilitation. LC 87-154. 468p. 1987. lib. bdg. 55.00 (*0-89862-702-8*) Guilford Pr.

***Meier, Marci.** A Fitting Bar Mitzvah. (Illus.). (YA). 1995. pap. text ed. 12.95 (*965-229-127-7*, Pub. by Gefen Pub Hse IS) Gefen Bks.

Meier, Matt S. Mexican American Biographies: A Historical Dictionary, 1836-1987. LC 87-12025. 300p. 1988. text ed. 55.00 (*0-313-24521-5*, MMX/, Greenwood Pr) Greenwood.

Meier, Matt S., comp. Bibliography of Mexican American History. LC 83-18585. x, 500p. 1984. text ed. 69.50 (*0-313-23776-X*, MBI/, Greenwood Pr) Greenwood.

Meier, Matt S. & Ribera, Feliciano. Mexican Americans, American Mexicans: From Conquistadors to Chicanos. rev. ed. LC 93-3385. (American Century Ser.). 1994. 10.95 (*0-8090-1559-5*) Hill & Wang.

Meier, Matt S. & Rivera, Feliciano, eds. Dictionary of Mexican American History. LC 80-24750. (Illus.). 472p. 1981. text ed. 49.95 (*0-313-21203-1*, NMD/, Greenwood Pr) Greenwood.

Meier, Matt S., ed. see McWilliams, Carey.

Meier, Michael. A Quick Reference Guide to Using Early Recollections in Treating Personality Disorders. LC 87-92202. (Orig.). (C). 1988. pap. text ed. write for info. (*0-945628-00-5*) Psychol Conslt Pub.

Meier, Moritz H. & Schomann, Georg F. Der Attische Process. Vlastos, Gregory, ed. LC 78-19370. (Morals & Law in Ancient Greece Ser.). (GER & GRE.). 1979. reprint ed. lib. bdg. 61.95 (*0-405-11561-X*) Ayer.

Meier, Nancy. Operating Room Policy & Procedure Guideline Manual. 1991. student ed 80.00 (*1-879575-10-8*) Acad Med Sys.

— Operating Room Policy & Procedures. 1993. 145.00 (*1-879575-35-3*) Acad Med Sys.

Meier, Nicholas, jt. auth. see Close, Daryl.

Meier, Norman C., ed.

Meier, P. Consejos-Padres De Ninos-Preescolar (Advice to Parents of Preschoolers) (SPA.). Date not set. 1.79 (*1-56063-334-4*, 497427) Editorial Unilit.

— Tu Puedes Evitar el Divorcio (You Can Avoid Divorce) (SPA.). Date not set. 1.50 (*1-56063-156-2*, 490490) Editorial Unilit.

Meier, Paul. Meditating for Success. Mack, Jane, ed. 25p. (Orig.). 1985. pap. 3.99 (*0-8010-6207-1*) Baker Bk.

Meier, Paul & Meier, Richard. Family Foundations. 96p. (Orig.). 1981. pap. 7.99 (*0-8010-6122-9*) Baker Bk.

Meier, Paul, jt. auth. see Houmes, Dan.

Meier, Paul, et al. Filling the Holes in Our Souls: Caring Groups That Build Lasting Relationships. 1992. 15.99 (*0-8024-2589-5*) Moody.

Meier, Paul, et al, eds. Bruised & Broken: Understanding & Healing Psychological Problems. LC 92-6988. 240p. 1992. 16.99 (*0-8010-6292-6*) Baker Bk.

Meier, Paul D. Christian Child Rearing & Personality Development. LC 76-57501. 1977. pap. 7.99 (*0-8010-6016-8*) Baker Bk.

— You Can Measure Your Spiritual Health. 32p. (Orig.). 1989. pap. 1.99 (*0-8010-6254-3*) Baker Bk.

— You Can Save Your Marriage. 15p. 1988. reprint ed. pap. 1.99 (*0-8010-6237-3*) Baker Bk.

Meier, Paul D. & Burnett, Linda. A Mother's Choice: Day Care or Home Care? 160p. 1989. pap. 7.99 (*0-8010-6145-8*) Baker Bk.

Meier, Paul D., jt. auth. see Minirth, Frank B.

Meier, Paul D., et al. Child-Rearing & Personality Development. 2nd ed. LC 93-23808. 256p. 1993. 12.99 (*0-8010-6305-1*) Baker Bk.

— Introduction to Psychology & Counseling: Christian Perspective & Applications. 2nd ed. LC 91-9525. (Illus.). 353p. 1991. text ed. 29.99 (*0-8010-6275-6*) Baker Bk.

Meier, Peg. Bring Warm Clothes: Letters & Photos from Minnesota's Past. LC 81-11236. (Illus.). 340p. (Orig.). 1981. pap. 14.95 (*0-932272-06-1*) Neighbors Pub.

— Coffee Made Her Insane: And Other Nuggets from Old Minnesota Newspapers. (Illus.). 314p. 1988. pap. 14.95 (*0-933387-01-6*) Neighbors Pub.

— The Last of the Tearoom Ladies: And Other Minnesota Tales. (Illus.). 240p. (Orig.). 1990. pap. 9.95 (*0-933387-02-4*) Neighbors Pub.

— Too Hot, Went to Lake: Seasonal Photos from Minnesota's Past. (Illus.). (Orig.). 1993. pap. 24.95 (*0-933387-03-2*) Neighbors Pub.

Meier, Peg & Wood, Dave. The Pie Lady of Winthrop: And Other Minnesota Tales. (Illus.). 244p. (Orig.). 1985. pap. 8.95 (*0-933387-00-8*) Neighbors Pub.

Meier, Peter & Munasinghe, Mohan. Incorporating Environmental Concerns into Power Sector Decision-Making: A Case Study of Sri Lanka. LC 93-45458. (Environment Paper Ser.: No. 6). 176p. 1994. write for info. (*0-8213-2746-1*) World Bank.

Meier, Peter, jt. auth. see Munasinghe, Mohan.

Meier, Peter C. & Zund, Richard E. Statistical Methods in Analytical Chemistry. LC 92-27288. (Chemical Analysis Ser.: Vol. 123). 352p. 1993. text ed. 64.95 (*0-471-58454-1*, Wiley-Interscience) Wiley.

Meier, R. The Comparison of Scientific & Technological Policies of Community Member States, EUR 14107. 53p. 1992. pap. 7.00 (*92-826-3656-9*, CD-NA-14107-EN-C, Pub. by Europ Com) UNIPUB.

Meier, R. H., III, jt. ed. see Atkins, D. J.

Meier, Rabbi L. Jewish Values in Psychotherapy: Essays on Vital Issues on the Search for Meaning. LC 88-178. 200p. (Orig.). (C). 1988. lib. bdg. 52.00 (*0-8191-6928-5*); pap. text ed. 19.50 (*0-8191-6929-3*) U Pr of Amer.

Meier, Regula A. Liechtenstein. (World Bibliographical Ser.). 1993. lib. bdg. 63.00 (*1-85109-201-3*) ABC-CLIO.

Meier, Regula S. & Ramsey, Donna. Guten Tag Study Worksheets. (Illus.). (C). 1978. student ed 3.50 (*0-8354-2501-0*) Intl Film.

Meier, Richard. Richard Meier, Architect, Vol. 2. LC 90-48765. (Illus.). 432p. 1991. 60.00 (*0-8478-1320-7*); pap. text ed. 42.50 (*0-8478-1321-5*) Rizzoli Intl.

Meier, Richard, jt. auth. see Meier, Paul.

Meier, Richard, et al. Sex in the Christian Marriage. 2nd ed. (Life Enrichment Ser.). 144p. 1988. pap. 5.99 (*0-8010-6204-7*) Baker Bk.

Meier, Richard L. Urban Futures Observed: In the Asian Third World. LC 79-28624. (Policy Studies on International Development). 256p. 1980. 78.00 (*0-08-025954-5*, Pergamon Pr) Elsevier.

Meier, Robert F. Crime & Society. 512p. 1989. teacher ed write for info. (*0-318-63866-5*, H17718); text ed. 45.00 (*0-205-11770-8*, H17700) Allyn.

Meier, Robert F., ed. Major Forms of Crime. (Criminal Justice System Annuals Ser.: Vol. 21). 320p. (Orig.). (C). 1984. pap. text ed. 24.00 (*0-8039-2095-4*) Sage.

— Theoretical Methods in Criminology. LC 84-27716. 247p. reprint ed. pap. 70.40 (*0-8357-4831-6*, 2037768) Bks Demand.

Meier, Robert F., jt. auth. see Clinard, Marshall B.

Meier, Robert F., jt. auth. see Geis, Gilbert.

Meier, Robert F., jt. auth. see Miethe, Terance D.

Meier, Robert J., et al, eds. Evolutionary Models & Studies in Human Diversity. (World Anthropology Ser.). xiv, 376p. 1978. 58.50 (*90-279-7640-6*) Mouton.

Meier-Ruge, W., ed. CNS Aging & Its Neuropharmacology: Experimental & Clinical Aspects. (Interdisciplinary Topics in Gerontology Ser.: Vol. 15). (Illus.). 1979. pap. 70.50 (*3-8055-2980-5*) S Karger.

— Die Dementielle Hirnerkrankung im Alter. (Geriatrie fuer die Taegliche Praxis Ser.: Vol. 3). viii, 216p. 1993. pap. 25.75 (*3-8055-4509-6*) S Karger.

— Dementing Brain Disease in Old Age. (Teaching & Training in Geriatric Medicine Ser.: Vol. 3). viii, 216p. 1993. pap. 29.00 (*3-8055-4478-2*) S Karger.

— The Elderly Patient in General Practice. (Teaching & Training in Geriatric Medicine Ser.: Vol. 1). viii, 256p. 1988. pap. 29.00 (*3-8055-4476-6*) S Karger.

— Le Malade Age en Pratique Medicale. (Geriatrie en Pratique Quotidienne Ser.: Vol. 1). viii, 256p. 1990. pap. 29.00 (*3-8055-5292-0*) S Karger.

— Patologie Vascolari Cerebrali Dell'Anziano. (Insegnamento E Formazione in Medicina Geriatrica Ser.: Vol. 2). viii, 188p. 1991. pap. 22.50 (*3-8055-5365-X*) S Karger.

— I Paziente Anziano nella Pratica Medica. viii, 256p. 1990. pap. 29.00 (*3-8055-5286-6*) S Karger.

— Vascular Brain Disease in Old Age. (Teaching & Training in Geriatric Medicine Ser.: Vol. 2). viii, 188p. 1989. pap. 22.50 (*3-8055-4477-4*) S Karger.

— Vaskulaere Hirnerkrankung im Alter. (Geriatrie fuer die Taegliche Praxis Ser.: Vol. 2). viii, 188p. 1989. pap. 19.25 (*3-8055-4508-8*) S Karger.

Meier-Ruge, W., ed. see Workshop on Advances in Experimental Pharmacology of Hydergine Basel, December 1976.

Meier, Sam. The Messenger in the Ancient Semitic World. LC 88-31164. (Harvard Semitic Museum Monographs). 283p. 1989. 14.95 (*1-55540-289-5*, 04 00 45) Scholars Pr GA.

Meier, Samuel A. Speaking of Speaking: Marking Direct Discourse in the Hebrew Bible. LC 92-16149. (Supplements to Vetus Testamentum Ser.: Vol. 46). xvi, 383p. 1992. 83.00 (*90-04-09602-7*) E J Brill.

Meier, Scott & Davis, Susan. Elements of Counseling. 2nd ed. 96p. (C). 1993. pap. 10.95 (*0-534-19428-1*) Brooks-Cole.

Meier, Scott T. The Chronic Crisis in Psychological Measurement & Assessment: A Historical Survey. (Illus.). 290p. 1994. text ed. 54.95 (*0-12-488440-7*) Acad Pr.

Meier, Shirley. Shadow's Daughter. 1991. mass mkt. 4.99 (*0-671-72096-1*) Baen Bks.

Meier, Shirley, jt. auth. see Stirling, S. M.

Meier, Shirley, et al. Shadow's Son. 1991. mass mkt. 4.99 (*0-671-72091-0*) Baen Bks.

Meier, Susan. Stand-In Mom. (Romance Ser.). 1994. pap. 2.75 (*0-373-19022-0*, 1-19022-2) Harlequin Bks.

— Temporarily Hers. 1995. mass mkt. 2.99 (*0-373-19109-X*, 1-19109-7) Silhouette.

Meier, Terry R., jt. auth. see Campbell, Dianna S.

***Meier, Thomas J.** Ed Tangen, the Pictureman: A Photographic History of the Boulder Region, Early Twentieth Century. (Illus.). 384p. (Orig.). 1994. 39.95 (*0-9641297-0-1*); pap. 29.95 (*0-9641297-1-X*) Boulder Creek.

Meier, Verena, jt. ed. see Ernste, Huib.

Meier, W. M. & Olson, D. H. Atlas of Zeolite Structure Types. 3rd ed. 112p. 1992. pap. 29.95 (*0-7506-9331-2*) Buttrwrth-Heinemann.

***Meierhofer, Maynard C.** A Simple Way to Solve the Health Care Crisis: Both the Health Care & the Cost of Health Care. Date not set. 12.95 (*0-533-11352-0*) Vantage.

Meierotto, Brigid, jt. auth. see Bukowiecki, Angeline.

Meiers, Marion, jt. auth. see McGregor, Robert.

Meiers, Michael. Was Jonestown a CIA Experiment: A Review of the Evidence. LC 88-30698. (Studies in American Religion: Vol. 35). (Illus.). 575p. 1988. 119.95 (*0-88946-013-2*) E Mellen.

An Asterisk (*) at the beginning of an entry indicates that the title is appearing in BIP for the first time.

Meiggs, Russell. The Athenian Empire. (Illus.). 1979. reprint ed. pap. 36.00 (*0-19-814843-7*) OUP.

Meiggs, Russell & Lewis, David M., eds. A Selection of Greek Historical Inscriptions to the End of the Fifth Century B.C. rev. ed. 344p. 1989. pap. 32.00 (*0-19-814487-3*) OUP.

Meiggs, Russell, jt. auth. see Bury, J. B.

Meigh, A. C. Cone Penetration Testing: Methods & Interpretation. (Illus.). 141p. 1987. text ed. 39.95 (*0-408-02446-1*) Buttrwrth-Heinemann.

Meighan, et al. A Sociology of Educating. 2nd ed. 448p. 1986. pap. text ed. 24.95 (*0-304-31587-7*) Cassell.

Meighan, C. W. & Scalise, J. L., eds. Obsidian Dates IV: A Compendium of Obsidian Hydration Determinations Made at the UCLA Obsidian Hydration Laboratory. LC 76-623273. (Monograph: No. 29). (Illus.). 512p. 1988. pap. 10.00 (*0-917956-61-3*) UCLA Arch.

Meighan, Clement W. Archaeology for Money. LC 86-24607. (Illus.). 151p. (Orig.). (C). 1986. pap. text ed. 10. 95 (*0-937523-01-1*) Wormwood Pr.

Meighan, Clement W. & Riddell, Francis A. The Maru Cult of the Pomo Indians: A California Ghost Dance Survival. 134p. 1972. 12.50 (*0-916561-51-8*) Southwest Mus.

Meighan, Clement W., jt. auth. see Sanger, Kay K.

Meighan, S. Spence. Principals of Health Care: (Parables from the Theater of Operations) Bullard, Oral, ed. (Illus.). 112p. (Orig.). 1991. pap. 12.50 (*0-911518-84-3*) Touchstone Oregon.

Meighan, Thomas. An Investigation of the Self Concept of Blind & Visually Handicapped Adolescents. LC 79-155921. 49p. reprint ed. pap. 25.00 (*0-685-16085-8*, 2027351) Bks Demand.

Meighen, Arthur. The Greatest Englishman of History. LC 76-51374. (Studies in Shakespeare: No. 24). 1977. lib. bdg. 40.95 (*0-8383-2136-4*) M S G Haskell Hse.

Meigs. The Box Closet. (NFS Canada Ser.). Date not set. pap. 13.95 (*0-88922-253-3*, Pub. by Talonbooks CN) InBook.

— Critical History of Children's Literature. 1987. 19.95 (*0-02-583900-4*) Macmillan.

— Lily Briscoe: A Self-Portrait. (NFS Canada Ser.). Date not set. pap. 15.95 (*0-88922-195-2*, Pub. by Talonbooks CN) InBook.

— The Medusa Head. (NFS Canada Ser.). Date not set. pap. 12.95 (*0-88922-210-X*, Pub. by Talonbooks CN) InBook.

Meigs, A. James & Goodman, John C. Federal Deposit Insurance Corp. A Case for Radical Reform. 1990. pap. 10.00 (*0-943802-58-X*, 155) Natl Ctr Pol.

Meigs, A. James, jt. auth. see Goodman, John C.

Meigs, Anna S. Food, Sex & Pollution: A New Guinea Religion. 195p. (C). 1984. text ed. 30.00 (*0-8135-0968-8*) Rutgers U Pr.

— Food, Sex & Pollution: A New Guinea Religion. 196p. (C). 1988. pap. text ed. 15.00 (*0-8135-1306-5*) Rutgers U Pr.

— Food, Sex, & Pollution: A New Guinea Religion. LC 82-12202. 215p. reprint ed. pap. 61.30 (*0-7837-5677-1*, 2059104) Bks Demand.

Meigs, Cornelia. Invincible Louisa. LC 68-21174. (Illus.). (J). (gr. 7 up). 1968. 17.95 (*0-316-56590-3*) Little.

— Invisible Louisa. (J). (gr. 4-7). 1988. pap. 2.95 (*0-590-44818-8*) Scholastic Inc.

— Swift Rivers. (Newbery Honor Roll Ser.). (Illus.). 288p. (Orig.). (J). (gr. 4-7). 1994. reprint ed. pap. 5.95 (*0-8027-7419-9*) Walker & Co.

Meigs, Henry. Gate of the Tigers. 448p. 1993. mass mkt. 4.99 (*1-55817-727-2*, Pinnacle NY) Windsor NY.

Meigs, John, ed. The Cowboy in American Prints. LC 82-76487. 1985. reprint ed. pap. 24.95 (*0-8040-0878-7*) Swallow.

Meigs, Mary. In the Company of Strangers. (Illus.). 176p. (Orig.). Date not set. pap. 12.95 (*0-88922-294-0*, Pub. by Talonbooks CN) InBook.

Meigs, Montgomery C. Slide Rules & Submarines: American Scientists & Subsurface Warfare in World War 2. LC 90-5793. (Illus.). 295p. 1990. per. 9.00 (*0-16-018591-2*, S/N 008-020-01193-2) USGPO.

Meigs, Robert F. Accounting: The Basis for Business Decisions. 9th ed. 1992. text ed. write for info. (*0-07-041385-1*); Acctg. worksheets, Group A problems, Chapters 1-15. write for info. (*0-07-043066-7*); Acctg. worksheets, Group B problems, Chapters 1-15. write for info. (*0-07-043068-3*) McGraw.

— Accounting: The Basis for Business Decisions. 9th ed. 1992. Acctg. worksheets, Group A problems, Chapters 14-26. write for info. (*0-07-043067-5*); Acctg. worksheets, Group B problems, Chapters 14-26. write for info. (*0-07-043069-1*) McGraw.

— Accounting: The Basis for Business Decisions. 9th ed. 1993. Acctg. cycle application, Facts-by-FAX. pap. text ed. write for info. (*0-07-043071-3*); Acctg. cycle application, Color Copy Co. pap. text ed. write for info. (*0-07-043072-1*) McGraw.

— Accounting: The Basis for Business Decisions. 9th ed. 1993. Study guide. student ed, pap. text ed. write for info. (*0-07-043063-2*) McGraw.

— Accounting: The Basis for Business Decisions. 9th ed. 1993. Acctg. cycle application, Next Dimension; Acctg. cycle application, Echo Paint Co. (0-07-043098-5). pap. text ed. write for info. (*0-07-043092-6*) McGraw.

— Financial Accounting. 8th rev. ed. LC 94-21842. 1994. text ed. write for info. (*0-07-043344-5*) McGraw.

Meigs, Robert F. & Meigs, Walter B. Accounting: The Basis for Business Decisions. 8th ed. 1990. 43.95 (*0-685-54081-2*); CYMA General Ledger Pkg. (3 1/2" version). pap. text ed. 18.63 (*0-07-835516-8*) McGraw.

— Financial Accounting. 7th ed. 1992. text ed. write for info. (*0-07-042319-9*) McGraw.

— Financial Accounting. 7th ed. 1992. Study guide. student ed, pap. text ed. write for info. (*0-07-042259-1*) McGraw.

— Financial Accounting, Set A. 7th ed. 1992. write for info. (*0-07-042323-7*) McGraw.

— Financial Accounting, Set B. 7th ed. 1992. write for info. (*0-07-042324-5*) McGraw.

Meigs, Robert F., jt. auth. see Meigs, Walter B.

Meigs, Walter B. & Meigs, Robert F. Accounting: The Basis for Business Decisions. (Illus.). 1136p. (C). 1985. Demo disk, TSR 80. disk write for info. (*0-07-041617-6*); Demo disk, Apple II+. Apple II write for info. (*0-07-041616-8*) McGraw.

— Accounting: The Basis for Business Decisions, Seventh Edition. Visual Classroom Displays. 7th ed. 1988. pap. text ed. write for info. (*0-07-074326-6*) McGraw.

— Financial Accounting. 6th ed. 1989. Accounting worksheets. write for info. (*0-07-041884-5*) McGraw.

Meigs, Walter B., jt. auth. see Meigs, Robert F.

Meigs, William M. The Growth of the Constitution in the Federal Convention of 1787: An Effort to Trace the Origin & Development of Each Separate Clause from Its First Suggestion in that Body to the Form Finally Approved Containing also a Fac-simile of a Heretofore Unpublished Manuscript of the First Draft of the Instrument Made for Use in the Committee of Detail. 374p. 1987. reprint ed. text ed. 37.50 (*0-8377-2436-8*) Rothman.

— Life of Charles Jared Ingersoll. LC 71-127194. (American Scene Ser.). 1970. reprint ed. lib. bdg. 42.50 (*0-306-70041-7*) Da Capo.

— Life of John Caldwell Calhoun, 2 vols. in 1. LC 75-127195. (American Scene Ser.). 1970. reprint ed. lib. bdg. 89.50 (*0-306-70042-5*) Da Capo.

— Life of Thomas Hart Benton. LC 71-126599. (American Scene Ser.). 1970. reprint ed. lib. bdg. 65.00 (*0-306-70043-3*) Da Capo.

— Relation of the Judiciary to the Constitution. LC 73-124896. (American Constitutional & Legal History Ser). 1971. reprint ed. lib. bdg. 35.00 (*0-306-71988-6*) Da Capo.

Meij, A. W., jt. ed. see Luijten, Ger.

Meijboom, Alfred P. & Prins, Corien, eds. The Law of Information Technology in Europe 1992: A Comparison with the USA. (Computer - Law Ser.: Vol. 9). 1991. pap. 67.00 (*90-6544-554-4*) Kluwer Law Tax Pubs.

Meijboom, B. R. Planning in Decentralized Firms. (Lecture Notes in Economics & Mathematical Systems Ser.: Vol. 289). x, 168p. 1987. pap. 33.90 (*0-387-17795-7*) Spr-Verlag.

Meijboom, Hajo U. A History & Critique of the Origin of the Marcan Hypothesis, 1835-1866: A Contemporary Report Rediscovered. Kiwiet, John J., ed. & tr. by. (New Gospel Studies: No. 8). 190p. 1992. 25.00 (*0-86554-407-7*, MUP/H330) Mercer Univ Pr.

Meijer, Anton, ed. Systems Network Architecture: A Tutorial. 224p. (C). 1987. text ed. 225.00 (*0-273-02842-1*, Pub. by Pitman Pubng UK) St Mut.

Meijer, Anton & Peeters, Paul. Computer Network Architectures. 350p. (C). 1982. pap. text ed. 225.00 (*0-273-02845-6*, Pub. by Pitman Pubng UK) St Mut.

— Computer Network Architectures. LC 82-22165. (Electrical Engineering, Telecommunications, & Signal Processing Ser.). 396p. (C). 1995. text ed. write for info. (*0-7167-8075-5*, Computer Sci Pr) W H Freeman.

Meijer, Cor J. W., et al, eds. New Perspectives on Integration & Special Education: A Six-Country Study. LC 93-10754. 1994. write for info. (*0-415-08336-2*) Routledge.

Meijer, D. J., ed. Natural Phenomena: Their Meaning, Depiction & Description in the Ancienct Near East. 316p. 1993. pap. 48.50 (*0-444-85759-1*, North Holland) Elsevier.

Meijer, Emile. Treasures from the Rijksmuseum, Amsterdam. LC 84-52612. (Illus.). 160p. 1985. pap. 25. 00 (*0-85667-216-5*) Scala Books.

Meijer, Fik J. A History of Seafaring in the Classical World. LC 86-17854. (Illus.). 256p. 1986. text ed. 39.95 (*0-312-00075-8*) St Martin.

Meijer, Fik J. & Van Nijf, Onno. Trade, Transport & Society in the Ancient World: A Sourcebook. LC 91-46010. 272p. 1992. 69.95 (*0-415-00344-X*, A7613); pap. 16.95 (*0-415-00345-8*, A7617) Routledge.

***Meijer, Fred.** Fred Meijer, in His Own Words. LC 94-42705. 1994. pap. write for info. (*0-8028-7900-4*) Eerdmans.

Meijer, G. C. & Herwaarden, A. W., eds. Thermal Sensors. (Sensors Ser.). 230p. 1994. 150.00 (*0-7503-0220-8*) IOP Pub.

***Meijer, Gerrit, ed.** New Perspectives on Austrian Economics. LC 94-32065. 272p. 1995. 69.95x (*0-415-12283-X*, C0482) Routledge.

Meijer, Hugo. The Pentose Phosphate Pathway in Skeletal Muscle under Patho-Physiological Conditions: A Combined Histochemical & Biochemical Study. (Progress in Histochemistry & Cytochemistry Ser.: Vol. 22, No. 2). 80p. (Orig.). 1991. pap. text ed. 90.00 (*1-56081-308-3*); 77.00 (*0-685-54390-0*, Pub. by Gustav Fischer Verlag) VCH Pubs.

Meijer, J. M. Knowledge & Revolution: The Russian Colony in Zuerich (1870-1873); A Contribution to the Study of Russian Populism. 1955. pap. 79.50 (*0-317-07649-3*) Elliots Bks.

Meijer, Jan M., ed. Dutch Contributions to the Eighth International Congress of Slavists. iv, 425p. 1979. pap. 82.00x (*90-272-2010-7*) Benjamins North Am.

Meijer, Jan M., ed. see Dostoyevsky, Fyodor.

Meijer, Marinus J. Introduction to Modern Criminal Law in China. LC 76-29206. (Studies in Chinese Government & Law). 224p. 1976. reprint ed. text ed. 55.00 (*0-313-26964-5*, U6964, Greenwood Pr) Greenwood.

— Murder & Adultery in Late Imperial China: A Study of Law & Morality. LC 90-47710. (Sinica Leidensia Ser.: No. 25). x, 137p. 1991. 34.50 (*90-04-09273-0*) E J Brill.

***Meijer, Martijn.** Borderline Adolescents. 141p. 1995. pap. 26.50 (*90-5170-338-4*, Pub. by Thesis Pubs NE) IBD Ltd.

Meijer, O. G. & Roth, K., eds. Complex Movement Behaviour: The Motor-Action Controversy. (Advances in Psychology Ser.: Vol.50). 584p. 1988. 115.50 (*0-444-70389-6*, North Holland) Elsevier.

Meijer, P. A. The Ninth Treatise of the Enneads: A Running & Analytical Commentary. 350p. 1991. write for info. (*0-318-69020-9*) Benjamins North Am.

— Plotinus on the Good or the One (Enneads Vol. 9) An Analytical Commentary. (Amsterdam Classical Monographs (ACM): Vol. I). xv, 381p. 1992. pap. 69.00 (*90-5063-082-0*, Pub. by Gieben NE) Benjamins North Am.

Meijer, P. A., jt. ed. see Bos, E. P.

Meijer, P. H., ed. Group Theory & Solid State Physics. (International Science Review Ser.). 304p. 1964. text ed. 190.00 (*0-677-00530-X*) Gordon & Breach.

— Quantum Statistical Mechanics. (Documents on Modern Physics Ser.). 182p. (Orig.). 1966. text ed. 145.00 (*0-677-01310-8*); pap. text ed. 99.00 (*0-677-01315-9*) Gordon & Breach.

Meijer, Reinder P. Literature of the Low Countries. 416p. (C). 1978. 85.00 (*0-85950-099-3*, Pub. by S Thornes Pubs UK); pap. 59.00 (*0-85950-094-2*, Pub. by S Thornes Pubs UK) St Mut.

— Literature of the Low Countries: A Short History of Dutch Literature in the Netherlands & Belgium. 1978. text ed. 39.50 (*0-8057-3431-7*); pap. 12.95 (*0-89197-825-9*) Irvington.

Meijer, Reinder P., ed. see Smit, Jacob.

Meijere, A., ed. Small Ring Compounds in Organic Synthesis III. (Topics in Current Chemistry Ser.: Vol. 144). (Illus.). 210p. 1988. 129.00 (*0-387-18368-X*) Spr-Verlag.

Meijering, E. P. Athanasius: De Incarnatione Verbi: Einleitung, Ubersetzung, Kommentar. 431p. (Orig.). (GER.). (C). 1989. pap. 83.00 (*90-5063-023-5*, Pub. by Gieben NE) Benjamins North Am.

— Augustine: De Fide et Symbolo: Introduction, Translation, Commentary. 197p. (Orig.). (C). 1987. pap. 35.00 (*90-70265-78-8*, Pub. by Gieben NE) Benjamins North Am.

— F. C. Baur Als Patristiker: Die Bedeutung Seiner Geschichtsplilosophie und Quellenforschung. 183p. (Orig.). (GER.). (C). 1986. pap. 35.00 (*90-70265-68-0*, Pub. by Gieben NE) Benjamins North Am.

— Die Geschichte der Christlichen Theologie Im Urteil J. L. Von Mosheims. 460p. 1995. pap. 69.00x (*90-5063-437-0*, Pub. by Gieben NE) Benjamins North Am.

— Von Den Kirchenvatern Zu Karl Barth: Das Altkirchliche Dogma in der "Kerchlichen Dogmatik" 513p. (GER.). 1993. pap. 83.00 (*90-5063-126-6*, Pub. by Gieben NE) Benjamins North Am.

Meijering, Roos. Literary & Rhetorical Theories in Greek Scholia. xi, 327p. (C). 1987. 52.00 (*90-6980-011-X*, Pub. by Egbert Forsten NE) Benjamins North Am.

Meijers, Daniel. Ascetic Hasidism in Jerusalem: The Guardian-of-the-Faithful Community of Mea Shearim. LC 91-41067. (Studies in Judaism in Modern Times: Vol. 10). viii, 142p. 1992. 51.50 (*90-04-09562-4*) E J Brill.

Meijler, A. P. Automation in Anesthesia: A Relief? (Illus.). 210p. 1987. pap. 60.00 (*0-387-18204-7*) Spr-Verlag.

Meikle, Henry W. Scotland & the French Revolution. LC 68-56255. xix, 317p. 1969. reprint ed. 39.50 (*0-678-00588-5*) Kelley.

Meikle, Jeffrey. Design in the Contemporary World: A Paper Prepared from the Proceedings of the Stanford Design Forum 1988. 100p. (Orig.). 1989. write for info. (*0-318-65097-5*) Pentagram Design.

***Meikle, Jeffrey L.** American Plastic: A Cultural History. LC 95-15187. 1995. pap. write for info. (*0-8135-2235-8*) Rutgers U Pr.

— American Plastic: A Cultural History. LC 95-15187. (Illus.). 500p. (C). 1995. text ed. 49.95 (*0-8135-2234-X*) Rutgers U Pr.

— Twentieth Century Limited: Industrial Design in America, 1925-1939. LC 79-17072. 249p. 1981. pap. 22. 95 (*0-87722-246-0*) Temple U Pr.

***Meikle, Scott.** Aristotle's Economic Thought. 200p. 1995. 36.00 (*0-19-815002-4*) OUP.

— Essentialism in the Thought of Karl Marx. LC 85-5130. 195p. 1985. 36.95 (*0-912050-75-6*) Open Court.

***Meikle, W. Eric & Parker, Sue T.** Naming Our Ancestors: An Anthology of Hominid Taxonomy. (Illus.). 254p. (Orig.). (C). 1994. pap. text ed. 12.95x (*0-88133-799-4*) Waveland Pr.

Meikleham, Robert. A Dictionary of Architecture, 3 vols., Set. 1980. lib. bdg. 500.00 (*0-8490-3122-2*) Gordon Pr.

Meiklejohn, Alexander. Education Between Two Worlds. LC 71-167385. (Essay Index Reprint Ser.). 1977. reprint ed. 22.95 (*0-8369-2565-3*) Ayer.

— Experimental College. LC 75-165724. (American Education, Ser, No. 2). 1977. reprint ed. 33.95 (*0-405-03712-0*) Ayer.

— Freedom & the College. LC 75-99641. (Essay Index Reprint Ser.). 1977. 21.95 (*0-8369-1990-4*) Ayer.

— Liberal College. LC 79-89203. (American Education: Its Men, Institutions & Ideas, Ser. 1). 1975. reprint ed. 18. 95 (*0-405-01441-4*) Ayer.

— Political Freedom: The Constitutional Powers of the People. LC 78-27616. 166p. 1979. reprint ed. text ed. 35.00 (*0-313-20907-3*, MEPF, Greenwood Pr) Greenwood.

Meiklejohn, Donald. Freedom & the Public: Public & Private Morality in America. LC 65-23650. 175p. reprint ed. pap. 49.90 (*0-317-52007-5*, 2027401) Bks Demand.

Meiklejohn, J. M., tr. see Kant, Immanuel.

Meiksin, Steve. Complete Guide to Active Filter Design Op Amps & Passive Components. 224p. 1989. pap. text ed. 38.00 (*0-13-159971-2*) P-H.

Meikson, Z. H. & Thackray, Philip C. Electronic Design with Off-the-Shelf Integrated Circuits. 220p. 1980. 27.95 (*0-13-250282-8*, Parker Publishing Co) P-H.

— Electronic Design with Off-the-Shelf Integrated Circuits. 2nd ed. LC 83-26905. (Illus.). 448p. 1987. 14.95 (*0-13-250549-5*, Busn); text ed. 39.95 (*0-13-250291-7*, Busn) P-H.

***Meil, Joanne.** New World Plants & Their Uses: A Guide to Selected Literature & Genetic Resources 1980-1993. (Illus.). 39p. (Orig.). (C). 1995. pap. text ed. 25.00 (*0-7881-1613-4*) Diane Pub.

Meilach, Dona, jt. auth. see Davis, M. Edward.

***Meilach, Dona Z.** The Best Bagels Are Made at Home. (Illus.). 176p. (Orig.). 1995. pap. 8.95 (*1-55867-131-5*, Nitty Gritty Ckbks) Bristol Pub Ent CA.

— Contemporary Stone Sculpture. LC 71-108070. (Illus.). 224p. 1987. pap. 19.95 (*0-88740-089-2*) Schiffer.

— Dynamics of Presentation Graphics. 2nd ed. 326p. 1990. pap. 30.00 (*1-55623-229-2*) Irwin Prof Pubng.

— Looking Great on Video. LC 92-44957. 200p. 1993. 25.00 (*1-55623-738-3*) Irwin Prof Pubng.

— Marinades: Make Ordinary Foods Extraordinary. rev. ed. (Illus.). 176p. 1995. pap. 8.95 (*1-55867-119-6*, Nitty Gritty Ckbks) Bristol Pub Ent CA.

— Word Processing for Business Users. LC 92-43863. (Barron's Educational Ser.). 1993. pap. 19.95 (*0-8120-1466-9*) Barron.

Meilach, Dona Z. & Mandel, Elias. Doctor Talks to Five to Eight Year Olds. (Illus.). 1988. pap. 5.50 (*0-318-37509-5*) Budlong.

Meilach, Dona Z., jt. auth. see Birch, William G.

Meilach, Michael, ed. There Shall Be One Christ. (Spirit & Life Ser.). 1968. 2.50 (*0-686-11576-7*) Franciscan Inst.

***Meilaender.** Limits of Love: Some Theological Explorations. 1992. pap. text ed. 12.95 (*0-271-00790-7*) Pa St U Pr.

Meilaender, Gilbert. Faith & Faithfulness: Basic Themes in Christian Ethics. LC 90-50966. (C). 1991. text ed. 22.95 (*0-268-00982-1*) U of Notre Dame Pr.

— The Limits of Love: Some Theological Explorations. LC 87-42548. 156p. 1992. 30.00 (*0-271-00611-0*); pap. text ed. 12.95 (*0-271-00862-8*) Pa St U Pr.

— Morality in Plague Time. 1989. pap. 3.99 (*0-570-04526-6*, 12-3133) Concordia.

***Meilaender, Gilbert C.** Body, Soul, & Bioethics. LC 95-17486. (C). 1996. text ed. 21.95 (*0-268-00698-9*) U of Notre Dame Pr.

— Faith & Faithfulness: Basic Themes in Christian Ethics. LC 90-50966. (C). 1992. pap. text ed. 11.95 (*0-268-00983-X*) U of Notre Dame Pr.

— Friendship: A Study in Theological Ethics. LC 81-50459. (Revisions: A Series of Books on Ethics). 128p. 1985. pap. text ed. 7.95 (*0-268-00969-4*) U of Notre Dame Pr.

Meilaender, Gilbert C., Jr. The Theory & Practice of Virtue. LC 83-40598. 208p. (C). 1984. text ed. 18.95 (*0-268-01852-9*); pap. text ed. 10.95 (*0-268-01853-7*) U of Notre Dame Pr.

Meiland, Jack W. College Thinking: How to Get the Best out of College. 224p. (Orig.). 1981. pap. 5.99 (*0-451-62655-9*, Ment) NAL-Dutton.

Meiland, Jack W. & Krausz, Michael, eds. Relativism: Cognitive & Moral. LC 81-19834. 272p. 1982. pap. 12. 95 (*0-268-01612-7*) U of Notre Dame Pr.

Meile, B. Verhaltensauffaellige Schueler. (Sozialmedizinische und Paedagogische Jugendkunde Ser.: Band 16). xii, 84p. 1982. pap. 18.50 (*3-8055-3552-X*) S Karger.

Meile, Larry, jt. ed. see Heineke, Janelle.

Meilgaard & Carr. Sensory Evaluation Techniques. 1987. 99.50 (*0-8493-5431-5*, TA418, CRC Reprint) Franklin.

Meilgaard, Morten C., et al. Sensory Evaluation Techniques. 2nd rev. ed. 1991. 95.00 (*0-8493-4280-5*, TA418) CRC Pr.

Meilhac, Henri & Halevy, Lucovic. The Brazilian. Shapiro, Norman R., tr. (Tour De Farce Ser.: Vol. 3). 56p. (Orig.). 1987. pap. 6.95 (*0-936839-59-7*) Applause Theatre Bk Pubs.

***Meili.** Those Who Know. Date not set. per. 16.95 (*0-920897-03-7*, Pub. by NeWest Pr CN) InBook.

Meilikhov, Evgenii Z., jt. ed. see Grigoriev, Igor S.

Meiling, W. & Stary, F. Nanosecond Pulse Techniques. 430p. 1968. text ed. 342.00 (*0-677-61490-X*) Gordon & Breach.

Meilinger, Phillip S. Hoyt S. Vandenberg: The Life of a General. LC 88-45097. (Illus.). 294p. 1989. 29.95 (*0-253-32862-4*) Ind U Pr.

Meilland, Alain. Meilland: A Life in Roses. Keating, Richard C. & Keating, L. Clark, trs. LC 83-14996. (Illus.). 176p. 1984. 24.95 (*0-8093-1111-9*) S Ill U Pr.

Meillassoux, Claude. The Anthropology of Slavery: The Womb of Iron & Gold. Dasnois, Alide, tr. 1991. lib. bdg. 49.95 (*0-226-51911-2*); pap. text ed. 18.95 (*0-226-51912-0*) U Ch Pr.

— Urbanization of an African Community. LC 84-45538. (American Ethnological Society Monographs: No. 45). 1988. reprint ed. 30.00 (*0-404-62943-1*) AMS Pr.

Meillassoux, Claude, ed. Maidens, Meal & Money. Edholm, Felicity, tr. LC 79-52834. (Themes in the Social Sciences Ser.). 200p. 1981. pap. 22.95 (*0-521-29708-7*) Cambridge U Pr.

Meillet, A. Comparative Method in Historical Linguistics. Ford, G. B., Jr., tr. 1967. pap. 26.50 (*0-685-00758-8*) Adlers Foreign Bks.

Meillet, A., jt. auth. see Ernout, A.

Meillet, Antoine. Altarmenisches Elementarbuch. LC 80-24325. (Anatolian & Caucasian Studies). 228p. 1980. reprint ed. 50.00 (*0-88206-043-0*) Caravan Bks.

*__Meillet, Antoine & Buck, George C.__ Introduction a l'Etude Comparative des Langues Indo-Europeennes. LC 64-64958. (Alabama Linguistic & Philological Ser.: No. 3). 536p. (FRE.). 1964. pap. 152.80 (*0-7837-8394-9*, 2059205) Bks Demand.

Meillon, Ross S., jt. auth. see Reading, Chris M.

Meilman, Philip, jt. auth. see Grayson, Paul.

Meilstrup, Jon W., ed. Imaging Atlas of the Normal Gallbladder & Its Variants. LC 93-44006. 160p. 1994. 125.00 (*0-8493-4788-2*) CRC Pr.

Meima, Karla L., jt. auth. see Grant, Christin N.

*__Meimon, Y., et al, eds.__ Recent Advances in Geomechanical, Geotechnical & Geo Environmental Engineering: Proceding of the Joint U. S.-France Workshop. (Illus.). 190p. (C). 1993. pap. text ed. 35.00 (*2-7108-0644-4*) Technip.

Mein. Diagnosis & Management of Ocular Motility Disorders. 2nd ed. 413p. 1991. 165.00 (*0-632-02736-3*) Blackwell Sci.

Mein, Annemmieke. The Art of Annemieke Mein: Wildlife Artist in Textiles. (Illus.). 160p. 1995. 50.00 (*1-879504-03-0*, 403-0) A Schwartz & Co.

Mein, Eric, ed. see Hunt, Anne E.

Mein, Eric, ed. see Hunt, Anne.

Mein, R. G., jt. auth. see McMahon, T. A.

Meinardi, H., et al, eds. Quantitative Assessment in Epilepsy Care. LC 93-26823. (NATO ASI Series A, Life Sciences: Series A, Vol. 255). 214p. 1993. 69.50 (*0-306-44620-0*, Plenum Pr) Plenum.

Meinardus, Gunter & Nurnberger, Gunter. Delay Equations, Approximation, & Application. (International Series of Numerical Mathematics: No. 74). 356p. 1985. lib. bdg. 105.00 (*0-8176-1733-7*) Birkhauser.

Meinardus, Gunter, jt. ed. see Collatz, Lothar.

Meinardus, Otto. The Holy Family in Egypt: In the Steps of the Tradition. 1987. pap. 12.50 (*977-424-129-0*, Pub. by Am Univ Cairo Pr UA) Col U Pr.

— Monks & Monasteries of the Egyptian Deserts. rev. ed. 200p. 1989. pap. 20.00 (*977-424-188-6*, Pub. by Am Univ Cairo Pr UA) Col U Pr.

Meinardus, Otto F. St. John of Patmos & the Seven Churches of the Apocalypse. LC 78-51245. (In the Footsteps of the Saints Ser.). (Illus.). 160p. 1979. 17.50 (*0-89241-070-1*); pap. 6.95 (*0-89241-043-4*) Caratzas.

— St. Paul in Ephesus & the Cities of Galatia & Cyprus. LC 78-51246. (In the Footsteps of the Saints Ser.). (Illus.). 160p. 1979. 17.50 (*0-89241-071-X*); pap. 6.95 (*0-89241-044-2*) Caratzas.

— St. Paul in Greece. LC 78-51244. (In the Footsteps of the Saints Ser.). 160p. 1979. 17.50 (*0-89241-072-8*); pap. 6.95 (*0-89241-045-0*) Caratzas.

— St. Paul's Last Journey. LC 78-51247. (In the Footsteps of the Saints Ser.). (Illus.). 160p. 1979. 17.50 (*0-89241-073-6*); pap. 6.95 (*0-89241-046-9*) Caratzas.

Meinbach, Anita, et al. The Complete Guide to Thematic Units: Creating the Integrated Curriculum. (Illus.). 250p. (Orig.). (C). 1995. pap. text ed. 28.95 (*0-926842-42-0*) CG Pubs Inc.

Meinbach, Anita M., jt. auth. see Rothlein, Liz.

Meinberg, Sherry L. Into the Hornets Nest: An Incredible Look at Life in an Inner City School. Parker, Diane, ed. LC 92-50866. 250p. 1993. pap. 11.95 (*0-88247-976-8*, 976) R & E Pubs.

Meinck, Fritz & Mohle, Helmut. Elsevier's Dictionary of Water & Sewage Engineering in German, English, French & Italian: Woerterbuch fur das Wasserfach und Abwasserfach. 4th ed. 661p. (ENG, FRE, GER & ITA.). 1993. 395.00 (*0-8288-0961-5*, M 7889) Fr & Eur.

Meinck, Fritz & Mohle, K. Dictionary of Water & Sewage Engineering. 2nd rev. ed. 738p. (ENG, FRE, GER & ITA.). 1977. 197.50 (*0-444-99811-X*) Elsevier.

Meinders, LaDonna K. Leaves in the Wind. LC 89-81374. (Illus.). 152p. (J). 1989. 15.95 (*0-934188-31-9*) Evans Pubns.

Meindl, James D. Micropower Circuits. LC 68-28502. (Illus.). 258p. reprint ed. pap. 73.60 (*0-317-08756-8*, 2010178) Bks Demand.

Meindl, James D., ed. Brief Lessons in High Technology. (Portable Stanford Book Ser.). 249p. 1991. 12.95 (*0-916318-41-9*) Stanford Alumni Assn.

Meine, Curt. Aldo Leopold: His Life & Work. LC 87-40367. (Illus.). 654p. 1988. 35.00 (*0-299-11490-2*) U of Wis Pr.

— Aldo Leopold: His Life & Work. LC 87-40367. (Illus.). 654p. 1991. reprint ed. pap. 21.95 (*0-299-11494-5*) U of Wis Pr.

Meine, Franklin J. Tall Tales of the Southwest. 1988. reprint ed. lib. bdg. 49.00 (*0-7812-0188-8*) Rprt Serv.

— Tall Tales of the Southwest. LC 78-166809. (Illus.). 1971. reprint ed. 79.00 (*0-403-01424-7*) Scholarly.

*__Meine, Franklin J., ed.__ The Crockett Almanacs: Nashville Series, 1835-1838. 1955. 25.00 (*0-614-04638-6*) Caxton Club.

Meinecke, Friedrich. The Age of German Liberation, 1795-1815. Paret, Peter & Fischer, Helmut, trs. LC 74-79767. Orig. Title: Das Zeitalter der Deutschen Erhebung. 1977. 45.00 (*0-520-02792-2*); pap. 13.00 (*0-520-03454-6*) U CA Pr.

— The Warfare of a Nation. 1977. 59.95 (*0-8490-2807-8*) Gordon Pr.

Meinecke, Kalani, tr. see Landgraf, Anne K.

*__Meinecke, Michael.__ Patterns of Stylistic Change in Islamic Architecture: Local Traditions vs. Migrating Artists. LC 95-5508. (Hagop Kevorkian Series on Near Eastern Art & Civilization). 1996. write for info. (*0-8147-5492-9*) NYU Pr.

Meineke, A. Ethnikon: A Geographical Lexicon on Ancient Cities, Peoples, Tribes & Toponyms. vi, 817p. (GRE.). (C). 1992. pap. text ed. 40.00 (*0-89005-411-8*) Ares.

Meineke, August. Analecta Alexandrina. vii, 440p. 1964. reprint ed. write for info. (*0-318-70975-9*, Pub. by Georg Olms GW) Lubrecht & Cramer.

— Poetarum Comicorum Graecorum Fragmenta. x, 807p. 1989. reprint ed. write for info. (*3-487-09213-1*, Pub. by Georg Olms GW) Lubrecht & Cramer.

Meinel, Aden B. & Meinel, Marjorie P. Applied Solar Energy: An Introduction. 400p. (C). 1976. text ed. write for info. (*0-201-04719-5*) Addison-Wesley.

— Sunsets, Twilights, & Evening Skies. (Illus.). 173p. (C). 1991. pap. 22.95 (*0-521-40647-1*) Cambridge U Pr.

Meinel, Aden B., et al. Catalog of Emission Lines in Astrophysical Objects. 2nd ed. 169p. reprint ed. pap. 48.20 (*0-317-26813-9*, 2023480) Bks Demand.

Meinel, C. Modified Branching Programs & Their Computational Power. (Lecture Notes in Computer Science Ser.: Vol. 370). vi, 132p. 1989. pap. 27.00 (*0-387-51340-X*) Spr-Verlag.

Meinel, Hans. A Course in Scientific German. 248p. 1972. 32.75 (*3-19-001103-6*) Adlers Foreign Bks.

Meinel, Marjorie P., jt. auth. see Meinel, Aden B.

*__Meiners, Arthur C.__ Fundamentals of the Acquisition Process. 257p. (Orig.). (C). 1995. pap. text ed. 38.50 (*0-87411-755-0*) Copley Pub.

Meiners, Harry P., et al. Laboratory Physics. 2nd ed. 560p. 1987. Net. pap. text ed. write for info. (*0-471-03675-7*) Wiley.

*__Meiners, Phyllis A. & Sanford, Greg A.__ Church Philanthropy for Native Americans & Other Minorities: A Guide to Multicultural Funding from Religious Sources. (Illus.). 350p. 1994. pap. 118.95 (*0-9633694-3-1*) CRC Pub CO.

— National Directory of Church Philanthropy. (Illus.). 400p. Date not set. pap. write for info. (*0-9633694-4-X*) CRC Pub CO.

— National Directory of Philanthropy for Native Americans. LC 92-72997. 160p. 1994. pap. 69.95 (*0-9633694-0-7*) Corp Res Cnslts.

Meiners, Phyllis A., jt. auth. see Tun-Atz, Hilary H.

Meiners, R. K. Journeying Back to the World: Poems. LC 74-30339. (Breakthrough Bks.). 88p. 1975. 14.95 (*0-8262-0173-3*) U of Mo Pr.

— Last Alternatives: Allen Tate. LC 72-4614. (American Literature Ser.: No. 49). 1972. reprint ed. lib. bdg. 75.00 (*0-8383-1594-1*) M S G Haskell Hse.

Meiners, Roger E. & Amacher, Ryan C., eds. Federal Support of Higher Education. LC 89-10189. 360p. (C). 1989. text ed. 29.95 (*0-943852-76-5*); pap. text ed. 15.95 (*0-943852-78-1*) Prof World Peace.

Meiners, Roger E. & Yandle, Bruce, eds. The Economic Consequences of Liability Rules: In Defense of Common Law Liability. LC 91-185. 256p. 1991. text ed. 59.95 (*0-89930-649-7*, MQS/, Quorum Bks) Greenwood.

— Regulation & the Reagan Era. LC 89-7594. (Independent Studies in Political Economy). 250p. (C). 1989. 49.50 (*0-8419-1174-6*); pap. 19.95 (*0-8419-1271-8*) Holmes & Meier.

— Taking the Environment Seriously. (Political Economy Forum Ser.). 288p. (C). 1993. text ed. 42.50 (*0-8476-7873-3*) Rowman.

Meiners, Roger E., jt. auth. see Clarkson, Kenneth W.

Meiners, Roger E., et al. The Legal Environment of Business. 5th ed. Fenton, ed. LC 93-33086. 825p. (C). 1993. text ed. 65.75 (*0-314-02690-8*) West Pub.

Meiners, Wim. Godspeed Thirteen. LC 93-60912. 170p. 1994. pap. 7.95 (*1-55523-655-3*) Winston-Derek.

Meinert, Curtis L. Clinical Trials: Design, Conduct & Analysis. (Monographs in Epidemiology & Biostatistics: No. 8). (Illus.). 1986. text ed. 85.00 (*0-19-503568-2*) OUP.

Meinert, David L. Energy Conservation in Housing: A Collection of Data on Energy-Efficient Housing Approaches. 146p. 1990. pap. 13.95 (*0-533-08331-1*) Vantage.

Meinert, Roland G., et al. Issues in Social Work: A Critical Analysis. LC 93-32125. 208p. 1994. text ed. 49.95 (*0-86569-209-2*, Auburn Hse) Greenwood.

Meinhardt, Carolyn & Verno, Ralph. Business Applications Using the IBM PC: Wordperfect, dBaseII-III, Lotus 1-2-3, & Data Transfer Between Applications. 384p. (C). 1987. pap. text ed. 26.95 (*0-685-14442-9*) McGraw.

Meinhardt, F. Untersuchungen Zur Genetik Des Fortpflanzungsverhaltens und der Fruchtkoerper- und Antibiotikabildung Des Basidiomyceten Agrocybe Aegerita. (Bibliotheca Mycologica Ser.: No. 75). (Illus.). 128p. (GER.). 1981. pap. text ed. 24.00 (*3-7682-1275-0*) Lubrecht & Cramer.

*__Meinhardt, H.__ Algorithmic Beauty of Shells. 1995. disk 39.95 (*0-387-57842-0*) Spr-Verlag.

— Models of Biological Pattern Formation. 1982. text ed. 119.00 (*0-12-488620-5*) Acad Pr.

Meinhardt, P. Company Law in Europe. 3rd ed. 656p. 1981. text ed. 104.95 (*0-566-02245-1*) Ashgate Pub Co.

Meinhardt, Peter & Davis, Nigel. Company Law in Great Britain. 196p. 1982. text ed. 55.95 (*0-566-02389-X*) Ashgate Pub Co.

Meinho, Ulrike & Richardson, Kay, eds. Text, Discourse & Context: Representations of Poverty in Britain. LC 93-50744. (Real Language Ser.). 1994. write for info. (*0-582-10214-6*, Pub. by Longman Grp UK); pap. write for info. (*0-582-10213-8*, Pub. by Longman Grp UK) Longman.

Meinhof, Carl. Die Dichtung der Afrikaner. (B. E. Ser.: No. 43). (GER.). 1911. 22.00 (*0-8115-2994-0*) Periodicals Srv.

— Introduction to the Study of African Languages. Werner, A., tr. LC 75-172719. reprint ed. 34.00 (*0-404-07955-5*) AMS Pr.

Meinhof, Carl, et al, eds. Deutsche Kolonialsprachen, 5 vols., Vols. 1-5. (B. E. Ser.: No. 177). 1972. 18.00 (*0-685-73993-7*) Periodicals Srv.

— Deutsche Kolonialsprachen Vol. 1: Die Sprache der Herero in Deutsch-Sudwest-Afrika, 1937, 5 vols. (B. E. Ser.: No. 177). 1937. 18.00 (*0-8115-3087-6*) Periodicals Srv.

— Deutsche Kolonialsprachen Vol. 3: Die Sprache der Haussa in Zentalafrika, 5 vols. (B. E. Ser.: No. 177). 1972. Vol. 3: Die Sprache der Haussa in Zentalafrika. 18.00 (*0-685-73994-5*) Periodicals Srv.

— Deutsche Kolonialsprachen Vol. 5: Die Sprache der Jaund in Kamerun, 5 vols. (B. E. Ser.: No. 177). 1972. Vol. 5: Die Sprache der Jaunde in Kamerun. 18.00 (*0-685-73995-3*) Periodicals Srv.

Meinhold. Child Psychology: Development & Behavior Analysis. 304p. (C). 1993. pap. text ed. 38.95 (*0-8403-8253-7*) Kendall-Hunt.

*__Meinhold, Charles B., intro.__ Advising the Public about Radiation Emergencies: A Document for Public Comment. (NCRP Commentaries Ser.). 25p. (Orig.). Date not set. pap. text ed. 15.00 (*0-929600-38-X*) NCRP Pubns.

— Considerations Regarding the Unintended Radiation Exposure of the Embryo, Fetus or Nursing Child. (Commentaries Ser.). 24p. (Orig.). Date not set. pap. text ed. 15.00 (*0-929600-36-3*) NCRP Pubns.

— Dose Control at Nuclear Power Plants: National Council on Radiation Protection and Measurements. (Report Ser.: No. 120). 138p. (Orig.). 1994. pap. text ed. 20.00 (*0-929600-39-8*) NCRP Pubns.

— An Introduction to the Efficacy of Diagnostic Radiology. (NCRP Report Ser.: No. 121). 50p. (Orig.). 1995. pap. text ed. 25.00 (*0-929600-40-1*) NCRP Pubns.

— Limitation of Exposure to Ionizing Radiation. (Report Ser.: No. 116). 70p. (Orig.). 1993. pap. text ed. 25.00 (*0-929600-30-4*) NCRP Pubns.

— Maintaining Radiation Protection Records. (Report Ser.: No. 114). 75p. (Orig.). 1992. pap. text ed. 20.00 (*0-929600-27-4*) NCRP Pubns.

— Misadministration of Radioactive By-Product Material in Medicine - Scientific Background. (Commentary Ser.: No. 7). 63p. 1991. pap. text ed. 15.00 (*0-929600-22-3*) NCRP Pubns.

— A Practical Guide to the Determination of Human Exposure to Radio Frequency Fields. (Report Ser.: No. 119). 200p. (Orig.). 1993. pap. 25.00 (*0-929600-35-5*) NCRP Pubns.

— Radiation Exposure & High Altitude Flight. (NCRP Commentaries Ser.). 22p. (Orig.). Date not set. pap. text ed. 20.00 (*0-929600-44-4*) NCRP Pubns.

— Radiation Protection in Medicine. (Report Ser.: No. 114). 250p. (Orig.). 1992. pap. text ed. 20.00 (*0-929600-29-0*) NCRP Pubns.

— Radiation Protection in the Mineral Extraction Industry. (Report Ser.: No. 118). 1993. pap. text ed. 20.00 (*0-929600-33-9*) NCRP Pubns.

— Radiation Science & Societal Decision Making. (NCRP Proceedings Ser.: No. 15). 270p. (Orig.). Date not set. pap. text ed. 25.00 (*0-929600-37-1*) NCRP Pubns.

— Radioactive & Mixed Waste - Risk As a Basis for Waste Classification. (Symposium Proceedings Ser.: No. 2). 217p. (Orig.). Date not set. pap. text ed. 25.00 (*0-929600-43-6*) NCRP Pubns.

— Research Needs for Radiation Protection. (Report Ser.: No. 117). 1993. pap. text ed. 20.00 (*0-929600-32-0*) NCRP Pubns.

— Risk Estimates for Radiation Protection. (Report Ser.: No. 115). 120p. (Orig.). 1993. pap. text ed. 20.00 (*0-929600-34-7*) NCRP Pubns.

— Uncertainty in NCRP Screening Models: An Evaluation of NCRP Commentary. (Commentary Ser.: No. 8). (Illus.). 60p. Date not set. pap. text ed. 20.00 (*0-929600-28-2*) NCRP Pubns.

*__Meinhold, Charles B., pref.__ Dose Limits for Individuals Who Receive Exposure from Radionuclide Therapy Patients. (NCRP Commentaries Ser.). 21p. (Orig.). Date not set. pap. text ed. 20.00 (*0-929600-42-8*) NCRP Pubns.

Meinhold, H., jt. auth. see Schwenkhagen, H.

Meinhold, Margit. Sri Lanka Phrasebook. 80p. (Orig.). 1987. pap. 2.95 (*0-908086-94-6*) Lonely Planet.

Meinhold, Richard J. Beyond the Sound of Cannon: Military Strategy in the 1990s. LC 91-50943. 200p. 1992. lib. bdg. 32.50x (*0-89950-697-6*) McFarland & Co.

Meinick, Ana, jt. auth. see Lomnitz, Larissa.

Meinig, D. W. Imperial Texas: An Interpretive Essay in Cultural Geography. 145p. 1969. pap. 10.95 (*0-292-73807-2*) U of Tex Pr.

— On the Margins of the Good Earth. 246p. (C). 1989. pap. text ed. 40.00 (*0-89771-022-3*, Pub. by Bob Mossel AT) St Mut.

— The Shaping of America: A Geological Perspective on 500 Years of American History, Vol. 2: Continental America, 1800-1867. (Illus.). 656p. (C). 1993. 50.00 (*0-300-05658-3*) Yale U Pr.

— Shaping of America, Vol. 1: A Geographical Perspective on 500 Years of History. LC 85-17962. 512p. (C). 1988. reprint ed. 19.95x (*0-300-03882-8*) Yale U Pr.

— Southwest: Three Peoples in Geographical Change, 1600-1970. (Historical Geography of North America Ser.). (Orig.). (C). 1971. pap. text ed. 16.95 (*0-19-501289-5*) OUP.

Meinig, D. W., ed. The Interpretation of Ordinary Landscapes. (Illus.). 1979. pap. text ed. 19.95 (*0-19-502536-9*) OUP.

Meinig, Donald W. On the Margins of the Good Earth. LC 62-7266. (Monograph Ser.: No. 2). 1972. 10.00 (*0-89291-081-X*) Assn Am Geographers.

Meinig, George E. New Trition: How to Achieve Optimum Health. (Illus.). 326p. (Orig.). 1988. pap. write for info. (*0-945196-08-3*) Bion Pub.

— Root Canal Cover-up. 2nd ed. Koonce, Charlene & Lovendale, Mark, eds. LC 93-72133. (Illus.). 257p. 1994. pap. 19.95 (*0-945196-14-8*) Bion Pub.

Meinikov, O. English-Russian Astronomical Dictionary. 504p. (ENG & RUS.). 1980. 45.00 (*0-569-06519-4*, Pub. by Collets UK) St Mut.

— English-Russian Dictionary of Astronomy. 504p. (ENG & RUS.). 1980. write for info. (*0-8288-0772-8*) Fr & Eur.

*__Meinikov, Yuri A.__ Green's Functions Method in Applied Mechanics. (Topics in Engineering Ser.). 260p. 1995. 108.00 (*1-56252-311-2*) Computational Mech MA.

*__Meining, Donald W.__ The Great Columbia Plain: A Historical Geography, 1805-1910. LC 68-11044. (Weyerhaeuser Environmental Classic Ser.). (Illus.). 598p. (C). 1995. pap. 19.95 (*0-295-97485-0*) U of Wash Pr.

Meininger, ed. see De Balzac, Honore.

Meininger, Jut. Success Through Transactional Analysis. 224p. 1974. pap. 3.50 (*0-451-12637-8*, Sig) NAL-Dutton.

Meininger, Peter L., jt. ed. see Goodman, Steven M.

Meininger, Richard C., ed. Effects of Aggregates & Mineral Fillers on Asphalt Mixture Performance. LC 92-31159. (Special Technical Publication Ser.: Vol. 1147). (Illus.). 360p. 1992. text ed. 58.00 (*0-8031-1468-0*, 04-011470-08) ASTM.

Meininger, Thomas A. The Formation of Nationalist Bulgarian Intelligentsia, 1835-1878. McNeill, William H. & Jelavich, Charles, eds. (Modern European History Ser.). 552p. 1988. lib. bdg. 20.00 (*0-8240-8028-9*) Garland.

Meinke, Albert H., Jr. Mountain Troops & Medics: Wartime Stories of a Frontline Surgeon in the U. S. Ski Troops. LC 92-64065. 370p. 1992. 19.95 (*0-9633742-0-6*) Rucksack Pub.

Meinke, Peter. Howard Nemerov. LC 68-64753. (University of Minnesota Pamphlets on American Writers Ser.: No. 70). 48p. (Orig.). reprint ed. pap. 25.00 (*0-7837-2873-5*, 2057582) Bks Demand.

— Liquid Paper: New & Selected Poems. LC 91-50108. (Poetry Ser.). 120p. (C). 1991. 29.95 (*0-8229-3681-X*); pap. 12.95 (*0-8229-5455-9*) U of Pittsburgh Pr.

— The Night Train & the Golden Bird. LC 76-43966. (Pitt Poetry Ser.). 79p. reprint ed. pap. 25.00 (*0-685-15969-8*, 2026316) Bks Demand.

— Night Watch on the Chesapeake. LC 86-25040. (Poetry Ser.). 96p. 1987. pap. 10.95 (*0-8229-5390-0*) U of Pittsburgh Pr.

— The Piano Tuner. LC 85-28864. (Flannery O'Connor Award for Short Fiction Ser.). 176p. 1986. 15.95 (*0-8203-0844-7*) U of Ga Pr.

— The Piano Tuner. LC 85-28864. (Flannery O'Connor Award for Short Fiction Ser.). 168p. 1994. pap. 11.95 (*0-8203-1645-8*) U of Ga Pr.

Meinke, William, jt. auth. see Lucas, David O.

*__Meinkoff.__ Treasure Island. 1995. 24.95 (*0-8057-8804-2*, Twayne) Macmillan.

Meinkohn, D. & Haken, H., eds. Dissipative Structures in Transport Processes & Combustion: Interdisciplinary Seminar, Bielefeld, 17-21 July, 1989. (Synergetics Ser.: Vol. 48). (Illus.). 256p. 1990. 71.00 (*0-387-52751-6*) Spr-Verlag.

Meinkoth, Norman A., jt. auth. see Audubon Society Staff.

Meins, Jan. Bouquet for Murder. (Illus.). 106p. 1987. pap. 13.95 (*0-914546-74-0*) Rose Pub.

— Murder in Little Rock. 1989. mass mkt. 4.50 (*0-312-92025-3*) St Martin.

Meinsy, Timothy, jt. auth. see Oberer, Walter.

Meintel, Deirdre. Race, Culture & Portuguese Colonialism in Cabo Verde. (Foreign & Comparative Studies Program, African Ser.: No. 41). (Orig.). 1984. pap. text ed. 12.50 (*0-915984-66-0*) Syracuse U Foreign Comp.

Meintjes, Ria & Athey, Jackie. The Bride's Choice. LC 79-52243. (Continental's Creative Cake Ser.). (Illus.). 64p. (Orig.). 1979. pap. 4.95 (*0-916096-22-X*) Books Bakers.

Meintjes, Stephen & Jacques, Michael. Trial of Chaka Dlamini. 120p. 1990. 6.00 (*0-9583105-1-3*, Pub. by Amagi Bks SA) Schalkenbach.

Meints, Graydon M. Along the Tracks: A Directory of Named Places on Michigan Railroads. LC 87-405797. 1987. 25.00 (*0-916699-11-0*); pap. 15.00 (*0-916699-12-9*) CMU Clarke Hist Lib.

— Michigan Railroads & Railroad Companies. LC 92-32966. (C). 1993. 35.00 (*0-87013-318-7*) Mich St U Pr.

Meinwald, Constance C. Plato's Parmenides. 208p. 1991. 39.95 (*0-19-506445-3*) OUP.

Meinzen-Dick, Ruth & Svendsen, Mark, eds. Future Directions for Indian Irrigation. 475p. 1991. 33.00 (*0-89629-316-5*); 24.00 (*0-87006-988-8*); 8.40 (*0-87006-987-X*) Intl Food Policy.

Meinzer, Wyman. The Roadrunner. LC 92-33693. (Illus.). 128p. 1993. 37.50 (*0-89672-243-0*); pap. 19.95 (*0-89672-244-9*) Tex Tech Univ Pr.

Meir Ai-Nai-Yim. Polychrome Historical Haggadah. (Illus.). 40.00 (*0-686-10317-3*) J Freedman Liturgy.

Meir, Avinoan, jt. ed. see Stern, Eliahu.

Meir Bar-Am. The Fateful Mission. 180p. 1986. 10.95 (*0-87306-420-8*); pap. 7.95 (*0-87306-421-6*) Feldheim.

Meir, Gabriella M. Diagnosis of Mental Disorders: Medical Subject Analysis with Research Bibliography. LC 84-45651. 150p. 1985. 37.50 (*0-88164-228-2*); pap. 29.50 (*0-88164-229-0*) ABBE Pubs Assn.

Meir, Keith. The Vigilant Truth. Ingram, tr. 1993. 12.95 (*1-880416-78-6*) NW Pub.

Meir, Mira. Alina: A Russian Girl Comes to Israel. Shapiro, Zeva, tr. (Illus.). 48p. (J). (gr. 2-4). 1982. 9.95 (*0-8276-0208-1*) JPS Phila.

*__Meir, Richard.__ Richard Meir Sculpture. LC 94-5348. (Illus.). 1994. write for info. (*0-8478-1849-7*) Rizzoli Intl.

An Asterisk (*) at the beginning of an entry indicates that the title is appearing in BIP for the first time.

Meir, Shoshana B. The Evolution of the Modern Jewish School System in Israel. (TWEC World Education Monographs). 25p. 1977. 2.50 (*0-685-05145-5*) I N Thut World Educ Ctr.

***Meir, Yehyda Ben.** Civil-Military Relations in Israel. LC 94-33142. 1995. write for info. (*0-231-09684-4*) Col U Pr.

***Meire, H. B. & Farrant, P.** Basic Clinical Ultrasound. LC 94-40651. 1994. pap. text ed. 39.95 (*0-471-91691-9*) Wiley.

Meire, Hylton, et al, eds. Clinical Ultrasound: A Comprehensive Text, 4 vols., Set. (Illus.). 3072p. 1993. text ed. 595.00 (*0-443-04846-0*) Churchill.

***Meirelles, Janet. Diabetes Is Not a Piece of Cake: Prescribed for Family, Friends & Co-workers of Folks with Diabetes. LC 94-75824. (Illus.). 1994. pap. 15.95 (*1-884929-75-3*) Lincoln Pubng.**
THIS YEAR MORE THAN 650,000 PEOPLE WILL BE DIAGNOSED WITH DIABETES. DIABETES IS NOT A PIECE OF CAKE...(1-884929-75-3), $15.95, is the FIRST BOOK anyone newly diagnosed with diabetes should buy or receive! It's the ONLY book for friends, family, co-workers & supervisors. 288 great pages. DIABETES... has the latest information, plus over 300 diabetics told this nurse-author their true stories: Kira's paramedics; The $200.00 sandwich; When Jo cuddles-- give her sugar; The hostage in Lebanon with diabetes. What you need to know about diabetes--whether you have it or not, including a chapter "Do I have it, will I get it?" 24 pages of great recipes. Recommended by physicians & diabetics: "My husband read it & finally understood." "Thanks for the recipe for fat-free, sugar-free cheesecake." "The glossary & index are great helps." (Ask us for details). Available to the trade through IPG, Pacific Pipeline & Ingram Books. For additional information from the Publisher call (800) BOOKS-4-U. Due to requests from readers, the 128 page DIABETES IS NOT A PIECE OF CAKE COOKBOOK (1-884929-82-6), $11.75, has just been completed.
Publisher Provided Annotation.

— Diabetes is Not a Piece of Cake Cookbook. 128p. (Orig.). 1995. pap. 11.75 (*1-884929-82-6*) Lincoln Pubng.

Meirelles, R. M., et al, eds. Clinical Endocrinology: Proceedings of the 18th Brazilian Congress of Endocrinology & Metabolism, Rio de Janeiro, Brazil, 12-17 June, 1988. (International Congress Ser.: No. 793). 450p. 1988. 136.00 (*0-444-81039-0*, Excerpta Medica) Elsevier.

Meireran, Sigmund, tr. see Sanne, Karl U.

Meiring, Bernard J. Educational Aspects of the Legislation of the Councils of Baltimore, 1829-1884. 1978. 28.95 (*0-405-10844-3*, 11821) Ayer.

Meiring, Steven P., et al. A Core Curriculum: Making Mathematics Count for Everyone. Hirsch, Christian R., ed. LC 92-6996. (Curriculum & Evaluation Standards for School Mathematics Addenda Ser.). (Illus.). 150p. (Orig.). 1992. pap. 17.00 (*0-87353-328-3*) NCTM.

Meirleir, K., jt. ed. see Osteaux, M.

Meirmanov, Anvarbek M. The Stephan Problem. Kegel et al, eds. Niezgodka, Marek & Crowley, Anna, trs. (Expositions in Mathematics Ser.: No. 3). ix, 245p. (C). 1992. lib. bdg. 92.95 (*3-11-011479-8*) De Gruyter.

***Meirose, Jim.** Tree: Spirit Deer. Smith, Artemis, ed. & illus. by. (On-Demand Collectors' Editions Ser.). 900p. 1988. per. 100.00x (*1-878998-26-9*) Savant Garde.

Meirovitch, Leonard. Analytical Methods in Vibrations. 576p. (C). 1967. write for info. (*0-02-380140-9*) Macmillan.

— Computational Methods in Structural Dynamics. 1980. lib. bdg. 74.50 (*90-286-0580-0*) Kluwer Ac.

— Dynamics & Control of Structures. 425p. 1990. text ed. 89.95 (*0-471-62858-1*) Wiley.

— Elements of Vibration Analysis. 2nd ed. 624p. (C). 1986. text ed. write for info. (*0-07-041342-8*) McGraw.

— Introduction to Dynamics & Control. LC 84-20938. 392p. 1985. Net. text ed. write for info. (*0-471-87074-9*); teacher ed 15.00 (*0-471-82282-5*) Wiley.

— Methods of Analytical Dynamics. 1970. text ed. write for info. (*0-07-041455-6*) McGraw.

***Meirovitz, Marco, et al.** Thinkability: A Practical Program to Improve Thinking Skills Using Games. 1995. teacher ed 89.00 (*0-570-04012-4*) L Erlbaum Assocs.

— Thinkability: A Practical Program to Improve Thinking Skills Using Games, 10 wkbks., Set. 1995. student ed 119.50 (*0-570-04017-5*); 149.00 (*0-570-04018-3*) L Erlbaum Assocs.

— Thinkability: A Practical Program to Improve Thinking Skills Using Games, Set, incl. 10 wkbks. & 5 game kits. 1995. teacher ed 239.00 (*0-570-04027-2*) L Erlbaum Assocs.

Meirowitz, Claire, jt. ed. see Kershen, Harry.

Meis, Jeanne M. & Enzinger, Franz M. Atlas of Soft Tissue Tumors. (C). 1993. disk 500.00 (*1-56815-019-9*) Image Premast.

Meis, John D. Taste for Tuscany. 1993. 27.50 (*1-55859-466-3*) Abbeville Pr.

Meis, M. Indian Women & Patriarchy. 113p. 1979. 23.95 (*0-318-37057-3*) Asia Bk Corp.

Meis, Reinhard. Pocket Watches. LC 86-63367. (Illus.). 316p. 1987. 50.00 (*0-88740-084-1*) Schiffer.

***Meisalas, S. & Whitley, A.** The Kurds. Date not set. write for info. (*0-679-42389-3*) Random.

Meisami, ed. Handbook of Human Growth & Developmental Biology, Vol. 2, Pt. A. 1990. Vol. 2 Pt. A, 1989. 216.95 (*0-8493-3184-6*, QP187) CRC Pr.

— Handbook of Human Growth & Developmental Biology, Vol. 2, Pt. B. 1990. Vol. 2 Pt. B, 1990. 216.95 (*0-8493-3185-4*, RJ131) CRC Pr.

— Handbook of Human Growth & Developmental Biology, Vol. III, Pt. A. 1990. Vol. III Pt. A, 1990. 130.95 (*0-8493-3186-2*, RJ131) CRC Pr.

— Handbook of Human Growth & Developmental Biology, Vol. III, Pt. B. 1990. Vol. III Pt. B, 1990. 130.95 (*0-8493-3187-0*, RJ131) CRC Pr.

Meisami, Esmail & Timiras, Paola S., eds. Handbook of Human Growth & Development, Vol. I: Neural, Sensory, Motor & Integrative Development, 3 pts., Pt. C: Factors Influencing Brain Development. 192p. 1988. 125.95 (*0-8493-3183-8*, RJ131) CRC Pr.

— Handbook of Human Growth & Development, Vol. I: Neural, Sensory, Motor & Integrative Development, 3 pts., Pt. A: Developmental Neurobiology. 240p. 1988. 158.95 (*0-8493-3181-1*, RJ131) CRC Pr.

— Handbook of Human Growth & Development, Vol. I: Neural, Sensory, Motor & Integrative Development, 3 pts., Pt. B: Sensory, Motor & Integrative Development. 240p. 1988. 180.95 (*0-8493-3182-X*, RJ131) CRC Pr.

Meisami, Esmail, ed. see International Symposium on Developmental Neurobiology Staff.

Meisami, Julie S. Medieval Persian Court Poetry. (Illus.). 384p. 1987. text ed. 55.00 (*0-691-06598-5*) Princeton U Pr.

Meisami, Julie S., ed. & tr. The Sea of Precious Virtues: A Medieval Islamic Mirror for Princes. LC 88-27858. 468p. 1990. lib. bdg. 39.95 (*0-87480-313-6*) U of Utah Pr.

Meisami, Julie S., ed. see Nizami.

Meisburger, W. F. History of Papa Frog. LC 93-74950. (Illus.). 24p. (J). (ps-3). 1994. pap. 4.95 (*0-943864-72-0*) Davenport.

Meisei Publications Staff. Educational Facilities. (Illus.). 224p. 1994. 89.95 (*4-87246-293-9*, Pub. by Meisei Co Ltd JA) Bks Nippan.

— Industrial Design Workshop: The Creative Process Behind Product Design. (Illus.). 224p. 1993. 115.00 (*4-87246-258-0*, Pub. by Meisei Co Ltd JA) Bks Nippan.

— Medical Facilities. (Illus.). 224p. 1994. 89.95 (*4-87246-294-7*, Pub. by Meisei Co Ltd JA) Bks Nippan.

— New Hotel Architecture. (Illus.). 400p. 1993. 115.00 (*4-87246-282-3*, Pub. by Meisei Co Ltd JA) Bks Nippan.

— Visual Merchandising & Display. (Illus.). 224p. 1993. 85.00 (*4-87246-281-5*, Pub. by Meisei Co Ltd JA) Bks Nippan.

Meisel, A., et al. X-Ray Spectra & Chemical Binding. (Chemical Physics Ser.: Vol. 37). (Illus.). 465p. 1989. 139.00 (*0-387-13325-9*) Spr-Verlag.

Meisel, Alan. The Right to Die. (Medico-Legal Library). 573p. 1989. text ed. 125.00 (*0-471-84687-2*) Wiley.

— The Right to Die, No. 2. suppl. ed. (Medico-Legal Library). 573p. 1993. 78.00 (*0-471-59701-5*) Wiley.

Meisel, Allen D., et al. Atlas of Osteoarthritis. LC 83-253444. 208p. reprint ed. pap. 59.30 (*0-7837-2727-5*, 2043107) Bks Demand.

***Meisel, Andy.** Menopaws. 64p. 1995. pap. 9.95 (*0-89815-780-3*) Ten Speed Pr.

Meisel, Anthony C. & Del Mastro, M. L., trs. The Rule of St. Benedict. LC 74-33611. 120p. 1975. mass mkt. 5.50 (*0-385-00948-8*, Image Bks) Doubleday.

Meisel, Burt. No! I Can't Afford It. LC 81-80557. 184p. 1981. pap. 9.75 (*0-87218-016-6*) Natl Underwriter.

Meisel, C. Julius, ed. Mainstreaming Handicapped Children: Outcomes, Controversies, & New Directions. 312p. (C). 1986. text ed. 59.95 (*0-89859-582-7*) L Erlbaum Assocs.

Meisel, F., jt. auth. see Harvey, Brian W.

Meisel, Frank, jt. auth. see Harvey, Brian.

Meisel, Irwin B. The Whole World Is Out or Busy. LC 86-61182. (Illus.). 174p. (Orig.). 1986. pap. 15.95 (*0-87218-048-4*) Natl Underwriter.

Meisel, J. M., ed. Two First Languages - Early Grammatical Development in Bilingual Children. (Studies on Language Acquisition: No. 10). iv, 318p. 1990. pap. 83.10 (*3-11-013133-1*) Mouton.

Meisel, Jacqueline. South Africa at the Crossroads. LC 94-8350. (Headliners Ser.). (Illus.). 64p. (J). (gr. 5-8). 1994. lib. bdg. 15.90 (*1-56294-511-4*) Millbrook Pr.

Meisel, James H. The Genesis of George Sorel: An Account of His Formative Period Followed by a Study of His Influence. LC 82-11860. 320p. 1982. reprint ed. text ed. 65.00 (*0-313-23658-5*, MEGS, Greenwood Pr) Greenwood.

Meisel, James H., pref. The Myth of the Ruling Class: Gaetano Mosca & the "Elite" LC 80-13080. xiv, 432p. 1980. reprint ed. text ed. 65.00 (*0-313-22346-7*, MEMR, Greenwood Pr) Greenwood.

Meisel, Janet. Barons of the Welsh Frontier: The Corbet, Pantulf, & Fitz Warin Families, 1066-1272. LC 80-10273. 251p. reprint ed. pap. 71.60 (*0-7837-6886-9*, 2046716) Bks Demand.

Meisel, Jerome. Principles of Electromechanical-Energy Conversion. LC 82-6540. 656p. 1984. reprint ed. lib. bdg. 49.50 (*0-89874-495-4*) Krieger.

Meisel, John, jt. ed. see Laponce, Jean.

Meisel, Judi & Meisel, Tony. The Peanut Butter Cookbook: From Soup to Nuts with America's Favorite Spread. (Illus.). 48p. 1993. 4.98 (*0-8317-7097-X*) Smithmark.

Meisel, Juergen M. & Pam, Martin D., eds. Linear Order & Generative Theory. (Current Issues in Linguistic Theory Ser.: No. 7). ix, 512p. 1979. 94.00x (*90-272-0908-1*) Benjamins North Am.

Meisel, Jurgen M., ed. The Acquisition of Verb Placement: Functional Categories & V2 Phenomena in Language Acquisition. LC 92-23956. (Studies in Theoretical Psycholinguistics: Vol. 16). 464p. (C). 1992. lib. bdg. 147.00 (*0-7923-1906-0*) Kluwer Ac.

— Bilingual First Language Acquisition: French & German Grammatical Development. LC 94-23215. (Language Acquisition & Language Disorders (LALD) Ser.: No. 7). 250p. 1994. lib. bdg. 70.00x (*1-55619-242-8*) Benjamins North Am.

— Bilingual First Language Acquisition: French & German Grammatical Development. LC 94-23215. (Language Acquisition & Language Disorders (LALD) Ser.: No. 7). 1994. pap. 29.95x (*1-55619-243-6*) Benjamins North Am.

Meisel, Louis & Cooper, Joseph, eds. Political Parties: Development & Decay. LC 76-46782. (Sage Electoral Studies Yearbook: Vol. 4). 344p. reprint ed. pap. 98.10 (*0-317-08816-5*, 2021927) Bks Demand.

Meisel, Louis K., sel. Photorealism Since Nineteen Eighty. LC 92-21997. (Illus.). 368p. 1993. 95.00 (*0-8109-3720-4*) Abrams.

Meisel, Martin. Realizations: Narrative, Pictorial, & Theatrical Arts of the Nineteenth Century. LC 82-12292. (Illus.). 471p. 1984. 75.00x (*0-691-06553-5*) Princeton U Pr.

— Shaw & the Nineteenth Century Theater. LC 75-25495. (Illus.). 477p. 1976. reprint ed. text ed. 87.50 (*0-8371-8416-9*, MESN, Greenwood Pr) Greenwood.

Meisel, Paul, jt. auth. see Spielman, Patrick.

Meisel, Perry. The Absent Father: Virginia Woolf & Walter Pater. LC 79-19289. 1980. text ed. 37.00 (*0-300-02401-0*) Yale U Pr.

— The Myth of the Modern: A Study in British Literature & Criticism after 1850. LC 87-10617. 266p. 1987. text ed. 35.00 (*0-300-03946-8*) Yale U Pr.

— The Myth of the Modern: A Study in British Literature & Criticism after 1850. 266p. (C). 1989. reprint ed. pap. 15.00 (*0-300-04560-3*) Yale U Pr.

— Thomas Hardy: The Return of the Repressed; a Study of the Major Fiction. LC 77-182211. (Yale College Ser.: No. 12). 189p. reprint ed. pap. 53.90 (*0-8357-8349-9*, 2033824) Bks Demand.

Meisel, Susan L., ed. see Vanhyning, Memory L.

Meisel, Tony. Cruising under Sail & Power. 272p. 1990. text ed. 35.00 (*0-02-583935-7*) Macmillan.

— Under Sail. 1982. 24.95 (*0-02-583940-3*) Macmillan.

Meisel, Tony, jt. auth. see Meisel, Judi.

Meisel, Wayne, ed. Men about Men: A Guide for Women & Men. (Gift Editions Ser.). 64p. 1992. 7.99 (*0-88088-427-4*) Peter Pauper.

Meisel, Wayne & Wolf, Maura, eds. Light One Candle: Quotes for Hope & Action. (Gift Editions Ser.). (Illus.). 64p. 1991. 7.99 (*0-88088-357-X*) Peter Pauper.

Meiselas, Susan, ed. Chile: From Within. 1990. 39.95 (*0-393-02817-8*) Norton.

Meiselman, David & Shapiro, Eli. The Measurement of Corporate Sources & Uses of Funds. (Technical Papers: No. 18). 301p. 1964. reprint ed. 78.30 (*0-87014-424-3*) Natl Bur Econ Res.

Meiselman, David I. Welfare Reform & the Carter Public Service Employment Program: A Critique. LC 77-95219. 1978. pap. 2.50 (*0-916770-05-2*) Law & Econ U Miami.

Meiselman, David J. Attorney Malpractice Law & Procedure. LC 79-89562. 1980. 135.00 (*0-685-59903-5*) Clark Boardman Callaghan.

Meiselman, Karin C. Incest: A Psychological Study of Causes & Effects with Treatment Recommendations. LC 78-62557. 382p. reprint ed. pap. 108.90 (*0-7837-6513-4*, 2045625) Bks Demand.

— Incest: A Psychological Study of the Causes & Effects with Treatment Recommendations. LC 78-62557. (Classics Ser.). 388p. 1992. reprint ed. pap. 21.00 (*1-55542-441-4*) Jossey-Bass.

— Resolving the Trauma of Incest: Reintegration Therapy with Survivors. LC 89-43302. (Social & Behavioral Science Ser.). 342p. 1990. 31.95x (*1-55542-219-5*) Jossey-Bass.

Meiselman, M. Jewish Woman in Jewish Law. (Library of Jewish Law & Ethics: Vol. 6). pap. 12.95 (*0-87068-329-2*) Ktav.

***Meisels, Alexander.** Cytopathology of the Uterine Cervix, Set. 1991. sl. 200.00 (*0-89189-341-5*) Am Soc Clinical.

— Cytopathology of the Uterine Cervix. LC 90-309. (Illus.). 1991. 145.00 (*0-89189-299-0*) Am Soc Clinical.

Meisels, Alexander & Morin, Carol. Pathology of the Uterine Cervix. LC 90-309. (Illus.). 334p. 1991. 125.00 (*0-685-54502-4*) Am Soc Clinical.

Meisels, M. & Shapiro, E. R. Tradition & Innovation in Psychoanalytic Education: Clark Conference on Psychoanalytic Training for Psychologists. 312p. 1990. 59.95 (*0-8058-0386-6*) L Erlbaum Assocs.

Meisels, Murray, jt. ed. see Lane, Robert C.

Meisels, Penina & Cronin, Michael. Polo. (Illus.). 112p. 1992. 50.00 (*0-00-637796-3*) Collins SF.

— Polo. limited ed. (Illus.). 112p. 1992. 150.00 (*0-00-255030-X*) Collins SF.

Meisels, Samuel J. Developmental Screening in Early Childhood: A Guide. 3rd ed. LC 89-61119. 58p. 1989. pap. text ed. 4.50 (*0-935989-27-7*, NAEYC#121) Natl Assn Child Ed.

Meisels, Samuel J. & Shonkoff, Jack P., eds. Handbook of Early Childhood Intervention. (Illus.). 720p. (C). 1990. pap. 34.95 (*0-521-38777-9*) Cambridge U Pr.

Meisels, Samuel J. & Wiske, Martha S. Early Screening Inventory. (C). 1983. 43.95 (*0-8077-6080-3*) Tchrs Coll.

Meisenheimer, Adel. Song Crafters Tool Kit: The Basics, Special Gospel Music Edition, Vol. I. 1987. Multi-media print/cassette. audio 39.95 (*0-944582-00-1*) Song Crafters.

Meisenheimer, Adel, ed. Song Crafters Tool Kit, the Basic, Vol. I. 1987. Multi-media print/cassette. audio 39.95 (*0-944582-02-8*) Song Crafters.

Meisenheimer, Adel, ed. see Boitos, Myra E.

Meisenheimer, Claire G. Improving Quality: A Guide to Effective Programs. LC 91-38796. 576p. 1992. 59.00 (*0-8342-0234-4*) Aspen Pub.

— Quality Assurance for Home Health Care. 288p. 1989. 69.00 (*0-8342-0026-0*) Aspen Pub.

Meisenheimer, Jim. Forty-Seven Ways to Sell Smarter. 144p. 1993. pap. 19.95 (*0-9637479-0-8*) Helbern Grp.

Meisenheimer, Klaus & Roser, Hermann-Josef, eds. Hot Spots in Extragalactic Radio Sources. (Lecture Notes in Physics Ser.: Vol. 327). xii, 301p. 1989. 48.00 (*0-387-50993-3*) Spr-Verlag.

Meisenheimer, Klaus, jt. auth. see Roser, Hermann-Josef.

Meisenheimer, Sharon. Color Days. (J). (gr. k-3). 1988. pap. 8.99 (*0-8224-1641-7*) Fearon Teach Aids.

— Special Ways with Ordinary Days. (J). (gr. k-3). 1988. pap. 13.99 (*0-8224-6347-4*) Fearon Teach Aids.

Meisenhelder, Janice B. & LaCharite, Christopher L. Comfort in Caring: Nursing the Person with HIV Infection. 300p. (C). 1989. text ed. 29.50 (*0-673-52004-8*) Lippincott.

Meisenhelder, Susan E. Wordsworth's Informed Reader: Structures of Experience in His Poetry. LC 86-28169. 280p. 1988. 27.50 (*0-8265-1218-6*) Vanderbilt U Pr.

Meisenzahl, Hilda. Meisen Breeding Manual. LC 73-84517. (Other Dog Bks.). (Illus.). 128p. 1975. 8.95 (*0-87714-017-0*) Denlingers.

— Meisen Poodle Manual. LC 73-84516. (Breed Bks.). (Illus.). 160p. 1974. 9.95 (*0-87714-016-2*) Denlingers.

Meiser, jt. auth. see Laidler.

Meiser, Edith & Giacoia, Frank. Sherlock Holmes: The Red Headed League & Other Stories. Mason, Tom, ed. (Illus.). 132p. 1991. pap. 17.95 (*0-944735-68-1*) Malibu Graphics.

— Sherlock Holmes, Vol. 1: The Classic Comic Strips. (Illus.). 140p. 1989. pap. 17.95 (*0-944735-15-0*) Malibu Graphics.

Meiser, Joy. Bed & Breakfast Guide to Rhode Island, 1990-1992. 6th ed. (Illus.). 110p. 1990. pap. 4.95 (*0-685-31413-8*) Bed Brkfst RI.

Meiser, Kenneth. Tenant-Landlord. (Illus.). 90p. 1989. pap. 35.00 (*0-685-14672-3*) NJ Inst CLE.

Meiser, Louis K. Photorealism. 1989. pap. 39.98 (*0-8109-8092-4*) Abrams.

Meiser, Mary. Good Writing! LC 94-12808. 1994. pap. text ed. 28.00 (*0-02-380155-7*) Allyn.

Meiser, Mary J., jt. auth. see Maxwell, Rhoda J.

Meish, Charles, jt. auth. see Margulias, Ivan.

Meisinger, J. J., et al, eds. Nitrification Inhibitors: Potentials & Limitations. (Illus.). 129p. 1980. pap. 7.50 (*0-89118-063-X*) Am Soc Agron.

Meisinger, Richard J., Jr. College & University Budgeting: An Introduction for Faculty & Academic Administrators. 2nd ed. LC 94-20513. 1994. 60.00 (*0-915164-94-9*) NACUBO.

Meisl, Josef. Haskalah: Geschichte der Aufklarungsbewegung unter den Juden in Russland. Katz, Steven, ed. LC 79-7147. (Jewish Philosophy, Mysticism & History of Ideas Ser.). 1980. reprint ed. lib. bdg. 23.95 (*0-405-12277-2*) Ayer.

***Meisler, Alan.** Flower Children: Thirty Original Victorian Postcards from the World-Class Meisler Collection. (Original Victorian Postcard Book Series from the World-Class Meisler Collection). (Illus.). 34p. (Orig.). 1994. pap. 8.95 (*1-886584-01-X*) Sentimental Times.

— Vegetable People: Thirty Original Victorian Postcards from the World-Class Meisler Collection. (Original Victorian Postcard Book Series from the World-Class Meisler Collection). (Illus.). 34p. (Orig.). 1994. pap. 8.95 (*1-886584-00-1*) Sentimental Times.

Meisler, Andy, jt. auth. see McCorvey, Norma.

Meisler, Jules. Effective Psychotherapy for Patient & Therapist. LC 91-2881. 208p. 1991. text ed. 49.95 (*0-275-93985-5*, C3985, Praeger Pubs) Greenwood.

Meisles. Art of Polo. Date not set. pap. 12.99 (*0-517-11151-9*) Random Hse Value.

Meislich, Herbert. Three Thousand Solved Problems in Organic Chemistry. (Schaum's Solved Problems Ser.). 1993. pap. text ed. 22.95 (*0-07-056424-8*) McGraw.

Meislich, Herbert, et al. Schaum's Outline of Organic Chemistry. 2nd ed. (Schaum's Outline Ser.). 1991. pap. text ed. 13.95 (*0-07-041458-0*) McGraw.

Meislin, Bernard. Jewish Law in American Trials & Tribunals. 25.00 (*0-87068-460-4*) Ktav.

Meislin, Harvey W. & Dresnick, Stephen J. Skills & Procedures of Emergency & General Medicine. 250p. 1981. text ed. 31.50 (*0-8359-7009-4*, Reston) P-H.

Meisner, jt. auth. see Paolini.

Meisner, Arnold. Desert Storm Sea War. (Illus.). 128p. 1991. pap. 9.98 (*0-87938-562-6*) Motorbooks Intl.

Meisner, Arnold, jt. auth. see Bailey, Dennis.

Meisner, Gary. Instant Keyboard: Quick & Easy Instruction for the Impatient Student! (Illus.). 136p. (Orig.). 1987. pap. 9.95 (*0-88188-624-6*, 00183575) H Leonard.

— Instant Scale & Chord Guide for Keyboards. (Instant Keyboard Ser.). (Illus.). 64p. (Orig.). 1990. pap. 4.95 (*0-7935-0008-7*, 00290166) H Leonard.

Meisner, Gary, ed. The Richard Rodgers Collection. LC 90-52955. (Composer Ser.). (Illus.). 320p. (Orig.). 1990. pap. 19.95 (*0-7935-0033-8*, 00490422) H Leonard.

Meisner, Janet N. The Jewish Tradition & Humanistic Education. (Area Studies Resource Guides). 45p. 1984. 4.50 (0-685-09435-9) I N Thut World Educ Ctr.

Meisner, Maurice. Mao's China: A History of the People's Republic. LC 76-51566. (Transformation of Modern China Ser.). 1979. pap. text ed. 10.95 (0-02-920810-6) Free Pr.

— Mao's China & after. enl. rev. ed. 1986. text ed. 29.95 (0-02-920870-X); pap. 16.95 (0-02-920880-7) Free Pr.

— Marxism, Maoism & Utopianism: Eight Essays. 276p. 1982. 13.95 (0-299-08420-5) U of Wis Pr.

Meisner, Maurice, jt. ed. see Dirlik, Arif.

Meisner, Sanford & Longwell, Dennis. Sanford Meisner on Acting. LC 86-46187. 1987. pap. 11.00 (0-394-75059-4, Vin) Random.

Meisner, Ulf-G, ed. Effective Field Theories of the Standard Model: Proceedings of the Workshop, Dobogoko, Hungary, 22-26 August 1991. LC 92-9939. 500p. 1992. text ed. 95.00 (981-02-1001-9) World Scientific Pub.

***Meisonnier, Etienne.** Dictionnaire des Medicaments Veterinaires et des Parapharmacies Animales. 6th ed. 1328p. (FRE.). 1992. pap. 110.00 (0-7859-8659-6, 286326091x) Fr & Eur.

Meiss, J. D., jt. auth. see MacKay, R. S.

Meiss, J. D., jt. auth. see Mackay, R. S.

Meiss, James D., jt. auth. see Hazeltine, Richard D.

Meiss, Kathleen A. Work, Welfare & Social Work Practice: A Study of Theoretical & Practice Relationships with Applications from Occupational Social Work. (Stockholm Studies in Social Work: No. 6). 253p. (Orig.). 1991. pap. 52.50x (91-22-01411-X, Pub. by Almqv & Wiksell SW) Coronet Bks.

Meiss, Millard. French Painting in the Time of Jean, Duke of Berry: The Limbourgs & Their Contemporaries, 2 vols., Set. LC 73-90120. (Illus.). 1975. 110.00 (0-8076-0734-7) Braziller.

— Giotto & Assisi. LC 60-9443. (Walter W. S. Cook Alumni Lecture Ser.: 1959). 80p. reprint ed. pap. 25.00 (0-317-09361-4, 2050841) Bks Demand.

— Painting in Florence & Siena after the Black Death: The Arts, Religion & Society in the Mid-Fourteenth-Century. 1976. pap. 19.95x (0-691-00312-2) Princeton U Pr.

— The Tres Riches Heures of Jean, Duke of Berry. LC 73-90120. (Illus.). 290p. pap. 24.95 (0-8076-1220-0); boxed 100.00 (0-8076-0512-3) Braziller.

Meiss, Millard & Kirsch, Edith W., intros. The Visconti Hours. LC 75-75371. (Illus.). 264p. 1972. boxed 100.00 (0-8076-0651-0) Braziller.

Meiss, Millard & Thomas, Marcel, intros. The Rohan Master. LC 73-77880. (Illus.). 247p. 1973. boxed 100.00 (0-8076-0690-1) Braziller.

Meiss, Millard, jt. auth. see Tintori, Leonetto.

Meissel, Chris. Young Children Rap to Learn about Famous African-Americans. Keeling, Jan, ed. (Illus.). 80p. (Orig.). (J). 1993. pap. text ed. 8.95 (0-86530-265-0) Incentive Pubns.

***Meissner.** Florida Law Enforcement Manual, 2 vols., Set. 1988. pap. 24.00 (0-614-05821-X) Michie Butterworth.

Meissner, Bill. Hitting into the Wind: A Collection of Short Stories. LC 93-24772. 1994. 19.00 (0-679-42929-8) Random.

Meissner, Bill & Driscoll, Jack. Twin Sons of Different Mirrors: Poems in Dialogue. LC 89-3106. 64p. (Orig.). 1989. pap. 6.95 (0-915943-35-2) Milkweed Ed.

Meissner, Boris. The Communist Party of the Soviet Union. Reshetar, John S., Jr., ed. Holling, Fred, tr. LC 75-27684. (Foreign Policy Research Institute Ser.: No. 4). 276p. 1976. reprint ed. text ed. 59.75 (0-8371-8461-4, MECP) Greenwood.

Meissner, C. Latin Phrase Book. Auden, H. W., tr. 338p. 1989. reprint ed. pap. text ed. 15.95 (0-89341-567-7, Longwood Academic) Hollowbrook.

Meissner, C., jt. auth. see American Vacuum Society Inc. Staff.

Meissner, Frank. Seeds of Change: Stories of IDB Innovation in Latin America. 132p. (Orig.). (C). 1991. pap. text ed. 15.95 (0-940602-39-3) IADB.

— Technology Transfer in the Developing World: The Case of the Chile Foundation. LC 87-36127. 177p. 1988. text ed. 49.95 (0-275-92926-4, C2926, Praeger Pubs) Greenwood.

***Meissner, Franz-Joseph.** Langenscheidts Woerterbuch der Ungangssprache Franzoesisch. 245p. (FRE & GER.). 1992. 39.95 (0-7859-8389-9, 3468201583) Fr & Eur.

Meissner, H. G. Strategic International Marketing. (Illus.). 260p. 1990. 69.00 (0-387-52254-9) Spr-Verlag.

Meissner, Larry, jt. ed. see Patrick, Hugh T.

***Meissner, Loren P.** FORTRAN 90. 492p. 1996. pap. 41.95 (0-534-93372-6) PWS Pubs.

Meissner, Loren P. & Organick, Elliot I. FORTRAN 77: Featuring Structured Programming. 3rd ed. LC 78-74689. (C). 1980. pap. text ed. 32.25 (0-201-05499-X) Addison-Wesley.

Meissner, M. & Pohl, R. O., eds. Phonon Scattering in Condensed Matter VII: Proceedings of the Seventh International Conference. (Solid-State Sciences Ser.: Vol. 112). 1993. 109.00 (0-387-56395-4); write for info. (3-540-56395-4) Spr-Verlag.

***Meissner, Paul A.** Florida Law Enforcement Manual. 592p. (C). 1994. pap. text ed. 49.00 (0-9645280-0-2) P A Meissner.

Meissner, R. & Bortfeld, R. K., eds. DEKORP-Atlas. (Illus.). 390p. 1990. 96.00 (0-387-52512-2) Spr-Verlag.

Meissner, R., et al, eds. Continental Lithosphere: Deep Seismic Reflections. (Geodynamics Ser.: Vol. 22). 452p. 1991. 55.00 (0-87590-522-6, GD0225226) Am Geophysical.

Meissner, Rolf. The Continental Crust: A Geophysical Approach. (International Geophysics Ser.). 1986. text ed. 121.00 (0-12-488950-6); pap. text ed. 63.00 (0-12-488951-4) Acad Pr.

Meissner, Virginia. Cross Country Ski Tours in Central Oregon. (Illus.). 192p. (Orig.). 1984. pap. 7.95 (0-9613755-1-5) Meissner Bks.

— Day Hikes in Central Oregon. 126p. 1981. pap. 6.95 (0-9613755-0-7) Meissner Bks.

— Hiking Central Oregon & Beyond. 400p. 1987. pap. 11.95 (0-9613755-2-3) Meissner Bks.

Meissner, W. W. Ignatius of Loyola: The Psychology of a Saint. (Illus.). 528p. (C). 1992. 40.00 (0-300-05156-5) Yale U Pr.

— Ignatius of Loyola: The Psychology of a Saint. 529p. 1994. pap. 18.00 (0-300-06079-3) Yale U Pr.

— Psychoanalysis & Religious Experience. LC 83-51296. 254p. 1986. pap. 15.00 (0-300-03751-1, Y-599) Yale U Pr.

— Thy Kingdom Come: Psychoanalytic Perspectives on the Messiah & the Millennium. (Orig.). 1995. pap. 24.95 (1-55612-750-2) Sheed & Ward MO.

— Treatment of Patients in the Borderline Spectrum. LC 88-10526. 644p. 1995. pap. 50.00 (1-56821-495-2) Aronson.

Meissner, Werner. Philosophy & Politics in China: The Controversy over Dialectical Materialism in the 1930's. LC 89-51664. 230p. 1990. 39.50 (0-8047-1772-9) Stanford U Pr.

Meissner, William A. Atlas of Tumor Pathology: Tumors of the Thyroid Gland. (Second Ser.: Fascicle 4, Supplement). (Illus.). 52p. 1990. per., pap. 4.50 (0-16-001855-2, S/N 008-023-000) USGPO.

Meissner, William W. The Assault on Authority: Dialogue or Dilemma? LC 70-152878. 320p. reprint ed. pap. 91.20 (0-8357-8807-5, 2033465) Bks Demand.

— Internalization in Psychoanalysis. LC 80-13867. (Psychological Issues Monograph: No. 50). 279p. 1980. text ed. 35.00 (0-8236-2713-6) Intl Univs Pr.

— Life & Faith: Psychological Perspectives on Religious Experience. fac. ed. LC 85-8026. 328p. 1987. reprint ed. pap. 93.50 (0-7837-7782-5, 2047537) Bks Demand.

— Psychotherapy & the Paranoid Process. LC 85-15614. 432p. 1994. 60.00 (0-87668-752-4) Aronson.

— Psychotherapy & the Paranoid Process. LC 85-15614. 448p. 1994. reprint ed. pap. 40.00 (1-56821-013-2) Aronson.

— Treatment of Patients in the Borderline Spectrum. LC 88-10526. 640p. 1988. 55.00 (0-87668-917-9) Aronson.

— What Is Effective in Psychoanalytic Therapy: The Move from Interpretation to Relation. LC 90-14509. 216p. 1991. 32.50 (0-87668-572-6) Aronson.

Meissonnier, Juste A. Oeuvre de Juste Aurele Meissonnier: The Complete Suite of Engravings of His Designs. LC 69-16909. (Illus.). 1978. reprint ed. 54.95 (0-405-08785-3, Pub. by Blom Pubns UK) Ayer.

***Meister.** Advances in Enzymology & Other Related Areas of Molecular Biology, Vol. 70. Date not set. text ed. write for info. (0-471-04097-5) Wiley.

***Meister, ed.** Advances in Enzymology & Related Areas of Molecular Biology Vol. 71. Date not set. pap. text ed. write for info. (0-471-12648-9) Wiley.

***Meister & AIA Staff.** Archaeological...Bulletin (95) 128p. 1994. per., pap. text ed. 10.50 (0-7872-0303-3) Kendall-Hunt.

— Excavations Is Israel. 128p. 1994. per., pap. text ed. 28.00 (0-7872-0486-2) Kendall-Hunt.

Meister, Albert. Participation, Associations, Development & Change. Ross, Jack L., tr. (Illus.). 286p. 1984. 34.95 (0-87855-423-8) Transaction Pubs.

Meister, Alton. Advances in Enzymology & Related Areas of Molecular Biology, Vol. 67. 528p. 1993. text ed. 119.95 (0-471-58279-4) Wiley.

Meister, Alton, ed. Advances in Enzymology: And Related Areas of Molecular Biology, 6 vols., Vol. 60. 417p. 1992. text ed. 98.00 (0-471-81282-X) Wiley.

— Advances in Enzymology: And Related Areas of Molecular Biology, 6 vols., Vol. 61. 557p. 1992. text ed. 98.00 (0-471-81830-5) Wiley.

— Advances in Enzymology: And Related Areas of Molecular Biology, 6 vols., Vol. 62. 455p. 1992. text ed. 98.00 (0-471-61770-9) Wiley.

— Advances in Enzymology: And Related Areas of Molecular Biology, 6 vols., Vol. 63. 551p. 1990. text ed. 119.95 (0-471-50984-1) Wiley.

— Advances in Enzymology: And Related Areas of Molecular Biology, 6 vols., Vol. 64. 494p. 1991. text ed. 119.95 (0-471-50949-3) Wiley.

— Advances in Enzymology: And Related Areas of Molecular Biology, 6 vols., Vol. 65. 448p. 1992. text ed. 119.95 (0-471-52760-2) Wiley.

— Advances in Enzymology & Related Areas of Molecular Biology, Vol. 66. 334p. 1993. text ed. 135.00 (0-471-55769-2) Wiley.

— Advances in Enzymology & Related Areas of Molecular Biology, Vol. 68. 237p. 1994. text ed. 129.95 (0-471-31071-9) Wiley.

— Advances in Enzymology & Related Areas of Molecular Biology, Vol. 69. 1994. text ed. 136.95 (0-471-01767-1) Wiley.

Meister, Barbara. Art Song: The Marriage of Music & Poetry. LC 91-12788. 300p. (C). 1992. text ed. 35.00 (0-89341-635-5, Longwood Academic) Hollowbrook.

— Nineteenth-Century French Song: Faure, Chausson, Duparc & Debussy. LC 79-2171. 416p. 1980. 35.00 (0-253-34075-6) Ind U Pr.

Meister, Barbara, jt. auth. see Bullock, Waneta B.

Meister, Cary W. Historical Demography of the Pima & Maricopa Indians, 1846-1974, 2 vols. (Studies in Historical Demography). 775p. 1990. reprint ed. write for info. (0-8240-3364-7) Garland.

Meister, Charles. Fourteen Ninety-Two: People, Purity, & Power. LC 92-757. 400p. (C). 1995. text ed. 37.50 (0-89341-703-3) Hollowbrook.

Meister, Charles W. Chekhov Criticism, 1880 Through 1986. LC 88-42508. 360p. 1988. lib. bdg. 52.50x (0-89950-355-1) McFarland & Co.

— Dramatic Criticism: A History. LC 84-43222. 326p. 1985. lib. bdg. 28.50 (0-89950-155-9) McFarland & Co.

— The Founding Fathers. LC 87-42514. 432p. 1987. lib. bdg. 27.50x (0-89950-291-1) McFarland & Co.

Meister, David. Behavioral Foundations of System Development. 2nd ed. LC 83-19964. 392p. 1985. 49.50 (0-89874-703-1) Krieger.

— Conceptual Aspects of Human Factors. LC 88-32055. 296p. 1989. 45.00x (0-8018-3732-4) Johns Hopkins.

— Human Factors Testing & Evaluation. (Advances in Human Factors-Ergonomics Ser.: No. 5). 424p. 1986. 118.00 (0-444-42701-5) Elsevier.

Meister, Ernst. Room Without Walls: Selected Poems. Gugelberger, Georg M., ed. Orig. Title: Wandloser Raum. 64p. 1981. pap. 4.00 (0-88031-057-X) Invisible-Red Hill.

Meister, Gail. Help for New Teachers: Developmental Practices That Work. 97p. 1990. pap. 21.95 (1-56602-036-0) Research Better.

Meister, Gail, jt. auth. see Austin, Susan.

Meister, H. The Purification Problem for Constrained Games with Incomplete Information. (Lecture Notes in Economics & Mathematical Systems Ser.: Vol. 295). 140p. 1987. pap. 23.40 (0-387-18429-5) Spr-Verlag.

Meister, Jeanne C. Corporate Quality Universities: Lessons Learned from Programs That Produce Results. 276p. 1993. text ed. 40.00 (1-55623-790-1) Irwin Prof Pubng.

Meister, John, ed. see Law, William.

Meister, Michael, ed. Blessed Ambiguity: Brothers in the Church. LC 93-74489. (Seminar Ser.). 276p. (Orig.). 1994. pap. 15.00 (1-884904-00-9) Christian Brothers.

— Blessed Ambiguity: Brothers in the Church. 276p. (Orig.). (C). 1994. pap. 12.00 (0-944808-09-3) Lasallian Pubns.

***Meister, Michael F., ed.** The Declaration: Text & Contexts. (Christian Brothers Seminar, 1994 Ser.). 225p. (Orig.). 1995. pap. text ed. 10.00 (1-884904-05-X) Christian Brothers.

Meister, Michael W., pref. Making Things in South Asia: The Role of Artist & Craftsman. (Proceedings of the South Asia Seminar Ser.: No. 4). (Illus.). 216p. (Orig.). 1988. pap. 10.00 (0-936115-03-3) U Penn South Asia.

Meister, Michael W. & Dhaky, M. A., eds. Encyclopaedia of Indian Temple Architecture, Vol. I, Pt. 2: South India: Upper Dravidadesa, Early Phase, 2 bks., Set. (Illus.). 263p. 1989. 150.00 (0-691-17992-1) Princeton U Pr.

— Encyclopedia of Indian Temple Architecture, Vol. Two, Pt. 2: North India: Period of Early Maturity, c. AD 700-900, 2 vols. (Illus.). 475p. 1991. text ed. 150.00 (0-691-04094-X) Princeton U Pr.

Meister, Michael W., ed. see Coomaraswamy, Amanda K.

Meister, Michael W., et al, eds. Encyclopaedia of Indian Temple Architecture, Vol. II, Pt. 1: North India: Foundations of North Indian Style, 2 bks. (Illus.). 500p. 1988. Text 500p., Plates 400p. 150.00 (0-691-04053-2) Princeton U Pr.

Meister, Richard. Race & Ethnicity in Modern America. (Major Problems in American History Ser.). 1975. pap. text ed. 8.50 (0-669-91124-0) Heath.

Meister, Robert. Thinking Through Marx: Materialism & Political Identity. 320p. (C). 1991. pap. text ed. 17.95 (0-631-17746-9) Blackwell Pubs.

Meister, Robert, tr. see Fuchs, Peter.

Meister, Susan B., jt. ed. see Nightingale, Elena O.

Meister, Teddy. A Minute with Mother Goose, Vol. I. 1990. 7.95 (0-88047-197-2, 101) DOK Pubs.

— A Minute with Mother Goose, Vol. II. 1990. 7.95 (0-88047-198-0, 102) DOK Pubs.

— Pardon Me, but Your References Are Showing. (Illus.). 48p. (Orig.). (J). (gr. 4-8). 1991. pap. 6.50 (0-913853-20-8, 32530, Alleyside) Highsmith Pr.

Meister, Teddy & Simpson, Ann. Boardwork & Beyond. 1990. 10.95 (0-88047-212-X, 104) DOK Pubs.

Meister, Teddy & Simpson, Ann M. Independent Study Enrichment Projects: Ready-to-Use Projects. 272p. (J). (gr. 3-8). 1988. pap. text ed. 22.95 (0-87628-447-0) Ctr Appl Res.

Meister, Teddy, jt. auth. see Simpson, Ann.

Meisterfeld, C. W. Jelly Bean vs. Dr. Jekyll & Mr. Hyde: Written for the Safety of Our Children & the Welfare of Our Dogs. LC 89-91639. (Illus.). 176p. 1989. 19.95 (0-9601292-5-1) M R K.

— Psychological Dog Training: Behavior Conditioning with Respect & Trust. (Illus.). 232p. (Orig.). (YA). (gr. 6 up). 1991. pap. 19.80 (0-9601292-6-X) M R K.

— Tails' of a Dog Psychoanalyst. LC 78-58492. (Illus.). 1978. 15.95 (0-9601292-2-7) M R K.

Meisterfeld, C. W. & Pecci, Ernest F. Crazy Dogs-Crazy People: Looking at Behavior in Our Society. Blakely, Kristine & Steinmueller, Heidi, eds. LC 92-81548. (Illus.). 272p. 1993. 26.95 (0-9601292-7-8) M R K.

Meisterhans, Konrad. Grammatik Der Attischen Inschriften. xiv, 288p. 1971. reprint ed. write for info. (3-487-04079-4, Pub. by Georg Olms GW) Lubrecht & Cramer.

Meistrell, Lois. The New Dachshund. LC 75-30419. (Complete Breed Book Ser.). (Illus.). 288p. 1982. 25.95 (0-87605-107-7) Howell Bk.

Meitam, Carol, ed. see Birnholz, Mary B., et al.

Meites, Joseph, ed. Neuroendocrinology of Aging. LC 83-10937. 400p. 1983. 85.00 (0-306-41310-8, Plenum Pr) Plenum.

Meites, L. An Introduction to Chemical Equilibrium & Kinetics. (Pergamon Series on Analytical Chemistry: Vol. 2). 1981. text ed. 232.00 (0-08-023802-5, Pub. by Pergamon Repr UK) Franklin.

Meites, L. & Zuman, P. Handbook Series in Inorganic Electrochemistry, 6 vols., Set. LC 80-17900. 1,643.00 (0-8493-0360-5, CRC Reprint) Franklin.

— Handbook Series in Organic Electrochemistry, Vol. 3. LC 77-24273. 1978. 124.95 (0-8493-7223-2) CRC Pr.

Meites, Louis. Polarographic Techniques. 2nd ed. LC 65-19735. (Illus.). 769p. reprint ed. pap. 180.00 (0-685-23818-0, 2056598) Bks Demand.

Meites, Louis & Zuman, Petr. Handbook of Organic Electrochemistry, Vol. 5. 472p. 1982. 130.95 (0-8493-7225-9, QD272, CRC Reprint) Franklin.

— Handbook Series in Inorganic Electrochemistry, Vol. VI. 552p. 1983. 152.95 (0-8493-7226-7, QD272, CRC Reprint) Franklin.

Meites, Louis & Zuman, Petr, eds. Handbook Series in Inorganic Electrochemistry: (Eu-Mg), Vol. III. 488p. 1983. 103.95 (0-8493-0363-X, QD557, CRC Reprint) Franklin.

Meites, Louis, et al. Handbook of Inorganic Electrochemistry, Vol. VI: PM-SC. (CRC Handbook Series in Inorganic Electrochemistry). 544p. 1986. Vol. VI: (PM-SC), 544p. 95.00 (0-8493-0366-4, QD557, CRC Reprint) Franklin.

— Handbook of Inorganic Electrochemistry, Vol. VII: SC-TM. (CRC Handbook Series in Inorganic Electrochemistry). 512p. 1986. Vol. VII: (SC-TM), 512p. 104.95 (0-8493-0367-2, CRC Reprint) Franklin.

— Handbook Series in Inorganic Electrochemistry: (Ag-Co), Vol. I. 512p. 1980. 104.95 (0-8493-0361-3, QD557, CRC Reprint) Franklin.

— Handbook Series in Inorganic Electrochemistry: (Cr-Er), Vol. II. Zuman, Petr, ed. 560p. 1981. 104.95 (0-8493-0362-1, QD557, CRC Reprint) Franklin.

Meites, Louis, et al, eds. Handbook Series in Inorganic Electrochemistry, Vol. VIII. 552p. 1988. 141.95 (0-8493-0369-9, QD557) CRC Pr.

— Handbook Series in Inorganic Electrochemistry: (Mn-Np), Vol. IV. 536p. 1984. 104.95 (0-8493-0364-8, QD557, CRC Reprint) Franklin.

— Handbook Series in Inorganic Electrochemistry: (O-Pd), Vol. V. 552p. 1985. 104.95 (0-8493-0365-6, QD557, CRC Reprint) Franklin.

Meites, Samuel, ed. Otto Folin, America's First Clinical Biochemist. 428p. 1989. 55.00 (0-915274-48-5) Am Assn Clinical Chem.

— Pediatric Clinical Chemistry Reference (Normal) Values. 3rd ed. LC 88-7449. 352p. 1989. 45.00 (0-915274-47-7) Am Assn Clinical Chem.

Meites, Samuel, jt. ed. see Faulkner, Willard R.

Meitin, Alberta. Teaching Basic Ceramics. LC 90-63281. 54p. 1990. pap. text ed. 4.95 (0-916809-45-5) Scott Pubns MI.

Meitler, Carolyn L. Graphing Calculator Enhancement for Elementary Algebra: TI-81, Casio FX-7700G, & TI-85 Graphing Calculators. LC 92-39470. 1993. pap. text ed. write for info. (0-07-041369-X) McGraw.

— Graphing Calculator Enhancement for Intermediate Algebra: TI-81, Casio FX-7700G, & TI-85 Graphing Calculators. LC 92-35331. 1993. pap. text ed. write for info. (0-07-041370-3) McGraw.

— A Guide to TI Graphing Calculators. LC 94-32478. 1994. write for info. (0-07-041371-1) McGraw.

Meitler, Neal D. & La Porte, Linda M. Standard Accounting System for Lutheran Congregations. 1981. 6.95 (0-8100-0129-2, 21N2001) Northwest Pub.

***Meitus, Marty & Thorn, Patti.** Places to Go with Children in Colorado. LC 94-31351. 1995. write for info. (0-8118-0455-0) Chronicle Bks.

***Meixner, Barbara.** Suzuki Harp Ensemble Music. 29p. 1994. pap. text ed. 5.95 (0-87487-753-9) Summy-Birchard.

— Suzuki Piano Ensemble Music Vol. 1: 1 Piano, 4 Hands. 22p. 1995. pap. text ed. 6.95 (0-87487-749-0) Summy-Birchard.

— Suzuki Piano Ensemble Music Vol. 1: 2 Pianos, 4 Hands. 25p. 1995. pap. text ed. 6.95 (0-87487-750-4) Summy-Birchard.

— Suzuki Piano Ensemble Music Vol. 2: 2 Pianos, 4 Hands. 32p. 1995. pap. text ed. 6.95 (0-87487-751-2) Summy-Birchard.

— Suzuki Piano Ensemble Music Vols. 3-4: 2 Pianos, 4 Hands. 30p. 1995. pap. text ed. 6.95 (0-87487-752-0) Summy-Birchard.

Meixner, Elizabeth, jt. auth. see Cummings, Gerald R.

***Meixner, Laura L.** French Realist Painting & the Critique of American Society, 1865-1900. (Illus.). 320p. (C). 1995. 100.00 (0-521-46103-0) Cambridge U Pr.

Meizel, Janet E. Spanish for Medical Personnel. 1993. pap. 16.95 (1-56930-001-1) Skidmore Roth Pub.

— Your Food-Allergic Child: A Parent's Guide. LC 88-23592. (Illus.). 296p. (Orig.). 1988. pap. 9.95 (0-938179-16-0) Mills Sanderson.

Meizner, Israel & Bar-Ziv, Jacob. In Utero Diagnosis of Skeletal Disorders: An Atlas of Prenatal Sonographic & Postnatal Radiologic Correlation. LC 92-48449. 1993. 149.95 (0-8493-5130-8, R6629) CRC Pr.

Meja, Volker & Stehr, Nico, eds. Knowledge & Politics: The Sociology of Knowledge Dispute. 384p. 1990. 89.95 (0-415-02881-7, A4580) Routledge.

Meja, Volker, jt. ed. see Stehr, Nico.

Meja, Volker, et al, eds. Modern German Sociology: An Anthology. 536p. 1987. text ed. 76.00 (0-231-05854-3) Col U Pr.

Mejdal, Majp S., tr. see Koplowitz, George B., ed.

Mejdal, S., tr. see Koplowitz, George B. & Warren, Alan, eds.

Mejer, Jorgen. Diogenes Laertius & His Hellenistic Background. 119p. (Orig.). 1978. pap. text ed. 49.50x (3-515-02686-X) Coronet Bks.

Mejia, Arthur, jt. ed. see Thompson, J. A.

Mejia, Eileen. From Inside Our Mountain. (Illus.). 24p. (J). 1984. pap. 2.95 (0-87595-166-X) Oregon Hist.

An Asterisk (*) at the beginning of an entry indicates that the title is appearing in BIP for the first time.

Mejia, Elizabeth, et al. American Picture Show: A Cultural Reader. 240p. (C). 1991. pap. text ed. 18.25 (*0-13-029687-2*) P-H.
— Very Teachable Films. 224p. 1994. pap. 15.95 (*0-13-106824-5*) P-H.
Mejia, Elizabeth A. & O'Connor, Frederick. Five Star Films. LC 93-44648. 176p. 1994. pap. text ed. 15.75 (*0-13-035536-4*) P-H.
Mejia, Joan, jt. auth. see Genkos, Mary.
Mejias. Nuestro Espanol. (C). 1981. pap. text ed. write for info. (*0-13-033770-6*) P-H.
Mejias, Antonio. Refrigeration License Examinations. LC 93-6800. 1993. 25.00 (*0-671-86705-9*, Arco Test) P-H Gen Ref & Trav.
Mejias-Bikandi, Errapel, jt. auth. see Farrell, Patrick.
***Meju, Max A.** Geophysical Data Analysis: Understanding Inverse Problem Theory & Practice. LC 94-41168. (Course Notes Ser.: Vol. 6). 1994. pap. 25.00 (*1-56080-027-5*) Soc Expl Geophys.
Mekas, Jonas. I Had Nowhere to Go. (Illus.). 480p. (Orig.). 1991. pap. 14.95 (*0-9628181-0-0*) Black Thistle Pr.
Mekeirle, Joseph O. Multinational Corporations: The ECISM Guide to Information Sources. LC 78-62333. 480p. 1978. text ed. 125.00 (*0-275-90307-9*, C0307, Praeger Pubs) Greenwood.
Mekel, Adrienne M., jt. auth. see Duke, Daniel L.
Meketa, Charles & Meketa, Jacqueline. One Blanket & Ten Days Rations. Jackson, Earl & Dodson, Carolyn, eds. LC 79-67811. (Illus.). 112p. (Orig.). 1980. pap. 3.50 (*0-911408-54-1*) SW Pks Mnmts.
Meketa, Jackqueline D. From Martyrs to Murderers: The Old Southwest's Saints, Sinners, & Scalawags. LC 93-60808. (Illus.). 224p. (Orig.). 1993. 18.95 (*1-881325-09-1*); pap. 12.95 (*1-881325-08-3*) Yucca Tree Pr.
Meketa, Jacqueline, jt. auth. see Meketa, Charles.
Meketa, Ray. Luther Rector Hare. 1976. 23.95 (*0-8488-1097-X*) Amereon Ltd.
Mekjavic, Igor, et al, eds. Environmental Ergonomics: Sustaining Human Performance in Harsh Environments. 330p. 1988. 125.00 (*0-85066-400-4*) Taylor & Francis.
Mekler, A. H., jt. auth. see Eklof, P. C.
Mekler, Eva, jt. auth. see Schulman, Michael.
Mekler, Eva, jt. ed. see Schulman, Michael.
Mekler, S., ed. Academicorum Philosophorum Index Herculanensis. xxxvi, 135p. (GER.). 1958. write for info. (*3-296-10100-4*, Pub. by Georg Olms GW) Lubrecht & Cramer.
Mekouar, Mohamed A. Environmental Impact of Economic Incentives for Agricultural Production. (Legislative Studies: No. 38). 84p. 1990. pap. 12.00 (*92-5-102360-3*, F3603) UNIPUB.
Meksyn, D. New Methods in Laminar Boundary Layer Theory. LC 61-8790. 1961. 130.00 (*0-08-009439-2*, Pub. by Pergamon Repr UK) Franklin.
Mekula, Janice. Frozen Sunshine. LC 80-81596. (Illus.). 64p. 1980. 10.00 (*0-8187-0038-6*) Harlo Press.
***Mekz, Andrew K.** Knicks Grit: Words of Wisdom from the Brash, Bold, Big Hearted 1994 New York Knicks. Broussard, Anne E., ed. 52p. (Orig.). 1994. pap. 6.95 (*0-9640033-4-1*) Wit Press.
— Rangers Wit: Reflections, Retorts & Reminiscences from the Stanley Cup Champs. Broussard, Anne E., ed. (Orig.). 1994. pap. 6.95 (*0-9640033-6-8*) Wit Press.
— Rockets Wit: Words of Wisdom from the Captivating, Charismatic, Clutch NBA Champs. Broussard, Anne E., ed. (Orig.). 1994. pap. 5.95 (*0-9640033-5-X*) Wit Press.
Mel, Jeanne, ed. see Marrs, Samuel.
Mel, Peter. Christopher Columbus: Two Civilizations Come Together. (Illus.). 192p. (Orig.). 1992. pap. 14.92 (*1-882234-03-0*) Heritage CA.
Mel, W. Bartlett. Connectionist Robot Motion Planning: A Neurally-Inspired Approach to Visually-Guided Reaching. (Perspectives in Artificial Intelligence Ser.: Vol. 7). 165p. 1990. text ed. 49.95 (*0-12-490020-8*) Acad Pr.
Mela, D. J., ed. Dietary Fats: Determinants of Preference, Selection, & Consumption. LC 92-5798. 1992. write for info. (*1-85166-865-9*) Elsevier.
Melack, John M., ed. Saline Lakes. (Developments in Hydrobiology Ser.). (C). 1988. lib. bdg. 197.00 (*90-6193-648-9*) Kluwer Ac.
Melady, John. Escape from Canada! The Untold Story of German POWs in Canada. (Illus.). 210p. 1986. pap. 4.95 (*0-7715-9256-6*, Pub. by Stoddart Pubng CN) Genl Dist Srvs.
— Korea: Canada's Forgotten War. (Illus.). 219p. 1988. pap. 4.95 (*0-7715-9278-7*, Pub. by Stoddart Pubng CN) Genl Dist Srvs.
— Pilots. 272p. 1991. pap. 16.95 (*0-7710-5887-X*, Pub. by McClelland & Stewart CN) Firefly Bks Ltd.
Melady, Margaret B., jt. auth. see Melady, Thomas P.
Melady, Thomas P. The Ambassador's Story: The United States & the Vatican in World Affairs. LC 93-87230. 224p. 1994. 19.95 (*0-87973-702-6*, 702) Our Sunday Visitor.
— Burundi: The Tragic Years. LC 73-89357. (Illus.). 128p. reprint ed. pap. 36.50 (*0-8357-8822-9*, 2033470) Bks Demand.
Melady, Thomas P. & Melady, Margaret B. Uganda: The Asian Exiles. LC 76-10321. 96p. reprint ed. pap. 27.40 (*0-8357-7062-1*, 2033550) Bks Demand.
Melam, Lawrence E., jt. auth. see Brown, Steven R.
Melamed, Barbara, et al, eds. Child Health Psychology. 360p. 1987. pap. text ed. 24.95 (*0-8058-0085-9*) L Erlbaum Assocs.
***Melamed, Daniel R.** J. S. Bach & the German Motet. (Illus.). 224p. (C). 1995. write for info. (*0-521-41864-X*) Cambridge U Pr.
***Melamed, Daniel R., ed.** Bach Studies, No. 2. (Illus.). 304p. (C). 1995. write for info. (*0-521-47067-6*) Cambridge U Pr.
Melamed, Evelyn, jt. auth. see Minkoff, Harvey.
Melamed, Evelyn B., jt. auth. see Minkoff, Harvey.
Melamed, Ezra Z. Milon Arami-Ivri: Aramaic-Hebrew Dictionary. (ARC & HEB.). 25.95 (*0-685-63107-9*) Feldheim.
Melamed, Frances. Janova: Portrait of a Jewish Lithuanian Village in Revolutionary & Communist Russia 1914-1920. LC 75-38045. (Illus.). 229p. 1976. 12.50 (*0-917294-01-7*) Janova Pr.
Melamed, Leo. Leo Melamed on the Markets: Twenty Years of Financial History As Seen by the Man Who Revolutionized the Markets. 304p. 1992. text ed. 29.95 (*0-471-57524-0*) Wiley.
Melamed, Leo, ed. The Merits of Flexible Exchange Rates: An Anthology. 450p. (Orig.). (C). 1988. lib. bdg. 68.50 (*0-913969-14-1*, G Mason Univ Pr); pap. text ed. 35.00 (*0-913969-15-X*, G Mason Univ Pr) Univ Pub Assocs.
Melamed, Myron R. & Farrow, George M. Urologic Neoplasams: Proceedings of the Fiftieth Annual Anatomic Pathology Slide Seminar of the American Society of Clinical Pathologists. LC 86-32287. 150p. 1987. pap. text ed. 35.00 (*0-89189-222-2*) Am Soc Clinical.
Melamed, Myron R., et al, eds. Flow Cytometry & Sorting. 2nd ed. 832p. 1990. text ed. 124.95 (*0-471-56235-1*) Wiley.
***Melan, Eugene H.** Process Management: A Systems Approach to Total Quality. (Management Masters Ser.). (Illus.). 53p. 1995. 15.95 (*1-56327-074-9*) Prod Press.
— Process Management: Methods for Improving Products & Service. LC 92-27834. 1992. text ed. 35.00 (*0-07-041339-8*) McGraw.
Melanchthon. The Confessyon of the Fayth of the Germaynes in the Councell, 2 pts., Set. LC 76-57351. (English Experience Ser.: No. 771). 1977. reprint ed. lib. bdg. 39.00 (*90-221-0771-X*) Walter J Johnson.
Melanchthon, Philip. The Loci Communes of Philip Melanchthon. Hill, Charles L., tr. LC 83-45649. reprint ed. 32.50 (*0-404-19858-9*) AMS Pr.
— A Melanchthon Reader. Keen, Ralph, tr. (American University Studies: Theology & Religion: Ser. VII, Vol. 41). 296p. (C). 1988. text ed. 45.00 (*0-8204-0563-9*) P Lang Pubs.
— A Very Godly Defense, Defending the Marriage of Priests. Beuchame, L., tr. LC 76-25643. (English Experience Ser.: No. 199). 1969. reprint ed. 20.00 (*90-221-0199-1*) Walter J Johnson.
Melanchthon, Philipp. The Epistle of P. Melancton Made unto Kynge Henry the Eyght, for the Revokynge of the Six Artycles. Wesel, J. C., tr. LC 72-216. (English Experience Ser.: No. 336). 32p. 1971. reprint ed. 45.00 (*90-221-0336-6*) Walter J Johnson.
— Epistolae, Judicia, Consilia, Testimonia Aliorumque Ad Eum Epistolae Quae in Corpore Reformatorum Desiderantur. x, 614p. (GER.). 1975. reprint ed. write for info. (*3-487-05726-3*, Pub. by Georg Olms GW) Lubrecht & Cramer.
— The Justification of Man by Faith Only. Lesse, Nicholas, tr. LC 79-84123. (English Experience Ser.: No. 942). 204p. 1979. reprint ed. lib. bdg. 35.00 (*90-221-0942-9*) Walter J Johnson.
Melancon, Charlotte, tr. see Shemie, Bonnie.
Melancon, Michael. The Socialist Revolutionaries & the Russian Anti-War Movement, 1914-1917. 336p. 1991. 47.50 (*0-8142-0528-3*) Ohio St U Pr.
Melancon, Richard, jt. auth. see Mayer, Morris.
Meland, Bernard E. Essays in Constructive Theology: A Process Perspective. LC 87-82148. 329p. 1988. text ed. 31.95 (*0-913552-38-0*); pap. text ed. 18.95 (*0-913552-39-9*) Exploration Pr.
— Fallible Forms & Symbols: Discourses on Method in a Theology of Culture. LC 76-7868. 226p. reprint ed. pap. 64.50 (*0-685-16141-2*, 2026957) Bks Demand.
— Future of Empirical Theology. Braver, J. C., ed. LC 78-83980. (Essays in Divinity Ser.: Vol. 7). 1969. lib. bdg. 20.00 (*0-226-51955-4*) U Ch Pr.
— Reawakening of Christian Faith. LC 72-142670. (Essay Index Reprint Ser.). 1977. reprint ed. 18.95 (*0-8369-2663-3*) Ayer.
Melander, John M. & Lauersdorf, Lynn R., eds. Masonry: Design & Construction, Problems & Repair. LC 93-1147. (STP Ser.: Vol. 1180). (Illus.). 430p. 1993. 47.00 (*0-8031-1492-3*, 04-011800-60) ASTM.
Melander, Lars & Saunders, William H., Jr. Reaction Rates of Isotopic Molecules. LC 85-23200. 348p. 1987. reprint ed. 49.50 (*0-89874-940-9*) Krieger.
***Melandri, B.A., et al, eds.** Bioelectrochemistry IV: Nerve Muscle Function- Bioelectrochemistry, Mechanisms, Bioenergetics, & Control. (NATO ASI Series A, Life Sciences: 267). (Illus.). 370p. 1994. 115.00 (*0-306-44813-0*, Plenum Pr) Plenum.
Melaniphy, John C. Restaurant & Fast Food Site Selection. 400p. 1992. text ed. 49.95 (*0-471-55716-1*) Wiley.
Melanos, Jack. Rapunzel & the Witch. (J). 1950. 5.00 (*0-87602-186-0*) Anchorage.
— Sinbad & the Evil Genii. (Orig.). (J). (gr. k up). 1985. pap. 5.00 (*0-87602-251-4*) Anchorage.
Melanson, Leo. Winning Secrets of a Master Sports Bettor - Football. 32p. (Orig.). 1991. pap. 6.95 (*0-934650-19-5*) Sunnyside.
Melanson, Philip. Who Killed Martin Luther King? LC 93-19961. (Real Story Ser.). 96p. 1993. pap. 5.00 (*1-878825-11-9*) Odonian Pr.
— Who Killed Robert Kennedy? (Real Story Ser.). 96p. 1993. pap. 5.00 (*1-878825-12-7*) Odonian Pr.
Melanson, Philip & Oglesby, Carl. Assassination Trilogy, 3 vols., Set. 300p. 1993. pap. 15.00 (*1-878825-09-7*) Odonian Pr.
Melanson, Philip H. Martin Luther King Assassination: New Revelations on the Conspiracy & Cover-Up, 1968-1991. 232p. 1991. pap. 12.95 (*1-56171-037-7*, S P I Bks) Sure Sellers.
— The Murkin Conspiracy: An Investigation into the Assassination of Dr. Martin Luther King, Jr. LC 88-15262. 219p. 1989. text ed. 35.00 (*0-275-93029-7*, C3029, Praeger Pubs) Greenwood.
— Robert F. Kennedy Assassination: New Revelations on the Conspiracy & Cover-Up. 1994. pap. 14.95 (*1-56171-102-0*, S P I Bks) Sure Sellers.
— Robert F. Kennedy Assassination: New Revelations on the Conspiracy & Cover-Up. 1994. pap. 5.99 (*1-56171-324-4*, S P I Bks) Sure Sellers.
— Robert F. Kennedy Assassination: New Revelations on the Conspiracy & Cover-Up, 1968-1991. 1991. 19.95 (*1-56171-036-9*) Sure Sellers.
Melanson, Phillip H. Martin Luther King Assassination: New Revelations on the Conspiracy & Cover Up. 1994. pap. 5.99 (*1-56171-330-9*) Sure Sellers.
Melanson, Richard A. Reconstructing Consensus: American Foreign Policy since the Vietnam War. LC 90-39670. 240p. (Orig.). 1990. text ed. 65.00 (*0-312-05238-3*) St Martin.
— Reconstructing Consensus: American Foreign Policy since the Vietnam War. LC 90-39670. 241p. (Orig.). (C). 1990. pap. text ed. 14.00 (*0-312-04651-0*) St Martin.
— Writing History & Making Policy, Vol. VI: The Cold War, Vietnam, & Revisionism. LC 83-10362. (Exxon Education Foundation Series on Rhetoric & Political Discourse). 260p. (C). 1983. lib. bdg. 50.50 (*0-8191-3352-5*); pap. text ed. 21.00 (*0-8191-3353-1*) U Pr of Amer.
***Melanson, Richard A., ed.** Neither Cold War nor Detente? Soviet-American Relations in the 1980's. fac. ed. LC 81-16299. 253p. 1982. reprint ed. pap. 72.20 (*0-7837-7984-4*, 2047740) Bks Demand.
Melanson, Richard A. & Mayer, David, eds. Reevaluating Eisenhower: American Foreign Policy in the Fifties. LC 86-4363. (Illus.). 288p. 1987. 29.95 (*0-252-01340-9*); pap. 12.95 (*0-252-06067-9*) U of Ill Pr.
Melanson, Richard A. & Thompson, Kenneth W., eds. Foreign Policy & Domestic Consensus, Vol. II. LC 85-15655. (Credibility of Institutions, Policies & Leadership Ser.). 212p. (Orig.). 1985. lib. bdg. 46.00 (*0-8191-4865-2*) U Pr of Amer.
***Melara, Julio A.** Do You Have the Time for Success? 115p. 1994. pap. 10.00 (*0-9642430-0-8*) NOPG.
Melaragno, Michele G. Introduction to Shell Structures: The Art & Science of Vaulting. LC 90-41113. (Illus.). 352p. 1991. text ed. 65.00 (*0-442-23725-1*) Chapman & Hall.
— Quantification in Science. (Illus.). 224p. 1991. text ed. 47.95 (*0-442-00641-1*) Chapman & Hall.
Melaragno, Ralph J. Tutoring with Students: A Handbook for Establishing Tutorial Programs in Schools. LC 75-40045. 172p. 1976. pap. 27.95 (*0-87778-090-0*) Educ Tech Pubns.
Melaro, Constance. Bitter Harvest: The Odyssey of a Teacher. 1965. 12.95 (*0-8392-1148-1*) Astor-Honor.
Melas-Kyriazi, Lisa. Motif & Meaning. LC 87-71912. (Illus.). 30p. (Orig.). 1987. pap. 4.00 (*0-934358-18-4*) Fuller Mus Art.
***Melashenko, E. Lonnie & Crosby, Timothy E.** In the Presence of Angels: A Collection of Inspiring, True Angel Stories. LC 95-6966. 1995. pap. write for info. (*0-8163-1261-3*) Pacific Pr Pub Assn.
***Melashenko, E. Lonnie & McLarty, John.** An Insider's Guide to the Kingdom: The Beatitudes as a Map to Joy & Freedom. LC 95-13760. 1995. write for info. (*0-8163-1269-9*) Pacific Pr Pub Assn.
Melashenko, Lonnie & Crosby, Tim. Sex: The Myth & the Magic. LC 93-41886. 1993. pap. 1.95 (*0-8163-1214-1*) Pacific Pr Pub Assn.
Melasuo, Tuomo. National Movements & World Peace. 189p. 1990. text ed. 59.95 (*1-85628-079-9*, Pub. by Avebury Pub UK) Ashgate Pub Co.
Melaville, Atelia I., et al. Together We Can: A Guide for Crafting a Profamily System of Education & Human Services. Thompson, Bruce A., ed. 157p. (Orig.). (C). 1993. pap. text ed. 45.00 (*0-7881-0098-X*) Diane Pub.
Melazzo, Lucio, jt. ed. see Herzfeld, Michael.
Melba, Nellie. Melodies & Memories. LC 73-107821. (Select Bibliographies Reprint Ser.). 1977. 26.95 (*0-8369-5192-1*) Ayer.
— Melodies & Memories. LC 71-126694. reprint ed. 34.00 (*0-404-04287-2*) AMS Pr.
— Melodies & Memories. 339p. 1990. reprint ed. lib. bdg. 79.00 (*0-7812-9103-8*, 10103) Rprt Serv.
Melber, G., ed. see Brownell, David.
***Melberg, Arne.** Theories of Mimesis. (Literature, Culture, Theory Ser.: No. 12). 196p. (C). 1995. 54.95 (*0-521-45225-2*) Cambridge U Pr.
Melbin, Murray. Night As Frontier: Colonizing the World after Dark. 1987. text ed. 29.95 (*0-02-920940-4*) Free Pr.
Melbourne, Bertram L. Slow to Understand: The Disciples in Synoptic Perspective. LC 88-22771. 224p. (Orig.). (C). 1988. lib. bdg. 41.50 (*0-8191-7154-9*); pap. text ed. 22.50 (*0-8191-7155-7*) U Pr of Amer.
Melbourne, Howard, jt. auth. see Stubbings, Derrek.
Melbourne, Roy M. Conflict & Crises: A Foreign Service Story. LC 92-23345. 300p. (C). 1993. lib. bdg. 38.50 (*0-8191-8874-3*) U Pr of Amer.
Melby. Simplified Irrigation Design. 2nd ed. 1995. pap. 34.95 (*0-442-01822-3*) Van Nos Reinhold.
Melby, Alan K., jt. auth. see Makkai, Adam.
Melby, Christopher & Hyner, Gerald C. Exercise & Physical Fitness: A Personalized Approach. 116p. 1988. pap. text ed. 12.95 (*0-912855-83-5*) E Bowers Pub.
Melby, Christopher L., jt. auth. see Hyner, Gerald C.
Melby, Edward C., Jr. & Balk, Melvin W. Importance of Laboratory Animal Genetics: Health & Environment in Biomedical Research. 1984. text ed. 66.00 (*0-12-489520-4*) Acad Pr.
Melby, Edward C., Jr., ed. see Charles River International Symposium on Laboratory Animals Staff.
Melby, Eric D. Oil & the International System: The Case of France, 1918-1969. Bruchey, Stuart, ed. LC 80-2816. (Dissertations in European Economic History Ser.). (Illus.). 1981. lib. bdg. 42.95 (*0-405-14000-2*) Ayer.
Melby, Ernest O. The Education of Free Men. LC 77-1248. (Horace Mann Lecture Ser.). 75p. 1977. text ed. 49.50 (*0-8371-9501-2*, MEEF, Greenwood Pr) Greenwood.
Melby, Ernest O. & Puner, Morton, eds. Freedom & Public Education. LC 72-14106. (Essay Index Reprint Ser.). 1977. reprint ed. 18.95 (*0-518-10019-7*) Ayer.
Melby, James C., jt. ed. see Biglieri, Edward G.
Melby, John F. The Mandate of Heaven: A Record of Civil War, China 1945-49. LC 68-9736. (Illus.). 327p. reprint ed. pap. 93.20 (*0-317-11289-9*, 2014363) Bks Demand.
Melby, John F. & Straka, W. W., eds. Constantine Nabokov: Letters of a Russian Diplomat to an American Friend, 1906-1922. LC 88-11770. (Slavic Studies: Vol. 1). 430p. 1988. lib. bdg. 109.95 (*0-88946-014-0*) E Mellen.
Melby, Michelle, ed. see Palazzolo, Carl R.
Melby, Pete, jt. auth. see Martin, Edward C., Jr.
Melcer, Donald. Self Development Through Meditative Practice. 1983. pap. 4.50 (*0-916786-70-6*, Saint George Pubns) R Steiner Col Pubns.
Melcher, Harold & Melcher, Joan. The Way to Greece. LC 84-18400. (Illus.). 113p. (Orig.). 1984. pap. 8.95 (*0-87233-077-X*) Bauhan.
Melcher, James R., jt. auth. see Woodson, Herbert H.
Melcher, Joan. Watering Hole: A User's Guide to Montana Bars. (Illus.). 128p. 1980. pap. text ed. 7.95 (*0-938314-00-9*) Am Wrld Geog.
Melcher, Joan, jt. auth. see Melcher, Harold.
Melcher, Marguerite F. Shaker Adventure. 319p. 1986. pap. 9.95 (*0-937942-08-1*) Shaker Mus.
Melcher, Michael. Parallel to the Shore. (Illus.). 19p. (Orig.). 1992. pap. 5.00 (*0-926935-68-2*) Runaway Spoon.
Melcher, Pierson F. The Flame & the Phoenix: The Education of a Schoolmaster. LC 93-20996. 451p. 1994. pap. 15.95 (*0-9630071-1-4*) Windhover CO.
— Year of Wonder: 1968: Reflections on Travel. rev. ed. LC 91-27393. 176p. (Orig.). 1991. pap. 6.95 (*0-9630071-0-6*) Windhover CO.
Melcher, Robert A., et al. Music for Study. 3rd ed. 256p. 1988. pap. write for info. (*0-318-62256-4*) P-H.
Melcher, Robert A. & Warch, Willard F. Music for Advanced Study. (Orig.). 1965. pap. text ed. write for info. (*0-13-607317-4*) P-H.
Melchers, Bernard. Traditional Chinese Cut-Paper Designs. LC 77-88654. (Pictorial Archive Ser.). (Illus.). 1978. reprint ed. pap. 4.95 (*0-486-23581-5*) Dover.
Melchers, F. & Potter, M., eds. Mechanisms in B-Cell Neoplasia. (Current Topics in Microbiology & Immunology Ser.: Vol. 132). (Illus.). 390p. 1986. 93.00 (*0-387-17048-0*) Spr-Verlag.
Melchers, F., jt. ed. see Potter, M.
Melchers, F., et al, eds. Lymphocyte Hybridomas: Second Workshop. (Illus.). 1979. 31.00 (*0-387-09670-1*) Spr-Verlag.
— Progress in Immunology, Vol. VII. (Illus.). 1408p. 1989. 168.00 (*0-387-51053-2*) Spr-Verlag.
***Melchers, Gunnel & Johannesson, Nils-Lennart, eds.** Nonstandard Varieties of Language. (Stockholm Studies in English: No. 84). 220p. 1994. pap. 32.50 (*91-22-01635-X*, Pub. by Almqv & Wiksell SW) Coronet Bks.
Melchers, R. E. & Stewart, M. G., eds. Probabalistic Risk & Hazard Assessment. 253p. 1994. 80.00 (*90-5410-349-3*, Pub. by A A Balkema NE) Ashgate Pub Co.
Melchert, Norman. The Great Conversation: A Historical Introduction to Philosophy. 595p. (C). 1991. text ed. 44.95 (*0-87484-952-7*) Mayfield Pub.
— The Great Conversation: A Historical Introduction to Philosophy. 2nd ed. LC 94-21855. 658p. (C). 1995. 44.95 (*1-55934-360-5*) Mayfield Pub.
— The Great Conversation: A Historical Introduction to Philosophy, Vol. I. 2nd ed. LC 94-34907. 344p. (C). 1995. pap. text ed. 27.95 (*1-55934-476-8*) Mayfield Pub.
— The Great Conversation: A Historical Introduction to Philosophy, Vol. II. 2nd ed. 408p. (C). 1995. text ed. 27.95 (*1-55934-477-6*) Mayfield Pub.
— Who's to Say: A Dialogue on Relativism. LC 94-21086. 96p. (C). 1994. lib. bdg. 24.95 (*0-87220-272-0*); pap. text ed. 4.95 (*0-87220-271-2*) Hackett Pub.
Melchert, Paul A. & Roebke, John. A Will Is Not Enough: A Helpful Guide for Your Family. (Illus.). 24p. (Orig.). 1993. write for info. (*0-9638509-0-3*) Waconia Pubng.
Melchert, Wanda R. Machine Sewn Rag Baskets. 64p. 1994. 11.95 (*0-9641199-0-0*) Desert Cntry.
Melchett, Sonia. Passionate Quests: Five Modern Women Travelers. 224p. (Orig.). 1992. pap. 13.95 (*0-571-12946-3*) Faber & Faber.
***Melchionda, N., et al, eds.** Recent Advances in Obesity & Diabetes Research. LC 83-19133. (Serono Symposia Publications from Raven Press: No. 8). (Illus.). Date not set. reprint ed. pap. 126.00 (*0-7837-9530-0*, 2060279) Bks Demand.
Melchior, Arne. There Is Something Wonderful Happening in Denmark. 1987. 14.95 (*0-8184-0429-9*) Carol Pub Group.
Melchior, Claus, ed. see Joyce, James.
Melchior, Debra. Organize Your Home! (Illus.). 270p. 1992. pap. 9.95 (*1-55850-119-3*) Adams Pubng.

Melchior, H., ed. Bildgebende Systeme in der Urologie. (Beitraege zur Urologie Ser.: Vol. 4). (Illus.). xiv, 386p. (GER.). 1986. 173.75 (3-8055-4335-2) S Karger.

Melchior, H. & Sollberger, A. Optical Communication. 1984. 113.00 (0-444-86797-X, 1-505-83) Elsevier.

Melchior, Paul, ed. IUGG Union Lectures. (Special Publications). 1992. 15.00 (0-87590-461-0) Am Geophysical.

— Seismic Activity in Western Europe: With Particular Consideration to the Liege Earthquake of November 8, 1983. 1984. lib. bdg. 136.50 (90-277-1889-X) Kluwer Ac.

Melchior, Paul, ed. see International Astronomical Union Staff.

Melchior, William T. Insuring Public School Property. LC 75-177068. (Columbia University. Teachers College. Contributions to Education Ser.: No. 168). reprint ed. 37.50 (0-404-55168-8) AMS Pr.

Melchiori, Gerlinda S., ed. Alumni Research: Methods & Applications. LC 85-645339. (New Directions for Institutional Research Ser.: No. IR 60). 1988. 16.95 (1-55542-889-4) Jossey-Bass.

Melchiori, Giorgio. Shakespeare's Garter Plays: Edward Third to Merry Wives of Windsor. LC 93-48123. (C). 1994. write for info. (0-87413-518-4) U Delaware Pr.

— The Tightrope Walkers: A Greenwood Archival Edition. LC 73-14036. 277p. 1974. reprint ed. text ed. 65.00 (0-8371-7141-5, METW, Greenwood Pr) Greenwood.

— The Whole Mystery of Art: Pattern into Poetry in the Work of W. B. Yeats. LC 72-12553. (Illus.). 306p. 1978. text ed. 35.00 (0-8371-6719-1, MEMA, Greenwood Pr) Greenwood.

Melchiori, Giorgio, ed. see Shakespeare, William.

Melchiorre, C. & Giannella, M. Highlights in Receptor Chemistry. 1984. 113.00 (0-444-80569-9, I-175-84) Elsevier.

Melchiorre, C. & Giannella, M., eds. Recent Advances in Receptor Chemistry: Proceedings of the 6th Camerino-Noordwijkerhout Symposium, Camerino, Italy,6-10 Sept., 1987. (Pharmacochemistry Library: No. 11). 334p. 1988. 120.50 (0-444-42965-4) Elsevier.

Melchiorre, Sherry, jt. auth. see Lotery, Fran.

Melchiorri, F. Gamow Cosmology: Proceedings of the International School of Physics, "Enrico Fermi" Course LXXXVI, Villa Monastero, Italy, 13-23 July, 1982. Ruffini, Remo, ed. (Enrico Fermi International Summer School of Physics Ser.: Vol. 68). 548p. 1987. 148.75 (0-444-87004-0, North Holland) Elsevier.

Melchiorri, F., jt. ed. see Audouze, Jean.

Melchoir, Daniel C. & Bassett, R. L., eds. Chemical Modeling of Aqueous Systems II. LC 89-28446. (ACS Symposium Ser.: No. 416). (Illus.). 538p. 1989. 94.95 (0-8412-1729-7) Am Chemical.

***Melchoir, H., et al, eds.** Gynecology & Obstretics. LC 94-3787. (Fibrin Sealing in Surgical & Nonsurgical Fields Ser.: Vol. 7). 1994. 54.00 (0-387-58227-4) Spr-Verlag.

Melchoir, P. The Tides of the Planet Earth. 2nd ed. LC 82-16567. (Illus.). 648p. 1983. 264.00 (0-08-026248-1, Pub. by Pergamon Repr UK) Franklin.

***Melchor, Lisa P.** Italian-American Artists, 1945-1968: A Limited Survey, Works on Paper. (Illus.). 48p. (Orig.). 1994. pap. text ed. 7.50 (1-885998-01-5) Hunter College.

Mel'cuk, Igor, ed. Dictionnaire Explicatif et Combinatoire du Francais Contemporain (DECFC), Vol. 1: Recherches Lexico-Semantiques. 172p. (FRE.). 1984. 44.00x (2-7606-0658-9, Pub. by Les Presses CN) Benjamins North Am.

— Dictionnaire Explicatif et Combinatoire du Francais Contemporain (DECFC), Vol. 2: Recherches Lexico-Semantiques. 344p. (FRE.). 1988. 89.00x (2-7606-0804-2, Pub. by Les Presses CN) Benjamins North Am.

— Dictionnaire Explicatif et Combinatoire du Francais Contemporain (DECFC), Vol. 3: Recherches Lexico-Semantiques. 325p. (FRE.). 1992. 65.00x (2-7606-1559-6, Pub. by Les Presses CN) Benjamins North Am.

Mel'cuk, Igor A. Dependency Syntax: Theory & Practice. LC 86-14542. (Suny Series in Linguistics). 428p. 1987. 89.50 (0-88706-450-7); pap. 34.95 (0-88706-451-5) State U NY Pr.

— Studies in Dependency Syntax. Roberge, Paul T., ed. Stern, Lev, tr. (Linguistica Extranea: Studia Ser.: Studia 2). 172p. 1979. pap. 5.50 (0-89720-001-2) Karoma.

Mel'cuk, Igor A., jt. auth. see Gladkij, Aleksej V.

Mel'cuk, Igor K. & Pertsov, Nikolai V. Surface Syntax of English: A Formal Model within the Meaning-Text Framework. LC 86-6884. (Linguistic & Literary Studies in Eastern Europe: No. 13). xv, 526p. 1986. 190.00x (90-272-1515-4) Benjamins North Am.

Melczer, William. The Pilgrim's Guide to Santiago de Compostela. LC 93-18623. (Historical Travel Ser.). (Illus.). 368p. (Orig.). 1993. pap. 17.50 (0-934977-25-9) Italica Pr.

Meldal-Johnsen, Trevor. For Women Only. 1990. mass mkt. 4.50 (1-55817-346-3, Pinnacle NY) Windsor NY.

— Mistresses. 1988. mass mkt. 4.50 (1-55817-109-6, Pinnacle NY) Windsor NY.

Meldau, Fred J. The Prophets Still Speak: Messiah in Both Testaments. LC 88-80834. 1988. 4.95 (0-915540-41-X) Frnds Israel.

Meldehout, M. & Seneor, R. Mathematical Physics: Eighth International Congress. 892p. 1987. pap. 43.00 (9971-5-0209-7) World Scientific Pub.

Melden, A. I. Ethical Theories: A Book of Readings with Revisions. 2nd ed. 1967. text ed. write for info. (0-13-290122-6) P-H.

— Rights & Persons. LC 77-80180. 1978. pap. 10.00 (0-520-03839-8) U CA Pr.

— Rights in Moral Lives: A Historical-Philosophical Essay. 1988. 35.00 (0-520-06275-2) U CA Pr.

Melden, A. I., ed. Essays in Moral Philosophy. LC 58-10483. 288p. 1966. pap. 8.00 (0-295-74049-3, WP20) U of Wash Pr.

Melder, Keith. Hail to the Candidate: Presidential Campaigns from Banners to Broadcasts. LC 91-5179. (Illus.). 224p. 1992. 39.95 (1-56098-177-6); pap. 19.95 (1-56098-178-4) Smithsonian.

Melder, O. M., jt. ed. see Starosolszky, O.

Meldin, Madeleine. The Tender Bud: A Physician's Journey Through Breast Cancer. LC 92-49967. 232p. 1993. 23.95 (0-88163-157-4) Analytic Pr.

Meldman & Petrie. Federal Taxation Practice & Procedure. 4th ed. 736p. 1992. 55.00 (0-685-66990-4, 4727) Commerce.

Meldman, Louis W. Mystical Sex: Love, Ecstasy & the Mystical Experience. LC 90-33641. 256p. (Orig.). 1990. pap. 9.95 (0-943173-70-1) Harbinger AZ.

Meldman, M. & Eysenck, Hans J. Diseases of Attention & Perception. LC 78-112614. (International Series of Monographs in Experimental Social Psychology: Vol. 10). 1970. 106.00 (0-08-006870-7, Pub. by Pergamon Repr UK) Franklin.

Meldolesi, J., jt. ed. see Clementi, F.

***Meldolesi, Luca.** Discovering the Possible: The Surprising World of Albert O. Hirschman. LC 94-42834. (C). 1995. text ed. 34.95x (0-268-00877-9) U of Notre Dame Pr.

Meldrum, B. Excitatory Amino Acid Antagonists. 1991. 125.00 (0-632-02737-1) Blackwell Sci.

Meldrum, Barbara H. Sophus K. Winther. LC 82-74094. (Western Writers Ser.: No. 60). (Illus.). 52p. (Orig.). 1983. pap. 3.95 (0-88430-034-X) Boise St U W Writ Ser.

Meldrum, Barbara H., ed. Old West - New West: Centennial Essays. LC 92-29828. 352p. (Orig.). (C). 1993. 36.00 (0-89301-166-5); pap. 29.95 (0-89301-163-0) U of Idaho Pr.

— Under the Sun: Myth & Realism in Western American Literature. LC 85-50609. (Illus.). vi, 231p. 1986. 22.50 (0-87875-303-6) Whitston Pub.

Meldrum, Brian S., et al, eds. Excitatory Amino Acids. (Fidia Research Foundation Symposium Ser.: Vol. 5). 816p. 1991. 192.50 (0-88167-701-9) Raven.

Meldrum, D. H. Fighting Fire with Foam: Basics of Effective Systems. 1979. 3.50 (0-686-25956-4, TR 79-2) Society Fire Protect.

Meldrum, David S., ed. see Galt, John.

Meldrum, Douglas G. The Night Two Thousand Men Came to Dinner: And Other Appetizing Anecdotes. (Illus.). 160p. 1994. text ed. 16.95 (0-02-583960-8, Scribners) S&S Trade.

Meldrum, Helen. Interpersonal Communication in Pharmaceutical Care. LC 93-31220. 180p. 1994. lib. bdg. 39.95 (1-56024-866-1) Haworth Pr.

Meldrum, Sandie. Traditional Candlewicking. (Illus.). 96p. (Orig.). 1994. pap. 15.95 (0-86417-564-7, Pub. by Kangaroo Pr AT) Seven Hills Bk.

Mele, Alfred, jt. ed. see Heil, John.

***Mele, Alfred R.** Autonomous Agents: From Self-Control to Autonomy. 352p. 1995. text ed. 45.00 (0-19-509454-9) OUP.

— Irrationality: An Essay on Akrasia, Self-Deception, & Self-Control. 200p. 1992. pap. 16.95 (0-19-508001-7) OUP.

— Springs of Action: Understanding Intentional Behavior. 288p. 1992. 42.00 (0-19-507114-X) OUP.

Mele, Alfred R., jt. ed. see Heil, John.

Mele, Audre. Polluting for Pleasure. LC 92-43498. 224p. 1993. 22.95 (0-393-03510-7) Norton.

Mele, Jim. The Calculation of Two. 68p. 1982. pap. 3.95 (0-916696-21-9) Cross Country.

— An Oracle of Love. 24p. 1976. pap. 1.00 (0-916696-01-4) Cross Country.

— The Sunday Habit. 1978. pap. 3.00 (0-916696-07-3) Cross Country.

Mele, Joan F., tr. see Baudelaire, Charles.

Mele, M., jt. ed. see Creazza, G.

Mele, Michael, ed. see Tise, Larry E.

Mele, P. E. Ceylon. (Illus.). 90p. lib. bdg. 9.95 (0-8288-3932-8) Fr & Eur.

Mele, Pietro F. Tibet. (Illus.). 80p. 1988. 14.95 (0-937938-63-7) Snow Lion Pubns.

Melear, Lawrence. Educator's Guide to Drug Prevention. (Illus.). 165p. 1990. teacher ed 48.00 (0-945207-00-X) Melear.

Melebea, jt. auth. see Calisto.

***Melegari, Vezio.** My First Book: A Journey Around the World. (J). 1994. 9.99 (0-517-12054-2) Random Hse Value.

Meleby, Hassan, tr. see Ranciere, Jacques.

Meleis, Afaf Ibrahim. Theoretical Nursing: Development & Progress. 2nd ed. (Illus.). 544p. 1990. text ed. 36.95 (0-397-54823-0) Lippincott.

Melek, Jacques. California Apartment Ownership: Orange County, 16 vols., Set. (Orig.). 1983. write for info. (0-318-56682-6) J Melek.

— California Apartment Ownership: San Bernandino County, Set. (Orig.). 1983. pap. 48.00 (0-942330-18-8) J Melek.

— California Apartment Ownership: San Bernandino County, Vol 1. (Orig.). 1983. pap. 480.00 (0-942330-19-6) J Melek.

— California Commercial Industrial Directories, 60 Vols., No. 32. (Plumas Ser.). 200p. (Orig.). 1982. pap. write for info. (0-942330-53-6) J Melek.

— California Commercial Industrial Directories, No. 33. (Riverside Ser.). 200p. (Orig.). 1983. 96.00 (0-686-35962-3); pap. write for info. (0-942330-54-4) J Melek.

— California Commercial Industrial Directories: Alamedia, No. 1. 200p. (Orig.). 1983. 96.00 (0-942330-22-6) J Melek.

— California Commercial Industrial Directories: Alamedia, Set. 200p. (Orig.). 1983. pap. 48.00 (0-686-35979-8) J Melek.

— California Commercial Industrial Directories: Alpine, No. 2. 150p. (Orig.). 1983. 96.00 (0-942330-23-4) J Melek.

— California Commercial Industrial Directories: Amador, No. 3. 200p. (Orig.). 1983. 96.00 (0-942330-24-2) J Melek.

— California Commercial Industrial Directories: Butte, Vol 4. 200p. (Orig.). 1983. 96.00 (0-942330-25-0) J Melek.

— California Commercial Industrial Directories: Calaveras, Vol. 5. 150p. (Orig.). 1983. 96.00 (0-942330-27-7) J Melek.

— California Commercial Industrial Directories: Central Sierra Counties, Vol. 7. 200p. (Orig.). 1983. 96.00 (0-686-35977-1) J Melek.

— California Commercial Industrial Directories: Contra Costa, Vol. 6. 200p. (Orig.). 1983. 96.00 (0-942330-28-5) J Melek.

— California Commercial Industrial Directories: Del Norte, Vol. 8. 200p. (Orig.). 1983. 96.00 (0-942330-29-3) J Melek.

— California Commercial Industrial Directories: El Dorado, Vol. 9. 150p. (Orig.). 1983. 96.00 (0-942330-30-7) J Melek.

— California Commercial Industrial Directories: Fresno, No. 10. 200p. (Orig.). 1982. pap. write for info. (0-942330-31-5) J Melek.

— California Commercial Industrial Directories: Fresno, Set. 200p. (Orig.). 1982. pap. 48.00 (0-685-05927-8) J Melek.

— California Commercial Industrial Directories: Glenn, No. 11. 200p. (Orig.). 1983. 96.00 (0-942330-32-3) J Melek.

— California Commercial Industrial Directories: Humboldt, No. 12. 200p. (Orig.). 1983. 96.00 (0-942330-33-1) J Melek.

— California Commercial Industrial Directories: Imperial, No. 13. 200p. (Orig.). 1983. 96.00 (0-942330-34-X) J Melek.

— California Commercial Industrial Directories: Inyo, No. 14. 200p. (Orig.). 1983. 96.00 (0-942330-35-8) J Melek.

— California Commercial Industrial Directories: Kern, No. 15. 200p. (Orig.). 1983. 96.00 (0-942330-36-6) J Melek.

— California Commercial Industrial Directories: Kings, No. 16. 200p. (Orig.). 1983. 96.00 (0-942330-37-4) J Melek.

— California Commercial Industrial Directories: Lake, No. 17. 200p. (Orig.). 1983. 96.00 (0-942330-38-2) J Melek.

— California Commercial Industrial Directories: Lassen, No. 18. 200p. (Orig.). 1983. pap. 96.00 (0-685-05926-X) J Melek.

— California Commercial Industrial Directories: Los Angeles, No. 19. 200p. (Orig.). 1983. pap. write for info. (0-942330-40-4) J Melek.

— California Commercial Industrial Directories: Madera, No. 20. 200p. (Orig.). 1983. 96.00 (0-942330-41-2) J Melek.

— California Commercial Industrial Directories: Marin, No. 21. 200p. (Orig.). 1983. 96.00 (0-686-98669-5); pap. write for info. (0-942330-42-0) J Melek.

— California Commercial Industrial Directories: Mariposa, No. 22. 200p. (Orig.). 1983. pap. write for info. (0-942330-43-9) J Melek.

— California Commercial Industrial Directories: Mendocino, No. 23. 200p. (Orig.). 1983. pap. write for info. (0-318-56681-8) J Melek.

— California Commercial Industrial Directories: Merced, No. 24. 200p. (Orig.). 1983. pap. write for info. (0-318-56680-X) J Melek.

— California Commercial Industrial Directories: Modoc, No. 25. 200p. (Orig.). 1983. pap. write for info. (0-942330-46-3) J Melek.

— California Commercial Industrial Directories: Mono, No. 26. 200p. (Orig.). 1983. pap. write for info. (0-942330-47-1) J Melek.

— California Commercial Industrial Directories: Monterey, No. 27. 200p. (Orig.). 1983. pap. write for info. (0-942330-48-X) J Melek.

— California Commercial Industrial Directories: Napa, No. 28. 200p. (Orig.). 1983. 96.00 (0-685-05925-1) J Melek.

— California Commercial Industrial Directories: Nevada, No. 29. 150p. 1983. pap. write for info. (0-942330-50-1) J Melek.

— California Commercial Industrial Directories: Northern Sierra Counties, No. 59. 200p. (Orig.). 1983. 96.00 (0-942330-80-3) J Melek.

— California Commercial Industrial Directories: Northern State Counties, No. 58. 200p. (Orig.). 1983. 96.00 (0-686-98787-X); pap. write for info. (0-942330-79-X) J Melek.

— California Commercial Industrial Directories: Orange, No. 30. 200p. (Orig.). 1983. 96.00 (0-942330-51-X) J Melek.

— California Commercial Industrial Directories: Placer, No. 31. 150p. (Orig.). 1983. pap. write for info. (0-942330-52-8) J Melek.

— California Commercial Industrial Directories: San Benito, No. 35. 200p. 1983. pap. write for info. (0-942330-56-0) J Melek.

— California Commercial Industrial Directories: San Bernardino, No. 36. 200p. (Orig.). 1983. pap. write for info. (0-942330-57-9) J Melek.

— California Commercial Industrial Directories: San Diego, No. 37. 200p. 1983. pap. write for info. (0-942330-58-7) J Melek.

— California Commercial Industrial Directories: San Francisco, No. 38. 200p. (Orig.). 1983. pap. write for info. (0-942330-59-5) J Melek.

— California Commercial Industrial Directories: San Joaquin, Vol. 39. 200p. (Orig.). 1983. 96.00 (0-942330-60-9) J Melek.

— California Commercial Industrial Directories: San Luis Obispo, No. 40. 200p. (Orig.). 1983. pap. 96.00 (0-942330-61-7) J Melek.

— California Commercial Industrial Directories: San Mateo, No. 41. 200p. (Orig.). 1983. 96.00 (0-942330-62-5) J Melek.

— California Commercial Industrial Directories: Sanislaus, No. 50. 200p. (Orig.). 1983. 96.00 (0-942330-71-4) J Melek.

— California Commercial Industrial Directories: Santa Barbara, No. 42. 200p. (Orig.). 1983. pap. 96.00 (0-942330-63-3) J Melek.

— California Commercial Industrial Directories: Santa Clara, No. 43. 200p. (Orig.). 1983. 96.00 (0-942330-64-1) J Melek.

— California Commercial Industrial Directories: Santa Cruz, No. 44. 200p. (Orig.). 1983. 96.00 (0-942330-65-X) J Melek.

— California Commercial Industrial Directories: Shasta, No. 45. 200p. (Orig.). 1983. 96.00 (0-942330-66-8) J Melek.

— California Commercial Industrial Directories: Sierra, No. 46. 150p. 1982. 96.00 (0-942330-67-6) J Melek.

— California Commercial Industrial Directories: Siskiyou, No. 47. 200p. 1983. 96.00 (0-942330-68-4) J Melek.

— California Commercial Industrial Directories: Solano, No. 48. 200p. (Orig.). 1983. pap. 96.00 (0-942330-69-2) J Melek.

— California Commercial Industrial Directories: Sonoma, No. 49. 200p. (Orig.). 1983. 96.00 (0-942330-70-6) J Melek.

— California Commercial Industrial Directories: Tehama, No. 51. 200p. (Orig.). 1983. 96.00 (0-942330-72-2) J Melek.

— California Commercial Industrial Directories: Trinity, No. 52. 200p. 1983. 96.00 (0-942330-73-0) J Melek.

— California Commercial Industrial Directories: Tulane, No. 53. 150p. (Orig.). 1983. 96.00 (0-942330-74-9) J Melek.

— California Commercial Industrial Directories: Tuolumne, No. 54. 200p. (Orig.). 1983. 96.00 (0-942330-75-7) J Melek.

— California Commercial Industrial Directories: Ventura, No. 55. 200p. (Orig.). 1983. 96.00 (0-942330-76-5) J Melek.

— California Commercial Industrial Directories: Yuba, No. 54. 200p. (Orig.). 1983. 96.00 (0-942330-78-1) J Melek.

— Cancer: Acute & Chronic Deleterious Effects of the Present Conventional Medical Therapy to Cancer Patients. 600p. (Orig.). 1984. pap. text ed. 19.95 (0-942330-04-8, Sunbright Bks) J Melek.

— Cancer: Affinity & Pool of Iron from the Red Blood Cells by the Highly Acidic Chromosomal Nucleic Acid of Cancer Cell As the Source of Energy of Cancer Cell & Loss of Weight by Cancer Patient. 400p. (Orig.). 1984. pap. text ed. 8.95 (0-942330-07-2, Sunbright Bks) J Melek.

— Cancer: All the Hazards & Risks You Cannot Afford to Take & the Preventive Natural, Universal Approaches to Prevention of This Dreadful Disease. (Illus.). 600p. (Orig.). 1984. pap. 19.95 (0-685-09129-5, Sunbright Bks) J Melek.

— Cancer: Allergic Induced Immune Response Effect on Cancer Cells. 600p. (Orig.). pap. text ed. 24.95 (0-685-09130-9, Sunbright Bks) J Melek.

— Cancer: An Iotragenic Environmental Disease-the Cause & Effect. 600p. (Orig.). 1984. pap. text ed. 24.95 (0-685-09132-5, Sunbright Bks) J Melek.

— Cancer: Calcification Effect of Cancer Cell Membrane with Calcium Hydroxide Solution in Cure & Control of Cancer. (Illus.). 300p. (Orig.). 1984. pap. text ed. 24.95 (0-685-09136-8, Sunbright Bks) J Melek.

— Cancer: Constant, Continuous Titration of Calcium Bicarbonate Solution Effect of Calcification Shell on the Membrane of Cancer Cells. 500p. (Orig.). 1984. pap. text ed. 24.50 (0-685-09137-6, Sunbright Bks) J Melek.

— Cancer: Egg-Shell Formation on Cancer Cell. (Illus.). 500p. (Orig.). 1984. pap. text ed. 19.95 (0-942330-05-6, Sunbright Bks) J Melek.

— Cancer: Iron Supplement & Increase Iron Rich Food. (Illus.). 250p. (Orig.). 1984. pap. text ed. 8.95 (0-685-09145-7, Sunbright Bks) J Melek.

— Cancer-Anaphylactic: The Jacques Melek Cytokinetic Induced Respond Immune Response & Molecular Theory Effect on Cancer Cells. 600p. (Orig.). 1984. pap. 24.95 (0-942330-03-X, Sunbright Bks) J Melek.

— Cancer-Biological Theory of Jacques Melek: Concepts of the Mechanism & Production of the First Cancer Cell. 250p. (Orig.). 1984. pap. text ed. 9.50 (0-685-09134-1, Sunbright Bks) J Melek.

— Cancer Oxidation. 300p. (Orig.). 1984. pap. text ed. 8.95 (0-685-09146-5, Sunbright Bks) J Melek.

— The Court Fox. 500p. 1983. pap. 24.95 (0-942330-49-8, Sunrise Pubns) J Melek.

— Lyrics of Love: Vol. 1, Songs & Poems. LC 81-85773. 120p. 1981. pap. 6.00 (0-686-96966-9, Sunrise Pubns) J Melek.

— Lyrics of Love: Vol. 1, Songs & Poems, 1. 120p. 1981. write for info. (0-318-56567-6, Sunrise Pubns) J Melek.

— Risks & Hazards You Cannot Afford. (Illus.). (Orig.). 1984. pap. 8.95 (0-685-08399-3, Sunrise Pubns) J Melek.

Melek, Jacques, jt. auth. see American Medical Association Staff.

Meleka, Fikri M. Dimensions of the Cancer Problem. xii, 144p. 1983. pap. 39.25 (3-8055-3622-4) S Karger.

Melekhin, V. N., jt. auth. see Kapitza, S. P.

Melen, Roger & Buss, Dennis, eds. Charge-Coupled Devices: Technology & Applications. LC 76-20887. 424p. 1977. 49.95 (0-87942-083-9, PC00802) Inst Electrical.

Melena, Elpis, pseud., jt. auth. see Garibaldi, Giuseppe.

Melendez, Andres A., ed. Libro de Concordia. (SPA.). 1989. 19.95 (0-570-09902-1, 16-1009) Concordia.

An Asterisk (*) at the beginning of an entry indicates that the title is appearing in BIP for the first time.

Melendez, Carlos, jt. auth. see Oquli, Ramon.

Melendez-Carrucini, G. & Melendez-Lugo, Ruben H. Ingreso Tributable: Inclusiones & Doctrinas. (Illus.). 742p. (SPA.). 1990. text ed. 75.00 (*1-878186-00-0*) Inst Cont PR.

Melendez, Concha. Complete Works of Concha Melendez, 5 vols., Set. (Puerto Rico Ser.). 1979. lib. bdg. 1,000.00 (*0-8490-2889-2*) Gordon Pr.

Melendez, Edgardo. El Movimiento Anexionista en Puerto Rico. 1993. pap. 16.95 (*0-8477-0186-7*) U of PR Pr.

— Puerto Rico's Statehood Movement. LC 88-10249. (Contributions in Political Science Ser.: No. 220). 212p. 1988. text ed. 45.00 (*0-313-26131-8*, MPH/, Greenwood Pr) Greenwood.

Melendez, Edgardo, jt. ed. see Melendez, Edwin.

Melendez, Edgardo, et al, eds. Hispanics in the Labor Force: Issues & Policies. (Environment, Development, & Public Policy: Public Policy & Social Services Ser.). (Illus.). 320p. 1991. 54.50 (*0-306-43799-6*, Plenum Pr) Plenum.

Melendez, Edwin & Melendez, Edgardo, eds. Colonial Dilemma: Critical Perspectives on Contemporary Puerto Rico. 350p. (Orig.). 1992. 40.00 (*0-89608-442-6*); pap. 16.00 (*0-89608-441-8*) South End Pr.

Melendez, Edwin & Uriarte, Miren, eds. Latino Poverty & Economic Development in Massachusetts. LC 93-34381. 212p. (Orig.). 1994. pap. 14.95 (*0-87023-894-9*) U of Mass Pr.

Melendez, Esteban N. Plantas Venenosas De Puerto Rico. 290p. (SPA.). 1990. pap. 12.75 (*0-8477-2341-0*) U of PR Pr.

Melendez, Francisco. Leopold's Dream. (Illus.). 80p. 1993. 19.95 (*0-8109-3563-5*) Abrams.

— The Mermaid & the Major: or, the True Story of the Invention of the Submarine. (Illus.). 64p. (J). 1991. 24.95 (*0-8109-3619-4*) Abrams.

Melendez, Guillermo. Seeds of Promise: The Prophetic Church in Central America. 1990. pap. 6.95 (*0-377-00204-6*) Friendship Pr.

Melendez, Jesus P. Concertos on Market Street. 79p. 1993. lib. bdg. 11.95 (*0-9626355-2-9*) Kemetic Images.

Melendez-Lugo, Ruben H., jt. auth. see Melendez-Carrucini, G.

Melendez, Marianne, jt. auth. see Rossant, Colette.

Melendez, Sarah E., jt. auth. see Ambert, Alba N.

Melendez, Tony & White, Mel. Tony Melendez "A Gift of Hope" 1989. 13.95 (*0-318-42499-1*) Harper SF.

Melendez Valdes, Juan. Poesias. Real Ramos, Cesar, ed. (Nueva Austral Ser.: Vol. 217). (SPA.). 1991. pap. text ed. 24.95x (*84-239-7217-8*) Elliots Bks.

— Poesias Ineditas de Juan Melendez Valdes. Rodriguez Monino, Antonio, ed. 259p. (SPA.). 1968. pap. 100.00 (*0-614-00218-4*) Elliots Bks.

Melendez, Winifred. The Universities of Puerto Rico: A Historical, Sociological & Cultural Study Including a Directory of Puerto Rico Scholars. 1979. lib. bdg. 250.00 (*0-8490-1247-3*) Gordon Pr.

Melendo, R. P., jt. auth. see Gallego, J. F.

Melendres, C., jt. ed. see Gutierrez, C.

Melendres, C. A., ed. Synchrotron Techniques in Interfacial Electrochemistry: Proceedings of the NATO Advanced Research Workshop, Funchal, Madeira, Portugal, December 14-18, 1992. (NATO Advanced Science Institutes C: Mathematical & Physical Sciences Ser.). 500p. (C). 1994. lib. bdg. 199.00 (*0-7923-2844-2*) Kluwer Ac.

Melenski, Aaron, ed. see Arpante, Barbara A.

Melentiev, A. & Rudenko, Yu N. Energy Reviews: Scientific & Engineering Problems of Energy Systems Reliability, Vol. 3. (Soviet Technology Reviews Ser.: Vol. 3). 350p. (C). 1987. reprint ed. text ed. 310.00 (*3-7186-0281-4*) Gordon & Breach.

Melentiev, L. A., ed. Energy Reviews: Nuclear Power Systems. (Soviet Technology Reviews Ser.: Vol. 1). 344p. 1982. text ed. 355.00 (*3-7186-0071-4*) Gordon & Breach.

— Unified Gas Supply System of the U. S. S. R., Vol. 2. (Soviet Technology Reviews Ser.: Vol. 2). 328p. 1985. text ed. 312.00 (*3-7186-0152-4*) Gordon & Breach.

Meleny, John C. The Public Life of Aedanus Burke: Revolutionary Republican in Post-Revolutionary South Carolina. 318p. 1989. text ed. 39.95 (*0-87249-610-4*) U of SC Pr.

Meler, Marta, ed. see Keiffer, Ann.

Meler, Vjekoslav. The Slavonic Pioneers of California. LC 68-57133. 1968. reprint ed. pap. 8.00 (*0-88247-121-X*) Ragusan Pr.

Melese & Katz. Thermal & Flow Design of Helium-Cooled Reactors. 432p. 1985. 59.00 (*0-89448-027-8*, 300019) Am Nuclear Soc.

Melese-D'Hospital, G., jt. auth. see Howe, J. P.

Meleshko, V. V. & Konstantinov, M. Yu. Vortex Dynamics & Chaotic Phenomena. 300p. 1995. text ed. 61.00 (*981-02-0871-5*) World Scientific Pub.

Melet-Sanson, J. Fouquet. (Artists Watercolor Ser.). (Illus.). (gr. 10-12). 1978. 14.95 (*0-8120-5280-3*) Barron.

Meletiou, Frances T. Frolic on Cape Cod. 1993. 7.95 (*0-8062-4584-0*) Carlton.

Meletis, E. I. & Bruemmer, S. M., eds. Parkins Symposium on Fundamental Aspects of Stress Corrosion Cracking. (Illus.). 585p. 1992. 150.00 (*0-87339-186-1*, 448) Minerals Metals.

Meletis, E. I., jt. ed. see Sagues, A. A.

Meleton, Marcus P., Jr. Nice Guys Don't Get Laid. rev. ed. LC 93-83581. 112p. 1993. pap. 7.95 (*0-9635826-0-7*) Sharkbait Pr.

Meleton, Marcus P., jt. auth. see Dunlop, Eileen.

***Meleton, Maruce.** Hunting for Lawyers: A Modest Proposal. LC 95-92039. 128p. (Orig.). 1995. pap. 9.95 (*0-9635826-2-3*) Sharkbait Pr.

Meleze-Modrzejewski, Joseph. Statut Personnel et Liens de Famille dans les Droits de l'Antiquite. (Collected Studies: Vol. 411). 320p. 1993. 89.95 (*0-86078-376-6*, Pub. by Variorum UK) Ashgate Pub Co.

Melfa, Frank A. Bodybuilding a Realistic Approach: How You Can Have a Great Body. LC 94-66492. (Illus.). 315p. (Orig.). 1995. pap. 15.95 (*0-9641640-5-1*) Power Writings.

— Bodybuilding a Realistic Approach: How You Can Have a Great Body. LC 94-66492. (Illus.). 315p. (Orig.). 1995. text ed. 23.95 (*0-9641640-4-3*) Power Writings.

***Melfi, Mary.** A Dialogue with Masks. 80p. 1995. lib. bdg. 25.00 (*0-8095-4537-3*) Borgo Pr.

— Infertility Rites. 182p. 1991. pap. 15.00 (*0-920717-51-9*) SPD-Small Pr Dist.

Melfi, Rudy C. Permar's Oral Embryology & Microscopic Anatomy: A Textbook for Students in Dental Hygiene. 9th ed. LC 93-5248. (Illus.). 1993. 32.95 (*0-8121-1659-3*) Williams & Wilkins.

***Melford, S. J. & Anysas, J. A.** Identifying a Liquid Using Physical Properties. Neidig, H. A., ed. (Modular Laboratory Program in Chemistry Ser.). 11p. (C). 1994. pap. text ed. 1.25x (*0-87540-440-5*) Chem Educ Res.

Melger, Boy, pseud. Lantana Malangii: Kembang Tembelehan Boyhood Impressions. (Illus.). 107p. (Orig.). 1991. pap. write for info. (*0-9622463-5-2*) B Melger.

— Lantana Malangii: Kembang Tembelehan Jeugd Impressies. (Illus.). 90p. (Orig.). (DUT.). 1991. pap. write for info. (*0-9622463-4-4*) B Melger.

Melger, Boyd A., pseud. High Bloodpressures, Infarction, Diagrams. LC 88-92898. (Illus.). 63p. (Orig.). 1988. pap. write for info. (*0-9622463-0-1*) B Melger.

Melger, Boyd A., see Boy Melger, pseud..

Melger, Boyd A., see Dyob Re'lem, pseud..

Melger, Boyd A., jt. auth. see Re'lem, Dyob.

Melger, Boyd A., see Dyob Re'lem, pseud..

Melges, Buddy & Mason, Charles. Sailing Smart: Winning Techniques, Tactics & Strategies. LC 82-15557. (Illus.). 208p. 1987. pap. 9.95 (*0-8050-0351-7*, Owl) H Holt & Co.

Melhado, Evan M. Jacob Berzelius: The Emergence of His Chemical System. LC 81-7593. 360p. 1981. reprint ed. 45.00 (*0-299-08970-3*) U of Wis Pr.

Melhado, Evan M. & Frangsmyr, Tore, eds. Enlightenment Science in the Romantic Era: The Chemistry of Berzelius & Its Cultural Setting. (Illus.). 250p. (C). 1992. 54.95 (*0-521-41775-9*) Cambridge U Pr.

Melham, T. F. Higher Order Logic & Hardware Verification. (Tracts in Theoretical Computer Science Ser.: No. 31). (Illus.). 225p. (C). 1993. 42.95 (*0-521-41718-X*) Cambridge U Pr.

Melham, T. F., jt. ed. see Gordon, M. J.

***Melham, Thomas F. & Camilleri, Juanito, eds.** Higher Order Logic Theorum Proving & Its Application: Proceedings of the Seventh International Workshop, Valletta, Malta, September 19-22, 1994. (Lecture Notes in Computer Science: Vol. 859). 1994. 62.00 (*3-540-58450-1*) Spr-Verlag.

— Higher Order Logic Theorum Proving & Its Application: Proceedings of the Seventh International Workshop, Valletta, Malta, September 19-22, 1994, 859. LC 94-35140. (Lecture Notes in Computer Science). 1994. 62.00 (*0-387-58450-1*) Spr-Verlag.

Melham, Tom. Alaska's Wildlife Treasures. LC 94-8008. 200p. 1994. 16.00 (*0-87044-977-X*) Natl Geog.

Melheim, Rich. One Hundred One Ways to Get Your Adult Children to Move Out (& Make Them Think It Was Their Idea) (Illus.). 76p. (Orig.). 1994. pap. 9.95 (*0-9635106-2-5*) Creat Outlet.

***Melheim, Richard A.** Lust. 1994. 19.95 (*0-9635106-3-0*) Creat Outlet.

— Unfinished Business: Saddam Hussein, George Bush, & an American Arab in Military Intelligence Who Knew Too Much. 240p. 1992. 20.00 (*0-9635106-0-6*) Creat Outlet.

Melhem, D. H. Blight. LC 94-13017. (Illus.). 160p. 1995. 21.95 (*0-7145-4274-1*) Riverrun NY.

— Heroism in the New Black Poetry: Introductions & Interviews. LC 89-22756. (Illus.). 288p. 1990. 32.00 (*0-8131-1709-7*) U Pr of Ky.

— Heroism in the New Black Poetry: Introductions & Interviews. LC 89-22756. (Illus.). 288p. 1990. pap. text ed. 14.00 (*0-8131-0807-1*) U Pr of Ky.

— Reaching Exercises: The IWWG Workshop Book. LC 81-67876. 1981. reprint ed. 10.95 (*0-935468-04-8*) Dovetail.

— Rest in Love. 2nd ed. 109p. (YA). 1995. reprint ed. pap. 9.95 (*0-913057-22-3*) Dovetail.

Melhem, G. Advanced Consequence Modelling. (Chemical Engineering Ser.). 1991. text ed. write for info. (*0-442-00755-8*) Van Nos Reinhold.

Melhem, R., ed. Parallel & Distributed Computing & Systems. (Conference Proceedings Ser.). 400p. 1992. write for info. (*1-880843-02-1*) Int Soc Comp App.

Melhnyk-Limnytchenko, P. Vasyl. Lysh ty odna Potrapysh nas spasty. 214p. (UKR.). 1977. pap. 15.00 (*0-686-48392-8*) Slavia Lib.

Melhorn, W. N. & Kempton, J. P., eds. Geology & Hydrogeology of the Teays-Mahomet Bedrock Valley System. (Special Paper Ser.: No. 258). (Illus.). 136p. 1991. pap. 36.25 (*0-8137-2258-6*) Geol Soc.

Melhuish, Edward & Moss, Peter. Day Care for Young Children: International Perspectives. (Illus.). 235p. 1990. 66.00 (*0-415-01746-7*, A4839); pap. 19.95 (*0-415-01747-5*, A4843) Routledge.

Melhuish, Edward, jt. ed. see Moss, Peter.

Melhuish, J., jt. auth. see Capes, W.

Meli, Domenico B. Equivalence & Priority: Newton Versus Leibniz: Including Leibniz's Unpublished Manuscripts on the Principia. LC 92-18967. (Illus.). 320p. 1993. 82.50 (*0-19-853945-2*, Clarendon Pr) OUP.

Meli, Francis. South Africa Belongs to Us: A History of the ANC. LC 88-39946. (Illus.). 290p. 1989. pap. 14.95 (*0-253-28591-7*) Ind U Pr.

Meli, Giovanni. Don Chisciotti & Sanciu Panza. Sbrocchi, Leonard G., ed. (Biblioteca di Quaderni d'Italianistica Ser.: Vol. 2). (Illus.). 324p. (Orig.). 1986. pap. 20.00 (*0-317-04132-0*, Pub. by Can Soc Ital Stu CN) Speedimpex.

— Moral Fables. Sbrocchi, Leonard G., ed. Cipolla, Gaetano, tr. & intro. by. (Biblioteca di Quaderni d'Italianistica Ser.: Vol. 6). (Illus.). 146p. (Orig.). 1988. pap. 20.00 (*0-9691979-5-0*, Pub. by Can Soc Ital Stu CN) Speedimpex.

— Moral Fables & Other Poems: A Bilingual (Sicilian/English) Anthology. Cipolla, Gaetano, ed. & tr. by. LC 94-47001. (Poets of Arba Sicula Ser.: Vol. 3). (ENG & ITA.). 1995. write for info. (*1-881901-07-6*) LEGAS.

Melia, Daniel F., jt. ed. see Matonis, A. T.

Melia, Jinx. Breaking into the Boardroom. 1989. mass mkt. 4.50 (*0-312-91649-3*) St Martin.

***Melia, Paul, ed.** David Hockney. LC 94-42848. (Critical Introductions to Art Ser.). 1995. text ed. write for info. (*0-7190-4404-9*, Pub. by Manchester Univ Pr UK); text ed. write for info. (*0-7190-4405-7*, Pub. by Manchester Univ Pr UK) St Martin.

Melia, Paul, ed. see Luckhardt, Ulrich.

Melia, Pius. The Origin, Persecutions, & Doctrines of the Waldenses from Documents: Many Now for the First Time Collected & Edited. LC 77-84716. reprint ed. 27.50 (*0-404-16122-7*) AMS Pr.

Melia, Richard P. Vocational Rehabilitation: Its Relationship to Vocational Education. 16p. 1986. 2.75 (*0-318-22246-9*, OC 120) Ctr Educ Trng Employ.

Melia, Tamara M. Damn the Torpedoes: A Short History of U. S. Naval Mine Countermeasures, 1777-1991. (Contributions to Naval History Ser.: No. 4). (Illus.). 209p. (C). 1991. pap. 10.00 (*0-945274-07-6*) Naval Hist Ctr.

Melia, Trevor & Ryder, Nova. Lucifer State. 2nd ed. (Illus.). 208p. (C). 1991. per. 15.95 (*0-8403-6847-X*, 40305701) Kendall-Hunt.

— Lucifer State: A Novel Approach to Rhetoric. 208p. (C). 1994. pap. text ed., spiral bd. 14.95 (*0-8403-9505-1*) Kendall-Hunt.

Melia, Trevor, jt. ed. see Simons, Herbert W.

Melica, F., ed. AIDS & Reproduction. (Illus.). xii, 196p. 1992. 135.25 (*3-8055-5481-8*) S Karger.

Melich, Anna, jt. auth. see Reif, Karlheinz.

Melich, Timothy F. Walk with Me. LC 89-51347. 61p. 1990. pap. 5.95 (*1-55523-266-3*) Winston-Derek.

Melichar, G., et al, eds. Invasives und nichtinvasives Monitoring von Atmung, Beatmung, Kreislauf, und Stoffwechsel. (Beitraege zur Intensiv und Notfallmedizin Ser.: Vol. 4). (Illus.). viii, 260p. 1986. 60.00 (*3-8055-4267-4*) S Karger.

Melicher, Ronald W., jt. auth. see Welshans, Merle T.

Melick, Harry C. The Manor of Fordham & Its Founder. LC 50-11879. (Illus.). 234p. reprint ed. pap. 66.70 (*0-7837-5584-8*, 2045376) Bks Demand.

Melick, Mary E., jt. auth. see Reiss, Barry S.

Melick, Ray. Roll Tide Roll: The Story of Alabama's National Championship Season. LC 93-84959. (Illus.). 250p. 1993. 19.95 (*0-915611-79-1*) Sagamore Pub.

Melick, Richard R., Jr. The New American Commentary, Vol. 32: Philippians, Colossians, Philemon, No. 40. 1991. 27.99 (*0-8054-0132-6*, 4201-32) Broadman.

Melick, Richard R., Jr., jt. ed. see Garrett, Duane A.

Meligari, Linda E., ed. see Wayne, Bill.

Melikian, Anahid. Byron & the East. 1977. 19.95 (*0-8156-6049-9*, Am U Beirut) Syracuse U Pr.

Melikian, Anahid, ed. see Smith, Byron P.

Melikian, Richard G. The Armenian Answer to the Armenian Question. (Illus.). 48p. 1987. pap. 4.95 (*0-317-56056-5*) Best West Pr.

Melikov, Edward, et al. Soviet Defense Decision-Making: An Integrated View, Vol. II. (Illus.). 331p. (Orig.). 1989. pap. text ed. 125.00 (*1-55831-100-9*) Delphic Associates.

Melilli, jt. ed. see Behal.

Melilli, Albert S. & Nisbett, Edward G., eds. Residual & Unspecified Elements in Steel. LC 89-32224. (Special Technical Publication Ser.: No. STP 1042). (Illus.). 320p. 1989. text ed. 64.00 (*0-8031-1259-9*) ASTM.

Melilli, Albert S., jt. ed. see Nisbett, E. G.

Melillo, Gaetano, et al, eds. Respiratory Allergy: Advances in Clinical Immunology & Pulmonary Medicine. LC 93-15160. (International Congress Ser.: Vol. 1007). 1993. write for info. (*0-444-89679-1*) Elsevier.

Melillo, Jerry, jt. auth. see Aber, John D.

Melin, Charlotte, jt. auth. see Zorach, Cecile.

Melin, Jane. Getting the Most Out of IBM Hollywood. 1991. pap. 24.95 (*0-13-345182-8*) Brady Compu Bks.

Melin, Nancy J., ed. The Serials Collection: Organization & Administration. LC 82-81133. (Current Issues in Serials Management Ser.: No. 1). 1982. 30.00 (*0-87650-140-4*) Pierian.

Melin, Nancy J. & Lisanti, Suzana. Essential Guide to the Library IBM PC. Incl. Vol. 1. Hardware: Set-Up & Expansion. LC 85-10535. 1985. (*0-88736-033-5*); Vol. 2. Operating System: PC-DOS. LC 85-10535. 1985. (*0-88736-034-3*); Vol. 3. Library Application Software. LC 85-10535. 1985. (*0-88736-035-1*); Vol. 4. Data Communications: Going Online. LC 85-10535. 1986. (*0-88736-036-X*); Vol. 5. Buying & Installing Generic Software for Library Use. LC 85-10535. 1986. (*0-88736-037-8*); LC 85-10535. 34.95 (*0-317-38262-4*) Mecklermedia.

***Melina, Branna C.** The Almost No Fat Holiday Cookbook: Festive Vegetarian Recipes. 192p. 1995. 12.95 (*1-57067-009-9*) Book Pub Co.

Melina, Lois R. Adoption: An Annotated Bibliography, Vol. 10. LC 86-31964. (Reference Books on Family Issues: Vol. 10). 314p. 1987. lib. bdg. 42.00 (*0-8240-8942-1*, SS374) Garland.

— Making Sense of Adoption: A Parent's Guide. LC 89-45106. 256p. (Orig.). 1989. pap. 13.00 (*0-06-096319-0*, PL 6319, PL) HarpC.

— Raising Adopted Children. 1986. pap. 12.00 (*0-06-096039-6*, PL) HarpC.

Melina, Lois R. & Roszia, Sharon K. The Open Adoption Experience: A Complete Guide for Adoptive & Birth Families - From Making the Decision Through the Child's Growing Years. LC 92-56254. 288p. 1993. pap. 11.00 (*0-06-096957-1*, PL) HarpC.

***Melina, Vesanto, et al.** Becoming Vegetarian: The Complete Guide to Adopting a Healthy Vegetarian. 262p. 1995. 14.95 (*1-57067-013-7*) Book Pub Co.

Melinek, Menachem, jt. ed. see Mullahy, Patrick.

Melinkov, V. N., jt. ed. see De Sabbata, Venzo.

Melino, G., et al, eds. Biochemistry of Neuroectodermal Tumors. (Clinical Chemistry & Enzymology Communications Ser.). 180p. 1990. pap. text ed. 182.00 (*3-7186-5019-3*) Gordon & Breach.

Melion, Walter, jt. ed. see Kuchler, Susanne.

Melion, Walter S. Shaping the Netherlandish Canon: Karel Van Mander's Schilder-Boeck. LC 91-2806. (Illus.). 282p. 1992. 45.00 (*0-226-51959-7*) U Ch Pr.

Melion, Walter S., jt. ed. see Barnes, Susan J.

Meliopoulos. Power System Grounding & Transients: An Introduction. (Electrical Engineering & Electronics Ser.: Vol. 50). 472p. 1988. 160.00 (*0-8247-7908-8*) Dekker.

Melious, Jean O. Land Banking Revisited: Massachusetts Breaks the Mold. (Land Policy Roundtable Ser.: No. 107). 51p. (Orig.). 1986. pap. text ed. 5.25 (*1-55844-107-7*) Lincoln Inst Land.

Melish, John. Surveys for Travellers, Emigrants & Others. LC 75-22829. (America in Two Centuries Ser.). 1976. 33.95 (*0-405-07701-7*) Ayer.

Melish, John H. Bishop Paul Jones: Witness for Peace. 2nd ed. 56p. 1992. pap. 2.95 (*0-88028-128-6*, 1159) Forward Movement.

Melissa, Ma P., ed. see Rajneesh, Osho.

Melissinos. Ten Minute Addresses. pap. 4.00 (*0-88053-356-0*, S411) Macoy Pub.

Melissinos, Adrian C. Experiments in Modern Physics. 1966. text ed. 59.00 (*0-12-489850-5*) Acad Pr.

— Principles of Modern Technology. (Illus.). 300p. (C). 1990. pap. 34.95 (*0-521-38965-8*) Cambridge U Pr.

— Principles of Modern Technology. (Illus.). 300p. (C). 1990. 84.95 (*0-521-35249-5*) Cambridge U Pr.

Melissinos, Adrian C., jt. auth. see Das, Ashok.

Melitz, Leo L. The Opera Goers' Complete Guide. Salinger, Richard, tr. LC 80-2293. reprint ed. 54.50 (*0-404-18859-1*) AMS Pr.

Melius, Ken, ed. see Kersten, John.

Melius, Kenneth W. National Forest Campground Guide. LC 82-51299. (Illus.). 310p. 1983. pap. 9.95 (*0-9610130-0-1*) Melius Pub.

Melius, Kenneth W., ed. see Melius, Michael M.

Melius, Michael M. Cloud Peak Primitive Area: Trail Guide, History & Photo Odyssey. Melius, Kenneth W., ed. LC 93-60487. (Illus.). 120p. (Orig.). 1993. pap. 11.95 (*0-937603-12-0*) Melius Pub.

— Plants & Animals Rare in South Dakota: A Field Guide. LC 87-50402. (Illus.). 120p. (Orig.). 1987. pap. 3.00 (*0-937603-05-8*) Melius Pub.

— True: Notes from Journeys in South Dakota. LC 91-52925. (Illus.). 130p. 1991. 15.00 (*0-937603-11-2*, Tensleep Pubns); pap. 8.00 (*0-937603-10-4*, Tensleep Pubns) Melius Pub.

Melius, Paul, jt. auth. see Friedman, Michael E.

***Meliza, Raymond W.** How to Find a Job (12 Simple Techniques) (Illus.). 16p. 1994. pap. 2.50 (*1-884241-30-1*) Energeia Pub.

— Time Management for High School Students. (Illus.). 8p. 1994. pap. 2.50 (*0-9626591-9-3*) Energeia Pub.

Melkanoff, Michel A., jt. auth. see Chang, Chao-Hwa.

Melke, Sabine. Cichlids from Lake Malawi & Tanganyika, Success with. (Illus.). 192p. 1993. 24.95 (*0-86622-489-0*, TT030) TFH Pubns.

Melkers, Julia, jt. ed. see Bozeman, Barry.

Melkman, Alan V. How to Handle Major Customers Profitably. 160p. 1979. text ed. 69.95 (*0-566-02097-1*) Ashgate Pub Co.

Melkman, R., ed. The Construction of Objectivity: A New Look at the First Months of Life. (Contributions to Human Development Ser.: Vol. 19). (Illus.). xiv, 130p. 1988. 79.25 (*3-8055-4746-3*) S Karger.

Melko, Matthew. Nature of Civilizations. LC 69-15527. (Extending Horizons Ser.). (Illus.). 224p. (C). 1969. 4.95 (*0-87558-044-0*) Porter Sargent.

— Peace in Our Time. 217p. 1990. 24.95 (*1-55778-055-2*) Prof World Peace.

Melko, Matthew & Scott, Leighton R., eds. The Boundaries of Civilizations in Space & Time. LC 87-10718. (Illus.). 480p. (Orig.). (C). 1987. pap. text ed. 37.00 (*0-8191-6493-3*) U Pr of Amer.

Melko, Matthew, jt. auth. see Cargan, Leonard.

Melko, Matthew, et al. Millfield on Saturday: Searching for Community in a Metropolitan Village. LC 93-40796. 154p. 1994. write for info. (*1-882090-09-8*); pap. 18.50 (*1-882090-10-1*) Wright State Univ Pr.

Melkonian, Carole, tr. see Nhat Hanh, Thich.

Melkonian, Haigazoun, tr. see Koushagian, Torkom.

Melkonian, Markar. The Weapon of Theory: A Post-Cold-War Primer on Marxism. 170p. 1994. pap. 12.00 (*0-9641569-0-3*) Sardarabad.

Melkonian, Martin, jt. ed. see Silver, Marc L.

An Asterisk (*) at the beginning of an entry indicates that the title is appearing in BIP for the first time.

Melkonian, Michael & Dring, Matthew J., eds. Algal Cell Motility. (Current Phycology Ser.). 192p. 1991. 42.00 (*0-412-02431-4*, A4037, Chap & Hall NY) Chapman & Hall.

Melkonian, Michael, ed. see Geider, Richard J. & Osborne, Bruce A.

Melkonian, Michael, et al, eds. The Cytoskeleton of Flagellate & Ciliate Protists. (Illus.). v, 167p. 1992. 128.00 (*0-387-82294-1*) Spr-Verlag.

Melkonian, Monte. The Right to Struggle. 2nd ed. 240p. 1994. pap. 20.00 (*0-9641569-1-1*) Sardarabad.

Melkote, R. Srinivas. Communication for Development in the Third World: Theory & Practice from 1950's to 1990's. 252p. (C). 1991. text ed. 29.95 (*0-8039-9683-7*); pap. text ed. 14.95 (*0-8039-9684-5*) Sage.

Melkote, Rama S., ed. Regional Organisations: A Third World Perspective. 220p. 1990. text ed. 27.95 (*81-207-1130-0*, Pub. by Sterling Pubs II) Apt Bks.

Melkote, Rama S. & Rao, A. Narasimha. International Relations. enl. rev. ed. Sharma, B. A. & Reddy, K. Madhusudan, eds. xi, 404p. 1992. 40.00 (*81-207-1410-5*, Pub. by Sterling Pubs II) Apt Bks.

Mell, Donald C., Jr., ed. English Poetry, 1660-1800: A Guide to Information Sources. LC 73-16974. (American Literature, English Literature, & World Literatures in English Information Guide Ser.: Vol. 40). 520p. 1982. 68.00 (*0-8103-1230-1*) Gale.

Mell, Donald C., Jr., et al, eds. Contemporary Studies of Swift's Poetry. LC 79-21610. (Illus.). 240p. 1980. 35.00 (*0-87413-173-1*, 173) U Delaware Pr.

— Man, God, & Nature in the Enlightenment. LC 87-51123. (Studies in Literature, 1500-1800: No. 2). 1989. 36.00 (*0-937191-03-5*); pap. 14.95 (*0-937191-13-2*) Colleagues Pr Inc.

Mell, George. Writing Antiques. (Album Ser.: No. 54). (Illus.). 32p. 1988. pap. text ed. 5.25 (*0-85263-519-2*, Pub. by Shire Pubns UK) Lubrecht & Cramer.

Mell, Jan. The Atlantic Gray Whale. LC 89-7868. (Gone Forever Ser.). (Illus.). 48p. (J). (gr. 5-6). 1989. text ed. 12.95 (*0-89686-458-8*, Crstwood Hse) Silver Burdett Pr.

— Grand Canyon. LC 88-18707. (National Parks Ser.). (Illus.). 48p. (J). (gr. 4-5). 1988. text ed. 13.95 (*0-89686-406-5*, Crstwood Hse) Silver Burdett Pr.

— Scorpion. LC 89-28273. (Wildlife Ser.). (Illus.). 48p. (J). (gr. 5). 1990. text ed. 12.95 (*0-89686-520-7*, Crstwood Hse) Silver Burdett Pr.

Mell, Ulrich. Neue Schoepfung: Eine Traditionsgeschichtliche und Exegetische Studie zu einem soteriologischen Grundsatz Paulinischer Theologie. (Beiheft zur Zeitschrift fuer die Neuetestamentliche Wissenschaft Ser.: No. 56). xv, 436p. (GER.). (C). 1989. lib. bdg. 119.25x (*3-11-011831-9*) De Gruyter.

Mella, Cesar T. A Priest to the World & Other Prose Works. 77p. (Orig.). 1984. pap. 6.25 (*971-10-0180-2*, Pub. by New Day Pub PH) Cellar.

Mella, Dorothee L. Candle Power: A Game of Light. 48p. 1992. pap. 4.95 (*0-9636345-0-X*) Domel.

— Functional Color A to Z: Energy Power of Colors. 56p. 1994. pap. 4.95 (*0-9636345-2-6*) Domel.

— The Language of Color. (Illus.). 128p. (Orig.). 1988. pap. 9.99 (*0-446-38781-9*) Warner Bks.

— Stone Power. 1988. pap. 12.99 (*0-446-38696-0*) Warner Bks.

Mella, Dorothee L. & Lusson, Michelle. GEM Pharmacy: Nature's Mineral Supports. 56p. 1992. pap. 4.95 (*0-9636345-1-8*) Domel.

Mella, Piero. Diccionario Enciclopedico De Contabilidad. 1989. 39.95 (*0-7859-6504-1*) Fr & Eur.

Mellado De Hunter, Elena. Anglicimos Profesionales De Puerto Rico. LC 80-17935. (Coleccion Mente y Palabra). 204p. (SPA.). 1981. 6.00 (*0-8477-0578-1*); pap. 5.20 (*0-8477-0579-X*) U of PR Pr.

Mellado de Hunter, Elena. El Estoicismo de Angel Ganivet. (UPREX, Estudios Literarios Ser.: No. 10). 193p. (C). 1972. pap. 1.50 (*0-8477-0010-0*) U of PR Pr.

Mellado, Joaquin & Aldana, Maria J., eds. Eulogius von Cordoba-Concordantia in Eulogium Cordubensem. (Alpha-Omega, Reihe B Ser.: Bd. VI). viii, 645p. (GER.). 1993. write for info. (*3-487-09657-9*, Pub. by Georg Olms GW) Lubrecht & Cramer.

Mellado, Ramon. Puerto Rico y Occidente. 6th ed. (UPREX, Ensayo Ser.: No. 31). 189p. (C). 1973. pap. 1.50 (*0-8477-0031-3*) U of PR Pr.

Mellah, Fawzi. Elissa. 188p. 1990. 19.95 (*0-7043-2704-X*, Pub. by Quartet UK) Interlink Pub.

Mellan, I. Industrial Plasticizers. LC 62-8734. 1963. 129.00 (*0-08-010144-5*, Pub. by Pergamon Repr UK) Franklin.

***Mellan, Olivia.** Money Harmony. 1995. pap. 9.95 (*0-8027-7456-3*) Walker & Co.

— Money Harmony: Resolving Money Conflicts in Your Life & Relationships. LC 93-37876. 256p. 1994. 19.95 (*0-8027-1285-1*) Walker & Co.

***Mellan, Olivia & Christie, Sherry.** Overcoming Overspending. 160p. 1995. 16.95 (*0-8027-1309-2*) Walker & Co.

Mellanby, K. Scabies. 87p. 1972. 20.00 (*0-317-07173-4*) St Mut.

Mellanby, K., ed. Air Pollution, Acid Rain & the Environment. 126p. 1989. pap. 72.00 (*1-85166-222-7*) Elsevier.

Mellanby, K., jt. auth. see Perring, F. H.

Melland, Frank H. In Witchbound Africa. (Illus.). 316p. 1967. reprint ed. 35.00 (*0-7146-1044-5*, Pub. by F Cass Pubs UK) Intl Spec Bk.

Mellander, Deane. B & O Thunder in the Allegheniés. (Carstens Hobby Bks.: No. C-45). (Illus.). 80p. 1983. pap. 12.95 (*0-911868-45-3*, C45) Carstens Pubns.

Mellander, Deane, jt. auth. see Carstens, Harold H.

Mellander, Erik & Jansson, Leif. CONRAD: A Maximum Likelihood Program for Estimation of Non-Linear Simultaneous Equations Models. 94p. (Orig.). 1987. pap. 55.00x (*91-7204-283-4*, Pub. by Industriens SW) Coronet Bks.

Mellander, Klas. The Power of Learning: Fostering Employee Growth. LC 92-47432. 225p. 1993. text ed. 20.00 (*1-55623-893-2*) Irwin Prof Pubng.

Mellar, Harvey, et al, eds. Learning with Artificial Worlds: Computer Based Modelling in the Curriculum. LC 94-11536. 218p. 1994. 85.00x (*0-7507-0312-1*, Falmer Pr); pap. 29.00x (*0-7507-0313-X*, Falmer Pr) Taylor & Francis.

Mellard, Charles W., Jr. Introduction to Business Programming Using Pascal: A Structured Problem-Solving Approach. 416p. (C). 1987. pap. write for info. (*0-675-20547-6*, Merrill Pub Co) Macmillan.

Mellard, Evelyn. In the Circles of Time. (Illus.). 120p. 1975. 15.00 (*0-685-58282-5*) A Jones.

Mellard, James C. & Wilcox, James C. The Authentic Writer: Freshman Rhetoric & Composition. 1977. pap. text ed. 14.00 (*0-669-85639-8*) Heath.

Mellard, James M. Doing Tropology: Analysis of Narrative Discourse. LC 86-11370. 192p. 1987. 24.95 (*0-252-01356-5*) U of Ill Pr.

— The Exploded Form: The Modernist Novel in America. LC 79-25993. 224p. 1980. 24.95 (*0-252-00801-4*) U of Ill Pr.

— Using Lacan, Reading Fiction. 264p. 1991. 36.50 (*0-252-01786-2*); pap. 14.95 (*0-252-06173-X*) U of Ill Pr.

Mellard, Rudolph. Along the Way with Horses & Me. (Illus.). 165p. 1975. 15.00 (*0-685-58281-7*) A Jones.

— Stagecoach 22-San Antonio-El Paso Line. (Illus.). 1977. 15.00 (*0-685-87381-1*) A Jones.

— The Track of the Albatross. (Illus.). 1974. 15.00 (*0-685-50194-9*) A Jones.

***Mellars, Paul.** The Neanderthal Legacy: An Archaeological Perspective from Western Europe. LC 95-4300. 1995. write for info. (*0-691-03493-1*) Princeton U Pr.

Mellars, Paul, ed. The Emergence of Modern Humans: An Archaeological Perspective. 576p. 1991. 68.50 (*0-8014-2614-6*) Cornell U Pr.

— Excavations on Oronsay: Prehistoric Ecology on a Small Island. (Illus.). 200p. 1987. 50.00 (*0-85224-544-0*, Pub. by Edinburgh U Pr UK) Col U Pr.

Mellars, Paul & Stringer, Christopher, eds. The Human Revolution: Behavioural & Biological Perspectives on the Origins of Modern Humans. (Illus.). 690p. 1990. 69.50 (*0-691-08539-0*) Princeton U Pr.

Mellars, Paul, jt. ed. see Dibble, Harold L.

Mellberg, James R. & Ripa, Louis W. Fluoride in Preventive Dentistry. (Illus.). 288p. 1983. text ed. 80.00 (*0-86715-102-1*) Quint Pub Co.

***Mellberg, William F.** Famous Airliners: Seventy Years of Aviation & Transport Progress. (Illus.). 180p. (Orig.). 1994. pap. text ed. 14.95 (*1-882663-02-0*) Plymouth MI.

Melle, Julie. My 911 Book for Help. LC 92-71606. (Illus.). 16p. (J). (ps-6). 1992. pap. text ed. 9.99 (*1-881402-00-2*) CA Storybook.

Melle, Ulrich. Das Wahrnehmungsproblam und Seine Verwandlung in Phanomenologischer Einstellung. 1983. lib. bdg. 74.50 (*90-247-2761-8*) Kluwer Ac.

Melle, Ulrich, ed. Edmund Husserl: Vorlesungen uber Ethik und Wertlehre, 1908-1914. (C). 1988. lib. bdg. 276.50 (*90-247-3708-7*) Kluwer Ac.

Melleby, Alexander. Y's Way to a Healthy Back. LC 82-14474. (Illus.). 192p. 1982. pap. 11.95 (*0-8329-0147-4*) New Win Pub.

Mellema, Gregory. Beyond the Call of Duty: Supererogation, Obligation & Offence. LC 90-45680. (SUNY Series in Ethical Theory). 226p. (C). 1991. 59.50 (*0-7914-0737-3*); pap. 19.95 (*0-7914-0738-1*) State U NY Pr.

— The Bottom Line: Making Christian Choices in the Marketplace. LC 94-22303. (Issues in Christian Living Ser.). 1994. pap. 6.50 (*1-56212-064-6*) CRC Pubns.

— Individuals, Groups, & Shared Moral Responsibility. (American University Studies: Philosophy: Ser. V, Vol. 61). 224p. (C). 1988. text ed. 33.50 (*0-8204-0855-7*) P Lang Pubs.

Mellen, Barbara. She Walks in Beauty: Jennifer, a Celebration of Life. (Illus.). 80p. (Orig.). 1993. pap. 10.00 (*0-9636524-0-0*) B Mellen.

Mellen, Diana L. Yesterday: The Hampton, McCracken, Longwith, Mabry, & Wells Families. (Illus.). vi, 324p. (Orig.). 1991. pap. 26.00 (*1-55613-505-X*) Heritage Bk.

Mellen, George W. Argument on the Unconstitutionality of Slavery, Embracing an Abstract of the Proceedings of the National & State Conventions on This Subject. LC 70-172720. reprint ed. 34.50 (*0-404-00089-4*) AMS Pr.

Mellen, J. Hellman & Hammett. Date not set. 23.00 (*0-06-018339-X*, HarpT) HarpC.

Mellen, Jaon. Kay Boyle: Author of Herself. LC 94-654. 1994. 35.00 (*0-374-18098-9*) FS&G.

Mellen, Joan. Bob Knight: His Own Man. 384p. 1989. mass mkt. 5.99 (*0-380-70809-4*) Avon.

— Bob Knight: His Own Man. 1988. 17.95 (*1-55611-100-2*) D I Fine.

— Filmguide to The Battle of Algiers. LC 73-75787. (Indiana University Press Filmguide Ser.: No. 8). 92p. reprint ed. pap. 26.30 (*0-8357-9210-2*, 2017629) Bks Demand.

Mellen, Philip. Gerhart Hauptmann: Religious Syncretism & Eastern Religions. (American University Studies: Germanic Languages & Literature: Ser. I, Vol. 24). 328p. (Orig.). 1983. pap. text ed. 30.55 (*0-8204-0060-2*) P Lang Pubs.

Mellen, Philip, jt. auth. see Von Peter Sprengel, Herausgegeben.

Mellen, Rachel. The Handy Book to English Genealogy. 3rd ed. (Illus.). 228p. (Orig.). 1990. pap. 15.00 (*1-55613-359-6*) Heritage Bk.

Mellen, Stephanie. A Bear in the Chair. LC 94-75065. (Illus.). 50p. (J). (gr. k-2). 1994. pap. 6.95 (*0-9637414-1-1*) Meltec.

— The Crystal Rabbit. LC 93-91632. (Illus.). 52p. 1993. pap. 7.00 (*0-9637414-0-3*) Meltec.

— The Golden Angel. LC 94-79576. (Illus.). 64p. 1995. pap. 7.00 (*0-9637414-2-X*) Meltec.

Mellen, Stephanie, jt. auth. see Polakiewicz, David M.

Mellencamp, Patricia. High Anxiety: Catastrophe, Scandal, Age, & Comedy. LC 91-46255. (Arts & Politics of the Everyday Ser.). (Illus.). 448p. 1992. 39.95 (*0-253-33744-5*); pap. 18.95 (*0-253-20735-5*, MB-735) Ind U Pr.

— Indiscretions: Avant-Garde Film, Video, & Feminism. LC 89-45804. (Theories of Contemporary Culture Ser.). 254p. 1990. 29.95 (*0-253-33743-7*); pap. 12.95 (*0-253-20587-5*, MB-587) Ind U Pr.

Mellencamp, Patricia, ed. Logics of Television: Essays in Cultural Criticism. LC 89-46004. (Theories of Contemporary Culture Ser.). 318p. 1990. 35.00 (*0-253-33617-1*); pap. 14.95 (*0-253-20582-4*, MB-582) Ind U Pr.

Mellencamp, Patricia & Rosen, Philip T., eds. Cinema Histories, Cinema Practices. LC 83-22457. 220p. (C). 1984. text ed. 42.95 (*0-313-27037-6*, U7037); pap. text ed. 17.95 (*0-313-27003-1*, P7003) Greenwood.

Mellencamp, Patricia, jt. ed. see Heath, Stephen.

Mellenkopf, John H. New York City in the 1980's: A Social, Economic, & Political Atlas. LC 93-25096. 1992. 50.00 (*0-13-616293-2*) S&S Trade.

Mellenthin, F. W. Von. Panzer Battles: A Study of the Employment of Armor in the Second World War. Turner, L. C., ed. Betzler, H., tr. LC 56-5997. (Illus.). 404p. 1956. pap. 18.95 (*0-8061-1802-4*) U of Okla Pr.

Meller, Eric, illus. Rabbit Who Overcame Fear: A Jataka Tale. (Jataka Tales Ser.). 32p. (Orig.). (J). (gr. k-4). 1991. 15.95 (*0-89800-212-5*); pap. 7.95 (*0-89800-211-7*) Dharma Pub.

Meller, Helen. Patrick Geddes: Social Evolutionist & City Planner. LC 93-4323. (Geography, Environment & Planning Ser.). 1994. pap. write for info. (*0-415-10393-2*) Routledge.

Meller, Hugh. London Cemeteries: An Illustrated Guide & Gazetteer. 3rd ed. (Illus.). 368p. 1993. 33.95 (*0-85967-997-7*, Pub. by Scolar Pr UK) Ashgate Pub Co.

***Meller, Michael N.** International Patent Litigation: A Country-by-Country Analysis with 94 Supplement. 1994. ring bd. 250.00 (*0-87179-830-1*) BNA.

— International Patent Litigation: A County-by-County Analysis, 1994. suppl. ed. 1994. text ed. 95.00 (*0-87179-380-6*) BNA.

Meller, Patricio. Adjustment & Equity in Chile. 102p. (Orig.). 1992. pap. 31.00 (*92-64-13619-3*) OECD.

— Efficiency Frontiers for Industrial Establishments of Different Sizes. (Explorations in Economic Research Three Ser.: No. 3). 28p. 1976. reprint ed. 35.00 (*0-685-61402-6*) Natl Bur Econ Res.

Meller, Patricio, ed. The Latin American Development Debate: Neostructuralism, Neomonetarism, & Adjustment Processes. (Series in Political Economy & Economic Development in Latin America). 220p. (C). 1991. text ed. 51.00 (*0-8133-7971-7*) Westview.

Meller, Patricio, jt. ed. see Blomstrom, Magnus.

Meller, Patricio, jt. ed. see Engel, Eduardo.

Meller, Rosine. The Contemporary French Writers. 1972. 59.95 (*0-87968-940-4*) Gordon Pr.

Meller, Susan, intro. Giftwraps by Artists: French Flowers: 19th-Century Textile Designs. (Illus.). 1989. pap. 14.95 (*0-8109-2961-9*) Abrams.

Meller, Susan & Elffers, Joost. Textile Designs: Two Hundred Years of European & American Patterns for Printed Fabrics. (Illus.). 464p. 1991. 65.00 (*0-8109-3853-7*) Abrams.

Meller, Walter C. A Knight's Life in the Days of Chivalry. LC 78-63506. (Illus.). 328p. reprint ed. 38.50 (*0-404-17155-9*) AMS Pr.

Mellerio, Andre. Odilon Redon. LC 67-27461. (Graphic Art Ser.). 1968. reprint ed. lib. bdg. 95.00 (*0-306-70975-9*) Da Capo.

Mellerio, Louis. Lexique De Ronsard. lxxv, 250p. 1974. reprint ed. write for info. (*3-487-05248-2*, Pub. by Georg Olms GW) Lubrecht & Cramer.

Mellerowicz, H. Der Kreislauf des Jugendlichen bei Arbeit und Sport. 2nd ed. (Illus.). viii, 60p. 1980. pap. 13.00 (*3-8055-1140-X*) S Karger.

Mellerowicz, H., jt. ed. see Loellgen, H.

Mellers, Barbara A. & Baron, Jonathan, eds. Psychological Perspectives on Justice: Theory & Applications. LC 92-27263. (Series on Judgment & Decision Making). (Illus.). 336p. (C). 1993. 54.95 (*0-521-43199-9*) Cambridge U Pr.

Mellers, Wilfrid. Caliban Reborn: Renewal in Twentieth-Century Music. LC 79-14238. (Music Reprint Ser.). 1979. reprint ed. lib. bdg. 29.50 (*0-306-79569-8*) Da Capo.

— Francis Poulenc. (Oxford Studies of Composers Ser.). (Illus.). 208p. 1995. reprint ed. pap. 18.95 (*0-19-816338-X*) OUP.

— Francois Couperin & the French Classical Tradition. 2nd rev. ed. 544p. 1987. 45.00 (*0-571-13983-3*) Faber & Faber.

— Percy Grainger. (Studies of Composers). (Illus.). 176p. 1992. 49.95 (*0-19-816269-3*); pap. 22.00 (*0-19-816270-7*) OUP.

— Percy Grainger. braille ed. 419p. 1994. text ed., vinyl bd. 33.52 (*1-56956-426-4*, BR9300) W A T Braille.

***Mellersh, H. E.** Chronology of Ancient World, 10,000 B.C. to A.D. 799. LC 94-30474. 1994. 70.00 (*0-13-326422-X*) S&S Trade.

***Mellert, Robert.** Seven Ethical Theories. 172p. 1995. pap. text ed. 17.44 (*0-7872-0567-2*) Kendall-Hunt.

Mellett, Dorothy W. Gravestone Art in Rockland County, New York. LC 90-85609. (Illus.). 160p. (Orig.). 1991. pap. 22.50 (*0-9630484-0-6*) Hudson Valley.

Mellett, H. J., jt. auth. see Edwards, J. R.

Mellett, Howard, jt. auth. see Edwards, Dick.

Mellett, Howard, et al. Financial Management in the NHS: A Manager's Handbook. LC 93-34382. 1993. write for info. (*0-412-47320-8*, Chap & Hall NY) Chapman & Hall.

Mellett, J. S. Paleobiology of North American Hyaenodon (Mammalia Creodonta) Szalay, F. S., ed. (Contributions to Vertebrate Evolution Ser.: Vol. 1). 1977. 60.00 (*3-8055-2379-3*) S Karger.

Mellett, Jennifer. Texas Limitations Manual, 1987-1993. suppl. ed. 650p. 1993. 85.00 (*0-685-17764-5*) Butterworth Legal Pubs.

Mellett, Jennifer N. Texas Limitations Manual, 1987-1993. 650p. 1993. pap. 95.00 (*0-409-25254-9*) Michie Butterworth.

— Texas Personal Injury Law. 1020p. 1994. ring bd. 170.00 (*0-409-25659-5*) Michie Butterworth.

— Texas Probate Code Manual. 1200p. 1994. ring bd. 175.00 (*0-614-05979-8*) Michie Butterworth.

— Texas Probate Code Manual, 1984-1993, 2 vols. 1040p. 1991. ring bd. 135.00 (*0-409-26177-7*) Butterworth Legal Pubs.

— Texas Probate Code Manual, 1984-1993, 2 vols. suppl. ed. 1040p. 1993. 49.00 (*0-685-46136-X*) Butterworth Legal Pubs.

Mellett, Jennifer N., suppl. Texas Personal Injury Law, 1981-1992, 2 vols. 2nd suppl. ed. 1024p. 1993. 45.00 (*0-685-74466-3*) Butterworth Legal Pubs.

— Texas Personal Injury Law, 1981-1992, 2 vols., Set. 2nd ed. 1024p. ring bd. 170.00 (*0-409-25621-8*) Butterworth Legal Pubs.

Mellett, M. & Edwards, E., eds. Introduction to Accounting for the Banking Certificate. (C). 1989. 90.00 (*0-85297-274-1*, Pub. by Inst Bankers UK) St Mut.

Mellett, M., jt. ed. see Edwards, E.

Mellett, Peter. Mididictionary of Science. LC 92-40594. (C). 1993. write for info. (*0-19-211680-0*) OUP.

Mellett, Peter, ed. Learning & Psychosomatic Approach to the Nature & Treatment of Illness: 18th Annual Conference of the Society for Psychosomatic Research. 1977. pap. 53.00 (*0-08-020881-9*, Pergamon Pr) Elsevier.

Mellett, Peter & Rossiter, Jane. Air on the Move. LC 92-14719. (Science Through Cookery Ser.). (J). 1993. 13.23 (*0-531-14244-2*) Watts.

— Food Energy. LC 92-11238. (Science Through Cookery Ser.). (J). 1993. lib. bdg. 13.23 (*0-531-14247-7*) Watts.

— Hot & Cold. LC 92-5141. (Science Through Cookery Ser.). (Illus.). 32p. (J). (gr. 5-8). 1993. lib. bdg. 13.23 (*0-531-14236-1*) Watts.

— Liquids in Action. LC 92-7649. (Science Through Cookery Ser.). (Illus.). 32p. (J). (gr. 5-8). 1993. lib. bdg. 13.23 (*0-531-14235-3*) Watts.

Mellett, Peter, jt. ed. see Christie, Margaret.

Mellett, Peter G., jt. ed. see Christie, Margaret J.

Mellgren, ed. Intracellular Calcium Dependent Proteolipis. 1990. 190.00 (*0-8493-6570-8*, QP609) CRC Pr.

Mellgren, R. L., ed. Animal Cognition & Behavior. (Advances in Psychology Ser.: Vol. 13). 514p. 1983. 92.50 (*0-444-86627-2*, 1-122-83, North Holland) Elsevier.

Melli, P. & Brebbia, C. A., eds. Supercomputing in Engineering Structures. LC 88-63525. 305p. 1989. 72.00 (*0-945824-07-6*) Computational Mech MA.

Melli, P. & Zannetti, P., eds. Environmental Modelling. LC 91-73784. (Computational Engineering Ser.). 392p. 1992. 155.00 (*1-56252-053-9*) Computational Mech MA.

Mellichamp, Leslie. We Thought at Least the Roof Would Fall. LC 87-2231. (Illus.). 128p. (Orig.). 1987. pap. 5.95 (*0-936015-07-1*) Pocahontas Pr.

Mellick, Andrew D., Jr. The Story of an Old Farm: or Life in New Jersey in the Eighteenth Century. (Illus.). 778p. 1993. reprint ed. pap. text ed. 47.00 (*0-685-70375-4*) Heritage Bk.

— The Story of an Old Farm: Or Life in New Jersey in the 18th Century: With a Genealogical Appendix. 742p. 1991. reprint ed. lib. bdg. 75.00 (*0-8328-2248-5*) Higginson Bk Co.

Mellick, J. S. The Passing Guest: A Biography of Henry Kingsley. LC 83-3285. 350p. 1983. text ed. 35.00 (*0-312-59777-0*) St Martin.

Mellick, J. S., ed. see Kingsley, Henry.

Mellier, Y., et al, eds. Gravitational Lensing: Proceedings of a Workshop Held in Toulouse, France, September 13-15, 1989. (Lecture Notes in Physics, Monographs: Vol. 360). xv, 315p. 1990. 46.00 (*0-387-52648-X*) Spr-Verlag.

Mellin, Bob. Waterhole: How to Dig Your Own Well. LC 91-72454. (Illus.). 75p. (Orig.). 1992. pap. 8.95 (*0-935902-21-X*) Balboa Pub.

Mellin, Jeanne. Illustrated Horseback Riding for Beginners. pap. 5.00 (*0-87980-196-4*) Wilshire.

— The Morgan Horse. rev. ed. (Illus.). 288p. 1986. 19.95 (*0-8289-0590-8*) Viking Penguin.

— Morgan Horse Handbook. 1980. 10.95 (*0-8289-0390-5*) Viking Penguin.

Mellin, Laurel. Shapedown: Weight Management Program for Adolescents. 4th ed. LC 86-71125. (Illus.). 124p. (Orig.). 1987. Parent's Guide 124pp. 16.95 (*0-935902-09-0*); Instr's. Guide 288pp. teacher ed 29.95 (*0-935902-08-2*); Teen wkbk. 215pp. student ed 16.95 (*0-935902-07-4*) Balboa Pub.

Mellin, Laurel M. Shapedown: Weight Management Program for Children. LC 88-70316. (Illus.). 1989. 16.95 (*0-685-74220-2*) Balboa Pub.

An Asterisk (*) at the beginning of an entry indicates that the title is appearing in BIP for the first time.

— Shapedown: Weight Management Program for Children. 3rd ed. LC 88-70316. (Illus.). 216p. 1989. teacher ed 16. 95 (*0-935902-14-7*) Balboa Pub.

— Shapedown: Weight Management Program for Children, Level 1, Ages 6-8. 2nd ed. LC 88-70316. (Illus.). 138p. 1989. write for info. (*0-935902-15-5*) Balboa Pub.

— Shapedown: Weight Management Program for Children, Level 2, Ages 9-12. 3rd ed. LC 88-70316. (Illus.). 124p. 1989. write for info. (*0-935902-16-3*) Balboa Pub.

— Y. E. S.: Shapedown Youth Evaluation Scale. 2nd rev. ed. LC 86-71116. (Illus.). 269p. 1986. write for info. (*0-935902-10-4*) Balboa Pub.

Melling, D. J. Understanding Plato. (Illus.). 190p. 1987. pap. text ed. 13.95 (*0-19-289116-2*) OUP.

Melling, Frank. Complete Book of Motocross. 1987. 29.95 (*0-85429-473-2*, Pub. by G T Foulis Ltd) Haynes Pubns.

Melling, J. K. Discovering London's Guilds & Liveries. 1989. pap. 25.00 (*0-85263-971-6*, Pub. by Shire UK) St Mut.

***Melling, John K.** Murder Done to Death: Parody & Pastiche in Detective Fiction. LC 95-15442. 1995. write for info. (*0-8108-3034-5*) Scarecrow.

Melling, John K., jt. auth. see Dickson, Carter.

Melling, John K., jt. auth. see Messenger, Elizabeth.

Melling, Maggie, jt. auth. see Fritchie, Rennie.

Melling, Orla. The Druid's Tune. rev. ed. (Illus.). 195p. (J). (gr. 7 up). 1993. pap. 9.95 (*0-86278-285-6*, Pub. by OBrien Pr IE) Dufour.

Melling, P. J., jt. auth. see Marshall, A. R.

Melling, Phil & Roper, Jon. America, France & Vietnam: Cultural History & Ideas of Conflict. 250p. 1991. text ed. 63.95 (*1-85628-072-1*, Pub. by Avebury Pub UK) Ashgate Pub Co.

Melling, Philip H. Vietnam in American Literature: The Puritan Heritage. (Twayne's Literature & Society Ser.: No. 1). 256p. 1990. text ed. 20.95 (*0-8057-8850-6*, Pub. by Royal Botanic Garden UK) Macmillan.

Mellinger, George B., ed. Environmental & Waste Management Issues in the Ceramic Industry. LC 93-47662. (Ceramic Transactions Ser.: Vol. 39). 463p. 1994. 69.00 (*0-944904-71-8*, TRANS039) Am Ceramic.

Mellinger, J., ed. Animal Nutrition & Transport Processes, No. 1: Nutrition in Wild & Domestic Animals. (Comparative Physiology Ser.: Vol. 5). viii, 288p. 1990. 204.00 (*3-8055-5157-6*) S Karger.

Mellinger, Martha. Little Ones Praise. 1981. pap. 4.35 (*0-87813-518-9*) Christian Light.

***Mellinger, Philip J.** Race & Labor in Western Copper: The Fight for Equality, 1896-1918. LC 94-18730. 270p. 1995. 40.00x (*0-8165-1477-1*) U of Ariz Pr.

Mellinghoff, Tilman, jt. auth. see Watkin, David.

Mellink, Machteld J. A Hittite Cemetery at Gordion. LC 58-1735. (University of Pennsylvania, University Museum, Anthropological Publications). 130p. reprint ed. pap. 37.10 (*0-317-29808-9*, 2052012) Bks Demand.

Mellink, Machteld J., ed. Troy & the Trojan War: A Symposium Held at Bryn Mawr College, October 1984. (Bryn Mawr Archaeological Monographs). (Illus.). xii, 101p. (Orig.). (C). 1986. pap. text ed. 10.00 (*0-929524-59-4*) Bryn Mawr Commentaries.

Mellinkoff, David. The Conscience of a Lawyer. 304p. 1988. reprint ed. text ed. 20.00 (*0-314-28402-8*) West Pub.

— Dictionary of American Legal Usage. 708p. 1993. reprint ed. text ed. 39.95 (*0-314-00068-2*) West Pub.

— Dictionary of American Legal Usage. 703p. (C). 1993. reprint ed. pap. text ed. 24.00 (*0-314-01060-2*) West Pub.

— The Language of the Law. 526p. 1973. pap. 26.00 (*0-316-56627-6*) Little.

— Legal Writing: Sense & Nonsense. 242p. (C). 1991. reprint ed. pap. text ed. 18.00 (*0-314-63275-1*) West Pub.

Mellinkoff, Ruth. The Devil at Isenheim: Reflections of Popular Belief in Grunewald's Altarpiece. (Discovery Ser.: No. 1). 100p. 1988. 48.00 (*0-520-06204-3*) U CA Pr.

— The Horned Moses in Medieval Art & Thought. LC 77-85450. (California Studies in the History of Art: No. XIV). (Illus.). 1970. 47.50 (*0-520-01705-6*) U CA Pr.

— The Mark of Cain. LC 80-18589. (Quantum Bks.: No. 20). 128p. 1981. 32.00 (*0-520-03969-6*) U CA Pr.

— Outcasts: Signs of Otherness in Northern European Art of the Late Middle Ages, 2 vols. (California Studies in the History of Art: No. 32). 1994. 195.00 (*0-520-07815-2*) U CA Pr.

***Mellion, Morris B., ed.** Office Sports Medicine. 2nd ed. (Illus.). 400p. 1995. 47.00 (*1-56053-120-7*) Hanley & Belfus.

— Sports Medicine Secrets: Questions You Will Be Asked on Rounds, in the Clinic, & on Oral Exams. (Secrets Ser.). (Illus.). 450p. (Orig.). 1993. pap. text ed. 35.95 (*1-56053-074-X*) Hanley & Belfus.

Mellion, Morris B., jt. ed. see Kobayashi, Roger H.

Mellis, Charles J. Committed Communities: Fresh Streams for World Missions. LC 76-53548. 138p. reprint ed. pap. 6.95 (*0-87808-426-6*, WCL426-6) William Carey Lib.

Mellis, James & Thomaneck, J. K., eds. Politics, Government & Society in the German Democratic Republic: Basic Documents. 373p. 1989. 68.00 (*0-85496-247-6*) Berg Pubs.

Mellish. Evaluation of Clinical Nursing. 1987. 15.95 (*0-409-10256-3*) Buttrwrth-Heinemann.

— Introduction to Ethos of Nursing. 1989. pap. 19.95 (*0-409-10007-2*) Buttrwrth-Heinemann.

— Preparing the Nursing Assistant. 1991. 24.95 (*0-409-10918-5*) Buttrwrth-Heinemann.

Mellish & Brink. Teaching the Practice of Nursing. 3rd ed. 1991. pap. 34.95 (*0-409-11154-6*) Buttrwrth-Heinemann.

Mellish, C. S., jt. auth. see Clocksin, W. F.

Mellish, Chris, jt. ed. see Hallam, John.

Mellish, J. M. Basic History of Nursing. 2nd ed. 120p. 1990. pap. text ed. 19.95 (*0-409-10011-0*) Buttrwrth-Heinemann.

— Unit Teaching & Administration for Nurses. 2nd ed. (Illus.). 268p. 1988. pap. text ed. 34.95 (*0-409-11200-3*) Buttrwrth-Heinemann.

Mellish, Joseph, tr. see Schiller, Friedrich.

***Mellitt, B., et al, eds.** Computers in Railways IV Vol. 1: Railway Design & Management. LC 94-72459. (Comprail Ser.: Vol. 4). 1994. 226.00 (*1-56252-282-5*) Computational Mech MA.

— Computers in Railways IV Vol. 2: Railway Operations. LC 94-72459. (Comprail Ser.: Vol. 4). 1994. 193.00 (*1-56252-283-3*) Computational Mech MA.

Mellizo, Carlos. Una Cuestion de Tiempo: Relatos. LC 90-86071. (Coleccion Hispanica - Narrativa Ser.: No. 1). 93p. (Orig.). (SPA.). 1991. pap. 9.95 (*0-89729-591-9*) Ediciones.

— Historia de Sonia y Otras Historias. LC 87-70083. 104p. 1987. pap. 9.00 (*0-916950-74-3*) Biling Rev-Pr.

***Mellman, Martin, et al.** Accounting for Effective Decision Making: A Manager's Guide to Corporate, Financial & Cost Reporting. LC 94-3720. 650p. (C). 1994. text ed. 50.00 (*1-55623-066-4*) Irwin Prof Pubng.

Mello, J. M., jt. auth. see Hastings, N. A.

***Mello, Jeffrey A.** AIDS & the Law of Workplace Discrimination. LC 94-29703. (C). 1994. text ed. 54.00 (*0-8133-2295-2*) Westview.

Mello, M. Chaves de. Portuguese - English, English - Portuguese Legal Dictionary: Diccionario Juridico. 3rd ed. 515p. (ENG & POR.). 1987. pap. 95.00 (*0-8288-0401-X*, F51280) Fr & Eur.

Mello, Nancy K., ed. Advances in Substance Abuse, Vol. 4. 300p. (Orig.). 1991. 88.00 (*1-85302-080-X*, Pub. by J Kingsley Pubs UK) Taylor & Francis.

Mello, Nancy K., jt. ed. see Mendelson, Jack H.

Mello, Nancy K., jt. auth. see Mendelson, Jack.

Mello, P., jt. ed. see Lamma, E.

Mello, Robert A. The Last Stand of the Red Spruce. LC 87-82039. (Illus.). 199p. (Orig.). 1987. pap. 14.95 (*0-933280-37-8*) Island Pr.

Melloan, Maryanne. Rock & Roll Revealed: The Outrageous Lives of Rock's Biggest Stars. (Illus.). 120p. 1993. 14.98 (*0-8317-5159-2*) Smithmark.

Mellody, Peggy. The Los Angeles Food Guide: The Food Lover's Ultimate Resource. 256p. 1992. 14.00 (*0-517-57563-9*, C P Pubs) Crown Pub Group.

Mellody, Peggy, jt. auth. see Noyes, Diane D.

Mellody, Peggy, jt. auth. see Zimmerman, Linda.

Mellody, Pia. Breaking Free. 1989. pap. 16.00 (*0-06-250590-4*, PL) HarpC.

Mellody, Pia, et al. Facing Codependence: What It Is, Where It Comes from, How It Sabotages Our Lives. LC 88-45662. 224p. 1989. pap. 13.00 (*0-06-250589-0*) Harper SF.

— Facing Love Addiction: Giving Yourself the Power to Change the Way You Love. LC 91-55289. 192p. 1992. pap. 12.00 (*0-06-250604-8*) Harper SF.

Mellon. Storytelling & the Art of Imagination. 1992. pap. 13.95 (*1-85230-339-5*) Element MA.

Mellon, Andrew W. Taxation: The People's Business. LC 73-2521. (Big Business; Economic Power in a Free Society Ser.). 1973. reprint ed. 19.95 (*0-405-05101-8*) Ayer.

Mellon, Constance A. Bibliographic Instruction: The Second Generation. 204p. 1987. lib. bdg. 29.50 (*0-87287-563-6*) Libs Unl.

— Naturalistic Inquiry for Library Science: Methods & Applications for Researach, Evaluation & Teaching. LC 89-27276. (Contributions in Librarianship & Information Science Ser.: No. 64). 218p. 1990. text ed. 55.00 (*0-313-25653-5*, MNC/) Greenwood.

Mellon-Elibol, Patricia. Having a Baby in Your Forties: An Intimate, Touching Account of a Career Minded Woman Adjusting to Becoming a Mother. 128p. (Orig.). 1992. pap. 9.95 (*0-8119-0752-X*) LIFETIME.

Mellon Institute Staff. Influence of Solute Elements & Thermoelastic Martensites on the Strength & Super-Elasticity of Copper-Based Alloys. 64p. 1967. 9.60 (*0-317-34530-3*, 86) Intl Copper.

Mellon, James, ed. Bullwhip Days: The Slaves Remember. (Illus.). 480p. 1990. pap. 14.00 (*0-380-70884-1*) Avon.

***Mellon, John C.** Mark as a Recovery Story: Alcoholism & the Rhetoric of Gospel Mystery. LC 94-24082. 1995. write for info. (*0-252-02165-7*) U of Ill Pr.

Mellon, Kathy. Social Breakdown. 212p. (Orig.). 1990. pap. 9.95 (*0-935539-02-6*) Heroica Bks.

Mellon, Marget, jt. auth. see Rissler, Jane.

Mellon, Paul & Baskett, John. Reflections in a Silver Spoon: A Memoir. (Illus.). 440p. 1992. 27.00 (*0-688-09723-5*) Morrow.

Mellon, R. H. Larimer, McMasters & Allied Families. (Illus.). 196p. 1990. reprint ed. lib. bdg. 39.00 (*0-8328-1482-2*); reprint ed. pap. 31.00 (*0-8328-1483-0*) Higginson Bk Co.

***Mellon, Steve & Baker, Don.** Evansville - Then & Now. Baumann, J. Bruce, ed. (Illus.). 112p. 1995. text ed. 29. 95 (*1-884850-06-5*) Scripps Howard.

***Mellon, Steve & Noyes, Charlene.** Sacramento: Then & Now. Baumann, J. Bruce, ed. (Illus.). 128p. Date not set. 29.95 (*1-884850-04-9*) Scripps Howard.

***Mellon, Thomas.** Thomas Mellon & His Times. (Illus.). 560p. (C). 1995. pap. 22.95 (*0-8229-5572-5*) U of Pittsburgh Pr.

— Thomas Mellon & His Times. 2nd rev. ed. (Illus.). 536p. (C). 1994. 35.00 (*0-8229-3777-8*) U of Pittsburgh Pr.

Mellon, W. Giles, jt. auth. see Bernstein, Samuel J.

Mellone, Michael. The Cachet Identifier of U. S. Cacheted First Day Covers. (Illus.). 1977. pap. 6.95 (*0-89794-004-0*) FDC Pub.

— Mellone's Specialized Cachet Catalogue of First Day Covers of the 1940's, 2vols. 2nd ed. (Illus.). 1979. pap. 8.95 (*0-89794-019-9*) FDC Pub.

— Mellon's Specialized Cachet Catalog of First Day Covers of the 1950's, 2 vols. 1984. pap. 8.95 (*0-685-73681-4*); pap. 8.95 (*0-685-73682-2*) FDC Pub.

Mellone, Michael, ed. see Newton, Barry.

Mellone, Michael, jt. auth. see Planty, Earl.

Mellone, Michael, ed. see Roessler, A. C.

***Mellone, Michael A.** Scott 95 U. S. First Day Cover Catalogue & Checklist. 1994. pap. 6.95 (*0-89487-199-4*) Scott Pub Co.

Mellone, Sydney H. Western Christian Thought in the Middle Ages. 1977. lib. bdg. 250.00 (*0-8490-2816-7*) Gordon Pr.

Melloni, B. J. Illustrated Dictionary of Medicine: Diccionario de Medicina Ilustrado. (Illus.). 650p. (SPA.). 1982. 75.00 (*0-8288-1868-1*, S29945) Fr & Eur.

Melloni, B. J., et al. Anatomy & Physiology, 4 bks. 1971. 100.00 (*0-07-076420-4*); Bk. 1. text ed. 100.00 (*0-07-076421-2*); Bk. 2. text ed. 100.00 (*0-07-076422-0*); Bk. 3. text ed. 100.00 (*0-07-076423-9*); Bk. 4. text ed. 100.00 (*0-07-076424-7*) McGraw.

— Melloni's Illustrated Review of Human Anatomy. LC 65-11216. (Illus.). 268p. 1988. text ed. 24.50 (*0-397-50956-1*, Lippincott Medical) Lippincott.

Mellonie, Bryan & Ingpen, Robert. Lifetimes: The Beautiful Way to Explain Death to Children. 48p. 1983. pap. 9.95 (*0-553-34402-1*) Bantam.

Mellor, A. M. Design of Modern Turbine Combustors. (Combustion Ser.). 557p. 1990. text ed. 237.00 (*0-12-490055-0*) Acad Pr.

Mellor, Alec. Strange Masonic Stories. (Illus.). xii, 184p. 1985. pap. 11.95 (*0-88053-082-0*, M-313) Macoy Pub.

Mellor, Alfred, et al. Mellor Meigs & Howe: A Monograph of the Work of Mellor Meigs & Howe. LC 90-47377. (American Architectural Classics Ser.). (Illus.). 228p. 1992. reprint ed. 85.00 (*1-878650-01-7*) Archit CT.

Mellor, Allec. Dictionnaire de la Franc-Maconnerie et des Francs-Macons. 324p. (FRE.). 1989. reprint ed. pap. 49. 95 (*0-7859-4834-1*) Fr & Eur.

Mellor, Anne K. English Romantic Irony. LC 80-10687. 228p. (C). 1980. 25.50 (*0-674-25690-5*) HUP.

— Mary Shelley: Her Life, Her Fiction, Her Monsters. (Illus.). 350p. 1988. 35.00 (*0-415-02591-5*); pap. 14.95 (*0-415-90147-2*) Routledge.

— Romanticism & Gender. LC 92-22902. 256p. 1992. 45.00 (*0-415-90111-1*, A3136, Routledge NY); pap. 14.95 (*0-415-90664-4*, A7604, Routledge NY) Routledge.

Mellor, Anne K., ed. Romanticism & Feminism. LC 87-45406. 244p. 1988. 39.95 (*0-253-35083-2*); pap. 12.95 (*0-253-20462-3*, MB-462) Ind U Pr.

Mellor, Bernard. Lugard in Hong Kong: Empires, Education & a Governor at Work, 1907-1912. (Illus.). 232p. 1992. 68.50 (*962-209-316-7*, Pub. by Hong Kong Univ Pr HK) Coronet Bks.

— The University of Hong Kong: An Informal History, 2 vols., Set. (Illus.). 428p. 1980. 87.50 (*962-209-023-0*, Pub. by Hong Kong Univ Pr HK) Coronet Bks.

Mellor, Bernard, jt. auth. see Blunden, Edmund C.

Mellor, Bernard, jt. auth. see Blunden, Edmund.

Mellor, Constance. How to Be Healthy, Wealthy & Wise. 112p. (C). 1976. pap. 8.95 (*0-8464-1023-0*) Beekman Pubs.

— Natural Remedies for Common Ailments. 134p. 1980. 17. 95 (*0-8464-1073-7*) Beekman Pubs.

Mellor, Corinne. Clark the Toothless Shark: A Pop-up Pull-Tab Book. (Illus.). 20p. (J). (ps-3). 1994. 14.95 (*0-307-17606-1*, Artsts Writrs) Western Pub.

***Mellor, D. H.** The Facts of Causation. 256p. 1995. 39.95 (*0-415-09779-7*, B3181) Routledge.

— The Matter of Chance. LC 70-152629. 203p. reprint ed. pap. 57.90 (*0-317-27988-2*, 2025592) Bks Demand.

Mellor, D. H., ed. Prospects for Pragmatism. 270p. 1981. 44.95 (*0-521-22548-5*) Cambridge U Pr.

— Science, Belief & Behavior. LC 79-41614. (Illus.). 240p. 1980. 47.95 (*0-521-22960-X*) Cambridge U Pr.

Mellor, David. A Paradise Lost: The Neo-Romantic Imagination In. (Illus.). 144p. (C). 1987. reprint ed. pap. 45.00 (*0-85331-532-9*, Pub. by Lund Humphries UK) Antique Collect.

— The Sixties Art Scene in London. (Illus.). 240p. (C). 1993. pap. 35.00 (*0-7148-2910-2*, Pub. by Phaidon Press UK) Chronicle Bks.

***Mellor, David & Garner, Philippe.** Cecil Beaton: Photographs 1920-1970. (Illus.). 320p. Date not set. 75. 00 (*0-8212-2180-9*) Bulfinch Pr.

***Mellor, David A.** Arthur Tress: Requiem for a Paperweight. Glenn, Constance W., ed. & intro. by. (Illus.). 16p. (Orig.). 1994. pap. 10.00 (*0-936270-33-0*) CA St U LB Art.

***Mellor, David Allan.** David Levinthal: Dark Light--Photographs 1984-1994. (Illus.). 48p. 1995. pap. 17.50 (*0-907879-43-8*) Dist Art Pubs.

Mellor, David H. Matters of Metaphysics. (Illus.). 328p. (C). 1991. 54.95 (*0-521-41117-3*) Cambridge U Pr.

Mellor, David H., ed. Ways of Communicating: The Darwin College Lectures, 1989. (Illus.). 208p. (C). 1991. 32.95 (*0-521-37074-4*) Cambridge U Pr.

***Mellor, Don.** Climbing in the Adirondacks: A Guide to Rock & Ice Routes. 3rd ed. (Illus.). 320p. Date not set. pap. 24.95 (*0-935272-79-8*) ADK Mtn Club.

— Climbing in the Adirondacks: A Guide to Rock & Ice Routes in Adirondack Park. (Illus.). 240p. (Orig.). 1986. pap. 15.95 (*0-685-11832-0*) Lake Placid Climb.

— Climbing in the Adirondacks: A Guide to Rock & Ice Routes in Adirondack Park. suppl. ed. (Illus.). 240p. (Orig.). 1986. Supplement. 4.50 (*0-9615992-1-9*) Lake Placid Climb.

Mellor, Eloise. Youth: Open the Door. 1969. 5.00 (*0-685-01385-5*); pap. 3.00 (*0-87516-114-6*) DeVorss.

Mellor, Grant. Flying Tinsel. (Illus.). 136p. (J). (gr. 5-8). 1993. pap. text ed. 12.95 (*0-938587-33-1*) Cuisenaire.

Mellor, Helen. Patrick Geddes: Social Evolutionist & City Planner. (Geography, Environment & Planning Ser.). 384p. 1990. 79.95 (*0-415-00938-3*, A4098) Routledge.

Mellor, J. D. Fundamentals of Freeze Drying. 1979. text ed. 184.00 (*0-12-490050-X*) Acad Pr.

Mellor, J. E. Falconry Notes by Mellor. 1972. 15.00 (*0-914802-07-0*) Falcon Head Pr.

Mellor, James, jt. auth. see Kitchin, David.

Mellor, Joanna, jt. auth. see Rzetelny, Harriet.

Mellor, John. The Art of Pilotage. (Illus.). 192p. 1990. 27.50 (*0-924486-04-X*) Sheridan.

— Boat Handling under Power. (Illus.). 190p. 1993. pap. 16. 50 (*0-924486-43-0*) Sheridan.

— Cruising Skipper. 96p. (C). 1990. text ed. 59.00 (*0-906754-71-2*, Pub. by Fernhurst Bks UK) St Mut.

— Log Book for Cruising under Sail. 96p. (C). 1990. text ed. 59.00 (*0-906754-62-3*, Pub. by Fernhurst Bks UK) St Mut.

— The Sailing Cruiser Manual. (Illus.). 196p. 1989. 26.50 (*0-911378-87-1*) Sheridan.

— A Small Boat Guide to the Rules of the Road: The Collision Regulations Simplified. 64p. (C). 1990. text ed. 59.00 (*0-906754-54-2*, Pub. by Fernhurst Bks UK) St Mut.

— Young Crew. (Illus.). 165p. 1994. pap. 19.95 (*1-85310-373-X*) Voyageur Pr.

Mellor, John W. Economics of Agricultural Development. LC 66-19491. (Illus.). 418p. 1970. pap. 16.95 (*0-8014-9102-9*) Cornell U Pr.

— The New Economics of Growth: A Strategy for India & the Developing World. (Twentieth Century Fund Study Ser.). 350p. 1976. pap. 16.95 (*0-8014-9188-6*) Cornell U Pr.

***Mellor, John W., ed.** Agriculture on the Road to Industrialization. (International Food Policy Research Institute Ser.). 488p. 1994. text ed. 57.50x (*0-8018-5012-6*) Johns Hopkins.

Mellor, John W. & Ahmed, Raisuddin, eds. Agricultural Price Policy for Developing Countries. LC 87-26862. 352p. 1988. text ed. 35.00 (*0-8018-3586-0*) Johns Hopkins.

Mellor, John W. & Desai, Gunvant M., eds. Agricultural Change & Rural Poverty: Variations on a Theme by Dharm Narain. LC 85-50. 256p. 1985. 28.50 (*0-8018-3275-6*) Johns Hopkins.

Mellor, John W., jt. auth. see Desai, Bhupat M.

Mellor, John W., et al, eds. Accelerating Food Production in Sub-Saharan Africa. LC 86-10684. 448p. 1987. text ed. 39.50 (*0-8018-3390-6*) Johns Hopkins.

Mellor, M. Joanna, jt. ed. see Getzel, George S.

Mellor, M. Joanna, jt. ed. see Getzel, George.

Mellor, Mary. Breaking the Boundaries: Towards a Feminist Green Socialism. 308p. 1993. pap. 15.95 (*1-85381-200-5*, Pub. by Virago Pr UK) Trafalgar.

Mellor, Mary, et al. Worker Cooperatives in Theory & Practice. 192p. 1988. 90.00 (*0-335-15863-3*, Open Univ Pr); pap. 32.00 (*0-335-15862-5*, Open Univ Pr) Taylor & Francis.

Mellor, Ronald. Tacitus. LC 92-10601. 1992. 25.00 (*0-415-90665-2*, A7603, Routledge NY) Routledge.

— Tacitus. 200p. 1994. pap. 16.95 (*0-415-91002-1*, B4411) Routledge.

Mellor, Ronald, ed. From Augustus to Nero: The First Dynasty of Imperial Rome. LC 88-42899. (Illus.). 435p. (C). 1990. 20.00 (*0-87013-281-4*) Mich St U Pr.

— Tacitus: The Classical Heritage. LC 95-6076. (Classical Heritage & Garland Reference Library of the Humanities: No. 1633). 1995. write for info. (*0-8153-0933-3*) Garland.

Mellor, Roy. Nation, State & Territory: A Political Geography. 224p. 1989. 49.50 (*0-415-02287-8*) Routledge.

Mellor, Roy & Smith, E. Alistair. Europe: A Geographical Survey of the Continent. LC 78-10171. (Illus.). 208p. 1979. text ed. 40.50 (*0-231-04708-8*) Col U Pr.

Mellor, Stephen, jt. auth. see Therriault, Daniel.

Mellor, Stephen J. & Shalaer, Sally. Object Life Cycles: Modeling the World in States. 288p. 1991. pap. text ed. 40.00 (*0-13-629940-7*) P-H.

Mellor, Stephen J. & Shlaer, Sally. Object Oriented Systems Analysis: Modeling the World in Data. (Illus.). 192p. (C). 1988. pap. text ed. 44.00 (*0-13-629023-X*) P-H.

Mellor, Stephen J., jt. auth. see Ward, Paul T.

Mellor, Stuart, jt. auth. see Read, Michael D.

Mellor, Tony, jt. auth. see Ellis, Steve.

Mellors, Colin, jt. auth. see Copperthwaite, Nigel.

Mellors, Colin, et al. Directory of Language Training & Services for Business: A Guide to Resources in Further & Higher Education. 500p. 1993. 74.50 (*0-415-09998-6*, B2530) Routledge.

Mellos, Koula. Perspectives on Ecology: A Critical Essay. LC 88-18183. 140p. 1988. text ed. 39.95 (*0-312-02417-7*) St Martin.

Mellott, Douglas W., Jr. Marketing: Principles & Practices. (Illus.). 1978. teacher ed write for info. (*0-318-55518-2*, Reston) P-H.

— New Product Planning Management of the Marketing-R & D Interface: An Annotated Bibliography. LC 76-57928. (American Marketing Association Bibliography Ser.: No. 26). 51p. reprint ed. pap. 25.00 (*0-317-20071-2*, 2023353) Bks Demand.

Mellott, Jack. West Virginia University. (Illus.). 112p. 1987. 37.50 (*0-916509-13-3*) Harmony Hse Pub LO.

Mellott, Jack, photos. Historic Ships of America. (Illus.). 216p. 1995. 49.95 (*0-943231-44-2*) Howell Pr VA.

— Northwestern University. (First Edition Ser.). (Illus.). 112p. 1988. 39.00 (*0-916509-46-X*) Harmony Hse Pub LO.

Mellott, Richard, jt. auth. see Woodson, Yoko.

Mellow, James R. Hemingway: A Life Without Consequences. (Illus.). 720p. 1993. pap. 16.35 (*0-201-62620-9*) Addison-Wesley.

— Hemingway: A Life Without Consequences. (Illus.). 576p. 1992. 30.00 (*0-395-37777-3*) HM.

***Mellowe, Clancey & Spiezio, E. A.** A Symphony of Love. 168p. 1994. 16.95 (*1-57087-059-4*) Prof Pr NC.

Mellown, Elgin W. A Descriptive Catalogue of the Bibliographies of Twentieth Century British Poets, Novelists & Dramatists. 2nd enl. rev. ed. LC 79-193301. 414p. 1978. 22.50 (*0-87875-137-8*) Whitston Pub.

Mellown, Elgin W., jt. auth. see Hoy, Peter C.

Mellown, Robert. The University of Alabama: A Guide to the Campus. LC 87-26205. (Illus.). 128p. 1988. pap. 8.50 (*0-8173-0395-2*) U of Ala Pr.

Mellows, A. R. Taxation for Executors & Trustees. 7th ed. 1993. U.K. pap. 101.00 (*0-406-62401-1*) Butterworth Legal Pubs.

Mellows, Clayton R. Absenteeism, Work Loss & Illness Behavior: Medical Analysis Index with Reference Bibliography. LC 85-47855. 150p. 1987. 39.50 (*0-88164-384-X*); pap. 34.50 (*0-88164-385-8*) ABBE Pubs Assn.

— Behavioral Sciences: Research & Subject Analysis with Reference Bibliography. LC 85-48099. 150p. 1987. 44.50 (*0-88164-470-6*); pap. 39.50 (*0-88164-471-4*) ABBE Pubs Assn.

— Health Insurance for Aged & Disabled, Title 18: Index of Modern Information. LC 88-47572. 150p. 1988. 39.50 (*0-88164-824-8*); pap. 34.50 (*0-88164-825-6*) ABBE Pubs Assn.

— Sex Counseling - Guidelines, Assessment & Treatment: Index of Modern Authors & Subjects with Guide for Rapid Research. LC 90-56284. 160p. 1991. 44.50 (*1-55914-350-9*); pap. 39.50 (*1-55914-351-7*) ABBE Pubs Assn.

— Workman's Compensation: Index of Modern Information. LC 88-47986. 150p. 1989. 44.50 (*1-55914-064-X*); pap. 39.50 (*1-55914-065-8*) ABBE Pubs Assn.

Mellows, F. Russellism: The Latest Blasphemy: Millions-Now-Living-Will-Never-Die-Ism. 23p. 1988. reprint ed. pap. 1.95 (*1-883858-50-X*) Witness CA.

Mellows, Joan. A Different World. large type ed. 1989. 17.95 (*0-7089-2077-2*) Ulverscroft.

— The Marriage Trap. large type ed. 455p. 1989. 17.95 (*0-7089-1935-9*) Ulverscroft.

Mellows, Mary. A Lamp for Orchid. 126p. 1986. pap. 22.00 (*0-7223-1987-8*, Pub. by A H S Ltd UK) St Mut.

Melloy, Kristine J., jt. auth. see Zirpoli, Thomas J.

Mellstrom. Protective Gloves for Occupational Use. 1994. 99.95 (*0-8493-7359-X*, RL244) CRC Pr.

Melluish, T. W., jt. auth. see Kinchin Smith, F.

Melluish, T. W., jt. auth. see Smith, F. K.

Melly, Brian W. Comparison of Several Computer Hydraulics Programs for the IBM PC & Compatibles. 1987. 7.50 (*0-318-23463-7*, TR87-1) Society Fire Protect.

Melly, Diana, ed. see Rhys, Jean.

Melly, George. Paris & the Surrealists. LC 90-72121. (Illus.). 160p. 1992. pap. 22.50 (*0-500-27638-2*) Thames Hudson.

— Towards Laughter: Paintings by Maggi Hambling. (Illus.). 64p. (C). 1993. pap. 27.50 (*0-85331-647-3*, Pub. by Lund Humphries UK) Antique Collect.

Melly, George, jt. contrib. see Gooding, Mel.

Melly, Peter J., jt. auth. see Ringerbach, Paul T.

***Melmad, Laura K.** The First Song Ever Sung. LC 94-44591. (Illus.). (J). 1995. 5.99 (*0-14-055457-2*) Puffin Bks.

Melman, A. G. & Woudstra, N. Solid Oxide Fuel Cell Systems Study, Vol. 2. 288p. 1991. pap. 35.00 (*92-826-1962-1*, CD-NB-13103-EN-C) UNIPUB.

Melman, Billie. Women & the Popular Imagination in the Twenties: Flappers & Nymphs. LC 87-4652. 208p. 1988. text ed. 35.00 (*0-312-00744-2*) St Martin.

— Women's Orients: English Women & the Middle East, 1718-1918 Sexuality, Religion & Work. 440p. 1995. pap. text ed. 16.95x (*0-472-08279-5*) U of Mich Pr.

— Women's Orients: Englishwomen & the Middle East, 718-1918 Sexuality, Religion & Work. LC 91-32433. 440p. (C). 1992. text ed. 39.50 (*0-472-10332-6*) U of Mich Pr.

Melman, Steven A., et al. Skin Diseases of Dogs & Cats: A Guide for Pet Owners & Professionals. LC 94-94063. 250p. 1994. pap. 29.99 (*0-9640295-0-2*) DermaPet.

***Melman, Y.** The New Israelis. 1994. pap. 4.99 (*0-517-13188-9*) Random.

Melman, Yossi. The Master Terrorist: The True Story Behind Abu Nidal. Himmelstein, Shmuel, tr. LC 86-10820. 216p. 1986. 16.95 (*0-915361-52-3*) Modan-Adama Bks.

— The Master Terrorist: The True Story Behind Abu-Nidal. 296p. 1987. pap. 3.95 (*0-380-70428-5*) Avon.

— The New Israelis: An Intimate View of a Changing People. 320p. 1992. 19.95 (*1-55972-129-4*, Birch Ln Pr) Carol Pub Group.

Melman, Yossi & Raviv, Dan. Behind the Uprising: Israelis, Jordanians, & Palestinians. LC 89-7486. (Contributions in Political Science Ser.: No. 238). 264p. 1989. text ed. 55.00 (*0-313-26787-1*, MBU/, Greenwood Pr) Greenwood.

— Friends in Deed: Inside the U. S.-Israel Alliance. LC 93-42416. (Illus.). 560p. 1995. pap. 14.95 (*0-7868-8090-2*) Hyperion.

Melman, Yossi, jt. auth. see Raviv, Dan.

Melmed. The Pituitary. (Illus.). 800p. 1994. 150.00 (*0-86542-126-9*) Blackwell Sci.

Melmed, Laura. The Rainbabies. LC 91-16877. (Illus.). 32p. (J). (gr. 1 up). 1992. 15.00 (*0-688-10755-9*); lib. bdg. 14.93 (*0-688-10756-7*) Lothrop.

Melmed, Laura K. First Song Ever Sung. LC 91-28528. (J). (ps-3). 1993. 16.00 (*0-688-08230-0*); lib. bdg. 15.93 (*0-688-08231-9*) Lothrop.

— I Love You As Much... LC 92-27677. (Illus.). (J). 1993. write for info. (*0-688-11718-X*); lib. bdg. write for info. (*0-688-11719-8*) Lothrop.

— Prince Nautilus. LC 93-37432. (Illus.). (J). 1994. write for info. (*0-688-04566-9*); lib. bdg. write for info. (*0-688-04567-7*) Lothrop.

Melmed-Sanjak, Jolyne, et al, eds. Recovery or Relapse in the Global Economy: Comparative Perspectives on Restructuring in Central America. LC 93-17117. 256p. 1993. text ed. 57.95 (*0-275-94605-3*, C4605, Praeger Pubs) Greenwood.

Melmed, Schlomo, jt. ed. see Robbins, R. J.

Melmed, Shlomo, ed. Molecular & Clinical Advances in Pituitary Disorders - 11993: Proceedings of the 3rd International Pituitary Congress. 400p. 1993. pap. 30.00 (*0-9637943-0-2*) Endocrine Res.

Melmon, Kenneth L., et al. Melmon & Morrelli's Clinical Pharmacology: Basic Principles in Therapeutics. 3rd ed. (Illus.). 1141p. 1992. pap. text ed. 57.00 (*0-07-105385-9*) Hlth Prof Div.

Melmon, Kenneth L., et al, eds. Clinical Pharmacology. 3rd ed. 1991. 79.51 (*0-08-040305-0*, Pub. by PPI UK); pap. 42.51 (*0-08-040644-0*, Pub. by PPI UK) McGraw.

Melmoth, Sebastian. Degas. 1993. 5.98 (*1-55521-826-1*) Bk Sales Inc.

— Egon Schiele. 1994. 5.98 (*0-7858-0208-8*) Bk Sales Inc.

— Klimt. 1994. 5.98 (*0-7858-0211-8*) Bk Sales Inc.

Melnechuk, Theodore, jt. ed. see Baxter, Claude F.

Melnick. Old Testament. (Book Notes Ser.). (C). 1985. pap. 2.50 (*0-8120-3531-3*) Barron.

Melnick, Arthur. Space, Time, & Thought in Kant. (C). 1989. lib. bdg. 137.00 (*0-7923-0135-8*) Kluwer Ac.

Melnick, Ben. LAN Administrator Handbook. Rinzler, Alan & Gancher, David, eds. (Illus.). 188p. 1991. pap. 18.95 (*0-9627212-1-2*) Computer CA.

Melnick, Ben, jt. auth. see Garwood, Anne.

Melnick, Daniel C. Fullness of Dissonance: Modern Fiction & the Aesthetics of Music. LC 93-8332. 1994. write for info. (*0-8386-3525-3*) Fairleigh Dickinson.

Melnick, Gregory. Icon Painter's Notebook: An Anthology of Source Materials. 1994. write for info. (*0-87903-819-5*) Oakwood Pubns.

***Melnick, Gregory, ed. & tr.** Iconographer's Sketchbook, Vol. 2. (Tyulin Collection). 250p. 1995. per. 14.95 (*1-879038-22-6*) Oakwood Pubns.

Melnick, J. L., ed. Enteric Viruses in Water. (Monographs in Virology: Vol. 15). (Illus.). x, 238p. 1984. 131.25 (*3-8055-3803-0*) S Karger.

— Progress in Medical Virology, Vol. 12. 1970. 69.00 (*3-8055-0409-8*) S Karger.

— Progress in Medical Virology, Vol. 13. 1971. 88.00 (*3-8055-1181-7*) S Karger.

— Progress in Medical Virology, Vol. 14. 1972. 76.00 (*3-8055-1291-0*) S Karger.

— Progress in Medical Virology, Vol. 16. (Illus.). 1973. 78.50 (*3-8055-1601-0*) S Karger.

— Progress in Medical Virology, Vol. 17. 400p. 1974. 78.50 (*3-8055-1642-8*) S Karger.

— Progress in Medical Virology, Vol. 20. (Illus.). 400p. 1975. 79.25 (*3-8055-2161-8*) S Karger.

— Progress in Medical Virology, Vol. 22. 250p. 1976. 95.25 (*3-8055-2315-7*) S Karger.

— Progress in Medical Virology, Vol. 23. (Illus.). 1977. 88.00 (*3-8055-2423-4*) S Karger.

— Progress in Medical Virology, Vol. 24. (Illus.). 1978. 86.50 (*3-8055-2810-8*) S Karger.

— Progress in Medical Virology, Vol. 25. (Illus.). 1979. 71.75 (*3-8055-2978-3*) S Karger.

— Progress in Medical Virology, Vol. 26. (Illus.). viii, 240p. 1980. 119.25 (*3-8055-0702-X*) S Karger.

— Progress in Medical Virology, Vol. 28. (Illus.). x, 234p. 1982. 118.50 (*3-8055-2983-X*) S Karger.

— Progress in Medical Virology, Vol. 29. (Illus.). x, 246p. 1984. 118.50 (*3-8055-3618-6*) S Karger.

— Progress in Medical Virology, Vol. 31. (Illus.). x, 234p. 1984. 131.25 (*3-8055-3909-6*) S Karger.

— Progress in Medical Virology, Vol. 33. (Illus.). viii, 182p. 1986. 119.25 (*3-8055-4155-4*) S Karger.

— Progress in Medical Virology, Vol. 34. (Illus.). x, 206p. 1987. 138.50 (*3-8055-4468-5*) S Karger.

— Progress in Medical Virology, Vol. 35. (Illus.). viii, 220p. 1988. 159.25 (*3-8055-4711-0*) S Karger.

— Progress in Medical Virology, Vol. 36. (Illus.). viii, 210p. 1989. 151.25 (*3-8055-4834-6*) S Karger.

— Progress in Medical Virology, Vol. 39. (Illus.). x, 270p. 1992. 213.00 (*3-8055-5428-1*) S Karger.

— Progress in Medical Virology, Vol. 40. (Illus.). viii, 224p. 1993. 212.00 (*3-8055-5600-4*) S Karger.

— Viruses, Oncogenes & Cancer. (Progress in Medical Virology Ser.: Vol. 32). (Illus.). viii, 224p. 1985. 134.50 (*3-8055-3976-2*) S Karger.

Melnick, J. L. & Hummeler, K., eds. Progress in Medical Virology, Vol. 30. (Illus.). viii, 212p. 1984. 124.00 (*3-8055-3851-0*) S Karger.

Melnick, J. L. & Khan, N. C., eds. Human Immunodeficiency Virus: Innovative Techniques for Isolation & Identification of HIV & for Monitoring of AIDS Patients. (Monographs in Virology: Vol. 18). viii, 130p. 1990. 107.25 (*3-8055-5182-7*) S Karger.

Melnick, J. L. & Maupas, P., eds. Hepatitis B Virus & Primary Liver Cancer. (Progress in Medical Virology Ser.: Vol. 27). (Illus.). viii, 212p. 1981. 100.00 (*3-8055-1784-X*) S Karger.

Melnick, J. L., ed. see Becker, I.

Melnick, J. L., ed. see Hotchin, J.

Melnick, J. L., ed. see Lonberg-Holm, K. & Philipson, L.

Melnick, J. L., ed. see Tinsley, T. W. & Harrap, K. A.

Melnick, Joseph L., ed. Progress in Medical Virology, Vol. 37. (Illus.). x, 250p. 1990. 181.75 (*3-8055-5077-4*) S Karger.

Melnick, Joseph L., ed. see International Congress for Virology Staff.

Melnick, Joseph L., jt. ed. see Ras, V. Shalapati.

Melnick, Michael & Jorgenson, Ronald, eds. Developmental Aspects of Craniofacial Dysmorphology. LC 79-2487. (Alan R. Liss Ser.: Vol. 15, No. 8). 1979. 19.00 (*0-685-42252-6*) March of Dimes.

Melnick, Michael, et al, eds. Clinical Dysmorphology of Oral-Facial Structures. LC 81-19816. 543p. reprint ed. pap. 154.80 (*0-8357-7871-1*, 2036288) Bks Demand.

Melnick, Mimi. Manhole Covers. (Illus.). 272p. 1994. 39.95x (*0-262-13302-4*) MIT Pr.

Melnick, R. Shep. Between the Lines: Interpreting Welfare Rights. 344p. (C). 1994. 36.95 (*0-8157-5664-X*); pap. 16.95 (*0-8157-5663-1*) Brookings.

— Regulation & the Courts: The Case of the Clean Air Act. LC 83-7694. 404p. 1983. 36.95 (*0-8157-5662-3*); pap. 16.95 (*0-8157-5661-5*) Brookings.

Melnick, Sharon, jt. ed. see Beilenson, Evelyn L.

Melnick, V. & Dubler, N., eds. Alzheimer's Dementia: Dilemmas in Clinical Research. LC 85-11740. (Contemporary Issues in Biomedicine, Ethics, & Society Ser.). 344p. 1985. 49.50 (*0-89603-067-9*) Humana.

Melnicoe, William B. & Mennig, Jan. Elements of Police Supervision. 2nd ed. 336p. (C). 1978. text ed. write for info. (*0-02-476000-5*) Macmillan.

Melnicove, Bettye F. The New Webster's Crossword Puzzle Dictionary. 1985. mass mkt. 4.99 (*0-449-20896-6*, Crest) Fawcett.

Melnik, Jan. How to Open & Operate a Home-Based Secretarial Services Business: An Unabridged Guide. unabridged ed. LC 93-42697. 224p. 1994. pap. 14.95 (*1-56440-398-X*) Globe Pequot.

Melnik, Peg, jt. auth. see Fish, Tim.

Melnik, Y. P., ed. Precambrian Banded Iron Formations: Physicochemical Conditions of Formations. (Developments in Precambrian Geology Ser.: Vol. 5). 310p. 1982. 105.25 (*0-444-41934-9*) Elsevier.

Melnikoff, Pamela. The Star & the Sword. LC 94-5813. (Illus.). 140p. (J). (gr. 3 up). 1994. 8.95 (*0-8276-0528-5*) JPS Phila.

Melnikoff, Tatyana, ed. see Wakoski, Diane, et al.

Melnikov, G. P. Systemology & Linguistic Aspects of Cybernetics. (Studies in Cybernetics: Vol. 16). 456p. 1988. text ed. 326.00 (*2-88124-665-6*) Gordon & Breach.

Mel'nikov, N. P. Engineering Design & Structural Analysis of Nuclear Reactors. 592p. 1967. text ed. 138.00 (*0-7065-0426-7*, Pub. by Keter Pub IS) Coronet Bks.

Melnikova-Levigne, Sonia, jt. auth. see Soltes, Ori Z.

***Melnuczuk, Askold.** What Is Told. 216p. 1995. pap. 11.95 (*0-571-19865-1*) Faber & Faber.

Melnychuk, Taras. From Behind Prison Bars. LC 82-50025. (Ukrainian Ser.). 83p. 1982. pap. 3.25 (*0-914834-48-7*) Smoloskyp.

Melnyczuk, Askold. What Is Told: A Novel. LC 93-42837. 216p. 1994. 21.95 (*0-571-19830-9*) Faber & Faber.

Melnyczuk, Askold, ed. Agni: Issue Focuses on State Control & the Arts. 322p. (C). 1990. write for info. (*0-318-66933-1*) New Cambrdge.

— Agni: The Used World. 312p. (Orig.). (C). 1989. pap. write for info. (*0-318-66934-X*) New Cambrdge.

Melnyk & Narasimhan. Computer Integrated Manufacturing: A Source Book. 344p. 1990. 49.95 (*1-55822-051-8*) Am Prod & Inventory.

***Melnyk, George.** Beyond Alienation: Political Essays on the West. 122p. (Orig.). 1993. pap. text ed. 13.95x (*1-55059-060-X*) Temeron Bks.

Melnyk-Limnychenko, Vasyl. W zatyshnim tsarstvi moikh dum: Vybrani Tvory. (Ukrainian Ser.). 261p. 1983. pap. 20.00 (*0-317-17114-3*) Slavia Lib.

Melnyk, Steven A. & Carter, Phillip L. Production Activity Control: A Practical Guide. (APICS Series in Production Management). 200p. 1987. text ed. 45.00 (*0-87094-970-5*) Irwin Prof Pubng.

— Shop Floor Control Principles & Practices & Case Studies. LC 87-72180. 535p. 1987. pap. text ed. 60.00 (*0-935406-95-6*) Am Prod & Inventory.

Melnyk, Steven A., et al. Shop Floor Control. LC 85-70568. 1985. 45.00 (*0-87094-628-5*) Irwin Prof Pubng.

Melo, L. F., et al, eds. Biofilms - Science & Technology. LC 92-34848. (NATO Advanced Study Institutes Series E, Applied Sciences: Vol. 223). 1992. lib. bdg. 262.00 (*0-7923-2022-0*) Kluwer Ac.

— Fouling Science & Technology. (C). 1988. lib. bdg. 251.50 (*90-247-3729-X*) Kluwer Ac.

Meloan, Becky, jt. auth. see Bryant, Kim.

Meloan, Clifton E. Instrumental Analysis Using Spectroscopy. LC 68-20179. (Medical Technology Ser.: No. 1). 178p. reprint ed. pap. 50.80 (*0-317-09062-3*, 2050349) Bks Demand.

Meloan, Clifton E., jt. auth. see Pomeranz, Yeshajahu.

Meloan, Taylor W. & Graham, John L., eds. International & Global Marketing: Concepts & Cases. LC 94-17867. (Series in Marketing). 640p. (C). 1994. 34.95 (*0-256-15723-5*) Irwin.

Melocarro, Lynne, ed. see Johnson, Samuel & Knight, Ellis C.

Meloche, Joseph. Introductory CD ROM Searching: The Key to Effective Ondisc Searching. LC 92-44616. (Illus.). 175p. 1994. lib. bdg. 39.95 (*1-56024-412-7*) Haworth Pr.

Melodia, Thomas V., jt. auth. see Malinowski, Stanley B.

***Melody, A. Love Is in the Earth - A Kaleidoscope of Crystals Update: The Reference Book Describing the Metaphysical Properties of the Mineral Kingdom. Jackson, R. R., ed. LC 94-61710. (Illus.). 728p. (Orig.). 1995. pap. 18.95 (*0-9628190-3-4*) Earth-Love Pub Hse.**

LOVE IS IN THE EARTH - A KALEIDOSCOPE OF CRYSTALS UPDATE, by Melody is the update of her first book LOVE IS IN THE EARTH - A KALEIDOSCOPE OF CRYSTALS & a sequel to LOVE IS IN THE EARTH - LAYING-ON-OF-STONES (a working-manual) & LOVE IS IN THE EARTH - MINERALOGICAL PICTORIAL (which contains 984 full colour photographs of the minerals discussed in the previous books). Released January 13, 1995, this UPDATED! REFERENCE book (over 700 pages) describes the metaphysical properties of the mineral kingdom, & supplies geologic, scientific, & metaphysical information for the major population of the mineral kingdom. It is designed as a comprehensive encyclopediae, alphabetized & indexed, addressing the properties of OVER 800 UNIQUE MINERALS & OVER 45 CONFIGURATIONS OF QUARTZ CRYSTAL, it includes "new" minerals discussed in LOVE IS IN THE EARTH - LAYING-ON-OF-STONES or photographed &/or included in LOVE IS IN THE EARTH - MINERALOGICAL PICTORIAL. It further provides definitions of terminology, astrological sign indications for each mineral, & the numerological vibratory rate for each mineral. The originally published edition was known as THE GRANDMASTER OF CRYSTAL BOOKS & THE FINAL WORD IN CRYSTAL BOOKS TO DATE. All LOVE IS IN THE EARTH... books may be ordered from distributors only. ***Publisher Provided Annotation.***

— Love Is in the Earth - Laying-on-the-Stones: The Journey Continues. Jackson, R. R. & Augustine, L., eds. LC 91-771320. (Illus.). 273p. (Orig.). 1992. pap. 12.95 (*0-9628190-1-8*) Earth-Love Pub Hse.

— Love Is in the Earth - Mineralogical Pictorial: Treasures of the Earth. Jackson, Bob, ed. LC 93-73772. (Illus.). 416p. (Orig.). 1994. pap. 27.95 (*0-9628190-2-6*) Earth-Love Pub Hse.

Melody, David, tr. see Bak, Samuel.

Melody, Michael E. The Apache. (Indians of North America Ser.). (Illus.). 112p. (J). (gr. 5 up). 1989. 17.95 (*1-55546-689-3*); pap. 9.95 (*0-7910-0352-3*) Chelsea Hse.

Melody, William H. Children's Television: The Economics of Exploitation. LC 73-80079. 176p. reprint ed. pap. 50.20 (*0-8357-8069-4*, 2033825) Bks Demand.

Melody, William H., et al, eds. Culture, Communication, & Dependency: The Tradition of H. A. Innis. LC 80-21189. (Communication & Information Science Ser.). 264p. (C). 1981. text ed. 55.00 (*0-89391-065-1*); pap. 29.50 (*0-89391-079-1*) Ablex Pub.

Meloe, Torleif. United States Control of Petroleum Imports: A Study of the Federal Government's Role in the Management of Domestic Oil Supplies. Bruchey, Stuart, ed. LC 78-22701. (Energy in the American Economy Ser.). (Illus.). 1979. lib. bdg. 28.95 (*0-405-12003-6*) Ayer.

Melograno, Vincent J. & Klinzing, James E. Orientation to Total Fitness. 4th ed. 240p. 1992. per. 17.95 (*0-8403-6745-7*) Kendall-Hunt.

Melohm, Tom. The New Partnership: Bringing Out the Best in Your People, Customers, Profits, & Yourself. LC 93-61781. 265p. 1994. 22.00 (*0-939246-57-0*) Oliver Wight.

Melon, jt. auth. see Laguerre.

Melon, jt. auth. see Rosa-Nieves.

Melon Diaz, Esther. La Narrativa De Marta Brunet. (UPREX, Literarios Ser.: No. 41). 272p. (C). 1975. pap. 1.50 (*0-8477-0041-0*) U of PR Pr.

Melon, Esther, jt. auth. see Laguerre, Enrique.

Melonakos, C. M. Tracting Made Easy. 48p. 1987. 3.95 (*0-9616024-1-4*) Paramount Bks.

Melonakos, Christine. Turn Your Little Ones into Book of Mormon Whiz Kids. LC 90-85979. 167p. (Orig.). 1991. pap. 14.98 (*0-88290-407-8*) Horizon Utah.

Melonakos, Kathleen. Saunders Pocket Reference for Nurses. 2nd ed. LC 94-20443. (Illus.). 656p. 1994. pap. text ed. 21.95 (*0-7216-4459-7*) Saunders.

Melone, Albert P. Researching Constitutional Law. (C). 1990. pap. text ed. 25.00 (*0-673-52086-2*) HarpCollege.

***Melone, Joseph J.** Collectively Bargained Multi-Employer Pension Plans. (C). 1963. 11.50 (*0-256-00654-7*) Irwin.

***Melone, Mark, illus.** The Mystery Believed, Pt. 1. (Light for Life Ser.). 112p. (Orig.). 1995. pap. text ed. 9.95 (*1-887158-07-3*) Educ Services.

Meloni, C., et al. Say the Right Thing! 1982. pap. text ed. 15.76 (*0-201-10205-6*) Addison-Wesley.

An Asterisk (*) at the beginning of an entry indicates that the title is appearing in BIP for the first time.

Meloni, Francesco. Severini's Graphic Work. limited ed. (Illus.). 218p. (ITA.). 1982. 275.00 (*1-55660-001-1*) A Wofsy Fine Arts.

Melosh. Physician's Hand. (C). 1982. 18.95 (*0-87722-290-8*) Temple U Pr.

Melosh, Barbara. Engendering Culture: Manhood & Womanhood in New Deal Public Art & Theater. LC 90-9948. (New Directions in American Art Ser.). (Illus.). 312p. (C). 1991. 60.00 (*0-87474-720-1*); pap. 24.95 (*0-87474-721-X*) Smithsonian.

Melosh, Barbara, ed. Gender & American History since 1890. (Re-writing Histories Ser.). 1993. 49.95 (*0-415-07675-7*, A7385) Routledge.

— Gender & Twentieth Century American History. (Re-writing Histories Ser.). 208p. 1993. pap. 15.95 (*0-415-07676-5*, A7389) Routledge.

Melosh, H. J. Impact Cratering: A Geologic Process. (Oxford Monographs on Geology & Geophysics: No. 11). (Illus.). 256p. 1988. 65.00 (*0-19-504284-0*) OUP.

Melosh, Robert J. Structural Engineering Analysis by Finite Elements. 384p. 1990. boxed 53.00 (*0-13-855701-2*) P-H.

Melosi. Coping with Abundances. 1985. pap. text ed. write for info. (*0-07-554666-3*) McGraw.

Melosi, Martin V. Garbage in the Cities: Refuse, Reform, & the Environment, 1880-1980. LC 81-40399. (Environmental History Ser.: No. 4). (Illus.). 286p. 1982. 32.50 (*0-89096-119-0*) Tex A&M Univ Pr.

— Garbage in the Cities: Refuse, Reform, & the Environment, 1880-1980. 268p. (C). 1981. reprint ed. pap. 21.95 (*0-534-10714-1*) Intl Thomson.

— Thomas A. Edison & the Modernization of America. (Library of American Biography). 224p. 1995. reprint ed. pap. 15.95 (*1-886746-27-3*) Talman Pub.

— Thomas Edison & the Modernization of America. (C). 1990. pap. text ed. 16.00 (*0-673-39625-8*) HarpCollege.

Melosi, Martin V., ed. Urban Public Policy: Historical Modes & Methods. LC 93-15358. (Issues in Public Policy Ser.: No. 3). 206p. 1993. pap. 13.95 (*0-271-01093-2*) Pa St U Pr.

Melossi, Dario. The State of Social Control: A Sociological Study of Concepts of State & Social Control in "The Making of Democracy" LC 89-77987. 200p. 1990. text ed. 49.95 (*0-312-04634-0*) St Martin.

Melott, Cheryll, ed. see Kuthumy, Aeoliah.

Melott, Ronald K. Is Energy Conservation Firesafe? 1978. 2.50 (*0-686-12081-7*, TR 78-8) Society Fire Protect.

Meloun, Milan, et al. Chemometrics in Instrumental Analysis, Vol. 1: Solved Problems by IBM PC. 500p. 1992. write for info. (*0-13-126376-5*) P-H.

Meloy, Betty T. Idaho Museum Guide. (Illus.). 72p. (Orig.). 1989. pap. 5.95 (*0-9623630-0-6*) B T Meloy.

Meloy, Ellen. Raven's Exile. 1994. 22.50 (*0-8050-2497-2*) H Holt & Co.

— Raven's Exile: A Season on the Green River. (Illus.). 272p. 1995. pap. 12.95 (*0-8050-3807-8*, Owl) H Holt & Co.

Meloy, Glenn R., ed. Innovative Powerhouse Design: Proceedings of a Session Sponsored by the Energy Division. 42p. 1985. 12.00 (*0-87262-505-2*) Am Soc Civil Eng.

Meloy, J. Reid. The Psychopathic Mind: Origins, Dynamics, & Treatment. LC 88-3454. 496p. 1988. 50.00 (*0-87668-922-5*) Aronson.

— The Psychopathic Mind: Origins, Dynamics, & Treatment. LC 88-3454. 496p. 1992. reprint ed. pap. 40.00x (*0-87668-311-1*) Aronson.

— Violent Attachments. LC 92-10469. 384p. 1992. 42.50 (*0-87668-537-8*) Aronson.

Meloy, J. Reid, jt. auth. see Gacono, Carl B.

Meloy, J. Reid, et al. Clinical Guidelines for Involuntary Outpatient Treatment. Smith, Harold H., Jr., ed. LC 89-43652. (Practitioner's Resource Ser.). 78p. (Orig.). 1990. pap. 14.70 (*0-943158-45-1*, GGIBP) Pro Resource.

Meloy, Judith. Writing the Qualitative Dissertation: Understanding by Doing. 128p. 1993. text ed. 29.95 (*0-8058-1416-7*); pap. 14.95 (*0-8058-1417-5*) L Erlbaum Assocs.

Meloy, Mark. Eastern Montana Mountain Ranges: Islands on the Prairie. (Montana Geographic Ser.: No. 13). (Illus.). 104p. (Orig.). 1986. pap. 13.95 (*0-938314-24-6*) Am Wrld Geog.

Melpomene Institute for Women's Health Research Staff. The Bodywise Woman. LC 93-22710. (Illus.). 304p. 1990. pap. 13.95 (*0-87322-551-1*, PMEL0551) Human Kinetics.

***Melrose, A. R.** The Pooh Dictionary. LC 95-6033. (Illus.). (J). 1995. 17.99 (*0-525-45395-4*, DCB) Dutton Child Bks.

Melrose Abbey Staff. Chronica De Mailros. Stephenson, Joseph, ed. LC 73-172721. (Bannatyne Club, Edinburgh. Publications: No. 49). reprint ed. 37.50 (*0-404-52759-0*) AMS Pr.

— Liber Sancte Marie De Melros, 2 Vols, Set. Innes, Cosmo, ed. LC 77-172722. (Bannatyne Club, Edinburgh. Publications: No. 56). reprint ed. 115.00 (*0-404-52910-0*) AMS Pr.

Melrose, D. B. Instabilities in Space & Laboratory Plasmas. (Illus.). 360p. 1986. 74.95 (*0-521-30541-1*) Cambridge U Pr.

— Instabilities in Space & Laboratory Plasmas. (Illus.). 360p. 1989. pap. 34.95 (*0-521-37962-8*) Cambridge U Pr.

— Plasma Astrophysics: Nonthermal Processes in Diffuse Magnetized Plasmas, Vol. 2: Astrophysical Applications, 2 vols., Vol. 2. 714p. 1980. Set. text ed. 372.00 (*0-677-03490-3*); text ed. 272.00 (*0-677-02130-5*) Gordon & Breach.

— Plasma Astrophysics: Nonthermal Processes in Diffuse Magnetized Plasmas, Vol.1: The Emission, Absorption & Transfer of Waves in Plasmas. 280p. 1980. text ed. 207.00 (*0-677-02340-5*) Gordon & Breach.

Melrose, Dianna. Bitter Pills: Medicines & the Third World Poor. 277p. (C). 1982. pap. text ed. 40.00 (*0-85598-065-6*, Pub. by Oxfam Pubns UK) St Mut.

— Nicaragua: The Threat of a Good Example? 80p. (C). 1985. pap. text ed. 21.00 (*0-85598-070-2*, Pub. by Oxfam Pubns UK) St Mut.

Melrose, Donald B. & McPhedran, R. C. Electromagnetic Processes in Dispersive Media. (Illus.). 400p. (C). 1991. 89.95 (*0-521-41025-8*) Cambridge U Pr.

Melrose, Georgiana. A Strange Occupation. 128p. 1989. 30.00 (*0-7223-2200-3*, Pub. by A H S Ltd UK) St Mut.

Melrose, Jennifer. To a Good Home Only. 230p. 1987. 60.00 (*1-85200-009-0*, Pub. by United Writers Pubns UK) St Mut.

Melrose, John & Melrose, Krisan K. BUCOMCO: A Business Communication Simulation. 2nd ed. LC 93-38289. 1993. write for info. (*1-56118-530-2*) Paradigm MN.

***Melrose, Ken.** Making the Grass Greener on Your Side: A CEO's Journey of Leading by Serving. 250p. 1995. 24.95 (*1-881052-21-4*) Berrett-Koehler.

Melrose, Krisan K., jt. auth. see Melrose, John.

Melrose, Richard. The Atiyah-Patodi-Singer Index Theorem. LC 93-1405. (Research Notes in Mathematics Ser.). 392p. (C). 1993. text ed. 59.95 (*1-56881-002-4*) AK Peters.

***Melrose, Richard B.** Geometric Scattering Theory. (Stanford Lectures: No. 1). (Illus.). 121p. (C). Date not set. write for info. (*0-521-49673-X*); pap. write for info. (*0-521-49810-4*) Cambridge U Pr.

Melrose, Robin. The Communicative Syllabus: A Systematic Functional Approach to Language Teaching. 224p. 1992. text ed. 59.00 (*0-86187-137-5*, Pub. by Pinter Pubs UK) St Martin.

Melrose, Susan. A Semiotics of the Dramatic Text. LC 93-17914. (New Directions in Theatre Ser.). 1994. text ed. 39.95 (*0-312-10086-8*) St Martin.

Mels, Reinhard, jt. auth. see Lane, Gerd R.

Melsa, James L. & Sage, Andrew P. An Introduction to Probability & Stochastic Processes. (Illus.). 448p. 1973. pap. text ed. 54.00 (*0-13-034850-3*) P-H.

Melsen, Birte, ed. Current Controversies in Orthodontics. (Illus.). 368p. 1991. text ed. 98.00 (*0-86715-174-9*) Quint Pub Co.

Melsher, Kenneth J., jt. ed. see McDowell, James K.

Melson, jt. auth. see Jaffe.

Melson, Charles. Marine Force Recon, 1940-1990. (Elite Ser.). (Illus.). 64p. 1994. pap. 12.95 (*1-85532-391-5*, 9470, Pub. by Osprey UK) Stackpole.

Melson, Charles D. Vietnam Marines 1965-73. (Elite Ser.: No. 43). (Illus.). 64p. pap. 12.95 (*1-85532-251-X*, 9458, Pub. by Osprey UK) Stackpole.

Melson, Gail F., jt. ed. see Fogel, Alan.

***Melson, Gordon A. & Figgis, Brian N., eds.** Transition Metal Chemistry Vol. 9 - 1985. fac. ed. LC 65-27431. 320p. 1985. pap. 91.20 (*0-7837-8638-7*, 2027127) Bks Demand.

— Transition Metal Chemistry, Vol. 8: 1982. LC 65-27431. (Illus.). 478p. 1982. reprint ed. pap. 136.30 (*0-7837-0915-3*, 2041220) Bks Demand.

Melson, James. The Golden Boy. LC 91-34576. 230p. 1992. lib. bdg. 32.95 (*1-56024-243-4*); pap. 14.95 (*1-56023-015-0*) Harrington Pk.

Melson, Kathryn A. Practice Problems for Dosage Calculations. 1991. teacher ed 11.00 (*0-8273-4401-5*); text ed. 13.95 (*0-8273-4400-7*) Delmar.

Melson, Kathryn A., jt. auth. see Jaffe, Marie S.

Melson, Robert. Revolution & Genocide: On the Origins of the Armenian Genocide & the Holocaust. LC 91-47944. 384p. 1992. 29.95 (*0-226-51990-2*) U Ch Pr.

Melson, William G., jt. auth. see Mason, Brian H.

Meltabarger, P. J. The Ballad of Padre Island, Vol. 1. Samuelson, Arnold & Samuelson, Billie, eds. (Illus.). 28p. (Orig.). (J). (gr. 1-5). 1987. pap. text ed. 3.95 (*0-923133-00-3*) JM Pub.

— The Karankawa Indians, Pt. 2. Samuelson, Arnold & Samuelson, Billie, eds. (Ballad of Padre Island Ser.). (Illus.). 28p. (Orig.). (J). (gr. 1-5). 1988. pap. text ed. 3.95 (*0-923133-01-1*) JM Pub.

— Livingston: The Pedigreed Pooch of Padre Island. Samuelson, Arnold & Samuelson, Billie, eds. (Illus.). 150p. (YA). (gr. 7-10). 1988. 19.95 (*0-923133-02-X*) JM Pub.

Melter, R. A., jt. auth. see Tomescu, I.

Meltesen, Clarence R. Roads to Liberation from Oflag 64. 2nd ed. LC 90-91707. (Illus.). 535p. 1990. 20.00 (*0-9627005-0-9*) C R Meltesen.

Melton. Directory of Religious Organizations in the U. S. 3rd ed. 1992. 130.00 (*0-8103-9890-7*, 072216) Gale.

— Software Measurement: Understanding Software Engineering. 1995. pap. (*0-412-55180-2*) Chapman & Hall.

Melton, A., ed. Mathematical Foundations of Programming Semantics. (Lecture Notes in Computer Science Ser.: Vol. 239). vi, 395p. 1986. pap. 42.00 (*0-387-16816-8*) Spr-Verlag.

***Melton, A. C.** The Mycota: A Comprehensive Treatise on Fungi As Experimental Systems for Basic & Applied Research. Esser, K. & Lemke, P. A., eds. 648p. 1995. 214.00 (*0-387-58003-4*) Spr-Verlag.

***Melton, Alan.** Caring Beyond Words. 128p. (Orig.). 1995. pap. write for info. (*1-57312-012-X*) Smyth & Helwys.

Melton, Charles E. Ancient Diamond Time Capsules: Secrets of Life & the World. (Illus.). 167p. 1985. 9.95 (*0-9614901-0-1*); pap. 5.95 (*0-9614901-2-8*) Melton-Giardini Bk.

— Principles of Mass Spectrometry & Negative Ions. LC 72-134445. 327p. reprint ed. pap. 93.20 (*0-685-16246-X*, 2027111) Bks Demand.

Melton, Dana D. & Ledbetter, Frances M. Hooked on Games. (Illus.). 150p. (Orig.). (J). (gr. k-6). 1989. pap. 9.95 (*0-685-29409-9*) Hooked Games.

Melton, David. A Boy Called Hopeless. LC 86-27557. (Illus.). 231p. (J). (gr. 4-8). 1986. reprint ed. lib. bdg. 13.95 (*0-933849-32-X*) Landmark Edns.

— A Boy Called Hopeless. LC 86-27557. (Illus.). 232p. (J). (gr. 4 up). 1986. reprint ed. pap. 5.95 (*0-933849-07-9*) Landmark Edns.

— How to Capture Live Authors & Bring Them to Your Schools. LC 85-81416. 1986. pap. 15.95 (*0-933849-03-6*) Landmark Edns.

— The One & Only Autobiography of Ralph Miller: The Dog Who Knew He Was A Boy. LC 86-27551. (Illus.). 104p. (J). (gr. 2-6). 1986. reprint ed. pap. 5.95 (*0-933849-05-2*) Landmark Edns.

— The One & Only Autobiography of Ralph Miller: The Dog Who Knew He Was a Boy. LC 86-27551. (Illus.). 90p. (J). (gr. 2-6). 1987. reprint ed. lib. bdg. 13.95 (*0-933849-30-3*) Landmark Edns.

— The One & Only Second Autobiography of Ralph Miller: The Dog Who Knew He Was a Boy. LC 86-27556. (Illus.). 116p. (J). (gr. 2-6). 1986. reprint ed. lib. bdg. 13.95 (*0-933849-31-1*) Landmark Edns.

— The One & Only Second Autobiography of Ralph Miller: The Dog Who Knew He Was a Boy. LC 86-27556. (Illus.). 128p. (J). (gr. 2-6). 1986. reprint ed. pap. 5.95 (*0-933849-06-0*) Landmark Edns.

— Todd. (Gentle Revolution Ser.). (Illus.). 266p. 1985. 13.95 (*0-936676-52-3*) Better Baby.

— Todd - the Story of a Brain-Injured Child. rev. ed. 173p. 1984. write for info. (*0-936676-54-X*) Better Baby.

— Written & Illustrated by... LC 85-50637. 1985. pap. 15.95 (*0-933849-00-1*) Landmark Edns.

Melton, David, comp. Images of Greatness: A Celebration of Life. LC 87-26300. (Illus.). 64p. (YA). (gr. 4 up). 1987. 15.95 (*0-933849-11-7*) Landmark Edns.

Melton, David, jt. auth. see Teachers of the School District of Independence, Missouri Staff.

Melton, Douglas A., ed. Antisense RNA & DNA. LC 88-205987. (Current Communications in Molecular Biology Ser.). 161p. reprint ed. pap. 45.90 (*0-7837-6439-1*, 2046439) Bks Demand.

Melton, Gary B. Child Advocacy: Psychological Issues & Interventions. LC 83-2255. 242p. 1983. 45.00 (*0-306-41156-3*, Plenum Pr) Plenum.

Melton, Gary B., ed. Adolescent Abortion: Psychological & Legal Issues. LC 85-31812. (Children & the Law Ser.). xiii, 152p. 1986. 25.00 (*0-8032-3094-X*) U of Nebr Pr.

— The Individual, the Family, & Social Good: Personal Fulfillment in Times of Change. (Nebraska Symposium on Motivation Ser.: No. 42). 401p. (C). 1995. pap. text ed. 20.00 (*0-8032-8221-4*) U of Nebr Pr.

— The Individual, the Family & Social Good: Personal Fulfillment in Times of Change. (Symposium on Motivation Ser.: No. 42). 401p. 1995. text ed. 35.00 (*0-8032-3187-3*) U of Nebr Pr.

— Legal Reforms Affecting Child & Youth Services. LC 82-6204. (Child & Youth Services Ser.: Vol. 5, Nos. 1 & 2). 150p. 1983. text ed. 49.95 (*0-86656-105-6*); pap. text ed. 19.95 (*0-86656-216-8*) Haworth Pr.

— Nebraska Symposium on Motivation, 1985: The Law as a Behavioral Instrument. LC 53-11655. (Nebraska Symposium on Motivation Ser.: Vol. 33). xxvii, 291p. 1986. 30.00 (*0-8032-3100-8*); pap. 14.95 (*0-8032-8132-3*) U of Nebr Pr.

— Neighbors Helping Neighbors: A New National Strategy for the Protection of Children. 196p. (Orig.). (C). (gr. 12 up). 1994. pap. text ed. 60.00 (*0-7881-0859-X*) Diane Pub.

— Reforming the Law: Impact of Child Development Research. LC 87-31. (Guilford Law & Behavior Ser.). 307p. 1987. lib. bdg. 40.00 (*0-89862-278-6*) Guilford Pr.

Melton, Gary B. & Barry, Frank D., eds. Protecting Children from Abuse & Neglect: Foundations for a New National Strategy. LC 94-18298. 451p. 1994. lib. bdg. 40.00 (*0-89862-265-4*, 2265) Guilford Pr.

Melton, Gary B., jt. ed. see Childs, Alan W.

Melton, Gary B., et al. Community Mental Health Centers & the Courts: An Evaluation of Community-Based Forensic Services. LC 84-25751. viii, 169p. 1985. 24.00 (*0-8032-3083-4*) U of Nebr Pr.

— Psychological Evaluations for the Courts: A Handbook for Mental Health Professionals & Lawyers. LC 86-26992. (Perspectives on Law & Behavior Ser.). 511p. 1987. lib. bdg. 50.00 (*0-89862-276-X*) Guilford Pr.

Melton, Gary B., et al, eds. Children's Competence to Consent. LC 82-18631. (Critical Issues in Social Justice Ser.). 286p. 1983. 49.50 (*0-306-41069-9*, Plenum Pr) Plenum.

Melton, H. Keith. CIA Special Weapons & Equipment: Spy Devices of the Cold War. (Illus.). 128p. 1994. pap. 11.95 (*0-8069-8733-2*) Sterling.

— OSS Special Weapons & Equipment: Spy Devices of WW II. LC 90-22118. (Illus.). 128p. 1992. pap. 11.95 (*0-8069-8239-X*) Sterling.

Melton, Henry. Clean Slate Word Processing for the TRS-80. 1983. write for info. (*0-318-57972-3*) Macmillan.

Melton, Hollis, ed. see Clark, VeVe A., et al.

***Melton, Hope & Roehlkepartain, Eugene C.** Finding a Focus: Rethinking the Public Sector's Role in Building Assets in Youth. (Everyone's an Asset-Builder Ser.). 1995. pap. 4.50 (*1-57482-332-9*) Search Inst.

Melton, Howard C. Poems to Glorify God. LC 88-51891. 44p. 1989. pap. 5.95 (*1-55523-213-2*) Winston-Derek.

Melton, Howard E. Melton Art Reference Library, 2 vols., Set, Vols. 1 & 2. 390p. 1993. Set, Vol 1, A Directory of 28,000 Artists & Their Museums; Vol. 2, A Directory of 1,125 Museums & t. ring bd., spiral bd. 195.00 (*0-9640163-0-3*) Melton Art Ref.

Melton, J. Gordon. Biographical Dictionary of American Cult & Sect Leaders. LC 83-48226. (Library of Social Sciences). 354p. 1986. lib. bdg. 50.00 (*0-8240-9037-3*, SS212) Garland.

— The Churches Speak Series, Issue 1. 150p. 1989. pap. text ed. 39.00 (*0-8103-7218-5*) Gale.

— The Churches Speak Series, Issue 2. 1989. pap. text ed. 39.00 (*0-8103-7219-3*) Gale.

— The Churches Speak Series, Issue 3. 1989. pap. text ed. 39.00 (*0-8103-7220-7*) Gale.

— The Churches Speak Series, Issue No. 4. 150p. 1989. pap. text ed. 39.00 (*0-8103-7221-5*) Gale.

— The Cult Controversy: A Guide to Sources. (Religious Information Systems Ser.: Vol. 6). 325p. 1992. 45.00 (*0-8153-0860-4*, H1601) Garland.

— Dir of Religious Organizations In The U. S. 3rd ed. 1992. 125.00 (*0-685-48433-5*) Gale.

— Encyclopedia of American Religions. 4th ed. 1992. 180.00 (*0-8103-6904-4*) Gale.

— Encyclopedia of American Religions. 5th ed. 1996. 180.00 (*0-8103-7714-4*) Gale.

— Encyclopedia of American Religions. 6th ed. 1900. 180.00 (*0-8103-8417-5*) Gale.

— Encyclopedia of American Religions: Rel Creeds 2. 2nd ed. 1993. 140.00 (*0-8103-5491-8*) Gale.

— Encyclopedia of American Religions: Rel Creeds 3. Date not set. 140.00 (*0-8103-7841-8*) Gale.

— Encyclopedic Handbook of Cults in America. rev. ed. LC 92-11540. (Religious Information Systems Ser.: Vol. 7). 424p. 1992. pap. 18.95 (*0-8153-1140-0*) Garland.

— Encyclopedic Handbook of Cults in America. 2nd rev. ed. LC 92-11540. (Religious Information Systems Ser.: Vol. 7). 424p. 1992. 65.00 (*0-8153-0502-8*, H#SS797) Garland.

— National Directory of Churches, Synagogues, & Other Houses of Worship, 4 Vols., Vol. 4. Krol, John, ed. 2400p. 1993. 310.00 (*0-8103-8989-4*, 101773) Gale.

— National Directory of Churches, Synagogues, & Other 1 Houses of Worship, Vol. 1: Northeastern States. Krol, John, ed. 600p. 1993. 85.00 (*0-8103-8990-8*, 101774) Gale.

— National Directory of Churches, Synagogues, & Other 1 Houses of Worship, Vol. 2: Midwestern States, Vol. 2. Krol, John, ed. 600p. 1993. 85.00 (*0-8103-8991-6*, 101775) Gale.

— National Directory of Churches, Synagogues, & Other 1 Houses of Worship, Vol. 3: Southern States, Vol. 3. Krol, John, ed. 600p. 1993. 85.00 (*0-8103-8992-4*, 101776) Gale.

— National Directory of Churches, Synagogues, & Other 1 Houses of Worship, Vol. 4: Western States, Vol. 4. Krol, John, ed. 600p. 1993. 85.00 (*0-8103-8993-2*, 101777) Gale.

— New Age Almanac. 1990. pap. 16.95 (*0-8103-9402-2*) Visible Ink Pr.

— New Age Encyclopedia. 2nd ed. Date not set. 59.50 (*0-8103-7610-5*) Gale.

— Religious Bodies in the United States: A Directory. LC 91-41564. (Religious Information Systems Ser.: Vol. 1). 340p. 1992. 55.00 (*0-8153-0806-X*, H#1568) Garland.

— Religious Leaders of American: A Biographical Guide to Founders & Leaders of Religious Bodies, Churches, & Spiritual Groups in North America. 2nd ed. 700p. Date not set. 79.95 (*0-8103-8878-2*, 008162) Gale.

— The Vampire Book: The Encyclopedia of the Undead. 1994. pap. 16.95 (*0-8103-2295-1*) Visible Ink Pr.

Melton, J. Gordon, ed. American Religious Creeds, Vols. 1-3: An Essential Compendium of More Than 450 Statements of Belief & Doctrine, 3 vols. LC 90-47872. 1992. reprint ed. Vol. 1, 349p. pap. 14.95 (*0-89243-487-2*, Triumph Books); reprint ed. Vol. 2, 323p. pap. 14.95 (*0-89243-488-0*, Triumph Books); reprint ed. Vol. 3, 201p. pap. 14.95 (*0-89243-489-9*, Triumph Books); reprint ed. Set. pap. 39.95 (*0-89243-490-2*, Triumph Books) Liguori Pubns.

— The Beginnings of Astrology in America. (Cults & New Religions Ser.: Vol. 3). 504p. 1990. reprint ed. 101.00 (*0-8240-4364-2*) Garland.

— Christian Science. (Cults & New Religions Ser.: Vol. 12). 528p. 1990. reprint ed. 93.00 (*0-8240-4373-1*) Garland.

— The Churches Speak Series, Issue 5. 1990. pap. 39.00 (*0-8103-7646-6*) Gale.

— The Churches Speak Series, Issue 6. 175p. 1991. 39.00 (*0-8103-7647-4*) Gale.

— The Churches Speak Series, Issue 7. 175p. 1991. 39.00 (*0-8103-7648-2*) Gale.

— The Churches Speak Series, Issues 5-8. 1990. pap. 77.00 (*0-8103-7658-X*) Gale.

— The Churches Speak Series, Set. 1989. pap. 95.00 (*0-8103-7158-8*, 30144-99728) Gale.

— Cults & New Religions: Sources for the Study of Nonconventional Religious Groups in Nineteenth & Twentieth-Century America, 22 vols., Set. 1992. 2,420.00 (*0-8153-0000-X*) Garland.

— Encyclopedia of American Religions: Religious Creeds 1. 816p. 1987. 125.00 (*0-8103-2132-7*) Gale.

— The Encyclopedia of American Religions, Vols. 1- 3: A Comprehensive Study of the Major Religious Groups in the United States & Canada, 3 vols., Set. LC 91-11412. 1991. reprint ed. pap. 39.95 (*0-89243-497-X*, Triumph Books) Liguori Pubns.

— The Encyclopedia of American Religions, Vols. 1- 3: A Comprehensive Study of the Major Religious Groups in the United States & Canada, 3 vols., Vol. 1. LC 91-11412. 460p. 1991. reprint ed. pap. 14.95 (*0-89243-494-5*, Triumph Books) Liguori Pubns.

— The Encyclopedia of American Religions, Vols. 1- 3: A Comprehensive Study of the Major Religious Groups in the United States & Canada, 3 vols., Vol. 2. LC 91-11412. 460p. 1991. reprint ed. pap. 14.95 (*0-89243-495-3*, Triumph Books) Liguori Pubns.

— The Encyclopedia of American Religions, Vols. 1- 3: A Comprehensive Study of the Major Religious Groups in the United States & Canada, Vol. 3. LC 91-11412. 434p. 1991. reprint ed. pap. 14.95 (*0-89243-496-1*, Triumph Books) Liguori Pubns.

— The Origins of Theosophy: Annie Besant - The Atheist Years. (Cults & New Religions Ser.: Vol. 5). 408p. 1990. reprint ed. 101.00 (*0-8240-4366-9*) Garland.

— Religious Leaders of America. 750p. 1991. 90.00 (*0-8103-4921-3*) Gale.

— Rosicrucianism in America. (Cults & New Religions Ser.: Vol. 4). 521p. 1990. reprint ed. 103.00 (*0-8240-4365-0*) Garland.

— Spiritualism I: Spiritualist Thought. (Cults & New Religions Ser.: Vol. 1). 488p. 1990. reprint ed. 87.00 (*0-8240-4362-6*) Garland.

— Spiritualism II: The Movement. (Cults & New Religions Ser.: Vol. 2). 456p. 1990. reprint ed. 112.00 (*0-8240-4363-4*) Garland.

— Theosophy I: The Inner Life of Theosophy. (Cults & New Religions Ser.: Vol. 6). 424p. 1990. reprint ed. 80.00 (*0-8240-4367-7*) Garland.

— Theosophy II: Controversial & Polemical Pamphlets. (Cults & New Religions Ser.: Vol. 7). 576p. 1990. reprint ed. 107.00 (*0-8240-4368-5*) Garland.

— The Unification Church, Vol. II. (Cults & New Religions Ser.: Vol. 16). 600p. 1990. reprint ed. 165.00 (*0-8240-4490-8*) Garland.

— The Unification Church, Vol. III: Outreach. (Cults & New Religions Ser.). 616p. 1990. reprint ed. 176.00 (*0-8240-4491-6*) Garland.

Melton, J. Gordon & Gordon, J. The New Age Encyclopedia: A Compendium of Information on the Beliefs, Concepts, Terms, People, & Organizations Related to Higher Consciousness, Spiritual Development, Holistic Health & Other Topics. 1990. pap. text ed. 65.00 (*0-8103-7159-6*) Gale.

Melton, J. Gordon & Koszegi, Michael A. Religious Information Sources: A Worldwide Guide. LC 91-47697. (Religious Information Systems Ser.: Vol. 2). 581p. 1992. 75.00 (*0-8153-0859-0*, H#1593) Garland.

Melton, J. Gordon & Lucas, Phillip. Encyclopedia of Religious Broadcasting. Stickney, Arthur H., ed. (Illus.). 416p. 1996. 64.95 (*0-89774-902-2*, 2148) Oryx Pr.

Melton, J. Gordon & Poggi, Isotta. Magic, Witchcraft, & Paganism in America: A Bibliography. 2nd ed. LC 91-45867. (Religious Information Systems Ser.: Vol. 3). 422p. 1992. 65.00 (*0-8153-0499-4*, SS#723) Garland.

Melton, J. Gordon, ed. see Hepper, F. Nigel.

Melton, J. Gordon, jt. ed. see Koszegi, Michael A.

Melton, J. Gordon, jt. ed. see Lewis, James R.

Melton, J. Gordon, jt. auth. see Pruter, Karl.

Melton, Jack W., Jr. & Pawl, Lawrence E. Introduction to Field Artillary Ordinance, 1861-1865. 175p. 1993. pap. 20.00 (*0-9635861-4-9*) Kennesaw Mtn.

Melton, James & Keenan, Matthew. The Socially Responsive Portfolio: Balancing Politics & Profits in Institutional Money Management. 275p. 1993. 45.00 (*1-55738-501-7*) Probus Pub Co.

Melton, James E. Vital Enthusiasm. LC 82-81903. 232p. 1983. 12.95 (*0-9604752-1-4*) Global Pubns CA.

— Your Right to Fly. LC 80-82961. (Illus.). 218p. 1979. pap. 8.95 (*0-9604752-0-6*) Global Pubns CA.

Melton, James V., tr. see Brunner, Otto.

***Melton, Jim & Simon, Alan.** Object-Oriented SQL. 1995. 39.95 (*1-55860-303-4*) Morgan Kaufmann.

— Understanding the New SQL: A Complete Guide. 450p. 1992. pap. 36.95 (*1-55860-245-3*) Morgan Kaufmann.

Melton, John. Astrologaster: or The Figvre-Caster. LC 92-550. (Augustan Reprints Ser.: No. 174X (1975)). reprint ed. 12.00 (*0-404-70173-6*, BF1681) AMS Pr.

Melton, L. Joseph, III, jt. ed. see Riggs, B. Lawrence.

***Melton, L. R.** An Introductory Guide to Information Sources in Physics. fac. ed. LC 79-313118. (Illus.). 48p. 1978. reprint ed. pap. 25.00 (*0-7837-8011-7*, 2047767) Bks Demand.

Melton, Lisa & Ladizinsky, Eric. Fifty Nifty Science Experiments. 64p. (J). (ps-3). 1992. pap. 3.95 (*0-929923-92-8*) Lowell Hse.

Melton, Lisa T. The Man Who Climbed the Mountain. 360p. 1989. 25.00 (*0-9623449-0-7*) M Okada Assn.

Melton, Luke. The Complete Loran-C Handbook. (Illus.). 228p. 1987. pap. text ed. 16.95 (*0-87742-225-7*) Intl Marine.

— The Complete LORAN-C Handbook. 1987. pap. text ed. 18.95 (*0-07-155210-3*) McGraw.

***Melton, Melanie.** Will Black Holes Devour the Universe? And 100 Other Questions & Answers about Astronomy. 1994. pap. 14.95 (*0-913135-20-8*) Kalmbach.

Melton, Reginald F. Instructional Models for Course Design & Development. LC 81-5538. (Illus.). 198p. 1982. 34.95 (*0-87778-178-8*) Educ Tech Pubns.

Melton, Robert G., et al, eds. AAS - AIAA Spaceflight Mechanics Meeting. LC 57-43769. (Advances in the Astronautical Sciences Ser.: Vol. 82 I & II). (Illus.). 1993. lib. bdg. 240.00 (*0-87703-368-4*, Pub. by Am Astro Soc); fiche 15.00 (*0-87703-369-2*, Pub. by Am Astro Soc) Univelt Inc.

Melton, Terry W., jt. ed. see Eckhardt, Robert B.

Melton, Timothy. For Black Men Who Have Considered Living... 48p. 1991. 4.95 (*1-877610-05-4*) Sea Island.

Melton, Victoria, ed. see Williams, Stephen J. & Sanchez, Julianne P.

Melton, W. F. The Rhetoric of John Donne's Verse. 1972. 59.95 (*0-8490-0953-7*) Gordon Pr.

Meltsner, Arnold J. Policy Analysis in the Bureaucracy. LC 74-30529. 1976. pap. 18.00 (*0-520-05746-5*) U CA Pr.

Meltsner, Arnold J., et al. Political Feasibility of Reform in School Financing: The Case of California. LC 72-92461. (Special Studies in U. S. Economic, Social & Political Issues). 1973. 36.50 (*0-685-70526-9*) Irvington.

Meltsner, Arnold J. Rules for Rulers: The Politics of Advice. 208p. 1990. 24.95 (*0-87722-685-7*) Temple U Pr.

Meltsner, Arnold J., ed. Politics & the Oval Office: Towards a Presidential Governance. 332p. 1981. 32.95 (*0-87855-428-9*); pap. 18.95 (*0-685-07094-8*) Transaction Pubs.

Meltsner, Susan. Body & Soul: A Guide to Lasting Recovery from Compulsive Eating & Bulimia. LC 93-4094. 240p. (Orig.). 1993. pap. 12.00 (*0-89486-903-5*, 5098A) Hazelden.

Meltsner, Susan, jt. auth. see Elliott, Miriam.

Meltz, Noah M. Industrial Relations Theory: Its Nature, Scope, & Pedagogy. Adams, Roy J., ed. LC 93-9898. (Institute of Management & Labor Relations Ser.: No. 4). (Illus.). 408p. 1993. Alk. paper. 42.50 (*0-8108-2678-X*) Scarecrow.

Meltz, Noah M., et al. Sharing the Work: An Analysis of the Issues in Worksharing & Jobsharing. LC 81-188245. 98p. reprint ed. pap. 28.00 (*0-317-39707-9*, 2055826) Bks Demand.

Meltzer. Filtration in the Pharmaceutical Industry. (Advances in Parenteral Science Ser.: Vol. 3). 1120p. 1987. 250.00 (*0-8247-7519-8*) Dekker.

— Intensive Coronary Care. (C). 1995. pap. text ed. 35.95 (*0-614-03656-9*) Appleton & Lange.

— Politics of Plagiarism. (C). 1990. lib. bdg. 34.95 (*0-226-51967-8*); pap. text ed. 14.95 (*0-226-51968-6*) U Ch Pr.

Meltzer & Dracup. Meltzer's Intensive Coronary Care. 5th ed. (C). 1995. pap. text ed. 35.95 (*0-8385-4276-X*) Appleton & Lange.

Meltzer, A. H., jt. ed. see Brunner, K. W.

Meltzer, Adolph. Breath of Life: The Life & Work of Dr. Samuel James Meltzer. 1993. 18.95 (*0-533-09572-7*) Vantage.

Meltzer, Albert, ed. A New World in Our Hearts: The Faces of Spanish Anarchism. 1979. pap. 4.50 (*0-932366-00-7*) Black Thorn Bks.

Meltzer, Allan H. Keynes's Monetary Theory: A Different Interpretation. (Illus.). 368p. (C). 1989. 59.95 (*0-521-30615-9*) Cambridge U Pr.

— Money, Credit & Policy. (Economists of the Twentieth Century Ser.). 544p. 1995. 74.95 (*1-85898-208-1*, Pub. by E Elgar Pub UK) Ashgate Pub Co.

— U. S. Leadership & Postwar Progress. LC 93-24884. (Occasional Papers: No. 42). 1993. pap. 9.95 (*1-55815-254-7*) ICS Pr.

Meltzer, Allan H., jt. auth. see Brunner, Karl.

Meltzer, Allan H., jt. auth. see Ott, David J.

Meltzer, Allan H., et al. Political Economy. (Illus.). 240p. 1991. 38.00 (*0-19-505624-8*) OUP.

Meltzer, Allan M., jt. ed. see Brunner, Karl.

Meltzer, Annabelle H., jt. auth. see Rothwell, Kenneth S.

Meltzer, B. N., et al. Symbolic Interactionism: Genesis, Varieties & Criticisms. (Monographs in Social Theory). 1977. reprint ed. pap. 13.95 (*0-7100-8056-5*, RKP) Routledge.

Meltzer, Bernard D. Supplement Labor '88. 1988. pap. 12.95 (*0-316-56649-7*) Little.

Meltzer, Bernard D. & Henderson, Stanley D. Labor Law: Cases, Materials & Problems. 3rd ed. LC 84-81751. (C). 1985. 52.00 (*0-316-56647-0*) Little.

— Statutory Supplement to Labor Law: Cases, Materials & Problems. LC 84-81751. (C). 1985. pap. 11.95 (*0-316-56648-9*) Little.

Meltzer, Daniel J. & Shapiro, David L. Federal Courts & the Federal System: 1993 Supplement. 3rd ed. (University Casebook Ser.). 216p. 1993. pap. text ed. 11.50 (*1-56662-102-X*) Foundation Pr.

— Judicial Code & Rules of Procedure in the Federal Courts, Student's Edition. rev. ed. 775p. 1993. pap. text ed. 18.95 (*1-56662-090-2*) Foundation Pr.

— The Judicial Code & Rules of Procedure in the Federal Courts, 1994. rev. ed. 738p. 1994. pap. text ed. 18.95 (*1-56662-177-1*) Foundation Pr.

Meltzer, David. The Agency Trilogy. (Orig.). 1994. pap. 12.95 (*1-56333-216-7*) Masquerade.

— Arrows: Selected Poetry, 1957-1992. LC 94-26540. 180p. (Orig.). (C). 1994. 25.00 (*0-87685-939-2*); pap. 13.00 (*0-87685-938-4*) Black Sparrow.

— Arrows: Selected Poetry, 1957-1992, signed ed. deluxe ed. LC 94-26540. 180p. (Orig.). (C). 1994. 30.00 (*0-87685-940-6*) Black Sparrow.

— The Art - The Veil. (Illus.). 64p. 1982. pap. 5.00 (*0-87924-040-7*) Membrane Pr.

— Blue Rags. 1974. 5.00 (*0-685-48375-4*); pap. 1.50 (*0-685-48377-0*) Oyez.

— Blue Rags. deluxe ed. 1974. 15.00 (*0-685-48376-2*) Oyez.

— The Eyes, the Blood. (Orig.). 1973. pap. 3.00 (*0-914726-13-7*) Mudra.

— Harps. 1974. 5.00 (*0-685-56671-4*); pap. 2.00 (*0-685-56672-2*) Oyez.

— Journal of the Birth. 1967. pap. 0.50 (*0-685-04670-2*) Oyez.

— The Name: Selected Poetry 1973-1983. LC 84-454. 160p. (Orig.). 1984. pap. 8.50 (*0-87685-491-9*) Black Sparrow.

— The Name: Selected Poetry 1973-1983, signed ed. deluxe ed. LC 84-454. 160p. (Orig.). 1984. 20.00 (*0-87685-492-7*) Black Sparrow.

— ORF. 1993. reprint ed. pap. text ed. 6.95 (*1-56333-110-1*) Masquerade.

— Six. LC 76-40038. (Illus.). 130p. (Orig.). 1976. pap. 4.00 (*0-87685-270-3*) Black Sparrow.

— Two-Way Mirror. 1977. 6.95 (*0-685-80005-9*); 2.95 (*0-685-80006-7*) Oyez.

— Under. (Orig.). 1995. pap. 12.95 (*1-56333-290-6*) Masquerade.

Meltzer, David, ed. Reading Jazz. LC 92-44561. 300p. (Orig.). 1993. pap. 14.95 (*1-56279-038-2*) Mercury Hse Inc.

— Tree: Five, the Snake, the Apple. (Illus.). 200p. (Orig.). 1975. pap. 10.00 (*0-686-10822-1*) Tree Bks.

— Tree: Four, Raa. (Illus.). (Orig.). 1974. pap. 10.00 (*0-686-17262-0*) Tree Bks.

— Tree: Six, Messiah. (Illus.). (Orig.). 1978. pap. 10.00 (*0-686-31720-3*) Tree Bks.

— Tree: Three, Shekinah. (Illus.). (Orig.). 1973. pap. 10.00 (*0-686-27969-7*) Tree Bks.

— Tree: Two, Yetzirah. (Illus.). (Orig.). 1972. pap. 10.00 (*0-686-27968-9*) Tree Bks.

Meltzer, David & Duncan, Robert. Wallace Berman: Retrospective. LC 78-70599. (Illus.). 118p. (Orig.). 1978. pap. 22.50 (*0-911291-03-2*) Fellows Cont Art.

Meltzer, David J. Search for the First Americans. LC 93-29453. 1993. write for info. (*0-89599-035-0*) Smithsonian Bks.

Meltzer, David J. & Dunnell, Robert C., eds. The Archaeology of William Henry Holmes. LC 91-27847. (Illus.). 736p. (Orig.). (C). 1992. pap. text ed. 34.95 (*1-56098-152-0*) Smithsonian.

Meltzer, David J., jt. auth. see Dillehay, Thomas D.

Meltzer, David J., jt. ed. see Mead, Jim I.

Meltzer, David J., et al, eds. American Archaeology Past & Future: A Celebration of the Society for American Archaeology, 1935-1985. LC 85-600308. (Illus.). 480p. (C). 1986. 39.95 (*0-87474-692-2*, MEAA) Smithsonian.

Meltzer, Edmund S., jt. ed. see Hick, John.

Meltzer, Edmund S., ed. see Murnane, William J.

Meltzer, Eric, jt. ed. see Hulbert, Mark.

Meltzer, Francoise. Hot Property: The Stakes & Claims of Literary Originality. LC 93-6275. (C). Date not set. pap. write for info. (*0-226-51976-7*) U Ch Pr.

— Hot Property: The Stakes & Claims of Literary Originality. LC 93-6275. (C). 1994. 27.50 (*0-226-51975-9*) U Ch Pr.

— Salome & the Dance of Writing: Portraits of Mimesis in Literature. LC 86-24983. (Illus.). xii, 226p. (C). 1987. 24.95 (*0-226-51971-6*) U Ch Pr.

— Salome & the Dance of Writing: Portraits of Mimesis in Literature. LC 86-24893. xii, 226p. 1989. reprint ed. pap. text ed. 14.95 (*0-226-51972-4*) U Ch Pr.

— The Trial(s) of Psychoanalysis. 296p. 1988. lib. bdg. 28.00 (*0-226-51969-4*); pap. text ed. 13.95 (*0-226-51970-8*) U Ch Pr.

Meltzer, Francoise, tr. see Poulet, Georges.

Meltzer, H. Y. & Nerozzi, D. Current Practices & Future Developments in the Pharmacotherapy of Mental Disorders. (International Congress Ser.: Vol. 941). 1991. 134.50 (*0-444-81402-7*) Elsevier.

Meltzer, Herbert Y., ed. Novel Antipsychotic Medications. 288p. 1992. 94.50 (*0-88167-893-7*) Raven.

Meltzer, Howard, et al. Disabled Children: Services, Transport & Education. 162p. 1989. pap. 35.00 (*0-11-691266-9*, HM2669) UNIPUB.

Meltzer, Jack. Metropolis to Metroplex: The Social & Spatial Planning of Cities. LC 83-49195. 216p. (C). 1984. text ed. 35.00x (*0-8018-3152-0*); pap. text ed. 12.95x (*0-8018-3153-9*) Johns Hopkins.

Meltzer, James D., jt. auth. see Shands, Harley C.

Meltzer, Judith, et al, eds. Policy Options in Long-Term Care. LC 81-10445. (C). 1981. pap. text ed. 12.50 (*0-226-51974-0*) U Ch Pr.

Meltzer, Lisa. One-Two-Three Look at Me. (Baby Shaped Board Bks.). (Illus.). 28p. (J). (ps). 1990. 2.95 (*0-02-689486-6*) Checkerboard.

Meltzer, Lynn J., ed. Strategy Assessment & Instruction for Students with Learning Disabilities: From Theory to Practice. LC 91-48272. 424p. 1993. text ed. 38.00 (*0-89079-540-1*, 5194) PRO-ED.

Meltzer, Marilyn & Palau, Susan M. Reading & Study Strategies for Nursing Students. (Illus.). 567p. 1993. pap. text ed. 26.50 (*0-7216-4483-X*) Saunders.

Meltzer, Maxine. Pups Speak Up. LC 92-33687. (Illus.). 32p. (J). (ps-3). 1994. text ed. 14.95 (*0-02-766710-3*, Bradbury S&S) S&S Childrens.

Meltzer, Milton. All Times, All Peoples: A World History of Slavery. LC 79-2810. (Illus.). 80p. (J). (gr. 5-9). 1980. lib. bdg. 15.89 (*0-06-024187-X*) HarpC Child Bks.

— The Amazing Potato: A Story in Which the Incas, Conquistadors, Marie Antoinette, Thomas Jefferson, Wars, Famines, Immigrants, & French Fries All Play a Part. LC 91-29610. (Illus.). 128p. (J). (gr. 3-7). 1992. 15.00 (*0-06-020806-6*); lib. bdg. 14.89 (*0-06-020807-4*) HarpC Child Bks.

— American Politics: How It Really Works. LC 88-26635. (Illus.). 192p. (YA). (gr. 7 up). 1989. 12.95 (*0-688-07494-4*) Morrow Jr Bks.

— The American Revolutionaries: A History in Their Own Words. LC 86-47846. (Illus.). 256p. (YA). (gr. 7 up). 1987. lib. bdg. 14.89 (*0-690-04643-X*, Crowell Jr Bks) HarpC Child Bks.

— American Revolutionaries: A History in Their Own Words 1750-1800. LC 86-47846. (Trophy Bk.). (Illus.). 224p. (YA). (gr. 7 up). 1993. pap. 6.95 (*0-06-446145-9*, Trophy) HarpC Child Bks.

— Andrew Jackson: And His America. (Illus.). 208p. (YA). (gr. 7-12). 1993. lib. bdg. 17.43 (*0-531-11157-1*) Watts.

— Benjamin Franklin: The New American. LC 88-17015. (Illus.). 288p. (J). (gr. 6-9). 1988. lib. bdg. 16.38 (*0-531-10582-2*) Watts.

— The Black Americans: A History in Their Own Words. rev. ed. LC 83-46160. (Illus.). 320p. (YA). (gr. 7 up). 1984. lib. bdg. 15.89 (*0-690-04418-6*, Crowell Jr Bks) HarpC Child Bks.

— The Black Americans: A History in Their Own Words, 1619-1983. rev. ed. LC 83-46160. (Trophy Nonfiction Bk.). (Illus.). 320p. (YA). (gr. 7 up). 1987. pap. 9.95 (*0-06-446055-X*, Trophy) HarpC Child Bks.

— A Book about Names. LC 83-45241. (Illus.). 128p. (YA). (gr. 7 up). 1984. lib. bdg. 14.89 (*0-690-04381-3*, Crowell Jr Bks) HarpC Child Bks.

— Bread & Roses: The Struggle of American Labor, 1865-1911. LC 67-19485. 1977. pap. 3.95 (*0-451-62396-7*, Ment) NAL-Dutton.

— Bread & Roses: The Struggle of American Labor, 1865-1915. (Library of American History). (Illus.). 192p. (YA). 1990. 17.95 (*0-8160-2371-9*) Facts on File.

— Brother, Can You Spare a Dime. 192p. (YA). (gr. 7). 1977. pap. 3.95 (*0-451-62442-4*, ME2178, Ment) NAL-Dutton.

— Brother, Can You Spare a Dime: The Great Depression 1929-1933. (Library of American History). (Illus.). 144p. (YA). 1990. 16.95 (*0-8160-2372-7*) Facts on File.

— Cheap Raw Material: How Our Youngest Workers Are Exploited & Abused. LC 93-31478. (Illus.). 192p. (J). (gr. 7 up). 1994. 14.99 (*0-670-83128-X*) Viking Child Bks.

— Columbus & the World Around Him. LC 89-24764. (YA). (gr. 9-12). 1990. lib. bdg. 16.38 (*0-531-10899-6*) Watts.

— Columbus & the World Around Him. braille ed. 245p. (J). 1991. vinyl bd. 19.60 (*1-56956-213-X*, BR8496) W A T Braille.

— Crime in America. LC 90-5698. 176p. (YA). (gr. 7 up). 1990. 12.95 (*0-688-08513-X*) Morrow Jr Bks.

— Dorothea Lange: Life Through the Camera. 64p. (J). (gr. 2-6). 1986. pap. 4.50 (*0-14-032105-5*, Puffin) Puffin Bks.

— George Washington & the Birth of Our Nation. LC 86-9222. 176p. (YA). (gr. 9-12). 1986. lib. bdg. 15.33 (*0-531-10253-X*) Watts.

— Gold: The True Story of Why People Search for It, Mine It, Trade It, Fight for It, Mint It, Display It, Steal It, & Kill for It. LC 92-44497. (Illus.). 176p. (J). (gr. 3-7). 1993. 15.00 (*0-06-022983-7*); lib. bdg. 14.89 (*0-06-022984-5*) HarpC Child Bks.

— Hold Your Horses! A Feedbag Full of Fact & Fable. LC 95-2983. (Illus.). 160p. (J). (gr. 3-7). 1995. 14.95 (*0-06-024477-1*); lib. bdg. 14.89 (*0-06-024478-X*) HarpC Child Bks.

— The Jewish Americans: A History in Their Own Words. LC 81-43886. (Illus.). 192p. (J). (gr. 5 up). 1982. lib. bdg. 14.89 (*0-690-04228-0*, Crowell Jr Bks) HarpC Child Bks.

— Jewish Life from Eastern Europe to America: The Lost World & the Discovered World. 1995. write for info. (*1-56821-433-2*) Aronson.

— Mark Twain Himself. LC 92-42530. 1993. 12.99 (*0-517-01248-0*, Pub. by Wings Bks) Random Hse Value.

— Mary McCleod Bethune. (Women of Our Time Ser.). (Illus.). (J). (gr. 2-6). 1988. pap. 3.50 (*0-317-69647-5*, Puffin) Puffin Bks.

— Mary McLeod Bethune. 1988. pap. 3.99 (*0-14-032219-1*, Puffin) Puffin Bks.

— Never to Forget: The Jews of the Holocaust. LC 75-25409. (YA). (gr. 7 up). 1976. lib. bdg. 15.89 (*0-06-024175-6*) HarpC Child Bks.

— Never to Forget: The Jews of the Holocaust. LC 75-25409. (Trophy Nonfiction Bk.). (Illus.). 240p. (YA). (gr. 7 up). 1991. pap. 6.95 (*0-06-446118-1*, Trophy) HarpC Child Bks.

— Poverty in America. LC 85-31963. 128p. (J). (gr. 7 up). 1986. 15.00 (*0-688-05911-2*) Morrow Jr Bks.

— Rescue: The Story of How Gentiles Saved Jews in the Holocaust. LC 87-47816. (Illus.). 224p. (YA). (gr. 7 up). 1988. lib. bdg. 15.89 (*0-06-024210-8*) HarpC Child Bks.

— Rescue: The Story of How Gentiles Saved Jews in the Holocaust. LC 87-47816. (Trophy Nonfiction Bk.). (Illus.). 176p. (YA). (gr. 7 up). 1991. pap. 6.95 (*0-06-446117-3*, Trophy) HarpC Child Bks.

— Slavery: A World History. (Illus.). 584p. 1993. reprint ed. pap. 19.95 (*0-306-80536-7*) Da Capo.

— Starting from Home: A Writer's Beginnings. (Illus.). 160p. (YA). (gr. 7 up). 1991. pap. 3.95 (*0-14-032299-X*, Puffin) Puffin Bks.

— The Teaching of Non-Fiction in Elementary & Secondary Classrooms: Essays by Milton Meltzer. Saul, Wendy, ed. (Language & Literacy Ser.). 216p. (C). 1994. text ed. 38.00x (*0-8077-3378-4*); pap. text ed. 17.95x (*0-8077-3377-6*) Tchrs Coll.

— Theodore Roosevelt & His America. LC 94-17369. (Illus.). 208p. (YA). (gr. 9-12). 1994. lib. bdg. 17.43 (*0-531-11192-X*) Watts.

— Thomas Jefferson: The Revolutionary Aristocrat. LC 91-15943. (Non-Fiction Ser.). (Illus.). 256p. (YA). (gr. 9-12). 1991. lib. bdg. 17.43 (*0-531-11069-9*) Watts.

— Underground Man. 261p. (J). (gr. 3-7). 1990. pap. 4.95 (*0-15-292846-4*, Odyssey) HarBrace.

— Underground Man. 261p. (J). (gr. 3-7). 1990. 14.95 (*0-15-200617-6*, Gulliver Bks) HarBrace.

— Voices from the Civil War: A Documentary History of the Great American Conflict. LC 88-34067. (Illus.). 224p. (YA). (gr. 7 up). 1989. lib. bdg. 14.89 (*0-690-04802-5*, Crowell Jr Bks) HarpC Child Bks.

— Voices from the Civil War: A Documentary of the Great American Conflict. LC 88-34067. (Trophy Nonfiction Bk.). (Illus.). 224p. (J). (gr. 6 up). 1992. pap. 6.95 (*0-06-446124-6*, Trophy) HarpC Child Bks.

— Who Cares? Millions Do-- LC 94-4082. (J). 1994. 15.95 (*0-8027-8324-4*); Reinforced. lib. bdg. 16.85 (*0-8027-8325-2*) Walker & Co.

— Winnie Mandela: The Soul of South Africa. (Women of Our Time Ser.). (Illus.). (J). (gr. 2-6). 1987. reprint ed. pap. 4.50 (*0-14-032181-0*, Puffin) Puffin Bks.

Meltzer, Milton, ed. Frederick Douglass, in His Own Words. LC 94-14524. (Illus.). 1995. write for info. (*0-15-229492-9*) HarBrace.

Meltzer, Milton & Harding, Walter. Thoreau Profile. 1969. reprint ed. pap. 4.00 (*0-912130-01-6*) Thoreau Found.

Meltzer, Milton, ed. see Child, Lydia M.

Meltzer, Milton, jt. auth. see Hughes, Langston.

An Asterisk (*) at the beginning of an entry indicates that the title is appearing in BIP for the first time.

Meltzer, Morton F. Information, the Ultimate Management Resource: How to Find, Use, & Manage It. LC 81-66222. 223p. reprint ed. pap. 63.60 (*0-317-28149-6*, 2055749) Bks Demand.

Meltzer, Otto & Kahrstedt, Ulrich. Geschichte der Karthager, 3 vols., 1. LC 75-7330. (Roman History Ser.). (GER.). 1975. reprint ed. 50.95 (*0-405-07106-X*) Ayer.

— Geschichte der Karthager, 3 vols., 2. LC 75-7330. (Roman History Ser.). (GER.). 1975. reprint ed. 51.95 (*0-405-07107-8*) Ayer.

— Geschichte der Karthager, 3 vols., 3. LC 75-7330. (Roman History Ser.). (GER.). 1975. reprint ed. 51.95 (*0-405-07108-6*) Ayer.

— Geschichte der Karthager, 3 vols., Set. LC 75-7330. (Roman History Ser.). (GER.). 1975. reprint ed. 150.95 (*0-405-07105-1*) Ayer.

Meltzer, Peter D., jt. auth. see Mariani, John F.

Meltzer, R. S. & Roelandt, Jos R. Contrast Echocardiography. 1982. lib. bdg. 149.50 (*90-247-2531-3*) Kluwer Ac.

Meltzer, Richard. The Aesthetics of Rock. 1987. pap. 11.95 (*0-306-80287-2*) Da Capo.

— Gulcher: Post-Rock Cultural Pluralism in America (1649-1993) 1990. pap. 9.95 (*0-8065-1197-4*, Citadel Pr) Carol Pub Group.

— The Night (Alone) A Novel. LC 95-13822. 1995. 21.95 (*0-316-56652-7*) Little.

— Post-Natal Trash. (Caned Out: The Authorized Autobiography of Richard Meltzer Ser.). 30p. (Orig.). 1984. pap. 3.95 (*0-89807-103-8*) Illuminati.

— Prickly Heat & Cold. (Caned Out: The Authorized Autobiography of Richard Meltzer Ser.). 64p. (Orig.). 1984. pap. 5.95 (*0-89807-106-2*) Illuminati.

— Richard Meltzer's Guide to the Ugliest Buildings of Los Angeles. 40p. (Orig.). 1984. pap. 4.95 (*0-89807-116-X*) Illuminati.

Meltzer, Richard & Tosches, Nick. Frankie, Pt. 1. (Talltales Ser.). 18p. 1984. pap. 1.95 (*0-89807-120-8*) Illuminati.

— Frankie, Part Two. (Talltales Ser.). (Orig.). 1987. pap. 1.95 (*0-89807-128-3*) Illuminati.

Meltzer, Richard S., et al, eds. Noninvasive Cardiac Imaging: Recent Developments. (Illus.). 404p. (C). 1988. 75.00 (*0-87993-314-3*) Futura Pub.

Meltzer, Robert. Biomedical & Clinical Instrumentation: Fast Tracking from Concept Through Production in a Regulated Environment. 274p. 1993. 98.50 (*0-935184-50-3*) Interpharm.

Meltzer, Ronald I., jt. ed. see Welch, Claude E., Jr.

Meltzer, Sol. Herb Gardening in Texas. 2nd ed. 104p. (Orig.). 1992. pap. 11.95 (*0-88415-043-7*) Gulf Pub.

Meltzer, Steve. Photographing Your Craftwork: A Hands-On Guide for Craftspeople. LC 86-2970. (Crafts Business Bks.). (Illus.). 144p. (Orig.). 1986. pap. 9.95 (*0-88089-012-6*) Madrona Pubs.

— Photographing Your Craftwork: A Hands-on Guide for Craftspeople. 2nd ed. 136p. 1993. reprint ed. pap. 12.95 (*0-934026-81-5*) Interweave.

***Meltzer, Theodore H.** High Purity Water Preparation. LC 92-85421. 833p. 1993. 125.00 (*0-927188-02-3*) Tall Oaks Pub.

Meltzer, Tom. Princeton Review Student Access Guide to the Best 286 Colleges 1995. 1994. pap. 18.00 (*0-679-75344-3*, Villard Bks) Random.

Meltzer, Yale L. Expanded Plastics & Related Products: Developments since 1978. LC 83-12165. (Chemical Technology Review Ser.: No. 221). (Illus.). 262p. 1984. 36.00 (*0-8155-0955-3*) Noyes.

Meltzoff, Sarah K. & Lipuma, Edward S. A Japanese Fishing Joint Venture: Worker Experience & National Development in the Solomon Islands. (ICLARM Technical Reports: No. 12). (Illus.). 63p. (Orig.). 1983. pap. text ed. 10.90 (*0-89955-386-9*, Pub. by ICLARM PH) Intl Spec Bk.

Meluch, R. M. Chicago Red. 1990. pap. 4.95 (*0-451-45034-5*, ROC) NAL-Dutton.

Melugin, R. K. & Pierce, W. G., eds. Cryogenic Optical Systems & Instruments, No. 3. 1988. 59.00 (*0-8194-0008-4*, 973) SPIE.

Melugin, R. K. & Pruitt, G. R. Cryogenic Optical Systems & Instruments IV, Vol. 1340. 1990. 62.00 (*0-8194-0401-2*) SPIE.

Melugin, Roy F. Formation of Isaiah 40-55. (Beiheft 141 zur Zeitschrift fuer die Alttestamentliche Wissenschaft Ser.). (C). 1976. text ed. 83.85 (*3-11-005820-0*) De Gruyter.

***Melum, Mara M. & Collett, Casey.** Breakthrough Leadership: Achieving Organizational Alignment Through Hoshin Planning. LC 94-48029. 1995. write for info. (*1-55648-133-0*) AHPI.

Melum, Mara M. & Sinioris, Marie K. Total Quality Management: The Health Care Pioneers. LC 92-11056. 404p. 1992. 69.00 (*1-55648-089-X*, 169410) AHPI.

Melusky, Joseph A. The Constitution: Our Written Legacy. LC 89-18963. 338p. (Orig.). 1991. 27.50 (*0-89464-334-7*); pap. 21.50 (*0-89464-550-1*) Krieger.

Melusky, Joseph A. & Ridgway, Whitman H. The Bill of Rights: Our Written Legacy. 268p. (C). 1993. text ed. 26.50 (*0-89464-533-1*); pap. 18.50 (*0-89464-827-6*) Krieger.

Melvern, Linda. Last Resort. 1992. pap. write for info. (*0-679-41218-2*) McKay.

Melvile, Hermann. Typee: A Peep at Polynesian Life. 1976. 24.95 (*0-8488-0581-X*) Amereon Ltd.

Melville, A. Resource Strategies in the 90s: Trends in ARL University Libraries. (Occasional Papers). 50p. 1994. pap. 25.00 (*0-918006-72-4*) ARL.

Melville, A. D., tr. see Ovid.

Melville, A. D., tr. see Statius.

Melville, Annabelle, jt. ed. see Kelly, Elin M.

Melville, Annabelle M. Elizabeth Bayley Seton. 1976. text ed. 25.00 (*0-684-14735-1*, Scribners) S&S Trade.

— Louis William DuBourg. LC 86-2934. 568p. (C). Date not set. write for info. (*0-8294-0529-1*, Campion Bks) Loyola Univ Pr.

— Louis William DuBourg, Set, Vols. I-II. LC 86-2934. 1096p. (C). Date not set. 34.95 (*0-8294-0501-1*, Campion Bks) Loyola Univ Pr.

Melville, Annette & Simmon, Scott. Film Preservation, 1993: A Report on America Film Preservation in the Film Industry & Public-Nonprofit Organizations. LC 93-21925. 1993. write for info. (*0-8444-0803-4*) Lib Congress.

***Melville, Annette & Simon, Scott, eds.** Redefining Film Preservation: A National Plan: Recommendations of the Librarian of Congress in Consultation with the National Film Preservation Board. LC 94-29345. 1994. write for info. (*0-8444-0819-0*) Lib Congress.

Melville, Antony, tr. see Jarry, Alfred.

Melville, Arabella. Natural Hormone Health: Drug-Free Ways to Manage Your Life. 176p. 1993. reprint ed. pap. 10.00 (*0-7225-2815-9*) Thorsons SF.

Melville, Arthur. With Eyes to See: A Journey from Religion to Spirituality. 352p. 1992. pap. 13.95 (*0-913299-85-5*) Stillpoint.

Melville, Charles & Smith, eds. Christians & Moors in Spain, Vol. 3: Arabic Sources (711-1501) (Hispanic Classics Ser.). 1992. 49.95 (*0-85668-449-X*, Pub. by Aris & Phillips UK); pap. write for info. (*0-85668-450-3*, Pub. by Aris & Phillips UK) David Brown.

***Melville, Chuck.** Felicia: Melari's Wish. (Illus.). 184p. (Orig.). 1995. pap. 14.95 (*1-883847-09-5*) MU Press.

Melville, Douglas, ed. see Ames, Joseph B.

Melville, Douglas, ed. see Anderson, Olof W.

Melville, Douglas, ed. see Arnold, Edwin L.

Melville, Douglas, ed. see Atkins, Frank.

Melville, Douglas, ed. see Bennet, Robert A.

Melville, Douglas, ed. see Bennett, Gertrude B.

Melville, Douglas, ed. see Blackwood, Algernon.

Melville, Douglas, ed. see Bramah, Ernest.

Melville, Douglas, ed. see Bruce, Muriel.

Melville, Douglas, ed. see Burton, Alice E.

Melville, Douglas, ed. see Chambers, Robert W.

Melville, Douglas, ed. see Channing, Mark.

Melville, Douglas, ed. see Chester, George R.

Melville, Douglas, ed. see Clock, Herbert & Boetzel, Eric.

Melville, Douglas, ed. see Coblentz, Stanton A.

Melville, Douglas, ed. see Constantine, Murray.

Melville, Douglas, ed. see Cook, William W.

Melville, Douglas, ed. see Cowan, Frank.

Melville, Douglas, ed. see De Comeau, Alexander.

Melville, Douglas, ed. see Dunn, Allan J.

Melville, Douglas, ed. see Eddison, Eric R.

Melville, Douglas, ed. see Fleckenstein, Alfred C.

Melville, Douglas, ed. see Fyne, Neal.

Melville, Douglas, ed. see Gillmore, Inez H.

Melville, Douglas, ed. see Gompertz, Martin L.

Melville, Douglas, ed. see Green, Fitzhugh.

Melville, Douglas, ed. see Gregory, Jackson.

Melville, Douglas, ed. see Griffith, George.

Melville, Douglas, ed. see Guthrie, Thomas A.

Melville, Douglas, ed. see Haggard, H. Rider.

Melville, Douglas, ed. see Haldane, Charlotte.

Melville, Douglas, ed. see Harris, Burland.

Melville, Douglas, ed. see Hartmann, Franz.

Melville, Douglas, ed. see Hodder, William R.

Melville, Douglas, ed. see Kingsmill, Hugh.

Melville, Douglas, ed. see Knowles, Vernon.

Melville, Douglas, ed. see Kummer, Frederic A.

Melville, Douglas, ed. see Large, E. C.

Melville, Douglas, ed. see Le Queux, William T.

Melville, Douglas, ed. see Leroux, Gaston.

Melville, Douglas, ed. see Lindsay, David.

Melville, Douglas, ed. see Linklater, Eric.

Melville, Douglas, ed. see London, Jack.

Melville, Douglas, ed. see Marshall, Sidney J.

Melville, Douglas, ed. see McHugh, Vincent.

Melville, Douglas, ed. see Merritt, Abraham.

Melville, Douglas, ed. see Morris, Kenneth.

Melville, Douglas, ed. see Murray, G. G.

Melville, Douglas, ed. see Owen, Frank.

Melville, Douglas, ed. see Potter, Margaret H.

Melville, Douglas, jt. ed. see Reginald, R.

Melville, Douglas, ed. see Rolfe, Frederick W., et al.

Melville, Douglas, ed. see Rosynyaine, J. H.

Melville, Douglas, ed. see Savile, Frank.

Melville, Douglas, ed. see Scott, G. Firth.

Melville, Douglas, ed. see Sheldon-Williams, Miles.

Melville, Douglas, ed. see Sinclair, Upton.

Melville, Douglas, ed. see Todd, Ruthven.

Melville, Douglas, ed. see Vivian, Charles E.

Melville, Douglas, ed. see Wells, H. G.

Melville, E. H. Residence at Sierra Leone. 336p. 1968. reprint ed. 35.00 (*0-7146-1837-3*, Pub. by F Cass Pubs UK) Intl Spec Bk.

Melville, Elinor G. A Plague of Sheep: Environmental Consequences of the Conquest of Mexico. (Studies in Environment & History). (Illus.). 240p. (C). 1994. 54.95 (*0-521-42061-X*) Cambridge U Pr.

Melville, H. Ancestry of John Whitney, Who Emigrated from London in 1635, & Settled in Watertown, Mass., the First of the Name in America & the One from Whom a Great Majority of the Whitneys in the U. S. Are Descended. (Illus.). 313p. 1989. reprint ed. lib. bdg. 48.50 (*0-8328-1262-5*); reprint ed. pap. 38.50 (*0-8328-1263-3*) Higginson Bk Co.

Melville, Henry. Veritas: Revelation of Mysteries Biblical, Historical, & Social, by Means of the Mediann & Persian Laws. 160p. 1993. reprint ed. pap. 17.95 (*1-56459-396-7*) Kessinger Pub.

Melville, Herman. Apple Tree Table: And Other Sketches. (BCL1-PS American Literature Ser.). 329p. 1992. reprint ed. lib. bdg. 89.00 (*0-7812-6793-5*) Rprt Serv.

— Apple-Tree Table & Other Sketches. LC 70-88907. 329p. 1969. reprint ed. text ed. 35.00 (*0-8371-2245-7*, MEAT, Greenwood Pr) Greenwood.

— Bartleby & Benito Cereno. 112p. 1990. pap. 1.00 (*0-486-26473-4*) Dover.

— Bartleby the Scrivener & Benito Cereno, Notes. 1992. pap. 3.95 (*0-8220-0220-5*) Cliffs.

— Battle-Pieces & Aspects of the War. LC 60-5042. 1979. reprint ed. lib. bdg. 50.00 (*0-8201-1252-6*) Schol Facsimiles.

— Battle-Pieces & Aspects of the War. 282p. 1995. reprint ed. pap. 13.95 (*0-306-80655-X*) Da Capo.

— Billy Budd. Bd. with The Encantadas (Airmont Classics Ser.). (J). (gr. 9 up). 1966. Set pap. 1.75 (*0-8049-0116-3*, CL-116) Airmont.

— Billy Budd: And Other Stories. 416p. 1993. pap. 4.95 (*0-460-87205-2*, Everyman's Classic Lib) C E Tuttle.

— Billy Budd & Other Stories. (Classics Ser.). 416p. 1986. mass mkt. 6.95 (*0-14-039053-7*, Penguin Classics) Viking Penguin.

— Billy Budd & Other Tales. 336p. 1961. pap. 2.50 (*0-451-52237-0*, Sig Classics) NAL-Dutton.

— Billy Budd Readalong. (Illustrated Classics Collection 5). 64p. 1994. audio, pap. 13.50 (*1-56103-617-X*) Lake Pub Co.

— Billy Budd, Sailor. Hayford, Harrision & Sealts, Merton M., Jr., eds. LC 62-17135. (Orig.). 1962. pap. 7.95 (*0-226-32132-0*, P99) U Ch Pr.

— Billy Budd, Sailor & Other Stories. (Bantam Classics Ser.). 288p. (gr. 7-12). 1982. 3.95 (*0-553-21274-5*) Bantam.

— Billy Budd, Sailor, & Other Stories. Beaver, Harold, ed. Incl. Cock-a-Doodle-Doo. 1968. (*0-318-55012-1*); Encantada. 1968. (*0-318-55013-X*); Bell Tower. 1968. (*0-318-55014-8*); Benito Cereno. 1968. (*0-318-55015-6*); John Marr. 1968. (*0-318-55016-4*); Daniel Orme. 1968. (*0-318-55017-2*); (English Library). 466p. 1968. Set pap. 2.50 (*0-14-043029-6*) Viking Penguin.

— Catskill Eagle. (Illus.). 32p. (J). (ps-3). 1991. 15.95 (*0-399-21857-2*, Philomel Bks) Putnam Pub Group.

— Clarel, 2 vols. 1972. 400.00 (*0-87968-875-0*) Gordon Pr.

— Clarel. Hayford, Harrison et al, eds. (Northwestern-Newberry Edition of the Writings of Herman Melville: Vol. 12). 893p. 1991. 82.95 (*0-8101-0906-9*); pap. 24.95 (*0-8101-0907-7*) Northwestern U Pr.

— Collected Poems. (BCL1-PS American Literature Ser.). 548p. 1993. reprint ed. lib. bdg. 99.00 (*0-7812-6987-3*) Rprt Serv.

— Collected Poems (except Clarel) annot. ed. Vincent, Howard P., ed. (Complete Works of Herman Melville Ser.). reprint ed. pap. write for info. (*0-87532-007-4*) Hendricks House.

— Confidence Man. (Airmont Classics Ser.). (J). (gr. 11 up). 1966. pap. 1.95 (*0-8049-0121-X*, CL-121) Airmont.

— Confidence Man. (C). 1971. pap. text ed. 9.95 (*0-393-09968-7*) Norton.

— The Confidence Man. 24.95 (*0-89190-890-0*, Am Repr) Amereon Ltd.

— The Confidence Man. 1964. mass mkt. 4.95 (*0-452-00894-8*, Mer) NAL-Dutton.

— The Confidence-Man. Hayford, Harrison et al, eds. (Northwestern-Newberry Edition of the Writings of Herman Melville: Vol. 10). 518p. 1984. 49.95 (*0-8101-0324-9*); pap. 18.95 (*0-8101-0325-7*) Northwestern U Pr.

— The Confidence-Man. Tanner, Tony & Dugdale, John, eds. (World's Classics Ser.). (Illus.). 408p. 1989. pap. 7.95 (*0-19-281824-4*) OUP.

— The Confidence-Man. 400p. 1991. mass mkt. 8.95 (*0-14-044547-1*, Penguin Classics) Viking Penguin.

— The Confidence Man. annot. ed. Foster, Elizabeth S., ed. (Complete Works of Herman Melville Ser.). 1979. 29.95 (*0-87532-009-0*) Hendricks House.

— The Confidence-Man. 260p. 1990. reprint ed. lib. bdg. 21.95 (*0-89966-714-7*) Buccaneer Bks.

— Confidence-Man: His Masquerade. Franklin, H. Bruce, ed. LC 66-30445. 1967. pap. 6.95 (*0-672-60986-X*, LL13, Bobbs) Macmillan.

— Correspondence. Horth, Lynn, ed. (Northwestern-Newberry Edition of the Writings of Herman Melville: Vol. 14). (Illus.). 924p. (Orig.). 1993. 89.95 (*0-8101-0981-6*); pap. 29.95 (*0-8101-0995-6*) Northwestern U Pr.

— Encantadas: or Enchanted Isles. (BCL1-PS American Literature Ser.). 118p. 1993. reprint ed. lib. bdg. 69.00 (*0-7812-6988-1*) Rprt Serv.

— Family Correspondence of Herman Melville. Paltsits, Victor H., ed. (American Literature Ser.: No. 49). 1976. lib. bdg. 75.00 (*0-8383-2111-9*) M S G Haskell Hse.

— Great Short Works. 19.75 (*0-8446-0798-3*) Peter Smith.

— Great Short Works of Herman Melville. 1970. pap. 8.00 (*0-06-083094-8*) HarpC.

— Herman Melville: Authentic Anecdotes of Old Zack. Starosciak, Kenneth, ed. & intro. by. 1973. reprint ed. pap. 5.00 (*0-686-02647-0*) K Starosciak.

— Israel Potter. Reagar, Daniel, ed. (Masterworks of Literature Ser.). 1995. pap. 12.95 (*0-8084-0476-8*) NCUP.

— Israel Potter. Hayford, Harrison et al, eds. LC 82-81178. (Northwestern-Newberry Edition of the Writings of Herman Melville: Vol. 8). 401p. 1982. 49.95 (*0-8101-0552-7*); pap. 18.95 (*0-8101-0553-5*) Northwestern U Pr.

— Israel Potter: His Fifty Years of Exile. rev. ed. Hennig, Cohen, ed. LC 90-56158. 505p. 1991. 60.00 (*0-8232-1322-6*) Fordham.

— Israel Potter: His Fifty Years of Exile. Cohen, Hennig, ed. LC 90-56158. (Illus.). 505p. 1994. reprint ed. pap. 19.95 (*0-8232-1323-4*) Fordham.

— Israel Potter: His Fifty Years of Exile. (BCL1-PS American Literature Ser.). 301p. 1992. reprint ed. lib. bdg. 89.00 (*0-7812-6794-3*) Rprt Serv.

— Journal of a Visit to Europe & the Levant, 1856-57. Horsford, Howard C., ed. LC 75-27655. (Princeton Studies in English Ser.: No.35). (Illus.). 299p. 1976. reprint ed. text ed. 35.00 (*0-8371-8448-7*, MEJV, Greenwood Pr) Greenwood.

— Journals. Horsford, Howard & Horth, Lynn, eds. (Northwestern-Newberry Edition of the Writings of Herman Melville: Vol. 15). (Illus.). 683p. 1989. 69.95 (*0-8101-0822-4*); pap. 24.95 (*0-8101-0823-2*) Northwestern U Pr.

— Mardi. (FRE.). 1983. pap. 20.95 (*0-7859-4190-8*) Fr & Eur.

— Mardi. Hillway, Tyrus, ed. (Masterworks of Literature Ser.). 1973. 25.95 (*0-8084-0016-9*); pap. 18.95 (*0-8084-0017-7*) NCUP.

— Mardi. Hayford, Harrison et al, eds. LC 67-21602. (Northwestern-Newberry Edition of the Writings of Herman Melville: Vol. 3). 1970. 69.95 (*0-8101-0015-0*); pap. 24.95 (*0-8101-0014-2*) Northwestern U Pr.

— Mardi. annot. ed. Wright, Nathalia, ed. (Complete Works of Herman Melville Ser.). 1990. 29.95 (*0-87532-015-5*) Hendricks House.

— Mardi & a Voyage Thither, 2 vols., Set. (BCL1-PS American Literature Ser.). 1992. reprint ed. lib. bdg. 150.00 (*0-7812-6795-1*) Rprt Serv.

— Moby-Dick. Lee, A. Robert, ed. 512p. 1993. pap. 3.95 (*0-460-87307-5*, Everyman's Classic Lib) C E Tuttle.

— Moby Dick: Or, the Whale. Tanner, Tony, ed. (World's Classics Ser.). 656p. 1988. pap. 4.95 (*0-19-281780-9*) OUP.

— Moby Dick: Or the Whale. LC 92-50222. 1992. 20.00 (*0-679-60010-8*, Modern Lib) Random.

— Moby-Dick or, the Whale. Parker, Hershel & Tanselle, G. Thomas, eds. (Northwestern-Newberry Edition of the Writings of Herman Melville: Vol. 6). 1043p. (C). 1988. 89.95 (*0-8101-0268-4*); pap. 29.95 (*0-8101-0269-2*) Northwestern U Pr.

— Moby Dick, or the Whale. annot. ed. Mansfield, Luther & Vincent, Howard P., eds. (Complete Works of Herman Melville Ser.). 909p. 1962. 29.95 (*0-87532-001-5*) Hendricks House.

— Moby-Dick: or The Whale. rev. ed. (Illus.). 624p. 1992. 9.95 (*0-14-039084-7*, Penguin Classics) Viking Penguin.

— Moby-Dick, or The Whale. LC 81-40320. (Illus.). 600p. 1981. reprint ed. 45.00 (*0-520-04354-5*); reprint ed. pap. 16.00 (*0-520-04548-3*); reprint ed. boxed 375.00 (*0-520-04549-1*) U CA Pr.

— Moby Dick Readalong. (Illustrated Classics Collection 1). 64p. 1994. audio, pap. 13.50 (*1-56103-434-7*) Lake Pub Co.

— Monarch Moby Dick. 1976. pap. 3.95 (*0-671-00623-1*) S&S Trade.

— Omoo. 1976. 21.95 (*0-8488-1098-8*) Amereon Ltd.

— Omoo. Hayford, Harrison et al, eds. LC 67-11991. (Northwestern-Newberry Edition of the Writings of Herman Melville: Vol. 2). 380p. 1968. 49.95 (*0-8101-0162-9*); pap. 18.95 (*0-8101-0160-2*) Northwestern U Pr.

— Omoo. (BCL1-PS American Literature Ser.). 299p. 1992. reprint ed. lib. bdg. 79.00 (*0-7812-6796-X*) Rprt Serv.

— Omoo: Adventures in the South Seas. (Pacific Basin Bks.). 220p. (Orig.). 1985. pap. 14.95 (*0-7103-0133-2*, Pub. by Kegan Paul Intl UK) Routledge Chapman & Hall.

— Piazza Tales. Reagan, Daniel, ed. (Masterworks of Literature Ser.). 1994. 14.95 (*0-8084-0443-1*) NCUP.

— The Piazza Tales. 19.95 (*0-89190-877-3*, Am Repr) Amereon Ltd.

— Piazza Tales. (BCL1-PS American Literature Ser.). 250p. 1993. reprint ed. lib. bdg. 79.00 (*0-7812-6989-X*) Rprt Serv.

— The Piazza Tales & Other Prose Pieces, 1839-60. Parker, Hershel & Tanselle, G. Thomas, eds. (Northwestern-Newberry Edition of the Writings of Herman Melville: Vol. 9). (Illus.). 847p. (C). 1987. 82.95 (*0-8101-0550-0*); pap. 24.95 (*0-8101-0551-9*) Northwestern U Pr.

— Pierre. Hayford, Harrison et al, eds. (Northwestern-Newberry Edition of the Writings of Herman Melville: Vol. 7). 435p. 1972. 49.95 (*0-8101-0266-8*); pap. 18.95 (*0-8101-0267-6*) Northwestern U Pr.

— Pierre, or the Ambiguities. annot. ed. Murray, Henry A., ed. (Complete Works of Herman Melville Ser.). 608p. 1962. 29.95 (*0-87532-003-1*) Hendricks House.

— Poems of Herman Melville. Robillard, Douglas, ed. (Masterworks of Literature Ser.). 1976. pap. 13.95 (*0-8084-0417-2*) NCUP.

— Redburn. Hayford, Harrison et al, eds. (Northwestern-Newberry Edition of the Writings of Herman Melville: Vol. 4). 384p. 1972. 49.95 (*0-8101-0013-4*); pap. 18.95 (*0-8101-0016-9*) Northwestern U Pr.

— Redburn. Beaver, Harold, ed. (English Library). 448p. 1977. mass mkt. 8.95 (*0-14-043105-5*, Penguin Classics) Viking Penguin.

— Redburn. (BCL1-PS American Literature Ser.). 346p. 1993. reprint ed. lib. bdg. 89.00 (*0-7812-6990-3*) Rprt Serv.

— Redburn ou Sa Premiere Croisiere. (FRE.). 1980. pap. 13.95 (*0-7859-4142-8*) Fr & Eur.

— Redburn, White-Jacket, Moby-Dick. Tanselle, G. Thomas, ed. Incl. White-Jacket; Or the World in a Man-of-War. LC 82-18677. 1983. (*0-318-63068-0*); Moby-Dick; Or the Whale. LC 82-18677. 1983. (*0-318-63069-9*); LC 82-18677. 1436p. 1983. 35.00 (*0-940450-09-7*) Library of America.

— Selected Tales & Poems. 27.95 (*0-89190-681-9*, Am Repr) Amereon Ltd.

— Selected Tales & Poems. Chase, Richard, ed. 417p. (C). 1950. pap. text ed. 19.75 (*0-03-008140-8*) HB Coll Pubs.

M

— Shorter Novels of Herman Melville. (Black & Gold Library). 1978. pap. 10.95 (*0-87140-122-3*) Liveright.

— Taipi. (FRE.). 1984. pap. 17.95 (*0-7859-4199-7*) Fr & Eur.

— Timoleon. 1972. 35.00 (*0-8490-1215-5*) Gordon Pr.

— Typee. (Airmont Classics Ser.). (J). (gr. 10 up). 1965. pap. 1.50 (*0-8049-0053-1*, CL-53) Airmont.

— Typee. 293p. 1993. pap. 3.95 (*0-460-87276-1*, Everyman's Classic Lib) C E Tuttle.

— Typee. 1964. pap. 5.95 (*0-451-52518-3*, CE1854, Sig Classics) NAL-Dutton.

— Typee. Hayford, Harrison et al, eds. LC 67-11990. (Northwestern-Newberry Edition of the Writings of Herman Melville: Vol. 1). (Illus.). 374p. (C). 1968. 49.95 (*0-8101-0161-0*); pap. 18.95 (*0-8101-0159-9*) Northwestern U Pr.

— Typee. Woodcock, George, ed. (English Library). 1972. mass mkt. 9.95 (*0-14-043070-9*, Penguin Classics) Viking Penguin.

— Typee. 300p. 1990. reprint ed. lib. bdg. 25.95 (*0-89966-715-5*) Buccaneer Bks.

— Typee: Four Months Residence in the Marquesas Islands. (Pacific Basin Bks.). 300p. (Orig.). 1985. pap. 14.95 (*0-7103-0132-4*, Pub. by Kegan Paul Intl UK) Routledge Chapman & Hall.

— Typee, Omoo, Mardi. Tanselle, G. Thomas, ed. Incl. Omoo: A Narrative of Adventures in the South Seas. LC 81-18600. 1982. (*0-318-63066-4*); Mardi; And a Voyage Thither. LC 81-18600. 1982. (*0-318-63067-2*); LC 81-18600. 1333p. 1982. 29.95 (*0-940450-00-3*) Library of America.

— White Jacket. 1979. mass mkt. 4.95 (*0-452-00955-3*, Meridian Bks) NAL-Dutton.

— White-Jacket. Hayford, Harrison et al, eds. LC 67-21603. (Northwestern-Newberry Edition of the Writings of Herman Melville: Vol. 5). 499p. 1970. 49.95 (*0-8101-0257-9*); pap. 18.95 (*0-8101-0258-7*) Northwestern U Pr.

— White-Jacket. LC 88-2650. (Classics of Naval Literature Ser.). 736p. 1988. reprint ed. 32.95 (*0-87021-788-7*) Naval Inst Pr.

— White-Jacket: Or the World in a Man of War. 1991. pap. 6.95 (*0-19-281828-7*) OUP.

— Works of Herman Melville. LC 87-14445. 736p. 1987. 9.98 (*0-517-65084-3*) Random Hse Value.

Melville, Jame. Body Wore Brocade. 1994. mass mkt. 4.99 (*0-449-22189-X*) Fawcett.

Melville, James. The Body Wore Brocade. large type ed. (Ulverscroft Ser.). 304p. 1994. 20.95 (*0-7089-3064-6*) Ulverscroft.

— The Body Wore Brocade: A Superintendent Otani Mystery. 224p. 1992. text ed. 20.00 (*0-684-19413-9*, Scribners) S&S Trade.

— The Bogus Buddha. large type ed. (Keating's Choice Ser.). 249p. 1992. 21.95 (*1-85089-569-4*, Pub. by ISIS UK) Transaction Pubs.

— The Chrysanthemum Chain. large type ed. 370p. 1982. 21.95 (*0-7089-0758-X*) Ulverscroft.

— Death of a Daimyo. large type ed. 256p. 1986. 21.95 (*0-7089-1462-4*) Ulverscroft.

— Diary. LC 70-172723. (Bannatyne Club, Edinburgh. Publications: No. 34). reprint ed. 32.50 (*0-404-52740-X*) AMS Pr.

— The Imperial Way. 304p. 1987. reprint ed. pap. 3.95 (*0-449-21374-9*, Crest) Fawcett.

— Memoirs of His Own Life. LC 74-172724. (Maitland Club, Glasgow. Publications: No. 21). reprint ed. 64.50 (*0-404-52718-3*) AMS Pr.

— The Ninth Netsuke. large type ed. 320p. 1986. 21.95 (*0-7089-1404-7*) Ulverscroft.

— Sayonara, Sweet Amaryllis. large type ed. 304p. 1986. 21.95 (*0-7089-1433-0*) Ulverscroft.

— A Tarnished Phoenix. large type ed. (Adventure Suspense Ser.). 432p. 1992. 21.95 (*0-7089-2666-5*) Ulverscroft.

***Melville, Jennie.** Dead Set. (WWL Mystery Ser.). 1995. mass mkt. 3.99 (*0-373-26174-8*, 1-26174-2) Harlequin Bks.

— Death in the Family. 1995. 21.00 (*0-312-11772-8*, Pub. by Thomas Dunne Bks) St Martin.

— Footsteps in the Blood. large type ed. LC 94-2047. 1994. pap. 17.95 (*0-7862-0189-4*) Thorndike Pr.

— Footsteps in the Blood: A Charmain Daniels Mystery. 192p. 1993. 17.95 (*0-312-09813-8*, Pub. by Thomas Dunne Bks) St Martin.

— Whoever Has the Heart. large type ed. LC 94-7116. 330p. 1994. lib. bdg. 17.95 (*0-7862-0207-6*) Thorndike Pr.

— Whoever Has the Heart: A Charmain Daniels Mystery. 224p. 1994. 19.95 (*0-312-11099-5*, Pub. by Thomas Dunne Bks) St Martin.

— Witching Murder. (Lythway Adult Ser.). 280p. 1991. text ed. 20.50 (*0-7451-1374-5*, Pub. by Chivers Pr UK) Chivers N Amer.

Melville, John. Crystal-Gazing & the World of Clairvoyance. 87p. 1968. reprint ed. spiral bd. 4.40 (*0-7873-1269-X*) Mokelumne.

Melville, K. F., ed. Guide to Coal Contracts, 1991. 731p. 1991. pap. 237.00 (*0-685-47990-0*) Pasha Pubns.

Melville, Keith. Marriage & Family Today. 3rd ed. 492p. (C). 1983. text ed. write for info. (*0-318-57008-4*) Random.

— Marriage & Family Today. 4th ed. 512p. (C). 1988. text ed. write for info. (*0-07-554748-1*) McGraw.

Melville, Keith, jt. auth. see Bird, Gloria.

Melville, Lawrence. The Fair Land of Gowrie. 1987. 60.00 (*0-900323-20-5*, Pub. by W Culross & Son Ltd UK) St Mut.

Melville, Leinani. Children of the Rainbow: The Religions, Legends & Gods of Pre-Christian Hawaii. LC 69-17715. (Illus.). 1969. pap. 7.95 (*0-8356-0002-5*, Quest) Theos Pub Hse.

Melville, Leslie W. Forms & Agreements on Intellectual Property & International Licensing, 3 vols., Set. 3rd ed. LC 78-17576. 1979. ring bd. 375.00 (*0-685-00782-0*) Clark Boardman Callaghan.

Melville, M., jt. auth. see Melville, T.

Melville, Margarita B., ed. Mexicanas at Work in the United States. (Mexican American Studies Monograph: No. V). (Orig.). (C). 1988. pap. text ed. 11.95 (*0-939709-04-X*) Univ Houston Mex Amer.

Melville, Mary H. The Temporary Worker in the Nuclear Power Industry: An Equity Analysis. LC 81-65590. (CENTED Monographs: No. 1). (Illus.). 70p. 1981. pap. text ed. 5.00 (*0-939436-00-0*) Ctr Tech Environ.

Melville, Michael L. The Story of the Lovat Scouts. 118p. 1981. 90.00 (*0-7152-0474-2*) St Mut.

***Melville, Stephen & Readings, Bill, eds.** Vision & Textuality. LC 94-39995. 1995. write for info. (*0-8223-1630-7*); pap. write for info. (*0-8223-1644-7*) Duke.

Melville, T. & Melville, M. Guatemala: The Politics of Land Ownership. LC 70-143523. 1971. 24.95 (*0-02-920840-8*) Free Pr.

Melville, Tom. Cricket for Americans: Playing & Understanding the Game. LC 92-7488. 214p. 1993. 25.95 (*0-87972-606-7*) Bowling Green Univ.

Melville, William L. Leven & Melville Papers. LC 78-172725. (Bannatyne Club, Edinburgh. Publications: No. 77). reprint ed. 67.50 (*0-404-52798-1*) AMS Pr.

Melvin, A. Natural Gas: Basic Science & Technology. (Illus.). 224p. 1987. 83.00 (*0-85274-478-1*) IOP Pub.

Melvin, B. L. & Smith, E. N. Rural Youth: Their Situation & Prospects. LC 71-165687. (Research Monograph Ser.: Vol. 15). 1971. reprint ed. lib. bdg. 22.50 (*0-306-70347-5*) Da Capo.

Melvin, Billy A. Free Will Baptist Minister's Manual. 1974. ring bd. 10.95 (*0-89265-024-9*) Randall Hse.

Melvin, Billy A., jt. auth. see O'Donnell, J. D.

Melvin, Bruce L. Rural Youth on Relief. LC 74-37899. (Select Bibliographies Reprint Ser.). 1977. reprint ed. 20.95 (*0-8369-6737-2*) Ayer.

— Rural Youth on Relief. LC 78-165686. (Research Monograph Ser.: Vol. 11). 1971. reprint ed. lib. bdg. 19.50 (*0-306-70343-2*) Da Capo.

Melvin, Bruce L. & Smith, Elna N. Youth in Agricultural Villages. LC 79-165603. (Research Monograph Ser.: Vol. 21). 1971. reprint ed. lib. bdg. 19.50 (*0-306-70353-X*) Da Capo.

Melvin, Don, jt. auth. see Kunerth, Jeff.

Melvin, Eric. Plan - Predict - Prevent: How to Reinvest in Public Buildings. (Special Report Ser.: No. 62). 83p. (Orig.). 1992. pap. text ed. 50.00 (*0-917084-11-X*) Am Public Works.

Melvin, Frances. The Boughs of Innocence. large type ed. 356p. 1983. 15.95 (*0-7089-1005-X*) Ulverscroft.

— Camberwell Beauty. large type ed. 352p. 1984. 15.95 (*0-7089-1105-6*) Ulverscroft.

Melvin, Frank E. Napoleon's Navigation System. LC 79-135721. reprint ed. 47.50 (*0-404-04288-0*) AMS Pr.

Melvin, George F., jt. auth. see Albert, Dave.

Melvin, J. L., ed. Evaporites, Petroleum & Mineral Resources. (Developments in Sedimentology Ser.: No. 50). 556p. 1991. 120.00 (*0-444-88680-X*) Elsevier.

Melvin, Jackie, ed. see Deaver, Korra.

Melvin, Jackie, ed. see Selling, Bernard.

Melvin, James R. The Effects of Energy Price Changes on Commodity Prices, Interprovincial Trade & Employment. LC 76-27870. (Ontario Economic Council Research Studies: No. 3). (Illus.). 112p. reprint ed. pap. 32.00 (*0-8357-3999-6*, 2036699) Bks Demand.

— Interregional Effects of Canadian Tariffs & Transportation Policy. (Ontario Economic Council Research Studies). 151p. 1987. pap. text ed. 12.95 (*0-8020-6630-5*) U of Toronto Pr.

— Trade in Services: A Theoretical Analysis. 195p. 1989. pap. text ed. 29.95 (*0-88645-090-X*, Pub. by Inst Res Pub CN) Ashgate Pub Co.

Melvin, Jeanne L. Rheumatic Disease in the Adult & Child: Occupational Therapy & Rehabilitation. 3rd ed. LC 88-38279. (Illus.). 607p. (C). 1989. 54.95 (*0-8036-6137-1*) Davis Co.

— Scleroderma: Caring for Your Hands & Face. (Illus.). 32p. 1994. pap. text ed. write for info. (*1-56900-006-9*) Am Occup Therapy.

Melvin, John, jt. ed. see Nahum, Alan.

Melvin, Julia, jt. ed. see Olney, R. J.

Melvin, Maureen. Paws for Pasta. (Illus.). 64p. 1993. pap. 13.95 (*1-85592-629-6*, Pub. by Chapmans UK) Trafalgar.

Melvin, Maureen A. Electrophoresis. (Analytical Chemistry by Open Learning Ser.). 127p. 1987. pap. text ed. 49.95 (*0-471-91375-8*) Wiley.

Melvin, Michael. International Money & Finance. 4th ed. LC 94-17773. 275p. (C). 1995. text ed. 39.00 (*0-673-99207-1*) HarpCollege.

Melvin, Michael, jt. auth. see Boyes, William.

Melvin, Michael, jt. auth. see Husted, Steven L.

Melvin, Michael H. International Money & Finance. 2nd ed. 240p. (C). 1990. text ed. 32.75 (*0-06-044472-X*) HarpCollege.

— International Money & Finance. 3rd ed. (C). 1991. text ed. 58.50 (*0-06-500277-6*) HarpCollege.

Melvin, Michael H., jt. auth. see Husted, Steven.

Melvin, Michael H., jt. auth. see Husted.

Melvin, Michael T., jt. auth. see Darby, Michael R.

Melvin, Particia M., ed. American Community Organizations: A Historical Dictionary. LC 86-9961. 252p. 1986. text ed. 59.95 (*0-313-24053-1*, MLV/, Greenwood Pr) Greenwood.

Melvin, Patricia M. The Organic City: Urban Definition & Community Organization, 1880-1920. LC 87-13322. 240p. 1987. 26.00 (*0-8131-1585-X*) U Pr of Ky.

Melvin, Patricia M., jt. auth. see Miller, Zane L.

Melvin, Robert. Profiles in Flowers: The Story of San Diego County Floriculture. Ecke, Paul, Jr., ed. 168p. 1989. write for info. (*0-318-65326-5*) P Ecke Ranch Pr.

Melvin, Shelley & Stone, Marilyn. Snack to Your Heart's Content! The Low-Fat, Low-Cholesterol, Low-Calorie Quick & Easy Cookbook. (Illus.). 192p. (Orig.). 1990. pap. 9.95 (*0-937404-32-2*) Triad Pub FL.

Melvin, William H. First Day of Forever & One Hundred Additional Poems. 110p. 1989. per., pap. 7.95 (*0-89697-308-5*) Intl Univ Pr.

Melvoin, Richard I. New England Outpost: War & Society in Colonial Deerfield. 368p. 1992. pap. 12.95 (*0-393-30808-1*) Norton.

Melvold, Robert W., et al. Sorbents for Liquid Hazardous Substance Cleanup & Control. LC 87-31550. (Pollution Technology Review Ser.: No. 150). (Illus.). 154p. 1988. 36.00 (*0-8155-1159-0*) Noyes.

Melwani, Murli D. Critical Essays on Indo-Anglian Themes. (Greybird Ser.). 1976. 5.00 (*0-89253-128-2*) Ind-US Inc.

— Deep Roots. (Writers Workshop Bluebird Ser.). 56p. 1975. 8.00 (*0-88253-524-2*); pap. text ed. 4.80 (*0-88253-523-4*) Ind-US Inc.

— Stories of a Salesman. 1976. lib. bdg. 8.00 (*0-89253-084-7*); 6.75 (*0-89253-268-8*) Ind-US Inc.

Melyan, Gary G. & Wen-kuang Chu. The Pocket I-Ching. LC 88-50327. (Illus.). 182p. 1988. reprint ed. pap. 6.95 (*0-8048-1566-6*) C E Tuttle.

Melyan, Wesley R. & Bonetti, Lee. Rolling Thunder: July 1965-December 1966. 149p. 1993. reprint ed. pap. 17.50x (*0-923135-70-7*) Dalley Bk Service.

Melynk, Steven A. & Narasimhan, Ram. Computer Integrated Manufacturing: Guidelines & Applications from Industrial Leaders. (APICS Series in Production Management). 378p. 1991. 50.00 (*1-55623-538-0*) Irwin Prof Pubng.

***Melzack, Ronald, ed.** Pain Measurement & Assessment. fac. ed. LC 82-40296. (Illus.). 311p. Date not set. pap. 88.70 (*0-7837-7506-7*, 2047000) Bks Demand.

Melzack, Ronald & Wall, Patrick D. The Challenge of Pain. rev. ed. 352p. 1989. pap. 10.00 (*0-14-015660-7*, Penguin Bks) Viking Penguin.

Melzack, Ronald, jt. ed. see Turk, Dennis C.

Melzack, Ronald, jt. ed. see Wall, Patrick D.

Melzak, Z. A. Bypasses: A Simple Approach to Complexity. 262p. (C). 1983. lib. bdg. 51.95 (*0-471-86854-X*) Krieger.

— Companion to Concrete Mathematics, Vol. 1: Mathematical Techniques & Various Applications. LC 72-14171. (Wiley Series in Pure & Applied Mathematics). 284p. reprint ed. pap. 81.00 (*0-317-08619-7*, 2022492) Bks Demand.

— Companion to Concrete Mathematics, Vol. 2: Mathematical Ideas, Modeling & Applications. LC 72-14171. 432p. reprint ed. pap. 123.20 (*0-317-08554-9*, 2055165) Bks Demand.

Melzer, Annabelle. Dada & Surrealist Performance. (PAJ Bks.). 312p. (C). 1994. pap. text ed. 14.95 (*0-8018-4845-8*) Johns Hopkins.

Melzer, Annabelle H. Latest Rage the Big Drum: Dada & Surrealist Performance. LC 80-22656. (Studies in the Fine Arts: The Avant-Garde: No. 7). (Illus.). 290p. reprint ed. pap. 82.70 (*0-8357-1639-2*, 2070231) Bks Demand.

Melzer, Arthur M. The Natural Goodness of Man: On the System of Rousseau's Thought. 368p. 1990. lib. bdg. 51.00 (*0-226-51978-3*); pap. text ed. 18.95 (*0-226-51979-1*) U Ch Pr.

***Melzer, Arthur M., et al, eds.** History & the Idea of Progress. 272p. 1995. 37.50x (*0-8014-2986-2*) Cornell U Pr.

— History & the Idea of Progress. 272p. 1995. pap. 14.95x (*0-8014-8182-1*) Cornell U Pr.

— Technology in the Western Political Tradition. 352p. 1993. 38.50 (*0-8014-2724-X*); pap. 15.95 (*0-8014-8006-X*) Cornell U Pr.

Melzer, Dorothy G. Introduction & Computations for Gases. LC 80-25594. (AIChEMI Modular Instruction F Ser.: Vol. 1: Material & Energy Balances). 51p. 1981. pap. 44.00 (*0-8169-0175-9*, J-6) Am Inst Chem Eng.

Melzer, John T. Fourteen Days to Field Spanish. 60p. 1985. pap. 7.95 (*0-317-01524-9*, Pub. by Univ Ed PE) Wordsmith Auburn.

Melzer, Manfred, et al. The East Germany Economy. Jeffries, Ian & Breuning, Eleanor, eds. 300p. 1987. lib. bdg. 72.50 (*0-7099-1469-5*, Pub. by Croom Helm UK) Routledge Chapman & Hall.

Melzer, Marilyn, jt. auth. see Palau, Susan M.

Melzer, Milton, ed. Lincoln, in His Own Words. LC 92-17431. (Illus.). 240p. (J). 1993. 22.95 (*0-15-245437-3*) HarBrace.

— Lincoln, in His Own Words. limited ed. LC 92-17431. (Illus.). 240p. (J). 1993. 150.00 (*0-15-245438-1*) HarBrace.

Melzer, Richard. Contrasting Views about New Mexico History. 200p. (C). 1994. pap. text ed. 20.00 (*1-878045-39-3*) Whittier Pubns.

— Madrid Revisited: Life & Labor in a New Mexican Mining Camp in the Years of the Great Depression. LC 76-18599. (Illus.). 1976. 15.00 (*0-89016-025-2*); pap. 10.00 (*0-89016-024-4*) Lightning Tree.

Melzer, Richard, jt. ed. see Meerbaum, Samuel.

Melzer, Sara E. & Rabine, Leslie W., eds. Rebel Daughters: Women & the French Revolution. (University of California Humanities Research Institute Ser.). (Illus.). 288p. 1992. pap. 16.95 (*0-19-507016-X*) OUP.

Melzer, Tom. Princeton Review: The Three Hundred Best American Colleges. 1992. pap. 16.00 (*0-679-73866-5*, Villard Bks) Random.

Melzer, Werner. Beekeeping: An Owner's Manual. 1989. pap. 5.95 (*0-8120-4089-9*) Barron.

Melzi, Robert C. Bantam Italian Dictionary. 1984. mass mkt. 5.99 (*0-553-27947-5*) Bantam.

Melzian, H. I., jt. auth. see Westermann, Diedrich.

Members of ESRC Inner Cities Research Programme Staff & Hausner, Victor A., eds. Urban Economic Change: Five City Studies. (ESRC Inner Cities Research Programme Ser.: No. 2). (Illus.). 280p. 1988. 65.00 (*0-19-823280-2*) OUP.

Members of Poetry Workshop Staff. Festival of Poetry, Bk. 1: Anthology of Poems by Members of Margaret Tyler's Scottsdale Library Poetry Workshop. 64p. (Orig.). 1989. pap. 2.50 (*0-9622775-0-9*) Tyler-Balstrode.

Members of TFCE Staff. Texas Temptations. 350p. 1993. 12.00 (*0-9637300-0-2*) TX Assn Fmly.

Members of the Arta Rehabilitation Center. Rock Bottom: Beyond Drug Addiction. Cornelis, Jakob, tr. 61p. 1990. pap. 12.95 (*1-869890-11-6*, 1300, Pub. by Hawthorn Press UK) Anthroposophic.

Members of the Department of Otolaryngology Staff, et al. The Management of Voice Disorders. (Illus.). 256p. (Orig.). (C). 1994. 55.00x (*1-56593-311-7*, 0464) Singular Publishing.

Members of the International Food, Wine & Travel Writers Association Staff. Windows to the World: Inside Look at Food, Wine & Travel. KaSaker, Ray & Jackson, D. K., eds. (Illus.). 254p. 1989. 7.98 (*0-9621891-1-1*) D & A Pub CA.

Members of the Society Staff. Proceedings: Papers from the 6th Regional Meeting. 588p. 1970. pap. 6.00 (*0-914203-01-0*) Chicago Ling.

Membrane Processes for Industry Symposium Staff. Proceedings of the Membrane Processes for Industry Symposium, May 19-20, 1986. Feazel, Charles E. & Lacey, Robert E., eds. LC 66-30620. (Illus.). 268p. 1966. pap. 5.00 (*0-940824-00-0*) S Res Inst.

Meme-Fun Dai, tr. see Graham, Billy.

Memed, Orhan. Seventeenth-Century English Keyboard Music: Benjamin Cosyn. LC 92-43441. (Outstanding Dissertations in Music from British Universities Ser.). 480p. 1993. 134.00 (*0-8153-0949-X*) Garland.

Memedovic, Olga. On the Theory & Measurement of Comparative Advantage: An Empirical Analysis of Yugoslav Trade in Manufactures with the OECD Countries, 1970-1986. (Tinbergen Institute Ser.). 360p. 1994. pap. 30.00 (*90-5170-251-5*, Pub. by Thesis Pubs NE) IBD Ltd.

Memelink, Mary, ed. see Hamernik, Marcia.

Memering, W. Dean. Prentice Hall Guide to Research Writing. 2nd ed. 384p. (C). 1989. pap. text ed. write for info. (*0-13-774480-3*) P-H.

Memering, W. Dean, jt. auth. see Howell, James F.

Memering, W. Dean, jt. auth. see O'Hare, Frank.

Memhard, Polly H., jt. auth. see Hunter, Laura R.

Memmer, Wayne. Tiger: A True Champion. LC 91-62540. 56p. 1992. 6.95 (*0-944957-32-3*) Rivercross Pub.

Memmi, Albert. Agar. (FRE.). 1984. pap. 10.95 (*0-7859-4210-6*) Fr & Eur.

— The Colonizer & the Colonized. rev. ed. LC 90-24035. 208p. 1991. pap. 14.00 (*0-8070-0301-8*) Beacon Pr.

— Desert Ou la Vie et les Aventures de Joubair Ouali El-Mammi. (Folio Ser.: No. 2034). (FRE.). 1989. pap. 10.95 (*2-07-038122-6*) Schoenhof.

— Jews & Arabs. Levieux, Eleanor, tr. LC 75-10697. 224p. 1975. 9.95 (*0-87955-327-8*); pap. 7.95 (*0-87955-328-6*) O'Hara.

— The Pillar of Salt: A Novel. LC 91-16952. 352p. 1992. reprint ed. pap. 14.00 (*0-8070-8327-5*) Beacon Pr.

— Scorpion. (Folio Ser.: No. 1715). 270p. (FRE.). 1986. pap. 10.95 (*2-07-037715-6*) Schoenhof.

— The Scorpion. 2nd ed. LC 79-114950. 242p. 1975. reprint ed. 9.95 (*0-87955-908-X*); reprint ed. pap. 7.95 (*0-87955-906-3*) O'Hara.

— Statue de Sel. (Folio Ser.: No. 206). 377p. (FRE.). 1984. pap. 9.95 (*2-07-036206-X*) Schoenhof.

Memmler, Ruth L., et al. The Human Body in Health & Disease. 7th ed. (Illus.). 432p. 1992. 33.50 (*0-397-54884-2*); pap. 28.50 (*0-397-54885-0*) Lippincott.

— Structure & Function of the Human Body. 5th ed. (Illus.). 336p. 1992. 31.50 (*0-397-54882-6*); pap. 27.95 (*0-397-54883-4*) Lippincott.

— Workbook to Accompany Structure & Function of. 5th ed. 256p. 1992. pap. 15.95 (*0-397-54944-X*) Lippincott.

— Workbook to Accompany the Human Body in Health & Disease. 7th ed. (Illus.). 320p. 1992. pap. 16.95 (*0-397-54943-1*) Lippincott.

***Memon, Ali N.** The Islamic Nation: Status & Future of Muslims in the New World Order. LC 95-6017. 272p. 1995. pap. 15.00 (*0-9627854-7-4*) Writers Inc.

Memon, Muhammad U. Ibn Taimaya's Struggle Against Popular Religion with an Annotated Translation of His Kitab Iqtida Assirat Al Mustaquin Mukhalafat Ashab Al-Jahim. (Religion & Society Ser.: No. 1). 1976. text ed. 74.70 (*90-279-7591-4*) Mouton.

Memon, Muhammad U., ed. & tr. The Tale of the Old Fisherman: Contemporary Urdu Short Stories. 176p. 1991. 25.00 (*0-89410-681-3*); pap. 11.00 (*0-89410-682-1*) Three Continents.

Memon, Muhammad U., tr. see Hussein, Abdullah.

***Memon, Siddique G.** Tomb of the Kalhora Chiefs at Hyderabad. (Illus.). 100p. 1995. 49.95 (*0-19-577502-3*) OUP.

Memorial Hospital Junior Auxiliary Easton Maryland Staff. A Cook's Tour of the Eastern Shore. 2nd ed. LC 59-15724. (Illus.). 386p. 1959. pap. 13.95 (*0-87033-001-2*, Tidewtr Pubs) Cornell Maritime.

Memorial Sloan-Kettering Cancer Center. International Alumni Directory, 1986-1988. Wood, Denise D., ed. 1986. 50.00 (*0-911315-01-2*) Memorial Sloan-Kettering.

Memories Magazine Staff. Yearbook Memories. 1990. mass mkt. 9.95 (*0-385-41625-3*) Doubleday.

Memory, J. D., jt. auth. see Stejskal, E. O.

An Asterisk (*) at the beginning of an entry indicates that the title is appearing in BIP for the first time.

*Memphis Orff Specialists. The World Sings: Visas to Our Musical World for Voices & Orff Instruments. Bennett, Michael D., ed. (Illus.). 1991. audio write for info. (0-934017-15-8) Memphis Musicraft.

Memrey, Paul W. Surrealism in Literature. 236p. 1983. 10.95 (0-935539-08-5) Heroica Bks.

Memry, Paul. The Mannequin. 208p. (Orig.). 1991. pap. 9.95 (0-935539-05-0) Heroica Bks.

Men Against Patriarchy Staff. Off Their Backs... And on Our Own Two Feet. 32p. 1983. pap. 3.45 (0-86571-028-7) New Soc Pubs.

Men, Hunbatz. Secrets of Mayan Science - Religion. LC 89-6637. (Illus.). 160p. (Orig.). 1989. pap. 10.95 (0-939680-63-7) Bear & Co.

Mena, B., et al, eds. Advances in Rheology: Proceedings of the Ninth International Congress on Rheology Acapulco, Mexico, October 8-13, 1984, 4 vols. 1985. pap. 300.00 (0-444-99576-5) Elsevier.

Mena, Cesar A. Historia de la Medicina en Cuba II: Ejercicios y Ensenanza de las Ciencias Medicas en la Epoca Colonial. LC 91-76473. (Coleccion Cuba y Sus Jueces Ser.). (Illus.). 380p. (Orig.). (SPA.). 1993. pap. 39.00 (0-89729-646-X) Ediciones.

— Historia de la Odontologia en Cuba: Cuba Comunista y en el Exilio 1959-1983, Vol. IV. LC 81-652235. (Coleccion Cuba y Sus Jueces Ser.). (Illus.). 752p. (Orig.). (SPA.). 1984. pap. 33.00 (0-89729-344-4) Ediciones.

— Historia de la Odontologia en Cuba: Vol. 1, Periodo Colonial(1492-1898), Vol. I. LC 81-65235. (Coleccion Cuba y Sus Jueces Ser.). (Illus.). 394p. (Orig.). (SPA.). 1981. pap. 29.00 (0-89729-293-6) Ediciones.

— Historia de la Odontologia en Cuba: Vol. 2, Intervencion Norteamericana, 1899-1902, 1906-1909, 3 vols. LC 81-65235. (Coleccion Cuba y Sus Jueces Ser.). (Illus.). 293p. (Orig.). (SPA.). 1982. pap. 29.00 (0-89729-310-X) Ediciones.

— Santa Apolonia (Patrona Dental) LC 86-80092. (Illus.). 79p. (Orig.). (SPA.). 1985. pap. 10.00 (0-89729-388-6) Ediciones.

Mena, Cesar A. & Cobelo, Armando F. Historia de la Medicina en Cuba, Vol. 1: Hospitales y Centros Beneficos en Cuba Colonial. LC 91-76473. (Coleccion Cuba y Sus Jueces Ser.). (Illus.). 717p. (Orig.). (SPA.). 1992. pap. 49.00 (0-89729-624-9) Ediciones.

Mena, Fernando de, tr. see Lopez Estrada, Francisco, ed.

*Mena, Hector R. Costa Rica Postal Catalogue. 216p. 1994. 12.00 (0-9645247-2-4) SCRC.

— Index to Costa Rican Philatelic Literature, Pt. II. vi, 59p. 1993. 5.00 (0-9645247-1-6) SCRC.

Mena, Patricio V. A Revision of the Genus Arcytophyllum (Rubiaceae: Hedyotideae) LC 90-6284. (Memoirs Ser.: No. 60). (Illus.). 26p. 1990. pap. 7.25 (0-89327-355-4) NY Botanical.

Mena Star Staff. Polk County, Arkansas. (Illus.). 307p. 1988. 50.00 (0-88107-124-2) Curtis Media.

*Menache, Alberto & Sher, Richard. Windows Animation Festival CD: A Digital Tour of the Best Animated Movies for Your Multimedia PC. 130p. 1994. cd-rom, pap. 32.95 (0-18-783970-0) Waite Group Pr.

Menache, Sophia. The Vox Dei: Communications in the Middle Ages. (Communication & Society Ser.). (Illus.). 368p. 1990. 45.00 (0-19-504916-0) OUP.

Menacker, Julius. School Law: Theoretical & Case Perspectives. 480p. (C). 1987. text ed. write for info. (0-13-793753-9) P-H.

Menage, Giles. The History of Women Philosophers. Zedler, Beatrice H., tr. 132p. (Orig.). 1985. pap. text ed. 17.00 (0-8191-4272-7) U Pr of Amer.

Menage, Ronald H. The Practical Book of Greenhouse Gardening. 168p. 1983. 7.95 (0-312-63461-7) St Martin.

— The Practical Book of Greenhouse Gardening. (Illus.). 168p. 1991. pap. 17.95 (0-7063-6751-0, Pub. by Ward Lock UK) Sterling.

Menage, V. L., ed. see Wittek, Paul.

Menager, Leon-Robert. Hommes et Institutions de l'Italie Normande. (Collected Studies: No. CS136). 372p. (FRE.). (C). 1981. reprint ed. lib. bdg. 69.95 (0-86078-082-1, Pub. by Variorum UK) Ashgate Pub Co.

Menaghan, Elizabeth G., jt. auth. see Parcel, Toby L.

Menaker, Austin H., jt. auth. see Kutz, Kenneth J.

Menaker, Daniel. The Old Left. 1987. 15.95 (0-394-54678-4) Knopf.

Menaker, Donald. Family Trees. limited ed. Lott, Clarinda H., ed. (Illus.). 1983. 2.00 (0-932616-12-7) New Poets Chestnut Hills.

*Menaker, Esther. The Freedom to Inquire: Self Psychological Perspectives on Women's Issues, Masochism, & the Therapeutic Relationship. LC 94-49182. 1995. 42.50 (1-56821-475-8) Aronson.

— Misplaced Loyalties. LC 94-24042. (History of Ideas Ser.). 1995. pap. write for info. (1-56000-816-4) Transaction Pubs.

— Otto Rank. (C). 1986. pap. text ed. 15.00 (0-231-05117-4) Col U Pr.

Menaker, Esther & Menaker, William. Ego in Evolution. (Psychoanalysis: Examined & Re-Examined Ser.). 280p. 1984. reprint ed. lib. bdg. 32.50 (0-306-76236-6) Da Capo.

Menaker, Michael, ed. Extraretinal Photoreception in Circadian Rhythms & Related Phenoma: Proceedings of a Symposium, Vancouver. 1976. pap. 26.00 (0-08-020965-3, Pergamon Pr) Elsevier.

Menaker, William, jt. auth. see Menaker, Esther.

Menaldi, J. L., jt. auth. see Garroni, M. G.

Menand, Louis. Discovering Modernism: T. S. Eliot & His Context. 224p. 1988. pap. 14.95 (0-19-505717-1) OUP.

Menander. Comedies. (Loeb Classical Library: No. 132). 582p. 1979. text ed. 18.95 (0-674-99147-8) HUP.

— The Dyskolos. (Orig.). 1984. mass mkt. 6.00 (0-452-00865-4, Mer) NAL-Dutton.

— Four Plays: The Hero - Epitrepontes - Periceiromene - Samia. (College Classical Ser.). (GRE.). (C). 1981. text ed. 32.50 (0-89241-364-6); pap. text ed. 16.00 (0-89241-113-9) Caratzas.

— Reliquiae Selectae. rev. ed. Sandbach, F. H., ed. (Oxford Classical Texts Ser.). 376p. 1990. 29.95 (0-19-814737-6) OUP.

— Das Schiedsgericht. Von Wilamowitz-Moellendorff, Ulrich, ed. viii, 219p. 1974. write for info. (3-296-14600-8, Pub. by Georg Olms GW) Lubrecht & Cramer.

Menander of Athens. Menander, the Principal Fragments. Allinson, Frank G., tr. LC 70-109789. 539p. 1970. reprint ed. text ed. 65.00 (0-8371-4279-2, MEFR, Greenwood Pr) Greenwood.

Menander, Turner E. Girl from Samos or The In-Laws. (C). 1972. pap. 17.50 (0-485-12019-4, Pub. by Athlone Pr UK) Humanities.

Menapace, John, photos. Letter in a Klein Bottle. LC 84-80980. 1984. 25.00 (0-912330-56-2) Jargon Soc.

Menarchik, Douglas. Powerlift - Getting to Desert Storm: Strategic Transportation & Strategy in the New World Order. LC 93-2857. 216p. 1993. text ed. 52.95 (0-275-94642-8, C4642, Praeger Pubs) Greenwood.

Menard, Christine. Bright & Bold Bulletin Boards. 64p. 1993. pap. 9.95 (0-913853-32-1, 32543, Alleyside) Highsmith Pr.

Menard, David. USAF Plus Fifteen: A Photo History 1947-1962. LC 92-63123. (Illus.). 144p. (Orig.). 1993. pap. 24.95 (0-88740-483-9) Schiffer.

Menard, David W. Colors & Markings of the F-100 Super Sabre. (Colors & Markings Ser.: Vol. 23, Pt. 2). 64p. 1992. pap. 12.95 (0-8306-3947-0, 24547) TAB Bks.

— F-100 Super Sabre. (Colors & Markings Ser.: Vol. 14). (Illus.). 1990. pap. 12.95 (0-8306-8538-3) TAB Bks.

— F-100 Super Sabre Pt. 2. (Colors & Markings Ser.: Vol. 21). 1994. pap. 15.95 (0-89024-193-7) Kalmbach.

Menard, Eusebe. At All Times, in Every Age. 122p. 1977. 2.95 (0-8199-0663-8, Frncscn Herld) Franciscan Pr.

Menard, H. W. The Ocean of Truth: A Personal History of Global Tectonics. LC 85-43300. (Geology & Paleontology Ser.). (Illus.). 470p. 1986. text ed. 49.50 (0-691-08414-9) Princeton U Pr.

— Oceanic Islands. LC 86-6573. 230p. 1995. text ed. write for info. (0-7167-5017-1) W H Freeman.

Menard, Henry W. Science: Growth & Change. LC 77-156138. (Illus.). 227p. reprint ed. pap. 64.70 (0-7837-4171-5, 2059020) Bks Demand.

*Menard, Louis. Dictionary of Accounting & Financial Management. 994p. 1994. write for info. (0-7859-8752-5) Fr & Eur.

— Dictionary of Accounting & of Financial Management. (ENG & FRE.). 1994. 156.60 (0-7859-8886-6) Fr & Eur.

*Menard, Mathilde. Dictionnaire des Termes Economiques. 94p. (FRE.). 1990. pap. 15.95 (0-7859-7890-9, 2501014154) Fr & Eur.

Menard, Orville D. Political Bossism in Mid-America: Tom Dennison's Omaha, 1900-1933. LC 88-33697. (Illus.). 360p. (C). 1989. lib. bdg. 50.00 (0-8191-7342-8) U Pr of Amer.

Menard, Russell R., jt. auth. see McCusker, John J.

*Menard, Scott. Applied Logistic Regression Analysis. (Quantitative Applications in the Social Science Ser.: Vol. 108). 96p. (C). 1995. pap. 9.95 (0-8039-5757-2) Sage.

— Longitudinal Research. (Quantitative Applications in the Social Sciences Ser.: Vol. 76). (Illus.). 96p. 1991. pap. 9.95 (0-8039-3753-9) Sage.

Menard, Shirley W., ed. The Clinical Nurse Specialist: Perspectives on Practice. 1987. pap. text ed. 29.95 (0-8273-4311-6) Delmar.

Menard-Warwick, Julia & Menard-Warwick, Peter. Letters Home: A Year in Nicaragua. 96p. (Orig.). 1989. pap. 7.95 (0-918957-07-9) Pika Oregon.

Menard-Warwick, Peter, jt. auth. see Menard-Warwick, Julia.

Menardon, M. Encyclopedie de l'Automobile; le Moteur a Explosion: Encyclopedia of the Automobile; the Internal Combustion Engine. 240p. (FRE.). 1980. pap. 95.00 (0-8288-4696-0, M14350) Fr & Eur.

Menaria, Rajendra. Environmental Conservation & Planning. 1989. 22.50 (81-7024-259-2, Pub. by Ashish II) S Asia.

Menarini, Piero, ed. see Garcia Lorca, Federico.

*Menary, Roland W. Opinions. 56p. 1995. pap. 7.00 (0-614-03659-3) Dorrance.

Menasce, Daniel A. Capacity Planning: A Practical Approach. 1993. disk 44.00 (0-685-70954-X) P-H.

Menasce, Daniel A., et al. Capacity Planning & Performance Modeling: From Mainframes to Client-Server Systems. LC 93-43464. 432p. 1994. 50.33 (0-13-035494-5) P-H.

Menasche, Lionel. Writing a Research Paper. LC 83-12492. (Pitt Series in English As a Second Language). (Illus.). 144p. 1984. pap. 13.95 (0-472-08119-5) U of Mich Pr.

Menasche, Lionel, jt. auth. see Furey, Patricia R.

Menase, Lev. Art Treasures of Slovenia. 208p. 1981. 131.00 (0-317-57218-0, Pub. by Collets UK) St Mut.

Menash, Thomas O., ed. Superconductor Engineering. LC 92-9161. (AIChE Symposium Ser.: No. 287, Vol. 88). 1992. 75.00 (0-8169-0567-3) Am Inst Chem Eng.

*Menasha. Emergency Preparedness & First Aid Guide. 1994. pap. text ed. 12.95 (0-9639782-0-9) Priority One.

Menashe, Samuel. Collected Poems. 220p. 1986. pap. 12.95 (0-915032-43-0) Natl Poet Foun.

Menashri, David. Education & the Making of Modern Iran. LC 91-55567. 376p. 1992. 47.50 (0-8014-2612-X) Cornell U Pr.

— Iran: A Decade of War & Revolution. LC 90-4787. 424p. 1990. 47.50 (0-8419-0949-0); pap. 24.95 (0-8419-0950-4) Holmes & Meier.

*Mench, Joy A., ed. The Well-Being of Birds in Laboratory & Field Research. 1995. write for info. (0-614-06553-4) Scientists Ctr.

Mench, Joy A. & Krulisch, Lee, eds. Canine Research Environment. LC 89-62910. 82p. 1989. 30.00 (0-685-59680-X) Scientists Ctr.

— Well-Being of Non Human Primates in Research. LC 89-62911. 86p. 30.00 (0-685-59682-6) Scientists Ctr.

Mench, Joy A. & Mayer, Stephen J., eds. The Well-Being of Agricultural Animals in Biomedical & Agricultural Research. LC 91-67050. (Illus.). 112p. 1991. 45.00 (0-685-59681-8) Scientists Ctr.

Menchaca, Frank. Nicolo G - & the Days of November. LC 90-84969. 56p. (Orig.). 1990. pap. 4.95 (0-9628159-0-X) Front Rm.

*Menchaca, Martha. The Mexican Outsiders: A Community History of Marginalization & Discrimination in California. LC 94-46190. 1995. write for info. (0-292-75173-7); pap. write for info. (0-292-75174-5) U of Tex Pr.

Mencher, A. G., ed. Management & Technology: An Anglo-American Exchange of Views. 96p. (C). 1972. 43.00 (0-08-018748-X, Pub. by Pergamon Repr UK) Franklin.

Mencher, Elaine, jt. ed. see Robinson, Ian.

Mencher, George T., jt. ed. see Gerber, Sanford E.

Mencher, Georges T., ed. see Nova Scotia Conference on Early Identification of Hearing Loss Staff.

Mencher, Joan & Okongwu, Anne, eds. Where Did All the Men Go? Female-Headed - Female-Supported Households in Cross-Cultural Perspective. LC 92-39725. (Women in Cross-Cultural Perspective Ser.). 282p. (C). 1993. pap. text ed. 42.00 (0-8133-8540-7) Westview.

*Mencher, Melvin. Basic Media Writing. 480p. (C). 1995. write for info. (0-697-27002-5); pap. write for info. (0-697-27001-7) Brown & Benchmark.

— Basic Media Writing. 4th ed. 480p. (C). 1993. student ed write for info. (0-697-08666-6); pap. text ed. write for info. (0-697-08664-X) Brown & Benchmark.

— Basic News Writing. 3rd ed. 512p. (C). 1989. pap. write for info. (0-697-04284-7) Brown & Benchmark.

— News Reporting & Writing. 6th ed. LC 93-35024. 634p. 1994. write for info. (0-697-13937-9); pap. 41.32 (0-697-13935-2) Brown & Benchmark.

Menchik, Mark D. Individual Equilibrium-Seeking Behavior: A Definition & a Test. (Discussion Paper Ser.: No. 33). 1969. pap. 10.00 (1-55869-056-5) Regional Sci Res Inst.

— Residential Environmental Preferences & Choice: Some Preliminary Empirical Results Relevant to Urban Form. (Discussion Paper Ser.: No. 46). 1971. pap. 10.00 (1-55869-108-1) Regional Sci Res Inst.

Menchin, Robert S. New Work Opportunities for Older Americans. 1993. pap. text ed. 14.00 (0-13-370016-X) P-H.

Menchine, Ron. A Picture Postcard History of U. S. Baseball. LC 92-16270. (Illus.). 128p. (Orig.). 1992. pap. 14.95 (0-930256-21-2) Almar.

Menchini, Pat. The Beatrix Potter Knitting Book. 128p. 1988. 19.95 (0-7232-3457-4) Warne.

Menchu, Rigoberta. I, Rigoberta Menchu: An Indian Woman in Guatemala. Wright, Ann, tr. 252p. 1985. 44.95 (0-86091-083-0, Pub. by Verso UK); pap. 13.95 (0-86091-788-6, A0663, Pub. by Verso UK) Routledge Chapman & Hall.

*Mencia, Mario. The Fertile Prison: Fidel Castro in Batista's Jails. (Illus.). 250p. 1994. pap. 15.95 (1-875284-08-7, Pub. by Ocean Pr AT) Talman.

*Mencik, J. Strength & Fracture of Glass & Ceramics. (Glass & Science Technology Ser.: Vol. 12). 358p. 1992. 122.75 (0-444-98685-5) Elsevier.

Mencius. Works of Mencius. 1990. pap. 11.95 (0-486-26375-4) Dover.

Menck, Herman & Smart, Charles, eds. Central Cancer Registries: Design, Management, & Use. LC 94-1853. 1994. text ed. 45.00 (3-7186-0579-1) Gordon & Breach.

— Central Cancer Registries: Design, Management & Use. 1994. pap. text ed. 20.00 (3-7186-0587-2) Gordon & Breach.

Menck, Karl W., ed. see Holthus, Manfred, et al.

Mencken, August. The Railroad Passenger Car: An Illustrated History of the First Hundred Years, with Accounts by Contemporary Passengers. LC 57-13290. 223p. reprint ed. pap. 63.60 (0-317-11162-0, 2002915) Bks Demand.

Mencken, H. L. The American Language. 1977. pap. 22.95 (0-394-73315-0) Knopf.

— American Language Abridged. McDavid, Raven I., Jr., ed. 1963. 35.00 (0-394-40081-X) Knopf.

— American Scene: A Reader. Cairns, Huntington, ed. 1965. 20.00 (0-394-43594-X) Knopf.

— Book of Burlesques. 1971. reprint ed. 49.00 (0-403-00666-X) Scholarly.

— A Book of Prefaces. (BCL1-PS American Literature Ser.). 283p. 1992. reprint ed. lib. bdg. 79.00 (0-7812-6612-2) Rprt Serv.

— A Choice of Days. Calligan, Edward L., ed. LC 81-40084. 368p. 1981. pap. 7.95 (0-394-74760-7, Vin) Random.

— Days of H. L. Mencken: Three Volumes in One: Happy Days, Newspaper Days, & Heathen Days. 925p. 1990. 29.95 (0-88029-417-5) Dorset Pr.

— The Diary of H. L. Mencken. Fecher, Charles A., ed. LC 89-2523. (Illus.). 544p. 1990. 30.00 (0-394-56877-X) Knopf.

— Diary of H. L. Mencken. Fecher, Charles A., ed. LC 90-50174. 512p. 1991. pap. 16.95 (0-679-73176-8, Vin) Random.

— The Editor, the Bluenose, & the Prostitute: H. L. Mencken's History of the "Hatrack" Censorship Case. Bode, Carl, ed. 1988. 29.95 (0-911797-40-8) R Rinehart.

— The Editor, the Bluenose, & the Prostitute: H. L. Mencken's History of the "Hatrack" Censorship Case. limited ed. Bode, Carl, ed. 1988. 65.00 (0-911797-48-3) R Rinehart.

— Friedrich Nietzsche. 280p. (C). 1993. pap. 21.95 (1-56000-649-8) Transaction Pubs.

— George Bernard Shaw: His Plays. LC 75-30843. (George Bernard Shaw Ser.: No. 92). 1975. lib. bdg. 75.00 (0-8383-2073-2) M S G Haskell Hse.

— H. L. Mencken on Music: A Selection of His Writings on Music Together with an Account of H. L. Mencken's Musical Life. 222p. 1990. reprint ed. lib. bdg. 69.00 (0-7812-9177-1) Rprt Serv.

— Mencken Chrestomathy. 1982. pap. 19.00 (0-394-75209-0) Pantheon.

— My Life As Author & Editor. 1993. 30.00 (0-679-41315-4) Knopf.

— My Life As Author & Editor. 1995. pap. 16.00 (0-679-74102-X, Vin) Random.

— The Philosophy of Friedrich Nietzsche. 325p. 1989. pap. 11.00 (0-939482-24-X) Noontide.

— A Second Mencken Chrestomathy. Teachout, Terry, ed. LC 94-12087. 1995. 30.00 (0-679-42829-1) Knopf.

— Thirty-Five Years of Newspaper Work. Hobson, Fred et al, eds. LC 94-2077. 1994. 34.95 (0-8018-4791-5) Johns Hopkins.

— Vintage Mencken. 1955. pap. 5.95 (0-394-70025-2) Random.

— Vintage Mencken. LC 89-40542. 1990. pap. 10.00 (0-679-72895-3, Vin) Random.

Mencken, H. L., ed. New Dictionary of Quotations on Historical Principles from Ancient & Modern Sources. 1942. 74.50 (0-394-40079-8) Knopf.

Mencken, H. L., jt. auth. see Fante, John.

Mencken, H. L., jt. auth. see La Monte, Robert R.

Mencken, H. L., jt. ed. see Nathan, George J.

Menconi, Al. Everything You Need to Know about Rock Music: Curriculum Guide. 40p. 1987. student ed, pap. 4.95 (0-942925-02-5) New Song Pub.

Menconi, Al & Hart, Dave. The Hot Two Hundred. Atkinson, Mike, ed. 16p. (Orig.). 1987. pap. 2.00 (0-942925-00-9) New Song Pub.

— Today's Music: A Window to Your Child's Soul. LC 89-34267. 1990. 12.99 (1-55513-257-X, 32573, LifeJourney) Chariot Family.

Menconi, Stephen J., jt. auth. see Bronson, Gary.

Menconi, Steve, ed. see Bronson, Gary J. & Silver, Howard I.

Menconi, Steve, jt. auth. see Bronson, Gary.

Menczel, J., et al, eds. Osteoporosis: Proceedings of an International Symposium Held at the Jerusalem Osteoporosis Center in June, 1981. LC 81-19822. (Illus.). 452p. reprint ed. pap. 128.90 (0-317-58625-4, 2029637) Bks Demand.

Menczer, Bela. Tensions of Order & Freedom: Catholic Political Thought, 1789-1848. 210p. (C). 1993. text ed. 32.95 (1-56000-133-X) Transaction Pubs.

Menczer, Leonard F., jt. auth. see Wolfe, Richard J.

Menczer, Leonard F., jt. ed. see Wolfe, Richard J.

Mendall, Howard L. & Aldous, Clarence M. The Ecology & Management of the American Woodcock. (Illus.). 201p. 1984. reprint ed. 17.95 (0-936075-02-3) Gunnerman Pr.

*Mende, Barbara. How to Get a Job Through Want Ads. Date not set. pap. 12.95 (0-931790-96-4) Brick Hse Pub.

Mende, Emilie. Pictorial Family Tree of Brass Instruments in Europe Since the Early Middle Ages. (Illus.). (ENG, FRE & GER.). 1978. 20.00 (2-88039-003-6) Brass Pr.

Mende, Kazuko, jt. auth. see Morishige, Reiko.

Mende, Matthias. Baldung (Hans) The Graphic Work. (Illus.). 336p. (GER.). 1978. 125.00 (1-55660-168-9) A Wofsy Fine Arts.

Mende, W., jt. auth. see Peschel, M.

Mendel, et al. Fort Johnson: A Historic Structure Report. 54p. (Orig.). 1977. pap. 7.00 (0-9608694-1-7) Montgomery Hist.

Mendel, Alfred O. Personality in Handwriting: A Step-by-Step Guide to Unlocking Hidden Talents & Desires In... 1990. pap. 14.95 (0-87877-153-0) Newcastle Pub.

Mendel, Arthur. Vision & Violence. 350p. (C). 1992. text ed. 32.50 (0-472-10275-3) U of Mich Pr.

Mendel, Arthur, tr. see Bekker, Paul.

Mendel, Arthur, tr. see Einstein, Alfred.

Mendel, Arthur, jt. auth. see Howard, John T., Jr.

Mendel, Arthur P. Michael Bakunin: Roots of Apocalypse. LC 81-5168. 528p. 1981. text ed. 59.95 (0-275-91699-5, C1699, Praeger Pubs) Greenwood.

Mendel, Carol. San Diego: City & County. 7th ed. (Illus.). 96p. 1990. pap. 6.95 (0-935179-12-7) Carol Mendel.

— San Diego on Foot. 8th ed. (Illus.). 96p. 1990. pap. 6.95 (0-935179-13-5) Carol Mendel.

Mendel, Donald J. The Oahe Sub-District: A Case Study in Water Resources Administration. 1963. 1.00 (1-55614-074-6) U of SD Gov Res Bur.

Mendel, G. Versuche ueber Pflanzenhybriden. 1966. reprint ed. pap. 12.00 (3-7682-0013-2) Lubrecht & Cramer.

Mendel, Gregor. Experiments in Plant-Hybridisation. LC 67-9611. 48p. 1968. pap. 8.50 (0-674-27800-3) HUP.

Mendel, J. M. Maximum-Likelihood Deconvolution. (Illus.). xiv, 227p. 1989. 61.00 (0-387-97208-0) Spr-Verlag.

Mendel, Jerry. Kalman Filtering & Other Digital Estimation Techniques. (Illus.). 1987. student ed, audio 398.00 (0-87942-462-1, HL0407-7) Inst Electrical.

— Prelude to Neural Networks, A: Adaptive & Learning Systems. 1993. text ed. 41.25 (0-685-70703-2) P-H.

Mendel, Jerry M. Discrete Techniques of Parameter Estimation: The Equation Error Formulation. (Control & Systems Theory Ser.: Vol. 1). 408p. 1973. 150.00 (0-8247-1455-5) Dekker.

An Asterisk (*) at the beginning of an entry indicates that the title is appearing in BIP for the first time.

M

— Lessons in Estimation Theory for Signal Processing, Communication & Control. 2nd ed. LC 94-15781. (Signal Processing Ser.). 1995. text ed. 70.00 (*0-13-120981-7*) P-H.

— Optimal Seismic Deconvolution: An Estimation Based Approach. LC 82-22739. (Monograph). 1983. text ed. 85.00 (*0-12-490780-6*) Acad Pr.

Mendel, Jerry M., ed. Adaptive & Learning Systems: A Prelude to Neural Networks. LC 93-39097. 464p. 1993. pap. text ed. 30.60 (*0-13-147448-0*) P-H Gen Ref & Trav.

Mendel, Kathleen L. Affirming Cosmic Unity: Awakening Universal Spirituality. Brethauer, Candy K., ed. LC 93-71317. 64p. (Orig.). (C). 1993. pap. 6.10 (*1-878142-31-3*) Telstar TX.

— Ancestral Shadows: The Native American Spirit. LC 94-60585. (Illus.). 30p. (Orig.). (C). 1994. pap. 5.20 (*1-878142-17-8*) Telstar TX.

— Ancient Hearts Whisper: Egyptian Love Poetry. Brethauer, Candy K., ed. & pref. by. LC 92-97166. 36p. (Orig.). (C). 1992. pap. 5.20 (*1-878142-28-3*) Telstar TX.

— Ankh - Eternal Light: Eternal Light. LC 94-60587. (Illus.). 40p. (Orig.). (C). 1994. pap. 6.10 (*1-878142-38-0*) Telstar TX.

— Calliope Garden. Brethauer, Candy K., ed. LC 91-77829. 40p. (Orig.). (C). 1992. pap. 5.20 (*1-878142-25-9*) Telstar TX.

— Coyote Solitude: A Wilderness Meditation. Brethauer, Candy K., ed. LC 92-71827. 20p. (Orig.). (YA). 1993. pap. 4.30 (*1-878142-32-1*) Telstar TX.

— Create Empowering Affirmations & Spiritual Petitions. 40p. (Orig.). 1995. student ed 10.15 (*0-614-06622-0*); student ed, pap. 10.15 (*1-878142-42-9*) Telstar TX.

— Creation's Unending Cycles. 40p. (Orig.). 1995. student ed 10.15 (*0-614-06623-9*); student ed, pap. 10.15 (*1-878142-40-2*) Telstar TX.

— Gateways. Brethauer, Candy K., ed. LC 91-77549. 46p. (Orig.). (C). 1992. pap. 5.20 (*1-878142-27-5*) Telstar TX.

— Into a Silhouette. LC 90-70182. 52p. 1990. pap. 4.00 (*0-9624384-5-6*) Telstar TX.

— Journey into Physical-Spiritual Self. 40p. (Orig.). 1995. student ed 10.15 (*0-614-06624-7*); student ed, pap. 10.15 (*1-878142-39-9*) Telstar TX.

— Nature Icons: Coral Reef. (Illus.). 40p. (Orig.). 1995. student ed 15.10 (*1-878142-14-3*) Telstar TX.

— Nature Icons...Coral Reef. (Illus.). 40p. (Orig.). 1995. student ed, pap. 15.10 (*1-878142-43-7*) Telstar TX.

— Red Mound: Celestial Light. (Illus.). 40p. (Orig.). (C). 1994. pap. 6.10 (*1-878142-36-4*) Telstar TX.

— Silent Stones Sacred Light: Sacred Light. LC 94-60584. (Illus.). 40p. (Orig.). (C). 1994. pap. 6.10 (*1-878142-37-2*) Telstar TX.

— Whispering Clay. Brethauer, Candy K., ed. LC 92-71598. (Illus.). 30p. (Orig.). (J). 1992. pap. 6.10x (*1-878142-29-1*) Telstar TX.

Mendel, Kathleen L., ed. Lions, Lizards & Ladybugs. LC 89-51485. (Illus.). 80p. (J). (gr. k-6). 1989. pap. 9.95 (*0-9624384-2-1*) Telstar TX.

— Sentinel. LC 90-70012. (Illus.). 146p. (Orig.). 1990. pap. 12.95 (*0-9624384-4-8*) Telstar TX.

Mendel, Kathleen L., jt. auth. see Flavin, Patrick L.

Mendel, Kathleen L., ed. see Marrs, John.

Mendel, Kathleen L., ed. see Quinn, Dawn & Malachowski, Cindy.

***Mendel, Matthew P.** The Male Survivor: The Impact of Sexual Abuse. 264p. 1994. 42.00 (*0-8039-5441-7*) Sage.

— The Male Survivor: The Impact of Sexual Abuse. 1994. pap. 18.95 (*0-8039-5442-5*) Sage.

***Mendel-Reyes, Meta.** Reclaiming Democracy: The Sixties in Politics & Memory. 240p. 1995. 19.95 (*0-415-91134-6*, B4901, Routledge NY) Routledge.

***Mendel, Richard A.** Prevention or Pork? A Hard Headed Look at Youth-Oriented Anti-Crime Programs. 33p. 1995. pap. text ed. write for info. (*1-887031-50-2*) Am Youth Policy.

***Mendel, Roberta.** At Random: A Book of Wisdom: Epigrams, Witticisms, & Interesting Definitions. (Books for Browsers Ser.). 24p. (Orig.). 1994. pap. 7.00 (*0-936424-03-6*) Pin Prick.

— Bits & Pieces: Forms, Leases, Applications, & Addenda for Landlords. (Real Estate Venture Ser.). (Orig.). Date not set. pap. 19.95 (*0-936424-13-3*) Pin Prick.

— Epigrams to Live & Die By. (Sketchbook Ser.). (Illus.). 36p. (Orig.). 1981. pap. 7.00 (*0-936424-08-7*) Pin Prick.

— The First Book of Whimsy: Bits of Almost-Haiku & Other Things. (Books for Browsers Ser.). (Illus.). 24p. (Orig.). 1994. pap. 7.00 (*0-936424-00-1*) Pin Prick.

— How to Buy & Sell a Business Enterprise. (Real Estate Venture Ser.). (Orig.). Date not set. pap. 19.95 (*0-936424-14-1*) Pin Prick.

— Jewish Poems. (Holocaust Ser.). 48p. (Orig.). 1984. pap. text ed. 7.00 (*0-936424-09-5*, 009) Pin Prick.

— Philosophical Mutterings About Things of Some Importance. (Sketchbook Ser.). (Illus.). 24p. (Orig.). 1980. pap. 7.00 (*0-936424-05-2*) Pin Prick.

— The Pin Prick Press Annual Index of Serial & Chapbook Publications, 1980. 27p. (Orig.). 1981. pap. 3.00 (*0-936424-07-9*) Pin Prick.

— The Second Book of Whimsey: Word Paintings, Political Grotesqueries, & Other Things. (Books for Browsers Ser.). (Illus.). 24p. (Orig.). 1994. pap. 7.00 (*0-936424-01-X*) Pin Prick.

— A Survival Manual for the Independent Woman Traveler. LC 82-80695. 128p. (Orig.). 1982. pap. 12.95 (*0-936424-06-0*) Pin Prick.

— Taking the Pain Out of Purchasing Property. (Real Estate Venture Ser.). (Orig.). Date not set. pap. 19.95x (*0-936424-12-5*) Pin Prick.

— The Third Book of Whimsey: Poignant Fragments, Serpentine Thoughts, & Other Things. (Books for Browsers Ser.). 24p. (Orig.). 1994. pap. 7.00 (*0-936424-02-8*) Pin Prick.

— Women's Prisms. (Xantippe Ser.). 24p. (Orig.). 1994. pap. 7.00 (*0-936424-04-4*) Pin Prick.

— Writing for Me. (Scribbler Ser.). 6p. (Orig.). 1984. pap. 5.00 (*0-936424-11-7*) Pin Prick.

— Writing for Me. rev. ed. (Scribbler Ser.). 6p. (Orig.). 1994. pap. 5.00 (*0-936424-15-X*) Pin Prick.

Mendel, S., tr. see Hauff, Wilhelm.

Mendel, Werner M. Treating Schizophrenia. LC 88-46080. (Social & Behavioral Sciences Ser.). 264p. 1989. 32.95x (*1-55542-151-2*) Jossey-Bass.

Mendel, Werner M., et al. Schizophrenia: The Experience & Its Treatment. LC 76-20083. (Jossey-Bass Behavioral Science Ser.). 192p. reprint ed. pap. 54.80 (*0-8357-4995-9*, 2037928) Bks Demand.

Mendele Moykher-Sforim. Mendele Moykher-Sforim Selected Works: The Three Great Classic Writers of Modern Yiddish Literature, Vol. 1. rev. ed. Zuckerman, Marvin S. et al, eds. LC 90-63397. (Illus.). 448p. (C). 1991. 34.50 (*0-934710-23-6*) J Simon.

Mendeleyev, William, jt. auth. see Nasibova, Aida.

Mendell, Dale. Early Female Development: Current Psychoanalytic Views. 303p. (C). 1982. text ed. 30.00 (*0-88331-135-6*) Luce.

***Mendell, Dale, ed.** Body & Self: An Exploration of Early Female Development. LC 94-32618. 276p. 1995. pap. text ed. 30.00 (*1-56821-396-4*) Aronson.

Mendell, Edward. A Bevy of Beasts: The Enchanting Animals of Borneo, Belize & Beyond. 144p. 1995. 50.00 (*0-9515863-1-9*, Pub. by Mendell Pubng UK) Atrium Pubs.

— Wildlife Odyssey: A Photographer's Travelogue. (Illus.). 1995. 50.00 (*0-9515863-0-0*, Pub. by Mendell Pubng UK) Atrium Pubs.

Mendell, Elizabeth L. Romanesque Sculpture in Saintonge. (Illus.). 1940. 150.00 (*0-685-89780-X*) Elliots Bks.

Mendell, Jay S. & Pessolano, F. John, eds. Nonextrapolative Methods in Business Forecasting: Scenarios, Vision, & Issues Management. LC 84-18093. (Illus.). ix, 222p. 1985. text ed. 59.95 (*0-89930-066-9*, MHF/, Quorum Bks) Greenwood.

Mendell, K. E. On Grandma's Porch. LC 89-52224. 147p. 1990. pap. 6.95 (*1-55523-321-X*) Winston-Derek.

Mendell, Lorne M., jt. ed. see Binder, Marc D.

***Mendell, Marguerite & Nielsen, Klas, eds.** Europe: Central & East. (Critical Perspectives on Historic Issues Ser.: Vol. 6). 200p. 1995. 48.99 (*1-895431-91-3*); pap. 19.99 (*1-895431-90-5*) Paul & Co Pubs.

Mendell, Marguerite & Salee, Daniel, eds. The Legacy of Karl Polanyi: Market, State & Society at the End of the Twentieth Century. LC 90-33974. 260p. 1991. text ed. 35.00 (*0-312-04783-5*) St Martin.

Mendell, Marguerite, jt. ed. see Cangiani, Michele.

Mendell, Michael J. Unfinished Business. Van Treese, James B., ed. 220p. 1995. pap. 8.95 (*1-56901-175-3*) NW Pub.

Mendell, Olga K., tr. see Hammond, Anna & Matunis, Joe.

Mendell, Ronald L. How to Do Financial Asset Investigations: A Practical Guide for Private Investigators, Collections Personnel, & Asset Recovery Specialists. LC 94-769. (Illus.). 180p. (C). 1994. text ed. 41.95x (*0-398-05907-1*) C C Thomas.

— How to Do Financial Asset Investigations: A Practical Guide for Private Investigators, Collections Personnel, & Asset Recovery Specialists. LC 94-769. (Illus.). 180p. 1994. pap. 25.95 (*0-398-06285-4*) C C Thomas.

Mendell, Rosalind B. & Mincer, Allen I., eds. Frontiers in Cosmic Physics: Symposium in Memory of Serge Alexander Korff. LC 92-18248. (Annals Ser.: Vol. 655). 1992. write for info. (*0-89766-721-2*); pap. write for info. (*0-89766-722-0*) NY Acad Sci.

Mendell, W. W., ed. Lunar Bases & Space Activities of the Twenty-First Century. LC 86-50. (Illus.). 865p. (C). 1986. 20.00 (*0-942862-02-3*) Lunar & Planet Inst.

Mendeloff, Albert & Dunn, James P. Digestive Diseases. LC 71-158432. (Vital & Health Statistics Monographs, American Public Health Association). (Illus.). 190p. 1971. 26.50 (*0-674-20580-4*) HUP.

Mendeloff, John. The Dilemma of Toxic Substance Regulation: How Overregulation Causes Underregulation. (Regulation of Economic Activity Ser.: No. 17). 450p. 1988. 42.00 (*0-262-13230-3*) MIT Pr.

Mendelowitz, Daniel M. Children Are Artists: An Introduction to Children's Art for Teachers & Parents. rev. ed. (Illus.). xiv, 158p. (C). 1963. 22.50 (*0-8047-0450-3*); pap. 10.95 (*0-8047-0451-1*) Stanford U Pr.

— Drawing. LC 80-50905. (Illus.). xvi, 464p. 1980. reprint ed. 39.50 (*0-8047-1089-9*) Stanford U Pr.

— A History of American Art. 2nd ed. LC 71-111303. (C). 1973. pap. text ed. 46.75 (*0-03-089475-1*) HB Coll Pubs.

Mendelowitz, Daniel M. & Wakeham, Duane A. A Guide to Drawing. 4th ed. LC 87-3466. (Illus.). 304p. (C). 1988. pap. text ed. 41.25 (*0-03-007312-X*) HB Coll Pubs.

— A Guide to Drawing. 5th ed. 336p. (C). 1993. pap. text ed. 43.00 (*0-03-055487-X*) SCP.

Mendels. Sinequan: Doxepin HC1. (International Congress Ser.: No. 385). 1976. pap. 24.75 (*0-444-15215-6*, Excerpta Medica) Elsevier.

Mendels, Doron. Land of Israel As a Political Concept in Hasmonean Literature: Recourse to History in Second Century B.C. Claims to the Holy Land. 200p. 1987. text ed. 63.50 (*3-16-145147-3*, Pub. by J C B Mohr GW) Coronet Bks.

— Rise & Fall of Jewish Nationalism: Jewish & Christian Ethnicity in Ancient Palestine. 1992. 35.00 (*0-385-26126-8*) Doubleday.

Mendels, Franklin F. Industrialization & Population Pressure in Eighteenth-Century Flanders. Bruchey, Stuart, ed. LC 80-2817. (Dissertations in European Economic History Ser.). (Illus.). 1981. lib. bdg. 35.95 (*0-405-14001-0*) Ayer.

Mendels, J., ed. Psychobiology of Affective Disorders. (Illus.). viii, 220p. 1981. pap. 31.25 (*3-8055-1400-X*) S Karger.

Mendels, Joseph & Secunda, Stephen K. Lithium in Medicine. 228p. 1972. text ed. 149.00 (*0-677-14480-6*) Gordon & Breach.

Mendels, Ora. A Taste for Treason. 1990. 17.95 (*1-55972-047-6*, Birch Ln Pr) Carol Pub Group.

— A Taste for Treason. 273p. 1993. reprint ed. pap. 5.50 (*1-56171-197-7*, S P I Bks) Sure Sellers.

Mendelsohn, A. Pocket Guide to Job Interviewing. rev. ed. Chavez, Joseph, ed. 45p. (J). (gr. 8 up). 1981. text ed. 1.50 (*0-918443-00-8*, AJDBI101) Job Data.

Mendelsohn, Charles J., jt. auth. see Friedman, William F.

Mendelsohn, E., ed. Algebraic & Geometric Combinatorics. 378p. 1982. pap. 125.75 (*0-444-86365-6*, I-194-82, North Holland) Elsevier.

Mendelsohn, Elliot. Introduction to Mathematical Logic. 3rd ed. LC 86-11084. (Mathematics Ser.). 341p. (C). 1987. boxed 53.50 (*0-534-06624-0*) Chapman & Hall.

Mendelsohn, Erich. Amerika: Bilderbuch Tines Architekten. LC 76-40319. (Architecture & Decorative Art Ser.). (GER.). 1977. reprint ed. lib. bdg. 55.00 (*0-306-70830-2*) Da Capo.

— Erich Mendelsohn: Complete Works of the Architect. (Illus.). 252p. 1992. reprint ed. 39.95 (*0-910413-91-6*) Princeton Arch.

— Mendelsohn's Amerika: 82 Photographs. LC 93-2259. 1993. reprint ed. pap. 11.95 (*0-486-27591-4*) Dover.

— Russia-Europe-America: An Architectural Cross Section. 248p. 1989. 74.00 (*0-8176-2279-9*) Birkhauser.

Mendelsohn, Everett. Heat & Life: The Development of the Theory of Animal Heat. LC 64-16067. 222p. reprint ed. pap. 63.30 (*0-7837-5937-1*, 2045736) Bks Demand.

Mendelsohn, Everett, ed. see American Friends Service Committee.

Mendelsohn, Everett, ed. see Maasen, Sabine.

Mendelsohn, Everett I. Sciences & Cultures: Anthropological & Historical Studies of the Sciences. Elkana, Yahuda, ed. 330p. 1981. lib. bdg. 62.00 (*90-277-1234-4*) Kluwer Ac.

Mendelsohn, Everett I. & Nowotny, Helga, eds. Science Between Utopia & Dystopia, 1984. (Sociology of the Sciences Yearbook Ser.: No. 8). 310p. 1984. lib. bdg. 98.00 (*90-277-1719-2*); pap. text ed. 50.00 (*90-277-1721-4*) Kluwer Ac.

Mendelsohn, Everett I., jt. ed. see Grene, Marjorie.

Mendelsohn, Everett I., et al, eds. Human Aspects of Biomedical Innovation. LC 74-160027. (Studies in Technology & Society). 246p. 1971. 39.00 (*0-674-41331-8*) HUP.

— The Social Production of Scientific Knowledge. (Sociology of the Sciences Yearbook Ser.: Vol. 1). 1977. pap. text ed. 44.50 (*90-277-0776-6*) Kluwer Ac.

Mendelsohn, Ezra. The Jews of East Central Europe Between the World Wars. LC 81-48676. (Illus.). 320p. 1983. 35.00 (*0-253-33160-9*); pap. 14.95 (*0-253-20418-6*, MB-418) Ind U Pr.

— On Modern Jewish Politics. (Studies in Jewish History). (Illus.). 184p. 1993. 39.95 (*0-19-503864-9*); pap. 14.95 (*0-19-508319-9*) OUP.

— Zionism in Poland: The Formative Years, 1915-1926. LC 81-10301. 384p. 1981. reprint ed. pap. 110.30 (*0-7837-3324-0*, 2057729) Bks Demand.

Mendelsohn, Ezra, ed. Studies in Contemporary Jewry, Vol. III: Jews & Other Ethnic Groups in a Multi-Ethnic World. (Illus.). 360p. 1987. 38.00 (*0-19-504896-2*) OUP.

— Studies in Contemporary Jewry, Vol. IX: Modern Jews & Their Musical Agendas. (Illus.). 352p. 1994. 45.00 (*0-19-508617-1*) OUP.

Mendelsohn, Ezra & Cohen, Richard I., eds. Studies in Contemporary Jewry Vol. 6: Art & Its Uses: The Visual Image & Modern Jewish Society. (Illus.). 416p. 1990. 45.00 (*0-19-506188-8*) OUP.

Mendelsohn, Ezra & Shatz, Marshall S., eds. Imperial Russia, Seventeen Hundred to Nineteen Seventeen: State, Society, Opposition Essays in Honor of Marc Raeff. 331p. 1989. text ed. 35.00 (*0-87580-143-9*) N Ill U Pr.

Mendelsohn, F. A. & Paxinos, George T., eds. Receptors in the Human Nervous System. (Illus.). 258p. 1991. text ed. 85.00 (*0-12-490830-6*) Acad Pr.

Mendelsohn, F. A., jt. ed. see Doyle, A. E.

Mendelsohn, Geoffrey, et al. Diagnosis & Pathology of Endocrine Diseases. LC 65-8956. (Illus.). 624p. 1988. text ed. 98.00 (*0-397-50731-3*, Lippincott Medical) Lippincott.

Mendelsohn, Harold. Mass Entertainment. 1966. pap. 14.95x (*0-8084-0218-8*) NCUP.

Mendelsohn, Harvey, tr. see Szondi, Peter.

Mendelsohn, Henry N. An Author's Guide to Social Work Journals. 3rd ed. LC 90-20573. 284p. 1992. 26.95 (*0-87101-219-7*) Natl Assn Soc Wkrs.

Mendelsohn, Isaac. Slavery in the Ancient Near East: A Comparative Study of Slavery in Babylonia, Assyria, Syria & Palestine, from the Middle of the Third Millennium to the End of the First Millenium. LC 78-6962. 162p. 1978. reprint ed. text ed. 45.00 (*0-313-20499-3*, MESA) Greenwood.

Mendelsohn, Jack. Being Liberal in an Illiberal Age: Why I am a Unitarian Universalist. rev. ed. LC 84-45717. 202p. 1985. reprint ed. pap. 14.00 (*0-8070-1801-5*, BP 693) Beacon Pr.

— Being Liberal in an Illiberal Age: Why I Am Unitarian Universalist. 1995. pap. 15.00 (*1-55896-332-4*) Unitarian Univ.

— Channing: The Reluctant Radical. 2nd ed. 1986. reprint ed. pap. 10.00 (*0-933840-28-4*, Skinner Hse Bks) Unitarian Univ.

— Channing: The Reluctant Radical. LC 79-17863. (Illus.). 308p. 1980. reprint ed. text ed. 59.75 (*0-313-22101-4*, MECH, Greenwood Pr) Greenwood.

Mendelsohn, John. Jewish Emigration: The SS St. Louis Affair & Other Cases. LC 81-80315. (Holocaust Ser.: Vol. 7). 274p. 1982. lib. bdg. 20.00 (*0-8240-4881-4*) Garland.

Mendelsohn, John, ed. Covert War, 18 vols. 6150p. 1989. 1,065.00 (*0-8153-0021-2*) Garland.

***Mendelsohn, John, et al.** The Molecular Basis of Cancer. (Illus.). 640p. 1994. text ed. 130.00 (*0-7216-6483-0*) Saunders.

Mendelsohn, L., ed. see Lenin, Vladimir I.

***Mendelsohn, Lotte.** Healthy Mexican Regional Cookery: A Culinary Travelogue. (Regional Cooking Ser.: No. 2). (Illus.). 288p. (Orig.). 1995. pap. 16.50 (*1-883280-06-0*) Font & Ctr Pr.

Mendelsohn, Lotte & Lazzaro, Bea. Italian Regional Cookery - A Culinary Travelogue: More Than 300 Authentic Regional Recipes Adapted to the New World Kitchen. LC 93-25341. (Illus.). 360p. 1993. reprint ed. pap. 15.95 (*1-883280-00-1*) Font & Ctr Pr.

Mendelsohn, M. The Guide to Franchising. 3rd ed. LC 78-40961. 1982. text ed. 28.00 (*0-08-025845-X*, Pergamon Pr) Elsevier.

— International Franchising: An Overview: Selection of Papers Presented at the SBL Conference Held in Toronto, October 1983, Organized by SBL-Section on Business Law, International Bar Association. LC 84-10139. 1984. 92.50 (*0-444-87548-4*, I-317-84, North Holland) Elsevier.

Mendelsohn, M. S. The Debt of Nations: A Twentieth Century Fund Paper. (International Debt Ser.). 67p. (Orig.). (C). 1984. pap. 7.00 (*0-87078-158-8*) TCFP-PPP.

Mendelsohn, Mark L. Civil Service Psychological & Psychiatric Tests. 160p. 1990. pap. 10.95 (*0-13-136912-1*) P-H.

***Mendelsohn, Martin.** The Guide to Franchising. 5th ed. 352p. 1992. text ed. 85.00 (*0-304-32406-X*) Cassell.

— The Guide to Franchising. 5th ed. 352p. 1993. pap. text ed. 32.50 (*0-304-32814-6*) Cassell.

Mendelsohn, Martin, ed. Franchising in Europe. 432p. 1992. text ed. 85.00 (*0-304-31978-3*) Cassell.

— Franchising in Europe. 432p. 1993. pap. text ed. 32.50 (*0-304-32812-X*) Cassell.

Mendelsohn, Martin, jt. auth. see Freiwald, Aaron.

Mendelsohn, Mortimer, ed. Genes, Cancer & Radiation Protection. (Proceedings Ser.: No. 13). 350p. (Orig.). 1992. pap. text ed. 25.00 (*0-929600-24-X*) NCRP Pubns.

***Mendelsohn, Mortimer L., et al, eds.** Biomarkers & Occupational Health: Progress & Perspectives. 335p. (Orig.). (C). 1995. text ed. 54.95 (*0-309-05187-8*) Natl Acad Pr.

Mendelsohn, Oliver & Baxi, Upendra, eds. The Rights of Subordinated Peoples. 350p. 1994. 14.95 (*0-19-563329-6*) OUP.

Mendelsohn, Pam. Happier by Degrees. LC 79-19380. 320p. (Orig.). 1986. reprint ed. pap. 8.95 (*0-89815-161-9*) Ten Speed Pr.

Mendelsohn, Patrick, jt. ed. see Lewis, Robert.

Mendelsohn, Richard. Sammy Marks: "The Uncrowned King of the Transvaal" LC 90-28333. (Illus.). 320p. 1991. text ed. 39.95 (*0-8214-0998-0*); pap. 19.95 (*0-8214-0999-9*) Ohio U Pr.

Mendelsohn, Richard L. & Schwartz, Lewis M. Basic Logic. 320p. (C). 1986. pap. text ed. write for info. (*0-13-062548-5*) P-H.

Mendelsohn, Robert S. Confessions of a Medical Heretic. 208p. 1990. reprint ed. pap. 12.95 (*0-8092-4131-5*) Contemp Bks.

— How to Raise a Healthy Child in Spite of Your Doctor. 304p. 1987. mass mkt. 5.99 (*0-345-34276-3*) Ballantine.

— Immunizations: The Terrible Risks Your Children Face That Your Doctor Won't Reveal. Chatz, Vera, ed. 100p. (Orig.). (C). 1993. reprint ed. pap. 18.00 (*0-9626646-9-3*) Second Opinion.

Mendelsohn, Roy. How Can Talking Help? An Introduction to the Technique of Analytic Therapy. LC 91-35243. 328p. 1992. 40.00 (*0-87668-503-3*) Aronson.

Mendelsohn, Roy M. Leaps: Facing Risks in Offering a Constructive Therapeutic Response When Unusual Measures Are Necessary. LC 90-22584. 320p. 1992. 40.00 (*0-87668-566-1*) Aronson.

— The Manifest Dream & Its Use in Therapy. LC 89-18361. 272p. 1990. 35.00 (*0-87668-766-4*) Aronson.

— The Synthesis of Self, 4 vols., Vol. 1. LC 87-25798. (Illus.). 370p. 1987. 55.00 (*0-306-42711-7*, Plenum Med Bk) Plenum.

— The Synthesis of Self, 4 vols., Vol. 2. LC 87-25798. (Illus.). 272p. 1987. 45.00 (*0-306-42712-5*, Plenum Med Bk) Plenum.

— The Synthesis of Self, 4 vols., Vol. 3. LC 87-25798. (Illus.). 392p. 1987. 49.50 (*0-306-42713-3*, Plenum Med Bk) Plenum.

— The Synthesis of Self, 4 vols., Vol. 4. LC 87-25798. (Illus.). 266p. 1987. 49.50 (*0-306-42714-1*, Plenum Med Bk) Plenum.

Mendelsohn, Samuel. The Criminal Jurisprudence of the Jews. (Studies in Jewish Jurisprudence: Vol. 6). 280p. (C). 1991. 25.00 (*0-87203-122-5*) Hermon.

Mendelsohn, Steven. Financing Adaptive Technology: A Guide to Sources & Strategies for Blind & Visually Impaired Users. LC 87-90669. 206p. 1987. pap. text ed. 28.95 (*0-944249-00-0*); audio 20.00 (*0-944249-02-7*); Apple II 20.00 (*0-944249-03-5*) Smiling Interface.

An Asterisk (*) at the beginning of an entry indicates that the title is appearing in BIP for the first time.

— Financing Adaptive Technology: A Guide to Sources & Strategies for Blind & Visually Impaired Users. braille ed. LC 87-90669. 206p. 1987. 20.00 (*0-944249-01-9*) Smiling Interface.

Mendelsohn, Steven B. Tax Options & Strategies for People with Disabilities. 276p. 1993. 34.95 (*0-939957-55-8*); pap. 19.95 (*0-939957-36-1*) Demos Vermande.

— Tax Options & Strategies for People with Disabilities. 1993. digital audio 19.95 (*0-939957-65-5*); disk 19.95 (*0-939957-66-3*) Demos Vermande.

Mendelson, Alan. Philo's Jewish Identity. LC 88-33719. (Brown Judaic Studies). 171p. 1989. 30.95 (*1-55540-307-7*, 14 01 61) Scholars Pr GA.

— Secular Education in Philo of Alexandria. (Monographs of the Hebrew Union College: No. 7). 128p. 1981. 20.00 (*0-87820-406-7*) Hebrew Union Coll Pr.

Mendelson, Alexander. Plasticity: Theory & Application. LC 68-12718. (Macmillan Series in Applied Mechanics). 367p. reprint ed. pap. 104.60 (*0-317-10993-6*, 2003540) Bks Demand.

— Plasticity: Theory & Application. LC 82-21231. 368p. (C). 1983. reprint ed. lib. bdg. 39.50 (*0-89874-582-9*) Krieger.

Mendelson, Anne. Biography of Rombauer Becker. Date not set. 17.95 (*0-8050-2904-4*) H Holt & Co.

Mendelson, E., tr. see Kushner, B.

Mendelson, E., tr. see Sanin, Nikolai A.

Mendelson, E. Michael. Sangha & State in Burma: A Study of Monastic Sectarianism & Leadership. Ferguson, John P., ed. LC 75-13398. (Illus.). 416p. 1975. 55.00 (*0-8014-0875-X*) Cornell U Pr.

Mendelson, Edward. Early Auden. 432p. 1983. pap. text ed. 16.95 (*0-674-21986-4*) HUP.

— W. H. Auden: 1907-1973. (Illus.). 64p. (Orig.). 1976. pap. 11.00 (*0-87104-264-9*) NY Pub Lib.

Mendelson, Edward, ed. Selected Poems of W. H. Auden. 1990. pap. 12.00 (*0-679-72483-4*, Vin) Random.

— W. H. Auden: Collected Poems. 1976. 39.95 (*0-394-40895-0*) Random.

Mendelson, Edward, ed. see Auden, W. H. & Kallman, Chester.

Mendelson, Edward, ed. see Auden, W. H.

Mendelson, Edward, jt. auth. see Bloomfield, B. C.

Mendelson, Edward, jt. ed. see Seidel, Michael.

Mendelson, Elliot. Boolean Algebra & Switching Circuits. (Schaum's Outline Ser.). 1970. pap. text ed. 11.95 (*0-07-041460-2*) McGraw.

— Schaum's Outline of Beginning Calculus. (Schaum's Outline Ser.). 384p. 1985. pap. text ed. 12.95 (*0-07-041465-3*) McGraw.

Mendelson, Elliot, jt. auth. see Ayres, Frank, Jr.

*__Mendelson, George.__ Psychiatric Aspects of Personal Injury Claims. (Illus.). 296p. 1988. pap. 33.95 (*0-398-06286-2*) C C Thomas.

— Psychiatric Aspects of Personal Injury Claims. (Illus.). 296p. (C). 1988. text ed. 55.95x (*0-398-05411-8*) C C Thomas.

Mendelson, Jack & Mello, Nancy K. Medical Diagnosis & Treatment of Alcoholism. (Illus.). 656p. 1992. text ed. 62.00 (*0-07-041491-2*) Hlth Prof Div.

Mendelson, Jack H., ed. Experimentally Induced Chronic Intoxication & Withdrawal in Alcoholics. (Journal of Studies on Alcohol: Suppl. No. 2). 1964. 5.00 (*0-911290-00-1*) Rutgers Ctr Alcohol.

Mendelson, Jack H. & Mello, Nancy K., eds. The Encyclopedia of Psychoactive Drugs Ser., 32 Vols., Set. (Illus.). 3328p. 1989. lib. bdg. 606.40 (*1-55546-202-2*) Chelsea Hse.

Mendelson, Jill, ed. see Sugar, Peter.

Mendelson, Lee. Rock-a-Bye Snoopy. (World of Snoopy Ser.). (Illus.). 26p. (J). (ps up). 1986. 12.95 (*1-55578-011-3*) Worlds Wonder.

— Snoopy & the Great Pumpkin. (World of Snoopy Ser.). (Illus.). 26p. (J). (ps up). 1986. 12.95 (*1-55578-006-7*) Worlds Wonder.

— Snoopy at the Dog Show. (World of Snoopy Ser.). (Illus.). 26p. (J). (ps up). 1986. 12.95 (*1-55578-008-3*) Worlds Wonder.

— Snoopy Goes Camping. (World of Snoopy Ser.). (Illus.). 26p. (J). (ps up). 1986. 12.95 (*1-55578-002-4*) Worlds Wonder.

— Snoopy Hits the Beach. (World of Snoopy Ser.). (Illus.). 26p. (J). (ps up). 1986. 12.95 (*1-55578-004-0*) Worlds Wonder.

— Snoopy, Spike & the Cat Next Door. (World of Snoopy Ser.). (Illus.). 26p. (J). (ps up). 1986. 12.95 (*1-55578-010-5*) Worlds Wonder.

— Snoopy's America. (World of Snoopy Ser.). (Illus.). 26p. (J). (ps up). 1986. 12.95 (*1-55578-007-5*) Worlds Wonder.

— Snoopy's Band. (World of Snoopy Ser.). (Illus.). 26p. (J). (ps up). 1986. 12.95 (*1-55578-009-1*) Worlds Wonder.

— Snoopy's Baseball Game. (World of Snoopy Ser.). (Illus.). 26p. (J). (ps up). 1986. 12.95 (*1-55578-012-1*) Worlds Wonder.

— Snoopy's Birthday Party. (World of Snoopy Ser.). (Illus.). 26p. (J). (ps up). 1986. 12.95 (*1-55578-001-6*) Worlds Wonder.

— Snoopy's Land of Make Believe. (World of Snoopy Ser.). (Illus.). 26p. (J). (ps up). 1986. 12.95 (*1-55578-003-2*) Worlds Wonder.

— Snoopy's Show & Tell. (World of Snoopy Ser.). (Illus.). 26p. (J). (ps up). 1986. 12.95 (*1-55578-005-9*) Worlds Wonder.

— Snoopy's Talent Show. (World of Snoopy Ser.). (Illus.). 26p. (J). (ps up). 1986. 12.95 (*1-55578-000-8*) Worlds Wonder.

Mendelson, Lee, et al. Red Riding Hood. write for info. (*0-318-58236-8*) P-H.

Mendelson, M. E., jt. auth. see Loscalzo, J.

Mendelson, Morton J. Becoming a Brother: A Child Learns about Life, Family & Self. (Illus.). 272p. 1993. pap. 9.95x (*0-262-63146-6*) MIT Pr.

Mendelson, Myer. Psychoanalytic Concepts of Depresssion. 2nd ed. 368p. 1993. pap. 40.00 (*1-56821-132-5*) Aronson.

Mendelson, Phyllis C., jt. ed. see Hall, Sharon K.

Mendelson, Ralph. Where Did I Put My Glasses? How You Can Improve Your Memory As You Grow Older. 348p. 1993. 24.95 (*0-9635556-0-X*) Segno Bks.

Mendelson, Robert. Complete Book of Parenting. 1991. 9.99 (*0-517-05670-4*) Random Hse Value.

Mendelson, Sara Heller. The Mental World of Stuart Women: Three Studies. LC 87-5972. 248p. 1987. lib. bdg. 30.00x (*0-87023-591-5*) U of Mass Pr.

Mendelson, Steve, illus. & ret. The Emperor's New Clothes. LC 91-42606. 32p. (J). 1992. 14.95 (*1-55670-232-9*) Stewart Tabori & Chang.

Mendelson, W. B. Human Sleep: Research & Clinical Care. LC 87-7372. (Illus.). 456p. 1987. 65.00 (*0-306-42627-7*, Plenum Med Bk) Plenum.

Mendelson, Wallace. Judicial Review & Party Politics. (Reprint Series in Social Sciences). (C). 1993. reprint ed. pap. text ed. 1.00 (*0-8290-2759-9*, PS-201) Irvington.

— Justices Black & Frankfurter: Conflict in the Court. 2nd ed. LC 61-5781. 165p. reprint ed. pap. 47.10 (*0-317-28142-9*, 2024100) Bks Demand.

Mendelssohn-Bartholdy, C., ed. see Mendelssohn-Bartholdy, Felix.

Mendelssohn-Bartholdy, F. Goethe & Mendelssohn. LC 70-122622. (Studies in German Literature: No. 13). 1970. reprint ed. lib. bdg. 49.95 (*0-8383-0902-X*) M S G Haskell Hse.

Mendelssohn-Bartholdy, Felix. Letters from Italy & Switzerland. Wallace, Lady, tr. LC 70-114866. (Select Bibliographies Reprint Ser.). 1977. 26.95 (*0-8369-5271-5*) Ayer.

— Letters of Felix Mendelssohn-Bartholdy from 1833-1847. Mendelssohn-Bartholdy, Paul & Mendelssohn-Bartholdy, C., eds. LC 73-114867. (Select Bibliographies Reprint Ser.). 1977. 29.95 (*0-8369-5272-3*) Ayer.

Mendelssohn-Bartholdy, Karl. Geschichte Griechenlands von der Eroberung Konstantinopels Durch die Turken im Jahre 1453 Bis Auf Unsere Tage, 2 vols. (GER.). Date not set. Vol. I: Von der Eroberung Konstantinopels durch die Turken bis zur Seeschlacht bei Navarin; xiv, 545. write for info. (*0-318-70437-4*, Pub. by Georg Olms GW); Vol. II: Von der Ubernahme der Verwaltung durch Kapodistrias bis zur Grobjahrigkeit des Konigs Otto;. write for info. (*0-318-70438-2*, Pub. by Georg Olms GW) Lubrecht & Cramer.

— Geschichte Griechenlands von der Eroberung Konstantinopels Durch die Turken im Jahre 1453 Bis Auf Unsere Tage, 2 vols., Set. (GER.). Date not set. write for info. (*0-318-70436-6*, Pub. by Georg Olms GW) Lubrecht & Cramer.

Mendelssohn-Bartholdy, Paul, ed. see Mendelssohn-Bartholdy, Felix.

Mendelssohn, F. Bartholdy. The Music Composed for Shakespeare's A Midsummer Night's Dream. 1976. lib. bdg. 59.95 (*0-8490-2307-6*) Gordon Pr.

Mendelssohn, Fanny, jt. auth. see Mendelssohn, Felix.

Mendelssohn, Felix. Complete Chamber Music for Strings. Rietz, Julius, ed. 1978. reprint ed. pap. 12.95 (*0-486-23679-X*) Dover.

— Complete Works for Pianoforte Solo, 2 vols., 1. 416p. 1975. pap. 10.95 (*0-486-23136-4*) Dover.

— Complete Works for Pianoforte Solo, 2 vols., 2. 416p. 1975. pap. 10.95 (*0-486-23137-2*) Dover.

— Letters of Felix Mendelssohn to Ignaz & Charlotte Moscheles. Moscheles, Felix, ed. & tr. by. LC 77-107822. (Select Bibliographies Reprint Ser.). 1977. 29.95 (*0-8369-5217-0*) Ayer.

— Letters of Felix Mendelssohn to Ignaz & Charlotte Moscheles. Moscheles, Felix, ed. LC 76-173116. (Illus.). 1972. reprint ed. 30.95 (*0-405-08786-1*, Pub. by Blom Pubns UK) Ayer.

— Major Orchestral Works in Full Score. 406p. 1976. pap. 16.95 (*0-486-23184-4*) Dover.

Mendelssohn, Felix & Mendelssohn, Fanny. Mendelssohn - Twenty-Four Songs (for High Voice) Paton, John G., ed. 96p. (Orig.). (C). 1992. pap. 9.95 (*0-88284-499-7*, 3387) Alfred Pub.

— Mendelssohn - Twenty-Four Songs (for Medium Voice) Paton, John G., ed. 96p. (Orig.). (C). 1992. pap. 9.95 (*0-88284-523-3*, 3388) Alfred Pub.

Mendelssohn, J., jt. auth. see Pfeiffer, A.

Mendelssohn, K. The Quest for Absolute Zero. 280p. 1977. pap. 39.00 (*0-85066-119-6*) Taylor & Francis.

Mendelssohn, Moses. Jerusalem: Or on Religious Power & Judaism. Arkush, Allan, tr. LC 83-40015. (Illus.). 262p. 1983. pap. 16.95 (*0-87451-264-6*) U Pr of New Eng.

— Love Letters to His Bride. Regan, Frauke, tr. (Illus.). 120p. 1991. 21.95 (*0-941062-55-4*) Begos & Rosenberg.

— Phaedon; or, the Death of Socrates. LC 73-2219. (Jewish People; History, Religion, Literature Ser.). 1973. reprint ed. 24.95 (*0-405-05282-0*) Ayer.

Mendelssohn, S. Judaic or Semitic Legends & Customs Amongst South African Natives. 1976. lib. bdg. 59.95 (*0-8490-2111-1*) Gordon Pr.

Mendelssohn, Sidney. The Jews of Africa, Especially in the 16th & 17th Centuries. 1972. 59.95 (*0-8490-0446-2*) Gordon Pr.

— The Jews of Asia: Especially in the Sixteenth & Seventeenth Centuries. LC 77-87612. (Illus.). 256p. reprint ed. 37.50 (*0-404-16436-6*) AMS Pr.

*__Mendenhall, Beverly.__ Reflections of Jade. 360p. (Orig.). Date not set. pap. 9.95 (*0-7610-0185-9*) NW Pub.

Mendenhall, Charles. The Air Racer. rev. ed. (Illus.). 200p. 1994. pap. 19.95 (*0-933424-01-9*) Specialty Pr.

Mendenhall, Charles A. The Gee Bees Racers: A Legacy of Speed. (Illus.). 190p. 1994. pap. 19.95 (*0-933424-05-1*) Voyageur Pr.

Mendenhall, Corwin. Submarine Diary. 272p. 1990. 18.95 (*0-945575-34-3*) Algonquin Bks.

Mendenhall, Doris A., jt. ed. see Fredericksen, Burton B.

Mendenhall, George E. The Syllabic Inscriptions from Byblos. 194p. 1986. text ed. 40.00 (*0-8156-6077-4*, Am U Beirut) Syracuse U Pr.

— The Tenth Generation: The Origins of the Biblical Tradition. 266p. 1973. pap. 13.95x (*0-8018-1654-8*) Johns Hopkins.

Mendenhall, Harlan H., jt. auth. see Lockwood, Brocton.

Mendenhall, John. American Trademarks 1930-1950, Vol. 2. (Illus.). 160p. reprint ed. pap. text ed. 22.50 (*0-88108-112-4*) Art Dir.

— British Trademarks of the 1920s & 1930s. (Illus.). 130p. 1989. pap. 14.95 (*0-87701-577-5*) Chronicle Bks.

— Character Trademarks. (Illus.). 132p. (Orig.). 1990. pap. 14.95 (*0-87701-752-2*) Chronicle Bks.

— French Trademarks: The Art Deco Era. (Illus.). 144p. (Orig.). 1991. pap. 16.95 (*0-87701-853-7*) Chronicle Bks.

— High Tech Trademarks. LC 85-61876. 160p. 1985. 19.95 (*0-88108-024-1*) Art Dir.

— High Tech Trademarks, No. 2. LC 85-61876. 160p. 1988. 27.50 (*0-88108-058-6*) Art Dir.

— Nederland Trademarks 1900-1950. LC 94-79354. (Illus.). (Orig.). 1995. pap. text ed. 17.95 (*0-88108-150-7*) Art Dir.

Mendenhall, John, ed. American Trade Marks, 1930-1950, Vol. 1. LC 83-7316. (Illus.). 160p. 1991. reprint ed. pap. text ed. 22.50 (*0-88108-095-0*) Art Dir.

— American Trademarks 1930-1950, Vol. 3. LC 86-81966. 160p. 1991. text ed. 24.95 (*0-88108-080-2*) Art Dir.

— Scan This Book. LC 91-77465. (Illus.). 120p. 1991. pap. text ed. 14.95 (*0-88108-099-3*) Art Dir.

Mendenhall, Karen. Making the Most of the Temporary Employment Market. 176p. (Orig.). 1993. pap. 9.95 (*1-55870-285-7*) Betterway Bks.

Mendenhall, M., ed. Tactical Missile Aerodynamics: Prediction Methodology. (PAAS Ser.: Vol. 142). 700p. 1992. 79.95 (*1-56347-016-0*, V-142) AIAA.

Mendenhall, Mark & Oddou, Gary. Readings & Cases in International Human Resource Management. 437p. (C). 1991. pap. 31.95 (*0-534-92332-1*) Intl Thomson.

*__Mendenhall, Mark & Oddou, Gary, eds.__ Readings & Cases in International Human Resources Management. 2nd ed. LC 94-37700. 1995. pap. 27.95 (*0-538-84737-9*) S-W Pub.

*__Mendenhall, Mark E., et al.__ Global Management. LC 94-28076. (Illus.). 600p. (C). 1994. text ed. 44.95 (*1-55786-635-X*) Blackwell Pubs.

Mendenhall, Michael J. Davy Crockett & the Unconstitutional Welfare State. LC 90-81995. 43p. 1990. pap. 4.00 (*0-9625954-1-1*) Inst Cons Res.

Mendenhall, Michael J., ed. The Constitution of the United States of America: The Definitive Edition. 44p. (Orig.). (C). 1991. pap. 2.00 (*0-9625954-0-3*) Inst Cons Res.

Mendenhall, Ruth D. Backpack Cookery. (Illus.). 1974. 2.95 (*0-910856-22-2*) La Siesta.

— Backpack Techniques. (Illus.). 1984. 1.95 (*0-910856-24-9*) La Siesta.

Mendenhall, Ruth D., jt. auth. see Prater, Yvonne.

Mendenhall, Thomas, jt. auth. see Howard, James.

Mendenhall, Thomas C. The Harvard-Yale Boat Race, 1852-1924: And the Coming of Sport to the American College. (Illus.). 386p. 1993. 49.95 (*0-913372-64-1*) Mystic Seaport.

Mendenhall, W. C. Three Hundred Twenty Desert Watering Places in Southeastern California & Southwestern Nevada. 104p. 19.95 (*0-913814-62-8*) Nevada Pubns.

Mendenhall, Willam & Beaver, Robert J. A Brief Course in Business Statistics. LC 94-17706. 654p. 1995. text ed. 37.95 (*0-534-25290-7*) Intl Thomson.

Mendenhall, William. Beginning Statistics: A to Z. 525p. (C). 1993. text ed. 51.95 (*0-534-19122-3*) Intl Thomson.

— Statistics for Engineering & the Sciences. 3rd ed. 963p. (C). 1991. write for info. (*0-02-380552-8*) Dellen Pub.

Mendenhall, William & Beaver, Robert. A Course in Business Statistics. 3rd ed. 800p. 1992. text ed. 57.95 (*0-534-92989-3*) Intl Thomson.

— A Course in Business Statistics. 3rd ed. 800p. 1992. pap. 16.95 (*0-534-92996-6*) Intl Thomson.

Mendenhall, William & Beaver, Robert J. Introduction to Probability & Statistics. 8th ed. 848p. (C). 1991. text ed. 55.95 (*0-534-92409-3*); student ed 20.95 (*0-534-92551-0*); teacher ed 14.95 (*0-534-92548-0*) Intl Thomson.

— Introduction to Probability & Statistics. 9th ed. 704p. 1994. text ed. 58.95 (*0-534-20886-X*) Intl Thomson.

Mendenhall, William & Sincich, Terry. A Second Course in Business Statistics: Regression Analysis. 4th ed. LC 92-31637. 880p. (C). 1993. text ed. write for info. (*0-02-380520-X*) Dellen Pub.

— Statistics for Engineering & the Sciences. 4th ed. LC 94-41303. 1995. text ed. 75.00 (*0-02-380581-1*) P-H.

Mendenhall, William, jt. auth. see Ott, R. Lyman.

Mendenhall, William, et al. Mathematical Statistics with Applications. 4th ed. 752p. (C). 1990. text ed. 59.95 (*0-534-92026-8*) Intl Thomson.

— Statistics for Management & Economics. 7th ed. LC 92-30933. 1062p. 1993. text ed. 58.95 (*0-534-93299-1*) Intl Thomson.

Mender, D. The Myth of Neuropsychiatry: A Look at Paradoxes, Physics & the Human Brain. (Illus.). 255p. (C). 1994. 26.95 (*0-306-44652-9*, Plenum Pr) Plenum.

Mender, Mona. Music Manuscript Preparation: A Concise Guide. LC 90-8373. (Illus.). 222p. 1991. 29.50 (*0-8108-2294-6*) Scarecrow.

Mendershausen, Horst. Changes in Income Distribution During the Great Depression. LC 75-19726. (National Bureau of Economic Research Ser.). (Illus.). 1975. reprint ed. 20.95 (*0-405-07604-5*) Ayer.

— Changes in Income Distribution During the Great Depression. (Studies in Income & Wealth: No. 7). 191p. 1946. reprint ed. 49.70 (*0-87014-162-7*); reprint ed. mic. film 24.90 (*0-685-61265-1*) Natl Bur Econ Res.

— Coping with the Oil Crisis: French & German Experiences. LC 75-35485. 127p. reprint ed. pap. 36.20 (*0-7837-3048-9*, 2023807) Bks Demand.

Mendes, A. J. Marques. Economic Integration & Growth in Europe. 160p. 1986. 49.95 (*0-7099-4664-3*, Pub. by Croom Helm UK) Routledge Chapman & Hall.

*__Mendes, Bob.__ Vengeance: Prelude to Saddam's War. Smittenaar, H. S., tr. 298p. 1995. pap. 9.95 (*1-881164-71-3*) Intercont VA.

Mendes, Chico & Gross, Tony. Fight for the Forest: Chico Mendes in His Own Words. rev. ed. (Latin America Bureau Ser.). (Illus.). 128p. (C). 1992. pap. text ed. 10.00 (*0-85345-866-9*, Pub. by Lat Am Bur UK) Monthly Rev.

Mendes de Leon, Pablo M., jt. ed. see Masson-Zwaan, Tanja L.

Mendes-Flohr, Paul. Divided Passions: Jewish Intellectuals & the Experience of Modernity. LC 89-22557. 450p. 1991. 42.95 (*0-8143-2030-9*) Wayne St U Pr.

— From Mysticism to Dialogue: Martin Buber's Transformation of German Social Thought. LC 88-20689. 193p. 1989. 32.95 (*0-8143-2028-7*); pap. 15.95 (*0-8143-2029-5*) Wayne St U Pr.

Mendes-Flohr, Paul, ed. Gershom Scholem: The Man & His Work. (SUNY Series in Judaica, Hermeneutics, Mysticism, & Religion). 127p. (C). 1994. 39.50 (*0-7914-2125-2*); pap. 12.95 (*0-7914-2126-0*) State U NY Pr.

— Philosophy of Franz Rosenzweig. LC 86-40552. (Tauber Institute Ser.: No. 8). (Illus.). 272p. 1987. text ed. 35.00 (*0-87451-398-7*) U Pr of New Eng.

Mendes-Flohr, Paul & Reinharz, Jehuda, eds. The Jew in the Modern World: A Documentary History. 2nd ed. (Illus.). 704p. (C). 1995. 55.00 (*0-19-507452-1*); pap. text ed. 28.00 (*0-19-507453-X*) OUP.

Mendes-Flohr, Paul R. & Reinharz, Jehuda. The Jew in the Modern World: A Documentary History. 1980. 37.50 (*0-19-502631-4*) OUP.

Mendes-Flohr, Paul R., ed. see Buber, Martin.

Mendes-Flohr, Paul R., jt. auth. see Cohen, Arthur A.

Mendes-Flohr, Paul R., jt. ed. see Cohen, Arthur A.

Mendes, Guy. Another Page, Bk. 1. (Another Page TV Ser.). 118p. 1988. student ed 6.95 (*0-910475-46-6*) KET.

— Another Page, Bk. 2. (Another Page TV Ser.). 167p. 1988. student ed 6.95 (*0-910475-47-4*) KET.

— Another Page, Bk. 3. (Another Page TV Ser.). 124p. 1988. student ed 6.95 (*0-910475-48-2*) KET.

— Another Page, Bk. 4. (Another Page TV Ser.). 142p. 1988. student ed 6.95 (*0-910475-49-0*) KET.

— Another Page, Bk. 5. (Another Page TV Ser.). 132p. 1988. student ed 6.95 (*0-910475-50-4*) KET.

— Light at Hand: Photographs 1970-85. LC 85-81724. (Illus.). 64p. 1986. 18.50 (*0-917788-30-3*) Gnomon Pr.

Mendes, H. Pereira. Looking Ahead: Twentieth Century Happenings. LC 79-154451. (Utopian Literature Ser.). 1976. reprint ed. 29.95 (*0-405-03533-0*) Ayer.

Mendes, Joel, jt. ed. see Rosen, Howard.

Mendes, Manuel, ed. J. Manuel Gallego. (Illus.). 96p. (ENG & SPA.). 1993. pap. 28.95 (*0-685-74554-6*) Rizzoli Intl.

Mendes, Peter. Clandestine Erotic Fiction in English 1800-1930: A Bibliographic Study. 497p. 1993. 124.95 (*0-85967-919-5*, Pub. by Scolar Pr UK) Ashgate Pub Co.

Mendes, R. V., jt. auth. see Garrido, M. S.

Mendes, Reva. Words for the Quiet Moments. 35p. 1973. reprint ed. pap. 2.00 (*0-87516-185-5*) DeVorss.

Mendes, Richard. Prose & Cons. 128p. 1993. pap. 8.95 (*1-880365-41-3*) Prof Pr NC.

Mendes, Valerie, jt. auth. see Wilcox, Claire.

*__Mendex-Vigo, Marisa.__ Training in the Retail Trade in Spain: Report for the Force Programme CEDEFOP. 99p. 1994. pap. 11.00 (*92-826-7498-3*, HX80-93-945ENC, Pub. by Europ Com) UNIPUB.

*__Mendez, Jr.__ El Que Sigue. LC 94-61480. (Coleccion Humor: No. 1). (Illus.). 86p. (Orig.). (SPA.). 1994. pap. 9.95 (*0-89729-659-1*) Ediciones.

Mendez, A. Diccionario Tecnico de la Industria del Petroleo y Derivados: Technical Dictionary of Petroleum & Petroleum Products Industry. 588p. (ENG, FRE & SPA.). 1980. 95.00 (*0-8288-0715-9*, S37582) Fr & Eur.

Mendez, Adriana. Cubans in America. LC 93-14339. (In America Ser.). (Illus.). 72p. (J). (gr. 5 up). 1994. lib. bdg. 17.50 (*0-8225-1953-4*, Lerner Publctns); pap. 5.95 (*0-8225-1039-1*, Lerner Publctns) Lerner Group.

Mendez, Carlos M. Critica al Poder Politico. LC 81-67847. (Illus.). 269p. (Orig.). (SPA.). 1981. pap. 14.95 (*0-89729-298-7*) Ediciones.

— El Manifiesto Democrata. LC 82-71115. (Coleccion Cuba y Sus Jueces Ser.). 40p. (Orig.). (SPA.). 1982. pap. 2.00 (*0-89729-313-4*) Ediciones.

Mendez, Carmen, jt. auth. see Rizzo, Ann-Marie.

Mendez, Clark R. Onetti y la Fidelidad a las Reglas del Juego. 188p. (Orig.). (SPA.). (C). 1992. lib. bdg. 39.50 (*0-8191-8889-1*); pap. text ed. 24.50 (*0-8191-8890-5*) U Pr of Amer.

Mendez, David. Dynamic Methods of Teaching the Word. 114p. (Orig.). 1989. pap. 9.00 (*1-56428-005-5*) Logos Intl Pub.

— The Gospel of John: The Living Word. 72p. (Orig.). 1989. pap. 9.00 (*1-56428-009-8*) Logos Intl Pub.

— La Gran Brecha Entre el Catolicismo Romano y Cristo. 31p. (Orig.). 1990. pap. 2.00 (*1-56428-011-X*) Logos Intl Pub.

— Guide to Power in Worship. 102p. (Orig.). 1989. pap. 9.00 (*1-56428-008-X*) Logos Intl Pub.

— Holy Spirit Renewal: The Roots of Revival. 53p. (Orig.). 1988. pap. 6.00 (*1-56428-006-3*) Logos Intl Pub.
— Marriage & Family Relationships. 116p. (Orig.). 1989. pap. 9.00 (*1-56428-007-1*) Logos Intl Pub.
— A Panorama of the New Testament. 93p. (Orig.). 1990. pap. 9.00 (*1-56428-004-7*) Logos Intl Pub.
— Psychology & Biblical Counseling. 58p. (Orig.). 1990. pap. 9.00 (*1-56428-015-2*) Logos Intl Pub.
— The Research Paper Made Easy. 29p. (Orig.). (C). 1990. pap. 3.00 (*1-56428-012-8*) Logos Intl Pub.
— Sickness: Physical, Mental or Demons? 16p. (Orig.). 1989. pap. 4.00 (*1-56428-013-6*) Logos Intl Pub.
— Sociology & Christianity. 55p. (Orig.). 1989. pap. 8.00 (*1-56428-003-9*) Logos Intl Pub.
— Speaking the Word to Modern Man. 72p. (Orig.). 1983. pap. 9.00 (*1-56428-001-2*) Logos Intl Pub.
— Urban Strategies: Bringing the Gospel to the Cities. 72p. (Orig.). 1990. pap. 8.00 (*1-56428-000-4*) Logos Intl Pub.
Mendez, David & Chant, Ken. Gifts of the Holy Spirit. 57p. 1990. pap. 7.00 (*1-56428-016-0*) Logos Intl Pub.
— Theological Themes on the Holy Spirit. 100p. (Orig.). 1990. pap. 7.00 (*1-56428-002-0*) Logos Intl Pub.
Mendez, David, jt. auth. see Allison, Dale.
Mendez, David, jt. auth. see Herald, Ivan.
Mendez, E. E. & Von Klitzing, K., eds. Physics & Applications of Quantum Wells & Superlattices. (NATO ASI Series B, Physics: Vol. 170). (Illus.). 442p. 1988. 120.00 (*0-306-42823-7*, Plenum Pr) Plenum.
Mendez, Eugenio F. Cronicas De Puerto Rico: Desde la Conquista Hasta Nuestros Dias, 1493-1955. 2nd ed. (C). reprint ed. pap. 8.00 (*0-8477-0811-X*) U of PR Pr.
— Identity & Culture. (Puerto Rico Ser.). 1979. lib. bdg. 59.95 (*0-8490-2943-0*) Gordon Pr.
Mendez-Faith, Kienzle. Habla Espanol? 4th annot. ed. Price, Julia, ed. (Illus.). 614p. (SPA.). (C). 1990. teacher ed write for info. (*0-03-013918-X*) HB Coll Pubs.
— Habla Espanol? 4th ed. Price, Julia, ed. (Illus.). 614p. (SPA.). (C). 1990. teacher ed 35.00 (*0-03-022795-2*); text ed. 45.25 (*0-03-014158-3*); audio write for info. (*0-03-026658-0*); 45.25 (*0-03-030012-6*); write for info. (*0-03-026229-1*) HB Coll Pubs.
Mendez-Faith, Teresa. Contextos: Literarios Hispanoamericanos. 228p. (C). 1986. pap. text ed. 25.50 (*0-03-063844-5*) HB Coll Pubs.
— Panoramas Literarios: Hispanoamerica. 416p. (SPA.). (C). 1995. pap. text ed. write for info. (*0-669-21805-7*) Heath.
Mendez-Faith, Teresa & Gill, Mary M. Habla Espanol? Essentials. 4th ed. 440p. (ENG & SPA.). (C). 1989. pap. text ed. 21.50 (*0-03-020732-0*) HB Coll Pubs.
— Habla Espanol? Essentials. 4th ed. 440p. (ENG & SPA.). (C). 1991. text ed. 41.25 (*0-03-055147-1*); 232.75 (*0-03-020728-2*); write for info. (*0-318-69168-X*) HB Coll Pubs.
— Habla Espanol? The Essentials. 5th ed. LC 93-36981. 1993. text ed. 43.00 (*0-15-500650-9*) HB Coll Pubs.
Mendez-Faith, Teresa, jt. auth. see Kienzle, Beverly M.
Mendez-Faith, Teresa, et al. Habla Espanol? An Introductory Course. 5th ed. (Illus.). 600p. (C). 1993. teacher ed write for info. (*0-03-075908-0*); text ed. 46.75 (*0-03-074997-2*) HB Coll Pubs.
Mendez, Jose L. Como Leer a Garcia Marquez: Una Interpretacion Sociologica. LC 89-5381. 224p. (Orig.). 1992. pap. text ed. 12.50 (*0-8477-3640-7*) U of PR Pr.
— Introduccion a la Sociologia de la Literatura. LC 80-25694. (Coleccion Mente y Palabra). 143p. 1982. 5.50 (*0-8477-0580-3*); pap. 5.00 (*0-8477-0581-1*) U of PR Pr.
Mendez, Juan. Spanish Grammar. LC 90-56014. (HarperCollins College Outline Ser.). 320p. (Orig.). 1991. pap. 12.00 (*0-06-467129-1*, Harper Ref) HarpC.
Mendez-Leite, L. El Cine Norteamericano. 1976. lib. bdg. 250.00 (*0-8490-1630-4*) Gordon Pr.
Mendez Luengo, Ernesto. Llanto Por un Lobo Muerto. (Nueva Austral Ser.: Vol. 49). (SPA.). 1991. pap. text ed. 24.95x (*84-239-1849-1*) Elliots Bks.
Mendez, Luis F. Julian del Casal: Estudio Comparativo de Prosa y Poesia. LC 78-70499. (Coleccion Polymita Ser.). 1979. pap. 10.00 (*0-89729-213-8*) Ediciones.
Mendez, M. Albert, jt. auth. see Russell, Lee.
Mendez, M. E. Por Favor Ayudame a Cambiar (Free to Be Me) (SPA.). Date not set. 2.49 (*0-945792-23-9*, 498046) Editorial Unilit.
Mendez, Miguel. The Dream of Santa Maria de las Piedras. Foster, David W., tr. LC 89-61106. 194p. 1989. 22.00 (*0-916950-98-0*); pap. 13.00 (*0-916950-99-9*) Biling Rev-Pr.
— Peregrinos de Aztlan. LC 90-27640. (Clasicos Chicanos - Chicano Classics Ser.: No. 6). 192p. 1991. pap. 13.00 (*0-927534-14-2*) Biling Rev-Pr.
— Pilgrims in Aztlan. Foster, David W., tr. LC 92-23636. 184p. 1992. 24.00 (*0-927534-22-3*); pap. 14.00 (*0-927534-23-1*) Biling Rev-Pr.
***Mendez, Miguel A.** Evidence: The California Code & the Federal Rules, a Problem Approach. (American Casebook Ser.). 515p. (C). 1995. text ed. write for info. (*0-314-06686-1*) West Pub.
Mendez, Phil. The Black Snowman. (Illus.). (J). (gr. 2-5). 1989. 14.95 (*0-590-40552-7*) Scholastic Inc.
— The Black Snowman. (Illus.). 48p. (J). 1991. pap. 4.95 (*0-590-44873-0*, Blue Ribbon Bks) Scholastic Inc.
Mendez, Prudencio. Paraguay, the Democratic Revolution: Why the Colorados. (C). 1993. pap. text ed. 2.00 (*0-9625497-0-3*) P Mendez.
Mendez, Ramon T. Costumbre Nacionales 1809-1883. (Illus.). (SPA.). 1978. lib. bdg. 35.00 (*0-8288-3941-7*) Fr & Eur.
Mendez, Raul H., ed. Visualization in Supercomputing. (Illus.). 224p. 1990. 49.50 (*0-387-97149-1*) Spr-Verlag.
Mendez, Raul H. & Orszag, S. A. Japanese Supercomputing. (Lecture Notes in Engineering Ser.: Vol. 36). (Illus.). 150p. 1988. pap. 42.00 (*0-387-96765-6*) Spr-Verlag.
Mendez, Ruben P. International Public Finance: Global Relations in a New Perspective. 320p. (C). 1992. pap. text ed. 26.00 (*0-19-507195-6*) OUP.
Mendez-Villarrubia, Jose M., jt. auth. see LaBruzza, Anthony.
Mendez, William & Hixon, Charles. UFO Contact at Pascagoula. (Factbooks Ser.). (Illus.). 274p. 1983. lib. bdg. 14.95 (*0-960858-6-6*) UFO Photo.
***Mendgen, Eva.** In Perfect Harmony: Picture & Frame 1850-1920. (Illus.). 336p. (C). 1995. 70.00 (*0-295-97478-8*) U of Wash Pr.
Mendgen, K. & Lesemann, D. E., eds. Electron Microscopy of Plant Pathogens. (Illus.). 352p. 1990. 154.00 (*0-387-52777-X*) Spr-Verlag.
Mendham, John & Derek, David. Classical Methods, Pt. 1. LC 86-28142. (Analytical Chemistry by Open Learning Ser.). 373p. 1987. pap. text ed. 63.95 (*0-471-91363-4*) Wiley.
Mendham, John, et al. Classical Methods, Vol. 2. (Analytical Chemistry by Open Learning Ser.). 351p. 1987. pap. text ed. 54.95 (*0-471-91365-0*) Wiley.
Mendheim, Beverly. Ritchie Valens, The First Latino Rocker. LC 87-71700. 176p. 1987. pap. 14.00 (*0-916950-79-4*) Biling Rev-Pr.
Mendieta, Eduardo, ed. Karl-Otto Apel: Selected Essays, Vol. 1: Towards a Transcendental Semiotics. LC 93-12057. 288p. (C). 1994. text ed. 55.00 (*0-391-03807-9*) Humanities.
Mendieta, Eduardo, ed. see Apel, Karl-Otto.
Mendieta, Eduardo, ed. see Dussel, Enrique.
Mendillo, M., jt. ed. see Brenning, N.
Mendillo, M., jt. auth. see Haerendel, G.
Mendiones, Ruchira, jt. ed. see Anderson, Benedict R.
Mendiones, Ruchira, tr. see Anderson, Benedict R. & Mendiones, Ruchira, eds.
Mendiones, Ruchira C., jt. auth. see Jones, Robert B.
Mendis, G. C. The Early History of Ceylon. (Illus.). 120p. 1986. reprint ed. 14.00 (*0-8364-1743-7*, Pub. by Manohar Bk Srv II) S Asia.
Mendis, Garrett C. The Early History of Ceylon & Its Relations with India & Other Foreign Countries. LC 70-179224. (Illus.). 103p. reprint ed. 29.50 (*0-404-54851-2*) AMS Pr.
Mendis, Patrick. Human Environment & Spatial Relationships in Agricultural Production: The Case Study of Sri Lanka & Other Tea Producing Countries. LC 91-43603. (American University Studies: Economics: Ser. XVI, Vol. 8). 256p. (C). 1992. text ed. 48.95 (*0-8204-1735-1*) P Lang Pubs.
***Mendis, W. M.** The Saga of an Entrepreneur: The Story of Mendis Special. 1995. 16.95 (*0-533-10941-8*) Vantage.
Menditto, Joseph & Kirsch, Debbie. Genetic Engineering, DNA & Cloning: A Bibliography in the Future of Genetics. LC 82-50417. 790p. 1982. 50.00 (*0-87875-241-2*) Whitston Pub.
Mendizabal. Oxford English & Spanish Computer Dictionary: Diccionario Oxford De Informatica. 2nd ed. 450p. (ENG & SPA.). 1986. 125.00 (*0-8288-0256-4*, S8231) Fr & Eur.
Mendizabal, A. The Martyrdom of Spain: Origin of a Civil War. 1972. 59.95 (*0-8490-0587-6*) Gordon Pr.
Mendizabal, Juan C., jt. auth. see Erro-Orthmann, Nora.
Mendl, James W., jt. auth. see Machann, Clinton.
Mendl, James W., Jr., jt. ed. see Machann, Clinton.
***Mendl, Wolf.** Japan's Asia Policy: Regional Security & Global Interests. LC 94-48165. 1995. 55.00 (*0-415-09648-0*) Routledge.
— The Study of War As a Contribution to Peace. LC 82-83955. (Orig.). (C). 1983. pap. 3.00 (*0-87574-247-5*) Pendle Hill.
***Mendle, Michael.** Dangerous Positions: Mixed Government, the Estates of the Realm & the Making of the Answer to the XIX Propositions. LC 83-4798. 269p. 1985. pap. 76.70 (*0-7837-8395-7*, 2059206) Bks Demand.
— Henry Parker & the English Civil War: The Political Thought of the Public's 'Privado' (Cambridge Studies in Early Modern British History). 230p. (C). Date not set. write for info. (*0-521-48227-5*) Cambridge U Pr.
Mendler, Allen N. What Do I Do When...? How to Achieve Discipline with Dignity in the Classroom. 136p. (Orig.). 1992. pap. 18.95 (*1-879639-21-1*) Natl Educ Serv.
Mendler, Allen N., jt. auth. see Curwin, Richard L.
Mendler, Edward C. Massachusetts Conveyancers' Handbook. 3rd ed. LC 83-83043. 1984. 110.00 (*0-318-01918-3*) Lawyers Cooperative.
— Massachusetts Conveyancers' Handbook. 3rd suppl. ed. LC 83-83043. 1993. Suppl. 1993. 54.00 (*0-317-03246-1*) Lawyers Cooperative.
***Mendleson, Alan & Michelson, Joan, eds.** From Bergen-Belsen to Baghdad: The Letters of Alex Aronson. 176p. 1995. lib. bdg. 39.00 (*0-8095-4946-8*) Borgo Pr.
Mendleson, Eliot. Schaum's Three Thousand Solved Problems in Calculus. rev. ed. 1992. pap. text ed. 19.95 (*0-07-041523-4*) McGraw.
Mendlewicz, J. New Trends in Suicide Prevention. Wilmotte, J., ed. (Bibliotheca Psychiatrica Ser.: No. 162). (Illus.). vi, 106p. 1982. pap. 38.50 (*3-8055-3430-2*) S Karger.
Mendlewicz, J., ed. Genetics & Psychopharmacology. (Modern Problems of Pharmacopsychiatry Ser.: Vol. 10). viii, 132p. 1975. 46.50 (*3-8055-2117-0*) S Karger.
— Psychoneuroendocrinology & Abnormal Behavior. (Advances in Biological Psychiatry Ser.: Vol. 5). (Illus.). vi, 130p. 1980. pap. 46.50 (*3-8055-0599-X*) S Karger.
Mendlewicz, J. & Hippius, H., eds. Genetic Research in Psychiatry: C.I.N.P. President's Workshop, 2nd, Munchner Genetikgesprache, September 12-15, 1991. (Illus.). 280p. 1992. 83.00 (*0-387-54827-0*) Spr-Verlag.
Mendlewicz, J. & Racagni, G., eds. Target Receptors for Anxiolytics & Hypnotics: From Molecular Pharmacology to Therapeutics. (International Academy for Biomedical & Drug Research Ser.: Vol. 3). (Illus.). vi, 162p. 1992. 140.00 (*3-8055-5602-0*) S Karger.
Mendlewicz, J. & Shopsin, Baron, eds. Genetic Aspects of Affective Illness: Current Concepts. LC 79-11827. 1979. text ed. 29.95 (*0-88331-146-1*) Luce.
Mendlewicz, J. & Van Praag, H. M., eds. Childhood Psychopharmacology: Current Concepts. (Advances in Biological Psychiatry Ser.: Vol. 2). (Illus.). 1978. pap. 31.25 (*3-8055-2901-5*) S Karger.
Mendlewicz, J. & Van Praag, Herman M. Biological Rhythms & Behavior. (Advances in Biological Psychiatry Ser.: Vol. 11). (Illus.). iv, 150p. 1983. pap. 79.25 (*3-8055-3672-0*) S Karger.
Mendlewicz, J. & Van Praag, Herman M., eds. Management of Depressions with Monoamine Precursors. (Advances in Biological Psychiatry Ser.: Vol. 10). (Illus.). vi, 202p. 1983. pap. 100.00 (*3-8055-3645-3*) S Karger.
Mendlewicz, J., ed. see Alcoholism Symposium Staff.
Mendlewicz, J., et al, eds. Depressive Illness. (Advances in Biological Psychiatry Ser.: Vol. 7). (Illus.). viii, 244p. 1981. pap. 59.25 (*3-8055-2482-X*) S Karger.
— New Pharmacological Approaches to the Therapy of Depressive Disorders. (International Academy for Biomedical & Drug Research Ser.: Vol. 5). (Illus.). vi, 196p. 1993. 178.50 (*3-8055-5746-9*) S Karger.
Mendlovitz, Saul H. The Struggle for a Just World Order: An Agenda of Inquiry & Praxis for the 1980's. 23p. 1982. pap. 10.95 (*0-911646-26-4*) Transaction Pubs.
Mendlovitz, Saul H., jt. ed. see Walker, R. B.
Mendlowitz, Benjamin, photos. The Book of Wooden Boats. LC 92-10533. (Illus.). 192p. 1992. 50.00 (*0-393-03417-8*) Norton.
— Wood, Water, & Light: A Celebration of Classic Wooden Boats. (Illus.). 1989. 100.00 (*0-393-03332-5*) Norton.
— Wood, Water, & Light: A Celebration of Classic Wooden Boats. deluxe limited ed. (Illus.). 1989. boxed 100.00 (*0-318-37480-3*) Norton.
Mendlowitz, Edward. The Biggest Mistakes Taxpayers Make & How to Avoid Them. 220p. 1984. 14.95 (*0-13-077074-4*); pap. 6.95 (*0-13-077066-3*) P-H.
Mendola, Rich. I Am. (Bible Study Ser.). 1986. 2.95 (*0-317-04071-5*); teacher ed 3.95 (*0-317-04072-3*) Intl Students Inc.
Mendola, Sharon. Design Workbook. 80p. (C). 1993. pap. text ed., spiral bd. 16.95 (*0-8403-8454-8*) Kendall-Hunt.
— Design Workbook. 80p. (C). 1995. spiral bd. 16.95 (*0-7872-0617-2*) Kendall-Hunt.
Mendon, Laurie. Rocky Mountain National Park Trail Guide & Journal. LC 94-66661. 216p. 1994. pap. 12.95 (*0-9641329-6-6*) Pinnacle KS.
Mendonca, Manuel, jt. auth. see Kanungo, Rabindra N.
Mendonca, Manuel, jt. ed. see Kanungo, Rabindra N.
Mendonca, Manuel, jt. auth. see Kanungo, Rabindra.
Mendonqa, Augustine. Rotal Anthology: An Annotated Index of Rotal Decisions from 1971-1988. 771p. 1992. 45.00 (*0-943616-59-X*) Canon Law Soc.
***Mendoza.** Acentric Labyrinth. 1995. text ed. 26.95 (*1-85230-640-8*) Element MA.
Mendoza, Andres De, jt. auth. see Almansa, Andres De.
Mendoza, Carlos. Earth Refugees of the Aquarian Age. 130p. (Orig.). 1982. pap. text ed. 4.95 (*0-686-38949-2*) C Mendoza.
— Rendezvous. LC 92-90877. 250p. (Orig.). 1992. pap. 10.00 (*0-9608420-1-2*) C Mendoza.
Mendoza, Carlos, jt. auth. see Paley, Karl.
Mendoza, Celia, tr. see Edge, Findley B.
Mendoza, Daniel. The Memoirs of the Life of Daniel Mendoza. Magriel, Paul, ed. LC 74-29507. (Modern Jewish Experience Ser.). (Illus.). 1975. reprint ed. 20.95 (*0-405-06734-8*) Ayer.
Mendoza De Mann, Wilma, tr. see Hunter, Emily.
Mendoza, E., jt. auth. see Weber, R. L.
Mendoza, E. Feliciano. Juana de Ibarbourou: Oficio de Poesia. LC 80-20020. (Mente y Palabra Ser.). (Illus.). xi, 370p. (SPA.). 1981. 8.00 (*0-8477-0572-2*); pap. 7.20 (*0-8477-0573-0*) U of PR Pr.
Mendoza, Eduardo. The City of Marvels. Molloy, Bernard, tr. 432p. 1988. 19.95 (*0-15-118040-7*) HarBrace.
— The Truth about the Savolta Case: A Novel. Mac Adam, Alfred, tr. LC 91-53086. 400p. 1992. 25.00 (*0-679-40949-1*) Pantheon.
— La Verdad Sobre el Caso Savolta. 17th ed. 432p. (SPA.). 1992. pap. 17.95 (*0-7859-0578-2*, S29407) Fr & Eur.
Mendoza, George. Fishing the Morning Lonely. (Illus.). 1974. 7.95 (*0-88395-029-4*) Freshet Pr.
— Hunter I Might Have Been. (Illus.). (J). (gr. 3-5). 1968. 10.95 (*0-8392-3064-8*) Astor-Honor.
— The Hunter I Might Have Been. (Illus.). 48p. (J). (gr. 3-6). 1989. reprint ed. pap. 6.95 (*0-89815-333-6*) Ten Speed Pr.
— Norman Rockwell Illustrated Cookbook. 1989. 17.95 (*0-685-33408-2*); pap. 9.99 (*0-517-69581-2*) Random Hse Value.
— Piece of String. (Illus.). 1965. 10.95 (*0-8392-1160-0*) Astor-Honor.
Mendoza, George & Wilson, Gahan. Hairticklers. (Illus.). 128p. (J). (gr. 5 up). 1989. reprint ed. 13.95 (*0-89815-332-8*); reprint ed. pap. 8.95 (*0-89815-330-1*) Ten Speed Pr.
Mendoza, George, jt. auth. see Lendl, Ivan.
Mendoza, George, jt. auth. see Snead, Sam.
Mendoza, Jonathan. Official Doom Survivor's Strategies & Secrets. LC 94-66139. 305p. 1994. pap. 19.99 (*0-7821-1546-2*) Sybex.
— Unofficial Guide to Doom Two Hell on Earth. LC 94-69698. 1994. pap. 14.99 (*0-7821-1659-0*) Sybex.
***Mendoza, Jonathan, et al.** The Lost Episodes of DOOM. 1995. disk 16.99 (*0-7821-1674-4*) Sybex.
Mendoza, Kenneth. Talking Books: Ethnopoetics, Translation, Text. LC 93-23760. (Studies in English & American Literature, Linguistics & Culture). xi, 102p. 1993. 38.95 (*1-879751-78-X*) Camden Hse.
Mendoza, Kenneth, jt. ed. see Timm, Eitel.
Mendoza, L. Spanish American Cookbook. 1974. lib. bdg. 69.95 (*0-685-51363-7*) Revisionist Pr.
Mendoza, Lydia. Lydia Mendoza: A Family Autobiography. LC 92-45111. 400p. 1993. text ed. 32.95 (*1-55885-065-1*); pap. 17.95 (*1-55885-066-X*) Arte Publico.
***Mendoza, Manuel & Napoli, Vincent.** Systems of Society: An Introduction to Social Science. 6th ed. 780p. (C). 1995. pap. text ed. write for info. (*0-669-39319-3*) Heath.
Mendoza, Manuel G. & Napoli, Vince. Systems of Society: An Introduction to Social Science. 5th ed. LC 89-81182. 740p. (C). 1990. pap. text ed. 26.00 (*0-669-19717-3*); Instr.'s guide. teacher ed 2.00 (*0-669-19718-1*) Heath.
Mendoza, Marcela, tr. see Sullivan, Jim & Roberts, Phil.
***Mendoza, Meyra S. & Rosegrant, Mark W.** Pricing Behavior in Philippine Corn Markets: Implications for Market Efficiency. LC 95-8312. (International Food Policy Research Institute Research Report Ser.: Vol. 101). 1995. write for info. (*0-89629-104-9*) Intl Food Policy.
Mendoza, Patrick. Song of Sorrow: Massacre at Sand Creek. LC 93-93930. 180p. 1993. teacher ed 2.75 (*0-9636362-1-9*); pap. 10.95 (*0-9636362-0-0*) Willow Wind.
Mendoza, Ramon G. Outside Humanity: A Study of Kafka's Fiction. 310p. (Orig.). (C). 1986. lib. bdg. 48.00 (*0-8191-5515-2*); pap. text ed. 26.00 (*0-8191-5516-0*) U Pr of Amer.
Mendoza, Rene, jt. auth. see Clarke, David J., IV.
Mendoza, Richard H., jt. ed. see Martinez, Joe L., Jr.
Mendoza, Sally P., jt. ed. see Barchas, Patricia R.
Mendoza, Sally P., jt. ed. see Mason, William A.
Mendoza, Thomas J. Appellations. 1993. 8.75 (*0-8062-4540-9*) Carlton.
***Mendoza, Tony.** Dogs: A Postcard Book. (Illus.). 32p. (Orig.). 1995. pap. 8.95 (*0-88496-397-7*) Capra Pr.
— Ernie: A Photographer's Memoir. LC 85-11313. (Illus.). 64p. (Orig.). 1985. pap. 6.95 (*0-88496-240-7*) Capra Pr.
— Ernie: A Photographer's Memoir. LC 89-733. (Illus.). 64p. (Orig.). (C). 1988. reprint ed. lib. bdg. 23.00x (*0-8095-4011-8*) Borgo Pr.
— Ernie's Postcard Book. LC 89-9797. 30p. (Orig.). 1989. pap. 6.95 (*0-88496-294-6*) Capra Pr.
Mendoza, Vicente T. Canciones Mexicanas. 126p. 1948. 3.00 (*0-318-14245-7*) Hispanic Inst.
Mendras, Henri. Social Change in Modern France: Towards a Cultural Anthropology of the Fifth Republic. 256p. (C). 1991. 59.95 (*0-521-39108-3*); pap. 17.95 (*0-521-39998-X*) Cambridge U Pr.
Mendrinos, Roxanne. Building Information Literacy Using High Technology: A Guide for Schools & Libraries. (Illus.). 170p. 1994. pap. text ed. 25.00 (*1-56308-032-X*) Libs Unl.
Mendus, Susan. Toleration & the Limits of Liberalism. LC 88-34576. (Issues in Political Theory Ser.). 192p. (C). 1989. text ed. 49.95 (*0-391-03621-1*) Humanities.
Mendus, Susan, ed. Justifying Toleration. 250p. 1988. 54.95 (*0-521-34302-X*) Cambridge U Pr.
Mendus, Susan & Edwards, David, eds. On Toleration. 164p. 1988. 45.00 (*0-19-827529-3*) OUP.
Mendus, Susan & Rendall, Jane. Sexuality & Subordination: Interdisciplinary Studies of Gender in the Nineteenth Century. 256p. 1989. 49.50 (*0-415-01368-2*); pap. 14.95 (*0-415-01369-0*) Routledge.
Mendus, Susan, jt. ed. see Bell, J. M.
Mendus, Susan, jt. ed. see Horton, John.
Mendus, Susan, jt. ed. see Kennedy, Ellen.
Mendyk, Dennis, ed. Living in the Reader's World, 4 bks., Bk. 1. (Adult Reading Ser.: Levels 2-6). (Illus.). 160p. 1988. pap. text ed. 6.30 (*0-8428-9514-0*) Cambridge Bk.
— Living in the Reader's World, 4 bks., Bk. 2. (Adult Reading Ser.: Levels 2-6). (Illus.). 160p. 1988. pap. text ed. 6.00 (*0-8428-9515-9*) Cambridge Bk.
— Living in the Reader's World, 4 bks., Bk. 4. (Adult Reading Ser.: Levels 2-6). (Illus.). 160p. 1988. pap. text ed. 6.00 (*0-8428-9517-5*) Cambridge Bk.
Mendyk, Dennis, ed. see Cyzyk, Janet L.
Mendyk, Stanley A. Speculum Britanniae: Regional Study, Antiquarianism, & Science in Britain to 1700. (Illus.). 432p. 1989. 45.00 (*0-8020-5744-6*) U of Toronto Pr.
Mene, Cesar A. Historia de la Odontologia en Cuba: Vol. 3, Periodo Repubicano 1940-1958, 3 vols. LC 81-65235. (Coleccion Cuba y Sus Jueces Ser.). (Illus.). 293p. (Orig.). (SPA.). 1982. pap. 29.00 (*0-89729-311-8*) Ediciones.
***Menear, Pauline & Hawkins, Terry.** Stage Management & Theater Administration. rev. ed. (Theater Manuals Ser.). (Illus.). 128p. 1995. reprint ed. pap. 14.95 (*0-7148-2516-6*, Pub. by Phaidon Press UK) Chronicle Bks.
Menear, Pauline, jt. auth. see Hawkins, Terry.
Menebroker, Ann, et al, eds. Landing Signals: An Anthology of Sacramento Poets. (Illus.). 256p. (Orig.). 1986. pap. 20.00 (*0-914485-09-1*); audio (*0-914485-11-3*) Trill Pr.
Menedez, Josefa, et al. Words of Love. LC 84-51596. 95p. (Orig.). 1985. reprint ed. pap. 5.00 (*0-89555-244-2*) TAN Bks Pubs.
Meneely, A. Howard. War Department, 1861. LC 72-127434. (Columbia University. Studies in the Social Sciences: No. 300). 1970. reprint ed. 27.50 (*0-404-51300-X*) AMS Pr.
Meneely, Frank T., jt. auth. see Bennett, John J.

M

An Asterisk (*) at the beginning of an entry indicates that the title is appearing in BIP for the first time.

Meneely, Janie. Santa & the Skipjack. (Illus.). 32p. (J). (gr. k-6). 1991. write for info. (*0-9618461-1-9*) BaySailor Bks.

***Menefee, Campbell A.** Historical & Descriptive Sketchbook of Napa, Sonoma, Lake, & Mendocino. 268p. 1994. 29. 95 (*1-885852-00-2*) J D Stevenson.

Menefee, Christine, jt. ed. see Mountaingrove, Jean.

Menefee, Craig. Harnessing DOS Batch File & Co. 1993. pap. 34.95 (*0-679-79048-9*) Random.

***Menefee, Craig & Bailes, Lenny.** Byte Guide to Optimizing Windows 95. 1995. pap. text ed. 29.95 (*0-07-882120-7*) Osborne-McGraw.

Menefee, Mark, jt. ed. see Needham, Helen C.

Menefee, Samuel P. Wives for Sale: An Ethnographic Study of British Popular Divorce. 1981. text ed. 29.95 (*0-312-88629-2*) St Martin.

Menefee, Sarah. The Blood about the Heart. LC 91-58997. 80p. (Orig.). 1992. pap. 10.95 (*0-915306-53-0*) Curbstone.

— I'm Not Thousandfurs. LC 85-48297. 64p. (Orig.). 1986. pap. 8.00 (*0-915306-59-X*) Curbstone.

Menefee, Selden C. Vocational Training & Employment of Youth. LC 70-166953. (Research Monograph Ser.: Vol. 25). 1971. reprint ed. lib. bdg. 22.50 (*0-306-70357-2*) Da Capo.

Meneghini, Carlo & Bonifazi, E. An Atlas of Pediatric Dermatology. (Illus.). 172p. 1986. 44.95 (*0-8151-5759-2*, GZM-1, Yr Bk Med Pubs) Mosby Yr Bk.

Meneghini, Giuseppe. Algae Italianae e Dalmatiche illustrata. (Illus.). 1970. 55.00 (*90-6123-094-2*) Lubrecht & Cramer.

Meneghini, Robert & Kozu, Toshiaka. Spaceborne Weather Radar. (Radar Library). 208p. 1990. text ed. 59.00 (*0-89006-382-6*) Artech Hse.

Meneguzzi, M., et al, eds. Turbulence & Nonlinear Dynamics in MHD Flows: Proceedings of the Workshop on Turbulence & Nonlinear Dynamics in MHD Flows, Cargese, France, July 4-8, 1988. 300p. 1989. 95.00 (*0-444-87396-1*, North Holland) Elsevier.

Menelaus, Malcolm B. The Orthopaedic Management of Spina Bifida Cystica. 2nd ed. LC 79-40044. (Current Problems in Orthopaedics Ser.). 227p. reprint ed. pap. 64.70 (*0-8357-3375-0*, 2039621) Bks Demand.

Menelaus, Malcolm B., ed. The Management of Limb Inequality. (Current Problems in Orthopaedics Ser.). (Illus.). 236p. 1991. text ed. 115.00 (*0-443-04298-5*) Churchill.

Menell, Jeff. Howard Stern: Big Mouth. 192p. 1993. mass mkt. 4.99 (*1-55817-796-5*, Pinnacle NY) Windsor NY.

Menell, Zoe, ed. see Musgrave, Beatrice.

Menell, Zoe, jt. ed. see Musgrave, Beatrice.

Menen, Audrey. The Abode of Love. 176p. 1990. mass mkt. 6.95 (*0-14-012346-6*, Penguin Bks) Viking Penguin.

— The Ramayana: As Told by Audrey Menen. LC 72-598. 276p. 1972. reprint ed. text ed. 49.50 (*0-8371-6181-9*, VARA, Greenwood Pr) Greenwood.

Menendez, Al & Menendez, Shirley. Maryland Trivia. LC 92-6746. 192p. (Orig.). 1992. pap. 5.95 (*1-55853-164-5*) Rutledge Hill Pr.

Menendez, Al & Menendez, Shirley, comps. New Jersey Trivia. LC 93-12564. 192p. (Orig.). 1993. pap. 5.95 (*1-55853-223-4*) Rutledge Hill Pr.

Menendez, Al, jt. auth. see Doerr, Edd.

Menendez, Albert J. Christmas in the White House. LC 83-3629. (Illus.). 128p. 1983. 12.00 (*0-664-21392-8*, Westminster) Westminster John Knox.

— The December Dilemma: Christmas in American Public Life. 104p. (Orig.). 1988. pap. 6.95 (*0-9617164-1-X*) AURF.

— December Wars: Religious Symbols & Ceremonies in the Public Square. 170p. 1993. 19.95 (*0-87975-857-0*) Prometheus Bks.

— John F. Kennedy: Catholic & Humanist. LC 78-68139. 144p. 1979. 23.95x (*0-87975-109-6*) Prometheus Bks.

— Visions of Reality: What Fundamentalist Schools Teach. LC 92-33260. 152p. (Orig.). (C). 1993. pap. 14.95 (*0-87975-802-3*) Prometheus Bks.

Menendez, Albert J., jt. auth. see Doerr, Edd.

Menendez, Antonio V. Power & Television in Latin America: The Dominican Case. LC 92-383. 208p. 1992. text ed. 49.95 (*0-275-94275-9*, C4275, Praeger Pubs) Greenwood.

Menendez, Aurelio. Access to Basic Infrastructure by the Urban Poor. (Economic Development Institute Policy Seminar Report Ser.: No. 28). 96p. 1991. 7.95 (*0-8213-1815-2*, 11815) World Bank.

— Estimating Capital & Operating Costs in Urban Transportation Planning. LC 92-9806. 200p. 1993. text ed. 49.95 (*0-275-94219-8*, C4219, Praeger Pubs) Greenwood.

Menendez-Botet, Celia & Rose, Herbert N., eds. Impact of AIDS on the Clinical Chemistry Laboratory: Paper from a Workshop Sponsored by the Safe Laboratory Practices Committe of the American Association for Clinical Chemistry at the 1990 AACC National Meeting. 28p. 1990. 15.00 (*0-915274-57-4*) Am Assn Clinical Chem.

Menendez-Botet, Celia J. & St Germain, Jean M., eds. Hazardous Waste: Facts & Fallacies. 64p. 1990. 20.00 (*0-915274-55-8*) Am Assn Clinical Chem.

Menendez, Emilio. Lecciones de Derecho de Familia. LC 76-961. 393p. (Orig.). (SPA.). (C). 1981. 9.60 (*0-8477-3018-2*); pap. 7.50 (*0-8477-3007-7*) U of PR Pr.

— Lecciones de Teoria General del Derecho. LC 79-16559. 262p. (SPA.). 1980. pap. text ed. 7.20 (*0-8477-3017-4*) U of PR Pr.

Menendez, Enrique C. Only the Wind. Armas, Jose, ed. Hernandez, Frances, tr. (Illus.). 182p. 1980. 9.00 (*0-918358-05-1*); pap. 7.00 (*0-686-64685-1*) Pajarito Pubns.

Menendez, J. Alberb, ed. The Catholic Novel: An Annotated Bibliography. LC 88-1718. (Reference Library of the Humanities). 344p. 1988. lib. bdg. 48.00 (*0-8240-8534-5*) Garland.

Menendez, James N., et al. Guide to Understanding Design Documentation in Trusted Systems. 40p. 1989. pap. 2.25 (*0-16-001510-3*, S/N 008-000-00518-4) USGPO.

Menendez, Josefa. Christ's Appeal for Love. Keppel, L., tr. 1975. reprint ed. pap. 5.50 (*0-89555-013-X*) TAN Bks Pubs.

— I Wait for You: Jesus' Lament Over Man's Indifference (Excerpts from the Way of Divine Love) 32p. (Orig.). 1985. pap. 0.75 (*0-89555-285-X*) TAN Bks Pubs.

— The Way of Divine Love. LC 79-112493. 504p. 1972. reprint ed. pap. 17.50 (*0-89555-030-X*) TAN Bks Pubs.

— The Way of Divine Love. 506p. 1981. reprint ed. pap. 8.50 (*0-89555-276-0*) TAN Bks Pubs.

***Menendez, Lyle.** The Private Diary of Lyle Menendez: In His Own Words! (Illus.). 288p. 1995. 17.95 (*0-7871-0474-4*) Dovebks.

Menendez, Manuela, ed. see Schoolcraft, Robert.

Menendez Pidal, Ramon. Antologia de Prosistas Espanoles, No. 110. 261p. (SPA.). 1978. 10.95 (*0-8288-8556-7*, S2322) Fr & Eur.

— La Crisis del Siglo XVII. Vargas, V. F. et al, eds. (Historia de Espana Ser.: Vol. 24). 796p. (SPA.). 1992. 195.00 (*0-7859-0561-8*, 842394994X) Fr & Eur.

— La Espana de Fernanado the Seventh: La Guerra de la Independencia y los Origenes del Regimen Constitucional. Gallego, M. A., ed. (Historia de Espana Ser.: Vol. 33). 1036p. (SPA.). 1992. 195.00 (*0-7859-0560-X*, 842394980X) Fr & Eur.

— La Espana de los Reyes Catolicos: La Edificacion del Estado y la Politica Exterior. Fernandez, L. S. & Alvarez, M. F., eds. (Historia de Espana Ser.: Vol. 19). 810p. (SPA.). 1992. 195.00 (*0-7859-0559-6*, 842394820X) Fr & Eur.

— Espana Primitiva: Prerromana. Almagro, M. et al, eds. (Historia de Espana Ser.: Vol. 3). (SPA.). 1992. 195.00 (*0-7859-0557-X*, 842394803X) Fr & Eur.

— Los Espanoles en la Historia. (Nueva Austral Ser.: Vol. 182). (SPA.). 1991. pap. text ed. 24.95x (*84-239-1982-X*) Elliots Bks.

— Estudios Literarios, No. 28. 212p. (SPA.). 1968. write for info. (*0-318-69890-0*) Fr & Eur.

— Flor Nueva de Romances Viejos. (Nueva Austral Ser.: Vol. 202). (SPA.). 1991. pap. text ed. 12.95x (*84-239-7202-X*) Elliots Bks.

— Historia De Espana, 37 vols., Set. (SPA.). 1992. write for info. (*0-7859-0510-3*, 8423948005) Fr & Eur.

— Historia De Espana, Vol. 1: Espana Primitiva: la Prehistoria. Pacheco, F. H. et al, eds. 1000p. (SPA.). 1992. 195.00 (*0-7859-0511-1*, 8423948013) Fr & Eur.

— Historia De Espana, Vol. 11: La Espana Cristiana De los Siglos VII al XI: Vol. 1 (722-1037) Sanchez-Albornoz, Claudio, ed. 886p. (SPA.). 1992. 195.00 (*0-7859-0531-6*, 8423949818) Fr & Eur.

— Historia De Espana, Vol. 12: Los Reinos Cristianos En los Siglos XI y XII: Vol. I, Economias, Sociedades, Instituciones. Pastor, R. & Carles, M., eds. 478p. (FRE.). 1992. 195.00 (*0-7859-0516-2*, 8423948129) Fr & Eur.

— Historia De Espana, Vol. 14: Expansion Peninsular y Mediterranea (1212-1350): la Corona De Castilla. Fontes, J. T. et al, eds. 660p. (SPA.). 1992. 195.00 (*0-7859-0517-0*, 8423948153) Fr & Eur.

— Historia De Espana, Vol. 15: Expansion Peninsular y Mediterranea (1212-1350): el Reino De Navarra, la Corona De Aragon, Portugal. Lacarra, J. M. et al, eds. 660p. (SPA.). 1992. 195.00 (*0-7859-0520-0*, 8423948242) Fr & Eur.

— Historia De Espana, Vol. 16: La Crisis De la Reconquista (1350-1410) Fernandez, L. S. & Campistol, J. R., eds. 862p. (SPA.). 1992. 195.00 (*0-7859-0518-9*, 8423948161) Fr & Eur.

— Historia De Espana, Vol. 18: La Espana De los Reyes Catolicos: la Bases Del Reinado, la Guerra De Sucesion, la Guerra De Granada. Fernandez, L. S. & Carriazo, J., eds. 1046p. (SPA.). 1992. 195.00 (*0-7859-0519-7*, 8423948196) Fr & Eur.

— Historia De Espana, Vol. 2: Espana Primitiva: la Protohistoria. Almagro, M. & Bellido, A. G., eds. 720p. (SPA.). 1992. 195.00 (*0-7859-0512-X*, 8423948021) Fr & Eur.

— Historia De Espana, Vol. 20: El Siglo XVI. Alvarez, M. F., ed. 778p. (SPA.). 1992. 195.00 (*0-7859-0521-9*, 8423948277) Fr & Eur.

— Historia De Espana, Vol. 21: La Espana De Carlos V: el Hombre, la Politica Espanola y la Politica Europea. Alvarez, M. F., ed. 1072p. (SPA.). 1992. 195.00 (*0-7859-0522-7*, 8423948285) Fr & Eur.

— Historia De Espana, Vol. 22: Felipe II: el Hombre y la Politica, Vol I 1556-1568. Fernandez, L. S. & Fernandez de Retana, eds. 868p. (SPA.). 1992. 195.00 (*0-7859-0523-5*, 8423948307) Fr & Eur.

— Historia De Espana, Vol. 23: Felipe II: el Hombre y la Politica, Vol. II 1569-1598. Fernandez, L. S. & Fernandez de Retana, eds. 920p. (SPA.). 1992. 195.00 (*0-7859-0524-3*, 8423948315) Fr & Eur.

— Historia De Espana, Vol. 25: La Espana De Felipe III. Bustamente, C. P., ed. 660p. (SPA.). 1992. 195.00 (*0-7859-0525-1*, 8423948323) Fr & Eur.

— Historia De Espana, Vol. 26: La Espana De Felipe IV. Tomas y Valiente, F. et al, eds. 880p. (SPA.). 1992. 195. 00 (*0-7859-0526-X*, 8423948331) Fr & Eur.

— Historia De Espana, Vol. 27: El Siglo Del Quijote (1580-1680): Vol. I, Religion, Filosofia, Ciencia. Martin, M. A. et al, eds. 913p. (SPA.). 1992. 195.00 (*0-7859-0536-7*, 8423949907) Fr & Eur.

— Historia De Espana, Vol. 28: El Siglo De Quijote (1580-1680): Vol. II, las Letras, las Artes. 879p. (SPA.). 1992. 195.00 (*0-7859-0537-5*, 8423949915) Fr & Eur.

— Historia De Espana, Vol. 29: La Epoca De los Primeros Borbones: la Nueva Monarquia (1700-1759) Sanchez, F. C. et al, eds. 778p. (SPA.). 1992. 195.00 (*0-7859-0527-8*, 8423948374) Fr & Eur.

— Historia De Espana, Vol. 30: La Epoca De los Primeros Borbones: la Cultura Espanola Entre el Barroco y la Illustracion (1680-1759) Stiffoni, G. et al, eds. 557p. (SPA.). 1992. 195.00 (*0-7859-0528-6*, 8423948382) Fr & Eur.

— Historia De Espana, Vol. 31: La Epoca De la Ilustracion: el Estado y la Cultura (1759-1808) Recio, L. M. et al, eds. 1088p. (SPA.). 1992. 195.00 (*0-7859-0529-4*, 8423948390) Fr & Eur.

— Historia De Espana, Vol. 32: La Epoca De la Ilustracion: las Indias y la Politica Exterior. Rikles, C. D. et al, eds. 904p. (SPA.). 1992. 195.00 (*0-7859-0530-8*, 8423949796) Fr & Eur.

— Historia De Espana, Vol. 34: La Era Isabelina y el Sexenio Democratico (1834-1874) Villarroya, J. T. et al, eds. 1208p. (SPA.). 1992. 195.00 (*0-7859-0532-4*, 8423949826) Fr & Eur.

— Historia De Espana, Vol. 35: La Epoca Del Romanticismo (1808-1874): Origenes, Religion, Filosofia, Ciencia. Juretschke, H. et al, eds. 786p. (SPA.). 1992. 195.00 (*0-7859-0538-3*, 8423949923) Fr & Eur.

— Historia De Espana, Vol. 37: La Comienzos del Siglo XX: la Problacion, la Economia, la Sociedad (1898-1931) Delgado, J. L. et al, eds. 782p. (SPA.). 1992. 195.00 (*0-7859-0535-9*, 8423949850) Fr & Eur.

— Historia De Espana, Vol. 4: Espana Romana: la Conquista y la Explotacion Economia. rev. ed. Duque, Angel M. & Martinez, J. M., eds. 762p. (SPA.). 1992. 195.00 (*0-7859-0533-2*, 8423949834) Fr & Eur.

— Historia De Espana, Vol. 5: Espana Romana: la Sociedad, el Derecho y la Cultura. rev. ed. Manjarres, J. M. et al, eds. 764p. (SPA.). 1992. 195.00 (*0-7859-0534-0*, 8423949842) Fr & Eur.

— Historia De Espana, Vol. 6: Espana Visigoda: las Invasiones, las Sociedades, la Iglesia. Diaz, M. C. et al, eds. 596p. (SPA.). 1992. 195.00 (*0-7859-0540-5*, 8423949958) Fr & Eur.

— Historia De Espana, Vol. 8: Espana Musulmana (711-1031): la Conquista, el Emirato, el Califato. Levi-Provencal, E., ed. 568p. (SPA.). 1992. 195.00 (*0-7859-0513-8*, 8423948064) Fr & Eur.

— Historia De Espana, Vol. 9: Espana Musulmana (711-1031): Instituciones y Vida Social e Intelectual. Levi-Provencal, E., ed. 862p. (SPA.). 1992. 195.00 (*0-7859-0514-6*, 8423948072) Fr & Eur.

— La Lengua Castellana en el Siglo XVII. (Nueva Austral Ser.: Vol. 208). (SPA.). 1991. pap. text ed. 24.95x (*84-239-7208-9*) Elliots Bks.

— Poesia Juglaresca & Juglares. Origenes de las Literaturas Romanicas. (Nueva Austral Ser.: No. 159). (SPA.). 1991. pap. text ed. 39.95x (*84-239-1959-5*) Elliots Bks.

— Los Trastamaras de Castilla y Aragon en el Siglo XV. Fernandez, L. S. et al, eds. (Historia de Espana Ser.: Vol. 17). 1026p. (SPA.). 1992. 195.00 (*0-7859-0558-8*, 842394817X) Fr & Eur.

— Visigoda: La Monarquia, la Cultura, las Artes. Prendes, J. M., ed. (Historia de Espana Ser.: Vol. 7). 510p. (SPA.). 1992. 195.00 (*0-7859-0545-6*, 9423949966) Fr & Eur.

Menendez Pidal, Ramon & Riquer, Martin D., intros. Cantar De Mio Cid: Texto Antiguo De Ramon Menendez Pidal Version Moderna De Alfonso Reyes. (Nueva Austral Ser.: No. 20). (SPA.). 1991. pap. text ed. 24.95x (*84-239-1820-3*) Elliots Bks.

Menendez Pidal, Ramon, et al. Historia de Espana: 26. El Siglo del Quijote (1580-1680), Vol. II: Las Letras, las Artes. 879p. 1992. 189.50x (*84-239-4991-5*) Elliots Bks.

Menendez, Shirley, jt. auth. see Menendez, Al.

Menendez, Shirley, jt. comp. see Menendez, Al.

Meneray, Wilbur E. & Favrot, Anne, eds. The Favrot Family Papers, Vol. IV: A Documentary Chronicle of Early Louisiana. Hampshire, Carole & Smith, Snn, trs. Date not set. write for info. (*0-87409-005-9*) Tulane Univ.

Meneses, Eloise H., jt. auth. see Hiebert, Paul G.

Menestrier, Claude-Francois. Traite des tournois, joustes, carrousels et autres spectacles publics. LC 76-43926. (Music & Theatre in France in the 17th & 18th Centuries Ser.). reprint ed. 84.50 (*0-404-60174-X*) AMS Pr.

Menetra, Louis. Journal of My Life. Roche, Daniel, ed. Goldhammer, Arthur, tr. 400p. 1986. text ed. 40.50 (*0-231-06128-5*) Col U Pr.

— Journal of My Life: The Autobiography of Jacques-Louis Menetra. Goldhammer, Arthur, tr. 400p. 1989. pap. text ed. 17.00 (*0-231-06129-3*) Col U Pr.

Menez, Annie R. Why the Kalaw Wears a Casque & Other Stories for Children. (Illus.). 34p. (Orig.). (J). (gr. 1-3). 1993. pap. 3.00 (*971-10-0494-1*, Pub. by New Day Pub PH) Cellar.

Menez, Ernani G., jt. auth. see Phillips, Ronald C.

Menez, Herminia Q. Folklore Communication Among Filipinos in California. Dorson, Richard M., ed. LC 80-733. (Folklore of the World Ser.). 1981. lib. bdg. 26.95 (*0-405-13320-0*) Ayer.

Menezes, Alfred J. Elliptic Curve Public Key Cryptosystems. LC 93-10961. (International Series in Engineering & Computer Science, VLSI, Computer Architecture, & Digital Screen Processing: Vol. 234). 144p. (C). 1993. lib. bdg. 79.95 (*0-7923-9368-6*) Kluwer Ac.

Menezes, Alfred J., ed. see Gao, XuHong & Mullin, Ronald C.

***Menezes, Arnold H. & Sonntag, Volker K.** Principles of Spinal Surgery, 2 vols., Set. (Illus.). 1995. text ed. 295.00 (*0-07-059662-X*) Hlth Prof Div.

Menezes, Mary N., ed. Amerindians in Guyana, 1803-1873: A Documentary History. 314p. 1979. 40.00 (*0-7146-3054-3*, Pub. by F Cass Pubs UK) Intl Spec Bk.

Meng, Alexander C., jt. auth. see Bischko, Johannes.

Meng, Brita, jt. auth. see Somogyi, Stephan.

Meng, C. I., et al, eds. Auroral Physics. (Illus.). 600p. (C). 1991. 140.00 (*0-521-38049-9*) Cambridge U Pr.

Meng Chu Zhou & DiCesare, Frank. Petri Net Synthesis for Discrete Event Control of Manufacturing Systems. LC 92-36721. (International Series in Engineering & Computer Science, VLSI, Computer Architecture, & Digital Screen Processing). 256p. 1992. lib. bdg. 95.50 (*0-7923-9289-2*) Kluwer Ac.

Meng, Frank P. I Don't Believe This World: Why I Am an Iconoclast. 220p. (Orig.). 1988. pap. 10.00 (*0-9619707-0-7*) Venice Pr.

Meng, S. M. Tsungli Yamen: Its Organization & Functions. LC 62-53393. (East Asian Monographs: No. 13). 151p. 1962. pap. 11.00 (*0-674-91095-8*) HUP.

Meng, Tan L. Insurance Law in Singapore. xliv, 600p. 1988. 179.00 (*0-409-99560-6*) Butterworth Legal Pubs.

— The Law in Singapore on Carriage of Goods by Sea. lv, 509p. 1986. 173.00 (*9971-70-049-2*) Butterworth Legal Pubs.

Meng, Teresa H. & Malik, Sharad, eds. Asynchronous Circuit Design for VLSI Signal Processing. LC 93-33160. 184p. (C). 1994. lib. bdg. 115.00 (*0-7923-9397-X*) Kluwer Ac.

***Meng, Wang.** The Butterfly & Other Stories. 215p. 1995. lib. bdg. 23.00 (*0-8095-4504-7*) Borgo Pr.

— The Stubborn Porridge & Other Stories. Hong, Zhu, tr. & intro. by. 180p. 1994. 18.50 (*0-8076-1353-3*) Braziller.

Meng, Zhaoqian, ed. Metrology for Quality Control in Production (IAP) Proceedings of the IMEKO TC 14 International Symposium on Metrology for Quality Control in Production, Beijing, China, 9-12 May 1989, No. 2. (International Academic Publishers Ser.). 382p. 1989. 110.00 (*0-08-037515-4*, Pergamon Pr) Elsevier.

Mengarini, Gregory. Selish or Flat-Head Grammar. LC 10-30201. (Library of American Linguistics: No. 2). reprint ed. 42.75 (*0-404-50982-7*) AMS Pr.

Mengas, Peter. The Doll Hospital. 1989. pap. 3.95 (*0-685-25351-1*) St Thomas.

Menge, H., et al, eds. Helicobacter Pylori 1990: Proceedings of the Second International Symposium on Helicobacter Pylori Bad Nauheim, August 25-26th, 1989. (Illus.). 299p. 1991. 64.00 (*0-387-52616-1*) Spr-Verlag.

Menge, Hermann. Langenscheidt German & Ancient Greek Pocket Dictionary: Langenscheidt Taschenwoerterbuch Altgriechisch. 1027p. (GER & GRE.). 1986. 49.95 (*0-8288-0510-5*, F19902) Fr & Eur.

— Langenscheidt Pocket Latin Dictionary: Langenscheidt Taschenwoerterbuch Lateinisch. 35th ed. 1036p. (GER & LAT.). 1983. 45.00 (*0-8288-1028-1*, F58022) Fr & Eur.

Menge, Hermann & Guthling, O. Langenscheidt Grosswoerterbuch Altgriechisch-Deutsch: Ancient Greek & German. 24th ed. 762p. (GER & GRE.). 1981. 135.00 (*0-8288-0509-1*, F 19904) Fr & Eur.

— Langenscheidt Large German-Latin Dictionary: Langenscheidt Grosswoerterbuch Deutsch-Latein. 13th ed. 740p. (GER & LAT.). 1982. 95.00 (*0-8288-1026-5*, F58000) Fr & Eur.

— Langenscheidt Large Latin-German Dictionary: Langenscheidt Grosswoerterbuch Lateinisch-Deutsch. 21th ed. 813p. (GER & LAT.). 1981. 95.00 (*0-8288-1027-3*, F57990) Fr & Eur.

Menge, R. & Preuss, S. Lexicon Caesarianum. (GER.). 1972. 175.00 (*0-8288-6405-5*, M-7284) Fr & Eur.

Menge, Walter O. & Fischer, Carl H. The Mathematics of Life Insurance. 2nd ed. LC 65-12855. (C). 1965. text ed. 12.95 (*0-914004-00-X*) Ulrich.

***Mengel, Elias F., Jr., ed.** Poems on Affairs of State: Augustan Satirical Verse, 1660-1714 Vol. 2: 1678-1681. 575p. 1965. 150.00 (*0-300-00766-3*) Elliots Bks.

Mengel, Ewald. On First Looking into Arden's Goethe: Adaptations & Translations of Classical German Plays for the Modern English State. 208p. 1994. 59.95 (*1-879751-84-4*) Camden Hse.

Mengel, Gail E. The Homework Organizer: Assignment Notebook & Guide. 96p. (YA). (gr. 7-12). 1991. 9.95 (*0-9631705-0-3*) Get Organized.

Mengel, J. Dansk-Italiensk Ordborg: Danish-Italian Dictionary. 660p. (DAN & ITA.). 1979. 39.95 (*0-8288-4724-X*, M1292) Fr & Eur.

Mengel, K. & Pilbeam, D. J., eds. Nitrogen Metabolism in Plants. (Proceedings of the Phytochemical Society of Europe Ser.: No. 33). (Illus.). 250p. 1992. 89.00 (*0-19-857752-4*) OUP.

Mengel, Mark B., ed. Principles of Clinical Practice: An Introductory Textbook. (Illus.). 436p. 1991. 37.50 (*0-306-43847-X*, Plenum Med Bk) Plenum.

Mengel, Mark B. & Schweibert, L. Peter. Ambulatory Medicine: Primary Care of Families. (Illus.). 690p. 1993. pap. text ed. 26.00 (*0-8385-1294-1*, A1294-6) Appleton & Lange.

Mengel, Robert M. Birds of Kentucky. American Ornithologists' Union Staff, ed. 581p. 1965. 15.00 (*0-943610-03-6*) Am Ornithologists.

Mengel, Robert M., ed. Papers in Vertebrate Paleontology Honoring Robert Warren Wilson. LC 84-71697. (Special Publications CMNH Ser.: No. 9). (Illus.). 192p. (Orig.). 1984. pap. 25.00 (*0-935868-09-7*) Carnegie Mus.

Mengel, Robert M., ed. see Daly, Eleanor.

Mengel, Robert M., jt. auth. see Jenkinson, Marion A.

Mengel, Robert M., jt. auth. see Tordoff, Harrison B.

Mengel, Wolfgang, jt. ed. see Fonkalsrud, Eric W.

Mengelkoch, Louise, ed. Native American Wisdom. LC 91-21315. (Classic Wisdom Collection). 128p. 1991. 12.95 (*0-931432-78-2*) New Wrld Lib.

M

Menger, Anton. Right to the Whole Produce of Labour: The Origin & Development of the Theory of Labour's Claim to the Whole Product of Industry. LC 68-54737. (Reprints of Economic Classics Ser.). cxviii, 271p. 1970. reprint ed. lib. bdg. 39.50 (0-678-00714-4) Kelley.

Menger, F. M. & Mandell, L. Electronic Interpretation of Organic Chemistry: A Problems-Oriented Text. LC 79-21718. 224p. 1980. pap. text ed. 27.50 (0-306-40391-9, Plenum Pr) Plenum.

Menger, Fredric M. Problems in Organic Reaction Mechanisms. LC 68-28060. (Appleton-Century-Crofts Series in Chemistry). 128p. reprint ed. pap. 36.50 (0-317-26294-7, 2055691) Bks Demand.

Menger, Karl. Kurventheorie. 2nd rev. ed. LC 63-11314. 1968. 18.95 (0-8284-0172-1) Chelsea Pub.

— Morality, Decisions, & Social Organization Toward a Logic of Ethics. Mulder, Henk L., ed. Van Der Schalie, E., tr. LC 74-81941. (Vienna Circle Collection: No. 6). 100p. 1974. lib. bdg. 62.00 (90-277-0318-3); pap. text ed. 33.00 (90-277-0319-1) Kluwer Ac.

— Reminiscences of the Vienna Circle & the Mathematical Colloquium. Golland, Louise, ed. LC 94-5014. (Vienna Circle Collection: Vol. 20). 272p. (C). 1994. pap. text ed. 24.50 (0-7923-2873-6) Kluwer Ac.

— Reminiscences of the Vienna Circle & the Mathematical Colloquium. Golland, Louise, ed. LC 94-5014. (Vienna Circle Collection: Vol. 20). 272p. (C). 1994. lib. bdg. 88.50 (0-7923-2711-X) Kluwer Ac.

— Selected Papers in Logic & Foundations, Didactics, & Economics. (Vienna Circle Collection: No. 10). 1979. lib. bdg. 117.00 (90-277-0320-5); pap. text ed. 64.00 (90-277-0321-3) Kluwer Ac.

Menger, Lucy. Theodore Sturgeon. LC 81-40468. (Recognitions Ser.). 144p. (C). 1981. 19.95 (0-8044-2618-X, F Ungar Bks) Continuum.

Menger, M. D., jt. ed. see Messmer, K.

Menger, Matt. Slowly Climbs the Sun. LC 72-96835. 1973. 5.50 (0-685-42651-3) Guild Bks.

— Valley of Mekong. 1970. 4.95 (0-685-79412-1); pap. 3.95 (0-685-79413-X) Guild Bks.

Mengerink, William C. Hand in Hand: Funding Strategies for Human Service Agencies. 115p. 1992. text ed. 40.00 (0-930807-37-5, 600317) Fund Raising.

Mengert, et al. Institution of Education. 1992. 22.55 (0-536-58222-X) Ginn Pr.

Mengert, Jim, jt. auth. see Linver, Sandy.

***Mengert, Terry, et al.** Emergency Medical Therapy. 4th ed. LC 94-39975. (Illus.). 800p. 1995. pap. text ed. write for info. (0-7216-5162-3) Saunders.

Menges. How to Make Injection Molds. 1987. 74.95 (0-02-947570-8) Macmillan.

Menges, Constantine. The Twilight Struggle: The Soviet Union v. the United States Today. 428p. (C). 1991. 39.75 (0-8447-3701-1) Am Enterprise.

Menges, Constantine, ed. Russia & the New Independent States: The Political & Economic Transitions. 300p. (C). 1994. lib. bdg. 57.00 (0-8191-9550-2); pap. text ed. 24.00 (0-8191-9551-0) U Pr of Amer.

Menges, Constantine C. The Future of Germany & the Atlantic Alliance. 297p. (C). 1991. 24.95 (0-8447-3731-3) Am Enterprise.

Menges, Constantine C., ed. Transitions from Communism in Russia & Eastern Europe: Analysis & Perspectives. LC 93-6192. 320p. 1993. 61.00 (0-8191-9296-1); pap. 24.50 (0-8191-9297-X) U Pr of Amer.

Menges, Georg & Mohren, Paul. How to Make Injection Molds. 400p. (C). 1986. text ed. 79.50 (1-56990-061-2) Hanser-Gardner.

— How to Make Injection Molds. 2nd ed. 540p. (C). 1993. text ed. 109.50 (1-56990-062-0) Hanser-Gardner.

Menges, Georg, et al, eds. Experts Systems in Production Engineering. (Lecture Notes in Engineering Ser.: Vol. 29). iv, 239p. 1987. pap. 39.00 (0-387-17927-5) Spr-Verlag.

Menges, Gunter, ed. Information, Inference & Decision. LC 73-91432. (Theory & Decision Library: No. 1). 1974. lib. bdg. 70.00 (90-277-0422-8); pap. text ed. 45.50 (90-277-0423-6) Kluwer Ac.

Menges, Karl, ed. see Herder, Johann G.

Menges, Karl, et al, eds. Herder Yearbook, Vol. 1. (Studies in German Literature, Linguistics & Culture). 220p. 49.50 (1-879751-22-4) Camden Hse.

Menges, Matthew C. The Concept of Univocity Regarding the Predication of God & Creature According to William Ockham. (Philosophy Ser.). 1952. 8.00 (0-686-11539-2) Franciscan Inst.

Menges, Patricia. How to Use Lotus 1-2-3, Rel. 3.4. Wolf, Charles R., ed. 99p. (Orig.). 1993. pap. text ed. 125.00 (1-56562-026-7) OneOnOne Comp Trng.

Menges, Patricia, ed. see Wolf, Charles R.

Menges, Patricia A. How to Use dBASE III Plus. Rinehart, Janice S., ed. (Illus.). 108p. 1986. 225.00 (0-917792-36-X) OneOnOne Comp Trng.

— Using MS-DOS on a Hard Disk. 80p. (Orig.). 1988. pap. text ed. 175.00 (0-917792-61-0); audio write for info. (0-318-64966-7) OneOnOne Comp Trng.

Menges, Patricia A., ed. see Dravilas, Paul.

Menges, Patricia A., ed. see Levin, David S.

Menges, Patricia A., ed. see Pinnacle Communications Staff.

Menges, Patricia A., ed. see Young, Natalie B.

***Menges, Phil.** Beyond Revolution: The Guide to Complete Political & Social Reform. 260p. (Orig.). 1994. pap. 14.95 (0-9643663-0-4) Outside NY.

Menges, Robert J. & Mathis, B. Claude. Key Resources on Teaching, Learning, Curriculum, & Faculty Development: A Guide to the Higher Education Literature. LC 88-42794. (Higher Education Ser.). 424p. 1988. 45.00 (1-55542-118-0) Jossey-Bass.

Menges, Robert J. & Svinicki, Marilla D., eds. College Teaching: From Theory to Practice. LC 85-644763. (New Directions for Teaching & Learning Ser.: No. TL 45). 1991. 16.95 (1-55542-799-5) Jossey-Bass.

***Menges, Robert J. & Wermer, Maryellen, eds.** Bitter Teaching & Learning in College: Using Scholarship to Improve Practice. (Higher & Adult Education Ser.). 1995. 32.95 (0-7879-0133-4) Jossey-Bass.

***Menges, Tracey, ed.** The Annual Directory of American & Canadian Bed & Breakfasts, 1996 Edition. (Illus.). 1502p. (Orig.). 1995. pap. 19.95 (1-55853-367-2) Rutledge Hill Pr.

Mengham, Rod. The Idiom of the Time: The Writings of Henry Green. LC 82-9716. 220p. 1983. 64.95 (0-521-24813-2) Cambridge U Pr.

— On Language: Descent from the Tower of Babel. LC 93-49656. Orig. Title: Descent of Language. 1994. reprint ed. 24.95 (0-316-56671-3) Little.

Menghi, A. Nuovo Dizionario di Terminologia Giuridica: New Dictionary of Legal Terms. (ITA.). 1979. pap. 49.95 (0-8288-4830-0, M9654) Fr & Eur.

Mengin, Robert. No Laurels for De Gaulle. Allen, Jay, tr. LC 78-179734. (Biography Index Reprint Ser.). 1977. reprint ed. 24.95 (0-8369-8102-2) Ayer.

Mengisteab, Kidane. Ethiopia: Failure of Land Reform & Agricultural Crisis. LC 90-32335. (Contributions in Afro-American & African Studies: No. 137). 240p. 1990. text ed. 55.00 (0-313-27423-1, MFJ, Greenwood Pr) Greenwood.

***Mengisteab, Kidane & Logan, Ikubolajeh, eds.** Beyond Economic Liberalization in Africa: Structural Adjustment & the Alternatives. (Illus.). 320p. (C). 1995. text ed. 59.95 (1-85649-293-1, Pub. by Zed Books UK) Humanities.

— Beyond Economic Liberalization in Africa: Structural Adjustment & the Alternatives. (Illus.). 320p. (C). 1995. pap. 25.00 (1-85649-294-X, Pub. by Zed Books UK) Humanities.

Mengle, Kathy. Tools for Healing: Working Toward Harmony & Balance. LC 84-72359. (Illus.). 172p. (Orig.). 1985. pap. 10.95 (0-87516-548-6) DeVorss.

Menhart, W. H., et al. Atlas of Cancer Incidence in the Former German Democratic Republic, 1978-1982. (IARC Scientific Publications: No. 106). (Illus.). 384p. 1993. pap. 95.00 (92-832-2106-0) OUP.

Menhennet, Alan. Romantic Movement. (Literary History of Germany Ser.: Vol. 6). 276p. 1981. 58.50 (0-389-20104-9, N6878) B&N Imports.

Menhennet, Alan, tr. see Hasek, Jaroslav.

Menhennet, David & Palmer, John. Parliament in Perspective. LC 67-73291. 1967. 16.95 (0-8023-1125-3) Dufour.

Menhinick, Edward F. The Freshwater Fishes of North Carolina. (Illus.). vi, 227p. (C). 1991. 34.70 (0-9628949-0-7) NC Wildlife.

Menhinick, G. Grampian Cookbook. 89p. 1984. pap. 6.00 (0-08-032420-7, Pergamon Pr) Elsevier.

***Menhinick, Oliver N.** Plant Propagation: Insight, Fundamentals & Techniques. (Illus.). 1990. 30.00 (0-948251-74-3, Pub. by Picton UK) St Mut.

Menick, jt. auth. see Burget.

Menick, Jim. Lingo. 336p. 1992. pap. 10.95 (0-88184-812-3) Carroll & Graf.

Menicucci, David F. Catholic Home & School Association Guidebook. 108p. (Orig.). 1990. pap. 6.00 (1-55833-058-5) Natl Cath Educ.

Menicucci, Wayne. The Rookie Card Collector. (Illus.). 42p. (Orig.). 1987. pap. 4.95 (0-942755-57-X) Diamond M Bks.

***Menier, Juan A.** Cuba Por Dentro: El Minint. LC 93-74509. (Coleccion Cuba y sus Jueces). 173p. (Orig.). (SPA.). 1994. pap. 18.00 (0-89729-718-0) Ediciones.

Menikoff, Barry. Robert Louis Stevenson & 'The Beach of Falesa' A Study in Victorian Publishing with the Original Text. LC 82-61072. (Illus.). 216p. 1984. 32.50 (0-8047-1162-3) Stanford U Pr.

Menikoff, Barry, ed. see Stevenson, Robert Louis.

Menin, Ben, et al. The Power of Point-of-Purchase Advertising. 304p. 1992. 69.95 (0-8144-5018-0) AMACOM.

***Meninger.** The Loving Search for God: Contemplative Prayer & the Cloud of Unknowing. 120p. 1995. pap. text ed. 11.95 (0-8264-0851-6) Continuum.

Meninger, William. Ten-Twelve Monastery Road. (Illus.). (Orig.). 1989. pap. 5.95 (0-932506-73-9) St Bedes Pubns.

Meninger, William A. Loving Search for God: Contemplative Prayer & "The Cloud of Unknowing" 120p. (C). 1994. 14.95 (0-8264-0682-3) Continuum.

Menissier, F., jt. auth. see King, J. W.

Menitove, Jay, jt. ed. see Snyder, Edward L.

***Menjou, Adolphe.** It Took Nine Tailors. (American Autobiography Ser.). 238p. 1995. reprint ed. lib. bdg. 79.00 (0-7812-8591-7) Rprt Serv.

Menk, Patricia H. To Live in Time: The Sesquicentennial History of Mary Baldwin College. 500p. 1992. write for info. (0-9633486-0-4) M Baldwin Coll.

Menkart, Deborah & Sunshine, Catherine A., eds. Caribbean Connections: Puerto Rico. LC 90-62779. (Caribbean Connections: Classroom Resources for Secondary Schools Ser.). (Illus.). 108p. (Orig.). 1990. pap. text ed. 12.00 (1-878554-04-2) Netwrk of Educ.

Menkart, Deborah, jt. ed. see Sunshine, Catherine A.

Menkart, Deborah, jt. ed. see Sunshine, Catherine H.

Menke, Anne M., tr. see Kristeva, Julia.

Menke, Arnold S., ed. The Semiaquatic & Aquatic Hemiptera of California (Heteroptera: Hemiptera) LC 77-91755. (Bulletin of the California Insect Survey Ser.: Vol. 21). 178p. reprint ed. pap. 50.80 (0-317-30426-7, 2024935) Bks Demand.

Menke, Christoph & Fazzari, P. Gregory. Improving Electric Power Utility Efficiency: Issues & Recommendations. LC 94-4995. (Technical Paper, Energy Ser.: No. 243). 52p. 1994. write for info. (0-8213-2801-8) World Bank.

Menke, Sophronia R. Selected Writings of Sophronia Robinson Menke. LC 93-80370. 97p. 1993. Incl. My Childhood Memories; Reflections from the Past--also written by Veronica Voss & William F. A. spiral bd. 20.00 (0-317-05608-5) J R Menke.

Menke, Tony. Fun with the Electric Bass. (Fun Bks.). 1993. 3.95 (0-87166-442-9, 93349) Mel Bay.

Menke, Werner. History of the Trumpet of Bach & Handel. Abraham, Gerald, tr. LC 86-2316. (Research Ser.: No. 12). (Illus.). 156p. 1986. text ed. 12.00 (0-914282-32-8) Brass Pr.

— History of the Trumpet of Bach & Handel. rev. ed. Abraham, Gerald, tr. (Blair Academy Ser.). (Illus.). 141p. 1972. reprint ed. text ed. 6.00 (0-914282-04-2) Brass Pr.

— History of the Trumpet of Bach & Handel. 1988. reprint ed. lib. bdg. 49.00 (0-7812-0365-1) Rprt Serv.

— History of the Trumpet of Bach & Handel. 1981. reprint ed. lib. bdg. 109.00 (0-403-01620-7) Scholarly.

— Hymn Tune Names: Their Sources & Significance. 1988. reprint ed. lib. bdg. 59.00 (0-7812-0196-9) Rprt Serv.

Menke, William. Geophysical Data Analysis: Discrete Inverse Theory. rev. ed. 289p. 1989. text ed. 61.00 (0-12-490921-3) Acad Pr.

Menke, William & Abbott, Dallas. Geophysical Theory. 1990. text ed. 47.50 (0-231-06792-5) Col U Pr.

Menkel, Helen S., jt. auth. see Spicer, W. A.

Menken, Adah I. Infelicia. 1972. 59.95 (0-87968-418-6) Gordon Pr.

— Infelicia. LC 70-178479. (Black Heritage Library Collection). 1977. reprint ed. 20.95 (0-8369-8928-7) Ayer.

***Menken, Alan.** Colors of the Wind. (Illus.). 48p. 1995. 9.95 (0-7868-6151-7) Hyperion.

Menken, Daniel L. Faith, Hope, & the Corporation: Sharpening Your Business Philosophy & Business Ethics. LC 88-90733. (Illus.). 208p. (Orig.). 1988. 19.95 (0-929295-00-5); pap. 14.95 (0-929295-01-3) Phrontisterion.

Menken, Jane, ed. World Population & U. S. Policy: The Choices Ahead. (American Assembly Book Ser.). 255p. 1986. pap. 8.95 (0-393-30399-3) Norton.

Menken, John. Grandpa's Gizmos. Skaggs, Keith A., ed. (Pennant Ser.). (Illus.). 28p. (Orig.). (J). (gr. 2-6). 1992. pap. 4.95 (0-89084-663-4) Bob Jones Univ Pr.

Menken, John, ed. The Tent of Meeting Texts. (Illus.). 134p. (Orig.). 1985. pap. 8.00 (0-9615531-0-3) Tent Meeting.

Menken, Maarten J. Second Thessalonians: Facing the End with Sobriety. LC 93-33187. (New Testament Readings Ser.). 176p. 1994. 49.95x (0-415-09504-2, B3952, Routledge NY); pap. 13.95 (0-415-09505-0, B3956, Routledge NY) Routledge.

Menken, S. B., ed. Proceedings of the Eighth International Symposium on Insect-Plant Relationships. (Series Entomologica). 440p. (C). 1993. lib. bdg. 157.50 (0-7923-2099-9) Kluwer Ac.

Menkes. Neurologic Signs & Symptoms in Children. 1991. 27.95 (0-8151-5857-2, Yr Bk Med Pubs) Mosby Yr Bk.

Menkes-Ivry, Vivienne. Paris up Close: District to District, Street by Street. 160p. 1992. pap. 12.95 (0-8442-9452-7, Passport Bks) NTC Pub Grp.

Menkes-Ivry, Vivienne & Eperon, Arthur. Paris. (Passport's Regional Guides of France Ser.). (Illus.). 192p. 1991. reprint ed. pap. text ed. 16.95 (0-8442-9942-1, Passport Bks) NTC Pub Grp.

Menkes, John H. Textbook of Child Neurology. 4th ed. LC 90-5894. (Illus.). 832p. 1990. text ed. 96.50 (0-8121-1266-0) Williams & Wilkins.

— Textbook of Child Neurology. 5th ed. LC 94-13052. 1994. write for info. (0-683-05920-3) Williams & Wilkins.

Menkin, Eva L., jt. auth. see Weininger, Ben.

Menking, Stanley J. & Wendland, Barbara. God's Partners: Lay Christains at Work. LC 93-30829. 164p. 1993. pap. 13.00 (0-8170-1196-X) Judson.

Menko, Fred H. Genetics of Colorectal Cancer for Clinical Practice. LC 92-48226. (Development in Oncology Ser.: Vol. 72). 196p. (C). 1993. lib. bdg. 107.00 (0-7923-2100-6) Kluwer Ac.

Menkus, Belden & Ruthberg, Zella, eds. Control Objectives: Controls in a Computer Environment. 132p. 1991. 49.95 (0-9629440-1-7) EDP Assn.

Menkveld, Paul A. Origin & Role of the European Bank for Reconstruction & Development. 192p. (C). 1991. lib. bdg. 85.00 (1-85333-626-2, Pub. by Graham & Trotman UK) Kluwer Ac.

Menkveld, R., et al. Atlas of Human Sperm Morphology. (Illus.). 136p. 1991. 145.00 (0-683-05925-4) Williams & Wilkins.

Menlewicz, J., et al, eds. Serotonin in Affective Disorders. (Advances in Biological Psychiatry Ser.: Vol. 14). (Illus.). vi, 90p. 1984. 43.25 (3-8055-3898-7) S Karger.

***Menlo, Rosemary & Haney, Shirley.** Communication, Compromise & Commitment. 88p. (YA). (gr. 7-12). 1994. pap. write for info. (1-57515-045-X) PPI Pubng.

Menlowe, Michael A. The Duty to Rescue: The Jurisprudence of Aid. (Applied Legal Philosophy Ser.). 224p. 1994. 57.95 (1-85521-396-6, Pub. by Dartmth Pub UK) Ashgate Pub Co.

Menlowm, Michael, jt. ed. see Matthews, Eric.

Menmuir, Ruth, ed. see Dixon, Sheila A. & Crowell, Richard D.

Menn, Christian. Prestressed Concrete Bridges. 512p. 1990. 179.00 (0-8176-2414-7) Birkhauser.

Menn, Don, ed. Secrets from the Masters: Conversations with 40 Great Guitar Players. (Illus.). 295p. (Orig.). 1992. pap. 19.95 (0-87930-260-7) Miller Freeman.

Menn, Lise & Obler, Loraine K., eds. Agrammatic Aphasia: A Cross-Language Narrative Sourcebook, 1. LC 89-18418. 2100p. 1990. write for info. (1-55619-025-5) Benjamins North Am.

— Agrammatic Aphasia: A Cross-Language Narrative Sourcebook, 2. LC 89-18418. 2100p. 1990. write for info. (1-55619-026-3) Benjamins North Am.

— Agrammatic Aphasia: A Cross-Language Narrative Sourcebook, 3. LC 89-18418. 2100p. 1990. write for info. (1-55619-027-1) Benjamins North Am.

— Agrammatic Aphasia: A Cross-Language Narrative Sourcebook, Set. LC 89-18418. 2100p. 1990. 690.00 (1-55619-024-7) Benjamins North Am.

***Menn, Lise, et al.** Non-Fluent Aphasia in a Multilingual World. LC 95-14639. (Studies in Speech Pathology & Clinical Linguistics: No. 5). 160p. 1995. lib. bdg. 65.00x (1-55619-391-2); pap. 24.95x (1-55619-392-0) Benjamins North Am.

Menn, Stephen. Plato As God As Nous. LC 94-15845. 112p. (C). 1995. pap. 24.95x (0-8093-1970-5) S Ill U Pr.

Menna, F., ed. Therapeutic Effects in Ocular Lesions Obtained by Systemic & Topical Administration of an Activator of the Oxygen Metabolism. (Journal: Ophthalmologica: Vol. 180, Suppl. 1). (Illus.). vi, 92p. 1980. 26.50 (3-8055-1686-X) S Karger.

***Menna, Larry, ed.** Sports in North America Vol. 2: A Documentary History. 1995. 95.00 (0-87569-136-6) Academic Intl.

Menne. Exogenous Dermatoses: Environmental Dermatitis. 1990. 115.00 (0-8493-5969-4, RC593) CRC Pr.

Menne, A., ed. Logico-Philosophical Studies. Glover, Horace S., tr. 136p. 1962. lib. bdg. 45.50 (90-277-0082-6) Kluwer Ac.

Menne, Albert. Zur Modernen Deutung der Aristotelischen Logik, Bd. V: Jan Lukasiewicz, Uber Den Statz Des Widerspruchs Bei Aristoteles. Date not set. write for info. (0-318-71267-9, Pub. by Georg Olms GW) Lubrecht & Cramer.

Menne, Albert & Offenberger, Niels. Zur Modernen Deutung der Aristotelischen Logik, Bd. I: Uber den Folgerungsbegriff in der Aristotelischen Logik. 220p. (GER.). 1982. write for info. (3-487-07265-3, Pub. by Georg Olms GW) Lubrecht & Cramer.

— Zur Modernen Deutung der Aristotelischen Logik, Bd. II: Formale und Nicht-Formale Logik Bei Aristoteles. 262p. (GER.). 1985. write for info. (3-487-07266-1, Pub. by Georg Olms GW) Lubrecht & Cramer.

— Zur Modernen Deutung der Aristotelischen Logik, Bd. III: Modallogik und Mehrwertigkeit. 322p. (GER.). 1988. write for info. (3-487-07267-X, Pub. by Georg Olms GW) Lubrecht & Cramer.

***Menne-Haritz, Angelika, ed.** Information Handling in Offices & Archives: Symposium on the Impact of Information Technologies, Marburg 17th-19th October 1991. 197p. 1993. 50.00 (3-598-11146-0) K G Saur.

Menne, Torkil & Maibach, Howard I., eds. Hand Eczema. LC 93-19124. (Series in Dermatology: Clinical & Basic Science). 336p. 1993. 95.00 (0-8493-7355-7, RL251) CRC Pr.

Mennear. Cadmium Toxicity. (Modern Pharmacology-Toxicology Ser.: Vol. 15). 240p. 1979. 125.00 (0-8247-6766-7) Dekker.

Mennel, Robert M. Thorns & Thistles: Juvenile Delinquents in the United States, 1825-1940. LC 72-95187. 259p. reprint ed. pap. 73.90 (0-317-41775-4, 2025640) Bks Demand.

Mennell, John M. Back Pain: Diagnosis & Treatment Using Manipulative Techniques. 226p. 1960. 46.95 (0-316-56667-5) Little.

— Joint Pain: Diagnosis & Treatment Using Manipulative Techniques. 178p. 1964. 42.95 (0-316-56668-3) Little.

— The Musculoskeletal System: Differential Diagnosis from Symptoms & Physical Signs. LC 91-4866. 208p. 1991. 69.00 (0-8342-0255-7) Aspen Pub.

Mennell, John M., jt. auth. see Zohn, David A.

Mennell, Robert L. Wills & Trusts in a Nutshell. 2nd ed. (Nutshell Ser.). 339p. 1994. pap. text ed. 16.00 (0-314-04025-0) Foundation Pr.

— Wills & Trusts in a Nutshell. LC 79-11590. (Nutshell Ser.). 392p. 1993. reprint ed. pap. text ed. 15.00 (0-8299-2042-0) West Pub.

Mennell, Robert L. & Boykoff, Thomas M. Community Property in a Nutshell. 2nd ed. (Nutshell Ser.). 432p. (C). 1993. reprint ed. pap. text ed. 17.50 (0-314-68355-0) West Pub.

***Mennell, Stephen.** All Manners of Food: Eating & Tasting in England & France from the Middle Ages to the Present. 2nd ed. 1995. pap. write for info. (0-252-06490-9) U of Ill Pr.

— Norbert Elias: An Introduction. LC 92-8515. reprint ed. pap. 24.95 (0-631-18264-0) Blackwell Pubs.

Mennell, Stephen, et al. The Sociology of Food & Eating. LC 92-50680. (Special Issue of Current Sociology Ser.). (Illus.). 160p. (C). 1993. text ed. 55.00 (0-8039-8839-7); pap. text ed. 19.95 (0-8039-8838-9) Sage.

Mennell, William. British Economy. 1964. pap. 12.00 (0-8464-0211-4) Beekman Pubs.

Mennella, Roxanna. Roxanna Mennella, in Search of a Song, Vol. 6. Fisher, Barbara & Spiegel, Richard, eds. 40p. (Orig.). (J). (gr. 4-7). 1984. pap. 2.00 (0-934830-32-0) Ten Penny.

— Roxanna Mennella, in Search of a Song: Inner Clockwork, Vol. 8. Fisher, Barbara, ed. (Illus.). 10p. (Orig.). (J). (gr. 5-9). 1985. pap. 2.00 (0-934830-36-3) Ten Penny.

Mennella, Roxanna, jt. auth. see Wilkins, Sarah.

An Asterisk (*) at the beginning of an entry indicates that the title is appearing in BIP for the first time.

M

Mennella, Roxanna, et al. Fairies, Elves & Gnomes. (Illus.). 32p. (Orig.). (J). (gr. 3-8). 1985. pap. 2.00 (*0-934830-38-X*, Waterways Project) Ten Penny.

Mennema, J., et al, eds. Atlas of the Netherlands Flora: Extinct & Very Rare Species, No. 1. (Illus.). 266p. 1980. lib. bdg. 117.00 (*90-6193-605-5*) Kluwer Ac.

Mennen, Ingrid. One Round Moon & a Star for Me. LC 93-9628. (Illus.). 32p. (J). (ps-2). 1994. 14.95 (*0-531-06804-8*); lib. bdg. 14.99 (*0-531-08654-2*) Orchard Bks Watts.

Mennen, Ingrid & Daly, Niki. Somewhere in Africa. LC 91-19379. (Illus.). 32p. (J). (ps-3). 1992. 14.00 (*0-525-44848-9*, DCB) Dutton Child Bks.

Mennen, Stacey, ed. see Dimattia, Dominic.

Mennes, John. Musarum Deliciae & Wit Restor'd. LC 85-1977. 1985. 50.00 (*0-8201-1404-9*) Schol Facsimiles.

Mennes, L. B., jt. ed. see Koekkoek, Ad.

Mennes, L. B., jt. ed. see Kol, Jacob.

Mennes, Loet B. & Stoutjesdijk, Ardy. Multicountry Investment Analysis. LC 85-45104. (Planning of Investment Programs: No. 4). 240p. 1986. pap. text ed. 14.95 (*0-8018-3141-5*) Johns Hopkins.

Mennick, Simon, jt. auth. see Briazack, Norman J.

Mennicke, Victor. From Private to Pastor. 1994. pap. 8.95 (*1-55673-848-X*) CSS OH.

***Mennig, Gunter.** Wear in Plastics Processing: How to Understand, Protect & Avoid. 436p. (C). 1995. text ed. write for info. (*1-56990-137-6*) Hanser-Gardner.

Mennig, Jan, jt. auth. see Melnicoe, William B.

Mennim, Eleanor. Transit Circle: Biography of William Simms, 1793-1860. (C). 1989. pap. 35.00 (*1-85072-101-7*, Pub. by W Sessions UK) St Mut.

Menning, Bruce W. Bayonets Before Bullets: The Imperial Russian Army, 1861-1914. LC 92-8233. (Indiana-Michigan Series in Russian & East European Studies). (Illus.). 416p. (C). 1992. 35.00 (*0-253-33745-3*) Ind U Pr.

Menning, Carol B. Charity & State in Late Renaissance Italy: The Monte di Pieta of Florence. LC 92-56788. 352p. 1993. 51.95 (*0-8014-2773-8*) Cornell U Pr.

Menning, Marion. Us Four: A Senator, His Family, Their Brain-injured Child. (Illus.). 160p. 1986. pap. write for info. (*0-9615632-0-6*) Alpha Pub MN.

Menning, Viiu. Great Dancers. (Illus.). (Orig.). (J). (gr. 8). 1978. pap. 3.95 (*0-88388-065-2*) Bellerophon Bks.

Menninger, Bonar. Mortal Error. 1992. mass mkt. 5.99 (*0-312-92989-7*) St Martin.

***Menninger, Edwin A.** Fantastic Trees. rev. ed. (Illus.). 320p. 1995. pap. 29.95 (*0-88192-324-9*) Timber.

Menninger Foundation, Children's Division Staff. Disturbed Children: Examination & Assessment Through Team Process. LC 68-54941. (Jossey-Bass Behavioral Science Ser.). 318p. reprint ed. pap. 90.70 (*0-317-41977-3*, 2025677) Bks Demand.

Menninger Foundation, Topeka, Kansas Staff. Catalog of the Menninger Clinic Library, 4 vols., Set. 1972. lib. bdg. 435.00 (*0-8161-0961-3*, Hall Library) G K Hall.

Menninger, Karl. Number Words & Number Symbols: A Cultural History of Numbers. Broneer, Paul, tr. (Illus.). 496p. 1992. reprint ed. pap. 15.95 (*0-486-27096-3*) Dover.

— The Vital Balance: The Life Process in Mental Health & Illness. 1983. 21.25 (*0-8446-6077-9*) Peter Smith.

Menninger, Karl & Holzman, Philip. Theory of Psychoanalytic Technique. 2nd ed. LC 94-71264. 224p. 1995. pap. 30.00 (*1-56821-266-6*) Aronson.

Menninger, Karl A. Love Against Hate. LC 42-50183. 310p. 1959. pap. 10.95 (*0-15-653892-X*, Harvest Bks) HarBrace.

— Man Against Himself. LC 38-5962. 429p. 1956. pap. 10. 95 (*0-15-656514-5*, Harvest Bks) HarBrace.

Menninger, Richard E. Israel & the Church in the Gospel of Matthew Vol. 162. LC 93-2496. (American University Studies: No. VII). 204p. (C). 1994. text ed. 42.95 (*0-8204-2242-8*) P Lang Pubs.

Menninger, Roy W., jt. auth. see Gabbard, Glen O.

Menninger, W. Walter & Hannah, Gerald, eds. The Chronic Mental Patient-II. LC 87-1085. 224p. 1987. text ed. 33. 00 (*0-88048-278-8*) Am Psychiatric.

Menninger,, ed. see American Psychiatric Association Staff.

Mennis, Edmund A. How the Economy Works: An Investor's Guide to Tracking the Economy. 1991. pap. 13.95 (*0-13-401035-3*, Busn) P-H.

Mennonite Church Staff. Mennonite Confession of Faith. LC 63-22593. 32p. (Orig.). 1963. pap. 1.50 (*0-8361-1314-4*) Herald Pr.

Menocal, Maria R. Shards of Love: Exile & the Origins of the Lyric. LC 93-26530. 312p. 1994. lib. bdg. 49.95 (*0-8223-1405-3*); pap. text ed. 18.95 (*0-8223-1419-3*) Duke.

— Writing in Dante's Cult of Truth: From Borges to Boccaccio. LC 90-45998. 232p. 1991. lib. bdg. 37.00 (*0-8223-1104-6*); pap. text ed. 16.95 (*0-8223-1117-8*) Duke.

Menocal, Narcisco G. Architecture As Nature: The Transcendentalist Idea of Louis Sullivan. (Illus.). 256p. 1981. 29.50 (*0-299-08150-8*) U of Wis Pr.

Menocal, Narcisco G., ed. see Wright, John L.

Menocal, Narciso G., ed. Wright Studies Vol. 1: Taliesin 1911-1914. (Illus.). 160p. (C). 1991. 39.95 (*0-8093-1624-2*); pap. 19.95 (*0-8093-1625-0*) S Ill U Pr.

Menolascino, Frank & Egger, Michael L. Medical Dimensions of Mental Retardation. LC 76-16503. (Illus.). xxiv, 477p. 1978. 25.00 (*0-8032-0900-2*) U of Nebr Pr.

Menolascino, Frank J. & Stark, Jack A., eds. Handbook of Mental Illness in the Mentally Retarded. LC 84-13263. 472p. 1984. 75.00 (*0-306-41648-4*, Plenum Pr) Plenum.

Menolascino, Frank J., ed. see Fletcher, Robert J.

Menolascino, Frank J., jt. auth. see McGee, J. J.

Menon, jt. auth. see Paal.

Menon, A. G. A Systematic Monograph of the Tongue Soles of the Genus Cynoglossus Hamilton-Buchanan (Pisces, Cynoglossidae) LC 76-608109. (Smithsonian Contributions to Zoology Ser.: No. 238). 133p. reprint ed. pap. 38.00 (*0-317-28685-4*, 2055286) Bks Demand.

Menon, B. P. World Orders. (Writers Workshop Blackbird Ser.). 32p. 1978. 6.00 (*0-86578-056-0*) Ind-US Inc.

Menon, Bhashkar P. Bridges Across the South: Technical Cooperation among Developing Countries. (Policy Studies). 1980. text ed. 56.00 (*0-08-024645-1*, Pergamon Pr); pap. text ed. 18.00 (*0-08-024646-X*, Pergamon Pr) Elsevier.

— Global Dialogue: The New International Economic Order. 1977. text ed. 56.00 (*0-08-021498-3*, Pub. by Pergamon Repr UK) Franklin.

Menon, Dilip M. Caste, Nationalism, & Communism in South India: Malabar, 1900-1948. LC 93-6609. (Cambridge South Asian Studies: No. 55). (Illus.). 200p. (C). 1994. 54.95 (*0-521-41879-8*) Cambridge U Pr.

Menon, Geeta. Social Integration, Age Groups, & Attitudes Towards Euthanasia. LC 91-22335. (Studies on Elderly in America). 128p. 1991. 40.00 (*0-8153-0522-2*) Garland.

Menon, H. G. TQM in New Product Manufacturing. 1992. text ed. 42.00 (*0-07-041532-3*) McGraw.

Menon, K. P. A Dictionary of Kathakali. (Illus.). 80p. 1981. text ed. 15.95 (*0-86131-046-2*, Pub. by Orient Longman Ltd II) Apt Bks.

— A Dictionary of Kathakali. (Illus.). 80p. 1979. 14.95 (*0-318-36308-9*) Asia Bk Corp.

— Memories & Musings. 361p. 1979. 14.95 (*0-318-36594-4*) Asia Bk Corp.

Menon, K. S. Style Book: For Journalists & Writers. 132p. 1990. text ed. 18.95 (*81-220-0183-1*, Pub. by Konark Pubs Pvt Ltd II) Advent Bks Div.

Menon, Kreshna. The Law of Property. (Orient Longman Law Library). 556p. 1980. pap. text ed. 18.95 (*0-86125-516-X*, Pub. by Orient Longman Ltd II) Apt Bks.

Menon, M. K., et al, eds. Postgraduate Obestetrics & Gynacology. xiii, 504p. (C). 1982. text ed. 30.00 (*0-86131-303-8*, Pub. by Orient Longman Ltd II) Apt Bks.

Menon, N. C. Mother of Battles: Saddam's Folly. (Illus.). 181p. 1992. text ed. 25.00 (*81-220-0254-4*, Pub. by Konark Pubs Pvt Ltd II) Advent Bks Div.

Menon, Narayana, tr. see Pillai, Thakazhi S.

***Menon, P. K.** The Law of Recognition in International Law: Basic Principles. LC 94-33966. 1994. write for info. (*0-7734-9109-0*) E Mellen.

— The Law of Treaties Between States & International Organizations. LC 92-22554. 264p. 1992. text ed. 89.95 (*0-7734-9590-8*) E Mellen.

— The Succession of States in Respect to Treaties, State Property, Archives, & Debts. LC 90-22575. (Studies in World Peace: Vol. 6). 265p. 1991. lib. bdg. 89.95 (*0-88946-263-1*) E Mellen.

— The United Nations Efforts to Control Arms in Outer Space: A Brief History with Key Documents. LC 87-24727. (Studies in World Peace: Vol. 1). 212p. 1989. lib. bdg. 89.95 (*0-88946-587-8*) E Mellen.

Menon, P. K., jt. ed. see Kodiline, Gilbert.

Menon, R. R., tr. see Kuttykrishnan, P. C.

Menon, R. Rabindranath. Dasavatara & Other Poems. (Redbird Ser.). 1976. lib. bdg. 5.00 (*0-89253-118-5*); 4.00 (*0-89253-148-7*) Ind-US Inc.

— Seventy Seven Poems. (Writers Workshop Redbird Ser.). 78p. 1975. 14.00 (*0-88253-630-3*); pap. text ed. 4.80 (*0-88253-629-X*) Ind-US Inc.

— Shadows in the Sun. 1976. 8.00 (*0-89253-813-9*); 4.80 (*0-89253-814-7*) Ind-US Inc.

— Straws in the Wind. (Writers Workshop Redbird Ser.). 1975. 12.00 (*0-88253-650-8*); pap. text ed. 4.80 (*0-88253-649-4*) Ind-US Inc.

Menon, Rajan. Soviet Power & the Third World. 1986. 35. 00 (*0-300-03500-4*) Yale U Pr.

— Soviet Power & the Third World. LC 85-40988. 272p. (C). 1989. reprint ed. pap. 16.00 (*0-300-04489-5*) Yale U Pr.

Menon, Rajan & Nelson, Daniel N. Limits to Soviet Power. LC 86-45368. 240p. (C). 1989. text ed. 40.00 (*0-669-13226-8*) Free Pr.

Menon, Raman V. K., tr. see Michaud, J., ed.

***Menon, Ramarkrishnan.** Writing to Learn Mathematics: Student Journals & Student Constructed Questions. 1993. pap. 45.00 (*0-7300-2059-2*, Pub. by Deakin Univ AT) St Mut.

Menon, Ritu, jt. ed. see Butalia, Urvashi.

Menon, Sathis. The C Workbook. 288p. 1993. pap. text ed. write for info. (*0-07-041576-5*) McGraw.

Menon, T. K. A Primer of Malayalam Literature. (C). 1990. text ed. 15.00 (*81-206-0603-5*, Pub. by Asian Educ Servs II) S Asia.

Menon, T. K., ed. see Padmanabha, K. P.

Menon, Vapal P. The Story of the Integration of the Indian States. LC 72-4282. (World Affairs Ser.: National & International Viewpoints). (Illus.). 542p. 1972. reprint ed. 36.95 (*0-405-04575-1*) Ayer.

Menorah Medical Center Auxiliary Cookbook Committee. Gourmet Garden Cookbook. 2nd ed. Bold, Ellyn & Schultz, Cathy, eds. (Illus.). 505p. 1983. reprint ed. 10. 00 (*0-9614735-0-9*) Menorah Med.

Menorah Park Residents Staff & R. H. Myers Tenants Staff. Cameo Recollections: From Generation to Generation. 100p. 1991. pap. text ed. 5.00 (*0-9631040-0-4*) Menorah Pk Ctr Age.

Menos, Dennis. Arms over Diplomacy: Reflections on the Persian Gulf War. LC 91-44450. 192p. 1992. text ed. 45. 00 (*0-275-94160-4*, C4160, Praeger Pubs) Greenwood.

— The Superpowers & Nuclear Arms Control: Rhetoric & Reality. LC 89-36700. 192p. 1990. text ed. 49.95 (*0-275-93458-6*, C3458, Praeger Pubs) Greenwood.

Menotti, Gian-Carlo. Amahl & the Night Visitors. LC 84-27196. (Illus.). 64p. (J). (ps up). 1986. 15.00 (*0-688-05426-9*); lib. bdg. 14.88 (*0-688-05427-7*) Morrow Jr Bks.

Menow, Sue, ed. see Bloomfield, Dick.

Men's Garden Clubs of America Staff. A to Z Hints for the Vegetable Gardener: From the 10,000 Members of the Men's Garden Clubs of America. LC 75-39519. (Illus.). 128p. 1977. reprint ed. pap. 7.95 (*0-88266-106-X*, Garden Way Pub) Storey Comm Inc.

Men's Health Books Staff, et al. Age Erasers for Men: Hundreds of Fast & Easy Ways to Beat the Years. (Illus.). 500p. 1994. 27.95 (*0-87596-213-0*) Rodale Pr Inc.

Men's Health Magazine Editors. How a Man Stays Young. LC 92-30477. 1993. pap. 14.95 (*0-87596-156-8*) Rodale Pr Inc.

— Men's Health: A Guide to Staying Young. 1995. reprint ed. 7.98 (*1-56731-069-9*, MJF Bks) Fine Comms.

Mensa, Dean L. High Resolution Radar Cross-Section Imaging. (Artech House Radar Library). 250p. 1991. text ed. 79.00 (*0-89006-389-3*) Artech Hse.

MENSA Publications Staff. MENSA Presents Number Puzzles for Math Geniuses. 1993. pap. 13.00 (*0-8129-2214-X*, Times Bks) Random.

— MENSA Presents Word Puzzles for Language Geniuses. 1993. pap. 13.00 (*0-8129-2213-1*, Times Bks) Random.

Mensa UK Puzzle Editors. Intelligent Puzzles. 160p. 1995. pap. 7.95 (*0-572-01806-1*) Atrium Pubs.

Mensah, J. T. & Soule, Larry. Re-Claiming Wasted Lands for Our Future: Man's Proven Ability to Green Out the Wasteland Areas of Our Planet. (Illus.). 176p. 1993. pap. 14.95 (*0-8059-3342-5*) Dorrance.

Mensah, Joe R. Trials & Tribulations of a Man. 1991. 13.95 (*0-533-08970-0*) Vantage.

Mensch, Barbara. D. H. Lawrence & the Authoritarian Personality. LC 90-45272. 284p. 1991. text ed. 39.95 (*0-312-05558-7*) St Martin.

— The Last Waterfront: The People of South Street. LC 84-18779. (Illus.). 188p. 1985. 20.00 (*0-88191-012-0*) Freundlich.

Mensch, Elizabeth & Freeman, Alan. The Politics of Virtue: Is Abortion Debatable? LC 92-41302. 279p. 1993. lib. bdg. 39.95 (*0-8223-1331-6*); pap. 14.95 (*0-8223-1349-9*) Duke.

Mensch, Elizabeth & Freeman, Alan, eds. Property Law, 2 vols., 1. LC 92-33815. (International Library of Essays in Law & Legal Theory: Vol. 14). 1992. write for info. (*0-8147-5488-0*) NYU Pr.

— Property Law, 2 vols., 2. LC 92-33815. (International Library of Essays in Law & Legal Theory: Vol. 14). 1992. write for info. (*0-8147-5489-9*) NYU Pr.

— Property Law, 2 vols., Set. LC 92-33815. (International Library of Essays in Law & Legal Theory: Vol. 14). 1992. 250.00 (*0-8147-5475-9*) NYU Pr.

Mensch, James R. The Gospel According to St. John: Philosophical Perspectives. LC 91-38847. (American University Studies: Philosophy: Ser. V, Vol. 121). 219p. (C). 1992. text ed. 40.95 (*0-8204-1583-9*) P Lang Pubs.

— Intersubjectivity & Transcendental Idealism. LC 87-18047. (SUNY Series in Contemporary Continental Philosophy). 430p. 1988. 64.50 (*0-88706-751-4*); pap. 21.95 (*0-88706-752-2*) State U NY Pr.

— The Question of Being in Husserl's Logical Investigations. 1981. lib. bdg. 80.00 (*90-247-2413-9*) Kluwer Ac.

Mensching, Glenn E., Jr. & Mensching, Teresa B., eds. Coping with Information Illiteracy: Bibliographic Instruction for the Information Age. (Library Orientation Ser.: No. 20). 1990. pap. 35.00 (*0-87650-267-2*) Pierian.

Mensching, James & Adams, Dennis. Managing an Information System. 320p. (C). 1990. text ed. write for info. (*0-13-552746-5*) P-H.

Mensching, Teresa B., ed. Reaching & Teaching Diverse Library User Groups. (Library Orientation Ser.: No. 19). 169p. 1989. pap. 35.00 (*0-87650-258-3*) Pierian.

Mensching, Teresa B. & Stanger, Keith J., eds. Bibliographic Instruction & Computer Database Searching. (Library Orientation Ser.: No. 17). 173p. 1988. pap. 35.00 (*0-87650-251-6*) Pierian.

Mensching, Teresa B., jt. ed. see Bunge, Mary B.

Mensching, Teresa B., jt. ed. see Mensching, Glenn E., Jr.

Mensching, Wilhelm. Conscience. LC 61-16821. (Orig.). 1961. pap. 3.00 (*0-87574-117-7*) Pendle Hill.

Mensh, Elaine & Mensh, Harry. The IQ Mythology: Class, Race, & Inequality. 160p. (C). 1991. 19.95 (*0-8093-1666-8*) S Ill U Pr.

Mensh, Harry, jt. auth. see Mensh, Elaine.

***Mensier, Paul.** Dictionnaire des Huiles Vegetales. 771p. (FRE.). 1957. pap. 165.00 (*0-7859-7964-6*, 2720504211) Fr & Eur.

Mensing, Steve. Apache Warrior. 1981. pap. 2.25 (*0-89083-836-4*) Zebra.

— Gold in the Black Hills. (Orig.). 1993. 13.00 (*0-86025-203-5*, Pub. by Ian Henry Pubns UK) Empire Pub Srvs.

— Hell Riders. large type ed. (Linford Western Library). 272p. (Orig.). 1985. pap. 11.95 (*0-7089-6083-9*, Traiitree Bookshop) Ulverscroft.

Mensky, M. B. Continuous Quantum Measurements & Path Integrals. (Illus.). 188p. 1993. 95.00 (*0-7503-0228-3*) IOP Pub.

Men'Sov, D. E. Limits of Indeterminacy in Measure of T-Means of Subseries of a Trigonometric Series. LC 81-14992. (Steklov Institute of Mathematics Ser.: No. 149). 56p. 1981. 34.00 (*0-8218-3043-0*, STEKLO-149) Am Math.

Ment, David & Donovan, Mary S. The People of Brooklyn: A History of Two Neighborhoods. LC 80-65107. (Brooklyn Rediscovery Booklet Ser.). (Illus.). 87p. 1980. pap. 3.50 (*0-933250-04-5*) Bklyn Educ.

Ment, David, jt. auth. see Brown, Joshua.

Ment, Merriam. First Start in Spanish Activity. 1987. pap. 7.95 (*0-8442-7532-8*) NTC Pub Grp.

***Menta, Ed.** The Magic World Behind the Curtain: Andrei Serban in the American Theatre. LC 94-22375. (Artists & Issues in the Theatre, 1051-9718: Vol. 5). 1995. write for info. (*0-8204-2640-7*) P Lang Pubs.

Mentasi, Rosa B. Venetian Glass 1890-1990. (Illus.). 208p. 1992. 95.00 (*88-7743-119-9*, Pub. by Arsenale Editrice IT) Antique Collect.

***Mentch, Roger.** Writer's Verb Dictionary. 137p. (Orig.). 1994. pap. text ed. 7.95 (*0-9645001-0-8*) R Mentch.

Mentel, James, jt. auth. see Hartmann, Pamela.

Mentemeier, Samuel H., ed. see Labo, James A.

***Menten.** Where Is Heaven: Children's Wisdom on Facing Death. 1995. 12.95 (*1-56138-525-5*) Running Pr.

Menten, Ted. After Goodbye: How to Begin Again after the Death of Someone You Love. LC 93-85506. 128p. 1994. 12.95 (*1-56138-295-7*) Running Pr.

— Baby Bears, Bunnies & Other Little Critters. 1985. pap. 3.50 (*0-486-24782-1*) Dover.

— Cut & Use Stencil Bunny Rabbit. (J). 1985. pap. 5.95 (*0-486-24909-3*) Dover.

— Decorative Labels for Home Canning. 1975. pap. 4.95 (*0-486-23219-0*) Dover.

— Easy to Duplicate News Designs. 1988. pap. 4.50 (*0-486-25216-7*) Dover.

— Favorite Storybook Characters. 1987. pap. 4.95 (*0-486-25448-8*) Dover.

— Folk Art Cut & Use Stencils. (J). 1985. pap. 4.95 (*0-486-24838-0*) Dover.

— Gentle Closings: How to Say Goodbye to Someone You Love. LC 91-52787. 128p. 1992. 12.95 (*1-56138-004-0*) Running Pr.

— Make Your Own Teddy bear Calendar Coloring Book. (Illus.). (J). 1991. pap. 2.50 (*0-486-26911-6*) Dover.

— Ships & Boats Punch Out Stencils. (J). 1986. pap. 3.50 (*0-486-25049-0*) Dover.

— Teddy Bear-Cut & Use Stencils. (J). 1983. pap. 5.95 (*0-486-24595-0*) Dover.

— Teddy Bear Lover's Companion. LC 90-85506. (Illus.). 160p. (Orig.). 1991. 9.98 (*1-56138-021-0*) Courage Bks.

— Teddy Bear Punch Out Stencils. (J). 1985. pap. 3.50 (*0-486-24832-1*) Dover.

— Teddy Bear Sticker Paper Doll. (Illus.). (J). (gr. k-3). 1991. pap. 1.00 (*0-486-26235-9*) Dover.

— Teddy Bear Stickers & Seals. 1985. 3.50 (*0-486-24928-X*) Dover.

— Where Is Heaven: Children's Wisdom on Facing Death. 288p. 1995. 12.95 (*1-56138-547-6*) Running Pr.

Menten, Ted, comp. The Teddy Bear Lover's Postcard Book. (Postcard Book Ser.). (Illus.). 64p. (Orig.). (J). 1988. pap. 7.95 (*0-89471-646-8*) Running Pr.

Menten, Theodore. Art Deco Cut & Use Stencils. (J). 1977. pap. 4.95 (*0-486-23551-3*) Dover.

— The Art Deco Style in Household Objects, Architecture, Sculpture, Graphics, Jewelry. (Illus.). (Orig.). 20.50 (*0-8446-4586-9*) Peter Smith.

— Art Nouveau Decorative Ironwork: One Hundred & Fifty Photographic Illustrations. (Illus.). 144p. 1981. pap. 7.95 (*0-486-23986-1*) Dover.

— Clown Masks Punch Out Stencils. (Toy Bks.). (Illus.). 16p. 1984. pap. 3.50 (*0-486-24633-7*) Dover.

— Ready-to-Use Art Deco Borders. 64p. (Orig.). 1985. pap. 4.50 (*0-486-24967-0*) Dover.

— Ready-to-Use Art Nouveau Borders. (Illus.). 64p. (Orig.). 1983. pap. 4.50 (*0-486-24431-8*) Dover.

— Ready-to-Use Art Nouveau Small Frames & Borders. 64p. (Orig.). 1985. pap. 4.50 (*0-486-24975-1*) Dover.

— Ready-to-Use Banners. (Clip Art Ser.). (Illus.). 1979. pap. 4.50 (*0-486-23899-7*) Dover.

— Ready-to-Use Teddy Bear Illustrations. 64p. (Orig.). 1985. pap. 4.50 (*0-486-24943-3*) Dover.

— Victorian Fashion Paper Dolls from Harper's Bazar, 1867-1898. (J). 1979. pap. 3.95 (*0-486-23453-3*) Dover.

Menten, Theodore, ed. Advertising Art in the Art Deco Style. LC 74-27703. (Pictorial Archive Ser.). (Illus.). 153p. 1975. pap. 8.95 (*0-486-23164-X*) Dover.

— The Art Deco Style in Household Objects, Architecture, Sculpture, Graphics, Jewelry. (Illus.). 192p. (Orig.). 1972. pap. 9.95 (*0-486-22824-X*) Dover.

— Art Nouveau & Early Art Deco Type & Design. (Pictorial Archive Ser.). (Illus.). 96p. (Orig.). 1972. pap. 4.95 (*0-486-22825-8*) Dover.

— Chinese Cut Paper Designs. LC 75-22240. (Pictorial Archive Ser.). (Illus.). 96p. (Orig.). 1975. pap. 5.95 (*0-486-23198-4*) Dover.

— Japanese Border Designs. LC 75-13124. (Pictorial Archive Ser.). Orig. Title: Kodai Moshiki Zuko. (Illus.). 93p. 1975. reprint ed. pap. 3.95 (*0-486-23180-1*) Dover.

— Ready-to-Use Arrows. (Clip Art Ser.). (Illus.). 1979. pap. 4.50 (*0-486-23783-4*) Dover.

— Ready-to-Use Borders. (Clip Art Ser.). (Illus.). 1979. pap. 4.50 (*0-486-23782-6*) Dover.

— Ready-to-Use Headlines. (Clip Art Ser.). 1979. pap. 4.50 (*0-486-23454-1*) Dover.

Menten, Theodore, ed. see Beardsley, Aubrey.

Menten, Theodore, ed. see Clusius, Carolus.

Menten, Theodore, ed. see Munting, Abraham.

Menten, Theodore, ed. see Stolpe, Hjalmar.

Menteshashvili, Z. R., jt. auth. see Garsevanishvili, V. R.

Menteshavili, Avtandil. Trouble in the Caucasus. (Illus.). 107p. (C). 1994. lib. bdg. 39.00 (*1-56072-177-4*) Nova Sci Pubs.

M

Mentienne, A. La Decouverte de la Photographie en 1839. Bunnell, Peter C. & Sobieszek, Robert A., eds. LC 76-23037. (Sources of Modern Photography Ser.). (FRE.). 1979. reprint ed. lib. bdg. 15.95 (0-405-09600-3) Ayer.

Menting, Peter. The Last Crusade. LC 92-3346. 148p. (Orig.). 1993. pap. 14.95 (0-86534-158-3) Sunstone Pr.

Mention, Philippe & Ramio, Christian. Cartridges of the Gras System. LC 88-82737. (Illus.). 147p. 1988. 37.95 (0-939683-02-4) Armory Pubns.

Menton, Seymour. Latin America's New Historical Novel. LC 93-787. (Texas Pan American Ser.). 240p. (C). 1993. text ed. 30.00 (0-292-75157-5) U of Tex Pr.

— Prose Fiction of the Cuban Revolution. (Latin American Monographs: No. 37). 364p. reprint ed. pap. 103.80 (0-8357-7713-8, 2036070) Bks Demand.

— The Spanish American Short Story: A Critical Anthology. LC 76-7765. (Latin American Studies Center, UCLA: No. 49). 1980. pap. 16.00 (0-520-04641-2) U CA Pr.

Menton, Seymour & Herrera-Sobek, Maria, eds. Saga de Mexico. LC 91-33663. 348p. 1991. pap. 20.00 (0-927534-11-8) Biling Rev-Pr.

Menton, Seymour, tr. see Cepeda Samudio, Alvaro.

Menton, Seymour, jt. ed. see Martins, Wilson.

Mentor Circle of Poets Staff. One Score & Two Years of Uncommon Fanfare: Anthology of Award-Winning Poems from the Annual Poetry Contests Sponsored by the North American Mentor Magazine, 1964-1985. LC 85-52334. xii, 244p. 1986. pap. 16.50 (0-87423-040-3) Westburg.

Mentor, Steven, ed. see Gray, Chris H.

Mentor Technologies Staff. Mentor Notes - Software Learning Made Easy: Advanced WordPerfect. (Illus.). 152p. 1991. 69.95 (1-56494-001-2) Mentor Tech.

— Mentor Notes - Software Learning Made Easy: Intermediate Lotus 1-2-3. (Illus.). 169p. 1991. 69.95 (1-56494-003-9) Mentor Tech.

— Mentor Notes - Software Learning Made Easy: Introduction to Lotus 1-2-3. (Illus.). 127p. 1991. 69.95 (1-56494-002-0) Mentor Tech.

— Mentor Notes - Software Learning Made Easy: Introduction to OS-2 2.0. (Illus.). 150p. 1992. 69.95 (1-56494-005-5) Mentor Tech.

— Mentor Notes - Software Learning Made Easy: Introduction to Windows. (Illus.). 211p. 1991. 69.95 (1-56494-004-7) Mentor Tech.

— Mentor Notes - Software Learning Made Easy: Introduction to WordPerfect. (Illus.). 116p. 1991. 69.95 (1-56494-000-4) Mentor Tech.

Mentre, Paul. The Fund, Commercial Banks & Member Countries. (Occasional Papers: No. 26). 39p. 1984. pap. 5.00 (1-55775-067-X) Intl Monetary.

Mentschikoff, Soia & Stotzky, Irwin R. The Theory & Craft of American Law. LC 80-70678. 1981. write for info. (0-8205-0211-1, 382); teacher ed write for info. (0-8205-0212-X) Bender.

Mentz, H. E. Pathophysiology in the Medical Sciences. 1983. text ed. 23.95 (0-409-09711-X) Buttrwrth-Heinemann.

Mentzer. Principles of Optical Circuit Engineering. (Optical Engineering Ser.: Vol. 26). 264p. 1990. 125.00 (0-8247-8202-X) Dekker.

Mentzer, ed. Integrated Optical Circuit Engineering, No. V. 1987. 59.00 (0-89252-870-2, 835) SPIE.

Mentzer, Diane. Your One Year Diet Diary: An Easy to Keep Daily Record of Your Successes. Elletro Productions Staff, ed. 72p. (Orig.). 1992. pap. 6.95 (0-88247-928-8, 928) R & E Pubs.

Mentzer, M. A., ed. Integrated Optical Circuit Engineering VI, Vol. 993. 1988. 59.00 (0-8194-0028-9) SPIE.

Mentzer, Michael. World of Owen Gromme. 240p. 1991. pap. 29.95 (1-55971-130-2, 0123) NorthWord.

Mentzer, Raymond A., Jr. Blood & Belief: Family Survival & Confessional Identity among the Provincial Huguenot Nobility. LC 93-25955. 288p. 1994. 32.95 (1-55753-041-6) Purdue U Pr.

***Mentzer, Raymond A., ed.** Sin & the Calvinists: Morals Control & the Consistory in the Reformed Tradition. LC 94-25541. (Sixteenth Century Essays & Studies: Vol. 32). 1995. write for info. (0-940474-34-4) Sixteenth Cent.

Mentzer, Richard C. The Core Package. Longdom, Danny G., ed. LC 79-23416. (Instructional Design Library). 124p. 1980. 23.95 (0-87778-141-9) Educ Tech Pubns.

Mentzer, William C. & Wagner, Gail M., eds. The Hereditary Hemolytic Anemias. (Illus.). 475p. 1989. text ed. 85.00 (0-443-08242-1) Churchill.

— The Hereditary Hemolytic Anemias. fac. ed. LC 88-23751. (Illus.). 488p. 1989. reprint ed. pap. 139.10 (0-7837-7889-9, 2047645) Bks Demand.

Mentzer, William C., Jr., ed. see Isaacs, David.

MENU Staff. The Software Catalog: Science & Engineering. 4th ed. 720p. 1987. pap. 73.75 (0-444-01228-1) Elsevier.

Menuez, Doug & Kounalakis, Markos. Defying Gravity: The Making of Newton. Livingston, Julie, ed. (Illus.). 224p. 1993. 29.95 (0-941831-94-9) Beyond Words Pub.

Menuhin, Yehudi, et al. Violin & Viola. (Illus.). 1976. write for info. (0-318-54251-X); pap. 9.95 (0-685-03273-6) Macmillan.

Menut, Albert D. Dostoevsky & Existentialism: With Reflections on the "Grand Inquisitor" 100p. 1972. 7.50 (0-87291-044-X) Coronado Pr.

Menut, Albert D., tr. Nicole Oresme: Highlights from His French Commentary on Aristotle's Politics. 237p. 1979. 15.00 (0-87291-132-2) Coronado Pr.

Menut, Albert D., ed. see Oresme, Nicole.

Menville, Douglas. A Historical & Critical Survey of the Science Fiction Film. LC 74-16509. (Science Fiction Ser.). 177p. 1977. 16.95 (0-405-06330-X) Ayer.

— Under Egypt: A Novel. LC 88-34592. 300p. (C). Date not set. lib. bdg. write for info. (0-89370-838-0); pap. write for info. (0-89370-938-7) Borgo Pr.

— The Work of Ross Rocklynne: An Annotated Bibliography & Guide. Clarke, Boden, ed. LC 88-34360. (Bibliographies of Modern Authors Ser.: No. 17). 70p. (C). 1989. lib. bdg. 20.00x (0-8095-0511-8); pap. 10.00x (0-8095-1511-3) Borgo Pr.

Menville, Douglas, ed. see Ainsworth, William H.

Menville, Douglas, ed. see Arlen, Michael.

Menville, Douglas, ed. see Barringer, Leslie.

Menville, Douglas, ed. see Benson, Edward F.

Menville, Douglas, ed. see Blackwood, Algernon.

Menville, Douglas, ed. see Boothby, Guy.

Menville, Douglas, ed. see Burrage, Alfred M.

Menville, Douglas, ed. see Campbell, Praed.

Menville, Douglas, ed. see Carew, Henry.

Menville, Douglas, ed. see Carnegie, James.

Menville, Douglas, ed. see Coppard, Alfred E.

Menville, Douglas, ed. see Crawford, Francis M.

Menville, Douglas, ed. see Dalton.

Menville, Douglas, ed. see De La Mare, Walter J.

Menville, Douglas, ed. see Doughty, Francis W.

Menville, Douglas, ed. see Erckmann, Emile & Erckmann, Alexandre.

Menville, Douglas, ed. see Ewers, Hanns H.

Menville, Douglas, ed. see Fielding, Henry.

Menville, Douglas, ed. see Gautier, Theophile.

Menville, Douglas, ed. see Griffith, George.

Menville, Douglas, ed. see Hadley, George.

Menville, Douglas, ed. see Haggard, H. Rider.

Menville, Douglas, ed. see Harvey, William F.

Menville, Douglas, ed. see Hecht, Ben.

Menville, Douglas, ed. see Heron-Allen, Edward.

Menville, Douglas, ed. see Holmes, Oliver Wendell.

Menville, Douglas, ed. see Housman, Clemence.

Menville, Douglas, ed. see Ingram, Eleanor M.

Menville, Douglas, ed. see James, Montague R.

Menville, Douglas, ed. see Keller, David H.

Menville, Douglas, ed. see Machen, Arthur.

Menville, Douglas, ed. see MacKay, Mary.

Menville, Douglas, ed. see Marrat, Florence.

Menville, Douglas, ed. see Moresby, Lily & Beck, Adams.

Menville, Douglas, ed. see Morris, William.

Menville, Douglas, ed. see Odell, Eric.

Menville, Douglas, ed. see O'Donnell, Elliot.

Menville, Douglas, ed. see Paget, Violet.

Menville, Douglas, ed. see Paine, Albert B.

Menville, Douglas, ed. see Phillpotts, Eden.

Menville, Douglas, ed. see Powys, John C.

Menville, Douglas, jt. ed. see Reginald, R.

Menville, Douglas, ed. see Reynolds, George W.

Menville, Douglas, ed. see Sicard, Clara.

Menville, Douglas, ed. see Stewart, Mary L.

Menville, Douglas, ed. see Viereck, George S.

Menville, Douglas, ed. see Vivan, Charles E.

Menville, Douglas, ed. see Wakefield, Herbert R.

Menville, Douglas, ed. see Ward, Arthur S.

Menville, Douglas, ed. see Whiting, Sydney.

Menville, Douglas A. & Reginald, R. Things to Come: An Illustrated History of the Science Fiction Film. LC 83-8789. 212p. 1983. reprint ed. lib. bdg. 31.00x (0-89370-019-3) Borgo Pr.

Meny, Yves. Government & Politics in Western Europe: Britain, France, Italy, Germany. 2nd ed. Knapp, Andrew, ed. Lloyd, Janet, tr. LC 92-42261. (Comparative European Politics Ser.). 1993. 46.00 (0-19-827885-3); pap. 18.95 (0-19-827886-1) OUP.

Meny, Yves & Wright, Vincent, eds. The Politics of Steel: Western Europe & the Steel Industry in the Crisis Years (1974-1984) (European University Institute, Series C (Political & Social Science): No. 7). x, 812p. 1986. lib. bdg. 242.35 (0-89925-194-3) De Gruyter.

— The Politics of Steel: Western Europe & the Steel Industry in the Crisis Years (1974-1984) (European University Institute, Series C (Political & Social Science): No. 7). x, 812p. 1986. lib. bdg. 242.35 (3-11-010517-9) De Gruyter.

Meny, Yves, jt. auth. see Duhamel, Olivier.

Menyuk, Paula. The Development of Speech. LC 74-173981. (Studies in Communicative Disorders). 1972. pap. text ed. 2.15 (0-672-61276-3, Bobbs) Macmillan.

— Language & Maturation. 1977. pap. 8.95 (0-262-63075-3) MIT Pr.

— Language Development: Knowledge & Use. (C). 1988. text ed. 51.00 (0-673-39740-8) HarpCollege.

— Sentences Children Use. (Press Research Monographs: No. 52). 176p. 1972. pap. 8.95 (0-262-63043-5) MIT Pr.

***Menyuk, Paula, et al.** Early Language Development in Full-Time & Premature Infants. 264p. 1995. 59.95 (0-8058-1772-7) L Erlbaum Assocs.

— Early Language Development in Full-Time & Premature Infants. 264p. 1995. pap. 24.50 (0-8058-1773-5) L Erlbaum Assocs.

Menz, Fredric C. & Stevens, Sarah A., eds. Economic Opportunities in Freer U. S. Trade with Canada. LC 90-34463. 203p. (C). 1991. 59.50 (0-7914-0530-3); pap. 19.95 (0-7914-0531-1) State U NY Pr.

Menz, K. M. Rainfed Rice Production in the Philippines: A Combined Agronomic Economic Study. 90p. (C). 1989. text ed. 120.00 (0-949511-73-0, Pub. by ACIAR) St Mut.

Menz, K. M. & Fleming, E. M. Economic Prospects for Vanilla in the South Pacific. (C). 1989. text ed. 46.00 (0-949511-89-7, Pub. by ACIAR) St Mut.

Menz, K. M., jt. auth. see Ryland, G. J.

Menz, Kenneth M. Rice Production in Sri Lanka: A Combined Agronomic-Economic Study in the Intermediate & Dry Zones. (C). 1990. text ed. 100.00 (1-86320-022-3, Pub. by ACIAR) St Mut.

Menza, Claudia. Cage of Wild Cries. 1991. pap. 12.95 (0-88962-445-3) Riverrun NY.

— The Lunatics Ball. 108p. 1995. lib. bdg. 33.00 (0-8095-4856-9) Borgo Pr.

Menze, Ernest A., ed. see Herder, Johann G.

Menze, Ernest A., tr. see Kinder, Herman & Hilgemann, Werner.

***Menzefricke, Ulrich.** Statistics for Managers. 650p. 1995. text ed. 56.95 (0-534-23538-7) Intl Thomson.

Menzel. Cytoskeleton of the Algae. 1992. 199.95 (0-8493-6679-8, QK565) CRC Pr.

— Fingerprint Detection with Lasers. 120p. 1980. 65.00 (0-8247-6974-0) Dekker.

Menzel, ed. Fluorescence Detection. 213p. 1987. 50.00 (0-89252-778-1, 743) SPIE.

— Fluorescence Detection, No. II. 1988. 45.00 (0-89252-945-8, 910) SPIE.

Menzel, Adolf. Hellenika. Vlastos, Gregory, ed. LC 78-19372. (Morals & Law in Ancient Greece Ser.). (GER & GRE.). 1979. reprint ed. lib. bdg. 17.95 (0-405-11562-8) Ayer.

Menzel, Barbara J. Would You Rather? LC 81-6810. (Illus.). 32p. (J). (ps-3). 1982. 16.95 (0-89885-076-2) Human Sci Pr.

Menzel, David W., ed. Ocean Processes: U. S. Southeast Continental Shelf: A Summary of Research Conducted in the South Atlantic Bight under the Auspices of the U. S. Department of Energy from 1977 to 1991. LC 93-13553. 112p. 1993. pap. 27.00 (0-87079-598-8, DE93010744); fiche 12.50 (0-87079-599-6, DE93010744) DOE.

Menzel, Donald H. Fundamental Formulas of Physics, 2 vols, 1. 2nd ed. (Illus.). 1960. pap. text ed. 8.95 (0-486-60595-7) Dover.

— Fundamental Formulas of Physics, 2 vols, 2. 2nd ed. (Illus.). 1960. pap. text ed. 10.95 (0-486-60596-5) Dover.

— Mathematical Physics. 1953. pap. text ed. 8.00 (0-486-60056-4) Dover.

Menzel, Donald H., ed. Radio Noise Spectrum. LC 60-7997. (Illus.). 191p. 1960. 25.50 (0-674-74675-9) HUP.

Menzel, Donald H., ed. see Martin, Martha E.

Menzel, Donald H., jt. auth. see Pasachoff, Jay M.

Menzel, E. R., ed. Fluorescence Detection, No. 3: 1989 Los Angeles Symposium - OE-LASE '89 (January 1989) (Proceedings Ser.: Vol. 1054). 238p. 1989. 62.00 (0-8194-0089-0) SPIE.

Menzel, E. Roland. An Introduction to Lasers, Forensic Lights & Fluorescent Fingerprint Detection. LC 91-76835. (Illus.). 55p. (Orig.). (C). 1991. pap. 14.95 (0-9622305-6-1, 8-5043) Lightning Powder.

Menzel-Gerrie, Sharon. Careers in Comedy. LC 93-4962. (J). 1993. 14.95 (0-8239-1517-4); pap. 9.95 (0-8239-1713-4) Rosen Group.

Menzel, H., jt. ed. see Chadwick, K.

***Menzel, Lois.** Celia. 1995. pap. 4.50 (0-449-22342-6) Fawcett.

Menzel, Lois J. At Daggers Drawn. 1989. pap. 2.95 (0-449-21601-2) Fawcett.

— Ruled by Passion. (Regency Romance Ser.). 240p. (Orig.). 1992. pap. 3.95 (0-449-21789-2, Crest) Fawcett.

Menzel, Paul T. Strong Medicine: The Ethical Rationing of Health Care. 256p. 1990. 35.00 (0-19-505710-4) OUP.

Menzel, Peter. Material World: A Global Family Portrait. LC 94-8588. (Illus.). 256p. 1994. pap. 30.00 (0-87156-437-8) Sierra.

Menzel, Peter & Sierra Club Staff. Material World: A Global Family Portrait. LC 94-8588. (Illus.). 256p. 1995. pap. 20.00 (0-87156-430-0) Sierra.

***Menzel, Roland.** Laser Spectroscopy: Techniques & Applications. LC 94-5323. (Practical Spectroscopy Ser.: 18). 1994. 135.00 (0-8247-9265-3) Dekker.

Menzel, Roy A. Hometown on the River. (Illus.). 160p. (Orig.). 1989. pap. 10.00 (0-685-30428-0) Tall Pine Bks.

Menzel, Sewall H. Bullets vs. Ballots: Political Violence & Revolutionary War in El Salvador, 1970-1991. (University of Miami North-South Center Ser.). 92p. (C). 1993. pap. text ed. 14.95 (1-56000-689-7) Transaction Pubs.

— Bullets vs. Ballots: Political Violence & Revolutionary War in El Salvador, 1970-1991. LC 94-772. 1994. write for info. (1-56000-757-5) Transaction Pubs.

Menzel, Suzanne. A201 Lab Manual: Exercises in C. (C). 1993. student ed 14.00 (1-881592-28-6) Hayden-McNeil.

Menzel Symposium on High Pressure Steam Curing Staff. Menzel Symposium on High Pressure Steam Curing. Kuenning, W. H., ed. LC 77-186848. (ACI Publication Ser.: No. SP-32). (Illus.). 296p. reprint ed. pap. 84.40 (0-7837-5216-4, 2044947) Bks Demand.

Menzel, Theophil, tr. see Andrae, Tor.

Menzel, Winston. Estuarine & Marine Bivalve Mollusk Culture. (Illus.). 432p. 1991. 239.00 (0-8493-4936-2, SH370) CRC Pr.

***Menzer, Joe & Graeff, Burt.** CAVS: From Fitch to Fratello. (Illus.). 250p. 1994. 23.95 (1-57167-006-8) Sagamore Pub.

Menzer, Michael. Fond du Lac: A Gift of the Glacier County. 200p. 1991. lib. bdg. 29.95 (0-9631213-0-8) Fond Du Lac CHS.

Menzer, Robert E., jt. ed. see Ragsdale, Nancy N.

Menzies. The Development of Early Christian Pneumatology. (JSNT Supplement Ser.). 370p. (C). 1991. 40.00 (1-85075-306-7, Pub. by Sheffield Acad UK) CUP Services.

— Glacial Environments: Processes Sediments & Landforms. 1994. pap. text ed. write for info. (0-08-040273-9, Pergamon Pr) Elsevier.

— Modern Glacial Environments: Processes, Dynamics & Sediments. 1994. text ed. 115.01 (0-08-042422-8, Pergamon Pr); pap. text ed. 42.01 (0-08-042421-X, Pergamon Pr) Elsevier.

Menzies, A., ed. see Baur, Ferdinand C.

Menzies, Edna. Storytime. (Illus.). 128p. (J). (gr. 1-3). 1993. pap. 5.95 (1-879224-15-1) Mailbox.

Menzies, Heather. The Rail Road's Not Enough. 318p. 1978. 11.95 (0-7720-1226-1, Pub. by Stoddart Pubng CN) Genl Dist Srvs.

Menzies, J. & Rose, J., eds. Drumlin Symposium: Proceedings of the Drumlin Symposium-First International Conference on Geomorphology, Manchester, 16-18 September 1985. 362p. 1987. text ed. 105.00 (90-6191-792-1, Pub. by A A Balkema NE) Ashgate Pub Co.

Menzies, Linda. Teen's Guide to Business: The Secret to a Successful Enterprise. (YA). 1992. pap. 7.95 (0-942361-50-4) MasterMedia Ltd.

Menzies, Linda, et al. A Teen's Guide to Business: The Secrets to a Successful Enterprise. large type ed. LC 93-30254. (Teen Scene Ser.). (YA). (gr. 9-12). 1993. 15.95 (0-7862-0061-8) Thorndike Pr.

Menzies, Lucy, ed. Life As Prayer: And Other Papers of Evelyn Underhill. LC 91-18022. 240p. 1991. reprint ed. pap. 12.95 (0-8192-1576-7) Morehouse Pub.

Menzies, Martin & Haekesworth, Chris. Mantle Metasomatism. (Press Geology Ser.). 1987. text ed. 137.00 (0-12-491080-7) Acad Pr.

Menzies, Nicholas K. Forest & Land Management in China since the Seventeenth Century. (Studies on the Chinese Economy). 200p. 1994. text ed. 75.00 (0-312-10254-2) St Martin.

Menzies, Nicholas K., jt. auth. see Daniels, Christian.

Menzies, Robert. The Riches of His Grace. 175p. 1956. 9.50 (0-227-67583-5) Attic Pr.

Menzies, Robert G. Central Power in the Australian Commonwealth: An Examination of the Growth of Commonwealth Power in the Australian Federation. LC 67-28061. (Virginia Legal Studies). 208p. reprint ed. pap. 59.30 (0-8357-8061-9, 2033973) Bks Demand.

Menzies, Robert J. Survival of the Sanest: Order & Disorder in a Pretrial Psychiatric Clinic. 310p. 1989. text ed. 40.00 (0-8020-5827-2); pap. text ed. 18.95 (0-8020-6737-9) U of Toronto Pr.

Menzies, Robert J., et al. Abyssal Environment & Ecology of the World Oceans. LC 72-8780. 488p. 1973. 37.50 (0-471-59440-7, Wiley) Krieger.

***Menzies, S. W., et al.** Atlas of the Surface Microscopy of Pigmented Skin Tumors. (Illus.). 208p. 1995. text ed. 98.00 (0-07-470206-8) Hlth Prof Div.

Menzies, William W. Anointed to Serve: The Story of the Assemblies of God. LC 79-146707. (Illus.). 440p. 1971. 15.95 (0-88243-465-9, 02-0465) Gospel Pub.

— Understanding the Times of Christ. LC 91-70704. 128p. 1991. reprint ed. pap. 2.95 (0-88243-622-8, 02-0622) Gospel Pub.

Menzies, William W. & Horton, Stanley H., eds. Bible Doctrines: A Pentecostal Perspective. enl. rev. ed. LC 92-43219. 304p. 1993. 19.95 (0-88243-318-0) Gospel Pub.

Menzinsky, Georg & Blomberg, Erik. Sweden: Lion Type Stamps 1862-1872 & Ring Type Stamps 1872-1892. Stone, Lauson et al, eds. Ahman, Sven, tr. (Illus.). 123p. (Orig.). 1985. pap. text ed. 17.50 (0-936493-05-4) Scand Philatelic.

Menzinsky, Georg, et al. Sweden: Skilling Banco Stamps, 1855-1858. Stone, Lauson et al, eds. Ahman, Sven, tr. Bd. with Black Local Stamp & 1862 Provisional of Local Stamp Type. 41p. (Illus.). 91p. (Orig.). 1985. Set pap. text ed. 17.50 (0-936493-06-2) Scand Philatelic.

Menzione, A. & Scribano, A. Calorimetry in High Energy Physics: Proceedings. 696p. 1994. text ed. 124.00 (981-02-1672-6) World Scientific Pub.

Meo, L., et al. The Arab Boycott of Israel. (Other Works Ser.: No. 2). 35p. (Orig.). 1976. pap. text ed. 2.00 (0-937694-12-6) Assn Arab-Amer U Grads.

Meo, Leila. Lebanon, Improbable Nation: A Study in Political Development. LC 75-46621. 246p. 1976. reprint ed. text ed. 59.75 (0-8371-8727-3, MELE, Greenwood Pr) Greenwood.

— U. S. Strategy in the Gulf. (Monograph Ser.: No. 14). 130p. (Orig.). 1981. pap. 6.00 (0-937694-50-9) Assn Arab-Amer U Grads.

Meo, Mel, jt. auth. see Grochowski, Nita.

Meopham, Brian. Commercial Guide to F. I. D. I. C. Conditions of Contract. (Waterlow Practitioner's Library). 352p. 1986. 69.00 (0-08-039234-2, K130, Pergamon Pr) Elsevier.

— Commercial Guide to GC-Works-1 Conditions of Contract. (Waterlow Practitioner's Library). 336p. 1985. 59.00 (0-08-039233-4, Pergamon Pr) Elsevier.

— Commercial Guide to I. C. E. Conditions Contract. (Waterlow Practitioner's Library). 336p. 1985. 59.00 (0-08-039232-6, Pergamon Pr) Elsevier.

Mep, Alan D. & Ulrich, Heidi. Partners for Prosperity: The Groups of Seven & the European Community: The Group of Seven & the European Community. 53p. (Orig.). (C). 1994. pap. text ed. 35.00x (0-7881-0687-2) Diane Pub.

Mepham, John. Virginia Woolf. LC 92-22238. (Criticism in Focus Ser.). 1992. text ed. 29.95 (0-312-08603-2) St Martin.

— Virginia Woolf: A Literary Life. LC 91-9081. (Literary Lives Ser.). 240p. 1991. text ed. 29.95 (0-312-06204-4) St Martin.

Mepham, Lydie, jt. intro. see Elliott, David.

Mepham, M. J. Accounting in Eighteenth Century Scotland. Brief, Richard P., ed. (Foundations of Accounting Ser.: No. 11). 666p. 1988. 25.00 (0-8240-6117-9) Garland.

Mepham, Michael S. Computation in Language Text Analysis. LC 75-305923. 242p. reprint ed. pap. 69.00 (0-317-20580-3, 2024591) Bks Demand.

Mepham, T. B. Physiology of Lactation. LC 86-8504. 100p. 1987. 113.00 (0-335-15152-3); pap. 48.00 (0-335-15151-5) Wiley.

An Asterisk (*) at the beginning of an entry indicates that the title is appearing in BIP for the first time.

— Physiology of Lactation. 224p. 1991. text ed. 144.95 (*0-471-93246-9*, Wiley-Liss); pap. text ed. 74.95 (*0-471-93247-7*, Wiley-Liss) Wiley.

Mepham, T. B., ed. Biochemistry of Lactation. 500p. 1983. 169.75 (*0-444-80489-7*) Elsevier.

Mepham, Virginia, jt. auth. see Molloy, William.

Mepsted, Joyce. Your Child Needs You: A Positive Approach to Down's Syndrome. (Illus.). 96p. (Orig.). 1988. pap. 20.00 (*0-7463-0511-7*, Pub. by Northcote House UK) Trans-Atl Phila.

Mera, H. Pueblo Designs: One Hundred Seventy-Six Illustrations of the Rain Bird. 1970. reprint ed. pap. 5.95 (*0-486-22073-7*) Dover.

***Mera, H. P.** Pueblo Indian Embroidery. LC 94-34722. (Illus.). 80p. 1995. pap. text ed. 6.95 (*0-486-28418-2*) Dover.

— Spanish-American Blanketry: Its Relationship to Aboriginal Weaving in the Southwest. LC 87-12715. (Illus.). 96p. (Orig.). 1987. pap. 14.95 (*0-933452-22-5*) Schol Am Res.

Mera, Harry P. Reconnaissance & Excavation in Southeastern New Mexico. LC 39-14217. (AAA. Memoirs Ser.: No. 51). 1938. 15.00 (*0-527-00550-9*) Periodicals Srv.

— Style Trends in Pueblo Pottery in the Rio Grande & Little Colorado Cultural Areas from the Sixteenth to the Nineteenth Century. LC 76-43776. (Laboratory of Anthropology, Memoirs: Vol. 3). reprint ed. write for info. (*0-404-15630-4*) AMS Pr.

Meral, Jean. Paris in American Literature. Long, Laurette, tr. LC 88-33910. xii, 284p. (C). 1989. 42.50 (*0-8078-1803-8*) U of NC Pr.

Merandonk, M. Basic Gurkhali Dictionary. 1991. 34.00 (*0-7855-0266-1*, Pub. by Ratna Pustak Bhandar) St Mut.

Merani, Alberto L. Dictionary of Child Psychiatry & Psychology: Diccionario de Psicologia y Psiquiatria Infantil. 176p. (ENG, GER, ITA & SPA.). 1983. 28.50 (*0-8288-2221-2*, S39839) Fr & Eur.

— Dictionary of Psychology: Diccionario de Psicologia. 5th ed. 280p. (SPA.). 1985. write for info. (*0-7859-4968-2*) Fr & Eur.

Meranto, Philip. Politics of Federal Aid to Education in 1965: A Study in Political Innovation. LC 67-16846. (Orig.). 1967. pap. 12.95x (*0-8156-2107-8*) Syracuse U Pr.

Merari, Ariel, ed. On Terrorism & Combating Terrorism. LC 84-22037. 208p. 1985. text ed. 45.00 (*0-313-27047-3*, U7047); pap. text ed. 19.95 (*0-313-27061-9*, P7061) Greenwood.

Meras, Phyllis. Exploring Rhode Island: A Visitor's Guide to the Ocean State. 82p. 1984. pap. 4.95 (*0-685-10922-4*) Providence Journ.

— The Mermaids of Chenonceaux: And 828 Other Stories. 352p. 1982. 16.95 (*0-312-92525-5*) St Martin.

— A Yankee Way with Wood. rev. ed. LC 93-14589. 1993. pap. 18.95 (*0-936399-49-X*) Berkshire Hse.

***Meras, Phyllis & Gannon, Tom.** Rhode Island: An Explorer's Guide. (Explorer's Guide Ser.). (Illus.). 272p. (Orig.). 1995. pap. 16.00 (*0-88150-308-8*) Countryman.

Merashi, Mehdi. Persian, Contemporary Spoken, Vol. 2. 119p. 1994. 14.95 (*0-88432-793-0*); digital audio 185.00 (*0-88432-792-2*) Audio-Forum.

Meraviglia-Crivelli, Graf. Wappen des Boemischen Adels. 316p. (CZE & GER.). 1990. reprint ed. 152.00 (*0-317-03842-7*) Szwede Slavic.

Meraw, Ken, ed. see Ahoy, Christopher K. & King, Frederick W.

Meray, jt. auth. see Aczel.

Meray, Tibor, jt. auth. see Aczel, Tamas.

***Merbreier, Carter & Capus Riley, Linda.** Television: What's Behind What You See. (Illus.). 40p. Date not set. 16.00 (*0-374-37388-4*) FS&G.

Merbs, C. & Miller, R., eds. Health & Disease in the Prehistoric Southwest. (Anthropological Research Papers: No. 34). (Illus.). xix, 402p. 1985. 25.00 (*0-685-73910-4*) AZ Univ ARP.

Merbury, Charles. A Briefe Discourse of Royall Monarchie, Wherunto Is Added a Collection of Italian Proverbes, Etc. LC 70-38209. (English Experience Ser.: No. 474). 94p. 1972. reprint ed. 14.00 (*90-221-0474-5*) Walter J Johnson.

Mercadal, Dennis. Dictionary of Artificial Intelligence. 1990. pap. 39.95 (*0-442-00451-6*) Van Nos Reinhold.

Mercadante, Saverio. Il Bravo: Libretto by Gaetano Rossi & Others, after James Fenimore Cooper & Anicet Bourgeois. Music by Saverio Mercadante. LC 89-753690. (Italian Opera 1810-1840 Ser.: Vol. 21). 368p. 1990. 124.00 (*0-8240-6570-0*) Garland.

— Elena Da Feltre. Gossett, Philip, ed. (Italian Opera Ser., 1810-1840). 1985. 92.00 (*0-8240-6569-7*) Garland.

— Elisa E Claudio & Excerpts From L'Apoteosi D'Ercole. Gossett, Philip, ed. (Italian Opera Ser., 1810-1840). 1990. 124.00 (*0-8240-6563-8*) Garland.

— Il Guiramento. Gosset, Philip, ed. (Italian Opera Ser., 1810-1840). 245p. 1986. 92.00 (*0-8240-6567-0*) Garland.

Mercadel, Walter F. Stutsbear & the Bionic Busboy: My Secret Diary So Stay Out Unless You Are My Friend This Means You. (Orig.). 1994. pap. 8.95 (*0-9634332-1-0*) Lithodendron.

Mercado. Developing Large Software Systems. 1995. pap. 37.00 (*0-442-01847-9*) Van Nos Reinhold.

Mercado, Carol. A Voice from the Grave. 160p. (Orig.). 1994. mass mkt. 4.99 (*0-7865-0013-1*) Diamond.

Mercado-Gardner, Juanita. No Code Database Design with Access 2.0. (Illus.). (Orig.). 1994. pap. 35.00 (*1-56686-153-5*) Brady Compu Bks.

Mercado, Julio. Del Camino. 120p. (SPA.). 1923. 1.00 (*0-318-14254-6*) Hispanic Inst.

***Mercado, Leonardo N.** The Fillipino Mind. LC 94-28262. (Cultural Heritage & Contemporary Change, Philippine Philosophical Studies: 8). 1994. 45.00 (*1-56518-063-1*); pap. 17.50 (*1-56518-064-X*) Coun Res Values.

Mercado, Mario R. The Evolution of Mozart's Pianistic Style. LC 91-8696. (Illus.). 272p. (C). 1992. 34.95 (*0-8093-1690-0*) S Ill U Pr.

Mercado, Monina A., ed. People Power: An Oral & Photographic History of the Philippines Revolution of 1986. (Illus.). (Orig.). 1987. pap. 19.95 (*0-86316-131-6*) Writers & Readers.

Mercado, O. A. An Atlas of Foot Surgery, Vol. II: Rear Foot Surgery. 75.00 (*0-940542-04-8*) Carolando.

— An Atlas of Podiatric Surgery: Forefoot Surgery, Vol. 1. (Illus.). 290p. 1980. 75.00 (*0-940542-03-X*) Carolando.

— Mercado Atlas of Foot Anatomy. Orig. Title: An Atlas of Podiatric Anatomy. (Illus.). 1995. spiral bd. 50.00 (*0-940542-05-6*) Carolando.

***Mercado, Sergio R.** Baile de Mascaras. 1995. pap. 14.95 (*0-679-76334-1*, Vin) Random.

Mercadoocasio, Gwen. How to Draw Comics. LC 94-1837. (J). 1994. pap. 5.95 (*0-681-00424-X*) Longmeadow Pr.

Mercat Press Staff. The Handbook to Edinburgh. 251p. (C). 1987. pap. 40.00 (*0-901824-88-7*, Pub. by Mercat Pr Bks UK) St Mut.

Mercatante, Anthony. The Facts on File Encyclopedia of World Mythology & Legend. (Illus.). 807p. 1988. 95.00 (*0-8160-1049-8*) Facts on File.

***Mercatante, Anthony S.** Who's Who in Egyptian Mythology. 2nd ed. Bianchi, Robert Steven, ed. 256p. 1995. 32.50 (*0-8108-2967-3*) Scarecrow.

Merced de Mendez, Ana T. Luceros de Amor. (Illus.). 100p. 1990. write for info. (*0-9627442-0-4*) A T Merced de Mendez.

Merced, Stoka A., jt. auth. see Brenner, R.

Mercedes, M., illus. Marian Prayers. 128p. 1986. pap. write for info. (*0-933820-06-2*) Marian Fathers.

***Mercedes, Sari.** Portraits in Pen. (Illus.). 100p. 1995. pap. 10.00 (*0-9647225-0-X*) Sari.

Mercenier, Jean & Srinivasan, T. N., eds. Applied General Equilibrium & Economic Development. 376p. 1993. text ed. 59.50 (*0-472-10382-2*) U of Mich Pr.

Mercer, jt. auth. see Herberman.

Mercer, jt. auth. see Reid.

Mercer, A. D. Progress in the Understanding & Prevention of Corrosion: Tenth European Corrosion Congress. Costa, J. M., ed. 960p. 1993. 240.00 (*0-901716-36-7*, Pub. by Inst Materials UK) Ashgate Pub Co.

Mercer, A. D., jt. ed. see McIntyre, P.

Mercer, A. S. Banditti of the Plains. LC 54-5940. (Western Frontier Library: No. 2). (Illus.). 1975. reprint ed. pap. 10.95 (*0-8061-1315-4*) U of Okla Pr.

Mercer, Alan D. Corrosion in Seawater Systems. 176p. 1991. text ed. write for info. (*0-13-388703-0*) P-H.

— Implementable Marketing Research. 256p. 1992. pap. text ed. 48.00 (*0-13-457532-6*) P-H.

Mercer, Alan D., et al. Operational Distribution Research. 196p. 1978. pap. 31.00 (*0-85066-168-4*) Taylor & Francis.

Mercer, Alex. Disease, Mortality & Population in Transition. 1991. text ed. 69.00 (*0-7185-1344-4*, Pub. by Pinter Pubs UK) St Martin.

Mercer, Ann R., jt. auth. see Mercer, Cecil D.

Mercer, Basil W., jt. auth. see Dawson, Gaynor W.

***Mercer, Bill.** Singing the Clay: Pueblo Pottery of the Southwest, Yesterday & Today. LC 95-5191. 1995. pap. write for info. (*0-931537-18-5*) Cincinnati Mus.

Mercer, Blaine & Covey, Herbert C. Theoretical Frameworks in the Sociology of Education. 139p. 1980. pap. 11.95 (*0-87073-855-0*) Schenkman Bks Inc.

Mercer, Blaine & Hey, Steven. People in Schools. LC 80-13278. 382p. 1981. 24.95 (*0-685-04511-0*); pap. text ed. 18.95 (*0-87073-857-7*) Schenkman Bks Inc.

Mercer, Calvin R. Norman Perrin's Interpretation of the New Testament. Mabee, Charles, ed. LC 84-27335. (Studies in American Biblical Hermeneutics). 192p. 1986. 24.95 (*0-86554-219-8*, MUP-H197) Mercer Univ Pr.

***Mercer, Cavalie.** Journal of the Waterloo Campaign. 416p. 1995. reprint ed. pap. 15.95 (*0-306-80651-7*) Da Capo.

Mercer, Cecil D. Students with Learning Disabilities. 4th ed. (Illus.). 688p. (C). 1992. text ed. write for info. (*0-02-380540-4*) Macmillan.

Mercer, Cecil D. & Mercer, Ann R. Teaching Students with Learning Problems. 4th ed. LC 92-21059. 720p. (C). 1992. pap. write for info. (*0-02-380561-7*, Merrill Pub Co) Macmillan.

Mercer, David. High-Level Selling: Techniques for Managing the Complex Sale. 224p. 1989. 26.95 (*0-87201-829-6*) Gulf Pub.

— Managing the External Environment: A Strategic Perspective. 312p. (C). 1992. text ed. 60.00 (*0-8039-8628-9*); pap. text ed. 24.00 (*0-8039-8629-7*) Sage.

— Marketing. 608p. (C). 1992. pap. text ed. 32.95 (*0-631-17631-4*) Blackwell Pubs.

— Marketing. 2nd ed. (Illus.). 576p. (C). 1995. pap. write for info. (*0-631-19638-2*) Blackwell Pubs.

— Mercer: Two Plays. 256p. 1995. pap. 15.95 (*0-413-65200-9*, Pub. by Methuen UK) Heinemann.

— No Limits to Love. 69p. 1988. pap. 8.95 (*0-413-48260-X*, A0191) Heinemann.

— A Question of Balance: Conflict over Natural Resources Development in Australia. 340p. 1991. pap. 43.00 (*1-86287-056-X*, Pub. by Federation Pr AU) W W Gaunt.

— A Question of Balance: Natural Resources Conflict Issues in Australia. 2nd ed. 350p. 1995. pap. 39.00 (*1-86287-163-9*, Pub. by Federation Pr AU) W W Gaunt.

Mercer, David & Laing, Stuart. Mercer: Plays One. (Methuen World Dramatists Ser.). 362p. (Orig.). (C). 1990. pap. 13.95 (*0-413-63450-7*, A0462, Pub. by Methuen UK) Heinemann.

***Mercer, Dean, et al.** Hugs 'n Kisses Couples Coupon Book. 1995. pap. write for info. (*0-9646365-0-6*) Idea Fifty-Seven Pubns.

Mercer, Deborah B., jt. auth. see Burkhart, Joyce L.

***Mercer, Dorothy D.** Injury: Learning to Live Again. 192p. 1994. lib. bdg. 33.00x (*0-8095-5918-8*) Borgo Pr.

Mercer, Dorothy L. Injury: Learning to Live Again. LC 94-1058. 192p. 1994. pap. 12.95 (*0-934793-54-9*) Pathfinder CA.

Mercer, E. I. & Alexander, P. Keratin & Keratinization: An Essay in Molecular Biology. LC 60-53516. (International Series of Monographs on Pure & Applied Mathematics: Vol. 12). 1961. 134.00 (*0-08-009548-8*, Pub. by Pergamon Repr UK) Franklin.

Mercer, E. I., jt. auth. see Goodwin, T. W.

***Mercer, Edward, et al.** Experiments in General Chemistry. 1994. per. 12.50 (*0-88252-168-3*) Paladin Hse.

Mercer, Ginger, jt. auth. see Bach, Bob.

***Mercer, Helen.** Constructing a Competitive Order: The Hidden History of British Anti-Trust Policies. (Illus.). 288p. (C). 1995. 59.95 (*0-521-41292-7*) Cambridge U Pr.

Mercer, Helen, et al, eds. Labour Government & Private Industry: The Experience of the 1945-51 Governments. 240p. 1992. 60.00 (*0-7486-0339-5*, Pub. by Edinburgh U Pr UK) Col U Pr.

Mercer, Henry C. Dating of Old Houses. (Illus.). 28p. 1976. reprint ed. pap. 2.00 (*0-910302-03-0*) Bucks Co Hist.

Mercer, Ian. Crystals. (British Museum of Natural History Ser.). (Illus.). 60p. 1990. pap. text ed. 9.95 (*0-674-17914-5*) HUP.

Mercer, Ian, jt. auth. see Van Rose, Susanna.

Mercer, James L. Public Management in Lean Years: Operating in a Cutback Management Environment. LC 92-15782. 288p. 1992. text ed. 55.00 (*0-89930-357-9*, MEB, Quorum Bks) Greenwood.

— Strategic Planning for Public Managers. LC 90-47590. 240p. 1991. text ed. 55.00 (*0-89930-355-2*, MSZ/, Quorum Bks) Greenwood.

Mercer, James L. & Philips, Ronald J. Public Technology: Key to Improved Government Productivity. LC 80-69693. 287p. reprint ed. pap. 81.80 (*0-317-27065-6*, 2023538) Bks Demand.

Mercer, James L., et al. Managing Urban Government Services: Strategies, Tools, & Techniques for the Eighties. LC 81-66228. 256p. reprint ed. pap. 73.00 (*0-317-20781-4*, 2023912) Bks Demand.

Mercer, James W. DNAPL Site Evaluation. LC 93-18972. 1994. 59.95 (*0-87371-977-8*, TD1066) Lewis Pubs.

Mercer, James W., jt. auth. see Anderson, Stephen F.

Mercer, Jane R. Labeling the Mentally Retarded: Clinical & Social System Perspectives on Mental Retardation. 1973. pap. 15.00 (*0-520-02428-1*) U CA Pr.

Mercer, Jean. To Everything There Is a Season: Development in the Context of the Lifespan. 584p. (Orig.). (C). 1991. lib. bdg. 71.00 (*0-8191-8391-1*); pap. text ed. 30.00 (*0-8191-8392-X*) U Pr of Amer.

Mercer, Jerry L. Being Christian: A United Methodist Vision for the Christian Life. LC 93-72074. 104p. 1993. pap. 9.95 (*0-88177-125-2*, DR125) Discipleship Res.

Mercer, John. The Informational Film. LC 80-54273. (Illus.). 200p. (C). 1981. pap. text ed. 6.80 (*0-87563-197-5*) Stipes.

— An Introduction to Cinematography. (Illus.). (C). 1979. spiral bd. 12.80 (*0-87563-168-1*) Stipes.

Mercer, John E. Alchemy, Its Science & Romance. LC 79-8617. (Illus.). reprint ed. 27.50 (*0-404-18481-2*) AMS Pr.

***Mercer, Jonathan.** Reputation & International Politics. (Studies in Security Affairs). 264p. 1996. 35.00 (*0-8014-3055-0*) Cornell U Pr.

Mercer, Joyce A. Behind the Mask of Adolescent Satanism. LC 91-72991. (Illus.). 160p. 1991. pap. 9.95 (*0-925190-22-5*) Fairview Press.

***Mercer, Judy.** Fast Forward. Chernoff, Dona, ed. 352p. 1995. 22.00 (*0-671-89960-0*) PB.

Mercer, Julia E. Bermuda Settlers of the Seventeenth Century: Genealogical Notes From Bermuda. LC 82-81220. 276p. 1982. reprint ed. 20.00 (*0-8063-0987-3*) Genealog Pub.

Mercer, June. The Clearing Mist. large type ed. 320p. 1987. 16.95 (*0-7089-1668-6*) Ulverscroft.

— Death-Line. large type ed. 304p. 1987. 16.95 (*0-7089-1614-7*) Ulverscroft.

Mercer, K. Lynne, jt. auth. see Cross, Patricia C.

Mercer, Kobena. Welcome to the Jungle: New Positions in Black Cultural Studies. LC 93-48150. 1994. 49.95 (*0-415-90634-2*); pap. 16.95 (*0-415-90635-0*) Routledge.

Mercer, Laurie F. & Singer, Jennifer. Opportunity Knocks-Using PR. LC 88-43402. 192p. 1989. pap. text ed. 14.95 (*0-8019-7884-X*) Chilton.

Mercer, Lloyd J. E. H. Harriman: Master Railroader. Perkins, Edwin, ed. (Twayne's Evolution of American Business Ser.: No. 3). 1985. text ed. 23.95 (*0-8057-9802-1*, 605, Twayne) Macmillan.

Mercer, M. Ray, jt. auth. see Butler, Kenneth M.

***Mercer, Mayer.** Frog Where Are You. (J). 1994. pap. 4.50 (*0-14-054632-4*) Dial Bks Young.

Mercer, Michael W. Hire the Best...& Avoid the Rest. 176p. 1993. 19.95 (*0-8144-0207-0*) AMACOM.

— How Winners Do It: High Impact Skills for Your Career Success. LC 93-46384. 1994. pap. text ed. 9.95 (*0-13-335696-5*) P-H.

— How Winners Do It: High Impact Skills for Your Career Success. LC 93-46384. 1994. write for info. (*0-13-335704-X*) P-H.

— Turning Your Human Resources Department into a Profit Center. LC 88-48024. 265p. 1989. 59.95 (*0-8144-5841-6*) AMACOM.

Mercer, Mick. Gothic Rock Black Book. (Illus.). 96p. 1988. pap. 17.95 (*0-7119-1546-6*, OP44866) Omnibus NY.

Mercer, Morris A., Jr. To All My Friends. (Illus.). 64p. (Orig.). 1986. pap. write for info. (*0-9617362-0-8*) M A Mercer.

***Mercer, Neil.** The Guided Construction of Knowledge: Talk Amongst Teachers & Learners. 160p. 1995. 48.00 (*1-85359-263-3*, Pub. by Multilingual Matters UK); pap. 15.95 (*1-85359-262-5*, Pub. by Multilingual Matters UK) Taylor & Francis.

Mercer, Neil, ed. Language & Literacy from an Educational Perspective, Vol. 1. (Language Studies). 244p. 1988. 90.00 (*0-335-10275-1*, Open Univ Pr); pap. 32.00 (*0-335-15553-7*, E815, Open Univ Pr) Taylor & Francis.

— Language & Literacy from an Educational Perspective: In School, E815 vol. II. 224p. 1988. 90.00 (*0-335-10293-X*, Open Univ Pr); pap. 32.00 (*0-335-15558-8*, Open Univ Pr) Taylor & Francis.

Mercer, Neil, jt. auth. see Edwards, Derek.

Mercer, Nelda & Orringer, Carl. Grocery Shopping Guide: A Consumer's Manual for Selecting Foods Lower in Dietary Saturated Fat & Cholesterol. rev. ed. LC 89-170947. 223p. 1989. pap. 14.95 (*0-9624147-0-0*) U MI MedSport.

***Mercer, Paul.** Directory of British Political Organizations. 2nd ed. 450p. 1995. pap. 150.00 (*1-56159-146-7*, Stockton Pr) Groves Dictionaries.

Mercer, Peter. Hamlet & the Acting of Revenge. LC 86-82701. 277p. (C). 1987. text ed. 33.95 (*0-87745-171-0*) U of Iowa Pr.

***Mercer, R. B.** Industrial Control Wiring. LC 94-22819. (Illus.). 112p. 1995. 14.95 (*0-7506-0933-8*) Buttrwrth-Heinemann.

Mercer, R. J. Causewayed Enclosures. 1989. pap. 25.00 (*0-7478-0064-2*, Pub. by Shire UK) St Mut.

Mercer, Ramona. Parents at Risk. LC 90-35580. 320p. 1990. 33.95 (*0-8261-7240-7*) Springer Pub.

***Mercer, Ramona T.** Becoming a Mother: Research on Maternal Role Identity from Rubin to the Present. LC 95-2601. (Focus on Women Ser.: Vol. 18). (Illus.). 352p. 1995. write for info. (*0-8261-8970-9*) Springer Pub.

— First-Time Motherhood: Experiences from Teens to Forties. 400p. 1986. 39.95 (*0-8261-5160-4*) Springer Pub.

Mercer, Ramona T., et al. Transitions in a Woman's Life: Major Life Events in Developmental Context. (Focus on Women Ser.). 224p. 1989. 27.95 (*0-8261-6560-5*) Springer Pub.

Mercer, Richard, jt. auth. see Hungerford, Thomas W.

Mercer, Rick. Computing Fundamentals with C Plus Plus: Using, Modifying & Implementing Object Classes. 1995. pap. 34.95 (*0-938661-72-8*) Franklin Beedle.

— Problem Solving & Program Implementation Using Turbo Pascal: Versions 4.0 to 6.0. LC 91-10125. (Illus.). 758p. (C). 1992. pap. text ed. 40.95 (*0-938661-15-9*) Franklin Beedle.

Mercer, Roger, ed. Farming Practices in Prehistoric Britain. 245p. 1981. 26.50 (*0-85224-501-7*, Pub. by Edinburgh U Pr UK) Col U Pr.

Mercer, Rosemary, tr. Deep Words: Miura Baien's System of Natural Philosophy. LC 90-21719. (Philosophy of History & Culture Ser.: No. 4). (Illus.). x, 216p. 1991. 65.75 (*90-04-09351-6*) E J Brill.

Mercer, S. A. Egyptian Hieroglyphic Grammar: With Vocabularies, Exercises, Chrestomathy. viii, 184p. 1980. 15.00 (*0-89005-203-4*) Ares.

Mercer, Samuel A. Assyrian Grammar. LC 22-17308. (Columbia University. Oriental Studies: No. 29). reprint ed. 15.00 (*0-404-50519-8*) AMS Pr.

— Ethiopic Liturgy. LC 76-141034. reprint ed. 47.50 (*0-404-04308-9*) AMS Pr.

— Handbook of Egyptian Hieroglyphs. 175p. (Orig.). 1993. pap. 16.95 (*0-87052-102-0*) Hippocrene Bks.

— Sumero-Babylonian Sign List. LC 18-16548. (Columbia University. Oriental Studies: No. 14). reprint ed. 21.50 (*0-404-50504-X*) AMS Pr.

Mercer, Samuel A. & Hallock, Frank H., eds. The Tell El-Amarna Tablets, 2 vols., Set. LC 78-72764. (Ancient Mesopotamian Texts & Studies). (Illus.). 942p. 1983. reprint ed. 145.00 (*0-404-18216-X*) AMS Pr.

Mercer, Sherry L., jt. auth. see Wattenbarger, James L.

Mercer, Steve, ed. see Miller, Randy, et al.

***Mercer-story, Eugenia.** Sea Condor - Dusty Son. 62p. 1994. pap. 12.95 (*1-879980-06-1*) Magick Mirror.

Mercer, Susan O., ed. Women As They Age: Challenge, Opportunity & Triumph. LC 88-34803. (Journal of Women & Aging: Vol. 1, Nos. 1-3). (Illus.). 415p. 1989. text ed. 59.95 (*0-86656-805-0*); pap. text ed. 19.95 (*0-86656-873-5*) Haworth Pr.

Mercer, Susan O., et al. Geriatric Case Practice in the Nursing Home. (Geriatric Case Practice Training Ser.: Vol. 1). (Illus.). 280p. 1991. 46.00 (*0-8039-2916-1*); pap. 22.95 (*0-8039-2917-X*) Sage.

Mercer, Tony. Chronometer Makers of the World. (Illus.). 291p. 1991. 75.00 (*0-7198-0240-7*, Pub. by NAG Press UK) Antique Collect.

Mercer, William W., jt. ed. see Keeling, David A.

Mercer, Z. Christopher. Valuing Financial Institutions. 656p. 1992. 72.50 (*1-55623-379-5*) Irwin Prof Pubng.

Merchan, M. A., et al, eds. The Mammalian Cochlear Nuclei: Organization & Function. (NATO ASI Series A, Life Sciences: Vol. 239). (Illus.). 511p. (C). 1993. 125.00 (*0-306-44406-2*, Plenum Pr) Plenum.

Merchand, H. Latinoamerica En Dos Mil Conciertos. 122p. (SPA.). 1974. 5.00 (*0-8288-7063-2*) Fr & Eur.

***Merchandise Staff.** Messipes. Date not set. write for info. (*0-679-87426-7*) Random.

Merchant, Alexander N. From Barter to Slavery: The Economic Relations of Portuguese & Indians in the Settlement of Brazil, 1500-1580. LC 78-64184. (Johns Hopkins University. Studies in the Social Sciences. Thirtieth Ser. 1912: 1). reprint ed. 11.50 (*0-404-61292-X*) AMS Pr.

Merchant, B., jt. ed. see Gershwin, M. Eric.

Merchant, Carolyn. Death of Nature. 1990. pap. 13.00 (*0-06-250595-5*) Harper SF.

— Earthcare: Women & the Environment. 288p. 1995. 59.95x (*0-415-90887-6*, B3088, Routledge NY); pap. 16.95 (*0-415-90888-4*, B3092, Routledge NY) Routledge.

— Ecological Revolutions: Nature, Gender, & Science in New England. LC 89-30945. (H. Eugene & Lillian Youngs Lehman Ser.). (Illus.). xviii, 380p. (C). 1989. 39.95 (*0-8078-1858-5*); pap. 14.95 (*0-8078-4254-0*) U of NC Pr.

— Radical Ecology: The Search for a Livable World. LC 92-12542. (Revolutionary Thought - Radical Movements Ser.). (Illus.). 288p. 1992. 49.95 (*0-415-90649-0*, A7614, Routledge NY); pap. 14.95 (*0-415-90650-4*, A7618, Routledge NY) Routledge.

Merchant, Carolyn, ed. Major Problems in American Environmental History: Documents & Essays. (Major Problems in American History Ser.). 544p. (C). 1993. pap. text ed. write for info. (*0-669-24993-9*) Heath.

Merchant, Carolyn & Gottleib, Roger, eds. Ecology. LC 94-3090. (Key Concepts in Critical Theory Ser.). (C). 1994. pap. 17.50 (*0-391-03795-1*) Humanities.

Merchant, Christina S., jt. auth. see Constantino, Cathy A.

Merchant, Darlene A. Treating Abused Adolescents: A Program for Providing Individual & Group Therapy. 1990. pap. text ed. 14.95 (*1-55691-017-7*) Learning Pubns.

Merchant, Ella, jt. auth. see Jones, Alice I.

Merchant, Gloria. The Tail of the Dragon & Other Works. write for info. (*0-932298-41-9*) Tri-State Pr Corp.

Merchant, H. D., ed. see AIME Metallurgical Society Staff.

Merchant, H. D., ed. see Metallurgical Society of AIME Staff.

Merchant, H. D., ed. see Metallurgical Society Staff.

Merchant, H. D., ed. see Minerals, Metals & Materials Society Staff.

Merchant, H. D., et al, eds. Aluminum Alloys for Packaging. (Illus.). 352p. 1993. 68.00 (*0-87339-221-3*, 465) Minerals Metals.

— Continuous Casting of Non-Ferrous Metals & Alloys. LC 89-60887. (Illus.). 304p. 1989. 95.00 (*0-87339-096-2*, 355) Minerals Metals.

Merchant, Harish D. Problems in Material Science. 486p. 1972. text ed. 304.00 (*0-677-13450-9*) Gordon & Breach.

— Recent Research on Cast Iron. LC 66-28072. 842p. 1968. text ed. 387.00 (*0-677-11000-6*) Gordon & Breach.

Merchant, Ismail. Ismail Merchant's Florence. LC 93-36471. 1994. 39.95 (*0-8109-3639-9*) Abrams.

— Ismail Merchant's Passionate Meals: The New Indian Cuisine for Fearless Cooks & Adventurous Eaters. LC 93-37147. (Illus.). 288p. 1994. 27.50 (*0-7868-6015-4*) Hyperion.

— Ismail Merchant's Passionate Meals: The New Indian Cuisine for Fearless Cooks & Adventurous Eaters. (Illus.). 288p. 1996. pap. 14.95 (*0-7868-8129-1*) Hyperion.

Merchant, James A., ed. Occupational Respiratory Diseases. (DHHS Publication NIOSH Ser.: No. 86-102). (Illus.). 851p. 1986. 47.00 (*0-16-002526-5*, S/N 017-033-00425-1) USGPO.

Merchant, Kenneth A. Fradulent & Questionable Financial Reporting: A Corporate Perspective. LC 87-80813. 88p. 1987. 6.00 (*0-910586-64-0*) Finan Exec.

— Rewarding Results: Motivating Profit Center Managers. 1989. text ed. 35.00 (*0-07-103258-4*) McGraw.

Merchant, Linda K., jt. ed. see Dupuis, Mary M.

Merchant, M. N. Quranic Laws. pap. 10.50 (*0-933511-30-2*) Kazi Pubns.

Merchant, Moelwyn. A Bundle of Papyrus. 124p. (C). 1989. pap. 22.00x (*0-86383-544-9*, Pub. by Gomer Pr UK) St Mut.

— Fire from the Heights. (Princeton Theological Monograph Ser.: No. 27). 126p. (Orig.). 1991. pap. 10.00 (*1-55635-011-2*) Pickwick.

— Inherit the Land. 203p. (C). 1991. pap. 21.00x (*0-86383-817-0*, Pub. by Gomer Pr UK) St Mut.

— Jeshua, Nazareth to Jerusalem. (Princeton Theological Monograph Ser.: No. 26). xviii, 426p. (Orig.). 1991. pap. 15.00 (*1-55635-010-4*) Pickwick.

Merchant, Moelwyn, ed. Breaking the Code. (C). 1975. 30.00 (*0-85088-327-X*, Pub. by Gomer Pr UK) St Mut.

— Fragments of a Life. 367p. (C). 1990. 48.00x (*0-86383-647-X*, Pub. by Gomer Pr UK) St Mut.

Merchant, Pat. Proceeding Without Anecdotal Details of Imagery. (Orig.). 1992. pap. 16.00 (*0-913412-62-7*) Brandon Hse.

Merchant, Paul, ed. Wendell Berry. (American Authors Ser.). 250p. (Orig.). 1991. 24.95 (*0-917652-89-4*); pap. 14.95 (*0-917652-88-6*) Confluence Pr.

***Merchant, Ronald.** Basic Business Math & Electronic Calculators. 384p. (C). 1995. pap. text ed. 32.95 (*0-89863-189-0*) Star Pub CA.

— Basic Business Math & Electronic Calculators. 4th ed. 306p. 1989. pap. text ed. 29.95 (*0-89863-130-0*) Star Pub CA.

— Business Math with Electronic Accuracy. 320p. (C). 1987. pap. text ed. 29.95 (*0-89863-107-6*) Star Pub CA.

— Calculator Proficiency. 144p. 1989. pap. text ed. 14.95 (*0-89863-123-8*) Star Pub CA.

Merchant, W. D. Home on the Hill: A Bombay Girlhood. (Illus.). 160p. (Orig.). 1992. text ed. 22.00 (*0-89410-712-7*); pap. text ed. 10.50 (*0-89410-713-5*) Three Continents.

Merchant, W. M., ed. see Shakespeare, William.

Merchant, W. Moelwyn. R. S. Thomas. LC 89-49708. 83p. 1990. 15.00 (*1-55728-162-9*) U of Ark Pr.

Merchant, W. Moelwyn, ed. see Marlowe, Christopher.

Merchant, William M. Creed & Drama: An Essay in Religious Drama. LC 66-23222. 127p. reprint ed. pap. 36.20 (*0-685-17063-2*, 2027867) Bks Demand.

***Merchanthouse, Don C.** I Remember When: A Collection of Verses. Roberts, Rachel, ed. (Illus.). 95p. (Orig.). 1995. pap. 10.00 (*0-9635294-1-2*) Auburn-Cord-Duesenberg.

Merchuk, J. C., jt. auth. see Asenjo, Juan A.

Mercia, Leonard S. Raising Poultry the Modern Way. rev. ed. Foster, Kimberly, ed. LC 89-45738. (Illus.). 240p. 1990. pap. 9.95 (*0-88266-577-4*, Garden Way Pub) Storey Comm Inc.

— Raising Your Own Turkeys. LC 81-6353. (Illus.). 144p. (Orig.). 1981. pap. 8.95 (*0-88266-253-8*, Garden Way Pub) Storey Comm Inc.

Mercie, Christine. Sons of God. 1954. pap. 5.95 (*0-87516-059-X*) DeVorss.

Mercier. Practical Orthopedics. 520p. 1991. pap. 49.00 (*0-8151-5865-3*, Yr Bk Med Pubs) Mosby Yr Bk.

Mercier, B. An Introduction to the Numerical Analysis of Spectral Methods. (Lecture Notes in Physics Ser.: Vol. 318). v, 154p. 1989. 31.00 (*0-387-51106-7*) Spr-Verlag.

— Lectures on Topics in Finite Element Solution of Elliptic Problems. (Tata Institute Lectures on Mathematics Ser.). (Illus.). 191p. 1980. pap. 24.00 (*0-387-09543-8*) Spr-Verlag.

Mercier, C. Petrochemical Industry & Possibilities of Its Establishment in Developing Countries. 202p. 1966. text ed. 241.00 (*0-677-61370-9*) Gordon & Breach.

Mercier, C. & Cantarelli, C., eds. Pasta & Extrusion Cooked Foods: Some Technological & Nutritional Aspects. 212p. 1986. 57.75 (*0-85334-417-5*, Pub. by Elsevier Applied Sci UK) Elsevier.

Mercier, C. A. Astrology in Medicine. 1972. 35.00 (*0-87968-672-3*) Gordon Pr.

Mercier, Cathyrn M., jt. auth. see Bloom, Susan P.

Mercier, Charles & Rieber, Robert W. Criminal Responsibility. (Historical Foundations of Forensic Psychiatry & Psychology Ser.). 256p. 1980. reprint ed. lib. bdg. 27.50 (*0-306-76064-9*) Da Capo.

Mercier, Cheryl G. Bulimia. 20p. 1990. 2.95 (*1-56456-024-4*, 226) W Gladden Found.

— Childhood Eating Disorders. 20p. 1990. 2.95 (*1-56456-022-8*, 227) W Gladden Found.

Mercier, Cheryl G. & Brown, Waln K. Anorexia Nervosa. 20p. 1989. 2.95 (*1-56456-023-6*, 223) W Gladden Found.

***Mercier, Claude.** Petrochemical Industries the Possibilities of Its Establishment in the Developing Countries. (Illus.). 202p. (C). 1966. text ed. 31.00 (*2-7108-0058-6*) Technip.

Mercier, Francois. Recollections of the Youkon. Yarborough, Linda F., ed. (Alaska Historical Commission Studies in History: No. 188). (Illus.). 1986p. (Orig.). 1986. pap. 10.00 (*0-943712-19-X*) Alaska Hist.

***Mercier, Geselle, tr.** Botero in Chicago. (Illus.). 64p. (Orig.). (SPA.). 1994. pap. 20.00 (*0-938903-17-9*) Chi Ofc Fine Arts.

Mercier, J., ed. Anticonvulsant Drugs, 1. LC 72-8044. (C). 1973. 173.00 (*0-08-016840-X*, Pub. by Pergamon Repr UK) Franklin.

— Anticonvulsant Drugs, 2. LC 72-8044. (C). 1973. 272.00 (*0-08-017245-8*, Pub. by Pergamon Repr UK) Franklin.

Mercier, J. Denis & Brown, Waln K. Building Family Communication. 20p. 1992. 2.95 (*1-56456-071-6*, 270) W Gladden Found.

Mercier, Jacques. Ethiopian Magic Scrolls. Molinaro, Ursule, tr. LC 78-9330. (Illus.). 1979. pap. 12.95 (*0-8076-0897-1*) Braziller.

— Petit Dictionnaire Franco-Belge, Belgo-Francais: Mots et Expressions Usuels. 286p. (FRE.). 1990. 49.95 (*0-7859-8175-6*, 2871760098) Fr & Eur.

Mercier, Jean. Lexique Anglais-Francais du Compteur D'electricite: Principes et Pieces Composantes. 42p. (ENG & FRE.). 1973. pap. 9.95 (*0-8288-6312-1*, M-6407) Fr & Eur.

— Lexique Anglais-Francais du Programmateur De Cuisiniere: Fonctionnement et Pieces Composantes. 29p. (ENG & FRE.). 1973. pap. 9.95 (*0-8288-6313-X*, M-6406) Fr & Eur.

Mercier, Jean & Belanger, Francine. Vocabulary of Metal Working: Vocabulaire du Travail des Metaux en Fauilles, Barres, Tubes et Profils. 99p. (ENG & FRE.). 1984. pap. 9.95 (*0-8288-1916-5*, M4663) Fr & Eur.

***Mercier, Laurie & Buckendorf, Madeline.** Using Oral History in Community History Projects. (Pamphlet Ser.: Vol. 4). (Orig.). 1992. pap. text ed. 8.00 (*0-615-00633-7*) Oral Hist.

Mercier, Louis S. Memoirs of the Year Two Thousand Five Hundred. Hooper, W., tr. LC 68-56258. xi, 360p. 1973. reprint ed. 45.00 (*0-678-00915-5*) Kelley.

Mercier, Louis-Sebastien. Du Theatre. xvi, 372p. 1973. reprint ed. write for info. (*3-487-04908-2*, Pub. by Georg Olms GW) Lubrecht & Cramer.

— Memoirs of the Year Twenty-Five Hundred. LC 77-6804. 360p. 1977. 35.00 (*0-8398-2380-0*) Ultramarine Pub.

— Le Nouveau Paris, 6 pts. in 3. xxxviii, 1486p. reprint ed. write for info. (*0-318-71379-9*, Pub. by Georg Olms GW) Lubrecht & Cramer.

— Oeuvres Dramatiques, 2 vols. in 1. 726p. 1984. reprint ed. write for info. (*3-487-07477-X*, Pub. by Georg Olms GW) Lubrecht & Cramer.

Mercier, M., ed. Criteria (Dose Effect Relationships) for Organichlorine Pesticides: Report of a Working Group of Experts Prepared for the Commission of the European Communities. 400p. 1981. pap. 171.00 (*0-08-023441-0*, Pub. by Pergamon Repr UK) Franklin.

Mercier, Mary. Johnny No-Trump. 1968. pap. 4.75 (*0-8222-0598-X*) Dramatists Play.

Mercier, Pierre, jt. auth. see Barral, Jean-Pierre.

Mercier, R., ed. see Cesaire, Aime.

Mercier, R., ed. see Dadie, Bernard B.

Mercier, Sheryl, jt. auth. see Hoover, Evalyn.

Mercier, Vivian. Beckett - Beckett: The Classic Study of a Modern Genius. 256p. 1995. pap. 12.95 (*0-285-63010-5*, Pub. by Souvenir UK) Atrium Pubs.

— Modern Irish Literature: Sources & Founders. Dillon, Eilis, ed. LC 93-24542. 384p. (C). 1994. 48.00 (*0-19-812074-5*, Clarendon Pr) OUP.

***Merck, Bobbie J.** Delay Is Not Denial. 83p. (Orig.). (C). 1994. pap. text ed. 5.95 (*0-929263-08-1*) Great Love Church Intl.

— Hope. 123p. (Orig.). (C). 1992. pap. text ed. 6.95 (*0-929263-05-7*) Great Love Church Intl.

— Power of the Secret Place. 78p. (Orig.). 1990. pap. text ed. 5.95 (*0-929263-03-0*) Great Love Church Intl.

— Spoiling Python's Schemes. 217p. (Orig.). (C). 1991. pap. text ed. 8.95 (*0-929263-02-2*) Great Love Church Intl.

Merck, Dohme, jt. auth. see Merck, Sharp.

Merck, E. & Bruker, eds. Merck FT-IR Atlas: A Collection of FT-IR Spectra, Pt. 1. LC 87-29140. 1174p. 1988. lib. bdg. 730.00 (*0-89573-488-5*) VCH Pubs.

Merck, Mandy, ed. Pervisions: Deviant Readings by Mandy Merck. 1993. 49.95 (*0-415-90791-8*, B0635, Routledge NY); pap. 13.95 (*0-415-90792-6*, B0639, Routledge NY) Routledge.

Merck, Mandy, ed. see Screen Editorial Collective Staff.

Merck, Robert M. Deck the Halls: Treasures of Christmas Past. 96p. 1992. 21.95 (*1-55859-267-9*) Abbeville Pr.

Merck, Sharp & Dohme. The Merck Manual for Veterinarians: El Manual Merck de Veterinaria. 2nd ed. 1386p. (SPA.). 1981. 75.00 (*0-8288-2389-8*, S39845) Fr & Eur.

Merck, Sharp & Merck, Dohme. Merck Manual: El Manual Merck. 7th ed. (SPA.). 1986. 75.00 (*0-8288-1869-X*, S37592) Fr & Eur.

Merck, Wilson. Review of Imagery Uses in Twentieth Century Literature. (Orig.). 1990. pap. 9.90 (*0-913412-15-5*) Brandon Hse.

Merckel, Curt. Die Ingenieurtechnik Im Alterthum. xix, 658p. 1969. reprint ed. write for info. (*0-318-70783-7*, Pub. by Georg Olms GW) Lubrecht & Cramer.

Merckx, R., jt. ed. see Mulongoy, K.

Mercure, Michael. Encyclopedia of Revenge. 126p. 1989. 49.95 (*0-926395-00-9*) Anchor Maryland.

— Encyclopedia of Revenge: The Most Devastating Book Ever Published. rev. ed. (Illus.). 128p. 1992. pap. 19.95 (*0-926395-08-4*) Anchor Maryland.

Mercuri, Carmela. Beauty & the Beast: Story with Music. (Illus.). 24p. (Orig.). (YA). (gr. 8-12). 1976. pap. 4.95 (*0-935474-24-2*) Carousel Pubns Ltd.

— The Best of Vaudeville 3. (Dear Teacher, I've Always Wanted to Play the Piano Ser.). (Illus.). 32p. (Orig.). 1982. pap. 4.95 (*0-935474-05-6*, CAR1122) Carousel Pubns Ltd.

— Christmas Songs 1. (Dear Teacher, I've Always Wanted to Play the Piano Ser.). (Illus.). 32p. (Orig.). 1982. pap. 4.95 (*0-935474-04-8*, CAR1111) Carousel Pubns Ltd.

— Classical Themes: Level Two, Themes 4. (Dear Teacher, I've Always Wanted to Play the Piano Ser.). (Illus.). 32p. (Orig.). 1982. pap. 4.95 (*0-935474-07-2*, CAR1133) Carousel Pubns Ltd.

— Classical Themes: Level Two, Themes 5. (Dear Teacher, I've Always Wanted to Play the Piano Ser.). (Illus.). 32p. (Orig.). 1982. pap. 3.95 (*0-685-73593-1*, CAR1134) Carousel Pubns Ltd.

— Music Theory in Practice, Bk. 1. 32p. 1984. pap. 4.95 (*0-935474-01-3*) Carousel Pubns Ltd.

— My First Theory Book: Note Names for Coloring. (Illus.). 32p. (Orig.). (J). (gr. 1-6). 1987. pap. text ed. 4.95 (*0-935474-20-X*) Carousel Pubns Ltd.

— Popular Folks Songs 1. (Dear Teacher. I've Always Wanted to Play the Piano Ser.). (Illus.). 32p. (Orig.). 1982. pap. 4.95 (*0-935474-02-1*, CAR1100) Carousel Pubns Ltd.

— The Recorder Book: The Beginners Recorder Book. (Illus.). (Orig.). 1993. pap. 4.95 (*0-935474-23-4*) Carousel Pubns Ltd.

— Toot-in-Time Band: Introducing Children to the World of Music. (Illus.). (Orig.). (J). (gr. 1-6). 1993. pap. 10.95 (*0-935474-21-8*) Carousel Pubns Ltd.

Mercuri, Carmela, ed. Modes in All Keys for Piano. (Orig.). 1993. pap. 4.95 (*0-935474-22-6*) Carousel Pubns Ltd.

Mercuri, Carmela, ed. see Mozart, Wolfgang Amadeus.

Mercurialis-Hieronymus. De Arte Gymnastica, Libre Sex. Tanis, Norman E., ed. (Northridge Facsimile Ser.: Pt. X). 1978. pap. 5.00 (*0-937048-09-7*) CSUN.

***Mercurio, Carl & Schwartz, Natalie.** Yellow Pages 2000: Forecast & Analysis. Elwell, Chris, ed. (Illus.). 324p. 1994. write for info. (*0-88709-070-2*) Simba Info Inc.

Mercurio, Carl, ed. see Skory, Michael.

***Mercurio, Gian & Peschel, Max.** The Guide to Trading Posts & Pueblos. (Illus.). 72p. (Orig.). 1994. pap. 8.95 (*0-9627377-2-0*) Lonewolf Pub.

— Mesa Verde: Fuerher Durch Den Nationalpark. Glosser, Margie, tr. (Illus.). (Orig.). (Ger.). 1991. pap. 4.95 (*0-9627377-0-4*) Lonewolf Pub.

***Mercurio, Gian & Peschel, Maxymilian L.** Mesa Verde: A Complete Guide. (Illus.). 50p. (Orig.). 1992. pap. 4.95 (*0-9627377-1-2*) Lonewolf Pub.

Mercurio, Helen C. The Miracle Santa's Beard. Mercurio, Mary M., ed. 29p. (J). 1985. 12.00 (*0-9616079-0-4*) Tiffany Pub.

Mercurio, John. NY Yankee Records: A Year-by-Year Collection of Baseball Stats & Stories. 104p. 1993. reprint ed. pap. 4.99 (*1-56171-215-9*, S P I Bks) Sure Sellers.

Mercurio, John A. Babe Ruth's Incredible Records & the Forty-Five Players Who Broke Them. 192p. (Orig.). 1993. pap. 5.50 (*1-56171-221-3*, S P I Bks) Sure Sellers.

— Boston Red Sox Records. 1993. pap. 4.99 (*1-56171-219-1*) Sure Sellers.

— Boston Red Sox Records. 112p. 1993. reprint ed. pap. 4.99 (*1-56171-222-1*, S P I Bks) Sure Sellers.

— Major League Baseball Records: A Year-by-Year Rundown of Season & Career Records. 1993. pap. 11.99 (*1-56171-224-8*, S P I Bks) Sure Sellers.

— Official Profiles - BB Hall-Famers. 1994. 10.99 (*1-56171-216-7*) Sure Sellers.

Mercurio, Joseph A. Caning: Educational Rite & Tradition. LC 72-85385. (Segregated Settings & the Problems of Change Ser.: No. 4). 189p. 1972. text ed. 25.00x (*0-8156-8081-3*) Syracuse U Pr.

Mercurio, Louis, illus. Instant Travel Art: Vol. 1: Cruises. (Instant Travel Art Ser.). 48p. 1982. pap. text ed. 18.95 (*0-916032-17-5*) Delmar.

Mercurio, Mary M., ed. see Mercurio, Helen C.

Mercurio, Robert, tr. see Zoja, Luigi.

Mercurio, Roger. The Passionists. (Religious Orders Ser.). 192p. (Orig.). 1992. pap. text ed. 18.95 (*0-8146-5725-7*) Liturgical Pr.

Mercuro, Nicholas, ed. Taking Property & Just Compensation: Lew & Economics Perspectives of the Takings Issue. (Recent Economic Thought Ser.). 240p. (C). 1992. lib. bdg. 78.00 (*0-7923-9233-7*) Kluwer Ac.

Mercuro, Nicholas, jt. ed. see Leonhard, Alan T.

Mercuro, Nicholas, jt. auth. see Ryan, Timothy.

Mercuro, Nicholas, et al. Ecology, Law & Economics: The Simple Analytics of Natural Resource & Environment Economics. LC 94-17739. (Illus.). 212p. (Orig.). (C). reprint ed. lib. bdg. 49.50 (*0-8191-9593-6*); reprint ed. pap. text ed. 32.50 (*0-8191-9594-4*) U Pr of Amer.

Mercy, Deborah. Frostbite & Other Cold Injuries. 2nd ed. (Fisheries Safety & Survival Ser.: No. 7). 19p. reprint ed. pap. 4.00 (*1-56612-008-X*) AK Sea Grant CP.

***Merdeka Thien-Ly Huong Do.** Caodaiism an Introduction: Cao Dai Indigenous Vietnamese Religion. LC 94-74876. 106p. 1994. pap. text ed. write for info. (*0-9644543-0-0*) Cao Dai Temple.

Merdinger & Rosenfeld. Even If You Can't Carry a Tune. 1984. pap. 18.95 (*0-8384-2713-8*, Newbury) Heinle & Heinle.

Mere, Gallogo, tr. see Woodbury, Michael A., ed.

Meredeen, M. Managing Industrial Conflict: Seven Major Disputes. (C). 1989. 160.00 (*0-09-173226-3*, Pub. by S Thornes Pubs UK) St Mut.

Meredith. Atlas of Ophthalmic Surgery Vol. IV: Vitreo-Ret. 192p. 1994. 95.00 (*0-8016-6798-4*) Mosby Yr Bk.

— The Calling. 124p. Date not set. pap. 5.99 (*1-886820-03-1*) Meredith WA.

— Love Across Time. 1995. mass mkt. 4.99 (*0-312-95409-3*) St Martin.

— Note Book of an Unknown Writer. 143p. Date not set. pap. text ed. 4.99 (*1-886820-02-3*) Meredith WA.

— Poetry of Meredith. 55p. Date not set. pap. 2.99 (*1-886820-01-5*) Meredith WA.

— Strange Valentine. 168p. Date not set. pap. 5.99 (*1-886820-00-7*) Meredith WA.

— Women's Nutrition & Health. 1995. write for info. (*0-8493-4563-4*) CRC Pr.

— X(PLORE) Version 4 for MS-DOS Compatible Computers 3.5. 1993. text ed. write for info. (*0-13-014226-3*) P-H.

Meredith, ed. The Environmentalist's Bookshelf. 272p. 1993. text ed. 40.00 (*0-8161-7359-1*, Hall Reference) Macmillan.

Meredith, jt. auth. see Jampol.

Meredith, et al. AAAS Science & Technology Policy Yearbook 1991. 432p. 1991. 19.95 (*0-87168-427-6*, 91-34S) AAAS.

Meredith, Anne. Love's Timeless Hope. 1994. mass mkt. 4.99 (*0-312-95273-2*) St Martin.

Meredith, Barbara, jt. auth. see Lewis, Jane.

Meredith Books Staff. Better Homes & Gardens Complete Guide to Home Repair, Maintenance, & Improvement. 1994. pap. 19.95 (*0-696-20328-6*) Meredith Bks.

— Bread Book. 1994. 29.95 (*0-696-02564-7*) Meredith Bks.

— Do-It-Yourself. 1994. 21.95 (*0-696-20001-5*) Meredith Bks.

— Forever Friends. Date not set. 24.95 (*0-696-02397-0*) Meredith Bks.

— Lullaby Quilts for Babies & Dolls. Date not set. 24.95 (*0-696-02381-4*) Meredith Bks.

***Meredith, Burgess.** So Far, So Good. large type ed. LC 94-39559. 1995. 22.95 (*0-7862-0368-4*) Thorndike Pr.

— So Far, So Good: A Memoir. 1994. 22.95 (*0-316-56717-5*) Little.

Meredith, C., tr. see Andreades, Andreas M.

Meredith, Carol, jt. auth. see Prosser, Alex.

Meredith, Christopher. Griffri. 1992. 30.00 (*1-85411-059-4*) Dufour.

— Shifts. LC 88-83234. 214p. 1988. 28.00 (*0-907476-91-0*, Pub. by Poetry Wales Pr UK); pap. 12.95 (*0-907476-92-9*, Pub. by Poetry Wales Pr UK) Dufour.

— Snaring Heaven. 80p. 1990. pap. 13.95 (*1-85411-026-8*, Pub. by Seren Bks UK) Dufour.

— This. (Poetry Wales Poets Ser.: Vol. 1). 41p. 1985. pap. 7.95 (*0-907476-39-2*, Pub. by Poetry Wales Pr UK) Dufour.

Meredith, Christopher, jt. ed. see Huzzard, Ron.

Meredith Corporation, Better Homes & Gardens Staff. At the Zoo. (Max the Dragon Project Book Ser.). (Illus.). 32p. (J). (ps-12). 1991. reprint ed. lib. bdg. 10.95 (*1-878363-30-1*) Forest Hse.

An Asterisk (*) at the beginning of an entry indicates that the title is appearing in BIP for the first time.

— Bird Buddies. (Max the Dragon Project Book Ser.). (Illus.). 32p. (J). (ps-12). 1991. reprint ed. lib. bdg. 10.95 (*1-878363-31-X*) Forest Hse.
— Make Believe. (Max the Dragon Project Book Ser.). (Illus.). 32p. (J). (ps-12). 1991. reprint ed. lib. bdg. 10.95 (*1-878363-32-8*) Forest Hse.
— On the Farm. (Max the Dragon Project Book Ser.). (Illus.). 32p. (J). (ps-12). 1991. reprint ed. lib. bdg. 10.95 (*1-878363-33-6*) Forest Hse.
Meredith Corporation-Better Homes & Gardens Staff. At the Circus. (Max the Dragon Project Book Ser.). (Illus.). 32p. (J). (ps-12). 1991. lib. bdg. 10.95 (*1-878363-57-3*) Forest Hse.
— Let's Go Exploring. (Max the Dragon Project Book Ser.). (Illus.). 32p. (J). (ps-12). 1991. lib. bdg. 10.95 (*1-878363-58-1*) Forest Hse.
— Trains & Railroads. (Max the Dragon Project Book Ser.). (Illus.). 32p. (J). (ps-12). 1991. lib. bdg. 10.95 (*1-878363-59-X*) Forest Hse.
— Water Wonders. (Max the Dragon Project Book Ser.). (Illus.). 32p. (J). (ps-12). 1991. lib. bdg. 10.95 (*1-878363-60-3*) Forest Hse.
***Meredith, D. R.** The Homefront Murders. (Southwest Mysteries Ser.). 1994. mass mkt. 4.99 (*0-345-38050-9*) Ballantine.
Meredith, Dale D., et al. Design & Planning of Engineering Systems. (Civil Engineering & Engineering Mechanics Ser.). (Illus.). 384p. 1973. Reference ed. 34.95 (*0-685-03823-8*) P-H.
— Design & Planning of Engineering Systems. 2nd ed. (Illus.). 352p. (C). 1984. text ed. 76.00 (*0-13-200189-6*) P-H.
Meredith, David & Dyster, Barrie. Australia in the International Economy in the Twentieth Century. (Illus.). 352p. (C). 1990. 74.95 (*0-521-33496-9*); pap. 29. 95 (*0-521-33689-9*) Cambridge U Pr.
Meredith, David, jt. auth. see Havinden, Michael.
Meredith, Dawn, jt. auth. see Koonin, Steven E.
Meredith, Doris R. Murder by Reference. 272p. 1991. pap. 3.95 (*0-345-36861-4*) Ballantine.
— Murder by Sacrilege. 1993. mass mkt. 4.99 (*0-345-37693-5*) Ballantine.
— Reckoning. 1993. mass mkt. 4.99 (*0-06-100685-8*, Harp PBks) HarpC.
— The Sheriff & the Branding Iron Murders. 160p. 1986. pap. 2.95 (*0-380-70050-6*) Avon.
— The Sheriff & the Branding Iron Murders. 159p. 1985. 14. 95 (*0-8027-4050-2*) Walker & Co.
— The Sheriff & the Folsom Man Murders. 208p. 1987. pap. 2.95 (*0-380-70364-5*) Avon.
— The Sheriff & the Folsom Man Murders. 192p. 1987. 16. 95 (*0-8027-5663-8*) Walker & Co.
— Sheriff & the Panhandle Murders. 1991. mass mkt. 3.99 (*0-345-36951-3*) Ballantine.
— The Sheriff & the Pheasant Hunt Murders. 1993. mass mkt. 4.50 (*0-345-36948-3*) Ballantine.
— Time Too Late. 1993. mass mkt. 4.99 (*0-06-100566-5*, Harp PBks) HarpC.
Meredith, Doris R., ed. Murder by Impulse. 288p. 1988. mass mkt. 3.99 (*0-345-34671-8*) Ballantine.
Meredith, Elaine C. A Lifetime of Poetry. (Illus.). 221p. (Orig.). 1986. pap. 25.00 (*0-9614058-1-3*) Southco.
Meredith, Ellen. Listening In: Dialogues with the Wiser Self. LC 93-77564. 304p. (Orig.). 1993. pap. 14.95 (*0-9636073-5-9*) Horse Mtn Pr.
***Meredith, Fred.** Tempting Fortune: The Way Business Really Works. Piper, David, ed. 144p. 1995. 37.00 (*0-8095-4862-3*) Borgo Pr.
Meredith, G. Small Business Management in Australia. 2nd ed. 352p. 1982. 18.50 (*0-07-451006-1*) McGraw.
Meredith, G., et al. The Practice of Entrepreneurship. ix, 196p. 1982. text ed. 24.00 (*92-2-102839-9*); pap. text ed. 18.00 (*92-2-102846-1*) Intl Labour Office.
***Meredith, Gary.** Colonization Strategies & Secrets. 1995. 12.99 (*0-7821-1672-8*) Sybex.
Meredith, George. The Adventures of Harry Richmond. Hergenhan, L. T., ed. LC 78-88088. xxxviii, 613p. 1970. 35.00 (*0-8032-0712-3*) U of Nebr Pr.
— Diana of the Crossways. reprint ed. lib. bdg. 79.00 (*0-7812-0098-9*) Rprt Serv.
— Diana of the Crossways. LC 70-145177. 1971. reprint ed. 89.00 (*0-403-01105-1*) Scholarly.
— The Egoist. 1986. mass mkt. 5.95 (*0-452-00820-4*, Mer) NAL-Dutton.
— The Egoist. Woodstock, George, ed. (English Library). 1979. pap. 10.95 (*0-14-043034-2*, Penguin Classics) Viking Penguin.
— The Egoist. Adams, Robert M., ed. (Critical Editions Ser.). (C). 1979. pap. text ed. 11.95 (*0-393-09171-6*) Norton.
— The Egoist: a Comedy in Narrative. Harris, Margaret, ed. (World's Classics Ser.). 602p. 1992. pap. 9.95 (*0-19-281817-1*) OUP.
— Letters of George Meredith, 2 vols., Set. (BCL1-PR English Literature Ser.). 1992. reprint ed. lib. bdg. 150. 00 (*0-7812-7594-6*) Rprt Serv.
— The Ordeal of Richard Feverel: A Story of a Father & Son. 480p. 1983. reprint ed. pap. 8.95 (*0-486-24463-6*) Dover.
— The Poems of George Meredith, Set. Bartlett, Phyllis B., ed. LC 73-77142. 1978. 155.00 (*0-300-01283-7*) Yale U Pr.
— Selected Poems. Hough, Graham G., ed. LC 79-2564. 95p. 1980. reprint ed. text ed. 42.50 (*0-313-22034-4*, MESP, Greenwood Pr) Greenwood.
— Short Stories. rev. ed. LC 73-144162. (Short Story Index Reprint Ser.). 1977. reprint ed. 20.95 (*0-8369-3777-5*) Ayer.
— The Tragic Comedians: A Study in a Well-Known Story. (Revised Edition) LC 74-29508. (Modern Jewish Experience Ser.). 1975. reprint ed. 17.95 (*0-405-06735-6*) Ayer.
— Works, 29 vols., Set. (BCL1-PR English Literature Ser.). 1992. reprint ed. lib. bdg. 2,610.00 (*0-7812-7593-8*) Rprt Serv.
Meredith, Gertrude E. The Descendants of Hugh Amory, 1605-1805, British & American. (Illus.). 373p. 1988. reprint ed. lib. bdg. 68.50 (*0-8328-0216-6*); reprint ed. pap. 58.50 (*0-8328-0217-4*) Higginson Bk Co.
Meredith, Gina, jt. auth. see Hartwig, Laurie.
Meredith, Gloria E. & Arbuthnott, Gordon W., eds. Morphological Investigations of Single Neurons in Vitro. LC 93-10269. (IBRO Handbook Series: Methods in the Neurosciences: No. 16). 193p. 1993. pap. text ed. 92.95 (*0-471-93928-5*) Wiley.
Meredith, H. O., jt. ed. see Dickinson, G. Lowes.
Meredith, H. V. Physical Growth of White Children. (SRCD M: Vol. 1, No. 2). 1936. pap. 15.00 (*0-527-01487-7*) Periodicals Srv.
Meredith, Henry. Account of the Gold Coast of Africa. (Illus.). 264p. 1967. 35.00 (*0-7146-1039-9*, Pub. by F Cass Pubs UK) Intl Spec Bk.
Meredith, Henry, ed. see Scarlatti, Alessandro.
***Meredith, Howard.** Dancing on Common Ground: Tribal Cultures & Alliances on the Southern Plains. LC 94-23557. (Illus.). 288p. 1995. 29.95 (*0-7006-0694-7*) U Pr of KS.
— Modern American Indian Tribal Government & Politics: An Interdisciplinary Study. 169p. 1993. pap. 16.95 (*0-912586-76-1*) Navajo Coll Pr.
Meredith, Howard & Milan, Virginia E. A Cherokee Vision of Eloh' Proctor, Wesley, tr. 37p. (CHR & ENG.). 1981. pap. 8.00 (*0-940392-04-6*) Indian U Pr OK.
Meredith, Howard L., jt. auth. see Newkumet, Vynola B.
Meredith, Isabel. A Girl among the Anarchists. LC 92-12212. xiv, 302p. (C). 1992. 35.00 (*0-8032-3168-7*); pap. 9.95 (*0-8032-8190-0*) U of Nebr Pr.
Meredith, J. Folk Songs of Australia, Vol. 2. 326p. 1988. pap. 24.95 (*0-86840-098-X*, Pub. by New South Wales Univ Pr AT) Intl Spec Bk.
Meredith, J. & Anderson, H. Folk Songs of Australia, Vol. 1. 297p. 1988. pap. 24.95 (*0-86840-002-5*, Pub. by New South Wales Univ Pr AT) Intl Spec Bk.
Meredith, J. C., tr. see Kant, Immanuel.
Meredith, J. M. Meredith's Second Book of Bible Lists. LC 83-3807. 192p. (Orig.). 1983. pap. 6.99 (*0-87123-319-3*) Bethany Hse.
Meredith, Jack, jt. auth. see Turban, Efraim.
Meredith, Jack R. The Management of Operations. 3rd ed. 1987. 25.00 (*0-471-54352-7*); Net. write for info. (*0-471-85582-0*) Wiley.
— The Management of Operations. 4th ed. 800p. (C). 1992. Net. text ed. write for info. (*0-471-50909-4*) Wiley.
Meredith, Jack R. & Mantel, Samuel J. Project Management: A Managerial Approach. 2nd ed. 624p. 1989. Net. text ed. write for info. (*0-471-61787-3*) Wiley.
— Project Management: A Managerial Approach. 3rd ed. LC 94-33876. (Series in Production-Operations Management). 1995. text ed. write for info. (*0-471-01626-8*) Wiley.
Meredith, Jack R., jt. auth. see Turban, Efraim.
Meredith, Jill, jt. ed. see Bruzelius, Caroline.
Meredith, Joel L. Meredith's Book of Bible Lists. LC 80-14486. 288p. (Orig.). 1980. text ed. 8.99 (*0-87123-023-2*, 210023) Bethany Hse.
Meredith, John. Dinkum Aussie Rhyming Slang. 72p. 1993. 8.95 (*0-86417-333-4*, Pub. by Kangaroo Pr AT) Seven Hills Bk.
— The Wild Colonial Boy: Bushranger Jack Donahoe, 1806-1830. (Studies in Australian Folklore: No. 3). (Illus.). 102p. (Orig.). 1985. reprint ed. pap. 12.95 (*0-908247-04-4*) Legacy Books.
Meredith, John & Gillespie, Rollo. Duke of the Outback: The Adventures of a Shearer Named Tritton. (Studies in Australian Folklore: No. 5). 132p. (Orig.). 1985. reprint ed. pap. 12.95 (*0-908247-10-9*) Legacy Books.
Meredith, John & Whalan, Rex. Frank the Poet. (Studies in Australian Folklore: No. 1). (Illus.). 71p. 1985. reprint ed. pap. 11.95 (*0-9596490-6-9*) Legacy Books.
Meredith, Joseph. Hunter's Moon: Poems from Boyhood to Manhood. LC 92-41085. 122p. 1993. 18.95 (*1-877770-83-3*); pap. 12.50 (*1-877770-84-1*); audio 12. 95 (*1-877770-85-X*) Time Being Bks.
Meredith, Joseph C. The CAI Author-Instructor: An Introduction & Guide to the Preparation of Computer-Assisted Instruction Materials. LC 70-125876. 144p. 1971. 24.95 (*0-87778-014-5*) Educ Tech Pubns.
***Meredith, Kenneth T.** You Are with Me: A Personal Story of God's Sustaining Grace. 80p. Date not set. per., pap. 6.95 (*0-8341-1551-4*, 91801) Beacon Hill.
***Meredith, Laurence.** Original Mercedes-Benz SL - Restoration Guide. (Illus.). 128p. 1995. 34.95 (*1-870979-66-4*, Pub. by Bay View Bks UK) Motorbooks Intl.
— The Original VW Beetle. (Illus.). 112p. 1994. 34.95 (*1-870979-46-X*, Pub. by Bay View Bks UK) Motorbooks Intl.
Meredith, Lawrence. Essential VW Karmann-Ghia. (Essential Ser.). (Illus.). 80p. 1994. pap. 12.95 (*1-870979-52-4*, Pub. by Bay View Bks UK) Motorbooks Intl.
— Original Porsche 356: The Restoration Guide. (Illus.). 96p. 1995. pap. 34.95 (*1-870979-58-3*, Pub. by Bay View Bks UK) Motorbooks Intl.
Meredith, M. Alex, jt. auth. see Stein, Barry E.
Meredith, Marcia. Mirabeau Plantation. 352p. (Orig.). 1980. pap. 2.50 (*0-89083-596-9*) Zebra.
Meredith, Marilyn. Cooking for a Big Family & Large Groups. (Illus.). 112p. 1990. pap. 7.95 (*0-929935-05-5*) Countrywomans Pr.
— The Demon Fire. 197p. 1984. 6.95 (*0-89697-132-5*) Intl Univ Pr.
— Two Ways West. 352p. 1994. pap. 9.95 (*1-56901-149-4*) NW Pub.
— When the Cook Camps Out. (Illus.). 112p. (Orig.). 1990. pap. 7.95 (*0-929935-03-9*) Countrywomans Pr.
Meredith, Martin. In the Name of Apartheid: South Africa in the Postwar Era. LC 88-45044. 320p. 1988. 25.00 (*0-06-430163-X*, HarpT) HarpC.
Meredith, Mary, ed. see Demou, Doris B.
Meredith, Michael. Meeting the Brownings. (Illus.). 128p. (Orig.). 1986. pap. 17.50 (*0-930252-19-5*) Browning Inst.
Meredith, Michael, intro. A Centenary Selection from Robert Browning's Poetry. LC 89-34659. (Illus.). xvi, 196p. 1989. 24.00 (*0-930252-25-X*); pap. 12.75 (*0-930252-26-8*) Browning Inst.
Meredith, Michael C. & Humphrey, Rita S., eds. More Than Friend: The Letters of Robert Browning to Katharine de Kay Bronson. LC 85-51046. (Illus.). lxxx, 192p. 1985. 25.00 (*0-911459-06-5*) Wedgestone Pr.
Meredith, N., tr. see Couture, Pascale & Prieur, Benoit.
Meredith-Owens. Mesair Ussuara: Tezkere of Asik Celebi. (Gibb Memorial New Ser.: Vol. 24). 1971. 70.00 (*0-7189-0200-9*, Pub. by Aris & Phillips UK) David Brown.
Meredith, P. Instruments of Communication. 1966. 264.00 (*0-08-010663-3*, Pub. by Pergamon Repr UK) Franklin.
Meredith, P. L. Space Law: a Case Study for the Practitioner: Implementing a Telecommunications Satellite Business Concept. 408p. (C). 1992. lib. bdg. 156.50 (*0-7923-1786-6*) Kluwer Ac.
Meredith, Paul. Government, Schools & the Law. LC 91-18088. 224p. 1992. 69.95 (*0-415-03658-5*, A5035) Routledge.
Meredith, Paul, jt. auth. see Landin, Leslie.
Meredith, Peter & Tailby, John, eds. Staging of Religious Drama in Europe in the Middle Ages: Texts & Documents in English Translation. 2nd ed. (Early Drama, Art & Music Ser.: No. 4). 1989. reprint ed. 24. 95 (*0-918720-23-0*) Medieval Inst.
Meredith, Philip & Beattie, Alan. Sex Education: Political Issues in Britain & Europe. 250p. (C). 1989. lib. bdg. 49. 95 (*0-415-00604-X*) Routledge.
Meredith Press Staff. An American Sampler: Gifts of Nature. 1994. 22.95 (*0-696-20036-8*) Meredith Bks.
— Fabulous Napkin Folds. 72p. 1993. 14.95 (*0-696-02399-7*) Meredith Bks.
— Folk Art Quilts. 112p. Date not set. 19.95 (*0-696-02396-2*) Meredith Bks.
— Forty Fabulous Afghans. 168p. 1993. 22.95 (*0-696-02357-1*) Meredith Bks.
— Miniature Quilts. 168p. 1994. 24.95 (*0-696-02579-5*) Meredith Bks.
— Storybook Cross-Stitch. 168p. 1994. 24.95 (*0-696-02385-7*) Meredith Bks.
— Successful Machine Quilting. 224p. 1994. 24.95 (*0-696-02400-4*) Meredith Bks.
— Victorian Patchwork & Quilting. 144p. 1994. 22.95 (*0-696-20079-1*) Meredith Bks.
Meredith, R. The Structures & Properties of Fibres. 85p. 1975. 70.00 (*0-686-63798-4*) St Mut.
— Structures & Properties of Fibres, Vol. 7, No. 4. 85p. (C). 1974. pap. text ed. 90.00 (*0-685-36067-9*, Pub. by Textile Institue UK) St Mut.
Meredith, R. & Hearle, J. W., eds. Physical Methods of Investigating Textiles. LC 59-13795. (Illus.). 441p. reprint ed. pap. 125.70 (*0-317-10818-2*, 2011955) Bks Demand.
Meredith, R. Alan, jt. auth. see Anderson, C. Dixon.
Meredith, R. J., jt. auth. see Metaxas, A. C.
Meredith, Rebecca, jt. auth. see Doty, Betty.
Meredith, Robert C. & Fitzgerald, John D. Structuring Your Novel: From Basic Idea to Finished Manuscript. LC 70-170126. 240p. 1993. reprint ed. pap. 11.00 (*0-06-273170-X*, Harper Ref) HarpC.
Meredith, Roy. Mr. Lincoln's Camera Man: Mathew B. Brady. LC 73-92262. (Illus.). 384p. 1974. reprint ed. pap. 15.95 (*0-486-23021-X*) Dover.
— Mr. Lincoln's Camera Man: Matthew B. Brady. 2nd rev. ed. (Illus.). 26.50 (*0-8446-5224-5*) Peter Smith.
— World of Matthew Brady. 1988. 9.99 (*0-517-21640-X*) Random Hse Value.
Meredith, Ruby F., jt. ed. see O'Kunewick, James P.
Meredith, Russell, jt. auth. see Howard, Michaela.
Meredith, S. & Mosely, F. Help Your Child Learn, Number Skills. (Parents' Guides Ser.). (Illus.). 48p. 1989. lib. bdg. 13.96 (*0-88110-412-4*, Usborne); pap. 6.95 (*0-7460-0314-5*, Usborne) EDC.
Meredith, S. & Tahta, S. Starting Point Science, Vol. 3. (Illus.). 96p. (J). (gr. 2-7). 1992. 12.95 (*0-7460-0970-4*, Usborne) EDC.
Meredith, S., jt. auth. see Gee, R.
Meredith, Scott, ed. Bar Five: A Roundup of Best Western Stories. LC 79-75782. (Short Story Index Reprint Ser.). 1977. 20.95 (*0-8369-3007-X*) Ayer.
— Bar One: Roundup of Best Western Stories. LC 79-75782. (Short Story Index Reprint Ser.). 1977. 20.95 (*0-8369-3032-0*) Ayer.
— Bar Six: Roundup of Best Western Stories. LC 79-75782. (Short Story Index Reprint Ser.). 1977. 20.95 (*0-8369-3056-8*) Ayer.
— Bar Three: Roundup of Best Western Stories. LC 79-75782. (Short Story Index Reprint Ser.). 1977. 20.95 (*0-8369-3055-X*) Ayer.
— Bar Two: Roundup of Best Western Stories. LC 79-75782. (Short Story Index Reprint Ser.). 1977. 20.95 (*0-8369-3033-9*) Ayer.
Meredith, Scott, jt. ed. see Wodehouse, P. G.
Meredith, Sheena. Eczema, the Natural Way. (Natural Way Ser.). 1994. pap. 5.95 (*1-85230-493-6*) Element MA.
Meredith, Sue. Why Are People Different? (Starting Point Science Ser.). (Illus.). 24p. (J). (gr. 1-5). 1993. lib. bdg. 11.96 (*0-88110-642-9*, Usborne); pap. 3.95 (*0-7460-1014-1*, Usborne) EDC.
Meredith, Susan H. Nature Walk. 2nd ed. (Illus.). 25p. (J). 1995. pap. text ed. 5.95 (*1-880666-09-X*) Oughten Hse.
— Wonder Walk. (Illus.). 25p. (Orig.). (J). 1995. pap. text ed. 7.95 (*1-880666-02-2*) Oughten Hse.
Meredith, Sydney. Fitness Unfolding: How to Begin & Maintain a Quality, Healthy Lifestyle. Tips, Guidelines, & Resources. 233p. (Orig.). 1991. pap. 13.95 (*0-911107-01-0*) Markbks.
Meredith, T. J., et al. Antidotes for Poisoning by Cyanide. LC 93-32558. (IPCS-CEC Evaluation of Antidotes Ser.: No. 2). 201p. (C). 1994. 54.95 (*0-521-45458-1*) Cambridge U Pr.
— Antidotes for Poisoning by Paracetamol. (IPCS-CES Evaluation of Antidotes Ser.: No. 3). (Illus.). 109p. (C). 1995. 49.95 (*0-521-49576-8*) Cambridge U Pr.
— Naloxone, Flumazenil & Dantrolene As Antidotes. LC 93-32098. (IPCS-CEC Evaluation of Antidotes Ser.: Vol. 1). 110p. (C). 1994. 42.95 (*0-521-45459-X*) Cambridge U Pr.
Meredith, Ted J. Northwest Wine: Winegrowing Alchemy along the Pacific Ring of Fire. 4th ed. (Illus.). 224p. 1990. pap. 14.95 (*0-936666-05-6*) Nexus WA.
— Northwest Wine Companion. LC 88-60743. 160p. (Orig.). 1988. pap. 8.95 (*0-936666-04-8*) Nexus WA.
Meredith, William. Love Letter from an Impossible Land. LC 70-144748. (Yale Series of Younger Poets: No. 42). reprint ed. 18.00 (*0-404-53842-8*) AMS Pr.
Meredith, William, ed. Poets of Bulgaria. 1988. pap. 16.95 (*0-948259-39-6*) Dufour.
— Poets of Bulgaria. Levertov, Denise et al, trs. 150p. 1985. 25.00 (*0-87775-189-7*) Unicorn Pr.
— Poets of Bulgaria. Levertov, Denise et al, trs. 150p. 1985. pap. 10.00 (*0-87775-190-0*) Unicorn Pr.
Meredith, William, jt. ed. see Harteis, Richard.
Meredith, Willis C., jt. auth. see Margeton, Stephen G.
Mereine, Richard, et al. Employee Dismissal in Victoria & NSW. 200p. 1990. 65.00 (*1-875263-08-X*, Blckstone AT) W W Gaunt.
Merejkowski, Demitri. The Death of the Gods. Trench, Herbert, tr. & intro. by. LC 82-82473. 464p. 1987. reprint ed. pap. 15.50 (*0-8334-0021-5*, Spir Lit Lib) Garber Comm.
Merejkowski, Dimitri. Dostoievsky. LC 73-21712. (Studies in Dostoyevsky: No. 86). (C). 1974. lib. bdg. 49.95 (*0-8383-1816-9*) M S G Haskell Hse.
Merek, Jack. Blackbird. 368p. 1992. mass mkt. 5.99 (*0-446-36192-5*) Warner Bks.
— Target Stealth. LC 88-40095. 352p. 1990. mass mkt. 4.95 (*0-446-34843-0*) Warner Bks.
Merel, Henri. Germinal: Une Documentation Integrale. 326p. 1993. 60.00 (*0-85261-248-6*, Pub. by Univ of Glasgow UK) St Mut.
Merello, Barbara S., tr. see Amado, Jorge.
Merelman, Richard M. Making Something of Ourselves: On Culture & Politics in the United States. LC 83-5959. 200p. (C). 1984. pap. 12.00 (*0-520-04915-2*) U CA Pr.
— Partial Visions: Culture & Politics in Britain, Canada, & the United States. LC 91-9089. 300p. (Orig.). (C). 1991. lib. bdg. 40.00 (*0-299-12990-X*); pap. 15.95 (*0-299-12994-2*) U of Wis Pr.
— Representing Black Culture: Race & Cultural Politics in the United States. 288p. 1995. pap. 16.95 (*0-415-91075-7*, B4660) Routledge.
— Representing Black Culture: Race & Cultural Politics in the United States. 288p. 1995. 59.95 (*0-415-91074-9*, B4656) Routledge.
Merelman, Richard M., ed. Language, Symbolism, & Politics. 311p. (C). 1992. text ed. 61.00 (*0-8133-8581-4*) Westview.
Merenbach, Dennis G. & Stephen, Anthony. How to Be an Expert Witness: Credibility in Oral Testimony. (Illus.). 64p. (Orig.). 1993. pap. 8.95 (*1-56474-048-X*) Fithian Pr.
Merenbloom, Elliot Y. The Team Process: A Handbook for Teachers. 3rd enl. ed. 168p. (C). 1991. pap. text ed. 18. 00 (*1-56090-054-7*) Natl Middle Schl.
Mereness, Newton D., jt. auth. see Alsop, George.
Mereness, Newton D., jt. auth. see Leland, G. Waldo.
Merenstein & Gardner. Handbook of Neonatal Intensive Care. 2nd ed. (Illus.). 752p. 1989. pap. 35.95 (*0-8016-3415-6*) Mosby Yr Bk.
Merenstein, Gerald B., ed. Handbook of Neonatal Intensive Care. 3rd ed. LC 92-48492. 688p. 1993. pap. 37.95 (*0-8016-6702-X*) Mosby Yr Bk.
Merenstein, Gerald B., et al. Handbook of Pediatrics. 17th ed. (Illus.). 1100p. 1994. pap. 26.00 (*0-8385-3657-3*, A3657-2) Appleton & Lange.
Meres, Francis. Palladis Tamia. LC 72-9751. reprint ed. 35. 00 (*0-404-04309-7*) AMS Pr.
— Palladis Tamia. LC 39-10093. 1978. reprint ed. 50.00 (*0-8201-1188-0*) Schol Facsimiles.
Meresco, Donald. New Light on the Rapture. LC 80-67028. (Orig.). 1980. pap. 6.95 (*0-937078-00-X*) Bible Light.
Mereste, U., jt. auth. see Liivaku, U.
Mereu, R. F., et al, eds. Properties & Processes of Earth's Lower Crust, IUGG 6. (Geophysical Monograph Ser.: Vol. 51). 338p. 1989. 32.00 (*0-87590-456-4*) Am Geophysical.
***Mereweather-Thompson, Cornelius.** Christian Approaches to Dialogue with Other Faith Communities. LC 94-47432. 148p. 1995. text ed. 69.95 (*0-7734-8979-7*, Mellen Univ Pr) E Mellen.
Merewether, F. H. A Tour Through the Famine Districts of India. 1986. reprint ed. 34.00 (*0-8364-1615-5*, Pub. by Usha II) S Asia.

M

Merezhkovsky, Dimitri & Allen, Paul M. Atlantis-Europe: The Secret of the West. LC 71-157506. 456p. 1989. reprint ed. pap. 16.50 (*0-89345-243-2*, Steinerbks) Garber Comm.
Merezhkovsky, Dmitri S. Tolstoi As Man & Artist. LC 69-13996. 310p. 1970. reprint ed. text ed. 59.75 (*0-8371-4098-6*, METO, Greenwood Pr) Greenwood.
Merezhkovsky, Dmitry. Malen'Kaya Tereza. LC 84-22518. 208p. pap. 9.50 (*0-938920-43-X*) Hermitage.
Merezhkhovsky, D. S. & Hippius, Z. H. Dante, Boris Godunov, D. Merezhkovsky & Z. Hippius: Kinostsenariy, Predislovie T. Pachmuss. (Alternate Currents Ser.). 210p. (Orig.). (RUS.). 1991. pap. 20.00 (*0-922792-50-X*) Gnosis Pr.
Merfield, LeAnn. Surrounded by Wild Hogs. Van Treese, James B., ed. 30p. (J). 1994. pap. 6.95 (*1-56901-135-4*) NW Pub.
MERG Policy Group. Making Democracy Work: A Framework for Macroeconomic Policy in South Africa. 360p. 1994. pap. 16.95 (*1-86808-183-4*) OUP.
Mergal, Angel M., jt. ed. see Williams, George H.
Mergal Llera, Angel M. Federico Degetau. (Puerto Rico Ser.). 1979. lib. bdg. 59.95 (*0-8490-2916-3*) Gordon Pr.
Mergal, Margaret Z. Communication for Business. 238p. 1974. pap. 2.50 (*0-8477-2610-X*) U of PR Pr.
— Speech Improvement: Tapescripts for Business English Three-Zero-One. 2nd ed. 112p. 1979. pap. 3.50 (*0-8477-2611-8*) U of PR Pr.
Mergal, Margaret Z., ed. see Flechas, Genaro.
Mergault, Jean. Apollo Larousse French-English, English-French Dictionary: Dictionnaire Larousse Apollo Francais-Anglais-Francais. 1028p. (ENG & FRE.). 1993. 23.95 (*0-7859-4734-5*) Fr & Eur.
— New Larousse Adonis French-English-French. 532p. 1987. pap. write for info. (*0-7859-4735-3*) Fr & Eur.
— Nouveau Dictionnaire Larousse: Mars French-English, English-French. 478p. (ENG & FRE.). 1989. 49.95 (*0-7859-7651-5*, 2034016211) Fr & Eur.
Mergen, Bernard. Play & Playthings: A Reference Guide. LC 82-6139. (American Popular Culture Ser.). (Illus.). 288p. 1982. text ed. 59.95 (*0-313-22136-7*, MGT/, Greenwood Pr) Greenwood.
— Recreational Vehicles & Travel: A Resource Guide. LC 84-28974. (American Popular Culture Ser.). ix, 222p. 1985. text ed. 59.95 (*0-313-23672-0*, MER/, Greenwood Pr) Greenwood.
Mergen, Bernard, ed. Cultural Dimensions of Play, Games, & Sport. LC 86-10563. (Association for the Anthropological Study of Play: Vol. 10). (Illus.). 224p. 1986. text ed. 38.00x (*0-87322-078-1*, BMER0078) Human Kinetics.
Mergener, Robert. College Algebra: A Functions Approach. 5th ed. 480p. 1993. per. 49.95 (*0-8403-7764-9*) Kendall-Hunt.
Mergener, Robert J. Trigonometry: A Functions Approach. 304p. 1989. per. 29.95 (*0-8403-5308-1*) Kendall-Hunt.

Mergenhagen, Paula. Targeting Transitions: Marketing to Consumers During Life Changes. LC 93-73829. 253p. (Orig.). 1994. 39.95 (*0-936889-29-2*); pap. 29.95 (*0-936889-30-6*) American Demo. Millions of individuals go through major life transitions each year. Life transitions include graduating, getting married or remarried, becoming parents & grandparents, changing careers, getting divorced, moving, becoming caregivers & retiring. Once you understand the characteristics of people in transition, you can begin to discover the marketing opportunities created by life change. ALSO FROM AMERICAN DEMOGRAPHIC BOOKS: THE INSIDER'S GUIDE TO DEMOGRAPHIC KNOW-HOW: How to Find, Analyze & Use Information About Your Customers, 3rd edition (ISBN 0-936889-24-1; 1993, $49. 95); THE AMERICAN FORECASTER ALMANAC: 1994 BUSINESS EDITION (ISBN 0-936889-26-8; 1994, $29.95); HEALTH CARE CONSUMERS IN THE 1990s: A Handbook of Trends, Techniques, & Information Sources for Health Care Executives (ISBN 0-936889-18-7; 1993, $42.50); TARGETING FAMILIES: Marketing To & Through the New Family Structures (ISBN 0-936889-22-5, 1993, $39.50); THE BABY BUST: A Generation Comes of Age (ISBN 0-936889-20-9, 1993, $39.50); SEASONS OF BUSINESS: The Marketer's Guide to Consumer Behavior (ISBN 0-936889-12-8, 1991, $34.95); BEYOND MIND GAMES: The Marketing Power of Psychographics (ISBN 0-936889-08-X, 1991, $34.95); SELLING THE STORY: The Layman's Guide to Collecting & Communicating Demographic Information (ISBN 0-936889-14-4, 1992, $24.95; DESKTOP MARKETING: Lessons from America's Best (ISBN 0-936889-09-8, 1991, $39. 95); CAPTURING CUSTOMERS: How to Target the Hottest Markets of the 1990s (ISBN 0-936889-08-X, 1990, $34.95). American Demographic Books, P.O. Box 68, Ithaca, NY 14851. To order call: 1-800-828-1133. ***Publisher Provided Annotation.***

Mergenhagen, Stephan E. & Rosan, Burton, eds. Molecular Basis of Oral Microbial Adhesion. LC 84-20504. 242p. reprint ed. pap. 69.00 (*0-7837-4041-7*, 2043871) Bks Demand.
Mergenthaler, E. Textbank Systems. (Lecture Notes in Medical Informatics Ser.: Vol. 27). vi, 177p. 1985. pap. 31.00 (*0-387-15974-6*) Spr-Verlag.
***Mergner, T. & Hlavacka, F., eds.** Multisensory Control of Posture. (Illus.). (C). 1995. write for info. (*0-306-45101-8*, Plenum Pr) Plenum.
Merguet, H. Lexikon Zu Den Philosophischen Schriften Cicero's: Mit Angabe Saemtlicher Stellen, 3 vols., Set. (GER & LAT.). 1987. reprint ed. lib. bdg. 575.00 (*3-487-00052-0*, Pub. by Georg Olms GW) Lubrecht & Cramer.
Merguet, Hugo. Handlexikon Zu Cicero. Bd. 7. pap. write for info. (*0-318-70790-X*, Pub. by Georg Olms GW) Lubrecht & Cramer.
— Handlexikon Zu Cicero. Vol. 7. 816p. 1962. reprint ed. write for info. (*0-318-72050-7*, Pub. by Georg Olms GW) Lubrecht & Cramer.
— Lexikon Zu Den Philosophischen Schriften Ciceros, 3 vols., Set. 1971. reprint ed. write for info. (*0-318-72052-3*, Pub. by Georg Olms GW) Lubrecht & Cramer.
— Lexikon Zu Den Reden Des Cicero, 4 vols., Set. (Lexikon Zu den Schriften Cicero's Ser.: Teil 1). 3513p. 1973. write for info. (*3-487-05028-5*, Pub. by Georg Olms GW) Lubrecht & Cramer.
— Lexikon Zu Den Reden des Cicero, 4 vols., Set. 1962. reprint ed. write for info. (*0-318-72051-5*, Pub. by Georg Olms GW) Lubrecht & Cramer.
— Lexikon Zu Den Schriften Casars, 2 vols., Set. iv, 1142p. 1963. reprint ed. write for info. (*0-318-71175-3*, Pub. by Georg Olms GW); reprint ed. write for info. (*0-318-72049-3*, Pub. by Georg Olms GW) Lubrecht & Cramer.
— Lexikon Zu Den Schriften Casars. Entwicklung. Bd. 28-29. pap. write for info. (*0-318-70798-5*, Pub. by Georg Olms GW) Lubrecht & Cramer.
— Lexikon Zu Vergilius. Vol. 36. 786p. 1969. reprint ed. write for info. (*0-318-72053-1*, Pub. by Georg Olms GW) Lubrecht & Cramer.
— Lexikon Zu Vergilius Mit Angabe Samtlicher Stellen. Bd. 48. pap. write for info. (*0-318-70800-0*, Pub. by Georg Olms GW) Lubrecht & Cramer.
— Lexikon Zu Vergilius Mit Angabe Samtlicher Stellen. 786p. 1969. reprint ed. write for info. (*0-318-71176-1*, Pub. by Georg Olms GW) Lubrecht & Cramer.
— Lexikon Zu Vergilius Mit Angabe Samtlicher Stellen. Bd. 36. 786p. (GER.). 1969. reprint ed. pap. write for info. (*0-318-70519-2*, Pub. by Georg Olms GW); reprint ed. pap. write for info. (*0-318-71177-X*, Pub. by Georg Olms GW) Lubrecht & Cramer.
Mergui, Raphael & Simonnot, Philippe. Israel's Ayatollahs: Meir Kahane & the Far Right in Israel. 204p. 1990. 39. 95 (*0-86356-142-X*, Pub. by Saqi Books UK); pap. 14.95 (*0-86356-054-7*, Pub. by Saqi Bks UK) Interlink Pub.
Merha, Lester. Cheyenne Manhunt. (Orig.). 1980. pap. 1.75 (*0-8439-0742-8*) Dorchester Pub Co.
Merhav, M. Technological Dependence, Monopoly & Growth. 1969. 97.00 (*0-08-012754-1*, Pub. by Pergamon Repr UK) Franklin.
Merhige. The Richmond School Decision. LC 72-83394. pap. 6.00 (*0-912008-02-4*) Equity & Excel.
Meriage, Lawerence P. Russia & the First Serbian Revolution, 1804-1813. (Modern European History Ser.). 312p. 1987. lib. bdg. 15.00 (*0-8240-8058-0*) Garland.
***Meriam & Kraige.** Engineering Mechanics Dynamics & Engineering Mechanics Dynamics Problem Supplement. 1994. text ed. write for info. (*0-471-12407-9*) Wiley.
Meriam, J. L. & Kraige, L. G. Engineering Mechanics: SI-English Version, 2 vols., Vol. 1: Statics. 3rd ed. 544p. (C). 1992. text ed. write for info. (*0-471-90294-2*) Wiley.
— Engineering Mechanics: SI-English Version, 2 vols., Vol. 2. 3rd ed. 752p. (C). 1992. text ed. write for info. (*0-471-60293-0*) Wiley.
— Engineering Mechanics: SI-English Version, 2 vols., Vol. 2. 3rd ed. (C). 1992. Combined ed., Net. text ed. write for info. (*0-471-60295-7*) Wiley.
— Engineering Mechanics Statics & Problem Supplement. 1994. text ed. write for info. (*0-471-12183-5*) Wiley.
Meriam, James L. Statics. 2nd ed. LC 71-136719. (Illus.). 394p. reprint ed. pap. 112.30 (*0-317-08359-7*, 2019288) Bks Demand.
Meriam, Junius L. Normal School Education & Efficiency in Teaching. LC 77-177071. (Columbia University. Teachers College. Contributions to Education Ser.: No. 1). reprint ed. 37.50 (*0-404-55001-0*) AMS Pr.
Meriam, Lewis, jt. auth. see Bachman, George W.
Meriam-Webster Staff. Merriam-Webster's Collegiate Dictionary. 10th deluxe ed. LC 93-20206. 1600p. 1993. 29.95 (*0-87779-711-0*) Merriam-Webster Inc.
Merian, E., et al. Carcinogenic & Mutagenic Metal Compounds: Environmental & Analytical Chemistry & Biological Effects. (Current Topics In Environmental & Toxicological Chemistry Ser.: Vol. 8). 537p. 1985. text ed. 197.00 (*2-88124-022-4*) Gordon & Breach.
— Carcinogenic & Mutagenic Metal Compounds 2. 544p. 1988. text ed. 125.00 (*2-88124-663-X*) Gordon & Breach.
Merian, E., et al, eds. Chemistry & Fate of Organophosphorus Compounds: Selected Papers from the Workshop, The Free University, Amsterdam, June 18-19, 1986. (Current Topics In Environmental & Toxicological Chemistry Ser.: Vol. 12). xviii, 210p. 1987. text ed. 74.00 (*2-88124-215-4*) Gordon & Breach.
Merian, Ernest, ed. Metals & Their Compounds in the Environment: Occurrence, Analysis, Biological Relevance. LC 90-12615. 1438p. 1991. lib. bdg. 250.00 (*0-89573-562-8*) VCH Pubs.
Merian, Maria S. Flowers, Butterflies & Insects: All One Hundred Fifty-Four Engravings. 1991. pap. 10.95 (*0-486-26636-2*) Dover.
Meriani, S. & Palmonari, C., eds. Zirconia 'Eighty-Eight - Advances in Zirconia Science & Technology: Proceedings of the International Conference Held in Bologna, Italy, 16-17 December 1988, Organized by the Italian Ceramic Center of Bologna with Sponsorship. 382p. 1989. 101.00 (*1-85166-396-7*) Elsevier.
Meriaux, J. Etude Analytique et Comparative de la Vegetation Aquatique D'Etangs et Marais du Nord de la France. (Valle de la Sensee et Bassin Houillier du Nord-Pas-de-Calais) (Offprint from Documents Phytosociolgique Ser.). (FRE.). 1979. pap. 35.00 (*3-7682-1238-6*) Lubrecht & Cramer.
Mericq, Luis H. Antarctica: Chile's Claim. LC 86-23570. (Illus.). 137p. (Orig.). 1987. pap. 3.50 (*0-16-001657-6*, S/N 008-020-01103-7) USGPO.
Merida, Carlos. Carlos Merida: Graphic Works 1915-1981. (Illus.). (ENG & SPA.). 1981. pap. 5.00 (*0-89192-337-3*, Ctr Inter-Am Rel) Interbk Inc.
— Modern Mexican Artists: Critical Notes. LC 68-22931. (Essay Index Reprint Ser.). 1977. 23.95 (*0-8369-0701-9*) Ayer.
Meriden Britannia Co. Staff. The Meriden Britannia Silver-Plate Treasury: The Complete Catalog of 1886-87. (Antiques Ser.). (Illus.). 464p. 1983. reprint ed. pap. 24. 95 (*0-486-24364-8*) Dover.
Merideth, Laurence. VW Bus Custom Handbook. (Illus.). 128p. 1994. pap. 15.95 (*1-870979-47-8*, Pub. by Bay View Bks UK) Motorbooks Intl.
Merideth, Lee W. Civil War Times: 30 Year Comprehensive Index, April 1959 - February 1989. LC 90-62096. 228p. (Orig.). 1990. pap. 29.95 (*0-9626237-0-9*) Hist Indexes.
Merideth, Lee W., ed. Guide to Civil War Periodicals, 1991, Vol. I. LC 91-77550. 368p. (Orig.). 1991. 37.00 (*0-9626237-2-5*); pap. 32.00 (*0-9626237-1-7*) Hist Indexes.
Merideth, Robert. The Politics of the Universe: Edward Beecher, Abolition, & Orthodoxy. LC 68-21869. 1968. 17.50 (*0-8265-1123-6*) Vanderbilt U Pr.
Meridian Editors. The New American Desk Encyclopedia. 3rd rev. ed. LC 93-43754. (Illus.). 1376p. 1994. pap. 18. 95 (*0-452-01109-4*, Mer) NAL-Dutton.
Meridian Education Corporation Staff. The Nine to Five Survival Guide. (Illus.). 29p. (Orig.). 1993. (*1-56191-278-6*); pap. 3.50 (*1-56191-277-8*) Meridian Educ.
— Now Serving ... Every Customer. (Illus.). 29p. (Orig.). 1993. (*1-56191-284-0*); pap. 3.50 (*1-56191-285-9*) Meridian Educ.
— The Seven Day Professional Image Update. (Illus.). 50p. (Orig.). 1993. teacher ed (*1-56191-281-6*); student ed, pap. 3.50 (*1-56191-280-8*) Meridian Educ.
— Ten Basics of Business Etiquette. (Illus.). 4p. (Orig.). 1993. teacher ed (*1-56191-275-1*); pap. 3.50 (*1-56191-276-X*) Meridian Educ.
Merieux, Ch, ed. see International Symposium on Requirements for Poultry Virus Vaccines Staff.
Merila, Edith. Liability Insurance: The Purchaser's Guide. 36p. 1986. 5.00 (*0-932622-08-9*) Ctr Public Rep.
Merill, David W. & Reid, Roger H. Personal Styles & Effective Performance: Making Your Style Work for You. LC 80-70389. (Illus.). 284p. 1983. pap. 14.95 (*0-8019-6899-2*) Chilton.
Merill, Elmer D. Index Rafinesquianus: The Plant Names Published by C. S. Rafinesque with Reductions, & a Consideration of His Methods, Objectives & Attainments. Cohen, I. Bernard, ed. LC 79-7984. 1980. reprint ed. lib. bdg. 28.95 (*0-405-12566-6*) Ayer.
Merillat, H. C. Land & the Constitution in India. LC 79-127362. (Studies of the South Asian). 337p. reprint ed. 96.10 (*0-8357-9066-5*, 2015389) Bks Demand.
Merillat, Herbert C. Guadalcanal Remembered. 1990. pap. 3.95 (*0-380-76102-5*) Avon.
Merillat, Herbert L. Island: A History of the First Marine Division on Guadalcanal, August 7 - December 9, Nineteen Forty-Two. LC 79-18779. reprint ed. 25.00 (*0-89201-067-3*) Zenger Pub.
Merillot, J. M. 117 et al, jt. ed. see Jackson, D. V.
Merimee, Prosper. Les Ames du Purgatoire. 192p. (FRE.). 1973. 10.95 (*0-7859-0078-0*, M2466) Fr & Eur.
— Carmen & Other Tales. Jotcham, Nicholas, ed. & tr. by. (World's Classics Ser.). 400p. 1989. pap. 9.95 (*0-19-282242-X*) OUP.
— Carmen et Autres Nouvelles. (Illus.). 1965. write for info. (*0-318-63444-9*) Fr & Eur.
— Carmen et Treize Autres Nouvelles. (Folio Ser.: No. 560). (Illus.). 1965. pap. 9.95 (*2-07-036560-3*) Schoenhof.
— Carmen, Les Ames du Purgatoire. (FRE.). 1983. pap. 10. 95 (*0-7859-2969-X*, 2080702637) Fr & Eur.
— Le Carrosse du Saint-Sacrement. 256p. (FRE.). 1989. 18. 95 (*0-7859-1574-5*, 2903638225) Fr & Eur.
— Chronique du Regne de Charles Neuf. Josserand, Pierre, ed. (FRE.). 1979. pap. 4.95 (*0-7859-1446-3*, 2211054609) Fr & Eur.
— Colomba. (Coll. GF). 247p. (FRE.). 1992. pap. 11.95 (*0-7859-4765-5*) Fr & Eur.
— Colomba et Autre Nouvelles. (FRE.). 1973. pap. 10.95 (*0-7859-3064-7*) Fr & Eur.
— Correspondance, 17 tomes. Parturier, ed. Incl. 1832-1835(FRE.). 1972. pap. 50.00 (*0-7859-1522-2*, 2708926012); 1836-1840(FRE.). 658p. 1964. pap. 50.00 (*0-7859-1523-0*, 2708926020); 1844-1846(FRE.). 584p. 1943. pap. 45.00 (*0-7859-1524-9*, 2708926047); 1847-1849(FRE.). 567p. 1945. pap. 45.00 (*0-7859-1525-7*, 2708926055); 1850-1852(FRE.). 492p. 1946. pap. 40.00 (*0-7859-1526-5*, 2708926063); 1853-1855(FRE.). 560p. 1947. pap. 45.00 (*0-7859-1527-3*, 2708926071); 1856-1858(FRE.). 1964. pap. 50.00 (*0-7859-1611-3*, 270892608X); 1859-1860(FRE.). 574p. 1955. pap. 45.00 (*0-7859-1528-1*, 2708926098); 1860-1861(FRE.). 450p. 1961. pap. 35.00 (*0-7859-1529-X*, 2708926101); 1862-1863(FRE.). 596p. 1962. pap. 45.00 (*0-7859-1612-1*); 1864-1865(FRE.). 607p. 1964. pap. 52.00 (*0-7859-1530-3*, 2708926128); 1866-1867(FRE.). 650p. 1958. pap. 55.00 (*0-7859-1531-1*, 2708926136); 1868-1869(FRE.). 712p. 1960. pap. 60.00 (*0-7859-1532-X*, 2708926144); 1870(FRE.). 256p. 1960. pap. 25.00 (*0-7859-1533-8*, 2708926152); Supplement(FRE.). 468p. 1961. pap. 35.00 (*0-7859-1534-6*, 2708926160); Tome XVII. Supplement, Additions et Corrections, Index et Tables. (FRE.). 538p. 1962. pap. 50.00 (*0-685-35900-X*, 2708926179); (FRE.). 1964. Set pap. write for info. (*0-318-51970-4*) Fr & Eur.
— Etudes sur les Arts du Moyen-Age. (Illus.). 282p. (FRE.). 1967. pap. 10.95 (*0-7859-1391-2*, 2080101692) Fr & Eur.
— Lettres a Fanny Lagden. 12.50 (*0-686-54756-X*) Fr & Eur.
— Lokis. 164p. 19.95 (*0-686-54757-8*) Fr & Eur.
— Notes d'un Voyage En Corse, 1840. 110p. (FRE.). 1989. pap. 19.95 (*0-7859-1559-1*, 2876600358) Fr & Eur.
— Nouvelles Completes: Carmen et Treize Autres Nouvelles, 2 vols. Josserand, Pierre, ed. 1974. pap. 12.95 (*0-7859-2880-4*) Fr & Eur.
— Nouvelles Completes, Vol. 1: Colomba et 10 Autres Nouvelles. (FRE.). 1976. pap. 12.95 (*0-7859-3387-5*) Fr & Eur.
— Romans et Nouvelles, 2 tomes, Set. Parturier, ed. (Coll. Prestige). 69.90 (*0-685-34944-6*) Fr & Eur.
— Romans et Nouvelles: Charles IX; Mateo Falcone; Vision de Charles IX; Enlevement de la Redoute; Tamango; Federico, 2 tomes. Parturier, ed. 318p. (FRE.). 1969. pap. 29.95 (*0-7859-4875-9*, F68021) Fr & Eur.
— Tamango: Mateo Falcone et Autres Nouvelles. (FRE.). 1983. pap. 10.95 (*0-7859-2983-5*) Fr & Eur.
— Theatre: Romans et Nouvelles. (FRE.). 1979. lib. bdg. 110.00 (*0-8288-3566-7*, F68014) Fr & Eur.
— Theatre: Romans et Nouvelles. rev. ed. 54.95 (*0-686-56540-1*) Fr & Eur.
— Theatre de Clara Gazul. (FRE.). 1968. 7.95 (*0-7859-0028-4*, F68310) Fr & Eur.
— La Venus d'Ile et Autres Nouvelles: Dossier de Lectures. (FRE.). 1982. pap. 10.95 (*0-7859-2980-0*) Fr & Eur.
— La Venus d'Ille: Les Ames du Purgatoire. (Illus.). 135p. (FRE.). 1991. pap. 8.95 (*0-7859-4691-8*) Fr & Eur.
Merimee, Prosper & Auzas, Pierre M. Notes de Voyage. 785p. (FRE.). 1989. 89.95 (*0-7859-1560-5*, 2876600366) Fr & Eur.
Merimee, Prosper & Connes, Georges. Etudes Anglo-Americaines. 369p. (FRE.). 1930. pap. 79.95 (*0-7859-5382-5*) Fr & Eur.
Merimee, Prosper & Jourda, Pierre. Colomba. (Folio Ser.: No. 819). 188p. (FRE.). 1947. 10.95 (*2-07-036819-X*) Schoenhof.
— Colomba - Mateo Falcone. 188p. (FRE.). 1989. reprint ed. pap. 10.95 (*0-7859-3227-5*, 2266030728) Fr & Eur.
— La Jacquerie. (Horizons et Visages Ser.). 462p. 1931. pap. 79.95 (*0-7859-5384-1*) Fr & Eur.
Merimee, Prosper & Levaillant, Maurice. Mosaique. 530p. (FRE.). 1933. pap. 105.00 (*0-7859-0026-8*, F68008) Fr & Eur.
Merimee, Prosper & Mongault, Henri. Etudes de Litterature Russe: Gogol, Tourguenev..., Vol. 2. 608p. (FRE.). 1932. pap. 79.95 (*0-7859-5383-3*) Fr & Eur.
Merimee, Prosper & Trahard, Pierre. Lettre a Francisque Michel, 1848-1870. 238p. (FRE.). 1930. pap. 79.95 (*0-7859-5385-X*) Fr & Eur.
Merin, S., ed. see Jerusalem Conference on Impaired Vison in Childhood Staff.
Merin, Saul. Inherited Eye Diseases: Diagnosis & Clinical Management. 528p. 1991. 195.00 (*0-8247-7410-8*) Dekker.
Mering, T. A., jt. auth. see Adrianov, O. S.
Meringer, Rudolf & Mayer, Carl. Versprechen und Verlesen: Eine Psychologisch-Linguistische Studie. (Classics in Psycholinguistics Ser.: No. 2). liv, 207p. 1978. 65.00x (*90-272-0973-1*) Benjamins North Am.
Meringolo, Denise D., jt. auth. see Mayo, Edith P.
Meringolo, Vince, ed. see Technical Association of the Pulp & Paper Industry Staff.
Merington, Marguerite, ed. The Custer Story: The Life & Intimate Letters of General George A. Custer & His Wife Elizabeth. LC 86-19301. (Illus.). xii, 339p. 1987. reprint ed. pap. 11.95 (*0-8032-8138-2*, Bison Books) U of Nebr Pr.
***Merini, Alda.** A Rage of Love. Verdicchio, Pasquale, tr. (Prose Ser.: No. 30). 96p. 1995. 12.00 (*1-55071-013-3*) Guernica Editions.
***Merini, Rafika.** Two Major Francophone Women Writers: Assia Djebar & Leila Sebbar. LC 94-30420. (Francophone Cultures & Literatures Ser.: Vol. 5). 1995. write for info. (*0-8204-2635-0*) P Lang Pubs.
Merino. Diccionario de Dudas del Ingles. 4th ed. (ENG & SPA.). 1990. write for info. (*0-7859-3701-3*, 8428318123) Fr & Eur.
Merino, Ana, jt. auth. see Merino, Jose.

Merino, Barbara. Business Income & Price Levels: The Accounting, Legal, & Political Views. Brief, Richard P., ed. LC 80-1460. (Dimensions of Accounting Theory & Practice Ser.). 1980. lib. bdg. 31.95 (0-405-13482-7) Ayer.

Merino, Barbara J., et al, eds. Language & Culture in Learning: Teaching Spanish to Native Speakers of Spanish. LC 93-26831. 290p. 1994. 88.00 (0-7507-0230-3, Falmer Pr); pap. 26.00 (0-7507-0231-1, Falmer Pr) Taylor & Francis.

***Merino-Bustamante, Jose.** Diccionario Auxiliar del Traductor Espanol-Ingles. 2nd ed. 240p. 1991. pap. 39. 95 (0-7859-5041-9) Fr & Eur.

— Vocabulario Ingles-Espanol, Espanol-Ingles. 8th ed. 192p. (ENG & SPA.). 1990. pap. write for info. (0-7859-5082-6) Fr & Eur.

Merino, Donald N., jt. auth. see Lang, Hans J.

***Merino, Elias M., ed.** DX Centers: Donors in AlGaAs & Related Compounds. (Defect & Diffusion Forum Ser.: Vol. 108). (Illus.). 186p. (C). 1994. text ed. 96.00 (3-908450-03-9, Pub. by Trans Tech SZ) LPS Dist Ctr.

Merino, Hugo Z., jt. auth. see Petras, James F.

***Merino, J.** English-Spanish Dictionary of Word Usage. (ENG & SPA.). 1990. pap. 28.00 (0-7859-8959-5) Fr & Eur.

— English-Spanish Dictionary of Word Usage. 304p. 1990. pap. 28.00 (84-283-1812-3) IBD Ltd.

— Spanish-English - English-Spanish Thematic Dictionary. 597p. 1977. pap. 15.00 (84-283-0918-3) IBD Ltd.

Merino, Jose & Merino, Ana. Spanish-English Dictionary of Common Expressions. 187p. 1991. pap. 25.00 (84-86623-39-1) IBD Ltd.

Merino, Jose M. The Gold of Dreams. Lane, Helen, tr. 224p. (YA). (gr. 7 up). 1992. 14.95 (0-374-32692-4) FS&G.

— Gold of Dreams. (YA). 1994. pap. 4.95 (0-374-42584-1, Sunburst Bks) FS&G.

— La Orilla Oscura. 1995. pap. 16.95 (0-679-76348-1, Vin) Random.

Merino, Jose Maria. Beyond the Ancient Cities. Lane, Helen, tr. LC 93-35482. (J). 1994. 16.00 (0-374-34307-1) FS&G.

Merino-Rodriguez, Manuel, ed. Lexicon of Plant Pests & Diseases. (Elsevier Lexica Ser.: Vol. 7). 351p. (ENG, FRE, GER, ITA, LAT & SPA.). 1966. 95.00 (0-444-40393-0) Elsevier.

Merinoff, Linda, see Peg Bundy, pseud..

Merisotis, Jamie P., ed. The Changing Dimensions of Student Aid. LC 85-644752. (New Directions for Adult & Continuing Education Ser.: No. ACE 74). 1991. 16.95 (1-55542-790-1) Jossey-Bass.

Merisotis, Jamie P., jt. ed. see Lee, John B.

Merit Books Inc. Staff, ed. see Smith, Neil.

Merit, Don. Excellence in Customer Service Within the Graphic Arts Industry: A Nuts & Bolts Approach to Quality Customer Service Within the Printing Trade. 32p. (Orig.). (C). 1991. pap. 9.95 (0-933600-06-2) Graph Arts Pub.

Meritt, Benjamin D. Inscriptions from the Athenian Agora. (Excavations of the Athenian Agora Picture Bks.: No. 10). (Illus.). 32p. 1966. pap. 3.00 (0-87661-610-4) Am Sch Athens.

Meritt, Benjamin D. & Traill, John S. Inscriptions: The Athenian Councillors. LC 54-5697. (Athenian Agora Ser.: Vol. 15). (Illus.). xii, 486p. 1974. 55.00 (0-87661-215-X) Am Sch Athens.

Meritt, Benjamin D., et al. The Athenian Tribute Lists, Vol. 3. LC 75-10396. xx, 366p. 1968. reprint ed. 35.00 (0-87661-913-8) Am Sch Athens.

Meritt, Herbert D. Some of the Hardest Glosses in Old English. xiv, 130p. 1968. 22.50 (0-8047-0620-4) Stanford U Pr.

Meritt, Lucy S. History of the American School of Classical Studies at Athens, 1939-1980. LC 83-22495. (Illus.). xv, 411p. 1984. 15.00 (0-87661-942-1) Am Sch Athens.

Meritt, Roy D., comp. Dictionary of Coal Science & Technology. LC 86-31143. (Illus.). 384p. 1987. 48.00 (0-8155-1124-8) Noyes.

Merivale, Herman. Lectures on Colonization & Colonies Delivered Before the University of Oxford in 1839, 1840, & 1841. 2nd ed. LC 67-25954. (Reprints of Economic Classics Ser.). xix, 685p. 1967. reprint ed. 49. 50 (0-678-00273-8) Kelley.

Merivale, Patricia. Pan, the Goat-God: His Myth in Modern Times. LC 69-12729. (Harvard Studies in Comparative Literature: No. 30). 319p. reprint ed. pap. 91.00 (0-685-20534-7, 2029996) Bks Demand.

Meriweather, James, ed. Flags in the Dust. LC 90-25146. (William Faulkner Annotations to Novels Ser.). 209p. 1991. 22.00 (0-8240-4391-X) Garland.

Meriweather, Mary B. Illustrated Bulletin Boards. (Illus.). 58p. (Orig.). 1992. pap. 6.95 (1-56794-031-5, C2280) Star Bible.

Meriwether, Colyer. History of Higher Education in South Carolina, with a Sketch of the Free School System. LC 75-187369. (Illus.). 283p. 1972. reprint ed. 16.50 (0-87152-097-4) Reprint.

***Meriwether, Dan.** The Macintosh Web Browser Kit. Date not set. text ed. 29.95 (0-471-11818-4) Wiley.

Meriwether, David. My Life in the Mountains & on the Plains: The Newly Discovered Autobiography. Griffen, Robert A., ed. LC 65-11240. (American Exploration & Travel Ser.: 46). 324p. reprint ed. pap. 92.40 (0-317-26252-1, 2052132) Bks Demand.

***Meriwether, Elizabeth A.** Recollections of Ninety-Two Years 1824-1916. LC 94-23586. (Illus.). 256p. (Orig.). 1994. pap. 14.95 (0-939009-84-6) EPM Pubns.

Meriwether, J. W., ed. Atmospheric Sciences in Antartica. 366p. 1989. 22.00 (0-685-38493-4) Am Geophysical.

Meriwether, Louise. Daddy Was a Number Runner. LC 86-9019. 240p. 1986. pap. 10.95 (0-935312-57-9) Feminist Pr.

— Fragments of the Ark. Rosenman, Jane, ed. 352p. 1995. pap. 10.00 (0-671-79948-7, WSP) PB.

Meriwether, Robert L. The Expansion of South Carolina: 1729-1765. LC 73-16348. (Perspectives in American History Ser.: No. 17). (Illus.). viii, 294p. 1974. reprint ed. lib. bdg. 39.50 (0-87991-345-2) Porcupine Pr.

Merk, Ann & Merk, Jim. Clouds. LC 94-13324. (Weather Report Ser.). (J). (gr. 2 up). 1994. write for info. (0-86593-389-8) Rourke Corp.

— Rain, Snow, & Ice. LC 94-13325. (Weather Report Ser.). (J). (gr. 3 up). 1994. write for info. (0-86593-390-1) Rourke Corp.

— Storms. LC 94-13321. (Weather Report Ser.). (J). (gr. 3 up). 1994. write for info. (0-86593-386-3) Rourke Corp.

— Studying Weather. LC 94-13320. (Weather Report Ser.). (J). (gr. 3 up). 1994. write for info. (0-86593-385-5) Rourke Corp.

— The Weather & Us. LC 94-13322. (Weather Report Ser.). (J). (gr. 3 up). 1994. write for info. (0-86593-387-1) Rourke Corp.

— Weather Signs. LC 94-13323. (Weather Report Ser.). (J). (gr. 3 up). 1994. write for info. (0-86593-388-X) Rourke Corp.

Merk, Frederick. Economic History of Wisconsin During the Civil War Decade. LC 72-180453. 414p. 1971. reprint ed. 10.00 (0-87020-117-4) State Hist Soc Wis.

— Manifest Destiny & Mission in American History. 304p. (Orig.). (C). 1995. pap. text ed. 14.95 (0-674-54805-1) HUP.

— Manifest Destiny & Mission in American History. (Orig.). 1966. pap. text ed. 4.95 (0-07-553693-5) McGraw.

— The Oregon Question: Essays in Anglo-American Diplomacy & Politics. LC 67-14345. 441p. reprint ed. pap. 126.30 (0-7837-2300-8, 2057388) Bks Demand.

Merk, Frederick & Merk, Lois B. Fruits of Propaganda in the Tyler Administration. LC 79-135547. 269p. 1971. 23.95 (0-674-32676-8) HUP.

— Manifest Destiny & Mission in American History: A Reinterpretation. LC 82-25146. ix, 265p. (C). 1983. reprint ed. text ed. 41.50 (0-313-23844-8, MERM, Greenwood Pr) Greenwood.

Merk, Frederick, ed. see Simpson, George.

Merk, H. F., jt. auth. see Bickers, D. R.

Merk, Jim, jt. auth. see Merk, Ann.

Merk, Lois B., jt. auth. see Merk, Frederick.

Merk, Otto & Wolter, Michael, eds. Im Zeichen des Kreuzes: Aufsatze von Erich Dinkler. (Beiheft zur Zeitschrift fuer die Neuetestamentliche Wissenschaft Ser.: No. 61). x, 578p. (GER.). (C). 1992. lib. bdg. 167. 70 (3-11-013017-3) De Gruyter.

Merkatz, Irwin R. & Thompson, Joyce E., eds. New Perspectives on Prenatal Care. 656p. 1990. 79.00 (0-685-48200-6) Elsevier.

Merkatz, Irwin R., et al, eds. New Perspectives on Prenatal Care. 670p. 1990. 79.00 (0-685-45394-4) Elsevier.

Merke, F. History & Iconography of Endemic Goitre & Cretinism. 330p. 1984. 68.00 (3-456-81189-6) Hogrefe & Huber Pubs.

Merkel-Holguin, Lisa A. & Sobel, Audrey J. The Child Welfare Stat Book 1993. 1993. 32.95 (0-87868-531-6) Child Welfare.

Merkel, Ingrid, jt. ed. see Debus, Allen G.

Merkel, J. Die Vegetation in Gebiet des Messtischblattes 6434 Hersbruck. (Dissertationes Botanicae Ser.: No. 51). (Illus.). 176p. (GER.). 1980. pap. text ed. 30.00 (3-7682-1235-1) Lubrecht & Cramer.

Merkel, Jayne. In Its Place: The Architecture of Carl Strauss & Ray Roush. (Illus.). 60p. 1985. pap. 15.95 (0-917562-36-4) Contemp Arts.

— Michael Graves & Riverbend: A Summer Pavillion for the Cincinnati Symphony Orchestra. (Illus.). 1987. 15.95 (0-917562-33-X) Contemp Arts.

Merkel, Jeanne S. Nine Boats & Nine Kids: A True Chronicle. LC 84-19422. (Illus.). 162p. (Orig.). 1984. 14. 95 (0-931447-01-1); pap. 9.95 (0-931447-00-3) Ledge Bks.

Merkel, Judi K., ed. Indiana State Fair Cookbook: Hoosier Heritage Edition. 246p. 1993. spiral bd. 17.95 (0-89730-230-3, State Fair Bks) Blue-Rib Grp.

***Merkel, Keith W. & Hoffman, Robert S.** Proceedings of the California Felgrass Symposium, Chula Vista, CA, May 27 & 28, 1988. 78p. 1990. pap. 17.50 (0-931950-02-3) Sweetwater River Pr.

***Merkel, Richard A.** Well Log Formation Evaluation. (Continuing Education Course Note Ser.: No. 14). (Illus.). vi, 82p. 1979. pap. 9.00 (0-89181-163-X) AAPG.

Merkel, Robert A., jt. auth. see Boggs, Donald L.

Merkel, Robert S. Textile Product Serviceability: By Specification. 400p. (C). 1991. write for info. (0-02-380565-X) Macmillan.

Merkel, Stephanie, tr. see Khakhina, Liya N.

Merkel, Susan L. Certifiably Bulimic. LC 91-14993. 136p. 1991. pap. 12.95 (0-942963-15-6) Distinctive Pub.

Merkelio, R., ed. see Ovid.

Merken, Melvin. Physical Science with Modern Applications. 4th ed. 576p. (C). 1989. text ed. 48.00 (0-03-023363-1) SCP.

Merken, Robert B. Zombie Jamboree. LC 86-745. write for info. (0-688-01949-8, Quill) Morrow.

Merker, Hannah. Listening. 192p. 1994. 20.00 (0-06-017054-9, HarpT) HarpC.

— Listening: Ways of Hearing in a Silent World. 208p. 1995. pap. 12.00 (0-06-092592-2, PL) HarpC.

Merker, Laura, et al. The Clinical Career Ladder: Planning & Implementation. 176p. 1985. pap. 19.95 (0-8261-4611-2) Springer Pub.

Merker, Milton, jt. ed. see Shen, Benjamin S.

Merkert, Joern, ed. David Smith: Sculpture & Drawings. (Illus.). 192p. 1986. 60.00 (3-7913-0793-2, Pub. by Prestel) TeNeues.

Merkert, Joern, jt. ed. see Nash, Steven A.

Merkhofer, Miley W. Decision Science & Social Risk Management. (C). 1986. lib. bdg. 97.50 (90-277-2275-7) Kluwer Ac.

Merkhoher, Miley W., jt. auth. see Covello, Vincent T.

Merkies, A. H. Selection of Models by Forecasting Intervals. Van Holten-De Wolff, M., tr. LC 73-83565. 1973. lib. bdg. 62.00 (90-277-0342-6) Kluwer Ac.

Merkin, Richard, intro. Jazz Age: As Seen Through the Eyes of Ralph Barton, Miguel Covarrubias & John Held, Jr. (Illus.). 1968. 2.50 (0-911517-56-1, 63-56465) Mus of Art RI.

Merkin, Rober. Tolley's Insurance Handbook. 350p. (C). 1994. 105.00 (0-85459-806-5) St Mut.

Merkin, Robert. Arbitration Law. 1991. ring bd. 390.00 (1-85044-367-X) Lloyds London Pr.

— Richards & Butler on Latent Damage. (C). 1987. 390.00 (0-685-32752-3, Pub. by Witherby & Co UK) St Mut.

— Richards Butler on Latent Damage. 1987. 90.00 (1-85044-128-6) Lloyds London Pr.

Merkin, Robert M. Essays in Memory of Professor F. H. Lawson. Wallington, Peter, ed. 1986. 58.00 (0-406-50030-4, U.K.) Butterworth Legal Pubs.

Merkitch, Warren. Beachcomber's Handbook. 1984. 4.00 (0-89316-605-7) Exanimo Pr.

Merkl, Peter H. German Unification in the European Context. LC 92-31665. 464p. (C). 1993. 65.00 (0-271-00921-7); pap. 18.95 (0-271-00922-5) Pa St U Pr.

— Political Violence under the Swastika: 581 Early Nazis. 1975. 99.50 (0-691-07561-1); pap. 29.95 (0-691-10028-4) Princeton U Pr.

— Political Violence under the Swastika: 581 Early Nazis. LC 74-12143. 751p. 1975. reprint ed. pap. 180.00 (0-7837-8593-3, 2049408) Bks Demand.

Merkl, Peter H., ed. The Federal Republic of Germany at Forty. 496p. 1989. 55.00x (0-8147-5445-7); pap. 22.50x (0-8147-5446-5) NYU Pr.

— The Federal Republic of Germany at Forty-Five: Union without Unity. LC 94-7526. 400p. 1994. 55.00 (0-8147-5514-3); pap. 20.00 (0-8147-5515-1) NYU Pr.

— New Local Centers in Centralized States. (Illus.). 356p. (Orig.). 1985. lib. bdg. 57.00 (0-8191-4535-1); pap. text ed. 29.00 (0-8191-4536-X) U Pr of Amer.

— Political Violence & Terror: Motifs & Motivations. LC 85-24505. 400p. 1986. 48.00 (0-520-05605-1) U CA Pr.

Merkl, Peter H. & Smart, Ninian, eds. Religion & Politics in the Modern World. 296p. 1983. pap. 16.50 (0-8147-5393-0) NYU Pr.

Merkl, Peter H. & Weinberg, Leonard, eds. Encounters with the Contemporary Radical Right. LC 92-31974. (New Directions in Comparative Politics Ser.). 277p. 1993. text ed. 72.00 (0-8133-1445-3) Westview.

— Encounters with the Contemporary Radical Right. (New Directions in Comparative Politics Ser.). 277p. (C). 1993. pap. text ed. 21.50 (0-8133-1446-1) Westview.

Merkl, Peter H., jt. ed. see Lawson, Kay.

Merkle, Charles L., ed. JTEC Panel Report on Space & Transatmospheric Propulsion Technology. (JTEC Panel Reports). xviii, 211p. 1990. pap. write for info. (1-883712-22-X, JTEC) Intl Tech Res.

Merkle, George, jt. auth. see Vermont Historical Society Staff.

Merkle, John C. Abraham Joshua Heschel: Exploring His Life & Thought. 184p. 1985. text ed. 19.95 (0-02-920970-6) Macmillan.

— The Genesis of Faith: The Depth Psychology of Abraham Joshua Heschel. 291p. 1985. text ed. 21.95 (0-02-920990-0) Macmillan.

Merkle, Judith. Committed by Choice. 158p. (Orig.). 1993. 9.95 (0-8146-2072-8) Liturgical Pr.

Merkle-Scotland, Mary, jt. auth. see Ekstrom, Reynolds.

Merkle, Sebastian, ed. Die Matrikel der Universitat Wurzburg, 1582-1830, 2 vols., Pt. 1. (Alumni of German Universities Ser.). 1990. reprint ed. 130.00 (0-8115-3811-7) Periodicals Srv.

Merkley, Christopher. Biography of Christopher Merkley: Written by Himself. LC 70-38363. (Select Bibliographies Reprint Ser.). 1977. reprint ed. 16.95 (0-8369-6780-1) Ayer.

Merkley, Jay Peter. Marksmanship with Rifles: A Basic Guide. 2nd ed. (Illus.). 67p. (C). 1984. pap. text ed. 5. 95x (0-89641-141-9) American Pr.

Merkley, Paul. The Greek & Hebrew Orgins of Our Idea of History. LC 87-11136. (Toronto Studies in Theology: Vol. 32). 312p. 1987. lib. bdg. 99.95 (0-88946-777-3) E Mellen.

— Italian Tonaries. (Wissenschaftliche Abhandlungen-Musicological Studies: Vol. 48). 246p. (ENG.). 1988. 60. 00 (0-931902-57-6) Inst Mediaeval Mus.

— Modal Assignment in Northern Tonaries. (Wissenschaftliche Abhandlungen-Musicological Studies: Vol. 56). 1992. lib. bdg. 100.00 (0-931902-72-X) Inst Mediaeval Mus.

— Reinhold Niebuhr: A Political Account. 304p. 1975. 29. 95 (0-7735-0216-5, Pub. by McGill CN) U of Toronto Pr.

— Reinhold Niebuhr: A Political Account. LC 76-351874. 303p. reprint ed. pap. 86.40 (0-7837-6912-1, 2046742) Bks Demand.

Merkley, Paul, jt. auth. see Bailey, Terence.

Merkley, Paul, jt. ed. see Gillingham, Bryan.

Merkley, Steve R., jt. ed. see Billings, Beverley.

Merkli, R., jt. auth. see Margairaz, A.

Merkling, Helet, jt. auth. see Greenberg, Marcia.

Merklinger. Indian Islamic Architecture: Deccan 1347-1686. 1981. 75.00 (0-85668-193-8, Pub. by Aris & Phillips UK) David Brown.

Merklinger, Harold, ed. Progress in Underwater Acoustics. 816p. 1987. 145.00 (0-306-42552-1, Plenum Pr) Plenum.

Merklinger, Philip M. Philosophy, Theology, & Hegel's Berlin Philosophy of Religion, 1821-1827. 250p. 1993. 59.50 (0-7914-1491-4); pap. 19.95 (0-7914-1492-2) State U NY Pr.

Merkow, L. P. & Slifkin, M., eds. Oncogenic Adenoviruses. (Progress in Experimental Tumor Research Ser.: Vol. 18). 1973. 78.50 (3-8055-1348-8) S Karger.

Merkow, M. S. Breaking Through Technical Jargon. 1990. pap. 23.95 (0-442-00151-7) Van Nos Reinhold.

Merks, J. W. Sampling & Weighting of Bulk Solids. (Bulk Materials Handling Ser.: Vol. 4). 1985. 68.00 (0-87849-053-1, Pub. by Trans Tech GW) LPS Dist Ctr.

Merkur, Dan. Gnosis: An Esoteric Tradition of Mystical Visions & Unions. LC 92-35390. (SUNY Series in Western Esoteric Traditions). 397p. (C). 1993. 59.50 (0-7914-1619-4); pap. 19.95 (0-7914-1620-8) State U NY Pr.

Merkur, Daniel. Becoming Half Hidden: Shamanism & Initiation among the Inuit. LC 92-16453. 376p. 1992. 57.00 (0-8153-0783-7, H1559) Garland.

— Powers Which We Do Not Know: The Gods & Spirits of the Inuit. LC 91-6394. 288p. (C). 1991. pap. text ed. 19. 95 (0-89301-148-7) U of Idaho Pr.

Merkuriev, S. P., jt. auth. see Fadeev, L. D.

Merkx, Gilbert W., jt. ed. see Elkin, Judith L.

Merlan, F., ed. see Merlan, Philip.

Merlan, Francesca. Mangarayi. (Descriptive Grammars Ser.). 264p. 1986. pap. 72.50 (0-7099-3567-6, Pub. by Croom Helm UK) Routledge Chapman & Hall.

Merlan, Francesca & Rumsey, Alan. Ku Waru: Language & Segmentary Politics in the Western Nebilyer Valley, Papua New Guinea. (Studies in the Social & Cultural Foundations of Language). (Illus.). 224p. (C). 1991. 69. 95 (0-521-32339-8) Cambridge U Pr.

Merlan, Francesca C. A Grammar of Wardaman: A Language of the Northern Territory of Australia. LC 93-36161. (Grammar Library: No. 11). xxi, 621p. (C). 1994. lib. bdg. 218.70 (3-11-012942-6) Mouton.

Merlan, Philip. Kleine Philosophische Schriften. Merlan, F., ed. (Collectanea Ser.: Bd. XX). xiv, 849p. 1976. write for info. (3-487-05727-1, Pub. by Georg Olms GW) Lubrecht & Cramer.

Merle, tr. see Bowman, Robert P.

Merle d'Aubigne, Jean H. History of the Reformation of the Sixteenth Century, 5 vols., Set. White, H., tr. LC 83-45666. reprint ed. 225.00 (0-404-19816-3) AMS Pr.

Merle d'Augbine, Jean H. History of the Reformation in Europe in the Time of Calvin, 8 vols., Set. Cates, W. L., tr. LC 83-45624. reprint ed. 395.00 (0-404-19842-2) AMS Pr.

Merle-Fishman, Carole, jt. auth. see Katsh, Shelley.

Merle, M., jt. ed. see Benichoux, R.

Merle, Marcel. The Sociology of International Relations. Parkin, Dorothy, tr. LC 86-26360. 429p. 1987. 69.95 (0-907582-44-3); pap. 19.95 (0-907582-45-1) Berg Pubs.

Merle, Pierre. Robert Dictionnaire des Mots Contemporains. 232p. (FRE.). 1989. pap. 14.95 (0-7859-4759-0, M2320) Fr & Eur.

Merle, Robert. Derriere la Vitre. (FRE.). 1974. pap. 15.95 (0-7859-4038-3) Fr & Eur.

— Les Hommes Proteges. 440p. (FRE.). 1989. pap. 15.95 (0-7859-4317-X, 2070381463) Fr & Eur.

— L' Ile. (FRE.). 1974. pap. 17.95 (0-7859-4030-8) Fr & Eur.

— Malevil. (FRE.). 1983. pap. 19.95 (0-7859-4179-7) Fr & Eur.

— La Mort Est Mon Metier. (FRE.). 1976. pap. 11.95 (0-7859-4058-8) Fr & Eur.

— Oscar Wilde. LC 79-8071. (FRE.). reprint ed. 43.50 (0-404-18381-6) AMS Pr.

— Vittoria. 1990. 19.95 (0-15-193915-2) HarBrace.

— Vittoria. large type ed. LC 90-29258. 724p. 1991. reprint ed. lib. bdg. 20.95 (1-56054-122-9) Thorndike Pr.

— Week-End a Zuydcoote. 256p. (FRE.). 1976. pap. 10.95 (0-7859-4057-X, 2070367754) Fr & Eur.

Merleau-Ponty, M. Eloge de la Philosophie, et Autres Essais. (FRE.). 1989. pap. 18.95 (0-7859-2816-2) Fr & Eur.

— Phenomenologie de la Perception. (FRE.). 1976. pap. 28. 95 (0-7859-2747-6) Fr & Eur.

— Phenomenology of Perception. Smith, Colin J., tr. (C). 1981. pap. 32.50 (0-391-02551-1) Routledge.

— Reumes de Cours au College de France, 1952-60. (FRE.). 1982. pap. 16.95 (0-7859-2737-9) Fr & Eur.

— La Structure du Comportement. (FRE.). 1990. pap. 21.95 (0-7859-3015-9) Fr & Eur.

— Structure of Behavior. Fisher, Alden, tr. 288p. 1983. reprint ed. pap. 19.50 (0-8207-0163-7) Duquesne.

— Le Visible et l'Invisible: Notes de Travail. (FRE.). 1979. pap. 22.95 (0-7859-2744-1) Fr & Eur.

Merleau-Ponty, Maurice. Adventures of the Dialectic. Bien, Joseph J., tr. LC 72-96697. (Studies in Phenomenology & Existential Philosophy). 237p. (C). 1973. 29.95 (0-8101-0404-0); pap. 17.95 (0-8101-0596-9) Northwestern U Pr.

— Consciousness & the Acquisition of Language. Silverman, Hugh J., tr. LC 73-76807. (Studies in Phenomenology & Existential Philosophy). 108p. (C). 1973. 26.95 (0-8101-0417-2); pap. 12.95 (0-8101-0597-7) Northwestern U Pr.

— Eloge de la Philosophie et Autres Essais. (Folio Essais Ser.: No. 118). (FRE.). pap. 14.95 (2-07-032510-5) Schoenhof.

— Humanism & Terror: An Essay on the Communist Problem. LC 71-84797. 1969. pap. 17.00x (0-8070-0277-1, BPA6) Beacon Pr.

— In Praise of Philosophy & Other Essays. Edie, James & O'Neill, John, trs. 199p. 1988. reprint ed. pap. 14.95 (0-8101-0796-1) Northwestern U Pr.

An Asterisk (*) at the beginning of an entry indicates that the title is appearing in BIP for the first time.

— Oeil et l'Esprit. (Folio Essais Ser.: No. 13). 92p. (FRE.). 1985. pap. 9.95 (*2-07-032290-4*) Schoenhof.

— Phenomenologie de la Perception. (Tel Ser.). 531p. (FRE.). 1945. pap. 23.95 (*2-07-029337-8*) Schoenhof.

— Phenomenology of Perception: An Introduction. 416p. 1995. pap. 19.95 (*0-415-04556-8*, C0559) Routledge.

— Primacy of Perception. Edie, James M., ed. Cobb, William et al, trs. (Studies in Phenomenology & Existential Philosophy). 228p. 1964. 29.95 (*0-8101-0165-3*); pap. 14.95 (*0-8101-0164-5*) Northwestern U Pr.

— The Prose of the World. Lefort, Claude, ed. O'Neill, John, tr. LC 72-96699. (Studies in Phenomenology & Existential Philosophy). 154p. (C). 1973. text ed. 29.95 (*0-8101-0412-1*); pap. 14.95 (*0-8101-0615-9*) Northwestern U Pr.

— Sense & Non-Sense. Dreyfus, Herbert L. & Dreyfus, Patrica A, trs. (Studies in Phenomenology & Existential Philosophy). 193p. 1964. 32.95 (*0-8101-0167-X*); pap. 15.95 (*0-8101-0166-1*) Northwestern U Pr.

— Signs. McCleary, Richard C., tr. (Studies in Phenomenology & Existential Philosophy). 355p. 1964. pap. 17.95 (*0-8101-0253-6*) Northwestern U Pr.

— Struktur des Verhaltens. (Phaenomenologisch-Psychologische Forschungen Ser.: Vol. 13). xxvi, 278p. (C). 1976. text ed. 75.40 (*3-11-004469-2*) De Gruyter.

— Visible & the Invisible. Lingis, Alphonso, tr. LC 68-30125. (Studies in Phenomenology & Existential Philosophy). 282p. 1969. 26.95 (*0-8101-0026-6*); pap. 17.95 (*0-8101-0457-1*) Northwestern U Pr.

— Visible et l'Invisible. (Tel Ser.). 360p. (FRE.). 1964. pap. 17.95 (*2-07-028625-8*) Schoenhof.

— Vorlesungen I: Schrift fuer die Kandidatur Am College De France: Lob der Philosophie; Vorlesungszusammenfassungen (College De France 1952-1960) Die Humanwissenschaften und die Phaenomenologie. Metraux, Alexandre, tr. (Phaenomenologisch-Psychologische Forschungen Ser.: No. 9). (GER.). (C). 1972. 115.40 (*3-11-001823-3*) De Gruyter.

*__Merli, Giorgio.__ Breakthrough Management: How to Convert Objectives into Results. 1995. text ed. 39.95 (*0-471-95351-2*) Wiley.

— Co-Makership: The New Supply Strategy for Manufacturers. Lubin, J., tr. LC 91-3436. 265p. 1991. 40.00 (*0-915299-84-4*) Prod Press.

Merli, P. G. & Vittori, M. Electron Microscopy in Materials Science: Proceedings of the International School. 500p. 1993. text ed. 121.00 (*981-02-0924-X*) World Scientific Pub.

Merlihan, James, ed. Philadelphia Images: Philadelphia People, Places & Pastimes by Artists from the University of the Arts. LC 90-71312. (Illus.). 184p. 1990. 40.00 (*0-9627916-0-1*) Univ of Arts Pr.

Merlin. Early History of King Arthur, 2 vols., Pts. I & IV. Wheatley, H. B., ed. (EETS, OS Ser.: Nos 10, 21, 36, 112). 1972. reprint ed. 70.00 (*0-527-00010-8*) Periodicals Srv.

— Early History of King Arthur, 2 vols., Pts. II & III. Wheatley, H. B., ed. (EETS, OS Ser.: Nos 10, 21, 36, 112). 1972. reprint ed. 70.00 (*0-527-00011-6*) Periodicals Srv.

Merlin, Ann, jt. auth. see Dumond, K. J.

Merlin, Arnaud, jt. auth. see Bergerot, Franck.

*__Merlin, Christa.__ Snowflame. large type ed. 304p. 1995. 23.95 (*0-7089-3224-X*) Ulverscroft.

Merlin, Christa, ed. Forever Eden. large type ed. (Dales Romance Ser.). 280p. 1993. pap. 16.95 (*1-85389-369-2*, Medcom-Trainex) Ulverscroft.

Merlin, Mark. Natural History of Marijuana. 1994. pap. 14.95 (*0-932551-15-7*) Quick Am Pub.

Merlin, Mark D. On the Trail of the Ancient Opium Poppy. LC 80-70994. (Illus.). 320p. 1984. 50.00 (*0-8386-3097-9*) Fairleigh Dickinson.

Merlin, Pierre & Choay, Francoise. Dictionnaire de l'Urbanisme et de l'Amenagement. 744p. (FRE.). 1988. 195.00 (*0-8288-2359-6*, M 414) Fr & Eur.

Merlin, Samuel, ed. Big Powers & the Present Crisis in the Middle East. LC 68-8864. 201p. 1975. 22.50 (*0-8386-7349-X*) Fairleigh Dickinson.

Merlin-Walch, Olivier & Amoros Rica, Narciso. Dictionnaire Juridique, Diccionario Juridico: French - Spanish, Spanish - French. 3rd ed. 933p. (FRE & SPA.). 1993. 195.00 (*0-7859-1078-6*, S36030) Fr & Eur.

Merlin-Walch, Olivier & Rica, Amoros. Diccionario Juridico Frances-Espanol-Frances. 800p. (FRE & SPA.). 1986. 175.00 (*0-8288-0407-9*, S 36030) Fr & Eur.

*__Merling, David & Geraty, Lawrence T., eds.__ Hesban after 25 Years. LC 94-77622. (Illus.). xxiv, 379p. (Orig.). 1994. pap. 14.95 (*0-9642060-0-5*) Inst of Archaeol.

Merlini, L., et al, eds. Current Concepts in Childhood Spinal Muscular Atrophy. (Illus.). 227p. 1989. 101.00 (*0-387-82131-7*) Spr-Verlag.

Merlini, Marco P., ed. Surgery of the Arteria Profunda Femuralis. LC 94-12558. 1994. write for info. (*0-387-58067-0*) Spr-Verlag.

*__Merlis, Brian.__ Brooklyn - The Way It Was. 250p. Date not set. 39.95 (*1-878741-21-7*); pap. 24.95 (*1-878741-20-9*) Israelowitz Pub.

— Welcome Back to Brooklyn. 172p. 19.95 (*1-878741-14-4*) Israelowitz Pub.

Merlis, Mark. American Studies. LC 94-6593. 1994. 21.95 (*0-395-68992-9*) HM.

Merlo, Alida V. Women, Law & Social Control. 324p. (C). 1994. pap. write for info. (*0-02-380567-6*) Macmillan.

Merlo, Alida V., jt. ed. see Benekos, Peter J.

*__Merlo, Catherine M.__ Legacy of a Shared Vision: The History of Calcot. 192p. 1995. lib. bdg. 29.95 (*0-9645117-0-3*) Calcot.

Merlo, Juan C. Y Equipo. Diccionario Enciclopedico: El Ateneo. 3rd ed. (SPA.). 995.00 (*0-7859-0709-2*, S-33045) Fr & Eur.

Merlo, Vicente A. Diccionario de Historia Eclesiastica de Espana, Vol. 3. 2nd ed. 128p. 1990. pap. 15.95 (*0-7859-5157-1*) Fr & Eur.

— Diccionario de Historia Eclesiastica de Espana, Vol. 4. 4th ed. 224p. 1990. pap. 14.95 (*0-7859-5158-X*, S19856) Fr & Eur.

Merlonghi, Ferdianando, jt. auth. see Merlonghi, Franca C.

Merlonghi, Ferdinando, jt. auth. see Merlonghi, Franca C.

Merlonghi, Ferdinando, et al. Oggi in Italia: A First Course in Italian. 2nd ed. LC 81-85378. 1982. reel tape 270.00 (*0-685-42421-9*) HM.

Merlonghi, Franca, et al. Racconti di oggi. (C). 1991. write for info. (*0-395-55423-3*) HM Soft Schl Col Div.

— Oggi in Italia. 4th ed. (C). 1991. write for info. (*0-395-43223-5*) HM Soft Schl Col Div.

Merlonghi, Franca C. & Merlonghi, Ferdianando. Andiamo Avanti: Attualita e Racconti. 200p. (C). 1991. pap. text ed. write for info. (*0-13-036542-4*) P-H.

Merlonghi, Franca C. & Merlonghi, Ferdinando. Andiamo Avanti! Lingua e Cultura. 352p. (C). 1992. pap. text ed. write for info. (*0-13-031451-X*) P-H.

Merlonghi, Franca C., jt. auth. see Valencia, Pablo.

Merluzzi, Thomas V., ed. see Glass, Carol R. & Genest, Myles.

Merluzzi, Thomas V., et al, eds. Cognitive Assessment. LC 80-24870. (Guilford Clinical Psychology & Psychotherapy Ser.). (Illus.). 548p. reprint ed. pap. 156.20 (*0-7837-0689-8*, 2041022) Bks Demand.

*__Merluzzi, Vincent J. & Adams, Julian, eds.__ The Search for Anti-Inflammatory Drugs: Case Histories from Concept to Clinic. LC 95-1583. 1995. write for info. (*0-8176-3685-4*) Birkhauser.

Merluzzi, Vincent J., jt. ed. see Adams, Julian.

Merlyn, Vaughan, et al. Development & Effectiveness: Strategies for IS Organizational Transition. LC 93-6045. (Ernst & Young Information Management Ser.). 300p. 1994. text ed. 45.00 (*0-471-58954-3*) Wiley.

Mermall, Thomas. The Rhetoric of Humanism: Spanish Culture After Ortega y Gasset. LC 76-45293. 1976. lib. bdg. 17.00 (*0-916950-02-6*); pap. 11.00 (*0-916950-16-6*) Biling Rev-Pr.

Mermel, Anita & Simons, Judy. Women & World Development: An Education & Action Guide for Making Global Connections in Your Community. OEF International Staff, ed. LC 89-7220. 92p. (Orig.). 1991. pap. 16.00 (*0-912917-21-0*) UNIFEM.

*__Mermel, Virginia L. & DuPuy, Nancy.__ Focus on Nutrition. LC 94-36731. 1994. write for info. (*0-8016-7261-9*) Mosby Yr Bk.

Mermelstein, Max, et al. Inside the Cocaine Cartel: The Riveting Eyewitness Account of Life Inside the Colombian Cartel. 336p. 1993. reprint ed. pap. 5.99 (*1-56171-254-X*, S P I Bks) Sure Sellers.

Mermelstein, Mel. By Bread Alone: The Story of A-4685. LC 78-1206. (Illus.). 290p. 1981. pap. 8.95 (*0-686-86305-4*) M Mermelstein.

— By Bread Alone: The Story of A-4685. 2nd ed. LC 78-1206. (Illus.). 290p. 1981. 12.95 (*0-9606534-0-6*, 7901) M Mermelstein.

Mermet, Charles & Marfault, Jean. Les Dagues Du III Reich. 2nd ed. (Illus.). 212p. 35.00 (*2-86551-003-4*) Johnson Ref Bks.

Mermet, Jean P., ed. Fundamentals & Standards in Hardware Description Languages: Proceedings of the NATO Advanced Study Institute, In Ciocco, Barga, Italy, April 16-26, 1993. LC 93-20899. (NATO Advanced Science Institutes Series C: Mathematical & Physical Sciences). 480p. (C). 1993. lib. bdg. 160.00 (*0-7923-2513-3*) Kluwer Ac.

Mermet, Michel, jt. ed. see Henry, Jean-Pierre.

Mermier, Guy, ed. Contemporary Readings of Medieval Literature. LC 81-50963. (Michigan Romance Studies: Vol. 8). 226p. (Orig.). 1989. pap. 9.00 (*0-939730-07-3*) Mich Romance.

— Synopsis, Nineteen Ninety-One to Ninety-Two, Vol. 3. 124p. 1993. text ed. 49.95 (*0-7734-9237-2*) E Mellen.

Mermier, Guy & Boilly-Widmer, Yvette. Explication de Texte: Theorie et Pratique. LC 93-18841. 206p. 1993. pap. 29.95 (*0-7734-9261-5*) E Mellen.

Mermier, Guy, jt. ed. see Vaquero, Mercedes.

Mermier, Guy R., ed. Courtly Romance: A Collection of Essays. LC 84-60235. (Medieval & Renaissance Monograph Ser.: Vol. 6). 320p. reprint ed. pap. 91.20 (*0-318-34986-8*, 2030826) Bks Demand.

Mermier, Guy R., tr. Le Jeu D'Adam le Bocu D'Arras - The Play of Adam the Hunchback from Arras. LC 93-50731. 76p. 1993. 49.95 (*0-7734-9142-2*) E Mellen.

— A Medieval Book of Beasts: Pierre de Beauvais' Bestiary Followed by a Diplomatic Transcription of the Malines (Mechelen) Manuscript of Pierre de Beauvais, Short Version, & with in Appendix, an English Translation of the Cambrai Bestiary. LC 91-37833. (Illus.). 364p. 1991. lib. bdg. 99.95 (*0-7734-9629-7*) E Mellen.

— The Romance of Jehan De Paris - Le Romant De Jehan De Paris. LC 92-45566. (Studies in French Literature: Vol. 15). 120p. 1993. text ed. 59.95 (*0-7734-9225-9*) E Mellen.

— La Vie de Saint Alexis - The Old French Text & Its Translation into English & Modern French As The Life of Saint Alexis. LC 93-50730. 108p. 1994. 59.95 (*0-7734-9140-6*) E Mellen.

Mermier, Guy R. & Dubruck, Edelgard E. Fifteenth Century Studies, Vols 1, 2, 3, 4, 5, 6, 7, 8, 9, pap. write for info. (*0-318-61242-9*, 2027023) Bks Demand.

Mermier, Guy R., ed. see Fifteenth-Century Studies Staff.

Mermier, Martha B. Coping with Severe Mental Illness: Families Speak Out. LC 93-20490. (Studies in Health & Human Services: Vol. 23). 212p. 1993. text ed. 89.95 (*0-7734-9285-2*) E Mellen.

*__Mermilliod, Jean-Claude & Mermilliod, Monique.__ Catalog of Mean UBV Data on Stars. 1994. write for info. (*0-387-94355-2*); write for info. (*3-540-94355-2*) Spr-Verlag.

Mermilliod, Monique, jt. auth. see Mermilliod, Jean-Claude.

Mermin, Dorothy. Elizabeth Barrett Browning: The Origins of a New Poetry. LC 88-28680. (Women in Culture & Society Ser.). 320p. 1989. pap. text ed. 15.95 (*0-226-52039-0*) U Ch Pr.

— Godiva's Ride: Women of Letters in England, 1830-1880. LC 92-45186. (C). 1993. 35.00 (*0-253-33749-6*); pap. 12.95 (*0-253-20824-6*) Ind U Pr.

Mermin, N. David. Boojums All the Way Through: Communicating Science in a Prosaic Age. (Illus.). 200p. (C). 1990. 59.95 (*0-521-38231-9*); pap. 19.95 (*0-521-38880-5*) Cambridge U Pr.

— Space & Time in Special Relativity. (Illus.). 240p. (C). 1989. reprint ed. pap. text ed. 18.95 (*0-88133-420-0*) Waveland Pr.

Mermin, N. David, jt. auth. see Ashcroft, Neil W.

Mermin, Samuel. Jurisprudence & Statecraft: The Wisconsin Development Authority & Its Implications. LC 63-15054. 264p. reprint ed. pap. 75.30 (*0-317-41625-1*, 2021141) Bks Demand.

— Law & the Legal System: An Introduction. 2nd ed. LC 81-83102. 361p. (C). 1982. pap. 23.00 (*0-316-56731-0*) Little.

*__Mermut, A. R., ed. & pref.__ Layer Charge Characteristics of 2:1 Silicate Clay Minerals. (CMS Workshop Lectures: Vol. 6). (Illus.). 144p. (C). 1994. pap. text ed. 12.00 (*1-881208-07-9*) Clay Minerals.

Mermut, Ahmed R., jt. ed. see Miedema, Rienk.

Merne. Handbook of Medical English Usage. 240p. (GER.). 1989. pap. text ed. 45.95 (*0-433-21250-0*) Buttrwrth-Heinemann.

Merne, John G. Handbook of Celtic Ornament: Complete Course in Construction-Development of Celtic Art. (Illus.). 103p. 1989. pap. 10.95 (*0-85342-403-9*, Pub. by Mercier Pr IE) Dufour.

Merne, Oscar, jt. auth. see Roche, Richard.

Mernissi, Fatima. Beyond the Veil: Male-Female Dynamics in Modern Muslim Society. rev. ed. LC 86-46034. 224p. 1987. 25.00 (*0-253-31162-4*); pap. 8.95 (*0-253-20423-2*, MB-423) Ind U Pr.

— Doing Daily Battle: Interviews with Moroccan Women. Lakeland, Jo, tr. LC 88-34211. 224p. (C). 1989. text ed. 35.00 (*0-8135-1417-7*); pap. text ed. 15.00 (*0-8135-1418-5*) Rutgers U Pr.

— Dreams of Trespass: Tales of a Harem Girlhood. LC 93-39523. (Illus.). 1994. 22.12 (*0-201-62649-7*) Addison-Wesley.

— The Forgotten Queens of Islam. 230p. 1992. text ed. 24.95 (*0-8166-2438-0*) U of Minn Pr.

— Islam & Democracy: Fear of the Modern World. Lakeland, Mary J., tr. 300p. 1992. 23.99 (*0-201-60883-9*) Addison-Wesley.

— Islam & Democracy: Fear of the Modern World. (Illus.). 208p. 1993. pap. 10.53 (*0-201-62483-4*) Addison-Wesley.

— The Veil & the Male Elite: A Feminist Interpretation of Women's Rights in Islam. (Illus.). 240p. 1992. pap. 12.45 (*0-201-63221-7*) Addison-Wesley.

— Women & Islam: An Historical & Theological Enquiry. (C). 1991. 22.50x (*81-85107-71-8*, Pub. by Kali for Women II) S Asia.

— Women in Emergent Morocco: Changes & Continuities. 1982. 15.00 (*0-933184-40-9*) Flame Intl.

Mernit, Susan. Everything You Need to Know about Changing Schools. (Need to Know Library). (YA). (gr. 7-12). 1992. lib. bdg. 15.95 (*0-8239-1326-0*) Rosen Group.

— Tree Climbing. 60p. (Orig.). 1981. pap. 3.00 (*0-87924-036-9*) Membrane Pr.

Mernitz, Scott. Mediation of Environmental Disputes: A Sourcebook. LC 80-7503. 230p. 1980. text ed. 55.00 (*0-275-90523-3*, C0523, Praeger Pubs) Greenwood.

Mero, L. Ways of Thinking: The Limits of Rational Thought & Artificial Intelligence. 260p. (C). 1990. text ed. 61.00 (*981-02-0266-0*); pap. text ed. 30.00 (*981-02-0267-9*) World Scientific Pub.

Merod, Jim. The Political Responsibility of the Critic. LC 86-47977. 288p. 1987. 34.50 (*0-8014-1976-X*); pap. 14.95 (*0-8014-9555-5*) Cornell U Pr.

Meron, Theodor. Henry's Wars & Shakespeare's Laws: Perspectives on the Law of War in the Later Middle Ages. 256p. 1994. 35.00 (*0-19-825811-9*) OUP.

— Human Rights & Humanitarian Norms As Customary Law. 280p. 1991. reprint ed. pap. 29.95 (*0-19-825745-7*) OUP.

— Human Rights in Internal Strife: Their International Protection. 185p. (C). 1987. 120.00 (*0-949009-04-0*, Pub. by Grotius Pubns UK) St Mut.

— Human Rights Law-Making in the United Nations: A Critique of Instruments & Processes. 350p. 1987. 85.00 (*0-19-825549-7*) OUP.

Meron, Theodor, ed. Human Rights in International Law: Legal & Policy Issues, 2 vols. in 1. 608p. 1986. pap. text ed. 38.00 (*0-19-825540-3*) OUP.

Meron, Tyrus. The Edge of Darkness. LC 90-82184. (C). 1991. 15.95 (*1-56062-037-4*) CIS Comm.

Meroney, Howard. Poems Made & Remade. 1966. pap. 10.00 (*0-685-62615-6*) Atlantis Edns.

Meroney, John W. Word Processing Applications in Practice. 3rd ed. LC 93-44960. 1995. pap. 15.95 (*0-538-62529-5*) S-W Pub.

Meroni, Rudolf, jt. ed. see Campbell, Dennis.

Meronuck, Richard, jt. auth. see Christensen, Clyde M.

Merot, Alain. Nicolas Poussin. (Illus.). 336p. 1990. 125.00 (*1-55859-120-6*) Abbeville Pr.

Merquior, J. G. Foucault. 1987. 35.00 (*0-520-06076-8*); pap. 11.00 (*0-520-06062-8*) U CA Pr.

— From Prague to Paris: A Critique of Structuralist & Post-Structuralist Thought. 286p. 1987. text ed. 50.00 (*0-318-41515-1*, A0890, Pub. by Verso UK); pap. text ed. 14.95 (*0-86091-860-2*, A0641, Pub. by Verso UK) Routledge Chapman & Hall.

— Liberalism Old & New. Roth, Michael, ed. (Studies in Intellectual & Cultural History: No. 1). 208p. 1991. text ed. 24.95 (*0-8057-8602-3*, Twayne); pap. 11.95 (*0-8057-8627-9*, Twayne) Macmillan.

Merran, S. CT & MRI Radioanatomy. (Illus.). 320p. 1991. 140.00 (*0-7506-1060-3*) Buttrwrth-Heinemann.

Merrell, Barbara. Sign of Death. (YA). (gr. 7 up). 1981. pap. 2.50 (*0-89083-781-3*) Zebra.

Merrell, Betty. Baptist Woman Manual. 96p. (Orig.). (SPA.). 1988. pap. text ed. 2.95 (*0-936625-49-X*) Womans Mission Union.

— Baptist Women Manual. rev. ed. (Illus.). 96p. 1988. pap. text ed. 2.95 (*0-936625-26-0*) Womans Mission Union.

Merrell, Bruce, ed. see Muir, John.

Merrell, David J. The Adaptive Seascape: The Mechanism of Evolution. LC 93-29841. 1994. 34.95 (*0-8166-2348-1*) U of Minn Pr.

— Ecological Genetics. LC 81-14789. (Illus.). 512p. (C). 1981. text ed. 39.95 (*0-8166-1019-3*) U of Minn Pr.

Merrell, Floyd. Pararealities: The Nature of Our Fictions & How We Know Them. (Purdue University Monographs in Romance Languages: No. 12). xii, 170p. 1983. 44.00x (*90-272-1722-X*) Benjamins North Am.

— Semiosis in the Postmodern Age. LC 94-21557. (Illus.). 360p. 1995. 37.95 (*1-55753-055-6*) Purdue U Pr.

— Semiotic Foundations: Steps Toward An Epistemology of Written Texts. LC 81-48631. (Illus.). 191p. 1982. pap. 54.50 (*0-7837-3718-1*, 2057896) Bks Demand.

— A Semiotic Theory of Texts. (Approaches to Semiotics Ser.: No. 70). x, 234p. 1985. 77.35 (*0-89925-035-1*) Mouton.

— Sign, Textuality, World. LC 91-26984. (Advances in Semiotics Ser.). (Illus.). 288p. 1992. text ed. 37.50 (*0-253-33748-8*) Ind U Pr.

— Signs Becoming Signs: Our Perfusive, Pervasive Universe. LC 90-49160. (Advances in Semiotics Ser.). (Illus.). 264p. 1991. 39.95 (*0-253-33746-1*) Ind U Pr.

— Unthinking Thinking: Jorge Luis Borges, Mathematics, & the New Physics. LC 90-20128. (Illus.). 320p. 1991. 29.50 (*1-55753-011-4*) Purdue U Pr.

Merrell, Floyd, jt. ed. see Anderson, Myrdene.

Merrell, Henry. The Autobiography of Henry Merrell: Industrial Missionary to the South. Skinner, James L., III, ed. LC 90-10919. (Illus.). 592p. 1991. 50.00 (*0-8203-1253-3*) U of Ga Pr.

Merrell, James H. The Catawbas. (Indians of North America Ser.). (Illus.). 112p. (YA). (gr. 5 up). 1989. 17.95 (*1-55546-694-X*) Chelsea Hse.

— The Indians' New World: Catawbas & Their Neighbors from European Contact Through the Era of Removal. LC 88-22658. (Illus.). xviii, 382p. (C). 1989. 37.50 (*0-8078-1832-1*) U of NC Pr.

— The Indians' New World: Catawbas & Their Neighbors from European Contact Through the Era of Removal. (C). 1991. pap. text ed. 10.95 (*0-393-96017-X*) Norton.

Merrell, James H., jt. ed. see Richter, Daniel K.

Merrell, Kenneth W. Assessment of Behavioral, Emotional, & Social Problems: Direct & Objective Methods for Use with Children & Adolescents. LC 93-19109. 288p. (C). 1994. boxed, text ed. 56.95 (*0-8013-1107-1*, 79565) Longman.

— Preschool & Kindergarten Behavior Scales. LC 94-12893. 60p. 1994. 19.95 (*0-88422-152-0*) Clinical Psych.

Merrell, Patricia. Art & Craft of Applique, Bk. 1: Sew Quick, Sew Easy. 24p. 1990. pap. 9.95 (*1-883504-01-5*) Sew-Art Int.

— Art & Craft of Applique, Bk. 2: Those Crazy Birds & Other Designs. 2nd ed. 32p. 1993. reprint ed. pap. 9.95 (*1-883504-02-3*) Sew-Art Int.

— Creative Fabric Embellishment. 60p. 1993. pap. 12.95 (*1-883504-12-0*) Sew-Art Int.

— Renaissance Thread Methods & Ideas. 24p. 1992. pap. 6.95 (*1-883504-00-7*) Sew-Art Int.

*__Merrell, Susan.__ The Accidental Bond: The Power of Sibling Relationships. LC 94-48375. 1995. 23.00 (*0-8129-2211-5*, Times Bks) Random.

Merrell, V. Dallas. Huddling: The Informal way to Management Success. LC 78-31941. 224p. reprint ed. pap. 63.90 (*0-317-09599-4*, 2022621) Bks Demand.

Merrell-Wolff, Franklin. Franklin Merrell-Wolff's Experience & Philosophy: A Personal Record of Transformation & a Discussion of Transcendental Consciousness: Containing His Philosophy of Consciousness Without an Object & His Pathways Through to Space. LC 93-30880. 445p. (C). 1994. reprint ed. 59.50 (*0-7914-1963-0*); reprint ed. pap. 19.95 (*0-7914-1964-9*) State U NY Pr.

— Transformations in Consciousness: The Metaphysics & Epistemology. 384p. (C). 1995. text ed. 59.50x (*0-7914-2675-0*); pap. 19.95x (*0-7914-2676-9*) State U NY Pr.

Merrens, Matthew R., jt. ed. see Brannigan, Gary G.

*__Merrett, Alicia.__ Make Your Own Teddy Bear: Everything You Need to Create Your Very Own Bear. (Miniature Kit Ser.). (Illus.). 48p. 1995. pap. 9.95 (*1-56138-541-7*) Running Pr.

— The Teddy Bear Kit. (Illus.). 48p. 1994. 19.95 (*0-312-11119-3*, Pub. by Thomas Dunne Bks) St Martin.

*__Merrett, Christopher.__ A Culture of Censorship: Secrecy & Intellectual Repression in South Africa. LC 94-32888. 1995. 18.95 (*0-86554-455-7*) Mercer Univ Pr.

An Asterisk (*) at the beginning of an entry indicates that the title is appearing in BIP for the first time.

— State Censorship & the Academic Process in South Africa. (Occasional Papers: No. 192). 1991. pap. 5.00 (*0-685-56565-3*) U of Ill Lib Info Sci.

Merrett, Frank. Encouragement Works Best: Positive Approaches to Classroom Management. 144p. 1993. pap. 25.00 (*1-85346-254-3*, Pub. by D Fulton UK) Taylor & Francis.

— Improving Reading: A Teacher's Guide to Peer-Tutoring. 112p. 1994. pap. 19.95x (*1-85346-326-4*, Pub. by D Fulton UK) Taylor & Francis.

Merrett, John. Famous Voyages in Small Boats. 1957. 22.95 (*0-87599-073-8*) S G Phillips.

Merrett, P., ed. see Platnick, Norman I.

Merrett, Patricia & Butcher, Ronald, eds. Hunting Journal 1852-1856. 1991. pap. 24.95 (*0-86980-788-9*, Pub. by Univ Natal Pr SA) Intl Spec Bk.

Merrett, T. G., jt. ed. see Said El Shami, A.

Merri, ed. see Hasbin, Almost A.

Merriam, Alan P. African Music on LP: An Annotated Discography. LC 72-111629. 214p. reprint ed. pap. 61.00 (*0-8357-5238-0*, 2010272) Bks Demand.

— An African World: The Basongye Village of Lupupa Ngye. LC 74-377. (Illus.). 384p. 1974. 25.00 (*0-253-30280-3*) Ind U Pr.

— Anthropology of Music. 358p. 1964. pap. 16.95 (*0-8101-0607-8*) Northwestern U Pr.

— Bibliography of Jazz. LC 75-127282. (Roots of Jazz Ser.). 1970. reprint ed. lib. bdg. 22.50 (*0-306-70036-0*) Da Capo.

— Congo, Background of Conflict. LC 61-11381. (Northwestern University African Studies Ser.: No. 6). (Illus.). 386p. reprint ed. 110.10 (*0-8357-9451-2*, 2016714) Bks Demand.

— Ethnomusicology of the Flathead Indians. LC 68-100257. (Viking Fund Publications in Anthropology: No. 44). 435p. reprint ed. pap. 124.00 (*0-317-09687-7*, 2006398) Bks Demand.

Merriam, C. Hart, ed. The Dawn of the World: Myths & Tales of the Miwok Indians of California. LC 92-42566. x, 273p. 1993. 30.00 (*0-8032-3164-4*); pap. 9.95 (*0-8032-8193-5*) U of Nebr Pr.

Merriam, C. Hart, ed. see Woiche, Istet.

Merriam, C. W. Automated Design of Control Systems. LC 73-86001. 356p. 1975. text ed. 195.00 (*0-677-04440-2*) Gordon & Breach.

Merriam, Charles. History of Sovereignty since Rousseau. 1972. 59.95 (*0-8490-0348-2*) Gordon Pr.

Merriam, Charles E. American Political Ideas. LC 70-97887. reprint ed. 20.00 (*0-404-04310-0*) AMS Pr.

— American Political Ideas. LC 68-56259. 481p. 1969. reprint ed. 45.00 (*0-678-00511-7*) Kelley.

— Chicago: A More Intimate View of Urban Politics. LC 71-112579. (Rise of Urban America Ser.). 1976. reprint ed. 24.95 (*0-405-02467-3*) Ayer.

— Four American Party Leaders. (History - United States Ser.). 104p. 1992. reprint ed. lib. bdg. 69.00 (*0-7812-6191-0*) Rprt Serv.

— Four American Party Leaders: Henry Ward Beecher Foundation Lectures, Amherst College. LC 67-23247. (Essay Index Reprint Ser.). 1977. 14.95 (*0-8369-0702-7*) Ayer.

— The History of American Political Theories. 1973. 59.95 (*0-8490-0317-2*) Gordon Pr.

Merriam, Charles E., Jr. History of the Theory of Sovereignty since Rousseau. LC 76-76667. (Columbia University. Studies in the Social Sciences: No. 33). reprint ed. 21.50 (*0-404-51033-7*) AMS Pr.

Merriam, Charles E. The Role of Politics in Social Change. LC 83-1490. 149p. 1983. reprint ed. text ed. 49.75 (*0-313-23852-9*, MERO, Greenwood Pr) Greenwood.

Merriam, Clinton H. The Classification & Distribution of the Pit River Indian Tribes of California. LC 76-43779. (Smithsonian Miscellaneous Collections: Vol. 78, No. 3). reprint ed. write for info. (*0-404-15633-9*) AMS Pr.

— The Mammals of the Adirondack Region, Northwestern New York: Introductory Chapter Treating of the Location & Boundaries of the Region, Its Geological History, Topography, Climate, General Features, Botany & Faunal Position. LC 73-17832. (Natural Sciences of America Ser.). 320p. 1974. reprint ed. 23.95 (*0-405-05750-4*) Ayer.

Merriam, Clinton H., ed. An-Nik-a-Del: The History of the Universe As Told by the Modes-Se Indians of California. LC 76-43777. reprint ed. write for info. (*0-404-15632-0*) AMS Pr.

Merriam, Daniel F., ed. Capture, Management & Display of Geological Data: With Special Emphasis on Energy & Mineral Resources. LC 76-56893. 1977. pap. 50.00 (*0-08-021422-3*, Pergamon Pr) Elsevier.

— Computer Assisted Instruction in Geology: Proceedings of the 4th Geochautauqua, Syracuse University, 1975. 1976. pap. 50.00 (*0-08-021040-6*, Pergamon Pr) Elsevier.

— Computer Software for the Geosciences: Proceedings of the Geochautauqua, 5th, 1976. LC 77-30468. 1977. pap. 50.00 (*0-08-022090-8*, Pergamon Pr) Elsevier.

— Current Trends in Geomathematics. (Computer Applications in the Earth Sciences Ser.). (Illus.). 334p. 1988. 75.00 (*0-306-43087-8*, Plenum Pr) Plenum.

— Management, Analysis & Display of Geoscience Data: Proceedings of the First Annual Conference, Golden, CO, January 27-29, 1982. 60p. 1983. pap. 57.00 (*0-08-030248-3*, Pergamon Pr) Elsevier.

— Quantitative Stratigraphic Correlation: Proceedings of the 6th Geochautauqua, Syracuse University, October 1977. (Illus.). 112p. 1979. pap. 50.00 (*0-08-023979-X*, Pergamon Pr) Elsevier.

— Quantitative Techniques for the Analysis of Sediments. 1976. 82.00 (*0-08-020613-1*, Pub. by Pergamon Repr UK) Franklin.

— Recent Advances in Geomathematics: An International Symposium. 1978. 145.00 (*0-08-022095-9*, Pergamon Pr) Elsevier.

Merriam, Daniel F. & Kurzl, Hans, eds. Use of Microcomputers in Geology. LC 92-29735. (Computer Applications in the Earth Sciences Ser.). 1992. 85.00 (*0-306-44310-4*, Plenum Pr) Plenum.

Merriam, Daniel F., jt. ed. see Gaal, G.

Merriam, Daniel F., jt. auth. see Gill, Dan.

Merriam, Daniel F., jt. ed. see Hanley, J. T.

Merriam, Daniel F., jt. ed. see Harff, Jan.

Merriam, Dena, jt. auth. see Finn, David.

Merriam, Dwight, et al, eds. Inclusionary Zoning Moves Downtown. LC 84-61997. 223p. (Orig.). 1985. lib. bdg. 33.95 (*0-918286-37-9*) Planners Pr.

Merriam, Eve. Bam, Bam, Bam. LC 94-20300. (Illus.). 32p. (J). 1995. 14.95 (*0-8050-3527-3*) H Holt & Co.

— Blackberry Ink. LC 84-16633. (Illus.). 40p. (J). (ps-2). 1985. 15.00 (*0-688-04150-7*); lib. bdg. 13.93 (*0-688-04151-5*) Morrow Jr Bks.

— Blackberry Ink. Cohn, Amy, ed. LC 84-16633. (Illus.). 40p. (J). (ps up). 1994. reprint ed. pap. 4.95 (*0-688-13080-1*, Mulberry) Morrow.

— Chortles: New & Selected Wordplay Poems. LC 88-29129. (Illus.). 64p. (J). (gr. 3-7). 1989. 11.95 (*0-688-08152-5*) Morrow Jr Bks.

— The Christmas Box. LC 85-5666. (Illus.). 32p. (J). (ps-3). 1985. 15.00 (*0-688-05255-X*); lib. bdg. 14.93 (*0-688-05256-8*) Morrow Jr Bks.

— A Conversation Against Death. 25p. 1991. 3.95 (*0-930194-24-1*) Ctr Thanatology.

— Daddies at Work. (Illus.). 32p. (J). (ps-2). 1991. pap. 2.50 (*0-671-73276-5*, Litl Simon S&S) S&S Childrens.

— Embracing the Dark: Poetry. Whitman, Ruth, ed. 80p. (Orig.). 1994. pap. 13.00 (*1-882329-04-X*) Garden St Pr.

— Fighting Words. (Illus.). 32p. (J). (gr. k up). 1992. 15.00 (*0-688-09676-X*); lib. bdg. 14.93 (*0-688-09677-8*) Morrow Jr Bks.

— Fresh Paint: New Poems. LC 85-23742. (Illus.). 48p. (J). (gr. 5 up). 1986. text ed. 13.95 (*0-02-766860-6*, Mac Bks Young Read) S&S Childrens.

— Goodnight to Annie. LC 92-7111. (Illus.). 32p. (J). (ps-1). 1992. 14.95 (*1-56282-205-5*); lib. bdg. 14.89 (*1-56282-206-3*) Hyprn Child.

— Goodnight to Annie: An Alphabet Lullaby. LC 92-7111. (Illus.). 32p. (J). (ps-2). 1994. pap. 4.95 (*0-7868-1005-X*) Hyprn Ppbks.

— Halloween ABC. LC 86-23772. (Illus.). 32p. (J). (gr. k up). 1987. text ed. 14.95 (*0-02-766870-3*, Mac Bks Young Read) S&S Childrens.

— Higgle Wiggle: Happy Rhymes. LC 92-29795. (Illus.). 40p. (J). (ps up). 1994. 15.00 (*0-688-11948-4*); lib. bdg. 14.93 (*0-688-11949-2*) Morrow Jr Bks.

— The Hole Story. (Illus.). (J). (gr. 3 up). 1995. 16.00 (*0-671-88353-4*, S&S Bks Young Read) S&S Childrens.

— The Inner City Mother Goose. LC 93-19735. (Illus.). (J). 1996. pap. 15.00 (*0-671-88033-0*, S&S Bks Young Read) S&S Childrens.

— Mommies at Work. (Illus.). (J). (ps-2). 1989. pap. 5.95 (*0-671-64386-X*, S&S Bks Young Read) S&S Childrens.

— Mommies at Work. (J). (ps-3). 1991. pap. 2.95 (*0-671-73275-7*, Litl Simon S&S) S&S Childrens.

— A Poem for a Pickle: Funnybone Verses. LC 88-22047. (Illus.). 40p. (J). (gr. k up). 1989. 12.95 (*0-688-08137-1*); lib. bdg. 12.88 (*0-688-08138-X*) Morrow Jr Bks.

— Shhh! LC 92-44110. (Illus.). (YA). (gr. 4 up). 1993. pap. 14.00 (*0-671-79816-2*, S&S Bks Young Read) S&S Childrens.

— The Singing Green: New & Selected Poems for All Seasons. LC 91-31205. (Illus.). 112p. (J). (gr. 3 up). 1992. 14.00 (*0-688-11025-8*) Morrow Jr Bks.

— The Singing Green: New & Selected Poems for All Seasons. braille ed. 86p. 1994. pap. text ed. 6.88 (*1-56956-564-3*, BR9515) W A T Braille.

— Thinking of You. (Illus.). 40p. 1991. lib. bdg. 7.95 (*0-8378-0372-1*) Gibson.

— Train Leaves the Station. LC 91-28009. (Illus.). 32p. (J). (ps-00). 1992. 14.95 (*0-8050-1934-0*, B Martin BYR) H Holt & Co.

— Train Leaves the Station. (Illus.). (J). (PS-3). 1994. pap. 5.95 (*0-8050-3547-8*) H Holt & Co.

— Twelve Ways to Get to Eleven. LC 92-25810. (Illus.). 40p. (J). (ps-1). 1993. pap. 14.00 (*0-671-75544-7*, S&S Bks Young Read) S&S Childrens.

— Where Is Everybody? LC 88-19800. (Illus.). (J). (ps-1). 1992. pap. 14.95 (*0-671-64964-7*, S&S Bks Young Read); pap. 4.95 (*0-671-77821-8*, S&S Bks Young Read) S&S Childrens.

— Wise Woman & Her Secret. LC 90-42406. (J). 1991. pap. 15.00 (*0-671-72603-X*, S&S Bks Young Read) S&S Childrens.

— You Be Good & I'll Be Night: Jump-on-the-Bed-Poems. LC 87-24859. (Illus.). 40p. (J). (ps-2). 1988. 16.00 (*0-688-06742-5*); lib. bdg. 15.93 (*0-688-06743-3*) Morrow Jr Bks.

Merriam, Eve, ed. Growing up Female in America: Ten Lives. LC 86-47761. (Illus.). 308p. 1987. reprint ed. pap. 15.00 (*0-8070-7009-2*, BP-737) Beacon Pr.

Merriam, Eve, ret. That Noodlehead Epaminondas. (Illus.). (J). 1992. reprint ed. pap. 8.95 (*0-89966-962-X*) Buccaneer Bks.

Merriam, Frederick R. Fundamentals of Biology Laboratory Guide. 160p. 1989. spiral bd. 14.95 (*0-8403-5240-9*) Kendall-Hunt.

Merriam, George R. & Lipsett, Mortimer B., eds. Catechol Estrogens. 300p. 1983. text ed. 98.00 (*0-89004-892-4*) Raven.

Merriam, George S. Life & Times of Samuel Bowles, 2 vols., Set. LC 76-108512. 1970. reprint ed. 49.00 (*0-403-00220-6*) Scholarly.

— Negro & the Nation. LC 75-95441. (Studies in Black History & Culture: No. 54). 1970. reprint ed. lib. bdg. 75.00 (*0-8383-0994-1*) M S G Haskell Hse.

Merriam, George S., ed. see Bowles, Samuel.

Merriam, H. G., ed. see Linderman, Frank B.

Merriam, John L. & Keller, Jack. Farm Irrigation System Evaluation. 300p. 1978. 12.50 (*0-317-34779-9*) Irrigation.

Merriam, Kendall. Medvedb's Journal. 32p. 1991. pap. 5.00 (*0-942396-64-2*) Blackberry ME.

Merriam, Raymond. Arizona Minerals & How to Find Them. (Illus.). 73p. (Orig.). 1995. pap. 4.95 (*0-918080-40-1*) Treas Chest Bks.

Merriam, Robert L. ABC of Revolution. (Illus.). 52p. (Orig.). 1976. pap. 1.75 (*0-686-32502-8*) R L Merriam.

— Abigail Challenges the Telephone Company. (Illus.). 8p. (Orig.). (J). (ps-6). 1972. pap. 1.50 (*0-686-32483-8*) R L Merriam.

— The Ancient Art of Skating. (Illus.). 25p. 1957. pap. 1.50 (*0-686-33162-1*) R L Merriam.

— Curious Emily. (Illus.). 29p. 1980. pap. 2.00 (*0-686-32487-0*) R L Merriam.

— The Darling Twins. (Illus.). 25p. (Orig.). 1976. pap. 2.00 (*0-686-32493-5*) R L Merriam.

— The Energy Crisis. (Illus.). 7p. (Orig.). 1974. pap. 2.00 (*0-686-32494-3*) R L Merriam.

— Eunice Williams. (Illus.). 32p. (Orig.). 1984. 35.00 (*0-918507-58-8*) R L Merriam.

— Helen Childs Boyden. (Illus.). 32p. 1989. 35.00 (*0-317-99671-1*) R L Merriam.

— J. Hamilton Rose. (Illus.). 29p. (Orig.). 1979. pap. 2.00 (*0-686-32488-9*) R L Merriam.

— John Carson. (Illus.). 23p. (Orig.). 1977. pap. 2.00 (*0-686-37766-4*) R L Merriam.

Merriam, Robert L. Lucy Terry Prince. (Illus.). 32p. 1983. 35.00 (*0-686-40220-0*) R L Merriam.

Merriam, Robert L. Maple Sugar. (Illus.). 32p. (Orig.). 1982. 35.00 (*0-685-05823-9*); pap. 2.50 (*0-686-35762-0*) R L Merriam.

— Moses Washington. (Illus.). 31p. 1978. pap. 2.00 (*0-686-32489-7*) R L Merriam.

— Pleasant Beth. (Illus.). 24p. (Orig.). 1975. pap. 2.00 (*0-686-32490-0*) R L Merriam.

— Santa Claus' Snack. (Illus.). 14p. (J). (ps-6). 1970. pap. 2.00 (*0-686-32491-9*) R L Merriam.

— Six Vignettes. (Illus.). 38p. 1981. 2.00 (*0-686-32492-7*) R L Merriam.

— The Stories of the Ants. (Illus.). 19p. (Orig.). 1981. pap. 2.00 (*0-686-32495-1*) R L Merriam.

Merriam, Sharan, jt. ed. see Elias, John L.

Merriam, Sharan B. Adult Development: Implications for Adult Education. 39p. 1984. 4.75 (*0-318-22018-0*, IN282) Ctr Educ Trng Employ.

— Case Study Research in Education: A Qualitative Approach. LC 88-42795. (Education-Higher Education Ser.: No. HE). 248p. 1991. pap. 18.95 (*1-55542-359-0*) Jossey-Bass.

— Case Study Research in Education: A Qualitative Approach. LC 88-42795. (Illus.). 246p. reprint ed. pap. 70.20 (*0-7837-6523-1*, 2045635) Bks Demand.

— Selected Writings on Philosophy & Adult Education. 2nd ed. LC 94-24355. (C). 1995. pap. write for info. (*0-89464-887-X*) Krieger.

— Themes of Adulthood Through Literature. 1983. pap. text ed. 21.95 (*0-8077-2731-8*) Tchrs Coll.

***Merriam, Sharan B., ed.** An Update on Adult Learning Theory. LC 85-644750. (New Directions for Adult & Continuing Education Ser.: No. 57). 116p. (Orig.). 1993. pap. 16.95 (*1-55542-684-0*) Jossey-Bass.

Merriam, Sharan B. & Caffarella, Rosemary S. Learning in Adulthood: A Comprehensive Guide. LC 90-47292. (Higher & Adult Education Ser.). 398p. 1991. 32.95 (*1-55542-312-4*) Jossey-Bass.

Merriam, Sharan B. & Clark, M. Carolyn. Lifelines: Patterns of Work, Love, & Learning in Adulthood. LC 91-10280. (Social & Behavioral Science Ser.). 280p. 1991. 29.95 (*1-55542-364-7*) Jossey-Bass.

Merriam, Sharan B. & Cunningham, Phyllis M., eds. The Handbook of Adult & Continuing Education. LC 89-45601. (Higher Education Ser.). 750p. 1989. 55.00x (*1-55542-161-X*) Jossey-Bass.

Merriam, Sharan B. & Simpson, Edwin L. A Guide to Research for Educators & Trainers of Adults. 2nd ed. 218p. (C). 1994. lib. bdg. 25.50 (*0-89464-849-7*) Krieger.

Merriam, Sharan B., jt. auth. see Darkenwald, Gordon G.

Merriam, Sharon, ed. The Research-To-Practice Dilemma. 13p. 1987. 3.00 (*0-318-23414-9*, OC123) Ctr Educ Trng Employ.

Merriam, Sharon, jt. auth. see Elias, John L.

Merriam, Thornton W. The Relations Between Scholastic Achievement in a School of Social Work & Six Factors in Students Background. LC 70-177072. (Columbia University. Teachers College. Contributions to Education Ser.: No. 616). reprint ed. 37.50 (*0-404-55616-7*) AMS Pr.

Merriam, Thornton W., jt. auth. see Knight, Frank H.

***Merriam-Webster, ed.** Webster's New Complete Thesaurus. LC 95-16737. 1995. write for info. (*0-8317-1543-X*) Smithmark.

Merriam-Webster Editorial Staff. Merriam-Webster's School Thesaurus. LC 88-26859. 704p. 1989. 14.95 (*0-87779-178-3*) Merriam-Webster Inc.

— Webster's Compact Dictionary of Synonyms. LC 86-33138. 384p. 1987. 5.95 (*0-87779-186-4*) Merriam-Webster Inc.

— Webster's Compact Rhyming Dictionary. LC 86-33165. 400p. 1987. 5.95 (*0-87779-185-6*) Merriam-Webster Inc.

— Webster's Compact Writers Guide. LC 86-28650. 336p. 1987. 5.95 (*0-87779-187-2*) Merriam-Webster Inc.

— Webster's Legal Speller. LC 76-9633. 368p. 1978. 5.95 (*0-87779-038-8*) Merriam-Webster Inc.

— Webster's New Geographical Dictionary. (Illus.). 1408p. 1988. 24.95 (*0-87779-446-4*) Merriam-Webster Inc.

— Webster's Official Crossword Puzzle Dictionary. LC 81-38341. 768p. 1981. 15.95 (*0-87779-021-3*) Merriam-Webster Inc.

Merriam-Webster Editorial Staff, ed. Webster's Compact Dictionary. LC 87-21956. 432p. 1987. 5.95 (*0-87779-488-X*) Merriam-Webster Inc.

— Webster's Guide to Abbreviations. LC 83-15286. 400p. 1985. 5.95 (*0-87779-072-8*) Merriam-Webster Inc.

— Webster's Medical Speller. 2nd ed. LC 87-26947. 400p. 1987. 5.95 (*0-87779-137-6*) Merriam-Webster Inc.

Merriam-Webster Editors. The Merriam-Webster Thesaurus. 672p. 1989. mass mkt., pap. 4.99 (*0-87779-902-4*) Merriam-Webster Inc.

Merriam-Webster Staff. Addenda Section 1993: A Supplement to Webster's Third New International Dictionary. 1993. pap. 5.00 (*0-87779-100-7*) Merriam-Webster Inc.

— The Merriam-Webster Compact Reference Set: Compact Dictionary, Synonyms, Writer's Guide, Quotations. deluxe ed. 1992. 34.95 (*0-87779-283-6*) Merriam-Webster Inc.

— The Merriam-Webster Company Reference Set: Compact Dictionary, Writers Guide, Synonyms, Quotations. 1993. pap. 24.95 (*0-87779-282-8*) Merriam-Webster Inc.

— The Merriam-Webster Concise Handbook for Writers. LC 91-27326. 320p. 1991. pap. 8.95 (*0-87779-602-5*) Merriam-Webster Inc.

— The Merriam-Webster Dictionary of Quotations. 512p. 1992. mass mkt., pap. 4.99 (*0-87779-904-0*) Merriam-Webster Inc.

— The Merriam-Webster New Book of Word Histories. 544p. 1991. pap. 9.95 (*0-87779-603-3*) Merriam-Webster Inc.

— The Merriam-Webster Thesaurus, Home & Office Edition. LC 91-11462. 704p. 1991. pap. 7.95 (*0-87779-601-7*) Merriam-Webster Inc.

— Merriam-Webster's Biographical Dictionary. rev. ed. LC 94-43025. 1184p. 1995. 27.95 (*0-87779-743-9*) Merriam-Webster Inc.

— Merriam Webster's Collegiate Dictionary. 10th deluxe ed. LC 93-20206. 1600p. 1993. Deluxe. 24.95 (*0-87779-710-2*) Merriam-Webster Inc.

— Merriam Webster's Collegiate Dictionary. 10th ed. LC 93-20206. 1600p. 1993. Laminated cover. 19.95 (*0-87779-707-2*); Unindexed. 20.95 (*0-87779-708-0*); 22.95 (*0-87779-709-9*) Merriam-Webster Inc.

— Merriam-Webster's Desk Dictionary. rev. ed. LC 95-5824. 896p. 1994. mass mkt. 12.95 (*0-87779-911-3*) Merriam-Webster Inc.

— Merriam-Webster's Dictionary of Basic English. 736p. 1995. pap. 7.95 (*0-87779-605-X*) Merriam-Webster Inc.

— Merriam-Webster's Dictionary of Synonyms. 944p. 1994. 21.95 (*0-87779-341-7*) Merriam-Webster Inc.

— Merriam-Webster's Elementary Dictionary. (School Ser.). (Illus.). 608p. (J). (gr. 4-6). 1986. text ed. 14.95 (*0-87779-575-4*) Merriam-Webster Inc.

— Merriam-Webster's Everyday Language Reference Set: Dictionary, Thesaurus, Vocabulary Builder. 1994. mass mkt., pap. 15.99 (*0-87779-970-9*) Merriam-Webster Inc.

— Merriam-Webster's Guide to Punctuation & Style. 320p. 1995. mass mkt. 4.99 (*0-87779-912-1*) Merriam-Webster Inc.

— Merriam-Webster's Intermediate Dictionary No. 79. (School Ser.). (Illus.). 960p. (YA). (gr. 7-9). 1994. text ed. 14.95 (*0-87779-479-0*) Merriam-Webster Inc.

— Merriam-Webster's Medical Dictionary. 800p. 1995. mass mkt. 6.99 (*0-87779-914-8*) Merriam-Webster Inc.

— Merriam-Webster's Pocket Guide to Punctuation. 320p. Date not set. 3.95 (*0-87779-502-9*) Merriam-Webster Inc.

***Merriam Webster Staff.** Merriam-Webster's Pocket Guide to Synonyms. 368p. 1995. 3.95 (*0-87779-501-0*) Merriam-Webster Inc.

Merriam-Webster Staff. Merriam-Webster's Premium Gift Set: Merriam Webster's Collegiate Dictionary & Collegiate Thesaurus. 1993. boxed 45.00 (*0-87779-712-9*) Merriam-Webster Inc.

— Merriam-Webster's Rhyming Dictionary. 384p. 1995. mass mkt. 4.99 (*0-87779-913-X*) Merriam-Webster Inc.

— Merriam-Webster's School Dictionary. 1184p. 1994. 15.95 (*0-87779-380-8*) Merriam-Webster Inc.

— Merriam-Webster's Secretarial Handbook. 3rd ed. LC 96-10632. 608p. 1993. 15.95 (*0-87779-236-4*) Merriam-Webster Inc.

— Merriam-Webster's Word Histories. LC 93-22569. 544p. 1993. 21.95 (*0-87779-148-1*) Merriam-Webster Inc.

— The Official Scrabble Players Dictionary. 2nd ed. LC 90-13314. 704p. 1991. 17.95 (*0-87779-120-1*) Merriam-Webster Inc.

— The Official Scrabble Players Dictionary. 2nd ed. 640p. 1993. mass mkt., pap. 5.99 (*0-87779-908-3*) Merriam-Webster Inc.

— Webster's Basic English Dictionary. LC 83-13709. 608p. 1990. 14.95 (*0-87779-150-3*) Merriam-Webster Inc.

— Webster's Third New International Dictionary. deluxe ed. LC 93-10630. 2783p. 1986. 100.00 (*0-87779-202-X*) Merriam-Webster Inc.

Merriam-Webster Staff, ed. Webster's Legal Secretaries Handbook. (Illus.). 672p. 1981. 14.95 (*0-87779-034-5*) Merriam-Webster Inc.

— Webster's Medical Desk Dictionary. LC 93-7965. 816p. 1993. 24.95 (*0-87779-125-2*) Merriam-Webster Inc.

— Webster's Medical Desk Dictionary. deluxe ed. LC 93-7965. 816p. 1993. 27.95 (*0-87779-126-0*) Merriam-Webster Inc.

***Merriam-Webster Staff & Encyclopaedia Britannica Staff.** Merriam-Webster's Encyclopedia of Literature. LC 94-42741. 1248p. 1995. 39.95 (*0-87779-042-6*) Merriam-Webster Inc.

Merrians, Deborah. I Can Read About Earthquakes & Volcanoes. LC 74-24966. (Illus.). (J). (gr. 2-4). 1975. pap. 2.50 (*0-89375-067-0*) Troll Assocs.

— I Can Read about Earthquakes & Volcanoes. LC 95-5944. (Illus.). 48p. (J). (gr. k-3). 1995. lib. bdg. 11.89 (*0-8167-3648-0*); pap. text ed. 4.95 (*0-8167-3649-9*) Troll Assocs.

— I Can Read About Insects. LC 76-54493. (Illus.). (J). (gr. 2-5). 1977. pap. 2.50 (*0-89375-040-9*) Troll Assocs.

— I Can Read About Spiders. LC 76-54576. (Illus.). (J). (gr. 2-5). 1977. pap. 2.50 (*0-89375-043-3*) Troll Assocs.

Merrick, A., tr. see Sor, Ferdinand.

Merrick, Barbara L. & Williams, Alicia C., eds. Middleborough, Massachusetts, Vital Records, Vol. 1. 487p. 1986. text ed. 35.00 (*0-942445-00-7*) MA Soc Mayflower Descendants.

— Middleborough, Massachusetts, Vital Records, Vol. 2. 360p. 1990. text ed. 35.00 (*0-942445-01-5*) MA Soc Mayflower Descendants.

Merrick, Beverly. Closing the Gate. Zarucchi, Roy & Page, Carolyn, eds. (Illus.). 48p. (Orig.). 1993. pap. 7.95 (*1-879205-41-6*) Nightshade Pr.

Merrick, David. Coal Combustion & Conversion Technology. 1984. 107.25 (*0-444-00933-7*) Elsevier.

Merrick, David, ed. Energy: Present & Future Options, Vol. 2. LC 80-41416. 394p. 1984. text ed. 162.95 (*0-471-90416-3*, Wiley-Interscience) Wiley.

Merrick, David & Marshall, Richard, eds. Energy: Present & Future Options, Vol. 1. LC 80-41416. (Illus.). 354p. reprint ed. pap. 100.90 (*0-685-20748-X*, 2030389) Bks Demand.

Merrick, Dorothy D. A Framework for Seventeenth Century Plymouth. (Pilgrim Society Notes Ser.: No. 12). 1963. 2.00 (*0-940628-18-X*) Pilgrim Soc.

Merrick, Elliot. Northern Nurse. (Illus.). 336p. 1994. reprint ed. pap. 14.00 (*0-88150-299-5*, Countryman Classics) Countryman.

Merrick, Elliott. Green Mountain Farm. 1978. 5.95 (*0-9603324-0-5*) Sherry Urie.

— The Long Crossing & Other Labrador Stories. LC 91-32226. (Illus.). 158p. (Orig.). (C). 1992. pap. 13.95 (*0-89101-074-2*) U Maine Pr.

— True North. LC 88-38068. (Illus.). x, 378p. 1989. reprint ed. pap. 9.95 (*0-8032-8164-1*) U of Nebr Pr.

Merrick, Fred. Down on the Farm: A Story of Stanford Football. LC 75-12202. (College Sports Book Ser.). 1975. 12.95 (*0-87397-070-5*) Strode.

Merrick, G. B. Genealogy of the Merrick-Merick-Myrick Family of Massachusetts, 1636-1902. (Illus.). 502p. 1989. reprint ed. lib. bdg. 83.00 (*0-8328-0867-9*); reprint ed. pap. 75.00 (*0-8328-0869-5*) Higginson Bk Co.

***Merrick, Gordon.** The Lord Won't Mind. 256p. 1995. reprint ed. pap. 9.95 (*1-55583-290-3*) Alyson Pubns.

— The Strumpet Wind. 256p. 1992. reprint ed. lib. bdg. 18.95 (*0-89966-892-5*) Buccaneer Bks.

Merrick, Janna C. & Blank, Robert H., eds. The Politics of Pregnancy: Policy Dilemmas in the Maternal-Fetal Relationship. LC 93-5723. (Women & Politics Ser.: Vol. 13, Nos. 3 & 4). (Illus.). 245p. 1993. lib. bdg. 39.95 (*1-56024-478-X*); pap. 14.95 (*1-56023-047-9*) Haworth Pr.

Merrick, Janna C., jt. auth. see Blank, Robert H.

Merrick, Jeffrey, intro. Early Modern European History: Selected Course Outlines & Reading Lists from Leading American Colleges & Universities. 3rd enl. ed. LC 88-17406. (History Syllabi Ser.). 300p. (C). 1988. pap. 16.95 (*0-910129-93-2*) Wiener Pubs Inc.

Merrick, Jeffrey W. & Medlin, Dorothy, eds. Andre Morellet (1727-1819) in the Republic of Letters & the French Revolution. LC 94-12273. (Eighteenth Century French Intellectual History Ser.: Vol. 2). 272p. (C). 1995. text ed. 57.95 (*0-8204-2494-3*) P Lang Pubs.

Merrick, Paul. Revolution & Religion in the Music of Liszt. (Illus.). 350p. 1987. 79.95 (*0-521-32627-3*) Cambridge U Pr.

Merrick, Paul, ed. see Bureloff, Morris, et al.

Merrick, R. Valve Selection & Specification. 1990. text ed. 69.95 (*0-442-31870-7*) Chapman & Hall.

***Merrick, Robert G.** The Stand-Alone Inventor: A Bible for Builders of Better Mousetraps. 256p. (Orig.). 1995. pap. write for info. (*0-9643832-0-9*) Lee Pubng.

Merrick, Sandra. Whole Language Units for Holidays. (Illus.). 112p. (Orig.). (ps-1). 1992. student ed 10.95 (*1-55734-019-6*) Tchr Create Mat.

— Whole Language Units for Math. (Whole Language Units Ser.). (Illus.). 144p. 1993. student ed 12.95 (*1-55734-200-8*) Tchr Create Mat.

— Whole Language Units for Nursery Rhymes. Goldfluss, Karen, ed. (Illus.). 112p. (Orig.). 1992. student ed 10.95 (*1-55734-020-X*) Tchr Create Mat.

Merrick, Thomas W. & Graham, Douglas H. Population & Economic Development in Brazil: Eighteen Hundred to the Present. LC 78-20523. 408p. 1979. text ed. 50.00 (*0-8018-2182-7*) Johns Hopkins.

Merrick, William, ed. see Cornesky, Robert, et al.

Merrick, William C. Property Management Systems: A Guide to Implementation & Staff Training. (Illus.). 80p. 1989. pap. 69.95 (*0-912150-10-6*) Magna Pubns.

Merrick, William G. Tan Vat. LC 93-83571. 124p. (Orig.). 1992. pap. 8.50 (*0-9635951-0-5*) Piedmont Coll.

Merricks, Paul, jt. ed. see Jones, Peter.

Merridale, Catherine & Ward, Chris, eds. Perestroika: The Historical Perspective. 256p. 1991. pap. 15.95 (*0-340-55789-3*, A6288, Pub. by E Arnold UK) Routledge Chapman & Hall.

Merrifield, et al. American History Reader, Vol. 1. 256p. (C). 1991. pap. text ed. 18.95 (*0-8403-7063-6*) Kendall-Hunt.

— American History Reader, Vol. II. 352p. (C). 1992. pap. text ed. 19.95 (*0-8403-7880-7*) Kendall-Hunt.

Merrifield, Bruce. Life During a Golden Age of Peptide Chemistry: The Concept & Development of Solid-Phase Peptide Synthesis. LC 92-42159. (Profiles, Pathways, & Dreams Ser.). (Illus.). 297p. 1993. 24.95 (*0-8412-1842-0*) Am Chemical.

Merrifield, Calvin & Merrifield, Rebecca. Call Me Ret Man & Have a Ball: Comic Book. 1979. For 10. 4.50 (*0-917476-13-1*) Inst Rational-Emotive.

Merrifield, D. Bruce. Strategic Analysis, Selection, & Management of R & D Projects. LC 77-14599. (AMA Management Briefing Ser.). 54p. reprint ed. pap. 25.00 (*0-317-29944-1*, 2051699) Bks Demand.

***Merrifield, Doris F.** Deutsche Wirtschaftssprache Fir Amerikaner. 3rd ed. 1994. disk, pap. text ed. write for info. (*0-471-10788-3*) Wiley.

— Deutsche Wirtschaftssprache fur Amerikaner. 2nd ed. 282p. 1989. Net. text ed. write for info. (*0-471-61374-6*); Net. audio write for info. (*0-471-50238-3*); audio 19.95 (*0-471-50237-5*) Wiley.

— Deutsche Wirtschaftssprache Fur Amerikaner. 3rd ed. 1994. text ed. write for info. (*0-471-30947-8*) Wiley.

— Praktische Anleitung Zur Interpretation Von Dichtung. LC 81-40127. 246p. (Orig.). 1982. pap. text ed. 21.50 (*0-8191-2054-5*) U Pr of Amer.

Merrifield, Doris F., jt. auth. see Haas, Werner.

Merrifield, Fred, ed. Modern Religious Verse & Prose: An Anthology. LC 79-51964. (Granger Poetry Library). 1980. reprint ed. 32.50 (*0-89609-186-4*) Roth Pub Inc.

Merrifield, Gladys. Twentieth Reunion & Other Poems. limited ed. LC 84-70671. (Living Poets' Library Ser.: No. 31). 1984. 5.00 (*0-934218-31-5*) Dragons Teeth.

— Windows on Manhattan. (Living Poets' Library Ser.). 1986. pap. 5.00 (*0-934218-33-1*) Dragons Teeth.

Merrifield, Heyoehkah. Magical Art. LC 87-401423. (Illus.). (Orig.). (C). 1986. pap. 12.95 (*0-945122-00-4*) Rain Bird Pubs.

Merrifield, Heyoka. Sacred Art Sacred Earth: Transformative Art - Birthing a New Myth. (Illus.). 144p. (Orig.). (YA). 1994. pap. 19.95 (*0-945122-01-2*) Rain Bird Pubs.

Merrifield, Kathy. A Christian Cline: Observations about Life & God. 250p. (Orig.). 1992. pap. write for info. (*0-9630692-1-7*) Selaginella.

— The Oregon Gull Identification Workbook. 38p. 1991. pap. 9.95 (*0-9630692-0-9*) Selaginella.

Merrifield, Leroy S., et al. Labor Relations Law: Cases & Materials. 8th ed. (Contemporary Legal Education Ser.). 1002p. 1989. Statutory Appendix. 10.00 (*0-87473-442-8*); text ed. 42.00 (*0-87473-429-0*) Michie Butterworth.

Merrifield, Michael. Colorado Gonzo Rides Vol. 1: A Mountain Biker's Guide to Colorado's Best Single Track Trails. LC 91-71647. 192p. 1991. pap. write for info. (*0-9628867-0-X*) Blue Clover.

Merrifield, Ralph. The Archaeology of Ritual & Magic. (Illus.). 224p. (C). 1988. 25.00 (*0-941533-25-5*); pap. 15.95 (*0-941533-26-3*) New Amsterdam Bks.

Merrifield, Rebecca, jt. auth. see Merrifield, Calvin.

Merrifield, Richard E., jt. auth. see Simmons, Howard.

Merrifield, Scott. North Sulawesi Language Survey. (Language Data Asia-Pacific Ser.: No. 15). (Orig.). Date not set. pap. write for info. (*1-55671-000-3*); fiche write for info. (*1-55671-984-1*) Summer Instit Ling.

Merrifield, William, et al, eds. Gods, Heroes, Kinsmen: Ethnographic Studies from Irian Jaya, Indonesia. LC 83-80231. (International Museum of Cultures Publications: No. 17). 300p. (Orig.). 1983. pap. 16.00 (*0-88312-112-3*); fiche 16.00 (*0-88312-991-4*) Summer Instit Ling.

Merrifield, William R. Proto Otomanguean Kinship. LC 80-50558. (International Museum of Cultures Publications: No. 11). 400p. (Orig.). 1981. fiche 20.00 (*0-88312-982-5*) Summer Instit Ling.

Merrifield, William R., ed. Five Amazonian Studies: On Worldview & Cultural Change. LC 85-80411. (International Museum of Cultures Publications: No. 19). (Illus.). 96p. (Orig.). 1985. pap. text ed. 11.00 (*0-88312-174-3*); fiche 4.00 (*0-88312-256-1*) Summer Instit Ling.

— South American Kinship: Eight Kinship Systems from Brazil & Colombia. LC 85-80410. (International Museum of Cultures Publications: No. 18). (Illus.). 132p. (Orig.). 1985. pap. 12.00 (*0-88312-173-5*); fiche 8.00 (*0-88312-255-3*) Summer Instit Ling.

Merrifield, William R. & Rensch, Calvin R., eds. Syllables, Tone, & Verb Paradigms. (Publications in Lingustics: No. 95). 130p. (Orig.). 1990. pap. 10.00 (*0-88312-105-0*); fiche 6.00 (*0-88312-630-3*) Summer Instit Ling.

Merrifield, William R., ed. see Anderson, Judi L.

Merrifield, William R., ed. see Powlison, Paul S.

Merrifield, William R., ed. see Price, Norman.

Merrifield, William R., ed. see Rensch, Calvin R.

Merrifield, William R., ed. see Rupp, James E.

Merrifield, William R., jt. ed. see Shin Ja Hwang.

Merrifield, William R., et al, eds. Laboratory Manual for Morphology & Syntax. rev. ed. 291p. 1987. pap. text ed. 16.00 (*0-88312-785-7*); fiche 20.00 (*0-88312-381-9*) Summer Instit Ling.

Merrigan, John J., jt. auth. see Guy, Edward T.

Merrigan, M. W., jt. auth. see Amrhein, James E.

Merrigan, Michael W., jt. auth. see Amrhein, J. E.

Merrigan, Terrence. Clear Heads & Holy Hearts: The Religious & Theological Ideal of John Henry Newman. (Louvain Theological & Pastoral Monographs). 272p. (Orig.). 1991. pap. 24.99 (*0-8028-0567-1*) Eerdmans.

Merriam, Robert L. A Christmas Legend. (Illus.). 9p. (Orig.). 1970. pap. 1.50 (*0-686-32485-4*) R L Merriam.

Merril, Carl R., ed. see Kroc Foundation Conference Staff.

Merril, Thomas F. Allen Ginsberg. rev. ed. (United States Authors Ser.: No. 161). 168p. 1988. text ed. 21.95 (*0-8057-7510-2*, Twayne) Macmillan.

***Merril, William L.** A Calculator Tutorial. (Illus.). 1994. pap. text ed. 8.95 (*0-914534-11-4*) Stokes.

Merrilees, Cynthia & Haack, Pamela. Write on Target. (Illus.). 63p. 1992. reprint ed. pap. 8.95 (*0-9627389-2-1*, Crystal Spgs) Soc Dev Educ.

Merrill, A. L., jt. auth. see Schwamb, P.

Merrill, A. Marion & Sprague, Grace E. Contemporary Verse. LC 72-8281. (Granger Index Reprint Ser.). 1977. reprint ed. 45.95 (*0-8369-6392-X*) Ayer.

Merrill, A. Roger & Merrill, Rebecca R. Connections: Quadrant II Time Management. 2nd rev. ed. 152p. 1989. 16.95 (*0-9622363-0-6*) IPCL.

Merrill, A. Roger, jt. auth. see Covey, Stephen R.

Merrill, Arch. Land of the Senecas. LC 86-13446. (Arch Merrill's New York Ser.: vol. 8). (Illus.). 168p. 1986. reprint ed. pap. 9.95 (*0-932334-82-2*, NY36042, Empire State Bks) Hrt of the Lakes.

— A River Ramble. (Arch Merrill's New York Ser.). (Illus.). 200p. 1995. pap. 9.95 (*1-55787-005-5*, Empire State Bks) Hrt of the Lakes.

— Rochester Sketchbook. LC 86-25741. (Arch Merrill's New York Ser.: Vol. 5). (Illus.). 192p. 1986. reprint ed. pap. 9.95 (*0-932334-84-9*, NY36039, Empire State Bks) Hrt of the Lakes.

— Shadows on the Wall. LC 87-24477. (Arch Merrill's New York Ser.: Vol. 11). (Illus.). 168p. 1987. reprint ed. pap. 9.95 (*1-55787-000-4*, NY36045, Empire State Bks) Hrt of the Lakes.

— Slim Fingers Beckon. LC 86-33602. (Arch Merrill's New York Ser.: Vol. 10). (Illus.). 204p. 1987. reprint ed. pap. 9.95 (*0-932334-86-5*, NY36044, Empire State Bks) Hrt of the Lakes.

— Southern Tier, Vol. I. LC 86-7694. (Arch Merrill's New York Ser.: Vol. 12). (Illus.). 240p. 1986. reprint ed. pap. 9.95 (*0-932334-46-6*, NY36046, Empire State Bks) Hrt of the Lakes.

— Southern Tier II. (Arch Merrill's New York Ser.). (Illus.). 200p. 1994. pap. 9.95 (*1-55787-006-3*, Empire State Bks) Hrt of the Lakes.

— Stagecoach Towns. (Arch Merrill's New York Ser.: Vol. 6). 208p. 1991. reprint ed. pap. 9.95 (*1-55787-002-0*, 76040, Empire State Bks) Hrt of the Lakes.

— The Towpath. (Arch Merrill's New York Ser.: Vol. 4). (Illus.). 208p. 1989. reprint ed. pap. 9.95 (*1-55787-001-2*, 76038, Empire State Bks) Hrt of the Lakes.

— The Underground, Freedom's Road, & Other Upstate Tales. LC 93-24251. 1995. pap. 9.95 (*1-55787-004-7*, Empire State Bks) Hrt of the Lakes.

— Upstate Echos. (Arch Merrill's New York Ser.: Vol. 9). (Illus.). 168p. 1992. reprint ed. pap. 9.95 (*1-55787-003-9*, 76043, Empire State Bks) Hrt of the Lakes.

— The White Woman & Her Valley. LC 87-434. (Arch Merrill's New York Ser.: Vol. 14). (Illus.). 228p. 1987. reprint ed. pap. 9.95 (*0-932334-88-1*, NY36048, Empire State Bks) Hrt of the Lakes.

Merrill, Arthur A. Battle of White Plains. (Illus.). (YA). (gr. 7 up). 1976. pap. 3.00 (*0-911894-27-6*) Analysis.

— Behavior of Prices on Wall Street. 2nd rev. ed. (Illus.). 147p. 1984. 35.00 (*0-911894-49-7*) Analysis.

— Chess Openings Simplified. 1974. pap. 3.75 (*0-911894-24-1*) Analysis.

— Circumpolar Constellations. (Illus.). 1962. pap. 3.00 (*0-911894-37-3*) Analysis.

— Filtered Waves, Basic Theory. LC 77-77420. (Illus.). 1977. 15.00 (*0-911894-36-5*) Analysis.

— Fitting Linear & Curvilinear Regression Lines with a Pocket Calculator. 1978. pap. 3.00 (*0-911894-40-3*) Analysis.

— Log Scale Construction. 29p. pap. 4.00 (*0-911894-31-4*) Analysis.

— Merrill MW Waves. (Illus.). 1979. 20.00 (*0-911894-44-6*) Analysis.

— Remembering Names: Improvement Is Easy. (Illus.). 57p. 1985. 9.75 (*0-911894-50-0*) Analysis.

— Revolutionary War: An Outline & Calendar. (Illus.). (YA). (gr. 7 up). 1976. pap. 2.00 (*0-911894-35-7*) Analysis.

Merrill, Arthur L. United Theological Seminary of the Twin Cities: An Ecumenical Venture. LC 92-41819. (Illus.). 340p. 1993. text ed. 99.95 (*0-7734-9201-1*) E Mellen.

Merrill, Arthur L. & Overholt, Thomas W., eds. Scripture in History & Theology: Essays in Honor of J. Coert Rylaarsdam. LC 77-12106. (Pittsburgh Theological Monographs: No. 17). 1977. pap. 10.00 (*0-915138-32-8*) Pickwick.

Merrill, Barbara. Learn about Teaching from Children: An Outstanding Guide for All early Childhood Educators. 5th ed. (Illus.). 53p. 5.00 (*0-9613271-1-1*) RAEYC.

***Merrill, Bill J.** Go to the Light. 280p. 1995. pap. 8.95 (*1-56901-791-3*) NW Pub.

Merrill, Boynton, Jr. A Bestiary. LC 75-3549. (Illus.). 72p. 1976. 10.00 (*0-8131-1329-6*) U Pr of Ky.

— Jefferson's Nephews: A Frontier Tragedy. LC 87-19005. 480p. 1987. reprint ed. pap. 20.00 (*0-8131-0173-5*) U Pr of Ky.

Merrill, Byron R., et al, comps. Heavens Are Open: Sperry Symposium on the Doctrine & Covenants, 1992. LC 93-16876. viii, 326p. 1993. 14.95 (*0-87579-741-5*) Deseret Bk.

Merrill, Caroline, jt. auth. see Merrill, John.

Merrill, Charles. Emily's Year. 1992. pap. 7.95 (*0-917320-34-4*) Mho & Mho.

— The Great Ukrainian Partisan Movement & Other Tales of the Eisenhower Years. LC 83-11758. 245p. (Orig.). 1983. pap. 10.95 (*0-87233-071-0*) Bauhan.

Merrill, Christopher. From the Faraway Nearby: Georgia O'Keeffe As Icon. 1993. pap. 16.30 (*0-201-62476-1*) Addison-Wesley.

— The Grass of Another Country: A Journey Through the World of Soccer. LC 93-4022. 160p. 1993. 20.00 (*0-8050-2771-8*) H Holt & Co.

— Grass of Another Country: A Journey Through the World of Soccer. 1994. pap. 12.95 (*0-8050-3591-5*) H Holt & Co.

— Only Nails Remain. 1996. 20.00 (*0-8050-3049-2*) H Holt & Co.

— Watch Fire. 1994. pap. 14.00 (*1-877727-43-1*) White Pine.

Merrill, Christopher, ed. The Forgotten Language: Contemporary Poets & Nature. 200p. (Orig.). 1991. pap. 15.95 (*0-87905-376-3*) Gibbs Smith Pub.

Merrill, Christopher, tr. Anxious Moments: Prose Poems by Ales Debeljak. 1994. 12.00 (*1-877727-35-0*) White Pine.

Merrill, Christopher, jt. ed. see Bradbury, Ellen.

Merrill, Christopher, jt. ed. see Buckley, Christopher.

Merrill, Claire. A Seed Is a Promise. (J). 1990. pap. 2.50 (*0-590-43454-3*) Scholastic Inc.

Merrill, Dale T., ed. see Merrill, Jane P. & Sunderland, Karen M.

Merrill, Daniel D. Augustus De Morgan & the Logic of Relations. (New Synthese Historical Library). 272p. 1990. lib. bdg. 126.50 (*0-7923-0758-5*) Kluwer Ac.

Merrill, Daniel D., jt. auth. see Grimm, Robert H.

Merrill, Daniel D., ed. see Oberlin Colloquium in Philosophy Staff.

***Merrill, David W.** Life Is a Test & You Will Pass. (Illus.). 40p. 1995. pap. 9.95 (*1-879418-96-7*) Audenreed Pr.

Merrill, Dawn. Senior Care Directory. rev. ed. (Illus.). 256p. 1987. pap. text ed. 2.00 (*0-941335-00-3*) Senior Media.

Merrill, Dean. Wait Quietly: Devotions for a Busy Parent. LC 94-11854. 224p. 1994. pap. 9.99 (*0-8423-7917-7*) Tyndale.

Merrill, Dennis. Bread & the Ballot: The United States & India's Economic Development, 1947-1963. LC 90-50012. (Illus.). xvi, 282p. (C). 1990. 45.00 (*0-8078-1920-4*) U of NC Pr.

Merrill, Dennis J., jt. auth. see Paterson, Thomas G.

Merrill, E. D. A Commentary on Loureiro's "Flora Cochinchinensis" 1935. pap. 10.00 (*0-934454-24-8*) Lubrecht & Cramer.

— A Flora of Manila. 1968. reprint ed. 72.00 (*3-7682-0548-7*) Lubrecht & Cramer.

— Polynesian Botanical Bibliography, 1773-1935. (BMB Ser.: No. 144). 1937. 30.00 (*0-527-02252-7*) Periodicals Srv.

Merrill, E. D. & Walker, E. H. A Bibliography of Eastern Asiatic Botany: Supplement 1. 1960. 45.00 (*0-934454-11-6*) Lubrecht & Cramer.

Merrill, Eliphalet & Merrill, Phinehas. Gazetteer of the State of New Hampshire. 251p. 1987. reprint ed. pap. 17.50 (*1-55613-073-2*) Heritage Bk.

Merrill, Elmer D. Plantae Elmerianae Borneenses. LC 29-219. (University of California Publications in Social Welfare: Vol. 15). 320p. reprint ed. pap. 91.20 (*0-685-23621-8*, 2014751) Bks Demand.

Merrill, Elmer T., ed. Catullus. (College Classical Ser.). (LAT.). 1988. reprint ed. text ed. 32.50 (*0-89241-023-X*); reprint ed. pap. text ed. 16.00 (*0-89241-381-6*) Caratzas.

Merrill, Elmer T., ed. see Catullus, Gaius V.

Merrill, Eugene H. Deuteronomy. LC 94-12543. (New American Commentary Ser.: Vol. 4). 480p. 1994. 27.99 (*0-8054-0104-0*, 4201-04) Broadman.

— Kingdom of Priests: A History of Old Testament Israel. LC 87-30853. 1988. 27.99 (*0-8010-6220-9*) Baker Bk.

Merrill, Frances & Merrill, Mason. Among the Nudists. LC 72-9664. reprint ed. 37.00 (*0-404-57475-0*) AMS Pr.

— Nudism Comes to America. LC 72-9773. reprint ed. 45.00 (*0-404-57476-9*) AMS Pr.

Merrill, Francis, tr. see Guerin, Daniel.

Merrill, Frederic, ed. Oregon Rules of Civil Procedure Handbook, 1992. 600p. 1992. pap. 39.50 (*0-409-24969-6*) Butterworth Legal Pubs.

Merrill, Frederick T. Japan & the Opium Menace. Grob, Gerald N., ed. LC 80-1264. (Addiction in America Ser.). 1981. reprint ed. lib. bdg. 18.95 (*0-405-13607-2*) Ayer.

Merrill, Fredric R. The Oregon Rules of Civil Procedure in the Courts. 194p. (Orig.). 1988. pap. text ed. 18.50 (*0-317-92497-4*) Oregon Law Inst.

Merrill, G. D. History of Androscoggin County. (Illus.). 893p. 1989. reprint ed. lib. bdg. 94.00 (*0-8328-0561-0*) Higginson Bk Co.

Merrill, Gary & Mathewson, Mark. The Grilling Buddies. (Illus.). 64p. (Orig.). 1993. ring bd. 8.95 (*1-879432-05-6*) Explorers Guide Pub.

Merrill, George. Studies in Comparative Jurisprudence & the Conflict of Laws. xii, 247p. 1985. reprint ed. lib. bdg. 30.00 (*0-8377-0850-8*) Rothman.

— Studies in Comparative Jurisprudence & the Conflict of Laws. LC 33-33040. (Historical Reprints in Jurisprudence & Classical Legal Literature Ser.). xii, 247p. 1984. reprint ed. lib. bdg. 45.00 (*0-89941-340-4*, 303440) W S Hein.

Merrill, George P. First One Hundred Years of American Geology. (Illus.). 773p. 1969. reprint ed. lib. bdg. 20.00 (*0-02-849180-7*) Lubrecht & Cramer.

Merrill, George P. & Albritton, Claude C., eds. Contributions to a History of American State Geological & Natural History Surveys. LC 77-6529. (History of Geology Ser.). (Illus.). 1978. reprint ed. lib. bdg. 54.95 (*0-405-10450-2*) Ayer.

Merrill, George R., photos. Reflections: Psychological & Spiritual Images of the Heart. (Illus.). 1990. pap. 6.95 (*0-8091-3127-7*) Paulist Pr.

Merrill, Georgia D. History of Carroll County, New Hampshire. LC 73-181351. (Illus.). 1103p. 1991. reprint ed. 59.50 (*0-912274-13-1*) Picton Pr.

An Asterisk (*) at the beginning of an entry indicates that the title is appearing in BIP for the first time.

***Merrill, Georgia D., ed.** Allegany County & Its People: A Centennial Memorial History of Allegany County, Also, Histories of the Towns of the County. (Illus.). 951p. 1995. reprint ed. lib. bdg. 95.00 (*0-8328-4707-0*) Higginson Bk Co.

— History of Carroll County, New Hampshire. (Illus.). 987p. 1993. reprint ed. lib. bdg. 99.50 (*0-8328-3170-0*) Higginson Bk Co.

Merrill, Ginette, ed. see Howells, Elinor M.

Merrill, Henry A. Alexander Gifford, or, Vi'let's Boy: A Story of Negro Life. LC 72-1821. (Black Heritage Library Collection). 1977. reprint ed. 31.95 (*0-8369-9036-6*) Ayer.

Merrill, Horace S. Bourbon Democracy of the Middle West, 1865-1896. LC 53-8592. (Americana Library Ser.: No. 2). (Illus.). 1969. reprint ed. 20.00 (*0-295-97857-0*, AL2); reprint ed. pap. 10.00 (*0-295-95032-3*, ALP2) U of Wash Pr.

— William Freeman Vilas: Doctrinaire Democrat. 310p. 1992. reprint ed. text ed. 15.00 (*0-87020-269-3*) State Hist Soc Wis.

***Merrill, Hugh.** Esky: The Early Years at Esquire. LC 94-39575. (Illus.). 220p. (C). 1995. 27.95 (*0-8135-2165-3*) Rutgers U Pr.

Merrill, Irving R., ed. Bound for Idaho: The 1864 Trail Journal of Julius Merrill. LC 87-38315. (Illus.). 160p. (Orig.). 1989. pap. 13.95 (*0-89301-124-X*) U of Idaho Pr.

***Merrill, J. E., ed.** The Role of Microglial Cells & Astrocytes in Pathology. (Journal: Vol. 16, No. 3-4, 1994). (Illus.). 124p. 1995. pap. 46.50 (*3-8055-6086-9*) S Karger.

Merrill, J. L., ed. History of Alworth, New Hampshire: With the Proceedings of the Centennial Anniversary, Genealogical Records & Register of Farms. (Illus.). 306p. 1988. reprint ed. lib. bdg. 36.00 (*0-8328-0039-2*, NH0037) Higginson Bk Co.

Merrill, James. The Changing Light at Sandover. LC 81-70062. (Illus.). 512p. 1983. 25.00 (*0-689-11282-3*, Atheneum S&S) S&S Trade.

— The Changing Light at Sandover: A Poem. 1993. pap. 16.00 (*0-679-74736-2*) Knopf.

— The Diblos Notebook. LC 94-9180. 160p. 1994. reprint ed. pap. 9.95 (*1-56478-064-3*) Dalkey Arch.

— A Different Person. LC 94-7687. 288p. 1994. pap. 14.00 (*0-06-251079-7*) Harper SF.

— A Different Person: A Memoir. LC 92-37974. 1993. 12.50 (*0-679-42317-6*) Knopf.

— From the First Nine: Poems 1946-1976. LC 81-70062. 192p. 1982. pap. 14.95 (*0-689-11281-5*) Macmillan.

— The Inner Room: Poems. LC 88-45265. 112p. 1988. 16.95 (*0-394-57248-3*); pap. 8.95 (*0-679-72049-9*) Knopf.

— New Selected Poems. 1992. pap. 24.50 (*0-679-41082-1*) McKay.

— Santorini: Stopping the Leak. (Metacom Limited Edition Ser.: No. 8). 24p. 1982. 37.50 (*0-911381-07-4*) Metacom Pr.

— A Scattering of Salts. 1995. 20.00 (*0-679-44158-1*) Knopf.

— Selected Poems, 1946-1985. 1993. pap. 15.00 (*0-679-74731-1*) Knopf.

Merrill, James M. Battle Flags South: Story of the Civil War Navies on Western Waters. LC 71-86652. 334p. 1975. 32.50 (*0-8386-7448-8*) Fairleigh Dickinson.

***Merrill, Jane.** Monday Through Friday: Day Care Alternatives. fac. ed. LC 82-3364. 236p. 1982. reprint ed. pap. 67.30 (*0-7837-8260-8*, 2049038) Bks Demand.

Merrill, Jane P. & Sunderland, Karen M. Set for Life: Eat More - Weigh Less - Feel Terrific! rev. ed. (Illus.). 326p. 1991. pap. 16.95 (*0-685-48503-X*) Sunrise Pubs.

— Set for Life: Eat More, Weigh Less, Feel Terrific. 2nd ed. Merrill, Dale T., ed. (Illus.). 350p. (Orig.). 1988. pap. 16.95 (*0-9621168-2-3*) Sunrise Pubs.

***Merrill, J.C.** The Road to Health Care Reform: Designing a System that Works. 313p. (C). 1994. 29.95 (*0-306-44770-3*, Plenum Pr) Plenum.

Merrill, Jean. The Girl Who Loved Caterpillars. (Illus.). 32p. (J). (ps up). 1992. lib. bdg. 14.95 (*0-399-21871-8*, Philomel Bks) Putnam Pub Group.

— The Pushcart War. 224p. (J). 1987. mass mkt. 3.99 (*0-440-47147-8*, YB) Dell.

— The Pushcart War. LC 84-43131. (Illus.). 224p. (J). (gr. 5-8). 1992. lib. bdg. 14.89 (*0-06-020822-8*) HarpC Child Bks.

— Seraphina. 224p. (Orig.). 1980. pap. 1.75 (*0-449-50124-8*, Coventry) Fawcett.

— The Toothpaste Millionaire. LC 73-22055. (Illus.). 96p. (J). (gr. 2-5). 1974. 14.95 (*0-395-18511-4*) HM.

— Toothpaste Millionaire. (J). (gr. 4-7). 1993. pap. 4.95 (*0-395-66954-5*) HM.

Merrill, Jeffrey C., ed. Mental Health Services in the United States & England: Struggling for Change: Collected Papers Prepared for the Joint United States-England Conference on Mental Health Services Princeton, New Jersey, February 25-28, 1990. LC 91-61190. (Illus.). 160p. (Orig.). 1991. pap. write for info. (*0-942054-03-2*) R W Johnson Found.

Merrill, Jo Lynne, jt. auth. see Robertson, Charles H.

Merrill, Joan. Camcorder Video: Shooting & Editing Techniques. 320p. 1991. pap. text ed. write for info. (*0-13-110925-1*) P-H.

Merrill, John. Canal Walks, Vol. 1: Derbyshire & Nottinghamshire. 1986. 25.00 (*0-907496-30-X*, Pub. by JNM Pubns UK) St Mut.

— Circular Walks in Western Peakland. 48p. 1986. 25.00 (*0-907496-44-X*, Pub. by JNM Pubns UK) St Mut.

— D. P. R. Korea: Politics, Economics & Society. (Marxist Regimes Ser.). 220p. 1987. 47.50 (*0-86187-424-2*, Pub. by Pinter Pubs UK); pap. 17.50 (*0-86187-425-0*, Pub. by Pinter Pubs UK) St Martin.

— Korea: The Peninsular Origins of the War. LC 85-40990. (Illus.). 240p. 1989. 36.50 (*0-87413-300-9*) U Delaware Pr.

— Long Circular Walks in the Peak District. 64p. 1986. 25.00 (*0-907496-42-3*, Pub. by JNM Pubns UK) St Mut.

— North Yorkshire Moors Challenge Walk - 24 Miles. 32p. 1986. 29.00 (*0-907496-36-9*, Pub. by JNM Pubns UK) St Mut.

— Peak District Challenge Walk - 25 Miles. 32p. 1987. 29.00 (*0-907496-43-1*, Pub. by JNM Pubns UK) St Mut.

— The River's Way. 36p. 1986. 40.00 (*0-907496-41-5*, Pub. by JNM Pubns UK) St Mut.

— Touring the Peak District & Derbyshire by Car. 60p. 1989. 50.00 (*0-907496-22-9*, Pub. by JNM Pubns UK) St Mut.

— Turn Right at Death Valley. 1986. 30.00 (*0-907496-26-1*, Pub. by JNM Pubns UK) St Mut.

Merrill, John & Merrill, Caroline. Sketches of Historic Bennington, Vermont. (Illus.). 104p. reprint ed. pap. 13.50 (*1-55613-662-5*) Heritage Bk.

Merrill, John C. The Dialectic in Journalism: Toward a Responsible Use of Press Freedom. LC 88-7851. 259p. 1993. pap. text ed. 62.95 (*0-8071-1889-3*) La State U Pr.

— Global Journalism: Survey of International Communication. 2nd ed. 448p. (C). 1991. pap. text ed. 32.50 (*0-8013-0512-8*, 78345) Longman.

— Global Journalism: Survey of International Communication. 3rd ed. LC 94-22482. 480p. (C). 1995. pap. text ed. 33.95 (*0-8013-1438-0*) Longman.

— The Imperative of Freedom. 2nd ed. 246p. (C). 1990. reprint ed. lib. bdg. 42.00 (*0-932088-45-7*) Freedom Hse.

— The Imperative of Freedom. 246p. (C). 1990. reprint ed. pap. text ed. 27.25 (*0-932088-44-9*) Freedom Hse.

— Legacy of Wisdom: Great Thinkers & Journalism. LC 94-14357. 200p. 1994. 24.95x (*0-8138-2041-3*) Iowa St U Pr.

Merrill, John C., ed. see Dennis, Everette E.

Merrill, John C., et al. Modern Mass Media. 2nd ed. (C). 1994. text ed. 30.75 (*0-673-99025-7*) HarpCollege.

Merrill, John N. Arkwright of Cromford. 36p. 1987. 25.00 (*0-907496-35-0*, Pub. by JNM Pubns UK) St Mut.

— Customs of the Peak District & Derbyshire. 48p. 1987. 25.00 (*0-907496-34-2*, Pub. by JNM Pubns UK) St Mut.

— Derbyshire Inns - An A to Z Guide. 120p. 1987. 25.00 (*0-907496-71-7*, Pub. by JNM Pubns UK) St Mut.

— Derbyshire Punishment. 60p. 1987. 29.00 (*0-907496-33-4*, Pub. by JNM Pubns UK) St Mut.

— Halls & Castles of the Peak District & Derbyshire. 96p. 1987. 25.00 (*0-907496-72-5*, Pub. by JNM Pubns UK) St Mut.

— Hike to Be Fit...Strolling with John. 32p. 1987. 45.00 (*0-907496-51-2*, Pub. by JNM Pubns UK) St Mut.

— The John Merrill Walk Record Book. 72p. 1987. 40.00 (*0-907496-47-4*, Pub. by JNM Pubns UK) St Mut.

— John Merrill's Dark Peak Challenge - 24 Miles. 32p. 1987. 29.00 (*0-907496-66-0*, Pub. by JNM Pubns UK) St Mut.

— John Merrill's Lakeland Challenge Walk - 18 Miles. 32p. 1987. 29.00 (*0-907496-50-4*, Pub. by JNM Pubns UK) St Mut.

— John Merrill's Staffordshire Moorland Challenge Walk - 22 Miles. 32p. 1987. 35.00 (*0-907496-67-9*, Pub. by JNM Pubns UK) St Mut.

— John Merrill's Yorkshire Dales Challenge Walk - 23 Miles. 32p. 1987. 55.00 (*0-907496-28-8*, Pub. by JNM Pubns UK) St Mut.

— Legends of Derbyshire. 2nd ed. (Illus.). 71p. (Orig.). (J). (gr. 6 up). 1975. pap. 3.00 (*0-913714-15-1*) Legacy Books.

— Lost Industries of Derbyshire. 120p. 1987. 35.00 (*0-907496-32-6*, Pub. by JNM Pubns UK) St Mut.

— Peak District End to End Walks - 23 & 24 Miles. 52p. 1987. 29.00 (*0-907496-39-3*, Pub. by JNM Pubns UK) St Mut.

— The Peak District...Something to Remember Her By. (Illus.). 96p. (C). 1989. 50.00 (*0-907496-53-9*, Pub. by JNM Pubns UK) St Mut.

— Turn Right at Land's End. 208p. (C). 1989. 39.00 (*0-907496-74-1*, Pub. by JNM Pubns UK) St Mut.

— Winster - A Visitor's Guide. 20p. 1987. 45.00 (*0-907496-21-0*, Pub. by JNM Pubns UK) St Mut.

— With Mustard on My Back. 76p. (Orig.). 1985. pap. 23.00 (*0-907496-27-X*) St Mut.

Merrill, John R. Using Computers in Physics. LC 80-5681. 271p. 1980. pap. text ed. 23.00 (*0-8191-1134-1*) U Pr of Amer.

***Merrill, Joseph.** Cases in Cost Accounting. 224p. (C). 1994. pap. text ed., ring bd. 19.95 (*0-8403-9445-4*) Kendall-Hunt.

— The History of Amesbury & Merrimac, Massachusetts. LC 78-5866. (Illus.). 1978. reprint ed. 37.50 (*0-917890-08-6*) Heritage Bk.

— History of Amesbury, Mass., Including the First Seventeen Years of Salisbury, to the Separation in 1654; & Merrimac, from Its Incorporation in 1876. (Illus.). 451p. 1989. reprint ed. lib. bdg. 43.50 (*0-8328-0800-8*, MA0002) Higginson Bk Co.

Merrill, K., ed. see Wergeland, Agnes M.

Merrill, Kathleen & Rinder, Lawrence. Sophie Calle: Proofs. LC 93-39485. 1993. pap. 10.00 (*0-944722-16-4*) Hood Mus Art.

Merrill, Kathryn L. & Christian, Kristy L. In Jesus' Time: Teaching Bible History to Children of All Ages. LC 92-34224. (Illus.). 280p. 1993. pap. 16.95 (*0-935834-93-1*) Rainbow Books.

Merrill Library, Special Collections Dept. Staff. Name Index to the Library of Congress Collection of Mormon Diaries. LC 75-636249. (Western Text Society Ser.: Vol. 1, No. 2). 395p. reprint ed. pap. 112.60 (*0-8357-6231-9*, 2034606) Bks Demand.

Merrill, Linda. An Ideal Country: Paintings by Dwight William Tryon in the Freer Gallery of Art. LC 90-35669. (Illus.). 200p. 1990. text ed. 45.00 (*0-87451-538-6*); pap. 22.50 (*0-87451-539-4*) U Pr of New Eng.

— A Pot of Paint: Aesthetics on Trial in Whistler vs. Ruskin. LC 91-10802. (Illus.). 448p. (C). 1992. text ed. 35.00 (*1-56098-101-6*) Smithsonian.

— A Pot of Paint: Aesthetics on Trial in Whistler vs. Ruskin. LC 91-10802. (Illus.). 448p. 1993. reprint ed. pap. 19.95 (*1-56098-300-0*) Smithsonian.

***Merrill, Linda, ed.** With Kindest Regards: The Correspondence of James McNeill Whistler & Charles Lang Freer, 1890-1903. LC 94-48202. 1995. write for info. (*1-56098-532-1*) Smithsonian.

Merrill, Linda & Ridley, Sarah. The Princess & the Peacocks: Or, the Story of the Room. LC 92-72019. (Illus.). 32p. (J). (gr. k-4). 1993. 14.95 (*1-56282-327-2*); lib. bdg. 14.89 (*1-56282-328-0*) Hyprn Child.

Merrill, Linda, jt. auth. see Lawton, Thomas.

Merrill, Lisa, jt. auth. see Borisoff, Deborah.

Merrill, Lois J., jt. ed. see Forbes, Malcolm H.

Merrill, M. A., jt. auth. see Terman, Lewis M.

Merrill, M. David. Instructional Design Theory. Twitchell, David G., ed. LC 93-45441. 450p. 1994. 39.95 (*0-87778-275-X*) Educ Tech Pubns.

Merrill, M. David, et al. Teaching Concepts: An Instructional Design Guide. 2nd ed. LC 92-15348. (Illus.). 232p. 1992. 34.95 (*0-87778-247-4*) Educ Tech Pubns.

— TICCIT. Langdon, Danny G., ed. LC 79-24448. (Instructional Design Library). 144p. 1980. 23.95 (*0-87778-160-5*) Educ Tech Pubns.

Merrill, Madeline & Merrill, Richard. Dolls & Toys at the Essex Institute. LC 76-40405. (E.I. Museum Booklet Ser.). 1976. 5.95 (*0-88389-066-6*, Essx Institute) Peabody Essex Mus.

Merrill, Marlene D., ed. Growing up in Boston's Gilded Age: The Journal of Alice Stone Blackwell, 1872-1874. (Illus.). 272p. (C). 1990. 30.00 (*0-300-04777-0*) Yale U Pr.

Merrill, Marlene D., jt. ed. see Lasser, Carol.

Merrill, Mary L., et al. A Light Unto My Path. (Illus.). 185p. 1981. reprint ed. 10.00 (*0-686-33180-X*) Pathway Pubns.

Merrill, Mary P. Financial Planning in the Bank. Johns, Rebecca B., ed. (Illus.). 380p. 1990. text ed. 55.00 (*0-89982-364-5*) Am Bankers.

Merrill, Mason, jt. auth. see Merrill, Frances.

Merrill, Milton R. Reed Smoot: Apostle in Politics. (Western Experience Ser.). 500p. 1989. 37.50 (*0-87421-127-1*) Utah St U Pr.

— Reed Smoot: Apostle in Politics. LC 89-22621. (Western Experience Ser.). reprint ed. pap. 127.40 (*0-7837-9254-9*, 2049994) Bks Demand.

Merrill, Nancy O. A Concise History of Glass Represented in the Chrysler Museum Glass Collection. LC 89-63529. (Illus.). 227p. 1989. pap. 45.00 (*0-940744-58-9*) Chrysler Museum.

— Contemporary Glass: Virginia & North Carolina Artists. (Illus.). 16p. 1979. pap. 1.00 (*0-940744-23-6*) Chrysler Museum.

Merrill-Oldham, J. Managing a Library Binding Program. 159p. 1993. pap. 15.00 (*0-918006-68-6*) ARL.

Merrill-Oldham, J., et al. Preservation Program Models. 54p. 1991. pap. 40.00 (*0-918006-20-1*) ARL.

Merrill-Oldham, Jan. Conservation & Preservation of Library Materials. LC 82-1875. 1982. pap. text ed. 10.00 (*0-917590-07-4*) Univ Conn Lib.

Merrill-Oldham, Jan & Parisi, Paul. Guide to the Library Binding Institute Standard for Library Binding. LC 90-44329. 1990. pap. 15.00 (*0-8389-3391-2*) ALA.

Merrill, Orin S. Mysterious Scott: The Monte Cristo of Death Valley. LC 72-93067. (Illus.). 216p. 1972. reprint ed. pap. 8.50 (*0-912494-10-7*) Chalfant Pr.

Merrill, Pat, ed. see Puryear, Anne.

Merrill, Pat, ed. see Puryear, Herbert B.

Merrill, Paul F., et al. Computers in Education. 2nd ed. 384p. (C). 1991. pap. text ed. 42.00 (*0-205-13391-6*) Allyn.

Merrill, Peter T., jt. auth. see Birnbaum, Henrik.

Merrill, Phinehas, jt. auth. see Merrill, Eliphalet.

Merrill, R. B. Proceedings of the Sixth Lunar Science Conference. 1975. 1,539.00 (*0-08-020566-6*, Pub. by Pergamon Repr UK) Franklin.

Merrill, R. Dale. The Church Business Meeting. LC 68-28075. 1968. pap. 8.00 (*0-8170-0409-2*) Judson.

Merrill, Rebecca R., jt. auth. see Merrill, A. Roger.

Merrill, Richard, jt. auth. see Merrill, Madeline.

Merrill, Richard A., jt. auth. see Hutt, Peter B.

Merrill, Richard A., jt. auth. see Mashaw, Jerry L.

Merrill, Robert. Critical Essays on Kurt Vonnegut. (Critical Essays on American Literature Ser.). 248p. 1989. text ed. 45.00 (*0-8161-8893-9*) G K Hall.

— Joseph Heller. (United States Authors Ser.). 165p. 1987. text ed. 20.95 (*0-8057-7492-0*, TUSAS 512, Twayne) Macmillan.

— Norman Mailer. (United States Authors Ser.). 1978. lib. bdg. 16.95 (*0-8057-7254-5*, Twayne) Macmillan.

— Norman Mailer. rev. ed. (Twayne's United States Authors Ser.). 160p. 1992. text ed. 23.95 (*0-8057-3967-X*, Twayne) Macmillan.

— Sir Thomas Malory & the Cultural Crisis of the Late Middle Ages. LC 86-27318. (American University Studies: English Language & Literature: Ser. IV, Vol. 39). 469p. (C). 1987. text ed. 59.00 (*0-8204-0303-2*) P Lang Pubs.

Merrill, Robert, ed. Ethics-Aesthetics. (Post Modern Positions Ser.: Vol. 1). 1988. lib. bdg. 22.96 (*0-944624-00-6*); pap. text ed. 11.95 (*0-944624-01-4*) Maisonneuve Pr.

Merrill, Robert, jt. ed. see Brown, David J.

Merrill, Robert, jt. ed. see Foerstel, Lenora.

Merrill, Robert K., ed. Source & Migration Processes & Evaluation Techniques. (Treatise of Petroleum Geology, Handbook of Petroleum Geology Ser.). (Illus.). 213p. 1991. 18.00 (*0-89181-600-3*) AAPG.

Merrill, Ron. The Ideas of Ayn Rand. LC 91-11283. 203p. (C). 1991. 34.95 (*0-8126-9157-1*); pap. 16.95 (*0-8126-9158-X*) Open Court.

***Merrill, Ronald E. & Sedgwick, Henry D.** The New Venture Handbook: Everything You Need to Know to Start & Run Your Own Business. 304p. 1995. pap. 18.95 (*0-8144-7892-1*) AMACOM.

— The New Venture Handbook: Everything You Need to Know to Start & Run Your Own Business. LC 86-47818. 366p. reprint ed. pap. 104.40 (*0-7837-4237-1*, 2043926) Bks Demand.

Merrill, Ruth E. Plants Used in Basketry by the California Indians. (Illus.). 1980. reprint ed. 6.95 (*0-686-77544-9*) Acoma Bks.

Merrill, S. East of the Jordan. 256p. 1986. 350.00 (*1-85077-089-1*, Darf Pubs Ltd) St Mut.

— Making Multicandidate Elections More Democratic. 1988. 35.00 (*0-691-07770-3*) Princeton U Pr.

***Merrill, Samuel.** Newspaper Libel. (Handbook for the Press Ser.). 304p. 1995. lib. bdg. 37.50x (*0-8377-2476-7*) Rothman.

Merrill, Sarah A., et al. Abeunt Studia in Mores: A Festschrift for Helga Doblin on Philosophies of Education, & Personal Learning in the Humanities & Moral Sciences. 364p. (C). 1990. text ed. 38.00 (*0-8204-1224-4*) P Lang Pubs.

Merrill, Selah. Ancient Jerusalem. Davis, Moshe, ed. LC 77-70724. (America & the Holy Land Ser.). (Illus.). 1977. reprint ed. lib. bdg. 44.95 (*0-405-10267-4*) Ayer.

Merrill, Stuart. Pastels in Prose. 1975. 250.00 (*0-87968-310-4*) Gordon Pr.

— Une Voix dans la Foule. 1972. 250.00 (*0-8490-1267-8*) Gordon Pr.

Merrill, Susan C., ed. Occupational Therapy Across Cultural Boundaries: Theory, Practice & Professional Development. LC 91-36744. (Occupational Therapy in Health Care Ser.). 116p. 1992. lib. bdg. 29.95 (*1-56024-223-X*) Haworth Pr.

Merrill, Susan C., intro. Occupational Therapy & Psychosocial Dysfunction. LC 92-30263. (Occupational Therapy in Health Care Ser.: Vol. 8, Nos. 2 & 3). (Illus.). 247p. 1992. lib. bdg. 39.95 (*1-56024-330-9*); pap. text ed. 19.95 (*1-56024-331-7*) Haworth Pr.

Merrill, Thomas F. The Poetry of Charles Olson: A Primer. LC 81-40341. 224p. 1982. 32.50 (*0-87413-196-0*) U Delaware Pr.

— William Perkins 1558-1602, English Puritanist--His Pioneer Works on Casuistry: Discourse on Conscience & the Whole Treatise of Cases of Conscience. xx, 242p. 1966. text ed. 49.50 (*90-6004-115-1*, Pub. by B De Graaf NE) Coronet Bks.

Merrill, Tim, jt. auth. see Library of Congress, Federal Research Division Staff.

Merrill, Tim L. Guyana & Belize Country Studies: Area Handbook. 2nd ed. LC 93-10956. (Department of the Army, Area Handbook Ser.). 1993. 22.00 (*0-8444-0778-X*) Lib Congress.

Merrill, Tim L., ed. see Federal Research Division Staff.

Merrill, Toni. Activities for the Aged & Infirm: A Handbook for the Untrained Worker. (Illus.). 392p. 1979. 57.95 (*0-398-01294-6*) C C Thomas.

— Activities for the Aged & Infirm: A Handbook for the Untrained Worker. (Illus.). 392p. 1979. pap. 33.95 (*0-398-06287-0*) C C Thomas.

Merrill, Virginia H., jt. auth. see Newman, Thelma R.

Merrill, Walter M. Against Wind & Tide: A Biography of Wm. Lloyd Garrison. LC 63-10871. (Illus.). 407p. reprint ed. pap. 116.00 (*0-7837-1718-0*, 2057247) Bks Demand.

Merrill, Walter M., ed. see Garrison, William L.

Merrill, William. Code for Classifiers: Principles Governing the Consistent Placing of Books in a System of Classification. 2nd ed. 189p. reprint ed. pap. 53.90 (*0-317-26287-4*, 2024259) Bks Demand.

Merrill, William L. An Investigation of Ethnographic & Archaeological Specimens of Mescalbeans (Sophora secundiflora) in American Museums. (Technical Reports: No. 6). (Illus.). 1977. pap. 2.00 (*0-932206-15-8*) U Mich Mus Anthro.

— Raramuri Souls: Knowledge & Social Process in Northern Mexico. LC 87-62623. (Ethnographic Inquiry Ser.). (Illus.). 248p. (C). 1988. 29.95 (*0-87474-684-1*) Smithsonian.

Merrill, William M., ed. Beyond Fantasy. 215p. 16.95 (*0-9618391-0-4*) Inland Pub.

Merrills, J. & Fisher, J. Pharmacy Law & Practice. 384p. 1994. pap. 34.95 (*0-632-03232-4*, Pub. by Blckwell Sci Pubns UK) Blackwell Sci.

***Merrills, J. G.** The Development of International Law by the European Court of Human Rights. 2nd ed. (Melland Schill Monographs in International Law). 272p. 1995. text ed. 24.95 (*0-7190-4560-6*, Pub. by Manchester Univ Pr UK) St Martin.

— International Dispute Settlement. enl. ed. 310p. (C). 1991. pap. 85.00 (*0-949009-94-6*, Pub. by Grotius Pubns UK) St Mut.

Merrills, J. G., jt. auth. see Robertson, A. H.

Merrill's Marauders Association. History of Merrill's Marauders. LC 87-71198. 128p. 1987. 49.95 (*0-938021-14-1*) Turner Pub KY.

Merrim, Stephanie. Logos & the Word. LC 83-47648. (Utah Studies in Literature & Linguistics: Vol. 23). 106p. 1983. pap. 13.70 (*0-8204-0003-3*) P Lang Pubs.

Merrim, Stephanie, ed. Feminist Perspectives on Sor Juana Ines de la Cruz. LC 90-36787. (Latin American Literature & Culture Ser.). 189p. (C). 1991. text ed. 22.95 (0-8143-2215-8) Wayne St U Pr.

Merriman, Brian. Midnight Court. 1987. pap. 16.95 (0-85342-658-9) Dufour.

— Midnight Court. O'Connor, Frank, tr. 1990. 19.95 (0-86278-189-2, Pub. by OBrien Pr IE) Dufour.

— Midnight Court: A New Translation by Cosslett O'Cuinn. (Illus.). 87p. 1982. pap. 16.95 (0-685-25950-1, Pub. by Mercier Pr IE) Dufour.

— Midnight Court: Cuirt an Mhean-Oiche. 1990. pap. 7.95 (0-85342-244-3) Dufour.

— The Midnight Court & the Adventures of a Luckless Fellow. Ussher, Percy A., tr. LC 75-28825. (Illus.). 80p. reprint ed. 24.50 (0-404-13817-9) AMS Pr.

Merriman, Brigid O. Searching for Christ: The Spirituality of Dorothy Day. LC 93-23827. (Studies in American Catholicism: Vol. 13). (C). 1994. text ed. 29.95 (0-268-01750-6) U of Notre Dame Pr.

***Merriman, Chad.** Blood on the Sun. 1994. 15.95 (0-7451-4615-5, Gunsmoke) Chivers N Amer.

— Hard Country. large type ed. 1975. 12.00 (0-85456-364-4) Ulverscroft.

Merriman, D. & Thorpe, L. M., eds. The Connecticut River Ecological Study: The Impact of a Nuclear Power Plant. LC 76-11293. (AFS Monograph Ser.: No. 1). 252p. 1976. pap. 10.50 (0-913235-12-1) Am Fisheries Soc.

Merriman, D., jt. ed. see Davis, J. D.

Merriman, D., jt. ed. see Sears, M.

Merriman, David. The Control of Municipal Budgets: Toward the Effective Design of Tax & Expenditure Limitations. LC 87-2495. 180p. 1987. text ed. 55.00 (0-89930-217-3, MTM/, Quorum Bks) Greenwood.

Merriman, Henry S. Young Mistley. Van Thal, Herbert, ed. 1966. 12.95 (0-685-09212-7); pap. 8.95 (0-304-93090-3) Dufour.

Merriman, John, ed. Consciousness & Class Experience in 19th Century Europe. LC 79-16032. 261p. (C). 1980. 33.50 (0-8419-0444-8); pap. 16.95 (0-8419-0610-6) Holmes & Meier.

— French Cities in the Nineteenth Century: Class, Power, & Urbanization. LC 81-2520. 256p. 1982. 31.95 (0-8419-0464-2) Holmes & Meier.

Merriman, John M. The Margins of City Life: Explorations on the French Urban Frontier, 1815-1851. (Illus.). 336p. 1991. 49.95 (0-19-506438-0) OUP.

— The Red City: Limoges & the French Nineteenth Century. (Illus.). 352p. 1989. reprint ed. pap. 18.95 (0-19-505682-5) OUP.

***Merriman, Linda M. & Tollafield, David R., eds.** Assessment of the Lower Limb. LC 94-44955. 1995. write for info. (0-443-05030-9) Churchill.

Merriman, Lyle, jt. comp. see Voxman, Himie.

Merriman, Margarita. A New Look at Sixteenth-Century Counterpoint. LC 81-40924. (Illus.). 230p. (Orig.). 1982. lib. bdg. 56.00 (0-8191-2391-9) U Pr of Amer.

Merriman, Marion & Lerude, Warren. American Commander in Spain: Robert Hale Merriman & the Abraham Lincoln Brigade. LC 86-1360. (Wilbur S. Shepperson Series in History & Humanities: No. 21). (Illus.). 272p. 1986. 29.95 (0-87417-106-7) U of Nev Pr.

Merriman, Nick. Early Humans. LC 88-13431. (Eyewitness Bks.). (Illus.). 64p. (J). (gr. 5 up). 1989. 16.00 (0-394-82257-9); lib. bdg. 16.99 (0-394-92257-3) Knopf Bks Yng Read.

— The Peopling of London: Fifteen Thousand Years of Settlement from Overseas. (Illus.). 256p. 1994. pap. 25.00 (0-904818-59-4) U of Wash Pr.

Merriman, Nick, tr. see Bourdieu, Pierre & Darbel, Alain.

Merriman, P. A. & Browitt, C. W., eds. Natural Disasters: Protecting Vulnerable Communities. 600p. 1993. 134.00 (0-7844-1936-1) Am Soc Civil Eng.

Merriman, Paul. Investing for a Lifetime: Paul Merriman's Guide to Mutual Fund Strategies. 250p. 1991. text ed. 30.00 (1-55623-485-6) Irwin Prof Pubng.

Merriman, Raymond. The Gold Book: Geocosmic Correlations to Gold Price Cycles. Robertson, Arlene, ed. 320p. (Orig.). 1982. 95.00 (0-685-06095-0); pap. 15.00 (0-930706-13-7) Seek-It Pubns.

***Merriman, Raymond A.** Basic Principles of Geocosmic Signatures Related to Financial Market Timing. 63p. 1995. per. 12.95 (0-930706-22-6) Seek-It Pubns.

— Evolutionary Astrology: The Journey of the Soul Through States of Consciousness. 255p. 1991. per. 25.00 (0-930706-18-8) Seek-It Pubns.

— Merriman on Market Cycles: The Basics. 64p. 1994. per. 25.00 (0-930706-20-X) Seek-It Pubns.

— Solar Return Book of Prediction. (Illus.). 132p. 1977. per. 5.95 (0-930706-00-5) Seek-It Pubns.

— The Sun, the Moon & the Silver Market: Secrets of a Silver Trader. 112p. 1992. per. 75.00 (0-930706-19-6) Seek-It Pubns.

Merriman, Raymond A. & Woodsmall, John. FAR: The Financial Astrological Research Program for Market Timing. 60p. 1994. per. 10.00 (0-930706-21-8) Seek-It Pubns.

— FAR: The Financial Astrological Research Program for Market Timing. 1994. disk 595.00 (0-614-01222-8) Seek-It Pubns.

Merriman, Roger B. Life & Letters of Thomas Cromwell, 2 vols. Incl. Vol. 1. Life, Letters of 1535. 1902. (0-318-54855-0); Vol. 2-. Letters from 1536, Notes, Index. 1902. (0-318-54856-9); 1969. 85.00 (0-19-822305-6) OUP.

Merriman, William E. & Bowman, Laura L. The Mutual Exclusivity Bias in Children's Word Learning. (Monographs of the Society for Research in Child Development: No. 220). 126p. 1990. pap. text ed. 14.50 (0-226-52066-8) U Ch Pr.

Merriman, William E., jt. ed. see Tomasello, Michael.

Merrin, Jeredith. An Enabling Humility: Marianne Moore, Elizabeth Bishop, & the Uses of Tradition. LC 89-70037. 184p. (C). 1990. text ed. 35.00 (0-8135-1547-5); pap. text ed. 17.00 (0-8135-1623-4) Rutgers U Pr.

Merrin, Leona M. Standing Ovations...Devi Dja: Woman of Java. Baum, Mary, ed. (Illus.). 417p. (Orig.). 1990. pap. 8.95 (0-9624120-0-7) Lee & Lee Pub.

***Merrin, Robbin.** Corel Ventura 5 Quick & Easy. LC 94-69702. 200p. 1995. 16.99 (0-7821-1666-3) Sybex.

Merrin, Robin. CorelDRAW 5 Quick & Easy. LC 94-67201. 167p. 1994. pap. 19.99 (0-7821-1461-X) Sybex.

— Up & Running with XTreeGold 2. LC 91-65166. 144p. (Orig.). 1991. pap. 9.95 (0-89588-820-3) Sybex.

— WordPerfect 6 for DOS Instant Reference. LC 93-84820. 245p. 1993. pap. 9.95 (0-7821-1197-1) Sybex.

***Merrin, Robin & Armstrong, James.** The Mosaic Roadmap. 1995. 22.99 (0-7821-1698-1) Sybex.

Merringer, John, tr. see Colletti, Lucio.

Merrins. Golf for the Young. (J). 1983. pap. 9.95 (0-689-70659-6, Atheneum S&S) S&S Trade.

Merrins, Matther R., jt. ed. see Brannigan, Gary G.

Merrion, Daid R. Diesel Engine Design for the Nineties; Fortieth Buckendale Lecture: SAE International Congress & Exposition 1994. (Special Publications). 160p. 1994. pap. 15.00 (1-56091-463-7, SP-1011) Soc Auto Engineers.

Merrion, Margaret & Madsen, Clifford, eds. What Works: Instructional Strategies for Music Education. (Illus.). 132p. (Orig.). (C). 1989. pap. 13.50 (0-940796-61-9, 1501) Music Ed Natl.

***Merrion, Margaret & Rubin, Janet, comps.** Drama & Music: Creative Activities for Young Children. LC 94-24087. 192p. 1995. 18.95 (0-89334-236-X) Humanics Ltd.

Merrion, Margaret, jt. auth. see Rubin, Janet.

Merrion, Margaret D. & Vincent, Marilyn C. A Primer on Music for Non-Musician Educators. LC 88-60072. (Fastback Ser.: No. 270). 50p. (Orig.). 1988. pap. 1.25 (0-87367-270-4) Phi Delta Kappa.

Merrison, Lynne. Rice. (Foods We Eat Ser.). (Illus.). 32p. (J). (gr. 1-4). 1990. lib. bdg. 14.96 (0-87614-417-2, Carolrhoda) Lerner Group.

Merrison, Tim. Books. Stefoff, Rebecca, ed. LC 90-13868. (Media Story Ser.). (Illus.). 32p. (J). (gr. 4-8). 1991. lib. bdg. 17.26 (0-944483-96-8) Garrett Ed Corp.

— Comics & Magazines. Stefoff, Rebecca, ed. LC 90-13985. (Media Story Ser.). (Illus.). 32p. (J). (gr. 4-8). 1991. lib. bdg. 17.26 (0-944483-97-6) Garrett Ed Corp.

— Field Athletics. LC 90-27451. (Olympic Sports Ser.). (Illus.). 48p. (J). (gr. 6). 1991. text ed. 13.95 (0-89686-665-3, Crstwood Hse) Silver Burdett Pr.

— Movies. Stefoff, Rebecca, ed. LC 90-3964. (Media Story Ser.). (Illus.). 32p. (J). (gr. 4-8). 1991. lib. bdg. 17.26 (0-944483-94-1) Garrett Ed Corp.

Merriss, William E. & Griswold, David H. Composition Handbook. 3rd ed. 1985. pap. text ed. 8.50 (0-88334-084-4) Longman.

— A Composition Handbook. 3rd ed. (J). 1985. teacher ed 10.84 (0-8013-0074-6, 75738); pap. text ed. 17.28 (0-88334-186-7, 76152) Longman.

Merrit, A. Dwellers in the Mirage. 1993. reprint ed. lib. bdg. 18.95 (0-89968-407-6, Lghtyr Pr) Buccaneer Bks.

— The Moon Pool. 1993. reprint ed. lib. bdg. 18.95 (0-89968-408-4, Lghtyr Pr) Buccaneer Bks.

***Merrit, Chris.** Crossing the Border: The Canada-United States Boundary. (Borderlands Monograph Ser.: No. 5). 19-55p. (C). 1991. pap. text ed. 5.00 (0-614-04707-2) Canadian-Amer Ctr.

Merrit, Ella A., jt. ed. see Chenery, William L.

***Merrit, J. I., et al, eds.** The Best of Field & Stream: 100 Years of Great Writing From America's Premier Sporting Magazine. LC 94-37855. (Illus.). 352p. 1995. 25.00 (1-55821-288-4) Lyons & Burford.

Merrit, Jeffrey. Day by Day: The Fifties. (Day by Day Ser.). (Illus.). 1036p. 1979. 125.00 (0-87196-383-3) Facts on File.

Merrit, Roy D. Coal Overburden: Geological Characterization & Premine Planning. LC 83-13093. (Energy Technology Review Ser.: No. 88). (Illus.). 343p. 1984. 39.00 (0-8155-0964-2) Noyes.

Merrit, Walter. History for the League for Industrial Rights. LC 76-120852. (Civil Liberties in American History Ser.). 1970. reprint ed. lib. bdg. 22.50 (0-306-71961-4) Da Capo.

***Merrithew, Cathy.** The Shetland Sheepdog. (Owner's Guide to a Happy, Healthy Pet Ser.). 160p. Date not set. 12.95 (0-87605-385-1) Howell Bk.

***Merritt.** Face in the Abyss. 1994. pap. 3.99 (0-517-13515-9) Random.

— Year Book of Ultrasound, 1993. 328p. 1993. 75.00 (0-8151-6046-1, Yr Bk Med Pubs) Mosby Yr Bk.

— Year Book of Ultrasound, 1994. 328p. 1994. 75.00 (0-8151-6047-X, Yr Bk Med Pubs) Mosby Yr Bk.

— Year Book of Ultrasound, 1995. 328p. 1995. 75.00 (0-8151-6048-8, Yr Bk Med Pubs) Mosby Yr Bk.

— Year Book of Ultrasound, 1996. 350p. 1996. 75.00 (0-8151-6049-6, Yr Bk Med Pubs) Mosby Yr Bk.

— Yearbook of Ultrasound, 1991. 311p. 1991. 75.00 (0-8151-5893-9) Mosby Yr Bk.

— Yearbook of Ultrasound, 1992. 357p. 1992. 75.00 (0-8151-5892-0) Mosby Yr Bk.

Merritt & McEwen. Mass Spectronomy, Pt. A. (Practical Spectroscopy Ser.: Vol. 3). 304p. 1979. 145.00 (0-8247-6749-7) Dekker.

Merritt, A. Creep, Shadow, Creep! 1991. reprint ed. lib. bdg. 21.95 (1-56849-033-X) Buccaneer Bks.

— Dwellers in the Mirage. 288p. 1991. pap. 5.95 (0-02-022872-4, Pub. by Gebrueder Borntraeger GW) Macmillan.

— The Face in the Abyss. (Illus.). 1991. 30.00 (0-937986-01-1); 60.00 (0-937986-00-3) D M Grant.

— The Face in the Abyss. 288p. 1992. pap. 9.00 (0-02-022873-2, Pub. by Gebrueder Borntraeger GW) Macmillan.

— The Metal Monster. 224p. (Orig.). 1993. pap. 3.95 (0-88184-979-0) Carroll & Graf.

— The Metal Monster. (Orig.). 1991. reprint ed. lib. bdg. 21.95 (1-56849-081-X) Buccaneer Bks.

— Metal Monster. LC 73-13259. (Classics of Science Fiction Ser.). 209p. 1989. reprint ed. 20.00 (0-88355-114-4); reprint ed. pap. 10.00 (0-88355-143-8) Hyperion Conn.

— The Moon Pool. 448p. 1993. pap. 4.95 (0-88184-891-3) Carroll & Graf.

— Ship of Ishtar. limited ed. 1990. 35.00 (0-87505-355-6) Borden.

— The Ship of Ishtar. (Nucleus Science Fiction Ser.). 304p. 1991. reprint ed. pap. 4.95 (0-02-022871-6, Pub. by Gebrueder Borntraeger GW) Macmillan.

Merritt, Abraham. The Fox Woman & Other Stories. Reginald, R. & Melville, Douglas, eds. LC 77-84256. (Lost Race & Adult Fantasy Ser.). 1978. reprint ed. lib. bdg. 19.95 (0-405-11000-6) Ayer.

Merritt, Abraham & Bok, Hannes. The Fox Woman & the Blue Pagoda & the Black Wheel, 2 vols. in one. LC 75-46293. (Supernatural & Occult Fiction Ser.). 1976. reprint ed. lib. bdg. 23.95 (0-405-08153-7) Ayer.

Merritt, Andrew. Jesus Destroyed the Works of the Devil. Temperance Publishing House Staff, ed. (Illus.). 20p. (Orig.). 1993. pap. 2.95 (0-9637640-0-4) A & V Pub.

— The Marriage Enrichment Handbook: Godly Principles for a Successful Marriage. Temperance Publishing House Staff, ed. (Illus.). 197p. (Orig.). 1993. pap. 9.95 (0-9637640-1-2) A & V Pub.

Merritt, Anna J. & Merritt, Richard L., eds. Public Opinion in Occupied Germany: The OMGUS Surveys, 1945. LC 74-943397. (Illus.). 350p. reprint ed. pap. 99.80 (0-317-08637-5, 2020223) Bks Demand.

Merritt, Anna J., jt. ed. see Merritt, Richard L.

Merritt, Arthur T. Sixteenth-Century Polyphony: A Basis for the Study of Counterpoint. LC 39-25128. (Illus.). 232p. reprint ed. pap. 66.20 (0-7837-6086-8, 2059132) Bks Demand.

Merritt, Bruce. The Patmos Conspiracy. Pierce, Glen A., ed. LC 90-80821. 288p. (Orig.). 1990. pap. 9.95 (0-916035-38-7) Evangel Indiana.

Merritt, Cathleen, jt. auth. see Bernhard, Keith.

Merritt, Cathleen, jt. ed. see Williams, Warren.

Merritt, Charles, Jr. & McEwen, Charles N., eds. Mass Spectrometry, Part B. LC 78-24085. (Practical Spectroscopy Ser.: No. 3). (Illus.). 415p. reprint ed. pap. 118.30 (0-7837-0670-7, 2041005) Bks Demand.

Merritt, Christopher R., ed. Doppler Color Imaging. (Clinics in Diagnostic Ultrasound Ser.: Vol. 27). (Illus.). 282p. 1992. text ed. 134.95 (0-443-08763-6) Churchill.

Merritt Company Staff. OSHA Construction Manual. 1995. ring bd. 397.00 (1-56343-069-X) Merritt Co.

— OSHA Reference Manual. 1995. ring bd. 397.00 (0-930868-03-X) Merritt Co.

— Risk Management Manual. 1995. ring bd. 397.00 (0-930868-02-1) Merritt Co.

— Spanish Glossary of Insurance Terms. 2nd ed. 209p. 1994. 9.95 (0-930868-83-8) Merritt Co.

Merritt, D. Adventure in Prolog. Muchnick, S. S. & Schnupp, P., eds. (Compass International Ser.). xii, 186p. 1990. 39.00 (0-387-97315-X) Spr-Verlag.

— Building Expert Systems in Prolog. (Compass International Ser.). (Illus.). xv, 358p. 1989. 52.00 (0-387-97016-9) Spr-Verlag.

— Building Expert Systems Prolog. 1989. 169.00 (0-387-97015-0) Spr-Verlag.

— Merritt. rev. ed. 204p. 1991. reprint ed. lib. bdg. 43.50 (0-8328-2076-8); reprint ed. pap. 33.50 (0-8328-2077-6) Higginson Bk Co.

Merritt, David, ed. Dynamics of Dense Stellar Systems. (Illus.). (C). 1989. 64.95 (0-521-36432-9) Cambridge U Pr.

***Merritt, Davis.** Telling the News Is Not Enough: An Editor's Challenge to Journalism. (Communication Ser.). 152p. 1995. text ed. 36.00 (0-8058-1982-7); pap. 17.50 (0-8058-1983-5) L Erlbaum Assocs.

Merritt, Dennis. Reflection. LC 92-71914. (Illus.). 114p. (Orig.). 1993. pap. 9.95 (1-881674-00-2) Amziod.

Merritt, Douglas. Graphic Design for Television. (Illus.). 128p. 1993. pap. 29.95 (0-240-51326-6, Focal) Buttrwrth-Heinemann.

— Television Graphics: From Pencil to Pixel. (Illus.). 160p. 1987. text ed. 10.98 (0-442-26469-0) Van Nos Reinhold.

Merritt, Elizabeth. James Henry Hammond, 1807-1864. LC 78-64112. (Johns Hopkins University. Studies in the Social Sciences. Thirtieth Ser. 1912: 4). reprint ed. 17.50 (0-404-61227-X) AMS Pr.

Merritt, Emma. Beneath a Texas Star. 448p. 1991. mass mkt. 4.50 (0-8217-3334-6) Zebra.

— Comanche Bride. 480p. 1989. pap. 3.95 (0-8217-2549-1) Zebra.

— Emerald Ecstasy. 496p. 1986. pap. 3.95 (0-8217-1908-4) Zebra.

— Lady of Summer. 400p. (Orig.). 1995. mass mkt. 5.50 (0-380-77984-6) Avon.

— Lone Star Lovesong. 512p. 1988. pap. 3.95 (0-8217-2373-1) Zebra.

— Lord of Fire. 400p. (Orig.). 1994. mass mkt. 4.50 (0-380-77288-4) Avon.

— Lord of Thunder. 432p. (Orig.). 1994. mass mkt. 4.99 (0-380-77290-6) Avon.

— Masque of Jade. 1990. mass mkt. 4.50 (0-8217-2956-X) Zebra.

— Restless Flames. (Hologram Romances Ser.). 1987. pap. 3.95 (0-8217-2203-4) Zebra.

— Sweet Wild Love. 1989. mass mkt. 4.50 (0-8217-2834-2) Zebra.

— Texas Touch. 448p. 1992. mass mkt. 4.50 (0-8217-3845-3) Zebra.

— Viking Captive. 1992. mass mkt. 4.50 (0-8217-3626-4) Zebra.

Merritt, Frederick S. Building Design & Construction Handbook. 5th ed. 1994. text ed. 99.95 (0-07-041596-X) McGraw.

Merritt, Frederick S., ed. Manual del Ingeniero Civil. 3rd ed. 1992. text ed. 124.50 (0-07-104148-6) McGraw.

— Standard Handbook for Civil Engineers. 3rd ed. 1632p. 1983. text ed. 124.50 (0-07-041515-3) McGraw.

Merritt, Frederick S. & Ambrose, James E. Building Engineering & Systems Design. 2nd ed. (Illus.). 656p. 1989. text ed. 65.00 (0-442-20668-2) Chapman & Hall.

***Merritt, Frederick S., et al, eds.** Standard Handbook for Civil Engineers. 4th ed. LC 95-11425. 1995. text ed. 96.50 (0-07-041597-8) McGraw.

Merritt, H. Wayne. In Word & Deed: Understanding Moral Integrity in Paul. LC 92-42844. (Emory Studies in Early Christianity: Vol. 1). 189p. (C). 1993. text ed. 41.95 (0-8204-1103-5) P Lang Pubs.

Merritt, Hardy L., ed. see Boykin, Milton L.

Merritt, Helen. Modern Japanese Woodblock Prints: The Early Years. LC 89-27923. (Illus.). 344p. 1990. text ed. 46.00 (0-8248-1200-X) UH Pr.

Merritt, Helen & Yamada, Nanko. Guide to Modern Japanese Woodblock Prints. (Illus.). 384p. 1992. text ed. 90.00 (0-8248-1286-7) UH Pr.

Merritt, Herbert E. Hydraulic Control Systems. LC 66-28759. 358p. 1991. text ed. 99.95 (0-471-59617-5, Wiley-Interscience) Wiley.

***Merritt, Hiram H. & Yahr, Melvin D., eds.** H. Houston Merritt: Memorial Volume. fac. ed. LC 82-23106. (Illus.). 231p. Date not set. pap. 65.90 (0-7837-7199-1, 2047100) Bks Demand.

Merritt, Howard S. To Walk with Nature: The Drawings of Thomas Cole. LC 81-84873. (Illus.). 64p. (Orig.). 1981. pap. 5.00 (0-943651-11-5) Hudson Riv.

Merritt, J. & Fisher, Scott S., eds. Stereoscopic Displays & Applications. 1990. 62.00 (0-8194-0303-2, VOL. 1256) SPIE.

Merritt, J. I. Goodbye, Liberty Bell' A Son's Search for His Father's War. 1993. 18.95 (1-882090-08-X) Wright State Univ Pr.

— Goodbye, Liberty Belle: A Son's Search for His Father's War. LC 92-42784. (Illus.). 214p. (C). 1993. 24.50 (0-929090-08-X) Wright State Univ Pr.

Merritt, J. O., jt. ed. see Fisher, S. S.

Merritt, J. O., jt. auth. see Fisher, Scott S.

***Merritt, Jackie.** Accidental Bride. (Desire Ser.). 1995. pap. 3.25 (0-373-05914-0, 1-05914-6) Silhouette.

— Babe in the Woods. large type ed. (Desire Ser.). 1993. 17.95 (0-373-58804-6, Silhouette Lrg Print); pap. 16.95 (0-373-58904-2, Silhouette Lrg Print) Chivers N Amer.

— Hesitant Husband. (Desire Ser.). 1995. mass mkt. 3.25 (0-373-05935-3, 1-05935-1) Silhouette.

— The Lady & the Lumberjack. (Desire Ser.: No. 683). 1991. pap. 2.79 (0-373-05683-4) Harlequin Bks.

— A Man & a Million. 1995. mass mkt. 3.75 (0-373-09988-6, 1-09988-6) Silhouette.

— Montana Sky. (Silhouette Desire Ser.). 1993. mass mkt. 2.99 (0-373-05790-3, 5-05790-6) Silhouette.

— Mystery Lady. (Silhouette Desire Ser.). 1994. mass mkt. 2.99 (0-373-05849-7, 5-05849-0) Silhouette.

— Nevada Drifter. (Desire Ser.). 1994. mass mkt. 2.99 (0-373-05866-7, 1-05866-8) Silhouette.

— The Rancher Takes a Wife. (Montana Mavericks Ser.). 1994. mass mkt. 3.99 (0-373-50169-2, 1-50169-1) Harlequin Bks.

— Rebel Love. 1995. mass mkt. 3.25 (0-373-05965-5, 1-05965-8) Silhouette.

— Tennessee Waltz. (Silhouette Desire Ser.). 1993. pap. 2.89 (0-373-05774-1, 5-05774-0) Silhouette.

— The Widow & the Rodeo Man. (Montana Mavericks Ser.). 1994. mass mkt. 3.99 (0-373-50166-8, 1-50166-7) Silhouette.

— Wrangler's Lady. (Silhouette Desire Ser.). 1994. mass mkt. 2.99 (0-373-05841-1, 5-05841-7) Silhouette.

Merritt, John, jt ed. see Curthoys, Ann.

Merritt, John E., ed. see World Congress on Reading Staff.

Merritt, Jon. Empowering Children: A Parent's Guide to Building-in Success & Self-Esteem. 161p. 1990. pap. 8.95 (1-880360-01-2) Parent Res.

— A Parent's Primer: Seven Short Lessons in Child-Raising. 100p. 1991. pap. 8.95 (0-685-50035-7) Parent Res.

Merritt, Jon, jt. auth. see Bloch, Douglas.

Merritt, Joseph F. Guide to the Mammals of Pennsylvania. LC 87-40157. (Illus.). 448p. 1987. pap. 19.95 (0-8229-5393-5) U of Pittsburgh Pr.

Merritt, Joseph F., ed. Winter Ecology of Small Mammals. LC 84-72213. (Special Publication CMNH Ser.: No. 10). (Illus.). 390p. 1984. 47.50 (0-935868-10-0) Carnegie Mus.

***Merritt, Joseph F., et al, eds.** Advances in the Biology of Shrews. (Special Publications of CMNH Ser.: 18). x458p. (Orig.). 1994. pap. 40.00x (0-911239-44-8) Carnegie Mus.

Merritt, Justine. Journey. LC 93-10737. 144p. 1993. 22.00 (0-932727-68-9) Hope Pub Hse.

Merritt, King, jt. auth. see Crawley, Sharon J.

Merritt, LeRoy C., et al. Reviews in Library Book Selection. LC 58-62836. (Wayne State University Studies: Humanities: No. 3). 205p. reprint ed. pap. 58.50 (0-7837-3821-8, 2043641) Bks Demand.

Merritt, M. L., ed. see ERDA Technical Information Center Staff & ERDA Technical Information Center.

Merritt, Marion. Uphill Both Ways. LC 85-13349. (Illus.). 100p. 1985. pap. 6.95 (0-916897-05-2) Andrew Mtn Pr.

An Asterisk (*) at the beginning of an entry indicates that the title is appearing in BIP for the first time.

*Merritt, Michael L. Tests of Subsurface Storage of Freshwater at Hialeah, Dade County, Florida & Digital Simulation of the Salinity of Recovered Water. 2431. 1995. write for info. (0-615-00059-2) US Geol Survey.

Merritt, Nancy-Jo. Conozca las Leyes de Immigracion. 2nd ed. Castro, Maria C., tr. (Layman's Law Guides Ser.). 128p. 1994. pap. 8.95 (1-56414-090-3) Career Pr Inc.

— Understanding Immigration Law. 2nd ed. (Layman's Law Guides Ser.). 128p. 1994. pap. 8.95 (1-56414-089-X) Career Pr Inc.

— Understanding Immigration Law: How to Enter, Work & Live in the United States. 96p. 1992. pap. 9.95 (0-9630356-2-2) Makai.

*Merritt, Onera. An American Child. (American Autobiography Ser.). 192p. 1995. reprint ed. lib. bdg. 69.00 (0-7812-8592-5) Rprt Serv.

*Merritt, Patty & Wells, Rosie. Rosie Wells Enterprises' Official Price Guide for Precious Moments Applause Dolls. 88p. (Orig.). 1995. pap. 9.95 (1-886812-04-7) R Wells.

Merritt, Peggy. Snowcap. 117p. (Orig.). 1994. pap. 3.95 (0-943861-17-9) Lone Tree.

Merritt, Ray E., Jr. & Walley, Donald D. The Group Leader's Handbook: Resources, Techniques, & Survival Skills. (Illus.). (C). 1977. pap. text ed. 15.95 (0-87822-139-5, 1395) Res Press.

Merritt, Raymond W. & Ennico, Clifford R., eds. Corporate Counseling, Vols. One & Two, 2 vols. 1400p. 1988. 110.00 (0-942954-20-3) NYS Bar.

Merritt, Raymond W., ed. see Abramowitz, Elkan & Williamson, Allan P.

Merritt, Raymond W., ed. see Douglass, Catherine J. & Lieberman, Ellen.

Merritt, Raymond W., ed. see Manno, Christopher E. & Gartner, Steven J.

Merritt, Raymond W., ed. see New York State Bar Association Staff.

Merritt, Richard, ed. Foreign Policy. (C). 1974. pap. 12.00 (0-918592-09-7) Pol Studies.

Merritt, Richard F., jt. auth. see Miller, Susann C.

*Merritt, Richard L. Democracy Imposed: U. S. Occupation Policy & the German Public, 1945-1949. LC 95-4263. 1995. write for info. (0-300-06037-8) Yale U Pr.

— Foreign Policy Analysis. 176p. 1985. reprint ed. lib. bdg. 39.50 (0-8191-5145-9, Pol Studies) U Pr of Amer.

Merritt, Richard L., ed. Foreign Policy Analysis. 176p. 1975. boxed 32.95 (0-669-00251-8) Transaction Pubs.

— Foreign Policy Analysis. LC 75-27808. (Policy Studies Organization Ser.: No. 9). (Illus.). 175p. reprint ed. pap. 49.90 (0-8357-8880-6, 2033581) Bks Demand.

Merritt, Richard L. & Hanson, Elizabeth C. Science, Politics, & International Conferences: A Functional Analysis of the Moscow Political Science Congress. LC 88-18322. (GSIS Monograph in World Affairs). 1989. lib. bdg. 20.00 (1-55587-134-8) Lynne Rienner.

Merritt, Richard L. & Merritt, Anna J., eds. Living with the Wall: West Berlin, 1961-1985. LC 85-10234. (Duke Press Policy Studies). (Illus.). xiv, 242p. 1985. 37.00 (0-8223-0657-3) Duke.

Merritt, Richard L. & Pyszka, Gloria L. Students Political Scientists Handbook. 192p. 1975. pap. 13.95 (0-87073-251-X) Schenkman Bks Inc.

Merritt, Richard L., jt. ed. see Merritt, Anna J.

Merritt, Richard L., et al. International Event-Data Developments. 226p. 1993. text ed. 39.50 (0-472-10427-6) U of Mich Pr.

Merritt, Richard W. & Cummins, Kenneth W. Aquatic Insects of North America. 2nd ed. 768p. (C). 1995. pap. text ed. 69.95 (0-8403-7588-3) Kendall-Hunt.

Merritt, Richard W., jt. ed. see Kim, Ke Chung.

Merritt, Robert. Early Music & the Aesthetics of Ezra Pound: Hush of Older Song. LC 93-32242. 176p. 1993. 79.95 (0-7734-9371-9) E Mellen.

— To the Death. 320p. 1990. mass mkt. 4.50 (0-380-70904-X) Avon.

— To the Death. 276p. 1988. 17.95 (0-945167-04-0) British Amer Pub.

Merritt, Robert C. Extractive Metallurgy of Uranium. LC 71-157076. (Illus.). 576p. 1979. reprint ed. 12.00 (0-918062-10-1) Colo Sch Mines.

Merritt, Robert E., Jr. Guide to California Subdivision Sales Law. LC 74-620082. xi, 204p. 1974. 60.00 (0-88124-031-1, RE-31320); write for info. (0-685-08742-5) Cont Ed Bar-CA.

Merritt, Robert E. & Corey, Arthur. Christian Science & Liberty. LC 70-132847. 1970. 8.95 (0-87516-060-3) DeVorss.

Merritt, Robert E., et al. Understanding Development Regulations. 248p. (Orig.). 1994. pap. 26.00 (0-923956-19-0) Solano Pr.

Merritt, Roy D. Coal Exploration, Mine Planning, & Development. LC 85-25869. (Illus.). 464p. 1986. 64.00 (0-8155-1070-5) Noyes.

Merritt, Russell & Kaufman, J. B. Walt in Wonderland: The Silent Films of Walt Disney. 176p. (C). 1994. 39.95 (0-8018-4907-1) Johns Hopkins.

Merritt Staff & Greene, Thomas E. Glossary of Insurance Terms. 5th ed. 276p. 1994. pap. text ed. 14.95 (0-685-72803-X) Merritt Co.

Merritt Staff, jt. auth. see Greene, Thomas E.

*Merritt, Steve. How to Build Wealth with Your 401(K) Everything You Need to Know to Become More Than a Millionaire over the Course of Your Working Lifetime. 224p. 1995. pap. text ed. 35.00 (1-887063-00-5) Halyard Pr.

— How to Invest for Retirement Wealth. 240p. 1995. pap. text ed. 45.00 (1-887063-01-3) Halyard Pr.

— How to Invest in Mutual Funds for Wealth Accumulation. 224p. 1995. pap. text ed. 35.00 (1-887063-02-1) Halyard Pr.

Merritt, Susan H. Pinter in Play: Critical Strategies & the Plays of Harold Pinter. LC 90-31163. 367p. (C). 1990. text ed. 41.95 (0-8223-1040-6) Duke.

*Merritt, Sydney A. Guided Meditations for Children: 40 Scripts & Activities Based on Sunday Lectionary. LC 94-48152. 192p. (J). 1995. pap. 19.95 (0-89390-336-1) Resource Pubns.

— Guided Meditations for Children: 40 Scripts & Activities Based on the Sunday Lectionary. LC 94-48152. 184p. (Orig.). 1995. teacher ed, pap. 19.95 (0-89390-327-2) Resource Pubns.

Merritt, T. Allen, jt. auth. see Miller, Herbert C.

Merritt, Valerie J. California Probate Workflow Manual Vols. 1 & 2: March 1993 Update. rev. ed. Tom, Janette, ed. LC 79-53359. 268p. 1993. ring bd. 40.00 (0-88124-600-X, ES-31563) Cont Ed Bar-CA.

— California Probate Workflow Manual Vols. 1 & 2: October 1991 Update. rev. ed. Dworin, Christopher D., ed. LC 79-53359. 275p. 1991. ring bd. 45.00 (0-88124-437-6, ES-31562) Cont Ed Bar-CA.

Merritt, W. W., Sr. A History of Montgomery County, Iowa from the Earliest Days to 1906. (Illus.). 343p. 1994. reprint ed. lib. bdg. 35.00 (0-8328-3818-7) Higginson Bk Co.

Merritt, W. W. A History of the County of Montgomery (Iowa) (Illus.). 344p. 1993. reprint ed. lib. bdg. 39.50 (0-8328-3445-9) Higginson Bk Co.

Merritt, Wesley. Three Indian Campaigns. 24p. reprint ed. pap. 3.95 (0-8466-4037-6, 137) Shorey.

Merritt, William E. Where the Rivers Ran Backward. LC 88-22043. 304p. 1989. 24.95 (0-8203-1107-3) U of Ga Pr.

*Merriweather, Curtis A. How to Put on the Whole Armor of God. 38p. (Orig.). 1995. pap. 7.00 (0-9623431-3-7) Faith Christ Ch.

— How to Take Charge of Your Future. 56p. (Orig.). (C). 1994. pap. 5.95 (0-9623431-6-1) Faith Christ Ch.

— Life Is Your Choice. 18p. (Orig.). (C). 1989. pap. 1.00 (0-9623431-0-2) Faith Christ Ch.

— Taking the Shield of Faith. 45p. (Orig.). 1994. pap. 3.95 (0-9623431-5-3) Faith Christ Ch.

— Why Satan Wants To Steal God's Word from You. 29p. (Orig.). 1993. pap. 2.95 (0-9623431-4-5) Faith Christ Ch.

Merrix, Robert P. & Ranson, Nicholas, eds. Ideological Approaches to Shakespeare: The Practice of Theory. LC 92-29122. 312p. 1992. text ed. 99.95 (0-88946-079-5) E Mellen.

Merron. Riding the Wave. 1994. text ed. 29.95 (0-442-01803-7) Van Nos Reinhold.

Merrow, Bill, jt. auth. see Gamble, Jesse.

Merrow, O. E. Merrow: Henry Merrow of Reading, Massachusetts & His Descendants named Marrow, Marrow & Merry. (Illus.). 659p. 1991. reprint ed. lib. bdg. 108.00 (0-8328-1933-6); reprint ed. pap. 98.00 (0-8328-1934-4) Higginson Bk Co.

Merrow, William. VSE ESA: Performance Management & Fine Tuning. 1993. text ed. 49.00 (0-07-041753-9) McGraw.

— VSE ESA Concepts & Facilities. 1994. text ed. 50.00 (0-07-041777-6) McGraw.

Merrullo, Victor D. Arboriculture & the Law. (C). Date not set. text ed. write for info. (1-881956-01-6) Int Soc Arboricult.

Merry. Hong Kong Tenancy Law: An Introduction to the Law of Landlord & Tenant. 2nd ed. 1989. 124.00 (0-409-99576-2) Butterworth Legal Pubs.

— Invitation to Person Centered Psychology. 1994. 24.95 (1-56593-510-1, 1178) Singular Publishing.

Merry, Barbara. The Splicing Handbook. (Illus.). 112p. 1988. pap. text ed. 10.95 (0-87742-952-9) Intl Marine.

Merry, Barbara & Darwin, John. The Splicing Handbook: Techniques for Modern & Traditional Ropes. 1988. pap. text ed. 10.95 (0-07-156371-7) McGraw.

Merry, Barbara L. Menippean Elements in Paul Scarron's Roman Comique. LC 91-16266. (American University Studies: Romance Languages & Literature: Ser. II, Vol. 172). 132p. (C). 1992. text ed. 35.95 (0-8204-1578-2) P Lang Pubs.

Merry, Eleanor. I Am. 1972. 59.95 (0-8490-0380-6) Gordon Pr.

Merry, Eleanor C. Goethe's Approach to Colour. 45p. 1960. reprint ed. spiral bd. 4.95 (0-7873-0608-8) Mokelumne.

Merry, Eleanor C., tr. & illus. The Dream Song of Olaf Asteson. 2nd ed. 48p. 1988. pap. 12.95 (0-85440-706-5, Steinerbks) Anthroposophic.

Merry, Graeme. Two Interpretations from Central Park. 1994. 8.95 (0-533-10809-8) Vantage.

Merry, Harold. New Horizons for Democracy: Enhancing the Functional Efficiency & Social Harmony in Democratic States. 1992. 16.95 (0-533-10154-9) Vantage.

Merry, Henry J. The Constitutional System: The Group Character of the Elected Institutions. LC 86-15162. 225p. 1986. text ed. 49.95 (0-275-92185-9, C2185, Praeger Pubs) Greenwood.

— Five-Branch Government: The Full Measure of Constitutional Checks & Balances. LC 79-22499. 286p. reprint ed. pap. 81.60 (0-317-08726-6, 2022775) Bks Demand.

*Merry, John F., ed. History of Delaware County & Its People, 2 vols., Set. (Illus.). 901p. 1995. reprint ed. lib. bdg. 95.00 (0-8328-4671-6) Higginson Bk Co.

Merry, Karen, jt. ed. see Feeney, Mary.

Merry, Sally E. Getting Justice & Getting Even: Legal Consciousness among Working-Class Americans. (Language & Legal Discourse Ser.). (Illus.). 288p. 1990. lib. bdg. 40.00 (0-226-52068-4); pap. text ed. 19.95 (0-226-52069-2) U Ch Pr.

— Urban Danger: Life in a Neighborhood of Strangers. 278p. 1986. pap. 18.95 (0-87722-425-0) Temple U Pr.

Merry, Sally E. & Milner, Neal, eds. The Possibility of Popular Justice: A Case Study of Community Mediation in the United States. LC 93-23588. (Law, Meaning, & Violence Ser.). 450p. (C). 1993. text ed. 49.50 (0-472-10426-8) U of Mich Pr.

*Merry, Uri. Coping with Uncertainty: Insights from the New Sciences of Chaos, Self-Organization & Complexity. LC 94-16996. 209p. 1995. pap. text ed. 18.95 (0-275-95152-9) Greenwood.

Merry, Uri, jt. auth. see Levy, Amir.

Merry, Uria. Coping with Uncertainty: Insights from the New Sciences of Chaos, Self-Organization. LC 94-16996. 224p. 1995. text ed. 59.95 (0-275-94910-9, Praeger Pubs) Greenwood.

Merryfield, Merry. International Trade & Manpower Development: Policy Changes & Economic Realities in Nigeria. (Graduate Student Term Paper Co-Winner Ser.). 1983. pap. text ed. 2.00 (0-941934-44-6) Indiana Africa.

Merryfield, Merry M., ed. Lessons from Africa. (Illus.). 99p. 1989. pap. text ed. 12.00 (0-941339-07-6) Ind U SSDC.

Merryfield, Merry M. & Remy, Richard C., eds. Teaching about International Conflict & Peace. (SUNY Series, Theory, Research, & Practice in Social Education). 320p. (C). 1995. 64.50 (0-7914-2373-5); pap. 21.95x (0-7914-2374-3) State U NY Pr.

Merryman, Gregory K. Regulation of Corporate Political Activity. 3rd ed. (Corporate Practice Series Portfolio: No. 16). 1988. 92.00 (0-87179-998-7) BNA.

Merryman, J. H. The United States Life-Saving Service: Eighteen Eighty. Jones, William R., ed. (Illus.). 1981. pap. 5.95 (0-89646-071-1) Vistabooks.

Merryman, John H. The Civil Law Tradition: An Introduction to the Legal Systems of Western Europe & Latin America. 2nd ed. LC 84-50153. 184p. 1985. 27.50 (0-8047-1247-6); pap. 10.95 (0-8047-1248-4) Stanford U Pr.

Merryman, John H., ed. Stanford Legal Essays. LC 75-182. 480p. 1975. 49.50 (0-8047-0884-3) Stanford U Pr.

Merryman, John H. & Clark, David S. Comparative Law: Western European & Latin American Legal Systems. 2nd ed. (Contemporary Legal Education Ser.). 1993. 25.00 (0-685-48590-0) Michie Butterworth.

Merryman, John H. & Elsen, Albert E. Law, Ethics, & the Visual Arts, 2 vols., Set. 2nd ed. LC 79-65005. (Illus.). 960p. 1987. text ed. 109.95 (0-8122-8052-0) U of Pa Pr.

Merryman, Louis M. Fragrance of a New Dawn. 1991. pap. 3.95 (1-55673-287-2, 9120) CSS OH.

Merryweather, F. Somner. Bibliomania in the Middle Ages. 1977. lib. bdg. 59.95 (0-8490-1503-0) Gordon Pr.

— Bibliomania in the Middle Ages. rev. ed. Copinger, H. B., ed. LC 72-83748. 1972. reprint ed. 24.95 (0-405-08787-X, Pub. by Blom Pubns UK) Ayer.

Merryweather, James. York Music: The Story of a City's Music from 1304-1896. (C). 1988. 85.00 (1-85072-034-7, Pub. by W Sessions UK) St Mut.

Merryweather, Marilyn W. The Only Home They Ever Knew: Summit County & the Children's Home. (Illus.). 112p. 1991. text ed. write for info. (0-9621895-5-3) Summit Cty Hist Soc.

Mers, Gilbert. Working the Waterfront: The Ups & Downs of a Rebel Longshoreman. LC 88-2168. (Illus.). 308p. 1988. 19.95 (0-292-76022-1) U of Tex Pr.

Mersand, Joseph. American Drama, 1930-1940: Essays on Playwrights & Plays. LC 75-157968. (Essay Index Reprint Ser.). 1977. reprint ed. 18.95 (0-8369-2245-X) Ayer.

— Traditions in American Literature. (BCL1-PS American Literature Ser.). 247p. 1993. reprint ed. lib. bdg. 79.00 (0-7812-6566-5) Rprt Serv.

Mersand, Joseph & Griffith, Francis. Spelling the Easy Way. braille ed. 943p. 1991. vinyl bd. 75.44 (1-56956-317-9, BR8068) W A T Braille.

Merser, Cheryl. A Starter Garden: The Guide for the Horticulturally Hapless. (Illus.). 256p. (Orig.). 1994. pap. 14.00 (0-06-096933-4, PL) HarpC.

Mersereau, John, Jr. Russian Romantic Fiction. 270p. 1983. pap. 13.95 (0-88233-740-8) Ardis Pubs.

Mersereau, Russell M. & Smith, Mark J. Digital Filtering: A Computer Laboratory Textbook. LC 93-17580. 240p. (C). 1993. Net. pap. text ed. write for info. (0-471-51694-5) Wiley.

Mersereau, Russell M., jt. auth. see Smith, Mark J.

Mersereau, Shirley W., jt. auth. see Coerper, Lois H.

Mersey, Charles C. Chief Ministers of England, Nine Hundred Twenty to Seventeen Twenty. LC 67-30222. (Essay Index Reprint Ser.). 1977. 26.95 (0-8369-0703-5) Ayer.

— Chief Ministers of England, Nine Hundred Twenty to Seventeen Twenty. LC 67-30222. (Essay Index Reprint Ser.). reprint ed. lib. bdg. 23.00 (0-8290-0845-4) Irvington.

— Prime Ministers of Britain. LC 74-86772. (Essay Index Reprint Ser.). 1977. 36.95 (0-8369-1422-8) Ayer.

Mersey, Clive B. Viceroys & Governors-General of India, 1757-1947. LC 70-160925. (Biography Index Reprint Ser.). 1977. reprint ed. 21.95 (0-8369-8088-3) Ayer.

Mershchikova, I., tr. see Naumova, T. N.

*Mershon, Carol & Pasquino, Gianfranco, eds. Italian Politics: Ending the First Republic. LC 94-36048. (C). 1994. pap. text ed. 34.95 (0-8133-8893-7) Westview.

Mershon, Janet, ed. see Samuelson, Don W.

Mershon, Jerry L. Juvenile Justice, the Adjudicatory Process. LC 82-154236. (Juvenile Justice Textbook Ser.: No. 501). 73p. 1982. 7.50 (0-318-00253-1) Natl Juv & Family Ct Judges.

Merskey, Harold, ed. see Int'l Assoc. for the Study of Pain, Task Force on Taxonomy Staff.

Merskey, Harold, jt. auth. see Vaery, Henning.

Mersky, Peter. The Grim Reapers: Fighting Squadron 10 in WW II. 150p. 1986. pap. 10.95 (0-912173-09-2) Champlin Museum.

Mersky, Peter B. U. S. Marine Corps Aviation: Nineteen Twelve to the Present. LC 83-13290. (Illus.). 324p. 1983. 24.95 (0-933852-39-8) Nautical & Aviation.

Mersky, Ray M., jt. auth. see Jacobstein, J. Myron.

Mersky, Roy M., ed. Collecting & Managing Rare Law Books: Papers Presented at a Conference Celebrating the Dedication of the New Tarlton Law Library, the University of Texas at Austin School of Law, January 7-8, 1981. LC 81-18820. 568p. 1981. lib. bdg. 45.00 (0-87802-070-5) Glanville.

— Law Library Information Reports, 17 vols. 1994. write for info. (0-685-20019-1) Glanville.

— Louis Dembitz Brandeis 1856-1941 - A Bibliography: (Celebration of the 100th Anniversary of His Birth) (Yale Law Library Publications: No. 15). 44p. 1987. reprint ed. pap. 10.00 (0-8377-2437-6) Rothman.

Mersky, Roy M. & Jacobstein, J. Myron. Index to Periodical Articles Related to Law, Thirty Year Cumulation, Vols. 1-30: 1958-1988, 4 vols., Set. 1989. lib. bdg. 400.00 (0-87802-063-2) Glanville.

— Index to Periodical Articles Related to Law, 1979-1993. (Retrospective Cumulative Issues Ser.). 1990. Issue 4 cumulative. 45.00 (0-87802-055-1) Glanville.

Mersky, Roy M. & Jacobstein, J. Myron, eds. Supreme Court of the United States Hearings & Reports On Successful & Unsuccessful Nominations of Supreme Court Justices By the Senate Judiciary Committee: 1916-1990 & 1983 Supplement, 17 vols. in 39. LC 75-13630. (Illus.). 1977. spiral bd. 1,700.00 (0-685-73463-3) W S Hein.

— Supreme Court of the United States Hearings & Reports On Successful & Unsuccessful Nominations of Supreme Court Justices By the Senate Judiciary Committee: 1916-1990 & 1983 Supplement, 17 vols. in 39, Set. LC 75-13630. (Illus.). 1977. lib. bdg. 2,500.00 (0-930342-48-8, 301030) W S Hein.

Mersky, Roy M., ed. see Ballantine, Sergeant.

Mersky, Roy M., jt. auth. see Blaustein, Albert P.

Mersky, Roy M., ed. see Carson, Hampton L.

Mersky, Roy M., ed. see Cogswell, Robert E.

Mersky, Roy M., ed. see DeHart, William C.

Mersky, Roy M., ed. see Field, Moses.

Mersky, Roy M., ed. see Foulkes, William D.

Mersky, Roy M., ed. see Gasaway, Laura N., et al.

Mersky, Roy M., ed. see Goodenow, J. M.

Mersky, Roy M., jt. auth. see Jacobstein, J. Myron.

Mersky, Roy M., jt. auth. see Middleton, Kent.

Mersky, Roy M., ed. see Parker, Edward G.

Mersky, Roy M., ed. see Pollock, Frederick.

Mersky, Roy M., ed. see Pulling, Alexander.

Mersky, Roy M., ed. see Thorpe, William G.

Mersky, Roy M., ed. see Tiedeman, Christopher G.

Mersky, Roy M., et al, eds. Collecting & Managing Rare Law Books: Papers Presented at a Conference Celebrating the Dedication of the New Tarlton Law Library, the University of Texas at Austin School of Law, January 7-8, 1981. LC 81-18820. 568p. 1982. lib. bdg. 45.00 (0-379-20740-0) Oceana.

— Index to Periodical Articles Related to Law: Five-Year Cumulative Index: 1989-1993. 1994. lib. bdg. 125.00 (0-87802-068-3) Glanville.

Mersman, Hans, ed. see Mozart, Wolfgang Amadeus.

Mersmann. Crystallization Technology Handbook. 688p. 1995. 195.00 (0-8247-9233-5) Dekker.

Mersmann, A. B. & Schroll, S. E., eds. Fundamentals of Adsorption. LC 90-84745. 1007p. 1991. 110.00 (0-8169-0540-1) Am Inst Chem Eng.

Mersmann, Alfons B. & Scholl, Stephan E. Fundamentals of Adsorption. LC 90-84745. 500p. 1991. 50.00 (0-939204-43-6) Eng Found.

Mersmann, H., jt. auth. see Stanton, H.

Mersmann, Hans. Letters of Mozart. Bozman, M. M., tr. 278p. 1987. 16.95 (0-88029-087-0) Dorset Pr.

Merson. Britain Fascism & the Popular Front. (C). 1985. pap. 19.95 (0-85315-642-5, Pub. by Lawrence & Wishart UK) Humanities.

— Communist Resistance in Nazi Germany. (C). 1985. pap. 22.50 (0-85315-602-6, Pub. by Lawrence & Wishart UK) Humanities.

Merson, Annette. African Cookery. LC 86-40283. 80p. (Orig.). 1987. pap. 8.95 (1-55523-027-X) Winston-Derek.

Merson, Elizabeth, jt. auth. see Lough, John.

Merson, John. Genius That Was China. 1990. 29.95 (0-87951-397-7) Overlook Pr.

Merson, Richard L., jt. auth. see Loncin, Marcel.

*Merson, Stephen. Depression. (Ward Lock Family Health Guides Ser.). (Illus.). 80p. 1995. pap. 9.95 (0-7063-7395-2, Pub. by Ward Lock UK) Sterling.

*Merson, Stephen & Baldwin, David. Psychiatric Emergencies. (Oxford Handbooks in Emergency Medicine Ser.: Vol. 11). 140p. 1995. 65.00 (0-19-262478-4); pap. 29.95 (0-19-262477-6) OUP.

Merson, Willy, tr. see Woeller, Waltraud & Cassiday, Bruce.

Merte, H. J., ed. Genesis of Glaucoma. (Documenta Ophthalmologica Proceedings Ser.: No. 16). 1978. lib. bdg. 112.50 (90-6193-156-8) Kluwer Ac.

— Societas Ergophthalmologica Internationalis: 5th Symposium, Bordeux 1974. 6th Symposium, Hamburg 1976. 7th Symposium, Nagoya 1978. (Problems of Industrial Medicine in Ophthalmology Ser.: Vol. 5-7). (Illus.). xx, 760p. 1982. pap. 199.25 (3-8055-3003-X) S Karger.

Mertelsmann, jt. auth. see Levitt.

Mertelsmann, R., ed. Lymphohaematopoietic Growth Factors in Cancer Therapy II. LC 92-49430. 1993. 98.00 (0-387-55953-1) Spr-Verlag.

M

Mertelsmann, R. & Herrmann, F. Hematopoietic Growth Factors in Clinical Applications. 528p. 1990. 125.00 (0-8247-8203-8) Dekker.

Mertelsmann, R. & Veronesi, U., eds. Lymphohaematopoietic Growth Factors in Cancer Therapy. (EOS Monographs). (Illus.). vii, 90p. 1990. 51.00 (0-387-53086-X) Spr-Verlag.

Mertelsmann, R., jt. ed. see Hiddemann, W.

***Mertelsmann, Roland & Herrmann, Friedhelm, eds.** Hematopoietic Growth Factors in Clinical Applications. 2nd expanded rev. ed. LC 94-22881. 1994. 150.00 (0-8247-9268-8) Dekker.

Merten, Cyndie, jt. auth. see Apple, Daniel K.

Merten, Steven. I Love You, God. 446p. 1990. pap. 12.95 (0-939116-24-3) Frontier OR.

***Mertens.** Not the Cross, but the Crucified. 1993. pap. text ed. (0-8028-0571-X) Eerdmans.

***Mertens, Donna M. & McLaughlin, John.** Research Methods in Special Education. (Applied Social Research Methods Ser.: Vol. 37). 168p. 1994. 37.00 (0-8039-4808-5) Sage.

— Research Methods in Special Education. (Applied Social Research Methods Ser.: Vol. 37). 1994. pap. 16.95 (0-8039-4809-3) Sage.

Mertens, F. G., jt. ed. see Spatschek, D. H.

Mertens, Fredrik, ed. see Mitelman, Felix.

***Mertens, Jean-Francois, ed.** Game-Theoretic Methods in General Equilibrium Analysis: Proceedings of the NATO Advanced Study Institute on Long Island, NY, U. S. A., July 1-12, 1991. (NATO ASI Series D: Behavioural & Social Sciences). 272p. (C). 1994. lib. bdg. 117.00 (0-7923-3011-0) Kluwer Ac.

Mertens, R. P., jt. auth. see Van OverStraeten, R. J.

Mertens, Randy. Purr Diem: A Daily Calendar of Cats. 366p. (Orig.). 1994. spiral bd. 7.00 (1-882835-26-3) STA-Kris.

Mertens, Thomas R. Genetics Laboratory Investigations. 9th ed. 272p. (C). 1991. pap. write for info. (0-02-380595-1) Macmillan.

Mertens, Thomas R. & Hammersmith, Robert L. Genetics: Laboratory Investigations. 10th ed. LC 94-14275. 272p. (C). 1994. pap. write for info. (0-02-380601-X) Macmillan.

Mertens, Thomas R., jt. auth. see Winchester, A. M.

Mertens, William J., jt. auth. see Crump, David.

Mertens, Wim. American Minimal Music. (Illus.). 128p. reprint ed. pap. 12.50 (0-912483-15-6) Pro-Am Music.

Mertes, Harald, jt. auth. see Hollander, Neil.

Mertes, Jack, ed. see Versace, Dick.

Mertes, James D., jt. auth. see Kaiser, Ronald A.

Mertes, John E., jt. auth. see Wright, John S.

Mertig, Angela G., jt. ed. see Dunlap, Riley E.

Mertin, Josef. Early Music: Approaches to Performance Practice. Levarie, Siegmund, tr. (Music Ser.). 300p. 1986. lib. bdg. 29.50 (0-306-76286-2) Da Capo.

Mertin, Roger. Roger Mertin, Records 1976-1978. Desmarais, ed. LC 78-17219. 46p. 1978. pap. 3.95 (0-932026-02-8) Columbia College Chi.

Mertins, Detlef. Presence of Mies. LC 94-16259. (Illus.). 272p. (Orig.). 1994. pap. 19.95 (1-56898-013-2) Princeton Arch.

— Presence of Mies. LC 94-16259. (Illus.). 272p. (Orig.). 1995. disk 24.95 (1-56898-020-5); disk 24.95 (1-56898-021-3) Princeton Arch.

Mertins, J. W., jt. auth. see Coppel, H. C.

***Mertins, Lisa.** Ginkgo & Moon. LC 94-40960. (J). 1996. write for info. (0-395-73576-9) HM.

Mertlich, Robert. Goldfish: A Complete Introduction. 1988. pap. 5.95 (0-86622-350-9, CO-019S) TFH Pubns.

Mertner, Edgar, jt. auth. see Camden, William.

Merton. Bread in the Wilderness. 1986. pap. 5.95 (0-8146-0406-4) Liturgical Pr.

Merton, Andrew, comp. In Your Own Voice: A Writer's Reader. LC 94-9460. (C). 1994. 18.25 (0-06-501763-3) HarpCollege.

Merton, D. & Yun-Kan, Shio. China: The Land & Its People. rev. ed. LC 85-72107. (Countries Ser.). (Illus.). 48p. (J). (gr. 5 up). 1991. lib. bdg. 14.95 (0-382-24242-4) Silver Burdett Pr.

Merton, Don & Butler, David E. The Black Robin: Saving the World's Most Endangered Bird. (Illus.). 308p. 1993. pap. 45.00 (0-19-558260-8) OUP.

Merton, Manan & Duncan, Russell, eds. First Person Past, Vol. I: American Autobiographies. (Illus.). 310p. (Orig.). (C). 1993. pap. text ed. 13.50 (1-881089-22-3) Brandywine Press.

Merton, R. Science, Technology & Society in Seventeenth Century England. LC 79-82308. 1970. 48.00 (0-86527-178-X) Fertig.

Merton, Reginald. Magicians, Seers, & Mystics: Apollonius of Tyana; the Unknown Master of the Albigeneses; Christian Rosenkreutz & the Rosicrucians; Mystery of the Templars; Nicholas Flamen & the Philosophers Stone; Saint-German the Immortal; Madame Blavatsky & the Theosophists. Magre, Maurice, tr. 287p. 1994. pap. 19.95 (1-56459-432-7) Kessinger Pub.

Merton, Robert. Social Research & the Practicing Professions. 1982. text ed. 30.00 (0-89011-569-9); pap. 19.75 (0-685-05493-4) Abt Bks.

Merton, Robert C. Continuous-Time Finance. (Macroeconomics & Finance Ser.). (C). 1992. 29.95 (0-631-18508-9) Blackwell Pubs.

Merton, Robert E., jt. auth. see Chirot, Daniel.

Merton, Robert K. Focused Interview. 1989. pap. 12.95 (0-02-920980-3) Macmillan.

— The Focused Interview: A Manual of Problems & Procedures. 1990. text ed. 27.95 (0-02-920985-4); pap. 14.95 (0-02-920986-2) Free Pr.

— Mass Persuasion: The Social Psychology of a War Bond Drive. LC 77-136076. 210p. 1971. reprint ed. text ed. 49.75 (0-8371-5226-7, MEMP, Greenwood Pr) Greenwood.

Merton, Robert K. . On the Shoulders of Giants: A Shandean Postscript. LC 65-12859. (Illus.). 290p. 1967. pap. 4.95 (0-15-668781-X, Harvest Bks) HarBrace.

Merton, Robert K. On the Shoulders of Giants: A Shandean Postscript. LC 65-12859. (Illus.). 302p. 1985. 14.95 (0-15-169962-3) HarBrace.

— On the Shoulders of Giants: The Post-Italianate Edition. LC 92-43871. (Illus.). xxxii, 318p. (C). 1993. pap. 14.95 (0-226-52086-2) U Ch Pr.

— On Theoretical Sociology: Five Essays, Old & New. 1967. pap. 14.95 (0-02-921150-6) Free Pr.

— Puritanism, Pietism, & Science. (Reprint Series in Social Sciences). (C). 1993. reprint ed. pap. text ed. 2.30 (0-8290-2664-9, S-192) Irvington.

— The Role-Set: Problems in Sociological Theory. (Reprint Series in Sociology). (C). 1993. reprint ed. pap. text ed. 1.00 (0-8290-3696-2, S-193) Irvington.

— Social Research & the Practicing Professions. 300p. 1984. reprint ed. lib. bdg. 59.00 (0-8191-4111-9) U Pr of Amer.

— Social Structure & Anomie. (Reprint Series in Social Sciences). (C). 1993. reprint ed. pap. text ed. 1.00 (0-8290-3491-9, S-194) Irvington.

— Social Theory & Social Structure. LC 68-28789. 1968. text ed. 32.95 (0-02-921130-1) Free Pr.

— Sociological Ambivalence & Other Essays. LC 76-1033. (Illus.). 1976. pap. 19.95 (0-02-921120-4) Free Pr.

— The Sociology of Science: An Episodic Memoir. LC 79-9962. (Arcturus Books Paperbacks). 164p. 1979. pap. 7.95 (0-8093-0925-4) S Ill U Pr.

— The Sociology of Science: Theoretical & Empirical Investigations. Storer, Norman W., ed. LC 72-97623. 1979. pap. text ed. 19.95 (0-226-52092-7, P846) U Ch Pr.

— Varieties of Political Expression in Sociology. LC 72-81104. 239p. reprint ed. pap. 68.20 (0-685-15775-X, 2026782) Bks Demand.

Merton, Robert K., ed. Authority & the Individual. LC 73-14144. (Perspectives in Social Inquiry Ser.). 386p. 1974. reprint ed. 23.95 (0-405-05491-2) Ayer.

— Factors Determining Human Behavior. LC 73-14153. (Perspectives in Social Inquiry Ser.). 186p. 1974. reprint ed. 12.95 (0-405-05500-5) Ayer.

Merton, Robert K. & Lazarsfeld, Paul F., eds. Continuities in Social Research: Studies in the Scope & Method of the American Soldier. LC 73-14168. (Perspectives in Social Inquiry Ser.). 260p. 1978. reprint ed. 18.95 (0-405-05514-5) Ayer.

Merton, Robert K. & Nisbet, Robert A., eds. Contemporary Social Problems. 4th ed. 782p. (C). 1976. text ed. 40.00 (0-15-513793-X); International ed. write for info. (0-318-52965-3) HB Coll Pubs.

Merton, Robert K. & Riley, Matilda W., eds. Sociological Traditions from Generation to Generation: Glimpses of the American Experience. LC 79-26693. (Modern Sociology Ser.). (Illus.). (C). 1980. text ed. 39.50 (0-89391-034-1); pap. text ed. 22.50 (0-89391-061-9) Ablex Pub.

Merton, Robert K., ed. see Allison, Paul D.

Merton, Robert K., ed. see Angell, Robert C.

Merton, Robert K., ed. see Bales, Robert F.

Merton, Robert K., ed. see Barber, Bernard.

Merton, Robert K., ed. see Beaver, Donald D.

Merton, Robert K., ed. see Becker, Howard S.

Merton, Robert K., ed. see Birnbaum, Norman.

Merton, Robert K., ed. see Bittner, Egon.

Merton, Robert K., ed. see Bredemeier, Harry C.

Merton, Robert K., ed. see Breed, Warren.

Merton, Robert K., ed. see Caplovitz, David.

Merton, Robert K., ed. see Clark, Burton R.

Merton, Robert K., ed. see Cohen, Steven M.

Merton, Robert K., ed. see Cole, Stephen.

Merton, Robert K., ed. see Costner, Herbert L.

Merton, Robert K., ed. see Davis, Arthur K.

Merton, Robert K., ed. see Davis, Kingsley.

Merton, Robert K., ed. see Davison, W. Phillips.

Merton, Robert K., ed. see Devereux, Edward C., Jr.

Merton, Robert K., ed. see Duncan, Otis D.

Merton, Robert K., ed. see Elder, Glen H., Jr.

Merton, Robert K., ed. see Elkana, Yahuda, et al.

Merton, Robert K., ed. see Etzioni, Amitai.

Merton, Robert K., jt. auth. see Fischer, Claude S.

Merton, Robert K., ed. see Fleck, Ludwig.

Merton, Robert K., ed. see Friedman, Nathalie S.

Merton, Robert K., ed. see Ginsberg, Ralph B.

Merton, Robert K., ed. see Goode, Erich.

Merton, Robert K., ed. see Goss, Mary E.

Merton, Robert K., ed. see Hammond, Phillip E.

Merton, Robert K., ed. see Hill, Robert B.

Merton, Robert K., ed. see Hyman, Herbert H.

Merton, Robert K., jt. auth. see Janowitz, Morris B.

Merton, Robert K., ed. see Keller, Suzanne I.

Merton, Robert K., ed. see Keyfitz, Nathan.

Merton, Robert K., ed. see Kohn, Melvin L.

Merton, Robert K., ed. see Levine, Donald N.

Merton, Robert K., ed. see March, James G.

Merton, Robert K., ed. see Marsh, Robert M.

Merton, Robert K., ed. see Moore, Wilbert E.

Merton, Robert K., ed. see Mullins, Nicholas C.

Merton, Robert K., ed. see Nettler, Gwynne.

Merton, Robert K., ed. see Nisbet, Robert A.

Merton, Robert K., ed. see O'Gorman, Hubert J.

Merton, Robert K., ed. see Reskin, Barbara F.

Merton, Robert K., ed. see Rosenberg, Morris.

Merton, Robert K., ed. see Rossi, Alice S.

Merton, Robert K., ed. see Ryder, Norman B.

Merton, Robert K., ed. see Schuessler, Karl F.

Merton, Robert K., ed. see Short, James F., Jr.

Merton, Robert K., ed. see Sills, David L.

Merton, Robert K., jt. ed. see Sills, David L.

Merton, Robert K., jt. ed. see Sills, David.

Merton, Robert K., ed. see Simmons, Roberta G.

Merton, Robert K., ed. see Skolnick, Jerome H.

Merton, Robert K., ed. see Storer, Norman W.

Merton, Robert K., ed. see Stouffer, Samuel A.

Merton, Robert K., ed. see Strodtback, Fred L.

Merton, Robert K., ed. see Swanson, Guy E.

Merton, Robert K., ed. see Thielens, Wagner P., Jr.

Merton, Robert K., ed. see Trow, Martin A.

Merton, Robert K., ed. see Vidich, Arthur J.

Merton, Robert K., ed. see White, Harrison C.

Merton, Robert K., ed. see Wright, Charles R.

Merton, Robert K., ed. see Wrong, Dennis H.

Merton, Robert K., ed. see Yinger, Milton J.

Merton, Robert K., jt. ed. see Zuckerman, Harriet.

Merton, Robert K., et al, eds. Qualitative & Quantitative Social Research: Papers in Honor of Paul F. Lazarsfeld. LC 78-24752. 1979. text ed. 29.95 (0-02-920930-7) Free Pr.

— Reader in Bureaucracy. 1965. pap. 22.95 (0-02-921070-4) Free Pr.

— Student-Physician: Introductory Studies in the Sociology of Medical Education. LC 57-12526. (Commonwealth Fund Publications Ser). (Illus.). 372p. reprint ed. 106.10 (0-8357-9179-3, 2011023) Bks Demand.

Merton, Stephen. Mark Rutherford: (William Hale White) 189p. 1967. 49.50 (0-685-63213-X) Elliots Bks.

Merton, Thomas. The Ascent to Truth. LC 80-26736. 352p. 1981. pap. 9.95 (0-15-608682-4, Harvest Bks) HarBrace.

— The Asian Journal of Thomas Merton. Stone, Naomi B. et al, eds. LC 71-103370. (Illus.). 448p. 1973. pap. 12.95 (0-8112-0570-3, NDP394) New Directions.

— Cables to the Ace. 100p. 1986. 8.95 (0-87775-192-7) Unicorn Pr.

— The Climate of Monastic Prayer. (Cistercian Studies: No. 1). 154p. 1973. reprint ed. 7.95 (0-87907-801-4) Cistercian Pubns.

— The Collected Poems of Thomas Merton. LC 77-9902. 1088p. 1980. 37.50 (0-8112-0643-2); pap. 29.95 (0-8112-0769-2, NDP504) New Directions.

— Conjectures of a Guilty Bystander. LC 66-24311. 1968. pap. 12.00 (0-385-01018-4, Image Bks) Doubleday.

— Contemplative Prayer. 1971. reprint ed. mass mkt. 6.95 (0-385-09219-9, Image Bks) Doubleday.

— Courage for Truth. 1994. pap. 15.95 (0-15-600004-0) HarBrace.

— The Courage for Truth: Letters to Writers. Bochen, Christine M., ed. LC 92-37078. 1993. 25.00 (0-374-13055-8) FS&G.

— Disputed Questions. LC 79-14717. 310p. 1985. pap. 7.95 (0-15-626105-7, Harvest Bks) HarBrace.

— Eighteen Poems. limited ed. 1986. 200.00 (0-8112-1012-X) New Directions.

— Faith & Violence: Christian Teaching & Christian Practice. 1968. pap. 11.95 (0-268-00094-8) U of Notre Dame Pr.

— The Geography of Lograire. LC 78-88727. 1969. pap. 7.95 (0-8112-0098-1, NDP283) New Directions.

— Honorable Reader: Reflections on My Work. Daggy, Robert E., ed. 184p. 1991. reprint ed. pap. 9.95 (0-8245-1125-5) Crossroad NY.

— The Last of the Fathers: Saint Bernard of Clairvaux & the Encyclical Letter, Doctor Mellifluus. LC 81-4105. 128p. 1981. pap. 4.95 (0-15-649438-8, Harvest Bks) HarBrace.

— Life & Holiness. 1969. mass mkt. 8.00 (0-385-06277-X, D183, Image Bks) Doubleday.

— The Literary Essays of Thomas Merton. Hart, Patrick, ed. LC 84-2056. 1985. pap. 18.95 (0-8112-0931-8, NDP587) New Directions.

— Love & Living. Stone, Naomi B. & Hart, Patrick, eds. LC 79-14717. 304p. 1985. pap. 8.95 (0-15-653895-4, Harvest Bks) HarBrace.

— Modern Spirituality Series. 96p. 1990. pap. 4.95 (0-87243-174-6) Templegate.

— My Argument with the Gestapo: A Macaronic Journal. LC 69-20082. 256p. 1975. pap. 10.95 (0-8112-0586-X, NDP403) New Directions.

— Mystics & Zen Masters. 303p. 1986. pap. 12.00 (0-374-52001-1) FS&G.

— The New Man. 256p. 1978. pap. 11.00 (0-374-51444-5) FS&G.

— The New Man. 1983. 19.75 (0-8446-5987-8) Peter Smith.

— New Seeds of Contemplation. rev. ed. LC 61-17869. 1972. pap. 9.95 (0-8112-0099-X, NDP337) New Directions.

— No Man Is an Island. large type ed. 384p. 1986. pap. 15.95 (0-8027-2527-9) Walker & Co.

— No Man Is an Island. LC 78-7108. 264p. 1978. reprint ed. pap. 8.95 (0-15-665962-X, Harvest Bks) HarBrace.

— Opening the Bible. LC 85-24722. 96p. 1986. pap. 8.00 (0-8006-1910-2, 1-1910, Fortress Pr) Augsburg Fortress.

— Opening the Bible. 96p. 1970. pap. 4.95 (0-8146-0408-0) Liturgical Pr.

— Passion for Peace: The Social Essays. 360p. 1995. 29.95 (0-8245-1494-7) Crossroad NY.

— Praying the Psalms. 48p. 1956. pap. 2.95 (0-8146-0548-6) Liturgical Pr.

— Raids on the Unspeakable. LC 66-17823. 1970. pap. 9.95 (0-8112-0101-5, NDP213) New Directions.

— The Road to Joy: Letters to New & Old Friends. Daggy, Robert E., ed. 672p. 1989. 27.95 (0-374-25123-1) FS&G.

— Run to the Mountain: The Story of a Vocation. Hart, Patrick, ed. LC 94-43414. (Journals of Thomas Merton: Vol. 1). 1995. 27.50 (0-06-065474-0) Harper SF.

— Run to the Mountain: The Story of a Vocation. Hart, Patrick, ed. LC 94-43414. (Journals of Thomas Merton: Vol. 1). 1995. pap. 12.00 (0-06-065475-9) Harper SF.

— Seeds of Contemplation. LC 78-10255. 201p. 1979. reprint ed. text ed. 55.00 (0-313-20756-9, MESC, Greenwood Pr) Greenwood.

— Seeds of Contemplation. LC 86-8559. 208p. 1986. reprint ed. 18.95 (0-8112-0990-3) New Directions.

— Selected Poems. enl. ed. LC 67-23488. 1967. pap. 8.95 (0-8112-0100-7, NDP85) New Directions.

— The Seven Storey Mountain. 300p. 1991. reprint ed. lib. bdg. 22.95 (0-89966-864-X) Buccaneer Bks.

— The Seven Storey Mountain. LC 78-7109. 429p. 1978. reprint ed. pap. 12.00 (0-15-680679-7, Harvest Bks) HarBrace.

— The Seven Story Mountain. 528p. 1990. 15.95 (0-15-181354-X) HarBrace.

— The Sign of Jonas. LC 79-10283. 362p. 1979. pap. 10.95 (0-15-682529-5, Harvest Bks) HarBrace.

— The Silent Life. 178p. 1975. pap. 12.00 (0-374-51281-7) FS&G.

— Spiritual Direction & Meditation. 108p. 1960. pap. 4.95 (0-8146-0412-9) Liturgical Pr.

— The Spring of Contemplation: A Retreat at the Abbey of Gethsemani. 1992. 22.00 (0-374-12893-6) FS&G.

— Thomas Merton in Alaska: Prelude to the Asian Journal. LC 87-24028. (Illus.). 224p. 1989. 19.95 (0-8112-1048-0); pap. 9.95 (0-8112-1038-3, NDP652) New Directions.

— Thoughts in Solitude. 124p. 1976. pap. 7.00 (0-374-51325-2, Noonday) FS&G.

— Thoughts in Solitude. LC 92-50736. 168p. 1993. reprint ed. pap. 6.00 (0-87773-920-X, Sham Pocket Class) Shambhala Pubns.

— Thoughts on the East. LC 95-5377. (New Directions Bibelot Ser.). 96p. (Orig.). 1995. pap. 6.00 (0-8112-1293-9, NDP802) New Directions.

— A Vow of Conversation. 256p. 1988. 17.95 (0-374-28535-7) FS&G.

— The Waters of Siloe. LC 79-10372. 377p. 1979. pap. 12.00 (0-15-694954-7, Harvest Bks) HarBrace.

— The Way of Chuang Tzu. LC 65-27556. (Illus.). 1969. reprint ed. pap. 7.95 (0-8112-0103-1, NDP276) New Directions.

— The Way of Chuang Tzu. LC 91-50903. (Pocket Classics Ser.). 194p. 1992. reprint ed. pap. 6.00 (0-87773-676-6) Shambhala Pubns.

— Ways of the Christian Mystics. LC 94-8330. (Pocket Classics Ser.). 200p. 1994. pap. 6.00 (1-57062-030-X, Sham Pocket Class) Shambhala Pubns.

— What Is Contemplation? 80p. 1981. reprint ed. pap. 6.95 (0-87243-103-7) Templegate.

— The Wisdom of the Desert. LC 59-15021. 1970. pap. 6.95 (0-8112-0102-3, NDP295) New Directions.

— Zen & the Birds of Appetite. LC 68-25546. 1968. pap. 7.95 (0-8112-0104-X, NDP261) New Directions.

— Zen & the Birds of Appetite. LC 93-16313. (Pocket Classics Ser.). 304p. 1993. reprint ed. pap. 6.00 (0-87773-936-6) Shambhala Pubns.

Merton, Thomas, ed. Monks Pond: Thomas Merton's Little Magazine. LC 89-8918. (Illus.). 368p. 1989. text ed. 36.00 (0-8131-1694-5) U Pr of Ky.

Merton, Thomas, sel. The Wisdom of the Desert. LC 93-23927. (Pocket Classics Ser.). 120p. 1994. reprint ed. pap. 6.00 (0-87773-976-5) Shambhala Pubns.

Merton, Thomas & Lax, Robert. A Catch of Anti-Letters. LC 94-1262. (Illus.). 136p. (Orig.). 1994. pap. 9.95 (1-55612-712-X, LL1712) Sheed & Ward MO.

***Merton, Thomas & Ruether, Rosemary R.** At Home in the World: The Letters of Thomas Merton & Rosemary Radford Ruether. LC 95-10200. 110p. (Orig.). 1995. pap. text ed. 12.95 (1-57075-015-7) Orbis Bks.

Merton, Thomas, jt. auth. see Arnold, Eberhard.

Merton, Thomas, ed. see Gandhi, Mohandas.

Merton, Thomas, jt. auth. see Niles, John J.

Merton, Thomas, tr. see St. Augustine.

Merts, A. L., jt. ed. see Hauer, Allan.

Merttens, Ruth & Vass, Jeff. Sharing the Maths Cultures: IMPACT LEA Maths for Parents, Children & Teachers. 200p. 1990. 55.00 (1-85000-875-2, Falmer Pr); pap. 28.00 (1-85000-876-0, Falmer Pr) Taylor & Francis.

Merttens, Ruth & Vass, Jeff, eds. Partnerships in Maths: Parents & Schools: the IMPACT Project. LC 92-42864. 256p. 1993. pap. 35.00 (0-7507-0155-2, Falmer Pr); boxed 90.00 (0-7507-0154-4, Falmer Pr) Taylor & Francis.

***Mertvago, Peter.** Dictionary of One-Thousand Spanish Proverbs. 250p. (Orig.). 1995. pap. 14.95 (0-7818-0412-4) Hippocrene Bks.

— Dictionary of Russian Proverbs: Bilingual. 606p. 1994. 50.00 (0-7818-0283-0) Hippocrene Bks.

Mertz, Ann, ed. see Field, Gary G.

Mertz, B. A. Ansata Tarot. 36p. 1985. 15.00 (0-88079-296-5) US Games Syst.

Mertz, Barbara. Red Land, Black Land: Daily Life in Ancient Egypt. LC 89-17875. (Illus.). 386p. 1990. pap. 15.95 (0-87226-222-7) P Bedrick Bks.

— Temples, Tombs & Hieroglyphs: A Popular History of Ancient Egypt. LC 89-17911. (Illus.). 336p. 1990. pap. 15.95 (0-87226-223-5) P Bedrick Bks.

Mertz, Edwin T., ed. Quality Protein Maize. LC 92-71401. (Illus.). 294p. (Orig.). 1992. pap. 69.00x (0-913250-75-9) Am Assn Cereal Chem.

Mertz, Elizabeth & Parmentier, Richard A., eds. Signs in Society: Psychological & Socio-Cultural Studies in Semiotic Mediation. (Language, Thought & Culture Ser.). 1985. text ed. 72.00 (0-12-491280-X) Acad Pr.

Mertz, Harold J., jt. ed. see Backaitis, Stan.

Mertz, James J., tr. see Murphy, John P., ed.

***Mertz, Steven.** Sudden Death. (Orig.). 1995. pap. text ed. 4.99 (1-57297-032-4) Blvd Books.

Mertz, Walter. Trace Elements in Human & Animal Nutrition, Vol. 1. 5th ed. 480p. 1987. text ed. 119.00 (0-12-491251-6) Acad Pr.

An Asterisk (*) at the beginning of an entry indicates that the title is appearing in BIP for the first time.

— Trace Elements in Human & Animal Nutrition, Vol. 2. 5th ed. 1986. text ed. 99.00 (*0-12-491252-4*) Acad Pr.

Mertz, Walter & Cornatzer, W. E., eds. Newer Trace Elements in Nutrition. LC 70-157834. (Illus.). 451p. reprint ed. pap. 128.60 (*0-317-07852-6*, 2055015) Bks Demand.

Mertz, Werner. Watercolor Paper Handbook: A Selection Guide for Artists. (Illus.). 112p. 1991. 18.95 (*0-8230-5678-3*, Watsn-Guptill) Watsn-Guptill.

Mertzluff, Bonnie, et al. Math Learning Resources from Recyclables. (Illus.). 128p. (J). (ps-3). 1994. teacher ed, pap. 12.95 (*1-878279-70-X*, MM 1991) Monday Morning Bks.

Mertzlufft, Bonnie, et al. Language Arts Resources from Recycables. (Illus.). 128p. (J). (gr. k-3). 1994. pap. 12.95 (*1-878279-71-8*) Monday Morning Bks.

Mertzlufft, F. O., jt. ed. see Zander, R.

Mertzlufft, Nancy, jt. auth. see Leach, Diana.

Mertzweiller, Joseph K., jt. ed. see Caillet, Marie.

Merullo, Roland. Leaving Losapas. 304p. 1992. pap. 10.00 (*0-380-71750-6*) Avon.

— A Russian Requiem. LC 93-22526. 1993. 22.95 (*0-316-56789-2*) Little.

***Merusi, Donald.** Software Implementation Techniques: Writing Software in VMS, OS/2, UNIX & Windows NT. 2nd ed. LC 95-14929. 1995. write for info. (*1-55558-134-X*, Digital DEC) Buttrwrth-Heinemann.

Merusi, Donald E. Software Implementation Techniques: VMS, UNIX, OS-2, MS-DOS. (Programmer's Ser.). (Illus.). 700p. 1992. pap. 39.95 (*1-55558-090-4*, EY-J822E-DP) DEC.

Merva, George, jt. auth. see Patterson, Dan.

Mervan, Leroy. Your First Gerbil. (Illus.). 34p. (Orig.). 1991. pap. 1.95 (*0-86622-063-1*, YF-107) TFH Pubns.

***Mervin, Dana V.** The 5 Minute Mutual Fund Investor: A Basic Guide to Investing in Mutual Funds. 240p. 1995. 19.95 (*0-9641819-0-8*) M Systs Pubng.

Mervin, David. The Presidency & Ronald Reagan. 237p. (C). 1990. pap. text ed. 22.95 (*0-582-03493-0*, 78530) Longman.

Mervin, Sabrina & Prunhuber, Carol. Women: Around the World & Through the Ages. (Illus.). 240p. 1991. 34.95 (*1-56182-016-4*) Atomium Bks.

Mervis, Cynthia & Hynes, Angela. Love Potions: A Doctor's Guide to Aphrodisia. LC 92-35363. 288p. (Orig.). 1993. pap. 10.95 (*0-87477-724-0*, J P T-Putnam) Putnam Pub Group.

Mervyn, Len. Minerals & Your Health. LC 80-84442. 144p. 1981. 10.95 (*0-87983-242-8*) Keats.

— Minerals & Your Health. LC 80-84442. 176p. 1984. reprint ed. pap. 3.50 (*0-87983-402-1*) Keats.

— Vitamin E Updated. Passwater, Richard A. & Mindell, Earl R., eds. (Good Health Guide Ser.). 32p. (Orig.). 1983. pap. 1.45 (*0-87983-274-6*) Keats.

Mervyn, Leonard. Diccionario de Vitaminas. 240p. (CAT.). 1985. pap. write for info. (*0-7859-4920-8*) Fr & Eur.

— Heart Disease: Thorsons New Self-Help Series. 1990. pap. 3.95 (*0-7225-2256-8*) Thorsons SF.

***Merwald, Judith F., et al.** The Christmas Tree Ship. (Illus.). 17p. (Orig.). (J). (gr. 2-6). 1993. pap. 10.00 (*0-9643859-0-2*, 1) True Story.

Merwick, Donna. Boston Priests, Eighteen Forty-Eight to Nineteen Ten: A Study in Social & Intellectual Change. LC 72-79309. 292p. 1973. 32.00 (*0-674-07975-2*) HUP.

— Possessing Albany, 1630-1710: The Dutch & English Experiences. (Illus.). (C). 1990. 64.95 (*0-521-37386-7*) Cambridge U Pr.

Merwin, Charles L. Financing Small Corporations in Five Manufacturing Industries: 1926-36. Bruchey, Stuart & Carosso, Vincent P., eds. LC 78-18970. (Small Business Enterprise in America Ser.). (Illus.). 1979. reprint ed. lib. bdg. 17.95 (*0-405-11473-7*) Ayer.

— Financing Small Corporations in Five Manufacturing Industries, 1926-36. (Financial Research Program III: Studies in Business Financing: No. 2). 189p. 1942. reprint ed. 50.00 (*0-87014-130-9*); reprint ed. mic. film 26.00 (*0-685-61229-5*) Natl Bur Econ Res.

Merwin, Don, jt. auth. see Howells, John.

Merwin, J. Streamer-Fly Fishing. 1991. pap. 9.95 (*1-55821-099-7*) Lyons & Burford.

Merwin, John. The Battenkill. (Illus.). 160p. 1993. 22.95 (*1-55821-208-6*) Lyons & Burford.

— New American Trout Fishing. 335p. 1994. text ed. 30.00 (*0-02-584382-6*) Macmillan.

Merwin, John, ed. Stillwater Trout. (Illus.). 232p. (Orig.). 1988. pap. 13.95 (*0-941130-80-0*) Lyons & Burford.

Merwin, John, ed. see Wulff, Lee.

Merwin, R. E. & Vaillant, G. C. Ruins of Holmul, Guatemala. (Harvard University PMAE Monographs). 1974. reprint ed. 60.00 (*0-527-01160-6*) Periodicals Srv.

Merwin, Richard. Mega-Slank from Titanium. LC 92-12842. (Widgets Ser.). (J). (gr. 2). 1992. lib. bdg. 13.99 (*1-56239-151-8*) Abdo & Dghtrs.

Merwin, Samuel & Webster, Henry K. The Short-Line War. LC 67-29273. (Americans in Fiction Ser.). 340p. reprint ed. lib. bdg. 29.50 (*0-8398-1256-6*); reprint ed. pap. text ed. 5.95 (*0-89197-935-2*) Irvington.

Merwin, Sandra J. Real Self: The Inner Journey of Courage. 104p. (Orig.). 1991. pap. text ed. 7.95 (*0-9628522-0-1*) TigerLily Pr.

Merwin, W. S. Finding the Islands. LC 82-81481. 88p. 1982. pap. 6.00 (*0-86547-089-8*, North Pt Pr) FS&G.

— The First Four Books of Poems: Including a Mask for Janus, the Dancing Bear, Green with Beasts, the Drunk in the Furnace. LC 75-4079. 288p. (C). 1975. pap. 10.95 (*0-689-10694-7*, Atheneum S&S) S&S Trade.

— First Four Poems. 1989. 45.00 (*0-02-584381-8*) Macmillan.

— Houses & Travellers. 1994. pap. 12.95 (*0-8050-2872-2*) H Holt & Co.

— The Lost Upland. 1992. 22.00 (*0-679-40526-7*) Knopf.

— The Lost Upland: Stories of Southwest France. 320p. 1993. pap. 14.95 (*0-8050-2593-6*) H Holt & Co.

— Miner's Pale Children. 1994. pap. 12.95 (*0-8050-2870-6*) H Holt & Co.

— Poem of the Cid. 1975. pap. 10.00 (*0-452-01060-8*, Mer) NAL-Dutton.

— Poem of the Cid. 1989. pap. 8.95 (*0-452-00915-4*) NAL-Dutton.

— The Rain in the Trees. LC 87-46081. 96p. 1988. pap. 13.00 (*0-394-75858-7*) Knopf.

— The Real World of Manuel Cordova. (Illus.). 47p. 1993. write for info. (*0-9614597-9-4*) Ninja Pr.

— Regions of Memory: Uncollected Prose, 1949-1982. Folsom, Ed & Nelson, Cary, eds. LC 86-1358. 376p. 1987. 29.95 (*0-252-01241-0*) U of Ill Pr.

— The Second Four Books of Poems. LC 92-39320. 400p. (Orig.). 1993. pap. 14.00 (*1-55659-054-7*) Copper Canyon.

— Selected Poems. 288p. 1988. pap. 16.00 (*0-689-70736-3*, Pub. by Ctrl Bur voor Schimmel NE) Macmillan.

— Travels. Date not set. pap. 12.00 (*0-679-75277-3*) Random.

— Travels: Poems. LC 92-14917. 1992. 20.00 (*0-679-41890-3*) Knopf.

— Unframed Originals. 1994. pap. 12.95 (*0-8050-2871-4*) H Holt & Co.

— Unframed Originals: Recollections. LC 81-70063. 256p. 1983. 14.95 (*0-689-11284-X*, Atheneum S&S) S&S Trade.

Merwin, W. S., ed. The Essential Wyatt. (Essential Poets Ser.: Vol. 10). 128p. 1989. pap. 6.00 (*0-88001-180-7*) Ecco Pr.

Merwin, W. S., tr. Poem of the Cid. 1975. pap. 7.95 (*0-452-00790-9*, Mer) NAL-Dutton.

Merwin, W. S., jt. tr. see Brown, Clarence.

Merwin, W. S., tr. see Lorca, Federico G.

Merwin, W. S., jt. tr. see Mustard, Helen M.

Merwin, W. S., tr. see Neruda, Pablo.

Merwin-Webster. Calumet "K" LC 90-63345. (Illus.). 345p. 1993. reprint ed. 24.95 (*1-56114-145-3*) Second Renaissance.

Merwin, William. Mask for Janus. LC 76-144755. (Yale Series of Younger Poets: No. 49). reprint ed. 18.00 (*0-404-53849-5*) AMS Pr.

— The Restructuring of America: A Futurist Projection. 104p. (Orig.). 1991. pap. 9.95 (*0-932863-13-2*) Clarity Pr.

Merwin, William S., tr. see Euripides.

Merxmuller, H. Prodromus Einer Flora Von Sudwestafrika. (C). 1988. text ed. 720.00 (*0-685-22106-7*, Scientific) St Mut.

Meryl, Debra. Baby's Peek-a-Boo Album. (Lift-the-Flap Book Ser.). (Illus.). 24p. (J). (ps). 1989. 11.95 (*0-448-15375-0*, G&D) Putnam Pub Group.

Meryll, Jane, ed. see Yelin, Joy.

Meryman, Richard. Andrew Wyeth. (First Impressions Ser.). (Illus.). 92p. (YA). (gr. 7 up). 1991. 19.95 (*0-8109-3956-8*) Abrams.

***Merz.** Points of Cosmic Energy. 1995. pap. 13.95 (*0-85207-194-9*) Atrium Pubs.

Merz, Andrew K. Phillies Wit: Words of Wisdom from the Wild, Wacky, Wonderful '93 Phillies. Broussard, Anne E., ed. (Orig.). 1993. pap. 5.95 (*0-9640033-0-9*) Wit Press.

Merz, Blanche. Points of Cosmic Energy. (Illus.). 184p. (Orig.). Date not set. pap. 20.95 (*0-8464-4271-X*) Beekman Pubs.

Merz, Carol, jt. auth. see Lutz, Frank.

Merz, Charles. Centerville, U. S. A. LC 78-160943. (Short Story Index Reprint Ser.). 1977. reprint ed. 20.95 (*0-8369-3922-0*) Ayer.

Merz, E. Ultrasound in Obstetrics & Gynecology. (Illus.). 343p. 1990. text ed. 139.00 (*0-86577-376-9*) Thieme Med Pubs.

Merz, Erich R. Federal Republic of Germany R & D Programme. (Special Issue of the Journal Radioactive Waste Management & the Nuclear Fuel Cycle Ser.). 125p. 1986. pap. text ed. 84.00 (*3-7186-0336-5*) Gordon & Breach.

***Merz, Erich R., et al, eds.** Mixed Oxide Fuel (MOX) Exploitation & Destruction in Power Reactors: Proceedings of the NATO Advanced Research Workshop, Obninsk, Russia, October 16-19, 1994. LC 95-12380. (NATO Advanced Sciences Institutes: Vol. 2). 320p. (C). 1995. lib. bdg. 160.00 (*0-7923-3473-6*) Kluwer Ac.

Merz, John T. History of European Thought in the Nineteenth Century, Vols. 3 & 4. 16.50 (*0-8446-2579-5*) Peter Smith.

Merz, Kenneth M., Jr. & Le Grand, Scott M., eds. The Protein Folding Problem & Tertiary Structure Prediction. LC 93-41522. x, 581p. 1994. 99.00 (*0-8176-3693-5*) Birkhauser.

Merz, M., jt. ed. see Guttman, V.

Merz, M., jt. ed. see Marriott, J. B.

Merzbach, Uta, jt. ed. see Birkhoff, Garrett.

Merzbach, Uta C., comp. Carl Friedrich Gauss: A Bibliography. LC 83-20345. 551p. 1984. lib. bdg. 100.00 (*0-8420-2169-8*) Scholarly Res Inc.

Merzbach, Uta C., jt. auth. see Davis, Audrey B.

Merzbacher, Eugen. Quantum Mechanics. 2nd ed. LC 74-88316. 621p. (C). 1969. Net. text ed. write for info. (*0-471-59670-1*) Wiley.

***Merzel, Dennis G.** Beyond Sanity & Madness: The Way of Zen Master Dogen. 176p. (Orig.). 1994. pap. 14.95 (*0-8048-3035-5*) C E Tuttle.

Merzel, Dennis G. & Maezumi, Hakuyu T. The Eye Never Sleeps: Striking to the Heart of Zen. LC 90-52803. 176p. (Orig.). 1991. pap. 12.00 (*0-87773-569-7*) Shambhala Pubns.

Merzheevskaya, O. I. Larvae of Owlet Moths (Noctuidae) (C). 1988. 58.50 (*0-8364-2397-6*, Pub. by Oxford IBH II) S Asia.

Merzkirch, Wolfgang. Flow Visualization. 2nd ed. 260p. 1987. text ed. 69.00 (*0-12-491351-2*) Acad Pr.

Merzlak, Regina. Earth Tones. LC 93-46363. 64p. 1994. pap. 12.95 (*0-7734-2722-8*, Mellen Poetry Pr) E Mellen.

— Underlight: Poems. LC 92-44220. 64p. 1993. pap. 12.95 (*0-7734-2770-8*, Mellen Poetry Pr) E Mellen.

Merzljakov, Ju. I., jt. auth. see Kargapolov, M. I.

Merzlyakov, N. S., jt. auth. see Yaroslavskii, L. P.

Mesa, Aldo. Nolanaceae. LC 81-80613. (Flora Neotropica Monograph Ser.: No. 26). (Illus.). 198p. 1981. pap. 12.00 (*0-89327-233-7*) NY Botanical.

Mesa-Bains, Amalia. A Facilitator's Guide to Diversity in the Classroom: A Casebook for Teachers & Teacher Educators. Culbertson, Hugh M. & Chen, Ni, eds. LC 94-7060. (LEA's Communication Ser.). 400p. 1995. pap. 40.00 (*0-8058-1685-2*) L Erlbaum Assocs.

Mesa-Bains, Amalia & Bettelheim, Judith. Adaline Kent Award Exhibition, 1991 - Mildred Howard: Ten Little Children Standing in a Line (One Got Shot, & Then There Were Nine) (Illus.). 1991. pap. 5.00 (*0-930495-10-1*) San Fran Art Inst.

***Mesa-Bains, Amalia & Shulman, Judith H.** A Facilitator's Guide to Diversity in the Classroom: A Casebook for Teachers & Teacher Educators. LC 94-7060. 1994. student ed 21.00 (*0-8058-1688-7*) L Erlbaum Assocs.

— A Facilitator's Guide to Diversity in the Classroom: A Casebook for Teachers & Teacher Educators. LC 94-7060. 80p. 1994. pap. 14.95 (*0-8058-1430-2*) L Erlbaum Assocs.

Mesa-Bains, Amalia, jt. ed. see Shulman, Judith H.

Mesa-Bains, Amalia, et al. Ceremony of Memory: Contemporary Hispanic Spiritual & Ceremonial Art. (Illus.). 48p. (Orig.). 1988. pap. text ed. 15.00 (*0-685-21899-6*) CCA Santa Fe.

***Mesa, Cuevas.** Spanish-English - English-Spanish Commercial Dictionary. 255p. 1993. 49.95 (*968-842-422-6*) IBD Ltd.

Mesa-Lago, Carmelo. Ascent to Bankruptcy: Financing Social Security in Latin America. LC 89-35475. (Latin American Ser.). 318p. 1990. 49.95 (*0-8229-3600-3*) U of Pittsburgh Pr.

— Changing Social Security in Latin America: Toward Alleviating the Social Costs of Economic Reform. LC 93-38662. 220p. 1994. lib. bdg. 42.00 (*1-55587-486-X*) Lynne Rienner.

— Dialectica de la Revolucion Cubana del Idealism Carismatico al Pragmatismo Institucionalista. 244p. (SPA.). (C). 1979. pap. text ed. 18.95 (*84-359-0203-X*) Transaction Pubs.

— The Economy of Socialist Cuba: A Two-Decade Appraisal. LC 80-54570. 251p. reprint ed. pap. 71.60 (*0-7837-5868-5*, 2045587) Bks Demand.

— Financiamiento De la Atencion a la Salud en America Latina y el Caribe, Con Focalizacion En el Seguro Social. (EDI Seminar Paper Ser.: No. 42). 80p. 1989. 7.95 (*0-8213-1365-7*, 11365) World Bank.

— Portfolio Performance of Selected Social Security Institutes in Latin America. (Discussion Paper Ser.: No. 139). 79p. 1991. 7.95 (*0-8213-1954-X*, 11954) World Bank.

— Social Security & Prospects for Equity in Latin America. (Discussion Paper Ser.: No. 140). 150p. 1991. 9.95 (*0-8213-1955-8*, 11955) World Bank.

— Social Security in Latin America: Pressure Groups, Stratification, & Inequality. LC 77-15732. (Pitt Latin American Ser.). 372p. reprint ed. pap. 106.10 (*0-7837-2474-8*, 2042628) Bks Demand.

Mesa-Lago, Carmelo, ed. Cuba after the Cold War. LC 92-50847. (Latin American Ser.). 408p. (C). 1993. text ed. 49.95 (*0-8229-3749-2*); pap. text ed. 19.95 (*0-8229-5503-2*) U of Pittsburgh Pr.

— Cuban Studies, Vol. 16. LC 75-649635. 302p. 1986. 39.95 (*0-8229-3540-6*) U of Pittsburgh Pr.

— Cuban Studies, Vol. 18. LC 75-649635. (Latin American Ser.). 261p. (C). 1988. 39.95 (*0-8229-3593-7*) U of Pittsburgh Pr.

— Cuban Studies, Vol. 19. LC 75-649635. (Latin American Ser.). 384p. 1990. 39.95 (*0-8229-3626-7*) U of Pittsburgh Pr.

— Cuban Studies, Vol. 20. LC 75-649635. (Latin American Ser.). 256p. 1990. 39.95 (*0-8229-3649-6*) U of Pittsburgh Pr.

— Revolutionary Change in Cuba. LC 73-158190. 560p. reprint ed. pap. 159.60 (*0-7837-2473-X*, 2042627) Bks Demand.

Mesa-Lago, Carmelo & Beck, Carl, eds. Comparative Socialist Systems: Essays on Politics & Economics. LC 75-331585. 466p. reprint ed. pap. 132.90 (*0-8357-4638-0*, 2037569) Bks Demand.

Mesa-Lago, Carmelo, et al, eds. Cuban Studies, Vol. 17. LC 75-649635. 255p. 1987. 39.95 (*0-8229-3562-7*) U of Pittsburgh Pr.

Mesa, Rosa Q. Argentina. LC 73-180800. (Latin American Serial Documents Ser.: Vol. 5). 726p. reprint ed. pap. 180.00 (*0-8357-5729-3*, 2013547) Bks Demand.

— Bolivia. LC 73-180800. (Latin American Serial Documents Ser.: Vol. 6). 190p. reprint ed. pap. 54.20 (*0-8357-7336-1*, 2013552) Bks Demand.

— Brazil. LC 68-57259. (Latin American Serial Documents Ser.: Vol. 2). 365p. reprint ed. pap. 104.10 (*0-8357-7385-X*, 2013544) Bks Demand.

— Chile. LC 73-180800. (Latin American Serial Documents Ser.: Vol. 7). 359p. reprint ed. pap. 102.40 (*0-317-10752-6*, 2013549) Bks Demand.

— Colombia. LC 68-56197. (Latin American Serial Documents Ser.: Vol. 1). 150p. pap. 42.80 (*0-317-10293-1*, 2013543) Bks Demand.

— Cuba. LC 70-79480. (Latin American Serial Documents Ser.: Vol. 3). 225p. reprint ed. pap. 64.20 (*0-317-10224-9*, 2013545) Bks Demand.

— Ecuador. LC 73-180800. (Latin American Serial Documents Ser.: Vol. 8). 174p. reprint ed. pap. 49.60 (*0-317-10745-3*, 2013550) Bks Demand.

— Paraguay. LC 73-180800. (Latin American Serial Documents Ser.: Vol. 9). 93p. reprint ed. pap. 26.60 (*0-317-10336-9*, 2013551) Bks Demand.

— Peru. LC 73-180800. (Latin American Serial Documents Ser.: Vol. 10). 307p. reprint ed. pap. 87.50 (*0-317-10757-7*, 2013548) Bks Demand.

— Uruguay. LC 73-180800. (Latin American Serial Documents Ser.: Vol. 11). 193p. reprint ed. pap. 55.10 (*0-317-10313-X*, 2013553) Bks Demand.

— Venezuela. LC 73-180800. (Latin American Serial Documents Ser.: Vol. 12). 337p. reprint ed. pap. 96.10 (*0-317-10310-5*, 2013554) Bks Demand.

Mesarovic, Jovan, ed. Istria & Kvarnev. Biconic, Sonja, tr. 1.95 (*0-8184-0120-6*) Carol Pub Group.

Mesarovic, M. D. & Takahara, Y. Abstract Systems Theory. (Lecture Notes in Control & Information Sciences Ser.: Vol. 116). viii, 439p. 1989. pap. 70.00 (*0-387-50529-6*) Spr-Verlag.

Mesavage. En Cours de Route. 2nd ed. 1992. pap. 33.95 (*0-8384-3712-5*) Heinle & Heinle.

— En Cours de Route. 2nd ed. 1992. student ed, pap. 28.95 (*0-8384-3717-6*) Heinle & Heinle.

Mesbah, M. T., et al. Status of Women in Islam. vi, 57p. 1990. text ed. 10.95 (*0-685-35772-4*, Pub. by Radiant Pubs II) S Asia.

Mesbahi, Mohiaddin, ed. Central Asia & the Caucasus after the Soviet Union: Domestic & International Dynamics. LC 94-16204. 344p. 1994. lib. bdg. 49.95 (*0-8130-1307-0*); pap. text ed. 24.95 (*0-8130-1308-9*) U Press Fla.

— Russia & the Third World in the Post-Soviet Era. 376p. (C). 1994. lib. bdg. 49.95 (*0-8130-1270-8*); pap. text ed. 19.95 (*0-8130-1271-6*) U Press Fla.

Mesce, Bill, Jr. Four Day Shoot. 1993. pap. 7.95 (*0-9638760-0-7*) Generic Pubng.

Mesch, Abraham J., tr. see Hanover, Nathan.

Meschan, Isadore & Ott, David J. Introduction to Diagnostic Imaging. (Illus.). 416p. 1984. text ed. 55.95 (*0-7216-6277-3*) Saunders.

Meschel, Susan V., jt. auth. see Handler, Andrew.

Meschery, Joanne. Home & Away. 1994. 21.00 (*0-671-88419-0*) S&S Trade.

Meschi, Bob. Antique Wicker from the Heywood-Wakefield Catalog. LC 94-65608. (Illus.). 160p. (Orig.). 1994. pap. 19.95 (*0-88740-618-1*) Schiffer.

Meschia, Giacomo, jt. auth. see Battaglia, Frederick C.

Meschiari, M., et al. Geometry Seminar "Luigi Bianchi" II, 1984. (Lecture Notes in Mathematics Ser.: Vol. 1164). vi, 224p. 1985. pap. 34.10 (*0-387-16048-5*) Spr-Verlag.

Meschke, Gunther, jt. auth. see Mang, Herbert.

Meschke, Michael & Sorenson, Margareta. In Search of Aesthetics for the Puppet Theatre. (Illus.). 176p. (C). 1992. 35.00 (*81-207-1400-8*, Pub. by Sterling Pubs II) Apt Bks.

Meschler, Maurice. Life of St. Aloysius Gonzaga: Patron of Christian Youth. LC 84-52294. 348p. 1985. reprint ed. pap. 10.00 (*0-89555-275-2*) TAN Bks Pubs.

Meschter, W. Kyrel. Twentieth-Century Schwenkfelders: A Narrative History. 1984. pap. write for info. (*0-935980-03-2*) Schwenkfelder Lib.

Mescon, Michael & Bramlette, Carl A., Jr., eds. Man & the Future of Organizations, Vol. 6. LC 72-619550. (Franklin Foundation Lecture Ser.). 64p. 1977. pap. 8.50 (*0-88406-116-7*) GA St U Busn Pr.

Mescon, Michael & Mescon, Timothy. Showing up for Work & Other Keys to Business Success. (Illus.). 224p. 1988. 15.95 (*0-934601-45-3*) Peachtree Pubs.

Mescon, Michael H. Man & the Future of Organizations, Vol. 3. Bramlette, Carl A., Jr., ed. LC 72-619550. (Franklin Foundation Lecture Ser.). Orig. Title: Man & the Future of Organizations. 57p. (Orig.). 1974. pap. 8.50 (*0-88406-017-9*) GA St U Busn Pr.

— Man & the Future of Organizations, Vol. 4. Bramlette, Carl A., Jr., ed. LC 72-619550. (Franklin Foundation Lecture Ser.). Orig. Title: Man & the Future of Organizations. 64p. (Orig.). 1975. pap. 8.50 (*0-88406-101-9*) GA St U Busn Pr.

Mescon, Michael H. & Bramlette, Carl A., Jr. The Individual & the Future of Organizations, Vol. 8. LC 72-619550. (Franklin Foundation Lecture Ser.). 90p. 1979. pap. 8.50 (*0-88406-129-9*) GA St U Busn Pr.

Mescon, Michael H. & Bramlette, Carl A., Jr., eds. Individual & the Future of Organizations, Vol. 9. LC 72-619550. (Franklin Foundation Lecture Ser.). 52p. 1980. pap. 8.50 (*0-88406-139-6*) GA St U Busn Pr.

— Individual & the Future of Organizations, Vol. 10. LC 72-619550. (Franklin Foundation Lecture Ser.). 75p. 1981. pap. 8.50 (*0-88406-144-2*) GA St U Busn Pr.

— Individual & the Future of Organizations, Vol. 11. LC 72-619550. (Franklin Foundation Lecture Ser.). 64p. 1982. pap. 8.50 (*0-88406-145-0*) GA St U Busn Pr.

Mescon, Michael H., Jr., jt. ed. see Bramlette, Carl A., Jr.

Mescon, Michael H.

Mescon, Michael H., et al. Management. 3rd ed. 784p. (C). 1989. text ed. 71.00 (*0-06-044415-0*) HarpCollege.

— Memos to Management: There's Nothing Wrong with Serving a Lousy Cup of Coffee. LC 92-84007. 112p. 1993. 15.95 (*1-56352-066-4*) Longstreet Pr Inc.

Mescon, Timothy, jt. auth. see Mescon, Michael.

MESD School Health Services. School Emergencies Manual. 1992. 25.00 (*1-880118-05-X*) MESD Pr.

MESD School Health Services Staff. Communicable Disease Control Plan for School District Employees. 106p. 1992. student ed 25.00 (*1-880118-08-4*) MESD Pr.

An Asterisk (*) at the beginning of an entry indicates that the title is appearing in BIP for the first time.

— Communicable Disease Control Plan for School District Employees - Instructor Manual. 155p. 1992. student ed 50.00 (*1-880118-09-2*) MESD Pr.

— Practical Guidelines for Reducing the Risk of Communicable Disease in a School Setting. 1992. 7.50 (*1-880118-06-8*) MESD Pr.

Meselson, Matthew, ed. Chemical Weapons & Chemical Arms Control. LC 77-93266. 1978. pap. text ed. 3.00 (*0-87003-010-8*) Carnegie Endow.

Mesens, E. L. & Penrose, Roland, eds. London Bulletin Nineteen Thirty-Eight to Nineteen Forty, 2 Vols, Set. LC 77-96917. (Contemporary Art Ser.). (Illus.). 1970. reprint ed. 60.95 (*0-405-00733-7*) Ayer.

Mesera, F., et al, eds. Biomechanical Transport Processes. LC 90-4246. (NATO ASI Series A, Life Sciences: Vol. 193). (Illus.). 410p. 1990. 110.00 (*0-306-43676-0*, Plenum Pr) Plenum.

Meserole, Harrison T., ed. American Poetry of the Seventeenth Century. LC 85-21701. 576p. 1985. reprint ed. pap. text ed. 16.95 (*0-271-00418-5*) Pa St U Pr.

Meserole, Harrison T., jt. auth. see Bateson, F. W.

Meserole, Mike, ed. The Nineteen Ninety-Five Information Please Sports Almanac. (Illus.). 896p. 1994. pap. 10.95 (*0-395-66565-5*) HM.

***Meserve.** Playwright's Companion, 1995: A Practical Guide to Script Opportunities in the U. S. A. 1995. pap. text ed. 20.95 (*0-937657-17-4*) Feedbk Theabks & Prospero.

Meserve, Bruce E. Fundamental Concepts of Algebra. (Mathematics Ser.). 320p. 1982. reprint ed. pap. 8.95 (*0-486-61470-0*) Dover.

— Fundamental Concepts of Geometry. (Illus.). 352p. 1983. reprint ed. pap. 8.95 (*0-486-63415-9*) Dover.

Meserve, Bruce E., et al. Contemporary Mathematics. 4th ed. (Illus.). 720p. 1986. text ed. write for info. (*0-13-170127-4*) P-H.

— Introduction to Mathematics. 6th ed. 544p. (C). 1989. text ed. write for info. (*0-13-499104-4*) P-H.

Meserve, Harry C. The Practical Meditator. LC 80-15631. 137p. 1981. 27.95 (*0-87705-506-8*) Human Sci Pr.

Meserve, Mollie A. The Playwright's Companion 1993: A Practical Guide to Script Opportunities in the U. S. A. 1993. pap. 20.95 (*0-937657-14-X*) Feedbk Theabks & Prospero.

— The Playwright's Companion, 1994: A Practical Guide to Script Opportunitites in the U. S. A. 1993. pap. 20.95 (*0-937657-15-8*) Feedbk Theabks & Prospero.

— Professional Playscript Format Guidelines & Sample (Booklet) 1991. pap. 4.95 (*0-937657-13-1*) Feedbk Theabks & Prospero.

Meserve, Mollie A. & Meserve, Walter J. The Theatre Lover's Cookbook. 1992. pap. 9.95 (*0-937657-11-5*) Feedbk Theabks & Prospero.

— Who's Where in the American Theatre. 3rd ed. 1992. pap. 14.95 (*0-937657-10-7*) Feedbk Theabks & Prospero.

Meserve, Mollie A., jt. auth. see Meserve, Walter J.

Meserve, Ruth I., comp. Denis Sinor Bibliography. (Acadia Bibliographica Virorum Eruditorum Ser.: Fasc. g). 64p. 1986. 16.00 (*0-685-13255-2*) Eurolingua.

Meserve, Ruth I., jt. ed. see Meserve, Walter M.

Meserve, Walter J. Heralds of Promise: The Drama of the American People During the Age of Jackson, 1829-1849. LC 85-21846. (Contributions in American Studies: No.86). (Illus.). 282p. 1986. text ed. 55.00 (*0-313-25015-4*, MHP, Greenwood Pr) Greenwood.

— Outline History of American Drama. 2nd ed. 1994. pap. 19.95 (*0-937657-18-2*) Feedbk Theabks & Prospero.

Meserve, Walter J., ed. Playhouse America! A Directory of Theatres & Theatre Companies in the U. S. A. 350p. (Orig.). 1991. pap. 16.95 (*0-937657-08-5*) Feedbk Theabks & Prospero.

Meserve, Walter J. & Meserve, Mollie A. A Chronological Outline of World Theatre. 1992. 9.95 (*0-937657-12-3*) Feedbk Theabks & Prospero.

Meserve, Walter J., jt. auth. see Meserve, Mollie A.

***Meserve, Walter M. & Meserve, Ruth I., eds.** Modern Drama from Communist China. LC 77-92524. 368p. 1970. 24.95 (*0-8147-0302-X*) Boulevard.

Meserve, William N. Meserve Civil War Record: With the Intriguing War Story by Major William N. Meserve. Huebner, Richard A., ed. LC 87-23557. (Illus.). xxii, 290p. (C). 1988. 25.00 (*0-9619037-7-5*) RAH Pubns.

— Meserve Civil War Record: With the Intriguing War Story by Major William N. Meserve. deluxe limited ed. Huebner, Richard A., ed. LC 87-23557. (Illus.). xxii, 290p. (C). 1988. 45.00 (*0-9619037-6-7*) RAH Pubns.

Meservy, Jay. The Terrible, Horrible, Awful, Deplorable, Lovable, Little Troll. LC 91-41387. (Illus.). 32p. (J). (ps-2). 1992. pap. 6.95 (*0-89802-586-9*) Beautiful Am.

Mesfin, Daniel J. Exotic Ethiopian Cooking. LC 87-90854. 213p. 1987. 18.95 (*0-317-57587-2*); pap. 14.95 (*0-9616345-0-2*) Ethiopian Ent.

— Exotic Ethiopian Cooking: Society, Culture, Hospitality & Tradition in Ethiopia. expanded ed. LC 89-81056. (Illus.). 310p. (Orig.). 1990. pap. 14.99 (*0-9616345-1-0*) Ethiopian Ent.

— Exotic Ethiopian Cooking: Society, Culture, Hospitality & Traditions in Ethiopia. enl. rev. ed. LC 89-81056. (Illus.). 352p. (C). 1993. pap. 15.99 (*0-9616345-2-9*) Ethiopian Ent.

Meshcherskii, I. & Romicki, R. Collection of Problems of Mechanics. LC 63-15496. (International Series of Monographs on Pure & Applied Mathematics: Vol. 65). 1965. 220.00 (*0-08-010145-3*, Pub. by Pergamon Repr UK) Franklin.

Mesher, Alan. A Journey of Love. 180p. (Orig.). 1982. pap. 7.95 (*0-942082-01-X*) Quartus Bks.

Meshii, M., ed. Mechanical Properties of BCC Metals: Proceedings of the U. S. - Japan Seminar. LC 82-81287. (Conference Proceedings Ser.). (Illus.). 253p. reprint ed. pap. 72.20 (*0-318-39699-8*, 2052267) Bks Demand.

Meshinsky, Joanne. How to Choose a Nursing Home: A Guide to Quality Caring. 1991. pap. 7.95 (*0-380-76078-9*) Avon.

Meshkati, N., jt. ed. see Hancock, P. A.

Meshorer, Yaakov. Ancient Jewish Coinage: Persian Period Through Hasmonaeans, Set. Incl. Vol. 2. Herod the Great Through Bar Cochba. 1983. (*0-318-57910-3*); 184p. 1983. Set text ed. 150.00 (*0-89757-006-5*) Am Sch Orient Res.

Meshorer, Ya'akov. Sylloge Nummorum Graecorum: The Collection of the American Numismatic Society, Pt. 6: Palestine-South Arabia. (SNGANS Ser.). (Illus.). 108p. 1981. 100.00 (*0-89722-187-7*); 125.00 (*0-685-00307-8*) Am Numismatic.

Meshram, Pradip S. Early Caves of Maharashtra: A Cultural Study. (C). 1991. 46.00 (*81-85067-73-2*, Pub. by Sundeep II) S Asia.

Meshri, Indu D. & Ortoleva, Peter J., eds. Prediction of Reservoir Quality Through Chemical Modeling. (AAPG Memoir Ser.: No. 49). (Illus.). 175p. 1990. 69.00 (*0-89181-327-6*) AAPG.

Mesias, Gerardo. Electronics Theory & Practice. (Illus.). 224p. 1993. pap. write for info. (*0-7506-1679-2*) Butrwrth-Heinemann.

***Mesiats, Gennadii A., et al.** Pulsed Gas Lasers. LC 94-23266. Orig. Title: Impulsnye Gazovye Lazery. (ENG & RUS.). 1994. write for info. (*0-8194-1709-2*) SPIE.

Mesibov, G. B., jt. ed. see Schopler, E.

Mesibov, Gary B., jt. ed. see Schopler, Eric.

Mesibov, Gary B., et al. Adolescent & Adult Psychoeducational Profile, Vol. IV. LC 78-13415. (Individualized Assessment & Treatment for Autistic & Developmentally Disabled Children Ser.). (Illus.). 150p. (Orig.). 1987. pap. 49.00 (*0-89079-152-X*, 1425) PRO-ED.

Mesibov, Laurie L., comp. North Carolina Constitutional & Statutory Provisions with Respect to Higher Education. rev. ed. 403p. (C). 1988. pap. text ed. 16.00 (*1-56011-110-0*, 88.08) Institute Government.

***Mesic, Richard, et al.** Strategic Futures: Evolving Missions for Traditional Strategic Delivery Vehicles. LC 94-16172. (MR-375-DAG Ser.). (Illus.). 125p. (Orig.). 1995. pap. text ed. 15.00 (*0-8330-1617-2*) Rand Corp.

Mesic, Richard F., jt. auth. see Shaver, Russell D.

***Mesick, Cohen, Waite Architects Staff.** Historic Structure Report: Pennsylvania State Capitol, 2 vols., Set. 700p. 1994. write for info. (*0-9643048-0-5*) Capitol Preserv.

Mesick, Jane L. English Traveller in America, 1785-1835. 1971. reprint ed. 15.00 (*0-403-01106-X*) Scholarly.

— The English Traveller in America, 1785-1835. (BCL1 - U. S. History Ser.). 370p. 1991. reprint ed. lib. bdg. 89.00 (*0-7812-6376-X*) Rprt Serv.

Mesina, M., et al, eds. CIM Handbook: The Opportunities for Rationalization Opened up by the Acquisition & Integration of Computer Automation. Morris, Adrian, tr. LC 93-13855. 1994. 110.00 (*0-7506-0820-X*) Buttrwrth-Heinemann.

Mesinai, Susan Y., jt. auth. see Carlebach, Shlomo.

Mesirov, J. Very Large Scale Computation in the Twenty-First Century. (Miscellaneous Ser.: No. 25). xviii, 327p. 1991. 51.50 (*0-89871-279-3*) Soc Indus-Appl Math.

Mesirow, Kip. The Care & Use of Japanese Woodworking Tools. LC 78-60055. (Illus.). 1982. reprint ed. pap. 9.95 (*0-918036-08-9*) Woodcraft Supply.

Meske, C. P. Fish Aquaculture. Vogt, F., ed. (Illus.). 224p. 1985. pap. text ed. 68.00 (*0-08-024919-1*, Pergamon Pr) Elsevier.

Meskell, David. Racine: A Theatrical Reading. (Illus.). 296p. 1991. 72.00 (*0-19-815161-6*) OUP.

Meskill, Johanna M. A Chinese Pioneer Family: The Lins of Wu-feng, Taiwan, 1729-1895. LC 78-70308. (Studies of the East Asian Institute, Columbia University). (Illus.). 392p. 1986. text ed. 59.50 (*0-691-03124-X*); pap. text ed. 16.95x (*0-691-00808-6*) Princeton U Pr.

Meskill, John. Gentlemanly Interests & Wealth on the Yangtze Delta. (Association for Asian Studies Monograph). (Illus.). 270p. 1994. 32.00 (*0-924304-19-7*); pap. 16.00 (*0-924304-20-0*) Assn Asian Studies.

Meskill, John, tr. see Ch'oe, Pu.

Meskill, John T. An Introduction to Chinese Civilization. 699p. 1973. pap. text ed. 21.50 (*0-669-73502-7*) Heath.

Meskill, John T., intro. The Pattern of Chinese History: Cycles, Development or Stagnation. LC 82-18378. (Problems in Asian Civilizations Ser.). xx, 108p. 1983. reprint ed. text ed. 55.00 (*0-313-23739-5*, MEPC, Greenwood Pr) Greenwood.

***Meskimmon, Marsha & West, Sherer, eds.** Visions of the "Neue Frau" Women & the Visual Arts in Weimar Germany. (Illus.). 350p. (C). 1995. 76.95 (*1-85928-157-5*, Pub. by Scolar Pr UK) Ashgate Pub Co.

Meskin. Year Book of Dentistry, 1993. 450p. 1993. 59.95 (*0-8151-5876-9*, Yr Bk Med Pubs) Mosby Yr Bk.

— Year Book of Dentistry, 1994. 450p. 1994. 59.95 (*0-8151-5877-7*, Yr Bk Med Pubs) Mosby Yr Bk.

— Year Book of Dentistry, 1995. 450p. 1995. 59.95 (*0-8151-5878-5*, Yr Bk Med Pubs) Mosby Yr Bk.

— Year Book of Dentistry, 1996. 450p. 1996. 59.95 (*0-8151-5879-3*, Yr Bk Med Pubs) Mosby Yr Bk.

— Yearbook of Dentistry, 1991. 472p. 1991. 57.95 (*0-8151-1898-8*, Yr Bk Med Pubs) Mosby Yr Bk.

— Yearbook of Dentistry, 1992. 451p. 1992. 59.95 (*0-8151-5882-3*) Mosby Yr Bk.

Meskin, J. O., jt. ed. see Coutts, J.

***Mesko, Jim.** A-20 Havoc in Action. (Aircraft in Action Ser.). (Illus.). 50p. 1994. pap. 8.95 (*0-89747-317-5*) Squad Sig Pubns.

— A-26 Invader in Action. (Aircraft in Action Ser.). (Illus.). 50p. 1993. pap. 8.95 (*0-89747-296-9*, 1134) Squad Sig Pubns.

— Amtracs in Action. (Armor in Action Ser.). (Illus.). 50p. Date not set. pap. 8.95 (*0-89747-298-5*) Squad Sig Pubns.

— Armor in Vietnam: A Pictorial History. (Vietnam Studies Group). (Illus.). 80p. 1982. pap. 10.95 (*0-89747-126-1*, 6033) Squad Sig Pubns.

— FJ Fury in Action. (Aircraft in Action Ser.). (Illus.). 50p. 1990. pap. 8.95 (*0-89747-245-4*, 1103) Squad Sig Pubns.

— F3H Demon in Action. (Aircraft in Action Ser.). (Illus.). 50p. 1994. pap. 8.95 (*0-89747-308-6*) Squad Sig Pubns.

— Ground War - Desert Storm. (Desert Storm Ser.). (Illus.). 64p. 1991. pap. 10.95 (*0-89747-261-6*, 6122) Squad Sig Pubns.

— Ground War - Vietnam, Vol. 1. (Vietnam Studies Group). (Illus.). 80p. 1990. pap. 9.95 (*0-89747-251-9*, 6053) Squad Sig Pubns.

— Ground War - Vietnam, Vol. 2. (Vietnam Studies Group). (Illus.). 80p. 1992. pap. 9.95 (*0-89747-288-8*, 6057) Squad Sig Pubns.

— Hummer in Action. (Armor in Action Ser.). (Illus.). 50p. 1994. pap. 8.95 (*0-89747-323-X*) Squad Sig Pubns.

— M-3 Lee - Grant in Action. (Armor in Action Ser.). (Illus.). 50p. 1995. pap. 9.95 (*0-89747-346-9*) Squad Sig Pubns.

— M-2 - M-3 Bradley in Action. (Armor in Action Ser.). (Illus.). 50p. 1992. pap. 8.95 (*0-89747-280-2*, 2030) Squad Sig Pubns.

— M-41 Walker Bulldog in Action. (Armor in Action Ser.). (Illus.). 50p. 1991. pap. 8.95 (*0-89747-222-5*) Squad Sig Pubns.

— M-551 Sheridan in Action. (Armor in Action Ser.). (Illus.). 50p. 1990. pap. 8.95 (*0-89747-253-5*, 2028) Squad Sig Pubns.

— OV-10 Bronco in Action. (Aircraft in Action Ser.). (Illus.). 50p. 1995. pap. 9.95 (*0-89747-340-X*) Squad Sig Pubns.

Meskoob, Shahrokh. Iranian Nationality & the Persian Language: Roles of Government, Religion, & Sufism in Persian Prose Writing. Perry, John, ed. Hillmann, Michael, tr. 175p. (C). 1992. 29.95 (*0-934211-21-3*) Mage Pubs Inc.

Meskys, Edmund R., ed. The Once & Future Arthur. (Illus.). 72p. 1989. pap. 5.95 (*0-910619-03-4*) Niekas Pubns.

— The Once & Future Arthur. LC 89-7309. 72p. (C). 1989. reprint ed. lib. bdg. 25.00x (*0-8095-6851-9*) Borgo Pr.

Mesland, jt. auth. see Innocenti.

Mesle, Barbara J. & Mesle, C. Robert. Parenting Together. 1981. pap. 6.50 (*0-8309-0311-9*) Herald Hse.

Mesle, C. Robert. The Bible As Story & Struggle. 1989. pap. 8.50 (*0-8309-0525-1*) Herald Hse.

— Fire in My Bones: Reflection on Faith. 1984. pap. 19.00 (*0-8309-0387-9*) Herald Hse.

— John Hick's Theodicy: A Process Humanist Critique. LC 90-48509. 184p. 1991. text ed. 49.95 (*0-312-05706-7*) St Martin.

— Process Theology: A Basic Introduction. LC 93-9204. 160p. (Orig.). 1993. pap. 12.99 (*0-8272-2945-3*) Chalice Pr.

Mesle, C. Robert, jt. auth. see Mesle, Barbara J.

Mesler, Donald T., jt. auth. see Barenblat, Scot G.

Meslier, Jean. Superstition in All Ages. Knoop, Anna, tr. LC 77-161337. (Atheist Viewpoint Ser.). (Illus.). 346p. 1976. reprint ed. 25.95 (*0-405-03795-3*) Ayer.

— Le Testament, 3 vols. in 1. lxv, 1162p. 1974. reprint ed. write for info. (*3-487-05278-4*, Pub. by Georg Olms GW) Lubrecht & Cramer.

Meslier, Jean & Knoop, Anna, trs. Superstition in All Ages; Last Will & Testament; Common Sense. 339p. 1974. reprint ed. spiral bd. 9.35 (*0-7873-0609-6*) Mokelumne.

Meslier, Jean, jt. auth. see D'Holbach, Paul H.

Mesmer, Robert E., jt. auth. see Baes, Charles F., Jr.

Mesnard, Pierre. Desarrollo De la Filosofia Politica en el Siglo XVI. 643p. (SPA.). 1956. 3.00 (*0-8477-2805-6*) U of PR Pr.

Mesner, Susan, jt. ed. see Davison, Rebecca.

Mesnick, Denyse S., jt. auth. see Hewitt, Patricia J.

Mesnooh, Christopher J. Law & Business in France: A Guide to French Commercial & Corporate Law. LC 93-46936. 384p. (C). 1994. lib. bdg. 134.00 (*0-7923-2682-2*) Kluwer Ac.

Meso-American Indian Center Women's Committee, ed. Daughters of Abya Yala: Indigenous Women Regaining Control. LC 94-2780. (Illus.). 128p. 1994. 8.95 (*0-913990-09-4*) Book Pub Co.

Mesobov, Gary B., jt. ed. see Schopler, Eric.

Meson-, Photo-, & Electroproduction at Low & Intermediate Energies Symposium Staff. Proceedings of the Meson-, Photo-, & Electroproduction at Low & Intermediate Energies Symposium, Bonn, 1970. LC 25-9130. (Tracts in Modern Physics Ser.: Vol. 59). 1971. 65.00 (*0-387-05494-4*) Spr-Verlag.

Mesrobian, Armen Z. Prepare & Enjoy Creative Dental Retirement. LC 92-81607. 195p. 1992. spiral bd. 29.95 (*0-9632735-0-7*) EPS Excel Pub.

— Prepare & Enjoy Creative Retirement. LC 93-90246. (Illus.). 202p. (Orig.). 1993. per. 17.95 (*0-9632735-1-5*) EPS Excel Pub.

Mess, B., jt. auth. see Jozsa, R.

Mess, B., et al. Role of the Pineal Gland in the Regulation of Ovulation. (Studia Biologica Hungarica Ser.: No. 16). 104p. 1978. 39.00 (*0-569-08479-2*, Pub. by Collets UK) Pro-Am Music.

Mess, R., et al, eds. The Pineal Gland: Current State of Pineal Research. (Developments in Endocrinology Ser.: Vol. 16). 372p. 1985. 133.50 (*0-444-80629-6*) Elsevier.

Messadie, Gerald. Great Inventions Through History. (Compact Reference Ser.). (Illus.). 256p. (Orig.). 1992. pap. 9.95 (*0-550-17005-7*, Chambers LKC) LKC.

— Great Modern Inventions. (Compact Reference Ser.). (Illus.). 256p. (Orig.). 1992. pap. text ed. 9.95 (*0-550-17001-4*, Chambers LKC) LKC.

— Great Scientific Discoveries. (Compact Reference Ser.). (Illus.). 256p. (Orig.). 1992. pap. 9.95 (*0-550-17002-2*, Chambers LKC) LKC.

— A History of the Devil. Urda, John, ed. Romano, Marc, tr. 416p. 1996. 25.00 (*1-56836-081-9*) Kodansha.

Message, Gordon M. Practical Aspects of Gas Chromotography-Mass Spectrometry. LC 83-23475. 351p. 1984. text ed. 139.00 (*0-471-06277-4*, Wiley-Interscience) Wiley.

Messaline, Peter, jt. auth. see Newhouse, Miriam.

Messano, Bob. Songs & Activities for Best, Best Friends: A Complete Music Curriculum for Early Childhood. 256p. 1991. student ed, audio 24.95 (*0-87628-796-8*, 710117) Ctr Appl Res.

Messaris, Paul. Visual "Literacy" Image, Mind, & Reality. LC 93-26069. 208p. 1994. text ed. 62.00 (*0-8133-1667-7*) Westview.

— Visual "Literacy" Image, Mind, & Reality. LC 93-26069. 208p. (C). 1994. pap. text ed. 18.95 (*0-8133-1937-4*) Westview.

Messaros, David W., jt. auth. see Slutsky, Elliot.

Messe, Lawrence A., jt. auth. see Lane, Irving M.

Messec, Jerry. Charlston Stories: L4. McConochie, Jean, ed. (Regents Readers Ser.). (gr. 7-12). 1987. pap. text ed. 3.50 (*0-13-128257-3*, 20951) Prentice ESL.

Messec, Jerry, et al. English Spoken Here, Bk. 4: Life in the United States. (English Spoken Here (ESL) Ser.). (Illus.). 128p. 1988. student ed 3.95 (*0-8428-0857-4*); pap. text ed. write for info. (*0-8428-0853-1*); 25.00 (*0-8428-0847-7*) Cambridge Bk.

Messec, Jerry. An Ordinary Life: L3. McConochie, Jean, ed. (Regents Readers Ser.). (Illus.). 68p. (gr. 7-12). 1987. pap. text ed. 3.50 (*0-13-639816-2*, 20886) Prentice ESL.

Messec, Jerry & Kranich, Roger. English Spoken Here, Bk. 1: Getting Started. Schenk, Brian, ed. (English Spoken Here (ESL) Ser.). (Illus.). 160p. 1988. pap. text ed. write for info. (*0-8428-0850-7*); student ed 3.95 (*0-8428-0854-X*) Cambridge Bk.

— English Spoken Here, Bk. 2: Consumer Information. Holzer, Eva, ed. (English Spoken Here (ESL) Ser.). (Illus.). 128p. 1988. student ed 3.75 (*0-8428-0855-8*); pap. text ed. write for info. (*0-8428-0851-5*); 25.00 (*0-8428-0845-0*) Cambridge Bk.

— English Spoken Here, Bk. 3: Health & Safety. Schenk, Brian, ed. (English Spoken Here (ESL) Ser.). (Illus.). 128p. 1988. student ed 3.95 (*0-8428-0856-6*); pap. text ed. write for info. (*0-8428-0852-3*); 25.00 (*0-8428-0846-9*) Cambridge Bk.

Messec, Jerry, jt. auth. see Thiele, Margaret.

Messec, Jerry L., jt. auth. see Kranich, Roger E.

***Messegue, Maurice.** Die Krauterkuche: Ein Lexikon der Kuchenkrauter mit Uber 200 Franzoesischen Rezepten. (GER.). Date not set. 19.95 (*0-7859-8425-9*, 3548349005) Fr & Eur.

— Of People & Plants: The Autobiography of Europe's Most Celebrated Herbal Healer. 336p. (Orig.). 1991. pap. 12.95 (*0-89281-437-3*) Inner Tradit.

Messel, Harry. Highlights in Science: Lectures for 24th Science School. 232p. 1988. pap. text ed. 18.50 (*0-08-034430-5*, Pergamon Pr) Elsevier.

— Surveys of Tidal River Systems in the Northern Territory & Their Crocodile Populations. (Monograph Ser.: No. 15). (Illus.). 368p. 1982. 135.00 (*0-08-024831-4*, Pergamon Pr) Elsevier.

Messel, Harry, ed. The Biological Manipulation of Life. (Illus.). 352p. 1981. text ed. 44.00 (*0-08-024825-X*, Pergamon Pr); pap. text ed. 27.00 (*0-08-024824-1*, Pergamon Pr) Elsevier.

— Energy for Survival. (Illus.). 368p. 1979. text ed. 22.00 (*0-08-024794-6*, Pergamon Pr); pap. text ed. 17.00 (*0-08-024791-1*, Pergamon Pr) Elsevier.

— The Study of Populations. (Illus.). 266p. 1986. pap. text ed. 26.00 (*0-08-029877-X*, PPA) Elsevier.

Messel, Harry, jt. auth. see Butler, S.

Messel, Harry, jt. auth. see Elton, L. R.

Messel, Harry, et al. Surveys of Tidal River Systems in the Northern Territory & Their Crocodile Population. (Monograph Ser.: No. 1). (Illus.). 464p. 1982. 155.00 (*0-08-024819-5*, G135, Pergamon Pr) Elsevier.

— Surveys of Tidal River Systems in the Northern Territory & Their Crocodile Populations. (Monograph Ser.: No. 17). (Illus.). 92p. 1981. pap. 28.00 (*0-08-024818-7*, Pergamon Pr) Elsevier.

— Surveys of Tidal River Systems in the Northern Territory of Australia: Resurveys of the Tidal Waterways of Van Diemen Gulf & the Southern Gulf of Carpentaria 1984 & 1985. (Surveys of Tidal Rivers Ser.: No. 19). (Illus.). 118p. 1986. 86.00 (*0-08-029882-6*, PPA) Elsevier.

— Surveys of Tidal Waterways in the Kimberley Region, Western Australia & Their Crocodile Populations: Monograph 20 - Tidal Waterways of the Kimberley Surveyed During 1977, 1978 & 1986. (Surveys of Tidal Rivers Ser.: No. 20). 256p. 1988. 83.00 (*0-08-034429-1*, Pergamon Pr) Elsevier.

Messel, Harry, et al, eds. Crocodiles: An Action Plan for Their Conservation. 136p. 20.00 (*2-8317-0060-4*, Pub. by IUCN SZ) Island Pr.

— Surveys of Tidal River Systems in the Northern Territory & Their Crocodile Population: Monograph, No. 18. (Illus.). 308p. 1985. 135.00 (*0-08-029858-3*, Pergamon Pr) Elsevier.

Messell, J., jt. auth. see Guy, W.

Messenger, Ann. His & Hers: Essays in Restoration & Eighteenth-Century Literature. LC 86-7803. 288p. 1986. 31.00 (*0-8131-1575-2*) U Pr of Ky.

— Pastoral Tradition & the Female Talent: Studies in Augustan Poetry. (Studies in the Eighteenth Century: No. 25). 1993. write for info. (*0-404-63525-3*) AMS Pr.

An Asterisk (*) at the beginning of an entry indicates that the title is appearing in BIP for the first time.

— Woman & Poet in the Eighteenth Century: The Life of Mary Whateley Darwall (1738-1825) (Studies in the Eighteenth Century: No. 27). 1993. write for info. (0-404-63527-X) AMS Pr.

Messenger, Ann, ed. Gender at Work: Four Women Writers of the Eighteenth Century. LC 89-21449. 165p. (C). 1990. text ed. 29.95 (0-8143-2147-X) Wayne St U Pr.

Messenger, Ann, ed. see Knight, Ellis C.

Messenger, Betty. Picking up the Linen Threads: Life in Ulster's Mills. 265p. 1988. pap. 13.95 (0-85640-415-2, Pub. by Blackstaff Pr IE) Dufour.

*Messenger, Bill. The Power of Music: A Complete Music Activities Program for Older Adults. 96p. 1995. audio, spiral bd. 24.95 (1-878812-27-0) Hlth Prof Pr.

Messenger, Bill, jt. auth. see Abrignani, Catherine.

Messenger, Charles. For Love of Regiment: A History of British Infantry, 1660-1993, 2 vols. (Illus.). 576p. 1994. 87.50 (0-317-05762-6, Pub. by L Cooper Bks UK) Trans-Atl Phila.

— For Love of Regiment Vol. 1: A History of British Infantry, 1660-1993. (Illus.). 1994. 47.50 (0-85052-371-0, Pub. by L Cooper Bks UK) Trans-Atl Phila.

— For Love of Regiment Vol. 2: A History of British Infantry, 1660-1993. (Illus.). 1995. 47.50 (0-85052-422-9, Pub. by L Cooper Bks UK) Trans-Atl Phila.

— Hitler's Gladiator: The Life & Times of SS-Oberstgruppenfuhrer & General der Waffen-SS Sepp Dietrich. (Illus.). 245p. 1988. 32.00 (0-08-031207-1, Pub. by Brasseys UK) Brasseys Inc.

— The Last Prussian. (Biography of Field Marshal Gerd von Rundstedt Ser.). 400p. 1991. 24.95 (0-08-036707-0, Pub. by Brasseys UK) Brasseys Inc.

— Observers Tanks & Other Armored Vehicles. (Observer's Guide 1990-1991 Ser.). 255p. 1990. pap. 9.95 (0-7232-3701-8, Pub. by Penguin Bks Ltd UK) Motorbooks Intl.

Messenger, Charles, ed. Terriers in the Trenches: The Post Office Rifles at War, 1914-1918. 170p. (C). 1987. 100.00 (0-317-90379-9, Pub. by Picton UK) St Mut.

Messenger, Chris, jt. auth. see Walker, Chet.

Messenger, Christian K. Sport & the Spirit of Play in Contemporary American Fiction. 456p. 1990. text ed. 35.00 (0-231-07094-2) Col U Pr.

— Sports & the Spirit of Play in American Fiction: Hawthorne to Faulkner. LC 81-4843. 352p. 1983. text ed. 47.50 (0-231-05168-9); pap. text ed. 18.50 (0-231-05169-7) Col U Pr.

Messenger, David & Souter, John. How to Do Something about the Way You Feel. 1984. reprint ed. pap. 2.95 (0-87983-368-8) Keats.

Messenger, Dorothy R., jt. auth. see Messenger, Orville J.

Messenger, E. C., tr. see Guiraud, Jean.

Messenger, Elizabeth & Melling, John K. Publicity for Murder. (Black Dagger Crime Ser.). 200p. 1990. reprint ed. text ed. 16.50 (0-86220-777-0, Black Dagger) Chivers N Amer.

Messenger, George C. & Ash, Milton S. The Effects of Radiation on Electronic Systems. 2nd ed. (Illus.). 665p. 1992. text ed. 89.95 (0-442-23952-1) Van Nos Reinhold.

Messenger, Jack. Personal Excellence: A Guide to Getting the Most from Yourself & Others. LC 89-85531. 207p. 1989. 19.95 (0-939975-04-1) Exec Pr NC.

Messenger, Jannat. Lullaby & Goodnight: A Bedtime Book with Music. (Illus.). 12p. (J). (ps-1). 1988. pap. 10.95 (0-689-71268-5, Aladdin Paperbacks) S&S Childrens.

— Twinkle, Twinkle, Little Star: A Lullaby Book with Lights & Music. (Illus.). 12p. (J). (ps-1). 1987. pap. 11.95 (0-689-71136-0, Mac Bks Young Read) S&S Childrens.

Messenger, John C. Inis Beag: Isle of Ireland. 136p. 1983. reprint ed. pap. text ed. 8.95 (0-88133-051-5) Waveland Pr.

— Inis Beag Revisited: The Anthropologist as Observant Participator. (Illus.). 154p. (C). 1988. reprint ed. pap. text ed. 10.95 (0-88133-408-1) Sheffield WI.

Messenger, Joseph. Lost Circulation. 112p. 1981. 15.00 (0-87814-175-8, P4277) PennWell Bks.

Messenger, Ken. Clients As Individuals. (Skills for Caring Ser.). (Illus.). 48p. (Orig.). 1992. pap. text ed. 12.00 (0-443-04530-5) Churchill.

Messenger, Michael. Coalport, 1795-1926. (Illus.). 350p. 1993. 59.50 (1-85149-112-0) Antique Collect.

Messenger, Norman. Annabel's House. LC 88-60089. (Illus.). 28p. (J). 1989. 18.95 (0-531-05764-X) Orchard Bks Watts.

— Famous Faces. (Illus.). 24p. (J). (gr. 4-7). 1995. pap. 14.95 (1-56458-686-3) Dorling Kindersley.

— Making Faces. LC 92-52807. (Illus.). 16p. (J). 1993. 14.95 (1-56458-111-X) Dorling Kindersley.

*Messenger, Orville J. & Messenger, Dorothy R. Borrowed Time: A Surgeon's Struggle with Transfusion-Induced AIDS. 160p. 1995. lib. bdg. 37.00 (0-8095-4885-2) Borgo Pr.

Messenger, Phyllis M., ed. The Ethics of Collecting Cultural Property: Whose Culture? Whose Property? LC 89-36190. (Illus.). 292p. 1991. reprint ed. pap. 16.95 (0-8263-1281-0) U of NM Pr.

Messenger, Phyllis M., jt. auth. see Desmond, Lawrence G.

Messenger, Robert C., jt. auth. see Andrews, Frank M.

Messenger, Robert C., jt. auth. see Morgan, James N.

Messenger, Ruth E. Ethical Teachings in the Latin Hymns of Medieval England. LC 30-20975. (Columbia University. Studies in the Social Sciences: No. 321). reprint ed. 20.00 (0-404-51321-2) AMS Pr.

Messent, A. D., jt. auth. see Hill, D. J.

Messent, Jan. The Embroiderer's Workbook. (Color Craft Workbooks Ser.). (Illus.). 96p. 1988. pap. 14.95 (0-312-02121-6) St Martin.

— Have You Any Wool? rev. ed. pap. 19.95 (0-85532-768-5, Pub. by Search Pr UK) A Schwartz & Co.

— Have You Any Wool? The Creative Use of Yarn. (Illus.). 128p. 1987. pap. 14.95 (0-85532-584-4, Pub. by Search Pr UK) A Schwartz & Co.

— Knit the Christmas Story. 62p. 1989. 5.95 (0-8192-2085-X) Morehouse Pub.

— Knitted Gardens. (Illus.). 128p. (Orig.). 1992. pap. 22.50 (0-85532-732-4, Pub. by Search Pr UK) A Schwartz & Co.

— Knitted Historical Figures. (Illus.). 144p. (Orig.). 1993. pap. 24.95 (0-85532-747-2, Pub. by Search Pr UK) A Schwartz & Co.

— Wool 'n Magic: Creative Uses of Yarn...Knitting, Crochet, Embroidery. Dawson, Pam, ed. (Illus.). 144p. (YA). 1989. 32.95 (0-85532-614-X, Pub. by Search Pr UK) A Schwartz & Co.

Messent, Peter. Ernest Hemingway. LC 92-9005. (Modern Novelists Ser.). 192p. 1992. text ed. 29.95 (0-312-08126-X) St Martin.

— New Readings of the American Novel: Narrative Theory & Its Application. LC 90-8042. 336p. 1991. text ed. 45.00 (0-312-04653-7) St Martin.

Messer, Colin. How to Keep Your Datsun--Nissan Alive: A Manual of Step-by-Step Procedures for the Compleat Idiot. (Illus.). 544p. 1987. pap. 21.95 (0-912528-65-6) John Muir.

Messer, David J. The Development of Communication: From Social Interaction to Language. LC 93-42347. 1994. pap. text ed. write for info. (0-471-94421-1) Wiley.

— The Development of Communication: From Social Interaction to Language. LC 93-42347. 1994. text ed. 37.95 (0-471-94076-3) Wiley.

Messer, David J. & Turner, Geoffrey J., eds. Critical Influences on Child Language Acquisition & Development. LC 92-18461. 1993. text ed. 59.95 (0-312-08474-9) St Martin.

Messer-Davidow, Ellen, jt. ed. see Hartman, Joan E.

Messer-Davidow, Ellen, et al, eds. Knowledges: Historical & Critical Studies in Disciplinarity. LC 92-46606. (Knowledge, Disciplinarity & Beyond Ser.). 465p. 1993. 67.50 (0-8139-1428-0); pap. 19.95 (0-8139-1429-9) U Pr of Va.

*Messer, Donald E. Calling Church & Seminary into the 21st Century. 176p. 1995. 15.95 (0-687-01351-8) Abingdon.

— Christian Ethics & Political Action. 176p. 1984. pap. 13.00 (0-8170-1018-1) Judson.

Messer, Donald E., ed. Send Me? The Itineracy in Crisis. 208p. (Orig.). 1991. pap. 12.95 (0-687-37155-4) Abingdon.

Messer, Donald E., jt. auth. see Geis, Sally B.

Messer, Ellen & May, Kathryn E. Back Rooms: Voices from the Illegal Abortion Era. 234p. (C). 1994. pap. 16.95 (0-87975-876-7) Prometheus Bks.

Messer, H. J. Able Seaman RNVR. (C). 1989. 49.00 (0-86303-475-6) St Mut.

Messer, Mitchell H., et al. Managing Anger: A Handbook of Proven Techniques. 303p. 1992. pap. 18.95 (0-9636776-0-8) Anger Clinic.

Messer, Mithcell, jt. auth. see Anger Clinic Staff.

Messer, Pamela L. Biltmore Estate: Frederick Law Olmsted's Landscape Masterpiece. Hall, Kathryn L., ed. LC 93-60162. (Illus.). 336p. (Orig.). 1993. pap. 24.95 (1-56664-022-9) WorldComm.

Messer, Richard. Does God's Existence Need Proof? LC 92-45110. 180p. 1993. 35.00 (0-19-826747-9) OUP.

— Murder in the Family: Poems. 80p. (Orig.). 1995. pap. 8.95 (0-933087-37-3) Bottom Dog Pr.

Messer, Robert. Linear Algebra: Gateway to Mathematics. LC 93-21043. (C). 1994. 48.00 (0-06-501728-5) HarpCollege.

Messer, Robert L. The End of an Alliance: James F. Byrnes, Roosevelt, Truman, & the Origins of the Cold War. LC 81-7618. 304p. reprint ed. pap. 86.70 (0-7837-0307-4, 2040629) Bks Demand.

Messer, Sharon D. Kara. Woolsey, Raymond H., ed. 128p. 1989. pap. 7.95 (0-8280-0487-0) Review & Herald.

Messer, Stanley, jt. ed. see Arkowitz, Hal.

Messer, Stanley B., et al, eds. Hermeneutics & Psychological Theory, Vol. 2: Interpretative Perspectives on Personality, Psychotherapy, & Psychopathology. (Rutgers Symposia on Applied Psychology Ser.). 500p. (C). 1988. text ed. 50.00 (0-8135-1291-3); pap. text ed. 20.00 (0-8135-1292-1) Rutgers U Pr.

Messer, Thomas M. Acquisition Priorities: Aspects of Postwar Painting in Europe. LC 83-60337. (Illus.). 104p. (Orig.). 1983. pap. 12.95 (0-89207-041-2) S R Guggenheim.

— Fifty Years of Collecting: An Anniversary Selection. Painting Since World War II. (Fifty Years of Collecting: An Anniversary Selection: Vol. II). (Illus.). 147p. 1987. pap. 20.00 (0-89207-066-8) S R Guggenheim.

— Fifty Years of Collecting: An Anniversary Selection. Sculpture of the Modern Era. (Fifty Years of Collecting: An Anniversary Selection: Vol. III). (Illus.). 145p. (Orig.). 1987. pap. 20.00 (0-89207-065-X) S R Guggenheim.

— Kolar - Chiasmage: Selections from the Guggenheim. (Illus.). 20p. 1988. 4.00 (0-685-45726-5) Katonah Gal.

— Munch. (Masters of Art Ser.). (Illus.). 128p. 1986. 22.95 (0-8109-1415-8) Abrams.

— Sixty Works: The Peggy Guggenheim Collection. (Illus.). 68p. 1982. pap. 5.95 (0-89207-037-4) S R Guggenheim.

Messer, Thomas M., jt. ed. see Catlin, Stanton L.

Messer, Thomas M., jt. intro. see Waldman, Diane.

Messer, Thomas M., et al. Guida: Collezione Peggy Guggenheim. enl. rev. ed. (Illus.). 336p. (Orig.). (ITA.). 1986. 15.00 (0-89207-054-4) S R Guggenheim.

— Handbook: Peggy Guggenheim Collection. enl. rev. ed. (Illus.). 336p. (Orig.). 1986. 15.00 (0-89207-053-6) S R Guggenheim.

Messere, Kenneth, jt. ed. see Chiancone, Aldo.

Messerle, H. Dynamic Circuit Theory, Chapters 1-5. LC 63-22598. 1965. 160.00 (0-08-010469-X, Pub. by Pergamon Repr UK) Franklin.

Messerle, Hugo K. Magneto-Hydro-Dynamic Electrical Power Generation. LC 94-18580. (Energy Engineering Learning Package Ser.). 1994. pap. text ed. 34.95 (0-471-94252-9) Wiley.

Messerli Bolliger, Barbara E., et al. The Journal of Decorative & Propaganda Arts, No. 19: Swiss Theme Issue. (Illus.). 200p. (Orig.). 1993. pap. 25.00 (0-9631601-2-5) Wolfson Fnd D&P Arts.

Messerli, Bruno, jt. auth. see Ives, Jack D.

Messerli, Carlos R., jt. auth. see Pfatteicher, Philip H.

Messerli, Douglas. Along Without: A Fiction in Film for Poetry, Pt. 1: The Structure of Destruction. (Littoral Bks.). 1992. pap. 11.95 (1-55713-147-3) Sun & Moon CA.

— From the Other Side of the Century: A New American Poetry 1960-1990. (Sun & Moon Classics Ser.: No. 47). 1136p. (Orig.). (C). 1994. pap. 29.95 (1-55713-131-7) Sun & Moon CA.

— Maxims from My Mother's Milk. 69p. 1989. 12.95 (1-55713-031-0); pap. 8.95 (1-55713-047-7) Sun & Moon CA.

— Silence All Round Marked: An Historical Play in Hysteria Writ. (Blue Corner Drama: No. 4). 40p. (Orig.). 1991. pap. 5.95 (1-55713-125-2) Sun & Moon CA.

— The Walls Come True: An Opera for Spoken Voices. 200p. (Orig.). 1994. pap. 12.95 (1-55713-180-5) Sun & Moon CA.

Messerli, Douglas, ed. Fifty: A Celebration of Sun & Mood Classics, New Works by Friends. (Sun & Moon Classics Ser.: No. 50). 350p. 1994. 24.95 (1-55713-152-X); pap. 13.95 (1-55713-132-5) Sun & Moon CA.

— The Gertrude Stein Awards in Innovative American Poetry: 1993-1994. 225p. (Orig.). 1995. pap. 13.95 (1-55713-161-9) Sun & Moon CA.

— Language Poetries: An Anthology. LC 86-18173. 160p. 1987. 10.95 (0-8112-1006-5) New Directions.

— The Sun & Moon Guide to Eating Through Literature & Art. Bennett, Guy et al, trs. (Illus.). 216p. 1994. 29.95 (1-55713-178-3) Sun & Moon CA.

Messerli, Douglas & Fox, Howard N., eds. Index to Periodical Fiction in English, 1965-69. LC 76-42288. 790p. 1977. 49.50 (0-8108-0952-4) Scarecrow.

Messerli, Douglas, ed. see Barnes, Djuna.

Messerli, Franz. ABC's of Antihypertensive Therapy. 288p. 1994. write for info. (1-881063-03-8) Raven.

Messerli, Franz H. Current Clinical Practice. (Illus.). 1000p. 1987. text ed. 73.50 (0-7216-1460-4) Saunders.

Messerli, Franz H., ed. Cardiovascular Disease in the Elderly. (Developments in Cardiovascular Medicine Ser.). 1984. lib. bdg. 94.50 (0-89838-596-2) Kluwer Ac.

— Current Cardiovascular Drug Therapy. 2nd ed. LC 95-1013. 1995. text ed. write for info. (0-7216-4814-2) Saunders.

— Kidney in Essential Hypertension. (Developments in Cardiovascular Medicine Ser.). 1983. lib. bdg. 75.00 (0-89838-616-0) Kluwer Ac.

Messerli, Franz H., jt. ed. see Prichard, B. N.

Messerlin, Patrick A., jt. auth. see Finger, J. Michael.

*Messerly, John. Lock Block Logic. (Illus.). 90p. (J). (gr. 2-6). 1993. pap. text ed. 15.95 (0-9643700-0-X) Elmwood Pr.

*Messerly, John G. An Introduction to Ethical Theories. LC 94-23950. 166p. (Orig.). (C). 1994. pap. text ed. 22.50 (0-8191-9823-4) U Pr of Amer.

Messerschmidt. Gurungs of Nepal. 1991. write for info. (0-85668-032-X, Pub. by Aris & Phillips UK) David Brown.

Messerschmidt & Harthcock. Infrared Microspectroscopy: Theory & Applications. (Practical Spectroscopy Ser.: Vol. 6). 288p. 1988. 125.00 (0-8247-8003-5) Dekker.

Messerschmidt, James. Capitalism, Patriarchy & Crime: Toward a Socialist Feminist Criminology. LC 86-15608. 224p. 1986. 56.00 (0-8476-7496-7) Rowman.

Messerschmidt, James, jt. auth. see Beirne, Piers.

Messerschmidt, James W. Masculinities & Crime: Critique & Reconceptualization of Theory. LC 93-7809. 248p. (C). 1993. text ed. 55.00 (0-8476-7868-7); pap. text ed. 21.95 (0-8476-7869-5) Rowman.

Messerschmidt, Jim. The Trial of Leonard Peltier. LC 82-61152. 198p. 1983. 35.00 (0-89608-164-8); pap. 14.00 (0-89608-163-X) South End Pr.

Messerschmidt, Lowell. Bauern-Sensei. 1991. pap. 8.50 (1-55673-311-9, 7762) CSS OH.

*Messerschmidt, Robert G. & Harthcock, Matthew A., eds. Infrared Microspectroscopy: Theory & Applications. LC 88-10850. (Practical Spectroscopy Ser.: Vol. 6). (Illus.). 302p. 1988. pap. 86.10 (0-7837-8953-X, 2049666) Bks Demand.

Messerschmitt, David G., jt. auth. see Hong, Micheal.

Messerschmitt, David G., jt. auth. see Lee, Edward A.

Messerschmitt, Henri. Encyclopedie Permanente d'Agriculture Biologique, 3 vols., Set. 660p. (FRE.). 1974. 250.00 (0-8288-6041-6, M6408) Fr & Eur.

Messersmith, Ann M. & Miller, Judy L. Forecasting in Foodservice. 160p. 1991. Net. text ed. write for info. (0-471-52916-8) Wiley.

Messersmith, Dan W. The History of Mohave County to Nineteen Twelve. LC 91-62434. 230p. (C). 1991. pap. 15.95 (0-9630125-0-9) Mohave Cnty.

*Messervey, Julie M. The Inward Garden: Creating a Place of Beauty & Meaning. LC 94-27802. 1995. 35.00 (0-316-56792-2) Little.

Messiah, Albert. Quantum Mechanics, Vol. 1. 504p. 1963. pap. text ed. 66.95 (0-471-59766-X) Halsted Pr.

— Quantum Mechanics, Vol. 2. 632p. 1963. pap. text ed. 66.95 (0-471-59768-6) Halsted Pr.

Messick, Blanche P. Fresh Roasted Ice Cream. (Illus.). 175p. (Orig.). 1988. 10.95 (0-945913-17-6); pap. 8.95 (0-945913-16-8) Publishers Ink.

Messick, Brinkley. The Calligraphic State: Textual Domination & History in a Muslim Society. (Comparative Studies on Muslim Societies: No. 16). (C). 1992. 40.00 (0-520-07605-2) U CA Pr.

Messick, Dale. Brenda Starr: The Red-Headed Bombshell. (Illus.). 104p. 1989. pap. 12.95 (0-944735-30-4) Malibu Graphics.

Messick, David M. & Cook, Karen S., eds. Equity Theory: Psychological & Sociological Perspectives. LC 82-18941. 346p. 1983. text ed. 45.00 (0-275-91044-X, C1044, Praeger Pubs) Greenwood.

Messick, David M., jt. ed. see Borcherding, K.

Messick, David M., jt. auth. see Kramer, Roderick M.

Messick, Frederic M., comp. Primary Sources in European Diplomacy, 1914-1945: A Bibliography of Published Memoirs & Diaries. LC 87-186. (Bibliographies & Indexes in World History Ser.: No. 6). 243p. 1987. text ed. 65.00 (0-313-24555-X, MEU) Greenwood.

Messick, Hank. The Politics of Prosecution: Jim Thompson, Richard Nixon, Marje Everett, & the Trial of Otto Kerner. LC 77-15915. (Illus.). 253p. 1978. 10.95 (0-916054-64-0) Green Hill.

Messick, Judith, tr. see Skram, Amalie.

Messick, L. J. & Singh, R., eds. International Conference on Indium Phosphide & Related Materials for Advanced Electronic & Optical Devices, 1st: March 1989, Norman, OK. 660p. 1989. 92.00 (0-8194-0180-3, VOL. 1144) SPIE.

Messick, Linda S. Through My Day with the 'L' Sound. (Illus.). 120p. (Orig.). (J). (gr. k-6). 1975. pap. text ed. 6.95x (0-87015-212-2) Pacific Bks.

— Through My Day with the 'S' Sound. (Illus.). 120p. (Orig.). (J). (gr. k-6). 1975. pap. text ed. 6.95 (0-87015-214-9) Pacific Bks.

— Through My Day with the 'SH' Sound. (Illus.). 112p. (Orig.). (J). (gr. k-6). 1975. pap. text ed. 6.95 (0-87015-215-7) Pacific Bks.

Messick, Rosemary G. & Reynolds, Karen E. Middle Level Curriculum in Action. 266p. (Orig.). (C). 1992. pap. text ed. 33.95 (0-8013-0540-3, 78417) Longman.

Messick, Rosemary G., jt. auth. see Chapin, June R.

Messick, Samuel. Effectiveness of Coaching for the SAT: Review & Reanalysis from the Fifties to the FTC. 1988. 5.00 (0-317-67894-9) Educ Testing Serv.

— Individuality in Learning. LC 76-11886. 398p. reprint ed. pap. 113.50 (0-317-26072-3, 2023776) Bks Demand.

Messick, Samuel, jt. auth. see Jackson, Douglas H.

Messick, Samuel, jt. ed. see Wainer, Howard.

Messick, Tim. Cross Country Skiing in Yosemite. 80p. 1993. pap. 9.95 (0-934641-67-6) Chockstone Pr.

Messick, Wayne D., jt. auth. see Jonovic, Donald J.

Messick, William, ed. see Luong Si Hang.

Messick, William L. America's Fighting Presidents: Chief Executives Who Served Their Country Long Before They Entered the White House. LC 92-72196. 200p. (Orig.). 1992. pap. 18.50 (1-879560-14-3) Harbor Hse West.

Messick, William L., jt. auth. see Chaney, Earlyne.

Messier, J., et al, eds. Nonlinear Optical Effects in Organic Polymers. (C). 1989. lib. bdg. 134.00 (0-7923-0132-3) Kluwer Ac.

— Organic Molecules for Nonlinear Optics & Photonics. (C). 1991. lib. bdg. 174.00 (0-7923-1181-7) Kluwer Ac.

Messier, R., et al, eds. New Diamond Science & Technology, Proceedings of the Second International Conference: Materials Research Society Conference Proceedings, Vol. NDST-2. 1991. text ed. 70.00 (1-55899-111-5) Materials Res.

Messier, Ronald A., jt. ed. see Dajani-Shareel, Hadia.

Messiha & Tyner, eds. Alcoholism: A Perspective. LC 80-80209. 512p. 1980. 49.95 (0-915340-02-X) PJD Pubns.

Messiha, F. S. & Tyner, G. S., eds. Endocrinological Aspects of Alcoholism. (Progress in Biochemical Pharmacology Ser.: Vol. 18). (Illus.). xii, 232p. 1981. 124.00 (3-8055-2689-X) S Karger.

Messimer, Dwight. In the Hands of Fate: The Story of Patrol Wing Ten. LC 85-3069. (Illus.). 352p. 1985. 22.95 (0-87021-293-1) Naval Inst Pr.

Messimer, Dwight R. Escape. LC 93-11122. 288p. 1994. 29.95 (1-55750-578-0) Naval Inst Pr.

— The Merchant U-Boat: Adventures of the Deutschland, 1916-1918. LC 88-22786. (Illus.). 288p. 1988. 28.95 (0-87021-771-2) Naval Inst Pr.

*Messina, Annie. The Myrtle & the Rose. Bright, Jessie, tr. & intro. by. 180p. (Orig.). 1996. pap. write for info. (0-934977-45-3) Italica Pr.

Messina, Anthony M. Race & Party Competition in Britain. (Illus.). 216p. 1989. 52.00 (0-19-827534-X) OUP.

Messina, Anthony M., et al, eds. Ethnic & Racial Minorities in Advanced Industrial Democracies. LC 91-26374. (Contributions in Ethnic Studies: No. 29). 376p. 1992. text ed. 55.00 (0-313-27259-X, MEH/, Greenwood Pr) Greenwood.

Messina, Ben. Looking Naked. rev. ed. LC 90-85068. 63p. 1990. pap. 6.95 (0-87208-300-4) Island Pr Pubs.

Messina, Calogero. Sicilians Wanted the Inquisition. LC 92-43674. 1993. pap. write for info. (1-881901-01-7) LEGAS.

Messina, Constance G., jt. auth. see Messina, James J.

Messina, Edmund J. Cytology. LC 74-79836. (Allied Health Ser.). 1975. pap. 7.65 (0-672-61382-4, Bobbs) Macmillan.

Messina, G. & Hamza, M. H., eds. Computers & Their Applications for Development: Proceedings IASTED Symposium, Taormina, Italy, September 3-5, 1986. 222p. 1987. 55.00 (0-88986-098-X, 106) Acta Pr.

An Asterisk (*) at the beginning of an entry indicates that the title is appearing in BIP for the first time.

— Measurement, Signal Processing & Control - MECO '86: Proceedings IASTED Symposium, Taormina, Italy, September 3-5, 1986. 323p. 1986. 91.00 (*0-88986-096-3*, 105) Acta Pr.

Messina, James J. Tools for Communication. LC 91-77542. (Tools for Coping Ser.: Bk. 6). 60p. (Orig.). 1992. pap. text ed. 8.95 (*0-8403-7194-2*) Kendall-Hunt.

— Tools for Handling Control Issues, Bk. 8. LC 91-77544. (Tools for Coping Ser.: Bk. 8). 120p. 1992. pap. text ed. 13.95 (*0-8403-7196-9*) Kendall-Hunt.

— Tools for Handling Loss. LC 91-77539. (Tools for Coping Ser.: Bk. 3). 60p. (Orig.). 1992. pap. text ed. 8.95 (*0-8403-7191-8*) Kendall-Hunt.

Messina, James J., ed. Case Management Handbook. (Professional Handbook Ser.). 84p. (Orig.). 1982. pap. text ed. 11.00 (*0-931975-18-2*) Advanced Dev Sys.

Messina, James J., pref. Advanced Communication Skills Handbook. (Professional Handbook Ser.). 61p. (Orig.). 1982. pap. text ed. 10.00 (*0-931975-12-3*) Advanced Dev Sys.

— Basic Communication Skills Handbook. 53p. (Orig.). 1982. pap. text ed. 10.00 (*0-931975-11-5*) Advanced Dev Sys.

— The Burnout & Stress Management Handbook: Professional Handbook Ser. 78p. (Orig.). 1982. pap. text ed. 11.00 (*0-931975-14-X*) Advanced Dev Sys.

— Family Therapy Handbook. (Professional Handbook Ser.). 79p. (Orig.). 1982. pap. text ed. 11.00 (*0-931975-19-0*) Advanced Dev Sys.

— The Group Leader's Handbook. (Professional Handbook Ser.). 45p. (Orig.). pap. text ed. 7.00 (*0-931975-10-7*) Advanced Dev Sys.

— The Handbook of Readings for the Training of Consultants & Trainers. (Professional Handbook Ser.). 127p. (Orig.). 1982. pap. text ed. 16.00 (*0-931975-08-5*) Advanced Dev Sys.

— The Handbook of Trainer's Activities. (Professional Handbook Ser.). 100p. (Orig.). 1982. pap. text ed. 11.00 (*0-931975-09-3*) Advanced Dev Sys.

— The Human Services Counseling Skills. (Professional Handbook Ser.). 35p. (Orig.). 1982. pap. text ed. 7.00 (*0-931975-17-4*) Advanced Dev Sys.

— Personal Values Analysis Handbook. (Professional Handbook Ser.). 26p. (Orig.). 1982. pap. text ed. 7.00 (*0-931975-16-6*) Advanced Dev Sys.

— The Time Management Handbook. (Professional Handbook Ser.). 37p. (Orig.). 1982. pap. text ed. 7.00 (*0-931975-15-8*) Advanced Dev Sys.

— Tools for Parents of Children with Developmental Disabilities. (Tools-for-Coping Ser.). 98p. (Orig.). 1987. pap. text ed. 11.00 (*0-931975-07-7*) Advanced Dev Sys.

Messina, James J. & Messina, Constance G. Getting Parents Involved in the Exceptional Education Process. (Tools-for-Coping Ser.). 140p. (Orig.). 1988. pap. text ed. 11.00 (*0-931975-24-7*) Advanced Dev Sys.

— Getting Parents Involved in the Exceptional Education Process a Leader's Guide. (Tools for Coping Ser.). 32p. (Orig.). 1988. pap. text ed. 7.00 (*0-931975-25-5*) Advanced Dev Sys.

Messina, Jennifer. The Secrets of the Jennivine Restaurant Cookbook. 202p. 1992. pap. 12.95 (*0-9636478-0-6*) Jennivine.

***Messina, John.** Death of Innocents. Lake, Elizabeth, ed. LC 94-68377. 288p. (Orig.). 1995. pap. 10.95 (*0-89716-554-3*) P B Pubng.

Messina, John L. Hand Motor Vehicle Treatise Only. LC 89-25234. 1990. ring bd. 105.00 (*0-685-59921-3*) Clark Boardman Callaghan.

— Handling Motor Vehicle Accident Cases. LC 89-25234. 1990. ring bd. 135.00 (*0-685-58521-2*) Clark Boardman Callaghan.

— Handling Motor Vehicle Accident Cases: Forms. LC 90-1377. 1990. ring bd. 135.00 (*0-685-34581-5*) Clark Boardman Callaghan.

Messina, Kathlyn. The Sleeping Giant Reading Program. LC 82-83558. (Illus.). 160p. (Orig.). 1982. pap. 10.95 (*0-910569-00-2*) Hampton Court Pub.

Messina, Kathlyn & Dacquino, Vinny. Proud That I'm Still Me. (Illus.). 21p. (Orig.). 1992. 6.25 (*0-910569-02-9*); ring bd. 2.95 (*0-910569-03-7*); audio 12.95 (*0-685-60795-X*); audio 3.75 (*0-910569-01-0*); 2.60 (*0-910569-04-5*) Hampton Court Pub.

— Proud That I'm Still Me. LC 92-70002. (Illus.). 21p. (Orig.). (J). (ps-5). 1992. pap. 7.95 (*0-910569-05-3*) Hampton Court Pub.

Messina, Maria. A House in the Shadows. Shepley, John, tr. LC 89-60939. 133p. 1989. 15.95 (*0-910395-50-0*); pap. 9.95 (*0-910395-51-9*) Marlboro Pr.

Messina, Mark, et al. The Simple Soybean & Your Health. LC 93-43374. 272p. 1994. pap. 12.95 (*0-89529-611-X*) Avery Pub.

***Messina, Paul & Murli, Almerico, eds.** Practical Parallel Computing: Status & Prospects. fac. ed. LC 91-44139. 253p. 1991. reprint ed. pap. 72.20 (*0-7837-8279-9*, 2049060) Bks Demand.

Messina, Paul C. & Sterling, Thomas A. Systems Software & Tools for High Performance Computing Environments. xix, 160p. 1993. 5.00 (*0-89871-326-9*) Soc Indus-Appl Math.

Messina, Phillip. Anzio - Song of Destiny. 316p. 1992. pap. 5.95 (*0-935648-38-0*) Halldin Pub.

Messina, Robert J. The Covenant of 1996: Countdown the Last Seven Years. (Illus.). (Orig.). 1993. pap. text ed. 8.00 (*0-685-65628-4*) Hse of Asher.

— For Signs & for Seasons: How Forty-Eight Ancient Celestial Signs Identify Our Messiah. 303p. 1992. pap. text ed. write for info. (*0-9633250-4-3*) Hse of Asher.

***Messina, Susan S.** Adolescents & the HIV-AIDS Epidemic: Stemming the Tide. 41p. 1993. 15.00 (*1-55516-646-6*, 6646) Natl Conf State Legis.

Messina, Virginia, jt. auth. see Schumann, Kate.

Messina, William S. Statistical Quality Control for Manufacturing Managers. LC 86-34022. (Engineering Management Ser.). 331p. 1987. text ed. 79.95 (*0-471-85774-2*) Wiley.

Messineo, Melinda. Sociology of Marriage & the Family: Gender, Love & Property, Test Bank. 4th ed. LC 94-15709. (Series in Sociology). 500p. 1995. write for info. (*0-8304-1418-5*) Nelson-Hall.

***Messing, Bob.** The I Ching of Management. (Illus.). 160p. (Orig.). 1995. pap. 16.95 (*0-89334-242-4*, 2424032) Humanics Ltd.

— The Tao of Management: An Age Old Study for New Age Managers. LC 88-12913. (Illus.). 148p. 1989. lib. bdg. 26.95 (*0-89334-199-1*, 199-1) Humanics Ltd.

Messing, Gordon M. A Glossary of Greek Romany As Spoken in Agia Varvara (Athens) 175p. (Orig.). 1988. pap. 17.95 (*0-89357-187-3*) Slavica.

Messing, Gordon M., ed. see Smyth, Herbert W.

Messing, Margaret S. Adelma Goes Herbing. LC 93-94108. (Illus.). 64p. (Orig.). (J). 1994. pap. 6.00 (*1-56002-383-X*, Univ Edtns) Aegina Pr.

Messing, Michael. Miniaturauszeichnungen des III. Reiches. 86p. 1988. pap. 15.00 (*0-318-40080-4*) Johnson Ref Bks.

Messing, Patricia, jt. auth. see Coyle, Rena.

Messing, Robert. The Tao of Management. LC 88-12913. 148p. (Orig.). 1989. pap. 16.95 (*0-89334-111-8*) Humanics Ltd.

Messing, Simon D. The Story of the Falashas: "Black Jews" of Ethiopia. (Illus.). 134p. 1982. pap. 10.00 (*0-9615946-9-1*) S D Messing.

Messing, Simon D., ed. Target of Health in Ethiopia: A Holistic Reader in Applied Anthropology. 285p. 1973. text ed. 34.50 (*0-8422-5074-3*); pap. text ed. 16.95 (*0-8422-0261-7*) Irvington.

Messing, William, jt. ed. see Cristante, Valentino.

Messinger, Gary S. British Propaganda & the State in the First World War. LC 92-7433. 1993. text ed. 59.95 (*0-7190-3014-5*, Pub. by Manchester Univ Pr UK) St Martin.

Messinger, H., jt. auth. see Willman, H.

***Messinger, Jean G. & Rust, Mary J.** Faith in High Places: Historic Country Churches of Colorado. 240p. (Orig.). 1995. pap. text ed. 16.95 (*1-57098-013-6*) R Rinehart.

Messinger, Lisa. Why Should I Eat Better? Simple Answers to All Your Nutritional Questions. LC 92-33752. 160p. (Orig.). 1993. pap. 9.95 (*0-89529-508-3*) Avery Pub.

Messinger, Lisa & Paino, Jon. The Tofu Book: The New American Cuisine. LC 91-46079. (Illus.). 184p. (Orig.). 1991. pap. 10.95 (*0-89529-409-5*) Avery Pub.

Messinger, Lisa M. Abstract Expressionism: Works on Paper: Selections from the Metropolitan Museum of Art. LC 92-33802. (Illus.). 176p. 1993. 45.00 (*0-685-62556-7*); 45.00 (*0-8109-6424-4*) Abrams.

— Georgia O'Keeffe. LC 87-51295. (Illus.). 1988. pap. 17.95 (*0-500-27499-1*) Thames Hudson.

— James Brooks: A Quarter-Century of Work. LC 88-81869. (Illus.). 40p. (Orig.). 1988. pap. text ed. 9.00 (*1-879195-02-X*) Heckscher Mus.

***Messinger, Paul R.** The Marketing Paradigm: A Guide for General Managers. LC 94-41608. 1995. 24.95 (*0-538-84494-9*) S-W Pub.

Messinger Press Staff, ed. see Ayers, Charles.

Messinger, Sheldon L., ed. see Criminology Review Yearbook Staff.

Messite, Jacqueline, ed. see New York Academy of Medicine Staff.

Messiter, Arthur. History of the Choir & Music of Trinity Church. LC 72-137317. reprint ed. 37.50 (*0-404-04313-5*) AMS Pr.

Messler, Norbert. The Art Deco Skyscraper in New York. rev. ed. (Illus.). 224p. (C). 1986. text ed. 14.80 (*0-8204-0158-7*) P Lang Pubs.

— The Art Deco Skyscraper in New York, Vol. 25. (European University Studies: Ser. 28). 234p. 1983. 44.60 (*3-8204-7562-1*) P Lang Pubs.

Messler, Robert W., Jr. Joining of Advanced Materials. 560p. 1993. 125.00 (*0-7506-9008-9*) Buttrwrth-Heinemann.

Messman, H. C. & Tibbetts, T. E., eds. Elements of Briquetting & Agglomeration I. 109p. 10.00 (*0-920292-00-3*) Inst Briquetting.

Messmann, Frank J. Richard Payne Knight: The Twilight of Virtuosity. 1974. text ed. 33.50 (*90-279-2628-X*) Mouton.

Messmann, Richard R. Lost in Space Technical Manual. Schuster, Hal, ed. (Files Ser.: Vol.1). 68p. 7.95 (*1-55698-009-4*) Movie Pubs Servs.

Messmer, Catherine C. & Halcomb, C. Andrew. South Carolina's Low Country: A Past Preserved. (Illus.). 1988. 19.95 (*0-87844-070-4*) Sandlapper Pub Co.

Messmer, Dale, ed. see Dalton, Robb E.

***Messmer, Hans-Peter.** The Indispensable PC Hardware Book: Your Hardware Questions Answered. 2nd ed. LC 94-25279. (ENG & GER.). (C). 1995. text ed. 39.95 (*0-201-87697-3*) Addison-Wesley.

Messmer, Harold M., Jr. Staffing Europe: An Indispensable Guide to Hiring & Being Hired in the New Europe. LC 92-8702. 1992. 24.95 (*0-87491-994-0*) Acropolis.

Messmer, Heinz, ed. Restorative Justice on Trial: Pitfalls & Potentials of Victim-Offender Mediation: International Research Perspectives - Proceedings of the NATO Advanced Research Workshop on Conflict, Crime & Reconciliation: The Organization of Welfare Interventions in the Field of Restitutive Justice, Held in Il Ciocco, Lucca, Italy 8-12 April, 1991. 608p. (C). 1992. lib. bdg. 181.50 (*0-7923-1620-7*) Kluwer Ac.

Messmer, K., ed. Capillary Functions & White Cell Interaction. (Progress in Applied Microcirculation Ser.: Vol. 18). (Illus.). x, 138p. 1991. 114.50 (*3-8055-5397-8*) S Karger.

Messmer, K. & Fagrell, B., eds. Mikrozirkulation und arterielle Verschlusskrankheiten, Muenchen, November 1980. (Illus.). vi, 222p. 1982. pap. 39.25 (*3-8055-2417-X*) S Karger.

Messmer, K. & Hammersen, F., eds. Entzuendung und Rheologie der Leukozyten. (Illus.). x, 136p. 1985. pap. 57.00 (*3-8055-4071-X*) S Karger.

— Gastrointestinal Microcirculation. (Progress in Applied Microcirculation Ser.: Vol. 17). (Illus.). x, 222p. 1991. 179.25 (*3-8055-5176-2*) S Karger.

— Microcirculation & Inflammation: Vessel Wall, Inflammatory Cells, Mediator Interaction. (Progress in Applied Microcirculation Ser.: Vol. 12). xvi, 330p. 1987. pap. 120.00 (*3-8055-4552-5*) S Karger.

— Die Mikrozirkulation des Skelettmuskels. (Illus.). viii, 162p. 1985. pap. 59.25 (*3-8055-3919-3*) S Karger.

— Mikrozirkulation und Entzuendung: Beziehungen Zwischen Gefaesswand Entzuendungszellen und Mediatoren. (Illus.). xvi, 358p. 1988. pap. 120.00 (*3-8055-4656-4*) S Karger.

— Skeletal Muscle Microcirculation. (Mikrozirkulation in Forschung und Klinik; Progress in Applied Microcirculation Ser.: Vol. 5). (Illus.). vii, 148p. 1984. pap. 59.25 (*3-8055-3920-7*) S Karger.

— Struktur und Funktion Endothelialer Zellen. (Illus.). x, 150p. 1983. pap. 39.25 (*3-8055-3712-3*) S Karger.

— Vasomotion & Quantitative Kapillaroskopie. (Progress in Applied Microcirculation Ser.: Vol. 3). (Illus.). viii, 152p. 1984. pap. 65.75 (*3-8055-3809-X*) S Karger.

— White Cell Rheology & Inflammation. (Mikrozirkulation in Forschung und Klinik; Progress in Applied Microcirculation Ser.: Vol. 7). (Illus.). x, 124p. 1985. pap. 57.00 (*3-8055-4040-X*) S Karger.

Messmer, K. & Menger, M. D., eds. Liver Microcirculation & Hepatobiliary Function. (Progress in Applied Microcirculation Ser.: Vol. 19). (Illus.). viii, 172p. 1993. 149.00 (*3-8055-5701-9*) S Karger.

Messmer, K. & Stein, M., eds. Pathways in Applied Immunology: In Memoriam Walter Brendel. (Illus.). 152p. 1991. 31.00 (*0-387-53989-1*) Spr-Verlag.

Messmer, K., jt. ed. see Brendel, W.

Messmer, K., ed. see Hammersen, F.

Messmer, K., jt. ed. see Hammersen, F.

Messmer, K., et al, eds. European Society Surgical Research, 16th Congress, Garmisch-Partenkirchen, April 1981. (Journal: European Surgical Research: Vol. 13, Suppl. 1). (Illus.). viii, 104p. 1981. pap. 33.00 (*3-8055-2644-X*) S Karger.

— Microcirculation in Organ Transplantation. (Progress in Applied Microcirculation Ser.: Vol. 21). (Illus.). x, 126p. 1994. 129.75 (*3-8055-5849-X*) S Karger.

— Perspectives in Methodology for Study of the Microcirculation. (Progress in Applied Microcirculation Ser.: Vol. 6). (Illus.). vi, 160p. 1984. pap. 59.25 (*3-8055-3988-6*) S Karger.

Messmer, Max. Fifty Ways to Get Hired. LC 94-7520. 12.95 (*0-688-11566-7*) Morrow.

Messmer, Sara E., ed. see Chavers-Wright, Madrue.

Messner & Assman. Swimming Everyone. 2nd ed. 192p. 1992. pap. text ed. 12.95 (*0-88725-180-3*) Hunter Textbks.

Messner, Charles, tr. see Steuermann, Edward.

Messner, David, ed. Mastery Motivation in Early Childhood: Development, Measurement, & Social Processes. LC 93-7213. (International Library of Psychology). 288p. 1994. 65.00 (*0-415-06956-4*, B0898) Routledge.

Messner, Edward. Resilience Enhancement for the Resident Physician. 163p. 1993. pap. 7.95 (*0-929240-57-X*) Essential Med Info Syst Inc.

Messner, Edward, et al, eds. What Therapists Learn about Themselves & How They Learn It: Autognosis. LC 93-74196. 166p. 1994. pap. 25.00 (*1-56821-188-0*) Aronson.

Messner, Fred. The Business-to-Business Communications Handbook. 1991. 59.95 (*1-56318-001-4*) Assn Natl Advertisers.

Messner, George, intro. International Electronics Packaging Conference, 1985, Vol. 5. (Illus.). 627p. (Orig.). 1985. pap. text ed. 35.00 (*1-880433-04-4*, 9151-1) Intl Elect Pack.

— International Electronics Packaging Conference, 1986, Vol. 6. (Illus.). 882p. (Orig.). 1986. pap. text ed. 35.00 (*1-880433-05-2*, 9161-1) Intl Elect Pack.

— International Electronics Packaging Conference, 1987, Vol. 7, Pts. 1 & 2. (Illus.). 1096p. (Orig.). 1987. pap. text ed. 35.00 (*1-880433-06-0*, 9171-1) Intl Elect Pack.

Messner-Loebs, William. Epicurus the Sage Vol. 2: The Many Loves of Zeus, Vol. 2. Nevelow, Mark, ed. 48p. 1991. pap. 9.95 (*0-930289-91-9*, Piranha Pr) DC Comics.

— The Journey Saga, Bk. 2: "Bad Weather" 96p. 1990. 9.95 (*1-56097-029-4*) Fantagraph Bks.

Messner-Loebs, William, et al. Indiana Jones: The Fate of Atlantis: The Fate of Atlantis Collection. (Illus.). 112p. 1992. pap. 13.95 (*1-878574-36-1*) Dark Horse Comics.

Messner-Loebs, William F. Journey Saga, Bk. 1: Tall Tales. (Illus.). 96p. (Orig.). 1987. pap. 9.95 (*0-930193-28-8*) Fantagraph Bks.

Messner, Michael, jt. auth. see Kimmel, Michael S.

Messner, Michael A. Power at Play: Sports & the Problem of Masculinity. LC 91-28600. 256p. 1992. 15.00 (*0-8070-4104-1*) Beacon Pr.

— Power at Play: Sports & the Problem of Masculinity. 1995. pap. 14.00 (*0-8070-4105-X*) Beacon Pr.

Messner, Michael A. & Sabo, Don F., eds. Sport, Men, & the Gender Order: Critical Feminist Perspectives. LC 90-31880. (Illus.). 296p. 1990. text ed. 38.00 (*0-87322-281-4*, BMES0281) Human Kinetics.

Messner, Michael A. & Sabo, Donald F. Sex, Violence, & Power in Sports: Rethinking Masculinity. LC 94-18562. 216p. 1994. pap. 12.95 (*0-89594-688-2*) Crossing Pr.

Messner, Michael A. & Sabo, Donald F., eds. Sport, Men, & the Gender Order: Critical Feminist Perspectives. LC 90-31880. (Illus.). 296p. 1990. pap. 22.00x (*0-87322-421-3*, BMES0421) Human Kinetics.

Messner, Michael A., jt. comp. see Kimmel, Michael S.

Messner, Reinhold. All Fourteen Eight-Thousanders. Salkeld, Audrey, tr. (Illus.). 247p. 1988. 40.00 (*0-938567-05-5*) Cloudcap.

— Antarctica: Both Heaven & Hell. (Illus.). 400p. 1991. text ed. 35.00 (*0-89886-305-8*) Mountaineers.

— The Big Walls. (Illus.). 1978. 35.00 (*0-19-520062-4*) OUP.

— The Crystal Horizon: Across Tibet to Mount Everest. LC 88-63854. (Illus.). 300p. 1989. 32.00 (*0-89886-207-8*) Mountaineers.

— Reinhold Messner, Free Spirit: A Climber's Life. (Illus.). 288p. 1991. 24.95 (*0-89886-290-6*) Mountaineers.

— To the Top of the World. (Illus.). 1992. 32.00 (*0-89886-332-5*) Mountaineers.

Messner, Robert C. Leadership Development Through S.E.R.V.I.C.E. An Ongoing Program for Equipping Servant Leaders in the Church. 112p. (Orig.). (C). 1989. student ed 9.99 (*0-87403-567-8*, 3173) Standard Pub.

Messner, Stephen D., et al. Real Estate Investment & Taxation. 4th ed. 464p. 1990. text ed. 62.00 (*0-13-763053-0*) P-H.

Messner, Stephen D., jt. ed. see Clapp, John M.

Messner, Stephen D., et al. Marketing Investment Real Estate. 3rd ed. Berlin, Helene, ed. LC 81-86402. (Illus.). 546p. 1985. reprint ed. text ed. 22.95 (*0-913652-59-8*, BK. 139) Realtors Natl.

Messner, Steven F. & Rosenfeld, Richard. Crime & the American Dream. 130p. 1994. pap. 12.95 (*0-534-20106-7*) Intl Thomson.

Messner, Steven F., et al, eds. Theoretical Integration in the Study of Deviance & Crime: Problems & Prospects. LC 88-22441. (SUNY Series in Deviance & Social Control). 342p. 1989. 74.50 (*0-7914-0000-X*); pap. 24.95 (*0-7914-0001-8*) State U NY Pr.

Messner, William A. Profitable Purchasing Management: A Guide for Small Business Owners-Managers. LC 81-69367. 317p. reprint ed. pap. 90.40 (*0-317-27186-5*, 2023922) Bks Demand.

Messoner, Dale, ed. see Walter, Lori J.

***Messonnier, Shawn.** Exotic Pets: A Veterinary Guide for Owners. LC 94-21728. 1994. pap. 8.95 (*1-55622-381-1*, Rep of TX Pr) Wordware Pub.

— Your Puppy's First Year. LC 94-48892. 1995. 12.95 (*1-55622-386-2*, Seaside Pr) Wordware Pub.

Messora, N. Mastering Italian. (Mastering Languages Ser.). (Illus.). 360p. (Orig.). 1991. pap. 11.95 (*0-87052-057-1*); audio 12.95 (*0-87052-066-0*) Hippocrene Bks.

Messora, Noemi. Cassell's Contemporary Italian: A Handbook of Grammar, Current Usage, & Word Power. LC 93-18041. (Illus.). 528p. 1993. text ed. 25.00 (*0-02-584375-3*) Macmillan.

Messori, Vittorio, jt. auth. see Ratzinger, Joseph C.

MESSQ Staff. Middle East Military Balance, Vol. 1, Pt. 3. (Middle East Strategic Studies Quarterly: No. 8903). 176p. 1990. 40.50 (*0-08-040375-1*, Pergamon Pr) Elsevier.

***Messud, Clare.** When the World Was Steady. 270p. 1995. 19.95 (*0-9645611-0-7*) Granta USA.

***Mestdagh, Denis.** Fundamentals of Multiaccess Optical Fiber Networks. LC 94-29879. 1994. 77.00 (*0-89006-666-3*) Artech Hse.

Mestecky, Jiri, jt. ed. see McGhee, Jerry R.

***Mestecky, Jiri, et al, eds.** Advances in Mucosal Immunology Pts. A & B: Proceedings of the Seventh International Congress of Mucosal Immunology, Held in Prague, Czechoslovakia, August 16-21, 1992. (Advances in Experimental Medicine & Biology Ser.: Vol. 371). 1520p. 1995. 245.00 (*0-306-45012-7*) Plenum.

— Immunology of Milk & the Neonate. (Advances in Experimental Medicine & Biology Ser.: Vol. 310). (Illus.). 480p. 1992. 125.00 (*0-306-44105-5*, Plenum Pr) Plenum.

— Recent Developments in Mucosal Immunology, Pt. A. LC 87-14129. (Illus.). 1866p. 1987. 135.00 (*0-306-42614-5*, Plenum Pr) Plenum.

— Recent Developments in Mucosal Immunology, Pt. B. LC 87-14129. (Illus.). 1866p. 1987. 155.00 (*0-306-42775-3*, Plenum Pr) Plenum.

Mestenhauser, Josef A., et al, eds. Culture, Learning, & the Disciplines: Theory & Practice in Cross-Cultural Orientation. 184p. 1988. 18.00 (*0-912207-23-X*) NAFSA Washington.

Mester, C. S. & Tauber, R. T. Oral Communication Skills for Vo-Tech Students (A Competency-Based Approach) (Orig.). 1991. pap. 10.75 (*0-911168-79-6*) Prakken.

Mester, Cathy S. & Tauber, Robert T. Tecnicas De Comunicacion Oral Para Estudiantes De Vocacional Tecnica: Metodo Basado En la Practica De Estas Tecnicas Para Lograr Su Perfeccionamiento. Tellez, Francisco J. & De Paoli de Sales, Nanette, trs. 160p. (Orig.). (SPA.). 1992. pap. text ed. 10.75 (*0-911168-83-4*) Prakken.

Mester, Cathy S., jt. auth. see Tauber, Robert T.

Mester, Michael, jt. ed. see McIntire, Paul.

Mesters, Carlos. Defenseless Flower: A New Reading of the Bible. McDonagh, Francis, tr. LC 89-35761. 225p. 1989. pap. 14.95 (*0-88344-596-4*) Orbis Bks.

— God, Where Are You? An Introduction to the Bible. rev. ed. Drury, John & McDonagh, Francis, trs. LC 94-44034. 252p. 1995. reprint ed. pap. 14.95 (*0-88344-998-6*) Orbis Bks.

Mesterton, Eric. The Waste Land: Some Commentaries. LC 75-22205. (Studies in T. S. Eliot: No. 11). 1975. lib. bdg. 75.00 (*0-8383-2085-6*) M S G Haskell Hse.

***Mesterton-Gibbons, Michael.** A Concrete Approach to Mathematical Modelling. 2nd ed. LC 94-35535. 1995. text ed. 64.95 (*0-471-10960-6*) Wiley.

An Asterisk (*) at the beginning of an entry indicates that the title is appearing in BIP for the first time.

Mesterton-Gibbons, Michael. A Concrete Approach to Mathematical Modelling. (Illus.). 624p. (C). 1989. 49.95 (*0-201-12910-8*, Adv Bk Prog); 14.95 (*0-201-09099-6*, Adv Bk Prog) Addison-Wesley.

— An Introduction to Game Theoretic Modelling. (C). 1992. 44.95 (*0-201-55439-9*, Adv Bk Prog); pap. 34.95 (*0-201-55448-8*, Adv Bk Prog) Addison-Wesley.

Mesthene, Emmanuel. Mesthene: Technology & Social Change. LC 67-23043. (Orig.). (C). 1967. pap. write for info. (*0-672-60900-2*, CR14, Bobbs) Macmillan.

Mesthene, Emmanuel G. Technological Change: Its Impact on Man & Society. LC 76-106960. (Harvard Studies in Technology & Society). 127p. reprint ed. pap. 36.20 (*0-7837-3851-X*, 2043673) Bks Demand.

Mesthrie, Rajend. English in Language Shift: The History, Structure & Sociolinguistics of South African Indian English. (Illus.). 232p. (C). 1993. 69.95 (*0-521-41514-4*) Cambridge U Pr.

Mestmacker, Ernst J. Law & Economics of Transborder Telecommunications: A Symposium. (Law & Economics of International Telecommunications Ser.). 450p. 1987. 108.50 (*3-7890-1368-4*, Pub. by Nomos Verlags GW) Intl Bk Import.

Mestmacker, Ernst J., ed. Natural Gas in the Internal Market: A Review of Energy Policy. (International Energy & Resources Law & Policy Ser.). (C). 1993. lib. bdg. 136.00 (*1-85333-795-1*) Kluwer Ac.

Mestmacker, Ernst-Joachim, jt. ed. see Friedmann, Daniel.

Meston, Dougall, jt. auth. see Wigan, C. R.

Meston, M. C., et al, eds. Cooper's Scottish Legal Tradition. (C). 1989. 39.00 (*0-85411-045-3*) St Mut.

Meston, Michael C., ed. see Lord Cooper.

Meston, Zach & Arnold, J. Douglas. Awesome Sega Genesis Secrets 4. (Gaming Mastery Ser.). (Illus.). 352p. (YA). 1994. pap. 11.95 (*0-9624676-2-6*) Sandwich Islands.

— Awesome Super Nintendo Secrets, No. 2. (Gaming Mastery Ser.). (Illus.). 320p. (Orig.). 1993. pap. 11.95 (*0-9624676-7-7*) Sandwich Islands.

— Heimdall: Official Strategy Guide. (Gaming Mastery Ser.). (Illus.). 120p. (Orig.). 1994. pap. 12.95 (*1-884364-02-0*) Sandwich Islands.

— Popful Mail. (Gaming Mastery Ser.). (Illus.). 160p. (Orig.). 1995. pap. 16.95 (*1-884364-18-7*) Sandwich Islands.

— Vay: The Official Strategy Guide. (Gaming Mastery Ser.). (Illus.). 120p. (Orig.). 1994. pap. 12.95 (*1-884364-10-1*) Sandwich Islands.

Meston, Zach, jt. auth. see Arnold, J. Douglas.

Meston, Zach, jt. auth. see DeMaria, Rusel.

Meston, Zach, ed. see Sandwich Islands Publishing Staff.

Mestre, Jose P., jt. ed. see Cocking, Rodney R.

Mestrovic, Stjepan. The Barbarian Temperamental: Toward a Postmodern Critical Theory. LC 92-45836. 1993. write for info. (*0-415-08572-1*, Routledge NY) Routledge.

— The Coming Fin De Siecle: An Application of Durkheim's Sociology to Modernity & Postmodernism. 224p. 1991. 55.00 (*0-415-04838-9*, A5047) Routledge.

— The Coming Fin de Siecle: An Application of Durkheim's Sociology to Modernity & Postmodernism. LC 90-8468. 224p. 1992. pap. 15.95 (*0-415-08526-8*, A7610) Routledge.

Mestrovic, Stjepan G. The Balkanization of the West: The Confluence of Postmodernism & Postcommunism. LC 94-16377. 240p. 1994. 59.95x (*0-415-08754-6*, B3805); pap. 18.95 (*0-415-08755-4*, B3809) Routledge.

— Durkheim & Postmodern Culture. (Communication & Social Order Ser.). 203p. 1992. lib. bdg. 41.95 (*0-202-30439-6*); pap. text ed. 22.95 (*0-202-30440-X*) Aldine de Gruyter.

— Emile Durkheim & the Reformation of Sociology. LC 93-16886. 180p. (C). 1993. pap. 19.95 (*0-8476-7867-9*) Rowman.

— Habits of the Balkan Heart: Social Character & the Fall of Communism. LC 93-11072. 200p. 1993. pap. 14.95 (*0-89096-593-5*) Tex A&M Univ Pr.

Mestrovic, Stjepan G., et al. Habits of the Balkan Heart: Social Character & the Fall of Communism. LC 93-11072. (Illus.). 200p. 1993. 32.50 (*0-89096-556-0*) Tex A&M Univ Pr.

— The Road from Paradise: Prospects for Democracy in Eastern Europe. LC 92-32442. 224p. 1993. 28.00 (*0-8131-1827-1*) U Pr of Ky.

Mesulam, M. Marsel. Tracing Neural Connections with Horseradish Peroxidase. LC 81-14692. (IBRO Handbook Ser.: Methods in the Neurosciences). 251p. 1982. pap. text ed. 109.95 (*0-471-10029-3*, Wiley-Interscience) Wiley.

Mesulam, M-Marsel, ed. Principles of Behavioral Neurology. LC 84-28650. (Contemporary Neurology Ser.: No. 26). (Illus.). 405p. 1985. text ed. 68.00 (*0-8036-6151-7*) Davis Co.

— Principles of Behavioral Neurology, Set. LC 84-28650. (Contemporary Neurology Ser.: No. 26). (Illus.). 405p. 1985. 10.00 (*0-8036-6152-5*) Davis Co.

Mesyats, G. A. & Proskurovsky, D. I. Pulsed Electrical Discharge in Vacuum. (Atoms & Plasmas Ser.: Vol. 5). (Illus.). 310p. 1989. 95.00 (*0-387-50725-6*) Spr-Verlag.

Meszaros, E. Atmospheric Chemistry: Fundamental Aspects. (Studies in Environmental Science: Vol. 11). 202p. 1981. 64.00 (*0-444-99753-9*) Elsevier.

Meszaros, E., et al. Atmospheric Particles & Nuclei. (Illus.). 273p. (C). 1991. text ed. 38.00 (*963-05-5682-0*, Pub. by A K HU) Intl Spec Bk.

Meszaros, Erno. Global & Regional Changes in Atmospheric Composition. 1993. 59.95 (*0-87371-662-0*, QB879) Lewis Pubs.

Meszaros, Istvan. Beyond Capital: Toward a Theory of Transition. 700p. 1993. 22.00 (*0-85345-881-2*) Monthly Rev.

— Marx's Theory of Alienation. 352p. 35.00 (*0-87556-438-0*) Saifer.

— Marx's Theory of Alienation. 4th ed. (C). 1986. pap. 9.95 (*0-85036-191-5*, Pub. by Merlin Pr UK) Humanities.

— Necessity of Social Control. (C). 1972. pap. 7.50 (*0-85036-153-2*, Pub. by Merlin Pr UK) Humanities.

— The Power of Ideology. 640p. 1989. pap. 22.50 (*0-8147-5458-9*) NYU Pr.

— The Work of Sartre: Search for Freedom. (Modern Revivals in Philosophy Ser.). 288p. 1993. 59.95 (*0-7512-0272-X*, Pub. by Gregg Revivals UK) Ashgate Pub Co.

Meszaros, Mark W., ed. see Bilash, Borislaw, 2nd, et al.

Meszaros, Peter. High-Energy Radiation from Magnetized Neutron Stars. LC 91-27376. (Theoretical Astrophysics Ser.). (Illus.). 464p. 1992. pap. text ed. 39.95 (*0-226-52094-3*) U Ch Pr.

— High-Energy Radiation from Magnetized Neutron Stars. LC 91-27376. (Theoretical Astrophysics Ser.). (Illus.). 464p. 1992. lib. bdg. 98.00 (*0-226-52093-5*) U Ch Pr.

Met, Leon. Going Public: Quality Circles in the Public Sector, 2 vols., Set. 65p. 1984. 31.95 (*0-317-07126-2*) IAQC Pr.

Met, Philipe, tr. see Cole, Bruce K., ed.

Met, Philippe, tr. see Hoffman, Mark, et al.

Meta, Gruppo. Uno: Guida Per l'Insegnante. (Illus.). 154p. (C). 1994. pap. 29.95 (*0-521-46812-4*) Cambridge U Pr.

— Uno: Guida Per l'Insegnante, No. 3. (Illus.). 154p. (C). 1994. pap. 12.95 (*0-521-46816-7*) Cambridge U Pr.

— Uno: Guida Per l'Insegnante, Nos. 1 & 2. (Illus.). 154p. (C). 1994. pap. 19.95 (*0-521-46815-9*) Cambridge U Pr.

— Uno: Libro Degli Esercizi e Sintesi di Grammatica. (Illus.). 168p. (C). 1994. pap. 14.95 (*0-521-46813-2*) Cambridge U Pr.

— Uno: Libro Dello Studente. (Illus.). 216p. (C). 1994. pap. 16.95 (*0-521-46814-0*) Cambridge U Pr.

Meta Systems, Inc. Staff. Systems Analysis in Water Resources Planning. LC 75-290. (Illus.). 393p. 1975. text ed. 30.00 (*0-912394-13-7*) Water Info.

Metabooks, Inc. Staff. Escape, No. 3. (Orig.). 1986. pap. 2.25 (*0-685-43515-6*) Bantam.

Metaferia, Getachew & Shifferraw, Maigenet. The Ethiopian Revolution of 1974 & the Exodus of Ethiopia's Trained Human Resources. LC 91-48086. (African Studies: Vol. 24). 184p. 1992. lib. bdg. 79.95 (*0-7734-9458-8*) E Mellen.

Metailie, Anne-Marie, ed. Amerique Latine-Latin America: Catalogues et Inventaires. (Maison des Sciences de l'Homme, Service d'Echange d'Information Scientifiques Publications: No. 5). 1974. pap. 21.25 (*0-686-21808-6*) Mouton.

Metakides. Patras Logic Symposium. (Studies in Logic & the Foundations of Mathematics: Vol. 109). 392p. 1982. 87. 25 (*0-444-86476-8*, I-326-82, North Holland) Elsevier.

Metal-Corbin, Josie, jt. auth. see Corbin, David.

Metal Powder Industries Federation Staff. Compendium on Metal Injection Molding. (Illus.). 137p. reprint ed. pap. 39.10 (*0-7837-5162-1*, 2044891) Bks Demand.

— Copper Base Powder Metallurgy. Taubenblat, Pierre W., ed. LC 80-81464. (New Perspectives in Powder Metallurgy: Fundamentals, Methods, & Applications Ser.: No. 7). (Illus.). 227p. reprint ed. pap. 64.70 (*0-7837-5161-3*, 2044890) Bks Demand.

— Forging of Powder Metallurgy Preforms. LC 73-1768. (New Perspectives in Powder Metallurgy; Fundamentals, Methods, & Applications Ser.: No. 6). 399p. reprint ed. pap. 113.80 (*0-7837-2044-0*, 2042312) Bks Demand.

— Friction & Antifriction Materials. LC 74-127937. (Perspectives in Powder Metallurgy: Fundamentals, Methods, & Applications Ser.: No. 4). (Illus.). 350p. reprint ed. pap. 99.80 (*0-7837-5160-5*, 2044889) Bks Demand.

— Iron Powder Metallurgy: With an Introductory Chapter by Kempton H. Roll & Peter K. Johnson. LC 67-17375. (Perspectives in Powder Metallurgy: Fundamentals, Methods, & Applications Ser.: No. 3). 387p. reprint ed. pap. 110.30 (*0-7837-2043-2*, 2042311) Bks Demand.

— Metal Injection Molding: Preprint of a Seminar Held at the 1988 International Powder Metallurgy Conference, Orlando, Florida, June 7, 1988. (Illus.). 103p. reprint ed. pap. 29.40 (*0-7837-1563-3*, 2041855) Bks Demand.

— Prevention & Detection of Cracks in Ferrous P - M Parts: Preprint of a Seminar Held at the 1988 International Powder Metallurgy Conference, Orlando, Florida, June 10, 1988. 128p. reprint ed. pap. 36.50 (*0-7837-1742-3*, 2057275) Bks Demand.

— Properties, Evaluation & Testing of P-M Materials - Preprint of a Seminar Held at the 1988 International Powder Metallurgy Conference, Orlando, FL, June 8, 1988. (Illus.). 128p. reprint ed. pap. 36.50 (*0-7837-1564-1*, 2041856) Bks Demand.

— Secondary Operations: Preprint of a Seminar Held at the 1988 International Powder Metallurgy Conference, Orlando, Florida, June 6, 1988, Seminar Chairman: Reynold Sansoucy. 66p. reprint ed. pap. 25.00 (*0-7837-2212-5*, 2057274) Bks Demand.

Metalious, Grace. Peyton Place. 300p. 1991. reprint ed. lib. bdg. 32.95 (*0-89966-861-5*) Buccaneer Bks.

***Metallo, Frances R.** The Abacus: Its History & Its Applications. (Hi Map Ser.: No. 17). 60p. Date not set. pap. text ed. 11.99 (*0-614-05309-9*, HM 5617) COMAP Inc.

Metallurgical Society Staff. Modeling Environmental Effects on Crack Growth Processes: Proceedings of a Symposium Sponsored by the Corrosion & Environmental Effects & Mechanical Metallurgy Committee, Held at the Fall Meeting of the Metallurgical Society in Toronto, Canada, October 13-17, 1985. Jones, Russell H. & Gerberich, William W., eds. LC 86-12512. 393p. reprint ed. pap. 112.10 (*0-7837-4075-1*, 2052472) Bks Demand.

Metallurgical Society of AIME, High Temperature Alloys Committee. Superalloys Nineteen Eighty: Proceedings of the Fourth International Symposium on Superalloys. LC 80-36888. 750p. reprint ed. pap. 180.00 (*0-317-10322-9*, 2015493) Bks Demand.

Metallurgical Society of AIME Staff. Advanced Fibers & Composites for Elevated Temperatures: Proceedings of a Symposium Sponsored by the Metallurgical Society of AIME & the American Society for Metals Joint Composite Materials Committee at the 108th AIME Annual Meeting, New Orleans, Louisiana, February 20-21, 1979. Ahmad, I. & Noton, B. R., eds. LC 80-82650. (Metallurgical Society of AIME Conference Proceedings Ser.). 260p. reprint ed. pap. 74.10 (*0-8357-5124-4*, 2025899) Bks Demand.

— Advanced Processing Methods for Titanium: Casting, Forming, Machining, Welding: Proceedings of a Symposium Held at the TMS Fall Meeting, Louisville, Kentucky, October 13-15, 1981. Hasson, Dennis F. & Hamilton, C. H., eds. LC 82-60584. (Conference Proceedings Ser.). 323p. reprint ed. pap. 92.10 (*0-8357-2595-2*, 2052375) Bks Demand.

— Alternate Alloying for Environmental Resistance: Proceedings of the Symposium Sponsored by the Corrosion & Environmental Effects Committee of the Metallurgical Society of AIME & Held at the TMS-AIME Annual Meeting in New Orleans, Louisiana, from March 2-6, 1986. fac. ed. Smolik, G. R. & Banerji, S. K., eds. LC 86-31207. 497p. 1987. reprint ed. pap. 141.70 (*0-7837-8301-9*, 2049087) Bks Demand.

— Amorphous Materials: Modeling of Structure & Properties: Proceedings of Symposium Held at the Fall Meeting of the Metallurgical Society of AIME, St. Louis, Missouri, October 25-26, 1982. Vitek, V., ed. LC 83-61432. 355p. reprint ed. pap. 101.20 (*0-8357-2596-0*, 2052376) Bks Demand.

— Arsenic Metallurgy, Fundamentals & Applications: Proceedings of Symposium Sponsored by the TMS-AIME Physical Chemistry Committee & Mackay Mineral Research Institute, University of Nevada-Reno, at the 1988 TMS Annual Meeting & Exhibition, Phoenix, Arizona, January 25-28, 1988. Reddy, Ramana G. et al, eds. LC 87-43300. 544p. reprint ed. pap. 155.10 (*0-7837-1438-6*, 2052412) Bks Demand.

— Calculation of Phase Diagrams & Thermochemistry of Alloy Phases: Proceedings of a Symposium Held at the Fall Meeting, Milwaukee, Wisconsin, September 17-18, 1979. Chang, Y. A. & Smith, J. F., eds. LC 79-89675. 292p. reprint ed. pap. 83.30 (*0-8357-7966-1*, 2025907) Bks Demand.

— Case Hardened Steels: Microstructural & Residual Stress Effects: Proceedings of the Symposium Held at the 112th AIME Annual Meeting, Atlanta, Georgia, March 9, 1983. Diesburg, Daniel E., ed. LC 83-63326. 247p. reprint ed. pap. 70.40 (*0-8357-2598-7*, 2052378) Bks Demand.

— Chemical Metallurgy: A Tribute to Carl Wagner: Proceedings of a Symposium. Gokoen, Nev A., ed. LC 81-83779. (Conference Proceedings Ser.). 516p. reprint ed. pap. 147.10 (*0-685-23486-X*, 2029123) Bks Demand.

— Chemistry & Physics of Rapidly Solidified Materials: Proceedings of a Symposium Sponsored by the Chemistry & Physics of Metals Committee of the Metallurgical Society of AIME, St. Louis MO, October 26-27, 1982. Berkowitz, B. J. & Scattergood, R. O., eds. LC 83-61484. (Illus.). 323p. reprint ed. pap. 92.10 (*0-8357-5537-1*, 2035151) Bks Demand.

— Computer Control in Process Metallurgy: A Short Course Sponsored by TMS-AIME Held in Las Vegas, Nevada, February 20-21, 1976. 147p. reprint ed. pap. 41.90 (*0-317-10708-9*, 2004308) Bks Demand.

— Computer Modeling of Phase Diagrams: Proceedings of a Symposium Held at the Fall Meeting of the Metallurgical Society in Toronto, Canada, October 13-17, 1985. Bennett, L. H., ed. LC 86-19174. 427p. reprint ed. pap. 121.70 (*0-8357-2599-5*, 2052379) Bks Demand.

— Computer Modeling of Sheet Metal Forming Process: Theory, Verification, & Application, Proceedings of Symposium Sponsored by the Metallurgical Society & the TMS Detroit Section, Held at 12th Automotive Materials Symposium at Ann Arbor, Michigan, April 29-30, 1985. Wang, N. M. & Tang, S. C., eds. LC 85-26015. 302p. reprint ed. pap. 86.10 (*0-7837-1442-4*, 2052416) Bks Demand.

— Computer Simulation of Microstructural Evolution: Proceedings of Symposium Sponsored by the American Society for Metals Materials Science Division Computer Simulation Technical Activity, Held at the Fall Meeting, Toronto, Canada, October 13-17, 1985. Srolovitz, David J., ed. LC 86-8687. 260p. reprint ed. pap. 74.10 (*0-7837-1441-6*, 2052415) Bks Demand.

— Computer Usage in Materials Education: Proceedings of a Symposium. LC 85-18907. (Illus.). 149p. reprint ed. pap. 42.50 (*0-8357-4686-0*, 2052341) Bks Demand.

— Copper & Nickel Converters: Proceedings of a Symposium on Converter Operating Practices Sponsored by the TMS-AIME Pyrometallurgy Committee at the 108th AIME Annual Meeting in New Orleans, LA, February 19-21, 1979. Johnson, Robert E., ed. LC 79-87441. (Illus.). 411p. reprint ed. pap. 117.20 (*0-8357-3202-9*, 2052362) Bks Demand.

— Copper Smelting, an Update: Proceedings of a Symposium Held at the 111th AIME Annual Meeting, Dallas, Texas, February 14-18, 1982. George, David B. & Taylor, John C., eds. LC 81-86302. (Conference Proceedings Ser.). 353p. reprint ed. pap. 100.70 (*0-8357-2500-6*, 2052380) Bks Demand.

— Corrosion-Erosion Behavior of Materials: Proceedings of a Symposium - Sponsored by the TMS-AIME Corrosion Resistant Metals Committee & the Oxidation Activity Committee of American Society for Metals at the Fall Meeting of the Metallurgical Society of AIME, St. Louis, Missouri, October 17-18, 1978. Natesan, K., ed. LC 80-81518. (Illus.). 320p. reprint ed. pap. 91.20 (*0-8357-7563-1*, 2052327) Bks Demand.

— Corrosion of Metals Processed by Directed Energy Beams: Proceedings of a Symposium Sponsored by the Corrosion & Environmental Effects Committee. . . Held at the Fall Meeting of the Metallurgical Society of AIME, Louisville, KY, October 13, 1981. Clayton, Clive R. & Preece, Carolyn M., eds. LC 82-60586. (Conference Proceedings Ser.). (Illus.). 171p. reprint ed. pap. 48.80 (*0-8357-5538-X*, 2035152) Bks Demand.

— Creep-Fatigue-Environment Interactions: Proceedings of a Symposium. Pelloux, R. M. & Stoloff, N. S., eds. LC 80-82904. (Conference Proceedings Ser.). (Illus.). 202p. reprint ed. pap. 57.60 (*0-8357-5605-X*, 2056845) Bks Demand.

— Diffusion Analysis & Applications: Proceedings of a Symposium on Diffusion Analysis & Applications - Jointly Sponsored by the Minerals, Metals & Materials Society & the Atomic Transport Activities Committee of ASM, Held During the TMS Fall Meeting, September 25-29, 1988, Chicago, Illinois. Romig, A. D., Jr. & Dayananda, M. A., eds. LC 89-61029. 373p. reprint ed. pap. 106.40 (*0-7837-5640-2*, 2052492) Bks Demand.

— Dispersion Strengthened Aluminum Alloys: Proceedings of the Six-Session Symposium Held at the 1988 TMS Annual Meeting, Phoenix, Arizona, January 25-29, 1988. Kim, Y. W. & Griffith, W. M., eds. LC 88-60117. (Illus.). 804p. reprint ed. pap. 180.00 (*0-7837-6062-0*, 2052508) Bks Demand.

— Effects of Load & Thermal Histories on Mechanical Behavior of Materials: Proceedings of a Symposium Sponsored by the Mechanical Metallurgy & the Phase Transformation Committees of TMS-AIME, Held at the 1987 TMS-AIME Annual Meeting in Denver, Colorado, February 22-26, 1987. Liaw, P. K. & Nicholas, T., eds. LC 87-42887. 307p. reprint ed. pap. 87.50 (*0-7837-5641-0*, 2052493) Bks Demand.

— Electrometallurgy, Proceedings of the Extractive Metallurgy Division Symposium on Electrometallurgy Held in Cleveland, Ohio on December 2-3, 1968. 368p. reprint ed. pap. 104.90 (*0-317-10317-2*, 2001171) Bks Demand.

— The Electrorefining & Winning of Copper: Proceedings of the Symposium. Hoffman, J. E. et al, eds. LC 86-32430. (Illus.). 560p. reprint ed. pap. 159.60 (*0-8357-8665-X*, 2052308) Bks Demand.

— Embrittlement by the Localized Crack Environment: Proceedings of an International Symposium. Gangloff, R. P., ed. LC 84-61499. (Illus.). 501p. reprint ed. pap. 142. 80 (*0-8357-3203-7*, 2052363) Bks Demand.

— Energy Efficient Electrical Steels: Proceedings of a Symposium - Sponsored by the TMS-AIME Ferrous Metallurgy Committee. Marder, A. R. & Stephenson, E. T., eds. LC 81-80990. (Conference Proceedings Ser.). (Illus.). 225p. reprint ed. pap. 64.20 (*0-8357-5539-8*, 2035153) Bks Demand.

— Energy Reduction Techniques in Metal Electrochemical Processes: Proceedings of a Symposium. Bautista, R. G. & Wesely, R. J., eds. LC 85-14621. (Illus.). 506p. reprint ed. pap. 144.30 (*0-8357-5540-1*, 2035154) Bks Demand.

— Environment-Sensitive Fracture of Engineering Materials: Proceedings of a Symposium Held at the Fall Meeting of the Metallurgical Society of AIME in Chicago, Illinois, October 24-26, 1977. Foroulis, Z. A., ed. LC 79-84173. (Illus.). 670p. reprint ed. pap. 180.00 (*0-685-23526-2*, 2027911) Bks Demand.

— Extractive Metallurgy of Nickel & Cobalt: Proceedings of a Symposium Sponsored by the CuNiCo & Non-Ferrous Pyrometallurgy Committees of the Metallurgical Society, at the 117th TMS Annual Meeting, Phoenix, Arizona, January 25-28, 1988. Tyroler, G. P. & Landolt, C. A., eds. LC 88-60119. 575p. reprint ed. pap. 163.90 (*0-7837-5892-8*, 2052501) Bks Demand.

— Extractive Metallurgy of Refractory Metals: Proceedings of a Symposium Sponsored by the TMS-AIME Refractory Metals Committee & the Physical Chemistry of Extractive Metallurgy Committee at the 110th AIME Annual Meeting, Chicago, Illinois, February 22-26, 1981. Sohn, H. Y. et al, eds. LC 80-85213. (Conference Proceedings Ser.). (Illus.). 483p. reprint ed. pap. 137.70 (*0-685-20797-8*, 2030111) Bks Demand.

— Forming Limit Diagrams: Concepts, Methods, & Applications: a Reference Book on the Available Experimental & Analytical Methods for Determination of Forming Limit Diagrams. Wagoner, R. H. et al, eds. LC 89-61034. 351p. reprint ed. pap. 100.10 (*0-7837-5642-9*, 2052494) Bks Demand.

— Fracture: Interactions of Microstructure, Mechanisms & Mechanics: Proceedings of the Symposium Held at the 113th AIME Annual Meeting in Los Angeles, California, February 27-29, 1984. Wells, Joseph M. & Landes, John D., eds. LC 84-62213. (Conference Proceedings Ser.). 519p. reprint ed. pap. 148.00 (*0-8357-2506-5*, 2052386) Bks Demand.

— Fundamentals of Dual-Phase Steels: Proceedings of a Symposium. Kot, R. A. & Bramfitt, B. L., eds. LC 81-83951. (Conference Proceedings Ser.). (Illus.). 511p. reprint ed. pap. 145.70 (*0-8357-3204-5*, 2052364) Bks Demand.

An Asterisk (*) at the beginning of an entry indicates that the title is appearing in BIP for the first time.

— High Conductivity Copper & Aluminum Alloys: Proceedings of a Symposium - Sponsored by the Non-ferrous Metals Committee of the Metallurgical Society of AIME Held at the Annual Meeting of the Metallurgical Society in Los Angeles, CA, February 26-March 1, 1984. Ling, Evan & Taubenblat, Pierre W., eds. LC 84-61484. (Conference Proceedings - The Metallurgical Society of AIME Ser.). (Illus.). 197p. reprint ed. pap. 56.20 (0-8357-7564-X, 2052328) Bks Demand.

— High Temperature Nuclear Fuels. Holden, A. N., ed. LC 67-28245. (Metallurgical Society Conference Ser.: Vol. 42). 525p. reprint ed. pap. 149.70 (0-317-08161-6, 2001531) Bks Demand.

— High-Temperature Protective Coatings: Proceedings of a Symposium Sponsored by the Corrosion & Environmental Effects Committee of the Society...Held at the 112th AIME Annual Meeting, Atlanta, GA, March 7-8, 1983. Singhal, Subhash C., ed. LC 82-63096. (Conference Proceedings Ser.). (Illus.). 371p. pap. 105.80 (0-685-20541-X, 2030014) Bks Demand.

— Hydrometallurgical Reactor Design & Kinetics: Proceedings of a Symposium Held at the Metallurgical Society Annual Meeting, New Orleans, Louisiana, March 2-6, 1986. Bautista, Renato G. et al, eds. LC 86-23568. 467p. reprint ed. pap. 133.10 (0-8357-2508-1, 2052388) Bks Demand.

— ICCM-2: Proceedings of the 1978 International Conference on Composite Materials, April 16-20, 1978, Toronto, Canada. LC 76-12236. 1675p. reprint ed. pap. 180.00 (0-317-28199-2, 2022770) Bks Demand.

— International Conference on Composite Materials (ICCM-V) Conference Proceedings of the Fifth International Conference...San Diego, CA, July 29-August 1, 1985. Harrigan, W. C. et al, eds. LC 85-13827. (Illus.). 1759p. reprint ed. pap. 180.00 (0-685-20341-7, 2029782) Bks Demand.

— Ion Implantation Metallurgy: Proceedings of a Symposium Held as Part of the Annual Meeting of the Materials Research Society, Cambridge, 1979. Preece, C. M. & Hirvonen, J. K., eds. LC 80-82278. 203p. reprint ed. pap. 57.90 (0-317-27623-9, 2025064) Bks Demand.

— Light Metals, 1978 Vol. 1: Proceedings of Sessions 107th AIME Annual Meeting, Denver, Colorado. Miller, John J., ed. LC 78-50868. 407p. reprint ed. pap. 116.00 (0-685-23584-X, 2056317) Bks Demand.

— Light Metals, 1980: Proceedings of Technical Sessions. McMinn, Curtis J., ed. LC 72-623660. (Conference Proceedings - The Metallurgical Society of AIME Ser.). (Illus.). 1041p. reprint ed. pap. 180.00 (0-8357-5542-8, 2035156) Bks Demand.

— Light Metals, 1981: Proceedings of Technical Sessions Sponsored by the TMS Light Metals Committee. Bell, Gordon M., ed. LC 72-623660. 1072p. reprint ed. pap. 180.00 (0-317-28267-0, 2025448) Bks Demand.

— Light Metals, 1982: Proceedings of Technical Sessions Sponsored by the TMS Light Metals Committee at the 11th AIME Annual Meeting, Dallas, TX, February 14-18, 1982. Andersen, J. E., ed. LC 72-623660. (Illus.). 1182p. reprint ed. pap. 180.00 (0-8357-6598-9, 2035996) Bks Demand.

— Light Metals, 1986: Proceedings of the Technical Sessions, Vol. 1. Miller, R. E., ed. LC 85-31081. (Illus.). 1141p. reprint ed. pap. 180.00 (0-8357-8663-3, 2052306) Bks Demand.

— Light Metals, 1988: Proceedings of the Technical Sessions by the TMS Light Metals Committee at the 117th TMS Annual Meeting, Phoenix, Arizona, January 25-28, 1988. fac. ed. Boxall, Larry G., ed. LC 72-623660. (Illus.). 930p. 1987. reprint ed. pap. 180.00 (0-7837-8299-3, 2049085) Bks Demand.

— Mathematical Modeling of Materials Processing Operations: Proceedings of Symposium Held in Palm Springs, California, U. S. A., November 29-December 2, 1987 at the Fifth Extractive & Process Metallurgical Fall Meeting. Szekely, J. et al, eds. LC 87-42884. 1212p. reprint ed. pap. 180.00 (0-7837-1437-8, 2052411) Bks Demand.

— Mechanical Behavior of Metal-Matrix Composites: Proceedings of a Symposium Held at the 111th AIME Annual Meeting, Dallas, Texas, February 16-18, 1982. Hack, John E. & Amateau, Maurice F., eds. LC 83-61431. (Conference Proceedings Ser.). 363p. reprint ed. pap. 103.50 (0-8357-2594-4, 2052374) Bks Demand.

— Mechanical Behavior of Metal-Matrix Composites: Proceedings of a Symposium Sponsored by the Composite Materials Committee of the Metallurgical Society of AIME...Held at the 111th AIME Annual Meeting, Dallas, TX, February 16-18, 1982. Hack, John E. & Amateau, Maruice F., eds. LC 83-61431. (Conference Proceedings Ser.). (Illus.). 363p. reprint ed. pap. 103.50 (0-8357-6599-7, 2035997) Bks Demand.

— Mechanical Behavior of Rapidly Solidified Materials: Proceedings of a Symposium Held at the AIME Annual Meeting, New York City, NY, February 24-28, 1985. Sastry, Shankar M. & MacDonald, Bruce A., eds. LC 85-30989. 319p. reprint ed. pap. 91.00 (0-8357-2509-X, 2052389) Bks Demand.

— The Metal Science of Stainless Steel: Proceedings of a Symposium Held at the 107th AIME Annual Meeting, 1978. Collings, E. W. & King, H. W., eds. LC 79-84706. 220p. reprint ed. pap. 62.70 (0-317-28271-9, 2025449) Bks Demand.

— Metallic Multi-Layers & Epitaxy: Proceedings of a Symposium Co-Sponsored by the TMS Electronic Device Materials Committee (EDMC), & the ASM-MSD Electrical, Magnetic & Optical Phenomena Activity (EMOP), held at the Annual Meeting of the Metallurgical Society in Denver, Colorado, February 24-25, 1987. fac. ed. Hong, M. et al, eds. LC 87-42881. 291p. 1988. reprint ed. pap. 83.00 (0-7837-8303-5, 2049089) Bks Demand.

— Metallurgy of Continuous-Annealed Sheet Steel: Proceedings of a Symposium Sponsored by the Heat Treatment Committee & the Ferrous Metallurgy Committee of the Metallurgical Society of AIME, Held at the AIME Annual Meeting in Dallas, TX, February 15-16, 1982. Bramfitt, B. L. & Mangonon, P. L., Jr., eds. LC 82-61947. (Illus.). 407p. reprint ed. pap. 116.00 (0-8357-7506-2, 2035998) Bks Demand.

— Microstructural Control in Aluminum Alloys: Deformation, Recovery, & Recrystallization: Proceedings of a Symposium Held at the Annual Meeting of TMS in New York, February 27, 1985. Chia, E. Henry & McQueen, H. J., eds. LC 85-29842. 233p. reprint ed. pap. 66.50 (0-8357-2510-3, 2052390) Bks Demand.

— Modeling of Casting & Welding Processes: Proceedings of a Symposium. Brody, Harold D. & Apelian, Diran, eds. LC 81-83753. (Conference Proceedings Ser.). (Illus.). 567p. reprint ed. pap. 161.60 (0-685-20799-4, 2030124) Bks Demand.

— New Developments & Applications in Composites: Proceedings of a Symposium Fall Meeting in St. Louis, Missouri, October 16-17, 1978. Kuhlmann-Wilsdorf, Doris & Harrigan, William C., Jr., eds. LC 79-64414. 377p. reprint ed. pap. 107.50 (0-8357-2511-1, 2052391) Bks Demand.

— Niobium: Proceedings of the International Symposium... Held in San Francisco, CA, November 8-11, 1981. LC 83-63096. (Technology of Metallurgy Ser.: No. 5). (Illus.). 1269p. reprint ed. pap. 180.00 (0-8357-7507-0, 2035999) Bks Demand.

— Nondestructive Evaluation: Microstructural Characterization & Reliability Strategies: Proceedings of a Symposium Held at the TMS Fall Meeting, Pittsburgh, PA, October 5-9, 1980. Buck, Otto & Wolf, Stanley M., eds. LC 81-82177. 413p. reprint ed. pap. 117.80 (0-8357-2512-X, 2052392) Bks Demand.

— Novel Techniques in Metal Deformation Testing: Proceedings of a Symposium Sponsored by the Shaping & Forming Committee of the Metallurgical Society of AIME & the Process Modeling Committee of the American Society for Metals, Held at the Fall Meeting, St. Louis, Missouri, October 25-26, 1982. Wagoner, R. H., ed. LC 83-60514. (Conference Proceedings Ser.). 432p. reprint ed. pap. 123.20 (0-7837-1440-8, 2052414) Bks Demand.

— Phase Stability During Irradiation: Proceedings of a Symposium Sponsored by the Nuclear Metallurgy Committee at the Fall Meeting of the Metallurgical Society of AIME, Pittsburgh, PA, October 5-9, 1980. Holland, J. R. et al, eds. LC 81-82941. (Conference Proceedings Ser.). 629p. reprint ed. pap. 179.30 (0-8357-2513-8, 2052393) Bks Demand.

— Physical Metallurgy of Metal Joining: Proceedings of a Symposium. Kossowsky, Ram & Glicksman, M. E., eds. LC 80-82303. 278p. reprint ed. pap. 79.30 (0-317-26075-8, 2023772) Bks Demand.

— Process Mineralogy: Extractive Metallurgy, Mineral Exploration, Energy Resources: Proceedings of a Symposium Held at the 110th AIME Annual Meeting, Chicago, IL, February 22-26, 1981. Hausen, Donald M. & Park, Won C., eds. LC 81-82942. (Conference Proceedings Ser.). 727p. reprint ed. pap. 180.00 (0-8357-2516-2, 2052396) Bks Demand.

— Process Mineralogy Two: Applications in Metallurgy, Ceramics, & Geology: Proceedings of a Symposium Held at the AIME Annual Meeting in Dallas, Texas, February 14-18, 1982. Hagni, Richard D., ed. LC 82-61494. 517p. reprint ed. pap. 147.40 (0-8357-2517-0, 2052397) Bks Demand.

— Process Mineralogy VI: Proceedings of a Symposium Presented in Six Sessions on Process Mineralogy Held During the Metallurgical Society Annual Meeting, New Orleans, Louisiana, March 2-6, 1986. fac. ed. Hagni, Richard D., ed. LC 86-23576. 647p. 1986. reprint ed. pap. 180.00 (0-7837-8300-0, 2049086) Bks Demand.

— Process Mineralogy VII: Applications to Mineral Beneficiation Technology & Mineral Exploration, with Special Emphasis on Disseminated Carbonaceous Gold Ores: Proceedings of a Symposium Presented in Seven Sessions on Process Mineralogy Held During the Metallurgical Society Annual Meeting, Denver, Colorado, February 23-27, 1987. fac. ed. Vassiliou, Andreas H. et al, eds. LC 87-42880. 663p. 1987. reprint ed. pap. 180.00 (0-7837-8302-7, 2049088) Bks Demand.

— Processing & Properties for Powder Metallurgy Composites: Proceedings of a Symposium Sponsored by the P-M Committee of TMS-AIME Held at the Annual Meeting of the Metallurgical Society in Denver, Colorado, February 1987. Kunar, P. et al, eds. LC 87-43115. 180p. reprint ed. pap. 51.30 (0-7837-1439-4, 2052413) Bks Demand.

— Recycle & Secondary Recovery of Metals: Proceedings of the International Symposium on Recycle & Secondary Recovery of Metals & the Fall Extractive & Process Metallurgy Meeting. Taylor, Patrick R. et al, eds. LC 85-21792. (Illus.). 874p. reprint ed. pap. 180.00 (0-8357-7006-0, 2052275) Bks Demand.

— Structure & Deformation of Boundries: Proceedings of a Symposium "Phase Boundary Effects on Deformation" Sponsored by the Physical Metallurgy, Structural Materials & Mechanical Metallurgy Committees of the Metallurgical Society of AIME & the Flow & Fracture Activity of American Society for Metals Held at the 1985 TMS-AIME Fall Meeting, Toronto, Canada, October 13-17, 1985. fac. ed. Subramanian, K. N. & Imam, M. A., eds. LC 86-16420. 355p. reprint ed. pap. 101.20 (0-7837-8304-3, 2049090) Bks Demand.

— Sulfur Dioxide Control in Pyrometallurgy: Proceedings of a Symposium - Sponsored by the TMS-AIME Pyrometallurgical Committee at the 110th AIME Annual Meeting, Chicago, Illinois, February 22-26, 1981. Chatwin, Terrence D. & Kikumoto, Nobuo, eds. LC 81-80107. (Conference Proceedings - Metallurgical Society of AIME Ser.). (Illus.). 267p. reprint ed. pap. 76.10 (0-8357-3556-7, 2034259) Bks Demand.

— Superplastic Forming of Structural Alloys: Proceedings of a Symposium. Paton, N. E. & Hamilton, C. H., eds. LC 82-81860. 426p. reprint ed. pap. 121.50 (0-317-42099-2, 2026228) Bks Demand.

— Synthesis & Properties of Metastable Phases: Proceedings of a Symposium - Sponsored by the TMS-AIME Alloy Phases Committee at the Fall Meeting of the Metallurgical Society of AIME, Pittsburgh, PA, October 5-9, 1980. Machlin, E. S. & Rowland, T. J., eds. LC 80-85205. (Conference Proceedings Ser.). 203p. reprint ed. pap. 57.90 (0-8357-2519-7, 2052399) Bks Demand.

— Technology for Premium Quality Castings: Proceedings of a Symposium Sponsored by the TMS Solidification Committee & Held at the TMS Annual Meeting in Denver, Colorado, February 24-27, 1987. Dunn, E. & Durham, D. R., eds. LC 87-43112. 187p. reprint ed. pap. 53.30 (0-7837-5645-3, 2052497) Bks Demand.

— Technology of Continuously Annealed Cold-Rolled Sheet Steel: Proceedings of a Symposium Held at the TMS-AIME Fall Meeting in Detroit, MI, September 17-18, 1984. Pradhan, R., ed. LC 85-4776. (Conference Proceedings Ser.). 471p. reprint ed. pap. 134.30 (0-8357-2520-0, 2052400) Bks Demand.

— Textures in Non-Ferrous Metals & Alloys: Proceedings of a Symposium - Sponsored by the Non-Ferrous Metals Committee of the Metallurgical Society of AIME, Detroit, MI, September 19-20, 1984. Merchant, H. D. & Morris, J. G., eds. LC 85-11569. 239p. reprint ed. pap. 68.20 (0-8357-2521-9, 2052401) Bks Demand.

— Theory of Alloy Phase Formation: Proceedings of a Symposium-Sponsored by the TMS-AIME Alloy Phases Committee & the Chemistry & Physics of Metals Committee at the 10th AIME Annual Meeting, New Orleans, La., February 19-20, 1979. Bennett, L. H., ed. LC 80-80305. 535p. reprint ed. pap. 152.50 (0-317-26178-9, 2024264) Bks Demand.

— Titanium Rapid Solidification Technology: Proceedings for the Four Session Symposium on "Titanium, Rapid Solidification Technology," Sponsored by the Titanium Committee of the Metallurgical Society Held at the 1986 TMS-AIME Annual Meeting, New Orleans, Louisiana, March 2-6, 1986. Froes, F. H. & Eylon, D., eds. LC 86-19176. (Illus.). 339p. reprint ed. pap. 96.70 (0-7837-1969-8, 2052447) Bks Demand.

— Toughness Characterization & Specifications for HSLA & Structural Steels: Proceedings of a Symposium. Mangonon, P. L., ed. LC 79-52169. 394p. reprint ed. pap. 112.30 (0-317-42102-6, 2026227) Bks Demand.

— Water Quality Management for the Metals & Minerals Industries, a Short Course (In Conjunction with the 104th AIME Annual Meeting, New York, 1975) 147p. reprint ed. pap. 41.90 (0-317-10692-9, 2004307) Bks Demand.

Metallurgical Society of AIME Staff, et al. Rapidly Solidified Crystalline Alloys: Proceedings of a TMS-AIME Northeast Regional Meeting. Das, S. K. et al, eds. LC 85-28833. (Illus.). 331p. reprint ed. pap. 94.40 (0-8357-5544-4, 2035159) Bks Demand.

Metallurgical Society Staff. Computerized Metallurgical Databases: Proceedings of a Symposium, Held at the Fall Meeting of the Metallurgical Society in Cincinnati, Ohio, U. S. A., October 12-13, 1987. Cuthill, J. R. et al, eds. LC 87-43243. 205p. reprint ed. pap. 58.50 (0-7837-1451-3, 2052427) Bks Demand.

— Dislocations & Interfaces in Semiconductors: Proceedings of a Symposium "Dislocations & Interfaces in Semiconductors" Sponsored by the Electronic Device Materials Committee of TMS, Held at the 1988 TMS Annual Meeting, Phoenix, AZ, January 25-26, 1988. fac. ed. Rajan, Krishna et al, eds. LC 88-61505. (Illus.). 207p. 1988. pap. 59.00 (0-7837-8603-4, 2052534) Bks Demand.

— Formability & Metallurgical Structure: Proceedings of a Symposium Co-Sponsored by the Mechanical Metallurgy & Shaping & Forming Committees of TMS-AIME & Held in Orlando, Florida October 5-9, 1986 at the Fall Meeting of the Metallurgical Society. Sachdev, A. K. & Embury, J. D., eds. LC 87-15388. 393p. reprint ed. pap. 112.10 (0-7837-4073-5, 2052470) Bks Demand.

— Hot- & Cold-Rolled Sheet Steel: Proceedings of a Symposium Held at the TMS Fall Meeting in Cincinnati, Ohio, October 12-13, 1987 Sponsored by the Ferrous Metallurgy Committee of the Metallurgical Society. Pradhan, R. & Ludkovsky, G., eds. LC 88-60118. 407p. reprint ed. pap. 116.00 (0-7837-4074-3, 2052471) Bks Demand.

— Metal Transfer & Galling in Metallic Systems: Proceedings of a Symposium Sponsored by the Non-Ferrous Metals Committee of the Metallurgical Society & the Erosion & Wear G2 Committee of ASTM, Orlando, Florida, October 8-9, 1986. Merchant, H. D. & Bhansali, K. J., eds. LC 87-5740. 307p. reprint ed. pap. 87.50 (0-7837-4077-8, 2052474) Bks Demand.

— Microstructure, Fracture Toughness, & Fatigue Crack Growth Rate in Titanium Alloys: Proceedings of the 1987 TMS-AIME Annual Symposia on Effect of Microstructure on Fracture Toughness & Fatigue Crack Growth Rate in Titanium Alloys, Held at Marriott City Center, Denver, Colorado, 1987, February 24-25. Chakrabarti, A. K. & Chesnutt, J. C., eds. LC 87-42879. 281p. reprint ed. pap. 80.10 (0-7837-4071-9, 2052468) Bks Demand.

— Physical Modeling of Metalworking Processes: Proceedings of a Symposium Sponsored by the TMS-AIME Shaping & Forming Committee, Held at the TMS Annual Meeting in Denver, Colorado, February 24-27, 1987. Erman, E. & Semiatin, S. L., eds. LC 87-73245. 271p. reprint ed. pap. 77.30 (0-7837-1452-1, 2052428) Bks Demand.

— Processing & Applications of High Tc Superconductors: Proceedings of the Northeast Regional Meeting of the Metallurgical Society Held at Rutgers - the State University of New Jersey, May 9-11, 1988. Mayo, William E., ed. LC 88-62259. (Illus.). 269p. Date not set. reprint ed. pap. 76.70 (0-7837-9134-8, 2049934) Bks Demand.

— Semiconductor-Based Heterostructures: Interfacial Structure & Stability: Proceedings of the Northeast Regional Meeting of the Metallurgical Society, Sponsored by the New Jersey Chapter & the Materials Research Society, Held at AT & T Bell Laboratories, Murray Hill, New Jersey, May 1-2, 1986. Green, Martin L. et al, eds. LC 86-23799. (Illus.). 474p. reprint ed. pap. 135.10 (0-7837-4076-X, 2052473) Bks Demand.

Metallurgy Society of AIME Staff. Powder Metallurgy of Titanium Alloys: Proceedings of the Metallurgy Society of AIME, 109th, Las Vegas, Nevada, 1980. Froes, F. H. & Smugeresky, John E., eds. LC 80-83013. 319p. reprint ed. pap. 91.00 (0-317-42396-7, 2056069) Bks Demand.

Metastasio, Pietro. Three Melodramas. Fucilla, Joseph G., tr. LC 80-51017. (Studies in Romance Languages: No. 24). 164p. 1981. 18.00 (0-8131-1400-4) U Pr of Ky.

Metaxas, A. C. & Meredith, R. J. Industrial Microwave Heating. (Power Engineering Ser.: No. 4). 357p. 1983. pap. 119.00 (0-906048-89-3, P0004, Pub. by Peregrinus UK) Inst Elect Eng.

Metaxas, B. N. The Economics of Tramp Shipping. (Illus.). 268p. (C). 1971. text ed. 38.00 (0-485-11127-6, Pub. by Athlone Pr UK) Humanities.

Metaxas, Eric. The Boy & the Whale: A Christmas Fairy Tale. (Illus.). 48p. 1994. 14.95 (1-884506-15-1) Third Story.

— David & Goliath. (Greatest Stories Ever Told Ser.). (Illus.). 40p. (J). (gr. k up). 1993. audio 19.95 (0-88708-295-5, Rabbit); 14.95 (0-88708-294-7, Rabbit) S&S Childrens.

— The Fool & the Flying Ship. LC 91-40669. (We All Have Tales Ser.). (Illus.). 40p. (J). (gr. k up). 1992. audio 19.95 (0-88708-229-7, Rabbit); pap. 14.95 (0-88708-228-9, Rabbit) S&S Childrens.

— Jack & the Beanstalk. LC 91-14176. (We All Have Tales Book & Cassette Ser.). (Illus.). 40p. (J). (gr. k up). 1991. pap. 14.95 (0-88708-188-6, Rabbit); audio 19.95 (0-88708-189-4, Rabbit) S&S Childrens.

— King Midas & the Golden Touch. LC 91-40670. (We All Have Tales Ser.). (Illus.). 40p. (J). (gr. k up). 1992. pap. 14.95 (0-88708-234-3, Rabbit); audio 19.95 (0-88708-235-1, Rabbit) S&S Childrens.

— Puss in Boots. LC 92-7789. (We All Have Tales Ser.). (Illus.). 40p. (J). 1992. pap. 14.95 (0-88708-285-8, Rabbit); audio 19.95 (0-88708-286-6, Rabbit) S&S Childrens.

— Stormalong. LC 95-48132. (Illus.). (J). 1995. write for info. (0-689-80194-7, Mac Bks Young Read) S&S Childrens.

Metaxas, Eric, tr. see Andersen, Hans Christian.

Metaxas, Eric, tr. see Grimm, Jacob & Grimm, Wilhelm K.

Metaxes, Eric. The Birthday ABC. LC 93-46896. (J). 1995. 15.00 (0-671-88306-2, S&S Bks Young Read) S&S Childrens.

Metcald, jt. auth. see Metcalf.

Metcalf. I-57. 160p. 1988. 11.95 (0-942986-06-7) LongRiver Bks.

— Kinesiology. 672p. 1995. 49.95 (0-8016-7920-6) Mosby Yr Bk.

Metcalf & Metcald. Living Anatomy. 1991. write for info. (0-8151-5894-7, Yr Bk Med Pubs) Mosby Yr Bk.

Metcalf, et al. Cross-Sectional Anatomy & CT Scan Atlas. 1991. write for info. (0-8151-5896-3, Yr Bk Med Pubs) Mosby Yr Bk.

— How to Make Money in Your Own Small Business. 1982. pap. 25.95 (0-8359-2964-7, Reston) P-H.

Metcalf, et al, eds. Probate Records of the Province of New Hampshire, 2 vols., Vol. 1. (Illus.). 874p. 1989. reprint ed. pap. 40.00 (1-55613-236-0) Heritage Bk.

— Probate Records of the Province of New Hampshire, 2 vols., Vol. 2. (Illus.). 876p. 1989. reprint ed. pap. 40.00 (1-55613-237-9) Heritage Bk.

— Probate Records of the Province of New Hampshire, 2 vols., Vol. 3. (Illus.). 815p. 1989. reprint ed. pap. 37.50 (1-55613-238-7) Heritage Bk.

Metcalf & Eddy, Inc. Staff & Tchobanoglous, George. Wastewater Engineering: Collection & Pumping of Wastewater. (Water Resources & Engineering Ser.). (Illus.). 448p. (C). 1981. text ed. write for info. (0-07-041680-X) McGraw.

— Wastewater Engineering: Treatment, Disposal & Reuse. 3rd ed. Burton, Franklin L., ed. (Water Resources & Environmental Engineering Ser.). 1991. text ed. write for info. (0-07-041690-7) McGraw.

Metcalf, Alida C. Family & Frontier in Colonial Brazil: Santana de Parnaiba, 1580-1822. (C). 1992. 40.00 (0-520-07574-9) U CA Pr.

An Asterisk (*) at the beginning of an entry indicates that the title is appearing in BIP for the first time.

Metcalf, Allan A. Poetic Diction in the Old English Meters of Boethius. LC 72-94487. (De Proprietatibus Litterarum, Ser. Practica: No. 50). 164p. 1973. pap. text ed. 32.35 (*90-279-2537-2*) Mouton.
— Research to the Point. 224p. (C). 1991. pap. text ed. 14.75 (*0-15-576604-X*) HB Coll Pubs.
— Research to the Point. 2nd ed. 244p. (C). 1994. pap. text ed. 16.00 (*0-15-501481-1*) HB Coll Pubs.
Metcalf, Allan A. & Kerrigan, William J. Essentials of Writing to the Point. (Illus.). 125p. (Orig.). (C). 1994. pap. text ed. 14.00 (*0-15-501709-8*) HB Coll Pubs.
Metcalf, Allen, jt. auth. see Kerrigan, William J.
Metcalf, Andy & Humphries, Martin, eds. Sexuality of Men. (C). 1985. pap. text ed. 16.95 (*0-86104-638-2*) Westview.
Metcalf, B. W., et al, eds. Cellular Adhesion: Molecular Definition to Therapeutic Potential. (New Horizons in Therapeutics Ser.). (Illus.). 312p. (C). 1994. 79.50 (*0-306-44685-5*, Plenum Pr) Plenum.
Metcalf, Barbara D. Islamic Revival in British India: Deoband, 1860-1900. LC 81-47934. (Illus.). 400p. 1982. 55.00 (*0-691-05343-X*) Princeton U Pr.
Metcalf, Barbara D., ed. Moral Conduct & Authority: The Place of Adab in South Asian Islam. LC 83-1361. 350p. 1984. 55.00 (*0-520-04660-9*) U CA Pr.
Metcalf, Barbara D., ed. & tr. Perfecting Women: Maulana Ashraf Ali Thanawi's Bihishti Zewar. 1990. 42.00 (*0-520-06491-7*) U CA Pr.
Metcalf, Barbara D., tr. & comment. Perfecting Women: Maulana Ashraf 'Ali Thanawi's Bihishti Zewar. (C). 1992. pap. 16.00 (*0-520-08093-9*) U CA Pr.
Metcalf, Ben & Samuels, David. Not Really Gone with the Wind: The Epic Parody of Our Time. (Illus.). 160p. (Orig.). 1990. pap. 9.95 (*0-312-05144-1*) St Martin.
***Metcalf, Bryce.** Original Members & Other Officers Eligible to the Society of the Cincinnati 1783-1938. Davenport, Robert R., ed. 390p. 1994. text ed. 45.00 (*1-885943-03-2*) Eastwood Pubng.
Metcalf, C. W. Lighten Up: Let C. W. Metcalf Show You How to Be More Productive, Resilient, & Stress-Free by Taking Laughter Seriously. (Illus.). 256p. 1992. 19.18 (*0-201-56779-2*) Addison-Wesley.
Metcalf, C. W. & Felible, Roma. The Humor Option: Facilitator's Guide. 11p. (Orig.). 1987. student ed 15.00 (*0-685-45029-5*) C W Metcalf.
— The Humor Option: Skills for Surviving & Thriving. 32p. (Orig.). 1987. student ed 25.00 (*0-685-32630-6*) C W Metcalf.
— Lighten Up: Survival Skills for People under Pressure. (Illus.). 304p. 1993. pap. 9.57 (*0-201-62239-4*) Addison-Wesley.
Metcalf, Calvin S. Voices from the Bible: Dramatic Monologs in Worship. LC 90-53277. (Illus.). 144p. (Orig.). (YA). 1990. pap. 9.95 (*0-916260-70-4*, B173) Meriwether Pub.
Metcalf, D. M. Coins of South Germany in the Thirteenth Century. 1961. 15.00 (*0-685-51539-7*) S J Durst.
— The Origins of the Anastasian Currency Reform. (Illus.). vii, 105p. 1969. text ed. 36.50 (*0-317-54491-8*, Pub. by A M Hakkert SP) Coronet Bks.
— Thrymsas & Sceattas in the Ashmolean Museum, Vol. 1. (Illus.). 208p. 1995. 42.00 (*1-85444-047-0*, 047-1, Pub. by Ashmolean Mus UK) A Schwartz & Co.
— Thrymsas & Sceattas in the Ashmolean Museum, Vol. 2. (Illus.). 152p. 1995. 42.00 (*1-85444-066-7*, 066-7, Pub. by Ashmolean Mus UK) A Schwartz & Co.
— Thrymsas & Sceattas in the Ashmolean Museum, Vol. 3. (Illus.). 436p. 1995. 65.00 (*1-85444-067-5*, 067-5, Pub. by Ashmolean Mus UK) A Schwartz & Co.
Metcalf, Donald. Clonal Culture of Hemopoietic Cells: Techniques & Applications. 168p. 1984. pap. 63.75 (*0-444-80565-6*) Elsevier.
— The Hemopoietic Colony Stimulating Factors. 493p. 1984. 208.75 (*0-444-80564-8*) Elsevier.
— The Molecular Control of Blood Cells. LC 88-605. (Illus.). 192p. 1988. 37.00 (*0-674-58157-1*) HUP.
***Metcalf, Donald, et al.** Theories of Mimesis. (Literature, Culture, Theory Ser.: No. 12). 196p. (C). 1995. pap. 16.95 (*0-521-45856-0*) Cambridge U Pr.
***Metcalf, Donald & Nicola, Nicos A.** The Hemopoietic Colony-Stimulating Factors: From Biology to Clinical Applications. (Illus.). 260p. (C). 1995. 64.95 (*0-521-46158-8*) Cambridge U Pr.
Metcalf, Doris. African Americans: Their Impact on U. S. History. (Illus.). 240p. (J). (gr. 5-9). 1992. 16.95 (*0-86653-670-1*, GA1345) Good Apple.
— Thinking Upside Down. (Orig.). 1994. pap. text ed. 12.97 (*0-937659-34-7*) GCT.
Metcalf, Doris & Marson, Ron. Rocks & Minerals. (Task Cards Ser.). (Illus.). 88p. (YA). (gr. 7-12). 1989. teacher ed 16.00 (*0-941008-23-1*) Tops Learning.
Metcalf, Doris H. Portraits of Exceptional African American Scientists. (Illus.). 144p. (J). (gr. 4-8). 1994. 11.95 (*0-86653-800-3*, GA1492) Good Apple.
Metcalf, Eleanor M. Herman Melville, Cycle & Epicycle. LC 75-104230. 311p. 1970. reprint ed. text ed. 59.75 (*0-8371-3340-8*, MEHM, Greenwood Pr) Greenwood.
Metcalf, Esther R., jt. auth. see Metcalf, Robert L.
Metcalf, Eugene. Calligraphy Techniques & Uses. (Artist's Library). (Illus.). 64p. (Orig.). 1989. pap. 6.95 (*0-929261-10-0*, AL10) W Foster Pub.
Metcalf, Eugene & Hall, Michael. The Ties That Bind: Folk Art in Contemporary American Culture. Krause, Carolyn, ed. (Illus.). 84p. 1986. pap. 12.95 (*0-917562-45-3*) Contemp Arts.
Metcalf, Eugene & Schwindler, Gary. Contemporary American Folk, Naive & Outsider Art: Into the Mainstream? LC 89-64503. (Illus.). 80p. (Orig.). 1990. pap. 15.00 (*0-940784-13-0*) Miami Univ Art.
Metcalf, Eugene W., jt. ed. see Hall, Michael D.
Metcalf, Eva-Marie. Astrid Lindgren. LC 94-20503. (Twayne's World Author Ser.: No. 851). 184p. 1994. text ed. 22.95x (*0-8057-4525-4*, Twayne) Macmillan.
Metcalf, Fay. Teaching with Historic Places: A Series of Lesson Plans Produced by the National Park Service & the National Trust for Historic Preservation. LC 92-32149. 1992. write for info. (*0-89133-229-4*) Preservation Pr.
Metcalf, Florence E. A Peek at Japan: A Lighthearted Look at Japan's Language & Culture. 2nd rev. ed. (Illus.). 133p. (J). (gr. 1-5). 1992. reprint ed. pap. text ed. 14.95 (*0-9631684-3-6*) Metco Pub.
Metcalf, Frank J. American Psalmody. 2nd ed. LC 68-13274. (Music Reprint Ser.). (Illus.). 1968. reprint ed. lib. bdg. 19.50 (*0-306-71132-X*) Da Capo.
Metcalf, Fred, ed. The Penguin Dictionary of Jokes. 240p. 1994. 18.95 (*0-670-84269-9*, Viking) Viking Penguin.
— The Penguin Dictionary of Modern Humorous Quotations. 1988. pap. 12.50 (*0-14-007568-2*, Penguin Bks) Viking Penguin.
Metcalf, Gale, jt. auth. see Wallach, Joel.
Metcalf, Geoffrey. The Terrorist Killers. (Critic's Choice Paperbacks Ser.). 1988. pap. 3.95 (*1-55547-269-9*, Univ Books) Carol Pub Group.
Metcalf, George F. Making Waves in the Information & Space Age: Creativity & Management in the Electronic Age. LC 92-71416. (Illus.). 256p. 1992. 24.95 (*0-8323-0497-2*); pap. 14.95 (*0-8323-0498-0*) Binford Mort.
Metcalf, George R. Fair Housing Comes of Age. LC 87-17747. (Contributions in Political Science Ser.: No. 198). 256p. 1988. text ed. 55.00 (*0-313-24757-9*, MAH/, Greenwood Pr) Greenwood.
— From Little Rock to Boston: The History of School Desegregation. LC 82-15581. (Contributions to the Study of Education Ser.: No. 8). x, 292p. 1983. text ed. 42.95 (*0-313-23470-1*, MDS/, Greenwood Pr) Greenwood.
Metcalf, Harlan G. Gold on Mount Grace: Boyhood Adventures in Long-Ago Warwick. LC 85-72088. (Illus.). 64p. (Orig.). 1985. pap. 4.95 (*0-912395-06-0*) Millers River Pub Co.
— The Pioneer Book of Nature Crafts. Orig. Title: Whittlin, Whistlin & Thingama Jigs. 1977. reprint ed. pap. 4.95 (*0-8065-0568-0*, Citadel Pr) Carol Pub Group.
Metcalf, Harry L., jt. ed. see McGlynn, Thomas J.
Metcalf, Jane. Dowry of Uncommon Women: "She Married a Flying Officer & a Gentleman Which She Knew to Be an Enviable Thing." (Orig.). 1988. pap. 12.95 (*0-9619194-4-2*) X-Press Pubns.
Metcalf, Jane, jt. auth. see Curtis, Clive.
Metcalf, Jill. Autumn Leaves. 336p. (Orig.). 1993. mass mkt. 4.99 (*1-55773-892-0*) Diamond.
— Family Reunion. 320p. (Orig.). 1994. mass mkt. 4.99 (*0-7865-0011-5*) Diamond.
— Spring Blossom. (Homespun Ser.). 336p. (Orig.). 1992. mass mkt. 4.99 (*1-55773-751-7*) Diamond.
Metcalf, Jim. Jim Metcalf's Journal. (Illus.). 64p. 1974. 8.95 (*0-88289-035-2*) Pelican.
Metcalf, Jim, ed. see Hirsch, Bob.
Metcalf, John. The Lady Who Sold Furniture. 150p. (C). 1970. 20.00 (*0-920802-09-5*, Pub. by ECW Press CN) Genl Dist Srvs.
Metcalf, John, ed. The Bumper Book. 220p. (C). 1986. text ed. 22.00 (*0-920763-92-8*, Pub. by ECW Press CN); pap. text ed. 12.00 (*0-920763-91-X*, Pub. by ECW Press CN) Genl Dist Srvs.
— Carry on Bumping. 268p. (C). 1988. text ed. 26.00 (*1-55022-079-9*, Pub. by ECW Press CN); pap. text ed. 13.00 (*1-55022-080-2*, Pub. by ECW Press CN) Genl Dist Srvs.
Metcalf, John G., ed. Annals of the Town of Menden, Ma. 723p. 1993. reprint ed. lib. bdg. 72.00 (*0-8328-2885-8*) Higginson Bk Co.
***Metcalf, John W.** Developing a Profession of Librarianship in Australia: Travel Diaries & Other Papers. Rayward, W. Boyd, ed. LC 94-32935. 1995. write for info. (*0-8108-2944-4*) Scarecrow.
Metcalf, Julia A., et al. Laboratory Manual of Neutrophil Function. 206p. 1986. spiral bd. 38.00 (*0-88167-160-6*) Raven.
Metcalf, Keyes D. My Harvard Library Years, 1937-1955: A Sequel to Random Recollections of an Anachronism. Williams, Edwin E., ed. 320p. 1988. 25.00 (*0-674-59600-5*) HUP.
— Random Recollections of an Anachronism. 401p. 1980. 35.00 (*0-918414-02-4*) Readex Bks.
***Metcalf, Linda.** Counseling Toward Solutions: A Practical Solution-Focused Program for Working with Students. 1994. spiral bd. 29.95 (*0-87628-267-2*) Ctr Appl Res.
***Metcalf, Mark S.** From Deeply Within. 1995. 9.95 (*0-533-11163-3*) Vantage.
Metcalf, Michael. Effective FORTRAN 77. (Illus.). 1985. pap. 29.95 (*0-19-853709-3*) OUP.
— FORTRAN Optimization. rev. ed. (APIC Studies in Data Processing). 1985. text ed. 69.00 (*0-12-492482-4*) Acad Pr.
Metcalf, Michael, ed. The Riksdag: A History of the Swedish Parliament. 220p. 1988. text ed. 45.00 (*0-312-00784-1*) St Martin.
Metcalf, Michael & Reid, John. FORTRAN 90 Explained. (Illus.). 312p. 1990. pap. 29.95 (*0-19-853772-7*) OUP.
Metcalf, Michael F., tr. see Ruin, Olof.
Metcalf, Nancy P. Family Resorts of the Northeast: Carefree Vacations for All-Including Mom & Dad. LC 91-8211. 224p. 1991. pap. 12.95 (*0-88150-185-9*) Countryman.
Metcalf, Paul. Araminta & the Coyotes. 1990. pap. 10.00 (*0-912330-73-2*) Jargon Soc.
— The Assassination. 16p. 1979. pap. 2.00 (*0-930794-13-3*) Station Hill Pr.
— The Assassination. deluxe limited ed. 16p. 1979. 10.00 (*0-930794-78-8*) Station Hill Pr.
— Both. LC 81-86062. 1982. 15.00 (*0-912330-49-X*, Inland Bk) Jargon Soc.
— Genoa: A Telling of Wonders. 1965. 10.00 (*0-912330-01-5*, Inland Bk) Jargon Soc.
— Genoa: A Telling of Wonders. LC 91-23293. 197p. 1991. reprint ed. pap. 14.95 (*0-8263-1300-0*) U of NM Pr.
— Golden Delicious & Firebird. 76p. 1989. reprint ed. pap. 35.00 (*0-87924-055-5*) Membrane Pr.
— Louis the Torch. 56p. 1983. pap. 3.95 (*0-916696-20-0*) Cross Country.
— The Middle Passage. LC 75-21931. 1976. 7.50 (*0-912330-33-3*, Inland Bk) Jargon Soc.
— Mountaineers Are Always Free! 100p. 1991. 9.50 (*0-917453-21-2*) Bamberger.
— Three Plays. LC 92-85260. 138p. 1993. pap. 12.00 (*0-933598-46-7*) NC Wesleyan Pr.
— Three Plays. limited ed. LC 92-85260. 138p. 1993. pap. 20.00 (*0-933598-47-5*) NC Wesleyan Pr.
— U. S. Dept. of the Interior. LC 80-66485. (Illus.). 88p. (Orig.). 1980. pap. 8.50 (*0-917788-23-0*) Gnomon Pr.
— Where Do You Put the Horse? Essays. LC 86-71074. 168p. 1986. 20.00 (*0-916583-16-3*) Dalkey Arch.
— Where Do You Put the Horse? Essays. limited ed. LC 86-71074. 165p. 1986. 40.00 (*0-916583-95-3*) Dalkey Arch.
— Will West. 2nd ed. 76p. 1973. reprint ed. pap. 10.00 (*0-912846-03-8*) Bookstore Pr.
Metcalf, Paul, ed. Enter Isabel: The Herman Melville Correspondence of Clare Spark & Paul Metcalf. LC 91-21889. 107p. 1991. 19.95 (*0-8263-1299-3*) U of NM Pr.
Metcalf, Paul, jt. auth. see Faxon, Susan.
Metcalf, Paul, jt. ed. see Newhall, Nancy.
Metcalf, Paul, et al. Three Times Three. LC 88-62647. 96p. (Orig.). 1989. pap. 10.00 (*0-933598-11-4*) NC Wesleyan Pr.
Metcalf, Pauline C. Ogden Codman & the Decoration of Houses. LC 88-71607. (Illus.). 224p. 1989. 40.00 (*0-87923-777-5*) Godine.
Metcalf, Peter. A Borneo Journey into Death: Berawan Eschatology from Its Rituals. LC 82-8460. (Symbol & Culture Ser.). 299p. reprint ed. pap. 85.30 (*0-8357-3322-X*, 2039546) Bks Demand.
— Where Are You - Spirits: Style & Theme in Berawan Prayer. LC 88-31119. 368p. 1989. 39.95 (*0-87474-620-5*) Smithsonian.
Metcalf, Peter & Huntington, Richard. Celebrations of Death: The Anthropology of Mortuary Ritual. 2nd ed. (Illus.). 304p. (C). 1991. 64.95 (*0-521-41312-5*); pap. 17.95 (*0-521-42375-9*) Cambridge U Pr.
Metcalf, Priscilla, jt. auth. see Harding, Vanessa.
Metcalf, Robert L. Destructive & Useful Insects: Their Habits & Control. 5th ed. LC 92-18374. 1992. text ed. 79.95 (*0-07-041692-3*) McGraw.
Metcalf, Robert L. & Luckmann, William H. Introduction to Insect Pest Management. 2nd ed. LC 82-4794. (Environmental Science & Technology: A Wiley-Interscience Series of Texts & Monographs). 577p. 1982. text ed. 59.95 (*0-471-08547-2*, Wiley-Interscience) Wiley.
Metcalf, Robert L. & Luckmann, William H., eds. Introduction to Insect Pest Management. 3rd ed. LC 93-44141. (Environmental Science & Technology Ser.). 1994. text ed. 69.95 (*0-471-58957-8*, Wiley-Interscience) Wiley.
Metcalf, Robert L. & Metcalf, Esther R. Plant Kairomones in Insect Control. (Current Topics in Entomology Ser.). (Illus.). 128p. 1991. 35.00 (*0-412-01991-4*, A3593, Chap & Hall NY) Chapman & Hall.
Metcalf, Robert L., jt. ed. see Pitts, James, Jr.
Metcalf, Rosamond S. The Sugar Maple. LC 82-595. (Illus.). 40p. (J). (gr. 3-5). 1982. pap. 3.50 (*0-914016-87-3*) Phoenix Pub.
Metcalf, Slade R. & Bierstedt, Robin. Rights & Liabilities of Publishers, Broadcasters & Reporters, 2 vols. LC 82-16839. (Individual Rights Ser.). 1549p. 1982. text ed. 195.00 (*0-07-041685-0*) Shepards-McGraw.
Metcalf, Thomas R. The Aftermath of Revolt India, 1857-1870. 352p. (C). 1990. reprint ed. 25.00 (*81-85054-99-1*) Riverdale Co.
— Ideologies of the Raj. (New Cambridge History of India: Vol. III.4). (Illus.). 224p. (C). 1995. 44.95 (*0-521-39547-X*) Cambridge U Pr.
— An Imperial Vision: Indian Architecture & Britain's Raj. (Philip E. Lilienthal Imprint Ser.: No. 2). (Illus.). 316p. 1988. 48.00 (*0-520-06235-3*) U CA Pr.
Metcalf, Thomas R., ed. Modern India: An Interpretive Anthology. rev. ed. 208p. 1991. pap. text ed. 18.95 (*81-207-1121-1*, Pub. by Sterling Pubs II) Apt Bks.
— Modern India: An Interpretive Anthology. 2nd rev. ed. 208p. 1991. text ed. 45.00 (*81-207-0900-4*, Pub. by Sterling Pubs II) Apt Bks.
Metcalf, V. M., jt. auth. see Evans, D. R.
Metcalf, William E. The Cistophori of Hadrian. (Numismatic Studies: NS-15). (Illus.). 195p. 1980. 65.00 (*0-89722-004-8*) Am Numismatic.
— Roman Medallions, No. 1: Handbook. 29p. 1979. 2.50 (*0-685-72034-9*); boxed, sl. 9.95 (*0-685-72035-7*) Am Numismatic.
Metcalf, William E., ed. America's Gold Coinage. (Illus.). 132p. 1990. 15.00 (*0-89722-238-5*) Am Numismatic.
— Mnemata: Papers in Memory of Nancy M. Waggoner. (Illus.). 115p. 1991. write for info. (*0-89722-243-1*) Am Numismatic.
Metcalf, William E., jt. ed. see Hahn, Wolfgang.
Metcalf, Woodbridge. Introduced Trees of Central California. (California Natural History Guides Ser.: No. 27). (Illus.). 1969. pap. 8.00 (*0-520-01548-7*) U CA Pr.
— Native Trees of the San Francisco Bay Region. (California Natural History Guides Ser.: No. 4). (Orig.). 1959. pap. 9.00 (*0-520-00853-7*) U CA Pr.
***Metcalf, Zubie.** Allied Health Professions Career Planning Guide. (Planning Guide Ser.). 160p. (Orig.). (YA). (gr. 10 up). 1995. pap. 14.95 (*0-941406-53-9*) Betz Pub Co Inc.
Metcalfe. Accountancy. 1987. pap. 29.95 (*0-442-31749-2*) Chapman & Hall.
Metcalfe, et al. Food Allergy: Adverse Reactions to Food & Food Additives. (Illus.). 417p. 1991. 95.00 (*0-86542-094-7*) Blackwell Sci.
***Metcalfe, A. V.** Statistics in Engineering: A Practical Approach. 1994. pap. 26.95 (*0-412-49220-2*, Blackie & Son-Chapman NY) Routledge Chapman & Hall.
Metcalfe, Allan A. & Von Schneidemesser, Luanne. An Index by Region, Usage, & Etymology to the Dictionary of American Regional English, Vols. I & II. (Publications of American Dialect Society: Vol. 77). 208p. (C). 1993. pap. 16.00 (*0-8173-0694-3*) U of Ala Pr.
Metcalfe, Brent L., pref. New Approaches to the Book of Mormon: Explorations in Critical Methodology. LC 92-16269. (Essays on Mormonism Ser.). (Illus.). 460p. 1993. 26.95 (*1-56085-017-5*) Signature Bks.
Metcalfe, C. R. Anatomy of the Dicotyledons, Vol. III: Magnoliales, Illiciales, & Laurales, Sensu Armen Takhtainan. 2nd ed. (Illus.). 240p. 1987. 85.00 (*0-19-854593-2*) OUP.
Metcalfe, C. R. & Chalk, L., eds. Anatomy of the Dicotyledons, Vol. I: Systematic Anatomy of the Leaf & Stem, with a Brief History of the Subject. 2nd ed. (Illus.). 304p. 1988. reprint ed. pap. 49.95 (*0-19-854253-4*) OUP.
— Anatomy of the Dicotyledons, Vol. II: Wood Structure & Conclusion of the General Introduction. 2nd ed. (Illus.). 324p. 1989. reprint ed. pap. 55.00 (*0-19-854594-0*) OUP.
Metcalfe, C. R., ed. see Tomlinson, P. B.
Metcalfe, Dean D., jt. ed. see Kaliner, Michael A.
Metcalfe, Ed & Prichard, F. Elizabeth. Atomic Absorption & Emission Spectroscopy. (Analytical Chemistry by Open Learning Ser.). 289p. 1987. pap. text ed. 49.95 (*0-471-91385-5*) Wiley.
Metcalfe, Fray & Long, Maria. The Art of Continental Knitting. (Illus.). 69p. (Orig.). 1986. pap. text ed. 9.95 (*0-318-22298-1*) Merriway Co.
Metcalfe, Henry C., jt. auth. see Tead, Ordway, Jr.
Metcalfe, J. C. Bible & Counseling. 1966. pap. 2.50 (*0-947788-31-X*) Chr Lit.
— Bible & the Human Mind. 1979. pap. 2.25 (*0-947788-26-3*) Chr Lit.
— Bible & the Spirit Filled Life. 1970. pap. 3.25 (*0-947788-05-0*) Chr Lit.
— Christian Paganism. 1964. pap. 2.25 (*0-947788-27-1*) Chr Lit.
— God the Spirit. 1972. pap. 0.95 (*0-947788-71-9*) Chr Lit.
— Great Enemy. 1970. pap. 2.95 (*0-947788-17-4*) Chr Lit.
— In the Mould of the Cross. 1982. pap. 4.95 (*0-947788-03-4*) Chr Lit.
Metcalfe, J. S., et al, eds. The Barriers to Growth in Small Firms. 256p. 1989. lib. bdg. 66.00 (*0-415-00093-9*, A2504) Routledge.
Metcalfe, James, et al. Burwell & Metcalfe's Heart Disease & Pregnancy: Physiology & Management. 2nd ed. 408p. 1986. 125.00 (*0-316-56797-3*) Little.
Metcalfe, James J. Poem Portraits. 270p. 1992. reprint ed. lib. bdg. 29.95x (*0-89966-893-3*) Buccaneer Bks.
Metcalfe, Janet & Shimamura, Arthur P. Metacognition: Knowing about Knowing. (Illus.). 220p. 1994. 35.00 (*0-262-13298-2*, Bradford Bks) MIT Pr.
Metcalfe, John. Smoking Leg, & Other Stories. LC 74-152950. (Short Story Index Reprint Ser.). 1977. reprint ed. 20.95 (*0-8369-3828-3*) Ayer.
Metcalfe, Kathy & Olson, Myrle. Marginal & Footnote Poetry. 1977. pap. 3.95 (*0-910286-56-6*) Boxwood.
Metcalfe, L. D., jt. ed. see Ackman, R. G.
Metcalfe, Les & Richards, Sue. Improving Public Management. 240p. (C). 1987. text ed. 45.00 (*0-8039-8103-1*) Sage.
***Metcalfe, Mike.** Forecasting Profit. LC 94-22587. 368p. (C). 1995. lib. bdg. 110.00 (*0-7923-9482-8*) Kluwer Ac.
Metcalfe, Philip. Nineteen Thirty-Three. LC 87-92040. 316p. 1988. 22.00 (*0-932966-87-X*) Permanent Pr.
Metcalfe, R., et al. Porewater & Groundwater Geochemistry at the Down Ampney Fault Research Site. (Nuclear Science & Technology Ser.). (Illus.). 62p. 1993. pap. 11.00 (*92-826-5241-6*, CD-NA-14335-EN-C, Pub. by Europ Com) UNIPUB.
Metcalfe, Sheldon. Building a Speech. 416p. (C). 1991. pap. text ed. 21.50 (*0-03-023423-9*) HB Coll Pubs.
— CD-ROM Building a Speech: An Interactive Approach. (C). 1994. cd-rom write for info. (*0-697-23210-7*) Brown & Benchmark.
— CD-ROM Building a Speech: An Interactive Approach. (C). 1995. cd-rom write for info. (*0-697-27020-3*) Brown & Benchmark.
Metcalfe, Terry. Union Pacific Freight Cars, 1936-1951. (Illus.). 200p. 1989. per. 24.95 (*0-9623347-0-7*) Metcalfe Pubns.
Metcalfe, William, et al, eds. Understanding Canada. 624p. 1982. 55.00x (*0-8147-5382-5*) NYU Pr.
***Metcalfe, William L.** Contra Costa County Under the Vitascope. Tatam, Robert D., ed. (Illus.). 120p. 1994. pap. 14.99 (*0-9637954-1-4*) Highlnd Pubs.
Metcalkf, Jill. Lila's Dance. 1993. mass mkt. 4.99 (*1-55773-951-X*) Diamond.
Metchette, Glenna W. Catt & Willett Families of Sussex, England & British Columbia, Canada, 1905-1993. (Illus.). 132p. 1994. reprint ed. lib. bdg. 31.00 (*0-8328-4082-3*); reprint ed. pap. 21.00 (*0-8328-4083-1*) Higginson Bk Co.
Metchnikoff, E. Scientifically Soured Milk: Its Influence in Arresting Intestinal Putrefaction. 1991. lib. bdg. 69.00 (*0-8490-4298-4*) Gordon Pr.

An Asterisk (*) at the beginning of an entry indicates that the title is appearing in BIP for the first time.

Metchnikoff, Elie. The Nature of Man: Studies in Optimistic Philosophy. Kastenbaum, Robert, ed. Mitchell, P. Chalmers, tr. LC 76-19582. (Death & Dying Ser.). (Illus.). 1977. reprint ed. lib. bdg. 31.95 (0-405-09578-3) Ayer.
— The Prolongation of Life: Optimistic Studies. Kastenbaum, Robert, ed. Mitchell, P. Chalmers, tr. LC 76-19583. (Death & Dying Ser.). (Illus.). 1977. reprint ed. lib. bdg. 34.95 (0-405-09579-1) Ayer.
— Scientifically Soured Milk: Its Influence in Arresting Intestinal Putrefaction. 11p. 1969. reprint ed. spiral bd. 2.75 (0-7873-0610-X) Mokelumne.
Metchnikoff, Olga. Life of Elie Metchnikoff. LC 72-7248. (Select Bibliographies Reprint Ser.). 1977. reprint ed. 24.95 (0-8369-6949-9) Ayer.
Meteer, Marie W. Expressibility & the Problem of Efficient Text Planning. LC 92-21879. 1992. 65.00 (1-85567-022-4, Pub. by Pinter Pubs UK) St Martin.
***Meter, Leo.** Letters to Barbara. Agee, Joel, tr. (Illus.). 62p. 1995. 15.95 (0-87951-589-9) Overlook Pr.
Metes, George S., jt. auth. see Grenier, Raymond H.
Metes, Rozeta J., tr. see Focas, Spiridon G.
Metev, Simeon M. & Veiko, Vadim P. Laser-Assisted Microtechnology. LC 94-25834. (Series in Materials Science: Vol. 19). 1995. 69.00 (0-387-53925-5) Spr-Verlag.
Meteyard, Eliza. The Wedgwood Handbook. 1972. 250.00 (0-8490-1281-3) Gordon Pr.
Metford, Beatrix. Where China Meets Burma: Life & Travel in the Burma-China Border Lands. LC 77-87047. reprint ed. 23.50 (0-404-16844-2) AMS Pr.
Metford, J. C. The Christian Year. 144p. 1991. 16.95 (0-8245-1084-4) Crossroad NY.
— Dictionary of Christian Lore & Legend. LC 82-50815. (Illus.). 272p. 1991. pap. 14.95 (0-500-27373-1) Thames Hudson.
***Meth, Clifford.** Crib Death & Other Bedtime Stories. (Illus.). 70p. (Orig.). 1995. pap. write for info. (1-885591-76-4) Morris Pubng.
Meth, Richard L., et al. Men in Therapy: The Challenge of Change. (Guilford Family Therapy Ser.). 298p. 1991. reprint ed. lib. bdg. 35.00 (0-89862-104-6); reprint ed. pap. text ed. 18.95 (0-89862-485-1) Guilford Pr.
Metha, R. S. Autobiography of a Cheque. 136p. 1984. text ed. 15.00 (0-86590-274-7, Pub. by Sterling Pubs II) Apt Bks.
Metha, Rustum J. Masterpieces of Indo-Islamic Architecture. (Illus.). viii, 52p. 1981. text ed. 30.00 (0-86590-062-0, Pub. by Taraporevala II) Apt Bks.
Metham, John. The Works of John Metham. Craig, H., ed. (EETS, OS Ser.: No. 132). 1974. 44.00 (0-527-00129-5) Periodicals Srv.
Methe, David T. Technological Competition in Global Industries: Marketing & Planning Strategies for American Industry. LC 90-8908. 248p. 1990. text ed. 55.00 (0-89930-480-X, MTG/, Quorum Bks) Greenwood.
Metheny, Dorothy M. Hardy Heather Species. (Illus.). 186p. 1991. 39.95 (0-939116-31-6); pap. 24.95 (0-939116-29-4) Frontier OR.
Metheny, Jeffry A. The Athletic Hunter: Sports Medicine for Outdoorsman. (Illus.). 128p. (Orig.). 1992. pap. text ed. 12.95 (0-9634193-0-7) Double Guage.
Metheny, Norma M. Fluid & Electrolyte Balance: Nursing Considerations. 2nd ed. (Illus.). 416p. 1991. pap. 24.95 (0-397-54891-5) Lippincott.
Metherell, Victoria, jt. auth. see Chirouze, Yves.
Methlagl, jt. auth. see Konig, Christoph.
Methlie, L. B. & Sprague, Ralph H., Jr., eds. Knowledge Representation for Decision Support Systems: Proceedings of the IFIP WG 8.3 Working Conference, Durham, U. K., July 24-26, 1984. 268p. 1985. 59.00 (0-444-87739-8, North Holland) Elsevier.
Methlie, Leif B., jt. auth. see Klein, Michel.
Methodist Hospital Staff. Basic ECG Interpretation, Level 1. 256p. 1986. pap. 25.95 (0-8016-3401-6) Mosby Yr Bk.
Methodology Committee American Classical League Staff, ed. Expertis Credite. 18p. 1991. 2.00 (0-939507-29-3, B19) Amer Classical.
Methods & Solutions Staff. Calendars Unlimited. 1988. 49.95 (0-87280-544-1, 574, Asher-Gallant) Caddylak Systs.
— LetterLibrary. 1988. 79.00 (0-87280-543-3, 573, Asher-Gallant) Caddylak Systs.
Methold, Keith, et al. Puzzles for English Practice: PEP 1, 2 & 3, PEP 1. (English As a Second Lanugage Bk.). 1978. pap. text ed. 3.50 (0-582-55260-5) Longman.
— Puzzles for English Practice: PEP 1, 2 & 3, PEP 2. (English As a Second Lanugage Bk.). 1978. pap. text ed. 3.50 (0-582-55258-3) Longman.
— Puzzles for English Practice: PEP 1, 2 & 3, PEP 3. (English As a Second Lanugage Bk.). 1978. pap. text ed. 3.50 (0-582-55259-1) Longman.
— Understanding Technical English, 3 bks., Bk. 1. (English As a Second Language Bk.). (Illus.). 60p. 1975. pap. text ed. 4.95 (0-582-69032-3) Longman.
— Understanding Technical English, 3 bks., Bk. 2. (English As a Second Language Bk.). (Illus.). 60p. 1975. pap. text ed. 4.95 (0-582-69035-8) Longman.
— Understanding Technical English, 3 bks., Bk. 3. (English As a Second Language Bk.). (Illus.). 60p. 1980. pap. text ed. 4.95 (0-582-69036-6) Longman.
Methorst-Kuiper, A. J. Krishnamurti: A Biography. 1974. lib. bdg. 250.00 (0-87968-545-X) Krishna Pr.
Methot, June. Up & down the Beach. (Illus.). 208p. 1988. write for info. (0-318-64042-2) Whip Pubs.
Methuen, Phillip. Haynes Volvo 260 Series Owners Workshop Manual, No. 400: 1975-1982. 16.95 (1-85010-287-2) Haynes Pubns.
Methven, Andrew S. The Genus Clavariadelphus in North America. (Bibliotheca Mycologica Ser.: Vol. 138). 192p. 1990. pap. text ed. 62.50 (3-443-59039-X, Pub. by Cramer-Borntraeger GW) Lubrecht & Cramer.
Methven, Barbara. Basic Microwaving. rev. ed. LC 87-20082. (Microwave Cooking Library). (Illus.). 160p. 1988. 16.95 (0-86573-554-9) Cy De Cosse.
— Cool Quick Summer Microwaving. LC 89-28535. (Microwave Cooking Library). 160p. 1990. 16.95 (0-86573-568-9) Cy De Cosse.
— Fresh Food Favorites. LC 92-43040. (Microwave Cooking Library). 160p. 1993. 16.95 (0-86573-538-7) Cy De Cosse.
— Ground Beef Microwave Meals. LC 90-32951. (Microwave Cooking Library). 160p. 1990. 16.95 (0-86573-569-7) Cy De Cosse.
— Low-Fat Microwave Meals. LC 89-11962. (Microwave Cooking Library). 160p. 1989. 16.95 (0-86573-567-0) Cy De Cosse.
— Microwave Speed Meals. LC 90-46447. (Microwave Cooking Library). 160p. 1991. 16.95 (0-86573-570-0) Cy De Cosse.
— Microwaving Light & Healthy. rev. ed. LC 88-33484. (Microwave Cooking Library). 160p. 1989. 16.95 (0-86573-564-6) Cy De Cosse.
— Microwaving on a Diet. rev. ed. LC 88-38466. (Microwave Cooking Library). 160p. 1989. 16.95 (0-86573-562-X) Cy De Cosse.
— More Microwaving Secrets. LC 87-15450. (Microwave Cooking Library). (Illus.). 160p. 1987. 16.95 (0-86573-552-2) Cy De Cosse.
— One Hundred Ideas for Today's Chicken. LC 92-11260. (Microwave Cooking Library). 160p. 1992. 16.95 (0-86573-574-3) Cy De Cosse.
Methven, Barbara, ed. see Papy, Frank.
Meti, T. K. Agricultural Growth & Non-Agricultural Growth: Dynamics of National Development. 170p. 1989. write for info. (81-212-0272-8, Pub. by Gian Publng Hse II) S Asia.
Metil, Luana & Townsend, Jace. The Story of Karate: From Buddhism to Bruce Lee. LC 93-32006. (Sports Legacy Ser.). (Illus.). 112p. (YA). (gr. 5 up). 1995. lib. bdg. 22.95 (0-8225-3325-1, Lerner Publctns) Lerner Group.
***Metivie, Michel.** Semimartingales: A Course on Stochastic Processes. (Studies in Mathematics). 287p. 1982. 67.95 (0-89925-650-3) De Gruyter.
Metivier, Don. Metivier On: Saratoga, Glens Falls, Lake George, & the Adirondacks. LC 92-82550. (Illus.). 230p. 1992. 19.95 (0-915611-60-0) Sagamore Pub.
Metivier, Michel. Semimartingales: A Course on Stochastic Processes. (Studies in Mathematics). 287p. 1982. 67.95 (3-11-008674-3) De Gruyter.
Metivier, Michel & Pardoux, E., eds. Stochastic Differential Systems. (Lecture Notes in Control & Information Sciences Ser.: Vol. 69). ix, 310p. 1985. pap. 43.00 (0-387-15176-1) Spr-Verlag.
Metivier, Michel & Pellaumail, J. Stochastic Integration. LC 79-23096. (Probability & Mathematical Statistics Ser.). 1980. text ed. 69.00 (0-12-491450-0) Acad Pr.
Metivier, Michel & Watanabe, S., eds. Stochastic Analysis. (Lecture Notes in Mathematics Ser.: Vol. 1322). 197p. 1988. pap. 30.00 (0-387-19352-9) Spr-Verlag.
Metken, Gunter, text. Gauguin in Tahiti: The First Journey. (Schirmer's Visual Library). (Illus.). 104p. 1993. pap. 10.95 (0-393-30895-2) Norton.
Metland, Daphne. Getting It Right: Blender & Mixer Recipes. 1994. pap. 9.95 (0-572-01926-2, Pub. by W Foulsham UK) Trans-Atl Phila.
— Getting It Right: Food Processor Recipes. 1994. pap. 9.95 (0-572-01927-0, Pub. by W Foulsham UK) Trans-Atl Phila.
— New Recipes for Your Food Processor. 120p. 1992. 14.95 (0-572-01614-X, Pub. by W Foulsham UK) Trans-Atl Phila.
***Metler.** Medical Examination Review: Surgery (MEPC) 11th ed. (C). 1995. pap. text ed. 16.95 (0-8385-6195-0) Appleton & Lange.
Metlina, L. S. Mathematics in Preschool: An Aid for the Preschool Educator. Rachlin, Sidney L. & Rottenbucher, Terri, eds. Teller, Joan, tr. LC 91-17814. (Soviet Studies in Mathematics Education). (Illus.). 371p. (Orig.). 1991. pap. 25.00 (0-87353-333-X) NCTM.
Metlitskii, L. V., et al, eds. Controlled Atmosphere Storage of Fruits. Dhote, A. K., tr. 209p. (C). 1983. text ed. 46.00 (90-6191-413-2, Pub. by A A Balkema NE) Ashgate Pub Co.
Metlitzki, Dorothee. The Matter of Araby in Medieval England. LC 76-23678. 1977. 42.00 (0-300-02003-1) Yale U Pr.
Metlzer, Hagen. Structure of Indecomposable Modules. 96p. (C). 1986. 40.00 (0-685-46647-7, Pub. by Collets) St Mut.
Metochites, Theodorus. Miscellanea Philosophica et Historia Graece. Muller, C., ed. 854p. reprint ed. lib. bdg. 95.00 (0-685-13372-9, Pub. by A M Hakkert SP) Coronet Bks.
Metos, Thomas H. The Human Mind: How We Think & Learn. (Venture Bks.). (Illus.). 128p. (YA). (gr. 9-12). 1990. lib. bdg. 14.28 (0-531-10885-6) Watts.
Metos, Thomas H., jt. auth. see Belok, Michael V.
Metoyer, Patrick G. I'm Rattle-Me-Bones III, Esquire. LC 87-90349. (Illus.). 24p. (Orig.). (J). (gr. 1-6). 1988. pap. 3.95 (0-944523-02-1) Western Slope Pubns.
— No Bones! No Bones! LC 87-90350. (Illus.). 24p. (Orig.). (J). (gr. k-2). 1988. pap. 3.95 (0-944523-03-X) Western Slope Pubns.
Metra Consulting Staff. ASIAN: Business Opportunities Series. 300p. 1984. 334.00 (0-86033-248-9) G & T Inc.
— Nigeria. (Business Opportunity Reports Ser.). 300p. 1984. 378.00 (0-686-64703-3) G & T Inc.
Metrano, Art & Goldsmith, Lee. Twice Blessed: Art Metrano Laughs the Darkness Away. (Illus.). 148p. 1994. 19.95 (1-56796-060-X) WRS Group.
Metras, Gary. Destiny's Calendar. rev. ed. 75p. 1988. reprint ed. pap. 7.00 (0-938566-39-3) Adastra Pr.
— The Night Watches. 48p. 1981. 10.00 (0-938566-07-5); pap. 6.00 (0-938566-06-7) Adastra Pr.
— The Night Watches. deluxe limited ed. 48p. 1981. 25.00 (0-938566-08-3) Adastra Pr.
— Northampton Poem. 28p. 1990. pap. 10.00 (0-938566-45-8) Adastra Pr.
Metras, Gary, ed. The Adastra Reader: The Collected Chapbooks. LC 87-70119. (Illus.). 248p. (Orig.). 1987. pap. 10.00 (0-938566-32-6) Adastra Pr.
Metraux, Alexandre, tr. see Merleau-Ponty, Maurice.
Metraux, Alfred. The Ethnology of Easter Island. rev. ed. (Bulletin Ser.: No. 160). (Illus.). 432p. 1971. reprint ed. pap. 29.50 (0-910240-12-4) Bishop Mus.
— Myths of the Toba & Pilaga Indians of the Gran Chaco. LC 46-4565. (American Folklore Society Memoirs Ser.). 1974. reprint ed. 25.00 (0-527-01092-8) Periodicals Srv.
— Voodoo in Haiti. 1989. pap. 11.96 (0-8052-0894-1) Schocken.
***Metraux, Alfred, ed.** Native Tribes of Eastern Bolivia & Western Matto Grosso. (Bureau of American Ethnology Bulletins Ser.). 182p. 1995. lib. bdg. 79.00 (0-7812-4134-0) Rprt Serv.
Metraux, Daniel. The Japanese Economy & the American Businessman. LC 89-9404. (Studies in Business: Vol. 5). 250p. 1989. lib. bdg. 89.95 (0-88946-158-9) E Mellen.
— Taiwan's Political & Economic Growth in the Late Twentieth Century. LC 91-37670. 172p. 1991. lib. bdg. 79.95 (0-7734-9636-X) E Mellen.
Metraux, Daniel A. The History As Theology of Soka Gakkai: A Japanese New Religion. LC 88-1613. (Studies in Asian Thought & Religion: Vol. 9). 200p. 1988. lib. bdg. 89.95 (0-88946-055-8) E Mellen.
***Metraux, Guy P.** Sculptors & Physicians in Fifth-Century Greece: A Preliminary Study. (Illus.). 176p. 1995. 39.95 (0-7735-1231-4) U of Toronto Pr.
Metraux, Ruth W., jt. auth. see Ames, Louise B.
Metreaux, Rhoda, jt. auth. see Abel, Theodora M.
***Metress, Christopher, ed.** The Critical Response to Dashiell Hammett. LC 94-28713. (Critical Responses in Arts & Letters Ser.: No. 15). 304p. 1994. text ed. 59.95 (0-313-28938-7) Greenwood.
Metress, Eileen K., jt. auth. see Fulton, Gere B.
Metress, James F., jt. ed. see Brace, C. Loring.
Metress, Seamus P., jt. auth. see Kart, Cary S.
Metric System Committe of the American Congress on Surveying & Mapping. Metric Practice Guide for Surveying & Mapping. reprint ed. 4.90 (0-317-60440-6, G400) Am Congrs Survey.
Metrick, Sydney. Crossing the Bridge. 144p. (Orig.). 1994. pap. 11.95 (0-89087-738-6) Celestial Arts.
Metrick, Sydney B. I Do: A Guide to Creating Your Own Wedding Ceremony. 160p. 1992. pap. 11.95 (0-89087-679-7) Celestial Arts.
Metro, Andre. Dictionnaire Forestier Multilingue. 434p. (FRE.). 1976. 125.00 (0-8288-5651-6, M6409) Fr & Eur.
Metro Deaf Senior Citizens, Inc. Staff. Health Care Delivery to Hearing Impaired Patients: An Instructional Guide for Hospitals on Developing Policies & Procedures. Thomas, Margaret R. & Ancheta, Jocelyn, eds. 112p. 1984. 70.00 (0-9613623-0-8) Metro Deaf Senior.
Metro Deaf Senior Citizens, Inc. Staff, et al. Hearcare: An Instructional Guide for Long Term Care Facilities on Developing Policies & Procedures. 112p. 1985. 47.50 (0-9613623-1-6) Metro Deaf Senior.
Metro Files, Inc. Staff, ed. Cityfile: Atlanta. (City at Your Fingertips! Ser.). 475p. 1988. 35.00 (0-942619-11-0) Metro Files.
— Cityfile: Baltimore. (City at Your Fingertips! Ser.). 475p. 1988. 35.00 (0-942619-25-0) Metro Files.
— Cityfile: Boston - the City at Your Fingertips! 475p. Directory. 35.00 (0-942619-03-X) Metro Files.
— Cityfile: Chicago. (City at Your Fingertips! Ser.). 475p. 1988. 35.00 (0-942619-04-8) Metro Files.
— Cityfile: Cleveland. (City at Your Fingertips! Ser.). 475p. 1988. 35.00 (0-942619-12-9) Metro Files.
— Cityfile: Dallas. (City at Your Fingertips! Ser.). 475p. 1988. 35.00 (0-942619-08-0) Metro Files.
— Cityfile: Denver. 475p. 1988. 35.00 (0-942619-45-5) Metro Files.
— Cityfile: Houston. (City at Your Fingertips! Ser.). 475p. 1988. 35.00 (0-942619-07-2) Metro Files.
— Cityfile: Kansas City. 475p. 1988. 35.00 (0-942619-46-3) Metro Files.
— Cityfile: Los Angeles - the City at Your Fingertips! 475p. Directory. 35.00 (0-942619-02-1) Metro Files.
— Cityfile: Miami. (City at Your Fingertips! Ser.). 475p. 1988. 35.00 (0-942619-09-9) Metro Files.
— Cityfile: Minneapolis. (City at Your Fingertips! Ser.). 475p. 1988. 35.00 (0-942619-26-9) Metro Files.
— Cityfile: New York - the City at Your Fingertips! 475p. Directory. 35.00 (0-942619-00-5) Metro Files.
— Cityfile: Orange County, CA. 475p. 1988. 35.00 (0-942619-44-7) Metro Files.
— Cityfile: Peninsula. (City at Your Fingertips! Ser.). 475p. 1988. 35.00 (0-942619-29-3) Metro Files.
— Cityfile: Philadelphia. (City at Your Fingertips! Ser.). 475p. 1988. 35.00 (0-942619-06-4) Metro Files.
— Cityfile: Phoenix. 475p. 1988. 35.00 (0-942619-43-9) Metro Files.
— Cityfile: Pittsburgh. (City at Your Fingertips! Ser.). 475p. 1988. 35.00 (0-942619-27-7) Metro Files.
— Cityfile: San Diego. (City at Your Fingertips! Ser.). 475p. 1988. 35.00 (0-942619-10-2) Metro Files.
— Cityfile: San Francisco. (City at Your Fingertips! Ser.). 475p. 1988. 35.00 (0-942619-05-6) Metro Files.
— Cityfile: Seattle. (City at Your Fingertips! Ser.). 475p. 1988. 35.00 (0-942619-28-5) Metro Files.
— Cityfile: St. Louis. (City at Your Fingertips! Ser.). 475p. 1988. 35.00 (0-942619-13-7) Metro Files.
— Cityfile: Washington, D.C. - the City at Your Fingertips! 475p. Directory. 35.00 (0-942619-01-3) Metro Files.
— Food File: New York - the City's Finest Food Sources at Your Fingertips! 475p. 35.00 (0-942619-14-5) Metro Files.
Metro Resource Publications Staff. Do It Yourself Job Search Manual. (Keep it Simple Ser.). (Illus.). 176p. (Orig.). pap. 11.95 (0-945376-00-6) Metro Resrc Pubns.
— The Flawless Resume Kit. (Keep it Simple Ser.). (Illus.). 67p. (Orig.). 1989. pap. 8.95 (0-945376-01-4) Metro Resrc Pubns.
— The Job Search Competency Review & Exam. (Illus.). 85p. (Orig.). Date not set. pap. 10.00 (0-945376-98-7) Metro Resrc Pubns.
— Retraining: Twenty-First Century Key to Success. (Keep it Simple Ser.). (Illus.). 132p. (Orig.). Date not set. pap. 14.95 (0-945376-99-5) Metro Resrc Pubns.
Metro Staff. Democracy in Europe: The Evolving Role of Parliaments. Flinterman, Cees et al, eds. 111p. 1994. pap. 37.00 (90-6215-403-4, Pub. by Maklu Uitgevers BE) W W Gaunt.
Metropolis, N., jt. auth. see Louck, J. D.
Metropolis, N., ed. see Oppenheimer, J. Robert.
Metropolis, N. C., ed. see Applied Mathematics Symposium Staff.
Metropolis, Nicholas, ed. New Directions in Physics: The Los Alamos 40th Anniversary Volume. 292p. 1987. text ed. 72.00 (0-12-492155-8) Acad Pr.
Metropolis, Nicholas & Rota, Gian-Carlo, eds. A New Era in Computation. LC 93-8200. (Daedalus Special Issue Ser.). 262p. 1993. 13.95 (0-262-63154-7) MIT Pr.
Metropolis, Nicholas, jt. auth. see Hall, J.
Metropolis, Nicholas, et al, eds. A History of Computing in the Twentieth Century. LC 79-51683. 1980. text ed. 85.00 (0-12-491650-3) Acad Pr.
Metropolitan Anthony Khrapovitsky. The Christian Faith & War. (Orig.). 1973. pap. 0.50 (0-317-30278-7) Holy Trinity.
Metropolitan Court Judges Committee. Deprived Children: A Judicial Response: Seventy-Three Recommendations. 48p. 1986. 4.50 (0-318-23300-2) Natl Juv & Family Ct Judges.
Metropolitan Cyprian of Oropos & Fili. The Monastic Life: A Most Beneficial Dialogue Between an Orthodox Monk & a Contemporary Theologian. Hieromonk Auxentios, tr. 52p. (Orig.). 1988. pap. text ed. 5.00 (0-911165-11-8) Ctr Trad Orthodox.
***Metropolitan Cyprian Staff.** Do You Have a Ticket? Barker, Patrick G., tr. 56p. (Orig.). 1994. pap. text ed. 5.00 (0-911165-23-1) Ctr Trad Orthodox.
Metropolitan Dade County, Historic Preservation Division, OCED Staff & Chase, Charles E. Resourceful Rehab: A Guide for Historic Buildings in Dade County, Florida. (Illus.). (Orig.). 1987. pap. 9.95 (0-9618373-0-6) MDC-Hist Preserv Div.
Metropolitan Innocent of Moscow Staff. Indication of the Way into the Kingdom of Heaven. 48p. (Orig.). 1981. pap. 2.00 (0-317-30275-2) Holy Trinity.
Metropolitan Life Foundation Staff, jt. auth. see American Assoc. of School Administrators Staff.
Metropolitan Museum of Art. What Makes a Cassatt a Cassatt? (Illus.). 48p. (J). (gr. 5 up). 1994. 11.99 (0-670-85742-4) Viking Child Bks.
— What Makes a Goya a Goya? (Illus.). 48p. (J). (gr. 5 up). 1994. 11.99 (0-670-85743-2) Viking Child Bks.
— What Makes a Leonardo a Leonardo? (Illus.). 48p. (J). (gr. 5 up). 1994. 11.99 (0-670-85744-0) Viking Child Bks.
— What Makes a Picasso a Picasso? (Illus.). 48p. (J). (gr. 5 up). 1994. 11.99 (0-670-85741-6) Viking Child Bks.
***Metropolitan Museum of Art Staff.** Angels: A Book of Ornaments; Five Ornaments to Press Out. 1994. 9.95 (0-8118-0813-0) Chronicle Bks.
— Baby's First Year Calendar. (Illus.). 24p. (J). 1984. pap. 9.95 (0-684-18258-0, C Scribner Sons Young) S&S Childrens.
— The Bulletin of the Metropolitan Museum of Art, New York: Old Series, Nov. 1905-June 1942. 1968. 7.78 (0-405-02357-X, 16013) Ayer.
— The Bulletin of the Museum of Modern Art. 1967. 15.95 (0-405-18720-3, 15626) Ayer.
— Cat Alphabet Vol. 1. (Illus.). 60p. 1994. 8.95 (0-8212-2129-9) Bulfinch Pr.
— The Christmas Story: Told Through Paintings. (Illus.). 40p. 1990. 16.95 (0-15-200426-2) HarBrace.
— Computers & Their Potential Applications in Museums: A Conference. 23.95 (0-405-00014-6, 11652) Ayer.
— Fun with Hieroglyphs Stationary. 1991. 12.95 (0-670-84207-9) Viking Child Bks.
— Go in & out the Window: An Illustrated Songbook for Children. LC 87-752208. (Illus.). 144p. (J). (gr. k up). 1987. 24.95 (0-8050-0628-1, Bks Young Read) H Holt & Co.
— Jack & Belle Linsky Collection in the Metropolitan Museum of Art. 1994. 19.95 (0-8109-6463-5) Abrams.
— Liechtenstein: The Princely Collections. 1994. pap. 14.95 (0-8109-6481-3) Abrams.
— Life in America: A Special Loan Exhibition of Paintings Held During the Period of the New York World's Fair, April 24 to October 29. 1974. 18.95 (0-405-02261-1, 16138) Ayer.
— Metropolitan Museum Journal, Vols. 1-29. Burn, Barbara, ed. (Illus.). 60.00 (0-226-52125-7, Univ of Chicago Schl of) Metro Mus Art.
— Monet Postcard Book, Vol. 1. (Illus.). 124p. 1994. 17.95 (0-8212-2089-6); pap. 8.95 (0-8212-2088-8) Bulfinch Pr.

An Asterisk (*) at the beginning of an entry indicates that the title is appearing in BIP for the first time.

— Monet's Years at Giverny: Beyond Impressionism. LC 95-1153. 1995. write for info. (*0-8109-8138-6*, Abradale Pr) Abrams.

— The Music-Lovers's Birthday Book. (Illus.). 128p. 1987. boxed 14.95 (*0-317-61333-2*) Abrams.

— Perennial Pleasures. 1993. 10.00 (*0-517-59495-1*, Crown) Crown Pub Group.

— Publications of the Metropolitan Museum of Art on Microfiche, 1870 to the Present. (Monograph Ser.). 1800p. 1990. lib. bdg. 4,950.00 (*0-8161-1747-0*) G K Hall.

— Publications of the Metropolitan Museum of Art, 1965-1995: A Bibliography. LC 95-7065. 1995. write for info. (*0-87099-746-7*) Metro Mus Art.

— Quintessential Pleasures. 1993. 10.00 (*0-517-59428-5*, Crown) Crown Pub Group.

— Saints: A Book of Days. (Illus.). 120p. 1995. 14.95 (*0-8212-2173-6*) Bulfinch Pr.

— Time Line of Culture in the Nile Valley & Its Relationship to Other World Cultures. 1994. 10.95 (*0-8109-6474-0*) Abrams.

Metropolitan Museum of Art Staff, ed. Catalog of the Robert Goldwater Library of Primitive Art, 4 vols., Set. 1982. lib. bdg. 455.00 (*0-8161-0381-X*, Hall Library) G K Hall.

— Library Catalog of the Metropolitan Museum of Art, 48 vols., Set. 2nd enl. rev. ed. 1980. lib. bdg. 5,320.00 (*0-8161-0295-3*, Hall Library) G K Hall.

— Library Catalog of the Metropolitan Museum of Art, New York, 25 vols. suppl. ed. 1973. First Suppl. 1962. lib. bdg. 130.00 (*0-8161-0579-0*, Hall Library); Second Suppl. 1965. lib. bdg. 130.00 (*0-8161-0670-3*, Hall Library); Third Suppl. 1968. lib. bdg. 130.00 (*0-8161-0748-3*, Hall Library); Fourth Suppl. 1970. lib. bdg. 130.00 (*0-8161-0846-3*, Hall Library); Fifth Suppl. lib. bdg. 130.00 (*0-8161-0936-2*, Hall Library) G K Hall.

— Library Catalog of the Metropolitan Museum of Art, New York, 25 vols., Set. 1973. lib. bdg. 2,255.00 (*0-8161-0496-4*, Hall Library) G K Hall.

— Library Catalog of The Metropolitan Museum of Art (New York), Suppl. 6. 1977. lib. bdg. 130.00 (*0-8161-1126-X*) G K Hall.

— Library Catalog of The Metropolitan Museum of Art (New York), Suppl. 6. suppl. ed. 1977. lib. bdg. 240.00 (*0-8161-0028-4*) G K Hall.

Metropolitan Museum of Art Staff & Priest, Alan. Chinese Sculpture in the Metropolitan Museum of Art. 1974. 40. 95 (*0-405-02264-6*, 16141) Ayer.

Metropolitan Museum of Art Staff, jt. auth. see Kanter, Laurence B.

Metropolitan Museum Staff & Smith, Dian G. My New Baby & Me: A First Year Record Book for Big Brothers & Sisters. (Illus.). 48p. (Orig.). (J). 1987. pap. 10.95 (*0-684-18712-4*, C Scribner Sons Young) S&S Childrens.

Metropolitan of Moscow, Philaret Staff. Christ is Risen: The Paschal Sermons of Metropolitan Philaret of Moscow. 1991. pap. 5.95 (*0-89981-118-3*) Eastern Orthodox.

Metropolitan Opera Staff. The Metropolitan Opera Book of Days. (Illus.). 112p. 1994. 19.95 (*1-55550-899-5*) Universe.

Metropolitan Philaret of Moscow Staff. Catechism of the Orthodox Church. 1901. pap. 2.95 (*0-89981-009-8*) Eastern Orthodox.

— Comparison of the Differences in the Doctrines of Faith Between the Eastern & Western Churches. Pinkerton, Robert, tr. 1974. reprint ed. pap. 1.25 (*0-89981-011-X*) Eastern Orthodox.

Metropolitan Staff, ed. see Saliba, Philip & Allen, Joseph J.

Metropolitan Staff, ed. see Yavorsky, Stefan.

Metrowerks, Inc. Staff. Metrowerks Modula-2 Start Pak. (C). 1990. pap. write for info. (*0-02-380810-1*) Macmillan.

Mets, Lisa A., jt. ed. see Peterson, Marvin W.

Metsch, K. Linear Spaces with Few Lines. Dold, A. et al, eds. (Lecture Notes in Mathematics Ser.: Vol. 1490). xiii, 196p. 1991. pap. 32.00 (*0-387-54720-7*) Spr-Verlag.

Metschl, John, ed. see Milwaukee Public Museum.

Mett, Percy. Introduction to Computing. (Illus.). 408p. (Orig.). (C). 1990. pap. text ed. 35.00 (*0-333-39336-8*, Pub. by Macmill Press UK) Scholium Intl.

Mett, Percy, et al. The Specification & Design of Concurrent Systems. LC 93-44210. (McGraw-Hill International Series in Software Engineering). 1994. write for info. (*0-07-707966-3*) McGraw.

Metta, Vito, jt. auth. see Cotton, Delores.

Mettam, Roger. Power & Faction in Louis XIV's France. 280p. 1987. text ed. 59.95 (*0-631-15667-4*) Blackwell Pubs.

Mette, Hans J. Urkunden Dramatischer Auffuehrungen in Griechenland. (Texte und Kommentare Ser.: Vol. 8). (C). 1977. 134.60 (*3-11-006782-X*) De Gruyter.

Mette, Norbert, jt. ed. see Greinacher, Norbert.

Metteer, Michael, tr. see Girard, Rene.

Metteer, Michael, tr. see Kittler, Friedrich A.

Metter, E. Jeffrey, ed. Speech Disorders: Clinical Evaluation & Diagnosis. LC 84-23794. (Neurologic Illness: Diagnosis & Treatment Ser.). 256p. 1985. text ed. 40.00 (*0-89335-223-3*); audio 12.95 (*0-685-10331-5*) PMA Pub Corp.

— Speech Disorders: Clinical Evaluation & Diagnosis, Set. LC 84-23794. (Neurologic Illness: Diagnosis & Treatment Ser.). 256p. 1985. 49.95 (*0-685-10332-3*) PMA Pub Corp.

***Metter, Ellen.** Writer's Ultimate Research Guide. 352p. 1995. 19.99 (*0-89879-668-7*) Writers Digest.

***Metter, Israel.** The Fifth Corner of the Room. Date not set. pap. 11.00 (*0-00-271214-8*, Pub. by HarpC UK) HarpC.

Metternich, Clemens V. Memoirs of Prince Metternich, 1773-1835, 5 Vols, Set. LC 68-9611. 1970. reprint ed. 225.00 (*0-86527-128-3*) Fertig.

Mettes, L. & Zuman, P. Handbook Series in Organic Electrochemistry, 3 vols., Set. LC 77-24273. 878.00 (*0-8493-7220-8*, CRC Reprint) Franklin.

Mettger, Zak. Reconstruction: America after the Civil War. (Illus.). 96p. (J). 1994. 16.99 (*0-525-67490-X*, Lodestar Bks) Dutton Child Bks.

— Till Victory Is Won: Black Soldiers in the Civil War. (Illus.). 96p. (J). (gr. 5-9). 1994. 16.99 (*0-525-67412-8*, Lodestar Bks) Dutton Child Bks.

Mettger, Zak, jt. auth. see Vlanton, Elias.

Metting, F. Blaine, ed. Soil Microbial Ecology: Applications in Agricultural & Environmental Management. LC 92-26049. (Books in Soils, Plants & the Environment: Vol. 25). 165p. 1992. 165.00 (*0-8247-8737-4*) Dekker.

Mettinger, Arthur. Aspects of Semantic Opposition in English. (Studies in Lexicography & Lexicology). 216p. 1994. 39.95 (*0-19-824269-7*) OUP.

Mettinger, Tryggve. The Dethronement of Sabaoth: Studies in the Shen & Kabod Theologies. (Coniectanea Biblica. Old Testament Ser.: No. 18). 158p. (Orig.). 1982. pap. 41.00x (*0-317-65792-5*) Coronet Bks.

— King & Messiah: The Civil & Sacred Legitimation of the Israelite Kings. (Coniectanea Biblica. Old Testament Ser.: No. 8). 342p. (Orig.). 1976. pap. 58.00x (*91-40-04349-5*, Pub. by Liber Gleerup SW) Coronet Bks.

Mettinger, Tryggve N. In Search of God. Cryer, Frederick H., tr. LC 88-45335. (Illus.). 288p. 1988. text ed. 30.00 (*0-8006-0892-5*, 1-892, Fortress Pr) Augsburg Fortress.

Mettler, Barbara. Basic Movement Exercises. 1973. 18.50 (*0-912536-06-3*) Mettler Studios.

— Creative Dance in Kindergarten. 1976. pap. 3.50 (*0-912536-08-X*) Mettler Studios.

— Dance As an Element of Life. 1985. 15.00 (*0-912536-12-8*) Mettler Studios.

— Group Dance Improvisations. 1975. 15.00 (*0-912536-07-1*) Mettler Studios.

— The Nature of Dance As a Creative Art Activity. 1980. 12.50 (*0-912536-11-X*) Mettler Studios.

Mettler, Barbara, ed. Materials of Dance As a Creative Art Activity. 5th ed. 1979. 18.50 (*0-912536-10-1*) Mettler Studios.

Mettler, Darlene D. Sound & Sense: Musical Allusion & Imagery in the Novels of Iris Murdoch. LC 90-22130. (American University Studies: English Language & Literature: Ser. IV, Vol. 127). 169p. (C). 1991. text ed. 34.95 (*0-8204-1462-X*) P Lang Pubs.

Mettler, Felix. Wild Boar. McCown, Edna, tr. 224p. 1993. pap. 8.95 (*0-88064-153-3*) Fromm Intl Pub.

Mettler, Fred A., Jr. Imaging, Nineteen-Ninety. 1989. 125. 00 (*0-316-56829-5*) Little.

Mettler, Fred A. Radionuclide Imaging of the GI Tract. LC 85-21344. (Contemporary Issues in Nuclear Imaging Ser.: No. 2). (Illus.). 373p. 1986. reprint ed. pap. 106.40 (*0-7837-6811-7*, 2046643) Bks Demand.

Mettler, Fred A., ed. Radionuclide Bone Imaging & Densitometry. (Contemporary Issues in Nuclear Imaging Ser.: Vol. 4). (Illus.). 344p. 1988. text ed. 79.00 (*0-443-08546-3*) Churchill.

Mettler, Fred A., Jr., ed. Radionuclide Imaging of the GI Tract. (Contemporary Issues in Nuclear Imaging Ser.: Vol. 2). (Illus.). 363p. 1986. text ed. 57.00 (*0-443-08391-6*) Churchill.

Mettler, Fred A., Jr. & Guiberteau. Essentials of Nuclear Medicine Imaging. 3rd ed. (Illus.). 368p. 1990. text ed. 73.50 (*0-7216-3996-8*) Saunders.

Mettler, Fred A. & Upton, Arthur C. Medical Effects of Ionizing Radiation. 2nd ed. 464p. 1995. text ed. 125.00 (*0-7216-6646-9*) Saunders.

***Mettler, Fred A., et al.** Magnetic Resonance Imaging & Spectroscopy. fac. ed. LC 86-13620. (Illus.). 331p. 1986. reprint ed. pap. 94.40 (*0-7837-7823-6*, 2047579) Bks Demand.

Mettler, Fred A., Jr., et al, eds. Medical Management of Radiation Accidents. 400p. 1989. 144.00 (*0-8493-4865-X*, RA1231) CRC Pr.

Mettler, George. Down Home. 352p. (Orig.). 1981. pap. 2.95 (*0-449-14403-8*, GM) Fawcett.

— Red Magnolias. 1991. mass mkt. 4.95 (*1-55817-508-3*, Pinnacle NY) Windsor NY.

Mettler, Helen. The Co-Op & Condo Owner's Handbook: Everything You Have to Know about the Apartment You Own & Live In. LC 83-90305. 89p. (Orig.). 1983. pap. 7.95 (*0-9611254-0-3*) H R M Comm Inc.

Mettler, John J., Jr. Basic Butchering of Livestock & Game: Beef, Veal, Hogs, Lamb, Poultry, Rabbits, Venison. LC 85-70195. (Illus.). 208p. 1986. pap. 11.95 (*0-88266-391-7*, Garden Way Pub) Storey Comm Inc.

— Horse Sense: A Complete Guide to Horse Selection & Care. Burns, Deborah, ed. LC 88-82753. (Illus.). 160p. (Orig.). 1989. pap. 12.95 (*0-88266-545-6*, Garden Way Pub) Storey Comm Inc.

***Mettler, L., ed.** Endometriosis. 84p. 1994. pap. 19.00 (*1-85070-531-3*) Prthnon Pub.

Mettler, Lawrence E. & Billington, W. D., eds. Reproductive Immunology, Nineteen Eighty-Nine: Proceedings of the 4th International Congress, Kiel, 26-29 July, 1989. 352p. 1990. 115.50 (*0-444-81153-2*) Elsevier.

Mettler, Lawrence E., jt. ed. see Semm, K.

Mettler, Lawrence E., et al. Population Genetics & Evolution. 2nd ed. (Illus.). 448p. 1988. text ed. 67.00 (*0-13-685678-0*) P-H.

Mettler, Michael. The Proper Care of Dwarf Rabbits. (Illus.). 256p. 1992. text ed. 14.95 (*0-86622-443-2*) TFH Pubns.

Mettler, Molly, jt. auth. see FallCreek, Stephanie.

Mettler, Molly, jt. auth. see Kemper, Donald W.

Mettler, Molly, ed. see Kemper, Donald W., et al.

Mettler, Rene. The Rain Forest. (First Discovery Bks.). (Illus.). 24p. (J). (ps-2). 1994. 11.95 (*0-590-47728-5*, Cartwheel) Scholastic Inc.

Mettler, Rene, illus. & creator. Birds. LC 92-15956. (First Discovery Bks.). (J). 1993. 11.95 (*0-590-46367-5*) Scholastic Inc.

— Flowers. LC 92-15957. (First Discovery Bks.). (J). 1993. 11.95 (*0-590-46383-7*) Scholastic Inc.

***Mettler, Richard.** Cognitive Learning Theory & Cane Travel Instruction: A New Paradigm. LC 95-69567. 110p. 1995. pap. 10.00 (*0-9646058-0-5*) St NE DPI DRSVI.

Mettler, Shirley L. Disease Susceptibility: Medical Subject Analysis with Reference Bibliogrphy. LC 85-48180. 150p. 1987. 44.50 (*0-88164-968-6*); pap. 39.50 (*0-88164-969-4*) ABBE Pubs Assn.

— Disease Susceptibility: Medical Subject Analysis with Reference Bibliogrphy. rev. ed. LC 92-31212. 150p. 1992. 49.50 (*1-55914-896-9*); pap. 39.50 (*1-55914-897-7*) ABBE Pubs Assn.

Mettler, Stephen C., jt. ed. see Hutcheson, Lynn D.

Mettling, Stephen R. The Graduated Payment Mortgage (GPM) The Pledged Account Mortgage (PAM), the FLIP Mortgage. Bd. with Pledged Account Mortgage (PAM); Flip Mortgage. (Residential Financing Resource Library). 47p. (Orig.). 1982. Set pap. 6.50 (*0-88462-135-9*, 1905-15, Real Estate Ed) Dearborn Finan.

Mettling, Stephen R. & Cortesi, Gerald R. Modern Residential Financing Methods: Tools of the Trade. 2nd ed. 189p. (Orig.). 1989. pap. 19.95 (*0-88462-885-X*, 1557-1502) Dearborn Finan.

Mettrick, D. F. & Desser, S. S., eds. Parasites-Their World & Ours: Proceedings of the Fifth International Congress of Parasitology, Toronto, Canada, August 7-14, 1982. 465p. 1982. 106.25 (*0-444-80433-1*) Elsevier.

Mettrop, P. J., jt. ed. see Musaph, H.

Metts, Sandra, jt. auth. see Cupach, William R.

Metts, Wallis C. Your Faith on Trial. 180p. (Orig.). 1979. pap. 4.95 (*0-89084-112-8*) Bob Jones Univ Pr.

***Mettzer, Stanton L., et al.** Guide to Divorce Engagements, 2 vols., Set. 1994. ring bd. 125.00 (*1-56433-539-9*) Prctnrs Pub Co.

— Guide to Divorce Engagements, Vol. 1. 1994. ring bd. write for info. (*1-56433-540-2*) Prctnrs Pub Co.

— Guide to Divorce Engagements, Vol. 2. 1994. ring bd. write for info. (*1-56433-541-0*) Prctnrs Pub Co.

Mettzner, Susan, jt. auth. see Earle, Ralph.

Metuzals, J., ed. Electron Microscopy & Alzheimer's Disease. (Illus.). 1986. 10.00 (*0-911302-57-3*) San Francisco Pr.

Metwalli, S. M., jt. ed. see Shawki, G. S.

Metz & Stang. Physical Diagnosis. (Illus.). 502p. 1991. 35. 00 (*0-8016-3221-8*) Mosby Yr Bk.

Metz, Allan. Bill Clinton's Pre-Presidential Career: An Annotated Bibliography. LC 94-3017. (Bibliographies & Indexes in American History Ser.: Vol. 27). 248p. 1994. text ed. 59.95 (*0-313-29285-X*, Greenwood Pr) Greenwood.

Metz, Barbara & Burchill, John. The Enneagram & Prayer: Discovering Our True Selves Before God. 164p. 1987. pap. 11.95 (*0-87193-259-8*) Dimension Bks.

Metz, Bernd, ed. see Abuli, Sanchez.

Metz, Bernd, ed. see Baciliero, Paolo.

Metz, Bernd, ed. see Bilal, Enki.

Metz, Bernd, ed. see Bourgeon, Francois.

Metz, Bernd, ed. see Cabanes, Max.

Metz, Bernd, ed. see Cadelo, Silvio.

Metz, Bernd, ed. see Canossa, L.

Metz, Bernd, ed. see Castelli, Alfredo.

Metz, Bernd, ed. see Christin, Pierre.

Metz, Bernd, ed. see Crepax, Guido.

Metz, Bernd, ed. see De Sade, Marquis.

Metz, Bernd, ed. see Giardino, Vittorio.

Metz, Bernd, ed. see Giger, H. R.

Metz, Bernd, ed. see Gillon, Paul.

Metz, Bernd, ed. see Huppen, Hermann.

Metz, Bernd, ed. see Igort.

Metz, Bernd, ed. see Magnus.

Metz, Bernd, ed. see Manara, Milo.

Metz, Bernd, ed. see Mattioli, Massimo.

Metz, Bernd, ed. see Mattotti, Lorenzo.

Metz, Bernd, ed. see Max.

Metz, Bernd, ed. see Nazario.

Metz, Bernd, ed. see Paringaux, Philippe.

Metz, Bernd, ed. see Paringnaux, Philippe.

Metz, Bernd, ed. see Riera, Marti.

Metz, Bernd, ed. see Sampayo, Carlos.

Metz, Bernd, ed. see Schultheiss, Matthias.

Metz, Bernd, tr. see Schultheiss, Matthias.

Metz, Bernd, ed. see Segura, Antonio.

Metz, Bernd, ed. see Serpieri, Paolo E.

Metz, Bernd, ed. see Stevenson, Robert Louis.

Metz, Bernd, ed. see Tamburini, Stefano.

Metz, Bernd, ed. see Tamburini, Stefano, et al.

Metz, Bernd, ed. see Torres, Daniel.

Metz, Bernd, ed. see Trillo, Carlos.

Metz, Bernd, ed. see Varenne, Alex.

Metz, Charles B. & Monroy, Alberto. Biology of Fertilization: The Fertilization Response of the Egg, Vol. 3. 1985. text ed. 148.00 (*0-12-492603-7*) Acad Pr.

Metz, Charles B. & Monroy, Alberto, eds. Biology of Fertilization: General Principles, Sex Determination, Gonad & Germ Cell Growth & Differentiation, 2 vols., 1. 1985. text ed. 128.00 (*0-12-492601-0*) Acad Pr.

— Biology of Fertilization: General Principles, Sex Determination, Gonad & Germ Cell Growth & Differentiation, 2 vols., 2. 1985. text ed. 148.00 (*0-12-492602-9*) Acad Pr.

Metz, Christian. Film Language: A Semiotics of the Cinema. Taylor, Michael, tr. LC 73-90363. 288p. 1990. pap. text ed. 14.95 (*0-226-52130-3*) U Ch Pr.

— The Imaginary Signifier: Psychoanalysis & the Cinema. Britton, Celia et al, trs. LC 81-47551. 340p. 1982. 27.95 (*0-253-33105-6*); pap. 13.95 (*0-253-20380-5*, MB-380) Ind U Pr.

— Language & Cinema. Umiker-Sebeok, Donna J., tr. 1974. text ed. 64.65 (*90-279-2682-4*) Mouton.

***Metz, Clyde.** Molecular Geometry & Bonding. Neidig, H. A., ed. (Modular Laboratory Program in Chemistry Ser.). 16p. (C). 1988. pap. text ed. 1.25x (*0-87540-352-2*) Chem Educ Res.

— Schaum's Outline for Physical Chemistry. 2nd ed. 512p. 1988. pap. text ed. 14.95 (*0-07-041715-6*) McGraw.

— Schaum's Two Thousand Solved Problems in Physical Chemistry. (Shaum's Solved Problem Ser.). 672p. (C). 1989. pap. text ed. 21.95 (*0-07-041716-4*) McGraw.

Metz, Clyde, et al. Chemistry with Inorganic Qualitative Analysis. 3rd ed. 263p. (C). 1989. Instr's manual by Clyde Metz & John Williams, 263 pgs. teacher ed, pap. text ed. 12.00 (*0-15-506457-6*) HB Coll Pubs.

***Metz, Clyde R.** Models & the Crystalline State. Neidig, H. A., ed. (Modular Laboratory Program in Chemistry Ser.). 16p. (C). 1988. pap. text ed. 1.25x (*0-87540-351-4*) Chem Educ Res.

— Statistical Analysis of Experimental Density Data. Neidig, H. A., ed. (Modular Laboratory Program in Chemistry Ser.). 11p. (C). 1988. pap. text ed. 1.25x (*0-87540-353-0*) Chem Educ Res.

Metz, Don. Madame President. Warren, James A., ed. 450p. 1993. per., pap. 14.95 (*0-929827-10-4*) New Saga Pubs.

— New Compact House Designs: 27 Award-Winning Plans, 1,250 Square Feet Or Less. Watson, Ben, ed. LC 90-50608. (Illus.). 192p. 1991. 27.95 (*0-88266-667-3*); pap. 17.95 (*0-88266-666-5*) Storey Comm Inc.

Metz, Don, ed. The Compact House Book: Thirty-Three Prize Winning Designs One Thousand Square Feet or Less. 2nd ed. LC 83-8912. (Illus.). 208p. 1988. pap. 14. 95 (*0-88266-323-2*, Garden Way Pub) Storey Comm Inc.

Metz, Donald. Studies in Biblical Holiness. 290p. 1971. 15. 95 (*0-8341-0117-3*) Beacon Hill.

Metz, Donald L. Running Hot: Structure & Stress in Ambulance Work. 252p. 1984. reprint ed. lib. bdg. 41.50 (*0-8191-4069-4*) U Pr of Amer.

Metz, G. Harold. Sources of Four Plays Ascribed to Shakespeare. LC 88-4793. (Illus.). 528p. 1989. text ed. 48.00 (*0-8262-0690-5*) U of Mo Pr.

***Metz, Harold.** Business Builders: Success Strategies to Get Clients to Come to You. (Illus.). 208p. (Orig.). 1995. pap. text ed. 39.00 (*0-89447-314-X*) Cypress.

Metz, Helen C., ed. Iran: A Country Study. 4th ed. LC 88-600484. (Area Handbook Ser.). (Illus.). 378p. 1989. text ed. 17.00 (*0-16-001729-7*, S/N 008-020-01181-9) USGPO.

— Iraq: A Country Study. 4th ed. LC 89-13940. (Area Handbook Ser.). (Illus.). 332p. 1990. text ed. 16.00 (*0-16-022052-1*, S/N 008-020-01206-8) USGPO.

Metz, Helen C., ed. see Federal Research Division, Library of Congress Staff.

Metz, Helen C., ed. see Federal Research Division Staff.

Metz, Helen C., ed. see Library of Congress, Federal Research Div. Staff.

Metz, Helen C., ed. see Library of Congress Federal Research Division.

Metz, Helen C., ed. see Library of Congress, Federal Research Division Staff.

Metz, J. A. & Diekmann, O., eds. The Dynamics of Physiologically Structured Populations. (Lecture Notes in Biomathematics Ser.: Vol. 68). xii, 511p. 1986. pap. 70.00 (*0-387-16786-2*) Spr-Verlag.

Metz, Jerred. Angels in the House: Poems by Jerred Metz. deluxe ed. (Illus.). 1978. 75.00 (*0-685-27838-7*) Heron Pr.

— Halley's Comet, Nineteen Ten: Fire in the Sky. (Illus.). (Orig.). 1985. 13.95 (*0-933439-00-8*); pap. 8.95 (*0-933439-01-6*) Singing Bone Pr.

Metz, Johann B. & Haring, Hermann, eds. Resurrection or Reincarnation? (Concilium Ser.). 1993. write for info. (*0-88344-872-6*) Orbis Bks.

***Metz, Johann-Baptist & Moltmann, Jurgen.** Faith & the Future: Essays on Theology, Solidarity, & Modernity. LC 95-2532. (Concilium Ser.). 225p. (Orig.). 1995. pap. 18.95 (*1-57075-016-5*) Orbis Bks.

Metz, Johannes B. Poverty of Spirit. LC 68-31045. 56p. 1968. pap. 4.95 (*0-8091-1924-2*) Paulist Pr.

Metz, Johannes B., jt. auth. see Schillebeeckx, Edward.

Metz, John. The Fables of La Fontaine: Vocal Settings & Interpretations. LC 83-8272. (Juilliard Performance Guides Ser.: No. 2). 160p. 1986. lib. bdg. 47.00 (*0-918728-26-6*) Pendragon NY.

Metz, Karen S. Information Sources in Power Engineering. LC 75-32096. 114p. 1976. text ed. 42.95 (*0-8371-8538-6*, MPE/, Greenwood Pr) Greenwood.

Metz, Karen S., jt. auth. see Gabriel, Richard A.

Metz, Lance, ed. see Anderson, Elaine.

Metz, Lance, jt. ed. see Viest, Ivan.

Metz, Lance E. Sherman's Guide to Hugh Moore Park. LC 87-25622. 1988. pap. 3.00 (*0-930973-07-0*) Canal Hist Tech.

Metz, Lance E., jt. auth. see Bartholomew, Ann M.

Metz, Lance E., jt. auth. see Bartholomew, Craig L.

Metz, Leon. The Shooters. LC 76-21578. (Illus.). 300p. 1976. 19.95 (*0-930208-04-8*) Mangan Books TX.

Metz, Leon C. Border: The U. S. - Mexico Line. LC 89-60730. (Illus.). 480p. 1989. 29.95 (*0-930208-27-7*) Mangan Books TX.

— Dallas Stoudenmire: El Paso Marshal. LC 70-79109. (C). 1993. pap. 9.95 (*0-8061-2487-3*) U of Okla Pr.

M

— Desert Army: Fort Bliss on the Texas Border. rev. ed. LC 88-90910. (Illus.). 208p. 1988. text ed. 19.95 (*0-930208-25-0*) Mangan Books TX.

— El Paso Chronicles: A Chronological Record of Historical Events in El Paso, Texas. Mangan, Judy & Mangan, Frank, eds. (Illus.). 320p. (C). 1993. 24.95 (*0-930208-32-3*) Mangan Books TX.

— John Selman, Gunfighter. LC 79-6719. (Illus.). 272p. (C). 1992. pap. 12.95 (*0-8061-2419-9*) U of Okla Pr.

— Pat Garrett: The Story of a Western Lawman. LC 72-9261. (Illus.). 328p. 1983. pap. 15.95 (*0-8061-1838-5*) U of Okla Pr.

— Roadside History of Texas. Greer, Daniel, ed. (Roadside History Ser.). (Illus.). 489p. 1993. 30.00 (*0-87842-293-5*); pap. 15.00 (*0-87842-294-3*) Mountain Pr.

— Southern New Mexico Empire: First National Bank of Dona Ana Country. LC 90-61912. 1990. 21.00 (*0-930208-28-5*) Mangan Books TX.

— Turning Points in El Paso, Texas. LC 85-60638. (Illus.). 128p. 1985. 19.95 (*0-930208-18-8*) Mangan Books TX.

Metz, Mary H. Different by Design: The Context & Character of Three Magnet Schools. 288p. 1986. 29.95 (*0-7102-0071-4*, RKP) Routledge.

— Different by Design: The Context & Character of Three Magnet Schools. 288p. 1992. pap. 16.95 (*0-415-90521-4*, A6804) Routledge.

Metz, Mary S. Reflets du Monde Francais. 2nd ed. 1978. Cahiers d'Exercices. pap. text ed. write for info. (*0-07-041793-8*); Test package. pap. text ed. write for info. (*0-07-041794-6*) McGraw.

— Reflets du Monde Francais. 2nd ed. 1978. Instr's. manual. teacher ed, pap. text ed. write for info. (*0-07-041792-X*) McGraw.

Metz, Mary S. & Helstrom, Jo. Le Francais a Vivre. 4th ed. Rebisz, Jacqueline, ed. (Illus.). (gr. 9-12). 1978. text ed. 29.92 (*0-07-041755-5*) McGraw.

Metz, Mary S., jt. auth. see Helstrom, Jo.

Metz, Myrtle D. Of Haviland & Honey: A Colorado Girlhood, 1924-1947. 151p. 1992. 24.95 (*0-87108-814-2*); pap. 15.95 (*0-87108-825-8*) Pruett.

Metz, Pamela. The Tao of Learning. LC 93-1945. 176p. 1994. 16.95 (*0-89334-222-X*) Humanics Ltd.

***Metz, Pamela K.** The Tao of Learning: Lao Tzu's Tao Te Ching Adapted for a New Age. LC 93-1945. (Illus.). 160p. 1994. lib. bdg. 26.95 (*0-89334-243-2*, 2432052) Humanics Ltd.

***Metz, Pamela K. & Tobin, Jacqueline.** The Tao of Women. (Illus.). 192p. (Orig.). 1995. lib. bdg. 26.95 (*0-89334-245-9*, 2459X35); pap. 16.95 (*0-89334-237-8*, 2378X35) Humanics Ltd.

***Metz, Patricia A.** Determining Atomic Emission by Spectroscopy. 12p. (C). 1994. 1.25 (*0-614-05692-6*, STRC 449-9) Chem Educ Res.

Metz, Paul A. Metallogeny of the Fairbanks Mining District, Alaska & Adjacent Areas, 2 vols. LC 91-67232. (MIRL Report Ser.: No. 90). (Illus.). 455p. (Orig.). (C). 1991. pap. text ed. 24.00 (*0-911043-13-6*); fiche, pap. text ed. 41.00 (*0-685-56388-X*) UAKF Min Ind Res Lab.

Metz, R. A., ed. Applied Mining Geology: Problems of Sampling & Grade Control. LC 85-71945. 173p. reprint ed. pap. 49.40 (*0-8357-3414-5*, 2039671) Bks Demand.

Metz, Rene & Schlick, Jean, eds. Informal Groups in the Church: Papers of the Second Cerdic Colloquium, Strasbourg, May 13-15, 1971. O'Connell, Matthew J., tr. LC 75-25591. (Pittsburgh Theological Monographs: No. 7). 1975. pap. 5.25 (*0-915138-08-5*) Pickwick.

Metz, Rene, ed. see Cerdic Colloquium Staff.

Metz, Robert & Stasen, George. It's a Sure Thing: A Wry Look at Investing, Investors, & the World of Wall Street. LC 92-44803. (Illus.). 1993. text ed. 15.95 (*0-07-041778-4*) McGraw.

Metz, Robert J. & Benson, James W. Management & Education of the Diabetic Patient. (Illus.). 208p. 1988. pap. text ed. 32.50 (*0-7216-1945-2*) Saunders.

Metz, Robert J. & Larson, Eric B. Blue Book of Endocrinology. (Blue Book Ser.). 396p. 1985. pap. text ed. 32.50 (*0-7216-5638-2*) Saunders.

***Metz, Sara E.** Proof Positive: An Empirical Look at God's Fourth Dimension. 36p. (Orig.). 1995. pap. 7.00 (*0-9647074-0-3*) Metz Prods.

Metz, Warren. Change of Face & Pace. LC 82-90982. 1983. 12.95 (*0-87212-165-8*) Libra.

Metz, William. Newswriting: From Lead to "Thirty" 3rd ed. 336p. (C). 1990. pap. text ed. write for info. (*0-13-622267-6*) P-H.

Metz, William D. & Hammond, Allen L. The Science Report on Solar Energy in America. LC 78-69957. (AAAS Publication Ser.: No. 78-10). 256p. reprint ed. pap. 73.00 (*0-7837-0070-9*, 2040317) Bks Demand.

Metzbower, E. A., ed. Lasers in Materials Processing. LC 83-72954. (Conference Proceedings - American Society for Metals Ser.). (Illus.). 276p. reprint ed. pap. 78.70 (*0-8357-6183-5*, 2034319) Bks Demand.

Metzbower, Edward A., ed. see American Society for Metals Staff.

Metzdorf, Martha. The Ultimate Portfolio. (Illus.). 144p. 1991. 32.95 (*0-89134-370-9*, 30286) North Light Bks.

Metze, Leroy P., jt. auth. see Craig, James R.

Metzelaar, Lawrence C. Hands on Using MS DOS, WordPerfect, dBASE III Plus & Lotus 1-2-3. 500p. (C). 1991. spiral bd. 34.50 (*0-8053-4506-X*) Benjamin-Cummings.

Metzelaar, Lawrence C. & Fox. Hands-on Without Software. 2nd ed. Apt, Alan, ed. (C). 1990. pap. text ed. 27.95 (*0-8053-4502-7*) Benjamin-Cummings.

Metzelaar, Lawrence C. & Fox, Marianne B. Hands-on dBase IV. Baxter, Michelle, ed. 144p. (Orig.). (C). 1991. pap. text ed. 16.25 (*0-8053-4509-4*) Benjamin-Cummings.

— Using dBASE III Plus: Limited Use Version & Manual. 210p. (C). 1987. pap. text ed. 23.75 (*0-8053-6742-X*) Benjamin-Cummings.

Metzelaar, Lawrence C., jt. auth. see Fox, Marianne B.

Metzen, Gerhard, tr. see Amann, Herbert.

Metzenbaum, Shelley, jt. auth. see Coltman, Edward.

Metzer, Jacob. Some Economic Aspects of Railroad Development in Tsarist Russia. Bruchey, Stuart, ed. LC 77-77180. (Dissertations in European Economic History Ser.). 1978. lib. bdg. 20.95 (*0-405-10793-5*) Ayer.

Metzer, Patricia Ann. Federal Income Taxation of Individuals. 4th suppl. ed. LC 84-70791. 615p. 1984. 132.00 (*0-8318-0402-5*, B402/B496); Supplement, 1984, 134p. 19.00 (*0-685-57995-6*, B496) Am Law Inst.

Metzgar & Stinger. SN: Health Assessment. 2nd ed. 1993. 14.95 (*0-87434-614-2*) Springhouse Pub.

Metzgar, jt. auth. see Hawley.

Metzgar, Elizabeth, jt. auth. see Stinger, Karen.

Metzgen, Fred. Killing the Paper Dragon: Creating Business Advantage with EDI. (Illus.). 133p. 1990. 30.95 (*0-434-91316-2*) Buttrwrth-Heinemann.

Metzger, Barbara. Christmas Wishes. (Orig.). 1992. mass mkt. 3.99 (*0-449-22078-8*, Crest) Fawcett.

— Christmas Wishes. (Orig.). 1993. mass mkt. 3.99 (*0-449-45241-7*, Crest) Fawcett.

— Cupboard Kisses. 224p. 1989. pap. 3.50 (*0-449-21760-4*, Crest) Fawcett.

— An Early Engagement. 208p. (Orig.). 1990. pap. 3.50 (*0-449-21818-X*, Crest) Fawcett.

— Lady Whilton's Wedding. 1995. mass mkt. 4.50 (*0-449-22351-5*, Crest) Fawcett.

— Minor Indiscretions. 1991. pap. 3.95 (*0-449-21872-4*) Fawcett.

— Rake's Ransom. 224p. 1986. 15.95 (*0-8027-0911-7*) Walker & Co.

— Rake's Ransom. 1989. pap. 3.95 (*0-8217-2850-4*) Zebra.

— A Suspicious Affair. large type ed. LC 95-9788. 299p. 1995. reprint ed. pap. 18.95 (*0-7838-1297-3*) Hall.

Metzger, Barbara, jt. auth. see Schlank, Carol H.

Metzger, Bert & Colletti, Jerome. Does Profit Sharing Pay? LC 70-156486. 112p. 1971. 8.50 (*0-911192-19-0*, 1-006) Profit Sharing.

Metzger, Bert L. New Horizons for Capitalism: Post-ERISA Idea Papers. 37p. 1977. pap. 6.00 (*0-911192-28-X*) Profit Sharing.

— Profit Sharing as a Motivator. 24p. 1984. pap. text ed. 4.50 (*0-911192-36-0*) Profit Sharing.

Metzger, Bruce M. Breaking the Code: Understanding the Book of Revelation. LC 93-5954. 112p. 1993. pap. 6.95 (*0-687-42807-6*) Abingdon.

— Breaking the Code: Understanding the Book of Revelation: Leader Guide. LC 93-32696. 112p. 1993. pap. 3.95 (*0-687-76973-6*) Abingdon.

— Breaking the Code: Understanding the Book of Revelation: Video Set. 1993. teacher ed, vhs 39.95 (*0-687-76242-1*) Abingdon.

— The Early Versions of the New Testament. 1977. 35.00 (*0-19-826170-5*) OUP.

— Introduction to the Apocrypha. 1977. pap. 16.95 (*0-19-502340-4*) OUP.

— Lexical Aids for Students of New Testament Greek. 3rd ed. xi, 100p. 1969. pap. text ed. 5.65 (*0-9644891-0-4*) Theol Bk.

— Manuscripts of the Greek Bible: An Introduction to Paleography. (Illus.). (C). 1981. 45.00 (*0-19-502924-0*) OUP.

— The New Testament: Its Background, Growth & Content. enl. ed. 310p. 1983. 20.95 (*0-687-27914-3*) Abingdon.

— The Text of the New Testament. 3rd ed. (Illus.). 320p. (C). 1992. pap. text ed. 17.95 (*0-19-507297-9*) OUP.

Metzger, Bruce M. & Coogan, Michael D., eds. The Oxford Companion to the Bible. (Illus.). 932p. 1993. 49.95 (*0-19-504645-5*) OUP.

Metzger, Bruce M., et al, eds. The Making of the New Revised Standard Version of the Bible. viii, 92p. 1991. pap. 6.99 (*0-8028-0620-1*) Eerdmans.

Metzger, Carmel B. Oliver Discovers Friendly U. 1991. 6.95 (*0-88047-283-9*, D9014) DOK Pubs.

Metzger, Charles R. Emerson & Greenough: Transcendental Pioneers of an American Esthetic. LC 74-139140. 153p. (C). 1971. reprint ed. text ed. 59.75 (*0-8371-5756-0*, MEEG, Greenwood Pr) Greenwood.

— F. Scott Fitzgerald's Psychiatric Novel: Nicole's Case, Dick's Case. (American University Studies: American Literature: Ser. XXIV, Vol. 13). 387p. (C). 1989. text ed. 50.80 (*0-8204-1040-3*) P Lang Pubs.

— The Silent River: A Pastoral Elegy in the Form of a Recollection of Arctic Adventure. (Illus.). xi, 161p. (Orig.). 1984. pap. 7.95 (*0-9613094-0-7*) Omega LA.

***Metzger-Court, Sarah & Pascha, Werner, eds.** Japan's Socio-Economic Evolution: Continuity & Change. 288p. (C). 1995. text ed. 75.00 (*1-873410-39-5*, Pub. by Curzon Pr UK) Humanities.

Metzger, D. E. & Crawford, M. E., eds. Fundamental & Applied Heat Transfer Research for Gas Turbines Engines. (HTD Ser.: Vol. 226). 96p. 1992. 30.00 (*0-7918-1071-2*, G00715) ASME.

Metzger, Daniel L. Electronic Circuit Behavior. 2nd ed. (Illus.). 400p. (C). 1983. student ed 24.00 (*0-13-250191-0*); text ed. 52.00 (*0-13-250241-0*) P-H.

— Electronics for Your Future. (Illus.). (C). 1994. pap. text ed. 26.50 (*0-9639471-0-9*) Tech Trning.

— Electronics Pocket Handbook. (Illus.). 272p. 1982. pap. 14.95 (*0-13-251835-X*) P-H.

— Electronics Pocket Handbook. 2nd ed. 272p. 1991. pap. 16.95 (*0-13-252008-7*) P-H.

— Microcomputer Electronics: A Practical Approach to Hardware, Software, Trouble-Shooting & Interfacing. 748p. 1988. text ed. 72.00 (*0-13-579871-X*) P-H.

— Twenty-Two Microcomputer Projects to Build, Use & Learn. (Illus.). 272p. 1985. pap. 20.50 (*0-13-934712-7*) P-H.

Metzger, David. The Lost Cause of Rhetoric: The Relation of Rhetoric & Geometry in Aristotle & Lacan. LC 93-38231. 135p. (C). 1994. 29.95x (*0-8093-1855-5*) S Ill U Pr.

Metzger, Deena. Looking for the Faces of God. LC 89-23139. 96p. (Orig.). 1989. pap. 8.00 (*0-938077-23-6*) Parallax Pr.

— Sabbath among the Ruins: New Poems. 174p. 1992. pap. 10.00 (*0-938077-53-8*) Parallax Pr.

— Writing for Your Life: Discovering the Story of Your Life's Journey. LC 91-55323. 1992. pap. 13.00 (*0-06-250612-9*) Harper SF.

Metzger, Edward C. Ralph, First Duke of Montagu, 1638-1709. LC 86-23797. (Studies in British History: Vol. 2). 450p. 1986. 109.95 (*0-88946-452-9*) E Mellen.

Metzger, Elizabeth & Ashton-Jones, Evelyn, eds. Advanced Placement English: Theory, Politics & Pedagogy. 205p. (Orig.). 1989. pap. text ed. 18.50 (*0-86709-246-7*) Boynton Cook Pubs.

Metzger, Emily, jt. ed. see Pearson, John K.

Metzger, Erika & Metzger, Mic. Reading Andreas Gryphius: Critical Trends 1664-1993. (Studies in German Literature, Linguistics, & Culture). 168p. 1994. 55.95 (*1-57113-005-5*) Camden Hse.

Metzger, G., tr. see Franke, H. W.

Metzger, Helene. Chemistry. Michael, Colette V., tr. LC 91-16970. (Women in the Sciences Ser.: Vol. 1). 151p. (C). 1991. lib. bdg. 25.00 (*0-933951-38-8*) Locust Hill Pr.

Metzger, Henry, ed. FC Receptors & the Action of Antibodies. (Illus.). 368p. 1990. 49.00 (*1-55581-016-0*) Am Soc Microbio.

***Metzger, Jeffrey A., ed.** Claiming Your Place: How to Find Where You Fit in the Life of the Church. 1994. 5.99 (*0-7847-0284-5*, 11-40304) Standard Pub.

Metzger, Jon, jt. auth. see Lord, Suzanne.

Metzger, Lawrence. From Denial to Recovery: Counseling Problem Drinkers, Alcoholics, & Their Families. LC 87-45504. (Social & Behavioral Science Ser.). 326p. 1987. 27.95x (*1-55542-063-X*) Jossey-Bass.

Metzger, Linda, ed. Black Writers: A Selection of Sketches from Contemporary Authors. 600p. 1988. 89.00 (*0-8103-2772-4*) Gale.

— Contemporary Authors, Vol. 14. LC 81-640179. (New Revision Ser.). 528p. 1985. 122.00 (*0-8103-1943-8*) Gale.

— Contemporary Authors, Vol. 15. LC 81-640179. (New Revision Ser.). 450p. 1985. 122.00 (*0-8103-1944-6*) Gale.

— Contemporary Authors, Vol. 18. (New Revision Ser.: Vol. 18). 1986. 122.00 (*0-8103-1947-0*) Gale.

— Hispanic Writers: A Selection of Sketches from Contemporary Authors. 475p. 1990. 90.00 (*0-8103-7688-1*) Gale.

Metzger, Linda & Ryan, Alan. Hispanic Writers: Sketches from CA. 2nd ed. 1999. 90.00 (*0-8103-8377-2*) Gale.

Metzger, Linda & Straub, Deborah A. Contemporary Authors, Vol. 16. rev. ed. LC 81-640179. (New Revision Ser.). 483p. 1985. 122.00 (*0-8103-1945-4*) Gale.

Metzger, Linda & Straub, Deborah A., eds. Contemporary Authors, Vol. 17. rev. ed. (New Revision Ser.). 600p. 1986. 115.00 (*0-8103-1946-2*) Gale.

— Contemporary Authors, Vol. 19. (New Revision Ser.: Vol. 19). 600p. 1986. 122.00 (*0-8103-1948-9*) Gale.

— Contemporary Authors, Vol. 20. (New Revision Ser.: Vol. 20). 499p. 1987. 122.00 (*0-8103-1949-7*) Gale.

— Contemporary Authors, Vol. 21. (New Revision Ser.: Vol. 21). 507p. 1987. 122.00 (*0-8103-1975-6*) Gale.

Metzger, Lois. Barry's Sister. LC 93-7760. 240p. (J). (gr. 5 up). 1993. pap. 4.50 (*0-14-036484-6*, Puffin) Puffin Bks.

— Barry's Sister. LC 91-23738. 240p. (J). (gr. 5 up). 1992. text ed. 15.95 (*0-689-31521-X*, Atheneum Bks Young) S&S Childrens.

— Ellen's Case. LC 95-2707. 1995. 15.00 (*0-689-31934-7*, Atheneum Bks Young) S&S Childrens.

Metzger, Lore. One Foot in Eden: Modes of Pastoral in Romantic Poetry. LC 85-16462. xix, 274p. 1986. 34.95 (*0-8078-1678-7*) U of NC Pr.

Metzger, Mary & Whittaker, Cinthya P. This Planet Is Mine: Teaching Environmental Awareness & Appreciation to Children. 256p. (Orig.). 1991. 17.00 (*0-671-74817-3*, Fireside) S&S Trade.

Metzger, Mic, jt. auth. see Metzger, Erika.

Metzger, Michael, et al. Business Law & the Regulatory Environment: Concepts & Cases. 8th ed. 1792p. (C). 1991. text ed. 69.95 (*0-256-08700-8*, 02-0405-08) Irwin.

— Business Law & the Regulatory Environment - College of Charleston: Concepts & Cases. 8th ed. (C). 1992. text ed. 38.95 (*0-256-12138-9*) Irwin.

Metzger, Michael B., et al. Business Law & the Regulatory Environment: Concepts & Cases. 9th ed. LC 94-12503. (Irwin Legal Studies in Business Ser.). 1408p. (C). 1994. 69.95 (*0-256-14103-7*) Irwin.

— Business Law & the Regulatory Environment: Concepts & Cases. 9th ed. LC 94-12503. (Legal Studies in Business). 1995. pap. write for info. (*0-256-17191-2*) Irwin.

Metzger, Nancy. Harpsichord Technique: A Guide to Expressivity. LC 89-92256. 115p. (Orig.). (C). 1989. pap. 22.00 (*0-9624934-0-6*) Musica Dulce.

Metzger, Norman. The Health Care Supervisor's Handbook. 3rd ed. 272p. (C). 1988. 50.00 (*0-87189-757-1*) Aspen Pub.

Metzger, Norman, ed. Handbook of Health Care Human Resources Management. 2nd ed. 588p. 1990. 135.00 (*0-8342-0094-5*) Aspen Pub.

Metzger, Norman, jt. auth. see Bassett, Lawrence.

Metzger, Phil. Enliven Your Paintings with Light. (Elements of Painting Ser.). (Illus.). 144p. 1994. 27.95 (*0-89134-514-0*) North Light Bks.

— Perspective Without Pain. (Illus.). 144p. 1992. pap. 19.95 (*0-89134-446-2*, 30386) North Light Bks.

Metzger, Philip W. Managing a Programming Project. 2nd ed. (Illus.). 288p. 1981. text ed. 86.00 (*0-13-550772-3*) P-H.

— Managing Programming People: A Personal View. (Illus.). 160p. write for info. (*0-318-61856-7*) P-H.

Metzger, R. M., ed. Crystal Cohesion & Conformal Energies. (Topics in Current Physics Ser.: Vol. 26). (Illus.). 160p. 1981. 37.00 (*0-387-10520-4*) Spr-Verlag.

Metzger, R. M. & Boo, W. Proceedings of the Symposium on Solid State Chemistry: A Special Issue of the Journal Molecular Crystals & Liquid Crystals. 270p. 1984. text ed. 297.00 (*0-677-06485-3*) Gordon & Breach.

Metzger, R. M., et al, eds. Lower-Dimensional Systems & Molecular Electronics. (NATO ASI Series B, Physics: Vol. 248). (Illus.). 740p. 1990. 149.50 (*0-306-43826-7*, Plenum Pr) Plenum.

Metzger, R. S. A Master of the Century Past. LC 93-37721. 288p. 1995. 17.95 (*0-913720-87-9*) Beil.

Metzger, Rainell M., ed. see Metzger, Thomas F.

Metzger, Robert, ed. My Land is the Southwest: Peter Hurd Letters & Journals. LC 83-45101. (Illus.). 440p. 1983. 17.50 (*0-89096-156-5*) Tex A&M Univ Pr.

Metzger, Robert M., ed. High Temperature Superconductivity: The First Two Years. (International Conference Ser., Tuscaloosa, Alabama, 11-13 April 1988). 462p. 1989. text ed. 85.00 (*2-88124-299-5*) Gordon & Breach.

Metzger, Robert O. Developing a Consulting Practice. (Survival Skills for Scholars Ser.: Vol. 3). (Illus.). 108p. (C). 1993. text ed. 27.50 (*0-8039-5046-2*); pap. text ed. 12.95 (*0-8039-5047-0*) Sage.

— Profitable Consulting: Helping American Managers Face the Future. 144p. 1988. 17.26 (*0-201-09539-4*) Addison-Wesley.

Metzger, Robert O., jt. auth. see Greiner, Larry E.

Metzger, Robert P. Reagan: American Icon. LC 89-60966. (Illus.). 144p. 1989. pap. 34.95 (*0-8122-1302-5*) U of Pa Pr.

Metzger, Robert P., ed. Transforming Texts: Classical Images in New Contexts. LC 91-58592. 1993. write for info. (*0-8387-5216-0*) Bucknell U Pr.

Metzger, Stephen. Colorado Handbook. 2nd ed. LC 93-30739. (Illus.). 430p. (Orig.). 1994. pap. 17.95 (*1-56691-013-7*) Moon Pubns CA.

— New Mexico Handbook. 3rd ed. (Illus.). 375p. (Orig.). 1994. pap. 14.95 (*1-56691-015-3*) Moon Pubns CA.

Metzger, Thomas A. Escape from Predicament: Neo-Confucianism & China's Evolving Political Culture. LC 76-25445. 303p. 1986. pap. text ed. 16.00 (*0-231-03980-8*) Col U Pr.

— The Internal Organization of Ching Bureaucracy: Legal, Normative, & Communication Aspects. LC 72-96632. (Harvard Studies in East Asian Law: No. 7). 479p. reprint ed. pap. 136.80 (*0-7837-2301-6*, 2057389) Bks Demand.

— The Unification of China & the Problem of Public Opinion in the Republic of China in Taiwan. LC 92-10214. (Essays in Public Policy Ser.: No. 32). 1992. 5.00 (*0-8179-5372-8*) Hoover Inst Pr.

***Metzger, Thomas F.** Becoming a Political Pain in the Ass. (Illus.). 176p. (Orig.). 1995. pap. 12.95 (*0-931892-99-6*) B Dolphin Pub.

— Did Big Brother Give You Permission to Go Wee-Wee? (Illus.). 144p. (Orig.). 1994. pap. 12.95 (*0-931892-98-8*) B Dolphin Pub.

— Did Big Brother Give You Permission to Go Wee Wee? rev. ed. Metzger, Rainell M., ed. (Illus.). 144p. 1994. pap. 12.95 (*0-9641789-0-7*) Metzger Ent.

Metzger, W. James, jt. ed. see Page, Clive P.

Metzger, Walter P. Academic Freedom in the Age of the University. LC 61-2328. 232p. 1961. pap. text ed. 16.00 (*0-231-08512-5*) Col U Pr.

Metzger, Walter P., ed. The Academic Profession Series, 40 vols., Set. (Illus.). 1977. reprint ed. lib. bdg. 1,259.00 (*0-405-10000-0*) Ayer.

— The American Concept of Academic Freedom Information: A Collection of Essays & Reports-an Original Anthology. LC 76-55209. (Academic Profession Ser.). (Illus.). 1979. reprint ed. lib. bdg. 34.95 (*0-405-10037-X*) Ayer.

— The Constitutional Status of Academic Freedom. LC 76-55211. (Academic Profession Ser.). 1978. reprint ed. lib. bdg. 51.95 (*0-405-10038-8*) Ayer.

— The Constitutional Status of Academic Tenure: An Original Anthology. LC 76-52627. (Academic Profession Ser.). 1979. reprint ed. lib. bdg. 34.95 (*0-405-09982-7*) Ayer.

— Professors on Guard: The First AAUP Investigations. LC 76-55213. (Academic Profession Ser.). 1977. lib. bdg. 29.95 (*0-405-10040-X*) Ayer.

— Reader on the Sociology of the Academic Profession. LC 76-55212. (Academic Profession Ser.). 1979. reprint ed. lib. bdg. 56.95 (*0-405-10039-6*) Ayer.

Metzger, Walter P., ed. see Annan, Noel G.

Metzger, Walter P., ed. see Berdahl, Robert O.

Metzger, Walter P., ed. see Bleuel, Hans P.

Metzger, Walter P., ed. see Bowman, Claude C.

Metzger, Walter P., ed. see Busch, Alexander.

Metzger, Walter P., ed. see Caplow, Theodore & Reece, J. McGee.

Metzger, Walter P., ed. see Carnegie Foundation for the Advancement of Teaching Staff.

Metzger, Walter P., ed. see Cattell, J. McKeen.

Metzger, Walter P., ed. see Cheyney, Edward P.

Metzger, Walter P., ed. see Elliott, Orrin L.

Metzger, Walter P., ed. see Ely, Richard T.

Metzger, Walter P., ed. see Flach, Johannes.

Metzger, Walter P., ed. see Hall, G. Stanley.

Metzger, Walter P., ed. see Hardy, Godfrey H.

An Asterisk (*) at the beginning of an entry indicates that the title is appearing in BIP for the first time.

Metzger, Walter P., ed. see Kluge, Alexander.
Metzger, Walter P., ed. see Kotsching, Walter M.
Metzger, Walter P., ed. see Lazarsfeld, Paul F. & Thielens, Wagner P., Jr.
Metzger, Walter P., ed. see McLaughlin, Mary M.
Metzger, Walter P., ed. see Mims, Edwin.
Metzger, Walter P., ed. see Mitsch, Wolfgang, et al.
Metzger, Walter P., ed. see Neumann, Franz L., et al.
Metzger, Walter P., ed. see Pattison, Mark.
Metzger, Walter P., ed. see Pollard, Lucille A.
Metzger, Walter P., ed. see Proctor, Mortimer R.
Metzger, Walter P., ed. see Quincy, Joseph.
Metzger, Walter P., ed. see Ross, Edward A.
Metzger, Walter P., ed. see Rudy, S. Willis.
Metzger, Walter P., ed. see Slosson, Edwin E.
Metzger, Walter P., ed. see Smith, Goldwin.
Metzger, Walter P., ed. see Wiley, Malcolm W.
Metzger, Walter P., ed. see Winstanley, D. A.
Metzger, Walter P., jt. auth. see Yeomans, Henry A.
***Metzger, Wendell.** Ain't Nobody Here but Us Typewriters. 48p. (Orig.). 1993. 4.95 (*1-878116-29-0*) JVC Bks.
— He & She. 60p. (Orig.). 1994. 5.95 (*1-878116-23-1*) JVC Bks.
— Troping the Triad. (Illus.). 60p. (Orig.). 1994. 5.95 (*1-878116-24-X*) JVC Bks.
Metzger, Will. Tell the Truth. 2nd ed. LC 83-25304. 191p. (Orig.). 1981. pap. 10.99 (*0-87784-934-X*, 934) InterVarsity.
Metzi, Francisco. The People's Remedy: The Struggle for Health Care in El Salvador's War of Liberation. Carroll, Jean, tr. 224p. (C). 1988. pap. 8.00 (*0-85345-775-1*) Monthly Rev.
Metzidakis, Stamos. Repetition & Semiotics: Interpreting Prose Poems. LC 86-60801. 175p. 1986. 21.95 (*0-917786-41-6*) Summa Pubns.
Metzidakis, Stamos, ed. Understanding French Poetry: Essays for a New Millennium. LC 93-50527. (Reference Library of the Humanities: Vol. 1596). (Illus.). 304p. 1994. 45.00 (*0-8153-0841-8*, H1596) Garland.
Metzing, Dieter, ed. Frame Conceptions & Text Understanding. (Research in Text Theory Ser.: No. 5). 167p. (C). 1980. text ed. 54.65 (*3-11-008006-0*) De Gruyter.
Metzinger, D. J. Fundamentals of Technic. 5p. 1993. reprint ed. spiral bd. 4.40 (*0-7873-0611-8*) Mokelumne.
Metzinger, Sylvia V., comp. The Favrot Collection: A Catalogue of the Printed Material in the Howard-Tilton Memorial Library. 1978. pap. 4.00 (*0-9603212-1-7*) Tulane Univ.
Metzker, Issac. A Bintel Brief. 1990. pap. 10.00 (*0-8052-0980-8*) Schocken.
Metzker, Mary. Mary Metzker's Cooking Plain & Fancy: Cooking Plain & Fancy with Mary Metzker. AmBroc, Charles, ed. (Illus.). 100p. (Orig.). 1988. pap. 8.95 (*0-317-91230-5*) Jam Prodns PA.
Metzker, Ray. Sand Creatures. (Illus.). 56p. 1979. pap. 10.00 (*0-89381-051-7*) Aperture.
Metzler Baker, Joyce. Not by Might Nor by Power. LC 89-27002. (Illus.). 235p. 1990. pap. text ed. 9.95 (*0-87227-135-8*) Reg Baptist.
Metzler, Eric H. Annotated Checklist & Distribution Maps of the Royal Moths & Giant Silkworm Moths (Lepidoptera: Saturniidae) in Ohio. (Biological Notes Ser.). 1980. 3.00 (*0-86727-088-8*) Ohio Bio Survey.
Metzler, Howard C., jt. auth. see Fink, Norman S.
Metzler, Jack. River of Joy. 280p. (Orig.). 1993. text ed. 8.99 (*1-56043-658-1*) Destiny Image.
— Tachechena. 238p. 1992. text ed. 8.99 (*1-56043-655-7*) Destiny Image.
Metzler, James E. From Saigon to Shalom: The Pilgrimage of a Missionary in Search of a More Authentic Mission. LC 84-9313. (Missionary Studies: No. 11). 142p. reprint ed. pap. 40.50 (*0-7837-1191-3*, 2041721) Bks Demand.
Metzler, Jane M. Corporate Interaction with Five Urban Education Systems in Connecticut. (Urban Education Reports Ser.: No. 4). 21p. 1983. 2.50 (*0-685-09451-0*) I N Thut World Educ Ctr.
Metzler, Ken. Creative Interviewing. 2nd ed. 192p. (C). 1988. pap. text ed. write for info. (*0-13-189747-0*) P-H.
— Newsgathering. 2nd ed. 384p. 1985. pap. text ed. write for info. (*0-13-617002-1*) P-H.
— Newswriting Exercises. (Illus.). 288p. 1981. pap. text ed. write for info. (*0-13-617803-0*) P-H.
— Newswriting Exercises. 2nd ed. (Illus.). 224p. (C). 1986. pap. text ed. write for info. (*0-13-611641-8*) P-H.
Metzler, Kenneth J. & Tiner, Ralph W. Wetlands of Connecticut. (Report of Investigations Ser.: No. 13). (Illus.). 113p. (Orig.). 1992. pap. text ed. 12.95 (*0-942081-03-X*) CT DEP CGNHS.
Metzler, Lloyd A. Collected Papers. LC 79-184108. (Economic Studies: No. 140). (Illus.). 614p. 1973. 35.00 (*0-674-13775-2*) HUP.
Metzler, Lloyd A. & Haberler, Gottfried. International Monetary Policies. Wilkins, Mira, ed. LC 78-3938. (International Finance Ser.). 1979. reprint ed. lib. bdg. 17.95 (*0-405-11239-4*) Ayer.
***Metzler, Michael & Sebolt, Don.** The Interactive Learning Approach: Student Personal Workbook for Golf. (The Personalized Sport Instruction Ser.). 144p. (C). 1994. pap. text ed., spiral bd. 13.95 (*0-8403-9948-0*) Kendall-Hunt.
— The Interactive Learning Approach: Student Personal Workbook for Racquetball. (The Personalized Sport Instruction Ser.). 144p. (C). 1994. spiral bd. 13.95 (*0-8403-9954-5*) Kendall-Hunt.
— The Interactive Learning Approach: Student Personal Workbook for Tennis. (The Personalized Sport Instruction Ser.). 144p. (C). 1994. pap. text ed., spiral bd. 13.95 (*0-8403-9949-9*) Kendall-Hunt.
Metzler, Michael W. Instructional Supervision for Physical Education. LC 89-7461. (Illus.). 272p. 1990. text ed. 35.00x (*0-87322-254-7*, BMET0254) Human Kinetics.
Metzler, Rosemary M. Snooty the Fox. 28p. (J). 1993. pap. write for info. (*0-9637381-0-0*) Snooty Prods.
Metzler, Susan & Metzler, Van. Texas Mushrooms: A Field Guide. LC 91-2239. (Corrie Herring Hooks Ser.: No. 18). (Illus.). 358p. 1992. 39.95 (*0-292-75125-7*); pap. 19.95 (*0-292-75126-5*) U of Tex Pr.
***Metzler, Tom, et al.** The Princeton Review Student Access Guide to the Best 309 Colleges '96. 1995. pap. 18.00 (*0-679-76146-2*, Villard Bks) Random.
Metzler, Van, jt. auth. see Metzler, Susan.
Metzloff, jt. auth. see Patterson.
Metzloff, Thomas B., ed. Professional Responsibility Anthology. LC 94-15848. 1994. write for info. (*0-87084-573-X*) Anderson Pub Co.
Metzner, Clifton G., Jr. Water Quality Issues of the California-Baja California Border Region. (Border Issue Ser.). 1989. 10.00 (*0-317-93042-7*) SDSU Inst Reg Studies.
***Metzner, Edward P.** More Than a Soldier's War: Pacification in Vietnam. (Texas A&M University Military History Ser.: No. 47). (Illus.). 256p. (C). 1995. 29.95x (*0-89096-666-4*) Tex A&M Univ Pr.
Metzner, P. & Thuillier, A., eds. Sulphur Reagents in Organic Synthesis. (Best Synthetic Methods Ser.). (Illus.). 224p. 1994. boxed 75.00 (*0-12-690770-6*) Acad Pr.
Metzner, Ralph. The Well of Remembrance: Rediscovering the Earth Wisdom Myths of Northern Europe. 375p. 1994. pap. 16.00 (*1-57062-028-8*) Shambhala Pubns.
— The Well of Remembrance: Rediscovering the Earth Wisdom Myths of Northern Europe. 1995. 24.25 (*0-8446-6826-5*) Peter Smith.
Metzner, Ralph, jt. auth. see Leary, Timothy.
Metzner, Seymour. One-Minute Game Guide. LC 67-29157. (J). (gr. 1-6). 1968. pap. 5.99 (*0-8224-5070-4*) Fearon Teach Aids.
— World History in Juvenile Books: A Geographical & Chronological Guide. LC 72-11598. 356p. 1973. 25.00 (*0-8242-0441-7*) Wilson.
Metzner, Seymour, jt. auth. see Sharp, Richard M.
Metzner, Sheila. Color. 172p. 1991. 50.00 (*0-944092-15-2*) Twin Palms Pub.
— Color. limited ed. 172p. 1991. 150.00 (*0-944092-16-0*) Twin Palms Pub.
Meudt, Edna. Promised Land, the Life & Times of Henry Dodge, First Territorial Governor of Wisconsin: A Historical Drama. Westburg, John E., ed. LC 80-54737. 56p. 1980. pap. 20.00 (*0-87423-026-8*) Westburg.
— The Rose Jar: The Autobiography of Edna Meudt. (Illus.). 352p. 1990. 17.50 (*0-944133-07-X*) Nrth Cntry Pr.
Meudt, R., jt. auth. see Lutz, H.
Meudt, Werner J., ed. Strategies of Plant Reproduction. LC 82-11594. (Beltsville Symposia in Agricultural Research Ser.: No. 6). (Illus.). 400p. 1983. text ed. 66.50 (*0-86598-054-3*) Rowman.
Meuer, Teresa & Abramson, Betsy. A Family's Guide to Selecting, Financing & Asserting Rights in a Nursing Home. 31p. 1986. 15.00 (*0-932622-09-7*) Ctr Public Rep.
Meuer, Teresa, jt. auth. see Weisberger, June.
Meulders, Daniele, jt. auth. see Heimler, Alberto.
Meulders, Daniele, et al. Atypical Employment in the EC. (Illus.). 280p. (C). 1994. text ed. 57.95 (*1-85521-426-1*, Pub. by Dartmth Pub UK) Ashgate Pub Co.
— Position of Women on the Labour Market in the European Community. 216p. 1993. 57.95 (*1-85521-419-9*, Pub. by Dartmth Pub UK) Ashgate Pub Co.
Meulders-Klein, I. & Ekelaar, J. Family, State & Individual Economic Security, 2 vols. 1096p. 1988. Vol. 1, Family. write for info. (*0-318-65380-X*); Vol. 2, State. write for info. (*0-318-65381-8*) Kluwer Ac.
— Family, State & Individual Economic Security, 2 vols., Set. 1096p. 1988. lib. bdg. 118.00 (*90-6544-399-1*) Kluwer Ac.
Meulen, A. Ter, ed. Studies in Modeltheoretic Semantics. (Groningen-Amsterdam Studies in Semantics). x, 206p. 1983. pap. 36.95 (*90-70176-80-7*) Mouton.
Meulen, Henry. Individualist Anarchism. (Men & Movements in the History & Philosophy of Anarchism Ser.). 1979. lib. bdg. 250.00 (*0-87700-315-7*) Revisionist Pr.
***Meulen, V. Ter & Billeter, M. A., eds.** Measles Virus. (Currents Topics in Microbiology & Immunology Ser.: Vol. 191). 319p. 1995. 118.00 (*0-387-57389-5*) Spr-Verlag.
Meulen, V. Ter & Katz, M. B., eds. Slow Virus Infections of the Central Nervous System. LC 77-1570. 1977. 101.00 (*0-387-90188-4*) Spr-Verlag.
Meulenbeld, G. Jan & Wujastyk, Dominik, eds. Studies on Indian Medical History: Papers Presented at the International Workshop on the Study of Indian Medicine Held at the Wellcome Institute for the History of Medicine, Sept. 2-4, 1985. (Groningen Oriental Studies: Vol. II). 247p. (Orig.). (C). 1987. pap. 46.00 (*90-6980-015-2*, Pub. by Egbert Forsten NE) Benjamins North Am.
Meulenbelt, Anja, et al, eds. A Creative Tension: Key Issues of Socialist Feminism. 152p. (Orig.). 1984. 30.00 (*0-89608-237-7*); pap. 8.50 (*0-89608-236-9*) South End Pr.
Meulenberg, Matthew, intro. Food & Agribusiness Marketing in Europe. LC 93-34606. (Journal of International Food & Agribusiness Marketing). (Illus.). 216p. 1993. lib. bdg. 49.95 (*1-56024-474-7*) Haworth Pr.
Meulenkamp, Johan D., jt. ed. see Seibold, Eugen.
Meulenkamp, Wim, jt. auth. see Plumridge, Andrew.
Meuli, Judith, jt. auth. see Carabillo, Toni.
Meuller, Francis J. Elements of Algebra. 3rd ed. (Illus.). 496p. 1981. text ed. write for info. (*0-13-262469-9*) P-H.
***Meunier, A., ed.** Clays & Hydrosilicate Gels in Nuclear Fields: Proceedings of Symposium B, E-MRS Fall Conference, Strasbourg, France, 4-7 November, 1991. (European Materials Research Society Symposia Proceedings Ser.: 26). vi, 250p. 1992. 191.50 (*0-444-89570-1*) Elsevier.
Meunier, C., jt. auth. see Lochak, P.
Meunier, J. Physics of Amphiphilic Layers. Langevin, D. & Boccara, Nino, eds. (Proceedings in Physics Ser.: Vol. 21). (Illus.). 410p. 1987. 71.00 (*0-387-18255-1*) Spr-Verlag.
Meunier, Jacques & Savarin, A. M. The Amazonian Chronicles. rev. ed. Christensen, Carol, tr. LC 93-12724. 240p. 1994. reprint ed. 20.00 (*1-56279-053-6*) Mercury Hse Inc.
Meunier-Tardif, Ghislaine. Eye People, Ear People: Getting Along. Baxter, Edward, tr. 144p. (Orig.). 1988. pap. 9.95 (*1-55021-009-2*, Pub. by NC Press CN) U of Toronto Pr.
Meuninck. Natural Health with Medicine. 1992. 59.95 (*0-939865-18-1*) Media Methods.
Meuninck, Jill, ed. see Meuninck, Jim.
Meuninck, Jim. The Basic Essentials of Edible Wild Plants & Useful Herbs. LC 88-13354. (Basic Essentials Ser.). (Illus.). 72p. (Orig.). 1988. pap. 5.99 (*0-934802-41-6*) ICS Bks.
— Diving Opportunities for Fun & Profit: Over 100 Ways to Make Money Diving. Gunter, Claude & Meuninck, Jill, eds. (Illus.). 216p. (Orig.). 1986. pap. 9.95 (*0-939865-00-9*) Media Methods.
Meurant, Georges. Shoowa Design: African Textiles from the Kingdom of Kuba. (Illus.). 200p. 1986. 60.00 (*0-500-59733-2*) Thames Hudson.
Meurant, Gloria. My Worship Planner & Organizer. 1992. pap. 7.50 (*1-55673-439-5*, 9242) CSS OH.
Meurer, K. A. Mineralocorticoids & Hypertension. Kaufman, W. et al, eds. (International Boehringer Mannheim Symposia Ser.). (Illus.). 225p. 1983. pap. 51.00 (*0-387-12391-1*) Spr-Verlag.
Meurer, Michael R. Sealed Battery Selection for Designers & Users. 1995. text ed. 55.00 (*0-07-041824-1*) McGraw.
Meurig, H. & Thomas, W. O. Y Geiriadur Mawr: The Complete Welsh-English, English-Welsh Dictionary. Williams, S. J., ed. 859p. (ENG & WEL.). 1981. 75.00 (*0-8288-4684-7*, M-9434) Fr & Eur.
Meuris, Jacques. Magritte. (Illus.). 236p. 1991. 39.98 (*0-89660-015-7*, Artabras) Abbeville Pr.
— Magritte. Underwood, J. A., tr. (Illus.). 236p. 1990. 85.00 (*0-87951-409-4*) Overlook Pr.
Meurn, Robert J. Survival Guide for the Mariner. (Illus.). 240p. 1993. text ed. 25.00x (*0-87033-444-1*) Cornell Maritime.
— Watchstanding Guide for the Merchant Marine. LC 89-71208. (Illus.). 288p. 1990. text ed. 27.50 (*0-87033-409-3*) Cornell Maritime.
Meurn, Robert J., jt. auth. see Sauerbier, Charles L.
Meurois-Givaudan, Anne & Meurois-Givaudan, Daniel. Way of the Essenes: Christ's Hidden Life Remembered. 400p. 1993. reprint ed. pap. 16.95 (*0-89281-322-9*, Destiny Bks) Inner Tradit.
Meurois-Givaudan, Daniel, jt. auth. see Meurois-Givaudan, Anne.
Meury, George. My Father Forgot to Mention... 1994. 8.95 (*0-8062-4951-X*) Carlton.
Meuse, Leonard F. Succeeding at Business & Technical Presentations. 2nd ed. 192p. 1988. text ed. 42.50 (*0-471-62486-1*) Wiley.
Meusel, Heinrich, ed. Caesar - Lexicon Caesarianum, Vol. I. vi, 772p. 1958. write for info. (*3-296-11201-4*, Pub. by Georg Olms GW) Lubrecht & Cramer.
— Caesar - Lexicon Caesarianum, Vol. II, 1. xi, 648p. 1958. write for info. (*3-296-11202-2*, Pub. by Georg Olms GW) Lubrecht & Cramer.
— Caesar - Lexicon Caesarianum, Vol. II, 2. 674p. 1958. write for info. (*3-296-11203-0*, Pub. by Georg Olms GW) Lubrecht & Cramer.
Meusel, Johann G. Lexikon der Vom Jahre 1750-1800 Verstorbenen Teutschen Schriftsteller, 15 vols., Set. 1968. reprint ed. write for info. (*0-318-71929-0*, Pub. by Georg Olms GW) Lubrecht & Cramer.
— Teutsches Kunstlerlexikon, 3 vols. reprint ed. write for info. (*0-318-71930-4*, Pub. by Georg Olms GW) Lubrecht & Cramer.
Meusel, Johann G., jt. auth. see Hamberger, Georg C.
Meuser, F., et al, eds. Plant Polymeric Carbohydrates. 295p. 1994. 99.95 (*0-85186-645-X*, Pub. by Royal Soc Chem UK) CRC Pr.
Meuss, A. R., tr. see Eggstein, Kurt.
Meuss, A. R., tr. see Wolff, Otto.
Meuss, Anna R., tr. see Society for Cancer Research Staff.
Meuss, Anna R., tr. see Steiner, Rudolf.
Meutsch, D., jt. ed. see Zwaan, R. A.
Meutsch, Dietrich & Viehoff, Reinhold, eds. Comprehension of Literary Discourse: Results & Problems of Interdisciplinary Approaches. (Research in Text Theory Ser.: No. 13). vi, 259p. (C). 1988. lib. bdg. 103.10 (*0-89925-465-9*) De Gruyter.
— Comprehension of Literary Discourse: Results & Problems of Interdisciplinary Approaches. (Research in Text Theory Ser.: No. 13). vi, 259p. (C). 1988. lib. bdg. 103.10 (*3-11-011111-X*) De Gruyter.
Meuwissen, Tony, illus. Miniature Bookplates: Moonlight Magic. 1993. boxed 3.95 (*1-56138-245-0*) Running Pr.
Meuzelaar, H. L., ed. Advances in Coal Spectroscopy. (Modern Analytical Chemistry Ser.). (Illus.). 408p. 1991. 89.50 (*0-306-43796-1*, Plenum Pr) Plenum.
— Computer-Enhanced Analytical Spectroscopy, Vol. 2. LC 87-15883. (Modern Analytical Chemistry Ser.). (Illus.). 340p. 1990. 79.50 (*0-306-43276-5*, Plenum Pr) Plenum.
Meuzelaar, H. L. & Isenhour, Thomas L., eds. Computer-Enhanced Analytical Spectroscopy, Vol. 1. LC 87-15883. (Modern Analytical Chemistry Ser.). (Illus.). 288p. 1988. 75.00 (*0-306-42644-7*, Plenum Pr) Plenum.
Meuzelaar, H. L., et al. Pyrolysis Mass Spectrometry of Recent & Fossil Biomaterials. (Techniques & Instrumentation in Analytical Chemistry Ser.: Vol. 3). 294p. 1982. 89.75 (*0-444-42099-1*) Elsevier.
Mevers, Frank C. Composite Index to Volumes 14-17 (Revolutionary War Rolls) of the New Hampshire State Papers. 343p. (Orig.). 1993. pap. 24.00 (*1-55613-824-5*) Heritage Bk.
***Meville, Peter.** Do Cats Need Shrinks. 1994. 6.98 (*0-7858-0158-8*) Bk Sales Inc.
Mevissen, Gerd J., jt. ed. see Gail, Adalbert J.
Mevlendyke, Eve, jt. auth. see Lipman, Jean.
Mevorach, J., jt. auth. see Kinori, B. Z.
Mevrin, Dawn. Billiards: Official Rules & Records Book. 272p. (Orig.). 1993. pap. 9.99 (*1-56171-210-8*, S P I Bks) Sure Sellers.
Mew. The Law of Limitations. 336p. 1991. 75.00 (*0-409-80909-8*) Butterworth Legal Pubs.
***Mew Group Staff.** Exploring Statistics, Set. (Illus.). 86p. 1993. student ed, teacher ed 110.00 (*0-340-53158-4*, Pub. by Hodder & Stoughton Ltd UK) Lubrecht & Cramer.
Mewes, Julia, jt. auth. see Farhar, Barbara C.
Mewett & Manning. Criminal Law. 2nd ed. 816p. 1985. 120.00 (*0-409-84922-7*) Butterworth Legal Pubs.
Mewett, Alan & Manning, Morris. Mewett & Manning on Criminal Law. 3rd ed. 1150p. (C). 1994. boxed 150.00 (*0-409-90375-2*, CN) Butterworth Legal Pubs.
***Mewis, J. J., et al, eds.** Loss Prevention & Safety Promotion in the Process Industries: Proceedings of the 8th International Symposium, Antwerp, Belgium, June 6-9, 1995, 2 vols. LC 95-6875. 1995. write for info. (*0-444-82136-8*) Elsevier.
— Loss Prevention & Safety Promotion in the Process Industries: Proceedings of the 8th International Symposium, Antwerp, Belgium, June 6-9, 1995, Vol. 1. LC 95-6875. 1995. write for info. (*0-444-82131-7*) Elsevier.
— Loss Prevention & Safety Promotion in the Process Industries: Proceedings of the 8th International Symposium, Antwerp, Belgium, June 6-9, 1995, Vol. 2. LC 95-6875. 1995. write for info. (*0-444-82134-1*) Elsevier.
Mews, Siegfried. Critical Essays on Bertolt Brecht. (Critical Essays on World Literature Ser.). 280p. 1989. text ed. 45.00 (*0-8161-8844-0*) G K Hall.
— Essays on Brecht. LC 78-31157. (North Carolina. University. Studies in the Germanic Languages & Literatures: No. 79). reprint ed. 27.00 (*0-404-50954-1*) AMS Pr.
Mews, Siegfried, ed. The Fisherman & His Wife: Gunter Grass's The Flounder in Critical Perspective. LC 81-69878. (Studies in Modern Literature: No. 12). (Illus.). 1983. 32.50 (*0-404-61582-1*) AMS Pr.
Mews, Siegfried & Hardin, James. Dictionary of Literary Biography 128: 20th Century Italian Poets, Vol. 128. (Second Ser.). 1993. 128.00 (*0-8103-5387-3*) Gale.
Mews, Stuart, ed. Religion in Politics: A World Guide. 332p. 1990. lib. bdg. 75.00 (*1-55862-051-6*) St James Pr.
Mewshaw, Michael. Ladies of the Court. LC 92-1645. 1993. 22.00 (*0-517-58758-0*, Crown) Crown Pub Group.
— Money to Burn. 480p. 1988. mass mkt. 4.50 (*1-55817-060-X*, Pinnacle NY) Windsor NY.
— Money to Burn. 1990. mass mkt. 4.95 (*1-55817-408-7*, Pinnacle NY) Windsor NY.
— True Crime. 1993. reprint ed. mass mkt. 5.99 (*0-449-22132-6*) Fawcett.
Mewton, Conrad, jt. auth. see Coleman, Nigel.
Mexican American Cultural Center Staff, tr. see Galeron, Soledad, et al.
Mexican American Legal Defense & Educational Fund Staff, et al. The Rights of the Immigrant Poor: A Legal Analysis. 1983. write for info. (*0-318-59004-2*) Mex Am Legal.
Mexican Museum Staff. Leonora Carrington: The Mexican Years, 1943-1985. 1992. pap. 20.00 (*1-880508-00-1*) Mexican Museum.
Mey, Jacob L. An Introduction to Pragmatics. LC 93-19925. 336p. 1993. 49.95 (*0-631-18689-1*); pap. 19.95 (*0-631-18691-3*) Blackwell Pubs.
— Whose Language: A Study in the Linguistic-Pragmatics. LC 85-6123. (Pragmatics & Beyond Companion Ser.: Vol. 3). ix, 412p. 1985. 84.00x (*0-915027-61-5*); pap. 27.95x (*0-915027-57-7*) Benjamins North Am.
Mey, Jacob L., ed. Language & Discourse: Test & Protest. A Festschift for Petr Sgall. LC 86-6882. (Linguistic & Literary Studies in Eastern Europe: Vol. 19). xiii, 611p. 1986. 127.00x (*90-272-1525-1*) Benjamins North Am.
— Pragmalinguistics: Theory & Practice. (Janua Linguarum, Series Major: No. 85). 1979. text ed. 80.80 (*90-279-7757-7*) Mouton.
Mey, Vander Brenda J. & Neff, Ronald L. Incest As Child Abuse: Research & Applications. LC 86-91536. 229p. 1986. text ed. 55.00 (*0-275-92114-X*, C2114, Praeger Pubs) Greenwood.
Meyanathan, Saha D., ed. Industrial Structures & the Development of Small & Medium Enterprise Linkages: Examples from East Asia. LC 94-20988. (EDI Seminar Ser.). 1994. write for info. (*0-8213-2876-X*) World Bank.
— Managing Restructuring in the Textile & Garment Subsector: Examples from Asia. LC 93-50881. (EDI Seminar Ser.). 1994. write for info. (*0-8213-2768-2*) World Bank.
Meybeck, M., jt. ed. see Lerman, A.

M

An Asterisk (*) at the beginning of an entry indicates that the title is appearing in BIP for the first time.

Meybeck, Michel, et al, eds. Global Freshwater Quality: A First Assessment. 360p. 1990. pap. text ed. 74.95 (*0-631-17314-5*) Blackwell Pubs.

*__Meybloom, Paul G.__ The Nile Mosaic of Palestrina: Early Evidence of Egyptian Religion in Italy. 424p. 1994. text ed. 123.00 (*90-04-10137-3*) E J Brill.

Meyen, Edward L., ed. Exceptional Children in Today's Schools. 2nd ed. LC 90-60835. 538p. 1990. text ed. 43.95 (*0-89108-213-1*) Love Pub Co.

Meyen, Edward L. & Skrtic, Thomas M., eds. Special Education & Student Disability: Traditional, Emerging, & Alternative Perspectives. 4th ed. LC 92-74811. Orig. Title: Exceptional Children & Youth. (Illus.). 700p. 1994. text ed. 49.95 (*0-89108-231-X*) Love Pub Co.

Meyen, Edward L., et al, eds. Challenges Facing Special Education. LC 92-74810. 404p. 1993. pap. 29.95 (*0-89108-229-8*, 9305) Love Pub Co.

— Educating Students with Mild Disabilities. LC 92-74809. 426p. 1993. pap. 29.95 (*0-89108-230-1*, 9306) Love Pub Co.

— Effective Instructional Strategies for Exceptional Children. LC 87-83464. 522p. 1988. pap. text ed. 29.95 (*0-89108-201-8*) Love Pub Co.

Meyen, Franz J. A Botanist's Visit to Oahu in 1831. Pultz, Mary Anne, ed. Jackson, Astrid, tr. LC 81-7353. (Illus.). 90p. 1981. pap. 6.95 (*0-916630-23-4*) Pr Pacifica.

Meyen, Franz J., 3rd. Outlines of the Geography of Plants: Native Country, the Culture, & the Uses of the Principal Cultivated Plants on Which the Prosperity of Nations Is Based. Egerton, Frank N., ed. LC 77-74239. (History of Ecology Ser.). 1978. reprint ed. lib. bdg. 39.95 (*0-405-10408-1*) Ayer.

Meyendorff, Alexander F., jt. auth. see Kohn, S.

Meyendorff, Elizabeth, tr. see Ouspensky, Leonid.

Meyendorff, J., et al, eds. The Legacy of St. Vladimir: Byzantium, Russia, America. LC 90-32389. 324p. 1990. pap. 10.95 (*0-88141-078-0*) St Vladimirs.

Meyendorff, John. The Byzantine Legacy in the Orthodox Church. LC 82-797. 268p. (Orig.). 1982. pap. 10.95 (*0-913836-90-7*) St Vladimirs.

— Byzantine Theology: Historical Trends & Doctrinal Themes. 2nd rev. ed. LC 72-94167. viii, 243p. 1987. pap. 16.00 (*0-8232-0967-9*) Fordham.

— Byzantium & the Rise of Russia. LC 89-28011. 326p. 1989. reprint ed. pap. 14.95 (*0-88141-079-9*) St Vladimirs.

— Catholicity & the Church. LC 83-20218. (Illus.). 160p. (Orig.). 1983. pap. 8.95 (*0-88141-006-3*) St Vladimirs.

— Christ in Eastern Christian Thought. LC 75-31977. Orig. Title: Le Christ Dans la Theologie Byzantine. 248p. 1975. pap. 12.95 (*0-913836-27-3*) St Vladimirs.

— Gregory Palamas, The Triads. (Classics of Western Spirituality Ser.). 192p. 1982. pap. 19.95 (*0-8091-2447-5*) Paulist Pr.

— Imperial Unity & Christian Divisions, Vol. II: The Church 450-680 AD. LC 87-31433. 402p. 1990. 29.95 (*0-88141-056-X*); pap. 16.95 (*0-88141-055-1*) St Vladimirs.

— Living Tradition. LC 78-2031. 202p. 1978. pap. 8.95 (*0-913836-48-6*) St Vladimirs.

— Marriage: An Orthodox Perspective. LC 75-14241. 144p. 1975. pap. 8.95 (*0-913836-05-2*) St Vladimirs.

— St. Gregory Palamas & Orthodox Spirituality. (Illus.). 184p. 1974. pap. 11.95 (*0-913836-11-7*) St Vladimirs.

— Vision of Unity. LC 87-23495. 192p. (Orig.). 1987. pap. 8.95 (*0-88141-068-3*) St Vladimirs.

— Vvedenie v Sviatootecheskoe Bogoslovia. rev. ed. Volokhonsky, Larisa, tr. LC 85-61006. 359p. (RUS.). 1985. pap. 16.00 (*0-934927-00-6*) RBR.

— Witness to the World. LC 87-23493. 262p. (Orig.). 1987. pap. 8.95 (*0-88141-069-1*) St Vladimirs.

Meyendorff, John, jt. auth. see Fahey, Michael J.

Meyendorff, John, jt. ed. see McGinn, Bernard.

Meyendorff, M. F. Vospominanija: Memoirs. (Illus.). 432p. 1990. 18.00 (*0-9616413-6-3*) Multilingual.

Meyendorff, Paul. Russia, Ritual, & Reform: The Liturgical Reforms of Nikon in the 17th Century. 256p. (Orig.). 1991. pap. 14.95 (*0-88141-090-X*) St Vladimirs.

Meyendorff, Paul, tr. see Aslanoff, Catherine, ed.

Meyendorff, Paul, tr. see St. Germanus of Constantinople.

Meyenn, K. V., ed. Wolfgang Pauli: Scientific Correspondence with Bohr, Einstein, Heisenberg a. o. Part II: 1930-1939. (Sources in the History of Mathematics & Physical Sciences Ser.: Vol. 6). 800p. 1985. 179.00 (*0-387-13609-6*) Spr-Verlag.

Meyenn, K. V., jt. ed. see Hermann, A.

Meyer. Expert Systems in Factory Management. 1990. pap. text ed. 110.00 (*0-13-293473-6*) P-H.

— Five Speeches That Changed the World. 144p. (Orig.). 1994. pap. text ed. 9.95 (*0-8146-2282-8*) Liturgical Pr.

— Sappho's Raft. deluxe ed. 1990. pap. 30.00 (*0-912330-52-X*) Jargon Soc.

— Secondary & Functional Rhinoplasty: The Difficult Nose. 1988. text ed. 250.00 (*0-8089-1879-6*, Grune) Saunders.

— Tools 14: Technology of Object-Oriented Languages & Systems. 562p. (C). 1994. pap. text ed. 60.00 (*0-13-199415-8*) P-H.

Meyer, jt. auth. see Ciccione.

Meyer, jt. auth. see Jackins, Harvey.

Meyer, ed. see Moliere.

Meyer, jt. auth. see Spurgeon.

Meyer, et al. Critical Issues in the Lives of People with Severe Disabilities. LC 90-32081. 704p. 1991. text ed. 90.00 (*1-55766-048-4*) P H Brookes.

Meyer, A. Voltaire. 1972. 59.95 (*0-8490-1268-6*) Gordon Pr.

Meyer, A. & Orlando, S. German-Italian, Italian-German Technical Dictionary: Dizionario Tecnico Italiano-Tedesco-Italiano. 6th ed. 2912p. (ITA.). 1981. 125.00 (*0-8288-2122-4*, M8446) Fr & Eur.

— German-Italian Technical Dictionary of Architecture Nuclear Weapons & Civil Engineering: Technisches Worterbuch: Architektur, Atomwaffen, Bauwesen, Vol. 2. 6th ed. 1567p. (GER & ITA.). 1981. 95.00 (*0-8288-0883-X*, M7652) Fr & Eur.

— Italian-German Technical Dictionary of Architecture - Nuclear Weapons & Civil Engineering: Technisches Woerterbuch: Architektur, Atomwaffen, Bauwesen, Vol. 1. 6th ed. 1345p. (GER & ITA.). 1981. 95.00 (*0-8288-0882-1*, M7651) Fr & Eur.

Meyer, A. E., ed. The Hamburg Short Psychotherapy Comparison Experiment. (Psychotherapy & Psychosomatics Journal: Vol. 35, Nos. 2-3, 1981). (Illus.). 136p. 1981. 31.25 (*3-8055-3435-3*) S Karger.

Meyer, A. G. Transmission Development of TEXTRON Lycoming's Geared Fan Engines. (Fall Technical Meeting Papers 88FTM14). (Illus.). 10p. 1988. pap. text ed. 30.00 (*1-55589-519-0*) AGMA.

Meyer, A. R. & Taitslin, M. A., eds. Logic at Botik Eighty-Nine. (Lecture Notes in Computer Science Ser.: Vol. 363). x, 289p. 1989. pap. 37.00 (*0-387-51237-3*) Spr-Verlag.

Meyer-Abich, Klaus M. Revolution for Nature. Armstrong, Matthew, tr. (Philosophy & the Environment Ser.: No. 3). 160p. 1993. 25.00 (*0-929398-70-X*); pap. 15.95 (*0-929398-69-6*) UNTX Pr.

Meyer, Adolf. The Commonsense Psychiatry of Dr. Adolf Meyer: Fifty-Two Selected Papers. Lief, Alfred, ed. LC 73-2406. (Mental Illness & Social Policy; the American Experience Ser.). 1973. reprint ed. 46.95 (*0-405-05216-2*) Ayer.

Meyer, Adolf, jt. auth. see Gropius, Walter.

Meyer, Adolph E. Development of Education in the Twentieth Century. 2nd ed. LC 75-97332. 609p. 1969. reprint ed. text ed. 85.00 (*0-8371-2838-2*, MEET, Greenwood Pr) Greenwood.

— Grandmasters of Educational Thought. 302p. (C). 1975. text ed. write for info. (*0-07-041737-7*) McGraw.

— Modern European Educators & Their Work. LC 73-152197. (Essay Index Reprint Ser.). 1977. reprint ed. 20.95 (*0-8369-2246-8*) Ayer.

Meyer, Agnes E. Out of These Roots. Baxter, Annette K., ed. LC 79-8801. (Signal Lives Ser.). (Illus.). 1980. reprint ed. lib. bdg. 46.95 (*0-405-12848-7*) Ayer.

Meyer, Alain. La Condition Humaine de Malraux. 254p. (FRE.). 1991. pap. 15.95 (*0-7859-4530-X*, 207038442X) Fr & Eur.

*__Meyer, Albert J. & Sutter, David L.__ Growing Pastors, Growing People: Initiating Denomination-Wide Change in the Pastor-People Partnership. Date not set. pap. 8.00 (*1-56699-140-4*, OD110) Alban Inst.

Meyer, Albert J. & Vassiliou, Simos. The Economy of Cyprus. LC 62-8183. (Harvard Middle Eastern Studies: No. 5). (Illus.). 125p. reprint ed. pap. 35.70 (*0-7837-1522-6*, 2041799) Bks Demand.

Meyer, Albert R., et al, eds. Research Directions in Computer Science: an MIT Perspective. 516p. 1991. pap. 45.00 (*0-262-13257-5*) MIT Pr.

Meyer, Alfred G. Communism. 4th ed. 256p. (C). 1984. pap. text ed. 10.50 (*0-394-33163-X*) Random.

— The Feminism & Socialism of Lily Braun. LC 84-43077. (Illus.). 256p. 1986. 29.95 (*0-253-32169-7*) Ind U Pr.

Meyer, Alfred G., ed. see Braun, Lilian J.

Meyer, Alfred G., jt. ed. see Wolchik, Sharon L.

Meyer, Alfred W., jt. auth. see Speidel, Richard E.

Meyer, Alice, jt. auth. see Meyer, David.

Meyer, Alice, jt. ed. see Meyer, David.

Meyer, Allen & Nowak, Michael. The Signal Season of Dummy Hoy. 63p. 1992. pap. 5.95 (*1-56850-013-0*) Chicago Plays.

*__Meyer, Alvin & Meyer, Kitty.__ All Ears. Huiping, Cal, tr. (Illus.). 32p. (Orig.). (CHI.). 1995. pap. write for info. (*0-9645121-0-6*) US China Invest.

Meyer, Andy & Becker, Jim. Zero Calorie Desserts. LC 87-42741. (Illus.). 1988. pap. 4.95 (*0-89480-505-3*, 1505) Workman Pub.

Meyer, Annette E. Evolution of United States Budgeting: Changing Fiscal & Financial Concepts. LC 89-1890. 193p. 1989. text ed. 49.95 (*0-313-25868-6*, MEV, Greenwood Pr) Greenwood.

Meyer, Annie & Munro, Mary Lynn. A Coloring Cookbook for Children. 64p. (Orig.). (J). (gr. 1-6). 1974. pap. 3.95 (*0-89716-061-4*) P B Pubng.

Meyer, Annie N., ed. Woman's Work in America. LC 72-2615. (American Women Ser.: Images & Realities). 462p. 1980. reprint ed. 26.95 (*0-405-04469-0*) Ayer.

*__Meyer-Arendt, Jurgen R.__ Introduction to Classical & Modern Optics. 4th ed. LC 94-30562. 1994. text ed. 70.00 (*0-13-124356-X*) P-H.

Meyer-Arendt, Jurgen R., ed. Selected Papers on Schlieren Optics. LC 92-29545. (Milestone Ser.: Vol. MS 61). 1992. 62.00 (*0-8194-1048-9*); pap. 77.00 (*0-8194-1049-7*) SPIE.

Meyer, Art & Meyer, Jocele. Earthkeepers: Environmental Perspectives on Hunger, Poverty, & Injustice. LC 90-24473. 264p. (Orig.). 1991. pap. 12.95 (*0-8361-3544-X*) Herald Pr.

Meyer, Arthur W. The Rise of Embryology. LC 40-3220. (Illus.). 115p. reprint ed. pap. 30.00 (*0-318-39758-7*, 2033132) Bks Demand.

Meyer, B. Indoor Air Quality. 1982. text ed. write for info. (*0-201-05094-3*) Addison-Wesley.

Meyer, B., et al, eds. Formaldehyde Release from Wood Products. LC 86-14194. (ACS Symposium Ser.: No. 316). (Illus.). 240p. 1986. 54.95 (*0-8412-0982-0*) Am Chemical.

Meyer, B. E., tr. see Hoffding, Harald.

Meyer, B. H. History of Transportation in the United States Before 1860. 678p. 1993. reprint ed. lib. bdg. 109.00 (*0-7812-5217-2*) Rprt Serv.

Meyer-Baer, Kathi. Music of the Spheres & the Dance of Death. LC 83-18905. (Music Reprint Ser.). (Illus.). 376p. 1984. reprint ed. lib. bdg. 47.50 (*0-306-76224-2*) Da Capo.

Meyer, Balthasar H. Railway Legislation in the United States. LC 73-2523. (Big Business; Economic Power in a Free Society Ser.). 1973. reprint ed. 23.95 (*0-405-05102-6*) Ayer.

Meyer, Balthasar Henry. A History of the Northern Securities Case. LC 70-124898. (American Constitutional & Legal History Ser). 136p. 1972. reprint ed. lib. bdg. 24.50 (*0-306-71989-4*) Da Capo.

Meyer, Barbara & Katz, Lori. One Hundred One Super Uses for Tampon Applicators: A Helpful Guide for the Environmentally Conscious Consumer of Feminine Hygiene Products. LC 94-78293. (Illus.). 128p. (Orig.). 1995. pap. 9.95 (*0-9641907-0-2*) High Stress.

Meyer, Barbara F. Cooking for a Crowd Naturally: Over 200 Recipes for Large Groups & Institutions. 192p. (Orig.). pap. 29.95 (*0-9614339-0-6*) Stamlyn Pub Co.

— Earth, Water, Fire, Air: A Vegetarian Cookbook for the 90s. LC 91-17660. 1992. pap. 16.95 (*0-87131-678-1*) M Evans.

Meyer, Barbara F. & Cato, Bob. The Great Garlic Cookbook. LC 91-43496. 1992. pap. 14.95 (*0-87131-673-0*) M Evans.

Meyer, Beat. Urea-Formaldehyde Resins. (Illus.). 1979. text ed. write for info. (*0-201-04558-3*) Addison-Wesley.

Meyer, Ben F. Christus Faber: The Master-Builder & the House of God. (Princeton Theological Monograph Ser.: No. 29). (Orig.). 1992. pap. 27.50 (*1-55635-014-7*) Pickwick.

— Critical Realism in the New Testament. LC 88-31722. (Princeton Theological Monograph Ser.: No. 17). 225p. (Orig.). 1989. pap. 19.95 (*0-915138-97-2*) Pickwick.

— The Early Christians: Their World Mission & Self-Discovery. (Good News Studies: Vol. 16). 245p. 1986. pap. 12.95 (*0-8146-5542-4*) Liturgical Pr.

— One Loaf, One Cup: Ecumenical Studies of 1 Cor 11 & Other Eucharistic Texts. (New Gospel Studies: No. 6). 180p. 1992. 25.00 (*0-86554-398-4*, MUP/H324) Mercer Univ Pr.

— Reality & Illusion in the New Testament Scholarship: A Primer in Critical Realist Hermeneutics. 272p. (Orig.). 1994. pap. text ed. 16.95 (*0-8146-5771-0*, M Glazier) Liturgical Pr.

Meyer, Ben F. & Sanders, E. P., eds. Jewish & Christian Self-Definition, Vol. 3. 320p. (C). 1982. text ed. 26.95 (*0-334-00822-0*, SCM Pr) TPI PA.

Meyer, Ben F., jt. ed. see McEvenue, Sean E.

Meyer, Bernadine, jt. auth. see Kolasa, Blair J.

Meyer, Bernard S. Botany at the Ohio State University: The First One Hundred Years, No. 2. Reese, Karen J. & Sciulli, Veda M., eds. (Bulletin New Ser.: Vol. 6). 177p. 1983. 10.00 (*0-86727-096-9*) Ohio Bio Survey.

Meyer, Bertrand. Eiffel: The Environment. 250p. 1994. text ed. 38.00 (*0-13-245507-2*) P-H.

— Eiffel: The Language & Environment. 300p. 1991. pap. text ed. 38.00 (*0-13-247925-7*) P-H.

— Eiffel: The Libraries. 400p. 1994. text ed. 44.00 (*0-13-245499-8*) P-H.

— Intro Theory of Programming Languages. 550p. 1988. boxed 37.00 (*0-318-37858-2*) P-H.

— Object-Oriented Software Construction. 1988. text ed. 55.00 (*0-13-629049-3*) P-H.

Meyer, Bertrand, et al. Tools 11: Technology of Object-Oriented Languages & Systems. 1993. pap. text ed. 60.00 (*0-13-103979-2*) P-H.

Meyer, Bertrand. Tools 5: Technology of Object-Oriented Languages & Systems. 416p. 1991. pap. text ed. 67.00 (*0-13-923178-1*) P-H.

Meyer, Bertrand & Beziven, Jean. Tools 4: Technology of Object-Oriented Languages & Systems. 415p. 1991. pap. text ed. 74.00 (*0-13-923160-9*, 270609) P-H.

Meyer, Bertrand & Nerson, Jean-Marc, eds. Object-Oriented Applications. LC 93-11370. 1993. pap. text ed. 54.00 (*0-13-013798-7*) P-H.

Meyer, Bertrand, et al. Tools Seven. 448p. 1992. pap. text ed. 82.00 (*0-13-917436-2*) P-H.

— Tools 8. 1992. pap. text ed. 75.00 (*0-13-042441-2*) P-H.

Meyer, Beryl, jt. auth. see Klensch, Elsa.

Meyer, Bette E. Fort George Wright: Not Only When the Band Played. LC 93-32422. 1993. write for info. (*0-87770-525-9*) Ye Galleon.

Meyer, Beverly, jt. auth. see Parsons, Virgil.

Meyer, Blaire, et al, eds. The Road of Life. (Illus.). 70p. (Orig.). 1987. pap. 5.00 (*0-9615214-1-4*) Barton Cty Comm.

Meyer-Blanck, Michael. Leben, Leib & Liturgie: Die Praktische Theologie Wilhelm Staehlins. (Arbeiten zur Praktischen Theologie: Vol. 6). xiv, 465p. (GER.). (C). 1994. lib. bdg. 152.35 (*3-11-014364-X*) De Gruyter.

— Wort und Antwort: Geschichte und Gestaltung der Konfirmation am Beispiel der Ev.-luth. Landeskirche Hannovers. (Arbeiten zur Praktischen Theolgie Ser.: Bd. 2). xii, 338p. (GER.). (C). 1992. lib. bdg. 106.15 (*3-11-013258-3*, 248-91) De Gruyter.

Meyer, Bonney, jt. auth. see Grey, John.

Meyer, Bonnie J., et al. Memory Improved: Reading & Memory Enhancement Across the Life Span Through Strategic Text Structure. 264p. 1989. 49.95 (*0-8058-0111-1*) L Erlbaum Assocs.

Meyer-Botnarescue, Helen, jt. auth. see Machado, Jeanne M.

Meyer, Bradley J. Talk Is Cheap. 1993. 16.95 (*0-533-10467-X*) Vantage.

Meyer-Breiting, E & Burkhardt, A. Tumours of the Larynx. (Illus.). 240p. 1988. 187.00 (*0-387-16342-5*) Spr-Verlag.

*__Meyer, Brian.__ A-to-Z Bus Tour of Buffalo: A Kid's Guide. (Kid's Guide Ser.). 1993. pap. 3.50 (*1-879201-10-0*) Meyer Enter.

— Buffalo Bluff. 1988. pap. 13.95 (*0-9620314-5-3*) Meyer Enter.

— Hometown Heroes: Western New Yorkers in Desert Storm. 1992. pap. 5.95 (*1-879201-07-0*) Meyer Enter.

— Quotable Cuomo: The Mario Years. 1991. pap. 5.95 (*1-879201-03-8*) Meyer Enter.

— The World According to Griffin: End of an Era. 1993. pap. 5.95 (*1-879201-11-9*) Meyer Enter.

Meyer, Bruce & O'Riordan, Brian. In Their Words: Interviews with Fourteen Canadian Writers. (Illus.). 211p. (Orig.). 1984. pap. 12.95 (*0-88784-142-2*, Pub. by Hse of Anansi Pr CN) Genl Dist Srvs.

Meyer, Bruce F., jt. auth. see Missair, Alfredo R.

Meyer, Bruce L. Data Communications Practice. rev. ed. LC 73-85629. (ABC of the Telephone Ser.: Vol. 11). (Illus.). 68p. (C). 1988. pap. text ed. 21.95 (*1-56016-010-1*) ABC TeleTraining.

Meyer, C. & Nienhuis, H. Discharge Lamps. Van Rees Vellinga, E. F., tr. (Philips Technical Library). (Illus.). 312p. 1989. text ed. 120.00 (*90-201-2147-2*) Scholium Intl.

Meyer, C. A. Thermodynamic & Transport Properties of Steam. LC 67-3043. 363p. reprint ed. pap. 103.50 (*0-317-11072-1*, 2011011) Bks Demand.

Meyer, C. K., et al. The Guide to South Dakota Grant Assistance & Technical Services. 1975. 5.00 (*1-55614-044-4*) U of SD Gov Res Bur.

Meyer, C. Kenneth, et al. Social Indicators: An Aid to Public Policy Evaluation in State Government. 1979. 1.00 (*1-55614-114-9*) U of SD Gov Res Bur.

Meyer, C. Kenneth & Brown, Charles H. Practicing Public Management: A Casebook. 2nd ed. LC 88-60537. 250p. (C). 1988. pap. text ed. 16.00 (*0-312-00329-3*) St Martin.

Meyer, C. Kenneth, et al. An Assessment of Grant Information & Tracking Systems: A Look at Selected Agencies of South Dakota State Government. 1978. 5.00 (*1-55614-021-5*) U of SD Gov Res Bur.

— Direct Democracy in South Dakota: The People Conducting Their Own Business. 1979. 10.00 (*1-55614-033-9*) U of SD Gov Res Bur.

Meyer-Camberg, Ernst. Das Praktische Lexikon der Naturheilkunde: Practical Lexicon of Natural Healing. (GER.). 1977. pap. 45.00 (*0-8288-5514-5*, M7594) Fr & Eur.

Meyer, Carl D. & Plemmons, Richard J., eds. Linear Algebra, Markov Chains, & Queueing Models. LC 93-2100. (IMA Volumes in Mathematics & Its Applications Ser.: Vol. 48). (Illus.). 1993. 49.00 (*0-387-94085-5*); write for info. (*3-540-94085-5*) Spr-Verlag.

Meyer, Carl F. & Gibson, David W. Route Surveying & Design. 5th ed. (Illus.). (C). 1990. text ed. 67.50 (*0-7002-2524-2*) HarpCollege.

Meyer, Carl H. & Matyas, Stephen M. Cryptography: A New Dimension in Computer Data Security: A Guide for the Design & Implementation of Secure Systems. LC 82-2831. 755p. 1982. text ed. 124.00 (*0-471-04892-5*) Wiley.

Meyer, Carl S., ed. Moving Frontiers. 524p. 1986. pap. 17.95 (*0-570-04461-8*, 12-3069) Concordia.

Meyer, Carol. Glass from Quseir al-Qadim & the Indian Ocean Trade. LC 92-61543. (Studies in Ancient Oriental Civilization: No. 53). (Illus.). xxvi, 201p. 1991. pap. 35.00 (*0-918986-87-7*) Orientl Inst Pr IT.

Meyer, Carol B., ed. Analysis of Workers Compensation Laws, 1990. 64p. 1990. pap. 25.00 (*0-685-32871-6*) Natl Chamber Foun.

Meyer, Carol H. Assessment in Social Work Practice. 192p. (C). 1993. text ed. 27.50 (*0-231-07556-1*) Col U Pr.

— Clinical Social Work in the Eco-Systems Perspective. 1983. text ed. 32.00 (*0-231-05194-8*) Col U Pr.

— Social Work Practice. 2nd ed. LC 75-20949. (Illus.). 1976. pap. 18.95 (*0-02-921160-3*) Free Pr.

Meyer, Carol H., ed. Social Work with the Aging. rev. ed. LC 75-27193. (Readings in Social Work Ser.). 257p. 1986. pap. text ed. 21.95 (*0-87101-139-5*) Natl Assn Soc Wkrs.

*__Meyer, Carol H. & Mattaini, Mark, eds.__ Foundations of Social Work Practice: A Graduate Text. (C). 1995. lib. bdg. 34.95 (*0-87101-237-5*, 2375) Natl Assn Soc Wkrs.

*__Meyer, Carolyn.__ Drummers of Jericho. (J). 1995. 11.00 (*0-15-200441-6*); pap. 5.00 (*0-15-200190-5*) HarBrace.

— Killing the Kudu. LC 90-6089. 208p. (YA). (gr. 9 up). 1990. text ed. 14.95 (*0-689-50508-6*, McElderry) S&S Childrens.

— A Voice from Japan: An Outsider Looks In. (Illus.). 212p. (YA). (gr. 7 up). 1988. 14.95 (*0-15-200633-8*, Gulliver Bks) HarBrace.

— Voice from Japan: An Outsider Looks In. (YA). 1992. pap. 9.95 (*0-15-200634-6*) HarBrace.

— Voices of Northern Ireland: Growing up in a Troubled Land. LC 87-199. (Illus.). 212p. (YA). (gr. 7 up). 1987. 15.95 (*0-15-200635-4*, Gulliver Bks) HarBrace.

— Voices of Northern Ireland: Growing up in a Troubled Land. (YA). 1992. pap. 9.95 (*0-15-200636-2*) HarBrace.

— Voices of Northern Ireland: Growing Up in a Troubled Land. (YA). (gr. 7 up). 1992. pap. 9.95 (*0-15-200638-9*) HarBrace.

— Voices of South Africa: Growing up in a Troubled Land. LC 86-45059. 244p. (J). (gr. 7 up). 1986. 16.95 (*0-15-200637-0*) HarBrace.

— Where the Broken Heart Still Beats. LC 92-257. (Great Episodes Historical Ser.). (J). (gr. 4-7). 1992. 16.95 (*0-15-200639-7*); pap. 6.95 (*0-15-295602-6*) HarBrace.

— White Lilacs. LC 92-30503. (J). 1993. 10.95 (*0-15-200641-9*) HarBrace.

— White Lilacs. (J). (gr. 4-7). 1993. pap. 5.00 (*0-15-295876-2*, HB Juv Bks) HarBrace.

Meyer, Carolyn, comp. Rio Grande Stories. LC 93-33639. (J). 1994. 10.95 (*0-15-200548-X*); pap. 3.95 (*0-15-200066-6*) HarBrace.

An Asterisk (*) at the beginning of an entry indicates that the title is appearing in BIP for the first time.

Meyer, Carolyn & Gallenkamp, Charles. The Mystery of the Ancient Maya. LC 84-24209. (Illus.). 176p. (YA). (gr. 7 up). 1985. lib. bdg. 14.95 (0-689-50319-9, McElderry) S&S Childrens.
— The Mystery of the Ancient Maya. rev. ed. (J). 1994. 14.95 (0-689-50619-8, McElderry) S&S Childrens.
Meyer, Carolyn & Pickens, Kel. Multicultural Sing & Learn: Folk Songs & Monthly Activities. (Illus.). 144p. (J). (gr. k-5). 1994. 12.95 (0-86653-830-5, GA1522) Good Apple.
— Sing & Learn. (Illus.). 144p. (J). (ps-3). 1989. student ed 12.95 (0-86653-476-8, GA1078) Good Apple.
Meyer, Carolyn J. Human Development. 4th ed. 288p. (C). 1986. student ed write for info. (0-317-44275-9) P-H.
Meyer, Carolyn M. Suzuki Repertory Group Lessons for Violin & Viola. 84p. 1993. pap. text ed. 12.95 (0-87487-435-1) Summy-Birchard.
Meyer, Carrie A. Land Reform in Latin America: The Dominican Case. LC 88-39661. 142p. 1989. text ed. 49.95 (0-275-93202-8, C3202, Praeger Pubs) Greenwood.
Meyer, Carrie A., et al. Population Growth, Poverty, & Environmental Stress: Frontier Migration in the Philippines & Costa Rica. 90p. 1992. Large format. pap. 14.95 (0-915825-86-4, MEPPP) World Resources Inst.
***Meyer, Charles.** The Saints of God Murders. 256p. (Orig.). 1995. pap. text ed. 4.99 (0-425-14869-6, Prime Crime) Berkley Pub.
— Surviving Death: A Practical Guide to Caring for the Dying & the Bereaved. rev. ed. LC 91-65169. 144p. 1991. pap. 9.95 (0-89622-486-4) Twenty-Third.
Meyer, Charles & Kilbourn, W. Douglas, Jr. Accounting for Lawyers. 1994. student ed 30.00 (1-55917-002-6, 4318); audio 135.00 (1-55917-000-X) Natl Prac Inst.
Meyer, Charles E. Rituals of the First Four Grades Societatis Rosicruciana. 1993. pap. 9.95 (1-56459-364-9) Kessinger Pub.
Meyer, Charles F. Apposition in Contemporary English. (Studies in English Language). (Illus.). 152p. (C). 1992. 44.95 (0-521-39475-9) Cambridge U Pr.
Meyer, Charles F., jt. ed. see Aarts, Bas.
***Meyer, Charles H.** Accounting & Finance for Lawyers in a Nutshell. (Nutshell Ser.). 407p. 1994. pap. text ed. 17.00 (0-314-04763-8) West Pub.
— The Securities Exchange Act of 1934: Analyzed & Explained. 251p. 1994. reprint ed. lib. bdg. 35.00 (0-8377-2447-3) Rothman.
Meyer, Charles R. Art of Scrimshaw. 1976. 21.95 (0-8488-0293-4) Amereon Ltd.
— How to Be a Clown. 1976. 14.95 (0-8488-0295-0); pap. 8.95 (0-8488-0294-2) Amereon Ltd.
— How to Be a Juggler. 1976. 14.95 (0-8488-0297-7); pap. 10.95 (0-8488-0296-9) Amereon Ltd.
— How to Be a Juggler. (Ringling Brothers - Barnum & Bailey Book). (Illus.). (J). (gr. 4-7). 1977. 6.95 (0-679-20407-5) McKay.
— How to Be a Magician. 1976. 14.95 (0-8488-0299-3); pap. 10.95 (0-8488-0298-5) Amereon Ltd.
— How to Be an Acrobat. 1976. 14.95 (0-8488-0301-9); pap. 10.95 (0-8488-0300-0) Amereon Ltd.
Meyer, Charles S. Digital Audio Design Handbook. 110p. (C). 1994. pap. text ed. write for info. (0-9640361-1-8) NVision.
— 1995 Catalog of Products & Application Notes. (Illus.). 112p. (Orig.). (C). 1995. pap. 12.00 (0-614-05121-5) NVision.
Meyer, Charles W., ed. Social Security: A Critique of Radical Reform Proposals. 178p. 1987. text ed. 35.00 (0-669-14518-1) Free Pr.
Meyer, Charles W. & Wolff, Nancy. Social Security & Individual Equity: Evolving Standards of Equity & Adequacy. LC 92-25739. (Studies in Social Welfare Policies & Programs: No. 15). 208p. 1993. text ed. 49.95 (0-313-26459-7, MYC, Greenwood Pr) Greenwood.
Meyer, Christian, ed. Finite Elements Idealization for Linear Elastic Static & Dynamic Analysis of Structures in Engineering Practice. 454p. 1988. 44.00 (0-87262-628-8) Am Soc Civil Eng.
Meyer, Christian & Okamura, Hajime, eds. Finite Element Analysis of Reinforced Concrete Structures. (Seminar Proceedings Ser.). 696p. 1986. 55.00 (0-87262-549-4) Am Soc Civil Eng.
Meyer, Christine & Moosang, Faith. Living with the Land: Communities Restoring the Earth. (New Catalyst Bioregional Ser.). 144p. 1992. 34.95 (0-86571-250-6); pap. 9.95 (0-86571-251-4) New Soc Pubs.
Meyer, Christopher. Fast Cycle Time: How to Align Purpose, Strategy, & Structure for Speed. 288p. 1993. text ed. 29.95 (0-02-921181-6) Free Pr.
Meyer, Chuck. The Eighth Day Letters, Poems & Parables. 175p. (Orig.). 1991. pap. 8.95 (0-9631149-1-3) Stone Angel.
— Fast, Funny, & Forty. 170p. (Orig.). 1994. pap. 9.95 (0-9631149-3-X) Stone Angel.
— God's Laughter & Other Heresies. 2nd ed. 238p. 1992. pap. 9.95 (0-9631149-0-5) Stone Angel.
— The Gospel According to Bubba. (Illus.). 192p. (Orig.). 1992. pap. 9.95 (0-9631149-2-1) Stone Angel.
Meyer, Clarence. American Folk Medicine. LC 85-155364. 312p. 1985. reprint ed. pap. 9.95 (0-916638-10-3) Meyerbooks.
— Herbal Aphrodisiacs from World Sources. enl. ed. Meyer, David, ed. (Illus.). 156p. (Orig.). 1993. pap. 8.95 (0-916638-23-5) Meyerbooks.
— The Herbalist Almanac: Fifty Years of Herbal Knowledge. Meyer, David C., ed. (Illus.). 1977. pap. 9.95 (0-916638-02-2) Meyerbooks.
— Old Ways Rediscovered. Meyer, David C., ed. (Illus.). 156p. (Orig.). 1988. pap. 8.95 (0-916638-18-9) Meyerbooks.
— Onions: Condiment, Nutrient, Medicine. Meyer, David C., ed. (Illus.). 115p. (Orig.). 1993. pap. 8.95 (0-916638-16-2) Meyerbooks.
— Vegetarian Medicines. Meyer, David C., ed. (Illus.). 96p. (Orig.). 1981. pap. 5.95 (0-916638-06-5) Meyerbooks.
Meyer, Clarence, comp. Herbal Recipes. (Illus.). 1978. pap. 3.95 (0-916638-04-9) Meyerbooks.
— Sachets, Potpourri & Incense Recipes. (Illus.). 96p. (Orig.). 1986. pap. 3.95 (0-916638-13-8) Meyerbooks.
Meyer, Clarence, illus. Essential Oils of Herbs & Flowers: A Guide & Recipe Book. 100p. (Orig.). 1995. pap. write for info. (0-916638-14-6) Meyerbooks.
Meyer, Claudia. Donald Teague: A Life in Color. (Illus.). 144p. 1988. 75.00 (0-9620327-0-0); 300.00 (0-9620327-1-9) Nygard Pub.
Meyer, Conrad F. Plautus in the Convent. Howard, William G., tr. Bd. with Monk's Marriage. LC 64-20048. LC 64-20048. xiv, 133p. 1964. Set pap. 3.95 (0-8044-6503-7) Continuum.
— The Saint. Hauch, E. F., tr. 1976. reprint ed. 35.00 (0-86527-298-0) Fertig.
— The Saint: A Fictional Biography of Thomas Becket. Twaddell, W. F., tr. LC 77-7038. 137p. reprint ed. pap. 39.10 (0-685-20775-7, 2030027) Bks Demand.
— The Tempting of Pescara. Bell, C., tr. LC 75-4902. 184p. 1975. reprint ed. 35.00 (0-86527-313-8) Fertig.
Meyer, Corky & Ginter, Steve. Grumman Swing-Wing XF10F-1 Jaguar. (Naval Fighters Ser.: No. 26). (Illus.). 34p. (Orig.). 1993. pap. text ed. 6.95 (0-942612-26-4) Naval Fighters.
Meyer, Cynthia A., ed. see Knox, Carol R.
Meyer, D. Union Square Cafe Cookbook. 1994. 30.00 (0-06-017013-1, HarpT) HarpC.
Meyer, Damon, jt. auth. see Ingraham, Lloyd L.
Meyer, Dan. Account for Your Own Success: Everything You Need to Manage Your Own Business & Personal Finances. (Illus.). 176p. 1993. pap. 16.95 (0-932150-04-7) MCS.
Meyer, Dan & Williams, Tom. Painless Recordkeeping: For That Small or Sideline Business of Yours. (Illus.). 150p. 1985. pap. write for info. (0-932150-02-0) MCS.
Meyer, Dan, et al. To Know by Experience-Outward Bound North Carolina. 4th ed. LC 73-83707. 136p. 1979. reprint ed. 12.00 (0-932150-03-9) MCS.
Meyer, Daniel. Stephen A. Douglas & the American Union. LC 94-2381. 1994. pap. 10.00 (0-943056-21-7) Univ Chi Lib.
Meyer, Daniel E., et al, eds. Chemical Structure Software for Personal Computers. LC 88-8153. (ACS Professional Reference Bk.). (Illus.). xiv, 107p. 1988. 39.95 (0-8412-1538-3); pap. 24.95 (0-8412-1539-1) Am Chemical.
Meyer, Daniel P. & Mayer, Herbert A. Radar Target Detection: Handbook of Theory & Practice. (Electrical Science Ser.). 1973. text ed. 140.00 (0-12-492850-1) Acad Pr.
***Meyer, David.** Quiz Book. 130p. 1995. pap. 7.95 (1-56901-877-4) NW Pub.
Meyer, David, comp. Howard Thurston's Card Tricks: An Illustrated & Descriptive Checklist of Various Editions Covering a 50 Year Period. (Illus.). 48p. (Orig.). 1991. pap. 12.00 (0-916638-75-8) Meyerbooks.
Meyer, David & Meyer, Alice. The Ten Commandments: An Illustrated Bible Passage for Young Children. LC 90-71557. (Illus.). 40p. (Orig.). (J). (ps-4). 1991. pap. 11.95 (1-879099-02-0) Thy Word.
Meyer, David & Meyer, Alice, eds. First Corinthians Thirteen: An Illustrated Bible Chapter for Young Children. LC 90-71555. (Illus.). 48p. (Orig.). (J). (ps-4). 1990. audio, pap. 12.95 (1-879099-01-2) Thy Word.
— Isaiah Fifty-Three: An Illustrated Bible Chapter for Young Children. LC 91-90827. (Illus.). 40p. (Orig.). (J). (ps-4). 1992. digital audio 11.95 (1-879099-06-3) Thy Word.
— The Lord's Prayer: An Illustrated Bible Passage for Young Children. LC 91-90826. (Illus.). 32p. (Orig.). (J). (ps-4). 1991. audio 10.95 (1-879099-05-5) Thy Word.
— Psalm One Hundred Thirty-Nine: An Illustrated Bible Chapter for Young Children. LC 91-90825. (Illus.). 48p. (Orig.). (J). (ps-4). 1991. audio 12.95 (1-879099-03-9) Thy Word.
— Psalm Twenty-Three: An Illustrated Bible Chapter for Young Children. (Illus.). 32p. (Orig.). (J). (ps-4). 1990. audio 9.95 (1-879099-00-4) Thy Word.
Meyer, David, ed. see Houdini, Harry & Thurston, Howard.
Meyer, David, ed. see Meyer, Clarence.
Meyer, David B. Laboratory Guide for Human Histology. rev. ed. LC 85-15296. 134p. (Orig.). (C). 1985. pap. text ed. 15.95 (0-8143-1801-0) Wayne St U Pr.
Meyer, David C., ed. see Meyer, Clarence.
Meyer, David E. & Kornblum, Sylvan, eds. Attention & Performance XIV: Synergies in Experimental Psychology, Artificial Intelligence, & Cognitive Neuroscience a Silver Jubilee Vol. (Illus.). 1380p. 1993. 75.00x (0-262-13284-2) MIT Pr.
Meyer, David N. Day by Day Runner's Log. (Illus.). 138p. 1990. pap. 6.95 (0-681-40968-1) Longmeadow Pr.
Meyer, David P. Underemployment from a Human Perspective. 63p. 1985. 6.25 (0-317-01303-3, IN303) Ctr Educ Trng Employ.
Meyer, David R. Spatial Variation of Black Urban Households. LC 72-128466. (Research Papers Ser.: No. 129). 127p. 1970. pap. 12.00 (0-89065-036-5) U Chicago Comm Geo.
— Spatial Variation of Black Urban Households. LC 72-129455. (University of Chicago, Department of Geography, Research Paper Ser.: No. 129). 144p. reprint ed. pap. 41.10 (0-7837-0404-6, 2040725) Bks Demand.
Meyer, David S. A Winter of Discontent: The Nuclear Freeze & American Politics. LC 89-26588. 320p. 1990. text ed. 59.95 (0-275-93305-9, C3305, Praeger Pubs); pap. text ed. 16.95 (0-275-93306-7, B3306, Praeger Pubs) Greenwood.
Meyer de Schauensee, Rodolphe. A Guide to the Birds of South America. 463p. 1982. pap. 25.00 (0-87098-027-0) U of KS Mus Nat Hist.
Meyer, Deke. Advanced Fly Fishing for Steelhead. (Illus.). 160p. (Orig.). 1992. 34.95 (1-878175-11-4); pap. 24.95 (1-878175-10-6) F Amato Pubns.
— Float Tube Fly Fishing. (Illus.). 125p. (Orig.). 1989. pap. 11.95 (0-936608-71-4) F Amato Pubns.
— Saltwater Fly Tying Directory. (Illus.). 120p. 1995. pap. 34.95 (1-57188-020-8) F Amato Pubns.
— Tying Trout Flies: Twelve of the Best. (Illus.). 32p. 1993. pap. 8.95 (1-878175-40-8) F Amato Pubns.
— Tying Trout Nymphs: Twelve of the Best. (Illus.). 32p. 1994. pap. 9.95 (1-878175-87-4) F Amato Pubns.
Meyer-Denkmann, Gertrud. Experiments in Sound: New Directions in Musical Education for Young Children. Paynter, Elizabeth & Paynter, John, eds. LC 50-26923. 1977. pap. 25.00 (0-900938-49-8, UE26923) Eur-Am Music.
Meyer, Diane. GRASP: A Patient Information & Workload Management System. LC 78-60243. (Illus.). 192p. (Orig.). 1978. pap. 26.00 (0-932150-00-4) MCS.
— GRASP Too: Applications & Adaptations of the GRASP Nursing Workload Management System. LC 81-85753. (Illus.). 291p. 1981. pap. 32.00 (0-932150-01-2) MCS.
Meyer, Donald. The Positive Thinkers: Popular Religious Psychology from Mary Baker Eddy to Norman Vincent Peale & Ronald Reagan. 432p. 1988. pap. 17.95 (0-8195-6166-5, Wesleyan Univ Pr) U Pr of New Eng.
— The Protestant Search for Political Realism, 1919-1941. 2nd ed. LC 88-17509. 519p. 1988. pap. 19.95 (0-8195-6210-6, Wesleyan Univ Pr) U Pr of New Eng.
— Sex & Power: The Rise of Women in America, Russia, Sweden, & Italy. LC 87-6080. 749p. 1987. text ed. 45.00 (0-8195-5153-8, Wesleyan Univ Pr) U Pr of New Eng.
— Sex & Power: The Rise of Women in America, Russia, Sweden, & Italy. 2nd ed. LC 89-185748. 751p. 1989. pap. 24.95 (0-8195-6214-9, Wesleyan Univ Pr) U Pr of New Eng.
***Meyer, Donald, ed.** Uncommon Fathers: Reflections on Raising a Child with a Disability. 220p. (Orig.). (C). 1995. pap. 14.95 (0-933149-68-9) Woodbine House.
Meyer, Donald J. & Vadasy, Patricia F. Sibshops: Implementing Workshops for Brothers & Sisters of Children with Special Health & Developmental Needs. LC 94-8827. (Illus.). 256p. 1994. pap. 32.00 (1-55766-169-3) P H Brookes.
Meyer, Donald J., et al. Grandparent Workshops: How to Organize Workshops for Grandparents of Children with Handicaps. 100p. 1987. ring bd. 40.00 (0-295-96458-8) U of Wash Pr.
— A Handbook for the Fathers Program: How to Organize a Program for Fathers & Their Handicapped Children. 160p. 1985. ring bd. 50.00 (0-295-96255-0); The Fathers Program. sl. 225.00 (0-295-72028-X) U of Wash Pr.
Meyer, Doris. Victoria Ocampo: Against the Wind & the Tide. (Illus.). 348p. 1989. reprint ed. pap. 13.95 (0-292-78710-3) U of Tex Pr.
Meyer, Doris, ed. Lives on the Line: The Testimony of Contemporary Latin American Authors. LC 87-25522. 280p. 1988. 35.00 (0-520-06002-4); pap. 14.00 (0-520-06794-0) U CA Pr.
— Reinterpreting the Spanish American Essay: Women Writers of the 19th & 20th Centuries. LC 94-17119. (The Texas Pan American Ser.). 272p. (C). 1995. text ed. 37.50x (0-292-75167-2) U of Tex Pr.
— Rereading the Spanish American Essay: Translations of 19th & 20th Century Women's Essays. LC 95-3564. (The Texas Pan American Ser.). 1995. write for info. (0-292-75179-6); pap. write for info. (0-292-75182-6) U of Tex Pr.
Meyer, Doris & Fernandez-Olmos, Margarite, eds. Introductory Essays. (Contemporary Women Authors of Latin America Ser.: Vol. I). 103p. 1984. pap. 9.50 (0-930888-20-0) Brooklyn Coll Pr.
— New Translations. (Contemporary Women Authors of Latin America Ser.: Vol. II). 331p. 1984. pap. 12.50 (0-930888-21-9) Brooklyn Coll Pr.
Meyer, Doris, tr. see Campobello, Nellie.
Meyer, Duane. The Highland Scots of North Carolina, 1732-1776. LC 61-66281. xi, 218p. 1987. reprint ed. pap. 10.95 (0-8078-4199-4) U of NC Pr.
Meyer, E. E., ed. see WHO Staff.
Meyer, E. Gerald, jt. ed. see Niederhauser, Warren D.
Meyer, E. M., et al, eds. Novel Approaches to the Treatment of Alzheimer's Disease. LC 89-26615. (Advances in Behavioral Biology Ser.: No. 36). (Illus.). 400p. 1989. 110.00 (0-306-43402-4, Plenum Pr) Plenum.
— Treatment of Dementias: A New Generation of Progress. (Advances in Behavioral Biology Ser.: Vol. 40). (Illus.). 528p. (C). 1992. 115.00 (0-306-44228-0, Plenum Pr) Plenum.
Meyer, Eduard. Forschungen Zur Alten Geschichte, 2 vols. xiv, 879p. 1966. reprint ed. write for info. (0-318-70784-5, Pub. by Georg Olms GW) Lubrecht & Cramer.
— Forschungen Zur Alten Geschichte, Bd. I: Zur Alteren Geschichte. xiv, 879p. 1966. reprint ed. write for info. (0-318-70785-3, Pub. by Georg Olms GW) Lubrecht & Cramer.
— Forschungen Zur Alten Geschichte, Bd. II: Zur Geschichte des 5. Jahrh v. Chr. xiv, 879p. 1966. reprint ed. write for info. (0-318-70786-1, Pub. by Georg Olms GW) Lubrecht & Cramer.
— Theopompus Hellenika. xii, 291p. 1966. reprint ed. write for info. (0-318-70976-7, Pub. by Georg Olms GW) Lubrecht & Cramer.
Meyer, Edward. Machiavelli & the Elizabethan Drama. 1972. 59.95 (0-8490-0572-8) Gordon Pr.
***Meyer, Edward C., et al.** Who Will Lead? Senior Leadership in the United States Army. LC 94-34319. 296p. 1995. text ed. 59.95 (0-275-95041-7, Praeger Pubs) Greenwood.
Meyer, Ellen H., jt. ed. see DeMaria, Robert.
Meyer, Emily & Smith, Louise Z. The Practical Tutor. (Illus.). 368p. 1987. 42.00 (0-19-504109-7); pap. text ed. 18.95 (0-19-503865-7) OUP.
Meyer, Erika, et al. Elementary German, 3 Vols. 3rd ed. (C). 1976. text ed. 34.36 (0-395-19866-6) HM.
— Elementary German, 3 Vols. 3rd ed. (C). 1977. student ed, pap. 19.96 (0-395-19868-2) HM.
Meyer, Ernest A., jt. ed. see Erlandsen, Stanley L.
Meyer, Ernest A., et al, eds. Giardiasis. (Human Parasitic Diseases Ser.: No. 3). 650p. 1990. 220.75 (0-444-81258-X) Elsevier.
Meyer, Ernest L. Hey Yellowbacks: The War Diary of a Conscientious Objector. LC 75-143432. (Peace Movement in America Ser.). x, 209p. 1972. reprint ed. lib. bdg. 25.95 (0-89198-080-6) Ozer.
— Hey! Yellowbacks: The War Diary of a Conscientous Objector. (American Biography Ser.). 209p. 1991. reprint ed. lib. bdg. 69.00 (0-7812-8284-5) Rprt Serv.
Meyer, Ernst. English Chamber Music. LC 71-127181. (Music Ser.). (Illus.). 1971. reprint ed. lib. bdg. 39.50 (0-306-70037-9) Da Capo.
Meyer, Erwin & Neumann, Ernst-Georg. Physical & Applied Acoustics: An Introduction. 1972. text ed. 60.00 (0-12-493150-2) Acad Pr.
***Meyer, Esther da Costa.** The Work of Antonio Sant'Elia: Retreat into the Future. LC 94-39125. (Publications in the History of Art). 1995. write for info. (0-300-04309-0) Yale U Pr.
Meyer, Eugene. Chemistry of Hazardous Materials. (Illus.). 1977. text ed. 40.00 (0-13-129239-0) P-H.
Meyer, Eugene & Brady, Joseph V., eds. Research in the Psychobiology of Human Behavior. LC 78-24710. (Illus.). 160p. reprint ed. pap. 45.60 (0-8357-8303-0, 2034152) Bks Demand.
Meyer, Eugene L. Maryland Lost & Found: People & Places from Chesapeake to Appalachia. LC 85-24079. (Illus.). 256p. 1986. 16.95 (0-8018-3233-0) Johns Hopkins.
Meyer, Eugene L., jt. auth. see Niemeyer, Lucian.
Meyer, F. Israel: A Prince with God. Chao, Lorna, tr. (Meyer's Bible Characters Ser.). 1987. pap. write for info. (0-941598-37-3) Living Spring Pubns.
— Joseph: Beloved, Hated, Exalted. Chen, Ruth T., tr. (Meyer's Bible Characters Ser.). 1987. pap. write for info. (0-941598-38-1) Living Spring Pubns.
Meyer, F. A., ed. see Weizman Institute of Science Staff.
Meyer, F. B. Abraham. 1993. pap. 5.95 (0-87508-340-4) Chr Lit.
— Abraham. (SPA.). 5.50 (84-7228-678-9, 220001, Pub. by Edit Clie SP) TSELF.
— Amor Hasta Lo Sumo: Love on the Highest Plain. (SPA.). 7.95 (84-7228-800-5, 220025, Pub. by Edit Clie SP) TSELF.
— El Camino Hacia el Lugar Santisimo: The Way to the Holiest. (SPA.). 6.95 (84-7645-261-6, 223319, Pub. by Edit Clie SP) TSELF.
— Changed by the Master's Touch. 250p. 1985. pap. 5.99 (0-88368-169-2) Whitaker Hse.
— Choice Notes on the Psalms. LC 84-17109. (F. B. Meyer Memorial Library). 192p. 1984. pap. 7.99 (0-8254-3242-1) Kregel.
— Cinco Requisitos Esenciales Vida Crist. Secrets of Christian Living. (SPA.). 3.25 (84-7228-564-2, 220155, Pub. by Edit Clie SP) TSELF.
— Ciudadanos Del Cielo: Citizens of Heaven. (SPA.). 6.25 (84-7228-916-8, 223011, Pub. by Edit Clie SP) TSELF.
— Cristo En Isaias: Christ in Isaiah. (SPA.). 6.50 (84-7228-676-2, 220205, Pub. by Edit Clie SP) TSELF.
— David. 1992. pap. 5.95 (0-87508-342-0) Chr Lit.
— Devotional Commentary on Exodus. LC 78-9530. 476p. 1978. pap. 12.99 (0-8254-3244-8) Kregel.
— Devotional Commentary on Philippians. LC 78-59146. 262p. 1978. pap. 8.99 (0-8254-3227-8) Kregel.
— Elijah. 1992. pap. 5.95 (0-87508-343-9) Chr Lit.
— Ephesians. 1989. pap. 5.50 (0-87508-344-7) Chr Lit.
— F. B. Meyer Devotional Commentary. 648p. 1989. pap. 12.99 (0-8423-0941-1) Tyndale.
— Gospel of John. 1992. pap. 6.95 (0-87508-346-3) Chr Lit.
— Israel. 1982. pap. 5.95 (0-87508-347-1) Chr Lit.
— Jeremiah. 1993. pap. 5.95 (0-87508-355-2) Chr Lit.
— Jeremias, Sacerdote y Profeta: Jeremiah, Priest & Prophet. (SPA.). 5.50 (84-7228-675-4, 220503, Pub. by Edit Clie SP) TSELF.
— John the Baptist. 1993. pap. 5.95 (0-87508-345-5) Chr Lit.
— Jose el Amado: Joseph the Beloved One. (SPA.). 4.25 (84-7228-674-6, 220516, Pub. by Edit Clie SP) TSELF.
— Joseph. 1991. pap. 5.95 (0-87508-356-0) Chr Lit.
— Joshua. 1993. pap. 5.95 (0-87508-357-9) Chr Lit.
— Juan el Bautista: John the Baptist. (SPA.). 5.50 (84-7228-803-X, 222341, Pub. by Edit Clie SP) TSELF.
— Moises Siervo de Dios: Moses: Servant of God. (SPA.). 5.50 (84-7228-673-8, 220611, Pub. by Edit Clie SP) TSELF.
— Moses. 1991. pap. 5.95 (0-87508-354-4) Chr Lit.
— O Profeta da Esperanca. Orig. Title: The Prophet of Hope. (POR.). 1987. 5.95 (0-8297-1607-6) Life Pubs Intl.
— Old Testament Men of Faith. (World Classic Reference Library). 575p. 1995. reprint ed. 19.99 (0-529-10423-7) World Bible.

— Our Daily Walk. 1989. pap. 12.99 (*0-310-38731-0*) Zondervan.
— Pablo, Siervo de Jesucristo: Paul: Servant of God. (SPA.). 5.95 (*84-7228-801-3*, 222360, Pub. by Edit Clie SP) TSELF.
— Paul. 1993. pap. 5.95 (*0-87508-348-X*) Chr Lit.
— Paz, Perfecta Paz (Peace, Perfect Peace) large type ed. (SPA.). Date not set. 2.99 (*1-56063-339-5*, 494021) Editorial Unilit.
— Pedro: Pescador, Discipulo, Apostol: Apostol Peter. (SPA.). 5.50 (*84-7228-949-4*, 223055, Pub. by Edit Clie SP) TSELF.
— Peter. 1993. pap. 5.95 (*0-87508-349-8*) Chr Lit.
— Probado Por Fuego: Tested by Fire. (SPA.). 6.00 (*84-7228-795-5*, 222369, Pub. by Edit Clie SP) TSELF.
— Prophet of Hope. 157p. 1989. pap. 5.95 (*0-87508-358-7*) Chr Lit.
— Salmo del Pastor: The Shephard's Psalm. (SPA.). 4.25 (*84-7228-425-5*, 220792, Pub. by Edit Clie SP) TSELF.
— Samuel. 1991. pap. 5.95 (*0-87508-339-0*) Chr Lit.
— Saved & Kept. 1989. pap. 4.50 (*0-87508-350-1*) Chr Lit.
— The Secret of Guidance. Taniguchi, Ruth, tr. (CHI.). 1984. pap. write for info. (*0-941598-07-1*) Living Spring Pubns.
— The Secret of Guidance. 1987. pap. 0.40 (*9971-972-07-7*) OMF Bks.
— Secretos de la Direccion Divina: Secret of Guidance. (SPA.). 3.25 (*84-7228-585-5*, 220806, Pub. by Edit Clie SP) TSELF.
— Sermones Luminosos: Sermons to Enlighten. (SPA.). 4.95 (*84-7645-024-9*, 223093, Pub. by Edit Clie SP) TSELF.
— Shepherd Psalm. 1979. pap. 4.50 (*0-87508-351-X*) Chr Lit.
— Tried by Fire. 1992. pap. 6.95 (*0-87508-352-8*) Chr Lit.
— Vide y Luz de los Hombres: Light & Life of Men. (SPA.). 7.50 (*84-7228-802-1*, 222911, Pub. by Edit Clie SP) TSELF.
— Way into the Holiest. 1982. pap. 4.95 (*0-87508-353-6*) Chr Lit.
— Zacaras-el Profeta Esperanza: Zacarias-El Profeta de Esperanza. Orig. Title: The Prophet of Hope - Zechariah. 128p. (SPA.). 1986. 4.95 (*0-8297-0895-2*) Life Pubs Intl.

Meyer, Faith, ed. see Piche, Thomas.

Meyer, Francis D. Exercise Designed for the Aging. (Exercise & Care of Aging Body Ser.). (Illus.). 181p. 1985. pap. text ed. 5.95 (*0-9615720-0-0*) FDM Distributor.

Meyer, Frank. Line of Duty. Costa, Gwen, ed. LC 90-43991. 1992. pap. 15.95 (*0-87949-332-1*) Ashley Bks.

Meyer, Frank S., ed. African Nettle. LC 78-121488. (Essay Index Reprint Ser.). 1977. 24.95 (*0-8369-1764-2*) Ayer.

Meyer, Frank S., et al. Left, Right & Center: Essays on Liberalism & Conservatism in the United States. Goldwin, Robert A., ed. LC 70-156679. (Essay Index Reprint Ser.). 1977. reprint ed. 20.95 (*0-8369-2777-X*) Ayer.

Meyer, Franz O. Diving & Snorkeling Guide to Belize. 96p. 1990. 11.95 (*1-55992-033-5*, Pisces Bks) Gulf Pub.

Meyer, Franz S. Handbook of Ornament. 4th ed. (Illus.). 1892. pap. 8.95 (*0-486-20302-6*) Dover.

Meyer, Fred & Baker, Ralph, eds. Law Enforcement & Police Policy. (C). 1979. pap. 12.00 (*0-918592-31-3*) Pol Studies.
— State Policy Problems. 250p. 1993. text ed. 28.95 (*0-8304-1337-5*) Nelson-Hall.
— State Policy Problems. 1992. pap. 12.00 (*0-944285-28-7*) Pol Studies.

Meyer, Frederick A. Life Is a Trust. (Religious Ser.). 95p. 1986. 8.95 (*0-935087-09-5*) Wright Pub Co.

***Meyer, Frederick B.** Daily Prayers: A Classic Collection. LC 95-7979. Orig. Title: My Daily Prayer. 144p. 1995. 12.99 (*0-87788-169-3*) Shaw Pubs.
— The Gift of Suffering. LC 91-11658. 128p. (Orig.). 1991. reprint ed. 9.99 (*0-8254-3275-8*) Kregel.
— The Shepherd Psalm. LC 91-9805. 128p. 1991. reprint ed. pap. 8.99 (*0-8254-3276-6*) Kregel.

Meyer, Fredric B., ed. Sundt's Occlusive Cerebrovascular Disease. 2nd rev. ed. LC 94-18063. 1994. text ed. 150.00 (*0-7216-4911-4*) Saunders.

Meyer, Fredrich, et al, eds. Theory of Accretion Disks: Proceedings of the NATO Advanced Research Workshop Held in Garching, FRG March 6-10, 1989. (C). 1989. lib. bdg. 169.00 (*0-7923-0453-5*) Kluwer Ac.

Meyer, Friedrich. Maler Muller-Bibliographie. viii, 175p. 1974. reprint ed. write for info. (*3-487-05286-5*, Pub. by Georg Olms GW) Lubrecht & Cramer.

Meyer, G. & Morss, L. R., eds. Synthesis of Lanthanide & Actinide Compounds. (C). 1991. lib. bdg. 150.00 (*0-7923-1018-7*) Kluwer Ac.

Meyer, G., jt. ed. see Petry, S.

Meyer, G. Curt, jt. ed. see Hall, Linda K.

Meyer, G. E., jt. auth. see DeShazer, J. A.

***Meyer, G. J.** Executive Blues. LC 95-11984. 1995. 21.95 (*1-879957-22-1*, Franklin Sq Pr) Harpers Mag Found.

Meyer, G. J., jt. auth. see Searson, P. C.

Meyer, Gabriel. The Gospel of Joseph: A Father's Story. 172p. 1994. 19.95 (*0-8245-1406-8*) Crossroad NY.
— In the Shade of the Terebinth: Tales of a Night Journey. (Illus.). 144p. 1994. 14.95 (*0-939516-23-3*) Forest Peace.

Meyer, Gabriela, tr. see Gischler, Eberhard & Schlager, Wolfgang, eds.

Meyer, Gail M., jt. auth. see Grant, Gregory J.

Meyer, Galen. Abraham: Manual del Maestro. rev. ed. (SPA.). 1985. 3.00 (*1-55955-053-8*) CITE MI.
— Abraham: Trusting the God Who Calls. (Revelation Ser.). 1995. teacher ed 5.50 (*1-56212-088-3*) CRC Pubns.
— First & Second Thessalonians: Longing for the Lord. (Revelation Ser.). 1995. teacher ed 5.50 (*1-56212-089-1*) CRC Pubns.
— Hebrews: A Study Guide. LC 93-14321. (Revelation Series for Adults). 1993. write for info. (*1-56212-044-1*) CRC Pubns.
— Hebrews: Glimpsing the Glory. (Revelation Ser.). 1995. teacher ed 5.50 (*1-56212-087-5*) CRC Pubns.

Meyer, Gary J. Automating Personnel Operations: The Human Resource Manager's Guide to Computerization. 1984. ring bd. 76.50 (*1-55645-416-3*) Busn Legal Reports.

Meyer, George H. American Folk Art Canes: Personal Sculpture. LC 92-9714. (Illus.). 252p. 1992. 65.00 (*0-295-97200-9*) U of Wash Pr.

Meyer, George H., ed. Folk Artists Biographical Index. 650p. 1986. 80.00 (*0-8103-2145-9*) Gale.

Meyer, George W., ed. see Wordsworth, William.

Meyer, Gerald. Vito Marcantonio: Radical Politician, 1902-1954. LC 88-31669. (SUNY Series in American Labor History). 303p. 1989. 59.50 (*0-7914-0082-4*); pap. 19.95 (*0-7914-0083-2*) State U NY Pr.

Meyer, Gladys C. Softball for Girls & Women. (Illus.). 256p. 1982. 15.95 (*0-684-17458-8*, Scribners) S&S Trade.
— Softball for Girls & Women. (Illus.). 320p. 1984. pap. 11.00 (*0-684-18140-1*, Scribners) S&S Trade.

Meyer, H. J., jt. auth. see Heidrich, H.

Meyer, H. O. The Interaction Between Medium Energy Nucleons in Nuclei, Indiana University Cyclotron Facility, 1982: AIP Conference Proceedings, No. 97. LC 83-70649. 433p. 1983. lib. bdg. 38.50 (*0-88318-196-7*) Am Inst Physics.

Meyer, H. O., jt. ed. see Boyd, F. R.

Meyer, H. O., jt. ed. see Schwandt, P.

Meyer, Harding, jt. ed. see Vischer, Lukas.

Meyer, Harold E. Credit & Collection Letters That Get Results. 1994. pap. 14.95 (*0-13-123704-7*) P-H.
— Lifetime Encyclopedia of Letters. LC 82-13343. 403p. 1986. 29.95 (*0-13-536383-7*, Busn) P-H.
— Lifetime Encyclopedia of Letters. 1991. text ed. 34.95 (*0-13-529546-7*) P-H.

Meyer, Harold E. & Sievert, Scott A. Complete Credit & Collection Model Letter Book. 384p. 1990. 49.95 (*0-13-156126-X*) P-H.

Meyer, Harold J. Hanging Sam: A Military Biography of General Samuel T. Williams. LC 90-35952. (Illus.). 183p. (Orig.). 1990. pap. 16.95 (*0-929398-12-2*) UNTX Pr.

Meyer, Harvey K. & Meyer, Jessie H. Historical Dictionary of Honduras. LC 93-49521. (Latin American Historical Dictionaries Ser.: No. 25). 1994. 77.50 (*0-8108-2845-6*) Scarecrow.

Meyer, Hazel. The Gold in Tin Pan Alley. LC 77-7039. 258p. 1977. reprint ed. text ed. 59.75 (*0-8371-9694-9*, MEGO, Greenwood Pr) Greenwood.

Meyer, Helen C., jt. auth. see Machado, Jeanne M.

Meyer, Henry C. Airshipmen, Businessmen, & Politics, 1890-1940. LC 90-22345. (History of Aviation Ser.). (Illus.). 276p. (C). 1991. text ed. 45.00 (*1-56098-031-1*) Smithsonian.

Meyer, Henry I. The Face of Business. LC 79-55064. 282p. reprint ed. pap. 80.40 (*0-317-27304-3*, 2023551) Bks Demand.
— The Moving Force. LC 81-66231. 333p. reprint ed. pap. 95.00 (*0-317-19935-8*, 2023572) Bks Demand.

Meyer, Henry J., jt. auth. see Litwak, Eugene.

Meyer, Henry J., et al. Girls at Vocational High: An Experiment in Social Work Intervention. LC 65-16221. 212p. 1965. 29.95 (*0-87154-601-9*) Russell Sage.

Meyer, Henye. The Exiles of Crocodile Island. (ArtScroll Youth Ser.). (Illus.). 224p. (YA). (gr. 6-12). 1984. 13.95 (*0-89906-772-7*); pap. 10.95 (*0-89906-773-5*) Mesorah Pubns.

Meyer, Herb. A Kaskaskia Chronology. 8p. 1986. 2.00 (*0-913415-05-7*) Am Resources.

Meyer, Herb, jt. auth. see McNerney, Michael J.

Meyer, Herbert E. Hard Thinking: The Fusion of Politics & Sciences. 72p. 1993. 9.95 (*0-935166-08-4*) Storm King Pr.
— How to Write. 1991. pap. 5.95 (*0-935166-01-7*) Storm King Pr.
— Real-World Intelligence: Organized Information for Executives. 102p. 1991. pap. 9.95 (*0-935166-05-X*) Storm King Pr.

Meyer, Herbert E. & Meyer, Jill M. How to Write: Communicating Ideas & Information - New Edition. 2nd ed. 1993. pap. 6.95 (*0-935166-07-6*) Storm King Pr.

Meyer, Herman. The Poetics of Quotation in the European Novel. LC 65-17152. 288p. reprint ed. pap. 82.10 (*0-8357-3701-2*, 2036425) Bks Demand.

Meyer, I. Hotel & Restaurant Dictionary: Fachworterbuch Gaststatten-und Hotelwesen. 2nd ed. 208p. (ENG, FRE, GER & RUS.). 1981. 39.95 (*0-8288-1478-3*, M15242) Fr & Eur.

Meyer, Ian & Huggett, Richard. Geography: Theory in Practice, Bks. 1-3. 208p. (C). 1979. pap. write for info. (*0-318-64709-5*, Pub. by P Chapman Pub UK) St Mut.
— Geography: Theory in Practice, Bks. 1-3, Bk. 1. 208p. (C). 1979. pap. 32.00 (*0-06-318096-0*, Pub. by P Chapman Pub UK) St Mut.
— Geography: Theory in Practice, Bks. 1-3, Bk. 2. 208p. (C). 1979. pap. 32.00 (*0-06-318166-5*, Pub. by P Chapman Pub UK) St Mut.
— Geography: Theory in Practice, Bks. 1-3, Bk. 3. 208p. (C). 1979. pap. 32.00 (*0-685-74067-6*, Pub. by P Chapman Pub UK) St Mut.

***Meyer, Isaac.** Oldest Books in the World: An Account of the Religion, Wisdom, Philosophy, Ethics, Psychology, Manners, Proverbs, Sayings, Refinement, etc., of the Ancient Egyptians (1900) 540p. 1995. pap. 33.00 (*1-56459-486-6*) Kessinger Pub.
— Scarabs: The History, Manufacture, & Religious Symbolism of the Scarabaeus, in Ancient Egypt, Phoenicia, Sardinia, Etruria, Etc. 205p. 1995. pap. 17.95 (*1-56459-491-2*) Kessinger Pub.

Meyer, Isidore S. The Hebrew Exercises of Governor William Bradford. 1973. 4.00 (*0-940628-01-5*) Pilgrim Soc.

Meyer, J. Penny Banks; Mechanicals & Stills. LC 60-13061. (Illus.). 1960. pap. 10.50 (*0-87282-085-8*) Am Life Foun.

Meyer, J., et al, eds. Advances in Noninvasive Cardiology. (Developments in Cardiovascular Medicine Ser.). 1983. lib. bdg. 94.00 (*0-89838-576-8*) Kluwer Ac.

Meyer, J., jt. ed. see Sreebny, L. M.

Meyer, J., jt. ed. see Vaeth, J. M.

Meyer, J., jt. auth. see Van Der Hoek, W.

Meyer, J., et al, eds. Improvement of Myocardial Perfusion. (Developments in Cardiovascular Medicine Ser.). 1985. lib. bdg. 154.00 (*0-89838-748-5*) Kluwer Ac.
— The Structure & Function of Oral Mucosa. LC 83-19633. (Illus.). 300p. 1984. 125.00 (*0-08-028020-X*, Pub. by Pergamon Repr UK) Franklin.

Meyer, J. F., et al, eds. Dependable Computing for Critical Applications 2. (Dependable Computing & Fault-Tolerant Systems Ser.: Vol. 6). (Illus.). xvi, 442p. 1992. 119.00 (*0-387-82330-1*) Spr-Verlag.

Meyer, J. J. & Wieringa, R. J. Deontic Logic in Computer Science: Normative System Specification. 300p. 1994. text ed. 75.95 (*0-471-93743-6*) Wiley.

Meyer, J. L. & Vaeth, J., eds. The Lymphatic System & Cancer: Mechanisms & Clinical Management. (Frontiers of Radiation Therapy & Oncology Ser.: Vol. 28). (Illus.). x, 240p. 1994. 189.00 (*3-8055-5889-9*) S Karger.

Meyer, J. L. & Vaeth, J. M., eds. Organ Conservation in Curative Cancer Treatment: Indications, Contraindications, Methods. (Frontiers of Radiation Therapy & Oncology Ser.: Vol. 27). (Illus.). xii, 256p. 1993. 199.25 (*3-8055-5663-2*) S Karger.
— Radiotherapy-Chemotherapy Interactions in Cancer Therapy. (Frontiers of Radiation Therapy & Oncology Ser.: Vol. 26). (Illus.). x, 202p. 1992. 158.50 (*3-8055-5493-1*) S Karger.

Meyer, J. L., jt. ed. see Vaeth, J. M.

Meyer, J. S., et al. Cerebral Vascular Disease, Vol. 3. (International Congress Ser.: No. 532). 352p. 1981. 98.50 (*0-444-90197-3*, Excerpta Medica) Elsevier.

Meyer, J. S., et al, eds. Cerebral Vascular Disease: Proceedings of the World Federation of Neurology 13th International Salzburg Conference, Sept. 25-27, 1986, Vol. 6. (International Congress Ser.: No. 736). 254p. 1988. 108.75 (*0-444-80875-2*, Excerpta Medica) Elsevier.
— Cerebral Vascular Disease 5: Proceedings of the World Federation of Neurology 12th International Salzburg Conference, Sept. 26-29, 1984. (International Congress Ser.: No. 687). 392p. 1986. 122.75 (*0-444-80706-3*, Excerpta Medica) Elsevier.

Meyer, Jack. Common Sense Union: An Agenda for Social & Political Reform. 55p. (Orig.). 1994. pap. 6.00 (*0-9631727-2-7*) CSU Pubns.
— The In-Between: A Vision of World Peace. LC 92-70265. (Illus.). 325p. 1992. 22.00 (*0-9631727-0-0*) CSU Pubns.
— Washington, D. C. Monuments in Architectural & Historical Review. (Illus.). 21p. (Orig.). 1993. pap. 4.00 (*0-9631727-1-9*) CSU Pubns.

Meyer, Jack A. Wage-Price Standards & Economic Policy. LC 82-8810. (AEI Studies: No. 358). 88p. reprint ed. pap. 25.10 (*0-8357-4543-0*, 2037440) Bks Demand.

Meyer, Jack A., comp. An Annotated Bibliography of the Napoleonic Era: Recent Publications, 1945-1985. LC 87-7605. (Bibliographies & Indexes in World History Ser.: No. 8). 305p. 1987. text ed. 69.50 (*0-313-24901-6*, MNF, Greenwood Pr) Greenwood.

Meyer, Jack A., ed. Market Reforms in Health Care: Current Issues, New Directions, Strategic Decisions. LC 82-22678. (AEI Symposia Ser.: No. 82F). 352p. reprint ed. pap. 100.40 (*0-8357-4503-1*, 2037359) Bks Demand.

Meyer, Jack A., jt. auth. see Zedlewski, Sheila R.

Meyer, Jack A., et al. Passing the Health Care Buck: Who Pays the Hidden Cost? LC 83-12296. (AEI Ser.: No. 386). 63p. reprint ed. pap. 25.00 (*0-8357-4521-X*, 2037380) Bks Demand.
— Setting New Priorities in Health Care. (Illus.). 50p. (Orig.). 1993. pap. text ed. write for info. (*0-9629870-2-6*) Milbank Memorial.

Meyer, Jacky, tr. see Drechsel, Willem, et al, eds.

Meyer, James. Thirty Changing Meter Duets for Treble Clef Instruments. 41p. 1984. pap. 9.95 (*0-938170-05-8*) Wimbledon Music.

Meyer, James & Hardick, Lothar. Words of St. Francis. rev. ed. 1982. 15.00 (*0-8199-0833-9*, Frncsen Herld) Franciscan Pr.

Meyer, Jan. Parachuting Manual with Log for Accelerated Freefall. LC 91-6811. (Illus.). 36p. (Orig.). 1992. pap. 3.95 (*0-915516-79-9*) Para Pub.

Meyer, Jean. Plant Galls & Gall Inducers. Cheskin, S., tr. (Illus.). 292p. 1987. lib. bdg. 111.00 (*3-443-01023-7*) Lubrecht & Cramer.

Meyer, Jean, jt. intro. see Lambert-Lagace, Louise.

Meyer, Jean A. The Cristero Rebellion: The Mexican People Between Church & State, 1926-1929. LC 75-35455. (Cambridge Latin American Studies: No. 24). 272p. reprint ed. pap. 77.60 (*0-318-34823-3*, 2031692) Bks Demand.

Meyer, Jean-Arcady, jt. ed. see Roitblat, Herbert L.

Meyer, Jean-Arcady, et al. From Animals to Animates 2: Proceedings of the 2nd International Conference on Simulation of Adaptive Behavior. LC 93-12410. (Bradford Series in Complex Adaptive Systems). (Illus.). 536p. 1993. pap. 57.50 (*0-262-63149-0*, Bradford Bks) MIT Pr.

Meyer, Jean-Christophe. Barron's Junior Illustrated Dictionary - French-English. (Illus.). 180p. (ENG & FRE.). (J). (gr. 2 up). 1994. 14.95 (*0-8120-6458-5*) Barron.

Meyer, Jeffrey D., jt. auth. see Shock, Michael D.

Meyer, Jeffrey F. The Dragons of Tiananmen: Beijing As a Sacred City. Denny, Frederick M., ed. (Studies in Comparative Religion). (Illus.). 220p. 1991. text ed. 34.95 (*0-87249-739-9*) U of SC Pr.

Meyer, Jennifer. Quattro Pro for Windows: Self-Teaching Guide. 288p. 1992. pap. text ed. 19.95 (*0-471-56939-9*) Wiley.

Meyer, Jerome. The Bonsai Book of Practical Facts Plus Addenda. 5th ed. LC 90-38869. (Illus.). 128p. 1992. 17.95 (*0-945487-00-2*) Purchase Pub.
— Puzzle, Quiz & Stunt Fun. (Illus.). 250p. 1957. pap. 4.95 (*0-486-20337-9*) Dover.

Meyer, Jerry. The Clay Target Handbook. 220p. 1992. 22.95 (*1-55821-176-4*) Lyons & Burford.
— The Clay-Target Handbook. 224p. 1995. pap. 16.95 (*1-55821-415-1*) Lyons & Burford.
— The Sporting Clays Handbook. (Illus.). 140p. 1990. pap. 15.95 (*1-55821-066-0*) Lyons & Burford.

Meyer, Jessie H., jt. auth. see Meyer, Harvey K.

Meyer, Jill M., jt. auth. see Meyer, Herbert E.

Meyer, Jimmy E., jt. ed. see Van Tassel, David D.

Meyer, Joachim E. Death & Neurosis. Nunberg, Margarete, tr. LC 73-19951. 147p. (C). 1975. text ed. 25.00 (*0-8236-1130-2*) Intl Univs Pr.

Meyer, Jocele, jt. auth. see Meyer, Art.

Meyer, Johann J. Sexual Life in Ancient India. 1989. reprint ed. 32.00 (*81-208-0638-7*, Pub. by Motilal Banarsidass II) S Asia.

Meyer, John, jt. auth. see Amato, Joseph.

Meyer, John A. Lung Cancer Chronicles. LC 89-11000. (Illus.). 250p. (Orig.). 1990. 35.00 (*0-8135-1492-4*); pap. 10.95 (*0-8135-1493-2*) Rutgers U Pr.

Meyer, John C., Jr. Complaints of Police Corruption. (Criminal Justice Center Monographs). 1977. pap. text ed. 3.25x (*0-318-37489-7*) John Jay Pr.

***Meyer, John-Jules & Van der Hoek, Wiebe.** Epistemic Logic for AI & Computer Science. (Tracts in Theoretical Computer Science Ser.: No. 41). (Illus.). 360p. (C). Date not set. 54.95 (*0-521-46014-X*) Cambridge U Pr.

***Meyer, John L., ed.** 3D-Conformal Radiotherapy. (Frontiers of Radiation Therapy & Oncology Ser.: Vol. 29). (Illus.). x, 240p. 1995. 192.00 (*3-8055-6161-X*) S Karger.

Meyer, John L. & Shadle, Carolyn C. The Changing Outplacement Process: New Methods & Opportunities for Transition Management. LC 94-2988. 312p. 1994. text ed. 59.95 (*0-89930-890-2*, Quorum Bks) Greenwood.

Meyer, John R. Supplement to NBER Report Five: The Evaluation & Planning of Social Programs. 8p. reprint ed. 20.00 (*0-685-61349-6*) Natl Bur Econ Res.
— Supplement to NBER Report Fourteen: Transportation Solutions to the Energy "Crisis" 6p. reprint ed. 20.00 (*0-685-61392-5*) Natl Bur Econ Res.
— Supplement to NBER Report Twelve: Setting Environmental Standards: An Economist's View. 10p. reprint ed. 20.00 (*0-685-61368-2*) Natl Bur Econ Res.

Meyer, John R., ed. Techniques of Transport Planning. Vol. 1: Pricing & Project Evaluation. LC 79-108833. (Transport Research Program Ser.). 343p. 1971. 17.95 (*0-8157-5690-9*) Brookings.
— Techniques of Transport Planning. Vol. 2: Systems Analysis & Simulation Models, Transport Research Program. LC 79-108833. 1971. 22.95 (*0-8157-5040-4*) Brookings.

***Meyer, John R. & Foster, Carol F.** A Guide to the Frogs & Toads of Belize. (Illus.). (C). 1996. lib. bdg. write for info. (*0-89464-963-9*) Krieger.

Meyer, John R. & Gomez-Ibanez, Jose A. Autos, Transit, & Cities. LC 81-6477. (Twentieth Century Fund Report Ser.). 370p. reprint ed. pap. 105.50 (*0-7837-1523-4*, 2041800) Bks Demand.

Meyer, John R. & Morton, Alexander L. The U. S. Railroad Industry in the Post-World War II Period: A Profile. (Explorations in Economic Research Two Ser.: No. 4). 52p. 1975. reprint ed. 35.00 (*0-685-61387-9*) Natl Bur Econ Res.

Meyer, John R. & Oster, Clinton V., Jr. Deregulation & the Future of Intercity Passenger Travel. (Regulation of Economic Activity Ser.: No. 15). (Illus.). 366p. 1987. 39.95 (*0-262-13225-7*) MIT Pr.

Meyer, John R. & Weinberg, Daniel H. On the Classification of Economic Fluctuations. (Explorations in Economic Research Two Ser.: No. 2). 36p. 1975. reprint ed. 35.00 (*0-685-66195-4*) Natl Bur Econ Res.
— On the Classification of Economic Fluctuations: An Update. (Explorations in Economic Research Three Ser.: No. 4). 2p. 1976. reprint ed. 35.00 (*0-685-61407-7*) Natl Bur Econ Res.

Meyer, John R., jt. auth. see Gomez-Ibanez, Jose A.

Meyer, John R., jt. ed. see Kain, John F.

Meyer, John R., Jr., et al. Airline Deregulation: The Early Experience. LC 81-3620. 287p. 1981. text ed. 49.95 (*0-86569-078-2*, Auburn Hse) Greenwood.

Meyer, John R., et al. Economics of Competition in the Transportation Industries. LC 59-6160. (Economic Studies: No. 107). (Illus.). 377p. 1959. 27.00 (*0-674-23251-8*) HUP.
— Urban Transportation Problem. LC 65-13848. (Rand Corporation Research Studies). (Illus.). 427p. 1965. pap. 16.50 (*0-674-93121-1*) HUP.

Meyer, John S., et al, eds. Vascular & Multi-Infarct Dementia. (Illus.). 288p. 1988. 39.00 (*0-87993-323-2*) Futura Pub.

An Asterisk (*) at the beginning of an entry indicates that the title is appearing in BIP for the first time.

Meyer, John W. No Turning Back: On the Loose in China & Tibet. (Illus.). 328p. (Orig.). 1991. pap. 10.95 (*0-911627-13-8*) Neither-Nor Pr.

Meyer, John W. & Hannan, Michael T., eds. National Development & the World System: Educational, Economic, & Political Change, 1950-1970. LC 78-26986. 1979. lib. bdg. 27.00 (*0-226-52136-2*) U Ch Pr.

Meyer, John W. & Scott, W. Richard. Organizational Environments: Ritual & Rationality. (Illus.). 312p. (C). 1992. 46.00 (*0-8039-4468-3*); pap. 21.95 (*0-8039-4469-1*) Sage.

Meyer, John W., jt. ed. see Scott, W. Richard.

Meyer, Jon K., et al. Clinical Management of Sexual Disorders. 2nd ed. LC 86-20620. (Illus.). 408p. 1986. reprint ed. pap. text ed. 18.50 (*0-88048-265-6*, 48-265-6) Am Psychiatric.

Meyer, Jon K., et al, eds. Clinical Management of Sexual Disorders. 2nd ed. LC 86-20620. (Illus.). 405p. reprint ed. pap. 115.50 (*0-8357-4757-3*, 2037683) Bks Demand.

Meyer, Jorgen C. Pre-Republican Rome: An Analysis of the Cultural & Chronological Relations, 1000-500 B.C. (Analecta Romana Ser.: Suppl. XI). 210p. (Orig.). 1983. pap. 38.50 (*87-7492-434-6*, Pub. by Odense Universitets Forlag DK) Coronet Bks.

Meyer, Joseph E. The Herbalist. rev. ed. (Illus.). 304p. 1986. pap. text ed. 11.95 (*0-916638-00-6*) Meyerbooks.

— The Old Herb Doctor. 2nd rev. ed. (Illus.). 176p. 1984. pap. 8.95 (*0-916638-08-1*) Meyerbooks.

Meyer, Joseph R., ed. Analysis & Design of Pile Foundations: Proceedings of a Symposium Sponsored by the Geotechnical Engineering Division & a Session Sponsored by the Technical Council on Codes & Standards. 410p. 1984. 32.00 (*0-87262-427-7*) Am Soc Civil Eng.

Meyer, Josh, jt. auth. see Willis, Dan.

Meyer, Joyce. Tell Them I Love Them. 52p. (Orig.). 1988. pap. 3.00 (*0-944834-00-0*) Life Word-Meyer Ministries.

Meyer, Judith W. Diffusion of an American Montessori Education. LC 74-80719. (Research Papers Ser.: No. 160). 97p. 1975. pap. 12.00 (*0-89065-067-5*) U Chicago Comm Geo.

Meyer, Jurgen. Acoustics & Performance of Music. Bowsher, John & Westphal, Sibylle, trs. (Illus.). 240p. 100.26 (*0-933224-28-1*) Bold Strummer Ltd.

— Computer Aided Design. 1994. pap. 19.95 (*1-55755-243-6*) Abacus MI.

Meyer, Justin. Plain Talk about Fine Wine. LC 89-9995. (Illus.). 150p. (Orig.). 1989. pap. 9.95 (*0-88496-300-4*) Capra Pr.

— Plain Talk about Fine Wine. 160p. (Orig.). (C). 1989. reprint ed. lib. bdg. 27.00x (*0-8095-4062-2*) Borgo Pr.

Meyer, K. & Saari, D., eds. Hamiltonian Dynamical Systems. LC 88-26831. (CONM Ser.: No. 81). 270p. 1988. pap. 36.00 (*0-8218-5086-5*, CONM-81) Am Math.

Meyer, K. R. & Hall, G. R. Introduction to Hamiltonian Dynamical Systems & the N-Body Problem. (Applied Mathematical Sciences Ser.: Vol. 90). (Illus.). xii, 292p. 1991. 49.80 (*0-387-97637-X*) Spr-Verlag.

Meyer, K. R., jt. auth. see Hale, Jack.

Meyer, K. R., jt. auth. see Markus, L.

Meyer, K. R., et al, eds. Computer Aided Proofs in Analysis. (IMA Volumes in Mathematics & Its Applications Ser.: Vol. 28). (Illus.). 264p. 1990. 39.00 (*0-387-97426-1*) Spr-Verlag.

Meyer, Karl E., anno. & intro. Pundits, Poets & Wits: An Omnibus of American Newspaper Columns. annot. ed. (Illus.). 504p. 1991. reprint ed. pap. 13.95 (*0-19-507137-9*) OUP.

Meyer, Karl E., ed. Pundits, Poets, & Wits: An Omnibus of American Newspaper Columns. (Illus.). 500p. 1990. 29.95 (*0-19-506063-6*) OUP.

Meyer, Karl H. Altkirchenslavisch-Griechisches Worterbuch des Codex Supraliensis. (GRE.). 25.00 (*0-685-71713-5*) J J Augustin.

Meyer, Katharine M. & McElroy, Martin P., eds. Detroit Architecture: AIA Guide. rev. ed. LC 80-132260. (Illus.). 272p. 1980. pap. 13.95 (*0-8143-1651-4*) Wayne St U Pr.

Meyer, Katherine, jt. auth. see Seidler, John.

Meyer, Kathleen. How to Shit in the Woods. 96p. (Orig.). 1989. pap. 5.95 (*0-89815-319-0*) Ten Speed Pr.

— How to Shit in the Woods: An Environmentally Sound Approach to a Lost Art. 2nd ed. LC 94-18053. 1994. pap. 5.95 (*0-89815-627-0*) Ten Speed Pr.

— Little Bear Finds a Friend. (Happy Day Bks.). (Illus.). 32p. (J). (gr. k-2). 1991. 2.50 (*0-87403-815-4*, 24-03915) Standard Pub.

Meyer, Kathleen A. Bear, Your Manners Are Showing. Beegle, Shirley, ed. (Happy Day Bks.). (Illus.). 24p. (J). (ps-3). 1994. reprint ed. pap. 1.89 (*0-7847-0251-9*) Standard Pub.

— Father Serra: Traveler on the Golden Chain. LC 89-63335. (Illus.). 72p. (Orig.). (J). 1990. 9.95 (*0-87973-139-7*); pap. 6.50 (*0-87973-141-9*) Our Sunday Visitor.

— God's Gifts, 5 vols. Incl. Vol. 1. Seeing. 1986. (*0-687-15307-7*); Vol. 2. Hearing. 1986. (*0-687-15306-9*); Vol. 3. Smelling. 1986. (*0-687-15308-5*); Vol. 4. Tasting. 1986. (*0-687-15309-3*); Vol. 5. Touching. 1986. (*0-687-15310-7*); Vol. 2. Hearing. 1986. (*0-687-15306-9*); 16p. (Orig.). (J). (gr. 1-3). 1986. Set. Set pap. write for info. (*0-318-60470-1*) Abingdon.

— I Have a New Friend. LC 95-5803. (Illus.). (J). 1995. write for info. (*0-8120-6532-8*); pap. write for info. (*0-8120-9408-5*) Barron.

— Little Bear's Big Adventure. (Happy Day Bks.). (Illus.). 32p. (J). (gr. k-2). 1990. 2.50 (*0-87403-706-9*, 24-03906) Standard Pub.

— Tul-Tok-A-Na: The Small One. (Illus.). 32p. (Orig.). (J). (gr. 1-5). 1992. pap. 6.95 (*0-89992-105-1*) Coun India Ed.

Meyer, Kathryn C., jt. auth. see MacDonald, Michael G.

Meyer, Kay, ed. see Cota-Robles, Patricia D.

Meyer, Kay E. The Road to Harmony...Day-by-Day. (Illus.). 398p. (Orig.). 1993. 17.00 (*0-9637023-0-0*) Grp Avatar.

Meyer, Keith, jt. auth. see Carter, Grace.

Meyer, Keith G., jt. auth. see Pedersen, Donald B.

Meyer, Keith G., et al. Agricultural Law: Cases & Materials. LC 84-19692. (American Casebook Ser.). 931p. 1984. text ed. 51.00 (*0-314-85082-1*) West Pub.

Meyer, Ken, jt. auth. see Wanek, Nimi.

Meyer, Kenneth, jt. auth. see Beville, Mitchel J.

Meyer, Kenneth, jt. auth. see Clem, Alan L.

Meyer, Kenneth, et al. An Analysis of Social Indicator & Quality of Life Research. 10.00 (*1-55614-018-5*) U of SD Gov Res Bur.

— An Operation of State & Regional Indicators in Public Policy & Quality of Life Evaluation. 10.00 (*1-55614-075-4*) U of SD Gov Res Bur.

— Public Employee Turnover in State Government: Costs & Beneifits. 1978. 1.00 (*1-55614-100-9*) U of SD Gov Res Bur.

— Robbery-Related Assaults on Police: An Empirical Analysis of National Incidents. 1979. 1.00 (*1-55614-109-2*) U of SD Gov Res Bur.

— Simpco Land Use Planning Information System Design: What to Do When the Data Arrives. (Technical Report Ser.: No. 1). 1978. 5.00 (*1-55614-113-0*) U of SD Gov Res Bur.

Meyer, Kent, jt. auth. see Hopson, Jim.

Meyer, Kenton T. The Crumhorn: Its History, Design, Repertory, & Technique. LC 83-3463. (Studies in Musicology: No. 66). (Illus.). 295p. reprint ed. pap. 84.10 (*0-8357-1406-3*, 2070511) Bks Demand.

Meyer, Kirstine B. Die Entwickelung de Temperaturbegriffs Im Laufe der Zeiten (the Discovery of Temperature in the Course of Time) Cohen, I. Bernard, ed. LC 80-2134. (Development of Science Ser.). (Illus.). 1981. reprint ed. lib. bdg. 18.95 (*0-405-13886-5*) Ayer.

Meyer, Kitty, jt. auth. see Meyer, Alvin.

Meyer-Krahmer, F., jt. auth. see Hornschild, K.

Meyer-Krahmer, Frieder. Science & Technology in the Federal Republic of Germany. (Guides to World Science & Technology Ser.). 480p. 1990. 115.00 (*0-582-05439-7*, 076418-99584) Longman.

Meyer, Kuno. A Primer of Irish Metrics. LC 78-72640. (Celtic Language & Literature Ser.: Goidelic & Brythonic). 88p. 1984. reprint ed. 27.50 (*0-404-17569-4*) AMS Pr.

— Ueber die Aelteste Irische Dichtung. LC 78-72641. (Celtic Language & Literature Ser.: Goidelic & Brythonic). reprint ed. 57.50 (*0-404-17574-0*) AMS Pr.

Meyer, Kuno, ed. Cain Adamnain. (Anecdota Oxoniensia Ser.: No. 12). 1988. reprint ed. 37.50 (*0-404-63962-5*) AMS Pr.

— Cath Finntraga. (Anecdota Oxoniensia Ser.: No. 4). 1988. reprint ed. 47.50 (*0-404-63954-2*) AMS Pr.

— The Death Tales of the Ulster Heroes. LC 78-72612. (Royal Irish Academy. Todd Lecture Ser.: Vol. 14). reprint ed. 14.50 (*0-404-60574-5*) AMS Pr.

— Hail Brigit: An Old-Irish Poem on the Hill of Alenn. 1987. pap. 4.95 (*0-89979-040-2*) British Am Bks.

— Hibernica Minora. (Anecdota Oxoniensia Ser.: No. 8). 1988. reprint ed. 49.50 (*0-404-63958-5*) AMS Pr.

— The Instructions of King Cormac Mac Airt. LC 78-72613. (Royal Irish Academy. Todd Lecture Ser.: Vol. 15). reprint ed. 14.50 (*0-404-60575-3*) AMS Pr.

— Life of Colman Son of Luachan. LC 78-72616. (Royal Irish Academy. Todd Lecture Ser.: Vol. 17). reprint ed. 18.50 (*0-404-60577-X*) AMS Pr.

— The Triads of Ireland. LC 78-72688. (Royal Irish Academy. Todd Lecture Ser.: Vol. 13). reprint ed. 14.50 (*0-404-60573-7*) AMS Pr.

Meyer, Kuno, tr. Selections from Ancient Irish Poetry. LC 75-28829. reprint ed. 20.00 (*0-404-13819-5*) AMS Pr.

Meyer, Kuno, tr. see Imran Brain.

Meyer, Kurt. Bitches, Bastards & Lovers. LC 81-83570. 1983. 9.95 (*0-87212-157-7*) Libra.

— Duden Taschenbucher: Woerterbuch der Schweizerischen. 380p. (GER.). 1989. 29.95 (*0-7859-8350-3*, 3411041315) Fr & Eur.

Meyer, L. A. Sheet Metal Shop Practice. 4th ed. (Illus.). 316p. 1975. 21.96 (*0-8269-1902-2*) Am Technical.

***Meyer, Larry & Meyer, Paula.** Santa's Favorite Questions from Kids. Kramer, Cheryl, ed. LC 95-94434. 60p. (Orig.). (J). Date not set. pap. write for info. (*0-9646762-0-6*) Captain Blys.

Meyer, Larry L. The Complete Works of Marcus Uteris. LC 87-10325. 176p. 1987. 15.00 (*0-942273-03-6*) Calafia Pr.

— My Summer with Molly: The Journal of a Second Generation Father. LC 89-840. (Illus.). 192p. 1989. 16.95 (*0-942273-04-4*) Calafia Pr.

***Meyer, Laure.** Art & Craft in Africa: Everyday Life, Rituals, & Court Art. (Illus.). 208p. 1995. pap. 24.95 (*2-87939-098-2*) Stewart Tabori & Chang.

Meyer, Laurence H., ed. Improving Money Stock Control: Problems, Solutions & Consequences. 1982. lib. bdg. 40.50 (*0-89838-115-0*) Kluwer Ac.

Meyer, Leo, jt. auth. see Wray, Lynn.

Meyer, Leo A. Atomic Energy in Industry: A Guide for Tradesmen & Technicians. LC 62-21342. 128p. reprint ed. pap. 36.50 (*0-8357-5854-0*, 2004581) Bks Demand.

— Sheet Metal Layout. 2nd ed. (Illus.). 1979. text ed. 35.95 (*0-07-041731-8*) McGraw.

— Teach! Plain Talk about Teaching. 124p. (Orig.). 1992. text ed. 18.95 (*0-88069-014-3*) L A Meyer.

Meyer, Leonard B. Emotion & Meaning in Music. LC 56-9130. 1961. pap. text ed. 11.95 (*0-226-52139-7*, P56) U Ch Pr.

— Music, the Arts, & Ideas: Patterns & Predictions in Twentieth-Century Culture. xii, 342p. 1994. pap. text ed. 17.95 (*0-226-52143-5*) U Ch Pr.

— Style & Music: Theory, History, & Ideology. LC 89-31354. (Studies in the Criticism & Theory of Music). (Illus.). 386p. (C). 1989. text ed. 47.95x (*0-8122-8178-0*) U of Pa Pr.

Meyer, Leonard B., jt. auth. see Cooper, Grosvenor.

Meyer, Levin. Classic Hassidic Tales. 300p. 1985. 16.95 (*0-88029-035-8*) Dorset Pr.

Meyer, Lewis. Preposterous Papa: A Hilarious & Affectionate Portrait by His Son. 224p. 1992. pap. 10.95 (*0-312-08280-0*) St Martin.

Meyer, Linda. John Meyer Pants-on-Fire: Pilot Adventures. LC 94-65977. (Illus.). 15p. (J). (gr. k-2). 1994. pap. 14.95 (*0-9640577-0-0*) Sunshine Advent.

— Teenspeak: A Bewildered Parent's Guide to Teenagers. 144p. (YA). 1994. pap. 8.95 (*1-56079-338-4*) Petersons Guides.

Meyer, Linda D. Harriet Tubman: They Called Me Moses. LC 87-43308. (Biographies for Young Children Ser.). (Illus.). 32p. (Orig.). (J). (ps-4). 1988. lib. bdg. 16.95 (*0-943990-33-5*); pap. 5.95 (*0-943990-32-7*) Parenting Pr.

— Safety Zone. (Illus.). 32p. 1985. pap. 3.50 (*0-446-38238-8*) Warner Bks.

Meyer, Lois, et al. Transcription Skills for Business. 4th ed. LC 92-16455. 161p. 1993. pap. text ed. 18.00 (*0-13-928029-4*) P-H.

Meyer, Lorenzo. The Mexican Revolution & the Anglo-American Powers: The End of Confrontation & the Beginning of Negotiation. Del Castillo, Sandra, tr. (Research Report Ser.: No. 34). 40p. (Orig.). (C). 1985. pap. 5.00 (*0-935391-33-9*, RR-34) UCSD Ctr US-Mex.

Meyer, Lorenzo, jt. auth. see Camin, Aguilar.

Meyer, Lorenzo, jt. auth. see Vazquez, Josefina Z.

Meyer, Lorraine C. Your Boxer. LC 78-187777. (Your Dog Bk.). (Illus.). 128p. 1973. 13.95 (*0-87714-004-9*) Denlingers.

Meyer, Louis, ed. & pref. Eminent Hebrew Christians of the Nineteenth Century: Brief Biographical Sketches. LC 83-22013. (Texts & Studies in Religion: Vol. 17). 184p. 1983. lib. bdg. 79.95 (*0-88946-806-0*) E Mellen.

Meyer, Louis & Moyer, Ruth. Transcription Skills for Business. 3rd ed. 1988. pap. text ed. 23.95 (*0-471-85452-2*) P-H.

Meyer, Luanna H. & Evans, Ian M. Nonaversive Intervention for Behavior Problems: A Manual for Home & Community. LC 88-34151. 224p. (Orig.). (C). 1989. pap. text ed. 26.00 (*1-55766-018-2*, 0182) P H Brookes.

Meyer-Lubke, Wilhelm. Grammatik Der Romanischen Sprachen, 4 vols., Set. lxvi, 2391p. 1972. reprint ed. write for info. (*3-487-04236-3*, Pub. by Georg Olms GW) Lubrecht & Cramer.

Meyer, Luc. Left Bank Celebrity Cookbook. 187p. (Orig.). 1982. pap. 8.95 (*0-89716-064-9*) P B Pubng.

— Wave Me No Flags: Challenging the Twenty-First Century. 1995. pap. 11.95 (*0-533-11078-5*) Vantage.

Meyer, Lucy, ed. see Fowler, Alex D.

Meyer-Luebke, Wilhelm. Romanisches Etymologisches Woerterbuch. 5th ed. 1204p. (GER & ITA.). 1992. 395.00 (*0-8288-6419-5*, M-7604) Fr & Eur.

Meyer, Lukas H., jt. auth. see Doeker, Gunther.

Meyer, Lysle E. The Farther Frontier: Six Case Studies of Americans & Africa, 1848-1936. LC 90-50770. (Illus.). 272p. 1992. 45.00 (*0-945636-19-9*) Susquehanna U Pr.

***Meyer, M.** Meyer's Manual on Louisiana Real Estate. 1991. 80.00 (*0-87511-913-1*) Claitors.

Meyer, M. & Miller, E. Urban Transportation Planning. 544p. 1984. text ed. write for info. (*0-07-041752-0*) McGraw.

Meyer, M. & Piiper, J., eds. Pulmonary Gas Exchange. (Progress in Respiration Research Ser.: Vol. 21). (Illus.). xiv, 274p. 1986. 99.25 (*3-8055-4330-1*) S Karger.

Meyer, M. & Schaap, J., eds. Historiography of Women's Cultural Traditions. (Women's Studies). viii, 196p. 1986. pap. 46.15 (*90-6765-276-8*) Mouton.

Meyer, M. W. Change in Public Bureaucracies. LC 76-47193. (Illus.). 1979. 59.95 (*0-521-22670-8*) Cambridge U Pr.

Meyer, M. Wilhelm. The End of the World: The Destiny of Man & Our Planet. Wagner, Margaret, tr. (Science for the Workers Ser.). (Illus.). 140p. 1984. 12.95 (*0-88286-087-9*) C H Kerr.

Meyer, Madeleine & Pontikis, Vassilis, eds. Computer Simulation in Materials Science: Intermatomic Potentials, Simulation Techniques & Applications. 560p. (C). 1991. lib. bdg. 174.00 (*0-7923-1455-7*) Kluwer Ac.

Meyer, Maggi H. Changing. LC 84-62316. 90p. 1984. pap. 6.00 (*0-915727-10-2*) im-Press.

— In Thrall. 60p. 1992. per. 5.00 (*0-915727-12-9*) im-Press.

— Maggi: Three Faces of Poetry. 176p. 1988. per. 10.00 (*0-915727-11-0*) im-Press.

Meyer, Maggi H., ed. see McDaniel, Wilma E.

***Meyer, Manfred, ed.** Education Programmes on Television: Deficiencies, Support, Chances: Contributions to an International Symposium. (Communication Research & Broadcasting Ser.: Vol. 11). 283p. 1993. pap. 25.00 (*3-598-20210-5*) K G Saur.

Meyer, Manfred, jt. ed. see Lohr, Paul.

***Meyer, Marc.** The Search for Order Vol. 1: Landmarks of World Civilization. LC 93-73093. 432p. 1994. pap. text ed. 14.95 (*1-56134-230-0*) Dushkin Pub.

— The Search for Order Vol. 2: Landmarks of World Civilization. LC 93-73095. 448p. 1994. pap. text ed. 14.95 (*1-56134-231-9*) Dushkin Pub.

Meyer, Marc A. A Documentary History of Western Civilization: From Ancient Times to the Present. LC 89-9127. (Illus.). 514p. (Orig.). (C). 1989. pap. text ed. 55.00 (*0-8191-7509-9*) U Pr of Amer.

Meyer, Marc A., ed. The Culture of Christendom: Essays in Medieval History in Commemoration of Denis L. T. Bethell. LC 93-16356. 328p. 1993. boxed 60.00 (*1-85285-064-7*) Hambledon Press.

Meyer, Maren E. Coping with Medications. LC 92-25613. (Coping with Aging Ser.). (Illus.). (Orig.). (C). 1993. pap. text ed. 18.95 (*1-879105-67-5*) Singular Publishing.

Meyer, Marian. A Century of Progress: History of the New Mexico School for the Deaf. (Illus.). 1989. text ed. write for info. (*0-318-64812-1*) NM School Deaf.

— Mary Donoho: New First Lady of the Santa Fe Trail. LC 90-56218. (Illus.). 150p. (Orig.). 1991. pap. 10.95 (*0-941270-69-6*) Ancient City Pr.

Meyer, Marie, et al. Different Voices - Shared Vision: Male & Female in the Trinitarian Community. 96p. (Orig.). (C). Date not set. pap. text ed. 4.00 (*0-9633142-1-1*) Am Luth Pub Bur.

Meyer, Marie Z. Life's Tapestry. LC 94-60716. 212p. 1995. 8.95 (*1-55523-708-8*) Winston-Derek.

Meyer, Marilyn. Instructor's Manual with Test Bank & Transparency Masters to Accompany Martin - Parker, Mastering Today's Software, Spreadsheets with Quattro Pro 4.0. 2nd ed. 140p. (C). 1994. pap. text ed. 66.50 (*0-03-002904-X*) Dryden Pr.

— Introduction to Programming with Quickbasic-QBASIC (Generic) 1993. pap. text ed. 3.00 (*0-13-036724-9*) P-H.

***Meyer, Marjorie.** One Man's Vision: The Life of Automotive Pioneer. (Illus.). 200p. 1995. 19.95 (*1-878208-66-7*) Guild Pr IN.

Meyer, Mark. Classics: U. S. Aircraft of World War II. Howell, Ross A., Jr. & Valenzi, Kathleen D., eds. 1992. pap. 24.95 (*0-943231-41-8*) Howell Pr VA.

Meyer, Mark, photos. Classics: U. S. Aircraft of World War II. LC 87-80777. (Illus.). 224p. 1987. 45.00 (*0-916878-6-X*) Howell Pr VA.

— Wings. LC 83-51813. (Illus.). 144p. 1984. 19.98 (*0-934738-05-X*); pap. 12.98 (*0-934738-62-9*) Thomasson-Grant.

Meyer, Marlane. Etta Jenks. (Royal Court Writers Ser.). 63p. (Orig.). 1990. pap. 9.95 (*0-413-65160-6*, A0515, Pub. by Methuen UK) Heinemann.

Meyer, Marshall, et al. Limits to Bureaucratic Growth. (Studies in Organization: No. 3). x, 259p. 1985. 49.95 (*3-11-009865-2*) De Gruyter.

— Limits to Bureaucratic Growth. (Studies in Organization: No. 3). x, 259p. 1985. 49.95 (*0-89925-003-3*) De Gruyter.

Meyer, Marshall W. Theory of Organizational Structure. LC 76-56415. (Studies in Sociology). 1977. pap. text ed. 3.95 (*0-672-61193-7*, Bobbs) Macmillan.

Meyer, Marshall W. & Zucker, Lynne G. Permanently Failing Organizations. 180p. (C). 1989. text ed. 38.95 (*0-8039-3258-8*); pap. text ed. 19.50 (*0-8039-3259-6*) Sage.

Meyer, Marshall W., jt. auth. see Blau, Peter M.

Meyer, Marshall W., et al. Environments & Organizations. LC 76-50706. (Jossey-Bass Social & Behavioral Science Ser.). 423p. reprint ed. pap. 120.60 (*0-8357-4996-7*, 2037929) Bks Demand.

Meyer, Martha B. Martha's Memoirs: Fond Remembrances of a Lively Life. Meyer, Paul, ed. 110p. (Orig.). 1987. pap. 8.95 (*0-910303-08-8*) Writers Pub Serv.

Meyer, Martin A. History of the City of Gaza from the Earliest Times to the Present. LC 07-29749. (Columbia University. Oriental Studies: No. 5). reprint ed. 18.25 (*0-404-50495-7*) AMS Pr.

Meyer, Marvin. Secret Teachings of Jesus: Four Gnostic Gospels. 1986. pap. 9.00 (*0-394-74433-0*, Vin) Random.

Meyer, Marvin, ed. The Ancient Mysteries: A Sourcebook. LC 86-45022. (Illus.). 256p. (Orig.). 1987. pap. 16.00 (*0-06-065576-3*) Harper SF.

Meyer, Marvin, tr. & intro. The Gospel of Thomas: The Hidden Sayings of Jesus. LC 91-58913. 1992. 16.00 (*0-06-065581-X*) Harper SF.

Meyer, Marvin, et al, eds. Ancient Christian Magic: Coptic Texts of Ritual Power. LC 93-28832. 352p. 1994. pap. 15.00 (*0-06-065584-4*) Harper SF.

— Ancient Christian Magic: Coptic Texts of Ritual Power. LC 93-28832. 352p. 1994. 25.00 (*0-06-065578-X*) Harper SF.

***Meyer, Marvin C., et al.** Essentials of Parasitology. 6th ed. 320p. (C). 1995. spiral bd. write for info. (*0-697-15983-3*) Wm C Brown Pubs.

Meyer, Marvin W. The Letter of Peter to Philip. Kee, Howard C., ed. LC 80-28612. (Society of Biblical Literature Dissertation Ser.). (C). 1981. pap. text ed. 20.95 (*0-89130-463-0*, 06-01-53) Scholars Pr GA.

— Who Do People Say I Am? The Interpretation of Jesus in the New Testament Gospels. LC 82-24229. 95p. reprint ed. pap. 27.10 (*0-317-30155-1*, 2025337) Bks Demand.

Meyer, Mary. Fahrenheit 451: A Study Guide. (Novel-Ties Ser.). (J). 1984. teacher ed 14.95 (*0-88122-114-7*) Lrn Links.

Meyer, Mary & Booker, Jane. Eliciting & Analyzing Expert Judgment: A Practical Guide. (Knowledge Based Systems Ser.: Vol. 5). (Illus.). 452p. 1991. text ed. 61.00 (*0-12-493230-4*) Acad Pr.

Meyer, Mary C. Walking with Jesus. 80p. (Orig.). 1992. pap. 10.95 (*0-8361-3574-1*) Herald Pr.

Meyer, Mary C., et al. Sexual Harassment at Work. (Illus.). 256p. 1981. text ed. 17.50 (*0-89433-156-6*) Petrocelli.

Meyer, Mary K., jt. ed. see Filby, P. William.

Meyer, Max, ed. see Ebbinghaus, Hermann.

Meyer, Melissa L. The White Earth Tragedy: Ethnicity & Dispossession at a Minnesota Anishinaabe Reservation, 1889-1920. LC 93-23456. xviii, 333p. (C). 1994. text ed. 40.00 (*0-8032-3154-7*) U of Nebr Pr.

***Meyer, Mercer.** Just Grandma & Me. 1994. pap. 29.50 (*1-57135-002-0*) Living Bks.

— What Do You Do with a Kangaroo. (J). (ps-3). 1993. pap. 199.51 (*0-590-21034-3*) Scholastic Inc.

— What Do You Do with a Kangaroo? (J). (ps-3). 1993. pap. 19.95 (*0-590-72851-2*) Scholastic Inc.

Meyer, Merle, jt. auth. see Altmaier, Elizabeth M.

Meyer, Merle E., jt. auth. see Altmaier, Elizabeth M.

Meyer, Michael. Bedford Introduction to Literature. 1992. 19.95 (*0-312-07115-9*) St Martin.

— Bedford Introduction to Literature. 3rd ed. LC 92-52518. 2122p. (C). 1993. pap. text ed. 28.00 (*0-312-06546-9*, Bedford Bks) St Martin.

— Bedford Introduction to Literature. 3rd ed. LC 92-52518. 2122p. (C). 1993. pap. text ed. 8.50 (*0-312-07833-1*, Bedford Bks) St Martin.

— The Compact Bedford Introduction to Literature: Reading, Thinking, & Writing. 3rd ed. 1512p. 1993. pap. text ed. 21.00 (*0-312-08620-2*) St Martin.

— The Little, Brown Guide to Writing Research Papers. 3rd ed. LC 93-2297. (C). 1993. 10.50 (*0-673-52298-9*) HarpCollege.

— Of Problematology: Philosophy, Science & Language. Jamison, David, tr. 312p. 1995. pap. text ed. 18.95 (*0-226-52151-6*) U Ch Pr.

— The Politics of Music in the Third Reich. (American University Studies: History: Ser. IX, Vol. 49). 434p. 1989. text ed. 69.95 (*0-8204-0805-0*) P Lang Pubs.

— Several More Lives to Live: Thoreau's Political Reputation in America. LC 76-56622. (Contributions in American Studies: No. 29). 216p. 1977. text ed. 49.95 (*0-8371-9477-6*, MES/, Greenwood Pr) Greenwood.

— Thinking & Writing about Literature. 208p. (C). 1995. pap. text ed. 7.98 (*0-312-11166-5*) St Martin.

Meyer, Michael, ed. From Metaphysics to Rhetoric. (C). 1989. lib. bdg. 94.50 (*90-277-2814-3*) Kluwer Ac.

Meyer, Michael, tr. The Plays of Ibsen, Vols. III, IV. pap. 4.95 (*0-317-43114-5*) PB.

Meyer, Michael & Heisler. Topics in Respiratory & Comparative Physiology. 1987. pap. text ed. 60.00 (*0-89574-236-5*, Pub. by Gustav Fischer Verlag) VCH Pubs.

Meyer, Michael & Trussler, Simon, eds. File on Strindberg. (Methuen Writer-Files Ser.). 96p. 1988. pap. 9.95 (*0-413-55020-6*, A0104, Pub. by Methuen UK) Heinemann.

Meyer, Michael, jt. auth. see Cournand, Andre.

Meyer, Michael, ed. see Douglass, Frederick.

Meyer, Michael, tr. see Ibsen, Henrik.

Meyer, Michael, ed. see Keyes, Sidney.

Meyer, Michael, tr. see Strindberg, August.

Meyer, Michael, ed. see Thoreau, Henry D.

Meyer, Michael A. Jewish Identity in the Modern World. LC 89-70707. (Samuel & Althea Stroum Lectures in Jewish Studies). 120p. 1990. 20.00x (*0-295-97000-6*) U of Wash Pr.

— The Origins of the Modern Jew: Jewish Identity & European Culture in Germany, 1749-1824. LC 67-12384. (Waynebooks Ser.: No. 32). 250p. (C). 1972. reprint ed. pap. 14.95 (*0-8143-1470-8*) Wayne St U Pr.

— Response to Modernity: A History of the Reform Movement in Judaism. 508p. 1995. reprint ed. pap. text ed. 18.95 (*0-8143-2555-6*) Wayne St U Pr.

Meyer, Michael A., ed. & intro. Ideas of Jewish History. LC 87-13810. 374p. 1987. reprint ed. 29.95 (*0-8143-1950-5*); reprint ed. pap. 16.95 (*0-8143-1951-3*) Wayne St U Pr.

Meyer, Michael C. Huerta; a Political Portrait. LC 70-162343. 290p. reprint ed. pap. 82.70 (*0-7837-4653-9*, 2044377) Bks Demand.

— Mexican Rebel: Pascual Orozco & the Mexican Revolution, 1910-1915. LC 67-10667. (Illus.). 182p. reprint ed. pap. 51.90 (*0-7837-6758-7*, 2059157) Bks Demand.

— Water in the Hispanic Southwest: A Social & Legal History, 1550-1850. LC 83-24276. 189p. 1984. 29.95 (*0-8165-0825-9*) U of Ariz Pr.

Meyer, Michael C. & Sherman, William L. The Course of Mexican History. 5th ed. (Illus.). 768p. (C). 1995. 49.95 (*0-19-508979-0*); pap. text ed. 24.95 (*0-19-508980-4*) OUP.

Meyer, Michael C., jt. ed. see Esquenazi-Mayo, Roberto.

Meyer, Michael C., jt. ed. see Greenleaf, Richard E.

Meyer, Michael J. & Parent, William A., eds. The Constitution of Rights: Human Dignity & American Values. LC 91-55535. (Start to Read! Library Edition Ser.). 256p. 1992. 35.00 (*0-8014-2650-2*); pap. 14.95 (*0-8014-9950-X*) Cornell U Pr.

Meyer, Michael T. Thinking Writing. 320p. 1989. per. 22.95 (*0-8403-5165-8*) Kendall-Hunt.

Meyer, Michel. From Logic to Rhetoric. LC 86-26346. (Pragmatics & Beyond Ser.: Vol. VII, 3). ix, 147p. (Orig.). 1986. pap. 47.00x (*1-55619-002-6*) Benjamins North Am.

— Meaning & Reading: A Philosophical Essay On Language & Literature. (Pragmatics & Beyond Ser.: Vol. IV, No. 3). ix, 176p. (Orig.). 1983. 53.00x (*90-272-2515-X*) Benjamins North Am.

— Of Problematology: Philosophy, Science & Language. Jamison, David, tr. LC 94-46783. 1993. lib. bdg. 49.95 (*0-226-52150-8*) U Ch Pr.

— Rhetoric, Language, & Reason. LC 92-41696. (Literature & Philosophy Ser.). 192p. (C). 1994. 29.75 (*0-271-01057-6*); pap. text ed. 16.95 (*0-271-01058-4*) Pa St U Pr.

Meyer, Michel, ed. Questions & Questioning. (Foundations of Communication & Cognition Ser.). vi, 392p. (C). 1988. lib. bdg. 129.25 (*0-89925-088-2*) De Gruyter.

— Questions & Questioning. (Foundations of Communication & Cognition Ser.). vi, 392p. (C). 1988. lib. bdg. 129.25 (*3-11-010680-9*) De Gruyter.

Meyer, Mike, jt. intro. see Singer, E. A.

Meyer, Milford J. Pennsylvania Vehicle Code Annotated. 2nd ed. Hartz, Steven J., ed. LC 94-72323. 1994. ring bd. 98.50 (*0-318-41046-X*) Bisel Co.

Meyer, Milford J. & Zanan, Arthur S. Handbook of Civil Procedure in the State & Federal Courts of Pennsylvania. LC 82-71145. 1993. text ed. 63.00 (*0-317-03822-2*) Bisel Co.

— Pennsylvania Trial Advocacy. 288p. 1995. text ed. 52.50 (*0-317-03820-6*) Bisel Co.

— Pennsylvania Vehicle Negligence, 2 vols., Set. 1344p. 1994. ring bd. 125.00 (*0-317-03821-4*) Bisel Co.

***Meyer, Milton W.** Asia: A Concise History. 608p. (C). 1995. text ed. 64.50 (*0-8476-8068-1*) Rowman.

— China: A Concise History. 3rd ed. 288p. (C). 1994. lib. bdg. 45.00 (*0-8476-7953-5*); pap. text ed. 16.95 (*0-8226-3033-8*) Rowman.

— Japan: A Concise History. 3rd ed. 288p. (C). 1992. text ed. 45.00 (*0-8476-7771-0*); pap. text ed. 14.95 (*0-8226-3018-4*) Rowman.

— Modern Asia: A Concise History. 224p. (C). 1995. pap. text ed. 16.95 (*0-8476-8063-0*) Rowman.

— South Asia: A Short History of the Subcontinent. 2nd ed. (Quality Paperback Ser.: No. 34). 268p. (Orig.). 1976. pap. 10.00 (*0-8226-0034-X*) Littlefield.

Meyer, Miriam W. The Blind Guards of Easter Island. LC 77-14528. (Great Unsolved Mysteries Ser.). (Illus.). 48p. (J). (gr. 4 up). 1983. reprint ed. lib. bdg. 21.36 (*0-8172-1048-2*) Raintree Steck-V.

Meyer, Moe, ed. The Politics & Poetics of Camp. LC 93-18913. 1994. write for info. (*0-415-08247-1*); pap. write for info. (*0-415-08248-X*) Routledge.

Meyer, N. Dean & Boone, Mary E. The Information Edge. 2nd ed. 425p. 1989. 45.00 (*1-55623-279-9*) Irwin Prof Pubng.

— The Information Edge. 2nd ed. (Illus.). 406p. 1995. reprint ed. pap. 19.95 (*0-9641635-0-0*) NDMA Pubng.

Meyer, Nancy. Endangered Species Coloring-Learning Books Adventure Series. (Illus.). (J). (ps-3). 1993. write for info. (*1-883408-05-9*) Meyer Pub FL.

***Meyer, Naomi.** The Journey with Joshua: Educating my Autistic Child. 250p. Date not set. write for info. (*1-56062-256-3*); pap. write for info. (*1-56062-257-1*) CIS Comm.

Meyer, Nathan M. The Patmos Prediction. LC 89-63537. 261p. (Orig.). 1989. pap. 9.95 (*0-941241-04-1*) Prophecy Pubns.

Meyer, Nicholas. Canary Trainer: From the Memoirs of John H. Watson. 224p. 1995. pap. 10.00 (*0-393-31241-0*) Norton.

— The Seven-Percent Solution. large type ed. 1977. 12.00 (*0-7089-0052-6*) Ulverscroft.

— The West End Horror. large type ed. 1978. 12.00 (*0-7089-0098-4*) Ulverscroft.

— West End Horror: From the Memoris of John H. Watson. 1994. pap. 8.95 (*0-393-31153-8*) Norton.

Meyer, Nicholas, ed. The Canary Trainer: From the Memoirs of John H. Watson. LC 93-13149. 1993. 19.95 (*0-393-03608-1*) Norton.

— The Seven-Percent Solution: Being a Reprint from the Reminiscences of John H. Watson, M.D. 256p. 1993. pap. 9.95 (*0-393-31119-8*) Norton.

Meyer, Nicholas E. Magic in the Dark: A Young Viewer's History of the Movies. LC 85-13004. (Illus.). 284p. reprint ed. pap. 81.00 (*0-7837-5335-7*, 2045075) Bks Demand.

Meyer-Nieberg, P. Banach Lattices. (Universitext Ser.). xv, 395p. 1991. pap. 56.00 (*0-387-54201-9*) Spr-Verlag.

***Meyer, Norvan L.** History of the Mexico-United States Screwworm Eradication Program. Simpson, Ocleris, ed. 1995. 25.00 (*0-533-11313-X*) Vantage.

Meyer, O. & Klauser, R. Clavis Mediaevalis: Kleines Woerterbuch der Mittelalterforschung. 312p. (GER.). 1966. 75.00 (*0-8288-6699-6*, M-7323, Pub. by Harrassowitz) Fr & Eur.

Meyer, P. Energy Systems Analysis for Developing Countries. (Lecture Notes in Economics & Mathematical Systems Ser.: Vol. 222). vi, 344p. 1984. pap. 41.00 (*0-387-12879-4*) Spr-Verlag.

***Meyer, P., ed.** Gene Silencing in Higher Plants & Related Phenomena in Other Eukaryotes. (Currents Topics in Microbiology & Immunology Ser.: Vol. 197). 240p. 1995. 128.00 (*0-387-58236-3*) Spr-Verlag.

Meyer, P., jt. ed. see Godfraind, K.

Meyer, P., jt. ed. see Levy, Maurice.

Meyer, P. A. Quantum Probability for Probabilists. Dold, A. et al, eds. (Lecture Notes in Mathematics Ser.: Vol. 1538). 297p. 1993. pap. 43.00 (*0-387-56476-4*) Spr-Verlag.

Meyer, P. A., jt. ed. see Azema, J.

Meyer, P. A., jt. auth. see Dellacherie, C.

Meyer, P. A., ed. see Seminaire de Probabilites Staff.

***Meyer, Pat H.** 150 Smart Rules for Carefree Living. (Fingertip Bks.). 96p. (Orig.). 1995. mass mkt. 4.99 (*0-8010-6322-1*) Baker Bk.

Meyer, Patricia, ed. see Lempfrit, Honore-Timothee.

***Meyer, Paul.** Herdsboy. 220p. 1995. pap. 8.95 (*1-56901-582-1*) NW Pub.

Meyer, Paul, ed. see Meyer, Martha B.

Meyer, Paul L. Introductory Probability & Statistical Applications. 1970. pap. text ed. write for info. (*0-201-04857-4*) Addison-Wesley.

— Introductory Probability & Statistical Applications. 2nd ed. (C). 1970. text ed. 61.25 (*0-201-04710-1*) Addison-Wesley.

Meyer, Paul M. Juristische Papyri. 440p. 1980. 40.00 (*0-89005-188-7*) Ares.

Meyer, Paul M., jt. ed. see Mommsen, Theodor.

Meyer, Paul R., ed. Papers in Mathematics. (Annals Ser.: Vol. 321). (Orig.). 1979. 22.00 (*0-89766-025-0*); pap. write for info. (*0-89766-026-9*) NY Acad Sci.

Meyer, Paul R., Jr., ed. Surgery of Spine Trauma. (Illus.). 867p. 1989. text ed. 175.00 (*0-443-08122-0*) Churchill.

— Surgery of Spine Trauma. LC 88-23790. (Illus.). reprint ed. pap. 180.00 (*0-7837-9590-4*, 2060339) Bks Demand.

Meyer, Paula, jt. auth. see Meyer, Larry.

***Meyer, Pedro.** Truths & Fictions: A Journey from Documentary to Digital Photography. LC 94-79645. (Illus.). 136p. 1995. 40.00 (*0-89381-608-6*) Aperture.

Meyer, Peter. Awarding College Credit for Non-College Learning. LC 74-28918. (Jossey-Bass Series in Higher Education). 223p. reprint ed. pap. 63.60 (*0-8357-4952-5*, 2037884) Bks Demand.

— Jews in the Soviet Satellites. LC 79-97297. 1971. reprint ed. text ed. 59.75 (*0-8371-2621-5*, MEJS, Greenwood Pr) Greenwood.

— Medicalese: A Humorous Medical Dictionary. Graves, Catherine, ed. LC 93-74044. (Illus.). 96p. (Orig.). 1994. pap. 9.95 (*0-9628186-1-5*) Avian Cetacean.

Meyer, Peter & Fasenfest, David, eds. The Comparative Politics of Local Economic Development. (Orig.). 1991. pap. 12.00 (*0-944285-26-0*) Pol Studies.

Meyer, Peter, tr. see Adamov, Arthur.

Meyer, Peter, tr. see Anouilh, Jean.

Meyer, Peter B., ed. Comparative Studies in Local Economic Development: Problems in Policy Implementation. LC 92-35599. (Contributions in Economics & Economic History Ser.: No. 144). 240p. 1993. text ed. 59.95 (*0-313-28820-8*, GM8820, Greenwood Pr) Greenwood.

Meyer, Peter K. Nature Guide to the Carolina Coast: Common Birds, Crabs, Shells, Fish, & Other Entities of the Coastal Environment. LC 90-85396. (Illus.). (Orig.). 1991. pap. 13.95 (*0-9628186-0-7*) Avian Cetacean.

Meyer, Philip. Ethical Journalism: A Guide for Students, Practitioners, & Consumers. 272p. (C). 1993. reprint ed. pap. text ed. 24.00 (*0-8191-8332-6*) U Pr of Amer.

— The New Precision Journalism. LC 91-8860. (Illus.). 288p. 1991. 35.00 (*0-253-33790-9*); pap. 12.95 (*0-253-20664-2*, MB-664) Ind U Pr.

— The Newspaper Survival Book: An Editor's Guide to Marketing Research. LC 84-48042. (Illus.). 186p. 1985. 25.00 (*0-253-15835-4*) Ind U Pr.

— Precision Journalism: A Reporter's Introduction to Social Science Methods. 2nd ed. LC 79-2172. (Illus.). 444p. reprint ed. pap. 126.60 (*0-8357-6688-8*, 2056868) Bks Demand.

Meyer, Philip E., jt. auth. see Shillinglaw, Gordon.

Meyer, Philippe & Marche, Pierre. Blood Cells & Arteries in Hypertension & Atherosclerosis. (Atherosclerosis Reviews Ser.: Vol. 19). 300p. 1989. 163.50 (*0-88167-475-3*) Raven.

Meyer-Plath & Schneider, A. M. Die Landmauer von Konstantinopel, Part 2: Aufnahme, Beschreibung und Geschichte. (Denkmaeler Antiker Architektur Ser.: Vol. 8). (Illus.). x, 170p. (GER.). (C). 1978. reprint ed. 229.25 (*3-11-004992-9*) De Gruyter.

Meyer, Priscilla. Find What the Sailor Has Hidden: Vladmir Nabokov's "Pale Fire" LC 88-5589. 287p. 1988. text ed. 40.00 (*0-8195-5206-2*, Wesleyan Univ Pr) U Pr of New Eng.

Meyer, Priscilla, ed. Essays on Gogol: Logos & the Russian Word. (Studies in Russian Literature & Theory). 300p. 1992. 42.95 (*0-8101-1009-1*) Northwestern U Pr.

Meyer, Priscilla, jt. ed. see Fusso, Susanne.

Meyer, R., jt. auth. see Denecke, H. J.

Meyer, R., jt. auth. see Kempt, K.

Meyer, R., et al. Alcohol Reinforcement. 1991. 74.50 (*0-8176-3463-0*) Birkhauser.

Meyer, R. A., ed. see National Congress on Pressure Vessels & Piping Staff.

Meyer, R. Daniel, jt. auth. see Klotz, Jerome H.

Meyer, R. E., et al, eds. Neuropharmacology of Ethanol: New Approaches. 280p. 1991. 69.00 (*0-685-48688-5*) Spr-Verlag.

Meyer, R. F. The Band Director's Guide to Instrument Repair. LC 72-96638. (Illus.). 156p. 1973. pap. text ed. 12.95 (*0-88284-002-9*, 680) Alfred Pub.

Meyer, R. K., jt. auth. see Thisthlewaite, P. B.

Meyer, R. M. Essential Mathematics for Applied Fields. (Universitext Ser.). (Illus.). 555p. 1979. pap. 54.00 (*0-387-90450-6*) Spr-Verlag.

Meyer, Ralph, jt. ed. see Beck, William C.

Meyer, Ralph O. Old-Time Telephones! Restoration & Repair. LC 94-10484. 1994. pap. text ed. 19.95 (*0-07-041818-7*) TAB Bks.

— Old-Time Telephones! Restoration & Repair. LC 94-10484. 1994. text ed. 34.95 (*0-07-041817-9*) TAB Bks.

***Meyer, Randall K.** Digging up the Past. (Illus.). 595p. (Orig.). 1994. write for info. (*0-9641984-0-1*) NAP AL.

Meyer, Raymond, tr. see Ingarden, Roman.

Meyer, Raymond F. Backwoods Jazz in the Twenties. LC 88-64118. 120p. (Orig.). 1989. pap. 9.95 (*0-934426-19-8*) NAPSAC Reprods.

Meyer, Raymond W. Handbook of Polyester Molding Compounds & Molding Technology. 300p. 1987. text ed. 45.00 (*0-412-00771-1*, 9199, Chap & Hall NY) Chapman & Hall.

— Handbook of Pultrusion Technology. 220p. 1985. 32.50 (*0-412-00761-4*, NO. 9201, Chap & Hall NY) Chapman & Hall.

Meyer, Rene, ed. see Ryle, Gilbert.

Meyer, Rich. Thieves of Tharbad. (Illus.). 36p. (J). (gr. 10-12). 1985. 7.00 (*0-915795-35-3*, 8050) Iron Crown Ent Inc.

Meyer, Rich J., jt. ed. see Flurkey, Alan.

Meyer, Richard, jt. auth. see McDowell, Peggy.

Meyer, Richard A. & Brenner, Daeg S., eds. Nuclei off the Line of Stability. LC 86-25905. (ACS Symposium Ser.: No. 324). (Illus.). xvi, 518p. 1986. 104.95 (*0-8412-1005-5*, PA 414) Am Chemical.

Meyer, Richard A. & Paar, Vladimir. Symmetries & Nuclear Structure. (Nuclear Science Research Conference Ser.: Vol. 13). 640p. 1987. text ed. 149.00 (*3-7186-0400-0*) Gordon & Breach.

Meyer, Richard C. One Anothering: Biblical Building Blocks for Small Groups. Wade, Wally, ed. LC 90-46181. 160p. (Orig.). 1990. pap. 11.95 (*0-931055-73-3*, L621) LuraMedia.

Meyer, Richard D., jt. auth. see Holmberg, Kenneth.

Meyer, Richard E. Introduction to Mathematical Fluid Dynamics. 192p. 1982. reprint ed. pap. 4.95 (*0-486-61554-5*) Dover.

— Waves on Fluid Interfaces: Symposium. LC 83-11797. (Mathematics Research Center Symposium Ser.). 1983. text ed. 79.00 (*0-12-493220-7*) Acad Pr.

Meyer, Richard E., ed. Cemeteries & Gravemarkers: Voices of American Culture. LC 92-31114. (Illus.). 347p. (C). 1992. reprint ed. pap. text ed. 19.95 (*0-87421-160-3*) Utah St U Pr.

— Ethnicity & the American Cemetery. LC 92-74504. 239p. (C). 1993. 48.95 (*0-87972-600-8*); pap. 16.95 (*0-87972-601-6*) Bowling Green Univ.

— Markers: The Journal of the Association for Gravestone Studies. LC 81-642903. (Illus.). 235p. 1995. 32.50 (*1-878381-05-9*) Assn Gravestone Studies.

— Markers, Vol. Eleven: The Journal of the Association for Gravestone Studies. LC 81-642903. (Illus.). 233p. 1993. 32.50 (*1-878381-04-0*) Assn Gravestone Studies.

— Markers, Vol. X: The Journal of the Association for Gravestone Studies. LC 81-642903. (Illus.). 256p. 1992. pap. 32.50 (*1-878381-03-2*) Assn Gravestone Studies.

***Meyer, Richard F., ed.** Exploration for Heavy Crude Oil & Natural Bitumen. (AAPG Studies in Geology: No. 25). (Illus.). xiii, 731p. 1987. pap. 69.00 (*0-89181-031-5*) AAPG.

Meyer, Richard K., et al. MechWarrior. (BattleTech Ser.). (Illus.). 144p. (Orig.). 1991. pap. 15.00 (*0-931787-58-0*) FASA Corp.

Meyer, Richard M. Altgermanische Religionsgeschichte: History of Ancient Germanic Religion. Bolle, Kees W., ed. LC 77-79143. (Mythology Ser.). (GER.). 1978. reprint ed. lib. bdg. 54.95 (*0-405-10552-5*) Ayer.

Meyer, Richard N. Glass Oasis: And Other Love - Hate Poetry about Los Angeles. LC 91-90267. 57p. 1991. pap. write for info. (*0-9629451-0-2*) R M Concepts.

Meyer, Robert A. Assessment of Carbon-Carbon Composite Research in the Far East. 58p. (Orig.). (C). 1992. pap. text ed. 49.95 (*1-56806-021-1*) Diane Pub.

— Life's Tapestry: A Collection of Poems. (Illus.). 164p. 1993. 12.95 (*0-931541-14-X*) Mancorp Pub.

Meyer, Robert E. Managing Rural Development. (Bibliographies in Technology & Social Change Ser.: No. 2). (Illus.). 40p. (C). 1988. pap. 6.00 (*0-945271-05-0*) ISU-TSCP.

Meyer, Robert G. Case Studies in Abnormal Behavior. 2nd ed. 1987. text ed. 32.00 (*0-205-10472-X*, H0472-4) Allyn.

— Cases in Developmental Psychology & Psychopathology. 410p. 1989. pap. text ed. 28.00 (*0-205-11907-7*, H19078) Allyn.

— The Clinician's Handbook: Integrated Diagnostic, Assessment, & Intervention in Adult & Intervention in Adult & Adolescent Psychopathology. 3rd ed. LC 92-21932. 496p. 1992. boxed write for info. (*0-205-14230-3*) Allyn.

— The Complete Book of Softball: The Loonies' Guide to Playing & Enjoying the Game. LC 83-80707. (Illus.). 192p. (Orig.). 1984. pap. 14.95 (*0-88011-212-3*, PMEY0212) Human Kinetics.

— Practical Clinical Hypnosis: Technique & Applications. LC 92-20250. (Scientific Foundations of Clinical & Counseling Psychology Ser.). 1992. text ed. 35.00 (*0-669-27729-0*) Free Pr.

— Preparation for Board Certification & Licensing Examinations in Psychology: The Professional, Legal & Ethical Components. 184p. 1992. 29.00 (*0-9634417-0-1*) Monkestee Pr.

— Preparation for Licensing & Board Certification Examinations in Psychology: The Professional, Legal, & Ethical Components. 2nd ed. LC 94-23369. (Continuing Education in Psychiatry & Psychology Ser.: No. 4). 224p. 1995. pap. text ed. 24.95 (*0-87630-767-5*) Brunner-Mazel.

Meyer, Robert G., ed. Integrated Circuit Operational Amplifiers. LC 78-59635. 320p. 1978. 39.95 (*0-87942-116-9*, PC01065) Inst Electrical.

***Meyer, Robert G. & Deitsch, Sarah E.** The Clinician's Handbook: Integrated Diagnostics, Assessment, & Intervention in Adult & Adolescent Psychopathology. 4th ed. 1995. text ed. 66.95 (*0-205-17181-8*) Allyn.

Meyer, Robert G. & Salmon, Paul G. Abnormal Psychology. 2nd ed. 580p. (C). 1988. pap. text ed. 55.00 (*0-685-18688-1*, H11778); Instr's. manual. teacher ed, pap. text ed. 70.00 (*0-205-11177-7*, H11786) Allyn.

Meyer, Robert G., jt. auth. see Gray, Paul R.

Meyer, Robert G., jt. auth. see Kronenberger, William G.

Meyer, Robert G., jt. auth. see Kurke, Martin I.

Meyer, Robert G., jt. auth. see Smith, Steven R.

Meyer, Robert G., et al. Law for the Psychotherapist. (Professional Bks.). 1988. 34.95 (*0-393-70033-X*) Norton.

Meyer, Robert H., jt. auth. see Teske, Raymond H.

Meyer, Robert J. Consumer & Business Mathematics. 176p. 1985. pap. 10.00 (*0-668-05744-0*, Arco Test) P-H Gen Ref & Trav.

Meyer, Robert S. Peace Organizations Past & Present: A Survey & Directory. LC 88-42515. 280p. 1988. lib. bdg. 32.50x (*0-89950-340-3*) McFarland & Co.

Meyer, Robert T., ed. Palladius: Dialogue on the Life of St. John Chrysostom. (Ancient Christian Writers Ser.: No. 45). 1985. pap. 16.95 (*0-8091-0358-3*) Paulist Pr.

Meyer, Roberta. Childhood. LC 94-9418. 1994. write for info. (*0-07-061234-X*) McGraw.

— Listen to the Heart: Creating Intimate Families Through the Power of Unconditional Love. LC 88-40603. 208p. 1990. pap. 8.95 (*0-446-39134-4*) Warner Bks.

Meyer, Robin, jt. ed. see Robertson, David W.

***Meyer, Rochelle W.** Exploresorts. (Hi Map Ser.: No. 16). (Illus.). 60p. Date not set. teacher ed 11.99 (*0-614-05310-2*, HM 5616) COMAP Inc.

An Asterisk (*) at the beginning of an entry indicates that the title is appearing in BIP for the first time.

Meyer, Rochelle W. & Meyer, Walter. Play it Again Sam: Recurrence Equations & Recursion in Mathematics & Computer Science. Malkevitch, Joseph, ed. (Explorations in Mathematics Ser.). (Illus.). 114p. (Orig.). 1990. pap. text ed. 12.95 (*0-912843-17-9*) COMAP Inc.

Meyer, Roger E., ed. Psychopathology & Addictive Disorders. LC 85-30547. 384p. 1986. lib. bdg. 45.00 (*0-89862-680-3*) Guilford Pr.

Meyer, Rolf, jt. auth. see Pejcic, Bogdan.

Meyer, Ronald, tr. see Akhmatova, Anna.

Meyer, Ronald, ed. see Gogol, Nikolai V.

Meyer, Roy W. Everyone's Country Estate: A History of Minnesota's State Parks. LC 91-14407. (Illus.). 357p. 1991. 34.95 (*0-87351-265-0*); pap. 19.95 (*0-87351-266-9*) Minn Hist.

— History of the Santee Sioux: United States Indian Policy on Trial. rev. ed. LC 93-34329. (Illus.). xx, 507p. 1993. pap. 17.95 (*0-8032-8203-6*, Bison Books) U of Nebr Pr.

— The Middle Western Farm Novel in the Twentieth Century. LC 64-17221. viii, 265p. 1974. pap. 7.95 (*0-8032-5798-8*, Bison Books) U of Nebr Pr.

— The Village Indians of the Upper Missouri: The Mandans, Hidatsas, & Arikaras. LC 77-4202. 392p. reprint ed. pap. 111.80 (*0-7837-3034-9*, 2042903) Bks Demand.

Meyer, Rudolf. Explosives. 4th ed. 480p. 1992. pap. 100.00 (*1-56081-266-4*) VCH Pubs.

— Gramatica del Hebreo Biblico. (SPA.). 25.95 (*84-7645-324-8*, 223501, Pub. by Edit Clie SP) TSELF.

— Hebraische Grammatik: Mit Einem Bibliographischen Nachwort von Udo Rutersworden. (Studienbuch Ser.). iv, 552p. (Orig.). (GER.). (C). 1992. pap. text ed. 36.95 (*3-11-013694-5*) De Gruyter.

— The Wisdom of Fairy Tales. 267p. 1988. 19.95 (*0-88010-192-X*) Anthroposophic.

Meyer, Rudolph. Beitraege zur Geschichte von Text & Sprache des Alten Testaments Gesammelte Aufsaetze. (Beiheft zur Zeitschrift fuer die Alttestamentliche Wissenschaft Ser.: Bd 209). viii, 259p. (GER.). (C). 1993. lib. bdg. 129.25 (*3-11-013695-3*) De Gruyter.

Meyer, Russ, see Adolph A. Schwartz, pseud..

***Meyer, Russell.** Poetry: An Introduction. 544p. 1994. pap. text ed. 19.00 (*0-312-11698-5*) St Martin.

***Meyer, Russell & Mylan, Sheryl.** Voices & Visions: An Integrated Approach to Reading & Writing. 450p. 1995. pap. text ed. 25.27 (*0-312-08385-8*) St Martin.

Meyer, Russell J. The Faerie Queene: Educating the Reader. (Twayne's Masterwork Studies: No. 73). 168p. 1991. text ed. 21.95 (*0-8057-8076-9*, Pub. by Royal Botanic Garden UK); pap. 12.95 (*0-8057-8122-6*, Pub. by Royal Botanic Garden UK) Macmillan.

Meyer, Ruth K. David Black: An American Sculptor. (Illus.). (Orig.). 1985. pap. 3.00 (*0-915577-06-2*) Taft Museum.

— Minitab Guide to Statistics for Business & Economics. (General Business Statistics Texts Ser.). 400p. (C). 1991. pap. write for info. (*0-02-380926-4*) Dellen Pub.

— The Pines: Brad Davis. (Illus.). 10p. (Orig.). 1984. pap. 3.00 (*0-915577-04-6*) Taft Museum.

Meyer, Ruth K. & Krueger, David D. A Course in Modern Business Statistics, Minitap Computer Supplement. 2nd ed. (C). 1994. pap. write for info. (*0-02-380837-3*) Dellen Pub.

— Statistics for Business & Economics, Minitab Computer Supplement. 6th ed. 416p. (C). 1994. pap. write for info. (*0-02-380840-3*) Dellen Pub.

— Statistics, Minitab Computer Supplement. 6th ed. 352p. (C). 1994. pap. write for info. (*0-02-380833-0*) Dellen Pub.

Meyer, Ruth K., ed. see Chapman, Laura.

Meyer, Ruth K., jt. auth. see O'Hara, Catherine L.

MEyer, Ruth K., jt. auth. see Shanes, Eric.

Meyer, S. Animal Pests & How to Get the Upper Hand on 'Em. (Illus.). 175p. 1993. pap. 9.95 (*1-878488-91-0*) Quixote Pr IA.

— True Stories in the News: A Beginning Reader. 1987. pap. text ed. 14.24 (*0-582-90743-8*, 75252) Longman.

Meyer-Sabellek, W., et al. Blood Pressure Measurements. 340p. 1990. 80.00 (*0-387-91332-7*, 1915) Spr-Verlag.

***Meyer, Sam.** Paradoxes of Fame: The Francis Scott Key Story. (Illus.). 144p. 1995. write for info. (*1-885457-06-5*) Eastwind MD.

Meyer, Scott B. Proper Care of Marine Aquaria. (TW Ser.). (Illus.). 256p. 1992. 14.95 (*0-86622-347-9*, TW117) TFH Pubns.

Meyer, Sheila, ed. see Litherland, Janet.

Meyer, Stacie A., jt. auth. see Berdine, William H.

Meyer, Stephen, III. The Five Dollar Day: Labor Management & Social Control in the Ford Motor Company, 1908-1921. LC 80-22795. 249p. 1981. 44.50 (*0-87395-508-0*); pap. 14.95 (*0-87395-509-9*) State U NY Pr.

Meyer, Stephen. Stalin over Wisconsin: The Making & Unmaking of Militant Unionism, 1900-1950. LC 91-32610. 275p. (C). 1992. text ed. 45.00 (*0-8135-1798-2*) Rutgers U Pr.

Meyer, Stephen, jt. ed. see Lichtenstein, Nelson.

***Meyer, Stephen A.** Baseline Sampling for Netware. 512p. 1995. write for info. (*0-8493-9446-5*, 9446) CRC Pr.

Meyer, Stephen M. The Dynamics of Nuclear Proliferation. LC 83-17893. (Illus.). xvi, 230p. (C). 1986. pap. text ed. 8.95 (*0-226-52149-4*) U Ch Pr.

— Soviet Defense Decisionmaking: What Do We Know & What Do We Understand? (CISA Working Paper Ser.: No. 33). 72p. (Orig.). Date not set. pap. 10.00 (*0-86682-041-8*) Ctr Intl Relations.

— A Statistical Risk Model for Forecasting Nuclear Proliferation. (CISA Working Paper Ser.: No. 41). 29p. (Orig.). Date not set. pap. 10.00 (*0-86682-053-1*) Ctr Intl Relations.

Meyer, Steve. Being Kind to Animal Pests: A No-Nonsense Guide to Humane Animal Control with Cage Traps. 132p. 1991. 15.00 (*0-9630284-0-5*) Meyer Pub.

— Discovering Your Iowa Civil War Ancestry: A Practical Little How to Book on Finding the What's & Where's of Your Iowa Civil War Ancestors. 2nd ed. 64p. 1993. pap. 8.00 (*0-9630284-1-3*) Meyer Pub.

— Iowa Valor: A Compilation of Civil War Combat Experiences from Soldiers of the State Distinguished as Most Patriotic of the Patriotic. (Illus.). 528p. 1994. 37.50 (*0-9630284-3-X*) Meyer Pub.

IOWA VALOR tells the heroic involvement of Iowa's sons & fathers in their own words. Readers will experience the Civil War & learn of a state's involvement in the Civil War, of which little has been written, but of which there is much to be proud. Unknown to many, no state in the Union Army had a greater involvement than Iowa. From the very first skirmish at Monroe Station, Missouri, through the very last engagement at Horse Creek, Kansas, every major episode of the Civil War that Iowa troops were involved in is covered by using their first-hand accounts from letters, diaries, battle reports & war correspondence to newspapers. By using first- hand accounts, the book reveals the Civil War as actually seen & felt by soldiers & command officers who were actually there. IOWA VALOR also includes factual summaries about battles, Iowa Civil War Regiments & notable individuals, by Author Steve Meyer. Available from Meyer Publishing, Box 247, Garrison, IA 52229. Ph. 1-800-477-5046; FAX: 319-477-5042. Or from your local distributor. ***Publisher Provided Annotation.***

— Iowans Called to Valor: The Story of Iowa's Entry into the Civil War. (Illus.). 128p. (C). 1993. pap. 12.00 (*0-9630284-2-1*) Meyer Pub.

Meyer, Steve, ed. see Fahey, Bob D.

Meyer, Steven M., jt. auth. see McCafferty, Michael D.

Meyer, Stuart L. Data Analysis for Scientists & Engineers. 513p. (C). 1992. reprint ed. text ed. 75.00 (*0-9635027-1-9*); reprint ed. pap. text ed. 45.00 (*0-9635027-0-0*) Peer Mgmt Cnslts.

Meyer, Susan. America's Great Illustrators. 1988. 24.98 (*0-88365-645-0*) Galahad Bks.

Meyer, Susan E. Edgar Degas. LC 94-8420. (First Impressions Ser.). (J). 1994. write for info. (*0-8109-3220-2*) Abrams.

— Mary Cassatt. (First Impressions Ser.). (Illus.). 80p. (YA). (gr. 7 up). 1990. 19.95 (*0-8109-3154-0*) Abrams.

— Norman Rockwell's World War II: Impressions from the Homefront. 96p. 1991. pap. 20.00 (*0-9631011-0-2*) USAA.

Meyer, Susan E., jt. auth. see Demoney, Jerry.

Meyer, Susan E., ed. see Guptill, Arthur L.

Meyer, Susan E., ed. see Kinstler, Everett R.

Meyer, Susan J. Pasta Salads! LC 86-4215. (Specialty Cookbook Ser.). (Illus.). 146p. (Orig.). 1986. pap. 8.95 (*0-89594-190-2*) Crossing Pr.

Meyer, Susan S. Aristotle on Moral Responsibility: Character & Cause. Barnes, Jonathan, ed. (Issues in Ancient Philosophy Ser.). 216p. 1994. 49.95 (*0-631-18527-5*) Blackwell Pubs.

Meyer, Sylvan & Nash, Seymour C. Prostate Cancer: Making Survival Decisions. 224p. 1994. 19.95 (*0-226-56857-1*) U Ch Pr.

Meyer, Sylvia. Professional Table Service. 1991. text ed. 49. 95 (*0-442-23982-3*) Van Nos Reinhold.

Meyer, Ted. Body Count. 166p. 1982. 8.50 (*0-682-49840-8*) Mey-Hse Bks.

— The Citizens Club. 224p. (Orig.). 1983. pap. 2.50 (*0-9611140-0-2*) Mey-Hse Bks.

Meyer, Thomas. Bang Book. LC 76-137212. (Illus.). 1971. 12.50 (*0-912330-19-8*, Inland Bk); pap. 7.50 (*0-912330-20-1*, Inland Bk) Jargon Soc.

— Fourteen Poems. 24p. (Orig.). 1989. pap. 10.00 (*0-317-93709-X*) French Broad.

— Fourteen Poems. deluxe ed. 24p. (Orig.). 1989. 35.00 (*0-317-93710-3*) French Broad.

— Fourteen Poems. limited ed. 24p. (Orig.). 1989. 50.00 (*0-685-25581-6*) French Broad.

— Sappho's Raft (Le Rideau de la Mytilenienne) LC 81-86065. 105p. 1982. 20.00 (*0-912330-51-1*); pap. 12.50 (*0-912330-50-3*) Jargon Soc.

— Staves Calends Legends. 1979. 17.50 (*0-912330-36-8*, Inland Bk); pap. 10.00 (*0-912330-37-6*, Inland Bk) Jargon Soc.

***Meyer, Thomas F. & Woolf, D. R., eds.** The Rhetorics of Life-Writing in Early Modern Europe: Forms of Biography from Cassandra Fedele to Louis XIV. LC 95-1859. (Studies in Medieval & Early Modern Civilization). 1995. 54.50 (*0-472-10591-4*) U of Mich Pr.

Meyer, Timothy P., jt. auth. see Anderson, James A.

Meyer, Tommye Q., jt. auth. see Quarles, Mary D.

Meyer, U. A., jt. auth. see Jucker, Ernst.

Meyer, Urs, jt. ed. see Testa, Bernard.

Meyer, Ursula & Wolfson, Alice. Abenteur in Deutschland. (Illus.). (J). (gr. 9-12). 1976. pap. text ed. 4.75 (*0-88345-276-6*, 18485) Prentice ESL.

— Workbook in Everyday German. (J). (gr. 9-10). 1976. pap. text ed. 4.75 (*0-88345-277-4*, 18600) Prentice ESL.

Meyer, Ursula, jt. auth. see Kind, Uwe.

Meyer, Vendla, tr. see Thom, Rene.

Meyer, Verne, jt. auth. see Sebranek, Patrick.

Meyer, Veronica R. Practical High-Performance Liquid Chromatography. 2nd ed. LC 93-13731. 350p. 1994. pap. text ed. 49.95 (*0-471-94132-8*) Wiley.

— Practical HPLC. LC 87-37136. 310p. 1988. text ed. 100. 00 (*0-471-91140-2*) Wiley.

Meyer, Viktor E. & Black, Michael J., eds. Microsurgical Procedures. (Illus.). 268p. 1991. text ed. 115.00 (*0-443-03463-X*) Churchill.

Meyer, W., jt. ed. see Althoff, K. H.

Meyer, W., et al, eds. High Energy Spin Physics Workshops, Vol. 2: Proceedings of the International Symposium, 9th, Bonn, FRG, September 6-15, 1990. (Illus.). xiii, 393p. 1991. 69.00 (*0-387-54073-3*) Spr-Verlag.

Meyer, W. E. & Reichert, J., eds. Surface Characteristics of Roadways: International Research & Technologies, STP 1031. LC 90-35195. (Special Technical Publication (STP) Ser.). (Illus.). 600p. 1990. text ed. 99.00 (*0-8031-1391-9*, 04-010310-08) ASTM.

Meyer, W. E. & Walter, J. D., eds. Frictional Interaction of Tire & Pavement - STP 793. LC 82-72886. 330p. 1983. text ed. 30.00 (*0-8031-0231-3*, 04-793000-37) ASTM.

Meyer, Walter, jt. auth. see Meyer, Rochelle W.

Meyer, Walter J. Concepts of Mathematical Modeling. 1984. text ed. write for info. (*0-07-041747-4*) McGraw.

Meyer, Warren G., et al. Retail Marketing: For Employees, Managers & Entrepreneurs. 1988. text ed. 21.80 (*0-07-041698-2*); pap. text ed. 7.68 (*0-07-002457-X*); pap. text ed. 7.68 (*0-07-002458-8*) McGraw.

— Retailing Principles & Practices. 7th ed. LC 80-24885. (Illus.). 560p. (gr. 11-12). 1981. text ed. 25.16 (*0-07-041693-1*) McGraw.

Meyer, Wilhelm. Gesammelte Abhandlungen Zur Mittellateinischen Rhythmik, 3 vols., Set. 1181p. 1970. reprint ed. write for info. (*0-318-71268-7*, Pub. by Georg Olms GW) Lubrecht & Cramer.

Meyer, Wilhelm J. Die Franzosischen Drucker- und Verlegerzeichen des Fifteenth Jahrhunderts. Vol. 2. 171p. 1970. reprint ed. write for info. (*0-318-71463-9*, Pub. by Georg Olms GW) Lubrecht & Cramer.

— Die Franzosischen Drucker- und Verlegerzeichen des XV Jahrhunderts, Vol. 2. 171p. 1970. reprint ed. write for info. (*0-318-71846-4*, Pub. by Georg Olms GW) Lubrecht & Cramer.

Meyer, William. Creative Aging: Five Easy (?) Lessons. 1992. 5.00 (*1-877871-34-6*, 6815) Ed Ministries.

— Native Americans: The New Indian Resistance. LC 71-163221. (Little New World Paperbacks Ser.). 96p. reprint ed. pap. 27.40 (*0-317-28799-0*, 2020635) Bks Demand.

Meyer, William B. & Turner, B. L., II, eds. Changes in Land Use & Land Cover: A Global Perspective. (Illus.). 380p. (C). 1994. 49.95 (*0-521-47085-4*) Cambridge U Pr.

Meyer, William F. Life & Health Insurance Law. LC 72-76891. 1972. 125.00 (*0-685-59870-5*) Clark Boardman Callaghan.

Meyer, William H. Transnational Media & Third World Development: The Structure & Impact of Imperialism. LC 88-10239. (Contributions to the Study of Mass Media & Communications Ser.: No. 11). 146p. 1988. text ed. 49.95 (*0-313-26264-0*, MYN/, Greenwood Pr) Greenwood.

Meyer, William K. Advanced PICK Programming. (Illus.). 320p. 1989. 29.95 (*0-8306-2999-8*) TAB Bks.

Meyer, William T. Energy Economics & Building Design. 352p. 1983. text ed. 37.00 (*0-07-041751-2*) McGraw.

Meyer, William W. Nice Things about Growing Older. 68p. (Orig.). 1990. pap. 7.75 (*1-877871-11-7*, 3530) Ed Ministries.

Meyer, Y. Wavelets: Algorithms & Applications. (Miscellaneous Bks.: No. 38). xi, 133p. 1993. pap. 19.50 (*0-89871-309-9*) Soc Indus-Appl Math.

Meyer, Yves. Wavelets. (Studies in Advanced Mathematics: No. 37). 220p. (C). 1993. 59.95 (*0-521-42000-8*) Cambridge U Pr.

— Wavelets & Operators. (Cambridge Studies in Advanced Mathematics Ser.: No. 37). 240p. (C). 1995. pap. 27.95 (*0-521-45869-2*) Cambridge U Pr.

***Meyer, Yves & Coiffman, Ronald.** Wavelets & Operators Vol. 2: Calderon-Zygmund Operators & Multilinear Operators. (Studies in Advanced Mathematics: No. 48). (Illus.). 400p. (C). Date not set. write for info. (*0-521-42001-6*) Cambridge U Pr.

Meyer, Yves, et al, eds. Wavelets & Applications: Proceedings of the International Conference Marseille, France, May 1989. (Recherches en Mathematiques Appliquees - Research Notes in Applied Mathematics Ser.: Vol. 20). (Illus.). xii, 450p. 1992. pap. 79.00 (*0-387-54516-6*) Spr-Verlag.

Meyerbeer, Giacomo. Excerpts from the Early Italian Operas: Romilda e Constanza, 1817, Semiramide riconosciuta, 1819, Emma di Resburgo, 1819, Mrgherita d'Anjou, 1820 & L'esule di Granata, 1822, Vol. 23. LC 91-754851. (Italian Opera 1810-1840 Ser.). 308p. 1992. lib. bdg. 97.00 (*0-8240-6572-7*) Garland.

Meyerding, Jane. Everywhere House. LC 93-41740. 256p. (Orig.). 1993. pap. 9.95 (*0-934678-42-1*) New Victoria Pubs.

Meyerhof, Walter E. Elements of Nuclear Physics. 1967. text ed. write for info. (*0-07-041745-8*) McGraw.

Meyerhof, Walter E., jt. auth. see Eichler, Jorg.

Meyerhofer, Nicholas J. Germany & the United States Facing the Post-Communist World. (Orig.). (ENG & GER.). Date not set. pap. write for info. (*0-910973-06-7*) Arrowhead AZ.

***Meyerhofer, Nicholas J. & Webb, Karl E., eds.** Felix Mitterer: A Critical Introduction. LC 95-1618. (Studies in Austrian Literature, Culture, & Thought). 1995. 34.95 (*1-57241-010-8*) Ariadne CA.

Meyerhoff, A. A., jt. auth. see Khudoley, K. M.

Meyerhoff, Arthur A., et al. China: Stratigraphy, Paleogeography & Tectonics. (C). 1991. lib. bdg. 142.00 (*0-7923-0972-3*) Kluwer Ac.

Meyerhoff, Dirk. Traditioneller Stoff und Individuelle Gestaltung, Untersuchungen Zu Alkaios und Sappho. (Beitrage Zur Altertumswissenschaft Ser.: Band 3). viii, 264p. (GER.). 1984. write for info. (*3-487-07463-X*, Pub. by Georg Olms GW) Lubrecht & Cramer.

— Traditioneller Stoff und Individuelle Gestaltung. Untersuchungen Zu Alkaios und Sappho. Bd. 3. Date not set. write for info. (*0-318-70707-1*, Pub. by Georg Olms GW) Lubrecht & Cramer.

Meyerhoff, Hans, tr. see Friedlander, Paul.

Meyerhoff, M. A Parent's Guide to the Roots of Sibling Rivalry. (Changing Behavior Through Understanding Ser.). 20p. (Orig.). 1991. pap. 2.95 (*1-56456-055-4*) W Gladden Found.

Meyerhoff, Michael K. A Parents' Guide to Avoiding the Superbaby Syndrome. 20p. 1992. 2.95 (*1-56456-136-4*, 257) W Gladden Found.

— A Parent's Guide to Dealing with a Child's Anger During Infancy, Toddlerhood, & the Preschool Years. 20p. 1992. 2.95 (*1-56456-077-5*, 281) W Gladden Found.

— A Parent's Guide to Encouraging Imagination & Creativity During Early Childhood. 20p. 1992. 2.95 (*1-56456-057-0*, 259) W Gladden Found.

— A Parent's Guide to Enhancing Early Language Development. 20p. 1992. 2.95 (*1-56456-058-9*, 261) W Gladden Found.

— A Parent's Guide to Ensuring a Successful Day Care Experience for an Infant or Toddler. 20p. 1992. 2.95 (*1-56456-075-9*, 280) W Gladden Found.

— A Parents' Guide to Establishing an Effective Parenting Partnership. 20p. 1993. 2.95 (*1-56456-078-3*, 273) W Gladden Found.

— A Parent's Guide to Making a Home Safe & Suitable for an Infant or Toddler. 20p. 1992. 2.95 (*1-56456-074-0*, 279) W Gladden Found.

— A Parents' Guide to Making Sense of Developmental Milestone During Infancy & Toddlerhood. 20p. 1993. 2.95 (*1-56456-080-5*, 275) W Gladden Found.

— A Parent's Guide to Nurturing the Roots of Emotional Security & Self-Esteem. 20p. 1992. 2.95 (*1-56456-056-2*, 260) W Gladden Found.

— A Parents' Guide to Promoting Social Skill Development During Infancy & Toddlerhood. 20p. 1992. 2.95 (*1-56456-137-2*, 256) W Gladden Found.

— A Parents' Guide to Raising an Only-Child. 20p. 1993. 2.95 (*1-56456-079-1*, 274) W Gladden Found.

— A Parents' Guide to Raising Twins. 20p. 1993. 2.95 (*1-56456-08X-9*, 278) W Gladden Found.

— A Parents' Guide to Selecting Toys for Infants & Toddlers. 20p. 1992. 2.95 (*1-56456-135-6*, 258) W Gladden Found.

— A Parents' Guide to the Mind of the Infant & Toddler. 20p. 1993. 2.95 (*1-56456-081-3*, 276) W Gladden Found.

— A Parent's Guide to the Terrible Twos. (Changing Behavior Through Understanding Ser.). 20p. (Orig.). 1991. pap. text ed. 2.95 (*1-56456-054-6*) W Gladden Found.

— A Parents' Guide to the World of the New Born. 20p. 1993. 2.95 (*1-56456-082-1*, 277) W Gladden Found.

— A Parent's Guide to Toilet Training. (Changing Behavior Through Understanding Ser.). 20p. (Orig.). 1991. pap. text ed. 2.95 (*1-56456-053-8*) W Gladden Found.

***Meyerhoff, Paul, 2nd.** Sabotage Flight. LC 94-37177. (Illus.). 200p. (Orig.). (J). (gr. 5-9). 1995. pap. 9.95 (*0-931625-24-6*) DIMI Pr.

Meyerhoff, Robert W., ed. Manufacture of Superconducting Materials: An International Conference, 8-10 November, 1976, Port Chester, New York, Proceedings. LC 77-11148. (Materials-Metalworking Technology Ser.). (Illus.). 239p. reprint ed. pap. 68.20 (*0-317-09703-2*, 2019478) Bks Demand.

Meyerhoff, Roland & Gillespie, George H., eds. Supernovae Spectra: La Jolla Institute, 1980. (AIP Conference Proceedings Ser.: No. 63). 173p. 1980. lib. bdg. 18.25 (*0-88318-162-2*) Am Inst Physics.

Meyerhoff, William L. Diagnosis & Management of Hearing Loss. (Illus.). 182p. 1984. text ed. 51.50 (*0-7216-1307-1*) Saunders.

Meyerhoff, William L., ed. see Paparella, Michael M. & Shumrick, Donald A.

Meyerhuber, Carl I., Jr. Less Than Forever: The Rise & Decline of Union Solidarity in Western Pennsylvania, 1914-1948. LC 86-62504. 240p. 1987. 39.50 (*0-941664-27-9*) Susquehanna U Pr.

Meyering, Robert. Who Is Jesus? LC 93-49845. 1993. 3.95 (*1-56212-035-2*) CRC Pubns.

Meyering, Robert A. Genesis One-Eleven. (Five on One Ser.). 96p. (Orig.). 1986. teacher ed 9.50 (*0-930265-17-3*); student ed, pap. text ed. 5.25 (*0-930265-16-5*) CRC Pubns.

Meyering, Sheryl L. A Reader's Guide to the Short Stories of Willa Cather. LC 93-10381. (Reference Ser.). 304p. 1993. text ed. 60.00 (*0-8161-1834-5*, Hall Reference) Macmillan.

— Sylvia Plath: A Reference Guide, 1973-1988. (Reference Guides to Literature Ser.). 288p. 1989. text ed. 40.00 (*0-8161-8929-3*, Hall Reference) Macmillan.

An Asterisk (*) at the beginning of an entry indicates that the title is appearing in BIP for the first time.

Meyering, Sheryl L., ed. Charlotte Perkins Gilman: The Woman & Her Work. LC 88-27771. (Challenging the Literary Canon Ser.). 224p. 1991. 50.00 (*0-8357-1931-6*) Univ Rochester Pr.

Meyering, Theo C. Historical Roots of Cognitive Science. (C). 1989. lib. bdg. 94.50 (*0-7923-0349-0*) Kluwer Ac.

Meyerink, George. Appliance Service Handbook. 2nd ed. (Illus.). 572p. 1987. text ed. 76.00 (*0-13-038902-1*) P-H.

***Meyerowitz, Elliot M. & Somerville, Chris R., eds.** Arabidopsis. (Monographs: No. 27). (Illus.). 1270p. (C). 1994. 175.00 (*0-87969-428-9*) Cold Spring Harbor.

Meyerowitz, Jacob. Before the Beginning of Time. LC 93-86657. (Illus.). 336p. 1994. 35.00 (*0-9607034-1-1*) RRP Pub.

Meyerowitz, Joanne, ed. Not June Cleaver: Women & Gender in the Postwar America, 1945-1960. LC 93-26987. (Critical Perspectives on the Past Ser.). 368p. (C). 1994. text ed. 49.95 (*1-56639-170-9*); pap. 19.95 (*1-56639-171-7*) Temple U Pr.

Meyerowitz, Joanne J. Women Adrift: Independent Wage Earners in Chicago, 1880-1930. (Women in Culture & Society Ser.). (Illus.). xxiv, 224p. 1988. 29.95 (*0-226-52197-4*) U Ch Pr.

— Women Adrift: Independent Wage Earners in Chicago, 1880-1930. LC 87-22449. (Women in Culture & Society Ser.). (Illus.). xxiv, 224p. 1991. pap. text ed. 13.95 (*0-226-52198-2*) U Ch Pr.

Meyerowitz, Joel. Bay - Sky. (Illus.). 96p. 1993. 50.00 (*0-8212-2037-3*) Bulfinch Pr.

— Cape Light: Color Photographs by Joel Meyerowitz. MacDonald, Bruce K. & Ackley, Clifford, eds. 1979. pap. 29.95 (*0-87846-131-0*) Bulfinch Pr.

— George Balanchine's the Nutcracker. (Illus.). (J). 1993. 29.95 (*0-316-56921-6*) Little.

— A Summer's Day. LC 84-40642. (Illus.). 156p. 1987. pap. 17.95 (*0-8129-1195-4*, Times Bks) Random.

— A Summer's Day. limited ed. LC 84-40642. (Illus.). 156p. 1987. 750.00 (*0-8129-1194-6*, Times Bks); 750.00 (*0-8129-1196-2*, Times Bks) Random.

Meyerowitz, Joel, jt. auth. see Westerbeck, Colin.

Meyerowitz, Michael & Sanchez, Sam. The Graphic Designer's Basic Guide to the Macintosh. LC 89-81077. (Illus.). 144p. 1990. pap. 19.95 (*0-927629-06-2*, 30208) Allworth Pr.

Meyerowitz, Patricia. And a Little Child: Stories of Anyone. Strobel, Peter, tr. LC 81-52891. 52p. (ENG & GER.). 1982. pap. 5.00 (*0-9607034-0-3*) RRP Pub.

— Making Jewelry & Sculpture Through Unit Construction. (Illus.). 1978. reprint ed. pap. 5.95 (*0-486-23678-1*) Dover.

***Meyerowitz, Rael.** Transferring to America: Jewish Interpretations of American Dreams. (Series in Psychoanalysis & Culture & the Series in Modern Jewish Literature & Culture). 304p. (C). 1995. text ed. 59.50x (*0-7914-2607-6*); pap. text ed. 19.95x (*0-7914-2608-4*) State U NY Pr.

***Meyerowitz, Rick.** Elvis the Bulldozer. LC 95-12189. (J). 1995. write for info. (*0-679-86958-1*) Random.

Meyerowitz, Steve. Food Combining & Digestion: How to Get More Out of What You Eat. 2nd ed. 1992. reprint ed. pap. write for info. (*1-878736-50-7*) Sprout Hse.

— Food Combining & Digestion: How to Improve Your Digestion Without Being a Rocket Scientist. 120p. 1993. pap. 7.95 (*1-878736-57-4*) Sprout Hse.

— Juice Fasting & Detoxification: A Guide to Self-Healing & Detoxification. 3rd ed. 144p. 1992. reprint ed. pap. 8.95 (*1-878736-64-7*) Sprout Hse.

— Sprout It! One Week from Seed to Salad: How to Supply Your Own Organic Food Year Round from Stored Seed. 224p. 1993. pap. 10.95 (*1-878736-02-7*) Sprout Hse.

— Sproutman's Kitchen Garden Cookbook: Sprout Breads, Cookies, Salads, Soups & 250 Other Low Fat, Dairy-Free, Vegetarian Recipes. 336p. 1994. pap. 14.95 (*1-878736-84-1*) Sprout Hse.

— Water: The Pollution & Purification. 3rd ed. 1992. reprint ed. pap. write for info. (*1-878736-19-1*) Sprout Hse.

— Wheatgrass: Nature's Finest Medicine. 3rd ed. 1992. reprint ed. pap. write for info. (*1-878736-72-8*) Sprout Hse.

Meyerowitz, Steven. Marketer's Legal Guide: A Complete & Practical Source to Marketing, Sales, & Advertising. 507p. 1993. pap. 22.95 (*0-8103-9383-2*, 089158) Visible Ink Pr.

Meyerowitz, Steven, ed. An Ounce of Prevention: Marketing, Sales & Advertising Law for Non-Lawyers. 507p. 1993. 45.00 (*0-8103-8997-5*, 101780) Gale.

Meyerowitz, Theresa B. Israeli Journal. LC 92-54528. (C). 1993. write for info. (*0-8453-4845-0*, Cornwall Bks) Assoc Univ Prs.

— The Journal. LC 90-55330. (Illus.). 136p. 1992. 30.00 (*0-8453-4830-2*, Cornwall Bks) Assoc Univ Prs.

— The Poetic Canvas. LC 87-46429. (Illus.). 128p. 1989. 30.00 (*0-8453-4817-5*, Cornwall Bks) Assoc Univ Prs.

— William Meyerowitz: The Artist Speaks. LC 84-45010. (Illus.). 192p. 1986. 40.00 (*0-87982-513-8*) Art Alliance.

— William Meyerowitz: The Artist Speaks. LC 84-45010. (Illus.). 192p. 1986. 40.00 (*0-8453-4768-3*, Cornwall Bks) Assoc Univ Prs.

***Meyers.** High Constable. 1995. mass mkt. (*0-553-56889-2*) Bantam.

— Martial Arts Movies. 1985. 19.95 (*0-8065-0950-3*, Citadel Pr) Carol Pub Group.

— Meyers Enzyklopaedisches Lexikon, 25 vols. (GER.). 1973. 3,995.00 (*0-8288-6321-0*, M-7558) Fr & Eur.

— Meyers Grosses Handlexikon. 14th ed. 1072p. (GER.). 1985. 75.00 (*0-8288-1962-9*, M15509) Fr & Eur.

— Meyers Kontinente und Meere-Daten, Karten Die Enzyklopadie der Erde, 8 vols. (GER.). 1973. 625.00 (*0-7859-0118-3*, M7560) Fr & Eur.

— Meyers Large Pocket Lexicon: Meyers Grosses Taschenlexikon des Gesamten Wissens. 2nd ed. 8640p. (GER.). 1987. 350.00 (*0-8288-1963-7*, M15512) Fr & Eur.

— Meyers Physik-Lexikon: Meyers Physics Lexicon. (GER.). 1973. 85.00 (*0-8288-6323-7*, M-7561) Fr & Eur.

— Meyers Standardlexikon des Gesamtes Wissesns. 2nd ed. 1118p. (GER.). 1980. 45.00 (*0-8288-1964-5*, M7562) Fr & Eur.

— Registered Representative Stockbroker. 3rd ed. 1994. pap. 35.00 (*0-671-88314-3*, J K Lasser) P-H Gen Ref & Trav.

Meyers & Jones. Textbook of Liver & Biliary Surgery. (Illus.). 544p. 1990. text ed. 125.00 (*0-397-50774-7*) Lippincott.

Meyers, jt. auth. see Norton.

Meyers, et al. Shock-Wave & High-Strain-Rate Phenomena in Materials. (Mechanical Engineering Ser.: Vol. 77). 1184p. 1992. 250.00 (*0-8247-8579-7*) Dekker.

Meyers, Alan. Cocaine: A Treatment Guide for Counselors. 120p. (Orig.). 1988. pap. 9.95 (*0-937119-01-6*) Meyers Pub.

— Composing Experience. LC 94-28376. (C). 1995. 19.50 (*0-673-46928-X*) HarpCollege.

— Composing with Confidence. 2nd ed. (C). 1988. pap. text ed. 20.25 (*0-673-38166-8*) HarpCollege.

— Composing with Confidence. 3rd ed. LC 92-28465. (C). 1992. 32.50 (*0-673-46596-9*) HarpCollege.

— Writing with Confidence. 3rd ed. (C). 1987. 19.95 (*0-673-18728-4*) HarpCollege.

— Writing with Confidence. 4th ed. (C). 1991. text ed. 34.50 (*0-673-46444-X*) HarpCollege.

— Writing with Confidence, Form B. 4th ed. (C). 1993. text ed. 24.50 (*0-673-46801-1*) HarpCollege.

Meyers, Albert. Immigration of the Irish Quakers Into Pennsylvania, 1682-1750: With Their Early History in Ireland. LC 77-92027. (Illus.). xxii, 477p. 1994. reprint ed. 30.00 (*0-8063-0252-6*, 3980) Genealog Pub.

Meyers, Albert, ed. Organic Synthesis, Vol. 70. 336p. 1992. text ed. 54.95 (*0-471-57743-X*) Wiley.

Meyers, Amy, ed. After Midnight Stories, Bk. 4. large type ed. 1990. 21.95 (*0-7089-2290-2*) Ulverscroft.

Meyers-Anderson, Maribeth, jt. auth. see Gordon, David.

Meyers, Andrew W. & Craighead, W. Edward, eds. Cognitive Behavior Therapy with Children. LC 83-16116. (Applied Clinical Psychology Ser.). 514p. 1984. 75.00 (*0-306-41291-8*, Plenum Pr) Plenum.

Meyers, Annette. Blood on the Street. 1993. mass mkt. 4.99 (*0-553-29731-7*) Bantam.

— Murder: The Musical. 1994. 5.50 (*0-553-56785-3*) Bantam.

— These Bones Were Made for Dancin' A Smith & Wetzon Mystery. LC 95-909. 1995. 19.95 (*0-385-47653-1*) Doubleday.

Meyers, Arlen D. Biological Basis of Facial Plastic Surgery. (American Academy of Facial Plastic & Reconstructive Surgery Monograph). (Illus.). 216p. 1993. text ed. 59.00 (*0-86577-443-9*) Thieme Med Pubs.

Meyers, Arthur. The Cheyenne. (First Bks.). (Illus.). 64p. (J). (gr. 5-8). 1992. pap. 5.95 (*0-531-15636-2*) Watts.

Meyers, Arthur, jt. auth. see Slattery, Thomas.

Meyers, Augustus. Ten Years in the Ranks U. S. Army. Kohn, Richard H., ed. LC 78-22387. (American Military Experience Ser.). 1980. reprint ed. lib. bdg. 26.95 (*0-405-11864-3*) Ayer.

Meyers, Bert. The Wild Olive Tree, 2 vols. in one. Bd. with Blue Cafe. 118p. 1982. reprint ed. Set pap. 6.95 (*0-915572-67-2*) Panjandrum.

Meyers, Betty & Fellers, Frederick P., comps. Discographies of Commercial Recordings of the Cleveland Orchestra (1924-1977) and the Cincinnati Symphony Orchestra (1917-1977) LC 78-3122. 211p. 1978. text ed. 42.95 (*0-313-20375-X*, MDI/) Greenwood.

Meyers, Bob. Parenting Teenagers in the Nineteen Nineties. (Illus.). 148p. 1993. pap. 14.95 (*0-86431-121-4*, Pub. by Aust Coun Educ Res AT) Paul & Co Pubs.

***Meyers, Bryan.** Desktop Guide to CL Programming. LC 94-33312. (News 3X-400 Technical Reference Ser.). 205p. (Orig.). 1994. pap. 34.95 (*1-882419-07-3*) Duke Commns Intl.

— RPG IV Jump Start: Moving Ahead with the New RPG. 193p. (Orig.). 1995. pap. 39.95 (*1-882419-17-0*) Duke Commns Intl.

Meyers, Bryan & Riehl, Dan. AS-400 Control Language Programming. 550p. (C). 1993. pap. text ed. 65.00 (*1-882419-04-9*, Duke Pr) Duke Commns Intl.

Meyers, Burt, ed. see Leung, Donald, et al.

***Meyers, Burt R.** Antimicrobial Prescribing. 10th ed. 1995. write for info. (*1-884065-06-6*) Assocs in Med.

— Antimicrobial Therapy Guide. 10th ed. 1995. write for info. (*1-884065-00-7*) Assocs in Med.

Meyers, C., jt. auth. see Kharasch, N.

Meyers, C. E., et al. Primary Abilities at Mental Age Six. (SRCD M: Vol. 27, No. 1). 1962. pap. 14.00 (*0-527-01592-X*) Periodicals Srv.

Meyers, C. J., jt. auth. see Williams, H. R.

Meyers, Carol. Discovering Eve: Ancient Israelite Women in Context. 256p. 1991. reprint ed. pap. 10.95 (*0-19-506581-6*) OUP.

Meyers, Carol L. & Meyers, Eric M. Haggai, Zechariah 1-8. LC 85-20924. (Anchor Bible Ser.). (Illus.). 576p. 1987. pap. 40.00 (*0-385-14482-2*) Doubleday.

— Zechariah Nine-Fourteen: A New Translation with Introduction & Commentary. LC 92-34535. (Anchor Bible Ser.: Vol. 25C). 1993. 40.00 (*0-385-14483-0*, Anchor NY) Doubleday.

Meyers, Carol L. & O'Connor, M., eds. The Word of the Lord Shall Go Forth: Essays in Honor of David Noel Freedman in Celebration of His Sixtieth Birthday. LC 83-20589. (American Schools of Oriental Research Special Volume Ser.: No. 1). xviii, 742p. 1983. text ed. 45.00 (*0-931464-19-6*) Eisenbrauns.

Meyers, Carole T. Eating Out with the Kids in San Francisco & the Bay Area. rev. ed. LC 85-12752. (Eating Out with the Kids in the U. S. A. Ser.). (Illus.). 1985. pap. 7.95 (*0-917120-08-6*) Carousel Pr.

— How to Organize a Babysitting Cooperative & Get Some Free Time Away from the Kids. LC 76-12660. (Illus.). (Orig.). 1976. 8.95 (*0-917120-01-9*); pap. 3.95 (*0-917120-00-0*) Carousel Pr.

— Miles of Smiles: One Hundred One Great Car Games & Activities. (Illus.). 128p. (Orig.). (J). 1992. pap. 8.95 (*0-917120-11-6*) Carousel Pr.

— San Francisco Family Fun. (Illus.). 296p. (Orig.). 1990. pap. 12.95 (*0-917120-10-8*) Carousel Pr.

— Weekend Adventures for City-Weary People: Overnight Trips in Northern California. 4th rev. ed. LC 88-10869. (Illus.). 304p. 1989. pap. 11.95 (*0-917120-09-4*) Carousel Pr.

— Weekend Adventures for City-Weary People: Overnight Trips in Northern California. 5th rev. ed. (Illus.). 336p. 1993. pap. 13.95 (*0-917120-12-4*) Carousel Pr.

Meyers, Carole T., ed. The Family Travel Guide: An Inspiring Collection of Family-Oriented Vacations. 300p. (Orig.). 1994. pap. 14.95 (*0-917120-14-0*) Carousel Pr.

Meyers, Casey. Aerobic Walking: The Best & Safest Weight Loss & Cardiovascular Exercise for Everyone Overweight or Out of Shape. LC 87-40076. 224p. 1987. pap. 10.00 (*0-394-75440-9*, Vin) Random.

— Walking: A Complete Guide to the Complete Exercise. 1992. pap. 12.00 (*0-679-73777-4*, Vin) Random.

Meyers, Charles J., jt. auth. see Williams, Howard R.

Meyers, Charles J., et al. Water Resource Management: A Casebook in Law & Public Policy. 3rd ed. (University Casebook Ser.). 1063p. 1987. text ed. 35.95 (*0-88277-593-6*) Foundation Pr.

— Water Resource Management: A Casebook in Law & Public Policy, 1992 Supplement. 3rd ed. (University Casebook Ser.). 116p. 1991. pap. text ed. 7.95 (*0-88277-969-9*) Foundation Pr.

Meyers, Charlie. Colorado Ski Country. Hagmann, Marnie, ed. LC 86-82747. 104p. 1987. 14.95 (*0-937959-17-0*); pap. 14.95 (*0-937959-16-2*) Falcon Pr MT.

Meyers, Chet. Teaching Students to Think Critically: A Guide for Faculty in All Disciplines. LC 86-45627. (Higher Education Ser.). 146p. 1986. 26.95x (*1-55542-011-7*) Jossey-Bass.

Meyers, Chet & Jones, Thomas. Promoting Active Learning: Strategies for the College Classroom. LC 92-41685. (Higher & Adult Education Ser.). 224p. 1993. 26.95 (*1-55542-524-0*) Jossey-Bass.

Meyers, David, jt. auth. see Joseph, Eric D.

Meyers, David, jt. ed. see Miller, David C.

Meyers, David W. The Human Body & the Law. 2nd ed. LC 90-71394. 368p. 1991. 42.50 (*0-8047-1885-7*) Stanford U Pr.

Meyers, Diana T. Inalienable Rights: A Defense. LC 84-23007. 292p. 1986. text ed. 50.00 (*0-231-06034-3*); pap. text ed. 15.50 (*0-231-06035-1*) Col U Pr.

— Self, Society, & Personal Choice. 452p. 1989. text ed. 36.50 (*0-231-06418-7*) Col U Pr.

— Self, Society, & Personal Choice. 304p. 1991. pap. text ed. 19.50 (*0-231-06419-5*) Col U Pr.

Meyers, Diana T., jt. ed. see Kipnis, Kenneth.

Meyers, Diana T., et al. Kindred Matters: Rethinking the Philosophy of the Family. LC 92-54970. 336p. 1993. 41.50 (*0-8014-2594-8*); pap. 15.95 (*0-8014-9909-7*) Cornell U Pr.

Meyers, Donald I., jt. ed. see Glick, Robert A.

Meyers, Douglas, jt. auth. see Smith, Maggy.

Meyers, Eleanor S., ed. Envisioning the New City: A Reader on Urban Ministry. 336p. (Orig.). 1992. pap. 22.99 (*0-664-25315-6*) Westminster John Knox.

Meyers, Ellen, comp. Teachers Catalog of Creative Program Ideas. (Illus.). 128p. 1986. pap. 10.00 (*0-939229-00-5*) Impact II.

Meyers, Ellen, ed. New Teachers Handbook. (Illus.). 52p. 1988. pap. 8.50 (*0-939229-01-3*) Impact II.

— Teacher-Parent Partnerships Handbook. (Illus.). 64p. 1990. pap. 9.50 (*0-939229-02-1*) Impact II.

Meyers, Ellen & McIsaac, Paul, eds. How Teachers Are Changing Schools. (By Teachers, for Teachers Ser.). (Illus.). 100p. (Orig.). 1994. pap. 15.00 (*0-939229-05-6*) Impact II.

Meyers, Eric M., jt. auth. see Meyers, Carol L.

Meyers, Eric M., et al. Excavations at the Ancient Synagogue of Gush Halav. LC 90-47594. (Meiron Excavation Project Reports: No. 5). xx, 292p. 1990. 40.00 (*0-931464-59-5*) Eisenbrauns.

— Sepphoris. viii, 63p. 1992. pap. text ed. 14.95 (*0-9602686-9-3*, Ctr Judaic Studies) Eisenbrauns.

Meyers, Frank M. The Commanches. 400p. 1987. reprint ed. 35.00 (*0-942211-95-2*) Olde Soldier Bks.

Meyers, Frank S., jt. auth. see Holloway, Harry.

Meyers, Franklin G. & French, Joyce N. Preparing for the Test of Standard Written English. 80p. (gr. 10-12). 1985. teacher ed 8.99 (*0-89026-071-0*); pap. text ed. 8.49 (*0-89026-070-2*) Media Materials.

Meyers, Fred E. Motion & Time Study: Improving Work Methods & Management. 304p. 1992. text ed. 71.00 (*0-13-596081-9*) P-H.

— Plant Layout & Material Handling. 352p. 1993. text ed. 61.00 (*0-13-013475-9*) P-H.

— Technology of Industrial Plant Layout & Material Handling. 1993. text ed. 52.00 (*0-13-904426-4*) P-H.

Meyers, Frederic. European Coal Mining Unions: Structure & Function. (Monograph & Research Ser.: No. 7). 161p. 1961. 5.00 (*0-89215-009-2*) U Cal LA Indus Rel.

— Mexican Industrial Relations Viewed from the Perspective of the Mexican Labor Court. (Monograph & Research Ser.: No. 24). 103p. 1979. 5.00 (*0-89215-104-8*) U Cal LA Indus Rel.

— Ownership of Jobs: A Comparative Study. (Monograph & Research Ser.: No. 11). 114p. 1964. 5.00 (*0-89215-012-2*) U Cal LA Indus Rel.

— State & Government Employee Unions in France. LC 73-634398. (Comparative Studies in Public Employment Labor Relations Ser.). 1971. 10.00 (*0-87736-007-3*); pap. 5.00 (*0-87736-008-1*) U of Mich Inst Labor.

— Training in European Enterprises. (Monograph & Research Ser.: No. 14). 173p. 1969. 5.00 (*0-89215-015-7*) U Cal LA Indus Rel.

Meyers, Frederic, jt. ed. see Hildebrand, George H.

Meyers, Frederic, tr. see Watillon, Leon.

Meyers, Gary D. The Carpenter's Toolbox Manual. (On-the-Job Reference Ser.). 352p. 1989. pap. 10.95 (*0-13-115296-3*) P-H.

***Meyers, Genna.** It's Almost Tomorrow. 560p. Date not set. pap. 12.95 (*0-7610-0310-X*) NW Pub.

***Meyers, Gloria E.** A Municipal Mother: Portland's Lola Greene Baldwin, America's First Policewoman. LC 95-16780. 1995. write for info. (*0-87071-386-8*) Oreg St U Pr.

Meyers, H. Alan. Cocaine: The Users Guide to Self-Help Treatment. rev. ed. 1985. pap. 9.95 (*0-937119-00-8*) Meyers Pub.

Meyers, H. P. Introductory Solid State Physics. 500p. 1990. 79.00 (*0-85066-759-3*); pap. 39.50 (*0-85066-761-5*) Taylor & Francis.

Meyers, Harold B. Geronimo's Ponies. LC 88-63117. (National Novella Winner Ser.). 120p. (Orig.). 1989. pap. 7.95 (*0-933031-18-1*) Coun Oak Bks.

Meyers, Helen C., ed. Between Analyst & Patient: New Dimensions in Countertransference & Tranference. 280p. 1986. text ed. 32.50 (*0-88163-043-8*) Analytic Pr.

Meyers, J. Gordon & Lawyer, John. A Guidebook for Problem-Solving in Group Settings. (Illus.). 38p. 1986. 2.95 (*0-934134-62-6*) Sheed & Ward MO.

Meyers, J. Thomas. Chert Resources of the Lower Illinois Valley. (Reports of Investigations Ser.: No. 18). (Illus.). 42p. 1970. pap. 2.00 (*0-89792-042-2*) Ill St Museum.

Meyers, James P. The Educational System of Kenya. (ECE Presents Ser.). (Illus.). 100p. (C). 1993. pap. 21.00 (*1-883971-03-9*) Educ Credential.

Meyers, Jason. America. 1991. 29.99 (*0-517-69507-3*) Random Hse Value.

— Lessons from Leaders, Vol. 1: Politicians. (Illus.). 1985. pap. 4.95 (*0-913290-83-1*) Camaro Pub.

Meyers, Jean O., ed. see O'Gara, W. H.

Meyers, Jeffrey. The Biographer's Art. 288p. (C). 1989. 30.00 (*0-941533-52-2*) New Amsterdam Bks.

— D. H. Lawrence: A Biography. 445p. 24.95 (*0-685-39477-8*) Knopf.

— D. H. Lawrence: A Biography. 1992. pap. 14.00 (*0-679-73065-6*, Vin) Random.

— D. H. Lawrence & the Experience of Italy. LC 82-60261. 207p. reprint ed. pap. 59.00 (*0-7837-3006-3*, 2042935) Bks Demand.

— Edgar Allan Poe: Life & Legacy. 384p. 1992. text ed. 30.00 (*0-684-19370-1*, Scribners) S&S Trade.

— Edmund Wilson: A Biography. LC 94-37574. (Illus.). 576p. 1995. 35.00 (*0-395-68993-7*, P Davison Bk) HM.

— Homosexuality & Literature: 1890-1930. 1977. lib. bdg. 32.95 (*0-7735-0300-5*, Pub. by McGill CN) U of Toronto Pr.

— Homosexuality & Literature 1890-1930. 200p. (C). 1987. reprint ed. pap. 15.00 (*0-485-12054-2*, Pub. by Athlone Pr UK) Humanities.

— Katherine Mansfield: A Biography. LC 79-18885. (Illus.). 1980. pap. 10.50 (*0-8112-0834-6*, NDP543) New Directions.

— The Legacy of D. H. Lawrence: New Essays. 208p. 1987. text ed. 29.95 (*0-312-47804-6*) St Martin.

— A Reader's Guide to George Orwell. 192p. 1977. pap. 8.95 (*0-8226-0339-X*) Littlefield.

— Scott Fitzgerald: A Biography. (Illus.). 368p. 1994. 27.50 (*0-06-019036-1*, HarpT) HarpC.

— The Spirit of Biography. Litz, A. Walton, ed. LC 89-33823. (Studies in Modern Literature: No. 102). 315p. reprint ed. 89.80 (*0-8357-2001-2*, 2070745) Bks Demand.

— The Wounded Spirit: T. E. Lawrence's "Seven Pillars of Wisdom" 2nd ed. 220p. 1989. text ed. 39.95 (*0-312-02721-4*) St Martin.

— Wyndham Lewis: A Revaluation. 1980. 39.95 (*0-7735-0516-4*, Pub. by McGill CN) U of Toronto Pr.

Meyers, Jeffrey, ed. D. H. Lawrence & Tradition. LC 84-16175. 176p. 1985. lib. bdg. 25.00 (*0-87023-464-1*) U of Mass Pr.

— George Orwell: The Critical Heritage. (Critical Heritage Ser.). 432p. 1975. 69.50 (*0-7100-8255-X*, RKP) Routledge.

— Graham Greene: A Revaluation. 220p. 1989. text ed. 39.95 (*0-312-03230-7*) St Martin.

— Hemingway: The Critical Heritage. (Critical Heritage Ser.). 628p. 1982. 65.00 (*0-7100-0929-1*, RKP) Routledge.

— Robert Lowell: Interviews & Memoirs. 300p. 1988. 34.50 (*0-472-10089-0*) U of Mich Pr.

— T. E. Lawrence: Soldier, Writer, Legend: New Essays. LC 88-29720. 192p. 1989. text ed. 45.00 (*0-312-02770-2*) St Martin.

Meyers, Jim. How to Earn Money on Your Utility Bills. LC 93-78049. 85p. 1993. pap. 10.95 (*0-9636969-0-4*) ICDI Pubns.

Meyers, Jim, ed. see Otto, Helen T.

An Asterisk (*) at the beginning of an entry indicates that the title is appearing in BIP for the first time.

Meyers, Joel, jt. auth. see Parsons, Richard D.

Meyers, Joel, et al. Mental Health Consultation in the Schools: A Comprehensive Guide for Psychologists, Social Workers, Psychiatrists, Counselors, Educators, & Other Human Service Professionals. LC 79-83567. (Social & Behavioral Science Ser.). 262p. 1979. 32.95x (*0-87589-400-3*) Jossey-Bass.

Meyers, John, ed. see Bartleman, Frank.

Meyers, L. Donald. The Complete Outdoor Building Book: Patios, Decks, Fences, Landscaping, etc. 352p. 1991. text ed. 40.00 (*0-13-155276-7*) P-H.

— Designing & Building a Deck. (Illus.). 272p. 1988. text ed. 46.00 (*0-13-201816-0*) P-H.

Meyers, L. Donald & Demske, Richard. Expanding the Living Space in Your Home: A Guide to Remodeling Basements, Attics, Garages & Porches. 1976. 14.95 (*0-87909-228-9*, Reston) P-H.

***Meyers, L. Richard, ed.** Innovation in Resource Management: Proceedings of the Ninth Agriculture Sector Symposium. 290p. 1989. 17.95 (*0-614-02806-X*, 11282) World Bank.

Meyers, Larry F. Tax Tips & Strategies: Income Tax Hints Every Taxpayer Should Know, 1994. 2nd ed. (Illus.). 1993. pap. 14.95 (*0-9639166-0-2*) L Meyers Pubng.

— Tax Tips & Strategies: 1995 Edition. (Illus.). 160p. 1995. pap. 13.95 (*0-9639166-1-0*) L Meyers Pubng.

Meyers, Larry S. Baseball Blackbook, 1992: The Winning Edge for Serious Rotisserie. rev. ed. (Illus.). 225p. 1992. pap. 12.95 (*1-55958-141-7*) Prima Pub.

Meyers, Lester. High-Speed Math. 2nd ed. LC 74-23585. 556p. 1975. reprint ed. 49.50 (*0-88275-240-5*) Krieger.

Meyers, Lewis. Crosscurrents: Writing on the Stream of Reading. 462p. 1992. pap. text ed. write for info. (*0-669-21458-2*); Instr.'s ed. teacher ed write for info. (*0-669-21459-0*) Heath.

Meyers, Lillian. Living & Loving. 1977. pap. 3.95 (*0-911866-85-X*) LifeSprings Res.

Meyers, M. A. Dynamic Radiology of the Abdomen. (Illus.). 592p. 1988. 134.00 (*0-387-96624-2*) Spr-Verlag.

— Dynamic Radiology of the Abdomen: Normal & Pathologic Anatomy. 4th ed. (Illus.). 680p. 1993. write for info. (*3-540-94022-7*) Spr-Verlag.

Meyers, M. A., ed. Computed Tomography of the Gastrointestinal Tract. (Illus.). xiv, 279p. 1986. 149.00 (*0-387-96232-8*) Spr-Verlag.

Meyers, M. A. & Ghahremani, G. G., eds. Iatrogenic Gastrointestinal Complications. (Radiology of Iatrogenic Disorders Ser.). (Illus.). 307p. 1981. 128.00 (*0-387-90505-7*) Spr-Verlag.

Meyers, M. A. & Inal, O., eds. Frontiers in Materials Technologies: Materials Science Monongraphs Twenty-Six, Vol. 26. 574p. 1985. 164.00 (*0-444-42462-8*) Elsevier.

Meyers, M. F. Doctors' Marriages: A Look at the Problems & Their Solutions. 2nd ed. (Illus.). 1994. 32.50 (*0-306-44618-9*, Plenum Med Bk) Plenum.

Meyers, Maan. Dutchman. 1993. mass mkt. 4.99 (*0-553-56285-1*) Bantam.

— The Dutchman's Dilemma. LC 95-5207. 1995. 21.95 (*0-553-09705-9*) Bantam.

— The High Constable: An Historical Mystery. LC 94-474. 1994. 19.95 (*0-385-46984-5*) Doubleday.

— Kingsbridge Plot. 1994. pap. 4.99 (*0-553-56380-7*) Bantam.

Meyers, Madeleine, intro. Cherokee Nation: Life Before the Tears. LC 93-70437. (Perspectives on History Ser.). (Illus.). 64p. (Orig.). (YA). (gr. 5-12). 1993. pap. 4.95 (*1-878668-26-9*) Disc Enter Ltd.

— Forward into Light: The Struggle for Women's Suffrage. LC 93-70436. (Perspectives on History Ser.). (Illus.). 64p. (Orig.). (YA). (gr. 5-12). 1994. pap. 4.95 (*1-878668-25-0*) Disc Enter Ltd.

Meyers, Manny. The Troy Dossier. (Crime Court Mystery Ser.). 240p. 1986. reprint ed. pap. 2.95 (*0-8439-5006-4*) Dorchester Pub Co.

Meyers, Marc A. Dynamic Behavior of Materials. LC 93-33109. 1994. text ed. 79.95 (*0-471-58262-X*) Wiley.

Meyers, Marsha A. A Child's Fear: Vision of Hope. (J). 1993. pap. 12.95 (*0-9637083-9-2*) Myi-Way Prod.

Meyers, Marshall D., jt. ed. see Scully, Vincent.

Meyers, Marvin. Jacksonian Persuasion: Politics & Belief. rev. ed. viii, 232p. 1960. reprint ed. 32.50 (*0-8047-0505-4*) Stanford U Pr.

— Jacksonian Persuasion: Politics & Belief. rev. ed. viii, 232p. 1960. pap. 11.95 (*0-8047-0506-2*) Stanford U Pr.

Meyers, Marvin, ed. see Madison, James.

Meyers, Marvin H., ed. The Multiply Injured Patient with Complex Fractures. LC 83-9333. (Illus.). 434p. reprint ed. pap. 123.70 (*0-7837-1490-4*, 2057186) Bks Demand.

Meyers, Mary. Teaching to Diversity. 144p. 1994. pap. text ed. write for info. (*0-201-55547-6*) Addison-Wesley.

— Teaching to Diversity: Teaching & Learning in the Multi-Ethnic Classroom. LC 94-137. 1994. write for info. (*0-7725-1958-7*) Addison-Wesley.

Meyers, Mary A. A New World Jerusalem: The Swedenborgian Experience in Community Construction. LC 82-11997. (Contributions in American Studies: No. 65). (Illus.). xiii, 217p. 1983. text ed. 55.00 (*0-313-23602-X*, MNJ/, Greenwood Pr) Greenwood.

***Meyers, Matt.** Take Home Poems. LC 95-90080. 72p. (Orig.). 1995. pap. 4.95 (*0-9646336-0-4*) M Meyers.

Meyers, Melba. Naked Emotions. 72p. 1984. pap. 6.00 (*0-9612296-0-8*) Williams SC.

***Meyers, Michael.** Visual Basic Client - Server Development. (Illus.). 900p. (Orig.). 1995. pap. text ed. 49.99 (*0-7897-0099-9*) Que.

Meyers, Morton A. Dynamic Radiology of the Abdomen: Normal & Pathologic Anatomy. 4th ed. LC 93-16236. (Illus.). 680p. 1995. 149.00 (*0-387-94022-7*) Spr-Verlag.

Meyers, Patricia, jt. auth. see Cabrera, Roberto.

Meyers, Patrick. Feedlot. 1984. pap. 4.75 (*0-8222-0395-2*) Dramatists Play.

— K-2. 1983. pap. 4.75 (*0-8222-0606-4*) Dramatists Play.

Meyers, Paula, ed. see Fabiano, Diane F.

Meyers, Perla. Burpee's American Harvest Cookbooks: The Spring Garden. 1988. 8.95 (*0-317-64461-0*, Fireside) S&S Trade.

— Perla Meyers' Art of Seasonal Cooking. (Illus.). 608p. 1991. 27.50 (*0-671-64984-1*) S&S Trade.

— Perla Meyer's Peasant Kitchen. 1992. 20.50 (*0-8446-6497-9*) Peter Smith.

— The Spur of the Moment Cook. LC 93-33690. 1994. 25.00 (*0-688-11009-6*) Morrow.

Meyers, Philip. Registered Representative: Stockbroker's Exam. 2nd ed. (Illus.). 448p. 1992. pap. 35.00 (*0-13-770702-9*, Arco Test) P-H Gen Ref & Trav.

Meyers, Pieter, jt. ed. see Scott, David A.

Meyers, R. E. & Torrance, E. P. Imagining: Invitations to Think about the Future for Intermediate Grades. 63p. 1986. pap. 14.95 (*0-936386-37-1*) Creative Learning.

Meyers, Rawley. Daily Readings in Catholic Classics. LC 92-71959. 332p. (Orig.). 1992. pap. 14.95 (*0-89870-389-1*) Ignatius Pr.

Meyers, Ray C. & Goodban, Dale F. Spell It Right! 3rd rev. ed. 150p. 1989. pap. text ed. 12.95 (*0-917962-77-X*) T H Peek.

Meyers, Reva. Winning Career Strategies: For Student in Hospitality, Travel & Tourism. Parkerson, Janet & Witzman, Joseph E., eds. (Orig.). 1988. pap. write for info. (*0-935423-06-0*) Educ Pubns.

Meyers, Ric. Murder on the Air. (Illus.). 240p. 1989. 12.95 (*0-89296-977-6*) Mysterious Pr.

Meyers, Richard. S-F 2: A Pictorial History of Science Fiction Films from Roller Ball to Return of the Jedi. LC 83-20964. (Illus.). 1984. 19.95 (*0-8065-0875-2*, Citadel Pr) Carol Pub Group.

Meyers, Richard, jt. auth. see Bushnell, Richard.

Meyers, Richard, et al. From Bruce Lee to Ninja: Martial Arts Movies. (Illus.). 256p. 1986. reprint ed. pap. 14.95 (*0-8065-1009-9*, Citadel Pr) Carol Pub Group.

Meyers, Richard A. Pascal: The Software Fundamentals of Computer Science. 848p. 1992. pap. text ed. 56.00 (*0-13-725623-X*) P-H.

Meyers, Richard B. Automatic I. D. Questions & Answers. rev. ed. 1992. pap. 29.95 (*0-929870-08-5*) Advanstar Commns.

Meyers, Richard L., jt. ed. see Butler, James C.

Meyers, Robert A. Coal Desulfurization. LC 77-9928. (Illus.). 270p. reprint ed. pap. 77.00 (*0-8357-6059-6*, 2034552) Bks Demand.

Meyers, Robert A., ed. Coal Handbook. LC 81-7824. (Energy, Power, & Environment Ser.: No. 11). (Illus.). 868p. reprint ed. pap. 180.00 (*0-7837-5175-3*, 2044905) Bks Demand.

— Encyclopedia of Lasers & Optical Technology. 764p. 1990. text ed. 92.00 (*0-12-226693-5*) Acad Pr.

— Encyclopedia of Modern Physics. 773p. 1989. text ed. 104.00 (*0-12-226692-7*) Acad Pr.

— Encyclopedia of Physical Science & Technology, 15 vols., 1. 11000p. 1987. text ed. 217.00 (*0-12-226901-2*) Acad Pr.

— Encyclopedia of Physical Science & Technology, 15 vols., 2. 11000p. 1987. text ed. 217.00 (*0-12-226902-0*) Acad Pr.

— Encyclopedia of Physical Science & Technology, 15 vols., 3. 11000p. 1987. text ed. 217.00 (*0-12-226903-9*) Acad Pr.

— Encyclopedia of Physical Science & Technology, 15 vols., 4. 11000p. 1987. text ed. 217.00 (*0-12-226904-7*) Acad Pr.

— Encyclopedia of Physical Science & Technology, 15 vols., 5. 11000p. 1987. text ed. 217.00 (*0-12-226905-5*) Acad Pr.

— Encyclopedia of Physical Science & Technology, 15 vols., 6. 11000p. 1987. text ed. 217.00 (*0-12-226906-3*) Acad Pr.

— Encyclopedia of Physical Science & Technology, 15 vols., 7. 11000p. 1987. text ed. 217.00 (*0-12-226907-1*) Acad Pr.

— Encyclopedia of Physical Science & Technology, 15 vols., 8. 11000p. 1987. text ed. 217.00 (*0-12-226908-X*) Acad Pr.

— Encyclopedia of Physical Science & Technology, 15 vols., 9. 11000p. 1987. text ed. 217.00 (*0-12-226909-8*) Acad Pr.

— Encyclopedia of Physical Science & Technology, 15 vols., 10. 11000p. 1987. text ed. 217.00 (*0-12-226910-1*) Acad Pr.

— Encyclopedia of Physical Science & Technology, 15 vols., 11. 11000p. 1987. text ed. 217.00 (*0-12-226911-X*) Acad Pr.

— Encyclopedia of Physical Science & Technology, 15 vols., 12. 11000p. 1987. text ed. 217.00 (*0-12-226912-8*) Acad Pr.

— Encyclopedia of Physical Science & Technology, 15 vols., 13. 11000p. 1987. text ed. 217.00 (*0-12-226913-6*) Acad Pr.

— Encyclopedia of Physical Science & Technology, 15 vols., 14. 11000p. 1987. text ed. 217.00 (*0-12-226914-4*) Acad Pr.

— Encyclopedia of Physical Science & Technology, 15 vols., 15. 11000p. 1988. text ed. 197.00 (*0-12-226915-2*) Acad Pr.

— Encyclopedia of Physical Science & Technology, 15 vols., Set, Vols. 1-5, Index. 11000p. 1987. Set, incl. Vols. 1-15 & index. 2,500.00 (*0-685-18138-3*) Acad Pr.

— Encyclopedia of Physical Science & Technology, 15 vols., Set, Vols. 1-15, Index. 11000p. 1988. Set, incl. Vols. 1-15 & index. 2,500.00 (*0-317-58440-5*) Acad Pr.

— Encyclopedia of Physical Science & Technology, Set, Vols. 1-18. 2nd ed. (Illus.). 14080p. 1992. Set. text ed. 2,500.00 (*0-12-226930-6*) Acad Pr.

— Encyclopedia of Physical Science & Technology: 1989 Yearbook. 750p. 1988. text ed. 215.00 (*0-12-226916-0*) Acad Pr.

— Encyclopedia of Physical Science & Technology: 1990 Yearbook. 651p. 1989. text ed. 225.00 (*0-12-226917-9*) Acad Pr.

— Encyclopedia of Physical Science & Technology: 1991 Yearbook. 617p. 1990. text ed. 225.00 (*0-12-226918-7*) Acad Pr.

— Encyclopedia of Telecommunications. 525p. 1988. text ed. 85.00 (*0-12-226691-9*) Acad Pr.

— Handbook of Petroleum Refining Processes. 528p. 1986. 89.50 (*0-07-041763-6*, P7128) PennWell Bks.

Meyers, Robert G. The Likelihood of Knowledge. (C). 1988. lib. bdg. 70.00 (*90-277-2671-X*) Kluwer Ac.

Meyers, Robert J., & Associates Staff, et al. Oil Spill Response Guide. LC 89-38445. (Pollution Technology Review Ser.: No. 174). (Illus.). 314p. 1990. 45.00 (*0-8155-1221-X*) Noyes.

Meyers, Robin R. With Ears to Hear: Preaching As Self-Persuasion. LC 92-42040. 176p. (Orig.). 1993. pap. 12.95 (*0-8298-0951-1*) Pilgrim OH.

Meyers, Rochelle, jt. auth. see Ray, Michael L.

Meyers, Roy T. Strategic Budgeting. LC 94-3056. 250p. (C). 1994. text ed. 42.50 (*0-472-10362-8*) U of Mich Pr.

Meyers, Samuel M., ed. see Bradbury, William C.

***Meyers, Scott.** Downloaders Companion for Windows. 192p. 1994. disk, pap. 19.95 (*0-13-342254-2*) P-H.

— Effective C Plus Plus: Fifty Simple Ways to Improve Your Programs & Designs. (Illus.). 224p. 1992. pap. 26.95 (*0-201-56364-9*) Addison-Wesley.

— Effective C Plus Plus: Fifty More Ways to Improve Your Programs & Designs. 1995. pap. 25.95 (*0-201-63371-X*) Addison-Wesley.

Meyers, Spike, jt. auth. see Duchow, Paul G.

***Meyers Staff.** Bildwoerterbuch German-English-French, Vol. 29 Grosses Lexikon. 937p. (ENG, FRE & GER.). 1981. 275.00 (*0-7859-6917-9*) Fr & Eur.

— Deutsches Woerterbuch A-F: Meyers Enzyklopaedisches Lexikon, Vol. 30. 928p. (GER.). 1979. 275.00 (*0-7859-6918-7*) Fr & Eur.

— Deutsches Woerterbuch G-N: Meyers Enzyklopaedisches Lexikon, Vol. 31. 983p. 1980. 275.00 (*0-7859-6919-5*) Fr & Eur.

— Deutsches Woerterbuch O-Z: Meyers Enzyklopaedisches Lexikon, Vol. 32. 1087p. (GER.). 1981. 275.00 (*0-7859-7098-3*) Fr & Eur.

Meyers, Stephen L. Breezers: A Lighthearted History of the Open Trolley Car in America. Harris, Marion, ed. LC 93-33978. (Illus.). 184p. 1993. text ed. 56.00 (*0-933449-20-8*) Transport Trails.

Meyers, Steven. Notes from the San Juans. 160p. 1992. 18.95 (*1-55821-186-1*) Lyons & Burford.

Meyers, Steven J. Lime Creek Odyssey. LC 88-32705. (Illus.). 116p. 1989. 14.95 (*1-55591-037-8*) Fulcrum Pub.

— San Juan River Chronicle. (Illus.). 160p. 1994. 19.95 (*1-55821-277-9*) Lyons & Burford.

Meyers, Steven J., ed. see Sundance Publications, Ltd. Staff.

***Meyers, Susan.** Cricket Goes to the Dogs. LC 94-19829. (Always Friends Ser.). 128p. (J). (gr. 3-6). 1995. pap. text ed. 2.95 (*0-8167-3577-8*, Little Rainbow) Troll Assocs.

— Insect Zoo. (Illus.). 48p. (J). (gr. 3-7). 1991. 16.95 (*0-525-67325-3*, Lodestar Bks) Dutton Child Bks.

— Meg & the Secret Scrapbook. LC 94-19828. (Always Friends Ser.). 128p. (J). (gr. 3-6). 1995. pap. text ed. 2.95 (*0-8167-3578-6*, Little Rainbow) Troll Assocs.

Meyers, Susan & Lakin, Joan. Who Will Take the Children? A New Custody Option for Divorced Mothers & Fathers. LC 82-17847. 228p. 1983. write for info. (*0-672-52739-1*) Macmillan.

Meyers, Susan, ed. see Koosman, Jerry.

Meyers, Susan J., jt. auth. see Pellegrini, Robert J.

***Meyers, Terry L.** The Sexual Tensons of William Sharp: A Study of the Birth of Fiona Macleod, Incorporating Two Lost Works, Ariadne in Naxos & "Beatrice", 2. LC 94-29463. (Studies in Nineteenth Century British Literature). 1995. write for info. (*0-8204-2637-7*) P Lang Pubs.

Meyers, Thomas & Denies, Mark. Longterm & Peakscan: Neutron Activation Analysis Computer Programs. (Technical Reports: No. 2). (Illus.). 1972. pap. 1.00 (*0-932206-11-5*) U Mich Mus Anthro.

Meyers, Thomas A. Technical Analysis Course: A Winning Program for Investors & Traders. rev. ed. 1993. 47.50 (*1-55738-523-8*) Probus Pub Co.

Meyers, Thomas A., jt. auth. see Colby, Robert W.

Meyers, W. & Hayes, M. V., eds. China Policy: New Priorities & Alternatives. 96p. 1972. text ed. 76.00 (*0-677-12210-1*) Gordon & Breach.

— Conversion from War to Peace: Social, Economic, & Political Problems. 132p. 1973. text ed. 76.00 (*0-677-15220-5*) Gordon & Breach.

Meyers, W. & Rinard, eds. Making Activism Work. 110p. 1972. text ed. 76.00 (*0-677-04650-2*) Gordon & Breach.

Meyers, W., et al, eds. Justice in America. (New Priorities Library Ser.). 100p. 1972. text ed. 65.00 (*0-677-12380-9*) Gordon & Breach.

Meyers, Walter E., jt. auth. see Rippon, Michelle.

Meyers, Warren B. Who Is That? (Illus.). 1976. pap. 7.95 (*0-8065-0535-4*, Citadel Pr) Carol Pub Group.

Meyers, William. Vampires or Gods? 192p. (Orig.). 1993. pap. 15.00 (*0-9622937-5-X*) III Pub.

Meyers, William K. Forge of Progress, Crucible of Revolt: The Origins of the Mexican Revolution in La Comarca Lagunera. LC 94-4349. (Illus.). 304p. 1994. 39.95x (*0-8263-1470-8*) U of NM Pr.

Meyers, William R. The Evaluation Enterprise: A Realistic Appraisal of Evaluation Careers, Methods & Applications. LC 81-81961. (Jossey-Bass Social & Behavioral Science Ser.). 284p. reprint ed. pap. 81.00 (*0-8357-4997-5*, 2037930) Bks Demand.

***Meyers, William S.** Adolescence: A Time of Change. 20p. 1995. 2.95 (*1-56456-091-0*) W Gladden Found.

Meyerson, Arthur T., ed. Barriers to Treating the Chronic Mentally Ill. LC 87-646993. (New Directions for Mental Health Services Ser.: No. MHS 33). 1987. 17.95 (*1-55542-966-1*) Jossey-Bass.

Meyerson, Arthur T. & Fine, Theodora, eds. Psychiatric Disability: Clinical, Legal & Administrative Dimensions. LC 87-1069. 312p. 1987. text ed. 40.00 (*0-88048-210-9*, 8210) Am Psychiatric.

Meyerson, Arthur T. & Solomon, Phyllis, eds. New Developments in Psychiatric Rehabilitation. LC 87-646993. (New Directions for Mental Health Services Ser.: No. MHS 45). 1990. 17.95 (*1-55542-832-0*) Jossey-Bass.

Meyerson, B., et al, eds. Advances in Stereotactic & Functional Neurosurgery, Vol. 10. 200p. 1993. 132.00 (*0-387-82478-2*) Spr-Verlag.

Meyerson, Denise. False Consciousness. (Oxford Philosophical Monographs). 200p. 1991. 55.00 (*0-19-824819-9*, 11953) OUP.

Meyerson, E. Identity & Reality. ii, 496p. 1989. pap. text ed. 42.00 (*2-88124-349-5*) Gordon & Breach.

Meyerson, Emile. Explanation in the Sciences. 641p. (C). 1991. lib. bdg. 177.00 (*0-7923-1129-9*) Kluwer Ac.

— The Relativistic Deduction: Epistemological Implications of the Theory of Relativity with a Review by Albert Einstein. Sipfle, David A. & Sipfle, Mary A., trs. 290p. 1985. lib. bdg. 97.50 (*90-277-1699-4*) Kluwer Ac.

Meyerson, Eva M. The Impact of Ownership Structure & Executive Team Composition on Firm Performance: The Resolution of a Leadership Paradox. (Industrial Institute for Economic & Social Research Report Ser.). (Illus.). 170p. (Orig.). 1992. pap. 49.00x (*91-7204-395-4*, Pub. by Almqv & Wiksell SW) Coronet Bks.

Meyerson, Harold & Harburg, Ernie. Who Put the Rainbow in The Wizard of Oz? Yip Harburg, Lyricist. (Illus.). 550p. (C). 1993. 35.00 (*0-472-10482-9*) U of Mich Pr.

Meyerson, Joel, ed. Measuring Institutional Performance in Higher Education. 141p. (C). 1993. 29.95 (*1-56079-331-7*) Petersons Guides.

Meyerson, Joel, jt. auth. see Hanson, Katherine H.

Meyerson, Joel D. Images of a Lengthy War. LC 85-30813. (United States Army in Vietnam CMH Publication Ser.: No. 91-11). (Illus.). 232p. (Orig.). 1986. 22.00 (*0-16-001621-5*, S/N 008-020-01031-6); pap. 18.00 (*0-318-22398-8*, S/N 008-020-01032-4) USGPO.

Meyerson, Joel W. & Anderson, Richard, eds. Productivity & Higher Education: Improving the Effectiveness of Faculty, Facilities, & Financial Resources. LC 91-22290. 144p. 1992. 27.95 (*1-56079-090-3*) Petersons Guides.

Meyerson, Joel W., jt. auth. see Anderson, Richard E.

Meyerson, Joel W., jt. ed. see Anderson, Richard E.

Meyerson, Joel W., ed. see Hanson, Katherine H.

Meyerson, Joel W., jt. ed. see Massy, William F.

Meyerson, Julia. Tambo: Life in an Andean Village. (Illus.). 297p. 1990. text ed. 30.00 (*0-292-78077-X*); pap. 16.95 (*0-292-78078-8*) U of Tex Pr.

Meyerson, Mark D. The Muslims of Valencia in the Age of Fernando & Isabel: Between Coexistence & Crusade. LC 90-35502. (Illus.). 382p. 1991. 52.00 (*0-520-06888-2*) U CA Pr.

Meyerson, Martin & Banfield, Edward C. Boston: The Job Ahead. LC 66-14449. (Publication of the Joint Center for Urban Studies of the Massachusetts Institute of Technology & Harvard University). reprint ed. pap. 34.60 (*0-7837-4479-X*, 2044187) Bks Demand.

Meyerson, Martin & Winegrad, Dilys P. Gladly Learn & Gladly Teach: Franklin & His Heirs at the University of Pennsylvania, 1740-1976. LC 77-82383. 270p. 1978. 37.95 (*0-8122-7735-X*) U of Pa Pr.

Meyerson, Mitch, jt. auth. see Ashner, Laurie.

Meyerson, Paul G., jt. ed. see Adler, Gerald.

Meyerstein, E. H., ed. see Royal Society of Literature, United Kingdom Staff.

Meyerstein, F. Walter, jt. auth. see Brisson, Luc.

Meylach, Martin & Whited, Charles. Diving to a Flash of Gold. LC 73-116234. (Florida Classics Ser.). (Illus.). 382p. (Orig.). 1987. reprint ed. pap. 15.95 (*0-912451-16-5*) Florida Classics.

Meylan, B. A. & Butterfield, B. G. Three-Dimensional Structure of Wood: A Scanning Electron Microscope Study. (Illus.). 80p. (C). 1972. pap. text ed. 34.50x (*0-8156-5030-2*) Syracuse U Pr.

Meylan, Claude. L' Option Nucleaire et les Entreprises Suisses. (European University Studies: Economics & Management: Ser. 5, Vol. 446). 272p. (FRE.). 1983. 35.80 (*3-261-03281-2*) P Lang Pubs.

Meylan, G., jt. ed. see Djorgovski, S. G.

Meyland, Raymond. Flute. Clayton, Alfred, tr. LC 88-19443. (Illus.). 152p. 1988. 25.95 (*0-931340-15-2*, Amadeus Pr) Timber.

Meyn, Barbara. The Abalone Heart. Trusky, Tom, ed. LC 88-71465. (Ahsahta Press Modern & Contemporary Poets of the West Ser.). 75p. (Orig.). 1988. pap. 6.95 (*0-916272-37-0*) Ahsahta Pr.

Meyn, S. P. & Tweedie, R. L. Markov Chains & Stochastic Stability. (Communications & Control Engineering Ser.). (Illus.). xvi, 548p. 1994. 99.00 (*0-387-19832-6*) Spr-Verlag.

Meynell, Alice C. Ceres' Runaway & Other Essays. LC 67-30223. (Essay Index Reprint Ser.). 1977. 17.95 (*0-8369-0704-3*) Ayer.

— The Colour of Life & Other Essays on Things Seen & Heard. 1977. 11.95 (*0-8369-7231-7*, 8030) Ayer.

— Essays. LC 70-100251. 267p. 1970. reprint ed. text ed. 59.75 (*0-8371-2984-2*, MEES, Greenwood Pr) Greenwood.

— Hearts of Controversy. LC 68-57332. (Essay Index Reprint Ser.). 1977. 17.95 (*0-8369-0705-1*) Ayer.

— The Poems of Alice Meynell. Page, Frederick, ed. LC 78-59032. 1990. reprint ed. 27.00 (*0-88355-704-5*) Hyperion Conn.

— Prose & Poetry. LC 76-117824. (Essay Index Reprint Ser.). 1977. 20.95 (*0-8369-1983-1*) Ayer.

— Rhythm of Life: And Other Essays. LC 78-37794. (Essay Index Reprint Ser.). 1977. reprint ed. 17.95 (*0-8369-2613-7*) Ayer.

— Second Person Singular, & Other Essays. LC 68-55851. (Essay Index Reprint Ser.). 1977. 17.95 (*0-8369-0706-X*) Ayer.

Meynell, Alix. Public Servant, Private Woman. (Illus.). 288p. 1988. 39.95 (*0-575-04086-6*, Pub. by V Gollancz UK) Trafalgar.

Meynell, E. Portrait of William Morris. 1972. 59.95 (*0-8490-0881-6*) Gordon Pr.

Meynell, Everard. Life of Francis Thompson. (Illus.). 1971. reprint ed. 18.00 (*0-403-01107-8*) Scholarly.

— The Life of Francis Thompson. (BCL1-PR English Literature Ser.). 360p. 1992. reprint ed. lib. bdg. 89.00 (*0-7812-7504-0*) Rprt Serv.

Meynell, Hugo. The Art of Handel's Operas. LC 86-5406. (Studies in the History & Interpretation of Music: Vol. 1). 264p. 1986. lib. bdg. 89.95 (*0-88946-425-1*) E Mellen.

— An Introduction to the Philosophy of Bernard Lonergan. 236p. 1991. text ed. 35.00 (*0-8020-5869-8*); pap. text ed. 16.95 (*0-8020-6792-1*) U of Toronto Pr.

— Is Christianity True? LC 93-47617. 149p. (C). 1994. pap. text ed. 14.95 (*0-8132-0804-1*) Cath U Pr.

Meynell, Hugo, jt. ed. see McLean, George F.

Meynell, Hugo A. The Nature of Aesthetic Value. LC 85-2742. 158p. 1986. 49.50 (*0-88706-118-4*) State U NY Pr.

— The Theology of Bernard Lonergan. (Studies in Religion). (C). 1986. pap. 15.95 (*1-55540-016-7*, 01 00 42) Scholars Pr GA.

Meynell, Laurence. The Affair at Barwold. large type ed. 1990. 21.95 (*0-7089-2142-6*) Ulverscroft.

— The Fairly Innocent Little Man. (Mystery Ser.: No. 102). 1992. mass mkt. 3.99 (*0-373-26102-0*) Harlequin Bks.

— Hooky Gets the Wooden Spoon. 1991. reprint ed. mass mkt. 3.95 (*0-373-26077-6*) Harlequin Bks.

— The Secret of the Pit. large type ed. 336p. 1985. 15.95 (*0-7089-1328-8*) Ulverscroft.

— Silver Guilt. large type ed. 1989. 17.95 (*0-7089-2060-8*) Ulverscroft.

Meynell, Viola. Alice Meynell. LC 79-145182. (Illus.). 1971. reprint ed. 49.00 (*0-403-00804-2*) Scholarly.

Meynell, Viola, ed. see Barrie, James M.

Meynell, W., ed. see Thompson, Francis.

Meynell, Wilfred, ed. see Thompson, Francis.

Meynen, Emil. International Geographical Glossary. 1479p. (Orig.). (ENG, FRE & GER.). 1985. 350.00 (*0-8288-0957-7*, M 7600) Fr & Eur.

— Multilingual Dictionary of Technical Terms in Cartography. 2nd ed. 700p. (ENG, FRE, GER, RUS & SPA.). 1984. 135.00 (*0-8288-1464-3*, M7564) Fr & Eur.

Meynen, Emil, ed. Bibliography of Mono- & Multilingual Dictionaries & Glossaries of Technical Terms Used in Geography As Well As in Related Natural & Social Sciences. 266p. (Orig.). 1974. pap. 58.50 (*3-515-01846-8*) Coronet Bks.

Meyners, Eckart. Fit for Riding: Exercises for Riders & Vaulters. Herrmann, Elke, tr. LC 92-34931. (Illus.). 164p. 1992. pap. 18.95 (*0-939481-29-4*) Half Halt Pr.

Meyners, Robert & Wooster, Claire. Solomon's Sword: Clarifying Values in the Church. LC 77-9391. reprint ed. 27.40 (*0-8357-9028-2*, 2016408) Bks Demand.

Meynert, Lennart. Life Management - Live Better by Working Smarter. 160p. (C). 1989. pap. 70.00 (*0-948353-48-1*, Pub. by Oldcastle Bks UK) St Mut.

Meynert, Theodor. Psychiatry: A Clinical Treatise on Disease of the Fore-Brain Based Upon a Study of Its Structure, Functions and Nutrition. Sachs, H., tr. LC 78-72811. reprint ed. 27.50 (*0-404-60881-7*) AMS Pr.

Meynier, Gil, tr. see Daniel-Rops, Henry.

Meyr, Heinrich & Ascheid, Gerd. Synchronization in Digital Communications, Vol. 1: Phase-, Frequency-Locked Loops, & Amplitude Control. (Series in Telecommunications). 510p. 1990. text ed. 95.00 (*0-471-50193-X*) Wiley.

Meyriat, Jean, jt. ed. see Rokkan, Stein.

Meyrick, Bette. Cockies Is Convenient. 160p. (C). 1981. pap. 20.00x (*0-85088-615-5*, Pub. by Gomer Pr UK) St Mut.

— Invasion! 70p. (YA). 1991. pap. 23.00 (*0-86383-773-5*, Pub. by Gomer Pr UK) St Mut.

Meyrick, Ceri, ed. Bloodstream Seren Poets, No. 1: Seren Poets. 100p. 1989. pap. 13.95 (*1-85411-014-4*, Pub. by Poetry Wales Pr UK) Dufour.

Meyrick, Gustav. Wapurgisnacht. Mitchell, Michael, tr. (Studies in Austrian Literature, Culture, & Thought. Translation Ser.). 1993. pap. 12.50 (*0-929497-71-6*) Ariadne CA.

Meyrick, Kathryn. Hazel's Healthy Halloween. LC 90-46517. (J). 1989. 11.95 (*0-85953-296-8*); pap. 5.95 (*0-85953-308-5*) Childs Play.

— The Lost Music: Gustav Mole's War on Noise. LC 91-33555. (Illus.). (J). (ps-5). 1992. 11.95 (*0-85953-304-2*); pap. 5.95 (*0-85953-327-1*) Childs Play.

— Musical Life of Gustav Mole. LC 90-49100. (J). (ps-3). 1990. 11.95 (*0-85953-303-4*); pap. 5.95 (*0-85953-347-6*) Childs Play.

Meyrier, Chantal. Lexi-Hotel Francais-Anglais. 144p. 1993. pap. 22.95 (*0-7859-5637-9*, 2713512441) Fr & Eur.

Meyrinck, Gustav. Clockmaker. (Orig.). 1987. pap. 4.50 (*0-317-56165-0*) Rosycross Pr.

Meyrink, Gustav. The Angel of the West Window. Mitchell, Mike, tr. & intro. by. (Studies in Austrian Literature, Culture, & Thought. Translation Ser.). 421p. 1991. pap. 17.00 (*0-929497-44-9*) Ariadne CA.

— The Golem. (Dedalus European Classics Ser.). 307p. 1987. pap. 11.95 (*0-946626-75-8*, Pub. by Dedalus Bks UK) Hippocrene Bks.

— The Golem. Mitchell, Mike, tr. 262p. 1995. pap. 14.95 (*1-57241-014-0*) Ariadne Pr.

— The Golem. 224p. 1986. reprint ed. pap. 7.95 (*0-486-25025-3*) Dover.

— The Green Face. Mitchell, Mike, tr. (Studies in Austrian Literature, Culture, & Thought. Translation Ser.). 224p. 1993. pap. 14.99 (*0-929497-37-6*) Ariadne CA.

— The Opal & Other Stories. Mitchell, Michael, tr. (Studies in Austrian Literature, Culture, & Thought. Translation Ser.). 222p. 1994. pap. 14.95 (*0-929497-89-9*) Ariadne CA.

— The White Dominican. Mitchell, Michael, tr. (Studies in Austrian Literature, Culture, & Thought. Translation Ser.). 1994. pap. 12.95 (*0-929497-88-0*) Ariadne CA.

Meyrowitz, Alan L., ed. Foundations of Knowledge Acquisition: Machine Learning. (International Series in Engineering & Computer Science, VLSI, Computer Architecture, & Digital Screen Processing). 352p. (C). 1993. lib. bdg. 79.95 (*0-7923-9278-7*) Kluwer Ac.

Meyrowitz, Alan L., jt. ed. see Chipman, Susan.

Meyrowitz, Elliott W. The Prohibition of Nuclear Weapons under International Law. 350p. 1988. 75.00 (*0-941320-53-7*) Transnatl Pubs.

Meyrowitz, Joshua. No Sense of Place: The Impact of Electronic Media on Social Behavior. 512p. 1986. pap. 12.95 (*0-19-504231-X*) OUP.

Meyrowitz, Michael R., jt. auth. see Mauro, Joseph V.

Meyrowitz, Norman, ed. Object-Oriented Programming Systems, Languages & Applications - OOPSLA, '88: Proceedings of the 3rd ACM Conference on Object-Oriented Programming Systems, Languages & Applications. (Sigplan Notices Ser.: Vol. 23, No. 11). (Illus.). 390p. 1988. pap. text ed. 32.00 (*0-89791-284-5*, 548881) Assn Compu Machinery.

Meys, Marie-Jose, jt. auth. see Charra, Pierre-Jean.

Meys, W. J. Compound Adjectives in English & the Ideal Speaker-Listener. (Linguistic Ser.: Vol. 18). 226p. 1975. pap. 38.50 (*0-444-10780-0*, North Holland) Elsevier.

Meyskens, Jr., jt. auth. see Ritenbaugh.

Meyskens, F. L. & Prasad, K. N., eds. Modulation & Mediation of Cancer by Vitamins. (Illus.). x, 350p. 1983. 132.00 (*3-8055-3526-0*) S Karger.

Meyskens, Frank L., Jr. & Prasad, Kedar, eds. Vitamins & Cancer. LC 85-27134. (Experimental Biology & Medicine Ser.). 504p. 1986. 99.50 (*0-89603-094-6*) Humana.

Meyskens, Frank L., Jr., jt. ed. see Prasad, Kedar N.

Meystel, A. Autonomous Mobile Robots: Vehicle with Cognitive Control. (Series in Automation: Vol. 1). 600p. 1991. text ed. 87.00 (*9971-5-0088-4*); pap. text ed. 41.00 (*9971-5-0089-2*) World Scientific Pub.

Meystre, P. Elements of Quantum Optics. (Illus.). xiv, 484p. 1990. 44.50 (*0-387-52160-7*, 3867) Spr-Verlag.

Meystre, P. & Sargent, Murray, III. Elements of Quantum Optics. 2nd ed. (Illus.). xiv, 496p. 1991. 49.50 (*0-387-54190-X*) Spr-Verlag.

Meystre, P. & Scully, Marian O., eds. Quantum Optics, Experimental Gravitation, & Measurement Theory. LC 83-4159. (NATO ASI Series B, Physics: Vol. 94). (Illus.). 712p. 1983. 125.00 (*0-306-41354-X*, Plenum Pr) Plenum.

Meystre, Pierre, ed. Nonclassical Effects in Quantum Optics. 464p. 1991. 80.00 (*0-88318-784-1*) Am Inst Physics.

Meyyappan, M., ed. Computational Modeling in Semiconductor Processing. LC 94-17563. 1994. 89.00 (*0-89006-707-4*) Artech Hse.

*__Meyyappan, M., et al.__ Process Control, Diagnostics, & Modeling in Semiconductor Manufacturing I. 1995. pap. 62.00 (*1-56677-096-3*, PV 95-2) Electrochem Soc.

Meyzlisch, Saul, ed. A Child's Passover Haggadah. (Illus.). 76p. (J). (gr. 1-6). 1987. 9.95 (*0-915361-70-1*) Modan-Adama Bks.

Mez, Adam. Die Renaissance Des Islams. iv, 492p. 1968. reprint ed. write for info. (*0-318-71533-3*, Pub. by Georg Olms GW) Lubrecht & Cramer.

— The Renaissance of Islam. Bukhsl, Salahuddin K & Margoliovth, D. S., trs. LC 70-180361. reprint ed. 45.00 (*0-404-56293-0*) AMS Pr.

Mez, Carl. Lauraceae Americaneae Monographice Descrips. 1963. reprint ed. 48.00 (*3-7682-0171-6*) Lubrecht & Cramer.

Meza, Fernando A., comp. Percussion Discography: An International Compilation of Solo & Chamber Percussion Music. LC 89-28647. (Discographies Ser.: No. 36). 117p. 1990. text ed. 42.95 (*0-313-26867-3*, MPQ/, Greenwood Pr) Greenwood.

Mezaki, R. & Inoue, H., eds. Rate Equations of Solid-Catalyzed Reactions. 420p. 1991. text ed. 140.00 (*0-86008-481-7*, Pub. by U of Tokyo JA) Col U Pr.

Mezard, M., et al. Spin Glass Theory & Beyond. (Lecture Notes in Physics Ser.: Vol. 9). 476p. 1987. text ed. 99.00 (*9971-5-0115-5*); pap. text ed. 55.00 (*9971-5-0116-3*) World Scientific Pub.

Mezei, Gy. I., ed. see Lukacs, G.

Mezei, Louis M. Instrument Interfacing with Lotus: The Next Generation. LC 93-9471. (Laboratory Lotus Ser.). 1993. text ed. 73.00 (*0-13-156852-3*) P-H.

— Laboratory Lotus: A Guide to Instrument Interfacing. 336p. 1989. text ed. 70.00 (*0-13-519885-2*) P-H.

Mezei, Louis N. Practical Laboratory Information Management for Scientists & Engineers. (Laboratory Lotus Ser.). 320p. 1991. text ed. 50.00 (*0-13-678186-1*, 520806) P-H.

Mezel, Kathy, jt. ed. see Gerson, Carole.

Mezentseva, Charmian. Albrecht Durer: Selected Woodcuts from the Hermitage. 1976. 550.00 (*0-317-61185-2*, Pub. by Collets UK) Pro-Am Music.

Mezereny, Eugene. Cross Country Skiing in Southern California. (Illus.). 160p. (Orig.). 1993. pap. 14.00 (*1-879415-08-9*) Mtn n Air Bks.

— Los Angeles Hikes: The Best Day-Hikes in the Los Angeles Foothills & Nearby Areas. (Illus.). 304p. 1995. pap. 17.00 (*1-879415-10-0*) Mtn n Air Bks.

Mezerik, Avrahm G., jt. ed. see Bliven, Bruce, Jr.

Mezey, Gillian C. & King, Michael B., eds. Male Victims of Sexual Assault. 160p. 1993. reprint ed. pap. 24.95 (*0-19-262469-5*) OUP.

Mezey, Mathy D. & McGivern, Diane O., eds. Nurses, Nurse Practitioners: Evolution to Advanced Practice. LC 93-13719. 400p. 1993. 42.95 (*0-8261-7770-0*) Springer Pub.

Mezey, Mathy D., jt. auth. see Gould, David A.

Mezey, Mathy D., et al. Health Assessment of the Older Individual, Vol. 2. 2nd rev. ed. LC 92-49574. (Geriatric Nursing Ser.). 256p. 1993. 29.95 (*0-8261-2902-1*) Springer Pub.

Mezey, Mathy D., et al, eds. Nursing Homes & Nursing Care: Lessons from the Teaching Nursing Homes. 176p. 1988. 23.95 (*0-8261-6210-X*) Springer Pub.

Mezey, Michael L., jt. ed. see Olson, David M.

Mezey, P. G. Potential Energy Hypersurfaces. (Studies in Physical & Theoretical Chemistry: Vol. 53). 538p. 1987. 172.00 (*0-444-42887-9*) Elsevier.

Mezey, P. G., ed. New Developments in Molecular Chirality. 300p. (C). 1991. lib. bdg. 103.00 (*0-7923-1021-7*) Kluwer Ac.

Mezey, Paul G. Mathematical Modeling in Chemistry. 386p. 1991. text ed. 200.00 (*1-56081-148-X*) VCH Pubs.

— Shape in Chemistry: An Introduction to Molecular Shape & Topology. LC 93-15622. 1993. 75.00 (*0-89573-727-2*) VCH Pubs.

Mezey, Phil, jt. auth. see Mezey, Phiz.

Mezey, Phiz & Mezey, Phil. Multi-Image Design & Production. (Illus.). 176p. 1988. pap. 34.95 (*0-240-51740-7*, Focal) Buttrwrth-Heinemann.

Mezey, Robert. Evening Wind. LC 86-32462. (Wesleyan Poetry Ser.). 88p. 1987. 12.95 (*0-8195-2149-3*, Wesleyan Univ Pr) U Pr of New Eng.

Mezey, Robert, ed. The Collected Poems of Henri Coulette. 270p. 1990. 24.95 (*1-55728-144-0*); pap. 14.95 (*1-55728-145-9*) U of Ark Pr.

Mezey, Robert, jt. ed. see Berg, Stephen.

Mezey, Susan G. In Pursuit of Equality: Women, Public Policy, & the Federal Courts. 1991. text ed. 49.95 (*0-312-06520-5*) St Martin.

— In Pursuit of Equality: Women, Public Policy, & the Federal Courts. LC 90-63547. 320p. (C). 1991. pap. text ed. 15.00 (*0-312-03706-6*) St Martin.

— No Longer Disabled: The Federal Courts & the Politics of Social Security Disability. LC 87-31783. (Studies in Social Welfare Policies & Programs: No. 7). 208p. 1988. text ed. 49.95 (*0-313-25424-9*, MNL/, Greenwood Pr) Greenwood.

Mezgar, Istvan & Bertok, Peter, eds. Knowledge Based Hybrid Systems: Proceedings of the International Working Conference on Knowledge Based Hybrid Systems in Engineering & Manufacturing, Budapest, Hungary, 20-22 April 1993. LC 93-11626. (IFIP Transactions B: Applications in Technology Ser.: Vol. B-11). 1993. write for info. (*0-444-81484-1*, North Holland) Elsevier.

Mezger, Dorothea. Copper in the World Economy. LC 79-3883. 282p. 1980. 16.00 (*0-85345-544-9*); pap. 8.00 (*0-85345-545-7*) Monthly Rev.

Mezhenina, E. P. Dictionary of Eponymic Names of Diseases & Syndromes. 182p. 1982. 19.95 (*0-8288-1858-4*, M15443) Fr & Eur.

Mezhenkov, V. & Skelley, E., eds. Soviet Scene, Nineteen Eighty-Eight: A Selection of Articles & Interviews from the Soviet Press. (C). 1987. pap. 45.00 (*0-569-09093-8*, Pub. by Collets) St Mut.

Mezhov, V. I. Ukazatelk Bibliografii Azii: Vsia Azila, Iskliuichaia Sibir. Betger, E. K. & Svidina, E. D., eds. LC 92-60508. 225p. (RUS.). 1994. lib. bdg. 100.00 (*0-88354-364-8*) N Ross.

Mezias, Stephen J. Agenda-Setting at the FASB. LC 91-73315. 42p. (Orig.). 1993. 12.00 (*0-910586-84-5*) Finan Exec.

— Systematic Factors Behind Standard Setting. 80p. 1994. 15.00 (*1-885065-00-0*) Finan Exec.

Mezias, Stephen J. & Chung, Seungwha. Due Process & Participation at the FASB: A Study of the Comment Period. 50p. 1989. pap. 12.00 (*0-910586-77-2*, 085-89) Finan Exec.

Mezines, Basil J. Trade Associations & the Antitrust Laws. (Corporate Practice Portfolio Ser.: No. 32). 1983. 92.00 (*0-318-33054-7*) BNA.

Mezins, Nick. Revelations. Teasley, Jamie, ed. LC 89-51757. 689p. 1990. 16.95 (*1-55523-294-9*) Winston-Derek.

Mezirow, Jack. Transformative Dimensions of Adult Learning. LC 90-24155. (Higher & Adult Education Ser.). 269p. 1991. 30.95 (*1-55542-339-6*) Jossey-Bass.

Mezirow, Jack, et al. Fostering Critical Reflection in Adulthood: A Guide to Transformative & Emancipatory Learning. LC 89-39667. (Higher & Adult Education - Adult & Continuing Education Ser.). 416p. 1990. 36.95x (*1-55542-207-1*) Jossey-Bass.

— Last Gamble on Education. 206p. 1988. 10.95 (*0-318-36404-2*, AEA-1) A A A C E.

— Last Gamble on Education: Dynamics of Adult Basic Education - New Dimensions in Program Analysis. 206p. 1975. 13.00 (*0-88379-010-6*) A A A C E.

Mezneries, I. International Payments: With Special Regard to Monetary Systems. 265p. 1979. lib. bdg. 55.00 (*90-286-0119-8*) Kluwer Ac.

Mezo, Kathryn, jt. auth. see Mezo, Merle.

Mezo, Merle & Mezo, Kathryn. Inventors Patent Information Guide. LC 87-82938. 103p. 1987. 24.95 (*0-9619923-0-1*) Inventrs Motiv Enterp.

Mezo, Richard E. A Study of B. Traven's Fiction: The Journey to Solipaz. LC 92-46178. 212p. 1993. text ed. 89.95 (*0-7734-9838-9*, Mellen Univ Pr) E Mellen.

*__Mezu, Rose U.__ Songs of the Hearth. 64p. (Orig.). 1994. 35.00 (*0-87831-065-7*); pap. 20.00 (*0-87831-066-5*) Blck Acad Pr.

— Women in Chains: Abandonment in Love Relationships in the Fiction of Selected West African Writers. 252p. (Orig.). (C). 1994. text ed. 50.00 (*0-87831-169-6*); pap. text ed. 25.00 (*0-87831-170-X*) Blck Acad Pr.

Mezu, S. Okechukwu. Leopold Sedar Senghor et la defense et illustration de la civilisation noire. 19.50 (*0-685-36567-0*) Fr & Eur.

Mezvinsky, Marjorie M. A Woman's Place. 1994. 22.50 (*0-517-59713-6*) Crown Pub Group.

Mezzalira, L. & Winter, S., eds. Design Tools for The 90's: Fifteenth EUROMICRO Symp. on Microprocessing & Microprogramming (EUROMICRO 89), Cologne, FRG, 4-8 Sept., 1989. 852p. 1990. 141.00 (*0-444-88052-6*, North Holland) Elsevier.

Mezzalira, L., jt. ed. see Fay, D.

Mezzatesta, Michael, ed. Fables & Fantasies: From the Collection of Susan Kasen & Robert D. Summer. LC 88-70686. (Illus.). 48p. (Orig.). 1989. pap. text ed. 15.00 (*0-8223-0917-3*) Duke.

Mezzatesta, Michael P. Henri Matisse-Sculptor-Painter: A Formal Analysis of Selected Works. LC 84-80456. (Illus.). 150p. 1984. 38.00 (*0-912804-16-5*); pap. 19.95 (*0-912804-15-7*) Kimbell Art.

Mezzatesta, Michael P., intro. On the Edge: The Sculpture of Leonid Lerman. LC 88-70686. (Illus.). viii, 52p. (Orig.). 1989. pap. text ed. 15.00 (*0-8223-0918-1*) Duke.

Mezzetti, M., et al, eds. Large Scale Structure & Motions in the Universe. (C). 1988. lib. bdg. 157.50 (*0-7923-0082-3*) Kluwer Ac.

Mezzich, Juan & Zimmer, Ben, eds. Emergency Psychiatry. LC 88-13599. 475p. 1990. 60.00x (*0-8236-1647-9*) Intl Univs Pr.

Mezzich, Juan E., ed. Clinical Care & Information Systems in Psychiatry. LC 86-1193. (Clinical Insights Ser.). 145p. reprint ed. pap. 41.40 (*0-8357-7851-7*, 2036228) Bks Demand.

Mezzich, Juan E. & Berganza, Carlos E., eds. Culture & Psychopathology. 512p. 1984. text ed. 68.50 (*0-231-04874-2*) Col U Pr.

Mezzich, Juan E. & Solomon, Herbert. Taxonomy & Behavioral Science: Comparative Performance of Grouping Methods. (Quantitative Studies in Social Relations). 1980. text ed. 84.00 (*0-12-493340-8*) Acad Pr.

Mezzich, Juan E. & Von Cranach, Michael, eds. International Classification in Psychiatry: Unity & Diversity. (Illus.). 432p. 1988. 84.95 (*0-521-32754-7*) Cambridge U Pr.

Mezzich, Juan E., et al, eds. Psychiatric Diagnosis: A World Perspective. LC 93-46006. 1994. 98.00 (*0-387-94221-1*) Spr-Verlag.

— Psychiatric Epidemiology: Assessment Concepts & Methods. LC 93-13621. (Series in Psychiatry & Neuroscience). 560p. (C). 1994. text ed. 86.00 (*0-8018-4615-3*) Johns Hopkins.

Mezzrow, Mezz & Wolfe, Bernard. Really the Blues. 1990. pap. 14.95 (*0-8065-1205-9*, Citadel Pr) Carol Pub Group.

Mezzullo, Louis A. & Woolpert, Mark. Advising the Elderly Client, 3 vols., Set. LC 92-72717. 1992. ring bd. 395.00 (*0-685-59858-6*) Clark Boardman Callaghan.

MFOA Committee Staff. Public Employee Retirement Administration. 134p. 1977. 15.00 (*0-686-84367-3*) Municipal.

Mgebroff, A. Earl. Healthy & Whole: A Doctor Looks at Life & Faith. 224p. (Orig.). 1988. pap. 12.99 (*0-8272-1422-7*) Chalice Pr.

M'Gillivray, Duncan. The Fur Trade Journal of Duncan M'Gillivray, 1794-1795. 200p. 1989. 19.95 (*0-87770-470-8*) Ye Galleon.

M'Gonigle, R. Michael & Zacher, Mark W. Pollution, Politics, & International Law: Tankers at Sea. (Studies in International Political Economy: Vol. 2). 1979. pap. 13.00 (*0-520-04513-0*) U CA Pr.

M'Gowan, George, tr. see Von Meyer, Ernst.

Mhaskar, H. N. Weighted Polynomial Approximation. (Series on Decompositions & Approximation). 300p. 1995. text ed. 74.00 (*981-02-1312-3*) World Scientific Pub.

Mheara, Roisin N. In Search of Irish Saints. (Illus.). 160p. 1994. pap. 15.00 (*1-85182-138-4*, Pub. by Four Cts Pr IE) Intl Spec Bk.

Mhina, A. K. & Munishi, G. K. Understanding Africa's Food Problems: Social Policy Perspectives. (African Social Challenges Ser.: No. 1). 259p. 1991. lib. bdg. 60.00 (*0-905450-39-6*, Pub. by H Zell Pubs UK) Bowker-Saur.

Mhire, Herman. A Century of Vision: Louisiana Photography 1884-1984. Allain, Mathe, ed. Montel, Edmee, tr. (Illus.). 140p. (Orig.). (ENG & FRE.). 1986. pap. 20.00 (*0-936819-00-6*) USL Art Museum.

Mhire, Herman, ed. see Grootkerk, Paul.

*__Mhire, Herman, et al.__ Robert Russett: A Retrospective Survey. (Illus.). 100p. (Orig.). 1989. 20.00 (*0-614-06300-0*) USL Art Museum.

An Asterisk (*) at the beginning of an entry indicates that the title is appearing in BIP for the first time.

— Robert Russett: A Retrospective Survey. (Illus.). 84p. (Orig.). 1989. pap. write for info. (*0-936819-05-7*) USL Art Museum.

Mhlanga, Constance C., jt. ed. see Obudho, Robert A.

Mhley, Rita R. Woodmont Country Club: A Proud Tradition for the Nation's Capital. LC 88-50441. (Illus.). 168p. 1988. 30.00 (*0-9620503-0-X*) Woodmont Cntry Club.

Mhlophe, Gcina, et al. Have You Seen Zandile? 77p. (Orig.). 1990. pap. 9.95 (*0-435-08600-6*, 08600) Heinemann.

Mhone, Buy C. The Political Economy of a Dual Labor Market in Africa: The Copper Industry & Dependency in Zambia, 1929-1969. LC 80-70184. (Illus.). 256p. 1982. 34.50 (*0-8386-3063-4*) Fairleigh Dickinson.

MHS Library & Archives Staff. Genealogical Resources of the Minnesota Historical Society: A Guide. 2nd ed. LC 89-3305. (Illus.). 63p. 1993. reprint ed. pap. 6.95 (*0-87351-240-5*) Minn Hist.

MHS Staff. Split Rock Lighthouse. rev. ed. LC 92-8341. (Minnesota Historic Sites Pamphlet Ser.: No. 15). Orig. Title: Split Rock. (Illus.). 32p. 1993. pap. 7.50 (*0-87351-275-8*) Minn Hist.

Mhyre, Noel L. Testing for Electrical Safety in Hospitals. (Illus.). 27p. 1975. 2.00 (*0-917054-03-2*) Med Communications.

Mi Mi Khaing, Daw. Burmese Family. LC 76-6607. (Illus.). reprint ed. 22.50 (*0-404-15291-0*) AMS Pr.

Mi-pham, Lama. Calm & Clear. LC 73-79058. (Tibetan Translation Ser.: Vol. 1). (Illus.). 128p. 1973. pap. 12.95 (*0-913546-02-X*) Dharma Pub.

Mialaret, Gaston. Lexicon of Education: Lexique d'Education. 168p. (FRE.). 1981. pap. 12.95 (*0-8288-1389-2*, M14201) Fr & Eur.

— Vocabulaire de L'Education: Vocabulary of Education. 488p. (FRE.). 1979. 125.00 (*0-8288-4842-4*, M6410) Fr & Eur.

Miall, A. D. Principles of Sedimentary Basin Analysis. (Illus.). 550p. 1985. 48.50 (*0-387-90941-9*) Spr-Verlag.

— Principles of Sedimentary Basin Analysis. 2nd ed. (Illus.). 424p. 1990. 69.00 (*0-387-97119-X*) Spr-Verlag.

Miall, A. M. Book of Fortune Telling. 1989. 5.99 (*0-517-64730-3*) Random Hse Value.

Miall, Andrew D. & Tyler, Noel, eds. The Three-Dimensional Facies Architecture of Terrigenous Clastic Sediments & Its Implications for Hydrocarbon Discovery & Recovery. (Concepts in Sedimentology & Paleontology Ser.: No. 52). (Illus.). 310p. 1992. pap. 95.00 (*0-918985-94-3*) SEPM.

Miall, B., tr. see Garcia-Calderon, F.

Miall, Bernard, tr. see Aleksinskii, Grigorii A.

Miall, Bernard, tr. see Bernstein, Eduard.

Miall, Bernard, tr. see Cabaton, Antoine.

Miall, Bernard, tr. see Fabre, Jean H.

Miall, Bernard, tr. see Hamburger, Max.

Miall, Bernard, tr. see Rolland, Romain.

Miall, Bernard, tr. see Salvatorelli, Luigi.

Miall, David S., ed. Humanities & the Computer: New Directions. 232p. 1990. 55.00 (*0-19-824244-1*) OUP.

Miall, Hugh. The Peacemakers: Peaceful Settlement of Disputes Since 1945. LC 91-23418. 256p. 1992. text ed. 65.00 (*0-312-06879-4*) St Martin.

— Redefining Europe: New Patterns of Conflict & Cooperation. LC 94-15091. 1994. 55.00 (*1-85567-257-X*); pap. 22.00 (*1-85567-258-8*) St Martin.

— Shaping a New European Order. LC 93-38880. 1993. 14.95 (*0-87609-157-5*) Coun Foreign.

***Miall, Hugh, ed.** Minority Rights in Europe: Prospects for a Transnational Regime. LC 94-43273. 120p. 1994. 14.95 (*0-87609-172-9*) Coun Foreign.

Miall, Laurence M., jt. auth. see Miall, Stephen.

Miall, Stephen & Miall, Laurence M. Chemistry, Matter, & Life. LC 70-39099. (Essay Index Reprint Ser.). 1977. reprint ed. 23.95 (*0-8369-2703-6*) Ayer.

Miall, W. E. & Greenberg, Gillian. Mild Hypertension: An Account of the MRC Trial. (Illus.). 200p. 1987. 64.95 (*0-521-33293-1*) Cambridge U Pr.

Miamee, A. G. Nonstationary Stochastic Processes & Their Applications: Proceedings of the Workshop. 296p. 1992. text ed. 95.00 (*981-02-1076-0*) World Scientific Pub.

***Miami Hearld Staff.** The Miami Herald 1995 South Florida Outdoor Guide. Millman, Ken, ed. (Illus.). 304p. 1994. pap. 12.95 (*0-8362-8080-6*) Andrews & McMeel.

***Miami Herald Staff.** Florida Golf Guide: The Best Public Access Courses in Florida. 192p. 1995. pap. 9.95 (*0-8362-0568-5*) Andrews & McMeel.

— Marlins! Top of the First. 1993. pap. 12.95 (*0-8362-8054-7*) Andrews & McMeel.

— Miami: In Our Own Words. 200p. 1995. pap. 15.95 (*0-8362-0572-3*) Andrews & McMeel.

— Miami Herald Florida Outdoor Guide, 1990. 1990. pap. 6.95 (*0-942084-45-4*) SeaSide Pub.

— The Miami Herald Guide to South Florida's Best Restaurants. 268p. 1995. pap. 7.95 (*0-8362-0785-8*) Andrews & McMeel.

Miami Herald Staff, et al. The Papal Visit: John Paul II in Miami. (Illus.). 112p. (Orig.). 1987. pap. 8.95 (*0-942084-66-7*); pap. 8.95 (*0-942084-67-5*) SeaSide Pub.

***Miami Herald Staff.** Una Vida de Novela: Eva Peron, Marilyn Monroe y Grace Kelly. 176p. 1995. pap. 7.95 (*0-8362-7036-3*) Andrews & McMeel.

Miami Herald Staff & El Nuevo Herald Staff. The Big One: Hurricane Andrew: Photographs. Lyskowski, Roman & Rice, Steve, eds. LC 92-34754. (Illus.). 1992. pap. 19.95 (*0-8362-8012-1*) Andrews & McMeel.

Miami Herald Staff & El Nuevo Herald Staff, eds. Hurricanes: How to Prepare & Recover. (Illus.). 128p. (Orig.). 1993. pap. 9.95 (*0-8362-1718-7*) Andrews & McMeel.

***Miami Herald Staff & Nuevo Herald Staff.** Summit of the Americas: Three Historic Days. (Illus.). 96p. 1995. pap. 19.95 (*0-8362-7048-7*) Andrews & McMeel.

Miami Symposium on the Prediction of Behavior Staff. Aversive Stimulation: Proceedings of the Miami Symposium on the Prediction of Behavior, 1967. Jones, Marshall R., ed. LC 68-18946. (Illus.). 1968. 5.95 (*0-87024-077-3*) U of Miami Pr.

Miami Theory Collective Staff, ed. Community at Loose Ends. (Illus.). 165p. (Orig.). 1991. text ed. 39.95 (*0-8166-1921-2*); pap. text ed. 15.95 (*0-8166-1922-0*) U of Minn Pr.

Miami University, Hispanic American Institute Staff. University of Miami Hispanic-American Studies. McNicoll, R. E. & Owre, J. R., eds. LC 70-117825. (Essay Index Reprint Ser.). 1977. 23.95 (*0-8369-1997-1*) Ayer.

Miami Valley Health Foundation, Work for Hire Staff. Cooks Incorporated. LC 92-61200. 368p. 1992. 19.95 (*0-9633527-0-9*) Miami VHF.

Mian, M. A. Petroleum Engineering Handbook for the Practicing Engineer, Vol. 1. 627p. 1992. 125.95 (*0-87814-370-X*, P4445) PennWell Bks.

— Petroleum Engineering Handbook for the Practicing Engineer, Vol. 2. 688p. 1992. 125.95 (*0-87814-379-3*, P4510) PennWell Bks.

Mian, Q. Javed & Lerrick, Alison. Saudi Business & Labor Law: Its Interpretation & Application. 2nd ed. 450p. 1987. lib. bdg. 334.50 (*0-86010-573-3*) G & T Inc.

Mianbe Betoudji, Denis. Le Dieu Supreme et le Dieu Des Patriarches (Genesis 14, 18-20) (Religionswissenschaftliche Texte und Studien Ser.: No. 1). iv, 290p. 1986. write for info. (*3-487-07760-4*, Pub. by Georg Olms GW) Lubrecht & Cramer.

Miang, Tan J., jt. auth. see Natarajan, S.

Miano, Kabuya, jt. auth. see Gicheru, H. B.

Miano, T. M., ed. see Sixth International Meeting of the International Humic Substances Society Staff.

Mianyu, Q. & Changlong, Y., eds. China's Sports Medicine. (Medicine & Sport Science Ser.: Vol. 28). (Illus.). viii, 120p. 1989. 79.25 (*3-8055-4806-0*) S Karger.

Miao, Gong, et al, eds. China Coal Industry Yearbook: Nineteen Eighty-Three. Zunfang, Chen et al, trs. (China Coal Industry Yearbooks Ser.). (Illus.). 304p. 1984. text ed. 50.00 (*0-918062-61-6*, Pub. by Economic Info HK) Colo Sch Mines.

— China Coal Industry Yearbook Nineteen Eighty-Two. (China Coal Industry Yearbooks Ser.). (Illus.). 336p. 1983. text ed. 40.00 (*0-918062-60-8*, Pub. by Economic Info HK) Colo Sch Mines.

Miao, Ronald C. Early Medieval Chinese Poetry: The Life & Verse of Wang Ts'an (AD 177-217) 349p. (Orig.). 1982. pap. text ed. 67.50x (*3-515-03718-7*) Coronet Bks.

Miarka, Judy M. Classy Cat - Astrological Annotated Categorized Catalogue. 140p. 1993. 10.00 (*0-86690-395-X*, M3130-014) Am Fed Astrologers.

Miasek, Meryl A., ed. see Miller, Heather S.

Miasek, Meryl A., ed. see Schofield, Eileen.

Miaskowski, et al. Year Book of Oncology Nursing, 1994. 320p. 1994. 39.95 (*0-8151-6140-9*, Yr Bk Med Pubs) Mosby Yr Bk.

— Year Book of Oncology Nursing, 1995. 320p. 1995. 39.95 (*0-8151-6141-7*, Yr Bk Med Pubs) Mosby Yr Bk.

— Year Book of Oncology Nursing, 1996. 320p. 1996. 39.95 (*0-8151-6142-5*, Yr Bk Med Pubs) Mosby Yr Bk.

— Year Book of Oncology Nursing, 1997. 320p. 1997. 39.95 (*0-8151-6143-3*, Yr Bk Med Pubs) Mosby Yr Bk.

— Yearbook of Oncology Nursing, 1993. 320p. 1993. 39.95 (*0-8151-6139-5*) Mosby Yr Bk.

***Miaskowski, Christine, ed.** Oncology Nursing. LC 94-32089. (Plans of Care for Specialty Practice Ser.). 1995. 27.95 (*0-8273-6118-1*) Delmar.

Miasnikov, V. Ch'ing Empire & the Russian State in the 17th Century. 342p. (C). 1985. 80.00 (*0-685-31474-X*) St Mut.

Miastkowski, Stan, jt. auth. see Lent, Anne F.

Miatello, A. International Nuclear Agreements: A Quadra-Lingual Glossary. 391p. (ENG, FRE, GER & ITA.). 1988. 110.00 (*0-8288-7898-6*) Fr & Eur.

Miatello, Hugo. The Argentine. 1976. lib. bdg. 35.00 (*0-87968-656-1*) Gordon Pr.

***Mibashan, David.** Still...Life. 196p. 1995. 33.00 (*0-8095-4827-5*) Borgo Pr.

Micale, F. J., jt. ed. see Sharma, M. K.

Micale, Mark S. Approaching Hysteria: Disease & Its Interpretations. LC 94-16596. 1994. 29.95 (*0-691-03717-5*) Princeton U Pr.

Micale, Mark S., ed. Beyond the Unconscious: Essays of Henri F. Ellenberger in the History of Psychiatry. Dubor, Francoise, tr. 488p. 1993. text ed. 49.50 (*0-691-08550-1*) Princeton U Pr.

Micale, Mark S. & Porter, Roy, eds. Discovering the History of Psychiatry. LC 93-12244. 480p. 1994. Alk. paper. 47.50 (*0-19-507739-3*) OUP.

Micali, A., ed. Clifford Algebras & Their Applications in Mathematical Physics. 536p. (C). 1992. lib. bdg. 162.50 (*0-7923-1623-1*) Kluwer Ac.

Micali, Paul. The Lacy Techniques of Salesmanship. rev. ed. 182p. 1982. pap. 7.95 (*0-8015-9201-1*, Dutton) NAL-Dutton.

Micali, Silvio, jt. ed. see Preparata, Franco P.

Micallef, A. M. Texas Safari: World Class Big Game Hunting in the State of Texas. (Illus.). 256p. 1986. 25.00 (*0-9616868-0-4*) Clear Fork Ranch.

Micallef, Mary. Floods & Droughts. (Natural Disaster Ser.). (Illus.). 48p. (J). (gr. 4-8). 1985. student ed 7.95 (*0-86653-323-0*, GA 632) Good Apple.

— Listening: The Basic Connection. (Illus.). 96p. (J). (gr. 3-8). 1984. student ed 9.95 (*0-86653-188-2*, GA 555) Good Apple.

— Storms & Blizzards. (Natural Disaster Ser.). 48p. (J). (gr. 4-8). 1985. student ed 7.95 (*0-86653-321-4*, GA 683) Good Apple.

Micchelli, et al. Methods of Functional Analysis in Approximation Theory. (International Series of Numerical Mathematics: No. 76). 416p. 1986. 80.00 (*0-8176-1761-2*) Birkhauser.

Micchelli, C. A., jt. auth. see Dikshit, H. P.

***Micchelli, Charles A.** Mathematical Aspects of Geometric Modeling. LC 94-10478. (CBMS-NSF Regional Conference Series in Applied Mathematics: Vol. 65). 256p. 1995. pap. 37.50 (*0-89871-331-5*) Soc Indus-Appl Math.

Miccinello, A., ed. see Pierce, Jennifer E.

Micek, Joseph G., jt. ed. see Muehrcke, Robert C.

Miceli, ed. Real Time Signal Processing, No. IX. 287p. 1986. 50.00 (*0-89252-733-1*, 698) SPIE.

Miceli, A. P. Man with the Red Umbrella. 1974. 8.95 (*0-87511-603-5*) Claitors.

Miceli, Eve, jt. auth. see Lazar, Elysa.

Miceli, Marcia P. & Near, Janet P. Blowing the Whistle: The Organizational & Legal Implications for Companies & Their Employees. 224p. 1992. text ed. 27.95 (*0-669-19599-5*) Free Pr.

Miceli, Michael, ed. see American Institute of Certified Public Accountants Staff.

Miceli, Michael A., ed. see American Institute of Certified Public Accountants Staff.

Miceli, Monica, jt. auth. see Mostacchi, Masssimo.

Miceli, Vincent. The Antichrist. 297p. 1991. pap. 12.95 (*0-912141-02-6*) Roman Cath Bks.

— The Roots of Violence. LC 88-70610. 1989. 19.95 (*0-8158-0449-0*) Chris Mass.

Micelotta, Jeanette & Michaels, Deborah. Get Rid of Your Butt. LC 93-6405. 1994. 5.95 (*0-688-12982-X*) Hearst Bks.

***Micevych, Paul E. & Hammer, Ronald P., Jr., eds.** Neurobehavioral Effects of Sex Steroid Hormones. (Illus.). 350p. (C). 1995. 84.95 (*0-521-45430-1*) Cambridge U Pr.

Micgiel, John, tr. see Kersten, Krystyna.

Mich, Adele, tr. see Lem, Stanislaw.

Micha, Alexandre, jt. auth. see Chretien de Troyes.

Micha, D. A., jt. ed. see Levin, F. S.

Micha, David A., ed. Few-Body Systems & Multiparticle Dynamics. LC 87-72594. (Conference Proceeding Ser.: No. 162). 304p. 1987. lib. bdg. 60.00 (*0-88318-362-5*) Am Inst Physics.

Michael. Environmental Data Bases: Design, Implementation & Maintenance. 1991. 59.95 (*0-87371-422-9*, TD193) Lewis Pubs.

— Finding Your Soul Mate. (Illus.). 128p. (Orig.). 1992. pap. 9.95 (*0-87728-765-1*) Weiser.

— The Soul Mate Book for Gay & Lesbian People. 128p. (Orig.). 1994. pap. 9.95 (*0-87728-805-4*) Weiser.

Michael, jt. auth. see McGilp.

Michael, A. M. Irrigation: Theory & Practice. 801p. 1982. 90.00 (*0-7069-1513-5*) St Mut.

Michael, Aloysius. Radhakrishna on Hindu Moral Life & Action. 1979. 17.50 (*0-8364-0334-7*) S Asia.

Michael, Angie, ed. see Pooser, Doris.

Michael, Anthony. I Am the Wolf. 1993. 15.95 (*0-533-10396-7*) Vantage.

Michael, Arnold. Blessed among Women. reprint ed. write for info. (*0-318-61348-9*); reprint ed. pap. 8.95 (*0-318-21242-0*) Gray Pubns CA.

Michael, Bill. Art: Making a School Policy. (C). 1989. 69.00 (*1-85098-377-1*, Pub. by Jordanhill College UK) St Mut.

— Foundations of Writing, Pt. 1: Teachers Handbook. (C). 1989. 90.00 (*1-85098-136-1*, Pub. by Jordanhill College UK) St Mut.

— Purposeful Drawing. (C). 1989. 50.00 (*1-85098-189-2*, Pub. by Jordanhill College UK) St Mut.

Michael, Bill, ed. Letterforms: Parent's Guide. (C). 1989. 30.00 (*0-685-52523-6*, Pub. by Jordanhill College UK) St Mut.

Michael, Bill & Michael, Maureen. Foundations of Writing, Pt. 2: Teachers Handbook. (C). 1989. 40.00 (*1-85098-235-X*, Pub. by Jordanhill College UK) St Mut.

— From Bonfires to Christmas. (C). 1989. 60.00 (*1-85098-378-X*, Pub. by Jordanhill College UK) St Mut.

Michael, Cecil. Signs & Wonders. 1977. 10.95 (*0-87881-048-X*); pap. 7.95 (*0-87881-049-8*) Mojave Bks.

Michael, Chester P. Scripture Themes & Texts for Meditation & Study. 1981. reprint ed. pap. 3.00 (*0-685-11860-6*) Open Door Inc.

Michael, Chester P. & Norrisey, Marie C. Arise: A Christian Psychology of Love. 162p. (Orig.). 1981. pap. 3.95 (*0-940136-00-7*) Open Door Inc.

Michael, Christine. Looking Down from the Mountain Top: The Story of One Woman's Fight Against All Odds. Plaut, Mary, ed. LC 91-62562. (Illus.). 300p. 1992. pap. 24.95 (*0-9630571-0-3*) Spirit of Success.

***Michael, Christopher.** Ice House. LC 94-61225. Date not set. 9.95 (*1-884570-12-7*) Research Triangle.

Michael, Christopher & Ismail, Mohammed I. Statistical Modeling for Computer-Aided Design of MOS VLSI Circuits. LC 92-35702. (Kluwer International Series in Engineering & Computer Science). 208p. (C). 1993. lib. bdg. 70.00 (*0-7923-9299-X*) Kluwer Ac.

***Michael, Christopher D.** Innocence Afloat. 310p. 1995. pap. 9.95 (*0-7610-0034-8*) NW Pub.

Michael, Colette V. Negritude: An Annotated Bibliography. LC 88-8848. 315p. 1988. lib. bdg. 35.00 (*0-933951-15-9*) Locust Hill Pr.

— Sade: His Ethics & Rhetoric. (American University Studies: Romance Languages & Literature: Ser. II, Vol. 106). 249p. (C). 1989. text ed. 37.95 (*0-8204-0884-0*) P Lang Pubs.

Michael, Colette V., tr. see Metzger, Helene.

Michael Crummett Photography Staff & Bryan, Bill. Montana Indians: Yesterday & Today. rev. ed. (Montana Geographic Ser.: No. 11). (Illus.). 1995. pap. 14.95 (*1-56037-064-5*) Am Wrld Geog.

Michael, David, jt. auth. see Mills, Dick.

Michael, Diana L. Angel Prayers. 208p. 1993. pap. 12.95 (*0-9634910-4-0*) Trust Pub MN.

Michael Digest Group. The Michael Game: One Hundred & One Questions to Ask a Channel & More. 160p. 1988. pap. 7.95 (*0-941109-01-1*) Warwick Pr CA.

Michael, Donald N. On Learning to Plan & Planning to Learn. LC 73-7153. (Jossey-Bass Behavioral Science Ser.). 359p. reprint ed. pap. 102.40 (*0-8357-4701-8*, 2052356) Bks Demand.

Michael, Donald N., ed. The Future Society. 131p. 1970. 28.95 (*0-87855-068-2*); pap. text ed. 14.95 (*0-87855-565-X*) Transaction Pubs.

Michael, Duncan. How Skyscrapers Are Made. (How It Is Made Ser.). (Illus.). 32p. (YA). (gr. 5-12). 1987. 12.95 (*0-8160-1692-5*) Facts on File.

Michael, E. Handbuch fuer Pilzfreunde: Volume 4: Blaetterilze-Dunkelblaettler. 3rd ed. Kreisel, H, ed. (Illus.). 472p. 1985. text ed. 34.80 (*3-437-30349-X*) Lubrecht & Cramer.

— Handbuch fuer Pilzfreunde: Vol.1: Die wichtiggsten... Pilze. Kreisel, H., ed. (Illus.). 392p. (GER.). 1978. text ed. 30.50 (*3-437-30346-5*) Lubrecht & Cramer.

— Handbuch fuer Pilzfreunde: Vol.3: Blaetterpilze, Hellblaettler & Leistlings. Kreisel, H., ed. (Illus.). 464p. 1977. text ed. 34.80 (*3-437-30348-1*) Lubrecht & Cramer.

Michael, E., et al. Handbuch der Pilzfreunde, Vol. 1: Die Wichtigsten und Haeufigsten Pilze Mit Besonderer Beruecksichtigung der Giftpilze. (Illus.). 408p. (GER.). 1978. lib. bdg. 51.75 (*3-437-30436-4*, Pub. by G Fischer Verlag GW) Lubrecht & Cramer.

— Handbuch Fuer Buecherfreunde. 4th ed. (Illus.). 484p. (GER.). 1987. lib. bdg. 51.75 (*3-437-30531-X*, Pub. by G Fischer Verlag GW) Lubrecht & Cramer.

— Handbuch Fuer Buecherfreunde, Vol. 4: Blaetterpilze-Dunkelblaetter. 2nd ed. (Illus.). 488p. (GER.). 1985. lib. bdg. 55.50 (*3-437-30463-1*, Pub. by G Fischer Verlag GW) Lubrecht & Cramer.

— Handbuch Fuer Pilzfreinde, Vol. 6: Die Gattungen der Grosspilze Europas. Bestimmungsschluessel und Gesamt-Register to Vols. 1-5. 2nd ed. (Illus.). 310p. (GER.). 1988. lib. bdg. 36.00 (*3-437-30352-X*, Pub. by G Fischer Verlag GW) Lubrecht & Cramer.

— Handbuch Fuer Pilzfreunde, Vol. 5: Blaetterpilze - Milchlinge und Taeublinge. 2nd ed. (Illus.). 408p. (GER.). 1983. lib. bdg. 55.50 (*3-437-30750-9*, Pub. by G Fischer Verlag GW) Lubrecht & Cramer.

Michael, E. A. Locally Multiplicatively-Convex Topological Algebras. LC 52-42839. (Memoirs Ser.: No. 1/11). 82p. 1971. reprint ed. pap. 16.00 (*0-8218-1211-4*, MEMO 1/11) Am Math.

***Michael, E. J.** Queen of the Sun: A Modern Revelation. 1995. 18.00 (*0-06-251355-9*) Harper SF.

— Queen of the Sun: A Modern Revelation. 2nd rev. ed. (Illus.). 250p. 1995. pap. 12.95 (*0-9642147-8-4*) Mtn Rose Pubng.

Michael, E. J., tr. see Bethlem, Jaap & Knobbout, Charlotte E.

Michael, Emory H. Androcles & the Lion. LC 87-51492. (Illus.). 44p. (J). (gr. k-4). 1988. 6.95 (*1-55523-132-2*) Winston-Derek.

Michael, Ernest D., et al. Laboratory Experiences in Exercise Physiology. 1979. student ed 11.95 (*0-932392-05-9*) Mouvement Pubns.

Michael, F. & Sisavic, Irene. The Ultimate Travel Journal. LC 87-81868. 128p. (Orig.). 1987. 19.95 (*0-9619093-1-5*); 44.95 (*0-9619093-2-3*); pap. 9.95 (*0-9619093-0-7*) Florian Group.

Michael, Franz. China Through the Ages: History of a Civilization. 278p. (C). 1986. pap. text ed. 21.50 (*0-86531-726-7*) Westview.

— Mao Tse-Tung & the Perpetual Revolution. Cadenhead, I. E., Jr., ed. LC 77-24400. 1977. pap. text ed. 19.95 (*0-8120-5132-7*) Barron.

Michael, Franz & Chang, Chung-Li. The Taiping Rebellion: History, Vol. 1. (Publications on Asia of the Institute for Comparative & Foreign Area Studies: No. 14, Pt. 1). 256p. 1966. pap. 10.00 (*0-295-95244-X*) U of Wash Pr.

Michael, Gayl, ed. see Lancaster, Clay.

Michael, George. The Basic Book of Antiques & Collectibles. 3rd ed. LC 92-50189. (Illus.). 352p. 1992. pap. 17.95 (*0-87069-649-1*) Chilton.

— The Overlook Treasury of Federal Antiques. 1986. 22.95 (*0-87951-254-7*); pap. 10.95 (*0-87951-268-7*) Overlook Pr.

Michael, Henry N., ed. The Archaeology & Geomorphology of Northern Asia: Selected Works. LC 65-1456. (Arctic Institute of North America-Anthropology of the North; Translation from Russian Sources Ser.: No. 5). 528p. reprint ed. pap. 150.50 (*0-8357-5715-3*, 2019174) Bks Demand.

Michael, Henry N., ed. see Levin, Maksim G.

Michael, Henry N., tr. see Masson, V. M.

Michael, Henry N., ed. see Zagoskin, Lavrentii A.

Michael, Ian. English Grammatical Categories & the Tradition to 1800. 638p. 1971. 79.50 (*0-685-10581-4*) Cambridge U Pr.

— The Teaching of English: From the Sixteenth Century to 1870. (Illus.). 600p. 1987. 94.95 (*0-521-24196-0*) Cambridge U Pr.

Michael, Iris A. Healthy Breasts: Every Woman's Birthright! (Illus.). 152p. (Orig.). 1991. pap. text ed. 16.95 (*0-9627883-0-9*) Clarke Pub.

Michael, James. The Politics of Secrecy. 1979. 20.00 (*0-901108-80-4*, Pub. by NCCL UK) St Mut.

M

An Asterisk (*) at the beginning of an entry indicates that the title is appearing in BIP for the first time.

— Privacy & Human Rights: An International & Comparative Study, with Special Reference to Developments in Information Technology. LC 94-11932. 208p. 1994. 39.95 (1-85521-381-8, Pub. by Dartmth Pub UK) Ashgate Pub Co.

Michael, James J. From A to Z39.50: A Networking Primer. 176p. 1994. pap. 29.50 (0-88736-766-6) Mecklermedia.

Michael, Jamie. Dishwater Blue. 1993. 14.95 (0-533-10581-1) Vantage.

Michael, Jerome & Adler, Mortimer J. Crime Law & Social Science. LC 77-108235. (Criminology, Law Enforcement, & Social Problems Ser.: No. 118). 1971. reprint ed. 30.00 (0-87585-118-5) Patterson Smith.

Michael, Joel A., jt. ed. see Modell, Harold I.

Michael, John. Emerson & Skepticism: The Cipher of the World. LC 87-30267. 208p. 1988. text ed. 32.50x (0-8018-3597-6) Johns Hopkins.

— The Last Nightmare. 118p. (Orig.). 1988. pap. 7.95 (0-945644-00-0) Intl Pub Inc.

Michael, John A. Art & Adolescence: Teaching Art at the Secondary Level. LC 83-4147. (C). 1983. pap. text ed. 18.95 (0-8077-2743-1) Tchrs Coll.

Michael, John A., ed. The Lowenfeld Lectures: Viktor Lowenfeld on Art Education & Therapy. LC 80-29265. (Illus.). 420p. (C). 1982. text ed. 35.00 (0-271-00283-2) Pa St U Pr.

Michael, Judith. Inheritance. Grose, Bill, ed. 1989. mass mkt. 6.50 (0-671-68885-5) PB.

— Judith Michael, 3 vols. 1989. Boxed. boxed 15.40 (0-671-92230-0) PB.

— Judith Michael, 3 vols. 1990. boxed 17.40 (0-671-96370-8) S&S Trade.

— Possessions. Grose, Bill, ed. 1989. mass mkt. 6.50 (0-671-69383-2) PB.

— Pot of Gold. LC 93-14336. 1994. pap. 6.99 (0-671-88629-0) PB.

— Pot of Gold. LC 93-14336. 1993. 23.00 (0-671-70704-3) S&S Trade.

— Pot of Gold. LC 94-6739. 1994. 26.95 (1-56895-060-8) Wheeler Pub.

— Pot of Gold. 1994. pap. 209.70 (0-671-99160-4) PB.

— Pot of Gold. large type ed. LC 93-14336. 1994. write for info. (0-318-72544-4) Wheeler Pub.

— A Ruling Passion. large type ed. (General Ser.). 917p. 1991. text ed. 22.95 (0-8161-5092-3) G K Hall.

— Sleeping Beauty. 1994. pap. 6.99 (0-671-89959-7) PB.

— Sleeping Beauty: A Novel. large type ed. LC 92-17882. (General Ser.). 832p. 1992. lib. bdg. 23.95 (0-8161-5490-2); pap. 16.95 (0-8161-5491-0) G K Hall.

— A Tangled Web. large type ed. LC 95-2007. (Large Print Book Ser.). 1995. write for info. (1-56895-201-5) Wheeler Pub.

— Tangled Web: The Long Awaited Sequel to Deceptions. 464p. 1994. 23.00 (0-671-79879-0) S&S Trade.

Michael, Julia W. Native Nassau. 1977. lib. bdg. 59.95 (0-8490-2331-9) Gordon Pr.

Michael, Kasey. Anonymous Miss Addams. braille ed. 322p. 1992. vinyl bd. 25.76 (1-56956-038-2, BR8670) W A T Braille.

Michael, LaBlanc. Hotdogs,Heroes & Hooligans, 2 vols. 1994. 15.95 (0-8103-9748-X, Pub. by Graham & Trotman UK) Gale.

Michael, Linda. Big As Texas: The A to Z Tour of Texas Cities & Places. Lowdermilk, Karen, ed. LC 87-36793. (Illus.). 64p. (J). (gr. k-3). 1988. pap. 6.95 (0-937460-34-6) Hendrick-Long.

Michael, M. A., tr. see Hoff, Trygve J.

Michael, M. Luisa. House for Sale. 352p. 1991. pap. text ed. 21.95 (0-89420-282-0, 344044) Natl Book.

Michael, Marjorie & Baron, Virginia. A Woman's Journey. 30p. 1992. pap. 12.95 (0-9634822-0-3) MTwo Media.

***Michael, Mary.** The Art & Science of Cooking. 1995. 16.95 (0-8062-5265-0) Carlton.

Michael, Maureen, jt. auth. see Michael, Bill.

Michael, Maurice A. Traveller's Quest: Original Contributions Towards a Philosophy of Travel. LC 72-5673. (Essay Index Reprint Ser.). 1977. reprint ed. 24.95 (0-8369-7297-X) Ayer.

***Michael, Michaelis, ed.** Philosophy in Mind: The Place of Philosophy in the Study of Mind. (Philosophical Studies). 332p. (C). 1994. lib. bdg. 105.00 (0-7923-3143-5) Kluwer Ac.

Michael, Nancy. Don't Sweat It -- Paint It. (Illus.). 32p. (Orig.). 1987. pap. 6.95 (0-941284-42-5) J Shaw Studio.

— Pericles: An Annotated Bibliography. LC 87-17295. (Shakespeare Bibliographies Ser.: No. 13). 289p. 1987. lib. bdg. 23.00 (0-8240-9113-2, 424) Garland.

Michael, Nicholas. Armies of Medieval Burgundy 1364-1477. (Men-at-Arms Ser.: No. 144). (Illus.). 48p. pap. 11.95 (0-85045-518-9, 9076, Pub. by Osprey UK) Stackpole.

Michael, Norma, jt. auth. see Burton, Celia.

Michael, Payne. Intermediate Algebra. (Illus.). 541p. 1985. text ed. 54.75 (0-314-85285-9) West Pub.

Michael, Peter P. Multiple Sclerosis: A Dragon with a Hundred Heads. LC 79-10954. 1981. 22.95 (0-87949-170-1) Ashley Bks.

Michael, Prudence G. Don't Cry "Timber"! Genealogical Research Guide. 8th ed. LC 78-20129. 1987. pap. 6.95 (0-318-35186-2) P G Michael.

Michael, R. Blake. Origins of Virasaiva Sects: A Typological Analysis of Ritual & Associational Patterns in the Sunyasampadane. (C). 1992. 25.00 (81-208-0776-6, Pub. by Motilal Banarsidass II) S Asia.

Michael, R. G. Managed Aquatic Ecosystems. (Ecosystems of the World Ser.: No. 13). 166p. 1987. 107.75 (0-444-42517-9) Elsevier.

Michael Reese Hospital & Medical Center Staff. Nursing Care Plans: Nursing Diagnosis & Intervention. 2nd ed. 688p. 1990. spiral bd. 34.95 (0-8016-6238-9) Mosby Yr Bk.

Michael, Robert T. The Effect of Education on Efficiency in Consumption. (Occasional Papers: No. 116). 149p. 1972. 38.80 (0-87014-242-9) Natl Bur Econ Res.

***Michael, Robert T., et al.** Sex in America. 1995. pap. write for info. (0-446-67183-5) Warner Bks.

Michael, Robert T., jt. auth. see Lazear, Edward P.

Michael, Robert T., et al. Sex in America: A Definitive Survey. 1994. 22.95 (0-316-07524-8) Little.

Michael, Robert T., et al, eds. Pay Equity: Empirical Inquiries. 272p. 1989. pap. text ed. 27.95 (0-309-03978-9) Natl Acad Pr.

Michael, Roberts, ed. see Danford, Chamness.

Michael-Rushmer, Jane, jt. auth. see Finkbeiner-Zellmann, Peter.

Michael, Russ. Tales of the Ram. 160p. (Orig.). 1989. pap. 9.95 (0-945127-04-9) Upword Pr.

Michael, S. M. Culture & Urbanization. (C). 1989. 60.00 (81-210-0231-1, Pub. by Inter-India Pubns) S Asia.

Michael, Sami. Refuge. Grossman, Edward, tr. 376p. 1988. 22.50 (0-8276-0308-8) JPS Phila.

***Michael, Sarah.** Three Consort Songs, for Soprano & Treble, Tenor & Bass Viols. (Contemporary Consort Ser.: No. 6). 22p. 1994. 12.00 (1-56571-094-0) PRB Prods.

Michael, Scott W. Reef Sharks & Rays of the World: A Guide to Their Identification, Behavior, & Ecology. Hashagen, Ken & Bertsch, Hans, eds. LC 92-46402. (Illus.). 112p. (Orig.). (C). 1993. pap. 24.95 (0-930118-18-9) Sea Chall.

Michael, Simon. The Long Lie. 256p. 1993. lib. bdg. 18.00 (0-7278-4396-6) Severn Hse.

Michael, Susan, ed. see Berger, Bruce.

Michael, Tom, ed. see Wilhite, Robert.

Michael, Tom, jt. ed. see Wilhite, Robert.

Michael, Toni, jt. auth. see MacCormack, Dave.

Michael, V. P. Management for Managers. 1992. 35.00 (81-7040-448-7, Pub. by Himalaya II) Apt Bks.

***Michael, Valerie.** The Leatherworking Handbook: A Practical Illustrated Sourcebook of Techniques & Projects. (Illus.). 128p. 1995. pap. 17.95 (0-304-34511-3, Pub. by Cassell UK) Sterling.

Michael, Walther P. Measuring International Capital Movements. LC 74-160315. (National Bureau of Economic Research, Occasional Paper Ser.: No. 114). 160p. reprint ed. pap. 45.60 (0-317-09535-8, 2006220) Bks Demand.

— Measuring International Capital Movements. (Occasional Papers: No. 114). 160p. 1971. reprint ed. 40.00 (0-87014-229-1) Natl Bur Econ Res.

Michael, Wendy, et al. FDDI: An Introduction to Fiber Distributed Data Interface. (Networking & Data Communications Ser.). (Illus.). 209p. 1993. pap. 17.95 (1-55558-093-9, EY-J840E-DP, Digital DEC) Buttrwrth-Heinemann.

Michael, William B., ed. Teaching for Creative Endeavor: Bold New Venture. LC 76-6603. reprint ed. 45.00 (0-404-15292-9) AMS Pr.

Michael, William B., jt. auth. see Isaac, Stephen.

Michael, Wolfgang. Das Deutsche Drama Des Mittelalters. (Grundriss der Germanischen Philologie Ser.: Vol. 20). 304p. (C). 1971. 119.25 (3-11-003310-0) De Gruyter.

— England under George I, 2 Vols, Set. LC 79-123757. reprint ed. 115.00 (0-404-04314-3) AMS Pr.

Michael X. The Seven Golden Prophecies for the Year 2000. 81p. 1985. reprint ed. spiral bd. 11.00 (0-7873-0612-6) Mokelumne.

Michaeli. Extrusion Dies. 1986. 89.95 (0-02-949550-4) Macmillan.

Michaeli, W. Extrusion Dies. 400p. 1986. 100.00 (0-318-37722-5) T-C Pubns CA.

Michaeli, Walter. Extrusion Dies for Plastics & Rubber: Design & Engineering Computations. 340p. (C). 1992. text ed. 84.95 (1-56990-063-9) Hanser-Gardner.

— Plastics Processing: An Introduction. 224p. (C). 1995. pap. text ed. write for info. (1-56990-144-9) Hanser-Gardner.

Michaeli, Walter, jt. auth. see Potsch, Gerd.

Michaeli, Walter, et al. Introduccion a la Tecnologia de los Plasticos. 174p. (C). 1992. pap. text ed. write for info. (1-56990-175-9) Hanser-Gardner.

— Tecnologia de los Composites-Plasticos Reforzados. 182p. (C). 1992. pap. text ed. write for info. (1-56990-171-6) Hanser-Gardner.

— Training in Injection Molding. Alex, Kurt, tr. LC 95-11657. 172p. (C). 1995. pap. text ed. write for info. (1-56990-135-X) Hanser-Gardner.

— Training in Plastics Technology. LC 95-11658. 192p. (C). 1995. pap. text ed. write for info. (1-56990-134-1) Hanser-Gardner.

Michaelides, Stephen & Deluca, Michael. Dining In - Cleveland. (Dining in Ser.). 176p. (Orig.). 1982. pap. 8.95 (0-89716-034-7) P B Pubng.

Michaelis. Basic Michaelis English-Portuguese, Portuguese-English Dictionary: Dicionario Basico Michaelis Ingles-Portugues-Ingles. 856p. (ENG & POR.). 1985. 75.00 (0-8288-0493-1, M9285) Fr & Eur.

— Michaelis Business English - Portuguese Dictionary. 5th ed. 407p. 1992. 125.00 (0-7859-8713-4) Fr & Eur.

— New Illustrated Michaelis English-Portuguese Dictionary: Novo Michaelis Dicionario Ilustrado, Vol. 1. 41th ed. (Illus.). 1151p. (ENG & POR.). 1986. 75.00 (0-8288-0494-X, M14123) Fr & Eur.

— New Michaelis Portuguese-English Illustrated Dictionary: Novo Michaelis Dicionario Ilustrado, Vol. 2. 40th ed. (Illus.). 1327p. (ENG & POR.). 1986. 75.00 (0-8288-0495-8, M14122) Fr & Eur.

— Portuguese-English - English-Portuguese Pocket Dictionary (Brazilian) 792p. 1989. pap. 13.50 (85-06-01594-4, Pub. by Melhoramentos) IBD Ltd.

— Portuguese-English - English-Portuguese Practical Dictionary (Brazilian) 861p. 1992. 37.50 (85-06-01600-2) IBD Ltd.

— Small Michaelis English-Portuguese, Portuguese-English Dictionary: Pequeno Dicionario Michaelis: Ingles-Portugues, Portugues-Ingles. 642p. (ENG & POR.). 1980. pap. 22.95 (0-8288-0496-6, M9282) Fr & Eur.

Michaelis, A., jt. auth. see Jahn, O.

Michaelis, Anthony R., ed. Interdisciplinary Science Reviews Essay Annual: Volume 5, 1981. 350p. reprint ed. pap. 99.80 (0-685-10877-5, 2022543) Bks Demand.

Michaelis De Vasconcellos, Carolina. Cancioneiro Da Ajuda, 2 vols., Set. xxviii, 1925p. 1979. reprint ed. write for info. (3-487-06924-5, Pub. by Georg Olms GW) Lubrecht & Cramer.

— Randglossen Zum Altportugiesischen Liederbuch. Vol. 20, 25-28. xx, 400p. reprint ed. write for info. (0-318-71637-2, Pub. by Georg Olms GW) Lubrecht & Cramer.

Michaelis-Jena, Ruth, tr. see Woeller, Waltraud & Cassiday, Bruce.

Michaelis, Johann D. Dissertation on the Influence of Opinions on Language & of Language on Opinions. LC 72-147981. reprint ed. pap. 25.00 (0-404-08236-X) AMS Pr.

Michaelis, John U. Social Studies for Children. 10th ed. 448p. (C). 1991. text ed. 49.00 (0-205-13130-1) Allyn.

— Social Studies for Children: A Guide to Basic Instruction. 9th ed. (Illus.). 448p. (C). 1988. text ed. write for info. (0-13-818832-7) P-H.

Michaelis, John U. & Nelson, J. Secondary Social Studies Introduction, Curriculum, Evaluation. (Illus.). 1980. text ed. write for info. (0-13-797753-0) P-H.

Michaelis, John U. & Rushdoony, Haig A. Elementary Social Studies Handbook. 186p. (C). 1987. pap. text ed. 13.50 (0-15-521091-2, MR) HB Coll Pubs.

Michaelis, John U., jt. auth. see Gabelko, Nina H.

Michaelis, Karen L. Reporting Child Abuse: A Guide to Mandatory Requirements for School Personnel. Herman, Jerry J. & Herman, Janice L., eds. (Road Maps to Success Ser.). 70p. 1993. pap. 15.00 (0-8039-6100-6) Corwin Pr.

Michaelis, Karin. The Dangerous Age. 215p. 1991. reprint ed. 25.95 (0-8101-1015-6); reprint ed. pap. 10.95 (0-8101-1040-7) Northwestern U Pr.

Michaelis, Richard. Looking Further Forward: An Answer to Looking Backward. LC 72-154452. (Utopian Literature Ser.). 1971. reprint ed. 16.95 (0-405-03534-9) Ayer.

Michaelis, Ronald F. Old Domestic Base-Metal Candlesticks. (Illus.). 140p. 1993. reprint ed. 49.50 (0-902028-27-8) Antique Collect.

***Michaels.** Grey Beginning. 1995. mass mkt. 5.50 (0-06-100725-0) HarpC.

— Here I Stay. 1994. mass mkt. 5.50 (0-06-100726-9, Harp PBks) HarpC.

— Panda Bear Is Critical. 1982. 12.95 (0-02-584550-0) Macmillan.

— Passion of an Angel. 1995. pap. 5.99 (0-671-79342-X) S&S Trade.

Michaels, Alan. Suffix Obsession: A Dictionary of All Words Ending in Annual, Ennial, Anthropy, Archy, Cracy, Cide, Culture, Gamy, Gon, Hedron, Lagnia, Latry, Theism, Loquy, Machy, Mancy, Mania, Nym, Phagous, Vorous, Phany, Philia & Phobia. LC 92-50941. 196p. 1993. lib. bdg. 25.95 (0-89950-674-7) McFarland & Co.

Michaels, Alan S. Structures Strategic Planning: A Practical Guide to Formulating & Implementing Corporate, Business Unit & Cost Center Strategies. (Illus.). 324p. (Orig.). 1994. pap. write for info. (0-9641122-0-5) A S Michaels.

Michaels, Albert L., jt. ed. see Wilkie, James W.

***Michaels, Angie.** Best Impressions in Hospitality: Your Professional Image for Excellence. 200p. (Orig.). 1995. pap. 14.95 (1-57023-018-8) Impact VA.

Michaels, Art. The Outboard Boater's Book of Skills & Projects. 224p. 1993. pap. 17.95 (0-87742-310-5, 60292) Intl Marine.

***Michaels Art & Crafts Editors.** Crafters' Guide to Christmas 1994. 1994. pap. 9.95 (1-56530-163-3) Summit TX.

Michaels, Barbara. Ammie, Come Home. 256p. 1987. mass mkt. 5.99 (0-425-09949-0) Berkley Pub.

— Ammie, Come Home. 1979. pap. 1.95 (0-449-23926-8, Crest) Fawcett.

— Ammie, Come Home. large type ed. LC 93-13246. 1993. 18.95 (0-7927-1672-8, Eagle Lrg Print); pap. 17.95 (0-7927-1671-X, Eagle Lrg Print) Chivers N Amer.

— Be Buried in the Rain. 50p. 1987. mass mkt. 6.50 (0-425-09634-3) Berkley Pub.

— Black Rainbow. 1991. pap. 5.99 (0-425-12481-9) Berkley Pub.

— The Crying Child. 1989. mass mkt. 5.99 (0-425-11584-4) Berkley Pub.

— The Crying Child. large type ed. 1995. 20.95 (0-7862-0353-6) Thorndike Pr.

— The Dark on the Other Side. 1988. mass mkt. 6.50 (0-425-10928-3) Berkley Pub.

— The Dark on the Other Side. large type ed. LC 92-40548. 1993. 19.95 (0-7927-1526-8, Eagle Lrg Print); pap. write for info. (0-7927-1525-X, Eagle Lrg Print) Chivers N Amer.

— The Grey Beginning. 320p. 1990. pap. 190.40 (0-312-92260-4) Congdon & Weed.

— The Grey Beginning. large type ed. (Charnwood Large Print Ser.). 352p. 1995. 25.95 (0-7089-8842-3, Charnwood) Ulverscroft.

— The Grey Beginning. 288p. 1994. reprint ed. 20.00 (0-7278-4538-1) Severn Hse.

— Greygallows. 352p. 1993. mass mkt. 5.99 (0-425-13794-5) Berkley Pub.

— Greygallows. large type ed. LC 93-36516. 1994. 20.95 (0-7927-1742-2, Eagle Lrg Print) Chivers N Amer.

— Greygallows. large type ed. LC 93-36516. 1994. pap. 19.95 (0-7927-1741-4, Paragon Lrg Print) Chivers N Amer.

— Here I Stay. large type ed. LC 94-26172. 1994. 21.95 (0-7927-2172-1, Eagle Lrg Print); pap. 20.95 (0-7927-2171-3, Eagle Lrg Print) Chivers N Amer.

— House of Many Shadows. large type ed. 1981. 12.00 (0-7089-0666-4) Ulverscroft.

— Houses of Stone. 368p. 1993. 21.00 (0-671-68949-5) S&S Trade.

— Houses of Stone. large type ed. LC 93-40498. 1994. 21.95 (0-8161-5936-X, Studio Ser Audio) Thorndike Pr.

— Houses of Stone. large type ed. LC 93-40498. 1995. pap. 17.95 (0-8161-5937-8, Studio Ser Audio) Thorndike Pr.

— Houses of Stone. 400p. 1994. reprint ed. pap. text ed. 5.99 (0-425-14306-6) Berkley Pub.

— Into the Darkness. 1991. mass mkt. 5.99 (0-425-12892-X) Berkley Pub.

— Into the Darkness. large type ed. (General Ser.). 528p. 1991. lib. bdg. 19.95 (0-8161-5129-6, Large Print Bks); pap. 14.95 (0-8161-5130-X, Large Print Bks) Hall.

— The Master of Blacktower. 304p. Date not set. pap. text ed. 6.50 (0-425-14941-2) Berkley Pub.

— The Master of Blacktower. large type ed. LC 92-40906. (General Ser.). 397p. 1993. pap. 16.95 (0-8161-5647-6, Large Print Bks) Hall.

— Patriot's Dream. 352p. (Orig.). 1994. pap. text ed. 5.99 (0-425-13355-9) Berkley Pub.

— Patriot's Dream. large type ed. LC 93-49513. (Orig.). 1994. 22.95 (0-7927-2021-0, Eagle Lrg Print) Chivers N Amer.

— Patriot's Dream. large type ed. LC 93-49513. (Orig.). 1995. pap. 21.95 (0-7927-2020-2, Paragon Lrg Print) Chivers N Amer.

— Prince of Darkness. 240p. 1988. mass mkt. 5.99 (0-425-10853-8) Berkley Pub.

— Scattered Blossoms. 1992. 20.00 (0-685-53583-5) S&S Trade.

— The Sea King's Daughter. 1989. mass mkt. 4.99 (0-425-11306-X) Berkley Pub.

— The Sea King's Daughter. large type ed. 1993. pap. 16.95 (0-7927-1301-X, Paragon Lrg Print) Chivers N Amer.

— Search the Shadows. 1988. 6.50 (0-425-11183-0) Berkley Pub.

— Search the Shadows. LC 87-11565. 384p. 1987. text ed. 17.95 (0-689-11906-2, Atheneum S&S) S&S Trade.

— Shattered Silk. Warriner, Mercer, ed. 320p. 1988. mass mkt. 5.99 (0-425-10476-1) Berkley Pub.

— Smoke & Mirrors. 1990. mass mkt. 5.99 (0-425-11911-4) Berkley Pub.

— Smoke & Mirrors. 1989. 17.95 (0-318-37669-5) S&S Trade.

— Someone in the House. 1976. 18.95 (0-8488-0834-7) Amereon Ltd.

— Someone in the House. 1989. mass mkt. 5.99 (0-425-11389-2) Berkley Pub.

— Sons of the Wolf. 1989. mass mkt. 5.99 (0-425-11687-5) Berkley Pub.

— Sons of the Wolf. 1994. reprint ed. lib. bdg. 20.00 (0-7278-4665-5) Severn Hse.

— Stitches in Time. 1995. 22.00 (0-06-017763-2) HarpC.

— Stitches in Time. large type ed. 527p. 1995. reprint ed. 23.95 (0-7838-1356-2) Hall.

— Vanish with the Rose. 432p. 1993. mass mkt. 5.99 (0-425-13898-4) Berkley Pub.

— Vanish with the Rose. 1992. 17.00 (0-671-75594-3) S&S Trade.

— Vanish with the Rose. large type ed. LC 92-31899. (General Ser.). 548p. 1994. lib. bdg. 21.95 (0-8161-5660-3); pap. 16.95 (0-8161-5661-1) G K Hall.

— Wait for What Will Come. 1990. pap. 5.99 (0-425-12005-8) Berkley Pub.

— Wait for What Will Come. large type ed. 1992. pap. 14.95 (0-7927-0865-2, Paragon Lrg Print) Chivers N Amer.

— Walker in Shadows. 1992. mass mkt. 5.99 (0-425-13399-0) Berkley Pub.

— Wings of the Falcon. 1988. mass mkt. 5.99 (0-425-11045-1) Berkley Pub.

— Wings of the Falcon. 1978. pap. 1.95 (0-449-23750-8, Crest) Fawcett.

— Wings of the Falcon. 1995. reprint ed. lib. bdg. 20.00 (0-7278-4722-8) Severn Hse.

— Witch. 1989. mass mkt. 6.50 (0-425-11831-2) Berkley Pub.

— Witch. LC 94-26170. 1994. 21.95 (0-7927-2168-3, Eagle Lrg Print); pap. 20.95 (0-7927-2167-5, Eagle Lrg Print) Chivers N Amer.

— The Wizard's Daughter. 336p. (Orig.). 1995. pap. text ed. 5.99 (0-425-14642-1) Berkley Pub.

Michaels, Barbara L. Gertrude Kasebier. (Illus.). 208p. 1992. 45.00 (0-8109-3505-8) Abrams.

Michaels, Bonnie & McCarty, Elizabeth. Solving the Work-Family Puzzle. 268p. 1992. 25.00 (1-55623-627-1) Irwin Prof Pubng.

Michaels, Carol. Charade of Hearts. 1992. pap. 3.99 (1-55773-688-X) Diamond.

Michaels, Carolyn. Children's Book Collecting. LC 92-35088. (Illus.). xii, 202p. (C). 1993. lib. bdg. 35.00 (0-208-02267-8, Lib Prof Pubns) Shoe String.

Michaels, Carolyn & Leopold, Dennette C. Library Literacy Means Lifelong Learning. LC 84-10705. 388p. 1985. 29.00 (0-8108-1719-5) Scarecrow.

Michaels, Charles & Cohen, Ruth. Four-Three-Two-One Bridge Student Text. 5th rev. ed. 1986. pap. 2.95 (0-87643-008-6) Barclay Bridge.

An Asterisk (*) at the beginning of an entry indicates that the title is appearing in BIP for the first time.

Michaels, Charlie & Brown, Mike. Avoiding Wedding Aftershock or I Like You Even Better Now That I Know You. LC 90-81456. (Illus.). 160p. 1990. pap. 14.95 (0-9626525-0-4) Carmichael Ventures.
Michaels, Craig A., ed. Transition Strategies for Persons with Learning Disabilities. LC 94-2164. (Illus.). 284p. (Orig.). (C). 1994. pap. text ed. 32.50 (1-56593-165-3, 0476) Singular Publishing.
Michaels, David D. Basic Refraction Techniques. 188p. 1988. 31.50 (0-88167-471-0, 1941) Raven.
Michaels, Deborah, jt. auth. see Micelotta, Jeanette.
Michaels, Dia L., jt. auth. see Bumslag, Naomi.
Michaels, Elizabeth. Lord Barton's Honour. (Regency Romance Ser.). 1993. mass mkt. 2.99 (0-373-31201-6, 1-31201-6) Harlequin Bks.
Michaels, Elizabeth A. From a Silver Heart. Tolley, Carolyn, ed. 576p. (Orig.). 1993. mass mkt. 4.99 (0-671-76096-3) PB.
— A Jewel So Rare. Tolley, Carolyn, ed. 336p. (Orig.). 1992. mass mkt. 4.99 (0-671-72730-3) PB.
— Sweet Madness Mine. 400p. 1994. mass mkt. 4.50 (0-8217-4774-6) Zebra.
Michaels, Eric. Bad Aboriginal Art & Other Essays: Tradition, Media, & Technological Horizons. LC 93-5132. (Theory out of Bounds Ser.: No. 3). 296p. 1993. pap. 21.95 (0-8166-2341-4) U of Minn Pr.
Michaels, Fern. All She Can Be. 1991. reprint ed. 17.95 (0-7278-4139-4) Severn Hse.
— Beyond Tomorrow. 1994. mass mkt. 4.50 (0-373-48302-3, 5-48302-9) Silhouette.
— Captive Embraces. 1983. mass mkt. 4.95 (0-345-31353-4) Ballantine.
— Captive Innocence. 1982. mass mkt. 5.95 (0-345-30804-2) Ballantine.
— Captive Innocence. large type ed. (General Ser.). 425p. 1991. lib. bdg. 19.95 (0-8161-5122-9) G K Hall.
— Captive Passions. LC 76-56142. 1987. mass mkt. 5.95 (0-345-34683-1) Ballantine.
— Captive Passions. 448p. 1992. reprint ed. 22.00 (0-7278-4384-2) Severn Hse.
— Captive Secrets. (Orig.). 1991. mass mkt. 5.95 (0-345-34123-6) Ballantine.
— Captive Secrets. large type ed. (General Ser.). 415p. (Orig.). 1992. text ed. 20.95 (0-8161-5360-4, Large Print Bks) Hall.
— Captive Splendors. 1983. mass mkt. 5.99 (0-345-31648-7) Ballantine.
— Captive Splendors. 1994. 22.00 (0-685-73092-1) Severn Hse.
— Cinders to Satin. 1986. mass mkt. 5.99 (0-345-33952-5) Ballantine.
— Cinders to Satin. 512p. 1995. reprint ed. lib. bdg. 22.00 (0-7278-4502-0) Severn Hse.
— Dear Emily. 512p. 1995. mass mkt. 5.99 (0-8217-4952-8) Zebra.
— Delta Ladies. 1995. mass mkt. 5.99 (0-671-79917-7) PB.
— Desperate Measures. LC 94-27157. 1994. 22.00 (0-345-38440-7) Ballantine.
— Desperate Measures. large type ed. LC 94-34299. 1995. write for info. (0-7862-0337-4) Thorndike Pr.
— For All Their Lives. 1992. mass mkt. 5.99 (0-345-36592-5) Ballantine.
— For All Their Lives. large type ed. LC 92-14410. (General Ser.). 688p. 1992. text ed. 22.95 (0-8161-5361-2, Large Print Bks); pap. 16.95 (0-8161-5362-0, Large Print Bks) Hall.
— Free Spirit. (Love & Life Ser.). 224p. (Orig.). 1983. pap. 3.95 (0-345-30840-9) Ballantine.
— Golden Lasso. 1994. mass mkt. 4.50 (0-373-48297-3, 5-48297-1) Silhouette.
— Nightstar. (Best of the Best Ser.). 1993. mass mkt. 4.50 (0-373-48274-4, 5-48274-0) Silhouette.
— Paint Me Rainbows. 1994. pap. 4.99 (1-55166-003-2, 1-66003-4, Mira Bks) Harlequin Bks.
— Paint Me Rainbows. 1994. mass mkt. 4.50 (0-373-48316-3, 5-48316-9) Silhouette.
— Sea Gypsy. (Best of the Best Ser.). (C). 1993. mass mkt. 4.50 (0-373-48275-2, 5-48275-7) Silhouette.
— Seasons of Her Life. 1994. pap. 5.99 (0-345-36591-7) Ballantine.
— Seasons of Her Life. large type ed. LC 94-35472. 1994. write for info. (1-56895-154-X) Wheeler Pub.
— Serendipity. LC 94-19693. 1994. 22.00 (0-345-39271-X) Ballantine.
— Serendipity. Date not set. pap. write for info. (0-345-37328-6) Ballantine.
— Serendipity. large type ed. LC 94-33681. 682p. 1995. 22.95 (0-7862-0339-0) Thorndike Pr.
— Sins of Omission. 512p. 1989. mass mkt. 5.95 (0-345-34120-1) Ballantine.
— Sins of Omission. 1994. reprint ed. lib. bdg. 22.00 (0-7278-4670-1) Severn Hse.
— Sins of the Flesh. 448p. (Orig.). 1990. mass mkt. 5.95 (0-345-34122-8) Ballantine.
— Sins of the Flesh. 1994. pap. 8.95 (0-345-38662-0) Ballantine.
— Tender Warrior. 384p. (Orig.). 1982. mass mkt. 5.99 (0-345-30358-X) Ballantine.
— Tender Warrior. large type ed. 587p. 1995. reprint ed. 21.95 (0-7862-0497-4) Hall.
— Texas Fury. 1989. mass mkt. 5.99 (0-345-90182-7) Ballantine.
— Texas Fury. large type ed. LC 93-13197. 1993. 21.95 (1-56054-754-5) Thorndike Pr.
— Texas Heat. 640p. 1986. mass mkt. 5.99 (0-345-90181-9) Ballantine.
— Texas Heat. 1990. reprint ed. 19.95 (0-7278-4007-X) Severn Hse.
— Texas Rich. 640p. 1989. mass mkt. 5.95 (0-345-90180-0) Ballantine.
— Texas Rich. large type ed. LC 92-42501. (Americana Ser.). 921p. 1993. reprint ed. lib. bdg. 21.95 (1-56054-662-X) Thorndike Pr.
— Texas Sunrise. 1993. 19.00 (0-345-36776-6, Ballantine Trade) Ballantine.
— Texas Sunrise. 1994. mass mkt. 5.99 (0-345-36593-3) Ballantine.
— Texas Sunrise. large type ed. LC 93-13194. 1994. 21.95 (1-56054-755-3) Thorndike Pr.
— To Have & to Hold. LC 94-13758. 1994. 22.00 (0-345-38451-2) Ballantine.
— To Have & to Hold. large type ed. LC 94-34296. 529p. 1994. lib. bdg. 23.95 (0-7862-0336-6) Thorndike Pr.
— To Taste the Wine. (Orig.). 1987. mass mkt. 5.95 (0-345-30360-1) Ballantine.
— Valentina. 1983. mass mkt. 4.95 (0-345-31126-4) Ballantine.
— Whisper My Name. (Best of the Best Ser.). 1993. mass mkt. 4.50 (0-373-48273-6, 5-48273-2) Silhouette.
— Wild Honey. Tolley, Carolyn, ed. 336p. 1992. mass mkt. 5.50 (0-671-79390-X) PB.
Michaels, Gerald Y. & Goldberg, Wendy A., eds. The Transition to Parenthood: Current Theory & Research. (Cambridge Studies in Social & Emotional Development). (Illus.). 350p. 1993. 54.95 (0-521-35418-8) Cambridge U Pr.
Michaels, Gerald Y., jt. auth. see Goldstein, Arnold P.
Michaels, Grant. Body to Dye For. 1991. pap. 8.95 (0-312-05825-X) St Martin.
— Dead on Your Feet. 256p. 1993. 19.95 (0-312-09781-6) St Martin.
— Dead on Your Feet. 256p. 1994. 8.95 (0-312-11457-5, Stonewall Inn) St Martin.
— Love You to Death. 256p. 1992. 18.95 (0-312-07027-6) St Martin.
— Love You to Death. LC 92-37742. (Stonewall Inn Mysteries Ser.). 1993. 8.95 (0-312-08841-8) St Martin.
— Mask for a Diva. 272p. 1994. 20.95 (0-312-11462-1) St Martin.
Michaels, Ian, ed. see Shaw, George Bernard.
Michaels, Ian, ed. see Wilde, Oscar.
Michaels, J. Ramsey. Interpreting the Book of Revelation. LC 92-16597. 160p. 1992. pap. 9.99 (0-8010-6293-4) Baker Bk.
— John. (New International Biblical Commentary Ser.). 400p. 1989. pap. 9.95 (0-943575-14-1) Hendrickson MA.
— WBC, Vol. 49: First Peter. 337p. 1988. write for info. (0-8499-0248-7) Word Inc.
— WBT: First Peter. 114p. 1989. 9.99 (0-8499-0788-8) Word Inc.
Michaels, Jack V. & Wood, William P. Design to Cost for Affordability. 413p. 1989. text ed. 74.95 (0-471-60900-5) Wiley.
Michaels, Jan. Death on the Late Show. (Mystery Puzzler Ser.: No. 14). (Illus.). (Orig.). 1979. pap. 1.95 (0-89083-434-2) Zebra.
— Sing a Song of Murder. (Mystery Puzzler Ser.: No. 12). (Illus.). 1978. pap. 1.95 (0-89083-424-5) Zebra.
Michaels, Janet. Inside London. 1991. 9.99 (0-517-05877-4) Random Hse Value.
— Inside New York. 1991. 9.99 (0-517-05876-6) Random Hse Value.
— Inside Paris. 1991. 9.99 (0-517-05878-2) Random Hse Value.
— Inside Rome. 1991. 9.99 (0-517-05881-2) Random Hse Value.
— Inside Sydney. 1991. 9.99 (0-517-05879-0) Random Hse Value.
— Inside Venice. 1991. 9.99 (0-517-05880-4) Random Hse Value.
Michaels, Jennifer. Anarchy & Eros: Otto Gross' Impact on German Expressionist Writers. LC 83-80232. (Utah Studies in Literature & Linguistics: Vol. 24). 230p. (Orig.). (C). 1983. pap. text ed. 24.20 (0-8204-0000-9) P Lang Pubs.
Michaels, Jennifer E. Franz Jung: Expressionist, Dadaist, Revolutionary Outsider. (American University Studies: Germanic Languages & Literature: Ser. I, Vol. 70). 238p. (C). 1989. text ed. 35.50 (0-8204-0758-5) P Lang Pubs.
— Franz Werfel & the Critics. 168p. 1994. 52.95 (1-879751-99-2) Camden Hse.
Michaels, Joanna. Nun in the Closet. LC 94-2197. 200p. (Orig.). 1994. pap. 9.95 (0-934678-43-X) New Victoria Pubs.
***Michaels, Joanne.** The Joy of Divorce. LC 94-78914. (Illus.). 100p. 1995. 9.95 (0-9619429-2-4) JMB NY.
— Lets Take the Kids. 1990. pap. 9.95 (0-312-04050-4) St Martin.
— Let's Take the Kids Out to Eat in the Hudson Valley: Over 200 Restaurants from Westchester to Albany Including the Catskills & Saratoga Springs. 128p. (Orig.). 1991. pap. 9.95 (0-9619429-1-6) JMB NY.
Michaels, Joanne & Barile, Mary. Famous Woodstock Cooks: And Their Favorite Recipes. 2nd ed. (Illus.). 143p. (Orig.). 1994. pap. 14.95 (0-9619429-0-8) JMB NY.
Michaels, Joanne & Barile, Mary-Margaret. The Hudson Valley & Catskill Mountains: An Explorer's Guide. LC 92-39949. (Illus.). 240p. 1993. pap. 15.00 (0-88150-259-6) Countryman.
***Michaels, Joe.** A-6 Intruder in Action. (Aircraft in Action Ser.). (Illus.). 50p. Date not set. pap. 8.95 (0-89747-302-7) Squad Sig Pubns.
Michaels, Joe, et al. Prime of Your Life. LC 80-21205. 366p. reprint ed. pap. 104.40 (0-317-26073-1, 2025159) Bks Demand.
Michaels, Joel L. Legal Issues in the Fee-for-Service - Prepaid Medical Group. rev. ed. (Going Prepaid Ser.). 62p. (C). 1990. pap. text ed. 28.00 (0-933948-34-4, 946) Ctr Res Ambulatory.
Michaels, John G. & Rosen, Kenneth H. Applications of Discrete Mathematics. 1991. pap. text ed. write for info. (0-07-041823-3) McGraw.
Michaels, Judith. Sleeping Beauty. Grose, Bill, ed. 640p. 1992. reprint ed. mass mkt. 5.99 (0-671-78252-5) PB.
Michaels, Judy, jt. auth. see Stevens, Jared.
Michaels, Kasey. The Anonymous Miss Addams. 192p. (Orig.). 1989. pap. 2.95 (0-380-75668-4) Avon.
— The Belligerent Miss Boynton. 224p. (Orig.). 1982. pap. 2.95 (0-380-77073-3) Avon.
— The Bride of the Unicorn. 384p. (Orig.). 1993. mass mkt. 5.99 (0-671-73181-5, Pocket Star Bks) PB.
— The Chaotic Miss Crispino. 192p. (Orig.). 1991. mass mkt. 3.99 (0-380-76300-1) Avon.
— The Dad Next Door. 1995. mass mkt. 2.99 (0-373-19108-1, 1-19108-9) Silhouette.
— The Dubious Miss Dalrymple. 192p. 1990. pap. 2.95 (0-380-89908-6) Avon.
— The Haunted Miss Hampshire. 192p. (Orig.). 1992. mass mkt. 3.99 (0-380-76301-X) Avon.
— Husbands Don't Grow on Trees. 1995. mass mkt. 3.50 (0-373-52008-5) Silhouette.
— The Illusions of Love. Zion, Claire, ed. 368p. (Orig.). 1994. mass mkt. 5.50 (0-671-79340-3, Pocket Star Bks) PB.
— The Legacy of the Rose. Zion, Claire, ed. 448p. (Orig.). 1992. mass mkt. 5.50 (0-671-73180-7) PB.
— The Lurid Lady Lockport. 208p. (Orig.). 1984. pap. 2.95 (0-380-86231-X) Avon.
— Marriage in a Suitcase. (Silhouette Romance Ser.). 1993. pap. 2.75 (0-373-08949-X, 5-08949-5) Silhouette.
— A Masquerade in the Moonlight. 1994. mass mkt. 5.50 (0-671-79339-X) PB.
— The Mischievous Miss Murphy. (Regency Romance Ser.). 176p. 1987. pap. 2.95 (0-380-89907-8) Avon.
— Playful Lady Penelope. 192p. 1988. pap. 2.95 (0-380-75297-2) Avon.
— Prenuptial Agreement. large type ed. 215p. 1993. reprint ed. lib. bdg. 13.95 (1-56054-614-X) Thorndike Pr.
— The Questioning Miss Quinton. 176p. 1987. pap. 2.95 (0-380-75296-4) Avon.
— The Rambunctious Lady Royston. 224p. 1982. pap. 2.95 (0-380-81448-X) Avon.
— The Secrets of the Heart. Zion, Claire, ed. 384p. (Orig.). 1995. mass mkt. 5.99 (0-671-79341-1) PB.
— The Tenacious Miss Tamerlane. 192p. 1982. pap. 2.95 (0-380-79889-1) Avon.
— Timely Matrimony. (Silhouette Romance Ser.). 1994. pap. 2.75 (0-373-19030-1, 1-19030-5) Harlequin Bks.
— Uncle Daddy. (Silhouette Romance Ser.). 1993. pap. 2.69 (0-373-08916-3, 5-08916-4) Silhouette.
— The Wagered Miss Winslow. 192p. (Orig.). 1992. mass mkt. 3.99 (0-380-76302-8) Avon.
Michaels, Katherine. Crashing into the Wall of Vanity: Cosmetic Surgery Is It for You? 160p. 1992. pap. 6.95 (0-9634948-0-5, TX3346596) Equinox Prods.
Michaels, Kevin. AIDS Crisis: Impact On the Gay Subculture, Pt. 1. 130p. 1986. ring bd. 11.95 (0-939020-77-7) MLP Ent.
— AIDS Crisis: Impact on the Gay Subculture, Pt. 2. 110p. 1987. ring bd. 12.95 (0-939020-79-3) MLP Ent.
— The Gay Book of Etiquette. rev. ed. 113p. 1984. pap. 11.95 (0-939020-76-9) MLP Ent.
— The Heterosexual Trap. 120p. 1987. ring bd. 12.50 (0-939020-80-7) MLP Ent.
— Loud Speakers: The Great Personalities of Hard & Alternative Rock. (Illus.). 240p. (Orig.). 1995. pap. 12.95 (1-56790-037-2) Cool Hand Comms.
— Michaels on Gay Life, Vol. 1. 140p. (Orig.). 1986. ring bd., pap. 11.95 (0-939020-78-5) MLP Ent.
— Michaels on Gay Life, Vol. 2. 140p. (Orig.). 1987. ring bd. 12.95 (0-939020-81-5) MLP Ent.
Michaels, L. Atlas of Ear, Nose & Throat Pathology. (C). 1990. lib. bdg. 190.00 (0-7923-8934-4) Kluwer Ac.
Michaels, Larry. Easy Bible Object Talks. (Illus.). 48p. 1985. pap. 3.99 (0-87239-846-3, 2886) Standard Pub.
Michaels, Larry R. East Side Story: People & Places in the History of East Toledo. (Illus.). 208p. 1993. 14.95 (1-883829-11-9); pap. 9.95 (1-883829-12-7) Bihl Hse Pub.
Michaels, Laura. Tune in Tomorrow. 224p. (Orig.). 1992. pap. 2.95 (1-878702-81-5, Kismet) Meteor Pub.
Michaels, Leigh. The Anonymous Miss Addams. large type ed. (Orig.). 1991. pap. 17.95 (0-7927-0748-6, Curley Lrg Print) Chivers N Amer.
— The Best Made Plans. (Romance Ser.: No. 214). 1992. pap. 2.89 (0-373-03214-5) Harlequin Bks.
— Dating Games. (Romance Ser.). 1993. mass mkt. 2.99 (0-373-03290-0, 1-03290-3) Harlequin Bks.
— Deadline for Love. large type ed. 1991. 17.95 (0-7451-9994-1, AH028, Atlantic Lrg Print) Chivers N Amer.
— Un Duo Romantique. (Horizon Ser.). (FRE.). 1994. pap. 3.50 (0-373-39289-3, 1-39289-3) Harlequin Bks.
— Family Secrets: (Kids & Kisses) (Romance Ser.). 1994. mass mkt. 2.99 (0-373-03324-9, 1-03324-0) Harlequin Bks.
— House of Dreams. (Larger Print Ser.). 1995. pap. 2.99 (0-373-15589-1, 1-15589-4) Harlequin Bks.
— House of Dreams. (Romance Ser.). 1995. pap. 2.99 (0-373-03343-5, 1-03343-0) Harlequin Bks.
— Invitation to Love: (Sealed with a Kiss) (Romance Ser.). 1995. pap. 2.99 (0-373-03352-4, 1-03352-1) Harlequin Bks.
— Kiss Yesterday Goodbye. 1994. 3.59 (0-373-45165-2) Harlequin Bks.
— The Lake Effect. (Romance Ser.). 1993. mass mkt. 2.99 (0-373-03275-7, 1-03275-4) Harlequin Bks.
— Let Me Count the Ways. (Romance Ser.: No. 3023). 1989. pap. 2.50 (0-373-03023-1) Harlequin Bks.
— A Matter of Principle. (Romance Ser.: No. 3070). 1990. pap. 2.50 (0-373-03070-3) Harlequin Bks.
— Old School Ties. (Romance Ser.: No. 184). 1992. pap. 2.89 (0-373-03184-X, 1-03184-8) Harlequin Bks.
— Promise Me Tomorrow. (Romance Ser.: No. 141). 1991. pap. 2.75 (0-373-03141-6) Harlequin Bks.
— Safe in My Heart. (Romance Ser.). 1993. pap. 2.89 (0-373-03248-X, 1-03248-1) Harlequin Bks.
— A Singular Honeymoon. (Romance Ser.). 1994. mass mkt. 2.99 (0-373-03300-1, 1-03300-0) Harlequin Bks.
— Taming a Tycoon. (Romance Ser.). 1995. mass mkt. 2.99 (0-373-03367-2, 1-03367-9) Harlequin Bks.
— Temporary Measures. (Romance Ser.: No. 3160). 1991. pap. 2.79 (0-373-03160-2) Harlequin Bks.
— Ties That Bind. (Romance Ser.). 1993. pap. 2.89 (0-373-03263-3, 1-03263-0) Harlequin Bks.
— Traveling Man. 1994. 2.99 (0-373-03311-7) Harlequin Bks.
— An Uncommon Affair. (Romance Ser.: No. 3119). 1991. pap. 2.75 (0-373-03119-X) Harlequin Bks.
— The Unlikely Santa. 1995. pap. 2.99 (0-373-03388-5, 1-03388-5) Harlequin Bks.
— With No Reservations. large type ed. 1990. lib. bdg. 18.95 (0-263-12355-3, Pub. by Mills & Boon UK) Thorndike Pr.
***Michaels, Leonard.** A Cat. LC 94-25257. (Illus.). 1995. 14.95 (0-614-03361-6) Riverhead Bks.
— The Men's Club. LC 92-45612. 1993. pap. 10.00 (1-56279-039-0) Mercury Hse Inc.
— Sylvia. LC 92-16541. 144p. 1992. 10.00 (1-56279-029-3) Mercury Hse Inc.
— To Feel These Things. LC 92-45611. 144p. (Orig.). 1993. pap. 12.00 (1-56279-040-4) Mercury Hse Inc.
Michaels, Leonard, jt. ed. see Ricks, Christopher.
***Michaels, Leonard, et al, eds.** West of the West: Imagining California: An Anthology. 1995. 13.00 (0-520-20164-7) U CA Pr.
Michaels, Leslie & Chissick, S. S., eds. Asbestos: Properties, Applications, & Hazards, Vol. 1. LC 78-16535. (Illus.). 572p. reprint ed. pap. 163.10 (0-8357-5782-X, 2052252) Bks Demand.
***Michaels, Lorna.** The Reluctant Bodyguard. (Superromance Ser.). 1995. pap. 3.75 (0-373-70633-2, 1-70633-2) Harlequin Bks.
— The Reluctant Hunk. (Tempation Ser.: No. 523). 1995. mass mkt. 2.99 (0-373-25623-X, 1-25623-9) Harlequin Bks.
Michaels, Lynn. Aftershock. (Temptation Ser.). 1994. mass mkt. 2.99 (0-373-25581-0, 1-25581-9) Harlequin Bks.
— Molly & the Phantom. 1994. mass mkt. 2.99 (0-373-25611-6, 1-25611-4) Harlequin Bks.
— Nightwing. (Temptation Ser.). 1995. mass mkt. 3.25 (0-373-25642-6, 1-25642-9) Harlequin Bks.
Michaels, Mark. Blues Riffs for Guitar. (Illus.). 48p. 1978. pap. 9.95 (0-8256-2203-4, AM23532) Music Sales.
— Heavy Metal Riffs for Guitar. (Illus.). 104p. 1985. pap. 12.95 (0-8256-2329-4, AM37318) Music Sales.
— New Wave Riffs for the Guitar. (Illus.). 128p. 1985. pap. 12.95 (0-8256-2331-6, AM36995) Music Sales.
— Original Jeff Beck. (Illus.). 80p. 1985. pap. 11.95 (0-8256-2340-5, AM38357) Music Sales.
— Rock Riffs for Guitar, EFS171. (Illus.). 48p. 1984. pap. 9.95 (0-8256-2171-2, AM22211) Music Sales.
— Rockabilly Riffs for Guitar. (Illus.). 104p. 1985. pap. 12.95 (0-8256-2330-8, AM36948) Music Sales.
— Teach Yourself Rhythm Guitar. 64p. pap. 9.95 (0-8256-2201-8) Music Sales.
***Michaels, Melisa.** Skirmish. (YA). 1994. pap. 5.99 (0-7043-4906-X) Interlink Pub.
Michaels, Melisa C. Far Harbor. 256p. 1989. pap. 3.95 (0-8125-4581-8) Tor Bks.
— Floater Factor. 288p. 1988. pap. 3.50 (0-8125-4578-8) Tor Bks.
— Through the Eyes of the Dead. 192p. 1989. 17.95 (0-8027-5718-9) Walker & Co.
***Michaels, Mickey.** Survival Guide for Parents: How to Avoid Screwing up Your Kids or Losing Your Own Sanity. 125p. 1995. pap. 9.95 (0-9644761-1-8) Possibility Pr.
Michaels, Nancy. Helping Women Recover from Abortion. LC 88-10447. 224p. (Orig.). 1988. pap. 7.99 (0-87123-621-4) Bethany Hse.
***Michaels, Neal.** How to Use, Compile, Maintain, & Sell Mailing Lists. 32p. 1992. pap. 12.00 (0-915665-27-1) Premier Publishers.
Michaels, Neal, jt. auth. see Bates, Owen.
Michaels, Neal, jt. auth. see Stilson, Galen.
Michaels, Norman, jt. auth. see Steinbrunner, Christopher.
Michaels, Patrick J. Sound & Fury: The Science & Politics of Global Warming. 1992. 15.95 (0-932790-90-9) Cato Inst.
— Sound & Fury: The Science & Politics of Global Warming. LC 92-36264. 1992. 11.95 (0-932790-89-5) Cato Inst.
Michaels, Peter A. Heat. 1993. mass mkt. 4.99 (0-312-92886-6) St Martin.
Michaels, Ragini E. Facticity: A Door to Mental Health & Beyond. (Illus.). 256p. (Orig.). 1991. pap. 16.95 (0-9628686-0-4) Facticity Tr.
— Lions in Wait: A Road to Personal Courage. (Illus.). 282p. (Orig.). 1993. pap. 16.95 (0-9628686-1-2) Facticity Tr.
Michaels, Richard M. Transportation Planning & Policy Decision Making: Behavioral Science Contributions. LC 79-24820. 264p. 1980. text ed. 59.95 (0-275-90524-1, C0524, Praeger Pubs) Greenwood.
Michaels, Scott, ed. Freddy & Betty, Vol. 1. (Illus.). (J). (gr. 1-6). 1989. teacher ed 2.50 (0-317-93682-4) S Michaels Pub.
Michaels, Shirley, ed. see Craig, Rebecca T. & Wright, Barbara.

An Asterisk (*) at the beginning of an entry indicates that the title is appearing in BIP for the first time.

Michaels, Ski. The Baseball Bat. LC 85-14065. (Illus.). 48p. (Orig.). (J). (gr. 1-3). 1986. lib. bdg. 10.59 (*0-8167-0596-8*); pap. text ed. 3.50 (*0-8167-0597-6*) Troll Assocs.

— The Big Surprise. LC 85-14017. (Illus.). 48p. (J). (gr. 1-3). 1986. lib. bdg. 10.59 (*0-8167-0576-3*); pap. text ed. 3.50 (*0-8167-0577-1*) Troll Assocs.

— Felix, the Funny Fox. LC 85-14097. (Illus.). 48p. (Orig.). (J). (gr. 1-3). 1986. lib. bdg. 10.59 (*0-8167-0590-9*); pap. text ed. 3.50 (*0-8167-0591-7*) Troll Assocs.

— Fun in the Sun. LC 85-14055. (Illus.). 48p. (Orig.). (J). (gr. 1-3). 1986. lib. bdg. 10.59 (*0-8167-0568-2*); pap. text ed. 3.50 (*0-8167-0569-0*) Troll Assocs.

— Mystery of the Missing Fuzzy. LC 85-14084. (Illus.). 48p. (Orig.). (J). (gr. 1-3). 1986. lib. bdg. 10.59 (*0-8167-0646-8*); pap. text ed. 3.50 (*0-8167-0647-6*) Troll Assocs.

— Mystery of the Windy Meadow. LC 85-14019. (Illus.). 48p. (Orig.). (J). (gr. 1-3). 1986. lib. bdg. 10.59 (*0-8167-0630-1*); pap. text ed. 3.50 (*0-8167-0631-X*) Troll Assocs.

— One Hundred Two Animal Jokes. LC 91-30061. (Illus.). 64p. (J). (gr. 2-6). 1991. pap. text ed. 2.95 (*0-8167-2613-2*) Troll Assocs.

— One Hundred Two Creepy, Crawly Bug Jokes. LC 91-42737. (Illus.). 64p. (J). (gr. 2-6). 1992. pap. text ed. 2.95 (*0-8167-2745-7*) Troll Assocs.

— One Hundred Two Haunted House Jokes. LC 91-21891. (Illus.). 64p. (J). (gr. 2-6). 1991. pap. 2.95 (*0-8167-2578-0*) Troll Assocs.

— Something New to Do. LC 85-14021. (Illus.). 48p. (Orig.). (J). (gr. 1-3). 1986. lib. bdg. 10.59 (*0-8167-0634-4*); pap. text ed. 3.50 (*0-8167-0635-2*) Troll Assocs.

— Wake up, Sam! LC 85-14115. (Illus.). 48p. (Orig.). (J). (gr. 1-3). 1986. lib. bdg. 10.59 (*0-8167-0580-1*); pap. text ed. 3.50 (*0-8167-0581-X*) Troll Assocs.

Michaels, Theresa. Fire & Sword. 1994. mass mkt. 3.99 (*0-373-28843-3*, 1-28843-0) Harlequin Bks.

— Once a Maverick. (Historical Ser.). 1995. mass mkt. 4.50 (*0-373-28876-X*, 1-28876-0) Harlequin Bks.

— Once an Outlaw. 1995. pap. 4.50 (*0-373-28896-4*, 1-28896-8) Harlequin Bks.

Michaels, Tilde. Rabbit Spring. LC 87-18107. (Illus.). 85p. (J). (gr. 2-6). 1989. 11.95 (*0-15-200568-4*, Gulliver Bks) HarBrace.

Michaels, Walter B. The Gold Standard & the Logic of Naturalism: American Literature at the Turn of the Century. 257p. (Orig.). (C). 1987. 42.00 (*0-520-05981-6*); pap. 13.00 (*0-520-05982-4*) U CA Pr.

— Our America: Nativism, Modernism & Pluralism. LC 95-12117. (Post-Contemporary Interventions Ser.). 1995. write for info. (*0-8223-1700-1*) Duke.

Michaels, Walter B. & Pease, Donald E., eds. The American Renaissance Reconsidered. LC 84-47940. (Selected Papers from the English Institute; 1982-83, New Ser.: No. 9). 231p. reprint ed. pap. 65.90 (*0-8357-8020-1*, 2034118) Bks Demand.

— The American Renaissance Reconsidered. LC 84-47940. (Selected Papers from the English Institute; 1982-83, New Ser.: No. 9). 208p. 1989. reprint ed. pap. text ed. 12.95 (*0-8018-3937-8*) Johns Hopkins.

Michaels, Wanda I., jt. auth. see Ross, Ronald G.

***Michaels, William.** What Falls Away Is Always. 420p. (Orig.). Date not set. pap. 12.95 (*0-7610-0211-1*) NW Pub.

Michaelsen, J. La Guerra Espiritual (Spirit Wars) (SPA.). Date not set. 1.99 (*1-56063-185-6*, 498125) Editorial Unilit.

Michaelsen, Johanna. The Beautiful Side of Evil. LC 82-82240. 224p. (Orig.). 1982. pap. 8.99 (*0-89081-322-1*) Harvest Hse.

— Like Lambs to the Slaughter: Your Child & the Occult. 224p. (Orig.). 1989. pap. 9.99 (*0-89081-617-4*) Harvest Hse.

— Like Lambs to the Slaughter: Your Child & the Occult. 224p. (Orig.). 1992. mass mkt. 5.99 (*0-89081-965-3*) Harvest Hse.

Michaelsen, William B. Creating the American Presidency, 1775-1789. 208p. (Orig.). (C). 1987. lib. bdg. 44.50 (*0-8191-5806-2*); pap. text ed. 22.50 (*0-8191-5807-0*) U Pr of Amer.

Michaelson, Connie O. & Greenberg, Michael R. New Jersey Toward the Year Two Thousand: Employment Projections. 190p. 1978. pap. text ed. 14.95 (*0-88285-051-2*) Transaction Pubs.

***Michaelson, Gerald A.** Building Bridges to Customers. LC 95-12448. (Management Master Ser.: Vol. 15). (Illus.). 50p. 1995. 15.95 (*1-56327-094-3*) Prod Press.

— Winning the Marketing War: A Field Manual for Business Leaders. 272p. 1995. pap. 12.95 (*1-883999-04-9*) Pressmark Intl.

— Winning the Marketing War: A Field Manual for Business Leaders. LC 86-11115. 280p. 1995. pap. 9.95 (*0-8191-5781-3*) U Pr of Amer.

Michaelson, Gerlad. Fifty Ways to Close a Sale (& Keep the Customer for Life) LC 94-7519. 1994. 12.95 (*0-688-11567-5*) Morrow.

Michaelson, Greg. An Introduction to Functional Programming Through Lambda Calculus. (International Computer Science Ser.). (Illus.). 320p. (C). 1989. text ed. 27.95 (*0-201-17812-5*) Addison-Wesley.

Michaelson, Herbert B. How to Write & Publish Engineering Papers & Reports. 3rd ed. 240p. 1990. pap. 19.95 (*0-89774-650-3*) Oryx Pr.

Michaelson, Holly J., jt. auth. see Michaelson, Sylvia J.

Michaelson, James B. Puppies As a New Pet. 1991. pap. 5.95 (*0-86622-616-8*) TFH Pubns.

Michaelson, Karen L., ed. And the Poor Get Children: Radical Perspectives on Population Dynamics. LC 81-38389. 272p. 1981. 16.00 (*0-85345-552-X*); pap. 8.50 (*0-85345-553-8*) Monthly Rev.

Michaelson, Karen L., et al. Childbirth in America: Anthropological Perspectives. LC 87-37490. 320p. 1988. text ed. 49.95 (*0-89789-136-8*, Bergin & Garvey) Greenwood.

Michaelson, L. W. On My Being Dead & Other Stories. LC 83-81251. (Orig.). 1984. pap. 4.00 (*0-913123-02-1*) Galileo.

Michaelson, Menachem. Zvi Ribak: A Jewish Artist. Grant, Murray, ed. LC 91-52500. (Illus.). 162p. 1991. 80.00 (*0-88734-615-4*) Players Pr.

***Michaelson, Mike.** Adventure to Contarrian. Orig. Title: Lightyears. 118p. (Orig.). (J). 1994. spiral bd. 16.95 (*0-9635636-0-2*) Humanform Robot.

— Chicago's Best-Kept Secrets. LC 90-63162. (Illus.). 300p. (Orig.). 1991. pap. 9.95 (*0-8442-9636-8*, Passport Bks) NTC Pub Grp.

— Exploring the Capitol: A Self-Guided Tour Through the Halls of Congress. 48p. 1992. pap. 7.95 (*1-881846-03-2*) C-Span.

— London's Best Kept Secrets: And Views on Old Favorites. 1991. pap. 9.95 (*0-8442-9638-4*, Passport Bks) NTC Pub Grp.

— New York's Best-Kept Secrets. 300p. 1994. pap. 9.95 (*0-8442-9637-6*, Passport Bks) NTC Pub Grp.

Michaelson, Peter. Secret Attachments: Exposing the Roots of Addictions & Compulsions. LC 92-83750. 208p. 1993. pap. 14.95 (*1-882631-26-9*) Prospect FL.

— See Your Way to Self-Esteem: An In-Depth Study of the Causes & Cures of Low Self-Esteem. LC 92-62627. 210p. (Orig.). 1993. pap. 14.95 (*1-882631-25-0*) Prospect FL.

Michaelson, Sandra. The Emotional Catering Service: The Quest for Emotional Independence. LC 93-83821. 264p. 1993. pap. 15.95 (*1-882631-27-7*) Prospect FL.

Michaelson, Sidney, jt. auth. see Morton, A. Q.

Michaelson, Sol M. & Lin, James C. Biological Effects & Health Implications of Radiofrequency Radiation. 688p. 1987. 135.00 (*0-306-41580-1*, Plenum Pr) Plenum.

Michaelson, Sylvia. Man of the Spirit "Jesus in the Tomb" (Illus.). 92p. 1988. pap. 3.50 (*0-9617005-3-X*) Ministering Angel.

Michaelson, Sylvia J. Angel in the Midst "the Science of Healing in the Human Garden" 1988. pap. 4.95 (*0-317-91059-0*) Ministering Angel.

— Aquarius. (Illus.). 1987. pap. 3.00 (*0-9617005-2-1*) Ministering Angel.

— Leviathan the Fire-Breathing Dragon & "The Dangers of Christian Evolution in the Church", 2 bks., Set. 1990. pap. 12.00 (*0-9617005-7-2*) Ministering Angel.

— Lucifer the Beautiful "Angel Worship" (Illus.). 85p. 1988. pap. 5.95 (*0-9617005-5-6*) Ministering Angel.

— Mystery Mothers "The Immortal Prehistoric Gene Pool in Eden" & "The Upright Alien Sperm", 2 bks., Set. (Illus.). 1990. pap. 10.00 (*0-9617005-8-0*) Ministering Angel.

— The New World Order: "The Mark (Dollar Sign) of the Beast" (Illus.). 178p. (Orig.). 1991. pap. text ed. 14.95 (*1-879456-00-1*) Ministering Angel.

Michaelson, Sylvia J. & Michaelson, Holly J. Jacob's Ladder, "DNA the Gate Beautiful" (Illus.). 270p. 1989. pap. text ed. 10.00 (*0-9617005-1-3*) Ministering Angel.

— The Wonders Have Been Found. (Illus.). 224p. 10.00 (*0-9617005-0-5*) Ministering Angel.

Michaely, M. Trade, Income Levels & Dependence. (Studies in International Economics: Vol. 8). 188p. 1984. 69.25 (*0-444-86771-6*, I-191-84, North Holland) Elsevier.

Michaely, Michael. Balance-of-Payments Adjustment Policies: Japan, Germany, & the Netherlands. (Occasional Papers: No. 106). 122p. 1968. reprint ed. 31.80 (*0-87014-492-8*) Natl Bur Econ Res.

— Israel. LC 75-323600. (Foreign Trade Regimes & Economic Development Ser.: No. 3). 239p. reprint ed. pap. 68.20 (*0-8357-7579-8*, 2056900) Bks Demand.

— Israel. (Special Conference Series on Foreign Trade Regimes & Economic Development: No. 3). 239p. 1975. reprint ed. 62.20 (*0-87014-503-7*) Natl Bur Econ Res.

— The Responsiveness of Demand Policies to Balance of Payments: Postwar Patterns. (Studies in International Economic Relations: No. 5). 317p. 1971. reprint ed. 82.50 (*0-87014-221-6*) Natl Bur Econ Res.

Michaely, Michael, jt. auth. see Papageorgiou, Demetrios.

Michaios, A. C. Global Report on Student Well-Being, Vol. II: Family, Friends, Living Partner & Self-Esteem. (Recent Research in Psychology Ser.). x, 288p. 1991. pap. 54.00 (*0-387-97666-3*) Spr-Verlag.

Michal, Elva. RX: Intentional Teaching Enthusiasm Caplets for the Independent Music Teacher. 192p. 1991. per. 15.95 (*0-8403-6489-X*) Kendall-Hunt.

***Michalak, Beth, et al.** High Performance Teamwork. 48p. (Orig.). 1994. pap. text ed. 5.95 (*0-87425-991-6*) Human Res Dev Pr.

Michalak, Donald F. Competing Conceptions of American Foreign Policy. (C). 1991. text ed. 35.50 (*0-06-044431-2*) HarpCollege.

Michalak, Donald F. & Yager, Edwin G. Making the Training Process Work. LC 78-17907. (Continuing Management Education Ser.). (C). 1979. 18.95 (*0-06-044429-0*) HarpCollege.

Michalak, Joseph M., jt. auth. see Fiske, Edward B.

Michalak, Laurence O. & Salacuse, Jeswald W., eds. Social Legislation in the Contemporary Middle East. LC 86-18613. (Research Ser.: No. 64). (Illus.). xii, 381p. (C). 1986. pap. 15.50 (*0-87725-164-9*) U of Cal IAS.

Michalak, Patricia S. Herbs. LC 92-32758. (Rodale's Successful Organic Gardening Ser.). 1993. 24.95 (*0-87596-557-1*); pap. 14.95 (*0-87596-558-X*) Rodale Pr Inc.

Michalak, Patricia S. & Gilkeson, Linda A. Controlling Pests & Diseases. LC 93-6103. (Rodale's Successful Organic Gardening Ser.). 1994. 24.95 (*0-87596-611-X*); 14.95 (*0-87596-612-8*) Rodale Pr Inc.

Michalak, Patricia S. & Peterson, Cass. Vegetables. LC 92-31890. (Rodale's Successful Organic Gardening Ser.). (Illus.). 1993. 24.95 (*0-87596-563-6*); pap. 14.95 (*0-87596-564-4*) Rodale Pr Inc.

Michalczyk, John J. Andre Malraux's Espoir: The Propaganda-Art Film & the Spanish Civil War. LC 77-7308. (Romance Monographs: No. 27). 1977. 25.00 (*84-399-6811-6*) Romance.

— Costa-Gavras: The Political Fiction Film. (Illus.). 296p. 1984. 48.50 (*0-87982-029-2*) Art Alliance.

— The French Literary Filmmakers. LC 78-75171. (Illus.). 230p. 1980. 38.50 (*0-87982-027-6*) Art Alliance.

— The Italian Political Filmakers. LC 84-48807. (Illus.). 328p. 1986. 65.00 (*0-8386-3250-5*) Fairleigh Dickinson.

— Medicine, Ethics & the Third Reich: Historical & Contemporary Issues. LC 94-25916. (Illus.). 240p. (Orig.). 1994. pap. 19.95 (*1-55612-752-9*, LL1752) Sheed & Ward MO.

Michalek, Boleslaw & Turaj, Frank. The Modern Cinema of Poland. LC 87-45372. (Illus.). 224p. (Orig.). 1988. 35.00 (*0-253-33813-1*); pap. 12.95 (*0-253-20481-X*, MB-481) Ind U Pr.

Michalenko, Seraphim, jt. auth. see Flynn, Vinny.

Michalenko, Seraphim, tr. see Kowalska, Faustina.

Michalenko, Sophia. Mercy My Mission: Life of Sister Faustina H. Kowalska, S.M.D.M. Congregation of Marians of the Immaculate Conception, ed. LC 87-90692. 264p. 1987. pap. 10.95 (*0-944203-02-7*) Marian Pr.

Michalewicz, Z. S., tr. see Bork, B. A., ed.

Michalewicz, Zbigniew. Genetic Algorithms Plus Data Structures Equals Evolution Programs. Loveland, D. W. et al, eds. LC 92-19925. (Symbolic Computation - Artificial Intelligence Ser.). xiv, 250p. 1993. 49.00 (*0-387-55387-8*) Spr-Verlag.

— Genetic Algorithms Plus Data Structures Equals Evolution Programs. 2nd expanded ed. LC 94-25886. 1994. 39.00 (*0-387-58090-5*) Spr-Verlag.

— Statistical & Scientific Databases. (Computers & Their Applications Ser.). 1991. 59.00 (*0-13-850652-3*, 540503) P-H.

Michalewicz, Zbigniew, ed. Statistical & Scientific Database Management. (Lecture Notes in Computer Science Ser.: Vol. 420). v, 256p. 1990. pap. 32.70 (*0-387-52342-1*) Spr-Verlag.

Michalik, K., tr. see Bezwinska, J. & Czech, Danuta, eds.

Michalik, Wieslaw, jt. ed. see Gibb, Richard.

Michalk, D., jt. ed. see Huxtable, R.

Michalka, Wolfgang, jt. auth. see Lee, Marshall M.

Michalko, Michael. Thinkertoys: A Handbook of Creativity in Business. (Illus.). 320p. (Orig.). 1991. pap. 17.95 (*0-89815-408-1*) Ten Speed Pr.

— Thinkpak. 1994. pap. 11.95 (*0-89815-607-6*) Ten Speed Pr.

Michalkow, Janina. Nicholas Poussin. 164p. (GER.). 1980. 99.00 (*0-317-57329-2*, Pub. by Collets) St Mut.

Michalopoulos, Andre. Homer. (World Authors Ser.). 224p. 1966. text ed. 22.95 (*0-8057-2432-X*, Pub. by Royal Botanic Garden UK) Macmillan.

Michalopoulos, Andre, tr. see Averoff-Tossizza, Evangelos.

Michalopoulos, Constantine. Trade Issues in the New Independent States. LC 93-22695. (Studies of Economics in Transformation Paper: No. 7). 39p. 1993. 6.95 (*0-8213-2483-7*, 12483) World Bank.

Michalopoulos, Constantine & Tarr, David. Trade & Payments Arrangements for States of the Former U. S. S. R. LC 92-31863. (Studies of Economies in Transformation: No. 2). 53p. 1992. 6.95 (*0-8213-2260-5*, 12260) World Bank.

— Trade & Payments Arrangements for States of the Former U. S. S. R. (Studies of Economies in Transformation: No. 2R). 49p. (RUS.). 1993. 6.95 (*0-8213-2422-5*, 12422) World Bank.

***Michalopoulos, Constantine & Tarr, David, eds.** Trade in the New Independent States. LC 94-35297. (Studies of Economies in Transformation: No. 15). 1994. write for info. (*0-8213-3077-2*) World Bank.

Michalos, Alex C. Global Report on Student Well-Being: Employment, Finances, Housing & Transportation. (Recent Research in Psychology Ser.: Vol. 3). x, 306p. 1992. pap. 54.00 (*0-387-97948-4*) Spr-Verlag.

— Global Report on Student Well-Being: Religion, Education, Recreation & Health. (Recent Research in Psychology Ser.: Vol. 4). x, 304p. 1992. pap. 54.00 (*0-387-97949-2*) Spr-Verlag.

— Global Report on Student Well-Being, Vol. One: Life Satisfaction & Happiness. (Recent Research in Psychology Ser.). (Illus.). x, 253p. 1991. pap. 39.00 (*0-387-97460-1*) Spr-Verlag.

— North American Social Report: Economics, Religion, & Morality, Vol. 5. 1982. pap. text ed. 70.00 (*90-277-1358-8*) Kluwer Ac.

— North American Social Report, Vol. 1: A Comparative Study of the Quality of Life in Canada & Theusa from 1964 to 1974: Foundations, Populations & Health. 280p. 1980. pap. text ed. 56.50 (*90-277-1058-9*) Kluwer Ac.

— North American Social Report, Vol. 3: A Comparative Study of the Quality of Life in Canada & the U. S. A. from 1964 to 1974. 212p. 1981. pap. text ed. 56.50 (*90-277-1257-3*) Kluwer Ac.

— A Pragmatic Approach to Business Ethics. LC 94-45244. 248p. 1995. text ed. 36.95 (*0-8039-7084-6*); pap. text ed. 17.95 (*0-8039-7085-4*) Sage.

Michalos, Alex C., ed. North American Social Report, Vol. 2: A Comparative Study of the Quality of Life in Canada & the U. S. A. from 1964 to 1974: Crime, Justice, & Politics. 244p. 1980. pap. text ed. 56.50 (*90-277-1085-6*) Kluwer Ac.

Michalos, Alex C., ed. see Philosophy of Science Association Staff.

Michalove, Ed, jt. auth. see Delson, Donn.

Michalowicz, Jerzy, tr. see Kahane, David.

Michalowicz, Jerzy, tr. see Tory, Avraham.

Michalowski, Helen, jt. ed. see Cooney, Robert.

Michalowski, P., tr. see Amsterdamski, Stefan.

Michalowski, Piotr. The Lamentation over the Destruction of Sumer & Ur. LC 88-33386. (Mesopotamian Civilizations Ser.: Vol. 1). (Illus.). xvi, 219p. (C). 1989. text ed. 36.50 (*0-931464-43-9*) Eisenbrauns.

Michalowski, Piotr, tr. see Reiner, Erica, ed.

Michalowski, Radoslaw L., ed. Cold Regions Engineering. 408p. 1989. 40.00 (*0-87262-680-6*) Am Soc Civil Eng.

Michalowski, Raymond J. Order, Law & Crime. 500p. (C). 1984. pap. text ed. write for info. (*0-07-554450-4*) McGraw.

Michalowski, Stefan, jt. auth. see Harvey, John.

Michals, Duane. Eros & Thanatos. limited ed. (Illus.). 64p. 1992. 150.00 (*0-944092-21-7*); 45.00 (*0-944092-20-9*) Twin Palms Pub.

— Sleep & Dreams. (Illus.). 64p. 1984. pap. 11.95 (*0-912810-46-7*) Lustrum Pr.

— Upside down, Inside Out, & Backwards. 80p. (J). Date not set. pap. 19.95 (*0-685-68802-X*) Sonny Boy Bks.

Michalsen, Karen, ed. see Stoliar, Marda.

***Michalski.** Complete Book of Cocktails & Punches. 1995. 12.98 (*1-56138-477-1*) Courage Bks.

— Over Kries. (C). 1990. lib. bdg. 34.95 (*0-226-52316-0*) U Ch Pr.

***Michalski, Anna & Wallace, Helen.** The European Community: The Challenge of Enlargement. 1993. pap. 15.95 (*0-905031-56-3*) Brookings.

Michalski, L., et al. Temperature Measurement. (Series in Measurement Science & Technology: No. 1824). 514p. 1991. text ed. 159.00 (*0-471-92229-3*) Wiley.

Michalski, Ryszard & Tecuci, George, eds. Machine Learning: A Multi-Strategy Approach, Vol. 4. 500p. (Orig.). (C). 1993. 59.95 (*1-55860-251-8*) Morgan Kaufmann.

Michalski, Ryszard, jt. ed. see Kodratoff, Yves.

Michalski, Ryszard S., ed. Multistrategy Learning. LC 93-22647. (International Series in Engineering & Computer Science, VLSI, Computer Architecture, & Digital Screen Processing). 166p. (C). 1993. lib. bdg. 105.00 (*0-7923-9374-0*) Kluwer Ac.

Michalski, Ryszard S., et al, eds. Machine Learning: An Artificial Intelligence Approach, Vol. 1. LC 86-2953. (Illus.). 572p. 1986. reprint ed. 49.95 (*0-934613-09-5*) Morgan Kaufmann.

— Machine Learning: An Artificial Intelligence Approach, Vol. II. LC 82-10654. (Illus.). 738p. 1986. text ed. 49.95 (*0-934613-00-1*) Morgan Kaufmann.

Michalski, Sergiusz. The Reformation & the Visual Arts: The Protestant Image Question in Western & Eastern Europe. LC 92-13311. (Christianity & Society in the Modern World Ser.). 272p. 1993. 49.95 (*0-415-06512-7*, A7874) Routledge.

Michalski, Tilman, jt. auth. see Michalski, Ute.

Michalski, Ute & Michalski, Tilman. Wind Crafts. LC 89-49553. (Craft Bks.). (Illus.). 64p. (J). 1990. 15.45 (*0-516-09258-8*); pap. 8.95 (*0-516-49258-6*) Childrens.

Michalski, W., ed. The Future of Industrial Societies: Problems, Prospects, Solutions. 313p. 1978. lib. bdg. 74.50 (*90-286-0257-7*) Kluwer Ac.

Michalson, Gordon E., Jr. Fallen Freedom: Kant on Radical Evil & Moral Regeneration. 192p. (C). 1990. 54.95 (*0-521-38397-8*) Cambridge U Pr.

— Lessing's "Ugly Ditch" A Study of Theology & History. LC 84-42991. 224p. (C). 1985. 27.50 (*0-271-00385-5*) Pa St U Pr.

Michalson, Greg, ed. For Our Beloved Country: American War Diaries from the Revolution to the Persian Gulf. LC 93-2495. 1994. 27.50 (*0-87113-549-3*) Grove-Atltic.

Michalson, Karen. Victorian Fantasy Literature: Literary Battles with Church & Empire. LC 90-19302. (Studies in British Literature: Vol. 10). 308p. 1990. lib. bdg. 99.95 (*0-88946-378-6*) E Mellen.

Michalson, Linda, jt. ed. see Lewis, Michael.

Michalun, M. Varinia, jt. auth. see Michalun, Natalia.

Michalun, Natalia & Michalun, M. Varinia. Skin Care & Cosmetic Ingredients Dictionary. LC 93-33822. 328p. 1994. pap. 23.95 (*1-56253-125-5*) Milady Pub.

Michard, G., jt. auth. see Allegre, C. J.

Michard, Jean-Guy. The Reign of the Dinosaurs. (Discoveries Ser.). (Illus.). 144p. 1992. pap. 12.95 (*0-8109-2808-6*) Abrams.

Michard, L., jt. auth. see Lagarde, A.

Michas, jt. auth. see Reynolds.

Michaud, David L., jt. auth. see Macdonald, John M.

Michaud, Doris, jt. auth. see Michaud, Terry.

Michaud, E. Guillaume de Champeaux et les Ecoles de Paris. 2nd ed. (Medieval Studies Reprint Ser.). (FRE.). reprint ed. lib. bdg. 45.00 (*0-697-00011-7*) Irvington.

Michaud, Ellen, et al. Boost Your Brainpower. 1994. 9.98 (*1-56731-026-5*, MJF Bks) Fine Comms.

— Listen to Your Body: A Head-to-Toe Guide to More Than 400 Common Symptoms, Their Causes & Best Treatments. LC 87-26402. 544p. 1990. pap. 14.95 (*0-87857-918-4*, 05-358-1) Rodale Pr Inc.

— Total Health for Women: From Allergies & Back Pain to Overweight & PMS, the Best Preventive & Curative Advice for Over 100 Women's Health Problems. LC 95-9810. 1995. 27.95 (*0-87596-271-8*) Rodale Pr Inc.

Michaud, G. Guide France. 14.95 (*0-685-36082-2*) Fr & Eur.

An Asterisk (*) at the beginning of an entry indicates that the title is appearing in BIP for the first time.

— Nouveau Guide France: Manuel De Civilisation Francaise. (Hachette Ser.). (FRE.). pap. 26.95 (*2-01-015387-1*) Schoenhof.
— Nouveau Guide France: Manuel de Civilization Francaise. write for info. (*0-318-63623-9*) Fr & Eur.
— Nouveau Guide France: Manuel de Civilization Francaise. 2nd rev. ed. 1992. 34.95 (*0-8288-7899-4*, F695) Fr & Eur.
Michaud, G. & Tutukov, A., eds. Evolution of Stars: The Photospheric Abundance Connection. (C). 1991. lib. bdg. 127.00 (*0-7923-1127-2*); pap. text ed. 59.00 (*0-7923-1128-0*) Kluwer Ac.
Michaud, Gene, jt. ed. see Dittmar, Linda.
Michaud, J., ed. History of Mysore under Hyder Ali & Tippoo Sultan. Menon, Raman V. K., tr. 290p. 1986. reprint ed. 22.00 (*0-8364-1733-X*, Pub. by Manohar II) S Asia.
Michaud, Joseph F. Bibliotheque des croisades, 4 vols., Set. LC 76-29846. (FRE.). reprint ed. 325.00 (*0-404-15450-6*) AMS Pr.
— History of the Crusades, 3 Vols. Robson, W., tr. LC 72-172729. reprint ed. 195.00 (*0-404-04320-8*) AMS Pr.
Michaud, Joy & Hilverson, Karen. The Saturn-Pluto Phenomenon. 208p. 1993. pap. 11.95 (*0-87728-722-8*) Weiser.
***Michaud, Leon A.** The Legend of Simon of Cyrene. 224p. (Orig.). 1995. pap. 15.95 (*1-885001-07-X*) Via Press.
— Simon Was Black. 1992. 15.95 (*0-533-10167-0*) Vantage.
Michaud, Marc, ed. see Smith, Clark A.
Michaud, Marc A. & Joshi, S. T. Necronomicon Press: The First Ten, An Index & Brief History. (Orig.). 1986. pap. 1.95 (*0-940884-11-9*) Necronomicon.
***Michaud, Margaret A.** Dead End: Homeless Teenagers: A Multi-Service Approach. (Illus.). 137p. (Orig.). 1988. pap. 14.95 (*0-920490-81-6*) Temeron Bks.
Michaud, Michael A. Reaching for the High Frontier: The American Pro-Space Movement, 1972-84. LC 86-91456. 462p. 1986. text ed. 59.95 (*0-275-92151-4*, C2151, Praeger Pubs) Greenwood.
Michaud, Michael G. Cardinal Winds. limited ed. LC 92-81452. (Illus.). 28p. (Orig.). (C). 1992. 24.00 (*0-9620574-6-0*) MGM Pr.
— Flames of Hate in the City of Angels. (Illus.). 20p. (Orig.). (C). 1992. pap. 4.95 (*0-9620574-7-9*) MGM Pr.
— Giraffes on Horseback Salad. (Illus.). 48p. (Orig.). (C). 1994. pap. 7.95 (*1-882585-01-1*) MGM Pr.
— Giraffes on Horseback Salad. deluxe limited ed. (Illus.). 48p. (Orig.). (C). 1994. 40.00 (*1-882585-02-X*) MGM Pr.
— The Land of Open Hands. (Illus.). 20p. (Orig.). (C). 1991. pap. 25.00 (*0-9620574-4-4*) MGM Pr.
— Moribundo. LC 92-96944. (Illus.). 32p. (Orig.). (C). 1992. pap. 9.95 (*0-9620574-9-5*) MGM Pr.
— Moribundo. deluxe limited ed. LC 92-96944. (Illus.). 32p. (Orig.). (C). 1992. 50.00 (*0-9620574-8-7*) MGM Pr.
— Silly Me. LC 89-92010. 123p. (Orig.). 1989. pap. 8.95 (*0-9620574-1-X*) MGM Pr.
— Uncle Mike's Totally Cool Way Excellent Tasty Sweet & Real Fattening Heirloom Dessert Recipes in No Particular Order & Some Candy Recipes Too, Cookbook. LC 93-80824. (Illus.). 165p. (Orig.). (C). 1993. spiral bd. 25.00 (*1-882585-00-3*) MGM Pr.
— The World According to Natasha. (Illus.). 28p. (Orig.). (C). 1991. pap. 20.00 (*0-9620574-3-6*) MGM Pr.
— The World of Mirth. 31p. (Orig.). 1988. pap. 5.95 (*0-9620574-0-1*) MGM Pr.
Michaud, Michael G., ed. see Wood, Beatrice.
***Michaud, Patrick A.** Accident Prevention & OSHA Compliance. LC 94-44946. 320p. 1995. 65.00 (*1-56670-150-3*, L1150) Lewis Pubs.
Michaud, Paul J., jt. auth. see Norian, Nicole A.
Michaud, Regis. The American Novel To-Day: A Social & Psychological Study. LC 77-2571. 1977. reprint ed. fiche write for info. (*0-8371-9605-1*, Greenwood Pr); reprint ed. text ed. 59.75 (*0-8371-9553-5*, MIAN, Greenwood Pr); reprint ed. fiche write for info. (*0-8371-9606-X*, Greenwood Pr) Greenwood.
— The American Novel To-Day: A Social & Psychological Study. (BCL1-PS American Literature Ser.). 293p. 1992. reprint ed. lib. bdg. 79.00 (*0-7812-6641-6*) Rprt Serv.
— Emerson, the Enraptured Yankee. Boas, George, tr. LC 74-5374. reprint ed. 42.50 (*0-404-11538-1*) AMS Pr.
— Modern Thought & Literature in France. LC 67-23248. (Essay Index Reprint Ser.). 1977. 18.95 (*0-8369-0707-8*) Ayer.
Michaud, Roland & Michaud, Sabrina. Afghanistan. LC 89-51869. (Illus.). 132p. 1990. reprint ed. pap. 17.95 (*0-500-27393-6*) Thames Hudson.
Michaud, Rosemary. Sherlock Holmes & the Somerset Hunt. 200p. 1993. 25.00 (*0-86025-276-0*, Pub. by Ian Henry Pubns UK) Empire Pub Srvs.
Michaud, Sabrina, jt. auth. see Michaud, Roland.
Michaud, Sabrina, jt. auth. see Roland.
Michaud, Scott. The Life & Times of Gustav Likan. (Illus.). 192p. 1994. 49.95 (*1-880092-15-8*) Bright Bks TX.
Michaud, Stephen G. Lethal Shadow: The Inside Story of America's Most Dangerous Criminal. 360p. (Orig.). 1994. pap. 5.99 (*0-451-40530-7*, Onyx) NAL-Dutton.
Michaud, Stephen G. & Aynesworth, Hugh. If You Love Me, You Will Do My Will: The Stranger-than-Fiction Saga of a Trappist Monk, a Texas Widow, & Her Half-Billion Dollar Fortune. (Illus.). 1990. 19.95 (*0-393-02762-7*) Norton.
— Murderers Among Us: Unsolved Homicides, Mysterious Deaths & Killers at Large. 352p. 1991. pap. 4.99 (*0-451-17057-1*, Sig) NAL-Dutton.
— The Only Living Witness: A True Account of Homicidal Insanity. 1990. pap. 5.99 (*0-451-16372-9*, Sig) NAL-Dutton.
— Ted Bundy: Conversations with a Killer. 1990. pap. 5.99 (*0-451-16355-9*, Sig) NAL-Dutton.
Michaud, Susan, ed. see Lovecraft, H. P.
Michaud, Terry. How to Make & Sell Quality Teddy Bears. 1994. pap. 12.95 (*0-87588-416-4*) Hobby Hse.
— Teddy Tales: Bears Repeating, Too! (Illus.). 112p. 1989. 19.95 (*0-87588-349-4*) Hobby Hse.
Michaud, Terry & Michaud, Doris. Bears Repeating. (Illus.). 96p. 1985. 14.95 (*0-87588-263-3*, 3119) Hobby Hse.
— Contemporary Teddy Bear Price Guide: Artist & Manufacturers. 160p. 1992. pap. 16.95 (*0-87588-398-2*) Hobby Hse.
Michaud, Thomas C. Foot Orthoses & Other Forms of Conservative Foot Care. (Illus.). 270p. 1993. 80.00 (*0-683-05974-2*) Williams & Wilkins.
Michaudon, A., et al, eds. Nuclear Fission & Neutron-Induced Fission Cross-Sections. LC 80-41822. (Neutron Physics & Nuclear Data in Science & Technology Ser.: Vol. 1). (Illus.). 270p. 1981. 118.00 (*0-08-026125-6*, Pub. by Pergamon Repr UK) Franklin.
Michauo, Kathryn, ed. see Palazzolo, Carl R.
Michaux, jt. auth. see Pound.
Michaux, Agnes. Dictionnaire Misogyne. 1993. pap. 45.00 (*0-7859-5635-2*, 2709612585) Fr & Eur.
Michaux, Francois A. Travels to the West of the Allegheny Mountains in the States of Ohio, Kentucky & Tennessee. 1993. reprint ed. lib. bdg. 89.00 (*0-7812-5390-X*) Rprt Serv.
Michaux, Henri. Aileurs. (FRE.). 1986. pap. 11.95 (*0-7859-2802-2*) Fr & Eur.
— Barbare en Asie. (Imaginaire Ser.). 238p. (FRE.). 1986. pap. 15.95 (*2-07-070622-2*) Schoenhof.
— A Barbarian in Asia. Beach, Sylvia, tr. LC 86-5362. (Revived Modern Classics Ser.). 192p. 1986. reprint ed. pap. 7.95 (*0-8112-0991-1*, NDP622) New Directions.
— By Surprise. Hough, Randolph, tr. 112p. (Orig.). 1987. pap. 5.95 (*0-937815-05-5*) Hanuman Bks.
— Connaissance par les Gouffre. (FRE.). 1988. pap. 14.95 (*0-7859-2811-1*) Fr & Eur.
— Darkness Moves: An Henri Michaux Anthology, 1927-1984. Ball, David, tr. LC 92-12925. 1994. 30.00 (*0-520-07231-6*) U CA Pr.
— Deplacement Degagements: Spared, Displaced. Constantine, David & Constantine, Helen, trs. (Contemporary French Poets Ser.: No. 3). 192p. (ENG & FRE.). 1993. pap. 21.00 (*1-85224-135-7*, Pub. by Bloodaxe Bks UK) Dufour.
— Epreuves Exorcismes, 1940-44. (FRE.). 1989. pap. 10.95 (*0-7859-2815-4*) Fr & Eur.
— Face aux Verroux. (FRE.). 1992. pap. 14.95 (*0-7859-3383-2*) Fr & Eur.
— Ideograms in China. deluxe limited ed. Sobin, Gustaf, tr. LC 84-1006. 40p. 1984. 150.00 (*0-8112-0910-5*) New Directions.
— Meidosems: Poems & Lithographs. Jackson, Elizabeth R., tr. & intro. by. LC 92-27205. (Illus.). 184p. (Orig.). 1993. pap. 24.95 (*0-939952-13-0*); pap. write for info. (*0-939952-14-9*) Moving Parts.
— Miserable Miracle; La Mescaline. (FRE.). 1991. pap. 10.95 (*0-7859-3381-6*) Fr & Eur.
— Plume; Lointain Interieur. (FRE.). 1985. pap. 14.95 (*0-7859-3379-4*) Fr & Eur.
— Selected Writings of Henri Michaux. Ellmann, Richard, tr. LC 68-25545. (ENG & FRE.). 1968. 10.95 (*0-8112-0105-8*, NDP264) New Directions.
— La Vie dans les Plis. (FRE.). 1989. pap. 16.95 (*0-7859-2822-7*) Fr & Eur.
Michaux, Henri, et al. Translations: Experiments in Reading. Wellman, Don et al, eds. Simic, Charles et al, trs. (Illus.). 272p. (Orig.). 1983. pap. 12.00 (*0-942030-03-6*) O ARS.
Michaux, J. P. French-English - English-French Dictionary of Machine Tools. 179p. pap. 27.00 (*2-7080-0444-1*) IBD Ltd.
***Michaux, Jean-Pierre.** Dictionnaire de l'Outillage et de la Machine Outil: French-English, English-French. (ENG & FRE.). 1976. pap. 22.95 (*0-7859-7928-X*, 2708004441) Fr & Eur.
— Dictionnaire Selectif des arbres, des Plantes et des Fleurs. 1979. write for info. (*0-7859-7929-8*, 2-7080-0463-8) Fr & Eur.
Michaux, Louis A. Christmas: Make-Believe Or Discovery. Davies, Evan, ed. LC 88-92481. (Illus.). 65p. (Orig.). 1989. pap. 7.50 (*0-317-93408-2*) L A Michaux.
Micheals, Lee, ed. Briers Way. 69p. (C). 1990. 30.00 (*0-7223-2424-3*, Pub. by A H S Ltd UK) St Mut.
Micheaux, Oscar. The Case of Mrs. Wingate. 6th ed. LC 73-18593. (Illus.). reprint ed. 69.50 (*0-404-11404-0*) AMS Pr.
— Conquest: The Story of a Negro Pioneer. LC 75-89391. (Black Heritage Library Collection). 1977. 30.95 (*0-8369-8632-6*) Ayer.
— Conquest: The Story of a Negro Pioneer. 15.00 (*1-56675-019-9*) Mnemosyne.
— The Conquest: The Story of a Negro Pioneer. (Illus.). xxi, 332p. 1994. pap. 9.95 (*0-8032-8209-5*, Bison Books) U of Nebr Pr.
— The Homesteader: A Novel. (Illus.). ix, 533p. 1994. pap. 12.95 (*0-8032-8208-7*, Bison Books) U of Nebr Pr.
— The Masquerade: An Historical Novel. LC 73-18595. reprint ed. 49.50 (*0-404-11406-7*) AMS Pr.
— The Wind from Nowhere. LC 72-4810. (Black Heritage Library Collection). 1977. reprint ed. 35.95 (*0-8369-9109-5*) Ayer.
***Micheels.** Detectives. 1995. mass mkt. 5.50 (*0-312-95392-5*) St Martin.
Micheels, Peter A. The Detectives: Their Toughest Cases in Their Own Words. (Illus.). 288p. 1994. 21.95 (*0-312-09785-9*) St Martin.
Michejda, Christopher J., jt. ed. see Loeppky, Richard N.
Michel. Collecting Yelloware. 128p. 1992. pap. 16.95 (*0-89145-521-3*) Collector Bks.
Michel, ed. Histoire de l'Art, 8 tomes en 15. write for info. (*0-8288-7900-1*) Fr & Eur.
— Histoire de l'Art, 8 tomes en 15, Set. 175.00 (*0-685-36014-8*) Fr & Eur.
Michel & Company Staff. Happy Ever After! 1994. 6.95 (*0-8362-4714-0*) Andrews & McMeel.
— Happy Wishes Birthday Girl. 1994. 4.95 (*0-8362-3083-3*) Andrews & McMeel.
— A Mother Knows Just What to Do. (Illus.). 32p. 1995. 6.95 (*0-8362-4738-8*) Andrews & McMeel.
— Small Lullabies. 1994. 4.95 (*0-8362-3082-5*) Andrews & McMeel.
— Two Little Ladies. 1994. 6.95 (*0-8362-4715-9*) Andrews & McMeel.
Michel, A., jt. auth. see Miller, Richard.
Michel, A. N., et al. Associative Memory Using Artificial Neural Networks. 300p. 1995. text ed. 74.00 (*981-02-1581-9*) World Scientific Pub.
***Michel, A. R.** Clinical Biology of Sodium: The Physiology & Pathophysiology of Sodium in Mammals. LC 95-2407. 1995. write for info. (*0-08-840842-6*, Pergamon Pr) Elsevier.
Michel, Aime. Flying Saucers & the Straight-Line Mystery. LC 58-8787. (Illus.). 1958. 42.95 (*0-87599-077-0*) S G Phillips.
Michel, Albert, jt. auth. see Loth, Bernard.
Michel Albin Staff. Dictionnaire National des Communes de France. 40th ed. 1342p. (FRE.). 1992. 150.00 (*0-8288-6917-0*, 2226057242) Fr & Eur.
Michel, Allen & Shaked, Israel. The Complete Guide to a Successful Leveraged Buyout. 300p. 1987. text ed. 72.00 (*0-87094-891-1*) Irwin Prof Pubng.
Michel, Aloys A. The Indus Rivers: A Study of the Effects of Partition. LC 67-13444. 624p. reprint ed. pap. 177.90 (*0-317-29282-X*, 2022021) Bks Demand.
Michel, Andreas, tr. see Lyotard, Jean-Francois.
Michel, Andree. The Modernization of North African Families in the Paris Area. LC 72-184752. (New Babylon Studies in the Social Sciences: No. 16). (Illus.). 387p. (Orig.). 1974. pap. text ed. 34.75 (*90-279-7312-1*) Mouton.
Michel, Anthony M. & Herget, Charles J. Applied Algebra & Functional Analysis. LC 93-15006. Orig. Title: Mathematical Foundations in Engineering & Science. (Illus.). 496p. 1993. reprint ed. pap. 10.95 (*0-486-67598-X*) Dover.
***Michel, Anthony N. & Kaining Wang.** Qualitative Theory for Dynamical Systems. LC 94-35418. (Pure & Applied Mathematics Ser.: Vol. 186). 450p. 1994. 150.00 (*0-8247-9420-6*) Dekker.
Michel, Anthony N., jt. auth. see Liu, Derong.
Michel, Barbara N., jt. auth. see Michel, John L.
Michel-Beyerle, M. E., ed. Antennas & Reaction Centers of Photosynthetic Bacteria: Structure, Interactions & Dynamics. (Chemical Physics Ser.: Vol. 42). (Illus.). 384p. 1985. 71.00 (*0-387-16154-6*) Spr-Verlag.
— Reaction Centers of Photosynthetic Bacteria: Feldafing-II-Meeting. (Biophysics Ser.: Vol. 6). (Illus.). xiv, 469p. 1991. 110.00 (*0-387-53420-2*) Spr-Verlag.
Michel, C. Recueil D'inscriptions Grecques: Supplements, 1912-1927. 227p. 1976. 25.00 (*0-89005-110-0*) Ares.
Michel, C. Charles, jt. ed. see Renkin, Eugene M.
Michel, Charles. Recueil d'Inscriptions Grecques. (Subsidia Epigraphica Ser.). xxvi, 1000p. (GER.). 1976. reprint ed. write for info. (*3-487-05634-8*, Pub. by Georg Olms GW) Lubrecht & Cramer.
— Recueil d'Inscriptions Grecques: Supplement. (Subsidia Epigraphica Ser.). 106p. (GER.). 1976. reprint ed. write for info. (*3-487-06140-6*, Pub. by Georg Olms GW) Lubrecht & Cramer.
***Michel, Christian.** Kleines Psychologisches Woerterbuch. (GER.). Date not set. 39.95 (*0-7859-8368-6*, 3451040549) Fr & Eur.
Michel, Claude, jt. auth. see Vurpas, Anne-Marie.
Michel, D. J., ed. see Topical Conference on Ferritic Alloys for Use in Nuclear Energy Technologies Staff.
Michel Design Staff, illus. Age Before Beauty. (Petites Ser.). 80p. 1991. 4.95 (*0-88088-727-3*) Peter Pauper.
— Joy. (Petites Ser.). 1991. 4.95 (*0-88088-731-1*) Peter Pauper.
— Nature Lover's Notebook. (Journals). 96p. 1991. 9.95 (*0-88088-705-2*) Peter Pauper.
— Thanks. (Petites Ser.). 80p. 1991. 4.95 (*0-88088-743-5*) Peter Pauper.
Michel, Dieter, jt. auth. see Engelhardt, Gunter.
Michel, Diethelm. Untersuchungen zur Eigenart des Buches Qohelet. (Beiheft zur Zeitschrift fuer die Alttestamentliche Wissenschaft Ser.: No. 183). vii, 329p. (C). 1989. lib. bdg. 95.40 (*3-11-012161-1*) De Gruyter.
Michel, Donald E. Music Therapy: An Introduction, Including Music in Special Education. 2nd ed. (Illus.). 152p. (C). 1985. 24.95x (*0-398-05063-5*) C C Thomas.
Michel, Donald E. & Jones, Janet L. Music for Developing Speech & Language Skills in Children: A Guide for Parents & Therapists. (MMB Horizon Ser.: No. 9). 56p. (Orig.). 1991. pap. 9.95 (*0-918812-69-0*, ST 233) MMB Music.
Michel, Edouard. Flemish Painting in the Seventeenth Century. (Illus.). 45p. 1939. lib. bdg. 35.00 (*0-8288-3981-6*) Fr & Eur.
Michel, Emile. Rembrandt, 2 vols. 1972. 200.00 (*0-8490-0943-X*) Gordon Pr.
Michel, Ernest. Promises to Keep. LC 93-13550. 1993. 22.00 (*0-9623032-4-0*) Barricade Bks.
Michel, F. Vocabulary of Cooking Utensils. 39p. (ENG & FRE.). 1990. pap. 29.95 (*0-8288-9379-9*) Fr & Eur.
Michel, F. Curtis. Theory of Neutron Star Magnetospheres. (Theoretical Astrophysics Ser.). (Illus.). 576p. 1990. lib. bdg. 79.95 (*0-226-52330-6*); pap. text ed. 34.95 (*0-226-52331-4*) U Ch Pr.
Michel, France. English - French Vocabulary of Electronic Data Interchange. 37p. (ENG & FRE.). 1991. pap. 19.95 (*0-8288-9406-X*) Fr & Eur.
Michel, France, jt. auth. see Boivin, Gilles.
Michel, Francois. Water. LC 92-9715. (Illus.). (YA). 1993. write for info. (*0-688-11427-X*) Lothrop.
Michel, Francois, comp. Stendhal Fichier, 3 Vols, Set. 1970. lib. bdg. 330.00 (*0-8161-0583-9*, Hall Library) G K Hall.
Michel, Freda. A Curious Proposal. LC 68-21699. 224p. 1980. pap. 1.75 (*0-449-50071-3*, Coventry) Fawcett.
— The Machiavellian Marquess. 1979. pap. 1.75 (*0-449-50014-4*, Coventry) Fawcett.
Michel, Genevieve. The Rulers of Tikal: An Historical Reconstruction & Field Guide to the Stelae. (Illus.). 148p. (Orig.). (C). 1989. pap. 12.95 (*0-9626221-1-7*) Vista Pubns FL.
***Michel, George F. & Moore, Celia L.** Developmental Psychobiology: An Interdisciplinary Science. LC 94-47023. (Illus.). 508p. 1995. 50.00x (*0-262-13312-1*, Bradford Bks) MIT Pr.
Michel, Hartmut. Crystallization of Membrane Proteins. 208p. 1990. 104.00 (*0-8493-4816-1*, QP552) CRC Pr.
Michel, J. P. Dictionary of Earth Sciences: English-French, French-English. 2nd ed. 299p. 1992. pap. text ed. 94.95 (*0-471-93535-2*) Wiley.
Michel, J. P., jt. auth. see Fairbridge, Rhodes W.
Michel, Jean, jt. auth. see Digne, Francois.
***Michel, John L. & Michel, Barbara N.** Antiquing New York: The Guide to the Antique Dealers of New York. 1995. pap. write for info. (*0-231-10013-2*) Col U Pr.
***Michel, Joyce H.** I Can Jump! My Little Kindergarten Practice Reader. 2nd rev. ed. (I Can! Bks.). 20p. (J). (gr. k). 1991. reprint ed. 1.75 (*0-9647262-0-3*) I Can Bks.
— I Can Ride! A Practice Reader. 2nd rev. ed. (I Can! Bks.). 20p. (J). (gr. k-3). 1993. reprint ed. 1.75 (*0-9647262-1-1*) I Can Bks.
Michel, June, ed. see Gabriel, Michael L. & McCauley, Cleyburn L.
Michel, L., et al, eds. Spontaneous Symmetry Breakdown & Related Subjects: XXI Karpacz Winter School on Theoretical Physics, Poland, 1985. 504p. 1985. 78.00 (*9971-978-54-7*) World Scientific Pub.
Michel, Laurence A. & Sewall, Richard B., eds. Tragedy: Modern Essays in Criticism. LC 77-13779. 340p. 1978. reprint ed. text ed. 55.00 (*0-8371-9876-3*, MITR, Greenwood Pr) Greenwood.
Michel, Louis. Light: the Shape of Space: Designing with Space & Light. 1994. text ed. 59.95 (*0-442-01804-5*) Van Nos Reinhold.
Michel, M. & Dauphin, M. SPECS: Specification & Programming Environment for Communication Software. Reed, R. et al, eds. 364p. 1993. 143.00 (*0-444-89923-5*, North Holland) Elsevier.
Michel, Maher, et al. Essays Plans for Anaesthesia Exams. (Illus.). 192p. (Orig.). 1992. pap. text ed. 39.00 (*0-443-04395-7*) Churchill.
Michel, Marc. La Mission Marchand, Eighteen Ninety-Five to Eighteen Ninetey-Nine. (Monde d'Outre Mer Passe & Present, Etudes Ser.: No. 36). (Illus.). 1972. pap. 49.25 (*90-279-7153-6*) Mouton.
Michel, Mark. The Beginner's Guide to Real Estate Wealth. 1986. pap. 9.95 (*0-939383-04-7*) Omnibus Pr.
Michel, Mary E., jt. ed. see Broman, Sarah H.
Michel, P. & Saucier, Gabriele, eds. Logic & Architecture Synthesis: Proceedings of the IFIP TC10 Workshop, Paris, France, 30 May-1 June, 1990. 338p. 1991. 100.00 (*0-444-89023-8*, North Holland) Elsevier.
Michel, Pamela A. The Child's View of Reading: Understandings for Teachers & Parents. LC 93-24104. 156p. 1994. pap. 25.95 (*0-205-13784-9*, Longwood Div) Allyn.
Michel, Paula, ed. see Milne, Drucilla.
***Michel, Peter.** Faith & Dogma. 160p. Date not set. pap. 10.95 (*1-885394-13-6*) Bluestar Commun.
— Faith & Dogma: What the Pope Did Not Say. Date not set. pap. 10.95 (*0-614-04380-8*) Bluestar Commun.
— Krishnamurti-Love & Freedom: Approaching a Mystery. 208p. 1995. pap. text ed. 10.95 (*1-885394-00-4*) Bluestar Commun.
Michel, Petra, ed. The Synthesis Approach to Digital System Design. (International Series in Engineering & Computer Science, VLSI, Computer Architecture, & Digital Screen Processing). 432p. (C). 1992. lib. bdg. 102.00 (*0-7923-9199-3*) Kluwer Ac.
Michel, Pierre. James Gould Cozzens: An Annotated Checklist. LC 75-169068. (Serif Series: Bibliographies & Checklists: No. 22). 123p. reprint ed. pap. 35.10 (*0-7837-0565-4*, 2040909) Bks Demand.
Michel, Pierre, ed. see Rabelais, Francois.
Michel, Pierre A., jt. auth. see Hawawini, Gabriel.
Michel, R. & Arnal, D., eds. Laminar-Turbulent Transition: IUTAM Symposium, Toulouse, France, September 11-15, 1989. (International Union of Theoretical & Applied Mechanics Symposia Ser.). (Illus.). 704p. 1991. 139.00 (*0-387-52196-8*) Spr-Verlag.
Michel, R., et al, eds. Unsteady Turbulent Shear Flows: Proceedings. (International Union of Theoretical & Applied Mechanics Symposia Ser.). 450p. 1982. 64.00 (*0-387-11099-2*) Spr-Verlag.
***Michel, Randy.** Justice Gone Awry: The Arrest & Trials of Jesus Christ. 80p. (Orig.). (C). 1995. pap. 6.95 (*0-614-05253-X*) Wine Pr Pub.
Michel, Richard C., jt. auth. see Levy, Frank S.
Michel, Richard C., jt. ed. see Lewis, Gordon H.
Michel, Sam. Under the Light. 1991. 19.00 (*0-394-58723-5*) Knopf.
Michel, Sandra S. Visions to Keep. Syrja, Steven, ed. 320p. (Orig.). 1990. pap. 14.95 (*0-917178-20-3*) Lenape Pub.
Michel, Sandra S., ed. see Smith, Viola B.
Michel, Sandy. No More Someday. (Illus.). 1973. pap. 2.00 (*0-685-83571-5*) Lenape Pub.

An Asterisk (*) at the beginning of an entry indicates that the title is appearing in BIP for the first time.

— Thomas My Brother. 1981. pap. 4.00 (*0-917178-15-7*) Lenape Pub.
Michel, Sara, jt. auth. see Deur, Lynne.
Michel, Sonya, jt. ed. see Koven, Seth.
Michel, Steve. The Bob Dylan Concordance. 153p. 1992. pap. 29.95 (*0-9635031-0-3*) Rolling Tomes.
— MacWrite Pro Inside & Out. 1992. text ed. 24.95 (*0-07-881864-8*) Osborne-McGraw.
Michel, Steve & Coleman, Dale. Best Mac Tips Ever. 1993. pap. text ed. 19.95 (*0-07-881968-7*) McGraw.
***Michel-Thiriet, Philippe.** Marcel Proust Lexikon. 514p. (GER.). 1992. 125.00 (*0-7859-8407-0*, 3518403907) Fr & Eur.
Michel, Thomas F., tr. see Taymiyah, Ibn.
***Michel, Trudi.** Inside Tin Pan Alley. (American Autobiography Ser.). 172p. 1995. reprint ed. lib. bdg. 69.00 (*0-7812-8593-3*) Rprt Serv.
Michelangelo. The Complete Poems of Michelangelo. Tusiani, Joseph, tr. LC 86-71314. 217p. 1986. 30.00 (*0-7206-6616-3*, Pub. by P Owen Ltd UK) Dufour.
— Drawings of Michelangelo. Stone, Irving, ed. (Master Draughtsman Ser.). (Illus.). (Orig.). 1962. pap. 4.95 (*0-87505-176-6*) Borden.
— Life Drawings of Michelangelo. (Fine Art Ser.). (Illus.). 48p. 1980. pap. 3.95 (*0-486-23876-8*) Dover.
— Life, Letters & Poetry. Bull, George, ed. (World's Classics Ser.). 216p. 1987. pap. 8.95 (*0-19-281603-9*) OUP.
Michele C. Solitary Traveller. 20p. (Orig.). 1990. pap. 3.00 (*0-916397-13-0*) Manic D Pr.
Michele, P. M., jt. auth. see Daviau.
Michelet, Jon. Orion's Belt. large type ed. 528p. 1987. 16.95 (*0-7089-1689-9*) Ulverscroft.
Michelet, Jules. Histoire de la Revolution Francaise, 2 vols., Vol. 1. Walter, ed. (Pleiade Ser.). (FRE.). 74.95 (*2-07-010356-0*) Schoenhof.
— Histoire de la Revolution Francaise, 2 vols., Vol. 2. Walter, ed. (Pleiade Ser.). (FRE.). 78.95 (*2-07-010357-9*) Schoenhof.
— Jeanne d'Arc. (FRE.). 1974. pap. 10.95 (*0-7859-4011-1*) Fr & Eur.
— Jeanne d'Arc. (Folio Ser.: No. 441). 320p. (FRE.). 1974. pap. 8.95 (*2-07-036441-0*) Schoenhof.
— Joan of Arc. Guerard, Albert, tr. 1957. pap. 11.95 (*0-472-06122-4*, 122, Ann Arbor Bks) U of Mich Pr.
— Mer. (Folio Ser.: No. 1470). 416p. (FRE.). 1983. pap. 13.95 (*2-07-037470-X*) Schoenhof.
— The People. 1973. 200.00 (*0-8490-0810-7*) Gordon Pr.
— The People. McKay, John P., tr. & intro. by. LC 72-91078. 245p. 1973. pap. 11.95 (*0-252-00331-4*) U of Ill Pr.
— Satanism & Witchcraft. 352p. 1983. reprint ed. pap. 12.95 (*0-8065-0059-X*, 89, Citadel Pr) Carol Pub Group.
Michelett, jt. auth. see Debay, Yves.
Micheletti, Emma. Domenico Ghirlandaio. Brierley, Anthony, tr. (Library of Great Masters). (Illus.). 80p. (Orig.). 1990. pap. 12.99 (*1-878351-08-7*) Riverside NY.
Micheletti, Eric. Air War over the Gulf, No. 8: Europa Militaria. 1991. pap. 15.95 (*1-872004-21-0*) Motorbooks Intl.
Micheletti, Eric & Debay, Yves. Victory: Desert Storm. (Power Ser.). (Illus.). 128p. 1991. pap. 17.95 (*1-872004-31-8*) Motorbooks Intl.
Micheletti, G. F., ed. Flexible Manufacturing Systems. (Illus.). 420p. 1988. 146.00 (*0-387-18524-0*) Spr-Verlag.
Micheletti, Julie A., jt. auth. see Grimaldi, Paul L.
***Micheletti, Michele.** Civil Society & State Relations in Sweden. 212p. (C). 1995. boxed, pap. text ed. 59.95 (*1-85972-037-4*, Pub. by Avebury Pub UK) Ashgate Pub Co.
— The Swedish Farmers' Movement & Government Agricultural Policy. LC 89-16206. 227p. 1990. text ed. 55.00 (*0-275-93398-9*, C3398, Praeger Pubs) Greenwood.
Michelfelder, Diane P. & Palmer, Richard E., eds. Dialogue & Deconstruction: The Gadamer-Derrida Encounter. LC 88-24792. (SUNY Series in Contemporary Continental Philosophy). 352p. 1989. 59.50 (*0-7914-0008-5*); pap. 19.95 (*0-7914-0009-3*) State U NY Pr.
Micheli, L. French - English Dictionary of Home Automation. 260p. (ENG & FRE.). 1991. pap. 32.50 (*2-85608-042-1*) IBD Ltd.
— French-English Dictionary of Home Automation: Dictionnaire de la Domotique. 250p. (ENG & FRE.). 1991. pap. 59.95 (*0-8288-6969-3*, 2856080421) Fr & Eur.
Micheli, Lyle. Pediatric & Adolescent Sports Medicine. 218p. 1984. 62.95 (*0-316-56949-6*) Little.
Micheli, Lyle, et al, eds. Soviet-American Dance Medicine: Proceedings of the 1990 Glasnost Dance Medicine Conference & Workshops. (Illus.). 113p. (Orig.). 1991. pap. text ed. 9.95 (*0-88314-512-X*) AAHPERD.
***Micheli, Lyle J. & Jenkins, Mark.** The Sports Medicine Bible: Prevent, Detect, & Treat Your Sports Injuries Through the Latest Medical Techniques. LC 95-2316. 1995. pap. 20.00 (*0-06-273143-2*, PL) HarpC.
Micheli, Lyle J. & Jenkins, Mark D. Sportsense for the Young Athlete: A Parent's Guide to Fun & Safe Fitness for AA. 288p. 1990. pap. 9.95 (*0-395-56408-5*) HM.
Micheli, Lyle J., jt. auth. see Cantu, Robert C.
***Michelin.** Michelin France. 256p. 1995. 40.00 (*0-8212-2219-8*) Bulfinch Pr.
***Michelin Staf.** Spain Green Guide English Edition. Date not set. pap. 17.95 (*0-7859-7193-9*, 2061523013) Fr & Eur.
***Michelin Staff.** Alpes du Nord Green Guide. (FRE.). pap. 17.95 (*0-7859-7217-X*, 2067003011) Fr & Eur.
— Alpes du Sud Green Guide French Edition. (FRE.). Date not set. pap. 17.95 (*0-7859-7218-8*, 2060030218) Fr & Eur.
— Alsace et Lorraine Green Guide French Edition. (FRE.). Date not set. pap. 17.95 (*0-7859-7219-6*, 2067003720) Fr & Eur.
— Atlas Great Britain & Ireland. 6th ed. (Orig.). 1994. pap. 20.00 (*2-06-112106-3*) Michelin.
— Atlas of Great Britain & Ireland. (Orig.). 1994. spiral bd., pap. 20.00 (*2-06-112206-X*) Michelin.
— Austria Green Guide English. Date not set. pap. 17.95 (*0-7859-7183-1*, 2067015079) Fr & Eur.
— Auvergne Green Guide French Edition. (FRE.). Date not set. pap. 17.95 (*0-7859-7220-X*, 2067003046) Fr & Eur.
— Belgique Green Guide. (Orig.). (FRE.). Date not set. pap. 19.00 (*2-06-051101-1*, 511) Michelin.
— Belgique Green Guide French Edition. (FRE.). Date not set. pap. 17.95 (*0-7859-7208-0*, 2060411011) Fr & Eur.
— Benelux Red Guide. 1994. 24.95 (*0-7859-7164-5*, 2060060494) Fr & Eur.
— Benelux Red Guide. 1995. 24.00 (*2-06-006059-1*, 605) Michelin.
— Berry-Limousin Green Guide French Edition. (FRE.). Date not set. pap. 17.95 (*0-7859-7221-8*, 2067003054) Fr & Eur.
— Bourgogne Green Guide French Edition. (FRE.). Date not set. pap. 17.95 (*0-7859-7222-6*, 2067003070) Fr & Eur.
— Bretagne Green Guide French Edition. (FRE.). pap. 17.95 (*0-7859-7223-4*, 2060030943) Fr & Eur.
— Brittany Green Guide English Edition. Date not set. pap. 17.95 (*0-7859-7200-5*, 2067013149) Fr & Eur.
— Burgundy Green Guide English Edition. Date not set. pap. 17.95 (*0-7859-7201-3*, 2067013084) Fr & Eur.
— California Green Guide English Edition. Date not set. pap. 17.95 (*0-7859-7177-7*, 2061598013) Fr & Eur.
— Canada Green Guide English Edition. Date not set. pap. 17.95 (*0-7859-7176-9*, 2061517056) Fr & Eur.
— Canada Green Guide French Edition. (FRE.). Date not set. pap. 17.95 (*0-7859-7209-9*, 2067005162) Fr & Eur.
— Champagne-Ardennes Green Guide French Edition. (FRE.). Date not set. pap. 17.95 (*0-614-00370-9*, 206700316X) Fr & Eur.
— Chateaux de la Loire Green Guide French Edition. (FRE.). Date not set. pap. 17.95 (*0-7859-7225-0*, 2067003178) Fr & Eur.
— Chateaux de la Loire Green Guide Japanese Edition. (FRE.). Date not set. pap. 36.00 (*0-614-00390-3*, 440801303X) Fr & Eur.
— Chateaux of the Loire Green Guide. 3rd ed. (Orig.). Date not set. pap. 18.00 (*2-06-132203-4*, 1322) Michelin.
— Chateaux of the Loire Green Guide English Edition. Date not set. pap. 17.95 (*0-7859-7202-1*, 206701322X) Fr & Eur.
— Corse Green Guide French Edition. (FRE.). Date not set. pap. 17.95 (*0-7859-7226-9*) Fr & Eur.
— Cote d'Azur Green Guide French Edition. (FRE.). Date not set. pap. 17.95 (*0-7859-7227-7*, 2067003208) Fr & Eur.
— Deutschland Red Guide. 1994. 26.95 (*0-7859-7165-3*, 2060062497) Fr & Eur.
— Deutschland Red Guide. (Red Guide Ser.). 1995. 26.00 (*2-06-006259-4*, 625) Michelin.
— Dordogne Green Guide. 3rd ed. (Orig.). Date not set. pap. 18.00 (*2-06-132303-0*, 1323) Michelin.
— Dordogne Green Guide English Edition. Date not set. pap. 17.95 (*0-7859-7203-X*, 2067013238) Fr & Eur.
— England-West Green Guide English Edition. Date not set. pap. 17.95 (*0-7859-7184-X*, 2061562035) Fr & Eur.
— Espana Green Guide Spanish Edition. (FRE.). Date not set. pap. 19.95 (*0-7859-7249-8*, 2067045261) Fr & Eur.
— Espana-Portugal Red Guide. 1994. 24.95 (*0-7859-7166-1*, 2060063493) Fr & Eur.
— Espana-Portugal Red Guide. (Red Guide Ser.). 1995. 24.00 (*2-06-006359-0*, 635) Michelin.
— Euro-Disney Green Guide English Edition. Date not set. pap. 17.95 (*0-7859-7195-5*, 2067014811) Fr & Eur.
— Europe (Main Cities) Red Guide. 1994. 25.95 (*0-7859-7167-X*, 206007049X) Fr & Eur.
— Europe Red Guide. (Red Guide Ser.). 1995. 25.00 (*2-06-007059-7*, 705) Michelin.
— Europe Road Atlas. (FRE.). Date not set. spiral bd., pap. 29.95 (*0-7859-7252-8*, 060057749X); pap. 29.95 (*0-7859-7253-6*, 060057749X) Fr & Eur.
— Flanders, Picardy & Paris Region Green Guide English Edition. Date not set. pap. 17.95 (*0-7859-7204-8*, 2061344011) Fr & Eur.
— Flandres-Artois-Picardie Green Guide French Edition. (FRE.). Date not set. pap. 17.95 (*0-7859-7228-5*, 2067003380) Fr & Eur.
— France: Camping & Caravaning Red Guide. 1994. pap. 19.95 (*0-7859-7172-6*, 2060061490) Fr & Eur.
— France, Camping Caravaning. (Red Guide Ser.). 1995. 15.00 (*2-06-006159-8*, 615) Michelin.
— France Green Guide. (Orig.). (FRE.). Date not set. pap. 19.00 (*2-06-049001-4*, 490) Michelin.
— France Green Guide. 2nd ed. (Orig.). Date not set. pap. 19.00 (*2-06-149102-2*, 1491) Michelin.
— France Green Guide: Japanese Edition. (FRE & JPN.). Date not set. pap. 36.00 (*0-7859-7240-4*) Fr & Eur.
— France Green Guide English Edition. Date not set. pap. 17.95 (*0-7859-7196-3*, 2067014919) Fr & Eur.
— France Green Guide French Edition. (FRE.). Date not set. pap. 17.95 (*0-7859-7210-2*, 2060039010) Fr & Eur.
— France Red Guide. 1994. 24.95 (*0-7859-7168-8*, 2060664497) Fr & Eur.
— France Red Guide. (Red Guide Ser.). (Orig.). 1995. 25.00 (*2-06-006459-7*, 645) Michelin.
— France Road Atlas. (FRE.). Date not set. spiral bd., pap. 14.95 (*0-7859-7254-4*, 206700915X); pap. 29.95 (*0-7859-7255-2*, 206700915X) Fr & Eur.
— French Riviera Green Guide English Edition. Date not set. pap. 17.95 (*0-7859-7205-6*, 2067013351) Fr & Eur.
— Germany Green Guide English Edition. Date not set. pap. 17.95 (*0-7859-7185-8*, 2061504019) Fr & Eur.
— Gorges du Tarn Green Guide French Edition. (FRE.). Date not set. pap. 17.95 (*0-7859-7229-3*, 2060033721) Fr & Eur.
— Great Britain & Ireland Red Guide. 1994. 24.95 (*0-7859-7169-6*, 2060065496) Fr & Eur.
— Great Britain & Ireland Red Guide. (Red Guide Ser.). 1995. 24.00 (*2-06-006559-3*, 655) Michelin.
— Great Britain & Ireland Road Atlas. (FRE.). Date not set. pap. 29.95 (*0-7859-7256-0*, 2061122051); spiral bd., pap. 29.95 (*0-7859-7257-9*, 2061122051) Fr & Eur.
— Great Britain Green Guide English Edition. Date not set. pap. 17.95 (*0-7859-7186-6*, 2067015419) Fr & Eur.
— Greece Green Guide English Edition. 2nd ed. 1991. pap. 17.95 (*0-7859-7187-4*, 520) Fr & Eur.
— Greece Green Guide Japanese Edition. (FRE.). Date not set. pap. 36.00 (*0-7859-7241-2*, 4408013080) Fr & Eur.
— Green Guide Canada. (Orig.). (FRE.). 1994. pap. 19.00 (*2-06-051605-6*) Michelin.
— Ile de France Green Guide French Edition. (FRE.). Date not set. pap. 17.95 (*0-614-00376-8*, 206326IX) Fr & Eur.
— Ile de France Green Guide Japanese Edition. (FRE.). Date not set. pap. 36.00 (*0-614-00391-1*, 4408013021) Fr & Eur.
— Ireland Green Guide English Edition. Date not set. pap. 17.95 (*0-7859-7188-2*, 2067015354) Fr & Eur.
— Ireland Red Guide. 1994. pap. 12.95 (*0-7859-7175-0*, 2060071496) Fr & Eur.
— Ireland Red Guide. (Red Guide Ser.). 1995. 10.00 (*2-06-007159-3*, 715) Michelin.
— Italia Red Guide. 1994. 24.95 (*0-7859-7170-X*, 2060067499) Fr & Eur.
— Italia Red Guide. (Red Guide Ser.). 1995. 24.00 (*2-06-006759-6*, 675) Michelin.
— Italy Green Guide English Edition. Date not set. pap. 17.95 (*0-7859-7189-0*, 2067015346) Fr & Eur.
— Italy Green Guide Japanese Edition. (FRE.). Date not set. pap. 36.00 (*0-614-00388-1*, 4408013072) Fr & Eur.
— Italy Road Atlas. 2nd ed. (Orig.). Date not set. pap. 20.00 (*2-06-146502-1*, 1465) Michelin.
— Jura-Franche-Comte Green Guide French Edition. (FRE.). Date not set. pap. 17.95 (*0-7859-7231-5*, 2060034019) Fr & Eur.
— London Green Guide English Edition. Date not set. pap. 17.95 (*0-7859-7197-1*, 2061590012) Fr & Eur.
— London Red Guide. 1994. pap. 12.95 (*0-7859-7173-4*, 2060066492) Fr & Eur.
— London Red Guide. (Red Guide Ser.). 1995. 10.00 (*2-06-006659-X*, 665) Michelin.
— Maroc Green Guide French Edition. (FRE.). Date not set. pap. 17.95 (*0-7859-7212-9*, 2060054532) Fr & Eur.
— Mexico Green Guide English Edition. Date not set. pap. 17.95 (*0-7859-7180-7*, 2060157919) Fr & Eur.
— Mexico Green Guide Spanish Edition. (FRE.). Date not set. pap. 19.95 (*0-7859-7250-1*, 2067045806) Fr & Eur.
— Michelin Green Guide - Alpes du Nord. (FRE.). 14.95 (*0-8288-6171-4*) Fr & Eur.
— Michelin Green Guide - Alpes du Sud. (FRE.). 14.95 (*0-8288-6172-2*) Fr & Eur.
— Michelin Green Guide - Alsace et Lorraine (Vosges) (FRE.). 14.95 (*0-8288-6173-0*) Fr & Eur.
— Michelin Green Guide - Austria. 14.95 (*0-8288-6117-X*) Fr & Eur.
— Michelin Green Guide - Auvergne. (FRE.). 14.95 (*0-8288-6174-9*) Fr & Eur.
— Michelin Green Guide - Belgium - Luxemburg. (FRE.). 14.95 (*0-8288-6142-0*) Fr & Eur.
— Michelin Green Guide - Berry-Limousin. (FRE.). 14.95 (*0-8288-6176-5*) Fr & Eur.
— Michelin Green Guide - Bourgogne. (FRE.). 14.95 (*0-8288-6175-7*) Fr & Eur.
— Michelin Green Guide - Bretagne. (FRE.). 14.95 (*0-8288-6177-3*) Fr & Eur.
— Michelin Green Guide - Brittany. 14.95 (*0-8288-6133-1*) Fr & Eur.
— Michelin Green Guide - Burgundy. 14.95 (*0-8288-6134-X*) Fr & Eur.
— Michelin Green Guide - Canada. 14.95 (*0-8288-6103-X*); 14.95 (*0-8288-6143-9*) Fr & Eur.
— Michelin Green Guide - Champagne-Ardennes. (FRE.). 14.95 (*0-8288-6178-1*) Fr & Eur.
— Michelin Green Guide - Chateaux de la Loire. (FRE.). 14.95 (*0-8288-6179-X*) Fr & Eur.
— Michelin Green Guide - Chateaux of the Loire. 14.95 (*0-8288-6135-8*) Fr & Eur.
— Michelin Green Guide - Corse. (FRE.). 14.95 (*0-8288-6180-3*) Fr & Eur.
— Michelin Green Guide - Cote d'Azur. (FRE.). 14.95 (*0-8288-6181-1*) Fr & Eur.
— Michelin Green Guide - Dordogne. 14.95 (*0-8288-6136-6*) Fr & Eur.
— Michelin Green Guide - England - West Country. 14.95 (*0-8288-6118-8*) Fr & Eur.
— Michelin Green Guide - Espana. (SPA.). 14.95 (*0-8288-6194-3*) Fr & Eur.
— Michelin Green Guide - Flandres - Artois - Picardie. (FRE.). 14.95 (*0-8288-6182-X*) Fr & Eur.
— Michelin Green Guide - France. 14.95 (*0-8288-6119-6*); 14.95 (*0-8288-6144-7*) Fr & Eur.
— Michelin Green Guide - French Riviera. 14.95 (*0-8288-6137-4*) Fr & Eur.
— Michelin Green Guide - Germany. 14.95 (*0-8288-6120-X*) Fr & Eur.
— Michelin Green Guide - Gorges du Tarn. (FRE.). 14.95 (*0-8288-6183-8*) Fr & Eur.
— Michelin Green Guide - Holland. (FRE.). 14.95 (*0-8288-6145-5*) Fr & Eur.
— Michelin Green Guide - Ile de France. 14.95 (*0-8288-6138-2*); 14.95 (*0-8288-6184-6*) Fr & Eur.
— Michelin Green Guide - Jura - Franche Comte. (FRE.). 14.95 (*0-8288-6185-4*) Fr & Eur.
— Michelin Green Guide - London. 14.95 (*0-8288-6130-7*) Fr & Eur.
— Michelin Green Guide - Mexico. 14.95 (*0-8288-6114-5*); 14.95 (*0-8288-6195-1*) Fr & Eur.
— Michelin Green Guide - Morocco. (FRE.). 14.95 (*0-8288-6146-3*) Fr & Eur.
— Michelin Green Guide - New England. 14.95 (*0-8288-6101-3*); 14.95 (*0-8288-6147-1*) Fr & Eur.
— Michelin Green Guide - New York. (FRE.). 14.95 (*0-8288-6149-8*) Fr & Eur.
— Michelin Green Guide - New York City. 14.95 (*0-8288-6113-7*) Fr & Eur.
— Michelin Green Guide - Normandie Cotentin. (FRE.). 14.95 (*0-8288-6186-2*) Fr & Eur.
— Michelin Green Guide - Normandie Vallee Seine. (FRE.). 14.95 (*0-8288-6187-0*) Fr & Eur.
— Michelin Green Guide - Normandy Cotentin. 14.95 (*0-8288-6139-0*) Fr & Eur.
— Michelin Green Guide - Normandy Seine Valley. 14.95 (*0-8288-6140-4*) Fr & Eur.
— Michelin Green Guide - Paris. (FRE.). 14.95 (*0-8288-6170-6*) Fr & Eur.
— Michelin Green Guide - Perigord-Ouercy. (FRE.). 14.95 (*0-8288-6188-9*) Fr & Eur.
— Michelin Green Guide - Poitou-Vendee-Charente. (FRE.). 14.95 (*0-8288-6189-7*) Fr & Eur.
— Michelin Green Guide - Portugal. (SPA.). 14.95 (*0-8288-6196-X*) Fr & Eur.
— Michelin Green Guide - Provence. 14.95 (*0-8288-6141-2*); 14.95 (*0-8288-6190-0*) Fr & Eur.
— Michelin Green Guide - Pyrenees-Aouitaine. (FRE.). 14.95 (*0-8288-6191-9*) Fr & Eur.
— Michelin Green Guide - Pyrenees-Roussillon. (FRE.). 14.95 (*0-8288-6192-7*) Fr & Eur.
— Michelin Green Guide - Quebec Province. 14.95 (*0-8288-6115-3*); 14.95 (*0-8288-6148-X*) Fr & Eur.
— Michelin Green Guide - Scotland. 14.95 (*0-8288-6127-7*) Fr & Eur.
— Michelin Green Guide - Vallee du Rhone. (FRE.). 14.95 (*0-8288-6193-5*) Fr & Eur.
— Michelin Green Guide - Washington D. C. 14.95 (*0-8288-6116-1*) Fr & Eur.
— Michelin Green Guides - Great Britain. 14.95 (*0-8288-6121-8*) Fr & Eur.
— Michelin Green Guides - Greece. 14.95 (*0-8288-6122-6*) Fr & Eur.
— Michelin Green Guides - Ireland. 14.95 (*0-8288-6123-4*) Fr & Eur.
— Michelin Green Guides - Italy. 14.95 (*0-685-66129-6*) Fr & Eur.
— Michelin Green Guides - Netherlands. 14.95 (*0-8288-6125-0*) Fr & Eur.
— Michelin Green Guides - Paris. 14.95 (*0-8288-6131-5*) Fr & Eur.
— Michelin Green Guides - Portugal. 14.95 (*0-8288-6126-9*) Fr & Eur.
— Michelin Green Guides - Rome. 14.95 (*0-8288-6132-3*) Fr & Eur.
— Michelin Green Guides - Spain. 14.95 (*0-8288-6128-5*) Fr & Eur.
— Michelin Green Guides - Switzerland. 14.95 (*0-8288-6129-3*) Fr & Eur.
— Michelin Guide No. 305: Berry-Limousin. (Green Guides Ser.). (FRE.). 1990. pap. 16.95 (*0-7859-0220-1*, 2067003054) Fr & Eur.
— Michelin Guide No. 317: Chateaux de la Loire. (Green Guides Ser.). (FRE.). 1990. pap. 16.95 (*0-7859-0226-0*, 2067003178) Fr & Eur.
— Michelin Guide No. 341: Ile de France. (Green Guides Ser.). 1990. pap. 14.95 (*0-7859-0236-8*, 2060134110) Fr & Eur.
— Michelin Guide No. 355: Paris. (Green Guides Ser.). 1990. pap. 14.95 (*0-7859-0242-2*, 2060135516) Fr & Eur.
— Michelin Guide No. 370: Perigord-Quercy. (Green Guides Ser.). (FRE.). 1990. pap. 16.95 (*0-7859-0246-5*, 2067003704) Fr & Eur.
— Michelin Guide No. 371: Poitou-Vendee-Charente. (Green Guides Ser.). (FRE.). 1990. pap. 16.95 (*0-7859-0247-3*, 2067003712) Fr & Eur.
— Michelin Guide No. 517: Canada. (Green Guides Ser.). 1990. pap. 16.95 (*0-7859-0282-1*, 2060151732) Fr & Eur.
— Michelin Guide No. 543: London. (Green Guides Ser.). 1990. pap. 14.95 (*0-7859-0289-9*, 2060154359) Fr & Eur.
— Michelin Guide No. 555: Netherlands. (Green Guides Ser.). 1990. pap. 16.95 (*0-7859-0294-5*, 2060155517) Fr & Eur.
— Michelin Guide No. 562: England-The West Country. (Green Guides Ser.). 1990. pap. 14.95 (*0-7859-0297-X*, 206015622X) Fr & Eur.
— Michelin Guide No. 575: Scotland. (Green Guides Ser.). 1990. pap. 16.95 (*0-7859-0304-6*, 2060157528) Fr & Eur.
— Michelin Guide No. 579: Mexico. (Green Guides Ser.). 1990. pap. 16.95 (*0-7859-0306-2*, 2060157919) Fr & Eur.
— Michelin Guide, No. 301: Alpes Du Nord. (Green Guides Ser.). (FRE.). 1988. pap. 16.95 (*0-7859-0217-1*, 2067003011) Fr & Eur.
— Michelin Guide, No. 302: Alpes Du Sud. (Green Guides Ser.). (FRE.). 1988. pap. 16.95 (*0-7859-0218-X*, 2060030218) Fr & Eur.
— Michelin Guide, No. 304: Auvergne. (Green Guides Ser.). (FRE.). 1992. pap. 19.95 (*0-7859-0219-8*, 2067003046) Fr & Eur.

An Asterisk (*) at the beginning of an entry indicates that the title is appearing in BIP for the first time.

— Michelin Guide, No. 307: Bourgogne. (Green Guides Ser.). (FRE.). 1988. pap. 16.95 (*0-7859-0221-X*, 2067003070) Fr & Eur.

— Michelin Guide, No. 308: Burgundy. (Green Guides Ser.). 1992. pap. 19.95 (*0-7859-0222-8*, 2067013084) Fr & Eur.

— Michelin Guide, No. 309: Bretagne. (Green Guides Ser.). (FRE.). 1986. pap. 16.95 (*0-7859-0223-6*, 2060030943) Fr & Eur.

— Michelin Guide, No. 314: Brittanny. (Green Guides Ser.). 1992. pap. 19.95 (*0-7859-0224-4*, 2067013149) Fr & Eur.

— Michelin Guide, No. 316: Champagne-Ardennes. (Green Guides Ser.). (FRE.). 1992. pap. 19.95 (*0-7859-0225-2*, 2060031621) Fr & Eur.

— Michelin Guide, No. 319: Corse. (Green Guides Ser.). (FRE.). 1989. pap. 16.95 (*0-7859-0227-9*, 2060031915) Fr & Eur.

— Michelin Guide, No. 320: Cote d'Azur. (Green Guides Ser.). (FRE.). 1987. pap. 16.95 (*0-7859-0228-7*, 2060032016) Fr & Eur.

— Michelin Guide, No. 322: Chateaux of the Loire. (Green Guides Ser.). 1989. pap. 14.95 (*0-7859-0229-5*, 206701322X) Fr & Eur.

— Michelin Guide, No. 323: Dordogne - Description & Travel. (Green Guides Ser.). 1992. pap. 19.95 (*0-7859-0230-9*, 2067013238) Fr & Eur.

— Michelin Guide, No. 326: Ile de France - Descripton & Travel. (Green Guides Ser.). (FRE.). 1992. pap. 19.95 (*0-7859-0231-7*, 206003261X) Fr & Eur.

— Michelin Guide, No. 335: French Riviera. (Green Guides Ser.). 1988. pap. 14.95 (*0-7859-0232-5*, 2067013351) Fr & Eur.

— Michelin Guide, No. 337: Gorges du Tarn. (Green Guides Ser.). (FRE.). 1989. pap. 16.95 (*0-7859-0233-3*, 2060033721) Fr & Eur.

— Michelin Guide, No. 338: Flandres-Artois-Picardie. (Green Guides Ser.). (FRE.). 1988. pap. 16.95 (*0-7859-0234-1*, 2067003380) Fr & Eur.

— Michelin Guide, No. 340: Jura-Franche Comte. (Green Guides Ser.). (FRE.). 1992. pap. 19.95 (*0-7859-0235-X*, 2060034019) Fr & Eur.

— Michelin Guide, No. 346: Normandie Cotentin. (Green Guides Ser.). (FRE.). 1988. pap. 16.95 (*0-7859-0237-6*, 2060034612) Fr & Eur.

— Michelin Guide, No. 347: Normandie Vallee de la Seine. (Green Guides Ser.). (FRE.). 1988. pap. 16.95 (*0-7859-0238-4*, 206003471X) Fr & Eur.

— Michelin Guide, No. 349: Normandy Cotentin. (Green Guides Ser.). 1989. pap. 14.95 (*0-7859-0239-2*, 2060134919) Fr & Eur.

— Michelin Guide, No. 350: Normandy Seine Valley. (Green Guides Ser.). 1989. pap. 14.95 (*0-7859-0240-6*, 206013501X) Fr & Eur.

— Michelin Guide, No. 352: Paris. (Green Guides Ser.). (FRE.). 1989. pap. 16.95 (*0-7859-0241-4*, 2067003526) Fr & Eur.

— Michelin Guide, No. 362: Provence. (Green Guides Ser.). (FRE.). 1988. pap. 16.95 (*0-7859-0243-0*, 2060036216) Fr & Eur.

— Michelin Guide, No. 367: Pyrenees-Aquitaine. (Green Guides Ser.). (FRE.). 1989. pap. 16.95 (*0-7859-0244-9*, 2060036720) Fr & Eur.

— Michelin Guide, No. 368: Pyrenees-Roussillon. (Green Guides Ser.). (FRE.). 1989. pap. 16.95 (*0-7859-0245-7*, 2067003682) Fr & Eur.

— Michelin Guide, No. 372: Alsace et Lorraine, Vosges. (Green Guides Ser.). (FRE.). 1989. pap. 16.95 (*0-7859-0248-1*, 2060037247) Fr & Eur.

— Michelin Guide, No. 373: Vallee du Rhone. (Green Guides Ser.). (FRE.). 1989. pap. 16.95 (*0-7859-0249-X*, 2067003739) Fr & Eur.

— Michelin Guide, No. 375: Provence. (Green Guides Ser.). 1989. pap. 14.95 (*0-7859-0250-3*, 2067013750) Fr & Eur.

— Michelin Guide, No. 390: France. (Green Guides Ser.). (FRE.). 1989. pap. 16.95 (*0-7859-0251-1*, 2060039010) Fr & Eur.

— Michelin Guide, No. 481: Euro-Disney. (Green Guides Ser.). 1992. pap. 19.95 (*0-7859-0276-7*, 2067014811) Fr & Eur.

— Michelin Guide, No. 491: France. (Green Guides Ser.). 1992. pap. 19.95 (*0-7859-0277-5*, 2067014919) Fr & Eur.

— Michelin Guide, No. 503: Germany. (Green Guides Ser.). 1987. pap. 16.95 (*0-7859-0278-3*, 2060150337) Fr & Eur.

— Michelin Guide, No. 507: Austria. (Green Guides Ser.). 1992. pap. 19.95 (*0-7859-0279-1*, 2067015079) Fr & Eur.

— Michelin Guide, No. 510: Belgique-Luxembourg, French Edition. (Green Guides Ser.). (FRE.). 1992. pap. 19.95 (*0-7859-0280-5*, 2060051044) Fr & Eur.

— Michelin Guide, No. 516: Canada, French Edition. (Green Guides Ser.). (FRE.). 1987. pap. 16.95 (*0-7859-0281-3*, 2067005162) Fr & Eur.

— Michelin Guide, No. 520: Greece. (Green Guides Ser.). 1992. pap. 19.95 (*0-7859-0283-X*, 2067015206) Fr & Eur.

— Michelin Guide, No. 521: Spain. (Green Guides Ser.). 1987. pap. 16.95 (*0-7859-0284-8*, 2060152135) Fr & Eur.

— Michelin Guide, No. 526: Espana. (Green Guides Ser.). (SPA.). 1987. pap. 19.95 (*0-7859-0285-6*, 2067045261) Fr & Eur.

— Michelin Guide, No. 534: Italy. (Green Guides Ser.). 1989. pap. 16.95 (*0-7859-0286-4*, 2067015346) Fr & Eur.

— Michelin Guide, No. 535: Ireland. (Green Guides Ser.). 1992. pap. 19.95 (*0-7859-0287-2*, 2067015354) Fr & Eur.

— Michelin Guide, No. 541: Great Britain. (Green Guides Ser.). 1992. pap. 19.95 (*0-7859-0288-0*, 2067015419) Fr & Eur.

— Michelin Guide, No. 545: Maroc. (Green Guides Ser.). (FRE.). 1988. pap. 16.95 (*0-7859-0290-2*, 2060054532) Fr & Eur.

— Michelin Guide, No. 548: New York. (Green Guides Ser.). (FRE.). 1989. pap. 16.95 (*0-7859-0291-0*, 2067005480) Fr & Eur.

— Michelin Guide, No. 551: New York City. (Green Guides Ser.). 1992. pap. 19.95 (*0-7859-0292-9*) Fr & Eur.

— Michelin Guide, No. 553: Hollande. (Green Guides Ser.). (FRE.). 1992. pap. 19.95 (*0-7859-0293-7*, 2060055342) Fr & Eur.

— Michelin Guide, No. 557: Portugal. (Green Guides Ser.). 1989. pap. 16.95 (*0-7859-0295-3*, 2060155738) Fr & Eur.

— Michelin Guide, No. 559: Rome. (Green Guides Ser.). 1985. pap. 14.95 (*0-7859-0296-1*, 2067015591) Fr & Eur.

— Michelin Guide, No. 563: Switzerland. (Green Guides Ser.). 1988. pap. 16.95 (*0-7859-0298-8*, 206701563X) Fr & Eur.

— Michelin Guide, No. 565: Portugal. (Green Guides Ser.). (SPA.). 1988. pap. 19.95 (*0-7859-0299-6*, 2067045652) Fr & Eur.

— Michelin Guide, No. 568: Nouvelle Angleterre. (Green Guides Ser.). (FRE.). 1988. pap. 16.95 (*0-7859-0300-3*, 2060056829) Fr & Eur.

— Michelin Guide, No. 569: New England. (Green Guides Ser.). 1988. pap. 14.95 (*0-7859-0301-1*, 2067015699) Fr & Eur.

— Michelin Guide, No. 572: Province de Quebec. (Green Guides Ser.). (FRE.). 1992. pap. 19.95 (*0-7859-0302-X*, 2980083348) Fr & Eur.

— Michelin Guide, No. 573: Quebec Province. (Green Guides Ser.). 1992. pap. 19.95 (*0-7859-0303-8*, 2980083356) Fr & Eur.

— Michelin Guide, No. 577: Washington, D. C. (Green Guides Ser.). 1988. pap. 14.95 (*0-7859-0305-4*, 206701577X) Fr & Eur.

— Michelin Guide, No. 580: Mexico. (Green Guides Ser.). (SPA.). 1988. pap. 19.95 (*0-7859-0307-0*, 2060458013) Fr & Eur.

— Michelin Guide, No. 603: Benelux. (Red Guides Ser.). 1993. 23.95 (*0-7859-0310-0*, 2060060397) Fr & Eur.

— Michelin Guide, No. 613: Camping, France. (Green Guides Ser.). 1993. pap. 17.95 (*0-7859-0311-9*, 2060061393) Fr & Eur.

— Michelin Guide, No. 623: Deutschland. (Red Guides). 1993. 25.95 (*0-7859-0312-7*, 206006239X) Fr & Eur.

— Michelin Guide, No. 633: Espana-Portugal. (Red Guides). 1993. 23.95 (*0-7859-0313-5*, 2060063396) Fr & Eur.

— Michelin Guide, No. 643: France. (Red Guides). 1993. 24.95 (*0-7859-0314-3*, 2060064392) Fr & Eur.

— Michelin Guide, No. 653: Great Britain & Ireland. (Red Guides). 1993. 23.95 (*0-7859-0315-1*, 5060065399) Fr & Eur.

— Michelin Guide, No. 663: Greater London. (Red Guides). 1993. pap. 12.95 (*0-7859-0316-X*, 2060066395) Fr & Eur.

— Michelin Guide, No. 673: Italia. (Red Guides). 1993. 23.95 (*0-7859-0317-8*, 2060067391) Fr & Eur.

— Michelin Guide, No. 683: Paris & Environs. (Red Guides). 1993. pap. 12.95 (*0-7859-0318-6*, 2060068398) Fr & Eur.

— Michelin Guide, No. 703: Europe, Main Cities. (Red Guides). 1993. 24.95 (*0-685-63826-X*, 2030070392) Fr & Eur.

— Michelin Guide, No. 713: Ireland. (Red Guides). 1993. pap. 12.95 (*0-7859-0320-8*, 2060071399) Fr & Eur.

— Michelin Map No. 212: Brugge - Rotterdam - Antwerpen. (Road Maps with Tourist Index Ser.). 1990. pap. 7.95 (*0-7859-0190-6*, 2067002120) Fr & Eur.

— Michelin Map No. 214: Mons - Dinant - Luxembourg. (Road Maps with Tourist Index Ser.). 1990. pap. 7.95 (*0-7859-0191-4*, 2067002147) Fr & Eur.

— Michelin Map No. 230: Bretagne. (Main Roads Maps: France Ser.). 1990. pap. 9.95 (*0-7859-0197-3*, 2067002309) Fr & Eur.

— Michelin Map No. 231: Normandie. (Main Roads Maps: France Ser.). 1990. pap. 9.95 (*0-7859-0198-1*, 2067002317) Fr & Eur.

— Michelin Map No. 232: Loire Region (Pays de Loire) (Main Roads Maps: France Ser.). 1990. pap. 9.95 (*0-7859-0199-X*, 2067002325) Fr & Eur.

— Michelin Map No. 233: Poitou-Charentes. (Main Roads Maps: France Ser.). 1990. pap. 9.95 (*0-7859-0200-7*, 2067002333) Fr & Eur.

— Michelin Map No. 234: Aquitaine. (Main Roads Maps: France Ser.). 1990. pap. 9.95 (*0-7859-0201-5*, 2067002341) Fr & Eur.

— Michelin Map No. 235: Midi Pyrenees. (Main Roads Maps: France Ser.). 1990. pap. 9.95 (*0-7859-0202-3*, 206700235X) Fr & Eur.

— Michelin Map No. 236: Nord de la France. (Main Roads Maps: France Ser.). 1990. pap. 9.95 (*0-7859-0203-1*, 2067002368) Fr & Eur.

— Michelin Map No. 238: Centre France. (Main Roads Maps: France Ser.). 1990. pap. 9.95 (*0-7859-0205-8*, 2067002374) Fr & Eur.

— Michelin Map No. 239: Auvergne-Limousin. (Main Roads Maps: France Ser.). 1990. pap. 9.95 (*0-7859-0206-6*, 2067002392) Fr & Eur.

— Michelin Map No. 240: Languedoc - Roussillon. (Main Roads Maps: France Ser.). 1990. pap. 9.95 (*0-7859-0207-4*, 2067002406) Fr & Eur.

— Michelin Map No. 241: Champagne-Ardennes. (Main Roads Maps: France Ser.). 1990. pap. 9.95 (*0-7859-0208-2*, 2067002414) Fr & Eur.

— Michelin Map No. 242: Alsace et Lorraine. (Main Roads Maps: France Ser.). 1990. pap. 9.95 (*0-7859-0209-0*, 2067002422) Fr & Eur.

— Michelin Map No. 243: Bourgogne-Franche Comte. (Main Roads Maps: France Ser.). 1990. pap. 9.95 (*0-7859-0210-4*, 2067002430) Fr & Eur.

— Michelin Map No. 244: Rhone - Alpes. (Main Roads Maps: France Ser.). 1990. pap. 9.95 (*0-7859-0211-2*, 2067002449) Fr & Eur.

— Michelin Map No. 246: Vallee du Rhone. (Main Roads Maps: France Ser.). 1990. pap. 9.95 (*0-7859-0213-9*, 2067002465) Fr & Eur.

— Michelin Map No. 412: Central Germany. (Main Roads Maps Ser.). 1990. pap. 9.95 (*0-7859-0261-9*, 2067004123) Fr & Eur.

— Michelin Map No. 428: North West Italy. (Main Roads Maps Ser.). 1990. pap. 9.95 (*0-7859-0263-5*, 206700428X) Fr & Eur.

— Michelin Map No. 429: North East Italy. (Main Roads Maps Ser.). 1990. pap. 9.95 (*0-7859-0264-3*, 2067004298) Fr & Eur.

— Michelin Map No. 441: North West Spain. (Main Roads Maps Ser.). 1990. pap. 9.95 (*0-7859-0269-4*, 2067004417) Fr & Eur.

— Michelin Map No. 442: Northern Spain. (Main Roads Maps Ser.). 1990. pap. 9.95 (*0-7859-0270-8*, 2067004425) Fr & Eur.

— Michelin Map No. 443: North East Spain. (Main Roads Maps Ser.). 1990. pap. 9.95 (*0-7859-0271-6*, 2067004433) Fr & Eur.

— Michelin Map No. 444: Central Spain. (Main Roads Maps Ser.). 1990. pap. 9.95 (*0-7859-0272-4*, 2067004441) Fr & Eur.

— Michelin Map No. 445: Central-Eastern Spain. (Main Roads Maps Ser.). 1990. pap. 9.95 (*0-7859-0273-2*, 206700445X) Fr & Eur.

— Michelin Map No. 446: Southern Spain. (Main Roads Maps Ser.). 1990. pap. 9.95 (*0-7859-0274-0*, 2067004468) Fr & Eur.

— Michelin Map No. 450: Canary Islands. (Main Roads Maps Ser.). 1990. pap. 9.95 (*0-7859-0275-9*, 2067004501) Fr & Eur.

— Michelin Map No. 970: Europe. (Main Roads Maps Ser.). 1990. pap. 9.95 (*0-7859-0327-5*, 2067009702) Fr & Eur.

— Michelin Map No. 972: Algeria-Tunisia. (Main Roads Maps Ser.). 1990. pap. 9.95 (*0-7859-0328-3*, 2067009729) Fr & Eur.

— Michelin Map No. 975: Ivory Coast. (Main Roads Maps Ser.). 1990. pap. 9.95 (*0-7859-0329-1*, 2067009753) Fr & Eur.

— Michelin Map, No. 101: Outskirts of Paris. (Main Roads Maps: France Ser.). 1992. pap. 9.95 (*0-7859-0178-7*, 2067001019) Fr & Eur.

— Michelin Map, No. 102: Battle of Normandy. (WW Two Battlefields Ser.). 1992. Commemorative. pap. 12.95 (*0-7859-0179-5*, 206700102X) Fr & Eur.

— Michelin Map, No. 106: Environs of Paris. (Main Roads Maps: France Ser.). 1992. pap. 9.95 (*0-7859-0180-9*, 206700102X) Fr & Eur.

— Michelin Map, No. 11: Paris Atlas. (Main Roads Maps with Useful Addresses Ser.). 1988. pap. 14.95 (*0-7859-0130-2*, 206700011X) Fr & Eur.

— Michelin Map, No. 115: Cote d'Azur. (Main Roads Maps: France Ser.). 1992. pap. 9.95 (*0-7859-0181-7*, 2067001159) Fr & Eur.

— Michelin Map, No. 121: Great Britain & Ireland. (Road Atlases Ser.). pap. 39.95 (*0-7859-0339-9*, 2067011219) Fr & Eur.

— Michelin Map, No. 122: Great Britain & Ireland. (Road Atlases Ser.). spiral bd. 39.95 (*0-7859-0182-5*, 2067011227) Fr & Eur.

— Michelin Map, No. 129: Europe. (Road Atlases Ser.). 1992. spiral bd. 39.95 (*0-7859-0183-3*, 2067001299) Fr & Eur.

— Michelin Map, No. 133: Europe. (Road Atlases Ser.). 1992. 39.95 (*0-7859-0184-1*, 600571637) Fr & Eur.

— Michelin Map, No. 134: Europe. large type ed. (Road Atlases Ser.). 1992. Large format. pap. 39.95 (*0-7859-0185-X*, 600572595) Fr & Eur.

— Michelin Map, No. 135: Europe. (Road Atlases Ser.). 1992. Small format. pap. 39.95 (*0-7859-0186-8*, 600573214) Fr & Eur.

— Michelin Map, No. 14: Paris Atlas with Metro & Regional Connections. (Main Roads Maps Ser.). 1992. pap. 14.95 (*0-7859-0132-9*, 2067000144) Fr & Eur.

— Michelin Map, No. 15: Paris by Arrondissements. (Main Roads Maps Ser.). 1992. pap. 19.95 (*0-7859-0133-7*, 2067000152) Fr & Eur.

— Michelin Map, No. 170: Beaune - Macon - Evian. (Road Maps with Tourist Index Ser.). 1992. pap. 7.95 (*0-7859-0187-6*, 2067001701) Fr & Eur.

— Michelin Map, No. 171: La Rochelle - Royan - Bordeaux. (Road Maps with Tourist Index Ser.). 1992. pap. 7.95 (*0-7859-0188-4*, 206700171X) Fr & Eur.

— Michelin Map, No. 189: Evian - Annecy - Briancon. (Road Maps with Tourist Index Ser.). 1992. pap. 7.95 (*0-7859-0189-2*, 2067001892) Fr & Eur.

— Michelin Map, No. 213: Brussel - Oostende - Liege. (Road Maps with Tourist Index Ser.). 1992. pap. 7.95 (*0-7859-0340-2*, 2067002139) Fr & Eur.

— Michelin Map, No. 215: Luxembourg. (Road Maps with Tourist Index Ser.). 1992. pap. 7.95 (*0-7859-0192-2*, 2067002155) Fr & Eur.

— Michelin Map, No. 216: Neuchatel - Basel - St. Gallen. (Road Maps with Tourist Index Ser.). 1992. pap. 7.95 (*0-7859-0193-0*, 2067002163) Fr & Eur.

— Michelin Map, No. 217: Geneve - Bern - Andermatt. (Road Maps with Tourist Index Ser.). 1992. pap. 7.95 (*0-7859-0194-9*, 2067002171) Fr & Eur.

— Michelin Map, No. 218: Andermatt - St. Moritz - Bolzano-Bozen. (Road Maps with Tourist Index Ser.). 1992. pap. 7.95 (*0-7859-0195-7*, 206700218X) Fr & Eur.

— Michelin Map, No. 219: Aosta - Aoste - Zermatt - Milano. (Road Maps with Tourist Index Ser.). 1992. pap. 7.95 (*0-7859-0196-5*, 2067002199) Fr & Eur.

— Michelin Map, No. 237: Ile de France. (Main Roads Maps: France Ser.). 1988. pap. 9.95 (*0-7859-0204-X*, 2067002376) Fr & Eur.

— Michelin Map, No. 245: Provence-Cote d'Azur. (Main Roads Maps: France Ser.). 1988. pap. 9.95 (*0-685-64752-8*, 2067002457) Fr & Eur.

— Michelin Map, No. 263: Battle of Provence. (WW Two Battlefields Ser.). 1992. pap. 12.95 (*0-7859-0214-7*, 2067002635) Fr & Eur.

— Michelin Map, No. 264: Battle of Alsace. (WW Two Battlefields Ser.). 1992. pap. 12.95 (*0-7859-0215-5*, 2067002643) Fr & Eur.

— Michelin Map, No. 265: Victory Road. (WW Two Battlefields Ser.). 1992. pap. 12.95 (*0-7859-0216-3*, 2067002651) Fr & Eur.

— Michelin Map, No. 30: Lyon. (Specialized Maps Ser.). 1992. pap. 9.95 (*0-7859-0134-5*, 2067000306) Fr & Eur.

— Michelin Map, No. 31: Lyon with Index. (Specialized Maps Ser.). 1992. pap. 9.95 (*0-7859-0135-3*, 2067000314) Fr & Eur.

— Michelin Map, No. 40: Barcelona. (Main Roads Maps Ser.). 1992. pap. 9.95 (*0-7859-0136-1*, 2067040405) Fr & Eur.

— Michelin Map, No. 401: Scotland. (Main Roads Maps, Great Britain & Ireland Ser.). 1988. pap. 9.95 (*0-7859-0252-X*, 2067004018) Fr & Eur.

— Michelin Map, No. 402: Midlands-The North. (Main Roads Maps, Great Britain & Ireland Ser.). 1988. pap. 9.95 (*0-7859-0253-8*, 2067004026) Fr & Eur.

— Michelin Map, No. 403: Wales-West Country-Midlands. (Main Roads Maps, Great Britain & Ireland Ser.). 1988. pap. 9.95 (*0-7859-0254-6*, 2067004034) Fr & Eur.

— Michelin Map, No. 404: South East-Midlands-East Anglia. (Main Roads Maps, Great Britain & Ireland Ser.). 1992. pap. 9.95 (*0-7859-0255-4*, 2067004042) Fr & Eur.

— Michelin Map, No. 405: Ireland. (Main Roads Maps, Great Britain & Ireland Ser.). 1992. pap. 9.95 (*0-7859-0256-2*, 2067004050) Fr & Eur.

— Michelin Map, No. 407: Benelux. (Main Roads Maps Ser.). 1992. pap. 9.95 (*0-7859-0257-0*, 2067004077) Fr & Eur.

— Michelin Map, No. 408: Netherlands. (Main Roads Maps Ser.). 1989. pap. 9.95 (*0-7859-0258-9*, 2067004085) Fr & Eur.

— Michelin Map, No. 409: Belgium-Luxemburg. (Main Roads Maps Ser.). 1992. pap. 9.95 (*0-7859-0259-7*, 2067004093) Fr & Eur.

— Michelin Map, No. 41: Barcelona with Index. (Main Roads Maps Ser.). 1992. pap. 9.95 (*0-7859-0137-X*, 2067040413) Fr & Eur.

— Michelin Map, No. 411: Northern Germany. (Main Roads Maps Ser.). 1988. pap. 9.95 (*0-7859-0260-0*, 2067004115) Fr & Eur.

— Michelin Map, No. 413: Bavaria, Southern Germany. (Main Roads Maps Ser.). 1992. pap. 9.95 (*0-7859-0262-7*, 2067004131) Fr & Eur.

— Michelin Map, No. 430: Central Italy. (Main Roads Maps Ser.). 1992. pap. 9.95 (*0-7859-0265-1*, 2067004301) Fr & Eur.

— Michelin Map, No. 431: South Italy. (Main Roads Maps Ser.). 1992. pap. 9.95 (*0-7859-0266-X*, 206700431X) Fr & Eur.

— Michelin Map, No. 432: Sicily. (Main Roads Maps Ser.). 1992. pap. 9.95 (*0-7859-0267-8*, 2067004328) Fr & Eur.

— Michelin Map, No. 433: Sardinia. (Main Roads Maps Ser.). 1992. pap. 9.95 (*0-7859-0268-6*, 2067004336) Fr & Eur.

— Michelin Map, No. 51: Calais - Lille - Bruxelles. (Road Maps with Tourist Index Ser.). 1992. pap. 7.95 (*0-7859-0138-8*, 2067000519) Fr & Eur.

— Michelin Map, No. 52: Le Havre - Dieppe - Amiens. (Road Maps with Tourist Index Ser.). 1992. pap. 7.95 (*0-7859-0139-6*, 2067000527) Fr & Eur.

— Michelin Map, No. 53: Arras - Char. - Mex. - St. Quentin. (Road Maps with Tourist Index Ser.). 1992. pap. 7.95 (*0-7859-0140-X*, 2067000535) Fr & Eur.

— Michelin Map, No. 54: Cherbourg - Caen - Rouen. (Road Maps with Tourist Index Ser.). 1992. pap. 7.95 (*0-7859-0141-8*, 2067000543) Fr & Eur.

— Michelin Map, No. 55: Caen - Rouen - Paris. (Road Maps with Tourist Index Ser.). 1992. pap. 7.95 (*0-7859-0142-6*, 2067000551) Fr & Eur.

— Michelin Map, No. 56: Paris - Rheims - Chalons-sur-Marne. (Road Maps with Tourist Index Ser.). 1992. pap. 7.95 (*0-7859-0143-4*, 206700056X) Fr & Eur.

— Michelin Map, No. 57: Verdun - Metz - Wissembourg. (Road Maps with Tourist Index Ser.). 1992. pap. 7.95 (*0-7859-0144-2*, 2067000578) Fr & Eur.

— Michelin Map, No. 58: St. Brieuc - St. Malo - Rennes. 1992. pap. 7.95 (*0-7859-0145-0*, 2067000586) Fr & Eur.

— Michelin Map, No. 585: Valley of the Kings. (France Historical Ser.). 1992. pap. 9.95 (*0-7859-0308-9*, 2067005855) Fr & Eur.

— Michelin Map, No. 588: Treasure Houses of the Sun King. (France Historical Ser.). 1992. pap. 9.95 (*0-7859-0309-7*, 206700588X) Fr & Eur.

— Michelin Map, No. 59: Brest - Quimper - St. Brieuc. (Road Maps with Tourist Index Ser.). 1992. pap. 7.95 (*0-7859-0146-9*, 2067000594) Fr & Eur.

— Michelin Map, No. 60: Le Mans - Chartres - Paris. (Road Maps with Tourist Index Ser.). 1992. pap. 7.95 (*0-7859-0147-7*, 2067000608) Fr & Eur.

M

An Asterisk (*) at the beginning of an entry indicates that the title is appearing in BIP for the first time.

— Michelin Map, No. 61: Paris - Troyes - Chaumont. (Road Maps with Tourist Index Ser.). 1992. pap. 7.95 (0-7859-0148-5, 2067000616) Fr & Eur.

— Michelin Map, No. 62: Epinal - Nancy - Strasbourg. (Road Maps with Tourist Index Ser.). 1992. pap. 7.95 (0-7859-0149-3, 2067000624) Fr & Eur.

— Michelin Map, No. 63: Vannes - Le Baule - Angers. (Road Maps with Tourist Index Ser.). 1992. pap. 7.95 (0-7859-0150-7, 2067000632) Fr & Eur.

— Michelin Map, No. 64: Angers - Tours - Orleans. (Road Maps with Tourist Index Ser.). 1992. pap. 7.95 (0-7859-0151-5, 2067000640) Fr & Eur.

— Michelin Map, No. 65: Montargis - Auxerre - Dijon. (Road Maps with Tourist Index Ser.). 1992. pap. 7.95 (0-7859-0152-3, 2067000659) Fr & Eur.

— Michelin Map, No. 66: Dijon - Besancon - Mulhouse. (Road Maps with Tourist Index Ser.). 1992. pap. 7.95 (0-7859-0153-1, 2067000667) Fr & Eur.

— Michelin Map, No. 67: Nantes - Les Sables-de l'O. - Poitiers. (Road Maps with Tourist Index Ser.). 1992. pap. 7.95 (0-7859-0154-X, 2067000675) Fr & Eur.

— Michelin Map, No. 68: Niort - Poitiers - Chateauroux. (Road Maps with Tourist Index Ser.). 1992. pap. 7.95 (0-7859-0155-8, 2067000683) Fr & Eur.

— Michelin Map, No. 69: Bourges - Nevers - Macon. (Road Maps with Tourist Index Ser.). 1992. pap. 7.95 (0-7859-0156-6, 2067000691) Fr & Eur.

M

— Michelin Map, No. 72: Angouleme - Limoges - Gueret. (Road Maps with Tourist Index Ser.). 1992. pap. 7.95 (0-7859-0157-4, 2067000721) Fr & Eur.

— Michelin Map, No. 73: Clermont-FD - Vichy - Lyon. (Road Maps with Tourist Index Ser.). 1992. pap. 7.95 (0-7859-0158-2, 206700073X) Fr & Eur.

— Michelin Map, No. 74: Lyon - Chambery - Geneve. (Road Maps with Tourist Index Ser.). 1992. pap. 7.95 (0-7859-0159-0, 2067000748) Fr & Eur.

— Michelin Map, No. 75: Bordeaux - Perigueux - Tulle. (Road Maps with Tourist Index Ser.). 1992. pap. 7.95 (0-7859-0160-4, 2067000756) Fr & Eur.

— Michelin Map, No. 76: Aurillac - le Puy - St. Etienne. (Road Maps with Tourist Index Ser.). 1992. pap. 7.95 (0-7859-0161-2, 2067000764) Fr & Eur.

— Michelin Map, No. 77: Valence - Grenoble - Gap. (Road Maps with Tourist Index Ser.). 1992. pap. 7.95 (0-7859-0162-0, 2067000772) Fr & Eur.

— Michelin Map, No. 78: Bordeaux - Dax - Biarritz. (Road Maps with Tourist Index Ser.). 1992. pap. 7.95 (0-7859-0163-9, 2067000780) Fr & Eur.

— Michelin Map, No. 79: Bordeaux - Agen - Montauban. (Road Maps with Tourist Index Ser.). 1992. pap. 7.95 (0-7859-0164-7, 2067000799) Fr & Eur.

— Michelin Map, No. 80: Albi - Rodez - Nimes. (Road Maps with Tourist Index Ser.). 1992. pap. 7.95 (0-7859-0165-5, 2067000802) Fr & Eur.

— Michelin Map, No. 81: Montelimar - Avignon - Digne. (Road Maps with Tourist Index Ser.). 1992. pap. 7.95 (0-7859-0166-3, 2067000810) Fr & Eur.

— Michelin Map, No. 82: Mont-de-Marsan - Pau - Toulouse. (Road Maps with Tourist Index Ser.). 1992. pap. 7.95 (0-7859-0167-1, 2067000829) Fr & Eur.

— Michelin Map, No. 83: Carcassone - Montpellier - Nimes. (Road Maps with Tourist Index Ser.). 1992. pap. 7.95 (0-7859-0168-X, 2067000837) Fr & Eur.

— Michelin Map, No. 84: Marseille - Toulon - Nice. (Road Maps with Tourist Index Ser.). 1992. pap. 7.95 (0-7859-0169-8, 2067000845) Fr & Eur.

— Michelin Map, No. 85: Biarritz - Lourdes - Luchon. (Road Maps with Tourist Index Ser.). 1992. pap. 7.95 (0-7859-0170-1, 2067000853) Fr & Eur.

— Michelin Map, No. 86: Luchon - Andorre - Perpignan. (Road Maps with Tourist Index Ser.). 1992. pap. 7.95 (0-7859-0171-X, 2067000861) Fr & Eur.

— Michelin Map, No. 87: Vosges - Alsace. (Road Maps with Tourist Index Ser.). 1992. pap. 7.95 (0-7859-0172-8, 206700087X) Fr & Eur.

— Michelin Map, No. 88: Clermont - Ferrand - Lyon - St. Etienne. (Road Maps with Tourist Index Ser.). 1992. pap. 7.95 (0-7859-0173-6, 2067000888) Fr & Eur.

— Michelin Map, No. 90: Corse. (Road Maps with Tourist Index Ser.). 1992. pap. 7.95 (0-7859-0174-4, 206700090X) Fr & Eur.

— Michelin Map, No. 918: Northern France. (Specialized Maps Ser.). 1992. pap. 7.95 (0-7859-0321-6, 2067009184) Fr & Eur.

— Michelin Map, No. 919: Southern France. (Specialized Maps Ser.). 1992. pap. 7.95 (0-7859-0322-4, 2067009192) Fr & Eur.

— Michelin Map, No. 92: France. (Road Atlases Ser.). 1992. spiral bd. 39.95 (0-7859-0175-2, 600569179) Fr & Eur.

— Michelin Map, No. 953: Africa, North & West. (Main Roads Maps Ser.). 1988. pap. 9.95 (0-7859-0323-2, 2067009532) Fr & Eur.

— Michelin Map, No. 954: Africa, NE Including Egypt & Arabia. (Main Roads Maps Ser.). 1988. pap. 9.95 (0-7859-0324-0, 2067009540) Fr & Eur.

— Michelin Map, No. 955: Africa, Central & South Madagascar. (Main Roads Maps Ser.). 1988. pap. 9.95 (0-7859-0325-9, 2067009559) Fr & Eur.

— Michelin Map, No. 96: France. (Road Atlases Ser.). 1992. pap. 39.95 (0-7859-0176-0, 600571653) Fr & Eur.

— Michelin Map, No. 969: Morocco. (Main Roads Maps Ser.). 1992. pap. 9.95 (0-7859-0326-7, 2067009699) Fr & Eur.

— Michelin Map, No. 98: France. (Road Atlases Ser.). 1992. 39.95 (0-7859-0177-9, 060057167X) Fr & Eur.

— Michelin Map, No. 980: Greece. (Main Roads Maps Ser.). 1992. pap. 9.95 (0-7859-0330-5, 206700980X) Fr & Eur.

— Michelin Map, No. 984: Germany. (Main Roads Maps Ser.). 1988. pap. 9.95 (0-7859-0331-3, 2067009842) Fr & Eur.

— Michelin Map, No. 985: Scandinavia & Finland. (Main Roads Maps Ser.). 1988. pap. 9.95 (0-7859-0332-1, 2067009850) Fr & Eur.

— Michelin Map, No. 986: Great Britain & Ireland. (Main Roads Maps Ser.). 1992. pap. 9.95 (0-7859-0333-X, 2067009869) Fr & Eur.

— Michelin Map, No. 987: Germany - Austria - Benelux. (Main Roads Maps Ser.). 1992. pap. 9.95 (0-7859-0334-8, 2067009877) Fr & Eur.

— Michelin Map, No. 988: Italy. (Main Roads Maps Ser.). 1992. pap. 9.95 (0-7859-0335-6, 2067009885) Fr & Eur.

— Michelin Map, No. 989: France. (Main Roads Maps Ser.). 1992. pap. 9.95 (0-7859-0336-4, 2067009893) Fr & Eur.

— Michelin Map, No. 990: Spain & Portugal. (Main Roads Maps Ser.). 1992. pap. 9.95 (0-7859-0337-2, 2067009907) Fr & Eur.

— Michelin Map, No. 991: Yugoslavia. (Main Roads Maps Ser.). 1988. pap. 9.95 (0-7859-0338-0, 2067009915) Fr & Eur.

— Michelin Red Travel Guide - Camping - France. (ENG, FRE, GER & ITA.). 1992. 14.95 (0-685-66128-8) Fr & Eur.

— Michelin Red Travel Guide - Greater London. 1992. 8.95 (0-8288-6110-2) Fr & Eur.

— Michelin Road Atlas - Europe. pap. 19.95 (0-8288-6200-1) Fr & Eur.

— Michelin Road Atlas - Europe. large type ed. pap. 19.95 (0-8288-6201-X) Fr & Eur.

— Michelin Road Atlas - France. 29.95 (0-8288-6199-4) Fr & Eur.

— Michelin Road Atlas - France. large type ed. pap. 19.95 (0-8288-6198-6) Fr & Eur.

— Michelin Road Atlas - Great Britain - Ireland. 19.95 (0-8288-6197-8) Fr & Eur.

— Netherlands Green Guide. (Orig.). Date not set. pap. 19.00 (2-06-157401-7, 1574) Michelin.

— Netherlands Green Guide English Edition. Date not set. pap. 17.95 (0-7859-7190-4, 20600155517) Fr & Eur.

— New England Green Guide English Edition. Date not set. pap. 17.95 (0-7859-7178-5, 2061569064) Fr & Eur.

— New York City Green Guide English Edition. Date not set. pap. 17.95 (0-7859-7179-3, 2061551114) Fr & Eur.

— New York City Green Guide French Edition. (FRE.). Date not set. pap. 17.95 (0-7859-7215-3, 2067005480) Fr & Eur.

— New York City Green Guide Japanese Edition. (FRE.). Date not set. pap. 36.00 (0-614-00393-8, 4408013137) Fr & Eur.

— Normandie Contentin Green Guide French Edition. (FRE.). Date not set. pap. 17.95 (0-7859-7232-3, 2060034612) Fr & Eur.

— Normandie Vallee Seine Green Guide French Edition. (FRE.). Date not set. pap. 17.95 (0-614-00379-2, 206034 71X) Fr & Eur.

— Normandy Green Guide. Date not set. pap. 18.00 (2-06-134801-7, 1348) Michelin.

— Normandy Green Guide English Edition. Date not set. pap. 17.95 (0-7859-7206-4, 2061348017) Fr & Eur.

— Nouvelle Angleterre Green Guide. 4th ed. (Orig.). (FRE.). Date not set. pap. 18.00 (2-06-056804-8, 568) Michelin.

— Nouvelle Angleterre Green Guide French Edition. (FRE.). Date not set. pap. 17.95 (0-7859-7213-7, 2060056829) Fr & Eur.

— Parid & Environs Red Guide. 1994. pap. 12.95 (0-7859-7174-2, 2060068495) Fr & Eur.

— Paris & Environs Red Guide. (Red Guide Ser.). 1995. 10.00 (2-06-006859-2, 685) Michelin.

— Paris Green Guide English Edition. Date not set. pap. 17.95 (0-7859-7198-X, 2067013556) Fr & Eur.

— Paris Green Guide French Edition. (FRE.). Date not set. pap. 17.95 (0-7859-7216-1, 2067003526) Fr & Eur.

— Paris Green Guide Japanese Edition. (FRE.). Date not set. pap. 36.00 (0-614-00394-6) Fr & Eur.

— Paris North East Plan with Index. 9th ed. (Orig.). Date not set. pap. 10.00 (2-06-700020-9, 020) Michelin.

— Paris North West Plan with Index. 9th ed. (Orig.). Date not set. pap. 10.00 (2-06-700018-7, 018) Michelin.

— Paris South East Plan with Index. 7th ed. (Orig.). Date not set. pap. 10.00 (2-06-700024-1, 024) Michelin.

— Paris Southwest Plan with Index. 8th ed. (Orig.). Date not set. pap. text ed. 10.00 (2-06-700022-5, 022) Michelin.

— Perigord-Quercy Green Guide French Edition. 252p. 1989. pap. 17.95 (0-7859-7234-X, 2067003704) Fr & Eur.

— Poitou-Vendee-Charentes Green Guide French Edition. (FRE.). Date not set. pap. 17.95 (0-7859-7235-8, 2067003712) Fr & Eur.

— Portugal Green Guide. 5th ed. 1994. pap. 17.95 (0-7859-7191-2, 557) Fr & Eur.

— Portugal Green Guide Spanish Edition. (FRE.). Date not set. pap. 29.95 (0-7859-7251-X, 2067045652) Fr & Eur.

— Portugal Red Guide. (Red Guide Ser.). 1995. 10.00 (2-06-007259-X, 725) Michelin.

— Provence Green Guide. (FRE.). Date not set. pap. 17.95 (0-7859-7236-6, 2067003623) Fr & Eur.

— Provence Green Guide English Edition. Date not set. pap. 17.95 (0-7859-7207-2, 2067013750) Fr & Eur.

— Provence Green Guide Japanese Edition. (FRE.). Date not set. pap. 36.00 (0-614-00392-X, 4408013048) Fr & Eur.

— Pyrenees-Aquitaine Green Guide French Edition. (FRE.). Date not set. pap. 17.95 (0-7859-7237-4, 2067003674) Fr & Eur.

— Pyrenees-Roussillon Green Guide French Edition. (FRE.). Date not set. pap. 17.95 (0-7859-7238-2, 2067003682) Fr & Eur.

— Quebec Green Guide French Edition. (FRE.). Date not set. pap. 17.95 (0-7859-7214-5, 2067005723) Fr & Eur.

— Quebec (Province) Green Guide English Edition. Date not set. pap. 17.95 (0-7859-7181-5, 2067015737) Fr & Eur.

— Rome Green Guide English Edition. Date not set. pap. 17.95 (0-7859-7199-8, 2067015591) Fr & Eur.

— Scotland Green Guide English Edition. Date not set. pap. 17.95 (0-7859-7192-0, 2060157528) Fr & Eur.

— Spain & Portugal Road Atlas. (FRE.). Date not set. spiral bd., pap. 9.95 (0-7859-7258-7) Fr & Eur.

— Spain-Portugal Road Atlas. 2nd ed. (Orig.). Date not set. pap. 20.00 (2-06-146002-X, 1460) Michelin.

— Switzerland Green Guide English Edition. Date not set. pap. 17.95 (0-7859-7194-7, 206701563X) Fr & Eur.

— Switzerland Green Guide Japanese Edition. (FRE.). Date not set. pap. 36.00 (0-614-00389-X, 4408013064) Fr & Eur.

— Switzerland Red Guide. 1994. 24.95 (0-7859-7171-8, 2060069491) Fr & Eur.

— Switzerland Red Guide. (Red Guide Ser.). 1995. 24.00 (2-06-006959-9, 695) Michelin.

— Valle du Rhone Green Guide French Edition. (FRE.). Date not set. pap. 17.95 (0-7859-7239-0, 2067003739) Fr & Eur.

— Washington, D. C. Green Guide English Edition. Date not set. pap. 17.95 (0-7859-7182-3, 206701577X) Fr & Eur.

— Washington DC Green Guide. 2nd ed. (Orig.). Date not set. pap. 17.00 (2-06-157702-4, 1577) Michelin.

***Michelin Staff, ed.** Green Guide - Italy (English Language) 4th ed. (Orig.). 1995. pap. 19.00 (2-06-153404-X) Michelin.

Micheline, Jack. Imaginary Conversation with Jack Kerouac. 24p. (Orig.). 1989. pap. 5.00 (0-929730-07-0) Zeitgeist Pr.

— Last House in America. 1976. pap. 5.00 (0-915016-06-0) Second Coming.

— Outlaw of the Lowest Planet. (Orig.). Date not set. pap. 5.00 (0-929730-47-X) Zeitgeist Pr.

— River of Red Wine. 60p. 1986. reprint ed. pap. 6.95 (0-934953-04-X) Water Row Pr.

— Skinny Dynamite & Other Short Stories. Winans, A. D., ed. LC 79-63969. 96p. (Orig.). 1980. pap. 10.00 (0-915016-27-3) Second Coming.

Michelini, Ann N. Euripides & the Tragic Tradition. LC 86-40057. (Studies in Classics). 528p. 1988. text ed. 32.75 (0-299-10760-4) U of Wis Pr.

Michelinie, et al. The Aladdin Effect. 64p. 1985. 5.95 (0-87135-081-5) Marvel Entmnt.

— The Power of Iron Man. (Illus.). 160p. 1984. pap. 9.95 (0-87135-599-X) Marvel Entmnt.

Michelinie, David. The Avengers: Emperor Doom. (Illus.). 640p. 1990. pap. 9.95 (0-87135-256-7) Marvel Entmnt.

— Invasion of the Spider-Slayers: Spider-slayers. (Illus.). 112p. 1995. pap. 15.95 (0-7851-0100-4) Marvel Entmnt.

— Iron Man vs. Dr. Doom. 128p. 1994. pap. 12.95 (0-7851-0062-8) Marvel Entmnt.

— Spider-Man: Carnage. 1993. pap. 6.95 (0-87135-971-5) Marvel Entmnt.

— Spider-Man: The Return of Sinister Six. (Spider-Man Ser.). 144p. 1994. pap. 15.95 (0-7851-0043-1) Marvel Entmnt.

— Spider-Man: The Return of Venom. (Illus.). 1993. pap. 12.95 (0-87135-966-9) Marvel Entmnt.

— Spider-Man vs. Doctor Doom. (Illus.). 64p. 1995. pap. 5.95 (0-7851-0110-1) Marvel Entmnt.

— Venom: Lethal Protector. (Illus.). 144p. 1995. pap. 15.95 (0-7851-0107-1) Marvel Entmnt.

Michelinie, David & McFarlane, Todd. Spider-Man vs. Venom. 112p. 1992. pap. 12.95 (0-87135-616-3) Marvel Entmnt.

***Michelinie, David & Smith, Dean W.** Spider-Man: Carnage in New York. (Orig.). 1995. pap. text ed. 5.99 (1-57297-019-7) Blvd Books.

Michelinie, David, et al. Spider-Man: Cosmic Adventures. (Illus.). 1993. pap. 19.95 (0-87135-963-4) Marvel Entmnt.

— Spider-Man: The Assassin Nation Plot. (Illus.). 144p. 1992. pap. 14.95 (0-87135-889-1) Marvel Entmnt.

Michelis, Dennis. Mary of Nazareth. LC 92-34728. 1992. write for info. (0-917651-94-4) Holy Cross Orthodox.

— Ten Greek Popes. 1987. pap. 5.95 (0-937032-54-9) Light&Life Pub Co MN.

Michell. Design in the High Street. 1986. pap. 39.95 (0-85139-159-1, Butterwrth Archit) Buttrwrth-Heinemann.

— Successful Machine Quilting. 1995. pap. (0-696-20432-0) Meredith Bks.

— Veterinary Fluid Therapy. 1989. 79.95 (0-632-01407-5) Blackwell Sci.

Michell, A. R. The Advancement of Veterinary Science, Vol. 1: Veterinary Medicine Beyond 2000. (Advancement of Veterinary Science Ser.: Vol. 1). 240p. 1993. 66.50 (0-85198-759-1) CAB Intl.

— The Advancement of Veterinary Science, Vol. 2: Veterinary Education: the Future. (Advancement of Veterinary Science Ser.: Vol. 2). 240p. 1993. 66.50 (0-85198-760-5) CAB Intl.

— The Advancement of Veterinary Science, Vol. 3: History of the Healing Professions. (Advancement of Veterinary Science Ser.: Vol. 3). 140p. 1993. 47.50 (0-85198-761-3) CAB Intl.

Michell, A. R., ed. The Advancement of Veterinary Science, Vol. 4: Veterinary Science - Growth Points & Comparative Medicine. 225p. 1993. text ed. 66.50 (0-85198-762-1) CAB Intl.

Michell, David. A Boys War. 1988. pap. 6.95 (9971-972-71-9) OMF Bks.

— The Spirit of Eric Liddell: Olympic Athlete of "Chariots of Fire" 28p. 1992. pap. text ed. 2.95 (981-3009-06-3) OMF Bks.

Michell, Dorothy. More Australian Tales of Ghost & Fantasy. 207p. (C). 1990. 36.00 (0-947333-00-2, Pub. by Pascoe Pub AT) St Mut.

— Slave by Marriage. 179p. (C). 1990. 39.00 (0-947333-15-0, Pub. by Pascoe Pub AT) St Mut.

Michell, Dorothy, ed. Commie-The Girl Who Married the Butler: A Novella of the 19th Century Australia, 1953-93. 184p. (C). 1990. 36.00 (0-947333-01-0, Pub. by Pascoe Pub AT) St Mut.

Michell, E. B. Art & Practice of Hawking. (Illus.). 303p. 1983. pap. 25.00 (0-87556-656-1) Saifer.

Michell, Edward B. Siamese-English Dictionary. (ENG & THA.). 1977. reprint ed. 43.95 (0-518-19004-8) Ayer.

Michell, Frank. Annals of an Ancient Cornish Town: Redruth. (C). 1989. 65.00 (0-907566-85-5, Pub. by Dyllansow Truran UK) St Mut.

***Michell, George.** Architecture & Art of Southern India: Vijayanagara & the Successor States, 1350-1750. (New Cambridge History of India Ser.: No. I:6). (Illus.). 288p. (C). Date not set. write for info. (0-521-44110-2) Cambridge U Pr.

— The Hindu Temple: An Introduction to Its Meaning & Forms. (Illus.). 192p. 1988. pap. 14.95 (0-226-53230-5) U Ch Pr.

— The Royal Palaces of India. LC 93-60425. (Illus.). 232p. 1994. 50.00 (0-500-34127-3) Thames Hudson.

— The Vijayanagara Courtly Style. (C). 1992. 44.00 (81-85425-29-9, Pub. by Manohar II) S Asia.

Michell, George, ed. Ahmadabad. (C). 1988. 48.50 (81-85026-03-3, Pub. by Marg) S Asia.

— Architecture of the Islamic World: Its History & Social Meaning. LC 84-50341. (Illus.). 1984. 40.00 (0-500-34076-5) Thames Hudson.

— Architecture of the Islamic World: Its History & Social Meaning. LC 84-50341. (Illus.). 288p. 1995. pap. 29.95 (0-500-27847-4) Thames Hudson.

— Brick Temples of Bengal: From the Archives of David McCutchion. LC 82-3872. (Illus.). 450p. 1983. 125.00 (0-691-04010-9) Princeton U Pr.

— Temple Towns of Tamil Nadu. (Illus.). (C). 1993. 68.00 (81-85026-21-1, Pub. by Marg) S Asia.

Michell, George, jt. auth. see Eaton, Richard M.

Michell, Humphrey. Sparta: To Kryton tes Politeias ton Lakedaimonoin. LC 85-12537. x, 348p. 1985. reprint ed. text ed. 59.75 (0-313-24955-5, MISP, Greenwood Pr) Greenwood.

Michell, J. An Introduction to the Logic of Psychological Measurement. 200p. (C). 1990. text ed. 39.95 (0-8058-0566-4) L Erlbaum Assocs.

Michell, J. E., tr. see Scheidemann, Philip.

Michell, John. At the Center of the World: Polar Symbolism Discovered in Celtic, Norse & Other Ritualized Landscapes. LC 93-61809. (Illus.). 184p. 1994. 24.95 (0-500-01607-0) Thames Hudson.

— The Earth Spirit: Its Ways, Shrines, & Mysteries. (Art & Imagination Ser.). (Illus.). 1989. pap. 15.95 (0-500-81011-7) Thames Hudson.

— Megalithomania: Artists, Antiquarians & Archaeologists at the Old Stone Monuments. LC 81-69643. (Illus.). 168p. 1982. 33.95 (0-8014-1479-2) Cornell U Pr.

— The New View over Atlantis. LC 95-61466. (Illus.). 224p. (Orig.). 1995. pap. 17.95 (0-500-27312-X) Thames Hudson.

— Secrets of the Stones. (Illus.). 128p. 1989. pap. 10.95 (0-89281-337-7, Destiny Bks) Inner Tradit.

— A Traveler's Key to Sacred England. LC 87-46041. (Illus.). 1988. pap. 18.95 (0-394-55573-2) Knopf.

Michell, John & Rhone, Christine. Twelve-Tribe Nations & the Science of Enchanting the Landscape. LC 91-26915. (Illus.). 192p. (Orig.). 1991. 25.00 (0-933999-48-8); pap. 17.95 (0-933999-49-6) Phanes Pr.

— Twelve-Tribe Nations & the Science of Enchanting the Landscape. deluxe ed. LC 91-26915. (Illus.). 192p. (Orig.). 1991. 35.00 (0-933999-47-X) Phanes Pr.

Michell, Keith. Practically Macrobiotic. 1989. pap. 22.95 (0-89281-278-8) Inner Tradit.

Michell, Lewis. The Life & Times of the Right Honourable Cecil John Rhodes, 1853-1902, 2 vols. Wilkins, Mira, ed. LC 76-29768. (European Business Ser.). 1977. reprint ed. lib. bdg. 63.95 (0-405-09782-4) Ayer.

Michell, Marti. Holiday Scrap Crafts. 168p. 1992. 24.95 (0-696-02358-X) Meredith Bks.

Michell, Monica. Teacher's Guide to the Great American West. (Illus.). 24p. (Orig.). 1985. pap. 4.95 (0-935213-09-0) A M Huntington Art.

Michell, R. B., jt. auth. see Bradley, Robert F.

Michell, R. H., jt. ed. see Finean, J. B.

Michell, Robert. Golden Eagles. 313p. (C). 1990. pap. 48.00 (0-646-09558-7, Pub. by Boolarong Pubns AT) St Mut.

Michell, Robert H., et al, eds. Inositol Lipids in Cell Signalling. 534p. 1989. text ed. 146.00 (0-12-493860-4) Acad Pr.

Michell, Ronald. The Carews of Beddington. 129p. 1989. pap. 29.00 (0-317-47426-X, Pub. by Sutton Libs & Arts) St Mut.

Michell, Ronald H. The Carews of Beddington. (C). 1985. pap. 29.00 (0-907335-02-0, Pub. by Sutton Libs & Arts) St Mut.

Michell, S. J. Introduction to Fluid & Particle Mechanics. 1970. 148.00 (0-08-013313-4, Pub. by Pergamon Repr UK) Franklin.

Michell, Tony. From a Developing to a Newly Industrialised Country: The Republic of Korea, 1961-82. (Employment, Adjustment & Industrialisation Ser.: No. 6). xii, 180p. (Orig.). 1988. pap. 24.00 (92-2-106396-8) Intl Labour Office.

***Michelle, Lonnie.** How Kids Make Friends: Secrets for Making Lots of Friends, No Matter How Shy You Are. LC 95-60589. (Illus.). 64p. (Orig.). (J). (gr. 3-8). 1995. pap. 9.95 (0-9638152-1-0) Freedom Pubng.

An Asterisk (*) at the beginning of an entry indicates that the title is appearing in BIP for the first time.

Michelman, Hans J. & Soldatos, Panayotis, eds. European Integration: Theories & Approaches. LC 94-984. 118p. (Orig.). (C). 1994. pap. text ed. 24.50 (0-8191-9455-7) U Pr of Amer.

Michelman, Irving S. The Crisis Meters: Business Response to Social Crises. LC 73-4914. (Illus.). xviii, 418p. 1973. lib. bdg. 45.00 (0-678-01320-9) Kelley.

— The Moral Limitations of Capitalism. (Philosophy Ser.). 182p. 1994. 59.95 (1-85628-877-3, Pub. by Avebury Pub UK) Ashgate Pub Co.

Michelman, Jeffrey E. Lotus 1-2-3 Release 2.2 for Accounting. (Illus.). 568p. (C). 1990. teacher ed write for info. (1-878748-10-6); disk 56.75 (1-878748-00-9); disk 56.75 (1-878748-01-7); disk 31.00 (1-878748-56-4); disk 31.00 (1-878748-57-2) Course Tech.

— Lotus 1-2-3 Release 2.3 for Accounting: Principles. (Illus.). 400p. (C). 1992. teacher ed write for info. (1-56527-026-6); disk 53.35 (1-878748-81-5); disk 53.35 (1-878748-82-3); disk 24.95 (1-878748-83-1); disk 24.95 (1-878748-84-X) Course Tech.

Michelman, Stanley B., et al. The Private Adoption Handbook: A Step-by-Step Guide to the Legal, Emotional, & Practical Demands of Adopting a Baby. 1988. 18.95 (0-394-56629-7, Villard Bks) Random.

Michelmann, Hans J. Organisational Effectiveness in a Multinational Bureaucracy. LC 78-60532. 271p. 1979. text ed. 55.00 (0-275-90394-X, C0394, Praeger Pubs) Greenwood.

Michelmann, Hans J. & Soldatos, Panayotis. Federalism & International Relations: The Role of Subnational Units. 336p. 1991. 82.00 (0-19-827491-2) OUP.

Michelotti, Leo. Intermediate Classical Dynamics with Applications to Beam Physics. LC 93-9418. 352p. 1995. text ed. 59.95 (0-471-55384-0) Wiley.

Michelove, Leon D., ed. see International SAMPE Technical Conference Staff.

Michelow, Bryan J., jt. auth. see Hartrampf, Carl R., Jr.

Michelozzi, Betty N. Coming Alive from Nine to Five: The Career Search Handbook. 4th ed. 294p. (C). 1992. pap. text ed. 19.95 (1-55934-089-4) Mayfield Pub.

— Instructor's Manual for Coming Alive from Nine to Five: The Career Search Handbook. 4th ed. 294p. (C). 1992. teacher ed write for info. (1-55934-151-3) Mayfield Pub.

Michels. Retinal Detachment: Diagnosis & Management. (Illus.). 1152p. 1990. 160.00 (0-8016-3417-2) Mosby Yr Bk.

Michels, A., jt. ed. see Freymann, J. R.

Michels, Caroll. How to Survive & Prosper As an Artist: A Complete Guide to Career Management. 3rd rev. ed. 288p. 1992. pap. 11.95 (0-8050-1953-7, Owl) H Holt & Co.

Michels, Christine. Ascent to the Stars. 400p. (Orig.). 1994. pap. 4.99 (0-505-51933-X, Love Spell) Dorchester Pub Co.

— Danger's Kiss. 368p. (Orig.). 1994. mass mkt. 4.50 (0-8439-3694-0) Dorchester Pub Co.

— In Fugitive Arms. 448p. (Orig.). 1995. mass mkt., pap. text ed. 4.99 (0-505-52029-X) Dorchester Pub Co.

Michels, Denis. Champions of the Faith. 182p. 1986. pap. 7.95 (0-917651-23-5) Holy Cross Orthodox.

Michels, Dia L., jt. auth. see Baumslag, Naomi.

Michels, Eugene. The Beginnings: Physical Therapy & the APTA. (Illus.). 1979. pap. 6.00 (0-912452-03-X) Am Phys Therapy Assn.

Michels, Gloria. How to Make Yourself Famous: Secrets of a Professional Publicist. 2nd ed. 1994. pap. 12.95 (0-8038-9359-0) Hastings.

Michels, Greg. Governments of Alabama, 1989. (Governments of Your State Ser.). (Illus.). 1989. text ed. 150.00 (1-55507-312-3) Municipal Analysis.

— Governments of Arkansas, 1989. (Governments of Your State Ser.). (Illus.). 1989. text ed. 150.00 (1-55507-313-1) Municipal Analysis.

— Governments of California, 1989. (Governments of Your State Ser.). (Illus.). 1989. text ed. 150.00 (1-55507-314-X) Municipal Analysis.

— Governments of Colorado, 1989. (Governments of Your State Ser.). (Illus.). 1989. text ed. 150.00 (1-55507-315-8) Municipal Analysis.

— Governments of Connecticut, 1989. (Governments of Your State Ser.). (Illus.). 1989. text ed. 150.00 (1-55507-316-6) Municipal Analysis.

— Governments of Florida, 1989. (Governments of Your State Ser.). (Illus.). 1989. text ed. 150.00 (1-55507-317-4) Municipal Analysis.

— Governments of Georgia, 1989. (Governments of Your State Ser.). (Illus.). 1989. text ed. 150.00 (1-55507-318-2) Municipal Analysis.

Michels, Greg, ed. Alabama Government's Performance Standards, 1990. (Governments Performance Standards Ser.). (Illus.). 150p. 1990. text ed. 125.00 (1-55507-474-X) Municipal Analysis.

— Arkansas Governments Performance Standards, 1990. (Governments Performance Standards Ser.). (Illus.). 150p. 1990. text ed. 125.00 (1-55507-475-8) Municipal Analysis.

— California Governments Performance Standards, 1990. (Governments Performance Standards Ser.). (Illus.). 150p. 1990. text ed. 125.00 (1-55507-476-6) Municipal Analysis.

— The Carolinas Governments Performance Standards, 1990. (Governments Performance Standards Ser.). (Illus.). 150p. 1990. text ed. 125.00 (1-55507-508-8) Municipal Analysis.

— Colorado Governments Performance Standards, 1990. (Governments Performance Standards Ser.). (Illus.). 150p. 1990. text ed. 125.00 (1-55507-477-4) Municipal Analysis.

— Connecticut Governments Performance Standards, 1990. (Governments Performance Standards Ser.). (Illus.). 150p. 1990. text ed. 125.00 (1-55507-478-2) Municipal Analysis.

— Florida Governments Performance Standards, 1990. (Governments Performance Standards Ser.). (Illus.). 150p. 1990. text ed. 125.00 (1-55507-479-0) Municipal Analysis.

— Georgia Governments Performance Standards, 1990. (Governments Performance Standards Ser.). (Illus.). 150p. 1990. text ed. 125.00 (1-55507-480-4) Municipal Analysis.

— Governments of Alabama, 1985. (Governments of Your State Ser.). 1984. 150.00 (1-55507-041-8); text ed. 150.00 (0-317-38176-8) Municipal Analysis.

— Governments of Alabama, 1986. (Governments of Your State Ser.). 1985. text ed. 150.00 (1-55507-086-8) Municipal Analysis.

— Governments of Alabama 1989: Expert Edition. (Governments of Your State: Expert Ser.). (Illus.). 400p. 1989. text ed. 325.00 (1-55507-350-6) Municipal Analysis.

— Governments of Alabama 1990. (Governments of Your State Ser.). (Illus.). 400p. 1990. text ed. 150.00 (1-55507-398-0) Municipal Analysis.

— Governments of Alabama 1990: Expert Edition. (Governments of Your State: Expert Ser.). (Illus.). 400p. 1990. text ed. 325.00 (1-55507-436-7) Municipal Analysis.

— Governments of Alabama, 1991. (Governments of Your State Ser.). (Illus.). 400p. 1991. text ed. 150.00 (1-55507-522-3) Municipal Analysis.

— Governments of Arkansas, 1985. (Governments of Your State Ser.). 1984. text ed. 150.00 (1-55507-042-6) Municipal Analysis.

— Governments of Arkansas, 1986. (Governments of Your State Ser.). 1985. text ed. 150.00 (1-55507-087-6) Municipal Analysis.

— Governments of Arkansas 1989: Expert Edition. (Governments of Your State: Expert Ser.). (Illus.). 400p. 1989. text ed. 325.00 (1-55507-351-4) Municipal Analysis.

— Governments of Arkansas 1990. (Governments of Your State Ser.). (Illus.). 400p. 1990. text ed. 150.00 (1-55507-399-9) Municipal Analysis.

— Governments of Arkansas 1990: Expert Edition. (Governments of Your State: Expert Ser.). (Illus.). 400p. 1990. text ed. 325.00 (1-55507-437-5) Municipal Analysis.

— Governments of Arkansas, 1991. (Governments of Your State Ser.). (Illus.). 400p. 1991. text ed. 150.00 (1-55507-523-1) Municipal Analysis.

— Governments of California, 1985. (Governments of Your State Ser.). 1984. text ed. 150.00 (1-55507-043-4) Municipal Analysis.

— Governments of California, 1986. (Governments of Your State Ser.). 1985. text ed. 150.00 (1-55507-088-4) Municipal Analysis.

— Governments of California 1989: Expert Edition. (Governments of Your State: Expert Ser.). (Illus.). 400p. 1989. text ed. 325.00 (1-55507-352-2) Municipal Analysis.

— Governments of California 1990. (Governments of Your State Ser.). (Illus.). 400p. 1990. text ed. 150.00 (1-55507-400-6) Municipal Analysis.

— Governments of California 1990: Expert Edition. (Governments of Your State: Expert Ser.). (Illus.). 400p. 1990. text ed. 325.00 (1-55507-438-3) Municipal Analysis.

— Governments of California, 1991. (Governments of Your State Ser.). (Illus.). 400p. 1991. text ed. 150.00 (1-55507-524-X) Municipal Analysis.

— Governments of Colorado, 1985. (Governments of Your State Ser.). 1984. text ed. 150.00 (1-55507-044-2) Municipal Analysis.

— Governments of Colorado, 1986. (Governments of Your State Ser.). 1985. text ed. 150.00 (1-55507-089-2) Municipal Analysis.

— Governments of Colorado 1989: Expert Edition. (Governments of Your State: Expert Ser.). (Illus.). 400p. 1989. text ed. 325.00 (1-55507-353-0) Municipal Analysis.

— Governments of Colorado 1990. (Governments of Your State Ser.). (Illus.). 400p. 1990. text ed. 150.00 (1-55507-401-4) Municipal Analysis.

— Governments of Colorado 1990: Expert Edition. (Governments of Your State: Expert Ser.). (Illus.). 400p. 1990. text ed. 325.00 (1-55507-473-1) Municipal Analysis.

— Governments of Colorado, 1991. (Governments of Your State Ser.). (Illus.). 400p. 1991. text ed. 150.00 (1-55507-525-8) Municipal Analysis.

— Governments of Connecticut, 1985. (Governments of Your State Ser.). 1984. text ed. 150.00 (1-55507-045-0) Municipal Analysis.

— Governments of Connecticut, 1986. (Governments of Your State Ser.). 1985. text ed. 150.00 (1-55507-090-6) Municipal Analysis.

— Governments of Connecticut 1989: Expert Edition. (Governments of Your State: Expert Ser.). (Illus.). 400p. 1989. text ed. 325.00 (1-55507-354-9) Municipal Analysis.

— Governments of Connecticut 1990. (Governments of Your State Ser.). (Illus.). 400p. 1990. text ed. 150.00 (1-55507-402-2) Municipal Analysis.

— Governments of Connecticut 1990: Expert Edition. (Governments of Your State: Expert Ser.). (Illus.). 400p. 1990. text ed. 325.00 (1-55507-439-1) Municipal Analysis.

— Governments of Connecticut, 1991. (Governments of Your State Ser.). (Illus.). 400p. 1991. text ed. 150.00 (1-55507-526-6) Municipal Analysis.

— Governments of Florida, 1985. (Governments of Your State Ser.). 1984. text ed. 150.00 (1-55507-046-9) Municipal Analysis.

— Governments of Florida, 1986. (Governments of Your State Ser.). 1985. text ed. 150.00 (1-55507-091-4) Municipal Analysis.

— Governments of Florida 1989: Expert Edition. (Governments of Your State: Expert Ser.). (Illus.). 400p. 1989. text ed. 325.00 (1-55507-355-7) Municipal Analysis.

— Governments of Florida 1990. (Governments of Your State Ser.). (Illus.). 400p. 1990. text ed. 150.00 (1-55507-403-0) Municipal Analysis.

— Governments of Florida 1990: Expert Edition. (Governments of Your State: Expert Ser.). (Illus.). 400p. 1990. text ed. 325.00 (1-55507-440-5) Municipal Analysis.

— Governments of Florida, 1991. (Governments of Your State Ser.). (Illus.). 400p. 1991. text ed. 150.00 (1-55507-527-4) Municipal Analysis.

— Governments of Georgia, 1985. (Governments of Your State Ser.). 1984. text ed. 150.00 (1-55507-047-7) Municipal Analysis.

— Governments of Georgia, 1986. (Governments of Your State Ser.). 1985. text ed. 150.00 (1-55507-092-2) Municipal Analysis.

— Governments of Georgia 1989: Expert Edition. (Governments of Your State: Expert Ser.). (Illus.). 400p. 1989. text ed. 325.00 (1-55507-356-5) Municipal Analysis.

— Governments of Georgia 1990. (Governments of Your State Ser.). (Illus.). 400p. 1990. text ed. 150.00 (1-55507-404-9) Municipal Analysis.

— Governments of Georgia 1990: Expert Edition. (Governments of Your State: Expert Ser.). (Illus.). 400p. 1990. text ed. 325.00 (1-55507-441-3) Municipal Analysis.

— Governments of Georgia, 1991. (Governments of Your State Ser.). (Illus.). 400p. 1991. text ed. 150.00 (1-55507-528-2) Municipal Analysis.

— Governments of Illinois, 1985. (Governments of Your State Ser.). 1984. text ed. 150.00 (1-55507-048-5) Municipal Analysis.

— Governments of Illinois, 1986. (Governments of Your State Ser.). 1985. text ed. 150.00 (1-55507-093-0) Municipal Analysis.

— Governments of Illinois, 1989. (Governments of Your State Ser.). (Illus.). 1989. text ed. 150.00 (1-55507-319-0) Municipal Analysis.

— Governments of Illinois 1989: Expert Edition. (Governments of Your State: Expert Ser.). (Illus.). 400p. 1989. text ed. 325.00 (1-55507-357-3) Municipal Analysis.

— Governments of Illinois 1990. (Governments of Your State Ser.). (Illus.). 400p. 1990. text ed. 150.00 (1-55507-405-7) Municipal Analysis.

— Governments of Illinois 1990. (Governments of Your State: Expert Ser.). (Illus.). 1990. text ed. 325.00 (1-55507-442-1) Municipal Analysis.

— Governments of Illinois, 1991. (Governments of Your State Ser.). (Illus.). 400p. 1991. text ed. 150.00 (1-55507-529-0) Municipal Analysis.

— Governments of Indiana, 1985. (Governments of Your State Ser.). 1984. text ed. 150.00 (1-55507-049-3) Municipal Analysis.

— Governments of Indiana, 1986. (Governments of Your State Ser.). 1985. text ed. 150.00 (1-55507-094-9) Municipal Analysis.

— Governments of Indiana, 1989. (Governments of Your State Ser.). (Illus.). 1989. text ed. 150.00 (1-55507-320-4) Municipal Analysis.

— Governments of Indiana 1989: Expert Edition. (Governments of Your State: Expert Ser.). (Illus.). 400p. 1989. text ed. 325.00 (1-55507-358-1) Municipal Analysis.

— Governments of Indiana 1990. (Governments of Your State Ser.). (Illus.). 400p. 1990. text ed. 150.00 (1-55507-406-5) Municipal Analysis.

— Governments of Indiana 1990: Expert Edition. (Governments of Your State: Expert Ser.). (Illus.). 400p. 1990. text ed. 325.00 (1-55507-443-X) Municipal Analysis.

— Governments of Indiana, 1991. (Governments of Your State Ser.). (Illus.). 400p. 1991. text ed. 150.00 (1-55507-530-4) Municipal Analysis.

— Governments of Iowa, 1985. (Governments of Your State Ser.). 1984. text ed. 150.00 (1-55507-050-7) Municipal Analysis.

— Governments of Iowa, 1986. (Governments of Your State Ser.). 1985. text ed. 150.00 (1-55507-095-7) Municipal Analysis.

— Governments of Iowa, 1989. (Governments of Your State Ser.). (Illus.). 1989. text ed. 150.00 (1-55507-321-2) Municipal Analysis.

— Governments of Iowa 1989: Expert Edition. (Governments of Your State: Expert Ser.). (Illus.). 400p. 1989. text ed. 325.00 (1-55507-359-X) Municipal Analysis.

— Governments of Iowa 1990. (Governments of Your State Ser.). (Illus.). 400p. 1990. text ed. 150.00 (1-55507-407-3) Municipal Analysis.

— Governments of Iowa 1990: Expert Edition. (Governments of Your State: Expert Ser.). (Illus.). 400p. 1990. text ed. 325.00 (1-55507-444-8) Municipal Analysis.

— Governments of Iowa, 1991. (Governments of Your State Ser.). (Illus.). 400p. 1991. text ed. 150.00 (1-55507-531-2) Municipal Analysis.

— Governments of Kansas, 1985. (Governments of Your State Ser.). 1984. text ed. 150.00 (1-55507-051-5) Municipal Analysis.

— Governments of Kansas, 1986. (Governments of Your State Ser.). 1985. text ed. 150.00 (1-55507-096-5) Municipal Analysis.

— Governments of Kansas, 1989. (Governments of Your State Ser.). (Illus.). 1989. text ed. 150.00 (1-55507-322-0) Municipal Analysis.

— Governments of Kansas 1989: Expert Edition. (Governments of Your State: Expert Ser.). (Illus.). 400p. 1989. text ed. 325.00 (1-55507-360-3) Municipal Analysis.

— Governments of Kansas 1990. (Governments of Your State Ser.). (Illus.). 400p. 1990. text ed. 150.00 (1-55507-408-1) Municipal Analysis.

— Governments of Kansas 1990: Expert Edition. (Governments of Your State: Expert Ser.). (Illus.). 400p. 1990. text ed. 325.00 (1-55507-445-6) Municipal Analysis.

— Governments of Kansas, 1991. (Governments of Your State Ser.). (Illus.). 400p. 1991. text ed. 150.00 (1-55507-532-0) Municipal Analysis.

— Governments of Kentucky, 1985. (Governments of Your State Ser.). 1984. text ed. 150.00 (1-55507-052-3) Municipal Analysis.

— Governments of Kentucky, 1986. (Governments of Your State Ser.). 1985. text ed. 150.00 (1-55507-097-3) Municipal Analysis.

— Governments of Kentucky, 1989. (Governments of Your State Ser.). (Illus.). 1989. text ed. 150.00 (1-55507-323-9) Municipal Analysis.

— Governments of Kentucky 1989: Expert Edition. (Governments of Your State: Expert Ser.). (Illus.). 400p. 1989. text ed. 325.00 (1-55507-361-1) Municipal Analysis.

— Governments of Kentucky 1990. (Governments of Your State Ser.). (Illus.). 400p. 1990. text ed. 150.00 (1-55507-409-X) Municipal Analysis.

— Governments of Kentucky 1990: Expert Edition. (Governments of Your State: Expert Ser.). (Illus.). 400p. 1990. text ed. 325.00 (1-55507-446-4) Municipal Analysis.

— Governments of Kentucky, 1991. (Governments of Your State Ser.). (Illus.). 400p. 1991. text ed. 150.00 (1-55507-533-9) Municipal Analysis.

— Governments of Louisiana, 1985. (Governments of Your State Ser.). 1984. text ed. 150.00 (1-55507-053-1) Municipal Analysis.

— Governments of Louisiana, 1986. (Governments of Your State Ser.). 1985. text ed. 150.00 (1-55507-098-1) Municipal Analysis.

— Governments of Louisiana, 1989. (Governments of Your State Ser.). (Illus.). 1989. text ed. 150.00 (1-55507-324-7) Municipal Analysis.

— Governments of Louisiana 1989: Expert Edition. (Governments of Your State: Expert Ser.). (Illus.). 400p. 1989. text ed. 325.00 (1-55507-362-X) Municipal Analysis.

— Governments of Louisiana 1990. (Governments of Your State Ser.). (Illus.). 400p. 1990. text ed. 150.00 (1-55507-410-3) Municipal Analysis.

— Governments of Louisiana 1990: Expert Edition. (Governments of Your State: Expert Ser.). (Illus.). 400p. 1990. text ed. 325.00 (1-55507-447-2) Municipal Analysis.

— Governments of Louisiana, 1991. (Governments of Your State Ser.). (Illus.). 400p. 1991. text ed. 150.00 (1-55507-534-7) Municipal Analysis.

— Governments of Maine, 1985. (Governments of Your State Ser.). 1984. text ed. 150.00 (1-55507-054-X) Municipal Analysis.

— Governments of Maine, 1986. (Governments of Your State Ser.). 1985. text ed. 150.00 (1-55507-099-X) Municipal Analysis.

— Governments of Maine, 1989. (Governments of Your State Ser.). (Illus.). 1989. text ed. 150.00 (1-55507-325-5) Municipal Analysis.

— Governments of Maine 1989: Expert Edition. (Governments of Your State: Expert Ser.). (Illus.). 400p. 1989. text ed. 325.00 (1-55507-363-8) Municipal Analysis.

— Governments of Maine 1990. (Governments of Your State Ser.). (Illus.). 400p. 1990. text ed. 150.00 (1-55507-411-1) Municipal Analysis.

— Governments of Maine 1990: Expert Edition. (Governments of Your State: Expert Ser.). (Illus.). 400p. 1990. text ed. 325.00 (1-55507-448-0) Municipal Analysis.

— Governments of Maine, 1991. (Governments of Your State Ser.). (Illus.). 400p. 1991. text ed. 150.00 (1-55507-535-5) Municipal Analysis.

— Governments of Massachusetts, 1986. (Governments of Your State Ser.). 1985. text ed. 150.00 (1-55507-100-7) Municipal Analysis.

— Governments of Massachusetts, 1989. (Governments of Your State Ser.). (Illus.). 1989. text ed. 150.00 (1-55507-326-3) Municipal Analysis.

— Governments of Massachusetts 1989: Expert Edition. (Governments of Your State: Expert Ser.). (Illus.). 400p. 1989. text ed. 325.00 (1-55507-364-6) Municipal Analysis.

— Governments of Massachusetts 1990. (Governments of Your State Ser.). (Illus.). 400p. 1990. text ed. 150.00 (1-55507-412-X) Municipal Analysis.

— Governments of Massachusetts 1990: Expert Edition. (Governments of Your State: Expert Ser.). (Illus.). 400p. 1990. text ed. 325.00 (1-55507-449-9) Municipal Analysis.

— Governments of Massachusetts, 1991. (Governments of Your State Ser.). (Illus.). 400p. 1991. text ed. 150.00 (*1-55507-536-3*) Municipal Analysis.
— Governments of Massachusetts,1985. (Governments of Your State Ser.). 1984. text ed. 150.00 (*1-55507-055-8*) Municipal Analysis.
— Governments of Michigan, 1985. (Governments of Your State Ser.). 1984. text ed. 150.00 (*1-55507-056-6*) Municipal Analysis.
— Governments of Michigan, 1986. (Governments of Your State Ser.). 1985. text ed. 150.00 (*1-55507-101-5*) Municipal Analysis.
— Governments of Michigan, 1989. (Governments of Your State Ser.). (Illus.). 1989. text ed. 150.00 (*1-55507-327-1*) Municipal Analysis.
— Governments of Michigan 1989: Expert Edition. (Governments of Your State: Expert Ser.). (Illus.). 400p. 1989. text ed. 325.00 (*1-55507-365-4*) Municipal Analysis.
— Governments of Michigan 1990. (Governments of Your State Ser.). (Illus.). 400p. 1990. text ed. 150.00 (*1-55507-413-8*) Municipal Analysis.
— Governments of Michigan 1990: Expert Edition. (Governments of Your State: Expert Ser.). (Illus.). 400p. 1990. text ed. 325.00 (*1-55507-450-2*) Municipal Analysis.
— Governments of Michigan, 1991. (Governments of Your State Ser.). (Illus.). 400p. 1991. text ed. 150.00 (*1-55507-537-1*) Municipal Analysis.
— Governments of Minnesota, 1985. (Governments of Your State Ser.). 1984. text ed. 150.00 (*1-55507-057-4*) Municipal Analysis.
— Governments of Minnesota, 1986. (Governments of Your State Ser.). 1985. text ed. 150.00 (*1-55507-102-3*) Municipal Analysis.
— Governments of Minnesota, 1989. (Governments of Your State Ser.). (Illus.). 1989. text ed. 150.00 (*1-55507-328-X*) Municipal Analysis.
— Governments of Minnesota 1989: Expert Edition. (Governments of Your State: Expert Ser.). (Illus.). 400p. 1989. text ed. 325.00 (*1-55507-366-2*) Municipal Analysis.
— Governments of Minnesota 1990. (Governments of Your State Ser.). (Illus.). 400p. 1990. text ed. 150.00 (*1-55507-414-6*) Municipal Analysis.
— Governments of Minnesota 1990: Expert Edition. (Governments of Your State: Expert Ser.). (Illus.). 400p. 1990. text ed. 325.00 (*1-55507-451-0*) Municipal Analysis.
— Governments of Minnesota, 1991. (Governments of Your State Ser.). (Illus.). 400p. 1991. text ed. 150.00 (*1-55507-538-X*) Municipal Analysis.
— Governments of Missisippi, 1989. (Governments of Your State Ser.). (Illus.). 1989. text ed. 150.00 (*1-55507-329-8*) Municipal Analysis.
— Governments of Mississippi, 1985. (Governments of Your State Ser.). 1984. text ed. 150.00 (*1-55507-058-2*) Municipal Analysis.
— Governments of Mississippi, 1986. (Governments of Your State Ser.). 1984. text ed. 150.00 (*1-55507-103-1*) Municipal Analysis.
— Governments of Mississippi 1989: Expert Edition. (Governments of Your State: Expert Ser.). (Illus.). 400p. 1989. text ed. 325.00 (*1-55507-367-0*) Municipal Analysis.
— Governments of Mississippi 1990. (Governments of Your State Ser.). (Illus.). 400p. 1990. text ed. 150.00 (*1-55507-415-4*) Municipal Analysis.
— Governments of Mississippi 1990: Expert Edition. (Governments of Your State: Expert Ser.). (Illus.). 400p. 1990. text ed. 325.00 (*1-55507-452-9*) Municipal Analysis.
— Governments of Mississippi, 1991. (Governments of Your State Ser.). (Illus.). 400p. 1991. text ed. 150.00 (*1-55507-539-8*) Municipal Analysis.
— Governments of Missouri, 1986. (Governments of Your State Ser.). 1985. text ed. 150.00 (*1-55507-104-X*) Municipal Analysis.
— Governments of Missouri, 1989. (Governments of Your State Ser.). (Illus.). 1989. text ed. 150.00 (*1-55507-330-1*) Municipal Analysis.
— Governments of Missouri 1989: Expert Edition. (Governments of Your State: Expert Ser.). (Illus.). 400p. 1989. text ed. 325.00 (*1-55507-368-9*) Municipal Analysis.
— Governments of Missouri 1990. (Governments of Your State Ser.). (Illus.). 400p. 1990. text ed. 150.00 (*1-55507-416-2*) Municipal Analysis.
— Governments of Missouri 1990: Expert Edition. (Governments of Your State: Expert Ser.). (Illus.). 400p. 1990. text ed. 325.00 (*1-55507-453-7*) Municipal Analysis.
— Governments of Missouri, 1991. (Governments of Your State Ser.). (Illus.). 400p. 1991. text ed. 150.00 (*1-55507-540-1*) Municipal Analysis.
— Governments of Nebraska, 1985. (Governments of Your State Ser.). 1984. text ed. 150.00 (*1-55507-060-4*) Municipal Analysis.
— Governments of Nebraska, 1986. (Governments of Your State Ser.). 1985. text ed. 150.00 (*1-55507-105-8*) Municipal Analysis.
— Governments of Nebraska, 1989. (Governments of Your State Ser.). (Illus.). 1989. text ed. 150.00 (*1-55507-331-X*) Municipal Analysis.
— Governments of Nebraska 1989: Expert Edition. (Governments of Your State: Expert Ser.). (Illus.). 400p. 1989. text ed. 325.00 (*1-55507-369-7*) Municipal Analysis.
— Governments of Nebraska 1990. (Governments of Your State Ser.). (Illus.). 400p. 1990. text ed. 150.00 (*1-55507-417-0*) Municipal Analysis.
— Governments of Nebraska 1990: Expert Edition. (Governments of Your State: Expert Ser.). (Illus.). 400p. 1990. text ed. 325.00 (*1-55507-454-5*) Municipal Analysis.
— Governments of Nebraska, 1991. (Governments of Your State Ser.). (Illus.). 400p. 1991. text ed. 150.00 (*1-55507-541-X*) Municipal Analysis.
— Governments of New Jersey, 1985. (Governments of Your State Ser.). 1984. text ed. 150.00 (*1-55507-061-2*) Municipal Analysis.
— Governments of New Jersey, 1986. (Governments of Your State Ser.). 1985. text ed. 150.00 (*1-55507-106-6*) Municipal Analysis.
— Governments of New Jersey, 1989. (Governments of Your State Ser.). (Illus.). 1989. text ed. 150.00 (*1-55507-332-8*) Municipal Analysis.
— Governments of New Jersey 1989: Expert Edition. (Governments of Your State: Expert Ser.). (Illus.). 400p. 1989. text ed. 325.00 (*1-55507-370-0*) Municipal Analysis.
— Governments of New Jersey 1990. (Governments of Your State Ser.). (Illus.). 400p. 1990. text ed. 150.00 (*1-55507-418-9*) Municipal Analysis.
— Governments of New Jersey 1990: Expert Edition. (Governments of Your State: Expert Ser.). (Illus.). 400p. 1990. text ed. 325.00 (*1-55507-455-3*) Municipal Analysis.
— Governments of New Jersey, 1991. (Governments of Your State Ser.). (Illus.). 400p. 1991. text ed. 150.00 (*1-55507-542-8*) Municipal Analysis.
— Governments of New York, 1985. (Governments of Your State Ser.). 1984. text ed. 150.00 (*1-55507-062-0*) Municipal Analysis.
— Governments of New York, 1986. (Governments of Your State Ser.). 1985. text ed. 150.00 (*1-55507-107-4*) Municipal Analysis.
— Governments of New York, 1989. (Governments of Your State Ser.). (Illus.). 1989. text ed. 150.00 (*1-55507-333-6*) Municipal Analysis.
— Governments of New York 1989: Expert Edition. (Governments of Your State: Expert Ser.). (Illus.). 400p. 1989. text ed. 325.00 (*1-55507-371-9*) Municipal Analysis.
— Governments of New York 1990. (Governments of Your State Ser.). (Illus.). 400p. 1990. text ed. 150.00 (*1-55507-419-7*) Municipal Analysis.
— Governments of New York 1990: Expert Edition. (Governments of Your State: Expert Ser.). (Illus.). 400p. 1990. text ed. 325.00 (*1-55507-456-1*) Municipal Analysis.
— Governments of New York, 1991. (Governments of Your State Ser.). (Illus.). 400p. 1991. text ed. 150.00 (*1-55507-543-6*) Municipal Analysis.
— Governments of North Dakota, 1985. (Governments of Your State Ser.). 1984. text ed. 150.00 (*1-55507-063-9*) Municipal Analysis.
— Governments of North Dakota, 1986. (Governments of Your State Ser.). 1985. text ed. 150.00 (*1-55507-108-2*) Municipal Analysis.
— Governments of North Dakota, 1989. (Governments of Your State Ser.). (Illus.). 1989. text ed. 150.00 (*1-55507-334-4*) Municipal Analysis.
— Governments of North Dakota 1989: Expert Edition. (Governments of Your State: Expert Ser.). (Illus.). 400p. 1989. text ed. 325.00 (*1-55507-396-4*) Municipal Analysis.
— Governments of North Dakota 1990. (Governments of Your State Ser.). (Illus.). 400p. 1990. text ed. 150.00 (*1-55507-420-0*) Municipal Analysis.
— Governments of North Dakota 1990: Expert Edition. (Governments of Your State: Expert Ser.). (Illus.). 400p. 1990. text ed. 325.00 (*1-55507-457-X*) Municipal Analysis.
— Governments of North Dakota, 1991. (Governments of Your State Ser.). (Illus.). 400p. 1991. text ed. 150.00 (*1-55507-544-4*) Municipal Analysis.
— Governments of Ohio, 1985. (Governments of Your State Ser.). 1984. text ed. 150.00 (*1-55507-064-7*) Municipal Analysis.
— Governments of Ohio, 1986. (Governments of Your State Ser.). 1985. text ed. 150.00 (*1-55507-109-0*) Municipal Analysis.
— Governments of Ohio, 1989. (Governments of Your State Ser.). (Illus.). 1989. text ed. 150.00 (*1-55507-335-2*) Municipal Analysis.
— Governments of Ohio 1989: Expert Edition. (Governments of Your State: Expert Ser.). (Illus.). 400p. 1989. text ed. 325.00 (*1-55507-372-7*) Municipal Analysis.
— Governments of Ohio 1990. (Governments of Your State Ser.). (Illus.). 400p. 1990. text ed. 150.00 (*1-55507-421-9*) Municipal Analysis.
— Governments of Ohio 1990: Expert Edition. (Governments of Your State: Expert Ser.). (Illus.). 400p. 1990. text ed. 325.00 (*1-55507-458-8*) Municipal Analysis.
— Governments of Ohio, 1991. (Governments of Your State Ser.). (Illus.). 400p. 1991. text ed. 150.00 (*1-55507-545-2*) Municipal Analysis.
— Governments of Oklahoma, 1985. (Governments of Your State Ser.). 1984. text ed. 150.00 (*1-55507-065-5*) Municipal Analysis.
— Governments of Oklahoma, 1986. (Governments of Your State Ser.). 1985. text ed. 150.00 (*1-55507-110-4*) Municipal Analysis.
— Governments of Oklahoma, 1989. (Governments of Your State Ser.). (Illus.). 1989. text ed. 150.00 (*1-55507-336-0*) Municipal Analysis.
— Governments of Oklahoma 1989: Expert Edition. (Governments of Your State: Expert Ser.). (Illus.). 400p. 1989. text ed. 325.00 (*1-55507-373-5*) Municipal Analysis.
— Governments of Oklahoma 1990. (Governments of Your State Ser.). (Illus.). 400p. 1990. text ed. 150.00 (*1-55507-422-7*) Municipal Analysis.
— Governments of Oklahoma 1990: Expert Edition. (Governments of Your State: Expert Ser.). (Illus.). 400p. 1990. text ed. 325.00 (*1-55507-459-6*) Municipal Analysis.
— Governments of Oklahoma, 1991. (Governments of Your State Ser.). (Illus.). 400p. 1991. text ed. 150.00 (*1-55507-546-0*) Municipal Analysis.
— Governments of Pennsylvania, 1985. (Governments of Your State Ser.). 1984. text ed. 150.00 (*1-55507-066-3*) Municipal Analysis.
— Governments of Pennsylvania, 1986. (Governments of Your State Ser.). 1985. text ed. 150.00 (*1-55507-111-2*) Municipal Analysis.
— Governments of Pennsylvania, 1989. (Governments of Your State Ser.). (Illus.). 1989. text ed. 150.00 (*1-55507-337-9*) Municipal Analysis.
— Governments of Pennsylvania 1989: Expert Edition. (Governments of Your State: Expert Ser.). (Illus.). 400p. 1989. text ed. 325.00 (*1-55507-374-3*) Municipal Analysis.
— Governments of Pennsylvania 1990. (Governments of Your State Ser.). (Illus.). 400p. 1990. text ed. 150.00 (*1-55507-423-5*) Municipal Analysis.
— Governments of Pennsylvania 1990. (Governments of Your State: Expert Ser.). (Illus.). 1990. text ed. 325.00 (*1-55507-460-X*) Municipal Analysis.
— Governments of Pennsylvania, 1991. (Governments of Your State Ser.). (Illus.). 400p. 1991. text ed. 150.00 (*1-55507-547-9*) Municipal Analysis.
— Governments of South Dakota, 1985. (Governments of Your State Ser.). 1984. text ed. 150.00 (*1-55507-067-1*) Municipal Analysis.
— Governments of South Dakota, 1986. (Governments of Your State Ser.). 1985. text ed. 150.00 (*1-55507-112-0*) Municipal Analysis.
— Governments of South Dakota, 1989. (Governments of Your State Ser.). (Illus.). 1989. text ed. 150.00 (*1-55507-338-7*) Municipal Analysis.
— Governments of South Dakota 1989: Expert Edition. (Governments of Your State: Expert Ser.). (Illus.). 400p. 1989. text ed. 325.00 (*1-55507-375-1*) Municipal Analysis.
— Governments of South Dakota 1990. (Governments of Your State Ser.). (Illus.). 400p. 1990. text ed. 150.00 (*1-55507-424-3*) Municipal Analysis.
— Governments of South Dakota 1990: Expert Edition. (Governments of Your State: Expert Ser.). (Illus.). 400p. 1990. text ed. 325.00 (*1-55507-461-8*) Municipal Analysis.
— Governments of South Dakota, 1991. (Governments of Your State Ser.). (Illus.). 400p. 1991. text ed. 150.00 (*1-55507-548-7*) Municipal Analysis.
— Governments of Tennessee, 1985. (Governments of Your State Ser.). 1984. text ed. 150.00 (*1-55507-068-X*) Municipal Analysis.
— Governments of Tennessee, 1989. (Governments of Your State Ser.). (Illus.). 1989. text ed. 150.00 (*1-55507-339-5*) Municipal Analysis.
— Governments of Tennessee 1989: Expert Edition. (Governments of Your State: Expert Ser.). (Illus.). 400p. 1989. text ed. 325.00 (*1-55507-376-X*) Municipal Analysis.
— Governments of Tennessee 1990. (Governments of Your State Ser.). (Illus.). 400p. 1990. text ed. 150.00 (*1-55507-425-1*) Municipal Analysis.
— Governments of Tennessee 1990: Expert Edition. (Governments of Your State: Expert Ser.). (Illus.). 400p. 1990. text ed. 325.00 (*1-55507-462-6*) Municipal Analysis.
— Governments of Tennessee, 1991. (Governments of Your State Ser.). (Illus.). 400p. 1991. text ed. 150.00 (*1-55507-549-5*) Municipal Analysis.
— Governments of Texas, 1985. (Governments of Your State Ser.). 1984. text ed. 150.00 (*1-55507-069-8*) Municipal Analysis.
— Governments of Texas, 1986. (Governments of Your State Ser.). 1985. text ed. 150.00 (*1-55507-114-7*) Municipal Analysis.
— Governments of Texas, 1989. (Governments of Your State Ser.). (Illus.). 1989. text ed. 150.00 (*1-55507-340-9*) Municipal Analysis.
— Governments of Texas 1989: Expert Edition. (Governments of Your State: Expert Ser.). (Illus.). 400p. 1989. text ed. 325.00 (*1-55507-377-8*) Municipal Analysis.
— Governments of Texas 1990. (Governments of Your State Ser.). (Illus.). 400p. 1990. text ed. 150.00 (*1-55507-426-X*) Municipal Analysis.
— Governments of Texas 1990: Expert Edition. (Governments of Your State: Expert Ser.). (Illus.). 400p. 1990. text ed. 325.00 (*1-55507-463-4*) Municipal Analysis.
— Governments of Texas, 1991. (Governments of Your State Ser.). (Illus.). 400p. 1991. text ed. 150.00 (*1-55507-550-9*) Municipal Analysis.
— Governments of the Carolinas, 1985. (Governments of Your State Ser.). 1984. text ed. 150.00 (*1-55507-075-2*) Municipal Analysis.
— Governments of the Carolinas, 1986. (Governments of Your State Ser.). 1985. text ed. 150.00 (*1-55507-120-1*) Municipal Analysis.
— Governments of the Carolinas, 1989. (Governments of Your State Ser.). (Illus.). 1989. text ed. 150.00 (*1-55507-346-8*) Municipal Analysis.
— Governments of the Carolinas 1989: Expert Edition. (Governments of Your State: Expert Ser.). (Illus.). 400p. 1989. text ed. 325.00 (*1-55507-383-2*) Municipal Analysis.
— Governments of the Carolinas 1990. (Governments of Your State Ser.). (Illus.). 400p. 1990. text ed. 150.00 (*1-55507-432-4*) Municipal Analysis.
— Governments of the Carolinas 1990: Expert Edition. (Governments of Your State: Expert Ser.). (Illus.). 400p. 1990. text ed. 325.00 (*1-55507-469-3*) Municipal Analysis.
— Governments of the Carolinas, 1991. (Governments of Your State Ser.). (Illus.). 400p. 1991. text ed. 150.00 (*1-55507-556-8*) Municipal Analysis.
— Governments of the Northeast, 1985. (Governments of Your State Ser.). 1984. text ed. 150.00 (*1-55507-076-0*) Municipal Analysis.
— Governments of the Northeast, 1986. (Governments of Your State Ser.). 1985. text ed. 150.00 (*1-55507-123-6*) Municipal Analysis.
— Governments of the Northeast, 1989. (Governments of Your State Ser.). (Illus.). 1989. text ed. 150.00 (*1-55507-349-2*) Municipal Analysis.
— Governments of the Northeast 1989: Expert Edition. (Governments of Your State: Expert Ser.). (Illus.). 400p. 1989. text ed. 325.00 (*1-55507-384-0*) Municipal Analysis.
— Governments of the Northeast 1990. (Governments of Your State Ser.). (Illus.). 400p. 1990. text ed. 150.00 (*1-55507-435-9*) Municipal Analysis.
— Governments of the Northeast 1990: Expert Edition. (Governments of Your State: Expert Ser.). (Illus.). 400p. 1990. text ed. 325.00 (*1-55507-472-3*) Municipal Analysis.
— Governments of the Northeast, 1991. (Governments of Your State Ser.). (Illus.). 400p. 1991. text ed. 150.00 (*1-55507-558-4*) Municipal Analysis.
— Governments of the Northwest, 1985. (Governments of Your State Ser.). 1984. text ed. 150.00 (*1-55507-078-7*) Municipal Analysis.
— Governments of the Northwest, 1986. (Governments of Your State Ser.). 1985. text ed. 150.00 (*1-55507-121-X*) Municipal Analysis.
— Governments of the Northwest, 1989. (Governments of Your State Ser.). (Illus.). 1989. text ed. 150.00 (*1-55507-347-6*) Municipal Analysis.
— Governments of the Northwest 1989: Expert Edition. (Governments of Your State: Expert Ser.). (Illus.). 400p. 1989. text ed. 325.00 (*1-55507-386-7*) Municipal Analysis.
— Governments of the Northwest 1990. (Governments of Your State Ser.). (Illus.). 400p. 1990. text ed. 150.00 (*1-55507-433-2*) Municipal Analysis.
— Governments of the Northwest 1990: Expert Edition. (Governments of Your State: Expert Ser.). (Illus.). 400p. 1990. text ed. 325.00 (*1-55507-470-7*) Municipal Analysis.
— Governments of the Northwest, 1991. (Governments of Your State Ser.). (Illus.). 400p. 1991. text ed. 150.00 (*1-55507-557-6*) Municipal Analysis.
— Governments of the West, 1985. (Governments of Your State Ser.). 1984. text ed. 150.00 (*1-55507-077-9*) Municipal Analysis.
— Governments of the West, 1986. (Governments of Your State Ser.). 1985. text ed. 150.00 (*1-55507-122-8*) Municipal Analysis.
— Governments of the West, 1989. (Governments of Your State Ser.). (Illus.). 1989. text ed. 150.00 (*1-55507-348-4*) Municipal Analysis.
— Governments of the West 1989: Expert Edition. (Governments of Your State: Expert Ser.). (Illus.). 400p. 1989. text ed. 325.00 (*1-55507-385-9*) Municipal Analysis.
— Governments of the West 1990. (Governments of Your State Ser.). (Illus.). 400p. 1990. text ed. 150.00 (*1-55507-434-0*) Municipal Analysis.
— Governments of the West 1990: Expert Edition. (Governments of Your State: Expert Ser.). (Illus.). 400p. 1990. text ed. 325.00 (*1-55507-471-5*) Municipal Analysis.
— Governments of the West, 1991. (Governments of Your State Ser.). (Illus.). 400p. 1991. text ed. 150.00 (*1-55507-559-2*) Municipal Analysis.
— Governments of Vermont, 1985. (Governments of Your State Ser.). 1984. text ed. 150.00 (*1-55507-070-1*) Municipal Analysis.
— Governments of Vermont 1986. (Governments of Your State Ser.). 1985. text ed. 150.00 (*1-55507-115-5*) Municipal Analysis.
— Governments of Vermont, 1989. (Governments of Your State Ser.). (Illus.). 1989. text ed. 150.00 (*1-55507-341-7*) Municipal Analysis.
— Governments of Vermont 1989: Expert Edition. (Governments of Your State: Expert Ser.). (Illus.). 400p. 1989. text ed. 325.00 (*1-55507-378-6*) Municipal Analysis.
— Governments of Vermont 1990. (Governments of Your State Ser.). (Illus.). 400p. 1990. text ed. 150.00 (*1-55507-427-8*) Municipal Analysis.
— Governments of Vermont 1990: Expert Edition. (Governments of Your State: Expert Ser.). (Illus.). 400p. 1990. text ed. 325.00 (*1-55507-464-2*) Municipal Analysis.
— Governments of Vermont, 1991. (Governments of Your State Ser.). (Illus.). 400p. 1991. text ed. 150.00 (*1-55507-551-7*) Municipal Analysis.
— Governments of Virginia, 1985. (Governments of Your State Ser.). 1984. text ed. 150.00 (*1-55507-071-X*) Municipal Analysis.

— Governments of Virginia, 1986. (Governments of Your State Ser.). 1985. text ed. 150.00 (*1-55507-116-3*) Municipal Analysis.

— Governments of Virginia, 1989. (Governments of Your State Ser.). (Illus.). 1989. text ed. 150.00 (*1-55507-342-5*) Municipal Analysis.

— Governments of Virginia 1989: Expert Edition. (Governments of Your State: Expert Ser.). (Illus.). 400p. 1989. text ed. 325.00 (*1-55507-379-4*) Municipal Analysis.

— Governments of Virginia 1990. (Governments of Your State Ser.). (Illus.). 400p. 1990. text ed. 150.00 (*1-55507-428-6*) Municipal Analysis.

— Governments of Virginia 1990: Expert Edition. (Governments of Your State: Expert Ser.). (Illus.). 400p. 1990. text ed. 325.00 (*1-55507-465-0*) Municipal Analysis.

— Governments of Virginia, 1991. (Governments of Your State Ser.). (Illus.). 400p. 1991. text ed. 150.00 (*1-55507-552-5*) Municipal Analysis.

— Governments of Washington, 1985. (Governments of Your State Ser.). 1984. text ed. 150.00 (*1-55507-072-8*) Municipal Analysis.

— Governments of Washington, 1986. (Governments of Your State Ser.). 1985. text ed. 150.00 (*1-55507-117-1*) Municipal Analysis.

— Governments of Washington, 1989. (Governments of Your State Ser.). (Illus.). 1989. text ed. 150.00 (*1-55507-343-3*) Municipal Analysis.

— Governments of Washington 1989: Expert Edition. (Governments of Your State: Expert Ser.). (Illus.). 400p. 1989. text ed. 325.00 (*1-55507-380-8*) Municipal Analysis.

— Governments of Washington 1990. (Governments of Your State Ser.). (Illus.). 400p. 1990. text ed. 150.00 (*1-55507-429-4*) Municipal Analysis.

— Governments of Washington 1990: Expert Edition. (Governments of Your State: Expert Ser.). (Illus.). 400p. 1990. text ed. 325.00 (*1-55507-466-9*) Municipal Analysis.

— Governments of Washington, 1991. (Governments of Your State Ser.). (Illus.). 400p. 1991. text ed. 150.00 (*1-55507-553-3*) Municipal Analysis.

— Governments of West Virginia, 1985. (Governments of Your State Ser.). 1984. text ed. 150.00 (*1-55507-073-6*) Municipal Analysis.

— Governments of West Virginia, 1986. (Governments of Your State Ser.). 1985. text ed. 150.00 (*1-55507-118-X*) Municipal Analysis.

— Governments of West Virginia, 1989. (Governments of Your State Ser.). (Illus.). 1989. text ed. 150.00 (*1-55507-344-1*) Municipal Analysis.

— Governments of West Virginia 1989: Expert Edition. (Governments of Your State: Expert Ser.). (Illus.). 400p. 1989. text ed. 325.00 (*1-55507-381-6*) Municipal Analysis.

— Governments of West Virginia 1990. (Governments of Your State Ser.). (Illus.). 400p. 1990. text ed. 150.00 (*1-55507-430-8*) Municipal Analysis.

— Governments of West Virginia 1990: Expert Edition. (Governments of Your State: Expert Ser.). (Illus.). 400p. 1990. text ed. 325.00 (*1-55507-467-7*) Municipal Analysis.

— Governments of West Virginia, 1991. (Governments of Your State Ser.). (Illus.). 400p. 1991. text ed. 150.00 (*1-55507-554-1*) Municipal Analysis.

— Governments of Wisconsin, 1989. (Governments of Your State Ser.). (Illus.). 1989. text ed. 150.00 (*1-55507-345-X*) Municipal Analysis.

— Governments of Wisconsin 1989: Expert Edition. (Governments of Your State: Expert Ser.). (Illus.). 400p. 1989. text ed. 325.00 (*1-55507-382-4*) Municipal Analysis.

— Governments of Wisconsin 1990. (Governments of Your State Ser.). (Illus.). 400p. 1990. text ed. 150.00 (*1-55507-431-6*) Municipal Analysis.

— Governments of Wisconsin 1990: Expert Edition. (Governments of Your State: Expert Ser.). (Illus.). 400p. 1990. text ed. 325.00 (*1-55507-468-5*) Municipal Analysis.

— Governments of Wisconsin, 1991. (Governments of Your State Ser.). (Illus.). 400p. 1991. text ed. 150.00 (*1-55507-555-X*) Municipal Analysis.

— Illinois Governments Performance Standards, 1990. (Governments Performance Standards Ser.). (Illus.). 150p. 1990. text ed. 125.00 (*1-55507-481-2*) Municipal Analysis.

— Indiana Governments Performance Standards, 1990. (Governments Performance Standards Ser.). (Illus.). 150p. 1990. text ed. 125.00 (*1-55507-482-0*) Municipal Analysis.

— Iowa Governments Performance Standards, 1990. (Governments Performance Standards Ser.). (Illus.). 150p. 1990. text ed. 125.00 (*1-55507-483-9*) Municipal Analysis.

— Kansas Governments Performance Standards, 1990. (Governments Performance Standards Ser.). (Illus.). 150p. 1990. text ed. 125.00 (*1-55507-484-7*) Municipal Analysis.

— Kentucky Governments Performance Standards, 1990. (Governments Performance Standards Ser.). (Illus.). 150p. 1990. text ed. 125.00 (*1-55507-485-5*) Municipal Analysis.

— Louisiana Governments Performance Standards, 1990. (Governments Performance Standards Ser.). (Illus.). 150p. 1990. text ed. 125.00 (*1-55507-486-3*) Municipal Analysis.

— Maine Governments Performance Standards, 1990. (Governments Performance Standards Ser.). (Illus.). 150p. 1990. text ed. 125.00 (*1-55507-487-1*) Municipal Analysis.

— Massachusetts Governments Performance Standards, 1990. (Governments Performance Standards Ser.). (Illus.). 150p. 1990. text ed. 125.00 (*1-55507-488-X*) Municipal Analysis.

— Michigan Governments Performance Standards, 1990. (Governments Performance Standards Ser.). (Illus.). 150p. 1990. text ed. 125.00 (*1-55507-489-8*) Municipal Analysis.

— Minnesota Governments Performance Standards, 1990. (Governments Performance Standards Ser.). (Illus.). 150p. 1990. text ed. 125.00 (*1-55507-490-1*) Municipal Analysis.

— Mississippi Governments Performance Standards, 1990. (Governments Performance Standards Ser.). (Illus.). 150p. 1990. text ed. 125.00 (*1-55507-491-X*) Municipal Analysis.

— Missouri Governments Performance Standards, 1990. (Governments Performance Standards Ser.). (Illus.). 150p. 1990. text ed. 125.00 (*1-55507-492-8*) Municipal Analysis.

— Nebraska Governments Performance Standards, 1990. (Governments Performance Standards Ser.). (Illus.). 150p. 1990. text ed. 125.00 (*1-55507-493-6*) Municipal Analysis.

— New Jersey Governments Performance Standards, 1990. (Governments Performance Standards Ser.). (Illus.). 150p. 1990. text ed. 125.00 (*1-55507-494-4*) Municipal Analysis.

— New York Governments Performance Standards, 1990. (Governments Performance Standards Ser.). (Illus.). 150p. 1990. text ed. 125.00 (*1-55507-495-2*) Municipal Analysis.

— North Dakota Governments Performance Standards, 1990. (Governments Performance Standards Ser.). (Illus.). 150p. 1990. text ed. 125.00 (*1-55507-496-0*) Municipal Analysis.

— The Northeast Governments Performance Standards, 1990. (Governments Performance Standards Ser.). (Illus.). 150p. 1990. text ed. 125.00 (*1-55507-511-8*) Municipal Analysis.

— The Northwest Governments Performance Standards, 1990. (Governments Performance Standards Ser.). (Illus.). 150p. 1990. text ed. 125.00 (*1-55507-509-6*) Municipal Analysis.

— Ohio Governments Performance Standards, 1990. (Governments Performance Standards Ser.). (Illus.). 150p. 1990. text ed. 125.00 (*1-55507-497-9*) Municipal Analysis.

— Oklahoma Governments Performance Standards, 1990. (Governments Performance Standards Ser.). (Illus.). 150p. 1990. text ed. 125.00 (*1-55507-498-7*) Municipal Analysis.

— Pennsylvania Governments Performance Standards, 1990. (Governments Performance Standards Ser.). (Illus.). 150p. 1990. text ed. 125.00 (*1-55507-499-5*) Municipal Analysis.

— South Dakota Governments Performance Standards, 1990. (Governments Performance Standards Ser.). (Illus.). 150p. 1990. text ed. 125.00 (*1-55507-500-2*) Municipal Analysis.

— Tennessee Governments Performance Standards, 1990. (Governments Performance Standards Ser.). (Illus.). 150p. 1990. text ed. 125.00 (*1-55507-501-0*) Municipal Analysis.

— Texas Governments Performance Standards, 1990. (Governments Performance Standards Ser.). (Illus.). 150p. 1990. text ed. 125.00 (*1-55507-502-9*) Municipal Analysis.

— Vermont Governments Performance Standards, 1990. (Governments Performance Standards Ser.). (Illus.). 150p. 1990. text ed. 125.00 (*1-55507-503-7*) Municipal Analysis.

— Virginia Governments Performance Standards, 1990. (Governments Performance Standards Ser.). (Illus.). 150p. 1990. text ed. 125.00 (*1-55507-504-5*) Municipal Analysis.

— Washington Governments Performance Standards, 1990. (Governments Performance Standards Ser.). (Illus.). 150p. 1990. text ed. 125.00 (*1-55507-505-3*) Municipal Analysis.

— The West Governments Performance Standards, 1990. (Governments Performance Standards Ser.). (Illus.). 150p. 1990. text ed. 125.00 (*1-55507-510-X*) Municipal Analysis.

— West Virginia Governments Performance Standards, 1990. (Governments Performance Standards Ser.). (Illus.). 150p. 1990. text ed. 125.00 (*1-55507-506-1*) Municipal Analysis.

— Wisconsin Governments Performance Standards, 1990. (Governments Performance Standards Ser.). (Illus.). 150p. 1990. text ed. 125.00 (*1-55507-507-X*) Municipal Analysis.

Michels, Gregg, ed. Governments of Tennessee, 1986. (Governments of Your State Ser.). 1985. text ed. 150.00 (*1-55507-113-9*) Municipal Analysis.

— Governments of Wisconsin, 1986. (Governments of Your State Ser.). 1985. text ed. 150.00 (*1-55507-119-8*) Municipal Analysis.

Michels, Jeanne & Murphy, Phyllis. The Queen of Bingo. 1994. pap. 4.75 (*0-8222-1417-2*) Dramatists Play.

Michels, Joanne, ed. see Baums, Roosevelt.

Michels, Kenneth M., jt. ed. see DeHaven-Smith, Lance.

Michels, Leo. A Basic Math Approach to Concepts of Chemistry. 5th ed. 343p. 1993. pap. 30.95 (*0-534-20622-0*) Brooks-Cole.

Michels, Leo, jt. auth. see Roberts, Keith.

Michels, Penny & Tropea, Judith. A Day in the Life of a Beekeeper. LC 90-11078. (Day in the Life of...Ser.). (Illus.). 32p. (J). (gr. 4-8). 1991. lib. bdg. 11.79 (*0-8167-2206-4*); pap. text ed. 2.95 (*0-8167-2207-2*) Troll Assocs.

Michels, Robert. Political Parties. LC 61-18564. 1966. pap. text ed. 16.95 (*0-02-921250-2*) Free Pr.

Michels, Robert, jt. auth. see MacKinnon, Roger A.

Michels, Roberto. First Lectures in Political Sociology. De Grazia, Alfred, tr. LC 73-14172. (Perspectives in Social Inquiry Ser.). 184p. 1978. reprint ed. 16.95 (*0-405-05515-3*) Ayer.

— Il Proletariato E la Borghesia Nel Movimento Socialista Italiano: Saggio Di Scienza Sociografico-Politica: Proletariat & Bourgeoisie Within the Socialist Movement: a Sociographic Political Essay. LC 74-25769. (European Sociology Ser.). 404p. 1975. reprint ed. 33.95 (*0-405-06523-X*) Ayer.

Michels, Ronald G. Vitreous Surgery. (Illus.). 126p. 1982. 25.00 (*0-317-94081-3*) Am Acad Ophthal.

Michels, Tilde. Sophie the Rag Picker. (Illus.). (J). (gr. k-1). 1962. 10.95 (*0-8392-3036-2*) Astor-Honor.

— Who's That Knocking at My Door? (Illus.). 28p. (J). (ps-3). 1986. 10.95 (*0-8120-5732-5*) Barron.

— Who's That Knocking at My Door? (Illus.). 28p. (J). (ps-3). 1992. pap. 4.95 (*0-8120-1486-3*) Barron.

Michelsen, John. Chevy Performance. 1981. 16.95 (*0-931472-07-5*) Motorbooks Intl.

Michelsen, Neil F. The American Book of Tables. 128p. 1976. pap. 9.95 (*0-917086-03-1*) ACS Pubns.

— The American Ephemeris: 1901 to 1930. (American Ephemeris Ser.). 368p. 1980. pap. 14.95 (*0-917086-12-0*) ACS Pubns.

— The American Ephemeris: 1931 to 1980 & Book of Tables. 2nd ed. LC 76-11919. 740p. 1982. 29.95 (*0-917086-01-5*) ACS Pubns.

— The American Ephemeris: 1981 to 1990. (American Ephemeris Ser.). 128p. 1977. pap. 9.95 (*0-917086-10-4*) ACS Pubns.

— The American Ephemeris: 1991 to 2000. (American Ephemeris Ser.). 128p. 1980. pap. 9.95 (*0-917086-21-X*) ACS Pubns.

— American Ephemeris for the Twentieth Century Revised 1900 to 2000 At: Noon. 5th rev. ed. (American Ephemeris Ser.). 608p. 1992. pap. 19.95 (*0-935127-20-8*) ACS Pubns.

— The American Heliocentric Ephemeris for 1901-2000. (American Ephemeris Ser.). 608p. (Orig.). 1982. pap. 24.95 (*0-917086-36-8*) ACS Pubns.

— American Midpoint Ephemeris: 1991-1995. (American Ephemeris Ser.). 60p. 1991. pap. 9.95 (*0-935127-17-8*) ACS Pubns.

— The American Sidereal Ephemeris, 1976-2000. (American Ephemeris Ser.). 320p. (Orig.). 1981. pap. 19.50 (*0-917086-30-9*) ACS Pubns.

— Tables of Planetary Phenomena. 2nd rev. ed. 260p. 1993. pap. 24.95 (*0-935127-31-3*) ACS Pubns.

Michelsen, Neil F., comp. American Ephemeris for the Twentieth Century Revised 1900 to 2000 At: Midnight. 5th rev. ed. (American Ephemeris Ser.). 608p. 1994. pap. 19.95 (*0-935127-19-4*) ACS Pubns.

— The American Ephemeris for the Twenty-First Century: 2001 to 2050 At: Midnight Only. 2nd ed. (American Ephemeris Ser.). 304p. (Orig.). 1992. pap. 16.95 (*0-935127-00-3*) ACS Pubns.

Michelsen, Neil F., ed. The Koch Book of Tables. 128p. (Orig.). 1985. pap. 9.95 (*0-917086-79-1*) ACS Pubns.

Michelsen, Sofus S., jt. auth. see Watermeyer, Basil.

Michelsohn, Arie M., jt. ed. see Raizen, Senta A.

Michelsohn, Marie-Louise, jt. auth. see Lawson, H. Blaine, Jr.

Michelson. Color Atlas of Uveitis Diagnosis. 2nd ed. 158p. 1992. 75.00 (*0-8151-5872-6*) Mosby Yr Bk.

***Michelson, A. A.** Studies in Optics. LC 95-10180. 1995. pap. write for info. (*0-486-68700-7*) Dover.

Michelson, A. M. & Bannister, J. V., eds. Life Chemistry Reports, Vol. 1, Pt. 1. 56p. 1982. pap. text ed. 65.00 (*3-7186-0185-0*) Gordon & Breach.

— Life Chemistry Reports, Vol. 1, Pt. 2. 108p. 1982. pap. text ed. 50.00 (*3-7186-0186-9*) Gordon & Breach.

— Life Chemistry Reports, Vol. 2. 95p. 1983. pap. text ed. 48.00 (*3-7186-0199-0*) Gordon & Breach.

— Life Chemistry Reports, Vol. 2. 82p. 1984. pap. text ed. 42.00 (*3-7186-0220-2*) Gordon & Breach.

Michelson, A. M., jt. ed. see Bannister, J. V.

Michelson, Annette. Drawing into Film: Directors' Drawings. LC 93-83854. (Illus.). 104p. (Orig.). 1993. pap. write for info. (*1-878283-30-8*) PaceWildenstein.

Michelson, Annette, ed. see Vertov, Dziga.

Michelson, Annette, et al, eds. October: The First Decade. (Illus.). 450p. 1987. 37.50 (*0-262-13222-2*) MIT Pr.

Michelson, Arnold M. & Levesque, Allen H. Error-Control Techniques for Digital Communication. LC 84-15327. 465p. 1985. text ed. 105.00 (*0-471-88074-4*, Wiley-Interscience) Wiley.

***Michelson, Bruce.** Mark Twain on the Loose: A Comic Writer & the American Self. LC 94-35579. 280p. 1995. lib. bdg. 45.00x (*0-87023-966-X*); pap. 16.95 (*0-87023-967-8*) U of Mass Pr.

— Wilbur's Poetry: Music in a Scattering Time. LC 90-20353. 272p. (C). 1991. lib. bdg. 33.50 (*0-87023-741-1*) U of Mass Pr.

Michelson, Carmen & Davis, Mary-Ann. The Knitters Guide to Sweater Design. LC 87-46352. 430p. 1904. 29.95 (*0-934026-33-5*) Interweave.

Michelson, Court. Michelson's Book of World Baseball Records. 184p. (Orig.). 1985. pap. 9.95 (*0-934175-00-4*) Sports Rec.

Michelson, D. Electrostatic Atomization. (Illus.). 164p. 1990. 76.00 (*0-85274-235-5*) IOP Pub.

Michelson, Derrick O. Fachworterbuch Textil. 136p. (ENG & GER.). 49.95 (*3-87150-106-9*, M-7404) Fr & Eur.

Michelson, Derrick O. & Wagner, G. Textile Dictionary: Fachwoerterbuch Textil. 4th ed. 120p. (FRE & GER.). 1987. 49.95 (*0-8288-0744-2*, M 7404) Fr & Eur.

Michelson, Frida. I Survived Rumbuli. Goodman, Wolf, tr. 224p. 1981. 10.95 (*0-89604-029-1*); pap. 5.95 (*0-89604-030-5*) Holocaust Pubns.

— Rumbuli. Goodman, Wolf, tr. 224p. 1983. reprint ed. 10.95 (*0-686-95085-2*); reprint ed. pap. 5.95 (*0-686-99459-0*) ADL.

Michelson, Joan & Gee, Sue, eds. Coming Late to Motherhood: Twenty Women Tell Their Stories. LC 86-16801. 284p. 1986. lib. bdg. 27.00x (*0-8095-7016-5*) Borgo Pr.

Michelson, Joan, jt. ed. see Mendleson, Alan.

Michelson, John L., ed. see Technical Association of the Pulp & Paper Industry Staff.

Michelson, Joseph B. & Nozik, Robert. Surgical Treatment of Ocular Inflammatory Disease. LC 65-9277. (Illus.). 304p. 1988. text ed. 59.00 (*0-397-50763-1*, Lippincott Medical) Lippincott.

Michelson, Karin. A Comparative Study of Lake-Iroquoian Accent. (C). 1988. lib. bdg. 114.50 (*1-55608-054-9*) Kluwer Ac.

Michelson, Karin, jt. ed. see Gerdts, Donna B.

Michelson, Larry & Ascher, Michael L., eds. Anxiety & Stress Disorders: Cognitive-Behavioral Assessment & Treatment. LC 86-29585. 624p. 1987. lib. bdg. 62.00 (*0-89862-693-5*) Guilford Pr.

Michelson, Larry, jt. ed. see Edelstein, Barry A.

Michelson, Larry, et al. Social Skills Assessment & Training with Children: An Empirically Based Handbook. 276p. 1983. 59.50 (*0-306-41234-9*, Plenum Pr) Plenum.

Michelson, Larry, et al, eds. Future Perspectives in Behavior Therapy. LC 81-10689. (Applied Clinical Psychology Ser.). 366p. 1981. 59.50 (*0-306-40680-2*, Plenum Pr) Plenum.

Michelson, M. J., ed. Comparative Pharmacology, 2 vols., Set. 1008p. (C). 1973. 420.00 (*0-08-016389-0*, Pub. by Pergamon Repr UK) Franklin.

Michelson, M. J. & Ziemel, E. V. Acetylcholine: An Approach to the Molecular Mechanism of Action. LC 73-11271. 252p. 1973. 110.00 (*0-08-017159-1*, Pub. by Pergamon Repr UK) Franklin.

Michelson, Maureen R. Rose Hills, a Place to Remember. Maze, Dessie L. & Durko, Sandy V., eds. LC 89-90901. 112p. 1989. 60.00 (*0-9622358-1-4*) Rose Hills Pubns.

— Rose Hills, a Place to Remember. limited ed. Maze, Dessie L. & Durko, Sandy V., eds. LC 89-90901. 112p. 1989. Limited edition. 200.00 (*0-9622358-0-6*) Rose Hills Pubns.

— Women & Work: In Their Own Words. 2nd ed. 1994. pap. 14.95 (*0-939165-23-6*) NewSage Press.

Michelson, P. F. & Hu En-ke, eds. Experimental Gravitational Physics: Proceedings of the Int'l Symposium on Experimental Gravitational Physics. 570p. (Orig.). (C). 1988. pap. 66.00 (*9971-5-0516-9*) World Scientific Pub.

Michelson, Paul E. Conflict & Crisis: Romanian Political Development, 1861-1871. McNeill, William H. & Jelavich, Charles, eds. (Modern European History Ser.). 300p. 1987. lib. bdg. 15.00 (*0-8240-8029-7*) Garland.

Michelson, Peter. Pacific Plainsong, Nos. I-XIII. LC 77-95077. (Illus.). 136p. 1987. reprint ed. pap. 6.95 (*0-9614644-1-0*) Another Chicago Pr.

— Speaking the Unspeakable: A Poetics of Obscenity. LC 91-46954. (SUNY Series, The Margins of Literature). 312p. 1992. 74.50 (*0-7914-1223-7*); pap. 24.95 (*0-7914-1224-5*) State U NY Pr.

Michelson, Peter, pref. Pacific Plainsong I-XIII. LC 77-95077. (Illus.). 1978. pap. 4.95 (*0-89681-000-3*) Brillig Works.

Michelson, Richard. Did You Say Ghosts? LC 92-30134. (Illus.). 32p. (J). (ps up). 1993. text ed. 14.95 (*0-02-766915-7*, Mac Bks Young Read) S&S Childrens.

Michelson, Sonia. Easy Classic Guitar Solos for Children. 1993. 4.95 (*1-56222-193-0*, 94488) Mel Bay.

— New Dimensions in Classical Guitar for Children. (J). 1993. 7.95 (*1-56222-115-9*, 94537); audio 9.98 (*1-56222-259-7*, 94537) Mel Bay.

Michelson, Stuart. Investment Management: Instructor's Manual. 200p. (C). 1993. pap. text ed. 10.75 (*0-03-030033-9*) Dryden Pr.

Michelson, Susan & Plotkin, Stanley A., eds. Multidisciplinary Approach to Understanding Cytomegalovirus Disease: Proceedings of the Fourth International Cytomegalovirus Workshop: Multidisciplinary Approaches to Understanding CMV Disease, Paris, France, 19-21 April 1993. LC 93-26857. (International Congress Ser.: No. 1032). 1993. 150.00 (*0-444-81699-2*, Excerpta Medica) Elsevier.

***Michelson, Truman.** Contributions to Fox Ethnology. (Bureau of American Ethnology Bulletins Ser.). 168p. 1995. lib. bdg. 79.00 (*0-7812-4085-9*) Rprt Serv.

— Contributions to Fox Ethnology. reprint ed. 39.00 (*0-403-03571-6*) Scholarly.

— Contributions to Fox Ethnology - II. (Bureau of American Ethnology Bulletins Ser.). 183p. 1995. lib. bdg. 79.00 (*0-7812-4095-6*) Rprt Serv.

— Fox Miscellany. (Bureau of American Ethnology Bulletins Ser.). 124p. 1995. lib. bdg. 79.00 (*0-7812-4114-6*) Rprt Serv.

— Fox Miscellany. reprint ed. 29.00 (*0-403-08986-7*) Scholarly.

— Notes on the Buffalo-Head Dance of the Bear Gens of the Fox Indians. reprint ed. 29.00 (*0-403-03668-2*) Scholarly.

— Notes on the Buffalo-Head Dance of the Thunder Gens of the Fox Indians. (Bureau of American Ethnology Bulletins Ser.). 94p. 1995. lib. bdg. 79.00 (*0-7812-4087-5*) Rprt Serv.

— Notes on the Fox Wapanowiweni. (Bureau of American Ethnology Bulletins Ser.). 195p. 1995. lib. bdg. 79.00 (*0-7812-4105-7*) Rprt Serv.

— Owl Sacred Pack of the Fox Indians. (Bureau of American Ethnology Bulletins Ser.). 83p. 1995. lib. bdg. 79.00 (*0-7812-4072-7*) Rprt Serv.
***Michelson, Truman, ed.** Observations on the Thunder Dance of the Bear Gens of the Fox Indians. (Bureau of American Ethnology Bulletins Ser.). 73p. 1995. lib. bdg. 79.00 (*0-7812-4089-1*) Rprt Serv.
— Ojibwa Texts, 2 vols. LC 73-3542. (American Ethnological Society Publications: No. 7). reprint ed. 96. 50 (*0-404-58157-9*) AMS Pr.
Michelson, Truman, tr. Kickapoo Tales. LC 73-3544. (American Ethnological Society Publications: No. 9). reprint ed. 24.00 (*0-404-58159-5*) AMS Pr.
Michelson, William. Public Policy in Temporal Perspective. 1978. pap. text ed. 22.00 (*90-279-7824-7*) Mouton.
Michelson, William, et al. The Child in the City: Vol. 2: Changes & Challenges. 1979. pap. 15.95 (*0-8020-6338-1*) U of Toronto Pr.
Michelucci, R. V., ed. see Russo, John A.
Michelucci, Robert V. The Collector's Guide to Monster, Science Fiction & Fantasy Film Magazines. LC 85-82030. (Illus.). 250p. (Orig.). 1988. pap. 9.95 (*0-911137-06-8*) Imagine.
Michelucci, Robert V., ed. see Ackerman, Forrest J.
Michelucci, Robert V., ed. see Russo, John.
Michelucci, Robert V., ed. see Savini, Tom.
Michelucci, Robert V., ed. see Smith, Dick.
***Michener.** Mexico. 7.99 (*0-517-13739-9*) Random Hse Value.
Michener, Charles. Stone Roberts: Paintings & Drawings. LC 93-6930. (Illus.). 64p. 1993. pap. 24.95 (*0-8109-2550-8*) Abrams.
— Stone Roberts: Paintings & Drawings. LC 93-6930. 1993. write for info. (*0-8109-3773-5*) Abrams.
Michener, Charles D. The Social Behavior of the Bees. LC 73-87379. 464p. 1974. 45.00 (*0-674-81175-5*) Belknap Pr.
Michener, Charles D., et al. The Bee Genera of North & Central America (Hymenoptera: Apoidea) LC 92-31000. (Illus.). 304p. (C). 1994. 45.00 (*1-56098-256-X*) Smithsonian.
***Michener, Dorothy.** Creating Connections: Learning to Appreciate Diversity. Britt, Leslie, ed. (Illus.). 96p. (Orig.). (J). (gr. 3-6). 1995. pap. text ed. 9.95 (*0-86530-310-X*, 1P310-0) Incentive Pubns.
— The Green Team: Winning Ideas & Activities to Promote Environmental Awareness. Britt, Leslie, ed. (Illus.). 160p. (Orig.). 1993. teacher ed 12.95 (*0-86530-271-5*) Incentive Pubns.
Michener, Dorothy & Muschlitz, Beverly. Bulletin Board Bonanza. (Illus.). 96p. (J). (gr. 2-6). 1981. pap. 7.95 (*0-86530-028-3*, IP-283) Incentive Pubns.
— Filling the Gaps. LC 83-80963. (Illus.). 96p. (gr. 2-6). 1983. pap. text ed. 8.95 (*0-86530-076-3*, IP-763) Incentive Pubns.
— Teacher's Gold Mine. LC 79-89646. (Illus.). 224p. 1979. pap. text ed. 10.95 (*0-913916-83-8*, IP 83-8) Incentive Pubns.
— Teacher's Gold Mine II: More Ideas & Activities for Creative Teaching. (Illus.). 160p. (Orig.). 1992. pap. text ed. 12.95 (*0-86530-150-6*, 83-9) Incentive Pubns.
Michener, Ezra. A Retrospect of Early Quakerism: Being Extracts from the Records of Philadelphia Yearly Meeting & the Meetings Composing It. LC 91-66330. 434p. 1991. text ed. 35.00 (*0-9629841-0-8*) Cool Spring.
Michener, Gail R., jt. ed. see Murie, Jan O.
Michener, H. Andrew & DeLamater, John D. Social Psychology. (Illus.). 688p. (C). 1993. text ed. 51.00 (*0-15-500760-2*) HB Coll Pubs.
Michener, H. Andrew, et al. Social Psychology. 2nd ed. 664p. (C). 1990. text ed. 46.75 (*0-15-581446-X*); pap. text ed. 3.00 (*0-15-581447-8*) HB Coll Pubs.
Michener, James A. Alaska. 1088p. 1989. mass mkt. 6.99 (*0-449-21726-4*, Crest) Fawcett.
— Alaska. 1994. mass mkt. 6.99 (*0-449-45313-8*, Crest) Fawcett.
— Alaska. LC 87-43232. 1100p. 1988. 22.00 (*0-394-55154-0*) Random.
— The Bridge at Andau. 224p. 1985. mass mkt. 5.99 (*0-449-21050-2*, Crest) Fawcett.
— Bridges at Toko-Ri. 1953. 16.95 (*0-394-41780-1*) Random.
— The Bridges at Toko-Ri. 1984. mass mkt. 5.95 (*0-449-20651-3*, Crest) Fawcett.
— Caravans. 1986. mass mkt. 6.95 (*0-449-21380-3*, Crest) Fawcett.
— Caravans. 1963. 29.95 (*0-394-41849-2*) Random.
— Caribbean. 832p. 1992. mass mkt. 6.95 (*0-449-21749-3*, Crest) Fawcett.
— Caribbean: A Novel. 1989. 22.95 (*0-394-56561-4*) Random.
— Centennial. 1987. mass mkt. 6.99 (*0-449-21419-2*, Crest) Fawcett.
— Centennial. 1994. mass mkt. 6.99 (*0-449-45269-7*, Crest) Fawcett.
— Centennial. 1974. 40.50 (*0-394-47970-X*) Random.
— Chesapeake. 1986. mass mkt. 6.95 (*0-449-21158-4*, Crest) Fawcett.
— Chesapeake. LC 78-2892. 1978. 45.00 (*0-394-50079-2*) Random.
— The Covenant. 1987. mass mkt. 6.95 (*0-449-21420-6*, Crest) Fawcett.
— The Covenant. LC 80-5315. (Spanish Literary Reader Ser.). 1980. 39.95 (*0-394-50505-0*) Random.
— Creatures of the Kingdom. 1995. pap. write for info. (*0-449-22092-3*) Fawcett.
— Creatures of the Kingdom. large type ed. LC 93-44109. 1994. 25.95 (*1-56895-054-3*) Wheeler Pub.
— Creatures of the Kingdom: Stories of Animals & Nature. 1993. 22.00 (*0-679-41367-7*) Random.
— Drifters. 1986. mass mkt. 5.95 (*0-449-21353-6*) Fawcett.
— Drifters. 1971. 29.95 (*0-394-46200-9*) Random.
— The Eagle & the Raven. LC 90-9684. (Illus.). 228p. (J). 1990. 19.95 (*0-938349-57-0*) State House Pr.
— Eagle & the Raven. 1991. mass mkt. 4.95 (*0-8125-1301-0*) Tor Bks.
— Fires of Spring. 1987. mass mkt. 5.95 (*0-449-21470-2*) Fawcett.
— The Floating World. (Illus.). 472p. 1983. reprint ed. pap. 13.95 (*0-8248-0873-8*) UH Pr.
— Hawaii. 1986. mass mkt. 6.99 (*0-449-21335-8*, Crest) Fawcett.
— Hawaii. 1994. mass mkt. 6.95 (*0-449-45268-9*, Crest) Fawcett.
— Hawaii. 1959. 45.00 (*0-394-42797-1*, Vin) Random.
— Iberia: Spanish Travels & Reflections. LC 67-22623. (Illus.). 1968. 29.95 (*0-394-42982-6*) Random.
— Iberia: Spanish Travels & Reflections. (Illus.). 960p. 1984. reprint ed. mass mkt. 6.95 (*0-449-20733-1*, Crest) Fawcett.
— James A. Michener on the Social Studies. (Bulletin Ser.: No. 85). 118p. 1991. pap. 14.95 (*0-87986-060-X*) Nat Coun Soc Studies.
— James A. Michener's Writer's Handbook. 1992. pap. 15. 00 (*0-679-74126-7*) Random.
— James Michener, 2 vols. in 1. LC 92-42529. 1993. 14.99 (*0-517-09151-8*, Pub. by Wings Bks) Random Hse Value.
— Journey. 1994. mass mkt. 5.99 (*0-449-21847-3*) Fawcett.
— Journey. 1989. 25.00 (*0-394-57826-0*); pap. 15.95 (*0-394-57892-9*) Random.
— Journey. large type ed. LC 89-48690. 344p. 1990. reprint ed. bds. 18.95 (*0-89621-935-6*) Thorndike Pr.
— Kent State What Happened & Why. 1985. mass mkt. 5.95 (*0-449-20273-9*) Fawcett.
— Legacy. 1988. mass mkt. 5.95 (*0-449-21641-1*, Crest) Fawcett.
— Legacy. LC 87-42644. 184p. 1988. pap. 15.95 (*0-394-57272-6*) Random.
— Legacy. limited ed. LC 87-42644. 184p. 1988. 100.00 (*0-394-56526-6*) Random.
— Literary Reflections. 1995. pap. 4.99 (*0-8125-5052-8*) Forge NYC.
— Literary Reflections: Michener on Michener, Hemingway, Capote, & Others. LC 93-32356. (Illus.). 224p. 1993. 21. 95 (*1-880510-06-5*) State House Pr.
— Literary Reflections: Michener on Michener, Hemingway, Capote, & Others. limited ed. LC 93-32356. (Illus.). 224p. 1993. 125.00 (*1-880510-07-3*) State House Pr.
— Mexico. 1994. mass mkt. 6.99 (*0-449-22187-3*, Crest) Fawcett.
— Mexico. LC 92-50151. 1992. 25.00 (*0-679-41649-8*) Random.
— Mexico. large type ed. LC 92-50238. 1992. 25.00 (*0-679-74329-4*) Random.
— Mexico. limited ed. 1992. 125.00 (*0-679-41844-X*) Random.
— A Michener Miscellany: 1950-1970. Hibbs, Ben, ed. 1973. 12.95 (*0-394-47948-3*, Readrs Digest Pr) Random.
— Miracle in Seville. LC 94-10187. 1995. 25.00 (*0-685-72068-3*) Random.
— My Lost Mexico. LC 92-26953. (Illus.). 165p. 1992. 24. 95 (*0-938349-93-7*) State House Pr.
— My Lost Mexico. 224p. 1993. mass mkt. 4.99 (*0-8125-3437-9*) Tor Bks.
— My Lost Mexico. limited ed. LC 92-26953. (Illus.). 165p. 1992. 125.00 (*0-938349-94-5*) State House Pr.
— The Novel. 1992. mass mkt. 5.99 (*0-449-22143-1*, Crest) Fawcett.
— The Novel. 1991. 22.50 (*0-679-40133-4*) Random.
— The Novel. large type ed. 704p. 1991. 24.50 (*0-679-40348-5*) Random.
— Poland. 1984. mass mkt. 6.95 (*0-449-20587-8*, Crest) Fawcett.
— Poland. LC 83-4477. 556p. 1983. 35.00 (*0-394-53189-2*) Random.
— The Quality of Life. 1994. reprint ed. lib. bdg. 24.95 (*1-56849-311-8*) Buccaneer Bks.
— Rascals in Paradise. 384p. 1987. mass mkt. 5.95 (*0-449-21459-1*, Crest) Fawcett.
— Recessional. 1994. 25.00 (*0-679-43612-X*) Random.
— Recessional. 1994. 125.00 (*0-679-43828-9*); pap. 24.00 (*0-679-75691-4*) Random.
— Return to Paradise. 1984. mass mkt. 5.99 (*0-449-20650-5*, Crest) Fawcett.
— Return to Paradise. 1951. 24.95 (*0-394-44291-1*) Random.
— Sayonara. 1983. mass mkt. 5.95 (*0-449-20414-6*, Crest) Fawcett.
— Source. 1986. mass mkt. 6.99 (*0-449-21147-9*, Crest) Fawcett.
— Source. 1965. 45.00 (*0-394-44630-5*) Random.
— South Pacific. Hague, M., ed. (Performing Arts Ser.). (J). 1992. 16.95 (*0-15-200618-4*, Gulliver Bks) HarBrace.
— Space. 1983. mass mkt. 5.95 (*0-449-20379-4*, Crest) Fawcett.
— Space. 1982. 17.95 (*0-394-50555-7*) Random.
— Space. (Illus.). 640p. 1985. 15.95 (*0-394-55041-2*) Random.
— Sports in America. 1987. mass mkt. 4.95 (*0-449-21450-8*, Crest) Fawcett.
— Sports in America. LC 75-40549. 1976. 15.95 (*0-394-40646-X*) Random.
— Tales of the South Pacific. 1984. mass mkt. 5.95 (*0-449-20652-1*, Crest) Fawcett.
— Tales of the South Pacific. 1980. 16.95 (*0-02-584490-3*) Macmillan.
— Tales of the South Pacific. 336p. 1987. text ed. 35.00 (*0-02-584540-3*, Scribners) S&S Trade.
— Texas. 1994. mass mkt. 6.99 (*0-449-45314-6*, Crest) Fawcett.
— Texas. 1995. mass mkt. 6.99 (*0-449-21092-8*, Crest) Fawcett.
— The Watermen. (Illus.). 1979. 12.95 (*0-394-50660-X*) Random.
— The World Is My Home. limited ed. 1992. 125.00 (*0-679-41118-6*) McKay.
— The World Is My Home: A Memoir. large type ed. 1991. pap. 19.00 (*0-679-73981-5*) Random.
— The World Is My Home: Memoirs. 512p. 1992. 25.00 (*0-679-40134-2*) Random.
Michener, James A., ed. Hokusai Sketchbooks: Selections from the Manga. LC 58-9983. (Illus.). 286p. 1958. 65.00 (*0-8048-0252-1*) C E Tuttle.
Michener, James A. & Kings, John. Six Days in Havana. (Illus.). 144p. 1989. 24.95 (*0-292-77629-2*) U of Tex Pr.
Michener, James S., jt. auth. see Hemingway, Ernest.
Michener, John. The Back to the City Movement & the Possibilities of Increasing Racial & Economic Integration. 50p. 1978. 3.50 (*0-318-15819-1*) Natl Neighbors.
Michener, R., jt. auth. see Lajtha, K.
***Michener, Roger, ed.** The Balance of Freedom: Political Economy, Law, & Learning. LC 94-38254. 288p. (C). 1995. text ed. 34.95x (*0-943852-73-0*) Prof World Peace.
— The Balance of Freedom: Political Economy, Law, & Learning. LC 94-38254. 288p. (C). 1995. pap. text ed. 17.95x (*0-943852-74-9*) Prof World Peace.
— Nationality, Patriotism, & Nationalism. LC 93-36087. 256p. 1994. text ed. 34.95x (*0-943852-65-X*) Prof World Peace.
— Nationality, Patriotism, & Nationalism. LC 93-36087. 256p. (C). 1994. pap. text ed. 17.95x (*0-943852-66-8*) Prof World Peace.
Michener, William K., et al, eds. Environmental Information Management & Analysis: Ecosystem to Global Scales. LC 94-1213. (Applications in Geographic Information Systems Ser.). 1994. 99.00 (*0-7484-0123-7*, Pub. by Tay Francis Ltd UK) Taylor & Francis.
Michenfelder, John D. Anesthesia & the Brain: Clinical, Functional, Metabolic, & Vascular Correlates. (Illus.). 215p. 1988. text ed. 65.00 (*0-443-08628-1*) Churchill.
Michenfelder, John D., jt. ed. see Cucchiara, Roy F.
Michette, A., et al, eds. X-Ray Microscopy Three. (Optical Sciences Ser.: Vol. 67). (Illus.). 419p. 1992. 100.00 (*0-387-53605-1*) Spr-Verlag.
Michette, A. G. & Buckley, C., eds. X-Ray Science & Technology. (Illus.). 376p. 1993. 58.00 (*0-7503-0233-X*) IOP Pub.
Michette, Alan G. Optical Systems for Soft X-Rays. 320p. 1986. 85.00 (*0-306-42320-0*, Plenum Pr) Plenum.
Michie, A. Coordination of Building Services: Design Stage Methods. (C). 1982. 42.00 (*0-86022-150-4*, Pub. by Build Servs Info Assn UK) St Mut.
Michie, A. & Wix, J. Computer Draughting. (C). 1983. 63. 00 (*0-86022-111-3*, Pub. by Build Servs Info Assn UK) St Mut.
— An Overview of Computers in the Building Service Industry. (C). 1983. 63.00 (*0-86022-106-7*, Pub. by Build Servs Info Assn UK) St Mut.
Michie, Allan A. & Graebner, Walter, eds. Their Finest Hour: The War in the First Person. LC 41-2009. 213p. reprint ed. pap. 60.80 (*0-317-28769-9*, 2051682) Bks Demand.
Michie, Aruna N., ed. Rural Poverty & Public Policy in the United States. (Orig.). 1986. pap. 12.00 (*0-918592-93-3*) Pol Studies.
***Michie Butterworth Editorial Staff.** Hawaii Court Rules Annotated, 1994 Edition. annot. ed. 1994. pap. 30.00 (*1-55834-041-6*) Michie Butterworth.
— Illinois Criminal Practice Law & Rules Annotated, 1993 Edition. Date not set. pap. 30.00 (*0-614-05844-9*) Michie Butterworth.
— Illinois Federal Court Rules Annotated, 1994 Edition. Date not set. pap. 20.00 (*0-614-05845-7*) Michie Butterworth.
— Illinois State Court Rules Annotated, 1994 Edition. 1994. pap. 25.00 (*0-614-05847-3*) Michie Butterworth.
— Indiana Court Rules Annotated, 1994 Editon. 1994. pap. 42.50 (*1-55834-042-4*) Michie Butterworth.
— Instructions for Virginia & West Virginia. 3rd ed. 1987. 120.00 (*0-614-05857-0*) Michie Butterworth.
— Instructions for Virginia & West Virginia, 3 vols., Set. 3rd ed. 1987. 135.00 (*0-614-05856-2*) Michie Butterworth.
— Kentucky Corporations Laws & Rules, 1992 Edition. 1992. 12.00 (*0-614-05871-6*) Michie Butterworth.
— Kentucky Rules Annotated, 1994-95 Edition. 1411p. 1994. pap. 45.00 (*0-87473-853-9*) Michie Butterworth.
— Maryland Rules, 1994 Edition, 2 vols., Set. Date not set. pap. 50.00 (*1-55834-043-2*) Michie Butterworth.
— Michie on Banks & Banking, 1955-1992, 13 vols., Set. suppl. ed. 1994. 440.00 (*0-87215-034-8*) Michie Butterworth.
— Nevada Court Rules Annotated, 1994 Edition. 1994. pap. 40.00 (*1-55834-044-0*) Michie Butterworth.
— New Mexico Rules Annotated, 1994 Edition. Date not set. pap. 45.00 (*1-55834-045-9*) Michie Butterworth.
— North Dakota Court Rules Annotated, 1994-95 Edition. Date not set. 50.00 (*0-87473-870-9*) Michie Butterworth.
— Rhode Island Court Rules Annotated, 1994 Edition. Date not set. 45.00 (*1-55834-089-0*) Michie Butterworth.
— South Dakota Court Rules, 1994 Edition. Date not set. pap. 50.00 (*1-55834-144-7*) Michie Butterworth.
— Tennessee Court Rules Annotated. 1993. pap. 42.00 (*0-87473-881-4*) Michie Butterworth.
— Tennessee Jurisprudence, 29 vols., Set. 1991. 1,800.00 (*0-87215-503-X*) Michie Butterworth.
— Tennessee Private Acts Index. 652p. 1984. 75.00 (*0-614-05976-3*) Michie Butterworth.
— Utah Court Rules Annotated, 1994 Edition. Date not set. pap. 65.00 (*1-55834-092-0*) Michie Butterworth.
— Virginia Rules Annotated, 1994 Edition. Date not set. 40. 00 (*1-55834-047-5*) Michie Butterworth.
— Washington Rules of Court Annotated, 1994 Edition. Date not set. 50.00 (*1-55834-178-1*) Michie Butterworth.
— West Virginia Court Rules, 1994 Edition. Date not set. pap. 47.00 (*1-55834-050-5*) Michie Butterworth.
— What's It Worth? A Guide to Personal Injury Awards & Settlements, 1993 Edition. 979p. 1993. pap. 75.00 (*1-55834-096-3*) Michie Butterworth.
Michie Butterworth Editorial Staff & Harriman, D. P. Wyoming Court Rules Annotated. 973p. 1991. ring bd. 85.00x (*0-87473-733-8*) Michie Butterworth.
Michie Butterworth Editorial Staff & Munger, J. P. Michie's Jurisprudence of Virginia & West Virginia with 1991 Cumulative Supplement, 46 vols., Set. rev. ed. 1993. 1,200.00 (*0-87215-128-X*) Michie Butterworth.
Michie Butterworth Staff. Consolidated Index: Consolidated Index 1994. (New Hampshire Practice Ser.). 450p. 1992. pap. 47.00 (*1-56257-269-5*) Michie Butterworth.
Michie Company, jt. auth. see Publisher's Staff.
Michie Company Editoral Staff. Delaware Corporation Law, Limited Partnership Act & Business Trust Act, 1991-92. 440p. 1991. 17.00 (*0-87473-741-9*) Michie Butterworth.
Michie Company Editorial Staff. Alabama Rules Annotated. 1549p. 1992. pap. 37.50 (*0-87473-839-3*) Michie Butterworth.
— Annotated Rules of North Carolina. 1116p. 1992. 35.00 (*0-87473-866-0*) Michie Butterworth.
— Arkansas Criminal Code. (State Practice Publications Ser.). 1088p. 1991. pap. 35.00 (*0-87473-530-0*) Michie Butterworth.
— Code of Virginia, 1950, 25 vols. write for info. (*0-318-54327-3*) Michie Butterworth.
— Code of Virginia, 1950, 25 vols., Set. write for info. (*0-87215-137-9*) Michie Butterworth.
— Delaware Code Annotated, Revised 1974, 21 vols. write for info. (*0-318-54328-1*) Michie Butterworth.
— Delaware Code Annotated, Revised 1974, 21 vols., Set. write for info. (*0-87215-247-2*) Michie Butterworth.
— General Statutes of North Carolina, Annotated, 24 vols., Set. write for info. (*0-87215-132-8*) Michie Butterworth.
— Idaho Civil Rules: Pocket Edition. 306p. 1992. pap. 20.00 (*0-87473-920-9*) Michie Butterworth.
— Idaho Court Rules, 1992 Edition. (State Practice Publications Ser.). 1992. 37.50 (*0-87473-905-5*) Michie Butterworth.
— Idaho Criminal Rules: Pocket Edition. 306p. 1992. pap. 25.00 (*0-87473-922-5*) Michie Butterworth.
— Indiana Alcoholic Beverage Law & Rules, 1992: Annotated. 313p. 1992. pap. 12.50 (*0-685-62337-8*) Michie Butterworth.
— Indiana Court Rules Annotated. 1504p. 1992. 40.00 (*0-87473-851-2*) Michie Butterworth.
— Indiana Criminal & Traffic Law Manual. 1001p. 1992. pap. 22.50 (*0-685-62338-6*) Michie Butterworth.
— Maryland Code of 1957, 37 vols., Set. write for info. (*0-87215-129-8*) Michie Butterworth.
— Michie on Banks & Banking, 1955-1992, 11 vols. Suppl. & Regulations of Board Governors of the Federal Reserve System. 180.00 (*0-87473-831-8*) Michie Butterworth.
— Michie's Jurisprudence of Virginia & West Virginia with 1991 Cumulative Supplement, 45 vols. rev. suppl. ed. 1991. Cumulative supplement 1991. 260.00 (*0-87473-908-X*) Michie Butterworth.
— Police, Crimes & Offenses & Motor Vehicle Laws of Virginia, 2 vols., Set. 1992. 80.00 (*0-685-62339-4*); 80.00 (*0-685-62355-6*) Michie Butterworth.
— Rhode Island Court Rules Annotated, 1991-92. 1216p. pap. 45.00 (*0-87473-729-X*) Michie Butterworth.
— Tennessee Jurisprudence, 29 vols. 185.00 (*0-87473-901-2*) Michie Butterworth.
— Tennessee Private Acts Index. suppl. ed. 652p. 1991. Suppl. 1991. 17.50 (*0-87215-870-5*) Michie Butterworth.
— Tennessee Private Acts Index, Incl. 1991 Suppl. 652p. 1984. 75.00 (*0-87215-812-8*) Michie Butterworth.
— Virginia Rules Annotated. 1461p. 1992. pap. 40.00 (*0-87473-875-X*) Michie Butterworth.
Michie Company Editorial Staff, ed. Arkansas Court Rules, 1992. (State Practice Publications Ser.). 1218p. 1992. 32. 50 (*0-87473-842-3*) Michie Butterworth.
Michie Company Editorial Staff, jt. auth. see Indiana Judges Association, Civil Instructions Committee Staff.
Michie Company Staff. Alabama Criminal Code. 1991. pap. 29.00 (*0-87473-529-7*) Michie Butterworth.
— Alabama Motor Vehicle Laws. 1991. 25.00 (*0-87473-521-1*) Michie Butterworth.
— Arizona Revised Statutes, 1991, 4 vols., Set. pap. 120.00 (*0-87473-675-7*) Michie Butterworth.
— West Virginia Court Rules Annotated. 1309p. 1992. 45.00 (*0-87473-879-2*) Michie Butterworth.
Michie Company Staff, ed. Drugs in Litigation: Damage Awards Involving Prescription & Nonprescription Drugs. 1075p. 1992. 60.00 (*0-87473-969-1*) Michie Butterworth.
Michie, D., et al, eds. Machine Learning, Neural & Statistical Classification. LC 94-7096. (Artificial Intelligence Ser.). 304p. 1994. text ed. 50.00 (*0-13-106360-X*) P-H Gen Ref & Trav.
Michie, Donald. Expert Systems in a Microelectronic Age. 287p. 1980. 30.00 (*0-85224-493-2*, Pub. by Edinburgh U Pr UK) Col U Pr.
— Machine Intelligence & Related Topics. 328p. 1982. text ed. 100.00 (*0-677-05560-9*) Gordon & Breach.
Michie, Donald, ed. Introductory Readings in Expert Systems. (Studies in Cybernetics: Vol. 1). 256p. 1982. text ed. 46.00 (*0-677-16350-9*) Gordon & Breach.
Michie, Donald & Rhoads, David. Mark As Story: An Introduction to the Narrative of a Gospel. LC 81-43084. 176p. 1982. pap. 12.00 (*0-8006-1614-6*, Fortress Pr) Augsburg Fortress.

 An Asterisk (*) at the beginning of an entry indicates that the title is appearing in BIP for the first time.

M

Michie, Donald M., ed. A Critical Edition of "The True Chronicle History of King Lear & His Three Daughters, Gonorill, Ragan & Cordella" LC 91-31663. (Renaissance Imagination Ser.). 256p. 1992. 72.00 (*0-8153-0456-0*) Garland.

Michie, Elsie B. Outside the Pale: Cultural Exclusion, Gender Difference, & the Victorian Woman Writer. LC 93-2458. (Reading Women Writing Ser.). 208p. 1993. 34.95 (*0-8014-2831-9*); pap. 13.95 (*0-8014-8085-X*) Cornell U Pr.

Michie, Helena. The Flesh Made Word: Female Figures & Women's Bodies. (Illus.). 192p. 1990. reprint ed. pap. 15. 95 (*0-19-506081-4*) OUP.

— Sororophobia: Differences among Women in Literature & Culture. (Illus.). 256p. 1992. 36.00 (*0-19-507387-8*) OUP.

Michie, James & Kavanagh, Patrick J., eds. The Oxford Book of Short Poems. 1986. 30.00 (*0-19-214135-X*); pap. 9.95 (*0-685-10547-4*) OUP.

Michie, James, tr. see Euripides.

Michie, James, tr. see Horace.

Michie, James, jt. ed. see Kavanagh, Patrick J.

Michie, James, tr. see Martial.

Michie, James L. Richmond Hill Plantation, Eighteen Ten to Eighteen Sixty-Eight: The Discovery of Antebellum Life on a Waccamaw Rice Plantation. LC 89-24298. (Illus.). xx, 204p. 1990. 24.95 (*0-87152-441-4*) Reprint.

Michie, Jonathan. The Economics of Restructuring & Intervention. 240p. 1991. text ed. 69.95 (*1-85278-346-X*, Pub. by E Elgar Pub UK) Ashgate Pub Co.

Michie, Jonathan, ed. The Economic Legacy 1979-1992. (Illus.). 391p. 1993. text ed. 64.95 (*0-12-494060-9*); pap. text ed. 29.95 (*0-12-494061-7*) Acad Pr.

***Michie, Jonathan & Smith, James G., eds.** Managing the Global Economy. (Illus.). 300p. 1995. pap. text ed. 24.95 (*0-19-828968-5*) OUP.

— Managing the Global Economy. (Illus.). 300p. 1995. text ed. 69.00 (*0-19-828969-3*) OUP.

Michie, Jonathon & Smith, John G., eds. Unemployment in Europe. (Illus.). 384p. 1994. pap. text ed. 29.95 (*0-12-494065-X*) Acad Pr.

Michie, Peter S. The Life & Letters of Emory Upton. Kohn, Richard H., ed. LC 78-22388. (American Military Experience Ser.). 1980. reprint ed. lib. bdg. 40.95 (*0-405-11865-1*) Ayer.

Michie, R. C., intro. Commercial & Financial Services, 11 vols. LC 93-43743. (Industrial Revolutions Ser.). 1994. 1,200.00 (*0-631-18123-7*) Blackwell Pubs.

Michie, R. Emmett, ed. see Davis, Norm.

Michigan Association of Municipal Attorneys Staff, jt. auth. see Michigan Municipal League Staff.

Michigan Department of Health Staff. Ground Water Heat Pump Installations in Michigan. 23p. 1983. pap. 3.75 (*1-56034-015-0*, K020) Natl Water Well.

Michigan Intercollegiate Athletic Association Staff. Celebrating a Century of the Student Athlete: A 100-Year History of the Oldest Collegiate Athletic Conference in the United States. Renner, Thomas L., ed. (Illus.). 206p. (Orig.). (C). 1988. 20.00 (*0-317-93624-7*); pap. 15.00 (*0-317-93625-5*) MI IAA.

Michigan Judicial Institute Staff. Michigan Criminal Procedure Benchbook. LC 92-74196. 276p. 1992. ring bd. 85.00 (*0-685-65664-0*, 92-024) U MI Law CLE.

Michigan Judicial Institute Staff & Michigan Probate Judges, Blue-Ribbon Committee Staff. Probate Court Benchbooks, 3 vols., 1. LC 90-84059. 1032p. 1990. pap. 65.00 (*0-685-39000-4*, 90-031) U MI Law CLE.

— Probate Court Benchbooks, 3 vols., 2. LC 90-84059. 1032p. 1990. pap. 65.00 (*0-685-39001-2*, 90-032) U MI Law CLE.

— Probate Court Benchbooks, 3 vols., 3. LC 90-84059. 1032p. 1990. pap. 65.00 (*0-685-39002-0*, 90-033) U MI Law CLE.

Michigan Legal Services Staff & National Health Law Program Staff. Health Law: Training of Trainers. 706p. 1985. 35.00 (*0-685-23177-1*, 41,209) NCLS Inc.

Michigan Legislative Council Staff. Michigan Administrative Code Nineteen Seventy-Nine: 1992 Annual Supplement. Peters, Roger W., ed. 1993. pap. 36.00 (*1-878210-05-X*) Legis Serv Bur.

— Michigan Administrative Code, 1979: 1989 Annual Supplement. Peters, Roger W., ed. 1071p. 1990. pap. 26. 50 (*1-878210-02-5*) Legis Serv Bur.

— Michigan Administrative Code 1979: 1993 Annual Supplement. Peters, Roger, ed. 1994. pap. 33.00 (*1-878210-07-6*) Legis Serv Bur.

— Michigan Administrative Code 1979: 1994 Annual Supplement. Peters, Roger, ed. 1995. pap. write for info. (*1-878210-08-4*) Legis Serv Bur.

— Michigan Administrative Code 1979, 1990 Annual Supplement. Peters, Roger W., ed. 1991. pap. 30.00 (*1-878210-03-3*) Legis Serv Bur.

— Michigan Manual 1991-1992. rev. ed. (Illus.). 1135p. 1991. 15.00 (*1-878210-04-1*) Legis Serv Bur.

Michigan Legislative Council Staff & Peters, Roger W. Michigan Manual 1993-1994. (Illus.). 1108p. 1993. 15. 00 (*1-878210-06-8*) Legis Serv Bur.

Michigan Municipal League Staff. Directory of Michigan Municipal Officials. 1994. 35.00 (*0-318-19475-9*) MI Municipal.

— Disorderly Conduct. (Ordinance Analysis Ser.: No. 20). 1985. pap. 5.00 (*0-317-01203-7*) MI Municipal.

— Glossary of Municipal Terms. 1992. 15.00 (*0-317-05702-2*) MI Municipal.

— Junk Yard & Second-Hand Dealers Ordinance Analysis. (Ordinance Analysis Ser.: No. 8). 1986. pap. 5.00 (*0-317-00870-6*) MI Municipal.

— Meetings: Minutes & Agendas. 1992. 15.00 (*0-317-05704-9*) MI Municipal.

— Parking Violations Bureaus. (Technical Topics Ser.: No. 35). 1987. pap. 5.00 (*0-317-00874-9*) MI Municipal.

— Private Swimming Pools. (Technical Topics Ser.: No. 26). 1987. pap. 5.00 (*0-317-00873-0*) MI Municipal.

— Salaries & Wages in Michigan Municipalities over 1,000 Population. (Information Bulletin Ser.: No. 109). 1993. 45.00 (*0-318-19474-0*) MI Municipal.

— Special Assessment Procedures for Cities & Villages. (Ordinance Analysis Ser.: No. 11). 1987. pap. 12.50 (*0-317-00871-4*) MI Municipal.

Michigan Municipal League Staff & Michigan Association of Municipal Attorneys Staff. Handbook for Municipal Attorneys in Michigan. 1993. 100.00 (*0-317-05716-2*) MI Municipal.

Michigan Municipal League Staff, ed. see Hannah, Susan B.

Michigan Papyri Staff. Michigan Papyri (P. Mich. XII) LC 71-649942. (American Studies in Papyrology: No. 14). 142p. reprint ed. pap. 40.50 (*0-7837-5486-8*, 2045251) Bks Demand.

— Michigan Papyri XIV. McCarren, Vincent P., ed. LC 71-649942. (American Studies in Papyrology: No. 22). 110p. reprint ed. pap. 31.40 (*0-7837-5491-4*, 2045256) Bks Demand.

***Michigan Press Staff.** Greek-English Dictionary of Science & Technological Terms. 569p. (ENG & GRE.). Date not set. 95.00 (*0-7859-9054-2*) Fr & Eur.

Michigan Probate Judges, Blue-Ribbon Committee Staff, jt. auth. see Michigan Judicial Institute Staff.

***Michigan Sea Grant Staff.** Lightning & Boats. (Illus.). 9p. 1995. pap. 1.00 (*1-885756-00-3*, MICHU-SG89-700) MI Sea Grant.

Michigan State Bar Special Committee on Standard Criminal Jury Instructions Staff. Michigan Criminal Jury Instructions, 3 vols. 2nd ed. LC 89-82310. 1500p. 1991. 75.00 (*0-685-58877-7*, 92-030); disk write for info. (*0-318-68094-7*) U MI Law CLE.

— Michigan Criminal Jury Instructions, 3 vols., Set. 2nd ed. LC 89-82310. 1500p. 1991. ring bd. 210.00 (*0-685-38202-8*, 76-010) U MI Law CLE.

Michigan State University, East Lansing Staff. Dictionary Catalog of the G. Robert Vincent Library. 1974. lib. bdg. 85.00 (*0-8161-1149-9*, Hall Library) G K Hall.

Michigan State University, Institute of Public Utilities, Staff. Adjusting to Regulatory, Pricing & Marketing Realities: Proceedings of the Institute of Public Utilities Annual Conference, 14th, Williamsburg, VA, 1982. LC 83-62894. (MSU Public Utilities Papers). 781p. reprint ed. pap. 180.00 (*0-8357-5100-7*, 2029405) Bks Demand.

Michigan State University, Institute of Public Utilities Conference Staff. Alternatives to Traditional Regulation: Options for Reform: Proceedings of the Institute of Public Utilities Nineteenth Annual Conference. Trebing, Harry M. & Mann, Patrick C., eds. LC 88-83141. (MSU Public Utilities Papers: No. 1987). 616p. reprint ed. pap. 175.60 (*0-7837-6268-2*, 2045980) Bks Demand.

Michigan State University, Institute of Public Utilities Staff. Assessing New Pricing Concepts in Public Utilities: Proceedings of the Institute of Public Utilities Ninth Annual Conference. Trebing, Harry M., ed. LC 78-620031. (MSU Public Utilities Papers). (Illus.). 528p. reprint ed. pap. 150.50 (*0-8357-5805-2*, 2056383) Bks Demand.

Michigan State University, Project Physnet Staff. Introduction to Physics, Vol. I. (C). 1993. pap. text ed. 30.00 (*1-881592-34-0*) Hayden-McNeil.

— Introduction to Physics, Vol. II. (C). 1993. pap. text ed. 30.00 (*1-881592-21-9*) Hayden-McNeil.

— Principles of Physics, Vol. II. (C). 1993. pap. text ed. 35. 00 (*1-881592-36-7*) Hayden-McNeil.

Michigan State University Staff. Visions of the Universe. (C). 1993. student ed 13.00 (*1-881592-08-1*) Hayden-McNeil.

Michigan State University Staff, Project Physnet Staff. Principles of Physics, Vol. I. (C). 1993. pap. text ed. 35. 00 (*1-881592-35-9*) Hayden-McNeil.

Michigan Supreme Court Committee on Standard Jury Instructions Staff. Michigan Standard Jury Instructions - Civil, 2 vols. 2nd ed. LC 81-80665. 1100p. 1981. ring bd. 140.00 (*0-685-39007-1*, 81-101) U MI Law CLE.

— Michigan Standard Jury Instructions - Civil, 2 vols. 2nd suppl. ed. LC 81-80665. 1100p. 1993. pap. 45.00 (*0-685-47731-2*, 93-013) U MI Law CLE.

Michigan Technological University Staff. Composition Variations of Incragrind for Large Sections. 60p. 1970. 9.00 (*0-317-34501-X*, 78) Intl Copper.

Michigan United Conservation Clubs Staff. Great Lakes Nature Guide. rev. ed. 1978. pap. 1.95 (*0-933112-05-X*) Mich United Conserv.

— Michigan County Maps & Outdoor Guide. 1977. pap. 11. 95 (*0-933112-04-1*) Mich United Conserv.

— Michigan's Fifty Best Fishing Lakes: The State's Top Inland Waters. 1982. pap. 6.95 (*0-933112-06-8*) Mich United Conserv.

— The Wildlife Chef. 2nd rev. ed. 1986. pap. 5.95 (*0-933112-02-5*) Mich United Conserv.

Michigan University Conference on Aging Staff. Aging & the Economy: Proceedings of the Michigan University Conference on Aging, 1962. Orbach, Harold L. & Tibbitts, Clark, eds. LC 63-13714. 249p. reprint ed. pap. 71.00 (*0-8357-5259-3*, 2055636) Bks Demand.

Michigan University, Department of English Staff. Studies in Shakespeare, Milton & Donne. LC 65-15881. (Studies in English Literature: No. 33). 1972. reprint ed. lib. bdg. 75.00 (*0-8383-0638-1*) M S G Haskell Hse.

Michigan University, Institute of Science & Technology, Industrial Development Division Staff. R & D for Small & Medium-Sized Firms: Proceedings of a Symposium at the University of Michigan, October 25,1966. Armstrong, John M., ed. LC 67-20367. (Illus.). 112p. reprint ed. pap. 32.00 (*0-317-10638-4*, 2012297) Bks Demand.

Michigan University Press Staff, jt. auth. see Marias, Julian.

Michigan University, Survey Research Center Staff. Five Thousand American Families: Patterns of Economic Progress, 5 vols., Vol. 1. LC 74-620002. 446p. reprint ed. pap. 127.20 (*0-7837-5693-3*, 2044997) Bks Demand.

— Five Thousand American Families: Patterns of Economic Progress, 5 vols., Vol. 2. LC 74-620002. 382p. reprint ed. pap. 108.90 (*0-7837-5694-1*) Bks Demand.

— Five Thousand American Families: Patterns of Economic Progress, 5 vols., Vol. 3. LC 74-620002. 496p. reprint ed. pap. 141.40 (*0-7837-5695-X*) Bks Demand.

— Five Thousand American Families: Patterns of Economic Progress, 5 vols., Vol. 4. LC 74-620002. 535p. reprint ed. pap. 152.50 (*0-7837-5696-8*) Bks Demand.

— Five Thousand American Families: Patterns of Economic Progress, 5 vols., Vol. 5. LC 74-620002. 534p. reprint ed. pap. 152.20 (*0-7837-5698-4*) Bks Demand.

— Five Thousand American Families: Patterns of Economic Progress, Vol. 6. LC 74-620002. 502p. reprint ed. pap. 143.10 (*0-7837-5697-6*, 2044997) Bks Demand.

— Five Thousand American Families: Patterns of Economic Progress, Vol. 7. LC 74-620002. 391p. reprint ed. pap. 111.50 (*0-7837-5699-2*) Bks Demand.

— Five Thousand American Families: Patterns of Economic Progress, Vol. 8. LC 74-620002. 458p. reprint ed. pap. 130.60 (*0-7837-5700-X*) Bks Demand.

— Five Thousand American Families: Patterns of Economic Progress, Vol. 9. LC 74-620002. 546p. reprint ed. pap. 155.70 (*0-7837-5701-8*) Bks Demand.

— Five Thousand American Families: Patterns of Economic Progress, Vol. 10. LC 74-620002. 442p. reprint ed. pap. 126.00 (*0-7837-5702-6*) Bks Demand.

Michigan University, William L. Clements Library Staff. Guide to the Manuscript Collections in the William L. Clements Library. Peckham, Howard H., ed. LC 42-20545. 419p. reprint ed. pap. 119.50 (*0-317-29302-8*, 2055639) Bks Demand.

Michihiko Ike, jt. auth. see Masanori Fujita.

Michiko Ishikawa, ed. see Creme, Benjamin.

Michilinie, et al. Revenge of the Living Monolith. 80p. 1985. 9.95 (*0-87135-083-1*) Marvel Entmnt.

Michio Hoshino. The Grizzly Bear Family Book. Colligan-Taylor, Karen, tr. (Illus.). 52p. (J). (gr. 2 up). 1993. 15. 95 (*0-88708-309-9*, Picture Book Studio) S&S Childrens.

Michio Kushi, et al. Raising Healthy Kids: A Book of Child Care & Natural Family Health. LC 93-46170. 1994. pap. 14.95 (*0-89529-578-4*) Avery Pub.

Michiyoshi, Itaru, jt. ed. see Jones, Owen C.

Michka, Nikolas & Michka, Vera. Azbuka. (Illus.). 70p. (RUS.). (YA). 1994. write for info. (*1-885024-00-2*) Slavic Christian.

Michka, Nikolas, ed. see Kuschnir, Vera.

Michka, Nikolas, ed. see Michka, Vitaly.

Michka, Vera, ed. see Kuschnir, Vera.

Michka, Vera, jt. auth. see Michka, Nikolas.

Michka, Vera, ed. see Salov-Astakhov.

Michka, Vitaly. Inside the New Russia. Michka, Nikolas et al, eds. (Illus.). 330p. (Orig.). 1994. pap. write for info. (*1-885024-17-7*) Slavic Christian.

Michka, Vitaly, tr. see Cambron, Mark.

Michka, Vitaly, tr. see Halsey, John.

Michl, Josef & Bonacic-Koutecky, Vlasta. Organic Photochemistry & Electronic Structure. 475p. 1990. text ed. 94.95 (*0-471-89626-8*) Wiley.

Michl, Josef, jt. auth. see Klessinger, Martin.

Michl, Josef, jt. auth. see Thulstrup, Erik W.

Michler, G. O. & Ringel, C. M. Representation Theory of Finite Groups & Finite-Dimensional Algebras. (Progress in Mathematics Ser.: Vol. 95). 532p. 1991. 83.50 (*0-8176-2604-2*) Spr-Verlag.

***Michler, Ralf & Lopsinger, Lutz W., eds.** Salvador Dali: Catalogue Raisonne of Prints II Lithographs & Wood Engravings 1956-1980, 2 vols., Set. (Illus.). 192p. 1995. text ed. 120.00 (*3-7913-1602-8*) Pegasus.

Michler, Ralf, jt. ed. see Lopsinger, Lutz W.

Michlin, S. G. & Prossdorf, S. Singular Integral Operators. Bottcher, A. & Lehmann, R., trs. (Illus.). 540p. 1987. 59. 00 (*0-387-15967-3*) Spr-Verlag.

Michlo, George. The Push of Gravity. (Illus.). 1993. 15.50 (*0-533-09133-0*) Vantage.

Michlovitz, Susan L., jt. auth. see Behrens, Barbara J.

***Michlovitz, Susan L., et al, eds.** Thermal Agents in Rehabilitation. 3rd ed. (Contemporary Perspectives in Rehabilitation Ser.). (Illus.). 330p. (C). 1995. 36.00 (*0-8036-0044-5*) Davis Co.

***Michman, Jozeph.** Gothic Turrets on a Corinthian Building: Dutch Jewry During the Emancipation Period (1787-1814) 200p. 1994. 29.50 (*90-5356-090-4*) IBD Ltd.

Michman-Melkman, Joseph, jt. ed. see Ramras-Rauch, Gila.

Michman, Ronald D. Lifestyle Market Segmentation. LC 90-24530. 232p. 1991. text ed. 55.00 (*0-275-93159-5*, C3159, Praeger Pubs) Greenwood.

— Marketing to Changing Consumer Markets: Environmental Scanning. 188p. 1983. text ed. 49.95 (*0-275-91045-8*, C1045, Praeger Pubs) Greenwood.

Michna, H. The Human Macrophage-System Activity & Functional Morphology. (Bibliotheca Anatomica Ser.: No. 31). (Illus.). xii, 84p. 1988. 75.25 (*3-8055-4641-6*) S Karger.

Michna, Horst, jt. ed. see Tenniswood, Martin.

Michnik, Adam. The Church & the Left. Ost, David, ed. 280p. (C). 1992. 24.95 (*0-226-52424-8*) U Ch Pr.

— Letters from Prison & Other Essays. Latynski, Maya, tr. LC 85-1196. (Societies & Culture in East-Central Europe Ser.: No. 2). 371p. 1986. pap. 15.00 (*0-520-06175-6*) U CA Pr.

Michno, Dennis G. A Manual for Acolytes: The Duties of the Server at Liturgical Celebrations. LC 80-81096. (Illus.). (Orig.). 1981. pap. 4.95 (*0-8192-1272-5*) Morehouse Pub.

— Priest's Handbook: The Ceremonies of the Church. 2nd ed. LC 86-12664. (Illus.). 304p. 1986. 32.50 (*0-8192-1390-X*) Morehouse Pub.

Michno, Gregory. The Mystery of E Troop: The Gray Horse Company at the Little Bighorn. 352p. 1994. pap. 15.00 (*0-87842-304-4*) Mountain Pr.

Michno, Michael J., jt. auth. see Pilato, Louis A.

Michnovicz, Jon J. & Klein, Diane S. How to Reduce Your Risk of Breast Cancer. 256p. 1994. 21.95 (*0-446-51751-8*) Warner Bks.

— How to Reduce Your Risk of Breast Cancer. 1996. pap. write for info. (*0-446-67104-5*) Warner Bks.

Michod, Richard E. Eros & Evolution: A Natural Philosophy of Sex. LC 94-13158. 241p. (C). 1995. 24.00 (*0-201-40754-X*) Addison-Wesley.

Micholson, Mavis. Martha Jane & Me: A Girlhood in Wales. (Illus.). 288p. 1992. 34.95 (*0-7011-3355-4*, Pub. by Chatto & Windus UK) Trafalgar.

Micholson-Smith, Donald, tr. see Laplanche, Jean & Pontalis, J-B.

Michon, Georges. The Franco Russian Alliance, 1891-1917. LC 68-9610. 1969. reprint ed. 48.50 (*0-86527-072-4*) Fertig.

Michon, Gerard P. KeyLISP: The Language (Apple II Version) 424p. (Orig.). (C). 1987. pap. 39.00 (*0-937185-01-9*); disk 149.00 (*0-937185-00-0*, A2KL01) XPrime.

Michon, J. A. & Jackson, J. L. Time, Mind & Behavior. (Illus.). 340p. 1985. 86.00 (*0-387-15444-2*) Spr-Verlag.

Michon, J. A., et al, eds. Handbook of Psychonomics, 2 Vols., 1. 1979. 143.75 (*0-444-85109-7*, North Holland) Elsevier.

— Handbook of Psychonomics, 2 Vols., 2. 1979. 143.75 (*0-444-85194-1*, North Holland) Elsevier.

Michon, John A. Traffic Education for Young Pedestrians: A Selection of Papers Adapted from the Proceedings of the 1978 OECD Workshop on Training Objectives for Child Pedestrians. (Accident Analysis & Prevention Ser.: No. 13). 138p. 1983. pap. 31.00 (*0-08-030224-6*, Pergamon Pr) Elsevier.

Michon, John A., ed. Generic Intelligent Driver Support. 266p. 1993. 75.00 (*0-7484-0069-9*, Pub. by Tay Francis Ltd UK) Taylor & Francis.

— Soar: a Cognitive Architecture in Perspective: A Tribute to Allen Newell. (Studies in Cognitive Systems). 260p. (C). 1992. lib. bdg. 94.00 (*0-7923-1660-6*) Kluwer Ac.

Michor, P. W. Manifolds of Differentiable Mappings. (Shiva Mathematics Ser.: 3). 160p. (Orig.). 1980. pap. text ed. 16.95 (*0-906812-03-8*) Birkhauser.

Michor, Peter, jt. ed. see Gindinkin, Simin.

Michor, Peter W., et al. Natural Operators in Differential Geometry. LC 92-45829. 1993. 89.00 (*0-387-56235-4*) Spr-Verlag.

Michotte, Edmond. Richard Wagner's Visit to Rossini. Weinstock, Herbert, tr. Bd. with Evening at Rossini's in Beau-Sejour. LC 68-16706. LC 68-16706. 1982. Set pap. 4.95 (*0-226-52443-4*) U Ch Pr.

Michra, Bharat. Eminent Blind Persons of the World. xiii, 168p. 1992. 18.00 (*81-7024-500-1*, Pub. by Ashish Pub Hse II) Nataraj Bks.

Michrina, Barry P. Pennsylvania Mining Families: The Search for Dignity in the Coal Fields. LC 93-19826. (Illus.). 200p. 1993. 24.00 (*0-8131-1850-6*) U Pr of Ky.

***Michrina, Barry P. & Richards, CherylAnne.** Person to Person: Fieldwork, Dialogue, & the Hermenutic Method. 192p. 1996. text ed. 49.50x (*0-7914-2833-8*); pap. text ed. 16.95x (*0-7914-2834-6*) State U NY Pr.

Michta, Andrew. East Central Europe after the Warsaw Pact: Security Dilemmas in the 1990s. LC 91-33126. (Contributions in Political Science Ser.: No. 296). 208p. 1992. text ed. 55.00 (*0-313-27886-5*, MRU/, Greenwood Pr) Greenwood.

— An Emigre Reports: Fridrikh Neznansky on Mikhail Gorbachev, 1950-58. 64p. (Orig.). 1985. pap. text ed. 100.00 (*1-55831-062-2*) Delphic Associates.

Michta, Andrew & Passafiume, John F. Selected Developments in Soviet Airborne Computer Technology, 1958-1977. 76p. (Orig.). 1986. pap. text ed. 100.00 (*1-55831-065-7*) Delphic Associates.

Michta, Andrew, ed. see Edelman, Felix.

Michta, Andrew, ed. see Firdman, Eric.

Michta, Andrew, ed. see Freidzon, Sergei.

Michta, Andrew, ed. see Greenberg, Karl.

Michta, Andrew, ed. see Khazatsky, Vily.

Michta, Andrew, ed. see Neznansky, Fridrikh.

Michta, Andrew, ed. see Peysakhovich, Vladimir.

Michta, Andrew, ed. see Polsky, Yury.

Michta, Andrew, ed. see Prutkovsky, Alexander.

Michta, Andrew, ed. see Steinhaus, Alexander.

Michta, Andrew, ed. see Tesler, Edward.

Michta, Andrew A. The Government & Politics of Postcommunist Europe. LC 93-43073. 248p. 1994. text ed. 65.00 (*0-275-94406-9*, Praeger Pubs); pap. text ed. 19.95 (*0-275-94866-8*, Praeger Pubs) Greenwood.

— Post-Communist Eastern Europe, Crisis & Reform. Prizel, Ilya, ed. 240p. 1992. text ed. 39.95 (*0-312-07564-2*) St Martin.

— Red Eagle: The Army in Polish Politics, 1944-1988. (Publication Ser.: No. 386). 280p. (C). 1989. 27.95 (*0-8179-8861-0*); pap. 18.95 (*0-8179-8862-9*) Hoover Inst Pr.

Michta, Andrew A., jt. ed. see Prizel, Ilya.

Michta, Andrew A., ed. see Vysotsky, George.

Michunas, Lynn. Kalculator Kids. 64p. (J). (gr. 3-7). 1982. 8.95 (*0-86653-076-2*, GA 410) Good Apple.

Michwitz, Gunnar. Die Kartellfunktionen der Zunfte und Ihre Bedeutung bei der Entstehung des Zunftwesens: Eine Studie in Spatantiker und mittelalterlicher Wirtschaftsgeschichte. Finley, Moses, ed. LC 79-4993. (Ancient Economic History Ser.). (GER.). 1979. reprint ed. lib. bdg. 25.95 (*0-405-12379-5*) Ayer.

M

An Asterisk (*) at the beginning of an entry indicates that the title is appearing in BIP for the first time.

M

Micich, Paul, illus. The Littlest Angel. LC 91-2442. 32p. (J). (ps-2). 1991. 16.95 (*0-8249-8516-8*, Ideals Child) Hambleton-Hill.

Micikas, Basney, jt. auth. see McDonald, Joseph.

Mick, Astrid, tr. see Heselhaus, Ralf.

Mick, Colin K. & Possony, Stefan T. Working Smart: How to Use Microcomputers to Do Useful Work. 1984. 25.95 (*0-07-041784-9*) McGraw.

Mick, Lawrence E. Penance: The Once & Future Sacrament. 96p. 1988. pap. 4.95 (*0-8146-1573-2*) Liturgical Pr.

— The RCIA: Renewing the Church As an Initiating Assembly. 102p. 1989. pap. 4.95 (*0-8146-1787-5*) Liturgical Pr.

— Sourcebook for Sundays & Seasons 1995: An Almanac for Parish Liturgy. Tufano, Victoria, ed. (Illus.). 240p. (Orig.). 1994. pap. 10.00 (*1-56854-031-0*, SSS95) Liturgy Tr Pubns.

— Sourcebook for Sundays & Seasons 1996. (Illus.). 240p. (Orig.). 1995. pap. 10.00 (*1-56854-066-3*, SSS96) Liturgy Tr Pubns.

— Understanding the Sacraments Today. 148p. (Orig.). 1987. pap. 5.95 (*0-8146-1567-8*) Liturgical Pr.

Mick, Stephen S., jt. ed. see Wyszewianski, Leon.

Mick, Stephen S., et al. Innovations in Health Care Delivery: Insights for Organization Theory. LC 90-4840. (Health-Management Ser.). 303p. 1990. 34.95 (*1-55542-281-0*) Jossey-Bass.

Mickaelian, Art. The MIDI Connection - A Beginner's Guide. pap. 7.95 (*0-685-75238-0*) Cherry Lane.

Mickaharic, Draja. A Century of Spells. 1989. pap. 8.95 (*0-942272-17-X*) Original Pubns.

— A Century of Spells. 160p. 1988. pap. 8.95 (*0-87728-647-7*) Weiser.

— The Practice of Magic: An Introductory Guide to the Art. 176p. (Orig.). 1995. pap. 9.95 (*0-87728-807-0*) Weiser.

— Spiritual Cleansing. 1987. pap. 5.95 (*0-942272-09-9*) Original Pubns.

— Spiritual Cleansing. LC 81-70348. 112p. 1982. pap. 5.95 (*0-87728-531-4*) Weiser.

***Micke, Warren, ed.** Almond Production Manual. (Illus.). 200p. 1995. pap. write for info. (*1-879906-22-8*, 3364) ANR Pubns CA.

Micke, William E., jt. auth. see Cohen, Steven.

Mickel, Earl E. Turkey Callmakers Past & Present Mick's Picks: Stories & History of Callmakers. LC 93-91846. (Illus.). 280p. (Orig.). 1994. pap. text ed. 23.00 (*0-9640164-0-0*) E E Mickel.

Mickel, Emanuel J. Ganelon, Treason, & the Chanson de Roland. LC 89-16058. 191p. 1989. lib. bdg. 28.50 (*0-271-00680-3*) Pa St U Pr.

Mickel, Emanuel J., Jr., ed. The Shaping of Text: Style, Imagery, & Structure in French Literature, Essays in Honor of John Porter Houston. LC 91-58183. 168p. (C). 1993. 32.50 (*0-8387-5227-6*) Bucknell U Pr.

Mickel, Emanuel J., jt. ed. see Nelson, Jan A.

Mickel, Emanuel J., tr. see Verne, Jules.

Mickel, Emmanuel, ed. see Thuroczy, Janos.

Mickel, J. T. & Beitel, J. M. Pteridophyte Flora of Oaxaca, Mexico. LC 88-12474. (Memoirs Ser.: Vol. 46). (Illus.). 568p. (C). 1988. text ed. 90.00 (*0-89327-323-6*) NY Botanical.

Mickel, J. T., et al. Liebmann's Mexican Ferns. LC 87-24791. (Contributions from the New York Botanical Garden Ser.: Vol. 19). 350p. 1987. pap. 27.75 (*0-89327-324-4*) NY Botanical.

Mickel, John T. Ferns for American Gardens. LC 93-13552. (Illus.). 416p. 1994. text ed. 60.00 (*0-02-584491-1*) Macmillan.

Mickel, John T., et al. Ferns & Fern Allies. 256p. (C). 1979. spiral bd. write for info. (*0-697-04771-7*) Wm C Brown Pubs.

Mickel, Stanley. Reading Chinese Newspapers: Tactics & Skills. 250p. (CHI.). 1991. pap. text ed. 21.95 (*0-88710-165-8*) Yale Far Eastern Pubns.

***Mickelbury, Penny.** Night Songs: A Gianna Maglione Mystery. 1995. pap. 10.95 (*1-56280-097-3*) Naiad Pr.

Mickelsen, A. Berkeley. Interpreting the Bible. 1963. 24.99 (*0-8028-3192-3*) Eerdmans.

Mickelsen, A. Berkeley & Mickelsen, Alvera M. Understanding Scripture: How to Read & Study the Bible. LC 92-7905. 160p. 1992. pap. 9.95 (*0-943575-84-2*) Hendrickson MA.

Mickelsen, Alvera, ed. Women, Authority & the Bible. LC 86-7158. 304p. (Orig.). 1986. pap. 14.99 (*0-87784-608-1*, 608) InterVarsity.

Mickelsen, Alvera, jt. auth. see Mickelsen, Berkeley.

Mickelsen, Alvera M., jt. auth. see Mickelsen, A. Berkeley.

Mickelsen, Berkeley & Mickelsen, Alvera. The Picture Bible Dictionary. LC 93-8472. 1993. 16.99 (*0-7814-0133-X*, Bible Discovery) Chariot Family.

Mickelsen, Berkley, jt. auth. see Mickelsen, Alvera.

Mickelsen, William C., ed. & tr. Hugo Riemann's Theory of Harmony. Bd. with History of Music Theory, Book III. LC 76-15366. LC 76-15366. xvi, 263p. 1977. 22.50 (*0-8032-0891-X*) U of Nebr Pr.

Mickelsen, William C. & Riemann, Hugo. Hugo Riemann's Theory of Harmony: a Study & History of Music Theory, Book III. LC 76-15366. 279p. reprint ed. pap. 79.60 (*0-8357-7772-3*, 2036132) Bks Demand.

Mickelson, Alan R. Guided Wave Optics. 1993. text ed. 64.95 (*0-442-00715-9*) Van Nos Reinhold.

— Physical Optics. (Illus.). 320p. 1992. text ed. 64.95 (*0-442-00614-4*) Van Nos Reinhold.

— Theory of Optical Communications. 1992. text ed. write for info. (*0-442-00714-0*) Van Nos Reinhold.

Mickelson, B. & Barr, N. Fish & Fisheries: Alaska Sea Week Curriculum Series Grade 5. (Report Ser.: No. 83-07). (Illus.). 172p. 1983. teacher ed, pap. 11.50 (*1-56612-017-9*) AK Sea Grant CP.

Mickelson, Belle. Animals of the Seas & Wetlands: Alaska Sea Week Curriculum Series II. (Alaska Sea Grant Report: No. 85-11). (Illus.). 220p. (Orig.). teacher ed, pap. 12.00 (*1-56612-015-2*) AK Sea Grant CP.

— Discovery, an Introduction: Alaska Sea Week Curriculum Series. (Alaska Sea Grant Report: No. 83-06). (Illus.). 130p. (Orig.). 1993. reprint ed. teacher ed, pap. 6.50 (*1-56612-019-5*) AK Sea Grant CP.

Mickelson, Bonnie S. Hollyhocks & Radishes: Mrs. Chard's Almanac Cookbook. LC 89-90856. (Illus.). 1989. 26.95 (*0-9622412-1-0*); pap. 19.95 (*0-9622412-0-2*) Pickle Point.

Mickelson, Bonnie S., ed. The Overlake School Cookbook: The Little Blue Book of Great Recipes. rev. ed. (Illus.). 192p. reprint ed. 13.95 (*0-9622412-6-1*) Pickle Point.

— Private Collection, 2 vols., Set. boxed 35.95 (*0-685-65601-2*) Pickle Point.

— A Recipe Treasury. (Illus.). 80p. 1992. ring bd. 19.95 (*0-9622412-2-9*) Pickle Point.

Mickelson, Bonnie S., ed. see Junior League of Palo Alto Staff.

Mickelson, Bonnie S., ed. see Overlake School Staff.

Mickelson, Elliott S. Quality Program Handbook. (Illus.). 157p. 1991. pap. 19.95 (*0-87389-096-5*) ASQC Qual Pr.

Mickelson-Gaughan, Joan, ed. Milestones in Western Civilization: Selected Readings, Vol. 1: Ancient Greece Through the Middle Ages. LC 90-46171. (Illus.). 447p. 1990. 49.50 (*0-8108-2188-5*) Scarecrow.

Mickelson-Gaughan, Joan, intro. Milestones in Western Civilization, Selected Readings, Vol. 2: The Renaissance Through Waterloo. LC 90-46171. 439p. 1991. 47.50 (*0-8108-2508-2*) Scarecrow.

Mickelson, James S., jt. auth. see Haynes, Karen S.

Mickelson, Marlys. Biking in Vikingland. rev. ed. 1993. pap. 7.95 (*0-934860-00-9*) Adventure Pubns.

— Seat Yourself: A Complete Guide to Twin Cities Arenas, Auditoriums & Theaters. 2nd ed. (Illus.). 76p. 1990. reprint ed. pap. 8.95 (*0-9620610-1-8*) Adventure Pubns.

Mickelson, Paul. Comlete Book of Wedding Music for Alto Saxophone. 1993. 7.95 (*0-685-64581-9*, 94370) Mel Bay.

— Complete Book of Wedding Music for Clarinet - Tenor Saxophone. 1993. 7.95 (*0-685-64604-1*, 94372) Mel Bay.

— Complete Book of Wedding Music for Flute or Violin. 1993. 7.95 (*0-87166-757-6*, 94368) Mel Bay.

— Complete Book of Wedding Music for Trombone. 1993. 7.95 (*0-685-64611-4*, 94371) Mel Bay.

— Complete Book of Wedding Music for Trumpet. 1993. 7.95 (*0-87166-759-2*, 94369) Mel Bay.

— Praise Him with Piano & Organ. 1993. 6.95 (*0-685-64710-2*, 94215) Mel Bay.

— With This Ring. 1993. 7.95 (*1-56222-200-7*, 94596) Mel Bay.

Mickelson, Peter G. Natural History of Alaska's Prince William Sound & How to Enjoy It. (Illus.). 210p. (Orig.). (C). 1989. pap. 9.95 (*0-317-93866-5*) AK Wild Wings.

Mickelson, Phillip J. Illustrated Ski-Doo Snowmobile Buyer's Guide. (MBI Illustrated Buyer's Guide Ser.). (Illus.). 160p. 1994. pap. 16.95 (*0-87938-871-4*) Motorbooks Intl.

Mickelson, Sig. America's Other Voice: The Story of Radio Free Europe & Radio Liberty. LC 83-13659. 288p. 1983. text ed. 55.00 (*0-275-91722-3*, C1722, Praeger Pubs) Greenwood.

— From Whistle Stop to Sound Bite: Four Decades of Politics & Television. LC 89-3554. 196p. 1989. text ed. 49.95 (*0-275-92351-7*, C2351, Praeger Pubs); pap. text ed. 16.95 (*0-275-92632-X*, B2632, Praeger Pubs) Greenwood.

— The Northern Pacific Railroad & the Selling of the West: A Nineteenth-Century Public Relations Venture. (Prairie Plains Ser.). (Illus.). 232p. 1993. pap. 12.95 (*0-931170-54-0*) Ctr Western Studies.

Mickelson, Sig & Teran, Elena M., eds. The First Amendment - The Challenge of New Technology. LC 88-19037. 136p. 1989. text ed. 39.95 (*0-275-93088-2*, C3088, Praeger Pubs) Greenwood.

Mickelsson, J. & Pekonen, O., eds. Topological & Geometrical Methods in Field Theory: Proceedings of the 2nd International Symposium, Turku, Finland, 26 May-1 June 1991. 448p. 1992. text ed. 109.00 (*981-02-0961-4*) World Scientific Pub.

Mickenberg, David & Zabo, George. Impressionism - Post-Impressionism: Nineteenth & Twentieth-Century Paintings from the Robert Lehman Collection of the Metropolitan Museum of Art. 1983. pap. text ed. 10.00 (*0-911919-00-7*) Okla City Art.

Mickenberg, David, et al. Songs of Glory: Medieval Art from 900-1500. 400p. (Orig.). 1985. pap. text ed. 20.00 (*0-911919-01-5*) Okla City Art.

Mickens, Ed. The One Hundred Best Companies for Gay Men & Lesbians. Isaacson, Dana, ed. 320p. (Orig.). 1994. pap. 12.00 (*0-671-87479-9*) PB.

Mickens, R. Difference Equations. 2nd ed. 1990. text ed. 49.95 (*0-442-00136-3*) Chapman & Hall.

Mickens, Ronald E. An Introduction to Nonlinear Oscillations. LC 80-13169. (Illus.). 320p. (C). 1981. 105.00 (*0-521-22208-7*) Cambridge U Pr.

— Nonstandard Finite Difference Models of Differential Equations. 250p. 1993. text ed. 61.00 (*981-02-1458-8*) World Scientific Pub.

Mickens, Ronald E., ed. Mathematics & Science. 352p. (C). 1990. pap. 32.00 (*981-02-0234-2*) World Scientific Pub.

Mickey, M. P. Cowrie Shell Miao of Kweichow. (Harvard University Peabody Museum of Archaeology & Ethnology Papers). 1972. reprint ed. pap. 15.00 (*0-527-01282-3*) Periodicals Srv.

Mickey Old Coyote & Smith, Helene. Apsaalooka: The Crow Nation Then & Now. rev. ed. Snyder, Catherine, ed. LC 92-82527. (Illus.). 251p. (Orig.). 1993. pap. 24.95 (*0-945437-11-0*) MacDonald-Sward.

Mickey, Paul A. Breaking Free from Wedlock Deadlock: Popular Myths That Cause, Christian Truths That Cure. LC 88-72131. 192p. (Orig.). 1988. pap. 7.95 (*0-917851-16-1*) Bristol Hse.

— Of Sacred Worth. LC 91-6681. 112p. 1991. pap. 7.95 (*0-687-28405-8*) Abingdon.

Mickiewicz, Adam. Konrad Wallenrod & Grazyna. Suboczewski, Irene, tr. LC 89-16529. 130p. 1989. 38.00 (*0-8191-7556-0*) U Pr of Amer.

— Pan Tadeus. Mackenzie, Kennety R., tr. 600p. 1992. pap. 19.95 (*0-7818-0033-1*) Hippocrene Bks.

Mickiewicz, Ellen. Media & the Russian Public. LC 80-21544. 176p. 1981. text ed. 42.95 (*0-275-90682-5*, C0682, Praeger Pubs) Greenwood.

— Split Signals: Television & Politics in the Soviet Union. (Communication & Society Ser.). 304p. 1990. reprint ed. pap. 9.95 (*0-19-506319-8*) OUP.

Mickiewicz, Ellen P. International Security & Arms Control. Koldowicz, Roman, ed. LC 86-15073. 184p. 1986. text ed. 55.00 (*0-275-92186-7*, C2186, Praeger Pubs) Greenwood.

***Mickle.** Replacing Dad. 1995. mass mkt. 4.99 (*0-312-95413-1*) St Martin.

Mickle, James E. Taxonomy of Specimens of the Pennsylvanian-Age Marattialean Fern Psaronius from Ohio & Illinois. (Scientific Papers: Vol. XIX). (Illus.). vii, 64p. (Orig.). 1984. pap. 5.00 (*0-89792-101-1*) Ill St Museum.

Mickle, M. M. & Da Costa, Francisco. Say It in Portuguese. (Orig.). 1954. pap. 2.50 (*0-486-20809-5*) Dover.

Mickle, Shelley F. The Queen of October. 308p. 1989. 15.95 (*0-945575-21-1*) Algonquin Bks.

— The Queen of October. 320p. 1992. pap. 8.95 (*1-56512-003-5*, 72003, Frnt Porch PB) Algonquin Bks.

— Replacing Dad. 1993. 16.95 (*1-56512-017-5*) Algonquin Bks.

Mickle, Steven M., jt. auth. see Hillman, Rich.

Mickleborough, Neil, jt. auth. see Gilbert, R. I.

Mickleburgh, John. Consumer Protection. 1979. U.K. pap. 32.00 (*0-903486-49-0*) Butterworth Legal Pubs.

Micklebury, Penny. Keeping Secrets: A Gianna Maglione Mystery. 240p. 1994. pap. 9.95 (*1-56280-052-3*) Naiad Pr.

Micklem, Caryl, ed. A Call to Prayer: Public Worship Through the Christian Year. 176p. (Orig.). 1993. pap. 12.99 (*0-8028-1523-5*) Eerdmans.

Micklem, Caryl, et al. Duty & Delight: Routley Remembered. Leaver, Robin A. et al, eds. LC 85-60220. 310p. 1985. 19.95 (*0-916642-27-5*, 782) Hope Pub.

Micklem, Nathaniel. National Socialism & the Roman Catholic Church. LC 78-63696. (Studies in Fascism: Ideology & Practice). (Illus.). 280p. reprint ed. 31.00 (*0-404-16957-0*) AMS Pr.

— Prayers & Praises. 1982. reprint ed. pap. 3.95 (*0-7152-0541-2*) Outlook.

— The Theology of Politics. 1977. 13.95 (*0-8369-7119-1*, 7953) Ayer.

***Micklem, Niel.** The Nature of Hysteria. LC 95-18320. 1996. write for info. (*0-415-12186-8*) Routledge.

Mickler, Ernest M. Sinkin Spells, Hot Flashes, Fits & Cravins. (Illus.). 192p. 1988. 19.95 (*0-89815-269-0*); spiral bd. 14.95 (*0-89815-268-2*) Ten Speed Pr.

— White Trash Cooking. 100p. 1986. spiral bd. 12.95 (*0-912330-59-7*) Jargon Soc.

— White Trash Cooking. 1986. 19.95 (*0-89815-207-0*); spiral bd. 14.95 (*0-89815-189-9*) Ten Speed Pr.

Mickler, Latrell. Indigo. abr. ed. 340p. 1995. pap. 9.95 (*1-56901-518-X*) NW Pub.

Mickler, Michael L. A History of the Unification Church in America 1959-1974: Emergence of a National Movement. LC 93-27146. (Cults & Nonconventional Religious Groups Ser.). 240p. 1993. 56.00 (*0-8153-1138-9*) Garland.

Mickler, Patricia F. The Micklers of Florida. LC 91-91931. (Illus.). xiv, 230p. 1991. 25.00 (*0-913122-57-2*) Mickler Hse.

Mickler, Robert A., jt. ed. see Fox, Susan.

Mickles, Morgan, jt. auth. see Breitling, Wolf.

Micklethwait, Lucy, creator & sel. I Spy Two Eyes: Numbers in Art. LC 92-35641. (Illus.). 48p. (J). (ps up). 1993. 19.00 (*0-688-12640-5*); lib. bdg. 18.93 (*0-688-12642-1*) Greenwillow.

Micklethwait, Lucy, sel. A Child's Book of Art: Great Pictures, First Words. LC 93-54320. (Illus.). 64p. (J). (gr. k up). 1993. 16.95 (*1-56458-203-5*) Dorling Kindersley.

— I Spy: An Alphabet in Art. LC 91-42212. (Illus.). 64p. (J). 1992. 19.00 (*0-688-11679-5*) Greenwillow.

— I Spy a Lion: Animals in Art. LC 93-30017. 48p. (J). 1994. 19.00 (*0-688-13230-8*); lib. bdg. 18.93 (*0-688-13231-6*) Greenwillow.

Micklewright, M., jt. auth. see Atkinson, A. B.

Mickley, Linda D., jt. ed. see Fox, M. W.

Mickley, Linda D., ed. see Fox, Michael A.

Mickley, M. F. Mickley: Genealogy of the Mickley Family of America, with a Brief General Record of the Michelet Family of Metz & Some Interesting & Valuable Correspondence, Biographical Sketches, Obits & History Memorabilia. (Illus.). 182p. 1991. reprint ed. lib. bdg. 37.50 (*0-8328-1707-4*); reprint ed. pap. 27.50 (*0-8328-1708-2*) Higginson Bk Co.

Mickley, Tracy, et al. Tips, Traps, & Techniques for TBBS. LC 93-85639. 300p. 1993. pap. 29.95 (*1-879705-02-8*) PC Info Grp.

Micklin, Michael, jt. ed. see Olsen, Marvin E.

Micklitz, Hans W. & Reich, Norbert. Legal Aspects of European Space Policy. 151p. 1989. pap. 30.50 (*3-7890-1875-9*, Pub. by Nomos Verlags GW) Intl Bk Import.

***Micklitz, Hans-W., et al, eds.** Federalism & Responsibility: A Study on Product Safety Law & Practice in the European Community. LC 94-32777. (European Business Law & Practice Ser.). 1994. lib. bdg. 120.00 (*1-85966-102-5*) Kluwer Ac.

Micklos, John, Jr. Leonard Nimoy: A Stars Trek. LC 87-32457. (Taking Part Ser.). (Illus.). 64p. (J). (gr. 3 up). 1988. text ed. 13.95 (*0-87518-376-X*, Dillon Silver Burdett) Silver Burdett Pr.

Micklus, Robert. The Comic Genius of Dr. Alexander Hamilton. LC 89-22468. 232p. 1990. text ed. 28.00x (*0-87049-633-6*) U of Tenn Pr.

***Micklus, Robert, ed.** The Tuesday Club: A Shorter Edition of the History of the Ancient & Honorable Tuesday Club by Dr. Alexander Hamilton. LC 94-20542. (Maryland Paperback Bookshelf Ser.). (Illus.). 360p. 1995. 48.50x (*0-8018-5008-8*); pap. 16.95x (*0-8018-4968-3*) Johns Hopkins.

Micklus, Robert, ed. see Hamilton, Alexander.

Mickolus, Edward F. International Terrorism: Attributes of Terrorist Events, 1968-1977 (ITERATE 2) LC 82-82385. 1982. write for info. (*0-89138-927-X*, ICPSR 7947) ICPSR.

— Terrorism, 1988-1991: A Chronology of Events & a Selectively Annotated Bibliography. LC 92-46525. (Bibliographies & Indexes in Military Studies: No. 6). 928p. 1993. text ed. 125.00 (*0-313-28970-0*, GR8970, Greenwood Pr) Greenwood.

— Transnational Terrorism: A Chronology of Events, 1968-1979. LC 79-6829. xxxviii, 967p. 1980. text ed. 105.00 (*0-313-22206-1*, MTT/, Greenwood Pr) Greenwood.

Mickolus, Edward F., comp. The Literature of Terrorism: A Selectively Annotated Bibliography. LC 80-541. xi, 553p. 1980. text ed. 95.00 (*0-313-22265-7*, MLT/, Greenwood Pr) Greenwood.

Mickolus, Edward F. & Flemming, Peter A., eds. Terrorism Nineteen Eighty to Nineteen Eighty-Seven: A Selectively Annotated Bibliography. LC 87-32275. (Bibliographies & Indexes in Law & Political Science Ser.: No. 8). 328p. 1988. text ed. 59.50 (*0-313-26248-9*, MKT/) Greenwood.

Micks, Marianne H. Loving the Questions: An Exploration of the Nicene Creed. LC 93-22816. 125p. 1993. pap. 9.95 (*1-56101-081-2*) Cowley Pubns.

— Loving the Questions: An Exploration of the Nicene Creed. LC 93-22816. 144p. (C). 1993. pap. 10.00 (*1-56338-072-2*) TPI PA.

Mickunas, Algis, tr. see Gebser, Jean.

Mickunas, Algis, jt. intro. see Kramer, Eric M.

Mickunas, Algis, jt. auth. see Pilotta, Joseph J.

Mickunas, Algis, jt. auth. see Stewart, David.

Mickunas, Algis, tr. see Stroker, Elisabeth.

Mickunes, Algis, jt. auth. see Stewart, David.

Mickwitz, Gunnar. Geld und Wirtschaft im Romischen Reich des vierten Jahrhunderts N. Chr. Finley, Moses, ed. LC 79-4991. (Ancient Economic History Ser.). (GER.). 1979. reprint ed. lib. bdg. 25.95 (*0-405-12380-9*) Ayer.

***Micky, Lloyd G. & Smith, Helene.** Flag & Emblem of the Apsaalooka Native. Snyder, Catherine, ed. LC 94-48414. (Illus.). 77p. (Orig.). 1995. pap. 9.95 (*0-945437-17-X*) MacDonald-Sward.

Mico, Jose, tr. see Reuter, Paul.

Mico, Paul R. Developing Your Community-Based Organization: With Special Emphasis on Community Economic Development Organizations & Community Action Agencies. LC 80-53828. (Illus.). 160p. 1981. pap. text ed. 9.95 (*0-89914-004-1*) Third Party Pub.

Micocci, Harriet. Captain Orkle's Treasure. (Illus.). (J). (gr. 3-7). 1961. 10.95 (*0-8392-3003-6*) Astor-Honor.

Micolean, Tyler, jt. auth. see Moore, James.

Micolo, Anthony M. Practical Supervision: How to Organize for Effectiveness. Bruce, Stephen E., ed. 332p. 1987. ring bd. 63.71 (*1-55645-427-9*) Busn Legal Reports.

***Micone, Marco.** Beyond the Ruins. MacDougall, Jill, tr. (Drama Ser.: No. 10). 78p. 1995. 10.00 (*0-920717-86-1*) Guernica Editions.

Micou, Paul. Music Programme. 1990. 16.95 (*1-55972-023-9*, Birch Ln Pr) Carol Pub Group.

Micozzi & Moon. Macronutrients: Investigating Their Role in Cancer. 496p. 1992. 190.00 (*0-8247-8593-2*) Dekker.

Micozzi, jt. auth. see Moon.

Micozzi, Marc C. Postmortem Change in Human & Animal Remains: A Systematic Approach. (Illus.). 136p. 1991. text ed. 32.95x (*0-398-05747-8*) C C Thomas.

— Postmortem Change in Human & Animal Remains: A Systematic Approach. (Illus.). 136p. 1991. pap. 18.95 (*0-398-06288-9*) C C Thomas.

Micro Analysis & Design Staff. Micro SAINT User's Guide. (Version 2.0 Ser.). 1986. text ed. 50.00 (*0-937197-01-7*) Micro Analysis.

— Micro SAINT User's Guide. rev. ed. (Version 2.2 Ser.). 1986. text ed. 50.00 (*0-937197-05-X*) Micro Analysis.

— Micro SAINT User's Guide: Version 2.1. 1986. 50.00 (*0-937197-03-3*) Micro Analysis.

— Micro SAINT User's Guide: Version 3.0. 1987. 60.00 (*0-317-64493-9*) Micro Analysis.

Micro Magazine Staff. Exploring Assembly Language Programming on Your Commodore 64. write for info. (*0-318-58227-9*) P-H.

— Exploring Character Graphics on Your Commodore 64. write for info. (*0-318-58228-7*) P-H.

— Mastering Your Atari Through Eight BASIC Projects. write for info. (*0-318-58229-5*) P-H.

— Mastering Your Commodore 64 Through Eight BASIC Projects. write for info. (*0-318-58230-9*) P-H.

An Asterisk (*) at the beginning of an entry indicates that the title is appearing in BIP for the first time.

Microbiological Standardization, Permanent Section Staff, ed. Brucellosis: Proceedings of the International Symposium on Standardization & Control of Vaccines & Reagents, 24, Tunise & Bourse du Travail, 1968. (Immunobiological Standardization Symposia Ser.: Vol. 12). 1970. 24.00 (*3-8055-0634-1*) S Karger.

Microcase Corporation Staff. MicroCase Analysis System Reference Manual: Version 3. (Illus.). 400p. 1994. pap. 24.95 (*0-922914-21-4*) MicroCase.

Microcase Corporation Staff & Stark, Rodney. Doing Sociology: An Introduction Through Microcase. 160p. 1993. Version 3.5". 3.5 hd 19.95 (*0-534-19525-3*); Version 5.25". 5.25 hd 19.95 (*0-534-19524-5*) Intl Thomson.

Microcosmos-B. U. Staff. The Microcosmos Curriculum Guide to Exploring Microbial Space. 480p. 1993. boxed 41.95 (*0-8403-8515-3*) Kendall-Hunt.

Microlytics, Inc. Staff. Pocket Word Finder Thesaurus. 1990. mass mkt. 4.99 (*0-671-68613-5*) PB.

MicroMotion Staff, et al. Mastering Forth. 216p. 1985. pap. 17.95 (*0-317-37785-X*) S&S Trade.

Microprocessor Report Newsletter Staff. Understanding RISC Microprocessors. 1993. pap. 79.95 (*1-56276-159-5*) Ziff-Davis.

— Understanding X86 Microprocessors. 1993. pap. 49.95 (*1-56276-158-7*) Ziff-Davis.

Microref. Lotus 1-2-3 with Template. 1986. pap. 19.95 (*0-913365-05-X*) Microref Educ Systs.

— Microref For MS & PC-DOS. 1986. pap. 19.95 (*0-913365-09-2*) Microref Educ Systs.

Microref Educational Systems Staff. MICROREF 1993 Guide Series. (Illus.). (Orig.). 1993. spiral bd., pap. 99.75 (*1-56351-098-7*) Microref Educ Systs.

Microref Staff. Quattro Pro 1.0-2.0 Quick Ref. 1991. pap. 19.95 (*0-913365-89-0*) Microref Educ Systs.

— WordPerfect for Windows Quick Reference. 1992. pap. 19.95 (*1-56351-072-3*) Microref Educ Systs.

— WordPerfect for Windows Quick Reference Version 5.1 & 5.2. 1993. pap. 14.95 (*1-56351-207-6*) Microref Educ Systs.

— WordStar 4.0-6.0 Quick Reference Guide. 1990. pap. 19.95 (*0-01-336561-4*) Microref Educ Systs.

Micros, Marianne. Al Purdy: An Annotated Bibliography. 277p. (C). 1980. pap. text ed. 9.00 (*0-920763-61-8*, Pub. by ECW Press CN) Genl Dist Srvs.

MicroSift Staff. The Evaluator's Guide for Microcomputer-Based Instructional Packages. rev. ed. 48p. (Orig.). 1986. pap. 4.00 (*0-924667-07-9*) Intl Society Tech Educ.

***Microsoft Corporation.** Microsoft Windows NT 3.5: Guidelines for Security, Audit & Control. LC 94-24468. 286p. 1994. 49.95 (*1-55615-814-9*) Microsoft.

— Microsoft Windows 95 Help Developer's Kit. 1995. disk, pap. 49.95 (*1-55615-892-0*) Microsoft.

— OLE Programmer's Reference Library: Creating Programmable 32-Bit Applications with OLE Automation, 2. 2nd ed. 1995. pap. 24.95 (*1-55615-851-3*) Microsoft.

— OLE Programmer's Reference Library: Working with 32-Bit Windows Objects, 1. 2nd ed. 1100p. 1995. pap. 29.95 (*1-55615-850-5*) Microsoft.

Microsoft Corporation Staff. The Developer's Guide to Plug 'n Play: The Official Guide to Designing Hardware for Windows. 300p. 1994. disk 29.95 (*1-55615-642-1*) Microsoft.

— Field Guide to Microsoft Excel for the Macintosh. 1993. pap. 9.95 (*1-55615-580-8*) Microsoft.

— Field Guide to Microsoft Works for Windows. 1993. pap. 9.95 (*1-55615-620-0*) Microsoft.

— Macros for the Microsoft Office. 1993. pap. 29.95 (*1-55615-591-3*) Microsoft.

***Microsoft Corporation, Staff.** Mastering Microsoft Access. 1995. 99.95 (*1-55615-912-9*) Microsoft.

— Mastering Microsoft Visual BASIC. 1995. pap. 99.95 (*1-55615-913-7*) Microsoft.

— Mastering Microsoft Windows 95 User Interface Design. 1995. 99.95 (*1-55615-874-2*) Microsoft.

— Mastering Object-Oriented Programming. 1995. 99.95 (*1-55615-914-5*) Microsoft.

Microsoft Corporation Staff. Microsoft Access for Windows Step by Step. 2nd ed. 1994. pap. 29.95 (*1-55615-593-X*) Microsoft.

***Microsoft Corporation, Staff.** Microsoft Excel Developer's Kit. 3rd ed. 1995. 49.95 (*1-55615-879-3*) Microsoft.

Microsoft Corporation Staff. Microsoft Excel for the Macintosh Step by Step. 2nd ed. 336p. 1992. pap. 29.95 (*1-55615-479-8*) Microsoft.

— Microsoft Excel Software Development Kit. 2nd ed. 1994. pap. 49.95 (*1-55615-632-4*) Microsoft.

***Microsoft Corporation, Staff.** Microsoft Excel Worksheet Function Reference. 2nd ed. 1995. 22.95 (*1-55615-878-5*) Microsoft.

Microsoft Corporation Staff. Microsoft Excel 4.0 Software Development Kit. LC 92-25955. 1992. disk, pap. 39.95 (*1-55615-521-2*) Microsoft.

***Microsoft Corporation, Staff.** Microsoft Excel/Visual BASIC Programmer's Guide for Windows 95. 1995. 24.95 (*1-55615-819-X*) Microsoft.

— Microsoft Excel/Visual BASIC Reference. 2nd ed. 1995. 29.95 (*1-55615-920-X*) Microsoft.

***Microsoft Corporation Staff.** Microsoft Foundation Class Library Reference. 1994. 44.95 (*1-55615-801-7*) Microsoft.

— Microsoft ODBC 2.0 Programmer's Reference & SDK Guide: For Microsoft Windows & Windows NT. LC 94-5039. 1994. 24.95 (*1-55615-658-8*) Microsoft.

***Microsoft Corporation, Staff.** Microsoft Office for Windows 95 Resource Kit. 1995. 49.95 (*1-55615-818-1*) Microsoft.

***Microsoft Corporation Staff.** Microsoft OLE Custom Control Developer's Kit. 1994. 22.95 (*1-55615-805-X*) Microsoft.

***Microsoft Corporation, Staff.** Microsoft Sourcebook for the Help Desk. 1995. 39.95 (*1-55615-927-7*) Microsoft.

***Microsoft Corporation Staff.** Microsoft Visual C Language References. 1994. 22.95 (*1-55615-804-1*) Microsoft.

— Microsoft Visual C Plus Plus User's Guide. 1994. pap. 24.95 (*1-55615-800-9*) Microsoft.

***Microsoft Corporation, Staff.** Microsoft Visual C++ Programmer's Reference: Microsoft Foundation Class Library Reference, 3. 1995. 29.95 (*1-55615-922-6*) Microsoft.

— Microsoft Visual C++ Programmer's Reference: Microsoft Visual C++ Programming with MFC, 2. 1995. pap. 29.95 (*1-55615-921-8*) Microsoft.

— Microsoft Visual C++ Programmer's Reference: Microsoft Visual C++ Run-Time Library Reference, 5. 1995. pap. 24.95 (*1-55615-924-2*) Microsoft.

— Microsoft Visual C++ Programmer's Reference: Microsoft Visual C++ User's Guide, 1. 1995. pap. 29.95 (*1-55615-915-3*) Microsoft.

— Microsoft Visual C++ Programmer's Reference: Microsoft Visual C/C++ Language Reference, 6. 1995. pap. 27.95 (*1-55615-925-0*) Microsoft.

— Microsoft Visual C++ Programmer's Reference Part 2: Microsoft Foundation Class Library Reference, 4. 1995. 29.95 (*1-55615-923-4*) Microsoft.

Microsoft Corporation Staff. Microsoft Windows Guide to Programming. 1990. pap. 29.95 (*1-55615-308-2*) Microsoft.

— Microsoft Windows 95 Resource Kit. LC 95-1475. 1995. write for info. (*1-55615-867-X*) Microsoft.

— Microsoft Windows NT Resource Kit: The Information & Tools You Need to Become a Windows NT Expert, Version 3.5 for Workstation & Advanced Server Editions, 4 vols., Set. 2nd ed. 1994. disk 199.95 (*1-55615-657-X*) Microsoft.

— Microsoft Windows Programmer's Reference. 1990. pap. 39.95 (*1-55615-309-0*) Microsoft.

— Microsoft Windows Programming Tools. 1990. pap. 24.95 (*1-55615-310-4*) Microsoft.

— Microsoft Windows 3.1 Programmer's Reference Library. (Microsoft Windows Programmer's Reference Library). 592p. (Orig.). 1992. pap. 29.95 (*1-55615-452-6*) Microsoft.

— Microsoft Windows 3.1 Programmer's Reference Library, 6 vols., Set. (Orig.). Date not set. 147.00 (*1-55615-423-2*) Microsoft.

— Microsoft Windows 3.1 Programmers Reference, Vol. 1: Overview. (Microsoft Windows Programmer's Reference Library). 520p. (Orig.). 1992. pap. 29.95 (*1-55615-453-4*) Microsoft.

— Microsoft Windows 3.1 Programmers Reference, Vol. 2: Functions. (Microsoft Windows Programmer's Reference Library). 1008p. (Orig.). 1992. pap. 39.95 (*1-55615-463-1*) Microsoft.

— Microsoft Windows 3.1 Programmers Reference, Vol. 3: Messages, Structures, & Macros. (Microsoft Windows Programmer's Reference Library). 624p. (Orig.). 1992. pap. 29.95 (*1-55615-464-X*) Microsoft.

— Microsoft Windows 3.1 Programmer's Reference, Vol. 4: Resources. (Microsoft Windows Programmer's Reference Library). 352p. (Orig.). 1992. pap. 22.95 (*1-55615-494-1*) Microsoft.

— Microsoft Windows 3.1 Programming Tools. 280p. (Orig.). 1992. pap. 22.95 (*1-55615-454-2*) Microsoft.

— Microsoft Win32 Programmer's Reference Vol. 1. LC 94-42920. 1995. write for info. (*1-55615-686-3*) Microsoft.

— Microsoft Win32 Programmer's Reference Library, 5 vols., Set. Date not set. 95.00 (*1-55615-750-9*) Microsoft.

***Microsoft Corporation, Staff.** Microsoft Word Developer's Kit. 3rd ed. 1995. pap. 49.95 (*1-55615-880-7*) Microsoft.

Microsoft Corporation Staff. Microsoft Word Technical Reference. 1990. 22.95 (*1-55615-290-6*) Microsoft.

— Microsoft Word 6 for Windows Resource Kit. LC 93-41594. 1994. pap. 39.95 (*1-55615-720-7*) Microsoft.

— The MS-DOS Encyclopedia. LC 87-21452. 1600p. 1989. 134.95 (*1-55615-174-8*); pap. 69.95 (*0-685-18700-4*) Microsoft.

— MS Windows 95 Resource Kit. 1995. disk, pap. 49.95 (*1-55615-678-2*) Microsoft.

— Object Linking & Embedding Programmer's Reference. LC 92-30346. 1992. pap. 27.95 (*1-55615-539-5*) Microsoft.

— Optimizing Windows NT, Vol. 4. 608p. 1994. disk 39.95 (*1-55615-655-3*) Microsoft.

— Programmer's Guide to Microsoft Windows 95. LC 95-13785. 1995. pap. text ed. 27.95 (*1-55615-834-3*) Microsoft.

— Programmer's Guide to Pen Services for Microsoft Windows 95. LC 95-1474. 1995. 27.95 (*1-55615-835-1*) Microsoft.

— Programming with MFC. LC 94-30463. 1994. pap. 29.95 (*1-55615-802-5*) Microsoft.

MicroSoft Corporation Staff. Windows Interface. 1992. pap. 39.95 (*1-55615-439-9*) Microsoft.

Microsoft Corporation Staff. Windows NT Messages, Vol. 3. 624p. 1994. 39.95 (*1-55615-654-5*) Microsoft.

— Windows NT Network Resource Guide, Vol. 2. 240p. 1994. 39.95 (*1-55615-656-1*) Microsoft.

— Windows NT Resource Guide, Vol. 1. 1024p. 1994. 49.95 (*1-55615-653-7*) Microsoft.

***Microsoft Corporation, Staff.** The Windows 95 Internet Kit. 1995. disk, pap. 29.95 (*1-55615-885-8*) Microsoft.

***Microsoft Educational Services, Staff.** Microsoft Windows NT Training, 2 vols. Date not set. pap. 199.95 (*1-55615-864-5*) Microsoft.

Microsoft Press Staff. Field Guide to Microsoft Excel for Windows. 1993. pap. 9.95 (*1-55615-579-4*) Microsoft.

— Field Guide to Microsoft Word for Windows. 1993. pap. 9.95 (*1-55615-577-8*) Microsoft.

— Field Guide to the Internet. (Illus.). 1994. pap. 9.95 (*1-55615-822-X*) Microsoft.

— Introducing Windows 95. 1995. pap. 12.95 (*1-55615-860-2*) Microsoft.

— Microsoft Press Computer Dictionary. 1990. pap. 24.95 (*1-55615-231-0*) Microsoft.

— Microsoft Press Computer Dictionary: The Comprehensive Standard for Business, School, Library, & Home. 2nd ed. LC 93-29868. 1993. pap. 19.95 (*1-55615-597-2*) Microsoft.

— MS Excel 5.0 Worksheet Function Reference. LC 93-23635. 1993. pap. 12.95 (*1-55615-637-5*) Microsoft.

MicroSoft Staff. GUI Guide. 1993. pap. 29.95 (*1-55615-538-7*) Microsoft.

— MicroSoft Access Step by Step. 1993. pap. 34.95 (*1-55615-482-8*) Microsoft.

— MicroSoft LAN Manager for Windows NT. 1993. pap. 39.95 (*1-55615-543-3*) Microsoft.

— MicroSoft Win32 Programmers Guide, Vol. 1. 1993. pap. 29.95 (*1-55615-515-8*) Microsoft.

— MicroSoft Win32 Programmers Guide, Vol. 2. 1993. pap. 29.95 (*1-55615-516-6*) Microsoft.

— MicroSoft Win32 Programmers Reference, Vol. 1. 1993. pap. 39.95 (*1-55615-517-4*) Microsoft.

— MicroSoft Win32 Programmers Reference, Vol. 2. 1993. pap. 39.95 (*1-55615-518-2*) Microsoft.

— MicroSoft Win32 Programmers Reference, Vol. 3. 1993. pap. 29.95 (*1-55615-519-0*) Microsoft.

— MicroSoft Word for MS-DOS Step by Step. 1993. pap. 29.95 (*1-55615-520-4*) Microsoft.

— Microsoft Word for the Macintosh Step by Step. 1992. disk, pap. 29.95 (*1-55615-558-1*) Microsoft.

Microsurgery Workshop Staff. Ophthalmic Microsurgery: Proceedings of the Workshop on Microsurgery, Singapore, May 1977. Ratnam, S. S. et al, eds. (Advances in Ophthalmology Ser.: Vol. 36). (Illus.). 1977. 94.50 (*3-8055-2782-9*) S Karger.

Microsymposia on Macromolecules. Macromolecular Chemistry: Proceedings. Sedlacek, B., ed. Incl. No. 12 & 13. Prague, 1973. (Illus.). 1974. 123.00 (*0-08-020790-1*); (International Union of Pure & Applied Chemistry Ser.). write for info. (*0-318-55177-2*, Pub. by Pergamon Repr UK) Franklin.

Microsymposium Staff. Radiological Aspects of Renal Transplantation: Proceedings of the Microsymposium, Nymegen, 1977. Penn, William, ed. (Radiologia Clinica et Biologica Ser.: Vol. 47, No. 1). (Illus.). 1977. 15.75 (*3-8055-2844-2*) S Karger.

Microtrend, Inc. Staff. C Language on the IBM PC. 1984. 14.95 (*0-685-08090-0*) P-H.

***Micrsoft Corporation Staff.** Microsoft Visual C Run-Time Library Reference. LC 94-30464. 1994. 22.95 (*1-55615-803-3*) Microsoft.

Micucci, Charles. The Life & Times of the Apple. LC 90-22779. (Illus.). 32p. (J). (gr. k-3). 1992. 15.95 (*0-531-05939-1*); lib. bdg. 15.99 (*0-531-08539-2*) Orchard Bks Watts.

— The Life & Times of the Apple. LC 90-22779. (Illus.). 32p. (J). (gr. k-3). 1995. pap. 5.95 (*0-531-07067-0*) Orchard Bks Watts.

— A Little Night Music. LC 88-505. (Illus.). 32p. (J). (ps-3). 1989. 10.95 (*0-688-07900-8*); lib. bdg. 10.88 (*0-688-07901-6*) Morrow Jr Bks.

Micucci, Charles, illus. & text. Life & Times of the Honey Bee. LC 93-8135. 32p. (J). (ps-3). 1995. 13.95 (*0-395-65968-X*) Ticknor & Flds Bks Yng Read.

Micula, Gheorghe & Pavel, Paraschiva. Differential & Integral Equations Through Practical Problems & Exercises. LC 92-22561. (Kluwer Texts in the Mathematical Sciences Ser.: Vol. 7). 408p. (C). 1992. lib. bdg. 150.00 (*0-7923-1890-0*) Kluwer Ac.

Miculka, Jean H. Let's Talk Business: A Speech Communication Text. 4th ed. 416p. 1993. pap. 21.95 (*0-538-70575-2*) S-W Pub.

Miczo, Alexander. Digital Logic Testing & Simulation. 480p. (C). 1985. Net. text ed. write for info. (*0-471-60365-1*); 10.00 (*0-471-60422-4*) Wiley.

Mid-America Spectroscopy Symposium (16th: 1965, Chicago). Developments in Applied Spectroscopy: Proceedings of the Sixteenth Annual Mid-America Spectroscopy Symposium Held in Chicago, IL, June 14-17, 1965, Vol. 5. Pearson, L. R. & Grove, E. L., eds. LC 61-17720. 516p. reprint ed. pap. 147.10 (*0-685-15709-1*, 2026293) Bks Demand.

Midda, Sara. Growing up & Other Vices. Kovalchick, Sally, ed. (Illus.). 32p. (J). 1994. 13.95 (*1-56305-728-X*) Workman Pub.

— In & Out of the Garden. LC 81-40501. (Illus.). 128p. 1984. 19.95 (*0-89480-193-7*, 344) Workman Pub.

— Sara Midda's South of France: A Sketch Book. LC 90-50369. 1990. 18.95 (*0-89480-763-3*, 1763) Workman Pub.

***Middaugh, Michael F., et al.** Strategies for the Practice of Institutional Research: Concepts, Resources, & Applications. 124p. (C). 1994. pap. text ed. 14.95 (*1-882393-04-X*) Assn Instl Res.

***Middaugh, Robert C., Jr.** Exercises in Celestial Navigation. (Illus.). 56p. (Orig.). (C). 1994. pap. text ed. 17.50 (*1-879778-24-6*, BK-0312) Marine Educ.

— Exercises in Coastwise Navigation. (Illus.). 61p. 1986. pap. text ed. 17.50 (*1-879778-33-5*, BK-556) Marine Educ.

Middelburg, Cornelis A. Logic & Specifiction: Extending VDM-SL for Advanced Formal Specification. LC 92-38105. 1993. write for info. (*0-412-48680-6*) Chapman & Hall.

Middelhoek, S. & Audet, S., eds. Physics of Silicon Sensors. (Microelectronics & Signal Processing Ser.). 376p. 1989. text ed. 97.00 (*0-12-495051-5*) Acad Pr.

Middelhoek, S., jt. ed. see Ciureanu, P.

Middelton-Moz, Jane. Children of Trauma: Rediscovering Your Discarded Self. (Orig.). 1989. pap. 9.95 (*1-55874-014-7*) Health Comm.

— Shame & Guilt: Masters of Disguise. 1990. pap. 8.95 (*1-55874-072-4*) Health Comm.

— Will to Survive: Affirming the Positive Power of the Human Spirit. LC 92-13302. 1992. 14.95 (*1-55874-231-X*) Health Comm.

Middelton-Moz, Jane & Dwinell, Lorie. After the Tears: Reclaiming the Personal Losses of Childhood. 146p. (Orig.). 1986. pap. 7.95 (*0-932194-36-2*) Health Comm.

Middendorf. Design of Devices & Systems. 2nd rev. ed. 528p. 1990. 65.00 (*0-8247-8281-X*) Dekker.

— What Every Engineer Should Know about Inventing. (What Every Engineer Should Know Ser.: Vol. 7). 168p. 1981. 55.00 (*0-8247-7497-3*) Dekker.

Middendorf, jt. auth. see Engelmann.

Middendorf, jt. auth. see Thorpe, James F.

Middendorf, John, jt. auth. see Long, John.

Middendorff, Wolf. Effectiveness of Punishment, Especially in Relation to Traffic Offenses. (New York University Criminal Law Education & Research Center Monograph: Vol. 5). xii, 129p. 1968. 12.50 (*0-8377-0826-5*) Rothman.

Middendorp, Kooiman-van, jt. auth. see Maria, Gerarda.

Middione, Carlo. The Food of Southern Italy. LC 87-15406. (Cookbook Library). (Illus.). 330p. 1987. 29.95 (*0-688-05042-5*) Morrow.

Middle East Executive Reports, Ltd. Staff. Arab Investors Sourcebook. Hearn, William, ed. 650p. 1989. pap. 345.00 (*0-915797-01-1*) Intl Exec Reports.

Middle East Watch Staff. Empty Reforms: Saudi Arabia's New Basic Laws. Human Rights Watch Staff, ed. LC 92-18857. 68p. (Orig.). 1992. pap. 7.00 (*1-56432-068-5*) Hum Rts Watch.

— Hidden Death: Land Mines & Civilian Casualties in Iraqi Kurdistan. Human Rights Watch Staff, ed. LC 92-19398. 78p. (Orig.). 1992. pap. 7.00 (*1-56432-067-7*) Hum Rts Watch.

— Human Rights in Iraq. 194p. 1991. pap. 15.00 (*0-929692-47-0*, M E Watch) Hum Rts Watch.

— Human Rights in Syria. LC 90-84055. 254p. 1990. pap. 15.00 (*0-929692-69-1*, M E Watch) Hum Rts Watch.

— The Israeli Army & the Intifada: Policies that Contribute to the Killings. LC 90-83440. 232p. 1990. pap. 15.00 (*0-929692-66-7*, M E Watch) Hum Rts Watch.

Middle, Hara G., jt. auth. see Middle, Howard.

Middle, Howard & Middle, Hara G. Conversational Greek in Seven Days. (Language in Seven Days Ser.). (Illus.). 96p. 1991. audio 12.95 (*0-8442-4502-X*, Passport Bks); pap. 5.95 (*0-8442-4503-8*, Passport Bks) NTC Pub Grp.

Middle, P., tr. see Schmidt, W. J. & Keil, A.

Middlebrook, Charlie. Life's Seasons Pass Quickly. (Illus.). 64p. 1985. write for info. (*0-318-60269-5*) Clear Fork Pub.

Middlebrook, David. The Old One. LC 73-80996. 180p. 1974. 18.95 (*0-913522-01-5*); pap. 10.95 (*0-913522-02-3*) Union Pr CA.

Middlebrook, Diane, jt. auth. see Lippard, Lucy.

Middlebrook, Diane W. Anne Sexton. LC 92-50093. 1992. pap. 14.00 (*0-679-74182-8*, Vin) Random.

— Anne Sexton: A Biography. (Illus.). 448p. 1991. 24.95 (*0-395-35362-9*, P Davison Bk) HM.

— Gin Considered As a Demon. LC 82-84116. 70p. (Orig.). 1983. pap. 3.95 (*0-941692-04-3*) Elysian Pr.

Middlebrook, Diane W. & Yalom, Marilyn, eds. Coming to Light: American Women Poets in the Twentieth Century. (Women & Culture Ser.). 240p. 1985. pap. text ed. 15.95 (*0-472-08061-X*) U of Mich Pr.

Middlebrook, Diane W., ed. see Sexton, Anne.

***Middlebrook, Kevin J.** The Paradox of Revolution: Labor, the State, & Authoritarianism in Mexico. LC 94-29470. 424p. 1994. text ed. 59.95x (*0-8018-4922-5*); pap. text ed. 18.95x (*0-8018-5148-3*) Johns Hopkins.

— Political Liberalization in an Authoritarian Regime: The Case of Mexico. (Research Report Ser.: No. 41). 36p. (Orig.). (C). 1985. pap. 5.00 (*0-935391-40-1*, RR-41) UCSD Ctr US-Mex.

Middlebrook, Kevin J., ed. Unions, Workers, & the State in Mexico. (U. S. - Mexico Contemporary Perspectives Ser.: No. 2). 246p. 1991. 19.95 (*1-878367-02-1*) UCSD Ctr US-Mex.

Middlebrook, Kevin J., et al, eds. Politics of Economic Restructuring in Mexico. (U.S.-Mexico Contemporary Perspectives Ser.: No. 7). 400p. 21.95 (*1-878367-18-8*) UCSD Ctr US-Mex.

Middlebrook, Kevin J. & Rico, Carlos, eds. The U. S. & Latin America in the 1980s: Contending Perspectives on a Decade of Crisis. LC 85-40359. (Latin American Ser.). (Illus.). 640p. (Orig.). 1986. 75.00 (*0-8229-3518-X*); pap. 19.95 (*0-8229-6087-7*) U of Pittsburgh Pr.

Middlebrook, L. F. Register of the Middlebrook Family, Descendants of Joseph Middlebrook of Fairfield, Connecticut. (Illus.). 411p. 1989. reprint ed. lib. bdg. 69.50 (*0-8328-0870-9*); reprint ed. pap. 61.50 (*0-8328-0871-7*) Higginson Bk Co.

***Middlebrook, Martin.** Arnhem 1994: The Airborne Battle. 1994. text ed. 34.95 (*0-8133-2498-X*) Westview.

— Boston at War. (C). 1989. text ed. 35.00 (*0-902662-62-7*, Pub. by R K Pubns UK); pap. text ed. 21.00 (*0-685-65762-0*, Pub. by R K Pubns UK) St Mut.

— The Catholic Church in Boston. (C). 1989. text ed. 35.00 (*0-902662-65-1*, Pub. by R K Pubns UK); pap. text ed. 21.00 (*0-685-65759-0*, Pub. by R K Pubns UK) St Mut.

— The Nuremberg Raid, 30-31 March 1944. (Illus.). 400p. 1993. pap. 14.00 (*0-14-014668-7*, Penguin Bks) Viking Penguin.

— The Peenemunde Raid. LC 82-17850. (Illus.). 272p. 1983. write for info. (*0-672-52759-6*) Macmillan.

— The Schweinfurt-Regensburg Mission: American Raids on 17 August 1943. (Illus.). 384p. 1990. pap. 10.95 (*0-14-006678-0*, Penguin Bks) Viking Penguin.

Middlebrook, Patricia N. Social Psychology & Modern Life. 2nd ed. 620p. 1980. text ed. write for info. (*0-07-553675-7*) McGraw.

***Middlebrook, Ron.** Backpacker's Songbook. (Illus.). 200p. 1994. pap. 5.50 (*0-931759-85-4*) Centerstream Pub.

— Bass Guitar Chord Chart. 4p. 1985. pap. 2.50 (*0-931759-01-3*, 286) Centerstream Pub.

— The Illustrated Guitar. 86p. 1988. reprint ed. pap. text ed. 9.95 (*0-931759-28-5*) Centerstream Pub.

— Power Rhythm Chording. rev. ed. (Illus.). 56p. (YA). (gr. 8 up). 1995. disk, pap. text ed. 17.95 (*0-931759-96-X*) Centerstream Pub.

— Songs Around the Campfire. (Illus.). 168p. (YA). 1994. pap. 24.95 (*0-931759-86-2*) Centerstream Pub.

— Songs of the Cowboy. 96p. (Orig.). 1991. 12.95 (*0-931759-46-3*) Centerstream Pub.

Middlebrook, Ron, comp. Songs of the Trail. (Illus.). 112p. 1992. pap. 14.95 (*0-931759-67-6*, 00000152, Ctrstream) H Leonard.

Middlebrook, Ron, ed. Marvin's Favorite Halloween Songs. 36p. (C). 1985. pap. text ed. 6.95 (*0-931759-07-2*) Centerstream Pub.

Middlebrook, Stanley M. & Pinnick, Alfred W. How Malaya Is Governed. 2nd ed. LC 73-179225. (Illus.). reprint ed. 22.50 (*0-404-54852-0*) AMS Pr.

Middlebrook, Stephen. Annual Reporting under the Federal Securities Laws. LC 83-7484. (Corporate Practice Ser.: No. 33). 1983. 92.00 (*1-55871-243-7*) BNA.

Middlebrook, William T. How to Estimate the Building Needs of a College or University: A Demonstration of Methods Developed At the University of Minnesota. LC 56-11614. 181p. reprint ed. pap. 51.60 (*0-317-29448-2*, 2055891) Bks Demand.

***Middlebrooks, Carl K.** The Biannual Book of Brass Models. 122p. 1995. pap. write for info. (*0-9646066-0-7*) CMC Pub VA.

Middlebrooks, Charlotte. VAX FORTRAN. 1984. text ed. 32.00 (*0-8359-8245-9*, Reston); pap. text ed. write for info. (*0-8359-8243-2*, Reston) P-H.

Middlebrooks, David J., jt. auth. see Lehr, Richard I.

Middlebrooks, E. Joe, jt. auth. see Eisenberg, Talbert N.

Middlebrooks, Florence L. Blue Ribbon Cookbook. LC 79-15295. 1980. 22.95 (*0-87949-160-4*) Ashley Bks.

Middlebrooks-Hutcherson, Gracie. How Many Vehicles Can You Name? I Can Name These Objects! Can You? What Animals Do You See?, 3 vols. Clowney, Earle D., tr. (Illus.). (Orig.). (ENG & SPA.). (J). 1992. audio write for info. (*1-882485-06-8*) Enhance Your Chlds.

— How Many Vehicles Can You Name? I Can Name These Objects! Can You? What Animals Do You See?, 3 vols., Set. Clowney, Earle D., tr. (Illus.). (Orig.). (ENG & SPA.). (J). 1992. 25.00 (*1-882485-05-X*); pap. 12.00 (*1-882485-07-6*) Enhance Your Chlds.

Middlecamp, Catherine, jt. auth. see Kean, Elizabeth.

Middleditch, Alison, jt. auth. see Oliver, Jean.

Middleditch, B. S. Analytical Artifacts: GS., MS, HPLC, TLC, & PC. 1028p. 1989. 254.00 (*0-444-87158-6*) Elsevier.

Middleditch, B. S. & Amer, A. M. Kuwaiti Plants. (Studies in Plant Science: Vol. 2). 1991. 143.75 (*0-444-89215-X*) Elsevier.

Middleditch, Brian S., et al. Mass Spectrometry of Priority Pollutants. LC 80-14953. 320p. 1981. 75.00 (*0-306-40505-9*, Plenum Pr) Plenum.

***Middleditch, Leigh B., Jr. & Sinclair, Kent.** Virginia Civil Procedure. 2nd ed. 1024p. 1992. 90.00 (*1-55834-003-3*) Michie Butterworth.

***Middleditch, Michael.** The Paris Mapguide. 64p. 1995. pap. 7.95 (*0-14-046962-1*, Penguin Bks) Viking Penguin.

— The Penguin London Mapguide. (Illus.). 48p. 1988. mass mkt. 5.95 (*0-14-046821-8*, Penguin Bks) Viking Penguin.

— Penguin London Mapguide. 1983. mass mkt. 4.95 (*0-14-046596-0*, Penguin Bks) Viking Penguin.

— The Penguin London Mapguide: The Essential Guide. rev. ed. (Illus.). 48p. 1993. mass mkt. 6.95 (*0-14-046954-0*, Penguin Bks) Viking Penguin.

— Penguin Map of North America. 1987. pap. 9.95 (*0-14-051186-5*, Penguin Bks) Viking Penguin.

Middlehurst, Barbara M. & Aller, Lawrence H., eds. Nebulae & Interstellar Matter. LC 66-13879. (Stars & Stellar Systems Ser.: Vol. 7). (Illus.). 1968. lib. bdg. 60. 00 (*0-226-45959-4*) U Ch Pr.

Middlehurst, Jack & Harrison, Roger. Practical Filter Design. 240p. 1994. Incl. disk. pap. text ed. 41.00 (*0-13-719980-5*) P-H.

Middlehurst, Robin. Leading Academics. LC 93-14563. 192p. 1994. 95.00 (*0-335-09989-0*, Open Univ Pr); pap. 34.00 (*0-335-09988-2*, Open Univ Pr) Taylor & Francis.

Middlehurst, Tony. Harley-Davidson. (Illus.). 112p. 1993. 14.98 (*0-8317-4393-X*) Smithmark.

— Harley-Davidson. (Illus.). 112p. 1995. 14.98 (*0-8317-4293-3*) Smithmark.

Middlekauff & Shubik. International Food Regulation Handbook: Policy - Science - Law. (Food Science & Technology Ser.: Vol. 34). 600p. 1989. 189.00 (*0-8247-7909-6*) Dekker.

Middlekauff, Robert. Ancients & Axioms: Secondary Education in Eighteenth-Century New England. LC 79-165725. (American Education Ser, No. 2). 1979. reprint ed. 23.95 (*0-405-03713-9*) Ayer.

— The Glorious Cause: The American Revolution, 1763 to 1789. (Oxford History of the United States Ser.). (Illus.). 736p. 1982. 39.95 (*0-19-502921-6*) OUP.

— The Glorious Cause: The American Revolution, 1763 to 1789. (Oxford History of the United States Ser.). (Illus.). 736p. 1985. pap. 17.95 (*0-19-503575-5*) OUP.

Middlekauff, Woodrow S. & Lane, Robert S. Adult & Immature Tabanidae (Diptera) of California. LC 78-66042. (Bulletin of the California Insect Survey Ser.: No. 22). (Illus.). 105p. reprint ed. pap. 30.00 (*0-8357-5119-8*, 2032897) Bks Demand.

***Middlekauff, Woodrow W.** A Revision of the Sawfly Family Orussidae for North & Central America (Hymenoptera: Symphyta, Orussidae) LC 83-1397. (University of California Publications in Entomology: No. 101). 58p. 1983. pap. 25.00 (*0-7837-7493-1*, 2049215) Bks Demand.

Middleman, Ruth, ed. Activities & Action in Groupwork. LC 83-309. (Social Work with Groups Ser.: Vol. 6, No. 1). 105p. 1983. text ed. 29.95 (*0-86656-228-1*) Haworth Pr.

Middleman, Ruth R. A Study Guide for ACSW Certification. 2nd ed. LC 87-17329. 53p. 1987. 12.95 (*0-87101-150-6*) Natl Assn Soc Wkrs.

— A Study Guide for ACSW Certification. 3rd ed. 84p. (C). 1994. lib. bdg. 15.95 (*0-87101-241-3*, 2413) Natl Assn Soc Wkrs.

Middleman, Ruth R. & Wood, Gail G., eds. Teaching Secrets: The Technology of Teaching Social Work Education. LC 91-27072. (Journal of Teaching in Social Work). (Illus.). 149p. 1991. lib. bdg. 29.95 (*1-56024-213-2*) Haworth Pr.

Middleman, Ruth R. & Wood, Gale G. Skills for Direct Practice in Social Work. 176p. 1990. text ed. 37.00 (*0-231-05508-0*); pap. text ed. 15.50 (*0-231-05509-9*) Col U Pr.

Middleman, Ruth R., jt. auth. see Wood, Gale G.

Middleman, Stanley. The Flow of High Polymers: Continuum & Molecular Rheology. LC 67-29460. 255p. reprint ed. pap. 72.70 (*0-685-16166-8*, 2056298) Bks Demand.

— Fundamentals of Polymer Processing. (C). 1977. text ed. write for info. (*0-07-041851-9*) McGraw.

— Modeling Axisymmetric Flows: Dynamics of Films, Jets, & Drops. (Illus.). 336p. 1995. text ed. write for info. (*0-12-494950-9*) Acad Pr.

Middleman, Stanley & Hochberg, Arthur K. Process Engineering Analysis in Semiconductor Fabrication. (Illus.). 672p. 1992. text ed. write for info. (*0-07-041853-5*) McGraw.

Middlemas, Keith. Diplomacy of Illusion: The British Government & Germany, 1937-1939. (Modern Revivals in History Ser.). 510p. 1992. 62.50 (*0-7512-0009-3*, Pub. by Gregg Revivals UK) Ashgate Pub Co.

— Power, Competition & the State: Britain in Search of Balance 1940-1961, Vol. 1. 404p. (C). 1987. text ed. 14. 78 (*0-8179-8491-7*) Hoover Inst Pr.

Middlemas, Robert K. Clydesiders: A Left-Wing Struggle for Parliamentary Power. LC 66-2916. (Illus.). 307p. 1965. 39.50 (*0-678-08040-2*) Kelley.

Middlemiss, F. A., et al. Faunal Provinces in Space & the Time, Vol. 4. (Liverpool Geological Society & the Manchester Geological Association Ser). 246p. 1980. text ed. 115.00 (*0-471-27751-7*) Wiley.

Middlemiss, Howard, jt. auth. see Cockshott, Peter.

Middlemiss, Robert. The Lofoten Run. (Orig.). 1979. pap. 1.95 (*0-449-14283-3*, GM) Fawcett.

Middlemist, R. Dennis, et al. Personnel Management: Jobs, People, & Logic. (Illus.). 592p. (C). 1983. text ed. write for info. (*0-13-659003-9*) P-H.

Middlemore, S. G., tr. see Burchhardt, Jacob.

Middles, Mick. The Smiths: The Complete Story. rev. ed. (Illus.). 128p. 1988. pap. 14.95 (*0-7119-1427-3*, OP43389) Omnibus NY.

Middlestadt, Pamela, ed. The Reimbursement Manual: How To Get Paid for Your Advanced Practice Nursing Services. LC 93-9420. 186p. 1993. 44.95 (*1-55810-085-7*, NP-84) Am Nurses Pub.

***Middlesworth, E. M. & Massoud, H.** ULSI Science & Technology: Fifth International Symposium. 1995. 59.00 (*1-56677-099-8*, PV 95-5) Electrochem Soc.

Middlesworth, Nancy, tr. see Mitchell, Donald D.

Middletn, David L., jt. auth. see Caldwell, Harry B.

***Middleton.** Encyclopedia of Sub-Saharan Africa. 1995. 295. 00 (*0-13-279936-7*) P-H.

— New York Times Acrostics Vol. 5. 1995. pap. 8.00 (*0-8129-2537-8*, Times Bks) Random.

Middleton & Tsang. Spelling the Written Word, Bk. B. (Administrator's Guide SD100). 64p. 1984. per. 17.90 (*0-8403-3191-6*) Kendall-Hunt.

— Spelling the Written Word, SD100: Administrators Guide, Bk. D. 64p. 1984. per. 17.90 (*0-8403-3193-2*) Kendall-Hunt.

Middleton, jt. auth. see Pollock.

Middleton, jt. auth. see Wilcock.

Middleton, et al. Allergy: Principles & Practice, No. 4. 1793p. 1993. 199.00 (*0-8016-6427-6*) Mosby Yr Bk.

Middleton, Alex L., jt. ed. see Perrins, Christopher.

Middleton, Arthur. Globes of the Western World. (Illus.). 224p. 1991. 95.00 (*0-85667-395-1*) Sothebys Pubns.

Middleton, Arthur P. Anglican Maryland, 1692-1792. LC 92-13669. 1992. write for info. (*0-89865-841-1*) Donning Co.

— Annapolis on the Chesapeake. (Illus.). 80p. (Orig.). 1988. 39.95 (*0-933101-13-9*); pap. 24.95 (*0-933101-14-7*) Legacy Pubns.

— New Wine in Old Skins: Liturgical Change & the Setting of Worship. LC 88-8908. 133p. (Orig.). 1988. pap. 9.95 (*0-8192-1432-9*) Morehouse Pub.

— Tobacco Coast. LC 84-47962. (Maryland Paperback Bookshelf Ser.). 528p. (C). 1984. reprint ed. pap. 16.95x (*0-8018-2534-2*) Johns Hopkins.

Middleton, Barth & Middleton, Sally. Living God's Way. (Illus.). 64p. (J). (gr. k-6). 1985. pap. text ed. 11.99 (*1-55976-031-1*) CEF Press.

— Loving God's Way. (Illus.). 55p. (J). (gr. k-6). 1988. pap. text ed. 7.50 (*1-55976-033-8*) CEF Press.

Middleton, Bernard C. A History of English Craft Bookbinding Technique. 328p. (C). 1988. 130.00 (*0-946323-13-5*, Pub. by New Holland Pubs UK) St Mut.

***Middleton, Betty J.** Special Times: Honoring Our Jewish & Christian Heritages for Gades 1 & 2. 208p. 1994. 30.00 (*1-55896-281-6*) Unitarian Univ.

Middleton, Bill, ed. North American Commuter Rail, 1994. (Illus.). 64p. 1994. pap. 9.95 (*0-685-72278-3*) Interurban.

Middleton, C. The Famous Historie of Chinon of England. (EETS, OS Ser.: No. 165). 1972. reprint ed. 35.00 (*0-527-00162-7*) Periodicals Srv.

Middleton, Charles R. & Rosovsky, Henry M. One Hundred Years of Arts & Sciences: A Centennial Reaffirmation. 32p. 1994. pap. 8.95 (*0-87081-336-6*) Univ Pr Colo.

Middleton, Christopher. Anasphere. enl. rev. ed. (Burning Deck Poetry Ser.). 1978. 20.00 (*0-930900-54-5*) Burning Deck.

— The Historie of Heaven. LC 76-57400. (English Experience Ser.: No. 816). 1977. reprint ed. lib. bdg. 5.00 (*0-685-05281-8*) Walter J Johnson.

— Munich up Close. (Illus.). 144p. 1993. pap. 12.95 (*0-8442-9454-3*, Passport Bks) NTC Pub Grp.

— Nonsequences: Self Poems. (Orig.). (C). 1966. pap. text ed. 1.95 (*0-393-04228-6*) Norton.

— Razzmatazz. 1976. 17.50 (*0-935072-02-0*) W T Taylor.

— Woden Dog. deluxe ed. (Burning Deck Poetry Ser.). 32p. (Orig.). 1982. boxed 20.00 (*0-930901-06-1*) Burning Deck.

Middleton, Christopher, ed. & tr. Goethe, Johann Wolfgang von: Collected Works, Vol. 1: Selected Poems. Hamburger, Michael et al, trs. LC 82-5492. xxxix, 298p. (ENG & GER.). 1983. 40.00 (*3-518-03053-1*, Pub. by Suhr Verlag GW) Intl Bk Import.

Middleton, Christopher & Garza-Falcon, Leticia, trs. Anadalusion Poems. 124p. 1993. 40.00 (*0-87923-887-9*) Godine.

Middleton, Christopher, tr. see Grass, Gunter.

Middleton, Christopher, ed. see Gustafsson, Lars.

Middleton, Christopher, tr. see Hofmann, Gert.

Middleton, Christopher, tr. see Kuoni, Carin & Walser, Robert.

Middleton, Christopher, ed. see Von Goethe, Johann W.

Middleton, Christopher, tr. see Walser, Robert.

Middleton, Christopher, tr. see Wolf, Christa.

Middleton, D., jt. ed. see Dyer, P.

Middleton, D. H. Airspeed: The Company & Its Aeroplanes. 216p. (C). 1988. 120.00 (*0-86138-009-6*, Pub. by T Dalton UK) St Mut.

Middleton, David. Ancient Forests: A Celebration of North America's Old-Growth Wilderness. (Illus.). 108p. (Orig.). 1992. pap. 16.95 (*0-87701-814-6*) Chronicle Bks.

— The Burning Fields. LC 90-49724. 64p. 1991. pap. 7.95 (*0-8071-1639-4*) La State U Pr.

— An Introduction to Statistical Communication Theory. 1140p. 1987. reprint ed. 65.95 (*0-932146-15-5*) Peninsula CA.

— Topics in Communications Theory. 126p. 1987. reprint ed. 19.95 (*0-932146-14-7*) Peninsula CA.

Middleton, David & Edwards, Derek, eds. Collective Remembering. (Inquiries in Social Construction Ser.). 240p. (C). 1990. text ed. 47.50 (*0-8039-8234-8*); pap. text ed. 18.95 (*0-8039-8235-6*) Sage.

***Middleton, David & Pearson, David.** The New Key to Ecuador & the Galapagos. LC 95-60705. (New Key Travel Ser.). (Illus.). 408p. (Orig.). 1995. pap. 14.95 (*1-56975-040-8*) Ulysses Pr.

Middleton, David, ed. see Finlay, John.

Middleton, David, ed. see Newton, Willis & Newton, Joe.

Middleton, David L., jt. auth. see Richmond, Kent D.

Middleton, Don, ed. Composite Materials in Aircraft Structures. 1990. text ed. 190.00 (*0-470-21511-9*) Halsted Pr.

Middleton, Dorothy. Victorian Lady Travellers. (Illus.). 182p. 1992. reprint ed. pap. 11.00 (*0-89733-063-3*) Academy Chi Pubs.

Middleton, Drew. Air War-Vietnam. 17.00 (*0-318-04272-X*) Ayer.

Middleton, Drew & Brown, Gene. Southeast Asia. (Great Contemporary Issues Ser.). 27.95 (*0-405-13399-5*) Ayer.

Middleton, Gayle. The Christmas Spirit. (Illus.). 16p. 1989. pap. 12.95 (*0-685-29047-6*, 51034) Willitts Designs.

— Glim the Glorious or How the Little Folk Bested the Gubgoblins. LC 86-2978. (Illus.). 64p. (J). (gr. k-5). 1987. 12.95 (*0-394-88081-1*) Knopf Bks Yng Read.

— The Legend of Catlantis. (Illus.). 112p. 1989. text ed. 24. 95 (*0-685-29046-8*, 47025) Willitts Designs.

Middleton, George. Diana Does It. 1961. pap. 4.75 (*0-8222-0306-5*) Dramatists Play.

— Embers & Other One-Act Plays: With the Failures, the Gargoyle, in His House, Madonna, the Man Masterful. LC 77-70359. (One-Act Plays in Reprint Ser.). 1977. reprint ed. 15.00 (*0-8486-2020-8*) Roth Pub Inc.

— These Things Are Mine. (American Autobiography Ser.). 448p. 1995. reprint ed. lib. bdg. 99.00 (*0-7812-8594-1*) Rprt Serv.

Middleton, Gerard V., ed. Primary Sedimentary Structures & Their Hydrodynamic Interpretation: A Symposium. LC 76-219474. (Society of Economic Paleontologists & Mineralogists, Special Publication Ser.: No. 12). 272p. reprint ed. pap. 77.60 (*0-317-27158-X*, 2024738) Bks Demand.

Middleton, Gerard V. & Southard, John B. Mechanics of Sediment Movement: Lecture Notes for Short Course No. 3, Sponsored by the Eastern Section of the Society of Economic Paleontologists & Mineralogists, & Given in Providence, Rhode Island, March 13-14, 1984. 2nd ed. (SEPM Short Course Ser.: No. 3, 1984). 411p. reprint ed. pap. 117.20 (*0-7837-2417-9*, 2042554) Bks Demand.

Middleton, Gerard V. & Wilcock, Peter R. Mechanics in the Earth & Environmental Sciences. (Illus.). 500p. (C). 1994. 89.95 (*0-521-44124-2*); pap. 34.95 (*0-521-44669-4*) Cambridge U Pr.

Middleton, Gordon K., Jr. Good News for Hurting Hearts: Breaking the Code. 64p. (Orig.). (YA). 1994. pap. 4.95 (*0-9641534-0-8*) GKM Pubng.

Middleton, Grace, jt. auth. see Pannbacker, Mary.

Middleton, Harry. The Bright Country: A Fisherman's Return to Trout, Wild Water, & Himself. 320p. 1993. 22.00 (*0-671-75859-4*) S&S Trade.

— The Earth Is Enough: Growing up in a World of Fly Fishing, Trout, & Old Men. 270p. Date not set. pap. 15. 00 (*0-87108-874-6*) Pruett.

— LBJ: The White House Years. 1990. 45.00 (*0-8109-1191-4*) Abrams.

— On the Spine of Time: An Angler's Love of the Smokies. 240p. 1992. pap. 10.00 (*0-671-75569-2*, Fireside) S&S Trade.

— Rivers of Memory. LC 92-38119. 90p. 1993. 18.95 (*0-87108-835-5*) Pruett.

— The Starlight Creek Angling Society. (Illus.). 57p. 1993. 90.00 (*0-9620609-5-X*) Meadow Run Pr.

Middleton, Hayden & Heater, Derek, eds. The Atlas of Modern History. (Illus.). 64p. (YA). (gr. 7 up). 1991. bds. 15.95 (*0-19-831677-1*) OUP.

Middleton, Haydn. Island of the Mighty. (Oxford Myths & Legends Ser.). 80p. (J). (gr. 5-8). 1987. 20.00 (*0-19-274133-0*) OUP.

— Son of Two Worlds. 208p. 1989. mass mkt. 5.95 (*0-345-36217-9*) Ballantine.

Middleton, Henry. The Last East Indian Voyage. LC 74-25700. (English Experience Ser.: No. 307). 1971. reprint ed. 20.00 (*90-221-0307-2*) Walter J Johnson.

Middleton, Ian. Pet Shop. (Pacific Writers Ser.). 188p. (C). 1990. pap. 9.95 (*0-685-63026-9*, A0480, Pub. by Heinemann Reed NZ) Heinemann.

Middleton, J. & Pande, G. N., eds. Numeta 85, Numerical Methods in Engineering, Theory & Applications: Proceedings of an International Conference Swansea, UK, 7-11 January 1985, 2 vols., Set. 1084p. (C). 1985. text ed. 300.00 (*90-6191-577-5*, Pub. by A A Balkema NE) Ashgate Pub Co.

Middleton, J., jt. ed. see Pande, G. N.

Middleton, J. Richard, jt. auth. see Walsh, Brian J.

Middleton, Jeff. Illustrated DOS Computing. (Illus.). 48p. (Orig.). 1990. pap. 29.95 (*0-8464-4322-8*) Beekman Pubs.

Middleton, Jo A. Willa Cather's Modernism: A Study of Style & Technique. LC 89-45407. 1990. 36.50 (*0-8386-3385-4*) Fairleigh Dickinson.

Middleton, John. The Central Tribes of the North-Eastern Bantu. LC 76-44758. reprint ed. 27.50 (*0-404-15952-4*) AMS Pr.

— Lugbara of Uganda. 2nd ed. 1993. pap. write for info. (*0-15-500622-3*) HB Coll Pubs.

— The Lugbara of Uganda. (Illus.). 96p. (Orig.). (C). 1983. reprint ed. pap. text ed. 7.95 (*0-88133-028-0*) Waveland Pr.

— Lugbara Religion: Ritual & Authority among an East African People. LC 60-51074. 294p. reprint ed. pap. 83. 80 (*0-317-28622-6*, 2055387) Bks Demand.

— Lugbara Religion: Ritual & Authority among East African People. LC 86-21889. (Illus.). 294p. 1987. reprint ed. pap. 15.95 (*0-87474-667-1*) Smithsonian.

— The World of the Swahili: An African Mercantile Civilization. (Illus.). 320p. (C). 1992. text ed. 32.50 (*0-300-05219-7*) Yale U Pr.

— The World of the Swahili: An African Mercantile Civilization. (Illus.). 266p. 1994. pap. 16.00 (*0-300-06080-7*) Yale U Pr.

Middleton, John, ed. Magic, Witchcraft, & Curing. LC 75-44038. (Sourcebooks in Anthropology: No. 7). 358p. 1976. pap. 13.95 (*0-292-75031-5*) U of Tex Pr.

— Myth & Cosmos: Readings in Mythology & Symbolism. LC 75-43817. (Sourcebooks in Anthropology: No. 5). 382p. 1976. pap. 17.95 (*0-292-75030-7*) U of Tex Pr.

Middleton, John & Campbell, Jane. Zanzibar, Its Society & Politics. LC 84-29046. (Illus.). 71p. 1985. reprint ed. text ed. 49.75 (*0-313-24739-0*, MIZA, Greenwood Pr) Greenwood.

Middleton, John & Demsky, Terry. Vocational Education & Training: A Review of World Bank Investment. (Discussion Paper Ser.: No. 51). 142p. 1989. 9.95 (*0-8213-1225-1*, 20051) World Bank.

Middleton, John & Kershaw, Greet. The Central Tribes of the North-Eastern Bantu: The Kikuyu Including Embu, Meru, Mere, Chuka, Mwimbi, Tharaka, & the Kamba of Kenya. LC 76-351844. (Ethnographic Survey of Africa: East Central Africa Ser.: Pt. 5). 108p. pap. 30.80 (*0-8357-6962-3*, 2039022) Bks Demand.

Middleton, John, jt. auth. see Adhikarya, Ronny.

Middleton, John, ed. see De Vere Allen, James.

Middleton, John, et al. Skills Training for Productivity: Vocational Education & Training in Developing Countries. (World Bank Publication Ser.). (Illus.). 376p. 1993. 37.95 (*0-19-520887-0*, 60887) OUP.

Middleton, Judy. Sussex Ghosts. 96p. 1987. 30.00 (*0-905392-90-6*) St Mut.

Middleton, K. J., jt. auth. see Wright, G. C.

Middleton, Katharine & Hess, Mary A. The Art of Cooking for the Diabetic. LC 77-23701. 384p. 1979. 15.95 (*0-685-01188-7*); pap. 11.95 (*0-8092-7222-9*) Contemp Bks.

Middleton, Katharine, jt. auth. see Hess, Mary A.

***Middleton, Kathleen.** Communication & Anger Management. (Comprehensive Health for Middle Grades Ser.). (J). (gr. 6-9). 1996. 24.00 (*1-56071-465-4*, H567) ETR Assocs.

Middleton, Kathleen, jt. ed. see Cortese, Peter.

An Asterisk (*) at the beginning of an entry indicates that the title is appearing in BIP for the first time.

Middleton, Kathleen, ed. see Post, Jory & McPherson, Carole.

Middleton, Kent & Mersky, Roy M. Freedom of Expression: A Collection of Best Writings. LC 81-83405. ix, 504p. 1981. lib. bdg. 52.00 (*0-89941-104-5*, 302320) W S Hein.

***Middleton, Kent R. & Chamberlin, Bill F.** Key Cases in the Law of Public Communication. LC 94-26567. 320p. (C). 1995. per., pap. text ed. 18.75 (*0-8013-1387-2*) Longman.

Middleton, Lamar. Revolt, U. S. A. LC 68-29232. (Essay Index Reprint Ser.). (Illus.). 1977. reprint ed. 20.95 (*0-8369-0708-6*) Ayer.

Middleton, Lamar, jt. auth. see Young, Klyde H.

Middleton, Lee T. Hearts of Fire: Soldier Women of the Civil War, Vol. I. 2nd deluxe ed. (Illus.). 250p. (C). 1993. Smyth sewn & signed. 19.95 (*1-882755-00-6*) Taylor Rader.

Middleton, Lorna. Prediction or Premonition - Coincidence Be Damned. 94p. (C). 1989. text ed. 50.00 (*0-946270-80-5*, Pub. by Pentland Pr UK) St Mut.

Middleton, Marcia S. & Katz, Bill, eds. Information & Referral in Reference Services. LC 88-2916. (Reference Librarian Ser.: No. 21). (Illus.). 259p. 1988. text ed. 49. 95 (*0-86656-693-7*) Haworth Pr.

Middleton, Margaret M. Violence-Psychological, Medical & Legal Aspects: A Subject Analysis & Research Index with Bibliography. LC 83-71660. 142p. 1985. 44.50 (*0-88164-022-0*); pap. 39.50 (*0-88164-023-9*) ABBE Pubs Assn.

Middleton, Michael L. Cop: A True Story. 256p. 1994. 19. 95 (*0-8092-3736-9*) Contemp Bks.

Middleton, Michael R. Data Analysis Using Excel 5.0. 200p. 1995. pap. 15.95 (*0-534-22122-X*) Intl Thomson.

***Middleton, Mike.** Cop: A True Story. 288p. 1995. pap. 12. 95 (*0-8092-3437-8*) Contemp Bks.

Middleton, Mildred. Spelling the Written Word: Administration Guide, Bk. A. 2nd ed. 1985. per. 17.90 (*0-8403-3190-8*) Kendall-Hunt.

Middleton, Mildred & Tsang, Eddie. Spelling the Written Word, Bk. C. (Administrator's Guide SD100). 64p. 1984. per. 17.90 (*0-8403-3192-4*) Kendall-Hunt.

— Spelling the Written Word, SD100, Bk. D. 200p. (gr. 10). 1984. per. 5.90 (*0-8403-3198-3*) Kendall-Hunt.

Middleton, Mildred L. Learning to Spell: Student Edition, Bk. 2. 112p. (gr. 8 up). 1984. per. 5.90 (*0-8403-3199-1*) Kendall-Hunt.

Middleton, Mildred L. & Tsang, Eddie. Learning to Spell: Administrator's Guide, Bk. 2. 64p. 1984. per. 17.90 (*0-8403-3194-0*) Kendall-Hunt.

Middleton, N. The British Constitution. (C). 1978. Incl. 3 filmstrips & cassette. audio, flmstrp 430.00 (*0-86158-641-7*, Pub. by S Thornes Pubs UK) St Mut.

— Ways of Life. (C). 1981. 280.00 (*0-86158-627-1*, Pub. by S Thornes Pubs UK) St Mut.

Middleton, Ned. Diving Belize. (Illus.). 128p. (Orig.). 1994. pap. 18.95 (*1-881652-01-7*) Aqua Quest.

— Ten Years Underwater. (Illus.). 136p. (C). 1990. 100.00 (*0-907151-43-4*, Pub. by IMMEL Pubng UK) St Mut.

Middleton, Neil, et al. The Tears of the Crocodile: From Rio to Reality in the Developing World. LC 93-5266. 228p. (C). 1993. text ed. 70.00 (*0-7453-0764-7*); pap. text ed. 19.95 (*0-7453-0765-5*) Westview.

Middleton, Nicholas J., jt. auth. see Thomas, David S. G.

Middleton, Nicholas J., jt. auth. see Thomas, David S.

Middleton, Nicholas J., jt. auth. see Thomas, David S.G.

Middleton, Nick. Atlas of Environmental Issues. (World Contemporary Issues Ser.). (Illus.). 64p. (YA). (gr. 6 up). 1989. 16.95 (*0-8160-2023-X*) Facts on File.

— Atlas of Social Issues. (World Contempoary Issues Ser.). (Illus.). 64p. (YA). 1990. 16.95 (*0-8160-2024-8*) Facts on File.

— Atlas of the Natural World. (World Contemporary Issues Ser.). (Illus.). 64p. (YA). 1990. 16.95 (*0-8160-2131-7*) Facts on File.

— Atlas of World Issues. (World Contemporary Issues Ser.). (Illus.). 64p. (YA). (gr. 6 up). 1989. 16.95 (*0-8160-2022-1*) Facts on File.

— Southern Africa. LC 94-18330. (Country Fact Files Ser.). (J). 1995. lib. bdg. write for info. (*0-8114-2785-4*) Raintree Steck-V.

Middleton, Norman G. Imaginative Healing: Using Imagery for Growth & Change. Elletro Productions Staff, ed. LC 93-12861. 200p. 1993. pap. 11.95 (*1-56875-043-9*) R & E Pubs.

Middleton, Pat. Discover! America's Great River Road: A Guide to the Heritage, Natural History, & Recreational Resources of the Upper Mississippi River Valley. LC 88-82228. (Illus.). 224p. (Orig.). (J). (gr. 4-12). 1990. pap. 11.95 (*0-9620823-0-9*) Heritage WI.

— Discover! America's Great River Road, Vol. 1 (WI, IA, MN, IL) A Guide to the Heritage, Natural History, & Recreational Resources of the Upper Mississippi River Valley. (Illus.). 224p. (Orig.). 1991. pap. 11.95 (*0-9620823-3-3*) Heritage WI.

— Mississippi River Activity Guide. (Illus.). 32p. (J). (gr. 4-7). 1993. pap. 5.50 (*0-9620823-5-X*) Heritage WI.

Middleton, Pat, ed. see Dearing, Shirley.

Middleton, Peter. The Inward Gaze: Masculinity & Subjectivity in Modern Subject. LC 92-9321. 240p. 1992. 69.95 (*0-415-07327-8*, A7965); pap. 15.95 (*0-415-07328-6*, A7969) Routledge.

— A Selected Flute Discography: Long-Playing & Compact Disk Classical Recordings, 1948-1990. 2000p. 1995. 25. 00 (*0-9627940-0-7*) Cornell Pr.

Middleton, Quinn B. Spirited Desserts: A Collection of Luscious Desserts Prepared with Liquors & Liqueurs. (Illus.). 100p. 1990. spiral bd. 10.95 (*0-9628029-0-5*) Q B Middleton.

Middleton, R. Studying Popular Music. 1990. 95.00 (*0-335-15276-7*, Open Univ Pr); pap. 39.00 (*0-335-15275-9*, Open Univ Pr) Taylor & Francis.

Middleton, R. W., jt. auth. see Benner, C. S.

Middleton, Richard. The Bells of Victory: The Pitt-Newcastle Ministry & the Conduct of the Seven Year's War, 1757-1762. 251p. 1985. 69.95 (*0-521-26546-0*) Cambridge U Pr.

— Colonial America: A History, 1607-1760. (Illus.). 436p. 1992. pap. 19.95 (*1-55786-259-1*) Blackwell Pubs.

Middleton, Robert. Negotiating on Non-Tariff Distortions of Trade: The EFTA Precedents. LC 74-19885. 208p. (C). 1975. text ed. 32.50 (*0-312-56315-9*) St Martin.

Middleton, Robert G. Bob Middleton's Handbook of Electronic Time-Savers & Shortcuts. 416p. 1987. text ed. 29.95 (*0-13-079559-3*) P-H.

— Bob Middleton's Handbook of Electronic Time-Savers & Shortcuts. 400p. 1988. pap. 16.95 (*0-13-055708-0*) P-H.

— How to Use DC Voltmeters. 1991. 28.80 (*0-13-430729-1*, 420301) P-H.

— New Digital Troubleshooting Techniques: A Complete, Illustrated Guide. LC 83-16157. 280p. 1986. 34.95 (*0-13-612275-2*, Busn) P-H.

— New Handbook of Troubleshooting Techniques for Microprocessors & Microcomputers. LC 84-9916. (Illus.). 293p. 1984. text ed. 39.95 (*0-13-613464-5*, Busn) P-H.

— New Ways to Use Test Meters: A Modern Guide to Electronic Servicing. 256p. 1986. 22.95 (*0-13-616169-3*, Busn) P-H.

— Practical Electricity. 4th ed. 512p. 1988. text ed. 22.50 (*0-02-584561-6*, Audel) Macmillan.

— Troubleshooting Electronic Equipment Without Service Data. LC 83-13772. (Illus.). 303p. 1986. 34.95 (*0-13-931097-5*, Scrbrough Hse) Madison Bks UPA.

— Troubleshooting Electronics Equipment Without Service Data. 2nd ed. 320p. 1989. text ed. 62.00 (*0-13-931164-5*) P-H.

Middleton, Robin & Watkin, David. Neoclassical & Nineteenth Century Architecture: The Diffusion & Development of Classicism & the Gothic Revival, Vol. II. LC 87-42632. (History of World Architecture Ser.). (Illus.). 224p. 1987. 29.95 (*0-8478-0851-3*) Rizzoli Intl.

— Neoclassical & Nineteenth Century Architecture: The Enlightenment in France & in England, Vol. I. LC 87-42631. (History of World Architecture Ser.). (Illus.). 224p. 1987. 29.95 (*0-8478-0850-5*) Rizzoli Intl.

Middleton, Roger. Towards the Managed Economy: Keynes, the Treasury & the Fiscal Policy Debate of the 1930's. 288p. 1985. 70.00 (*0-416-35830-6*, 9523) Routledge Chapman & Hall.

Middleton, Sally, jt. auth. see Middleton, Barth.

Middleton, Stanley. An After Dinner's Sleep. large type ed. 448p. 1988. 15.95 (*0-7089-1903-0*) Ulverscroft.

— Catalysts. 266p. 1995. 26.00 (*0-09-178494-8*, Pub. by Hutchinson UK) Trafalgar.

— Changes & Chances. 215p. 1991. 18.95 (*1-56131-004-2*) New Amsterdam Bks.

— Entry into Jerusalem. LC 88-31300. 172p. (C). 1988. 16. 95 (*0-941533-46-8*) New Amsterdam Bks.

— Recovery. large type ed. 1990. 21.95 (*0-7089-2242-2*) Ulverscroft.

— Vacant Places. 238p. (C). 1990. 16.95 (*0-941533-78-6*) New Amsterdam Bks.

— Vacant Places. 1992. 9.95 (*1-56131-036-0*) New Amsterdam Bks.

— Valley of Decision. LC 87-20323. 214p. 1987. 15.95 (*0-941533-08-5*) New Amsterdam Bks.

Middleton, Stephen. The Black Laws in the Old Northwest: A Documentary History. LC 91-47063. (Contributions in Afro-American & African Studies: No. 152). 464p. 1993. text ed. 55.00 (*0-313-28016-9*, MKL, Greenwood Pr) Greenwood.

— Ohio & the Antislavery Activities of Attorney Salmon Portland Chase, 1830-1849. LC 90-35912. (Distinguished Studies in American Legal & Constitutional History: Vol. 18). 184p. 1990. reprint ed. 48.00 (*0-8240-2516-4*) Garland.

Middleton, Sue. Educating Feminists: Life Histories & Pedagogy. LC 92-43007. (Athene Ser.). 224p. (C). 1993. text ed. 39.00 (*0-8077-3234-6*); pap. text ed. 17.95 (*0-8077-3233-8*) Tchrs Coll.

Middleton, Susan. Here Today. (Illus.). 144p. 1991. 35.00 (*0-8118-0041-5*); pap. 22.95 (*0-8118-0028-8*) Chronicle Bks.

Middleton, Susan & Liittschwager, David. Witness: Endangered Species of North America. LC 93-48877. (Illus.). 256p. 1994. 50.00 (*0-8118-0282-5*); pap. 29.95 (*0-8118-0258-2*) Chronicle Bks.

Middleton, Teresa, ed. Virtual Worlds - Real Challenges: Papers from SRI's 1991 Conference on Virtual Reality. (Illus.). 145p. 1992. pap. 35.00 (*0-88736-870-0*) Mecklermedia.

Middleton, Thomas. The Bridgewater Manuscript of Thomas Middleton's A Game at Chess (1624) Howard-Hill, T. H., ed. LC 94-18381. 148p. 1994. text ed. 69.95 (*0-7734-9113-9*) E Mellen.

— The Changeling. LC 65-24538. 144p. 1966. pap. text ed. 18.95 (*0-8122-7524-1*) U of Pa Pr.

— A Chaste Maid in Cheapside. Brissenden, Alan, ed. (New Mermaid Ser.). (C). 1976. pap. text ed. 4.95 (*0-393-90023-1*) Norton.

— Five Plays: A Trick to Catch the Old One, The Revenger's Tragedy, A Chaste Maid in Cheapside, Women Beware Women, The Changeling. Loughrey, Bryan & Taylor, Neil, eds. 496p. 1988. pap. 9.95 (*0-14-043219-1*, Penguin Classics) Viking Penguin.

— A Game at Chesse. (BCL1-PR English Literature Ser.). 172p. 1992. reprint ed. lib. bdg. 69.00 (*0-7812-7254-8*) Rprt Serv.

— A Game at Chesse. (BCL1-PR English Literature Ser.). 172p. 1992. reprint ed. lib. bdg. 69.00 (*0-7812-7266-1*) Rprt Serv.

— The Ghost of Lucrece. reprint ed. 29.00 (*0-403-07246-8*) Somerset Pub.

— Ghost of Lucrece. reprint ed. lib. bdg. 79.00 (*0-7812-0249-3*) Rprt Serv.

— Harper's Magazine Acrostic Puzzle Book. 1993. ring bd. 8.95 (*1-879957-12-4*, Franklin Sq Pr) Harpers Mag Found.

— Harper's Magazine Acrostic Puzzle Book. 2nd ed. 1995. ring bd. 8.95 (*1-879957-23-X*) Harpers Mag Found.

— Hengist, King of Kent: Or the mayor of Queensborough. 1988. reprint ed. lib. bdg. 75.00 (*0-7812-0230-2*) Rprt Serv.

— A Mad World, My Masters. Henning, Standish, ed. LC 65-10544. (Regents Renaissance Drama Ser.). 131p. reprint ed. pap. 37.40 (*0-8357-7877-0*, 2036295) Bks Demand.

— Michaelmas Term. Levin, Richard, ed. LC 66-17765. (Regents Renaissance Drama Ser.). 165p. reprint ed. pap. 47.10 (*0-7837-0147-0*, 2040436) Bks Demand.

— No Wit, No Help Like a Woman's. Johnson, Lowell E., ed. LC 74-33673. (Regents Renaissance Drama Ser.). xxiv, 144p. 1976. 17.95 (*0-8032-0300-4*) U of Nebr Pr.

— S&S Crostics Number 111. 1994. pap. 7.00 (*0-671-87193-5*, Fireside) S&S Trade.

— Thomas Middleton: With an Introduction by Algernon Charles Swinburne, 2 vols. (BCL1-PR English Literature Ser.). 1992. reprint ed. lib. bdg. 150.00 (*0-7812-7253-X*) Rprt Serv.

— Thomas Middleton: With an Introduction by Algernon Charles Swinburne, 2 vols., Set. (BCL1-PR English Literature Ser.). 1992. reprint ed. lib. bdg. 150.00 (*0-7812-7265-3*) Rprt Serv.

— The Witch. Schafer, Elizabeth, ed. LC 94-25850. (C). 1994. pap. text ed. write for info. (*0-393-90073-8*) Norton.

— The Witch (From Bodeian Ms Malone 12) From Bodeian Manuscript Malone 12. Drees, L. & De Vocht, H., eds. (Material for the Study of the Old English Drama Ser.: No. 2, Vol. 18). 1974. reprint ed. pap. 11.00 (*0-8115-0311-9*) Periodicals Srv.

— Women Beware Women. Mulryne, J. R., ed. (Revels Plays Ser.). 201p. 1988. reprint ed. text ed. 12.95 (*0-7190-1614-2*, Pub. by Manchester Univ Pr UK) St Martin.

— Works, 8 vols., Set. Bullen, A. H., ed. (BCL1-PR English Literature Ser.). 1992. reprint ed. lib. bdg. 720.00 (*0-7812-7264-5*) Rprt Serv.

— Works of Thomas Middleton, 8 Vols, Set. Bullen, A. H., ed. LC 78-181958. reprint ed. 360.00 (*0-404-04330-5*) AMS Pr.

Middleton, Thomas, ed. Simon & Schuster Crostics, No. 112. 1994. pap. 7.00 (*0-671-89711-X*, Fireside) S&S Trade.

Middleton, Thomas & Dekker, Thomas. The Roaring Girl. Mulholland, Paul, ed. (Revels Plays Ser.). 1990. text ed. 18.95 (*0-7190-1630-4*, Pub. by Manchester Univ Pr UK) St Martin.

— Roaring Girl. LC 71-133654. (Tudor Facsimile Texts. Old English Plays Ser.: No. 130). reprint ed. 49.50 (*0-404-53430-9*) AMS Pr.

Middleton, Thomas & Rowley, William. The Changeling. Williams, George W., ed. LC 65-15340. xxiv, 112p. 1966. pap. 6.95x (*0-8032-5281-1*, Bison Books) U of Nebr Pr.

— A Fair Quarrel. Price, George R., ed. LC 74-33674. (Regents Renaissance Drama Ser.). xxviii, 138p. 1976. 17.95 (*0-8032-0299-7*) U of Nebr Pr.

— A Fair Quarrel. Holdsworth, R. V., ed. (New Mermaid Ser.). (C). 1976. pap. text ed. 4.95 (*0-393-90029-0*) Norton.

Middleton, Thomas & Rowley, Wm. The Changeling. Bawcutt, N. W., ed. (Revels Plays Ser.). 140p. 1988. text ed. 14.95 (*0-7190-1610-X*, Pub. by Manchester Univ Pr UK) St Martin.

Middleton, Thomas H. Crostics, No. 104. 1990. pap. 6.95 (*0-671-72354-5*) S&S Trade.

— A Game at Chess, No. 1624. Howard-Hill, Trevor H., ed. (Malone Society Ser.: No. 150). 1991. 45.00 (*0-19-729027-2*) OUP.

— The New York Times Acrostic Omnibus, Vol. 3. 1994. pap. 8.50 (*0-8129-2362-6*, Times Bks) Random.

— The New York Times Acrostic Puzzles, Vol. 4. 64p. (Orig.). 1985. 8.50 (*0-8129-1116-4*, Times Bks) Random.

— Simon & Schuster Crostics, No. 83. 1980. 3.95 (*0-686-61340-6*, 25464) S&S Trade.

— Simon & Schuster Crostics, No. 108. 1992. pap. 7.00 (*0-671-79180-X*, Fireside) S&S Trade.

— Simon & Schuster Crostics, No. 110. 1993. pap. 7.00 (*0-671-87192-7*, Fireside) S&S Trade.

— Simon & Schuster Crostics Series, No. 105. 1991. pap. 6.95 (*0-671-74046-6*, Fireside) S&S Trade.

— Simon & Schuster's Crostics, No. 106. 64p. 1991. pap. 6.95 (*0-671-74923-4*, Fireside) S&S Trade.

— Simon & Schuster's Crostics, No. 107. 1992. pap. 6.99 (*0-671-77854-4*) S&S Trade.

— Simon & Schuster's Crostics, No. 109. 1993. pap. 7.00 (*0-671-86410-6*, Fireside) S&S Trade.

— Simon & Schuster's Crostics Treasury Series, No. 2: A New Collection of 75 Scintillating Challenges - Selected from America's Premier Puzzle Series. 96p. 1992. pap. 6.95 (*0-671-75850-0*, Fireside) S&S Trade.

— Simon & Schuster's Crostics Treasury Series, No. 3. 1994. 7.00 (*0-671-87221-4*, Fireside) S&S Trade.

— Simon & Schuster's Super Crostics Book No. 3. 256p. 1995. pap. 9.00 (*0-671-51132-7*, Fireside) S&S Trade.

— Simon & Schuster's Super Crostics Book Series, No. 2. 224p. 1993. pap. 9.00 (*0-671-79789-1*, Fireside) S&S Trade.

Middleton, Thomas H., ed. The New York Times Acrostic Puzzle Omnibus, Vol. 1. 1992. 8.50 (*0-8129-1993-9*, Times Bks) Random.

— The New York Times Acrostic Puzzle Omnibus, Vol. 2. 1992. 8.00 (*0-8129-1994-7*, Times Bks) Random.

— The New York Times Acrostic Puzzles, Vol. 1. 64p. (Orig.). 1983. spiral bd., pap. 8.50 (*0-8129-1064-8*, Times Bks) Random.

— The New York Times Acrostic Puzzles, Vol. 2. 64p. (Orig.). 1983. spiral bd., pap. 8.50 (*0-8129-1065-6*, Times Bks) Random.

Middleton, Tim, jt. ed. see Giles, Judy.

Middleton, Tom. The Book of Maidenhead. 1977. 40.00 (*0-86023-006-6*) St Mut.

Middleton, Victor. Marketing in Travel & Tourism. 308p. 1988. pap. 29.95 (*0-434-91254-9*) Buttrwrth-Heinemann.

— Marketing in Travel & Tourism. 2nd ed. 308p. 1994. pap. 22.50 (*0-7506-0973-7*) Buttrwrth-Heinemann.

Middleton, W. E. Scientific Revolution. 96p. 1965. pap. 11. 95 (*0-87073-851-8*) Schenkman Bks Inc.

Middleton, W. E., tr. see Bouguer, Pierre.

Middleton, W. E. Knowles. The Experimenters: A Study of the Accademia del Cimento. LC 77-142816. (Illus.). 431p. (ITA.). reprint ed. pap. 122.90 (*0-8357-9271-4*, 2015692) Bks Demand.

Middleton, William. Manhattan Gateway. Drury, George, ed. (Illus.). (Orig.). Date not set. write for info. (*0-89024-177-5*) Kalmbach.

Middleton, William D. From Bullets to Bart. Carlson, Norman, ed. LC 88-70491. (Bulletin Ser.: No. 127). (Illus.). 176p. 1989. 35.00 (*0-915348-27-6*) Central Electric.

— The Time of the Trolley: The Street Railway from Horsecar to Light Rail, Vol. 1. LC 87-21112. (Illus.). 420p. 1987. 42.95 (*0-87095-098-3*) Gldn West Bks.

— Traction Classics: The High Speed & Deluxe Interurban Cars, Vol. 2. LC 83-18482. (Illus.). 230p. 1985. 38.95 (*0-87095-089-4*) Gldn West Bks.

Middleton, William D. & Lawson, Thomas L., eds. Anatomy & MRI of the Joints: A Multiplanar Atlas. (Illus.). 316p. 1989. text ed. 153.50 (*0-88167-455-9*) Raven.

Middleton, William E. The History of the Barometer. LC 64-10942. 511p. reprint ed. pap. 145.70 (*0-317-08446-1*, 2003887) Bks Demand.

— A History of the Theories of Rain & Other Forms of Precipitation. LC 66-15982. (Watts History of Science Library Ser.). 231p. reprint ed. pap. 65.90 (*0-317-26524-5*, 2024059) Bks Demand.

— A History of the Thermometer & Its Use in Meteorology. LC 66-23978. 262p. reprint ed. pap. 74.70 (*0-317-51975-1*, 2027376) Bks Demand.

— Invention of the Meteorological Instruments. LC 68-31640. (Illus.). 377p. reprint ed. pap. 107.50 (*0-317-41686-3*, 2025853) Bks Demand.

— Vision Through the Atmosphere. 264p. reprint ed. pap. 75.30 (*0-317-08955-2*, 2014366) Bks Demand.

***Middleton, William J.** It's about Time. 47p. 1994. pap. 4.00 (*1-886467-00-5*) WJM Press.

— Professor McGee's Solution. 31p. 1994. pap. 4.00 (*1-886467-01-3*) WJM Press.

***Middleton, William J. & Stanbrough, Harvey.** Partners in Rhyme: The Best of Bill Middleton & Harvey Stanbrough. 52p. (Orig.). Date not set. pap. 5.00 (*1-886467-05-6*) WJM Press.

***Middleton, William J. & Stanbrough, Harvey E.** Partners in Rhyme. 65p. 1995. pap. 7.50 (*1-886467-04-8*) WJM Press.

Middleton, William S. Values in Modern Medicine. LC 72-1379. (Illus.). 321p. reprint ed. pap. 91.50 (*0-8357-4751-4*, 2037673) Bks Demand.

Middleton, Katherine, jt. auth. see Hess, Mary A.

Midegeley, Magdelina. TRB Culture: The First Farmers of the North European Plain. (Illus.). 424p. 1992. text ed. 95.00 (*0-7486-0378-6*, Pub. by Edinburgh U Pr UK) Col U Pr.

Midelfort, H. C. Mad Princes of Renaissance Germany. LC 93-39116. (Studies in Early Modern German History). (Illus.). 224p. (C). 1994. 22.95 (*0-8139-1500-7*) U Pr of Va.

Midelfort, H. C., tr. see Blickle, Peter.

Midelfort, H. C. Erik, ed. see Moeller, Bernard.

Midelfort, H. Erik. Witch Hunting in Southwestern Germany, 1562-1684: The Social & Intellectual Foundations. LC 75-183891. 320p. 1972. 39.50 (*0-8047-0805-3*) Stanford U Pr.

***Midence, Kenny & Elander, James.** Sickle Cell Disease: A Psychosocial Approach. 1994. 39.95 (*1-870905-14-8*) Scovill Paterson.

Midford, Paul, jt. auth. see Youtz, David.

Midgaard, J. Norway, Brief History. (Tanum of Norway Tokens Ser.). 1989. pap. 32.50 (*82-03-16182-0*, N441) Vanous.

Midgeley, Magdelina. TRB Culture: The First Farmers of the North European Plain. (Illus.). 424p. 1992. 95.00 (*0-7486-0348-4*, Pub. by Edinburgh U Pr UK) Col U Pr.

Midgely, Derek & Torrance, Kenneth E. Potentiometric Water Analysis. 2nd ed. 586p. 1991. text ed. 195.00 (*0-471-92983-2*) Wiley.

Midgely, John. The Goodness of Beans. LC 92-13768. (Illus.). 1992. 12.00 (*0-679-41624-2*) Random.

— The Goodness of Garlic. LC 92-14507. (Illus.). 1992. 12. 00 (*0-679-41626-9*) Random.

— The Goodness of Olive Oil. LC 92-13767. 1992. 12.50 (*0-679-41627-7*) Random.

— The Goodness of Peppers. LC 93-4404. (Goodness of Ser.). 1993. 12.00 (*0-679-42680-9*) Random.

— The Goodness of Potatoes & Other Roots. LC 92-13766. 1992. 12.00 (*0-679-41625-0*) Random.

Midgett, Elwin W. Accounting Primer. 1968. pap. 3.50 (*0-451-62500-5*, Ment) NAL-Dutton.

An Asterisk (*) at the beginning of an entry indicates that the title is appearing in BIP for the first time.

Midgett, Matthew, ed. see Bulen, James A. & Bridgman, Charles.

Midgette, Nancy S. To Foster the Spirit of Professionalism: Southern Scientists & State Academies of Science. LC 91-7765. (History of American Science & Technology Ser.). 272p. (C). 1991. 32.50 (*0-8173-0549-1*) U of Ala Pr.

Midgley, Claire. Women Against Slavery: The British Campaigns 1780-1870. LC 91-45790. 256p. 1992. 69.95 (*0-415-06669-7*, A7889) Routledge.

Midgley, David, ed. The German Novel in the Twentieth Century: Beyond Realism. 207p. 1993. text ed. 49.95 (*0-312-10062-0*) St Martin.

Midgley, David A. Barron's How to Prepare for the College Board Achievement Test - CBAT: American History & Social Studies. 8th ed. 480p. 1990. Metric Converter. pap. 11.95 (*0-8120-4376-6*) Barron.

Midgley, David A. & Lefton, Phillip. How to Prepare for SAT II: American History & Social Studies. 9th ed. LC 93-5987. (SAT II: Subject Test Preparation Manuals Ser.). (YA). 1994. pap. 11.95 (*0-8120-1757-9*) Barron.

Midgley, Derek & Torrance, Kenneth. Potentiometric Water Analysis. LC 77-7213. 421p. reprint ed. pap. 120.00 (*0-685-20723-4*, 2030512) Bks Demand.

Midgley, E. B. The Ideology of Max Weber: A Thomist Critique. LC 82-16445. 182p. (C). 1983. text ed. 42.00 (*0-389-20343-2*, 07187) B&N Imports.

Midgley, Graham, ed. see Bunyan, John.

Midgley, J. R. Lawyers' Professional Liability. 208p. 1992. pap. write for info. (*0-7021-2675-6*, Pub. by Juta SA) W W Gaunt.

***Midgley, James.** Social Development. 192p. (C). 1995. 65.00 (*0-8039-7772-7*) Sage.

— Social Development. 192p. (C). 1995. pap. 21.95 (*0-8039-7773-5*) Sage.

Midgley, James & Glennerster, Howard, eds. The Radical Right & the Welfare State. 208p. (C). 1991. text ed. 59.00 (*0-389-20976-7*) B&N Imports.

Midgley, James, jt. auth. see Hardiman, Margaret.

Midgley, James, jt. ed. see Karger, Howard J.

Midgley, James, et al. Community Participation, Social Development & the State. 200p. 1986. 42.50 (*0-416-39820-0*, 1014); pap. 15.95 (*0-416-39830-8*, 1038) Routledge Chapman & Hall.

Midgley, Jane. The Women's Budget. (Illus.). 1987. 3.00 (*0-9506968-0-3*) WILPF.

Midgley, John. Culinary Herbs - Basil: A Sprig of Basil. (Illus.). 48p. 1994. 8.95 (*0-8212-2097-7*) Bulfinch Pr.

— Culinary Herbs - Coriander: A Sprig of Coriander. (Illus.). 48p. 1994. 8.95 (*0-8212-2098-5*) Bulfinch Pr.

— Culinary Herbs - Mint: A Sprig of Mint. (Illus.). 48p. 1994. 8.95 (*0-8212-2099-3*) Bulfinch Pr.

— Culinary Herbs - Parsley: A Sprig of Parsley. (Illus.). 48p. 1994. 8.95 (*0-8212-2096-9*) Bulfinch Pr.

— The Goodness of Grains. 1994. 12.00 (*0-679-43359-7*) Random.

— The Goodness of Vinegars. LC 93-48529. (Goodness of Ser.). (Illus.). 1994. 12.00 (*0-679-43360-0*) Random.

— 100 Fast Noodles. (Illus.). 160p. 1995. pap. 19.95 (*1-85793-573-X*, Pub. by Pavilion UK) Trafalgar.

— 100 Great Snacks. (Illus.). 144p. 1995. pap. 22.95 (*1-85793-222-6*, Pub. by Pavilion UK) Trafalgar.

Midgley, John, jt. auth. see Wood, Stephen.

Midgley, John M. & Midgley, Susan V. A Decision to Love: A Marriage Preparation Program. LC 92-80388. 144p. (Orig.). 1992. pap. 6.50 (*0-89622-514-3*) Twenty-Third.

Midgley, Jon, jt. auth. see Mays, Elaine.

Midgley, Leslie. How Many Words Do You Want? Richardson, Stewart, ed. 320p. 1989. 19.95 (*1-55972-015-8*, Birch Ln Pr) Carol Pub Group.

Midgley, Mary. Animals & Why They Matter. LC 83-17933. 160p. (C). 1984. 18.00 (*0-8203-0704-1*); pap. 10.00 (*0-8203-0756-4*) U of Ga Pr.

— Beast & Man: The Roots of Human Nature. LC 95-7506. 1995. 15.95 (*0-415-12740-8*) Routledge.

— Beast & Man: The Roots of the Human Nature. 400p. 1995. pap. 17.95 (*0-415-10445-9*, C0560) Routledge.

— Biological & Cultural Evolution. 23p. 1984. pap. 4.00 (*0-904674-08-8*, Pub. by Octagon Pr UK) ISHK Bk Service.

— Can't We Make Moral Judgements? (Mind Matters Ser.). 192p. (C). 1993. pap. text ed. 16.95 (*0-312-08726-8*) St Martin.

— The Ethical Primate: Humans, Freedom & Morality. LC 94-8485. 208p. 1994. 29.95 (*0-415-09530-1*, B0130) Routledge.

— Evolution As a Religion: Strange Hopes & Stranger Fears. 192p. 1986. pap. text ed. 12.95 (*0-416-39660-7*, 9513) Routledge Chapman & Hall.

— Science As Salvation: A Modern Myth & Its Meaning. LC 91-30984. 1992. 25.00 (*0-415-06271-3*, A7063) Routledge.

— Wickedness. 232p. 1986. pap. 9.95 (*0-7448-0053-6*, 0053W) Routledge Chapman & Hall.

— Wickedness: A Philosophical Essay. 208p. 1984. 35.00 (*0-7100-9759-X*, RKP) Routledge.

— Wisdom, Information & Wonder: What Is Knowledge For? 272p. 1989. 27.50 (*0-415-02829-9*) Routledge.

— Wisdom, Information & Wonder: What is Knowledge For? 272p. 1991. pap. 14.95 (*0-415-02830-2*, A5460) Routledge.

***Midgley, Michael.** Butterworths Taxation Library, 3 vols., Set. Date not set. ring bd. write for info. (*0-409-66128-7*, NZ) Butterworth Legal Pubs.

***Midgley, Michael & Andrew, Lee.** Butterworths Commercial Service, 2 vols., Set. Date not set. ring bd. write for info. (*0-409-68100-8*, NZ) Butterworth Legal Pubs.

Midgley, Peter. Urban Transport in Asia: An Operational Agenda for the 1990s. LC 93-20905. (Technical Paper, Asia Technical Department Ser.: No. 224). 110p. 1994. write for info. (*0-8213-2624-4*) World Bank.

Midgley, S. J., et al, eds. Casuarina Ecology, Management & Utilization: Proceedings of an International Workshop, Canberra, Australia 17-21 August 1981. (Illus.). 286p. (Orig.). 1983. pap. text ed. 35.00 (*0-643-03463-3*, Pub. by CSIRO AT) Intl Spec Bk.

Midgley, Susan V., jt. auth. see Midgley, John M.

Midhat, Ali H. The Life of Midhat Pasha. LC 73-6290. (Middle East Ser.). 1973. reprint ed. 24.95 (*0-405-05348-7*) Ayer.

MIDI Staff. Interactive Blues Jam for Keyboard. (Illus.). 1993. pap. 14.95 (*0-8256-1361-2*) Music Sales.

— Interactive Rock Jams for Keyboard. (Illus.). 1993. pap. 14.95 (*0-8256-1365-5*) Music Sales.

***Midkiff, Ruby B. & Thomasson, Rebecca D.** A Practical Approach to Using Learning Styles in Math Instruction. LC 93-5643. (Illus.). 132p. 1993. pap. 19.95 (*0-398-06289-7*) C C Thomas.

— A Practical Approach to Using Learning Styles in Math Instruction. LC 93-5643. (Illus.). 132p. (C). 1993. text ed. 34.95x (*0-398-05888-1*) C C Thomas.

Midlam, Don S. Flight of the Lucky Lady. (Illus.). 216p. 1954. 12.95 (*0-8323-0091-8*) Binford Mort.

Midlarksy, Elizabeth & Kahana, Eva. Altruism & the Elderly. (Library of Social Research: Vol. 196). 320p. 1994. 49.95 (*0-8039-2768-1*); pap. 24.00 (*0-8039-2769-X*) Sage.

Midlarsky & Vasquez. From Rivalry to Cooperation. (C). 1993. text ed. 21.50 (*0-06-501081-7*) HarpCollege.

Midlarsky, Manus I. The Onset of World War. (Studies in International Conflict: No. 1). 320p. (C). 1990. 55.00 (*0-04-497004-8*); pap. text ed. 19.95 (*0-04-497005-6*) Routledge Chapman & Hall.

Midlarsky, Manus I., ed. Handbook of War Studies. 352p. 1989. text ed. 55.00 (*0-04-497055-2*) Routledge Chapman & Hall.

— Handbook of War Studies. LC 92-46397. 372p. 1993. pap. text ed. 17.95 (*0-472-08224-8*) U of Mich Pr.

— Inequality & Contemporary Revolutions. (Monograph Series in World Affairs: Vol. 22, Bk. 2). (Illus.). 184p. (Orig.). 1986. pap. 9.95 (*0-87940-081-1*) Monograph Series.

— The Internationalization of Communal Strife. (Studies in International Conflict). (Illus.). 240p. 1992. 55.00 (*0-415-08408-3*, A7988) Routledge.

Midmore, Peter. Input-Output Models & the Agricultural Sector. 148p. 1991. text ed. 68.95 (*1-85628-223-6*, Pub. by Avebury Pub UK) Ashgate Pub Co.

Midolle, et al. Florid & Unusual Alphabets. LC 75-30175. (Pictorial Archive Ser.). 96p. 1976. reprint ed. pap. 6.95 (*0-486-23304-9*) Dover.

***Midroni & Bilbao.** Nerve Biopsy in Peripheral Neuropathy. 400p. 1995. 125.00 (*0-7506-9552-8*, Focal) Buttrwrth-Heinemann.

***Midura, Daniel W. & Glover, Donald R.** More Team Building Challenges. LC 95-8965. (Illus.). 128p. (Orig.). 1995. pap. write for info. (*0-87322-785-9*, BMID0785) Human Kinetics.

Midura, Daniel W., jt. auth. see Glover, Donald R.

Midura, Edmund M., ed. Blacks & Whites: The Urban Communication Crisis. LC 70-148676. Orig. Title: Why Aren't We Getting Through?. (Illus.). pap. 6.95 (*0-87491-316-0*) Acropolis.

Midwest Living Staff. Favorite Recipes from Great Midwest Cooks. 144p. 1992. 19.95 (*0-696-01978-7*) Meredith Bks.

— Midwest Living All-Time Best Recipes. 180p. 1994. 9.95 (*0-696-20225-5*) Meredith Bks.

— Midwest Living 20 Great Weekend Getaways: Favorite Driving Tours from the Editors of Midwest Living Magazine. 148p. 1994. pap. 11.95 (*0-696-20277-8*) Meredith Bks.

Midwest Plan Service Engineers Staff. Agricultural Sprinkler Irrigation Systems for Humid Regions. Midwest Plan Service Staff, ed. LC 93-48730. (Illus.). (Orig.). 1995. pap. write for info. (*0-89373-077-7*, MWPS-30) MidWest Plan Serv.

— Beef Housing & Equipment Handbook. 4th ed. MWPS Staff, ed. LC 85-28358. (Illus.). 1987. pap. 7.00 (*0-89373-068-8*, MWPS-6) MidWest Plan Serv.

— Conservation Tillage Systems & Management. LC 92-37291. (Illus.). (Orig.). 1992. pap. 15.00 (*0-89373-088-2*, MWPS-45) MidWest Plan Serv.

— Designs for Glued Trusses. 4th ed. LC 80-39547. (Illus.). 84p. 1981. pap. 7.00 (*0-89373-051-3*, MWPS-9) MidWest Plan Serv.

— Farm Buildings Wiring Handbook. 2nd ed. LC 91-21159. (Illus.). 63p. 1992. pap. 10.00 (*0-89373-085-8*, MWPS-28) MidWest Plan Serv.

— Farm Shop Plans Book. rev. ed. LC 94-38735. (Illus.). 32p. (Orig.). 1994. pap. 10.00 (*0-89373-091-2*, MWPS-26) MidWest Plan Serv.

— Grain Drying, Handling & Storage Handbook. 2nd ed. MWPS Staff, ed. LC 86-12751. (Illus.). 1987. pap. 7.00 (*0-89373-071-8*, MWPS-13) MidWest Plan Serv.

— Heating, Cooling & Tempering Air for Livestock Housing. LC 90-34153. 1991. 6.00 (*0-89373-076-9*, MWPS-34) MidWest Plan Serv.

— Home & Yard Improvements Handbook. LC 78-4505. (Illus.). 100p. 1978. pap. 9.00 (*0-89373-034-3*, MWPS-21) MidWest Plan Serv.

— Horse Housing & Equipment Handbook. (Illus.). 60p. 1971. pap. 7.00 (*0-89373-009-2*, MWPS-15) MidWest Plan Serv.

— Livestock Waste Facilities Handbook. 3rd ed. Church, Glenn A., II, ed. LC 93-7384. (Illus.). 112p. 1993. pap. 8.00 (*0-89373-089-0*, MWPS-18) MidWest Plan Serv.

— Low Temperature & Solar Grain Drying Handbook. LC 80-12869. (Illus.). 86p. 1980. pap. 6.00 (*0-89373-048-3*, MWPS-22) MidWest Plan Serv.

— Natural Ventilating Systems for Livestock Housing. Midwest Plan Service Staff, ed. LC 89-14544. (Illus.). 32p. 1989. pap. 5.00 (*0-89373-074-2*, MWPS-33) MidWest Plan Serv.

— Onsite Domestic Sewage Disposal Handbook. LC 81-18994. (Illus.). 40p. (Orig.). (C). 1982. pap. 6.00 (*0-89373-053-X*, MWPS-24) MidWest Plan Serv.

— Private Water Systems Handbook. 4th ed. LC 79-19040. (Illus.). 72p. 1979. pap. 7.00 (*0-89373-045-9*, MWPS-14) MidWest Plan Serv.

— Solar Livestock Housing Handbook. LC 82-20889. (Illus.). 88p. (Orig.). 1983. pap. 7.00 (*0-89373-056-4*, MWPS-23) MidWest Plan Serv.

— Structures & Environment Handbook. 11th rev. ed. LC 76-27983. (Illus.). 658p. 1987. pap. text ed. 25.00 (*0-89373-057-2*) MidWest Plan Serv.

— Swine Housing & Equipment Handbook. 4th ed. LC 82-2292. (Illus.). 112p. 1983. pap. 8.00 (*0-89373-054-8*, MWPS-8) MidWest Plan Serv.

Midwest Plan Service Personnel, ed. see Friday, William H., et al.

Midwest Plan Service Staff, jt. auth. see Bickert, W. G.

Midwest Plan Service Staff, ed. see Midwest Plan Service Engineers Staff.

Midwest Research Institute Staff. Development of Heat-Stable Electrocoating Resins with Improved Insulation Properties. 49p. 1970. 7.35 (*0-317-34512-5*, 170) Intl Copper.

— New Applications for Copper & Copper Compounds. 109p. 1974. 16.35 (*0-317-34538-9*, 229) Intl Copper.

— Studies to Evaluate the Potential for Improvements in Biological & Chemical Characteristics of Potable Water Transported in Copper Pipe. 26p. 1984. write for info. (*0-318-60414-0*) Intl Copper.

Midwestern Mechanics Conference Staff. Developments in Mechanics: Proceedings of the Midwestern Mechanics Conference, 7th, Michigan State University, 1961, Vol. 1. Lay, J. E. & Malvern, L. E., eds. LC 61-17719. 636p. reprint ed. pap. 180.00 (*0-317-09036-4*, 2019387) Bks Demand.

***Midwinter, A. & McVicar, M.** Size & Efficiency Debate: Public Library Authorities in a Time of Change. 90p. 1994. pap. 45.00 (*1-85604-148-4*, LAP1484, Pub. by Europ Com) UNIPUB.

Midwinter, Arthur & Monaghan, Claire. From Rates to Poll Tax: Local Government Finance in the Thatcher Era. 176p. 1993. text ed. 65.00 (*0-7486-0402-2*, Pub. by Edinburgh U Pr UK); pap. text ed. 30.00 (*0-7486-0403-0*, Pub. by Edinburgh U Pr UK) Col U Pr.

Midwinter, Eric. The Development of Social Welfare in Britain. LC 93-21335. (C). 1994. 79.00 (*0-335-19105-3*, Open Univ Pr); pap. 23.00 (*0-335-19104-5*, Open Univ Pr) Taylor & Francis.

Midwinter, J. E. & Guo, Y. L. Optoelectronics & Lightwave Technology. 300p. 1992. text ed. 89.95 (*0-471-92934-4*) Wiley.

Midwinter, J. E., et al, eds. Optical Technology & Wideband Local Networks. (Royal Society Discussion Ser.). (C). 1991. 69.95 (*0-521-39004-4*) Cambridge U Pr.

Midwinter, John E. Optical Fibers for Transmission. LC 91-4636. 428p. 1992. reprint ed. 66.50 (*0-89464-595-1*) Krieger.

Midwinter, John E., ed. Photonics in Switching, 2 vols., Set. LC 92-38764. (Quantum Electronics - Principles & Applications Ser.). (Illus.). 352p. 1993. 139.90 (*0-12-496050-2*) Acad Pr.

— Photonics in Switching, 2 vols., Vol. 1. LC 92-38764. (Quantum Electronics - Principles & Applications Ser.). (Illus.). 374p. 1993. text ed. 69.95 (*0-12-496051-0*) Acad Pr.

— Photonics in Switching, 2 vols., Vol. 2. LC 92-38764. (Quantum Electronics - Principles & Applications Ser.). (Illus.). 352p. 1993. text ed. 69.95 (*0-12-496052-9*) Acad Pr.

Midwinter, John E., jt. ed. see Hinton, H. Scott.

Midwinter, John E., jt. auth. see Zernike, Frits.

Midwood, Barton A. Bennett's Angel. Plimpton, George, ed. 224p. 1989. 17.95 (*0-945167-15-6*) British Amer Pub.

Miech, Marilyn, jt. auth. see McClay, Shirley Atwater.

Miech, R. J. Calculus with MathCAD. 183p. (C). 1991. pap. 27.95 (*0-534-15481-6*) PWS Pubs.

Miechenbau. Stress Inoculation Training. (Practitioner Guidebook Ser.). (C). 1985. pap. 19.95 (*0-205-14418-7*, H4418, Longwood Div) Allyn.

Mieczkowski, Bogdan. Dysfunctional Bureaucracy: A Comparative & Historical Perspective. 312p. (Orig.). (C). 1991. lib. bdg. 51.00 (*0-8191-8393-8*); pap. text ed. 24.00 (*0-8191-8394-6*) U Pr of Amer.

— The Rot at the Top: Dysfunctional Bureaucracy in Academia. 252p. (Orig.). (C). 1995. lib. bdg. 44.50 (*0-8191-9844-7*); pap. text ed. 29.50 (*0-8191-9845-5*) U Pr of Amer.

— Social Services for Women in Eastern Europe. (ASN Series in Issues Studies (U. S. S. R. & East Europe): No. 3). 128p. (Orig.). (C). 1982. pap. 9.50 (*0-910895-00-7*) Assn Study Nat.

— Transportation in Eastern Europe. (East European Monographs: No. 38). 240p. 1978. text ed. 47.00 (*0-914710-31-1*) East Eur Quarterly.

Mieczkowski, Bogdan, ed. Eastern European Transportation: Systems & Modes. (Developments in Transportation Studies: No. 2). 366p. 1980. lib. bdg. 87.50 (*90-247-2390-6*) Kluwer Ac.

Mieczkowski, Bogdan & Zinam, Oleg. Bureaucracy, Technology, Ideology: Quality of Life East & West. LC 84-71093. (Issue Studies (U. S. S. R. & East Europe): No. 5). 463p. (Orig.). 1984. pap. 28.00 (*0-910895-02-3*) Assn Study Nat.

Mieczkowski, Thomas M. Drugs, Crime, & Social Policy. 416p. (C). 1991. pap. text ed. 48.00 (*0-205-13205-7*) Allyn.

***Miedema, MaeJean.** The Mystery Flag. (Wee Write Bks.: No. 16). (Illus.). 33p. (J). (ps-3). 1995. 32.95 (*1-884987-53-2*); lib. bdg. 17.95 (*1-884987-51-6*); pap. 7.95 (*1-884987-52-4*) WeWrite.

Miedema, Rienk & Mermut, Ahmed R., eds. Annotated Bibliography on Soil Micromorphology, 1968-1986. 250p. (Orig.). 1990. pap. text ed. 50.00 (*0-85198-681-1*) CAB Intl.

***Miedema, Siebren, et al, eds.** The Politics of Human Science. 229p. 1995. pap. 19.95 (*90-5487-095-8*) Paul & Co Pubs.

Mieder, Wolfgang. As Sweet As Apple Cider: Vermont Expressions. LC 88-12464. (Illus.). 72p. (Orig.). 1988. pap. 5.95 (*0-933050-58-5*) New Eng Pr VT.

— Howl Like a Wolf: Animal Proverbs. LC 93-86688. (Illus.). 95p. (Orig.). 1993. pap. 6.95 (*1-881535-08-8*) New Eng Pr VT.

— International Proverb Scholarship: An Annotated Bibliography, Supplement I, 1800-1981. LC 90-3049. (Folklore Bibliographies Ser.: Vol. 15). 454p. 1990. 54.00 (*0-8240-4037-6*, 1230) Garland.

— International Proverb Scholarship: An Annotated Bibliography Supplement II, 1982-1991. LC 90-3049. (Folklore Bibliographies Ser.: Vol. 20). 959p. 1993. 95.00 (*0-8153-1133-8*, H1655) Garland.

— Love: Proverbs of the Heart. LC 89-63662. (Illus.). 80p. (Orig.). 1989. pap. 6.95 (*0-933050-63-1*) New Eng Pr VT.

— Not By Bread Alone: Proverbs of the Bible. LC 90-63099. (Illus.). 80p. (Orig.). 1990. pap. 6.95 (*0-933050-86-0*) New Eng Pr VT.

— Prentice Hall Encyclopedia of World Proverbs. 1993. pap. 18.95 (*0-13-556218-X*) P-H.

— The Prentice-Hall Encyclopedia of World Proverbs: A Treasury of Wit & Wisdom. 1986. 34.95 (*0-13-695586-X*) P-H.

— Proverbs Are Never Out of Season: Popular Wisdom in the Modern Age. LC 92-25051. (Illus.). 304p. 1993. 25.00 (*0-19-507728-8*) OUP.

— Salty Wisdom: Proverbs of the Sea. LC 90-52966. (Illus.). 64p. (Orig.). 1990. pap. 6.95 (*0-933050-82-8*) New Eng Pr VT.

— Talk Less & Say More: Vermont Proverbs. LC 86-50974. (Illus.). 64p. (Orig.). 1986. pap. 6.95 (*0-933050-42-9*) New Eng Pr VT.

— Tradition & Innovation in Folk Literature. LC 86-21206. (Illus.). 315p. 1987. text ed. 35.00 (*0-87451-387-1*) U Pr of New Eng.

— Yankee Wisdom: New England Proverbs. LC 89-61223. (Illus.). 72p. (Orig.). 1989. pap. text ed. 6.95 (*0-933050-73-9*) New Eng Pr VT.

Mieder, Wolfgang, comp. Wise Words: Essays on the Proverb. LC 94-3960. (Folklore Casebooks Ser.: Vol. 6). 608p. 1994. 75.00 (*0-8153-0942-2*, H1638) Garland.

Mieder, Wolfgang, ed. Disenchantments: An Anthology of Modern Fairy Tale Poetry. LC 84-40592. (Illus.). 221p. 1985. pap. 13.95 (*0-87451-440-1*) U Pr of New Eng.

***Mieder, Wolfgang & Bryan, George B., eds.** The Proverbial Winston S. Churchill: An Index to Proverbs in the Works of Sir Winston Churchill. LC 95-2464. (Bibliographies & Indexes in World History: Vol. 38). 448p. 1995. text ed. 79.50 (*0-313-29433-X*, Greenwood Pr) Greenwood.

Mieder, Wolfgang & Dundes, Alan, eds. The Wisdom of Many: Essays on the Proverb. LC 94-16235. 346p. 1994. reprint ed. 45.00 (*0-299-14360-0*); reprint ed. pap. 19.95 (*0-299-14364-3*) U of Wis Pr.

Mieder, Wolfgang & Kingsbury, Stewart A., eds. A Dictionary of Wellerisms. 208p. 1994. 24.95 (*0-19-508318-0*) OUP.

Mieder, Wolfgang, jt. ed. see Bryan, George B.

Mieder, Wolfgang, tr. see Von Ebner-Eschenbach, Marie.

Mieder, Wolfgang, et al, eds. Dictionary of American Proverbs. 736p. 1991. 55.00 (*0-19-505399-0*) OUP.

Miedzian, Myriam. Boys Will Be Boys: Breaking the Link Between Masculinity & Violence. 1992. mass mkt. 10.00 (*0-385-42254-7*, Anchor NY) Doubleday.

Miedzinski, Charles. The In-Between World of Paul Klee. LC 88-6068. (Illus.). 28p. (Orig.). 1988. pap. 7.95 (*0-918471-13-3*) San Fran MOMA.

Miedzyrzecka, Daniela, tr. see Kott, Jan.

Miege, Bernard. The Capitalization of Cultural Production. 168p. 1989. pap. 13.95 (*0-88477-025-7*) Intl General.

***Mieghem, Timothy V.** Implementing Supplier Partnerships: How to Lower Costs & Improve Service. 1994. 69.95 (*0-13-180365-4*) P-H.

Miehe, Georg. Langtang Himal. Flora & Vegetation Als Klimaanzeiger & - Zeugen Im Himalaya. a Prodromus of the Vegetation Ecology of the Himalayas. (Dissertationes Botanicae Ser.: Vol. 158). 530p. (ENG & GER.). 1990. lib. bdg. 155.00 (*3-443-64070-2*, Pub. by Cramer-Borntraeger GW) Lubrecht & Cramer.

Miehe, Georg. Vegetationsgeographische Untersuchungen im Dhaulagiri-und Annapurna-Himalaya, 2 vols. (Dissertationes Botanicae Ser.: No. 66). (Illus.). 500p. 1982. lib. bdg. 90.00 (*3-7682-1356-0*) Lubrecht & Cramer.

Miehe, Patrick K., comp. The Robert Lowell Papers at the Houghton Library, Harvard University: A Guide to the Collection. LC 90-45082. (Bibliographies & Indexes in American Literature Ser.: No. 12). 240p. 1990. text ed. 85.00 (*0-313-27692-7*, HLW, Greenwood Pr) Greenwood.

Miehe, Sabine. Vegetation Ecology of the Jebel Marra Massif in the Semiarid Sudan. (Dissertationes Botanicae Ser.: Vol. 113). (Illus.). 208p. 1988. pap. text ed. 84.50 (*3-443-64025-7*) Lubrecht & Cramer.

Miehm, Grant, jt. auth. see Verheiden, Mark.

An Asterisk (*) at the beginning of an entry indicates that the title is appearing in BIP for the first time.

Miel, Alice, et al. Individualizing Reading Practices. LC 58-8337. (Practical Suggestions for Teaching Ser.: No. 14). 101p. reprint ed. pap. 28.80 (*0-8357-2761-0*, 2039886) Bks Demand.

Miel, Jan. Pascal & Theology. LC 75-93822. 236p. reprint ed. pap. 67.30 (*0-318-34949-3*, 2030746) Bks Demand.

Mielants, H. & Veys, E. M., eds. Spondylarthropathies: Involvement of the Gut: Proceedings of the First Conference, Ghent, September 10-13, 1986. (International Congress Ser.: No. 720). 456p. 1987. 149.75 (*0-444-80894-9*) Elsevier.

Mielczarek, Eugenie V., et al, eds. Biological Physics. LC 93-3280. (Key Papers in Physics). 1993. write for info. (*0-88318-855-4*) Am Inst Physics.

Mields, Hugh. Federally Assisted New Communities: New Dimensions in Urban Development. LC 73-78874. (Urban Land Institute, ULI Landmark Report Ser.). 287p. reprint ed. pap. 81.80 (*0-317-20035-6*, 2023242) Bks Demand.

Miele, A. Flight Mechanics: Theory of Flight Paths. 1962. 175.00 (*0-08-009722-7*, Pub. by Pergamon Repr UK) Franklin.

Miele, A. & Salvetti, A., eds. Applied Mathematics in Aerospace Science & Engineering. (Mathematical Concepts & Methods in Science & Engineering Ser.: Vol. 44). (Illus.). 500p. (C). 1994. 110.00 (*0-306-44754-1*, Plenum Pr) Plenum.

Miele, Mark. The Dumbbell Book: Fitness Without a Gym. 112p. 1992. pap. 11.95 (*1-880680-01-7*) Sand Dllr Fl.

Mieli, Aldo. Science Arabe & Son Role Dans l'Evolution Scientifique Mondiale. (Medieval Studies Reprint Ser.). (FRE.). reprint ed. lib. bdg. 44.00 (*0-697-00044-3*) Irvington.

Mielke, A. Hamiltonian & Lagrangian Flows on Center Manifolds: With Applications to Elliptic Variational Problems. Dold, A. et al, eds. (Lecture Notes in Mathematics Ser.: Vol. 1489). (Illus.). x, 140p. 1991. pap. 24.00 (*0-387-54710-X*) Spr-Verlag.

Mielke, A., jt. auth. see Kirchgassner, K.

***Mielke, Arthur J.** Christians, Feminists, & the Culture of Pornography. 154p. (C). 1994. lib. bdg. 44.00 (*0-8191-9764-5*); pap. text ed. 28.50 (*0-8191-9765-3*) U Pr of Amer.

Mielke, Bruce. Integrated Computer Graphics. Westby, ed. 419p. (C). 1991. text ed. 65.25 (*0-314-78431-4*) West Pub.

Mielke, Dan & Holstedt, Peggy. Alcohol & Drug Abuse Prevention Education in Oregon: K-12 Infused Lesson Guide. (Illus.). 762p. (Orig.). (C). 1993. pap. text ed. 49.95 (*0-7881-0081-5*) Diane Pub.

***Mielke, Dee.** The Unseen Scars. 1995. 8.95 (*0-8062-5182-4*) Carlton.

Mielke, Howard. Patterns of Life: Biogeography of a Changing World. (Illus.). 370p. 1989. 75.00 (*0-04-574032-1*); pap. 29.95 (*0-04-574033-X*) Routledge Chapman & Hall.

Mielke, James H., jt. ed. see Crawford, Michael H.

Mielke, James H., jt. auth. see Gilbert, Robert I., Jr.

Mielke, Judy. Native Plants for Southwestern Landscapes. LC 93-12092. (Illus.). 384p. (Orig.). (C). 1993. text ed. 39.95 (*0-292-75553-8*); pap. 22.95 (*0-292-75147-8*) U of Tex Pr.

Mielke, K. L., jt. auth. see Adler, N. W.

Mielke, Robert. The Riddle of the Painful Earth: Suffering & Society in W. D. Howell's Major Writings of the Early 1890's. (Illus.). 214p. (Orig.). 1994. lib. bdg. 57.00 (*0-943549-16-7*) TJU Pr.

Mielnik, Edward M. Metalworking Science & Engineering. 1991. text ed. write for info. (*0-07-041904-3*); Solutions manual. text ed. write for info. (*0-07-041905-1*) McGraw.

Mielziner, Moses. Introduction to the Talmud. 4th ed. LC 68-29908. 1969. reprint ed. 27.50 (*0-8197-0156-4*); reprint ed. pap. 16.95 (*0-8197-0015-0*) Bloch.

Mier, jt. auth. see Atkins.

Mier, Avinoam, jt. auth. see Stern, Eliahu.

Mier, J. G., et al. Fracture Processes in Concrete, Rock & Ceramics: Proceedings of the International RILEM-ESIS Conference. 1100p. 1991. write for info. (*0-412-43080-0*, E & FN Spon) Routledge Chapman & Hall.

Mier-Jedrzejowicz, Wlodek. Extend Your HP-41. (Illus.). 670p. (Orig.). (C). 1985. pap. 26.95 (*0-9510733-0-3*, 621) EduCALC Pubns.

— Tips & Programs for the HP-32S. (Illus.). 81p. (Orig.). (C). 1988. pap. text ed. 7.95 (*0-937637-05-X*, 2014) EduCALC Pubns.

Mier, Paul D. & Van de Kerkhof, Peter C., eds. Textbook of Psoriasis. LC 85-16669. (Illus.). 292p. 1986. text ed. 156.00 (*0-443-03210-6*) Churchill.

***Mier, R. J. & Brower, T. J.** Pediatric Orthopedics: A Guide for the Primary Care Physician. (Critical Issues in Developmental & Behavioral Pediatrics Ser.). (Illus.). 317p. 1994. 45.00 (*0-306-44796-7*, Plenum Med Bk) Plenum.

Mier, Robert. Social Justice & Local Development Policy. (Illus.). 256p. 1993. 49.95 (*0-8039-4947-2*); pap. 24.00 (*0-8039-4948-0*) Sage.

Mier, Robert, jt. auth. see Bingham, Richard D.

Mierhof, Annette. The Dried Flower Book: Growing, Picking, Drying Arranging. (Illus.). 96p. 1981. pap. 13.50 (*0-525-47700-4*, Dutton) NAL-Dutton.

Miermont, Jacques. A Dictionary of Family Therapy. Jenkins, Hugh, ed. Turner, Chris, tr. (Illus.). 600p. (C). 1994. text ed. 95.00 (*0-631-17048-0*) Blackwell Pubs.

Miernyk, William H. Elements of Input-Output Analysis. (Orig.). 1965. pap. text ed. write for info. (*0-394-30393-8*) Random.

— Illusions of Conventional Economics. 185p. 1982. 18.00 (*0-937058-14-9*) West Va U Pr.

Miers, Charles, ed. The New York City Marathon: Twenty Five Years, 1969-1994. LC 94-10396. 176p. 1994. 35.00 (*0-8478-1815-2*) Rizzoli Intl.

Miers, David. Compensation for Criminal Injuries. 1990. U.K. text ed. 90.00 (*0-406-12324-1*) Butterworth Legal Pubs.

Miers, David, jt. auth. see Twining, William.

Miers, Earl S. Lincoln Day-by-Day. 1988. 45.00 (*0-89029-542-5*) Morningside Bkshop.

— The Web of Victory: Grant at Vicksburg. LC 84-9717. (Illus.). 320p. 1984. pap. 11.95 (*0-8071-1199-6*) La State U Pr.

Miers, Earl S. & Ellis, Richard, eds. Bookmaking & Kindred Amenities. LC 70-80392. (Essay Index Reprint Ser.). 1977. 20.95 (*0-8369-1045-1*) Ayer.

Miers, Earl S., jt. auth. see Angle, Paul.

Miers, Earl S., ed. see LeConte, Emma.

Miers, Horst E. Lexikon des Geheimwissens. (GER.). 125.00 (*0-8288-7901-X*, M7214) Fr & Eur.

— Lexikon des Geheimwissens. deluxe ed. (GER.). 125.00 (*3-7626-0028-7*, M-7214) Fr & Eur.

Miers, John. Travels in Chili & La Plata, 2 Vols, Set. LC 76-128416. reprint ed. 115.00 (*0-404-04317-8*) AMS Pr.

Miers, Richenda. Scotland: Highlands & Islands. 4th ed. (Cadogan Guides Ser.). (Illus.). 512p. 1994. pap. 17.95 (*1-56440-461-7*) Globe Pequot.

— Scotland: Highlands & Islands. (Cadogan Guides Ser.). (Illus.). 320p. 1994. pap. 14.95 (*0-947754-86-5*) Globe Pequot.

Miers, Suzanne & Kopytoff, Igor, eds. Slavery in Africa: Historical & Anthropological Perspectives. LC 76-53653. (Illus.). 494p. 1977. 35.00 (*0-299-07330-0*) U of Wis Pr.

— Slavery in Africa: Historical & Anthropological Perspectives. LC 76-53653. (Illus.). 494p. 1979. pap. 16.50 (*0-299-07334-3*) U of Wis Pr.

Miers, Suzanne & Roberts, Richard L., eds. End of Slavery in Africa. LC 88-40192. 448p. 1988. pap. text ed. 16.95 (*0-299-11554-2*) U of Wis Pr.

Miers, Suzanne, jt. ed. see Jaschok, Maria.

Mierse, William E., jt. auth. see Hanfmann, George M.

Mierswa, Richard, jt. auth. see Mierswa, Ruth.

Mierswa, Ruth & Mierswa, Richard. Ray-Centered Astrology. LC 84-90404. 1986. 16.00 (*0-87212-185-2*) Libra.

Mierzecki, R. The Historical Development of Chemical Concepts. 296p. (C). 1991. lib. bdg. 154.50 (*0-7923-0915-4*) Kluwer Ac.

Mierzejewski, Alfred C. The Collapse of the German War Economy, 1944-1945: Allied Air Power & the German National Railway. LC 88-4777. xxi, 285p. (C). 1988. 39.95 (*0-8078-1792-9*) U of NC Pr.

Mierzejewski, D. L. Fundamentals of Chemistry. (Illus.). 410p. 1982. ring bd. 149.50 (*0-87683-212-5*) GP Pub.

Mierzwa, Joseph W. The Twenty-First Century Family Legal Guide. 448p. 1994. pap. 19.95 (*0-9637285-0-4*) Prose Assocs.

Mies, Maria. Patriarchy & Accumulation on a World Scale: Women in the International Division of Labour. 260p. (C). 1986. text ed. 49.95 (*0-86232-341-X*, Pub. by Zed Books UK); pap. 17.50 (*0-86232-342-8*, Pub. by Zed Books UK) Humanities.

Mies, Maria & Shiva, Vandana. Ecofeminism: Reconnecting a Divided World. 288p. (C). 1993. text ed. 55.00 (*1-85649-155-2*, Pub. by Zed Books UK); pap. 19.95 (*1-85649-156-0*, Pub. by Zed Books UK) Humanities.

Mies, Paul. Beethoven's Sketches: An Analysis of His Style Based on a Study of His Sketch-Books. 198p. 1990. reprint ed. lib. bdg. 59.00 (*0-7812-9044-9*) Rprt Serv.

Miescher, P A., jt. ed. see Muller-Eberhard, H. J.

***Miescher, Peter A., ed.** Systemic Lupus Erythematosus. LC 95-1128. 240p. 1995. 92.00 (*0-387-59039-0*) Spr-Verlag.

Miescke, Lori. Christian Crafts from Construction Paper. (Christian Craft Ser.). 64p. (J). (ps-5). 1992. 8.95 (*0-86653-707-4*, SS2843, Shining Star Pubns) Good Apple.

Miesel, Sandra. Against Time's Arrow: The High Crusade of Poul Anderson. LC 78-14913. (Milford Series: Popular Writers of Today: Popular Writers of Today: Vol. 18). 64p. 1978. lib. bdg. 20.00 (*0-89370-124-6*); pap. 10.00 (*0-89370-224-2*) Borgo Pr.

Miesel, Victor. Ludwig Meidner: An Expressionist Master. (Illus.). 71p. 1978. pap. 6.00 (*0-912303-16-6*) Michigan Mus.

Miesel, William P. The Creative Card Magic of William P. Miesel. LC 80-80275. (Illus.). 178p. 1980. 20.00 (*0-9604016-0-1*) Unikorn Magik.

Miesen, Bere M., jt. ed. see Jones, Gemma M.

Miesse, Frank. Chinese Herbs Made Easy. 20p. pap. 2.95 (*0-913923-64-8*) Woodland UT.

Miessler, Gary L. & Tarr, Donald A. Inorganic Chemistry. 480p. 1991. text ed. 77.00 (*0-13-465659-8*) P-H.

Miessner, B. F. On the Early History of Radio Guidance. (Illus.). 1964. 7.50 (*0-911302-00-X*) San Francisco Pr.

Mieszkowski, Gretchen. The Reputation of Criseyde, 1155-1500. (Connecticut Academy of Arts & Sciences Ser., Trans.: Vol. 43). 1971. pap. 39.50 (*0-685-22886-X*) Elliots Bks.

Mieszkowski, Peter & Straszheim, Mahlon, eds. Current Issues in Urban Economics. LC 78-14947. 605p. reprint ed. pap. 172.50 (*0-7837-4780-2*, 2044535) Bks Demand.

Mieszkowski, Peter, jt. ed. see McLure, Charles E., Jr.

Mieth, Dietmar & Cahill, Lisa S., eds. Migrants & Refugees: The Moral Challenge. (Concilium Ser.). 1993. write for info. (*0-88344-873-4*) Orbis Bks.

Mieth, Dietmar, jt. ed. see Cahill, Lisa S.

Miethe, Terance D. & Meier, Robert F. Crime & Its Social Context: Toward an Integrated Theory of Offenders, Victims, & Situations. LC 93-24503. (SUNY Series in Deviance & Social Control). 209p. 1994. 57.50x (*0-7914-1901-0*); pap. 18.95x (*0-7914-1902-9*) State U NY Pr.

Miethe, Terry & Flew, Antony G. Does God Exist? A Believer & an Atheist Debate. LC 91-70040. 224p. (Orig.). 1991. pap. 12.95 (*0-06-065579-8*) Harper SF.

Miethe, Terry & Habermas, Gary. Why Believe? God Exists: Rethinking the Case for God & Christianity. (C). 1993. 16.99 (*0-89900-608-6*) College Pr Pub.

Miethe, Terry L. Augustinian Bibliography, 1970-1980: With Essays on the Fundamentals of Augustinian Scholarship. LC 82-6173. xxiii, 218p. 1982. text ed. 59.95 (*0-313-22629-6*, MIA/, Greenwood Pr) Greenwood.

— Compact Dictionary of Doctrinal Words. LC 88-12161. 224p. (Orig.). 1988. reprint ed. pap. 8.99 (*0-87123-678-8*, 210678) Bethany Hse.

Miethe, Terry L. & Bourke, Vernon J., comps. Thomistic Bibliography, 1940-1978. LC 80-1195. xxii, 318p. 1980. text ed. 49.95 (*0-313-21991-5*, MTH/, Greenwood Pr) Greenwood.

Miettinen, Asko, jt. auth. see Donckels, Rik.

Miettinen, Jukka O. Classical Dance & Theatre in South-East Asia. (Illus.). 200p. 1993. 75.00 (*0-19-588595-3*) OUP.

Miettinen, Olli S. Theoretical Epidemiology: Principles of Occurrence Research in Medicine. LC 85-3697. 354p. 1985. text ed. 48.50 (*0-8273-4313-2*) Delmar.

Mietzer, Dick. The Subsidized Muse: Public Support for the Arts in the United States. (Modern Revivals in Economics Ser.). 300p. 1993. 59.95 (*0-7512-0142-1*, Pub. by Gregg Pub UK) Ashgate Pub Co.

Mieville, Claudia, tr. see Guarnieri, Patrizia.

Miewald, Robert D., ed. Nebraska Government & Politics. LC 83-3684. (State Politics & Government Ser.). xiv, 230p. 1984. 21.00 (*0-8032-3078-8*); pap. 12.95 (*0-8032-8113-7*) U of Nebr Pr.

Miewald, Robert D. & Longo, Peter J. The Nebraska State Constitution: A Reference Guide. LC 92-21359. (Reference Guides to the State Constitutions of the United States Ser.: No. 13). 240p. 1993. text ed. 65.00 (*0-313-27947-0*, MNG, Greenwood Pr) Greenwood.

Miewald, Robert D. & Steinman, Michael, eds. Problems in Administrative Reform. LC 83-15399. (Illus.). 280p. 1984. 34.95 (*0-88229-747-3*) Nelson-Hall.

Miezitis, S. Creating Alternatives to Depression: Assessment, Intervention, & Prevention. LC 91-861. (Illus.). 448p. 1992. pap. text ed. 37.00 (*0-88937-039-7*) Hogrefe & Huber Pubs.

Miezo, Peggy M. Parenting Children with Disabilities. 1983. 49.75 (*0-8247-1090-8*) Phoenix Soc.

Miffleton, Jack. Sunday's Child: A Planning Guide for Liturgies with Both Children & Adults. 64p. (Orig.). 1989. pap. 7.50 (*0-912405-62-7*) Pastoral Pr.

Mifflin, R., jt. ed. see Lemarechale, C.

Mifflin, Ray, jt. auth. see Weeks-Mifflin, Mary.

Mifflin, Theodore E., et al. Diagnostic Molecular Biology. 1992. text ed. 47.50 (*0-07-041933-7*) McGraw.

Miflin, B. J. Oxford Surveys of Plant Molecular Biology, Vol. 7. (Illus.). 342p. 1991. pap. 50.00 (*0-19-857750-8*) OUP.

Miflin, B. J., ed. Oxford Surveys of Plant Molecular & Cell Biology, Vol. 1. (Illus.). (Orig.). 1985. pap. 45.00 (*0-19-854151-1*) OUP.

— Oxford Surveys of Plant Molecular & Cell Biology, Vol. 3: 1986. (Illus.). 482p. (Orig.). 1987. pap. 45.00 (*0-19-854202-X*) OUP.

— Oxford Surveys of Plant Molecular & Cell Biology, Vol. 5: 1988. (Illus.). 224p. (Orig.). 1989. pap. 45.00 (*0-19-854238-0*) OUP.

— Oxford Surveys of Plant Molecular & Cell Biology, Vol. 6: 1989. (Illus.). 322p. 1990. pap. 45.00 (*0-19-857735-4*) OUP.

Miflin, B. J. & Miflin, H. F., eds. Oxford Surveys of Plant Molecular & Cell Biology, Vol. 4: 1987. (Illus.). 380p. (Orig.). 1988. pap. 45.00 (*0-19-854233-X*) OUP.

Miflin, B. J., et al, eds. The Biochemistry of Plants Vol. 16: A Comprehensive Treatise, Intermediary Nitrogen Metabolism. 402p. 1990. text ed. 160.00 (*0-12-675416-0*) Acad Pr.

Miflin, H. F., jt. ed. see Miflin, B. J.

Mifsud, Alfred. Knights Hospitallers of the Venerable Tongue of England in Malta. LC 78-63348. (Crusades & Military Orders Ser.: Second Series). (Illus.). reprint ed. 59.50 (*0-404-17009-9*) AMS Pr.

***Mifsud, Manwel.** Loan Verbs in Maltese: A Descriptive & Comparative Study. LC 94-43608. (Studies in Semitic Languages & Linguistics: Vol. 21). 1994. 92.75 (*90-04-10091-1*) E J Brill.

Migaki, George, jt. ed. see Montali, Richard J.

Migaki, George, jt. ed. see Ribelin, William E.

Migala, Joseph. Polish Radio Broadcasting in the United States. 320p. 1987. text ed. 42.00 (*0-88033-112-7*, 216) East Eur Quarterly.

Migan, Helen. Nell's Story of Long Ago. LC 92-84106. 60p. (J). (gr. 2-6). 1993. pap. 5.95 (*1-55523-593-X*) Winston-Derek.

Migas, Abraham I. Kevod Elohim. 1979. 30.95 (*0-405-12616-6*) Ayer.

***Migdail, Karen I. & Youngs, Maralee, eds.** 1995 Medical Quality Management Sourcebook. 524p. 1994. 145.00 (*1-881393-32-1*) Faulkner & Gray.

Migdal, A. B. Qualitative Methods in Quantum Theory. Leggett, Anthony J., tr. (Advanced Book Classics Ser.). 1977. 29.95 (*0-685-42004-3*, Adv Bk Prog) Addison-Wesley.

Migdal, A. B., tr. see Krylov, Nikolai S.

Migdal, Arkadii B. & Krainov, Vladimir P. Approximation Methods of Quantum Mechanics. Schensted, Irene V., tr. 150p. 1968. 6.00 (*0-911014-06-3*) Neo Pr.

Migdal, Joel, jt. auth. see Kimmerling, Baruch.

Migdal, Joel S. Palestinian Society & Politics. LC 79-84002. (Center for International Affairs at Harvard University Ser.). 1980. 45.00 (*0-691-07615-4*) Princeton U Pr.

— Peasants, Politics, & Revolution: Pressures Toward Political & Social Change in the Third World. LC 74-2972. 368p. 1974. pap. 16.95 (*0-691-02177-5*) Princeton U Pr.

— Peasants, Politics, & Revolution: Pressures Toward Political & Social Change in the Third World. LC 74-2972. 311p. reprint ed. pap. 88.70 (*0-8357-7889-4*, 2036308) Bks Demand.

— Strong Societies & Weak States: State-Society Relations & State Capabilities in the Third World. (Illus.). 344p. 1988. 49.50 (*0-691-05669-2*); pap. 14.95 (*0-691-01073-0*) Princeton U Pr.

Migdal, Joel S., jt. auth. see Kimmerling, Baruch.

Migdal, Joel S., et al. Palestinian Society & Politics. LC 79-84002. 308p. reprint ed. pap. 87.80 (*0-8357-2553-7*, 2040244) Bks Demand.

Migdal, Joel S., et al, eds. State Power & Social Forces: Domination & Transformation in the Third World. LC 93-48757. (Studies in Comparative Politics). 320p. (C). 1994. pap. 19.95 (*0-521-46734-9*) Cambridge U Pr.

— State Power & Social Forces: Domination & Transformation in the Third World. LC 93-48757. (Studies in Comparative Politics). 320p. (C). 1994. 59.95 (*0-521-46166-9*) Cambridge U Pr.

Migdal, S., ed. see Hughes, R.

Migdal, S., jt. ed. see Hughes, R.

Migdal, Sy, jt. auth. see Stallone, James.

Migdalski, E. C. & Fichter, G. S. Fresh & Salt Water Fishes of the World. (Illus.). 320p. 1990. 17.99 (*0-517-41670-0*) Random Hse Value.

Migdalski, Edward C. The Inquisitive Angler. 1991. 27.95 (*1-55821-132-2*) Lyons & Burford.

Migdoll, Ivor. Field Guide to the Butterflies of Southern Africa. (C). 1988. 110.00 (*1-85368-002-8*, 314, Pub. by New Holland Pubs UK) St Mut.

Migel, J. Michael, ed. The Masters on the Dry Fly. (Illus.). 246p. 1989. reprint ed. pap. 14.95 (*1-55821-031-8*) Lyons & Burford.

Migel, J. Michael & Wright, Leonard M., eds. The Masters on the Nymph. LC 84-62783. (Illus.). 272p. 1985. pap. 16.95 (*0-941130-96-7*) Lyons & Burford.

Migel, Parmenia. The Ballerinas: From the Court of Louis XIV to Pavlova. (Quality Paperbacks Ser.). (Illus.). 1980. reprint ed. pap. 6.95 (*0-306-80115-9*) Da Capo.

— Great Ballet Prints of the Romantic Era. (Illus.). 19.00 (*0-8446-5905-3*) Peter Smith.

— Great Ballet Prints of the Romantic Era: 109 Illustrations, Including 9 in Full Color. (Illus.). 128p. (Orig.). 1981. pap. 9.95 (*0-486-24050-9*) Dover.

Migel, Parmenia, ed. see Picasso, Pablo.

Migeod, Frederick W. H. The Languages of West Africa, 2 vols. LC 72-3001. (Black Heritage Library Collection). 1977. reprint ed. 69.95 (*0-8369-9076-5*) Ayer.

Miggins, Edward M., jt. ed. see Campbell, Thomas F.

Mighell, John. Miller's Antiques Checklist: Clocks. (Illus.). 1993. 13.95 (*1-85732-945-7*, Pub. by Millers Pubns UK) Antique Collect.

Mighell, Ronald L. & Black, J. D. Interregional Competition in Agriculture: With Special Reference to Dairy Farming in the Lake States & New England. LC 51-11577. (Economic Studies: No. 89). (Illus.). 334p. 1951. 22.50 (*0-674-46050-2*) HUP.

Mighetto, Lisa. Muir among the Animals: The Wildlife Writings of John Muir. LC 86-3914. (Illus.). 256p. 1989. pap. 10.00 (*0-87156-607-9*) Sierra.

— Wild Animals & American Environmental Ethics. LC 91-16910. (Illus.). 215p. (Orig.). 1991. lib. bdg. 35.00 (*0-8165-1160-8*); pap. 17.95 (*0-8165-1266-3*) U of Ariz Pr.

Mighill, Benjamin P. & Blodgette, George B. The Early Records of the Town of Rowley Massachusetts 1639-1672. 496p. 1984. reprint ed. 35.00 (*0-917890-41-8*) Heritage Bk.

Migiel, Marilyn. Gender & Genealogy in Tasso's "Gerusalemme Liberata" LC 93-32355. 204p. 1993. text ed. 89.95 (*0-7734-9392-1*) E Mellen.

Migiel, Marilyn & Schiesari, Juliana, eds. Refiguring Woman: Perspectives on Gender & the Italian Renaissance. LC 90-55736. 304p. 1991. 38.95 (*0-8014-2538-7*); pap. 14.95 (*0-8014-9771-X*) Cornell U Pr.

Migliaccio, Janice C. Follow Your Heart's Vegetarian Soup Cookbook. LC 82-21822. (Illus.). 128p. (Orig.). 1983. pap. 7.95 (*0-88007-131-1*) Woodbridge Pr.

Migliaresi. Biomedical Applications of Composites. 1992. write for info. (*0-8493-6548-1*) CRC Pr.

Migliaresi, C., et al, eds. Polymers in Medicine: Proceedings of the 3rd International Conf., Porot Cervo, 9-13 June, 1987, Vol. III. (Progress in Biomedical Engineering Ser.: No. 5). 248p. 1988. 92.50 (*0-444-43003-2*) Elsevier.

Migliaro, A. & Jain, Chaman L. An Executive's Guide to Econometric Forecasting. 2nd ed. 147p. 1987. pap. 26.95 (*0-932126-14-6*) Graceway.

Migliaro, Al & Jain, Chaman L. An Executive's Guide to Econometric Forecasting. 74p. (C). 1983. pap. 26.95 (*0-932126-10-3*) Graceway.

Migliaro, Al & Jain, Chaman L., eds. Understanding Business Forecasting: A Manager's Guide. 234p. (Orig.). 1985. pap. 27.95 (*0-932126-12-X*) Graceway.

Migliaro, Marco W. Glossary of Stationary Battery Terminology. Alber, Glenn, ed. (Illus.). 56p. (Orig.). 1992. 18.95 (*0-9635109-0-8*) Alber Technol.

Miglio, L., jt. ed. see Stella, A.

Migliore, Daniel L. Faith Seeking Understanding: An Introduction to Christian Theology. LC 91-13551. xiv, 306p. (C). 1991. pap. 18.99 (*0-8028-0601-5*) Eerdmans.

Migliore, Daniel L., ed. The Lord's Prayer. 152p. (Orig.). 1993. pap. 12.99 (*0-8028-0119-6*) Eerdmans.

Migliore, Henry R. Common Sense Management. 108p. (Orig.). 1986. pap. 6.95 (*1-56292-515-6*, HB515) Honor Bks OK.

M

— Personal Action Planning. 96p. (Orig.). 1988. pap. 5.95 (*1-56292-514-8*, HB514) Honor Bks OK.
Migliore, R. Henry. Common Sense Management. 100p. (Orig.). 1990. pap. 11.95 (*0-87683-633-3*) GP Pub.
— Personal Action Planning. 100p. (Orig.). 1990. pap. 11.95 (*0-87683-637-6*) GP Pub.
— Strategic Planning & Management. 256p. 1990. pap. 25.95 (*0-87683-630-9*) GP Pub.
— Strategic Planning for Churches & Ministries. 1988. pap. 7.95 (*1-56292-513-X*) Honor Bks OK.
Migliore, R. Henry & Thrun, Walt. The Management of Production: A Productivity Approach. 400p. 1990. 34.95 (*0-87683-631-7*) GP Pub.
Migliore, R. Henry, et al. Church & Ministry Strategic Planning: From Concept to Success. LC 93-17360. (Illus.). 172p. 1994. lib. bdg. 34.95 (*1-56024-346-5*) Haworth Pr.
— Strategic Planning for Not-for-Profit Organizations. LC 93-17360. (Illus.). 209p. 1994. lib. bdg. 29.95 (*1-56024-919-6*) Haworth Pr.
Migliore, Sally A., jt. ed. see Butterworth, Amy S.
Migliorini, Andy. Airport Pocket Guide: United States Edition. (Illus.). 186p. (C). 1992. pap. 14.95 (*0-943265-17-7*) AM Data Services.
Migliorini, B., et al, eds. DOP: Dizionario d'Ortografia e di Pronunzia. 755p. 1981. 95.00 (*0-913298-62-X*) S F Vanni.
Migliorini, Mario. Kennel Building & Management. LC 87-21435. (Illus.). 208p. 1987. 27.95 (*0-87605-656-7*) Howell Bk.
Miglis, John. Killing Eyes. 1984. pap. 2.50 (*0-449-12637-4*) Fawcett.
Mignani, Rigo, jt. auth. see Bernardo, Aldo S.
Mignani, Rigo, ed. see Herbert, George.
Mignani, Rigo, tr. see Ruiz, Juan.
Mignani, Rigo, et al. A Concordance to Juan Ruiz's "Libro De Buen Amor" (State University of New York Press Ser.: Vol. SU4). 328p. 1977. 18.00 (*0-87395-322-3*) MRTS.
Mignano, Andrew J., Jr., jt. auth. see Weinstein, Carol S.
Migneault, Robert L., jt. auth. see Baldwin, David A.
Migneco, Ronald & Biel, Timothy L. The Crash of 1929. LC 89-33556. (World Disasters Ser.). (Illus.). 64p. (J). (gr. 5-8). 1989. lib. bdg. 14.95 (*1-56006-007-7*) Lucent Bks.
Mignery, Herb. Best of Mignery. Cornhuskers Press Staff, ed. LC 85-70978. 1985. pap. text ed. 15.95 (*0-933909-01-2*) Cornhusker Pr.
— Fourteen Carrot Mignery. Daniels, Jeremy L., ed. (Illus.). 109p. 1990. 29.95 (*0-933909-04-7*); pap. 15.95 (*0-933909-05-5*) Cornhusker Pr.
— Western Horseman Collection of Mignery Cartoons. Cornhusker Press Staff, ed. LC 90-86357. 1991. pap. 24.95 (*0-933909-06-3*) Cornhusker Pr.
Mignie, Sophie, tr. see Smarandache, Florentin.
Mignin, Robert J., jt. ed. see Reed, Keith A.
Migniuolo, Frances W., jt. ed. see De Lyon, Hilary.
***Mignola, Mike & Byrne, John.** Hellboy Bk. 1: Seed of Destruction. (Illus.). 128p. 1994. pap. 17.95 (*1-56971-038-4*) Dark Horse Comics.
— Hellboy Bk. 1: Seed of Destruction. deluxe limited ed. (Illus.). 136p. 1995. 99.95 (*1-56971-051-1*) Dark Horse Comics.
Mignolli, Marisa. Hosanna to You, Jesus! A Palm Sunday Experience. (Illus.). 32p. (Orig.). (J). (ps-3). 1993. pap. 3.95 (*0-8198-3368-1*) Pauline Bks.
***Mignolo, Walter D.** The Darker Side of the Renaissance: Literacy, Territoriality, & Colonization. (Illus.). 400p. 1995. text ed. 39.50x (*0-472-10327-X*) U of Mich Pr.
Mignolo, Walter D., jt. ed. see Boone, Elizabeth H.
Mignon, Charles, ed. see Cather, Willa.
Mignon, Charles W. Emerson's Essays Notes. 1975. pap. 3.75 (*0-8220-0429-1*) Cliffs.
Mignon, Charles W., ed. see Taylor, Edward.
Mignon, M. & Jensen, R. T., eds. Endocrine Tumors of the Pancreas. (Frontiers of Gastrointestinal Research Ser.: Vol. 23). (Illus.). xii, 482p. 1995. 297.75 (*3-8055-5953-4*) S Karger.
Mignon, Molly R. Dictionary of Concepts in Archaeology. LC 92-43151. (Reference Sources for the Social Sciences & Humanities Ser.: No. 13). 384p. 1993. text ed. 89.50 (*0-313-24659-9*, MID, Greenwood Pr) Greenwood.
Mignone, Emilio F. Witness to the Truth: The Complicity of Church & Dictatorship in Argentina. Berryman, Phillip, tr. LC 88-1448. 180p. reprint ed. pap. 51.30 (*0-8357-2686-X*, 2040222) Bks Demand.
***Mignone, Mario B.** Italy Today: A Country in Transition. LC 94-5280. (Studies in Modern European History: Vol. 16). 272p. (C). 1995. pap. text ed. 29.95 (*0-8204-2659-8*) P Lang Pubs.
Mignosa, Charles, ed. see McGill, Ormond.
Mignotte, M. Mathematics for Computer Algebra. xiv, 346p. 1991. 42.00 (*0-387-97675-2*) Spr-Verlag.
Migone, L., ed. Urinary Proteins. (Contributions to Nephrology Ser.: Vol. 26). (Illus.). viii, 124p. 1981. pap. 66.50 (*3-8055-1848-X*) S Karger.
Migueis, Jose R. A Man Smiles at Death with Half a Face. Monteiro, George, tr. & intro. by. LC 90-38976. 109p. 1990. 15.95 (*0-87451-503-3*) U Pr of New Eng.
— Steerage & Ten Other Stories. LC 82-84530. (Illus.). 224p. (Orig.). 1983. pap. 6.00 (*0-943722-06-3*) Gavea-Brown.
Miguel, Byron. Seis Dias de Noviembre: El Fusilamiento de los Estudiantes de Medicina. LC 90-84963. (Coleccion Cuba y Sus Jueces Ser.). (Illus.). 96p. (Orig.). (SPA.). 1990. pap. 9.95 (*0-89729-586-2*) Ediciones.
Miguel de Cervantes, Saavedra. El Ingenioso Hidalgo Don Quijote De la Mancha. (SPA.). 1989. 7.95 (*0-8288-2561-0*) Fr & Eur.
Miguel-Munoz, Elias. En Estas Tierras: In This Land. LC 88-64102. 142p. 1989. pap. 11.00 (*0-916950-92-1*) Biling Rev-Pr.
Miguelez, Armando & Sandoval, Maria. Juaja: Metado Integral de Espanol Para Bilingues. (Illus.). 352p. (SPA.). (C). 1987. pap. text ed. write for info. (*0-13-509258-2*) P-H.
Miguens, Jose E., jt. ed. see Turner, Frederick C.
Miguez-Bonino, Jose, ed. Faces of Jesus: Latin American Christologies. Barr, Robert R., tr. LC 83-19375. 192p. 1984. pap. 16.95 (*0-88344-129-2*) Orbis Bks.
***Mihailescu, Calin-Andrei & Hamarneh, Walid, eds.** Fiction Updated: Theories of Fictionality in Contemporary Criticism. (Theory - Culture Ser.). 384p. 1995. 60.00 (*0-8020-0576-4*) U of Toronto Pr.
— Fiction Updated: Theories of Fictionality in Contemporary Criticism. (Theory - Culture Ser.). 384p. 1995. pap. 24.95 (*0-8020-6995-9*) U of Toronto Pr.
Mihailidi, A. English-Serbocroat Dictionary of Chemical Technology. 2nd rev. ed. 544p. (C). 1985. 195.00 (*0-685-46838-0*, Pub. by Collets) St Mut.
Mihailidi, Agapi. English-Serbocroatian Dictionary of Chemical Engineering: Hemijsko-Tehnoloski Recnik Englesko-Srpskohrvatski. 544p. (ENG & SER.). 1985. 49.95 (*0-8288-0174-6*, F108040) Fr & Eur.
Mihailovic, Kosta. Regional Development: Experiences & Prospects in Eastern Europe. Kuklinski, Antoni, ed. LC 71-163631. (Illus.). 225p. 1972. text ed. 27.50 (*90-279-7945-6*) Mouton.
Mihailovich, Vasa D. First Supplement to a Comprehensive Bibliography of Yugoslav Literature in English 1981-1985. 338p. (Orig.). 1989. pap. 18.95 (*0-89357-188-1*) Slavica.
— Second Supplement to "A Comprehensive Bibliography of Yugoslav Literature in English" 1986-1990. 301p. (Orig.). 1992. pap. 19.95 (*0-89357-230-6*) Slavica.
Mihailovich, Vasa D., ed. Contemporary Yugoslav Poetry. LC 77-22865. (Iowa Translations Ser.). 290p. reprint ed. pap. 82.70 (*0-317-42148-4*, 2025936) Bks Demand.
— Modern Russian Literature. (Library of Literary Criticism). 440p. 1972. 75.00 (*0-685-62302-5*, F Ungar Bks) Continuum.
— White Stones & Fir Trees: An Anthology of Contemporary Slavic Literature. LC 74-32519. 603p. 1977. 50.00 (*0-8386-1194-X*) Fairleigh Dickinson.
Mihailovich, Vasa D., prod. Say It in Serbo-Croatian. (Say It Ser.). 160p. 1987. pap. 3.95 (*0-486-25261-2*) Dover.
Mihailovich, Vasa D. & Matejic, Mateja. A Comprehensive Bibliography of Yugoslav Literature in English, 1593-1980. xii, 586p. 1984. 29.95 (*0-89357-136-9*) Slavica.
Mihailovich, Vasa D., jt. auth. see Holton, Milne.
Mihailovich, Vasa D., jt. auth. see Milivojevic, Dragan.
Mihailovich, Vasa D., ed. see Njegos, Petar P.
Mihailovich, Vasa D., et al, eds. Modern Slavic Literatures. Incl. Vol. 1. Russian Literature. 1972. 60.00 (*0-8044-3176-0*); Vol. 2. Bulgarian, Czechoslovak, Polish, Ukrainian, & Yugoslav Literatures. 1976. 60.00 (*0-8044-3177-9*); (Library of Literary Criticism). 1972. Set. 120.00 (*0-8044-3175-2*) Continuum.
Mihajlov, Mihajlo, et al. Underground Notes. 2nd ed. Ivusic, Maria M. & Ivusic, Christopher, trs. LC 80-65723. 208p. 1982. reprint ed. lib. bdg. 20.00 (*0-89241-132-5*); reprint ed. pap. 6.95 (*0-89241-131-7*) Caratzas.
Mihalache, A. N., jt. auth. see Catuneanu, V. M.
Mihalakis, Diana & Bertrand, Marlene C. Kindercize. (Illus.). 69p. 1987. pap. 19.00 (*0-317-90482-5*) Kindercize Mktg.
Mihalap, Hope. Where There's Hope: There's Life & Laughter. Johnson, Judith A., ed. (Illus.). 215p. (Orig.). 1994. pap. 15.00 (*0-9611354-6-8*) T Knox Pub.
Mihalas, D. & Winkler, Karl-Heinz A., eds. Radiation Hydrodynamics in Stars & Compact Objects. (Lecture Notes in Physics Ser.: Vol. 255). vi, 454p. 1986. 59.00 (*0-387-16764-1*) Spr-Verlag.
Mihalas, Dimitri. Cantata for Six Lives & Continuo. Pursifull, Carmen M., ed. (Hawk Production Ser.). 41p. (Orig.). 1992. pap. 5.00 (*0-932884-98-9*) Red Herring.
— Dream Shadows. Pursifull, Carmen M., ed. 53p. (Orig.). 1994. pap. 5.00 (*1-881900-02-9*) Hawk Prods.
— If I Should Die Before I Wake. Pursifull, Carmen M., ed. 43p. (Orig.). Date not set. pap. 5.00 (*1-881900-00-2*) Hawk Prods.
— Life Matters. Pursifull, Carmen M., ed. 63p. (Orig.). 1995. pap. 5.00 (*1-881900-03-7*) Hawk Prods.
Mihalenko, Alyson E. Worms, Cocoons, & Butterflies. 1994. pap. 12.95 (*0-533-10825-X*) Vantage.
Mihalic, Slavko. Atlantis: Selected Poems, Nineteen Fifty-Three to Nineteen Eighty-Two. Simic, Charles & Kastmiler, Peter, trs. LC 83-81610. 48p. 1984. pap. 5.00 (*0-912678-61-5*, Greenfld Rev Pr) Greenfld Rev Lit.
Mihalich, Joseph C. Existentialism & Thomism. (Orig.). pap. 0.95 (*0-685-19401-9*, 77, Citadel Pr) Carol Pub Group.
— Existentialism & Thomism. (Quality Paperback Ser.: No. 170). 91p. (Orig.). (C). 1969. reprint ed. pap. 6.95 (*0-8226-0170-2*) Littlefield.
— Sports & Athletics: Philosophy in Action. LC 82-3736. 236p. 1982. pap. 12.95 (*0-685-52029-3*) Rowman.
Mihalik & Tschantz. Semistability of Amalgamated Products & HNN-Extensions. 86p. 1992. 24.00 (*0-8218-2531-3*) Am Math.
Mihalik, Paul A. Patagonia Profile. (Illus.). 93p. (Orig.). (J). (gr. 7-12). 1985. pap. text ed. 9.95 (*0-9615916-0-9*) Padre Pio Pubs.
Mihaly, Eugene. A Song to Creation: A Dialogue with a Text. (Jewish Perspectives Ser.: No. 1). 108p. 1988. reprint ed. pap. 6.00 (*0-87820-503-9*) Hebrew Union Coll Pr.
Mihaly, Lauren, ed. New York Party Directory. 2nd ed. (Illus.). 72p. 1986. 9.95 (*0-933255-00-4*) NY Party Pub Ass.
Mihalyi, Louis. More Nature, Nuture, Nostalgia. 1989. pap. 9.95 (*0-932052-79-7*) North Country.
Mihalyi, Martha. The Woman in the Glass House Speaks. (Illus.). 40p. (Orig.). (C). 1989. pap. write for info. (*0-318-65553-5*) Stone & Water Pr.
Mihalyi, Peter. Socialist Investment Cycles: Analysis in Retrospect. LC 92-31351. (International Studies in Economics & Econometrics). 1992. lib. bdg. 109.00 (*0-7923-1973-7*) Kluwer Ac.
Mihalyka & Wilson. Graven Stones: Inscriptions from Accomack County, VA Liberty & Parksley Cemeteries. 3rd ed. (Illus.). 324p. 1992. pap. 28.50 (*1-55613-551-3*) Heritage Bk.
***Mihalyka, Jean M.** Marriages: Northampton County, VA. (1660-1854). 177p. (Orig.). 1995. reprint ed. pap. text ed. 16.50 (*0-7884-0166-1*) Heritage Bk.
— Marriages of Northampton County, Virginia, 1660-1 to 1854. 199p. (Orig.). 1991. pap. 16.50 (*1-55613-459-2*) Heritage Bk.
Mihanovich, C. S. Americanization of the Croats in St. Louis, Missouri During the Past Thirty Years. LC 75-146895. 1971. reprint ed. pap. 8.00 (*0-88247-122-8*) Ragusan Pr.
Mihanovich, Clement S., jt. comp. see Werth, Alvin.
Mihara, Yoshiaki, ed. Agricultural Meteorology of Japan. LC 74-78859. (East-West Center Book Ser.). 225p. reprint ed. pap. 64.20 (*0-7837-3985-0*, 2043815) Bks Demand.
Mihashi, H., et al, eds. Fracture Toughness & Fracture Energy Test Methods for Concrete & Rock: Proceedings of the International Workshop Sendai, 12 - 14 October 1988. (Illus.). 640p. (C). 1989. text ed. 160.00 (*90-6191-988-6*, Pub. by A A Balkema NE) Ashgate Pub Co.
Mihelic, Duean. The Political Element in the Port Geography of Trieste. LC 69-18024. (Research Papers Ser.: No. 120). 104p. 1969. pap. 12.00 (*0-686-67195-3*) U Chicago Comm Geo.
Mihelic, Dusan. The Political Element in the Port Geography of Trieste. LC 69-18024. (University of Chicago, Department of Geography, Research Paper Ser.: No. 120). (Illus.). 117p. reprint ed. pap. 33.40 (*0-7837-0397-X*, 2040718) Bks Demand.
***Mihelich, Emil.** Running Clear. 350p. 1995. pap. 9.95 (*1-56901-775-1*) NW Pub.
Mihesuah, Devon A. Cultivating the Rosebuds: The Education of Women at the Cherokee Female Seminary, 1851-1909. LC 92-5845. (Illus.). 240p. (C). 1993. 35.95 (*0-252-01953-9*) U of Ill Pr.
***Mihevc, John.** The Market Tells Them So: The World Bank & Economic Fundamentalism in Africa. (Illus.). 320p. (C). 1995. text ed. 59.95 (*1-85649-327-X*, Pub. by Zed Books UK) Humanities.
— The Market Tells Them So: The World Bank & Economic Fundamentalism in Africa. (Illus.). 320p. (C). 1995. pap. 22.50 (*1-85649-328-8*, Pub. by Zed Books UK) Humanities.
***Mihevic.** Where a White Dog Smiles. 1991. 5.00 (*0-614-04744-7*) Royal Fireworks.
***Mihevic, Demetra.** When the Barred Owl Calls. 189p. (Orig.). (YA). 1995. pap. 5.00 (*0-88092-131-5*) Royal Fireworks.
— When the Barred Owl Calls. 189p. (Orig.). (YA). 1995. lib. bdg. 15.00 (*0-88092-132-3*) Royal Fireworks.
Mihich, E. & Eckhardt, S., eds. Design of Cancer Chemotherapy. (Antibiotics & Chemotherapy Ser.: Vol. 28). (Illus.). x, 194p. 1980. 71.25 (*3-8055-0411-X*) S Karger.
Mihich, E. & Schimke, R. T., eds. Apoptosis. (Pezcoller Symposium Ser.: Vol. 5). (Illus.). 283p. (C). 1994. text ed. 89.50 (*0-306-44733-9*, Plenum Pr) Plenum.
Mihich, Enrico, ed. Biological Responses in Cancer: Progress Toward Potential Applications, Vol. 1. LC 82-18041. 322p. 1982. 85.00 (*0-306-41146-6*, Plenum Pr) Plenum.
— Biological Responses in Cancer: Progress Toward Potential Applications, Vol. 2. LC 82-18041. 258p. 1984. 79.50 (*0-306-41583-6*, Plenum Pr) Plenum.
— Biological Responses in Cancer: Progress Toward Potential Applications; Vol. 4. LC 82-18041. 270p. 1985. 79.50 (*0-306-42044-9*, Plenum Pr) Plenum.
Mihich, Enrico & Sakurai, Yoshio, eds. Biological Responses in Cancer: Progress Toward Potential Applications, Vol. 3: Immunomodulation by Anticancer Drugs. LC 84-18041. 230p. 1985. 79.50 (*0-306-41879-7*, Plenum Pr) Plenum.
Mihich, Enrico, jt. ed. see Hemler, Martin E.
Mihm, Madelyn T. Sentence by Sentence: A Basic Rhetoric, Reader & Grammar. 375p. (C). 1989. pap. text ed. 18.75 (*0-15-579672-0*); teacher ed, pap. text ed. 6.75 (*0-15-579673-9*) HB Coll Pubs.
Mihm, Martin C., Jr. & Googe, Paul. Problematic Pigmented Lesions: A Case Method Approach. LC 89-12216. (Illus.). 543p. 1990. text ed. 98.00 (*0-8121-1261-X*) Williams & Wilkins.
Mihopoulos, Effie. Languid Love Lyrics. (Offset Offshoot: No. 16). 70p. 1993. pap. 8.00 (*0-941240-18-5*) Ommation Pr.
— The Moon Cycle. (Offset Offshoot Ser.: No. 14). 8.00 (*0-941240-17-7*) Ommation Pr.
Mihopoulos, Effie, ed. Dancers: Eight Stories about the Dance. 1986. 4.00 (*0-941240-08-8*) Ommation Pr.
— Dancers II: Eight Stories about the Dance. (Dialogues on Dance Ser.: No. 8). 70p. 1987. 6.00 (*0-941240-10-X*) Ommation Pr.
Mihoubi, Bachir, tr. see Atias, Christian.
***Mihule, Jaroslav.** Bohuslav Martinu. (20th Century Composers Ser.). (Illus.). 240p. 1995. pap. 19.95 (*0-7148-3171-9*, Pub. by Phaidon Press UK) Chronicle Bks.
Mihura, M. Tres Sombreros de Copa - Maribel y la Extrana Familia. 11th ed. 206p. (SPA.). 1988. pap. 10.95 (*0-7859-5137-7*) Fr & Eur.
Mihura, Miguel. The Independent Act: Two Plays by Miguel Mihura (Sublime Decision! & The Enchanting Dorotea) Koppenhaver, John H. & Nelson, Susan, trs. 118p. pap. 16.00 (*0-939980-16-9*) Trinity U Pr.
— Melocoton en Almibar - Ninette y un Senor de Murcia. 7th ed. 204p. (SPA.). 1989. pap. 11.95 (*0-7859-5136-9*) Fr & Eur.
— Tres Sombreros de Copa. Tordera, Antonio, ed. (Nueva Austral Ser.: Vol. 63). (SPA.). 1991. pap. text ed. 11.95 (*84-239-1863-7*) Elliots Bks.
— Tres Sombreros de Copa. 15th ed. 136p. (SPA.). 1991. pap. 11.95 (*0-7859-5135-0*) Fr & Eur.
Mihyo, Paschal. Non - Market Controls & the Accountability of Public Enterprises in Tanzania. 186p. 1994. 20.00 (*0-88936-701-9*, IDRC7019, Pub. by IDRC CN) UNIPUB.
Miido, Helis. The Integrated Medical Library. (Illus.). 200p. 1991. 79.95 (*0-8493-0182-3*, Z65) CRC Pr.
Miikkulainen, Risto. Subsymbolic Natural Language Processing: An Integrated Model of Scripts, Lexicon, & Memory. LC 92-37285. (Neural Network Modeling & Connectionism Ser.). 422p. (C). 1993. 50.00 (*0-262-13290-7*, Bradford Bks) MIT Pr.
Miiller, Kathryn M. Did My First Mother Love Me? A Story for an Adopted Child. (Illus.). 48p. (Orig.). (J). (ps-3). 1994. 12.95 (*0-930934-85-7*) Morning Glory.
Mijakovs'kyj, Volodymyr. Unpublished & Forgotten Writings: Editor's Text in English. Antonovych, Marc, ed. (Sources of Modern History of the Ukraine Ser.). (Illus.). 516p. (UKR.). 1984. 30.00 (*0-916381-02-1*) Ukrainian Arts Sci.
Mijalkovic, S., jt. auth. see Joppich, W.
Mijares, David P. Modern Samurai Training. (Illus.). 100p. (Orig.). (YA). 1989. pap. 9.95 (*0-9623400-0-6*) Group M Probelications.
Mijatev, K. Bulgaria: Mediaeval Wall Paintings. (UNESCO World Art Ser.). (Illus.). 96p. (C). 1961. text ed. 300.00 (*0-685-47837-8*, Pub. by Collets) St Mut.
Mijatovic, Elodie. Serbian Folk Lore. Denton, W., ed. LC 68-56477. 1972. reprint ed. 24.95 (*0-405-08788-8*, Pub. by Blom Pubns UK) Ayer.
Mijatovic, M. Hadronic Mechanics & Nonpotential Interaction. 371p. 1989. 129.00 (*0-941743-72-1*) Nova Sci Pubs.
Mijere, Nsolo J. African Refugees & Human Rights in Host Countries: The Long Term Demographic, Environmental, Economic, Social, & Psychological Impacts of Angolan Refugees in Zambia. 1994. 16.95 (*0-533-10621-4*) Vantage.
Mijeski, Kenneth J., ed. The Nicaraguan Constitution of 1987: English Translation & Commentary. LC 90-47132. (Monographs in International Studies, Latin America Ser.: No. 17). 350p. (Orig.). (C). 1991. pap. 25.00 (*0-89680-165-9*) Ohio U Pr.
Mijia, A., jt. ed. see Bankowski, Z.
Mijnhardt, Wijnand W., jt. ed. see Jacob, Margaret C.
Mijs, W. J., ed. New Methods for Polymer Synthesis. (Illus.). 346p. 1992. 75.00 (*0-306-43871-2*, Plenum Pr) Plenum.
Mijs, W. J. & De Jonge, C. R. H., eds. Organic Syntheses by Oxidation with Metal Compounds. 879p. 1986. 155.00 (*0-306-41999-8*, Plenum Pr) Plenum.
Mijs, Wim, jt. ed. see Muller, Sam.
Mijuskovic, Ben. Contingent Immaterialism: Meaning, Freedom, Time & Mind. 214p. (Orig.). 1984. pap. 30.00 (*90-6032-254-1*, Pub. by B R Gruener NE) Benjamins North Am.
Mijuskovic, Ben L. Loneliness. 1988. pap. 9.00 (*0-87212-226-3*) Libra.
Mijuskovic, Vera, jt. auth. see Fiser, Ana.
***Mika, J. R. & Banasiak, J.** Singularly Perturbed Evolution Equations with Applications to Kinetic Theory. (Series on Advances in Mathematics for Applied Sciences). 250p. 1995. text ed. 61.00 (*981-02-2125-8*) World Scientific Pub.
Mika, Jim. Writing with Confidence: A Composition Program for High School Juniors & Seniors. (Illus.). 160p. 1993. pap. text ed. 11.95 (*0-9639717-0-0*) Jennifer Pubng.
Mika, Jozsef & Torok, Tibor. Analytical Emission Spectroscopy: Fundamentals. enl. rev. ed. Floyd, P. A., ed. Nemes, Laszlo, tr. LC 74-196239. (Illus.). 533p. reprint ed. pap. 152.00 (*0-8357-5455-3*, 2025724) Bks Demand.
Mika, Karin. Making Sense of the Citator: A Manual & Workbook. 112p. (C). 1991. spiral bd. 14.95 (*0-8403-6824-0*) Kendall-Hunt.
Mika, Stephen. Microcomputers for Building Surveyors. (C). 1986. text ed. 50.00 (*0-85406-309-9*, Pub. by Surveyors Pubns) St Mut.
Mikael'an, Galina, jt. auth. see Akhmanova, Olga.
Mikaelian, Andrei L. Optical Methods for Information Technologies. LC 94-11785. 1994. 125.00 (*0-89864-070-9*) Allerton Pr.
Mikaelian, Martin. Art Gallery of Armenia. 160p. 1984. 90.00 (*0-317-61212-3*, Pub. by Collets UK) Pro-Am Music.
Mikaelsen, Ben. Rescue Josh McGuire. LC 91-71386. 272p. (YA). (gr. 5-9). 1991. 14.95 (*1-56282-099-0*); lib. bdg. 14.89 (*1-56282-100-8*) Hyprn Child.
— Rescue Josh McGuire. LC 91-71386. 272p. (J). (gr. 5-9). 1993. pap. 4.50 (*1-56282-523-2*) Hyprn Ppbks.
— Sparrow Hawk Red. LC 92-53458. 224p. (J). (gr. 5-9). 1993. 14.95 (*1-56282-387-6*); lib. bdg. 14.89 (*1-56282-388-4*) Hyprn Child.
— Sparrow Hawk Red. 192p. (J). (gr. 5-9). 1994. pap. 4.50 (*0-7868-1002-5*) Hyprn Ppbks.
— Stranded. LC 94-27069. 288p. (J). (gr. 4-8). 1995. 15.95 (*0-7868-0072-0*); lib. bdg. 15.89 (*0-7868-2059-4*) Hyprn Child.
Mikail. Moh's Micrographic Surgery. (Illus.). 432p. 1991. text ed. 145.00 (*0-7216-3415-X*) Saunders.

M

An Asterisk (*) at the beginning of an entry indicates that the title is appearing in BIP for the first time.

Mikal, Alan. Exploring Boston Harbor. (Illus.). 128p. 1973. 10.95 (*0-8158-0303-6*) Chris Mass.

***Mikal, Elizabeth J.** Until Darkness Holds No Fear. 350p. 1995. pap. 17.95 (*1-883862-08-6*) Bks Beyond Brdrs.

Mikalac, Miriam, jt. auth. see Carter, Eneida.

Mikalachki, Albert. Change Process in Sport & Physical Education Management. Zeigler, Earle F. & Leyshon, Glynn, eds. (Stipes Monograph Series on Sport & Physical Education Management). 37p. (Orig.). 1988. pap. text ed. 3.80 (*0-87563-317-X*) Stipes.

Mikalson, Jon D. Athenian Popular Religion. LC 82-25616. xiv, 142p. (C). 1987. reprint ed. pap. 11.95 (*0-8078-4194-3*) U of NC Pr.

— Honor Thy Gods: Popular Religion in Greek Tragedy. LC 91-50282. xvi, 360p. (C). 1992. 45.00 (*0-8078-2005-9*); pap. 14.95 (*0-8078-4348-2*) U of NC Pr.

— The Sacred & Civil Calendar of the Athenian Year. LC 74-25622. 240p. reprint ed. pap. 68.40 (*0-8357-2784-X*, 2039910) Bks Demand.

Mikami, Riichiro & Hosoda, Yutaka, eds. Sarcoidosis. 413p. 1981. 74.50 (*0-86008-295-4*, Pub. by U of Tokyo JA) Col U Pr.

Mikami, Y. The Development of Mathematics in China & Japan. 2nd ed. LC 74-6716. 383p. 1974. text ed. 29.50 (*0-8284-0149-7*) Chelsea Pub.

Mikanagi, K., et al, eds. Purine & Pyrimidine Metabolism in Man VI, 2 pts., Pt. A. (Illus.). 574p. 1989. 120.00 (*0-306-43233-1*, Plenum Pr) Plenum.

— Purine & Pyrimidine Metabolism in Man VI, 2 pts., Pt. B. (Illus.). 566p. 1989. 120.00 (*0-306-43234-X*, Plenum Pr) Plenum.

— Purine & Pyrimidine Metabolism in Man VI, 2 pts., Set. (Illus.). 1989. 210.00 (*0-685-44617-4*, Plenum Pr) Plenum.

Mikasinovich, Branko, ed. Modern Yugoslav Satire. LC 79-83730. (Illus.). (Orig.). 1979. 20.00 (*0-89304-029-0*, CCC117); pap. 12.00 (*0-89304-030-4*) Cross-Cultrl NY.

Mikasinovich, Branko, jt. ed. see Barkan, Stanley H.

Mikasinovich, Branko, tr. see Popa, Vasco.

Mikdadi, Faysal. Gamal Abdel Nasser: A Bibliography. LC 91-21168. (Bibliographies of World Leaders Ser.: No. 5). 164p. 1991. text ed. 55.00 (*0-313-28119-X*, MKG, Greenwood Pr) Greenwood.

— Margaret Thatcher: A Bibliography. LC 92-38071. (Bibliographies of British Statesmen Ser.: No. 18). 288p. 1993. text ed. 85.00 (*0-313-28288-9*, MKE/) Greenwood.

Mikdashi, Zuhayr. The International Politics of Natural Resources. LC 75-38002. (Illus.). 248p. 1976. 35.00 (*0-8014-1001-0*) Cornell U Pr.

— Transnational Oil: Issues, Policies & Perspectives. LC 85-30364. 280p. 1986. text ed. 39.95 (*0-312-81482-8*) St Martin.

Mikdashi, Zuhayr, ed. Bankers' & Public Authorities' Management of Risks: Proceedings of the Second International Banking Colloquium Held by the Ecole des Hautes Etudes Commerciales de l'Universite de Lausanne. 225p. 1990. text ed. 49.95 (*0-312-03621-3*) St Martin.

— Financial Strategies & Public Policies: Banking, Insurance, & Industry. LC 92-34120. 1993. text ed. 69.95 (*0-312-09113-3*) St Martin.

Mikdashi, Zuhayr, jt. ed. see Iffland, Charles.

Mike, jt. auth. see A. Jay.

Mike Brynes & Associates Staff. Bumper-to-Bumper: The Diesel Mechanics Student's Guide to Tractor-Trailer Operations. (Illus.). x, 242p. (Orig.). (C). 1993. pap. text ed. 21.90 (*0-9621687-4-2*, B2BMSG) M Byrnes & Assocs.

Mike Brynes & Associates Staff. Bumper to Bumper: La Guia Completa Para Operaciones de Autotransporte de Carga. Pedrero, Manuel, tr. (Illus.). xii, 610p. (Orig.). (SPA.). (C). 1993. pap. text ed. 39.00 (*0-9621687-3-4*, GUIA) M Byrnes & Assocs.

— Bumper-to-Bumper: The Instructor's Guide. (Illus.). xii, 448p. (C). 1992. Incls. The complete Guide to Tractor-Trailer Operations, 545p. 110.00 (*0-9621687-2-6*, B2BIG) M Byrnes & Assocs.

***Mike, Dr., pseud.** Francis A. Frog's First & Last Picnic. LC 95-60380. (Illus.). 24p. (Orig.). (J). (gr. k-3). 1995. pap. 6.00 (*0-9639450-1-7*) Joy Ent.

Mike, Hi. Laugh a Little! 1993. pap. 12.95 (*0-533-10630-3*) Vantage.

***Mike, Jan.** Juan Bobo & the Horse of Seven Colors: A Puerto Rican Legend. LC 95-11765. (Legends of the World Ser.). (Illus.). 32p. (J). (gr. 1-4). 1995. lib. bdg. 11.89 (*0-8167-3745-2*); pap. text ed. 2.95 (*0-8167-3746-0*) Troll Assocs.

— New Mexico, Land of Enchantment Alphabet Book. (Illus.). 32p. (Orig.). (J). (gr. k-5). 1993. pap. 7.95 (*0-918080-55-X*) Treas Chest Bks.

— La Zariguerya y el Gran Creador de Fuego - Opossum & the Great Filmmaker: Una Leyenda Mexicana. LC 92-36459. (J). (gr. 4-7). 1993. lib. bdg. 11.89 (*0-8167-3125-X*); pap. 3.95 (*0-8167-3073-3*) Troll Assocs.

Mike, Jan & Lowmiller, Cathie. Bizagolaa: An Apache Girl. (Illus.). 32p. (Orig.). (J). (gr. k-6). 1995. 3.95 (*0-918080-46-0*, 20976) Treas Chest Bks.

— Chana: An Anasazi Girl. 32p. (Orig.). (J). (gr. k-4). 1995. 3.95 (*0-918080-61-4*, 20977) Treas Chest Bks.

Mike, Jan & Mike, Samuel, illus. Desert Seasons. 32p. (J). (gr. k-8). 1995. 7.95 (*0-918080-49-5*, 20975) Treas Chest Bks.

Mike, Jan M. Gift of the Nile: An Ancient Egyptian Legend. LC 92-5826. (Legends of the World Ser.). (Illus.). 32p. (J). (gr. 2-5). 1992. lib. bdg. 11.89 (*0-8167-2813-5*); pap. text ed. 3.95 (*0-8167-2814-3*) Troll Assocs.

— Opossum & the Great Firemaker: A Mexican Legend. LC 92-36459. (Legends of the World Ser.). (Illus.). 32p. (J). (gr. 2-5). 1993. teacher ed 3.95 (*0-8167-3056-3*); lib. bdg. 11.89 (*0-8167-3055-5*) Troll Assocs.

Mike, Jan M. & Lowmiller, Cathie. Dolii: A Navajo Girl. (Illus.). 32p. (J). (gr. k-6). 1995. 3.95 (*0-918080-54-1*, 20978) Treas Chest Bks.

— Kachi: A Hopi Girl. (Illus.). 32p. (J). (gr. k-6). 1995. 3.95 (*0-918080-47-9*, 20979) Treas Chest Bks.

Mike Murach & Assoc., Inc. Staff. The Least You Need to Know about DOS Instructor's Guide. 2nd ed. 1993. ring bd. 250.00 (*0-911625-82-8*) M Murach & Assoc.

— The Least You Need to Know about Lotus 1-2-3 Instructor's Guide. 1993. ring bd. 150.00 (*0-911625-72-0*) M Murach & Assoc.

— The Least You Need to Know about WordPerfect Instructor's Guide. 1993. ring bd. 150.00 (*0-911625-73-9*) M Murach & Assoc.

Mike, Samuel, jt. illus. see Mike, Jan.

Mikell, Gwendolyn. Cocoa & Chaos in Ghana. 288p. 1992. pap. 18.95 (*0-88258-153-8*) Howard U Pr.

Mikels, Elaine. Just Lucky I Guess: From Closet Lesbian to Radical Dyke. LC 93-71778. 385p. (Orig.). 1993. pap. text ed. 12.95 (*0-9637257-1-8*) Desert Crone.

— Just Lucky I Guess: From Closet Lesbian to Radical Dyke. 2nd ed. (Orig.). 1994. pap. 12.95 (*0-9637257-2-6*) Desert Crone.

***Mikels, Jennifer.** Child of Mine. 1995. mass mkt. 3.75 (*0-373-09993-2*, 1-09993-6) Silhouette.

— Denver's Lady. (Silhouette Special Edition Ser.). 1994. mass mkt. 3.50 (*0-373-09870-7*, 5-09870-2) Silhouette.

— Jake Ryker's Back in Town. (Special Edition Ser.). 1994. mass mkt. 3.50 (*0-373-09929-0*, 1-09929-0) Silhouette.

— Sara's Father. (Special Edition Ser.). 1995. pap. 3.75 (*0-373-09947-9*, 1-09947-2) Silhouette.

— Your Child, My Child. 1993. mass mkt. 3.39 (*0-373-09807-3*, 5-09807-4) Silhouette.

Mikelsons, Arnolds, jt. auth. see Bilinskis, Ivars.

***Mikes, Anthony P.** Lifeblood: A Three-Hundred-Sixty-Five Day-a-Year New Business Plan for Small Agencies. (Illus.). 255p. (Orig.). Date not set. pap. 49.95 (*0-9626971-1-7*) Second Wind.

— The Small Agency Survival Manual: How to Emerge Victorious from the Advertising Battleground. 224p. (Orig.). Date not set. pap. 49.95 (*0-9626971-0-9*) Second Wind.

Mikes, George. How to Be a Brit: A Mikes Minibus, 3 vols. in 1. Bd. with How to Be an Alien.; How to Be Inimitable.; How to Be Decadent. (Illus.). 1984. 19.95 (*0-233-97724-4*, Pub. by A Deutsch UK) Trafalgar.

— How to Be a Yank: And More Wisdom. (Illus.). 120p. 1988. 19.95 (*0-233-98145-4*, Pub. by A Deutsch UK) Trafalgar.

— How to Be Poor. (Illus.). 144p. 1984. 17.95 (*0-233-97541-1*, Pub. by A Deutsch UK) Trafalgar.

Mikes, Jay. Basketball FundaMENTALS: A Complete Mental Training Guide. LC 86-19133. (Illus.). 272p. 1987. text ed. 21.00 (*0-88011-281-6*, PMIK0281) Human Kinetics.

— Basketball FundaMENTALS: Complete Mental Training Guide. 272p. 1987. pap. 16.95 (*0-88011-442-8*, PMIK0442) Human Kinetics.

Mikes, O. High-Performance Liquid Chromatography of Biopolmers & Bioligomers, Part A: Principles, Materials, & Techniques. (Journal of Chromatography Library: Vol. 41A). 380p. 1988. 146.25 (*0-444-42951-4*) Elsevier.

— High-Performance Liquid Chromatography of Biopolymers & Biooligomers: Part B - Separation of Individual Compound Classes. (Journal of Chromatography Library: No. 41B). 722p. 1988. 184.75 (*0-444-43034-2*) Elsevier.

Mikes, Petr. In the Tracks of the Dead. Keys, Kerry S. & Boeke, Wanda, trs. (Illus.). 33p. 1993. pap. 5.00 (*0-930502-08-6*) Pine Pr.

Mikes, Steven. Visual Programming Tools for X. 1994. pap. 34.00 (*0-13-954132-2*) P-H.

— X Window Program Design & Development. 1991. pap. 26.95 (*0-201-55077-6*) Addison-Wesley.

— X Windows Developer's Technical Reference. 800p. 1989. pap. 34.95 (*0-201-52370-1*) Addison-Wesley.

Mikesell, Margaret & Vaughan, V. Othello: An Annotated Bibliography. LC 89-25852. (Shakespeare Bibliographies Ser.: Vol. 20). 976p. 1990. 109.00 (*0-8240-2749-3*, 964) Garland.

***Mikesell, Elizabeth A.** Legacy: Gifts from a Grandmother. 66p. 1995. pap. 6.00 (*0-918949-68-8*) Papier-Mache Press.

***Mikesell, James H.** Fate Worse Than Death: And Other Hospital Stories. LC 95-16217. 1995. write for info. (*0-929925-30-0*) Univ SD Pr.

Mikesell, Janice H. A Survivor's Manual: A Book of Poems. 52p. (Orig.). 1990. reprint ed. pap. 8.00 (*0-9621112-1-X*) Hens Teeth.

Mikesell, Janice H. & Richardson, Marilyn, eds. Women, Houses & Home: An Anthology of Prose, Poetry & Photography. (Illus.). 52p. reprint ed. pap. 8.00 (*0-9621112-3-6*) Hens Teeth.

Mikesell, Janice H., ed. see Harlan, John L. & Harlan, Katherine C.

Mikesell, John L. Fiscal Administration: Analysis & Applications for the Public Sector. 3rd ed. 510p. (C). 1991. text ed. 50.95 (*0-534-13638-9*) Intl Thomson.

— Fiscal Administration: Analysis & Applications for the Public Sector. 4th ed. LC 94-4547. 594p. 1995. text ed. 51.95 (*0-534-24606-0*) Intl Thomson.

Mikesell, John L., jt. auth. see Due, John F.

Mikesell, Lillie A., ed. see Stewart, Judith K.

Mikesell, Marvin W. Northern Morocco: A Cultural Geography. LC 84-29028. vi, 135p. 1985. reprint ed. text ed. 55.00 (*0-313-23865-0*, MNOR, Greenwood Pr) Greenwood.

Mikesell, Marvin W., ed. Geographers Abroad: Essays on the Problems & Prospects of Research in Foreign Areas. LC 73-87829. (Research Papers Ser.: No. 152). 296p. 1973. pap. 12.00 (*0-89065-059-4*) U Chicago Comm Geo.

Mikesell, Raymond. World Copper Industry. 1979. pap. 19.95x (*0-8018-2270-X*) Johns Hopkins.

Mikesell, Raymond & Williams, Larry. International Banks & the Environment: From Growth to Sustainability - An Unfinished Agenda. LC 91-30504. (Illus.). 386p. 1992. 30.00 (*0-87156-640-0*) Sierra.

Mikesell, Raymond F. The Bretton Woods Debates: A Memoir. LC 94-8984. (Essays in International Finance Ser.: No. 192). 1994. 8.00 (*0-88165-099-4*) Princeton U Int Finan Econ.

— Economic Development & the Environment. (Global Development & the Environment Ser.). 192p. 1992. text ed. 75.00 (*0-7201-2138-8*, Mansell Pub) Cassell.

— Foreign Investment in Copper Mining: Case Studies of Mines in Peru & Papua New Guinea. LC 75-11356. (Resources for the Future Ser.). (Illus.). 166p. 1975. 18.00 (*0-8018-1750-1*) Johns Hopkins.

— Foreign Investment in Copper Mining: Case Studies of Mines in Peru & Papua New Guinea. LC 75-11356. 166p. reprint ed. pap. 47.40 (*0-317-20609-5*, 2024150) Bks Demand.

— Foreign Investment in the Petroleum & Mineral Industries: Case Studies of Investor-Host Country Relations. LC 79-123860. 477p. reprint ed. pap. 136.00 (*0-317-26215-7*, 2052113) Bks Demand.

— The Global Copper Industry: Problems & Prospects. 176p. 1988. lib. bdg. 65.00 (*0-7099-3508-0*) Routledge Chapman & Hall.

— New Patterns of World Mineral Development. LC 79-90054. (British-North American Committee Ser.). 116p. 1980. 5.00 (*0-89068-049-3*) Natl Planning.

— Nonfuel Minerals: Foreign Dependence & National Security. LC 86-27247. (Illus.). 269p. reprint ed. pap. 76.70 (*0-7837-4719-5*, 2059071) Bks Demand.

— Petroleum Company Operations & Agreements in the Developing Countries. LC 83-43265. 148p. 1984. pap. text ed. 20.00 (*0-915707-07-1*) Resources Future.

— Supplement to NBER Report Fifteen: The Eurocurrency Market & the Recycling of Petrodollars. 9p. reprint ed. 20.00 (*0-685-61394-1*) Natl Bur Econ Res.

— The World Copper Industry: Structure & Economic Analysis. 393p. 1979. pap. 19.95 (*0-8018-2210-6*) Resources Future.

Mikesell, Raymond F. & Furth, J. Herbert. Foreign Dollar Balances & the International Role of the Dollar. (Studies in International Economic Relations: No. 8). 141p. 1974. 36.70 (*0-87014-262-3*) Natl Bur Econ Res.

***Mikesell, Richard H., et al, eds.** Integrating Family Therapy: Handbook of Family Psychology & Systems Theory. 576p. 1995. text ed. 59.95 (*1-55798-280-5*, 431-7450) Am Psychol.

Mikesell, Sarah. Opportunities in Veterinary Medicine. (Opportunities in...Ser.). (Illus.). 160p. 1993. 13.95 (*0-8442-4059-1*, VGM Career Bks); pap. 10.95 (*0-8442-4060-5*, VGM Career Bks) NTC Pub Grp.

Mikesell, Shirley K. Early Settlers of Montgomery County, Ohio: Genealogical Abstracts from Common Pleas Court Records. 317p. (Orig.). 1992. pap. 25.00 (*1-55613-601-3*) Heritage Bk.

— Early Settlers of Montgomery County, Ohio: Genealogical Abstracts from Land Records, Tax Lists, & Biographical Sketches. viii, 241p. (Orig.). 1991. pap. 21.50 (*1-55613-495-9*) Heritage Bk.

— Early Settlers of Montgomery County, Ohio, Vol. III: Genealogical Abstracts from Marriage & Divorce Records, 1803-1827, Early Deeds Recorded Late, Election Abstracts, Obituary of an Early Settler. viii, 208p. (Orig.). 1993. pap. text ed. 19.00 (*1-55613-751-6*) Heritage Bk.

Mikesell, Susan, ed. see Mayans, Ernesto.

Mikesell, Suzanne, ed. see Gilbert, Isabel.

Mikesell, Suzanne, ed. see Mutke, Peter H.

Mikesell, Suzanne, ed. see Robinson, James W.

Mikesell, Suzanne, ed. see Tebbetts, Charles.

Mikesh, Robert & Abe, Shorzoe. Japanese Aircraft, Nineteen Hundred Ten to Nineteen Forty-One. (Putnam Aviation Ser.). (Illus.). 320p. 1990. 45.00 (*1-55750-563-2*) Naval Inst Pr.

Mikesh, Robert C. Albatros D. Va: German World War I Fighter. LC 80-36711. (Famous Aircraft of the National Air & Space Museum Ser.: No. 4). (Illus.). (Orig.). 1980. pap. 12.95 (*0-87474-633-7*, MIALP) Smithsonian.

— Broken Wings of the Samurai: The Destruction of the Japanese Air Force. (Illus.). 199p. 1993. 36.95 (*1-55750-083-5*) Naval Inst Pr.

— Excalibur III: Story of a P-51 Mustang. LC 78-606028. (Famous Aircraft of the National Air & Space Museum Ser.: No. 1). (Illus.). 76p. 1978. pap. 12.95 (*0-87474-635-3*) Smithsonian.

— Japanese Aircraft: Code Names & Designations. LC 92-85346. (Illus.). 192p. (Orig.). 1993. pap. 14.95 (*0-88740-447-2*) Schiffer.

— Japan's World War II Balloon Bomb Attacks on North America. 1990. pap. 9.95 (*0-87474-911-5*) Smithsonian.

— Zero: Japan's Legendary WWII Fighter. (Illus.). 128p. 1994. pap. 19.95 (*0-87938-915-X*) Motorbooks Intl.

Mikesh, Robert C. & Tagaya, Osamu. Moonlight Interceptor: Japan's "Irving" Night Fighter. LC 84-23506. (Famous Aircraft of the National Air & Space Museum Ser.: No. 8). (Illus.). 112p. (Orig.). 1985. pap. 10.95 (*0-87474-689-2*, MIMLP) Smithsonian.

***Miketta, Patricia L.** Rape: How to Fight, Prevent, Use Protective Psychology or Later Identify Rapists. 3rd rev. ed. LC 90-56286. 230p. 1995. 44.50 (*0-7883-0454-2*); pap. 39.50 (*0-7883-0455-0*) ABBE Pubs Assn.

Mikhail, E. H. An Annotated Bibliography of Modern Anglo-Irish Drama. LC 80-51874. 306p. 1981. 20.00 (*0-87875-201-3*) Whitston Pub.

— Bibliography of Modern Irish Drama, 1899-1970. LC 72-1373. 63p. 1972. 25.00 (*0-295-95229-6*) U of Wash Pr.

— Brendan Behan: An Annotated Bibliography of Criticism. 117p. 1980. text ed. 44.00 (*0-06-494826-9*, N6595) B&N Imports.

— Contemporary British Drama, 1950-1976. 147p. 1976. 20.00 (*0-87471-854-6*) Rowman.

— Lady Gregory: An Annotated Bibliography of Criticism. LC 81-50702. 269p. (C). 1981. 20.00 (*0-87875-216-1*) Whitston Pub.

— A Research Guide to Modern Irish Dramatists. LC 78-69874. 1979. 10.00 (*0-87875-166-1*) Whitston Pub.

— Sean O'Casey: A Bibliography of Criticism. LC 76-37007. 164p. 1972. text ed. 30.00 (*0-295-95167-2*) U of Wash Pr.

— Sean O'Casey & His Critics: An Annotated Bibliography, 1916-1982. LC 84-14166. (Author Bibliographies Ser.: No. 67). 362p. 1985. 32.50 (*0-8108-1747-0*) Scarecrow.

Mikhail, E. H., ed. The Abbey Theatre: Interviews & Recollections. LC 86-3407. 220p. 1986. 59.00 (*0-389-20616-4*, N8174) B&N Imports.

— Goldsmith: Interviews & Recollections. LC 93-13921. 1993. text ed. 49.95 (*0-312-10193-7*) St Martin.

— James Joyce: Interviews & Recollections. LC 88-18177. 304p. 1990. text ed. 45.00 (*0-312-02416-9*) St Martin.

— Sheridan: Interviews & Recollections. LC 88-35562. (Illus.). 200p. 1990. text ed. 39.95 (*0-312-03013-4*) St Martin.

Mikhail, E. H., ed. see Behan, Brendan.

Mikhail, Edward, jt. auth. see Anderson, James.

Mikhail, Maged S., jt. auth. see Morgan, G. Edward, Jr.

Mikhail, Mona N. Mafouz & Idris: Studies in Arabic Short Fiction. 272p. (C). 1992. text ed. 45.00 (*0-8147-5474-0*) NYU Pr.

Mikhail, Raouf S. & Robens, Erich. Microstructure & Thermal Analysis of Solid Surfaces. LC 82-17507. (Wiley Heyden Publication Ser.). 506p. reprint ed. pap. 144.30 (*0-7837-3237-6*, 2043256) Bks Demand.

Mikhailov. Applied Mechanics Vol. 4: Soviet Review. 1994. write for info. (*0-8493-9329-9*) CRC Pr.

Mikhailov, A. A., ed. Physics of Stars & Stellar Systems, 2 Vols., Set. 856p. 1969. text ed. 201.50 (*0-7065-0654-5*, Pub. by Keter Pub IS) Coronet Bks.

— Physics of the Solar System. 406p. 1966. text ed. 100.00 (*0-7065-0404-6*, Pub. by Keter Pub IS) Coronet Bks.

— Radio Astronomy. 332p. 1967. text ed. 86.50 (*0-7065-0443-7*, Pub. by Keter Pub IS) Coronet Bks.

Mikhailov, A. I., et al. Scientific Communications & Informatics. Burger, Robert H., tr. LC 83-81012. xxix, 402p. (C). 1984. text ed. 55.50 (*0-87815-046-3*) Info Resources.

Mikhailov, A. S. Foundations of Synergetics: Distributed Active Systems. LC 93-43340. (Synergetics Ser.: Vol. 51). 1994. write for info. (*3-540-57299-6*) Spr-Verlag.

— Foundations of Synergetics: Distributed Active Systems. 2nd ed. LC 93-43340. (Synergetics Ser.: Vol. 51). 1994. 79.00 (*0-387-57299-6*) Spr-Verlag.

— Foundations of Synergetics One: Distributed Active Systems. Haken, H., ed. (Synergetics Ser.: Vol. 51). (Illus.). 208p. 1990. 69.00 (*0-387-52775-3*) Spr-Verlag.

Mikhailov, A. S. & Loskutov, A. Yu. Foundations of Synergetics Two: Complex Patterns. Haken, H., ed. (Synergetics Ser.: Vol. 52). (Illus.). viii, 210p. 1991. 79.00 (*0-387-53448-2*) Spr-Verlag.

Mikhailov, A. S., jt. ed. see Haken, H.

Mikhailov, A. V., jt. auth. see Ivanov-Kholodny, G. S.

Mikhailov, B. M. & Bubnov, Yu N. Organoboron Compounds in Organic Synthesis. xxxiv, 781p. 1984. text ed. 394.00 (*3-7186-0113-3*) Gordon & Breach.

Mikhailov, G. A. Minimization of Computational Costs of Non-Analogue Monte Carlo Methods. 220p. (C). 1992. text ed. 43.00 (*981-02-0707-7*) World Scientific Pub.

— Optimization of Weighted Monte Carlo Methods. Glowinski, R. et al, eds. Sabelfeld, K. K., tr. (Computational Physics Ser.). 220p. 1992. 91.00 (*0-387-53005-3*) Spr-Verlag.

Mikhailov, G. K. & Parton. Applied Mechanics & Soviet Reviews, Vol. 1. 1989. 197.00 (*0-89116-718-8*) Taylor & Francis.

— Applied Mechanics, Soviet Reviews, Vol. 2: Stability & Analytical Mechanics. 1990. 178.00 (*0-89116-720-X*) Hemisp Pub.

Mikhailov, G. K. & Parton, V. Z. Fluid Mechanics. (Applied Mechanics: Soviet Reviews Ser.: Vol. 3). 500p. 1991. 145.00 (*0-89116-719-6*) CRC Pr.

Mikhailov, G. K. & Parton, V. Z., eds. Applied Mechanics: Soviet Reviews, Vol. 2: Electromagnetoelasticity. 360p. 1990. 145.00 (*0-685-40762-4*) Hemisp Pub.

Mikhailov, G. K., jt. ed. see Koiter, W. T.

Mikhailov, K. & Smirnov, G. Portrait Miniatures from the Collection of the Russian Museum. (Seventeenth to Early Twentieth Centuries Ser.). 1979. 39.00 (*0-317-14316-6*, Pub. by Collets UK) Pro-Am Music.

Mikhailov, K. V., et al. Polymer Concretes & Their Structural Uses. Parameswaran, V. S., ed. (Russian Translation Ser.: No. 91). (Illus.). 326p. (C). 1991. text ed. 95.00 (*90-6191-110-9*, Pub. by A A Balkema NE) Ashgate Pub Co.

Mikhailov, M. D. & Ozisik, M. N. Unified Analysis & Solutions of Heat & Mass Diffusion. LC 93-34237. (Illus.). 524p. 1994. reprint ed. pap. text ed. 15.95 (*0-486-67876-8*) Dover.

Mikhailov, M. D. & Ozisik, M. Necati. Heat Transfer Solver. 160p. 1991. pap. text ed. 36.60 (*0-13-388802-9*, 340101) P-H.

Mikhailov, N. Book about Russia in the Union of Equals. 254p. (C). 1988. 80.00 (*0-685-31682-3*, Pub. by Collets UK) Pro-Am Music.

An Asterisk (*) at the beginning of an entry indicates that the title is appearing in BIP for the first time.

Mikhailov, N. A. Pavel Korin. 102p. 1982. pap. 14.00 (*0-317-57405-1*, Pub. by Collets UK) St Mut.

Mikhailov, V. A. Neptunium. (Analytical Chemistry of the Elements Ser.). 244p. reprint ed. pap. text ed. 62.50 (*0-7065-1264-2*, Pub. by Keter Pub IS) Coronet Bks.

Mikhailov, Y., jt. auth. see Luikov, A.

Mikhailova, Tatyana A., jt. auth. see Rozhkov, Anatoly S.

Mikhailovskii, A. B. Electromagnetic Instabilities in an Inhomogeneous Plasma. (Plasma Physics Ser.). (Illus.). 320p. 1992. 118.00 (*0-7503-0182-1*) IOP Pub.

— Theory of Plasma Instabilities, 2 vols. Incl. Vol. 1. Instabilities of a Homogeneous Plasma. LC 73-83899. 308p. 1974. 59.50 (*0-306-17181-3*, Consultants); Vol. 2. Instabilities of an Inhomogeneous Plasma. LC 73-83899. 332p. 1974. 59.50 (*0-306-17182-1*, Consultants); LC 73-83899. (Studies in Soviet Science, Physical Sciences). 1974. write for info. (*0-318-55302-3*, Consultants) Plenum.

Mikhailovskii, A. B., tr. see Leontovich, M. A., ed.

Mikhailovsky, V. Uchenije o Pravoslavnom Bogosluzhenii. 146p. reprint ed. pap. text ed. 6.00 (*0-317-30287-6*) Holy Trinity.

***Mikhalchishin, Adrian & Pein, Malcom.** The Exchange Grunfeld. 160p. 1995. 19.95 (*1-85744-056-0*, Pub. by Cadogan Books UK) Macmillan.

***Mikhalev, Alexander A. & Zolotykh, Andrej A.** Combinatorial Aspects of Lie Superalgebras. LC 95-15995. 1995. write for info. (*0-8493-8960-7*) CRC Pr.

Mikheev, M. I., jt. ed. see Karvonen, M.

Mikheeva, G. V., jt. auth. see Nitkina, N. V.

Mikheeva, G. V., jt. ed. see Nitkina, N. V.

Mikhejev, A. V., jt. auth. see Frumkina, R. M.

Mikhelson, M. & Longo, V. G. Pharmacology of Conditioning, Learning, & Retention. LC 64-15320. (Proceedings of the International Pharmacological Meeting, Prague, August 1963 Ser.). 1965. 160.00 (*0-08-010803-2*, Pub. by Pergamon Repr UK) Franklin.

Mikheyev, Dimitry. The Soviet Perspective on the Strategic Defense Initiative. LC 87-2323. (Foreign Policy Report Ser.). xii, 95p. 11.95 (*0-317-65162-5*) Inst Foreign Policy Anal.

Mikheyev, Dmitry. The Rise & Fall of Gorbachev. 178p. (Orig.). (C). 1992. pap. text ed. 12.95 (*1-55813-041-1*) Hudson Instit IN.

Mikheyev, Sergei M., tr. see Berezhkov, Valentin M.

Mikhin, N. M., jt. auth. see Kragel'skii, I. V.

Mikhin, V. Western Expansionism in the Persian Gulf. (C). 1988. 17.50 (*0-8364-2448-4*, Pub. by Allied II) S Asia.

Mikhlin, A. & Armstrong, A. Integral Equations: Application Certain Problems Mechanics Math Physics Tech. LC 57-13328. (International Series Mono in Pure & Applied Biology: Vol. 4). 1957. 146.00 (*0-08-010535-1*, Pub. by Pergamon Repr UK) Franklin.

Mikhlin, S. & Whyte, W. Multidimensional Singular Integrals & Integral Equations. LC 64-21900. (International Series Mono on Pure & Applied Mathematics: Vol. 83). 1965. 113.00 (*0-08-010852-0*, Pub. by Pergamon Repr UK) Franklin.

Mikhlin, S. G. Approximation on a Rectangular Grid: With Application to Finite Element Methods & Other Problems, No. 4. (Mechanics Analysis Ser.). 235p. 1979. lib. bdg. 74.50 (*90-286-0008-6*) Kluwer Ac.

— Linear Integral Equations. (Russian Monographs & Texts on the Physical Sciences). 240p. 1961. text ed. 121.00 (*0-677-20320-9*) Gordon & Breach.

Mikhlin, Solomon G. Constants in Some Inequalities of Analysis. LC 84-13108. 107p. 1986. text ed. 59.95 (*0-471-90559-3*) Wiley.

— Error Analysis in Numerical Processes. (Pure & Applied Mathematics: A Wiley-Interscience Series of Texts, Monographs & Tracts: No. 1237). 283p. 1991. text ed. 145.00 (*0-471-92133-5*) Wiley.

Miki, Fujio. Haniwa. Rosenfield, John, ed. Barnes, Gina, tr. LC 73-88477. (Arts of Japan Ser.: Vol. 8). (Illus.). 144p. 1974. 15.00 (*0-8348-2714-X*) Weatherhill.

Miki, Roy. The Prepoetice of William Carlos Williams: Kora in Hell. LC 83-15551. (Studies in Modern Literature: No. 32). (Illus.). 223p. reprint ed. pap. 63.60 (*0-8357-1476-4*, 2070563) Bks Demand.

— Random Access File. 96p. 1995. pap. 9.95 (*0-88995-130-6*, Pub. by Red Deer CN) BookWorld Dist.

Mikics, David. The Limits of Moralizing: Pathos & Subjectivity in Spenser & Milton. 1994. write for info. (*0-8387-5285-3*) Bucknell U Pr.

Mikio Sumiya & Koji Taira, eds. An Outline of Japanese Economic History, 1603-1940: Major Works & Research Findings. LC 79-670232. 386p. reprint ed. pap. 110.10 (*0-7837-6270-4*, 2045982) Bks Demand.

Mikiro, Sasaki. Demented Flute: Selected Poems, 1967-1986. Fitzsimmons, Thomas, ed. Elliott, William I. et al, trs. (Asian Poetry in Translation: Japan Ser.: No. 9). 64p. (Orig.). 1988. lib. bdg. 14.50 (*0-942668-15-4*); pap. 9.50 (*0-942668-14-6*) Katydid Bks.

***Mikkelsen, Britha.** Methods for Development Work & Research: A Guide for Practioners. LC 95-5373. (Illus.). 250p. 1995. 35.00 (*0-8039-9229-7*); pap. 16.95 (*0-8039-9230-0*) Sage.

Mikkelsen, Edwin J., jt. auth. see Brown, Phil.

Mikkelsen, John. Hoping Against Hope: A Selection of Modern Day Healing Miracles. LC 93-84110. (Orig.). 1993. pap. 12.95 (*0-9636935-0-6*) Step Stone NY.

Mikkelsen, M. A. The Bishop Hill Colony: A Religious, Communistic Settlement in Henry County, Illinois. LC 72-187466. (American Utopian Adventure Ser.). 167p. 1973. reprint ed. lib. bdg. 29.50 (*0-87991-014-3*) Porcupine Pr.

Mikkelsen, Michael A. The Bishop Hill Colony. LC 78-63808. (Johns Hopkins University. Studies in the Social Sciences. Thirtieth Ser. 1912: 1). reprint ed. 11.50 (*0-404-61071-4*) AMS Pr.

Mikkelsen, Nina. Virginia Hamilton. LC 94-621. (Twayne's United States Authors Ser.). 200p. 1994. text ed. 22.95 (*0-8057-4010-4*, Twayne) Macmillan.

Mikkelson, Gerald, tr. see Rasputin, Valentin.

Mikkelson, Holly. The Interpreter's Companion. 2nd ed. (Illus.). 368p. (ENG & SPA.). 1993. pap. 35.00 (*1-880594-07-2*, IC2) Acebo.

— The Interpreter's Edge: Practical Exercises in Court Interpreting. Willis, Jim & Alvarez, Norma, eds. 224p. (Orig.). (ENG & SPA.). (C). 1992. pap. 20.00 (*1-880594-04-8*, IE-A) Acebo.

— The Interpreter's Edge Instructor's - Self-Study Notes. Willis, Jim & Alvarez, Norma, eds. 86p. (Orig.). (ENG & SPA.). (C). 1992. pap. 20.00 (*1-880594-05-6*, IE-B) Acebo.

— The Interpreter's Edge Self-Study Package, 2 bks., Set. Willis, Jim & Alvarez, Norma, eds. (SPA.). (C). 1992. audio, pap. 60.00 (*0-614-04751-X*) Acebo.

— The Interpreter's Edge Turbo Supplement: Advanced Exercises in Court Interpreting. Willis, Jim & Alvarez, Norma, eds. 94p. (Orig.). (ENG & SPA.). (C). 1993. pap. text ed. 45.00 (*1-880594-08-0*, IET) Acebo.

— The Interpreter's RX: A Training Program for Spanish/English Medical Interpreting. (Illus.). 262p. (SPA.). (C). 1994. pap. 55.00 (*1-880594-11-0*, 1RX) Acebo.

Mikkelson, Holly & Willis, Jim. The Interpreter's Edge, Generic Edition: Practical Exercise in Court Interpreting. 160p. (Orig.). (C). 1993. audio, pap. 55.00 (*1-880594-06-4*, EG) Acebo.

— The Interpreter's Edge, Generic Edition: Practical Exercise in Court Interpreting. (Orig.). (KOR.). (C). 1993. audio 100.00 (*0-614-04752-8*) Acebo.

Mikkelson, Shirley, ed. All My Tomorrows, Vol. I. (Illus.). 148p. (Orig.). 1993. pap. 24.95 (*0-943536-73-1*) Quill Bks.

— All My Tomorrows, Vol. II. (Illus.). 148p. (Orig.). 1993. pap. 24.95 (*0-943536-74-X*) Quill Bks.

— All My Tomorrows, Vol. III. (Illus.). 148p. (Orig.). 1993. pap. 24.95 (*0-943536-75-8*) Quill Bks.

— Dusting off Dreams, Vol. I. (Illus.). 152p. (Orig.). 1994. pap. 24.95 (*0-943536-81-2*) Quill Bks.

— Dusting off Dreams, Vol. II. (Illus.). 152p. (Orig.). 1994. pap. 24.95 (*0-943536-82-0*) Quill Bks.

— Dusting off Dreams, Vol. III. (Illus.). 152p. (Orig.). 1994. pap. 24.95 (*0-943536-83-9*) Quill Bks.

— Echoes from the Silence, Vol. I. (Illus.). 156p. (Orig.). 1995. pap. 24.95 (*0-943536-94-4*) Quill Bks.

— Echoes from the Silence, Vol. II. (Illus.). 156p. (Orig.). 1995. pap. 24.95 (*0-943536-95-2*) Quill Bks.

— Echoes from the Silence, Vol. III. (Illus.). 156p. (Orig.). 1995. pap. 24.95 (*0-943536-96-0*) Quill Bks.

Mikkola, Donald E., jt. ed. see Schlesinger, Mark E.

Mikkola, Heimo. Owls of Europe. LC 83-71804. (Illus.). 400p. 1983. 40.00 (*0-931130-10-7*) Harrell Bks.

Miklas, Christine L., ed. see American Indian Lawyer Training Program, Inc., Staff & American Indian Resources Institute Staff.

Miklich, Carol L. Feeding the New American Family. (Illus.). 300p. (Orig.). 1994. pap. 19.95 (*0-9640966-0-9*) B & C Pubng.

Miklos, Erwin. Training-in-Common for Educational, Public, & Business Administrators. 55p. (Orig.). (C). 1972. pap. text ed. 1.25 (*1-55996-115-5*, W114) Univ Council Educ Admin.

Miklos, George, jt. auth. see John, Bernard.

Miklosko, J., ed. Fast Algorithms & Their Implementation on Specialized Parallel Computers. (Special Topics in Supercomputing Ser.: No. 5). 266p. 1989. 77.00 (*0-444-70141-9*, North Holland) Elsevier.

Miklovic, Daniel T. Real-Time Control Networks. LC 93-13670. (Resources for Measurement & Control Ser.). 277p. 1993. 65.00 (*1-55617-231-1*) Instru Soc.

Miklowitz. Past Forgiving. (YA). 1995. 15.00 (*0-671-88442-5*, S&S Bks Young Read) S&S Childrens.

Miklowitz, Gloria. The Killing Boy. (YA). 1993. pap. 3.50 (*0-553-56037-9*) Bantam.

Miklowitz, Gloria D. Anything to Win. 1990. reprint ed. pap. 3.50 (*0-440-20732-0*, LFL) Dell.

— Desperate Pursuit. (J). (gr. 7 up). 1992. mass mkt. 3.99 (*0-553-29746-5*, Starfire) Bantam.

— The War Between the Classes. (J). (gr. 6 up). 1986. pap. 3.99 (*0-440-99406-3*, LFL) Dell.

Miklowitz, J. The Theory of Elastic Waves & Waveguides. (Applied Mathematics & Mechanics Ser.: Vol. 22). 618p. 1978. 131.00 (*0-7204-0551-3*, North Holland) Elsevier.

— Theory of Elastic Waves & Waveguides. (Applied Mathematics & Mechanics Ser.: Vol. 22). 1984. pap. 50.50 (*0-444-87513-1*, I-189-84, North Holland) Elsevier.

Miklowitz, Julius, ed. Wave Propagation in Solids. LC 72-101230. 189p. reprint ed. pap. 53.90 (*0-317-08536-0*, 2010125) Bks Demand.

Miklusack-Cooper, Cindy. Living in Hope. LC 90-2611. 324p. (Orig.). 1991. pap. 12.95 (*0-89087-629-0*) Celestial Arts.

Miknis, Francis P. & McKay, John F., eds. Geochemistry & Chemistry of Oil Shales. LC 83-11801. (ACS Symposium Ser.: No. 230). 576p. 1983. lib. bdg. 65.95 (*0-8412-0799-2*) Am Chemical.

Miko, Chris J. & Weilant, Edward. Opinions 1990, No. 4 Cum. 1991. 99.00 (*0-8103-7804-3*) Gale.

Miko, Chris J. & Weilant, Edward, eds. Opinions '90: Extracts from Public Opinion Surveys & Polls Conducted by Business, Government, & News Organizations, 4 Issues. (Illus.). 150p. 1990. Three quarterlies, 150p. ea. pap. text ed. 129.00 (*0-8103-7800-0*) Gale.

Miko Hino. Water Quality & Its Control. (Hydraulic Structures Design Manual Ser.: Vol. 5). (Illus.). 262p. 1994. text ed. 110.00 (*90-5410-123-7*, Pub. by A A Balkema NE) Ashgate Pub Co.

Miko, Stephen J. Toward Women in Love: The Emergence of a Lawrentian Aesthetic. LC 73-151583. (Yale Studies in English: No. 177). 309p. reprint ed. pap. 88.10 (*0-8357-8354-5*, 2033827) Bks Demand.

Mikohailov. Super-Hypersonic Aerodynamic & Heat Transfer. 1992. 167.95 (*0-8493-9309-4*, TL571) CRC Pr.

Mikojkovic-Djuric, Jelena. Aspects of Soviet Culture: Voices of Glasnost 1960-1990. 180p. 1991. text ed. 25.00 (*0-88033-204-2*) Col U Pr.

Mikola, Tibor. Die Alten Postpositionen des Nenzischen Juraksamojedischen. (Janua Linguarum, Series Practica: No. 240). 242p. 1975. pap. text ed. 53.50 (*90-279-3087-2*) Mouton.

Mikolajczak. Algebraic & Structural Automata Theory. (Annals of Discrete Mathematics Ser.: Vol. 44). 1991. 143.00 (*0-444-87458-5*, ADM 44) Elsevier.

Mikolajczy, P. & Paszkowski, B. Electronic Universal Vade-Mecum: Electron Valves & Semiconductor Devices, 2 vols., Set. LC 60-53074. 1964. 267.00 (*0-08-010739-7*, Pub. by Pergamon Repr UK) Franklin.

Mikolajczyk, Andrzej. Polish Museums: Anglo-Saxon & Later Medieval British Coins. (Sylloge of Coins of the British Isles British Academy Ser.: Vol. 37). (Illus.). 88p. 1988. 55.00 (*0-19-726063-2*) OUP.

Mikolajczyk, Stanislaw. The Rape of Poland. LC 73-141282. (Illus.). 309p. 1972. reprint ed. text ed. 65.00 (*0-8371-5879-6*, MIRP, Greenwood Pr) Greenwood.

Mikolajewska, Joanna, et al, eds. The Symbiotic Phenomenon. (C). 1988. lib. bdg. 140.00 (*90-277-2723-6*) Kluwer Ac.

Mikolas, Barbara S. Pool of Water: New Age Reflections. (Illus.). 128p. (Orig.). 1989. pap. 7.95 (*1-877633-01-1*) Luthers.

Mikolas, M. Real Functions, Abstract Spaces & Orthogonal Series. 400p. Date not set. 58.00 (*963-05-6652-4*, Pub. by A K HU) Intl Spec Bk.

***Mikolas, Mark.** Nature Walks in Southern Vermont. (Illus.). 288p. 1995. pap. 12.95 (*1-878239-47-3*) AMC Books.

Mikolaycak, C., ed. see Hopkins, Lee B.

Mikolaycak, Charles. Babushka: An Old Russian Folktale. LC 84-500. (Illus.). 32p. (J). (ps-3). 1984. lib. bdg. 15.95 (*0-8234-0520-6*); pap. 5.95 (*0-8234-0712-8*) Holiday.

— Orpheus. (J). 1992. 19.95 (*0-15-258804-3*, HB Juv Bks) HarBrace.

Mikolaycak, Charles, illus. Bearhead: A Russian Folktale. LC 91-55026. 32p. (J). (ps-3). 1991. lib. bdg. 15.95 (*0-8234-0902-3*) Holiday.

— A Gift from Saint Nicholas. LC 87-8797. 32p. (J). (ps-3). 1988. lib. bdg. 15.95 (*0-8234-0674-1*) Holiday.

— He Is Risen: The Easter Story. LC 84-15869. 32p. (J). (gr. 4-6). 1985. lib. bdg. 15.95 (*0-8234-0547-8*) Holiday.

Mikoletsky, Loren, ed. Allgemeines Verwaltungsarchiv, Archiv der Republik, Vienna. LC 94-45841. (Archives of the Holocaust Ser.: Vol. 21). 435p. 1995. 125.00 (*0-8240-6465-8*) Garland.

Mikolowski, Ken. Big Enigmas. 77p. (Orig.). 1990. pap. 7.50 (*0-9622474-4-8*) Past Tents Pr.

Mikolyzk, Thomas A., comp. Langston Hughes: A Bio-Bibliography. LC 90-3613. (Bio-Bibliographies in Afro-American & African Studies: No. 2). 312p. 1990. text ed. 45.00 (*0-313-26895-9*, MLK/, Greenwood Pr) Greenwood.

— Oscar Wilde: An Annotated Bibliography. LC 93-14052. (Bibliographies & Indexes in World Literature Ser.: No. 38). 496p. 1993. text ed. 75.00 (*0-313-27597-1*, MOT/, Greenwood Pr) Greenwood.

Mikos, A. G., et al, eds. Biomaterials for Drug & Cell Delivery, Vol. 331: Materials Research Society Symposium Proceedings. 1994. text ed. 78.00 (*1-55899-230-8*) Materials Res.

— Polymers in Medicine & Pharmacy. (Symposium Proceedings Ser.: Vol. 394). 1995. text ed. 78.00 (*1-55899-297-9*) Materials Res.

***Mikos, Michael J.** Polish Renaissance Literature: An Anthology. (Illus.). 275p. 1995. 24.95 (*0-89357-257-8*) Slavica.

Mikos, Michael J., tr. Medieval Literature of Poland: An Anthology. LC 91-24676. (Library of Medieval Literature: Vol. 82B). (Illus.). 286p. 1992. 37.00 (*0-8153-0408-0*, GLML82B) Garland.

Mikos, Pal. The Collections of the Budapest Museum of Applied Arts. 376p. 1981. 165.00 (*0-317-57235-0*, Pub. by Collets UK) St Mut.

Mikoshiba, Nobuo, jt. ed. see Hasiguti, Ryukiti R.

Mikotowicz, Tom. Oliver Smith: A Bio-Bibliography. LC 93-21635. (Bio-Bibliographies in the Performing Arts Ser.: No. 43). 264p. 1993. text ed. 59.95 (*0-313-28709-0*, Greenwood Pr) Greenwood.

Mikotowicz, Tom, ed. Theatrical Designers: An International Biographical Dictionary. LC 91-28086. 360p. 1992. text ed. 69.50 (*0-313-26270-5*, MZT/, Greenwood Pr) Greenwood.

***Miksanek, Tony.** Murmurs: The Story of a Stethoscope. 123p. 1995. 13.95 (*0-9646089-0-1*) Illusions Pr.

Miksche, Ferdinand O. The Failure of Atomic Strategy & a New Proposal for the Defence of the West. LC 76-27852. 224p. 1977. reprint ed. text ed. 55.00 (*0-8371-9023-1*, MIFA, Greenwood Pr) Greenwood.

— Secret Forces: The Technique of Underground Movements. LC 73-110273. (Illus.). 181p. 1971. reprint ed. text ed. 49.75 (*0-8371-4499-X*, MISF, Greenwood Pr) Greenwood.

Miksic, John. Borobudur. (Illus.). 160p. 1991. 69.50 (*0-945971-31-1*) Periplus.

— Borobudur: Golden Tales of the Buddhas. (Illus.). 160p. 1990. 45.00 (*0-945971-15-X*) Periplus.

— Vertellingen Van de Buddha: Borobudur. (Illus.). 160p. 1991. 4.95 (*0-945971-25-7*) Periplus.

Miksicek, Barbara, et al. In the Line of Duty: St. Louis Police Officers Who Made the Ultimate Sacrifice. 340p. 1991. write for info. (*0-934426-41-4*) NAPSAC Reprods.

Mikula, G., jt. ed. see Lerner, M. J.

Mikulan, K., jt. auth. see Thomas, N.

Mikulas, William L. The Way Beyond. LC 87-40131. (Illus.). 150p. (Orig.). 1987. pap. 7.95 (*0-8356-0625-2*, Quest) Theos Pub Hse.

Mikulas, William L., ed. Psychology of Learning: Readings. LC 77-8234. 1977. text ed. 37.95 (*0-88229-226-9*) Nelson-Hall.

Mikulecky, Bea. A Short Course in Teaching Reading Skills. (Illus.). 1990. pap. text ed. 24.95 (*0-201-50079-5*) Addison-Wesley.

Mikulecky, Bea & Jeffries, Linda. Reading Power. (Illus.). (C). 1986. text ed. 21.94 (*0-201-15865-5*) Addison-Wesley.

Mikulecky, Donald C. Applications of Network Thermodynamics to Problems in Biomedical Engineering. LC 92-30771. (Monographs in Biomedical Engineering). 1992. 80.00 (*0-8147-5490-2*) NYU Pr.

Mikulecky, Donald C. & Clarke, Alexander M., eds. Biomedical Engineering: Opening Doors, Set. (Monographs in Biomedical Engineering). 296p. 1990. 85.00 (*0-8147-7908-5*) NYU Pr.

Mikulecky, Larry & Drew, Rad A. On the Job: Activity Book II. (On the Job Ser.). 80p. (Orig.). 1988. pap. text ed. 4.00 (*0-8428-0164-2*) Cambridge Bk.

— On the Job: Book 1. (On the Job Ser.). 144p. (Orig.). 1988. pap. text ed. 6.00 (*0-8428-0160-X*) Cambridge Bk.

— On the Job: Book 3. (On the Job Ser.). 144p. (Orig.). 1988. pap. text ed. 6.00 (*0-8428-0162-6*) Cambridge Bk.

Mikulecky, Larry, jt. auth. see Stricht, Thomas G.

Mikuleky, Maureen P. & Ledford, Cathleen. Computers in Nursing: Hospital & Clinical Applications. 280p. (C). 1988. pap. text ed. 32.25 (*0-201-15908-2*) Addison-Wesley.

Mikulincer, M. Human Learned Helplessness: A Coping Perspective. (Series in Social - Clinical Psychology). (Illus.). 365p. (C). 1994. 45.00 (*0-306-44743-6*, Plenum Pr) Plenum.

Mikulski, Florian A. Managing Your Vendors: The Business of Buying Technology - A Complete Management Handbook for the Procurement of Technology from Vendors, Principles, Processes & Procedures, with a Case Study. LC 93-4395. 307p. 1993. text ed. 41.00 (*0-13-221060-6*) P-H.

Mikulsky, K. Lenin's Teaching on the World Economy. Riordan, Jim, tr. 1975. 25.00 (*0-8464-0560-1*) Beekman Pubs.

***Mikuriya, Tod.** Excerpts from the Indian Hemp Commission Report. 48p. 1995. 9.95 (*0-86719-420-0*) Last Gasp.

Mikuriya, Tod H., ed. Marijuana: Medical Papers, 1839-1972. LC 72-87736. 23.50 (*0-9600704-1-9*); pap. 15.00 (*0-685-48562-5*) Medi-Comp.

Mikus, Joseph A. Beyond Deterrence: From Power Politics to World Public Order. (American University Studies: Political Science: Ser. X, Vol. 15). 219p. (C). 1988. text ed. 33.00 (*0-8204-0699-6*) P Lang Pubs.

Mikusinski, Jan. Operational Calculus, Vol. 1. 2nd ed. (International Series on Pure & Applied Mathematics: Vol. 109). (Illus.). 320p. 1983. 141.00 (*0-08-025071-8*, Pub. by Pergamon Repr UK) Franklin.

— Operational Calculus, Vol. 2. 2nd ed. (International Series on Pure & Applied Mathematics: Vol. 110). (Illus.). 240p. 1987. 118.00 (*0-08-026479-4*) Franklin.

Mikusinski, Jan & Mikusinski, Piotr. An Introduction to Analysis: From Number to Integral. 290p. 1993. Net. text ed. write for info. (*0-471-58988-8*) Wiley.

Mikusinski, Jan, jt. auth. see Hartman, S.

Mikusinski, Piotr, jt. ed. see Debnath, Lokenath.

Mikusinski, Piotr, jt. auth. see Mikusinski, Jan.

Mikusko, M. Brady. Sourcebook of Oral Histories of Trade Union & Working in the United States. (Program on Workers Culture Ser.). 94p. 1982. pap. 6.50 (*0-87736-348-X*) U of Mich Inst Labor.

Milacic, V. R., ed. Intelligent Manufacturing Systems II, 2 vols., Set. 306p. 1988. 166.75 (*0-444-42997-2*) Elsevier.

Milacic, V. R. & Stanic, J., eds. Computer Integrated Quality System in CIM Systems: Proceedings of the IFIP TC5 - WG5.3 Working Conference, Belgrade, Yugoslavia, 20-23 June, 1989. 362p. 1990. 89.75 (*0-444-88562-5*, North Holland) Elsevier.

Miladinovic, Tomislav. Woerterbuch der Elektrotechnik und Elektronik: German & Russian Dictionary of Electronics & Electrical Engineering. (GER & RUS.). 1970. 175.00 (*0-8288-6561-2*, M-7016) Fr & Eur.

Milady. Milady's Art & Science of Nail Technology. 3rd rev. ed. 256p. 1992. pap. 21.95 (*1-56253-089-5*) Milady Pub.

Milady Editors. Exam Reviews in Hair Structure & Chemistry. 1977. 12.95 (*0-87350-135-7*) Milady Pub.

— Practical Beauty Culture Workbook. (Illus.). 1985. 16.00 (*0-87350-378-3*); teacher ed 23.95 (*0-87350-351-1*) Milady Pub.

— Standard Textbook of Professional Barber Styling. 1983. text ed. 34.50 (*0-87350-501-8*) Milady Pub.

— Texto General de Cosmetologia. (SPA.). 1986. student ed 4.50 (*0-87350-879-3*) Milady Pub.

— Van Dean Manual. rev. ed. (Illus.). 1990. text ed. 32.50 (*0-87350-516-6*) Milady Pub.

— Van Dean Practical Workbook. (Illus.). 1975. teacher ed 23.95 (*0-87350-524-7*); pap. 15.50 (*0-87350-518-2*) Milady Pub.

— Van Dean Theory Workbook. (Illus.). 1975. teacher ed 24.95 (*0-87350-523-9*); pap. 15.50 (*0-87350-519-0*) Milady Pub.

— Workbook for Professional Barber Styling. 1984. 17.50 (*0-87350-503-4*); teacher ed 23.95 (*0-87350-500-X*) Milady Pub.

An Asterisk (*) at the beginning of an entry indicates that the title is appearing in BIP for the first time.

Milady Publishing Co. Staff. Guide to Cosmetology Licensing 1991. LC 82-641642. 160p. 36.95 (*0-87350-398-8*) Milady Pub.

Milady Publishing Company Staff. Answers to Milady's Professional Barber-Styling Workbook. rev. ed. 193p. 1993. 23.95 (*1-56253-147-6*) Milady Pub.

— Answers to Milady's Workbook for Hair Structure & Chemistry Simplified. rev. ed. 86p. 1993. 21.50 (*1-56253-152-2*) Milady Pub.

— Hair Structure & Chemistry Exam Review. 2nd ed. Morehouse, Jayne, ed. 55p. 1993. pap. text ed. 12.95 (*1-56253-153-0*) Milady Pub.

— Lesson Plans to Accompany Milady's Standard Textbook of Cosmetology. 404p. 1994. teacher ed, text ed. 49.95 (*1-56253-234-0*) Milady Pub.

— Milady's Art & Science of Nail Technology. 224p. (SPA.). 1993. pap. text ed. 24.95 (*1-56253-156-5*) Milady Pub.

— Milady's Art & Science of Nail Technology - Exam Review. 65p. (SPA.). 1993. pap. text ed. 7.95 (*1-56253-181-6*) Milady Pub.

— Milady's Standard Textbook of Cosmetology Practical Workbook. rev. ed. 273p. 1994. text ed. 15.50 (*1-56253-218-9*) Milady Pub.

— Milady's Standard Textbook of Cosmetology Practical Workbook-Answer Key. rev. ed. 273p. 1994. teacher ed, text ed. 26.00 (*1-56253-219-7*) Milady Pub.

— Milady's Standard Textbook of Cosmetology Theory Workbook. rev. ed. 130p. 1994. text ed. 15.50 (*1-56253-220-0*) Milady Pub.

— Milady's Standard Textbook of Cosmetology Theory Workbook-Answer Key. rev. ed. 130p. 1994. teacher ed, text ed. 26.00 (*1-56253-221-9*) Milady Pub.

— Milady's Standard Textbook of Cosmetology, 1991. 544p. 1991. 25.50 (*1-56253-008-9*); 1.00 (*1-56253-004-6*); text ed. 34.50 (*1-56253-001-1*); pap. text ed. 31.50 (*1-56253-003-8*); student ed, disk 1,495.00 (*0-87350-817-3*); trans. 99.95 (*0-87350-924-2*); trans. 145.00 (*0-87350-922-6*); vhs 160.00 (*0-87350-659-6*); disk write for info. (*0-87350-995-1*); disk 1,495.00 (*0-87350-815-7*); disk 1,495.00 (*0-87350-816-5*); 5.50 (*1-56253-059-3*); 7.50 (*1-56253-018-6*); 10.95 (*0-87350-443-7*) Delmar.

— Revision Del Examen De Estado De Cosmetologia - State Exam Review for Cosmetology. (SPA.). 1992. student ed 11.50 (*1-56253-099-2*) Milady Pub.

— Standard Textbook for Professional Barber-Styling: Lesson Plans. rev. ed. 184p. 1993. 43.95 (*1-56253-163-8*) Milady Pub.

— Standard Textbook for Professional Barber-Styling: State Exam Review. rev. ed. 152p. 1993. pap. text ed. 10.50 (*1-56253-144-1*) Milady Pub.

— State Exam Review for Cosmetology. 126p. 1994. pap. 11.00 (*1-56253-237-5*) Milady Pub.

— State Exam Review for Nail Technology. 63p. 1993. pap. text ed. 7.95 (*1-56253-170-0*) Milady Pub.

— Texto General De Cosmetologia. 576p. (SPA.). 1992. pap. 29.50 (*1-56253-093-3*) Milady Pub.

— Texto General De Cosmetologia, Respuestas a las Preguntas de Repaso. 19p. (SPA.). 1992. teacher ed write for info. (*1-56253-143-3*) Milady Pub.

— Workbook for Milady's Hair Structure & Chemistry Simplified. rev. ed. 86p. 1993. 16.00 (*1-56253-151-4*) Milady Pub.

***Milady Publishing Company Staff & Edgerton, Leslie.** Milady's Guide to Becoming a Financially Solvent Salon. LC 95-16204. 1996. write for info. (*1-56253-211-1*) Milady Pub.

Milady Publishing Company Staff, jt. auth. see Sheahan, Maura.

Milakovich, Michael, jt. auth. see Humphrey, John A.

***Milakovich, Michael E.** Improving Serivce Quality: Achieving High Performance in the Public & Private Sectors. 320p. 1995. 39.95 (*1-884015-45-X*) St Lucie Pr.

Milakovich, Michael E., jt. auth. see Gordon, George J.

Milam & Ketcham, Katherine. Under the Influence - Myths-Realities-Alcoholism. 1984. mass mkt. 5.99 (*0-553-27487-2*) Bantam.

Milam, Edward E. & Crumbley, D. Larry. Estate Planning, after the 1976 Tax Reform Act. LC 78-970. 240p. reprint ed. pap. 68.40 (*0-317-20739-3*, 2023896) Bks Demand.

Milam, Edward E., jt. auth. see Crumbley, D. L.

Milam, Edward E., jt. auth. see Crumbley, D. Larry.

Milam, Edward E., jt. auth. see Sellers, James H.

***Milam, June M.** Big Decisions. Gilmer, Chris & Nelson, Laura L., eds. (Drugless Douglass Tales Ser.). (Illus.). 20p. (J). (ps-k). 1994. pap. text ed. 42.95 (*1-884307-15-9*); student ed, pap. text ed. 4.95 (*1-884307-16-7*) Dev Res Educ.

— Flying Around. Gilmer, Chris & Nelson, Laura L., eds. (Drugless Douglass Tales Ser.). (Illus.). 20p. (J). (ps-k). 1994. pap. text ed. 42.95 (*1-884307-17-5*); student ed, pap. text ed. 4.95 (*1-884307-18-3*) Dev Res Educ.

— I've Got an Idea. Gilmer, Chris, ed. (Drugless Douglass Tales Ser.). (Illus.). 20p. (J). (ps). 1994. student ed 4.95 (*1-884307-08-6*) Dev Res Educ.

— I've Got an Idea. Gilmer, Chris, ed. (Drugless Douglass Tales Ser.). (Illus.). 20p. (J). (ps-00). 1994. pap. text ed. 24.95 (*1-884307-07-8*) Dev Res Educ.

— Rainy Days. Gilmer, Chris & Peaster, Laura L., eds. (Drugless Douglass Tales Ser.). (Illus.). 20p. (J). (ps-00). 1994. student ed 4.95 (*1-884307-12-4*); pap. 42.95 (*1-884307-11-6*) Dev Res Educ.

— The Short Cut. Gilmer, Chris, ed. (Drugless Douglass Tales Ser.). (Illus.). 20p. (J). (ps). 1994. pap. text ed. 42.95 (*1-884307-05-1*); student ed 4.95 (*1-884307-06-X*) Dev Res Educ.

— A Terrible Thing. Gilmer, Chris & Nelson, Laura L., eds. (Drugless Douglass Tales Ser.). (Illus.). 20p. (J). (ps-k). 1994. 4.95 (*1-884307-14-0*); pap. text ed. 42.95 (*1-884307-13-2*) Dev Res Educ.

Milam, June M. & Gaston, Kathy. All by Myself. Gilmer, Chris & Wilson, Amy L., eds. (Drugless Douglass Tales Ser.). (Illus.). 24p. (Orig.). (J). (ps-00). 1993. pap. text ed. 42.95 (*1-884307-00-0*); student ed 4.95 (*1-884307-01-9*) Dev Res Educ.

Milam, June M., jt. auth. see Gilmer, Chris.

Milam, June M., et al. The Drugless Douglas Tales Series, 9 vols., Set. Wilson, Amy L., ed. (Illus.). (Orig.). (J). (ps-k). 1994. pap. 431.10 (*1-884307-02-7*) Dev Res Educ.

Milam, Lorenzo W. Cripple Liberation Front Marching Band Blues. 222p. 1992. 14.95 (*0-917320-10-7*); pap. 9.95 (*0-917320-09-3*) Mho & Mho.

— CripZen: A Manual for Survival. 254p. 1993. 17.95 (*0-917320-02-6*); pap. 12.95 (*0-917320-03-4*) Mho & Mho.

— The Radio Papers: From KRAB to KCHU-Essays on the Art & Practice of Radio Transmission. (Twenty-Five Years of Community Broadcasting Ser.). (Illus.). 224p. 1986. pap. 9.95 (*0-917320-19-0*) Mho & Mho.

— Sex & Broadcasting: A Handbook on Building a Radio Station for the Community. (Illus.). 375p. 1988. pap. 12.95 (*0-917320-01-8*) Mho & Mho.

Milam, Mary A. Right Side Up. 239p. (Orig.). 1991. pap. 5.95 (*0-9631187-0-6*) Marigold Pub.

— Right Side Up. 54p. (Orig.). 1994. pap. 3.95 (*0-9631187-1-4*) Marigold Pub.

Milam, Melody J., jt. auth. see Harris, Jerry L.

Milamed, Susan, jt. auth. see Schwartz, Rosaline.

Milan, Albert R. Breast Self-Examination. LC 79-56529. (Illus.). 128p. 1980. pap. 3.50 (*0-89480-124-4*, 419) Workman Pub.

Milan, Deanne. Developing Reading Skills. 4th ed. LC 94-7827. 1994. pap. text ed. write for info. (*0-07-041914-0*) McGraw.

— Improving Reading Skills. 3rd ed. LC 95-14560. (C). 1995. write for info. (*0-07-041930-2*) McGraw.

Milan, Deanne K. Developing Reading Skills. 416p. (C). 1983. pap. text ed. write for info. (*0-394-32789-6*) Random.

— Developing Reading Skills. 3rd ed. 496p. 1991. pap. text ed. write for info. (*0-07-041901-9*) McGraw.

— Improving Reading Skills. 2nd ed. 480p. 1992. pap. text ed. write for info. (*0-07-041906-X*); write for info. (*0-07-041907-8*) McGraw.

Milan, June M. Just a Little Lie. Gilwer, Chris, ed. (Drugless Douglass Tales Ser.). (Illus.). 20p. (J). (ps-00). 1993. pap. text ed. 42.95 (*1-884307-03-5*); student ed 4.95 (*0-685-70993-0*) Dev Res Educ.

Milan, Luys. Libro de Musica de Vihuela de Mano Intitulado el Maestro. (Publikationen Alterer Musik Ser.: No. II). xxx, 382p. 1976. reprint ed. write for info. (*3-487-00629-4*, Pub. by Georg Olms GW) Lubrecht & Cramer.

Milan, Michael. The Squad: The U.S. Government's Secret Alliance with Organized Crime. (Illus.). 1989. 19.95 (*0-933503-36-9*) Sure Sellers.

Milan, Michael A., jt. auth. see Ayllon, Teodoro.

Milan, Sara. Czech for English Speaking Students. 600p. 1988. 100.00 (*0-569-06362-0*, Pub. by Collets UK) Pro-Am Music.

***Milan, Victor.** CLD (Collective Landing Detachment) 304p. (Orig.). 1995. mass mkt. 5.50 (*0-380-77734-7*, AvoNova) Avon.

— Close Quarters. 288p. (Orig.). 1994. pap. 4.99 (*0-451-45378-6*, ROC) NAL-Dutton.

— From the Depths. (Star Trek Ser.: No. 66). 288p. (Orig.). 1993. mass mkt. 5.50 (*0-671-86911-6*) PB.

— Red Sands. 416p. (Orig.). 1993. mass mkt. 4.99 (*0-446-35840-1*) Warner Bks.

— War in Tethyr. (The Nobles Ser.). 320p. (Orig.). 1995. pap. 4.95 (*0-7869-0184-5*) TSR Inc.

Milan, Virginia E., jt. auth. see Meredith, Howard.

Milan Women's Bookstore Collective Staff. Sexual Difference: A Theory of Social-Symbolic Practice. (Theories of Representation & Difference Ser.). 160p. 1990. 25.00 (*0-253-33826-3*); pap. 10.95 (*0-253-20605-7*, MB-605) Ind U Pr.

Milanese, M., et al, eds. Robustness in Identification & Control. (Applied Information Technology Ser.). (Illus.). 350p. 1989. 75.00 (*0-306-43251-X*, Plenum Pr) Plenum.

Milanesi, Enza. Bulfinch Guide to Carpets: How to Identify, Classify, & Evaluate Antique Carpets & Rugs. (Illus.). 192p. 1993. 19.95 (*0-8212-2057-8*) Bulfinch Pr.

Milani, A., et al. Non-gravitational Perturbations & Satellite Geodesy. (Illus.). 136p. 1987. 75.00 (*0-85274-538-9*) IOP Pub.

Milani, A., et al, eds. Asteroids, Comets, & Meteors 1993: Proceedings of the 160th Symposium of the International Astronomical Union, Held in Belgirate, Italy, June 14-18, 1993. LC 94-16936. (International Astronomical Union Symposia Ser.). 503p. (C). 1994. lib. bdg. 147.50 (*0-7923-2880-9*); pap. text ed. 75.00 (*0-7923-2881-7*) Kluwer Ac.

Milani, Abbas, tr. see Irani, Manuchehr.

Milani, Farzaneh. Veils & Words: The Emerging Voices of Iranian Women Writers. LC 91-28640. (Contemporary Issues in the Middle East Ser.). 320p. 1992. text ed. 39.95x (*0-8156-2557-X*); pap. 16.95 (*0-8156-0266-9*) Syracuse U Pr.

***Milani, Mohsen.** The Making of Iran's Islamic Revolution. (C). 1994. pap. text ed. 21.95 (*0-8133-8476-1*) Westview.

— The Making of Iran's Islamic Revolution. (C). 1994. text ed. 62.00 (*0-8133-8475-3*) Westview.

***Milani, Myrna M.** The Art of Veterinary Practice: A Guide to Client Communication. LC 94-40919. 312p. 1995. text ed. 29.95 (*0-8122-3260-7*) U of Pa Pr.

— The Body Language & Emotion of Cats. LC 87-5772. 288p. 1987. 18.95 (*0-688-06786-7*) Morrow.

— Body Language & Emotion of Cats. 1993. pap. 12.00 (*0-688-12840-8*, Quill) Morrow.

— Body Language & Emotion of Dogs. 1993. pap. 12.00 (*0-688-12841-6*, Quill) Morrow.

— The Body Language & Emotions of Dogs. LC 86-8449. 288p. 1986. 17.95 (*0-688-06239-3*) Morrow.

Milani, Myrna M. & Smith, Brian R. A Primer of Rotational Physics. LC 84-13518. (Rational Physics Ser.). (Illus.). (Orig.). 1985. 15.00 (*0-943290-02-3*); pap. 10.00 (*0-943290-01-5*) Fainshaw Pr.

— Rotational Physics: The Principles of Energy. LC 85-16305. (Rotational Physics Ser.). (Illus.). (Orig.). 1986. pap. 12.00 (*0-943290-03-1*) Fainshaw Pr.

Milani, Myrna M., jt. auth. see Smith, Brian R.

Milani, Terrence E. & Johnston, J. William, eds. The College Union in the Year Two Thousand. LC 85-644751. (New Directions for Student Services Ser.: No. SS 58). 100p. 1992. 16.95 (*1-55542-762-6*) Jossey-Bass.

Milanich, Jerald T. Archaeology of Pre-Columbian Florida. LC 93-36888. (Illus.). 496p. (C). 1994. lib. bdg. 49.95 (*0-8130-1272-4*); pap. 24.95 (*0-8130-1273-2*) U Press Fla.

— Florida Indians & the Invasion from Europe. LC 95-7951. (Illus.). 304p. 1995. 29.95 (*0-8130-1360-7*) U Press Fla.

Milanich, Jerald T., ed. Earliest Hispanic - Native American Interactions in the American Southeast. LC 91-17734. (Spanish Borderlands Sourcebooks Ser.: Vol. 12). 528p. 1991. 76.00 (*0-8240-1951-2*) Garland.

— The Hernando de Soto Expedition. LC 90-29269. (Spanish Borderlands Sourcebooks Ser.: Vol. 11). 496p. 1991. 72.00 (*0-8240-1950-4*) Garland.

Milanich, Jerald T. & Hudson, Charles. Hernando de Soto & the Indians of Florida. LC 92-22868. (Columbus Quincentenary Series - Ripley P. Bullen). (Illus.). 312p. 1993. 34.95 (*0-8130-1170-1*) U Press Fla.

Milanich, Jerald T. & Milbrath, Susan, eds. First Encounters: Spanish Explorations in the Caribbean & the United States, 1492-1570. (Ripley P. Bullen Monographs Ser.: No. 9). (Illus.). 232p. 1989. lib. bdg. 49.95 (*0-8130-0946-4*); pap. 23.95 (*0-8130-0947-2*) U Press Fla.

Milanich, Jerald T. & Proctor, Samuel, eds. Tacachale: Essays on the Indians of Florida & Southeastern Georgia During the Historic Period. LC 94-6039. (Ripley P. Bullen Ser.). 232p. 1994. pap. text ed. 18.95 (*0-8130-1297-X*) U Press Fla.

Milanich, Jerald T., et al. McKeither Weeden Island: The Culture of Northern Florida, A.D. 200-900. (New World Archaeological Record Ser.). 1984. text ed. 63.00 (*0-12-495970-9*) Acad Pr.

Milanino, R., et al, eds. Copper & Zinc in Inflammation. (Inflammation & Drug Therapy Ser.). 160p. (C). 1989. lib. bdg. 70.50 (*0-7462-0079-X*) Kluwer Ac.

Milano, Carol. Hers: The Wise Woman's Guide to Starting a Business on 2,000 Dollars or Less. 208p. (Orig.). 1991. pap. 12.95 (*0-9607118-7-2*) Allworth Pr.

Milano, Carol, jt. auth. see Hutchinson, Betty.

Milano, Carol, jt. auth. see Lewis, William.

Milano, Dominic, ed. Synthesizer Programming. (Keyboard Magazine Synthesizer Library). (Illus.). 120p. (Orig.). 1987. pap. 14.95 (*0-88188-550-9*, HL00183703) H Leonard.

Milano, Geraldine B., jt. auth. see Mayott, Clarence W.

Milano, Jim, jt. auth. see Brogan, Patrick.

Milano, L. Mozan, No. 2: The Epigraphic Finds of the Sixth Season. (Mesopotamian Studies: No. 5-1). (Illus.). 34p. (C). 1991. pap. text ed. 8.25 (*0-89003-276-9*) Undena Pubns.

Milano, Paolo, ed. see Dante Alighieri.

Milanova, D. Swedish-Russian Dictionary. 760p. (RUS & SWE.). 1973. 59.95 (*0-8288-6331-8*, M-9077) Fr & Eur.

Milanovic, Branko. Liberalization & Entrepreneurship: Dynamics of Reform in Socialism & Capitalism. LC 89-4196. 200p. 1989. 57.95 (*0-87332-568-0*) M E Sharpe.

Milanovic, Branko, jt. ed. see Hillman, Arye L.

Milanovic, Petar J. Karst Hydrogeology. LC 80-54287. 1981. 32.00 (*0-918334-36-5*) WRP.

Milanovich, Norma, et al. We, the Arcturian's. LC 90-82682. (Illus.). 336p. (Orig.). 1990. pap. 14.95 (*0-9627417-0-1*) Athena NM.

***Milanovich, Norma J. & McCune, Shirley.** The Light Shall Set You Free. LC 94-78618. Date not set. student ed write for info. (*0-9627417-1-X*); write for info. (*0-9627417-5-2*); pap. write for info. (*0-9627417-7-9*) Athena NM.

Milanovich, Norma J., jt. auth. see Grier, Paula.

Milanowski, Stephen & Tarte, Bob. Duplicity. LC 91-65127. (Illus.). 42p. 1992. 22.95 (*0-942159-11-X*) U of Wash Pr.

Milarch, Christopher G. Day by Day in Advent: Devotions for the Season. LC 90-29126. (Illus.). 32p. (Orig.). 1991. pap. 4.99 (*0-8066-2556-2*, 10-25562) Augsburg Fortress.

Milard, A. & Chisholm, J. Early Civilizations. (Illustrated World History Ser.). (Illus.). 96p. (YA). 1992. lib. bdg. 16.96 (*0-88110-438-8*); pap. 10.95 (*0-7460-0328-5*) EDC.

Milardo, Robert M., ed. Families & Social Networks. LC 87-20462. (New Perspectives on Family Ser.). 237p. reprint ed. pap. 67.60 (*0-7837-6595-9*, 2046160) Bks Demand.

Milavec, Aaron. Exploring Scriptural Sources. 224p. (Orig.). 1994. pap. 19.95 (*1-55612-706-5*) Sheed & Ward MO.

— A Pilgrim Experiences the World's Religions. LC 84-9024. (Mellen Lives Ser.: Vol. 1). 96p. 1984. pap. 34.95 (*0-88946-010-8*) E Mellen.

— To Empower As Jesus Did: Acquiring Spiritual Power through Apprenticeship. LC 82-6466. (Toronto Studies in Theology: Vol. 9). 345p. (C). 1982. lib. bdg. 99.95 (*0-88946-966-0*) E Mellen.

Milavsky, J. Ronald, et al. Television & Aggression: Results of a Panel Study. (Quantitative Studies in Social Relations). 493p. 1982. text ed. 59.00 (*0-12-495980-6*) Acad Pr.

Milazzo, Dino. Getting the Most Out of Your VCR & Planning Your Home Entertainment System. (Illus.). 192p. (Orig.). 1992. pap. 12.95 (*0-9633138-3-5*) Inamar.

Milazzo, G., ed. Energetics & Technology of Biological Elimination of Wastes. (Studies in Enviornmental Science: Vol. 9). 252p. 1981. 87.25 (*0-444-41900-4*) Elsevier.

Milazzo, G. & Blank, Martin, eds. Bioelectrochemistry III: Charge Separation Across Biomembranes. (Ettore Majorana International Science Series, Life Sciences: Vol. 51). (Illus.). 348p. 1990. 95.00 (*0-306-43606-X*, Plenum Pr) Plenum.

Milazzo, G., ed. see Blank, Martin.

Milazzo, G., jt. auth. see Herington, E.

Milazzo, Giulio, ed. Topics in Bioelectrochemistry & Bioenergetics, 2 vols., 4. LC 76-18231. 356p. reprint ed. pap. 101.50 (*0-685-20645-9*, 2030431) Bks Demand.

— Topics in Bioelectrochemistry & Bioenergetics, 2 vols., 5. LC 76-18231. 356p. reprint ed. pap. 91.00 (*0-685-44058-3*, 2030431) Bks Demand.

Milazzo, Guilio & Caroli, Sergio. Tables of Standard Electrode Potentials. LC 77-8111. 437p. reprint ed. pap. 124.60 (*0-685-20767-6*, 2030411) Bks Demand.

Milazzo, Lee, ed. Conversations with Joyce Carol Oates. LC 89-16673. (Literary Conversations Ser.). 144p. 1989. 37.50 (*0-87805-411-1*); pap. 15.95 (*0-87805-412-X*) U Pr of Miss.

Milazzo, Matteo J. The Chetnik Movement & the Yugoslav Resistance. LC 74-24384. 219p. reprint ed. pap. 62.50 (*0-7837-2187-0*, 2042525) Bks Demand.

Milazzo, Richard, ed. Beauty & Critique. LC 82-50165. 176p. (Orig.). 1983. pap. text ed. 8.00 (*0-939858-01-0*) T S L Pr.

Milazzo, Richard, ed. see Ball, Pam, et al.

Milazzo, Richard, ed. see Gillespie, Abraham L.

Milazzo, Richard, ed. see Marsicano, Ed.

Milbank, Alison. Daughters in the House: Modes of the Gothic in Victorian Fiction. LC 91-27231. 256p. 1992. text ed. 45.00 (*0-312-07168-X*) St Martin.

Milbank, Alison, ed. see Radcliffe, Ann.

Milbank, Caroline R. Couture: The Great Designers. LC 85-2827. (Illus.). 432p. 1985. 85.00 (*0-941434-51-6*) Stewart Tabori & Chang.

— New York Fashion: The Evolution of American Style. (Illus.). 304p. 1989. 49.50 (*0-8109-1388-7*) Abrams.

Milbank, John. The Religious Dimension in the Thought of Giambattista Vico 1668-1744, Pt. 1: The Early Metaphysics. LC 91-32629. (Studies in the History of Philosophy: Vol. 23). 364p. 1991. lib. bdg. 99.95 (*0-7734-9694-7*) E Mellen.

— The Religious Dimension in the Thought of Giambattista Vico (1668-1744), Vol. 11: Language, Law & History. LC 91-32629. 292p. 1993. text ed. 89.95 (*0-7734-9215-1*) E Mellen.

— Theology & Social Theory: Beyond Secular Reason. (Signposts in Theology Ser.). 448p. 1993. pap. text ed. 24.95 (*0-631-18948-3*) Blackwell Pubs.

***Milbank, Richard.** Emperors & Barbarians: The Expanding World. (J). (gr. 4-7). 1994. 15.95 (*0-688-13907-8*, Tambourine Bks) Morrow.

***Milbank, Samuel L. & Fox, Daniel M., intros.** Federalism in Health Reform: Views from the States That Could Not Wait. (Illus.). 27p. 1994. pap. text ed. write for info. (*0-9629870-6-9*) Milbank Memorial.

Milbank, Samuel L. & Fox, Daniel M., prefs. The States That Could Not Wait: Lessons for Health Reform from Florida, Hawaii, Minnesota, Oregon & Vermont. 19p. (Orig.). 1993. pap. text ed. write for info. (*0-9629870-1-8*) Milbank Memorial.

Milbank, Tweed, Hadley & McCloy Law Firm Staff. Creditors Workout Strategies. 152.00 (*0-685-69622-7*, BBWR) Warren Gorham & Lamont.

Milbauer, Asher Z. & Watson, Donald G., eds. Reading Philip Roth. 225p. 1988. text ed. 32.50 (*0-312-00934-8*) St Martin.

Milberg, Doris. Hooray for Hollywood: Trivia & Puzzles for Those Today Who Remember Yesterday. 54p. (Orig.). 1994. pap. 8.95 (*1-879633-16-7*) Eldersong.

— Repeat Performances: A Guide to Hollywood Movie Remakes. 232p. 1990. pap. 12.95 (*0-911747-21-4*) Broadway Pr.

Milberg, William, ed. The Megacorp & Macrodynamics: Essays in Memory of Alfred Eichner. LC 90-26733. 230p. (C). 1992. 51.95 (*0-87332-782-9*); pap. text ed. 25.95 (*0-87332-783-7*) M E Sharpe.

Milberg, William & Bartholomew, Philip F., eds. Research in International Business & Finance, Vol. 9. 1991. 73.25 (*1-55938-234-1*) Jai Pr.

— Research in International Business & Finance, Vol. 8: Prospects for Canadian-United States Economic Relations under Free Trade. 240p. 1990. 73.25 (*1-55938-050-0*) Jai Pr.

Milbert, Jacques. Picturesque Itinerary of the Hudson River & Peripheral Parts of North America. LC 67-29606. (American Environmental Studies). 1971. reprint ed. 26.95 (*0-405-02678-1*) Ayer.

Milbourn, Evelyn, jt. auth. see Milbourn, Maurice.

Milbourn, Maurice & Milbourn, Evelyn. Understanding Miniature British Pottery & Porcelain, 1730-the Present Day. (Understanding Ser.). (Illus.). 184p. 1983. 29.50 (*0-907462-30-8*) Antique Collect.

M

An Asterisk (*) at the beginning of an entry indicates that the title is appearing in BIP for the first time.

Milbrandt, Ben. EDI (Electronic Data Interchange) - Making Business More Efficient. LC 87-2669. 80p. (Orig.). (C). 1987. pap. 25.00 (0-944952-00-3) Data Interchange Standards Assn.

Milbrath, Lester W. Environmentalists: Vanguard for a New Society. LC 83-24250. (SUNY Series in Environmental Public Policy). 180p. 1985. 59.50 (0-87395-887-X); pap. 19.95 (0-87395-888-8) State U NY Pr.

— Envisioning a Sustainable Society: Learning Our Way Out. LC 88-37558. (SUNY Series in Environmental Public Policy). 403p. 1989. 59.50 (0-7914-0162-6); pap. 19.95 (0-7914-0163-4) State U NY Pr.

— The Washington Lobbyists. LC 76-5789. (Illus.). 431p. 1976. reprint ed. text ed. 105.00 (0-8371-8802-4, MIWL, Greenwood Pr) Greenwood.

— Washington Lobbyists Survey, 1956-1957. 1972. write for info. (0-89138-054-X) ICPSR.

Milbrath, Lester W. & Goel, M. I. Political Participation: How & Why Do People Get Involved in Politics? (Illus.). 236p. (C). 1982. reprint ed. pap. text ed. 23.00 (0-8191-2647-0) U Pr of Amer.

Milbrath, Lester W., et al, eds. The Politics of Environmental Policy. LC 75-27013. (Sage Contemporary Social Science Issues Ser.: No. 18). 136p. reprint ed. pap. 38.80 (0-317-09728-8, 2021932) Bks Demand.

M

Milbrath, Susan. Study of Olmec Sculptural Chronology. LC 79-89248. (Studies in Pre-Columbian Art & Archaeology: No. 23). (Illus.). 75p. 1979. pap. 10.00 (0-88402-093-2) Dumbarton Oaks.

Milbrath, Susan, jt. ed. see Milanich, Jerald T.

Milburn, B. A. Curious Cases: A Collection of American & English Decisions Selected for Their Readability. (Illus.). xvi, 441p. 1985. reprint ed. lib. bdg. 37.50 (0-8377-0819-2) Rothman.

Milburn, Douglas. Houston, A Self-Portrait. (Illus.). 192p. 1986. 35.00 (0-917001-04-4) Herring Pr.

Milburn, Frank. The Emperor of Games. LC 93-5157. 1994. pap. 30.00 (0-394-57161-4) Knopf.

Milburn, G. J., jt. auth. see Walls, D. F.

Milburn, G. J., jt. auth. see Walls, D.

Milburn, Geoffrey, jt. auth. see Barrow, Robin.

Milburn, Geoffrey, et al, eds. Re-Interpreting Curriculum Research: Images & Arguments. 200p. 1989. 70.00 (1-85000-504-4, Falmer Pr); pap. 33.00 (1-85000-505-2, Falmer Pr) Taylor & Francis.

Milburn, George. Catalogue. LC 87-5432. 312p. 1987. reprint ed. lib. bdg. 18.95 (0-940827-00-X) Davenport NYC.

— No More Trumpets & Other Stories. LC 79-134968. (Short Story Index Reprint Ser.). 1977. 20.95 (0-8369-3699-X) Ayer.

— Oklahoma Town. LC 72-134969. (Short Story Index Reprint Ser.). 1977. 15.95 (0-8369-3700-7) Ayer.

Milburn, J. A., jt. ed. see Zimmermann, M. H.

Milburn, JoAnne F., jt. auth. see Cartledge, Gwendolyn.

Milburn, JoAnne F., jt. ed. see Cartledge, Gwendolyn.

Milburn, Josephine F. British Business & Ghanaian Independence. LC 76-50681. 166p. reprint ed. pap. 47.40 (0-8357-6741-8, 2035396) Bks Demand.

Milburn, Joyce & Smith, Lynette. The Natural Childbirth Book. LC 81-4647. 192p. (Orig.). 1981. pap. 7.99 (0-87123-399-1) Bethany Hse.

***Milburn, Kate.** I Only Ask for Yesterday's Encore. (Illus.). 84p. (Orig.). 1994. pap. text ed. 10.00 (0-9638316-0-7) Renais Pr.

Milburn, Leigh H. Progressed Horoscope Simplified. 180p. 1936. 14.00 (0-86690-131-0, M1339-014) Am Fed Astrologers.

Milburn, Lonna, contrib. Building a Cancer Information Network in Texas: A Demonstration in the Heart of Texas Region. (Special Project Report Ser.). 277p. 1989. pap. 10.00 (0-89940-864-8) LBJ Sch Pub Aff.

Milburn, Michael. Such Silence. LC 88-34011. (Alabama Poetry Ser.). 80p. 1989. pap. 9.95 (0-8173-0430-4) U of Ala Pr.

***Milburn, Michael & Oelbermann, Maren.** Electromagnetic Fields & Your Health. 208p. 1994. pap. 12.00 (0-921586-30-2, Pub. by New Star Bks CN) InBook.

Milburn, Robert L. Early Christian Art & Architecture. (C). 1988. 60.00 (0-520-06326-0) U CA Pr.

— Early Christian Art & Architecture. (Illus.). 336p. 1991. pap. 28.00 (0-520-07412-2) U CA Pr.

— Early Christian Interpretations of History. LC 79-21671. 221p. 1980. reprint ed. text ed. 55.00 (0-313-22157-X, MIEA, Greenwood Pr) Greenwood.

Milburn, Thomas W. & Watman, Kenneth H., eds. On the Nature of Threat: A Social Psychological Analysis. LC 80-20814. 160p. 1981. text ed. 45.00 (0-275-90683-3, C0683, Praeger Pubs) Greenwood.

Milby, Robert V. Plastics Technology. (Illus.). 576p. 1973. text ed. 46.95 (0-07-041918-3) McGraw.

Milby, T. H., jt. auth. see Johnson, Forrest L.

Milch, J. R., jt. auth. see Chang, W.

Milch, Jerome, jt. auth. see Feldman, Elliot J.

Milch, Robert. Aeneid Notes. 1982. pap. 3.95 (0-8220-0119-5) Cliffs.

— Aeschylus' Agamemnon Notes. 1965. pap. 4.25 (0-8220-0128-4) Cliffs.

— Aristotle's Ethics Notes. (Orig.). 1966. pap. 4.25 (0-8220-0889-0) Cliffs.

— Faust Notes. 1965. pap. 4.25 (0-8220-0479-8) Cliffs.

— Oedipus the King, Oedipus at Colonus, Antigone: Notes. (Orig.). 1965. pap. 3.75 (0-8220-0708-8) Cliffs.

Milch, Robert A. Palliative Pain & Symptom Management for Children & Adolescents. 29p. 1985. pap. 7.95 (0-317-61842-3) Child Hospice VA.

Milch, Robert J. Euripides' Electra & Medea Notes. 1965. pap. 3.75 (0-8220-0424-0) Cliffs.

— Idylls of the King Notes. 1964. pap. 4.50 (0-8220-0636-7) Cliffs.

— Iliad Notes. 1986. pap. 3.75 (0-8220-0645-6) Cliffs.

— Odyssey Notes. 1966. pap. 3.95 (0-8220-0921-8) Cliffs.

Milchard, Les J. To Heaven Via Walthamstow. (C). 1989. pap. 29.00 (0-7223-2268-2, Pub. by A H S Ltd UK) St Mut.

Milchhoefer, A. Ancient Athens, Piraeus & Phaleron: Schriftquellen Zur Topographie Von Athen. 156p. 1977. 20.00 (0-89005-215-8) Ares.

***Milchman, Alan & Rosenberg, Alan, eds.** Martin Heidegger & the Holocaust. 352p. (C). 1996. text ed. 60.00 (0-391-03925-3) Humanities.

***Milcovich, Suellyn K. & Dunn-Long, Barbara.** Diabetes Mellitus: A Practical Handbook. 6th rev. ed. LC 94-23731. 1995. pap. 12.95 (0-923521-31-3) Bull Pub.

Milcsik, Margie. Cupid Computer. LC 91-46152. 128p. (J). (gr. 3-7). 1992. reprint ed. pap. 3.95 (0-689-71569-2, Aladdin Paperbacks) S&S Childrens.

Mild, Mary L., ed. Songs of Miriam: A Women's Book of Devotions. LC 93-45872. 1994. 7.00 (0-8170-1207-9) Judson.

Mild, Warren. Joseph Highmore of Holborn Row: Biography of 18th Century British Portrait Painter. LC 90-91935. (Illus.). 490p. 1990. 48.00 (0-9627517-0-7) Mild Assocs.

Milde, Kurt. Neorenaissance in Der Deutschen Architektur des 19 Jahrhunderts. 352p. (GER.). 1981. 168.00 (0-317-57326-8, Pub. by Collets UK) St Mut.

Milde, L., jt. ed. see Hohlbaum, G. G.

Milde, M. H., et al, eds. Index Annual Report-Northern Nut Growers Association, 1910-1975. 152p. 1983. 7.50 (0-9602248-1-5) N Nut Growers.

Milde, W. & Schuder, W., eds. De Captu Lectoris: Wirkungen Des Buches in 15. und 16. Jahrhundert Dargestellt an Ausgewahlten Handschriften und Drucken. xii, 313p. (C). 1988. lib. bdg. 161.55 (0-89925-498-5) De Gruyter.

— De Captu Lectoris: Wirkungen Des Buches in 15. und 16. Jahrhundert Dargestellt an Ausgewahlten Handschriften und Drucken. xii, 313p. (C). 1988. lib. bdg. 161.55 (3-11-009989-6) De Gruyter.

***Mildenball, Cheryl.** Summer of Enlightment. Date not set. pap. 5.95 (0-352-32937-8, London Bridge) Genl Dist Srvs.

Mildenberg, Leo. The Coinage of the Bar Kokhba War: Typos VI. 1984. 95.00 (3-7941-2634-3) Numismatic Fine Arts.

Mildenberg, Leo & Hurter, Silvia, eds. The Arthur S. Dewing Collection of Greek Coins, 2 Vols. (ACNAC (American Coins in North American Collections)). (Illus.). 336p. 1985. boxed 120.00 (0-89722-206-7) Am Numismatic.

Mildenberger, Friedrich. Theorie der Theologie: Enzyklopaedie als Methodenlehre. 164p. (GER.). 1972. 19.95 (0-8288-6424-1, M-7094) Fr & Eur.

Milder, Ben. The Good Book Says. 145p. 1995. 20.95 (1-56809-013-7); pap. 14.50 (1-56809-014-5) Time Being Bks.

Milder, Benjamin & Rubin, Melvin L. The Fine Art of Prescribing Glasses Without Making a Spectacle of Yourself. 2nd ed. (Illus.). 544p. 1991. text ed. 78.00 (0-937404-02-0) Triad Pub FL.

Milder, John, jt. auth. see Snow, Robbie.

Milder, Robert. Critical Essays on Melville's "Billy Budd" (Critical Essays on American Literature Ser.). 264p. (C). 1989. text ed. 45.00 (0-8161-8889-0) G K Hall.

— Reimagining Thoreau. (Cambridge Studies in American Literature & Culture: No. 85). 350p. (C). 1995. 54.95 (0-521-46149-9) Cambridge U Pr.

***Mildice, Paul J.** Le Juif Terrible. LC 93-94307. 96p. (Orig.). 1994. pap. 9.00 (1-56002-424-0, Univ Edtns) Aegina Pr.

***Mildmay, Eroica.** Lucker & Tiffany Peel Out. 1994. pap. 12.99 (1-85242-285-8) Serpents Tail.

Mildmay, Grace. With Faith & Physic: The Life of a Tudor Gentlewoman - Lady Grace Mildmay, 1552-1620. Pollock, Linda, ed. 179p. 1994. 55.00 (1-85585-071-0) Trafalgar.

Mildner, Gerard C., jt. auth. see Salins, Peter D.

***Mildon, Marsha.** Fighting for Air. (Illus.). 200p. (Orig.). 1995. pap. text ed. 10.95 (0-934678-69-3) New Victoria Pubs.

Mildren, Ken & Hicks, Peter, eds. Information Sources in Engineering. 3rd ed. 600p. 1995. 100.00 (1-85739-057-1) Bowker-Saur.

Milea, Ioan, tr. see Freud, Sigmund.

Mileaf, Harry. Electricity One-Seven. 2nd rev. ed. 1072p. 1978. 49.95 (0-8104-5952-3) Sams.

Mileck, Joseph. Hermann Hesse: Biography & Bibliography, 2 vols. 1977. 95.00 (0-520-02756-6) U CA Pr.

— Hermann Hesse: Life & Art. LC 76-48020. 1978. pap. 13.00 (0-520-04152-6) U CA Pr.

— Hermann Hesse & His Critics. LC 72-10899. (North Carolina. University. Studies in the Germanic Languages & Literatures: No. 21). reprint ed. 34.00 (0-404-50921-5) AMS Pr.

Mileck, Joseph, ed. see Hesse, Hermann.

Mileham, James W. The Conspiracy Novel: Structure & Metaphor in Balzac's Comedie Humaine. LC 81-68004. (French Forum Monographs: No. 31). 142p. (Orig.). 1982. pap. 9.95 (0-917058-30-5) French Forum.

Mileiko, S. T., jt. ed. see Kelly, Anthony.

***Mileikovskii, I. E. & Trushin, S. I.** Analysis of Thin-Walled Structures. (Russian Translations Ser.: No. 108). (Illus.). 196p. (ENG.). (C). 1994. text ed. 85.00 (90-5410-250-0, Pub. by A A Balkema NE) Ashgate Pub Co.

***Milekic & Tappan, eds.** Ebner's Connective Tissue Manipulation for Bodyworkers. (Illus.). (C). 1995. lib. bdg. write for info. (0-89464-736-9) Krieger.

Milener, Eugene D. Oneonta: The Development of a Railroad Town. LC 83-61205. 576p. 1983. 14.50 (0-9610682-0-5) E D Milener.

Milenkovic, Dragen, jt. auth. see Mori, Takeo.

Milenkovic, Milan, jt. ed. see Furht, Borko.

Milenkovitch, Deborah D. Plan & Market in Yugoslav Economic Thought. LC 78-140534. (Russian & East European Studies: No. 9). 333p. reprint ed. 95.00 (0-8357-9440-7, 2011104) Bks Demand.

Milenkovitch, Michael M. Milovan Djilas: An Annotated Bibliography, 1928-1975. LC 76-20364. 50p. reprint ed. pap. 25.00 (0-317-10711-9, 2016499) Bks Demand.

Milepost Editors. Alaska A to Z: The Most Comprehensive Book of Facts & Figures Ever Compiled about Alaska. (Illus.). 200p. (Orig.). 1993. pap. 9.95 (1-878425-75-7) Vernon Pubns.

— The Alaska Wilderness Guide. 7th rev. ed. (Illus.). 508p. 1993. pap. 16.95 (1-878425-50-1) Vernon Pubns.

Miler, I. The Immunity of the Foetus & Newborn Infant. 1983. lib. bdg. 89.00 (90-247-2610-7) Kluwer Ac.

***Milera, Laura.** The Flavor of Cuba: Traditional Recipes from the Cuban Kitchen. 200p. 1995. pap. text ed. 23.95 (0-9642941-7-6) Royal Palm Pr.

Miles. More Sex & Drugs & Rock 'n Roll. (Illus.). 96p. 1985. pap. 14.95 (0-7119-1462-1, OP44676) Omnibus NY.

— Permanent Retirement. 1994. pap. 3.99 (0-517-13426-8) Random.

— Pink Floyd: A Visual Documentary. rev. ed. (Illus.). 120p. 1982. pap. 17.95 (0-399-41001-5, Perigree Bks) Berkley Pub.

— Sex & Drugs & Rock 'n Roll. (Illus.). 96p. 1985. pap. 15.95 (0-7119-0110-4, OP41953) Omnibus NY.

— Zappa, a Visual Documentary. Date not set. pap. 19.95 (0-7119-3099-6) Omnibus NY.

Miles, comp. The Beatles: In Their Own Words. (Illus.). 128p. 1978. pap. 15.95 (0-86001-540-8, OP40419) Omnibus NY.

— Bob Dylan: In His Own Words. (Illus.). 128p. pap. 15.95 (0-86001-542-4, OP40393) Omnibus NY.

— Bob Dylan in His Own Words. (Illus.). 128p. Date not set. pap. 12.95 (0-7119-3219-0) Omnibus NY.

— Bowie in His Own Words. (Illus.). 128p. 1980. pap. 15.95 (0-86001-645-5, OP40567) Omnibus NY.

— John Lennon: In His Own Words. (Illus.). 128p. 1980. pap. 15.95 (0-86001-816-4, OP41060) Omnibus NY.

— Mick Jagger: In His Own Words. (Illus.). 128p. pap. 15.95 (0-86001-930-6, OP41268) Omnibus NY.

Miles & Mabbett, Andy. Pink Floyd: Twenty-First Anniversary Edition. (Illus.). 156p. 1988. pap. 19.95 (0-7119-1444-3, OP40583) Omnibus NY.

Miles, jt. auth. see Bracegirdle.

Miles, A. E. & Grigson, C., eds. Colyer's Variations & Diseases of the Teeth of Animals. 2nd ed. (Illus.). 850p. 1990. 390.00 (0-521-25273-3) Cambridge U Pr.

Miles, A. J. Tournament Chess, Vol. 6. 176p. 1983. pap. 21.95 (0-08-029721-8, Pergamon Pr) Elsevier.

Miles, A. J., ed. see Chandler, M.

Miles, A. J., jt. ed. see Chandler, M.

Miles, A. Marie. Bible: Chain of Truth. 168p. (J). (gr. 5 up). pap. 2.00 (0-686-29101-8) Faith Pub Hse.

Miles, A. R. Introduccion Popular Estudio S. Escrit. A Layman's Introduction. (SPA.). 6.95 (84-7228-909-5, 220498, Pub. by Edit Clie SP) TSELF.

Miles, A. W. & Tanner, K. E., eds. Strain Measurement in Biomechanics. (Illus.). 212p. (C). 1992. text ed. 69.95 (0-412-43270-6, A6906) Chapman & Hall.

Miles, Agnes. The Neurotic Woman: The Role of Gender in Psychiatric Illness. 224p. 1988. pap. 16.50 (0-8147-5463-5) NYU Pr.

— Women, Health & Medicine. 224p. 1991. pap. 29.00 (0-335-09905-X, Open Univ Pr) Taylor & Francis.

Miles, Alan. Dictionary of Classical Ballet in Labanotation. 108p. (Orig.). 1995. pap. 15.00 (0-932582-17-6) Dance Notation.

— Labanotation Workbook, Vol. I. 64p. (C). 1995. pap. 12.00 (0-932582-18-4) Dance Notation.

Miles, Albert S. College Law. LC 87-61790. (Illus.). 121p. (Orig.). (C). 1987. pap. 19.95 (0-943487-01-3) Sevgo Pr.

Miles, Alexander. Devil's Island: Colony of the Damned. (Illus.). 224p. 1988. pap. 9.95 (0-89815-275-5) Ten Speed Pr.

Miles, Alfred H., ed. Poets & the Poetry of the Nineteenth Century, 12 Vols. Set. rev. ed. LC 16-2291. reprint ed. 780.00 (0-404-05120-0) AMS Pr.

Miles, Alice. Every Girl's Duty: The Diary of a Victorian Debutante. (Illus.). 256p. 1993. 34.95 (0-233-98755-X, Pub. by A Deutsch UK) Trafalgar.

Miles, Allan. Labanotation for Ballet Dancers. 2nd ed. (Illus.). 47p. (Orig.). (C). 1984. reprint ed. pap. text ed. 15.00 (0-9602002-7-4) Ray Cook.

— Labanotation Workbook, Vol. I. 64p. 1970. pap. 12.00 (0-685-18018-2) Princeton Bk Co.

— Labanotation Workbook, Vol. II. 64p. (C). 1984. pap. 12.00 (0-932582-19-2) Dance Notation.

— Labanotation Workbook, Vol. II. 64p. 1990. pap. 12.00 (0-317-56647-4) Princeton Bk Co.

Miles, Andrew, jt. auth. see Savage, Mike.

Miles, Andrew, jt. ed. see Vincent, David.

Miles, Andrew, et al, eds. Melatonin: Clinical Perspectives. (Illus.). 304p. 1988. 80.00 (0-19-261652-8) OUP.

Miles, Angela. Integrative Feminisms: Building a Global Vision, 1960s to 1990s. LC 92-33164. (Perspectives on Gender Ser.). 256p. 1995. 55.00 (0-415-90756-X, B0252, Routledge NY); pap. 16.95 (0-415-90757-8, B0256, Routledge NY) Routledge.

Miles, Anthony. First Steps to Winning Chess. 1992. pap. 14.95 (0-945806-08-6) Summit CA.

Miles, Archie. The Malvern Hills: Travels Through Elgar Country. (Classic Country Connections Ser.). (Illus.). 144p. 1992. 34.95 (1-85145-731-3, Pub. by Pavilion UK) Trafalgar.

— The Malvern Hills: Travels Through Elgar Country. (Classic Country Companions Ser.). (Illus.). 144p. 1993. pap. 17.95 (1-85145-868-9, Pub. by Pavilion UK) Trafalgar.

Miles, Austin. Don't Call Me Brother: A Ringmaster's Escape from the Pentacostal Church. (Illus.). 331p. (C). 1989. 23.95 (0-87975-507-5) Prometheus Bks.

— Setting the Captives Free: Victims of the Church Tell Their Stories. 239p. (C). 1990. 21.95 (0-87975-617-9) Prometheus Bks.

Miles, Barbara. Play with Me: Crafts for Preschoolers. (Illus.). (Orig.). (ps). 1990. pap. 12.98 (0-88290-367-5) Horizon Utah.

Miles, Barry. Ginsberg. 1989. 24.95 (0-318-41502-X) S&S Trade.

— Two Lectures on the Work of Allen Ginsberg. LC 93-36395. (Turret Papers). 1993. 20.00 (0-935061-54-1) Contemp Res.

— William Burroughs: El Hombre Invisible. LC 92-38285. (Illus.). 272p. 1994. pap. 12.95 (0-7868-8018-X) Hyperion.

Miles, Barry, jt. ed. see Maynard, Joe.

***Miles, Bebe.** Wildflower Perennials for Your Garden: A Detailed Guide to Years of Bloom for America's Native Heritage. (American Garden Classics Ser.). (Illus.). 320p. 1996. pap. 14.95 (0-8117-2660-6) Stackpole.

Miles, Benard J. Hydroxybenzoic Acids--Index of New Information & Medical Research Bible. 150p. 1994. 44.50 (0-7883-0094-6); pap. 39.50 (0-7883-0095-4) ABBE Pubs Assn.

Miles, Bernard. Favorite Tales from Shakespeare. (Illus.). 128p. (J). (gr. 4-7). 1993. reprint ed. 14.95 (1-56288-257-0) Checkerboard.

— Robin Hood: His Life & Legend. LC 79-64615. (Illus.). 128p. (J). (gr. 4 up). 12.95 (1-56288-412-3) Checkerboard.

— Well-Loved Tales from Shakespeare. LC 85-63829. (Illus.). 128p. (J). (gr. 2 up). 1986. 12.95 (0-528-82758-8) Checkerboard.

***Miles, Betty.** Hey I'm Reading. (J). 1995. 16.99 (0-679-95644-1) Random.

— How to Read: A Book for Beginners. LC 93-25884. (J). 1995. 12.00 (0-679-85644-7) Knopf.

— I Would If I Could. 120p. (J). (gr. 3-6). 1983. pap. 2.95 (0-380-63438-4, Camelot) Avon.

— Just the Beginning. 148p. (J). (gr. 3 up). 1978. pap. 2.50 (0-380-01913-2, Camelot) Avon.

— Maudie & Me & the Dirty Book. 140p. (J). (gr. 4-7). 1981. pap. 2.95 (0-380-55541-7, Camelot) Avon.

— Maudie & Me & the Dirty Book. LC 79-19783. 144p. (J). (gr. 4-7). 1989. pap. 2.95 (0-394-82595-0, Bullseye Bks) Random Bks Yng Read.

— The Real Me. 124p. (J). (gr. 4-7). 1978. pap. 2.75 (0-380-00347-3, Camelot) Avon.

— Save the Earth: An Action Handbook for Kids. LC 90-46514. (Illus.). 128p. (Orig.). (J). (gr. 5 up). 1991. pap. 6.95 (0-679-81731-X) Knopf Bks Yng Read.

— The Secret Life of the Underwear Champ. LC 80-15651. (Books for Young Readers Ser.). (Illus.). 128p. (J). (gr. 3-7). 1981. pap. 3.99 (0-394-84563-3, Silver Creek) Random Bks Yng Read.

— Sink or Swim. 208p. (YA). (gr. 3-7). 1987. pap. 2.95 (0-380-69913-3, Camelot) Avon.

— The Trouble with Thirteen. LC 78-31678. (J). (gr. 4-7). 1979. lib. bdg. 12.99 (0-394-93930-1) Knopf Bks Yng Read.

— The Trouble with Thirteen. LC 78-31678. 112p. (J). (gr. 3-7). 1989. reprint ed. pap. 2.95 (0-394-82043-6) Knopf Bks Yng Read.

Miles, Betty T., et al. The Miles Chart Display, 2 vols. 1980. 163.95 (0-405-19072-7, 19805) Ayer.

— Miles Chart Display of Popular Music: Vol 1: Top 100, 1955-1970. 3rd ed. (Illus.). 1979. reprint ed. lib. bdg. 95.00 (0-913920-03-7) Convex Indus.

Miles, Brian J., jt. ed. see Vogelzang, Nicholas J.

Miles-Brown, John. Acting: A Drama Studio Source Book. 110p. 1987. pap. 14.95 (0-7206-0632-2, Pub. by P Owen Ltd UK) Dufour.

— Directing Drama. LC 87-60978. (Illus.). 172p. 1980. pap. 18.95 (0-7206-0688-8, Pub. by P Owen Ltd UK) Dufour.

— Speech for the Speaker. LC 89-81770. 128p. 1990. pap. 18.95 (0-7206-0726-4, Pub. by P Owen Ltd UK) Dufour.

Miles, C. Indian & Eskimo Artifacts of North America. (Illus.). 12.99 (0-517-00142-X) Random Hse Value.

Miles, C., jt. auth. see Fallding, H.

Miles, C. W., jt. auth. see Seabrooke, W.

Miles, Calvin. Calvin's Christmas Wish. (Illus.). 32p. (J). (ps-3). 1993. 13.99 (0-670-84295-8) Viking Child Bks.

— When Dreams Came True. Literacy Volunteers of New York City Staff, ed. (New Writers' Voices Ser.). (Illus.). 64p. (Orig.). 1990. pap. text ed. 3.50 (0-929631-18-8, Signal Hill) New Readers.

Miles, Candice, ed. see Golden, Harris.

Miles, Cara. Lord of the Night. 384p. (Orig.). 1993. mass mkt. 4.50 (0-380-76453-9) Avon.

— Love Me with Fury. 384p. (Orig.). 1991. mass mkt. 4.50 (0-380-76450-4) Avon.

— Promise Me Forever. 1992. mass mkt. 4.50 (0-380-76451-2) Avon.

— Surrender to the Fury. 384p. (Orig.). 1992. mass mkt. 4.50 (0-380-76452-0) Avon.

***Miles, Carol, comp.** 1995 ABACUS Expanded: ABA's Financial Survey of Member Bookstores Based on 1993 Operations. (Illus.). 128p. (Orig.). 1995. pap. 50.00 (1-879923-11-4) Booksellers Pub.

Miles, Cassie. Are You Lonesome Tonight? (Intrigue Ser.). 1994. mass mkt. 2.99 (0-373-22269-6, 1-22269-4) Harlequin Bks.

— Borrowed Time. (American Romance Ser.). 1995. pap. 3.50 (0-373-16574-9, 1-16574-5) Harlequin Bks.

— Buffalo McCloud. (American Romance Ser.). 1995. pap. 3.50 (*0-373-16567-6*, 1-16567-9) Harlequin Bks.
— Don't Be Cruel. (Intrigue Ser.). 1994. mass mkt. 2.99 (*0-373-22285-8*, 1-22285-0) Harlequin Bks.
— Full Steam. 224p. (Orig.). 1990. pap. 2.75 (*1-878702-09-2*, Kismet) Meteor Pub.
— Heartbreak Hotel. (Intrigue Ser.). 1993. mass mkt. 2.99 (*0-373-22237-8*, 1-22237-1) Harlequin Bks.
— Mysterious Vows: (Mail Order Bride) (Intrigue Ser.). 1995. mass mkt. 3.50 (*0-373-22320-X*, 1-22320-5) Harlequin Bks.
— The Suspect Groom. (Intrigue Ser.). 1995. mass mkt. 3.50 (*0-373-22332-3*, 1-22332-0) Harlequin Bks.

Miles, Celia H. Writing Technical Reports. 1992. text ed. write for info. (*0-07-024608-4*) McGraw.

Miles, Chris. Business Traveler's Atlas. (Illus.). 208p. 1992. pap. 12.95 (*0-13-095217-6*, H M Gousha) P-H Gen Ref & Trav.

Miles, Claudia, ed. see Curry, Jerri.

Miles, Clement A. Christmas Customs & Traditions: Their History & Significance. (Illus.). 19.75 (*0-8446-5484-1*) Peter Smith.
— Christmas Customs & Traditions: Their History & Significance. LC 76-9183. (Illus.). 1976. reprint ed. pap. 6.95 (*0-486-23354-5*) Dover.
— Christmas in Ritual & Tradition: Christian & Pagan. 1977. lib. bdg. 59.95 (*0-8490-1618-5*) Gordon Pr.
— Christmas in Ritual & Tradition: Christian & Pagan. LC 89-29299. (Illus.). 400p. 1990. reprint ed. lib. bdg. 42.00 (*1-55888-896-9*) Omnigraphics Inc.

Miles, Curtis & Rauton, Jane. Thinking Tools. 2nd ed. Savige, Katherine, ed. LC 87-219. (Illus.). 371p. (C). 1990. pap. text ed. 29.95 (*0-943202-23-X*) H & H Pub.

Miles, D. & Neale, R. Building for Tomorrow: International Experience in Construction Industry Development. vii, 238p. (Orig.). 1991. pap. 24.00 (*92-2-107284-3*) Intl Labour Office.

Miles, D. K., jt. auth. see Chowdhury, G.

Miles, D. K., jt. auth. see Hall, S. G.

Miles, Dale A., et al. Basic Principles of Oral & Maxillofacial Radiology. (Illus.). 240p. 1992. pap. text ed. 35.50 (*0-7216-3471-0*) Saunders.
— Oral & Maxillofacial Radiology: Radiologic - Pathologic Correlations. (Illus.). 352p. 1991. text ed. 55.50 (*0-7216-3070-7*) Saunders.
— Radiographic Imaging for Dental Auxiliaries. 2nd ed. LC 92-17230. (Illus.). 336p. 1993. pap. text ed. 36.95 (*0-7216-6729-5*) Saunders.

Miles, Daniel J, jt. auth. see Mukes, Martin J.

Miles, Darrell & Bigley, William. Quantity Cooking: Tested Recipes for Twenty or More. LC 75-46351. (Cookbook Ser.). Orig. Title: Dare to Excel in Cooking. (Illus.). 64p. 1976. reprint ed. pap. 3.95 (*0-486-23318-9*) Dover.

Miles, David. Housing Financial Markets & the Wider Economy. LC 94-17863. (Financial Economics & Quantitative Analysis Ser.). 1995. text ed. 60.00 (*0-471-95210-9*) Wiley.
— Testing for Short-Termism in the U.K. Stock Market. fac. ed. (Bank of England, Economics Division, Working Paper Ser.). 42p. 1992. reprint ed. pap. 25.00 (*0-7837-8335-3*, 2049122) Bks Demand.

Miles, David, jt. auth. see Cunliffe, Barry.

Miles, David, jt. auth. see Mackie, Karl.

Miles, David H. Hofmannsthal's Novel, Andreas: Memory & Self. LC 70-155001. (Princeton Essays in European & Comparative Literature Ser.). 242p. reprint ed. pap. 69.00 (*0-8357-3425-0*, 2039683) Bks Demand.

Miles, Delos. Church Growth - A Mighty River. LC 80-67352. 1991. pap. 6.99 (*0-8054-6227-9*) Broadman.
— Introduction to Evangelism. LC 82-73078. (C). 1983. 24.99 (*0-8054-6239-2*) Broadman.
— Testifica! Como Superar Obstaculos que Impiden la Evangelizacion Personal (Overcoming Barriers to Witnessing) Gonzalez, Jorge A., tr. 128p. (Orig.). (SPA.). 1991. pap. 4.25 (*0-311-13850-0*) Casa Bautista.

Miles, Don C., et al. Trackside: Preserving Railroad Station Warehouse Districts: A Comparative Study of Seven Cities. Kreisman, Lawrence, ed. (Illus.). 140p. (Orig.). 1988. pap. write for info. (*0-9621572-0-1*) City Tacoma Hist Preserv.

Miles, Don E. Signs of the Nineties: The Poet. (Illus.). 108p. (Orig.). 1992. pap. 12.50 (*0-9635478-0-1*) Marked Tree.

Miles, Donald. Broadcast News Handbook. LC 75-2550. 1975. teacher ed 2.75 (*0-672-21198-X*, Bobbs); pap. 9.95 (*0-672-21183-1*, Bobbs) Macmillan.

Miles, Dorothy. Church of Our Fathers: The Story of Old St. Michaels. 2nd ed. MacDonald, Alexander, ed. 112p. (Orig.). 1984. reprint ed. pap. write for info. (*0-318-65391-5*) D Miles.
— Dreams of Glory: A Family Saga. 300p. (Orig.). 1989. 15.00 (*0-9623631-0-3*); pap. 8.00 (*0-9623631-1-1*) D Miles.
— Gestures-Poetry in Sign Language. Joyce, John, ed. LC 76-55854. (Illus.). 1976. pap. 9.00 (*0-917002-12-1*) Joyce Media.
— The Revival of a Marblehead Mansion. MacDonald, Alexander, ed. 35p. 1982. reprint ed. pap. write for info. (*0-318-65392-3*) D Miles.

Miles, Douglas G., jt. auth. see Ryan, Tim.

Miles, Douglas L., ed. Water-Rock Interaction (WRI-Six) Proceedings of the International Symposium, Malvern, UK, 3 - 8 August 1989. (Illus.). 838p. (C). 1989. text ed. 130.00 (*90-6191-970-3*, Pub. by A A Balkema NE) Ashgate Pub Co.

Miles, Dudley. Francis Place, 1771-1854: The Life of a Remarkable Radical. LC 87-35324. 256p. 1988. text ed. 39.95 (*0-312-01953-X*) St Martin.

Miles, E. & Allen, S., eds. The Law of the Sea & Ocean Development Issues in the Pacific Basin: 15th Annual Conference Proceeding. 638p. 1983. 18.00 (*0-911189-06-8*) Law Sea Inst.

Miles, E., jt. ed. see Miles, T. R.

Miles, Edward L. Organizational Arrangements to Facilitate Global Management of Fisheries. LC 73-20844. (Resources for the Future, Program of International Studies of Fishery Arrangements, Paper: No. 4). 35p. reprint ed. pap. 25.00 (*0-317-26473-7*, 2023808) Bks Demand.
— Science, Politics, & International Ocean Management: The Uses of Scientific Knowledge in International Negotiations. LC 87-81999. (Policy Papers in International Affairs Ser.: No. 33). (Illus.). viii, 70p. 1987. pap. 6.50 (*0-87725-533-4*) U of Cal IAS.

Miles, Edward L., ed. The Management of World Fisheries: Implications of Extended Coastal State Jurisdiction. 344p. 1990. 30.00 (*0-295-96854-0*) U of Wash Pr.

Miles, Edward L. & Treves, Tullio, eds. The Law of the Sea: New Worlds, New Discoveries, 26th Conference Proceedings. 500p. Date not set. 58.00 (*0-911189-26-2*) Law Sea Inst.

Miles, Edward L., jt. ed. see Kuribayashi, Tadao.

Miles, Edward L., et al. Atlas of Marine Use in the North Pacific Region. LC 81-675743. (Illus.). 107p. 1982. 180.00 (*0-520-04433-9*) U CA Pr.
— Nuclear Waste Disposal under the Seabed: Assessing the Policy Issues. LC 85-80007. (Policy Papers in International Affairs Ser.: No. 22). (Illus.). xii, 112p. 1985. pap. 7.50 (*0-87725-522-9*) U of Cal IAS.

Miles, Edward L., et al, eds. Natural Resources Economics & Policy Applications: Essays in Honor of James A. Crutchfield. 448p. 1986. 30.00 (*0-295-96345-X*) U of Wash Pr.

Miles, Edwin A. Jacksonian Democracy in Mississippi. LC 78-107415. (American Scene Ser.). 1970. reprint ed. lib. bdg. 29.50 (*0-306-71884-7*) Da Capo.

***Miles, Elaine.** The Bangor Dyslexia Teaching System. 2nd ed. 96p. 1992. 34.95 (*1-879105-72-1*, 0427) Singular Publishing.
— Many Hands: Making a Communal Quilt. (Illus.). 75p. (Orig.). 1982. 6.95 (*0-936810-02-5*) R&E Miles.
— Patchwork Year: A Datebook. (Illus.). 128p. 1983. pap. 4.95 (*0-936810-03-3*) R&E Miles.

Miles, Elaine, jt. auth. see Miles, T. R.

Miles, Elizabeth, illus. Goldilocks & the Three Bears. (Children's Classics Ser.). (J). 1991. 6.95 (*0-8362-4900-3*) Andrews & McMeel.

Miles, Elizabeth B. The Elizabeth B. Miles Collection: English Silver. LC 75-37418. (Illus.). 145p. 1976. pap. 12.00 (*0-317-13587-2*) Wadsworth Atheneum.

***Miles, Ellen G.** American Paintings of the Eighteenth Century. LC 94-37473. (Collection of the National Gallery of Art, Systematic Catalogue Ser.). 1994. write for info. (*0-89468-210-5*) Natl Gallery Art.
— Saint-Memin & the Neoclassical Profile Portrait in America. LC 94-15239. (Illus.). 512p. 1994. 95.00 (*1-56098-411-2*) Smithsonian.

Miles, Ellen G., ed. The Portrait in Eighteenth-Century America. LC 90-50995. (Illus.). 168p. (C). 1993. 49.50 (*0-87413-437-4*) U Delaware Pr.

Miles, Ellen G. & Saunders, Richard H. American Colonial Portraits, 1700-1776. LC 87-600059. (Illus.). 356p. (C). 1987. pap. 37.50 (*0-87474-695-7*) Smithsonian.

Miles, Elton. Stray Tales of the Big Bend. LC 92-39729. (Centennial Series of the Association of Former Students: No. 47). (Illus.). 160p. 1993. 25.00 (*0-89096-534-X*); pap. 12.50 (*0-89096-542-0*) Tex A&M Univ Pr.
— Tales of the Big Bend. LC 76-17977. (Illus.). 200p. 1995. pap. 12.50 (*0-89096-360-6*) Tex A&M Univ Pr.

Miles, Emma B. Spirit of the Mountains. LC 75-19222. (Tennesseana Editions Ser.). (Illus.). 250p. 1975. reprint ed. 26.00x (*0-87049-181-4*); reprint ed. pap. 15.00x (*0-87049-465-1*) U of Tenn Pr.

Miles, Eustace. Life after Life: The Theory of Reincarnation. 180p. 1985. pap. 16.50 (*0-89540-126-6*, SB-126) Sun Pub.

Miles, F. A. & Wallman, J., eds. Visual Motion & Its Role in the Stabilization of Gaze. LC 92-32805. (Reviews of Oculomotor Research Ser.: Vol. 5). 1992. 272.00 (*0-444-81195-8*) Elsevier.

Miles, Fern H. Captive Community: Life in a Japanese Internment Camp, 1941-1945. LC 87-61092. viii, 192p. (Orig.). 1987. pap. 8.95 (*0-9618895-0-0*) Mossy Creek Pr.

***Miles, Gary B.** Livy: Reconstructing Early Rome. 256p. 1995. 35.00x (*0-8014-3060-7*) Cornell U Pr.

Miles, George. Go West & Grow up with the Country: An Exhibition of Nineteenth-Century Guides to the American West in the Collections of the American Antiquarian Society. (Illus.). 47p. (Orig.). 1991. pap. 13.00 (*0-944026-30-3*) Am Antiquarian.
— Wills, Probate & Administration. 200p. 1993. 34.00 (*1-85431-295-2*, Pub. by Blackstone Pr UK) W W Gaunt.

***Miles, George & Denyer, Paulene.** Wills, Probate & Administration, Vol. 1. 352p. 1994. pap. text ed. 34.00 (*1-85431-370-3*, Blckstone AT) W W Gaunt.

Miles, George C. The Coinage of the Arab Amirs of Crete. (Numismatic Notes & Monographs: 160). (Illus.). 95p. 1960. pap. 12.00 (*0-89722-059-5*) Am Numismatic.

Miles, George H. A Review of Hamlet. LC 77-172730. reprint ed. 29.50 (*0-404-04324-0*) AMS Pr.

Miles, Guy, ed. Voices from the Countryside. LC 77-4404. (Illus.). 1977. 6.95 (*0-916224-13-9*) Banyan Bks.

Miles, H., tr. see Bunin, Ivan A.

Miles, H. B. Some Factors Affecting Attainment at 18: A Study of Examination Performance in British Schools. (Illus.). 1979. 67.00 (*0-08-024678-8*, Pub. by Pergamon Repr UK) Franklin.

Miles, Hamish, tr. see Bunin, Ivan A.

Miles, Hamish, tr. see Maurois, Andre.

Miles, Hamish, ed. see Painter, William M.

Miles, Hamish, tr. see Villiers De l'Isle-Adam, Jean M.

Miles, Hamish S., tr. see Pierre-Quint, Leon.

Miles, Harold. Bad Ol' Boy. LC 93-2059. 384p. 1993. 22.50 (*0-89603-267-1*) Humana.
— The Devil & Uncle Will. LC 90-49274. 1991. 17.95 (*0-89603-197-7*) Humana.

Miles, Henry A. Lowell, As It Was, & As It Is. LC 72-5063. (Technology & Society Ser.). (Illus.). 234p. 1976. reprint ed. 18.95 (*0-405-04714-2*) Ayer.

Miles, Herbert J. Sexual Happiness in Marriage. 1987. pap. 8.99 (*0-310-29221-2*) Zondervan.

Miles, Hugh & Salisbury, Mike. Kingdom of the Ice Bear: A Portrait of the Arctic. (Illus.). 192p. 1986. 24.95 (*0-292-70393-7*) U of Tex Pr.

Miles, I. & Irvine, J., eds. The Poverty of Progress: Changing Ways of Life in Industrial Societies. LC 81-17779. (Illus.). 275p. 1982. 150.00 (*0-08-028906-1*, K110, Pub. by Pergamon Repr UK) Franklin.

Miles, Ian, jt. auth. see Cole, Sam.

Miles, Ian, et al. Information Horizons: The Long Term Social Implications of New Information Technology. 320p. 1988. text ed. 59.95 (*1-85278-041-X*, Pub. by E Elgar Pub UK) Ashgate Pub Co.

Miles, Isabel S. & Rostami, S. Multicomponent Polymer Systems. LC 92-22235. (Polymer Science & Technology Ser.). 435p. 1992. text ed. 105.00 (*0-470-21951-3*) Wiley.

Miles, J. Ships, Sailors & the Sea. 1989. 13.96 (*0-88110-365-9*, Usborne) EDC.
— Ships, Sailors & the Sea. 1989. 7.95 (*0-7460-0285-8*, Usborne) EDC.

Miles, J. & Walton, D. W., eds. Primary Succession on Land. LC 92-35652. 309p. 1993. 65.00 (*0-632-03547-1*) Blackwell Sci.

Miles, J., et al, eds. Temporal & Spatial Patterns of Vegetation Dynamics. (Advances in Vegetation Science Ser.). (C). 1989. lib. bdg. 175.50 (*0-7923-0103-X*) Kluwer Ac.

Miles, J. C. First Book of the Keyboard. (First Music Ser.). (Illus.). 64p. (J). (gr. 2 up). 1993. lib. bdg. 14.96 (*0-88110-622-4*); pap. 8.95 (*0-7460-0962-3*) EDC.

Miles, J. F., jt. auth. see Harris, C. J.

***Miles, Jack.** God: A Biography. LC 94-30153. 446p. 1995. 27.50 (*0-679-41833-4*) Knopf.

Miles, Jacob R., 3rd, ed. see Williams, Bob.

***Miles, James G.** Five Trillion Dollars & Ever Deeper in Debt. 1994. pap. 9.95 (*0-8062-5151-4*) Carlton.
— Pay Any Price. 288p. 1989. 19.95 (*0-9627006-0-6*, TXU 350 632) J G Miles.

Miles, James M. Georgia Civil War Sites. (Illus.). 140p. (Orig.). 1987. pap. 8.95 (*0-941907-00-7*) J & R Graphics.

Miles, James W., jt. ed. see Laird, Marshall.

Miles, Jennifer A. Illustrated Glossary of Petroleum Geochemistry. (Illus.). 152p. 1994. reprint ed. pap. 21.95 (*0-19-854849-4*) OUP.

Miles, Jerry L. Sir Walter Raleigh: A Reference Guide. (Reference Guides to Literature Ser.). 148p. (C). 1986. text ed. 40.00 (*0-8161-8596-4*, Hall Reference) Macmillan.

Miles, Jim. Fields of Glory: A History & Tour Guide of the Atlanta Campaign. LC 89-6389. (Illus.). 192p. 1989. pap. 14.95 (*1-55853-023-1*) Rutledge Hill Pr.
— Paths to Victory: A History & Tour Guide of the Stone's River, Chickamauga, Chattanooga, Knoxville, & Nashville Campaigns. LC 91-29167. (Civil War Campaign Ser.). (Illus.). 224p. (Orig.). 1991. pap. 12.95 (*1-55853-126-2*) Rutledge Hill Pr.
— Piercing the Heartland. (Civil War Campaign Ser.). (Illus.). 224p. (Orig.). 1991. pap. 12.95 (*1-55853-104-1*) Rutledge Hill Pr.
— River Unvexed: A History & Tour Guide to the Campaign for the Mississippi River. LC 93-35025. 1994. pap. 24.95 (*1-55853-210-2*) Rutledge Hill Pr.
— To the Sea: A History & Tour Guide of Sherman's March. LC 89-24232. (Illus.). 224p. (Orig.). 1989. pap. 18.95 (*1-55853-047-9*) Rutledge Hill Pr.

***Miles, John.** A Most Deadly Retirement: A Laura Michaels Mystery. 246p. 1995. 22.95 (*0-8027-3258-5*) Walker & Co.
— Murder in Retirement: A Laura Michaels Mystery. LC 93-25234. 1994. 19.95 (*0-8027-3246-1*) Walker & Co.
— A Permanent Retirement. LC 92-12985. 230p. 1992. 19.95 (*0-8027-1243-6*) Walker & Co.
— Stoppers: How to Put an End to Meetings, Monologues, Conferences, Discussions, Telephone Calls, Debates, Filibusters, Boring Parties, & Anything That Lasts Too Long. LC 93-6277. 64p. (Orig.). 1994. pap. 6.95 (*0-687-39639-5*) Abingdon.
— Ten O'Clock Scholar: A Johnnie Baker Mystery. 1996. 19.95 (*0-8027-3273-9*) Walker & Co.

Miles, John & Moore, Carolynne. Practical Knowledge Based Systems in Conceptual Design. LC 92-46682. 1993. 116.00 (*0-387-19823-7*) Spr-Verlag.

Miles, John & Morris, Tom. Operation Nightfall. LC 74-17665. 224p. 1975. 6.95 (*0-672-52085-0*, Bobbs) Macmillan.

***Miles, John C.** Guardians of the Parks: A History of the NPCA. LC 95-134. 400p. 1995. 29.95 (*1-56032-446-5*) Taylor & Francis.

Miles, John C., ed. Treasury of Animal Stories. LC 90-11158. (Illus.). 96p. (J). (gr. 2-5). 1991. lib. bdg. 14.89 (*0-8167-2240-4*); pap. text ed. 6.95 (*0-8167-2241-2*) Troll Assocs.
— Treasury of Christmas. LC 90-39372. (Illus.). 96p. (J). (gr. 2-5). 1991. lib. bdg. 14.89 (*0-8167-2236-6*); pap. text ed. 6.95 (*0-8167-2237-4*) Troll Assocs.

Miles, John C. & Priest, Simon. Adventure Education. LC 90-71690. 473p. 1991. pap. 31.95 (*0-910251-39-8*) Venture Pub PA.

Miles, John C., ed. see Dempsey, Michael.

Miles, John J. Health Care & Antitrust Law, 4 vols., Set. LC 92-5626. (Health Law Ser.). 1992. ring bd. 475.00 (*0-87632-831-1*) Clark Boardman Callaghan.

Miles, John J., jt. auth. see Proser, Phillip A.

Miles, John R. Retroversion & Text Criticism: The Predictability Syntax in an Ancient Translation from Greek to Ethropic. (Society of Biblical Literature Septuagint & Cognate Studies Ser.). (C). 1985. 23.95 (*0-89130-878-4*, 06-04-17); pap. 15.95 (*0-89130-879-2*) Scholars Pr GA.

Miles, John W. The Potential Theory of Unsteady Supersonic Flow. LC 59-564. (Cambridge Monographs on Mechanics & Mathematics). 234p. reprint ed. pap. 66.70 (*0-317-10245-1*, 2050772) Bks Demand.

Miles, Jonathan. Backgrounds to David Jones: A Study in Sources & Drafts. xii, 232p. 1990. 40.00 (*0-7083-1051-6*, Pub. by U of Wales UK) Bks Intl VA.
— Eric Gill & David Jones at Capel-Y-Ffin. 1992. 35.00 (*1-85411-051-9*); pap. 15.95 (*1-85411-052-7*) Dufour.

Miles, Josephine. Civil Poems. 1966. pap. 1.00 (*0-685-29875-2*) Oyez.
— Fields of Learning. 1968. pap. 1.00 (*0-685-04667-2*) Oyez.
— The Primary Language of Poetry in the Sixteen Forties. LC 78-11614. (Univ. of California Publications in English: Vol. 19, No. 1). (Illus.). 160p. 1979. reprint ed. text ed. 38.50 (*0-313-20661-9*, MIPP, Greenwood Pr) Greenwood.
— The Primary Language of Poetry in the 1740's & 1840's. LC 83-45454. reprint ed. 27.50 (*0-404-20177-6*) AMS Pr.

Miles, Julia, ed. Playwriting Women: Seven Plays from the Women's Project. 300p. (C). 1993. pap. 17.95 (*0-435-08617-0*, 08617) Heinemann.
— Women Heroes: Six Short Plays from the Women's Project. 256p. 1987. pap. 6.95 (*0-936839-22-8*) Applause Theatre Bk Pubs.
— Women's Project Two: Five New Plays by Women. LC 84-81624. 1984. 21.95 (*0-933826-73-7*) PAJ Pubns.
— Womenswork: Five New Plays from the Women's Project. 356p. (Orig.). 1989. pap. 10.95 (*1-55783-029-0*) Applause Theatre Bk Pubs.

Miles, Kathy. The Rocking-Stone. (Poetry Wales Poets Ser.: No. 10). 48p. (Orig.). 1988. pap. 8.95 (*0-907476-86-4*, Pub. by Poetry Wales Pr UK) Dufour.

Miles, Keith. Double Eagle. large type ed. 355p. 1992. 21.95 (*0-7505-0337-8*) Ulverscroft.

Miles, Keith A. Flagstick. large type ed. 333p. 1994. 18.95 (*0-7505-0601-6*) Ulverscroft.

Miles, L., jt. auth. see Craft, M.

Miles, Laughton E. & Broughton, Roger J. Medical Monitoring in the Home & Work Environment. 352p. 1990. 99.50 (*0-88167-595-4*) Raven.

Miles, Laurie, et al. Black Hit Woman. 224p. (Orig.). 1983. pap. 2.25 (*0-87067-221-5*, BH221) Holloway.

Miles, Lawrence W., Jr. The California Auto Dealer Legal Manual. 200p. 1993. pap. 75.00 (*0-9635978-0-9*) Clairidge Pr.
— Law of the Car: Everything You Ever Wanted to Know about Buying, Owning, & Selling a Vehicle. 175p. 1993. pap. text ed. write for info. (*0-9635978-1-7*) Clairidge Pr.

Miles, Lee. Heat Pumps - Theory & Service. 397p. 1993. text ed. 43.95 (*0-685-70403-3*) Delmar.

***Miles, Lee A.** Fine Tuning Air Conditioning Systems & Heat Pumps. Turpin, Joanna, ed. LC 94-50363. (Illus.). 104p. (Orig.). 1995. pap. 21.95 (*0-912524-96-0*) Busn News.

***Miles, Lena.** Country Reds. 90p. 1994. write for info. (*0-9642054-0-8*) High Ridge.

Miles, Leo W. High Pressure: A Pipeliner's Story. (Illus.). 179p. (C). 1988. 17.95 (*0-9622105-0-1*) Raton Bks.

Miles, Leona, ed. see Hamilton, Mary M.

Miles, Linda. Linda Miles Practice Dynamics. 160p. 1986. 24.95 (*0-87814-301-7*, D4256) PennWell Bks.

Miles, Linda & Wilson, Betty. The Complete Field Guide to Kitty Cat Positions. LC 92-40530. 128p. 1993. 6.95 (*0-681-41788-9*) Longmeadow Pr.

Miles, Linda B., ed. see Richmond, Elmore, Jr.

Miles, Lion G., ed. The Hessians of Lewis Miller. (Illus.). 66p. 1983. pap. 15.00 (*0-939016-07-9*) Johannes Schwalm Hist.

***Miles, Lisa.** Dinosaurs. (Hotshots Ser.). (Illus.). 32p. (J). (gr. 1 up). 1995. pap. 2.95 (*0-7460-2277-8*, Usborne) EDC.
— Lettering. (Hotshots Ser.). (Illus.). 32p. (J). (gr. 1 up). 1995. pap. 2.95 (*0-7460-2274-3*, Usborne) EDC.

Miles, M. Scott. Confronting a World Gone Wrong: Eight Sections from Elijah's Life on Being God's Person for God's Purposes. LC 92-2290. (Orig.). 1992. pap. 5.99 (*1-56476-023-5*, Victor Books) SP Pubns.
— Someone in My Corner. 144p. 1995. pap. 5.99 (*1-56476-409-5*, 3-3409, Victor Books) SP Pubns.
— When the Walls Are Closing In. 132p. (Orig.). 1993. pap. 5.99 (*1-56476-104-5*, Victor Books) SP Pubns.

Miles, Malcolm. Art for Public Places: Critical Essays. (Illus.). 244p. 1991. pap. 18.95 (*0-9506783-8-4*, Pub. by Winchester Schl Art Pr UK) Paul & Co Pubs.

Miles, Marc A. Devaluation, the Trade Balance, & the Balance of Payments. LC 78-7550. (Business Economics & Finance Ser.: No. 11). 160p. reprint ed. pap. 45.60 (*0-7837-0632-4*, 2040976) Bks Demand.

Miles, Marcia, jt. auth. see Reed, Vicki A.

Miles, Margaret. Carnal Knowing: Female Nakedness & Religious Meaning in the Christian West. LC 90-55679. 272p. 1991. pap. 15.00 (*0-679-73401-5*, Vin) Random.

Miles, Margaret, ed. see Johnston, Ralph C., Jr.

Miles, Margaret R. Desire & Delight: A New Reading of Augustine's Confessions. 120p. 1992. 15.95 (*0-8245-1163-8*) Crossroad NY.

M

An Asterisk (*) at the beginning of an entry indicates that the title is appearing in BIP for the first time.

— Image As Insight: Visual Understanding in Western Christianity & Secular Culture. LC 85-47528. (Illus.). 200p. 1985. pap. 17.00 (0-8070-1007-3) Beacon Pr.
— Practicing Christianity: Critical Perspectives for an Embodied Christianity. 224p. 1990. pap. 12.95 (0-8245-1022-4) Crossroad NY.
Miles, Margaret R., ed. see Wilkins, Walter J.
Miles, Margot. The Old Tennant. 127p. (C). 1988. 39.00 (0-7316-4200-7) St Mut.
Miles, Marshall. Stronger Competitive Bidding. LC 92-70047. 324p. (Orig.). 1992. pap. 14.95 (1-877908-03-7) Lawrence & Leong Pub.
Miles, Martin J. Investment Math Made Easy. 303p. 1986. text ed. 22.95 (0-13-503244-X, Busn) P-H.
— Real Estate Investor's Complete Handbook. LC 82-351. 572p. 1982. 49.95 (0-13-763086-7, Busn) P-H.
— Vest Pocket Real Estate Advisor. 544p. 1989. pap. 24.95 (0-13-945064-5) P-H.
— Vest-Pocket Real Estate Advisor. 560p. 1990. pap. 12.95 (0-13-964941-7) P-H.
Miles, Mary. Nantucket Etcetera. (Illus.). 196p. (Orig.). 1989. pap. 12.00 (0-9623188-1-7) Yesterdays Island.
— Nantucket Gam. LC 93-71134. 192p. 1993. write for info. (0-9636885-1-0); pap. write for info. (0-9636885-2-9) Faraway Pub.
— What's So Special about Nantucket? LC 98-71418. (Illus.). 36p. (J). (ps up). 1993. lib. bdg. 17.00 (0-9636885-0-2) Faraway Pub.
— Yesterday's & Today's Island. (Illus.). 200p. (Orig.). 1989. pap. write for info. (0-318-65208-0) Yesterdays Island.
Miles, Mary A., ed. see Zabel, Craig.
Miles, Mary D. Stress. (Lifesearch Ser.). 64p. (Orig.). 1994. pap. 4.95 (0-687-77876-X) Abingdon.
Miles, Matthew B. & Huberman, A. Michael. Qualitative Data Analysis: An Expanded Sourcebook. 2nd ed. (C). 1994. text ed. 65.00 (0-8039-4653-8); pap. text ed. 32.00 (0-8039-5540-5) Sage.
Miles, Matthew B., jt. auth. see Gold, Barry A.
Miles, Matthew B., jt. auth. see Huberman, A. Michael.
Miles, Matthew B., jt. auth. see Louis, Karen S.
Miles, Matthew B., jt. auth. see Weitzman, Eben.
Miles, Michael W. The Odyssey of the American Right. 1980. 30.00 (0-19-502774-4) OUP.
Miles, Mike E., jt. auth. see Wurtzebach, Charles H.
***Miles, Mike E., et al.** Real Estate Development Principles & Process. 450p. 1991. text ed. 53.95 (0-87420-712-6, R23) Urban Land.
Miles, Miska. Annie & the Old One. (Illus.). (J). (gr. 1-3). 1972. lib. bdg. 14.95i (0-316-57117-2, Joy St Bks) Little.
— Annie & the Old One. (Illus.). (J). (gr. 1-3). 1985. reprint ed. mass mkt. 7.95 (0-316-57120-2) Little.
— Gertrude's Pocket. (Illus.). (J). (gr. 2-5). 1984. 15.25 (0-8446-6164-3) Peter Smith.
Miles, Nelson A. Nelson A. Miles: A Documentary Biography of His Military Career, 1861-1903. Pohanka, Brian C. & Carroll, John M., eds. LC 84-72715. (Frontier Military Ser.: Vol. 13). (Illus.). 327p. 1986. 35.00 (0-87062-159-9) A H Clark.
— Personal Recollections & Observations of General Nelson A. Miles. rev. ed. LC 68-23812. (American Scene Ser.). (Illus.). 1969. reprint ed. lib. bdg. 69.50 (0-306-71020-X) Da Capo.
— Personal Recollections & Observations of General Nelson A. Miles, 2 vols., Set. LC 91-39603. (Illus.). xvii, 591p. 1992. reprint ed. pap. 23.90 (0-8032-8182-X, Bison Books) U of Nebr Pr.
— Personal Recollections & Observations of General Nelson A. Miles, 2 vols., Vol. 1. LC 91-39603. (Illus.). vi, 319p. 1992. reprint ed. pap. 11.95 (0-8032-8180-3, Bison Books) U of Nebr Pr.
— Personal Recollections & Observations of General Nelson A. Miles, 2 vols., Vol. 2. LC 91-39603. (Illus.). xxi, 272p. 1992. reprint ed. pap. 11.95 (0-8032-8181-1, Bison Books) U of Nebr Pr.
— Serving the Republic: Memoirs of the Civil & Military Life of Nelson A. Miles. LC 74-147786. (Select Bibliographies Reprint Ser.). 1977. reprint ed. 28.95 (0-8369-5632-X) Ayer.
Miles, P., et al, eds. Reflections on the 1988-1990 March of the Living. (Illus.). 139p. (Orig.). (C). 1991. pap. 15.00 (0-930029-05-4) Central Agency.
Miles, Pamela S., et al. Obstetrics & Gynecology. LC 94-3805. (Oklahoma Notes Ser.). (Illus.). 240p. 1994. pap. 16.95 (0-387-94184-3) Spr-Verlag.
Miles, Patricia H., jt. auth. see Bracegirdle, Brian.
Miles, Patrick, ed. & tr. Chekhov on the British Stage. LC 92-26037. (Illus.). 270p. (C). 1993. 59.95 (0-521-38467-2) Cambridge U Pr.
Miles, Patrick, tr. see Chekhov, Anton.
Miles, Patrick, jt. auth. see Westfall, Tanja.
Miles, Paul A. The Dawning. abr. ed. Ingram, tr. 238p. 1995. pap. 8.95 (1-56901-247-4) NW Pub.
Miles, Peter. A Gift of Observation. 92p. (C). 1988. 75.00 (0-7212-0794-4, Pub. by Regency Press) St Mut.
— Wuthering Heights. (Critics Debate Ser.). 96p. (C). 1990. text ed. 35.00 (0-333-38516-0, Pub. by Macmillan UK) Humanities.
Miles, Peter & Smith, Malcolm. Cinema, Literature & Society: Elite & Mass Culture in Interwar Britain. (Film Ser.). 272p. 1987. lib. bdg. 35.00 (0-7099-3363-0, Pub. by Croom Helm UK) Routledge Chapman & Hall.
Miles, Peter, ed. see Smollett, Tobias.
Miles, Peter, ed. see Trollope, Anthony.
Miles, Preston. Speech Power. Pei, Mario, ed. 59p. 1983. pap. text ed. 99.95 (1-55678-024-9) Learn Inc.
Miles, R. & Chalmers, A. Progress in Transputer & Occam Research. LC 94-75912. 229p. 1994. pap. 69.50 (90-5199-163-0) IOS Press.
Miles, R. E., jt. ed. see Snowden, C. M.
Miles, R. S., et al. The Design of Educational Exhibits. (Illus.). 224p. (C). 1982. text ed. 44.95 (0-04-069002-4) Routledge Chapman & Hall.
— The Design of Educational Exhibits. 2nd ed. (Illus.). 208p. 1988. pap. text ed. 29.95 (0-04-445078-8) Routledge Chapman & Hall.
Miles, Raymond C. How to Price a Business. LC 81-13270. 133p. 1982. text ed. 64.95 (0-87624-211-5, Inst Busn Plan) P-H.
Miles, Raymond E. Fit, Failure & the Hall of Fame. 1994. text ed. 24.95 (0-02-921265-0) Free Pr.
Miles, Raymond E. & Snow, Charles C. Organizational Strategy: Structure & Process. (Management Ser.). (Illus.). 1978. text ed. write for info. (0-07-041932-9) McGraw.
Miles, Richard. Elizabeth Keith: the Printed Works (1917-1939) A Catalogue Raisonne. (Illus.). 80p. 1991. 60.00 (1-877921-08-4); pap. 27.50 (1-877921-07-6) Pacific Asia.
— Prints of Paul Jacoulet. (Illus.). 140p. (C). 1982. pap. text ed. 25.50 (0-903697-13-0) Pacific Asia.
— Watercolors of Paul Jacoulet. (Illus.). 84p. 1989. 60.00 (1-877921-02-5); pap. 27.50 (1-877921-01-7) Pacific Asia.
Miles, Richard, jt. auth. see Traub, Roger D.
***Miles, Robert.** Anne Radcliffe: The Great Enchantress. 208p. 1995. text ed. 49.95 (0-7190-3828-6, Pub. by Manchester Univ Pr UK); text ed. 19.95 (0-7190-3829-4, Pub. by Manchester Univ Pr UK) St Martin.
— Capitalism & Unfree Labor: Anomaly or Necessity. 256p. 1989. 55.00 (0-422-79250-0, A0712); pap. 18.95 (0-685-26092-5, A3795) Routledge Chapman & Hall.
— Capitalism & Unfree Labour: Anomaly or Necessity? 256p. 1987. lib. bdg. 49.50 (0-422-61730-X, Routledge NY) Routledge Chapman & Hall.
— Gothic Writing, 1764-1850: A Genealogy. LC 92-26012. 256p. 1993. 62.50 (0-415-07748-6, B0368) Routledge.
— Racism. 158p. 1989. pap. 11.95 (0-415-01809-9) Routledge.
— Racism after 'Race' Relations. LC 92-47079. 1993. write for info. (0-415-07453-3, Routledge NY); pap. write for info. (0-415-10034-8, Routledge NY) Routledge.
— Racism & Migrant Labour: A Critical Text. 206p. (Orig.). 1983. pap. 14.95 (0-7100-9212-1, RKP) Routledge.
***Miles, Robert & Thranhardt, Dietrich.** Migration & European Integration: The Dynamics of Inclusion & Exclusion. 224p. 1994. 38.50 (0-8386-3613-6) Fairleigh Dickinson.
Miles, Robert, jt. ed. see Monteith, Moira.
Miles, Robert, et al. Prose Style: A Contemporary Guide. 2nd ed. 224p. (C). 1990. pap. text ed. write for info. (0-13-713181-X) P-H.
Miles, Robert H. Managing the Corporate Social Environment. (Illus.). 304p. 1987. pap. 25.95 (0-13-550872-X) P-H.
Miles, Robert H. & Randolph, W. Alan. The Organization Game: A Simulation. 2nd ed. (C). 1985. pap. text ed. 16.75 (0-673-16654-6) HarpCollege.
Miles, Robert H., et al. The Organization Game. 3rd ed. (C). 1993. 17.00 (0-673-46861-5) HarpCollege.
Miles, Robert W. That Frenchman, John Calvin. LC 83-45625. reprint ed. 29.00 (0-404-19843-0) AMS Pr.
Miles, Roger & Zavala, Lauro. Towards the Museum of the Future: New European Perspectives. LC 93-12788. 1993. write for info. (0-415-09498-4) Routledge.
Miles, Rogers B. Science, Religion & Belief: The Clerical Virtuosi of the Royal Society of London, 1663-1687. LC 91-16763. (American University Studies: Theology & Religion: Ser. VII, Vol. 106). 207p. 1993. 41.95 (0-8204-1564-2) P Lang Pubs.
Miles, Rosalind. Ben Jonson: His Craft & Art. 272p. (C). 1990. text ed. 70.50 (0-389-20944-9) B&N Imports.
— Ben Jonson: His Craft & Art. 256p. 1990. 55.00 (0-415-05578-4, A4913) Routledge.
— Ben Jonson: His Life & Work. 288p. 1986. 55.00 (0-7102-0838-3, 08383, RKP) Routledge.
— I Elizabeth: The Word of a Queen, a Novel. LC 93-43947. 1994. 25.00 (0-385-47160-2) Doubleday.
— Women's History of the World. LC 88-39598. 320p. 1990. reprint ed. pap. 13.00 (0-06-097317-X, PL) HarpC.
***Miles, S. Johnston.** The Preacherman & the Godlight. 290p. 1995. pap. 8.95 (0-7610-0013-5) NW Pub.
Miles, S. Phillip. Rubicon. (Illus.). 40p. 1994. pap. 7.95 (1-884778-03-8) Old Mountain.
Miles, Sally. Alfi & the Dark. LC 88-1043. (Illus.). 32p. (J). (ps-1). 1988. 13.95 (0-87701-527-9) Chronicle Bks.
Miles, Sam. Guilt Free Gourmet: Food That Tastes "Too Good" to Be "Good for You", Vol. 1. 422p. 1994. 39.95 (0-9641843-0-3) Wellness.
Miles, Samuel B. Countries & Tribes of the Persian Gulf. 634p. 1994. 100.00 (1-873938-56-X, Pub. by Garnet Pubng Ltd UK) Paul & Co Pubs.
Miles, Sara, ed. see Jordan, June.
Miles, Sara, tr. see Rugama, Leonel, et al.
Miles, Sarah, ed. see Benjamin, Medea & Freeman, Andrea.
Miles, Scott. Families Growing Together. 144p. 1990. pap. text ed. 2.00 (0-89693-821-2) SP Pubns.
Miles, Sian, ed. & tr. Simone Weil: An Anthology. LC 86-9242. 304p. 1986. pap. 12.95 (1-55584-021-3) Grove-Atltic.
Miles, Sian, ed. see Sand, George.
Miles, Sian, tr. see Sand, George.
Miles, Simon. Reasons Why. (C). 1989. 24.95 (1-871058-04-X, Pub. by Dragonheart Pr UK) St Mut.
Miles, Steven & Gomez, Carlos. Protocols for Elective Use of Life Sustaining Treatments: A Design Guide. 176p. 1989. 25.95 (0-8261-6700-4) Springer Pub.
Miles, Susan G. Adoption Literature for Children & Young Adults: An Annotated Bibliography. LC 91-31854. (Bibliographies & Indexes in Sociology Ser.: No. 21). 232p. 1991. text ed. 45.00 (0-313-27606-4, MBK/, Greenwood Pr) Greenwood.
***Miles, T. R.** Dyslexia: The Pattern of Difficulties. 2nd ed. 315p. 1993. text ed. 34.95 (0-614-00860-3, 0548) Singular Publishing.
— Dyslexia: The Pattern of Difficulties. 2nd ed. 315p. 1993. pap. 34.95 (1-56593-249-8, 0548) Singular Publishing.
Miles, T. R., ed. Understanding Dyslexia. (C). 1988. 60.00 (1-871458-07-2, Pub. by Bath Educ Pubs UK) St Mut.
Miles, T. R. & Miles, E., eds. Dyslexia & Mathematics. 128p. 1991. 59.95 (0-415-06480-5, A6178); pap. 13.95 (0-415-04987-3, A5962) Routledge.
Miles, T. R. & Miles, Elaine. Dyslexia: A Hundred Years On. 176p. 1990. 80.00 (0-335-09541-0, Open Univ Pr); pap. 25.00 (0-335-09540-2, Open Univ Pr) Taylor & Francis.
— Help for Dyslexic Children. 116p. 1983. pap. 9.95 (0-416-33740-6, NO. 3829) Routledge Chapman & Hall.
***Miles, T. R. & Varma, V., eds.** Dyslexia & Stress. 200p. 1995. pap. 49.95 (1-56593-593-4, 1214) Singular Publishing.
Miles, T. R., jt. auth. see Harzem, Peter.
Miles, T. R., jt. ed. see Pavlidis, George T.
Miles, Thomas H. Critical Thinking & Writing for Science & Technology. 345p. (C). 1990. pap. text ed. 25.50 (0-15-516156-3); pap. text ed. 1.50 (0-15-516157-1) HB Coll Pubs.
— Guide to Building Sensible Phrases with Noun Strings & Unit Modifiers. 59p. Date not set. pap. text ed. 15.00 (0-914548-78-6) Soc Tech Comm.
Miles, Thomas H., tr. see Lao Tzu.
Miles, Thomas R., jt. auth. see Gilroy, Dorothy E.
Miles, Tim R. Dyslexia at College. 160p. 1987. 12.95 (0-416-39670-4) Routledge Chapman & Hall.
Miles, Timothy R., jt. auth. see Pavlidis, George T.
Miles, Tom. Ad-Libbing Poems, 1978-1986. LC 87-71905. 50p. (Orig.). 1987. pap. 3.75 (0-938711-01-6) Tecolote Pubns.
Miles, Tony. Carp Fishing: Expert Advice for Beginners. (Fishing Facts Ser.). (Illus.). 96p. 1992. pap. 13.95 (1-85223-474-1, Pub. by Crowood Pr UK) Trafalgar.
— Pike Fishing: Expert Advice for Beginners. (Fishing Facts Ser.). (Illus.). 96p. 1992. pap. 13.95 (1-85223-475-X, Pub. by Crowood Pr UK) Trafalgar.
Miles, Vera. Practical Four-Shaft Weaving. (Illus.). 50p. 1979. pap. 11.95 (0-85219-128-6, Pub. by Batsford UK) Trafalgar.
***Miles, Victoria.** Bald Eaglets. (Illus.). 24p. (Orig.). (J). (gr. 1-4). 1995. pap. text ed. 5.95 (1-55143-028-2) Orca Bk Pubs.
— Cougar Kittens. (Illus.). 24p. (Orig.). (J). (gr. 1-4). 1995. pap. 5.95 (1-55143-026-6) Orca Bk Pubs.
— Sea Otter Pup. (Illus.). 24p. (Orig.). (J). (gr. 1-4). 1993. pap. 5.95 (1-55143-002-9) Orca Bk Pubs.
— Spotted Owlets. (Illus.). 24p. (Orig.). (J). (gr. 1-4). 1993. pap. 5.95 (1-55143-004-5) Orca Bk Pubs.
Miles, Walter F., jt. auth. see Montgomery, Richard H.
Miles, Walter R., et al. Science in Progress, Fourth Series. Baitsell, George A., ed. LC 78-37534. (Essay Index Reprint Ser.). 1977. reprint ed. 46.95 (0-8369-2529-7) Ayer.
Miles, Wilfred. Military Operations, France & Belgium, 1916, Vol. II. (Great War Ser.: No. 19). (Illus.). 654p. reprint ed. 49.95 (0-89839-169-5) Battery Pr.
***Miles, Wilfrid.** Military Operations, France & Belgium, 1916 Vol. II: Maps & Appendices. (Great War Ser.: No. 34). 135p. 1994. reprint ed. 39.95 (0-89839-207-1) Battery Pr.
— Military Operations, France & Belgium, 1917: The Battle of Cambrai. (Great War Ser.: No. 13). (Illus.). 432p. reprint ed. 39.95 (0-89839-162-8) Battery Pr.
Miles, William. The Image Makers: A Bibliography of American Presidential Campaign Biographies. LC 79-19472. 272p. 1979. 25.00 (0-8108-1252-5) Scarecrow.
— Songs, Odes, Glees, & Ballads: A Bibliography of American Presidential Campaign Songsters. LC 90-44938. (Music Reference Collection Ser.: No. 27). 256p. 1990. text ed. 55.00 (0-313-27697-8, MGI, Greenwood Pr) Greenwood.
Miles, William, comp. The People's Voice: An Annotated Bibliography of American Presidential Campaign Newspapers, 1828-1984. LC 87-11969. (Bibliographies & Indexes in American History Ser.: No. 6). 272p. 1987. text ed. 69.50 (0-313-23976-2, MPN/) Greenwood.
Miles, William, jt. auth. see Burns, Khephra.
Miles, William F. Elections & Ethnicity in French Martinique: A Paradox in Paradise. LC 85-16737. 302p. 1985. text ed. 65.00 (0-275-90031-2, C0031, Praeger Pubs) Greenwood.
— Hausaland Divided: Colonialism & Independence in Nigeria & Niger. LC 93-31669. (Wilder House Series in Politics, History, & Culture). (Illus.). 392p. 1994. 49.95 (0-8014-2855-6) Cornell U Pr.
— Imperial Burdens: Countercolonialism in Former French India. LC 93-50213. 255p. 1994. lib. bdg. 45.00 (1-55587-511-4) Lynne Rienner.
Miles, Wyndham D., ed. American Chemists & Chemical Engineers. LC 76-192. 544p. 1976. 32.95 (0-8412-0278-8) Am Chemical.
Miles, Wyndham D. & Gould, Robert F., eds. American Chemists & Chemical Engineers. 364p. 1994. lib. bdg. 20.00 (0-9640255-0-7) Gould Bks.
Milesius, Timotheus. Die Perser. (Wissenschaftliche Veroffentlichungen der Deutschen Orient-Gesellschaft Ser.: Heft 3). 126p. 1973. reprint ed. write for info. (3-487-05049-8, Pub. by Georg Olms GW) Lubrecht & Cramer.
Mileski, Maureen, jt. auth. see Black, Donald.
Milestone, Wayne D., ed. Reliability, Stress Analysis & Failure Prevention Methods in Mechanical Design: International Conference on Reliability, Stress Analysis & Failure Prevention, 1980, San Francisco, CA. LC 80-66039. 327p. reprint ed. pap. 93.20 (0-317-58253-4, 2056393) Bks Demand.
Mileti, Dennis S. & Fitzpatrick, Colleen. The Great Earthquake Experiment: Risk Communication & Public Action. LC 91-19576. 149p. (C). 1993. pap. text ed. 39.00 (0-8133-8369-2) Westview.
Mileti, Dennis S., et al. Earthquake Prediction Response & Options for Public Policy. (Program on Environment & Behavior Monograph Ser.: No. 31). 190p. (Orig.). (C). 1981. pap. 8.00 (0-685-28105-1) Natural Hazards.
Miletich, John J. Acid Rain in Canada: A Selected Bibliography. LC 83-15159. (CPL Bibliographies Ser.: No. 124). 1983. 6.00 (0-86602-124-8) CPL Biblios.
— AIDS: A Multimedia Sourcebook. LC 92-39121. 288p. 1993. pap. text ed. 15.95 (0-89789-362-X, Greenwood Pr) Greenwood.
— Retirement-Planning & Adjustment: A Selected Bibliography. (CPL Bibliographies Ser.: No. 117). 53p. 1983. 9.00 (0-86602-117-5) Coun Plan Librarians.
— Treatment of Cocaine Abuse: An Annotated Bibliography. LC 91-35403. (Bibliographies & Indexes in Medical Studies: No. 9). 256p. 1992. text ed. 55.00 (0-313-27839-3, MTQ/, Greenwood Pr) Greenwood.
Miletich, John J., comp. AIDS: A Multimedia Sourcebook. LC 93-10830. (Bibliographies & Indexes in Medical Studies: No. 10). 288p. 1993. text ed. 59.95 (0-313-28669-8) Greenwood.
— Airline Safety: An Annotated Bibliography. LC 90-13988. (Bibliographies & Indexes in Psychology Ser.: No. 7). 240p. 1990. text ed. 59.95 (0-313-27391-X, MRS/, Greenwood Pr) Greenwood.
— Police, Firefighter & Paramedic Stress: An Annotated Bibliography. LC 89-28649. (Bibliographies & Indexes in Psychology Ser.: No. 6). 239p. 1990. text ed. 59.95 (0-313-26682-4, MOF/, Greenwood Pr) Greenwood.
— Retirement: An Annotated Bibliography. LC 86-9933. (Bibliographies & Indexes in Geronotology Ser.: No. 2). 164p. 1986. text ed. 42.95 (0-313-24815-X, MRI/, Greenwood Pr) Greenwood.
— States of Awareness: An Annotated Bibliography. LC 88-24733. (Bibliographies & Indexes in Psychology Ser.). 320p. 1988. text ed. 55.00 (0-313-26194-6, MSR, Greenwood Pr) Greenwood.
— Work & Alcohol Abuse: An Annotated Bibliography. LC 87-23619. (Bibliographies & Indexes in Sociology Ser.: No. 12). 272p. 1987. text ed. 55.00 (0-313-25689-6, MWR/, Greenwood Pr) Greenwood.
***Miletich, John J., ed.** Depression: A Multimedia Sourcebook. LC 95-4194. (Bibliographies & Indexes in Medical Studies: Vol. 11). 240p. 1995. text ed. 69.50 (0-313-29374-0, Greenwood Pr) Greenwood.
Miletich, John S. The Bugarstica: Bilingual Anthology of the Earliest Extant South Slavic Folk Narrative Song. (Illinois Medieval Monographs: No. III). 384p. 1990. 34.95 (0-252-01711-0) U of Ill Pr.
Miletich, Leo N. Broadway's Prize-Winning Musicals: An Annotated Guide for Libraries & Audio Collectors. LC 92-4125. 255p. 1993. pap. 14.95 (1-56023-018-5) Harrington Pk.
— Broadway's Prize-Winning Musicals: An Annotated Guide for Libraries & Audio Collectors. LC 92-4125. (Illus.). 222p. 1993. lib. bdg. 39.95 (1-56024-288-4) Haworth Pr.
— Dan Stuart's Fistic Carnival. (Illus.). 280p. 1994. 29.50 (0-89096-614-1); pap. 14.95 (0-89096-615-X) Tex A&M Univ Pr.
Mileur, Jean-Pierre. The Critical Romance: The Critic As Reader, Writer, Hero. LC 89-40533. 272p. (Orig.). 1990. text ed. 39.50 (0-299-12410-X); pap. text ed. 15.00 (0-299-12414-2) U of Wis Pr.
— Literary Revisionism & the Burden of Modernity. LC 84-2768. 1985. 45.00 (0-520-05236-6) U CA Pr.
Mileur, Jerome M., ed. Polity: The Journal of the Northeastern Political Science Association. (Illus.). 200p. 1992. lib. bdg. 35.00 (0-317-00292-9) NE Poli Sci.
Mileur, Jerome M. & Sulzner, George T. Campaigning for the Massachusetts Senate: Electioneering Outside the Political Limelight. LC 73-85898. 208p. 1974. pap. 14.95 (0-87023-140-5) U of Mass Pr.
Mileur, Jerome M., jt. ed. see White, John K.
Milev, Geo. Road to Freedom. LC 87-82775. 1990. pap. 16.95 (0-948259-45-0) Dufour.
Milewski, jt. auth. see Katz.
Milewski, B. Supersymmetry & Supergravity, 1983: Proceedings of the XIX Winter School & Workshop on Theoretical Physics, Karpacz, Poland, February 14-26, 1983. 588p. (C). 1983. 98.00 (9971-950-23-5); pap. 52.00 (9971-950-97-9) World Scientific Pub.
Milewski, John V., ed. see Adams, John, et al.
Milewski, John V., jt. ed. see Katz, Harry S.
Milewski, John W., jt. auth. see Katz, Harry S.
Milewski, Stanley E., jt. auth. see Swastek, Joseph.
Milewski, Tadeusz. Introduction to the Study of Language. 1973. pap. text ed. 34.75 (90-279-2598-4) Mouton.
***Miley, E. J., Jr., illus.** I Was So Stupid. (Wee Write Bks.: No. 23). 50p. (J). (ps-3). 1995. lib. bdg. 18.95 (1-884987-78-8) WeWrite.
— I Was So Stupid. (Wee Write Bks.: No. 23). 50p. (J). (ps-3). 1995. pap. 8.95 (1-884987-79-6) WeWrite.
— I Was So Stupid. (Wee Write Bks.: No. 23). 50p. (J). (ps-3). 1995. 32.95 (1-884987-80-X) WeWrite.
Miley, George H. Direct Conversion of Nuclear Radiation Energy. LC 70-155742. (ANS Monographs). 532p. 1970. 40.00 (0-89448-004-9, 300003) Am Nuclear Soc.
— Fusion Energy Conversion. LC 75-44554. (Nuclear Science Technology Ser.). (Illus.). 1976. text ed. 46.00 (0-89448-008-1, 300009) Am Nuclear Soc.

An Asterisk (*) at the beginning of an entry indicates that the title is appearing in BIP for the first time.

*Miley, George H., ed.** Laser Interaction & Related Plasma Phenomena. (AIP Conference Proceedings Ser.: No. 318). 696p. 1994. text ed. 150.00x (*1-56396-324-8*) Am Inst Physics.

Miley, George H. & Hora, H., eds. Laser Interaction & Related Plasma Phenomena, Vol. 10. (Illus.). 688p. (C). 1993. 145.00 (*0-306-44353-8*, Plenum Pr) Plenum.

Miley, George H., jt. ed. see Hora, H.

Miley, George H., jt. ed. see Hora, Heinrich.

Miley, Jeanie. Becoming Fire: Experience the Presence of Jesus Every Day. LC 93-11922. 272p. (Orig.). 1993. pap. 9.99 (*0-8007-5479-4*) Revell.

— Shared Splendor. LC 91-17222. 192p. 1991. 12.99 (*0-8007-1659-0*) Revell.

Miley, Jerry D. Night Is Colder Than Autumn. (Original Poetry Ser.). 20p. 1991. 3.00 (*0-916397-18-1*) Manic D Pr.

— Standing in Line. 20p. (Orig.). 1990. pap. 3.00 (*0-916397-08-4*) Manic D Pr.

Miley, John. Systematic Theology, 2 vols., Set. 1108p. 1989. reprint ed. 39.95 (*0-943575-09-5*) Hendrickson MA.

Miley, Karla K., jt. auth. see DuBois, Brenda L.

*Miley, Karla K., et al.** Generalist Social Work Practice: An Empowering Approach. 2nd ed. LC 94-23337. 1995. pap. text ed. write for info. (*0-205-15617-7*) Allyn.

Miley, Lorene. I Looked for a Man...& Found One. 1983. pap. 6.95 (*0-89265-088-5*) Randall Hse.

Miley, Michael. StuffIt Deluxe User's Guide 3.0. Schargel, David, ed. (Illus.). 290p. 1992. 120.00 (*1-878777-03-3*) Aladdin Systs.

Miley, Michael & Schargel, David. StuffIt SpaceSaver User's Guide 1.0. (Illus.). 36p. 1992. 59.95 (*1-878777-04-1*) Aladdin Systs.

Miley, W. N. & Oosterhuis, D. M., eds. Nitrogen Nutrition of Cotton. 115p. 1990. 15.00 (*0-89118-105-9*) Am Soc Agron.

Milford. The Hand. 3rd ed. (Illus.). 512p. 1988. text ed. 89.00 (*0-8016-3345-1*) Mosby Yr Bk.

Milford, Bryan, jt. auth. see Coen, Patricia.

Milford Conference Staff. Social Case Work, Generic & Specific: An Outline: a Report of the Milford Conference. LC 74-83097. (Studies in the Practice of Social Work: No. 2). 102p. reprint ed. pap. 29.10 (*0-7837-5365-9*, 2045129) Bks Demand.

Milford, H. S., ed. see Cowper, William.

Milford, H. S., ed. see Hunt, Leigh.

Milford, Humphrey S., ed. Selected Modern English Essays. LC 80-29398. (World's Classics, Second Ser.). x, 342p. 1981. reprint ed. text ed. 65.00 (*0-313-22763-2*, MISE, Greenwood Pr) Greenwood.

Milford, Judy G. Are You Sure This Is Mine? A Search for God & Truth. 1990. pap. 11.95 (*0-88347-261-9*) Thomas More.

Milford, Nancy. Zelda. LC 66-20742. (Illus.). 464p. 1983. pap. 15.00 (*0-06-091069-0*, CN 1069, PL) HarpC.

Milfull, John. Why Germany? National Socialist Antisemitism & the European Context. 264p. 1993. 54.95 (*0-85496-315-4*) Berg Pubs.

Milfull, John, ed. The Attractions of Fascism: Social Psychology & Aesthetics of the "Triumph of the Right" LC 89-28950. 326p. 1990. 68.00 (*0-85496-613-7*) Berg Pubs.

Milgate, Murray, ed. Capital & Employment. (Studies Political Economy Ser.). 1983. text ed. 85.00 (*0-12-496250-5*) Acad Pr.

— Critical Issues in Social Thought. 244p. 1989. text ed. 72.00 (*0-12-496248-3*) Acad Pr.

Milgate, Murray & Stimson, Shannon C. Ricardian Politics. 176p. 1992. text ed. 35.00 (*0-691-04278-0*) Princeton U Pr.

Milgate, Murray, ed. see Eatwell, John.

Milgram, James R., ed. Algebraic & Geometric Topology, 2 pts., Pt. 1. 3rd ed. LC 78-14304. (Proceedings of Symposia in Pure Mathematics Ser., Humboldt State University, Arcata, CA, July 29-August 16, 1974: Vol. 32). 412p. 1989. 36.00 (*0-8218-1432-X*, PSPUM 32.1) Am Math.

— Algebraic & Geometric Topology, 2 pts., Pt. 2. 3rd ed. LC 78-14304. (Proceedings of Symposia in Pure Mathematics Ser., Humboldt State University, Arcata, CA, July 29-August 16, 1974: Vol. 32). 322p. 1989. 36.00 (*0-8218-1433-8*, PSPUM 32.2) Am Math.

— Algebraic & Geometric Topology, 2 pts., Set. 3rd ed. LC 78-14304. (Proceedings of Symposia in Pure Mathematics Ser., Humboldt State University, Arcata, CA, July 29-August 16, 1974: Vol. 32). 734p. 1989. 60.00 (*0-8218-1473-7*, PSPUM 32) Am Math.

*Milgram, James W.** Abraham Lincoln Illustrated Envelopes & Letter Paper. (Illus.). 272p. 1984. 21.95 (*0-9614018-0-X*) Northbrook Pub.

— Radiologic & Histologic Pathology of Nontumorous Diseases of Bones & Joints, 2 vols., Set. Gruhn, John G., ed. (Illus.). 1382p. 1990. 199.00 (*0-9614018-1-8*) Northbrook Pub.

— Radiologic & Histologic Pathology of Nontumorous Diseases of the Bones & Joints, 2 vols., Set. (Illus.). 1406p. 1991. 395.00 (*0-8121-1371-3*) Williams & Wilkins.

Milgram, James W., et al. Vessel Named Markings on United States Inland & Ocean Waterways 1810-1890. Hahn, Charless & Stral, Harold M., eds. (Illus.). 832p. 1984. 99.00 (*0-916675-00-9*) Collectors Club IL.

Milgram, Morris. The Challenge of Open Housing: Good Neighborhood. 248p. 1977. 8.00 (*0-318-15820-5*, O-2) Natl Neighbors.

Milgram, Norman, ed. Stress & Coping in Time of War: Generalizations from the Israeli Experience. LC 86-9715. (Psychosocial Stress Ser.: No. 7). 420p. 1986. 49.95 (*0-87630-430-7*) Brunner-Mazel.

Milgram, R. James, jt. auth. see Madsen, Ib.

Milgram, Richard J., jt. auth. see Adem, Alejandro.

*Milgram, Roberta M.** Teaching Gifted & Talented Learners in Regular Classrooms. (Illus.). 316p. 1989. pap. 35.95 (*0-398-06290-0*) C C Thomas.

— Teaching Gifted & Talented Learners in Regular Classrooms. (Illus.). 316p. (C). 1989. text ed. 62.95 (*0-398-05557-2*) C C Thomas.

Milgram, Roberta M. & Runco, Mark, eds. Counseling Gifted & Talented Children: A Guide for Teachers, Counselors, & Parents. (Creativity Research Ser.). 288p. 1991. text ed. 47.50 (*0-89391-724-9*); pap. text ed. 24.95 (*0-89391-773-7*) Ablex Pub.

Milgram, Roberta M., et al, eds. Teaching & Counseling Gifted & Talented Adolescents: An International Learning Style Perspective. LC 92-35348. 296p. 1993. text ed. 55.00 (*0-275-93640-6*, C3640, Praeger Pubs) Greenwood.

Milgram, Roger. Milgrim on Licensing. 1991. write for info. (*0-8205-1743-7*) Bender.

Milgram, Stanley. Obedience to Authority. 225p. 1983. pap. text ed. 13.00 (*0-06-131983-X*, TB1983, Torch) HarpC.

Milgram, Stanley, et al. The Individual in a Social World: Essays & Experiment. 2nd ed. 345p. 1992. text ed. write for info. (*0-07-041936-1*) McGraw.

Milgran, Gail G. & Griffin, Thomas. What, When, & How to Talk to Students About Alcohol & Other Drugs. 86p. (Orig.). 1986. pap. 10.00 (*0-89486-336-3*, 5191A) Hazelden.

Milgrim, Roger M. Milgrim on Trade Secrets, 4 vols., Set. 1967. ring bd. write for info. (*0-8205-1738-0*) Bender.

Milgrim, Sally-Anne. Plays to Play with in Class. LC 85-60244. (Illus.). 216p. (Orig.). 1985. pap. text ed. 10.95 (*0-89390-060-5*) Resource Pubns.

Milgrim, Shirley. Haym Salomon: Liberty's Son. LC 75-17349. (Illus.). 120p. (J). (gr. 5-8). 1975. 9.95 (*0-8276-0073-9*) JPS Phila.

— Pathways to Independence: Discovering Independence National Historical Park. LC 73-89767. (Illus.). 128p. 1975. 12.95 (*0-85699-101-5*) Chatham Pr.

Milgrin, David. Why Benny Barks: A Step One Book. LC 93-47102. (Step into Reading Bks.: Step 1). (Illus.). 32p. (Orig.). (J). (ps-1). 1994. lib. bdg. 7.99 (*0-679-96157-7*); pap. 3.99 (*0-679-86157-2*) Random Bks Yng Read.

Milgrom, Al. Spider-Man: Round Robin. 144p. 1994. pap. 15.95 (*0-7851-0027-X*) Marvel Entmnt.

Milgrom, Elie, jt. ed. see Joosen, Wouter.

Milgrom, F., ed. see International Convocation on Immunology Staff.

Milgrom, F., et al, eds. Antibodies: Protective, Destructive & Regulatory Role: Ninth International Convocation on Immunology, Amherst, N.Y., June 1984. (Illus.). xiv, 462p. 1985. 300.00 (*3-8055-3990-8*) S Karger.

— Principles of Immunological Diagnosis in Medicine. LC 80-20724. (Illus.). 536p. reprint ed. pap. 152.80 (*0-8357-7650-6*, 2056976) Bks Demand.

Milgrom, Felix & Flanagan, Thomas D., eds. Medical Microbiology. LC 82-1261. (Illus.). 762p. reprint ed. pap. 180.00 (*0-7837-2581-7*, 2042740) Bks Demand.

Milgrom, Jacob. The JPS Torah Commentary: Numbers. 520p. 1990. 50.00 (*0-8276-0329-0*) JPS Phila.

— Leviticus 1-16. 1991. 45.00 (*0-385-11434-6*) Doubleday.

— Studies in Levitical Terminology: Vol. 1, The Encroacher & the Levite. The Term Aboda. LC 76-626141. (Univeraity of California Publications. Near Eastern Studies: Vol. 14). 120p. reprint ed. pap. 34.20 (*0-317-10194-3*, 2021380) Bks Demand.

Milgrom, Jo. Handmade Midrash: Workshops in Visual Theology. LC 91-29181. (Illus.). 150p. 1992. reprint ed. text ed. 37.50 (*0-8276-0394-0*); reprint ed. pap. text ed. 25.00 (*0-8276-0406-8*) JPS Phila.

Milgrom, Paul & Roberts, John. Economics, Organization & Management. 600p. 1992. text ed. 73.00 (*0-13-224650-3*) P-H.

Milgroom, Mike, ed. Visual Elements Three: Marks & Patterns. (Design Sourcebook Ser.). (Illus.). 1990. pap. 19.99 (*0-935603-40-9*, 30212) Rockport Pubs.

*Milhailovich, Vasa D., ed.** DLB 147: South Slavic Writers Before World War II. 368p. 1994. 112.00 (*0-8103-5708-9*) Gale.

Milham, C. G. Gallant Pelham, American Extraordinary. 1976. 20.95 (*0-8488-1099-6*) Amereon Ltd.

Milham, Charles G. Gallant Pelham. 250p. 1988. reprint ed. 25.00 (*0-942211-63-4*) Olde Soldier Bks.

Milhaud, Darius. My Happy Life. Evans, Donald & Palmer, Christopher, trs. 380p. 1994. 25.00 (*0-7145-2957-5*) M Boyars Pubs.

— Notes Without Music. LC 72-87419. (Music Ser.). (Illus.). 1970. reprint ed. lib. bdg. 49.50 (*0-306-71565-1*) Da Capo.

Milhaud, G., jt. ed. see Jaffiol, C.

Milhaud, Gaston. Les Philosophes-Geometres de la Grece: Platon & Ses & Predecesseurs. LC 75-13280. (History of Ideas in Ancient Greece Ser.). (FRE.). 1976. reprint ed. 26.95 (*0-405-07323-2*) Ayer.

Milhaven, Annie L., ed. Sermons Seldom Heard: Women Proclaim Their Lives. 240p. (Orig.). 1991. pap. 15.95 (*0-8245-1066-6*) Crossroad NY.

Milhaven, J. Giles. Good Anger: We Love More Than We Think We Do. LC 89-61217. 224p. 1989. pap. 12.95 (*1-55612-264-0*) Sheed & Ward MO.

Milhaven, John G. Hadewijch & Her Sisters: Other Ways of Loving & Knowing. LC 92-31369. (SUNY Series, The Body in Culture, History, & Religion). 171p. (C). 1993. 49.50 (*0-7914-1541-4*); pap. 16.95 (*0-7914-1542-2*) State U NY Pr.

Milheim, William, comp. Artificial Intelligence & Instruction: A Selected Bibliography. LC 89-23662. (Educational Technology Selected Bibliography Ser.: Vol. 1). 55p. 1989. 19.95 (*0-87778-220-2*) Educ Tech Pubns.

Milheim, William D. Computer-Based Simulations in Education & Training: A Selected Bibliography. LC 92-32545. (Educational Technology Selected Bibliography Ser.: Vol. 8). 60p. (Orig.). 1992. pap. 19.95 (*0-87778-254-7*) Educ Tech Pubns.

Milheim, William D., ed. Authoring-Systems Software for Computer-Based Training. LC 93-40880. (Illus.). 200p. 1994. 37.95 (*0-87778-274-1*) Educ Tech Pubns.

Milheim, William D., ed. see Clemente, Rebecca & Bohlin, Roy M.

Milheim, William D., ed. see Huyvaert, Sarah H. & Huyvaert, Thomas R.

Milheim, William D., ed. see Lamb, Annette.

Milheim, William D., ed. see Maddux, Cleborne D.

Milheim, William D., ed. see McLellan, Hilary.

Milheim, William D., ed. see Tennyson, Robert D. & Anderson, Ronald O.

Milhorat, Thomas H. Cerebrospinal Fluid & the Brain Edemas. (Illus.). 172p. (C). 1987. 45.00 (*0-944809-00-6*) NeuroSci Soc NY.

Milhorn, H. T., Jr. Chemical Dependence: Diagnosis, Treatment & Prevention. (Illus.). 352p. 1990. 87.00 (*0-387-97292-7*) Spr-Verlag.

— Drug & Alcohol Abuse: The Authoritative Guide for Parents, Teachers, & Counselors. (Illus.). 325p. 1994. 27.95 (*0-306-44640-5*, Plenum Pr) Plenum.

Milhous, Enid, jt. auth. see Refnes, Vera.

Milhous, Judith. Thomas Betterton & the Management of Lincoln's Inn Fields, 1695-1708. LC 78-21017. 318p. 1979. 25.95 (*0-8093-0906-8*) S Ill U Pr.

Milhous, Judith & Hume, Robert D., eds. Producible Interpretation: Eight English Plays, 1675-1707. LC 84-5634. (Illus.). 352p. 1979. text ed. 35.00 (*0-8093-1167-4*) S Ill U Pr.

— Vice Chamberlain Coke's Theatrical Papers, 1706-1715. LC 81-5616. 319p. 1982. 28.95 (*0-8093-1024-4*) S Ill U Pr.

Milhous, Katherine. The Egg Tree. LC 50-6817. (Illus.). 32p. (J). (gr. 1-4). 1971. text ed. 13.95 (*0-684-12716-4*, C Scribner Sons Young) S&S Childrens.

— The Egg Tree. LC 91-15854. (Illus.). 32p. (J). (gr. k-3). 1992. pap. 4.95 (*0-689-71568-4*, Aladdin Paperbacks) S&S Childrens.

Milhous, Katherine & Dalgiesh, Alice. The Turnip: An Old Russian Folktale. (Illus.). 32p. (J). (ps-3). 1990. 14.95 (*0-399-22229-4*, Philomel Bks) Putnam Pub Group.

Mili, Ali, et al. Computer Program Construction. 384p. (C). 1994. text ed. 55.00 (*0-19-509236-8*) OUP.

Miliaras, E. S., ed. see American Society of Mechanical Engineers Staff.

*Miliband.** Socialism for a Skeptical Age. 200p. 1995. 64.95x (*1-85984-947-4*, C0494, Pub. by Verso UK); pap. 18.95 (*1-85984-057-4*, C0495, Pub. by Verso UK) Routledge Chapman & Hall.

Miliband, David, ed. Reinventing the Left. 250p. 1995. text ed. 49.95 (*0-7456-1390-X*); pap. text ed. 19.95 (*0-7456-1391-8*) Blackwell Pubs.

Miliband, David, jt. ed. see Glyn, Andrew.

Miliband, Ralph. Capitalist Democracy in Britain. (C). 1984. pap. 12.95 (*0-19-285137-3*) OUP.

— Class Power & State Power: Political Essays. 311p. 1985. pap. text ed. 14.95 (*0-86091-773-8*, Pub. by Verso UK) Routledge Chapman & Hall.

— Divided Societies: Class Struggle in Contemporary Capitalism. 288p. 1990. 49.95 (*0-19-827535-8*) OUP.

— Divided Societies: Class Struggle in Contemporary Capitalism. 288p. 1991. reprint ed. pap. 16.95 (*0-19-285234-5*, 9048) OUP.

— Marxism & Politics. (Marxist Introductions Ser.). 1978. pap. 9.95 (*0-19-876062-0*) OUP.

*Miliband, Ralph & Panitch, Leo, eds.** Between Globalism & Nationalism: Socialist Register 1994. 288p. (Orig.). (C). 1994. pap. text ed. 18.00 (*0-85345-907-X*, Pub. by Merlin UK) Monthly Rev.

— New World Order? Socialist Register, 1992. 360p. (C). 1992. pap. text ed. 18.00 (*0-85345-855-3*) Monthly Rev.

— Real Problems - False Solutions: Socialist Register 1993. 288p. 1993. 18.00 (*0-85345-882-0*) Monthly Rev.

— The Socialist Register, 1990: The Retreat of the Intellectuals. 384p. (C). 1990. text ed. 60.00 (*0-85036-395-0*, Pub. by Merlin Pr UK) Humanities.

— The Socialist Register, 1992: New World Order? (Socialist Register Ser.). 400p. (C). 1992. text ed. 60.00 (*0-85036-427-2*, Pub. by Merlin Pr UK) Humanities.

— The Socialist Register, 1993. 256p. (C). 1993. text ed. 60.00 (*0-85036-431-0*, Pub. by Merlin Pr UK) Humanities.

— Socialist Register 1994: Between Globalism & Nationalism. 356p. (C). 1994. text ed. 60.00 (*0-85036-441-8*, Pub. by Merlin Pr UK) Humanities.

Miliband, Ralph & Saville, John, eds. The Socialist Register: 1977. 276p. 1977. pap. 5.95 (*0-85345-435-3*) Monthly Rev.

— The Socialist Register: 1978. 338p. 1978. pap. 5.95 (*0-85345-453-1*) Monthly Rev.

— Socialist Register, 1980. (C). 1980. text ed. 12.95 (*0-85036-266-0*, Pub. by Merlin Pr UK); pap. 7.50 (*0-85036-267-9*, Pub. by Merlin Pr UK) Humanities.

— Socialist Register 1983. (C). 1983. text ed. 15.95 (*0-85036-309-8*, Pub. by Merlin Pr UK); pap. 8.50 (*0-85036-310-1*, Pub. by Merlin Pr UK) Humanities.

Miliband, Ralph, et al, eds. Conservatism in Britain & America: Rhetoric & Reality. (Socialist Register Ser.). 528p. (C). 1987. pap. 12.00 (*0-85345-730-1*, Pub. by Merlin UK) Monthly Rev.

— Revolution Today: Aspirations & Realities: Socialist Register 1989. 336p. (Orig.). (C). 1989. pap. 15.00 (*0-85345-784-0*) Monthly Rev.

— Socialist Register, 1988. 460p. (C). 1988. text ed. 60.00 (*0-85036-354-3*, Pub. by Merlin Pr UK) Humanities.

— The Socialist Register, 1989: Revolution Today: Aspirations & Realities. 320p. (C). 1989. text ed. 60.00 (*0-85036-376-4*, Pub. by Merlin Pr UK) Humanities.

— The Socialist Register, 1991: The Communist Experience & Its Lessons. 400p. (C). 1991. text ed. 60.00 (*0-85036-419-1*, Pub. by Merlin Pr UK) Humanities.

Milicevic, Barbara. Your Spiritual Child. (Illus.). 96p. 1984. pap. 7.00 (*0-87516-528-1*) DeVorss.

Milicevic, J. English-Serbocroat Dictionary of Engineering. 266p. (C). 1986. 180.00 (*0-685-58756-8*, Pub. by Collets) St Mut.

*Milich.** Centenarian Women. 1995. 26.95 (*0-8057-9131-0*, Twayne); pap. 14.95 (*0-8057-9132-9*, Twayne) Macmillan.

Milich, E., et al. European Communities Oil & Gas Technological Development Projects: Second Status Report. 264p. 1984. lib. bdg. 76.50 (*0-86010-616-0*) G & T Inc.

Milich, Edzia F. God Had a Reason. (Illus.). 116p. 1993. pap. 20.00 (*0-9636347-0-4*) Rose Pub CA.

*Milich, Melissa.** Can't Scare Me! (J). (ps-3). 1995. 14.95 (*0-385-31052-8*) Doubleday.

Milicivec, Jovan. Serbocroatian-English Dictionary of Mechanical Engineering. 250p. (ENG & SER.). 1986. 39.95 (*0-8288-0656-X*, F 14125) Fr & Eur.

Milicivek, Jovan. English-Serbocroatian Dictionary of Mechanical Engineering. 266p. (ENG & SER.). 1986. 29.95 (*0-8288-0657-8*, F 14124) Fr & Eur.

Milidantri, Mary Ann. Hurray for Today, Level 1. 1979. pap. 4.50 (*0-8497-5601-4*, WE1.) Kjos.

— Hurray for Today, Level 2. 1979. pap. 4.50 (*0-8497-5602-2*, WE2) Kjos.

Milik, Jozef T., jt. auth. see De Vaux, Roland.

Milin, Irene & Milin, Mike. How to Buy & Manage Rental Properties: The Milin Method of Real Estate Management for the Small Investor. 1988. pap. 11.00 (*0-671-64423-8*, Fireside) S&S Trade.

Milin, Isaak M. Univalent Functions & Orthonormal Systems. LC 77-1198. (Translations of Mathematical Monographs: Vol. 49). 202p. 1977. 62.00 (*0-8218-1599-7*, MMONO-49) Am Math.

Milin, Mike, jt. auth. see Milin, Irene.

Milinar, Zdravji. Local Government & Rural Development in Yugoslavia. (Special Series on Rural Local Government: No. 18). 136p. pap. 3.50 (*0-86731-104-5*) Cornell CIS RDC.

Milindapanha. The Milindapanho, Being Dialogues Between King Milinda & the Buddhist Sage: The Pali Text to Which Has Now Been Appended a General Index...& An Index of Gathas. reprint ed. 42.00 (*0-404-17348-9*) AMS Pr.

Milingo, Emmanuel. The World in Between: Christian Healing & the Struggle for Spiritual Survival. LC 84-191633. 144p. (Orig.). reprint ed. pap. 41.10 (*0-7837-5520-1*, 2045290) Bks Demand.

Milinowski, Marta. Teresa Carreno "By the Grace of God" LC 76-58931. (Music Reprint Ser.). 1977. reprint ed. lib. bdg. 45.00 (*0-306-70870-1*) Da Capo.

*Milio, Frank & Loffredo, William.** Qualitative Tests for Amino Acids & Proteins. 12p. (C). 1995. 1.25 (*0-614-05691-8*, REAC 448-0) Chem Educ Res.

*Milio, Frank R. & Loffredo, William M.** Qualitative Testing for Lipids. Neidig, H. A., ed. (Modular Laboratory Program in Chemistry Ser.). 16p. (C). 1994. pap. text ed. 1.25x (*0-87540-447-2*) Chem Educ Res.

Milio, Frank R., et al. Experiments in Chemistry. 3rd ed. 300p. (C). 1991. pap. text ed. 31.00 (*0-03-053488-7*) SCP.

Milio, Nancy. Ninety-Two Twenty-Six Kercheval: The Storefront That Did Not Burn. 1970. pap. 15.95 (*0-472-06180-1*, 180, Ann Arbor Bks) U of Mich Pr.

— Nutrition Policy for Food-Rich Countries: A Strategic Analysis. LC 89-43482. (Series in Contemporary Medicine & Public Health). 256p. 1990. text ed. 42.50 (*0-8018-3951-3*) Johns Hopkins.

Milioni, B., jt. auth. see Toledo, F.

Milios, Ray. Working Together Against Racism. LC 94-1023. (Library of Social Activism). (J). 1994. 14.95 (*0-8239-1840-8*) Rosen Group.

*Milios, Rita.** Anorexia & Bulimia. 87p. (YA). (gr. 7-12). 1993. pap. write for info. (*1-57515-030-1*) PPI Pubng.

— Bears, Bears Everywhere. (Rookie Reader Ser.). (J). (ps-2). 1988. lib. bdg. 10.35 (*0-516-02085-4*); pap. 2.95 (*0-516-42085-2*) Childrens.

— A Desert Cactus Comes to Life. LC 92-12895. (Beginning Science Ser.). 24p. (J). (ps-3). Date not set. 11.95 (*1-56065-168-7*) Capstone Pr.

— Donde Esta Pedro? Sneaky Pete. LC 89-34666. (Rookie Reader Ser.). (Illus.). 32p. (SPA.). (J). (ps-2). 1991. lib. bdg. 10.35 (*0-516-32092-0*); pap. 2.95 (*0-516-52092-X*) Childrens.

— Dreams Journal. 48p. 1995. ring bd. 9.95 (*0-9641657-2-4*) Tools for Transform.

— The Hungry Billy Goat. LC 88-673. (Rookie Reader Ser.). (Illus.). 32p. (J). (ps-2). 1989. lib. bdg. 10.35 (*0-516-02090-0*); pap. 2.95 (*0-516-42090-9*) Childrens.

— I Am. LC 87-5163. (Rookie Reader Ser.). (Illus.). 32p. (J). (ps-2). 1987. lib. bdg. 10.35 (*0-516-02081-1*); pap. 2.95 (*0-516-42081-X*) Childrens.

— Imagi-size: Activities to Exercise Your Students' Imaginations. (Illus.). 80p. (J). (gr. k-4). 1993. pap. 8.95 (*1-880505-05-3*) Pieces of Lrning.

— Independent Living. Rosen, Ruth, ed. (Life Skills Library). (YA). (gr. 7-12). 1992. 13.95 (*0-8239-1454-2*) Rosen Group.

— Intuition Log Book. 96p. 1995. ring bd. 9.95 (*0-9641657-3-2*) Tools for Transform.

— Mean Words. LC 92-10837. (Illus.). 32p. (J). (ps-2). Date not set. 11.95 (*1-56065-163-6*) Capstone Pr.

M

— Osos, osos, aqui y alli: (Bears, Bears, Everywhere) LC 87-33780. (Rookie Reader Ser.). (Illus.). 32p. (ENG & SPA.). (J). (ps-2). 1989. pap. 2.95 (*0-516-52085-7*) Childrens.

— Planetary Initiation. LC 94-60531. 128p. 1995. pap. 9.95 (*0-9641657-0-8*) Tools for Transform.

— Shopping Savvy. Rosen, Ruth, ed. (Life Skills Library). (YA). (gr. 7-12). 1992. 13.95 (*0-8239-1455-0*) Rosen Group.

— Sneaky Pete. LC 89-34666. (Rookie Reader Ser.). (Illus.). 32p. (J). (ps-2). 1989. lib. bdg. 10.35 (*0-516-02092-7*); pap. 2.95 (*0-516-42092-5*) Childrens.

— Tools for Transformation. LC 94-60530. 128p. 1995. pap. 9.95 (*0-9641657-1-6*) Tools for Transform.

— The Value of Trust. Rosen, Ruth, ed. (Encyclopedia of Ethical Behavior Ser.). (YA). (gr. 7-12). 1991. lib. bdg. 15.95 (*0-8239-1285-X*) Rosen Group.

— Yo Soy (I Am) LC 87-5163. (Rookie Reader Ser.). 32p. (SPA.). (J). (ps-2). 1990. pap. 2.95 (*0-516-52081-4*) Childrens.

***Milios, Rita & King, Marcia.** Cigarette Smoking. 88p. (YA). (gr. 7-12). 1994. pap. write for info. (*1-57515-044-1*) PPI Pubng.

Milis, Ludo. Angelic Monks & Earthly Men: Monasticism & Its Meaning in Medieval Society. (Illus.). 192p. (C). 1992. text ed. 50.00 (*0-85115-303-8*) Boydell & Brewer.

Milisauskas, Sarunas. Early Neolithic Settlement & Society at Olszanica. (Memoirs Ser.: No. 19). xx, 320p. (Orig.). 1986. pap. 20.00 (*0-915703-03-3*) U Mich Mus Anthro.

Military History Magazine Staff. Desert Storm. 176p. 1991. 34.95 (*0-943231-46-9*) Empire Pr.

— Military History's Magazine Tenth Anniversary Index. Kelly, C. Brian, ed. (Illus.). (Orig.). (C). 1994. pap. text ed. 21.95 (*1-884641-03-2*) Empire Pr.

Militello, Frederick C. & Davis, Henry A. The Empowered Organization: Redefining the Roles & Practices of Finance. LC 94-70916. (Illus.). 225p. (Orig.). 1994. pap. 35.00 (*0-910586-95-0*) Finan Exec. Today, companies are downsizing not just to cut costs, but because they are redefining their boundaries. Rather than focusing primarily on external forces, such as competition, companies are looking within to define principles & values that will help them develop their own unique capabilities. In embracing new corporate values - most of which describe how people should work together - practices, attitudes & behaviors also had to change. This research report documents how nine companies in a variety of industries articulated corporate principles & values, & how their finance functions responded to the challenge of organizational change. Case study companies include: CoreStates Financial; Corning; W. L. Gore; Harley-Davidson; Geo. E. Keith; Herman Miller; Silicon Graphics, Inc.; Steelcase & Levi Strauss & Co. Excellent supplemental reading for students in business management programs. Order from: Professional Book Distributors, P.O. Box 6996, Alpharetta, GA 30239-6996. Call (404) 751-1986 or FAX (404) 442-5114. ***Publisher Provided Annotation.***

— Foreign Exchange Risk Management: A Survey of Corporate Practices. LC 94-70913. 180p. (Orig.). 1995. pap. text ed. 35.00 (*0-910586-94-2*) Finan Exec. The volatility of European currency rates after a period of relative stability has brought a new focus to foreign exchange rate exposure management issues. Corporations of all sizes source & sell in overseas markets & compete both at home & abroad with foreign companies. As a result, derivatives such as currency swaps, futures & options, which came into common use just over a decade ago, have become a permanent fixture. Corporate treasury departments concerned with foreign exchange are working less as independent units & are more involved with business unit managers. The researchers surveyed the foreign exchange practices of 22 corporations to illustrate the best practices for the benefit of companies of all sizes in a variety of industries & to highlight the most important issues for the corporate financial officer. Glossary & biliography included. Excellent supplementary reading for courses in international business & accounting. Order from: Professional Book Distributors, P.O. Box 6996, Alpharetta, GA 30239-6996. Call (404) 751-1986 or FAX (404) 442-5114. ***Publisher Provided Annotation.***

***Militello, Joseph.** Winning with the Thoroughbreds: "A Race Fans' Guide to Handicapping & History" (Illus.). 284p. 1994. pap. 14.95 (*0-9641634-0-3*) J Militello.

Militky, J., et al. Modified Polyester Fibres. (Textile Science & Technology Ser.: Vol. 10). 264p. 1991. 136.00 (*0-444-98735-5*) Elsevier.

Militz, Annie R. Concentration. 84p. 1972. reprint ed. spiral bd. 2.20 (*0-7873-0614-2*) Mokelumne.

— The Renewal of the Body. 166p. 1972. reprint ed. spiral bd. 6.60 (*0-7873-0613-4*) Mokelumne.

Miliukov, Paul N. Outlines of Russian Culture: The Origins of Ideology. Wieczynski, Joseph L., tr. Bd. with Two Worlds of Paul Miliukov. LC 74-81632. LC 74-81632. (Russian Ser.: Vol. 19, Pt. 1). 1974. 24.50 (*0-87569-056-4*) Academic Intl.

Miliukov, Pavel N. Bolshevism: An International Danger; Its Doctrine & Its Practice Through War & Revolution. LC 79-2915. 303p. 1981. reprint ed. 25.75 (*0-8305-0084-7*) Hyperion Conn.

Milius, John. The Wind & Lion. 16.95 (*0-88411-454-6*, Aeonian Pr) Amereon Ltd.

***Milius, Patti, et al, illus.** West of the Rockies: From Campfire to Candlelight. 360p. 1994. 17.95 (*0-9641314-0-4*) JSLOGJ.

Milivojevic, Dragan & Mihailovich, Vasa D. Yugoslav Linguistics in English: A Bibliography 1900-1980. 122p. (Orig.). 1990. pap. 14.95 (*0-89357-213-6*) Slavica.

Milivojevic, Dragan, jt. auth. see Matejic, Mateja.

Milivojevic, Dragan D. Current Russian Phonemic Theory 1952-1962. LC 75-108142. (Janua Linguarum, Ser. Minor: No. 78). (Orig.). 1970. pap. text ed. 16.15 (*3-10-800273-2*) Mouton.

Milivojevic, Marko. The Debt Rescheduling Process. LC 85-18342. 300p. 1986. text ed. 45.00 (*0-312-18898-6*) St Martin.

— Descent into Chaos: Yugoslavia's Worsening Crisis. (C). 1989. 35.00 (*0-907967-08-6*, Pub. by Inst Euro Def & Strat UK) St Mut.

— Yugoslavia's Military Industries. 1992. write for info. (*0-275-93769-0*, C3769, Praeger Pubs) Greenwood.

Milivojevic, Marko & Maurer, Pierre. Swiss Neutrality & Security: Armed Forces, National Defence & Foreign Policy. LC 89-28949. 272p. 1991. 55.00 (*0-85496-608-0*) Berg Pubs.

Milivojevic, Marko, et al, eds. Yugoslavia's Security Dilemmas: Army Forces, National Defence & Foreign Policy. LC 87-23081. 332p. 1988. 72.00 (*0-85496-149-6*) Berg Pubs.

Miljan, Toivo. The Political Economy of North-South Relations. 712p. 1987. pap. 29.95 (*0-921149-11-5*) Broadview Pr.

Miljan, Toivo, et al. Food & Agriculture in Global Perspective: Discussions in the Committee of the Whole of the United States. (Illus.). 260p. 1980. 74.00 (*0-08-025550-7*, Pergamon Pr) Elsevier.

Miljanic, P. N., jt. auth. see Moore, W. J.

Miljkovic, Tajana. Student's Russian & Serbocroatian Pocket Dictionary: Ruso-Hrvatski Ili Srpski I Hrvatsko Ili Srpskoruski Dzepni Rjecnik Za Osnovn. 496p. (RUS & SER.). 1984. pap. 19.95 (*0-8288-1641-7*, F114890) Fr & Eur.

Milke, J., jt. auth. see Klote, J.

Milkereit, Joanne & Higdon, Hal. The Runner's Cookbook. LC 78-58058. (Illus.). 324p. 1979. spiral bd. 16.95 (*0-89037-145-8*) Anderson World.

Milkias, Paulos. Ethiopia: A Comprehensive Bibliography. (Reference Bks.). 650p. 1989. text ed. 85.00 (*0-8161-9066-6*, Hall Reference) Macmillan.

Milkins, Colin S. Fish. LC 91-6726. (Weird & Wonderful Ser.). (Illus.). 32p. (J). (gr. 2-6). 1993. 14.95 (*1-56847-008-8*) Thomson Lrning.

— Fish. (Weird & Wonderful Ser.). (Illus.). 32p. (J). (gr. 2-5). 1995. reprint ed. pap. 5.95 (*1-56847-305-2*) Thomson Lrning.

Milkis, Sidney M. The President & the Parties: The Transformation of the American Party System since the New Deal. LC 92-42965. 429p. (C). 1993. 49.95 (*0-19-506620-0*); pap. 19.95 (*0-19-508425-X*) OUP.

Milkis, Sidney M. & Nelson, Michael. The American Presidency: Origins & Development, 1776-1993. LC 93-43358. 1993. pap. 25.95 (*0-87187-766-X*) Congr Quarterly.

— The American Presidency: Origins & Development, 1776-1993. 2nd ed. LC 93-43358. 1993. 37.95 (*0-87187-949-2*) Congr Quarterly.

Milkis, Sidney M., jt. auth. see Harris, Richard A.

Milkman, Harvey B. & Shaffer, Howard J., eds. The Addictions: Multidisciplinary Perspectives & Treatments. LC 84-47871. 224p. 1984. text ed. 37.95 (*0-669-08739-4*) Free Pr.

Milkman, Harvey B. & Sunderwirth, Stanley. Craving for Ecstasy: The Consciousness & Chemistry of Escape. 1987. text ed. 29.95 (*0-669-12337-4*); pap. 13.95 (*0-669-15281-1*) Free Pr.

— Pathways to Pleasure: The Consciousness & Chemistry of Optimal Living. 200p. 1993. text ed. 19.95 (*0-02-921273-1*) Free Pr.

Milkman, Ruth. Gender at Work: The Dynamics of Job Segregation by Sex During World War II. LC 86-7001. (Working Class in American History Ser.). 232p. 1987. pap. 10.95 (*0-252-01357-3*) U of Ill Pr.

— Japan's California Factories: Labor Relations & Economic Globalization. (Monograph & Research Ser.: No. 55). 130p. 1991. pap. 11.00 (*0-89215-171-4*) U Cal LA Indus Rel.

Milkman, Ruth, ed. Women, Work & Protest: A Century of U. S. Women's History. 320p. (Orig.). 1985. pap. 14.95 (*0-7100-9940-1*, RKP) Routledge.

Milko, et al. The Practical Law Manual to Consumer Legal Affairs: Featuring Hyatt Legal Services' Home Lawyer Software. 1992. pap. 45.00 (*0-679-74287-5*) Random.

Milko, George. Everyday Contracts Protecting Your Rights: A Step-by-Step Guide. 1991. 10.00 (*0-679-73058-3*) McKay.

— Real Estate. (Random House Practical Law Manual Ser.). 165p. 1990. pap. write for info. (*0-679-72980-1*) HALT DC.

***Milkoff, Shirley.** Jackson Elwood. 1995. 8.95 (*0-8062-5225-1*) Carlton.

Milkoff, Shirley H. Emma. 1995. 8.95 (*0-8062-4989-7*) Carlton.

Milkon, Phyllis A. Cooking Healthy with BCV's Shortcuts: Delicious Recipes Lower in Fat - Cholesterol - Sodium with No Refined Sugar Plus Nutrient Data. LC 91-73959. 250p. 1991. pap. write for info. (*0-9630025-1-1*) Burgess Creat.

Milkovich, Barbara A. & Cramer, Esther, eds. Early Businesses in Orange County: A Selection of Stories about the Creators of County Commerce. (Orange Countiana Ser.: Vol. V). (Illus.). 256p. 1992. 17.97 (*1-881860-00-0*); text ed. 29.95 (*0-685-60658-9*); pap. 13.17 (*1-881860-01-9*); pap. text ed. 21.95 (*0-685-60659-7*) Orange Cnty Hist.

Milkovich, George T. & Boudreau, John W. Human Resource Management. 6th ed. 832p. (C). 1991. Text with 5.25 inch diskette. disk 64.95 (*0-256-09148-X*, 11-3323-06); Text with 3.5 inch diskette. disk 61.95 (*0-256-09659-7*, 11-3407-06); Text alone. text ed. 59.95 (*0-256-08153-0*, 11-1081-06) Irwin.

— Human Resource Management. 7th ed. LC 93-17923. 832p. (C). 1993. text ed. 63.95 (*0-256-11608-3*) Irwin.

Milkovich, George T. & Newman, Jerry M. Compensation. 3rd ed. 736p. (C). 1990. text ed. 59.95 (*0-256-07671-5*) Irwin.

— Compensation. 4th ed. LC 92-27604. 656p. (C). 1992. text ed. 64.95 (*0-256-10527-8*) Irwin.

Milkovich, George T., et al. Cases in Compensation. 5th ed. 100p. (C). 1994. pap. text ed. write for info. (*0-945601-02-6*) Compensation.

— Compensation. 5th ed. LC 95-16253. 656p. (C). 1995. text ed. 64.95 (*0-256-14145-2*) Irwin Prof Pubng.

Milkovich, George T., et al, eds. Pay for Performance: Evaluating Performance Appraisal & Merit Pay. 224p. 1991. 24.95 (*0-309-04427-8*) Natl Acad Pr.

Milkowitz, Michael. Good-Bye Tomorrow. braille ed. 202p. 1990. Braille. vinyl bd. 16.16 (*1-56956-246-6*, BR8310) W A T Braille.

***Milkowski, Bill.** Jaco: The Extraordinary & Tragic Life of Jaco Pastorius, the "World's Greatest Bass Player" (Illus.). 224p. 1995. 22.95 (*0-87930-361-1*) Miller Freeman.

Milkowski, Jandra, jt. auth. see Zulauf, Sander W.

Mill, Anna J. Medieval Plays in Scotland. LC 68-56497. 1972. reprint ed. 26.95 (*0-405-08789-6*, Pub. by Blom Pubns UK) Ayer.

Mill, C. Rheology of Disperse Systems: Proceedings Conference British Society of Rheology Univ Coll, Swansea 9-57. LC 59-9833. 1959. 100.00 (*0-08-013454-8*, Pub. by Pergamon Repr UK) Franklin.

Mill, Christine. Norman Collie: A Life in Two Worlds: Mountain Explorer & Scientist, 1859-1942. (Aberdeen University Press Bks.). (Illus.). 256p. 1987. text ed. 30.00 (*0-08-032456-8*, Pub. by Aberdeen U Pr) Macmillan.

Mill, Cyril R. Activities for Trainers: Fifty Useful Designs. LC 80-50465. 226p. 1980. pap. 34.95 (*0-88390-159-5*) Pfeiffer & Co.

Mill, Dick. How to Have a Happy Marriage. 96p. 1993. pap. 3.99 (*0-88368-223-0*) Whitaker Hse.

Mill, Harriet T., jt. auth. see Mill, John Stuart.

Mill Hunk Herald Editors. Overtime: Ten Years of Punching Out with the Mill Hunk Herald (1977-87) 208p. (Orig.). 1990. pap. 12.95 (*0-931122-55-4*) West End.

Mill, James. Analysis of the Phenomena of the Human Mind, 2 vols. 2nd ed. (C). 1986. reprint ed. Set. pap. 29.95 (*0-935005-54-4*) Lincoln-Rembrandt.

— Analysis of the Phenomena of the Human Mind, 2 vols. in 1. Findlater, A. et al, eds. xxvii, 856p. 1982. reprint ed. 128.70 (*3-487-07243-2*, Pub. by Georg Olms GW) Lubrecht & Cramer.

— Elements of Political Economy. 3rd ed. (C). 1986. reprint ed. lib. bdg. 15.95 (*0-935005-55-2*); reprint ed. pap. text ed. 9.75 (*0-935005-56-0*) Lincoln-Rembrandt.

— Elements of Political Economy. 3rd ed. 311p. 1971. reprint ed. 48.10 (*3-487-04192-8*, Pub. by Georg Olms GW) Lubrecht & Cramer.

— Essay of the Impolicy of a Bounty on the Exportation of Grain & on the Principles Which Ought to Regulate the Commerce of Grain. LC 66-19693. 70p. 1966. reprint ed. 19.50 (*0-678-00152-9*) Kelley.

— Essay on Government. Shields, Currin V., ed. (gr. 9 up). 1955. pap. 2.95 (*0-672-60215-6*, LLA47, Bobbs) Macmillan.

— Essays on Government, Jurisprudence, Liberty of the Press & Law of Nations Reprinted from the Supplement to the Encyclopaedia Britannica. LC 86-7454. 1986. reprint ed. 29.50 (*0-678-00297-5*) Kelley.

— Overproduction & Unemployment. 1971. 250.00 (*0-685-26310-X*) Revisionist Pr.

— Political Writings. Ball, Terence, ed. (Cambridge Texts in the History of Political Thought Ser.). 304p. (C). 1992. 59.95 (*0-521-38323-4*); pap. 18.95 (*0-521-38748-5*) Cambridge U Pr.

Mill, James, jt. auth. see Mill, John Stuart.

Mill, John S., ed. see Bentham, Jeremy.

Mill, John Stuart. Autobiography. Robson, John H., ed. 240p. 1990. pap. 9.95 (*0-14-043316-3*, Penguin Classics) Viking Penguin.

— Autobiography of John Stuart Mill. LC 24-27691. 240p. (C). 1960. pap. text ed. 15.50 (*0-231-08506-0*) Col U Pr.

— Autobiography of John Stuart Mill. Stillinger, Jack, ed. (C). 1957. pap. 9.96 (*0-395-05120-7*, RivEd) HM.

— Collected Works. 1972. 600.00 (*0-87968-893-9*) Gordon Pr.

— Considerations on Representative Government. (Great Books in Philosophy). 365p. 1991. pap. 6.95 (*0-87975-670-5*) Prometheus Bks.

— Dissertations & Discussions, 2 vols. LC 72-94. (Studies in Philosophy: No. 40). 1972. reprint ed. lib. bdg. 150.00 (*0-8383-1400-7*) M S G Haskell Hse.

— Earlier Letters, 1812-1848, 2 Vols, Set. Mineka, Francis E., ed. LC 65-109962. (Collected Works of John Stuart Mill). 1963. 75.00 (*0-8020-5123-5*) U of Toronto Pr.

— The Early Draft of John Stuart Mill's Autobiography. Stillinger, Jack, ed. LC 61-62769. 226p. reprint ed. pap. 64.50 (*0-317-08848-3*, 2013333) Bks Demand.

— Essays on Economics & Society, 2 vols., Vol. 1. Robson, J. M., ed. LC 68-56473. (Collected Works of John Stuart Mill: No. 4-5). reprint ed. pap. 115.00 (*0-685-16017-3*, 2026407) Bks Demand.

— Essays on Economics & Society, 2 vols., Vol. 2. Robson, J. M., ed. LC 68-56473. (Collected Works of John Stuart Mill: No. 4-5). reprint ed. pap. 112.50 (*0-685-16018-1*) Bks Demand.

— Essays on England, Ireland, & the Empire. Robson, John M., ed. (Collected Works of John Stuart Mill: Vol. 6). 744p. 1982. 75.00 (*0-8020-5572-9*) U of Toronto Pr.

— Essays on Equality, Law, & Education. Robson, John M., ed. (Collected Works of John Stuart Mill: No. XXI). 592p. 1984. 70.00 (*0-8020-5629-6*) U of Toronto Pr.

— Essays on Ethics, Religion & Society. Robson, J. M., ed. (Collected Works of John Stuart Mill: Vol. 10). 720p. reprint ed. pap. 180.00 (*0-317-41695-2*, 2037648) Bks Demand.

— Essays on French History & Historians. Robson, John M., ed. (Collected Works of John Stuart Mill: No. XX). 656p. 1985. 75.00 (*0-8020-2490-4*) U of Toronto Pr.

— Essays on Philosophy & the Classics. Robson, J. M., ed. LC 63-25976. (Collected Works of John Stuart Mill: No. 11). (Illus.). 680p. reprint ed. pap. 180.00 (*0-8357-4732-8*, 2037649) Bks Demand.

— Essays on Politics & Culture. Himmelfarb, Gertrude, ed. 24.50 (*0-8446-0801-7*) Peter Smith.

— Essays on Some Unsettled Questions of Political Economy. 2nd ed. LC 68-25642. (Reprints of Economic Classics Ser.). vi, 164p. 1968. reprint ed. 29.50 (*0-678-00390-4*) Kelley.

— An Examination of Sir William Hamilton's Philosophy. Robson, John M., ed. LC 63-25976. (Collected Works of John Stuart Mill). 1979. 60.00 (*0-8020-2329-0*) U of Toronto Pr.

— John Mill's Boyhood Visit to France: Being a Journal & Notebook. LC 60-4877. 165p. reprint ed. pap. 47.10 (*0-317-08748-7*, 2014367) Bks Demand.

— John Stuart Mill's Philosophy of Scientific Method. 1974. pap. 12.95 (*0-317-30541-7*) Free Pr.

— Later Letters: Eighteen Forty-Nine to Eighteen Seventy-Three, 4 vols, Set. Mineka, Francis E. & Lindley, Dwight N., eds. LC 75-163833. (Collected Works of John Stuart Mill). 1972. 125.00 (*0-8020-5261-4*) U of Toronto Pr.

— The Logic of the Moral Sciences. 144p. 1987. pap. 8.00 (*0-8126-9053-2*) Open Court.

— Mill on Bentham & Coleridge. LC 82-15854. 168p. (C). 1983. reprint ed. text ed. 42.50 (*0-313-23740-9*, MIOB, Greenwood Pr) Greenwood.

— Miscellaneous Writings. Robson, J. M., ed. & intro. by. (Collected Works of John Stuart Mill: Vol. 31). 462p. 1989. text ed. 85.00 (*0-8020-2728-8*) U of Toronto Pr.

— On Liberty. Rapaport, Elizabeth, ed. LC 77-26848. (HPC Classics Ser.). 139p. (C). 1978. lib. bdg. 22.50 (*0-915144-44-1*); pap. text ed. 3.95 (*0-915144-43-3*) Hackett Pub.

— On Liberty. Castell, Alburey, ed. LC 47-3494. (Crofts Classics Ser.). 128p. (C). 1947. pap. text ed. write for info. (*0-88295-056-8*) Harlan Davidson.

— On Liberty. Shields, Currin V., ed. 1956. pap. write for info. (*0-672-60234-2*, LLA61) Macmillan.

— On Liberty. LC 85-63408. (Great Books in Philosophy). 129p. pap. 4.95 (*0-87975-336-6*) Prometheus Bks.

— On Liberty. 1982. mass mkt. 7.95 (*0-14-043207-8*, Penguin Classics) Viking Penguin.

— On Liberty. Spitz, David, ed. (Critical Editions Ser.). (C). 1975. pap. text ed. 7.95 (*0-393-09252-6*) Norton.

— On Liberty: Freedom of Speech. 120p. 1990. reprint ed. 30.00 (*1-877981-06-0*); reprint ed. pap. 22.00 (*1-877981-12-5*) Becoming-One.

— On Liberty: With the Subjection of Women & Chapters on Socialism. Collini, Stefan, ed. (Cambridge Texts in the History of Political Thought Ser.). 260p. (C). 1989. pap. 7.95 (*0-521-37917-2*) Cambridge U Pr.

— On Liberty: With the Subjection of Women & Chapters on Socialism. Collini, Stefan, ed. (Cambridge Texts in the History of Political Thought Ser.). 260p. (C). 1989. 39.95 (*0-521-37015-9*) Cambridge U Pr.

— On Liberty & Other Essays. Gray, John, ed. (World's Classics Ser.). 632p. 1991. pap. 6.95 (*0-19-282208-X*) OUP.

— On Liberty & Utilitaranism. 1992. 15.00 (*0-679-41329-4*, Everymans Lib) Knopf.

— On Liberty & Utilitarianism. 1993. mass mkt. 4.95 (*0-553-21414-4*) Bantam.

— On Socialism. (Great Books in Philosophy). 146p. (Orig.). 1988. pap. 7.95 (*0-87975-404-4*) Prometheus Bks.

An Asterisk (*) at the beginning of an entry indicates that the title is appearing in BIP for the first time.

— Principles of Political Economy. Winch, Donald, ed. (Classics Ser.). 400p. 1986. pap. 10.95 (*0-14-043260-4*, Penguin Classics) Viking Penguin.
— Principles of Political Economy. LC 93-28404. (World's Classics Ser.). 512p. (C). 1994. pap. 9.95 (*0-19-283081-3*) OUP.
— Principles of Political Economy. (Reprints of Economic Classics Ser.). liii, 1013p. 1987. reprint ed. 57.50 (*0-678-00073-5*); reprint ed. pap. 27.95 (*0-678-01453-1*) Kelley.
— Public & Parliamentary Speeches, 2 vols. (Collected Works of John Stuart Mill: Nos. XXVIII-XXIX). 760p. 1988. 135.00 (*0-8020-2693-1*) U of Toronto Pr.
— Sobre la Libertad & Comentarios a Tocqueville. Negro Pavon, Dalmacio, ed. Garcia Cay, Cristina, tr. (Nueva Austral Ser.: Vol. 183). (SPA.). 1991. pap. text ed. 24. 95x (*84-239-1983-8*) Elliots Bks.
— The Subjection of Women. LC 88-1762. (HPC Classics Ser.). 128p. (C). 1988. lib. bdg. 22.50 (*0-87220-055-8*); pap. text ed. 4.75 (*0-87220-054-X*) Hackett Pub.
— The Subjection of Women. Mansfield, Sue, ed. LC 76-3318. (Crofts Classics Ser.). 136p. (C). 1980. pap. text ed. write for info. (*0-88295-116-5*) Harlan Davidson.
— The Subjection of Women. LC 85-63407. (Great Books in Philosophy). 106p. 1986. pap. 4.95 (*0-87975-335-8*) Prometheus Bks.
— Subjection of Women. 1970. pap. 7.95 (*0-262-63038-9*) MIT Pr.
— System of Logic. 8th ed. (C). 1986. reprint ed. lib. bdg. 31.95 (*0-935005-29-3*); reprint ed. pap. text ed. 21.95 (*0-935005-34-X*) Lincoln-Rembrandt.
— Theism. Taylor, Richard, ed. 1957. pap. 2.25 (*0-672-60238-5*, Bobbs) Macmillan.
— Three Essays on Religion. LC 76-130995. reprint ed. 23. 45 (*0-404-04325-9*) AMS Pr.
— Utilitarianism. Sher, George, ed. LC 78-74450. (HPC Classics Ser.). 80p. (C). 1979. pap. text ed. 3.50 (*0-915144-41-7*) Hackett Pub.
— Utilitarianism. 1974. pap. 10.95 (*0-452-00970-7*, Mer) NAL-Dutton.
— Utilitarianism. LC 86-62704. (Great Books in Philosophy). 83p. pap. 4.95 (*0-87975-376-5*) Prometheus Bks.
— Utilitarianism. Warnock, Mary, ed. Bd. with On Liberty.; Essay on Bentham.; Selected Writings of Jeremy Bentham & John Austin. Set mass mkt. 6.95 (*0-452-00598-1*, F598, Mer) NAL-Dutton.
— Utilitarianism, On Liberty, Considerations on Representative Government. Williams, Geraint, ed. 512p. 1993. pap. 6.95 (*0-460-87346-6*, Everyman's Classic Lib) C E Tuttle.
— Writings on India, Vol. 30. Robson, John M. et al, eds. (Collected Works of John Stuart Mill). 340p. 1990. text ed. 90.00 (*0-8020-2717-2*) U of Toronto Pr.
Mill, John Stuart & Bentham, Jeremy. Utilitarianism & Other Essays. Ryan, Alan, ed. 352p. 1987. pap. 9.95 (*0-14-043272-8*, Penguin Classics) Viking Penguin.
Mill, John Stuart & Mill, Harriet T. Essays on Sex Equality. Rossi, Alice S., ed. LC 78-133381. (Orig.). 1970. pap. 12.95 (*0-226-52546-5*, P420) U Ch Pr.
Mill, John Stuart & Mill, James. James & John Stuart Mill on Education. LC 78-27822. 208p. 1979. reprint ed. text ed. 35.00 (*0-8371-4282-2*, MIOE, Greenwood Pr) Greenwood.
Mill, John Stuart, jt. auth. see Carlyle, Thomas.
Mill, John Stuart, jt. auth. see Wollstonecraft, Mary.
Mill, Robert C. Tourism: The International Business. 336p. 1990. text ed. 63.00 (*0-13-926296-2*) P-H.
Mill, Robert C. & Morrison, Alastair M. The Tourism System: An Introductory Text. 2nd ed. 512p. 1992. text ed. 63.00 (*0-13-923145-5*) P-H.
Mill, Susan W., et al. Indexed Bibliography on the Flowering Plants of Hawaii. LC 88-17257. 216p. 1989. text ed. 25.00 (*0-8248-1169-0*) UH Pr.
Mill, Wendy C. Repetitive Strain Industry. 128p. 1994. pap. 8.00 (*0-7225-2919-8*) Thorsons SF.
Millais, John E. The Parables of Our Lord & Savior Jesus Christ. 7.75 (*0-8446-5225-3*) Peter Smith.
Millais, John E., illus. Parables of Our Lord & Savior Jesus Christ. LC 74-20328. 128p. 1975. pap. 4.95 (*0-486-20494-4*) Dover.
Millais, John G. Life & Letters of Sir John Everett Millais, President of the Royal Academy, 2 Vols, Set. LC 72-148280. reprint ed. 124.50 (*0-404-04326-7*) AMS Pr.
Millais, Raoul. Elijah & Pin-Pin. LC 91-20032. (Illus.). 48p. (J). (ps-1). 1992. pap. 14.00 (*0-671-75543-9*, S&S Bks Young Read) S&S Childrens.
Millam, Michael J. Reaction Guide for Organic Chemistry. 204p. (C). 1989. pap. text ed. 9.00 (*0-669-13248-9*) Heath.
— Reaction Guide for the Brief Organic Chemistry Course. 185p. (C). 1989. pap. text ed. 9.50 (*0-669-13247-0*) Heath.
Millan, Alonso. Plan Manzanares. 85p. (SPA.). 1967. 1.00 (*0-8288-7154-X*) Fr & Eur.
Millan, Gordon. A Throw of the Dice: The Life of Stephane Mallarme. LC 93-40180. 1994. 35.00 (*0-374-27707-9*) FS&G.
Millan, Millan M., jt. ed. see Gryning, Sven-Erik.
Millan, V. Mexico Reborn. 1976. 59.95 (*0-8490-2250-9*) Gordon Pr.
Millan, W. H., jt. auth. see Rogers, J. W.
Millane, R. P., et al, eds. Frontiers in Carbohydrate Research, No. 1: Food Applications: Proceedings of a Conference, Held at Purdue University, West Lafayette, IA, 13-15 Sept., 1988. 298p. 1990. 63.00 (*1-85166-446-7*) Elsevier.
***Millang.** I Love Cheesecake: A Family Guide to Nature. 1995. pap. text ed. 7.95 (*1-885061-07-2*) Adventure Pubns.
Millang, Steve, jt. auth. see Scelsa, Greg.
Millang, Theresa. Best of Cajun-Creole Recipes. 1992. pap. 5.95 (*0-934860-93-9*) Adventure Pubns.
— Best of Chili Recipes. 1993. spiral bd., pap. 5.95 (*0-934860-08-4*) Adventure Pubns.
Millang, Theresa, ed. see McDaniel, Effie.
Millar, Alan. Reasons & Experience. 238p. 1991. 69.00 (*0-19-824270-0*) OUP.
Millar, Alejandra, tr. see Zollars, Jean A.
***Millar, Anthony P.** Sports Injuries & Their Management. 2nd ed. (Illus.). 151p. (C). 1994. pap. text ed. 35.00 (*0-8036-0077-1*) Davis Co.
Millar, D. D., jt. ed. see Brennan, M. H.
Millar, D. D., jt. auth. see Cram, L. E.
Millar, Delia. Royal Estates of Britain. (Illus.). 152p. 1991. 75.00 (*0-8109-3756-5*) Abrams.
Millar, Donald. The Messel ERA: The History of the School of Physics & its Science Foundation with the University of Sydney 1952-1987. 176p. 1987. 11.75 (*0-317-66359-3*, Pergamon Pr) Elsevier.
Millar, Donald, jt. auth. see Swash, Mary.
Millar, Ernest, tr. see Mukasa, Ham.
Millar, Fergus. The Emperor in the Roman World. LC 76-20059. 696p. 1977. 79.95 (*0-8014-1058-4*) Cornell U Pr.
— The Emperor in the Roman World. LC 76-20059. 696p. 1992. pap. 23.95 (*0-8014-8049-3*) Cornell U Pr.
— The Roman Near East, 31 B. C. - A. D. 337. LC 93-18174. 617p. 1993. 47.50 (*0-674-77885-5*) HUP.
Millar, Fergus, ed. The Roman Empire & Its Neighbours. 2nd ed. LC 81-326. 376p. 1981. 49.50 (*0-8419-0711-0*) Holmes & Meier.
***Millar, Fergus G.** The Roman Near East: 31 B. C.-A. D. 337. (Illus.). 617p. 1995. pap. text ed. 19.95 (*0-674-77886-3*, MILROX) HUP.
***Millar, Garnet W. E.** Paul Torrance: The Gentle Genius of Georgia, An Authorized Biography. 1995. write for info. (*1-56750-172-9*); pap. write for info. (*1-56750-173-7*) Ablex Pub.
Millar, Gavin, jt. auth. see Reisz, Karel.
Millar, Geoffrey T., jt. auth. see Dhillon, Baljean.
Millar, Gilbert J. Tudor Mercenaries & Auxiliaries, 1485-1547. LC 79-22164. (Illus.). 223p. 1980. 28.50 (*0-8139-0818-3*) U Pr of Va.
***Millar, Heather.** China's Tang Dynasty. (Cultures of the Past Ser.). 80p. (J). (gr. 5-8). 1995. lib. bdg. write for info. (*0-7614-0074-5*, Benchmark NY) Marshall Cavendish.
***Millar, Ian.** Riding High: Ian Miller's World of Show Jumping. 1990. 35.00 (*0-7710-5872-1*, Pub. by McClelland & Stewart CN) Firefly Bks Ltd.
***Millar, James R.** The ABCs of Soviet Socialism. LC 80-24196. 230p. 1981. reprint ed. pap. 65.60 (*0-7837-8080-X*, 2047833) Bks Demand.
Millar, James R., ed. Cracks in the Monolith: Party Power in the Brezhnev Era. LC 92-9300. (Contemporary Soviet - Post Soviet Politics Ser.). 256p. 1992. 62.95 (*0-87332-885-X*) M E Sharpe.
— Politics, Work, & Daily Life in the U. S. S. R. A Survey of Former Soviet Citizens. (Illus.). 400p. 1987. pap. 29. 95 (*0-521-34890-0*) Cambridge U Pr.
Millar, James R. & Wolchik, Sharon L., eds. Social Legacies of Communism. (Woodrow Wilson Center Press Ser.). 350p. (C). 1994. 69.95 (*0-521-46182-0*); pap. 18.95 (*0-521-46748-9*) Cambridge U Pr.
Millar, Jane. Poverty & the Lone-Parent Family: The Challenge to Social Policy. 216p. 1989. text ed. 59.95 (*0-566-05770-0*) Ashgate Pub Co.
Millar, Jim. Handbook of Hawaiian Machine - Made Soda Bottles. (Illus.). 114p. (Orig.). 1988. pap. 14.00 (*1-56046-211-6*) Interact Pubs.
Millar, John. Observations Concerning the Distinction of Ranks in Society. LC 78-67536. reprint ed. 34.50 (*0-404-17199-0*) AMS Pr.
Millar, John F. Classical Architecture in Renaissance Europe: 1419-1585. LC 86-50560. (Illus.). 250p. (Orig.). 1987. 36.00 (*0-934943-07-9*); pap. 24.00 (*0-934943-06-0*) Thirteen Colonies Pr.
— A Complete Life of Christ. LC 85-51584. (Illus.). 180p. (Orig.). 1986. 16.00 (*0-934943-04-4*); pap. 9.00 (*0-934943-01-X*) Thirteen Colonies Pr.
— Country Dances of Colonial America. LC 90-49922. (Illus.). 160p. (Orig.). 1990. pap. 20.00 (*0-934943-28-1*) Thirteen Colonies Pr.
— Handbook on the Founding of Australia 1788. LC 87-50807. (Illus.). 128p. 1987. pap. 16.00 (*0-934943-19-2*) Thirteen Colonies Pr.
— Ships of the American Revolution. Knill, Harry, ed. (Illus.). 48p. (Orig.). 1976. pap. 3.95 (*0-88388-036-9*) Bellerophon Bks.
Millar, John R., jt. auth. see Liberti, Lorenzo.
***Millar, Joy.** Higher Ground. 300p. 1996. pap. 9.95 (*0-7610-0504-8*) NW Pub.
Millar, Kenneth, jt. auth. see Hancock, Molly R.
Millar, Margaret. An Air That Kills. 247p. 1985. pap. 4.95 (*0-930330-23-4*) Intl Polygonics.
— Ask Me for Tomorrow. 1991. pap. 8.95 (*1-55882-115-5*) Intl Polygonics.
— Banshee. 202p. 1985. reprint ed. pap. 5.95 (*0-930330-14-5*) Intl Polygonics.
— Beast in View. LC 83-80874. 251p. 1983. reprint ed. pap. 4.95 (*0-930330-07-2*) Intl Polygonics.
— Beyond This Point Are Monsters. 213p. pap. 4.95 (*0-930330-31-5*) Intl Polygonics.
— The Birds & the Beasts Were There. 242p. (C). 1991. reprint ed. lib. bdg. 29.00x (*0-8095-4081-9*) Borgo Pr.
— The Birds & the Beasts Were There. LC 90-21649. 242p. 1991. reprint ed. pap. 10.95 (*0-88496-324-1*) Capra Pr.
— The Cannibal Heart. 207p. 1985. pap. 4.95 (*0-930330-32-3*) Intl Polygonics.
— The Fiend. LC 84-80231. 244p. 1984. reprint ed. pap. 5.95 (*0-930330-10-2*) Intl Polygonics.
— Fire Will Freeze. (Library of Crime Classics). 200p. 1987. pap. 5.95 (*0-930330-59-5*) Intl Polygonics.
— The Iron Gates. LC 87-82440. 192p. 1987. reprint ed. pap. 4.95 (*0-930330-67-6*) Intl Polygonics.
— The Listening Walls. 236p. 1986. 5.95 (*0-930330-52-8*) Intl Polygonics.
— Mermaid. 220p. pap. 8.95 (*1-55882-114-7*) Intl Polygonics.
— The Murder of Miranda. 20.95 (*0-89190-156-6*, Am Repr) Amereon Ltd.
— The Murder of Miranda. LC 88-82355. 240p. 1988. reprint ed. pap. 4.95 (*0-930330-95-1*, Lib Crime Classics) Intl Polygonics.
— Rose's Last Summer. 223p. 1985. pap. 4.95 (*0-930330-26-9*) Intl Polygonics.
— Spider Webs. 323p. 1988. pap. 5.95 (*0-930330-76-5*) Intl Polygonics.
— A Stranger in My Grave. 310p. 1990. reprint ed. pap. 7.95 (*1-55882-066-3*) Intl Polygonics.
— Vanish in an Instant. LC 89-85721. 245p. reprint ed. pap. 7.95 (*1-55882-051-5*, Lib Crime Classics) Intl Polygonics.
— Wall of Eyes. 224p. 1986. pap. 4.95 (*0-930330-42-0*) Intl Polygonics.
Millar, Martin. The Good Fairies of New York. 224p. 1992. pap. 13.95 (*1-85702-076-6*, Pub. by Fourth Estate UK) Trafalgar.
Millar, Mary. Assessing Information Needs Module 1: Facilitator's Guide. (Primary Health Care Management Advancement Programme (PHC MAP) Modules Ser.). 55p. 1993. pap. text ed. write for info. (*1-882839-08-0*) Aga Khan Fnd.
— Assessing the Quality of Management Module 7: Facilitator's Guide. (Primary Health Care Management Advancement Programme (PHC MAP) Modules Ser.). 47p. 1993. pap. text ed. write for info. (*1-882839-13-7*) Aga Khan Fnd.
— Cost Analysis Module 8: Facilitator's Guide. (Primary Health Care Management Advancement Programme (PHC MAP) Modules Ser.). 53p. 1993. pap. text ed. write for info. (*1-882839-14-5*) Aga Khan Fnd.
— Sustainability Analysis Module 9: Facilitator's Guide. (Primary Health Care Management Advancement Programme (PHC MAP) Modules Ser.). 55p. 1993. pap. text ed. write for info. (*1-882839-16-1*) Aga Khan Fnd.
Millar, Oliver. The Victorian Pictures in the Collection of Her Majesty the Queen. (Pictures in the Collection of Her Majesty the Queen). (Illus.). 736p. (C). 1993. 325. 00 (*0-521-26522-3*) Cambridge U Pr.
Millar, Pamela, ed. see Ching Hai.
Millar, Perry S. & Baar, Carl. Judicial Administration in Canada. LC 82-173244. (Canadian Public Administration Series - Collection Administration Publique Canadienne). 476p. reprint ed. pap. 135.70 (*0-7837-1019-4*, 2041330) Bks Demand.
Millar, Rob, et al. Professional Interviewing. (International Series on Communication Skills). (Illus.). 224p. 1991. 74. 50 (*0-415-04084-1*, A6293); pap. 18.95 (*0-415-04085-X*, A6297) Routledge.
Millar, Robert. Policing the Miners Strike. Fine, Ben, ed. (C). 1985. text ed. 49.95 (*0-85315-632-8*, Pub. by Lawrence & Wishart UK); pap. 19.95 (*0-85315-633-6*, Pub. by Lawrence & Wishart UK) Humanities.
Millar, Robert W., tr. see Garofalo, Raffaele.
Millar, Robin, ed. Doing Science: Images of Science in Science Education. 250p. 1989. 65.00 (*1-85000-506-0*, Falmer Pr); pap. 32.50 (*1-85000-507-9*, Falmer Pr) Taylor & Francis.
Millar, Susan B. Bugis Weddings: Rituals of Social Location in Modern Indonesia. LC 89-62006. (Monograph Ser.: No. 29). (Illus.). 236p. (Orig.). (C). 1989. pap. 17.50 (*0-944613-06-3*); pap. 11.50 (*0-685-30762-X*) UC Berkeley Ctrs SE Asia.
Millar, Susanna. Understanding & Representing Space: Theory & Evidence from Experiments with Blind & Sighted Children. LC 94-10299. (Illus.). 240p. 1994. 65. 00 (*0-19-852142-1*, Old Oregon Bk Store) OUP.
Millar, T. B. & Walter, James, eds. Asian-Pacific Security after the Cold War. 144p. (Orig.). 1993. pap. 24.95 (*1-86373-398-1*, Pub. by Allen Unwin AT) Paul & Co Pubs.
Millar, T. J. & Williams, David A., eds. Rate Coefficients in Astrochemistry. (C). 1988. lib. bdg. 129.50 (*90-277-2752-X*) Kluwer Ac.
Millar, T. J., jt. ed. see James, R. A.
Millar, T. J., jt. ed. see Williams, D. A.
Millar, Victor. On the Management of Professional Service Firms. 50p. 1991. pap. text ed. 10.00 (*0-916654-69-9*) Kennedy Pubns.
Millar, W. P., jt. auth. see Gidney, R. D.
Millard. The Age of Revolutions. (Picture History Ser.). (Illus.). (J). (gr. 4-9). 1979. lib. bdg. 13.96 (*0-88110-112-5*, Usborne); pap. 6.95 (*0-86020-263-1*, Usborne) EDC.
— Crusaders, Aztecs & Samurai. (Picture History Ser.). (Illus.). (J). (gr. 4-6). 1978. lib. bdg. 13.96 (*0-88110-110-9*, Usborne); pap. 6.95 (*0-86020-194-5*, Usborne) EDC.
— Eponyms Assyrian Empire. 1991. write for info. (*0-85668-109-1*, Pub. by Aris & Phillips UK) David Brown.
— Essential Histopathology. 1990. pap. 46.95 (*0-632-02238-8*) Blackwell Sci.
— Exploration & Discovery. (Picture History Ser.). (Illus.). (J). (gr. 4-9). 1979. lib. bdg. 13.96 (*0-88110-111-7*, Usborne); pap. 6.95 (*0-86020-261-5*, Usborne) EDC.
— The First Civilization. (Picture History Ser.). (Illus.). (J). (gr. 4-9). 1977. lib. bdg. 13.96 (*0-88110-107-9*, Usborne); pap. 6.95 (*0-86020-138-4*, Usborne) EDC.
— Rewriting of America's History. Date not set. 13.99 (*0-88985-092-5*, Pub. by Horizon Books CN) Chr Pubns.
— Warriors & Seafarers. (Picture History Ser.). (Illus.). (J). (gr. 4-9). 1977. lib. bdg. 13.96 (*0-88110-108-7*, Usborne); pap. 6.95 (*0-86020-140-6*, Usborne) EDC.
— World History, Book Of. (Picture History Ser.). (Illus.). 195p. (J). (gr. 3-9). 1986. 24.95 (*0-86020-959-8*) EDC.
***Millard, ed.** Trade Associations & Professional Bodies of the United Kingdom. 12th ed. 648p. 1994. text ed. 150. 00 (*1-873477-21-X*, Gale Res Intl) Gale.
Millard, jt. auth. see Ash.
Millard, jt. auth. see Evans.
Millard, A. Round the World Cookbook. (Illus.). 48p. (J). 1993. pap. 7.95 (*0-7460-0966-6*, Usborne) EDC.
Millard, A. & Peach, S. The Greeks. (Illustrated World History Ser.). (Illus.). 96p. (YA). 1990. lib. bdg. 16.96 (*0-88110-415-9*); pap. 10.95 (*0-7460-0342-0*) EDC.
Millard, A., jt. auth. see Evans, C.
Millard, A., et al. Ancient World. (Illustrated World History Ser.). (Illus.). 288p. (YA). (gr. 7-12). 1992. pap. 24.95 (*0-7460-1233-0*) EDC.
Millard, A. J. A Technological Lag: Diffusion of Electrical Technology in England, 1879-1914. McNeill, William H. & Stansky, Peter, eds. (Modern European History Ser.). 264p. 1987. lib. bdg. 15.00 (*0-8240-7823-3*) Garland.
Millard, A. R., jt. ed. see Wiseman, D. J.
Millard, A. R., et al, eds. Faith, Tradition, & History: Old Testament Historiography in Its Near Eastern Context. LC 94-2529. xiv, 354p. 1994. text ed. 34.50 (*0-931464-82-X*) Eisenbrauns.
Millard, Alan. Discoveries from the Time of Jesus. 1990. 29. 95 (*0-7459-1207-9*) Lion USA.
— Equality: A Man's Claim. abr. ed. 680p. 1995. pap. 14.95 (*1-56901-342-X*) NW Pub.
— First Kings - Second Chronicles. (Bible Study Commentaries Ser.). 126p. 1985. pap. 4.95 (*0-87508-155-X*) Chr Lit.
***Millard, Allan.** The Eponyms of the Assyrian Empire 910-612 B. C. (State Archives of Assyria Studies). xvi, 155p. 1994. pap. text ed. 36.50x (*951-45-6715-3*, Pub. by Neo-Assyrian Text FI) Eisenbrauns.
***Millard, Andre.** America on Record: A History of Recorded Sound. (Illus.). 416p. (C). 1995. 59.95 (*0-521-47544-9*); pap. 17.95 (*0-521-47556-2*) Cambridge U Pr.
— Edison & the Business of Innovation. (Johns Hopkins Studies in the History of Technology; New Ser.). 408p. (C). 1993. reprint ed. pap. text ed. 22.95 (*0-8018-4730-3*) Johns Hopkins.
Millard, Anne. Eric the Red: The Vikings Sail the Atlantic. LC 93-26113. (Beyond the Horizons Ser.). (J). 1994. lib. bdg. 22.80 (*0-8114-7252-3*) Raintree Steck-V.
— Eyewitness Atlas of Ancient Worlds. (Illus.). 64p. (J). (gr. 5 up). 1994. write for info. (*1-56458-679-0*) Dorling Kindersley.
— How People Lived. LC 92-54315. (See & Explore Library). (Illus.). 64p. (J). (gr. 3-7). 1993. 12.95 (*1-56458-237-X*) Dorling Kindersley.
Millard, Bob. Country Music: 70 Years of America's Favorite Music. LC 92-56276. (Illus.). 416p. (Orig.). 1993. pap. 20.00 (*0-06-273244-7*, Harper Ref) HarpC.
— Country Music What's What: The Fan's Guide to the People, Places & Things of Country Music. LC 95-12614. (Illus.). 1995. 18.00 (*0-06-273334-6*, PL) HarpC.
— Judds. 1992. mass mkt. 4.50 (*0-312-95014-4*) St Martin.
— Music City U. S. A. A Guide to Nashville & Tennessee. LC 92-54686. (Illus.). 224p. (Orig.). 1993. pap. 13.00 (*0-06-273229-3*, Harper Ref) HarpC.
Millard, Brian J. Winning on the Stock Market: Low Risk & High-Profit Strategies for Investors. LC 93-14742. 205p. (Orig.). 1994. pap. text ed. 30.50 (*0-471-93881-5*) Wiley.
Millard, Catherine. A Children's Companion Guide to America's History. LC 93-78892. (Illus.). 96p. (Orig.). (J). 1993. student ed 10.99 (*0-88965-102-7*, Pub. by Horizon Books CN) Chr Pubns.
— God's Signature over the Nation's Capital. (Illus.). 176p. (Orig.). 1988. pap. 6.95 (*0-936369-17-5*) Son-Rise Pubns.
— The Rewriting of America's History. LC 91-73175. (Illus.). 1991. 13.99 (*0-88965-092-6*, Pub. by Horizon Books CN) Chr Pubns.
Millard, D. O. Applied Anatomy of the Lymphatics. 278p. 1964. reprint ed. spiral bd. 19.25 (*0-7873-0615-0*) Mokelumne.
Millard, D. Ralph, Jr. Cleft, 3 vols., Set. 1983. 630.00 (*0-316-57148-2*) Little.
— Cleft Craft: Alveolar & Palatal Deformities, Vol. III. 1980. 235.00 (*0-316-57139-3*) Little.
— Cleft Craft: Bilateral & Rare Deformities, Vol. 2. 1977. 235.00 (*0-316-57138-5*) Little.
— Cleft Craft: The Evolution of Its Surgery, Vol. 1: The Unilateral Deformity. 1976. 235.00 (*0-316-57137-7*) Little.
— Principalization of Plastic Surgery. 1986. 235.00 (*0-316-57153-9*) Little.
Millard, David. The Joy of Watercolor. (Illus.). 144p. 1992. reprint ed. pap. 18.95 (*0-8230-2566-7*, Watsn-Guptill) Watsn-Guptill.
Millard, Edward. Export Marketing for a Small Handicraft Business. 128p. (Orig.). (C). 1992. pap. text ed. 40.00 (*0-85598-174-1*, Pub. by Oxfam Pubns UK) St Mut.
Millard, Elaine. Developing Readers in the Middle Years. LC 93-29245. (English, Language & Education Ser.). 1994. 23.00 (*0-335-19071-5*, Open Univ Pr) Taylor & Francis.
Millard, Elizabeth. Criminal Trial Preparation. (Illus.). 204p. 1992. pap. 35.00 (*0-685-14628-6*) NJ Inst CLE.
Millard, Frances. The Anatomy of a New Poland: Post-Communist Politics in Its First Phase. (Studies of Communism in Transition). 272p. 1994. 59.95 (*1-85278-924-7*, Pub. by E Elgar Pub UK) Ashgate Pub Co.
Millard, Frances, jt. auth. see Ball, Alan R.

M

An Asterisk (*) at the beginning of an entry indicates that the title is appearing in BIP for the first time.

Millard, Graham. Commissioning Hospital Buildings. (King Edward's Hospital Fund Ser.). 1975. pap. text ed. 19.95 (*0-8464-0260-2*) Beekman Pubs.

Millard, Gregory. Geechies. 1992. pap. 5.95 (*0-88378-092-5*) Third World.

Millard, J. M. Yang-Baxter Equations in Paris: Proceedings of the Conference. 300p. 1993. text ed. 95.00 (*981-02-1343-3*) World Scientific Pub.

Millard, Kenneth. Edwardian Poetry. (Oxford English Monographs). 208p. 1992. 55.00 (*0-19-812225-X*) OUP.

Millard, Kent. Spiritual Gifts. (Lifesearch Ser.). 64p. (Orig.). 1994. pap. 4.95 (*0-687-77866-2*) Abingdon.

Millard, L. Adult Learners: Study Skills & Teaching Methods. (C). 1981. 40.00 (*1-85041-010-0*, Pub. by Univ Nottingham UK) St Mut.

Millard, Lisa S. Expressions of Life. (Illus.). (Orig.). 1989. pap. write for info. (*0-318-66296-5*) LSM Enterprises.

Millard, Margaret. Casenotes of a Medical Astrologer. rev. ed. 208p. 1984. pap. 7.95 (*0-87728-606-X*) Weiser.

Millard, Mary. Shattered Secrets. 408p. (Orig.). 1992. pap. 16.95 (*0-9624022-5-7*) Venture Bk Pubns.

Millard, P., tr. see Belokurov, V. V. & Shirov, D. V.

Millard, Patricia. Trade Associations & Professional Bodies of the United Kingdom. 8th ed. 600p. 1987. 78.00 (*0-08-033390-7*, Pergamon Pr) Elsevier.

— Trade Associations & Professional Bodies of the United States. 7th ed. 1984. 46.00 (*0-08-023024-5*, Pergamon Pr) Elsevier.

Millard, Patricia, ed. Trade Associations & Professional Bodies of the United Kingdom. 9th ed. LC 88-19516. (Trade Association & Professional Bodies Ser.). 530p. 1988. 40.00 (*0-08-034876-9*, Pergamon Pr) Elsevier.

Millard, Peter J. How to Buy an Established Business (Without Losing Your Shirt) Lobley, Steven J., ed. LC 85-82087. 52p. (Orig.). 1985. pap. 7.50 (*0-9615795-5-2*) Ledena Pub.

Millard, R., jt. auth. see Flintoff, F.

Millard, R. S. Road Building in the Tropics. (TRL State of the Art Review Ser.: No. 9). 322p. 1993. pap. 55.00 (*0-11-551062-1*, HM10621, Pub. by HMSO UK) UNIPUB.

Millard, Richard J., jt. ed. see Ware, Mark E.

Millard, Richard M. Today's Myths & Tomorrow's Realities: Overcoming Obstacles to Academic Leadership in the Twenty-First Century. LC 91-11251. (Higher & Adult Education Ser.). 340p. 1991. 32.95 (*1-55542-361-2*) Jossey-Bass.

Millard, Rodney J. The Master Spirit of the Age: Canadian Engineers & the Politics of Professionalism, 1887-1922. 236p. 1988. 37.50 (*0-8020-2652-4*) U of Toronto Pr.

Millard, Scott, jt. auth. see Johnson, Eric A.

Millard, Scott, ed. see Walheim, Lance.

Millard, Sue. The Complete Book of Candlewick Embroidery. (Illus.). 96p. 1994. pap. 14.95 (*1-85368-150-4*, Pub. by New Holland Pubs UK) Sterling.

— Creative Candlewicking for the Home. 96p. (C). 1988. 100.00 (*1-85368-069-9*, Pub. by New Holland Pubs UK) St Mut.

— Traditional Country Needlecraft. 1995. 14.99 (*0-517-12107-7*) Random Hse Value.

— Traditional Country Needlecrafts: Creative Guide to Embroidery, Candlewicking, Smocking, Quilting, Working with Lace. LC 94-28035. 1995. 12.99 (*0-517-12108-5*) Random Hse Value.

Millares Carlos, Agustin. Tratado de Paleografia Espanola, 3 vols., 1-Texto. 3rd ed. 1176p. 1989. write for info. (*0-318-65348-6*) Elliots Bks.

— Tratado de Paleografia Espanola, 3 vols., 2-Laminas. 3rd ed. 1176p. 1989. write for info. (*0-318-65349-4*) Elliots Bks.

— Tratado de Paleografia Espanola, 3 vols., 3-Laminas. 3rd ed. 1176p. 1989. write for info. (*0-318-65350-8*) Elliots Bks.

— Tratado de Paleografia Espanola, 3 vols., Set. 3rd ed. 1176p. 1989. 975.00 (*84-239-4986-9*) Elliots Bks.

Millares Vazquez, Manuel, tr. see McNeill, William H.

***Millas.** El Desorden de Tu Nombre: The Disorder of Your Name. 1995. pap. 12.50 (*0-679-76091-1*, Vin) Random.

Millas, Aristides J. Seventy Years of Miami Architecture: Commercial & Institutional Architecture in Dade County. LC 91-70266. (Illus.). 96p. (Orig.). 1991. pap. 14.95 (*1-880511-01-0*) Bass Museum.

Millasich, James, see James Britton, pseud..

***Millau, Christian.** Guide Gault Millau France 1994. 799p. (FRE.). 1994. 69.95 (*0-614-00404-7*, 2902968701) Fr & Eur.

— Guide Gault Millau Paris 1994. 720p. (FRE.). 1994. 59.95 (*0-614-00403-9*, 2902968396) Fr & Eur.

Millay, Edna St. Vincent. Collected Lyrics. LC 75-6348. 304p. 1981. pap. 12.00 (*0-06-090863-7*, CN863, PL) HarpC.

— Collected Poems. LC 75-6348. 1992. reprint ed. lib. bdg. 35.95x (*0-89968-266-9*, Lghtyr Pr) Buccaneer Bks.

— Collected Poems. Millay, Norma, ed. LC 75-6348. 760p. (YA). 1981. reprint ed. pap. 22.50 (*0-06-090889-0*, CN-889, PL) HarpC.

— Collected Sonnets. LC 83-48369. 176p. 1988. pap. 11.00 (*0-06-091091-7*, CN 1091, PL) HarpC.

— Renascence & Other Poems. LC 72-3092. (Granger Index Reprint Ser.). 1977. reprint ed. pap. 13.95 (*0-8369-8245-2*) Ayer.

— Renascence & Other Poems. (Thrift Editions Ser.). (Illus.). 64p. reprint ed. pap. 1.00 (*0-486-26873-X*) Dover.

Millay, Norma, ed. see Millay, Edna St. Vincent.

***Millberg, Karen.** Flight Against the Wind. (American Autobiography Ser.). 182p. 1995. reprint ed. lib. bdg. 69.00 (*0-7812-8595-X*) Rprt Serv.

Millberg, Richard S. Myocardial Infarction with Diagnosis: Subject Analysis with Bibliography. LC 87-47629. 160p. 1987. 44.50 (*0-88164-560-5*); pap. 39.50 (*0-88164-561-3*) ABBE Pubs Assn.

Millcroft, Robert J., jt. auth. see Sydlaske, Janet M.

Mille, Carol E. Which Translation Do You Prefer. 1975. pap. 1.95 (*0-915374-52-8*, 52-8) Rapids Christian.

***Millea, Janice & Zinser, Charles I.** Outdoor Recreation: United States National Parks, Forests & Public Lands. LC 94-38100. 1995. text ed. 69.95 (*0-471-05373-2*) Wiley.

Millea, Nicholas. Settlements. LC 93-24680. (Young Geographer Ser.). (Illus.). 32p. (J). (gr. 4-6). 1993. 14.95 (*1-56847-057-6*) Thomson Lrning.

Milledge, A., jt. auth. see Whittome, S.

Millen, Bruce H. The Political Role of Labor in Developing Countries. LC 79-29735. x, 148p. 1980. reprint ed. text ed. 52.50 (*0-313-22286-X*, MIPO, Greenwood Pr) Greenwood.

Millen, Nina. Children's Games from Many Lands. LC 65-24039. (Illus.). 194p. reprint ed. pap. 55.30 (*0-7837-1952-3*, 2042169) Bks Demand.

***Millen, Patricia E.** Bare Trees: Zadock Pratt, Master Tanner & the Story of What Happens to the Catskill Mountain Forests. (Illus.). 112p. (Orig.). 1995. pap. 11.95 (*1-883789-05-2*) Blk Dome Pr.

Millen-Posner, Barbara, jt. auth. see Hyman, Jane.

Millen, Ronald F. & Wolf, Robert E. Heroic Deeds & Mystic Figures: A New Reading of Rubens' Life of Maria de' Medici. (Illus.). 296p. 1990. text ed. 60.00 (*0-691-04065-6*) Princeton U Pr.

***Millen, Timothy M., et al.** Lead Isotopes from the Upper Mississippi Valley District: A Regional Perspective. LC 95-7133. (Evolution of Sedimentary Basins--Illinois Basin Ser., Vol. B: Bulletins Ser.: Vol. 2094). 1996. write for info. (*0-615-00673-6*) US Geol Survey.

Millender, Dharathula H. Crispus Attucks: Black Leader of Colonial Patriots. LC 86-10779. (Childhood of Famous Americans Ser.). (Illus.). 192p. (J). (gr. 2-6). 1986. reprint ed. pap. 3.95 (*0-02-041810-8*, Aladdin Paperbacks) S&S Childrens.

— Martin Luther King, Jr. Young Man with a Dream. LC 86-10739. (Childhood of Famous Americans Ser.). (Illus.). 192p. (J). (gr. 2-6). 1986. reprint ed. pap. 3.95 (*0-02-042010-2*, Aladdin Paperbacks) S&S Childrens.

Millender, Lewis H., et al, eds. Occupational Disorders of the Upper Extremity. (Illus.). 308p. 1992. text ed. 63.00 (*0-443-08797-0*) Churchill.

***Millenson, J. R.** Mind Matters: Psychological Medicine in Holistic Practice. (Illus.). 330p. (C). 1995. pap. text ed. 29.95 (*0-939616-21-1*) Eastland.

Millenson, Susan F. Sir John Soane's Museum. LC 86-24926. (Architecture & Urban Design Ser.: No. 18). (Illus.). 202p. reprint ed. pap. 57.60 (*0-8357-1766-6*, 2070611) Bks Demand.

Miller. Air Conditioners: Home & Commercial. 1986. 15.95 (*0-02-501930-9*) Macmillan.

— Banner O'Brien. 1995. mass mkt. 5.99 (*0-671-53422-X*) PB.

— Blood Diseases of Infancy & Childhood. 6th ed. (Illus.). 992p. 1989. 99.00 (*0-8016-3914-X*) Mosby Yr Bk.

— Book of Jargon. 1982. 16.95 (*0-02-584960-3*) Macmillan.

— Cardiac Radiology - The Requisites. 384p. 1993. 65.00 (*0-8016-6478-0*) Mosby Yr Bk.

— Childbearing Family, No. 2. 1983. 30.50 (*0-316-57338-8*) Little.

— Choosing College Major in Education. 1979. 10.95 (*0-679-50957-7*); pap. 5.95 (*0-679-50958-5*) McKay.

— Civil War Sea Battles. 1995. 24.95 (*0-938289-52-7*) Combined Bks.

— Clinical Ophthalmology for the Postgraduate. 599p. 1987. 160.00 (*0-7236-0754-0*, Pub. by John Wright UK) Buttrwrth-Heinemann.

— Conquering Asthma. Date not set. 14.95 (*1-55664-139-7*) Mosby Yr Bk.

— Corbin's Fancy. 1995. mass mkt. 5.99 (*0-671-53421-1*) PB.

— Death Comes to Dinner: Scene of the Crime, No. 1. 1995. pap. (*0-590-56871-X*) Scholastic Inc.

— Economics Today. 8th ed. 944p. (C). 1993. text ed. 45.75 (*0-06-502273-4*); Student guide. student ed 15.25 (*0-06-501466-9*) HarpCollege.

— Everlasting Love. 1995. mass mkt. 5.99 (*0-671-52150-0*) PB.

— Eye of the Octopus. 1995. pap. 9.99 (*0-8024-2729-4*) Moody.

— From Ritual to Repertoire: A Systems Approach to Cognitive Development with Disordered Children. (Personality Processes Ser.). 521p. 1989. text ed. 74.95 (*0-471-84897-2*) Wiley.

— Go to Bed! LC 92-54958. 1995. pap. text ed. 5.99 (*1-56402-509-8*) Candlewick Pr.

— Greenland. (World Bibliographical Ser.). 1991. lib. bdg. 55.00 (*1-85109-139-4*) ABC-CLIO.

— Introduction to AutoCAD. 1995. pap. text ed. write for info. (*0-8053-6420-X*) Benjamin-Cummings.

— Introduction to Plastics & Composites. 555p. 1995. write for info. (*0-8247-9663-2*) Dekker.

— Just Kate. 1995. mass mkt. 4.99 (*1-55166-055-5*, Mira Bks) Harlequin Bks.

— Memory's Embrace. 1995. mass mkt. 5.99 (*0-671-53420-3*) PB.

— Miniature Pinschers. 1995. (*0-7938-1081-7*) TFH Pubns.

— Monsters. (World of the Unknown Ser.). (Illus.). 32p. (J). (gr. k-6). 1977. pap. 5.95 (*0-685-73598-2*) EDC.

— Most of My Patients Are Animals. 1986. pap. 3.95 (*0-312-90511-4*) St Martin.

— My Darling Melissa. 1995. mass mkt. 5.99 (*0-671-53419-X*) PB.

— Nursing Care of Older Adults: Theory & Practice. (Illus.). 688p. 1990. text ed. 32.50 (*0-673-39795-5*) Lippincott.

— One Thousand & One Ideas for English Papers. 1994. pap. 10.00 (*0-671-88766-1*) P-H Gen Ref & Trav.

— People & Their Planet: A Textbook of Environmental Science. (Illus.). 640p. 1991. 39.95 (*0-8016-3301-X*) Mosby Yr Bk.

— Pictures of a Childhood. 1995. pap. (*0-452-01158-2*, Mer) NAL-Dutton.

— Plastic Products Design Handbook: Processes & Design for Processes, Pt. B. (Mechanical Engineering Ser.: Vol. 8). 392p. 1983. 140.00 (*0-8247-1886-0*) Dekker.

— Rants. 1995. (*0-385-47804-6*) Doubleday.

— Sabbath Shiurim, I. 1979. 13.95 (*0-87306-993-5*) Feldheim.

— Sabbath Shiurim, II. 1979. 13.95 (*0-686-67019-1*) Feldheim.

— Sales Training: ASTD Trainer's Sourcebook. 1995. pap. text ed. 39.95 (*0-07-053436-5*) McGraw.

— Selecting & Implementing Educational Software. 1986. text ed. 30.95 (*0-205-10468-1*, H04682) Allyn.

— Soviet Navy. LC 88-11327. (Soviet Military Power Ser.). (Illus.). 48p. (J). (gr. 3-8). 1988. lib. bdg. 18.60 (*0-86625-336-X*); lib. bdg. 13.95 (*0-685-58300-7*) Rourke Corp.

— Soviet Rocket Forces. LC 88-11367. (Soviet Military Power Ser.). (Illus.). 48p. (J). (gr. 3-8). 1988. lib. bdg. 18.60 (*0-86625-333-5*); lib. bdg. 13.95 (*0-685-58297-3*) Rourke Corp.

— Soviet Submarines. (Soviet Military Power Ser.). (Illus.). 48p. (J). (gr. 3-8). 1987. lib. bdg. 18.60 (*0-86625-332-7*); lib. bdg. 13.95 (*0-685-58296-5*) Rourke Corp.

— The Stress Solution. 1994. mass mkt. 5.99 (*0-671-75311-8*) PB.

— Surviving Joy. 1995. 21.50 (*1-55611-448-6*) D I Fine.

— War at Sea: A Naval History of World War II. 1995. 32.50 (*0-684-80380-1*) S&S Trade.

— Year Book of Anesthesia, 1993. 400p. 1993. 64.95 (*0-8151-5985-4*, Yr Bk Med Pubs) Mosby Yr Bk.

— Year Book of Anesthesia, 1994. 400p. 1994. 64.95 (*0-8151-5986-2*, Yr Bk Med Pubs) Mosby Yr Bk.

— Year Book of Anesthesia, 1995. 400p. 1995. 64.95 (*0-8151-5987-0*, Yr Bk Med Pubs) Mosby Yr Bk.

— Year Book of Anesthesia, 1996. 400p. 1996. 64.95 (*0-8151-5988-9*, Yr Bk Med Pubs) Mosby Yr Bk.

— Year Book of Plastic & Reconstructive Surgery, 1994. 320p. 1994. 64.95 (*0-8151-6041-0*, Yr Bk Med Pubs) Mosby Yr Bk.

— Year Book of Plastic & Reconstructive Surgery, 1995. 320p. 1995. 64.95 (*0-8151-6042-9*, Yr Bk Med Pubs) Mosby Yr Bk.

— Year Book of Plastic & Reconstructive Surgery, 1996. 341p. 1996. 64.95 (*0-8151-6043-7*, Yr Bk Med Pubs) Mosby Yr Bk.

— Year Book of Plastic, Reconstructive, & Aesthetic Surgery, 1991. 325p. 1991. 57.95 (*0-8151-6038-0*, Yr Bk Med Pubs) Mosby Yr Bk.

— Yearbook of Anesthesia, 1990. 376p. 1990. 57.95 (*0-8151-5927-7*, Yr Bk Med Pubs) Mosby Yr Bk.

— Yearbook of Anesthesia, 1991. 398p. 1991. 57.95 (*0-8151-5926-9*) Mosby Yr Bk.

— Yearbook of Anesthesia, 1992. 466p. 1992. 59.95 (*0-8151-5938-2*) Mosby Yr Bk.

— Yearbook of Plastic, Reconstructive, & Aesthetic Surgery, 1992. 350p. 1992. 59.95 (*0-8151-6039-9*) Mosby Yr Bk.

— Yearbook of Plastic, Reconstructive & Aesthetic Surgery, 1993. 336p. 1993. 64.95 (*0-8151-6040-2*) Mosby Yr Bk.

— Yearbook of Plastic Surgery, 1990. 336p. 1990. 57.95 (*0-8151-6037-2*, Yr Bk Med Pubs) Mosby Yr Bk.

— Your Own Magic Puzzle Show. 1995. pap. (*0-590-25994-6*) Scholastic Inc.

Miller, ed. Proceedings of the 26th Annual Simulation Symposium. LC 71-149514. 348p. 1993. pap. text ed. 80.00 (*0-8186-3620-3*, ANS26-1) Soc Computer Sim.

Miller & Felszeghy. Engineernig Features of the Santa Barbara Earthquake of August 13, 1978. 129p. 1978. 12.00 (*0-685-14399-6*) Earthquake Eng.

Miller & Grasso. Partial Prosthodontics. 3rd ed. (Illus.). 525p. (C). 1991. 56.95 (*1-55664-182-6*) Mosby Yr Bk.

Miller & Kopeika, eds. Optical, Infrared, & Millimeter Wave Propagation Engineering. 1988. 59.00 (*0-89252-961-X*, 926) SPIE.

Miller & Kulman. Auto Accident Law & Practice, 4 vols. 1988. Updates available. ring bd. write for info. (*0-8205-1158-7*, 158) Bender.

Miller & Palenik. Infection Control & Hazardous Materials Management. 250p. 1993. pap. 24.95 (*0-8016-6932-4*) Mosby Yr Bk.

Miller & Rowlands. The Physiologic Basis of Modern Surgical Care. (Illus.). 1208p. 1987. text ed. 99.00 (*0-8016-3421-0*) Mosby Yr Bk.

Miller, jt. auth. see Cummings.

Miller, jt. auth. see Dowben.

Miller, jt. auth. see Gunning.

Miller, jt. auth. see Hatfield.

Miller, jt. auth. see Humi.

Miller, jt. auth. see McPherson.

Miller, jt. auth. see Reedy.

Miller, jt. auth. see Robinson.

Miller, jt. auth. see Sexton.

Miller, jt. auth. see Shephard.

Miller, jt. auth. see Traugott.

Miller, jt. auth. see Yu.

***Miller, et al.** Basic College Mathematics. 4th ed. (C). 1994. text ed. 51.50 (*0-673-46741-4*) HarpCollege.

— Basic College Mathematics. 4th ed. (C). 1994. student ed, text ed. 12.50 (*0-673-99064-8*) HarpCollege.

— Daredevil - Punisher: Child's Play. 64p. 1988. 4.95 (*0-87135-351-2*) Marvel Entmnt.

— General & Oral Pathology for the Dental Hygienist. 450p. 1993. pap. 34.95 (*0-8016-7024-1*) Mosby Yr Bk.

— Laboratory Evaluation of Pulmonary Function. 1987. 26.50 (*0-397-58574-8*) Lippincott.

— Laboratory Manual in General Zoology. 3rd ed. 124p. (C). 1987. student ed 17.95 (*0-88725-078-5*) Hunter Textbks.

***Miller & Zaucha Staff.** The Color PC: Production Techniques. (Illus.). 400p. (Orig.). 1995. pap. 40.00 (*1-56830-179-0*) Alpha Bks IN.

Miller, A. & Litvinov, I., trs. Anton Chekhov Collected Works, 5 vols. 2266p. 1990. 59.95 (*0-8285-5000-X*) Firebird NY.

Miller, A., jt. ed. see Cunliffe, W. J.

Miller, A., jt. ed. see Eason, R. W.

Miller, A., ed. see Elm, B.

Miller, A., jt. auth. see McCullough, D.

***Miller, A., et al, eds.** Nonlinear Optical Materials & Devices for Applications in Information Technology: Proceedings of the NATO Advanced Study Institute, Erice, Sicily, Italy, July 13-26, 1993. LC 95-11664. (NATO ASI Ser., Series C: Applied Sciences: Vol. 289). 372p. (C). 1995. lib. bdg. 179.00 (*0-7923-3457-4*) Kluwer Ac.

Miller, A. B. Cervical Cancer Screening Programmes: Managerial Guidelines. (Illus.). viii, 50p. 1992. pap. 10.80 (*92-4-154447-3*) World Health.

Miller, A. B., ed. Diet & the Aetiology of Cancer. (ESO Monographs). (Illus.). 84p. 1989. 62.00 (*0-387-50681-0*) Spr-Verlag.

Miller, A. B., jt. ed. see Day, N. E.

Miller, A. B., jt. ed. see Prorok, P. C.

Miller, A. B., et al, eds. Cancer Screening. 300p. (C). 1991. 99.95 (*0-521-41041-X*) Cambridge U Pr.

Miller, A. Browne. The Day Care Dilemma: Critical Concerns for American Families. LC 89-26684. (Illus.). 328p. 1990. 23.95 (*0-306-43435-0*, Plenum Insight) Plenum.

— Working Dazed: Why Drugs Pervade the Workplace & What Can Be Done about It. LC 91-7247. (Illus.). 340p. 1991. 26.95 (*0-306-43765-1*, Plenum Insight) Plenum.

Miller, A. Carolyn & Punsalan, Victoria J., comps. Refereed & Nonrefereed Economic Journals: A Guide for Publishing Opportunities. LC 87-25158. 269p. 1988. text ed. 65.00 (*0-313-25857-0*, MPB/, Greenwood Pr) Greenwood.

Miller, A. G. Walt Disney's Bambi Gets Lost. (Disney's Wonderful World of Reading Ser.: No. 2). (J). (ps-3). 1973. lib. bdg. 4.99 (*0-394-92520-3*) Random Bks Yng Read.

Miller, A. G., rev. The Boatswain's Manual. rev. ed. (C). 1987. 84.00 (*0-85174-475-3*, Pub. by Brwn Son Ferg) St Mut.

***Miller, A. G. & Cope, T. A., eds.** Flora of the Arabian Peninsula & Socotra, Vol. 1. (Illus.). 600p. 1994. 95.00 (*0-7486-0475-8*, Pub. by Edinburgh U Pr UK) Col U Pr.

Miller, A. I., ed. Sixty-Two Years of Uncertainty: Historical, Philosophical, & Physical Inquiries into the Foundations of Quantum Mechanics. (NATO ASI Series B, Physics: Vol. 226). (Illus.). 320p. 1990. 89.50 (*0-306-43608-6*, Plenum Pr) Plenum.

Miller, A. J., et al, eds. Foodborne Listeriosis. (Topics in Industrial Microbiology Ser.: Vol. 2). 220p. 1990. 181.25 (*0-444-81186-9*) Elsevier.

Miller, A. M. From Delos to Delphi: A Literary Study of the Homeric Hymn to Apollo. (Mnemosyne Ser.: Supplement 93). xii, 130p. 1986. pap. 27.50 (*90-04-07674-3*) E J Brill.

Miller, A. T., jt. auth. see Durand, John.

Miller, A. V., tr. see Hegel, Georg W.

Miller, A. W. The Destroyers. (Orig.). 1980. pap. 1.75 (*0-8439-0738-X*) Dorchester Pub Co.

Miller, Aaron. In the Eye. 8.00 (*0-89253-700-0*); 4.80 (*0-89253-701-9*) Ind-US Inc.

Miller, Aaron D. The Arab States & the Palestine Question: Between Ideology & Self-Interest. LC 86-931. (Washington Papers: No. 120). 114p. 1986. text ed. 45.00 (*0-275-92215-4*, C2215, Praeger Pubs); pap. text ed. 14.95 (*0-275-92216-2*, B2216, Praeger Pubs) Greenwood.

— Search for Security: Saudi Arabian Oil & American Foreign Policy, 1939-1949. xvlii, 320p. 1991. pap. 14.95 (*0-8078-4324-5*) U of NC Pr.

Miller, Abraham H., ed. Terrorism, the Media, & the Law. LC 82-11020. 232p. 1982. lib. bdg. 30.00 (*0-941320-04-9*) Transnatl Pubs.

Miller Accounting Staff. Miller's Comprehensive Nineteen Eighty-Seven GAAS Guide. 1987. 42.00 (*0-317-64875-6*); pap. 32.00 (*0-317-64876-4*) HarBrace.

Miller, Adam, jt. auth. see Card, Emily.

Miller, Adam D. Forever Afternoon: Poems. LC 94-3903. (Lotus Poetry Ser.: Vol. 2). 1994. pap. 10.00 (*0-87013-354-3*) Mich St U Pr.

Miller, Adam L., jt. auth. see Card, Emily W.

Miller, Adam W. Introduction to the New Testament. rev. ed. 1984. pap. 3.95 (*0-87162-141-X*, D2403) Warner Pr.

— Introduction to the Old Testament. 1981. pap. 3.95 (*0-87162-193-2*, D2401) Warner Pr.

Miller, Adolph. Converting for Flexible Packaging: A Primer. LC 93-61005. 185p. 1993. pap. text ed. 49.00 (*1-56676-061-5*) Technomic.

Miller, Agnes, jt. auth. see Stapledon, Olaf.

Miller, Alain O., ed. Advanced Research on Animal Cell Technology. (NATO Advanced Science Institutes Series C: Mathematical & Physical Sciences). (C). 1988. lib. bdg. 162.00 (*0-7923-0031-9*) Kluwer Ac.

Miller, Alan. El ABC del AutoCad Version 11. 348p. 1992. pap. text ed. 25.95 (*968-6346-35-X*, Pub. by Ventura Ediciones MX) Computer & Tech.

— ABCs of DOS 6.2. LC 94-66291. 350p. 1994. pap. 19.99 (*0-7821-1590-X*) Sybex.

Miller, Alan, jt. auth. see Moore, Curtis.

Miller, Alan, et al. Growing Power: Bioenergy for Development & Industry. LC 85-62028. 112p. (Orig.). 1986. pap. 10.00 (*0-915825-14-7*) World Resources Inst.

Miller, Alan C., et al. The Disposable Woman. Ashton, Sylvia, ed. LC 77-77865. 1977. 22.95 (*0-87949-077-2*) Ashley Bks.

Miller, Alan J. Socially Responsible Investing: How to Invest with Your Conscience. 250p. 1991. 19.95 (*0-13-156183-9*) NY Inst Finance.

— Standard & Poor's 401K Planning Guide: Every Employee's Guide to Making 401K Decisions. LC 94-40808. 1995. pap. text ed. 12.95 (*0-07-042197-8*) McGraw.

— Standard & Poor's 401K Planning Guide: Every Employee's Guide to Making 401K Decisions. LC 94-40808. 1995. text ed. 27.95 (*0-07-042196-X*) McGraw.

— Subset Selection in Regression. (Monographs on Statistics & Applied Probability: No. 40). 224p. 1990. 47.50 (*0-412-35380-6*, A3897) Chapman & Hall.

Miller, Alan L., ed. see Hori, Ichiro.

Miller, Alan R. El ABC del DOS 4. 270p. 1991. pap. text ed. 22.95 (*968-6346-09-0*, Pub. by Ventura Ediciones MX) Computer & Tech.

— El ABC del DOS 5. 264p. 1992. pap. text ed. 22.95 (*968-6346-33-3*, Pub. by Ventura Ediciones MX) Computer & Tech.

— The ABCs of AutoCAD Release 12. LC 92-61600. 316p. 1992. pap. 22.95 (*0-7821-1038-X*) Sybex.

Miller, Alan S. Gaia Connections: An Introduction to Ecology, Ecoethics, & Economics. 288p. (C). 1990. lib. bdg. 57.00 (*0-8476-7655-2*); pap. text ed. 17.95 (*0-8476-7656-0*) Rowman.

***Miller, Alan W.** The Atlas of Virginia State General Elections, 1980 Through 1994. LC 95-75541. (Illus.). 137p. (Orig.). 1995. pap. 29.95 (*0-9645318-0-1*) Klipsan Pr.

— God of Daniel S: In Search of the American Jew. (Brown Classics in Judaica Ser.). 260p. 1986. reprint ed. pap. text ed. 22.50 (*0-8191-5047-9*) U Pr of Amer.

***Miller, Alan W., ed.** Atlas of California Presidential Elections by Country: 1932-1992. LC 95-77908. (Illus.). 135p. (Orig.). 1995. pap. 29.95 (*0-9645318-2-8*) Klipsan Pr.

— Atlas of the 1994 California General Election: Statewide Offices & Measures by County. LC 95-77910. (Illus.). 133p. (Orig.). 1995. pap. text ed. 29.95 (*0-9645318-1-X*) Klipsan Pr.

Miller, Albert, et al. Elements of Meteorology. 4th ed. LC 82-61242. (Illus.). 443p. reprint ed. pap. 126.30 (*0-318-39709-9*, AU00367) Bks Demand.

Miller, Albert G. Captain Whopper. (Illus.). (J). (gr. 3-7). 1968. 10.95 (*0-8392-3058-3*) Astor-Honor.

— More Captain Whopper Tales. (Illus.). (J). (gr. 3-7). 1968. 10.95 (*0-8392-3060-5*) Astor-Honor.

Miller, Albert J. Confrontation, Conflict & Dissent: A Bibliography of a Decade of Controversy, 1960-1970. LC 78-189440. 567p. 1972. 35.00 (*0-8108-0490-5*) Scarecrow.

— Diagnosis of Chest Pain. (Illus.). 240p. 1988. text ed. 72.00 (*0-88167-400-1*) Raven.

Miller, Alden H. & Stebbins, Robert C. The Lives of Desert Animals in Joshua Tree National Monument. 1974. 42.00 (*0-520-00866-9*) U CA Pr.

Miller, Alden H., jt. auth. see Grinnell, Joseph.

Miller, Alex. Ancestor Game. 320p. 1994. 24.00 (*1-55597-217-9*) Graywolf.

Miller, Alex, jt. auth. see Dess, Gregory G.

Miller, Alfred C. Descendants & Related Families of Kerrs Creek, Rockbridge County, Virginia, Vol. 1. 1991. lib. bdg. write for info. (*0-9624215-1-0*) A C Miller.

— Descendants & Related Families of Kerrs Creek, Rockbridge County, Virginia, Vol. 2. 1991. lib. bdg. write for info. (*0-9624215-2-9*) A C Miller.

— Descendants & Related Families of Kerrs Creek, Rockbridge County, Virginia, Vol. 3. 1991. lib. bdg. write for info. (*0-9624215-3-7*) A C Miller.

— One Time Around & Beyond. 591p. 1990. 46.50 (*0-9624215-0-2*) A C Miller.

Miller, Alfred E., tr. see Plaass, Peter.

Miller, Alice. Banished Knowledge: Facing Childhood Injury. 1991. mass mkt. 10.00 (*0-385-26762-2*, Anchor NY) Doubleday.

— Breaking down the Wall of Science: The Liberating Experience of Facing the Painful truth. 192p. 1993. pap. 10.00 (*0-452-01111-6*, Plume) NAL-Dutton.

— The Drama of the Gifted Child: The Search for True Self. rev. ed. LC 80-50535. Orig. Title: Prisoners of Childhood. 144p. 1994. reprint ed. pap. 11.00 (*0-465-01693-6*) Basic.

— For Your Own Good: Hidden Cruelty in Child-Rearing & the Roots of Violence. Hannum, Hildegarde & Hannum, Hunter, trs. 1990. pap. 10.00 (*0-374-52269-3*, Noonday) FS&G.

— Index to the Works of Immanuel Velikovsky, Vol. 1. 1977. 25.00 (*0-917994-08-6*) Kronos Pr.

— Pictures of a Childhood. 1995. pap. 14.95 (*0-452-27482-6*, Plume) NAL-Dutton.

— Prisoners of Childhood. LC 80-50535. 128p. 1981. 18.00 (*0-465-06347-0*) Basic.

— Thou Shalt Not Be Aware: Society's Betrayal of the Child. 1986. pap. 8.95 (*0-452-00801-8*, Plume) NAL-Dutton.

— Thou Shalt Not Be Aware: Society's Betrayal of the Child. LC 85-32084. 336p. 1991. pap. 11.95 (*0-452-00929-4*, Mer) NAL-Dutton.

— Untouched Key: Tracing Childhood Trauma in Creativity & Destructiveness. 1991. 9.95 (*0-385-26764-9*, Anchor NY) Doubleday.

***Miller, Alice D.** All Our Lives. 1994. reprint ed. lib. bdg. 21.95x (*1-56849-519-6*) Buccaneer Bks.

— Not for Love. 1994. reprint ed. lib. bdg. 21.95x (*1-56849-518-8*) Buccaneer Bks.

— Welcome Home. 1994. reprint ed. lib. bdg. 21.95x (*1-56849-524-2*) Buccaneer Bks.

— The White Cliffs. 74p. 1987. reprint ed. lib. bdg. 19.95 (*0-89966-615-9*) Buccaneer Bks.

Miller, Alistair & Callander, Robin. Obstetrics Illustrated. 4th ed. (Illus.). 483p. 1989. pap. text ed. 39.95 (*0-443-04016-8*) Churchill.

***Miller, Allan.** A Passion for Acting: Exploring the Creative Process. Weiler, Fred, ed. (Illus.). 206p. (Orig.). (C). Date not set. pap. 16.95 (*0-9644844-0-4*) Dynmic Prod.

— A Passion for Acting: Exploring the Creative Process. 208p. (Orig.). 1992. pap. 16.95 (*0-8230-8254-7*, Back Stage Bks) Watsn-Guptill.

Miller, Allan, ed. see Larson, Russ.

***Miller, Allan R.** Yankee on the Prairie: Howard R. Barnard, Pioneer Educator. (Illus.). 216p. 1995. pap. 15.95 (*0-89745-184-8*) Sunflower U Pr.

***Miller, Allan W. & LaFountain, Julie, eds.** Greenberg's Pocket Price Guide American Flyer S Gauge, 1995 Edition: American Flyer S Gauge. 11th ed. 56p. 1994. pap. 8.95 (*0-89778-737-4*) Greenberg Bks.

***Miller, Allan W., et al, eds.** Greenberg's Pocket Price Guide to Lionel Trains 1901-1995: Lionel Trains 1901-1995. 15th ed. 208p. 1994. pap. 9.95 (*0-89778-396-4*) Greenberg Bks.

Miller, Allen O. & Osterhaven, M. Eugene, trs. Heidelberg Catechism. LC 62-20891. 1963. pap. 4.95 (*0-8298-0060-3*) Pilgrim OH.

Miller, Allen R., et al. The Reorganization of the Joint Chiefs of Staff: A Critical Analysis. LC 86-28384. (Foreign Policy Reports). 1986. 9.95 (*0-685-17972-9*) Inst Foreign Policy Anal.

Miller, Alois M. & Kozloff, Max. Filmstills: Emotions Made in Hollywood. (Illus.). 224p. (Orig.). 1993. pap. 29.95 (*3-89322-492-0*, Pub. by Edition Cantz GW) Dist Art Pubs.

Miller, Alton, jt. auth. see Warfield, William.

***Miller, Alyce.** The Nature of Longing. 240p. 1995. pap. 10.00 (*0-393-31379-4*, Norton Paperbks) Norton.

— The Nature of Longing: Stories by Alyce Miller. LC 94-7582. (Flannery O'Connor Award for Short Fiction Ser.). 264p. 1994. 19.95 (*0-8203-1674-1*) U of Ga Pr.

Miller, Amy B. & Fuller, Persis W., eds. The Best of Shaker Cooking. LC 92-30875. 482p. 1993. reprint ed. pap. 12.00 (*0-02-035045-7*, Collier S&S) S&S Trade.

***Miller, Amy J.** The Pioneer Doctor in the Ozarks White River Country. rev. ed. (Illus.). 165p. 1994. pap. 15.80 (*0-9643894-0-1*) Delphi Assocs.

Miller, Andrea W., jt. auth. see Grant, Richard D., Jr.

Miller, Andrew, ed. Depressive Disorders & Immunity. LC 89-4. (Progress in Psychiatry Ser.). 187p. 1989. text ed. 23.95 (*0-88048-291-5*) Am Psychiatric.

— Don't Hang Up. LC 92-24845. (C). 1992. write for info. (*0-929925-20-3*) Univ SD Pr.

Miller, Andrew, jt. ed. see Lane, David A.

Miller, Andrew, et al. Rethinking Work Experience. 280p. 1991. 70.00 (*1-85000-895-7*, Falmer Pr); pap. 31.00 (*1-85000-896-5*, Falmer Pr) Taylor & Francis.

***Miller, Andrew B.** Church History Publishing Kit. 80p. 1994. ring bd. 25.00 (*1-881576-28-0*) Providence Hse.

***Miller, Andrew H.** Novels Behind Glass: Commodity Culture & Victorian Narrative. (Literature, Culture, Theory Ser.: No. 17). (Illus.). 232p. (C). 1995. write for info. (*0-521-47133-8*) Cambridge U Pr.

Miller, Andrew M. Plato: Ion. 2nd ed. 1984. pap. text ed. 6.00 (*0-929524-27-6*) Bryn Mawr Commentaries.

Miller, Angela. The Empire of the Eye: Landscape Representation & American Cultural Politics, 1825-1875. LC 92-37226. (Illus.). 320p. (C). 1993. 37.50 (*0-8014-2830-0*) Cornell U Pr.

Miller, Angela, jt. auth. see Norman, David.

Miller, Angelyn. The Enabler: When Helping Harms the Ones You Love. 128p. (Orig.). 1990. mass mkt. 4.95 (*0-345-36848-7*) Ballantine.

Miller, Anita, ed. Complete Transcripts of the Clarence Thomas-Anita Hill Hearings: October 11, 12, 13, 1991. 450p. 1994. pap. 22.95 (*0-89733-408-6*) Academy Chi Pubs.

Miller, Anita, ed. & intro. Four Classic Ghostly Tales. 250p. 1993. pap. 10.00 (*0-89733-398-5*) Academy Chi Pubs.

Miller, Anita & Greenberg, Hazel, eds. The Equal Rights Amendment: A Bibliographic Study. LC 76-24999. xxvii, 367p. 1976. text ed. 79.50 (*0-8371-9058-4*, ERA/, Greenwood Pr) Greenwood.

Miller, Anita, tr. see Haasse, Hella S.

Miller, Anita, ed. see Haasse, Hella S.

Miller, Anita, tr. see Haasse, Hella.

Miller, Anita, ed. see Hare, Augustus.

Miller, Anita, jt. auth. see Weimann, Jeanne M.

Miller, Ann, ed. see Johnson, Patricia M.

Miller, Ann K. Engineering Quality Software: Defect Detection & Prevention. LC 92-16345. 1992. pap. write for info. (*0-201-63432-5*) Addison-Wesley.

Miller, Ann L. Antebellum Orange. (Illus.). 200p. 1988. 27.50 (*0-943522-14-5*) Moss Pubns VA.

Miller, Ann R., et al, eds. Work, Jobs, & Occupations: A Critical Review of the Dictionary of Occupational Titles. LC 80-24653. 455p. reprint ed. pap. 129.70 (*0-7837-1639-7*, 2041932) Bks Demand.

Miller, Anna M. The Buyer's Guide to Affordable Antique Jewelry: How to Find, Buy, & Care for Fabulous Antique Jewelry. LC 92-37557. 1993. 9.95 (*0-8065-1411-6*) Carol Pub Group.

— Cameos Old & New. LC 90-47269. (Illus.). 168p. 1991. text ed. 42.95 (*0-442-00278-5*) Chapman & Hall.

— Gems & Jewelry Appraising: Techniques of Professional Practice. (Illus.). 208p. 1988. text ed. 42.95 (*0-442-26467-4*) Chapman & Hall.

— Illustrated Guide to Jewelry Appraising. 1989. text ed. 42.95 (*0-442-31944-4*) Chapman & Hall.

— Illustrated Guide to Jewelry Appraising: Antique, Period & Modern. 1994. 47.50 (*0-412-98931-X*, Blackie & Son-Chapman NY) Routledge Chapman & Hall.

Miller, Anna M. & Sinkankas, John. Standard Catalog of Gem Values. 2nd ed. (Illus.). 288p. 1994. pap. 24.00 (*0-945005-16-4*) Geoscience Pr.

Miller, Anne, jt. auth. see Heynes, Michael.

Miller, Anne, jt. auth. see Madden, T. O., Jr.

Miller, Anne, jt. auth. see Mair, Douglas.

Miller, Anne I. Independent Theatre in Europe, Eighteen Eighty-Seven to the Present. LC 65-27914. 1972. 30.95 (*0-405-08790-X*, Pub. by Blom Pubns UK) Ayer.

Miller, Anneliese H. A Calendar of Memories. 1991. 15.95 (*0-533-09601-4*) Vantage.

Miller, Anthony B., jt. ed. see Chamberlain, Jocelyn.

Miller, Anthony R. Pupil Transportation Management: School Bus Operations, Personnel Management for Transportation Managers & Supervisors. LC 88-61377. 210p. (Orig.). (C). 1988. pap. text ed. 15.75 (*0-929298-00-4*) Ramsburg & Roth Pubs.

Miller, Ariel, jt. ed. see Cohen, Irun R.

***Miller, Arij & Miller, Simon.** The Indian Community of Colonial Mexico: Fifteen Essays on Land Tenure, Corporate Organizations, Ideology & Village Politics. (CEDLA Latin America Studies (CLAS): No. 58). 338p. 1990. pap. 32.00 (*90-70280-33-7*, Pub. by Thesis Pubs NE) IBD Ltd.

Miller, Arlene, jt. auth. see Shelly, Judith A.

Miller, Arlene D. What's What. Gilbert, Carol, ed. (Illus.). 21p. (Orig.). (J). (ps-6). 1985. pap. 4.00 (*0-9614209-0-1*) Adam Pub Co.

Miller, Arthur. After the Fall. 1964. pap. 4.75 (*0-8222-0010-4*) Dramatists Play.

— After the Fall. (Plays Ser.). 1980. pap. 7.95 (*0-14-048162-1*, Penguin Bks) Viking Penguin.

— The American Clock. 1981. pap. 4.75 (*0-8222-0027-9*) Dramatists Play.

— The American Clock & Archbishop's Ceiling. 176p. 1989. pap. 8.95 (*0-8021-3127-1*) Grove-Atltic.

— The Archbishop's Ceiling. 1985. pap. 4.75 (*0-8222-0064-3*) Dramatists Play.

— Broken Glass. 1995. pap. 4.75 (*0-8222-1413-X*) Dramatists Play.

— Broken Glass. 96p. 1994. pap. 7.95 (*0-14-048095-1*) Viking Penguin.

— Broken Glass & the Last Yankee: Two Plays by Arthur Miller. 192p. 1994. 9.99 (*1-56865-104-X*, GuildAmerica) Dblday Bk Music.

— Craniomandibular Muscles: Their Role in Function & Form. (Illus.). 256p. 1991. 121.00 (*0-8493-4873-0*, QP325) CRC Pr.

— The Creation of the World & Other Business. 1973. pap. 4.75 (*0-8222-0249-2*) Dramatists Play.

— Crucible. 1976. pap. 7.95 (*0-14-048138-9*, Penguin Bks) Viking Penguin.

— The Crucible. (Orig.). 1953. pap. 4.75 (*0-8222-0255-7*) Dramatists Play.

— The Crucible. 160p. (Orig.). 1994. pap. 64.95 (*0-14-024277-5*, Penguin Bks) Viking Penguin.

— The Crucible. 176p. 1995. 7.95 (*0-14-018964-5*, Penguin Classics) Viking Penguin.

— Crucible: Text & Criticism. Weales, Gerald, ed. LC 73-119776. (Viking Critical Library: No. 7). 1977. pap. text ed. 14.00 (*0-14-015507-4*, Viking) Viking Penguin.

— Danger: Memory! Two Plays: I Can't Remember Anything; Clara. LC 86-29402. 96p. 1987. pap. 5.95 (*0-8021-5176-0*) Grove-Atltic.

— Danger: Memory! I Can't Remember Anything, & Clara: Two Related One-Act Plays. 1987. pap. 4.75 (*0-8222-0268-9*) Dramatists Play.

— Death of a Salesman. 17.95 (*0-89190-729-7*, Am Repr) Amereon Ltd.

— Death of a Salesman. 1952. pap. 4.75 (*0-8222-0290-5*) Dramatists Play.

— Death of a Salesman. 1976. pap. 7.95 (*0-14-048134-6*, Penguin Bks) Viking Penguin.

— Death of a Salesman: Text & Criticism. Weales, Gerald, ed. (Viking Critical Library: No. 2). 1977. pap. text ed. 13.95 (*0-14-015502-3*, Viking) Viking Penguin.

— Elegy for a Lady. 1982. pap. 2.75 (*0-8222-0356-1*) Dramatists Play.

— Everybody Wins. 144p. 1990. pap. 7.95 (*0-8021-3200-6*) Grove-Atltic.

— Homely Girl, a Life, 2 vols., Set. (Illus.). 1992. 125.00 (*0-935875-10-7*) P Blum Edit.

— Homely Girl, a Life: And Other Stories. LC 95-14267. 96p. 1995. 12.95 (*0-670-86541-9*, Viking) Viking Penguin.

— Incident at Vichy. 1966. pap. 4.75 (*0-8222-0564-5*) Dramatists Play.

— Incident at Vichy. (Plays Ser.). 80p. 1985. pap. 8.00 (*0-14-048193-1*, Penguin Bks) Viking Penguin.

— The Last Yankee. 96p. (Orig.). 1994. pap. 7.50 (*0-14-048151-6*, Penguin Bks) Viking Penguin.

— The Last Yankee - Full Length. 1993. 4.75 (*0-8222-1337-0*) Dramatists Play.

— The Last Yankee - One Act. 1991. pap. 2.75 (*0-8222-0641-2*) Dramatists Play.

— Monarch Death of a Salesman. 1976. pap. 3.95 (*0-671-00688-6*) S&S Trade.

— The Obedience Experiments: A Case Study of Controversy in Social Science. LC 85-25723. 305p. 1986. text ed. 59.95 (*0-275-92012-7*, C2012, Praeger Pubs) Greenwood.

— People, Products & Progress: The Durametallic Story. (Illus.). 256p. 1992. 24.95 (*0-9626408-6-7*) Priscilla Pr.

— Playing for Time. 1985. 5.45 (*0-87129-267-X*, P59) Dramatic Pub.

— The Price. 1969. pap. 4.75 (*0-8222-0911-X*) Dramatists Play.

— The Price. (Plays Ser.). 128p. 1985. mass mkt. 7.95 (*0-14-048194-X*, Penguin Bks) Viking Penguin.

— The Price: A Play. LC 68-14982. 119p. 1968. 14.95 (*0-910278-38-5*) Boulevard.

— The Ride Down Mount Morgan. 96p. (Orig.). 1992. pap. 7.00 (*0-14-048236-9*, Penguin Bks) Viking Penguin.

— The Ride Down Mt. Morgan. deluxe limited ed. 1992. 80.00 (*0-89366-237-2*) Ultramarine Pub.

— Some Kind of Love Story. 1983. pap. 2.75 (*0-8222-1053-3*) Dramatists Play.

— Spain. (Places & Peoples of the World Ser.). (Illus.). 112p. (J). (gr. 5 up). 1989. lib. bdg. 14.95 (*1-55546-795-4*) Chelsea Hse.

— A View from the Bridge. 1956. pap. 4.75 (*0-8222-1209-9*) Dramatists Play.

— A View from the Bridge. (Plays Ser.). 1977. mass mkt. 7.95 (*0-14-048135-4*, Penguin Bks) Viking Penguin.

Miller, Arthur, jt. auth. see Bate, Michele.

Miller, Arthur, jt. auth. see Friedanthal, Jack.

Miller, Arthur, ed. see Ibsen, Henrik.

Miller, Arthur, jt. auth. see Miller, Warren.

Miller, Arthur, jt. auth. see Nesbit, Robert.

Miller, Arthur, et al. The Misfits: An Original Screenplay, Directed by John Huston. Garrett, George P. et al, eds. LC 71-135273. (Film Scripts Ser.). (Illus.). 1989. pap. 19.95 (*0-89197-850-X*) Irvington.

— Poetry & Film: Two Symposiums. 1973. pap. 3.50 (*0-910664-24-2*) Gotham.

Miller, Arthur F. & Mattson, Ralph T. The Truth about You. 1989. pap. 11.95 (*0-89815-194-5*) Ten Speed Pr.

Miller, Arthur G. Maya Rulers of Time: A Study of Architectural Sculpture at Tikal, Guatemala. LC 86-7010. (Illus.). 96p. reprint ed. pap. 27.40 (*0-685-24018-5*, 2031611) Bks Demand.

— The Mural Painting of Teotihuacan. LC 72-97208. (Illus.). 193p. 1973. 35.00 (*0-88402-049-5*) Dumbarton Oaks.

— On the Edge of the Sea: Mural Painting at Tancah-Tulum, Quintana Roo, Mexico. LC 81-15278. (Illus.). 164p. 1982. 35.00 (*0-88402-105-X*) Dumbarton Oaks.

— The Painted Tombs of Oaxaca, Mexico: Living with the Dead. LC 94-23474. (RES Monographs on Antropology & Aesthetics). 1995. write for info. (*0-521-45110-8*) Cambridge U Pr.

Miller, Arthur G., ed. In the Eye of the Beholder: Contemporary Issues in Stereotyping. LC 81-11849. 542p. 1982. text ed. 49.95 (*0-275-90861-5*, C0861, Praeger Pubs) Greenwood.

Miller, Arthur H. Presidential Campaigning & America's Self Images. LC 94-27733. 300p. 1994. text ed. 55.00 (*0-8133-1885-8*) Westview.

***Miller, Arthur H. & Gronbeck, Bruce E., eds.** Presidential Campaigning & America's Self Images. LC 94-27733. (C). 1994. pap. text ed. 19.95 (*0-8133-8899-6*) Westview.

Miller, Arthur H., et al, eds. Public Opinion & Regime Change: The New Politics of Post-Soviet Societies. 310p. (C). 1992. pap. text ed. 50.00 (*0-8133-1503-4*) Westview.

Miller, Arthur I. Early Quantum Electrodynamics: A Sourcebook. 320p. (C). 1994. 59.95 (*0-521-43169-7*) Cambridge U Pr.

— Frontiers of Physics: Nineteen Hundred to Nineteen Eleven Selected Essays. 316p. 1986. lib. bdg. 57.50 (*0-8176-3203-4*) Birkhauser.

— Imagery in Scientific Thought: Creating 20th-Century Physics. 320p. 1984. 34.50 (*0-8176-3196-8*) Birkhauser.

Miller, Arthur K. The Cephalopods of the Bighorn Formation of the Wind River Mountains of Wyoming. (Connecticut Academy of Arts & Sciences Ser., Trans.: Vol. 31). 1932. pap. 100.00 (*0-685-44358-2*) Elliots Bks.

Miller, Arthur P., Jr. Park Ranger Guide to Wildlife. LC 89-39934. (Park Ranger Guides Ser.: Bk. 1). (Illus.). 224p. (Orig.). 1990. pap. 12.95 (*0-8117-2289-9*) Stackpole.

Miller, Arthur P., Jr. & Miller, Marjorie L. Park Ranger Guide to Rivers & Lakes: What to See & Learn on America's Freshwaters. LC 90-10291. (Park Ranger Guides Ser.). (Illus.). 224p. (Orig.). 1991. pap. 10.95 (*0-8117-3038-7*) Stackpole.

— Park Ranger Guide to Seashores: Discover Sea Life along the Coasts' Marshes, Bays, & Beaches. LC 91-34258. (Park Ranger Guides Ser.). (Illus.). 240p. 1992. pap. 12.95 (*0-8117-3039-5*) Stackpole.

Miller, Arthur R. & Davis, Michael H. Intellectual Property, Patents, Trademarks & Copyright in a Nutshell. 2nd ed. (Nutshell Ser.). 437p. 1990. pap. text ed. 17.00 (*0-314-75738-4*) West Pub.

Miller, Arthur R. & Gossman, Thomas L. Business Law: Text with Cases. (C). 1989. text ed. 66.50 (*0-673-38413-6*) HarpCollege.

Miller, Arthur R., jt. auth. see Wright, Charles A.

Miller, Arthur S. A Capacity for Outrage: The Judicial Odyssey of J. Skelly Wright. LC 83-22761. (Contributions in American Studies: No. 74). (Illus.). xiv, 242p. 1984. text ed. 59.95 (*0-313-23304-7*, MSW/, Greenwood Pr) Greenwood.

— Corporations & Society: Power & Responsibility. Samuels, Warren J., ed. LC 86-19451. (Contributions in American Studies: No. 88). 343p. 1987. text ed. 69.50 (*0-313-25072-3*, SCI/, Greenwood Pr) Greenwood.

— Democratic Dictatorship: The Emergent Constitution of Control. LC 80-25424. (Contributions in American Studies: No. 54). xvi, 268p. 1981. text ed. 55.00 (*0-313-22836-1*, MDD/, Greenwood Pr) Greenwood.

— The Modern Corporate State: Private Governments & the American Constitution. LC 75-35350. (Contributions in American Studies: No. 23). 269p. 1976. text ed. 45.00 (*0-8371-8589-0*, MCS/, Greenwood Pr) Greenwood.

— Politics, Democracy & the Supreme Court: Essays on the Frontier of Constitutional Theory. LC 85-5604. (Contributions in American Studies: No. 83). viii, 368p. 1985. text ed. 65.00 (*0-313-24831-1*, MLP/, Greenwood Pr) Greenwood.

An Asterisk (*) at the beginning of an entry indicates that the title is appearing in BIP for the first time.

— The Secret Constitution & the Need for Constitutional Change. LC 87-235. (Contributions in American Studies: No. 90). 189p. 1987. text ed. 49.95 (0-313-25745-0, MCG/, Greenwood Pr) Greenwood.
— The Supreme Court: Myth & Reality. LC 77-91106. (Contributions in American Studies: No. 38). xvii, 288p. 1978. text ed. 55.00 (0-313-20046-7, MSC/, Greenwood Pr) Greenwood.
— Toward Increased Judicial Activism: The Political Role of the Supreme Court. LC 81-20201. (Contributions in American Studies: No. 59). xii, 355p. 1982. text ed. 39.95 (0-313-23305-5, MIO/, Greenwood Pr) Greenwood.
Miller, Arthur S., ed. On Courts & Democracy: Selected Nonjudicial Writings of J. Skelly Wright. LC 83-22810. (Contributions in American Studies: No. 75). xvi, 291p. 1984. text ed. 55.00 (0-313-23938-X, MDE/, Greenwood Pr) Greenwood.
Miller, Arthur S. & Bowman, Jeffrey H. Death by Installments: The Ordeal of Willie Francis. LC 88-3124. (Contributions in Legal Studies: No. 44). 189p. 1988. text ed. 49.95 (0-313-26009-5, MDN/, Greenwood Pr) Greenwood.
Miller, Arthur S. & Feinrider, Martin, eds. Nuclear Weapons & Law. LC 84-4482. (Contributions in Legal Studies: No. 31). (Illus.). xiii, 415p. 1984. text ed. 75.00 (0-313-24206-2, MNW/, Greenwood Pr) Greenwood.
Miller, Audrey. Writing Reaction Mechanisms in Organic Chemistry. (Illus.). 488p. 1992. pap. text ed. 42.50 (0-12-496711-6) Acad Pr.
Miller, B. Organic Chemistry: The Basis of Life. 1980. write for info. (0-8053-7071-4) Addison-Wesley.
Miller, B. D. Local Warning System Definition. LC 70-141214. 147p. 1970. 19.50 (0-403-04519-3) Scholarly.
Miller, B. J. Old Rags & Bones. 88p. 1994. pap. 9.95 (0-8059-3491-X) Dorrance.
Miller, Barbara. The Endangered Sex: Neglect of Female Children in Rural North India. LC 81-3226. (Illus.). 192p. 1981. 29.95 (0-8014-1371-0) Cornell U Pr.
Miller, Barbara & Yepa, Debra, eds. Masked Spirits: New Work from the Institute of American Indian Arts. (IAIA Anthology Ser.: No. 3). 72p. 1991. pap. 6.00 (1-881396-02-9) IOA Indian Arts.
Miller, Barbara, jt. auth. see Fitzgerald, Thomas.
Miller, Barbara, jt. auth. see Newman, Marsha.
Miller, Barbara D., ed. Sex & Gender Hierarchies. (Publications of the Society for Psychological Anthropology). (Illus.). 376p. (C). 1993. 74.95 (0-521-41297-8); pap. 22.95 (0-521-42368-6) Cambridge U Pr.
Miller, Barbara S. Bhagavad-Gita: Krishna's Counsel in Time of War. 1991. mass mkt. 9.00 (0-553-35340-3) Bantam.
— Gitagovinda of Jayadeva: Love Songs of the Dark Lord. (C). reprint ed. 11.50 (0-685-54515-6, Pub. by Motilal Banarsidass II) S Asia.
Miller, Barbara S., ed. Love Song of the Dark Lord: Jayadeva's Gitagovinda. LC 76-13165. (Translations from the Oriental Classics Ser.). 125p. 1977. pap. text ed. 14.50 (0-231-04029-6) Col U Pr.
— Masterworks of Asian Literature in Comparative Perspective: A Guide for Teaching. LC 93-24473. (Columbia Project on Asia in the Core Curriculum Ser.). 616p. (C). 1994. text ed. 65.00 (1-56324-257-5, East Gate Bk); pap. text ed. 22.50 (1-56324-258-3, East Gate Bk) M E Sharpe.
— The Powers of Art: Patronage in Indian Culture. (Illus.). 340p. 1992. 16.95 (0-19-562842-X) OUP.
Miller, Barbara S., tr. The Bhagavad-Gita: Krishna's Counsel in Time of War. LC 86-13725. (Illus.). 176p. 1986. text ed. 28.00 (0-231-06468-3) Col U Pr.
Miller, Barbara S., tr. & intro. The Bhagavad-Gita. 176p. (Orig.). 1986. mass mkt. 4.50 (0-553-21365-2, Bantam Classics) Bantam.
Miller, Barbara S., tr. Phantasies of a Love-Thief: The Caurapancasika Attributed to Bilhana. LC 77-122947. (Studies in Oriental Culture: No. 6). 233p. 1971. text ed. 41.00 (0-231-03451-2) Col U Pr.
Miller, Barbara S., tr. see Bhartrihari & Bilhana.
Miller, Barbara S., jt. auth. see Gordon, Leonard A.
Miller, Barbara S., ed. see Kramrisch, Stella.
Miller, Barbara S., et al, eds. The Theater of Memory: Three Plays of Kalidasa. LC 83-26362. (Translations from the Oriental Classics Ser.). 384p. (Orig.). 1984. text ed. 53.00 (0-231-05838-1); pap. text ed. 19.50 (0-231-05839-X) Col U Pr.
Miller, Barnett. The Palace School of Muhammad the Conqueror. LC 73-6291. (Middle East Ser.). 1973. reprint ed. 20.95 (0-405-05349-5) Ayer.
Miller, Barnette. Beyond the Sublime Porte. LC 79-111774. reprint ed. 62.50 (0-404-04329-1) AMS Pr.
Miller, Barry. From Existence to God: A Contemporary Philosophical Argument. 224p. 1992. 42.50 (0-415-07006-6, A6527) Routledge.
Miller, Barry E. & Miller, Donald E. How to Interpret Financial Statements for Better Business Decisions. LC 90-55206. 352p. 1990. 59.95 (0-8144-5940-4) AMACOM.
Miller, Barry I., jt. auth. see Miller, Kathryn S.
Miller, Basil. Charles G. Finney. LC 77-2813. 144p. 1969. pap. 4.99 (0-87123-061-5) Bethany Hse.
— Florence Nightingale. LC 87-71602. (Women of Faith Ser.). 128p. 1987. reprint ed. pap. 4.99 (0-87123-985-X) Bethany Hse.
— George Muller: Man of Faith. 160p. 1972. reprint ed. pap. 4.99 (0-87123-182-4) Bethany Hse.
— The Holy Spirit. 1990. reprint ed. pap. 6.99 (0-88019-259-3) Schmul Pub Co.
— John Wesley. (Men of Faith Ser.). 144p. 1969. reprint ed. pap. 4.99 (0-87123-272-3) Bethany Hse.
— Mary Slessor. LC 85-71477. 144p. 1985. reprint ed. pap. 4.99 (0-87123-849-7) Bethany Hse.
— William Carey. LC 85-71476. 154p. 1985. reprint ed. pap. 4.99 (0-87123-850-0) Bethany Hse.
Miller, Basil, comp. Beautiful Poems on Jesus. LC 68-58826. (Granger Index Reprint Ser.). 1977. 19.95 (0-8369-6029-7) Ayer.
***Miller, Beatrice.** Musically Mixed. 32p. 1995. pap. text ed. 5.95 (0-87487-746-6) Summy-Birchard.
Miller, Ben, ed. The Advanced Card & Identification Technology Sourcebook, 1994. 192p. (Orig.). 1993. pap. 125.00 (1-878413-02-3) Warfel & Miller.
Miller, Benjamin. IC "Smart" Card Industry Directory, 1990. (IC "Smart" Card Industry Directory Ser.: No. 4). (Illus.). 88p. (Orig.). 1990. pap. 65.00 (0-685-29785-3) Warfel & Miller.
— When Opponents Cooperate: Great Power Conflict & Collaboration in World Politics. 376p. 1994. text ed. 49.50x (0-472-10458-6) U of Mich Pr.
Miller, Benjamin, jt. auth. see Hartstein, Jacob I.
***Miller, Benjamin F.** Encyclopedia & Dictionary of Medicine, Nursing & Allied Health. 5th ed. 1992. 18.70 (0-7216-3456-7) Saunders.
— Poems: Partly Medical. (Countway Library Associates Historical Publication: No. 4). 85p. 1978. 9.95 (0-686-23786-2) F A Countway.
Miller, Benjamin L. Biometric Industry Directory, 1990. 5th ed. (Illus.). 90p. 1990. pap. 65.00 (1-878413-00-7) Warfel & Miller.
— Smart Card Industry Directory, 1990. 4th ed. (Illus.). 100p. 1990. pap. 65.00 (1-878413-01-5) Warfel & Miller.
Miller, Benjamin S. Ranch Life in Southern Kansas & the Indian Territory, As Told by a Novice: How a Fortune Was Made in Cattle. LC 75-111. (Mid-American Frontier Ser.). 1975. reprint ed. 19.95 (0-405-06878-6) Ayer.
Miller, Benjamin S. & Singewald, Joseph T. The Deposits of South America. Wilkins, Mira, ed. LC 76-29758. (European Business Ser.). (Illus.). 1977. reprint ed. lib. bdg. 51.95 (0-405-09773-5) Ayer.
Miller, Berkeley & Canak, William. New Labor, New Laws: Public Sector Collective Bargaining Laws. 200p. (C). 1996. text ed. 35.00 (0-8133-0689-2) Westview.
Miller, Bernard. Thermal Analysis: Proceedings of the Seventh International Conference on Thermal Analysis, 2 vols. 1530p. 1982. text ed. 230.00 (0-471-26243-9) Wiley.
Miller, Bernard, ed. see International Conference on Thermal Analysis Staff.
Miller, Bert. Mathematics for Business. (Illus.). 294p. 1986. teacher ed 12.99 (0-86601-545-9); student ed 4.99 (0-86601-546-9); text ed. 18.49 (0-86601-544-2) Media Materials.
Miller, Bert & Rogers, Chris. Plain Talk about Money. (Illus.). 111p. 1989. text ed. 15.95 (0-9607256-6-0) Rich Pub Co.
Miller, Bertha M. & Field, Elinor W., eds. Newbery Medal Books, 1922-1955. LC 55-13968. (Illus.). 458p. 1955. 22.95 (0-87675-396-9) Horn Bk.
Miller, Bertha M., et al, eds. Illustrators of Children's Books: 1946-1956, Vol. 2. LC 57-31264. (Illus.). 229p. 1958. 28.95 (0-87675-016-1) Horn Bk.
Miller, Bessie M. Legal Secretary's Complete Handbook. 3rd ed. (Illus.). 1986. 27.95 (0-13-528562-3, Busn) P-H.
Miller, Bessie M., jt. auth. see Doris, Lillian.
Miller, Beth, ed. Women in Hispanic Literature: Icons & Fallen Idols. LC 81-14663. 480p. 1983. 45.00 (0-520-04291-3); pap. 14.00 (0-520-04367-7) U CA Pr.
Miller, Beth A. Emma: A Story of Need. LC 90-71983. 211p. 1992. pap. 10.00 (1-56002-043-1) Aegina Pr.
Miller, Beth A., ed. see Grind, Chance E.
Miller, Bette L. & Wilmshurst, Ann L. Parents As Volunteers in the Classroom. 2nd rev. ed. LC 75-21027. (Illus.). 100p. 1984. spiral bd. 14.95 (0-88247-728-5) R & E Pubs.
Miller, Betty. The Amish in Switzerland & Other European Countries. 1978. pap. 1.50 (0-685-46025-8) O R Miller.
— Amish Pioneers of the Walnut Creek Valley. 1978. pap. 2.50 (0-685-87375-7) O R Miller.
— Exposing Satan's Devices. (Overcoming Life Ser.). 104p. 1991. pap. 5.00 (1-57149-008-6) Christ Unltd.
— Exposing Satan's Devices Workbook. (Overcoming Life Ser.). 213p. 1993. pap. 10.00 (1-57149-009-4) Christ Unltd.
— Extremes or Balances? (Overcoming Life Ser.). 52p. 1994. pap. 5.00 (1-57149-014-0) Christ Unltd.
— Extremes or Balances Workbook. (Overcoming Life Ser.). 1995. pap. 10.00 (1-57149-015-9) Christ Unltd.
— Healing of the Spirit, Soul & Body. (Overcoming Life Ser.). 60p. 1994. pap. 5.00 (1-57149-010-8) Christ Unltd.
— Healing of the Spirit, Soul & Body Workbook. (Overcoming Life Ser.). 1995. pap. 10.00 (1-57149-011-6) Christ Unltd.
— Keys to the Kingdom. (Overcoming Life Ser.). 56p. 1994. pap. 5.00 (1-57149-006-X) Christ Unltd.
— Keys to the Kingdom Workbook. (Overcoming Life Ser.). 1995. pap. 10.00 (1-57149-007-8) Christ Unltd.
— Mark of God or Mark of the Beast. (End Times Ser.). 112p. 1991. pap. 5.00 (1-57149-019-1) Christ Unltd.
— Neither Male Nor Female. (Overcoming Life Ser.). 70p. 1994. pap. 5.00 (1-57149-012-4) Christ Unltd.
— Neither Male Nor Female Workbook. (Overcoming Life Ser.). 1995. pap. 10.00 (1-57149-013-2) Christ Unltd.
— The Pathway into the Overcomer's Walk. (Overcoming Life Ser.). 92p. 1994. pap. 5.00 (1-57149-016-7) Christ Unltd.
— The Pathway into the Overcomer's Walk Workbook. (Overcoming Life Ser.). 1995. pap. 10.00 (1-57149-017-5) Christ Unltd.
— Personal Spiritual Warfare. (End Times Ser.). 92p. 1991. pap. 5.00 (1-57149-018-3) Christ Unltd.
— Prove All Things. (Overcoming Life Ser.). 44p. 1994. pap. 5.00 (1-57149-000-0) Christ Unltd.
— Prove All Things Workbook. (Overcoming Life Ser.). 1995. pap. 10.00 (1-57149-001-9) Christ Unltd.
— Sign Language House. 32p. (J). 1984. 4.50 (0-915035-03-0, 4162) Dawn Sign.
— The True God. (Overcoming Life Ser.). 46p. 1994. pap. 5.00 (1-57149-002-7) Christ Unltd.
— The True God Workbook. (Overcoming Life Ser.). 1995. pap. 10.00 (1-57149-003-5) Christ Unltd.
— The Will of God. (Overcoming Life Ser.). 50p. 1994. pap. 5.00 (1-57149-004-3) Christ Unltd.
— The Will of God Workbook. (Overcoming Life Ser.). 1995. pap. 10.00 (1-57149-005-1) Christ Unltd.
Miller, Betty, jt. auth. see Thomas, Virginia.
Miller, Betty A. & Miller, Oscar R. Bixel Family History: Descendants of Abraham Bixel & Magdalena Schumacher, 1843-1984. (Illus.). 94p. 1984. pap. 7.50 (0-317-17479-7) O R Miller.
— Cornelius Jansen Family History, 1822-1973. (Illus.). 73p. 1974. pap. 4.50 (0-685-64818-4) O R Miller.
Miller, Betty D., jt. auth. see Miller, Kent.
Miller, Beverly, jt. auth. see Bradbury, Jim.
Miller, Beverly, ed. see Penson-Ward, Betty.
Miller, Bill. Alley Strewn Phrases. 56p. (Orig.). 1986. pap. 5.00 (0-940584-04-2) Gull Bks.
— Insiders Guide to Cruise Discounts. LC 89-20357. (Illus.). 127p. (Orig.). 1989. pap. 9.95 (0-9624019-1-9) Ticket Adventure.
— Sacramento, D. C. A Political Lampoon. LC 88-30886. 192p. 1988. 15.95 (0-929473-00-0); pap. 8.95 (0-317-91079-5) Erin Pr Inc.
— The Ways of Wisdom: Great Thoughts from Great Thinkers. 64p. 1992. pap. 4.95 (0-9630439-4-3) Bayrock.
***Miller, Bill & Caligiuri, Tony.** Modern Bird Hunting. LC 89-63989. (Hunter's Information Ser.). 328p. 1990. write for info. (0-914697-27-7) N Amer Outdoor Grp.
Miller, Bill, ed. see Burch, Monte.
Miller, Bill, jt. ed. see Cohn, Howard.
Miller, Bill, ed. see Helgeland, Glenn.
Miller, Bill, ed. see Lapinski, Mike, et al.
Miller, Bill, ed. see Miller, Mary F.
Miller, Bill, jt. ed. see Vail, Mike.
Miller, Bill R., jt. auth. see Pesti, Gene M.
Miller, Billie M. Soo Ling: The Story of the Silkworm. Luna, Rose Mary, tr. (Illus.). 12p. (ENG & SPA.). (J). 1991. 12.00 (1-878742-01-9); pap. 6.00 (1-878742-02-7) Kidship Assoc.
Miller, Bjorn & Wiberg, Hakan, eds. Non-Offensive Defence for the Twenty-First Century. LC 93-48369. (C). 1994. text ed. 52.50 (0-8133-2073-9) Westview.
***Miller, Blair.** American Silent Film Comedies: An Illustrated Encyclopedia of Persons, Studios & Terminology. 288p. 1995. lib. bdg. 42.50x (0-89950-929-0) McFarland & Co.
Miller, Bob. Conversations with God. 106p. (Orig.). 1992. pap. 5.95 (0-9634161-0-3) Vanquish Pubns.
— One Hundred Personal Effectiveness Traps & Their Solutions. Morgan, Jane, ed. (Illus.). 206p. (Orig.). 1987. pap. 15.00 (0-318-22780-0) Universal Lrn Ctr.
— One Thousand One Tips to Increase Your Effectiveness. Morgan, Jane, ed. 184p. (Orig.). 1987. pap. 20.00 (0-318-23120-4) Universal Lrn Ctr.
— One Thousand One Tips to Increased Effectiveness: PracticalTips Techniques & Ideas to Save You Time & Get More Done in Your Busy Day. Morgan, Jane, ed. 192p. (Orig.). 1987. pap. 20.00 (0-318-22828-9) Universal Lrn Ctr.
— Time Rides the River. Spelius, Carol & Spelius, Wayne, eds. 75p. 1993. 7.95 (0-941363-27-9) Lake Shore Pub.
— You Have My Word on It. Allen, Kathleen, ed. (Illus.). 100p. (Orig.). 1995. pap. 5.95 (0-9634161-1-1) Vanquish Pubns.
Miller, Bob & Miller, Sue. Amish Country Cookbook. (Illus.). 296p. (Orig.). 1981. pap. 11.99 (0-934998-00-0) Bethel Pub.
— The Amish-Country Cookbook, Vol. 2. 320p. 1986. spiral bd. 11.99 (0-934998-23-X) Bethel Pub.
— Amish Country Cookbook, Vol. 3. 320p. (Orig.). 1993. spiral bd., pap. 11.99 (0-934998-49-3) Bethel Pub.
Miller, Bob W. Higher Education & the Community College. 2nd ed. LC 84-5277. (Illus.). 298p. 1984. pap. text ed. 24.00 (0-8191-3973-4) U Pr of Amer.
Miller, Bob W., et al, eds. Leadership in Higher Education: A Handbook for Practicing Administrators. LC 82-15579. xxi, 585p. 1983. text ed. 89.50 (0-313-22263-0, MHE/, Greenwood Pr) Greenwood.
Miller, Bonnie J., jt. auth. see Le Peau, Phyllis J.
Miller, Boyd. Copy Editing: Making Good Writing Better. 64p. 1992. pap. text ed. 5.95 (0-9615971-1-9) Wordpix Serv.
— Veteran's Return to a Battlefield: Where 29th Division Fought near Aachen. (Illus.). 36p. 1985. 4.00 (0-9615971-0-0) Wordpix Serv.
***Miller, Bradford.** A Man from Seneca Falls: A Personal Account of a Search Through Myth & History for What It Means to Be a White Man Today. (Elizabeth Cady Stanton, Frederick Douglass, & the Women's Rights Convention of 1848) 192p. (Orig.). 1995. pap. 17.95 (0-940262-68-1) Lindisfarne Pr.
Miller, Branda, jt. ed. see Irmas, Deborah.
***Miller, Brandon M.** Buffalo Gals: Women of the Old West. (Illus.). 88p. (YA). (gr. 5 up). 1995. lib. bdg. 18.95 (0-8225-1730-2) Lerner Group.
Miller, Brenda V. Heavenly Bread: Spiritual Food for Hungry Souls. 150p. 1995. pap. 7.95 (0-9635630-0-9) Global Promise.
Miller, Brent, jt. auth. see Duvall, Evelyn M.
Miller, Brent C. Family Research Methods. LC 86-964. (Family Studies Text Ser.: Vol. 4). (Illus.). 160p. (Orig.). (C). 1986. text ed. 37.00 (0-8039-2143-8); pap. text ed. 16.95 (0-8039-2144-6) Sage.
Miller, Brent C. & Olson, David H., eds. Family Studies Review Yearbook, Vol. 3. LC 83-643783. (Illus.). 616p. reprint ed. pap. 175.60 (0-7837-1128-X, 2041658) Bks Demand.
Miller, Brent C., et al, eds. Preventing Adolescent Pregnancy: Model Programs & Evaluations. (Focus Editions Ser.: Vol. 140). (Illus.). 304p. 1992. 49.95 (0-8039-4390-3); pap. 24.95 (0-8039-4391-1) Sage.
Miller, Brian J. South Wales Railways at the Grouping. 96p. (C). 1989. 75.00 (0-905928-55-5, Pub. by D Brown & Sons Ltd UK) St Mut.
Miller, Brown. Water & Shadows. 1969. pap. 6.00 (0-912136-15-4) Twowindows Pr.
***Miller, Bruce, photos.** Albert Paley: Organic Logic. LC 94-65751. (Illus.). 60p. (Orig.). 1994. pap. text ed. 25.00 (1-881658-10-4) P J Gallery.
***Miller, Bruce A.** Children at the Center: Implementing the Multiage Classroom. LC 94-34054. xii, 123p. 1994. 15.95 (0-86552-130-1) U of Oreg ERIC.
Miller, Bruce E. The Arts & the Basis of Education. 134p. (Orig.). (C). 1993. lib. bdg. 39.50 (0-8191-9127-2); pap. text ed. 17.50 (0-8191-9128-0) U Pr of Amer.
Miller, Bruce J., jt. ed. see Anderson-Miller, Julia.
Miller, Bruce K., jt. auth. see Wolf, Arthur D.
Miller, Bruce W., III. Chumash: A Picture of Their World. (Illus.). 136p. (Orig.). 1988. pap. 8.95 (0-944627-51-X) Sand River Pr.
— The Gabrielino: A Southern California Indian Tribe. 132p. (Orig.). 1991. pap. 7.95 (0-944627-90-0) Sand River Pr.
Miller, Bruce W. & Widess, Jim. The Caner's Handbook: A Descriptive Guide...for Restoring Cane...Furniture. LC 91-60690. (Illus.). 148p. 1991. pap. 18.95 (0-937274-60-7) Lark Books.
— The Caner's Handbook: A Descriptive Guide...for Restoring Cane...Furniture. LC 91-60690. 143p. 1991. reprint ed. lib. bdg. 45.00x (0-8095-7611-2) Borgo Pr.
Miller, Bruce W., jt. auth. see Weis, William L.
Miller, Bryan. The New York Times Guide to Restaurants in New York City. LC 86-5896. 448p. 1987. pap. 12.95 (0-8129-1313-2, Times Bks) Random.
— The New York Times Guide to Restaurants in New York City. rev. ed. (Illus.). 448p. 1988. pap. 12.95 (0-8129-1735-9, Times Bks) Random.
— New York Times Guide to Restaurants in New York City: 1993-1994. 1992. pap. 15.00 (0-8129-1859-2, Times Bks) Random.
— New York Times Guide to Restaurants in New York City, 1993-94. 1992. pap. 15.00 (0-8129-2089-9, Times Bks) Random.
Miller, Bryan, jt. auth. see Franey, Pierre.
Miller, Bryane K. Dignified Departure: A Complete National Outline for Preparing All Necessary Documents to Control Your Death or That of a Loved One. Elletro Productions Staff, ed. LC 93-7541. 225p. (Orig.). 1993. pap. 11.95 (1-56875-059-5) R & E Pubs.
Miller, Burnett, jt. auth. see Zimmer, William.
Miller-Busschau, Kristin. Flirting with Frypans: Cook Book for Men. (Illus.). (C). 1993. pap. text ed. 14.95 (1-881116-21-2) Black Forrest Pr.
Miller, Butch & Smith, Steve. Short Track Driving Techniques. (Illus.). 80p. (Orig.). 1991. pap. text ed. 10.95 (0-936834-65-X) S S Autosports.
Miller, Buzz & Marriett, Jane. Not for Love Alone: Labanotation Score. (Educational Performance Collection). 80p. 1986. pap. write for info. (0-932582-50-8) Dance Notation.
Miller, Byron, ed. see Schwalbe, Donna.
Miller, Byron E. Object Oriented Design Made Easy! LC 93-78275. (Illus.). 1993. pap. 19.95 (0-9636637-6-3) Impatience Pubns.
Miller, C. Clinical Epidemiology & Biostatistics. (National Medical Ser.). 340p. 1992. 24.00 (0-683-06206-9) Williams & Wilkins.
Miller, C. & Parks, J. E., eds. Resonance Ionization Spectroscopy, 1992: Proceedings of the 6th International Symposium on Resonance Ionization Spectroscopy & Its Applications, Santa Fe, New Mexico, 24-29 May 1992. (Institute of Physics Conference Ser.: No. 128). (Illus.). 376p. 1992. 150.00 (0-7503-0230-5) IOP Pub.
Miller, C., jt. ed. see Juhasz, S.
Miller, C., jt. auth. see Miller, H.
Miller, C., jt. ed. see Rea, G.
Miller, C. Arden. Maternal Health & Infant Survival. 2nd ed. LC 91-62010. 52p. 1991. reprint ed. pap. text ed. 7.50 (0-943657-14-8) Zero To Three.
Miller, C. Arden & Moos, Merry-K., eds. Local Health Departments: Fifteen Case Studies. LC 81-68703. 528p. 1981. 12.00 (0-87553-094-X, 061) Am Pub Health.
Miller, C. Arden, jt. auth. see Williams, Bret C.
Miller, C. Arden, et al. Monitoring Children's Health: Key Indicators. 2nd ed. 176p. 1989. 17.50 (0-87553-162-8) Am Pub Health.
***Miller, C. C.** The Adventures of the Streetsboro Bear. (Illus.). 47p. (Orig.). (J). 1995. pap. 9.95 (0-9645652-0-X) Bright Side Bks.
— Fifty Years among the Bees. (Illus.). 328p. 1980. reprint ed. pap. 8.95 (0-931308-05-4) Molly Yes.
Miller, C. D. Food Values of Poi, Taro, & Limu. (BMB Ser.: No. 37). 1969. reprint ed. pap. 15.00 (0-527-02140-7) Periodicals Srv.
Miller, C. D. & White, David. EMT Basic National Standards Review Self Test. 208p. 1992. pap. text ed. write for info. (0-318-68768-2) P-H.
Miller, C. Eugene & Steinlage, Forrest F. Der Turner Soldat: A Turner Soldier in the Civil War; Germany to Antietam. LC 88-70880. (Illus.). 135p. 1988. 13.95 (0-9620368-0-3) Calmar Pubns.
Miller, C. J. Contempt of Court. 2nd ed. (Illus.). 552p. 1991. reprint ed. pap. 45.00 (0-19-825684-1) OUP.

An Asterisk (*) at the beginning of an entry indicates that the title is appearing in BIP for the first time.

— Miller Product Liability & Safety Encyclopedia, 2 binders, Set. U.K. ring bd. 390.00 (*0-406-29629-4*, UK) Butterworth Legal Pubs.

Miller, C. J. & Harvey, Brian W. Consumer & Trading Law - Cases & Materials. 1985. 100.00 (*0-406-01260-1*); pap. 62.00 (*0-406-01261-X*, U.K.) Butterworth Legal Pubs.

Miller, C. John. Outgrowing the Ingrown Church. 176p. 1986. pap. 10.99 (*0-310-28411-2*, 12815P) Zondervan.

— Repentance & Twentieth Century Man. (Orig.). 1993. pap. 4.95 (*0-87508-334-X*) Chr Lit.

***Miller, C. L.** Jewel Tea: Sales & Houseware Collectibles. (Illus.). 280p. 1995. 49.95 (*0-88740-898-2*) Schiffer.

— The Jewel Tea Company: Its History & Products. LC 94-65854. (Illus.). 288p. 1994. 39.95 (*0-88740-634-3*) Schiffer.

Miller, C. L., ed. Eet Smakelijk, 12 Bks. 2nd ed. (Illus.). 589p. 1976. 108.00 (*0-9612710-0-0*) Holland Jr Welfare.

Miller, C. William. Benjamin Franklin's Philadelphia Printing: A Descriptive Bibliography. LC 72-83464. (Memoirs Ser.: Vol. 102). 1974. 50.00 (*0-87169-102-7*, M102-MIC) Am Philos.

Miller, Calvin. Apples, Snakes & Bellyaches. 1990. write for info. (*0-8499-0690-3*) Word Inc.

— Apples, Snakes & Bellyaches. (J). (gr. 4-7). 1993. pap. 10.99 (*0-8499-3526-1*) Word Inc.

— A Covenant for All Seasons: The Marriage Journey. LC 95-7593. 192p. 1995. 14.99 (*0-87788-386-6*) Shaw Pubs.

— The Empowered Communicator: Seven Keys to Unlocking an Audience. LC 94-1951. 1994. 17.99 (*0-8054-1144-5*) Broadman.

— The Empowered Leader: Ten Keys to Staying on Top in the Church. LC 94-12752. 1996. 17.99 (*0-8054-1145-3*) Broadman.

— Guardians of the Singreale. rev. ed. LC 93-44479. (Singreale Chronicles Ser.). 240p. (Orig.). 1994. reprint ed. pap. 9.99 (*0-89107-773-1*) Crossway Bks.

— Marketplace Preaching: How to Return the Sermon to Where It Belongs. LC 94-32754. 192p. (Orig.). 1995. pap. 12.99 (*0-8010-6320-5*) Baker Bk.

— Once upon a Tree. 160p. 1991. 13.99 (*0-8010-6050-8*) Baker Bk.

— The Philippian Fragment. Kam, May C., tr. 139p. (CHI.). 1985. pap. 5.00 (*1-56582-080-0*) Christ Renew Min.

— Requiem for Love. 1989. write for info. (*0-8499-0687-3*) Word Inc.

— Sed de Significado: Thirst for Meaning. (SPA.). 3.25 (*84-7228-195-7*, 220813, Pub. by Edit Clie SP) TSELF.

— Servidumbre del Yoga: Transcendental Hesitation. (SPA.). 5.50 (*84-7228-544-8*, 220812, Pub. by Edit Clie SP) TSELF.

— The Singer. LC 74-20097. 152p. (Orig.). 1975. pap. 8.99 (*0-87784-639-1*, 639) InterVarsity.

— The Singer Trilogy. (Illus.). 496p. reprint ed. pap. 16.99 (*0-8308-1321-7*, 1321) InterVarsity.

— Spirit, Word & Story. 246p. 1989. write for info. (*0-8499-0691-1*) Word Inc.

— The Star Riders of Ren. rev. ed. LC 93-45810. (Singreale Chronicles Ser.). 256p. 1994. reprint ed. pap. 9.99 (*0-89107-774-X*) Crossway Bks.

— Symphony in Sand. 1990. 12.99 (*0-8499-0688-1*) Word Inc.

— The Table of Inwardness. LC 84-9134. 120p. (Orig.). 1984. pap. 7.99 (*0-87784-832-7*, 832) InterVarsity.

— Walking with the Angels: The Valiant Papers & the Philippian Fragment. LC 94-7402. (Illus.). 222p. 1994. reprint ed. 15.99 (*0-8010-6308-6*) Baker Bk.

— War of the Moonrhymes. rev. ed. (Singreale Chronicles Ser.). 240p. (Orig.). 1994. reprint ed. pap. 9.99 (*0-89107-775-8*) Crossway Bks.

— When the Aardvark Parked on the Ark, & Other Poems. LC 95-13082. (Illus.). (J). 1995. write for info. (*0-8499-3699-3*) Word Pub.

Miller, Calvin C. Boris Yeltsin: First President of Russia. LC 94-16562. (Champions of Freedom Ser.). (Illus.). 190p. (YA). (gr. 6 up). 1995. 18.95 (*1-883846-08-0*) M Reynolds.

Miller, Calvin M., et al. Optical Fiber Splices & Connectors: Theory & Methods. LC 86-1439. (Optical Engineering Ser.: No. 10). (Illus.). 440p. reprint ed. pap. 125.40 (*0-7837-4424-2*, 2052484) Bks Demand.

***Miller, Cameron & Falla, Dominique.** Woodlore. LC 94-27987. (J). 1995. 14.95 (*0-395-72034-6*) Ticknor & Flds Bks Yng Read.

Miller, Carey D., et al. Fruits of Hawaii: Description, Nutritive Value, & Recipes. 4th ed. 1976. pap. 7.95 (*0-8248-0448-1*) UH Pr.

***Miller, Carl.** Stages of Desire: Male & Female Homosexuality in British & American Theatre. (Lesbian & Gay Studies). 256p. 1995. 60.00 (*0-304-32815-4*) Cassell.

Miller, Carl V., jt. auth. see Ehlen-Miller, Margaret.

***Miller, Carlos.** Belize. 450p. Date not set. pap. 12.95 (*0-7610-0223-5*) NW Pub.

Miller, Carman. Painting the Map Red: Canada & the South African War, 1899-1902. 592p. 1992. 47.95 (*0-7735-0913-5*, Pub. by McGill CN) U of Toronto Pr.

Miller, Carol. What Students Can Tell Us about the Multicultural Classroom. Bridwell-Bowles, Lillian & Batchelder, Susan, eds. (Technical Report Ser.: No. 1). 7p. (Orig.). (C). 1992. pap. 2.00 (*1-881221-04-0*) U Minn Ctr Interdis.

Miller, Carol & Rivera, Guadalupe. The Winged Prophet from Hermes to Quetzalcoatl: An Introduction to the Mesoamerican Deities Through the Tarot. (Illus.). 448p. (Orig.). 1994. pap. 17.95 (*0-87728-799-6*) Weiser.

Miller, Carol, jt. auth. see Evans, Carolyn.

Miller, Carol, jt. auth. see Wirtshafter, Donald.

Miller, Carol, et al. Laboratory Manual for Concepts of Physical Activity. 5th ed. 112p. 1992. spiral bd. 9.95 (*0-8403-7556-5*) Kendall-Hunt.

— Laboratory Manual for Concepts of Physical Activity. 6th ed. 112p. (C). 1994. pap. text ed., spiral bd. 10.36 (*0-8403-9559-0*) Kendall-Hunt.

Miller, Carol A. Nursing Care for Older Adults: Theory & Practice. 2nd ed. LC 94-10140. 1994. write for info. (*0-397-55086-3*) Lippincott.

Miller, Carol E. Disciples of Jesus, Beginner-Primary Teacher. 1984. pap. 2.25 (*0-915374-47-1*) Rapids Christian.

— Teaching Junior High. 1980. pap. 2.95 (*0-915374-23-4*) Rapids Christian.

— Teaching Toddlers. 1971. pap. 2.95 (*0-915374-22-6*, 22-6) Rapids Christian.

— The Ten Commandments: Youth & Adult Student. 1971. pap. 1.00 (*0-915374-45-5*) Rapids Christian.

— Ten Commandments: Youth & Adult Teacher. 1991. 2.50 (*0-915374-37-4*) Rapids Christian.

— Under the Sun & in the Heavenlies: Youth & Adult Teacher. 1985. 2.00 (*0-915374-49-8*) Rapids Christian.

Miller, Carol J., ed. International Association of Logopaedics & Phoniatrics, 19th Congress, Edinburgh 1983: Abstracts. (Journal: Folia Phoniatrica: Vol. 35, No. 3-4). 96p. 1983. pap. 29.00 (*3-8055-3730-1*) S Karger.

Miller, Carol P. & Wheeler, Robert. Cleveland: A Concise History, 1796-1990. LC 89-24580. (Encyclopedia of Cleveland History Ser.). (Illus.). 208p. 1990. 29.95 (*0-253-33841-7*); pap. 10.95 (*0-253-20572-7*, MB-572) Ind U Pr.

Miller, Carole A., ed. see Seklemian, M.

Miller, Caroline. Lamb in His Bosom. 1991. lib. bdg. 21.95 (*1-56849-057-7*) Buccaneer Bks.

— Lamb in His Bosom. LC 92-38286. (Modern Southern Classics Ser.). 368p. 1993. 24.95 (*1-56145-074-X*); pap. 13.95 (*1-56145-075-8*) Peachtree Pubs.

Miller, Caroline, ed. see Krasner, A. M.

Miller, Caroline A. Bright Words for Dark Days: Meditations for Women Who Get the Blues. LC 94-15934. 1994. pap. 8.95 (*0-553-37181-9*) Bantam.

— My Name Is Caroline. Cohn, Leigh, ed. LC 87-19852. 288p. 1991. reprint ed. pap. 12.95 (*0-936077-07-7*) Gurze Bks.

***Miller, Carolyn G.** Creating Miracles: Understanding the Experience of Divine Intervention. Carleton, Nancy, ed. LC 94-48620. 312p. 1995. pap. 12.95 (*0-915811-62-6*) H J Kramer Inc.

Miller, Carolynne L. Indiana Sources for Genealogical Research in the Indiana State Library. 200p. 1984. 20.00 (*0-87195-079-0*) Ind Hist Soc.

Miller-Catchpole, Robin, jt. auth. see Bezkorovainy, Anatoly.

Miller, Catherine & Abu-Manga, Al-Amin. Language Change & National Integration: Rural Migrants in Khartoum. 208p. 1994. pap. 25.00 (*0-86372-171-0*, Pub. by Ithaca UK) Paul & Co Pubs.

Miller, Catherine G. Carscape: A Parking Handbook. (Illus.). 121p. (Orig.). 1988. pap. 30.00 (*0-945387-00-8*, TL175.M55) Wshngtn St Pr.

Miller Center Commission Staff. Transferring Responsibility: The Dangers of Transition: Report of the Miller Center Commission on Presidential Transitions & Foreign Policy. LC 86-5536. 9.00 (*0-8191-5344-3*) U Pr of Amer.

Miller, Char. Selected Writings of Hiram Bingham - Missionary to the Hawaiian Islands, 1814-1869: To Raise the Lord's Banner. LC 88-11790. (Studies in American Religion: Vol. 31). 550p. 1988. lib. bdg. 119.95 (*0-88946-675-0*) E Mellen.

Miller, Char, ed. Missions & Missionaries in the Pacific. LC 85-5074. (Symposium Ser.: Vol. 14). 136p. 1986. lib. bdg. 69.95 (*0-88946-705-6*) E Mellen.

Miller, Char & Sanders, Heywood T., eds. Urban Texas: Politics & Development. (Southwestern Studies: No. 8). (Illus.). 224p. 1989. pap. 15.95 (*0-89096-397-5*) Tex A&M Univ Pr.

Miller, Charles. Lobbying: Understanding & Influencing the Corridors of Power. 2nd ed. 250p. 1989. text ed. 39.95 (*0-631-17212-2*) Blackwell Pubs.

Miller, Charles, et al, eds. Process & Procedures: A Guide to Visa Processing at U. S. Consulates & Embassies. 324p. (Orig.). 1992. pap. 60.00 (*1-878677-32-2*) Amer Immi Law Assn.

Miller, Charles A. A Catawba Assembly. LC 73-84983. (Illus.). 250p. 1973. pap. 7.00 (*0-9606522-0-5*) Trackaday.

— Isn't That Lewis Carroll? LC 83-51809. (Illus.). 126p. 1984. pap. 3.95 (*0-9606522-1-3*) Trackaday.

— Jefferson & Nature. 320p. (C). 1993. reprint ed. pap. text ed. 14.95 (*0-8018-4729-X*) Johns Hopkins.

Miller, Charles C., ed. History of Allen County, Ohio & Representative Citizens. (Illus.). 872p. 1993. reprint ed. lib. bdg. 89.00 (*0-8328-2784-3*) Higginson Bk Co.

***Miller, Charles D.** Abundant Life. 200p. Date not set. pap. 7.95 (*1-56901-576-7*) NW Pub.

Miller, Charles D., et al. Intermediate Algebra: A Text-Workbook: Alternate Approach. LC 94-12271. (C). 1995. 36.25 (*0-673-99313-2*) HarpCollege.

Miller, Charles D. & Lial, Margaret L. Fundamentals of Trigonometry. (C). 1986. text ed. 29.00 (*0-673-15868-3*) HarpCollege.

Miller, Charles D. & Salzman, Stanley A. Business Mathematics: A Programmed Approach, Bk. 2. (C). 1981. pap. text ed. 22.50 (*0-673-15426-2*) HarpCollege.

— Business Mathematics: A Programmed Approach, Bk. 1. (C). 1980. pap. text ed. 17.25 (*0-673-15347-9*) HarpCollege.

Miller, Charles D., jt. auth. see Lial, Margaret L.

Miller, Charles D., jt. auth. see Liall, Margaret L.

Miller, Charles D., et al. Basic College Math: Student Solution Manual. 3rd ed. (C). 1990. 19.00 (*0-673-46280-3*) HarpCollege.

— Basic College Math Text Workbook. 3rd ed. (C). 1990. pap. text ed. 55.50 (*0-673-46279-X*) HarpCollege.

— Business Mathematics. 6th ed. LC 93-22140. 636p. (C). 1993. pap. text ed. 51.00 (*0-673-46742-2*) HarpCollege.

— Business Mathematics. 6th ed. LC 93-22140. 636p. (C). 1993. Instr.'s ed. teacher ed 7.20 (*0-673-99052-4*) HarpCollege.

— Business Mathematics. 6th ed. LC 93-22140. 636p. (C). 1994. Sale tutorial, IBM. 12.00 (*0-673-99119-9*); Sale tutorial, Mac. 12.00 (*0-673-99120-2*) HarpCollege.

— Business Mathematics, Bk. 1: A Programmed Approach. LC 79-24513. 223p. reprint ed. pap. 63.60 (*0-7837-4050-6*, 2043880) Bks Demand.

— Economics of Public Issues. 9th ed. (C). 1992. 22.50 (*0-06-501336-0*) HarpCollege.

— Fundamentals of College Algebra. 4th ed. (C). 1993. text ed. 60.50 (*0-673-46743-0*) HarpCollege.

— Fundamentals of College Algebra. 4th ed. (C). 1994. Solutions manual. teacher ed 14.25 (*0-673-46992-1*) HarpCollege.

— Fundamentals of College Algebra. 4th ed. (C). 1994. Sale tutorial, Mac. 12.00 (*0-673-99110-5*) HarpCollege.

— Fundamentals of Trigonometry. 2nd ed. (C). 1990. text ed. 58.50 (*0-673-38961-8*) HarpCollege.

— Intermediate Algebra: A Text - Workbook. 5th ed. LC 94-11108. (C). 1995. 50.00 (*0-673-46744-9*) HarpCollege.

— Intermediate Algebra: Text-Workbook. 4th ed. (C). 1990. pap. text ed. 56.50 (*0-673-46272-2*); 19.00 (*0-673-46273-0*) HarpCollege.

— Introduction to Algebra, a Test & Workbook. 4th ed. (C). 1990. pap. text ed. 56.50 (*0-673-46270-6*); 13.50 (*0-673-46271-4*) HarpCollege.

— Introductory Algebra: A Text - Workbook. 5th ed. LC 94-11107. (C). 1994. text ed. 50.00 (*0-673-46745-7*) HarpCollege.

— Mathematical Ideas. 7th ed. LC 93-1955. 828p. (C). 1993. text ed. 56.50 (*0-673-46738-4*) HarpCollege.

— Mathematical Ideas. 7th ed. LC 93-1955. 828p. (C). 1993. CLAST Guide. 14.50 (*0-673-99095-8*) HarpCollege.

— Mathematical Ideas. 7th ed. LC 93-1955. 828p. (C). 1994. Sale tutorial, IBM. 12.00 (*0-673-99115-6*); Sale tutorial, Mac. 12.00 (*0-673-99116-4*) HarpCollege.

Miller, Charles E. As Rain That Falls: Homiletic Reflections for the Weekdays of Advent & Lent. LC 88-13963. 150p. 1988. pap. 7.95 (*0-8189-0535-2*) Alba.

— Making Holy the Day: A Commentary in the Liturgy of the Hours. 1976. 0.95 (*0-89942-410-4*, 410/04) Catholic Bk Pub.

— Mother & Disciple: A Devout Discourse on the Blessed Virgin Mary. LC 89-32761. 108p. (Orig.). 1989. pap. 4.95 (*0-8189-0548-4*) Alba.

— Opening the Treasures: A Book of Daily Homily Meditations. LC 81-19095. (Illus.). 557p. 1982. pap. 16.95 (*0-8189-0424-0*) Alba.

— Ordained to Preach: A Theology & Practice of Preaching. LC 92-16295. 236p. (Orig.). 1992. pap. 12.95 (*0-8189-0637-5*) Alba.

— Where the Road Leads. LC 94-90225. 320p. (Orig.). 1995. pap. 10.00 (*1-56002-473-9*, Univ Edtns) Aegina Pr.

***Miller, Charles E., ed.** Together in Prayer: Learning to Love the Liturgy of the Hours. LC 94-23025. 124p. (Orig.). 1994. pap. 9.95 (*0-8189-0712-6*) Alba.

Miller, Charles F., 3rd. On Group-Theoretic Decision Problems & Their Classification. (Annals of Mathematics Studies: No. 68). 1971. 25.00 (*0-691-08091-7*) Princeton U Pr.

Miller, Charles M., et al. Visa Processing Guide: Process & Procedures at U. S. Consulates & Embassies. 2nd ed. 465p. 1993. pap. text ed. 72.00 (*1-878677-56-X*) Amer Immi Law Assn.

Miller, Charles W., Jr. Stake Your Claim! The Tale of America's Enduring Mining Laws. (Illus.). 1991. 34.95 (*0-87026-080-4*) Westernlore.

Miller, Charles W. Today's Technology in Bible Prophecy. (Illus.). 512p. (Orig.). 1990. pap. 10.00 (*0-9627032-0-6*) TIP MI.

Miller, Charles W., ed. see DOE Technical Information Center Staff.

Miller, Charly D. Home Meds. 176p. 1991. pap. text ed. 12.00 (*0-89303-180-1*, 740802) P-H.

Miller, Charly D. & White, David. EMT - Paramedic National Standards Review Self Test. LC 92-49915. write for info. (*0-89303-955-1*) Brady Compu Bks.

— EMT - Paramedic National Standards Review Self Test. 2nd ed. LC 94-18794. 432p. 1994. pap. 19.00 (*0-89303-720-6*) P-H.

***Miller, Charly D., et al.** 1994 Revised EMT-Basic National Standards Review Self Test. rev. ed. LC 95-16025. 1996. write for info. (*0-8359-4948-6*, Reston) P-H.

***Miller, Chip E.** Marketing Research Workbook. 200p. 1995. pap. 17.75 (*0-314-04737-9*) West Pub.

Miller, Chris, jt. auth. see Hale, Mary.

Miller, Christina G. & Berry, Louise A. Acid Rain. LC 86-8605. (Illus.). 128p. (YA). (gr. 7 up). 1986. lib. bdg. 12.98 (*0-671-60177-6*, Julian Messner) Silver Burdett Pr.

— Coastal Rescue: Preserving Our Seashores. LC 88-27520. (Illus.). 128p. (J). (gr. 5-9). 1989. text ed. 14.95 (*0-689-31288-1*, Atheneum Bks Young) S&S Childrens.

— Jungle Rescue: Saving the New World Tropical Rain Forests. LC 90-1150. (Illus.). 128p. (J). (gr. 5-9). 1991. text ed. 14.95 (*0-689-31487-6*, Atheneum Bks Young) S&S Childrens.

Miller, Christine M. & McKinney, Bruce C., eds. Governmental Commission Communication. LC 93-17118. (Praeger Series in Political Communication). 248p. 1993. text ed. 55.00 (*0-275-94223-6*, C4223, Praeger Pubs) Greenwood.

Miller, Christopher, ed. Ion Channel Reconstitution. LC 86-4900. 600p. 1986. 120.00 (*0-306-42136-4*, Plenum Pr) Plenum.

Miller, Christopher L. Blank Darkness: Africanist Discourse in French. LC 85-1157. (Illus.). xii, 268p. 1986. pap. text ed. 13.95 (*0-226-52622-4*) U Ch Pr.

— Blank Darkness: Africanist Discourse in French. LC 85-1157. (Illus.). xii, 268p. 1986. lib. bdg. 30.00 (*0-226-52621-6*) U Ch Pr.

— Prophetic Worlds: Indians & Whites on the Columbia Plateau. 180p. (C). 1985. text ed. 35.00 (*0-8135-1084-8*) Rutgers U Pr.

— Theories of Africans: Francophone Literature & Anthropology in Africa. (Black Literature & Culture Ser.). (Illus.). 360p. 1990. pap. text ed. 19.95 (*0-226-52802-2*) U Ch Pr.

— Theories of Africans: Francophone Literature & Anthropology in Africa. (Black Literature & Culture Ser.). (Illus.). 360p. 1990. lib. bdg. 49.95 (*0-226-52801-4*) U Ch Pr.

Miller, Chuck. Ahora Que Soy Cristiano: Now That I Am a Christian, Vol. 1. (SPA.). 3.95 (*84-7228-489-1*, 220013, Pub. by Edit Clie SP) TSELF.

— Ahora Que Soy Cristiano: Now That I Am a Christian, Vol. 2. (SPA.). 3.95 (*84-7228-490-5*, 220014, Pub. by Edit Clie SP) TSELF.

— How in the Morning: Poems 1962-1988. Sklar, Morty, ed. LC 88-16062. (Outstanding Author Ser.: No. 5). 80p. 1988. 12.75 (*0-930370-32-5*) Spirit That Moves.

— How in the Morning: Poems 1962-1988. deluxe ed. Sklar, Morty, ed. LC 88-16062. (Outstanding Author Ser.: No. 5). 80p. 1988. 25.00 (*0-930370-34-1*); Signed A-Z. per. 7.00 (*0-930370-33-3*) Spirit That Moves.

— Northern Fields: New & Selected Poems. (Orig.). 1994. pap. 11.95 (*1-56689-014-4*) Coffee Hse.

Miller, Chuck, jt. auth. see Underwood, Tim.

Miller, Chuck, jt. ed. see Underwood, Tim.

Miller, Cindy F. & Slossburg, Wendy J. Au Pair American Style. 150p. (Orig.). 1986. pap. 5.95 (*0-915765-35-7*) Natl Pr Bks.

Miller, Clare. Eight Minute Makeovers: Your Most Beautiful Face for Every Occasion. (Illus.). 172p. 1984. 15.95 (*0-87491-736-0*) Acropolis.

Miller, Clarence H., ed. see More, Thomas.

Miller, Clarence W. The Funeral Book. Jacobs, Pamela D., ed. LC 94-18601. 96p. 1994. pap. 7.95 (*1-885003-02-1*) R D Reed Pubs.

Miller-Clark, Denise, ed. New Chicago Photographers. (Illus.). 32p. 1984. 10.00 (*0-932026-13-3*) Columbia College Chi.

Miller-Clark, Denise, pref. Linda Connor: Spiral Journey: Photographs 1967-1990. 70p. 1990. pap. 25.00 (*0-932026-21-4*) Columbia College Chi.

Miller, Claude. Fat & Fed Up: Challenge to Weight Control. 1970. 5.95 (*0-8184-0031-5*) Carol Pub Group.

Miller, Claudia S., jt. auth. see Ashford, Nicholas A.

Miller, Clifford, jt. auth. see Pearson, Hilary.

Miller, Clive & Domoney, Lynette. Unemployment & Social Services. (C). 1988. 60.00 (*0-685-28600-2*, Pub. by Natl Inst Soc Work) St Mut.

Miller, Clive & Scott, Tony. Strategies & Tactics: Planning & Decision Making in Social Services Fieldwork Teams. (C). 1984. 49.00 (*0-685-28591-X*, Pub. by Natl Inst Soc Work); 59.00 (*0-685-40352-1*, Pub. by Natl Inst Soc Work); 60.00 (*0-902789-32-5*, Pub. by Natl Inst Soc Work); 75.00 (*0-7855-0073-1*, Pub. by Natl Inst Soc Work) St Mut.

Miller, Clive, jt. auth. see Flynn, Norman.

Miller, Clive, jt. auth. see Scott, Tony.

Miller, Clive, et al. Everyday Community Care: A Manual for Managers. (C). 1991. 75.00 (*0-902789-73-2*, Pub. by Natl Inst Soc Work) St Mut.

Miller, Clyde. Commentary on First & Second Kings. LC 88-72271. (Living Word Ser.). 416p. 1992. 27.95 (*0-89112-188-9*) Abilene Christ U.

Miller, Clyde L., tr. see DeCusa, Nicolas.

Miller, Colin, ed. see Christian Parenting Staff.

Miller, Connie. Feminist Research Methods: An Annotated Bibliography. LC 91-3792. (Bibliographies & Indexes in Women's Studies Ser.: No. 13). 288p. 1991. text ed. 59.95 (*0-313-26029-X*, MFT, Greenwood Pr) Greenwood.

Miller, Connie, jt. ed. see Leppa, Carol J.

Miller, Conrad & Maloney, E. S. Your Boat's Electrical System. rev. ed. LC 88-11002. (Illus.). 512p. 1988. 18.95 (*0-688-08132-0*, Hearst Marine Bks) Morrow.

Miller, Constance & Campbell, Kay. From the Ashes: A Head Injury Self-Advocacy Guide. (Illus.). 107p. (Orig.). 1987. student ed 23.00 (*0-9636594-0-5*); pap. write for info. (*0-318-62771-X*) Phoenix Seattle.

Miller, Constance, tr. see Gyatso, Losang K.

***Miller, Constance O.** Gazehounds: The Search for Truth. deluxe ed. (Illus.). 184p. 1995. pap. 30.00 (*0-614-04524-X*) Donald R Hoflin.

Miller, Constance O. & Gilbert, Edward M., Jr. The New Complete Afgan Hound. rev. ed. (Illus.). 288p. 1988. 25.95 (*0-87605-001-1*) Howell Bk.

Miller, Cookie, ed. see Blumin, Barbara.

Miller-Cory House Museum Staff. Pleasures of Colonial Cooking. (Illus.). xviii, 168p. 1982. pap. text ed. 9.95 (*0-911020-06-3*) NJ Hist Soc.

Miller, Craig K. Baby Boomer Spirituality: Ten Essential Values of a Generation. LC 91-72143. 192p. 1992. pap. 12.95 (*0-88177-106-6*, DR106) Discipleship Res.

— Encounters with Jesus. LC 92-70576. 88p. 1992. pap. 7.95 (*0-88177-113-9*, DR113) Discipleship Res.

Miller, Craig S., jt. auth. see Langlais, Robert P.

Miller, Crane S. & Hyslop, Richard S. California: The Geography of Diversity. LC 82-73744. (Illus.). 255p. 1983. pap. 29.95 (*0-87484-441-X*) Mayfield Pub.

Miller, Cristanne. Emily Dickinson: A Poet's Grammar. 256p. 1989. pap. 13.95 (*0-674-25036-2*) HUP.

An Asterisk (*) at the beginning of an entry indicates that the title is appearing in BIP for the first time.

— Marianne Moore: Questions of Authority. LC 95-7167. 320p. (C). 1995. text ed. 35.00 (0-674-54862-0) HUP.

Miller, Cristanne, jt. ed. see Keller, Lynn.

***Miller, Crow.** Let's Get Growing: A Dirt-Under-the-Nails Primer on Raising Vegetables, Fruits & Flowers Organically. (Illus.). 388p. 1995. 23.95 (0-87596-640-3) Rodale Pr Inc.

— Rodale's Garden Answers-Vegetables, Fruits & Herbs: At-a-Glance Solutions for Every Gardening Problem. Bradley, Fern M., ed. (Illus.). 384p. 1995. 27.95 (0-87596-639-X) Rodale Pr Inc.

Miller, Cynthia, tr. see Molina, Felipe S., ed.

Miller, Cynthia A., ed. Journal of the Senate of Virginia: Session of 1798-99. v, 92p. 1977. 10.00 (0-88490-010-X) VA State Lib.

Miller, Cynthia P. Challenges of the Heart. LC 90-21432. (Illus.). 144p. (Orig.). (YA). 1991. pap. 6.99 (0-932581-79-X) Word Aflame.

Miller, D., ed. Clinical Light Damage to the Eye. (Illus.). 180p. 1987. 142.00 (0-387-96451-7) Spr-Verlag.

Miller, D., jt. auth. see Farmer, R.

Miller, D., jt. ed. see Littlewood, B.

Miller, D., et al. Domination & Resistance. (One World Archaeology Ser.). 352p. 1989. text ed. 65.00 (0-04-445022-2) Routledge Chapman & Hall.

Miller, D. A. Bringing Out Roland Barthes. 1992. pap. 13.00 (0-520-07948-5) U CA Pr.

— Forbidden Knowledge...Or Is It. 256p. 1994. pap. 10.00 (0-939513-75-7) Joy Pub SJC.

— Narrative & Its Discontents: Problems of Closure in the Traditional Novel. 318p. 1989. pap. text ed. 15.95 (0-691-01458-2) Princeton U Pr.

— The Novel & the Police. 1988. pap. 13.00 (0-520-06746-0) U CA Pr.

Miller, D. A., jt. auth. see Barthes, Roland.

Miller, D. B. Peasants & Politics: Grass Roots Reactions to Change in Asia. (Illus.). 1979. text ed. 27.50 (0-312-59993-5) St Martin.

Miller, D. Carey. The Acquisition & Protection of Ownership. 408p. 1986. 24.00 (0-7021-1777-3, Pub. by Juta SA); pap. 20.00 (0-7021-2366-8, Pub. by Juta SA) W W Gaunt.

Miller, D. Douglas & Highsmith, Anne L., comps. Heinrich Schutz: A Bibliography of the Collected Works & Performing Editions. LC 86-7610. (Music Reference Collection Ser.: No. 9). 295p. 1986. text ed. 47.95 (0-313-24884-2, MHZ/) Greenwood.

Miller, D. F. & Aubin, L. X. St. Alphonsus Liguori: Bishop, Confessor, Founder of the Redemptorist & Doctor of the Church. LC 87-51071. Orig. Title: Saint Alphonsus Mary de' Liquori - Founder, Bishop, & Doctor (1696-1780). 388p. 1987. reprint ed. pap. 15.00 (0-89555-329-5) TAN Bks Pubs.

Miller, D. M., ed. Developments in Integrated Circuit Testing. (Perspectives in Computing Ser.: Vol. 18). 440p. 1988. text ed. 66.00 (0-12-496735-3) Acad Pr.

Miller, D. M., et al, eds. Tectonic & Stratigraphic Studies in the Eastern Great Basin. (Memoir Ser.: No. 157). (Illus.). 333p. 1983. 7.50 (0-8137-1157-6) Geol Soc.

Miller, D. Patrick. A Little Book of Forgiveness: Challenges & Meditations for Anyone with Something to Forgive. LC 93-49780. 96p. 1994. 12.95 (0-670-85406-9, Viking) Viking Penguin.

Miller, D. Patrick, jt. auth. see Rusk, Tom.

Miller, D. S. Discharge Characteristics. (Hydraulic Structures Design Manual Ser.: Vol. 8). (Illus.). 270p. (C). 1994. 110.00 (90-5410-180-6, Pub. by A A Balkema NE) Ashgate Pub Co.

— Internal Flow Systems. 2nd rev. ed. 364p. (C). 1990. 79.00 (0-947711-77-5, Pub. by BHRA Fluid UK) Air Sci Co.

Miller, Dale, ed. Logic Programming: Proceedings of the '93 International Symposium, Vancouver, British Columbia, October 26-29, 1993, Reports & Notes. (Logic Programming Ser.). (Illus.). 400p. 1993. 75.00 (0-262-63152-0) MIT Pr.

Miller, Dale & Miller, Patricia. The Gospel of Mark As Midrash on Earlier Jewish & New Testament Sacred Literature. LC 90-32887. (Studies in Bible & Early Christianity: Vol. 21). 408p. 1990. lib. bdg. 109.95 (0-88946-621-1) E Mellen.

Miller, Dale E., jt. auth. see Ching, Francis D.

Miller, Dan & Nam, Park B. The Fundamentals of Pa Kua Chang: The Methods of Lu Shui-Tien As Taught by Park Bok Nam. 204p. 1993. pap. 19.95 (1-883175-01-1) High View Pubns.

Miller, Dan, jt. auth. see Cartnell, Tim.

Miller, Dan, et al, eds. Critical Paths: Blake & the Argument of Method. LC 87-13514. (Illus.). xii, 382p. (C). 1987. lib. bdg. 50.50 (0-8223-0751-0); pap. text ed. 21.95 (0-8223-0792-8) Duke.

Miller, Dan B. Erskine Caldwell: The Journey from Tobacco Road: a Biography. LC 93-48924. 1994. 30.00 (0-679-42931-X) Knopf.

Miller, Dana R., ed. see Kopystens'kyj, Zaxarija.

Miller, Daniel. Artefacts As Categories: A Study of Ceramic Variability in Central India. (New Studies in Archaeology). (Illus.). 250p. 1985. 64.95 (0-521-30522-5) Cambridge U Pr.

— Material Culture & Mass Consumption. (Social Archaeology Ser.). 256p. 1991. pap. 21.95 (0-631-18001-X) Blackwell Pubs.

— Modernity, an Ethnographic Approach: Dualism & Mass Consumption in Trinidad. LC 93-23406. 1994. 49.95 (0-85496-916-0); pap. 19.95 (0-85496-917-9) Berg Pubs.

— Starting a Small Restaurant: A Guide to Excellence in the Purveying of Public Victuals. rev. ed. LC 83-6188. 224p. (Orig.). 1983. pap. 11.95 (0-916782-37-9) Harvard Common Pr.

***Miller, Daniel, ed.** Acknowledging Consumption. LC 94-37293. (Material Cultures Ser.). (Illus.). 304p. 1995. 65.00x (0-415-10688-5, C0226); pap. 19.95 (0-415-10689-3, C0227) Routledge.

— Unwrapping Christmas. (Studies in the Anthropology of Cultural Forms). (Illus.). 284p. 1993. 35.00 (0-19-827903-5) OUP.

— Unwrapping Christmas. (Oxford Studies in Social & Cultural Anthropology). (Illus.). 256p. 1995. pap. 19.95 (0-19-828066-1) OUP.

— Worlds Apart: Modernity Through the Prism of the Local. LC 94-46805. (Uses of Knowledge Ser.). 1995. 40.00 (0-415-10788-1); pap. 14.99 (0-415-10789-X) Routledge.

***Miller, Daniel, et al, eds.** Domination & Resistance. (One World Archaeology Ser.). (Illus.). 352p. 1995. pap. 25.00 (0-415-12254-6, C0587) Routledge.

Miller, Daniel C., jt. auth. see Demuth, Donald L.

Miller, Daniel J. & Lea, Robert N. Guide to the Coastal Marine Fishes of California. 249p. 1972. reprint ed. pap. 7.50 (0-931876-13-3, 4065) ANR Pubns CA.

Miller, Daniel L., jt. auth. see Partridge, Arthur D.

Miller, Daniel R., ed. Coming of Age: Protestantism in Contemporary Latin America. (Calvin College Ser.: Vol. I). 265p. (Orig.). Date not set. lib. bdg. 53.00 (0-8191-9406-9); pap. text ed. 22.50 (0-8191-9407-7) U Pr of Amer.

Miller, Daniel W. The Unseen Universe: Of Mind & Matter. LC 93-73063. (Illus.). 325p. (Orig.). 1993. pap. 12.95 (0-9638055-0-9) Beyond Realm.

Miller, Danny, jt. auth. see Kets de Vries, Manfred F.

Miller, Danny, jt. auth. see Quintana, Kathy.

Miller, Danny L., ed. see Pace, Mildred M.

Miller, Dare. Dog Master System. LC 75-36106. 19.95 (0-686-22367-5); pap. 9.95 (0-686-22368-3) Dog Master.

Miller, Darla. First Steps Toward Cultural Difference: Socialization in Infant-Toddler Day Care. 112p. 1989. 16.95 (0-87868-351-8) Child Welfare.

***Miller, Darla F.** Positive Child Guidance. 352p. 1995. pap. 25.95 (0-8273-5878-4) Delmar.

***Miller, Darlene.** Your Share, Your Clothes & You: Secrets of a Successful Wardrobe. rev. ed. (Illus.). 80p. 1994. 14.95 (0-9642936-0-9) Clothes For You.

Miller, Darlis A. Across the Plains in 1864 with Additional Paymaster Samuel C. Staples. 96p. 1980. pap. text ed. 20.00 (0-89126-098-6) MA-AH Pub.

— Captain Jack Crawford: Buckskin Poet, Scout, & Showman. LC 93-8611. (Illus.). 384p. 1993. 45.00x (0-8263-1449-X) U of NM Pr.

Miller, Dave. Brewing the World's Great Beers: A Step-By-Step Guide. Watson, Ben, ed. LC 91-50605. 160p. 1992. 22.95 (0-88266-776-9); pap. 12.95 (0-88266-775-0) Storey Comm Inc.

— Classic Bear Style Series: Continental Pilsener. (Classic Beer Style Ser.). (Illus.). 102p. 1990. pap. 11.95 (0-937381-20-9) Brewers Pubns.

— The Complete Handbook of Home Brewing. Clarkson, Sarah M., ed. LC 87-46447. 256p. 1988. 19.95 (0-88266-522-7, Garden Way Pub); pap. 11.95 (0-88266-517-0, Garden Way Pub) Storey Comm Inc.

— Dave. (Illus.). 144p. 1994. pap. 7.95 (0-8092-3626-5) Contemp Bks.

— Dave Miller's New Homebrewing Guide. LC 95-13385. 296p. 1995. pap. 14.95 (0-88266-905-2) Storey Comm Inc.

— Singing & New Testament Worship. 1994. pap. 4.95 (0-89137-144-3) Quality Pubns.

***Miller, Dave & Blum, Kenneth.** Overload: Attention Deficit Disorder & the Addictive Brain. 192p. 1995. pap. 9.95 (0-8362-0460-3) Andrews & McMeel.

Miller, Dave, ed. see St. Claire, Mary.

Miller, David. Apple ProDOS Data Files: A Basic Tutorial. (Illus.). 232p. 1985. 18.95 (0-8359-0134-3, Reston) P-H.

— Commodore One Twenty-Eight File Programming. (Illus.). 300p. (Orig.). (C). 1987. 21.95 (0-8306-0205-4, 2805) TAB Bks.

— Commodore 128 Data File Program. 1991. 24.95 (0-8306-6429-7) TAB Bks.

— Commodore 64 Data Files: A Basic Tutorial. (Illus.). 1986. 17.95 (0-8359-0791-0, Reston) P-H.

— Critical Rationalism: A Restatement & Defence. 275p. 1994. 44.95 (0-8126-9197-0); pap. 19.95 (0-8126-9198-9) Open Court.

— Dark Eden: The Swamp in Nineteenth-Century American Culture. (Cambridge Studies in American Literature & Culture: No. 43). (Illus.). (C). 1990. 59.95 (0-521-37553-3) Cambridge U Pr.

— Don't Mention the War: Northern Ireland, Propaganda & the Media. (C). 1994. pap. text ed. 17.95 (0-7453-0836-8, Pub. by Pluto Pr UK) Westview.

— Don't Mention the War: Northern Ireland, Propaganda & the Media. (C). 1994. text ed. 69.95 (0-7453-0835-X) Westview.

— Macintosh Data Files. (Illus.). 232p. 14.95 (0-685-09444-8) P-H.

— Market, State, & Community: Theoretical Foundations of Market Socialism. 376p. 1991. pap. 29.95 (0-19-827864-0) OUP.

— Modern Submarine Hunters. (New Illustrated Guide Ser.). (Illus.). 160p. 1992. 5.98 (0-8317-5060-X) Smithmark.

— Modern Tanks & Fighting Vehicles. (New Illustrated Guide Ser.). (Illus.). 160p. 1992. 5.98 (0-8317-5056-1) Smithmark.

— Olympic Revolution: The Authorised Biography of Juan Antonio Samaranch. (Illus.). 192p. 1992. 34.95 (1-85145-768-2, Pub. by Pavilion UK) Trafalgar.

— Olympic Revolution: The Olympic Biography of Juan Antonio Samaranch. (Illus.). 284p. 1995. pap. 16.95 (1-85793-403-2, Pub. by Pavilion UK) Trafalgar.

— On Nationality. (Oxford Political Theory Ser.). 168p. 1995. 24.95 (0-19-828047-5) OUP.

— Primavera. deluxe ed. (Burning Deck Poetry Chapbooks Ser.). 1979. pap. 10.00 (0-930900-63-4) Burning Deck.

— Sebastian Coe - Born to Run: A Life in Athletics. (Illus.). 272p. 1993. pap. 19.95 (1-85793-091-6, Pub. by Pavilion UK) Trafalgar.

— Social Justice. 1979. pap. 24.95 (0-19-824621-8) OUP.

— Stromata. (Poetry Ser.). 64p. (Orig.). 1994. pap. 8.00 (0-930901-96-7, PR9619.3.M47S77) Burning Deck.

— Stromata. deluxe ed. (Poetry Ser.). 64p. (Orig.). 1994. pap. 15.00 (0-930901-97-5) Burning Deck.

— Submarines of the World. 198p. 1992. 30.00 (0-517-58666-5, Orion Bks) Crown Pub Group.

— Unity. 32p. (Orig.). 1981. pap. 3.00 (0-935162-03-8) Singing Horse.

— W. H. Hudson & the Elusive Paradise. 240p. 1990. text ed. 45.00 (0-312-03698-1) St Martin.

— World's Navies. 1992. 14.99 (0-517-05241-5) Random Hse Value.

— The Wreck of the Isabella. (Illus.). 272p. 1995. 25.00 (1-55750-768-6) Naval Inst Pr.

***Miller, David, ed.** Blackwell Encyclopedia of Political Thought. 1991. pap. 27.95 (0-631-17944-5) Blackwell Pubs.

— Liberty. (Oxford Readings in Politics & Government Ser.). 232p. 1991. 58.00 (0-19-878041-9, 12225); pap. 18.95 (0-19-878042-7) OUP.

Miller, David & Effler, James M. Dynamic Airbrush. (Illus.). 168p. 1987. 29.95 (0-89134-190-0, 7492) North Light Bks.

Miller, David & Martin, Diana. Getting Started in Airbrush. (Illus.). 128p. (Orig.). 1993. pap. 22.95 (0-89134-479-9, 30514) North Light Bks.

Miller, David & Ridefort, Gerard. Weapons of the Elite Forces. (New Illustrated Guide Ser.). (Illus.). 160p. 1992. 5.98 (0-8317-5057-X) Smithmark.

***Miller, David & Walzer, Michael, eds.** Pluralism, Justice, & Equality. 312p. 1995. text ed. 59.00 (0-19-827937-X) OUP.

— Pluralism, Justice, & Equality. 312p. 1995. pap. text ed. 19.95 (0-19-828008-4) OUP.

Miller, David, jt. ed. see Bonasso, Pete.

Miller, David, ed. see Chambers, Maggie.

Miller, David, tr. see Cuza-Male, Belkis.

Miller, David, jt. auth. see Miller, Merlene.

Miller, David, ed. see Pilling, Ron.

Miller, David, ed. see Popper, Karl.

Miller, David, jt. auth. see Stegmaier, Mark J.

Miller, David C., ed. American Iconology: New Approaches to Nineteenth-Century Art & Literature. LC 92-46082. (Illus.). 360p. 1993. 40.00 (0-300-05478-5) Yale U Pr.

Miller, David C. & Meyers, David, eds. Comparative & Historical Essays in Scots Law. 232p. 1992. U.K. pap. 60.00 (0-406-00877-9) Butterworth Legal Pubs.

Miller, David C. & Pouilliard, James, eds. The Relevance of Albert Schweitzer at the Dawn of the Twenty-First Century. 168p. (C). 1992. lib. bdg. 29.50 (0-8191-8525-6) U Pr of Amer.

Miller, David C., jt. ed. see Liao, Thomas T.

Miller, David D. From Pascal to FORTRAN 77: Applications for Scientists & Engineers. 287p. (C). 1987. pap. text ed. 23.00 (0-15-529175-0) SCP.

— From Pascal to FORTRAN 77: Applications for Scientists & Engineers. 287p. (C). 1987. pap. text ed. 6.75 (0-15-529176-9) SCP.

— VAX-VMS Operating Systems Concepts. (VAX-VMS Ser.). (Illus.). 550p. 1991. text ed. 44.95 (1-55558-065-3, EY-F590E-DP, Digital DEC) Buttrwrth-Heinemann.

***Miller, David E.** Great Salt Lake: Past & Present. 5th rev. ed. Eckman, Lawrence L. & Eckman, Anne M., eds. (Illus.). 50p. (Orig.). 1994. pap. 5.00 (0-9639924-0-6) Utah Hist Atlas.

— Hole in the Rock. Eckman, Lawrence L. & Eckman, Anne M., eds. (Illus.). 231p. (C). Date not set. reprint ed. pap. 11.95 (0-9639924-1-4) Utah Hist Atlas.

— Hole in the Rock: An Epic in the Colonization of the Great American West. 2nd ed. LC 66-22142. (Illus.). 261p. reprint ed. pap. 74.40 (0-8357-6426-5, 2035794) Bks Demand.

— Living Trust Handbook. 1991. pap. 20.00 (0-9627178-0-0) D E Miller Law.

— Occupational Safety, Health, & Fire Index: A Source Guide to Voluntary & Obligatory Regulations, Codes Standards & Publications. LC 76-12285. (Occupational Safety & Health Ser.: Vol. 1). 224p. reprint ed. pap. 63.90 (0-685-15932-9, 2027823) Bks Demand.

Miller, David F., et al. Look Before You Leap into Business! LC 92-31639. 32p. 1995. 5.95 (0-87576-164-X) Pilot Bks.

Miller, David H. The Alaska Treaty. (Alaska History Ser.: No. 18). (Illus.). 1981. 18.00 (0-919642-95-0) Limestone Pr.

— Custer's Fall: The Indian Side of the Story. 288p. 1992. pap. 10.95 (0-452-01095-0, Mer) NAL-Dutton.

— Energy at the Surface of the Earth: An Introduction to the Energetics of Ecosystems. (International Geophysics Ser.). 1981. pap. text ed. 65.00 (0-12-497152-0) Acad Pr.

— Snow Cover & Climate in the Sierra Nevada, California. LC 55-9597. (University of California Publications in Social Welfare: Vol. 11). 226p. reprint ed. pap. 64.50 (0-317-29516-0, 2021271) Bks Demand.

— Water at the Surface of the Earth: Student Edition. LC 82-13769. (International Geophysics Ser.). (C). 1982. pap. text ed. 66.00 (0-12-496752-3) Acad Pr.

Miller, David J. & Hersen, Michel, eds. Research Fraud in the Behavioral & Biomedical Sciences. 272p. 1992. text ed. 49.95 (0-471-52068-3) Wiley.

Miller, David K. Measurement by the Physical Educator: Why & How. (Illus.). 328p. 1988. text ed. write for info. (0-697-14820-3) Brown & Benchmark.

— Measurement by the Physical Educator: Why & How. 2nd ed. 400p. 1994. boxed write for info. (0-697-16621-X) Brown & Benchmark.

Miller, David K. & Allen, T. Earl. Fitness: A Lifetime Commitment. 4th ed. 320p. (C). 1990. pap. write for info. (0-02-381273-7) Macmillan.

— Fitness: A Lifetime Commitment. 5th ed. (Illus.). 352p. (C). 1994. pap. write for info. (0-02-381292-3) Macmillan.

Miller, David L. Introduction to Collective Behavior. (Illus.). 342p. (C). 1989. reprint ed. pap. text ed. 18.95 (0-88133-436-7) Waveland Pr.

— Jung & the Bible, Vol. 1. 160p. 1995. 15.95 (0-8264-0809-5) Continuum.

— The Poem's Two Bodies: The Poetics of the 1590 Faerie Queene. 312p. 1991. text ed. 47.50 (0-691-06744-9); pap. text ed. 14.95 (0-691-01512-0) Princeton U Pr.

Miller, David L. & Dunlop, Alexander, eds. Approaches to Teaching Spenser's The Faerie Queene. LC 94-5713. (Approaches to Teaching World Literature Ser.: Vol. 50). 200p. (Orig.). 1994. lib. bdg. 37.50 (0-87352-723-2, AP50C); pap. 18.00 (0-87352-724-0, AP50P) Modern Lang.

Miller, David L., jt. ed. see Jay, Gregory S.

Miller, David L., ed. see Mead, George H.

Miller, David L., jt. ed. see Puligandla, Ramakrishma.

Miller, David L., et al, eds. The Production of English Renaissance Culture. (Illus.). 336p. 1994. 37.50 (0-8014-2961-7); pap. 15.95 (0-8014-8201-1) Cornell U Pr.

Miller, David M. Frank Herbert. Schlobin, Roger C., ed. LC 80-20880. (Starmont Reader's Guide Ser.: Vol. 5). 70p. 1980. lib. bdg. 20.00 (0-916732-16-9); pap. 10.00 (0-916732-07-X) Borgo Pr.

— John Milton: Poetry. (English Authors Ser.: No. 242). 200p. 1978. text ed. 23.95 (0-8057-6724-X, Pub. by Royal Botanic Garden UK) Macmillan.

***Miller, David M. & Busby, Cathy, eds.** Jurassic Magmatism & Tectonics of the North American Cordillera. (Special Paper Ser.: No. 299). (Illus.). 1995. pap. write for info. (0-8137-2299-3) Geol Soc.

Miller, David M. & Jordan, J. Modern Submarine Warfare. (Modern Combat Ser.). (Illus.). 208p. 1988. 14.99 (0-517-64647-1) Random Hse Value.

Miller, David N. Bibliography of Isaac Bashevis Singer 1924-1949. LC 83-47647. 315p. (Orig.). (C). 1984. pap. text ed. 28.95 (0-8204-0002-5) P Lang Pubs.

— Fear of Fiction: Narrative Strategies in the Works of Isaac Bashevis Singer. LC 84-16448. (SUNY Series in Modern Jewish Literature & Culture). 169p. 1985. 59.50 (0-88706-009-9); pap. 19.95 (0-88706-010-2) State U NY Pr.

— Recovering the Canon: Essays on Isaac Bashevis Singer. (Studies in Judaism in Modern Times: Vol. 8). xxii, 154p. 1986. 35.50 (90-04-07681-6) E J Brill.

Miller, David N., jt. ed. see Lambropoulos, Vassilis.

Miller, David R. Breaking Free! Rescuing Families from the Clutches of Legalism. LC 91-35648. 176p. 1992. pap. 9.99 (0-8010-6288-8) Baker Bk.

— Counseling Single Parents: Meeting the Challenges of Single Parent Families. LC 93-46347. 1994. 15.99 (0-8499-1062-5) Word Inc.

— Help! I'm Not a Perfect Parent: Overcoming the Guilty-Parent Syndrome. 1991. pap. 8.99 (0-89636-301-5, LifeJourney) Chariot Family.

— Parent Power - Godly Influence in an Age of Weakness. LC 87-73391. 185p. (Orig.). 1988. pap. 8.99 (0-89636-245-0, LifeJourney) Chariot Family.

— A Parent's Guide to Adolescents: Understanding Your Teenager. LC 88-84156. 192p. (Orig.). 1989. pap. 8.99 (0-89636-254-X, LifeJourney) Chariot Family.

— Single Moms, Single Dads: Help & Hope for the One-Parent Family. LC 90-80336. 1992. pap. 8.99 (0-89636-269-8, AC 217, LifeJourney) Chariot Family.

Miller, David S., jt. auth. see Keyes, Thomas R.

Miller, David W. Church, State, & Nation in Ireland, 1898-1921. LC 72-95453. 589p. reprint ed. pap. 167.90 (0-318-34735-0, 2031992) Bks Demand.

— The Courts' View of Regulation at the Federal Energy Regulatory Commission, 2 vols. LC 89-147208. 1048p. 1988. ring bd. 170.00 (0-685-29078-6) Norland Pr.

— Dead Lawyers & Other Pleasant Thoughts. LC 92-56804. 96p. 1993. pap. 9.95 (0-679-74441-X) Random.

— Waste Disposal Effects on Ground Water: A Comprehensive Survey of the Occurrence & Control of Ground-Water Contamination Resulting from Waste Disposal Practices. LC 78-65680. (Illus.). 512p. 1980. reprint ed. pap. 18.00 (0-912722-01-0) Prem Press.

Miller, David W. & Starr, Martin K. Structure of Human Decisions. (Orig.). 1967. pap. text ed. write for info. (0-13-854687-8) P-H.

Miller, Dawn. David Robinson: Backboard Admiral. (Sports Achievers Ser.). (Illus.). 64p. (J). (gr. 4-9). 1991. lib. bdg. 13.50 (0-8225-0494-4, Lerner Publctns) Lerner Group.

— David Robinson: Backboard Admiral. (J). (gr. 4-9). 1992. pap. 4.95 (0-8225-9600-8, Lerner Publctns) Lerner Group.

Miller, Dawn, jt. auth. see Rupp, Keith.

Miller, Dayton C. Catalogue of Books & Literary Material Relating to the Flute & Other Musical Instruments. 1988. reprint ed. lib. bdg. 59.00 (0-7812-0679-0) Rprt Serv.

— Catalogue of Books & Literary Material Relating to the Flute & Other Musical Instruments, with Annotations. LC 72-181210. 29.00 (0-403-01621-5) Scholarly.

— The Science of Musical Sounds. 2nd ed. LC 76-181211. 286p. 1926. reprint ed. 59.00 (0-403-01622-3) Scholarly.

An Asterisk (*) at the beginning of an entry indicates that the title is appearing in BIP for the first time.

— The Science of Musical Sounds. 286p. 1990. reprint ed. lib. bdg. 69.00 (*0-7812-9127-5*) Rprt Serv.

Miller, Dayton C., tr. see Boehm, Theobold.

Miller, Dean F. The Case for School-Based Health Clinics. LC 90-60219. (Fastback Ser.: No. 300). 40p. (Orig.). (C). 1990. pap. 1.25 (*0-87367-300-X*) Phi Delta Kappa.

— Dimensions of Community Health. 3rd ed. 536p. (C). 1992. pap. write for info. (*0-697-10121-5*) Brown & Benchmark.

— Dimensions of Community Health. 4th ed. 512p. (C). 1995. pap. text ed. write for info. (*0-697-15262-6*) Brown & Benchmark.

— Safety: Principles & Issues. 320p. (C). 1995. boxed write for info. (*0-697-10943-7*) Brown & Benchmark.

Miller, Dean F. & Telljohan, Susan. Health Education in the Elementary School. 400p. (C). 1992. pap. text ed. write for info. (*0-697-11157-1*) Brown & Benchmark.

***Miller, Dean F. & Telljohann, Susan.** Health Education in the Elementary School. 432p. (C). 1995. pap. write for info. (*0-697-15256-1*) Brown & Benchmark.

Miller, Debbie S. A Caribou Journey. LC 93-9777. (Illus.). (J). (gr. 2-5). 1994. 15.95 (*0-316-57380-9*) Little.

— Midnight Wilderness: Journeys in Alaska's Arctic National Wildlife Refuge. LC 89-27634. (Illus.). 224p. 1990. 19.95 (*0-87156-715-6*) Sierra.

***Miller, Debby, et al.** Sound Patterns for Primary Children. (Illus.). 98p. 1988. teacher ed 8.95 (*1-886131-29-5*, SP) Math Lrning.

Miller, Debora J., jt. auth. see Nelson, John D.

Miller, Deborah. Coping When a Parent Is Gay. Rosen, Ruth, ed. (Coping Ser.). (YA). (gr. 7-12). 1993. 15.95 (*0-8239-1404-6*) Rosen Group.

— Coping with Incest. rev. ed. (J). (gr. 4-7). 1995. 15.95 (*0-8239-1949-8*) Rosen Group.

— I Will Burn Candles. 64p. 1995. pap. 8.95 (*1-896209-16-5*, Pub. by Bayeux Arts CN) Trafalgar.

Miller, Deborah & Ostrove, Karen. Fins & Scales: A Kosher Tale. LC 90-24388. (Illus.). 32p. (J). (gr. 1-3). 1992. 8.95 (*0-929371-25-9*) Kar Ben.

Miller, Deborah H. & Myers, Stewart, eds. Frontiers of Finance: The Batterymarch Fellowship Papers. (Illus.). 600p. 1991. text ed. 79.95 (*1-55786-085-8*) Blackwell Pubs.

Miller, Deborah U. My Siddur. (Illus.). 35p. (J). (gr. k-2). 1984. pap. text ed. 4.50 (*0-87441-389-3*) Behrman.

— Only Nine Chairs-A Tall Tale for Passover. LC 82-80035. (Illus.). 40p. (J). (ps-3). 1982. pap. 5.95 (*0-930494-13-X*) Kar Ben.

Miller, Debra, ed. Billy Name: Stills from the Warhol Films. (Illus.). 128p. 1994. pap. 29.95 (*3-7913-1367-3*, Pub. by Prestel) TeNeues.

Miller, Debra L. EC, 1992: A Commerce Department Analysis of European Community Directives, Vol. 3. 261p. 1990. per., pap. 13.00 (*0-16-021263-4*, S/N 003-009-005) USGPO.

— Principles for Health Care Reform. (CSIS Report Ser.). 52p. (Orig.). (gr. 13). 1994. pap. 10.00 (*0-89206-269-X*) CSI Studies.

Miller, Debra L., ed. EC, 1992, Vol. 1: A Commerce Department Analysis of European Community Directives. 181p. (Orig.). 1989. pap. 10.00 (*0-685-33672-7*, S/N 003-009-00557-4) USGPO.

— EC, 1992, Vol. 2: A Commerce Department Analysis of European Community Directives. 179p. (Orig.). 1989. pap. 9.50 (*0-16-000365-2*, S/N 003-009-00564-7) USGPO.

Miller, Dee. How Little We Knew. LC 93-85849. 224p. 1993. pap. 9.99 (*0-933451-18-0*) Prescott Pr.

Miller, Delbert C. Handbook of Research Design & Social Measurement. 5th ed. 400p. (C). 1991. 95.00 (*0-8039-4219-2*); pap. 39.95 (*0-8039-4220-6*) Sage.

— International Community Power Structures: Comparative Studies of Four World Cities. LC 74-85093. (Illus.). 342p. reprint ed. 97.50 (*0-8357-9219-6*, 2055211) Bks Demand.

***Miller, Dell M.** Re*Union: Healing Our Victim & Offender Patterns. (Illus.). 151p. (Orig.). (C). 1993. pap. 9.95 (*0-9641650-0-7*) Serenity Pubns.

***Miller, Denis R., et al, eds.** Blood Diseases of Infancy & Childhood: In the Tradition of C. H. Smith. 7th ed. LC 94-30133. 1994. write for info. (*0-8151-6137-9*) Mosby Yr Bk.

***Miller, Dennis & Hunt, Amelia.** Changing Lives: A Practical Guide to a Spiritually Powerful Youth Ministry. Prin, John, ed. (Illus.). 280p. (Orig.). (C). 1989. pap. text ed. 26.95 (*0-9627730-0-X*) CD Publshng.

Miller, Dennis P. Visual Project Planning & Scheduling: A Personal Approach to Project Management. Cascella, Christine, ed. (Illus.). 254p. (Orig.). (C). 1994. pap. text ed. 39.95 (*0-9640630-1-8*) Fifteenth St Pr.

Miller, Derek. The Age Between: Adolescence & Therapy. rev. ed. LC 83-3893. 456p. 1986. 45.00 (*0-87668-639-0*) Aronson.

— Attack on the Self: Adolescent Behavioral Disturbances & Their Treatment. LC 93-74780. 352p. 1994. pap. 35.00 (*1-56821-214-3*) Aronson.

Miller, Derek, et al. Miller, Reiter & Robbins: Three New Poets. 1991. 15.00 (*0-914610-96-1*); pap. 9.00 (*0-914610-95-3*) Hanging Loose.

Miller, Deyanne F., jt. auth. see Braund, Kathryn.

Miller, Diane, ed. see Tracy, Denise D.

Miller, Diane, et al. Dental Office Hazard Communication. rev. ed. (Illus.). 103p. (C). 1989. bmax, vhs 65.00 (*0-317-93907-6*) Hascom Inc.

— Dental Office Hazard Communication. 2nd rev. ed. (Illus.). 103p. (C). 1989. ring bd. 95.00 (*0-317-93906-8*) Hascom Inc.

Miller, Dickinson S. Philosophical Analysis & Human Welfare. Easton, Loyd D., ed. LC 75-4832. (Philosophical Studies: No. 3). x, 335p. 1975. lib. bdg. 112.50 (*90-277-0566-6*) Kluwer Ac.

Miller, Dolores E., jt. auth. see Miller, Jerome H.

Miller, Don. B Movies. 384p. 1987. mass mkt. 4.95 (*0-345-34710-2*) Ballantine.

— Calculator Explorations & Problems. (J). 1992. pap. 10.95 (*0-201-48038-7*) Addison-Wesley.

— Calculator Explorations & Problems. 108p. (J). (gr. 5-12). 1979. pap. text ed. 10.95 (*0-914040-75-8*) Cuisenaire.

— The Carr Creek Legacy. 1995. 14.95 (*0-533-11186-2*) Vantage.

— Euphoria vs. Ecstasy: How to "Get a Life" 175p. 1992. pap. 13.95 (*0-9635165-3-1*) Gate Prods.

— I Love Chocolate. LC 88-83286. (Illus.). 130p. (Orig.). 1988. pap. 8.95 (*0-938711-06-7*) Tecolote Pubns.

— The Intrepid Journey of a Timid Tourist. LC 91-90034. 160p. 1991. pap. 11.95 (*0-9628975-1-5*) Eldon Pr.

— Mental Math & Estimation. 80p. (J). (gr. 3-8). 1992. pap. text ed. 9.95 (*0-938587-30-7*) Cuisenaire.

— Pet Owner's Guide to the English Springer Spaniel. LC 95-11925. 1995. write for info. (*0-87605-920-5*) Howell Bk.

— Problem Solving Explorations. (Illus.). 150p. (C). 1993. pap. write for info. (*0-02-381302-4*) Macmillan.

— Problem Solving Study Guide to Accompany Mathematics for Elementary Teachers. 3rd ed. (Illus.). 256p. (C). 1994. pap. write for info. (*0-02-381304-0*) Macmillan.

***Miller, Don & Miller, Kathleen.** Bible Memory Verse Games for Children: 50 Fun & Creative Activities to Help Kids Learn - & Remember - God's Word. 72p. (J). Date not set. per., pap. 7.95 (*0-8341-1539-5*, 93151) Beacon Hill.

Miller, Don & Naraine, Bishnu. Problem Solving Challenges. 114p. Date not set. pap. text ed. 12.00 (*1-883547-06-7*) Tricon Pub.

Miller, Don, et al. The Hollywood Corral: A Comprehensive B-Western Roundup. Smith, M. P. & Hulse, Ed, eds. (Illus.). 485p. 1992. 59.95 (*1-880756-03-X*) Riverwood Pr.

Miller, Don A., jt. auth. see Beaver, Marion L.

Miller, Don C., jt. auth. see Cohen, Stan B.

Miller, Don E. Drug Wars: The Final Battle: Rescuing America from Drug Violence. LC 94-66003. (Illus.). 406p. (Orig.). 1994. pap. 9.95 (*0-9640695-0-4*) Speranza Prods.

Miller, Don M., jt. auth. see Canavos, George C.

Miller, Donald A. Songs in the Night: How to Have Peace under Pressure. 1992. 1.19 (*0-87509-489-9*) Chr Pubns.

Miller, Donald B. Managing Professionals in Research & Development. LC 86-7283. (Management Ser.). 427p. 1986. 40.95 (*1-55542-000-1*) Jossey-Bass.

Miller, Donald C. Ghost Towns of Montana. LC 72-95496. (Illus.). 177p. 1981. pap. 16.95 (*0-87108-606-9*) Pruett.

— Ghosts of the Black Hills. LC 79-87462. (Illus.). 72p. 1979. pap. 3.95 (*0-933126-07-7*) Pictorial Hist.

Miller, Donald C., jt. auth. see Davis, Arnold R.

***Miller, Donald E.** The Gospel & Mother Goose. fac. ed. LC 87-5180. (Illus.). 133p. (Orig.). 1994. pap. 38.00 (*0-7837-7345-5*, 2047298) Bks Demand.

— A Self-Instruction Guide Through Brethren History. fac. ed. (Church of the Brethren, Heritage Learning Program Ser.). 108p. 1994. pap. 30.80 (*0-7837-7346-3*, 2047299) Bks Demand.

— The Wing-Footed Wanderer: Conscience & Transcendence. LC 77-1503. reprint ed. 45.60 (*0-8357-9032-0*, 2016421) Bks Demand.

Miller, Donald E. & Miller, Lorna T. Survivors: An Oral History of the Armenian Genocide. LC 92-18439. 1993. 25.00 (*0-520-07984-1*) U CA Pr.

Miller, Donald E. & Relkin, Donald B. Improving Credit Practice. LC 70-119384. 367p. reprint ed. pap. 104.60 (*0-317-09935-3*, 2051517) Bks Demand.

Miller, Donald E., jt. auth. see Miller, Barry E.

Miller, Donald E., jt. auth. see Seltser, Barry J.

Miller, Donald E., jt. auth. see Seymour, Jack L.

Miller, Donald F. The Reason of Metaphor: A Study in Politics. 268p. (C). 1992. text ed. 29.95 (*0-8039-9410-9*) Sage.

Miller, Donald G. On This Rock: A Commentary on First Peter. LC 93-30951. (Princeton Theological Monograph Ser.: No. 34). 1993. pap. 30.00 (*1-55635-020-1*) Pickwick.

— The Scent of Eternity: The Life of Harris Elliott Kirk. LC 89-35945. (Illus.). xvi, 730p. (C). 1990. 31.95 (*0-86554-332-1*, MUP/H246) Mercer Univ Pr.

Miller, Donald G., ed. The Hermeneutical Quest: Essays in Honor of James Luther Mays on His Sixty-Fifth Birthday. LC 86-833. (Princeton Theological Monograph Ser.: No. 4). 1986. pap. 24.00 (*0-915138-86-7*) Pickwick.

Miller, Donald G, tr. see Bovon, Francois & Rouiller, Gregoire, eds.

Miller, Donald G., et al. P. T. Forsyth: The Man, the Preacher's Theologian & Prophet for the Twentieth Century. (Pittsburgh Theological Monographs: No. 36). 1981. pap. 15.00 (*0-915138-48-4*) Pickwick.

Miller, Donald L. Lewis Mumford: A Life. LC 91-29646. (Illus.). 672p. 1992. pap. 24.95 (*0-8229-5907-0*) U of Pittsburgh Pr.

Miller, Donald L., ed. The Lewis Mumford Reader. 400p. 1995. reprint ed. pap. 19.95 (*0-8203-1695-4*) U of Ga Pr.

Miller, Donald L. & Sharpless, Richard E. The Kingdom of Coal: Work, Enterprise, & Ethnic Communities in the Mine Fields. LC 85-1153. (Illus.). 382p. (C). 1985. pap. text ed. 24.95 (*0-8122-1201-0*) U of Pa Pr.

Miller, Donald M. & Tindall, Donald R. Ciguatera Seafood Toxins. (Illus.). 378p. 1990. 133.00 (*0-8493-6073-0*, QP632) CRC Pr.

Miller, Donald S., jt. auth. see Catt, Stephen E.

Miller, Donna. Mothers & Others Be Aware. 228p. 1986. pap. 12.95 (*0-934263-13-2*) Res Bks.

Miller, Dorcas S. Berry Finder: A Guide to Native Plants with Fleshy Fruits for Eastern North America. 62p. 1986. pap. 2.50 (*0-912550-14-7*) Nature Study.

— Good Food for Camp & Trail: All-Natural Recipes for Delicious Meals Outdoors. LC 92-38281. 190p. 1993. pap. 14.95 (*0-87108-811-8*) Pruett.

— The Stop Junk Mail Book. (Illus.). 62p. (Orig.). 1991. pap. 6.95 (*0-9628753-0-9*) Georgetwn ME.

— Track Finder. (Guide to Mammal Tracks of Eastern North America Ser.). (Illus.). 62p. 1981. pap. 2.50 (*0-912550-12-0*) Nature Study.

— Winter Weed Finder: A Guide to Dry Plants in Winter. (Illus.). 62p. 1989. pap. 2.50 (*0-912550-17-1*) Nature Study.

Miller, Doris I. & Nelson, Richard C. Biomechanics of Sport: A Research Approach. LC 73-3173. (Health Education, Physical Education, & Recreation Ser.). 273p. reprint ed. pap. 77.90 (*0-8357-7249-7*, 2056571) Bks Demand.

Miller, Doris P. Tales of a Tourist, or What Trip Was That & Who Are All These People? 1993. 15.95 (*0-533-10624-9*) Vantage.

***Miller, Dorothy.** Perfect Pair. 1994. pap. 14.95 (*0-944101-14-3*) New Pittsburgh.

— Runaways, Illegal Aliens in Their Own Land: Implications for Service. LC 79-11682. (Praeger Special Studies). 224p. 1980. text ed. 55.00 (*0-275-90525-X*, C0525, Praeger Pubs) Greenwood.

— A Song for Grandmother. Steel, Mary B., ed. 187p. (Orig.). 1990. pap. 9.95 (*1-878993-00-3*) Jeremiah Pubs.

— What Happened? My Experience with Divorce. (Illus.). 61p. (Orig.). 1987. pap. 2.95 (*0-936625-10-4*, New Hope AL) Womans Mission Union.

Miller, Dorothy, jt. auth. see Matriscrana, Patrick.

Miller, Dorothy C. Helping the Strong: An Exploration of the Needs of Families Headed by Women. (Illus.). 105p. reprint ed. pap. 30.00 (*0-7837-6542-8*, 2045679) Bks Demand.

— Women & Social Welfare: A Feminist Analysis. LC 89-16207. 191p. 1990. text ed. 45.00 (*0-275-92973-6*, C2973, Praeger Pubs) Greenwood.

— Women & Social Welfare: A Feminist Analysis. 192p. 1992. pap. text ed. 14.95 (*0-275-94384-4*, B4384, Praeger Pubs) Greenwood.

Miller, Dorothy C., ed. Americans Nineteen Forty-Two to Nineteen Sixty-Three: Six Group Exhibitions. LC 71-169312. (Museum of Modern Art Publications in Reprint). (Illus.). 560p. 1972. 71.95 (*0-405-01581-X*) Ayer.

Miller, Dorothy C. & Barr, Alfred H., Jr., eds. American Realists & Magic Realists. LC 77-86431. (Museum of Modern Art Publications in Reprint). (Illus.). 1969. reprint ed. 12.95 (*0-405-01539-9*) Ayer.

Miller, Dorothy C., jt. auth. see Mather, Eleanore P.

Miller, Dorothy C., jt. auth. see Soby, James T.

***Miller, Dorothy E.** The Long Summer. 35p. (J). 1994. lib. bdg. 9.00 (*0-9638844-1-7*) Miller & Seymour.

— The Manuscript of a Black Caucasian. 137p. 1993. pap. text ed. 14.99 (*0-685-69286-8*) Miller & Seymour.

— The Manuscript of a Black Caucasian. 151p. 1994. lib. bdg. 14.99 (*0-9638844-0-9*) Miller & Seymour.

Miller, Douglas. Henry David Thoreau. Scott, John A., ed. (Makers of America Ser.). (Illus.). 144p. (YA). (gr. 6-10). 1991. lib. bdg. 16.95 (*0-8160-2478-2*) Facts on File.

— The Landsknechts. (Men-at-Arms Ser.: No. 58). (Illus.). 48p. pap. 11.95 (*0-85045-258-9*, 9010, Pub. by Osprey UK) Stackpole.

— The Swiss at War 1300-1500. (Men-at-Arms Ser.: No. 94). (Illus.). 48p. pap. 11.95 (*0-85045-334-8*, 9030, Pub. by Osprey UK) Stackpole.

Miller, Douglas, ed. & tr. Goethe, Johann Wolfgang von: Collected Works, Vol. 12: Scientific Studies. (Illus.). xix, 344p. 1987. 40.00 (*3-518-02969-X*, Pub. by Suhr Verlag GW) Intl Bk Import.

Miller, Douglas, jt. auth. see Brown, Sallie.

Miller, Douglas, tr. see Hobbin, Enno.

Miller, Douglas B. & Shipp, R. Mark. An Akkadian Handbook: Paradigms, Helps, Logograms, & Sign Lists. 1995. pap. text ed. write for info. (*0-931464-86-2*) Eisenbrauns.

Miller, Douglas E., jt. auth. see Brown, Sallie A.

***Miller, Douglas K., et al.** Quality Improvement in Geriatric Care. 144p. 1995. write for info. (*0-8261-8840-0*) Springer Pub.

Miller, Douglas T. Birth of Modern America, 1820-1850. LC 79-114173. (Illus.). 1970. pap. 10.83 (*0-672-63509-7*) Pegasus.

— Frederick Douglass & the Fight for Freedom. (Makers of America Ser.). (Illus.). 144p. (J). (gr. 5 up). 1988. 16.95 (*0-8160-1617-8*) Facts on File.

— Frederick Douglass & the Fight for Freedom. 1993. pap. 8.95 (*0-8160-2996-2*) Facts on File.

Miller, Douglas W., jt. auth. see Calfior, Fred J.

Miller, Dudley G. Radioactivity & Radiation Detection. LC 70-146446. (Illus.). 122p. 1972. text ed. 114.00 (*0-677-01490-2*) Gordon & Breach.

Miller, Dusty. Women Who Hurt Themselves: A Book of Hope & Understanding. LC 93-4720. 224p. 1994. 22.00 (*0-465-09220-9*) Basic.

— Women Who Hurt Themselves: A Book of Hope & Understanding. 288p. 1995. pap. 12.00 (*0-465-09219-5*) Basic.

***Miller, Dwayne.** Surface Electron Transfer Processes. LC 94-22662. 1995. write for info. (*1-56081-036-X*) VCH Pubs.

Miller, Dwight C. Marcantonio Franceschini & the Liechtensteins: Prince Johan Adam Andreas & the Decoration of the Liechtenstein Garden Palace at Rossau-Vienna. (Cambridge Studies in the History of Art). (Illus.). 288p. (C). 1991. 130.00 (*0-521-36503-1*) Cambridge U Pr.

Miller, Dwight M., jt. ed. see Walch, Timothy.

Miller, E. Engineering with Plastics & Composites. 1990. text ed. write for info. (*0-442-20624-0*) Van Nos Reinhold.

— F-Animals. 96p. 1994. pap. text ed. 9.95 (*1-877978-70-1*, FLF Pr) Woldt.

— Melanges de Litterature Grecque. 491p. reprint ed. lib. bdg. 125.00 (*0-685-13371-0*, Pub. by A M Hakkert SP) Coronet Bks.

Miller, E., ed. Foundations of Child Psychiatry. 1968. 298.00 (*0-08-011826-7*, Pub. by Pergamon Repr UK) Franklin.

Miller, E., jt. auth. see Meyer, M.

Miller, E. B. Bataan Uncensored. 439p. 1991. reprint ed. pap. 13.95 (*0-9631642-0-1*) Milit Hist Soc MN.

Miller, E. C., Jr. Toward a Fuller Vision: Orthodoxy & the Anglican Experience. LC 84-61015. 188p. (Orig.). 1984. pap. 8.95 (*0-8192-1351-9*) Morehouse Pub.

Miller, E. E., et al, eds. Growth Hormone & Somatomedins During Lifespan. (Illus.). 260p. 1993. write for info. (*3-540-56690-2*) Spr-Verlag.

Miller, E. Ethelbert. First Light: New & Selected Poems. 144p. (Orig.). 1994. write for info. (*0-318-72767-6*) Black Classic.

— In Search of Color Everywhere: A Collection of Africa-American Poetry. 1994. 24.95 (*1-55670-339-2*) Stewart Tabori & Chang.

— Where Are the Love Poems for Dictators? LC 86-62885. (Illus.). (Orig.). 1987. pap. 7.95 (*0-940880-16-4*) Open Hand.

Miller, E. L. Questions That Matter. 2nd ed. 1987. text ed. write for info. (*0-07-042182-X*); Study disk, Apple. Apple II write for info. (*0-07-042177-3*) McGraw.

Miller, E. Lorraine. Free with Biz Bee. LC 77-82754. (Miller Enterprises Self-Help Bks.). (Illus.). (J). (gr. k up). 1977. 6.50 (*0-89566-350-3*) Miller Ent.

— Friendship. LC 77-79105. (Aware Bear Ser.). (Illus.). (J). (ps up). 1977. 5.00 (*0-89566-000-8*) Miller Ent.

— Rooney Crooney's Second Chance. LC 77-88334. (Miller Enterprises Self-Help Bks.). (Illus.). (J). (ps-4). 1978. per. 6.50 (*0-89566-351-1*) Miller Ent.

Miller, E. Robert, jt. auth. see Lapides, Paul D.

***Miller, E. S.** R.I.P. A Poem. Hickok, Gloria V., ed. 24p. (Orig.). 1994. pap. 2.50 (*1-884235-04-2*) Helicon Nine Eds.

Miller, E. Willard. The College of Earth & Mineral Sciences at Penn State. (Illus.). 400p. 1992. 45.00 (*0-271-00796-6*) Pa St U Pr.

— Pennsylvania: Keystone to Progress. LC 86-9207. (Illus.). 640p. 1986. 34.95 (*0-89781-171-2*) Preferred Mktg.

Miller, E. Willard, ed. A Geography of Pennsylvania. LC 94-575. 416p. 1995. 75.00 (*0-271-01017-7*); pap. text ed. 25.00 (*0-271-01342-7*) Pa St U Pr.

***Miller, E. Willard & Miller, Ruby M.** America in International Trade. 300p. 1995. 39.50 (*0-87436-770-0*) ABC-CLIO.

— Doing Business in & with Latin America: An Information Sourcebook. (Sourcebook Series in Business & Management). 128p. 1987. 35.00 (*0-89774-308-3*) Oryx Pr.

— Energy & American Society. (Contemporary World Issues Ser.). 418p. 1993. lib. bdg. 39.50 (*0-87436-689-5*) ABC-CLIO.

— Environmental Hazards: Air Pollution. (Contemporary World Issues Ser.). 250p. (C). 1989. lib. bdg. 39.50 (*0-87436-528-7*) ABC-CLIO.

— Environmental Hazards: Radioactive Materials & Wastes: A Handbook for Reference & Research. (Contemporary World Issues Ser.). 298p. 1990. lib. bdg. 39.50 (*0-87436-234-2*) ABC-CLIO.

— Water Quality & Availability: A Reference Handbook. LC 92-33057. (Contemporary World Issues Ser.). 1992. lib. bdg. 39.50 (*0-87436-647-X*) ABC-CLIO.

Miller, E. Willard & Miller, Rudy M. Environmental Hazards: Toxic Wastes & Hazardous Materials. (Contemporary World Issues Ser.). 175p. 1991. lib. bdg. 39.50 (*0-87436-596-1*) ABC-CLIO.

Miller, E. Willard, jt. ed. see Majumdar, Shyamal K.

Miller, Ed L. Believing in God: Statements on Faith & Reason. LC 92-41719. (Illus.). 220p. (Orig.). (C). 1997. pap. write for info. (*0-02-381192-7*) Macmillan.

— God & Reason: A Historical Approach to Philosophical Theology. 224p. (C). 1972. pap. write for info. (*0-02-381270-2*) Macmillan.

— God & Reason: A Historical Approach to Philosophical Theology. 2nd ed. 256p. (C). 1994. pap. write for info. (*0-02-381261-3*) Macmillan.

— Questions that Matter. 3rd ed. 624p. (C). 1992. teacher ed write for info. (*0-318-72123-6*); text ed. write for info. (*0-07-042187-0*); MAC. disk write for info. (*0-318-72126-0*); IBM 5-1/4". 5.25 hd write for info. (*0-318-72125-2*); Apple. Apple II write for info. (*0-318-72124-4*) McGraw.

— Questions That Matter: An Invitation to Philosophy. LC 92-43671. 448p. (C). 1993. pap. text ed. write for info. (*0-07-042191-9*) McGraw.

Miller, Ed L., ed. Good News in History: Essays in Honor of Professor Bo Reicke. LC 93-17977. (Homage Ser.). 212p. 1993. 44.95 (*1-55540-882-6*, 001617) Scholars Pr GA.

Miller, Edgar. Abnormal Aging: The Psychology of Senile & Presenile. LC 76-28175. 176p. 1992. reprint ed. pap. 50.20 (*0-8357-5006-X*, 2022408) Bks Demand.

— Recovery & Management of Neuropsychological Impairments. fac. ed. LC 83-21582. 185p. 1984. reprint ed. pap. 52.80 (*0-7837-8286-1*, 2049068) Bks Demand.

Miller, Edgar & Cooper, Peter J. Adult Abnormal Psychology. (Illus.). 400p. 1988. text ed. 89.00 (*0-443-03513-X*) Churchill.

M

An Asterisk (*) at the beginning of an entry indicates that the title is appearing in BIP for the first time.

Miller, Edgar & Morley, Stephen, eds. Investigating Abnormal Behavior. (Weidenfeld Modern Psychology Ser.). 343p. 1986. pap. text ed. 34.50 (*0-86377-053-3*) L Erlbaum Assocs.

Miller, Edgar & Morris, Robin. The Psychology of Dementia. LC 93-5046. (Clinical Psychology Ser.). 300p. 1994. text ed. 46.95 (*0-471-92776-7*) Wiley.

Miller, Edgar G., Jr. American Antique Furniture, 2 Vols, 1. (Illus.). 1966. pap. 19.95 (*0-486-21599-7*) Dover.

— American Antique Furniture, 2 Vols, 2. (Illus.). 1966. pap. 19.95 (*0-486-21600-4*) Dover.

Miller, Edith S., pseud. Occult Theocracy. 741p. 18.00 (*0-913022-37-3*) Angriff Pr.

Miller, Edmund. Exercises in Style. 4th ed. 68p. (C). 1984. pap. 4.00 (*0-9600486-3-4*) Edmund Miller.

— Fucking Animals: A Book of Poems. 67p. (Orig.). 1973. pap. 5.00 (*0-9600486-2-6*) Edmund Miller.

— George Herbert's Kinships. vi, 140p. (Orig.). 1993. pap. text ed. 19.00 (*1-55613-793-1*) Heritage Bk.

— The Happiness Cure: And Other Poems. (Illus.). 32p. (Orig.). (C). 1993. pap. text ed. 5.00 (*1-878173-35-9*) Birnham Wood.

— Leavings. (C). 1995. pap. text ed. 5.00 (*1-878173-41-3*) Birnham Wood.

— The School for Coeds. 1972. pap. 1.25 (*0-9600486-1-8*) Edmund Miller.

Miller, Edmund & DiYanni, Robert. Like Season 'd Timber: New Essays on George Herbert. (Seventeenth-Century Texts & Studies). 396p. 1988. text ed. 55.95 (*0-8204-0466-7*) P Lang Pubs.

Miller, Edmund K., et al, eds. Computational Electromagnetics: Frequency - Domain Method of Moments. LC 91-12159. (Illus.). 528p. (C). 1992. 69.95 (*0-87942-276-9*, PC02709) Inst Electrical.

Miller, Edna. Duck Duck. (Treehouse Bks.). (J). (ps-3). 1981. pap. 3.95 (*0-685-03845-9*) P-H.

— Exploring Ctos. 1991. pap. text ed. 35.80 (*0-13-297342-1*) P-H.

— Mousekin Finds a Friend. LC 67-18924. (Illus.). 32p. (J). (gr. k-4). 1987. pap. 5.95 (*0-671-66973-7*, S&S Bks Young Read) S&S Childrens.

— Mousekin's ABCs. LC 72-176159. (Illus.). 32p. (J). (gr. k-4). 1974. pap. 5.95 (*0-671-66473-5*, S&S Bks Young Read) S&S Childrens.

— Mousekin's Christmas Eve. LC 65-25244. (Illus.). 32p. (J). (gr. k-4). 1972. pap. 5.95 (*0-671-66479-4*, S&S Bks Young Read) S&S Childrens.

— Mousekin's Close Call. LC 77-27571. (Illus.). (J). (gr. k-3). 1980. 9.95 (*0-13-604207-4*, Pub. by Treehouse Paperback) P-H.

— Mousekin's Easter Basket. LC 86-22511. (Illus.). 32p. (J). (ps-3). 1989. pap. 12.95 (*0-671-66803-X*, S&S Bks Young Read); pap. 5.95 (*0-671-67439-0*, S&S Bks Young Read) S&S Childrens.

— Mousekin's Fables. (Illus.). 28p. (J). (ps-3). 1982. 11.95 (*0-13-604165-5*) P-H.

— Mousekin's Family. (Illus.). (J). (gr. k-3). 1972. lib. bdg. 9.95 (*0-13-604462-X*, Pub. by Treehouse Paperback) P-H.

— Mousekin's Family. LC 69-12673. (Illus.). 32p. (J). (gr. k-4). 1972. pap. 5.95 (*0-671-66477-8*, S&S Bks Young Read) S&S Childrens.

— Mousekin's Frosty Friend. LC 89-29892. (Illus.). 32p. (J). (gr. k-4). 1990. pap. 14.00 (*0-671-70445-1*, S&S Bks Young Read) S&S Childrens.

— Mousekin's Golden House. LC 64-16429. (Illus.). 32p. (J). (gr. k-4). 1971. pap. 5.95 (*0-671-66972-9*, S&S Bks Young Read) S&S Childrens.

— Mousekin's Golden House. LC 87-32111. (J). (ps-3). 1990. pap. 14.00 (*0-671-66282-1*, S&S Bks Young Read) S&S Childrens.

— Mousekin's Lost Woodland. LC 91-4201. (Illus.). 40p. (J). (ps-3). 1992. pap. 14.00 (*0-671-74938-2*, S&S Bks Young Read) S&S Childrens.

— Mousekin's Thanksgiving. (Illus.). 32p. (J). (ps-3). 1988. pap. 5.95 (*0-671-66859-5*, S&S Bks Young Read) S&S Childrens.

— Mousekin's Thanksgiving. (J). 1985. pap. 12.95 (*0-671-66470-0*) S&S Trade.

— Mousekin's Woodland Sleepers. (J). 1987. 11.95 (*0-13-604505-7*) P-H.

— Patches Finds a New Home. (Illus.). (J). (ps-4). 1989. pap. 12.95 (*0-671-66266-X*, S&S Bks Young Read) S&S Childrens.

— Patches Finds a New Home. LC 87-32355. (Illus.). 40p. (J). (gr. k-4). 1993. pap. 5.95 (*0-671-79677-1*, S&S Bks Young Read) S&S Childrens.

— Scamper. 1993. pap. 3.99 (*0-517-11066-0*) Random Hse Value.

— Scamper: A Gray Tree Squirrel. (Illus.). 32p. (J). (gr. k-3). 1991. lib. bdg. 14.95 (*0-945912-12-9*) Pippin Pr.

Miller, Edward. Portrait of a College. 160p. 1993. pap. 21.00 (*1-85183-052-9*, Silent Bks) St Mut.

— Textiles: Properties & Behavior. (Illus.). 192p. 1984. pap. 34.95 (*0-7134-7235-9*, Pub. by Batsford UK) Trafalgar.

Miller, Edward, ed. The Agrarian History of England & Wales, Vol. 3, 1350-1500. (Illus.). 750p. (C). 1991. 150.00 (*0-521-20074-1*) Cambridge U Pr.

— Plastics Products Design Handbook, Pt. A: Materials & Components. LC 81-9730. (Mechanical Engineering Ser.: No. 10). (Illus.). 615p. reprint ed. pap. 175.30 (*0-7837-4083-2*, 2052480) Bks Demand.

***Miller, Edward, ed. & intro.** Ready to Learn: How Schools Can Help Kids Be Healthier & Safer. (Harvard Education Letter Reprint Ser.: No. 2). 100p. (Orig.). (C). 1995. pap. 15.00 (*1-883433-01-0*) Harvard Educ Rev.

***Miller, Edward & Hatcher, John.** Medieval England: Towns, Commerce, & Crafts, 1086-1348. LC 94-31297. (Social & Economic History of England Ser.). 488p. (C). 1996. text ed. 56.95 (*0-582-48548-7*, 77006); pap. text ed. 26.95 (*0-582-48549-5*, 77005) Longman.

Miller, Edward, jt. auth. see Ames, Nancy L.

Miller, Edward A., Jr. Gullah Statesman: Robert Smalls from Slavery to Congress, 1839-1915. LC 94-17937. 1994. write for info. (*1-57003-002-2*) U of SC Pr.

Miller, Edward A. History of Educational Legislation in Ohio from 1803 to 1850. LC 72-89204. (American Education: Its Men, Institutions & Ideas, Ser. 1). 1970. reprint ed. 13.95 (*0-405-01442-2*) Ayer.

Miller, Edward B. An Administrative Appraisal of the NLRB. 3rd ed. LC 80-85253. (Labor Relations & Public Policy Ser.: No.16). 169p. 1981. pap. 15.00 (*0-89546-029-7*) U PA Wharton Ctr Human Resc.

— Antitrust Laws & Employee Relations: An Analysis of Their Impact on Management & Union Policies. LC 84-48294. (Labor Relations & Public Policy Ser.: No. 26). 144p. 1984. pap. 20.00 (*0-89546-046-7*) U PA Wharton Ctr Human Resc.

Miller, Edward D. The Power Staff. abr. ed. 162p. 1995. pap. 7.95 (*1-56901-335-7*) NW Pub.

— The Role of Student Organizations in Vocational Education. 10p. 1983. 2.25 (*0-318-22195-0*, OC94) Ctr Educ Trng Employ.

Miller, Edward F. Influence of Gesenius on Hebrew Lexicography. LC 28-3581. (Columbia University. Contributions to Oriental History & Philology Ser.: No. 11). reprint ed. 14.00 (*0-404-50541-4*) AMS Pr.

***Miller, Edward G.** A Dark & Bloody Ground: The Hurtgen Forest & the Roer River Dams, 1944-1945. LC 94-45333. (Texas A&M University Military History Ser.: No. 42). (Illus.). 260p. (C). 1995. 29.95 (*0-89096-626-5*) Tex A&M Univ Pr.

Miller, Edward J. John Henry Newman on the Idea of Church. LC 87-61223. (Illus.). 200p. 1987. 29.95 (*0-915762-16-1*) Patmos Pr.

Miller, Edward J. & Wolensky, Robert P., eds. The Small City & Regional Community: Proceedings of the 1979 Conference, Vol. II. (Orig.). 1979. pap. text ed. 16.50 (*0-932310-01-X*) U of Wis-Stevens Point.

— The Small City & Regional Community: Proceedings of the 1981 Conference, Vol. IV. LC 79-644450. viii, 550p. (Orig.). (C). 1981. pap. text ed. 16.50 (*0-932310-03-6*) U of Wis-Stevens Point.

— The Small City & Regional Community: Proceedings of the 1984 Conference, Vol. VI. LC 79-644450. viii, 450p. (Orig.). (C). 1985. pap. text ed. 16.50 (*0-932310-06-0*) U of Wis-Stevens Point.

Miller, Edward J., jt. auth. see Wolensky, Robert P.

Miller, Edward J., jt. ed. see Wolensky, Robert P.

Miller, Edward M. U.S.S. Monitor: The Ship that Launched a Modern Navy. 1978. 24.95 (*0-915268-10-8*) Ayer.

Miller, Edward S. War Plan Orange: The U. S. Strategy to Defeat Japan, 1897-1945. LC 91-14361. (Illus.). 509p. 1991. 34.95 (*0-87021-759-3*) Naval Inst Pr.

Miller, Edwin H. Salem Is My Dwelling Place: A Life of Nathaniel Hawthorne. LC 91-14543. (Illus.). 648p. 1991. 37.95 (*0-87745-332-2*) U of Iowa Pr.

— Salem Is My Dwelling Place: A Life of Nathaniel Hawthorne. LC 91-14543. (Illus.). 648p. 1993. reprint ed. pap. 16.95 (*0-87745-381-0*) U of Iowa Pr.

— Walt Whitman's "Song of Myself" A Mosaic of Interpretations. LC 88-38069. 209p. 1989. pap. 19.95x (*0-87745-345-4*) U of Iowa Pr.

Miller, Edwin H., ed. Selected Letters of Walt Whitman. LC 89-20478. (Illus.). 340p. (Orig.). (C). 1990. pap. 19.95 (*0-87745-267-9*) U of Iowa Pr.

Miller, Edwin H., ed. see Whitman, Walt.

***Miller, Elaine.** Alabama Myths, Mysteries & Legends. 1995. pap. write for info. (*1-878561-36-7*) Seacoast AL.

Miller, Eleanor. One Hundred Reading Games & Activities: Fun Excerises for Teaching & Reinforcing Basic Reading Skills. LC 84-81873. 128p. (Orig.). 1986. pap. text ed. 19.95 (*0-918452-77-5*) Learning Pubns.

Miller, Eleanor M. Street Woman. (Women in the Political Economy Ser.). 216p. 1986. pap. 16.95 (*0-87722-509-5*) Temple U Pr.

Miller, Elinor & Genovese, Eugene D., eds. Plantation, Town, & County: Essays on the Local History of American Slave Society. LC 73-20359. 463p. reprint ed. pap. 132.00 (*0-317-09956-6*, 2022778) Bks Demand.

Miller, Elinor, tr. see Butor, Michel.

Miller, Elisa B. & Karp, Alexander, eds. The Russian Far East: A Reference Guide. (Orig.). 1994. pap. 37.50 (*0-9641286-0-8*) Russian Far East.

***Miller, Elizabeth B.** The Internet Resource Directory for K-12 Teachers & Librarians, 94-95. 100p. 1994. pap. text ed. 25.00 (*1-56308-337-X*) Libs Unl.

Miller, Elizabeth G., tr. see Balcells, Jacqueline.

Miller, Elizabeth G., tr. see Lindo, Hugo.

Miller, Elizabeth L. Get Rolling: The Beginner's Guide to In-Line Skating. LC 92-81185. (Illus.). 128p. (Orig.). 1992. pap. 10.00 (*0-9632196-2-6*) Pix & Pts.

— I Just Need More Time. (Illus.). 1984. 12.95 (*0-9610530-0-3*) Woman Time Mgmt.

Miller, Elizabeth R., comp. The American Revolution. (Illus.). 146p. (Orig.). 1991. pap. 14.50 (*1-55613-466-5*) Heritage Bk.

Miller, Elizabeth W., ed. The Negro in America: A Bibliography. 2nd enl. rev. ed. 373p. (C). 1970. pap. 16.50 (*0-674-60702-3*) HUP.

Miller, Elizabeth W., ed. see Mather, Cotton.

Miller, Ella M. A Woman & Her Home. LC 93-84461. 128p. 1993. reprint ed. pap. 6.95 (*0-89221-241-1*) New Leaf.

***Miller, Ellanita.** Never, Never Talk to Strangers. (Illus.). 16p. (J). (gr. 1-5). 1995. pap. 6.00 (*0-8059-3714-5*) Dorrance.

Miller, Ellen. Video: A Guide for Lawyers. LC 83-80276. 142p. 1983. 29.75 (*0-88238-063-X*) Law Arts.

Miller, Ellen, jt. auth. see Hansen, Orval.

Miller, Ellen, jt. auth. see Lindstrom, Peter.

Miller, Ellen C. Eastern Sketches: Notes of Scenery, Schools, & Tent Life in Syria & Palestine. Davis, Moshe, ed. (America & the Holy Land Ser.). 1977. reprint ed. lib. bdg. 23.95 (*0-405-10269-0*) Ayer.

Miller, Ellen S., jt. auth. see Freeberg, Ellen M.

Miller, Elliot & Samples, Kenneth B. The Cult of the Virgin: Catholic Mariology & the Apparitions of Mary. LC 92-4273. (Christian Research Institute Ser.). 192p. 1992. pap. 9.99 (*0-8010-6291-8*) Baker Bk.

Miller, Elliott. A Crash Course on the New Age Movement: Describing & Evaluating a Growing Social Force. 1989. 14.99 (*0-8010-6251-9*); pap. 10.99 (*0-8010-6248-9*) Baker Bk.

— The Jews of Sandor. (Illus.). 25p. (Orig.). (C). 1975. pap. 1.50 (*0-935982-21-3*, SMJ-01) Spertus Coll.

Miller, Elmer I. Legislature of the Province of Virginia. LC 08-1371. (Columbia University. Studies in the Social Sciences: No. 76). reprint ed. 32.50 (*0-404-51076-0*) AMS Pr.

***Miller, Elmer S.** Nurturing Doubt: From Missionary to Anthropologist in the Argentine Chaco. LC 94-30791. 248p. (C). 1995. pap. 17.50 (*0-252-06455-0*) U of Ill Pr.

Miller, Elwyn R., et al. Swine Nutrition. (Illus.). 696p. 1991. text ed. 85.00 (*0-409-90095-8*) Buttrwrth-Heinemann.

***Miller, Emery, ed.** User's Guide to Powder Coating. 2nd fac. ed. LC 87-61422. (Illus.). 300p. reprint ed. pap. 85.50 (*0-7837-8189-X*, 2047894) Bks Demand.

Miller, Emery P., ed. User's Guide to Powder Coating. LC 85-71675. (Illus.). 176p. reprint ed. pap. 50.20 (*0-8357-6481-8*, 2035852) Bks Demand.

Miller, Emily, ed. see Business of Your Own Staff.

Miller, Emma G. Clatsop County, Oregon: Its History, Legends & Industries. LC 57-13209. (Illus.). 334p. 1978. reprint ed. 14.95 (*0-8323-0034-9*) Binford Mort.

Miller, Emmanuel. Glossaire Grec-Latin de la Bibliotheque de Laon. No. 29-2. 230p. reprint ed. write for info. (*0-318-72054-X*, Pub. by Georg Olms GW) Lubrecht & Cramer.

Miller, Emmett E. Opening Your Inner "I" LC 87-14660. 296p. (Orig.). 1987. pap. 11.95 (*0-89087-642-8*) Celestial Arts.

— Self Imagery: Creating Your Own Good Health. rev. ed. LC 78-4529. 272p. (Orig.). 1986. pap. 8.95 (*0-89087-458-1*) Celestial Arts.

***Miller, Eric.** From Dependency to Autonomy: Studies in Organization & Change. 343p. 1993. pap. 42.00 (*1-85343-335-7*) Col U Pr.

Miller, Eric & Miller, Walden. Discovering CD-I. Davis, David F., ed. (Illus.). 178p. (Orig.). (C). 1991. pap. text ed. write for info. (*0-918035-02-3*, DCD68NA68BK) Microware Systs.

Miller, Eric J., ed. Task & Organization. LC 75-12606. (Wiley Series on Individuals, Groups & Organizations). 397p. reprint ed. pap. 113.20 (*0-318-35028-9*, 2030928) Bks Demand.

Miller, Erika T. Guide to Collections in the Archives & Special Collections on Women in Medicine at the Medical College of Pennsylvania. 69p. (Orig.). (C). 1987. 10.00 (*0-944542-00-X*) Med Coll PA ASCWM.

Miller, Erin-Aine, jt. ed. see Hinman, Felicitas.

Miller, Ernest C., ed. Conference Leadership: A Manual to Assist in the Development of Conference Leaders. rev. ed. LC 72-86426. (Illus.). 124p. reprint ed. pap. 35.40 (*0-317-09780-6*, 2050344) Bks Demand.

Miller, Ernest G., jt. auth. see Lyden, Fremont J.

Miller, Ernestine. The Sportswoman Daybook. (Illus.). 120p. 1993. 14.95 (*0-8109-3973-8*) Abrams.

Miller, Errol. Education for All: Caribbean Perspectives & Imperatives. 250p. (Orig.). (C). 1992. pap. text ed. 18.50 (*0-940602-45-8*) IADB.

— A Succession of Fine Lives. Bixby, Robert, ed. 36p. 1993. pap. 6.00 (*1-882983-04-1*) March Street Pr.

Miller, Erston V. & Munger, James I. Good Fruits & How to Buy Them. (Illus.). (Orig.). 1967. 4.95 (*0-910286-22-1*); pap. 3.95 (*0-910286-04-3*) Boxwood.

Miller, Ervin. The Microeconomic Effects of Monetary Policy. LC 77-17980. 1978. text ed. 29.95 (*0-312-53173-7*) St Martin.

Miller, Estelle B., jt. ed. see Kinoy, Barbara P.

Miller, Ethel H. Story of Quailwood. (Illus.). 48p. 1952. 4.95 (*0-912142-07-3*); pap. 2.00 (*0-912142-04-9*) White S Bks.

— White Saddle. 1934. 5.95 (*0-912142-02-2*); lib. bdg. 6.95 (*0-912142-01-4*); pap. 3.95 (*0-912142-03-0*) White S Bks.

Miller, Ethel M. Bibliography of Ohio Botany. (Bulletin Ser.: No. 27). 1932. 3.00 (*0-86727-026-8*) Ohio Bio Survey.

Miller, Eugene. Barron's Guide to Graduate Business Schools. 8th ed. 1992. pap. 14.95 (*0-8120-4863-6*) Barron.

— Guide to Graduate Business Schools. 9th ed. 1995. pap. 14.95 (*0-8120-1753-6*) Barron.

Miller, Eugene, jt. auth. see Thomas, Edmund J.

Miller, Eugene D., ed. Mexico in the 1990s: Liberalization & the State. 100p. (C). 1991. write for info. (*0-929972-05-8*) CUNY Bildner Ctr.

Miller, Eugene E. Voice of a Native Son: The Poetics of Richard Wright. LC 89-37374. 275p. 1990. 35.00 (*0-87805-399-9*) U Pr of Miss.

Miller, Eugene F., ed. see Hume, David.

Miller, Eugene L., Jr., jt. auth. see Arnold, Edwin T.

Miller, Ev. Close the Door So It Can't Get in Your Room. (Illus.). 52p. (Orig.). 1986. pap. 4.00 (*0-88680-265-2*) I E Clark.

— Dickerson for Senate. 1983. pap. 3.00 (*0-686-39594-8*) Eldridge Pub.

— A Dusty Echo. LC 88-93078. 42p. (Orig.). 1989. pap. 6.00 (*0-88734-219-1*) Players Pr.

— The Incredible Years. 78p. 1991. pap. 4.95 (*0-87129-092-8*, I45) Dramatic Pub.

— Morning Shows the Day. LC 93-48187. 60p. (Orig.). 1994. pap. 6.00 (*0-88734-246-9*) Players Pr.

— A Nice Day in the Park. 1984. pap. 1.75 (*0-912963-03-4*) Eldridge Pub.

— The Wonderful Western Hat. 1985. 2.50 (*0-87129-372-2*, W61) Dramatic Pub.

Miller, Evelyn. Airedale Terriers. (Illus.). 160p. 1989. 11.95 (*0-86622-674-5*, KW165) TFH Pubns.

— Budgies As a Hobby. (Save Our Planet Ser.). (Illus.). 98p. 1991. pap. 7.95 (*0-86622-416-5*, TT002) TFH Pubns.

— Fox Terriers. 1990. 11.95 (*0-86622-754-7*, KW-185) TFH Pubns.

— Miniature Pinschers. (Illus.). 160p. 1989. lib. bdg. 9.95 (*0-86622-872-1*, KW162) TFH Pubns.

Miller, Evelyn, et al. Reading & Language Arts for All Students: A Practical Guide for Content Area Teachers. 496p. (C). 1994. per. 46.95 (*0-8403-9309-1*) Kendall-Hunt.

Miller, Everitt L. & Cohen, Jay S. The American Garden Guidebook: West. LC 89-37897. 294p. 1989. pap. 9.95 (*0-87131-580-7*) M Evans.

— The American Garden Guidebook East. LC 87-6857. 294p. 1987. pap. 8.95 (*0-87131-499-1*) M Evans.

Miller, F. B. Miller Family: Descendants of Frank Miller. (Illus.). 174p. 1991. reprint ed. lib. bdg. 47.00 (*0-8328-2086-5*); reprint ed. pap. 37.00 (*0-8328-2087-3*) Higginson Bk Co.

Miller, F. D. & Kureth, E. C. Reflections of a Warrior. McCarthy, Paul, ed. 256p. 1992. reprint ed. mass mkt. 5.50 (*0-671-75396-7*) PB.

Miller, F. L. A Guide to Confession. (RUS.). 1992. 0.25 (*1-56036-032-1*) AMI Pr.

— Marian Spirituality of Pope John Paul the Second. 1992. pap. 0.50 (*1-56036-050-X*) AMI Pr.

— Mary - Catechist at Fatima. (SPA.). 1993. 1.50 (*1-56036-030-5*) AMI Pr.

— Mary & the Priesthood. (SPA.). 1993. 1.95 (*1-56036-031-3*) AMI Pr.

Miller, F. L., ed. see Thomas, D. V.

Miller, F. M. Chemistry: Structure & Dynamics. 1984. Instr's. manual. teacher ed write for info. (*0-07-041986-8*); Solutions supplement. write for info. (*0-07-041988-4*) McGraw.

Miller, F. P., et al, eds. Land Use Planning, Techniques & Policies. (Special Publication Ser.). 123p. 1984. pap. 12.00 (*0-89118-772-3*) Soil Sci Soc Am.

Miller, F. R., jt. auth. see Curtis, W. D.

Miller, F. Thornton. Juries & Judges vs. the Law: Virginia's Provincial Legal Perspective, 1783-1828. (Illus.). 192p. (C). 1994. text ed. 32.50 (*0-8139-1486-8*) U Pr of Va.

Miller, F. Thornton, ed. see Taylor, John.

Miller, Faren. The Illusionists. 1991. mass mkt. 4.95 (*0-446-36131-3*) Warner Bks.

Miller, Faye Y. & Coffey, Wayne. Winning Basketball for Girls. (Illus.). 160p. 1992. 19.95 (*0-8160-2769-2*); pap. 11.95 (*0-8160-2776-5*) Facts on File.

Miller, Florence & Rotella, Alexis K. Eleven Renga. (Illus.). 40p. 1993. 11.00 (*0-917951-27-1*) Jade Mtn.

Miller, Florence F. Hardscrabble Journey. 1994. 22.45 (*1-881591-09-3*) Grizzly Bear.

Miller, Florence S. A Legacy of Learning: The History of the West Chester Area Schools. 339p. 1994. text ed. 25.00 (*0-9640745-0-8*) W Chester Area.

Miller, Floyd C. Gods Maintenance Program for the New Creature. Biebel, Kenneth, ed. 61p. (Orig.). 1988. write for info. (*0-318-63719-7*) Prevailing Word Pubns.

Miller, Floyd J. The Search for a Black Nationality: Black Emigration & Colonization, 1787-1863. LC 75-4650. (Blacks in the New World Ser.). 311p. reprint ed. pap. 88.70 (*0-317-10832-8*, 2020247) Bks Demand.

Miller, Floyd J., ed. see Delany, Martin R.

Miller, Forrestt A. Dmitrii Miliutin & the Reform Era in Russia. LC 68-20545. 1968. 17.95 (*0-8265-1112-0*) Vanderbilt U Pr.

***Miller, Fraank.** Sin City Bk. 1: A Dame to Kill For. 2nd ed. (Illus.). 208p. 1994. pap. 15.00 (*1-56971-068-6*) Dark Horse Comics.

Miller, Frances. WordPerfect 5.1 - "Instant Replay" "On the Job" Quick Notes. 100p. 1994. pap. 20.00 (*0-9642135-1-6*) Good To Go.

Miller, Frances A. The Truth Trap. 1984. pap. 2.25 (*0-449-70096-8*, Juniper) Fawcett.

— The Truth Trap. 187p. (YA). 1986. reprint ed. pap. 3.95 (*0-449-70247-2*, Juniper) Fawcett.

Miller, Francesca. Latin American Women & the Search for Social Justice. LC 91-50371. (Illus.). 342p. 1991. text ed. 45.00 (*0-87451-557-2*); pap. 19.95 (*0-87451-558-0*) U Pr of New Eng.

Miller, Francis P. Man from the Valley: Memoirs of a Twentieth Century Virginian. LC 71-132255. (Illus.). 280p. reprint ed. pap. 79.80 (*0-8357-3867-1*, 2036599) Bks Demand.

Miller, Francis T. Lindbergh: His Story in Pictures. Gilbert, James B., ed. LC 79-7286. (Flight: Its First Seventy-Five Years Ser.). (Illus.). 1980. reprint ed. lib. bdg. 36.95 (*0-405-12195-4*) Ayer.

— Lindbergh: His Story in Pictures. (Illus.). 320p. 1989. reprint ed. pap. 15.00 (*0-910667-14-4*) Northstar Bks.

— Portrait Life of Lincoln. LC 76-133528. (Select Bibliographies Reprint Ser.). 1977. reprint ed. 28.95 (*0-8369-5560-9*) Ayer.

Miller, Frank. Batman: The Dark Night Returns. O'Neil, D. & Giordano, D., eds. 200p. 1986. pap. 12.95 (*0-930289-13-7*) DC Comics.

— Batman: Year One. Bruning, Richard, ed. 208p. 1988. pap. 9.95 (*0-930289-33-1*) DC Comics.

Miller, Frank, et al. Batman: The Dark Knight Returns. 1986. pap. 13.95 (*0-446-38505-0*) Warner Bks.

An Asterisk (*) at the beginning of an entry indicates that the title is appearing in BIP for the first time.

Miller, Frank. Casablanca: Fiftieth Anniversary Commemorative. Sunshine, Linda, ed. (Illus.). 224p. 1992. 29.95 (*1-878685-14-7*); pap. 19.95 (*1-878685-17-1*) Turner Pub GA.

— Censored Hollywood: Sex, Sin & Violence on Screen. LC 94-19982. 1994. 24.95 (*1-57036-116-9*); pap. 14.95 (*1-878685-55-4*) Turner Pub GA.

— Complete Frank Miller Batman. (Deluxe Leatherbound Ser.). (Illus.). 312p. 1989. 29.95 (*0-681-40969-X*) Longmeadow Pr.

— Daredevil: Love & War. (Illus.). 64p. 1986. 9.95 (*0-87135-172-2*) Marvel Entmnt.

— Daredevil: Man Without Fear. 160p. 1994. pap. 15.95 (*0-7851-0046-6*) Marvel Entmnt.

— Elektra, No. 16: Assassin. deluxe limited ed. Duffy, Jo, ed. (Illus.). 255p. 1989. ring bd. 39.95 (*0-936211-14-8*) Graphitti Designs.

— Give Me Liberty, Bk. 1. deluxe limited ed. (Illus.). 224p. 1995. 114.95 (*1-56971-045-7*) Dark Horse Comics.

— Give Me Liberty, Bk. 1. 2nd ed. (Illus.). 208p. 1994. pap. 19.95 (*1-56971-067-8*) Dark Horse Comics.

— Hard Boiled, Bk. 1. deluxe limited ed. (Illus.). 144p. 1995. 99.95 (*1-56971-049-X*) Dark Horse Comics.

— Ronin. Marx, Barry, ed. 302p. 1987. pap. 12.95 (*0-930289-21-8*) DC Comics.

— Ronin. 302p. 1987. pap. 12.95 (*0-446-38674-X*) Warner Bks.

— Sin City. deluxe limited ed. Prosser, Jerry, ed. (Illus.). 208p. 1992. 79.95 (*1-878574-82-5*) Dark Horse Comics.

— Sin City. rev. ed. Prosser, Jerry, ed. (Illus.). 208p. 1992. pap. 15.00 (*1-878574-59-0*) Dark Horse Comics.

— Sin City. rev. ed. Prosser, Jerry, ed. (Illus.). 208p. 1994. 25.00 (*1-56971-036-8*) Dark Horse Comics.

— Sin City, Bk. 1. (Illus.). 208p. 1994. 25.00 (*1-56971-048-1*) Dark Horse Comics.

— Sin City Bk. 1: A Dame to Kill For. deluxe limited ed. (Illus.). 216p. 1995. 90.00 (*1-56971-046-5*) Dark Horse Comics.

***Miller, Frank, ed. & text.** MGM Posters: The Golden Years. LC 94-26286. (Illus.). 1994. 24.95 (*1-57036-105-3*) Turner Pub GA.

Miller, Frank & Darrow, Geof. Hard Boiled Collection. Prosser, Jerry, ed. (Illus.). 128p. 1993. pap. 14.95 (*1-878574-58-2*) Dark Horse Comics.

Miller, Frank & Gibbons, Dave. Give Me Liberty - an American Dream, Vol. 1: Homes & Gardens. Stradley, Randy, ed. (Illus.). 48p. (Orig.). 1990. pap. 4.95 (*1-878574-09-4*) Dark Horse Comics.

— Give Me Liberty - an American Dream, Vol. 2: Travel & Entertainment. Stradley, Randy, ed. (Illus.). 48p. (Orig.). 1990. pap. 4.95 (*1-878574-10-8*) Dark Horse Comics.

— Give Me Liberty - an American Dream, Vol. 3: Health & Welfare. Stradley, Randy, ed. (Illus.). 48p. (Orig.). 1990. pap. 4.95 (*1-878574-11-6*) Dark Horse Comics.

— Give Me Liberty - An American Dream, Vol. 4: Death & Taxes. Stradley, Randy, ed. (Illus.). 48p. (Orig.). 1991. pap. 4.95 (*1-878574-12-4*) Dark Horse Comics.

— Give Me Liberty Collection. (Illus.). 216p. 1992. pap. 16.00 (*1-878574-26-4*) Dark Horse Comics.

Miller, Frank & Mazzucchelli, David. Batman: Year One. 1988. pap. 10.95 (*0-446-38923-4*) Warner Bks.

— Daredevil: Born Again. 176p. 1987. pap. 9.95 (*0-87135-297-4*) Marvel Entmnt.

Miller, Frank & Seinkiewicz, Bill. Elektra: Assassin. 264p. 1987. pap. 12.95 (*0-87135-309-1*) Marvel Entmnt.

Miller, Frank & Varley, Lynn. Elektra Lives Again. (Illus.). 96p. 1990. 24.95 (*0-87135-738-0*) Marvel Entmnt.

Miller, Frank, jt. auth. see Kagan, Olga.

Miller, Frank, et al. Daredevil: Gang War. (Illus.). 112p. 1992. pap. 12.95 (*0-87135-880-8*) Marvel Entmnt.

***Miller, Frank B.** Miller Family: An Address Delivered Before the Miller Re-Union at N. Waldoboro, Maine, Sept. 7, 1904, with Genealogy. (Illus.). 47p. 1995. reprint ed. lib. bdg. 20.00 (*0-8328-4561-2*); reprint ed. pap. 10.00 (*0-8328-4562-0*) Higginson Bk Co.

Miller, Frank C. Old Villages & a New Town: Industrialization in Mexico. rev. ed. (Illus.). 177p. (C). 1990. reprint ed. pap. text ed. 9.50 (*0-88133-487-1*) Waveland Pr.

***Miller, Frank C. & Miller, Wilma B.** Blueprint Reading for Heating, Ventilating & Air Conditioning. LC 95-1920. 1995. teacher ed, text ed. write for info. (*0-8273-6872-0*) Delmar.

***Miller-Frank, Felicia.** The Mechanical Song: Women, Voice, & the Artificial in Nineteenth-Century French Narrative. LC 94-34279. 1995. 35.00 (*0-8047-2381-8*) Stanford U Pr.

Miller, Frank J. Folklore for Stalin: Russian Folklore & Pseudofolklore in the Stalin Era. LC 90-21540. 192p. 1990. 57.95 (*0-87332-668-7*) M E Sharpe.

— A Handbook of Russian Verbs: Spravochnik po Russkim Glagolam. (Orig.). (ENG & RUS.). (C). 1989. pap. text ed. 15.95 (*0-87501-052-0*) Ardis Pubs.

— Reading & Speaking about Russian Newspapers. (Focus Text Ser.). 300p. (Orig.). (C). 1989. pap. text ed. 19.95 (*0-941051-05-6*) Focus Info Gr.

— Study Guide for Reading & Speaking about Russian Newspapers. (Focus Text Ser.). 1989. pap. text ed. 9.95 (*0-941051-06-4*) Focus Info Gr.

Miller, Frank N. Pathology, Review for New National Boards. LC 93-79828. 222p. 1993. pap. text ed. 25.00 (*0-9632873-3-8*) J & S Pub VA.

Miller, Frank W., et al. Criminal Justice Administration: Cases & Materials On. 4th ed. (University Casebook Ser.). 1265p. 1991. text ed. 44.50 (*0-88277-860-9*) Foundation Pr.

— Criminal Justice Administration: Cases & Materials, 1994 Supplement. 4th ed. (University Casebook Ser.). 129p. 1994. pap. text ed. 7.95 (*1-56662-209-3*) Foundation Pr.

— Criminal Justice Administration, 1993 Supplement to Cases & Materials On. 4th ed. (University Casebook Ser.). 91p. 1993. pap. text ed. 7.95 (*1-56662-091-0*) Foundation Pr.

— The Juvenile Justice Process. 3rd ed. LC 85-10268. (University Casebook Ser.). 1020p. 1985. text ed. 37.95 (*0-88277-243-0*) Foundation Pr.

— The Police Function. 5th ed. 640p. 1991. pap. text ed. 21.95 (*0-88277-881-1*) Foundation Pr.

— Prosecution & Adjudication. 4th ed. 1260p. 1991. pap. text ed. 22.25 (*0-88277-882-X*) Foundation Pr.

Miller, Franklin, Jr., et al. College Physics. 6th ed. 869p. (C). 1987. teacher ed 4.00 (*0-15-511747-5*); text ed. 61.25 (*0-15-511743-2*) SCP.

Miller, Fred. Music in Advertising. (Illus.). 104p. 1985. pap. 9.95 (*0-8256-2289-1*, AM61227) Music Sales.

— Studio Recording for Musicians. (Illus.). 144p. pap. 14.95 (*0-8256-4204-3*) Music Sales.

Miller, Fred, et al. Management & Organization Analysis of the Stockton Municipal Court Clerk-Administrator's Office. 195p. 1987. 12.00 (*0-685-33622-0*, WRO-087) Natl Ctr St Courts.

— Management Review of the Clerk's Office, Circuit & County Courts, 11th Judicial Circuit of Florida. 157p. 1989. 9.50 (*0-685-34853-9*, SERO-055) Natl Ctr St Courts.

— Organization, Management, & Technology Review for the Courts of the Commonwealth of the Northern Mariana Islands. 139p. 1991. 8.50 (*0-685-55332-9*, WRO131) Natl Ctr St Courts.

***Miller, Fred D., Jr.** Nature, Justice, & Rights in Aristotle's Politics. (Illus.). 384p. 1995. text ed. 65.00 (*0-19-824061-9*) OUP.

Miller, Fred D. Out of the Mouths of Babes: The Infant Formula Controversy. 98p. 1983. pap. 14.95 (*0-912051-01-9*) Transaction Pubs.

Miller, Fred D. & Smith, Nicholas D. Thought Probes. 2nd ed. 368p. (C). 1989. pap. text ed. write for info. (*0-13-920059-2*) P-H.

Miller, Fred D., jt. ed. see Keyt, David.

Miller, Fred H. & Harrell, Alvin C. The Law of Modern Payment Systems & Notes. 2nd ed. LC 92-22178. 1992. write for info. (*0-87084-562-4*) Anderson Pub Co.

Miller, Fred P. Christian Attitudes & Racial Problems. rev. ed. 60p. 1993. pap. 4.95 (*1-883116-03-1*) Moellerhaus.

— Revelation: A Panorama of the Gospel Age. 404p. 1991. pap. 19.95 (*1-883116-01-5*) Moellerhaus.

— Revelation: A Panorama of the Gospel Age. 2nd rev. ed. 424p. 1993. pap. text ed. 19.95 (*1-883116-00-7*) Moellerhaus.

— Thinking on Drinking: A New Look at an Old Question. 32p. 1990. pap. 3.50 (*1-883116-04-X*) Moellerhaus.

— Zechariah & Jewish Renewal: From Gloom to Glory. 255p. 1992. pap. 15.95 (*1-883116-02-3*) Moellerhaus.

Miller, Frederick H., jt. auth. see Stockton, John M.

Miller, Frederick H., et al. Practitioner's Guide to the Oklahoma Uniform Consumer Credit Code, 1990-1992. 490p. 1990. ring bd. 95.00 (*0-409-25146-1*) Butterworth Legal Pubs.

— Practitioner's Guide to the Oklahoma Uniform Consumer Credit Code, 1990-1992. suppl. ed. 490p. 1992. 52.50 (*1-56257-975-4*) Butterworth Legal Pubs.

Miller, Frederick L. Una Guia Para la Confesion. 1989. 0.25 (*0-911988-80-7*) AMI Pr.

— A Guide to Confession. 1989. 0.25 (*0-911988-79-3*) AMI Pr.

— Mary: Catechist at Fatima. 1991. 1.50 (*1-56036-010-0*) AMI Pr.

— Mary & the Priesthood. 55p. 1990. 1.95 (*0-911988-89-0*) AMI Pr.

— The Significance of Fatima: A Seventy-Five Year Perspective. 1993. 2.00 (*1-56036-078-X*) AMI Pr.

Miller, Frederick T., jt. auth. see Langton, Stuart.

Miller, Fredric M. Arranging & Describing Archives & Manuscripts. (Archival Fundamentals Ser.). 132p. 1990. pap. 25.00 (*0-931828-75-9*) Soc Am Archivists.

Miller, Fredric M., et al. Still Philadelphia: A Photographic History, 1890-1940. LC 82-19227. 312p. 1983. 24.95 (*0-87722-306-8*) Temple U Pr.

***Miller, Fredric M. & Gillette, Howard, Jr.** Washington Seen: A Photographic History, 1875-1965. LC 95-2948. (Illus.). 288p. 1995. 35.95 (*0-8018-4979-9*) Johns Hopkins.

Miller, Fredric M., et al. Philadelphia Stories: A Photographic History, 1920-1960. (Illus.). 336p. (C). 1988. 29.95 (*0-87722-551-6*) Temple U Pr.

***Miller, Freeman, et al.** Cerebral Palsy: A Complete Guide for Caregiving. LC 95-8826. (Health Book Ser.). (Illus.). 488p. 1995. 35.95 (*0-8018-5091-6*) Johns Hopkins.

Miller, G. Calculations for Examination Physics. (C). 1985. text ed. 65.00 (*0-85950-212-0*, Pub. by S Thornes Pubs UK) St Mut.

— DRUGS & the LAW: Detection, Recognition & Investigation. 1994. pap. 34.95 (*0-87526-398-4*) Gould.

Miller, G. A. Nucleon Resonances & Nucleon Structures: Institute for Nuclear Theory 1st Summer School. 400p. 1992. text ed. 95.00 (*981-02-0954-1*) World Scientific Pub.

Miller, G. E. & Fulop, T. Educational Strategies for the Health Professions. (Public Health Papers: No. 61). 1974. pap. 2.80 (*92-4-130061-2*) World Health.

Miller, G. Hindman. Ten Thousand Dreams Interpreted. 1988. 9.99 (*0-517-65834-8*) Random Hse Value.

Miller, G. J., jt. auth. see Miller, Norman E.

Miller, G. M. Historical Point of View in English Literary Criticism from 1570-1770. LC 67-30906. 160p. 1967. reprint ed. 45.00 (*0-87753-027-0*) Phaeton.

Miller, G. M., comp. Thudding Drums. LC 79-76948. (Granger Index Reprint Ser.). 1977. 19.95 (*0-8369-6030-0*) Ayer.

Miller, G. S., Jr. Characters & Probable History of the Hawaiian Rat. Bd. with Ectoparasites of Some Polynesian and Malaysian Rats of the Genus Rattus. (BMB Ser.). 1972. reprint ed. Set pap. 15.00 (*0-527-02117-2*) Periodicals Srv.

— The Families & Genera of Bats. 1967. reprint ed. 60.00 (*3-7682-0534-7*) Lubrecht & Cramer.

Miller, G. S. What, How & Do It! 205p. (C). 1989. text ed. 70.00 (*1-872795-41-2*, Pub. by Pentland Pr UK) St Mut.

Miller, G. Tyler, Jr. Chemistry: A Basic Introduction. 4th ed. 561p. (C). 1987. text ed. 49.95 (*0-534-06912-6*) Intl Thomson.

— Environment: Problems & Solutions. 150p. 1994. pap. 14.95 (*0-534-23394-5*) Intl Thomson.

— Environmental Science: Sustaining the Earth. 4th ed. 470p. (C). 1993. text ed. 54.95 (*0-534-17808-1*) Intl Thomson.

— Environmental Science: Working with the Earth. 5th ed. LC 94-1534. 540p. 1995. text ed. 54.95 (*0-534-21588-2*) Intl Thomson.

***Miller, G. Tyler.** Living in the Environment: Principles, Connections, & Solutions. 9th ed. LC 95-8559. (Biology Ser.). 1996. text ed. 59.95 (*0-534-23898-X*) Intl Thomson.

Miller, G. Tyler, Jr. Living in the Environment: An Introduction to Environmental Science. 7th ed. 705p. (C). 1992. text ed. 55.95 (*0-534-16560-5*) Intl Thomson.

— Living in the Environment: Problems, Connections, & Solutions. 8th ed. 701p. (C). 1994. text ed. 59.95 (*0-534-19950-X*) Intl Thomson.

— Sustaining the Earth: An Integrated Approach. 360p. 1994. pap. 31.95 (*0-534-21432-0*) Intl Thomson.

Miller, G. Tyler, Jr. & Lygre, David G. Chemistry: A Contemporary Approach. 3rd ed. 674p. (C). 1991. text ed. 51.95 (*0-534-14280-X*) Intl Thomson.

Miller, G. Wayne. Coming of Age. LC 94-20307. 1995. 22.00 (*0-679-42326-5*) Random.

— The Work of Human Hands: Surgical Wonder at Children's Hospital. LC 92-531. 1993. 23.00 (*0-679-40264-0*) Random.

Miller, G. William, ed. Regrowing the American Economy. LC 83-3171. 192p. 1983. 11.95 (*0-13-771022-4*); pap. 4.95 (*0-13-771014-3*) Am Assembly.

Miller, Gabriel. Clifford Odets. (Literature & Life Ser.). 192p. (C). (gr. 12). 1989. 19.95 (*0-8044-2632-5*) Continuum.

— Critical Essays on Clifford Odets. (Critical Essays on American Literature Ser.). 288p. (C). 1991. text ed. 45.00 (*0-8161-7300-1*, Hall Reference) Macmillan.

Miller, Gale. Enforcing the Work Ethic: Rhetoric & Everyday Life in a Work Incentive Program. LC 89-26319. (SUNY Series in the Sociology of Work). (Illus.). 252p. (C). 1991. 59.50 (*0-7914-0423-4*); pap. 19.95 (*0-7914-0424-2*) State U NY Pr.

Miller, Gale & Holstein, James A. Constructionist Controversies: Issues in Social Problems Theory. LC 92-36979. (Social Problems & Social Issues Ser.). 231p. 1993. pap. 23.95 (*0-202-30457-4*) Aldine de Gruyter.

Miller, Gale, jt. ed. see Holstein, James A.

Miller, Gary. Mind Bogglers for Juniors. 38p. (J). 1991. student ed 1.95 (*1-882449-00-2*) Messenger Pub.

***Miller, Gary D.** Ancient Scripts & Phonological Knowledge. LC 94-28635. (Current Issues in Linguistic Theory Ser.: No. 116). 1994. lib. bdg. 35.00 (*1-55619-570-2*) Benjamins North Am.

— Complex Verb Formation. LC 92-34479. (Current Issues in Linguistic Theory Ser.: No. 95). xix, 381p. 1993. 83.00x (*1-55619-156-1*) Benjamins North Am.

Miller, Gary E. The Meaning of General Education: The Emergence of a Curriculum Paradigm. LC 87-26739. 224p. reprint ed. pap. 63.90 (*0-7837-0988-9*, 2041294) Bks Demand.

Miller, Gary J. Cities by Contract: The Politics of Municipal Incorporation. 256p. 1981. 35.00x (*0-262-13164-1*) MIT Pr.

— Managerial Dilemmas: The Political Economy of Hierarchy. (Political Economy of Institutions & Decisions Ser.). (Illus.). 268p. (C). 1992. 59.95 (*0-521-37281-X*) Cambridge U Pr.

— Managerial Dilemmas: The Political Economy of Hierarchy. (Political Economy of Institutions & Decisions Ser.). (Illus.). 268p. (C). 1993. pap. 16.95 (*0-521-45769-6*) Cambridge U Pr.

Miller, Gary J., jt. auth. see Knott, Jack H.

Miller, Gary M. Modern Electronic Communication. 4th ed. LC 92-17273. 640p. 1993. text ed. 74.00 (*0-13-589201-5*) P-H.

— Modern Electronic Communications. 2nd ed. (Illus.). 592p. (C). 1983. text ed. 42.00 (*0-13-593152-5*) P-H.

Miller, Gary M. & Rotter, Joseph C. The Middle School Counselor. LC 83-24028. 246p. 1985. 29.50 (*0-910328-38-2*); pap. 17.50 (*0-910328-39-0*) Sulzburger & Graham Pub.

Miller, Gene. God's Saving Power. (Eagle Bible Ser.). 1989. pap. 2.50 (*0-87162-499-0*, D9151) Warner Pr.

Miller, Gene H. Microcomputer Engineering. 480p. 1993. text ed. 74.00 (*0-13-584475-4*) P-H.

Miller, Genevieve. Bibliography of the History of Medicine of the United States & Canada, 1939-1960. 1979. 37.95 (*0-405-10616-5*) Ayer.

— A Bibliography of the Writings of Henry E. Sigerist. LC 66-19764. 123p. reprint ed. pap. 35.10 (*0-8357-7205-5*, 2023831) Bks Demand.

Miller, Genevieve, ed. Letters of Edward Jenner & Other Documents Concerning the Early History of Vaccination. LC 82-21295. (Henry E. Sigerist Supplements to the Bulletin of the History of Medicine, New Ser.). 176p. (C). 1983. text ed. 28.50x (*0-8018-2962-3*) Johns Hopkins.

Miller, Geoffrey. The Black Glove. 254p. 1984. pap. 3.50 (*0-88184-080-7*) Carroll & Graf.

Miller, Geoffrey & Ramer, Jeanette C. Static Encephalopathies of Infancy & Childhood. 384p. 1992. 121.00 (*0-88167-872-4*) Raven.

Miller, Geoffrey F., jt. auth. see Baker, Christopher T.

Miller, Geoffrey P., jt. auth. see Macey, Jonathan R.

***Miller, Georg J., et al.** Pennsylvania Guide to Air Permitting & Enforcement: A Practical Guide to Compliance. 172p. 1995. 77.00 (*0-925773-20-4*) M Lee Smith.

Miller, George. Landscaping with Native Plants of Texas & the Southwest. LC 90-44298. (Illus.). 128p. (Orig.). 1991. pap. 19.95 (*0-89658-138-1*) Voyageur Pr.

***Miller, George, comp.** The Prentice Hall Reader. 4th ed. LC 94-32237. 593p. 1994. pap. text ed. write for info. (*0-13-079302-7*) P-H.

Miller, George, ed. Giving Children a Chance: The Case for More Effective National Policies. (Orig.). write for info. (*0-318-67253-7*) Ctr National Policy.

— Giving Children a Chance: The Case for More Effective National Policies. LC 88-35188. 246p. (Orig.). (C). 1989. lib. bdg. 37.25 (*0-944237-27-4*); pap. text ed. 21.00 (*0-944237-28-2*) Ctr National Policy.

Miller, George & Matthews, Hugoe. Richard Jefferies: A Bibliographical Study. 832p. 1993. 129.95 (*0-85967-918-7*, Pub. by Scolar Pr UK) Ashgate Pub Co.

Miller, George, jt. ed. see Smith, Frank.

Miller, George, jt. auth. see Stueart, Robert D.

Miller, George, jt. auth. see Tull, Delena.

Miller, George A. Language & Speech. 150p. (C). 1995. pap. text ed. 14.95 (*0-7167-1298-9*) W H Freeman.

— The Science of Words: A Scientific American Library Book. 250p. 1995. text ed. 32.95 (*0-7167-5027-9*) W H Freeman.

Miller, George A. & Johnson-Laird, Philip N. Language & Perception. 773p. 1987. pap. 17.95 (*0-674-50948-X*) Belknap Pr.

Miller, George A. & Lenneberg, Elizabeth, eds. Psychology & Biology of Language & Thought: Essays in Honor of Eric Lenneberg. 1978. text ed. 53.00 (*0-12-497750-2*) Acad Pr.

Miller, George A., jt. auth. see Chomsky, Noam.

Miller, George A., jt. ed. see Grusky, Oscar.

Miller, George A., jt. intro. see James, William.

Miller, George A., et al. Plans & the Structure of Behavior. (Illus.). 226p. (C). 1986. reprint ed. text ed. 24.95 (*0-937431-00-1*) Adams Bannister Cox.

Miller, George B., Jr., et al, comps. Puppetry Library: An Annotated Bibliography Based on the Batchelder-McPharlin Collection at the University of New Mexico. LC 80-23474. xxi, 171p. 1981. text ed. 42.95 (*0-313-21359-3*, HPL/, Greenwood Pr) Greenwood.

Miller, George E. Educating Medical Teachers. (Commonwealth Fund Publications). (Illus.). 243p. 1980. 25.00 (*0-674-23775-7*) HUP.

Miller, George F. Academy System of the State of New York. LC 76-89205. (American Education: Its Men, Institutions & Ideas, Ser., No. 1). 1977. reprint ed. 18.95 (*0-405-01443-0*) Ayer.

Miller, George H. Railroads & the Granger Laws. LC 75-138059. 308p. reprint ed. pap. 87.80 (*0-8357-4752-2*, 2037674) Bks Demand.

Miller, George H. & Gidbeau, Kenneth W. Residential Real Estate Appraisal: An Introduction to Real Estate Appraising. (Illus.). 1980. text ed. 29.67 (*0-13-774521-4*) P-H.

Miller, George H. & Gilbeau, Kenneth W. Residential Real Estate Appraisal. 2nd ed. (Illus.). 320p. (C). 1987. text ed. 51.00 (*0-13-762428-X*) P-H.

Miller, George H., jt. auth. see Ashley, Robert.

Miller, George H., et al. California Real Estate Appraisal: Residential Properties. 3rd ed. (Illus.). 304p. (C). 1987. text ed. 50.00 (*0-13-112558-3*) P-H.

— California Real Estate Appraisal: Residential Properties. 4th rev. ed. LC 94-40190. 1995. text ed. 42.67 (*0-13-312067-8*) P-H.

Miller, George L. Tantalum & Niobium. (Metallurgy of the Rarer Metals Ser.: 6). 789p. reprint ed. pap. 180.00 (*0-317-41849-1*, 2025734) Bks Demand.

Miller, George L. & Krumm, La Rue. The Whats, Whys, & Hows of Quality of Improvement. 1992. pap. 29.95 (*0-87389-183-X*) ASQC Qual Pr.

Miller, George N. The Strike of a Sex & Zugassent's Discovery: After the Sex Struck. LC 73-20636. (Sex, Marriage & Society Ser.). 124p. 1974. reprint ed. 19.95 (*0-405-05812-8*) Ayer.

Miller, George N., ed. see Noyes, John H.

Miller, George O. Texas Hill Country. (Illus.). 96p. 1991. 21.95 (*0-89658-164-0*) Voyageur Pr.

— Texas Parks & Campgrounds: A Vacation Guide. 3rd ed. (Texas Monthly Guidebook Ser.). 224p. 1995. pap. 14.95 (*0-87719-265-0*, 9265, Lone Star Bks) Gulf Pub.

— Texas Photo Safaris. LC 85-28814. (Illus.). 256p. 1986. pap. 14.95 (*0-932012-92-2*, Lone Star Bks) Gulf Pub.

Miller, George O., jt. auth. see Tull, Delena.

Miller, Gerald J. Government Financial Management Theory. (Public Administration & Public Policy Ser.: Vol. 43). 272p. 1991. 99.75 (*0-8247-7910-X*) Dekker.

Miller, Gerald R. An Introduction to Speech Communication. 2nd ed. LC 78-173982. 1972. pap. text ed. 3.95 (*0-672-61298-4*, SC7, Bobbs) Macmillan.

Miller, Gerald R. & Stiff, James B. Deceptive Communication: Many Questions & a Few Answers. (Series in Interpersonal Communication: Vol. 14). (Illus.). 160p. 1993. 49.95 (*0-8039-3484-X*); pap. 24.00 (*0-8039-3485-8*) Sage.

Miller, Gerald R., jt. ed. see Knapp, Mark L.

Miller, Gerald R., jt. ed. see Roloff, Michael E.

M

*Miller, Gerald V.** The Gay Male's Odyssey in the Corporate World: From Disempowerment to Empowerment. LC 94-47539. 163p. (C). 1995. lib. bdg. 39.95 (*1-56024-942-0*); pap. 14.95 (*1-56023-867-4*) Haworth Pr.

Miller, Gerlinde F. Die Bedeutu ng des Entwicklungsbeqriffs fuer Menschenbild und Dichtungstheorie bei Gottfried Benn. (New York University Ottendorfer Ser.: Vol. 29). 291p. 1988. text ed. 47.80 (*0-8204-0835-2*) P Lang Pubs.

Miller, Gilbert H. & Crooks, Alan F., eds. Major Modern Essayists. 2nd ed. LC 93-20970. 487p. 1994. pap. text ed. write for info. (*0-13-497983-4*) P-H.

Miller, Girard. Effective Budgetary Presentations: The Cutting Edge. LC 82-81886. (Illus.). 230p. 1982. 15.00 (*0-685-06405-0*); pap. 23.50 (*0-686-84268-5*); pap. 18.50 (*0-686-84269-3*) Municipal.

— A Public Investor's Guide to Money Market Instruments. LC 82-80937. (Illus.). 111p. 1982. pap. 13.00 (*0-686-84370-3*); pap. 11.00 (*0-686-84371-1*) Municipal.

Miller, Girard, jt. auth. see Government Finance, Officers Association Staff.

Miller, Girard, jt. auth. see Municipal Finance Officers Association Staff.

Miller, Glenn. Customer Service & Innovation in Libraries. 90p. 1995. pap. 12.00 (*0-917846-39-7*, 95614) Highsmith Pr.

Miller, Glenn A. & Pender, Robert H. Golf: A Target Sport. 2nd ed. (Illus.). 113p. (Orig.). 1991. pap. text ed. 8.95 (*0-89641-219-9*) American Pr.

Miller, Glenn T. Piety & Intellect: The Aims & Purposes of Ante-Bellum Theological Education. (Studies in Theological Education). 458p. 1990. 59.95 (*1-55540-470-7*) Scholars Pr GA.

Miller, Glenn W. & Skaggs, Jimmy M., eds. Metropolitan Wichita: Past, Present, & Future. LC 77-16690. x, 194p. 1978. pap. 12.95 (*0-7006-0169-4*) U Pr of KS.

Miller, Gloria. Above All, Don't Flush: Adventures in Valorous Living. LC 81-22035. 160p. (Orig.). 1982. pap. 7.95 (*0-916930-03-3*) Wistaria Pr.

Miller, Gloria B. Figure Sculpture in Wax & Plaster. Miller, Richard M., ed. 176p. 1987. reprint ed. pap. 8.95 (*0-486-25354-6*) Dover.

— The Thousand Recipe Chinese Cookbook. 1984. pap. 20.00 (*0-671-50993-4*, Fireside) S&S Trade.

***Miller, Gordon, ed. & photos.** Wisdom of the Earth: Visions of an Ecological Faith. (Wisdom of the Earth Ser.: Vol. 1). (Illus.). 160p. (Orig.). 1995. pap. 19.95 (*0-9647007-1-9*) Green Rock.

— Wisdom of the Earth: Visions of an Ecological Faith, 3 vols., Set. (Wisdom of the Earth Ser.: Vol. 1). (Illus.). (Orig.). Date not set. write for info. (*0-9647007-0-0*) Green Rock.

Miller, Gordon, jt. auth. see Dann, Kevin.

***Miller, Gordon L.** The History of Science. (Magill Bibliographies Ser.). 193p. 1992. 40.00 (*0-8108-2795-6*) Scarecrow.

Miller, Gordon P. Choosing a College. 165p. 1990. pap. 9.95 (*0-87447-333-0*) College Bd.

Miller, Graham. Calvin's Wisdom. 392p. 1992. 35.95 (*0-85151-624-6*) Banner of Truth.

— Treasury of His Promises. 386p. (Orig.). 1986. pap. 17.95 (*0-85151-472-3*) Banner of Truth.

Miller, Graham A., ed. Handbook of Cardiac Catheterization. (Illus.). 128p. 1990. pap. 39.95 (*0-632-02691-X*) Blackwell Sci.

Miller, Gregory, jt. auth. see Connell, Des W.

***Miller, Gregory A., ed.** The Behavioral High-Risk Paradigm in Psychopathology. LC 95-6678. (Series in Psychopathology). (Illus.). 304p. 1995. 98.00 (*0-387-94504-0*) Spr-Verlag.

***Miller, Gregory D., et al.** Handbook of Dairy Foods & Nutrition. 256p. 1994. 69.95 (*0-8493-8505-9*, 8505) CRC Pr.

***Miller, Gustavus H.** Dictionary of Dreams: An Alphabetical Journey Through the Images of Sleep. 1994. 9.98 (*0-8317-2297-5*) Smithmark.

Miller, Gwynelle W., jt. auth. see Miller, Sherman N.

Miller, H. Henry the Eighth English Nobility. 1989. pap. 19.95 (*0-631-16863-X*) Blackwell Pubs.

— Progress & Decline: Group in Evolution. LC 63-12997. 1963. 122.00 (*0-08-010831-8*, Pub. by Pergamon Repr UK) Franklin.

Miller, H. & McGuire, G. Evaluating Liberal Adult Education. 1961. 2.50 (*0-87060-034-6*, REP 125) Syracuse U Cont Ed.

Miller, H. & Miller, C. Evolution: From Stellar Dust to Technological Society. (C). 1975. pap. text ed. 8.80 (*0-87563-090-1*) Stipes.

Miller, H. & Rosenfeld, U., eds. Tenth Symposium on Latin-American Geosciences, Berlin 1986. (Zentralblatt Fuer Geologie Ser.). (Illus.). 368p. 1987. pap. 92.40 (*0-945345-26-7*, Pub. by Schweitzerbart'sche GW) Lubrecht & Cramer.

Miller, H. A. Electrical Installation Practice. 5th ed. LC 93-7062. 1993. write for info. (*0-632-03524-2*) Blackwell Sci.

Miller, H. A. & Whittier, H. O. Prodromus Florae Hepaticarum Polynesiae. (Bryophytorum Bibliotheca Ser.: Vol. 25). 422p. 1983. lib. bdg. 90.00 (*3-7682-1373-0*) Lubrecht & Cramer.

Miller, H. A., et al. Bryoflora of the Atolls of Micronesia. (Illus.). 1963. pap. 24.00 (*3-7682-5411-9*) Lubrecht & Cramer.

— Prodromus Florae Muscorum Polynesiae with a Key to Genera. 1978. lib. bdg. 65.00 (*3-7682-1115-0*) Lubrecht & Cramer.

Miller, H. G., et al. OSHA & State Employee Hazard Communications Program, 2 vols., Vols. 1-2. Knowles-McFarland, ed. 622p. 1985. 395.00 (*0-940394-16-2*) Labelmaster.

Miller, H. R. & Ravenel, D. C., eds. Algebraic Topology, Vol. 1286. (Lecture Notes in Mathematics Ser.). vii, 341p. 1987. pap. 45.30 (*0-387-18481-3*) Spr-Verlag.

Miller, H. R. & Witta, P. J., eds. Active Galactic Nuclei. (Lecture Notes in Physics Ser.: Vol. 307). xi, 438p. 1988. 53.00 (*0-387-19492-4*) Spr-Verlag.

Miller, H. Richard & Wiita, Paul J., eds. Variability of Active Galactic Nuclei. (Illus.). 416p. (C). 1991. 59.95 (*0-521-41295-1*) Cambridge U Pr.

Miller, Hal. The Abandoned Middle: The Ethics & Politics of Abortion in America. 80p. (Orig.). (C). 1988. pap. text ed. 5.50 (*0-317-01537-0*) Penumbra Press.

— The Abandoned Middle: The Ethics & Politics of Abortion in America. LC 88-90864. 92p. (Orig.). (C). 1988. pap. text ed. 7.95 (*0-929645-00-6*) Penumbra MA.

Miller-Hall, Mary. Deaf, Dumb, & Black: An Accounting of an Actual Life of a Family. 1994. 13.95 (*0-8062-4929-3*) Carlton.

Miller, Hannah E. Films in the Classroom: A Practical Guide. LC 78-21941. 313p. 1979. lib. bdg. 21.00 (*0-8108-1184-7*) Scarecrow.

— Films in the Classroom: A Practical Guide. LC 78-21941. 638p. reprint ed. pap. 180.00 (*0-317-52043-1*, 2027476) Bks Demand.

Miller, Harlan. Arguments, Arrows, Trees & Truth: A First Book in Logic & Language. 2nd ed. 242p. (C). 1980. pap. text ed. 8.65 (*0-89894-036-2*) Advocate Pub Group.

Miller, Harlan B. & Williams, William H., eds. Ethics & Animals. LC 82-21387. (Contemporary Issues in Biomedicine, Ethics, & Society Ser.). 416p. 1983. pap. 22.95 (*0-89603-053-9*) Humana.

Miller, Harold D., jt. ed. see Zimmerman, Sherwood E.

Miller, Harold G. New Zealand. LC 82-24157. (British Empire History Ser.). 156p. 1983. reprint ed. text ed. 49.75 (*0-313-22997-X*, MINZ, Greenwood Pr) Greenwood.

— Race Conflict in New Zealand, 1814-1865. LC 81-20183. (Illus.). xxvii, 328p. 1982. reprint ed. text ed. 52.50 (*0-313-23443-4*, MIRC, Greenwood Pr) Greenwood.

Miller, Harold L., ed. Wisconsin Progressives: The Charles McCarthy Papers: Guide to a Microfilm Edition. 38p. 1986. pap. 25.00 (*0-87020-235-4*) Chadwyck-Healey.

— Wisconsin Progressives: The John R. Commons Papers: Guide to a Microfilm Edition. 48p. 1986. pap. 25.00 (*0-87020-236-2*) Chadwyck-Healey.

— Wisconsin Progressives: The Richard T. Ely Papers: Guide to a Microfilm Edition. 78p. 1986. pap. 25.00 (*0-87020-233-8*) Chadwyck-Healey.

Miller, Harold L. & Aber, Lynn B., eds. Wisconsin Progressives: The Edward A. Ross Papers: Guide to a Microfilm Edition. 51p. 1986. pap. 25.00 (*0-87020-234-6*) Chadwyck-Healey.

Miller, Harold L., jt. ed. see Albert, Peter J.

Miller, Harrice S. Costume Jewelry: Identification & Price Guide. 2nd ed. 344p. (Orig.). 1994. pap. 15.00 (*0-380-77078-4*, Confident Collect) Avon.

— The Official Identification & Price Guide to Costume Jewelry. 512p. 1990. pap. 12.00 (*0-87637-787-8*, House of Collect) Ballantine.

Miller, Harriet P. Pioneer Colored Christians. LC 73-37313. (Black Heritage Library Collection). 1977. reprint ed. 22.95 (*0-8369-8950-3*) Ayer.

Miller, Harriett P., jt. auth. see Bell, Charles B.

Miller, Harry. Common Sense Book. 1987. mass mkt. 4.95 (*0-553-27789-8*) Bantam.

— Common Sense Book of Kitten & Cat Care. 144p. (Orig.). 1984. pap. 4.99 (*0-553-26805-8*) Bantam.

Miller, Harry, ed. see National Passive Solar Conference Staff.

Miller, Harry E. Banking Theories in the U. S. Before 1860. LC 78-182194. (Library of Money & Banking History). xi, 240p. 1972. reprint ed. lib. bdg. 35.00 (*0-678-00886-8*) Kelley.

Miller, Harry L. Understanding Group Behavior: A Discussion Guide. rev. ed. 99p. reprint ed. pap. 28.30 (*0-317-10607-4*, 2000637) Bks Demand.

Miller, Harvey R. & Cook, Michael L. A Practical Guide to the Bankruptcy Reform Act, 2 vols. 1400p. 1979. write for info. (*0-318-65476-8*, C00191) P-H.

Miller, Haskell. Let God Be God. (Orig.). 1988. pap. 5.80 (*1-55673-062-4*, 8859) CSS OH.

Miller, Haskell M. Who Sets the Standards? Behavior, Society, & the Church. LC 89-30360. 176p. (Orig.). (C). 1989. pap. 9.95 (*0-8298-0805-1*) Pilgrim OH.

Miller, Haynes R., et al, eds. Proceedings of the Northwestern Homotopy Theory Conference. LC 83-9941. (Contemporary Mathematics Ser.: Vol. 19). 454p. 1983. pap. text ed. 42.00 (*0-8218-5020-2*, CONM-19) Am Math.

***Miller, Hazen L.** Old Au Sable. 1974. 12.95 (*0-8028-7007-4*) Eerdmans.

Miller, Heather, et al. Language Lessons for the Cirriculum, 3 vols. (Illus.). 1991. First Grade Math. spiral bd. 27.95 (*1-55999-163-1*); First Grade Language Arts. spiral bd. 27.95 (*1-55999-164-X*); First Grade Science - Social Studies. spiral bd. 27.95 (*1-55999-165-8*) LinguiSystems.

— Language Lessons for the Cirriculum, 3 vols., Set. (Illus.). 1991. spiral bd. 74.85 (*1-55999-185-2*) LinguiSystems.

Miller, Heather G., et al, eds. AIDS: The Second Decade. 512p. 1990. pap. 39.95 (*0-309-04287-9*) Natl Acad Pr.

Miller, Heather R. Friends & Assassins: Poems. LC 92-35984. 64p. (C). 1993. text ed. 16.95 (*0-8262-0828-2*); pap. 9.95 (*0-8262-0829-0*) U of Mo Pr.

— Hard Evidence: Poems. LC 90-35051. 64p. 1990. 18.95 (*0-8262-0754-5*); pap. 9.95 (*0-8262-0751-0*) U of Mo Pr.

Miller, Heather S. Children & Gardens: An Annotated Bibliography of Children's Garden Books, 1829-1988. Miasek, Meryl A., ed. (CBHL Plant Bibliography Ser.). 60p. (Orig.). (J). pap. write for info. (*0-9621791-1-6*) CBHL Inc.

— Managing Acquisitions & Vendor Relations: A How-to-Do-It Manual. (How-to-Do-It Ser.). 196p. 1992. 39.95 (*1-55570-111-6*) Neal-Schuman.

Miller, Helen H. Captains from Devon: The Great Elizabethan Seafarers Who Won the World for England. LC 85-15712. (Illus.). 256p. 1985. 16.95 (*0-912697-27-X*) Algonquin Bks.

— The Case for Liberty. LC 65-16295. (Illus.). 270p. reprint ed. pap. 77.00 (*0-8357-3051-4*, 2039307) Bks Demand.

— Colonel Parke of Virginia: The Greatest Hector in the Town. (Illus.). 210p. 1989. 19.95 (*0-912697-87-3*) Algonquin Bks.

— George Mason, Gentleman Revolutionary. LC 75-1377. (Illus.). 404p. reprint ed. pap. 115.20 (*0-8357-3873-6*, 2036605) Bks Demand.

— Passage to America: Ralegh's Colonists Take Ship for Roanoke. (America's 400th Anniversary Ser.). (Illus.). xiv, 84p. 1986. reprint ed. pap. 5.00 (*0-86526-202-0*) NC Archives.

Miller, Helen L. Everyday Plays for Boys & Girls. LC 86-8884. (Orig.). (J). (gr. 1-6). 1986. pap. 12.00 (*0-8238-0274-4*) Plays.

— First Plays for Children. 295p. (J). (gr. 1-3). 1985. pap. 12.00 (*0-8238-0268-X*) Plays.

— Special Plays for Holidays. LC 86-9332. (Orig.). (J). (gr. 1-6). 1986. pap. 12.00 (*0-8238-0275-2*) Plays.

***Miller, Helena.** Magic Box. Grishaver, Joel L., ed. (Illus.). (Orig.). (J). (gr. k up). 1995. pap. text ed. 18.95 (*0-933873-92-1*) Torah Aura.

Miller, Henry. The Air-Conditioned Nightmare. LC 45-11390. 1970. pap. 10.95 (*0-8112-0106-6*, NDP302) New Directions.

— Aller Retour New York. LC 91-4029. (Revived Modern Classics Ser.). 96p. 1993. reprint ed. 15.95 (*0-8112-1193-2*); reprint ed. pap. 8.95 (*0-8112-1226-2*, NDP753) New Directions.

— Big Sur & the Oranges of Hieronymus Bosch. LC 57-5542. 1964. pap. 12.95 (*0-8112-0107-4*, NDP161) New Directions.

— Black Spring. 244p. 1989. pap. 10.95 (*0-8021-3182-4*) Grove-Atltic.

— Book of Friends. 1978. 42.50 (*0-911156-73-9*) Bern Porter.

— The Books in My Life. LC 71-88728. 1969. reprint ed. pap. 10.95 (*0-8112-0108-2*, NDP280) New Directions.

— California Missions: The Earliest Series of Views Made in 1856. Knill, Harry, ed. (Illus.). 64p. (Orig.). 1986. pap. 4.95 (*0-88388-119-5*) Bellerophon Bks.

— The Colossus of Maroussi. LC 58-9511. 1958. pap. 9.95 (*0-8112-0109-0*, NDP75) New Directions.

— The Cosmological Eye. LC 75-88729. 1969. reprint ed. pap. 12.95 (*0-8112-0110-4*, NDP109) New Directions.

— Crazy Crock: A Novel. 1992. pap. 9.95 (*0-8021-3293-6*) Grove-Atltic.

— A Devil in Paradise. LC 93-16389. (Bibelot Ser.). 128p. (Orig.). 1993. reprint ed. pap. 6.50 (*0-8112-1244-0*, NDP765) New Directions.

— Henry Miller, 3 vols. boxed set. Incl. Tropic of Cancer. (Orig.). 1979. (*0-318-52772-3*); Tropic of Capricorn. 1979. (*0-318-52773-1*); Black Spring. 1979. (*0-318-52774-X*); 1979. Set pap. 13.85 (*0-394-17094-6*, B430) Grove-Atltic.

— Henry Miller on Writing. Moore, Thomas H., ed. LC 64-10675. (Orig.). 1964. pap. 9.95 (*0-8112-0112-0*, NDP151) New Directions.

— Henry Miller Reader. Durrell, Lawrence, ed. LC 73-38712. (Essay Index Reprint Ser.). 1977. reprint ed. 22.95 (*0-8369-2664-1*) Ayer.

— Henry Miller Reader. Durrell, Lawrence, ed. LC 59-15022. 1969. reprint ed. pap. 12.95 (*0-8112-0111-2*, NDP269) New Directions.

— Henry Miller Stories, Essays, Travel Sketches. Fine, Antony, ed. (Illus.). 1994. 12.98 (*1-56731-009-5*, MJF Bks) Fine Comms.

— Henry Miller's Book of Friends: A Trilogy. LC 86-31691. 320p. (Orig.). 1987. pap. 9.95 (*0-88496-256-3*) Capra Pr.

— Henry Miller's Book of Friends: A Trilogy. LC 89-31049. 320p. (Orig.). (C). 1988. reprint ed. lib. bdg. 33.00x (*0-8095-4031-2*) Borgo Pr.

— Henry Miller's Hamlet Letters. Hargraves, Michael, ed. LC 88-34677. 186p. (Orig.). (C). 1988. reprint ed. lib. bdg. 27.00x (*0-8095-4058-4*) Borgo Pr.

— Into the Heart of Life: Henry Miller at One Hundred. Turner, Fredrick, ed. LC 91-29996. 224p. (Orig.). 1991. pap. 10.95 (*0-8112-1185-1*, NDP728) New Directions.

— Just Wild about Harry. LC 62-17269. 1979. pap. 7.95 (*0-8112-0724-2*, NDP479) New Directions.

— The Mezzotints. (Illus.). 40p. (C). 1993. 50.00 (*0-9634136-3-5*); 40.00 (*0-9634136-2-7*) R Jackson.

— Moloch: Or This Gentile World. 288p. 1993. pap. 12.00 (*0-8021-3372-X*) Grove-Atltic.

— My Bike & Other Friends. 1978. pap. 3.95 (*0-88496-076-5*) Capra Pr.

— Nexus: The Rosy Crucifixion III. 316p. 1987. pap. 11.95 (*0-8021-5178-7*) Grove-Atltic.

— The Nightmare Notebook. deluxe limited ed. LC 75-4746. (Illus.). 220p. 1975. 150.00 (*0-8112-0576-2*) New Directions.

— Nothing but the Marvelous: The Wisdoms of Henry Miller. Fielding, Blair, ed. LC 89-48703. (Illus.). 96p. 1990. pap. 12.95 (*0-88496-313-6*) Capra Pr.

— On the Fringe: The Dispossessed in America. 224p. 1991. text ed. 19.95 (*0-669-24905-X*) Free Pr.

— Plexus. (Orig.). 1987. pap. 9.95 (*0-394-62370-3*) Random.

— Plexus: The Rosy Crucifixion II. 640p. 1987. pap. 14.95 (*0-8021-5179-5*) Grove-Atltic.

— Printemps Noir. (FRE.). 1975. pap. 11.95 (*0-7859-4042-1*) Fr & Eur.

— Quiet Days in Clichy. 160p. 1987. pap. 9.95 (*0-8021-3016-X*) Grove-Atltic.

— Sexlet. 1994. 14.95 (*0-7145-3828-0*); pap. 9.95 (*0-7145-3844-2*) Riverrun NY.

— Sextet. LC 77-20795. (Illus.). 1977. pap. 7.95 (*0-88496-111-7*) Capra Pr.

— Sextet: His Later Writings under One Cover. LC 89-779. 188p. (C). 1988. reprint ed. lib. bdg. 27.00x (*0-8095-4046-0*) Borgo Pr.

— Sextet: Six Essays. LC 95-9979. (I.O. Evans Studies in the Philosophy & Criticism of Literature, 0271-9061: Vol. 29). 1995. write for info. (*0-8095-0903-2*); pap. write for info. (*0-8095-1903-8*) Borgo Pr.

— Sexus: The Rosy Crucifixion I. LC 86-35723. 506p. 1987. pap. 13.95 (*0-8021-5180-9*) Grove-Atltic.

— The Smile at the Foot of the Ladder. LC 58-11829. (Illus.). 64p. 1975. pap. 5.95 (*0-8112-0556-8*, NDP386) New Directions.

— Stand Still Like the Hummingbird. LC 62-10408. 1967. reprint ed. pap. 9.95 (*0-8112-0322-0*, NDP236) New Directions.

— The Time of the Assassins: A Study of Rimbaud. LC 55-12452. 1962. pap. 8.95 (*0-8112-0115-5*, NDP115) New Directions.

— Tropic of Cancer. 318p. 1987. pap. 11.95 (*0-8021-3178-6*) Grove-Atltic.

— Tropic of Cancer. LC 82-42868. 1983. 18.00 (*0-394-60435-0*, Modern Lib) Random.

— Tropic of Cancer. 1987. pap. 7.95 (*0-394-62375-4*) Random.

— Tropic of Capricorn. 348p. 1987. pap. 11.95 (*0-8021-5182-5*) Grove-Atltic.

— Tropic of Capricorn. 1987. pap. 7.95 (*0-394-62379-7*) Random.

— Tropique du Cancer. (FRE.). 1972. pap. 13.95 (*0-7859-3997-0*) Fr & Eur.

— Under the Roofs of Paris. LC 84-73204. Orig. Title: Opus Pistorum. 272p. 1985. pap. 10.00 (*0-8021-3183-2*) Grove-Atltic.

— Wisdom of the Heart. LC 41-28118. 1942. pap. 10.95 (*0-8112-0116-3*, NDP94) New Directions.

Miller, Henry & Schnellock, Emil. Letters to Emil. Wickes, George, ed. LC 88-36470. 192p. 1991. reprint ed. 21.95 (*0-8112-1092-8*); reprint ed. pap. 12.95 (*0-8112-1170-3*, NDP717) New Directions.

Miller, Henry & Stuhlmann, Gunther, eds. A Literate Passion: Letters of Anais Nin & Henry Miller, 1932-1953. 1987. 19.95 (*0-15-152729-6*) HarBrace.

Miller, Henry, jt. auth. see Briar, Scott.

Miller, Henry, jt. auth. see Durrell, Lawrence.

Miller, Henry, jt. auth. see Walford, Geoffrey.

Miller, Henry, et al. New York Practice Guide: Negligence, 4 vols. 1989. Updates. ring bd. write for info. (*0-8205-1521-3*) Bender.

Miller, Henry A. Practical Wiring in SI Units, Vol. 1. rev. ed. LC 68-57882. (Pergamon International Library, Electrical Engineering Division). 108p. 1975. pap. 48.00 (*0-08-019754-X*, Pub. by Pergamon Repr UK) Franklin.

Miller, Henry C. State Coinage of Connecticut. (Illus.). 1981. reprint ed. lib. bdg. 30.00 (*0-915262-64-9*) S J Durst.

***Miller, Henry D.** The Management of Change in Universities: Universities, State & Economy in Australia, Canada & the United Kingdom. LC 94-44549. 208p. 1994. 85.00x (*0-335-19089-8*, Open Univ Pr) Taylor & Francis.

Miller, Henry G. Settlement. (Art of Advocacy Ser.). 1983. Looseleaf updates available. write for info. (*0-8205-1041-6*) Bender.

***Miller, Henry I.** Is the Biodiversity Treaty a Bureaucratic Time Bomb? LC 94-43957. (Essays in Public Policy Ser.: No. 56). 1994. write for info. (*0-8179-5612-3*) Hoover Inst Pr.

Miller, Henry K., ed. see Fielding, Henry.

Miller, Henry M. Discovering Maryland's First City. (Archaeology Ser.: No. 2). (Illus.). 164p. 1986. pap. 16.00 (*1-878399-32-2*) Div Hist Cult Progs.

— The Search for the "City of St. Maries" (Archaeology Ser.: No. 1). (Illus.). 195p. 1983. pap. 16.00 (*1-878399-31-4*) Div Hist Cult Progs.

Miller, Henry W. The Paris Gun: The Bombardment of Paris & the Great German Offensives of 1918. 1972. 59.95 (*0-8490-0800-X*) Gordon Pr.

Miller, Herb. Actions Speak Louder Than Verbs. LC 88-22642. 128p. 1989. pap. 6.95 (*0-687-00712-7*) Abingdon.

— Building a Meaningful Life with the Carpenter's Twenty Megatruths. 108p. (Orig.). 1968. pap. write for info. (*0-937462-03-9*) Net Pr.

— Connecting with God: Fourteen Ways Churches Can Help People Grow Spiritually. LC 94-6697. (Effective Church Ser.). 144p. (Orig.). 1994. pap. 12.95 (*0-687-09405-4*) Abingdon.

— Developing a Vital Congregation. (Orig.). 1989. pap. write for info. (*0-937462-12-8*) Net Pr.

— How to Build a Magnetic Church. LC 86-28782. (Creative Leadership Ser.). 128p. 1987. pap. 11.95 (*0-687-17762-6*) Abingdon.

— Identifying Your Spiritual Giftabilities. 1988. Incl. videotape. vhs 39.95 (*0-318-32653-1*); pap. 12.95 (*0-937462-10-1*) Net Pr.

— Moving Toward a Biblical Theology of Evangelism: A Five-Session Study for Members of the Christian Church (Disciples of Christ) (Orig.). 1987. pap. 5.95 (*0-937462-08-X*) Net Pr.

— Vital Congregation. LC 90-31095. 1990. pap. 11.95 (*0-687-43796-2*) Abingdon.

Miller, Herb & Moore, Douglas V. Three Hundred Seed Thoughts: Illustrative Stories for Speakers. 157p. (Orig.). 1986. pap. 9.95 (*0-937462-01-2*) Net Pr.

Miller, Herb, ed. see Cueni, Robert.

Miller, Herb, ed. see Grimm, Eugene.

Miller, Herb, ed. see Lee, Robert A.

An Asterisk (*) at the beginning of an entry indicates that the title is appearing in BIP for the first time.

Miller, Herbert. Evangelism's Open Secrets. 2nd ed. LC 77-23468. 112p. 1985. pap. 7.99 (*0-8272-0805-7*) Chalice Pr.

— Fishing on the Asphalt. LC 83-10006. 208p. (Orig.). 1983. pap. 8.99 (*0-8272-1011-6*) Chalice Pr.

— Tools for Active Christians. LC 79-14795. (P.A.C.E. Ser.). (Orig.). 1979. pap. 9.99 (*0-8272-3624-7*) Chalice Pr.

Miller, Herbert A. School & the Immigrant. LC 71-129507. (American Immigration Collection, Ser. 2). 1980. reprint ed. 13.95 (*0-405-00561-X*) Ayer.

Miller, Herbert A., Jr. & Wasseman, Paul. Retirement Benefit Plans: An Information Sourcebook. (Sourcebook Series in Business & Management: No. 8). 224p. 1988. 43.50 (*0-89774-282-6*) Oryx Pr.

Miller, Herbert A., jt. auth. see Park, Robert E.

Miller, Herbert C. & Mattioli, Leone, eds. Clinical Problems in Pediatrics. LC 77-89459. 251p. reprint ed. pap. 71.60 (*0-8357-6760-4*, 2035421) Bks Demand.

Miller, Herbert C. & Merritt, T. Allen. Fetal Growth in Humans. LC 79-9974. (Illus.). 192p. reprint ed. pap. 54. 80 (*0-685-44471-6*, 2033001) Bks Demand.

Miller, Herbert E. & Mead, George C. CPA Review Manual. 5th ed. (Illus.). 1979. 38.50 (*0-685-03807-6*); text ed. 28.95 (*0-685-03808-4*) P-H.

***Miller, Herman L.** Lumbering in Early Twentieth Century Michigan: The Kneeland-Bigelow Company Experience. (Illus.). 86p. (Orig.). 1995. pap. 19.95 (*0-9645716-0-9*) Walnut Hll Pr.

***Miller, Hillis.** Preserving the Literary Heritage: The Final Report of the Scholarly Advisory Committee on Modern Language & Literature. 8p. 1991. pap. 10.00 (*1-887334-08-4*) Comm Preserv & Access.

Miller, Hobart G., et al. OSHA & State Employee Hazard Communication Program. 325p. 1988. teacher ed 295.00 (*0-940394-29-4*) Labelmaster.

Miller, Holly. How to Add More Than Pennies to Your Thoughts. 1990. pap. 7.95 (*0-87162-501-6*, D4318) Warner Pr.

Miller, Holly & Hensley, Dennis. How to Stop Living for the Applause: Help for Women Who Need to Be Perfect. 160p. (Orig.). (C). 1990. pap. 8.99 (*0-89283-642-3*, Vine Bks) Servant.

Miller, Holly G., jt. auth. see Hensley, Dennis E.

***Miller, Hope.** Hope's Mushroom Cookbook. 220p. (Orig.). 1994. pap. 19.95x (*0-614-00623-6*) Mad River.

Miller, Hope H., jt. auth. see Miller, Orson K., Jr.

Miller, Howard. Abraham Lincoln's Flag: We Won't Give up a Star. (Illus.). 26p. (J). (gr. 4-6). 1990. pap. text ed. 4.95 (*0-939631-19-9*) Thomas Publications.

— Trees. 3rd ed. (Pictured Key Nature Ser.). 276p. (C). 1978. spiral bd. write for info. (*0-697-04896-9*) Wm C Brown Pubs.

Miller, Howard A. & Lamb, Samuel H. Oaks of North America. (Illus.). 328p. 1984. 20.95 (*0-87961-136-7*); pap. 12.95 (*0-87961-137-5*) Naturegraph.

Miller, Howard S., jt. auth. see Corbett, Katharine T.

Miller, Howard W. How to Automate Your Computer Center: Achieving Unattended Operations. 1990. 44.95 (*0-471-58427-4*, GA3187) Wiley.

— How to Automate Your Computer Center: Achieving Unattended Operations. LC 89-24229. 360p. 1990. pap. 44.95 (*0-89435-318-7*) Wiley.

Miller, Hub. The Laminated Wood Boatbuilder: A Step by Step Guide for the Backyard Builder. 1993. pap. text ed. 22.95 (*0-07-042192-7*) McGraw.

Miller, Hubert J. Padre Miguel Hidalgo: Father of Mexican Independence. 77p. (Orig.). 1986. pap. text ed. write for info. (*0-938738-05-4*) U TX Pan Am Pr.

Miller, Hugh. Skin Deep. large type ed. 293p. 1993. 21.95 (*0-7505-0446-3*) Ulverscroft.

***Miller, Hugh, ed.** Best One-Act Plays of 1958-59. 255p. 1960. 14.95 (*0-910278-83-0*) Boulevard.

Miller, Hugh G. Isthmian Highway: A Review of the Problems of the Caribbean. LC 76-111725. (American Imperialism: Viewpoints of United States Foreign Policy, 1898-1941 Ser.). 1970. reprint ed. 26.95 (*0-405-02039-2*) Ayer.

— The Old Red Sandstone, or New Walks in an Old Field. Albritton, Claude C., Jr., ed. LC 77-6531. (History of Geology Ser.). (Illus.). 1978. reprint ed. lib. bdg. 37.95 (*0-405-10451-0*) Ayer.

— Scenes & Legends of the North of Scotland: Traditional History of Cromarty. 2nd rev. ed. Dorson, Richard M., ed. (International Folklore Ser.). 1977. reprint ed. lib. bdg. 41.95 (*0-405-10110-4*) Ayer.

— The Testimony of the Rocks: Or, Geology in Its Bearings on Two Theologies, Natural & Revealed. Gould, Stephen J., ed. LC 79-8336. (History of Paleontology Ser.). (Illus.). 1980. reprint ed. lib. bdg. 46.95 (*0-405-12720-0*) Ayer.

Miller, Hugh M. & Cockerell, Dale. History of Western Music. LC 90-56020. (HarperCollins College Outline Ser.). (Illus.). 320p. (Orig.). 1991. pap. 12.00 (*0-06-467107-0*, Harper Ref) HarpC.

Miller, Hugh M., et al. Introduction to Music. LC 90-56020. (HarperCollins College Outline Ser.). (Illus.). 320p. (Orig.). 1991. pap. 13.00 (*0-06-467108-9*, Harper Ref) HarpC.

Miller, Hugh T., jt. auth. see Fox, Charles F.

Miller, Ian, jt. auth. see Harrison, M. John.

Miller, Ian J. Gemini. 1986. 30.00 (*0-7223-2057-4*, Pub. by A H S Ltd UK) St Mut.

Miller, Ilene & Moore, Jane B., eds. Avenues of Love: An Intergenerational Activities Manual. 66p. (Orig.). 1991. pap. text ed. 10.95 (*0-685-57048-7*) Geriatric Educ.

Miller, Inabeth. Microcomputers & the Media Specialist: An Annotated Bibliography. 70p. 1981. 4.25 (*0-318-35503-5*, IR-57) ERIC Clear.

— Microcomputers in School Library Media Centers. LC 82-22361. 165p. 1984. pap. 24.95 (*0-918212-51-0*) Neal-Schuman.

Miller, Inabeth, jt. ed. see Willie, Charles V.

Miller, Ingrid W. Afro-Hispanic Literature: An Anthology of Hispanic Writers of Hispanic Ancestry. LC 91-84525. (Coleccion Ebano y Canela Ser.). 143p. (Orig.). 1991. pap. 19.00 (*0-89729-582-X*) Ediciones.

Miller, Iona, jt. auth. see Miller, Richard A.

Miller, Iona, jt. auth. see Miller, Richard.

Miller, Iris. Visions of Washington: Composite Plan of Urban Interventions. 1992. 68.00 (*0-9635710-0-1*) Iris Miller.

Miller, Iris & Busser, Robert A., eds. Urban Design: Visions & Reflections. 160p. (Orig.). (C). 1991. pap. text ed. write for info. (*0-9635710-1-X*) Iris Miller.

***Miller, Iris & Grim, Ronald, eds.** Capital Visions: Reflections on a Decade of Urban Design & a Look Ahead. (Illus.). v, 52p. (Orig.). (C). 1995. pap. text ed. write for info. (*0-8444-0882-4*) Lib Congress.

***Miller, Irvin.** Who's in Charge? How to Take Back Control of Your Health & Life. 358p. 1992. pap. 14.95 (*0-89716-454-7*) P B Pubng.

Miller, Irving. Burns for Bairns. (Illus.). (C). 1989. pap. text ed. 35.00 (*0-907526-46-2*, Alloway Pub) St Mut.

Miller, Irwin & Miller, Marylees. Statistical Methods for Quality: With Applications to Engineering & Management. LC 94-4684. 1994. text ed. 64.00 (*0-13-013749-9*) P-H.

Miller, Irwin, et al. Probability & Statistics for Engineers. 4th ed. 640p. (C). 1990. Casebound. text ed. write for info. (*0-13-712761-8*) P-H.

— Probability & Statistics for Engineers. 5th ed. LC 93-24611. 1993. text ed. 75.00 (*0-13-721408-1*) P-H.

Miller, Isabel. A Dooryard Full of Flowers. 192p. 1993. pap. 9.95 (*1-56280-029-9*) Naiad Pr.

— The Love of Good Women. 224p. 1986. pap. 8.95 (*0-930044-81-9*) Naiad Pr.

— Patience & Sarah. 1985. mass mkt. 5.99 (*0-449-21007-3*, Crest) Fawcett.

— Patience & Sarah. 224p. 1994. pap. 10.00 (*0-449-90930-1*, Columbine) Fawcett.

— Side by Side. 256p. 1990. pap. 9.95 (*0-941483-77-0*) Naiad Pr.

Miller, Isobel, jt. auth. see Miller, Kentalle.

***Miller, Ivan J. What Managed Care Is Doing to Outpatient Mental Health: A Look Behind the Veil of Secrecy. 49p. 1994. pap. 7.50 (*0-9645263-0-1*) Boulder Psychother.**

Dr. Miller explains how managed care is damaging the heart & soul of the profession of psychotherapy. He cuts through the complexity of the managed mental health care industry with explanations that can be easily understood by both professionals & consumers. His presentation is described as thoughtfully on target, calmly presented & devastatingly revealing of the illusions incumbent in managed care. Clear graphics & easy to understand style make reading this book effortless. This expose explains that inherent economic pressures within managed care make quality problems unavoidable. The many confusing practices of managed care are revealed as tools for "invisible rationing" of mental health care. Finally, he proposes constructive alternatives & innovative legislation to control the abuses of managed care. To order write or call: Boulder Psychotherapists' Press, Inc., 350 Broadway, Suite 210, Boulder, CO 80303, or call 303-444-1036. ***Publisher Provided Annotation.***

Miller, J. Religion in the Popular Prints 1600-1832. LC 85-5938. (English Satirical Print Ser.). 372p. 1986. lib. bdg. 100.00 (*0-85964-170-8*) Chadwyck-Healey.

Miller, J., ed. Telecommunications & Equity--Policy Research Issues: Proceedings of the Thirteenth Annual Telecommunications Policy Research Conference, Airlie House, Airlie, VA, 21-24 April 1985. 348p. 1986. pap. 102.75 (*0-444-70013-7*) Elsevier.

Miller, J., ed. see Gass, T. & Bennett, T.

Miller, J., jt. ed. see Morel, T.

Miller, J. A. William David Coolidge: Yankee Scientist. 224p. 1963. text ed. 76.00 (*0-677-65150-3*) Gordon & Breach.

Miller, J. A., jt. ed. see Crow, D. E.

Miller, J. Abbott, jt. auth. see Lupton, Ellen.

Miller, J. Abbott, jt. ed. see Lupton, Ellen.

Miller, J. Allen. Christian Doctrine: Lectures & Sermons. 1946. 1.75 (*0-934970-01-7*) Brethren Church.

Miller, J. C. & Haglund, R. F., Jr., eds. Laser Ablation, Mechanisms & Applications: Proceedings of a Workshop Held in Oak Ridge, Tennessee, U. S. A., 8-10 April 1991. (Lecture Notes in Physics Ser.: Vol. 389). viii, 362p. 1991. 58.00 (*0-387-97731-7*) Spr-Verlag.

Miller, J. C. & Miller, J. N. Statistics for Analytical Chemistry. 2nd ed. 227p. 1992. pap. write for info. (*0-13-845421-3*) P-H.

Miller, J. D. Commonwealth in the World. 3rd ed. LC 65-8789. (Illus.). 362p. 1965. 29.00 (*0-674-14700-6*) HUP.

— Norman Angell & the Futility of War: Peace & the Public Mind. LC 85-18378. 192p. 1986. text ed. 32.50 (*0-312-57773-7*) St Martin.

Miller, J. D. & Vincent, R. J., eds. Order & Violence: Hedley Bull & International Relations. (Illus.). 232p. 1990. 55.00 (*0-19-827555-2*) OUP.

Miller, J. D., jt. auth. see Carnwath, T.

Miller, J. D., jt. ed. see Carsten, M. E.

Miller, J. D., jt. ed. see Evans, L. T.

Miller, J. D., ed. see International Symposium on Hydrometallurgy Staff.

Miller, J. D., jt. ed. see Teasdale, G. M.

Miller, J. Dale. One Thousand Spanish Idioms. 2nd ed. LC 71-180253. 115p. 1972. pap. 7.95 (*0-8425-1513-5*) BYU Scholarly.

Miller, J. David & Trenholm, L., eds. Mycotoxins in Grain: Compounds Other Than Aflatoxin. LC 93-73623. (Illus.). 552p. 1994. 124.00 (*0-9624407-5-2*) Eagan Pr.

Miller, J. David, jt. auth. see Glanville, Jerry.

Miller, J. E. & Schmidt, F. E., Jr., eds. Slurry Erosion: Uses, Applications, & Test Methods. LC 87-920. (Special Technical Publication Ser.: No. 946). (Illus.). 274p. 1987. text ed. 48.00 (*0-8031-0941-5*, 04-946000-29) ASTM.

Miller, J. E., Jr., ed. see Whitman, Walt.

Miller, J. G. Family Property & Financial Provision. 3rd ed. 600p. 1993. 75.00 (*0-85459-750-6*, Pub. by Tolley Pubng UK) St Mut.

Miller, J. G., tr. see Drai, et al.

Miller, J. H. & Reznikoff, W. S., eds. The Operon. 2nd ed. LC 80-15490. (Monograph Ser.: No. 7). (Illus.). 469p. (Orig.). 1980. pap. text ed. 25.00 (*0-87969-133-6*) Cold Spring Harbor.

Miller, J. Hillis. Ariadne's Thread: Story Lines. 320p. (C). 1992. text ed. 37.50x (*0-300-05216-2*) Yale U Pr.

— The Ethics of Reading: Kant, de Man, Eliot, Trollope, James, & Benjamin. (Wellek Library Lectures). 137p. 1989. text ed. 33.00 (*0-231-06334-2*); pap. text ed. 15.50 (*0-231-06335-0*) Col U Pr.

— Fiction & Repetition: Seven English Novels. LC 81-6733. 260p. 1982. 25.00 (*0-674-29925-6*) HUP.

— Fiction & Repetition: Seven English Novels. 260p. 1985. pap. 12.95 (*0-674-29926-4*) HUP.

— The Form of Victorian Fiction. 151p. 1980. 17.50 (*0-934958-00-9*) Bellflower.

— Hawthorne & History: Defacing It. 160p. 1991. pap. 17. 95 (*0-631-17561-X*) Blackwell Pubs.

— Illustration. (Essays in Art & Culture Ser.). (Illus.). 168p. 1992. 37.50 (*0-674-44357-8*) HUP.

— Illustration. 1994. pap. 19.95 (*0-674-44358-6*) HUP.

— The Linguistic Moment: From Wordsworth to Stevens. 472p. 1987. pap. 19.95 (*0-691-01439-6*) Princeton U Pr.

— Theory Now & Then. LC 90-44884. 420p. 1991. text ed. 50.50 (*0-8223-1112-7*) Duke.

— Topographies. LC 94-25351. (Meridian Ser.). 1995. 49.50 (*0-8047-2378-8*); pap. 16.95 (*0-8047-2379-6*) Stanford U Pr.

— Tropes, Parables, Performatives: Essays on Twentieth-Century Literature. LC 90-44886. 288p. 1991. text ed. 50.50 (*0-8223-1111-9*) Duke.

— Victorian Subjects. LC 90-44885. 336p. 1991. text ed. 50. 50 (*0-8223-1110-0*) Duke.

Miller, J. Hillis, et al. Narrative Endings. (Ninteenth-Century Studies: Vol. 33, No. 1). 160p. reprint ed. pap. 45.60 (*0-685-23977-2*, 2031541) Bks Demand.

Miller, J. J., ed. Nasecode VII Transactions. (Illus.). 448p. (Orig.). (C). 1991. 170.00 (*1-873936-09-5*, Pub. by J & J Sci Pubs UK) Bks Intl VA.

— Nasecode VIII Transactions. (Illus.). 168p. (Orig.). (C). 1992. 95.00 (*1-873936-17-6*, Pub. by J & J Sci Pubs UK) Bks Intl VA.

Miller, J. Jefferson. Eighteenth Century Meissen Porcelain from the Margaret M. & Arthur J. Mourot Collection in the Virginia Museum. LC 82-17557. (Illus.). 68p. 1983. pap. 7.50 (*0-917046-13-7*) Va Mus Arts.

Miller, J. Jefferson, II. English Yellow-Glazed Earthenware. LC 73-21328. (Illus.). 1974. 35.00 (*0-87474-150-5*, MIEY) Smithsonian.

Miller, J. K., intro. Official Fair-Use Guidelines: Complete Texts of Four Official Documents Arranged for Use by Educators. 3rd ed. 1987. pap. 5.95 (*0-914143-11-5*, Copy Info Svc) Assn Ed Comm Tech.

Miller, J. Keith. Compelled to Control: Why Relationships Break Down & What Makes Them Well. 300p. 1992. 18. 95 (*1-55874-212-3*) Health Comm.

— Hope in the Fast Lane. 1991. mass mkt. 4.95 (*0-06-104049-5*, Harp PBks) HarpC.

— Hope in the Fast Lane: A New Look at Faith in a Compulsive World. LC 87-45189. 1990. pap. 12.00 (*0-06-065720-0*) Harper SF.

— A Hunger For Healing. 288p. 1992. pap. 12.00 (*0-06-065767-7*); student ed, pap. 12.00 (*0-06-065721-9*) Harper SF.

— Invitation to Life: God's Call to the Reluctant Believer. 1994. 17.95 (*1-56977-632-6*) McCracken Pr.

— Ten Minute Magic: Uncovering Your Goals & Achieving Them. 256p. 1994. 17.95 (*1-56977-630-X*) Cadell & Davies.

Miller, J. L., et al. Sentencing Reform: A Review & Annotated Bibliography. 147p. 1981. pap. write for info. (*0-89656-056-2*, R-061) Natl Ctr St Courts.

Miller, J. M. & Spelman, F. A., eds. Cochlear Implants. (Illus.). 350p. 1989. 139.00 (*0-387-97033-9*, 2956) Spr-Verlag.

Miller, J. M., jt. ed. see Hamburger, Joel I.

Miller, J. Martin, et al. Needle Biopsy of the Thyroid: Current Concepts. LC 82-16667. 304p. 1983. text ed. 89.50 (*0-275-91403-8*, C1403, Praeger Pubs) Greenwood.

Miller, J. Maxwell. The Old Testament & the Historian. Tucker, Gene M., ed. LC 75-10881. (Guides to Biblical Scholarship: Old Testament Ser.). 96p. 1976. pap. 8.00 (*0-8006-0461-X*, 1-461, Fortress Pr) Augsburg Fortress.

Miller, J. Maxwell, ed. Archaeological Survey of the Kerak Plateau. 354p. 1991. 115.00 (*1-55540-642-4*, 80 00 01) Scholars Pr GA.

Miller, J. Maxwell & Hayes, John H. A History of Ancient Israel & Judah. LC 85-11468. (Illus.). 524p. (C). 1986. 32.00 (*0-664-21262-X*, Westminster) Westminster John Knox.

Miller, J. Maxwell, jt. ed. see Hayes, John H.

Miller, J. Michael. Life's Greatest Grace: Why I Belong to the Catholic Church. LC 92-60314. 160p. (Orig.). 1993. pap. 9.95 (*0-87973-477-9*, 477) Our Sunday Visitor.

— Marian Apparitions & the Church. 16p. 1993. 1.50 (*0-87973-153-2*, 153) Our Sunday Visitor.

— The North Anna Campaign "Even to Hell Itself" May 21-26, 1864. (Virginia Civil War Battles & Leaders Ser.). (Illus.). 188p. 1989. 19.95 (*0-930919-71-8*) H E Howard.

Miller, J. Michael & Wentworth, Berttina B., eds. Methods for Quality Control in Diagnostic Microbiology. LC 85-3991. 368p. 1985. 45.00 (*0-87553-121-0*) Am Pub Health.

Miller, J. N. Standard Flourescence Spectra. 600p. 1995. text ed. 138.95 (*0-13-841636-2*) P-H.

Miller, J. N., jt. auth. see Miller, J. C.

Miller, J. P. Days of Wine & Roses. 1973. pap. 4.75 (*0-8222-0281-6*) Dramatists Play.

— Good Night, Little Rabbit. LC 85-62017. (Board Bks.). (Illus.). 7p. (J). (ps). 1986. bds. 3.95 (*0-394-87992-9*) Random Bks Yng Read.

— Learn about Colors with Little Rabbit. LC 84-6943. (Knee-High Bks.). (Illus.). (J). (ps-1). 1984. lib. bdg. 4.99 (*0-394-96671-6*) Random Bks Yng Read.

— Little Duckling's Surprise. LC 86-62052. (Illus.). 24p. (J). (ps-1). 1987. 4.95 (*0-394-88682-8*) Random Bks Yng Read.

— Little Rabbit Takes a Walk. LC 86-61525. (Book & Doll Packages Ser.). (Illus.). 24p. (J). (ps-1). 1987. pap. 5.95 (*0-394-88667-4*) Random Bks Yng Read.

— The People Next Door. adapted ed. 1969. pap. 4.75 (*0-8222-0884-9*) Dramatists Play.

— Yoo-Hoo Little Rabbit. LC 85-61529. (J). (ps). 1986. 3.99 (*0-394-87884-1*) Random Bks Yng Read.

Miller, J. P., illus. The Cow Says Moo. (Cloth Bks.). (J). (ps). 1979. 3.50 (*0-394-84131-X*) Random Bks Yng Read.

Miller, J. Philip. Numbers in Presence & Absence: A Study of Husserl's Philosophy of Mathematics. 1982. lib. bdg. 29.50 (*0-686-37593-9*) Kluwer Ac.

***Miller, J. R.** The Freethinker's Little Handbook: Ammunition in the Battle for Truth. 104p. 1995. spiral bd. 9.95 (*0-9636500-1-7*) Flying M Grp.

— How Professional Gamblers Beat the Pro Football Pointspread: A Step-by-Step Textbook Guide. (Illus.). 170p. 1993. student ed 24.95 (*0-9636500-0-9*) Flying M Grp.

— The Master's Blesseds: The Sermon on the Mount. pap. 2.99 (*0-87377-061-7*) GAM Pubns.

— The Nine Hundred & One Best Jokes There Ever Was. LC 91-24866. (Illus.). 192p. (Orig.). 1991. pap. 5.95 (*1-55853-122-X*) Rutledge Hill Pr.

— Roulette for the Weekend Gambler: How to Get in, Make Your Hit & Get Out a Winner. 86p. 1995. spiral bd. 7.95 (*0-9636500-2-5*) Flying M Grp.

— Secretos de una Vida Hermosa: Secrets of a Beautiful Life. (SPA.). 5.95 (*84-7645-007-9*, 223078, Pub. by Edit Clie SP) TSELF.

— Skyscrapers Hide the Heavens: A History of Indian-White Relations in Canada. (Illus.). 408p. 1991. pap. text ed. 20.95 (*0-8020-6869-3*) U of Toronto Pr.

Miller, J. R., ed. Sweet Promises: A Reader in Indian-White Relations in Canada. 448p. 1991. pap. text ed. 24.95 (*0-8020-6818-9*) U of Toronto Pr.

Miller, J. R. & Miller, T. A., eds. Insect-Plant Interactions: Plant Interactions. (Experimental Entomology Ser.). (Illus.). 350p. 1990. 99.00 (*0-387-96260-3*) Spr-Verlag.

Miller, J. Ronald. Prophet in the House. LC 93-73155. 171p. (Orig.). 1993. pap. 10.00 (*0-9638451-0-1*) Commun Church.

Miller, J. S. Astrophysics of Quasi-Stellar Objects & Active Galactic Nuclei. 519p. (C). 1985. text ed. 30.00 (*0-935702-21-0*) Univ Sci Bks.

Miller, J. Wesley, ed. Legal Laughs: A Joke for Every Jury. LC 93-79765. lii, 437p. 1993. reprint ed. 48.50 (*0-89941-854-6*, 307800) W S Hein.

Miller, J. William. Modern Playwrights at Work, Vol. 1. 1968. 12.00 (*0-573-69018-9*) French.

Miller, Jack. Healing Our Losses: A Journal for Working Through Your Grief. LC 92-41564. (Illus.). 104p. (Orig.). (C). 1993. pap. 10.95 (*0-89390-255-1*) Resource Pubns.

— The Important Steps That Take You to Health, Wealth & Happiness. 120p. Date not set. 19.95 (*1-882434-00-5*) Grp Commun.

— Menu Pricing & Strategy. 3rd ed. (Illus.). 224p. 1992. pap. 34.95 (*0-442-00692-6*) Van Nos Reinhold.

Miller, Jack, ed. Jews in Soviet Culture. 325p. 1983. 39.95x (*0-87855-495-5*) Transaction Pubs.

Miller, Jack & Walk, Mary. Personal Training Manual for the Hospital Industry. (Illus.). 176p. 1991. pap. 34.95 (*0-442-23534-8*) Van Nos Reinhold.

Miller, Jack, et al. Supervision in the Hospitality Industry. 2nd ed. (Service Management Ser.: No. 1416). 400p. 1992. Net. text ed. write for info. (*0-471-54904-5*) Wiley.

Miller, Jack E. & Hayes, David K. Basic Food & Beverage Cost Control. 400p. 1993. Net. text ed. write for info. (*0-471-57918-1*) Wiley.

Miller, Jack S. The Healing Power of Grief. 125p. 1985. pap. 7.95 (*0-914373-02-1*) Wieser & Wieser.

Miller, Jack V. Fat Hogs & Dead Dogs: How to Use Ideas, Inventions & Patents to Win the War for Your Markets & Profits. (Illus.). 255p. 1990. 24.95 (*1-879254-01-8*) Design Tech.

***Miller, Jack W., ed.** Addressing the Problems of Youth At-Risk: Approaches That Work. 237p. (Orig.). 1994. pap. 10.00 (*0-9640143-0-0*) GSU Coll Educ.

Miller, Jackie. The Not Just for Kids Coloring Book. 12p. (Orig.). 1990. pap. 1.50 (*0-945145-01-2*) Miller Family Pubns.

Miller, Jacqueline T. Poetic License: Authority & Authorship in Medieval & Renaissance Contexts. 192p. 1987. 45.00 (*0-19-504103-8*) OUP.

Miller, Jacqueline Y., ed. The Common Names of North American Butterflies. LC 91-21343. (Illus.). 192p. (Orig.). (C). 1992. pap. 15.95 (*1-56098-122-9*) Smithsonian.

Miller, Jacques-Alain. The Seminar of Jacques Lacan: The Ethics of Psychoanalysis, 1959-1960, Bk. 7. Porter, Dennis, tr. & notes by. 352p. 1992. 35.00 (*0-393-03357-0*) Norton.

Miller, Jacques-Alain, ed. The Seminar of Jacques Lacan, Bk. 1: Freud's Papers on Technique, 1953-1954. Forrester, John, tr. & notes by. 1991. pap. 14.95 (*0-393-30697-6*) Norton.

— The Seminar of Jacques Lacan, Bk. 2: The Ego in Freud's Theory & in the Technique of Psychoanalyis, 1954-1955. Tomaselli, Sylvana, tr. 1988. 24.95 (*0-393-01897-0*) Norton.

— The Seminar of Jacques Lacan, Bk. 2: The Ego in Freud's Theory & in the Technique of Psychoanalyis, 1954-1955. Tomaselli, Sylvana, tr. 1991. pap. 15.95 (*0-393-30709-3*) Norton.

Miller, Jacques-Alain, ed. see Lacan, Jacques.

Miller, James. Convergence: A Futuristic Thriller of Environmental Intrigue. 1994. pap. 5.50 (*1-56171-164-0*, S P I Bks) Sure Sellers.

— Democracy Is in the Streets: From Port Huron to the Siege of Chicago. LC 94-15547. 441p. 1994. pap. 14.95 (*0-674-19725-9*, MILDEX) HUP.

— The Detroit Yiddish Theater, 1920 to 1937. LC 67-16851. 196p. reprint ed. pap. 55.90 (*0-7837-3796-3*, 2043616) Bks Demand.

— Drilltype Two: Number & Special Character Drills. LC 77-80579. 1978. spiral bd. 9.96 (*0-02-830700-3*) Glencoe.

— Fluid Exchanges: Artists & Critics in the Age of AIDS. 496p. 1992. 50.00 (*0-8020-5892-2*); pap. 22.95 (*0-8020-6824-3*) U of Toronto Pr.

— Harlequin-Horace: or The Art of Modern Poetry. LC 92-25505. (Augustan Reprints Ser.: No. 178 (1976)). reprint ed. 12.00 (*0-404-70178-7*, PR3549) AMS Pr.

— History & Human Existence: From Marx to Merleau-Ponty. LC 78-51747. 1979. pap. 14.00 (*0-520-04779-6*) U CA Pr.

— Mable Mothers & Foster Son. 1995. 18.95 (*0-8062-5169-7*) Carlton.

— Measures of Wisdom: The Cosmic Dance in Classical & Christian Antiquity. 672p. 1986. 60.00 (*0-8020-2553-6*) U of Toronto Pr.

— The Passion of Michel Foucault. LC 93-39069. 1994. 14.95 (*0-385-47240-4*) Doubleday.

Miller, James, jt. auth. see Miller, Mary.

Miller, James, jt. auth. see Place, Irene.

Miller, James, see Adib Rashad, pseud..

Miller, James, tr. see Saumjan, S. K.

Miller, James, ed. see Wehrman, Robert.

Miller, James A. Quarternary History of the Sangamon River Drainage System, Central Illinois. (Reports of Investigations Ser.: No.27). (Illus.). 36p. 1973. pap. 2.00 (*0-89792-051-1*) Ill St Museum.

Miller, James A. & Macintyre, Ian G. Field Guidebook to the Reefs of Belize. (Third International Symposium on Coral Reefs Ser.). (Illus.). 36p. 1977. pap. 4.00 (*0-932981-41-0*) Univ Miami A R C.

Miller, James A., jt. auth. see Bookin-Weiner, Jerome B.

Miller, James A., jt. auth. see English, Paul W.

Miller, James A., jt. auth. see Westbrook, Charles.

Miller, James B. & Brown, Paul B. The Corporate Coach. LC 93-9669. (Illus.). 256p. 1993. 21.95 (*0-312-09262-8*) St Martin.

— The Corporate Coach: How to Build a Team of Loyal Customers & Happy Employees. 256p. 1994. reprint ed. pap. 12.00 (*0-88730-685-3*) Harper Busn.

Miller, James C. The Economist As Reformer: Revamping the FTC, 1981-1985. LC 89-6504. (AEI Studies: No. 489). 110p. (C). 1989. lib. bdg. 16.25 (*0-8447-3684-8*) U Pr of Amer.

Miller, James C., III. Fix the U. S. Budget! Reflections of an "Abominable No-Man" LC 93-40600. (Publication Ser.: No. 413). 176p. (C). 1994. pap. 19.95 (*0-8179-9212-X*) Hoover Inst Pr.

Miller, James C. Microcomputer Support of Commercial Lending: A Management Perspective. LC 85-18818. (Illus.). 80p. (Orig.). 1985. pap. text ed. 15.50 (*0-936742-25-9*) Robt Morris Assocs.

Miller, James C., III & Yandle, Bruce, eds. Benefit-Cost Analyses of Social Regulation: Case Studies from the Council on Wage & Price Stability. LC 79-876. 183p. reprint ed. pap. 52.20 (*0-8357-4436-1*, 2037270) Bks Demand.

Miller, James E., Jr. The American Quest for a Supreme Fiction: Whitman's Legacy in the Personal Epic. LC 78-15176. 1981. pap. text ed. 9.95 (*0-226-52612-7*) U Ch Pr.

Miller, James E. The Baseball Business: Pursuing Pennants & Profits in Baltimore. LC 89-36996. (Illus.). xii, 382p. (C). 1991. reprint ed. 29.95 (*0-8078-1876-3*); reprint ed. pap. 14.95 (*0-8078-4323-7*) U of NC Pr.

— From Elite to Mass Politics: Italian Socialism in the Giolittian Era, 1900-1914. LC 89-20043. 277p. 1990. 32.00 (*0-87338-395-8*) Kent St U Pr.

Miller, James E., Jr. Heritage of American Literature, 2 vols., Vol. I: Beginnings to the Civil War. 1240p. (C). 1990. pap. text ed. 29.50 (*0-15-535697-6*) HB Coll Pubs.

— Heritage of American Literature, 2 vols., Vol. II: Civil War to the Present. 2200p. (C). 1990. pap. text ed. 29.50 (*0-15-535698-4*) HB Coll Pubs.

— Leaves of Grass: America's Lyric-Epic of Self & Democracy. (Masterwork Studies). 160p. 1992. text ed. 21.95 (*0-8057-8089-0*, Twayne); pap. 12.95 (*0-8057-8565-5*, Twayne) Macmillan.

Miller, James E. The Passion of Michel Foucault. LC 92-35828. 528p. 1993. 27.50 (*0-671-69550-9*) S&S Trade.

— T. S. Eliot's Personal Waste Land: Exorcism of the Demons. LC 76-40424. 1977. 28.50 (*0-271-01237-4*) Pa St U Pr.

— The United States & Italy, 1940-1950: The Politics & Diplomacy of Stabilization. LC 85-10035. xv, 356p. 1986. 39.95 (*0-8078-1673-6*) U of NC Pr.

Miller, James E. & Miller, James E. Myth & Method: Modern Theories of Fiction. LC 60-12941. (Bison Book Ser.: No. BB105). 177p. reprint ed. pap. 50.50 (*0-685-20366-2*, 2029821) Bks Demand.

Miller, James E., Jr. & Regenstein, Helen. Walt Whitman. rev. ed. (Twayne's United States Authors Ser.: No. 20). 176p. (C). 1990. text ed. 22.95 (*0-8057-7600-1*, Pub. by Royal Botanic Garden UK) Macmillan.

Miller, James E., jt. auth. see Miller, James E.

Miller, James E., et al. Start with the Sun: Studies in the Whitman Tradition. LC 60-5493. (Bison Book Ser.: No. 165). 269p. reprint ed. pap. 76.70 (*0-7837-7047-2*, 2046858) Bks Demand.

Miller, James G. Living Systems. (Illus.). 1978. text ed. 62.95 (*0-07-042015-7*) McGraw.

— Living Systems. (Illus.). 1152p. (C). Date not set. pap. text ed. 39.95x (*0-87081-363-3*) Univ Pr Colo.

— The Pharmacology & Clinical Usefulness of Carisoprodol: A Symposium Sponsored by Wayne State University College of Medicine & the University of Michigan Medical School, Department of Postgraduate Medicine, held in Detroit, Michigan, July 1, 1959. LC 59-15115. 192p. reprint ed. pap. 54.80 (*0-7837-3656-8*, 2043527) Bks Demand.

Miller, James G., jt. auth. see Swanson, G. A.

Miller, James H. Grounding. 2nd ed. (ABC Pocket Guide for the Field Ser.). (Illus.). 40p. (C). 1988. pap. 6.95 (*1-56016-027-6*) ABC TeleTraining.

— Self-Supporting Scenery for Children's Theatre & Grown-Ups' Too. 4th ed. Zapel, Arthur L., ed. LC 81-84402. (Illus.). 120p. (C). 1982. pap. text ed. 9.95 (*0-916260-15-1*, B-105) Meriwether Pub.

— Self-Supporting Scenery for Children's Theatre & Grown-Ups' Too. 5th rev. ed. Zapel, Arthur L., ed. LC 81-84402. (Illus.). 120p. (C). 1993. reprint ed. pap. 10.95 (*0-916260-91-7*, B105) Meriwether Pub.

— Small Stage Sets on Tour. 2nd ed. Zapel, Arthur L. & Zapel, Theodore O., eds. LC 87-42872. 112p. (Orig.). 1987. pap. 9.95 (*0-916260-46-1*, B-102) Meriwether Pub.

— Stage Lighting in the Boondocks. 3rd ed. Zapel, Arthur L., ed. LC 87-42531. (Illus.). 64p. (Orig.). 1981. pap. text ed. 6.95 (*0-916260-11-9*, B-141) Meriwether Pub.

— Stage Lighting in the Boondocks. 4th rev. ed. Zapel, Arthur L., ed. (Illus.). 76p. (Orig.). 1995. pap. 9.95 (*1-56608-017-7*, B141) Meriwether Pub.

— Stagecraft for Christmas & Easter Plays: A Method of Simplified Staging for the Church. Zapel, Arthur & Zapel, Ted, eds. LC 89-49383. (Illus.). 80p. (Orig.). 1989. pap. 6.95 (*0-916260-64-X*, B-170) Meriwether Pub.

— Station Protectors. (ABC Pocket Guide for the Field Ser.). 44p. (Orig.). (C). 1983. pap. 6.95 (*1-56016-026-8*) ABC TeleTraining.

Miller, James K. The Road to Virginia City: The Diary of James Knox Polk Miller. LC 60-8750. (American Exploration & Travel Ser.: Vol. 30). (Illus.). 176p. 1989. pap. 9.95 (*0-8061-2163-7*) U of Okla Pr.

Miller, James M. Chromatography: Concepts & Contrasts. LC 87-16084. 297p. 1988. text ed. 65.95 (*0-471-84821-2*) Wiley.

— Genesis of Culture in the Ohio Valley, 1800-1825. 1993. reprint ed. lib. bdg. 89.00 (*0-7812-5391-8*) Rprt Serv.

— Genesis of Western Culture: The Upper Ohio Valley, 1800-1825. LC 77-87420. (American Scene Ser.). 1969. reprint ed. lib. bdg. 29.50 (*0-306-71566-X*) Da Capo.

— Separation Methods in Chemical Analysis. LC 74-13781. (Illus.). 319p. reprint ed. pap. 91.00 (*0-685-20442-1*, 2056454) Bks Demand.

Miller, James M., jt. auth. see Lehto, Mark R.

Miller, James M., et al. Instructions & Warnings: The Annotated Bibliography. LC 89-23362. (Warnings Ser.: Vol. 3). 395p. 1990. 45.00 (*0-940537-06-0*); disk 150.00 (*0-685-26954-X*) Fuller Tech.

Miller, James N., jt. auth. see Miller, Jane C.

Miller, James W. Beyond My Canopy. Asher, Ken, ed. LC 80-82869. 64p. (Orig.). 1980. write for info. (*0-9620151-0-5*); pap. write for info. (*0-9620151-1-3*) J W Miller.

Miller, James W., ed. see Gerstacker, Friedrich.

Miller, Jan W. Retouching Your Photographs. (Illus.). 144p. 1986. pap. 18.95 (*0-8174-3832-7*, Amphoto) Watsn-Guptill.

Miller, Jane. The Farm Alphabet Book. (Illus.). 32p. (J). (ps-2). 1987. pap. 2.95 (*0-590-31991-4*) Scholastic Inc.

— Farm Counting Book. (Illus.). 24p. (J). (ps-4). 1992. pap. 5.95 (*0-671-66552-9*, S&S Bks Young Read) S&S Childrens.

— Farm Noises. (Illus.). 24p. (J). (ps-4). 1992. pap. 5.00 (*0-671-75976-0*, S&S Bks Young Read) S&S Childrens.

— Seductions: Studies in Reading & Culture. (Convergences Ser.). 194p. (C). 1991. 24.95 (*0-674-79679-9*) HUP.

Miller, Jane, ed. Eccentric Propositions: Literature & the Curriculum. 224p. (Orig.). pap. 17.95 (*0-7100-9987-8*, RKP) Routledge.

Miller, Jane, jt. auth. see Bradshaw, Jonathan.

Miller, Jane, ed. see Kimball, Helen.

Miller, Jane A., jt. auth. see Benson, Dale S.

Miller, Jane A., ed. see Woodke, Dale.

Miller, Jane C. & Miller, James N. Statistics for Analytical Chemistry. 3rd ed. LC 93-4521. 256p. 1993. pap. text ed. 59.00 (*0-13-030990-7*) P-H.

Miller, Jane R. August Zero. LC 93-4137. 96p. (Orig.). 1993. 22.00 (*1-55659-060-1*); pap. 11.00 (*1-55659-061-X*) Copper Canyon.

— Working Time: Essays on Poetry, Culture, & Travel. LC 91-45197. (Poets on Poetry Ser.). 176p. (C). 1992. text ed. 39.50 (*0-472-09480-7*); pap. 13.95 (*0-472-06480-0*) U of Mich Pr.

Miller, Janeen, jt. auth. see Kueter, Roger A.

Miller, Janet L. Creating Spaces & Finding Voices: Teachers Collaborating for Empowerment. LC 89-36216. (SUNY Series, Teacher Preparation & Development). 204p. 1990. 59.50 (*0-7914-0281-9*); pap. 19.95 (*0-7914-0282-7*) State U NY Pr.

Miller, Janet R., jt. auth. see Gutknecht, Douglas B.

Miller, Janice. Final Thunder: A Novel. 1994. pap. 9.99 (*0-8024-2634-4*) Moody.

— This Blue Planet: Finding God in the Wonders of Nature. 1994. 18.99 (*0-8024-8181-7*) Moody.

***Miller, Janice & Kilpatrick, John.** Issues for Managers: An International Perspective. 57p. (C). 1987. teacher ed write for info. (*0-256-05763-X*) Irwin.

Miller, Janice, jt. auth. see Miller, Robert.

Miller, Janice J., jt. auth. see Miller, Robert R.

Miller, Janice M., jt. auth. see Ayres, H. Joseph.

Miller, Jason. That Championship Season. 1972. pap. 4.75 (*0-8222-1126-2*) Dramatists Play.

— Three One Act Plays by Jason Miller. 1972. pap. 4.75 (*0-8222-0759-1*) Dramatists Play.

Miller, Jay. The Delaware. LC 93-36670. (New True Bks.). (Illus.). 48p. (J). (gr. k-4). 1994. lib. bdg. 12.90 (*0-516-01053-0*) Childrens.

— Delaware. LC 93-36670. (J). (ps-2). 1994. pap. 4.95 (*0-516-41053-9*) Childrens.

— F-117 Stealth Fighter. (Aerofax Extras Ser.). (Illus.). 48p. 1991. pap. 9.95 (*0-933424-55-8*) Specialty Pr.

— Native Americans. (New True Bks.). (Illus.). 48p. (J). (gr. k-4). 1993. lib. bdg. 12.90 (*0-516-01192-8*); pap. 4.95 (*0-516-41192-6*) Childrens.

— Shamanic Odyssey: The Lushootseed Salish Journey to the Land of the Dead. Vane, Sylvia B., ed. LC 88-16761. (Anthropological Papers: No. 32). (Illus.). 217p. 1988. 39.95 (*0-87919-113-9*); pap. 28.95 (*0-87919-112-0*) Ballena Pr.

— Soviet Space. LC 91-65880. (Orig.). 1991. 35.00 (*0-9629867-0-4*); pap. 15.00 (*0-9629867-3-9*) Ft Worth Mus Sci Hist.

Miller, Jay, comp. Earthmaker: Tribal Stories from Native North America. LC 92-8581. 160p. (Orig.). 1992. pap. 10.95 (*0-399-51779-0*, Perigee Bks) Berkley Pub.

Miller, Jay & Eastman, Carol M., eds. The Tsimshian & Their Neighbors of the North Pacific Coast. LC 83-28364. (Illus.). 366p. 1985. 35.00 (*0-295-96126-0*) U of Wash Pr.

Miller, Jay, ed. see Dove, Mourning.

Miller, Jay, ed. see Mourning Dove.

***Miller, Jay, et al, comps.** Writings in Indian History, 1985-1990. LC 95-8776. (D'Arcy McNickle Center Bibliographies in American Indian History Ser.: Vol. 2). 1995. write for info. (*0-8061-2759-7*) U of Okla Pr.

Miller, Jayne. Too Much Trick or Treat. Thatch, Nancy R., ed. LC 91-14930. (Books for Students by Students Ser.). (Illus.). 26p. (J). (gr. k-4). 1991. lib. bdg. 14.95 (*0-933849-37-0*) Landmark Edns.

Miller, Jean. Prophets of Joy: A Spirituality for the Baptized. 1990. pap. 9.95 (*0-87193-268-7*) Dimension Bks.

Miller, Jean B. Toward a New Psychology of Women. 2nd ed. LC 86-47553. 143p. 1986. pap. 12.00 (*0-8070-2909-2*, BP 729) Beacon Pr.

Miller, Jean R. & Janosik, Ellen. Family Focused Care. (Illus.). 1979. text ed. 33.95 (*0-07-042060-2*) McGraw.

Miller, Jeanne. Improve Your Reading, Improve Your Job. Gerould, W. Philip, ed. LC 90-84075. (Fifty-Minute Ser.). (Illus.). (Orig.). 1991. pap. 9.95 (*1-56052-086-8*) Crisp Pubns.

Miller, Jeannette L. & Schafer, Elisabeth. Lunches to Go: Brown Bagging It. LC 91-90261. (Illus.). (Orig.). 1992. pap. 18.95 (*1-879776-00-6*) JEM Commns.

Miller, Jeff. Sunshine Shootouts: The Greatest Games Between Florida-Florida State, Florida State-Miami. LC 92-71793. (Illus.). 224p. 1992. 29.95 (*1-56352-043-5*) Longstreet Pr Inc.

Miller, Jeffery, ed. CWA at Fifty. (Illus.). 64p. 1988. pap. text ed. 5.00 (*0-9621092-0-7*) CWA.

Miller, Jeffery, ed. see Bowles, Paul.

Miller, Jeffrey. Paul Bowles: A Descriptive Bibliography. LC 84-10967. (Illus.). 327p. 1986. 50.00 (*0-87685-609-1*) Black Sparrow.

— Paul Bowles: A Descriptive Bibliography, signed ed. deluxe ed. LC 84-10967. (Illus.). 327p. 1986. 75.00 (*0-87685-610-5*) Black Sparrow.

Miller, Jeffrey, ed. see Bowles, Paul.

Miller, Jeffrey, jt. ed. see Koford, Kenneth.

Miller, Jeffrey, ed. see Suzuki, David T. & Griffiths, Tony.

Miller, Jeffrey G. & Colosi, Thomas R. Fundamentals of Negotiation. 75p. 1989. pap. 28.00 (*0-911937-28-5*) Environ Law Inst.

Miller, Jeffrey G., jt. auth. see Environmental Law Institute Staff.

Miller, Jeffrey G., jt. ed. see Klein, Janice A.

Miller, Jeffrey G., et al. Benchmarking Global Manufacturing: Understanding International Suppliers, Customers, & Competitors. (APICS Ser.). 443p. 1994. 47.50 (*1-55623-674-3*) Irwin Prof Pubng.

Miller, Jeffrey H. A Short Course in Bacterial Genetics: A Laboratory Manual & Handbook for Escherichia Coli & Related Bacteria, 2 vols., Set. (Illus.). 876p. 1992. student ed 110.00 (*0-87969-349-5*) Cold Spring Harbor.

— A Short Course in Bacterial Genetics: Handbook for Escherichia Coli & Related Bacteria. (Illus.). 1992. pap. 75.00 (*0-614-06575-5*) Cold Spring Harbor.

Miller, Jeffrey H., ed. Experiments in Molecular Genetics. LC 72-78914. (Illus.). 468p. 1972. 40.00 (*0-87969-106-9*) Cold Spring Harbor.

Miller, Jeffrey H., et al, eds. Methods in Enzymology, Vol. 204: Bacterial Genetic Systems. (Illus.). 706p. 1991. text ed. 99.00 (*0-12-182105-6*) Acad Pr.

Miller, Jeffrey H. & Calos, Michele P., eds. Gene Transfer Vectors for Mammalian Cells. LC 87-149603. (Current Communications in Molecular Biology Ser.). 179p. reprint ed. pap. 51.10 (*0-7837-1998-1*, 2042272) Bks Demand.

Miller, Jeffrey H., jt. auth. see Schele, Linda.

Miller, Jeffrey M. & Chambers, Larry. The Four Hundred One (k) Plan Management Handbook: A Guide for Sponsors & Their Advisors. 300p. 1992. 50.00 (*1-55738-465-7*) Probus Pub Co.

Miller, Jennifer. Coastal Affair. (Southern Exposure Ser.). (Illus.). 120p. (Orig.). 1982. pap. 4.00 (*0-943810-13-2*) Inst Southern Studies.

Miller, Jerome. The Way of Suffering: A Geography of Crisis. LC 88-4703. 215p. 1988. 10.95 (*0-87840-465-1*) Georgetown U Pr.

Miller, Jerome A. In the Throe of Wonder: Intimations of the Sacred in a Post-Modern World. LC 91-12723. 222p. (C). 1992. 59.50 (*0-7914-0953-8*); pap. 19.95 (*0-7914-0954-6*) State U NY Pr.

Miller, Jerome A., ed. NAB Study Guide: How to Prepare for the Nursing Home Administrators Examination. 240p. (C). 1992. pap. text ed. write for info. (*0-9635064-0-4*) Nat Asn Bds Exam.

***Miller, Jerome A. & Allen, James E., eds.** Directory of U. S. Colleges & Universities Offering a Curriculum in Long Term Care Administration & State Board Licensure Requirements for Nursing Home Administrators. 284p. (Orig.). (C). 1994. pap. 29.00 (*0-9635064-1-2*) Nat Asn Bds Exam.

Miller, Jerome G. Last One over the Wall: The Massachusetts Experiment in Closing Reform Schools. 279p. 1991. 39.50 (*0-8142-0534-8*) Ohio St U Pr.

— Last One over the Wall: The Massachusetts Experiment in Closing Reform Schools. 276p. 1993. pap. 19.95 (*0-8142-0605-0*) Ohio St U Pr.

Miller, Jerome H. & Miller, Dolores E. Gettysburg for Walkers Only: Four Auto-Free Tours of the Battlefield. (Illus.). 64p. (C). 1991. pap. text ed. 3.95 (*0-939631-38-5*) Thomas Publications.

Miller, Jerome K. Church Copyright Seminar. 1987. Incl. audio cassette. audio 24.87 (*0-914143-15-8*, Copy Info Svc) Assn Ed Comm Tech.

— Using Copyrighted Videocassettes in Classrooms, Libraries, & Training Centers. 2nd ed. LC 87-24572. (Copyright Information Bulletin Ser.: No. 3). 131p. 1988. 19.95 (*0-914143-14-X*, Copy Info Svc) Assn Ed Comm Tech.

— Video Copyright Permissions: A Guide to Securing Permission to Retain, Perform, & Transmit Television Programs Videotaped off the Air. (Copyright Information Bulletin Ser.: No. 5). 140p. 1989. 29.95 (*0-914143-13-1*, Copy Info Svc) Assn Ed Comm Tech.

Miller, Jerry, jt. auth. see Coyne, John.

Miller, Jerry L. Desktop Reference of Compliance Terms. 1990. pap. 30.00 (*1-55520-135-0*) Probus Pub Co.

Miller, Jewel. Whisper of Love. 176p. (Orig.). 1991. pap. 6.95 (*0-8361-3570-9*) Herald Pr.

Miller, Jill. Happy As a Dead Cat. 120p. (Orig.). 1993. pap. 6.95 (*0-7043-3898-X*, Pub. by Womens Pr UK) Interlink Pub.

Miller, Jim. The Big Fifty. large type ed. (Linford Western Library). 272p. (Orig.). 1988. pap. 11.95 (*0-7089-6602-0*, Linford) Ulverscroft.

— Border Marshal. 1993. mass mkt. 3.99 (*0-06-100706-4*, Harp PBks) HarpC.

— The Brass Boy. large type ed. (Linford Western Library). 1990. pap. 12.95 (*0-7089-6803-1*, Linford) Ulverscroft.

— Campaigning. large type ed. (Linford Western Library). 304p. (Orig.). 1988. pap. 11.95 (*0-7089-6487-7*, Linford) Ulverscroft.

— Carston's Law. Grad, Doug, ed. (Ex-Rangers Ser.: No. 9). 224p. (Orig.). 1993. pap. 3.50 (*0-671-74827-0*) PB.

— The Ex-Rangers: Ranger's Revenge, No. 1. 224p. 1990. pap. 2.95 (*0-671-66946-X*) PB.

— The Ex-Rangers: The Long Rope. large type ed. 1992. 18.95 (*0-7927-1312-5*, Curley Lrg Print); pap. 16.95 (*0-7927-1311-7*, Curley Lrg Print) Chivers N Amer.

— The Ex-Rangers, No. 11: South of the Border. 224p. (Orig.). 1993. mass mkt. 3.99 (*0-671-74829-7*) PB.

— Gone to Texas. 1984. pap. 2.50 (*0-449-13100-9*) Fawcett.

— Gone to Texas. 1990. 15.95 (*0-7278-4086-X*) Severn Hse.

— Gone to Texas. large type ed. (Linford Western Library). 320p. 1987. pap. 11.95 (*0-7089-6422-2*, Linford) Ulverscroft.

— Hell with the Hide Off. large type ed. LC 93-42948. 1994. 15.95 (*0-8161-5933-5*, Large Print Bks) Hall.

— Line Riders. 1994. mass mkt. 3.50 (*0-06-100705-6*, Harp PBks) HarpC.

— Mister Henry. large type ed. (Linford Western Library). 277p. (Orig.). 1989. pap. 11.95 (*0-7089-6679-9*, Linford) Ulverscroft.

An Asterisk (*) at the beginning of an entry indicates that the title is appearing in BIP for the first time.

— Orphan's Preferred. large type ed. (Linford Western Library). 304p. 1988. pap. 11.95 (0-7089-6493-1, Linford) Ulverscroft.
— Ranger's Revenge. large type ed. (Nightingale Ser.). 291p. 1991. pap. 14.95 (0-8161-5151-2, Nightingale) Hall.
— Riding Shotgun. large type ed. (Linford Western Library). 304p. 1987. pap. 11.95 (0-7089-6410-9, Linford) Ulverscroft.
— Shootout in Sendero. Grad, Doug, ed. (Ex-Rangers Ser.: No. 8). 224p. (Orig.). 1992. pap. 3.50 (0-671-74826-2) PB.
— Shootout in Sendero. large type ed. LC 93-138. (Orig.). 1993. 14.95 (0-8161-5776-6) G K Hall.
— Shotgun & Sagebrush. large type ed. 1990. pap. 12.95 (0-7089-6942-9, Trailtree Bookshop) Ulverscroft.
— The Six Hundred Mile Stretch. Grad, Doug, ed. (Ex-Rangers Ser.: No. 6). 224p. (Orig.). 1992. pap. 3.50 (0-671-74824-6) PB.
— Spencer's Revenge. large type ed. (Linford Western Library). 237p. 1989. pap. 11.95 (0-7089-6671-3, Linford) Ulverscroft.
— Stranger from Nowhere. Grad, Doug, ed. (Ex-Rangers Ser.: No. 10). 224p. (Orig.). 1993. mass mkt. 3.99 (0-671-74828-9) PB.
— That Damn Single Shot. 1988. pap. 2.95 (0-449-13317-6, GM) Fawcett.
— That Damn Single Shot. large type ed. 1990. pap. 12.95 (0-7089-6864-3, Trailtree Bookshop) Ulverscroft.
— War Clouds. (Orig.). 1990. 15.95 (0-7278-4079-7) Severn Hse.
Miller, Jim, jt. auth. see Brown, Keith.
Miller, Jim, ed. see Rolling Stone Press Staff.
Miller, Jim W. Brier, His Book. LC 87-82662. 80p. 1988. 16.00 (0-917788-35-4); pap. 10.50 (0-917788-34-6) Gnomon Pr.
— Copperhead Cane. O'Dell, Mary, ed. Dorsett, Thomas, tr. (Library Poetry Ser.). 80p. (GER.). 1995. 17.50 (0-9623666-5-X); pap. 11.95 (0-9623666-6-8) Green Rvr Writers.
— Copperhead Cane. deluxe ed. O'Dell, Mary, ed. Dorsett, Thomas, tr. (Library Poetry Ser.). 80p. (GER.). 1995. boxed 50.00 (0-614-01860-9) Green Rvr Writers.
— His First, Best Country. LC 92-75360. 224p. 1993. 18.50 (0-917788-54-0) Gnomon Pr.
— His First, Best Country. 224p. 1995. pap. 12.50 (0-917788-55-9) Gnomon Pr.
— The Mountains Have Come Closer. LC 80-80456. 1980. pap. 9.95 (0-913239-19-4) Appalach Consortium.
— Newfound. rev. ed. (J). Date not set. write for info. (0-917788-59-1) Gnomon Pr.
— Round & Round with Kahlil Gibran. LC 90-30378. 10p. (Orig.). 1990. pap. 4.00 (0-926487-05-1) Rowan Mtn Pr.
Miller, Jim W., ed. see Stuart, Jesse.
Miller, Jo, ed. see Long, Jeanne, et al.
Miller, Jo, ed. see Miller, Ray.
Miller, Jo, jt. ed. see Miller, Ray.
Miller, Jo Ann L., jt. ed. see Knudsen, Dean D.
Miller, Joan. Before Baby Arrives. 128p. 1995. pap. 6.95 (0-572-01655-7, Pub. by Foulsham UK) Atrium Pubs.
— One Girl's War. 156p. 1989. 15.95 (0-312-03410-5) St Martin.
— Taking the "Ouch" out of Headaches. 1983. 24.95 (0-9613786-0-3) J Miller.
— Your Baby's Development. 128p. 1995. pap. 6.95 (0-572-01657-3, Pub. by Foulsham UK) Atrium Pubs.
Miller, Joan, jt. auth. see Schwartz, Sue.
***Miller, Joan H. & Jones, Norman.** Organic & Compost-Based Growing Media for Tree Seedling Nurseries. LC 94-23707. (Technical Papers: No. 264). 1994. write for info. (0-8213-3039-X) World Bank.
Miller, Joan I. & Taylor, Bruce J. The Punctuation Handbook. 96p. (Orig.). 1989. pap. 4.95 (0-937473-14-6) Alcove Pub Co OR.
— The Thesis Writer's Handbook: A Complete One-Source Guide for Writers of Research Papers. (Illus.). 322p. 1989. pap. 12.95 (0-937473-12-X) Alcove Pub Co OR.
Miller, Joan M., jt. auth. see Chaya, Ruth K.
Miller, Joan M., et al. BASIC Programming for the Classroom & Home Teacher. 262p. (C). 1982. pap. text ed. 17.95 (0-8077-2728-8) Tchrs Coll.
Miller, Joan V. Auguste Rodin, Eighteen Forty to Nineteen Seventeen: B. G. Cantor Sculpture Center. Marotta, Gary, ed. (Illus.). 64p. (Orig.). 1981. pap. write for info. (0-939912-00-7) Cantor Art Found.
***Miller, Joanne L. & Eimas, Peter D., eds.** Speech, Language & Communication. 2nd ed. (Handbook of Perception & Cognition). (Illus.). 472p. 1995. text ed. 59.95 (0-12-497770-7) Acad Pr.
Miller, Joanne L., jt. ed. see Eimas, Peter D.
Miller, Joaquin. The Complete Poetical Works of Joaquin Miller. LC 72-4967. (Romantic Tradition in American Literature Ser.). 356p. 1978. reprint ed. 31.95 (0-405-04638-3) Ayer.
— Forty Nine: The Gold-Seekers of the Sierras. LC 78-104527. reprint ed. lib. bdg. 27.50 (0-8398-1258-2) Irvington.
— Joaquin Miller's Poems (The Bear Edition), 6 vols. LC 74-5238. reprint ed. 425.00 (0-404-11530-6) AMS Pr.
— Joaquin Miller's Poems (The Bear Edition), 6 vols., 1. LC 74-5238. reprint ed. write for info. (0-404-11531-4) AMS Pr.
— Joaquin Miller's Poems (The Bear Edition), 6 vols., 2. LC 74-5238. reprint ed. write for info. (0-404-11532-2) AMS Pr.
— Joaquin Miller's Poems (The Bear Edition), 6 vols., 3. LC 74-5238. reprint ed. write for info. (0-404-11533-0) AMS Pr.
— Joaquin Miller's Poems (The Bear Edition), 6 vols., 4. LC 74-5238. reprint ed. write for info. (0-404-11534-9) AMS Pr.
— Joaquin Miller's Poems (The Bear Edition), 6 vols., 5. LC 74-5238. reprint ed. write for info. (0-404-11535-7) AMS Pr.
— Joaquin Miller's Poems (The Bear Edition), 6 vols., 6. LC 74-5238. reprint ed. write for info. (0-404-11536-5) AMS Pr.
— Life Amongst the Modocs: Unwritten History. LC 85-52081. 447p. 1987. 19.95 (0-913522-13-9); pap. 12.95 (0-913522-12-0) Urion Pr CA.
— Life Amongst the Modocs: Unwritten History. LC 68-57540. (Muckrakers Ser.). 460p. reprint ed. lib. bdg. 24.50 (0-8398-1259-0) Irvington.
— Life Amongst the Modocs: Unwritten History. (Muckrakers Ser.). 460p. 1984. reprint ed. pap. 6.95 (0-8290-1565-5) Irvington.
— Poetical Works. (BCL1-PS American Literature Ser.). 587p. 1992. reprint ed. lib. bdg. 99.00 (0-7812-6798-6) Rprt Serv.
— Selected Writings of Joaquin Miller. Rosenus, Alan, ed. LC 73-88918. (Primary Source Book Ser.). (Illus.). 1976. 18.95 (0-913522-05-8); pap. 12.95 (0-913522-06-6) Urion Pr CA.
— Songs of the Sierras. LC 71-104528. 309p. reprint ed. lib. bdg. 36.50 (0-8398-1260-4) Irvington.
— True Bear Stories. LC 89-31044. 96p. (C). 1988. reprint ed. lib. bdg. 23.00x (0-8095-4051-7) Borgo Pr.
— True Bear Stories. Robertson, James, ed. LC 86-31688. (Illus.). 80p. 1987. reprint ed. pap. 7.95 (0-88496-259-8) Capra Pr.
Miller, Joe. Burst of Speed: Five Proven Techniques to Increase Your Speed. (Illus.). 144p. 1984. 15.95 (0-89651-705-5); pap. 8.95 (0-89651-706-3) B L Pub.
— The Nuts & Bolts a Novice Needs to Wire His New Home: The Bundle Saved Will Be His. (Illus.). 65p. (Orig.). 1986. pap. 9.95 (0-9616542-0-1) Joe Miller Pub.
Miller, Joe, intro. Great Song: The Life & Teachings of Joe Miller. 240p. (Orig.). 1993. pap. 16.00 (0-9618916-8-8) Maypop.
Miller, Joe A., ed. see Institute of Labor & Industrial Relations Staff.
Miller, Joel E., jt. auth. see Parella, Robert E.
Miller, Joel S., ed. Chemically Modified Surfaces in Catalysis & Electrolysis. LC 82-8731. (ACS Symposium Ser.: No. 192). 301p. 1982. lib. bdg. 43.95 (0-8412-0727-5) Am Chemical.
— Extended Linear Chain Compounds, Vol. 1. LC 81-17762. 498p. (C). 1981. 110.00 (0-306-40711-6, Plenum Pr) Plenum.
— Extended Linear Chain Compounds, Vol. 2. LC 81-17762. 532p. 1981. 110.00 (0-306-40712-4, Plenum Pr) Plenum.
— Extended Linear Chain Compounds, Vol. 3. LC 81-17762. 580p. 1983. 110.00 (0-306-40941-0, Plenum Pr) Plenum.
Miller, Joel S. & Epstein, Arthur J., eds. Synthesis & Properties of Low-Dimensional Materials, Vol. 313. (Annals Ser.). 828p. 1978. pap. 82.00 (0-89072-069-X) NY Acad Sci.
Miller, John. The Berkshires: A History & Guide. pap. write for info. (0-318-58334-8) Random.
— Christmas Stories. LC 92-46110. 224p. 1993. 17.95 (0-8118-0345-7) Chronicle Bks.
— Court Cases of Consequence. 84p. (Orig.). 1978. pap. text ed. 15.00 (1-886536-00-7) Elevator Wrld.
— Early Victorian New Zealand: A Study of Racial Tensions & Social Attitudes 1839-1852. LC 86-22845. (Illus.). 227p. 1986. reprint ed. text ed. 59.75 (0-313-25283-1, MIEV, Greenwood Pr) Greenwood.
— An Englishman's Home. 208p. 1987. 35.00 (0-905392-46-9) St Mut.
— First Power: The Inner Planet Trilogy. LC 89-51880. (Buck Rogers Bks.). (Illus.). 320p. (Orig.). 1990. pap. 3.95 (0-88038-840-4) TSR Inc.
— History of Erie County, Pennsylvania: A Narrative Account of Its Historical Progress, Its People & Its Principal Interests, 2 vols., Vol. I. (Illus.). 897p. 1992. reprint ed. lib. bdg. 89.00 (0-8328-1424-5) Higginson Bk Co.
— History of Erie County, Pennsylvania: A Narrative Account of Its Historical Progress, Its People & Its Principal Interests, 2 vols., Vol. II. (Illus.). 709p. 1992. reprint ed. lib. bdg. 78.50 (0-8328-1425-3) Higginson Bk Co.
— Implementing Activity-Based Costing in Daily Operations. Date not set. text ed. 37.95 (0-471-04003-7) Wiley.
— An Inquiry into the Present State of the Civil Law of England. viii, 533p. 1994. reprint ed. lib. bdg. 57.50 (0-8377-2449-X) Rothman.
— Memoirs of General Miller, in the Service of the Republic of Peru, 2 Vols, Set. 2nd ed. reprint ed. 135.00 (0-404-04339-9) AMS Pr.
— Mikhail Gorbachev & the End of Soviet Power. LC 92-29615. 210p. 1993. text ed. 59.95 (0-312-09080-3) St Martin.
— New Orleans Stories: Great Writers on the City. 1992. pap. 10.95 (0-8118-0059-8) Chronicle Bks.
Miller, John, ed. Absolutism in Seventeenth-Century Europe. LC 90-36375. 256p. 1991. text ed. 49.95 (0-312-04930-7) St Martin.
— Desert Light: Myths & Visions of the Great Southwest. LC 92-12828. 120p. 1992. pap. 18.95 (0-8118-0211-6) Chronicle Bks.
— Fish Tales: Stories from the Sea. LC 93-2665. (Illus.). 160p. 1993. 30.00 (0-8117-0619-2) Stackpole.
— Los Angeles Stories. 176p. (Orig.). 1991. pap. 10.95 (0-87701-822-7) Chronicle Bks.
— Nasecode IX Transactions: Selected Papers from the Ninth International Conference on the Numerical Analysis of Semi-conductor Devices & Integrated Circuits. (Compel Ser.: Vol. 12, No. 4). (Illus.). (Orig.). (C). 1993. pap. text ed. 120.00 (1-873936-30-3, Pub. by J & J Sci Pubs UK) Bks Intl VA.
— On Suicide: Great Writers on the Ultimate Question. 194p. 1993. pap. 10.95 (0-8118-0231-0) Chronicle Bks.
— San Francisco Stories: Great Writers on the City. LC 89-25337. 304p. (Orig.). 1990. pap. 11.95 (0-87701-669-0) Chronicle Bks.
Miller, John & Anderson, Genevieve, eds. Chicago Stories: Great Writers on the City. LC 92-20490. 256p. 1993. pap. 10.95 (0-8118-0164-0) Chronicle Bks.
Miller, John & Harwood, Kirsten, eds. Florida Stories: Tales from the Tropics. LC 93-327. 256p. 1993. pap. 10.95 (0-8118-0457-7) Chronicle Bks.
***Miller, John & Miller, Kirsten.** Istanbul. LC 94-34514. (Chronicles Abroad Ser.). 1995. write for info. (0-8118-0823-8) Chronicle Bks.
Miller, John & Miller, Kirsten, eds. Alaska Stories: Tales from the Wild Frontier. LC 94-15574. 1995. pap. 11.95 (0-8118-0675-8) Chronicle Bks.
— Cairo: Tales of the City. LC 93-1815. (Chronicles Abroad Ser.). 192p. 1994. 12.95 (0-8118-0492-5) Chronicle Bks.
— Hong Kong. LC 93-48091. (Chronicles Abroad Ser.). 256p. 1994. 12.95 (0-8118-0680-4) Chronicle Bks.
— In the Garden. LC 93-34672. (Illus.). 160p. 1994. 30.00 (0-8117-0906-X) Stackpole.
— Lust: Lascivious Love Stories & Passionate Poems. LC 93-28053. (Illus.). 144p. 1994. 14.95 (0-8118-0691-X) Chronicle Bks.
— The Moon Goddess. LC 95-12953. 1995. write for info. (0-8118-1128-X) Chronicle Bks.
— Moon Lore. LC 95-12955. 1995. write for info. (0-8118-1104-2) Chronicle Bks.
— Prague. LC 93-48953. (Chronicles Abroad Ser.). 256p. 1994. 12.95 (0-8118-0649-9) Chronicle Bks.
— St. Petersburg. LC 94-34287. (Chronicles Abroad Ser.). 1995. write for info. (0-8118-0879-3) Chronicle Bks.
— Somnium & Other Trips to the Moon. LC 95-12956. 1995. write for info. (0-8118-1129-8) Chronicle Bks.
— The Were-Wolf. LC 95-12954. 1995. write for info. (0-8118-1131-X) Chronicle Bks.
***Miller, John & Miller, Kisten, eds.** Texas Stories. LC 94-37904. 1995. pap. write for info. (0-8118-0845-9) Chronicle Bks.
Miller, John & Miller, Kristen, eds. Venice: Tales of the City. LC 93-13594. (Abroad Ser.). 176p. 1994. 12.95 (0-8118-0471-2) Chronicle Bks.
***Miller, John & Smith, Tim, eds.** San Francisco Thrillers: True Crimes & Dark Mysteries from the City by the Bay. LC 95-12957. 1995. write for info. (0-8118-1043-7) Chronicle Bks.
Miller, John, ed. see Anderson-Morgan, Genevieve.
Miller, John, ed. see Dollars & Sense Magazine Staff.
Miller, John, jt. auth. see Dosani, Majid.
Miller, John, jt. auth. see Gielgud, John.
Miller, John, ed. see Hemingway, Ernest.
Miller, John, jt. auth. see Kelley, Mike.
Miller, John, ed. see Koral, Randall.
Miller, John, ed. see Kuhlewind, Georg.
Miller, John, jt. auth. see Manoff, Tom.
Miller, John, jt. auth. see McAllister, Dawson.
***Miller, John, et al, eds.** European Dinantian Environments. fac. ed. LC 86-13323. (Geological Journal Special Issue Ser.: No. 12). (Illus.). 412p. 1994. pap. 117.50 (0-7837-7657-8, 2047410) Bks Demand.
***Miller, John A.** The Garcia File. 188p. 1995. pap. 7.95 (1-56901-498-1) NW Pub.

— Jackson Street: And Other Soldier Stories. LC 94-61157. 1995. 18.95 (0-9642949-3-1) Orloff Pr. "Mary Alice Goodman taught piano & lived on Jackson Street, in a house that surely cried at night." Hailed by Publishers Weekly as "an impressive first collection" & "memorable reading", & by Kirkus Reviews as "an impressively serious & professional debut" this fine collection of stories is an auspicious debut for North Carolina author John Miller. "These are stories that will absorb the reader, whether they have ever served in the military or not. Where has (Miller) been up until now, & when can we expect more?"--Southern Book Trade. Possessed of an extraordinary eye & ear for the patterns of Southern life & the rhythms of Southern speech, Miller draws us inexorably into the lives of his uncelebrated heroes. "To chance upon this brilliant collection & begin reading Miller's lyrical parade of magical sentences is like walking out to get the morning paper & finding the Hope diamond."--Hilton Head Island Packet. "(W)ell crafted & poignant."--The Missouri Review. Available from: Baker & Taylor, Pacific Pipeline, Parnassus Books Dist., or contact John Spencer, Orloff Press, (510) 548-3670. *Publisher Provided Annotation.*

— Master Builders of Sixty Centuries. LC 70-37524. (Essay Index Reprint Ser.). (Illus.). 1977. reprint ed. 23.95 (0-8369-2566-1) Ayer.
Miller, John A. & Neuzil, E. F. General Organic Chemistry. 1979. text ed. 23.00 (0-669-01885-6); student ed 12.00 (0-669-01887-2) Heath.
— Modern Experimental Organic Chemistry. 722p. (C). 1982. pap. text ed. 36.00 (0-669-03174-7); Instr.'s guide. teacher ed 2.00 (0-669-06160-3) Heath.
***Miller, John A., et al.** Progress in Simulation, Vol. 3. 320p. 1995. write for info. (0-89391-681-1) Ablex Pub.
Miller, John C. Federalist Era, Seventeen Eighty Nine to Eighteen-One. (New American Nation Ser.). (Illus.). 1963. pap. text ed. 14.00 (0-06-133027-2, TB 3027, Torch) HarpC.
— The First Frontier: Life in Colonial America. 284p. 1986. reprint ed. pap. text ed. 19.00 (0-8191-4977-2) U Pr of Amer.
— Origins of the American Revolution: With a New Introduction & Bibliography. (Illus.). xxii, 530p. 1959. 62.50 (0-8047-0593-3); pap. 18.95 (0-8047-0594-1) Stanford U Pr.
— Sam Adams: Pioneer in Propaganda. (Illus.). 437p. 1936. 52.50 (0-8047-0024-9); pap. 17.95 (0-8047-0025-7) Stanford U Pr.
— Triumph of Freedom, Seventeen Seventy-Five to Seventeen Eighty-Three. LC 78-23672. (Illus.). 718p. 1979. reprint ed. text ed. 75.00 (0-313-20779-8, MITF, Greenwood Pr) Greenwood.
— Triumph of Freedom, 1775-1783. (History - United States Ser.). 718p. 1993. reprint ed. lib. bdg. 109.00 (0-7812-4833-7) Rprt Serv.
— The Wolf by the Ears: Thomas Jefferson & Slavery. 336p. 1991. reprint ed. pap. 14.95 (0-8139-1365-9) U Pr of Va.
Miller, John C., ed. Laser Ablation: Principles & Aplications. LC 94-5045. (Series in Material Science: Vol. 48). 1994. 59.00 (0-387-57571-5) Spr-Verlag.
— Poe's Helen Remembers. LC 79-742. (Illus.). 528p. 1980. 35.00 (0-8139-0771-3) U Pr of Va.
Miller, John C. & Geohegan, David, eds. Laser Ablation: Mechanism & Applications-II. (AIP Conference Proceedings Ser.: No. 288). (Illus.). 456p. 1993. text ed. 150.00 (1-56396-226-8, AIP Pr) Am Inst Physics.
Miller, John D. & Rigby, T. H., eds. Disintegrating Monolith: Pluralist Trends in the Communist World. LC 66-5402. xiii, 264p. 1965. 37.50 (0-678-05188-7) Kelley.
Miller, John E. How to Start a Business Without a Bankroll. 128p. (Orig.). 1986. 55.00 (0-933203-00-4) Miller Money Mgmt.
— Laura Ingalls Wilder's Little Town: Where History & Literature Meet. LC 93-40632. (Illus.). 220p. 1994. 29.95x (0-7006-0654-8) U Pr of KS.
— Laura Ingalls Wilder's Little Town: Where History & Literature Meet. (Illus.). 220p. 1995. pap. 14.95 (0-7006-0713-7) U Pr of KS.
— Looking for History on Highway 14. LC 92-30506. (Illus.). 280p. (Orig.). 1993. pap. 15.95 (0-8138-1246-1) Iowa St U Pr.
— The Reciprocating Pump: Theory, Design & Use. 2nd ed. LC 91-2639. 316484p. (C). 1995. lib. bdg. 69.50 (0-89464-599-4) Krieger.
Miller, John E. & Halvorson, Mark J. The Way They Saw Us: The South Dakota State Historical Society Collection of Images from the Nineteenth-Century Illustrated Press. Koupal, Nancy T., ed. LC 89-50608. (Illus.). 64p. (Orig.). 1989. 6.95 (0-9622621-0-2) SD State Hist Soc.
Miller, John E., jt. auth. see Pawson, David L.
Miller, John F. Ovid Fasti Two. (Latin Commentaries Ser.). 102p. (Orig.). (C). 1985. pap. text ed. 7.00 (0-929524-46-2) Bryn Mawr Commentaries.
Miller, John G. The Battle to Save the Houston. McCarthy, Paul, ed. 264p. 1992. reprint ed. mass mkt. 4.99 (0-671-78621-0) PB.
— The Battle to Save the Houston, October 1944 to March 1945. LC 85-314. (Illus.). 226p. 1985. 24.95 (0-87021-276-1) Naval Inst Pr.
— The Bridge at Dong Ha. LC 89-2908. 224p. 1989. 24.95 (0-87021-020-3) Naval Inst Pr.
Miller, John G., jt. auth. see Mastin, Fred.
Miller, John H. Love Responds: Reflections on Christian Morality. 149p. (Orig.). 1990. pap. 7.00 (0-9626257-0-1) CBCCU Amer.
— Why We Act That Way. LC 47-354. reprint ed. pap. 56.00 (0-317-10045-9, 2001338) Bks Demand.
Miller, John H., intro. Curing World Poverty: The New Role of Property. (Illus.). 310p. (Orig.). 1994. pap. 15.00 (0-9626257-5-2) CBCCU Amer.
Miller, John H. & Gelfand, Michael, eds. Pediatric Nuclear Imaging. LC 93-38091. 1994. text ed. 99.95 (0-7216-3685-3) Saunders.
Miller, John H., tr. see Poupard, Paul C.
Miller, John J., III, ed. Juvenile Rheumatoid Arthritis. LC 78-55290. (Illus.). 280p. 1979. 35.00 (0-88416-189-7, Yr Bk Med Pubs) Mosby Yr Bk.
Miller, John J., jt. auth. see Leigh, Stephen.
Miller, John J., ed. see Metallurgical Society of AIME Staff.
Miller, John L. Principles of Infrared Technology: A Practical Guide to the State of the Art. LC 93-32092. 1994. text ed. 69.95 (0-442-01210-1) Van Nos Reinhold.
Miller, John M. Fingerpicking Gershwin. 1981. pap. 9.95 (0-8256-2215-8) Music Sales.
— Minnesota Legal Forms: Commercial Real Estate. 180p. 1982. disk, ring bd. 69.95 (0-917126-88-2) Butterworth Legal Pubs.
— Minnesota Legal Forms: Commercial Real Estate. 180p. 1993. disk, ring bd. 69.95 (0-614-05900-3) Michie Butterworth.

— Minnesota Legal Forms: Commercial Real Estate. suppl. ed. 180p. 1993. 35.00 (*0-685-70860-8*) Butterworth Legal Pubs.
— Minnesota Legal Forms: Commercial Real Estate. suppl. ed. 1993. ring bd. 35.00 (*0-614-03156-7*) Butterworth Legal Pubs.
Miller, John P. The Contemplative Practitioner: Meditation in Education & the Professions. LC 94-4767. 184p. 1994. text ed. 45.00 (*0-89789-401-4*, Bergin & Garvey) Greenwood.
— Creating Academic Settings: High Craft & Low Cunning: Memoirs. LC 91-90125. 247p. 1991. 17.00 (*0-9629010-0-8*) J Simeon Pr.
— Pricing of Military Procurements. (Yale Studies in National Policy Ser.: No. 2). 1949. 89.50 (*0-685-69842-4*) Elliots Bks.
Miller, John R., jt. auth. see Campbell, Luther.
Miller, John T. Ideology & Enlightenment: The Political & Social Thought of Samuel Taylor Coleridge. McNeill, William H. & Stansky, Peter, eds. (Modern European History Ser.). 336p. 1987. lib. bdg. 15.00 (*0-8240-7824-1*) Garland.
Miller, John W. The Definition of the Thing: With Some Notes on Language. (C). 1980. reprint ed. text ed. 20.00 (*0-393-01377-4*) Norton.
— The Definition of the Thing: With Some Notes on Language. 1983. reprint ed. pap. 6.50 (*0-393-30059-5*) Norton.
— In Defense of the Psychological. 192p. 1985. reprint ed. pap. 6.50 (*0-393-30226-1*) Norton.
— Meet the Prophets: A Beginner's Guide to the Books of the Biblical Prophets. 288p. 1987. pap. 13.95 (*0-8091-2899-3*) Paulist Pr.
— The Midworld of Symbols & Functioning Objects. 192p. 1982. reprint ed. 20.00 (*0-393-01579-3*) Norton.
— The Midworld of Symbols & Functioning Objects. 192p. 1984. reprint ed. pap. 6.95 (*0-393-30156-7*) Norton.
— The Origins of the Bible: Rethinking Canon History. LC 94-33902. (Theological Inquiries Ser.). 272p. 1995. pap. 18.95 (*0-8091-3522-1*) Paulist Pr.
— Paradox of Cause & Other Essays. 1990. pap. 10.95 (*0-393-30731-X*) Norton.
— The Philosophy of History with Reflections & Aphorisms. LC 80-29179. 192p. (C). 1981. reprint ed. text ed. 20.00 (*0-393-01464-9*) Norton.
Miller, John W. & McKenna, Michael. Teaching Reading in the Elementary Classroom. (C). 1989. text ed. 40.00 (*0-89787-521-4*) Gorsuch Scarisbrick.
Miller, John W., tr. see Goldoni, Carlo.
Miller, Johnny, jt. auth. see Gorden, Bill.
Miller, Jon. Pathways in the Workplace: The Effect of Race & Gender on Access to Organzational Resources. (American Sociological Assn. Rose Monograph Ser.). (Illus.). 160p. 1986. 54.95 (*0-521-32365-7*) Cambridge U Pr.
— The Social Control of Religious Zeal: A Study of Organizational Contradictions. LC 93-6030. (Arnold & Caroline Rose Monograph Series of the American Sociological Association). 240p. (C). 1994. text ed. 48.00 (*0-8135-2060-6*) Rutgers U Pr.
Miller, Jon, ed. Research on Child Language Disorders: A Decade of Progress. LC 89-25120. (Illus.). 413p. 1991. pap. text ed. 32.00 (*0-89079-408-1*, 1581) PRO-ED.
Miller, Jon, et al, eds. Contemporary Issues in Language Intervention: ASHA Reports, 12th. LC 82-50935. 340p. 1983. text ed. 42.50 (*0-910329-02-8*) Am Speech Lang Hearing.
Miller, Jon F. Assessing Language Production in Children: Experimental Procedures. (Illus.). 186p. (C). 1991. pap. text ed. 47.00 (*0-205-13546-3*) Allyn.
***Miller, Jon F. & Paul, Rhea.** The Clinical Assessment of Language Comprehension. LC 94-35065. 208p. 1994. spiral bd. 33.00 (*1-55766-176-6*) P H Brookes.
Miller, Jonathan. The Afterlife of Plays. (Distinguished Graduate Research Lecture Ser.: No. 5). 48p. 1992. 12. 50 (*1-879691-12-4*) SDSU Press.
— Darwin for Beginners. 1989. pap. 10.00 (*0-679-72511-3*) McKay.
— Don Giovanni: Myths of Seduction & Betrayal. 1991. pap. 10.95 (*0-8018-4332-4*) Johns Hopkins.
— The Human Body. Pelham, David, ed. LC 83-80311. (Illus.). (J). 1983. pap. 22.50 (*0-670-38605-7*) Viking Child Bks.
— Human Body. (J). (ps-3). 1994. 22.95 (*0-670-85570-7*) Viking Child Bks.
***Miller, Jonathan & Pelham, David.** The Facts of Life. rev. ed. (Illus.). 12p. 1995. 22.95 (*0-670-86553-2*, Viking Studio) Studio Bks.
Miller, Jonathan & Van Loon, Boris. Darwin for Beginners. 12.95 (*0-906495-95-4*) Writers & Readers.
Miller, Jonathan, jt. ed. see Durant, John.
Miller, Jonathan, jt. auth. see Lurie, Joe.
Miller, Jonathon D. Candida Yeast: The Battle in Your Body. (Orig.). 1986. pap. 2.50 (*0-935815-03-1*) Lifecircle.
— Changes: Adapting to Earth's Renewal. (Orig.). pap. 4.95 (*0-935815-07-4*) Lifecircle.
— The Fountain of Youth: Secrets of Health & Long Life. (Orig.). pap. 2.95 (*0-935815-05-8*) Lifecircle.
— Herbs & Iridology. rev. ed. (Illus.). (Orig.). 1985. pap. 4.95 (*0-935815-01-5*) Lifecircle.
— Holistic Healing. (Orig.). 1993. pap. 2.95 (*0-935815-04-X*) Lifecircle.
— Jonathon's Herbal: A Guide to Herbs for Health. rev. ed. 1986. pap. 2.50 (*0-935815-02-3*) Lifecircle.
— Nutrition, Health & Harmony. rev. ed. (Illus.). (Orig.). 1980. pap. 3.50 (*0-935815-00-7*) Lifecircle.
— Stress Control: Relaxation, Detoxification & Nutrition. (Orig.). 1993. pap. 2.95 (*0-935815-06-6*) Lifecircle.
Miller, Joni. True Grits: The Southern Foods Mail Order Catalog. LC 88-51583. (Illus.). 384p. (Orig.). 1990. pap. 10.95 (*0-89480-344-1*, 1344) Workman Pub.
Miller, Joni & Thompson, Lowry. Rubber Stamp Album. LC 78-7118. (Illus.). 216p. 1978. pap. 9.95 (*0-89480-045-0*, 211) Workman Pub.
Miller, Jordan Y. The Health Introduction to Drama. 3rd ed. LC 87-80582. 1047p. (C). 1988. pap. text ed. 14.00 (*0-669-14812-1*) Heath.
— The Heath Introduction to Drama. 4th ed. 1131p. (C). 1992. pap. text ed. write for info. (*0-669-24411-2*) Heath.
Miller, Jordan Y. & Frazer, Winifred L. American Drama Between the Wars: A Critical History. (Twayne's Critical History of American Drama Ser.). 280p. 1991. text ed. 24.95 (*0-8057-8950-2*, Twayne) Macmillan.
Miller, Joseph. The Descendants of Captain Thomas Carter of "Lyford", Lancaster County, Virginia, with Allied Families. (Illus.). 430p. 1989. reprint ed. lib. bdg. 77.50 (*0-8328-0376-6*); reprint ed. pap. 67.50 (*0-8328-0377-4*) Higginson Bk Co.
— Discovering Life in Christ. (Illus.). 62p. (C). 1989. teacher ed 2.95 (*0-87227-137-4*); student ed 2.95 (*0-87227-136-6*) Reg Baptist.
— Discovering Life in the Church. 94p. 1990. student ed 2.95 (*0-87227-141-2*); teacher ed, pap. 2.95 (*0-87227-142-0*) Reg Baptist.
— The Joys of Success. LC 79-87657. (Illus.). 1979. 6.00 (*0-912472-23-5*) Miller Bks.
— Republican Chaos: Campaigns from Truman Through Nixon. (Illus.). (C). 1980. 8.00 (*0-912472-24-3*) Miller Bks.
— Singer & Songs of the Church. reprint ed. lib. bdg. 75.00 (*0-7812-0770-3*) Rprt Serv.
— Wandering Gypsies. LC 72-87908. (Illus.). (J). (gr. 6-12). 1969. text ed. 10.00 (*0-912472-08-1*) Miller Bks.
Miller, Joseph, ed. Government & the People. 9th ed. 1977. text ed. 10.00 (*0-912472-04-9*) Miller Bks.
— Sears List of Subject Headings. 15th ed. LC 94-16705. 758p. 1994. lib. bdg. 49.00 (*0-8242-0858-7*) Wilson.
Miller, Joseph B., jt. auth. see Wood, Stephen.
Miller, Joseph C. Slavery & Slaving in World History: A Bibliography, 1900-1991. LC 93-36546. 576p. 1993. 90. 00 (*0-527-63660-6*) Kraus Intl.
— Way of Death: Merchant Capitalism & the Angolan Slave Trade, 1730-1830. LC 87-40368. (Illus.). 796p. (C). 1988. text ed. 35.00 (*0-299-11560-7*) U of Wis Pr.
Miller, Joseph L., Jr. How to Destroy God's Kingdom & Democracy at the Same Time: Case Study: Water Supply of Portland, Oregon. 59p. 1989. pap. text ed. 3.45 (*0-9614887-1-9*) DRC Graphics Serv.
— Nibbling Away at Our Citizenship Rights & Our Water Supply: Portland, Oregon's Bull Run-Little Sandy Rivers & U. S. Forest Service "Management" 16p. (Orig.). (C). 1994. pap. 9.25 (*0-9614887-3-5*) DRC Graphics Serv.
— What Good Is Free Speech in a Closet: A Story of Cover-up in Planning for Our Grandchildren's Drinking Water. (Illus.). 68p. 1985. pap. 4.75 (*0-9614887-0-0*) DRC Graphics Serv.
Miller, Joseph M., et al, eds. Readings in Medieval Rhetoric. LC 73-77857. 319p. reprint ed. pap. 91.00 (*0-8357-6690-X*, 2056870) Bks Demand.
Miller, Joseph S., jt. ed. see Osterbrock, Donald E.
Miller, Joshua. The Rise & Fall of Democracy in Early America, 1630-1789: The Legacy for Contemporary Politics. 128p. 1991. 22.50 (*0-271-00744-3*) Pa St U Pr.
Miller, Joy. Addictive Relationships: Reclaiming Your Boundaries. (Orig.). 1989. pap. 7.95 (*1-55874-003-1*) Health Comm.
— Celebrations for Your Inner Child: There Is Joy in Recovery - A 90-Day Program. 98p. (Orig.). 1992. pap. 6.95 (*1-55874-208-5*) Health Comm.
Miller, Joyce. A Home for Grandma. 1983. 8.50 (*0-686-39794-0*) Rod & Staff.
— War-Torn Valley. 256p. 1990. 8.10 (*0-317-02913-4*) Rod & Staff.
Miller, Joyce U., ed. see Miller, Raymond W. & Donahue, Roy L.
Miller, Judi. Cry in the Night. 224p. 1990. pap. 3.95 (*0-380-75699-4*) Avon.
— How to be Friends with a Boy - How to be Friends with a Girl. 96p. (YA). (gr. 5-9). 1990. pap. 2.50 (*0-590-42806-3*) Scholastic Inc.
— My Crazy Cousin Courtney. MacDonald, Pat, ed. 160p. (Orig.). (J). (gr. 4-6). 1993. pap. 2.99 (*0-671-73821-6*, Minstrel Bks) PB.
— My Crazy Cousin Courtney Comes Back. MacDonald, Pat, ed. 160p. (J). 1994. pap. 3.50 (*0-671-88734-3*, Minstrel Bks) PB.
— My Crazy Cousin Courtney Returns Again. MacDonald, Pat, ed. 160p. (Orig.). (J). 1995. pap. 3.50 (*0-671-88733-5*, Minstrel Bks) PB.
Miller, Judi B., jt. auth. see Taylor, Anita.
Miller, Judith. Antiques Directory: Furniture. 1988. 29.99 (*0-517-66190-X*) Random Hse Value.
— Miller's International Antiques Price Guide, 1991. LC 90-50073. 750p. 1991. 29.95 (*0-670-83540-4*, Viking Studio) Studio Bks.
— One, By One, By One: Facing the Holocaust. 1991. pap. 10.95 (*0-671-74034-2*, Touchstone Bks) S&S Trade.
— Period Fireplaces: A Practical Guide to Period-Style Decorating. (Illus.). 128p. 1995. 19.95 (*1-85732-397-1*, Pub. by Reed Illust Books UK) Antique Collect.
— Period Kitchens: A Practical Guide to Period-Style Decorating. (Illus.). 128p. 1995. 19.95 (*1-85732-398-X*, Pub. by Reed Illust Books UK) Antique Collect.
Miller, Judith & Miller, Martin. The American Country Companion. LC 93-28954. (Country Companion Ser.). 1994. 12.95 (*0-00-255367-8*) Collins SF.
— The Country Decorative Painting Companion. LC 94-24446. 1995. 12.95 (*0-00-255490-9*) Collins SF.
— International Country. 240p. 1990. 35.00 (*0-670-83543-9*, Viking Studio) Studio Bks.
— Miller's Antiques Checklist: Art Deco. LC 90-21226. (Illus.). 192p. 1991. 12.95 (*0-670-83956-6*, Viking Studio) Studio Bks.
— Miller's Antiques Checklist: Furniture. LC 90-21225. (Illus.). 192p. 1991. 12.95 (*0-670-83957-4*, Viking Studio) Studio Bks.
— Miller's Antiques Checklist: Porcelain. (Illus.). 192p. 1992. 12.95 (*0-670-83263-4*, Viking Studio) Studio Bks.
— Miller's Antiques Checklist: Victoriana. (Illus.). 192p. 1992. 12.95 (*0-670-83262-6*, Viking Studio) Studio Bks.
— Miller's Antiques Price Guide 1996. (Illus.). 808p. 1995. 35.00 (*1-85732-746-2*, Pub. by Millers Pubns UK) Antique Collect.
— Miller's Art Deco & Art Nouveau Review. (Illus.). 400p. Date not set. write for info. (*1-85732-685-7*, Pub. by Millers Pubns UK) Antique Collect.
— Miller's Collectables Price Guide, 1995-1996, Vol. VI. Murfin, Robert, ed. (Illus.). 496p. 1994. 25.00 (*1-85732-338-6*) Antique Collect.
— Miller's International Antique Price Guide, 1994. 1993. 29.95 (*1-85732-241-X*, Pub. by Millers Pubns UK) Antique Collect.
— Miller's Pocket Dictionary of Antiques: An Authoritative Reference Guide for Dealers, Collectors, & Enthusiasts. (Illus.). 160p. 1990. 10.95 (*0-85533-760-5*, Pub. by Millers Pubns UK) Antique Collect.
— Miller's Pocket Dictionary of Antiques: An Essential Reference for Dealers, Collectors, & Enthusiasts. LC 89-40680. (Illus.). 160p. 1990. pap. 9.95 (*0-670-83259-6*, Viking Studio) Studio Bks.
— Miller's Victorian Style: Creating Period Interiors for Contemporary Living. LC 92-40900. (Illus.). 240p. 1993. 40.00 (*0-670-84238-9*, Viking Studio) Studio Bks.
— Period Finishes & Effects. LC 92-5471. (Illus.). 180p. 1992. 40.00 (*0-8478-1569-2*) Rizzoli Intl.
Miller, Judith & Miller, Martin, comps. Miller's Pocket Antiques Fact File. 1988. pap. 8.95 (*0-670-82059-8*, Viking Studio) Studio Bks.
Miller, Judith & Miller, Martin, eds. Miller's Collectors Cars Price Guide 1993-1994. 3rd ed. (Illus.). 1993. 29.95 (*1-85732-095-6*, Pub. by Millers Pubns UK) Antique Collect.
— Miller's Picture Price Guide 1993, Vol. 1. (Illus.). 633p. 1992. 35.00 (*1-85732-981-3*, Pub. by Millers Pubns UK) Antique Collect.
— Miller's Picture Price Guide 1994. (Illus.). 1993. 35.00 (*1-85732-177-4*, Pub. by Millers Pubns UK) Antique Collect.
— Miller's Pocket Antiques Fact File: Essential Information for Dealers, Collectors, & Enthusiasts. (Illus.). 192p. 1993. 10.95 (*0-85533-689-7*, Pub. by Millers Pubns UK) Antique Collect.
— Miller's Understanding Antiques. (Illus.). 272p. 1993. pap. 19.95 (*1-85732-001-8*, Pub. by Millers Pubns UK) Antique Collect.
— Victorian Style: Creating Period Interiors for Contemporary Living. (Illus.). 240p. 1993. 45.00 (*1-85732-098-0*, Pub. by Millers Pubns UK) Antique Collect.
Miller, Judith & Miller, Mertin, eds. Miller's Collector's Cars Price Guide: Professional Handbook 1992-1993. (Illus.). 455p. 1993. 29.95 (*0-905879-74-0*, Pub. by Millers Pubns UK) Antique Collect.
Miller, Judith, ed. see Bly, John.
Miller, Judith, ed. see Davidson, Richard.
Miller, Judith, ed. see Knowles, Eric.
Miller, Judith, ed. see Lang, Gordon.
Miller, Judith, jt. auth. see Miller, Martin.
Miller, Judith, ed. see Pearson, Sue.
Miller, Judith A. Community-Based Long-Term Care. (Illus.). 320p. 1991. 45.00 (*0-8039-3918-3*); pap. 21.95 (*0-8039-3919-1*) Sage.
Miller, Judith C., jt. ed. see Stein, Alice M.
Miller, Judith D., jt. auth. see Jacobus, Lee A.
Miller, Judith F. Coping with Chronic Illness: Overcoming Powerlessness. 2nd ed. (Illus.). 442p. (C). 1992. pap. text ed. 24.95 (*0-8036-6192-4*) Davis Co.
Miller, Judith G. Francoise Sagan. (World Authors Ser.: No. 797). 152p. 1988. text ed. 22.95 (*0-8057-8228-1*, Pub. by Royal Botanic Garden UK) Macmillan.
— Theater & Revolution in France since 1968. LC 76-47500. (French Forum Monographs: No. 4). 169p. (Orig.). 1977. pap. 10.95 (*0-917058-03-8*) French Forum.
Miller, Judith G., jt. ed. see Makward, Christiane P.
Miller, Judy. Abstracts. (Illus.). 92p. (Orig.). 1988. pap. 11. 96 (*0-912833-11-4*) J Miller Pubns.
— Birds & Flowers. (Illus.). 112p. (Orig.). 1987. pap. 7.96 (*0-912833-00-9*) J Miller Pubns.
— Carousel. (Illus.). 68p. (Orig.). 1990. pap. 7.16 (*0-912833-13-0*) J Miller Pubns.
— Climb up to the Sunshine. 244p. 1993. 8.95 (*0-942341-06-6*) Dawn Pubns TX.
— Cups Running Over. 235p. 1985. 7.95 (*0-89225-278-2*) Dawn Pubns TX.
— Gifts for All Occasions. (Illus.). 104p. (Orig.). 1983. pap. 7.96 (*0-912833-01-7*) J Miller Pubns.
— Gifts II: For All Occasions. (Illus.). 104p. (Orig.). 1985. pap. 7.96 (*0-912833-03-3*) J Miller Pubns.
— God in My Day. 151p. 1994. 6.95 (*0-942341-09-0*) Dawn Pubns TX.
— Heart Against a Thorn. 60p. 1990. pap. 6.95 (*0-942341-03-1*) Dawn Pubns TX.
— Hold Gently This Bright Hour. 130p. (Orig.). 1988. pap. 5.95 (*0-942341-01-5*) Dawn Pubns TX.
— Holidays. (Illus.). 68p. 1990. pap. 7.16 (*0-912833-14-9*) J Miller Pubns.
— House Tours. (Illus.). 112p. (Orig.). 1984. pap. 7.96 (*0-912833-02-5*) J Miller Pubns.
— House Tours II. (Illus.). 96p. (Orig.). 1985. pap. 7.96 (*0-912833-04-1*) J Miller Pubns.
— House Tours III: International. (Illus.). 112p. (Orig.). 1987. pap. 12.76 (*0-912833-10-6*) J Miller Pubns.
— House Tours IV: International. (Illus.). 96p. (Orig.). Date not set. pap. 12.76 (*0-912833-12-2*) J Miller Pubns.
— It Only Takes a Spark. 167p. (Orig.). 1987. pap. 6.95 (*0-942341-00-7*) Dawn Pubns TX.
— Judy Miller Presents: Pattern Book 1. (Illus.). 80p. (Orig.). 1986. pap. 6.36 (*0-912833-06-8*) J Miller Pubns.
— Judy Miller Presents: Pattern Book 2. (Illus.). 80p. (Orig.). 1986. pap. 6.36 (*0-912833-07-6*) J Miller Pubns.
— Judy Miller Presents: Pattern Book 3. (Illus.). 80p. (Orig.). 1987. pap. 6.36 (*0-912833-08-4*) J Miller Pubns.
— Judy Miller Presents: Pattern Book 4. (Illus.). 80p. (Orig.). 1989. pap. 6.36 (*0-912833-09-2*) J Miller Pubns.
— New Day Dawning. 350p. (Orig.). 1989. pap. 10.95 (*0-942341-02-3*) Dawn Pubns TX.
— PB: SideLights. (Illus.). 72p. (Orig.). 1986. pap. 7.96 (*0-912833-05-X*) J Miller Pubns.
— The Power of Names: A Fascinating Study in the Psychology of Names. Bernard, Barry, ed. 211p. (Orig.). 1992. per. 11.95 (*0-9631327-0-9*) Cascade Spec.
— Ripples on the Water. 150p. (Orig.). 1990. pap. 7.95 (*0-942341-04-X*) Dawn Pubns TX.
— Seasons of Celebration. 146p. 1994. 6.95 (*0-614-04220-8*) Dawn Pubns TX.
— Seasons of the Heart. 126p. 1984. 6.95 (*0-89225-272-3*) Dawn Pubns TX.
— Songs in the Night. 500p. 1995. 12.95 (*0-942341-10-4*) Dawn Pubns TX.
***Miller, Judy & Parker, Farris.** Faithfully Yours. 159p. 1991. 7.95 (*0-942341-05-8*) Dawn Pubns TX.
Miller, Judy, jt. auth. see Daley, Dennis.
Miller, Judy L., jt. auth. see Messersmith, Ann M.
Miller, Julano. Life Line Series, 5 in 1 set, Set. (Illus.). 48p. (J). (gr. 3-9). 1985. pap. 17.00 (*0-87879-484-0*) High Noon Bks.
Miller, Julia, jt. auth. see Weathers, Michelle.
Miller, Julia K. Wild Animals: 1000 or More Places to See & Photograph Birds & Wildlife in the United States & Canada. (Illus.). 400p. 1990. pap. 18.95 (*0-937480-11-8*) Intl Resources.
Miller, Julian H. A Monograph of the World Species of Hypoxylon. LC 61-15571. 250p. reprint ed. pap. 71.30 (*0-318-34870-5*, 2031046) Bks Demand.
Miller, Julian J., ed. CRC Handbook of Ototoxicity. LC 84-20032. 336p. 1986. 145.00 (*0-8493-3215-X*, RF285, CRC Reprint) Franklin.
Miller, Julian S., ed. Isaac Watts Merrill's Journal, 1828-1878, 3 vols. (Illus.). 2500p. 1991. Vol. 1, 1-878651-14-5; Vol. 2, 1- 878651-15-3; Vol. 3, 1-878651-16-1. 100.00 (*1-878651-13-7*); Vol. 1, 1-878651-18-8; Vol. 2, 1- 878651-19-6; Vol. 3, 1-878651-20-X. pap. 65.00 (*1-878651-17-X*) HPL Pr.
Miller, Juliet V. The Family-Career Connection: A New Framework for Career Development. 49p. 1984. 5.50 (*0-318-22103-9*, IN288) Ctr Educ Trng Employ.
Miller, Juliet V. & Musgrove, Mary L., eds. Issues in Adult Career Counseling. LC 85-644750. (New Directions for Adult & Continuing Education Ser.: No. ACE 32). (Orig.). 1986. pap. 16.95x (*1-55542-983-1*) Jossey-Bass.
Miller, K., ed. Toxicological Aspects of Food. 458p. 1987. 128.00 (*1-85166-080-1*, Pub. by Elsevier Applied Sci UK) Elsevier.
Miller, K., jt. ed. see Leonard, B.
Miller, K., jt. auth. see Stevenson, D. M.
Miller, K., et al. Principles & Practice of Immunotoxicology. (Illus.). 379p. 1992. 195.00 (*0-632-02563-8*) Blackwell Sci.
— Second Year Evaluation of the Florida Public Guardianship Pilot Program. 1984. write for info. (*0-318-58137-X*) FSU CSP.
Miller, K. J. The International Karakoram Project, 2 vols., Vol. 1. 412p. 1984. 89.95 (*0-521-26339-5*) Cambridge U Pr.
Miller, K. J. & Brown, M. W., eds. Multiaxial Fatigue - STP 853. LC 85-7376. 750p. 1985. text ed. 88.00 (*0-8031-0444-8*, 04-85300030) ASTM.
Miller, K. J. & Smith, R. F. Mechanical Behaviour of Materials. 1980. 726.00 (*0-08-024739-3*, Pub. by Pergamon Repr UK) Franklin.
Miller, K. S., jt. auth. see Ingold, T. S.
Miller, Karen. Ages & Stages: Developmental Descriptions & Activities, Birth Through Eight Years. LC 85-25175. (Illus.). 153p. (C). 1985. pap. 12.95 (*0-910287-05-8*, RJ131.M54) TelShare Pub Co.
— More Things To Do with Toddlers & Twos. LC 90-70984. (Illus.). 212p. (Orig.). (C). 1990. pap. 12.95 (*0-910287-08-2*) TelShare Pub Co.
— The Outside Play & Learning Book: Activities for Young Children. Charner, Kathleen, ed. LC 88-82595. (Illus.). 256p. (Orig.). 1989. pap. 14.95 (*0-87659-117-9*) Gryphon Hse.
— Reiki I Manual. 2nd ed. 88p. (Orig.). 1993. pap. 12.95 (*0-9630439-5-1*) Bayrock.
— Reiki II Manual. 2nd ed. (Illus.). 124p. (Orig.). 1993. pap. 12.95 (*0-9630439-6-X*) Bayrock.
— Tales from a Reiki Seeker. 96p. (Orig.). 1995. pap. 12.95 (*0-9630439-8-6*) Bayrock.
— Things to Do with Toddlers & Twos. LC 92-184870. (Illus.). 168p. (C). 1984. pap. 12.95 (*0-910287-04-X*) TelShare Pub Co.
Miller, Karen, jt. auth. see Miller, Kevin.
Miller, Karen, et al. Elizabeth Cady Stanton: A Biography for Young Children. (Illus.). 32p. (J). (ps-2). 1995. 19.95 (*0-87659-176-4*) Gryphon Hse.
Miller, Karen P. Disciplines for Spiritual Growth. (Covenant Bible Study Ser.). 48p. (Orig.). 1989. pap. 3.95 (*0-87178-812-8*) Brethren.

An Asterisk (*) at the beginning of an entry indicates that the title is appearing in BIP for the first time.

Miller, Karen P., ed. see National Association of Insurance Commissioners Staff.

Miller, Karl. Authors. 234p. 1991. reprint ed. pap. 14.95 (*0-19-212277-0*) OUP.

*Miller, Karl V. & Marchinton, R. Larry, eds. Quality Whitetails: The Why & How of Quality Deer Management. (Illus.). 320p. 1995. 29.95 (*0-8117-1387-3*) Stackpole.

Miller, Kate. First Book of WordPerfect for Windows. 1993. 14.95 (*1-56761-132-X*) Alpha Bks IN.

— 10 Minute Guide to CC: Mail with CC: Mail Mobile. 160p. 1995. pap. text ed. 10.99 (*1-56761-587-2*) Alpha Bks IN.

— 10 Minute Guide to Lotus Notes: New Edition. (Illus.). 176p. (Orig.). 1995. pap. text ed. 10.99 (*1-56761-582-1*) Alpha Bks IN.

— 10 Minute Guide to WordPerfect Office. (Illus.). 160p. (Orig.). 1994. pap. 10.95 (*1-56761-474-4*) Alpha Bks IN.

— Your First Book of Windows 95. 300p. 1995. 19.99 (*1-56761-518-X*) Alpha Bks IN.

— 10 Minute Guide to cc: Mail with cc: Mobile. (Illus.). (Orig.). 1995. pap. text ed. 10.99 (*0-614-07357-X*) Alpha Bks IN.

Miller, Kate & Barnes, Kate. First Book of WordPerfect 6.0. (Illus.). 1993. pap. 19.95 (*1-56761-022-6*) Alpha Bks IN.

Miller, Kathaleen, ed. see Mohan, A. G.

*Miller, Katherine. Organizational Communication: Approaches & Processes. LC 94-28667. 353p. 1995. text ed. 32.95 (*0-534-20790-1*) Intl Thomson.

*Miller, Katherine B., et al. Strategies for Managing Ozone-Depleting Refrigerants: Confronting the Future. LC 94-32043. 1995. 34.95 (*0-935470-84-0*) Battelle.

Miller, Kathleen. Fair Share Divorce for Women. 248p. (Orig.). 1994. pap. write for info. (*0-9622269-7-1*) BookPartners.

— Fair Share Divorce for Women. 220p. (Orig.). 1994. pap. text ed. 15.95 (*1-885221-01-0*) BookPartners.

Miller, Kathleen, jt. auth. see Miller, Don.

Miller, Kathleen N. Mathematics for Business: College Course. 6th ed. 1987. text ed. 17.75 (*0-07-042061-0*) McGraw.

— Mathematics for Business: College Course. 6th ed. 1988. text ed. write for info. (*0-07-042129-3*) McGraw.

Miller, Kathleen N., jt. auth. see Peterson, David R.

Miller, Kathryn. Haunted Houses. 46p. 1986. reprint ed. pap. 3.45 (*0-87129-026-X*, H57) Dramatic Pub.

— A Thousand Cranes. 28p. (Orig.). 1990. pap. 3.45 (*0-87129-004-9*, T80) Dramatic Pub.

Miller, Kathryn C., comp. Fayette County, Pa: Gleanings. 98p. 1990. pap. text ed. 11.00 (*1-55856-029-7*) Closson Pr.

Miller, Kathryn M. Did My First Mother Love Me? A Story for an Adopted Child. (Illus.). 48p. (Orig.). (J). (ps-3). 1994. pap. 5.95 (*0-930934-84-9*) Morning Glory.

Miller, Kathryn S. Amelia Earhart. 1993. 3.45 (*0-87129-291-2*, A54) Dramatic Pub.

— Poe! Poe! Poe! (Illus.). 24p. (J). (gr. 4-12). 1984. pap. 2.50 (*0-88680-224-5*) I E Clark.

— The Shining Moment: (Musical) (J). 1989. Playscript. 5.00 (*0-87602-286-7*) Anchorage.

— You Don't See Me. 22p. 1986. reprint ed. pap. 3.45 (*0-87129-022-7*, Y15) Dramatic Pub.

Miller, Kathryn S. & Miller, Barry I. I'm A Celebrity! (Illus.). 32p. 1983. pap. 4.00 (*0-88680-088-9*) I E Clark.

*Miller, Kathy. His Hand in Mine. 270p. Date not set. pap. 8.95 (*0-7610-0349-5*) NW Pub.

Miller, Kathy, jt. auth. see Sanna, Lucy.

Miller, Kathy A., jt. auth. see Dunton, Sabina.

Miller, Kathy A., et al. Stress: Facilitator's Manual. (Well Aware About Health Risk Reduction Ser.). (Illus.). (Orig.). 1983. 35.00 (*0-943562-53-8*) Well Aware.

— Stress: Participant Workbook. (Well Aware About Health Risk Reduction Ser.). (Illus.). 120p. (Orig.). 1982. student ed 8.75 (*0-943562-54-6*) Well Aware.

*Miller, Kathy C. Character of the King. (Bible Study Series for Daughters of the King). 1994. pap. text ed. 4.95 (*0-89636-310-4*) Accent CO.

— Choices of the Heart. (Bible Study Series for Daughters of the King). 96p. 1993. pap. 4.95 (*0-89636-295-7*, AC244) Accent CO.

— Contentment. LC 93-71076. (Bible Study Series for Daughters of the King). 64p. 1993. pap. 4.95 (*0-89636-294-9*, AC243) Accent CO.

— Help for Hurting Moms...& Hurting Kids, Too! rev. ed. LC 90-3810. 160p. 1990. reprint ed. pap. 8.95 (*0-926284-02-9*) Evergreen MI.

— My Father in Me. (Bible Study Series for Daughters of the King). 1994. pap. text ed. 4.95 (*0-89636-309-0*) Accent CO.

— Your View of God ... God's View of You: Inspirational Devotions for Women. 136p. 1992. pap. 8.95 (*0-8341-1431-3*) Beacon Hill.

Miller, Kathy H. In the Interstices of the Tate: Edith Wharton's Narrative Strategies. LC 92-29801. (American University Studies: American Literature: Ser. XXIV, Vol. 47). 155p. (C). 1993. text ed. 38.95 (*0-8204-2041-7*) P Lang Pubs.

Miller, Keith. Habitation of Dragons: Daily Meditations for Men in Recovery. LC 92-3709. 192p. 1992. pap. 8.99 (*0-8007-5431-X*) Revell.

— Highway Home Through Texas. LC 93-84638. 96p. 1993. 12.95 (*1-55725-064-2*) Paraclete MA.

— A Second Touch. Kao, Samuel, tr. 202p. (CHI.). 1985. pap. 3.50 (*1-56582-090-8*) Christ Renew Min.

— Simple Surveying. (C). 1977. 21.00x (*0-907649-58-0*, Pub. by Expedit Advisory Centre UK) St Mut.

— Taste of New Wine. LC 93-82109. 1993. pap. 8.95 (*1-55725-059-6*); audio 14.95 (*1-55725-061-8*) Paraclete MA.

— Write from the Heart: From Idea to Publication of a Non-Fiction Book. 1993. student ed 8.95 (*1-55725-071-5*); student ed, vhs 79.95 (*1-55725-072-3*) Paraclete MA.

Miller, Keith W., jt. auth. see Roth, Sheldon H.

Miller-Keller, Andrea & Ravenal, John B. From the Collection of Sol LeWitt. LC 84-81616. (Illus.). 48p. 1984. 10.00 (*0-916365-13-1*) Ind Curators.

Miller, Kelly. Appeal to Conscience: America's Code of Caste, a Disgrace to Democracy. LC 71-89390. (Black Heritage Library Collection). 1977. 11.95 (*0-8369-8633-4*) Ayer.

— Appeal to Conscience: America's Code of Caste a Disgrace to Democracy. LC 69-18553. (American Negro: His History & Literature, Ser. No. 2). 1968. reprint ed. 11.95 (*0-405-01881-9*) Ayer.

— As to the Leopard's Spots. (African-American Chapbook Ser.). (Illus.). 32p. (Orig.). 1989. reprint ed. pap. 16.95 (*0-685-26488-2*) Dreamkeeper Pr.

— The Everlasting Stain. 1990. 25.00 (*0-87498-030-5*) Assoc Pubs DC.

— Out of the House of Bondage. LC 69-18554. (American Negro: His History & Literature, Ser. No. 2). 1969. reprint ed. 11.95 (*0-405-01882-7*) Ayer.

— Race Adjustment: Essays on the Negro in America. LC 77-89389. (Black Heritage Library Collection). 1977. 18. 95 (*0-8369-8634-2*) Ayer.

— Race Adjustment: Essays on the Negro in America. 15.00 (*1-56675-020-2*) Mnemosyne.

Miller, Kelly S., et al. Initial Public Offerings Annual, 1989. 969p. 1990. lib. bdg. 175.00 (*1-55888-314-2*) Omnigraphics Inc.

Miller, Ken. Always to Remember, Never to Forget Shantewa. 142p. (YA). (gr. 11 up). 1984. 7.95 (*0-942241-09-6*, 8683) Pubs Bk Sales.

— The Hamptons: Long Island's East End. (Illus.). 208p. 1993. 45.00 (*0-8478-1694-X*) Rizzoli Intl.

— Have You Kicked Your Horseshoer Today? A Consumer's Guide to Horseshoeing. LC 91-188948. (Illus.). 105p. 1992. 17.45 (*0-685-57468-7*) Treeline Pub.

— The Reluctant Missionary. (YA). (gr. 9 up). 1987. write for info. (*0-942241-01-0*) Pubs Bk Sales.

*Miller, Ken, photos. Open All Night Ken Miller. (Illus.). 118p. 1995. 40.00 (*0-87951-571-6*) Overlook Pr.

Miller, Kenn, jt. auth. see Chambers, Larry.

Miller, Kenneth. Energy & Life. Head, J. J., ed. LC 86-72192. (Carolina Biology Readers Ser.: No. 168). (Illus.). 16p. (Orig.). (YA). (gr. 10 up). 1988. pap. text ed. 2.75 (*0-89278-168-8*, 45-9768) Carolina Biological.

Miller, Kenneth & Ross, Bertram. An Introduction to the Fractional Calculus & Fractional Differential Equations. LC 93-9500. 384p. 1993. text ed. 79.95 (*0-471-58884-9*, Wiley-Interscience) Wiley.

Miller, Kenneth E. Anthology of Songs for the Solo Voice. 3rd ed. 320p. 1994. pap. text ed. 38.67 (*0-13-720558-9*) P-H.

— Denmark: A Troubled Welfare State. 224p. 1991. text ed. 49.00 (*0-8133-0834-8*) Westview.

— Principles of Singing: A Textbook for Voice Class or Studio. 2nd ed. 288p. (C). 1989. pap. text ed. write for info. (*0-13-712712-X*) P-H.

— Vocal Music Education. (Illus.). 352p. 1987. text ed. 57. 33 (*0-13-942996-4*) P-H.

Miller, Kenneth L. & Weidner, William A., eds. Handbook of Management of Radiation Protection Programs. 536p. 1986. 145.00 (*0-8493-3769-0*, RA569, CRC Reprint) Franklin.

— Handbook of Management of Radiation Protection Programs. 2nd ed. 1992. 145.00 (*0-8493-3770-4*, RA569) CRC Pr.

Miller, Kenneth R., ed. Advances in Cell Biology, Vol. 2. 1988. 73.25 (*0-89232-886-X*) Jai Pr.

Miller, Kenneth R., jt. auth. see Levine, Joseph S.

Miller, Kenneth R., jt. auth. see Levine, Joseph.

Miller, Kenneth S. Complex Stochastic Processes: An Introduction to Theory & Application. LC 73-18094. 252p. reprint ed. pap. 71.90 (*0-317-55523-5*, 2056328) Bks Demand.

— Elements of Modern Abstract Algebra. LC 74-6497. 198p. 1975. reprint ed. 17.50 (*0-88275-178-6*) Krieger.

— Partial Differential Equations. LC 87-16930. 262p. (C). 1987. reprint ed. lib. bdg. 27.50 (*0-89464-234-0*) Krieger.

— Partial Differential Equations in Engineering Problems. 1953. 47.00 (*0-13-650408-6*) P-H.

— Some Eclectic Matrix Theory. LC 85-18454. 140p. (C). 1987. lib. bdg. 16.00 (*0-89874-895-X*) Krieger.

Miller, Kenneth S. & Leskiw, Donald M. An Introduction to Kalman Filtering with Applications. LC 85-12606. 128p. 1987. lib. bdg. 18.50 (*0-89874-824-0*) Krieger.

Miller, Kenneth S. & Walsh, J. B. Advanced Trigonometry. abr. ed. LC 76-7918. 116p. (C). 1977. 13.00 (*0-88275-391-6*) Krieger.

Miller, Kenneth S., jt. auth. see Murray, Francis J.

Miller, Kent & Miller, Betty D. To Kill & Be Killed - Case Studies from Florida's Death Row. LC 88-32360. 118p. 1989. lib. bdg. 16.95 (*0-932727-24-7*); pap. 9.95 (*0-932727-23-9*) Hope Pub Hse.

*Miller, Kent C. Laying the Foundations of Ministry. (Healing Presence Ser.). 128p. (Orig.). 1994. pap. 29.95 (*0-89390-333-7*) Resource Pubns.

— Ministry to the Homebound. (Healing Presence Ser.). 120p. (Orig.). (C). 1995. pap. text ed. 29.95 (*0-89390-268-3*) Resource Pubns.

Miller, Kent C., jt. auth. see Burggrabe, Janice L.

Miller, Kent S. & Radelet, Michael L. Executing the Mentally Ill: The Criminal Justice System of the Case of Alvin Ford. (Illus.). 200p. 1993. 39.95 (*0-8039-5149-3*); pap. 17.95 (*0-8039-5150-7*) Sage.

Miller, Kentalle & Miller, Isobel. Retraining & Tradition: Skilled Worker in an Era of Change. 192p. 1975. 27.95 (*0-8464-1127-X*) Beekman Pubs.

Miller, Kenton R. Balancing the Scales: Managing Biodiversity at the Bioregional Level. large type ed. 150p. 1993. Large format. pap. 14.95 (*0-915825-85-6*, MIBSP) World Resources Inst.

Miller, Kenton R., jt. ed. see McNeely, Jeffrey A.

Miller, Kenton R., jt. auth. see Reid, Walter V.

Miller, Kerby & Wagner, Paul. Out of Ireland: The Story of Irish Emigration to America. LC 94-11475. (Illus.). 132p. (C). 1994. 24.95 (*1-880216-25-6*) Elliott & Clark.

Miller, Kerby A. Emigrants & Exiles: Ireland & the Irish Exodus to North America. 684p. 1985. 39.95 (*0-19-503594-1*) OUP.

— Emigrants & Exiles: Ireland & the Irish Exodus to North America. 704p. 1988. pap. 17.95 (*0-19-505187-4*) OUP.

*Miller, Kevin. Light That Whispers Morning. 88p. (Orig.). 1994. pap. 11.00 (*0-911287-16-7*) Blue Begonia.

Miller, Kevin & Miller, Karen. More Than You & Me. 270p. 1994. pap. 9.99 (*1-56179-217-9*) Focus Family.

Miller, Kirk. Landscape Workshop. (How to Draw & Paint Ser.). (Illus.). 32p. (Orig.). 1989. pap. 5.95 (*1-56010-000-1*, HT216) W Foster Pub.

Miller, Kirk M. Tort Actions under the General Municipal Law in N. Y. C. ring bd. 24.95 (*0-930137-79-5*) Looseleaf Law.

Miller, Kirsten, jt. auth. see Miller, John.

Miller, Kirsten, jt. ed. see Miller, John.

Miller, Kisten, jt. ed. see Miller, John.

Miller, Klara & Nicklin, Stephen, eds. Immunology of the Gastrointestinal Tract, 2 vols., Set. 336p. 1987. 259.90 (*0-8493-4310-0*, RC817) CRC Pr.

Miller, Klara, jt. auth. see Liddell, F. D.

Miller, Kristen, jt. ed. see Miller, John.

Miller, Kristie. Ruth Hanna McCormick: A Life in Politics, 1880-1944. LC 91-28230. 3533p. 1992. 27.50 (*0-8263-1333-7*) U of NM Pr.

Miller, Kristin. The Careless Quilter: Decide-As-You-Sew, Design-As-You-Go Quiltmaking. LC 94-7377. (Illus.). 260p. (Orig.). 1994. pap. 18.95 (*1-55853-296-X*) Rutledge Hill Pr.

*Miller, Kristine. Bed & Breakfast Southern California. rev. ed. 76p. 1994. pap. 5.95 (*1-56413-250-1*) Auto Club.

— Desert Areas. rev. ed. Van Wingerden, Judy, ed. 224p. 1994. pap. 7.95 (*1-56413-201-3*) Auto Club.

Miller, Kristine, ed. see Brown, Sandy S.

Miller, Kristine, ed. see Hart, Chris & Rowe, Monica.

Miller, Kristine, ed. see Hunter, R. Clark & Yago, George.

Miller, Kristine, ed. see Hunter, R. Clark.

Miller-Kritsberg, Ceci, jt. auth. see Lee, John.

Miller, L. Concurrent Engineering Design: Integrating Best Practices for Process Improvement. LC 92-85526. 319p. 1993. 60.00 (*0-87263-433-7*) SME.

Miller, L., et al, eds. Parallel Architectures for Data-Knowledge Base Systems. 400p. 1994. Microform. write for info. (*0-8186-6351-0*); pap. write for info. (*0-8186-6350-2*) IEEE Comp Soc.

Miller, L. Ann, jt. auth. see Ketcham, Katherine.

Miller, L. D., et al, eds. Remote Sensing & Geoinformation Systems as Related to Regional Planning of Health Services. (CPL Bibliographies Ser.: No. 51). 76p. 1981. 10.00 (*0-86602-051-9*) Coun Plan Librarians.

Miller, L. F. Thick Film Technology & Chip Joining. (Processes & Materials in Electronics Ser.). 228p. 1972. text ed. 109.00 (*0-677-03440-7*) Gordon & Breach.

Miller, L. Keith. Principles of Everyday Behavior Analysis. 2nd ed. LC 79-27797. 512p. (C). 1980. pap. 35.95 (*0-8185-0373-4*) Brooks-Cole.

Miller, L. L., et al, eds. Parallel Architectures for Data-Knowledge Base Systems. LC 94-15104. 616p. 1994. Casebound. text ed. 54.00 (*0-8186-6352-9*, BP06352) IEEE Comp Soc.

*Miller, L. R. Training Workhorses: Training Teamsters. (Illus.). 352p. (Orig.). 1994. pap. 24.95 (*1-885210-00-0*) Small Farmers.

— Training Workhorses: Training Teamsters. (Illus.). 352p. (Orig.). 1994. 43.95 (*1-885210-01-9*) Small Farmers.

Miller, L. S. & Brown, A. M. Criminal Evidence Laboratory: An Introduction to the Crime Laboratory. 2nd ed. LC 89-81937. (Illus.). 256p. (C). 1990. pap. text ed. 24.95 (*0-87084-564-0*) Anderson Pub Co.

Miller, L. S. & Mullin, J. B., eds. Electronic Materials: From Silicon to Organics. (Illus.). 470p. 1991. 110.00 (*0-306-43655-8*, Plenum Pr) Plenum.

*Miller, L. Scott. Accelerating the Educational Advancement of Minorities: A Nation-Building & Region-Building Imperative for America's Third Century. LC 94-31669. 1995. write for info. (*0-300-05793-8*) Yale U Pr.

Miller-Lachmann, Lyn. Hiding Places. 206p. (Orig.). (YA). (gr. 9-12). 1987. pap. 4.95 (*0-938961-00-4*, Stamp Out Sheep Pr) Sq One Pubs.

— Our Family, Our Friends, Our World: An Annotated Guide to Significant Multicultural Books for Children & Teenagers. 710p. 1992. 46.00 (*0-8352-3025-2*) Bowker.

Miller-Lachmann, Lyn, ed. Global Voices, Global Visions: A Core Collection of Multicultural Books. 590p. 1995. 52.00 (*0-8352-3291-3*) Bowker.

With the increasing realization that we are members of a truly global community comes great interest in the works of minority authors & scholars around the world. The first annotated bibliography with a fully global perspective, this comprehensive, one-volume guide lists some 1,600 of the best multicultural titles geared to a general adult readership. Compiled by the renowned author of OUR FAMILY, OUR FRIENDS, OUR WORLD--winner of the Denali Press Award--with individual chapters authored by prominent librarians, academics, & subject specialists, GLOBAL VOICES, GLOBAL VISIONS introduces & evaluates the literature of cultures & regions around the world: U.S./African Americans; U.S./Asian Americans; U.S./Latinos; U.S./Native Americans; Canada; Latin America & the Caribbean; Great Britain & Ireland; Western Europe; Eastern Europe; the Middle East; Africa; Central & Southern Asia; East Asia; Southeast Asia; Australia/New Zealand, & the Pacific. The literature discussed is available in English, & includes contemporary & historical fiction, poetry, drama, social science & history titles, essays, & biographical works. This unique guide also features an appendix of additional biographical, bibliographical, & critical resources, & author, title, & subject indexes. For use as a selection tool or as a general guide to the literatures of the world, GLOBAL VOICES, GLOBAL VISIONS is an essential purchase for libraries wishing to expand representation of different cultures & ethnicities. Each chapter features: * a map to help the reader locate the country/region * an introduction giving an overview of the region & culture & highlighting major events & themes * annotations divided into three groups: fiction, drama, & poetry; nonfiction; & biography. Each annotation describes the content of the book, its contribution, possible uses & audiences; & related works. * cross-references to other chapters where necessary. *Publisher Provided Annotation.*

M

Miller, Lafe, ed. see Burnette, Alma.

Miller, LaMar P., ed. Equality of Educational Opportunity: A Handbook for Research. LC 73-9244. (Studies in Education: No. 1). 1974. lib. bdg. 37.50 (*0-404-10535-1*) AMS Pr.

Miller, Larry. Holographic Golf: Uniting the Mind & Body to Improve Your Game. LC 93-15851. (Illus.). 112p. 1993. 15.00 (*0-06-017006-9*, HarpT) HarpC.

— Holographic Golf: Uniting the Mind & Body to Improve Your Game. 144p. 1995. pap. 10.00 (*0-06-092603-1*, PL) HarpC.

— King Odorant & His Flies. Anderson, David & Tronslin, Andrea, eds. (Illus.). 32p. (J). (ps up). 1995. 13.95 (*0-9641330-8-3*); pap. 8.95 (*0-9641330-7-5*) Portunus Pubng.

— Selling in Agribusiness. Lee, Jasper S., ed. (Career Preparation for Agriculture-Agribusiness Ser.). (Illus.). 1979. text ed. 16.96 (*0-07-041962-0*) McGraw.

Miller, Larry & Braswell, Michael. Human Relations & Police Work. 3rd rev. ed. 219p. (Orig.). (C). 1993. pap. text ed. 12.95 (*0-88133-725-0*) Waveland Pr.

Miller, Larry & Quilici, Alec. The Turbo C Survival Guide. (Illus.). 553p. 1989. pap. text ed. 29.95 (*0-471-61708-3*) Wiley.

Miller, Larry, ed. see Biebl, Andrew R., et al.

Miller, Larry, ed. see Bield, Andrew R. & McKeen, Gregory B.

Miller, Larry, ed. see Bischoff, William R., et al.

Miller, Larry, ed. see Cleveland, Grover A., et al.

Miller, Larry, ed. see DiTommaso, Elizabeth, et al.

Miller, Larry, ed. see Grasso, Albert L., et al.

Miller, Larry, ed. see Tommaso, Elizabeth D., et al.

Miller, Larry A. Wings of Blood. Van Treese, James B., ed. 420p. 1994. pap. 9.95 (*1-56901-041-2*) NW Pub.

*Miller, Larry L. Ohio Place-Names. LC 95-14555. 1996. write for info. (*0-253-32932-9*) Ind U Pr.

Miller, Larry S. Sansones's Police Photography. 3rd ed. LC 91-76957. (Illus.). (C). 1992. pap. text ed. write for info. (*0-87084-767-8*) Anderson Pub Co.

Miller, Larry S., et al. Human Evidence in Criminal Justice. 2nd ed. LC 83-221811. vii, 190p. 1985. 13.95 (*0-932930-56-5*) Pilgrimage Inc.

Miller, Laura, jt. auth. see Bartz, David.

Miller, Laurence. Freud's Brain: Neuropsychodynamic Foundations of Psychoanalysis. LC 91-16480. 276p. 1991. lib. bdg. 30.00 (*0-89862-762-1*) Guilford Pr.

— Psychotherapy of the Brain-Injured Patient: Reclaiming the Shattered Self. 256p. (C). 1993. 29.95 (*0-393-70158-1*) Norton.

Miller, Laurence H., jt. ed. see Goy, Peter A.

Miller, Lauri, ed. Promo Two: The Ultimate in Graphic Designer's & Illustrator's Promotion. (Illus.). 160p. 1992. 39.95 (*0-89134-451-9*, 30420) North Light Bks.

Miller, Laurie, jt. auth. see Krumn, Rob.

Miller, Lawrence. Samuel Beckett: The Expressive Dilemma. LC 91-45795. 192p. 1992. text ed. 45.00 (*0-312-07960-5*) St Martin.

— Whole System Architecture: Beyond Reengineering: A Guidebook for Designing Work Processes & Human Systems for High Performance Capabilities. 2nd ed. (Illus.). 320p. 1994. student ed, spiral bd. 49.95 (*0-9629679-2-0*) Miller Howard Cnslt.
Miller, Lawrence, jt. auth. see Howard, Jennifer.
Miller, Lawrence H. Advanced Programming: Design & Structure Using PASCAL. 624p. (C). 1986. write for info. (*0-318-61095-7*) Addison-Wesley.
— Programming & Problem Solving: A Second Course with Pascal. 624p. (C). 1986. teacher ed write for info. (*0-201-05579-1*); text ed. 39.75 (*0-201-05531-7*) Addison-Wesley.
Miller, Lawrence H. & Quilici, Alexander E. C Programming Language: An Applied Perspective. 340p. 1987. pap. text ed. 27.95 (*0-471-82560-3*) Wiley.
— The Joy of C: Programming in C. 2nd ed. 672p. (C). 1993. Net. pap. text ed. write for info. (*0-471-51333-4*) Wiley.
— Official Borland Turbo C Survival Guide. (Higher Education Ser.). 553p. 1989. Net. pap. text ed. write for info. (*0-471-60861-0*) Wiley.
— Programming in C. LC 85-26602. 193p. 1986. teacher ed 17.50 (*0-471-81876-3*) Wiley.
Miller, Lawrence M. American Spirit: Visions of a New Corporate Culture. 256p. 1985. mass mkt. 3.95 (*0-446-32710-7*) Warner Bks.
— Barbarians to Bureaucrats: Corporate Life Cycle Strategies. 1990. pap. 12.00 (*0-449-90526-8*) Fawcett.
— From Management to Leadership. (Management Master Ser.). (Illus.). 50p. 1995. 15.95 (*1-56327-103-6*) Prod Press.
Miller, Lee. The Seeds of Racism. 176p. 1988. 9.00 (*0-8059-3141-4*) Dorrance.
***Miller, Lee, ed.** From the Heart: Voices of the American Indian. LC 94-28492. 1995. 24.00 (*0-679-43549-2*) Knopf.
Miller, Lee, jt. auth. see Cattell, Hudson.
Miller, Lee E., jt. auth. see Warner, Michael A.
Miller, Lee G. Story of Ernie Pyle. LC 78-100169. 439p. 1970. reprint ed. text ed. 65.00 (*0-8371-3743-8*, MIEP, Greenwood Pr) Greenwood.
Miller, Lee O. Assignment Burma. 240p. 1986. reprint ed. pap. 2.95 (*0-8439-2408-X*) Dorchester Pub Co.
— The Outside Lawman. 192p. 1983. pap. 2.25 (*0-8439-2091-2*) Dorchester Pub Co.
Miller, Lee S., jt. auth. see Cattell, Hudson.
Miller, Lee T. Medical Student's Guide to Successful Residency Matching, 1994-1995. (Illus.). 112p. 1994. 9.95 (*0-683-05996-3*) Williams & Wilkins.
Miller, Len. Gambling Times Guide to Casino Games. (Illus.). 170p. (Orig.). 1983. pap. text ed. 5.95 (*0-685-01829-6*) Carol Pub Group.
— Gambling Times Guide to Casino Games, 1990. (Illus.). (Orig.). 1983. pap. text ed. 9.95 (*0-89746-071-5*) Gambling Times.
Miller, Lenore, jt. auth. see Walter, Carol.
Miller, Lenore H. The Nature Specialist: A Complete Guide to Program & Activities. 170p. 1986. pap. 24.95 (*0-87603-087-8*) Am Camping.
Miller, Leo. Ghost Stories. Costa, Gwen, ed. LC 91-33874. (YA). 1992. pap. 13.95 (*0-87949-358-5*) Ashley Bks.
— John Milton's Writings in the Anglo-Dutch Negotiations, 1651-1654. LC 92-33554. (Duquesne Studies: Language & Literature Ser.: Vol. 13). 364p. (C). 1992. text ed. 48.00 (*0-8207-0232-3*) Duquesne.
Miller, Leon C. How to Direct the High School Play. 1968. 14.95 (*0-87129-366-8*, H33) Dramatic Pub.
Miller, Leon H., jt. auth. see Dickey, John W.
Miller, Leon K. Musical Savants: Exceptional Skill in Mentally Retarded. 272p. (C). 1989. text ed. 59.95 (*0-8058-0034-4*) L Erlbaum Assocs.
Miller, Leonard A., et al, eds. Essentials of Basic Science in Surgery. LC 92-17502. 1992. 29.95 (*0-397-51168-X*) Lippincott.
Miller, Lesley. Cristobal Balenciaga. (Fashion Designers Ser.). (Illus.). 96p. (Orig.). 1994. pap. 25.95 (*0-8419-1344-7*) Holmes & Meier.
Miller, Leslie. Adios Mundo Cruel: Good Bye World. (SPA.). 4.25 (*84-7228-629-0*, 220004, Pub. by Edit Clie SP) TSELF.
— Hablaron Con Dios: They Talked with God. (SPA.). 3.95 (*84-7228-376-3*, 220439, Pub. by Edit Clie SP) TSELF.
— Hablaron Desde el Infierno: They Spoke from Hell. (SPA.). 5.50 (*84-7228-374-7*, 220441, Pub. by Edit Clie SP) TSELF.
— La Ira del Cordero del Apocalipsis: The Angry Lamb of Revelation. (SPA.). 5.25 (*84-7228-497-2*, 220502, Pub. by Edit Clie SP) TSELF.
— Todo Sobre los Angeles: All about Angels. (SPA.). 3.95 (*84-7228-101-9*, 220895, Pub. by Edit Clie SP) TSELF.
Miller, Leslie, jt. ed. see Emery, Robert W.
Miller, Leslie, et al, eds. Literature & Politics in Central Europe: Studies in Honour of Marketa Goetz-Stankiewicz. LC 93-1490. 180p. 1993. 59.95 (*1-879751-68-2*) Camden Hse.
Miller, Leslie A. Staying up for Love. (Carnegie Mellon Ser.). 68p. (Orig.). (C). 1990. pap. 9.95 (*0-88748-096-9*) Carnegie-Mellon.
— Ungodliness. LC 93-73475. (Poetry Ser.). 80p. (Orig.). 1994. 17.95 (*0-88748-172-8*); pap. 10.95 (*0-88748-173-6*) Carnegie-Mellon.
Miller, Leta E. & Cohn, Albert. Music in the Royal Society of London, 1660-1806. LC 87-344. (Detroit Studies in Music Bibliography: No. 56). xvii, 264p. 1987. 25.00 (*0-89990-032-1*) Info Coord.
Miller, Leta E., jt. auth. see Cohn, Albert.
Miller, Levi. Ben's Wayne. LC 89-32436. 168p. 1989. 14.95 (*0-934672-77-6*) Good Bks PA.
— Ben's Wayne. LC 89-32436. 168p. 1992. pap. 9.95 (*1-56148-061-4*) Good Bks PA.
— Our People: The Amish & Mennonites in Ohio. rev. ed. (Illus.). 64p. 1992. pap. 4.95 (*0-8361-3582-2*) Herald Pr.
Miller, Lew. Miracles Can Happen to You: Power of Visual Imagery. 3rd ed. LC 85-61118. 72p. (Orig.). 1986. reprint ed. pap. 5.45 (*0-9615752-0-4*); reprint ed. audio 10.00 (*0-9615752-1-2*) Milbeck Pr.
Miller, Lewis. Nursing in America. (C). 1989. 32.00 (*0-7223-2389-1*, Pub. by A H S Ltd UK) St Mut.
— Psychology of Interviewing. (C). 1989. 40.00 (*0-7223-2388-3*, Pub. by A H S Ltd UK) St Mut.
Miller-Lewis, S. Jill. Dressing Successfully, Vol. 1, No. 1. rev. ed. (Illus.). 52p. (Orig.). 1987. pap. 10.00 (*0-934155-00-3*) Miller Des.
— Fashions Throughout the Years: Vol. 1, No. 1. (Illus.). 65p. (Orig.). 1987. pap. 10.00 (*0-934155-01-1*) Miller Des.
— How to Become a Fashion Designer: A Guide on the Ins & Outs of Fashion Designing, Vol. 1, No. 1. (Illus.). 60p. (Orig.). 1987. pap. 10.00 (*0-934155-02-X*) Miller Des.
— Making Yourself Even More Beautiful, Vol. I, No. 1. (Illus.). 46p. (Orig.). 1987. pap. 8.00 (*0-934155-03-8*) Miller Des.
— Silk: The Luxurious Fabric, Vol. 1, No. 1. (Illus.). 34p. (Orig.). 1987. pap. text ed. 8.00 (*0-934155-04-6*) Miller Des.
Miller, Liam. Dolmen Book of Irish Stamps. 1986. 17.95 (*0-85105-453-6*, Pub. by Colin Smythe Ltd UK) Dufour.
Miller, Liam, jt. auth. see Hanley, Mary.
Miller, Libby & Rothlein, Liz. Read It Again! Introducing Literature to Young Children, Preschool - Kindergarten, Bk. 1. (Illus.). 112p. (Orig.). (J). (ps-00). 1991. pap. 9.95 (*0-673-36008-3*) GdYrBks.
— Read It Again! Preschool - Kindergarten, Bk. 2. (Illus.). 144p. (Orig.). (J). (ps-00). 1993. pap. 9.95 (*0-673-36042-3*) GdYrBks.
Miller, Lillian B. In Pursuit of Fame: Rembrandt Peale, 1778-1860. LC 92-18207. (Illus.). 320p. 1993. 60.00 (*0-295-97243-2*) U of Wash Pr.
Miller, Lillian B., ed. The Collected Papers of Charles Willson Peale & His Family. 1980. 1,500.00 (*0-527-99008-6*) Kraus Intl.
Miller, Lillian B. & Ward, David C., eds. New Perspectives on Charles Willson Peale: A 250th Anniversary Celebration. LC 90-39815. (Illus.). 432p. (C). 1991. 49.95 (*0-8229-3660-7*) U of Pittsburgh Pr.
Miller, Lillian B., ed. see Library of Congress Staff.
Miller, Lillian B., ed. see Peale, Charles W.
Miller, Lillian S., ed. see Peale, Charles W.
***Miller, Linda.** Towards Reading: Literacy Development in the Pre-School Years. LC 95-14679. (Re-Thinking Reading Ser.). 1995. text ed. write for info. (*0-335-19216-5*, Open Univ Pr); pap. text ed. write for info. (*0-335-19215-7*, Open Univ Pr) Taylor & Francis.
Miller, Linda, ed. see Chambers, Maggie.
Miller, Linda, jt. auth. see Hess, Karen M.
Miller, Linda, ed. see St. Claire, Mary.
Miller, Linda, et al. Manual of Laboratory Immunology. 2nd ed. LC 89-13712. (Illus.). 427p. 1991. pap. text ed. 45.50 (*0-8121-1319-5*) Williams & Wilkins.
Miller, Linda B. Shadow & Substance: Jimmy Carter & the Camp David Accords. (Pew Case Studies in International Affairs). 50p. (C). 1992. pap. text ed. 2.50 (*1-56927-433-9*) Geo U Inst Dplmcy.
— World Order & Local Disorder: The United Nations & Internal Conflicts. LC 67-16953. 245p. reprint ed. pap. 69.90 (*0-8357-7078-8*, 2033382) Bks Demand.
Miller, Linda B. & Smith, Michael J., eds. Ideas & Ideals: Essays on Politics in Honor of Stanley Hoffmann. LC 93-19809. 436p. 1993. text ed. 68.50 (*0-8133-1286-8*) Westview.
Miller, Linda F. An Introduction to the Literature & Personalities of the Bible. 89p. (YA). (gr. 7-12). 1985. 14.00 (*1-881678-10-5*) CRIS.
Miller, Linda L. Angelfire. Marrow, Linda, ed. 352p. 1991. mass mkt. 5.99 (*0-671-73765-1*) PB.
— Banner O'Brian. Marrow, Linda, ed. 1991. mass mkt. 5.99 (*0-671-73766-X*) PB.
— Caroline & the Raider. Marrow, Linda, ed. 368p. (Orig.). 1992. mass mkt. 5.99 (*0-671-67638-5*) PB.
— Corbin's Fancy. Marrow, Linda, ed. 320p. 1991. mass mkt. 5.99 (*0-671-73767-8*) PB.
— Daniel's Bride. Marrow, Linda, ed. 400p. (Orig.). 1992. mass mkt. 5.99 (*0-671-73166-1*) PB.
— Daniel's Bride. large type ed. LC 92-41556. (Popular Ser.). 504p. (Orig.). 1993. reprint ed. pap. 17.95 (*1-56054-619-0*) Thorndike Pr.
— Desire & Destiny. Marrow, Linda, ed. 320p. (Orig.). 1990. mass mkt. 5.99 (*0-671-70635-7*) PB.
— Emma & the Outlaw. Marrow, Linda, ed. 384p. (Orig.). 1991. mass mkt. 5.99 (*0-671-67637-7*) PB.
— Escape from Cabriz. large type ed. (Desire Ser.). 1993. 17.95 (*0-373-58813-5*, Silhouette Lrg Print); pap. 16.95 (*0-373-58913-1*, Silhouette Lrg Print) Chivers N Amer.
— Fletcher's Woman. (Tapestry Romance Ser.). 1991. mass mkt. 5.99 (*0-671-73768-6*) PB.
— For All Eternity. 352p. (Orig.). 1994. pap. 5.99 (*0-425-14456-9*) Berkley Pub.
— Forever & the Night. 1993. mass mkt. 5.50 (*0-425-14060-1*) Berkley Pub.
— Forever & the Night. large type ed. LC 93-39749. 1994. 19.95 (*0-7862-0068-5*) Thorndike Pr.
— Glory, Glory. large type ed. (Silhouette Desire Ser.). 1993. 17.95 (*0-373-58833-X*, Silhouette Lrg Print); pap. 16.95 (*0-373-58925-5*, Silhouette Lrg Print) Chivers N Amer.
— Lauralee. Marrow, Linda, ed. 1990. mass mkt. 5.99 (*0-671-70634-9*) PB.
— The Legacy. Marrow, Linda, ed. 336p. (Orig.). 1994. mass mkt. 5.99 (*0-671-79792-1*, Pocket Star Bks) PB.
— The Legacy. large type ed. LC 94-29353. 1995. write for info. (*0-7862-0326-9*) Thorndike Pr.
— Lily & the Major. Marrow, Linda, ed. 384p. (Orig.). 1990. mass mkt. 5.50 (*0-671-67636-9*) PB.
— Memory's Embrace. Marrow, Linda, ed. 320p. 1991. mass mkt. 5.99 (*0-671-73769-4*) PB.
— Moonfire. Marrow, Linda, ed. 384p. 1991. mass mkt. 5.99 (*0-671-73770-8*) PB.
— My Darling Melissa. Marrow, Linda, ed. 336p. 1991. mass mkt. 5.99 (*0-671-73771-6*) PB.
— Only Forever. 1995. pap. 4.99 (*1-55166-073-3*, 1-66073-7, Mira Bks) Harlequin Bks.
— Part of the Bargain. (Men Made in America Ser.). 1994. mass mkt. 3.59 (*0-373-45176-8*, 1-45176-4) Harlequin Bks.
— Pirates. Marrow, Linda, ed. 304p. 1995. 20.00 (*0-671-52732-0*) PB.
— Princess Annie. Marrow, Linda, ed. 480p. (Orig.). 1994. mass mkt. 5.99 (*0-671-79793-X*, Pocket Star Bks) PB.
— Ragged Rainbows. 1995. pap. 4.99 (*1-55166-059-8*, 1-66059-6, Mira Bks) Harlequin Bks.
— Ragged Rainbows. 1994. mass mkt. 4.50 (*0-373-48300-7*, 5-48300-3) Silhouette.
— Snowflakes on the Sea. 1994. mass mkt. 4.50 (*0-373-48303-1*, 5-48303-7) Silhouette.
— State Secrets. 1995. pap. 4.99 (*1-55166-014-8*, Mira Bks) Harlequin Bks.
— State Secrets. 1994. mass mkt. 4.50 (*0-373-48307-4*, 5-48307-8) Silhouette.
— Used-to-Be Lovers. 1995. mass mkt. 4.99 (*1-55166-037-7*, 1-66037-2, Mira Bks) Harlequin Bks.
— Wanton Angel. Marrow, Linda, ed. 352p. 1991. mass mkt. 5.99 (*0-671-73772-4*) PB.
— Willow. Marrow, Linda, ed. 320p. (Orig.). 1991. mass mkt. 5.99 (*0-671-73773-2*) PB.
— Yankee Wife. Marrow, Linda, ed. 368p. (Orig.). 1993. mass mkt. 5.99 (*0-671-73755-4*, Pocket Star Bks) PB.
Miller, Linda L., et al. Timeless. 272p. (Orig.). 1994. mass mkt. 4.99 (*0-425-13701-5*) Berkley Pub.
Miller, Linda M., ed. The Impact of the Media on Collective Bargaining. LC 80-65636. 92p. 1980. pap. 4.00 (*0-943001-16-1*) Am Arbitration.
***Miller, Linda M., et al, eds.** ABA Book Buyer's Handbook, 1994-1995. 846p. 1994. pap. write for info. (*1-879556-14-6*) ABA.
— ABA Book Buyer's Returns Handbook, 1994 to 1995. 342p. 1994. 50.00 (*1-879556-15-4*) ABA.
Miller, Linda P., ed. Letters from the Lost Generation: Gerald & Sara Murphy & Friends. LC 90-42139. (Illus.). 400p. (C). 1991. 27.95 (*0-8135-1642-0*) Rutgers U Pr.
— Letters from the Lost Generation: Gerald & Sara Murphy & Friends. LC 90-42139. (Illus.). 362p. 1993. pap. 15.95 (*0-8135-1966-7*) Rutgers U Pr.
Miller, Linda Patterson, jt. ed. see Miller, Randall M.
Miller, Linda R. Planning a Christian Wedding. 82p. 1992. ring bd. 12.95 (*0-940883-05-8*) Calvary Pubns.
Miller, Lindsay, jt. ed. see Gardner, David.
Miller, Linsday, jt. ed. see Nunan, David.
Miller, Lise, jt. auth. see Toothaker, Larry E.
Miller, Lise M., jt. auth. see Seranne, Ann.
Miller, Liz. Memorabilia: The Regional Prints of Jane Dunning Baldwin. 20p. 1989. pap. 2.95 (*0-910524-14-9*) Eastern Wash.
Miller, Liz & Burns, Carol. Easy Does It Cookbook. 1982. 9.95 (*0-9610530-1-1*) Woman Time Mgmt.
Miller, Liz, ed. see Wong, Thomas.
Miller, Lloyd E., Jr. The Profaners. rev. ed. 175p. (Orig.). 1995. pap. 4.95 (*0-9639322-1-7*) Literary Prods.
— Soul of the Shepherd. 175p. (Orig.). 1995. pap. 4.95 (*0-9639322-2-5*) Literary Prods.
— Tenth Stay at Midnight. (Prestige Classic Ser.). 104p. 1994. reprint ed. pap. 4.95 (*0-9639322-0-9*) Literary Prods.
— Trail to El Paso. (Western Classic Premier Bks.). 225p. (Orig.). 1995. pap. 4.95 (*0-9639322-3-3*) Literary Prods.
Miller, Lois N. Abstracts of Deeds, 1830-1838: Deed Book A, Washington County, AR. 166p. 1990. 31.50 (*1-878193-14-7*); pap. 25.00 (*1-878193-15-5*) L N Miller Geog Pubns.
— Index to Wills, 1828-1931 & Index to Probate Records A-K Book, 1836-1901. 165p. 1985. reprint ed. 30.00 (*1-878193-12-0*); reprint ed. pap. 22.00 (*1-878193-13-9*) L N Miller Geog Pubns.
— Marriages of Washington Co., Arkansas, 1845-71. 118p. (Orig.). 1982. 31.50 (*1-878193-00-7*); pap. 25.00 (*1-878193-01-5*) L N Miller Geog Pubns.
— Marriages of Washington Co., Arkansas, 1871-91. 194p. 1985. 27.00 (*1-878193-02-3*); pap. 22.00 (*1-878193-03-1*) L N Miller Geog Pubns.
— Marriages of Washington Co., Arkansas, 1930-41. 260p. 1990. 37.50 (*1-878193-10-4*); pap. 30.00 (*1-878193-11-2*) L N Miller Geog Pubns.
— Tax Records for Washington County, Arkansas, Real Estate & Personal Property, 1890. 317p. 1990. 42.50 (*1-878193-16-3*); pap. 34.00 (*1-878193-17-1*) L N Miller Geog Pubns.
Miller, Lois N., et al. Marriages of Washington Co., Arkansas, 1901-10. 166p. 1990. 31.50 (*1-878193-04-X*); pap. 25.00 (*1-878193-05-8*) L N Miller Geog Pubns.
— Marriages of Washington Co., Arkansas, 1911-21. 218p. 1990. 31.50 (*1-878193-06-6*); pap. 25.00 (*1-878193-07-4*) L N Miller Geog Pubns.
— Marriages of Washington Co., Arkansas, 1922-30. 156p. 1990. 31.50 (*1-878193-08-2*); pap. 25.00 (*1-878193-09-0*) L N Miller Geog Pubns.
Miller, Loren. Bishops: The Eternal Crusade. (Primal Order Ser.). 128p. 1994. pap. 12.95 (*1-880992-19-1*) Wizards Coast.
Miller, Lorna T., jt. auth. see Miller, Donald E.
***Miller, Louis.** Beacons of Light: Ecclesiastical Writers Cited in the Catechism. 64p. 1995. pap. 4.95 (*0-89243-784-7*) Liguori Pubns.
Miller, Louis & Einstein, Stanley, eds. Drugs & Society: Contemporary Social Issues. 317p. 1976. 34.95 (*0-87855-273-1*) Transaction Pubs.
Miller, Louis W. & Abell, John B. DRIVE (Distribution & Repair in Variable Environments) Design & Operation of the Ogden Prototype. LC 92-13079. 1992. write for info. (*0-8330-1243-6*, R-4158-AF) Rand Corp.
— Evaluations of Alternative Approaches to Central Stock Leveling. LC 95-2391. (MR-546-AF Ser.). 95p. 1995. pap. text ed. 15.00 (*0-8330-1632-6*) Rand Corp.
Miller, Louise. Career Portraits: Animals. LC 93-49056. (J). 1994. 13.95 (*0-8442-4359-0*, VGM Career Bks) NTC Pub Grp.
— Careers for Animal Lovers: And Other Zoological Types. LC 90-50725. (Careers for You Ser.). 160p. (Orig.). (YA). (gr. 7 up). 1991. pap. 9.95 (*0-8442-8125-5*, VGM Career Bks) NTC Pub Grp.
— Careers for Nature Lovers & Other Outdoor Types. (Careers for You Ser.). 130p. 1992. 12.95 (*0-8442-8132-8*, VGM Career Bks); pap. 9.95 (*0-8442-8133-6*, VGM Career Bks) NTC Pub Grp.
Miller, Lowell. Wholesale-By-Mail Catalog, 1995. 1994. pap. 16.00 (*0-06-273310-9*) HarpC.
***Miller, Lucien.** Masks of Fiction in Dream of the Red Chamber: Myth, Mimesis, & Persona. fac. ed. LC 75-23643. (Association for Asian Studies, Monographs & Papers: No. 28). 359p. 1994. pap. 102.40 (*0-7837-7674-8*, 2047427) Bks Demand.
Miller, Lucien, ed. & tr. South of the Clouds: Tales of Yunnan. Xu, Guo et al, trs. LC 93-36563. (McLellan Book Ser.). 342p. (C). 1994. 40.00 (*0-295-97293-9*); pap. 19.95 (*0-295-97348-X*) U of Wash Pr.
Miller, Lucille. Heidi. (J). 1936. 5.00 (*0-87602-136-4*) Anchorage.
Miller, Lucy J., ed. Developing Norm-Referenced Standardized Tests. LC 88-36502. (Physical & Occupational Therapy in Pediatrics Ser.: Vol. 9, No. 1). (Illus.). 205p. 1989. text ed. 39.95 (*0-86656-883-2*) Haworth Pr.
Miller, Lula, jt. auth. see Yoder, Elmina.
Miller, Luree. Literary Hills of San Francisco. (Literary Cities Ser.). (Illus.). 72p. (Orig.). 1992. pap. 8.95 (*0-913515-76-0*, Starrhill) Elliott & Clark.
— Literary Villages of London. LC 88-36889. (Literary Cities Ser.). (Illus.). 80p. (Orig.). 1989. pap. 8.95 (*0-913515-41-8*, Starrhill) Elliott & Clark.
— On Top of the World: Five Women Explorers in Tibet. LC 84-16619. (Illus.). 224p. 1984. reprint ed. pap. 10.95 (*0-89886-097-0*) Mountaineers.
Miller, Lyle L. Developing Reading Efficiency. 4th ed. LC 79-55778. 1980. pap. text ed. write for info. (*0-8087-3958-1*) Burgess MN Intl.
— Increasing Reading Efficiency. 5th ed. 352p. (C). 1984. pap. text ed. 23.50 (*0-03-062049-X*) HB Coll Pubs.
— Personalizing Reading Efficiency. 2nd ed. (C). 1981. pap. text ed. write for info. (*0-8087-3990-5*) Burgess MN Intl.
Miller, Lynda. The Smart Profile: A Qualitative Approach of Describing Learners & Designing Instruction. 94p. 1993. pap. 16.00 (*0-9636140-0-2*) Smart Alternat.
— What We Call Smart: A New Narrative for Intelligence & Learning. LC 92-40680. (School-Age Children Ser.). (Illus.). 191p. (Orig.). (C). 1993. pap. text ed. 34.95x (*1-879105-44-6*, 0228) Singular Publishing.
— Your Personal Smart Profile: A Qualitative Approach for Describing Yourself in Your Everyday Life. 134p. 1993. pap. 16.00 (*0-9636140-1-0*) Smart Alternat.
Miller, Lynda, jt. auth. see Wallach, Geraldine P.
***Miller, Lynda, et al.** Cultural Cobblestones: Teaching Cultural Diversity. (School Library Media Ser.: No. 4). (Illus.). 216p. (Orig.). 1994. 25.00 (*0-8108-2966-5*) Scarecrow.
***Miller, Lynda H.** Because I Can't Do Standup. 60p. 1995. pap. 7.95 (*1-56901-700-X*) NW Pub.
Miller, Lynda M. Glasgow, Virginia: One Hundred Years of Dreams. LC 92-8681. (Illus.). 208p. (Orig.). 1992. 35.00 (*0-9623572-5-1*) Rockbridge Pub.
Miller, Lynn. The Hand That Holds the Camera: Interviews with Women Film & Video Directors. LC 87-32871. 271p. 1988. lib. bdg. 45.00 (*0-8240-8530-2*) Garland.
Miller, Lynn A. Firstfruits Living: Giving God Our Best. LC 90-48699. 96p. (Orig.). 1991. pap. 5.95 (*0-8361-3543-1*) Herald Pr.
Miller, Lynn E. Managing Human Service Organizations. LC 88-35682. 256p. 1989. text ed. 55.00 (*0-89930-305-6*, MMN/, Quorum Bks) Greenwood.
Miller, Lynn F., jt. ed. see Boos, Florence.
Miller, Lynn F., jt. auth. see Comtois, M. F.
Miller, Lynn H. Global Order: Values & Power in International Politics. 3rd ed. LC 93-28749. 269p. (C). 1993. text ed. 58.00 (*0-8133-1743-6*); pap. text ed. 19.95 (*0-8133-1744-4*) Westview.
Miller, Lynn H., jt. auth. see Schuster, Jack H.
Miller, Lynn M. Maintaining Esthetic Restorations. Miller, Michael B., ed. (Illus.). 100p. (Orig.). 1989. pap. 25.00 (*0-9623707-0-3*) Reality TX.
Miller, Lynn R. Work Horse Handbook. (Illus.). 224p. 1983. pap. 16.45 (*0-9607268-0-2*, Scribners) S&S Trade.
Miller, Lynne, jt. auth. see Lieberman, Ann.
Miller, Lynne, jt. ed. see Lieberman, Ann.
Miller, Lynne D., jt. ed. see Dottin, Erskine S.
Miller, M. Plant Types One. (C). 1982. text ed. 55.00 (*0-7487-0189-3*, Pub. by S Thornes Pubs UK) St Mut.
— Plant Types Two. (C). 1985. text ed. 55.00 (*0-7487-0289-X*, Pub. by S Thornes Pubs UK) St Mut.
— Yom Tov Shiurim. LC 94-6787. 1994. 13.95 (*0-87306-673-1*) Feldheim.
Miller, M., ed. Control Technologies for Air Pollution. (C). 1991. text ed. 350.00 (*0-89771-590-X*, Pub. by Intl Bk Distr II) St Mut.
— Environmental Monitoring. (C). 1991. text ed. 350.00 (*0-89771-591-8*, Pub. by Intl Bk Distr II) St Mut.

An Asterisk (*) at the beginning of an entry indicates that the title is appearing in BIP for the first time.

— The Logic of Language Development in Early Childhood. King, R. T., tr. (Language & Communication Ser.: Vol. 3). (Illus.). 1979. 33.00 (*0-387-09606-X*) Spr-Verlag.

Miller, M. & Van Loon, V. Darwin for Beginners. 1990. pap. 30.00 (*0-04-573018-0*, Pub. by Northcote UK) St Mut.

Miller, M., tr. see Fisher, J., et al.

Miller, M., jt. auth. see Price, Wilson T.

Miller, M. C. Supplementum Inscriptionum Atticarum, VII. Date not set. 45.00 (*0-89005-533-5*, SIA07) Ares.

Miller, M. C., ed. Excerpta de Historia Macedonia Bks. VII-XII: Epitoma Historiarum Philippicarum. (Illus.). xxiii, 132p. (C). 1992. text ed. 25.00 (*0-89005-410-X*) Ares.

— Supplementum Inscriptionum Atticarum VI: The Latin Inscriptions of Athens & Attica. (Inscriptiones Atticae Ser.). (Illus.). viii, 189p. (LAT.). (C). 1992. text ed. 45.00 (*0-89005-532-7*) Ares.

Miller, M. C. & De Voto, J. Fortification of the Roman Camp: Polybius & PS-Hyginus. (Illus.). vi, 120p. (Orig.). (C). 1994. pap. text ed. 20.00 (*0-89005-518-1*) Ares.

Miller, M. C., ed. see Barber, G. L.

Miller, M. C., ed. see Hanno the Carthaginian.

Miller, M. C., III, et al. Mathematical Models in Medical Diagnosis. LC 81-5170. 206p. 1981. text ed. 59.95 (*0-275-91349-X*, C1349, Praeger Pubs) Greenwood.

Miller, M. Catherine. Flooding the Courtrooms: Law & Water in the Far West. LC 92-33048. (Law in the American West Ser.: Vol. 4). (Illus.). x, 256p. 1993. 45.00 (*0-8032-3153-9*) U of Nebr Pr.

Miller, M. Clinton & Knapp, Rebecca G. Evaluating Quality of Care: Analytic Procedures, Monitoring Techniques. LC 79-4482. 352p. 1979. 80.00 (*0-89443-091-2*) Aspen Pub.

***Miller, M. E.** The Comprehensive Classification of Fractures. 300p. 1994. 370.00 (*0-387-14150-2*); 370.00 (*0-387-14156-1*) Spr-Verlag.

Miller, M. I., jt. auth. see Snyder, D. L.

Miller, M. K. & Smith, G. D. Atom Probe Microanalysis: Principles & Applications to Materials Problems. (Monograph). 278p. 1989. text ed. 47.00 (*0-931837-99-5*) Materials Res.

***Miller, M. K., et al.** Atom Probe Field Ion Microscopy. (Monographs on the Physics & Chemistry of Materials). 544p. 1996. 120.00 (*0-19-851387-9*) OUP.

Miller, M. L. Dizzy from Fools. LC 85-9390. (Illus.). 32p. (J). (gr. 1 up). 1991. pap. 13.95 (*0-88708-004-9*, Picture Book Studio) S&S Childrens.

— Those Bottles! LC 93-19684. (Illus.). 32p. (J). (ps-3). 1994. 14.95 (*0-399-22607-9*, Putnam) Putnam Pub Group.

Miller, M. M., jt. ed. see Harwood, D. S.

Miller, M. R. & Davies, E. Key Facts in Infection. 38p. 1993. spiral bd. write for info. (*0-443-04993-9*) Churchill.

Miller, M. Sammye, ed. see James, L. Royal & James, Zenobia A.

Miller, Madelyn. Shop Aerobics Pocket Guide: How to Trim Fat from Your Budget & Your Waist. 32p. 1992. pap. text ed. 6.00 (*0-9632431-0-1*) M Miller Agency.

Miller, Madge. Alice in Wonderland. (J). 1953. 5.00 (*0-87602-104-6*) Anchorage.

— Hansel & Gretel. (J). 1954. 5.00 (*0-87602-135-6*) Anchorage.

— The Land of the Dragon. (J). 1946. 5.00 (*0-87602-148-8*) Anchorage.

— OPQRS, Etc. (Orig.). (J). (gr. 4 up). 1984. pap. 5.00 (*0-87602-246-8*) Anchorage.

— The Pied Piper of Hamelin. (J). 1951. 5.00 (*0-87602-174-7*) Anchorage.

— Pinocchio. (J). 1954. 5.00 (*0-87602-175-5*) Anchorage.

— The Princess & the Swineherd. (J). 1946. 5.00 (*0-87602-181-X*) Anchorage.

— Puss in Boots: Miniature Play. 37p. (Orig.). (J). 1954. 5.00 (*0-87602-184-4*) Anchorage.

— Robinson Crusoe. (J). (gr. 1-9). 1954. 5.00 (*0-87602-193-3*) Anchorage.

— The Unwicked Witch. (J). (gr. 1-7). 1964. 5.00 (*0-87602-216-6*) Anchorage.

Miller, Malcolm. Chartres Cathedral. (Illus.). 96p. (Orig.). 1991. pap. 14.95 (*1-878351-13-3*) Riverside NY.

Miller, Mara. Garden As an Art. LC 92-8162. 233p. 1993. 59.50 (*0-7914-1377-2*); pap. 19.95 (*0-7914-1378-0*) State U NY Pr.

***Miller, Marc.** The Color Mac. 2nd ed. 1995. pap. 45.00 (*1-56830-126-X*) Hayden.

— Fundamental Tennis. LC 93-48385. (Fundamental Sports Ser.). (Illus.). 64p. (J). (gr. 5-9). 1994. lib. bdg. 19.95 (*0-8225-3450-9*, Lerner Publctns) Lerner Group.

Miller, Marc, ed. Elections: Grassroots Strategies for Change. (Southern Exposure Ser.). (Illus.). 120p. (Orig.). 1984. pap. 4.00 (*0-943810-17-5*) Inst Southern Studies.

— Liberating Our Past. (Illus.). 120p. 1984. pap. 4.00 (*0-943810-18-3*) Inst Southern Studies.

Miller, Marc, intro. Waging Peace. (Southern Exposure Ser.). (Illus.). 120p. (Orig.). 1982. pap. 4.00 (*0-943810-14-0*) Inst Southern Studies.

Miller, Marc & Bond, Larry. Ship Forms. (Harpoon Ser.). (Illus.). (Orig.). 1988. pap. 8.00 (*0-943580-61-7*) Game Designers.

Miller, Marc, ed. see Bond, Larry.

Miller, Marc, jt. auth. see Zaucha, Randy.

Miller, Marc H., et al. Louis Armstrong: A Cultural Legacy. (Illus.). 248p. (C). 1994. 50.00x (*0-295-97382-X*); pap. 29.95 (*0-295-97383-8*) U of Wash Pr.

Miller, Marc L., jt. auth. see Kirk, Jerome.

Miller, Marc S. The Irony of Victory: World War II & Lowell, Massachusetts. LC 87-27212. 248p. 1988. 24.95 (*0-252-01505-3*) U of Ill Pr.

Miller, Marc S., jt. auth. see Families U. S. A. Staff.

Miller, Marc S., jt. auth. see Grover, Martha S.

Miller, Marc W. ASW Forms. (Harpoon Ser.). (Illus.). 49p. (Orig.). (YA). 1990. pap. 8.00 (*1-55878-057-2*) Game Designers.

— Fighting Ships. (MegaTraveller Ser.). (Illus.). 96p. (Orig.). (YA). 1990. pap. 10.00 (*1-55878-050-5*) Game Designers.

— Mega Traveller. Fugate, Joe, Sr. & Thomas, Gary L., eds. 104p. (Orig.). 1987. write for info. (*0-318-62777-9*); Player's Manual, 104 pgs. pap. 10.00 (*0-943580-38-2*); Referee's Manual, 104 pgs. pap. 10.00 (*0-943580-47-1*) Game Designers.

— Mega Traveller: Imperial Encyclopedia. Fugate, Joe, Sr. & Thomas, Gary L., eds. 96p. (Orig.). 1987. pap. 10.00 (*0-943580-48-X*) Game Designers.

— Rebellion Sourcebook. (MegaTraveller Ser.). (Illus.). 96p. (Orig.). 1988. pap. 10.00 (*0-943580-63-3*) Game Designers.

— Referee's Companion. (MegaTraveller Ser.). (Illus.). 96p. (Orig.). 1988. pap. 10.00 (*0-943580-71-4*) Game Designers.

— Sub Forms. (Harpoon Ser.). (Illus.). 49p. (Orig.). (YA). 1989. pap. 8.00 (*1-55878-019-X*) Game Designers.

Miller, Marc W., jt. auth. see Smith, Lester.

Miller, Marcia. The Waiting Heart. large type ed. LC 92-29019. 1993. 18.95 (*0-7927-1453-9*, Curley Lrg Print); pap. 16.95 (*0-7927-1452-0*, Curley Lrg Print) Chivers N Amer.

***Miller, Marcia & Lee, Martin.** Investigating with Pattern Blocks. 72p. 1995. pap. text ed. 8.95 (*0-938587-78-1*) Cuisenaire.

Miller, Marcia M. Post Card Views & Other Souvenirs. (Illus.). 64p. 1973. pap. 2.95 (*0-913270-24-5*) Sunstone Pr.

Miller, Marcus & Williamson, John. Targets & Indicators: A Blueprint for the International Coordination of Economic Policy. LC 87-22724. (Policy Analysis in International Economics Ser.: No. 22). 108p. (Orig.). (C). 1987. pap. 10.00 (*0-88132-051-X*) Inst Intl Eco.

Miller, Marcus, jt. ed. see Krugman, Paul R.

Miller, Marcus, et al. Blueprints for Exchange Rate Management. (Illus.). 329p. 1991. pap. text ed. 44.00 (*0-12-497061-3*) Acad Pr.

Miller, Marcus, et al, eds. Blueprints for Exchange Rate Management. 329p. 1989. text ed. 80.00 (*0-12-497060-5*) Acad Pr.

***Miller, Mardith K.** Building & Builders in Hispanic California 1769-1850. (Illus.). 231p. (Orig.). 1995. pap. 37.00 (*0-915076-12-8*) SW Mission.

***Miller, Marek.** Arystokracja. (Illus.). 270p. (POL.). 1994. 24.00 (*0-614-02646-6*) Szwede Slavic.

Miller, Margaret. Can You Guess? LC 92-29406. (Illus.). 40p. (J). (ps up). 1993. 16.00 (*0-688-11180-7*); lib. bdg. 13.93 (*0-688-11181-5*) Greenwillow.

— Guess Who? LC 93-26704. (Illus.). 40p. (J). 1994. 15.00 (*0-688-12783-5*); lib. bdg. 14.93 (*0-688-12784-3*) Greenwillow.

— My Five Senses. LC 93-1956. (J). 1994. 15.00 (*0-671-79168-0*, S&S Bks Young Read) S&S Childrens.

— Now I'm Big. (Illus.). 48p. (J). 1996. 15.00 (*0-688-14077-7*); lib. bdg. 14.93 (*0-688-14078-5*) Greenwillow.

— Where Does It Go? LC 91-30160. (Illus.). 40p. (J). (ps-4). 1992. 14.00 (*0-688-10928-4*); lib. bdg. 13.93 (*0-688-10929-2*) Greenwillow.

— Where's Jenna? LC 93-13981. (J). 1994. pap. 15.00 (*0-671-79167-2*, S&S Bks Young Read) S&S Childrens.

— Who Uses This? LC 89-30456. (Illus.). 40p. (J). (ps up). 1990. 12.95 (*0-688-08278-5*); lib. bdg. 12.88 (*0-688-08279-3*) Greenwillow.

— Whose Hat? LC 86-18324. (Illus.). 40p. (J). (ps-1). 1988. 14.00 (*0-688-06906-1*); lib. bdg. 13.93 (*0-688-06907-X*) Greenwillow.

— Whose Shoe? LC 90-38491. (Illus.). 40p. (J). (ps up). 1991. 13.95 (*0-688-10008-2*); lib. bdg. 13.88 (*0-688-10009-0*) Greenwillow.

Miller, Margaret, et al. Human Development. LC 92-13561. (Skills for Caring Ser.). (Illus.). 40p. (Orig.). 1992. pap. text ed. 12.00 (*0-443-04531-3*) Churchill.

Miller, Margaret J. Blockbuster Quilts. McGehee, Liz & Tucker, Shellie, eds. LC 90-15476. (Illus.). 168p. 1991. pap. 12.95 (*0-943574-75-7*) That Patchwork.

— Strips That Sizzle. Weiland, Barbara, ed. LC 92-8798. (Illus.). 112p. (Orig.). 1992. pap. 24.95 (*1-56477-009-5*, B141) That Patchwork.

Miller, Margarette S. Twenty-Three Words: A Biography of Francis Bellamy, Author of the Pledge of Allegiance. LC 79-9478. (Illus.). 400p. 1976. 15.00 (*0-686-15626-9*) Natl Bellamy.

Miller, Margery. Sound Business Bites: A Common Sense Approach to Customer Service & Management. 100p. (Orig.). 1994. pap. 10.00 (*1-884363-04-0*) Odenwald Pr.

Miller, Margery S. & Allan, Karen K. Reading the Newspaper: Middle Level. (Illus.). (Orig.). 1987. pap. text ed. 10.75 (*0-89061-480-6*) Jamestown Pubs.

Miller, Margery S., jt. auth. see Allan, Karen K.

Miller, Margery S., jt. auth. see Allen, Karen K.

Miller, Marguerite, jt. auth. see Kern, R. Fred.

Miller, Marguerite L., jt. auth. see Cochrane, Ruth T.

Miller, Maria G., tr. see Plaass, Peter.

***Miller, Marian A.** The Third World in Global Environmental Politics. LC 94-36484. 182p. 1995. lib. bdg. 40.00 (*1-55587-422-3*); pap. text ed. 17.95 (*1-55587-423-1*) Lynne Rienner.

Miller, Marianne M. Too Busy: A Days of the Week Story. Wray, Rhonda, ed. LC 93-11657. (Illus.). 36p. (Orig.). (J). (gr. k-3). 1993. pap. 9.95 (*0-916260-96-8*, B114) Meriwether Pub.

Miller, Marie S. New Dimensions in Floral Design. (Illus.). 173p. (Orig.). (C). 1981. text ed. 29.95 (*0-9606424-0-4*) M S Miller.

Miller, Marilyn. The Bridge at Selma. LC 84-40379. (Turning Points in American History Ser.). (Illus.). 64p. (J). (gr. 5 up). 1984. lib. bdg. 14.95 (*0-382-06826-2*); pap. 7.95 (*0-382-06973-0*) Silver Burdett Pr.

— D-Day. LC 84-40380. (Turning Points in American History Ser.). (Illus.). 64p. (J). (gr. 5 up). 1984. lib. bdg. 14.95 (*0-382-06825-4*) Silver Burdett Pr.

— The Trans-Continental Railroad. LC 85-40167. (Turning Points in American History Ser.). (Illus.). 64p. (J). (gr. 5 up). 1985. lib. bdg. 14.95 (*0-382-06824-6*); pap. 7.95 (*0-382-09912-5*) Silver Burdett Pr.

Miller, Marina C. Blurred Boundaries: My Therapist, My Friend. (Orig.). 1993. pap. 14.95 (*0-9636710-5-7*) Shades Of Gray.

Miller, Marion M. Great Debates in American History. 1970. reprint ed. 225.00 (*0-8108-0386-0*) Scarecrow.

Miller, Marjorie A. & Slavick, Patricia B. Introduction to Law Practice Management. 2nd ed. LC 93-29530. 1993. write for info. (*0-8205-0203-0*) Bender.

Miller, Marjorie L., jt. auth. see Miller, Arthur P., Jr.

Miller, Marjorie M. Isaac Asimov: A Checklist of Works Published in the United States. LC 72-76948. (Serif Series: Bibliographies & Checklists: No. 25). 114p. reprint ed. pap. 32.50 (*0-8357-5575-4*, 2035202) Bks Demand.

Miller, Mark. Bad Trips. (Encyclopedia of Psychoactive Drugs Ser.: No. 2). (Illus.). 112p. (YA). (gr. 5 up). 1987. lib. bdg. 19.95 (*1-55546-218-9*) Chelsea Hse.

— Conversing with Stones. 64p. (C). 1989. 50.00 (*0-685-41002-1*, Pub. by Five Islands Pr AT) St Mut.

— Conversing with Stones. (C). 1990. 55.00 (*0-86418-085-3*, Pub. by Pascoe Pub AT) St Mut.

— Coyote Cafe. (Illus.). 160p. 1989. 25.95 (*0-89815-245-3*) Ten Speed Pr.

— Coyote's Cool Juice Drinks Book. 1995. pap. 16.95 (*0-89815-654-8*) Ten Speed Pr.

— Dear Old Roanoke: A Sesquacentennial Portrait. (Illus.). 1992. 35.00 (*0-86554-366-6*, H303) Mercer Univ Pr.

— Great Chile Postcard Book. 160p. 1994. pap. 8.95 (*0-89815-577-0*) Ten Speed Pr.

— The Great Salsa Book. 152p. 1994. pap. 14.95 (*0-89815-517-7*) Ten Speed Pr.

— Internetworking: A Guide to Network Communications LAN to LAN; LAN to WAN. 2nd ed. 550p. 1995. pap. 34.95 (*1-55851-436-8*) M&T Bks.

— Jazz in Canada: Fourteen Lives. LC 82-243184. 255p. reprint ed. pap. 72.70 (*0-317-27010-9*, 2023652) Bks Demand.

— LAN Troubleshooting Handbook. 2nd ed. (Orig.). 1993. pap. 34.95 (*1-55851-301-9*) M&T Bks.

— Managing Internetworks with SNMP. 1993. disk, pap. 44.95 (*1-55851-304-3*) M&T Bks.

— Mount Washington: Baltimore Suburb. (Illus.). 84p. (Orig.). pap. 8.95 (*0-939928-00-0*) GBS Pubs.

— Police Patrol Operations. LC 95-67382. 500p. 1995. pap. 29.95 (*0-942728-59-9*) Copperhouse.

Miller, Mark, ed. Curbing Waste in a Throwaway World: Report of the Task Force on Solid Waste Management. (Consensus for Change Ser.). 72p. (Orig.). 1990. pap. text ed. 15.00 (*1-55877-115-8*) Natl Governor.

— Directory of Governors of the American States, Commonwealths & Territories 1991. (Illus.). 76p. (Orig.). 1991. pap. text ed. 8.95 (*1-55877-083-6*) Natl Governor.

— Directory of Governors of the American States, Commonwealths & Territories 1992. (Illus.). 76p. (Orig.). 1992. pap. text ed. 8.95 (*1-55877-142-5*) Natl Governor.

— Fiscal Survey of the States, April 1992. 51p. (Orig.). 1992. pap. text ed. 20.00 (*1-55877-150-6*) Natl Governor.

— Governors' Staff Directory. 75p. (Orig.). 1988. 7.50 (*1-55877-005-4*) Natl Governor.

— Governors' Staff Directory. 80p. (Orig.). 1989. pap. 7.50 (*1-55877-063-1*) Natl Governor.

— Governors' Staff Directory. 80p. (Orig.). 1990. pap. 7.50 (*1-55877-108-5*) Natl Governor.

— Governors' Staff Directory. 80p. (Orig.). 1990. pap. text ed. 7.50 (*1-55877-124-7*) Natl Governor.

— Governors' Staff Directory. 80p. (Orig.). 1991. pap. text ed. 7.50 (*1-55877-091-7*) Natl Governor.

— Governors' Staff Directory. 80p. (Orig.). 1991. pap. text ed. 7.50 (*1-55877-133-6*) Natl Governor.

— Governors' Staff Directory, April 1992. 80p. (Orig.). 1992. pap. 7.50 (*1-55877-148-4*) Natl Governor.

— Kids in Trouble: Coordinating Social & Correctional Service Systems for Youth. 50p. (Orig.). 1991. pap. text ed. 15.00 (*1-55877-094-1*) Natl Governor.

— Policy Positions, 1990-91. 350p. (Orig.). 1990. pap. text ed. 15.00 (*1-55877-123-9*) Natl Governor.

— Policy Positions, 1991-92. 350p. (Orig.). 1991. pap. text ed. 15.00 (*1-55877-131-X*) Natl Governor.

— Report of the Task Force on Domestic Markets. (America in Transition, the International Frontier Ser.). 40p. (Orig.). 1989. pap. text ed. 10.95 (*1-55877-048-8*) Natl Governor.

— Report of the Task Force on Foreign Markets. (America in Transition, the International Frontier Ser.). 42p. (Orig.). 1989. pap. text ed. 10.95 (*1-55877-043-7*) Natl Governor.

— Report of the Task Force on Research & Technology. (America in Transition, the International Frontier Ser.). 40p. (Orig.). 1989. pap. text ed. 10.95 (*1-55877-046-1*) Natl Governor.

— Report of the Task Force on Transportation Infrastructure. (America in Transition, the International Frontier Ser.). 40p. 1989. pap. text ed. 10.95 (*1-55877-050-X*) Natl Governor.

— Results in Education: 1990. 80p. (Orig.). 1990. pap. text ed. 12.50 (*1-55877-080-1*) Natl Governor.

— A World of Difference: Report of the Task Force on Global Climate Change. (Consensus for Change Ser.). 50p. (Orig.). 1990. pap. text ed. 15.00 (*1-55877-113-1*) Natl Governor.

Miller, Mark & Feinstein, Gerry, eds. Building Information Partnerships: Conference Proceedings, Anchorage, Alaska, May 5-9, 1990. 285p. (Orig.). 1991. pap. text ed. 20.00 (*1-55877-135-2*) Natl Governor.

Miller, Mark & Glass, Karen, eds. Report of the Task Force on International Education. (America in Transition, the International Frontier Ser.). 40p. (Orig.). 1989. pap. text ed. 10.95 (*1-55877-038-0*) Natl Governor.

Miller, Mark & Kiffen, Mark. Coyote's Pantry. 128p. 1993. 25.95 (*0-89815-494-4*) Ten Speed Pr.

Miller, Mark, ed. see Breyel, Janine.

Miller, Mark, ed. see Clarke, Marianne K. & Dobson, Eric N.

Miller, Mark, jt. ed. see Feinstein, Gerry R.

Miller, Mark, jt. ed. see Feinstein, Gerry.

Miller, Mark, ed. see Forrer, John.

Miller, Mark, jt. ed. see Glass, Karen.

Miller, Mark, ed. see National Governors' Association Staff.

Miller, Mark, ed. see O'Donnell, Christine & Thompson, Paul.

Miller, Mark, ed. see Shields, Evelyn.

***Miller, Mark, et al.** Mark Miller's Indian Market: Recipes from Santa Fe's Famous Coyote Cafe. 144p. 1995. 27.95 (*0-89815-620-3*) Ten Speed Pr.

Miller, Mark A. Analyzing Broadband Networks: Frame Relay, SMDS & ATM. LC 94-32690. (Network Troubleshooting Library). 522p. 1994. pap. 44.95 (*1-55851-389-2*) M&T Bks.

— Christopher Lee & Peter Cushing & Horror Cinema: A Filmography of Their 22 Collaborations. 480p. 1994. lib. bdg. 45.00 (*0-89950-960-6*) McFarland & Co.

— Internetworking: A Guide to Network Communications LAN to LAN LAN to WAN. (Illus.). 350p. (Orig.). 1991. pap. 34.95 (*1-55851-143-1*) M&T Bks.

— LAN Protocol Handbook. (Illus.). 400p. (Orig.). 1990. pap. 34.95 (*1-55851-099-0*) M&T Bks.

— LAN Troubleshooting Handbook. (Illus.). 309p. (Orig.). 1989. pap. 29.95 (*1-55851-054-0*) M&T Bks.

— Troubleshooting Internetworks: Tools, Techniques, & Protocols. (Illus.). 350p. (Orig.). 1991. pap. 34.95 (*1-55851-236-5*) M&T Bks.

— Troubleshooting TCP - IP: Analyzing the Protocols of the Internet. 608p. (Orig.). 1992. pap. 44.95 (*1-55851-268-3*) M&T Bks.

Miller, Mark C. Boxed In: The Culture of TV. (Illus.). 349p. 1988. pap. 14.95 (*0-8101-0792-9*) Northwestern U Pr.

— The High Priests of American Politics: The Role of Lawyers in American Political Institutions. LC 95-4360. 1995. write for info. (*0-87049-902-5*) U of Tenn Pr.

— Living Ethically in Christ: Is Christian Ethics Unique? LC 93-48502. (American University Studies: Vol. 173). 1994. write for info. (*0-8204-2386-6*) P Lang Pubs.

— Spectacle: Operation Desert Storm & the Triumph of Illusion. 320p. 1993. 22.00 (*0-671-78504-4*) S&S Trade.

Miller, Mark C., ed. Seeing Through Movies. 266p. 1990. pap. 10.36 (*0-679-72367-6*) Pantheon.

***Miller, Mark D., et al, eds.** Review of Sports Medicine & Arthroscopy. LC 94-22156. (Illus.). 1995. pap. text ed. 49.00 (*0-7216-5281-6*) Saunders.

Miller, Mark J. Employer Sanctions in Western Europe. LC 86-31739. (CMS Occasional Papers & Documentation Ser.). 67p. 1987. 9.95 (*0-934733-20-1*) Ctr Migration.

— Foreign Workers in Western Europe: An Emerging Political Force. LC 81-5853. 252p. 1981. text ed. 59.95 (*0-275-90684-1*, C0684, Praeger Pubs) Greenwood.

— Quest for Control: A Quarter Century of Immigration Reform in Industrial Democracies, 1964-1989. 224p. (C). 1929. pap. text ed. 25.00 (*0-8133-1030-X*) Westview.

***Miller, Mark J. & Denemark, Robert A.** International Migration & Theories of World Politics: Assessments & Lessons from the Western European Case. 1994. 9.95 (*0-934733-76-7*) Ctr Migration.

Miller, Mark J., jt. auth. see Castles, Stephen.

***Miller, Mark R., ed.** Governors' Staff Directory, October 1992. 80p. (Orig.). 1992. pap. text ed. 7.50 (*1-55877-167-0*) Natl Governor.

— Managing the Policy Agendy: Organizational Options for Governors. 56p. (Orig.). 1992. pap. text ed. 17.95 (*1-55877-164-6*) Natl Governor.

Miller, Mark R., jt. auth. see Miller, Rex.

Miller, Mark S. The Physically Handicapped. (Medical Disorders & Their Treatment Ser.). (Illus.). (YA). (gr. 6-12). 1994. 19.95 (*0-7910-0073-7*, Am Art Analog); pap. write for info. (*0-7910-0500-3*, Am Art Analog) Chelsea Hse.

Miller, Marlane, jt. auth. see Cherry, David.

Miller, Marlene. Business Guide to Print Promotion. LC 87-83397. (Illus.). 224p. (Orig.). 1988. pap. 19.95 (*0-945372-03-5*) Iris Comn Grp.

Miller, Marlene, jt. auth. see Gorski, Terence T.

***Miller, Marlin E., ed.** The Church's Peace Witness. 216p. 1994. pap. text ed. 14.99 (*0-8028-0555-8*) Eerdmans.

Miller, Marlin E., tr. see Trocme, Andre.

Miller, Marlis & Galey, Denise. Administration & Operation of the College Union, No. 1. 3rd ed. 108p. 1988. pap. 60.00 (*0-317-93265-9*) Assn Coll Unions Intl.

Miller, Marshall L. Bulgaria During the Second World War. LC 74-82778. 304p. 1975. 37.50 (*0-8047-0870-3*) Stanford U Pr.

Miller-Marshall, Mary, jt. auth. see Thompson, Douglas.

Miller, Martha. Kidney Disorders. (Medical Disorders & Their Treatment Ser.). (Illus.). (J). (gr. 6-12). 1992. 18.95 (*0-7910-0066-4*) Chelsea Hse.

Miller, Martha J. Pathophysiology: Principles of Disease. (Illus.). 528p. 1983. text ed. 54.50 (*0-7216-6337-0*) Saunders.

***Miller, Martha L.** Politics & Verbal Play: The Ludic Poetry of Angel Gonzalez. 1995. write for info. (*0-8386-3552-0*) Fairleigh Dickinson.

Miller, Martin, ed. Miller's International Antiques Price Guide, 1993. (Illus.). 750p. 1992. 30.00 (*0-670-84500-0*, Viking Studio) Studio Bks.

Miller, Martin & Miller, Judith. Period Design & Furnishing: A Sourcebook for Home Restoration. (Illus.). 1989. 30.00 (*0-517-57156-0*, Crown) Crown Pub Group.

— Period Details: A Sourcebook for House Restoration. (Illus.). 192p. 1993. pap. 22.00 (*0-517-88013-X*, Crown) Crown Pub Group.

Miller, Martin, ed. see Bly, John.

Miller, Martin, ed. see Davidson, Richard.

Miller, Martin, ed. see Knowles, Eric.

Miller, Martin, ed. see Lang, Gordon.

Miller, Martin, jt. auth. see Miller, Judith.

Miller, Martin, jt. comp. see Miller, Judith.

Miller, Martin, jt. ed. see Miller, Judith.

Miller, Martin, ed. see Pearson, Sue.

Miller, Martin A. HBJ Miller Comprehensive GAAP Guide, 1991: College Edition. 1116p. (C). 1990. pap. text ed. 32.00 (*0-15-529499-7*) HB Coll Pubs.

— Miller Comprehensive GAAP Guide. (Miller Accounting Ser.). 1000p. 1988. pap. 50.00 (*0-15-601790-3*); pap. 35.00 (*0-15-601791-1*) HarBrace.

— Miller Comprehensive GAAP Guide, 1990. 1989. pap. 40.00 (*0-685-33321-3*) HarBrace.

— Miller Comprehensive GAAS Guide, 1990. 1989. pap. 40.00 (*0-685-33322-1*) HarBrace.

— The Russian Revolutionary Emigres, Eighteen Twenty-Five to Eighteen Seventy. LC 86-2715. (Studies in Historical & Political Science: 104th Series, No. 2). 320p. 1986. text ed. 45.00x (*0-8018-3303-5*) Johns Hopkins.

Miller, Martin A. & Bailey, Larry P. HBJ Miller Comprehensive GAAS Guide, 1991: College Edition. 1520p. (C). 1990. pap. text ed. 32.00 (*0-15-529500-4*) HB Coll Pubs.

— Miller Comprehensive GAAS Guide. (Miller Accounting Ser.). 1400p. 1988. pap. 55.00 (*0-15-601792-X*); pap. 40.00 (*0-15-601793-8*) HarBrace.

Miller, Martin A., jt. auth. see Bailey, Larry P.

Miller, Martin A., jt. auth. see Williams, Jan R.

Miller, Martin B. Dictionary of Electronic Packaging, Microelectronic, & Interconnection Term. 186p. 1990. 39.95 (*0-9625930-0-1*) Technology Seminars.

Miller, Martin B., jt. auth. see Harper, Charles A.

Miller, Martin R., jt. auth. see Miller, Rex.

Miller, Marv. Suicide after Sixty: The Final Alternative. LC 79-4246. (Death & Suicide Ser.: Vol. 2). 128p. 1979. pap. 16.95 (*0-8261-2781-9*) Springer Pub.

Miller, Marvin. Mad Scientist's Secret: Amazing Adventure Puzzle Thrillers. (J). (gr. 5-7). 1994. pap. 2.50 (*0-590-49438-4*) Scholastic Inc.

— Whole Different Ballgame: The Sport & Business of Baseball. 1991. 21.95 (*1-55972-067-0*, Birch Ln Pr) Carol Pub Group.

— You Be the Detective. (J). (gr. 4-7). 1991. pap. 2.50 (*0-590-42731-8*) Scholastic Inc.

— You Be the Detective, No. II. (J). 1992. 2.50 (*0-590-45690-3*) Scholastic Inc.

— You Be the Jury: Courtroom Four. (J). 1992. 2.50 (*0-590-45723-3*, 066) Scholastic Inc.

— You Be the Jury: Courtroom Three. 96p. (J). (gr. 4 up). 1992. pap. 2.50 (*0-590-45724-1*) Scholastic Inc.

— You Be the Jury: Courtroom Two. (J). 1992. pap. 2.50 (*0-590-45727-6*) Scholastic Inc.

— You Be the Jury: Courtroom Two. (J). (gr. 4-7). 1992. pap. 2.50 (*0-590-45725-X*) Scholastic Inc.

— Your Own Christmas Magic Show. (J). 1993. pap. 6.95 (*0-590-47558-4*) Scholastic Inc.

— Your Own Super Magic Show. (J). 1993. pap. 4.95 (*0-590-33044-6*) Scholastic Inc.

Miller, Marvin D. Wunderlich's Salute: The Interrelationship of the German-American Bund, Camp Siegfried, Yaphank, Long Island, & the Young Siegfrieds & Their Relationship with American & Nazi Institutions. LC 82-62515. (Illus.). 336p. 1983. pap. 13.95 (*0-9610466-0-0*) Malamud-Rose.

Miller, Marvin J., intro. Computer Applications Mental Health, 1991: Education & Evaluation. LC 92-1541. (Computers in Human Services Ser.: Vol. 8, Nos. 3-4). (Illus.). 200p. 1992. text ed. 39.95 (*1-56024-279-5*); pap. text ed. 19.95 (*1-56024-353-8*) Haworth Pr.

***Miller-Marx, Kim.** I Have a Friendly Smile. (Illus.). 33p. (J). (gr. k-3). 1994. pap. 9.99 (*0-9644265-0-1*) K Miller-Marx.

Miller, Mary. Gray Power. 275p. 1982. 12.50 (*0-913218-72-3*); pap. 6.95 (*0-913218-71-5*) Dustbooks.

— Tales of Topanga. 144p. (Orig.). 1994. pap. 9.95 (*1-56474-068-4*) Fithian Pr.

Miller, Mary & Miller, James. Communications Skills at the Keyboard. 94p. (Orig.). 1986. pap. text ed. 13.95 (*0-273-04236-X*) Trans-Atl Phila.

Miller, Mary, jt. auth. see Schele, Linda.

Miller, Mary A. Junior Showmanship from Hand to Lead: The Complete Handbook for Junior Handlers. LC 94-1099. 120p. (J). 1994. pap. 9.95 (*0-931866-66-9*) Alpine Pubns.

Miller, Mary B. & Charlip, Remy. Handtalk Birthday: A Number & Story Book in Sign Language. LC 91-1967. (Illus.). 48p. (J). (ps-3). 1991. reprint ed. pap. 4.95 (*0-689-71531-5*, Aladdin Paperbacks) S&S Childrens.

Miller, Mary B., jt. auth. see Ancona, George.

Miller, Mary B., jt. auth. see Charlip, Remy.

Miller, Mary Beth & Ancona, George. Handtalk School. LC 90-24030. (Illus.). 32p. (J). (gr. k-6). 1991. text ed. 14.95 (*0-02-700912-2*, Mac Bks Young Read) S&S Childrens.

Miller, Mary C. Devotions for Living with Loss. 1991. 7.95 (*0-910452-72-5*) Covenant.

Miller, Mary E. The Art of Mesoamerica. LC 85-51916. (World of Art Ser.). (Illus.). 1986. pap. 14.95 (*0-500-20203-6*) Thames Hudson.

Miller, Mary E. & Taube, Karl. The Gods & Symbols of Ancient Mexico & the Maya. LC 92-80338. (Illus.). 240p. 1993. 34.95 (*0-500-05068-6*) Thames Hudson.

Miller, Mary F. How to Get a Job with a Cruise Line: Adventure - Travel - Romance, How to Sail Around the World on Luxury Cruise Ships & Get Paid for It. 3rd ed. (Illus.). 224p. 1994. pap. 14.95 (*0-9624019-6-X*) Ticket Adventure.

— How to Get a Job with a Cruise Line: Adventure-Travel-Romance - How to Sail Around the World on Cruise Ships & Get Paid for It. rev. ed. Miller, Bill, ed. LC 90-46720. 160p. (Orig.). 1992. pap. 14.95 (*0-9624019-4-3*) Ticket Adventure.

Miller, Mary J. Fast Forward. 144p. (J). (gr. 3-7). 1993. 14.99 (*0-670-84339-3*) Viking Child Bks.

— Going the Distance. 160p. (J). (gr. 3-7). 1994. 14.99 (*0-670-84815-8*) Viking Child Bks.

— Me & My Name. LC 92-20302. 128p. (J). (gr. 5 up). 1992. pap. 3.99 (*0-14-034374-1*) Puffin Bks.

— Upside Down. 121p. (J). (gr. 3-7). 1994. pap. 3.99 (*0-14-034624-4*) Puffin Bks.

Miller, Mary K. Mathematics for Nurses with Clinical Applications. LC 80-26040. 390p. (Orig.). (C). 1981. pap. 39.95 (*0-8185-0429-3*) Brooks-Cole.

Miller, Mary R. Children of the Salt River. LC 76-45149. (Language Science Monographs: Vol. 16). 1977. pap. 11.00 (*0-87750-206-4*) Res Inst Inner Asian Studies.

Miller, Mary S. Save Our Schools: 66 Things You Can Do to Improve Your School Without Spending an Extra Penny. LC 92-56416. 1993. pap. 8.00 (*0-06-250733-8*) Harper SF.

— School Book: Everything Parents Should Know about Their Child's Education. 1991. pap. 14.95 (*0-312-05508-0*) St Martin.

Miller, Maryann. Careers Inside the World of Homemaking & Parenting. LC 94-19045. (Careers & Opportunities Ser.). (YA). (gr. 9 up). 1994. 14.95 (*0-8239-1901-3*) Rosen Group.

— Coping with a Bigoted Parent. (Coping Ser.). (YA). (gr. 7-12). 1992. lib. bdg. 15.95 (*0-8239-1345-7*) Rosen Group.

— Coping with Weapons & Violence in School & on Your Streets. Rosen, Ruth, ed. (Coping Ser.). (YA). (gr. 7-12). 1993. 15.95 (*0-8239-1435-6*) Rosen Group.

— Drugs & Date Rape. LC 94-37824. (Drug Abuse Prevention Library). (J). 1995. 15.95 (*0-8239-2064-X*) Rosen Group.

— Drugs & Gun Violence. LC 95-5910. (Drug Abuse Prevention Library). (J). 1995. write for info. (*0-8239-2060-7*) Rosen Group.

— Everything You Need to Know about Dealing With the Police. LC 94-18526. (Illus.). 64p. (YA). (gr. 7-12). 1995. 15.95 (*0-8239-1875-0*) Rosen Group.

— Working Together Against Gun Violence. LC 94-1021. (Library of Social Activism). (J). 1994. 14.95 (*0-8239-1779-7*) Rosen Group.

— Your Best Foot Forward: Winning Strategies for the Job Interview. LC 93-44347. (J). 1994. 13.95 (*0-8239-1697-9*) Rosen Group.

Miller, Marylees, jt. auth. see Miller, Irwin.

Miller, Maureen. The Formation of a Medieval Church: Ecclesiastical Change in Verona, 950-1150. LC 92-54971. (Illus.). 264p. 1993. 35.95 (*0-8014-2837-8*) Cornell U Pr.

Miller, Maurice. Hearing Aids. LC 72-190707. (Studies in Communicative Disorders). (C). 1972. pap. write for info. (*0-672-61284-4*, Bobbs) Macmillan.

Miller, Maurice H., jt. auth. see Armbruster, Joan M.

Miller, Max J. & Love, Edgar J., eds. Parasitic Diseases: Treatment & Control. 352p. 1989. 180.00 (*0-8493-4922-2*, RC119) CRC Pr.

Miller, Max J., et al. Diagnosis & Treatment of Prevalent Diseases of North American Indian Populations. (American Indian Health Ser.: Vol. 2). 250p. 1974. text ed. 24.50 (*0-8422-7216-X*) Irvington.

Miller, May. The Clearing & Beyond. LC 73-93070. 1974. 7.50 (*0-910350-08-6*) Charioteer.

— Collected Poems. LC 88-83172. 235p. (YA). (gr. 7-12). 1989. 18.00 (*0-916418-70-7*) Lotus.

— Dust of Uncertain Journey. LC 75-40977. 67p. (YA). (gr. 9-12). 1975. pap. 5.00 (*0-916418-05-7*) Lotus.

— Halfway to the Sun. LC 81-50427. (Series Six). (Illus.). 50p. (Orig.). (J). (gr. 6). 1981. pap. text ed. 7.00 (*0-931846-17-X*) Wash Writers Pub.

— Halfway to the Sun. (Illus.). 52p. (Orig.). (J). (gr. 2-5). 1988. reprint ed. pap. 5.00 (*0-916418-75-8*) Lotus.

— The Ransomed Wait. LC 82-83856. 77p. (YA). (gr. 9-12). 1983. per. 4.50 (*0-916418-40-5*) Lotus.

Miller, Maynard M. & Marston, Richard A., eds. Environment & Society in the Manaslu-Ganesh Region of the Central Nepal Himalaya. (UW Publications Ser.). (Illus.). 110p. 1989. pap. 10.00 (*0-941570-10-X*) U of Wyoming.

Miller-McLemore, Bonnie. Also a Mother: Work & Family As Theological Dilemma. LC 93-44713. 224p. (Orig.). 1994. pap. 15.95 (*0-687-11020-3*) Abingdon.

Miller-McLemore, Bonnie J. Death, Sin & the Moral Life. LC 87-28872. (American Academy of Religion Academy Ser.). 357p. 1988. 31.95 (*1-55540-202-X*, 01 01 59); pap. 20.95 (*1-55540-203-8*) Scholars Pr GA.

Miller, Melanie A. Birds: A Guide to the Literature. LC 85-45116. (Reference Library of the Humanities: Vol. 680). 912p. 1986. lib. bdg. 86.00 (*0-8240-8710-0*) Garland.

Miller, Melinda J. & Rachfalski, Jane. Rainbow Dancer: Positive Thought, Imagery & Exercise for Self-Esteem, Inner Peace & Caring for the Earth. Van Wert, Johanna, ed. LC 92-80720. (Illus.). 119p. (Orig.). 1991. pap. 19.95 (*0-9631046-0-8*) Rainbow Dancer.

Miller, Melissa. The Dog I.Q. Test: For Dogs & Their Owners. 192p. 1994. 7.95 (*0-14-024020-9*, Penguin Bks) Viking Penguin.

Miller, Melissa A. Family Violence: The Compassionate Church Responds. 184p. (Orig.). 1994. pap. 9.95 (*0-8361-3654-3*) Herald Pr.

Miller, Melvia. An Apple a Day. (Illus.). 1990. 9.95 (*0-685-45575-0*) Holistic Rsch Exch.

— A Picture Speaks a Thousand Words. pap. 25.00 (*0-685-74228-8*) Holistic Rsch Exch.

Miller, Melville D., Jr. & Goldhill, Nancy. You & the Law in New Jersey: A Resource Guide. 384p. 1988. text ed. 38.00 (*0-8135-1342-1*); pap. 14.95 (*0-8135-1343-X*) Rutgers U Pr.

Miller, Melvin D. Principles & a Philosophy For Vocational Education. 250p. 1985. 17.00 (*0-318-17790-0*, SN48) Ctr Educ Trng Employ.

Miller, Melvin E. & Cook-Greuter, Susanne, eds. Transcendence & Mature Thought in Adulthood: The Further Reaches of Adult Development. 300p. (C). 1994. lib. bdg. 54.50 (*0-8476-7918-7*); pap. text ed. 22.95 (*0-8476-7919-5*) Rowman.

Miller, Melvin R. That Woman I Married. 104p. 1986. pap. 3.95 (*0-88144-061-2*) Christian Pub.

Miller, Merle. Plain Speaking: An Oral Biography of Harry S. Truman. 480p. 1986. pap. 6.99 (*0-425-09499-5*) Berkley Pub.

Miller, Merle & Cogley, John. Blacklisting: Two Key Documents. LC 78-161171. (History of Broadcasting: Radio to Television Ser.). 1980. reprint ed. 35.95 (*0-405-03579-9*) Ayer.

Miller, Merlene. Recovery Education: A Guide for Teaching Chemically Dependent People. 1992. pap. 3.50 (*0-8309-0565-0*) Herald Hse.

Miller, Merlene & Gorski, Terence. Lowering the Risk: A Self-Care Plan for Relapse Prevention. 31p. 1991. pap. 3.00 (*0-8309-0609-6*) Herald Hse.

Miller, Merlene & Gorski, Terence T. Family Recovery: Growing Beyond Addiction. 1982. pap. 6.50 (*0-8309-0369-0*) Herald Hse.

Miller, Merlene & Miller, David. Reversing the Weight Gain Spiral: The Groundbreaking Program for Lifelong Weight Control. 352p. (Orig.). 1993. pap. 10.00 (*0-345-36984-X*, Ballantine Trade) Ballantine.

Miller, Merlene, jt. auth. see Gorski, Terence T.

Miller, Merlene, jt. auth. see Gorski, Terrence.

Miller, Merlene, et al. Learning to Live Again: A Guide for Recovery from Chemical Dependency. rev. ed. 1992. pap. text ed. 12.50 (*0-8309-0619-3*) Herald Hse.

Miller, Mertin, jt. ed. see Miller, Judith.

Miller, Merton H. Financial Innovations & Market Volatility. (Illus.). 288p. 1991. text ed. 34.95 (*1-55786-252-4*) Blackwell Pubs.

Miller, Merton H. & Upton, Charles W. Macroeconomics: A Neoclassical Introduction. LC 73-90598. xvi, 368p. (C). 1986. pap. text ed. 16.95 (*0-226-52623-2*) U Ch Pr.

Miller, Merton H., jt. auth. see Fama, Eugene F.

Miller, Merton L. A Preliminary Study of the Pueblo of Taos, New Mexico. LC 74-7992. reprint ed. 31.50 (*0-404-11879-8*) AMS Pr.

Miller, Mervyn. Raymond Unwin: Architect & Planner - A Biography. (Illus.). 240p. 1992. text ed. 59.00 (*0-7185-1363-0*, Pub. by Pinter Pubs UK) St Martin.

Miller, Miamon. How to Play Romanian Folk Violin. Fraenkel, Eran, ed. (Illus.). 31p. (Orig.). (C). 1990. student ed 20.00 (*0-9626468-0-6*) Fuge Imaginea.

Miller, Miamon, ed. see Apan, Valeria.

Miller, Miamon, ed. see Saunders, Lawrence.

Miller, Michael. Dare to Live: A Guide to the Prevention & Understanding of Teenage Suicide & Depression. (YA). (gr. 7-12). 1989. pap. 9.95 (*0-941831-22-1*) Beyond Words Pub.

— Development of the Central Nervous System: Effects of Alcohol & Opiates. 360p. 1991. text ed. 159.95 (*0-471-56125-8*, Wiley-Liss) Wiley.

— Jackhammer. deluxe limited ed. 16p. 1972. pap. 10.00 (*0-914496-01-8*) Helikon NY.

— Managing an Inherited NetWare Network. 1995. 34.99 (*0-7821-1745-7*) Sybex.

— Ten Minute Guide to Norton Desktop for Windows. 1992. pap. 10.95 (*1-56761-025-0*) Alpha Bks IN.

— Therapeutic Hypnosis. LC 78-10405. 368p. 1979. 45.95 (*0-87705-341-3*) Human Sci Pr.

— What Are They Saying about Papal Primacy? (What Are They Saying about...Ser.). 128p. 1983. pap. 4.95 (*0-8091-2501-3*) Paulist Pr.

Miller, Michael A. Introduction to Digital & Data Communications. Conty, ed. 435p. (C). 1992. text ed. 67.50 (*0-314-93371-9*) West Pub.

Miller, Michael B. The Bon Marche: Bourgeois Culture & the Department Store. LC 80-36797. (Illus.). 295p. reprint ed. pap. 84.10 (*0-8357-8819-9*, 2032650) Bks Demand.

— Bon Marche: Bourgeois Culture & the Department Store, 1869-1920. (C). 1994. pap. 15.95 (*0-691-03494-X*) Princeton U Pr.

— A Physicians Guide to History & Physical Examination. 125p. (C). 1994. text ed. 40.00 (*0-9645229-0-X*); pap. text ed. 35.00 (*0-9645229-1-8*) MBM Pubns.

— Shanghai on the Metro: Spies, Intrigue, & the French Between the Wars. LC 93-34114. (C). 1994. 35.00 (*0-520-08519-1*) U CA Pr.

Miller, Michael B., ed. see Miller, Lynn M.

Miller, Michael D. Marine War Risks. 2nd ed. 369p. 1994. 150.00 (*1-85044-255-X*) Lloyds London Pr.

Miller, Michael F. Classical Greek & Roman Coins: The Investor's Handbook. LC 81-69260. (Illus.). 224p. 1982. 17.95 (*0-9607106-0-4*) Altara Group.

Miller, Michael J., jt. ed. see Flug, Phyllis O.

Miller, Michael J., et al, eds. Satellite Communications: Mobile & Fixed Services. LC 93-10183. (International Series in Engineering & Computer Science, VLSI, Computer Architecture, & Digital Screen Processing). 432p. (C). 1993. lib. bdg. 97.50 (*0-7923-9333-3*) Kluwer Ac.

Miller, Michael L. Absolute Beginner's Guide to Memory Management. 300p. 1993. disk, pap. 16.95 (*0-672-30282-9*) Sams.

— Oops! Excel: What To Do When Things Go Wrong. (Illus.). 300p. (Orig.). 1993. pap. 16.95 (*1-56529-169-7*) Que.

— Oops! What to Do When Things Go Wrong. (Illus.). 300p. (Orig.). 1992. pap. 14.95 (*1-56529-114-X*) Que.

— Oops! Windows: What To Do When Things Go Wrong. (Illus.). 320p. (Orig.). 1993. pap. 16.95 (*1-56529-180-8*) Que.

— Ten Minute Guide to Excel 4 Windows. 1992. pap. 10.95 (*0-672-30126-1*) Sams.

Miller, Michael L., jt. auth. see Dorpat, Theodore L.

Miller, Michael M. North Dakota Centennial Newspaper Index. 130p. 1991. write for info. (*0-9629777-0-5*) ND State Univ.

— Researching the Germans from Russia: An Annotated Bibliography of the "Germans from Russia Heritage Collection" LC 86-61716. 224p. 1987. 20.00 (*0-911042-34-2*) N Dak Inst.

Miller, Michael O. & Sales, Bruce D. The Law & Mental Health Professionals: Arizona. LC 86-10780. 367p. (Orig.). 1986. boxed 39.95 (*0-912704-50-0*) Am Psychol.

***Miller, Michael S. & Tiley, Larry P.** Manual of Canine & Feline Cardiology. 2nd ed. (Illus.). 528p. 1994. text ed. 55.00 (*0-7216-5940-3*) Saunders.

Miller, Michael T. Vagabond. 224p. 1990. 15.95 (*0-930545-11-7*) Maple Hill Pr.

— Vagabond. Teasley, Jamie, ed. LC 89-51801. 357p. 1990. pap. 15.95 (*1-55523-289-2*) Winston-Derek.

***Miller, Michael V.** Intimate Terrorism: The Deterioration of Erotic Life. LC 94-41704. 250p. 1995. 23.00 (*0-393-03759-2*) Norton.

Miller, Michele G. & Brantley, Clarice P. Basics of English. LC 92-16384. 1993. pap. 16.95 (*0-538-70559-0*) S-W Pub.

Miller, Michele G., jt. auth. see Brantley, Clarice P.

Miller, Michelle. Hunger in the First Person Singular: Stories of Desire & Power. LC 92-72299. (Illus.). 176p. (Orig.). 1993. pap. 9.00 (*0-938513-15-X*) Amador Pubs.

Miller, Michelle A., jt. auth. see Miller, Thomas I.

***Miller, Mike.** Easy Internet. 1994. disk, pap. 24.99 (*0-7897-0012-3*) Que.

— Oops. 3rd ed. 1994. pap. 19.99 (*1-56529-918-3*) Que.

— Oops! What to Do When Things Go Wrong. 2nd ed. (Illus.). 320p. (Orig.). 1993. pap. 16.95 (*1-56529-446-7*) Que.

— Using Norton Desktop 3 for Windows: Special Edition. 1993. pap. 27.95 (*1-56529-586-2*) Que.

— Using Prodigy. (Illus.). 384p. (Orig.). 1995. pap. 19.99 (*0-7897-0323-8*) Que.

— You're on the Air with Mike Miller. LC 74-78647. (Illus.). 155p. (Orig.). 1975. pap. 3.95 (*0-88435-001-0*) Chateau Pub.

Miller, Mike & Ackland, Laura. Oops! Wordperfect 6 for Windows. (Illus.). 320p. (Orig.). 1993. pap. 16.95 (*1-56529-460-2*) Que.

Miller, Mike & O'Hara, Shelley. Real Men Use DOS. 1992. pap. 16.95 (*1-56529-019-4*) Que.

***Miller, Mike & Que Staff.** Using CompuServe. 2nd ed. (Illus.). 400p. 1995. pap. 19.99 (*0-7897-0079-4*) Que.

Miller, Mike, jt. auth. see Weingarten, John.

Miller, Mildred B. & Snyder, Bascha G. Kosher Gourmet Cookbook. LC 94-1531. (Illus.). 320p. 1994. reprint ed. pap. 7.95 (*0-486-28155-8*) Dover.

Miller, Millie. Kinnikinnick: Rocky Mountain Flowers. (Pocket Nature Guides Ser.). 1980. pap. 5.95 (*0-933472-09-9*) Johnson Bks.

— Saguaro: Southwest Desert Flowers. (Pocket Nature Guides Ser.). (Illus.). (Orig.). 1982. pap. 5.95 (*0-933472-69-2*) Johnson Bks.

— Sierra: Sierra Mountain Flowers. (Pocket Nature Guides Ser.). (Illus.). 40p. (Orig.). 1981. pap. 5.95 (*0-933472-57-9*) Johnson Bks.

Miller, Millie & Nelson, Cyndi. Chanterelle: A Rocky Mountain Mushroom Book. (Pocket Nature Guides Ser.). (Illus.). 1986. pap. 5.95 (*0-933472-97-8*) Johnson Bks.

— Early Bird: Eastern Backyard Birds. (Illus.). (Orig.). 1990. pap. 5.95 (*1-55566-066-5*) Johnson Bks.

— Early Bird: Western Backyard Birds. (Illus.). (Orig.). 1991. pap. 5.95 (*1-55566-075-4*) Johnson Bks.

— Hummers: Hummingbirds of North America. (Pocket Nature Guides Ser.). (Illus.). 1987. pap. 5.95 (*1-55566-012-6*) Johnson Bks.

— Hummers: The Postcard Collection. (Illus.). 20p. 1992. 7.95 (*1-55566-092-4*) Johnson Bks.

— Painted Ladies: Butterflies of North America. (Illus.). 64p. (Orig.). 1993. pap. 5.95 (*1-55566-103-3*) Johnson Bks.

— Talons: North American Birds of Prey. (Pocket Nature Guides Ser.). (Illus.). 1989. pap. 5.95 (*1-55566-035-5*) Johnson Bks.

***Miller, Mina, ed.** The Nielsen Companion. (Illus.). 400p. 1995. 49.95 (*1-57467-004-2*, Amadeus Pr); pap. 24.95 (*1-57467-005-0*, Amadeus Pr) Timber.

Miller, Minnie T. Grandma's Tiny Kitty. 130p. (J). (gr. k-3). 1975. 5.95 (*0-87881-014-5*) Mojave Bks.

— Why the March Hare Went Mad & Other Stories. 55p. (J). (gr. k-4). 1972. 5.00 (*0-87881-002-1*) Mojave Bks.

An Asterisk (*) at the beginning of an entry indicates that the title is appearing in BIP for the first time.

Miller, Miranda. A Thousand & One Coffee Mornings: Scenes from Saudi Arabia. LC 89-81667. 142p. 1990. 28.00 (*0-7206-0761-2*, Pub. by P Owen Ltd UK) Dufour.

Miller, Miriam. A History of the Early Years of the Roman Catholic Diocese of Charlotte. LC 84-9645. (Illus.). 208p. 1984. 20.95 (*0-9624488-1-8*) Laney-Smith.

Miller, Miriam Y. & Chance, Jane, eds. Approaches to Teaching Sir Gawain & the Green Knight. LC 85-21548. (Approaches to Teaching World Literature Ser.: No. 9). xii, 256p. 1986. 37.50 (*0-87352-491-8*, AP09C); pap. text ed. 18.00x (*0-87352-492-6*, AP09P) Modern Lang.

Miller, Mitch, jt. auth. see Waldemar, Carla.

Miller, Mitchell H., Jr. Plato's "Parmenides" The "Conversion" of the Soul. LC 85-43301. 264p. 1986. 49.50 (*0-691-07303-1*) Princeton U Pr.

— Plato's Parmenides: The Conversion of the Soul. 314p. 1991. pap. 14.95 (*0-271-00803-2*) Pa St U Pr.

Miller, Mitchell W., jt. auth. see Cohen, Arnold B.

Miller, Moira. Oscar Mouse Finds a Home. (J). (ps-3). 1992. pap. 4.99 (*0-14-054682-0*) Viking Child Bks.

Miller, Molly, jt. auth. see Lawless, Jo.

Miller, Molly M. & Benson, Eric. LISP: Style & Design. (Illus.). 214p. (Orig.). (C). 1990. pap. 26.95 (*1-55558-044-0*, EY-C199E-DP, Digital DEC) Buttrwrth-Heinemann.

Miller, Monica M. Sexuality & Authority in the Catholic Church. LC 92-63037. 1994. write for info. (*0-940866-24-2*) U Scranton Pr.

Miller, Morris. Debt & Environment: Converging Crises. 260p. 1991. pap. 19.95 (*92-1-100457-8*) UN.

Miller, Morris & Janis, Arthur. Modern Bookkeeping & Accounting. 2nd ed. LC 72-109961. (gr. 10-12). 1973. teacher ed 8.48 (*0-02-830820-4*); text ed. 19.96 (*0-02-830790-9*); 48.76 (*0-02-830830-1*) Glencoe.

— Modern Bookkeeping & Accounting, Wkbk. I, Units 1-26. 2nd ed. LC 72-109961. (gr. 10-12). 1973. Workbook I (units 1-26). student ed 8.32 (*0-02-830800-X*) Glencoe.

— Modern Bookkeeping & Accounting, Wkbk. II, Units 27-45. 2nd ed. LC 72-109961. (gr. 10-12). 1973. Workbook II (units 27-45). student ed 8.32 (*0-02-830810-7*) Glencoe.

Miller, Morris E., jt. auth. see Fahner, Hal.

Miller, Morton A. Reading & Writing Short Essays. 3rd ed. 416p. (C). 1986. pap. text ed. write for info. (*0-07-554763-5*) McGraw.

— Reading & Writing Short Essays. 3rd ed. 405p. 1986. pap. text ed. write for info. (*0-318-55406-2*) Random.

Miller, Moshe, tr. Tomer Devorah. 1993. 12.95 (*0-944070-99-X*) Targum Pr.

— Tzipisa Leyeshua. 1993. 19.95 (*0-944070-97-3*) Feldheim.

Miller, Moshe, tr. see Cordevero, Moshe.

Miller, Moshe, tr. see Cordovero, Moshe.

Miller, Moshe L., tr. see Steinberg, Shalom D.

Miller, N. Single Parents by Choice: A Growing Trend in Family Life. (Illus.). 220p. (C). 1992. 24.95 (*0-306-44321-X*, Plenum Insight) Plenum.

Miller, N. Edd & Boyd, Stephen D. Public Speaking: A Practical Handbook. 136p. 1989. 9.95 (*0-89917-510-4*) Tichenor Pub.

Miller, N. G., ed. Advances in Bryology, Vol. 4: Bryophyte Systematics. (Illus.). 264p. 1991. pap. 112.00 (*3-443-52002-2*, Pub. by Cramer-Borntraeger GW) Lubrecht & Cramer.

Miller, N. S. The Pharmacology of Alcohol & Drugs of Abuse & Addiction. (Illus.). 312p. 1990. 76.00 (*0-387-97383-4*) Spr-Verlag.

Miller, N. S. & Gold, M. S. Alcohol. LC 91-2391. (Drugs of Abuse: A Comprehensive Series for Clinicians: Vol. 2). (Illus.). 260p. 1991. 37.50 (*0-306-43641-8*, Plenum Med Bk) Plenum.

Miller, Nadine. Iron & Lace. 224p. (Orig.). 1992. pap. 2.95 (*1-56597-030-6*, Kismet) Meteor Pub.

Miller, Nancy. Subject to Change: Women's Writing--Feminist Reading. (Gender & Culture Ser.). 185p. 1989. text ed. 41.00 (*0-231-06660-0*); pap. text ed. 16.00 (*0-231-06661-9*) Col U Pr.

Miller, Nancy, ed. see Chase, Harold S.

Miller, Nancy, jt. auth. see Rounds, Michael F.

Miller, Nancy B. Nobody's Perfect: Living & Growing with Children Who Have Special Needs. (Illus.). 272p. (Orig.). 1993. pap. 21.00 (*1-55766-143-X*) P H Brookes.

Miller, Nancy B., jt. auth. see Falk, R. Frank.

Miller, Nancy E. File Structures: With Ada. Apt, Alan, ed. (Illus.). 600p. (C). 1990. teacher ed 10.75 (*0-8053-0442-8*); teacher ed write for info. (*0-318-63300-0*); text ed. 51.75 (*0-8053-0440-1*); disk write for info. (*0-8053-0441-X*) Benjamin-Cummings.

— File Structures Using Pascal. 487p. 1987. teacher ed 10.75 (*0-8053-7083-8*) Benjamin-Cummings.

— File Structures Using Pascal. 487p. (C). 1987. text ed. 50.50 (*0-8053-7082-X*) Benjamin-Cummings.

Miller, Nancy E. & Cohen, Gene D., eds. Clinical Aspects of Alzheimer's Disease & Senile Dementia. (Aging Ser.: Vol. 15). 372p. 1981. text ed. 103.00 (*0-89004-326-4*) Raven.

— Schizophrenia & Aging: Schizophrenia, Paranoia, & Schizophreniform Disorders in Later Life. LC 87-14852. (Guilford Psychiatry Ser.). 367p. 1987. lib. bdg. 47.50 (*0-89862-228-X*) Guilford Pr.

Miller, Nancy E., jt. auth. see Petersen, Charles G.

Miller, Nancy E., et al, eds. Psychodynamic Treatment Research: A Handbook for Clinical Practice. LC 92-57904. 624p. 1993. text ed. 60.00 (*0-465-02877-2*) Basic.

***Miller, Nancy H. & Taylor, Craig B.** Lifestyle Management for Patients with Coronary Heart Disease. LC 95-177. (Current Issues in Cardiac Rehabilitation Ser.: No. 2). 128p. (Orig.). 1995. pap. text ed. write for info. (*0-87322-441-8*, BHOU0441) Human Kinetics.

Miller, Nancy K. French Dressing: Women, Men, & Ancient Regime Fiction. LC 94-16714. 1994. pap. 16.95 (*0-415-90322-X*, A4597, Routledge NY) Routledge.

— French Dressing: Women, Men, & Ancient Regime Fiction. LC 94-16707. 1995. 55.00 (*0-415-90321-1*, A4593, Routledge NY) Routledge.

— Getting Personal: Feminist Occasions & Other Autobiographical Acts. 224p. 1991. 39.95 (*0-415-90323-8*, A4600, Routledge NY); pap. 13.95 (*0-415-90324-6*, A4604, Routledge NY) Routledge.

— The Heroine's Text: Readings in the French & English Novel, 1722-1782. LC 79-28473. 1980. text ed. 37.50 (*0-231-04910-2*) Col U Pr.

Miller, Nancy K., ed. & intro. The Poetics of Gender. LC 85-29904. (Gender & Culture Ser.). 272p. 1987. text ed. 42.00 (*0-231-06310-5*); pap. text ed. 15.50 (*0-231-06311-3*) Col U Pr.

Miller, Nancy K., ed. see Awkward, Michael.

Miller, Nancy K., jt. ed. see DeJean, Joan.

Miller, Nancy K., jt. ed. see Heilbrun, Carolyn G.

Miller, Nancy K., jt. ed. see Heilbrun, Carolyn G.

Miller, Nancy K., ed. see Schor, Naomi.

Miller, Nancy K., ed. see Sedgwick, Eve K.

Miller, Naomi. Renaissance Bologna: A Study in Architectural Form & Content. (University of Kansas Humanistic Studies). 218p. (C). 1989. text ed. 39.95 (*0-8204-0885-9*) P Lang Pubs.

Miller, Naomi, ed. see Morgan, Keith.

Miller, Naomi F. & Gleason, Kathryn L., eds. The Archaeology of Garden & Field. (Illus.). 248p. (C). 1994. text ed. 28.95 (*0-8122-3244-5*) U of Pa Pr.

Miller, Naomi J. & Waller, Gary, eds. Reading Mary Wroth: Representing Alternatives in Early Modern England. LC 91-390. 256p. (C). 1991. 42.00x (*0-87049-709-X*); pap. text ed. 20.00x (*0-87049-710-3*) U of Tenn Pr.

Miller, Natalie. The Statue of Liberty. LC 91-44647. (Cornerstones of Freedom Ser.). (Illus.). 32p. (J). (gr. 3-6). 1992. lib. bdg. 12.30 (*0-516-06655-2*) Childrens.

— The Statue of Liberty. LC 91-44647. (Cornerstones of Freedom Ser.). (Illus.). 32p. (J). (gr. 3-6). 1993. pap. 3.95 (*0-516-46655-0*) Childrens.

— Story of the Star-Spangled Banner. LC 65-1221. (Cornerstones of Freedom Bks.). (Illus.). (J). (gr. 2-5). 1965. pap. 3.95 (*0-516-44636-3*) Childrens.

Miller, Nathan. FDR: An Intimate History. 576p. 1991. reprint ed. pap. 16.95 (*0-8191-8061-0*) Madison Bks UPA.

— The Naval Air War. 1982. pap. 2.95 (*0-89083-942-5*) Zebra.

— The Naval Air War, Nineteen Thirty-Nine to Nineteen Forty-Five. 21.95 (*0-405-13277-8*) Ayer.

— The Naval Air War, 1939-1945. LC 90-49699. (Illus.). 256p. 1991. 25.95 (*1-55750-564-0*) Naval Inst Pr.

— Sea of Glory: A Naval History of the American Revolution. (Illus.). 558p. 1992. reprint ed. 36.95 (*1-55750-577-2*) Naval Inst Pr.

— Stealing from America: A History of Corruption from Jamestown to Whitewater. 2nd ed. 450p. 1995. pap. 13.95 (*1-56924-820-6*) Marlowe & Co.

— Theodore Roosevelt: A Life. 1994. pap. 15.00 (*0-688-13220-0*, Quill) Morrow.

— The U. S. Navy: A History. rev. ed. LC 89-49709. 384p. 1990. reprint ed. pap. 10.95 (*0-688-08243-2*, Quill) Morrow.

Miller, Nathan, ed. see Loftus, John.

Miller, Neal E. & Dollard, John. Social Learning & Imitation. LC 78-23728. (Illus.). 341p. 1979. reprint ed. text ed. 35.00 (*0-313-20714-3*, MISL, Greenwood Pr) Greenwood.

Miller, Ned. Emmett's Snowball. LC 89-77787. (Illus.). 40p. (J). (ps-2). 1990. 14.95 (*0-8050-1394-6*, Bks Young Read) H Holt & Co.

Miller, Ned, ed. see Clarke, Richard.

Miller, Neil. Conversation in Portuguese: Points of Departure. 2nd rev. ed. LC 80-83025. (Illus.). 1980. pap. text ed. 7.95 (*0-9601444-2-0*) N Miller.

— Gay Life. 1992. write for info. (*0-679-41241-7*) McKay.

— Out in the World: Gay & Lesbian Life from Buenos Aires to Bangkok. LC 93-1300. (Vintage Departures Ser.). 1993. pap. 13.00 (*0-679-74551-3*, Vin) Random.

— Out of the Past: Gay & Lesbian History from 1869 to the Present. LC 94-10739. 1995. 16.00 (*0-679-74988-8*, Vin) Random.

— Walsh & Hoyt's Clinical Neuro-Ophthalmology, Vol. 1. 4th ed. (Illus.). 382p. 1982. lib. bdg. 115.00 (*0-683-06020-1*) Williams & Wilkins.

Miller, Neil, ed. Walsh & Hoyt's Clinical Neuro-Opthalmology, Vol. 3. 4th ed. 734p. 1988. 140.00 (*0-683-06022-8*) Williams & Wilkins.

Miller, Neil R. Walsh & Hoyt's Clinical Neuro-Ophthalmology, Vol. 5. 195.00 (*0-683-06024-4*) Williams & Wilkins.

— Walsh & Hoyt's Clinical Neuro-Ophthalmology, Vol. 4: Vascular Disease. 4th ed. (Illus.). 947p. 1991. 170.00 (*0-683-06023-6*) Williams & Wilkins.

— Walsh & Hoyt's Clinical Neuro-Opthalmology, Vol. 2. 4th ed. (Illus.). 750p. 1985. 135.00 (*0-683-06021-X*) Williams & Wilkins.

***Miller, Neil Z.** Vaccine Roulette: Gambling with Your Child's Life. 32p. (Orig.). 1995. pap. 5.95 (*1-881217-09-4*) New Atlantean.

— Vaccine Seminar: Critical Data for New Parents & Health Practitioners. 40p. (Orig.). 1995. pap. 6.95 (*1-881217-08-6*) New Atlantean.

— Vaccines - Are They Really Safe & Effective? A Parent's Guide to Childhood Shots. (Illus.). 80p. 1992. pap. 7.95 (*1-881217-10-8*) New Atlantean.

Miller, Nelson J., ed. International Conference on Aircraft Damage Assessment & Repair. (Illus.). 274p. (Orig.). 1991. pap. 62.50 (*0-85825-537-5*) Accents Pubns.

Miller, Newton W. & Navarre, Monty, eds. The Airguide Manual. 2nd ed. 1207p. 1987. pap. write for info. (*0-934754-01-2*) Airguide Pubns.

Miller, Nicholas R. Committees, Agendas, & Voting. LC 94-6282. (Fundamentals of Pure & Applied Economics Ser.). 1995. pap. text ed. 23.00 (*3-7186-5569-1*) Gordon & Breach.

Miller, Nick, jt. ed. see Stott, John.

Miller, Nicola. Soviet Relations with Latin America, 1959-1987. (Cambridge Soviet Paperbacks Ser.: No. 1). (Illus.). (C). 1990. pap. 16.95 (*0-521-35979-1*) Cambridge U Pr.

Miller, Nicola, jt. ed. see Biriotti, Maurice.

Miller, Nina. Heart of Hulda: A Biography. (Illus.). 142p. (Orig.). reprint ed. pap. 12.95 (*0-940151-07-3*) Statesman Exam.

Miller, Norbert & Salaquarda, Jorg, eds. Nietzsche - Briefweshsel, Kritische Gesamtausgabe: I, Abtielung, Vierter Band Nachbericht Zu Abteilung I: Briefe Von und An Friedrich Nietzsche Oktober 1849-April 1869. viii, 960p. (GER.). 1993. lib. bdg. 276.95 (*3-11-012277-4*) De Gruyter.

Miller, Norma. Tacitus: Annals XIV: A Companion to the Penguin Translation. 58p. 1987. 11.95 (*0-86292-238-0*, Pub. by Brstl Class Pr UK) Focus Info Gr.

Miller, Norma, intro. Plays & Fragments: Menander. 274p. 1988. mass mkt. 9.95 (*0-14-044501-3*, Penguin Classics) Viking Penguin.

***Miller, Norma L., ed.** The Healthy School Handbook: Conquering the Sick Building Syndrome & Other Environmental Hazards in & around Your School. LC 95-6345. 1995. write for info. (*0-8106-1863-X*, NEA Prof Lib) NEA.

Miller, Norma R., jt. auth. see Feingold, S. Norman.

***Miller, Norman.** IceSpy. 256p. 1995. 21.95 (*0-8338-0224-0*) M Jones.

Miller, Norman, ed. AIDS in Africa: The Social Impact & Policy Issues. LC 88-12750. (Studies in African Health & Medicine: Vol. 1). 350p. 1989. lib. bdg. 99.95 (*0-88946-187-2*) E Mellen.

***Miller, Norman, et al, eds.** Principles of Addiction Medicine: ASAM Review Course Syllabus. 1000p. 1994. 140.00 (*1-880425-02-5*) Am Soc Addict Med.

Miller, Norman & Brewer, Marilynn B. Groups in Contact: The Psychology of Desegregation. LC 83-9185. 316p. 1984. text ed. 54.00 (*0-12-497780-4*) Acad Pr.

Miller, Norman & Yeager, Rodger. Kenya: The Quest for Prosperity. 2nd ed. (Profiles - Nations of Contemporary Africa Ser.). 254p. 1993. text ed. 62.00 (*0-8133-8201-7*) Westview.

— Kenya: The Quest for Prosperity. 2nd ed. (Profiles - Nations of Contemporary Africa Ser.). 254p. (C). 1993. pap. text ed. 19.95 (*0-8133-8202-5*) Westview.

Miller, Norman, jt. ed. see Hertz-Lazarowitz, Rachel.

Miller, Norman C. Garcia Lorca's Poema del Cante Jondo. (Series A: Monagrafias, LXV). 226p. (C). 1978. 45.00 (*0-7293-0048-X*, Pub. by Tamesis Bks Ltd UK) Boydell & Brewer.

Miller, Norman E., ed. High Density Lipoproteins & Arteriosclerosis II: Proceedings of the Second International Workshop, Maidstone, UK, 6-8 Oct., 1988. (International Congress Ser.: No. 826). 340p. 1989. 102.75 (*0-444-81087-0*, Excerpta Medica) Elsevier.

Miller, Norman E. & Lewis, B., eds. Lipoproteins, Atherosclerosis & Coronary Heart Disease. (Metabolic Aspects of Cardiovascular Disease Ser.: Vol. 1). 214p. 1981. 53.50 (*0-444-80265-7*) Elsevier.

Miller, Norman E. & Miller, G. J. Clinical & Metabolic Aspects of High-Density Lipoproteins. (Metabolic Aspects of Cardiovascular Disease Ser.: Vol. 3). 1985. 206.25 (*0-444-80596-6*) Elsevier.

Miller, Norman E. & Tall, Alan R., eds. High Density Lipoproteins & Atherosclerosis III: Proceedings of the 3rd International Symposium on Plasma High Density Lipoproteins & Atherosclerosis, San Antonio, 4-6 March 1992. LC 92-49651. (International Congress Ser.: No. 1001). 1992. write for info. (*0-444-81442-6*, Excerpta Medica) Elsevier.

Miller, Norman E., jt. auth. see Richter-Heinrich, E.

Miller, Norman G. & Goebel, Paul R. The Buyer, Seller & Broker's Guide to Creative Home Finance. (Illus.). 464p. 1986. 14.95 (*0-13-109413-0*) P-H.

— Handbook of Mortgage Mathematics & Financial Tables. 2nd ed. 412p. 1989. pap. 26.67 (*0-13-380460-7*) P-H.

Miller, Norman G., jt. auth. see Goebel, Paul R.

Miller, Norman M. & Cave, Hugh B. I Took the Sky Road. LC 79-21830. reprint ed. 19.95 (*0-89201-089-4*) Zenger Pub.

Miller, Norman N., jt. auth. see Yeager, Rodger.

***Miller, Norman S.** Current Diagnosis & Treatment in Addiction Psychiatry. LC 94-32386. 1995. text ed. 54.95 (*0-471-56201-7*) Wiley.

Miller, Norman S., ed. Comprehensive Handbook of Drug & Alcohol Addiction. 1360p. 1991. 99.75 (*0-8247-8474-X*) Dekker.

***Miller, Norman S., ed. & intro.** Treating Alcohol & Drug Addictions: Methods & Outcomes for the Nineties. LC 94-22157. (Alcoholism Treatment Quarterly Ser.: Vol. 12, No. 2). (Illus.). 135p. 1994. lib. bdg. 39.95 (*1-56024-686-3*) Haworth Pr.

Miller, Norman S., ed. Treating Coexisting Psychiatric & Addictive Disorders: A Practical Guide. LC 94-4696. 1994. 24.95 (*0-89486-972-8*, 1499) Hazelden.

***Miller, Norman S., intro.** Treating Alcohol & Drug Addictions: Methods & Outcomes for the Nineties. LC 94-22157. (Alcoholism Treatment Quarterly Ser.: Vol. 12, No. 2). (Illus.). 135p. 1994. pap. 12.95 (*1-56023-064-9*) Haworth Pr.

***Miller, Norman S. & Gold, Mark S., eds.** Pharmacological Therapies for Drug & Alcohol Addictions. LC 94-3755. 1994. 150.00 (*0-8247-8979-2*) Dekker.

Miller, Norton G., ed. Advances in Bryology: Publication of the International Association of Bryologists. (Bryophyte Ultrastructure Ser.: Vol. 3). 281p. 1989. text ed. 80.00 (*3-443-52001-4*, Pub. by Gebrueder Borntraeger GW) Lubrecht & Cramer.

Miller, Nyle H. & Snell, Joseph W. Great Gunfighters of the Kansas Cowtowns, 1867-1886. LC 63-63480. (Illus.). vi, 494p. 1967. pap. 14.00 (*0-8032-5137-8*) U of Nebr Pr.

***Miller, O. Victor. One Man's Junk. George, Roberta & Phillips, Nancy, eds. 159p. (Orig.). 1995. pap. 10.00 (*0-9638364-1-2*) Snake Nation. Victor Miller draws on his 20 plus years of experience as a war veteran & a Georgia black-water diver to write a book about one man's experiences. Clyde Edgerton says: "As with the very best writers, Miller puts you so squarely into the action of his stories that you forget they are written. You are there. ONE MAN'S JUNK was this man's pleasure." Mary Hood says: "I read these stories with a blend of pity & terror--the true signs of wonder in art. Mr. Miller goes places the rest of us only suspect, cannot bear to experience for ourselves, & yet are only too glad to read about in headlines." Janice Daugharty says: "Vic Miller is one of the most innovative, intuitive Southern writers since Faulkner--on a par with Cormac McCarthy. Every word in ONE MAN'S JUNK has been weighed." Miller deals with mortality & masculinity. Sometimes hilarious, sometimes melancholy, but always 100 percent honest. Add to that a perfect bound, glossy cover & you have a book that will enhance any library. ONE MAN'S JUNK, 159p. short stories, $10, from Snake Nation Press, 110 #2 W. Force, Valdosta GA 31601. Available now. Wholesale rates for volume purchasers.** *Publisher Provided Annotation.*

Miller, Oaky. One Hundred One Ways to Dump on Your Ex! The All-Purpose Get Even! Book. (Illus.). 108p. (Orig.). 1986. pap. 5.95 (*0-930753-01-1*) Spect Ln Pr.

Miller, Olive B. Heroes, Outlaws & Funny Fellows of America. LC 72-96306. (Illus.). 332p. 1973. reprint ed. lib. bdg. 46.00 (*0-8154-0468-9*) Cooper Sq.

Miller, Olive T. Bird-Lover in the West. LC 76-125753. (American Environmental Studies). 1971. reprint ed. 19.95 (*0-405-02679-X*) Ayer.

Miller, Orlando W. The Frontier in Alaska & the Matanuska Colony. LC 74-82747. (Yale Western Americana Ser.: No. 26). 340p. reprint ed. pap. 96.90 (*0-7837-3303-8*, 2057705) Bks Demand.

Miller, Orson K., Jr. Mushrooms of North America. rev. ed. 1977. pap. 14.50 (*0-525-48226-1*, Dutton) NAL-Dutton.

Miller, Orson K., Jr. & Miller, Hope H. Gasteromycetes: Morphological & Developmental Features. 150p. (Orig.). 1988. pap. 24.95 (*0-916422-74-7*) Mad River.

Miller, Oscar J., et al. Recommended Publications for Legal Research, 1980. LC 86-17669. 1986. 37.50 (*0-8377-2529-1*) Rothman.

Miller, Oscar J. & Schwartz, Mortimer D. Recommended Publications for Legal Research, 1981. LC 87-10106. 1987. 37.50 (*0-8377-2533-X*) Rothman.

— Recommended Publications for Legal Research, 1983. LC 87-4837. 1987. 37.50 (*0-8377-2531-3*) Rothman.

— Recommended Publications for Legal Research, 1984. LC 86-3253. 1986. 37.50 (*0-8377-2528-3*) Rothman.

— Recommended Publications for Legal Research, 1985. LC 86-31543. 1987. 37.50 (*0-8377-2530-5*) Rothman.

— Recommended Publications for Legal Research, 1986. LC 87-12723. 1987. 37.50 (*0-8377-2532-1*) Rothman.

Miller, Oscar J. & Schwartz, Mortimer D., comps. Recommended Publications for Legal Research, 1979. (Orig.). 1985. pap. text ed. 37.50 (*0-8377-2527-5*) Rothman.

Miller, Oscar R., jt. auth. see Miller, Betty A.

Miller, Owen J., jt. ed. see Valdes, Mario J.

Miller, P. The Cooperative Extension Service: Paradoxical Servant. LC 73-8308. (Landmark Ser.: No. 2). 1973. pap. text ed. 2.00 (*0-87060-060-5*, LNH 2) Syracuse U Cont Ed.

— The Gardener's Dictionary. 1969. reprint ed. 120.00 (*3-7682-0613-0*) Lubrecht & Cramer.

— Project Cost Databanks. (Illus.). 116p. 1988. pap. text ed. 74.95 (*0-408-02630-8*) Buttrwrth-Heinemann.

Miller, P. B. L. A. 's Ninety-Nine Best Hole-in-the-Wall Restaurants: A Paul Wallach Guide. Ramirez, Lynette, ed. 1989. 6.95 (*0-9619156-2-5*) P Wallach.

Miller, P. C., ed. Resource Use by Chaparral & Matorral: A Comparison of Vegetation Function in Two Mediterranean Type Ecosystems. (Ecological Studies: Vol. 39). (Illus.). 416p. 1981. 106.00 (*0-387-90556-1*) Spr-Verlag.

Miller, P. L., ed. Selected Topics in Medical Artificial Intelligence. (Computers & Medicine Ser.). (Illus.). 220p. 1988. 60.00 (*0-387-96701-X*) Spr-Verlag.

Miller, P. L., ed. see Society for Experimental Biology (Great Britain).

M

Miller, P. M. Behavioral Treatment of Alcoholism. 1976. 88.00 (*0-08-019519-9*, Pub. by Pergamon Repr UK) Franklin.

Miller, P. R. & Pollard, H. L., eds. Multilingual Compendium of Plant Diseases, Vol. 2. LC 75-46932. 434p. 1977. 40.00 (*0-89054-020-9*) Am Phytopathol Soc.

Miller, P. Schuyler. Alicia in Blunderland. 10.00 (*1-880418-22-3*) D M Grant.

***Miller, Paddy J.** Lies in the Family Album. 288p. 1994. pap. 12.95 (*0-89896-291-9*) Larksdale.

Miller, Page P. A Claim to New Roles. LC 85-2249. (American Theological Library Association Monograph: No. 22). 253p. 1985. 25.00 (*0-8108-1809-4*) Scarecrow.

Miller, Page P., ed. Reclaiming the Past: Landmarks of Women's History. LC 91-46604. (Illus.). 256p. 1992. 35.00 (*0-253-33842-5*) Ind U Pr.

Miller, Pam, ed. see Applebaum, Susan.

Miller, Pamela. Fast Little Shoes. 40p. (Orig.). 1986. pap. 3.00 (*0-942582-11-X*) Erie St Pr.

— The McCord Museum Archives. (Illus.). 32p. 1992. pap. 14.95 (*0-7735-0965-8*, Pub. by McGill CN) U of Toronto Pr.

— Mysterious Coleslaw. 64p. (Orig.). (C). 1993. pap. 6.95 (*1-56439-020-9*) Ridgeway.

— The Vision Care Assistant: An Introductory Handbook. Corngold, Sally M., ed. 112p. (Orig.). 1990. lib. bdg. 15.00 (*0-929780-01-9*) VisionExtension.

Miller, Pamela, ed. Eighteen Seventy Census Index to Hamilton County, Ohio Including Cincinnati. (Illus.). 400p. 1988. lib. bdg. 235.00 (*0-945302-00-2*) Egeon Enterprises.

Miller, Pamela, et al. The McCord Family: A Passionate Vision. (Illus.). 140p. 1992. pap. 35.95 (*0-7735-0971-2*, Pub. by McGill CN) U of Toronto Pr.

Miller, Pamela C., jt. auth. see Anderson, Kathleen.

***Miller, Pamela J.** The Introductory Handbook for the Contact Lens Assistant. Corngold, Sally M., ed. (Illus.). 114p. (Orig.). (C). 1995. lib. bdg. write for info. (*0-929780-06-X*) VisionExtension.

Miller, Pamella, ed. see Kaplan, Levi.

Miller, Pat. Gabby Gourmet. 10th ed. 1992. pap. 7.95 (*0-918481-09-0*) TDF Pub.

— Gabby Gourmet - 1992. 9th ed. 1991. pap. 6.95 (*0-918481-08-2*) TDF Pub.

Miller, Pat, et al. The Serendipity Cookbook: The Best from New York's Incredible Dessert Emporium. LC 94-20351. (Illus.). 1994. 14.95 (*0-8065-1541-4*, Citadel Pr) Carol Pub Group.

Miller, Pat P. Script Supervising & Film Continuity. 2nd ed. (Illus.). 248p. 1990. pap. 29.95 (*0-240-80018-4*, Focal) Buttrwrth-Heinemann.

Miller, Patrice M., jt. ed. see Demick, Jack.

***Miller, Patricia.** Provisioning (How-to for Pleasure Boaters) 1995. 12.95 (*0-9638470-2-3*) Pt Loma Pubng.

— The Rolling Stones Are Just a Mirage. abr. ed. 160p. 1994. pap. 7.95 (*1-56901-215-6*) NW Pub.

Miller, Patricia, jt. auth. see Miller, Dale.

Miller, Patricia, jt. auth. see Rains, John.

Miller, Patricia C. Dreams in Late Antiquity: Studies in the Imagination of a Culture. LC 93-40363. 1994. 39.50 (*0-691-07422-4*) Princeton U Pr.

— Starting a Swan Dive. LC 93-18474. 64p. (Orig.). 1993. pap. 9.00 (*0-933532-91-1*) BkMk.

— Westport: Missouri's Port of Many Returns. LC 83-17523. (Illus.). 128p. 1983. 15.00 (*0-913504-82-3*) Lowell Pr.

Miller, Patricia D., ed. Fitness Programming & Physical Disability: Publication for Disabled Sports U. S. A. LC 94-4961. 232p. 1995. pap. text ed. 29.00x (*0-87322-434-5*, BMIL0434) Human Kinetics.

Miller, Patricia F. Sex Is Not a Four-Letter Word! Talking Sex with Children Made Easier. 176p. (Orig.). 1994. pap. 12.95 (*0-8245-1437-8*) Crossroad NY.

Miller, Patricia G. The Worst of Times. 336p. 1994. pap. 12.00 (*0-06-099512-2*, A Asher Bks) HarpC.

Miller, Patricia H. Theories of Development Psychology. 3rd ed. LC 92-37252. (C). 1995. pap. text ed. write for info. (*0-7167-2309-3*) W H Freeman.

Miller, Patricia S. & McDowelle, James O. Administering Preschool Programs in Public Schools: Practitioner's Handbook. LC 92-20133. (Illus.). 283p. (Orig.). (C). 1992. pap. text ed. 34.95x (*1-879105-78-0*) Singular Publishing.

Miller, Patrick, jt. auth. see Falk, Charles.

Miller, Patrick D. Deuteronomy. (Interpretation: a Bible Commentary for Preaching & Teaching Ser.). 276p. (Orig.). 1990. text ed. 22.00 (*0-8042-3105-2*) Westminster John Knox.

Miller, Patrick D., Jr. Interpreting the Psalms. LC 85-16258. 176p. 1986. pap. 14.00 (*0-8006-1896-3*, 1-1896, Fortress Pr) Augsburg Fortress.

Miller, Patrick D. They Cried to the Lord: The Form & Theology of Biblical Prayer. LC 94-10750. 1994. 40.00 (*0-8006-2768-7*, Fortress Pr); pap. 24.00 (*0-8006-2762-8*, Fortress Pr) Augsburg Fortress.

Miller, Patrick D. & Roberts, J. M. The Hand of the Lord: A Reassessment of the "Ark Narrative" of Samuel. LC 76-48737. (Johns Hopkins Near Eastern Studies). 128p. reprint ed. pap. 36.50 (*0-317-26633-0*, 2010959) Bks Demand.

Miller, Patrick D., ed. see Brueggemann, Walter.

Miller, Patrick D., Jr., et al, eds. Ancient Israelite Religion: Essays in Honor of Frank Moore Cross. LC 86-45919. 688p. (C). 1987. text ed. 50.00 (*0-8006-0831-3*, 1-831, Fortress Pr) Augsburg Fortress.

Miller, Patrizia & Fairbanks, Linda C. The Cat & the Old Rat. Barbee, S. Diane, ed. 24p. 1986. 20.00 (*0-938364-03-0*) Orirana Pr.

Miller, Patsy R. & Riley, Philip J. My Hollywood: When Both of Us Were Young - The Hunchback of Notre Dame, 2 vols., 1. LC 88-90728. (Ackerman Archives Ser.: Vol. 3). (Illus.). 428p. 1989. write for info. (*1-882127-02-1*) Magicimage Filmbooks.

— My Hollywood: When Both of Us Were Young - The Hunchback of Notre Dame, 2 vols., 2. LC 88-90728. (Ackerman Archives Ser.: Vol. 3). (Illus.). 428p. 1989. write for info. (*1-882127-01-3*) Magicimage Filmbooks.

— My Hollywood: When Both of Us Were Young - The Hunchback of Notre Dame, 2 vols., Set. LC 88-90728. (Ackerman Archives Ser.: Vol. 3). (Illus.). 428p. 1989. 39.95 (*0-685-30712-3*) Magicimage Filmbooks.

***Miller, Patti.** Writing Your Life: A Journey of Discovery. 1995. pap. 11.95 (*1-86373-641-7*) IPG Chicago.

Miller, Paul. Great Joy Coming Program Resources. 1984. 6.00 (*0-685-68500-4*, MC-53A) Lillenas.

— Jesse's Run. 180p. Date not set. pap. 7.95 (*0-7610-0322-3*) NW Pub.

Miller, Paul A. Lyric Texts & Lyric Consciousness: The Birth of a Genre from Archaic Greece to Augustan Rome. LC 93-21184. 208p. 1994. 55.00x (*0-415-10518-8*, B3151, Routledge NY) Routledge.

Miller, Paul B. & Redding, Rodney J. The FASB: The People, the Process, & the Politics. 2nd ed. 176p. (C). 1987. pap. text ed. 21.95 (*0-256-06265-X*) Irwin.

Miller, Paul B., jt. auth. see Larson, Kermit D.

Miller, Paul B., jt. auth. see Nelson, A. Thomas.

Miller, Paul B., et al. The FASB: The People, the Process, & the Politics. 3rd ed. LC 93-5703. 208p. (C). 1993. pap. text ed. 21.95 (*0-256-08276-6*) Irwin.

Miller, Paul C. & Gorman, Tom. Big League Business Thinking: The Heavy Hitter's Guide to Top Managerial Performance. LC 94-6310. 1994. write for info. (*0-13-289042-9*) P-H.

Miller, Paul D. Both Swords & Plowshares: Military Roles in the 1990s. LC 92-44040. 1992. 7.50 (*0-89549-095-1*) Inst Foreign Policy Anal.

— The Inter-Agency Process: Engaging America's Full National Security Capabilities. LC 93-17575. (National Security Papers: No. 11). 1993. 7.50 (*0-89549-097-8*) Inst Foreign Policy Anal.

— Leadership in a Transnational World: The Challenge of Keeping the Peace. LC 93-25820. (National Security Papers: No. 12). 1993. write for info. (*0-89549-098-6*) Inst Foreign Policy Anal.

Miller, Paul E. Down Beat's Yearbook of Swing. LC 78-6152. 183p. 1978. reprint ed. text ed. 35.00 (*0-313-20476-4*, MIYS, Greenwood Pr) Greenwood.

Miller, Paul E., ed. Esquire's Jazz Book: 1944-1946, 3 Vols. (Roots of Jazz Ser.). 1979. reprint ed. lib. bdg. 27.50 (*0-685-73546-X*); reprint ed. lib. bdg. 27.50 (*0-306-79525-6*); reprint ed. lib. bdg. 27.50 (*0-306-79526-4*); reprint ed. lib. bdg. 27.50 (*0-306-79527-2*) Da Capo.

— Esquire's Jazz Book: 1944-1946, 3 Vols., Set. (Roots of Jazz Ser.). 1979. reprint ed. lib. bdg. 75.00 (*0-306-79528-0*) Da Capo.

Miller, Paul F., jt. ed. see Baderschneider, Earl R.

Miller, Paul M. Christmas Comes to Lone Star Gulch. (J). 1989. 4.95 (*0-8341-9157-1*, BCMC-67); 29.95 (*0-685-68524-1*, MC-67C); audio 10.98 (*0-685-68525-X*, TA-9106C) Lillenas.

— Day Star Program Resources. 1986. 6.00 (*0-685-68656-6*, MB-567A) Lillenas.

— Developing the Church Drama Ministry. (Drama Topics Ser.). 1994. 8.95 (*0-8341-9127-X*, MP-513) Lillenas.

— Dinner Theatre: Entertaining Outreach. (Drama Topics Ser.). 1994. 8.95 (*0-8341-9056-7*, MP-510) Lillenas.

— Ebenezer, Jr. 1985. 4.95 (*0-685-68494-6*, MC-56); 10.98 (*0-685-68495-4*, TA-9064C) Lillenas.

— The Missing Jesus. 1985. 4.25 (*0-685-68587-X*, MC-262) Lillenas.

— Star Carols Program Resources. 1985. 6.00 (*0-685-72842-0*, MC-55A) Lillenas.

Miller, Paul M., comp. Ben, Hannah, & the Witness. 1987. 4.25 (*0-685-68588-8*, BCMC-267) Lillenas.

— Christmas Program Builder, No. 35. 1982. 4.25 (*0-685-68569-1*, MC-135) Lillenas.

— Christmas Program Builder, No. 36. 1983. 4.25 (*0-685-68568-3*, MC-136) Lillenas.

— Christmas Program Builder, No. 37. 1984. 4.25 (*0-685-68567-5*, MC-137) Lillenas.

— Christmas Program Builder, No. 38. 1985. 4.25 (*0-8341-9143-1*, MC-138) Lillenas.

— Christmas Program Builder, No. 39. 1986. 4.25 (*0-685-68565-9*, MC-139) Lillenas.

— Christmas Program Builder, No. 40. 1987. 4.25 (*0-685-68564-0*, MC-140) Lillenas.

— Christmas Program Builder, No. 41. 1988. 4.25 (*0-8341-9144-X*, MC-141) Lillenas.

— Christmas Program Builder, No. 42. 1989. 4.25 (*0-8341-9145-8*, MC-142) Lillenas.

— Christmas Program Builder, No. 43. 1990. 4.25 (*0-685-68561-6*, MC-143) Lillenas.

— Christmas Program Builder, No. 44. 1991. 4.25 (*0-685-68560-8*, MC-144) Lillenas.

— Christmas Program Builder, No. 45. 1992. 4.25 (*0-685-68559-4*, MC-145) Lillenas.

— Christmas Program Builder, No. 46. 1993. 4.25 (*0-685-72867-6*, MC-146) Lillenas.

— Christmas Program Builder, No. 47. 1994. 4.25 (*0-8341-9104-0*, MC-147) Lillenas.

— Christmas Program Builder: Resources for Inspiration, Outreach, & Fun. 1994. 4.25 (*0-8341-9053-2*, MP-110) Lillenas.

— The Christmas Script Book. 1988. 5.25 (*0-685-68584-5*, MC-270) Lillenas.

— Don't Miss the Pageant. 1983. 4.25 (*0-685-68599-3*, MC-257) Lillenas.

— Easter Program Builder, No. 17. 1982. 4.25 (*0-685-68666-3*, ME-117) Lillenas.

— Easter Program Builder, No. 18. 1984. 4.25 (*0-685-68665-5*, ME-118) Lillenas.

— Easter Program Builder, No. 19. 1986. 4.25 (*0-685-68664-7*, ME-119) Lillenas.

— Easter Program Builder, No. 21. 1990. 4.25 (*0-8341-9202-0*, ME-121) Lillenas.

— Easter Program Builder, No. 22. 1992. 4.25 (*0-8341-9203-9*, ME-122) Lillenas.

— Evangelistic Program Builder, No. 1. 1987. 5.25 (*0-685-74873-1*, MP-615) Lillenas.

— Evangelistic Program Builder, No. 2. 1994. 5.25 (*0-8341-9026-5*, MP-616) Lillenas.

— Home for Christmas. 1983. 4.25 (*0-685-68596-9*, MC-259) Lillenas.

— Lenten & Easter Drama Resources. 1982. 4.25 (*0-685-68678-7*, ME-227) Lillenas.

— Missionary Program Builder, No. 4. 1990. 4.25 (*0-685-68752-X*, MP-204) Lillenas.

— Mother's Day & Father's Day Program Builder, No. 7. 1985. 4.25 (*0-685-68764-3*, MP-307) Lillenas.

— Mother's Day & Father's Day Program Builder, No. 9. 1934. 4.25 (*0-685-72853-6*, MP-309) Lillenas.

— The Not Too Perfect Nativity Play. 1988. 4.25 (*0-685-68597-7*, MC-269) Lillenas.

— Senior Adult Program Builder, No. 1. 1985. 5.25 (*0-685-68743-0*, MP-627) Lillenas.

— Senior Adult Program Builder, No. 2. 1992. 5.25 (*0-685-68742-2*, MP-502) Lillenas.

— A Shepherd, a Wish, & Three Wise Men. 1982. 4.25 (*0-685-68590-X*, MC-256) Lillenas.

— Special Events in the Church Program Builder, No. 2. 1982. 5.25 (*0-8341-9111-3*, MP-612) Lillenas.

— Special Worship Resources. 1983. 5.25 (*0-685-68737-6*, MP-613) Lillenas.

— Troubled in Toyland. 1992. 5.25 (*0-685-71347-4*, MC-274) Lillenas.

— Whose Birthday? 1986. 4.25 (*0-8341-9151-2*, MC-263) Lillenas.

— Women's Program Builder, No. 2. 1985. 5.25 (*0-8341-9250-0*, MP-632) Lillenas.

— Women's Program Builder, No. 3. 1990. 5.25 (*0-685-68760-0*, MP-665) Lillenas.

Miller, Paul M., ed. Christmas Onstage! 1993. 5.25 (*0-685-72866-8*, MC-277) Lillenas.

— Son of the Highest. 1983. 5.25 (*0-685-68490-3*, MC-50); audio 10.98 (*0-685-68491-1*, TA-9044C) Lillenas.

— Star Quest. 1989. 5.95 (*0-685-68459-8*, MC-71); audio 10.98 (*0-685-68460-1*, TA-9118C) Lillenas.

Miller, Paul M. & Dunlop, Dan. Create a Drama Ministry. 1984. 9.95 (*0-685-69281-7*, MP-625) Lillenas.

***Miller, Paul M. & Stargel, Scott, comps.** Easter Program Builder, No. 23. 1994. 4.25 (*0-8341-9233-0*, ME-123) Lillenas.

Miller, Paul M. & Wyatt, Jeff. The Word in Worship. 1992. 9.95 (*0-685-68735-X*, MP-673) Lillenas.

Miller, Paul M., jt. auth. see Jackson, Chuck.

Miller, Paul W., ed. Seven Minor Epics of the English Renaissance. LC 67-10125. 1977. 50.00 (*0-8201-1034-5*) Schol Facsimiles.

Miller, Paul W., jt. auth. see Nelson, A. Tom.

Miller, Paule M. Parlons de Tout: Livre Pour Cours de Conversation Francaise. 278p. (C). 1990. reprint ed. 32.50 (*0-89464-495-5*) Krieger.

Miller, Paulette, tr. see Gaarder, Jostein.

Miller, Peggy, jt. auth. see Miller, Ron.

Miller, Peggy J. Amy, Wendy & Beth: Learning Language in South Baltimore. LC 81-11656. 208p. (C). 1982. text ed. 22.95x (*0-292-70357-0*) U of Tex Pr.

Miller, Peggy J., jt. ed. see Corsaro, William A.

Miller, Peggy J., jt. auth. see Haight, Wendy L.

Miller, Penny M. Kentucky Politics & Government: Do We Stand United? LC 93-23959. (Politics & Governments of the American States Ser.). xxx, 469p. 1994. 45.00 (*0-8032-3139-3*); pap. 18.95 (*0-8032-8206-0*) U of Nebr Pr.

Miller, Penny M. & Jewell, Malcolm E. Political Parties & Primaries in Kentucky. LC 89-70690. 336p. 1990. text ed. 35.00 (*0-8131-1753-4*) U Pr of Ky.

Miller, Penny M., jt. auth. see Jewell, Malcolm E.

Miller-Perrin, Cindy L., jt. auth. see Wurtele, Sandy K.

Miller, Perry. The American Puritans: Their Prose & Poetry. LC 81-10222. 360p. 1982. reprint ed. pap. text ed. 18.00 (*0-231-05419-X*) Col U Pr.

— Critiquing Approach to Expert Computer Advice: Attending. (Research Notes in Artificial Intelligence Ser.). 1984. 29.95 (*0-273-08665-0*) Morgan Kaufmann.

— Jonathan Edwards. LC 72-7877. (American Men of Letters Ser.). (Illus.). 348p. 1973. reprint ed. text ed. 59.50 (*0-8371-6551-2*, MIJE, Greenwood Pr) Greenwood.

— Life of the Mind in America: From the Revolution to the Civil War. LC 65-19065. 338p. 1970. reprint ed. pap. 12.95 (*0-15-651990-9*, Harvest Bks) HarBrace.

— The New England Mind: From Colony to Province. 528p. 1983. pap. 16.95 (*0-674-61301-5*) HUP.

— The New England Mind: The Seventeenth Century. 540p. 1983. pap. 16.95 (*0-674-61306-6*) HUP.

— The Raven & the Whale: The War of Words & Wits in the Era of Poe & Melville. LC 72-11741. 370p. 1973. reprint ed. text ed. 45.50 (*0-8371-6707-8*, MIRW, Greenwood Pr) Greenwood.

Miller, Perry, ed. Major Writers of America. abr. ed. 1052p. (C). 1966. Shorter ed. text ed. 36.00 (*0-15-554602-3*) HB Coll Pubs.

Miller, Perry, ed. see Edwards, Jonathan.

Miller, Perry, ed. see Helmbold, W. C.

Miller, Perry, ed. see Wise, John.

Miller, Perry, et al. In Search of Early America: The William & Mary Quarterly, 1943-1993. (Illus.). xii, 288p. (Orig.). 1993. pap. 14.95 (*0-910776-05-9*) Inst Early Am.

— Religion & Freedom of Thought. LC 78-128296. (Essay Index Reprint Ser.). 1977. 12.95 (*0-8369-2199-2*) Ayer.

Miller, Perry G. Errand into the Wilderness. LC 56-11285. 244p. 1956. pap. 12.95 (*0-674-26155-0*) Belknap Pr.

— Nature's Nation. LC 67-17316. 314p. 1967. 32.00 (*0-674-60550-0*) Belknap Pr.

Miller, Perry G., ed. Transcendentalists: An Anthology. LC 50-7360. 521p. 1950. pap. 18.50 (*0-674-90333-1*) HUP.

Miller, Peter. Domination & Power. 250p. 1987. lib. bdg. 39.95 (*0-7102-0624-0*, RKP) Routledge.

— Get Published, Get Produced: A Literary Agent's Tips on How to Sell Your Writing. 232p. 1990. 16.95 (*1-56171-007-5*) Sure Sellers.

— Media Power: How Your Business Can Profit from the Media. 192p. 1991. 19.95 (*0-7931-0269-3*, 5608-52) Dearborn Finan.

— Vermont People. (Illus.). 128p. 1990. 35.00 (*0-9628064-0-4*) VT People Proj.

Miller, Peter, ed. & intro. Yankee Weather Proverbs. (Illus.). 64p. (Orig.). 1992. pap. 3.95 (*0-9628064-1-2*) VT People Proj.

Miller, Peter, jt. auth. see Chang, Leon L.

Miller, Peter, jt. ed. see Hopwood, Anthony G.

Miller, Peter, ed. see Priestley, Joseph.

Miller, Peter, jt. auth. see Salmon, Francis.

Miller, Peter G. Buy Your First Home Now: A Practical Guide to Better Deals, Cheaper Mortgages & Bigger Tax Breaks for the First-Time Home Buyer. LC 89-45689. 224p. 1991. reprint ed. pap. 11.00 (*0-06-092051-3*, PL) HarpC.

— The Common-Sense Mortgage. 336p. 1995. pap. 13.00 (*0-06-273332-X*, Harper Ref) HarpC.

— How to Sell Your Home In Any Market: With or Without a Broker. LC 93-33066. 224p. 1994. 20.00 (*0-06-270087-1*, Harper Ref) HarpC.

— How to Sell Your Home in Any Market: With or Without a Broker. 240p. 1995. pap. 12.00 (*0-06-272058-9*, Harper Ref) HarpC.

— Successful Real Estate Investing in the 90's: A Practical Guide for the Small Investor. 288p. 1995. pap. 12.00 (*0-06-272062-7*) HarpC.

— Successful Real Estate Investing in the'90s. LC 94-19421. 1994. 18.00 (*0-06-270123-1*) HarpC.

Miller, Peter G. & Bregman, Douglas M. Successful Real Estate Negotiation. rev. ed. LC 93-31859. 320p. 1994. pap. 13.00 (*0-06-273264-1*, Harper Ref) HarpC.

Miller, Peter M. The Hilton Head Diet for Children & Teenagers. 176p. (Orig.). 1993. pap. 9.99 (*0-446-39337-1*) Warner Bks.

— The Hilton Head Metabolism Diet. 256p. 1986. mass mkt. 5.99 (*0-446-34528-8*) Warner Bks.

— The Hilton Head Over-35 Diet. 1990. mass mkt. 5.99 (*0-446-35861-4*) Warner Bks.

— The New Hilton Head Metabolism Diet. (Orig.). 1996. mass mkt. write for info. (*0-446-60325-2*) Warner Bks.

Miller, Peter M. & Nirenberg, Ted D., eds. Prevention of Alcohol Abuse. 536p. 1984. 95.00 (*0-306-41328-0*, Plenum Pr) Plenum.

Miller, Peter M. & Rankin, Howard. If I'm So Smart, Why Do I Eat Like This? 1989. mass mkt. 4.99 (*0-446-35746-4*) Warner Bks.

Miller, Peter N. Defining the Common Good: Empire, Religion & Philosophy in Eighteenth-Century Britain. (Ideas in Context Ser.: No. 29). 448p. (C). 1994. 69.95 (*0-521-44259-1*) Cambridge U Pr.

Miller, Phil. Life & Other Poems. (Petites Major Ser.). 42p. 1993. pap. 4.00 (*1-884754-03-1*) Potpourri Pubns.

— Media Law for Producers. 2nd ed. 267p. 1993. 45.00 (*0-86729-328-4*) Knowledge Indus.

Miller, Phil, jt. auth. see Deniston, Keith.

Miller, Philip. Hard Freeze. LC 93-44194. 64p. (Orig.). 1994. pap. 9.00 (*0-933532-96-2*) BkMk.

— Slivers: A Poem. Hickok, Gloria V., ed. 6p. (Orig.). 1994. pap. 2.50 (*1-884235-07-7*) Helicon Nine Eds.

Miller, Philip, intro. The Ring of Words: An Anthology of Song Texts. 544p. 1973. reprint ed. pap. 16.95 (*0-393-00677-8*) Norton.

***Miller, Philip & Devon, Molly.** Screw the Roses, Send Me the Thorns: The Romance & Sexual Sorcery of Sadomasochism. LC 95-79674. (Illus.). 283p. (Orig.). Date not set. pap. 24.95 (*0-9645960-0-8*) Mystic Rose.

Miller, Philip, ed. see McGhee, Laura, et al.

Miller, Philip E. Karaite Separatism in Nineteenth-Century Russia: Joseph Solomon Lutski's "Epistle of Israel's Deliverance" (Monographs of the Hebrew Union College: No. 16). 252p. 1993. 49.95 (*0-87820-415-6*) Hebrew Union Coll Pr.

Miller, Philip L. Vocal Music, Vol. 2. LC 78-94. (Guide to Long-Playing Records Ser.: Vol. 2). 381p. 1978. reprint ed. text ed. 55.00 (*0-313-20295-8*, GULP02, Greenwood Pr) Greenwood.

Miller, Phillip, jt. auth. see Elliott, Steven.

Miller, Phillip L., ed. see Brahms & Mahler.

Miller, Phyllis, jt. auth. see Norton, Andre.

Miller, Phyllis A. Managing Your Reading: Strategies & Techniques for Reading Smarter & Faster. (Illus.). 324p. (C). 1987. pap. text ed. 18.00 (*0-943311-00-4*) Read Devlpmt Resc.

— Managing your Reading Instruction Manual. 300p. 1988. ring bd. 55.00 (*0-943311-01-2*) Read Devlpmt Resc.

Miller, Phyllis B. AutoCAD for the Apparel Industry. LC 92-47249. 540p. 1994. pap. text ed. 34.95 (*0-8273-5224-7*) Delmar.

— Autocad for the Apparel Industry: Instructor's Guide. 64p. 1994. 15.00 (*0-8273-5928-4*) Delmar.

Miller, Phyllis B., ed. Report, Vol. 33. 1993. 25.00 (*0-935057-71-4*) OH Genealogical.

An Asterisk (*) at the beginning of an entry indicates that the title is appearing in BIP for the first time.

— Report, Vol. 34. 1994. 25.00 (0-935057-76-5) OH Genealogical.

Miller, Phyllis Z., jt. auth. see Fox, Karen L.

Miller-Pogacar, Anesa, jt. ed. see Berry, Ellen E.

Miller-Pogacar, Anesa, ed. see Epstein, Mikhail N.

Miller, Preston J., ed. The Rational Expectations Revolution: Readings from the Front Line. LC 93-5815. 292p. 1994. 45.00 (0-262-13297-4); pap. 23.00 (0-262-63155-5) MIT Pr.

Miller, R. Automated Guided Vehicles & Automated Manufacturing. 192p. 1987. 34.00 (0-87263-281-4) SME.

— Communication: Electricity & Electronics. 1976. 10.48 (0-13-153098-4); pap. text ed. 10.16 (0-13-153072-0) P-H.

— Communication: Industry & Careers. 1976. 10.16 (0-685-03796-7); pap. 10.14 (0-13-152967-6) P-H.

— Cortico-Hippocampal Interplay & the Representation of Contexts in the Brain. (Studies of Brain Function: Vol. 17). (Illus.). 288p. 1991. 70.00 (0-387-53109-2) Spr-Verlag.

Miller, R., ed. see Gass, T. & Bennett, T.

Miller, R., jt. ed. see Merbs, C.

Miller, R., jt. auth. see Semple, S. J.

Miller, R. B. An Introduction to the Physics of Intense Charged Particle Beams. LC 82-557. 362p. (C). 1982. 75.00 (0-306-40931-3, Plenum Pr) Plenum.

Miller, R. B. & Heiman, S. E. Conceptual Selling. (C). 1987. 190.00 (0-685-33724-3, Pub. by Witherby & Co UK) St Mut.

Miller, R. B. & Lyons, A. B., eds. Lyon Memorial: New York Families, Descendants from the Immigrant Thomas Lyon of Rye. (Illus.). 539p. 1989. reprint ed. lib. bdg. 89.00 (0-8328-0797-4); reprint ed. pap. 81.00 (0-8328-0798-2) Higginson Bk Co.

Miller, R. Baxter. The Art & Imagination of Langston Hughes. LC 89-5645. 160p. 1990. 18.00 (0-8131-1662-7) U Pr of Ky.

Miller, R. Baxter, ed. Black American Literature & Humanism. LC 80-5179. 128p. 1981. 14.00 (0-8131-1436-5) U Pr of Ky.

— Black American Poets Between Worlds, 1940-1960. LC 85-22644. (Tennessee Studies in Literature: Vol. 30). 206p. (C). 1986. text ed. 25.00x (0-87049-499-6); pap. 14.00x (0-87049-590-9) U of Tenn Pr.

Miller, R. Bruce, ed. Thinking Robots, an Aware Internet, & Cyberpunk Librarians: The 1992 LITA President's Program. LC 92-30742. (LITA President's Ser.). (Illus.). 1992. 22.00 (0-8389-7625-5) Lib Info Tech.

Miller, R. Bryan & Wade, L. G., Jr., eds. Annual Reports in Organic Synthesis 1976, Vol. 7. 1977. pap. text ed. 106.00 (0-12-040807-4) Acad Pr.

Miller, R. Bryan, jt. ed. see McMurray, John.

Miller, R. Bryan, jt. ed. see McMurry, John.

Miller, R. C. Moving into Management. 144p. 1985. 45.00 (0-631-14311-4) Blackwell Pubs.

Miller, R. Craig. Modern Design, 1890-1990, in the Metropolitan Museum of Art. (Illus.). 328p. 1990. 29.95 (0-87099-598-7) Metro Mus Art.

Miller, R. E. & Skucas, Jovitas. Radiological Examination of the Colon. 1983. lib. bdg. 251.50 (90-247-2666-2) Kluwer Ac.

Miller, R. E., ed. see Metallurgical Society of AIME Staff.

Miller, R. Edward. The Flaming Flame. 95p. (Orig.). (YA). (gr. 12). 1973. pap. 2.50 (0-945818-03-3) Peniel Pubns.

— I Looked & I Saw Mysteries. 106p. (YA). (gr. 12). 1988. reprint ed. pap. 3.50 (0-945818-01-7) Peniel Pubns.

— I Looked & I Saw the Lord. 95p. (Orig.). (YA). (gr. 12). 1988. reprint ed. pap. 3.50 (0-945818-00-9) Peniel Pubns.

— I Looked & I Saw Visions of God. 147p. (Orig.). (YA). (gr. 12). 1974. pap. 3.50 (0-945818-06-8) Peniel Pubns.

— I Looked & Saw the Heavens Opened... 96p. (Orig.). (YA). (gr. 12). 1972. pap. 3.50 (0-945818-05-X) Peniel Pubns.

— The Prince & the Three Beggars. 33p. (Orig.). (YA). (gr. 12). 1975. pap. 2.00 (0-945818-04-1) Peniel Pubns.

— Romance of Redemption. 213p. (Orig.). (YA). (gr. 10). 1990. pap. 7.95 (0-945818-09-2) Peniel Pubns.

— Secrets of the Kingdom. 180p. (Orig.). (YA). (gr. 10). 1989. pap. 5.25 (0-945818-08-4) Peniel Pubns.

— Thy God Reigneth. 58p. (YA). (gr. 12). 1964. pap. 2.50 (0-945818-02-5) Peniel Pubns.

— Victory in Adversity. 168p. (Orig.). (YA). (gr. 10). 1988. pap. 4.95 (0-945818-07-6) Peniel Pubns.

Miller, R. F., et al, eds. Gorbachev at the Helm: A New Era in Soviet Politics? 320p. 1987. lib. bdg. 47.50 (0-7099-5506-5, Pub. by Croom Helm UK) Routledge Chapman & Hall.

Miller, R. H. Handbook of Literary Research. LC 86-29812. xiv, 110p. 1987. 20.00 (0-8108-1959-7) Scarecrow.

— Handbook of Literary Research. 2nd ed. LC 94-44091. (Illus.). 119p. 1995. 22.50 (0-8108-2977-0) Scarecrow.

— Understanding Graham Greene. (Understanding Contemporary British Literature Ser.). 128p. (C). 1990. text ed. 34.95 (0-87249-704-6) U of SC Pr.

Miller, R. H., jt. ed. see Gastil, R. G.

Miller, R. K. The Placenta: Receptors, Pathology & Toxicology. Thiede, H., ed. 390p. 1981. text ed. 95.00 (0-275-91350-3, C1350, Praeger Pubs) Greenwood.

Miller, R. K., jt. ed. see Kaufmann, P.

Miller, R. Michael & Harper, Josephine M. The Psychic Energy Workbook: An Illustrated Course in Practical Psychic Skills. (Workbook Ser.). 112p. (Orig.). 1995. pap. 12.95 (0-85030-529-2) Sterling.

Miller, R. R. & Greenblatt, D. J., eds. Handbook of Drug Therapy. 1126p. 1979. pap. 49.75 (0-444-00253-7, North Holland) Elsevier.

Miller, R. S., jt. auth. see Leary, Mark R.

***Miller, R. S. Bud.** Covenant, God's Guarantee for Victorious Living. 1995. pap. 5.00 (1-57149-020-5) Christ Unltd.

***Miller, R. T.** Welding Skills. LC 94-29965. 1994. 28.96 (0-8269-3004-2) Am Technical.

***Miller, Raeburn.** The Comma after Love: Selected Poems of Raeburn Miller. Justice, Donald et al, eds. (Akron Series in Poetry). 107p. 1994. 24.95 (1-884836-03-8); pap. 12.95 (1-884836-04-6) U Akron Pr.

— Millenary. Katrovas, Richard & Cassin, Maxine, eds. LC 85-63468. (Journal Press Books: Louisiana Legacy). 88p. (Orig.). 1986. pap. 7.00 (0-938498-06-1) New Orleans Poetry.

Miller, Ralph. Estate Planning Primer. 1994. 99.00 (0-943293-05-7) ViewPlan.

— If You Care to, You Can. 128p. (Orig.). 1993. pap. text ed. 7.95 (0-9637344-5-8) Chadshana Pub.

Miller, Ralph, Sr. Sign Language Clowns. 32p. (J). 1983. 4.50 (0-915035-00-6, 4160) Dawn Sign.

Miller, Ralph & Withers, Bud. Ralph Miller: Spanning the Game. (Illus.). 222p. 1991. 19.95 (0-685-75066-3) Sagamore Pub.

Miller, Ralph R. & Spear, Norman E., eds. Information Processing in Animals: Conditioned Inhibition. 480p. (C). 1985. text ed. 89.95 (0-89859-506-1) L Erlbaum Assocs.

Miller, Ralph R., jt. ed. see Spear, Norman E.

***Miller, Ralph T.** Jehovah's Witnesses - Victims of Deception: How Investigation & Divine Intervention Led Us to Escape a Religious Cult. 160p. (Orig.). 1995. pap. 7.95 (0-9637448-1-X) Comments Friends.

Miller, Ramona, jt. auth. see Peterson, Ingrid.

Miller, Rand, jt. auth. see Miller, Robyn.

Miller, Randall K., jt. auth. see Keynes, Edward.

Miller, Randall M. The Cotton Mill Movement in Antebellum Alabama. LC 77-14771. (Dissertations in American Economic History Ser.). 1978. 30.95 (0-405-11049-9) Ayer.

Miller, Randall M., ed. The Afro-American Slaves: Community or Chaos? LC 80-24034. 152p. (Orig.). (C). 1981. pap. 9.50 (0-89874-078-9) Krieger.

— Dear Master: Letters of a Slave Family. LC 89-20536. (Illus.). 304p. 1990. reprint ed. pap. 15.95 (0-8203-1230-4) U of Ga Pr.

— The Kaleidoscopic Lens: How Hollywood Views Ethnic Groups. (Illus.). 222p. (C). 1980. lib. bdg. 25.95 (0-89198-120-9); pap. text ed. 15.95 (0-89198-121-7) Ozer.

— A "Warm & Zealous Spirit" John J. Zubly & the American Revolution, a Selection of His Writings. LC 81-22367. xii, 211p. 1982. 14.95x (0-86554-028-4, MUP-H29) Mercer Univ Pr.

***Miller, Randall M. & Cimbala, Paul A., eds.** American Reform & Reformers: A Biographical Dictionary. LC 95-16048. 1996. text ed. write for info. (0-313-28839-9, Greenwood Pr) Greenwood.

Miller, Randall M. & McKivigan, John R., eds. The Moment of Decision: Biographical Essays on American Character & Regional Identity. LC 93-30981. (Contributions in American History Ser.: No. 156). 256p. 1994. text ed. 59.95 (0-313-28635-3, Greenwood Pr) Greenwood.

Miller, Randall M. & Miller, Linda Patterson, eds. The Book of American Diaries. LC 94-17807. 512p. (Orig.). 1995. pap. 12.50 (0-380-76583-7) Avon.

Miller, Randall M. & Pozzetta, George E., eds. Shades of the Sunbelt: Essays on Ethnicity, Race, & the Urban South. LC 87-18164. (Contributions in American History Ser.: No. 128). 240p. 1988. text ed. 55.00 (0-313-25690-X, MET/, Greenwood Pr) Greenwood.

— Shades of the Sunbelt: Essays on Ethnicity, Race, & the Urban South. 240p. 1989. pap. text ed. 19.95 (0-8130-0956-1) U Press Fla.

Miller, Randall M. & Smith, John D., eds. Dictionary of Afro-American Slavery. LC 87-37543. 882p. 1988. text ed. 95.00 (0-313-23814-6, SMS/, Greenwood Pr) Greenwood.

Miller, Randall M., jt. auth. see Wakelyn, Jon L.

Miller, Randolph C., ed. Church & Organized Movements. LC 76-134115. (Essay Index Reprint Ser.). 1977. 20.95 (0-8369-1998-X) Ayer.

— Empirical Theology: A Handbook. 304p. (Orig.). 1993. pap. 18.95 (0-89135-088-8) Religious Educ.

— Theologies of Religious Education. 328p. (Orig.). 1995. pap. 19.95 (0-89135-096-9) Religious Educ.

Miller, Randy, et al. EMS Skill Sheets. Mercer, Steve, ed. 176p. (C). 1994. ring bd. 59.95 (1-884225-01-2) Communs Skills.

Miller, Ray. Building a Home Darkroom (KW-14), KW-14. LC 81-66622. (Kodak Workshop Ser.). (Illus.). 96p. 1991. pap. 13.95 (0-87985-746-3) Saunders Photo.

— Camaro! Chevy's Classy Chassis. (Chevy Chase Ser.: Vol. 4). (Illus.). 320p. 1981. 44.95 (0-913056-10-3) Evergreen Pr.

— Catalina! Wish You Were Here. Miller, Jo, ed. LC 93-71599. (Illus.). 96p. (Orig.). 1993. pap. 19.95 (0-913056-13-8) Evergreen Pr.

— Chevrolet: The Coming of Age, 1911-1942. LC 76-21060. (Chevy Chase Ser.: Vol. 1). (Illus.). 1976. 29.95 (0-614-03282-2) Evergreen Pr.

— Chevrolet: U. S. A. No. 1, 1946-1959. LC 76-12000. (Chevy Chase Ser.: Vol. 2). (Illus.). 1977. 44.95 (0-913056-07-3) Evergreen Pr.

— Eyes of Texas: Fort Worth - Brazos Valley. 2nd ed. (Illus.). 224p. 1991. pap. 17.95 (0-88415-005-4, 5005) Gulf Pub.

— Eyes of Texas: Travel Ft. Worth. 1992. 22.95 (0-88415-016-X) Gulf Pub.

— Eyes of Texas Travel Guide: Dallas-East Texas. (Illus.). 222p. 1978. pap. 9.95 (0-89123-060-2) Cordovan Pr.

— Eyes of Texas Travel Guide: Fort Worth-Brazos Valley. (Illus.). 218p. 1981. 13.95 (0-89123-098-X); pap. 9.95 (0-89123-097-1) Cordovan Pr.

— Eyes of Texas Travel Guide: Hill Country-Permian Basin. (Illus.). 214p. 1980. 13.95 (0-89123-070-X); pap. 9.95 (0-89123-071-8) Cordovan Pr.

— Eyes of Texas Travel Guide: Panhandle-Plains. (Illus.). 204p. 1982. 13.95 (0-89123-024-6); pap. 9.95 (0-89123-042-4) Cordovan Pr.

— Falcon! The New Size Ford. LC 82-90194. (Ford Road Ser.: Vol. 7). (Illus.). 320p. 1982. 44.95 (0-913056-11-1) Evergreen Pr.

— Houston-Gulf Coast. 2nd ed. (Eyes of Texas Travel Guides Ser.). (Illus.). 224p. 1987. pap. 10.95 (0-88415-225-1) Gulf Pub.

— Man Kidnapped by UFO for Third Time. Bixby, Robert, ed. 39p. 1994. pap. text ed. 6.00 (0-9624453-6-3) March Street Pr.

— Mustang Does It. LC 77-78278. (Ford Road Ser.: Vol. 6). 1978. lib. bdg. 44.95 (0-913056-09-X) Evergreen Pr.

— The Nifty 'Fifties' Fords: An Illustrated History of the Early Post-War Fords. LC 73-93879. (Ford Road Ser.: Vol. 5). (Illus.). 1974. 44.95 (0-913056-05-7) Evergreen Pr.

— Panhandle-Plains. (Eyes of Texas Travel Guides Ser.). (Illus.). 200p. 1982. pap. 9.95 (0-88415-210-3) Gulf Pub.

— Ray Miller's Galveston. (Illus.). 280p. 1983. 19.95 (0-89123-032-7) Cordovan Pr.

— Ray Miller's Galveston. 2nd ed. LC 92-36295. 304p. 1993. 29.95 (0-88415-092-5); pap. 18.95 (0-88415-091-7) Gulf Pub.

— Ray Miller's Houston. (Illus.). 248p. pap. 19.95 (0-89123-039-4) Cordovan Pr.

— Ray Miller's Texas Forts: A History & Guide. 240p. 1985. pap. 13.95 (0-89123-036-X) Cordovan Pr.

— Ray Miller's Texas Parks: A History & Guide. (Illus.). 248p. (Orig.). 1984. pap. 13.95 (0-89123-046-7) Cordovan Pr.

— San Antonio-Border. 2nd ed. (Eyes of Texas Travel Guides Ser.). (Illus.). 252p. 1988. pap. 10.95 (0-88415-234-0) Gulf Pub.

— Texas Forts: A History & Guide. (Eyes of Texas Travel Guides Ser.). (Illus.). 223p. 1985. pap. 13.95 (0-88415-215-4) Gulf Pub.

— Texas Parks: A History & Guide. (Eyes of Texas Travel Guides Ser.). (Illus.). 232p. 1984. pap. 13.95 (0-88415-217-0) Gulf Pub.

— Volkswagen Bug! The People's Car. (Autobahn Ser.: Vol. 1). (Illus.). 320p. 1984. 44.95 (0-913056-12-X) Evergreen Pr.

Miller, Ray & Embree, Glenn. Henry's Lady: An Illustrated History of the Model A Ford. LC 72-77244. (Ford Road Ser.: Vol. 2). (Illus.). 300p. 1972. 44.95 (0-913056-03-0) Evergreen Pr.

— The Real Corvette: An Illustrated History of Chevrolet's Sports Car. LC 75-8100. (Chevy Chase Ser.: Vol. 3). (Illus.). 320p. 1975. 44.95 (0-913056-06-5) Evergreen Pr.

— Thunderbird! An Illustrated History of the Ford T-Bird. LC 73-75630. (Ford Road Ser.: Vol. 4). (Illus.). 1973. 44.95 (0-913056-04-9) Evergreen Pr.

— The V-Eight Affair: An Illustrated History of the Pre-War Ford V-8. LC 70-174898. (Ford Road Ser: Vol. 3). (Illus.). 303p. 1972. pap. 29.95 (0-913056-02-2) Evergreen Pr.

Miller, Ray & Miller, Jo, eds. Hawaii! - Wish You Were Here. LC 93-91067. (Illus.). 96p. (Orig.). 1994. pap. 19.95 (0-913056-14-6) Evergreen Pr.

Miller, Ray, Jr., ed. see Bayer, Hans.

Miller, Ray, Jr., jt. auth. see McCloy, James F.

Miller, Raymond C., ed. Twentieth-Century Pessimism & the American Dream. LC 79-26081. (Franklin Memorial Lectures: No. 8). 118p. reprint ed. pap. 33.70 (0-7837-3802-1, 2043622) Bks Demand.

— Twentieth-Century Pessimism & the American Dream. LC 79-26081. (Franklin Memorial Lectures Ser.: Vol. VIII). (Illus.). ix, 104p. 1980. reprint ed. text ed. 38.50 (0-313-22122-7, MITW, Greenwood Pr) Greenwood.

***Miller, Raymond W. & Donahue, Roy L.** Soils in Our Environment. 7th rev. ed. Miller, Joyce U., ed. LC 94-44096. Orig. Title: Soils. 1995. text ed. 78.00 (0-13-095803-4) P-H.

Miller, Reese P. Principles of Philosophy. Miller, Valentine R. & Miller, Resse P., trs. (Orig.). 1984. pap. text ed. 44.50 (90-277-1754-0) Kluwer Ac.

Miller, Reese P., tr. see Descartes, Rene.

***Miller, Regina.** The Developmentally Appropriate Inclusive Childhood Classroom. LC 95-13337. 1995. write for info. (0-8273-7071-7) Delmar.

***Miller, Regina & Mixer, Jennifer.** Don't Pay Retail! Indiana's Discount Buying Guide. 275p. 1994. pap. 16.95 (1-878208-54-3) Guild Pr IN.

Miller, Resse P., tr. see Miller, Reese P.

Miller, Rex. Basic Electricity. (gr. 9-12). 1978. 10.64 (0-02-662580-6); pap. 8.56 (0-02-662570-9) Bennett IL.

— Butcher. Grad, Doug, ed. 320p. (Orig.). 1994. mass mkt. 5.50 (0-671-86882-9) PB.

— Chaingang. Grad, Doug, ed. 320p. (Orig.). 1992. mass mkt. 4.99 (0-671-74847-5) PB.

— The Electrician's Toolbox Manual. 352p. 1989. pap. 11.00 (0-13-247701-7) P-H.

— Electricity & Electronics. 2nd ed. 1991. teacher ed 14.00 (0-8273-4420-1); text ed. 27.95 (0-8273-4419-8) Delmar.

— Electricity for Heating, Air Conditioning & Refrigeration. 369p. (C). 1988. pap. text ed. 40.00 (0-15-520947-7); pap. text ed. 3.00 (0-15-520948-5) SCP.

— Electronics the Easy Way. 2nd ed. (Easy Way Ser.). 352p. 1988. pap. 9.95 (0-8120-4081-3) Barron.

— Fractional Horsepower Electric Motors. 1984. text ed. 15.95 (0-672-23410-6, Audel) Macmillan.

— Have Fun Playing the Market. (Illus.). 40p. 1995. pap. 7.00 (0-8059-3621-1) Dorrance.

— Industrial Electricity. (gr. 9-12). 1978. student ed 4.60 (0-02-664700-1) Bennett IL.

— Industrial Electricity. rev. ed. (gr. 9-12). 1982. text ed. 21.28 (0-02-664730-3) Bennett IL.

— Refrigeration & Air-Conditioning Technology. 1983. teacher ed 6.64 (0-02-665550-0); text ed. 26.00 (0-02-665540-3); student ed 6.64 (0-02-665560-8) Bennett IL.

— Residential Electrical Wiring. (Illus.). 300p. 1981. teacher ed 5.60 (0-02-665630-2); text ed. 15.96 (0-02-665620-5); student ed 6.40 (0-02-665640-X) Bennett IL.

— St. Louis Blues. limited ed. 160p. 1995. boxed 40.00 (0-940776-30-8) Maclay Assoc.

— Savant. Grad, Doug, ed. 320p. (Orig.). 1994. mass mkt. 5.99 (0-671-74848-3) PB.

— Small Electric Motors. 2nd ed. 436p. 1993. text ed. 30.00 (0-02-584975-1) Macmillan.

— Small Gasoline Engines. 3rd ed. 681p. 1993. text ed. 30.00 (0-02-584991-3) Macmillan.

Miller, Rex & Baker, Glenn E. Carpentry & Construction. 2nd ed. 1991. text ed. 42.95 (0-07-157669-X); pap. text ed. 34.95 (0-07-157668-1) McGraw.

— Carpentry & Construction. 2nd ed. (Illus.). 656p. 1991. 42.95 (0-8306-8678-9, 3678); pap. 29.95 (0-8306-3678-1) TAB Bks.

Miller, Rex & Culpepper, Fred. Math for Electricity-Electronics. 160p. 1980. pap. text ed. 10.64 (0-02-818220-0); 7.96 (0-02-818230-8) Glencoe.

Miller, Rex & Miller, Mark R. Electric Motor Controls. 464p. (C). 1991. text ed. write for info. (0-13-249376-4) P-H.

— Electronics the Easy Way. 3rd ed. LC 94-46445. 1995. write for info. (0-8120-9144-2) Barron.

Miller, Rex & Miller, Martin R. Mathematics for Electricians & Electronics Technicians. 1985. text ed. 14.95 (0-8161-1700-4, Audel) Macmillan.

Miller, Rex & Morrisey, Thomas J. Metal Technology. LC 74-77817. 1976. 22.39 (0-672-97623-4, Bobbs); teacher ed 3.67 (0-672-97625-0, Bobbs); 5.99 (0-672-97624-2, Bobbs) Macmillan.

Miller, Rex, ed. see Anderson, Edwin P.

Miller, Rex, jt. auth. see Baker, Glenn E.

Miller, Rex, jt. auth. see Fuller, Nelson.

Miller, Rhoda. Institutionalizing Peace: The Conception of the United States Institute for Peace & Its Role in American Political Thought. 191p. 1994. lib. bdg. 28.50 (0-89950-994-0) McFarland & Co.

Miller, Rich, jt. auth. see McAllister, Dawson.

Miller, Richard. California Traveler Ghost Towns: Remnants of the Mining Days. (American Traveler Ser.). (Illus.). 48p. (Orig.). 1992. pap. 4.95 (1-55838-124-4) R H Pub.

— English, French, German & Italian Techniques of Singing: A Study in National Tonal Preferences & How They Relate to Functional Efficiency. LC 76-58554. (Illus.). 275p. 1977. 27.50 (0-8108-1020-4) Scarecrow.

— Introduction to Differential Equations. 2nd ed. 640p. (C). 1991. text ed. write for info. (0-13-478264-X) P-H.

— The Structure of Singing: System & Art in Vocal Technique. (Illus.). 372p. 1986. text ed. 37.00 (0-02-872660-X) Schirmer Bks.

— To My Dear Slimeball: Secret Letters from a Senior Demon to His Slippery Sidekick. (Orig.). (YA). 1995. pap. 7.99 (1-56507-187-5) Harvest Hse.

— The Town & Country World of Golf. LC 92-13913. 224p. 1992. 45.00 (0-87833-805-5) Taylor Pub.

— The Town & Country World of Golf. limited ed. LC 92-13913. 224p. 1992. 100.00 (0-87833-798-9) Taylor Pub.

— Training Tenor Voices. 192p. 1993. text ed. 35.00 (0-02-871397-4) Schirmer Bks.

— Triumphant Journey: The Saga of Bobby Jones & the Grand Slam of Golf. LC 93-45456. 272p. 1994. reprint ed. pap. 10.95 (0-87833-851-9) Taylor Pub.

Miller, Richard, tr. Magritte - Torczyner: Letters Between Friends. LC 93-38902. 1994. 19.95 (0-8109-2568-0) Abrams.

Miller, Richard & Michel, A. Ordinary Differential Equations. 1981. text ed. 72.00 (0-12-497280-2) Acad Pr.

Miller, Richard & Miller, Iona. The Modern Alchemist: A Guide to Personal Transformation. (Illus.). 300p. (Orig.). 1994. pap. 14.95 (0-933999-37-2) Phanes Pr.

Miller, Richard & Walker, Terri C., eds. CIM & Manufacturing Automation Markets: 1992-1995. (Orig.). 1992. pap. text ed. 485.00 (1-881503-02-X) R K Miller Assocs.

Miller, Richard, tr. see Barthes, Roland.

Miller, Richard, tr. see Cesaire, Aime.

Miller, Richard, tr. see Giroud, Francoise & Levy, Bernard-Henry.

Miller, Richard, tr. see Hadas-Lebel, Mireille.

Miller, Richard, tr. see Le Guerer, Annick.

Miller, Richard, tr. see Locke, Ralph, ed.

Miller, Richard, tr. see Sarde, Michel.

Miller, Richard, tr. see Tilly.

***Miller, Richard A.** Beating Bad Breath: Your Complete Guide to Eliminating & Preventing Halitosis. (Illus.). 64p. (Orig.). Date not set. pap. 8.95 (1-56167-202-5) Am Literary Pr.

— The Magical & Ritual Use of Aphrodisiacs. (Illus.). 208p. (Orig.). 1992. pap. 9.95 (0-89281-402-0, Destiny Bks) Inner Tradit.

— The Magical & Ritual Use of Herbs. (Illus.). 144p. 1992. pap. 9.95 (0-89281-401-2, Destiny Bks) Inner Tradit.

— The Potential of Herbs As a Cash Crop. LC 85-70967. 230p. 1985. pap. 14.00 (0-911311-10-6) Halcyon Hse.

— The Potential of Herbs As a Cash Crop: How to Make a Living in the Country. (Illus.). 240p. (Orig.). 1992. pap. 12.95 (0-89815-472-3) Ten Speed Pr.

M

An Asterisk (*) at the beginning of an entry indicates that the title is appearing in BIP for the first time.

— El Uso Magico y Ritual de las Hierbas-The Magic & Ritual Use of Herbs. 1995. pap. 9.95 (0-89281-467-5) Inner Tradit.

Miller, Richard A. & Miller, Iona. Magical & Ritual Use of Perfumes. (Illus.). 224p. 1990. pap. 12.95 (0-89281-210-9, Destiny Bks) Inner Tradit.

Miller, Richard B. American Banking in Crisis: Views from 25 Leading Financial Services CEOs. 250p. 1989. text ed. 40.00 (1-55623-221-7) Irwin Prof Pubng.

— Bankers Almanac 1985. (Bankers Reference Ser.). 464p. reprint ed. pap. 132.30 (0-8357-5962-8, 2052181) Bks Demand.

— The Banker's Desk Book. 400p. 1990. text ed. 69.95 (0-13-058538-6) P-H.

— Interpretations of Conflict: Ethics, Pacificism, & the Just-War Tradition. LC 91-3044. 296p. 1991. pap. text ed. 17.95 (0-226-52796-4) U Ch Pr.

— Late, Great Citicorp. 1993. text ed. 21.95 (0-07-042340-7) McGraw.

— The PH Banking Yearbook. 564p. 1990. 89.95 (0-13-717323-7) P-H.

— Super Banking: Innovative Management Strategies That Work. 250p. 1988. 50.00 (1-55623-114-8) Irwin Prof Pubng.

Miller, Richard B., ed. War in the Twentieth Century: Sources in Theological Ethics. LC 92-2318. (Library of Theological Ethics). 320p. (Orig.). 1993. pap. 21.99 (0-664-25323-7) Westminster John Knox.

Miller, Richard C. & Solverson, John F. Student Lamps of the Victorian Era. (Illus.). 176p. (Orig.). 1992. pap. 34.95 (0-915410-86-9, 4012); write for info. (0-318-69706-8, 4014) Antique Pubns.

— Student Lamps of the Victorian Era. limited ed. (Illus.). 176p. (Orig.). 1992. 49.95 (0-915410-87-7, 4013) Antique Pubns.

Miller, Richard E., jt. ed. see McClellan, Keith.

***Miller, Richard F. & Mooney, Robert F. The Civil War: The Nantucket Experience. Oldham, Elizabeth, ed. (Illus.). 208p. (Orig.). 1994. pap. 14.95 (0-9627851-1-3) Wesco Pub MA. "For Civil War buffs & all who love Nantucket, Miller & Mooney have given us a treasure of a book. Reminding us that Nantucketers were there - at Antietam, at Fredericksburg, at Gettysburg - it's an important piece of scholarship, & a fascinating read." - Russell Baker. "A superb & detailed story of one company of Nantucket men during the Civil War - Excellent." - Warren Wilkinson, Civil War historian & author of Mother, May You Never See the Sights I Have Seen. A chronicle of the war years as lived by the people of Nantucket including the memoirs & diary of Josiah Fitch Murphey, a Nantucketer of the famed Harvard Regiment, who was at Fredericksburg, Chancellorsville, the Wilderness, Spotsylvania, & Petersburg. THE CIVIL WAR: THE NANTUCKET EXPERIENCE also contains detailed biographies of the 80 Nantucketers who served with the 20th Massachusetts. 216 pages, complete with photographs & notes. Softcover (available immediately) $14.95. Send check or money order to: Wesco Publishing, P.O. Box 1540, Nantucket, MA 02554.** *Publisher Provided Annotation.*

Miller, Richard H., ed. The Evolution of the Cold War: From Confrontation to Containment. LC 79-4258. (American Problem Studies). 144p. 1979. reprint ed. pap. text ed. 9.50 (0-88275-935-3) Krieger.

Miller, Richard I. The Assessment of College Performance. LC 79-83575. (Jossey-Bass Series in Higher Education). (Illus.). 392p. reprint ed. pap. 111.80 (0-8357-4912-6, 2037842) Bks Demand.

— Developing Programs for Faculty Evaluation: A Sourcebook for Higher Education. LC 73-12063. (Jossey-Bass Higher Education Ser.). 260p. reprint ed. pap. 74.10 (0-685-16167-6, 2027763) Bks Demand.

— Evaluating Faculty for Promotion & Tenure. LC 87-45499. (Higher & Adult Education Ser.). 275p. 1987. 34.95x (1-55542-069-9) Jossey-Bass.

— Evaluating Faculty Performance. LC 70-184958. (Jossey-Bass Higher Education Ser.). 161p. reprint ed. pap. 45.90 (0-685-20944-X, 2056556) Bks Demand.

— Major American Higher Education Issues in the Nineteen Ninety's. (Higher Education Policy Ser.: No. 9). 200p. 1990. 51.00 (1-85302-514-3, Pub. by J Kingsley Pubs UK) Taylor & Francis.

Miller, Richard I., ed. Applying the Deming Method to Higher Education. 133p. 1991. 27.00 (0-910402-98-1) Coll & U Personnel.

Miller, Richard I. & Holzapfel, Edward W., Jr., eds. Issues in Personnel Management. LC 85-644753. (New Directions for Community Colleges Ser.: No. CC 62). 1988. 16.95 (1-55542-913-0) Jossey-Bass.

Miller, Richard K. Artificial Intelligence Applications for Business Management. LC 86-46130. 300p. 1987. text ed. 110.00 (0-88173-032-7) Fairmont Pr.

— Artificial Intelligence Applications for Manufacturing. LC 86-46129. 500p. 1987. text ed. 110.00 (0-88173-031-9) Fairmont Pr.

— Design for Manufacturability - Assembly. 219p. 1990. pap. text ed. 955.00 (0-89671-111-0) SEAI Tech Pubns.

— Directory of Technical Magazines & Directories. 1982. text ed. 45.00 (0-915586-33-9) Fairmont Pr.

— Energy & Noise. 39.00 (0-915586-40-1) Fairmont Pr.

— Energy Conservation Marketing Handbook. 1982. text ed. 42.50 (0-915586-65-7) Fairmont Pr.

— Guide to the Noise Control Literature. 39.00 (0-915586-09-6) Fairmont Pr.

— Handbook of Selling to the U. S. Military. 1982. text ed. 39.00 (0-915586-63-0) Fairmont Pr.

— Industrial Robot Handbook: Case Histories of Effective Robot Use in 70 Industries. (Illus.). 686p. 1989. pap. 105.00 (0-442-23733-2) Chapman & Hall.

— Manufacturing Simulation. LC 89-17111. 178p. 1989. pap. text ed. 95.00 (0-88173-104-8) Fairmont Pr.

— Neural Networks. LC 89-17158. 302p. 1989. pap. text ed. 95.00 (0-88173-100-5) Fairmont Pr.

— Optical Computers: The Next Frontier in Computing, 2 vols. (Illus.). 276p. 1991. pap. text ed. 285.00 (0-89671-113-7) SEAI Tech Pubns.

— Remote Sensing, Noncontact Sensing, & Image Processing. 966p. 1991. pap. text ed. 485.00 (0-89671-109-9) SEAI Tech Pubns.

— Superconductors: Electronics & Computer Applications. LC 89-17028. 270p. 1989. pap. text ed. 95.00 (0-88173-103-X) Fairmont Pr.

— Waterjet Cutting. LC 88-45797. 165p. 1990. text ed. 62.95 (0-88173-068-8) Fairmont Pr.

Miller, Richard K., comp. Energy Conservation & Utilization in Foundries. 45.00 (0-915586-44-4) Fairmont Pr.

— Energy Conservation & Utilization in the Glass Industry. 45.00 (0-915586-48-7) Fairmont Pr.

Miller, Richard K., ed. Fifth Generation Computers. LC 86-45549. 220p. 1986. text ed. 54.95 (0-88173-050-5) Fairmont Pr.

Miller, Richard K. & Montone, Wayne V. Handbook of Acoustical Enclosures & Barriers. 33.00 (0-915586-06-1) Fairmont Pr.

Miller, Richard K. & Rupnow, Marcia. Aboveground Storage Tanks. (Survey on Technology & Markets Ser.: No. 215). 50p. 1994. pap. text ed. 200.00 (1-55865-246-9) Future Tech Surveys.

— Environmental Legal Services. (Survey on Technology & Markets Ser.: No. 223). 50p. 1993. pap. text ed. 200.00 (1-55865-253-1) Future Tech Surveys.

— Underground Storage Tanks. (Survey on Technology & Markets Ser.: No. 214). 50p. 1994. pap. text ed. 200.00 (1-55865-245-0) Future Tech Surveys.

— Waste-to-Energy. (Survey on Technology & Markets Ser.: No. 213). 50p. 1994. pap. text ed. 200.00 (1-55865-244-2) Future Tech Surveys.

Miller, Richard K. & Rupnow, Marcia E. Air Doors & Air Curtains. LC 90-83931. (Survey on Technology & Markets Ser.: No. 136). 50p. 1991. pap. text ed. 200.00 (1-55865-161-6) Future Tech Surveys.

— Air Duct Cleaning Services. (Survey on Technology & Markets Ser.: No. 221). 50p. 1993. pap. text ed. 200.00 (1-55865-252-3) Future Tech Surveys.

— Air Pollution Instrumentation. LC 90-83884. (Survey on Technology & Markets Ser.: No. 180). 50p. 1991. pap. text ed. 200.00 (1-55865-204-3) Future Tech Surveys.

— Asbestos Abatement Equipment. LC 90-83848. (Survey on Technology & Markets Ser.: No. 143). 50p. 1991. pap. text ed. 200.00 (1-55865-168-3) Future Tech Surveys.

— Asbestos Contracting Services. LC 90-83847. (Survey on Technology & Markets Ser.: No. 142). 50p. 1991. pap. text ed. 200.00 (1-55865-167-5) Future Tech Surveys.

— Asbestos Laboratory Services. LC 90-83849. (Survey on Technology & Markets Ser.: No. 144). 50p. 1991. pap. text ed. 200.00 (1-55865-169-1) Future Tech Surveys.

— Asphalt Recycling. LC 90-84379. (Survey on Technology & Markets Ser.: No. 173). 50p. 1991. pap. text ed. 200.00 (1-55865-225-6) Future Tech Surveys.

— Balers. LC 90-83888. (Survey on Technology & Markets Ser.: No. 184). 50p. 1991. pap. text ed. 200.00 (1-55865-208-6) Future Tech Surveys.

— Bioenergy Systems. LC 90-83926. (Survey on Technology & Markets Ser.: No. 126). 50p. 1991. pap. text ed. 200.00 (1-55865-149-7) Future Tech Surveys.

— Bioremediation. (Survey on Technology & Markets Ser.: No. 226). 50p. 1994. pap. text ed. 200.00 (1-55865-257-4) Future Tech Surveys.

— CFC Alternatives. LC 90-83916. (Survey on Technology & Markets Ser.: No. 110). 50p. 1991. pap. text ed. 200.00 (1-55865-133-0) Future Tech Surveys.

— CFC Recovery & Recycling Equipment. LC 90-83934. (Survey on Technology & Markets Ser.: No. 140). 50p. 1991. pap. text ed. 200.00 (1-55865-165-9) Future Tech Surveys.

— Chemical Storage Buildings. LC 90-83882. (Survey on Technology & Markets Ser.: No. 178). 50p. 1991. pap. text ed. 200.00 (1-55865-202-7) Future Tech Surveys.

— Chemical Storage Drums. (Survey on Technology & Markets Ser.: No. 156). 50p. 1991. 200.00 (1-55865-226-4) Future Tech Surveys.

— Chromatography, Gas. LC 90-83897. (Survey on Technology & Markets Ser.: No. 193). 50p. 1991. pap. text ed. 200.00 (1-55865-217-5) Future Tech Surveys.

— Cogeneration. (Survey on Technology & Markets Ser.: No. 207). 50p. 1993. pap. text ed. 200.00 (1-55865-238-8) Future Tech Surveys.

— Commercial Air Cleaning Systems. LC 90-83895. (Survey on Technology & Markets Ser.: No. 191). 50p. 1991. pap. text ed. 200.00 (1-55865-215-9) Future Tech Surveys.

— Commercial Lighting. (Survey on Technology & Markets Ser.: No. 209). 50p. 1993. pap. text ed. 200.00 (1-55865-240-X) Future Tech Surveys.

— Cooling Towers. LC 90-83921. (Survey on Technology & Markets Ser.: No. 117). 50p. 1991. pap. text ed. 200.00 (1-55865-140-3) Future Tech Surveys.

— Dataloggers. LC 90-83898. (Survey on Technology & Markets Ser.: No. 194). 50p. 1991. pap. text ed. 200.00 (1-55865-218-3) Future Tech Surveys.

— Demand Side Management. (Survey on Technology & Markets Ser.: No. 220). 50p. 1993. pap. text ed. 200.00 (1-55865-251-5) Future Tech Surveys.

— Electric & Magnetic Field Recovery. LC 90-83933. (Survey on Technology & Markets Ser.: No. 139). 50p. 1991. pap. text ed. 200.00 (1-55865-164-0) Future Tech Surveys.

— Electric Utilities: Executive Outlook. (Survey on Technology & Markets Ser.: No. 202). 50p. 1993. pap. text ed. 200.00 (1-55865-233-7) Future Tech Surveys.

— Emergency Lighting. LC 89-85437. (Survey on Technology & Markets Ser.: No. 129). 50p. 1991. pap. text ed. 200.00 (1-55865-152-7) Future Tech Surveys.

— Energy Efficient Motors. (Survey on Technology & Markets Ser.: No. 212). 50p. 1993. pap. text ed. 200.00 (1-55865-243-4) Future Tech Surveys.

— Energy Management & HVAC Software. LC 90-83908. (Survey on Technology & Markets Ser.: No. 103). 50p. 1991. pap. text ed. 200.00 (1-55865-126-8) Future Tech Surveys.

— Energy Management Consulting Services. LC 90-83914. (Survey on Technology & Markets Ser.: No. 106). 50p. 1991. pap. text ed. 200.00 (1-55865-129-2) Future Tech Surveys.

— Energy Management in Commercial Buildings. LC 90-83913. (Survey on Technology & Markets Ser.: No. 105). 50p. 1991. pap. text ed. 200.00 (1-55865-128-4) Future Tech Surveys.

— Energy Management, Industrial. LC 90-83912. (Survey on Technology & Markets Ser.: No. 104). 50p. 1991. pap. text ed. 200.00 (1-55865-127-6) Future Tech Surveys.

— Energy Management Systems. (Survey on Technology & Markets Ser.: No. 208). 50p. 1993. pap. text ed. 200.00 (1-55865-239-6) Future Tech Surveys.

— Energy Project Financing. LC 90-83924. (Survey on Technology & Markets Ser.: No. 120). 50p. 1991. pap. text ed. 200.00 (1-55865-143-8) Future Tech Surveys.

— Environmental & Waste Management Robotics. LC 90-83894. (Survey on Technology & Markets Ser.: No. 190). 50p. 1991. pap. text ed. 200.00 (1-55865-214-0) Future Tech Surveys.

— Environmental Consulting Services. (Survey on Technology & Markets Ser.: No. 219). 50p. 1993. pap. text ed. 200.00 (1-55865-250-7) Future Tech Surveys.

— Environmental Immunoassays. (Survey on Technology & Markets Ser.: No. 169). 50p. 1991. pap. text ed. 200.00 (1-55865-231-0) Future Tech Surveys.

— Environmental Noise Control. LC 90-83904. (Survey on Technology & Markets Ser.: No. 200). 50p. 1991. pap. text ed. 200.00 (1-55865-224-8) Future Tech Surveys.

— Environmental Software. (Survey on Technology & Markets Ser.: No. 217). 50p. 1993. pap. text ed. 200.00 (1-55865-248-5) Future Tech Surveys.

— Environmental Test Laboratories. (Survey on Technology & Markets Ser.: No. 222). 50p. 1994. pap. text ed. 200.00 (1-55865-256-6) Future Tech Surveys.

— Expert Systems. LC 90-83860. (Survey on Technology & Markets Ser.: No. 153). 50p. 1991. pap. text ed. 200.00 (1-55865-180-2) Future Tech Surveys.

— Fluidized Bed Boilers. LC 89-85439. (Survey on Technology & Markets Ser.: No. 131). 50p. 1991. pap. text ed. 200.00 (1-55865-154-3) Future Tech Surveys.

— Fuel Cells. LC 90-83923. (Survey on Technology & Markets Ser.: No. 119). 50p. 1991. pap. text ed. 200.00 (1-55865-142-X) Future Tech Surveys.

— Fume Hoods. LC 90-83928. (Survey on Technology & Markets Ser.: No. 133). 50p. 1991. pap. text ed. 200.00 (1-55865-158-6) Future Tech Surveys.

— Geographic Information Systems. (Survey on Technology & Markets Ser.: No. 233). 50p. 1994. pap. text ed. 200.00 (1-55865-264-7) Future Tech Surveys.

— Global Positioning Systems. LC 90-83857. (Survey on Technology & Markets Ser.: No. 152). 50p. 1991. pap. text ed. 200.00 (1-55865-177-2) Future Tech Surveys.

— Groundwater Remediation. (Survey on Technology & Markets Ser.: No. 228). 50p. 1994. 200.00 (1-55865-259-0) Future Tech Surveys.

— Hearing Protective Devices. LC 90-83902. (Survey on Technology & Markets Ser.: No. 198). 50p. 1991. pap. text ed. 200.00 (1-55865-222-1) Future Tech Surveys.

— Heat Pumps. LC 89-85430. (Survey on Technology & Markets Ser.: No. 122). 50p. 1991. pap. text ed. 200.00 (1-55865-145-4) Future Tech Surveys.

— Heat Recovery Equipment. LC 89-85431. (Survey on Technology & Markets Ser.: No. 123). 50p. 1991. pap. text ed. 200.00 (1-55865-146-2) Future Tech Surveys.

— HVAC - R CFC Recovery Equipment. (Survey on Technology & Markets Ser.: No. 210). 50p. 1993. pap. text ed. 200.00 (0-685-69519-0) Future Tech Surveys.

— HVAC & Energy Systems Water Treatment. LC 90-83929. (Survey on Technology & Markets Ser.: No. 134). 50p. 1991. pap. text ed. 200.00 (1-55865-159-4) Future Tech Surveys.

— Incinerator Construction. (Survey on Technology & Markets Ser.: No. 231). 50p. 1994. pap. text ed. 200.00 (1-55865-262-0) Future Tech Surveys.

— Independent Power Production. (Survey on Technology & Markets Ser.: No. 232). 50p. (Orig.). 1994. pap. text ed. 200.00 (1-55865-263-9) Future Tech Surveys.

— Indoor Air Quality. (Survey on Technology & Markets Ser.: No. 218). 50p. 1993. pap. text ed. 200.00 (1-55865-249-3) Future Tech Surveys.

— Industrial Air Pollution Control Equipment. LC 90-83885. (Survey on Technology & Markets Ser.: No. 181). 50p. 1991. pap. text ed. 200.00 (1-55865-205-1) Future Tech Surveys.

— Industrial Wastewater Treatment. (Survey on Technology & Markets Ser.: No. 229). 50p. 1994. 200.00 (1-55865-260-4) Future Tech Surveys.

— Infrared Heaters. LC 89-85433. (Survey on Technology & Markets Ser.: No. 125). 50p. (Orig.). 1991. pap. text ed. 200.00 (1-55865-148-9) Future Tech Surveys.

— Intelligent Buildings. LC 90-83911. (Survey on Technology & Markets Ser.: No. 102). 50p. (Orig.). 1991. pap. text ed. 200.00 (1-55865-125-X) Future Tech Surveys.

— Landfill Design & Construction. LC 90-83887. (Survey on Technology & Markets Ser.: No. 183). 50p. 1991. pap. text ed. 200.00 (1-55865-207-8) Future Tech Surveys.

— Landfill Methane Gas Recovery. LC 90-83892. (Survey on Technology & Markets Ser.: No. 188). 50p. 1991. pap. text ed. 200.00 (1-55865-212-4) Future Tech Surveys.

— Landfill Privatization. LC 90-83886. (Survey on Technology & Markets Ser.: No. 182). 50p. 1991. pap. text ed. 200.00 (1-55865-206-X) Future Tech Surveys.

— Lead Paint Abatement. LC 90-83850. (Survey on Technology & Markets Ser.: No. 145). 50p. 1991. pap. text ed. 200.00 (1-55865-170-5) Future Tech Surveys.

— Leak Detectors. (Survey on Technology & Markets Ser.: No. 216). 50p. 1993. pap. text ed. 200.00 (1-55865-247-7) Future Tech Surveys.

— Lechate Collection & Treatment Systems. LC 90-83891. (Survey on Technology & Markets Ser.: No. 187). 50p. 1991. pap. text ed. 200.00 (1-55865-211-6) Future Tech Surveys.

— Lining Systems & Containment Membranes. LC 90-83853. (Survey on Technology & Markets Ser.: No. 148). 50p. 1991. pap. text ed. 200.00 (1-55865-173-X) Future Tech Surveys.

— Medical Waste Management. LC 90-83866. (Survey on Technology & Markets Ser.: No. 161). 50p. 1991. pap. text ed. 200.00 (1-55865-186-1) Future Tech Surveys.

— Meteorological Instruments. LC 90-83899. (Survey on Technology & Markets Ser.: No. 195). 50p. 1991. pap. text ed. 200.00 (1-55865-219-1) Future Tech Surveys.

— Municipal & Industrial Composting. LC 90-83868. (Survey on Technology & Markets Ser.: No. 163). 50p. 1991. pap. text ed. 200.00 (1-55865-188-8) Future Tech Surveys.

— Municipal Wastewater Treatment. (Survey on Technology & Markets Ser.: No. 230). 50p. 1994. 200.00 (1-55865-261-2) Future Tech Surveys.

— Natural Gas: Executive Outlook. (Survey on Technology & Markets Ser.: No. 204). 50p. 1993. pap. text ed. 200.00 (1-55865-235-3) Future Tech Surveys.

— Natural Gas Vehicles. (Survey on Technology & Markets Ser.: No. 205). 50p. 1993. pap. text ed. 200.00 (1-55865-236-1) Future Tech Surveys.

— Neural Network. LC 90-83861. (Survey on Technology & Markets Ser.: No. 154). 50p. 1991. pap. text ed. 200.00 (1-55865-181-0) Future Tech Surveys.

— Occupancy Sensors. LC 89-85424. (Survey on Technology & Markets Ser.: No. 116). 50p. 1991. pap. text ed. 200.00 (1-55865-139-X) Future Tech Surveys.

— Oil Spill Prevention & Clean-Up. LC 90-83867. (Survey on Technology & Markets Ser.: No. 162). 50p. 1991. pap. text ed. 200.00 (1-55865-187-X) Future Tech Surveys.

— Outdoor Lighting Systems. LC 89-85436. (Survey on Technology & Markets Ser.: No. 128). 50p. 1991. pap. text ed. 200.00 (1-55865-151-9) Future Tech Surveys.

— Packaged Cogeneration Systems. LC 90-83915. (Survey on Technology & Markets Ser.: No. 108). 50p. 1991. pap. text ed. 200.00 (1-55865-131-4) Future Tech Surveys.

— Paper Recycling. LC 90-83878. (Survey on Technology & Markets Ser.: No. 174). 50p. 1991. pap. text ed. 200.00 (1-55865-198-5) Future Tech Surveys.

— PCBs. LC 90-83852. (Survey on Technology & Markets Ser.: No. 147). 50p. 1991. pap. text ed. 200.00 (1-55865-172-1) Future Tech Surveys.

— PET Recycling. LC 90-83876. (Survey on Technology & Markets Ser.: No. 171). 50p. 1991. pap. text ed. 200.00 (1-55865-196-9) Future Tech Surveys.

— Petroleum: Strategic Planning & Future Trends. LC 90-83932. (Survey on Technology & Markets Ser.: No. 138). 50p. 1991. pap. text ed. 200.00 (1-55865-163-2) Future Tech Surveys.

— Photovoltaics. LC 89-85417. (Survey on Technology & Markets Ser.: No. 109). 50p. 1991. pap. text ed. 200.00 (1-55865-132-2) Future Tech Surveys.

— PID Controllers. LC 89-85429. (Survey on Technology & Markets Ser.: No. 121). 50p. 1991. pap. text ed. 200.00 (1-55865-144-6) Future Tech Surveys.

— Protective Clothing. LC 90-83903. (Survey on Technology & Markets Ser.: No. 199). 50p. 1991. pap. text ed. 200.00 (1-55865-223-X) Future Tech Surveys.

— Radon. LC 90-83851. (Survey on Technology & Markets Ser.: No. 146). 50p. 1991. pap. text ed. 200.00 (1-55865-171-3) Future Tech Surveys.

— Respiratory Protection. LC 90-83901. (Survey on Technology & Markets Ser.: No. 197). 50p. 1991. pap. text ed. 200.00 (1-55865-221-3) Future Tech Surveys.

— Secondary Containment Systems. (Survey on Technology & Markets Ser.: No. 157). 50p. 1991. 200.00 (1-55865-227-2) Future Tech Surveys.

— Site Remediation. (Survey on Technology & Markets Ser.: No. 227). 50p. 1994. pap. text ed. 200.00 (1-55865-258-2) Future Tech Surveys.

An Asterisk (*) at the beginning of an entry indicates that the title is appearing in BIP for the first time.

— Sludge Management Equipment. LC 90-83900. (Survey on Technology & Markets Ser.: No. 196). 50p. 1991. pap. text ed. 200.00 (*1-55865-220-5*) Future Tech Surveys.

— Solar Screen Window Films. LC 90-83927. (Survey on Technology & Markets Ser.: No. 130). 50p. 1991. pap. text ed. 200.00 (*1-55865-153-5*) Future Tech Surveys.

— Solvent Recovery Equipment. LC 90-83881. (Survey on Technology & Markets Ser.: No. 177). 50p. 1991. pap. text ed. 200.00 (*1-55865-201-9*) Future Tech Surveys.

— Sorbents. LC 90-83873. (Survey on Technology & Markets Ser.: No. 168). 50p. 1991. pap. text ed. 200.00 (*1-55865-193-4*) Future Tech Surveys.

— Spectroscopy in Environmental & Occupational Health Applications. LC 90-83875. (Survey on Technology & Markets Ser.: No. 170). 50p. 1991. pap. text ed. 200.00 (*1-55865-195-0*) Future Tech Surveys.

— Standby Power Systems. LC 90-83920. (Survey on Technology & Markets Ser.: No. 115). 50p. 1991. pap. text ed. 200.00 (*1-55865-138-1*) Future Tech Surveys.

— Steam Traps. LC 89-85440. (Survey on Technology & Markets Ser.: No. 132). 50p. 1991. pap. text ed. 200.00 (*1-55865-155-1*) Future Tech Surveys.

— Stormwater Management. (Survey on Technology & Markets Ser.: No. 225). 50p. 1993. pap. text ed. 200.00 (*1-55865-255-8*) Future Tech Surveys.

— Thermal Energy Storage. (Survey on Technology & Markets Ser.: No. 206). 50p. 1993. pap. text ed. 200.00 (*1-55865-237-X*) Future Tech Surveys.

— UNIX Workstations. LC 90-83862. (Survey on Technology & Markets Ser.: No. 155). 50p. 1991. pap. text ed. 200.00 (*1-55865-182-9*) Future Tech Surveys.

— Used Tire Recycling & Resource Recovery. LC 90-83879. (Survey on Technology & Markets Ser.: No. 175). 50p. 1991. pap. text ed. 200.00 (*1-55865-199-3*) Future Tech Surveys.

— Utility Meter Reading Systems. LC 89-85445. (Survey on Technology & Markets Ser.: No. 137). 50p. 1991. pap. text ed. 200.00 (*1-55865-162-4*) Future Tech Surveys.

— Utility-Scale Energy Storage. LC 90-83919. (Survey on Technology & Markets Ser.: No. 114). 50p. 1991. pap. text ed. 200.00 (*1-55865-137-3*) Future Tech Surveys.

— Variable Frequency Motor Drives. (Survey on Technology & Markets Ser.: No. 211). 50p. 1993. pap. text ed. 200.00 (*1-55865-242-6*) Future Tech Surveys.

— Vibration Isolators. LC 90-83930. (Survey on Technology & Markets Ser.: No. 135). 50p. 1991. pap. text ed. 200.00 (*1-55865-160-8*) Future Tech Surveys.

— Virtual Reality. (Survey on Technology & Markets Ser.: No. 201). 50p. 1991. pap. text ed. 200.00 (*1-55865-232-9*) Future Tech Surveys.

— Waste Compactors. LC 90-83890. (Survey on Technology & Markets Ser.: No. 186). 50p. 1991. pap. text ed. 200.00 (*1-55865-210-8*) Future Tech Surveys.

— Waste Minimization & Pollution Prevention. (Survey on Technology & Markets Ser.: No. 224). 50p. 1993. pap. text ed. 200.00 (*1-55865-254-X*) Future Tech Surveys.

— Waste Oil Recycling & Resource Recovery. LC 90-83880. (Survey on Technology & Markets Ser.: No. 176). 50p. 1991. pap. text ed. 200.00 (*1-55865-200-0*) Future Tech Surveys.

— Waste Shredders. LC 90-83889. (Survey on Technology & Markets Ser.: No. 185). 50p. 1991. pap. text ed. 200.00 (*1-55865-209-4*) Future Tech Surveys.

— Water Quality Instrumentation. LC 90-83896. (Survey on Technology & Markets Ser.: No. 192). 50p. 1991. pap. text ed. 200.00 (*1-55865-216-7*) Future Tech Surveys.

— Wind Power. LC 90-83925. (Survey on Technology & Markets Ser.: No. 124). 50p. 1991. pap. text ed. 200.00 (*1-55865-147-0*) Future Tech Surveys.

Miller, Richard K. & Sell, George R. Volterra Integral Equations & Topological Dynamics. (Memoirs Ser.: No. 1/102). 67p. 1979. reprint ed. pap. 19.00 (*0-8218-1802-3*, MEMO 1/102) Am Math.

Miller, Richard K. & Supnow, Marcia E. Electric Vehicles. (Survey on Technology & Markets Ser.: No. 203). 50p. 1994. pap. text ed. 200.00 (*1-55865-234-5*) Future Tech Surveys.

***Miller, Richard K. & Thiede, Henry A., eds.** HIV, Perinatal Infections & Therapy: The Role of the Placenta. (Trophoblast Research Ser.: Vol. 8). 640p. 1995. text ed. 135.00 (*1-878822-45-4*) Univ Rochester Pr.

— Molecular Biology & Cell Regulation of the Placenta. (Trophoblast Research Ser.: Vol. 5). (Illus.). 488p. (C). 1991. 85.00 (*0-9630864-0-5*) Verav Med.

— Trophoblast Research, Vol. 2: Cellular Biology & Pharmacology of the Placenta, Techniques & Applications. LC 87-6934. 640p. 1987. 130.00 (*0-306-42563-7*, Plenum Med Bk) Plenum.

Miller, Richard K. & Thumann, Albert. Fundamentals of Noise Control Engineering. 2nd ed. 300p. 1989. text ed. 58.00 (*0-88173-091-2*) Fairmont Pr.

Miller, Richard K. & Walker, Matthew, eds. Superconductivity Update. LC 88-45796. 220p. 1990. pap. text ed. 95.00 (*0-88173-071-8*) Fairmont Pr.

Miller, Richard K. & Walker, Terri C. Active Noise Control. LC 88-81665. (Survey on Technology & Markets Ser.: No. 74). 50p. 1989. pap. text ed. 200.00 (*1-55865-073-3*) Future Tech Surveys.

— AI Programming Systems. LC 88-81893. (Survey on Technology & Markets Ser.: No. 95). 50p. 1989. pap. text ed. 200.00 (*1-55865-095-4*) Future Tech Surveys.

— Aquaculture. LC 88-80910. (Survey on Technology & Markets Ser.: No. 27). 50p. 1989. pap. text ed. 200.00 (*1-55865-026-1*) Future Tech Surveys.

— Array Processors. LC 88-81632. (Survey on Technology & Markets Ser.: No. 41). 50p. 1989. pap. text ed. 200.00 (*1-55865-040-7*) Future Tech Surveys.

— Artificial Neural Systems: A Survey on Technology & Markets, No. 11. LC 88-80489. 44p. 1989. pap. text ed. 200.00 (*1-55865-010-5*) Future Tech Surveys.

— Automated Guided Vehicles: A Survey on Technology & Markets. LC 88-80495. 50p. 1989. pap. text ed. 200.00 (*1-55865-002-4*) Future Tech Surveys.

— Automotive Sensors: A Survey on Technology & Markets, No. 67. LC 88-84057. (Survey on Technology & Markets Ser.: No. 67). 50p. 1989. pap. text ed. 200.00 (*1-55865-109-8*) Future Tech Surveys.

— Autonomous Vehicle Guidance Systems. LC 88-81887. (Survey on Technology & Markets Ser.: No. 90). 50p. 1989. pap. text ed. 200.00 (*1-55865-089-X*) Future Tech Surveys.

— Bioprocessing. LC 88-80910. (Survey on Technology & Markets Ser.: No. 26). 50p. 1989. pap. text ed. 200.00 (*1-55865-025-3*) Future Tech Surveys.

— Biosensors: A Survey on Technology & Markets, No. 16. LC 88-80900. (Survey on Technology & Markets Ser.: No. 16). 50p. 1989. pap. text ed. 200.00 (*1-55865-015-6*) Future Tech Surveys.

— Biotechnology in Animal Agriculture. LC 88-80913. (Survey on Technology & Markets Ser.: No. 25). 50p. 1989. pap. text ed. 200.00 (*1-55865-024-5*) Future Tech Surveys.

— Biotechnology in Plant Agriculture. LC 88-80908. (Survey on Technology & Markets Ser.: No. 24). 50p. 1989. pap. text ed. 200.00 (*1-55865-023-7*) Future Tech Surveys.

— CAD-CAM, CAE. LC 88-81648. (Survey on Technology & Markets Ser.: No. 57). 50p. 1989. pap. text ed. 200.00 (*1-55865-056-3*) Future Tech Surveys.

— Canadian CIM Markets. LC 88-84067. (Survey on Technology & Markets Ser.: No. 72). 50p. 1989. pap. text ed. 200.00 (*1-55865-119-5*) Future Tech Surveys.

— CD-ROM. LC 88-80905. (Survey on Technology & Markets Ser.: No. 21). 50p. 1989. pap. text ed. 200.00 (*1-55865-020-2*) Future Tech Surveys.

— Cellular Telephones. LC 88-81674. (Survey on Technology & Markets Ser.: No. 83). 50p. 1989. pap. text ed. 200.00 (*1-55865-082-2*) Future Tech Surveys.

— Chaos Fractals & Non-Linear Dynamic Systems. LC 88-80491. (Survey on Technology & Markets Ser.: No. 12). 50p. 1989. pap. text ed. 200.00 (*1-55865-011-3*) Future Tech Surveys.

— CIM Systems Integrators. LC 88-81657. (Survey on Technology & Markets Ser.: No. 66). 50p. 1989. pap. text ed. 200.00 (*1-55865-065-2*) Future Tech Surveys.

— Clean Room Robotics. LC 88-81637. (Survey on Technology & Markets Ser.: No. 46). 50p. 1989. pap. text ed. 200.00 (*1-55865-045-8*) Future Tech Surveys.

— Color Sensors & Instrumentation. LC 88-84060. (Survey on Technology & Markets Ser.: No. 85). 50p. 1989. pap. text ed. 200.00 (*1-55865-112-8*) Future Tech Surveys.

— Computer-Aided Software Engineering. LC 88-81631. (Survey on Technology & Markets Ser.: No. 40). 50p. 1989. pap. text ed. 200.00 (*1-55865-039-3*) Future Tech Surveys.

— Computer Integrated Manufacturing. LC 88-72187. (Survey on Technology & Markets Ser.: No. 34). 50p. 1989. pap. text ed. 200.00 (*1-55865-099-7*) Future Tech Surveys.

— Computer Workstations: A Survey on Technology & Markets, No. 7. LC 88-80485. 50p. 1988. pap. text ed. 200.00 (*1-55865-006-7*) Future Tech Surveys.

— Computers for Artificial Intelligence. LC 88-84063. (Survey on Technology & Markets Ser.: No. 91). 50p. 1989. pap. text ed. 200.00 (*1-55865-115-2*) Future Tech Surveys.

— Coordinate Measuring Machines. LC 88-81668. (Survey on Technology & Markets Ser.: No. 77). 50p. 1989. pap. text ed. 200.00 (*1-55865-076-8*) Future Tech Surveys.

— Database Engines. LC 88-81633. (Survey on Technology & Markets Ser.: No. 42). 50p. 1989. pap. text ed. 200.00 (*1-55865-041-5*) Future Tech Surveys.

— Decision Support Systems. LC 88-81884. (Survey on Technology & Markets Ser.: No. 93). 50p. 1989. pap. text ed. 200.00 (*1-55865-092-X*) Future Tech Surveys.

— Dextrous Robotic Hands. LC 88-80903. (Survey on Technology & Markets Ser.: No. 19). 50p. 1989. pap. text ed. 200.00 (*1-55865-018-0*) Future Tech Surveys.

— Diamond Films: A Survey on Technology & Markets, No. 14. LC 88-80492. 34p. 1989. pap. text ed. 200.00 (*1-55865-013-X*) Future Tech Surveys.

— Environmental Markets 1991-93. 435p. 1991. 285.00 (*0-89671-118-8*) SEAI Tech Pubns.

— Expert Systems in Manufacturing. LC 88-81886. (Survey on Technology & Markets Ser.: No. 92). 50p. 1989. pap. text ed. 200.00 (*1-55865-091-1*) Future Tech Surveys.

— Fault-Tolerant Computers. LC 88-81635. (Survey on Technology & Markets Ser.: No. 44). 50p. 1989. pap. text ed. 200.00 (*1-55865-043-1*) Future Tech Surveys.

— Fiber Optic LANS. LC 88-81643. (Survey on Technology & Markets Ser.: No. 52). 50p. 1989. pap. text ed. 200.00 (*1-55865-051-2*) Future Tech Surveys.

— Fiber Optic Sensors. LC 88-81651. (Survey on Technology & Markets Ser.: No. 60). 50p. 1989. pap. text ed. 200.00 (*1-55865-059-8*) Future Tech Surveys.

— Flat Panel Displays. LC 88-81655. (Survey on Technology & Markets Ser.: No. 64). 50p. 1989. pap. text ed. 200.00 (*1-55865-063-6*) Future Tech Surveys.

— Flexible Manufacturing Systems. LC 88-81645. (Survey on Technology & Markets Ser.: No. 54). 50p. 1989. pap. text ed. 200.00 (*1-55865-053-9*) Future Tech Surveys.

— Flow Sensors. LC 88-84053. (Survey on Technology & Markets Ser.: No. 32). 50p. 1989. pap. text ed. 200.00 (*1-55865-105-5*) Future Tech Surveys.

— FMS-CIM Systems Integration Handbook. LC 88-45791. 520p. 1989. pap. text ed. 95.00 (*0-88173-067-X*) Fairmont Pr.

— Four Eighty-Six Microprocessor Impact. LC 88-84066. (Survey on Technology & Markets Ser.: No. 96). 50p. 1989. pap. text ed. 200.00 (*1-55865-118-7*) Future Tech Surveys.

— Fuzzy Controllers. 82p. 1991. 285.00 (*0-89671-117-X*) SEAI Tech Pubns.

— Fuzzy Sets & Systems. LC 88-81895. (Survey on Technology & Markets Ser.: No. 94). 50p. 1989. pap. text ed. 200.00 (*1-55865-093-8*) Future Tech Surveys.

— Gallium Arsenide. LC 88-81650. (Survey on Technology & Markets Ser.: No. 59). 50p. 1989. pap. text ed. 200.00 (*1-55865-058-X*) Future Tech Surveys.

— Global Positioning System Applications. 156p. 1991. 285.00 (*0-89671-125-0*) SEAI Tech Pubns.

— High-Tc Superconductor Applications: A Survey on Technology & Markets, No. 4. LC 88-80490. 49p. 1988. pap. text ed. 200.00 (*1-55865-003-2*) Future Tech Surveys.

— Holography. LC 88-81642. (Survey on Technology & Markets Ser.: No. 51). 50p. 1989. pap. text ed. 200.00 (*1-55865-050-4*) Future Tech Surveys.

— Image Compression. 87p. 1991. 285.00 (*0-89671-122-6*) SEAI Tech Pubns.

— Indoor Air Quality. 244p. 1991. 285.00 (*0-89671-116-1*) SEAI Tech Pubns.

— Industrial Bioelectronics. LC 88-80907. (Survey on Technology & Markets Ser.: No. 23). 50p. 1989. pap. text ed. 200.00 (*1-55865-022-9*) Future Tech Surveys.

— Industrial Heat Processing Equipment. LC 88-80493. (Survey on Technology & Markets Ser.: No. 78). 50p. 1989. pap. text ed. 200.00 (*0-317-93535-6*) Future Tech Surveys.

— Industrial Noise Control Markets. LC 88-84059. (Survey on Technology & Markets Ser.: No. 68). 50p. 1989. pap. text ed. 200.00 (*1-55865-067-9*) Future Tech Surveys.

— Industrial Robots. LC 88-81646. (Survey on Technology & Markets Ser.: No. 55). 50p. 1989. pap. text ed. 200.00 (*1-55865-054-7*) Future Tech Surveys.

— Infrared Thermography. LC 88-84058. (Survey on Technology & Markets Ser.: No. 73). 50p. 1989. pap. text ed. 200.00 (*0-317-93534-8*) Future Tech Surveys.

— Integrated Optical Circuits. LC 88-81644. (Survey on Technology & Markets Ser.: No. 53). 50p. 1989. pap. text ed. 200.00 (*1-55865-052-0*) Future Tech Surveys.

— Interactive Multi-Media. 138p. 1991. 285.00 (*0-89671-121-8*) SEAI Tech Pubns.

— Knowledge-Based Systems: A Survey on Technology & Markets. LC 88-80493. 50p. 1989. pap. text ed. 200.00 (*1-55865-000-8*) Future Tech Surveys.

— Laboratory Robots. LC 88-81638. (Survey on Technology & Markets Ser.: No. 47). 50p. 1989. pap. text ed. 200.00 (*1-55865-046-6*) Future Tech Surveys.

— Laser Sensors. LC 88-72189. (Survey on Technology & Markets Ser.: No. 80). 50p. 1989. pap. text ed. 200.00 (*1-55865-097-0*) Future Tech Surveys.

— Learning & Automated Discovery in AI Systems. LC 88-81889. (Survey on Technology & Markets Ser.: No. 88). 50p. 1989. pap. text ed. 200.00 (*1-55865-087-3*) Future Tech Surveys.

— Machine Translation. LC 88-80494. (Survey on Technology & Markets Ser.: No. 2). 50p. 1989. pap. text ed. 200.00 (*1-55865-001-6*) Future Tech Surveys.

— Machine Vision. LC 88-80902. (Survey on Technology & Markets Ser.: No. 18). 50p. 1989. pap. text ed. 200.00 (*1-55865-017-2*) Future Tech Surveys.

— Magnetic Refrigeration: A Survey on Technology & Markets. LC 88-80922. (Survey on Technology & Markets Ser.: No. 38). 50p. 1989. pap. text ed. 200.00 (*1-55865-037-7*) Future Tech Surveys.

— Manufacturing Simulation. LC 88-72190. (Survey on Technology & Markets Ser.: No. 35). 50p. 1989. pap. text ed. 200.00 (*1-55865-096-2*) Future Tech Surveys.

— Manufacturing Software. LC 88-81640. (Survey on Technology & Markets Ser.: No. 49). 50p. 1989. pap. text ed. 200.00 (*1-55865-048-2*) Future Tech Surveys.

— MAP & Industrial LANS. LC 88-81647. (Survey on Technology & Markets Ser.: No. 56). 50p. 1989. pap. text ed. 200.00 (*1-55865-055-5*) Future Tech Surveys.

— Medical-Clinical Bioelectronics. LC 88-80906. (Survey on Technology & Markets Ser.: No. 22). 50p. 1989. pap. text ed. 200.00 (*1-55865-021-0*) Future Tech Surveys.

— Molecular Electronics. LC 88-81636. (Survey on Technology & Markets Ser.: No. 45). 50p. 1989. pap. text ed. 200.00 (*1-55865-044-X*) Future Tech Surveys.

— Multi-Sensor & Data Fusion. LC 88-81634. (Survey on Technology & Markets Ser.: No. 43). 50p. 1989. pap. text ed. 200.00 (*1-55865-042-3*) Future Tech Surveys.

— Natural Language & Voice Processing. LC 89-17105. 259p. 1989. pap. text ed. 95.00 (*0-88173-102-1*) Fairmont Pr.

— Natural Language Understanding. LC 88-81661. (Survey on Technology & Markets Ser.: No. 70). 50p. 1989. pap. text ed. 200.00 (*1-55865-069-5*) Future Tech Surveys.

— Non-Industrial Robotic Markets, No. 9. LC 88-80487. (Survey on Technology & Markets Ser.). 52p. 1989. pap. text ed. 200.00 (*1-55865-008-3*) Future Tech Surveys.

— Optical Computing. LC 88-81641. (Survey on Technology & Markets Ser.: No. 50). 50p. 1989. pap. text ed. 200.00 (*1-55865-049-0*) Future Tech Surveys.

— Optical Encoders & Resolvers. LC 88-84061. (Survey on Technology & Markets Ser.: No. 86). 50p. 1989. pap. text ed. 200.00 (*1-55865-113-6*) Future Tech Surveys.

— Parallel Processing. LC 89-17155. 284p. 1989. pap. text ed. 95.00 (*0-88173-101-3*) Fairmont Pr.

— Parallel Processing. 200p. 1991. 285.00 (*0-89671-128-5*) SEAI Tech Pubns.

— Parallel Processing: A Survey on Technology & Markets, No. 8. LC 88-80486. 32p. 1988. pap. text ed. 200.00 (*1-55865-007-5*) Future Tech Surveys.

— Pressure Sensors. LC 88-84054. (Survey on Technology & Markets Ser.: No. 48). 50p. 1989. pap. text ed. 200.00 (*1-55865-106-3*) Future Tech Surveys.

— Programmable Controllers. LC 88-81656. (Survey on Technology & Markets Ser.: No. 65). 50p. 1989. pap. text ed. 200.00 (*1-55865-064-4*) Future Tech Surveys.

— Radiation Detectors. LC 88-84052. (Survey on Technology & Markets Ser.: No. 31). 50p. 1989. pap. text ed. 200.00 (*1-55865-104-7*) Future Tech Surveys.

— Remote Sensing. LC 88-84059. (Survey on Technology & Markets Ser.: No. 81). 50p. 1991. pap. text ed. 200.00 (*1-55865-111-X*) Future Tech Surveys.

— RISC Architectures. LC 88-81639. (Survey on Technology & Markets Ser.: No. 87). 50p. 1989. pap. text ed. 200.00 (*1-55865-086-5*) Future Tech Surveys.

— Robotic Applications in Non-Industrial Environments. 311p. 1991. 285.00 (*0-89671-119-6*) SEAI Tech Pubns.

— Robotic, Vision & AI Applications in Agriculture. LC 88-81667. (Survey on Technology & Markets Ser.: No. 76). 50p. 1989. pap. text ed. 200.00 (*1-55865-075-X*) Future Tech Surveys.

— Sensor Markets 1991-95. 235p. 1991. 485.00 (*0-89671-115-3*) SEAI Tech Pubns.

— Shape Memory Alloys. LC 88-81888. (Survey on Technology & Markets Ser.: No. 89). 50p. 1989. pap. text ed. 200.00 (*1-55865-100-4*) Future Tech Surveys.

— Silicon Micromachining & Microstructures. LC 88-80901. (Survey on Technology & Markets Ser.: No. 17). 50p. 1989. pap. text ed. 200.00 (*1-55865-016-4*) Future Tech Surveys.

— Smart Cards. LC 88-80899. (Survey on Technology & Markets Ser.: No. 15). 50p. 1989. pap. text ed. 200.00 (*1-55865-014-8*) Future Tech Surveys.

— Smart Homes & Home Automation. LC 88-80904. (Survey on Technology & Markets Ser.: No. 20). 50p. 1989. pap. text ed. 200.00 (*1-55865-019-9*) Future Tech Surveys.

— Smart Power Chips. LC 88-81670. (Survey on Technology & Markets Ser.: No. 79). 50p. 1989. pap. text ed. 200.00 (*1-55865-078-4*) Future Tech Surveys.

— Smart Sensors. LC 88-81654. (Survey on Technology & Markets Ser.: No. 63). 50p. 1989. pap. text ed. 200.00 (*1-55865-062-8*) Future Tech Surveys.

— Solid State Cameras. LC 88-81662. (Survey on Technology & Markets Ser.: No. 71). 50p. 1989. pap. text ed. 200.00 (*1-55865-070-9*) Future Tech Surveys.

— Spatial Light Modulators. LC 88-80482. (Survey on Technology & Markets Ser.: No. 13). 50p. 1989. pap. text ed. 200.00 (*1-55865-012-1*) Future Tech Surveys.

— SQUID Sensors. LC 88-81653. (Survey on Technology & Markets Ser.: No. 62). 50p. 1989. pap. text ed. 200.00 (*1-55865-061-X*) Future Tech Surveys.

— Supercomputers. LC 88-82059. (Survey on Technology & Markets Ser.: No. 37). 50p. 1989. pap. text ed. 200.00 (*1-55865-036-9*) Future Tech Surveys.

— Superconductor Magnetic Energy Storage. LC 88-80923. (Survey on Technology & Markets Ser.: No. 39). 50p. 1989. pap. text ed. 200.00 (*1-55865-038-5*) Future Tech Surveys.

— Surface Mount Technology. LC 88-81649. (Survey on Technology & Markets Ser.: No. 58). 50p. 1989. pap. text ed. 200.00 (*1-55865-057-1*) Future Tech Surveys.

— Tactile Sensors: A Survey on Technology & Markets, No. 6. LC 88-80484. 54p. 1988. pap. text ed. 200.00 (*1-55865-005-9*) Future Tech Surveys.

— Temperature Sensors. LC 88-72188. (Survey on Technology & Markets Ser.: No. 30). 50p. 1989. pap. text ed. 200.00 (*1-55865-098-9*) Future Tech Surveys.

— Thin Film Sensors. LC 88-84057. (Survey on Technology & Markets Ser.: No. 61). 50p. 1989. pap. text ed. 200.00 (*1-55865-107-1*) Future Tech Surveys.

— Three-D Computing: Modeling, Image Processing, & Visualization. 246p. 1991. 285.00 (*0-89671-130-7*) SEAI Tech Pubns.

— Ultrasonic Sensors. LC 88-72189. (Survey on Technology & Markets Ser.: No. 82). 50p. 1989. pap. text ed. 200.00 (*0-317-93536-4*) Future Tech Surveys.

— Underground Storage Tanks. 226p. 1991. 285.00 (*0-89671-120-X*) SEAI Tech Pubns.

— UNIX. LC 88-82060. (Survey on Technology & Markets Ser.: No. 84). 50p. 1989. pap. text ed. 200.00 (*1-55865-083-0*) Future Tech Surveys.

— Vibration Sensors & Analyzers. LC 88-81666. (Survey on Technology & Markets Ser.: No. 75). 50p. 1989. pap. text ed. 200.00 (*1-55865-074-1*) Future Tech Surveys.

— Voice & Speech Processing. 293p. 1991. 285.00 (*0-89671-126-9*) SEAI Tech Pubns.

— Voice Processing. LC 88-81660. (Survey on Technology & Markets Ser.: No. 69). 50p. 1989. pap. text ed. 200.00 (*1-55865-068-7*) Future Tech Surveys.

— Waterjet Cutting: A Survey on Technology & Markets, No. 5. LC 88-80483. 36p. 1988. pap. text ed. 200.00 (*1-55865-004-0*) Future Tech Surveys.

— Workstation Trends of the 1990s. 212p. 1991. 285.00 (*0-89671-114-5*) SEAI Tech Pubns.

— X-Ray Machine Vision & Computed Tomography: A Survey on Technology & Markets, No. 10. LC 88-80488. 36p. 1988. pap. text ed. 200.00 (*1-55865-009-1*) Future Tech Surveys.

Miller, Richard K. & Walker, Terri C., eds. Computer Graphics & Advanced Computing Markets: 1992-1995. (Orig.). 1992. pap. text ed. 485.00 (*1-881503-04-6*) R K Miller Assocs.

— Environmental Markets: 1992-1995. (Orig.). 1992. pap. text ed. 485.00 (*1-881503-00-3*) R K Miller Assocs.

— Sensor & Instrumentation Markets: 1992-1995. (Orig.). 1992. pap. text ed. 485.00 (*1-881503-01-1*) R K Miller Assocs.

Miller, Richard K., jt. auth. see Barr, David F.

Miller, Richard K., ed. see Industrial Heating Equipment Association Staff.

Miller, Richard K., jt. auth. see Oviatt, Mark D.

Miller, Richard K., jt. auth. see Walker, Terri C.

Miller, Richard K., jt. auth. see Zeuch, Nello.

Miller, Richard K., et al. Neural Net Applications & Products. 347p. 1990. pap. 285.00 (*0-89671-107-2*) SEAI Tech Pubns.

M

Miller, Richard L. The Case for Legalizing Drugs. LC 90-7379. 264p. 1991. text ed. 21.95 (0-275-93459-4, C3459, Praeger Pubs) Greenwood.

— Environmental Short Shorts: Two Thousand Facts Arranged for Rapid Learning. 224p. (Orig.). (C). 1991. pap. 24.95 (1-881043-00-2) Legis Corp.

— Heritage of Fear: Illusion & Reality in the Cold War. 1988. 24.95 (0-8027-1021-2) Walker & Co.

— Nazi Justiz: Law of the Holocaust. LC 94-46176. 240p. 1995. text ed. 39.95 (0-275-94912-5, Praeger Pubs) Greenwood.

— New Directions in Hospital & Healthcare Facility Design. 1995. text ed. 75.00 (0-07-063014-3) McGraw.

— The Official Fajita Cookbook. 1988. pap. 12.95 (0-87719-112-3, Lone Star Bks) Gulf Pub.

— Under the Cloud: The Decades of Nuclear Testing. 550p. 1986. 24.95 (0-02-921620-6) Free Pr.

Miller, Richard M., ed. see Miller, Gloria B.

***Miller, Richard N.** International Direct Marketing. 1995. text ed. 44.95 (0-07-042356-3) McGraw.

Miller, Richard U., et al. The Impact of Collective Bargaining on Hospitals. LC 79-9401. 256p. 1979. text ed. 59.95 (0-275-90395-8, C0395, Praeger Pubs) Greenwood.

Miller, Richard W. Analyzing Marx: Morality, Power, & History. LC 84-42571. 240p. 1984. text ed. 55.00 (0-691-06613-2); pap. 14.95 (0-691-01413-2) Princeton U Pr.

— Fact & Method. 520p. 1987. text ed. 85.00 (0-691-07318-X); pap. text ed. 18.95 (0-691-02045-0) Princeton U Pr.

— Flow Measurement Engineering Handbook. 2nd ed. (Illus.). 1024p. 1989. text ed. 99.50 (0-07-042046-7) McGraw.

— Introduction to Logic. 9th ed. (Illus.). 290p. (C). 1994. student ed, pap. write for info. (0-02-381252-4) Macmillan.

— Moral Differences: Truth, Justice & Conscience in a World of Conflict. 416p. 1992. text ed. 69.50 (0-691-07409-7); pap. text ed. 18.95 (0-691-02092-2) Princeton U Pr.

— Mountain Directory for Truckers, RV, & Motorhome Drivers. 2nd ed. (Illus.). 117p. 1995. reprint ed. pap. 12.95 (0-9646805-0-5) R&R Pub.

Miller, Richareds T., jt. auth. see Henry, Robert G.

Miller, Rick. Bounty Hunter. LC 88-7168. (Early West Ser.). (Illus.). 256p. 1988. 21.95 (0-932702-41-4) Creative Texas.

— The Train Robbing Bunch. LC 82-22204. (Early West Ser.). (Illus.). 175p. 1983. 18.95 (0-932702-25-2); pap. 8.50 (0-932702-27-9) Creative Texas.

— The Train Robbing Bunch. deluxe ed. LC 82-22204. (Early West Ser.). (Illus.). 175p. 1983. ring bd. 75.00 (0-932702-26-0) Creative Texas.

Miller, Rickey. Kitchen Memories from My Childhood. (Illus.). 110p. 1994. text ed. 14.95 (0-9641543-0-7) Millers Three.

Miller, Rima. Team Planning for Educational Leaders. 79p. 1987. pap. 21.95 (1-56602-017-4) Research Better.

— Your Leadership Style. 62p. 1987. pap. 17.95 (1-56602-019-0) Research Better.

Miller, Rima, jt. auth. see Woods-Houston, Michele A.

Miller, Rita. Nutritional Services Policy & Procedures. 1993. 115.00 (1-879575-41-8) Acad Med Sys.

Miller, Rita, ed. Fresh from the Garden: Time Honored Recipes from the Readers of Texas Gardener. (Illus.). 186p. 1986. 19.95 (0-914641-05-0) TX Gardener Pr.

Miller, Rita S., ed. Brooklyn, U. S. A. (Brooklyn College Studies on Society in Change: No. 7). (Illus.). 1979. 20.00 (0-930888-02-2) Brooklyn Coll Pr.

Miller, Riva, jt. auth. see Bor, Robert.

Miller, Rob, des. Implementing Architecture: Exposing the Paradigm Surrounding the Implements & the Implementation of Architecture. 1988. 50.00 (0-932526-25-X) Nexus Pr.

Miller, Rob H. Shanghai Creek Fire. Bayes, Ronald H., ed. (Illus.). 1979. pap. 5.00 (0-932662-30-7) St Andrews NC.

Miller, Robert. Bob Miller's Precalc Helper. 1991. pap. text ed. 8.95 (0-07-042256-7) McGraw.

— Buffalo Soldiers. (Reflections of a Black Cowboy Ser.). (Illus.). 104p. (J). (gr. 4-7). 1992. lib. bdg. 12.95 (0-382-24080-4); pap. 4.95 (0-382-24085-5) Silver Burdett Pr.

— Calc I Helper. 1991. pap. text ed. 8.95 (0-07-042257-5) McGraw.

— Calc II Helper. 1991. pap. text ed. 8.95 (0-07-042258-3) McGraw.

— Cowboys. (Reflections of a Black Cowboy Ser.). (Illus.). 104p. (J). (gr. 4-7). 1992. lib. bdg. 12.95 (0-382-24079-0); pap. 4.95 (0-382-24084-7) Silver Burdett Pr.

— Flintnapping & Arrowhead Manufacture at Tell Hadidi, Syria. (Contributions in Anthropology & History Ser.: No. 4). 46p. 1985. 6.95 (0-317-41585-9) Milwaukee Pub Mus.

— Liability or Asset? A Policy for the Falkland Islands. (C). 1990. 45.00 (0-907967-80-9, Pub. by Inst Euro Def & Strat UK) St Mut.

— Lubricants & Their Applications. 224p. 1993. text ed. 37.00 (0-07-041992-2) McGraw.

— M. I. Hummel Album. 1994. 19.98 (0-88365-878-X) Galahad Bks.

— Meaning & Purpose in the Intact Brain: A Philosophical, Psychological, & Biological Account of Conscious Processes. (Illus.). 1982. 55.00 (0-19-857579-3) OUP.

— Mountain Men. (Reflections of a Black Cowboy Ser.). (Illus.). 104p. (J). (gr. 4-7). 1991. lib. bdg. 12.95 (0-382-24082-0); pap. 4.95 (0-382-24087-1) Silver Burdett Pr.

— Offshore UK: A Guide to Offshore Financial Centres. 200p. 1993. 90.00 (1-85573-117-7, Pub. by Woodhead Pubng UK) St Mut.

— Pioneers. (Reflections of a Black Cowboy Ser.). (Illus.). 104p. (J). (gr. 4-7). 1991. lib. bdg. 12.95 (0-382-24081-2); pap. 4.95 (0-382-24086-3) Silver Burdett Pr.

— Reflections of a Black Cowboy Series, 4 vols., Set. (Illus.). 416p. (J). (gr. 4-7). 1991. lib. bdg. 51.80 (0-382-24078-2); pap. 19.80 (0-382-24083-9) Silver Burdett Pr.

— Urban Forestry: Planning & Managing Urban Vegetation. (Illus.). 432p. 1987. text ed. 76.00 (0-13-939620-9) P-H.

Miller, Robert & Basten, Fred. Gringo. LC 14-251. 1980. 10.95 (0-9603490-0-6) Noble Hse.

***Miller, Robert & Miller, Janice.** Introduction to Business: An International Perspective. 61p. (C). 1987. teacher ed write for info. (0-256-05762-1) Irwin.

Miller, Robert & Weber, Gerard. Touchstone. 160p. 1987. pap. 9.95 (0-89505-450-7, 21102) Tabor Pub.

***Miller, Robert & Wilson, Kenneth.** Making & Enjoying Telescopes: 6 Complete Projects & a Stargazer's Guide. LC 95-4592. (Illus.). 160p. 1995. 24.95 (0-8069-1277-4, Lark Bks) Sterling.

Miller, Robert, jt. auth. see Robinson, Jerry.

Miller, Robert, jt. auth. see Weber, Gerard P.

Miller, Robert, jt. auth. see Weber, Gerard.

Miller, Robert A. August 1944. (Illus.). 300p. 1988. 17.95 (0-89141-316-2) Presidio Pr.

— The Federal Role in Education: New Directions in the Eighties. 192p. 1980. lib. bdg. 15.00 (0-318-03019-5); pap. 9.50 (0-318-03020-9) Inst Educ Lead.

Miller, Robert A., jt. auth. see Oberlander, Theodore M.

Miller, Robert B. Minitab Handbook for Business & Economics. rev. ed. 628p. 1990. pap. 22.95 (0-534-92478-6) Intl Thomson.

Miller, Robert B. & Wichern, Dean W. Intermediate Business Statistics. LC 76-51330. 516p. (C). 1977. text ed. 58.00 (0-03-089101-9) Dryden Pr.

Miller, Robert B., jt. auth. see Cryer, Jonathan D.

Miller, Robert B., et al. Conceptual Selling. 320p. 1989. pap. 13.99 (0-446-38906-4) Warner Bks.

— Strategic Selling. 320p. 1988. pap. 13.99 (0-446-38627-8) Warner Bks.

— Strategic Selling: The Unique Sales System Proven Successful by America's Best Companies. LC 84-25463. (Illus.). 352p. 1985. 19.95 (0-688-04313-5) Morrow.

— Successful Large Account Management. 240p. 1991. 25.00 (0-8050-1304-0) H Holt & Co.

— Successful Large Account Management. 240p. 1992. reprint ed. pap. 10.99 (0-446-39356-8) Warner Bks.

Miller, Robert D. Involuntary Civil Commitment of the Mentally Ill in the Post-Reform Era. 280p. 1987. 59.95 (0-398-05343-X) C C Thomas.

— Involuntary Civil Commitment of the Mentally Ill in the Post-Reform Era. 280p. 1987. pap. 34.95 (0-398-06291-9) C C Thomas.

— Problems in Hospital Law. 6th ed. LC 90-142. (Health Care Administration Ser.). 316p. (C). 1991. 52.00 (0-8342-0142-9) Aspen Pub.

— Spelling Games & Puzzles for Junior High. (Makemaster Bk.). (J). (gr. 6-8). 1976. pap. 9.99 (0-8224-6460-8) Fearon Teach Aids.

— Tommy the Toothbrush. (Illus.). 16p. (J). (gr. 2-4). 1982. write for info. (0-318-56644-3) Miller OH.

Miller, Robert D., ed. Legal Implications of Hospital Policies & Practices. LC 87-646993. (New Directions for Mental Health Services Ser.: No. MHS 41). 1989. 17.95 (1-55542-872-X) Jossey-Bass.

Miller, Robert E. Agni. (Writers Workshop Redbird Ser.). 1975. 8.00 (0-88253-492-0); pap. text ed. 4.80 (0-88253-491-2) Ind-US Inc.

— How to Compete Successfully in a Public Accounting Practice. 280p. 1987. text ed. 49.95 (0-13-402157-6, Busn) P-H.

Miller, Robert F. Careers Without College: Travel. Colton, Kitty, ed. 96p. (Orig.). (YA). (gr. 10-12). 1993. pap. 7.95 (1-56079-249-3) Petersons Guides.

— One Hundred Thousand Tractors: The MTS & the Development of Controls in Soviet Agriculture. LC 70-95929. (Russian Research Center Studies: No. 60). 439p. 1970. 37.00 (0-674-63875-1) HUP.

— Running a Meeting That Works. (Business Success Ser.). 96p. 1991. pap. 4.95 (0-8120-4640-4) Barron.

Miller, Robert F., ed. Development of Civil Society in Communist Systems. 176p. 1992. pap. text ed. 19.95 (1-86373-171-7, Pub. by Allen Unwin AT) Paul & Co Pubs.

Miller, Robert G. Statistical Prediction by Discriminant Analysis. (Meteorological Monograph Ser.: Vol. 4. No. 25). (Illus.). 54p. (Orig.). 1962. pap. 17.00 (0-933876-13-0) Am Meteorological.

***Miller, Robert H.** Buffalo Soldiers: The Story of Emanuel Stance. LC 94-28640. (Illus.). (J). 1994. 12.95 (0-382-24395-1); 12.95 (0-382-24400-1); lib. bdg. 14.95 (0-382-24391-9) Silver.

— Graham Greene: A Descriptive Catalog. LC 77-92925. 85p. reprint ed. pap. 25.00 (0-7837-5810-3, 2045477) Bks Demand.

— Inside an Embassy: The Political Role of Diplomats Abroad. LC 92-13193. (Martin F. Herz Series on United States Diplomacy). 1992. 37.95 (0-87187-714-7); pap. 25.95 (0-87187-713-9) Congr Quarterly.

— Power System Operation. 2nd ed. LC 82-24959. (Illus.). 224p. 1983. text ed. 59.95 (0-07-041975-2) McGraw.

— Power System Operation. 3rd ed. 1993. text ed. 43.00 (0-07-041977-9) McGraw.

— Reflections of a Black Cowboy. (Book: Vol. I). (Illus.). 9p. (Orig.). (J). (gr. 5-7). 1988. pap. text ed. 9.95 (0-929592-01-8) Waterline Prodns.

— The Story of Jean Baptiste Du Sable. (Illus.). 32p. (J). 1994. 12.95 (0-382-24402-8); lib. bdg. 14.95 (0-382-24392-7) Silver Pr.

— The Story of Nat Love. LC 93-46287. (Stories of the Forgotten West Ser.). (Illus.). (J). 1994. 12.95 (0-382-24398-6); lib. bdg. 14.95 (0-382-24389-7); pap. 4.95 (0-382-24393-5) Silver Pr.

— The Story of "Stagecoach" Mary Fields. LC 93-46286. (Stories of the Forgotten West Ser.). (Illus.). (J). 1994. write for info. (0-382-24394-3) Silver Pr.

— The Story of "Stagecoach" Mary Fields. (Illus.). 32p. (J). 1994. 12.95 (0-382-24399-4); lib. bdg. 14.95 (0-382-24390-0) Silver Pr.

— U. S. & Vietnam, 1787-1941. (Illus.). 323p. (Orig.). (C). 1994. pap. text ed. 50.00 (0-7881-0810-7) Diane Pub.

Miller, Robert H. & Wilson. Manual of Prehospital Emergency Medicine. 544p. 1992. 31.95 (0-8016-5791-1) Mosby Yr Bk.

***Miller, Robert J.** The Complete Gospels. annot. ed. LC 94-34585. 1994. pap. 18.00 (0-06-065587-9) Harper SF.

Miller, Robert J., ed. The Complete Gospels: Annotated Scholars Version. LC 91-35779. 320p. (C). 1991. 29.95 (0-944344-29-1) Polebridge Pr.

— The Complete Gospels: Annotated Scholars Version. 2nd rev. ed. LC 91-35779. 320p. (C). 1991. pap. 19.95 (0-944344-30-5) Polebridge Pr.

— The Complete Gospels: Annotated Scholars Version. 3rd expanded rev. ed. LC 94-34585. 480p. 1995. 28.00 (0-944344-45-3); pap. 18.00 (0-944344-49-6) Polebridge Pr.

Miller, Robert K. Carlyle's Life of John Sterling: A Study in Victorian Biography. LC 86-25062. (Nineteenth-Century Studies). 113p. reprint ed. pap. 32.30 (0-8357-1782-8, 2070564) Bks Demand.

— The Informed Argument. 2nd ed. 622p. (C). 1989. pap. text ed. 21.50 (0-15-541458-5) HB Coll Pubs.

— The Informed Argument: A Multidisciplinary Reader & Guide. 3rd ed. 640p. (C). 1992. pap. text ed. 21.50 (0-15-541456-9) HB Coll Pubs.

Miller, Robert K., ed. Great Short Works of Willa Cather. LC 88-45964. 384p. 1993. reprint ed. pap. 12.00 (0-06-092376-8, PL) HarpC.

Miller, Robert K. & Webb, Suzanne S. Motives for Writing. 549p. (C). 1992. pap. text ed. 24.95 (0-87484-974-8); teacher ed, pap. text ed. write for info. (0-87484-975-6) Mayfield Pub.

— Motives for Writing. 2nd ed. LC 94-30498. 559p. (C). 1994. pap. text ed. 24.95 (1-55934-468-7) Mayfield Pub.

— Teaching Motives for Writing: An Instructor's Manual to Accompany Motives for Writing. 2nd ed. Date not set. teacher ed write for info. (1-55934-469-5) Mayfield Pub.

Miller, Robert K., ed. see Cather, Willa.

Miller, Robert L. Linguistic Relativity Principle & Humboldtian Ethnolinguistics. LC 68-13340. (Janua Linguarum, Ser.). 1968. pap. text ed. 22.00 (90-279-0595-9) Mouton.

— M.I. Hummel: The Golden Anniversary Album. 1989. 19.98 (0-88365-745-7) Galahad Bks.

— Number One Price Guide to M. I. Hummel. 5th ed. 1992. pap. 15.95 (0-88486-068-X) Arrowood Pr.

— Number One Price Guide to M. I. Hummel: Figurines, Plates, Miniatures, & More. 1994. pap. 15.95 (0-88486-109-0, Bristol Park Bks) Arrowood Pr.

Miller, Robert L., ed. Flow-Induced Crystallization in Polymer Systems. (Midland Macromolecular Monographs: Vol. 6). 380p. 1979. text ed. 191.00 (0-677-12540-2) Gordon & Breach.

Miller, Robert L., et al. Acoustic Charge Transport: Device Technology & Applications. LC 92-10502. (Microwave Ser.). 606p. 1992. text ed. 85.00 (0-89006-520-9) Artech Hse.

Miller, Robert M. The Best of RMM. LC 86-73111. (Illus.). 239p. 1987. 26.50 (0-939674-18-1) Am Vet Pubns.

— Bishop G. Bromley Oxnam: Paladin of Liberal Protestantism. LC 90-42071. 608p. 1990. 29.95 (0-687-03564-3) Abingdon.

— Harry Emerson Fosdick: Preacher, Pastor, Prophet. LC 84-7168. (Illus.). 608p. 1985. 45.00 (0-19-503512-7) OUP.

— How Shall They Hear Without a Preacher? The Life of Ernest Fremont Tittle. LC 74-149031. 538p. reprint ed. pap. 153.40 (0-7837-0284-1, 2040605) Bks Demand.

— Imprint Training: Of the Newborn Foal. (Illus.). 144p. (Orig.). 1991. pap. 12.95 (0-911647-22-8) Western Horseman.

— More RMM: Who Has the Nine-Thirty Appointment? (Illus.). 192p. 1979. 24.50 (0-939674-12-2) Am Vet Pubns.

— The Revised Health Problems of the Horse. Vorhes, Gary, ed. (Illus.). 144p. (Orig.). 1987. pap. 12.95 (0-911647-13-9) Western Horseman.

— RMM: The Second Oldest Profession. LC 90-85392. (Illus.). 664p. 1990. 49.00 (0-939674-35-1) Am Vet Pubns.

— RMM Strikes Again. LC 84-72573. (Illus.). 192p. 1984. 25.50 (0-939674-16-5) Am Vet Pubns.

— Star Myths: Show-Business Biographies on Film. LC 83-14292. 416p. 1983. 32.50 (0-8108-1643-1) Scarecrow.

Miller, Robert M. & Groher, Michael E. Medical Speech Pathology. 396p. (C). 1989. text ed. 56.00 (0-8342-0112-7) Aspen Pub.

Miller, Robert M., jt. auth. see Byrge, Duane.

Miller, Robert P., ed. Chaucer: Sources & Backgrounds. (Illus.). (C). 1977. pap. text ed. 18.95 (0-19-502167-3) OUP.

Miller, Robert R. Mexico: A History. LC 84-28105. (Illus.). 384p. 1989. pap. 15.95 (0-8061-2178-5) U of Okla Pr.

— Shamrock & Sword: Saint Patrick's Battalion in the U. S.-Mexican War. LC 89-5252. (Illus.). 248p. 1989. 27.95 (0-8061-2204-8) U of Okla Pr.

Miller, Robert R., ed. Chronicle of Colonial Lima: The Diary of Josephe & Francisco Mugaburu, 1640-1697. LC 73-21221. (Illus.). 352p. 1975. 35.00 (0-8061-1134-8) U of Okla Pr.

— The Mexican War Journal & Letters of Ralph W. Kirkham. LC 90-41183. (Essays on the American West, Sponsored by Elma Dill Russell Spencer Foundation Ser.: No. 11). (Illus.). 168p. 1993. pap. 12.95 (0-89096-537-4) Tex A&M Univ Pr.

Miller, Robert R. & Miller, Janice J. Introduction to Business: An International Perspective. 224p. (C). 1987. pap. text ed. 19.50 (0-256-05628-5) Irwin.

Miller, Robert R. & Sumlinski, Mariusz A. Trends in Private Investment in Developing Countries, 1994: Statistics for 1970-92. (IFC Discussion Paper Ser.: No. 20). 56p. 1994. 6.95 (0-8213-2763-1, 12763) World Bank.

Miller, Robert R., ed. see Zeh, Frederick.

Miller, Robert S. Energy Conservation with Adhesives & Sealants. LC 85-27505. (Illus.). 170p. 1986. 9.95 (0-937558-13-3) Scharff Ltd.

Miller, Robert T. & Flowers, Ronald B., eds. Toward Benevolent Neutrality: Church, State, & the Supreme Court. 4th ed. LC 92-24655. 786p. 1992. 44.95 (0-918954-56-8) Baylor Univ Pr.

Miller, Robert W. Western Horse Behavior & Training. 336p. 1975. pap. 15.95 (0-385-08181-2, Dolp) Doubleday.

Miller, Roberta B. City & Hinterland: A Case Study of Urban Growth & Regional Developments. LC 78-55340. (Contributions in American History Ser.: No. 77). (Illus.). 179p. 1979. text ed. 45.00 (0-313-20524-8, MCH/, Greenwood Pr) Greenwood.

Miller, Roberta R., jt. ed. see Shimosato, Yukio.

Miller, Robin. Sugarbird Lady. large type ed. 318p. 1981. 12.00 (0-7089-0615-X) Ulverscroft.

— Talks with Jonathon - Bk. I: A Guide to Transformation. 156p. (Orig.). 1993. pap. 14.95 (1-881343-04-9) Channel One.

— Talks with Jonathon - Bk II: The Path of Love. 180p. 1994. 14.95 (1-881343-06-5) Channel One.

Miller, Robin F. The Brothers Karamazov: Worlds of the Novel. (Masterwork Studies). 160p. (C). 1992. text ed. 21.95 (0-8057-8060-2, Twayne) Macmillan.

— The Brothers Karamazov: Worlds of the Novel. (Masterwork Studies: No. 83). 160p. (C). 1992. pap. 12.95 (0-8057-8118-8, Twayne) Macmillan.

— Dostoevsky & The Idiot: Author, Narrator & Reader. LC 80-29496. 305p. 1981. 34.00 (0-674-21490-0) HUP.

***Miller, Robyn & Miller, Rand.** Myst: The Book of Atrus. (Illus.). 304p. 1995. 22.95 (0-7868-6159-2) Hyperion.

Miller, Rockley, ed. see Binder, Roberta H.

Miller, Rockley, ed. see DeBloois, Michael.

Miller, Rockley L. Compatibility of Interactive Videodisc Systems: Players, Controllers, Overlay Devices, Authoring Programs, Touch Screens, Integrated Systems. (Monitor Report Ser.). (Illus.). 150p. 1987. pap. 49.95 (0-938907-03-4) Future Syst.

— The U. S. Videodisc Market: Forecasts & Analysis to 1990. (Monitor Report Ser.). (Illus.). 300p. (Orig.). 1985. 795.00 (0-938907-01-8) Future Syst.

Miller, Rockley L. & Sayers, John H. Videodisc & Related Technologies: A Glossary of Terms. 80p. (Orig.). (C). 1986. pap. 7.95 (0-938907-02-6) Future Syst.

Miller, Rockley L., jt. auth. see Kasten, Alex S.

***Miller, Rodney E.** Institutionalizing Music: The Administration of Music Programs in Higher Education. LC 93-19769. (Illus.). 216p. 1993. pap. 25.95 (0-398-06292-7) C C Thomas.

— Institutionalizing Music: The Administration of Music Programs in Higher Education. LC 93-19769. (Illus.). 216p. (C). 1993. text ed. 41.95x (0-398-05874-1) C C Thomas.

Miller, Roger. Baltimore: A Portrait (An Address Book) (Illus.). 112p. 1986. 10.95 (0-911897-03-8) Image Ltd.

— Maryland a Portrait - An Address Book. (Illus.). 128p. 1988. 14.95 (0-911897-08-9) Image Ltd.

Miller, Roger, ed. & photos. Washington a Portrait. (Illus.). 144p. 1991. 34.50 (0-911897-20-8) Image Ltd.

Miller, Roger & Cote, Marcel. Growing the Next Silicon Valley: A Guide for Successful Regional Planning. LC 86-45880. 192p. 1987. text ed. 37.95 (0-669-14577-7) Free Pr.

Miller, Roger, et al. Baltimore: A Portrait. rev. ed. (Illus.). 128p. 1988. 19.95 (0-911897-15-1) Image Ltd.

— Baltimore: A Portrait. rev. ed. LC 88-81951. (Illus.). 128p. 1988. 34.50 (0-911897-01-1) Image Ltd.

Miller, Roger C., photos. Annapolis: A Portrait. (Illus.). 96p. 1987. 34.50 (0-911897-06-2) Image Ltd.

Miller, Roger C. & Pilling, R., photos. Tokyo: A Portrait. (Illus.). 128p. 1987. 34.50 (0-911897-05-4) Image Ltd.

Miller, Roger F. What Can I Say? LC 86-26868. 96p. (Orig.). 1987. pap. 4.99 (0-8272-4220-4) Chalice Pr.

Miller, Roger L. Economic Issues for Consumers. 5th ed. LC 86-24722. (Illus.). 526p. (C). 1987. text ed. 41.00 (0-314-30391-X) West Pub.

— Economic Issues for Consumers. 6th ed. Perlee, Clyde, ed. 517p. (C). 1990. reprint ed. text ed. 49.75 (0-314-56771-2) West Pub.

— Economics Today. 8th ed. LC 93-8233. (C). 1994. text ed. 42.00 (0-06-501465-0) HarpCollege.

— Economics Today. 8th ed. LC 95-8149. (C). 1995. write for info. (0-06-502544-X) HarpCollege.

— Economics Today: The Macro View. 8th ed. LC 93-8235. (C). 1994. 30.00 (0-06-501878-8) HarpCollege.

— Economics Today: The Micro View. 8th ed. LC 93-8234. (C). 1994. 30.00 (0-06-501877-X) HarpCollege.

— Modern Money & Banking. 640p. 1986. Instr's. manual. teacher ed write for info. (0-07-042164-1); Test bank. write for info. (0-07-042166-8) McGraw.

Miller, Roger L. & Benjamin, Daniel K. The Economics of Macro Issues. 7th ed. Perlee, Clyde, ed. 197p. (C). 1991. pap. text ed. 22.75 (0-314-92214-8) West Pub.
Miller, Roger L. & Cross, Frank B. The Legal & Regulatory Environment Today: Changing Perspectives for Business. LC 92-18824. 650p. (C). 1993. text ed. 65.75 (0-314-01046-7) West Pub.
Miller, Roger L. & Fishe, Raymond P. Microeconomics: Price Theory Practice. LC 94-21506. (Economics Ser.). (C). 1995. 65.00 (0-06-500526-0) HarpCollege.
Miller, Roger L. & Jentz, Gaylord A. Business Law Today. 2nd ed. Perlee, Clyde, ed. 894p. (C). 1991. text ed. 60.25 (0-314-74269-7) West Pub.
— Business Law Today: Text, Summarized Cases, Legal, Ethical, Regulatory, & International Environment. 3rd ed. Perlee, ed. LC 93-25927. 850p. (C). 1993. text ed. 67.00 (0-314-02582-0) West Pub.
— Business Law Today, Comprehensive Edition: Text, Cases, Legal, Ethical, Regulatory, & International Environment. 3rd ed. Perlee, ed. 620p. (C). Date not set. text ed. 70.75 (0-314-02851-X) West Pub.
— Business Law Today, the Essentials: Text, Summarized Cases, Legal, Ethical, Regulatory, & International Environment. 3rd ed. Perlee, ed. LC 93-37600. 620p. (C). 1993. text ed. 49.25 (0-314-02852-8) West Pub.
— Fundamentals of Business Law. 2nd ed. Perlee, Clyde, ed. LC 92-20019. 760p. (C). 1993. reprint ed. pap. text ed. 44.25 (0-314-01004-1) West Pub.
Miller, Roger L. & Pulsinelli, Robert. McGraw-Hill Principles of Economics Courseware, Vol. II. 1985. text ed. write for info. (0-07-079780-3) McGraw.
Miller, Roger L. & Pulsinelli, Robert W. Understanding Economics. (Illus.). 457p. (C). 1983. text ed. 48.75 (0-314-69669-5); teacher ed, pap. text ed. write for info. (0-314-71114-7); student ed, pap. text ed. 18.50 (0-314-71143-0) West Pub.
Miller, Roger L. & Stafford, Alan D. Economic Issues for Consumers. 7th ed. Perlee, ed. LC 93-8170. 500p. (C). 1994. text ed. 57.50 (0-314-02261-9) West Pub.
***Miller, Roger L. & Urisko, Mary S.** West's Paralegal Today: The Essentials--the Legal Team at Work. LC 94-37656. 500p. 1995. pap. text ed. 38.25 (0-314-04595-3) West Pub.
— West's Paralegal Today: The Legal Team at Work. LC 94-37650. 1000p. 1995. text ed. 50.75 (0-314-04360-8) West Pub.
Miller, Roger L. & VanHoose, David D. Modern Money & Banking. 3rd ed. LC 92-12189. 1993. text ed. write for info. (0-07-042335-0) McGraw.
— Modern Money & Banking. 3rd ed. LC 92-12189. 1993. pap. text ed. write for info. (0-07-042338-5) McGraw.
Miller, Roger L., jt. auth. see Cross, Frank B.
Miller, Roger L., jt. ed. see Manne, Henry G.
Miller, Roger L., et al. Personal Finance Today. (Illus.). 446p. (C). 1983. teacher ed, pap. text ed. write for info. (0-314-71112-0); student ed, pap. text ed. 19.00 (0-314-71113-9) West Pub.
— Personal Finance Today. 2nd ed. (Illus.). 446p. (C). 1983. text ed. 56.00 (0-314-69668-7) West Pub.
Miller, Roger R., ed. see Institute on Research Toward Improving Race Relations (1967: Warrenton, VA).
Miller, Roland E. Mappila Muslims of Kerala: A Study of Islamic Trends. 2nd enl. rev. ed. 389p. 1992. 37.50 (0-86311-270-6, Pub. by Orient Longman Ltd II) Apt Bks.
Miller, Roman & Brubaker, Beryl, eds. Bioethics & the Beginning of Life: An Anabaptist Perspective. LC 89-15266. 224p. (Orig.). 1989. pap. 15.95 (0-8361-3502-4) Herald Pr.
Miller, Ron. The Dream Machines: An Illustrated History of the Spaceship in Art, Science, & Literature. 744p. (Orig.). 1993. 112.50 (0-89464-039-9) Krieger.
— Extraordinary Voyages. 1976. 19.95 (0-8488-0712-X) Amereon Ltd.
— What Are Schools For? Holistic Education in American Culture. 2nd rev. ed. 208p. (Orig.). (C). 1992. pap. 16.95 (0-9627232-0-7) Holistic Educ Pr.
Miller, Ron, ed. Renewal of Meaning in Education: Responses to the Cultural & Ecological Crisis of Our Times. 160p. (Orig.). (C). 1993. pap. text ed. 18.95 (0-9627232-3-1) Holistic Educ Pr.
Miller, Ron, intro. New Directions in Education: Selections from Holistic Education Review. 400p. (Orig.). (C). 1991. pap. 18.95 (0-9627232-1-5) Holistic Educ Pr.
Miller, Ron & Miller, Peggy. Mines of the Mojave. 1992. 4.50 (0-910856-57-5) La Siesta.
Miller, Ron, jt. auth. see Haddock, Durwood.
Miller, Ron, jt. auth. see Hartmann, William K.
MIller, Ron
Miller, Ron
Miller, Ron J. The Medallion. Van Treese, James B., ed. 256p. (Orig.). 1993. pap. 8.95 (1-880416-40-9) NW Pub.
Miller, Ronald, jt. auth. see Colangelo, Robert.
Miller, Ronald B., ed. The Restoration of Dialogue: Readings in the Philosophy of Clinical Psychology. 676p. 1992. 59.95 (1-55798-157-4); pap. 39.95 (1-55798-166-3) Am Psychol.
Miller, Ronald D. Mines of the High Desert. rev. ed. (Illus.). 1992. 4.50 (0-910856-13-3) La Siesta.
— Paul Bailey & the Westernlore Press: The First 40 Years, with Annotated Bibliography. LC 83-51162. (Illus.). 1984. 25.00 (0-930704-16-9) Sagebrush Pr.
— Shady Ladies of the West. LC 64-25860. (Illus.). 18.95 (0-87026-023-5) Westernlore.
Miller, Ronald D., ed. Anesthesia, 2 vols., Set. 4th ed. (Illus.). 2700p. 1994. 195.00 (0-443-08906-X) Churchill.
— Anesthesia, 3 vols., Vol. 1. 2nd ed. LC 85-17446. 898p. reprint ed. pap. 160.00 (0-8357-4657-7, 2037589) Bks Demand.
— Anesthesia, 3 vols., Vol. 2. 2nd ed. LC 85-17446. 921p. reprint ed. pap. 180.00 (0-8357-4658-5) Bks Demand.
— Anesthesia, 3 vols., Vol. 3. 2nd ed. LC 85-17446. 899p. reprint ed. pap. 180.00 (0-8357-4659-3) Bks Demand.
Miller, Ronald D., jt. auth. see Stoelting, Robert K.
Miller, Ronald E. Further Results on Inter-Regional Feedback Effects in Input-Output Models: Supplement. (Discussion Paper Ser.: No. 7). 1966. pap. 10.00 (1-55869-049-2) Regional Sci Res Inst.
— Interregional Feedback Effects in Input-Output Models: Some Preliminary Results. (Discussion Paper Ser.: No. 7). 1965. pap. 10.00 (1-55869-061-1) Regional Sci Res Inst.
Miller, Ronald E. & Dossani, Nazir G. A Note on Degeneracy & Multiple Optima in Linear Programs. (Discussion Paper Ser.: No. 17). 1967. pap. 10.00 (1-55869-080-8) Regional Sci Res Inst.
Miller, Ronald E. & Sawers, David. The Technical Development of Modern Aviation. (Airlines History Project Ser.). reprint ed. 42.50 (0-404-19328-5) AMS Pr.
Miller, Ronald E., ed. see Polenske, Karen R. & Rose, Adam Z.
Miller, Ronald H. Dialogue & Disagreement: Franz Rosenzweig's Relevance to Contemporary Jewish-Christian Understanding. LC 89-35492. 234p. (Orig.). (C). 1990. lib. bdg. 57.00 (0-8191-7539-0) U Pr of Amer.
Miller, Ronald L. Personnel Policies for Museums: A Handbook for Management. 164p. pap. 16.00 (0-931201-05-5) Am Assn Mus.
Miller, Ronald S., jt. auth. see New Age Journal Editors.
Miller, Ronald S., jt. auth. see Schachter-Shalomi, Zalman.
Miller, Ronald W. Planning for Success: A Ten-Step Process for Setting & Achieving Your Goals in Life. (Illus.). 120p. (Orig.). 1990. pap. write for info. (0-9625695-0-X) New Pers Pub.
Miller, Ronnie. Following the Americans to the Persian Gulf: Canada, Australia, & the Development of the New World Order. LC 92-55107. Date not set. write for info. (0-8386-3536-9) Fairleigh Dickinson.
— From Lebanon to the Intifada: The Jewish Lobby & Canadian Middle East Policy. 128p. (Orig.). (C). 1990. lib. bdg. 40.50 (0-8191-7984-1); pap. text ed. 23.00 (0-8191-7985-X) U Pr of Amer.
Miller, Ronnie K. & McIntire, Paul, eds. ASNT Nondestructive Testing Handbook, Vol. 5: Acoustic Emission Testing. (Illus.). 604p. 1987. 121.25 (0-931403-02-2, 130) Am Soc Nondestructive.
Miller, Rory. Britain & Latin America in the Nineteenth & Twentieth Centuries. LC 92-35634. (Studies in Modern History). 228p. (C). 1993. text ed. 52.50 (0-582-21877-2, 79639) Longman.
— Britain & Latin America in the Nineteenth & Twentieth Centuries. LC 92-35634. (Studies in Modern History). 228p. (C). 1994. pap. text ed. 27.50 (0-582-49721-3, 79638) Longman.
Miller, Rosalie J. & Walker, Kay F. Perspectives on Theory for the Practice of Occupational Therapy. 2nd ed. Orig. Title: Six Perspectives on Theory for the Practice of Occupational Therapy. 300p. 1993. 47.00 (0-8342-0358-8, 20358) Aspen Pub.
Miller, Rosalind & Terwillegar, Jane. Commonsense Cataloging: A Cataloger's Manual. 4th rev. ed. 182p. 1990. 29.00 (0-8242-0789-0) Wilson.
Miller, Rose. The Old Barn. LC 92-35283. (Publish-a-Book Contest Ser.). (Illus.). 32p. (J). (gr. 2-6). 1992. lib. bdg. 19.97 (0-8114-3581-4) Raintree Steck-V.
— Old Barn. (J). (ps-3). 1994. pap. 4.95 (0-8114-7778-9) Raintree Steck-V.
Miller, Rose M. From Fear to Freedom: Living As Sons & Daughters of God. LC 94-13660. 224p. 1994. pap. 9.99 (0-87788-259-2) Shaw Pubs.
Miller, Rose M., jt. auth. see Stone, J. David.
Miller, Rosemary, jt. auth. see Lintott, Pam.
Miller, Ross. American Apocalypse: The Great Fire & the Myth of Chicago. LC 89-20338. (Illus.). 248p. 1990. 24.95 (0-226-52599-6) U Ch Pr.
Miller, Ross H., jt. auth. see Allen, Marshall B.
Miller, Ross M. Computer: Aided Financial Analysis. (Illus.). 480p. (C). 1990. text ed. 43.25 (0-201-12337-1) Addison-Wesley.
Miller, Roy A. The Footprints of the Buddha: An Eighth-Century Old Japanese Poetic Sequence. (American Oriental Ser.: Vol. 58). 1975. pap. 15.00 (0-940490-58-7) Am Orient Soc.
— Japanese Reader: Graded Lessons in the Modern Language. LC 62-9359. 250p. 1963. pap. 14.95 (0-8048-1647-6) C E Tuttle.
— Japan's Modern Myth: The Language & Beyond. LC 81-16213. 312p. 1982. 22.50 (0-8348-0168-X) Weatherhill.
— Nihongo: In Defence of Japanese. LC 85-23007. 260p. (C). 1986. text ed. 45.00 (0-485-11251-5, Pub. by Athlone Pr UK) Humanities.
— Studies in the Grammatical Tradition in Tibet. (Studies in the History of Linguistics: No. 6). xix, 142p. 1976. 39.00x (90-272-0897-2) Benjamins North Am.
Miller, Ruby M., jt. auth. see Miller, E. Willard.
Miller, Rudy M., jt. auth. see Miller, E. Willard.
Miller, Rupert, Jr. Simultaneous Statistical Inference. (Series in Statistics). (Illus.). 299p. 1991. 55.00 (0-387-90548-0) Spr-Verlag.
Miller, Rupert G., Jr. Survival Analysis. LC 81-4437. (Probability & Mathematical Statistics: Applied Probability & Statistics Section Ser.). 238p. 1981. pap. text ed. 69.95 (0-471-09434-X, Wiley-Interscience) Wiley.
Miller, Russell. Bare-Faced Messiah: A Biography of L. Ron Hubbard. 1988. 19.95 (0-8050-0654-0) H Holt & Co.
— The Larger Hope, Vol. 1. 25.00 (0-933840-00-4) Unitarian Univ.
— Larger Hope, Vol. 2. 1986. 25.00 (0-933840-25-X) Unitarian Univ.
— Nothing Less Than Victory. 1994. 27.50 (0-688-10209-3) Morrow.
Miller, Russell R., ed. Evaluations of New Antimicrobial Agents 1981-1984. LC 84-20726. (Pharmacotherapy Monograph: No. 1). (Illus.). 184p. (Orig.). 1985. pap. 50.00 (0-931591-00-7) Pharm Pubns.
— Evaluations of New Cardiovascular-Renal Drugs 1981-1984. LC 85-3545. (Pharmacotherapy Monograph: No. 2). (Illus.). 240p. (Orig.). 1985. pap. 60.00 (0-931591-01-5) Pharm Pubns.
— Evaluations of New Psychotherapeutic Drugs 1981-1984. LC 85-3515. (Pharmacotherapy Monograph: No. 3). (Illus.). 128p. (Orig.). 1985. pap. 40.00 (0-931591-02-3) Pharm Pubns.
Miller, Russell R., jt. auth. see Shuster, Albert H.
Miller, Russell V. Annotated Trade Practices Act. 14th ed. 770p. 1993. pap. 45.00 (0-455-21186-8, Pub. by Law Bk Co) W W Gaunt.
— Annotated Trade Practices Act 1991. 12th ed. liv, 520p. 1991. pap. 39.00 (0-455-21042-X, Pub. by Law Bk Co) W W Gaunt.
— Annotated Trade Practices Act 1994. 15th ed. 678p. 1994. pap. 45.00 (0-455-21239-2, Pub. by Sweet & Maxwll) W W Gaunt.
— Annotated Trade Practices Act, 1995. 16th ed. 680p. 1995. pap. 45.00 (0-455-21312-7, Pub. by Law Bk Co) W W Gaunt.
Miller, Ruth. California Divorce: Through the Legal Maze. (Illus.). 104p. (Orig.). 1988. pap. 9.95 (0-9620223-0-6) Beier & Assocs.
— Charleston Charlie. (Illus.). 32p. (J). 1994. pap. 3.95 (0-941711-00-5) Wyrick & Co.
Miller, Ruth & Parks, Sandy. Success Through Color Charisma. LC 83-73079. 133p. (Orig.). 1983. pap. 12.00 (0-916359-38-7) Color Charisma.
Miller, Ruth M. & Andrus, Ann T. Witness to History: Charleston's Old Exchange & Provost Dungeon. (Illus.). (J). (gr. 4 up). 1986. pap. 5.95 (0-87844-066-6) Sandlapper Pub Co.
Miller, Ruth M. & Lennor, Linda A. The Angel Oak Story. (Illus.). 1989. 5.00 (0-937684-26-0) Tradd St Pr.
Miller, Ryle, jt. auth. see McCullen, Geoffrey.
Miller, Ryle L., Jr. How to Write for the Professional Journals: A Guide for Technically Trained Managers. LC 87-32592. 189p. 1988. text ed. 49.95 (0-89930-254-8, MHT/, Quorum Bks) Greenwood.
Miller, S. Arete: Ancient Writers, Papyri, & Inscriptions on the History & Ideals of Greek Athletics & Games. 120p. 1979. pap. 12.50 (0-89005-313-8) Ares.
— Competitive Manufacturing. 1988. text ed. 44.95 (0-442-26395-3) Van Nos Reinhold.
Miller, S., jt. ed. see Lewis, M.
Miller, S. A., ed. Nutrition & Behavior. 320p. 1981. pap. 59.95 (0-89859-735-8) L Erlbaum Assocs.
Miller, S. Dennis. How to Write a Police Report. LC 92-36440. 148p. 1993. pap. text ed. 19.95 (0-8273-4728-6) Delmar.
Miller, S. M. & Ferge, Zsuzsa. The Dynamics of Deprivation. (Studies in Social Policy & Welfare). 330p. 1986. text ed. 68.95 (0-566-05137-0, Pub. by Avebury Pub UK) Ashgate Pub Co.
Miller, Sally M. From Prairie to Prison: The Life of Social Activist Kate Richards O'Hare. LC 93-12223. (Missouri Biography Ser.). (Illus.). 280p. (C). 1993. Alk. paper. 29.95 (0-8262-0898-3) U of Mo Pr.
— Victor Berger & the Promise of Constructive Socialism, 1910-1920. LC 72-175609. (Contributions in American History Ser.: No. 24). 390p. 1973. text ed. 59.95 (0-8371-6264-5, MVB/, Greenwood Pr) Greenwood.
***Miller, Sally M., ed.** American Labor in the Era of World War II. LC 94-24570. 240p. 1995. pap. text ed. 18.95 (0-275-95185-5, Praeger Pubs) Greenwood.
— The Ethnic Press in the United States: A Historical Analysis & Handbook. LC 85-31699. 459p. 1987. text ed. 89.50 (0-313-23879-0, MIE/, Greenwood Pr) Greenwood.
— Flawed Liberation: Socialism & Feminism. LC 80-1050. (Contributions in Women's Studies: No. 19). 240p. 1981. text ed. 55.00 (0-313-21401-8, MFL/, Greenwood Pr) Greenwood.
— John Muir: Life & Work. LC 93-10925. (Illus.). 335p. 1995. reprint ed. pap. text ed. 17.95 (0-8263-1594-1) U of NM Pr.
***Miller, Sally M. & Cornford, Daniela.** American Labor in the Era of World War II. LC 94-24570. (Contributions in Labor Studies Ser.: Vol. 45). 240p. 1995. text ed. 59.95 (0-313-29074-1) Greenwood.
Miller, Sally M., ed. see O'Hare, Kate R.
Miller, Sam F. Design Process: A Primer for Architectural & Interior Design. 240p. 1995. pap. 39.95 (0-442-01394-9) Van Nos Reinhold.
Miller, Samantha. Prostitutes Discuss Male Sexuality. 1996. pap. 12.95 (0-9627418-6-8, Smart Pubns) Hlth Freedom.
Miller, Sammy. Sammy Miller on Trials. (Illus.). 1971. 5.95 (0-393-60015-7) Norton.
Miller, Samuel. The Life of the Soul. large type ed. (Large Print Inspirational Ser.). 216p. 1986. pap. 12.95 (0-8027-2551-1) Walker & Co.
Miller, Samuel, jt. auth. see Crean, Hugh.
Miller, Samuel, tr. see Del Rio Garcia, Eduardo.
Miller, Samuel C. Neon Techniques & Handling: Handbook of Neon Sign & Cold Cathode Lighting. 1977. 27.95 (0-911380-41-8) ST Pubns.
Miller, Samuel D. An Aerospace Bibliography. (Reference Ser.). 341p. 1986. reprint ed. write for info. (0-912799-22-6) Off Air Force.
Miller, Samuel D., jt. auth. see Olson, Mary W.
Miller, Samuel F. Lectures on the Constitution of the United States. xxi, 765p. 1981. reprint ed. lib. bdg. 45.00 (0-8377-0836-2) Rothman.
***Miller, Samuel H.** The Life of the Soul. large type ed. 208p. 1995. pap. 9.95 (0-8027-2689-5) Walker & Co.
— Religion in a Technical Age. LC 68-17628. 158p. reprint ed. pap. 45.10 (0-7837-3848-X, 2043670) Bks Demand.
Miller, Samuel H. & Wright, G. Ernest, eds. The Roman Catholic-Protestant Colloquium, Ecumenical Dialogue at Harvard. LC 64-19583. 396p. 1964. 35.00 (0-674-23700-5) Belknap Pr.
Miller, Samuel L. History of the Town of Waldoboro, Maine. (Illus.). 281p. 1988. reprint ed. lib. bdg. 33.00 (0-8328-0034-1, ME0007) Higginson Bk Co.
Miller, Samuel O., jt. auth. see Dane, Barbara O.
Miller, Sandra. A Survey of Constantin Brancusi's Work. (Clarendon Studies in the History of Art). (Illus.). 256p. 1995. 65.00 (0-19-817514-0) OUP.
Miller, Sandra E., et al. Rural Resource Management: A Guide for Long-Term Planning. LC 93-38131. (Illus.). 312p. (C). 1994. text ed. 21.95 (0-8138-0686-0) Iowa St U Pr.
Miller, Sandra L., ed. see Libby, Gary R.
Miller, Sandra L., ed. see Poyner, Robin.
Miller, Sandra W. & Tulloch, Charlotte R., eds. Teaching Basic Skills Through Home Economics. 75p. (C). 1989. pap. text ed. 6.00 (0-911365-29-X, A261-08474) Home Econ Educ.
***Miller, Sandy.** Cerro Gordo, Illinois. (Illus.). 140p. 1989. 52.50 (0-88107-145-5) Curtis Media.
— Smart Girl. 160p. (YA). (gr. 7 up). 1982. pap. 2.25 (0-451-11887-1, Sig Vista) NAL-Dutton.
Miller, Sandy, ed. see Butler-Moore, Nylea & Krau, Carol F.
Miller, Sanford, ed. see S. U. N. Y. Brockport Conference Staff.
Miller, Sara E., jt. auth. see Hayat, M. A.
Miller, Sara S. Three Stories You Can Read to Your Dog. LC 93-38856. (J). 1995. 13.95 (0-395-69938-X) HM.
— What's in the Woods? An Outdoor Activity Book. (Illus.). (J). (gr. 3-6). 1995. pap. 11.95 (0-9646246-0-5) Cygnet Mill Bks.
Miller, Sarah F. & Smith, Susan K. Seven Springs Sampler: Herb Recipes from Historic Homes of Powder Springs, Georgia. (Illus.). 218p. (Orig.). 1991. pap. 17.50 (1-882063-12-0) Cottage Pr MA.
Miller, Sarah W. Bible Dramas for Older Boys & Girls. LC 75-95409. (J). (gr. 3-6). 1970. pap. 4.99 (0-8054-7506-0) Broadman.
— A Variety Book of Puppet Scripts. LC 78-57276. 1978. pap. 4.99 (0-8054-7515-X) Broadman.
Miller, Sarah W. & Madaris, Don L. Count on Us. Montgomery, Charles, ed. 44p. 1984. reprint ed. pap. 3.95 (0-916043-00-2) Light Hearted Pub Co.
Miller, Saul. Little Relaxation: On Being More Alive & at Ease. LC 90-43249. 1990. pap. 7.95 (0-88179-025-7) Hartley & Marks.
Miller, Scott. Loon Journal. (Illus.). 40p. (Orig.). (J). (gr. 4 up). 1989. pap. 5.98 (0-926147-01-3) Loonfeather.
Miller, Scott A. Developmental Research Methods. (Illus.). 464p. 1986. text ed. 54.00 (0-13-208133-4) P-H.
Miller, Scott D. & Berg, Insoo K. The Miracle Method: A Radically New Approach to Problem Drinking. 160p. 1995. 19.95 (0-393-03740-1) Norton.
Miller, Scott D., jt. auth. see Berg, Insoo K.
Miller, Scott S. & Guy, Thomas. Dealing with the IRS. (Illus.). 70p. 1992. pap. 8.95 (0-9631941-0-0) Creek Bend Pub.
Miller, Setphen B. NAC, Vol 18: Daniel. 576p. 1994. 27.99 (0-8054-0118-0, 4201-18) Broadman.
Miller, Seumas, jt. auth. see Freadman, Richard.
Miller, Sharon. Satin Roses. pap. 11.99 (0-87377-001-3) GAM Pubns.
— Transplanted Kids. pap. 6.95 (0-87377-010-2) GAM Pubns.
Miller, Sheila. I Can Trace a Rainbow. 1987. pap. 4.95 (9971-972-60-3) OMF Bks.
— Ian & the Gigantic Leafy Obstacle. 1983. pap. 2.95 (9971-83-790-0) OMF Bks.
— My Book about Hudson. 1975. pap. 2.95 (9971-972-20-4) OMF Bks.
Miller, Sheila & Murray, Ian. The Gods Must Be Angry. 34p. (J). (gr. 1-4). 1990. 2.95 (9971-972-93-X) OMF Bks.
Miller, Sheila, jt. ed. see Szur, Rolene.
Miller, Sheldon. Stealth Management: With Shared Goals They Will Hardly Know You Are Leading Them. LC 92-90895. (Illus.). 300p. 1993. 39.00 (0-9635316-0-3) Stealth Mgmt.
Miller, Sheldon I., jt. ed. see Frances, Richard J.
Miller, Shelley, comp. Serial Publications Available by Exchange: Mexico, Central America & Panama. (Bibliography & Reference Ser.: No. 29). vii, 86p. (Orig.). 1992. pap. 22.50 (0-917617-28-2) SALALM.
***Miller, Shelley & Sonntag-Grigera, Gabriela.** Serial Publications Available by Exchange: Caribbean Area. (Bibliography & Reference Ser.: No. 36). 48p. (Orig.). 1994. pap. 19.50 (0-917617-45-2) SALALM.
Miller, Sheri & Garber, Berry. Sounds Like Business: Improving English Pronunciation Skills in the Business World, Set 6. 77p. (C). 1994. audio write for info. (0-9640809-0-7) S Miller.
Miller, Sherman N. & Miller, Gwynelle W. Secrets of the Twenty-Five Year Happy Marriage. (Illus.). 110p. (Orig.). 1992. pap. text ed. write for info. (0-9635708-0-3, TXU534-407) Z James.
— Wedlock... The Common Sense Marriage. 224p. (Orig.). 1994. pap. 12.95 (0-9640915-6-9) S N M Pubng.
Miller, Sherod, ed. Marriages & Families: Enrichment Through Communication. LC 75-27012. (Sage Contemporary Social Science Issues Ser.: No. 20). 126p. reprint ed. pap. 36.00 (0-317-08969-2, 2021933) Bks Demand.
Miller, Sherod, et al. Connecting Instructor Manual. 256p. 1989. 45.00 (0-917340-17-5) Interpersonal Comm.

— Connecting Skills Workbook. 210p. (Orig.). 1989. student ed 11.95 (*0-917340-16-7*) Interpersonal Comm.
— Connecting with Self & Others. 312p. (Orig.). 1988. pap. text ed. 12.95 (*0-917340-15-9*) Interpersonal Comm.
— Couple Communication I: Talking Together. (Couple Communication Ser.). 1979. pap. 8.95 (*0-917340-09-4*); teacher ed, ring bd. 49.95 (*0-917340-06-X*) Interpersonal Comm.
— Straight Talk: A New Way to Get Close to Others by Saying What You Really Mean. 1982. pap. 4.95 (*0-451-15907-1*, Sig) NAL-Dutton.
— Talking & Listening Together: Couple Communication One. (Illus.). 160p. (C). 1991. pap. 11.95 (*0-917340-18-3*) Interpersonal Comm.
— Working Together: Productive Communication on the Job. (Illus.). 200p. 1985. teacher ed, text ed. 25.00 (*0-917340-14-0*); pap. 34.95 (*0-917340-11-6*) Interpersonal Comm.
Miller, Sherrill. The Sacred Earth. (Illus.). 246p. 1993. 49.50 (*0-8109-3831-6*) Abrams.
Miller, Sherry. The Day Happy E. Bunny Lost His Cotton Tail. (Illus.). 16p. (Orig.). (J). (gr. k-5). 1983. pap. 0.49 (*0-685-43303-X*) Double M Pub.
— Lost in the Arctic with Pal Bear. (Molly Character - Color Me Ser.: No. 2). (Illus.). 32p. (Orig.). (J). (gr. k-5). 1984. pap. 1.95 (*0-913379-01-8*) Double M Pub.
— Santa's Helper. LC 83-72493. (Molly Character - Color Me Ser.: No. 1). (Illus.). 32p. (Orig.). (J). (gr. k-5). 1983. pap. 1.95 (*0-913379-00-X*) Double M Pub.
— Snowskate Goes for Gold. (Molly Character - Color Me Ser.: No. 3). (Illus.). 32p. (Orig.). (J). (gr. k-5). 1984. pap. 1.95 (*0-913379-02-6*) Double M Pub.
Miller, Sherry C. Snowharry Takes a Vacation (with Arctic Friends) (Molly Character - Color Me Ser.: No. 4). (Illus.). 32p. (J). (gr. k-5). 1985. pap. write for info. (*0-913379-03-4*) Double M Pub.
Miller, Shirley & Welles, Lynn. Mexico West Cookbook. (Illus.). 1983. pap. 4.95 (*0-914622-05-6*) Baja Trail.
Miller, Shirley A. TemperaMysticism: Exploding the Temperament Theory. 176p. 1991. pap. 8.95 (*0-914984-30-6*) Starburst.
Miller, Shirley J. My House, Your House. (Illus.). 60p. (Orig.). (J). (gr. 2-6). 1993. pap. 6.95 (*1-878580-91-4*) Asylum Arts.
— School Days. (Illus.). 80p. (Orig.). (J). (gr. 2-6). 1993. pap. 6.95 (*1-878580-90-6*) Asylum Arts.
Miller, Shirley M., comp. Webster's New World Speller - Divider: Based upon Webster's New World Dictionary of the American Language, College Edition. 3rd ed. 1992. write for info. (*0-318-69384-4*, Websters New Wrld) P-H Gen Ref & Trav.
Miller, Sigmund. One Bright Day. 1952. pap. 4.75 (*0-8222-0852-0*) Dramatists Play.
***Miller, Simon.** Landlords & Haciendas in Modern Mexico: Essays in Radical Reappraisal. (CEDLA Latin America Studies (CLAS): No. 72). 200p. 1995. pap. 23.50 (*90-70280-95-7*, Pub. by Thesis Pubs NE) IBD Ltd.
Miller, Simon, jt. auth. see Miller, Arj.
Miller, Skip. Tidewater Fishing: The Complete Guide to Eastern Virginia Waters. LC 93-9061. 1993. pap. 9.99 (*1-56943-007-1*, Tribune) Contemp Bks.
Miller, Somi A. & Lake, Patricia. Thai Cooking Class. (Illus.). 96p. (Orig.). 1993. pap. 7.00 (*0-685-66882-7*, Pub. by Angus & Robertson AT) HarpC.
Miller, Stanford M. Two Thousand Hard to Locate Latin Forms. 18p. (Orig.). (LAT.). 1992. spiral bd. 2.20 (*0-939507-21-8*, B104) Amer Classical.
Miller, Stanton S. Environmental Monitoring. LC 76-54966. (ACS Reprint Collection Ser.). 207p. reprint ed. pap. 59.00 (*0-7837-1453-X*, 2052429) Bks Demand.
Miller, Stella G. Two Groups of Thessalian Gold. LC 77-80473. (University of California Publications in Social Welfare: No. 18). (Illus.). 126p. reprint ed. pap. 36.00 (*0-685-23997-7*, 2031581) Bks Demand.
Miller, Stephen. Excellence & Equity: The National Endowment for the Humanities. 202p. reprint ed. pap. 57.60 (*0-7837-5789-1*, 2045455) Bks Demand.
— Misguiding Lights? (Dialog Ser.). 1991. student ed, pap. 4.95 (*0-8341-1280-9*); teacher ed, pap. 3.95 (*0-8341-1279-5*) Beacon Hill.
— Protecting Restaurant Profits. 1988. pap. 36.95 (*0-86730-252-6*) Lebhar Friedman.
— Special Interest Groups in American Politics. LC 83-4691. 160p. 1983. 32.95 (*0-87855-485-8*) Transaction Pubs.
Miller, Stephen, jt. ed. see Perez, Janet.
Miller, Stephen A. General Zoology Laboratory Manual. 2nd ed. 352p. (C). 1991. spiral bd. write for info. (*0-697-01371-5*) Wm C Brown Pubs.
— General Zoology Laboratory Manual. 3rd ed. 352p. (C). 1993. spiral bd. write for info. (*0-697-13703-1*) Wm C Brown Pubs.
Miller, Stephen A. & Harley, John P. Zoology. 60p. (C). 1991. write for info. (*0-697-14072-5*); write for info. (*0-697-09928-8*) Wm C Brown Pubs.
— Zoology. (C). 1995. student ed write for info. (*0-697-25689-8*) Wm C Brown Pubs.
— Zoology. 2nd ed. 744p. (C). 1993. pap. text ed. write for info. (*0-697-13704-X*) Wm C Brown Pubs.
— Zoology. 2nd ed. 744p. (C). 1993. text ed. write for info. (*0-697-16952-9*); Study guide. student ed write for info. (*0-697-13706-6*) Wm C Brown Pubs.
— Zoology. 3rd ed. 752p. (C). 1995. pap. write for info. (*0-697-24373-7*) Wm C Brown Pubs.
— Zoology. 3rd ed. 752p. (C). 1995. text ed. write for info. (*0-697-24374-5*) Wm C Brown Pubs.
— Zoology, 1. 2nd ed. 744p. (C). 1993. pap. text ed. write for info. (*0-697-16953-7*) Wm C Brown Pubs.
— Zoology, 2. 2nd ed. 744p. (C). 1993. pap. text ed. write for info. (*0-697-16954-5*) Wm C Brown Pubs.
— Zoology, 3. 2nd ed. 744p. (C). 1993. pap. text ed. write for info. (*0-697-16955-3*) Wm C Brown Pubs.
— Zoology, 4. 2nd ed. 744p. (C). 1993. pap. text ed. write for info. (*0-697-20486-3*) Wm C Brown Pubs.
Miller, Stephen A. & Templin, Jay M. Student Study Guide to Accompany Zoology. 3rd ed. 256p. (C). 1995. spiral bd. write for info. (*0-697-26068-2*) Wm C Brown Pubs.
Miller, Stephen B. Historical Sketches of Hudson NY. 140p. 1985. reprint ed. 12.50 (*0-932334-75-X*, NY11031); reprint ed. pap. 8.95 (*0-932334-77-6*, NY11030) Hrt of the Lakes.
Miller, Stephen G. Arete: Greek Sports from Ancient Sources. LC 90-28646. (Illus.). 239p. 1991. 40.00 (*0-520-07508-0*); pap. 15.00 (*0-520-07509-9*) U CA Pr.
— Nemea: A Guide to the Site & Museum. 1990. 35.00 (*0-520-06590-5*); pap. 15.00 (*0-520-06799-1*) U CA Pr.
Miller, Stephen H., ed. Year Book of Plastic & Reconstructive Surgery, 1989. (Illus.). 328p. 1989. 57.95 (*0-8151-6036-4*, Yr Bk Med Pubs) Mosby Yr Bk.
Miller, Stephen J. Parson's Diseases of the Eye. 18th ed. (Illus.). 456p. 1990. text ed. 59.95 (*0-443-04230-6*) Churchill.
Miller, Stephen M. Beacon Small-Group Bible Studies, II Corinthians, Galatians: Reckless Freedom, Responsible Living. Wolf, Earl C., ed. 96p. (Orig.). 1985. pap. 3.95 (*0-8341-0957-3*) Beacon Hill.
— Duck Hunting on the Fox: Hunting & Decoy-Carving Traditions on the Mississippi Flyway. (Illus.). 144p. 1995. write for info. (*1-883953-11-1*) Midwest Trad.
— Early American Waterfowling, 1700's-1930. LC 86-23586. (Illus.). 256p. 1986. 27.95 (*0-8329-0438-4*, Winchester Pr) New Win Pub.
— Questions You Shouldn't Ask about Christianity. (Dialog Ser.). 124p. 1987. student ed, pap. 4.95 (*0-8341-1122-5*); teacher ed, pap. 3.95 (*0-8341-1123-3*) Beacon Hill.
Miller, Stephen P. An Act of God: Memories of Vietnam. rev. ed. 32p. (Orig.). (C). 1987. reprint ed. pap. 5.00 (*0-943285-00-3*) Nrthcst View Pr.
— Art Is Boring for the Same Reason We Stayed in Vietnam. (Post- & Pre-Everything Ser.). 120p. (Orig.). 1992. pap. 9.00 (*0-934450-50-1*) Unmuzzled Ox.
Miller, Stephen W. Cardiac Angiography. (Library of Radiology). 430p. 1984. 105.00 (*0-316-57367-1*) Little.
Miller, Steve. The Art of the Weathervane. LC 83-51742. (Illus.). 160p. 1984. 35.00 (*0-88740-005-1*) Schiffer.
— The Contemporary Christian Music Debate: Worldly Compromise or Agent of Renewal? LC 92-30629. 1993. 8.99 (*0-685-62282-7*) Tyndale.
— Experimental Design & Statistics. 2nd ed. (New Essential Psychology Ser.). 192p. 1984. pap. 8.95 (*0-416-34940-4*, NO. 9014) Routledge Chapman & Hall.
— Multivariate Design & Statistics. (New Essential Psychology Ser.). 224p. 1986. pap. 7.95 (*0-416-34930-7*, 1019) Routledge Chapman & Hall.
Miller, Steve A. How to Get the Most Out of Trade Shows. 177p. 1991. 29.95 (*0-8442-3193-2*, NTC Busn Bks) NTC Pub Grp.
Miller, Steven, jt. auth. see Chanin, Eileen.
Miller, Steven, jt. auth. see Fredericks, Marcel.
***Miller, Steven E.** Civilizing Cyberspace: Policy, Power & the Information Superhighway. (C). 1996. text ed. write for info. (*0-201-84760-4*) Addison-Wesley.
Miller, Steven E., ed. The Good Ideas Book: Tips & Techniques for Mastering 1-2-3 & Symphony. (Lotus Magazine Ser.). 1988. pap. 19.95 (*0-201-15664-4*) Addison-Wesley.
— The Macro Book: Expert Advice for 1-2-3 & Symphony Users. (Best of Lotus Magazine Ser.). 432p. 1988. pap. 21.95 (*0-201-15665-2*) Addison-Wesley.
— Strategy & Nuclear Deterrence: An International Security Reader. LC 84-42549. 312p. 1984. pap. 13.95x (*0-691-00597-4*) Princeton U Pr.
— The Worksheet Book: Buiding Skills for 1-2-3 & Symphony. (Best of Lotus Magazine Ser.). 400p. 1988. pap. 21.95 (*0-201-15039-5*) Addison-Wesley.
Miller, Steven E & Van Evera, Stephen, eds. Naval Strategy & National Security: An International Security Reader. 408p. 1988. text ed. 57.50 (*0-691-07775-4*) Princeton U Pr.
— Naval Strategy & National Security: An International Security Reader. LC 87-36108. 401p. reprint ed. pap. 114.30 (*0-8357-2550-2*, 2040241) Bks Demand.
— The Star Wars Controversy: An International Security Reader. (Illus.). 336p. 1986. text ed. 55.00x (*0-691-07713-4*) Princeton U Pr.
Miller, Steven E., jt. ed. see Arbatov, Alexei G.
Miller, Steven E., jt. ed. see Eden, Lynn.
Miller, Steven E., jt. ed. see Johnson, Teresa P.
Miller, Steven E., jt. ed. see Lynn-Jones, Sean M.
Miller, Steven E., jt. ed. see Matseiko, Youri.
Miller, Steven E., ed. see Van Evera, Stephen, et al.
Miller, Steven E., et al, eds. Military Strategy & the Origins of the First World War: An International Security Reader. rev. ed. 360p. 1991. pap. text ed. 16.95 (*0-691-02349-2*) Princeton U Pr.
— The Star Wars Controversy: An International Security Reader. LC 86-4280. (Illus.). 350p. reprint ed. pap. 99.80 (*0-8357-4201-6*, 2036980) Bks Demand.
Miller, Steven I. An Introduction to the Sociology of Education. 204p. 1978. text ed. 32.95 (*0-87073-395-8*); pap. text ed. 17.95x (*0-87073-396-6*) Transaction Pubs.
Miller, Steven I. & Fredericks, Marcel. Qualitative Research Methods: Social Epistemology & Practical Inquiry. LC 93-20936. 160p. (C). 1994. text ed. 44.95 (*0-8204-2326-2*) P Lang Pubs.
Miller, Steven I. & Morgan, Ronald R. An Introduction to the Social Psychology of Education: Implications for Learning & Instruction. 208p. 1983. 18.95 (*0-87073-632-9*); pap. 11.95 (*0-87073-633-7*) Schenkman Bks Inc.
Miller, Steven L. Economic Education for Citizenship. 85p. (Orig.). 1988. pap. 8.00 (*0-941339-06-8*) Ind U SSDC.
Miller, Steven M. Impacts of Industrial Robotics: Potential Effects on Labor & Costs Within the Metalworking Industries. LC 87-40151. (Economics of Technological Change Ser.). (Illus.). 352p. (C). 1989. pap. text ed. 19.95 (*0-299-10504-0*) U of Wis Pr.
Miller, Steven M., jt. auth. see Bereiter, Susan R.
Miller, Stewart, jt. ed. see George, Victor.
Miller, Stewart E. & Chynoweth, Alan G., eds. Optical Fiber Telecommunications. LC 78-20046. 1979. text ed. 99.00 (*0-12-497350-7*) Acad Pr.
Miller, Stewart E. & Kaminow, Ivan P., eds. Optical Fiber Telecommunications, Vol. II. 768p. 1988. text ed. 97.00 (*0-12-497351-5*) Acad Pr.
Miller, Stuart. Men & Friendship. 240p. 1992. pap. 8.95 (*0-87477-685-6*) J P Tarcher.
— Property Tax Legislation in the United States, 1976, 2 pts., Pt. 2. (Research & Information Ser.: No. 1). 1977. pap. 8.00 (*0-88329-031-6*) IAAO.
— Understanding Europeans. 272p. 1990. reprint ed. pap. 14.95 (*0-945465-77-7*) John Muir.
Miller, Stuart & Schlitt, Judith K. Interior Space: Design Concepts for Personal Needs. LC 85-6337. 192p. 1985. text ed. 49.95 (*0-275-90146-7*, C0146, Praeger Pubs) Greenwood.
— Interior Space: Design Concepts for Personal Needs. LC 85-6337. 192p. 1987. pap. text ed. 16.95 (*0-275-92824-1*, Praeger Pubs) Greenwood.
Miller, Stuart C. Benevolent Assimilation: The American Conquest of the Philippines, 1899-1903. LC 82-1957. 342p. 1984. reprint ed. pap. 17.00 (*0-300-03081-9*, Y-488) Yale U Pr.
— The Unwelcome Immigrant: The American Image of the Chinese, 1785-1882. LC 76-81763. 271p. reprint ed. pap. 77.30 (*0-685-23355-3*, 2032284) Bks Demand.
Miller, Stuart J., jt. auth. see Bartollas, Clemens.
Miller, Stuart W. Agricultural Land: Assessment, Taxation & Preservation. (Bibliographic Ser.). 44p. 1981. pap. 10.50 (*0-88329-048-0*) IAAO.
— Concise Dictionary of Acronyms & Initialisms. 192p. 1988. 24.95 (*0-8160-1577-5*) Facts on File.
— Property Taxation in the U. S. An Annotated Bibliography, Supplement No. 1. (Research & Information Ser.: No. 3-I). 82p. 1979. 14.50 (*0-88329-021-9*) IAAO.
***Miller, Sue.** The Distinguished Guest. large type ed. 1995. 26.95 (*1-56895-229-5*) Wheeler Pub.
— The Distinguished Guest: A Novel. 288p. 1995. 24.00 (*0-06-017673-3*) HarpC.
— Family Pictures. 1991. mass mkt. 5.99 (*0-06-109925-2*, Harp PBks) HarpC.
— For Love. 1994. mass mkt. 6.50 (*0-06-109161-8*, Harp PBks) HarpC.
— For Love. large type ed. LC 92-45877. 1993. 16.95 (*0-8161-5755-3*); pap. 16.95 (*0-8161-5756-1*) G K Hall.
— Good Mother. 1994. pap. 11.95 (*0-385-31243-1*, Delta) Dell.
Miller, Sue, intro. The Passage of Time. 255p. (Orig.). (C). 1993. pap. 8.95 (*0-933277-08-3*) Ploughshares.
Miller, Sue, jt. auth. see Miller, Bob.
Miller, Susan. Rescuing the Subject: A Critical Introduction to Rhetoric & the Writer. LC 88-18196. 212p. (C). 1989. text ed. 24.95 (*0-8093-1501-7*) S Ill U Pr.
— The Shame Experience. (Psychoanalytic Monographs: Vol. 1). 208p. 1993. reprint ed. pap. 24.95 (*0-88163-165-5*) Analytic Pr.
— Textual Carnivals: The Politics of Composition. LC 90-34244. 288p. (C). 1993. pap. 14.95 (*0-8093-1922-5*) S Ill U Pr.
— The Written World. 624p. (C). 1990. pap. text ed. 16.00 (*0-06-044526-2*) HarpCollege.
Miller, Susan, comp. Written Worlds: Reading & Writing Culture. 2nd ed. LC 92-18636. (C). 1992. 26.00 (*0-06-500585-6*) HarpCollege.
Miller, Susan, jt. ed. see Bennett, Bruce.
Miller, Susan, jt. auth. see Walter, Jeff.
***Miller, Susan B.** When Parents Have Problems: A Book for Kids. LC 94-45929. 94p. (C). 1995. text ed. 31.95x (*0-398-05989-6*); pap. text ed. 18.95x (*0-398-05990-X*) C C Thomas.
Miller, Susan E. When the Tulips Bloom. Burdge-Rezvan, Jereng, ed. (Illus.). 152p. (Orig.). 1993. pap. text ed. 12.95 (*1-880254-08-5*) Vista.
Miller, Susan G., tr. see As-Saffar, Muhammad.
Miller, Susan J. & Lefebvre, Philip. Miller's Standard Insurance Policies Annotated. 3rd ed. LC 93-197619. 1995. 495.00 (*0-9639112-0-1*) Legal Res Systs.
Miller, Susan M. Elijah. (Young Reader's Christian Library). (Illus.). (J). (gr. 3 up). per. 2.50 (*1-55748-189-X*) Barbour & Co.
— Esther. (Young Reader's Christian Library). (J). (gr. 3 up). 1992. per. 2.50 (*1-55748-260-8*) Barbour & Co.
— Hudson Taylor. (J). (gr. 3-10). 1993. pap. 4.95 (*1-55748-338-8*) Barbour & Co.
— Reading Too Soon: How to Understand & Help the Hyperlexic Child. 1993. pap. 14.95 (*0-9637921-0-5*) Ctr for Speech.
***Miller, Susan S.** Shame in Context. 1996. write for info. (*0-88163-209-0*) Analytic Pr.
Miller, Susann, ed. Porsche Year, 1982. (Illus.). 96p. 1982. 29.95 (*0-910597-00-6*); pap. 5.00 (*0-685-10125-8*) M M Pub Inc.
— Porsche Year, 1985-6. (Porsche Ser.). (Illus.). 96p. (Orig.). 1986. 40.00 (*0-915927-04-7*); pap. text ed. 18.95 (*0-915927-03-9*) M M Pub Inc.
Miller, Susann C. & Merritt, Richard F. Porsche Brochures & Sales Literature: A Sourcebook 1948-1965. rev. ed. 312p. 1985. reprint ed. 49.95 (*0-915927-02-0*) M M Pub Inc.
Miller, Susanna. Beans & Peas. (Foods We Eat Ser.). (Illus.). 32p. (J). (gr. 1-4). 1990. lib. bdg. 14.96 (*0-87614-428-8*, Carolrhoda) Lerner Group.
Miller, Susanne. Special Reading Problems: Some Helps Training Module-Trainer's Guide. rev. ed. 32p. 1983. audio 132.00 (*0-930713-47-8*) Lit Vol Am.
— Special Reading Problems Some Helps Tutor Notes. 9p. 1983. 2.00 (*0-930713-25-7*) Lit Vol Am.
Miller, Susanne, jt. auth. see Wilkins, Gloria.
***Miller, Susanne B.** Summon the Light Within: Daily Exercises & Meditations with Master Jesus. (Illus.). (Orig.). 1995. pap. 3.95 (*1-881217-11-6*) New Atlantean.
Miller, Susanne S. Prehistoric Mammals. (Illus.). (J). (ps-5). 1984. pap. 7.95 (*0-671-47976-8*, S&S Bks Young Read) S&S Childrens.
Miller, Suzanne M. & McCaskill, Barbara, eds. Multicultural Literature & Literacies: Making Space for Difference. LC 92-39543. (SUNY Series, Literacy, Culture, & Learning: Theory & Practice). 300p. (C). 1993. 59.50 (*0-7914-1645-3*); pap. 19.95 (*0-7914-1646-1*) State U NY Pr.
Miller, Suzanne S. Whales & Sharks. Klimo, Kate, ed. (Illus.). 48p. (J). 1982. pap. 9.95 (*0-671-45148-0*, S&S Bks Young Read) S&S Childrens.
Miller, Sylvia R. The Human Condition: The Way of the Infant, the Way of the Child, the Way of the Adult. LC 83-81968. (Illus.). 144p. 1983. 20.00 (*0-913504-80-7*) Lowell Pr.
— A Pictorial Memoir. LC 80-81146. (Illus.). 120p. 1980. 20.00 (*0-913504-57-2*) Lowell Pr.
Miller, T., ed. The Old English Version of Bede's Ecclesiastical History, Pt. II, No. 1. (EETS, OS Ser.: Vol. 110). 1974. reprint ed. 40.00 (*0-8115-3368-9*) Periodicals Srv.
Miller, T., et al. Subnormal Operators & Representations of Algebras of Bounded Analytic Functions & Other Uniform Algebras. LC 86-17381. (Memoirs of the American Mathematical Society Ser.: Vol. 63/354). 125p. 1986. pap. text ed. 26.00 (*0-8218-2415-5*, MEMO 63/354) Am Math.
Miller, T. A. Cuticle Techniques in Arthropods. (Experimental Entomology Ser.). (Illus.). 410p. 1980. 152.00 (*0-387-90475-1*) Spr-Verlag.
— Insect Neurophysiological Techniques. (Experimental Entomology Ser.). (Illus.). 1979. 99.00 (*0-387-90407-7*) Spr-Verlag.
Miller, T. A., ed. Neurohormonal Techniques in Insects. (Experimental Entomology Ser.). (Illus.). 282p. 1980. 108.00 (*0-387-90451-4*) Spr-Verlag.
Miller, T. A., jt. ed. see Bradley, T. J.
Miller, T. A., jt. ed. see Heinrichs, E. A.
Miller, T. A., jt. ed. see Hummel, H. E.
Miller, T. A., jt. ed. see Krysan, J. L.
Miller, T. A., jt. ed. see Miller, J. R.
Miller, T. A., jt. ed. see Strausfeld, N. J.
Miller, T. A., jt. ed. see Zalucki, M. P.
Miller, T. Franklin. Life & Teachings of Jesus. rev. ed. 1971. pap. 3.95 (*0-87162-114-2*, D5200) Warner Pr.
— Psalms that Sing. (Eagle Bible Ser.). 1989. pap. 2.50 (*0-87162-553-9*, D9155) Warner Pr.
***Miller, T. G.** Connor Quinn: Living on the Edge Case One. LC 93-92785. 96p. (Orig.). 1994. pap. 7.00 (*1-56002-372-4*, Univ Edtns) Aegina Pr.
Miller, T. J. Brushless Permanent-Magnet & Reluctance Motor Drives. (Monographs in Electrical & Electronic Engineering: No. 21). (Illus.). 244p. 1989. 64.00 (*0-19-859369-4*) OUP.
— Switched Reluctance Motors & Their Control. LC 92-82559. (Monographs in Electrical & Electronic Engineering: No. 31). 1993. 75.00 (*0-19-859387-2*, Clarendon Pr) OUP.
Miller, T. J., jt. auth. see Hendershot, J. R., Jr.
Miller, T. K. & Winston, R. B. Administration & Leadership in Student Affairs: Actualizing Student Development in Higher Education. 2nd ed. LC 90-81438. 864p. (Orig.). (C). 1991. 36.95 (*1-55959-022-X*) Accel Devel.
Miller, T. Michael. Alexandria & Alexandria (Arlington) County, Virginia Minister Returns & Marriage Bonds - 1801-1852. xii, 206p. (Orig.). 1987. pap. 12.00 (*1-55613-029-5*) Heritage Bk.
— Alexandria Virginia City Officialdom: 1749-1992. 146p. (Orig.). 1992. pap. 16.00 (*1-55613-611-0*) Heritage Bk.
— Artisans & Merchants of Alexandria, Virginia 1780-1820, Vol. 1. 428p. 1991. pap. 20.00 (*1-55613-389-8*) Heritage Bk.
— Artisans & Merchants of Alexandria, Virginia 1780-1820, Vol. 2. (Illus.). 545p. 1992. pap. 35.50 (*1-55613-598-X*) Heritage Bk.
— Murder & Mayhem: Criminal Conduct in Old Alexandria, Virginia, 1749-1900. xi, 206p. (Orig.). 1988. pap. 15.00 (*1-55613-115-1*) Heritage Bk.
— Pen Portraits of Alexandria, Virginia, 1739-1900. 401p. (Orig.). 1987. pap. 20.00 (*1-55613-061-9*) Heritage Bk.
Miller, T. Rothrock. Evaluating Orthopedic Disability: A Common Sense Approach. 2nd ed. 128p. 1987. pap. 32.95 (*0-87489-437-9*) Med Economics.
— A Ship Without a Name. 1992. 17.95 (*0-533-10204-9*) Vantage.
Miller, Tari V., jt. auth. see Rantz, Marilyn.
Miller, Ted. El Me Toco: He Touched Me. (SPA.). 3.25 (*84-7228-336-4*, 220345, Pub. by Edit Clie SP) TSELF.
Miller, Ted, ed. The Story from the Book. 544p. 1986. mass mkt. 4.95 (*0-8423-6677-6*) Tyndale.
***Miller, Ted R., et al.** Databook on Nonfatal Injury: Incidence, Costs, & Consequences. 200p. (C). 1994. lib. bdg. 48.50 (*0-87766-630-X*) Urban Inst.
Miller, Terence, jt. auth. see Prendergast, John.
Miller, Teresa & Pellowski, Anne. Joining In: An Anthology of Audience Participation Stories & How to Tell Them. Livo, Norma J., ed. 136p. (Orig.). (J). 1988. pap. text ed. 11.95 (*0-938756-21-4*) Yellow Moon.

M

An Asterisk (*) at the beginning of an entry indicates that the title is appearing in BIP for the first time.

Miller, Terry. Greenwich Village & How It Got That Way. 1990. 30.00 (*0-517-57322-9*, Crown) Crown Pub Group.
— Pines '79. LC 81-86675. (Gay Play Script Ser.). (Illus.). 131p. (Orig.). 1982. pap. 5.95 (*0-935672-06-0*) JH Pr.
Miller, Terry A. & Bondybey, V. E., eds. Molecular Ions: Spectroscopy, Structure & Chemistry. 1984. 74.50 (*0-444-86717-1*, I-438-83) Elsevier.
Miller, Terry E. Folk Music in America: A Reference Guide. LC 84-48014. (Reference Library of the Humanities). 448p. 1986. lib. bdg. 48.00 (*0-8240-8935-9*) Garland.
— Traditional Music of the Lao: Kaen Playing & Mawlum Singing in Northeast Thailand. LC 84-22538. (Contributions in Intercultural & Comparative Studies: No. 13). xv, 333p. 1985. text ed. 69.50 (*0-313-24765-X*, MKP/, Greenwood Pr) Greenwood.
Miller, Thelma R., jt. auth. see Klein, Roz.
Miller, Theodore. Kiplinger's Make Your Money Grow. rev. ed. 434p. 1993. pap. 14.95 (*0-938721-22-4*) Kiplinger Bks.
***Miller, Theodore J.** Kiplinger's Invest Your Way to Wealth. rev. ed. 1995. 25.00 (*0-8129-2642-0*, Times Bks) Random.
— Kiplinger's Invest Your Way to Wealth: How Ordinary People Can Accumulate Extraordinary Amounts. 1993. 23.95 (*0-938721-30-5*) Kiplinger Bks.
— Kiplinger's Make Your Money Grow. Date not set. pap. 15.00 (*0-8129-2658-7*, Times Bks) Random.
Miller, Theodore K. & Prince, Judith S. The Future of Student Affairs: A Guide to Student Development for Tomorrow's Higher Education. LC 76-19496. 238p. reprint ed. pap. 67.90 (*0-7837-6521-5*, 2045633) Bks Demand.
Miller, Theodore R. Graphic History of the Americas. LC 72-88215. 72p. (C). 1972. reprint ed. text ed. 16.50 (*0-88275-103-4*) Krieger.
Miller, Theodore R., jt. auth. see Schmidt, Waldemar A.
Miller, Thomas. Godfrey Malvern: Or, the Life of an Author. Browne, Hablot K., tr. LC 79-8174. (Illus.). reprint ed. 44.50 (*0-404-62051-5*) AMS Pr.
Miller, Thomas E. California Construction Defect Litigation: Residential & Commercial. 2nd ed. (Construction Law Library). 760p. 1992. text ed. 128.00 (*0-471-57266-7*) Wiley.
***Miller, Thomas F.** Minnesota Legal Forms: Creditors' Remedies. 190p. 1994. disk, ring bd. 69.95 (*0-614-05901-1*) Michie Butterworth.
— Minnesota Legal Forms: Creditors' Remedies, 1981-1993. (Minnesota Legal Forms Ser.). 200p. 1993. ring bd. 69. 95 (*0-917126-95-5*) Butterworth Legal Pubs.
— Minnesota Legal Forms: Creditors' Remedies, 1981-1993. suppl. ed. (Minnesota Legal Forms Ser.). 200p. 1994. ring bd. 39.00 (*0-685-74347-0*) Butterworth Legal Pubs.
Miller, Thomas G., Jr. The Cactus Air Force. deluxe ed. LC 69-15320. (Illus.). 242p. 1990. reprint ed, 55.00 (*0-934841-17-9*) Adm Nimitz Foun.
— The Cactus Air Force. LC 69-15320. (Illus.). 242p. 1990. reprint ed. 15.00 (*0-934841-18-7*) Adm Nimitz Foun.
Miller, Thomas I. & Miller, Michelle A. Citizen Surveys: How to Do Them, How to Use Them, What They Mean. (Special Report Ser.). 213p. 1991. pap. 38.00 (*0-87326-920-9*) Intl City-Cnty Mgt.
Miller, Thomas K. Sherlock Holmes on the Roof of the World. LC 88-34116. 75p. (C). 1988. reprint ed. lib. bdg. 25.00x (*0-89370-526-8*) Borgo Pr.
Miller, Thomas L. Texas Confederate Scrip Grantees. LC 85-71227. 165p. (Orig.). 1985. pap. 15.00 (*0-911317-38-4*) Ericson Bks.
Miller, Thomas P., ed. The Selected Writings of John Witherspoon. LC 89-29994. 320p. (C). 1990. 29.95 (*0-8093-1469-X*) S Ill U Pr.
***Miller, Thomas R.** Time Out: Leisure & Play. Glassman, Bruce, ed. (Our Human Family Ser.). (Illus.). 64p. (J). (gr. 4-8). 1995. lib. bdg. 18.95 (*1-56711-128-9*) Blackbirch.
***Miller, Thomas W., ed.** Children of Trauma: Stressful Life Events & Their Effects on Children & Adolescents. (Stress & Health Ser.: Monograph 8). 200p. 1995. text ed. 30.00 (*0-8236-0810-7*) Intl Univs Pr.
— Chronic Pain, Vol. I. 400p. 1990. 52.50x (*0-8236-0850-6*) Intl Univs Pr.
— Chronic Pain, Vol. II. 550p. 1990. 67.50x (*0-8236-0851-4*) Intl Univs Pr.
— Clinical Disorders & Stressful Life Events. (Stress & Health Ser.: Monograph 7). 297p. 1995. text ed. 42.00 (*0-8236-0910-3*) Intl Univs Pr.
— Stressful Life Events. (Stress & Health Ser.: No. 4). 838p. 1989. 75.00x (*0-8236-6165-2*, BN#00165) Intl Univs Pr.
— Theory & Assessment of Stressful Life Events. (Stress & Health Ser.: Monograph 6). 224p. 1995. text ed. 32.50 (*0-8236-6521-6*) Intl Univs Pr.
Miller, Thomas W., jt. auth. see Veltkamp, Lane J.
Miller, Tice L. Bohemians & Critics: American Theatre Criticism in the Nineteenth Century. LC 80-24430. x, 190p. 1981. 22.50 (*0-8108-1377-7*) Scarecrow.
Miller, Tice L., jt. ed. see Engle, Ron.
Miller, Tice L., jt. ed. see Wilmeth, Don B.
Miller-Tiedeman, Anna. How Not to Make It-& Succeed: Life on Your Own Terms. LC 84-60644. (Illus.). 1989. pap. 13.95 (*0-9613436-9-9*) Lifecareer Pr.
— Lifecareer: How It Can Benefit You. 2nd ed. Sherf, Terry, ed. LC 92-19764. 50p. 1992. pap. 6.95 (*0-9613436-8-0*) Lifecareer Pr.
— LIFECAREER: The Quantum Leap into a Process Theory of Career. 1988. pap. 9.95 (*0-9613436-3-X*) Lifecareer Pr.
Miller, Tim & Hendershot, James R., Jr. Switched Reluctance Motors & Their Controls. 300p. 1992. 150. 00 (*1-881855-02-3*) Magna Physics.
Miller, Tim, jt. auth. see Sharpton, Beth.
Miller, Tim D. Teens in Drama Ministry. (Drama Topics Ser.). 1994. 8.95 (*0-8341-9129-6*, MP-514) Lillenas.
Miller, Timothy. American Communes, 1860-1960. LC 89-27481. (Sects & Cults in America Ser.). 624p. 1990. 44. 00 (*0-8240-8470-5*, SS402) Garland.
— Following in His Steps: A Biography of Charles M. Sheldon. LC 87-5871. (Illus.). 304p. 1987. 35.00x (*0-87049-537-2*) U of Tenn Pr.
— The Hippies & American Values. LC 90-48062. (Illus.). 216p. (C). 1991. pap. 18.95 (*0-87049-694-8*) U of Tenn Pr.
— How to Want What You Have: Discovering the Magic & Grandeur of Everyday Existence. LC 94-12653. 1995. 19.95 (*0-8050-3317-3*) H Holt & Co.
— Practice to Deceive. 1991. 19.95 (*1-55611-251-3*) D I Fine.
Miller, Timothy, ed. America's Alternative Religions. LC 94-16605. (SUNY Series in Religious Studies). 440p. (C). 1995. text ed. 74.50 (*0-7914-2397-2*); pap. text ed. 24.95 (*0-7914-2398-0*) State U NY Pr.
— When Prophets Die: The Postcharismatic Fate of New Religious Movements. LC 90-44859. (SUNY Series in Religious Studies). 251p. (C). 1991. 59.50 (*0-7914-0717-9*); pap. 19.95 (*0-7914-0718-7*) State U NY Pr.
Miller, Timothy B. Just in the Nick of Time. LC 87-72303. 90p. (Orig.). (YA). (gr. 5 up). 1989. pap. 6.00 (*0-916383-48-2*) Aegina Pr.
Miller, Timothy J., ed. Reactive Power Control in Electric Systems. LC 82-10838. 381p. 1982. text ed. 135.00 (*0-471-86933-3*, Wiley-Interscience) Wiley.
Miller, Timothy S. The Birth of the Hospital in the Byzantine Empire. LC 84-26111. (Henry E. Sigerist Supplements to the Bulletin of the History of Medicine, New Ser.: No. 13). 304p. reprint ed. pap. 86.70 (*0-8357-6744-2*, 2035399) Bks Demand.
***Miller, Timothy S. & Nesbitt, John, eds.** Peace & War in Byzantium: Essays in Honor of George T. Dennis, S.J. LC 94-19723. 304p. 1995. 49.95 (*0-8132-0805-X*) Cath U Pr.
Miller, Toby. The Well-Tempered Self: Formations of the Cultural Subject. LC 93-13102. (C). 1994. text ed. 42.50 (*0-8018-4603-X*); pap. text ed. 14.95 (*0-8018-4604-8*) Johns Hopkins.
Miller, Tom. Angler's Guide to Baja California. (Illus.). 1987. pap. 7.95 (*0-914622-04-8*) Baja Trail.
— Baja Book 3: The Alltime Best-Selling Map Guide to Today's Baja California. 16th ed. 1992. pap. 12.95 (*0-914622-10-2*) Baja Trail.
— Copeland Killings. (Illus.). 304p. 1993. mass mkt. 4.99 (*1-55817-675-6*, Pinnacle NY) Windsor NY.
— Eating Your Way Through Baja. (Illus.). 1986. pap. 4.95 (*0-914622-07-2*) Baja Trail.
— On the Border: Portraits of America's Southwestern Frontier. LC 85-8698. 226p. 1985. reprint ed. pap. 12.95 (*0-8165-0943-3*) U of Ariz Pr.
— The Panama Hat Trail: A Journey to South America. LC 87-45913. (Departures Ser.). 272p. 1988. pap. 11.00 (*0-394-75774-2*, Vin) Random.
— This Path of Scattered Glass: A Collection of Poems. LC 92-84067. (Illus.). 96p. (Orig.). (YA). (gr. 7 up). 1993. pap. 6.95 (*1-878893-39-4*) Telcraft Bks.
— Trading with the Enemy: A Yankee Travels Through Castro's Cuba. 352p. 1992. text ed. 24.00 (*0-689-12094-X*, Pub. by Ctrl Bur voor Schimmel NE) Macmillan.
— The Unfair Advantage. 170p. (Orig.). 1986. pap. 13.95 (*0-9613034-1-7*) Unfair Advan Corp.
— Unfair Advantage. 170p. (Orig.). 1986. pap. 17.95 (*0-9613034-2-5*) Unfair Advan Corp.
Miller, Tom, ed. Arizona: The Land & the People. fac. ed. LC 86-4275. (Illus.). 303p. reprint ed. pap. 86.40 (*0-7837-6954-7*, 2046904) Bks Demand.
Miller, Tom & Hoffman, Carol. The Baja Book III. (Illus.). 1989. pap. 11.95 (*0-914622-08-0*) Baja Trail.
Miller, Tom, ed. see Conley, Robert J.
Miller, Tom, ed. see Givens, Charles J.
Miller, Tom, ed. see Goldberg, Lucianne.
Miller, Tom, ed. see Hare, Robert D.
Miller, Tom, ed. see McNamara, Eileen.
Miller, Tom, ed. see Rasberry, Salli & Elwyn, Padi S.
Miller, Tom, ed. see Schaum, Melita & Parrish, Karen.
Miller, Tom, ed. see Solway, Diane.
Miller, Tom, ed. see Wiatt, Carrie L.
Miller, Tom, ed. see Zuniga, Jose.
Miller, Trish, ed. see Clement, Brian R.
Miller, Tron. Gold Rocker Handbook. 1980. pap. 4.00 (*0-89316-619-7*); 6.00 (*0-686-70739-7*) Exanimo Pr.
Miller, Trudi C. Public Sector Performance: A Turning Point. LC 83-23895. 288p. 1984. 40.95 (*0-8018-3146-6*); pap. 45.00x (*0-8018-3147-4*) Johns Hopkins.
Miller, Trudy. Where to Find Everything for Practically Nothing in Chicagoland: A Bargain Hunters Guide to Resale & Thrift Shops. LC 87-82215. 170p. 1987. pap. 6.95 (*0-913587-02-8*) Second T Pub.
Miller, Ulrike. Persian Cats. 72p. 1990. pap. 5.95 (*0-8120-4405-3*) Barron.
Miller, Valentine R., tr. see Descartes, Rene.
Miller, Valentine R., tr. see Miller, Reese P.
Miller, Vassar. Approaching Nada. Lomax, Joseph J., ed. LC 77-20734. 1977. 15.00 (*0-930324-03-X*) Wings Pr.
— If I Could Sleep Deeply Enough. 1974. 6.95 (*0-87140-607-1*); pap. 2.50 (*0-87140-291-2*) Liveright.
— If I Had Wheels or Love: Collected Poems of Vassar Miller. LC 90-52660. 358p. 1991. 28.95 (*0-87074-315-5*); pap. 14.95 (*0-87074-316-3*) SMU Press.
— Small Change. Lomax, Joseph F. & Whitebird, J., eds. LC 77-20728. 1977. pap. 10.00 (*0-930324-00-5*) Wings Pr.
— Struggling to Swim on Concrete. Cassin, Maxine, ed. (Journal Press Books: Louisiana Legacy). (Illus.). 80p. (Orig.). 1984. pap. 7.00 (*0-938498-05-3*) New Orleans Poetry.
— Wage War on Silence: A Book of Poems. LC 60-13157. (Wesleyan Poetry Program Ser.: Vol. 8). 69p. 1960. 12. 95 (*0-8195-2008-X*, Wesleyan Univ Pr) U Pr of New Eng.
Miller, Vassar, ed. Despite This Flesh: The Disabled in Stories & Poems. 166p. 1985. 15.95 (*0-292-72449-7*); pap. 8.95 (*0-292-71550-1*) U of Tex Pr.
***Miller, Verna.** Lynn's Tree. 1995. 11.95 (*0-8062-5311-8*) Carlton.
Miller, Vernell K. Anywhere with You! 208p. (Orig.). 1989. pap. 8.95 (*0-8361-3505-9*) Herald Pr.
— Meditations for Adoptive Parents. (Illus.). 88p. (Orig.). 1992. pap. 6.95 (*0-8361-3606-3*) Herald Pr.
***Miller, Vernon.** Brethren Patriots Again: A Thirteen Session Study Guide Proposing Nonviolence As the Potential Power for the Continuing American Revolution. fac. ed. (Heritage Learning Program Ser.). 64p. 1994. pap. 25.00 (*0-7837-7347-1*, 2047300) Bks Demand.
Miller, Victor & Westerback, Mary. Interpretation of Topographic Maps. 416p. (C). 1989. pap. write for info. (*0-675-20919-6*, Merrill Pub Co) Macmillan.
Miller, Victor, jt. auth. see Dobson, Terry.
Miller, Vincent A. The Guidebook for Global Trainers. 400p. 1993. pap. 35.00 (*0-87425-245-8*) Human Res Dev Pr.
Miller, Viola, jt. auth. see Blodgett, Elizabeth.
Miller, Virginia. Eat Your Dinner! LC 91-58728. (Illus.). 32p. (J). (ps up). 1992. 14.95 (*1-56402-121-1*) Candlewick Pr.
— Eat Your Dinner! LC 91-58728. 32p. (J). (ps up). 1994. pap. 5.99 (*1-56402-368-0*) Candlewick Pr.
— Go to Bed! LC 92-54958. (Illus.). 32p. (J). (ps up). 1993. 14.95 (*1-56402-244-7*) Candlewick Pr.
— On Your Potty! LC 90-49221. (Illus.). 32p. (J). (ps up). 1991. 13.95 (*0-688-10617-X*); lib. bdg. 13.88 (*0-688-10618-8*) Greenwillow.
Miller, Virginia, jt. auth. see Waddell, Martin.
Miller, Virginia E. The Frieze of the Palace of the Stuccoes, Acanceh, Yucatan, Mexico. LC 91-13724. (Studies in Pre-Columbian Art & Archaeology: No. 31). (Illus.). 88p. 1991. 18.00 (*0-88402-195-5*) Dumbarton Oaks.
— The Role of Gender in Precolumbian Art & Architecture. LC 88-17316. (Illus.). 222p. (Orig.). (C). 1988. pap. text ed. 26.00 (*0-8191-7067-4*) U Pr of Amer.
***Miller, Virginia L. & Lewis, John G.** Interior Woodwork of Winchester, Virginia, 1750-1850, with Some History & Tales. 220p. 1994. text ed. 25.00 (*0-9642862-0-3*) Grim-Moore Hse.
Miller, Virginia L., et al, eds. Molecular Genetics of Bacterial Pathogenesis. LC 94-19193. 566p. 1994. 79.00 (*1-55581-082-9*) Am Soc Microbio.
Miller, Vousette T. Color Me Beautiful Color Me Black. (Illus.). 32p. (J). (ps-6). 1988. student ed 4.00 (*0-9619641-0-3*) Vous Etes Tres Belle.
— Poems by Shining Star: The Voice of Shining Star. 16p. (Orig.). (J). (ps-6). 1990. student ed, pap. write for info. (*0-9619641-1-1*) Vous Etes Tres Belle.
Miller, W. A History of the Greek People, 1821-1921. (Illus.). 1976. 20.00 (*0-916710-28-9*) Obol Intl.
Miller, W., Jr. On Lie Algebras & Some Special Functions of Mathematical Physics. (Memoirs of the American Mathematical Society Ser.: Vol. 50). 43p. 1987. reprint ed. 16.00 (*0-8218-1250-5*, MEMO/1/50C) Am Math.
Miller, W., Jr., ed. see Friedman, A.
Miller, W., jt. auth. see Huni, M., Jr.
Miller, W., et al, eds. Die Lumboischialgie. (Fortbildungskurse fuer Rheumatologie Ser.: Vol. 6). (Illus.). xii, 264p. 1982. pap. 57.75 (*3-8055-2207-X*) S Karger.
Miller, W. B., jt. auth. see Bissonnette, L. R.
Miller, W. D., jt. ed. see Matox, R. B.
Miller, W. E., jt. auth. see IFAC Symposium Staff.
Miller, W. F., Jr., jt. auth. see Lewis, E. E.
Miller, W. H. History & Genealogy of the Family of Miller, Woods, Harris, Wallace, Maupin, Oldham, Kavanaugh & Brown, & Others. (Illus.). 855p. 1989. reprint ed. lib. bdg. 136.00 (*0-8328-0872-5*); reprint ed. pap. 128.00 (*0-8328-0873-3*) Higginson Bk Co.
Miller, W. H., ed. Dynamics of Molecular Collisions, Pt. A. LC 76-12633. (Modern Theoretical Chemistry Ser.: Vol. 1). (Illus.). 318p. 1976. 85.00 (*0-306-33501-8*, Plenum Pr) Plenum.
— Dynamics of Molecular Collisions, Pt. B. LC 76-12633. (Modern Theoretical Chemistry Ser.: Vol. 2). (Illus.). 380p. 1976. 95.00 (*0-306-33502-6*, Plenum Pr) Plenum.
Miller, W. H., et al, eds. Fishes of the Upper Colorado River System: Present & Future. 131p. 1982. pap. 12.50 (*0-913235-27-X*) Am Fisheries Soc.
Miller, W. J. Dairy Cattle Feeding & Nutrition. LC 78-51234. (Animal Feeding & Nutrition Ser.). 1979. text ed. 80.00 (*0-12-497650-6*) Acad Pr.
— Geological History of New York. 130p. 1993. reprint ed. lib. bdg. 69.00 (*0-7812-5149-4*) Rprt Serv.
Miller, W. M. & Dinda, R. J., trs. Luther's Works, Vol. 20. LC 55-9893. 300p. 1973. 19.95 (*0-570-06420-1*, 15-1762) Concordia.
Miller, W. R. Estrogen & Breast Cancer. (Medical Intelligence Unit Ser.). 1995. write for info. (*1-57059-047-8*) R G Landes.
— Instructors & Their Jobs. 4th ed. (Illus.). 300p. 1990. pap. 32.96 (*0-8269-4163-X*) Am Technical.
Miller, W. Thomas, III & Sutton, Richard S. Neural Networks for Control. 450p. 1990. 60.00 (*0-262-13261-3*) MIT Pr.
Miller, W. Thomas, ed. see Werbos, Paul J.
Miller, W. Watts, ed. Socialism & the Law. 155p. (Orig.). 1992. pap. 48.50 (*3-515-06190-8*) Coronet Bks.
Miller, W. Wesley. Blain's Woods. Kratoville, Betty L., ed. (Meridian Bks.). (Illus.). 64p. (J). (gr. 3-9). 1989. lib. bdg. 4.95 (*0-87879-618-5*) High Noon Bks.
— Dark Secret. Kratoville, Betty L., ed. (Meridian Bks.). (Illus.). 64p. (J). (gr. 3-9). 1989. lib. bdg. 4.95 (*0-87879-620-7*) High Noon Bks.
Miller, Wade, jt. auth. see Shafer, Steven.
Miller, Walden, jt. auth. see Miller, Eric.
Miller, Wallace T. Introduction to Clinical Radiology. 1992. text ed. 43.95 (*0-07-105300-X*) McGraw.
Miller, Wallis, jt. ed. see Makela, Taisto.
Miller, Walter B. Lower Class Culture as a Generating Milieu of Gang Delinquency. (Reprint Series in Sociology). (C). 1993. reprint ed. pap. text ed. 1.00 (*0-8290-2623-1*, S-197) Irvington.
Miller, Walter B., jt. auth. see Bequaert, Joseph C.
Miller, Walter B., jt. ed. see Bissonnette, Luc R.
Miller, Walter B., jt. ed. see Kopeika, Norman S.
Miller, Walter B., jt. ed. see Vorontsov, Mikhail A.
Miller, Walter J. Arco SAT Verbal Workbook. 3rd ed. 1992. pap. 10.00 (*0-13-951963-7*, Arco Test) P-H Gen Ref & Trav.
— Making an Angel. LC 77-4747. 64p. (Orig.). 1977. pap. 3.95 (*0-918524-01-6*) Lintel.
— Monarch Notes: Dashiell Hammett's the Maltese Falcon, the Thin Man & Other Works. 128p. 1988. pap. 4.50 (*0-671-67128-6*, Arco Test) P-H Gen Ref & Trav.
Miller, Walter J. & Saidla, Leo E., eds. Engineers As Writers. LC 74-128279. (Essay Index Reprint Ser.). 1977. 26.95 (*0-8369-2000-7*) Ayer.
Miller, Walter J., tr. see Verne, Jules.
Miller, Walter J., et al. SAT Verbal Workbook. 4th ed. LC 93-3538. 1993. 10.00 (*0-671-86405-X*, Arco Test) P-H Gen Ref & Trav.
— SAT Verbal Workbook. 5th ed. LC 93-44287. 1994. pap. 10.00 (*0-671-88813-7*, Arco Test) P-H Gen Ref & Trav.
— SAT Verbal Workbook: Scholastic Aptitude Test. 3rd ed. 400p. 1992. pap. 10.00 (*0-685-51950-3*, Arco Test) P-H Gen Ref & Trav.
Miller, Walter M. A Canticle for Leibowitz. 1993. reprint ed. lib. bdg. 18.95 (*0-89969-353-3*, Lghtyr Pr) Buccaneer Bks.
Miller, Walter M., Jr. A Canticle for Leibowitz. 320p. 1984. mass mkt. 5.99 (*0-553-27381-7*, Bantam Classics) Bantam.
Miller, Walter M., Jr. & Greenberg, Martin H., eds. Beyond Armageddon. LC 85-80625. 387p. 1986. pap. 3.95 (*0-917657-96-9*) D I Fine.
***Miller, Walter W.** Taxation of Health & Welfare Benefits. 1000p. 1995. 150.00 (*0-7913-2085-5*) Warren Gorham & Lamont.
Miller, Wanda M. & Steeber de Orozco, Sharon. Reading Faster & Understanding More, Bk. I. 3rd ed. (C). 1989. pap. text ed. 32.00 (*0-673-39938-9*) HarpCollege.
— Reading Faster & Understanding More, Bk. II. 3rd ed. (C). 1989. pap. text ed. 32.00 (*0-673-39939-7*) HarpCollege.
Miller, Wanda M. & Steeber, Sharon. Reading Faster & Understanding More, Bk. III. (C). 1987. pap. text ed. 33. 50 (*0-673-39286-4*) HarpCollege.
Miller, Warren & Miller, Arthur. American National Election Study, 1976. LC 82-81969. 1982. reprint ed. write for info. (*0-89138-929-6*, ICPSR 7381) ICPSR.
Miller, Warren, et al. American National Election Study, 1972. LC 82-81968. 1982. reprint ed. boxed write for info. (*0-89138-928-8*, ICPSR 7010) ICPSR.
Miller, Warren A. Wine, Women, Warren, & Skis. 1993. pap. 9.95 (*0-9636144-0-1*) W Miller Prods.
Miller, Warren E. Without Consent: Mass-Elite Linkages in Presidential Politics. LC 88-3217. 200p. 1988. 22.00 (*0-8131-0550-1*) U Pr of Ky.
Miller, Warren E., ed. Cattle, Horses, Sky, & Grass: Cowboy Poetry of the Late Twentieth Century. LC 94-6724. (Illus.). 224p. 1994. 21.95 (*0-87358-570-4*); pap. 14.95 (*0-87358-578-X*) Northland AZ.
— Cattle, Horses, Sky, & Grass: Cowboy Poetry of the Late Twentieth Century. limited ed. LC 94-6724. (Illus.). 224p. 1994. 40.00 (*0-87358-579-8*) Northland AZ.
Miller, Warren E. & Levitin, Teresa E. Leadership & Change: Presidential Elections from 1952 to 1976. (Illus.). 320p. 1984. reprint ed. pap. text ed. 26.00 (*0-8191-3850-9*) U Pr of Amer.
Miller, Warren E. & Stokes, Donald E. Constituency Influence in Congress. (Reprint Series in Social Sciences). (C). 1993. reprint ed. pap. text ed. 1.00 (*0-8290-3691-1*, PS-404) Irvington.
Miller, Warren E. & Traugott, Santa A. American National Election Studies Data Sourcebook, 1952-1986. LC 89-7546. (Illus.). 400p. 1989. text ed. 44.50 (*0-674-02636-5*) HUP.
Miller, Warren E., jt. auth. see National Election Studies, Center for Political Studies Staff.
Miller, Warren E., jt. auth. see National Election Studies Center for Political Studies Staff.
Miller, Warren E., jt. auth. see National Election Studies Staff.
Miller, Warren E., et al. American National Election Studies Data Sourcebook, 1950-1978. 388p. 1980. 29.95 (*0-674-02634-9*) HUP.
— American National Election Study, 1974. LC 83-81218. 1983. reprint ed. write for info. (*0-89138-918-0*) ICPSR.
— American National Election Study, 1992: Pre - & Post-Election Survey (Enhanced with 1990 & 1991 Data), Vol. One: Introduction & 1990 Codebook Variables. LC 93-80826. 544p. 1993. write for info. (*0-89138-858-3*) ICPSR.

M

An Asterisk (*) at the beginning of an entry indicates that the title is appearing in BIP for the first time.

— American National Election Study, 1992: Pre - & Post-Election Survey (Enhanced with 1990 & 1991 Data), Vol. Three: Appendix, Notes, Frequency Addendum, & Questionnnaires. LC 93-80826. 632p. 1993. write for info. (0-89138-860-5) ICPSR.
— American National Election Study, 1992: Pre - & Post-Election Survey (Enhanced with 1990 & 1991 Data), Vol. Two: 1991 & 1992 Codebook Variables. LC 93-80826. 696p. 1993. write for info. (0-89138-859-1) ICPSR.
Miller, Wayne, et al. Graphing Calculator Activities for Finite Mathematics. 208p. (C). 1992. pap. 19.95 (0-534-17460-4) Brooks-Cole.
— Pass the TASP Test. Hackworth, Robert & Howland, Joseph, eds. (Illus.). 246p. 1989. pap. 9.95 (0-943202-33-7) H & H Pub.
Miller, Wayne C. The Biochemistry of Exercise & Metabolic Adaptation. 152p. (C). 1992. pap. text ed. write for info. (0-697-16707-0) Brown & Benchmark.
— The Non-Diet Diet. 160p. (C). 1991. pap. text ed. 17.95x (0-89582-222-9) Morton Pub.
Miller, Wayne L., et al. Graphing Calculator Activities for Algebra. 192p. 1992. pap. 17.95 (0-534-17463-9) Brooks-Cole.
— Graphing Calculator Activities for Applied Calculus. 192p. 1992. pap. 19.95 (0-534-17462-0) Brooks-Cole.
— Graphing Calculator Activities for Mathematical Analysis. 168p. (C). 1992. pap. 20.95 (0-534-17461-2) Brooks-Cole.
Miller, Wendell E. Forgiveness the Power & the Puzzles. LC 94-94384. 261p. (Orig.). 1994. text ed. 10.95 (0-9641441-0-7) ClearBrook.
Miller, Wendy. Around the World with God's Friends: Mission Education Activity Book - Elementary Grades. (Illus.). 24p. (Orig.). (J). (gr. 1-5). 1990. pap. text ed. 1.50 (1-877736-06-6, Mission Focus) MB Missions.
— Learning to Listen: A Guide for Spiritual Friends. LC 92-61441. 128p. 1993. pap. 8.95 (0-8358-0677-4) Upper Room Bks.
Miller, White Burkett, Center of Public Affairs Staff & University of Virginia Staff. Report of the Miller Center Commission on Presidential Disability & the Twenty-Fifth Amendment. 44p. (Orig.). (C). 1988. pap. text ed. 8.00 (0-8191-6893-9, Pub. by White Miller Center) U Pr of Amer.
Miller, Wick R. Newe Natekwinappeh: Shoshoni Stories & Dictionary. LC 72-612763. (Anthropological Papers: No. 94). 180p. reprint ed. pap. 51.30 (0-7837-2606-6, 2042770) Bks Demand.
— Newe Natekwinappeh: Shoshoni Stories & Dictionary. (Utah Anthropological Papers: No. 94). reprint ed. 24.00 (0-404-60694-6) AMS Pr.
Miller, Wick R., ed. see Sullivan, Thelma D.
Miller, Wilbur R. Revenuers & Moonshiners: Enforcing Federal Liquor Law in the Mountain South, 1865-1900. LC 90-49549. (Illus.). xii, 251p. 1991. 37.50 (0-8078-1959-X); pap. 13.95 (0-8078-4330-X) U of NC Pr.
Miller, Wilbur R., jt. auth. see McKnight Staff.
Miller, Wilford L. Wildlife of the Prairie. 1976. 8.95 (0-686-18906-X); pap. 5.95 (0-686-18907-8) Assoc Print.
Miller, Wilhelm, jt. auth. see Robbins, Allan.
Miller, William, Jr. The Great Luxury Liners, 1927-1952: A Photographic Record. (Illus.). 160p. 1981. pap. 10.95 (0-486-24056-8) Dover.
Miller, Willard, Jr. Symmetry & Separation of Variables. (Encyclopedia of Mathematics & Its Applications Ser.: No. 4). 1984. 64.95 (0-521-30224-2) Cambridge U Pr.
— Symmetry Groups & Their Applications. (Pure & Applied Mathematics Ser.: Vol. 50). 1972. text ed. 121.00 (0-12-497460-0) Acad Pr.
Miller, William. The Balkans: Rumania, Bulgaria, Serbia & Montenegro. LC 72-66. (Select Bibliographies Reprint Ser.). 1977. reprint ed. 30.95 (0-8369-9965-7) Ayer.
— Essays on the Latin Orient. LC 78-63360. (Crusades & Military Orders Ser.: Second Series). reprint ed. 72.50 (0-404-17024-2) AMS Pr.
Miller, William, Jr. The First Great Ocean Liners in Photographs: 180 Views, 1897-1927. (Antiques Ser.). 144p. (Orig.). 1984. pap. 11.95 (0-486-24574-8) Dover.
***Miller, William.** Frederick Douglass: The Last Day of Slavery. (Illus.). 32p. (J). (gr. 1 up). 1995. 14.95 (1-880000-17-2) Lee & Low Bks.
— A History of the Greek People (1821-1921) LC 83-45816. 1983. reprint ed. 27.50 (0-404-20178-4) AMS Pr.
— The Knee-High Man. LC 95-13150. (Illus.). 32p. (J). 1995. 13.95 (0-87905-634-7) Gibbs Smith Pub.
— The Latins in the Levant: A History of Frankish Greece. LC 75-41193. reprint ed. 72.50 (0-404-14689-9) AMS Pr.
Miller, William, Jr. Ocean Liners of the World. 1984. pap. 11.50 (0-915276-43-7) Quadrant Pr.
Miller, William. Old Faith: Poems. LC 92-15312. 64p. 1992. pap. 12.95 (0-7734-0042-7, Mellen Poetry Pr) E Mellen.
— Travels & Politics in the Near East. LC 70-135822. (Eastern Europe Collection Ser.). 1971. reprint ed. 33.95 (0-405-02764-8) Ayer.
— Vega: The Story of Marshall Miller of Oldham County, TX. (Illus.). 136p. (Orig.). 1995. pap. write for info. (1-885591-81-0) Morris Pubng.
— Zora Hurston & the Chinaberry Tree. LC 94-1291. (Illus.). 32p. (J). (gr. 1 up). 1994. 14.95 (1-880000-14-8) Lee & Low Bks.
Miller, William, ed. Men in Business: Essays on the Historical Role of the Entrepreneur. LC 78-21159. 389p. 1979. reprint ed. text ed. 35.00 (0-313-20867-0, MIME, Greenwood Pr) Greenwood.
Miller, William & Rockwood, D. Stephen, eds. College Librarianship. LC 80-25546. 290p. 1981. 29.50 (0-8108-1383-1) Scarecrow.
Miller, William, jt. auth. see Ballatore, Ron.
Miller, William, jt. auth. see Hof, Larry.
Miller, William, et al. Natural Analogue Studies in the Geological Disposal of Radioactive Wastes. LC 93-45535. (Studies in Environmental Science: Vol. 57). 1994. 168.50 (0-444-81755-7) Elsevier.
Miller, William A. Conversations. LC 80-54283. 96p. 1980. pap. 5.50 (0-934104-04-2) Woodland.
— The Joy of Feeling Good: Eight Keys to a Happy & Abundant Life. LC 86-20574. 192p. (Orig.). 1986. pap. 5.99 (0-8066-2236-9, 10-3601, Augsburg) Augsburg Fortress.
— Make Friends with Your Shadow: How to Accept & Use Positively the Negative Side of Your Personality. LC 80-67793. 144p. (Orig.). 1981. pap. 9.99 (0-8066-1855-8, 10-4238, Augsburg) Augsburg Fortress.
— Your Golden Shadow. 64p. 1993. pap. 5.00 (0-06-250639-0) Harper SF.
— Your Golden Shadow: Discovering & Fulfilling Your Undeveloped Self. LC 89-45184. 160p. 1992. reprint ed. pap. 9.00 (0-06-250553-X) Harper SF.
Miller, William A., jt. ed. see McLeod, Donald C.
Miller, William B. Easter & Hybrid Lily Production. Armitage, Allan M., ed. LC 91-19986. (Growers Handbook Ser.: Vol. 5). (Illus.). 126p. 1992. 12.95 (0-88192-205-6) Timber.
Miller, William B. & Schenk, Vicki L. All I Need to Know about Manufacturing I Learned in Joe's Garage: World Class Manufacturing Made Simple. 96p. (Orig.). 1993. pap. 9.95 (0-9630439-3-5) Bayrock.
— The Day I Learned about Quality in Joe's Garage: High Quality Made Simple. 128p. (Orig.). 1995. pap. 9.95 (0-9630439-7-8) Bayrock.
— Manufacturing Beyond Joe's Garage: Value Based Manufacturing. 128p. (Orig.). 1995. pap. 9.95 (0-9630439-9-4) Bayrock.
Miller, William C. Alvar Aalto: A Bibliography, No. 1190. 1976. 5.00 (0-686-19684-8) CPL Biblios.
— Creative Edge. 1989. pap. 15.95 (0-201-52401-5) Addison-Wesley.
— Dealing with Stress: A Challenge for Educators. LC 79-89540. (Fastback Ser.: No. 130). (Orig.). (C). 1979. pap. 1.25 (0-87367-130-9) Phi Delta Kappa.
— Quantum Quality: Quality Improvement Through Innovation, Learning, & Creativity. LC 93-12408. 208p. 1993. pap. 19.95 (0-527-91719-2) Qual Resc.
Miller, William D. Memphis During the Progressive Era, 1900-1917. LC 58-21437. 258p. reprint ed. 73.60 (0-685-15751-2, 2027518) Bks Demand.
— Pretty Bubbles in the Air: America in 1919. 248p. 1991. 29.95 (0-252-01823-0) U of Ill Pr.
— Valuing Banks & Thrifts. 1990. pap. 69.95 (1-55840-434-1) Exec Ent Pubns.
— Valuing Banks & Thrifts. 1994. pap. text ed. 69.95 (0-471-11292-5) Wiley.
Miller, William G. The Data of Jurisprudence. xiv, 477p. 1980. reprint ed. lib. bdg. 42.50 (0-8377-0835-4) Rothman.
— Lectures on the Philosophy of Law, Designed Mainly as an Introduction to the Study of International Law. xv, 432p. 1979. reprint ed. lib. bdg. 35.00 (0-8377-0834-6) Rothman.
Miller, William G., jt. comp. see Ash, Lee.
Miller, William H. The Chandris Liners. (Illus.). 80p. (Orig.). 1993. pap. text ed. 19.95 (0-9518656-2-5, Waterfront Pubns) Hallenbook.
Miller, William H., Jr. The Fabulous Interiors of the Great Ocean Liners in Historic Photographs. 160p. 1984. pap. 9.95 (0-486-24756-2) Dover.
— Great Cruise Ships & Ocean Liners from 1954 to 1986: A Photographic Survey. (Illus.). 128p. (Orig.). 1987. pap. 9.95 (0-486-25540-9) Dover.
Miller, William H. Miller on Managing: "Straight Talk on the Ups & Downs, Do's & Don'ts of Managing a Water Utility. (Illus.). 180p. (C). 1992. 19.95 (0-89867-619-3) Am Water Wks Assn.
— Modern Cruise Ships, 1965-1990: A Photographic Record. 1991. pap. 10.95 (0-486-26753-9) Dover.
Miller, William H., Jr. Pictorial Encyclopedia of Ocean Liners, 1860-1993: 402 Photographs. (Illus.). 192p. (Orig.). 1994. pap. 16.95 (0-486-28137-X) Dover.
Miller, William H. S. S. United States. (Illus.). 224p. 1991. 35.00 (0-393-03030-X) Norton.
Miller, William H., jt. auth. see Braynard, Frank O.
Miller, William H., jt. auth. see Duffy, Francis J.
Miller, William H., et al. More Leaves from the Copper Beeches. Starr, H. W. et al, eds. LC 76-244. (Illus.). 222p. 1976. 15.00 (0-915010-16-X) Sutter House.
Miller, William I. Bloodtaking & Peacemaking: Feud, Law, & Society in Saga Iceland. LC 89-77971. (Illus.). 416p. 1990. 29.95 (0-226-52679-8) U Ch Pr.
— Humiliation: And Other Essays on Honor, Social Discomfort, & Violence. 288p. 1993. 25.00 (0-8014-2881-5) Cornell U Pr.
— Humiliation: And Other Essays on Honor, Social Discomfort, & Violence. 288p. 1995. pap. 13.95x (0-8014-8117-1) Cornell U Pr.
Miller, William I., jt. auth. see Andersson, Theodore M.
Miller, William J., Jr. Crossing the Delaware: The Story of the Delaware Memorial Bridge. 114p. 1990. reprint ed. 9.95 (0-685-33045-1); reprint ed. pap. 5.95 (0-911293-06-X) Guage Corp.
— Crossing the Delaware: The Story of the Delaware Memorial Bridge, the Longest Twin Suspension Bridge in the World. Demerast, Kathy K., ed. LC 83-71879. (Illus.). 114p. 1983. 9.95 (0-911293-02-7); pap. 5.95 (0-911293-01-9) Guage Corp.
Miller, William J. From the Valley, I Couldn't See the Sun. 1991. 8.50 (0-533-09460-7) Vantage.
— Mapping for Stonewall: The Civil War Service of Jed Hotchkiss. LC 93-18611. (Illus.). 176p. 1993. 29.95 (1-880216-11-6) Elliott & Clark.
— The Training of an Army: Camp Curtin & the North's Civil War. LC 90-31770. (Illus.). 300p. (C). 1990. 27.95 (0-942597-15-X) White Mane Pub.
Miller, William J., Jr., jt. auth. see Broeg, Bob.
Miller, William J., et al, eds. The Peninsula Campaign of Eighteen Sixty-Two: Yorktown to the Seven Days, 2 vols., 2. (Campaign Chronicles Ser.). (Illus.). 238p. 1995. pap. 16.00 (1-882810-75-9) Savas Woodbury.
— The Peninsula Campaign of Eighteen Sixty-Two: Yorktown to the Seven Days, 2 vols., Set. (Campaign Chronicles Ser.). (Illus.). 208p. 1995. pap. 16.00 (1-882810-76-7, 106) Savas Woodbury.
— The Peninsula Campaign of Eighteen Sixty-Two: Yorktown to the Seven Days, 2 vols., Vols. 1-2. (Campaign Chronicles Ser.). (Illus.). 478p. 1995. 34.95 (1-882810-77-5) Savas Woodbury.
Miller, William L. The Business of May Next: James Madison & the Founding. (C). 1992. 27.50 (0-8139-1368-3) U Pr of Va.
— The Business of May Next: James Madison & the Founding. 312p. (C). 1994. pap. 10.95 (0-8139-1490-6) U Pr of Va.
— Electoral Dynamics. LC 76-19226. (C). 1978. text ed. 29.95 (0-312-24115-1) St Martin.
— The First Liberty: Religion & the American Republic. LC 85-40342. 416p. 1986. 24.95 (0-394-53476-X) Knopf.
— Irrelevant Elections? The Quality of Local Democracy in Britain. 280p. 1988. 59.00 (0-19-827572-2) OUP.
***Miller, William L. & Caird, Edward, eds.** Alternatives to Freedom: Arguments & Opinions. LC 94-28992. 264p. (C). 1995. pap. text ed. 19.95 (0-582-25130-3, 77018, Pub. by Longman UK) Longman.
Miller, William L., jt. auth. see Crabtree, Benjamin F.
Miller, William L., jt. ed. see Harrop, Martin.
Miller, William L., Jr., jt. auth. see Jacquet, Jay.
Miller, William L., et al. How Voters Change: The Nineteen Eighty-Seven British Election Campaign in Perspective. (Illus.). 320p. 1990. 77.00 (0-19-827342-8) OUP.
— Religion & the Public Good: A Bicentennial Forum. LC 88-13667. 139p. (C). 1989. 35.00 (0-86554-326-7, MUP/H276) Mercer Univ Pr.
Miller, William M. The Baha'i Faith: Its History & Teachings. LC 74-8745. (Illus.). 444p. 1984. pap. 11.95 (0-87808-137-2) William Carey Lib.
— A Christian's Response to Islam. 1976. pap. 4.99 (0-87552-335-8) Presby & Reformed.
Miller, William R. Lightened by Laughter. LC 91-75087. 56p. 1991. 7.95 (1-55523-458-5) Winston-Derek.
— Promised Land. LC 89-52125. 65p. 1990. 6.95 (1-55523-306-6) Winston-Derek.
— Second Spring. LC 92-80529. 109p. 1992. 8.95 (1-55523-511-5) Winston-Derek.
Miller, William R., ed. Contemporary American Protestant Thought: 1900-1970. LC 77-151612. 1973. pap. 9.65 (0-672-60140-0, AHS84, Bobbs) Macmillan.
Miller, William R. & Heather, Nick H., eds. Treating Addictive Behaviors: Processes of Change. (Applied Clinical Psychology Ser.). 450p. 1986. 62.50 (0-306-42248-4, Plenum Pr) Plenum.
***Miller, William R. & Jackson, Kathleen A.** Practical Psychology for Pastors. 2nd ed. LC 94-34115. 448p. 1994. pap. text ed. 56.00 (0-13-171829-0) P-H.
Miller, William R. & Jackson-Miller, Kathleen A. Practical Psychology for Pastors. (Illus.). 400p. 1985. 39.95 (0-13-692807-2) P-H.
Miller, William R. & Martin, John E., eds. Behavior Therapy & Religion: Integrating Spiritual & Behavioral Approaches to Change. (Focus Editions Ser.: Vol. 98). 200p. (C). 1988. text ed. 49.95 (0-8039-3203-0); pap. text ed. 24.95 (0-8039-3204-9) Sage.
Miller, William R. & Rollnick, Stephen. Motivational Interviewing: Preparing People to Change Addictive Behavior. LC 91-16597. 348p. 1991. lib. bdg. 35.00 (0-89862-566-1) Guilford Pr.
— Motivational Interviewing: Preparing People to Change Addictive Behavior. LC 91-16597. 348p. 1992. reprint ed. pap. text ed. 19.95 (0-89862-469-X) Guilford Pr.
Miller, William R., jt. ed. see Hester, Reid K.
Miller, William R., jt. auth. see McCrady, Barbara S.
Miller, William R., jt. auth. see Murray, William M.
Miller, William R., et al. Adjustment: The Psychology of Change. 608p. (C). 1990. Casebound. text ed. write for info. (0-13-004342-7) P-H.
— Motivational Enhancement Therapy Manual: A Clinical Research Guide for Therapists Treating Individuals with Alcohol Abuse & Dependence. 121p. (Orig.). (C). 1994. pap. text ed. 45.00x (0-7881-1476-X) Diane Pub.
Miller, William T. Mysterious Encounters at Mamre & Jabbok. (Brown Judaic Studies: No. 50). 252p. (C). 1984. 25.95 (0-89130-816-4, 14 00 50); pap. 19.95 (0-89130-817-2) Scholars Pr GA.
Miller, Wilma B., jt. auth. see Miller, Frank C.
***Miller, Wilma H.** Alternative Assessment Techniques for Reading & Writing. LC 95-826. 1995. spiral bd. 29.95 (0-87628-141-2) Ctr Appl Res.
— Complete Reading Disabilities Handbook. 356p. 1993. spiral bd. 29.95 (0-87628-249-4) Ctr Appl Res.
— The First R: Elementary Reading Today. 2nd ed. (Illus.). 256p. (C). 1983. reprint ed. pap. text ed. 17.95x (0-88133-054-X) Waveland Pr.
— Reading Comprehension Activities Kit. 1990. pap. text ed. 27.95 (0-87628-789-5) P-H.
— Reading Diagnosis Kit. 3rd ed. 1986. spiral bd. 24.95 (0-87628-720-8) Ctr Appl Res.
— Reading Diagnosis Kit. 3rd ed. 376p. 1986. pap. 27.95 (0-317-66024-1, Ctr Appl Res) P-H.
— Reading Teacher's Complete Diagnosis & Correction Manual. 256p. 1988. spiral bd. 29.95 (0-87628-772-0) Ctr Appl Res.
— Reading Teacher's Complete Diagnosis & Correction Manual. 296p. 1988. pap. 24.95 (0-318-35308-3) P-H.
Miller, Wolfgang. Dictionary of Polygraphy: Fachworterbuch Polygrafie. 1020p. (ENG, FRE, GER & RUS.). 1981. 175.00 (0-8288-2228-X, M11292) Fr & Eur.
Miller, Worth R. Oklahoma Populism: A History of the People's Party in the Oklahoma Territory. LC 87-40214. (Illus.). 304p. 1987. 28.95 (0-8061-2072-X) U of Okla Pr.
Miller, Wynne, ed. see Ratner-Gantshar, Barbara.
***Miller, Y.** What's Wrong with Being Happy. 1994. 17.95 (0-89906-121-4); pap. 14.95 (0-89906-122-2) Mesorah Pubns.
— What's Wrong with Being Human. 1992. 17.95 (0-89906-544-9); pap. 14.95 (0-89906-545-7) Mesorah Pubns.
Miller, Yisroel. Guardian of Eden, Pt. 1: In Search of the Jewish Woman. 1993. write for info. (0-318-72253-4) Feldheim.
— Guardian of Eden, Pt. 2: Letters to a Jewish Feminist. 1993. write for info. (0-318-72254-2) Feldheim.
— Guardian of Eden, 2 pts., Set. LC 93-34033. 1993. 14.95 (0-87306-659-6) Feldheim.
Miller, Yvette E. The Boom in Retrospect: A Reconsideration. Williams, Raymond L., ed. 248p. 1987. pap. 20.00 (0-318-42060-0) Lat Am Lit Rev Pr.
Miller, Yvette E., ed. The Fertile Rhythms: Contemporary Women Poets of Mexico. Hoeksema, Thomas & Enriquez, Romelia, trs. LC 89-13659. 126p. (ENG & SPA.). 1989. pap. 12.95 (0-935480-44-7) Lat Am Lit Rev Pr.
Miller, Yvette E. & Ross, Kathleen, eds. Scents of Wood & Silence: Short Stories by Latin American Women Writers. LC 91-30002. 220p. 1991. pap. 16.95 (0-935480-55-2) Lat Am Lit Rev Pr.
Miller, Yvette E. & Rossman, Charles, eds. Gabriel Garcia Marquez: Special Issue. 160p. 1985. pap. 16.00 (0-317-26520-2) Lat Am Lit Rev Pr.
Miller, Yvette E., ed. see Agosin, Marjorie.
Miller, Yvette E., ed. see Aguilar, Eduardo G.
Miller, Yvette E., ed. see Alegria, Fernando.
Miller, Yvette E., ed. see Bianco, Jose.
Miller, Yvette E., ed. see Bullrich, Silvina.
Miller, Yvette E., ed. see Caicedo, Andes.
Miller, Yvette E., ed. see Campos, Julieta.
Miller, Yvette E., ed. see Castellanos, Rosario.
Miller, Yvette E., ed. see Collyer, Jaime.
Miller, Yvette E., ed. see De la Cuesta, Barbara.
Miller, Yvette E., ed. see Delgado, Ana M.
Miller, Yvette E., ed. see Diaz Valcarcel, Emilio.
Miller, Yvette E., ed. see Donahue, Moraima.
Miller, Yvette E., jt. ed. see Estrada, Ezequiel M.
Miller, Yvette E., ed. see Galeana, Benita.
Miller, Yvette E., ed. see Galindo, Sergio.
Miller, Yvette E., ed. see Gomez de la Serna, Ramon.
Miller, Yvette E., ed. see Guerra, Lucia.
Miller, Yvette E., ed. see Hahn, Oscar.
Miller, Yvette E., jt. ed. see Jackson, Kenneth D.
Miller, Yvette E., ed. see Kanellos, Nicolas.
Miller, Yvette E., ed. see Levi, Enrique J.
Miller, Yvette E., ed. see Levinson, Luisa M.
Miller, Yvette E., ed. see Lindo, Hugo.
Miller, Yvette E., ed. see Mallea, Eduardo.
Miller, Yvette E., ed. see Martinez, Eliud.
Miller, Yvette E., ed. see Matute, Ana M.
Miller, Yvette E., ed. see Montes De Oca, Marco A.
Miller, Yvette E., ed. see Muniz-Huberman, Angelina.
Miller, Yvette E., ed. see Naranjo, Carmen.
Miller, Yvette E., ed. see Neruda, Pablo.
Miller, Yvette E., ed. see Nunes, Maria L.
Miller, Yvette E., ed. see Ortega, Julio.
Miller, Yvette E., ed. see Paoli, Francisco Matos.
Miller, Yvette E., ed. see Perez-Galdos, Benito.
Miller, Yvette E., ed. see Piglia, Ricardo.
Miller, Yvette E., ed. see Ponce, Manuel.
Miller, Yvette E., ed. see Samperio, Guillermo.
Miller, Yvette E., ed. see Sanchez, Marta.
Miller, Yvette E., ed. see Sarduy, Severo.
Miller, Yvette E., ed. see Schevill, Rudolph.
Miller, Yvette E., ed. see Valdivieso, Mercedes.
Miller, Yvette E., ed. see Vallejo, Cesar.
Miller, Yvette E., ed. see Zurita, Raul.
Miller, Zachary. Illustrated Vincent Buyer's Guide. LC 93-34190. (Illustrated Buyer's Guide Ser.). (Illus.). 128p. 1994. pap. text ed. 16.95 (0-87938-848-X) Motorbooks Intl.
***Miller, Zane L.** Suburb: Neighborhood & Community in Forest Park, Ohio, 1935-1976. fac. ed. LC 80-21828. (Twentieth-Century American Ser.). (Illus.). 296p. 1981. pap. 84.40 (0-7837-7686-1, 2047439) Bks Demand.
Miller, Zane L. & Melvin, Patricia M. Urbanization of Modern America: A Brief History. 2nd ed. 264p. (C). 1987. pap. text ed. 16.00 (0-15-593657-3) HB Coll Pubs.
Miller, Zane L. & Wade, Richard C. Boss Cox's Cincinnati: Urban Politics in the Progressive Era. LC 81-6346. (Urban Life in America Ser.). xii, 301p. 1981. reprint ed. text ed. 59.75 (0-313-22760-8, MIBC, Greenwood Pr) Greenwood.
Miller, Zane L., jt. ed. see Gillette, Howard, Jr.
Miller, Zell. Mountains Within Me. LC 85-19068. 176p. 1985. reprint ed. pap. 7.95 (0-87797-116-1) Cherokee.
Milleret, Margo & Eakin, Marshall C., eds. Homenagem a Alexandrino Severino: Essays on the Portuguese-Speaking World. 276p. (ENG & POR.). (C). 1993. text ed. 35.00 (0-924047-08-9); pap. 15.00 (0-924047-09-7) Host Pubns.
Millermaster, Ralph A., ed. Harwood's Control of Electric Motors. 4th ed. LC 87-16598. 512p. 1987. reprint ed. 59.50 (0-89464-242-1) Krieger.
Millero, Frank J. & Sohn, Mary L. Chemical Oceanography. 448p. 1991. 82.95 (0-8493-8840-6, GC111) CRC Pr.

Milleron, Jean-Claude, jt. auth. see Champsaur, Paul.

Millers, Antonia. Latvian Language for the Use of Students: Grammar, Vocabulary & Exercises. LC 79-89077. 170p. (ENG & LAV.). (C). 1979. 20.00 (*0-912852-26-7*) Echo Pubs.

***Millers, Elmer S., ed.** Nurturing Doubt: From Missionary to Anthropologist in the Argentine Chaco. LC 94-30791. 1995. write for info. (*0-252-02155-X*) U of Ill Pr.

Millers, John. Stock Index Futures & Options. LC 92-14697. 1993. text ed. 39.95 (*0-07-707461-0*) McGraw.

Millerson, Gerald. Effective TV Production. 3rd ed. LC 92-37229. (Media Manuals Ser.). (Illus.). 224p. 1993. pap. 19.95 (*0-240-51324-X*, Focal) Buttrwrth-Heinemann.

— Lighting for Video. 3rd ed. (Media Manuals Ser.). 156p. 1991. pap. 12.95 (*0-240-51303-7*) Buttrwrth-Heinemann.

— The Technique of Lighting for Television & Film. 3rd ed. (Library of Communication Techniques Ser.). 466p. 1991. 46.95 (*0-240-51299-5*) Buttrwrth-Heinemann.

— Technique of Television Production. 12th ed. (Illus.). 566p. (Orig.). 1989. pap. 39.95 (*0-240-51289-8*, Focal) Buttrwrth-Heinemann.

— TV Scenic Design Handbook. 3rd ed. 262p. 1989. pap. 34.95 (*0-240-51285-5*) Buttrwrth-Heinemann.

— Video Camera Techniques: A New Media Manual. 2nd ed. (Media Manuals Ser.). (Illus.). 160p. 1994. pap. 19.95 (*0-240-51225-1*, Focal) Buttrwrth-Heinemann.

— Video Camera Techniques: A New Media Manual. 2nd ed. LC 94-18429. (Media Manual Ser.). 160p. 1994. 19.95 (*0-240-51376-2*, Focal) Buttrwrth-Heinemann.

— Video Production Handbook. 2nd ed. LC 92-10611. (Illus.). 256p. (Orig.). 1992. pap. 25.00 (*0-240-51321-5*) Buttrwrth-Heinemann.

Milles, George. Health Careers & Medical Sciences. LC 74-79837. (Allied Health Ser.). 1975. pap. write for info. (*0-672-61384-0*) Macmillan.

Milles, James. Internet Handbook for Law Librarians. (Law Library Information Reports: Vol. 15). 64p. 1993. pap. text ed. 100.00 (*0-87802-093-4*) Glanville.

Milles, Lee. Heat Pumps - Theory & Service: Instructor's Guide. 68p. 1994. 12.00 (*0-8273-4957-2*) Delmar.

Millet & Dahl. The Capstone of Our Religion: Insights into the Doctrine & Covenants. 11.95 (*0-88494-684-3*) Bookcraft Inc.

Millet, jt. auth. see McConkie.

Millet, Allan R. & Maslowski, Peter. For the Common Defense: A Military History of the United States of America. enl. rev. ed. LC 94-5199. 1994. reprint ed. 27.95 (*0-02-921581-1*) Free Pr.

— For the Common Defense: A Military History of the United States of America. enl. rev. ed. LC 94-5199. 1994. reprint ed. pap. 22.95 (*0-02-921597-8*) Free Pr.

Millet, Allan R., et al. Military Effectiveness, Vol. II. 294p. (C). 1990. pap. text ed. 24.95 (*0-04-445844-4*) Routledge Chapman & Hall.

— Military Effectiveness, Vol. III. 391p. (C). 1990. pap. text ed. 24.95 (*0-04-445845-2*) Routledge Chapman & Hall.

Millet, C. & Millet, D., illus. Castles. LC 92-15955. (First Discovery Bks.). (J). 1993. 11.95 (*0-590-46377-2*) Scholastic Inc.

Millet, D., jt. illus. see Millet, C.

Millet, Francis D. Capillary Crime, & Other Stories. LC 72-157793. (Short Story Index Reprint Ser.). 1977. reprint ed. 20.95 (*0-8369-3905-0*) Ayer.

Millet, Gary W. & Rosenberg, Ralph G. Primer for Graphic Arts Profitability: A Money-Making Formula. 96p. (Orig.). 1992. pap. 14.95 (*1-881637-04-2*) Millet Grp.

Millet, Jean. La Belle Methode Ou l'Art De Bien Chanter. LC 71-126600. (Music Ser.). 76p. 1973. reprint ed. lib. bdg. 21.50 (*0-306-70044-1*) Da Capo.

Millet, John. Poetry Australia. 128p. (C). 1990. 80.00 (*0-909185-38-7*, Pub. by Pascoe Pub AT) St Mut.

— Tail Arse Charlie. 24p. 1984. pap. 2.00 (*0-317-07609-4*) Samisdat.

— The World Faces Johnny Tripod. 80p. 1992. pap. 8.00 (*0-909185-52-2*) Story Line.

***Millet, Olivier.** Dictionnaire Des Citations. 409p. (FRE.). 1992. pap. 16.95 (*0-7859-7859-3*, 2253061409) Fr & Eur.

Millet, Robert. Steadfast & Immovable: Striving for Spiritual Maturity. LC 92-18727. 166p. 1992. 11.95 (*0-87579-635-4*) Deseret Bk.

Millet, Robert, jt. comp. see Jackson, Kent P.

***Millet, Robert L.** Christ-Centered Living. 1994. 12.95 (*0-88494-934-6*) Bookcraft Inc.

— Joseph Smith: Selected Sermons on Writings. (Sources of American Spirituality Ser.). 1989. 24.95 (*0-8091-0427-X*) Paulist Pr.

— The Power of the Word: Saving Doctrines from the Book of Mormon. LC 93-44307. x, 342p. 1994. 14.95 (*0-87579-826-8*) Deseret Bk.

— The Promise of Perfection: Hope in the Here & Now. Date not set. write for info. (*0-614-07054-6*) Deseret Bk.

— Within Reach. LC 95-7681. 132p. 1995. 13.95 (*0-87579-968-X*) Deseret Bk.

***Millet, Robert L., comp.** Watch & Be Ready: Preparing for the Second Coming of the Lord. LC 94-27762. iv, 230p. 1994. 14.95 (*0-87579-911-6*) Deseret Bk.

Millet, Robert L., ed. Studies in Scripture: Acts to Revelation, Vol. 6. LC 87-70686. 303p. 1987. 14.95 (*0-87579-084-4*) Deseret Bk.

Millet, Robert L. & Jackson, Kent P., eds. Studies in Scripture, Vol. 1: The Doctrine & Covenants. 615p. 1989. reprint ed. 17.95 (*0-87579-274-X*) Deseret Bk.

Millet, Robert L. & McConkie, Joseph F. Our Destiny: The Call & Election of the House of Israel. 1993. 11.95 (*0-88494-888-9*) Bookcraft Inc.

Millet, Robert L., jt. ed. see Jackson, Kent P.

Millet, Robert L., jt. auth. see McConkie, Joseph F.

Millet, Sandra. Quilt as You Go. 2nd ed. (Illus.). 176p. 1993. pap. 19.95 (*0-8019-8357-6*) Chilton.

Millett, Allan R. The General: Robert L. Bullard & Officership in the U. S. Army, 1881-1925. LC 75-68. (Contributions in Military History Ser.: No. 10). (Illus.). 499p. 1975. text ed. 59.95 (*0-8371-7957-2*, MIG/, Greenwood Pr) Greenwood.

— In Many a Strife: General Gerald C. Thomas & the U. S. Marine Corps, 1917-1956. LC 92-31557. 456p. 1993. 49.95 (*0-87021-034-3*) Naval Inst Pr.

— Semper Fidelis: The History of the United States Marine Corps. enl. rev. ed. 800p. 1991. text ed. 35.00 (*0-02-921595-1*); pap. 19.95 (*0-02-921596-X*) Free Pr.

Millett, Allan R., ed. A Short History of the Vietnam War. LC 77-23623. 189p. reprint ed. pap. 54.50 (*0-7837-1758-X*, 2057294) Bks Demand.

Millett, Allan R. & Cooling, B. F. Doctoral Dissertations in Military Affairs. LC 72-186550. (Libraries Bibliography: No. 10). 1973. reprint ed. 7.50 (*0-686-20812-9*) KSU.

Millett, Allan R. & Maslowski, Peter. For the Common Defense: A Military History of the United States 1607-1983. (Illus.). 680p. 1984. text ed. 27.95 (*0-02-921580-3*) Free Pr.

Millett, Allan R. & Murray, Williamson, eds. Military Effectiveness, 3 vols. 1988. write for info. (*0-318-62728-0*) Routledge Chapman & Hall.

— Military Effectiveness, 3 vols., Vol. I: The First World War. 320p. 1988. 65.00 (*0-04-445053-2*) Routledge Chapman & Hall.

— Military Effectiveness, 3 vols., Vol. II: The Interwar Period. 320p. 1988. 65.00 (*0-04-445054-0*) Routledge Chapman & Hall.

— Military Effectiveness, 3 vols., Vol. III: The Second World War. 320p. 1988. 65.00 (*0-04-445055-9*) Routledge Chapman & Hall.

— Military Effectiveness, Vol. 1: The First World War. (Mershon Center Series on International Security & Foreign Policy). 384p. 1989. pap. text ed. 24.95 (*0-04-445578-X*) Routledge Chapman & Hall.

Millett, Allan R., jt. ed. see Murray, William.

Millett, Benignus. Four Franciscan Martyrs of Ireland. 1989. pap. 22.00 (*1-85390-161-X*, Pub. by Veritas IE) St Mut.

Millett, Craig B. In God's Image: Archetypes of Women in Scripture. Hardesty, Nancy, ed. LC 90-20578. 176p. (Orig.). 1990. pap. 3.95 (*0-931055-77-6*) LuraMedia.

Millett, Fred B. Reading Drama: A Method of Analysis with Selections for Study. LC 71-111110. (Play Anthology Reprint Ser.). 1977. reprint ed. 20.95 (*0-8369-8203-7*) Ayer.

Millett, Fred B. & Bentley, Gerald E. Art of the Drama. (Illus.). 1947. 64.50 (*0-89197-034-7*) Irvington.

Millett, Fred B., ed. see Webster, John.

Millett, J. D. The Works Progress Administration in New York City. LC 77-74950. (American Federalism-the Urban Dimension Ser.). 1978. reprint ed. lib. bdg. 23.95 (*0-405-10496-0*) Ayer.

Millett, John. Blue Dynamite. 100p. 1986. pap. 5.00 (*0-318-23493-9*) Samisdat.

— The Nine Lives of Big Meg O'Shannessy. 50p. (Orig.). 1989. pap. 9.95 (*0-934257-30-2*) Story Line.

Millett, John, jt. auth. see McGavin, P. A.

Millett, John D. Conflict in Higher Education: State Government Coordination vs. Institutional Independence. LC 83-24806. 307p. reprint ed. pap. 87.50 (*0-7837-6517-7*, 2045629) Bks Demand.

— Decision Making & Administration in Higher Education. LC 68-55383. 171p. reprint ed. pap. 48.80 (*0-685-16426-8*, 2027311) Bks Demand.

— New Structures of Campus Power. LC 77-82911. (Jossey-Bass Higher Education Ser.). 316p. reprint ed. pap. 90.10 (*0-685-20945-8*, 2056557) Bks Demand.

Millett, John D., jt. auth. see Macmahon, Arthur W.

Millett, John David. The Process & Organization of Government Planning. LC 76-38753. (FDR & the Era of the New Deal Ser.). 188p. 1972. reprint ed. lib. bdg. 29.50 (*0-306-70444-7*) Da Capo.

***Millett, K. C.** Random Knotting & Linking. (Series on Knots & Everything). 208p. 1994. text ed. 48.00 (*981-02-2005-7*) World Scientific Pub.

***Millett, Kate.** A. D. A Memoir. 256p. 1995. 23.00 (*0-393-03524-7*) Norton.

— Loony-Bin Trip. 1991. pap. 10.95 (*0-671-74028-8*, Touchstone Bks) S&S Trade.

— The Politics of Cruelty: An Essay on the Literature of Political Imprisonment. 288p. 1994. 23.00 (*0-393-03575-1*) Norton.

— The Politics of Cruelty: An Essay on the Literature of Political Imprisonment. 336p. 1995. pap. 13.00 (*0-393-31312-3*, Norton Paperbks) Norton.

— Sexual Politics. 1990. pap. 12.00 (*0-671-70740-X*) S&S Trade.

— Sita. 336p. 1992. pap. 11.00 (*0-671-73169-6*, Touchstone Bks) S&S Trade.

— Sita (50 Percent Nonreturnable) Date not set. 10.00 (*0-942986-07-5*) LongRiver Bks.

Millett, Kenneth C. Piecewise Linear Concordances & Isotopies. LC 74-18328. (Memoirs Ser.: No. 1/153). 73p. 1974. pap. 17.00 (*0-8218-1853-8*, MEMO 1/153) Am Math.

Millett, Larry. The Curve of the Arch: The Story of Louis Sullivan's Owatonna Bank. LC 84-25528. (Illus.). 205p. 1985. pap. 14.95 (*0-87351-182-4*) Minn Hist.

— Lost Twin Cities. LC 92-10460. (Illus.). 370p. 1992. pap. 29.95 (*0-87351-273-1*) Minn Hist.

Millett, Martin. The Romanization of Britain: An Essay in Archaeological Interpretation. 252p. (C). 1990. 69.95 (*0-521-36084-6*) Cambridge U Pr.

— The Romanization of Britain: An Essay in Archaeological Interpretation. (Illus.). 252p. (C). 1992. pap. 24.95 (*0-521-42864-5*) Cambridge U Pr.

Millett, Martin, jt. ed. see Blagg, Thomas.

Millett, Paul. Lending & Borrowing in Ancient Athens. 360p. (C). 1991. 74.95 (*0-521-37333-6*) Cambridge U Pr.

Millett, Peter, et al, eds. The Encyclopaedia of Forms & Precedents, 33 vols., Set. 5th ed. boxed 5,512.00 (*0-406-02360-3*) Butterworth Legal Pubs.

Millett, Richard & Will, W. Marvin, eds. The Restless Caribbean: Changing Patterns of International Relations. LC 78-19764. 330p. 1979. text ed. 55.00 (*0-275-90396-6*, C0396, Praeger Pubs) Greenwood.

Millett, Richard L., jt. auth. see Falcoff, Mark.

Millett, Robert. Magnifying Priesthood Power. LC 89-85213. 187p. reprint ed. 12.98 (*0-88290-037-4*) Horizon Utah.

Millett, Robert W. The Vultures & the Phoenix. LC 81-65877. (Illus.). 168p. 1983. 32.50 (*0-87982-039-X*) Art Alliance.

Millett, Stephen M. The Heirs of Somerled: The Historical Origins of the MacDougalls & MacDonalds, 1100-1500. 55p. 1990. pap. 9.95 (*0-9629741-1-0*) Scot Lore Pr.

— A Sourcebook on the Scottish Settlers of America, 1600-1800. (Illus.). ii, 63p. (Orig.). 1991. pap. text ed. 12.00 (*0-9629741-2-9*) Scot Lore Pr.

Millett, Stephen M. & Honton, Edward J. A Manager's Guide to Technology Forecasting & Strategy Analysis Methods. LC 91-13690. 112p. 1991. pap. 19.95 (*0-935470-63-8*) Battelle.

Millett, Timothy. Court of First Instance of the European Communities. 1991. 76.00 (*0-406-20222-2*, U.K.) Butterworth Legal Pubs.

Millette, James R., jt. ed. see Basu, Samarendra.

Millette, Robert & Gosine, Mahin. The Grenada Revolution: Why It Failed. 172p. (Orig.). 1985. pap. 10.00 (*0-933524-00-5*) Africana Res.

Milletti, Mario A. Voices of Experience: Fifteen Hundred Retired People Talk about Retirement. rev. ed. 208p. 1987. pap. 3.00 (*0-9613704-0-8*) Tchrs Insurance.

Millgard, Janie, ed. see Macduff, Nancy.

***Millgate, Irvine H.** The Human Side of Systems Engineering. Weaver, Joel W., ed. 238p. (Orig.). 1991. pap. 24.00 (*0-938919-21-0*) Six Lights.

— Power Lab. (Illus.). 262p. (Orig.). 1992. pap. 24.00 (*0-938919-14-8*) Six Lights.

— Power Lab: Creditability & Initiative. Weaver, Joel W., ed. (Illus.). 86p. (Orig.). 1994. pap. 18.00 (*0-938919-20-2*) Six Lights.

— Power Lab: For Children to Nurture the Human Spirit Project Think. Weaver, Joel W., ed. (Illus.). 324p. (Orig.). 1993. pap. 24.00 (*0-938919-19-9*) Six Lights.

— Power Lab: Seeking the Meaning of Mindsets. Weaver, Joel W., ed. (Illus.). 87p. (Orig.). (YA). (gr. 11 up). 1994. pap. 18.00 (*0-938919-28-8*) Six Lights.

— Power Lab: Seeking the Meaning of Outward Passage. Weaver, Joel W., ed. (Illus.). 109p. (Orig.). (YA). (gr. 9 up). 1994. pap. 18.00 (*0-938919-25-3*) Six Lights.

— Power Lab: Seeking Understanding. Weaver, Joel W., ed. (Illus.). 54p. (Orig.). (J). (gr. 4 up). 1994. pap. 18.00 (*0-938919-24-5*) Six Lights.

— Power Lab: What Have We Learned about Thinking? Weaver, Joel W., ed. (Illus.). 96p. (Orig.). 1994. pap. 18.00 (*0-938919-23-7*) Six Lights.

— Seeking the Meaning of the Management of "Relationships" Weaver, Joel W., ed. 115p. (Orig.). (YA). (gr. 11 up). 1994. pap. 18.00 (*0-938919-31-8*) Six Lights.

— Teacher-Manager Systems: Think & Learn & Grow While Nurturing the Human Spirit. (Illus.). 412p. 1991. 24.00 (*0-938919-05-9*) Six Lights.

Millgate, Irvine H. & Millgate, Rachel W., eds. The Common Language of Values & Ethics. rev. ed. (Illus.). 209p. 1987. pap. 18.00 (*0-938919-10-5*) Six Lights.

Millgate, Jane. Scott's Last Edition: A Study in Publishing History. (Illus.). 160p. 1987. 17.50 (*0-85224-541-6*, Pub. by Edinburgh U Pr UK) Col U Pr.

— Walter Scott: The Making of the Novelist. 223p. 1984. pap. 14.95 (*0-8020-6692-5*) U of Toronto Pr.

— Walter Scott: The Making of the Novelist. LC 84-243112. 237p. reprint ed. pap. 67.60 (*0-8357-4144-3*, 2036917) Bks Demand.

Millgate, Jane, ed. Editing Nineteenth-Century Fiction: Papers Given at the Thirteenth Annual Conference on Editorial Problems, University of Toronto, 4-5 November, 1977. LC 78-3393. (Conference on Editorial Problems Ser.: No. 13). 1987. 37.50 (*0-404-63663-2*) AMS Pr.

Millgate, Michael. The Achievement of William Faulkner. LC 88-37591. (Brown Thrasher Bks.). 360p. 1989. reprint ed. pap. 16.95 (*0-8203-1142-1*) U of Ga Pr.

— Testamentary Acts: Browning, Tennyson, James, Hardy. 224p. 1992. 49.95 (*0-19-811276-9*) OUP.

— Testamentary Acts: Browning, Tennyson, James, Hardy. 288p. 1995. reprint ed. pap. 19.95 (*0-19-818366-6*) OUP.

— Thomas Hardy: His Career As a Novelist. LC 94-9494. 1994. pap. write for info. (*0-312-12233-0*) St Martin.

Millgate, Michael, ed. New Essays on "Light in August" (American Novel Ser.). 160p. 1987. 27.95 (*0-521-30814-3*); pap. 11.95 (*0-521-31332-5*) Cambridge U Pr.

Millgate, Michael, ed. see Faulkner, William.

Millgate, Michael, ed. see Gosse, Edmund.

Millgate, Michael, ed. see Hardy, Thomas.

Millgate, Michael, ed. see Tennyson, Alfred.

Millgate, Rachel W., jt. ed. see Millgate, Irvine H.

Millgram, Abraham E. Concepts That Distinguish Judaism. Vol. 5. 1985. pap. 12.00 (*0-910250-00-6*) Bnai Brith Intl.

— Jerusalem Curiosities. (Illus.). 368p. 1990. 24.95 (*0-8276-0358-4*) JPS Phila.

— Jewish Worship. LC 77-151316. (Illus.). 674p. 1971. 22.50 (*0-8276-0003-8*) JPS Phila.

Millgram, Abraham E., ed. Concepts That Distinguish Judaism. (B'nai B'rith History of the Jewish People Ser.: Vol. V). 368p. (C). 1985. 20.00 (*0-910250-01-4*); pap. 12.00 (*0-685-67350-2*) Bnai Brith Intl.

Millham, Peter & Mason, Bruce. The White Book: A Guide to Addiction Recovery. 95p. 1989. pap. 12.95 (*0-9693296-0-1*) Gordon Soules Bk.

Millham, Spencer, et al. Access Disputes in Child-Care. (Illus.). viii, 118p. 1989. 48.95 (*0-566-05820-0*, Pub. by Gower UK); pap. text ed. 28.95 (*0-566-07087-1*, Pub. by Gower UK) Ashgate Pub Co.

— Lost in Care. 275p. 1986. text ed. 52.00 (*0-566-00998-6*) Ashgate Pub Co.

Millhauser, Steven. Little Kingdoms. 1993. 21.00 (*0-671-86890-X*) S&S Trade.

Millhiser, Marlys. Death of the Office Witch. LC 93-19365. 1993. 20.00 (*1-883402-02-6*) S&S Trade.

— Death of the Office Witch. 304p. 1995. pap. 5.95 (*0-14-024340-2*, Penguin Bks) Viking Penguin.

— Murder in a Hot Flash: A Charlie Greene Mystery. LC 94-27050. 1995. 21.00 (*1-883402-29-8*) S&S Trade.

— Nightmare Country. 320p. 1982. pap. 2.95 (*0-449-24522-5*, Crest) Fawcett.

— Willing Hostage. 256p. 1994. pap. 4.95 (*0-7867-0110-2*) Carroll & Graf.

Millhollin, Bonnie, jt. auth. see Blackett, Ruth.

Millhollin, Bonnie, jt. auth. see Sherves, Kathey L.

Millhouse, Barbara B. American Originals: Selections from Reynolda House, Museum of American Art. (Illus.). 136p. 1990. 45.00 (*0-685-54059-6*) Abbeville Pr.

Millhouse, Dorothy F. Harriett's Doll. 1991. 7.95 (*0-533-09507-7*) Vantage.

Millhouse, Nicholas, jt. auth. see Bowman, Margret.

Millhouse, O. Eugene. Central Nervous System: The Structural Basis of Human Neurobiology. 1991. pap. text ed. write for info. (*0-07-042314-8*) McGraw.

Millian, Louise B. Seasons & Its Weather, Variations & Mood Psychology: Index of New Information. 150p. 1994. 44.50 (*0-7883-0052-0*); pap. 39.50 (*0-7883-0053-9*) ABBE Pubs Assn.

Milliband, Ralph & Saville, J., eds. Socialist Register: Annuals: Nineteen Sixty-Eight to Nineteen Seventy-Eight. 35.00 (*0-87556-440-2*) Saifer.

— Socialists Register: Annuals: Nineteen Seventy-Nine to Nineteen Ninety-One. 35.00 (*0-685-73631-8*) Saifer.

Millican, Edward. One United People: The Federalist & the National Idea. LC 89-48254. 280p. 1990. text ed. 31.00 (*0-8131-1678-3*) U Pr of Ky.

Millican, Percy, ed. Index of Wills Proved in the Consistory Court of Norwich: 1550-1603. (British Record Society Index Library Ser.: Vol. 73-75). 1969. reprint ed. 79.00 (*0-8115-1513-3*) Periodicals Srv.

Millican, T. David. DBASE Dialect Software Engineering. 1994. text ed. write for info. (*0-442-00510-5*) Van Nos Reinhold.

— The dBase Dialects Software Engineering. 1991. text ed. 39.95 (*0-442-00254-8*) Van Nos Reinhold.

Millicap, J. Gordon. The Hyperactive Child with Minimal Brain Dysfunction. (Illus.). 1975. 31.00 (*0-8151-5911-0*, Yr Bk Med Pubs) Mosby Yr Bk.

— Learning Disabilities & Related Disorders: Facts & Current Issues. 1977. pap. 36.50 (*0-8151-5913-7*, Yr Bk Med Pubs) Mosby Yr Bk.

Millicer, Jan. When It Rains. LC 92-31136. (Voyages Ser.). (Illus.). (J). 1993. 2.50 (*0-383-03667-4*) SRA Schl Grp.

Millich, E., et al. New Technologies for the Exploration & Exploitation of Oil & Gas Resources, 2 vols., 1. (C). 1900. lib. bdg. 140.00 (*1-85333-058-2*) Kluwer Ac.

— New Technologies for the Exploration & Exploitation of Oil & Gas Resources, 2 vols., 2. (C). 1900. lib. bdg. 108.00 (*1-85333-059-0*) Kluwer Ac.

Millich, Frank. Interfacial Synthesis, Vol. 3: Recent Advances. LC 75-27750. (Illus.). 405p. reprint ed. pap. 115.50 (*0-7837-4723-3*, 2041285) Bks Demand.

Millich, Frank & Carraher, Charles E., Jr., eds. Interfacial Synthesis, Vol. 1: Fundamentals. LC 75-27750. (Illus.). 312p. reprint ed. pap. 89.00 (*0-7837-0979-X*, 2041285) Bks Demand.

— Interfacial Synthesis, Vol. 2: Polymer Applications & Technology. LC 75-27750. (Illus.). 560p. reprint ed. pap. 159.60 (*0-7837-0719-3*, 2041045) Bks Demand.

Millichap, Denzil, jt. auth. see Matthews, Paul.

Millichap, J. Gordon. Environmental Poisons in Our Food. LC 92-91280. (Illus.). 271p. 1993. 29.95 (*0-9629115-7-7*) PNB Pub.

— The Hyperactive Child with Minimal Brain Dysfunction: Questions & Answers. LC 75-17008. (Illus.). 179p. reprint ed. pap. 51.10 (*0-8357-6149-5*, 2034266) Bks Demand.

— Is Our Water Safe to Drink? A Guide to Drinking Water Hazards & Health Risks. LC 95-67490. (Illus.). 212p. 1995. 21.95 (*0-9629115-5-0*) PNB Pub.

— Progress in Pediatric Neurology. LC 91-90076. 598p. 1991. text ed. 57.95 (*0-9629115-0-X*) PNB Pub.

— Progress in Pediatric Neurology II. LC 94-66683. (Illus.). 550p. 1994. 64.95 (*0-9629115-8-5*) PNB Pub.

Millichap, J. Gordon, ed. Learning Disabilities & Related Disorders: Facts & Current Issues. LC 77-73607. (Illus.). 189p. reprint ed. pap. 53.90 (*0-8357-6186-X*, 2034265) Bks Demand.

Millichap, Joseph R. George Catlin. LC 77-76200. (Western Writers Ser.: No. 27). (Illus.). 48p. 1977. pap. 3.95 (*0-88430-051-X*) Boise St U W Writ Ser.

— Robert Penn Warren: A Study of the Short Fiction. LC 92-14380. (Twayne's Studies in Short Fiction: No. 39). 150p. 1992. text ed. 22.95 (*0-8057-8346-6*, Twayne) Macmillan.

Millichap, Nancy. Foster Care. LC 93-23237. (Changing Family Ser.). (Illus.). 128p. (YA). (gr. 9-12). 1994. lib. bdg. 14.49 (*0-531-11081-8*) Watts.

Millichip, Paul. The Travelling Painter: A Companion, Tutor & Guide. (Illus.). 224p. 1991. 34.95 (*0-7134-6451-8*, Pub. by Batsford UK) Trafalgar.

Millidge, Edward A. Esperanto-English Dictionary. (ENG & ESP.). 42.50 (*0-87557-018-6*, 018-6) Saphrograph.

Millier, Brett C. Elizabeth Bishop: Life & the Memory of It. LC 92-8548. 1993. 30.00 (*0-520-07978-7*) U CA Pr.

— Elizabeth Bishop: Life & the Memory of It. 1995. pap. 16.95 (*0-520-20345-3*) U CA Pr.

Milligan, jt. auth. see Palmeri.

***Milligan, Barry.** Pleasures & Pains: Opium & the Orient in Nineteenth-Century British Culture. 192p. (C). 1995. text ed. 29.50 (*0-8139-1571-6*) U Pr of Va.

Milligan, Bryce. Comanche Captive: You Are There. (Illus.). 156p. (YA). (gr. 5 up). 1989. pap. 3.95 (*0-87719-157-3*, Lone Star Bks) Gulf Pub.

— Daysleepers & Other Poems. LC 84-70036. 64p. (Orig.). 1984. pap. 6.95 (*0-931722-29-2*) Corona Pub.

— Lawmen: Stories of Men Who Tamed the West. LC 94-70797. (Disney's American Frontier Ser.: Bk. 14). (Illus.). 80p. (J). (gr. 1-4). 1994. lib. bdg. 12.89 (*0-7868-5005-1*); pap. 3.50 (*0-7868-4006-4*) Disney Pr.

— Litany Sung at Hell's Gate. (Illus.). x, 36p. (Orig.). 1990. pap. 8.00 (*0-913983-08-X*) M & A Edns.

— With the Wind, Kevin Dolan. LC 86-70018. (Multicultural Texas Ser.). (Illus.). 194p. (YA). (gr. 7 up). 1992. pap. 7.95 (*0-931722-45-4*) Corona Pub.

Milligan, Charles B. Spenser & the Table Round: A Study in the Contemporaneous Background for Spenser's Use of the Arthurian Legend. 1977. lib. bdg. 59.95 (*0-8490-2656-3*) Gordon Pr.

Milligan, David & Watts-Miller, William, eds. Liberalism, Citizenship, & Autonomy. LC 92-9982. (Avebury Series in Philosophy). 260p. 1992. 68.95 (*1-85628-280-5*, Pub. by Avebury Pub UK) Ashgate Pub Co.

Milligan, Debra. Marshmallow Autumn: Fire Safety. (Child Safety Ser.). (Illus.). 48p. 1986. 5.95 (*0-513-01830-1*) Denison.

Milligan, Debra T. Northstar. 272p. 1994. pap. 8.95 (*1-56901-446-9*) NW Pub.

Milligan, Don. Sex-Life: A Critical Commentary on the History of Sexuality. LC 92-36245. 169p. (C). 1993. text ed. 55.50 (*0-7453-0611-X*); pap. text ed. 15.95 (*0-7453-0612-8*) Westview.

Milligan, Edward H. Quakers & Railways. (C). 1988. 39.00 (*1-85072-099-1*, Pub. by W Sessions UK) St Mut.

Milligan, Edward T. The Looking Glass Self. LC 90-71969. (Illus.). 204p. (Orig.). 1992. pap. 9.95 (*1-56002-028-8*) Aegina Pr.

— On Linda: Love Loss & Renewal the Case for Human Organ Sharing. LC 91-50694. 200p. 1992. pap. 11.95 (*0-88247-898-2*, 898) R & E Pubs.

***Milligan, Elaine G.** Forever in His Presence. 125p. (Orig.). 1995. pap. 7.00 (*0-9646187-0-2*) Milligan Pub.

Milligan, G., ed. Signal Transduction: A Practical Approach. (Practical Approach Ser.). (Illus.). 192p. 1992. 70.00 (*0-19-963296-0*, IRL Pr); pap. 39.00 (*0-19-963295-2*, IRL Pr) OUP.

Milligan, G., et al, eds. G Proteins & Signal Transduction. (Biochemical Society Symposium Ser.: No. 56). 1990. 70.00 (*1-85578-001-1*, Pub. by Portland Pr Ltd UK) Ashgate Pub Co.

Milligan, G., jt. auth. see Moulton, J. H.

Milligan, George. Paul's Epistle to the Thessalonians. 306p. lib. bdg. 12.99 (*0-8254-5183-3*) Kregel.

— Selections from Greek Papyri. 152p. 1980. 20.00 (*0-89005-335-9*) Ares.

Milligan, George, ed. & tr. Selections from the Greek Papyri. LC 76-103654. (Select Bibliographies Reprint Ser.). 1977. 21.95 (*0-8369-5154-9*) Ayer.

Milligan, Graeme & Wakelam, Michael, eds. G-Proteins: Signal Transduction & Disease. (Illus.). 247p. 1992. text ed. 89.95 (*0-12-497515-1*) Acad Pr.

Milligan, Graeme, jt. ed. see Houslay, Miles D.

Milligan, H. V. Stephen Collins Foster. 1977. 250.00 (*0-87968-313-9*) Gordon Pr.

Milligan, Hugh H., ed. Tech Tips. (Illus.). 176p. (Orig.). 1993. teacher ed write for info. (*0-9635225-0-7*) Jensen Intercep.

Milligan, Ira. Understanding the Dreams You Dream. 280p. (Orig.). 1993. pap. 9.99 (*1-56043-761-8*) Destiny Image.

Milligan, J. E., rev. Brown's Signalling: How to Learn the International Code of Signals. rev. ed. (C). 1987. 66.00 (*0-85174-350-1*, Pub. by Brwn Son Ferg) St Mut.

Milligan, Jacquie. Lazy Day Adventure: Water Safety. (Child Safety Ser.). (Illus.). 48p. 1986. pap. 5.95 (*0-513-01832-8*) Denison.

— Spring Cleaning: Household Poisons. (Child Safety Ser.). (Illus.). 48p. 1986. 4.95 (*0-513-01829-8*) Denison.

***Milligan, Jane.** Snow. 220p. 1995. pap. 8.95 (*0-7610-0020-8*) NW Pub.

Milligan, John. The Resilient Pioneers: A History of the Elastic Rail Spike Company. (Illus.). 1977. 24.95 (*0-8464-0791-4*) Beekman Pubs.

Milligan, John D. Gunboats Down the Mississippi. LC 79-6119. (Navies & Men Ser.). (Illus.). 1980. reprint ed. lib. bdg. 30.95 (*0-405-13047-3*) Ayer.

Milligan, John E. Celestial Navigation by H. O. 249. LC 74-1464. (Illus.). 111p. 1974. pap. 7.50 (*0-87033-191-4*) Cornell Maritime.

Milligan, Lynda, jt. auth. see Smith, Nancy J.

Milligan, Lynda, jt. auth. see Smith, Nancy.

Milligan, Lynda S., jt. auth. see Smith, Nancy J.

Milligan, Martin, tr. see Marx, Karl.

Milligan, Maureen A., jt. ed. see More, Ellen S.

Milligan, Melba J. Diet - in Life, Food, Old Age & Research: Index of New Information with Authors & Subjects. 180p. 1993. 49.50 (*1-55914-842-X*); pap. 39.50 (*1-55914-843-8*) ABBE Pubs Assn.

— Diet - Investigations, Research & Results: Index of New Information with Authors & Subjects. 180p. 1993. 49.50 (*1-55914-844-6*); pap. 39.50 (*1-55914-845-4*) ABBE Pubs Assn.

— Food Mania & Over-Eating: Index of Modern Authors & Subjects with Guide for Rapid Research. LC 90-56314. 160p. 1991. 44.50 (*1-55914-416-5*); pap. 39.50 (*1-55914-417-3*) ABBE Pubs Assn.

— Physical Education & Training: Medical Subject Analysis with Bibliography. LC 84-45741. 150p. 1987. 37.50 (*0-88164-260-6*); pap. 34.50 (*0-88164-261-4*) ABBE Pubs Assn.

***Milligan, P.** Engima. Kahan, ed. (Illus.). 208p. 1995. pap. 19.95 (*1-56389-192-1*, Vertigo) DC Comics.

— Tank Girl Movie Adaptation. Young, A., ed. (Illus.). 64p. 1995. pap. 5.95 (*1-56389-219-7*, Vertigo) DC Comics.

Milligan, Peter. Catwoman Defiant. O'Neil, Dennis, ed. 48p. 1992. pap. 4.95 (*1-56389-071-2*) DC Comics.

Milligan, Robert H. Fetish Folk of West Africa. LC 73-116017. reprint ed. 47.50 (*0-404-00200-5*) AMS Pr.

Milligan, S. R., ed. The Oxford Reviews of Reproductive Biology, Vol. 13. (Illus.). 328p. 1991. 85.00 (*0-19-857761-3*) OUP.

— Oxford Reviews of Reproductive Biology, Vol. 14. (Illus.). 384p. 1992. 95.00 (*0-19-262241-2*) OUP.

— Oxford Reviews of Reproductive Biology, Vol. 15. (Illus.). 384p. 1993. 75.00 (*0-19-262346-X*) OUP.

— Oxford Reviews of Reproductive Biology, Vol. 11: 1989. (Illus.). 472p. 1989. 85.00 (*0-19-857649-8*) OUP.

Milligan, Sharlene, ed. see Plumb, Sally.

Milligan, Thomas B. The Concerto & London's Musical Culture in the Late Eighteenth Century. LC 83-5915. (Studies in Musicology: No. 69). 386p. reprint ed. pap. 110.10 (*0-8357-1441-1*, 2070512) Bks Demand.

***Milligan, Thomas B. & Graue, Jerald C.** Johann Baptist Cramer (1771-1858) A Thematic Catalogue of His Works. 1994. lib. bdg. 54.00 (*0-945193-41-6*) Pendragon NY.

***Milligan, Tony.** The Making of the Scottish Working Class: From Feudalism to Chartism. 1997. pap. 16.50 (*1-899438-21-1*, Pub. by Porcupine Bks UK) Humanities.

Milligan, V., jt. ed. see Brawner, C. O.

Milligan, V., ed. see International Conference on Stability in Open Pit Mining Staff.

Milligan, W. D., jt. auth. see Bowman, Arthur G.

Milligan, William. The Ascension & Heavenly Priesthood of Our Lord. 416p. 1977. reprint ed. 14.00 (*0-87921-034-6*) Attic Pr.

— Ascension of Christ. 385p. lib. bdg. 15.99 (*0-8254-5186-8*) Kregel.

Millikan, Larry E., jt. ed. see Parish, Lawrence C.

Millikan, Marilyn. Puppet Programs, No. 2. 1980. 6.50 (*0-685-68731-7*, MP-610) Lillenas.

Millikan, Max F., ed. National Economic Planning. (Universities-National Bureau Conference Ser.: No. 19). 423p. 1967. 110.00 (*0-87014-310-7*) Natl Bur Econ Res.

Millikan, Max F. & Rostow, Walt W. A Proposal: Key to an Effective Foreign Policy. LC 76-39842. 170p. 1977. reprint ed. text ed. 49.75 (*0-8371-9346-X*, MIAPR, Greenwood Pr) Greenwood.

Millikan, Robert A. The Autobiography of Robert A. Millikan. Cohen, I. Bernard, ed. LC 79-7975. (Three Centuries of Science in America Ser.). (Illus.). 1980. reprint ed. lib. bdg. 29.95 (*0-405-12558-5*) Ayer.

— The Electron: Its Isolation & Measurement & the Determination of Some of its Properties. DuMond, Jesse W., ed. LC 63-20910. 330p. reprint ed. pap. 94.10 (*0-317-08089-X*, 2019980) Bks Demand.

— Science & Life. LC 76-93360. (Essay Index Reprint Ser.). 1977. 17.95 (*0-8369-1307-8*) Ayer.

— Science & the New Civilization. LC 76-142671. (Essay Index Reprint Ser.). 1977. reprint ed. 20.95 (*0-8369-2418-5*) Ayer.

Millikan, Ruth G. White Queen Psychology & Other Essays for Alice. LC 92-24024. (Illus.). 420p. (C). 1993. 45.00 (*0-262-13288-5*, Bradford Bks) MIT Pr.

— White Queen Psychology & Other Essays for Alice. (Illus.). 400p. 1995. pap. 17.50 (*0-262-63162-8*, Bradford Bks) MIT Pr.

Milliken, Douglas L., jt. auth. see Milliken, William F.

Milliken, George A. Analysis of Messy Data, Vol. 1. 1992. pap. 39.95 (*0-442-01309-4*) Chapman & Hall.

— Analysis of Messy Data, Vol. 1: Designing Experiment. 1987. 47.95 (*0-317-63765-7*) Chapman & Hall.

Milliken, George A., jt. auth. see Johnson, Dallas E.

Milliken, J. G. & Taylor, G. Metropolitan Water Management. (Water Resources Monograph Ser.: Vol. 6). 180p. 1981. 10.00 (*0-87590-307-X*) Am Geophysical.

Milliken, Linda. Alphabet Patterns. (Illus.). 64p. (J). (ps-2). 1993. Grades ps-2. pap. text ed. 6.95 (*1-56472-008-X*) Edupress.

— Alphabet Pocket Fun: Letter Sound & Word Recognition Activities. (Illus.). 64p. 1994. student ed 6.95 (*1-56472-019-5*) Edupress.

— American Indian Activity Book: Art, Crafts, Cooking. 40p. 1980. pap. text ed. 4.95 (*1-56472-000-4*) Edupress.

— Classroom Kickoff. 304p. 1992. pap. text ed. 21.50 (*1-56472-001-2*) Edupress.

— Frontier American Activity Book: Art, Crafts, Cooking. (Illus.). (J). (gr. k-6). 1990. pap. text ed. 5.95 (*1-56472-017-9*) Edupress.

— Inexpensive Ideas for Classroom Environments. Celecia, Deneen, ed. (Illus.). 48p. 1994. student ed 6.95 (*1-56472-052-7*) Edupress.

— Literature Patterns. (Illus.). 112p. (J). (ps-2). 1993. Grades ps-2. pap. text ed. 11.95 (*1-56472-007-1*) Edupress.

— Low Cost Ways to Brighten Displays. Celecia, Deneen, ed. (Illus.). 48p. 1994. student ed 6.95 (*1-56472-051-9*) Edupress.

— Make Your Own Category Pictionary: Thematic Skillbuilder. (Illus.). 64p. 1994. student ed 6.95 (*1-56472-020-9*) Edupress.

— Make Your Own Spanish Category Pictionary: Thematic Skillbuilder. (Illus.). 64p. (J). (gr. k-2). 1994. student ed 6.95 (*1-56472-030-6*) Edupress.

— Medieval Times Activity Book. Celecia, Deneen, ed. (Illus.). 1995. student ed 5.95 (*1-56472-049-7*) Edupress.

— Medieval Times Photo Fun Activities. Celecia, Deneen, ed. (Illus.). 8p. (J). (gr. 3-6). 1995. 5.95 (*1-56472-050-0*) Edupress.

— Multicurricular Springboards & Starters. (Illus.). 144p. (Orig.). (J). (gr. k-6). 1993. Grades k-6. pap. text ed. 12.95 (*1-56472-010-1*) Edupress.

— Oodles of Writing Activities. 72p. 1990. pap. text ed. write for info. (*1-56472-002-0*) Edupress.

— Quick Learning Kits: Art & Literature. 96p. 1992. teacher ed 8.95 (*1-56472-004-7*) Edupress.

— Quick Learning Kits: Language & Social Studies. 96p. 1992. teacher ed 8.95 (*1-56472-005-5*) Edupress.

— Quick Learning Kits: Math & Science. 96p. 1992. teacher ed 8.95 (*1-56472-006-3*) Edupress.

— Scissor Skill Patterns. (Illus.). 72p. (J). (ps-2). 1993. Grades ps-2. pap. 7.95 (*1-56472-009-8*) Edupress.

— Seasonal & Holiday Springboards & Starters. (Illus.). 144p. (J). (gr. k-6). 1993. Grades k-6. pap. text ed. 12.95 (*1-56472-011-X*) Edupress.

— Spring Pick-a-Project. (Illus.). 52p. 1989. student ed 5.95 (*1-56472-038-1*) Edupress.

— Thematic Book Reports for Holidays: Literature Lists & Ready-to-Use Book Reports. (Illus.). 64p. 1994. student ed 6.95 (*1-56472-021-7*) Edupress.

— Thematic Book Reports for Math: Literature Lists & Ready-to-Use Book Reports. (Illus.). 64p. 1994. student ed 6.95 (*1-56472-022-5*) Edupress.

— Winter Pick-a-Project. (Illus.). 52p. (J). (gr. 1-5). 1989. student ed 5.95 (*1-56472-031-4*) Edupress.

— Word Banks, Bulletin Boards & More. (Illus.). 112p. 1993. pap. 10.95 (*1-56472-016-0*) Edupress.

Milliken, Linda, ed. see Brown, Karen & Engel, Holly.

Milliken, Linda, ed. see Celecia, Deneen.

Milliken, Linda, ed. see Engel, Holly & Brown, Karen.

Milliken, Linda, ed. see Hamman, Joyce.

Milliken, Linda, ed. see Loreen, Wendy.

Milliken, Mary E. Understanding Human Behavior: A Guide for Health Care Providers. 4th ed. LC 86-16758. 304p. (C). 1987. teacher ed 12.00 (*0-8273-2799-4*); pap. text ed. 25.95 (*0-8273-2797-8*) Delmar.

— Understanding Human Behavior: A Guide for Health Care Providers. 5th ed. LC 92-14880. 78p. 1993. teacher ed 12.00 (*0-8273-5475-4*); text ed. 28.50 (*0-8273-5474-6*); pap. text ed. 25.95 (*0-8273-5473-8*) Delmar.

***Milliken, Mary S.** City Cuisine. 1994. pap. 14.95 (*0-688-13177-8*) Hearst Bks.

Milliken, Mary S., et al. Mesa Mexicana. LC 93-43099. 1994. 17.95 (*0-688-10649-8*) Morrow.

***Milliken, Randall.** A Time of Little Choice: The Disintegration of Tribal Culture in the San Francisco Bay Area 1769-1810. Vane, Sylvia B., ed. (Ballena Press Anthropological Papers: No. 43). 400p. 1995. pap. 24.95 (*0-87919-131-7*) Ballena Pr.

— A Time of Little Choice: The Disintegration of Tribal Culture in the San Francisco Bay Area 1769-1810. Vane, Sylvia B., ed. (Ballena Press Anthropological Papers: No. 43). 400p. (C). 1995. 32.95 (*0-87919-132-5*) Ballena Pr.

Milliken, Stephen F. Chester Himes: A Critical Appraisal. LC 75-44081. 320p. reprint ed. pap. 91.20 (*0-7837-2356-3*, AU00421) Bks Demand.

***Milliken, William F. & Milliken, Douglas L.** Race Car Vehicle Dynamics. 1000p. 1994. 85.00 (*1-56091-526-9*, R146) Soc Auto Engineers.

Millikin, Donald D. Elementary Cryptography & Cryptanalysis. 140p. (Orig.). 1992. lib. bdg. 30.30 (*0-89412-174-X*); pap. 20.80 (*0-89412-173-1*) Aegean Park Pr.

Millikin, Jimmy A. Christian Doctrine for Everyman: Introduction to Baptist Beliefs. LC 78-10464. (Orig.). 1989. reprint ed. pap. 4.50 (*0-9621902-0-9*) KRB Bks.

Millili, Anthony T., jt. auth. see Ruben, Paul.

Milliman, Dan. The Inner Athlete: Realizing Your Fullest Potential. 2nd ed. Seymour, Dorothy, ed. 1994. pap. 11.95 (*0-913299-97-9*) Stillpoint.

Milliman, J. D. & Qingming, J., eds. Sediment Dynamics on the Changjiang Estuary & the Adjacent East China Sea: A Selection of Edited Papers from the International Symposium Held in Hangzhou, People's Republic of China, April 1983. 236p. 1985. pap. 44.00 (*0-08-030257-2*, Pergamon Pr) Elsevier.

Milliman, J. D. & Summerhays, C. P., eds. Upper Continental Margin Sedimentation off Brazil. (Contributions to Sedimentology Monograph: No. 4). (Illus.). 175p. 1975. pap. text ed. 55.25 (*3-510-57004-9*) Lubrecht & Cramer.

Milliman, John D., ed. Climatic Change & the Mediterranean. (Climatic Change & the Level of Seas Ser.). 550p. 1991. 120.00 (*0-340-55329-4*, A6222, Pub. by E Arnold UK) Routledge Chapman & Hall.

Milliman, John D. & Wright, W. Redwood, eds. The Marine Environment of the U. S. Atlantic Continental Slope & Rise. 1986. boxed 77.50 (*0-86720-066-9*) Jones & Bartlett.

Millin, D., et al, eds. The Social Implications of Robotics & Advanced Industrial Automation: Proceedings of the IFIP TC9 International Working Conference, Tel-Aviv, Israel, 14-16 December, 1987. 290p. 1989. 79.50 (*0-444-87320-1*, North Holland) Elsevier.

Millin, Laura J., ed. James Turrell: Four Light Installations. deluxe ed. LC 82-50224. 30p. 1982. Signed. 100.00 (*0-941104-03-6*) Real Comet.

Millin, Peggy T. Mary's Way: A Personal Story of Spiritual Growth & Transformation. 1991. pap. 8.95 (*0-89087-644-4*) Celestial Arts.

Millin, Sarah G. Mary Glenn. 1982. reprint ed. 20.00 (*0-89733-015-3*); reprint ed. pap. 8.95 (*0-89733-014-5*) Academy Chi Pubs.

Millinary Institute Staff. The Art & Craft of Ribbon Work. Nager, Sandra, ed. (Illus.). 120p. 1982. reprint ed. pap. 19.95 (*0-9617110-0-0*) Antiquity Pr.

***Milliner, E. Ramon.** The Conscoius State of Matter. (Illus.). 1995. pap. 29.95 (*0-615-00499-7*) Vantage.

Milliner, Michael. Contractors' Business Handbook: Accounting, Tax Management, Finance, Cost Control. (Illus.). 300p. 1988. 59.95 (*0-87629-105-1*, 67255) R S Means.

Milliner, Michael S. & Home Builder Press. Commercial Building: An Introduction for Home Builders. 208p. 1989. pap. 30.00 (*0-86718-329-2*) Home Builder.

Milling, Bryan E. The Basics of Finance: Financial Tools for Non-Financial Managers. LC 90-27684. 208p. 1991. pap. 14.95 (*0-942061-18-7*, Sourcebooks Trade); boxed 24.95 (*0-942061-25-X*, Sourcebooks Trade) Sourcebks.

— The Basics of Finance: Financial Tools for Non-Financial Managers. 2nd ed. 224p. 1995. pap. 14.95 (*1-57071-055-4*) Sourcebks.

— Cash Flow Problem Solver: Common Problems & Practical Solutions. 3rd ed. LC 91-29705. (Illus.). 282p. 1991. reprint ed. 32.95 (*0-942061-28-4*, Sourcebooks Trade); reprint ed. pap. 19.95 (*0-942061-27-6*, Sourcebooks Trade) Sourcebks.

— Financial Tools for the Non-Financial Executive. LC 82-70779. 215p. reprint ed. pap. 61.30 (*0-317-55810-2*, 2029391) Bks Demand.

— How to Get a Loan or Line of Credit for Your Business. LC 92-41609. (Small Business Sourcebooks Ser.). (Illus.). 1993. 17.95 (*0-942061-46-2*); pap. 8.95 (*0-942061-43-8*) Sourcebks.

Milling, P. M. & Zahn, E. O., eds. Computer-Based Management of Complex Systems. (Illus.). xiv, 648p. 1989. pap. 109.00 (*0-387-51447-3*, 3304) Spr-Verlag.

Millingrton, John. Pentominoes. 1993. pap. 6.95 (*0-906212-57-X*, Pub. by Tarquin UK) Parkwest Pubns.

Millington, A. C., ed. Environmental Change in Drylands: Biogeographical & Geomorphological Perspectives. LC 93-27489. (British Geomorphological Research Group Symposia Ser.). 1994. text ed. 74.95 (*0-471-94267-7*) Wiley.

Millington, A. I. The Penetration of EC Markets by U. K. Manufacturing Industry. 200p. 1988. text ed. 46.95 (*0-566-05409-4*, Pub. by Avebury Pub UK) Ashgate Pub Co.

Millington, Andrew C., et al, eds. Estimating Woody Biomass in Sub-Saharan Africa. LC 93-23481. 208p. 1994. 24.95 (*0-8213-2306-7*, 12306) World Bank.

— Estimating Woody Biomass in Sub-Saharan Africa. 208p. (FRE.). 1994. 24.95 (*0-8213-2507-8*, 12507) World Bank.

Millington, Barry. Wagner. rev. ed. (Illus.). 352p. 1992. pap. text ed. 13.95 (*0-691-02722-6*) Princeton U Pr.

Millington, Barry, ed. The Wagner Compendium: A Guide to Wagner's Life & Music. (Illus.). 432p. 1992. text ed. 35.00 (*0-02-871359-1*) Schirmer Bks.

Millington, Barry & Spencer, Stewart, eds. Wagner in Performance. (Illus.). 224p. (C). 1992. text ed. 30.00 (*0-300-05718-0*) Yale U Pr.

Millington, Barry, jt. auth. see Spencer, Stewart.

Millington, John. Tangrams. 1993. pap. 6.95 (*0-906212-56-1*, Pub. by Tarquin UK) Parkwest Pubns.

— Tropical Visions. (Illus.). 144p. 1988. text ed. 49.95 (*0-7022-2079-5*, Pub. by Univ Queensland Pr AT) Intl Spec Bk.

Millington, John P. John Dalton. LC 73-14966. (English Men of Letters Ser.: No. 6). reprint ed. 37.50 (*0-404-07896-6*) AMS Pr.

Millington, Jon. Curve Stitching. (Illus.). 96p. (Orig.). 1990. pap. 17.95 (*0-906212-65-0*, Pub. by Tarquin UK) Parkwest Pubns.

Millington, Joyce. Liverpool Friends Service Centre. (C). 1989. pap. 30.00 (*1-85072-123-8*, Pub. by W Sessions UK) St Mut.

Millington, Mark, jt. ed. see McGuirk, Bernard.

Millington, Mark I. An Analysis of the Short Stories of Juan Carlos Onetti: Fictions of Desire. LC 93-29918. 220p. 1993. text ed. 89.95 (*0-7734-9340-9*) E Mellen.

Millington, Richard H. Practicing Romance: Narrative Form & Cultural Engagement in Hawthorne's Fiction. 245p. 1992. text ed. 35.00 (*0-691-06876-3*) Princeton U Pr.

Millington, Susan. Nihongo Pera Pera: A User's Guide to Japanese Onomatopoeia. 152p. 1993. pap. 9.95 (*0-8048-1890-8*) C E Tuttle.

Millington, Thomas. Debt Politics after Independence: The Funding Conflict in Bolivia. (University of Florida Social Sciences Monographs: No. 79). (Illus.). 200p. 1992. lib. bdg. 29.95 (*0-8130-1140-X*) U Press Fla.

Million, Arthur B. & Dixon, Thomas W., Jr. Pere Marquette Power. Shaver, Carl W., ed. LC 85-70004. (Illus.). 224p. (Orig.). 1984. pap. 23.95 (*0-939487-06-3*) Ches & OH Hist.

Million, John W. State Aid to Railways in Missouri. Bruchey, Stuart, ed. LC 80-1331. (Railroads Ser.). (Illus.). 1981. reprint ed. lib. bdg. 27.95 (*0-405-13805-9*) Ayer.

***Million, Robert P.** Zapata: The Ideology of a Peasant Revolution. LC 94-31757. Date not set. pap. 7.50 (*0-7178-0710-X*) Intl Pubs Co.

Million, Rodney R., et al, eds. Management of Head & Neck Cancer: A Multidisciplinary Approach. 2nd ed. LC 93-18326. 913p. (C). 1993. 150.00 (*0-397-51208-2*) Lippincott.

An Asterisk (*) at the beginning of an entry indicates that the title is appearing in BIP for the first time.

Millionschikov, M., et al. Scientific & Technological Revolution: A Study of the Soviet Union, Capitalist, & Third World Countries. 279p. 1975. 25.00 (*0-8464-0818-X*) Beekman Pubs.

Milliot, Jim, comp. Micros at Work: Case Studies of Microcomputers in Libraries. LC 85-241. (Professional Librarian Ser.). 148p. 1985. pap. 31.50 (*0-86729-116-8*) Macmillan.

Milliron, Kerry, ed. see Pellicani, Luciano.

Millis, Bette R., jt. auth. see Mord, Jeanne.

***Millis, Christopher.** Impossible Mirrors. 72p. (Orig.). 1994. pap. 10.95 (*1-880286-18-1*) Singular Speech Pr.

Millis, Christopher, tr. The Dark of the Sun: Selected Poems of Umberto Saba. 126p. (C). 1994. lib. bdg. 34.50 (*0-8191-9330-5*) U Pr of Amer.

Millis, E. A., jt. auth. see Wilson, M. S.

Millis, Harry A. The Japanese Problem in the United States. Daniels, Roger, ed. LC 78-54828. (Asian Experience in North America Ser.). (Illus.). 1979. reprint ed. lib. bdg. 26.95 (*0-405-11285-8*) Ayer.

— Organized Labor. LC 74-22752. (Labor Movement in Fiction & Non-Fiction Ser.). reprint ed. 57.50 (*0-404-58504-3*) AMS Pr.

Millis, Harry A., ed. How Collective Bargaining Works: A Survey of Experience in Leading American Industries. LC 74-156436. (American Labor Ser., No. 2). 1978. reprint ed. 65.95 (*0-405-02933-0*) Ayer.

Millis, Harry A. & Brown, Emily C. From the Wagner Act to Taft-Hartley: A Study of National Labor Policy & Labor Relations. LC 50-7091. 734p. reprint ed. pap. 180.00 (*0-317-09623-0*, 2020123) Bks Demand.

Millis, R. L. & Franz, O. G., eds. Identification, Optimization, & Production of Optical Telescope Sites. Date not set. pap. text ed. write for info. (*0-9618288-0-3*) Lowell Observ.

Millis, R. M. Atlas of Breast Pathology. (Current Histopathology Ser.). 144p. 1983. lib. bdg. 155.50 (*0-85200-329-3*) Kluwer Ac.

Millis, Richard M., jt. ed. see Dutta, Sisir K.

Millis, Walter. Arms & Men: A Study of American Military History. LC 84-4711. 365p. (C). 1984. reprint ed. pap. 15.00 (*0-8135-0931-9*) Rutgers U Pr.

— The Marital Spirit. 444p. 1989. reprint ed. pap. 11.95 (*0-929587-07-3*, Elephant Paperbacks) I R Dee.

— The Martial Spirit. Kohn, Richard H., ed. LC 78-22389. (American Military Experience Ser.). (Illus.). 1980. reprint ed. lib. bdg. 37.95 (*0-405-11866-X*) Ayer.

— This Is Pearl: The United States & Japan, 1941. LC 77-138594. (Illus.). 384p. 1971. reprint ed. text ed. 65.00 (*0-8371-5795-1*, MITP, Greenwood Pr) Greenwood.

***Milliss, Roger.** Waterloo Creek. 1995. pap. 49.95 (*0-86840-326-1*, Pub. by New South Wales Univ Pr AT) Intl Spec Bk.

Millkie, Ron & Carlson, Ray. You Don't Have to Be Beautiful to Be a Model. LC 77-26794. 38p. 1986. pap. 3.50 (*0-87576-064-3*) Pilot Bks.

Millman, Anne, jt. auth. see Rokach, Allen.

***Millman, Dan.** The Laws of Spirit: Simple, Powerful Truths for Making Life Work. Carleton, Nancy, ed. 120p. 1995. 12.95 (*0-915811-64-2*) H J Kramer Inc.

— Life You Were Born to Live: A Guide to Finding Your Life Purpose. LC 93-77108. 468p. 1993. 20.00 (*0-915811-45-6*) H J Kramer Inc.

— The Life You Were Born to Live: A Guide to Finding Your Life Purpose. LC 93-77108. 468p. 1995. pap. 14.95 (*0-915811-60-X*) H J Kramer Inc.

— No Ordinary Moments: A Peaceful Warrior's Guide to Daily Life. Carleton, Nancy, ed. LC 92-9545. 324p. 1992. pap. 12.95 (*0-915811-40-5*) H J Kramer Inc.

— Quest for the Crystal Castle. LC 92-70302. (Illus.). 32p. (J). (ps-5). 1992. 13.95 (*0-915811-41-3*) H J Kramer Inc.

— Sacred Journey of the Peaceful Warrior. Carleton, Nancy, ed. LC 91-11234. 252p. 1991. 19.95 (*0-915811-34-0*); pap. 11.95 (*0-915811-33-2*) H J Kramer Inc.

— Secret of the Peaceful Warrior. San Souci, Robert, ed. LC 90-52636. (Illus.). 32p. 1991. 13.95 (*0-915811-23-5*) H J Kramer Inc.

— Way of the Peaceful Warrior: A Book That Changes Lives. rev. ed. LC 83-83240. 216p. (C). 1984. reprint ed. pap. 11.95 (*0-915811-00-6*) H J Kramer Inc.

***Millman, Don.** Economics: Making Good Choices. LC 95-12635. 1996. text ed. 27.95 (*0-538-84559-7*) S-W Pub.

Millman, Gregory J. The Floating Battlefield: Corporate Strategies in the Currency Wars. LC 89-77449. 224p. 1990. 24.95 (*0-8144-5987-0*) AMACOM.

— Vandal's Crown: How Market Vigilantes Are Remaking the Global Financial Order. 1995. 23.00 (*0-02-921287-1*) Free Pr.

Millman, Howard L., jt. auth. see Schaefer, Charles E.

Millman, Howard L., et al. Therapies for Adults. LC 82-48064. (Jossey-Bass Social & Behavioral Science Ser.). 544p. reprint ed. pap. 155.10 (*0-7837-0184-5*, 2040480) Bks Demand.

— Therapies for School Behavior Problems: A Handbook of Practical Interventions. LC 80-8318. (Social & Behavioral Science Ser.). 557p. 1980. 36.95x (*0-87589-483-6*) Jossey-Bass.

Millman, J., jt. auth. see Pauk, Walter.

Millman, Jack H., jt. auth. see Holt, Roger W.

Millman, Jacob. Microelectronics. 2nd ed. 1008p. 1987. text ed. write for info. (*0-07-042330-X*) McGraw.

Millman, Jason & Darling-Hammond, Linda, eds. The New Handbook of Teacher Evaluation: Assessing Elementary & Secondary School Teachers. 2nd ed. (Illus.). 448p. (C). 1989. text ed. 49.95 (*0-8039-3394-0*); pap. 25.00 (*0-8039-4523-X*) Sage.

Millman, Joan. The Effigy: Stories. 112p. 1990. 16.95 (*0-8262-0755-3*) U of Mo Pr.

Millman, Joan & Behrmann, Polly. Parents As Playmates: A Games Approach to the Preschool Years. LC 79-4547. 140p. 1979. pap. 18.95 (*0-87705-404-5*) Human Sci Pr.

Millman, Ken, ed. Florida Outdoor Guide, 1993. 300p. 1992. pap. write for info. (*0-9634818-0-0*) Keynoter Pub.

— South Florida Outdoor Guide, 1994. 300p. 1993. pap. write for info. (*0-9634818-1-9*) Keynoter Pub.

Millman, Ken, ed. see Miami Hearld Staff.

Millman, L., jt. auth. see Schaefer, Charles E.

Millman, Laurence. Parliament of Ravens. 32p. 1986. pap. 5.00 (*0-910477-03-5*) LoonBooks.

Millman, Lawrence. Hero Jesse. 196p. (C). 1994. reprint ed. pap. 13.95 (*0-87451-663-3*) U Pr of New Eng.

— A Kayak Full of Ghosts: Eskimo Tales. LC 87-11729. 200p. (Orig.). 1987. pap. 9.95 (*0-88496-267-9*) Capra Pr.

— A Kayak Full of Ghosts: Eskimo Tales. LC 89-31047. 208p. (Orig.). (C). 1988. reprint ed. lib. bdg. 27.00x (*0-8095-4040-1*) Borgo Pr.

— Last Places: A Journey in the North. 1990. 18.95 (*0-685-45106-2*) HM Soft-Ref Div.

— Last Places: A Journey in the North. 1991. 10.00 (*0-679-73456-2*, Vin) Random.

— Last Places: Journey. 1992. 10.00 (*0-685-59153-0*) McKay.

— Our Like Will Not Be There Again: Notes from the West of Ireland. 1992. pap. 12.00 (*1-877727-22-9*) White Pine.

— Wolverine Creates the World: Labrador Indian Tales. LC 92-46340. (Illus.). 160p. (Orig.). 1993. pap. 12.95 (*0-88496-363-2*) Capra Pr.

— The Wrong-Handed Man: Stories. LC 87-27200. 112p. (Orig.). 1988. pap. 10.95 (*0-8262-0674-3*) U of Mo Pr.

Millman, Lawrence W. Wolverine Creates the World: Labrador Indian Tales. (Illus.). 160p. (Orig.). (C). 1993. reprint ed. lib. bdg. 33.00x (*0-8095-4115-7*) Borgo Pr.

***Millman, M. C.** Cheery Bim Band No. 4: Color War! LC 94-70754. 150p. (YA). Date not set. write for info. (*1-56062-260-1*) CIS Comm.

— Cheery Bim Band No. 5: In the Spotlight! LC 94-60672. 141p. (J). (gr. 5-8). Date not set. 10.95 (*1-56062-265-2*) CIS Comm.

— Cheery Bim Band No. 6: Trumpet Trouble. LC 94-72546. 176p. (J). (gr. 5-8). 1994. 10.95 (*1-56062-271-7*) CIS Comm.

— Mind Your Own Business. LC 94-70753. 200p. (YA). Date not set. write for info. (*1-56062-264-4*) CIS Comm.

— Regards from Camp: Search Party Sunday, No. 4. LC 94-69038. 150p. (J). (gr. 5-8). Date not set. write for info. (*1-56062-284-9*) CIS Comm.

Millman, Maggie, jt. auth. see Downing, Taylor.

Millman, Malka. Too Tough to Care. 150p. (J). (gr. 6). Date not set. 8.95 (*1-56062-237-7*) CIS Comm.

Millman, Marcia. Warm Hearts & Cold Cash: The Intimate Dynamics of Families & Money. 240p. 1991. text ed. 27.95 (*0-02-921285-5*) Free Pr.

Millman, Mary & Bohn, Dave. Master of Line: John Winkler, American Etcher. LC 94-5208. (Illus.). 192p. 1994. 58.00 (*0-88496-358-6*) Capra Pr.

Millman, Michael, jt. auth. see Erwin, Richard.

Millman, Michael L. Politics & the Expanding Physician Supply. LC 78-73591. (Conservation of Human Resources Ser.: No. 11). (Illus.). 176p. 1980. text ed. 31.50 (*0-916672-84-0*) Rowman.

Millman, Mike, et al. Boat Fishing. (Illus.). 112p. 1992. pap. 24.95 (*1-85223-685-X*, Pub. by Crowood Pr UK) Trafalgar.

Millman, R. G. Auburn University Walking Tour Guide. 128p. 1991. pap. 9.95 (*0-8173-0523-8*) U of Ala Pr.

Millman, R. S. & Parker, George D. Geometry: A Metric Approach with Models. (Undergraduate Texts in Mathematics Ser.). (Illus.). 355p. 1981. 38.00 (*0-387-90610-X*) Spr-Verlag.

— Geometry: A Metric Approach with Models. 2nd ed. Ewing, J. H. et al, eds. (Undergraduate Texts in Mathematics Ser.). (Illus.). 352p. 1993. text ed. 39.00 (*0-387-97412-1*) Spr-Verlag.

— Geometry: A Metric Approach with Models. 2nd ed. (Undergraduate Texts in Mathematics Ser.). (Illus.). xiii, 370p. 1993. write for info. (*3-540-97412-1*) Spr-Verlag.

Millman, Richard S. & Parker, George D. Elements of Differential Geometry. LC 76-28497. (Illus.). 1977. text ed. write for info. (*0-13-264143-7*) P-H.

Millman, Val & Burchell, Helen, eds. Gender Issues in Secondary Education: Agenda for Change. 128p. 1989. pap. 29.00 (*0-335-09533-X*, Open Univ Pr) Taylor & Francis.

***Millmore, Paul.** South Downs Way. (National Travel Guide Ser.). (Illus.). 168p. Date not set. pap. 19.95 (*1-85410-099-8*, London Bridge) Genl Dist Srvs.

Millmoss, A. B., jt. auth. see Duensing, Edward.

Millner, Cork. Beefcake Bazaar. LC 90-52519. (Orig.). 1984. pap. 6.00 (*0-88734-208-6*) Players Pr.

— Cork Millner's Recipe of the Winemakers. 64p. 1986. pap. 6.50 (*0-87461-064-8*) McNally & Loftin.

— Portraits: Creative Conversations with Celebrities. (Illus.). 224p. 1994. 25.00 (*1-56474-087-0*) Fithian Pr.

— Write from the Start. rev. ed. 236p. 1994. pap. 9.95 (*1-56474-120-6*) Fithian Pr.

Millner, Fredrick L. The Operas of Johann Adolf Hasse. LC 79-11832. (Studies in Musicology: No. 2). (Illus.). 428p. reprint ed. pap. 122.00 (*0-685-20873-7*, 2070191) Bks Demand.

Millner, Nancy, jt. auth. see Corlett, Eleanor.

Millns, Susan, jt. ed. see Bridgeman, Jo.

Millodot, Michel. Diccionario de Optometria. 304p. 1990. write for info. (*0-7859-6039-2*, 8440464142) Fr & Eur.

— Dictionary of Optometry. 3rd ed. 208p. 1993. pap. 30.00 (*0-7506-0847-1*) Buttrwrth-Heinemann.

Milloff, Doug, jt. auth. see Dimino, Frank.

***Millon & Green.** Objective Psychodiagnostic Inventories. text ed. write for info. (*0-471-88315-8*) Wiley.

Millon, Henry A. Baroque & Rococo Architecture. LC 61-15492. (Great Ages of World Architecture Ser.). (Illus.). 127p. 1961. pap. 10.95 (*0-8076-0333-3*) Braziller.

— Studies in Art History I: Studies in Italian Art & Architecture. (Fifteenth - Eighteenth Centuries Ser.). (Illus.). 344p. 1980. 56.00 (*0-271-00457-6*) Am Acad Rome.

Millon, Henry A., ed. The Renaissance from Brunelleschi to Michelangelo. LC 94-65749. (Illus.). 800p. 1994. 85.00 (*0-8478-1828-4*) Rizzoli Intl.

Millon, Henry A. & Munshower, Susan S., eds. An Architectural Progress in the Renaissance & Baroque: Sojourns in & Out of Italy. (Papers in Art History: Vol. VIII). (Illus.). 929p. (Orig.). 1992. pap. 70.00 (*0-915773-07-4*) Penn St Univ Dept Art Hist.

Millon, Henry A. & Nochlin, Linda, eds. Art & Architecture in the Service of Politics. 1978. 70.00x (*0-262-13137-4*) MIT Pr.

Millon, Judith. St. Pauls Within-the-Walls: Rome, a History. LC 81-8055. 1982. 9.95 (*0-87233-058-3*) Bauhan.

Millon, Kim, jt. auth. see Millon, Marc.

Millon, Marc & Millon, Kim. Flavours of Korea. (Illus.). 242p. 1991. pap. 17.95 (*0-233-98635-9*, Pub. by A Deutsch UK) Trafalgar.

— Shopping for Food & Drink in Northern France & Belgium. (Illus.). 192p. 1995. pap. 16.95 (*1-85793-147-5*, Pub. by Pavilion UK) Trafalgar.

— Small Hotels & Restaurants in Northern France & Belgium. (Illus.). 192p. 1995. pap. 16.95 (*1-85793-148-3*, Pub. by Pavilion UK) Trafalgar.

— The Wine Roads of France. (Illus.). 416p. (Orig.). 1992. pap. 22.00 (*0-246-13749-5*, Pub. by HarpC UK) HarpC.

— The Wine Roads of Italy. (Illus.). 529p. 1993. pap. 22.00 (*0-246-13737-1*, Pub. by HarpC UK) HarpC.

— The Wine Roads of Spain. (Illus.). 424p. (Orig.). 1993. pap. 22.00 (*0-246-13871-8*, Pub. by HarpC UK) HarpC.

Millon, Rene, ed. see Sempowski, Martha L. & Spence, Michael W.

Millon, Theodore. Disorders of Personality: DSM-III: AXIS II. LC 80-28249. 458p. 1981. text ed. 64.95 (*0-471-06403-3*) Wiley.

— Modern Psychopathology: A Biosocial Approach to Maladaptive Learning & Functioning. (Illus.). 681p. 1983. reprint ed. text ed. 40.95 (*0-88133-020-5*) Waveland Pr.

— Personality & Psychopathology: Building a Clinical Science: Selected Papers of Theodore Millon. LC 95-10576. 1995. write for info. (*0-471-11685-8*) Wiley-Interscience.

— Toward a New Personology: An Evolutionary Model. (Series on Personality Processes). 200p. 1990. text ed. 34.95 (*0-471-51573-6*) Wiley.

Millon, Theodore, ed. Theories of Personality & Psychopathology. 3rd ed. LC 82-25843. 452p. (C). 1983. text ed. 41.25 (*0-03-062629-3*) HB Coll Pubs.

Millon, Theodore & Everly, George S., Jr. Personality & Its Disorders: A Biosocial Learning Approach. LC 84-21995. 291p. (C). 1985. Net. pap. text ed. write for info. (*0-471-87816-2*) Wiley.

Millon, Theodore & Klerman, Gerald L., eds. Contemporary Directions in Psychopathology: Toward the DSM-IV. LC 85-30549. 737p. 1986. lib. bdg. 79.95 (*0-89862-659-5*) Guilford Pr.

Millon, Theodore, et al, eds. Handbook of Clinical Health Psychology. LC 82-11236. 632p. 1982. 85.00 (*0-306-40932-1*, Plenum Pr) Plenum.

Millones, Luis & Pratt, Mary L. Amor Brujo: Images & Culture of Love in the Andes. LC 89-39918. (Foreign & Comparative Studies Program, Latin American Ser.: No. 10). (Illus.). (Orig.). (C). 1990. pap. text ed. 14.00 (*0-915984-33-4*) Syracuse U Foreign Comp.

***Millonig, Virginia L.** Today's Women - Before & after Menopause: Sex, Bones, Heart, Hot Flashes, Menopause "& Beyond" 300p. (Orig.). 1995. pap. text ed. 12.95 (*1-878028-23-5*) Hlth Lead Assoc.

Millonig, Virginia L., ed. see Celetano, Deborah, et al.

Millonig, Virginia L., ed. see Davis, et al.

Millonig, Virginia L., ed. see Diehl, Beth, et al.

Millonig, Virginia L., ed. see Edmonds, et al.

Millonig, Virginia L., ed. see Moran, Cathleen, et al.

Millonzi, Joel, jt. auth. see Ehrlich, Daniel J.

Millor, W. J., ed. see John of Salisbury.

Millot, Catherine. Horsexe: Essay on Transsexuality. 150p. 1990. pap. 10.00 (*0-936756-20-9*) Autonomedia.

Millot, Marc D., et al. The Day After...Study Nuclear Proliferation in the Post-Cold War, Vol. II: Main Report. LC 93-27731. 1993. write for info. (*0-8330-1424-2*, MR-253-AF) Rand Corp.

— The Day After...Study: Nuclear Proliferation in the Post-Cold War World, Vol. I: Summary Report. LC 93-33243. 1993. write for info. (*0-8330-1459-5*, MR-266-AF) Rand Corp.

Milloy, Jean & O'Rourke, Rebecca. The Woman Reader: Learning & Teaching Women's Writing. 176p. 1991. 55.00 (*0-415-00983-9*, A5698); pap. 15.95 (*0-415-00984-7*, A5699) Routledge.

Milloy, Nancy R. Breakdown of Speech: Causes & Remediation. (Therapy in Practice Ser.: No. 20). pap. 32.50 (*0-412-31550-5*) Chapman & Hall.

Millross, Janice & Speht, Alan. Utilization of the Cook-Freeze Catering System for School Meals. 212p. 1974. text ed. 30.00 (*0-685-51318-1*) Scholium Intl.

Millroy, Wendy L. An Ethnographic Study of the Mathematical Ideas of a Group of Carpenters. LC 91-39453. (Journal for Research in Mathematics Education Monograph Ser.: No. 5). (Illus.). 210p. (Orig.). 1992. pap. 7.50 (*0-87353-341-0*) NCTM.

***Mills.** The Big Blue Bottom Line: The Story Behind the Turnaround at IBM. Date not set. text ed. 27.95 (*0-471-11622-X*) Wiley.

— Blowout Prevention: Theory & Applications. 193p. 1988. text ed. 59.00 (*0-13-080193-3*) P-H.

— Color Atlas of Emergencies. 2nd ed. 1993. 99.95 (*0-8151-5912-9*, Yr Bk Med Pubs) Mosby Yr Bk.

— Deviated Drilling. 199p. 1988. text ed. 63.67 (*0-13-208315-9*) P-H.

— Placenames of Lancashire. 150p. 1991. text ed. 19.95 (*0-7134-5236-6*, Pub. by Batsford UK) Trafalgar.

— Space, Time, Quantum Physics. (C). 1995. pap. text ed. write for info. (*0-7167-2436-7*) W H Freeman.

Mills & O'Neill. Marshal Law: Fear & Loathing. 144p. 1990. pap. 14.95 (*0-87135-676-7*) Marvel Entmnt.

Mills, jt. auth. see Conti.

Mills, jt. auth. see Leoung.

Mills, A. D. A Dictionary of English Place Names. LC 92-43070. (C). 1993. pap. 6.99 (*0-19-283131-3*) OUP.

— Dorset Place Names. (C). 1989. 45.00 (*1-85455-065-9*, Pub. by Ensign Pubns & Print UK) St Mut.

Mills, A. E. The Acquisition of Gender. (Language & Communication Ser.: Vol. 20). (Illus.). 180p. 1986. 71.00 (*0-387-16740-4*) Spr-Verlag.

Mills, A. J. The Will to Live: The Battle of a Young Boy Against Muscular Dystrophy. 100p. 1992. pap. 7.95 (*0-9633921-0-7*) Humor Bks.

Mills, Adam. Cold Chills. (Twin Connection Ser.: No. 10). (J). (gr. 4 up). 1989. pap. 2.95 (*0-345-35929-1*) Ballantine.

— High-Tech Heist. (Twin Connection Ser.: No. 9). 144p. 1989. pap. 2.95 (*0-345-35928-3*) Ballantine.

Mills, Adelbert P. Materials of Construction, Their Manufacture & Properties. 6th ed. LC 55-73681. (Illus.). 662p. reprint ed. pap. 180.00 (*0-317-08337-6*, 2055132) Bks Demand.

Mills, Albert J. & Murgatroyd, Stephen J. Organizational Rules: A Framework for Understanding Organizational Action. 240p. 1990. 90.00 (*0-335-09908-4*, Open Univ Pr); pap. 32.00 (*0-335-09907-6*, Open Univ Pr) Taylor & Francis.

Mills, Albert J. & Tancred, Peta. Gendering Organizational Analysis. 336p. (C). 1992. text ed. 49.95 (*0-8039-4558-2*); pap. text ed. 22.50 (*0-8039-4559-0*) Sage.

Mills, Alden B. Hospital Public Relations Today. 1965. 12.75 (*0-917036-02-6*) Physicians Rec.

Mills, Alice S., jt. auth. see Joseph, Lou.

Mills, Allen. Fool for Christ: The Intellectual Politics of J. S. Woodsworth. 352p. 1991. text ed. 50.00 (*0-8020-2787-3*); pap. text ed. 18.95 (*0-8020-6842-1*) U of Toronto Pr.

Mills, Ami C. CIA Off Campus: Building the Movement Against Agency Recruitment & Research. 210p. (Orig.). 1991. 25.00 (*0-89608-404-3*); pap. 10.00 (*0-89608-403-5*) South End Pr.

Mills, Andrea. Caravan to Tiern. (Illus.). 1989. 8.95 (*0-940244-22-5*) Flying Buffalo.

Mills, Anita. Anita Mills Falling Stars. 384p. 1993. pap. 4.99 (*0-451-40365-7*, Topaz) NAL-Dutton.

— Autumn Rain. 384p. (Orig.). 1993. pap. 4.99 (*0-451-40328-2*, Onyx) NAL-Dutton.

— Comanche Moon. 384p. (Orig.). 1995. mass mkt. 4.99 (*0-451-40553-6*, Topaz) NAL-Dutton.

— Duel of Hearts. 240p. 1988. pap. 3.99 (*0-451-15713-3*, Sig) NAL-Dutton.

— The Duke's Double. 224p. (Orig.). 1988. pap. 3.99 (*0-451-15400-2*, Sig) NAL-Dutton.

— Hearts of Fire. 1989. pap. 4.99 (*0-451-40135-2*, Onyx) NAL-Dutton.

— Lady of Fire. 384p. 1987. pap. 4.99 (*0-451-40044-5*, Onyx) NAL-Dutton.

— The Rogue's Return. (Signet Regency Romance Ser.). 224p. 1992. 3.99 (*0-451-17258-2*) NAL-Dutton.

— Secret Nights. 384p. (Orig.). 1994. pap. 4.99 (*0-451-40481-5*, Topaz) NAL-Dutton.

Mills, Anita, et al. Cherished Moments. LC 93-47563. 1994. 17.95 (*0-681-45413-X*) Longmeadow Pr.

— Christmas Rogues: The Christmas Stranger; The Homecoming; Bayberry & Mistletoe. 1995. 4.99 (*0-373-83297-4*) Harlequin Bks.

Mills, Ann, ed. see Dadaji.

Mills, Anne, ed. The Acquisition of German: The Crosslinguistic Study of Language Acquisition. (Crosslinguistic Study of Language Acquisition Ser.). 136p. 1986. pap. 14.95 (*0-89859-841-9*) L Erlbaum Assocs.

Mills, Anne & Lee, Kenneth, eds. Health Economics Research in Developing Countries. LC 92-49379. (Oxford Medical Publications). (C). 1993. pap. write for info. (*0-19-262320-6*) OUP.

— Health Economics Research in Developing Countries. LC 92-49379. (Illus.). 384p. (C). 1993. 59.95 (*0-19-261620-X*) OUP.

Mills, Anne, jt. ed. see Lee, Kenneth.

***Mills, Anthony F.** Basic Heat & Mass Transfer. LC 94-28226. (Heat Transfer Ser.). 928p. (C). 1994. 72.95 (*0-256-16388-X*) Irwin.

— Heat & Mass Transfer. LC 94-146. (Irwin Heat Transfer Ser.). 1280p. (C). 1994. text ed. 89.95 (*0-256-11443-9*) Irwin Prof Pubng.

— Heat Transfer. 888p. (C). 1991. text ed. 69.95 (*0-256-07642-1*, 19-2997-01) Irwin.

***Mills, Antonia.** Eagle Down Is Our Law: Witsuwit'en Law, Feasts, and Land Claims. 256p. 1995. pap. 24.95 (*0-7748-0513-7*) U of Wash Pr.

Mills, Antonia & Slobodin, Richard, eds. Amerindian Rebirth: Reincarnation Belief among North American Indians & Inuit. (Illus.). 240p. 1994. 60.00 (*0-8020-2829-2*); pap. 19.95 (*0-8020-7703-X*) U of Toronto Pr.

Mills, Arlen C. Communicating the Appraisal: Small Residential Income Property Appraisal Report. (Communicating the Appraisal Ser.: No. 4). (Illus.). 150p. 1990. pap. 18.00 (*0-922154-01-5*) Appraisal Inst.

— Communicating the Appraisal: The Individual Condominium or PUD Unit Appraisal Report. 100p. 1988. pap. 18.00 (*0-911780-96-3*) Appraisal Inst.

Mills, Arlen C. & Mills, Dorothy Z. Communicating the Appraisal: The Uniform Residential Appraisal Report. 2nd ed. LC 93-48498. (Orig.). 1994. 25.00 (*0-922154-15-5*) Appraisal Inst.

Mills, Arthur. Management for Technologists. 272p. 1968. 28.00 (*0-8464-1425-2*) Beekman Pubs.

Mills, B. & Redford, A. H. Machinability of Engineering Materials. (Illus.). 200p. 1983. 54.00 (*0-85334-183-4*, Pub. by Elsevier Applied Sci UK) Elsevier.

Mills, Barbara F., ed. see Kanahele, George S.

***Mills, Barbara J. & Crown, Patricia L., eds.** Ceramic Production in the America Southwest. LC 95-8771. 1995. write for info. (*0-8165-1508-5*) U of Ariz Pr.

Mills, Barriss. Domestic Fables. 1971. 8.00 (*0-685-01006-6*) Elizabeth Pr.

— Roughened Roundnesses. 1976. 10.00 (*0-685-79208-0*); pap. 5.00 (*0-685-79209-9*) Elizabeth Pr.

— The Soldier & the Lady. 1975. 16.00 (*0-685-56232-8*); pap. 8.00 (*0-685-56233-6*) Elizabeth Pr.

— The Unheroic Muse. 1978. 20.00 (*0-686-59681-1*); pap. 8.00 (*0-686-59682-X*) Elizabeth Pr.

Mills, Barriss, tr. see Theokritus.

Mills, Bebe A., intro. Ert Moore: Experiences of a Pioneeer Educator. 74p. 1979. lib. bdg. 22.00 (*1-56475-181-3*); fiche write for info. (*1-56475-182-1*) U NV Oral Hist.

Mills, Bert. Budget Auto Restoration. (Illus.). 288p. 1990. pap. 24.95 (*0-87938-405-0*) Motorbooks Intl.

Mills, Betty. Seven Sisters Follow a Star: A P.E.O. Saga As Told Through Paper Dolls. 1987. pap. 8.95 (*0-89672-162-0*) Tex Tech Univ Pr.

Mills, Betty J. Amanda Goes West. LC 83-70168. (Amanda Ser.: Bk. I). (Illus.). 20p. (Orig.). 1983. pap. 5.95 (*0-89672-109-4*) Tex Tech Univ Pr.

— Amanda's Home on the Range. (Amanda Ser.: Bk. 3). (Illus.). 24p. 1984. pap. 6.95 (*0-89672-122-1*) Tex Tech Univ Pr.

— Amanda's New Life. (Amanda Ser.: Bk. 2). (Illus.). 20p. (Orig.). 1983. pap. 5.95 (*0-89672-112-4*) Tex Tech Univ Pr.

— Calico Chronicle: Texas Women & Their Fashions, 1830-1910. LC 84-52249. (Illus.). 192p. 1985. 25.95 (*0-89672-129-9*); pap. 15.95 (*0-89672-128-0*) Tex Tech Univ Pr.

— Flashes of Fashion: Eighteen Thirty to Nineteen Seventy-Two. Webber, Gale, ed. (Illus.). 192p. 1973. 10.00 (*0-911618-02-3*) West Tex Mus.

— Language of Lace. Earnshaw, Pat, ed. 35p. 1984. pap. 5.50 (*0-911618-09-0*) West Tex Mus.

Mills, Billy. Wokini: A Lakota Journey to Happiness & Self-Understanding. 1994. 17.50 (*0-517-59770-5*, Orion Bks) Random.

Mills, Billy, ed. Letters from Barcelona. (C). 1990. 23.00 (*0-948268-71-9*, Pub. by Dedalus Pr IE) St Mut.

Mills, Bronwyn. The Mexican War. Bowman, John, ed. (America at War Ser.). (Illus.). 128p. (YA). (gr. 6-12). 1992. lib. bdg. 17.95 (*0-8160-2393-X*) Facts on File.

— Thomas J. "Stonewall" Jackson. 1994. 8.98 (*0-681-45387-7*) Longmeadow Pr.

Mills, Bruce. Cultural Reformations: Lydia Maria Child & the Literature of Reform. LC 93-33745. 216p. 1994. 30.00 (*0-8203-1638-5*) U of Ga Pr.

Mills, Bruce & Carne, Barbara. A Basic Guide to Horse Care & Management. rev. ed. (Illus.). 304p. 1988. 18.95 (*0-87605-871-3*) Howell Bk.

Mills, Burt. Auto Restoration From Junker to Jewel. LC 79-24680. (Illus.). 291p. 1981. reprint ed. pap. 22.95 (*0-87938-098-5*) Motorbooks Intl.

Mills, C., jt. auth. see Burt, R. O.

Mills, C. A., ed. see Capgrave, John.

Mills, C. F., et al. TEMA Five: Trace Elements in Man & Animals. 977p. (C). 1985. text ed. 94.00 (*0-85198-533-5*) CAB Intl.

Mills, C. P. Industrial Disputes Law in Malaysia. 2nd ed. xl, 392p. 1984. 88.00 (*967-962-000-X*) Butterworth Legal Pubs.

Mills, C. Wright. The Middle Classes in Middle-Sized Cities: The Stratification & Political Position of Small Business & Whit. (Reprint Series in Social Sciences). (C). 1993. reprint ed. pap. text ed. 1.00 (*0-8290-2662-2*, S-198) Irvington.

— Power Elite. 1959. pap. 14.95 (*0-19-500680-1*) OUP.

— Situated Actions & Vocabularies of Motive. (Reprint Series in Sociology). (C). 1993. reprint ed. pap. text ed. 1.90 (*0-8290-2668-1*, S-200) Irvington.

— Sociological Imagination. 1967. reprint ed. pap. 8.95 (*0-19-500751-4*) OUP.

— White Collar: American Middle Classes. 1956. pap. 12.95 (*0-19-500677-1*) OUP.

Mills, C. Wright, jt. auth. see Gerth, Hans.

Mills, C. Wright, tr. see Weber, Max M.

***Mills, Cadman A.** Structural Adjustment in Sub-Saharan Africa. (EDI Policy Seminar Report Ser.: No. 18). 56p. (FRE.). 1989. 6.95 (*0-614-02853-1*, 11337) World Bank.

— Structural Adjustment in Sub-Saharan Africa: Ajustement Structurel en Afrique Subsaharienne. (EDI Policy Seminar Report Ser.). 56p. 1989. 6.95 (*0-8213-1336-3*, 11336) World Bank.

Mills, Cadman A. & Nallari, Raj. Analytical Approaches to Stabilization & Adjustment Programs. (EDI Seminar Paper Ser.: No. 44). 144p. 1992. 9.95 (*0-8213-1943-4*, 11943) World Bank.

Mills, Carl. American Grammar: Sound, Form, & Meaning. (American University Studies: Linguistics: Ser. XIII, Vol. 13). 475.p. (C). 1989. text ed. 67.95 (*0-8204-0952-9*) P Lang Pubs.

Mills, Carol & Mills, John, eds. Australasian Serials: Current Developments in Bibliography. LC 91-24326. (Australian & New Zealand Journal of Serials Librarianship). (Illus.). 93p. 1991. lib. bdg. 24.95 (*1-56024-195-0*) Haworth Pr.

Mills, Carol H., jt. auth. see Powell, Tag.

Mills, Catherine M., et al. Magnetic Resonance Imaging: Atlas of the Head, Neck & Spine. LC 87-29344. 305p. reprint ed. pap. 87.00 (*0-7837-2728-3*, 2043108) Bks Demand.

Mills, Charles. God's Special Promise to Me: A Devotional Book for Early Readers. LC 93-17945. (J). 1993. pap. 7.95 (*0-8163-1147-1*) Pacific Pr Pub Assn.

— The History of Chivalry. LC 78-63507. reprint ed. 32.00 (*0-404-17156-7*) AMS Pr.

— The Master's Touch. LC 93-6802. 1993. pap. 8.95 (*0-8280-0754-3*) Review & Herald.

— My Talents for Jesus; When I Grow Up. LC 92-26393. (J). 1993. pap. 8.95 (*0-8163-1115-3*) Pacific Pr Pub Assn.

— The Secret of Squaw Rock. LC 92-1660. 1992. write for info. (*0-8280-0700-4*) Review & Herald.

— Treasure of the Merrilee. LC 93-6803. 1993. pap. 4.95 (*0-8280-7117-9*) Review & Herald.

— The Tree of Mythology, Its Growth & Fruitage. 1976. lib. bdg. 59.95 (*0-8490-2765-9*) Gordon Pr.

— Voyager. LC 89-32337. 157p. reprint ed. pap. 44.80 (*0-7837-6401-4*, 2046117) Bks Demand.

— Voyager, II. Coffen, Richard, ed. 192p. (Orig.). (J). (gr. 5-8). 1991. pap. 9.95 (*0-8280-0595-8*) Review & Herald.

***Mills, Charles A.** Echoes of Manassas. 98p. 1988. pap. 6.75 (*1-886826-01-3*) Manassas Mus.

Mills, Charles E. The Quality Control Audit: A Management Evaluation Tool. 320p. 1989. text ed. 57.00 (*0-07-042428-4*) McGraw.

Mills, Charles K. Charles C. DeRudio. 1976. 14.95 (*0-8488-0582-8*, J M C & Co) Amereon Ltd.

— Roster of the Seventh Cavalry Campaigns. 1976. 24.95 (*0-8488-0012-5*, J M C & Co) Amereon Ltd.

Mills, Charles K., intro. General Sturgis & Brice's Crossroads: A Short Biography & Service Profile on the 7th Calvalry's Samuel D. Sturgis. (Guidon Monograph Ser.). (Illus.). 1985. 9.00 (*0-685-10875-9*, J M C & Co) Amereon Ltd.

Mills, Charles M. From Dusk to Dawn: Sermons for Lent & Easter: Cycle B Gospel Texts. LC 93-4024. 1993. pap. 7.95 (*1-55673-607-X*, 9332) CSS OH.

Mills, Charles M. & Buchheim, Durwood L. Homiletic Meditations, Cycle B, Vol. 2: Lent Through Ascension of Our Lord, First Reading & Gospel. LC 93-44100. 1994. pap. 14.50 (*1-55673-638-X*) CSS OH.

Mills, Charles P. Meet Your Zoning Hearing Board: A Zoning Handbook & Guide. LC 75-9523. 1975. spiral bd. 4.00 (*0-686-05762-7*) C P Mills.

Mills, Charles W. The Causes of World War Three. LC 75-31436. 172p. 1976. reprint ed. text ed. 49.75 (*0-8371-8513-0*, MICW, Greenwood Pr) Greenwood.

Mills, Charlotte, ed. see Barton, Lois.

Mills, Charlotte, ed. see Davis, Ruth B.

Mills, Charlotte, ed. see Pullen, Virginia A.

Mills, Chester W. New Men of Power: America's Labor Leaders. LC 68-56261. 323p. 1971. reprint ed. 39.50 (*0-678-00715-2*) Kelley.

Mills, Christina, tr. see Randall, Margaret.

Mills, Clark, tr. see Mallarme, Stephane.

Mills, Claudia. After Fifth Grade, the World! LC 88-26664. 128p. (J). (gr. 3-7). 1989. text ed., lib. bdg. 13.95 (*0-02-767041-4*, Mac Bks Young Read) S&S Childrens.

— After Fifth Grade, the World! (J). (gr. 3-7). 1991. reprint ed. pap. 2.95 (*0-380-70894-9*, Camelot) Avon.

— Cally's Enterprise. 128p. (J). (gr. 5 up). 1989. pap. 2.75 (*0-380-70693-8*, Camelot) Avon.

— Dinah for President. LC 91-34839. 128p. (J). (gr. 3-7). 1992. text ed. 13.95 (*0-02-766999-8*, Mac Bks Young Read) S&S Childrens.

— Dinah for President. LC 93-44668. 128p. (J). (gr. 3-7). 1994. pap. 3.95 (*0-689-71854-3*, Aladdin Paperbacks) S&S Childrens.

— Dinah Forever. LC 94-42136. 114p. (J). 1995. 14.00 (*0-374-31788-7*) FS&G.

— Dinah in Love. LC 93-19256. 144p. (J). (gr. 3-7). 1993. text ed. 13.95 (*0-02-766998-X*, Mac Bks Young Read) S&S Childrens.

— Dynamite Dinah. LC 89-13300. 128p. (J). (gr. 3-7). 1990. text ed. 13.95 (*0-02-767101-1*, Mac Bks Young Read) S&S Childrens.

— Dynamite Dinah. LC 91-20651. 128p. (J). (gr. 3-7). 1992. reprint ed. pap. 3.95 (*0-689-71591-9*, Aladdin Paperbacks) S&S Childrens.

— Gus & Grandpa. LC 95-13859. (Illus.). (J). 1996. write for info. (*0-374-32824-2*) FS&G.

— Hannah on Her Way. LC 90-46532. 160p. (J). (gr. 3-7). 1991. text ed. 13.95 (*0-02-767011-2*, Mac Bks Young Read) S&S Childrens.

— Hannah on Her Way. LC 92-42534. 160p. (J). (gr. 3-7). 1993. reprint ed. pap. 3.95 (*0-689-71754-7*, Aladdin Paperbacks) S&S Childrens.

— Phoebe's Parade. LC 93-21861. (Illus.). 32p. (J). (gr. k-3). 1994. text ed. 14.95 (*0-02-767012-0*, Mac Bks Young Read) S&S Childrens.

— Values & Public Policy. 700p. (C). 1991. pap. text ed. 29.50 (*0-15-594711-7*) HB Coll Pubs.

— A Visit to Amy-Claire. LC 91-280. (Illus.). 32p. (J). (gr. k-3). 1992. text ed. 14.95 (*0-02-766991-2*, Mac Bks Young Read) S&S Childrens.

— What about Annie? LC 84-20862. 128p. (J). (gr. 5 up). 1985. 9.95 (*0-8027-6573-4*) Walker & Co.

Mills, Claudia, ed. Values & Public Policy. 1992. pap. 29.50 (*0-317-05235-7*) IPPP.

Mills, Claudia, jt. ed. see Fullinwider, Robert K.

Mills, Claudia, jt. ed. see MacLean, Douglas.

Mills, Colin, jt. ed. see Meek, Margaret.

Mills-Courts, Karen. Poetry As Epitaph: Representation & Poetic Language. LC 89-13533. 352p. 1990. text ed. 42.50 (*0-8071-1568-1*); pap. text ed. 16.95 (*0-8071-1657-2*) La State U Pr.

***Mills, Craig.** King's Quest No. 1: The Floating Castle. 304p. (Orig.). 1995. pap. text ed. 7.99 (*1-57297-009-X*) Blvd Books.

Mills, Crystal S., jt. ed. see Untalan, Faye F.

Mills, D. Salmon in the Sea & New Enhancement Strategies. 1993. 85.00 (*0-85238-199-9*) Blackwell Sci.

Mills, D. & Vevers, G. The Tetra Encyclopedia of Freshwater Tropical Aquarium Fishes. rev. ed. (Illus.). 211p. 31.95 (*3-923880-89-8*, 16060) Tetra Pr.

Mills, D. L. Nonlinear Optics: Basic Concepts. (Illus.). viii, 184p. 1991. 39.50 (*0-387-54192-6*) Spr-Verlag.

Mills, D. M. X-Rays in Materials Analysis Two: Novel Applications & Recent Developments. 1992. 53.00 (*0-8194-0678-3*, 1550) SPIE.

Mills, D. Quinn. Labor-Management Relations. 3rd ed. (Management Ser.). 624p. (C). 1986. Instr's. manual. teacher ed write for info. (*0-07-042422-5*) McGraw.

— Rebirth of the Corporation. 336p. 1992. pap. text ed. 16.95 (*0-471-57919-X*) Wiley.

***Mills, Dale D.** Deliver Us from Squid Roe. LC 94-71494. 176p. (Orig.). 1995. pap. 7.50 (*1-56002-454-2*) Aegina Pr.

Mills, Daniel Q. Empowerment Imperative. 1994. pap. 14.95 (*0-87425-960-6*) Human Res Dev Pr.

— The Empowerment Imperative: Leader's Guide. 1994. ring bd. 75.00 (*0-87425-968-1*) Human Res Dev Pr.

— The Gem Principle: Six Steps to Creating a High Performance Organization. 256p. 1994. 18.00 (*0-939246-75-9*) Oliver Wight.

— Labor-Management Relations. 4th ed. 640p. 1989. text ed. write for info. (*0-07-042429-2*) McGraw.

— Labor-Management Relations. 5th ed. LC 93-21687. (Series in Management). 1993. text ed. write for info. (*0-07-042512-4*) McGraw.

Mills, David. The Idea of Loyalty in Upper Canada, 1784-1850. (Illus.). 256p. (C). 1988. text ed. 44.95 (*0-7735-0660-8*, Pub. by McGill CN) U of Toronto Pr.

— Overcoming Religion. 1980. pap. 3.95 (*0-8065-0742-X*, Citadel Pr) Carol Pub Group.

Mills, David, ed. The Chester Mystery Cycle: A New Edition with Modernised Spelling. (Medieval Texts & Studies: No. 9). 460p. 1992. text ed. 42.00 (*0-937191-29-9*); pap. text ed. 16.95x (*0-937191-27-2*) Colleagues Pr Inc.

— A Dictionary of English Place Names. 424p. 1992. 27.50 (*0-19-869156-4*) OUP.

Mills, David, jt. auth. see Lumiansky, Robert M.

Mills, David, jt. ed. see Lumiansky, Robert M.

Mills, David H., jt. auth. see Fretz, Bruce R.

Mills, Dean. Union on the King's Highway. LC 87-72772. (Campbell-Stone Heritage of Unity Ser.). 188p. 1987. 12.99 (*0-89900-286-2*) College Pr Pub.

Mills, Deanie F. Losers Weepers. 304p. (Orig.). 1994. pap. text ed. 4.99 (*0-515-11461-8*) Jove Pubns.

— Love Me Not. 384p. (Orig.). 1995. pap. text ed. 5.99 (*0-515-11607-6*) Jove Pubns.

Mills, Dennis, jt. ed. see Turner, Michael.

Mills, Derek. Ecology & Management of Atlantic Salmon. (Illus.). 368p. (C). 1989. 65.00 (*0-412-32140-8*, A3418); pap. text ed. 39.95 (*0-412-46020-3*, A6803) Chapman & Hall.

Mills, Derek, jt. auth. see Jeffries, Michael.

Mills, Diana. Crazy Hattie. (Illus.). 12p. (J). (gr. 3-7). 1986. pap. 7.95 (*0-9616555-0-X*) Berry Good Child Bks.

Mills, Dick. Aquarium Fish. LC 93-3155. (Eyewitness Handbks.). (Illus.). 304p. 1993. 29.95 (*1-56458-294-9*); Flexibinding. 17.95 (*1-56458-293-0*) Dorling Kindersley.

— Encyclopedia of the Marine Aquarium. (J). 1988. 12.99 (*0-517-63378-7*) Random Hse Value.

— A Fishkeeper's Guide to Community Fishes. rev. ed. (Illus.). 120p. 1991. 10.95 (*3-923880-52-9*, 16062) Tetra Pr.

— A Fishkeeper's Guide to Marine Fishes. write for info. (*0-318-59670-9*) S&S Trade.

— A Fishkeeper's Guide to the Marine Fishes. rev. ed. (Illus.). 120p. 1991. 10.95 (*3-923880-53-7*, 16064) Tetra Pr.

— A Fishkeeper's Guide to the Tropical Aquarium. rev. ed. (Illus.). 117p. 1991. 10.95 (*3-923880-51-0*, 16061) Tetra Pr.

— The Four Loves. (Orig.). 1983. pap. 0.98 (*0-685-06514-6*, HH-287) Harrison Hse.

— He Spoke & I Was Strengthened. 176p. pap. 4.99 (*0-88368-026-2*) Whitaker Hse.

— He Spoke & I Was Strengthened. rev. ed. 174p. 1973. pap. 6.95 (*0-9629011-0-5*) D Mills Minis.

— How to Have a Happy Marriage. 91p. (Orig.). 1985. pap. 2.95 (*0-89274-381-6*) Harrison Hse.

— Keeping Goldfish. (Illus.). 96p. (Orig.). 1986. pap. 9.95 (*0-7137-1693-2*, Pub. by Blandford Pr UK) Sterling.

— Keeping Goldfish: An Aquarium Guide. rev. ed. (Illus.). 96p. 1991. pap. 9.95 (*0-7137-2250-9*, Pub. by Blandford Pr UK) Sterling.

— Popular Guide to Tropical Aquarium Fish. 1993. 19.95 (*1-56465-109-6*, 16016) Tetra Pr.

— The Tetra Encyclopedia of the Marine Aquarium. (Illus.). 208p. 31.95 (*3-923880-94-4*, 16059) Tetra Pr.

— The Word Daily Devotional. rev. ed. (Student of the Word Ser.). 372p. 1990. pap. 8.95 (*0-89274-804-4*, HH804) Harrison Hse.

— You & Your Aquarium. 1986. pap. 15.00 (*0-394-72985-4*) Knopf.

Mills, Dick, comp. A Popular Guide to Garden Ponds. 1992. 17.95 (*1-56465-104-5*, 16012) Tetra Pr.

***Mills, Dick & Michael, David.** The Messiah & His Hebrew Alphabet. (Orig.). Date not set. pap. 9.95 (*0-9629011-1-3*) D Mills Minis.

Mills, Dixie, jt. auth. see Gardner, Mona J.

Mills, Dixie L., jt. auth. see Gardner, Mona J.

Mills, Donald, tr. see Albertini, Bianca & Bagnoli, Alessandra.

***Mills, Donna R.** Some Southern Balls (& Allied Families) 344p. 1993. lib. bdg. 38.00 (*0-931069-09-2*) Mills Historical.

Mills, Donna R., comp. The First Families of Louisiana Index. LC 92-81054. 105p. 1992. lib. bdg. 17.50 (*0-931069-07-6*) Mills Historical.

— Florida's Unfortunates: The Census, Dependent, Defective, & Delinquent Classes, 1880. LC 92-60783. 112p. 1993. lib. bdg. 19.50 (*0-931069-08-4*) Mills Historical.

Mills, Donna R., ed. Biographical & Historical Memoirs of Natchitoches Parish, Louisana, 1714-1890. LC 85-60815. 122p. 1985. reprint ed. pap. 15.00 (*0-931069-05-X*) Mills Historical.

Mills, Donna R., tr. & comp. Florida's First Families: Translated Abstracts of Pre-1821 Spanish Census. LC 91-6661. 201p. 1992. 22.00 (*0-931069-06-8*) Mills Historical.

Mills, Dorothy. Renaissance & Reformation Times. LC 83-45667. reprint ed. 55.00 (*0-404-19817-1*) AMS Pr.

Mills, Dorothy H. Dictionary for the Mental Health Professional: Psychiatrists, Psychologists. 250p. 1993. 24.95 (*0-8288-1871-1*, S50021) Fr & Eur.

— English & Spanish Dictionary for the Dental Professional. 255p. (ENG & SPA.). 1988. 24.95 (*0-8288-1870-3*, S50376) Fr & Eur.

Mills, Dorothy H., et al. Spanish Vocabulary & Structure for the Health Professional, Bk. 1. 2nd ed. LC 80-54900. (Illus.). 157p. (ENG & SPA.). (C). 1981. pap. text ed. 18.00 (*0-935356-02-9*) Mills Pub Co.

— Survival Spanish. 2nd ed. LC 90-91491. (Illus.). 175p. (Orig.). (ENG & SPA.). 1990. pap. text ed. 18.00 (*0-935356-12-6*) Mills Pub Co.

Mills, Dorothy Z., jt. auth. see Mills, Arlen C.

Mills, E. Andrew, ed. Supervision & Administration: Programs, Positions, Perspectives. (Illus.). 222p. (C). 1991. 20.00 (*0-937652-56-3*) Natl Art Ed.

Mills, E. S. & Nijkamp, Peter, eds. Handbook of Regional & Urban Economics, Vol. 2. 1987. 75.00 (*0-444-87970-6*) Elsevier.

Mills, E. S., jt. auth. see Nijkamp, Peter.

Mills, Earl. Dorothy Dandridge. rev. ed. (Orig.). (J). 1991. pap. 3.95 (*0-87067-580-X*) Holloway.

Mills, Edward D. National Exhibition Centre: Shop Window for the World. (Illus.). 120p. 1976. pap. 19.95 (*0-8464-0667-5*) Beekman Pubs.

Mills, Edward D., ed. Building Maintenance & Preservation: A Guide for Design & Management. 2nd ed. LC 93-45309. (Illus.). 240p. 1994. 74.95 (*0-7506-0900-1*) Buttrwrth-Heinemann.

Mills, Edwin S. The Burden of Government. 188p. 1986. text ed. 23.95 (*0-8179-8281-7*) Hoover Inst Pr.

— Studies in the Structure of the Urban Economy. LC 71-179873. (Resources for the Future Ser.). (Illus.). 162p. 1972. 15.95 (*0-8018-1367-0*); pap. 9.95 (*0-8018-1595-9*) Johns Hopkins.

Mills, Edwin S., ed. Economic Analysis of Environmental Problems: A Conference of the Universities - National Bureau Committee for Economic Research & Resources for the Future. LC 74-82378. 486p. reprint ed. pap. 138.60 (*0-8357-7570-4*, 2056891) Bks Demand.

Mills, Edwin S. & Becker, Charles M. Studies in Indian Urban Development. (World Bank Publication Ser.). 224p. 1986. 29.95 (*0-19-520507-3*) OUP.

Mills, Edwin S. & Byung-Nak Song. Urbanization & Urban Problems. (East Asian Monographs: No. 88). 329p. 1979. 17.50 (*0-674-93133-5*) HUP.

Mills, Edwin S. & Graves, Philip E. Economics of Environmental Quality. 2nd ed. (C). 1986. text ed. 19.95 (*0-393-95270-3*) Norton.

Mills, Edwin S. & Hamilton. Urban Economics. 5th ed. 480p. (C). 1993. text ed. 45.75 (*0-673-46867-4*) HarpCollege.

Mills, Edwin S. & McDonald, John F., eds. Sources of Metropolitan Growth. LC 91-8650. 331p. (C). 1992. 29.95 (*0-88285-135-7*) Ctr Urban Pol Res.

Mills, Edwin S., ed. see Universities-National Bureau Staff.

Mills, Elaine. The Cottage at the End of the Lane. LC 93-45748. (Illus.). 32p. (J). (ps-4). 1994. 15.00 (*0-517-59703-9*) Crown Bks Yng Read.

Mills, Elaine, jt. auth. see Wilkins, Verna A.

Mills, Elaine, jt. auth. see Wilkins, Verna.

Mills, Elaine L., ed. The Papers of John Peabody Harrington in the Smithsonian Institution, 1907-1957: Pt. 3, Southern California-Basin (microfilm w guidebook) 208p. 1986. mic. film (*0-318-60727-1*) Kraus Intl.

— The Papers of John Peabody Harrington in the Smithsonian Institution, 1907-1957: Pt. 3, Southern California-Basin (microfilm w guidebook), Pt. 4: Southwest. 208p. 1986. Pt. 4, Southwest. 2,900.00 (*0-685-13349-4*) Kraus Intl.

Mills, Elizabeth. In the Suzuki Style. LC 74-20230. (Illus.). 120p. 1974. 7.95 (*0-87297-023-X*); pap. 6.95 (*0-87297-024-8*) Diablo.

— Senoufo Phonology, Discourse to Syllable: A Prosodic Approach. LC 81-51057. (Publications in Lingustics: No. 72). 217p. 1984. fiche 12.00 (*0-88312-434-3*) Summer Instit Ling.

Mills, Elizabeth & Murphy, Therese, eds. The Suzuki Concept: An Introduction to a Successful Method for Early Music Education. (Illus.). 220p. 1973. 9.95 (*0-87297-002-7*); pap. 7.95 (*0-87297-003-5*) Diablo.

An Asterisk (*) at the beginning of an entry indicates that the title is appearing in BIP for the first time.

Mills, Elizabeth S., ed. Natchitoches Church Marriages, 1818-1850: Translated Abstracts from the Registers of St. Francois des Natchitoches, Louisiana. LC 84-9654. (Cane River Creole Ser.). vii, 216p. (Orig.). 1985. pap. 20.00 (*0-931069-04-1*) Mills Historical.

Mills, Enos A. Adventures of a Nature Guide & Essays in Interpretation. 2nd ed. Kiley, Enda M. & Goc, Michael J., eds. (Illus.). 248p. 1991. reprint ed. pap. 10.95 (*0-938627-12-0*) New Past Pr.

— The Grizzly. (Illus.). 1976. reprint ed. pap. 4.95 (*0-89174-006-6*) Comstock Edns.

— In Beaver World. LC 90-35730. (Illus.). xlii, 255p. 1990. reprint ed. pap. 9.95 (*0-8032-8172-2*, Bison Books) U of Nebr Pr.

— The Rocky Mountain Wonderland. LC 90-21151. (Illus.). liv, 436p. 1991. reprint ed. pap. 14.95 (*0-8032-8173-0*, Bison Books) U of Nebr Pr.

— The Spell of the Rockies. LC 89-33076. (Illus.). xxxii, 412p. 1989. pap. 11.50 (*0-8032-8163-3*, Bison Books) U of Nebr Pr.

— Wild Life on the Rockies. LC 87-30203. (Illus.). lvi, 317p. 1988. pap. 8.95 (*0-8032-8152-8*) U of Nebr Pr.

— Wild Life on the Rockies. fac. ed. LC 87-30203. (Illus.). 373p. 1988. reprint ed. pap. 106.40 (*0-7837-8105-9*, 2047908) Bks Demand.

Mills, Eric L. Biological Oceanography: An Early History, Eighteen Seventy to Nineteen Sixty. LC 89-33048. (Comstock Book Ser.). (Illus.). 368p. 1989. 51.50x (*0-8014-2340-6*) Cornell U Pr.

Mills, Ernestine, ed. see Shields, Frederic.

Mills, Eugene S. The Story of Elderhostel. LC 92-53864. (Illus.). 216p. 1993. 22.95 (*0-87451-599-8*); pap. 14.95 (*0-87451-600-5*) U Pr of New Eng.

Mills, F. E., jt. ed. see Cline, D. B.

Mills, F. John, ed. see Harding, Richard M.

Mills, Frederick C. The Anatomy of Prices, 1890-1940. (NBER Bulletin Ser.: No. 80). 1940. reprint ed. 20.00 (*0-685-61216-3*) Natl Bur Econ Res.

— Aspects of Manufacturing Operations During Recovery. (NBER Bulletin Ser.: No. 56). 1935. reprint ed. 20.00 (*0-685-61171-X*) Natl Bur Econ Res.

— Aspects of Recent Price Movements. (NBER Bulletin Ser.: No. 48). 1933. reprint ed. 20.00 (*0-685-61158-2*) Natl Bur Econ Res.

— The Behavior of Prices. LC 75-19729. (National Bureau of Economic Research Ser.). (Illus.). 1975. reprint ed. 47.95 (*0-405-07607-X*) Ayer.

— The Behavior of Prices. (General Ser.: No. 11). 598p. 1927. reprint ed. 155.50 (*0-87014-010-8*); reprint ed. mic. film 77.80 (*0-685-61141-8*) Natl Bur Econ Res.

— Changes in Physical Production, Industrial Productivity, & Manufacturing Costs, 1927-1932. (NBER Bulletin Ser.: No. 45). 1993. reprint ed. 20.00 (*0-685-61155-8*) Natl Bur Econ Res.

— Changes in Prices, Manufacturing Costs, & Industrial Productivity, 1929-1934. (NBER Bulletin Ser.: No. 53). 1934. reprint ed. 20.00 (*0-685-61166-3*) Natl Bur Econ Res.

— Contemporary Theories of Unemployment & of Unemployment Relief. LC 68-56670. (Columbia University. Studies in the Social Sciences: No. 93). reprint ed. 24.50 (*0-404-51183-X*) AMS Pr.

— Economic Tendencies in the United States: Aspects of Pre-War & Post-War Changes. LC 75-19727. (National Bureau of Economic Research Ser.). (Illus.). 1975. reprint ed. 54.95 (*0-405-07605-3*) Ayer.

— Economic Tendencies in the United States: Aspects of Pre-War & Post-War Changes. (General Ser.: No. 21). 664p. 1932. reprint ed. 160.00 (*0-87014-020-5*); reprint ed. mic. film 80.00 (*0-685-61153-1*) Natl Bur Econ Res.

— Employment Opportunities in Manufacturing Industries of the United States. (NBER Bulletin Ser.: No. 70). 1938. reprint ed. 20.00 (*0-685-61192-2*) Natl Bur Econ Res.

— Price-Quality Interactions in Business Cycles. LC 75-19728. (National Bureau of Economic Research Ser.). (Illus.). 1975. reprint ed. 19.95 (*0-405-07606-1*) Ayer.

— Price-Quantity Interactions in Business Cycles. (Twenty-Fifth Anniversary Ser.: No. 2). 152p. 1946. reprint ed. 41.10 (*0-87014-114-7*); reprint ed. mic. film 20.60 (*0-685-61263-5*) Natl Bur Econ Res.

— Prices in a War Economy: Some Aspects of the Present Price Structure of the United States. (Occasional Papers: No. 12). 104p. 1943. reprint ed. 27.10 (*0-87014-327-1*); reprint ed. mic. film 20.00 (*0-685-61244-9*) Natl Bur Econ Res.

— Prices in Recession & Recovery: A Survey of Recent Changes. (General Ser.: No. 31). 601p. 1936. reprint ed. 156.30 (*0-87014-030-2*); reprint ed. mic. film 78.20 (*0-685-61174-4*) Natl Bur Econ Res.

— Productivity & Economic Progress. (Occasional Papers: No. 38). 46p. 1952. reprint ed. 20.00 (*0-87014-353-0*) Natl Bur Econ Res.

— The Structure of Postwar Prices. (Occasional Papers: No. 27). 72p. 1948. reprint ed. 20.00 (*0-87014-342-5*); reprint ed. mic. film 20.00 (*0-685-61275-9*) Natl Bur Econ Res.

Mills, Frederick C. & Long, Clarence D. The Statistical Agencies of the Federal Government: A Report to the Commission on Organization of the Executive Branch of the Government. (General Ser.: No. 50). 215p. 1949. reprint ed. 60.40 (*0-87014-049-3*); reprint ed. mic. film 30.20 (*0-685-61276-7*) Natl Bur Econ Res.

Mills, Frederick V., Sr. Bishops by Ballot: An Eighteenth-Century Ecclesiastical Revolution. 1978. 22.95 (*0-19-502411-7*) OUP.

Mills, Fredrick E., ed. Advanced Accelerator Concepts: Proceedings from the International Symposium on Advanced Accelerator Concepts Held in Madison, Wisconsin, August 1986. (AIP Conference Proceedings Ser.: No. 156). 610p. 1987. 75.00 (*0-685-58860-2*) Am Inst Physics.

***Mills, Gareth.** On the Waterfront. 130p. 1994. pap. 30.00 (*1-85902-037-2*, Pub. by Gomer Pr UK) St Mut.

Mills, Gary B. The Forgotten People: Cane River's Creoles of Color. LC 77-452. (Illus.). xxx, 278p. 1977. pap. 11.95 (*0-8071-0287-3*) La State U Pr.

— Southern Loyalists in the Civil War: A Composite Directory of Case Files Created by the U. S. Commissioner of Claims, 1871-1880, Including Those Appealed to the War Claims Committee of the U. S. House of Representatives & the U. S. Court of Claims. 684p. 1994. 45.00 (*0-614-03819-7*, 3847) Genealog Pub.

Mills, Gary K. Quiet Moments Kid's Relaxation: A Guide to the Tape Series for Parents & Teachers. 27p. (Orig.). 1986. pap. 6.00 (*0-938669-07-9*) MediaHlth Pubns.

— Quiet Moments Kid's Relaxation: A Guide to the Tape Series for Parents & Teachers. Set. 27p. (Orig.). 1986. audio 20.00 (*0-938669-12-5*) MediaHlth Pubns.

— Quiet Moments Relaxation: A Guide to Deep Relaxation for Adults. LC 86-16464. (Illus.). 72p. (Orig.). 1986. pap. 10.00 (*0-938669-00-1*); audio 60.00 (*0-938669-11-7*) MediaHlth Pubns.

Mills, Geoffery, jt. ed. see Flinders, David.

Mills, Geoffrey. On the Board? 2nd ed. 256p. 1985. text ed. 24.95 (*0-04-658250-9*) Routledge Chapman & Hall.

Mills, Geoffrey, et al. Modern Office Management. 7th ed. 512p. 1986. pap. text ed. 35.00 (*0-273-02156-7*) Trans-Atl Phila.

Mills, Geoffrey E. A Consumer's Guide to School Improvement. (Trends & Issues Ser.). vi, 25p. (Orig.). 1990. 7.00 (*0-86552-101-8*) U of Oreg ERIC.

Mills, Geoffrey T., ed. see Rockoff, Hugh.

Mills, George. The House Sails Out of Sight of Home. (Samuel French Morse Poetry Prize Ser.). 64p. 1991. pap. text ed. 9.95 (*1-55553-113-X*) NE U Pr.

— A Judge & a Rope & Other Stories of Bygone Iowa. LC 94-27078. 1994. pap. 14.95 (*0-8138-0693-3*) Iowa St U Pr.

— Looking in Windows: Surprising Stories of Old Des Moines. LC 90-45892. (Illus.). 280p. 1991. 16.95 (*0-8138-1573-8*) Iowa St U Pr.

— The People of the Saints. (Illus.). 1967. 5.00 (*0-916537-30-7*, Taylor Museum) CO Springs Fine Arts.

— Rogues & Heroes from Iowa's Amazing Past. (Iowa Heritage Collection Ser.). (Illus.). 252p. 1994. reprint ed. pap. 8.95 (*0-8138-1446-4*) Iowa St U Pr.

Mills, George, jt. auth. see Aitken, John.

Mills, George H. History of the Sixteenth North Carolina Regiment in the Civil War. LC 91-78346. 88p. 1992. reprint ed. pap. 9.95 (*0-9622393-3-X*) Edmonston Pub.

Mills, George R. Go Big Red! The Story of a Nebraska Football Player. (Sport & Society Ser.). (Illus.). 272p. 1991. 19.95 (*0-252-01825-7*) U of Ill Pr.

Mills, George S. The Little Man with the Long Shadow: The Life & Times of Frederick M. Hubbell. LC 88-13117. (Iowa Heritage Collection). (Illus.). 272p. 1988. reprint ed. pap. 7.95 (*0-8138-0242-3*) Iowa St U Pr.

Mills, George T. Navaho Art & Culture. LC 83-5636. (Illus.). 273p. (C). 1983. reprint ed. text ed. 59.75 (*0-313-24008-6*, MINA, Greenwood Pr) Greenwood.

***Mills, Gerald D.** Safe Harbor Regulations. 200p. (Orig.). 1995. pap. 39.95 (*0-07-600782-0*) Hlthcare Mgmt Grp.

Mills, Glen E. Putting a Message Together. 2nd ed. LC 78-179367. Orig. Title: Message Preparation: Analysis & Structure. 1972. pap. 3.95 (*0-672-61299-2*, SC8, Bobbs) Macmillan.

Mills, Gordon & Walter, John. Technical Writing. 5th ed. 576p. (C). 1986. text ed. 32.00 (*0-03-062019-8*) HB Coll Pubs.

Mills, Gregory B. & Palmer, John L., eds. Federal Budget Policy in the Nineteen Eighties: Conference Volume. LC 84-7227. (Changing Domestic Priorities Ser.). 468p. (Orig.). 1984. pap. text ed. 32.50 (*0-87766-336-X*) Urban Inst.

Mills, Gretchen, et al. Discussing Death: A Guide to Death Education. LC 75-17885. 1976. 12.95 (*0-88280-026-4*); pap. 12.95 (*0-88280-027-2*) ETC Pubns.

Mills, H. E., et al. College Women & the Social Sciences. LC 74-152165. (Essay Index Reprint Ser.). 1977. reprint ed. 21.95 (*0-8369-2221-2*) Ayer.

Mills, H. Robert. Practical Astronomy: A User-Friendly Handbook for Skywatchers. (Illus.). 240p. 1994. 29.95 (*1-898563-02-0*) Paul & Co Pubs.

Mills, Harlan D. Software Productivity. LC 88-5099. (Illus.). 288p. 1988. reprint ed. pap. 25.00 (*0-932633-10-2*) Dorset Hse Pub Co.

Mills, Harlan D., et al. Principles of Information Systems Analysis & Design. 1986. text ed. 66.00 (*0-12-497545-3*) Acad Pr.

Mills, Harlow B., et al. A Century of Biological Research. Egerton, Frank N., 3rd, ed. LC 77-74240. (History of Ecology Ser.). (Illus.). 1978. reprint ed. lib. bdg. 17.95 (*0-405-10409-X*) Ayer.

Mills, Harriet C. Intermediate Reader in Modern Chinese, Vol. 1. 1967. pap. 22.95 (*0-8014-9825-2*) Cornell U Pr.

— Intermediate Reader in Modern Chinese, Vol. 3. 1967. pap. 22.95 (*0-8014-9827-9*) Cornell U Pr.

Mills, Heidi & Clyde, Jean A., eds. Portraits of Whole Language Classrooms: Learning for All Ages. LC 89-35937. (Illus.). 307p. (Orig.). 1990. pap. text ed. 21.50 (*0-435-08510-7*) Heinemann.

Mills, Heidi, et al. Looking Closely: Exploring the Role of Phonics in One Whole Language Classroom. (Illus.). 69p. (Orig.). 1992. pap. 11.95 (*0-8141-3031-3*) NCTE.

Mills, Helen. Commanding Sentences. 3rd ed. 378p. 1990. reprint ed. pap. text ed. 22.95 (*0-88133-524-X*) Sheffield WI.

Mills, Henery E. A Treatise Upon the Law of Eminent Domain. lxvii, 404p. 1982. reprint ed. lib. bdg. 35.00 (*0-8377-0841-9*) Rothman.

Mills, Howard. Working with Shakespeare. LC 93-13139. 224p. (C). 1993. lib. bdg. 49.50 (*0-389-21009-9*) B&N Imports.

Mills, Howard, ed. see Crabbe, George.

Mills, Howard, jt. auth. see Ellis, David.

Mills, Hugh L. Low Level Hell: A Scout Pilot in the Big Red One. 1993. mass mkt. 4.99 (*0-440-21549-8*) Dell.

Mills, Hugh L. & Anderson, Robert A. Low-Level Hell: A Scout Pilot in the Big Red One. 1992. 21.95 (*0-89141-433-9*) Presidio Pr.

Mills, J. Pergamon Dictionary of Art. LC 65-19836. 1965. 72.00 (*0-08-011043-6*, Pub. by Pergamon Repr UK) Franklin.

Mills, J. J., jt. auth. see Gorman, Gary E.

***Mills, J. J., et al.** Bliss Bibliographic Classification Class R: Politics & Public Administration. (Bliss Bibliographic Classification). 155p. 1995. 55.00 (*1-85739-077-6*) Bowker-Saur.

— Bliss Bibliographic Classification Class S: Law. (Bliss Bibliographic Classification Ser.). 225p. 1995. 60.00 (*1-85739-067-9*) Bowker-Saur.

Mills, J. R. Principles & Practice of Orthodontics. 2nd ed. LC 87-10291. (Dental Ser.). (Illus.). 294p. 1987. pap. text ed. 69.00 (*0-443-03608-X*) Churchill.

Mills, J. Warner. Mills' Constitutional Annotations: A Compendium of the Law Especially Applicable to State Constitutions, & Adapted to the Constitution of Colorado & Cross-Reference to the Constitutions of Other States. viii, 444p. 1991. lib. bdg. 55.00 (*0-8377-2441-4*) Rothman.

***Mills, Jack & Broughton, Vanda, eds.** Bliss Bibliographic Classification: Class A-AL: Philosophy & Logic. 2nd rev. ed. 56p. 1992. text ed. 65.00 (*1-85739-025-3*) Bowker-Saur.

— Bliss Bibliographic Classification: Class GR-GZ: Applied Biology & Agriculture. 2nd ed. 1992. write for info. (*0-408-70835-2*) Bowker-Saur.

— Bliss Bibliographic Classification: Class H: Anthropology, Human Biology & Life Sciences. 2nd ed. 326p. 1981. text ed. 67.00 (*0-408-70828-X*) Bowker-Saur.

— Bliss Bibliographic Classification: Class I: Psychology & Psychiatry. 62p. 1978. text ed. 35.00 (*0-408-70841-7*) Bowker-Saur.

— Bliss Bibliographic Classification: Class K: Society. 2nd ed. 167p. 1984. text ed. 61.00 (*0-408-70830-1*) Bowker-Saur.

— Bliss Bibliographic Classification: Class P: Religion, the Occult, Morals & Ethics. 2nd ed. 43p. 1977. text ed. 31.00 (*0-408-70832-8*) Bowker-Saur.

— Bliss Bibliographic Classification: Class T: Economics, Management of Economic Enterprises. 2nd ed. 36p. 1977. text ed. 95.00 (*0-408-70834-4*) Bowker-Saur.

— Bliss Bibliographic Classification: Class W: Fine Arts & Music. 2nd ed. 1995. write for info. (*0-408-70838-7*) Bowker-Saur.

— Bliss Bibliographic Classification: Class X-Z: Language & Literature. 2nd ed. 1995. write for info. (*0-408-70839-5*) Bowker-Saur.

— Bliss Bibliographic Classification: Introduction & Auxiliary Schedules. 2nd ed. 268p. 1992. 75.00 (*0-408-70865-4*) Bowker-Saur.

— Bliss Bibliographic Classification: Social Welfare and Criminology. 2nd ed. 200p. 1994. 50.00 (*1-85739-121-7*) Bowker-Saur.

Mills, Jackie. Sirena of Salado. (Illus.). 32p. (J). (gr. 2-7). 1991. 10.95 (*0-9629284-0-2*) Indian Trail.

***Mills, James.** Haywire. 416p. 1995. 23.95 (*0-446-51619-8*) Warner Bks.

— Haywire. 1996. mass mkt. write for info. (*0-446-60296-5*, Warner Vision) Warner Bks.

— The Power. 1990. 21.95 (*0-446-51393-8*) Warner Bks.

— The Power. 1992. mass mkt. 5.99 (*0-446-36127-5*) Warner Bks.

— The Truth about Peter Harley. 272p. 1983. pap. 2.95 (*0-345-29005-4*) Ballantine.

Mills, James D. The Art of Money Making. LC 73-2524. (Big Business; Economic Power in a Free Society Ser.). 1973. reprint ed. 28.95 (*0-405-05103-4*) Ayer.

Mills, James P. The Lhota Nagas. LC 76-44760. reprint ed. 41.50 (*0-404-15869-2*) AMS Pr.

— The Rengma Nagas. LC 76-44761. reprint ed. 59.50 (*0-404-15870-6*) AMS Pr.

Mills, James R. San Diego Where California Began. 5th rev. ed. (Illus.). 84p. 1985. pap. 4.95 (*0-918740-04-5*) San Diego Hist.

Mills, James W. Coping with Stress: A Guide to Living. LC 82-16044. 151p. 1982. pap. text ed. 16.95 (*0-471-87678-X*) Wiley.

Mills, Jane. Womanwords: A Dictionary of Words about Women. 1992. text ed. 24.95 (*0-02-921495-5*) Free Pr.

***Mills, Jane, ed.** Erotic Literature. 1995. pap. 16.00 (*0-06-272036-8*, Harper Ref) HarpC.

— Erotic Literature: Twenty-Four Centuries of Sensual Writing. LC 92-52543. (Illus.). 384p. 1993. 30.00 (*0-06-270057-X*, Harper Ref) HarpC.

Mills, Jane & Smith, Janet. Design Concepts: A Career Primer. (Illus.). 100p. 1984. pap. text ed. 17.50 (*0-87005-498-8*) Fairchild.

Mills, Jane J. First Cap'n General of Liberty Tree. LC 79-90388. 324p. 1979. pap. 5.95 (*0-935344-00-4*) Jupiter Bks.

Mills, Jane L. & Johnson, Larry D. Arnie's Surprise. LC 86-60363. (Search & Find Set Ser.: Level 2). (Illus.). 14p. (Orig.). (J). (ps). 1986. pap. 4.00 (*0-938155-05-9*) Read A Bol.

— Arnie's Surprise, 3 vols., Set. LC 86-60363. (Search & Find Set Ser.: Level 2). (Illus.). 14p. (Orig.). (J). (ps). 1986. pap. 12.00 (*0-685-13523-3*) Read A Bol.

— Build Like Me. LC 86-60362. (Building Set Ser.: Level 2). (Illus.). 13p. (Orig.). (J). (ps). 1986. pap. 4.00 (*0-938155-01-6*) Read A Bol.

— Build Like Me, 3 vols., Set. LC 86-60362. (Building Set Ser.: Level 2). (Illus.). 13p. (Orig.). (J). (ps). 1986. pap. 12.00 (*0-685-13524-1*) Read A Bol.

— Peek-a-Boo. LC 86-60380. (Search & Find Set Ser.: Level 1). (Illus.). 13p. (Orig.). (J). (ps). 1986. pap. 3.50 (*0-938155-04-0*); pap. 12.00 (*0-685-13530-6*) Read A Bol.

Mills, Jane L., jt. auth. see Johnson, Larry D.

Mills, Janet. Free of Dieting Forever. 208p. (Orig.). 1992. mass mkt. 4.99 (*0-446-36275-1*) Warner Bks.

— Free of Dieting Forever: Eight Steps to Achieve & Maintain Your Ideal Weight. 208p. (Orig.). 1991. pap. 9.95 (*1-878424-00-9*) Amber-Allen Pub.

Mills, Janet, ed. & intro. The Power of a Woman: Timeless Thoughts on a Woman's Inner Strengths. LC 93-45653. (Classic Wisdom Collection). 96p. 1994. 12.95 (*1-880032-39-2*) New Wrld Lib.

***Mills, Jason & Paradis, Adrian A.** Partnership for Excellence, 1969-1994: The History of EHV-Weidmann Industries, Inc. LC 94-39419. (Illus.). 120p. 1995. 30.00 (*0-914659-72-3*) Phoenix Pub.

Mills, Jean & Mills, Richard W., eds. Primary School People: Getting to Know Your Colleagues. LC 94-20730. 1995. write for info. (*0-415-11396-2*, Routledge NY) Routledge.

Mills, Jean, jt. ed. see Mills, Richard W.

Mills, Jeffrey P. Electromagnetic Interference Reduction in Electronic System. 350p. 1993. text ed. 57.00 (*0-13-463902-2*) P-H.

Mills, Jerry & Mitchell, Roy. General Chemistry Experiments. 2nd ed. (Illus.). 208p. (C). 1987. 21.95x (*0-89582-162-1*) Morton Pub.

Mills, Jerry L. Chemistry. 5th ed. 1993. Student Solutions Manual. pap. text ed. write for info. (*0-07-011004-2*) McGraw.

Mills, Jerry L. & Hampton, Michael D. Microscale & Macroscale Experiments for General Chemistry. 1991. pap. text ed. write for info. (*0-07-042442-X*) McGraw.

— Microscale Experiments for General Chemistry. 2nd ed. 1991. pap. text ed. write for info. (*0-07-042447-0*) McGraw.

Mills, Jerry L., jt. ed. see Rubin, Louis D., Jr.

Mills, Jo A. Command the Morning. 1989. pap. 6.25 (*0-89137-453-1*) Quality Pubns.

Mills, Jo Ann. Leaves Only. 1988. pap. 6.25 (*0-89137-447-7*) Quality Pubns.

— Making It. 1986. pap. 6.25 (*0-89137-439-6*) Quality Pubns.

Mills, Joe. A Mountain Boyhood. LC 87-30202. (Illus.). lvi, 311p. 1988. pap. 9.95 (*0-8032-8154-4*) U of Nebr Pr.

Mills, Joey. New Classic Beauty: A Step-by-Step Guide to Naturally Glamorous Makeup. LC 87-40185. 144p. 1987. 19.95 (*0-394-56433-2*, Villard Bks) Random.

Mills, John. Basketball Handbook. (Illus.). 65p. pap. 8.95 (*0-88839-042-4*) Hancock House.

— The Encyclopedia of Sculpture Techniques. (Illus.). 240p. 1990. 35.00 (*0-8230-1609-9*, Watsn-Guptill) Watsn-Guptill.

— Lizard in the Grass. 256p. (C). 1980. pap. text ed. 3.00 (*0-920802-26-5*, Pub. by ECW Press CN) Genl Dist Srvs.

— Robertson Davies & His Works. (Canadian Author Studies). 58p. (C). 1985. pap. text ed. 9.95 (*0-920802-65-6*, Pub. by ECW Press CN) Genl Dist Srvs.

— The Technique of Casting for Sculpture. (Illus.). 176p. 1990. 55.00 (*0-7134-6157-8*, Pub. by Batsford UK) Trafalgar.

— Three Months' Residence at Nablus: And an Account of the Modern Samaritans. LC 77-87610. reprint ed. 25.50 (*0-404-16434-X*) AMS Pr.

— Traction on the Grand. (Illus.). 96p. 10.00 (*0-317-05882-7*, Pub. by Boston Mills Pr CN) Genl Dist Srvs.

Mills, John & Corey, Lawrence, eds. Antiviral Chemotherapy: New Directions for Clinical Applications & Research, Vol. 3. LC 93-19985. (Illus.). 464p. (C). 1993. Alk. paper. text ed. 155.00 (*0-13-050717-2*) P-H.

Mills, John, jt. auth. see Branan, Carl.

Mills, John, jt. ed. see Mills, Carol.

Mills, John A. Arthritis: Diseases & Treatment, 3 vols., Set. 3rd ed. Incl. Bk. 2. Arthritis. 1977. pap. text ed. 18.50 (*0-89147-050-6*); Bk. 3. Anti-Inflammatory Therapy. (Illus.). 1977. pap. text ed. 16.50 (*0-89147-051-4*); 1977. Set pap. text ed. 48.00 (*0-89147-048-4*) CAS.

— Hamlet on Stage: The Great Tradition. LC 84-22461. (Contributions in Drama & Theatre Studies: No. 15). (Illus.). xv, 304p. 1985. text ed. 55.00 (*0-313-24660-2*, MIH/, Greenwood Pr) Greenwood.

— Language & Laughter: Comic Diction in the Plays of Bernard Shaw. LC 68-9339. 192p. reprint ed. pap. 54.80 (*0-317-26802-3*, 2024319) Bks Demand.

Mills, John F. Art for Our Children: A "Hands-off" Guide. 1991. pap. 16.95 (*0-86327-287-8*) Dufour.

— Top Knocker. 200p. (Orig.). 1990. pap. 9.95 (*0-86327-280-0*, Pub. by Wolfhound Pr IE) Dufour.

— Top Knockers. 210p. 1990. 24.95 (*0-86327-260-6*, Pub. by Wolfhound Pr IE) Dufour.

Mills, John M. Canadian Coastal & Inland Steam Vessels, 1809-1930. LC 79-91504. 135p. 1979. 28.00 (*0-913423-01-7*) Steamship Hist Soc.

Mills, John S. & White, Raymond. The Organic Chemistry of Museum Objects. 2nd ed. LC 93-32082. (Series in Conservation & Museology). 206p. 1994. 59.95 (*0-7506-1693-8*) Buttrwrth-Heinemann.

M

Mills, Joseph A. Father, I Give This Day to You: A Collection of Meditations & Commentaries. Battle, Stafford, ed. LC 90-91700. 87p. (Orig.). 1990. pap. text ed. 8.95 (*0-943454-08-5*) Jotarian.

— Goin' Off. 68p. (Orig.). 1982. pap. text ed. 5.25 (*0-943454-01-8*) Jotarian.

— When Love Speaks, Are You Listening? (Illus.). 100p. 1985. pap. 7.95 (*0-943454-02-6*) Jotarian.

Mills, Joy. One Hundred Years of Theosophy. 245p. (Orig.). 1987. pap. 9.95 (*0-8356-0235-4*, Quest) Theos Pub Hse.

Mills, Joy, ed. see Blavatsky, H. P.

Mills, Joyce, ed. see Nanji, Aisha.

Mills, Joyce C. Gentle Willow: A Story for Children about Dying. LC 93-22770. (Illus.). 32p. (J). (ps-3). 1993. 16.95 (*0-945354-54-1*); pap. 8.95 (*0-945354-53-3*) Magination Pr.

— Gentle Willow: A Story For Children about Dying. LC 93-38212. (J). (gr. 2 up). 1994. 17.27 (*0-8368-1070-8*) Gareth Stevens Inc.

— Little Tree: A Story for Children with Serious Medical Problems. LC 92-19654. (Illus.). 32p. (J). 1992. 16.95 (*0-945354-52-5*); pap. 8.95 (*0-945354-51-7*) Magination Pr.

— Stories of the Dreamwalkers. (Illus.). 48p. 1989. 48.95 (*0-944082-01-7*) Santa Fe Fine Art.

— Stories of the Dreamwalkers: Storyteller Edition. (Illus.). 48p. 1990. reprint ed. 48.00 (*0-944082-02-5*) Santa Fe Fine Art.

Mills, Joyce C. & Crowley, Richard J. Sammy the Elephant & Mr. Camel: A Story to Help Children Overcome Bedwetting While Discovering Self-Appreciation. LC 88-13581. (Illus.). 48p. (J). (gr. 1 up). 1988. pap. 16.95 (*0-945354-09-6*); pap. 8.95 (*0-945354-08-8*) Magination Pr.

— Therapeutic Metaphors for Children & the Child Within. LC 86-9700. 288p. 1986. 28.95 (*0-87630-429-3*); audio 14.95 (*0-87630-459-5*) Brunner-Mazel.

Mills, Joyce H., jt. auth. see Mills, Watson E.

Mills, Judy & Dombre, Irene. University of Toronto Doctoral Theses, 1897-1967: A Bibliography. LC 75-354611. 197p. reprint ed. pap. 56.20 (*0-317-41719-3*, 2055822) Bks Demand.

Mills, Juliet. Mind, Body & Soul in Balance. 1993. pap. 10.00 (*1-879371-45-6*) Pub Mills.

Mills, K. B. & Cronly, Dillon J., eds. Glaucoma: Proceedings of the Fourth International Symposium of the Northern Eye Institute, Manchester, U. K., 14-16 July 1988. LC 89-3964. (Vision & Visual Health Care Ser.: Vol. 4). (Illus.). 265p. 1989. 112.00 (*0-08-036150-1*, Pub. by Pergamon Repr UK) Franklin.

Mills, K. C. Review of ECSC Funded Research on Mould Powders, No. EUR 13177. 92p. 1991. pap. 12.00 (*92-826-0461-6*, CD-NA-13177-EN-C, Pub. by Europ Com) UNIPUB.

— Thermodynamic Data for Inorganic Sulphides, Selenides & Tellurides. LC 74-173939. 855p. reprint ed. pap. 180.00 (*0-317-08901-3*, 2051842) Bks Demand.

Mills, K. C., et al. Effect of Low Levels of Calcium on Weld Penetration. (EUR Ser.: No. 13962). 82p. 1993. pap. 13.00 (*92-826-4290-9*, CG-NA-13962-EN-C, Pub. by Europ Com) UNIPUB.

Mills, Katherine H., jt. auth. see Kilmann, Peter R.

Mills, Kathi. A Moment a Day: Practical Devotions for Today's Busy Women. LC 88-4360. 200p. 1988. pap. 7.99 (*0-318-32761-9*, 5419516) Regal.

Mills, Kathi, ed. see Briscoe, Jill & Briscoe, Stuart.

Mills, Kathi, ed. see Dobson, James.

Mills, Kathi, jt. auth. see Galloway, Dale.

Mills, Kathi, ed. see Getz, Gene & Getz, Elaine.

Mills, Kathi, jt. auth. see Grier, Rosey.

Mills, Kathi, ed. see Wright, H. Norman.

Mills, Kathleen, ed. see Brentano, Robyn & Georgia, Olivia.

***Mills, Kay.** From Pocahontas to Power Suits: Everything You Need to Know about Women's History in America. LC 94-34521. 272p. (Orig.). 1995. pap. 10.95 (*0-452-27152-5*, Plume) NAL-Dutton.

— A Place in the News: From the Women's Pages to the Front Page. (Illus.). 384p. 1990. text ed. 39.50 (*0-231-07416-6*); pap. text ed. 16.50 (*0-231-07417-4*) Col U Pr.

— This Little Light of Mine: The Life of Fannie Lou Hamer. LC 92-19713. 1993. 24.00 (*0-525-93501-0*) NAL-Dutton.

— This Little Light of Mine: The Life of Fannie Lou Hamer. (Illus.). 400p. 1994. pap. 12.95 (*0-452-27052-9*, Plume) NAL-Dutton.

Mills, Keith. Mountain Biking. 128p. 1989. pap. 15.95 (*0-8117-2315-1*) Stackpole.

Mills, Ken. A New Way to Fly: An Alternative Way to Achieve Freedom from Alcohol & Drugs. LC 87-60845. 184p. (Orig.). 1987. pap. text ed. 6.95 (*0-942267-00-1*) Profile Press.

Mills, Ken & Keith-Smith, Brian, eds. Georg Buchner - Tradition & Innovation: Fourteen Essays. LC 92-8268. (Bristol German Publications: Vol. 1). 276p. 1992. reprint ed. lib. bdg. 89.95 (*0-7734-1334-0*) E Mellen.

***Mills, Kenneth.** Applied Visual Merchandising. 3rd ed. 256p. 1994. text ed. 48.75 (*0-13-041989-3*) P-H.

Mills, Kenneth, et al. A Color Atlas of Low Back Pain. (Illus.). 92p. 1990. text ed. 39.00 (*0-8036-9858-5*) Davis Co.

Mills, Kenneth G. Anticipations. (Illus.). 141p. 1980. 17.95 (*0-919842-07-0*, KGOB5) Sun-Scape Ent.

— The Beauty Unfoldment: A Spontaneous Unfoldment. 1977. audio, pap. 10.95 (*0-919842-50-X*, KGOM3) Sun-Scape Ent.

— Embellishments. (Illus.). 150p. 1986. 17.95 (*0-919842-08-9*, KGOB6) Sun-Scape Ent.

— Freedom Is Found: A Spontaneous Unfoldment. 1991. pap. 10.95 (*0-919842-12-7*, KGOC30) Sun-Scape Ent.

— Given to Praise! An Array of Provocative Metaphysical-Philosophical Utterances. (Illus.). 152p. 1976. 17.95 (*0-919842-00-3*, KGOB1); lp 16.99 (*0-685-93126-9*, KBOM2) Sun-Scape Ent.

— The Golden Nail. (Illus.). 432p. (Orig.). 1993. pap. 29.95 (*0-919842-13-5*, KGOB9) Sun-Scape Ent.

— The Key: Identity. Limper, Mary G. & Brodie, Barry, eds. 432p. (Orig.). 1994. pap. 29.95 (*0-919842-16-X*, KGOB10) Sun-Scape Ent.

— The Key: Identity. Limper, Mary G. & Brodie, Barry, eds. (Illus.). 432p. (Orig.). 1994. 39.95 (*0-919842-18-6*, KGOB11) Sun-Scape Ent.

— Near to the Fire: A Spontaneous Unfoldment. 1979. pap. 10.95 (*0-919842-04-6*, KGOM11); audio (*0-318-55888-2*) Sun-Scape Ent.

— The New Land! Conscious Experience Beyond Horizons. (Illus.). 77p. 1978. pap. 8.95 (*0-919842-01-1*, KGOB2) Sun-Scape Ent.

— The Newness of the Unchanging: A Spontaneous Unfoldment, Set. 1978. audio, pap. 10.95 (*0-919842-02-X*, KGOM5) Sun-Scape Ent.

— Quickening Spirit of Radiance: A Spontaneous Unfoldment. 1990. audio 10.95 (*0-919842-10-0*, KGOC29) Sun-Scape Ent.

— The Seal of Approval: A Spontaneous Unfoldment. 1979. audio 10.95 (*0-919842-03-8*, KGOM9) Sun-Scape Ent.

— Surprises. (Illus.). 135p. 1980. 17.95 (*0-919842-06-2*, KGOB4) Sun-Scape Ent.

— Tyranny of Love. Leaper, Mary J. & MacQueen, Megan, eds. (Illus.). 432p. (Orig.). 1995. pap. 29.95 (*0-919842-17-8*) Sun-Scape Ent.

— A Word Fitly Spoken. (Illus.). 211p. 1980. 17.95 (*0-686-64679-7*, KGOB3); pap. 17.95 (*0-919842-05-4*) Sun-Scape Ent.

— Words of Adjustment. (Illus.). 130p. (Orig.). 1992. pap. 13.95 (*0-919842-09-7*, KGOB7) Sun-Scape Ent.

Mills, Kenneth H. & Paul, Judith E. Applied Visual Merchandising. (Illus.). 320p. (C). 1982. pap. text ed. write for info. (*0-13-043331-4*) P-H.

Mills, Kirk M. Kirk's Directory of California Golf. (Illus.). 1990. 11.95 (*0-9627273-0-X*) Mills & Assocs.

Mills, L., jt. auth. see Ibach, Harald.

Mills, L. E., ed. see Mac Farlane, Muriel.

Mills, L. H., jt. auth. see Darmesteter, James.

Mills, Larry W. & McDowell, Danny B. The Business Game. (C). 1987. 20.25 (*0-673-39026-8*) HarpCollege.

***Mills, Lauren.** The Dog Prince. LC 95-5302. (Illus.). (J). 1996. 15.95 (*0-316-57417-1*) Little.

— Fairy Wings. LC 92-37168. (J). 1995. 15.95 (*0-316-57397-3*) Little.

— The Rag Coat. (Illus.). (J). (ps-3). 1991. 15.95 (*0-316-57407-4*) Little.

Mills, Lauren, ret. Tatterhood & the Hobgoblins: A Norwegian Folktale, Vol. 1. (Illus.). (J). (ps-3). 1993. 15.95 (*0-316-57406-6*) Little.

Mills, Lawrence H. Avesta Eschatology: Compared with the Books of Daniel & Revelations. LC 74-24644. reprint ed. 29.50 (*0-404-12816-5*) AMS Pr.

— Dictionary of the Gathic Language of the Zend Avesta. LC 74-21253. (GAE.). reprint ed. 72.50 (*0-404-12804-1*) AMS Pr.

— Our Own Religion in Ancient Persia. LC 74-21262. reprint ed. 62.50 (*0-404-12811-4*) AMS Pr.

— Zarathushtra, Philo, the Achaemenids & Israel. LC 74-21261. reprint ed. 49.50 (*0-404-12815-7*) AMS Pr.

Mills, Lawrence H., ed. A Study of the Five Zarathushtrian (Zoroastrian) Gathas, 4 pts. in 1 vol., Pts. I-IV. LC 74-21252. reprint ed. 110.00 (*0-404-12803-3*) AMS Pr.

Mills, Lennox A. Southeast Asia: Illusion & Reality in Politics & Economics. LC 64-17805. 373p. reprint ed. pap. 106.40 (*0-8357-7030-3*, 2033271) Bks Demand.

Mills, Lenox A. Ceylon under British Rule, 1795-1932. 311p. 1964. 30.00 (*0-7146-2019-X*, Pub. by F Cass Pubs UK) Intl Spec Bk.

Mills, Letha. Little Rock: A Contemporary Portrait. 168p. 1990. 29.95 (*0-89781-290-5*) Preferred Mktg.

Mills, Liston M. Pastoral Theologian of the Year: Seward Heltner; Special Issue of Pastoral Psychology, Vol. 29, No. 1, No. 1. LC 80-82467. 112p. 1981. pap. 16.95 (*0-89885-068-1*) Human Sci Pr.

Mills, Louise, ed. see Haaland, Lynn.

Mills, Lynn, jt. auth. see Gibson, Rebecca.

Mills, M. & Standingford, S. Modern Office Management. 496p. (C). 1986. 130.00 (*0-685-39842-0*, Inst Pur & Supply) St Mut.

Mills, M. G. Kalahari Hyenas: Mammals. 288p. 1989. text ed. 75.00 (*0-04-445328-0*); pap. 21.95 (*0-04-445329-9*) Routledge Chapman & Hall.

Mills, Maldwyn, ed. Six Middle English Romances: The Sege of Melayne, Emare, Octavian, Sir Isumbras, Sir Gowther, Sir Amadace. 256p. 1993. pap. 9.95 (*0-460-87225-7*, Everyman's Classic Lib) C E Tuttle.

Mills, Maldwyn, intro. Yvain & Gawain, Sir Percyvell, The Anturs of Arthur. 256p. 1992. pap. text ed. 10.95 (*0-460-87077-7*, Everyman's Classic Lib) C E Tuttle.

Mills, Maldwyn, ed. see Chaucer, Geoffrey.

Mills, Maldwyn, et al, eds. Romance in Medieval England. 236p. (C). 1991. text ed. 71.00 (*0-85991-326-0*) Boydell & Brewer.

Mills, Margaret A. Oral Narrative in Afghanistan: The Individual in Tradition. Lord, Albert B., ed. LC 90-2960. (Folklore & Oral Tradition Ser.). 288p. 1990. lib. bdg. 98.00 (*0-8240-2871-6*) Garland.

— Rhetorics & Politics in Afghan Traditional Storytelling. LC 90-22019. (Publications of the American Folklore Society, Bibliographical & Special Ser.). 408p. (C). 1991. text ed. 33.95 (*0-8122-8199-3*) U of Pa Pr.

Mills, Margaret H., ed. Topics in Colloquial Russian. LC 90-20776. (American University Studies: Slavic Languages & Literature: Ser. XII, Vol. 11). 203p. (C). 1991. text ed. 36.95 (*0-8204-1251-1*) P Lang Pubs.

***Mills, Margie B. & Morrison, Carlton A.** Homebound: The Happy/Sad, Funny/Grim, Human Story of Homebound Patients & the Medical Professionals & Paraprofessionals Who Take Care of Them. LC 94-44405. 1994. write for info. (*0-86554-474-3*) Mercer Univ Pr.

Mills, Marlene C. Adolescent Self-Disclosure: Its Facilitation Through Themes, Therapeutic Techniques & Interview Conditions. LC 84-47529. (American University Studies: Psychology: Ser. VIII, Vol. 3). 198p. (C). 1985. text ed. 23.50 (*0-8204-0115-3*) P Lang Pubs.

Mills, Merope. Imaginative Brushwork. (Illus.). 96p. 1993. 20.00 (*1-86351-089-3*, Pub. by S Milner AT) Sterling.

— Imaginative Brushwork. (Milner Craft Ser.). (Illus.). 78p. 1995. pap. 14.95 (*1-86351-155-5*, Pub. by S Milner AT) Sterling.

Mills, Michael. David, Lion & Lamb. Sherer, Michael L., ed. (Orig.). 1988. pap. 7.10 (*1-55673-029-2*, 8814) CSS OH.

— Dirty Hands, Pure Hearts. 1985. 4.75 (*0-89536-724-6*, 5808) CSS OH.

Mills, Michael & Schiff, William. The Active Eye. 150p. 1989. student ed, pap. 10.00 (*1-56321-031-2*); vhs write for info. (*1-56321-034-7*); disk 99.00 (*1-56321-030-4*) L Erlbaum Assocs.

— The Active Eye, Set. 150p. 1989. pap. 750.00 (*1-56321-033-9*); pap. 99.00 (*1-56321-032-0*) L Erlbaum Assocs.

Mills, Michael P. Prevention, Health, & British Politics. 200p. 1993. 55.95 (*1-85628-190-6*, Pub. by Avebury Pub UK) Ashgate Pub Co.

Mills, Mike. The Politics of Dietary Change. 160p. 1992. text ed. 58.95 (*1-85521-226-9*, Pub. by Dartmth Pub UK) Ashgate Pub Co.

Mills, Miriam. Alternative Dispute Resolution in the Public Sector. (Political Science Ser.). 300p. 1991. 28.95 (*0-8304-1258-1*) Nelson-Hall.

Mills, Miriam, ed. Alternate Dispute Resolution & Public Policy. (Orig.). 1988. pap. 12.00 (*0-944285-01-5*) Pol Studies.

Mills, Miriam, jt. ed. see Blank, Robert.

Mills, Miriam, jt. auth. see Nagel, Stuart.

Mills, Miriam K., ed. Conflict: Resolution & Public Policy. LC 90-36780. (Contributions in Political Science Ser.: No. 262). 232p. 1990. text ed. 55.00 (*0-313-27519-X*, MRG, Greenwood Pr) Greenwood.

Mills, Miriam K. & Blank, Robert H., eds. Health Insurance & Public Policy: Risk, Allocation, & Equity. LC 91-43370. (Contributions in Political Science Ser.: No. 299). 252p. 1992. text ed. 55.00 (*0-313-28465-2*, MHX/, Greenwood Pr) Greenwood.

Mills, Miriam K. & Nagel, Stuart S., eds. Public Administration in China. LC 92-42675. (Contributions in Political Science Ser.: No. 323). 184p. 1993. text ed. 55.00 (*0-313-28847-X*, GM8847, Greenwood Pr) Greenwood.

Mills, Miriam K., jt. ed. see Blank, Robert H.

Mills, Miriam K., jt. auth. see Nagel, Stuart S.

Mills, Miriam K., jt. ed. see Nagel, Stuart S.

Mills, Mona. Horses & Other Animals. (How to Draw & Paint Ser.). (Illus.). 32p. (Orig.). 1989. pap. 5.95 (*0-929261-82-8*, HT165) W Foster Pub.

— Landscapes in Oil, No. 2. (How to Draw & Paint Ser.). (Illus.). 32p. (Orig.). 1989. pap. 5.95 (*0-929261-39-9*, HT167) W Foster Pub.

Mills, N. J. Plastics: Microstructure Properties & Applications. 2nd ed. 377p. 1994. pap. text ed. 52.95 (*0-470-22132-1*) Halsted Pr.

Mills, Nicolaus. Arguing Immigration. 1994. pap. 12.00 (*0-671-89558-3*, Touchstone Bks) S&S Trade.

— Crowd in American Literature. LC 86-3014. ix, 146p. 1986. text ed. 25.00 (*0-8071-1286-0*) La State U Pr.

— Legacy of Dissent. 1994. pap. 16.00 (*0-671-88879-X*, Touchstone Bks) S&S Trade.

— Like a Holy Crusade: Mississippi 1964 - the Turning of the Civil Rights Movement in America. 224p. 1992. 22.50 (*0-929587-96-0*) I R Dee.

— Like a Holy Crusade: Mississippi, 1964 - The Turning of the Civil Rights Movement in America. LC 93-11246. 228p. 1993. reprint ed. pap. 9.95 (*1-56663-026-6*) I R Dee.

Mills, Nicolaus, ed. Culture in an Age of Money: The Legacy of the 1980s in America. (Illus.). 256p. 1990. 22.50 (*0-929587-35-9*) I R Dee.

— Culture in an Age of Money: The Legacy of the 1980s in America. (Illus.). 256p. 1991. reprint ed. pap. 12.95 (*0-929587-71-5*, Elephant Paperbacks) I R Dee.

Mills, Nicolaus, intro. Debating Affirmative Action: Race, Gender, Ethnicity, & the Politics of Inclusion. LC 93-23253. 1994. 10.95 (*0-385-31221-0*, Delta) Dell.

Mills Novelty Company Staff. The Anatomy of a Vintage Slot Machine. Post, Dan R., ed. LC 74-26383. 48p. 1978. 12.95 (*0-911160-60-4*) Post Group.

***Mills, P.** God's World. (Chunky Pop up Book Ser.). (J). (ps). 1993. 3.99 (*0-7814-1513-6*) Cook.

— Mi Dia (My Day) (Figuras Que Aparecen (A Chunky Pop-up Bk.)). (SPA.). (J). Date not set. 3.50 (*1-56063-631-9*, 494604) Editorial Unilit.

— El Mundos De Dios (God's World) (Figuras Que Aparecen (Chunky Pop-up Bk.)). (SPA.). (J). Date not set. 3.50 (*1-56063-632-7*, 494606) Editorial Unilit.

— My Day. (Chunky Pop up Book Ser.). (J). (ps). 1993. 3.99 (*0-7814-1514-4*) Cook.

Mills, P., jt. auth. see McGrath, Philomena.

Mills, Pamela. DOS for WordPerfect Users. 1993. pap. 11.95 (*1-56052-216-X*) Crisp Pubns.

Mills, Pat & O'Neill, Kevin. Marshal Law: Blood Sweat & Fears Collection. (Illus.). 168p. 1993. pap. 15.95 (*1-878574-95-7*) Dark Horse Comics.

***Mills, Patricia.** On an Island in the Bay. LC 94-21533. (Illus.). 32p. (J). (gr. k-3). 1994. 14.95 (*1-55858-333-5*); lib. bdg. 14.88 (*1-55858-334-3*) North-South Bks NYC.

— Until the Cows Come Home. LC 92-31049. (Illus.). 32p. (J). (gr. k-3). 1993. 14.95 (*1-55858-190-1*); lib. bdg. 14.88 (*1-55858-191-X*) North-South Bks NYC.

Mills, Patricia J. Woman, Nature, & Psyche. LC 87-10408. 266p. 1987. 32.00 (*0-300-03537-3*) Yale U Pr.

Mills, Patrick L., jt. ed. see Dudukovic, Milorad P.

Mills, Patti A., tr. see Del Castillo, Diego.

Mills, Paul. The New Figurative Art of David Park. LC 89-7066. (Illus.). 128p. (C). 1989. reprint ed. lib. bdg. 47.00x (*0-8095-4069-X*) Borgo Pr.

Mills, Paul C. The New Figurative Art of David Park. LC 88-30247. (Illus.). 128p. 1989. 19.50 (*0-88496-295-4*) Capra Pr.

Mills, Perry, ed. see Shakespeare, William.

Mills, Perry F. Simply Cinema. 272p. 1989. per. 29.95 (*0-8403-5298-0*) Kendall-Hunt.

Mills, Peter. Daniel's Adventure with the Lions. (Bible Flap Bks.). 24p. (J). 1994. 7.95 (*0-687-10084-4*) Abingdon.

— David's Adventure with the Giant: (Bible Flap Book) (Illus.). 24p. (J). 1994. 7.95 (*0-687-10278-2*) Abingdon.

— Jonah's Adventure with the Big Fish: Bible Adventures. (Illus.). (J). 1991. bds. 8.99 (*0-8007-7121-4*) Revell.

Mills, Peter G. Blowout Prevention: Theory & Applications. LC 84-4507. (Illus.). 193p. 1984. 40.00 (*0-934634-78-5*) Intl Human Res.

— Deviated Drilling. LC 85-19731. (Illus.). 208p. 1986. text ed. 50.00 (*0-88746-063-1*) Intl Human Res.

Mills, Quinn D. Rebirth of the Corporation. 320p. 1991. text ed. 24.95 (*0-471-52220-1*) Wiley.

Mills, R. & Lobo, V. M. Self-Delusion in Electrolyte Solutions: A Critical Examination of Data Compiled from the Literature. (Physical Sciences Data Ser.: No. 36). 354p. 1989. 141.00 (*0-444-87288-4*) Elsevier.

Mills, R., jt. auth. see Stokes, R. H.

Mills, R. L. Propagators for Many-Particle Systems. 140p. 1969. text ed. 136.00 (*0-677-02040-6*) Gordon & Breach.

Mills, R. P. & Heijl, A., eds. Perimetry Update, 1990-1991. LC 91-14629. (Illus.). 585p. 1991. lib. bdg. 150.00 (*90-6299-075-4*, Pub. by Kugler NE) Kugler Pubns.

Mills, R. W. & Stiles, J. Finance for the General Manager: An Overview of Key Financial Principles & Perspectives. LC 93-44836. (Henley Management Ser.). 1994. write for info. (*0-07-707960-4*) McGraw.

Mills, Ralph J., Jr. Cry of the Human: Essays on Contemporary American Poetry. LC 74-14507. 295p. reprint ed. pap. 84.10 (*0-8357-9667-1*, 2019013) Bks Demand.

— Each Branch. 117p. 1987. 11.95 (*0-933180-89-6*) Spoon Riv Poetry.

— For a Day. 36p. 1985. pap. 3.00 (*0-933180-69-1*) Spoon Riv Poetry.

Mills, Ralph J. Living with Distance. (American Poets Continuum Ser.: No. 3). 1979. 18.00 (*0-918526-17-5*); pap. 10.00 (*0-918526-18-3*) BOA Edns.

Mills, Ralph J., Jr. A Man to His Shadow. (Juniper Bk. Ser.: No. 14). 1973. pap. 5.00 (*1-55780-013-8*) Juniper Pr WI.

Mills, Ralph J. Richard Eberhart. LC 66-63487. (University of Minnesota Pamphlets on American Writers Ser.: No. 55). 46p. (Orig.). reprint ed. pap. 25.00 (*0-7837-2872-7*, 2057583) Bks Demand.

Mills, Ralph J., Jr. A Window in Air. 88p. (Orig.). 1993. pap. 9.95 (*1-55921-073-7*, Asphodel Pr) Moyer Bell.

Mills, Ralph J., Jr., ed. see Ignatow, David.

Mills, Randell L. & Good, William R. Unification of Spacetime, the Forces, Matter & Energy. (Illus.). 224p. 1992. 25.00 (*0-9635171-0-4*) Hydrocat Power.

Mills, Reita. Don't Dump the Teacher. 1987. 8.95 (*0-533-07345-6*) Vantage.

— Santa's Ups & Downs. (YA). 1992. 6.95 (*0-533-10307-X*) Vantage.

Mills, Richard M. As Moscow Sees Us: American Politics & Society in the Soviet Mindset. 320p. 1990. 35.00 (*0-19-506260-4*) OUP.

Mills, Richard P., ed. Perimetry Update 1992-1993. LC 93-1932. 609p. 1993. 162.00 (*90-6299-094-0*) Kugler Pubns.

Mills, Richard P., ed. see International Perimetric Society Staff.

Mills, Richard W. Observing Children in the Primary Classroom: All in a Day. rev. ed. Orig. Title: Classroom Observation of Primary School Children. (Illus.). 170p. 1988. pap. text ed. 16.95 (*0-04-445176-8*) Routledge Chapman & Hall.

Mills, Richard W. & Mills, Jean, eds. Bilingualism in the Primary School: A Handbook for Teachers. LC 92-32058. 144p. 1993. 59.95 (*0-415-08860-7*, B0407); pap. write for info. (*0-415-08861-5*) Routledge.

Mills, Richard W., jt. ed. see Mills, Jean.

Mills, Rick W. & Reisdorff, James J. The High, Dry & Dusty: Memories of the Cowboy Line. (Illus.). 168p. 1992. 43.95 (*0-942035-20-8*); pap. 37.95 (*0-942035-27-5*) South Platte.

Mills, Robert. Memorial of Robert Mills. Date not set. pap. write for info. (*0-87770-411-2*) Ye Galleon.

Mills, Robert, ed. Mills' Atlas of 1825. 1979. reprint ed. 75.00 (*0-87844-021-6*) Sandlapper Pub Co.

Mills, Robert & Pedersen, John. A Flour Mill Sanitation Manual. LC 90-82381. (Illus.). 164p. (Orig.). 1990. pap. 36.00 (*0-9624407-1-X*) Eagan Pr.

Mills, Robert A. & Haines, Olin R., eds. National Outdoor Guides Directory. (Illus.). 434p. (Orig.). 1987. 12.95 (*0-944080-00-6*) Prof Guides Pub.

Mills, Robert E. The Cheyenne's Woman - the Kansan's Lady. (Kansan Double Edition Ser.). 416p. 1993. pap. 4.99 (*0-8439-3450-6*) Dorchester Pub Co.

— Dark World. (Star Quest Ser.: No. 4). 224p. (Orig.). 1982. pap. 2.25 (*0-8439-1178-6*) Dorchester Pub Co.

— Red Apache Sun; Judge Colt. (Kansan Ser.). 384p. 1992. pap. 4.50 (*0-8439-3373-9*) Dorchester Pub Co.

An Asterisk (*) at the beginning of an entry indicates that the title is appearing in BIP for the first time.

— Showdown at Hells Canyon; Across the High Sierra, 2 vols. in 1. (Kansan Ser.). 384p. 1992. pap. 4.50 (*0-8439-3342-9*) Dorchester Pub Co.

— Trail of Desire; Shootout at the Golden Slipper. (Kansan Double Edition Ser.). 432p. 1993. pap. 4.99 (*0-8439-3421-2*) Dorchester Pub Co.

— Warm Flesh & Hot Lead - Long, Hard Ride, 2 vols. in 1. (Kansan Double Edition Ser.). 416p. 1993. pap. 4.99 (*0-8439-3395-X*) Dorchester Pub Co.

***Mills, Robert K.** Implement & Tractor: Reflections on 100 Years of Farm Equipment. LC 86-81762. (Illus.). 512p. Date not set. text ed. 39.95 (*0-87288-566-6*, I&T 100) Intertec Pub.

***Mills, Robert L.** It Didn't Happen the Way You Think: The Lincoln Assassination: What the Experts Missed. (Orig.). 1995. pap. text ed. 17.00 (*0-7884-0119-X*) Heritage Bk.

Mills, Robin K. & Schultz, Jon S. South Carolina Legal Research Handbook. LC 75-21933. vi, 115p. 1976. lib. bdg. 32.00 (*0-930342-16-X*, 301040) W S Hein.

Mills, Roger. Badminton. (EP Sports Ser.). (Illus.). 1975. 6.95 (*0-7158-0595-9*) Charles River Bks.

***Mills, Roger C.** Realizing Mental Health. 207p. (Orig.). (C). 1995. pap. text ed. 12.99 (*0-945819-78-1*) Sulzburger & Graham Pub.

Mills, Roger F., ed. see Wojowasito, Soewojo.

***Mills, Ronald E.** Long-Term Care Investment Strategies: A Guide to Start-ups, Facility Conversions & Strategic Alliances. 200p. 1995. 55.00 (*1-55738-622-6*) Probus Pub Co.

Mills, S. E., comp. Underground Office Humor: Real Memos, Rude Faxes, Tasteless Jokes & Eye-Popping True Stories from the Workplace. LC 94-20043. 1994. 9.95 (*0-8065-1567-8*, Citadel Pr) Carol Pub Group.

Mills, Sara. Discourses of Difference: An Analysis of Women's Travel Writing & Colonialism. 208p. 1992. 55.00 (*0-415-04629-7*, A6766) Routledge.

— Discourses of Difference: An Analysis of Women's Travel Writing & Colonialism. (Illus.). 208p. 1993. pap. 16.95 (*0-415-09664-2*, B2566) Routledge.

— Feminist Stylistics. LC 94-22697. (Interface Ser.). (Illus.). 256p. 1995. pap. 16.95 (*0-415-05028-6*, A7884) Routledge.

— Feminist Stylistics. LC 94-22697. (Interface Ser.). (Illus.). 256p. 1995. 69.95x (*0-415-05027-8*, A7880) Routledge.

— Genering the Reader. 272p. 1994. pap. text ed. 32.50 (*0-13-302290-0*) P-H.

— Language & Gender: Interdisciplinary Perspectives. LC 95-12460. (C). 1995. pap. text ed. 17.95 (*0-582-22631-7*, Pub. by Longman UK) Longman.

Mills, Sara, tr. see Shen, Terry C.

Mills, Sara, et al. Feminist Readings - Feminists Reading. 304p. (C). 1989. pap. text ed. 12.95 (*0-8139-1243-1*) U Pr of Va.

***Mills, Scott A.** Stranded in the Philippines: Missionary Professor Organizes Resistance to the Japanese. (Illus.). 137p. (Orig.). 1994. pap. 12.50 (*971-10-0519-0*, Pub. by New Day Pub PH) Cellar.

Mills, Selwyn & Weisser, Max. The Odd Couple Syndrome: Resolving the Neat-Sloppy Dilemma. McNally, Catherine, ed. (Illus.). 160p. 1988. 14.95 (*0-944748-00-7*); pap. 10.95 (*0-944748-01-5*) Jameison Pub.

Mills, Sheila A. Rocky Mountain Kettle Cuisine Two. (Illus.). (Orig.). 1990. pap. 15.95 (*0-9628428-0-X*) Sheilas Good.

Mills, Simon. Britannic: The Last Titan. 56p. 1993. pap. 12.95 (*0-946184-71-2*, Waterfront Pubns) Hallenbook.

— The Dictionary of Modern Herbalism: The Complete Guide to Herbs & Herbal Therapy. 208p. 1985. pap. 10.95 (*0-89281-238-9*) Inner Tradit.

— Olympic: The Old Reliable. (Illus.). 64p. (Orig.). 1993. pap. 14.95 (*0-946184-79-8*, Waterfront Pubns) Hallenbook.

Mills, Simon Y. The Essential Book of Herbal Medicine. 704p. 1994. pap. 15.00 (*0-14-019309-X*, Penguin Bks) Viking Penguin.

— Out of the Earth: The Science & Practice of Herbal Medicine. 704p. 1992. 30.00 (*0-670-83565-X*, Arkana) Viking Penguin.

Mills, Smithson, jt. auth. see Brettel, Anna.

Mills, Stacey E. & Fechner, Robert E. Pathology of the Larynx: Atlases of the Pathology of the Head & Neck. LC 84-720142. 86p. 1985. sl. 100.00 (*0-89189-187-0*) Am Soc Clinical.

Mills, Stacey E., jt. auth. see Fechner, Robert E.

Mills, Stacey E., jt. ed. see Sternberg, Stephen S.

Mills, Stella, ed. The Collected Letters of Colin MacLaurin. 560p. (C). 1982. text ed. 35.00 (*0-906812-08-9*) Birkhauser.

***Mills, Stephanie.** In Service of the Wild: Restoring & Reinhabiting Damaged Land. LC 94-38094. 256p. 1995. 23.00 (*0-8070-8534-0*) Beacon Pr.

— Whatever Happened to Ecology? LC 89-6294. 1989. 18.95 (*0-87156-658-3*) Sierra.

Mills, Stephanie, ed. In Praise of Nature. LC 90-33875. 255p. 1990. 29.95 (*1-55963-035-3*); pap. 16.00 (*1-55963-034-5*) Island Pr.

Mills, Stephen & Williams, Roger. Public Acceptance of New Technologies. 368p. 1986. 55.00 (*0-7099-4319-9*, Pub. by Croom Helm UK) Routledge Chapman & Hall.

Mills, Stephen, ed. see Ickringill, Steve.

Mills, Steve, jt. auth. see Riemer, Pierce.

Mills, Steven, jt. auth. see Reimer, Pierce.

Mills, Susan W. Eight Hundred Forty-Nine Traditional Patchwork Patterns: A Pictorial Handbook. (Illus.). 160p. 1989. pap. 5.95 (*0-486-26003-8*) Dover.

Mills, T., III, et al. Instrumental Data for Drug Analysis, Set. 2nd ed. (Forensic & Police Science Ser.). 631p. 1991. 425.00 (*0-444-01630-9*) CRC Pr.

— Instrumental Data for Drug Analysis, Vol. 5. 2nd ed. (Forensic & Police Science Ser.). 631p. 1991. 120.00 (*0-444-01626-0*) CRC Pr.

Mills, T. C. Composite Monetary Indicators for the United Kingdom: Construction & Empirical Analysis. (Bank of England. Discussion Papers. Technical Ser.: No. 3). 72p. pap. 25.00 (*0-317-29022-3*, 2020428) Bks Demand.

Mills, Terence. The Econometric Analysis of Financial Time Series. LC 92-37624. 264p. (C). 1994. 49.95 (*0-521-41048-7*) Cambridge U Pr.

***Mills, Terence C.** The Econometric Modelling of financial Time Series. 256p. (C). 1995. pap. 19.95 (*0-521-42257-4*) Cambridge U Pr.

— Predicting the Unpredictable? Science & Guesswork in Financial Market Forecasting. (C). 1992. text ed. 59.95 (*0-255-36310-9*, Pub. by Inst Economic Affairs UK) St Mut.

— Time Series Techniques for Economists. 381p. (C). 1991. pap. 21.95 (*0-521-40574-2*) Cambridge U Pr.

Mills, Terry, III. Instrumental Data for Drug Analysis, 5 vols., 1. 2nd ed. 1992. 120.00 (*0-444-01281-8*) CRC Pr.

— Instrumental Data for Drug Analysis, 5 vols., 2. 2nd ed. 1992. 120.00 (*0-444-01282-6*) CRC Pr.

— Instrumental Data for Drug Analysis, 5 vols., 3. 2nd ed. 1992. 120.00 (*0-444-01283-4*) CRC Pr.

— Instrumental Data for Drug Analysis, 5 vols., 4. 2nd ed. 1992. 120.00 (*0-444-01284-2*) CRC Pr.

— Instrumental Data for Drug Analysis, 5 vols., 5. 2nd ed. 1992. 120.00 (*0-444-01271-0*, RS189) CRC Pr.

Mills, Terry, III & Roberson, J. Conrad. Instrumental Data for Drug Analysis. 2nd ed. LC 92-13539. (Forensic & Police Science Ser.). 1992. reprint ed. 125.00 (*0-8493-9521-6*, RS189) CRC Pr.

Mills, Thomas. Rediscovering Brooklyn History: A Guide to Research Collections. LC 78-65791. (Brooklyn Rediscovery Booklet Ser.). (Illus.). 35p. 1978. pap. 2.50 (*0-933250-00-2*) Bklyn Educ.

Mills, Thomas, et al. The Healthy Heart Gourmet. rev. ed. (Illus.). 268p. 1994. pap. 14.95 (*0-9620896-1-3*) Healthy Heart.

Mills, Thomas S. The Pilot's Reference to ATC Procedures & Phraseology. 2nd ed. (Illus.). 224p. 1987. pap. 19.95 (*0-935695-08-7*) Reavco Pub.

— The Pilot's Reference to ATC Procedures & Phraseology. 3rd ed. LC 89-10550. (Illus.). 296p. (C). 1991. pap. 24.95 (*0-935695-10-9*) Reavco Pub.

— The Pilot's Reference to ATC Procedures & Phraseology, 1986. LC 85-62754. (Illus.). 224p. (Orig.). 1986. pap. 19.95 (*0-935695-03-6*) Reavco Pub.

Mills, Thomas S. & Archibald, Janet S. The Pilot's Reference to ATC Procedures & Phraseology. 4th ed. (Illus.). 336p. (C). 1992. pap. 24.95 (*0-935695-05-2*) Reavco Pub.

Mills-Thornton, Serena G. Mentor Wisdom: Requisites for Living. Allen, Sharon, ed. (Illus.). 31p. (Orig.). (YA). 1993. write for info. (*0-9614338-0-9*) Ideas.

Mills, Velma, ed. see Eager, George B.

Mills, Watson. New Testament Greek: An Introductory Grammar. 2nd ed. LC 85-11540. 1989. lib. bdg. 79.95 (*0-88946-201-1*) E Mellen.

Mills, Watson E. A Bibliography of the Nature & Role of the Holy Spirit in Twentieth-Century Writings. LC 93-22748. 372p. 1993. text ed. 99.95 (*0-7734-2366-4*, Mellen Biblical Pr) E Mellen.

— Glossolalia: A Bibliography. LC 85-8987. (Studies in the Bible & Early Christianity: Vol. 6). 132p. 1989. lib. bdg. 69.95 (*0-88946-605-X*) E Mellen.

— Index to Periodical Literature on the Apostle Paul, 1960-1992. LC 93-7974. (New Testament Tools & Studies: Vol. 16). xx, 345p. 1993. 85.75 (*90-04-09674-4*) E J Brill.

— A Theological-Exegetical Approach to Glossolalia. 192p. (Orig.). 1985. pap. text ed. 19.50 (*0-8191-4527-0*) U Pr of Amer.

***Mills, Watson E., comp.** Bibliographies for Biblical Research: The Gospel of John. LC 93-30864. (New Testament Ser.: Vol. IV). 436p. Date not set. text ed. 169.95 (*0-7734-2400-8*) E Mellen.

— Bibliographies for Biblical Research: The Gospel of Luke. LC 93-30864. (New Testament Series: The Gospel of Luke: Vol. III). 416p. Date not set. text ed. 129.95 (*0-7734-2385-0*) E Mellen.

— Bibliographies for Biblical Research: The Gospel of Luke. LC 93-30864. (New Testament Series: The Gospel of Luke: Vol. III). 416p. Date not set. text ed. 169.95 (*0-7734-2402-4*) E Mellen.

— Bibliographies for Biblical Research: The Gospel of Mark. LC 93-30864. (New Testament Ser.: Vol. II). 552p. 1994. text ed. 169.95 (*0-7734-2398-2*) E Mellen.

***Mills, Watson E., ed.** Bibliographies for Biblical Research: The Gospel of Matthew. LC 93-30864. (New Testament Ser.: Vol. I). 304p. 1993. text ed. 129.95 (*0-7734-2396-6*) E Mellen.

Mills, Watson E., ed. & comp. Bibliographies for Biblical Research: The Gospel of John. LC 93-30864. (New Testament Ser.: Vol. IV). 436p. Date not set. text ed. 129.95 (*0-7734-2357-5*) E Mellen.

— Bibliographies for Biblical Research: The Gospel of Mark. LC 93-30864. (New Testament Ser.: Vol. II). 552p. 1994. text ed. 129.95 (*0-7734-2349-4*, Mellen Biblical Pr) E Mellen.

— Bibliographies for Biblical Research: The Gospel of Matthew. LC 93-30864. (New Testament Ser.: Vol. I). 304p. 1993. text ed. 169.95 (*0-7734-2347-8*, Mellen Biblical Pr) E Mellen.

Mills, Watson E., ed. Mercer Dictionary of the Bible. LC 89-13857. (Illus.). 1088p. (C). 1990. 35.00 (*0-86554-402-6*, MUP/H327) Mercer Univ Pr.

***Mills, Watson E & Mills, Joyce H.** An Index to Novum Testamentum Volumes 1-35 Vols. 1-35, Set. 256p. 1994. 48.75 (*90-04-10082-2*) E J Brill.

***Mills, Watson E., et al, eds.** Mercer Commentary on the Bible. LC 94-23638. 1994. 35.00 (*0-86554-406-9*) Mercer Univ Pr.

Mills, William. The Arkansas: An American River. LC 88-10607. (Illus.). 260p. (Orig.). 1988. 30.00 (*1-55728-043-6*); pap. 20.00 (*1-55728-044-4*) U of Ark Pr.

— Bears & Men: A Gathering. LC 86-7855. (Illus.). 168p. 1986. 24.95 (*0-912697-41-5*) Algonquin Bks.

— I Know a Place: Three Stories. (Illus.). 1976. 12.50 (*0-912960-08-6*) Nightowl.

— Properties of Blood. LC 91-29773. 112p. 1992. 19.95 (*1-55728-243-9*); pap. 9.95 (*1-55728-244-7*) U of Ark Pr.

— Stained Glass: Poems. fac. ed. LC 78-11893. 69p. 1979. reprint ed. pap. 25.00 (*0-7837-7808-2*, 2047564) Bks Demand.

— Those Who Blink. Novel. LC 85-24160. 177p. 1986. 14.95 (*0-8071-1270-4*) La State U Pr.

Mills, William, intro. John William Corrington: Southern Man of Letters. 280p. 1994. lib. bdg. 30.00 (*0-944436-20-X*) Univ Central AR Pr.

Mills, William C. Flint Ridge. (Archaeology, Ohio History, Prehistoric Indians Ser.). (Illus.). 80p. 1993. reprint ed. pap. 6.25 (*1-56651-093-7*) A W McGraw.

Mills, William J., jt. auth. see Seyer, Martin D.

Mills, William R., jt. auth. see West, Gary.

Mills, Willis N., Jr., jt. auth. see Lushington, Nolan.

Mills, Wright C. The Causes of World War Three. LC 85-14381. 188p. 1985. reprint ed. pap. 25.95 (*0-87332-357-2*) M E Sharpe.

Millsap, Larry & Ferl, Terry E. Descriptive Cataloging for AACR2 & USMARC: A How-to-Do-It Workbook for Librarians. (How-to-Do-It Ser.). 240p. 1991. 39.95 (*1-55570-098-5*) Neal-Schuman.

Millsap, Larry, jt. auth. see Ferl, Terry E.

Millsaps, Bridget B., jt. ed. see Baker, Barbara E.

Millsaps, Daniel & Washington International Arts Letter Editors. National Directory of Arts Support by Private Foundations, No. 5. LC 77-79730. (Arts Patronage Ser.: No. 12). 340p. (Orig.). 1983. 79.95 (*0-912072-13-X*) Wash Intl Arts.

— National Directory of Grants & Aid to Individuals in the Arts, International. 5th ed. LC 70-112695. (Arts Patronage Ser.: No. 11). 256p. (Orig.). 1983. 15.95 (*0-912072-12-1*) Wash Intl Arts.

Millsaps, Daniel, jt. auth. see Washington International Arts Letter Editors.

Millson, Cecilia. Tales of Old Wiltshire. 96p. 1987. 30.00 (*0-905392-12-4*) St Mut.

Millson, Cecilia. Old Berkshire Tales. 96p. 1987. 30.00 (*0-905392-69-8*) St Mut.

Millson, Cecillia. The History of Donnington Hospital. 83p. 1987. pap. 30.00 (*0-905392-51-5*) St Mut.

— Tales of Old Oxfordshire. 96p. 1987. pap. 30.00 (*0-905392-20-5*) St Mut.

Millspauch, Ben. Z Car: A Legend in Its Own Time. 1993. pap. 16.95 (*0-8306-4339-7*) TAB Bks.

Millspaugh, A. C. The American Task in Persia. LC 73-6293. (Middle East Ser.). 1973. reprint ed. 25.95 (*0-405-05350-9*) Ayer.

— Business Programming in C for DOS-Based Systems. 482p. (C). 1993. pap. text ed. 35.75 (*0-15-500139-6*) Dryden Pr.

— Instructor's Manual & Transparency Masters to Accompany Business Programming in C for DOS-Based Systems. 319p. (C). 1993. pap. text ed. 9.50 (*0-15-500946-X*) Dryden Pr.

Millspaugh, Arthur. Americans in Persia. LC 76-9837. (Politics & Strategy of World War II Ser.). 1976. reprint ed. lib. bdg. 37.50 (*0-306-70764-0*) Da Capo.

Millspaugh, Arthur Chester. Crime Control by the National Government. LC 70-168678. (American Constitutional & Legal History Ser). 306p. 1972. reprint ed. lib. bdg. 37.50 (*0-306-70418-8*) Da Capo.

Millspaugh, Ben. Aviation & Space Projects for Young Scientists. 1991. text ed. 16.95 (*0-07-157680-0*); pap. text ed. 9.95 (*0-07-157679-7*) McGraw.

— Aviation & Space Science Projects. (J). 1991. 16.95 (*0-8306-2157-1*); pap. 9.95 (*0-8306-2156-3*) TAB Bks.

— Z Car: A Legend in Its Own Time. 1991. 24.95 (*0-07-155392-4*) McGraw.

— Z Car: A Legend in Its Own Time. 1993. pap. 16.95 (*0-07-042596-5*) McGraw.

— Z Car: A Legend in Its Own Time. (Illus.). 208p. 1990. 24.95 (*0-8306-3536-X*, 3536) TAB Bks.

Millspaugh, Charles F. American Medicinal Plants: An Illustrated & Descriptive Guide to Plants Indigenous to & Naturalized in the United States Which Are Used in Medicine. LC 73-91487. (Illus.). 450p. 1974. reprint ed. pap. 15.95 (*0-486-23034-1*) Dover.

— Medicinal Plants: An Illustrated & Descriptive Guide to Plants Indigenous to & Naturalized in the United States Which Are Used in Medicine, 2 vols., Set. 1132p. 1980. lib. bdg. 200.00 (*0-8490-3103-6*) Gordon Pr.

Millstein, Barbara H. & Lowe, Sarah M. Consuelo Kanaga: An American Photographer. LC 91-35933. (Illus.). 224p. 1992. pap. 35.00 (*0-295-97228-9*) U of Wash Pr.

Millstein, Jeffrey, ed. see Levitin, Victor.

Millstein, Jeffrey A., ed. see Khibnik, Alexander I.

Millstein, Susan G., et al, eds. Promoting Adolescent Health. LC 92-22707. 1993. 60.00 (*0-19-507454-8*) OUP.

— Promoting the Health of Adolescents: New Directions for the Twenty-First Century. (Illus.). 424p. 1994. reprint ed. pap. 24.95 (*0-19-509188-4*) OUP.

***Millstone.** An Elementary Odyssey: Teaching Ancient Civilization Through Story. LC 94-48431. 300p. 1995. pap. text ed. 22.00 (*0-435-08841-6*) Heinemann.

Millu, Liana. Smoke over Birkenau. Schwartz, Lynne S., tr. LC 91-22973. 208p. 1991. 19.95 (*0-8276-0398-3*) JPS Phila.

Millus, Donald. Fishing the Southeast Coast. (Illus.). 1989. 14.95 (*0-87844-076-3*); pap. 9.95 (*0-87844-085-2*) Sandlapper Pub Co.

Millward. L' Oeuvre de Pierre Loti et l'Esprit Fin de Siecle. 9.50 (*0-685-34266-2*) Fr & Eur.

Millward, C. M. A Biography of the English Language. 432p. (C). 1989. text ed. 31.25 (*0-03-059431-6*) HB Coll Pubs.

Millward, Carl L., jt. auth. see Schwamm, Harry A.

Millward, Celia. Handbook for Writers. 2nd ed. 504p. (C). 1983. text ed. 20.75 (*0-03-062382-0*) HB Coll Pubs.

Millward, Pamela. Mother: A Novel of the Revolution. LC 76-78045. (Writing Ser.: No. 26). 64p. (Orig.). 1970. pap. 2.00 (*0-87704-015-X*) Four Seasons Foun.

***Millward, Robert & Singleton, John, eds.** The Political Economy of Nationalisation in Britain, 1920-50. (Illus.). 344p. (C). 1995. 59.95 (*0-521-45096-9*) Cambridge U Pr.

Millward, Robert, jt. auth. see Foreman-Peck, James.

Millward, Robert E., et al. Public Sector Economics. LC 82-4609. (Surveys in Economics Ser.). 293p. reprint ed. pap. 83.60 (*0-7837-1590-0*, 2041882) Bks Demand.

Millward, Stephen, jt. auth. see Hatch, David.

Millward, William G., jt. ed. see Mazzaoui, Michel M.

Millword, Michael T., jt. ed. see Glaeser, Phyllis S.

Milly, ed. see Proust, Marcel.

Millyard, Anne W., jt. auth. see Wilks, Rick J.

Milman, jt. auth. see Jawerth.

Milman, Donald & Goldman, George, eds. Techniques of Working with Resistance. LC 85-18653. 417p. 1986. 50.00 (*0-87668-616-1*) Aronson.

Milman, Harry, jt. auth. see Freeman, Gustave.

Milman, Harry A. & Elmore, Eugene, eds. Biomechanical Mechanisms & Regulations of Intercellular Communication. LC 87-61833. (Advances in Modern Environmental Toxicology Ser.). (Illus.). 325p. 1987. 65.00 (*0-911131-15-9*) Princeton Sci Pubs.

Milman, Harry A. & Weisburger, Elizabeth K. Handbook of Carcinogen Testing. LC 85-4930. (Illus.). 637p. 1985. 72.00 (*0-8155-1035-7*) Noyes.

Milman, Harry A. & Weisburger, Elizabeth K., eds. Handbook of Carcinogen Testing. 2nd ed. LC 94-15231. (Illus.). 855p. 1994. 98.00 (*0-8155-1356-9*) Noyes.

Milman, Henry H. History of Christianity from the Birth of Christ to the Abolition of Paganism in the Roman Empire, 3 Vols, Set. rev. ed. LC 78-172733. reprint ed. 210.00 (*0-404-04350-X*) AMS Pr.

— History of Latin Christianity, 9 Vols, Set. LC 71-172734. reprint ed. lib. bdg. 145.00 (*0-404-04360-7*) AMS Pr.

— The History of the Jews. 640p. 1986. 360.00 (*1-85077-133-2*, Darf Pubs Ltd) St Mut.

Milman, M. & Schonbek, T., eds. Harmonic Analysis & Partial Differential Equations: (Proceedings of a Conference) LC 90-34635. (CONM Ser.: Vol. 107). 129p. 1990. pap. text ed. 40.00 (*0-8218-5113-6*, CONM-107) Am Math.

Milman, Mario. Extrapolation & Optimal Decompositions: With Applications to Analysis. Dold, A. et al, eds. (Lecture Notes in Mathematics: Vol. 1580). 1994. 33.00 (*0-387-58081-6*) Spr-Verlag.

Milman, V. D., jt. ed. see Lindenstrauss, J.

Milman, Yoseph. Opacity in the Writings of Robbe-Grillet, Pinter, & Zach: A Study in the Poetics of Absurd Literature. LC 91-43258. (Studies in Comparative Literature: Vol. 18). 148p. 1992. lib. bdg. 69.95 (*0-7734-9701-3*) E Mellen.

Milmed, Bella K. Kant & Current Philosophical Issues: Some Modern Developments of His Theory of Knowledge. LC 61-8058. 272p. reprint ed. pap. 77.60 (*0-317-08912-9*, 2050213) Bks Demand.

Milmine, Georgine, jt. auth. see Cather, Willa.

Milne & Pistolesi. Quick Reference to Pathophysiology on Chest Radiog. 1992. 7.95 (*0-8016-7512-X*) Mosby Yr Bk.

— Reading the Chest Radiograph: A Physiologic Approach. (Illus.). 383p. 1992. 99.00 (*0-8016-3303-6*) Mosby Yr Bk.

Milne, A. A. Christopher Robin Gives Pooh a Party. (Pooh Jewelry Bks.). (Illus.). 32p. (J). (ps up). 1992. 13.95 (*0-525-44871-3*, DCB) Dutton Child Bks.

— Christopher Robin Gives Pooh a Party. (Illus.). 32p. (J). 1993. 4.99 (*0-525-45144-7*, DCB) Dutton Child Bks.

— Christopher Robin Leads an Expotition. (Illus.). 32p. (J). 1993. 4.99 (*0-525-45142-0*, DCB) Dutton Child Bks.

— Eeyore Loses a Tail. (Winnie-the-Pooh Storybks.). (Illus.). 32p. (J). 1993. 4.99 (*0-525-45137-4*, DCB) Dutton Child Bks.

— Eyeore Has a Birthday. (Illus.). 32p. (J). 1993. 4.99 (*0-525-45043-2*, DCB) Dutton Child Bks.

— House at Pooh Corner. (Illus.). (J). (gr. k up). 1985. 9.95 (*0-525-32302-3*, Dutton) NAL-Dutton.

— The House at Pooh Corner. (Illus.). 192p. (J). (ps up). 1988. 9.95 (*0-525-44444-0*, DCB) Dutton Child Bks.

— The House at Pooh Corner. LC 91-29462. (Illus.). 192p. (J). (ps up). 1991. Full-color Gift Edition. 20.00 (*0-525-44774-1*, DCB) Dutton Child Bks.

— The House at Pooh Corner. (Illus.). 192p. (J). 1992. pap. 3.99 (*0-14-036122-7*, Puffin) Puffin Bks.

— House at Pooh Corner: A Pop-Up Book. (Illus.). 12p. (J). (ps up). 1991. 13.99 (*0-525-44245-6*, DCB) Dutton Child Bks.

— The House on Pooh Corner - El Rincon de Puh. (SPA.). (J). 8.95 (*84-372-3013-6*) Santillana.

— I Think I Am a Tram - Mne Kazhetsia Chto Ia Tramvai. Greenhill, Rima, ed. Marshak, S et al, trs. LC 93-44475. (Illus.). 176p. (Orig.). (ENG & RUS.). (YA). 1994. pap. 9.00 (*1-55779-068-X*) Hermitage.

— Kanga & Baby Roo Come to the Forest. (Illus.). 32p. (J). 1993. 4.99 (*0-525-45141-2*, DCB) Dutton Child Bks.

— Le Meilleur des Ours. (FRE.). (J). (gr. 3-8). 9.95 (*0-685-23403-7*) Fr & Eur.

M

An Asterisk (*) at the beginning of an entry indicates that the title is appearing in BIP for the first time.

— Now We Are Six. (Illus.). 112p. (J). (ps up). 1988. 9.95 (*0-525-44446-7*, DCB) Dutton Child Bks.
— Now We Are Six. (Illus.). 112p. (J). (ps-6). 1992. 17.50 (*0-525-44960-4*, DCB) Dutton Child Bks.
— Now We Are Six. (Illus.). 112p. (J). 1992. pap. 3.99 (*0-14-036124-3*, Puffin) Puffin Bks.
— Piglet Is Entirely Surrounded by Water. (Illus.). 32p. (J). 1993. 4.99 (*0-525-45143-9*, DCB) Dutton Child Bks.
— Piglet Meets a Heffalump. (Illus.). 32p. (J). 1993. 4.99 (*0-525-45042-4*, DCB) Dutton Child Bks.
— The Poems & Hums of Winnie-the-Pooh. (Illus.). 10p. (J). (gr. 4-7). 1994. pap. 5.99 (*0-525-45205-2*, DCB) Dutton Child Bks.
— Pooh & Piglet Go Hunting. (Pooh Jewelry Bks.). (Illus.). 32p. (J). (ps up). 1992. 13.95 (*0-525-44872-1*, DCB) Dutton Child Bks.
— Pooh & Piglet Go Hunting. (Winnie-the-Pooh Storybks.). (Illus.). 32p. (J). 1993. 4.99 (*0-525-45136-6*, DCB) Dutton Child Bks.
— Pooh & Some Bees. (Illus.). 10p. (J). (ps up). 1987. 7.95 (*0-525-44339-8*, 0674-210, DCB) Dutton Child Bks.
— Pooh Goes Visiting. (Illus.). 10p. (J). (ps up). 1987. 7.95 (*0-525-44337-1*, 0674-210, DCB) Dutton Child Bks.
— Pooh Goes Visiting. (Winnie-the-Pooh Storybks.). (Illus.). 32p. (J). 1993. 4.99 (*0-525-45040-8*, DCB) Dutton Child Bks.
— The Pooh Story Book. LC 65-19580. (Illus.). 80p. (J). (gr. k-4). 1965. 13.99 (*0-525-37546-5*, DCB) Dutton Child Bks.

Milne, A. A., et al. Pooh's Bedtime Book. LC 80-65523. (Illus.). 48p. (J). (ps-3). 1980. 9.95 (*0-525-44895-0*, DCB) Dutton Child Bks.

Milne, A. A. Pooh's Library, 4 bks., Set. (Illus.). (J). (ps up). 1988. 39.95 (*0-525-44451-3*, DCB) Dutton Child Bks.
— Pooh's Library, 4 bks., Set. (Illus.). (J). 1992. boxed 16.00 (*0-14-095560-7*, Puffin) Puffin Bks.
— Pooh's Pot O'Honey, 4 vols., Set. (Alive Travel Ser.). (Illus.). (J). (ps up). 1985. boxed 10.95 (*0-525-37518-X*, DCB) Dutton Child Bks.
— Prince Rabbit. (Classic Short Stories Ser.). (J). 1991. lib. bdg. 13.95 (*0-88682-480-X*) Creative Ed.
— The Red House Mystery. reprint ed. lib. bdg. 18.95 (*0-89190-487-5*, Rivercity Pr) Amereon Ltd.
— The Songs of Winnie-the-Pooh. (Illus.). 10p. (J). (gr. 4-7). 1994. pap. 5.99 (*0-525-45206-0*, DCB) Dutton Child Bks.
— Two People. 22.95 (*0-89190-234-1*, Am Repr) Amereon Ltd.
— When We Were Very Young. (Illus.). 112p. (J). (ps up). 1988. 9.95 (*0-525-44445-9*, DCB) Dutton Child Bks.
— When We Were Very Young. (Illus.). 112p. (J). (ps-6). 1992. 17.50 (*0-525-44961-2*, DCB) Dutton Child Bks.
— When We Were Very Young. (Illus.). 112p. (J). 1992. pap. 3.99 (*0-14-036123-5*, Puffin) Puffin Bks.
— Winnie Ille Pu. Lenard, Alexander, tr. (Illus.). 160p. (LAT.). 1991. pap. 9.95 (*0-14-015339-X*, Penguin Bks) Viking Penguin.
— Winnie-Ille-Pu: A Latin Version of A. A. Milne's Winnie-the-Pooh. (Illus.). 120p. (LAT.). 1984. 10.00 (*0-525-24267-8*, 0971-290, Dutton) NAL-Dutton.
— Winnie l'Ourson. (Illus.). (FRE.). (J). (gr. 3-8). 9.95 (*0-685-23402-9*) Fr & Eur.
— Winnie-the-Pooh. (Illus.). 176p. (J). (ps up). 1988. 10.95 (*0-525-44443-2*, DCB) Dutton Child Bks.
— Winnie-the-Pooh. LC 91-26203. (Illus.). 176p. (J). (ps up). 1991. Full-color Gift Edition. 20.00 (*0-525-44776-8*, DCB) Dutton Child Bks.
— Winnie-the-Pooh. (Illus.). (J). (gr. 1-5). 1961. 9.95 (*0-525-43035-0*, Dutton) NAL-Dutton.
— Winnie-the-Pooh. (Illus.). 176p. (J). 1992. pap. 3.99 (*0-14-036121-9*, Puffin) Puffin Bks.
— Winnie the Pooh, 4 vols., Set. (J). 1992. boxed 75.00 (*0-525-45004-1*, DCB) Dutton Child Bks.
— Winnie-the-Pooh: A Pop-Up Book. (Illus.). 12p. (J). (ps up). 1984. 13.00 (*0-525-44119-0*, DCB) Dutton Child Bks.
— Winnie the Pooh & Some Bees. (Pooh Jewelry Bks.). (Illus.). 32p. (J). 1993. 13.99 (*0-525-45044-0*, DCB) Dutton Child Bks.
— Winnie the Pooh & Some Bees Storybooks. 128p. (J). (ps-2). 1993. pap. 4.99 (*0-525-45033-5*, DCB) Dutton Child Bks.
— Winnie-the-Pooh (Full-Musical) 1964. 5.00 (*0-87129-364-1*, W01) Dramatic Pub.
— The Winnie-the-Pooh Journal. (Illus.). 64p. (J). (ps up). 1986. 7.99 (*0-525-44237-5*, DCB) Dutton Child Bks.
— Winnie-the-Pooh Lift-the-Flap Rebus Book. (Illus.). 16p. (J). (ps-3). 1992. 12.99 (*0-525-44987-6*, DCB) Dutton Child Bks.
— Winnie-the-Pooh's Baby Book. (Illus.). 32p. (J). (gr. k up). 1994. 13.99 (*0-525-45298-2*) Dutton Child Bks.
— Winnie-the-Pooh's Calendar Book 1987. (J). (ps up). 1986. 4.95 (*0-525-44235-9*, Dutton) NAL-Dutton.
— Winnie-the-Pooh's Calendar Book 1988. (J). (ps up). 1987. spiral bd. 4.95 (*0-525-44311-8*, Dutton) NAL-Dutton.
— Winnie-the-Pooh's Calendar Book 1989. (Illus.). 32p. (J). (ps up). 1988. spiral bd. 5.95 (*0-525-44398-3*, Dutton) NAL-Dutton.
— Winnie-the-Pooh's Friendship Book. (Illus.). 48p. (J). (gr. 4-7). 1994. 8.99 (*0-525-45204-4*, DCB) Dutton Child Bks.
— Winnie-the-Pooh's Hundred Acre Wood: A Press-Out Model Book. (Illus.). 40p. (J). (gr. k up). 1994. 7.99 (*0-525-45341-5*) Dutton Child Bks.
— Winnie-the-Pooh's Little Book about Food. (Illus.). 10p. (J). (ps up). 1992. 4.95 (*0-525-44875-6*, DCB) Dutton Child Bks.
— Winnie-the-Pooh's Little Book about Friends. (Illus.). 10p. (J). (ps up). 1992. 4.95 (*0-525-44874-8*, DCB) Dutton Child Bks.
— Winnie-the-Pooh's Little Book about Parties. (Illus.). 10p. (J). (ps up). 1992. 4.95 (*0-525-44876-4*, DCB) Dutton Child Bks.
— Winnie-the-Pooh's Little Book about Weather. (Illus.). 10p. (J). (ps up). 1992. 4.95 (*0-525-44877-2*, DCB) Dutton Child Bks.
— Winnie-the-Pooh's Opposites. (Illus.). 32p. (J). (ps up). 1995. 9.99 (*0-525-45429-2*, DCB) Dutton Child Bks.
— Winnie the Pooh's Pop-up Theater Book. (Illus.). 12p. (J). 1993. 15.99 (*0-525-44990-6*, DCB) Dutton Child Bks.
— Winnie-the-Pooh's Revolving Picture Book. (Illus.). 12p. (J). (ps up). 1990. 13.99 (*0-525-44645-1*, DCB) Dutton Child Bks.
— Winnie-the-Pooh's Story Box, 10 bks., Set. (Illus.). (J). 1993. 49.90 (*0-525-45168-4*, DCB) Dutton Child Bks.
— Winnie-the-Pooh's Teatime Cookbook. LC 92-35650. (Illus.). 64p. (J). 1993. 8.99 (*0-525-45135-8*, DCB) Dutton Child Bks.
— Winnie-The-Pooh's Trivia Quiz Book. LC 93-39969. (Illus.). 48p. (J). 1994. 8.99 (*0-525-45265-6*, DCB) Dutton Child Bks.
— Winnie-the-Pooh's Visitors Book. (Illus.). 128p. (J). 1994. 13.99 (*0-525-45217-6*) Dutton Child Bks.
— Winniw-the-Pooh's Colors. (Illus.). 32p. (J). (ps up). 1995. 9.99 (*0-525-45428-4*, DCB) Dutton Child Bks.
— Winny de Puh. (SPA.). (J). 7.50 (*0-685-31015-9*) Santillana.
— Winny De Puh. (Illus.). 176p. (SPA.). (J). (ps-3). 1999. 11.00 (*0-525-44986-8*, DCB) Dutton Child Bks.
— The World of Christopher Robin. (Illus.). 256p. (J). (ps up). 1988. 17.50 (*0-525-44448-3*, DCB) Dutton Child Bks.
— World of Christopher Robin, Incl. World of Pooh. (J). (gr. 1-4). 1958. Boxed with "World of Pooh". boxed 29.95 (*0-525-43348-1*, Dutton) NAL-Dutton.
— The World of Pooh. (Illus.). 320p. (J). (ps up). 1988. 17.50 (*0-525-44447-5*, DCB) Dutton Child Bks.
— The World of Pooh. (Illus.). (J). (gr. 1-4). 1957. 13.95 (*0-525-43320-1*, 01258-370, Dutton) NAL-Dutton.
— The World of Pooh, Incl. World of Christopher. (Illus.). (J). (gr. 1-4). 1957. Incl. "World of Christopher". boxed 29.95 (*0-685-46952-2*, 01258-370, Dutton) NAL-Dutton.
— The World of Winnie-the-Pooh, 2 bks., Set. (Illus.). (J). (ps up). 1988. 35.00 (*0-525-44452-1*, DCB) Dutton Child Bks.

Milne, A. A., jt. auth. see Perry, Ruth.

Milne, A. J. M. Human Rights & Human Diversity: An Essay in the Philosophy of Human Rights. LC 86-5804. 186p. (C). 1986. 59.50 (*0-88706-366-7*); pap. 19.95 (*0-88706-367-5*) State U NY Pr.

Milne, Alan, ed. see United Kingdom Association for Legal & Social Philosophy.

Milne, Alasdair. DG: Memoirs of a British Broadcaster. (Illus.). 236p. 1989. 29.95 (*0-340-42772-8*, Pub. by H & S UK) Trafalgar.

Milne, Ann, jt. ed. see Folberg, Jay.

***Milne, Antony.** Beyond the Warming: The Hazards of Climate Prediction in the Age of Chaos. (Illus.). 192p. (Orig.). (C). 1995. pap. 14.95 (*1-85327-098-9*, Pub. by Prism Pr UK) Atrium Pubs.

Milne, Bill, jt. auth. see Blake, Kathy.

Milne, Brian, jt. auth. see Ennew, Judith.

Milne, Bruce. Know the Truth. LC 82-4711. 288p. 1982. pap. 12.99 (*0-87784-392-9*, 392) InterVarsity.
— The Message of John: Here is Your King! LC 93-8158. (Bible Speaks Today Ser.). 352p. (Orig.). 1993. pap. 14.99 (*0-8308-1233-4*, 1233) InterVarsity.
— Power Planning: Structuring Your Software Company for Success. LC 88-62380. 1989. disk 24.95 (*0-945264-04-6*) Resolution Busn Pr.

***Milne, Courtney.** Sacred Places in North America: A Journey of the Spirit. LC 94-44794. (Illus.). 128p. 1995. 27.50 (*1-55670-414-3*) Stewart Tabori & Chang.

Milne, David. MOS: Design & Manufacture. (Illus.). 260p. (Orig.). 1983. pap. 25.00 (*0-85224-415-0*, Pub. by Edinburgh U Pr UK) Col U Pr.
— The Scottish Office & Other Scottish Government Departments. LC 84-24792. (New Whitehall Ser.). v, 140p. 1986. reprint ed. text ed. 59.75 (*0-313-23655-0*, MISO, Greenwood Pr) Greenwood.

***Milne, David, frwd.** Butterworth's Handbook of Consolidated VAT Legislation. 1994. pap. write for info. (*0-406-04554-2*) Butterworth Legal Pubs.

Milne, David, et al, eds. Evolution of Complex & Higher Organisms: A Report Prepared by the Participants of Workshops Held at NASA Ames Research Center, Moffett Field, CA, July 1981, Jan. 1982, & May 1982. LC 85-7159. (NASA SP Ser.: No. 478). (Illus.). 112p. (Orig.). 1985. pap. 8.50 (*0-16-004186-4*, S/N 033-000-00951-8) USGPO.

Milne, David H. Marine Biology. LC 94-20337. 459p. 1995. pap. 49.95 (*0-534-16314-9*) Intl Thomson.

Milne, DeLane, ed. International Symposium on Microelectronics, 1992: Proceedings. (Illus.). 748p. (Orig.). 1992. pap. text ed. 30.00 (*0-930815-36-X*) Intl Soc Hybrid.
— ISHM '92 Proceedings. 700p. 1992. write for info. (*0-930815-35-1*) Intl Soc Hybrid.

Milne, Derek. Training Behaviour Therapists: Methods, Evaluation & Implementation with Parents, Nurses & Teachers. 324p. 1986. text ed. 29.95 (*0-914797-22-0*) Brookline Bks.

Milne, Derek, ed. Evaluating Mental Health Practice: Methods & Applications. 288p. 1987. lib. bdg. 69.50 (*0-7099-4626-0*, Pub. by Croom Helm UK) Routledge Chapman & Hall.

Milne, Douglas, jt. ed. see Haynes, Raymond.

Milne, Drew, jt. ed. see Eagelton, Terry.

***Milne, Drucilla.** The Amish of Harmony. King, Martha & Michel, Paula, eds. (Illus.). 134p. (Orig.). 1993. pap. 10.00 (*0-9638637-0-3*) D Milne.

Milne-Edwards, Henri. Introduction a la Zoologie General (Introduction to General Zoology) Cohen, I. Bernard, ed. LC 80-2137. (Development of Science Ser.). 1981. reprint ed. lib. bdg. 18.95 (*0-405-13892-X*) Ayer.

Milne, Elizabeth, et al. Mongolian People's Republic, 1991: Toward a Market Economy. LC 91-4710. (Occasional Paper Ser.: No. 79). viii, 81p. (Orig.). 1991. pap. 10.00 (*1-55775-207-9*) Intl Monetary.

Milne, Eric N., et al. Models & Techniques in Medical Imaging Research. LC 82-13141. 624p. 1983. text ed. 115.00 (*0-275-91404-6*, C1404, Praeger Pubs) Greenwood.

***Milne, Frank.** Finance Theory & Asset Pricing. (Vienna Institute for Advanced Studies Lecture Notes). (Illus.). 128p. 1995. text ed. 39.95 (*0-19-877397-8*); pap. text ed. 14.95 (*0-19-877398-6*) OUP.

Milne, G. J. The Fusion of Hardware Design & Verification: Proceedings of the IFIP WG10.2 Working Conference, Glasgow, Scotland, UK, 4-6 July, 1988. 502p. 1988. 107.75 (*0-444-70532-5*) Elsevier.

Milne, G. J. & Pierre, L., eds. Correct Hardware Design & Verification Methods: IFIP WG10.2 Advanced Research Working Conference CHARME '93, Arles, France, May 24-26, 1993. (Lecture Notes in Computer Science Ser.: Vol. 683). viii, 269p. 1993. pap. 44.00 (*0-387-56778-X*) Spr-Verlag.

Milne, G. J. & Subrahmanyam, P. A., eds. Formal Aspects of VLSI Design: Proceedings of the 1985 Edinburgh Workshop on VLSI, Edinburgh, Scotland, U. K., 30 June-2 July 1985. 214p. 1986. 84.75 (*0-444-70026-9*) Elsevier.

***Milne, G. W., ed.** Handbook of Data on Pesticides. 416p. 1994. 95.00 (*0-8493-2447-5*, 2447) CRC Pr.
— Properties of Pesticides: User's Guide. 40p. 1995. disk 250.00 (*0-8493-2448-3*, 2448) CRC Pr.

Milne, G. W., jt. auth. see Lide, David R.

Milne, G. W., jt. ed. see Lide, David R.

Milne, George. Formal Specification & Verification of Digital Systems. LC 93-29419. 1994. text ed. 40.00 (*0-07-707811-X*) McGraw.

Milne, George, ed. see Johnson, Samuel.

***Milne, George M.** Connecticut Woodlands: A Century's Story of the Connecticut Forest & Park Association. (Illus.). 160p. 1995. 30.00x (*0-914659-73-1*) Phoenix Pub.

***Milne, George McLean.** Connecticut Woodlands: A Century's Story of the Connecticut Forest & Park Association. LC 95-3080. 1995. 30.00 (*0-9619052-3-9*) CT Forest & Pk Assn.

Milne, Gordon. American Political Novel. 1972. pap. 11.95 (*0-8061-1050-3*) U of Okla Pr.
— Ports of Call: A Study of the American Nautical Novel. (Illus.). 132p. (C). 1987. lib. bdg. 35.50 (*0-8191-5673-6*); pap. text ed. 17.00 (*0-8191-5674-4*) U Pr of Amer.
— The Sense of Society: A History of the American Novel of Manners. 305p. 1977. 35.00 (*0-8386-1927-4*) Fairleigh Dickinson.

Milne, Gustav. From Roman Basilica to Medieval Market. 170p. 1992. pap. 44.95 (*0-11-290446-7*, HM8073, Pub. by HMSO UK) UNIPUB.
— The Port of Roman London. (Illus.). 176p. 1986. pap. 29.95 (*0-7134-4565-0*, Pub. by Batsford UK) Trafalgar.

Milne, H. F. How to Build a Small Two-Manual Chamber Pipe Organ. (Illus.). 1925. pap. 25.00 (*0-913746-03-7*) Organ Lit.
— The Reed Organ: Its Design & Construction. (Illus.). 168p. 1932. pap. 20.00 (*0-913746-02-9*) Organ Lit.

Milne, Hamish. Bartok. (Illustrated Lives of the Great Composers Ser.). (Illus.). 112p. 1987. pap. 14.95 (*0-7119-0260-7*, OP42464) Omnibus NY.

Milne, Hugh. Heart of Listening: A Visionary Approach to Craniosacral Work. 1995. pap. 40.00 (*1-55643-181-3*) North Atlantic.

Milne, J. G. Catalog of Alexandrian Coins. (Illus.). 1983. reprint ed. lib. bdg. 50.00 (*0-942666-20-8*) S J Durst.
— Greek & Roman Coins & the Study of History. (Illus.). 128p. 1980. 20.00 (*0-916710-80-7*) Obol Intl.
— A History of Egypt under Roman Rule. 3rd ed. (Illus.). xxiii, 331p. (C). 1994. text ed. 35.00 (*0-89005-510-6*) Ares.
— Inscriptiones Graecae Aegypti, No. 1: Cairo. xivi, 153p. 1976. 30.00 (*0-89005-111-9*) Ares.
— Surgical Instruments in Greek & Roman Times. (Illus.). 201p. 1991. 25.00 (*0-89005-127-5*) Ares.

Milne, J. S. Etale Cohomology. LC 79-84003. (Mathematical Ser.: No. 33). 1980. 55.00 (*0-691-08238-3*) Princeton U Pr.

Milne, James. London Book Window. LC 68-16957. (Essay Index Reprint Ser.). 1977. reprint ed. 18.95 (*0-8369-0709-4*) Ayer.
— Pages in Waiting. LC 74-93357. (Essay Index Reprint Ser.). 1977. 20.95 (*0-8369-1308-6*) Ayer.

Milne, James S. Arithmetic Duality Theorems. (Perspectives in Mathematics Ser.). 230p. 1986. text ed. 73.00 (*0-12-498040-6*) Acad Pr.

Milne, James S., jt. ed. see Clozel, Laurent.

Milne, John. Dead Birds. 208p. 1988. pap. 3.95 (*0-14-009704-X*, Penguin Bks) Viking Penguin.

Milne, John, jt. auth. see Fraser, Charles.

Milne, Judith. Flowers in Watercolour. (Illus.). 128p. 1993. 34.95 (*0-7134-6403-8*, Pub. by Batsford UK) Trafalgar.
— Wild Flowers in Watercolour. (Illus.). 128p. 1995. 29.95 (*0-7134-7380-0*, Pub. by Batsford UK) Trafalgar.

Milne, June. Kwame Nkrumah: The Conakry Years: His Life & Letters. LC 90-23173. 448p. (C). 1990. text ed. 60.00 (*0-901787-53-1*, Pub. by Panaf Bks UK); pap. 25.00 (*0-901787-54-X*, Pub. by Panaf Bks UK) Humanities.

Milne, Lorus J. & Milne, Margery. Understanding Radioactivity. LC 88-7382. (Illus.). 80p. (J). (gr. 4 up). 1989. lib. bdg. 14.95 (*0-689-31362-4*, Atheneum Bks Young) S&S Childrens.

Milne, Margery, jt. auth. see Milne, Lorus J.

Milne, Mary. Sunday Dismissals for RCIA Candidates & Catechumens. 242p. (Orig.). 1994. pap. text ed. 19.95 (*0-8146-2145-7*) Liturgical Pr.

Milne, Mary L. The Home of an Eastern Clan: A Study of the Palaungs of the Shan States. LC 77-87048. reprint ed. 30.75 (*0-404-16845-0*) AMS Pr.

Milne, Michael. Acompaname. 448p. 1991. pap. text ed. 34.95 (*0-8403-6857-7*) Kendall-Hunt.

Milne, P. H. Fish & Shellfish Farming in Coastal Waters. 1978. 70.00 (*0-685-63408-6*) St Mut.
— Underwater Acoustic Positioning Systems. LC 83-80348. 288p. 1983. 57.00 (*0-87201-012-0*) Gulf Pub.
— Underwater Engineering Surveys. LC 80-65129. (Illus.). 370p. 1980. 59.00 (*0-87201-884-9*) Gulf Pub.

Milne, Peter. Fish in a Barrel: Nick Cave & the Bad Seeds on Tour. (Illus.). 118p. reprint ed. pap. 22.00 (*1-880985-17-9*) Two Thirteen Sixty-one.

Milne, Peter C. Rhymes of the Times. LC 91-67930. 149p. (Orig.). 1993. pap. 9.00 (*1-56002-189-6*, Univ Edtns) Aegina Pr.

Milne, Peter H. BASIC Programs for Land Surveying. 420p. 1984. pap. 35.00 (*0-419-13010-1*, NO. 9086, E & FN Spon) Routledge Chapman & Hall.
— Computer Graphics for Surveying. 230p. 1987. text ed. 59.50 (*0-419-14080-8*, E & FN Spon); pap. text ed. 27.50 (*0-419-14070-0*, E & FN Spon) Routledge Chapman & Hall.
— Presentation Graphics for Engineering, Science & Business. (Illus.). 256p. 1991. 49.95 (*0-412-32050-9*, E & FN Spon); pap. write for info. (*0-412-32060-6*, E & FN Spon) Routledge Chapman & Hall.

Milne, R. G., ed. The Plant Viruses, Vol. 4: The Filamentous Plant Viruses. LC 88-15221. (Viruses Ser.). (Illus.). 440p. 1988. 95.00 (*0-306-42845-8*, Plenum Pr) Plenum.

Milne, R. S. & Ratnam, K. J. Malaysia: New States in a New Nation. (Studies in Commonwealth Politics & History: No. 2). 512p. 1973. 45.00 (*0-7146-2988-X*, Pub. by F Cass Pubs UK) Intl Spec Bk.

Milne, R. W., jt. auth. see Bramer, Max A.

Milne, Robert D. Into the Sun. (Illus.). 1980. 15.00 (*0-937986-41-0*) D M Grant.

Milne, Robert S. Opportunities in Travel Careers. LC 75-32612. (Illus.). (gr. 8 up). 1985. 13.95 (*0-8442-6215-3*, VGM Career Bks); pap. 10.95 (*0-8442-6216-1*, VGM Career Bks) NTC Pub Grp.
— Opportunities in Travel Careers. (Illus.). 160p. 1991. 13.95 (*0-8442-8568-4*, VGM Career Bks); pap. 10.95 (*0-8442-8569-2*, VGM Career Bks) NTC Pub Grp.

Milne, Seumas. The Enemy Within. 300p. 1993. 29.95 (*0-86091-461-5*, B2491, Pub. by Verso UK) Routledge Chapman & Hall.

Milne, T. A., et al. Sourcebook of Methods of Analysis for Biomass & Biomass Conversion Processes. 440p. 1990. 93.75 (*1-85166-527-7*) Elsevier.

Milne, Teddy. Anthony. LC 86-62446. 197p. (Orig.). (J). (gr. 5 up). 1986. pap. 5.00 (*0-938875-01-9*) Pittenbruach Pr.
— Cal Coolidge Doesn't Life Here Anymore: Glimpses of Northhampton MA. LC 94-74079. 1994. pap. 12.95 (*0-938875-33-7*) Pittenbruach Pr.
— The Candy Puzzle: An Alexa Powell Mystery. LC 89-60248. 172p. (J). (gr. 6-8). 1989. pap. 6.95 (*0-938875-16-7*) Pittenbruach Pr.
— Choose Love. LC 86-62021. 203p. 1986. pap. 10.95 (*0-938875-00-0*) Pittenbruach Pr.
— Christmas Serenity. 1990. pap. 3.50 (*0-938875-24-8*) Pittenbruach Pr.
— Compassionate Democracy - Next Steps in Self Government: Excerpts from 'Choose Love' 40p. 1987. pap. 3.95 (*0-938875-10-8*); student ed, pap. 4.95 (*0-685-67620-X*) Pittenbruach Pr.
— European Spoken Here. Date not set. write for info. (*0-938875-30-2*) Pittenbruach Pr.
— Instant Russian: An Easy Introduction to the Russian Language. LC 89-60249. 56p. 1989. pap. 3.60 (*0-938875-17-5*) Pittenbruach Pr.
— Is War Okay? 103p. 1991. student ed 10.95 (*0-685-69226-4*); pap. 9.95 (*0-938875-26-4*) Pittenbruach Pr.
— Kids Who Have Made a Difference. 34p. 1989. pap. 3.95 (*0-938875-21-3*) Pittenbruach Pr.
— Money, Power, & Responsibility: Common Sense for Today. LC 90-62776. 101p. 1990. pap. 9.95 (*0-938875-13-2*) Pittenbruach Pr.
— Mooncakes & Flower Beans, Adventures in China & Japan. 180p. 1993. pap. 12.50 (*0-938875-31-0*) Pittenbruach Pr.
— Peace Porridge - Where Now? 1995. pap. write for info. (*0-938875-32-9*) Pittenbruach Pr.
— Quote Quest: Something Different...for the Puzzle Buff. 43p. 1990. pap. 3.50 (*0-938875-25-6*) Pittenbruach Pr.
— Shambala Warriors: Non-Violent Fighters for Peace. LC 86-64054. (Illus.). 150p. (Orig.). (J). (gr. 4 up). 1987. pap. 7.95 (*0-938875-07-8*) Pittenbruach Pr.
— Solo Publishing. LC 90-63045. 100p. 1990. pap. 9.95 (*0-938875-23-X*) Pittenbruach Pr.
— War Is a Dinosaur, & Other Songs of Hope, Love & Weltschmerz. LC 86-64053. 96p. 1987. pap. 9.95 (*0-938875-04-3*) Pittenbruach Pr.

Milne, Thomas A., jt. ed. see Soltes, Ed J.

Milne-Thompson, L. M. Theoretical Aerodynamics. 430p. (C). 1973. reprint ed. pap. text ed. 9.95 (*0-486-61980-X*) Dover.

Milne-Thomson, L. M. The Calculus of Finite Difference. 2nd ed. LC 80-65906. xxiii, 558p. 1980. text ed. 29.50 (*0-8284-0308-2*) Chelsea Pub.

An Asterisk (*) at the beginning of an entry indicates that the title is appearing in BIP for the first time.

Milne-Thomson, Louis M. Russian-English Mathematical Dictionary: Words & Phrases in Pure & Applied Mathematics with Roots & Accents, Arranged for Easy Reference. LC 62-7217. (Mathematics Research Center, United States Army, University of Wisconsin Publication Ser.: No. 7). 205p. reprint ed. pap. 58.50 (*0-317-28131-3*, 2055742) Bks Demand.

Milne, Tom, ed. The Time Out Film Guide. (Illus.). 784p. 1990. pap. 14.95 (*0-14-012700-3*, Penguin Bks) Viking Penguin.

— The Time Out Film Guide. 784p. (Orig.). 1992. pap. 15.00 (*0-14-014592-3*, Penguin Bks) Viking Penguin.

— The Time Out Film Guide: The Definitive, A-Z Directory of over 10,000 Films. 3rd ed. 992p. 1994. pap. 20.00 (*0-14-017513-X*, Penguin Bks) Viking Penguin.

Milne, Tom & Willemen, Paul. The Overlook Film Encyclopedia: Horror. Hardy, Phil, ed. LC 93-23387. (Illus.). 496p. 1994. 50.00 (*0-87951-518-X*) Overlook Pr.

Milne, Tom, tr. see Eisenschitz, Bernard.

Milne, Tom, ed. see Godard, Jean-Luc.

Milne-Tyte, Robert. Bloody Jeffreys: The Hanging Judge. (Illus.). 208p. 1990. 34.95 (*0-233-98403-8*, Pub. by A Deutsch UK) Trafalgar.

Milne, W. S. Practical Bengali Grammar. (BEN & ENG.). 1992. 49.95 (*0-8288-8469-2*) Fr & Eur.

Milne Wallis, Timmon. Satyagraha: The Gandhian Approach to Nonviolent Social Change. 2nd ed. 100p. 1989. pap. 8.95 (*0-938875-18-3*) Pittenbruach Pr.

Milne, Wendy H. Making Your Own Jewelry: Creative Designs to Make & Wear. Balmuth, Deborah, ed. LC 94-4909. (Illus.). 96p. 1994. 18.95 (*0-88266-883-8*, Storey Pub) Storey Comm Inc.

Milne, William E. Numerical Calculus: Approximations, Interpolation, Finite Differences, Numerical Integration & Curve Fitting. LC 49-7739. 403p. reprint ed. pap. 114.90 (*0-7837-1421-1*, 2041776) Bks Demand.

— Numerical Solution of Differential Equations. 1970. reprint ed. pap. text ed. 8.95 (*0-486-62437-4*) Dover.

Milner. Diagnostic Picture Tests in Pediatrics. 2nd ed. 160p. 1991. pap. 14.95 (*0-8016-6292-3*) Mosby Yr Bk.

— Self-Assessment Picture Tests in Medicine: Pediatr. 176p. 1994. pap. 19.95 (*0-8151-5916-1*, Yr Bk Med Pubs) Mosby Yr Bk.

Milner, ed. Hospital Paediatrics. 2nd ed. (Illus.). 455p. (Orig.). 1992. pap. text ed. 69.95 (*0-443-04306-X*) Churchill.

Milner, A., ed. African Law Reports, Sierra Leone Series, 1950-1969, 5 vols., Set. LC 75-21503. 1972. 225.00 (*0-379-16003-X*) Oceana.

Milner, A. C. & Wilson, Trevor, eds. Australian Diplomacy: Challenges & Options for the Department of Foreign Affairs. LC 87-155223. (Australian Institute of International Affairs, Occasional Paper Ser.: No. 5). 98p. reprint ed. pap. 28.00 (*0-8357-6827-9*, 2035513) Bks Demand.

Milner, A. C., jt. auth. see Matheson, V.

***Milner, A. D.** Childhood Asthma. 2nd ed. 1994. 49.95 (*1-85317-110-7*) Scovill Paterson.

***Milner, A. D. & Goodale, M. A.** The Visual Brain in Action. (Oxford Psychology Ser.: No. 27). (Illus.). 230p. 1995. 55.00 (*0-19-852136-7*) OUP.

Milner, A. D. & Rugg, M. D. The Neuropsychology of Consciousness. (Foundations of Neuropsychology Ser.). (Illus.). 283p. 1992. text ed. 85.00 (*0-12-498045-7*); pap. 34.95 (*0-685-48692-3*) Acad Pr.

Milner, A. M. & Wood, James D., Jr., eds. Proceedings of the Second Glacier Bay Science Symposium. LC 90-5862. (Illus.). (C). 1990. pap. (*0-943475-03-1*) Natl Park GA.

Milner, A. R. & Wood, P. R., eds. Johne's Disease: Current Trends in Research, Diagnosis & Management. 1989. text ed. 50.00 (*0-643-04890-1*, Pub. by CSIRO AT) Intl Spec Bk.

Milner, Alan, ed. African Law Reports: Commercial Law Series, 1964, Vols. 1-2; 1965; 1966, Vols. 1-2; 1967, Vols. 1-3; 1968, Vols. 1-3; 1960, Vols. 1-3, 14 vols., Set. LC 67-26375. 1973. 630.00 (*0-379-13700-3*) Oceana.

Milner, Andrew. Contemporary Cultural Theory: An Introduction, Nos. 1-4. 192p. 1991. pap. 19.95 (*0-04-442292-X*, Pub. by Allen & Unwin Aust Pty AT) Paul & Co Pubs.

Milner, Andrew, et al, eds. Postmodern Conditions. LC 89-31934. 224p. 1990. 39.95 (*0-85496-591-2*) Berg Pubs.

***Milner, Angela, ed.** Dinosaurs. LC 95-12938. (Discoveries Ser.). (Illus.). 64p. (J). (gr. 4-7). 1995. write for info. (*0-7835-4765-X*) Time-Life.

Milner, Angela, jt. auth. see Gardom, Tom.

Milner, Anita C. Newspaper Genealogical Column Directory. rev. ed. x, 112p. (Orig.). 1992. pap. text ed. 14.00 (*1-55613-680-3*) Heritage Bk.

— Newspaper Indexes: A Location & Subject Guide for Researchers, Vol. I. LC 77-7130. 210p. 1977. 22.50 (*0-8108-1066-2*) Scarecrow.

— Newspaper Indexes: A Location & Subject Guide for Researchers, Vol. II. LC 77-7130. 203p. 1979. 22.50 (*0-8108-1244-4*) Scarecrow.

— Newspaper Indexes: A Location & Subject Guide for Researchers, Vol. III. LC 77-7130. 192p. 1982. 22.50 (*0-8108-1493-5*) Scarecrow.

Milner, Anne, jt. auth. see Harley, Geoff.

Milner, Anthony. The Invention of Politics in Colonial Malaya: Contesting Nationalism & the Expansion of the Public Sphere. (Illus.). 336p. (C). 1995. 59.95 (*0-521-46565-6*) Cambridge U Pr.

Milner, Anthony, jt. ed. see Herbert, Patricia.

Milner, C. Tatlin & the Russian Avant-Garde. (C). 1990. 375.00 (*0-685-34338-3*, Pub. by Collets); pap. 150.00 (*0-685-34339-1*, Pub. by Collets) St Mut.

Milner, Carol. Auditing ARM Portfolios: A Practical Guide. 50p. (Orig.). 1993. pap. 20.00 (*0-945359-19-5*) Mortgage Bankers.

Milner, Cate. France. LC 89-21783. (World in View Ser.). (Illus.). 96p. (YA). (gr. 6-12). 1990. lib. bdg. 24.26 (*0-8114-2427-8*) Raintree Steck-V.

Milner, Chris, ed. Export Promotion Strategies: Theory & Evidence from Developing Countries. 288p. 1990. 55.00 (*0-8147-5457-0*) NYU Pr.

Milner, Chris & Greenaway, David. An Introduction to International Economics. LC 78-40512. (Illus.). 272p. reprint ed. pap. 77.60 (*0-685-20294-1*, 2030328) Bks Demand.

Milner, Chris & Rayner, A. J., eds. Policy Adjustment in Africa: Case-Studies in Economic Development, Vol. 1. LC 91-33541. 280p. 1992. text ed. 75.00 (*0-312-07492-1*) St Martin.

Milner, Chris, jt. auth. see Greenaway, David.

Milner, Chris, jt. ed. see Llewelyn, David T.

Milner, Chris, jt. auth. see Williamson, John.

Milner, Clyde A., II. Major Problems in the History of the American West: Documents & Essays. LC 88-80718. (Major Problems in American History Ser.). 681p. (C). 1989. pap. text ed. 15.50 (*0-669-15134-3*) Heath.

— With Good Intentions: Quaker Work among the Pawnees, Otos, & Omahas in the 1870's. LC 81-16238. (Illus.). xvi, 246p. 1982. 25.00 (*0-8032-3066-4*) U of Nebr Pr.

Milner, Clyde A., II & O'Neil, Floyd A., eds. Churchmen & the Western Indians, 1820-1920. LC 85-40477. (Illus.). 272p. 1985. 26.95 (*0-8061-1950-0*) U of Okla Pr.

Milner, Clyde A., II, et al, eds. The Oxford History of the American West. (Illus.). 904p. 1994. 39.95 (*0-19-505968-9*) OUP.

Milner, D. & Vasiliou, V. Computer-Aided Engineering for Manufacture. 256p. 1987. text ed. 45.00 (*0-07-042427-6*) McGraw.

Milner, Dan & Kaplan, Paul. Songs of England, Ireland & Scotland: A Bonnie Bunch of Roses. (Illus.). 224p. 1983. pap. 17.95 (*0-8256-0248-3*, Oak) Music Sales.

Milner, David. Pediatrics. (Self-Assessment Picture Tests in Medicine Ser.). 148p. 1994. pap. 19.95 (*0-7234-1951-5*, Wolfe Pub) Mosby Yr Bk.

***Milner, E. R.** The Lives & Times of Bonnie & Clyde. LC 95-4305. (Illus.). 168p. (C). 1995. 24.95 (*0-8093-1977-2*) S Ill U Pr.

Milner, Esther. The Failure of Success: The Middle Class Crisis. LC 67-27951. 238p. 1968. 12.50 (*0-87527-054-9*) Green.

— The Failure of Success: The Middle-Class Crisis. 2nd ed. LC 67-27951. 238p. reprint ed. pap. 67.90 (*0-685-20345-X*, 2029791) Bks Demand.

Milner, Evgeny C., jt. auth. see Volkov, Vladimir.

Milner, Frank. Toulouse-Lautrec. (Gallery of Art Ser.). (Illus.). 176p. 1992. 19.98 (*0-8317-5449-4*) Smithmark.

Milner, G. Drugs & Driving: A Survey of the Relationship of Adverse Drug Reactions, & Drug-Alcohol Interaction to Driving Safety. Avery, G. S., ed. (Monographs on Drugs: Vol. 1). (Illus.). xi, 124p. 1972. 24.00 (*3-8055-1242-2*) S Karger.

Milner, G. B. Samoan Dictionary: Samoan-English, English-Samoan. 465p. 1992. text ed. 32.00 (*0-908597-12-6*, Pub. by Polynesian Soc) UH Pr.

Milner, G. W. & Phillips, G. Coulometry in Analytical Chemistry. 1968. 95.00 (*0-08-012439-9*, Pub. by Pergamon Repr UK) Franklin.

Milner, Gene. The Indiana High School Basketball Record Book. 144p. pap. 3.00 (*0-9613849-0-5*) Ind Basketball High Sch.

Milner, George. The Crime Against Marcella. large type ed. (Linford Mystery Library). 288p. 1988. pap. 11.95 (*0-7089-6622-5*, Linford) Ulverscroft.

— A Leavetaking. large type ed. (Linford Mystery Library). 276p. 1989. pap. 11.95 (*0-7089-6635-7*, Linford) Ulverscroft.

— Your Money & Your Life. large type ed. (Linford Mystery Library). 352p. 1988. pap. 11.95 (*0-7089-6514-8*, Trailtree Bookshop) Ulverscroft.

Milner, George, jt. auth. see Nodal, John.

Milner, George R. The East St. Louis Stone Quarry Site Cemetery. (American Bottom Archaeology Ser.: Selected FAI-270 Site Reports: Vol. 1). (Illus.). 192p. 1983. pap. 15.95 (*0-252-01060-4*) U of Ill Pr.

— The Julien (11-S-63) Site: A Mississippian Occupation. LC 84-602. (American Bottom Archaeology Ser.: Selected FAI-270 Site Reports: Vol. 7). (Illus.). 296p. 1984. pap. 19.95 (*0-252-01070-1*) U of Ill Pr.

— The Robinson's Lake (11-Ms-582) Site: Emergent Mississippian Occupation. LC 84-24107. (American Bottom Archaeology Ser.: Selected FAI-270 Site Reports: Vol. 10). (Illus.). 240p. 1985. pap. 16.95 (*0-252-01072-8*) U of Ill Pr.

— The Turner (11-S-50) & DeMange (11-S-447) Sites: A Mississippian Occupation. (American Bottom Archaeology Ser.: Selected FAI-270 Site Reports: Vol. 4). (Illus.). 256p. 1983. 17.95 (*0-252-01066-3*) U of Ill Pr.

Milner, George R., jt. auth. see Buikstra, Jane E.

Milner, George R., jt. ed. see Larsen, Clark S.

Milner, George W. The Principles & Applications of Polarography & Other Electroanalytical Processes. LC 57-3248. 757p. reprint ed. pap. 180.00 (*0-317-09850-0*, 2004947) Bks Demand.

Milner-Gulland, R. R., ed. Yevgeny Yevtushenko: Selected Poetry. 1963. 6.70 (*0-08-009808-8*, Pergamon Pr); pap. 5.15 (*0-08-009807-X*, Pergamon Pr) Elsevier.

Milner-Gulland, Robin & Dejevsky, Nikolai. Cultural Atlas of Russia & the Soviet Union. (Cultural Atlas Ser.). (Illus.). 240p. 1989. 45.00 (*0-8160-2207-0*) Facts on File.

Milner, Helen V. Resisting Protectionism: Global Industries & the Politics of International Trade. 268p. (C). 1989. 47.50 (*0-691-05676-0*); pap. text ed. 16.95 (*0-691-01074-9*) Princeton U Pr.

Milner, Helen V., jt. ed. see Baldwin, David A.

Milner, Henry. The Long Road to Reform: Restructuring Public Education in Quebec. 170p. (C). 1986. text ed. 44.95 (*0-7735-0563-6*, Pub. by McGill CN); pap. text ed. 24.95 (*0-7735-0564-4*, Pub. by McGill CN) U of Toronto Pr.

— Social Democracy & Rational Choice: The Scandanavian (sic) Experience & Beyond. LC 94-15094. (Illus.). 312p. 1995. 49.95 (*0-415-11699-6*, B4762) Routledge.

Milner, Ian, tr. see Holub, Miroslav.

Milner, Ian, tr. see Macek, Josef.

Milner, J. Edward. The Tree Book: The Indispensable Guide to Tree Facts, Crafts & Lore. (Illus.). 192p. 1994. 39.95 (*1-85585-132-6*) Trafalgar.

Milner, James B. Milner's Cases & Materials on Contracts. 3rd ed. Waddams, S. M., ed. LC 75-151396. 915p. reprint ed. pap. 180.00 (*0-7837-1049-6*, 2041361) Bks Demand.

Milner, Jarmila, tr. see Fischerova, Sylva.

Milner, Jean-Claude. For the Love of Language: L'Amour de la Langue. Banfield, Ann, tr. & intro. by. 150p. 1990. text ed. 39.95 (*0-312-03554-3*) St Martin.

Milner, Joe E. & Forrest, Earle R. California Joe: Noted Scout & Indian Fighter. LC 87-5908. (Illus.). viii, 396p. 1987. reprint ed. pap. 9.95 (*0-8032-8150-1*) U of Nebr Pr.

Milner, Joel S., ed. Neuropsychology of Aggression. 208p. (C). 1991. lib. bdg. 98.50 (*0-7923-1245-7*) Kluwer Ac.

Milner, John. Dictionary of Russian & Soviet Artists. (Illus.). 550p. 1993. 99.50 (*1-85149-182-1*) Antique Collect.

— Mondrian. (Illus.). 240p. 1992. 29.98 (*1-55859-400-0*) Abbeville Pr.

— Mondrian. rev. ed. (Illus.). 240p. (C). 1995. pap. 29.95 (*0-7148-3167-0*, Pub. by Phaidon Press UK) Chronicle Bks.

— The Studios of Paris: The Capital of Art in the Late Nineteenth Century. 256p. (C). 1990. reprint ed. pap. 26.50 (*0-300-04749-5*) Yale U Pr.

— The Studios of Paris: The Capital of Art in the Nineteenth Century. (C). 1988. 45.00 (*0-300-03990-5*) Yale U Pr.

— Vladimir Tatlin & the Russian Avant-Garde. LC 82-25923. (Illus.). 262p. reprint ed. pap. 74.70 (*0-7837-6219-4*, 2080229) Bks Demand.

Milner, Joseph O. & Milner, Lucy F. Bridging English. LC 92-33936. 512p. (C). 1993. pap. write for info. (*0-675-21412-2*, Merrill Pub Co) Macmillan.

Milner, Joseph O. & Pope, Carol A., eds. Global Voices: Culture & Identity in the Teaching of English. LC 93-41342. 229p. 1994. 22.95 (*0-8141-1855-0*) NCTE.

***Milner, Kathleen.** Reiki & Other Rays of Touch Healing. 2nd ed. (Healing Art Ser.). (Illus.). 152p. (Orig.). (C). 1995. pap. 15.95 (*1-886903-97-2*) K Milner.

Milner, Laurie. Royal Scots in the Gulf: First Battalion Royal Scots on Operation GRANBY 1990-1991. (Illus.). 256p. 1994. 42.50 (*0-85052-273-0*, Pub. by L Cooper Bks UK) Trans-Atl Phila.

Milner, Lucy F., jt. auth. see Milner, Joseph O.

Milner, M., jt. ed. see Hultin, H. O.

Milner, Marc. North Atlantic Run: The Royal Canadian Navy & the Battle for the Convoys. LC 85-60967. (Illus.). 326p. 1985. 24.95 (*0-87021-450-0*) Naval Inst Pr.

— The U-Boat Hunters: The Royal Canadian Navy & the Offensive Against Germany's Submarines. LC 94-66600. (Illus.). 280p. 1994. 29.95 (*1-55750-854-2*) Naval Inst Pr.

Milner, Marion. Hands of the Living God: An Account of a Psychoanalytic Treatment. LC 78-85201. (Illus.). 444p. 1969. text ed. 60.00 (*0-8236-2320-3*) Intl Univs Pr.

— The Suppressed Madness of Sane Men: Forty-Four Years of Exploring Psycho-Analysis. (Illus.). 250p. (C). 1987. lib. bdg. 49.50 (*0-422-61020-8*, Pub. by Tavistock UK); pap. 19.95 (*0-422-61690-7*, Pub. by Tavistock UK) Routledge Chapman & Hall.

Milner, Mordaunt. The Godolphin Arabian. 200p. 1990. 52.00 (*0-85131-476-7*, Pub. by J A Allen & Co UK) St Mut.

Milner, Morris, jt. auth. see Gowitzke, Barbara.

Milner, Murray, Jr. Status & Sacredness: A General Theory of Status Relations & An Analysis of Indian Culture. LC 93-20052. 1994. 60.00 (*0-19-508334-2*); pap. 24.95 (*0-19-508489-6*) OUP.

— Unequal Care: A Case Study of Interorganizational Relations. LC 80-15612. (Illus.). 224p. 1980. text ed. 49.00 (*0-231-05006-2*) Col U Pr.

Milner, N. P., tr. & intro. Vegetius: Epitome of Military Science. (Translated Texts for Historians Ser.). 182p. (Orig.). 1993. pap. text ed. 17.95 (*0-85323-228-8*, Pub. by Liverpool Univ Pr UK) U of Pa Pr.

Milner, Neal, jt. ed. see Merry, Sally E.

Milner, O. & Belcher, R. Analysis of Petroleum for Trace Elements. LC 63-19331. (International Series Mono on Analytical Chemistry: Vol. 14). 1963. 55.00 (*0-08-010448-7*, Pub. by Pergamon Repr UK) Franklin.

Milner, Oscar I. Successful Management of the Analytical Laboratory. 176p. 1991. 49.95 (*0-87371-438-5*, QD251) Lewis Pubs.

Milner, R. Retriever Training for the Duck Hunter. (Illus.). 168p. 1993. 21.95 (*0-940143-90-9*) Safari Pr.

Milner, Richard. Charles Darwin. (Makers of Modern Science Ser.). 128p. (J). (gr. 5 up). 1993. lib. bdg. 16.95 (*0-8160-2557-6*) Facts on File.

— Encyclopedia of Evolution: Humanity's Search for Its Origins. (Illus.). 498p. 1990. 45.00 (*0-8160-1472-8*) Facts on File.

— Encyclopedia of Evolution: Humanity's Search for Its Origins. (Illus.). 496p. 1993. pap. 25.00 (*0-8050-2717-3*) H Holt & Co.

Milner, Robert. A Menu for Manners. 39.95 (*0-935935-02-9*) Junction Pr.

— Retriever Training - A Better Way. 59.95 (*0-935935-01-0*) Junction Pr.

— Retriever Training for the Duck Hunter. (Illus.). 150p. 1985. reprint ed. 18.95 (*0-935935-00-2*) Junction Pr.

Milner, Robin & Tofte, Mads. Commentary on Standard ML. 160p. 1991. 30.00x (*0-262-13271-0*); pap. 19.95x (*0-262-63137-7*) MIT Pr.

Milner, Robin, et al. The Definition of Standard ML. 100p. 1990. 30.00 (*0-262-13255-9*); pap. 15.00 (*0-262-63132-6*) MIT Pr.

Milner, Roger. How's the World Treating You? 1967. pap. 4.75 (*0-8222-0541-6*) Dramatists Play.

Milner, Ronald, jt. ed. see King, Woodie.

Milner, Sonia. Sonia: Survival in War & Peace. LC 83-50758. 1983. pap. 8.95 (*0-88400-102-4*) Shengold.

Milner, Susan. The Dilemmas of Internationalism: French Syndicalism & the International Labour Movement, 1900-1914. LC 90-374. 268p. 1991. 65.00 (*0-85496-617-X*) Berg Pubs.

Milnes, A. G. Geology & Radwaste. 1985. text ed. 137.00 (*0-12-498070-8*); pap. text ed. 66.00 (*0-12-498071-6*) Acad Pr.

Milnes, Erin, ed. see Jaen, Nestor.

***Milnes, Lynne.** In a Victoria Garden. (Illus.). 120p. (Orig.). 1995. pap. 18.95 (*1-55143-031-2*) Orca Bk Pubs.

Milnes, Michelle, jt. auth. see Eckols, Steve.

Milnor, Andrew. Politics, Violence & Social Change in Northern Ireland. (Western Societies Papers). 73p. 1976. 11.95 (*0-8014-9628-4*) Cornell U Pr.

***Milnor, John.** John Milnor Collected Papers Vol. 1. (Illus.). x, 295p. 1994. text ed. 30.00 (*0-914098-30-6*) Publish or Perish.

— John Milnor, Collected Papers Vol. 2: The Fundamental Group. (Illus.). xii, 302p. 1995. text ed. 30.00 (*0-914098-31-4*) Publish or Perish.

Milnor, John W. Morse Theory. (Annals of Mathematics Studies: No. 51). (Orig.). 1963. pap. 32.50 (*0-691-08008-9*) Princeton U Pr.

— Singular Points of Complex Hypersurfaces. (Annals of Mathematics Studies: No. 61). 1969. pap. 27.50 (*0-691-08065-8*) Princeton U Pr.

— Topology from the Differentiable Viewpoint. LC 65-26874. (Illus.). 64p. 1965. pap. 6.95x (*0-8139-0181-2*) U Pr of Va.

Milnor, John W. & Stasheff, James D. Characteristic Classes. LC 72-4050. (Annals of Mathematics Studies: No. 76). 250p. 1973. 47.00 (*0-691-08122-0*) Princeton U Pr.

Milnor, Tilla, ed. see Brink, Raymond W.

Milnor, William R. Cardiovascular Physiology. (Illus.). 520p. 1990. 37.95 (*0-19-505884-4*) OUP.

Milo. Transformation of Human Epithelial Cells. 1992. 179.00 (*0-8493-6382-9*, RC280) CRC Pr.

Milo, ed. Transformation of Human Diploid Fibroblasts. 1990. 190.00 (*0-8493-4956-7*, RC268) CRC Pr.

Milo, Jack, jt. auth. see Day, Filomena T.

Milo, Mary. Guide to Beauty. LC 72-83736. (Family Circle Bks.). (Illus.). 160p. 1977. 12.95 (*0-405-09841-3*) Ayer.

Milo, Mary, jt. auth. see Family Circle Food Staff.

Milo, Ronald D. Immorality. LC 84-42564. 272p. 1984. text ed. 45.00 (*0-691-06614-0*) Princeton U Pr.

Milofsky, Carl. Testers & Testing: The Sociology of School Psychology. LC 88-28293. 304p. (C). 1989. text ed. 40.00 (*0-8135-1407-X*); pap. text ed. 15.00 (*0-8135-1408-8*) Rutgers U Pr.

Milofsky, Carl, ed. Community Organizations: Studies in Resource Mobilization & Exchange. (Yale Studies in Nonprofit Organizations). 320p. 1988. 55.00 (*0-19-504680-3*) OUP.

***Milofsky, David, ed.** Colorado Review: A Journal of Contemporary Literature. 200p. 1995. write for info. (*0-614-00687-2*) CO St U Ctr Literary.

— New Voices: Poetry & Fiction from Colorado State University. 300p. (C). 1994. pap. text ed. 10.00 (*1-885635-00-1*) CO St U Ctr Literary.

— New Voices: The Essay. 300p. (C). 1995. pap. text ed. 10.00 (*1-885635-01-X*) CO St U Ctr Literary.

Miloh, T. Mathematical Approaches in Hydrodynamics. (Miscellaneous Ser.: No. 24). xxi, 517p. 1991. pap. 72.50 (*0-89871-277-7*) Soc Indus-Appl Math.

Milojevic. Nonlinear Functional Analysis. (Lecture Notes in Pure & Applied Mathematics Ser.: Vol. 121). 288p. 1990. 125.00 (*0-8247-8255-0*) Dekker.

Milojicic, Dejan S. Load Distribution: Implementation for the Mach Microkernel. (Vieweg Advanced Studies in Computer Science). xx, 149p. 1994. 70.00 (*3-528-05424-7*, Pub. by Vieweg & Sohn GW) Ballen Bkslr.

***Milojkovic-Djuric, Jelena.** Panslavism & National Identity in Russia & in the Balkans, 1830-1880: Images of the Self & Others. 200p. 1994. 29.00 (*0-88033-291-3*) East Eur Quarterly.

— Tradition & Avant Garde. 1988. 42.00 (*0-685-42856-7*) East Eur Quarterly.

— Tradition & Avant Garde: Literature & Arts in Serbian Culture, 1900-1918. (East European Monographs: No. 234). 224p. 1988. text ed. 42.00 (*0-88033-131-3*) East Eur Quarterly.

— Tradition & Avante-Garde: The Arts in Serbian Culture Between the Two World Wars. 175p. 1984. text ed. 38.50 (*0-88033-052-X*) East Eur Quarterly.

Milon, Ellie. Two Hundred One Ways to Enjoy Your Dog. LC 89-18403. (Illus.). 291p. 1990. pap. 18.95 (*0-931866-33-2*) Alpine Pubns.

Milon, H., jt. ed. see Frigerio, Alberto.

***Milon, Walter J.** Integrating Economic & Ecological Indicators. LC 94-37882. 232p. 1995. text ed. 59.95 (*0-275-94983-4*, Praeger Pubs) Greenwood.

Milonas, Rolf. Fantasex: A Book of Erotic Games for the Adult Couple. rev. ed. 96p. (Orig.). 1983. pap. 10.00 (*0-399-50839-2*, Perigee Bks) Berkley Pub.

M

Milone, A. F., jt. ed. see Caglioti, G.

Milone, E. F. Light Curve Modeling of Eclipsing Binary Stars. LC 92-21532. 1992. 65.00 (*0-387-97946-8*) Spr-Verlag.

Milone, E. F., ed. Infrared Extinction & Standardization. (Lecture Notes in Physics Ser.: Vol. 341). iii, 79p. 1989. 41.00 (*0-387-51610-7*) Spr-Verlag.

Milone, Karen, illus. Beauty & the Beast. LC 81-612. 32p. (J). (gr. k-4). 1981. lib. bdg. 9.79 (*0-89375-464-1*); pap. text ed. 2.50 (*0-89375-465-X*) Troll Assocs.

— Still As a Star: A Book of Nighttime Poems. 32p. (J). (ps-3). 1989. 14.95 (*0-316-37272-2*) Little.

Milone, Michael N., Jr. Handwriting Skills, K-8. 64p. (gr. k-8). 1982. teacher ed 4.95 (*0-88085-018-3*); student ed 2.59 (*0-685-06079-9*) Zaner-Bloser.

Milone, Richard P. Hip Hop Astro Rap: A Creative Writing & Coloring Experience. 32p. 1993. pap. 20.00 (*0-9639808-0-7*) Classic Intl.

Milonni, P., et al. Chaos in Laser-Matter Interactions. 384p. 1987. text ed. 70.00 (*9971-5-0179-1*); pap. text ed. 37.00 (*9971-5-0180-5*) World Scientific Pub.

Milonni, P. W., jt. ed. see Grandy, Walter T., Jr.

Milonni, Peter W. The Quantum Vacuum: An Introduction to Quantum Electrodynamics. (Illus.). 522p. 1993. text ed. 75.00 (*0-12-498080-5*) Acad Pr.

Milonni, Peter W., jt. auth. see Eberly, Joseph H.

Milor, Vedat, ed. Changing Political Economies: Privatization in Post-Communist & Reforming Communist States. LC 93-34548. (Emerging Global Issues Ser.). 238p. 1994. lib. bdg. 42.00 (*1-55587-405-3*) Lynne Rienner.

Milora, Stanley L. & Tester, Jefferson W. Geothermal Energy As a Economic Source of Electric Power: Thermodynamics & Economic Design Criteria. LC 76-7008. 190p. 1976. 35.00 (*0-262-13123-4*) MIT Pr.

Miloradov, M., ed. Pollution of the Mediterranean Sea: Proceedings of An IAWPRC International Regional Conference Held in Split, Yugoslavia, 2-5 October 1985. (Water Science & Technology Ser.: No. 18). (Illus.). 338p. 1987. pap. 52.00 (*0-08-035578-1*, Pergamon Pr) Elsevier.

— Water Pollution Control in the Danube Basin. (Water Science & Technology Ser.: No. 22). (Illus.). 300p. 1990. pap. 130.00 (*0-08-040765-X*, Pergamon Pr) Elsevier.

Miloradovic, Z. English-Serbocroat & Serbocroat-English Grammatical Dictionary. 610p. (C). 1988. 140.00 (*0-89771-928-X*, Pub. by Collets) St Mut.

— English-Serbocroat & Serbocroat-English Grammatical Dictionary. 3rd ed. 610p. (C). 1988. 195.00 (*0-685-46892-5*, Pub. by Collets) St Mut.

Miloradovic, Zivan. English - Serbocroatian, Serbocroatian - English Dictionary: Englesko-Srpskohrvatski I Srpskohrvatsko-Engleski Recenicnik sa Primenjen. 658p. (ENG & SER.). 1987. 125.00 (*0-8288-0506-7*, F102240) Fr & Eur.

— French - Serbocroatian, Serbocroatian - French Dictionary: Francusko-Srpskohrvatsko-Francuski Recenicnik sa Primen. 600p. (FRE & SER.). 1987. 95.00 (*0-8288-1046-X*, F97180) Fr & Eur.

— Russian-Serbocroatian, Serbocroatian-Russian Dictionary & Grammatical Primer: Rusko-Srpskohrvatski i Srpskohrvatsko-Ruski Recenicnik sa Primenjenon Gramatik. 611p. (RUS & SER.). 1987. 95.00 (*0-8288-1056-7*, F114894) Fr & Eur.

Miloradovich, Milo. Cooking with Herbs & Spices. 320p. 1990. pap. 6.95 (*0-486-26177-8*) Dover.

— Growing & Using Herbs & Spices. 236p. 1986. reprint ed. pap. 5.95 (*0-486-25058-X*) Dover.

Miloradovitch, Hazelle, ed. see Lidl, Andreas.

Milord, Susan. Adventures in Art: Art & Crafts Experiences for 7- to 14-Year Olds. Williamson, Susan, ed. LC 90-39031. (Kids Can! Ser.: No. 3). (Illus.). 160p. (Orig.). (J). (gr. 2-8). 1990. pap. 12.95 (*0-913589-54-3*) Williamson Pub Co.

— Hands Around the World: Three Hundred Sixty-Five Creative Ways to Build Cultural Awareness & Global Respect. LC 92-21753. (Kids Can! Ser.: No. 7). (Illus.). 176p. (Orig.). (J). (gr. 1-8). 1992. pap. 12.95 (*0-913589-65-9*) Williamson Pub Co.

— The Kids' Nature Book: Three Hundred Sixty-Five Indoor - Outdoor Activities & Experiences. Williamson, Susan, ed. LC 89-14724. (Kids Can! Ser: No. 1). (Illus.). 160p. (Orig.). (J). (ps-3). 1989. pap. 12.95 (*0-913589-42-X*) Williamson Pub Co.

— Tales Alive! Ten Multicultural Folk Tales, with Art, Craft & Creative Experiences. (Illus.). 128p. (Orig.). (J). (gr. k-6). 1994. pap. 15.95 (*0-913589-79-9*) Williamson Pub Co.

Milos Acin, Kosta. Draza Mihailovic & Ravna Gora: Srpska KRV - Staljinova Vlast, 18 vols., Set. (Illus.). 300p. (SER.). 1990. write for info. (*0-318-66826-2*) Ravnogorski.

— Draza Mihailovic & Ravna Gora: Srpska KRV - Staljinova Vlast, 18 vols., Vol. XIV. (Draza Mihailovic & Ravna Gora Ser.). (Illus.). 300p. (SER.). 1990. pap. 25.00 (*0-931931-31-2*) Ravnogorski.

Milos, Jon. Through the Needle's Eye. Walker, Brenda, tr. 112p. (Orig.). 1990. pap. 19.95 (*0-948259-61-2*, Pub. by Forest Bks UK) Dufour.

Milosavljevic, Bosko, tr. see Jankovic, Branimir M.

Milosavljevic, Margot, tr. see Jankovic, Branimir M.

Milosavljevic, Petar, ed. Yugoslav Literary-Theoretical Thought, 2 vols., Set. 1992. write for info. (*90-272-1544-8*) Benjamins North Am.

— Yugoslav Literary-Theoretical Thought, 2 vols., Vol. 1: 1500-1955. xxi, 521p. 1992. 169.00 (*0-685-53304-2*) Benjamins North Am.

— Yugoslav Literary-Theoretical Thought, 2 vols., Vol. 2: 1955-1985. 400p. 1992. write for info. (*90-272-1543-X*) Benjamins North Am.

— Yugoslav Literary-Theoretical Thought, Vol. 1: 1500-1955. LC 90-1117. (Linguistic & Literary Studies in Eastern Europe: Vol. 32). xxi, 521p. 1990. 153.00 (*90-272-1538-3*) Benjamins North Am.

***Milosch, Joseph.** On the Wing. Thomas, Erikheath A., ed. (Illus.). 35p. (Orig.). 1995. pap. 5.00 (*0-9638412-1-1*) Drury Ln.

Milosh, Joseph E. The Scale of Perfection & the English Mystical Tradition. LC 66-22857. 226p. reprint ed. pap. 64.50 (*0-317-07863-1*, 2010975) Bks Demand.

Miloslav, Rechcigl. Handbook of Agricultural Productivity, Vol. II: Animal Productivity. 416p. 1981. 151.00 (*0-8493-3963-4*, S494, CRC Reprint) Franklin.

Miloslavski, I. Short Practical Russian Grammar. 244p. (ENG & RUS.). (C). 1988. 45.00x (*0-685-39367-4*) Collets.

Miloslavskii, I. G. Concise Practical Russian Grammar. 284p. (C). 1987. 50.00 (*0-317-92394-3*) St Mut.

Miloslavsky, Yury. Urban Romances. 1995. 22.95 (*0-87501-062-8*) Ardis Pubs.

Milostan, Harry. Enduring Poles. LC 76-42844. 1977. 7.95 (*0-918020-01-8*); pap. 4.95 (*0-918020-02-6*) Masspac Pub.

— The Errant Nun. LC 79-83634. (Illus.). 1979. pap. 9.00 (*0-918020-05-0*) Masspac Pub.

— Folksy Fables. LC 84-61017. (Illus.). 80p. (Orig.). 1984. pap. 4.00 (*0-918020-07-7*) Masspac Pub.

Milostan, Harry, ed. Parisville Poles. LC 77-77917. 1977. lib. bdg. 12.00 (*0-918020-03-4*) Masspac Pub.

Milosz, Czeslaw. Beginning with My Streets: Essays & Recollections. Levine, Madeline G., tr. 288p. 1992. 30.00 (*0-374-11010-7*) FS&G.

— The Captive Mind. 1992. 21.00 (*0-8446-6615-7*) Peter Smith.

— The Captive Mind. LC 89-40503. 272p. 1990. pap. 11.00 (*0-679-72856-2*, Vin) Random.

— Captive Mind. 1981. pap. 6.95 (*0-394-74724-0*) Random.

— Collected Poems. 528p. 1990. pap. 14.95 (*0-88001-174-2*) Ecco Pr.

— Emperor of the Earth: Modes of Eccentric Vision. LC 76-20005. 1977. 38.00 (*0-520-03302-7*); pap. 12.00 (*0-520-04503-3*) U CA Pr.

— Facing the River: New Poems. 1995. 22.00 (*0-88001-404-0*) Ecco Pr.

— The History of Polish Literature. rev. ed. LC 82-20227. 570p. (C). 1983. pap. 14.00 (*0-520-04477-0*) U CA Pr.

— Hymn O Perle: Hymn to the Pearl. (Michigan Slavic Materials Ser.: No. 21). 1982. 10.00 (*0-930042-45-X*) Mich Slavic Pubns.

— The Issa Valley. Iribarne, Louis, tr. 288p. 1982. pap. 13.00 (*0-374-51695-2*) FS&G.

— The Land of Ulro. Iribarne, Louis, tr. 287p. 1985. pap. 9.95 (*0-374-51937-4*) FS&G.

— Native Realm: A Search for Self-Definition. Leach, Catherine S., tr. 1981. pap. 14.00 (*0-520-04474-6*) U CA Pr.

— Postwar Polish Poetry: An Anthology. rev. ed. LC 82-16084. 180p. (C). 1983. pap. 12.00 (*0-520-04476-2*) U CA Pr.

— Provinces. 1991. 19.95 (*0-88001-317-6*) Ecco Pr.

— Provinces: Poems 1987-1991. Hass, Robert, tr. LC 92-44647. 1993. pap. 9.95 (*0-88001-321-4*) Ecco Pr.

— The Separate Notebooks. Hass, Robert & Pinsky, Robert, trs. 212p. 1983. 17.50 (*0-88001-031-2*) Ecco Pr.

— The Separate Notebooks. Hass, Robert et al, trs. 250p. 1986. 12.50 (*0-88001-116-5*) Ecco Pr.

— Utwory Poetyckie: Poems. 1976. 25.00 (*0-930042-22-0*) Mich Slavic Pubns.

— Visions from San Francisco Bay. Lourie, Richard, tr. 226p. 1982. 14.95 (*0-374-28488-1*) FS&G.

— The Witness of Poetry. (Charles Eliot Norton Lectures). 128p. 1984. pap. text ed. 7.95 (*0-674-95383-5*) HUP.

— A Year of the Hunter. Levine, Madeline G., tr. LC 93-49598. 1994. 27.50 (*0-374-29344-9*) FS&G.

— A Year of the Hunter. Levine, Madeline G., tr. 294p. Date not set. 12.00 (*0-374-52444-0*) FS&G.

Milosz, Czeslaw, ed. Piesn Niepodlegla-the Invincible Song. (Michigan Slavic Materials Ser.: No. 18). 1981. 10.00 (*0-930042-41-7*) Mich Slavic Pubns.

Milosz, Czeslaw & Hass, Robert. Unattainable Earth. 140p. 1986. 17.95 (*0-88001-098-3*) Ecco Pr.

Milosz, Czeslaw, tr. see Wat, Aleksander.

***Milosz, Czeslaw, et al.** O Rus! Studia Litteraria Slavica in Honorem Hugh McLean. Karlinsky, Simon et al, eds. 530p. (Orig.). (C). 1995. pap. 50.00 (*1-57201-008-8*) Berkeley Slavic.

Milosz, O. V. Amorous Initiation: A Novel of Sacred & Profane Love. 256p. 1993. 22.95 (*0-89281-418-7*) Inner Tradit.

Milotte, Alfred & Milotte, Elma. Toklat: The Story of an Alaskan Grizzly Bear. LC 87-26910. (Illus.). 124p. (Orig.). (gr. 4 up). 1987. pap. 9.95 (*0-88240-325-7*) Alaska Northwest.

Milotte, Elma, jt. auth. see Milotte, Alfred.

Milovanov, E. L. English-Russian Dictionary of Environmental Control. 338p. (ENG & RUS.). 1981. write for info. (*0-8288-1401-5*, M15790) Fr & Eur.

Milovanov, E. L. & Veistman, E. A., eds. English-Russian Dictionary of Environmental Control. 338p. (ENG & RUS.). 1981. 159.00 (*0-08-023576-X*, Pub. by Pergamon Repr UK) Franklin.

Milovanovic, Dragan. Postmodern Law & Disorder: Psychoanalytic Semiotics, Chaos & Juridic Exegeses. (Legal Semiotics Monographs Ser.: Vol. 3). 280p. 1992. 67.50 (*0-9513793-3-X*) W W Gaunt.

— Weberian & Marxian Analysis of Law: Development & Functions of Law in a Capitalist Mode of Production. 240p. 1989. text ed. 52.95 (*0-566-07000-6*, Pub. by Dartmth Pub UK) Ashgate Pub Co.

Milovanovic, Dragan, jt. ed. see Janikowski, W. Richard.

Milovanovic, G. V., et al. Topics in Polynomials: Extremal Problems, Inequalities, Zeros. 300p. 1994. text ed. 146.00 (*981-02-0499-X*) World Scientific Pub.

Milovanovic, R. & Elzer, P., eds. Experience with the Management of Software Projects, 1988. LC 89-26462. (IFAC Publication Ser.: No. 90). (Illus.). 106p. 1989. 51.00 (*0-08-036928-6*, Pergamon Pr) Elsevier.

Milovic, D. Stresses & Displacements for Shallow Foundations. LC 92-10556. (Developments in Geotechnical Engineering Ser.: Vol. 70). 1992. write for info. (*0-444-88349-5*) Elsevier.

Milovksy, A. Ancient Russian Cities. (Illus.). 226p. (C). 1986. 60.00 (*0-685-37533-1*, Pub. by Collets) St Mut.

Milovskii, A. Pure Spring: Craft & Craftsmen of the U. S. S. R. 256p. (C). 1987. text ed. 90.00 (*0-685-40315-7*, Pub. by Collets) St Mut.

Milovsky, A. Ancient Russian Cities: Moscow Raduga, 1986. (Illus.). 226p. (C). 1986. 60.00 (*0-685-32386-2*, Pub. by Collets UK) Pro-Am Music.

Milroy, E., ed. Role-Play: A Practical Guide. (Illus.). 150p. 1982. text ed. 22.00 (*0-08-025744-5*, R130, Pergamon Pr); pap. text ed. 17.90 (*0-08-025745-3*, R132, Pergamon Pr) Elsevier.

— World Literature on: Prazosin: An Evaluation of Its Clinical Efficacy & Safety in the Treatment of Benign Prostatic Hypertrophy. (Journal: Urologia Internationalis: Vol. 45, Suppl. 1, 1990). (Illus.). iv, 64p. 1990. pap. 27.25 (*3-8055-5181-9*) S Karger.

Milroy, Elizabeth & Owens, Gwendolyn. Painters of a New Century: The Eight & American Art. (Illus.). 256p. (Orig.). 1991. pap. 39.95 (*0-944110-08-8*) Milwauk Art Mus.

Milroy, James. Linguistic Variation & Change: On the Historical Sociolinguistics of English. (Language in Society Ser.). (Illus.). 256p. 1991. pap. 21.95 (*0-631-14367-X*) Blackwell Pubs.

Milroy, James & Milroy, Lesley. Authority in Language: Investigating Language Standardisation & Prescription. 2nd ed. 216p. 1991. pap. 16.95 (*0-415-06575-5*, A6387) Routledge.

Milroy, James & Milroy, Lesley, eds. Real English: The Grammar of English Dialects in the British Isles. LC 92-42775. (Real Language Ser.). 1993. write for info. (*0-582-08177-7*); pap. write for info. (*0-582-08176-9*) Longman.

Milroy, Lesley. Observing & Analysing Natural Language. 240p. (Orig.). (C). 1987. pap. text ed. 24.95 (*0-631-13623-1*) Blackwell Pubs.

***Milroy, Lesley & Muysken, Pieter, eds.** One Speaker, Two Languages: Cross-Disciplinary Perspectives on Code-Switching. 376p. (C). 1995. write for info. (*0-521-47350-0*); pap. write for info. (*0-521-47912-6*) Cambridge U Pr.

Milroy, Lesley, jt. auth. see Lesser, Ruth.

Milroy, Lesley, jt. auth. see Milroy, James.

Milroy, Lesley, jt. ed. see Milroy, James.

Milroy, Patrick. Ward Lock Family Health Guide: Sports Injuries. (Illus.). 80p. 1994. pap. 9.95 (*0-7063-7253-0*, Pub. by Ward Lock UK) Sterling.

Milroy, Wallace. Wallace Milroy's Malt Whisky Alamanac: A Taster's Guide. (Illus.). 144p. 1991. 10.95 (*0-312-06542-6*) St Martin.

Milsant, Jeanne. Micro-Computer & Computer Lexicon: Lexique d'Informatique et de Micro-Informatique. 176p. (ENG & FRE.). 1985. pap. write for info. (*0-7859-4925-9*) Fr & Eur.

Mil'Shteyn, Y. I., ed. see Scriabin, Alexander.

***Milsk, Nancy.** Empowered by God. 253p. Date not set. 9.99 (*0-88368-338-5*) Whitaker Hse.

Milsom, C. H. Guide to the Merchant Navy. (C). 1987. 36.00 (*0-85174-037-5*, Pub. by Brwn Son Ferg) St Mut.

Milsom, John. Field Geophysics. (Geological Society of London Professional Handbook Ser.: No. 1572). 182p. 1991. pap. text ed. 27.95 (*0-471-93248-5*) Wiley.

***Milsom, Kim.** Match Fishing: A Champion's Guide. (Illus.). 128p. 1995. 39.95 (*1-85223-791-0*, Pub. by Crowood Pr UK) Trafalgar.

Milsom, S. E. The Legal Framework of English Feudalism. LC 85-82332. (Cambridge Studies in English Legal History). 212p. 1986. reprint ed. lib. bdg. 55.00 (*0-912004-58-4*) W W Gaunt.

Milsom, S. F. Historical Foundations of the Common Law. 2nd ed. 1981. pap. 44.00 (*0-406-62503-4*, U.K.) Butterworth Legal Pubs.

Milsom, S. F., jt. auth. see Baker, J. H.

Milsom, S. F. C. Studies in the History of the Common Law. 368p. 1985. text ed. 60.00 (*0-907628-61-3*) Hambledon Press.

Milsom, Stroud. The Legal Framework of English Feudalism: The Maitland Lectures Given in 1972. LC 75-2351. (Cambridge Studies in English Legal History). 212p. reprint ed. pap. 60.50 (*0-318-34824-1*, 2031693) Bks Demand.

Milsome, John. Heroine of Newgate: Elizabeth Fry. 1982. pap. 3.95 (*0-87508-633-0*) Chr Lit.

— Sierra Leone. (Let's Visit Places & Peoples of the World Ser.). (Illus.). 96p. (J). (gr. 5 up). 1988. 14.95 (*0-7910-0106-7*) Chelsea Hse.

Milsome, John, jt. auth. see Damien of Molokai.

Milson, Fred. An Introduction to Community Work. 168p. 1974. 15.95 (*0-7100-7840-4*, RKP); pap. 15.95 (*0-7100-7841-2*, RKP) Routledge.

Milson, Menahem. A Sufi Rule for Novices: Kiteab Eadeab Al-Mureidein of Abeu Al-Najeib Al-Suhrawardei. abr. ed. LC 74-27750. (Harvard Middle Eastern Studies: No. 17). 99p. reprint ed. pap. 29.70 (*0-7837-4436-6*, 2057965) Bks Demand.

Milstead. Subject Access Systems. 1984. text ed. 59.00 (*0-12-498120-8*) Acad Pr.

Milstead, James A., ed. see Hardegree, Greg D.

***Milstead, Jessica.** ASIS Thesaurus of Information Science & Librarianship. 150p. 1994. pap. 34.95 (*0-938734-80-6*) Learned Info.

***Milstead, Jessica L. & Pajer, Beverly A.** Index to the Inventory of Records of the American Jewish Committee, 1906-80. LC 94-34400. 1994. write for info. (*0-87495-107-0*) Am Jewish Comm.

Milstead, Victoria. The Hidden Scarlet Sin. 56p. 1992. pap. 6.95 (*0-8059-3281-X*) Dorrance.

Milstein, jt. auth. see Wells.

***Milstein, G. N.** Numerical Integration of Stochastic Differential Equations. (Mathematics & Its Applications Ser.: Vol. 313). 169p. (C). 1994. lib. bdg. 86.50 (*0-7923-3213-X*) Kluwer Ac.

Milstein, Herbert E. Attorney-Client Privilege & the Work Product Doctrine: Corporate Applications. (Corporate Practice Ser.: No. 22). 1980. 92.00 (*1-55871-254-2*) BNA.

Milstein, Jeff, jt. auth. see Walker, Lester.

Milstein, Linda. Grandma's Jewelry Box. LC 91-66738. (Illus.). 24p. (J). (ps-3). 1992. 8.00 (*0-679-81973-8*) Random Bks Yng Read.

Milstein, Linda B. Amanda's Perfect Hair. LC 92-34314. (Illus.). 32p. (J). (ps up). 1993. 14.00 (*0-688-11153-X*, Tambourine Bks); lib. bdg. 13.93 (*0-688-11154-8*, Tambourine Bks) Morrow.

— Coconut Mon. LC 94-27171. (J). (gr. 1-8). 1995. write for info. (*0-688-12862-9*); write for info. (*0-688-12863-7*) Morrow.

— Giving Comfort: What You can Do When Someone You Love Is Ill. LC 93-32169. 128p. 1994. 6.95 (*0-14-023538-8*, Penguin Bks) Viking Penguin.

— Living in the Aftermath. Warren, Shirley, ed. 36p. 1995. pap. 5.50 (*1-877801-27-5*) Still Waters.

— Miami-Nanny Stories. LC 93-28680. (Illus.). (J). 1994. 16.00 (*0-688-11151-3*, Tambourine Bks); lib. bdg. 15.93 (*0-688-11152-1*, Tambourine Bks) Morrow.

***Milstein, Michael.** Wolf: Return to Yellowstone. (Illus.). 96p. (Orig.). 1995. pap. write for info. (*0-9627618-8-5*) Billings Gazette.

Milstein, Michael, et al. Internship Programs in Educational Administration: A Guide to Preparing Educational Leaders. 176p. (C). 1991. text ed. 41.95 (*0-8077-3080-7*); pap. text ed. 19.95 (*0-8077-3079-3*) Tchrs Coll.

Milstein, Mike M. Changing the Way We Prepare Educational Leaders: The Danforth Experience. 264p. 1993. 43.95 (*0-8039-6077-8*); pap. 21.95 (*0-8039-6078-6*) Corwin Pr.

— Restructuring Schools: Doing It Right. Herman, Jerry J. & Herman, Janice L., eds. LC 93-17872. (Road Maps to Success Ser.). 80p. (C). 1993. pap. 15.00 (*0-8039-6072-7*) Corwin Pr.

Milstein, Mike M., ed. Schools, Conflict, & Change. LC 79-20327. 320p. reprint ed. pap. 91.20 (*0-318-34884-5*, 2031205) Bks Demand.

Milstein, Mike M. & Jennings, Robert E. Educational Policy-Making & the State Legislature: The New York Experience. LC 78-185780. (Special Studies in U. S. Economic, Social & Political Issues). 1973. 39.00 (*0-275-28719-X*) Irvington.

Milstein, Nathan & Volkov, Solomon. From Russia to the West: The Musical Memoirs & Reminiscences of Nathan Milstein. Bouis, Antonina W., tr. LC 91-22222. (Illus.). 282p. 1991. reprint ed. pap. 14.95 (*0-87910-151-2*) Limelight Edns.

Milstein, Rachel. Miniature Painting in Ottoman Baghdad. (Islamic Art & Architecture Ser.: No. 5). (Illus.). 268p. (C). 1989. lib. bdg. 59.95 (*0-939214-60-1*) Mazda Pubs.

Milstein, Silvina. Arnold Schoenberg: Notes, Sets, Forms. (Music in the Twentieth Century Ser.). (Illus.). 208p. (C). 1992. 89.95 (*0-521-39049-4*) Cambridge U Pr.

Milstein, Stanley, tr. Jacques Joseph's Rhinoplasty & Facial Plastic Surgery with a Supplement on Mammaplasty. (Illus.). 855p. 1987. 395.00 (*0-9605972-1-2*) Columella Pr.

Milstein, Stanley, tr. see Politzer, Adam.

Milsten, David R. Will Rogers: An Appreciation. 1976. lib. bdg. 59.95 (*0-8490-2826-4*) Gordon Pr.

Milsum, J. Positive Feedback: General Systems Approach Positive - Negative Feedback & Causal. LC 68-17739. 1968. 80.00 (*0-08-012577-8*, Pub. by Pergamon Repr UK) Franklin.

Milt, Harry, jt. auth. see Custer, Robert L.

Milt, Harry, jt. auth. see Zane, Manuel D.

Milt, Harry, et al. North Georgia Mountains: A Comprehensive Guide to Shopping, Sightseeing, Activities, Restaurants, & Accommodations. SelpH, Alexa, ed. LC 92-19437. (Illus.). 352p. (Orig.). 1992. pap. 15.95 (*0-87797-236-2*) Cherokee.

Miltal, Al. Marilyn Had Hands Full of Eyes. (Orig.). 1989. pap. 5.00 (*0-941720-66-7*) Slough Pr TX.

Milteer, Lee. Feel & Grow Rich. 224p. 1993. 18.95 (*1-878901-88-5*) Hampton Roads Pub Co.

***Miltenburg, John.** Manufacturing Strategy: How to Formulate & Implement a Winning Plan. (Illus.). 300p. 1995. 45.00 (*1-56327-071-4*) Prod Press.

Milthorpe, F. L., ed. see Easter School in Agricultural Science (3rd: 1956: University of Nottingham) Staff.

Milting, Martha. My Best to You. 304p. 1985. pap. text ed. 11.95 (*0-9614455-5-6*) M Milting.

***Miltner, Robert.** Against the Simple. LC 94-33223. (Wick Poetry Chapbook Ser.: No. 6). 24p. (Orig.). 1995. pap. 3.00 (*0-87338-521-7*) Kent St U Pr.

— The Seamless Serial Hour. 1993. pap. 6.95 (*0-685-70583-8*) Pudding Hse Pubns.

***Milton.** Apes: They're Like Us. 7.99 (*0-679-97284-6*) Random.

— Inflation: Everyone's Problem. 4.95 (*0-8065-0320-3*, Citadel Pr) Carol Pub Group.

An Asterisk (*) at the beginning of an entry indicates that the title is appearing in BIP for the first time.

— Life Insurance Stocks: The Modern Gold Rush. 2.95 (0-8065-0322-X, Citadel Pr) Carol Pub Group.
— The Merchant of Venice (Shakespeare) (Book Notes Ser.). (C). 1985. pap. 2.95 (0-8120-3526-7) Barron.
— To Kill a Mockingbird (Lee) (Book Notes Ser.). (C). 1984. pap. 2.95 (0-8120-3446-5) Barron.
— Walden (Thoreau) (Book Notes Ser.). (C). 1984. pap. 2.50 (0-8120-3447-3) Barron.

Milton, jt. auth. see Bronte, Charlotte.

Milton, A. S., ed. Pyretics & Antipyretics. (Handbook of Experimental Pharmacology Ser.: Vol. 60). 715p. 1982. 327.00 (0-387-11511-0) Spr-Verlag.
— Temperature Regulation: Recent Physiological & Pharmacological Advances. LC 93-50550. (Advances in Pharmacological Sciences Ser.). xii, 376p. 1994. 101.00 (0-8176-2992-0) Birkhauser.

***Milton, Adrian.** Lavender Light: Daily Meditations for Gay Men in Recovery. LC 94-32616. 1995. write for info. (0-399-51939-4) Putnam Pub Group.

Milton, Anthony. Catholic & Reformed: The Roman & Protestant Churches in English Protestant Thought, 1600-1640. (Cambridge Studies in Early Modern British History). 640p. (C). 1995. 79.95 (0-521-40141-0) Cambridge U Pr.

Milton, Arthur. How Your Life Insurance Policies Rob You. LC 81-4679. 178p. (Orig.). 1983. 8.95 (0-8065-0768-3, Citadel Pr); pap. 4.95 (0-685-01099-6, Citadel Pr) Carol Pub Group.
— How Your Life Insurance Policies Rob You. (Orig.). 1990. pap. 8.95 (0-8065-1176-1, Citadel Pr) Carol Pub Group.
— Milton on America. 224p. 1987. 12.00 (0-8065-1039-0, Citadel Pr) Carol Pub Group.
— A Nation Saved. (Illus.). 192p. 1983. 10.00 (0-8065-0870-1, Citadel Pr) Carol Pub Group.
— Will Inflation Destroy America? 1977. 7.95 (0-8065-0608-3, Citadel Pr) Carol Pub Group.
— You Are Worth a Fortune. 1977. 6.95 (0-8065-0589-3, Citadel Pr) Carol Pub Group.

Milton, Barbara. A Small Cartoon. (Fiction Book Award Winner Ser.). 52p. (Orig.). 1983. pap. 5.95 (0-912527-00-5) Word Beat.

***Milton Bradley Company Staff.** Crocodile Dentist, No. 1. Date not set. write for info. (0-679-87411-9) Random.
— Memory, No. 1. Date not set. write for info. (0-679-87410-0) Random.

***Milton Bradley Staff.** Happy House-Milton Bradley Color with Reservations. 1994. 47.04 (0-679-86806-2) Random.

Milton, Brian, intro. MECH 'Ninety-One Australia: Engineering in a Competitive World, Conference 4: Energy: Resources, Usage, Conservation & the Environment. (Illus.). 163p. 1991. pap. 48.00 (0-85825-528-6, Pub. by Inst Engrs Aust-EA Bks AT) Accents Pubns.

Milton, Colin. Lawrence & Nietzsche: A Study in Influence. 264p. 1987. text ed. 37.90 (0-08-035067-4, Pub. by Aberdeen U Pr) Macmillan.

Milton, Corinne H. Corona: Bullfighter & Artist. LC 87-33677. (Illus.). 64p. (Orig.). 1988. pap. 16.95 (0-86534-119-2) Sunstone Pr.

Milton, David. As Peace Lay Dying. 1990. mass mkt. 4.95 (1-55817-321-8, Pinnacle NY) Windsor NY.
— Conspiracy of Mirrors. 1992. mass mkt. 4.99 (1-55817-564-4, Pinnacle NY) Windsor NY.
— Hyte Maneuver: What It Is, How to Prevent It, How to Stop It. 1989. pap. 3.95 (1-55817-178-9, Pinnacle NY) Windsor NY.
— The Politics of U. S. Labor: From the Great Depression to the New Deal. LC 80-8934. 189p. reprint ed. pap. 53.90 (0-7837-3915-X, 2043763) Bks Demand.

Milton, Earl R., ed. Recollections of a Fallen Sky: Velikovsky & Cultural Amnesia. 176p. 1992. pap. 12.00 (0-940268-28-0) Metron Pubns.

Milton, Earl R., jt. auth. see De Grazia, Alfred.

Milton, Francis. A Trilogy of Sonnets. 64p. (Orig.). 1993. pap. 2.95 (0-931888-46-8) Christendom Pr.

Milton, George F. Age of Hate: Andrew Johnson & the Radicals. (History - United States Ser.). 787p. 1992. reprint ed. lib. bdg. 109.00 (0-7812-6205-4) Rprt Serv.

Milton, Gladys. Why Not Me? The Story of Gladys Milton, Midwife. LC 92-38694. (Illus.). 128p. 1993. 9.95 (0-913990-97-3) Book Pub Co.

Milton, Graeme, jt. auth. see Kohn, Robert.

***Milton, Hal.** Going Public: A Practical Guide to Developing Personal Charisma. 150p. (Orig.). 1995. pap. 9.95 (1-55874-360-X, 360X) Health Comm.

Milton, Hilary. Escape from High Doom. Schwartz, Betty, ed. (Plot It Yourself Horror Stories Ser.: No. 5). (Illus.). 128p. (Orig.). (J). (gr. 3-7). 1984. lib. bdg. 5.97 (0-685-08595-3) S&S Trade.
— Fun House Terrors! (Plot It Yourself Horror Stories Ser.). (Illus.). 128p. (J). (gr. 3-7). 1984. pap. 2.95 (0-685-09678-5, Julian Messner) Silver Burdett Pr.

Milton, Howard. Packaging Design. (Issues in Design Ser.). (Illus.). 104p. (C). 1991. pap. 16.95 (0-85072-280-2, Pub. by Design Council Bks UK) Ashgate Pub Co.

Milton, J. R. South African Criminal Law & Procedure, Vol. II: Common Law Crimes. 2nd rev. ed. 965p. 1990. write for info. (0-7021-2378-1, Pub. by Juta SA) W W Gaunt.

Milton, J. R. & Burchell, J. M. Cases & Materials on Criminal Law. 752p. 1992. 45.00 (0-7021-2846-5, Pub. by Juta SA) W W Gaunt.

Milton, J. R. & Cowling, M. South African Criminal Law & Procedure, Vol. III: Statutory Offences. 2nd ed. 1988. ring bd. write for info. (0-7021-2036-7, Pub. by Juta SA) W W Gaunt.

Milton, J. R., jt. auth. see Burchell, J. M.

***Milton, J. S. & Arnold, Jesse C.** Introduction to Probability & Statistics: Principles & Applications for Engineering & the Computing Sciences. 3rd ed. LC 94-31189. 1994. text ed. write for info. (0-07-042623-6) McGraw.

Milton, J. S., jt. auth. see Myers, Raymond H.

Milton, J. Susan. Statistical Methods in the Biological & Health Sciences. 2nd ed. 1992. text ed. write for info. (0-07-042506-X) McGraw.

Milton, J. Susan & Arnold, Jesse. Probability & Statistics in the Engineering & Computer Sciences. 2nd ed. 672p. (C). 1990. text ed. write for info. (0-07-042353-9) McGraw.

Milton, John. Areopagatica. 80p. 1972. reprint ed. 15.00 (0-87556-219-1) Saifer.
— Areopagitica. Jebb, Richard C., ed. LC 72-170811. reprint ed. 22.50 (0-404-03556-6) AMS Pr.
— Areopagitica: Freedom of the Press. rev. ed. Ash, A. S., ed. LC 86-64056. (Humanist Classics Ser.). Orig. Title: Areopagitica. 48p. 1990. pap. 4.00 (0-942208-04-8) Bandanna Bks.
— Areopagitica & Of Education. Sabine, George H., ed. (Crofts Classics Ser.). 128p. 1951. pap. text ed. write for info. (0-88295-057-6) Harlan Davidson.
— Complete English Poems, of Education, Areopagitica. Campbell, Gordon, ed. 412p. 1993. pap. 12.95 (0-460-87275-3, Everyman's Classic Lib) C E Tuttle.
— Complete Poems. LC 92-52905. 1992. 20.00 (0-679-40997-1, Everymans Lib) Knopf.
— Complete Poetical Works. Bush, Douglas, ed. LC 65-2686. (Cambridge Editions Ser.). 1965. pap. 8.95 (0-395-07493-2) HM.
— Complete Poetical Works. Bush, Douglas, ed. LC 65-2686. (Cambridge Editions Ser.). (C). 1965. text ed. 45.56 (0-395-05574-1) HM.
— Complete Poetry of John Milton. Shawcross, John T., ed. LC 72-150934. 1971. reprint ed. pap. 11.95 (0-385-02351-0, Anchor NY) Doubleday.
— Comus. LC 94-13618. Orig. Title: A Mask at Ludlow Castle. (Illus.). (J). (gr. 1-8). Date not set. write for info. (0-8234-1146-X) Holiday.
— John Milton. Orgel, Stephen & Goldberg, Jonathan, eds. (Oxford Authors Ser.). (Illus.). 1000p. 1991. pap. 17.95 (0-19-281379-X) OUP.
— John Milton. Orgel, Stephen & Goldberg, Jonathan, eds. (Oxford Authors Ser.). (Illus.). 1000p. 1991. 58.00 (0-19-254188-9) OUP.
— John Milton: Selected Longer Poems. Davies, Tony, ed. (English Texts Ser.). 352p. 1991. pap. 13.95 (0-415-04946-6, A6053) Routledge.
— John Milton's Complete Poetical Works: Reproduced in Photograhic Facsimile. Fletcher, Harris F., ed. LC 44-1984. 461p. reprint ed. pap. 131.40 (0-317-29074-6, 2020211) Bks Demand.
— The Latin Poems of John Milton. (BCL1-PR English Literature Ser.). 382p. 1992. reprint ed. lib. bdg. 89.00 (0-7812-7377-3) Rprt Serv.
— A Maske: The Earlier Versions. Sprott, S. E., ed. LC 72-97784. 236p. reprint ed. pap. 67.30 (0-685-15906-X, 2026385) Bks Demand.
— Milton on Education. Ainsworth, Oliver M., ed. LC 75-112640. 22.5p. reprint ed. 19.00 (0-404-00298-6) AMS Pr.
— Milton on Education: The Tractate of Education with Supplementary Extracts from Other Writings of Milton. Ainsworth, Oliver M., ed. LC 70-145185. 1971. reprint ed. 18.00 (0-403-01110-8) Scholarly.
— Milton on Education, the Tractatte of Education. (BCL1-PR English Literature Ser.). 369p. 1992. reprint ed. lib. bdg. 89.00 (0-7812-7378-1) Rprt Serv.
— Milton's Dramatic Poems. 6th rev. ed. Bullough, Geoffrey & Bullough, Margaret, eds. LC 85-3986. 224p. (C). 1958. pap. 8.95 (0-485-61009-4, Pub. by Athlone Pr UK) Humanities.
— Odes, Pastorals, Masques. Broadbent, John et al, eds. LC 73-94355. (Milton for Schools & Colleges Ser.). 300p. 1975. pap. 22.95 (0-521-20456-9) Cambridge U Pr.
— Paradise Lost. Bd. with Paradise Regained. (Airmont Classics Ser.). (J). (gr. 11-p). 1968. Set pap. 2.50 (0-8049-0173-2, CL-173) Airmont.
— Paradise Lost. 395p. 1983. reprint ed. lib. bdg. 25.95 (0-89966-457-1) Buccaneer Bks.
— Paradise Lost. Bentley, Richard, ed. (Anglistica & Americana Ser.: Vol. 175). 415p. 1976. reprint ed. lib. bdg. 115.00 (3-487-06053-1, Pub. by Georg Olms GW) Lubrecht & Cramer.
— Paradise Lost, Bks. 1-2. Prince, F. T., ed. 1971. 8.95 (0-19-831912-6) OUP.
— Paradise Lost, Bks. 3 & 4. Potter, L. J. & Broadbent, John, eds. LC 75-36681. (Milton for Schools & Colleges Ser.). 200p. 1976. pap. 14.50 (0-521-21150-6) Cambridge U Pr.
— Paradise Lost, Bks. 5 & 6. Hodge, R. I. & MacCaffrey, I., eds. LC 75-8314. (Milton for Schools & Colleges Ser.). (Illus.). 176p. (C). 1975. pap. 14.50 (0-521-20796-7) Cambridge U Pr.
— Paradise Lost, Bks. 7 & 8. Aers, D. & Radzinowics, Mary Ann, eds. LC 77-181884. (Milton for Schools & Colleges Ser.). 200p. 1974. pap. 14.50 (0-521-20457-7) Cambridge U Pr.
— Paradise Lost, Set. Evans, J. M., ed. LC 72-87438. (Milton for Schools & Colleges Ser.). 208p. (C). 1973. pap. 14.50 (0-521-20067-9) Cambridge U Pr.
— Paradise Lost: An Authoritative Text, Backgrounds & Sources, Criticism. 2nd ed. Elledge, Scott, ed. LC 92-9988. (C). 1993. pap. text ed. 11.95 (0-393-96293-8) Norton.
— Paradise Lost: Modern Library College Editions. Madsen, William G., ed. (C). 1969. pap. text ed. write for info. (0-07-553668-4, 30997) McGraw.
— Paradise Lost & Other Poems. 1961. pap. 4.95 (0-451-62710-5, Ment) NAL-Dutton.
— Paradise Lost & Paradise Regained. Ricks, Christopher, ed. 1968. pap. 4.95 (0-451-52352-0, Sig Classics) NAL-Dutton.
— Paradise Lost, Bks. 1 & 2. Broadbent, John, ed. (Milton for Schools & Colleges Ser.). (gr. 11-12). 1972. pap. 14.50 (0-521-08298-6) Cambridge U Pr.
— Poems: The Sixteen Forty-Five Edition. Bd. with Essays in AnalysisLC 68-24444. LC 68-24444. 369p. 1968. reprint ed. 50.00 (0-87752-075-5) Gordian.
— Poems in English, 2 vols., Set. LC 27-273. (Illus.). 1968. reprint ed. 79.00 (0-403-00349-0) Scholarly.
— Poems in English, with Illustrations by William Blake, 2 vols., Set. (BCL1-PR English Literature Ser.). (Illus.). 1992. reprint ed. lib. bdg. 150.00 (0-7812-7375-7) Rprt Serv.
— The Poetical Works, 2 vols. Darbishire, Helen, ed. Incl. Vol. 1. Paradise Lost. 1953. 65.00 (0-19-811819-8); Vol. 2. Paradise Regained, Samson Agonistes, Poems Upon Several Occasions. 1955. 55.00 (0-19-811820-1); (Oxford English Texts Ser.). write for info. (0-318-54882-8) OUP.
— Poetical Works of John Milton, 6 Vols, 1. Brydges, Egerton, ed. LC 75-172735. (Illus.). reprint ed. write for info. (0-404-04381-X) AMS Pr.
— Poetical Works of John Milton, 6 Vols, 2. Brydges, Egerton, ed. LC 75-172735. (Illus.). reprint ed. write for info. (0-404-04382-8) AMS Pr.
— Poetical Works of John Milton, 6 Vols, 3. Brydges, Egerton, ed. LC 75-172735. (Illus.). reprint ed. write for info. (0-404-04383-6) AMS Pr.
— Poetical Works of John Milton, 6 Vols, 4. Brydges, Egerton, ed. LC 75-172735. (Illus.). reprint ed. write for info. (0-404-04384-4) AMS Pr.
— Poetical Works of John Milton, 6 Vols, 5. Brydges, Egerton, ed. LC 75-172735. (Illus.). reprint ed. write for info. (0-404-04385-2) AMS Pr.
— Poetical Works of John Milton, 6 Vols, 6. Brydges, Egerton, ed. LC 75-172735. (Illus.). reprint ed. write for info. (0-404-04386-0) AMS Pr.
— Poetical Works of John Milton, 6 Vols, Set. Brydges, Egerton, ed. LC 75-172735. (Illus.). reprint ed. 435.00 (0-404-04380-1) AMS Pr.
— Poetical Works of John Milton - with Notes of Various Authors 7 Vols, Set. 2nd ed. LC 71-115361. reprint ed. 525.00 (0-404-04370-4) AMS Pr.
— The Poetical Works of John Milton, with Notes of Various Authors, 7 vols., Set. (BCL1-PR English Literature Ser.). 1992. reprint ed. lib. bdg. 525.00 (0-7812-7376-5) Rprt Serv.
— Poetical Works of John Milton, with the Principal Notes of Various Commentators, 6 Vols, Set. LC 72-1734. (Illus.). reprint ed. 182.00 (0-404-04390-9) AMS Pr.
— Political Writings. Dzelainis, Martin, ed. Gruzelier, Claire, tr. (Cambridge Texts in the History of Political Thought Ser.). 304p. (C). 1991. 59.95 (0-521-34394-1); pap. 18.95 (0-521-34866-8) Cambridge U Pr.
— The Portable Milton. Bush, Douglas, ed. (Portable Library: No. 44). 1976. pap. 14.95 (0-14-015044-7, Penguin Bks) Viking Penguin.
— Samson Agonistes. Prince, F. T., ed. 1970. pap. 10.95 (0-19-831910-X) OUP.
— Samson Agonistes & Shorter Poems. Barker, A. E., ed. (Crofts Classics Ser.). 128p. 1950. pap. text ed. write for info. (0-88295-058-4) Harlan Davidson.
— Selected Poems. LC 92-29792. (Thrift Editions Ser.). 128p. 1993. reprint ed. pap. 1.00 (0-486-27554-X) Dover.
— Works, Vol. 2, Pt. 2. Patterson, Frank A., ed. LC 31-10596. 1931. text ed. 49.50 (0-231-08709-8) Col U Pr.

Milton, John, jt. auth. see Dore, Gustav.

Milton, John, tr. see Gadotti, Moacir.

Milton, John R. The Novel of the American West. LC 79-17713. xviii, 341p. 1980. 35.00 (0-8032-0980-0) U of Nebr Pr.
— South Dakota: A History. 1989. pap. 9.95 (0-393-30571-6) Norton.

Milton, John W. The Guppy Swim Book. 24p. 1990. 3.00 (0-87322-287-3, LYMC5088) Human Kinetics.

Milton, Joyce. Bats! Creatures of the Night. LC 92-43198. (All Aboard Reading Ser.). (Illus.). 48p. (J). (ps-1). 1993. 7.99 (0-448-40194-0, G&D); pap. 3.50 (0-448-40193-2, G&D) Putnam Pub Group.
— Bats & Other Creatures of the Night. (Picturebacks Ser.). (Illus.). 32p. (Orig.). (J). (ps-2). 1994. pap. 2.50 (0-679-86213-7) Random Bks Yng Read.
— Big Cats. LC 94-7361. (All Aboard Reading Ser.). (Illus.). (J). 1994. write for info. (0-448-40565-2, G&D) Putnam Pub Group.
— Big Cats. LC 94-7361. (All Aboard Reading Ser.). (Illus.). (J). 1994. pap. write for info. (0-448-40564-4, G&D) Putnam Pub Group.
— Dinosaur Days. LC 84-17861. (Step into Reading Bks.). (Illus.). 48p. (J). (gr. k-3). 1985. lib. bdg. 7.99 (0-394-97023-3); pap. 3.99 (0-394-87023-9) Random Bks Yng Read.
— Dinosaur Days. (Step into Reading Book & Cassette Library). 48p. (J). (gr. k-3). 1988. audio, pap. 6.99 (0-394-89774-9) Random Bks Yng Read.
— Don Quixote (Miguel de Cervantes) (Book Notes Ser.). (J). (gr. 9-12). 1985. pap. 2.50 (0-8120-3512-7) Barron.
— Loss of Eden: A Biography of Charles & Anne Morrow Lindbergh. 528p. 1994. pap. 13.00 (0-06-092482-9, PL) HarpC.
— Marching to Freedom: The Story of Martin Luther King Jr. (Orig.). (J). (gr. k-6). 1987. pap. 3.50 (0-440-45433-6, YB) Dell.
— Story of Hillary Rodham Clinton: First Lady of the United States. 1994. pap. 3.50 (0-440-40966-7) Dell.
— Whales: The Gentle Giants. LC 88-15616. (Step into Reading Bks.). (Illus.). 48p. (Orig.). (J). (gr. k-3). 1989. lib. bdg. 7.99 (0-394-99809-X); pap. 3.50 (0-394-89809-5) Random Bks Yng Read.
— Whales & Other Creatures of the Sea. LC 92-2409. (Pictureback Ser.). (Illus.). 32p. (J). (ps-4). 1993. pap. 2.50 (0-679-83899-6) Random Bks Yng Read.
— Wild, Wild Wolves. LC 90-8807. (Step into Reading Bks.). (Illus.). 48p. (Orig.). (J). (gr. 1-3). 1992. pap. 3.50 (0-679-81052-8) Random Bks Yng Read.
— Wild, Wild Wolves. LC 90-8807. (Step into Reading Bks.). (Illus.). 48p. (Orig.). (J). (gr. 1-3). 1992. lib. bdg. 7.99 (0-679-91052-2) Random Bks Yng Read.

Milton, K. A., et al, eds. Beyond the Standard Model II. 400p. (C). 1991. text ed. 118.00 (981-02-0569-4) World Scientific Pub.

Milton, Katherine. The Foraging Strategy of Howler Monkeys: A Study in Economics. LC 79-27380. (Illus.). 1980. text ed. 42.50 (0-231-04850-5) Col U Pr.

Milton, Kay, ed. Environmentalism: The View from Anthropology. LC 93-14815. (ASA Monographs: Vol. 32). 1993. 69.00 (0-415-09474-7); pap. 18.95 (0-415-09475-5) Routledge.

Milton, Kay, ed. see Yearly, Steven.

Milton, Kwasi. Hieroglyphics the Genesis of Writing. (Illus.). (Orig.). 1992. pap. 10.95 (1-56411-018-4) Untd Bros & Sis.

Milton, Leanne W., jt. ed. see Boland, Maeve A.

***Milton, Mary.** Cat Lips. (Illus.). 36p. (Orig.). 1994. pap. 5.00 (1-883348-05-6) Fresh Ink.

Milton, Nancy. The Giraffe That Walked to Paris. LC 91-31767. (Illus.). 32p. (J). (gr. k-4). 1992. 15.00 (0-517-58132-9); lib. bdg. 15.99 (0-517-58133-7) Crown Bks Yng Read.

Milton, Ohmer, et al. Making Sense of College Grades. LC 85-45910. (Jossey-Bass Higher Education Ser.). (Illus.). 309p. reprint ed. pap. 88.10 (0-7837-6519-3, 2045631) Bks Demand.

Milton, Peter. The Primacy of Touch: The Drawings of Peter Milton - A Catalogue Raisonne. LC 93-17551. (Illus.). 132p. 1993. 45.00 (1-55595-075-2) Hudson Hills.

***Milton, Richard.** Forbidden Science: Suppressed Research That Could Change Our Lives. 264p. 1995. 29.95 (1-85702-188-6, Pub. by Fourth Estate UK) Trafalgar.

Milton, Robert G., jt. auth. see Milton, Verneta J.

Milton, Rod. Portrait of a Mass Killer: Wade Frankum at Strathfield Plaza. 250p. 1994. 40.00 (1-875114-26-2, Bckstone AT) W W Gaunt.

Milton, Shirley, jt. auth. see Winters, Arthur.

Milton, Shirley F. & Winters, Arthur A. The Creative Connection: Advertising Copy & Idea Visualization. (Illus.). 200p. (C). 1981. text ed. 20.00 (0-87005-316-7) Fairchild.

Milton, Sybil. In Fitting Memory: The Art & Politics of Holocaust Memorials. LC 91-19603. (Illus.). 348p. 1991. 39.95 (0-8143-2066-X) Wayne St U Pr.

Milton, Sybil & Bogin, Frederick D., eds. American Jewish Joint Distribution Committee, New York, 2 vols., Set. LC 94-40786. (Archives of the Holocaust Ser.: Vol. 10). 1200p. 1995. 250.00 (0-8240-5492-X) Garland.

Milton, Sybil, jt. ed. see Friedlander, Henry.

Milton, Sybil, jt. ed. see Klemig, Roland.

Milton, Toby H., jt. ed. see Schmidtlein, Frank A.

Milton, Verneta J. & Milton, Robert G. Tips: The Imaginative Parent Succeeds. (Illus.). 202p. (Orig.). 1985. pap. 6.95 (0-9614763-9-7) Ink Illusions.

Miltoun, F. The Spell of Algeria & Tunisia. 554p. 1985. 300.00 (1-85077-060-3, Darf Pubs Ltd) St Mut.

***Miltowski, Robert E.** The New York, Ontario & West Railway & the Industry of Central New York State: Milk Cans, Mixed Trains & Motor Cars. (Illus.). x, 350p. Date not set. write for info. (0-9620844-6-8) Garrigues Hse.

Miltz, Arthur I. Discovery. (Art of Advocacy Ser.). 1982. Looseleaf Updates Avail. write for info. (0-8205-1044-0) Bender.

Miluck, Michael & Miluck, Nancy, eds. The Genoa-Carson Valley Book, 1991-92. 4th ed. (Illus.). 96p. 1992. pap. 3.00 (0-9606382-1-0) Dragon Ent.

Miluck, Nancy, jt. ed. see Miluck, Michael.

Miluck, Nancy B. Nevada: This Is Our Land. rev. ed. (Illus.). 200p. (Orig.). (YA). (gr. 7 up). 1994. reprint ed. pap. 15.00 (0-9606382-7-X) Dragon Ent.

Miluck, Nancy C. Nevada History Coloring Books: Nevada's Native Americans. (Illus.). 48p. (J). (gr. k-5). 1992. pap. text ed. 3.75 (0-9606382-4-5) Dragon Ent.
— Nevada History Coloring Books: The First Settlers. (Illus.). 48p. (J). (gr. k-6). 1993. pap. 3.75 (0-9606382-5-3) Dragon Ent.
— Nevada History Coloring Books: The 20th Century. (Illus.). 48p. (Orig.). (J). (gr. k-5). 1992. pap. text ed. 3.75 (0-9606382-3-7) Dragon Ent.

Milunsky, Aubrey. Heredity & Your Family's Health. LC 91-25343. 508p. 1991. reprint ed. pap. 18.95 (0-8018-4331-6) Johns Hopkins.

Milunsky, Aubrey, ed. Genetic Disorders & the Fetus: Diagnosis, Prevention & Treatment. 2nd ed. LC 86-20477. 924p. 1986. 125.00 (0-306-42301-4, Plenum Pr) Plenum.
— Genetic Disorders & the Fetus: Diagnosis, Prevention, & Treatment. 3rd rev. ed. (Illus.). 992p. 1992. text ed. 125.00 (0-8018-4413-4) Johns Hopkins.

Milunsky, Aubrey & Annas, George J., eds. Genetics & the Law, Vol. 3. LC 85-19347. 534p. 1985. 69.50 (0-306-41983-1, Plenum Pr) Plenum.

Milunsky, Aubrey, et al, eds. Advances in Perinatal Medicine, Vol. 1. LC 80-20701. 456p. 1981. 85.00 (0-306-40482-6, Plenum Med Bk) Plenum.
— Advances in Perinatal Medicine, Vol. 2. LC 80-20701. 400p. (C). 1982. 85.00 (0-306-40763-9, Plenum Med Bk) Plenum.

An Asterisk (*) at the beginning of an entry indicates that the title is appearing in BIP for the first time.

— Advances in Perinatal Medicine, Vol. 3. LC 80-20701. 272p. 1983. 85.00 (*0-306-41208-X*, Plenum Med Bk) Plenum.
— Advances in Perinatal Medicine, Vol. 4. LC 80-20701. 350p. 1985. 85.00 (*0-306-41840-1*, Plenum Med Bk) Plenum.
— Advances in Perinatal Medicine, Vol. 5. LC 80-20701. 298p. 1986. 89.50 (*0-306-42331-6*, Plenum Med Bk) Plenum.
Milutinovic, V. Microprogramming & Firmware Engineering. LC 88-46158. 410p. 1989. pap. 9.95 (*0-8186-0839-0*, 839) IEEE Comp Soc.
Milutinovic, V. M. Advanced Microprocessors & High-Level Language Computer Architecture. LC 85-80875. 597p. 1986. pap. 9.95 (*0-8186-0623-1*, 623) IEEE Comp Soc.
Milutinovic, V. M., ed. Computer Architecture: Concepts & Systems. 600p. 1988. 61.75 (*0-444-01019-X*) Elsevier.
Milutinovic, Veljko, jt. ed. see Tartalja, I.
Milutinovic, Veljko, jt. auth. see Tomasevic, Milo.
Milvy, Paul, ed. The Marathon: Physiological, Medical, Epidemiological, & Psychological Studies, Vol. 301. (Annals Ser.). 1090p. 1977. 77.00 (*0-89072-047-9*) NY Acad Sci.
Milward, Alan S. The New Order & the French Economy. (Modern Revivals in Economic & Social History Ser.). (Illus.). 502p. 1993. 74.95 (*0-7512-0146-4*, Pub. by Gregg Revivals UK) Ashgate Pub Co.
— The Reconstruction of Western Europe 1945-51. LC 83-17931. 500p. 1984. pap. 18.00 (*0-520-06035-0*) U CA Pr.
— War, Economy & Society: 1939-1945. LC 76-40823. (History of the World Economy in the Twentieth Century Ser.: Vol. 5). 1977. pap. 15.00 (*0-520-03942-4*) U CA Pr.
Milward, Alan S., et al. The European Rescue of the Nation-State. LC 92-11223. (C). 1993. 45.00 (*0-520-08137-4*) U CA Pr.
— The Frontier of National Sovereignty: History & Theory, 1945-1992. LC 92-36702. 248p. 1993. 59.95 (*0-415-08892-5*, B2350, Routledge NY) Routledge.
— The Frontier of National Sovereignty: History & Theory, 1945-1992. 248p. 1994. pap. 16.95 (*0-415-11784-4*, C0248) Routledge.
Milward, Burton, Jr. Kentucky Criminal Practice, 1 vol. 2nd ed. 442p. 1984. 65.00 (*0-8322-0044-1*) Banks-Baldwin.
Milward, G. R., jt. ed. see Pitt, G. J.
***Milward, Jane M.** Playing God's Melodies: The Psalms in Our Lives. 160p. 1993. 35.00 (*0-85439-465-6*, Pub. by St Paul Pubns UK) St Mut.
Milward-Oliver, Edward. Len Deighton: An Annotated Bibliography 1954-1985. 100p. 1988. 85.00 (*0-944166-02-4*) Santa Teresa Pr.
Milward, Peter. Biblical Influences in Shakespeare's Great Tragedies. LC 86-45543. 224p. 1987. 20.00 (*0-253-31198-5*) Ind U Pr.
— A Challenge to C. S. Lewis. LC 94-34812. 1995. write for info. (*0-8386-3568-7*) Fairleigh Dickinson.
— A Commentary on G. M. Hopkins' "The Wreck of the Deutschland" LC 90-25437. (Studies in British Literature: Vol. 13). 200p. 1992. reprint ed. lib. bdg. 79.95 (*0-88946-584-3*) E Mellen.
— A Commentary on the Sonnets of G. M. Hopkins. 200p. 1985. pap. 6.95 (*0-8294-0494-5*) Loyola Univ Pr.
Milward, Peter, comp. An Encyclopedia of Flora & Fauna in English & American Literature. LC 92-14298. 244p. 1992. lib. bdg. 89.95 (*0-7734-9539-8*) E Mellen.
Milward, Peter, ed. The Mediaeval Dimension in Shakespeare's Plays. LC 90-31081. (Studies in Renaissance Literature: Vol. 7). 156p. 1990. lib. bdg. 69.95 (*0-88946-116-3*) E Mellen.
— Shakespeare's Religious Background. 312p. 1985. reprint ed. 10.35 (*0-8294-0508-9*) Loyola Univ Pr.
Milward, Peter S. & Schoder, Raymond S., eds. Readings of the Wreck. 1976. 8.95 (*0-8294-0249-7*) Loyola Univ Pr.
Milward, R. S. Japan: The Past in the Present. 128p. 1987. pap. 75.00 (*0-904404-29-3*, Pub. by P Norbury Pubns Ltd UK) St Mut.
Milwaukee Brewers Baseball Club, Publicity Dept. Staff. Robin Yount: The Legend Lives On. (Illus.). 80p. Date not set. 19.00 (*0-9634967-0-0*) Milwauk BBC.
Milwaukee Public Museum. The Rudolph J. Nunnemacher Collection of Projectile Arms, 2 pts., 1. Metschl, John, ed. Bd. with Pt. 1. Long Arms.; Pt. 2. Short Arms. LC 74-111395. (Illus.). 1970. reprint ed. Set text ed. 75.00 (*0-8371-4627-5*, MPMO, Greenwood Pr) Greenwood.
— The Rudolph J. Nunnemacher Collection of Projectile Arms, 2 pts., Vol. 2. Metschl, John, ed. Bd. with Pt. 1. Long Arms.; Pt. 2. Short Arms. LC 74-111395. (Illus.). 1970. reprint ed. Set text ed. 75.00 (*0-8371-4628-3*, MPMP, Greenwood Pr) Greenwood.
— The Rudolph J. Nunnemacher Collection of Projectile Arms, 2 pts., Vol. 9. Metschl, John, ed. Bd. with Pt. 1. Long Arms.; Pt. 2. Short Arms. LC 74-111395. (Illus.). 1970. reprint ed. Set text ed. 125.00 (*0-8371-4626-7*, MPMN, Greenwood Pr) Greenwood.
Milwaukee Shops Inc. Staff. Hiawatha First of the Speedliners: C. M. St. P. & P. R. R. Equipment Built by: The Milwaukee Shops, 1934-1935. Solheim, Carl W. et al, eds. (Illus.). 134p. 1993. 64.95 (*0-9639029-0-3*) Milwaukee Shops.
***Milwee, William I., Jr.** Modern Marine Salvage. (Illus.). 720p. 1995. text ed. 50.00 (*0-87033-471-9*) Cornell Maritime.
Milwid, Beth. Working with Men: Women in the Workplace Talk about Sexuality, Success & Their Male Coworkers. 288p. (Orig.). 1992. mass mkt. 4.99 (*0-425-13482-2*) Berkley Pub.
Milwidsky, Benjamin M. & Gabriel, Delia M. Detergent Analysis: A Handbook for Cost-Effective Quality Control. LC 81-19840. (Illus.). 303p. 1989. reprint ed. 65.00 (*0-9608752-3-9*) Micelle Pr.
Milyukova, M. S., et al. Plutonium. (Analytical Chemistry of the Elements Ser.). 453p. 1970. text ed. 102.00 (*0-7065-0749-5*, Pub. by Keter Pub IS) Coronet Bks.
Milza, Pierre, jt. auth. see Berstein, Serge.
Mimep, jt. auth. see Galbiati, E.
Mimica, Jadran. Intimations of Infinity: The Cultural Meanings of the Iqwaye Counting System & Number. LC 87-22412. (Explorations in Anthropology Ser.). 195p. 1988. 49.95 (*0-85496-145-3*) Berg Pubs.
— Intimations of Infinity: The Mythopoeia of the Iqwaye Counting System & Number. 196p. 1992. pap. 16.95 (*0-85496-854-7*) Berg Pubs.
Mimms, Agneta, ed. see Technical Association of the Pulp & Paper Industry Staff.
***Mimms, Kenneth A. & Ross, Leon T.** African American Almanac: Day-by-Day Black History. 240p. 1995. lib. bdg. 29.95 (*0-89950-675-5*) McFarland & Co.
***Mimno, Pieter.** Developing Mission-Critical Applications: In Client Server Environment. 1996. text ed. 40.00 (*0-07-042364-4*) McGraw.
Mimno, Pieter R. CASE. 250p. 1994. text ed. 40.00i (*0-07-042326-1*) McGraw.
Mimoso, Adriana R. Modernism in the Puerto Rican Lyric. (Puerto Rico Ser.). 1979. lib. bdg. 59.95 (*0-8490-2973-2*) Gordon Pr.
Mimouni, Francis, jt. auth. see Tsang, Reginald C.
Mimouni, Rachid. The Ogre's Embrace. Eber, Shirley, tr. 224p. 1993. 19.95 (*0-7043-7043-3*, Pub. by Quartet UK) Interlink Pub.
Mims & Carr. Activities, Readings, & Skills for Teacher Support Specialists. 240p. (C). 1991. pap. text ed. 26.95 (*0-8403-6995-6*) Kendall-Hunt.
Mims, Amy, tr. see Kazantzakis, Helen.
***Mims, Cedric, et al, eds.** Pathogenesis of Infectious Disease. 4th ed. (Illus.). 416p. 1995. text ed. 45.00 (*0-12-498262-X*) Acad Pr.
Mims, Cedric A. The Pathogenesis of Infectious Disease. 3rd ed. 352p. 1987. text ed. 61.00 (*0-12-498260-3*); pap. text ed. 30.00 (*0-12-498261-1*) Acad Pr.
Mims, Cedric A., et al. Medical Microbiology. LC 93-19347. 1993. 35.95 (*0-397-44631-4*) Mosby Yr Bk.
— Viruses & Demyelinating Diseases. 1984. text ed. 95.00 (*0-12-498280-8*) Acad Pr.
Mims, Charles W., jt. auth. see Alexopoulos, Constantine J.
Mims, Edwin. The Advancing South: Stories of Progress & Reaction. (BCL1 - United States Local History Ser.). 319p. 1991. reprint ed. lib. bdg. 89.00 (*0-7812-6290-9*) Rprt Serv.
— Great Writers As Interpreters of Religion. LC 70-134116. (Essay Index Reprint Ser.). 1977. reprint ed. 19.95 (*0-8369-1988-2*) Ayer.
— History of Vanderbilt University. Metzger, Walter P., ed. LC 76-55185. (Academic Profession Ser.). (Illus.). 1977. reprint ed. lib. bdg. 41.95 (*0-405-10012-4*) Ayer.
— Sidney Lanier. 1972. 59.95 (*0-8490-1052-7*) Gordon Pr.
Mims, Ferm & Swenson, Melinda. Sexuality: A Nursing Perspective. 1979. pap. text ed. 25.95 (*0-07-042388-1*) McGraw.
Mims, Forrest, III. Engineer's Notebook. 1995. text ed. 69.95 (*0-07-021588-X*) McGraw.
Mims, Forrest M., II. The Forrest Mims Engineer's Notebook. 168p. 1992. pap. 14.95 (*1-878707-03-5*) HighText.
Mims, Forrest M., III. Siliconnections: Coming of Age in the Electronic Era. 240p. 1985. text ed. 16.95 (*0-07-042411-X*) McGraw.
Mims, Sam. No Americans Wanted. 1969. 3.95 (*0-87511-085-1*) Claitors.
— Toledo Bend. LC 74-186988. 1972. 12.95 (*0-911116-57-5*); pap. 9.95 (*0-911116-70-2*) Pelican.
— Trail of the Pack Peddler. 40p. pap. 2.00 (*0-911116-45-1*) Pelican.
Mims, Sam S. Rendezvous with Halley's Comet. (Illus.). 44p. (Orig.). 1985. pap. text ed. 4.95 (*0-936591-00-5*) Space News Pub.
Mimura, Goro, ed. Childhood & Juvenile Diabetes Mellitus. (Current Clinical Practice Ser.: No. 27). 258p. 1986. 106.25 (*4-900392-72-3*) Elsevier.
Mimura, Goro, et al, eds. Current Status of Diabetes Mellitus in East Asian: Proceedings of the 4th Japan-China Symposium on Diabetes Mellitus, Yokohama, 7-8 October, 1993. LC 94-15343. (International Congress Ser.: No. 1053). 1994. write for info. (*0-444-81758-1*) Elsevier.
Mimura, Goro & Zhisheng, Chi, eds. Recent Progress of Diabetes Mellitus in East Asia: Proceedings of the Third Japan-China Symposium, Shanghai, China, 11-12 October 1991. LC 92-49546. (International Congress Ser.: No. 997). 1992. write for info. (*0-444-88503-X*, Excerpta Medica) Elsevier.
Mimura, Goro, et al, eds. Diabetes Mellitus in East Asia: Proceedings of the 1st China-Japan Symposium on Diabetes Mellitus, Beijing, China, 5-6 May, 1987. (International Congress Ser.: No. 771). 406p. 1988. 118.00 (*0-444-80992-9*, Excerpta Medica) Elsevier.
— Lipids & Ischemic Heart Diseases: Proceedings of the Symposium on Lipids & Ischemic Heart Diseases, Tokyo, Japan; 5-6 December; 1983. (International Congress Ser.: No. 639). 138p. 1985. 92.00 (*0-444-80664-4*, Excerpta Medica) Elsevier.
Mimura, M., ed. Homotopy Theory & Related Topics. (Lecture Notes in Mathematics Ser.: Vol. 1418). vi, 241p. 1990. pap. 34.80 (*0-387-52246-8*) Spr-Verlag.
Mimura, M. & Nishida, T., eds. Recent Topics in Non-Linear Partial Differential Equations. (Mathematics Studies: Vol. 98). 1985. 74.50 (*0-444-87544-1*, North Holland) Elsevier.
— Recent Topics in Nonlinear PDE Four: Lecture Notes in Numerical & Applied Analysis, 10. (Mathematics Studies: No. 160). 244p. 1990. pap. 97.50 (*0-444-88087-9*, North Holland) Elsevier.
Mimura, M. & Toda, H. Topology of Lie Groups, I & II. LC 91-9459. 451p. 1991. 200.00 (*0-8218-4541-1*, MMONO-91) Am Math.
Mimura, M., jt. ed. see Masuda, K.
***Min, Anchee.** Katherine. LC 95-1973. 1995. write for info. (*1-57322-005-1*) Riverhead Bks.
— Red Azalea. 320p. 1995. pap. text ed. 6.99 (*0-425-14776-2*) Berkley Pub.
— Red Azalea. LC 93-9038. 320p. 1994. 22.00 (*0-679-42332-X*) Pantheon.
Min, Anselm K. Dialectic of Salvation: Issues in Theology of Liberation. LC 88-39150. 207p. (C). 1989. 64.50 (*0-88706-908-8*); pap. 21.95 (*0-88706-909-6*) State U NY Pr.
Min Chen. The Strategic Triangle & Regional Conflicts: Lessons from the Indochina Wars. LC 91-20699. 230p. 1992. lib. bdg. 38.50 (*1-55587-287-5*) Lynne Rienner.
Min Chen & Pan, Winston. Understanding the Process of Doing Business in China, Taiwan, & Hong Kong: A Guide for International Executives. LC 93-29328. 260p. 1993. 89.95 (*0-7734-9404-9*) E Mellen.
Min, David B. & Smouse, Thomas H., eds. Flavor Chemistry of Fats & Oils. 309p. 1985. 60.00 (*0-935315-12-8*) AOCS Pr.
— Flavor Chemistry of Lipid Foods. 488p. 1989. 85.00 (*0-935315-24-1*) AOCS Pr.
Min Education Staff. Courses of Study for SLC Exam, 1965: Expanded Outlines; Recommended Texts Included. 106p. 1965. 10.00 (*0-318-04183-9*) Am-Nepal Ed.
Min Kantrowitz & Associates Staff. Design Evaluation of Six Primary Care Facilities for the Purpose of Informing Future Design Decisions. 102p. 1993. pap. write for info. (*0-9638938-0-7*) Ctr for Hlth.
Min, Kellet I. Modern Informative Nursery Rhymes: American History, Book I. LC 89-91719. (Illus.). 64p. (Orig.). (J). (gr. 2-5). 1992. pap. 10.95 (*0-9623411-2-6*) Rhyme & Reason.
— Modern Informative Nursery Rhymes: General Science, Book I. LC 89-91719. (Illus.). 64p. (Orig.). (J). (gr. 2-5). 1993. pap. 10.95 (*0-9623411-4-2*) Rhyme & Reason.
— Modern Informative Nursery Rhymes: The Rationale. 176p. (Orig.). 1991. pap. 10.95 (*0-9623411-1-8*) Rhyme & Reason.
— Modern Informative Nursery Rhymes: Values. LC 89-91719. (General Science, American History Ser.: Bk. I). (Illus.). 32p. (Orig.). (J). (ps-3). 1989. pap. 7.95 (*0-9623411-3-4*) Rhyme & Reason.
Min, Laura. Mrs. Sato's Hens. 2nd ed. (Let Me Read Ser.). 8p. (J). (ps-2). 1994. text ed. 2.95 (*0-673-36193-4*) GdYrBks.
Min, P. & Klapisch, Robert, eds. New Applications of Accelerators & Nuclear Detectors to Medical Diagnosis. (Nuclear Science Applications Ser.: Sec. A, Vol. 3, No. 2). 192p. 1988. text ed. 107.00 (*3-7186-4825-3*) Gordon & Breach.
Min, Pyong G. Ethnic Business Enterprise: The Case of Korean Small Business in Atlanta. 200p. 1988. 19.50 (*0-934733-15-5*); pap. 14.50 (*0-934733-14-7*) Ctr Migration.
Min, T., ed. see American Society of Mechanical Engineers, Heat Transfer Division Staff.
Min Tu-ki. National Polity & Local Power: The Transformation of Late Imperial China. Kuhn, Philip A. & Brook, Timothy, eds. LC 87-36474. (Harvard-Yenching Institute Monograph: No. 27). 316p. 1990. 26.00 (*0-674-60225-0*) HUP.
***Min Zhou.** Chinatown: The Socioeconomic Potential of an Urban Enclave. (Conflicts in Urban & Regional Development Ser.). 300p. 1994. pap. write for info. (*0-614-03051-X*) Temple U Pr.
***Mina, Gianni.** An Encounter with Fidel: Interview with Fidel Castro. (Illus.). 273p. 1993. pap. 13.95 (*1-875284-21-4*, Pub. by Ocean Pr AT) Talman.
Mina, Hanna. Fragments of Memory: A Story of a Syrian Family. Kenny, Olive & Kenny, Lorne, trs. (Modern Middle East Literature in Translation Ser.). 180p. (C). 1993. pap. 11.95 (*0-292-75155-9*) U of Tex Pr.
Mina, M. V. Microevolution of Fishes. (C). 1991. 42.50 (*81-7087-060-7*, Pub. by Oxford IBH II) S Asia.
— Microevolution of Fishes: Evolutionary Aspects of Phenetic Diversity. Yablokov, A. V., ed. (Russian Translation Ser.: No. 79). (Illus.). 225p. (C). 1991. text ed. 85.00 (*90-6191-032-3*, Pub. by A A Balkema NE) Ashgate Pub Co.
Minachev, jt. auth. see Boreskov, G. K.
Minachev, Kh. M. & Shapiro, E. S. Catalyst Surface: Physical Methods of Studying. 375p. 1990. 76.95 (*0-8493-7532-0*, T) CRC Pr.
Minachin, V., tr. see Ilin, A. M.
Minachin, V. V., tr. see Sharko, V. V.
***Minadeo, Richard.** The Thematic Sophocles. viii, 200p. 1994. pap. 52.00x (*90-256-1056-0*, Pub. by A M Hakkert NE) Benjamins North Am.
Minahan, Anne, ed. Encyclopedia of Social Work, Set. 18th ed. LC 30-30948. 2396p. 1987. 90.00 (*0-87101-141-7*) Natl Assn Soc Wkrs.
***Minahan, James.** Nations Without States: A Historical Dictionary of Contemporary National Movements. LC 95-6626. 1996. text ed. write for info. (*0-313-28354-0*, Praeger Pubs) Greenwood.
***Minahan, John.** Abigail's Drum. (Illus.). 64p. (J). (gr. 2-5). 1995. lib. bdg. 14.95 (*0-945912-51-X*) Pippin Pr.
— Great Grave Robbery. 1989. 18.95 (*0-393-02721-X*) Norton.
— The Great Harvard Robbery: A Novel. 1988. 16.95 (*0-393-02605-1*) Norton.
— The Quiet American: A Biography of George R. Wackenhut. LC 93-80474. 800p. 1994. 29.95 (*0-9639395-0-5*) Intl Pub Grp.
Minahan, John A. Teaching Democracy: A Professor's Journal. 220p. 1993. 20.00 (*1-883285-01-1*) Delphinium.
— Word Like a Bell: John Keats, Music & the Romantic Poet. LC 91-29422. 232p. 1992. lib. bdg. 32.00 (*0-87338-453-9*) Kent St U Pr.
Minahan, John C., Jr. Nebraska Legal Forms: Bankruptcy. 230p. 1982. disk, ring bd. 85.00 (*0-685-49516-7*) Butterworth Legal Pubs.
— Nebraska Legal Forms: Bankruptcy. 230p. 1982. ring bd. 50.00 (*0-86678-029-7*) Michie Butterworth.
— Nebraska Legal Forms: Bankruptcy. suppl. ed. 230p. 1993. 42.50 (*1-56257-808-1*) Butterworth Legal Pubs.
Minahen, Charles D. Vortex-t: The Poetics of Turbulence. 200p. 1992. text ed. 28.50 (*0-271-00774-5*) Pa St U Pr.
***Minahen, Charles D., ed.** Figuring Things: Char, Ponge, & Poetry in the Twentieth Century. LC 94-70553. (French Forum Monographs: No. 84). 256p. (Orig.). 1994. pap. 24.95x (*0-917058-89-5*) French Forum.
Minai, Asghar T. Aesthetics, Mind, & Nature: A Communication Approach to the Unity of Matter & Consciousness. LC 92-36548. 352p. 1993. text ed. 69.50 (*0-275-94296-1*, C4296, Praeger Pubs) Greenwood.
— Design As Aesthetic Communication: Structuring Random-Order. (American University Studies: Fine Arts: Ser. XX, Vol. 9). 500p. (C). 1989. text ed. 67.95 (*0-8204-0815-8*) P Lang Pubs.
Minai, Yoshitaka, jt. auth. see Tominaga, Takeshi.
Minakata, H. Festschrift of the Symposium in Honor of Tetsuro Kobayaski. 264p. 1994. text ed. 67.00 (*981-02-1417-0*) World Scientific Pub.
Minakir, Pavel A. & Freeze, Gregory L., eds. The Russian Far East: An Economic Handbook. Freeze, Gregory L., tr. 544p. 1994. text ed. 150.00 (*1-56324-456-X*) M E Sharpe.
Minakuchi, Hiroya. In Search of Whales & Dolphins. (Illus.). 104p. 1995. 27.50 (*0-8050-1771-2*) H Holt & Co.
Minale, Marcello. Leader of the Pack. (Illus.). 224p. 1993. 60.00 (*1-870458-50-8*, Pub. by Elfande Art Pub UK) Bks Nippan.
Minami, K., et al, eds. Cardio-Thoracic Surgery: What Is New in Current Practice, Proceedings of the Second International Symposium, Bad Deynhausen, 5-7 September 1991. LC 92-9994. (International Congress Ser.: No. 985). 1992. write for info. (*0-444-89267-2*, Excerpta Medica) Elsevier.
Minami, Masahiko & Kennedy, Bruce P., eds. Language Issues in Literacy & Bilingual - Multicultural Education. LC 91-75438. (Reprint Ser.: No. 22). 572p. (Orig.). (C). 1991. pap. 29.95 (*0-916690-24-5*) Harvard Educ Rev.
Minami, N. Multiplicative Homology Operations & Transfer. LC 91-28757. (MEMO Ser.). 74p. 1991. 18.00 (*0-8218-2518-6*, MEMO 94/457) Am Math.
Minami, Ryoshin. The Economic Development of China: A Comparison with the Japanese Experience. Jiang, Wenran et al, trs. LC 93-15600. 262p. 1993. text ed. 45.00 (*0-312-10021-3*) St Martin.
— The Economic Development of Japan: A Quantitative Study. 2nd ed. Thompson, Ralph et al, trs. LC 93-10467. 1994. text ed. 45.00 (*0-312-09956-8*); pap. write for info. (*0-312-09958-4*) St Martin.
Minami, Ryoshin, jt. ed. see Kosobud, Richard F.
Minami, Ryoshin, et al, eds. Acquisition, Adaptation, & the Development of Technologies: Japan's Experience & Its Lessons. LC 94-12855. (Studies in Modern Japanese Enconomy). 1994. write for info. (*0-312-12241-1*) St Martin.
Minamiki, George. The Chinese Rites Controversy: From Its Beginnings to Modern Times. 1985. 15.95 (*0-8294-0457-0*) Loyola Univ Pr.
Minan, John H., jt. ed. see Folsom, Ralph H.
Minan, John H., jt. auth. see Lawrence, William H.
Minar, Barbara. Unrealistic Expectations. 156p. 1990. pap. text ed. 1.60 (*0-89693-542-6*) SP Pubns.
Minar, Barbra. Lamper's Meadow. LC 91-34151. 160p. (J). (gr. 4-7). 1992. pap. 6.99 (*0-89107-663-8*) Crossway Bks.
Minar, Edwin L., Jr. Early Pythagorean Politics in Practice & Theory. Vlastos, Gregory, ed. LC 78-19373. (Morals & Law in Ancient Greece Ser.). (ENG & GRE.). 1979. reprint ed. lib. bdg. 25.95 (*0-405-11563-6*) Ayer.
Minar, Edwin L., Jr., tr. see Burkert, Walter.
Minard, Bernie. Health Care Computer Systems for the 1990s: Critical Executive Decisions. LC 90-15620. 325p. 1991. text ed. 42.00 (*0-910701-67-9*, 0902) Health Admin Pr.
Minard, John S., ed. see Hubbard, J. Niles.
Minard, Rosemary, ed. Womenfolk & Fairy Tales. LC 74-26555. (Illus.). 176p. (J). (gr. 2-5). 1975. 16.95 (*0-395-20276-0*) HM.
Minarik, Elsa H. Percy & the Five Houses. (J). (ps-3). 1990. pap. 3.95 (*0-14-054209-4*, Puffin) Puffin Bks.
Minarik, Else. Father Bear Comes Home: (Papa Oso Vuele a Casa) (SPA.). (J). 9.95 (*84-204-3048-X*) Santillana.
— Little Bear - Osito. (SPA.). (J). 9.95 (*84-204-3044-7*) Santillana.
— Little Bear's Friends - Los Amigos de Osito. (SPA.). (J). 7.95 (*84-204-3049-8*) Santillana.
Minarik, Else H. Am I Beautiful? LC 91-32562. (Illus.). 24p. (J). (ps-4). 1992. 14.00 (*0-688-09911-4*); lib. bdg. 13.93 (*0-688-09912-2*) Greenwillow.
— Cat & Dog. LC 60-14998. (Early I Can Read Bk.). (Illus.). 32p. (J). (gr. k-2). 1960. lib. bdg. 14.89 (*0-06-024221-3*) HarpC Child Bks.
— Father Bear Comes Home. LC 59-5794. (Harper I Can Read Bk.). (Illus.). 64p. (J). (gr. k-3). 1959. 14.95 (*0-06-024230-2*); lib. bdg. 14.89 (*0-06-024231-0*) HarpC Child Bks.
— Father Bear Comes Home. LC 59-5794. (Trophy I Can Read Bk.). (Illus.). (J). (ps-3). 1978. pap. 3.50 (*0-06-444014-1*, Trophy) HarpC Child Bks.
— Father Bear Comes Home. LC 85-45260. (I Can Read Book & Casette Ser.). (Illus.). 64p. (J). (gr. k-3). 1995. audio 6.95 (*0-694-70010-X*) HarperAudio.

An Asterisk (*) at the beginning of an entry indicates that the title is appearing in BIP for the first time.

— It's Spring! LC 87-37202. (Illus.). 24p. (J). (ps up). 1989. 11.95 (*0-688-07619-X*); lib. bdg. 11.88 (*0-688-07620-3*) Greenwillow.
— Kiss for Little Bear. LC 57-9263. (Harper Early I Can Read Bk.). (Illus.). 32p. (J). (gr. k-3). 1968. 14.95 (*0-06-024298-1*); lib. bdg. 14.89 (*0-06-024299-X*) HarpC Child Bks.
— A Kiss for Little Bear. LC 68-16820. (Trophy Early I Can Read Bk.). (Illus.). 32p. (J). (ps-3). 1984. pap. 3.50 (*0-06-444050-8*, Trophy) HarpC Child Bks.
— Kiss for Little Bear. braille ed. 6p. (J). 1992. Braille. vinyl bd. 0.48 (*1-56956-271-7*, BR7951) W A T Braille.
— A Kiss for Little Bear. unabridged ed. (I Can Read Book Ser.). (Illus.). (J). (ps-3). 1991. digital audio 6.95 (*1-55994-263-0*, Caedmon) HarperAudio.
— Little Bear. (Harper I Can Read Bk.). (Illus.). 64p. (J). (gr. k-3). 1957. 14.00i (*0-06-024240-X*); lib. bdg. 14.89 (*0-06-024241-8*) HarpC Child Bks.
— Little Bear. LC 57-9263. (Trophy I Can Read Book & Cassette Set). (Illus.). 64p. (J). (gr. k-3). 1978. pap. 3.50 (*0-06-444004-4*, Trophy) HarpC Child Bks.
— Little Bear. unabridged ed. (I Can Read Book Ser.). (Illus.). (J). (ps-3). 1990. audio 6.95 (*1-55994-234-7*, Caedmon) HarperAudio.
— Little Bear, 3 bks., Set. (Trophy I Can Read Bk.). (Illus.). (J). (gr. k-3). 1992. Boxed set. pap. 10.50 (*0-06-444197-0*, Trophy) HarpC Child Bks.
— Little Bear's Friend. LC 60-6370. (Harper I Can Read Bk.). (Illus.). 64p. (J). (gr. k-3). 1960. 14.00i (*0-06-024255-8*); lib. bdg. 14.89 (*0-06-024256-6*) HarpC Child Bks.
— Little Bear's Friend. LC 60-6370. (Trophy I Can Read Book Ser.). (Illus.). 64p. (J). (ps-3). 1984. pap. 3.50 (*0-06-444051-6*, Trophy) HarpC Child Bks.
— Little Bear's Friend. unabridged ed. (I Can Read Book Ser.). (Illus.). (J). (ps-3). 1990. audio 6.95 (*1-55994-235-5*, Caedmon) HarperAudio.
— Little Bear's Visit. LC 61-11451. (Harper I Can Read Bk.). (Illus.). 64p. (J). (ps-3). 1961. 14.95 (*0-06-024265-5*); lib. bdg. 14.89 (*0-06-024266-3*) HarpC Child Bks.
— Little Bear's Visit. LC 61-11451. (Trophy I Can Read Bk.). (Illus.). 64p. (J). (gr. k-3). 1979. pap. 3.50 (*0-06-444023-0*, Trophy) HarpC Child Bks.
— Little Bear's Visit. unabridged ed. (I Can Read Book Ser.). (Illus.). (J). (ps-3). 1990. audio 6.95 (*1-55994-236-3*, Caedmon) HarperAudio.
— The Little Girl & the Dragon. LC 90-38495. (Illus.). 24p. (J). (ps up). 1991. 13.95 (*0-688-09913-0*); lib. bdg. 13.88 (*0-688-09914-9*) Greenwillow.
— No Fighting, No Biting! LC 58-5293. (Harper I Can Read Bk.). (Illus.). 64p. (J). (gr. k-3). 1958. 13.00 (*0-06-024290-6*); lib. bdg. 14.89 (*0-06-024291-4*) HarpC Child Bks.
— No Fighting, No Biting! LC 58-5293. (Trophy I Can Read Bk.). (Illus.). 64p. (J). (ps-3). 1978. pap. 3.50 (*0-06-444015-X*, Trophy) HarpC Child Bks.
— Osito. LC 69-14452. (Spanish I Can Read Bk.). (Illus.). 64p. (SPA.). (J). (ps-3). 1969. lib. bdg. 10.89 (*0-06-024244-2*) HarpC Child Bks.
— Percy & the Five Houses. LC 88-4804. (Illus.). 24p. (J). (gr. k up). 1989. 11.95 (*0-688-08104-5*); lib. bdg. 11.88 (*0-688-08105-3*) Greenwillow.
— Visita de Osito: (La Visita de Osito) (SPA.). (J). (gr. 1-6). pap. 9.50 (*84-204-3051-X*) Santillana.
— What If? LC 86-7649. (Illus.). 24p. (J). (ps-2). 1987. 11.75 (*0-688-06473-6*); lib. bdg. 11.88 (*0-688-06474-4*) Greenwillow.

Minarik, Etienne. Individual Motivation: Removing the Blocks to Creative Involvement. LC 91-28947. (Illus.). 263p. 1992. 30.00 (*0-915299-85-2*) Prod Press.

Minarik, John P., ed. Kicking Their Heels with Freedom. LC 80-71014. 80p. 1981. pap. 4.00 (*0-939406-00-4*) Acad Prison Arts.

Minarik, Joseph J. Making America's Budget Policy: From the 1980's to the 1990's. LC 89-27503. 248p. 1990. 46.95 (*0-87332-573-7*); pap. text ed. 20.95 (*0-87332-621-0*) M E Sharpe.
— Making Tax Choices. LC 85-5342. (Illus.). 180p. (Orig.). 1985. lib. bdg. 44.00 (*0-87766-382-3*) Urban Inst.

Minars, David. Accounting. (E Z 101 Study Keys Ser.). 144p. (Orig.). (C). 1992. pap. text ed. 5.95 (*0-8120-4738-9*) Barron.
— Business Start-ups: The Professional's Guide to Tax & Financial Strategies. 300p. 1987. text ed. 49.95 (*0-13-107707-4*) P-H.
— Shepard's-McGraw-Hill Tax Dictionary for Business. 1993. text ed. 29.95 (*0-07-042371-7*) McGraw.

Minars, David & Davidoff, Howard. Tax Penalties & Interest Handbook, 1990-1991. 340p. 1990. and Suppl. 12/91. 40.00. write for info. (*0-318-68638-4*) Butterworth Legal Pubs.
— Tax Penalties & Interest Handbook, 1990-1991. 340p. 1991. ring bd. 80.00 (*0-88063-748-X*) Michie Butterworth.

Minars, David, jt. auth. see Blond, Neil C.

Minarski, M. Testudines. (Encyclopedia of Paleoherpetology Ser.: Pt. 7). (Illus.). 130p. 1976. text ed. 70.00 (*3-437-30236-1*) Lubrecht & Cramer.

Minary, Ruth, jt. auth. see Moorman, Charles.

Minas, Anne. Gender Basics: Feminist Perspectives on Women & Men. 545p. (C). 1993. pap. 31.95 (*0-534-17814-6*) Intl Thomson.

Minasi, Dom. Musician's Manual for Chord Substitution. Gambino, Thomas, ed. 30p. (Orig.). (J). 1973. student ed, pap. 4.50 (*0-936519-03-7*) Sunrise Artistries.
— Principles of Harmonic Substitution. Gambino, Thomas, ed. 48p. (Orig.). 1979. student ed, pap. 8.95 (*0-936519-02-9*) Sunrise Artistries.
— Stress Points. Gambino, Thomas, ed. (Illus.). (Orig.). 1986. 9.95 (*0-936519-00-2*) Sunrise Artistries.

***Minasi, Mark.** The Complete PC Upgrade & Maintenance Guide. 1995. 34.99 (*0-7821-1660-4*) Sybex.
— Complete PC Upgrade & Maintenance Guide. 3rd ed. LC 93-87698. 807p. 1994. pap. 29.99 (*0-7821-1498-9*) Sybex.
— Guia Completa de Mantenimieato 4 Actualizacion de la PC. 760p. 1993. pap. text ed. 27.95 (*968-6346-76-7*, Pub. by Ventura Ediciones MX) Computer & Tech.
— The Hard Disk Survival Guide. LC 91-65408. 444p. 1991. pap. 29.95 (*0-89588-799-1*) Sybex.
— Inside OS - 2 Warp, Ver. 3. 1994. disk, pap. 39.99 (*1-56205-378-7*) New Riders Pub.
— Mastering Windows NT 3.5 Server. LC 94-69699. 950p. 1994. 44.99 (*0-7821-1622-1*) Sybex.
— The PC Upgrade & Maintenance Guide: Multimedia Edition. 1995. 49.99 (*0-7821-1738-4*) Sybex.
— The Secrets of Effective GUI Design. LC 93-87704. 225p. 1994. pap. 19.99 (*0-7821-1495-4*) Sybex.
— Secrets of Wing Commander Universe. LC 94-65691. 464p. 1994. pap. 19.99 (*0-7821-1505-5*) Sybex.
— Troubleshooting Windows. LC 92-62324. 442p. 1992. 27.95 (*0-7821-1115-7*) Sybex.

Minasian, Stanley M. Whales of Hawaii. 1991. pap. 5.95 (*0-9627803-0-8*) Hamilton West.

Minasian, Stanley M., jt. auth. see Balcomb, Kenneth C., III.

Minassian, John. Many Hills Yet to Climb. 300p. (Orig.). 1986. pap. write for info. (*0-936941-00-6*) Jim Cook.

Minassian, Martiros. Grammaire d'Armenien Oriental. LC 80-18625. (Anatolian & Caucasian Studies Ser.). 1980. 50.00 (*0-88206-040-6*) Caravan Bks.

Minatoya, Lydia. Talking to High Monks in the Snow: An Asian-American Odyssey. LC 91-50450. 288p. 1993. pap. 11.00 (*0-06-092372-5*, PL) HarpC.

***Minatra, MaryAnn.** The Heirloom. LC 94-30954. (Alcott Legacy Ser.: Bk. 3). (Orig.). 1995. pap. 9.99 (*1-56507-235-9*) Harvest Hse.
— The Masterpiece. LC 93-27042. (Alcott Legacy Ser.). 1994. pap. 9.99 (*1-56507-172-7*) Harvest Hse.
— The Tapestry. LC 92-20866. 1993. pap. 9.99 (*1-56507-037-2*) Harvest Hse.

Minault, Gail. The Khilafat Movement: Religious Symbolism & Political Mobilization in India. LC 81-4553. (Studies in Oriental Culture: No. 16). 288p. 1982. text ed. 42.00 (*0-231-05072-0*) Col U Pr.

Minault, Gail, ed. The Extended Family: Women in India. (C). 1989. reprint ed. 40.00 (*0-685-33289-6*, Pub. by Chanakya II) S Asia.
— Voices of Silent: English Translation of Hali's Majalis Un-Nissa & Chup Di Dad. 1986. 18.50 (*81-7001-018-7*, Pub. by Chanakya II) S Asia.

Minault, Gail, ed. see Douglas, Ian H.

***Minawer, Sidney J. & Shike, Moshe.** Liberese del Cancer. 1995. pap. 11.00 (*0-684-81332-7*) S&S Trade.

Minay, C. Recycling Disued Industrial Land in the Black Country: An Initial Assessment & Conference Transcript. (C). 1987. 29.00 (*0-685-30253-9*, Pub. by Oxford Polytechnic UK) St Mut.

Minay, C., ed. Implementation - View from an Ivory Tower. (C). 1980. 29.00 (*0-685-30299-7*, Pub. by Oxford Polytechnic UK) St Mut.

Minay, C. & Weston, J. The Future of Work Jobs in the Environment. (C). 1987. 35.00 (*0-685-30251-2*, Pub. by Oxford Polytechnic UK) St Mut.

Minaya-Rowe, Liliana F. A Comparison of Bilingual Education in Three Latin American Countries & in the United States. (TWEC World Education Monographs). 20p. 1980. 2.50 (*0-685-05137-4*) I N Thut World Educ Ctr.

Minc, Alain. The Great European Illusion. (Developmental Management Ser.). 256p. (C). 1992. text ed. 32.95 (*0-631-17695-0*) Blackwell Pubs.

Minc, Alain, jt. auth. see Nora, Simon.

Minc, Henryk. Nonnegative Matrices. LC 87-27416. (Discrete Mathematics Ser.). 206p. 1988. text ed. 103.00 (*0-471-83966-3*) Wiley.
— Permanents. (Encyclopedia of Mathematics & Its Applications Ser.: No. 6). 1984. 54.95 (*0-521-30226-9*) Cambridge U Pr.

Minc, Henryk, jt. auth. see Marcus, Marvin.

Minc, Rose. Lo Fantastico y lo Real en la Narrativa de Juan Rulfo y Guadalupe Duenas. LC 77-76932. (Senda de Estudios y Ensayos Ser.). (Illus.). (Orig.). (SPA.). 1977. pap. 9.95 (*0-918454-03-4*) Senda Nueva.

Minc, Rose S., ed. The Contemporary Latin American Short Story. LC 78-73619. (Senda de Estudios y Ensayos Ser.). (Orig.). (SPA.). 1979. pap. 9.95 (*0-918454-10-7*) Senda Nueva.

Minc, Rose S., ed. see Desnoes, et al.

Minc, Rose S., ed. see Fuentes, Carlos, et al.

Mincberg. WordPerfect for Windows Bundle. 1993. pap. 24.95 (*0-07-882020-0*) Osborne-McGraw.

Mincberg, Mella. WordPerfect Six: The Pocket Reference. 1993. pap. text ed. 9.95 (*0-07-881905-9*) Osborne-McGraw.
— WordPerfect Six Made Easy. 3rd ed. 1993. pap. text ed. 24.95 (*0-07-881895-8*) Osborne-McGraw.
— WordPerfect 5.1: The Pocket Reference. 1990. pap. text ed. 6.95 (*0-07-881662-9*) Osborne-McGraw.
— WordPerfect 5.1 Made Easy. 1990. pap. text ed. 24.95 (*0-07-881625-4*) Osborne-McGraw.
— WordPerfect 6 for Windows Made Easy. 1993. pap. text ed. 24.94 (*0-07-881925-3*) McGraw.

Mincer, Allen I., jt. ed. see Mendell, Rosalind B.

Mincer, Jacob. Schooling, Experience, & Earnings. (Studies in Human Behavior & Social Institutions: No. 2). 167p. 1974. 45.50 (*0-87014-265-8*) Natl Bur Econ Res.
— Studies in Human Capital, Vol. 1: The Collected Essays of Jacob Mincer. (Economists of the Twentieth Century Ser.). 448p. 1993. 89.95 (*1-85278-579-9*, Pub. by E Elgar Pub UK) Ashgate Pub Co.
— Studies in Labor Supply, Vol. 2: The Collected Essays of Jacob Mincer. (Economists of the Twentieth Century Ser.). 368p. 1993. 79.95 (*1-85278-578-0*, Pub. by E Elgar Pub UK) Ashgate Pub Co.

Mincer, Jacob, ed. Economic Forecasts & Expectations: Analysis of Forecasting Behavior & Performance. (Business Cycles Ser.: No. 19). 269p. 1969. text ed. 70.50 (*0-87014-202-X*) Natl Bur Econ Res.

Mincer, Jacob A. Supplement to NBER Report Eleven: Youth, Education, & Work. 7p. reprint ed. 20.00 (*0-685-61366-6*) Natl Bur Econ Res.

Minces, Juliet. House of Obedience: Women in Arab Society. Pallis, M., tr. 116p. (C). 1982. pap. 12.50 (*0-86232-063-1*, Pub. by Zed Books UK) Humanities.

Minces, Juliette. Veiled: Women in Islam. Berrett, A. M., tr. LC 93-28544. 176p. 1994. 35.00 (*0-9628715-5-9*) Blue Crane Bks.

Mincey, Melvin. Ward Street. (Illus.). 281p. (Orig.). 1994. pap. text ed. 8.95 (*0-9637969-0-9*) Mincey Pub Hse.
— The Worm That Never Dies. 2nd rev. ed. Abrims, Etelle, ed. Orig. Title: Ward Street. (Illus.). 223p. 1995. pap. 8.95 (*0-9637969-2-5*) Mincey Pub Hse.

Minch, John & Leslie, Thomas. The Baja Highway. (Illus.). 240p. 1991. write for info. (*0-9631090-0-6*) J Minch Assocs.

Minch, Stephen. By Forces Unseen: The Innovative Card Magic of Ernest Earick. (Illus.). 216p. 1993. 32.00 (*0-945296-09-6*) Hermetic Pr.

Minch, Stephen, ed. see Lesley, Ted.

Minchev, G., ed. Molecular Beam Epitaxy. 200p. 1991. text ed. 96.00 (*0-87849-614-9*, Pub. by Trans Tech GW) LPS Dist Ctr.

Minchin-Comm, Dorothy. Gates of Promise. Wheeler, Gerald, ed. 96p. (YA). (gr. 7 up). 1989. pap. 6.95 (*0-8280-0470-6*) Review & Herald.

Minchin, James. No Man Is an Island. 384p. 1987. text ed. 37.95 (*0-86861-906-X*) Routledge Chapman & Hall.
— No Man Is an Island. 2nd ed. 396p. 1991. pap. text ed. 17.95 (*0-04-400028-6*, Pub. by Allen & Unwin Aust Pty AT) Paul & Co Pubs.

***Minchinton, Jerry A.** Fifty-Two Things You Can Do to Raise Your Self-Esteem. 80p. (Orig.). 1995. pap. 6.50 (*0-9635719-6-6*) Arnford MO.
— Maximum Self-Esteem: The Handbook for Reclaiming Your Sense of Self-Worth. LC 92-76034. 256p. (Orig.). 1993. pap. 14.95 (*0-9635719-7-4*) Arnford MO.

Minchinton, Walter, et al, eds. Virginia Slave-Trade Statistics, 1698-1775. xvi, 218p. (Orig.). 1984. 45.00 (*0-88490-118-1*) VA State Lib.

Minchinton, Walter E., ed. Industrial South Wales 1750-1914: Essays in Welsh Economic History. LC 68-21451. (Illus.). xxxi, 264p. 1969. 35.00 (*0-678-05018-X*) Kelley.
— Industrial South Wales, 1750-1914: Essays in Welsh Economic History. 296p. 1969. 35.00 (*0-7146-1344-4*, Pub. by F Cass Pubs UK) Intl Spec Bk.

Minchom, Martin. The People of Quito, 1690-1810: Change & Unrest in the Underclass. (Dellplain Latin American Studies: No. 32). 297p. (C). 1993. pap. text ed. 49.95 (*0-8133-8831-7*) Westview.

Minciacchi, Diego, et al, eds. Thalamic Networks for Relay & Modulation. LC 93-21166. (Studies in Neuroscience). 1993. 150.00 (*0-08-042274-8*, Pergamon Pr) Elsevier.

Minckler & Buskirk. Glaucoma. (Illus.). 240p. 1991. text ed. 99.50 (*0-397-51069-1*) Lippincott.

Minckler, Leon S. Woodland Ecology: Environmental Forestry for the Small Owner. 2nd ed. (Illus.). 230p. 1980. pap. 15.95 (*0-8156-0154-9*) Syracuse U Pr.

Minckley, Barbara B. & Walters, Mary D., eds. Building Trust Relationships in Nursing. LC 83-19363. 131p. 1983. pap. 6.00 (*0-942146-04-2*) Midwest Alliance Nursing.

Minckley, Wendell L. & Deacon, James E., eds. Battle Against Extinction: Native Fish Management in the American West. LC 91-6977. (Illus.). 517p. 1991. 50.00 (*0-8165-1221-3*) U of Ariz Pr.

Minco, Marga. Empty House. LC 89-81668. 160p. 1990. 26.00 (*0-7206-0760-4*, Pub. by P Owen Ltd UK) Dufour.
— The Fall. Ringold, Jeannette K., tr. LC 90-80801. 112p. 1990. 25.00 (*0-7206-0789-2*, Pub. by P Owen Ltd UK) Dufour.
— Glass Bridge. Knecht, Stacey, tr. 111p. 1988. 21.00 (*0-7206-0719-1*, Pub. by P Owen Ltd UK) Dufour.
— The Other Side. Levitt, Ruth, tr. 144p. 1994. 30.00 (*0-7206-0908-9*, Pub. by P Owen Ltd UK) Dufour.

Mincoff, Elizabeth & Marriage, Margaret S. Pillow Lace: A Practical Handbook. 1981. 22.95 (*0-903585-10-3*) Robin & Russ.
— Pillow or Bobbin Lace: Technique, Patterns, History. (Illus.). 288p. 1987. reprint ed. pap. 7.95 (*0-486-25505-0*) Dover.

Mincoff, Elizabeth & Mincoff, Margaret S. Marriage Pillow or Bobbin Lace - Techniques, Patterns, History. 1988. 16.00 (*0-8446-6327-1*) Peter Smith.

Mincoff, Marco. Things Supernatural & Causeless: Shakespearean Romance. LC 92-53580. 136p. 1992. 28.50 (*0-87413-456-0*) U Delaware Pr.

Mincoff, Margaret S., jt. auth. see Mincoff, Elizabeth.

***Mincolla, Mark D. The Tao of Ch'i: Healing with the Unseen Life Force. (Illus.). 250p. (Orig.). (YA). Date not set. pap. 14.95 (*0-9632811-1-9*) Pennyroyal Pr.**
The TAO OF CH'I, HEALING WITH THE UNSEEN LIFE FORCE by Mark Dana Mincolla, Ph.D., is a profoundly innovative & inspirational work which explores the application of contemporized Chinese healing protocols as models for 21st century energy medicine. Phonetically pronounced as DOA OF CHEE, this title may be literally translated as "the way of energy." To the ancient Chinese however, Ch'i was no ordinary energy. Rather, it was described as the subtle universal energy which vivifies all living things. With subtle energy as his main theme, the author draws astonishing parallels between the metaphysics of ancient China & the physics of the modern west. We are emphatically reminded by the author that Ch'i, not unlike Einstein's "quanta," is the mystical unifying life force which represents the most vital common denominator of all living & healing. The book centers around a series of informal workshops where subjects were administered four uniquely adapted Chinese energy healing protocols. The author employed the bio-feedback technology of Kirlian (auric energy) photography in order to visually demonstrate the aura (human energy field) changes in subjects before & after administering the energy protocols. Also, inspired by ancient Eastern principles which contend that sound & light vibrations are the most powerful, primal form of energy medicine, the author has developed an innovative synchronized light & sound vibrational healing bath for use in these energy workshops. To order: Atrium Publishers, 1-800-275-2606, 3356 Coffey Ln., Santa Rosa, CA 95403. ***Publisher Provided Annotation.***

— The Wu Way: A Path to Natural Healing. 256p. (Orig.). 1992. pap. 10.95 (*0-9632811-0-0*) Pennyroyal Pr.

Mincu, Julian. Diabetic Macro- & Microangiopathy. LC 73-82434. (C). 1975. 150.00 (*3-11-004533-8*) De Gruyter.

Mincy, Ronald B., ed. Nurturing Young Black Males: Challenges to Agencies, Programs, & Social Policy. 250p. 1994. 19.95 (*0-87766-598-2*) Urban Inst.

Minczeski, John. Gravity. x, 67p. 1991. 16.50 (*0-89672-267-8*); pap. 9.50 (*0-89672-268-6*) Tex Tech Univ Pr.
— The Reconstruction of Light. LC 81-80546. (Minnesota Voices Project Ser.: No. 2). (Illus.). 80p. 1981. pap. 3.00 (*0-89823-023-3*) New Rivers Pr.

Minczeski, John, ed. Concert at Chopin's House: A Collection of Polish American Writing. 1987. pap. 11.95 (*0-89823-098-5*) New Rivers Pr.
— The Midnight Butterfly Sings. (Illus.). 164p. (Orig.). 1988. pap. 7.50 (*0-927663-01-5*) COMPAS.

Mind-Body Medical Institute Staff, et al. The Wellness Book: The Comprehensive Guide to Maintaining Health & Treating Stress-Related Illness. (Illus.). 352p. 1991. 21.95 (*1-55972-092-1*, Birch Ln Pr) Carol Pub Group.

***Minda, Gary.** Postmodern Legal Movements: Law & Jurisprudence at Century's End. LC 94-24934. 344p. 1995. 40.00 (*0-8147-5510-0*); pap. 18.50 (*0-8147-5511-9*) NYU Pr.

Minde, Ase, jt. auth. see Jennings, Sue.

Minde, Klaus & Minde, Regina. Infant Psychiatry: An Introduction Textbook. LC 85-14231. (Developmental Clinical Psychology & Psychiatry Ser.: No. 4). 197p. reprint ed. pap. 56.20 (*0-7837-6717-X*, 2046344) Bks Demand.

Minde, Regina, jt. auth. see Minde, Klaus.

Mindel, Charles H., Jr., ed. see Habenstein, Robert W. & Wright, Roosevelt.

Mindel, Charles H., Jr., et al, eds. Ethnic Families in America: Patterns & Variations. 3rd ed. 525p. 1988. pap. 27.75 (*0-444-01319-9*) P-H.

Mindel, Charles S., jt. auth. see Markides, Kyriacos C.

Mindel, Eugene D. & Vernon, McCay, eds. They Grow in Silence: Understanding Deaf Children & Adults. 2nd ed. LC 90-21666. (Illus.). 204p. (C). 1987. reprint ed. pap. text ed. 28.00 (*0-89079-325-5*, 1744) PRO-ED.

Mindeleff, Victor. A Study of Pueblo Architecture: Tusayan & Cibola Bureau of American Ethnology, 8th Annual Report. LC 88-43115. (Illus.). 426p. (C). 1989. pap. 19.95 (*0-87474-619-1*) Smithsonian.

Mindell. Dreambody in Relationships. 1987. pap. 9.95 (*0-7102-1072-8*, RKP) Routledge.
— Power Reading: Self Pace System for Mastering All Your Business Reading. 1993. pap. 14.95 (*0-13-753872-3*) P-H.

***Mindell, Amy.** Metaskills: The Spiritual Art of Therapy. 192p. (Orig.). 1994. pap. 12.95 (*1-56184-119-6*) New Falcon Pubns.

Mindell, Amy, jt. auth. see Mindell, Arnold.

***Mindell, Arnold.** Coma: The Dreambody Near Death. 144p. 1995. 10.95 (*0-14-019483-5*, Arkana) Viking Penguin.
— Dreambody: The Body's Role in Revealing the Self. LC 82-3239. 219p. (Orig.). 1982. 30.00 (*0-938434-05-5*); pap. 16.95 (*0-938434-06-3*) Sigo Pr.
— Dreambody in Relationships. 1988. pap. 10.00 (*0-14-019281-6*, Arkana) Viking Penguin.

— The Leader As Martial Artist: An Introduction to Deep Democracy. LC 91-55333. (Illus.). 176p. 1993. pap. 10.00 (0-06-250640-4) Harper SF.
— River's Way: The Process Science of the Dreambody. 176p. 1989. 10.95 (0-14-019124-0, Arkana) Viking Penguin.
— River's Way: The Process Science of the Dreambody. 176p. 1995. pap. 9.95 (0-14-019274-3, Penguin Bks) Viking Penguin.
— The Shaman's Body: A New Shamanism for Transforming Health, Relationships, & the Community. LC 92-56408. 176p. 1993. pap. 11.00 (0-06-250655-2) Harper SF.
— Sitting in the Fire: Large Group Transformation Using Conflict & Diversity. 200p. (Orig.). 1995. pap. 13.95 (1-887078-00-2) Lao Tse Pr.
— Work with a Dreaming Body. 1989. pap. 10.95 (0-14-019142-9, Arkana) Viking Penguin.
— Working on Yourself Alone: Inner Dreambody Work. (Illus.). 160p. 1990. pap. 9.95 (0-14-019201-8, Arkana) Viking Penguin.

Mindell, Arnold & Mindell, Amy. Riding the Horse Backwards: Process Work in Theory & Practice. 256p. (Orig.). 1992. pap. 10.00 (0-14-019320-0, Arkana) Viking Penguin.

Mindell, Earl. Dr. Earl Mindell's Live Longer & Feel Better with Vitamins & Minerals. LC 94-12737. 1994. pap. 4.95 (0-87983-652-0) Keats.
— Earl Mindell's Food As Medicine. 1994. 13.00 (0-671-79755-7, Fireside) S&S Trade.
— Earl Mindell's Herb Bible. 304p. (Orig.). 1992. pap. 13.00 (0-671-76122-6, Fireside) S&S Trade.
— Earl Mindell's New & Revised Vitamin Bible. 384p. 1989. mass mkt. 5.95 (0-446-35643-3) Warner Bks.
— Earl Mindell's Quick & Easy Guide to Good Health. 1982. pap. 2.95 (0-87983-271-1) Keats.
— Earl Mindell's Safe Eating. 288p. 1988. mass mkt. 5.99 (0-446-34670-5) Warner Bks.
— Earl Mindell's Shaping up with Vitamins. 256p. 1988. mass mkt. 5.99 (0-446-30952-4) Warner Bks.
— Earl Mindell's Soy Miracle. 1995. pap. 12.00 (0-671-89820-5, Fireside) S&S Trade.
— Earl Mindell's Vitamin Bible: Revised & Updated. 368p. 1991. mass mkt. 6.50 (0-446-36184-4) Warner Bks.
— Parents' Nutrition Bible: A Guide to Raising Healthy Children. rev. ed. LC 91-71698. Orig. Title: The Vitamin Bible for Kids. 256p. 1991. pap. 9.00 (1-56170-018-5, 137) Hay House.

Mindell, Earl, ed. see Bland, Jeffrey.
Mindell, Earl, ed. see Challem, Jack J.
Mindell, Earl, ed. see DiCyan, Erwin.
Mindell, Earl, ed. see Heinerman, John.
Mindell, Earl, ed. see Heyer, Albrecht A.
Mindell, Earl, ed. see Kugler, Hans.
Mindell, Earl, ed. see Lee, William H.
Mindell, Earl, ed. see Lee, William.
Mindell, Earl, ed. see Light, Marilyn.
Mindell, Earl, ed. see Passwater, Richard A.
Mindell, Earl, ed. see Rose, Jeanne.
Mindell, Earl, ed. see Rosenberg, Harold S.
Mindell, Earl, ed. see Wunderlich, Ray C. & Kalita, Dwight K.

Mindell, Earl L. Dr. Earl Mindell's Garlic: The Miracle Nutrient. LC 94-20651. 1994. pap. 4.95 (0-87983-649-0) Keats.

Mindell, Earl R. The Vitamin Robbers. Passwater, Richard, ed. (Good Health Guide Ser.). (Illus.). (C). 1983. pap. 2.50 (0-87983-275-4) Keats.

Mindell, Earl R., ed. see Garrison, Robert, Jr.
Mindell, Earl R., ed. see Goldbeck, Nikki.
Mindell, Earl R., ed. see Jones, Susan S.
Mindell, Earl R., ed. see Leviton, Richard.
Mindell, Earl R., ed. see Mervyn, Len.
Mindell, Earl R., ed. see Sloan, Sara.
Mindell, Earl R., ed. see Vogel, Jerome & Walsh, Richard.
Mindell, Jacalyn, jt. ed. see Helms, Janet E.

Mindell, Jodi A. Issues in Clinical Psychology. 352p. (C). 1993. pap. text ed. write for info. (0-697-16945-6) Brown & Benchmark.

***Mindell, Phyllis, ed.** A Woman's Guide to the Language of Success: Communicating with Confidence & Power. 1995. text ed. 27.95 (0-13-157207-5); pap. text ed. 14.95 (0-13-157215-6) P-H.

Minden, Karen. Bamboo Stone: The Evolution of a Chinese Medical Elite. (Illus.). 200p. (C). 1994. 45.00 (0-8020-0550-0) U of Toronto Pr.

***Minden, Karen & Wong, Poh-Kam, eds.** Developing Technology Managers in the Pacific Rim: Comparative Strategies. LC 95-15666. (Illus.). 272p. 1995. 59.95 (1-56324-618-X, East Gate Bk); pap. 24.95 (1-56324-619-8, East Gate Bk) M E Sharpe.

Minden, Katherine. Using Framemaker 2.0 for the Macintosh. 1990. pap. 22.95 (0-201-57026-2) Addison-Wesley.

Mindes, Gayle, jt. auth. see Berry, Carla F.

Mindess, Harvey. Makers of Psychology: The Personal Factor. 182p. 1988. 35.95 (0-89885-371-0, Plenum Insight); pap. 20.95 (0-89885-380-X) Human Sci Pr.

Mindess, Mary, jt. auth. see Feinburg, Sylvia G.

Mindess, S. & Shah, S., eds. Bonding in Cementitious Composites. (Symposium Proceedings Ser.: Vol. 114). 1988. text ed. 42.00 (0-931837-82-0) Materials Res.

Mindess, S. & Shah, S. P., eds. Cement-Based Composites: Strain Rate Effects on Fracture, Vol. 64. (Materials Research Society Symposium Proceedings Ser.). 1986. text ed. 36.00 (0-931837-29-4) Materials Res.

Mindess, S. & Skalny, J. P., eds. Fiber Reinforced Cementitious Materials: Materials Research Society Symposium Proceedings, Vol. 211. 286p. 1991. text ed. 52.00 (1-55899-103-4) Materials Res.

Mindess, Sidney & Young, J. Francis. Concrete. (Civil Engineering & Engineering Mechanics Ser.). 4488p. 1981. text ed. 87.00 (0-13-167106-5) P-H.

Mindess, Sidney, jt. ed. see Skalny, Jan.

Mindick, Burton. Social Engineering in Family Matters. LC 85-6595. 240p. 1985. text ed. 55.00 (0-275-90040-1, C0040, Praeger Pubs) Greenwood.

Mindiola, Tatcho, et al. Chicano-Mexicano Relations. (Mexican American Studies Monograph: No. IV). (Orig.). 1986. pap. text ed. 11.95x (0-939709-03-1) Univ Houston Mex Amer.

Mindlanguage Industries Staff. Angel. 80p. 1989. pap. text ed. 10.95 (0-8403-5542-4) Kendall-Hunt.

Mindlin, H. & Londgraf, R. W., eds. Use of Computers in the Fatigue Laboratory - STP 613. 172p. 1976. 20.00 (0-8031-0593-2, 04-613000-30) ASTM.

***MindShare, Inc. Staff.** Card Bus System Architecture. 1995. pap. write for info. (0-201-40997-6) Addison-Wesley.
— 80486 System Architecture. 3rd ed. (C). 1995. pap. 19.95 (0-201-40994-1) Addison-Wesley.
— ISA System Architecture. 3rd ed. (C). 1995. pap. 34.95 (0-201-40996-8) Addison-Wesley.
— PCI System Architecture. 3rd ed. (C). 1995. pap. 34.95 (0-201-40993-3) Addison-Wesley.
— PCMCIA System Architecture. 2nd ed. 1995. pap. 29.95 (0-201-40991-7) Addison-Wesley.
— Plug & Play System Architecture. 1995. pap. 29.95 (0-201-41013-3) Addison-Wesley.
— PowerPC System Architecture. 2nd ed. (C). 1995. pap. 34.95 (0-201-40990-9) Addison-Wesley.

***MindShare, Inc. Staff & Shanley, Tom.** EISA System Architecture. 2nd ed. LC 95-9829. 1995. pap. 24.95 (0-201-40995-X) Addison-Wesley.

***MindShare, Inc. Staff, et al.** Pentium Processor System Architecture. 2nd ed. LC 95-1804. 1995. pap. 29.95 (0-201-40992-5) Addison-Wesley.

Mindt, Nicole & Sullivan, CeCe. The Seattle Times Guide to Cooking Techniques. (Illus.). 64p. (Orig.). 1987. spiral bd. 4.95 (0-944912-00-1) Seattle Times.

Mine, Hisashi & Osaki, Shunji. Markovian Decision Processes. LC 70-116709. (Modern Analytic & Computational Methods in Science & Mathematics Ser.: No. 25). 152p. reprint ed. pap. 43.40 (0-685-15419-X, 2026264) Bks Demand.

Mine, K. Japanese-English-Russian Physics Dictionary. 886p. (C). 1982. 160.00 (0-685-36914-5, Pub. by Collets) St Mut.
— Japanese-English-Russian Physics Dictionary. 886p. (C). 1982. 160.00 (0-89771-922-0, Pub. by Collets) St Mut.

Mine, Kim. Japanese-English-Russian Physics Dictionary. 886p. (ENG, JPN & RUS.). 1982. 85.00 (0-8288-2245-X, M15369) Fr & Eur.
— Japanese-English-Russian Physics Dictionary. 886p. (ENG, JPN & RUS.). 1987. 150.00 (0-685-18396-3, Pub. by Collets) St Mut.

***Mine Ventilation Symposium Staff.** Mine Ventilation Symposium: Proceedings of the 1st, March 29-31, 1982, the University of Alabama, University (Tuscaloosa), Alabama. fac. ed. Hartman, Howard L., ed. LC 82-71996. (Illus.). 324p. 1982. reprint ed. pap. 92.40 (0-7837-7857-0, 2047616) Bks Demand.
— Proceedings of the 6th U. S. Mine Ventilation Symposium: June 21-23, 1993, Salt Lake City, Utah. fac. ed. LC 93-83949. (Illus.). 652p. 1993. reprint ed. pap. 180.00 (0-7837-7869-4, 2047626) Bks Demand.

***Minear.** Humanitarianism Under Siege: A Critical Review of Operation Lifeline Sudan. Date not set. per. 9.95 (0-932415-66-0) Red Sea Pr.

Minear, Keith. Water Analysis, Vol. 2. LC 82-1755. 1984. text ed. 138.00 (0-12-498302-2) Acad Pr.
— Water Analysis, Vol. 3. LC 82-1755. 1984. text ed. 146.00 (0-12-498303-0) Acad Pr.

Minear, Larry & Weiss, Thomas G. Humanitarian Action in Times of War: A Handbook for Practitioners. LC 93-9825. 120p. (Orig.). 1993. pap. text ed. 8.95 (1-55587-437-1) Lynne Rienner.
— Humanitarian Politics. Hoepli-Phalon, Nancy L., ed. (Headline Ser.: No. 304). (Illus.). 72p. (Orig.). 1995. pap. 5.95 (0-87124-162-5) Foreign Policy.
— Mercy under Fire: War & the Global Humanitarian Community. (C). 1995. pap. text ed. 17.95 (0-8133-2567-6) Westview.
— Mercy under Fire: War & the Global Humanitarian Community. 1995. text ed. 55.00 (0-8133-2566-8) Westview.

Minear, Larry, jt. auth. see Deng, Francis M.
Minear, Larry, jt. ed. see Weiss, Thomas G.

Minear, Mark. Richmond Eighteen Eighty-Seven: A Quaker Drama Unfolds. LC 87-7603. 150p. 1987. pap. 6.95 (0-913408-98-0) Friends United.

Minear, Paul S. Christians & the New Creation: Genesis Motifs in the New Testament. LC 93-42167. 176p. (Orig.). 1994. pap. 14.99 (0-664-25531-0) Westminster John Knox.
— The Golgotha Earthquake: Three Witnesses. 128p. (Orig.). 1995. pap. 11.95 (0-8298-1070-6) Pilgrim OH.

Minear, Ralph & Proctor, William. Kids' Symptoms: From Birth to Teens. 352p. (Orig.). 1992. pap. 12.50 (0-380-76228-5) Avon.

Minear, Ralph E. & Proctor, William. The Brain Food Diet for Children. LC 83-3798. 228p. 1984. write for info. (0-672-52755-3) Macmillan.

Minear, Richard H. Japanese Tradition & Western Law: Emperor, State, & Law in the Thought of Hozumi Yatsuka. LC 72-115478. (Harvard East Asian Ser.: No. 48). 259p. reprint ed. pap. 73.90 (0-7837-2063-7, 2042338) Bks Demand.
— Through Japanese Eyes. (Through Eyes Ser.). (C). 1981. teacher ed, pap. 9.90 (0-614-02975-9) Amer Forum.
— Through Japanese Eyes. 3rd rev. ed. Clark, Leon E., ed. (Illus.). 360p. 1994. pap. text ed. 21.95 (0-685-72889-7) CITE.
— Through Japanese Eyes. 3rd rev. ed. Clark, Leon E., ed. (Illus.). 360p. 1994. lib. bdg. 44.00 (0-938960-34-2) CITE.
— Through Japanese Eyes, 2 vols., Set. (Through Eyes Ser.). 298p. (C). 1981. pap. 19.95 (0-614-02974-0) Amer Forum.

Minear, Richard H., ed. Hiroshima: Three Witnesses. 338p. (Orig.). 1990. text ed. 49.50 (0-691-05573-4); pap. text ed. 16.95 (0-691-00837-X) Princeton U Pr.

Minear, Richard H., tr. see Sadako, Kurihara.

Minear, Roger & Keith, L. H., eds. Water Analysis, Vol. 1: Solution Control Parameters & Analysis Techniques of Inorganic Species. 1982. text ed. 95.00 (0-12-498301-4) Acad Pr.

***Minear, Roger A. & Amy, Gary.** Disinfection By-Products in Water Treatment: The Chemistry. 450p. 1995. write for info. (1-56670-136-8, L1136) Lewis Pubs.

Minear, Roger A., et al, eds. Applications of Molecular Biology in Environmental Chemistry. 272p. 1995. 95.00 (0-87371-951-4, L951) Lewis Pubs.

***Minear, Tish & Limon, Janet.** Discover Native America: Arizona Colorado New Mexico & Utah. (Illus.). 300p. (Orig.). 1995. pap. 16.95 (0-7818-0327-6) Hippocrene Bks.
— The Southwest: A Family Adventure. (U. S. A. Guides Ser.). 280p. (Orig.). 1990. pap. 16.95 (0-87052-640-5) Hippocrene Bks.

Mineau, Charles. The Flowers. (Illus.). 24p. (J). (ps-8). 1988. pap. 4.95 (0-88753-171-7, Pub. by Black Moss Pr CN) Firefly Bks Ltd.

Mineau, G. W., et al, eds. Conceptual Graphs for Knowledge Representation: Proceedings of the First International Conference on Conceptual Structures, ICCS 93, Quebec, Canada, August 4-7, 1993. (Lecture Notes in Artificial Intelligence Ser.: Vol. 699). ix, 451p. 1993. 65.00 (0-387-56979-0) Spr-Verlag.

Minehart, Tom & Heisig, James W. Remembering the Kanji: Hyperkanji! 114p. 1993. disk 160.00 (0-87040-917-4) Japan Pubns USA.

Mineka, Francis E., ed. see Mill, John Stuart.

Minelli, A. Biological Systematics: The State of the Art. LC 93-3578. 1993. write for info. (0-412-36440-9) Chapman & Hall.

Minelli, Alessandro, ed. Proceedings of the Seventh International Congress of Myriapodology. LC 89-9901. xv, 480p. 1989. 154.50 (90-04-08972-1) E J Brill.

Minelli, Allessandro. Great Book of the Animal Kingdom. 1993. 29.99 (0-517-08801-0) Random Hse Value.

Minelli, Fiorigio, jt. tr. see Browning, John.

Minelli, Giuseppe. Amphibians. (History of Life on Earth Ser.). (Illus.). 64p. (YA). 1987. 15.95 (0-8160-1557-0) Facts on File.
— Dinosaurs & Birds. (History of Life on Earth Ser.). (Illus.). 64p. (YA). 1988. 15.95 (0-8160-1559-7) Facts on File.
— The Evolution of Life. (History of Life on Earth Ser.). (Illus.). 64p. 1987. 15.95 (0-8160-1555-4) Facts on File.
— The History of Life on Earth Series, 6 vols., Set. (Illus.). 75.00 (0-8160-1566-X) Facts on File.
— Mammals. (History of Life on Earth Ser.). (Illus.). 64p. (YA). 1988. 15.95 (0-8160-1560-0) Facts on File.
— Marine Life. (History of Life on Earth Ser.). (Illus.). 64p. 1987. 15.95 (0-8160-1556-2) Facts on File.
— Reptiles. LC 86-32907. (History of Life on Earth Ser.). (Illus.). 64p. 1987. 15.95 (0-8160-1558-9) Facts on File.

***Minelli, Mark J.** Beyond Beer Goggles: Interactive Teaching Methods for Alcohol, Other Drugs & AIDS Prevention. 163p. (Orig.). (C). 1994. pap. text ed. 12.80 (0-87563-505-9) Stipes.
— Drug Abuse in Sports: A Student Course Manual. 2nd ed. 99p. (C). 1995. pap. text ed. 9.80 (0-87563-554-7) Stipes.

Minelli, Tali M. Chanukah Fun. Cohn, Amy, ed. (Illus.). (J). (gr. 1 up). 1995. pap. 6.95 (0-688-13560-9, Tupelo Bks) Morrow.

Minely, Ivy. Municipal Land Use. (Illus.). 311p. 1982. pap. 35.00 (0-685-14650-2) NJ Inst CLE.

Mineo, Higashi, jt. auth. see Tatsuhiro, Oshiro.

Miner. Indiana's Best. 1992. pap. 19.95 (0-7906-1018-3, Prompt Pubns) H W Sams.
— Malibu Summer. 1995. mass mkt. (0-590-20354-1) Scholastic Inc.
— Uranus. 1990. pap. write for info. (0-318-68273-7) P-H.

***Miner & Crane.** Human Resource Management: Readings. (C). 1995. text ed. 26.00 (0-06-500498-1) HarpCollege.

Miner, et al. Familial Alzheimer's Disease: Molecular Genetics & Clinical Perspectives. (Neurological Disease & Therapy Ser.: Vol. 3). 444p. 1989. 175.00 (0-8247-8068-X) Dekker.

***Miner, Brad, ed.** Good Order: Right Answers to Contemporary Questions. LC 94-3712. 1995. write for info. (0-671-88235-X, Touchstone Bks) S&S Trade.

Miner, Brad, jt. ed. see Sykes, Charles.

Miner, C. J., et al, eds. Semi-Insulating III-V Materials, Ixtapa, Mexico, 1992: Proceedings of the 7th Conference on Semi-Insulating III-V Materials, Ixtapa, Mexico, 21-24 April 1992. (Illus.). 360p. 1993. 130.00 (0-7503-0242-9) IOP Pub.

Miner, Charles. History of Wyoming (Valley, Pennsylvania) in a Series of Letters from Charles Minor to His Son William Penn Miner, Esq. 628p. 1991. reprint ed. pap. 35.00 (1-55613-455-X) Heritage Bk.

Miner, Clarence E. Ratification of the Federal Constitution by the State of New York. LC 68-56671. (Columbia University. Studies in the Social Sciences: No. 214). reprint ed. 16.50 (0-404-51214-3) AMS Pr.

Miner, Colleen. Together in the Kitchen. 1993. spiral bd. 7.50 (1-879127-25-3) Lighten Up Enter.
— Treat Yourself. (Illus.). 366p. 1992. spiral bd. 7.50 (1-879127-10-5) Lighten Up Enter.

Miner, Craig. The Corporation & the Indian: Tribal Sovereignty & Industrial Civilization in Indian Territory, 1865-1907. LC 88-40550. (Illus.). 252p. 1989. reprint ed. pap. 14.95 (0-8061-2205-6) U of Okla Pr.
— Grede of Milwaukee: Business Career of an Individualist. 300p. 1989. 22.50 (0-922820-06-6) Watermark Pr.
— West of Wichita: Settling the High Plains of Kansas, 1865-1890. (Illus.). viii, 304p. 1986. pap. 12.95 (0-7006-0364-6) U Pr of KS.
— Wolf Creek Station: Kansas Gas & Electric Company in the Nuclear Era. LC 93-14241. (Historical Perspectives on Business Enterprise Ser.). 1993. 39.50 (0-8142-0614-X) Ohio St U Pr.

Miner, Craig, ed. The Wichita Reader: A Collection of Writing about a Prairie City. (Illus.). 160p. 1992. 19.95 (1-880652-13-7) Wichita Eagle.

Miner, Craig, jt. auth. see Rowe, Frank.

Miner, Earl. Comparative Poetics: An Intercultural Essay on Theories of Literature. (Illus.). 286p. (C). 1990. text ed. 42.50 (0-691-06860-7); pap. text ed. 12.95 (0-691-01490-6) Princeton U Pr.
— An Introduction to Japanese Court Poetry. LC 68-17138. iv, 173p. 1968. 27.50 (0-8047-0635-2); pap. 10.95 (0-8047-0636-0) Stanford U Pr.
— Japanese Linked Poetry. LC 78-51182. 400p. 1978. pap. 18.95 (0-691-01368-3) Princeton U Pr.
— The Japanese Tradition in British & American Literature. LC 76-3698. 312p. 1976. reprint ed. text ed. 55.00 (0-8371-8818-0, MIJT, Greenwood Pr) Greenwood.

Miner, Earl, ed. & intro. English Criticism in Japan: Essays by Younger Japanese Scholars on English & American Literature. 1973. lib. bdg. 55.00 (0-691-06250-1) Princeton U Pr.

Miner, Earl, ed. Literary Uses of Typology from the Late Middle Ages to the Present. LC 76-45904. 1977. 65.00 (0-691-06327-3) Princeton U Pr.

Miner, Earl, intro. & sel. Poems on the Reign of William the Third. LC 92-22021. (Augustan Reprints Ser.: No. 166 (1974)). reprint ed. 12.00 (0-404-70166-3, PR565) AMS Pr.

Miner, Earl, ed. see Brady, Jennifer, et al.
Miner, Earl, tr. see Brower, Robert H.
Miner, Earl, jt. auth. see Brower, Robert H.
Miner, Earl, ed. see Konishi, Jin'ichi.

Miner, Earl, et al. The Princeton Companion to Classical Japanese Literature. LC 83-24475. (Illus.). 560p. 1985. pap. 18.95 (0-691-00825-6) Princeton U Pr.

***Miner, Earl R.** Literary Uses of Typology: From the Late Middle Ages to the Present. LC 76-45904. 429p. 1977. reprint ed. pap. 122.30 (0-7837-8177-6, 2047882) Bks Demand.
— The Monkey's Straw Raincoat & Other Poetry of the Basho School. LC 80-28811. (Princeton Library of Asian Translations). (Illus.). 400p. reprint ed. pap. 114.00 (0-8357-3711-X, 2036433) Bks Demand.
— The Restoration Mode from Milton to Dryden. LC 73-14865. 614p. reprint ed. pap. 175.00 (0-7837-0563-8, 2040907) Bks Demand.

Miner, Earl R., ed. Stuart & Georgian Moments: Clark Library Seminar Papers on Seventeenth & Eighteenth Century Literature. LC 78-100020. (Publications of the 17th & 18th Centuries Studies Group, UCLA: No. 3). 325p. reprint ed. pap. 92.70 (0-685-44492-9, 2031507) Bks Demand.

***Miner, Ed.** Past & Present of Greene County. (Illus.). 645p. 1995. reprint ed. lib. bdg. 67.00 (0-8328-4680-5) Higginson Bk Co.

Miner, Ernest. Living Thoughts. (Book of Inspirational Thoughts Ser.). 84p. 1985. 7.95 (0-935087-00-1) Wright Pub Co.

Miner, Ethel N. Hanson, Henson, Hinson, Hynson & Allied Families, Vol. 2: Early Records of the Southeast United States, AL, FL, GE, MS. 126p. (Orig.). 1993. pap. text ed. 20.00 (1-55613-828-8) Heritage Bk.
— Hanson, Henson, Hinson, Hynson & Allied Family Names: Early Records of the Midwest & Southwest United States. xi, 129p. 1993. pap. text ed. 22.50 (1-55613-737-0) Heritage Bk.
— Hanson, Henson, Hinson, Hynson & Allied Family Names Vol. V: Early Records of the Mid-Atlantic States (DE, D.C., MD, VA-WV) 174p. (Orig.). 1995. pap. text ed. write for info. (0-7884-0180-7) Heritage Bk.
— Hanson, Henson, Hinson, Hynson & Allied Family Names, Vol. 3: Early Records of the Carolinas. 124p. (Orig.). 1993. pap. text ed. 23.00 (1-55613-923-3) Heritage Bk.
— Hanson, Henson, Hinson, Hynson, & Allied Family Names, Vol. 4: Early Records of Kentucky & Tennessee. 150p. (Orig.). 1993. pap. text ed. 25.00 (1-55613-927-6) Heritage Bk.

Miner, Gary D., et al, eds. Caring for Alzheimer's Patients: A Guide for Family & Healthcare Providers. (Illus.). 308p. 1989. 22.95 (0-306-43199-8, Plenum Insight) Plenum.

Miner, Gayle F. & Comer, David J. Physical Data Acquisition for Digital Processing: Components, Parameters, & Specifications. 480p. 1992. text ed. 78.00 (0-13-209958-6) P-H.

Miner, Gordon S. & Broome, Stephen W. Soil Science Lab Notebook. 200p. 1940. spiral bd. 14.95 (0-8403-8860-8) Kendall-Hunt.

Miner, H. Craig. The Rebirth of the Missouri Pacific, 1956-1983. LC 83-45097. (Illus.). 258p. 1983. 19.50 (0-89096-159-X) Tex A&M Univ Pr.
— Wichita: The Early Years, 1865-80. LC 81-23138. (Illus.). xiv, 201p. 1982. 20.00 (0-8032-3077-X) U of Nebr Pr.
— Wichita - The Magic City. (Illus.). 210p. 1988. 24.95 (0-9621250-0-8) Wichita-Sedgwick Hist Mus.

Miner, H. Craig & Unrau, William E. The End of Indian Kansas: A Study of Cultural Revolution, 1854-1871. LC 77-4410. (Illus.). xiv, 182p. 1977. pap. 9.95 (*0-7006-0474-X*) U Pr of KS.

Miner, H. Craig, jt. auth. see Unrau, William E.

Miner, Horace. Body Ritual Among the Nacirema. (Reprint Series in Social Sciences). (C). 1993. reprint ed. pap. text ed. 1.30 (*0-8290-4182-6*, S-185) Irvington.

Miner, Jane C. Alcohol & Teens. LC 84-658. (Jem (High Interest-Low Reading Level) Ser.). (Illus.). 64p. (YA). (gr. 7-11). 1984. lib. bdg. 9.29 (*0-671-44890-0*, Julian Messner) Silver Burdett Pr.

— Winter Love Story. (YA). 1993. pap. 3.50 (*0-590-47610-6*) Scholastic Inc.

— Winter Love, Winter Wishes. (YA). 1994. pap. 3.95 (*0-590-48152-5*) Scholastic Inc.

Miner, John B. The Human Constraint: The Coming Shortage of Managerial Talent. 1974. text ed. 25.00 (*0-87179-215-X*) Organizat Meas.

— Industrial Organizational Psychology. 1992. text ed. write for info. (*0-07-042440-3*) McGraw.

— Intelligence in the United States: A Survey - with Conclusions for Manpower Utilization in Education & Employment. LC 72-11482. 180p. 1973. reprint ed. text ed. 49.75 (*0-8371-6667-5*, MIIU, Greenwood Pr) Greenwood.

— Motivation to Manage: A Ten Year Update on the "Studies in Management Education" Research. (Illus.). 1977. text ed. 25.00 (*0-917926-00-5*) Organizat Meas.

— People Problems: The Executive Answer Book. 1985. text ed. 25.00 (*0-394-55002-1*) Organizat Meas.

— Role Motivation Theories. LC 92-28816. (People & Organizations Ser.). (Illus.). 304p. 1993. 39.95 (*0-415-08486-5*, B0012, Routledge NY) Routledge.

— Role Motivation Theories. (People & Organizations Ser.). (Illus.). 376p. 1994. pap. 18.95 (*0-415-11994-4*, C03985) Routledge.

— Studies in Management Education. LC 65-16849. (Illus.). 1965. text ed. 25.00 (*0-317-99717-3*) Organizat Meas.

Miner, John B., ed. Administrative & Management Theory. (History of Management Thought Ser.). 456p. 1995. 112.95 (*1-85521-475-X*, Pub. by Dartmth Pub UK) Ashgate Pub Co.

***Miner, John B. & Crane, Donald P.** Human Resource Management: The Strategic Perspective. LC 94-33443. (C). 1995. 52.00 (*0-06-500496-5*) HarpCollege.

Miner, John B. & Luchsinger, Arlene E. Introduction to Management. 672p. (C). 1985. write for info. (*0-675-20390-2*, Merrill Pub Co) Macmillan.

Miner, John B., et al. The Practice of Management: Text, Readings & Cases. 832p. (C). 1985. write for info. (*0-675-20388-0*, Merrill Pub Co); pap. write for info. (*0-675-20391-0*, Merrill Pub Co) Macmillan.

Miner, John N. The Grammar Schools of Medieval England: A. F. Leach in Historiographical Perspective. 384p. (C). 1989. text ed. 55.00 (*0-7735-0634-9*, Pub. by McGill CN) U of Toronto Pr.

Miner, John W., jt. auth. see Gillis, Frank J.

Miner, Julia, illus. The Shepherd's Song: The Twenty-Third Psalm. LC 91-31067. 32p. (J). 1993. 14.99 (*0-8037-1196-4*) Dial Bks Young.

Miner, Kathleen R., jt. auth. see Krantzler, Nora J.

Miner, Kathleen R., jt. auth. see Stang, Lucas.

Miner, Kathleen R., jt. auth. see Thacker, Netha L.

Miner, Kathleen R., jt. auth. see Thacker, Netha.

Miner, Lenore & Guzman, Carol, eds. The New Mexico Directory of Hispanic Culture. 2nd ed. (Illus.). 171p. 1992. pap. 8.95 (*0-944725-02-3*) Hispanic Culture.

Miner, Lynn E. & Griffith, Jerry. Proposal Planning & Writing. LC 93-19948. 160p. 1993. pap. 29.50 (*0-89774-726-7*) Oryx Pr.

Miner, Lynn E., jt. auth. see Griffith, Jerry.

***Miner, M. Jane, et al.** Moving Toward Your Potential: The Athlete's Guide to Peak Performance. 157p. (Orig.). 1995. student ed, pap. 18.00 (*1-887476-01-6*) Perf Publns.

Miner, Madonne M. Insatiable Appetites: Twentieth-Century American Women's Bestsellers. LC 83-18331. (Contributions in Women's Studies: No. 48). ix, 158p. 1984. text ed. 47.95 (*0-313-23951-7*, MIN/, Greenwood Pr) Greenwood.

Miner, Margaret. Dictionary of Quotations from the Bible. 1990. pap. 4.95 (*0-451-16550-0*, Sig) NAL-Dutton.

— Resonant Gaps: Between Baudelaire & Wagner. LC 94-28793. 1995. write for info. (*0-8203-1709-8*) U of Ga Pr.

Miner, Margaret, ed. The New International Dictionary of Quotations. 2nd ed. 448p. 1993. 25.00 (*0-525-93599-1*, Dutton) NAL-Dutton.

— The New International Dictionary of Quotations. 2nd ed. 496p. 1994. 5.99 (*0-451-16673-6*, Sig) NAL-Dutton.

Miner, Margaret, jt. ed. see Rawson, Hugh.

Miner, Martha, ed. see Reid, C. W.

***Miner, Martha, et al.** College Class Piano. 78p. (C). 1993. teacher ed 25.00 (*1-881986-09-7*) Demibach Eds.

— Elementary Class Piano. (J). (gr. k-6). 1992. teacher ed 25.00 (*1-881986-11-X*) Demibach Eds.

— Reading Keyboard Music. Date not set. pap. text ed. 24.00 (*1-881986-16-0*) Demibach Eds.

— Reading Keyboard Music, Vol. 1. 49p. 1994. pap. text ed. 7.50 (*1-881986-13-6*) Demibach Eds.

— Reading Keyboard Music, Vol. 2. 45p. 1994. pap. text ed. 7.50 (*1-881986-14-4*) Demibach Eds.

— Reading Keyboard Music, Vol. 3. 45p. 1994. pap. text ed. 7.50 (*1-881986-15-2*) Demibach Eds.

— Supplementary Materials Guide. 7p. 1993. teacher ed 2.00 (*1-881986-18-7*) Demibach Eds.

— Supplementary Pieces, Vol. 1. 23p. (J). (gr. k-3). 1992. student ed 5.00 (*1-881986-04-7*) Demibach Eds.

— Written Work Papers, Set, Vol. 1, 2 & 3. 1993. student ed 5.00 (*1-881986-17-9*) Demibach Eds.

Miner, Myrtilla, jt. auth. see O'Connor, Ellen M.

Miner, Nagel T. The Golden Gate University Story, Vol. I. (Illus.). 320p. 1983. 20.00 (*0-943844-01-0*) Golden Gate Law.

Miner, Newton. Continuum. 64p. 1986. 6.95 (*0-317-42525-0*) Harlo Press.

Miner, Nikolay, jt. auth. see Donaldson, John.

Miner, O. Irene. Plants We Know. LC 81-9929. (New True Bks.). 48p. (J). (gr. k-4). 1981. lib. bdg. 12.90 (*0-516-01642-3*) Childrens.

Miner, Robert, ed. see Mother Earth News Editors.

Miner, Robert G. Flea Market Handbook: Making Money in Antiques. 2nd ed. LC 89-51677. 160p. 1990. pap. text ed. 12.95 (*0-87069-559-2*, Wallace-Hmestead) Chilton.

Miner, Robert G. & Early American Society Staff. Early Homes of Massachusetts: From Homes of Material Originally Published as the White Pine Series of Architectural Monographs. Whitehead, Russell F. & Brown, Frank C., eds. 1978. 16.95 (*0-405-10064-7*, 10408) Ayer.

Miner, Ron. Come Sit with Me: Sermons for Children. LC 81-10650. (Illus.). 96p. (Orig.). 1981. pap. 8.95 (*0-8298-0469-2*) Pilgrim OH.

Miner, Ron, jt. auth. see Benjamin, Don-Paul.

Miner, Ruth. Days to Celebrate. (Illus.). 50p. pap. 1.00 (*0-686-30389-X*) WILPF.

Miner, Sharon. The Delmarva Conspiracy. LC 92-72680. 136p. (YA). (gr. 7-9). 1993. 14.95 (*1-880851-06-7*) Greene Bark Pr.

Miner, Stephen M. Between Churchill & Stalin: The Soviet Union, Great Britain, & the Origins of the Grand Alliance. LC 88-4828. xi, 320p. (C). 1988. 39.95 (*0-8078-1796-1*) U of NC Pr.

***Miner, Steven M.** Between Churchill & Stalin: The Soviet Union, Great Britain, & the Origins of the Grand Alliance. LC 88-4828. reprint ed. pap. 95.00 (*0-7837-9015-5*, 2049767) Bks Demand.

Miner, Valerie. Blood Sisters: An Examination of Conscience. 224p. 1982. pap. 6.95 (*0-312-08462-5*) St Martin.

— Rumors from the Cauldron: Selected Essays, Reviews, & Reportage. 318p. (C). 1991. text ed. 39.50 (*0-472-09472-6*); pap. text ed. 13.95 (*0-472-06472-X*) U of Mich Pr.

— A Walking Fire. (SUNY Series, The Margins of Literature). 254p. 1994. 32.50 (*0-7914-2007-8*); pap. 18.95 (*0-7914-2008-6*) State U NY Pr.

Miner, Valerie, jt. ed. see Longino, Helen E.

Miner, W. N., ed. see World Metallurgical Congress Staff.

Miner, William M. & Hathaway, Dale E., eds. World Agricultural Trade: Building a Consensus. 218p. 1988. pap. text ed. 16.95 (*0-88645-071-3*) Inst Intl Eco.

Miner, William N., ed. Plutonium Nineteen-Seventy & Other Actinides: Proceedings of the 4th International Conference on Plutonium & Other Actinides, Santa Fe, New Mexico, October 5-9, 1970, Pt. I. (Nuclear Metallurgy Ser.: Vol. 17). reprint ed. Part I. pap. 133.00 (*0-317-10226-5*) Bks Demand.

— Plutonium Nineteen-Seventy & Other Actinides: Proceedings of the 4th International Conference on Plutonium & Other Actinides, Santa Fe, New Mexico, October 5-9, 1970, Pt. II. (Nuclear Metallurgy Ser.: Vol. 17). reprint ed. Part II. pap. 137.50 (*0-317-13005-6*) Bks Demand.

Mineral Processing Plant Design Symposium Staff. Mineral Processing Plant Design. 2nd ed. Mular, Andrew L. & Bhappu, Roshan B., eds. LC 79-57345. 960p. reprint ed. pap. 180.00 (*0-8357-3418-8*, 2039675) Bks Demand.

Minerals, Metals, & Materials Society Staff. Advances in Magnesium Alloys & Composites: Proceedings of a Symposium Sponsored by the International Magnesium Association & the Non-Ferrous Metals Committee, Held at the Annual Meeting of the Minerals, Metals, & Materials Society in Phoenix, Arizona, January 26, 1988. fac. ed. Paris, Henry G. & Hunt, W. H., eds. LC 88-60116. (Illus.). 153p. pap. 43.70 (*0-7837-6966-0*, 2052523) Bks Demand.

— Process Control & Automation in Extractive Metallurgy: Proceedings of an International Symposium. fac. ed. Partelpoeg, E. H. & Himmesoete, D. C., eds. LC 88-63685. (Illus.). 233p. pap. 66.50 (*0-7837-6968-7*, 2052525) Bks Demand.

— Process Mineralogy VIII: Applications of Mineralogy to Mineral Beneficiation Technology, Metallurgy, & Mineral Exploration & Evaluation, with Emphasis on Precious Metal Ores: Proceedings of a Symposium Presented in Six Sessions on Process Mineralogy Held During the Minerals, Metals & Materials Society Annual Meeting, Phoenix, Arizona, January 25-28, 1988. fac. ed. Carson, David J. & Vassiliou, Andreas H., eds. LC 88-63682. (Illus.). 405p. 1988. pap. 115.50 (*0-7837-8607-7*, 2052538) Bks Demand.

— Processing, Microstructure & Properties of HSLA Steels: Proceedings of International Symposium Held November 3-5, 1987 in Pittsburgh, Pennsylvania. DeArdo, Anthony J., Jr., ed. LC 88-62439. 523p. reprint ed. pap. 149.10 (*0-7837-1443-2*, 2052417) Bks Demand.

Minerals, Metals & Materials Society Staff. Computer Simulation of Electron Microscope Diffraction & Images: Proceedings of a Topical Symposium on Computer Simulation of Electron Microscope Diffraction & Images - Sponsored by the ASM-MSD Computer Simulation Committee, Held at the TMS Annual Meeting in Las Vegas, Nevada, February 28-March 3, 1989. fac. ed. Krakow, William & O'Keefe, Michael, eds. LC 89-61030. (Illus.). 283p. pap. 80.70 (*0-7837-6967-9*, 2052524) Bks Demand.

— Continuous Casting of Non-Ferrous Metals & Alloys: Proceedings of a Symposium, Sponsored by the Non-Ferrous Metals Committee of the Minerals, Metals, & Materials Society, Chicago, Illinois, September 28-29, 1988. Merchant, H. D. et al, eds. LC 89-60887. 305p. reprint ed. pap. 87.00 (*0-7837-5891-X*, 2052500) Bks Demand.

— Corrosion & Particle Erosion at High Temperatures: Proceedings of a Symposium Sponsored by the TMS-ASM Joint Corrosion & Environmental Effects Committee, Held at the 118th Annual Meeting of the Minerals, Metals & Materials Society in Las Vegas, Nevada, February 27-March 3, 1989. Srinivasan, V. & Vedula, K., eds. LC 89-60379. (Illus.). 651p. reprint ed. pap. 180.00 (*0-7837-6061-2*, 2052507) Bks Demand.

— Fundamental Relationships Between Microstructures & Mechanical Properties of Metal Matrix Composites: Proceedings of a Symposium Held During the TMS Fall Meeting, October 1-5, 1989, in Indianapolis, Indiana. Liaw, Peter K. & Gungor, M. N., eds. LC 89-60370. (Illus.). 862p. reprint ed. pap. 180.00 (*0-7837-6065-5*, 2052511) Bks Demand.

— Intelligent Processing of Materials: Proceedings of a Symposium Sponsored by the Process Control Committee of the Materials Design & Manufacturing Division, Held at the Fall Meeting of the Minerals, Metals & Materials Society in Indianapolis, Indiana, October 2-5, 1989. Wadley, Haydn N. & Eckhart, Eugene, Jr., eds. LC 90-61976. (Illus.). 465p. Date not set. reprint ed. pap. 132.60 (*0-7837-9137-2*, 2049937) Bks Demand.

— Light Metals, 1989: Proceedings of the Technical Sessions the TMS Light Metals Committee at the 118 TMS Annaul Meeting, Las Vegas, Nevada, February 27-March 3, 1989. Campbell, Paul G., Jr., ed. LC 72-623660. (Illus.). 1065p. Date not set. reprint ed. pap. 180.00 (*0-7837-9131-3*, 2049931) Bks Demand.

— Light Metals, 1990: Proceedings of the Technical Sessions Presented by the TMS Light Metals Committee at the 119th Annual Meeting, Anaheim, CA, February 18-22, 1990. LC 72-623660. (Illus.). 1063p. Date not set. reprint ed. pap. 180.00 (*0-7837-9132-1*, 2049932) Bks Demand.

— Light Metals, 1992: Proceedings of the Technical Sessions, Presented by the TMS Light Metals Committee at the 121st TMS Annual Meeting, San Diego, CA, March 1-5, 1992. Cutshall, Euel R., ed. LC 72-623660. (Illus.). 1427p. Date not set. reprint ed. pap. 180.00 (*0-7837-9130-5*, 2049930) Bks Demand.

— Magnetohydrodynamics in Process Metallurgy: Proceedings of a Symposium Sponsored by TMS Extraction & Processing Division, TMS Light Metals Division & the Iron & Steel Society, Held During the 1992 TMS Annual Meeting, San Diego, California, March 1-5, 1992. Szekely, J. et al, eds. LC 91-51129. (Illus.). 316p. Date not set. reprint ed. pap. 90.10 (*0-7837-9129-1*, 2049929) Bks Demand.

— Materials Processing in the Computer Age: Proceedings of an International Symposium Sponsored by TMS Synthesis & Analysis in Materials Processing Committee Held in New Orleans, Louisiana, USA, February 17 Through February 21, 1991 at the 120th TMS Annual Meeting & Exhibit. fac. ed. Voller, V. R. et al, eds. LC 90-64039. 474p. 1991. reprint ed. pap. 135.10 (*0-7837-8298-5*, 2049084) Bks Demand.

— Metal & Ceramic Matrix Composites: Processing, Modeling & Mechanical Behavior: Proceedings of an International Conference Held at the TMS Annual Meeting in Anaheim, California, February 19-22, 1990. Bhagat, Ram B. et al, eds. LC 89-63253. 682p. reprint ed. pap. 180.00 (*0-7837-6064-7*, 2052510) Bks Demand.

— Metallurgy of Vacuum-Degassed Steel Products: Proceedings of an International Symposium - Sponsored by the TMS Ferrous Metallurgy Committee & Held at the 1989 Fall Meeting in Indianapolis, Indiana, October 3-5. Pradhan, R., ed. LC 90-70808. (Illus.). 522p. Date not set. reprint ed. pap. 148.80 (*0-7837-9138-0*, 2049938) Bks Demand.

— Modeling the Deformation of Crystalline Solids: Proceedings of a Symposium Jointly Sponsored by the ASM-MSD Computer Simulation Committee & the TMS-AIME Shaping & Forming Committee, Held at the Annual Meeting of the Minerals, Metals & Materials Society in New Orleans, Louisiana, February 17-21, 1991. Lowe, Terry C. et al, eds. LC 91-62769. (Illus.). 700p. Date not set. reprint ed. pap. 180.00 (*0-7837-9139-9*, 2049939) Bks Demand.

— Precious Metals '89: Proceedings of an. fac. ed. LC 88-62441. (Illus.). 533p. 1988. pap. 152.00 (*0-7837-8606-9*, 2052537) Bks Demand.

— Rare Earths: Extraction, Preparation & Applications, Proceedings of a Symposium on Rare Earths, Extraction, Preparation & Applications Sponsored by the TMS Reactive Metals Committee, Held at the TMS Annual Meeting in Las Vegas, Nevada, February 27-March 2, 1989. Bautista, Renato G. & Wong, Morton M., eds. LC 88-42986. 415p. reprint ed. pap. 118.30 (*0-7837-5894-4*, 2052503) Bks Demand.

— Refractory Metals: State of the Art, 1988: Proceedings of a Symposium Held on Refractory Metals, State-of-the-Art, Sponsored by the TMS Refractory Metals Committee, Held During the TMS Fall Meeting, Chicago, Illinois, September 27, 1988. fac. ed. Kumar, P. & Ammon, R. L., eds. LC 89-60380. (Illus.). 207p. 1989. pap. 59.00 (*0-7837-8608-5*, 2052539) Bks Demand.

— Residues & Effluents: Processing & Environmental Considerations: Proceedings of an International Symposium Sponsored by Extraction & Process Division of TMS & the Iron & Steel Society at the 1992 TMS Annual Meeting, San Diego, California, U. S. A., March 1-5, 1992. Reddy, Ramana G. et al, eds. LC 91-51084. (Illus.). 915p. Date not set. reprint ed. pap. 180.00 (*0-7837-9136-4*, 2049936) Bks Demand.

— Simulation & Theory of Evolving Microstructures: Proceedings of a Symposium Sponsored by Computer Simulation Committee, Held at the Fall Meeting of the Minerals, Metals & Materials Society in Indianapolis, 2-5th October 1989. Anderson, M. P. & Rollett, A. D., eds. LC 90-61686. (Illus.). 299p. reprint ed. pap. 85.30 (*0-7837-6063-9*, 2052509) Bks Demand.

— Surface Modification Technologies IV: Proceedings of the Fourth International Conference Held in Paris, France, November 6-9, 1990. fac. ed. Sudarshan, T. S. et al, eds. LC 91-60269. (Illus.). 1032p. 1991. pap. 180.00 (*0-7837-8611-5*, 2052542) Bks Demand.

Minerbi, Luciano, et al, eds. Land Readjustment, the Japanese System: A Reconnaissance & a Digest. LC 85-31964. (Lincoln Institute of Land Policy Book Ser.). (Illus.). 284p. reprint ed. pap. 81.00 (*0-7837-5762-X*, 2045425) Bks Demand.

Minerbi, Sergio I. Vatican & Zionism: Conflict in the Holy Land, 1895-1925. Schwartz, Arnold, tr. (Studies in Jewish History). (Illus.). 272p. 1990. 30.00 (*0-19-505892-5*) OUP.

Minerick, Jerry. Mystic Mountain Memories, A Mother-Son Cookbook. (Illus.). 200p. 1993. spiral bd. 14.95 (*0-9626335-3-4*) C&G Pub CO.

Miners, J., et al, eds. Microsomes & Drug Oxidations, Vol. 7. 400p. 1988. 130.00 (*0-85066-361-X*) Taylor & Francis.

Miners, Norman J. The Government & Politics of Hong Kong. 5th ed. (Illus.). 352p. 1992. pap. 19.95 (*0-19-585425-X*) OUP.

Miners, Scott, ed. Give Yourself Health: Thoughts, Attitudes & Your Health. 160p. (Orig.). 1990. pap. 7.95 (*0-9625720-0-4*) Turning Pt WA.

Miners, Scott, ed. see Snyder, Jacqueline.

Miners, Scott E., ed. see Snyder, Jacqueline T.

Minerva & Hammond, Jane. Heavenly Parties: An Astrology Cookbook for Cosmic Entertaining. (Illus.). 164p. (Orig.). 1989. pap. 9.95 (*0-933174-67-5*) Wide World-Tetra.

Minerva - Internationales Verzeichnis Wissenschaftlicher Institutionen Staff. Forschungsinstitute. 33th ed. Schuder, Werner, ed. (C). 1972. 188.50 (*3-11-001953-1*); 146.15 (*3-11-002067-X*) De Gruyter.

***Mines, Allan H.** Respiratory Physiology. fac. ed. LC 80-5658. (Physiology Ser.). (Illus.). 176p. Date not set. pap. 50.20 (*0-7837-7518-0*) Bks Demand.

— Respiratory Physiology. 2nd fac. ed. LC 86-607. (Physiology Ser.). (Illus.). 176p. Date not set. pap. 47.60 (*0-7837-7282-3*, 2047024) Bks Demand.

— Respiratory Physiology. 3rd ed. LC 92-49692. (Series in Physiology). 192p. 1993. 72.50 (*0-88167-963-1*); pap. 34.00 (*0-88167-962-3*) Raven.

Mines, Allan H., jt. auth. see Goerke, Jon.

Mines, Antonio N., jt. ed. see Pauly, Daniel.

Mines, Antonio N., jt. ed. see Smith, Ian R.

Mines, Christopher W. Policy Development for Cellular Telephone Service in the United States & the United Kingdom, No. P-93-3. (Illus.). 58p. 1993. pap. text ed. write for info. (*1-879716-01-1*) Ctr Info Policy.

Mines, Jeanette. Reckless: A Teenage Love Story. 176p. 1983. pap. 2.95 (*0-380-83717-X*, Flare) Avon.

— Risking It. 160p. (YA). 1988. pap. 2.75 (*0-380-75401-0*, Flare) Avon.

Mines, Mattison. Public Faces, Private Voices: Community & Individuality in South India. LC 93-35609. 1994. 45.00 (*0-520-08478-0*) U CA Pr.

— Public Faces, Private Voices: Community & Individuality in South India. 1994. pap. 18.00 (*0-520-08479-9*) U CA Pr.

— The Warrior Merchants: Textiles, Trade, & Territory in South India. (Illus.). 192p. 1985. 64.95 (*0-521-26714-5*) Cambridge U Pr.

Mines, R., et al. A Course in Constructive Algebra. 360p. 1987. pap. 42.00 (*0-387-96640-4*) Spr-Verlag.

Mines, Richard. Developing a Community Tradition of Migration: A Field Study in Rural Zacatecas, Mexico & California Settlement Areas. (Monograph Ser.: No. 3). (Illus.). 219p. (Orig.). (C). 1981. pap. 15.00 (*0-935391-42-8*, MN-03) UCSD Ctr US-Mex.

Mines, Richard & Anzaldua, Ricardo. New Migrants vs. Old Migrants: Alternative Labor Market Structures in the California Citrus Industry. (Monograph Ser.: No. 9). 118p. (Orig.). (C). 1982. pap. 7.50 (*0-935391-47-9*, MN-09) UCSD Ctr US-Mex.

Mines, Robert A. Adult Cognitive Development: Methods & Models. LC 85-16969. 192p. 1985. text ed. 37.50 (*0-275-90012-6*, C0012, Praeger Pubs) Greenwood.

Minet, William & Waller, William C., eds.

Minett, Gunnel. Breath & Spirit: Rebirthing As a Healing Technique. 208p. 1994. pap. 15.00 (*1-85538-353-5*) Thorsons SF.

Minett, John, ed. Local Planning in the Netherlands & England: A Comparison of the Requirements & Procedures of the Two Systems. (C). 1979. 29.00 (*0-685-30302-0*, Pub. by Oxford Polytechnic UK) St Mut.

Minett, Steve. Power, Politics & Participation in the Firm. 236p. 1992. 68.95 (*1-85628-331-3*, Pub. by Avebury Pub UK) Ashgate Pub Co.

Minetti, L., et al, eds. Debates in Nephrology. (Contributions to Nephrology Ser.: Vol. 34). (Illus.). viii, 132p. 1982. pap. 71.25 (*3-8055-3535-X*) S Karger.

M

Minetti, Luigi, ed. The Kidney in Plasma Cell Dyscrasias. (Developments in Nephrology Ser.). (C). 1988. lib. bdg. 150.00 (*0-89838-385-4*) Kluwer Ac.
Minev, Nikolay & Berry, Jonathan. King's Indian Defense: Tactics, Ideas, Exercises. x, 106p. (Orig.). 1993. pap. 12. 95 (*1-879479-13-3*) ICE WA.
Minford. Handbook of Aluminum Bonding Technology & Data. 744p. 1993. 215.00 (*0-8247-8817-6*) Dekker.
Minford, J. Dean, ed. Treatise on Adhesion & Adhesives, Vol. 7. 528p. 1991. 199.00 (*0-8247-8112-0*) Dekker.
Minford, John, ed. A Little Primer of Tu Fu. Hawkes, David, tr. ix, 212p. (CHI & ENG.). 1990. reprint ed. pap. 9.50 (*962-7255-02-5*, Pub. by Renditions Papbk HK) SPD-Small Pr Dist.
Minford, John, tr. see Cao, Xueqin & Gao, E.
Minford, John, tr. see Cao Xueqin.
Minford, John, ed. see Hawkes, David.
Minford, John, tr. see Xueqin, Cao & E, Gao.
Minford, Patrick. Rational Expectations Macroeconomics: An Introductory Handbook. 2nd ed. (Illus.). 240p. (C). 1992. pap. 24.95 (*0-631-17788-4*) Blackwell Pubs.
— The Supply Side Revolution in Britain. 272p. 1991. text ed. 74.95 (*1-85278-426-1*, Pub. by E Elgar Pub UK) Ashgate Pub Co.
Ming, D. W., et al. Lunar Base Agriculture: Soils for Plant Growth. 276p. 1989. 24.00 (*0-89118-100-8*) Am Soc Agron.
Ming-Dao, Deng. Chronicles of Tao: The Secret Life of a Taoist Master. LC 92-56409. 640p. 1993. pap. 16.00 (*0-06-250219-0*) Harper SF.
Ming-han Ye & Tao Huang. Charm Physics. xii, 562p. 1988. text ed. 117.00 (*2-88124-233-2*) Gordon & Breach.
Ming, Julian L., jt. ed. see Postiglione, Gerard A.
Ming, Li, ed. Transformation of Science & Technology into Productive Power, 2 vols., Set. 2119p. 1991. 620.00 (*0-7484-0004-4*, Pub. by Tay Francis Ltd UK) Taylor & Francis.
Ming Li & Vitanyi, Paul M. An Introduction to Kolmogorov Compexity & Its Applications. LC 93-10430. (Texts & Monographs in Computer Science). 1994. 59.00 (*0-387-94053-7*) Spr-Verlag.
Ming-liang, Hsieh. Catalogue of the Special Exhibition of Ting Ware White Porcelain. 2nd ed. (Collections of the National Palace Museum, Taipei). 231p. 1987. reprint ed. boxed 54.50 (*957-562-123-9*) Heian Intl.
Ming, Lillie V. A Joy to Read. (Illus.). (Orig.). 1987. pap. 9.95 (*0-318-22520-4*) Health Is Wealth.
Ming-Pao News Reporters & Photographers. June Four: A Chronicle of the Chinese Democratic Uprising. LC 89-20260. (Illus.). 187p. (Orig.). 1989. pap. 7.50 (*1-55728-140-8*) U of Ark Pr.
Ming, Ruan. Hu Yao Bang on Turning Point of History. 134p. 1992. pap. text ed. 7.00 (*0-9625118-9-7*) World Scientific Pub.
Ming, Si-Chun. Atlas of Tumor Pathology: Tumors of the Esophagus & Stomach. (Second Ser.: Fascicle 7, Supplement). (Illus.). 70p. 1990. pap. 4.75 (*0-16-001859-5*, S/N 008-023-00097-2) USGPO.
Ming, Si-Chun, ed. Precursors of Gastric Cancer. LC 83-27025. 350p. 1984. text ed. 79.50 (*0-275-91444-5*, C1444, Praeger Pubs) Greenwood.
Ming, Sung & Tsu, Min. Never Alone: A Story of Survival under the Gang of Four. Harper, A. F., ed. 149p. 1985. pap. 6.95 (*0-8341-0848-8*) Beacon Hill.
Ming-Tao Wang, tr. see Yu, James C., ed.
Ming Tat Wong. The Medical Manual for Chinese Family. 200p. (CHI.). Date not set. pap. 18.00 (*0-9635700-0-5*) J Wong.
Ming, Virginia, jt. auth. see Ming, William.
Ming, William & Ming, Virginia. Biographical Gazetteer of Texas, 6 vols., Set. (Orig.). 1988. pap. 117.00 (*0-317-93433-3*) W M Morrison.
— Biographical Gazetteer of Texas, 6 vols., Vol. 1: A-B. (Orig.). 1988. Vol. 1, A-B. pap. 19.50 (*0-685-74070-6*) W M Morrison.
— Biographical Gazetteer of Texas, 6 vols., Vol. 2: C-F. (Orig.). 1988. Vol. 2, C-F. pap. 19.50 (*0-685-74071-4*) W M Morrison.
— Biographical Gazetteer of Texas, 6 vols., Vol. 3: G-J. (Orig.). 1988. Vol. 3, G-J. pap. 19.50 (*0-685-74072-2*) W M Morrison.
— Biographical Gazetteer of Texas, 6 vols., Vol. 4: K-M. (Orig.). 1988. Vol. 4, K-M. pap. 19.50 (*0-685-74073-0*) W M Morrison.
— Biographical Gazetteer of Texas, 6 vols., Vol. 5: N-Smiley. (Orig.). 1988. Vol. 5, N-Smiley. pap. 19.50 (*0-685-74074-9*) W M Morrison.
— Biographical Gazetteer of Texas, 6 vols., Vol. 6: Smith-Z. (Orig.). 1988. Vol. 6, Smith-Z. pap. 19.50 (*0-685-74075-7*) W M Morrison.
Ming, Yang J. Introduction to Ancient Chinese Weapons. LC 84-51052. (Illus.). 180p. pap. 8.95 (*0-86568-052-3*, 107) Unique Pubns.
Ming-Yi, Yang, illus. The Shell Woman & the King: A Chinese Folktale. LC 92-9583. 32p. (J). (gr. k-3). 1993. 13.99 (*0-8037-1394-0*); lib. bdg. 13.89 (*0-8037-1395-9*) Dial Bks Young.
Ming, Yuan, jt. auth. see Harding, Harry.
***Mingana, Alphonse.** The Yezidis: The Devil Worshippers of the Middle East; Their Beliefs & Sacred Books. Date not set. pap. 4.95 (*1-55818-231-4*, Sure Fire) Holmes Pub.
Mingarro, E., et al. Characterization of Clay (Bentonite) - Crushed Granite Mixtures to Build. 142p. 1991. pap. 15. 00 (*92-826-3066-8*, CD-NA-13666-EN-C) UNIPUB.
Mingat, Alain & Tan, Jee-Peng. Analytical Tools for Sector Work in Education. LC 87-46373. 224p. 1988. text ed. 25.95 (*0-8018-3672-7*) Johns Hopkins.
Mingat, Alain, jt. auth. see Jee-Peng Tan.
Mingay, G. E. Land & Society in England, 1750-1980. LC 94-1130. (Themes in British Social History Ser.). 288p. (C). 1994. pap. text ed. 21.95 (*0-582-49132-0*, 76879, Pub. by Longman UK) Longman.
— Rural Life in Victorian England. (Illus.). 224p. (C). 1991. text ed. 34.00 (*0-86299-539-6*) A Sutton Pub.
— A Social History of the English Countryside. 272p. 1991. 49.95 (*0-415-03408-6*, A4689) Routledge.
— The Transformation of Britain 1830-1939. (Making of Britain Ser.). (Illus.). 233p. (C). 1986. 49.95 (*0-7100-9762-X*, RKP) Routledge.
Mingay, G. E., ed. The Agrarian History of England & Wales, Vol. 6: 1750-1850. 1280p. 1989. 185.00 (*0-521-22726-7*) Cambridge U Pr.
— The Victorian Countryside, 2 vols. (Illus.). 1986. Vol. I, 380 pg. write for info. (*0-7102-0884-7*); Vol. II, 348 pg. write for info. (*0-7102-0886-3*) Routledge Chapman & Hall.
— The Victorian Countryside, 2 vols., Set. (Illus.). 1986. pap. 45.00 (*0-685-43559-8*, 88888) Routledge Chapman & Hall.
Mingay, G. E., jt. auth. see Bagwell, Philip S.
Mingay, J. M., ed. see Aristotle.
Minge, M. Ronald, et al. Mating. 352p. 1982. pap. 9.95 (*0-940162-01-6*) Red Lion.
Minge, Ward A. Acoma: Pueblo in the Sky. rev. ed. LC 91-20689. (Illus.). 262p. 1991. reprint ed. pap. 24.95 (*0-8263-1301-9*) U of NM Pr.
Mingei International Museum Staff. Precolumbian Flora & Fauna: Continuity of Plant & Animal Themes in Mesoamerican Art. Jennings, Jan et al, eds. LC 90-63119. (Illus.). 148p. 1991. pap. 35.00 (*0-914155-07-5*, U of Wash Pr) Mingei Intl Mus.
***Minger, Elda.** Baby by Chance: (New Arrival) (American Romance Ser.). 1995. mass mkt. 3.50 (*0-373-16584-6*, 1-16584-4) Harlequin Bks.
— Daddy's Little Dividend. (American Romance Ser.). 1993. mass mkt. 3.50 (*0-373-16489-0*, 1-16489-6) Harlequin Bks.
— Embrace the Night. 352p. (Orig.). 1994. mass mkt. 4.99 (*0-515-11373-5*) Jove Pubns.
— Teddy Bear Heir. (American Romance Ser.). 1994. mass mkt. 3.50 (*0-373-16531-5*, 1-6531-5) Harlequin Bks.
— Wed Again. (American Romance Ser.). 1993. mass mkt. 3.50 (*0-373-16510-2*, 1-16510-9) Harlequin Bks.
Minger, Miriam. Captive Rose. 384p. 1991. pap. 3.95 (*0-380-76311-7*) Avon.
— Defiant Impostor. 384p. (Orig.). 1992. mass mkt. 4.50 (*0-380-76312-5*) Avon.
— A Hint of Rapture. 400p. 1990. pap. 3.95 (*0-380-75863-6*) Avon.
— Pagan's Prize. 336p. (Orig.). 1993. mass mkt. 4.99 (*0-515-11014-0*) Jove Pubns.
— Stolen Splendor. 384p. (Orig.). 1989. pap. 3.95 (*0-380-75862-8*) Avon.
— Wild Angel. 352p. (Orig.). 1994. mass mkt. 4.99 (*0-515-11247-X*) Jove Pubns.
Minger, Ralph E. William Howard Taft & United States Foreign Policy: The Apprenticeship Years, 1900-1908. LC 75-6691. 253p. reprint ed. pap. 72.20 (*0-317-29034-7*, 2020228) Bks Demand.
***Mingers, John.** Self-Producing Systems: Implications & Applications of Autopoiesis. LC 94-43375. (Contemporary Systems Thinking Ser.). 240p. 1995. 49. 50 (*0-306-44797-5*, Plenum Pr) Plenum.
Minges, B., et al. Kerygma: the Bible in Depth: Leader's Guide. 330p. 1992. pap. 29.00 (*1-882236-00-9*) Kerygma Prog.
Minghella. Living with Dinosaurs: One Act Plays. (C). 1995. pap. write for info. (*0-413-64240-2*, A0504) Heinemann.
Minghella, Anthony. Interior; Room, Exterior; City. (Methuen New Theatrescripts Ser.). 130p. (Orig.). (C). 1989. pap. 12.95 (*0-413-61790-4*, A0407, Pub. by Methuen UK) Heinemann.
— Minghella: Plays One. 292p. 1992. pap. 15.95 (*0-413-66580-1*, A0659, Pub. by Methuen UK) Heinemann.
— Truly, Madly, Deeply. (Illus.). v, 58p. 1991. pap. 8.95 (*0-413-64000-0*, A0503, Pub. by Methuen UK) Heinemann.
Minghella, Anthony, ed. The Storyteller. 144p. (C). 1990. 45.00 (*1-85283-026-3*, Pub. by Boxtree Ltd UK) St Mut.
Minghi, Julian V., jt. auth. see Rumley, Dennis.
Mingilton, Jesse, jt. auth. see Dowall, David E.
Mingilton, Jesse, jt. auth. see Dowell, David E.
Mingione, Enzo. Fragmented Societies: A Sociology of Economic Life beyond the Market Paradigm. 432p. (C). 1991. text ed. 46.95 (*0-631-16399-9*) Blackwell Pubs.
— Social Conflict & the City. 1981. text ed. 32.50 (*0-312-73163-9*) St Martin.
Mingle, Ida. The Science & Art of Regeneration. 65p. 1984. reprint ed. spiral bd. 9.90 (*0-7873-0618-5*) Mokelumne.
— Science of Love with Key to Immortality, 2 vols., Set. 1976. reprint ed. spiral bd. 22.00 (*0-7873-0616-9*) Mokelumne.
— Spiritual Significance of the Body. 355p. 1993. reprint ed. spiral bd. 16.50 (*0-7873-0619-3*) Mokelumne.
— The Unfoldment of Man. 45p. 1987. reprint ed. spiral bd. 7.70 (*0-7873-0617-7*) Mokelumne.
Mingle, James R., et al. Challenges of Retrenchment: Strategies in Consolidating Programs, Cutting Costs, & Reallocating Resources. LC 81-47770. (Jossey-Bass Series in Higher Education). 416p. reprint ed. pap. 118. 60 (*0-8357-4865-0*, 2037797) Bks Demand.
Mingo, Jack. Couch Potato Guide to Life. 1988. pap. 3.50 (*0-380-75596-3*) Avon.
— How the Cadillac Got Its Fins. 1995. pap. 10.00 (*0-88730-753-1*) Harper Busn.
— How the Cadillac Got Its Fins: And Other True Tales from the Annals of Business & Marketing. LC 94-2392. 1994. 15.00 (*0-88730-677-2*) Harper Busn.
— How to Spit Nickels: And 101 Other Cool Tricks You Never Learned to Do As A Kid! (Illus.). 144p. 1993. pap. 8.95 (*0-8092-3724-5*) Contemp Bks.
— Magic Card Tricks: 50 Amazing Tricks You Can Do with a Magic Deck. (Illus.). 96p. 1995. pap. 12.95 (*0-8092-3446-7*) Contemp Bks.
***Mingos, D. M.** Essentials of Inorganic Chemistry 1. (Oxford Chemistry Primers Ser.: No. 28). (Illus.). 96p. (C). 1995. pap. text ed. 9.95 (*0-19-855848-1*) OUP.
Mingos, D. M., et al. Bond & Structure Models. (Structure & Bonding Ser.: Vol. 63). (Illus.). 190p. 1985. 69.00 (*0-387-15820-0*) Spr-Verlag.
Mingos, D. M. P., et al, eds. Chemical Hardness. LC 93-16082. (Structure & Bonding Ser.). 1993. write for info. (*3-540-56091-2*); 167.00 (*0-387-56091-2*) Spr-Verlag.
Mingotaud, Anne-Francoise, et al. Handbook of Monolayers, 2 vols., 1. (Illus.). 2726p. 1993. text ed. 87. 50 (*0-12-498305-7*) Acad Pr.
— Handbook of Monolayers, 2 vols., 2. (Illus.). 2726p. 1993. text ed. 87.50 (*0-12-498306-5*) Acad Pr.
— Handbook of Monolayers, 2 vols., Set, Vols. 1 & 2. (Illus.). 2726p. 1993. Set. text ed. 175.00 (*0-12-498304-9*) Acad Pr.
Mingotti, Antonio. Maria Cebotari, das Leben Einer Sangerin. Farkas, Andrew, ed. LC 76-29955. (Opera Biographies Ser.). (Illus.). (GER.). 1977. reprint ed. lib. bdg. 19.95 (*0-405-09696-8*) Ayer.
Mingovits, Victor. A Satan Worshiper's Guide to the American Northeast. 79p. (Orig.). 1991. pap. 4.95 (*0-9630465-9-4*) Watershed.
Mings, Stephen D. Nuclear Winter. (Illus.). 99p. (Orig.). 1991. pap. 6.95 (*0-913632-20-1*) All Things Pr.
***Mings, Turley.** Study of Economics: Principles, Concepts & Applications. 5th ed. (Illus.). 544p. 1995. 34.95 (*1-56134-303-X*) Dushkin Pub.
Mingst, Karen. The Ivory Trade. (Pew Case Studies in International Affairs). 50p. (C). 1993. pap. text ed. 2.50 (*1-56927-154-2*) Geo U Inst Dplmcy.
Mingst, Karen A. Politics & the African Development Bank. LC 90-30935. 216p. 1990. text ed. 26.00 (*0-8131-1754-2*) U Pr of Ky.
***Mingst, Karen A. & Karns, Margaret P.** The United Nations in the Post-Cold War Era. LC 95-5657. (Dilemmas in World Politics Ser.). (C). 1995. pap. text ed. 13.95 (*0-8133-2261-8*) Westview.
— The United Nations in the Post-Cold War Era. LC 95-5657. (Dilemmas in World Politics Ser.). (C). 1995. text ed. 49.95 (*0-8133-2260-X*) Westview.
Mingst, Karen A., jt. ed. see Karns, Margaret P.
Minguet, Charles, ed. see Gallegos, Romulo.
Minguez, E., jt. ed. see Velarde, G.
Mingus, Charles. Beneath the Underdog. LC 91-50277. 384p. 1991. pap. 13.00 (*0-679-73761-8*, Vin) Random.
— Charles Mingus: More Than a Fake Book. 160p. 1991. pap. 19.95 (*0-7935-0900-9*, 00673220) H Leonard.
Mingyu, Wu, jt. auth. see Lalkaka, R.
Mingyuan, Jin, ed. The Directory of Chinese Government Organs. Yanrui, Chang, tr. 944p. (CHI.). 1991. 108.00 (*962-7167-13-4*, Pub. by New China News UK) Cypress Co.
Minh-Ha, Trinh. When the Moon Waxes Red: Representation, Gender & Cultural Politics. (Illus.). 240p. 1991. 45.00 (*0-415-90430-7*, A5627, Routledge NY); pap. 14.95 (*0-415-90431-5*, A5631, Routledge NY) Routledge.
Minh-ha, Trinh T. Woman, Native, Other: Writing Postcoloniality & Feminism. LC 88-45455. (Illus.). 184p. 1989. 39.95 (*0-253-36603-8*); pap. 14.95 (*0-253-20503-4*, MB-503) Ind U Pr.
Minh-ha, Trinh T., jt. auth. see Bourdier, Jean-Paul.
***Minhinnett, Ray & Young, Bob.** The Story of the Fender Stratocaster: "Curves, Contours & Body Horns" a Celebration of the World's Greatest Guitar. LC 94-33586. (Illus.). 128p. 1995. 24.95 (*0-87930-349-2*) Miller Freeman.
***Minhinnick, Robert.** Hey Fatman. 64p. 1994. pap. 14.95 (*1-85411-110-8*, Pub. by Seren Bks UK) Dufour.
— The Looters. LC 89-82059. 72p. 1990. pap. 14.95 (*1-85411-019-5*, Pub. by Seren Bks UK) Dufour.
— Watching the Fire-Eater. 139p. 1993. pap. 15.95 (*1-85411-075-6*, Pub. by Seren Bks UK) Dufour.
— Watching the Fire Eater. 139p. 1993. pap. 15.95 (*0-685-67834-2*, Pub. by Seren Bks UK) Dufour.
Mini Book Staff. Getting Started: Recorder. 1990. 2.50 (*0-685-32163-0*, G162) Hansen Ed Mus.
— Getting Started: Tooter. 1990. 2.50 (*0-685-32162-2*, G163) Hansen Ed Mus.
Mini, Martin. Career Planning. 272p. (C). 1994. per., pap. text ed. 15.00 (*0-8403-9431-4*) Kendall-Hunt.
Mini, Piero V. John Maynard Keynes: A Study in the Psychology of Original Work. LC 93-48289. 1994. write for info. (*0-312-12137-7*) St Martin.
— Philosophy & Economics: The Origins & Development of Economic Theory. LC 74-7122. 1974. 24.95 (*0-8130-0381-4*) U Press Fla.
Minich, Elizabeth, jt. auth. see Porter, Catherine.
Minichiello, Robert J. Retailing Merchandising & Control: Concepts & Problems. 216p. (C). 1990. pap. text ed. 31. 95 (*0-256-06767-8*) Irwin.
Minichiello, Sharon. Retreat from Reform: Patterns of Political Behavior in Interwar Japan. LC 84-8535. 186p. 1984. text ed. 18.00 (*0-8248-0778-2*) UH Pr.
Minichino, Camille, jt. auth. see Heckman, Richard A.
Minick, N., tr. see Vygotsky, L. S.
Minick, Scott. Chinese Graphic Design. 1990. text ed. 19.95 (*0-442-30364-5*) Van Nos Reinhold.
Minieka, jt. ed. see Evans.
Minier, Elizabeth M., jt. auth. see Field, Dorothy M.
Minifie, Bernard W. Chocolate, Cocoa & Confectionary Science & Technology. 3rd ed. (Illus.). 544p. 1988. text ed. 99.95 (*0-442-26521-2*) Chapman & Hall.
Minifie, Fred D. Introduction to Communication Sciences & Disorders. LC 94-3135. (Illus.). 480p. (Orig.). (C). 1994. pap. text ed. 39.95x (*1-56593-202-1*, 0525) Singular Publishing.
Minifie, Fred D., et al. Student Workbook for Introduction to Communication Sciences & Disorders. (Illus.). 128p. (Orig.). (C). 1994. spiral bd. 24.95 (*1-56593-361-3*, 0690) Singular Publishing.
Minihan, Michael A., tr. see Mochulsky, Konstantin.
Minihofer. Czech-English Dictionary of Computer Science. (CZE & ENG.). 1990. 49.95 (*0-8288-7199-X*) Fr & Eur.
— English-Czech Dictionary of Computer Science. (CZE & ENG.). 1990. 49.95 (*0-8288-7200-7*) Fr & Eur.
— English-Czech Explanatory Dictionary of Computer Science. (CZE & ENG.). 1990. 49.95 (*0-8288-7201-5*) Fr & Eur.
Minihofer, D. Czech-English Dictionary of Computer Science. 2nd ed. 334p. 1990. 29.00 (*80-03-00169-2*) IBD Ltd.
— English-Czech Dictionary of Computer Science. 494p. 1990. reprint ed. 29.00 (*80-03-00302-4*) IBD Ltd.
Minihofer, O. & Kratochvilova, J. English-Czech Computer Dictionary. 494p. (C). 1986. 95.00 (*0-685-37171-9*, Pub. by Collets) St Mut.
— English-Czech Computer Dictionary. 494p. (C). 1990. 125.00 (*0-89771-910-7*, Pub. by Collets); text ed. 63.00 (*0-7855-0113-4*, Pub. by Collets) St Mut.
***Minihofer, Oldrich, et al.** English-Czech Dictionary of Data Processing, Telecommunications & Office Systems. 621p. (CZE & ENG.). 1994. pap. 45.00 (*80-901664-1-5*) IBD Ltd.
***Mining Unit, Industry & Energy Division Staff.** Strategy for African Mining. (Technical Paper Ser.: No. 181). 95p. (FRE.). 1992. 7.95 (*0-614-02852-3*, 12835) World Bank.
Minio-Paluello, L., ed. see Aristotle.
Minio-Paluello, L. Opuscula. The Latin Aristotle. xii, 590p. 1972. text ed. 95.00 (*0-317-54477-2*, Pub. by A M Hakkert SP) Coronet Bks.
Minio-Paluello, Lorenzo. Education in Fascist Italy. LC 78-63697. (Studies in Fascism: Ideology & Practice). (Illus.). 256p. reprint ed. 29.00 (*0-404-16958-9*) AMS Pr.
Minion, Ronald. The Protection Officer Training Manual. 5th ed. 70p. 1992. teacher ed 15.00 (*0-7506-9292-8*); pap. text ed. 34.95 (*0-7506-9291-X*) Buttrwrth-Heinemann.
***Minion, Ronald R., et al, eds.** Security Supervisor Training Manual. 192p. 1995. pap. 34.95 (*0-7506-9632-X*, Focal) Buttrwrth-Heinemann.
Minirth, et al. Love Hunger: Recovery from Food Addiction. 1991. pap. 12.00 (*0-449-14706-1*, GM) Fawcett.
Minirth, Frank. Before Burnout: Balanced Living for Busy People. 1989. pap. 8.99 (*0-8024-0879-6*) Moody.
— Christian Psychiatry. LC 76-57767. 1990. pap. 9.99 (*0-8007-5352-6*) Revell.
— Stress Factor: Thriving Emotionally & Spiritually in the Turbulant 90's. 1992. pap. 8.99 (*0-8024-9481-1*) Moody.
— Stress Factor: Thriving Emotionally & Spiritually in the Turbulant 90's. 1992. pap. 8.99 (*1-881273-02-4*) Northfield Pub.
Minirth, Frank, jt. auth. see Reese, Randy L.
Minirth, Frank, et al. Beating the Odds: Overcoming Life's Trials. (Life Enrichment Ser.). 128p. (Orig.). 1987. pap. 5.99 (*0-8010-6217-9*) Baker Bk.
— Happy Holidays: How to Beat the Holiday Blues. (Life Enrichment Ser.). 144p. (Orig.). 1990. pap. 7.99 (*0-8010-6272-1*) Baker Bk.
— The Healthy Christian Life. (Minirth-Meier Clinic Bible Study Ser.). (Orig.). 1988. pap. 12.99 (*0-8010-6232-2*) Baker Bk.
— One Hundred Ways to Overcome Depression. 128p. 1993. reprint ed. pap. 3.99 (*0-8007-8613-0*, Spire) Revell.
— Taking Control: New Hope for Substance Abusers & Their Families. 176p. (Orig.). 1988. pap. 7.99 (*0-8010-6234-9*) Baker Bk.
Minirth, Frank B. You Can Measure Your Mental Health. 1980. pap. 1.99 (*0-8010-6087-7*) Baker Bk.
***Minirth, Frank B. & Littleton, Mark.** You Can! LC 94-27191. 1994. write for info. (*0-8407-7749-3*) Nelson Comm.
Minirth, Frank B. & Meier, Paul D. Elige Ser Feliz! Velez, Jose S., tr. 208p. (Orig.). 1988. pap. 5.95 (*0-311-46113-1*) Casa Bautista.
— Happiness Is a Choice: Overcoming Depression. LC 78-62442. 1978. pap. 6.99 (*0-8010-6062-1*) Baker Bk.
— Happiness Is a Choice: The Symptoms, Causes, & Cures of Depression. 2nd ed. 240p. 1994. pap. 9.99 (*0-8010-6314-0*) Baker Bk.
Minirth, Frank B., et al. Ask the Doctors: Questions & Answers about Your Mental Health. LC 91-6905. 208p. 1991. 12.99 (*0-8010-6280-2*) Baker Bk.
— Beating the Clock: A Guide to Maturing Successfully. (Life Enrichment Ser.). 1986. pap. 3.99 (*0-8010-6205-5*) Baker Bk.
— How to Beat Burnout. (Orig.). 1986. pap. 7.99 (*0-8024-2314-0*) Moody.
— The Workaholic & His Family: An Inside Look. 144p. (Orig.). 1981. pap. 6.99 (*0-8010-6191-1*) Baker Bk.
Minis, Margaret D. I Don't Mind Suffering As Long As It Doesn't Hurt. 112p. (Orig.). 1995. pap. 8.95 (*0-8245-1438-6*) Crossroad NY.
Minisci, Francesco, ed. Free Radicals in Synthesis & Biology: Proceedings of the NATO Advanced Research Workshop Held in Bardolino (VR), Italy, May 8-13, 1988. (C). 1988. lib. bdg. 162.00 (*0-7923-0070-X*) Kluwer Ac.
Minish, Gary L., et al. Livestock Judging. (C). 1985. pap. text ed. 21.33 (*0-8359-4089-6*, Reston) P-H.

An Asterisk (*) at the beginning of an entry indicates that the title is appearing in BIP for the first time.

Minister, Edward. The Complete Guide to Practical Cutting (1853) 2nd enl. rev. ed. Shep, R. L., ed. LC 92-50696. (Illus.). 480p. 1993. pap. 31.95 (*0-914046-17-9*) R L Shep.

Minister of Information Staff. Republic of Tea Book of Tea & Herbs: A Guide to Appreciating the Virtues & Varietals Of. LC 93-31073. 1993. pap. 12.00 (*1-56426-570-6*) Cole Group.

Ministers of the Church of Scotland (Glasgow, 1840). Lectures on the Revival of Religion. 470p. 1980. 17.50 (*0-939464-37-3*) Labyrinth Pr.

Ministre du Travail et de la Main d'Oeuvre Staff, ed. Vocabulaire Francais-Anglais des Relations Professionnelles. 302p. (ENG & FRE.). 1972. pap. 37.50 (*0-686-57279-3*, M-4655) Fr & Eur.

Ministry & Nurture Committee Staff. The Wounded Meeting: Dealing with Difficult Behavior in Meeting for Worship. 60p. (Orig.). 1993. pap. text ed. 5.00 (*0-9620912-7-8*) Friends Genl Conf.

Ministry of Agriculture, Nature Management & Fisheries Staff, jt. auth. see International Society for Horticultural Science Staff.

Ministry of Chemical Industry, Scientific & Technical Information Research Institute Staff, ed. China Chemical Industry: World Chemical Industry Yearbook, 1987. 580p. 1987. lib. bdg. 275.00 (*0-89573-666-7*) VCH Pubs.

Ministry of Education, New Zealand Staff. Dancing with the Pen. 152p. 1992. pap. text ed. 25.00 (*0-478-05560-9*) R Owen Pubs.

***Ministry of Education of New Zealand Staff, ed.** Assessment: Policy to Practice. (Illus.). 52p. (Orig.). (C). 1994. pap. text ed. 12.95x (*1-878450-95-6*, Pub. by Lrning Media NZ) R Owen Pubs.

— The New Zealand Curriculum Framework. 28p. (Orig.). (C). 1994. pap. text ed. 12.95x (*1-878450-96-4*, Pub. by Lrning Media NZ) R Owen Pubs.

Ministry of Education Staff. Japanese Scientific Terms, English-Japanese-English: Oceanography. 186p. (ENG & JPN.). 1981. 75.00 (*0-8288-0421-4*, M 11209) Fr & Eur.

— Scientific Terms, Aeronautics: Japanese-English, English-Japanese. 235p. (ENG & JPN.). 1973. 39.95 (*0-8288-6328-8*, M-9347) Fr & Eur.

Ministry of Industry Staff. Swedish Industry & Industrial Policy 1985. (Illus.). 122p. (Orig.). 1985. pap. text ed. 115.00x (*91-38-82144-3*, Pub. by Almqv & Wiksell SW) Coronet Bks.

Ministry of Social Affairs & Employment Staff. Social Security in the Netherlands. 192p. 1990. pap. 24.00 (*90-6544-493-9*) Kluwer Law Tax Pubs.

Ministry on International Trade & Industry Staff. White Paper on International Trade: Japan 1993. 410p. 1993. 105.00 (*4-8224-0633-4*, Pub. by Japan External Trade JA) Gale.

— White Paper on International Trade Japan, 1994. 400p. 1994. pap. 120.00x (*4-8224-0669-5*) Taylor & Francis.

— The World Who's Who of Women: Japan 1993. 12th ed. 1200p. 1994. 195.00 (*0-948875-36-4*, Pub. by Melrose UK) Taylor & Francis.

Minitab Inc. Staff. Stat 101: Software for Statistics Instruction. 200p. (C). 1993. disk write for info. (*0-201-59087-5*); disk write for info. (*0-201-59088-3*) Addison-Wesley.

Minium, Dennis. Information Engineering. 368p. 1992. boxed 49.00 (*0-13-466079-X*) P-H.

***Minium, E. M., et al.** Elements of Statistical Reasoning: With IBM 3.5 Version Mystat. 1994. text ed. write for info. (*0-471-11704-8*) Wiley.

— Elements of Statistical Reasoning: With IBM 5.25 Version Mystat. 1994. text ed. write for info. (*0-471-11694-7*) Wiley.

— Elements of Statistical Reasoning: With MAC Mystat. 1994. text ed., disk write for info. (*0-471-11692-0*) Wiley.

— Elements of Statistical Reasoning with IBM 3.5 Version Mystat Set, Set. 1994. student ed, pap. text ed. write for info. (*0-471-12211-4*) Wiley.

Minium, Edward W. Statistical Reasoning in Psychology & Education. 2nd ed. 129p. 1978. teacher ed 4.00 (*0-471-04055-X*) Wiley.

— Statistical Reasoning in Psychology & Education. 3rd ed. 608p. (C). 1993. text ed. write for info. (*0-471-82188-8*) Wiley.

Minium, Edward W. & Clarke, Robert. Elements of Statistical Reasoning. LC 81-21843. 123p. (C). 1982. teacher ed 5.50 (*0-471-87590-2*); Net. text ed. write for info. (*0-471-08041-1*); Net. student ed write for info. (*0-471-86463-3*) Wiley.

— Elements of Statistical Reasoning: Study Guide Set. 3rd ed. 1989. Net. text ed. write for info. (*0-471-52622-3*) Wiley.

***Minium, Edward W., et al.** Statistical Reasoning in Psychology & Education. 3rd ed. 1993. text ed. write for info. (*0-471-00817-6*) Wiley.

Minjungseorim's Editorial Staff. Minjung's English-Korean & Korean-English Dictionary. LC 90-86010. (Illus.). 1554p. (Orig.). (ENG & KOR.). 1992. pap. 37.50 (*0-930878-02-7*) Hollym Intl.

Minjungseorim's Staff, ed. Essence English-Korean Dictionary: American Edition. LC 88-80990. 2731p. (ENG & KOR.). 1990. pap. 55.50x (*0-930878-79-5*) Hollym Intl.

— Essence Korean-English Dictionary: American Edition. LC 88-80991. 2510p. (ENG & KOR.). 1990. pap. 55.50x (*0-930878-80-9*) Hollym Intl.

Mink, Charles. Princess of the Everglades. LC 90-24998. 212p. 1991. 16.95 (*0-910923-98-1*) Pineapple Pr.

Mink, Claudia G. Cahokia: City of the Sun: Prehistoric Urban Center in the American Bottom. LC 92-81951. (Illus.). 80p. (Orig.). 1992. pap. text ed. 10.00 (*1-881563-00-6*) Cahokia MMS.

Mink, George, jt. auth. see Ballew, Julius R.

Mink, Gerd, jt. ed. see Schmitz, Franz-Juergan.

Mink, Gerd, jt. ed. see Schmitz, Franz-Jurgen.

Mink, Gwendolyn. Old Labor & New Immigrants in American Political Development: Union, Party & State, 1875-1920. LC 85-30963. 304p. 1986. 37.95 (*0-8014-1863-1*) Cornell U Pr.

— Old Labor & New Immigrants in American Political Development: Union, Party, & State, 1875-1920. LC 85-30963. 304p. 1990. reprint ed. pap. 15.95 (*0-8014-9680-2*) Cornell U Pr.

— The Wages of Motherhood: Inequality in the Welfare State, 1917-1942. 208p. 1995. 27.50x (*0-8014-2234-5*) Cornell U Pr.

Mink, Herman. Diccionario Tecnico Espanol-Aleman-Espanol. 6th ed. 1560p. 1989. 195.00 (*0-8288-2143-7*, S50189) Fr & Eur.

— Diccionario Tecnico, Tomo 1: Aleman-Espanol. 8th ed. 1908p. (GER & SPA.). 1991. 225.00 (*0-8288-5157-3*, S50190) Fr & Eur.

— Technical Dictionary: Diccionario Tecnico: Suplemento, Vol. 2. deluxe ed. 384p. (GER & SPA.). 1981. 59.95 (*0-8288-4437-2*, S50270) Fr & Eur.

Mink, Hermann. Diccionario Tecnico Espanol-Frances. 1356p. (FRE & SPA.). 1988. 195.00 (*0-7859-5825-8*, 8425414814) Fr & Eur.

— Diccionario Tecnico Frances-Espanol (French-Spanish Technical Dictionary) 3rd ed. 1152p. (FRE & SPA.). 1989. write for info. (*0-7859-5028-1*) Fr & Eur.

— Diccionario Tecnico Vol. 2 Espanol-Aleman. 7th ed. 1560p. 1991. 195.00 (*0-7859-5819-3*) Fr & Eur.

Mink, Jerrold H., et al. Magnetic Resonance Imaging of the Knee. LC 86-43229. (Illus.). 192p. reprint ed. pap. 54.80 (*0-7837-7122-3*, 2046951) Bks Demand.

— MRI of the Knee. 2nd ed. LC 92-17023. 502p. 1993. 136.50 (*0-88167-936-4*, 2417) Raven.

Mink, Joanna S. & Ward, Janet D. The Significance of Sibling Relationships in Literature. LC 92-75707. 174p. (C). 1993. 38.95 (*0-87972-612-1*); pap. 19.95 (*0-87972-613-X*) Bowling Green Univ.

Mink, JoAnna S. & Ward, Janet D., eds. Joinings & Disjoinings: The Significance of Marital Status in Literature. LC 91-70903. 200p. (C). 1992. lib. bdg. 39.95 (*0-87972-523-0*); pap. text ed. 19.95 (*0-87972-524-9*) Bowling Green Univ.

Mink, Joanna S., jt. auth. see Ward, Janet D.

Mink, Len. Gospel Duck. (Illus.). 20p. (J). (ps-5). 1988. reprint ed. pap. text ed. write for info. (*0-318-63671-9*) Mink Ministries.

— Gospel Duck Goes to School. (Illus.). 24p. (J). (ps-6). 1988. reprint ed. pap. text ed. write for info. (*0-318-63672-7*) Mink Ministries.

Mink, Louis O. A Finnegans Wake Gazetteer. LC 77-44443. 585p. reprint ed. pap. 166.80 (*0-685-44460-0*, 2056731) Bks Demand.

— Historical Understanding. Fay, Brian et al, eds. LC 87-47601. (Illus.). 312p. (C). 1987. 37.50 (*0-8014-1983-2*) Cornell U Pr.

— Mind, History, & Dialectic: The Philosophy of R. G. Collingwood. LC 87-6143. 287p. 1987. pap. 16.95 (*0-8195-6178-9*, Wesleyan Univ Pr) U Pr of New Eng.

Mink, Nelson G. How They Entered In. 1993. pap. 11.99 (*0-88019-307-7*) Schmul Pub Co.

Mink, Oscar. Change at Work: A Comprehensive Management Process for Transforming Organizations. (Management Ser.). 288p. 1993. 29.95 (*1-55542-587-9*) Jossey-Bass.

Mink, Oscar, et al. Developing High Performance People. (Illus.). 208p. 1993. pap. 24.95 (*0-201-56313-4*) Addison-Wesley.

— Groups at Work. LC 87-9081. (Techniques in Training & Performance Development Ser.). (Illus.). 279p. (C). 37.95 (*0-87778-196-6*) Educ Tech Pubns.

Mink, Oscar G., et al. Developing & Managing Open Organizations. LC 79-10195. 303p. 1991. pap. 19.95 (*0-318-21892-5*) Catapult Press.

— Developing & Managing Open Organizations: A Model & Methods for Maximizing Organizational Potential. 2nd ed. Stelzner, Karen I., ed. (Illus.). 303p. (C). 1991. reprint ed. pap. 19.95 (*0-685-66131-8*) Catapult Press.

— Open Organizations: A Model for Effectiveness, Renewal, & Intelligent Change. LC 94-22696. (Management Ser.). 176p. 1994. 29.95 (*0-7879-0028-1*) Jossey-Bass.

Mink, Stephen D. Poverty, Population, & the Environment. LC 92-43480. (Discussion Paper Ser.: No. 189). 49p. 1993. 6.95 (*0-8213-2328-8*, 12328) World Bank.

Mink, Walter D., jt. auth. see Rowe, Clarence J.

Mink, William. The Spot. Van Treese, James B., ed. 280p. 1993. pap. 8.95 (*1-56901-013-7*) NW Pub.

Minke, Gernot, jt. auth. see Grasser, Klaus.

Minkel, Margaret & Schutz, Ruth K. A Lamp in the Night: Domestic Violence from a Feminist Perspective. 100p. 1992. pap. 10.00 (*0-9634517-0-7*) M Minkel.

Minkema, Douglas D. System Thirty-four Teacher's Guide. 48p. (gr. 9-12). text ed. 110.00 (*0-9610582-7-7*) Apollo Com.

Minkema, Douglas D. & Carter, Gerald L. RPG II Programming. 2nd ed. (RPG II Programming-Advanced Topics Ser.). 1977. pap. text ed. 17.50 (*0-9610582-2-6*) Apollo Com.

— RPG II Programming Teacher's Guide. 175p. text ed. 55.00 (*0-9610582-5-0*) Apollo Com.

Minkema, Douglas D. & Pasquini, Mark T. RPG II Programming Advanced Topics. (RPG II Programming-Advanced Topics Ser.). 187p. 1977. pap. text ed. 14.50 (*0-9610582-3-4*) Apollo Com.

— RPG II Programming Advanced Topics Teacher's Guide. 210p. (gr. 9-12). text ed. 55.00 (*0-9610582-6-9*) Apollo Com.

Minkema, Douglas D., jt. auth. see Carter, Gerald L.

Minkema, Kenneth P., ed. The Sermon Notebook of Samuel Parris, 1689-1694. (Publications Ser.: Vol. 66). (Illus.). 322p. (C). 1993. text ed. 50.00 (*0-9620737-1-7*) Colonial MA.

Minkenberg, Michael. The New Right in Comparative Perspective: The United States & Germany. (Western Societies Papers). 90p. 1993. pap. 11.95 (*0-8014-9656-X*) Cornell U Pr.

Minker, Allen G., et al. Making the Criminal Record on Appeal. LC 82-201256. viii, 139p. 1981. 12.65 (*0-910039-06-2*) AZ Law Inst.

Minker, Jack, ed. Foundations of Deductive Databases & Logic Programming. (Illus.). 746p. (C). 1988. text ed. 44.95 (*0-934613-40-0*) Morgan Kaufmann.

Minker, Jack, jt. ed. see Gallaire, H.

***Minker, Margaret.** Medizinisches Woerterbuch. 320p. (GER.). 1992. 29.95 (*0-7859-8496-8*, 3809400580) Fr & Eur.

— Woerterbuch der Medizin. 399p. (GER.). 1991. 59.95 (*0-7859-8495-X*, 3806845352) Fr & Eur.

Minkes, A. L. & Nutall, C. S. Business Behavior & Management Structure. LC 84-27687. 221p. 1985. text ed. 32.50 (*0-312-10895-8*) St Martin.

Minkhlin, Solomon G. The Problem of the Minimum of a Quadratic Functional. Feinstein, A., tr. LC 64-24626. (Holden-Day Series in Mathematical Physics). 164p. reprint ed. pap. 46.80 (*0-317-09170-0*, 2016292) Bks Demand.

Minkiel, Stephen J. Man in Search of Man. 3rd ed. 220p. (C). 1988. ring bd. 12.00 (*0-945810-01-6*) Vincentian Fathers Erie.

Minkin, Barry. Econoquake: How to Survive & Prosper in the Coming Global Depression. 1992. 18.95 (*0-13-224866-2*) P-H.

Minkin, Jacob S. The Teachings of Maimonides. LC 87-70737. 448p. 1993. pap. 24.95 (*1-56821-039-6*) Aronson.

Minkin, Lewis. The Contentious Alliance: Trade Unions & the Labour Party. 752p. 1991. text ed. 95.00 (*0-7486-0301-8*, Pub. by Edinburgh U Pr UK) Col U Pr.

— The Contentious Alliance: Trade Unions & the Labour Party. 704p. 1993. pap. text ed. 30.00 (*0-7486-0404-9*, Pub. by Edinburgh U Pr UK) Col U Pr.

Minkin, Mary J., jt. auth. see Burg, Dale.

Minkin, Rita, tr. see Salaz, Ruben D.

Minkin, V. I., et al. Molecular Design of Tautomeric Compounds. (C). 1987. lib. bdg. 147.00 (*90-277-2478-4*) Kluwer Ac.

— Quantum Chemistry of Organic Compounds: Mechanisms of Reactions. (Illus.). xvi, 270p. 1990. 119.00 (*0-387-52530-0*) Spr-Verlag.

Minkin, Vladimir, et al. Aromaticity & Antiaromaticity: Electronic & Structural Aspects. 336p. 1994. text ed. 79.95 (*0-471-59382-6*, Wiley-Interscience) Wiley.

Minkkinen, Arno. Waterline. (Illus.). 112p. 1994. 40.00 (*0-89381-591-8*) Aperture.

Minkler, Gary. Philosophy of Goodness & Mercy. 150p. (Orig.). 1991. 18.50 (*0-9621618-3-7*) Magellan Bk.

Minkler, Gary & Minkler, Jing. Aerospace Coordinate Systems & Transformations. (Illus.). 306p. (C). 1990. 65.00 (*0-9621618-0-2*) Magellan Bk.

— CFAR. 300p. (Orig.). (C). 1988. pap. text ed. 65.00 (*0-685-24050-9*) Magellan Bk.

— CFAR: The Principles of Automatic Radar Detection in Clutter. (Illus.). 374p. (C). 1990. 68.00 (*0-9621618-1-0*) Magellan Bk.

— Theory & Application of Kalman Filtering. (Illus.). 608p. (C). 1990. 72.00 (*0-9621618-2-9*) Magellan Bk.

Minkler, Jing, jt. auth. see Minkler, Gary.

Minkler, Meredith & Estes, Carroll, eds. Critical Perspectives on Aging: The Political & Moral Economy of Growing Old. (Policy, Politics, Health & Medicine Ser.). 372p. 1991. text ed. 38.00 (*0-89503-076-4*); pap. text ed. 28.50 (*0-89503-075-6*) Baywood Pub.

Minkler, Meredith & Estes, Carroll L., eds. Readings in the Political Economy of Aging. (Policy, Politics, Health & Medicine Ser.: Vol. 6). 278p. (Orig.). 1984. pap. 26.00 (*0-89503-042-X*) Baywood Pub.

Minkler, Meredith & Roe, Kathleen M. Grandmothers As Caregivers: Raising the Children of the Crack Cocaine Epidemic. (Family Caregiver Applications Ser.: Vol. 2). (Illus.). 200p. (C). 1993. text ed. 44.00 (*0-8039-4846-8*); pap. text ed. 18.95 (*0-8039-4847-6*) Sage.

Minkler, Penny. Seeing Through Broccoli. (Illus.). 1993. 5.00 (*0-9619744-8-6*) Blue Light Pr.

Minkler, Wanda, ed. see Spencer, Emmett.

Minkoff. Biology. (Barron's E Z 101 Study Keys Ser.). 144p. 1991. pap. 5.95 (*0-8120-4569-6*) Barron.

***Minkoff, Debra C.** Organizing for Equality: The Evolution of Women's & Racial-Ethnic Organizations in America, 1955-1985. LC 94-46688. (Arnold & Caroline Rose Book Series of the American Sociological Association). 150p. (C). 1995. text ed. 48.00 (*0-8135-2208-0*) Rutgers U Pr.

Minkoff, Eli C. Evolutionary Biology. (Biology Ser.). (Illus.). 640p. (C). 1983. teacher ed write for info. (*0-201-15891-4*); text ed. 49.50 (*0-201-15890-6*) Addison-Wesley.

***Minkoff, Harvey, ed.** Approaches to the Bible: A Collection of Articles from Bible Review & Biblical Archaeology Review, 1978-1993, 2 vols., Set. (Illus.). (Orig.). (C). 1995. pap. text ed. 35.95 (*1-880317-21-4*, 7H84S) Biblical Arch Soc.

Minkoff, Harvey & Melamed, Evelyn. Exploring America: Perspectives on Critical Issues. (Illus.). 704p. (Orig.). (C). 1994. pap. text ed. 25.00 (*0-15-500981-8*) HarBrace.

Minkoff, Harvey & Melamed, Evelyn B. Visions & Revisions: Critical Reading & Writing. 480p. (C). 1989. pap. text ed. write for info. (*0-13-949884-2*) P-H.

Minkoff, Harvey, jt. ed. see Shanks, Hershel.

Minkoff, I. Materials Processes: A Short Introduction. (Illus.). 160p. (C). 1992. text ed. 69.00 (*0-387-18895-9*) Spr-Verlag.

— Solidification & Cast Structure. LC 85-9382. 240p. 1986. text ed. 245.00 (*0-471-90798-7*) Wiley.

Minkoff, John R. Signals, Noise & Active Sensors: Radar, Sonar & Laser Radar. 264p. 1992. text ed. 67.95 (*0-471-54572-4*) Wiley.

Minkoff, Kenneth & Drake, Robert, eds. Dual Diagnosis of Major Mental Illness & Substance Disorder. LC 87-646993. (New Directions for Mental Health Services Ser.: No. MHS 50). 1991. 17.95 (*1-55542-794-4*) Jossey-Bass.

Minkoff, Randy, jt. auth. see Santo, Ron.

Minkova, Donka. The History of Final Vowels in English: The Sound of Muting. LC 91-28082. (Topics in English Linguistics Ser.: No. 4). xii, 220p. 1991. lib. bdg. 72.35 (*3-11-012763-6*) Mouton.

Minkowich, Avram. Success & Failure in Israeli Elementary Education: An Evaluation Study with Special Emphasis on Disadvantaged Students. LC 80-19873. 539p. 1981. 49.95 (*0-87855-370-3*) Transaction Pubs.

Minkowitz, Martin, jt. auth. see De Carlo, Donald T.

Minkowski, A. & Monset-Couchard, M., eds. Physiological & Biochemical Basis for Perinatal Medicine. (Illus.). xiv, 370p. 1981. 125.00 (*3-8055-1283-X*) S Karger.

Minkowski, A. & Relier, J. P., eds. Journees Nationales de Neonatologie, XIVes, 1984. (Progres en Neonatologie Ser.: Vol. 4). (Illus.). vi, 306p. 1984. pap. 78.50 (*3-8055-3946-0*) S Karger.

Minkowski, A., ed. see Artificial Ventilation Symposium Staff.

Minkowski, Alexandre, jt. auth. see Evrard, Philippe.

Minkowski, Alexandre, jt. ed. see Kretchmer, Norman.

Minkowski, Hermann. Diophantische Approximationen. LC 56-13056. 19.95 (*0-8284-0118-7*) Chelsea Pub.

— Gesammelte Abhandlungen, 2 Vols. in 1. LC 66-28570. 75.00 (*0-8284-0208-6*) Chelsea Pub.

Minkowycz, W. J., et al. Handbook of Numerical Heat Transfer. LC 87-23100. 1024p. 1988. text ed. 175.00 (*0-471-83093-3*) Wiley.

Minks, A. K. & Harrewijn, P., eds. Aphids: Their Biology, Natural Enemies & Control. (World Crop Pests Ser.: Vol. 2A). 472p. 1987. 172.00 (*0-444-42630-2*) Elsevier.

— Aphids: Their Biology, Natural Enemies & Control, Vol. B. (World Crop Pests Ser.: Vol. 2B). 382p. 1988. 164.00 (*0-444-42798-8*) Elsevier.

— Aphids: Their Biology, Natural Enemies & Control, Vol. C. (World Crop Pests Ser.). 322p. 1990. 141.00 (*0-444-42799-6*) Elsevier.

Minks, Benton. One Hundred Greatest Hitters. 1988. 9.99 (*0-517-65611-6*) Random Hse Value.

Minks, Leah, jt. illus. see Minks, Louise.

Minks, Louise & Minks, Leah, illus. Memorial Hall Coloring Book. 24p. (Orig.). (J). (gr. 1-2). 1989. pap. 2.95 (*0-9612876-7-5*) Pocumtuck Valley Mem.

Minkus, Jerome B. The Branched Cyclic Covering of Two Bridge Knots & Links. LC 81-19099. (Memoirs of the American Mathematical Society Ser.: No. 35/255). 68p. 1982. pap. 16.00 (*0-8218-2255-1*, MEMO 35/255) Am Math.

Minlos, R. Many-Particle Hamiltonians: Spectra & Scattering. 194p. 1991. 75.00 (*0-8218-4104-1*, ADVSOV-5) Am Math.

Minlos, R., jt. auth. see Gelfand, I.

Minlos, R. A., jt. auth. see Malyshev, V. A.

Minmier, George. An Evaluation of the Zero-Base Budgeting System in Governmental Institutions. LC 75-22437. (Research Monograph: No. 68). 110p. 1975. pap. 25.00 (*0-88406-104-3*) GA St U Busn Pr.

Minn, Jay P., tr. see Loti, Pierre.

Minn, Loretta. Teach Speech. 64p. (J). (gr. 3-7). 1982. 8.95 (*0-86653-058-4*, GA 418) Good Apple.

Minn, Loretta B. Trek for Trivia. (Illus.). 48p. (J). (gr. 3-8). 1985. student ed 6.95 (*0-86653-291-9*, GA 646) Good Apple.

Minnaar, Maria, jt. auth. see Minnaar, Phillip.

***Minnaar, Phillip.** A Manual on Emu Farming. (Illus.). 44p. (Orig.). 1989. pap. 18.00 (*0-9643741-0-2*) Nyoni Pubng.

***Minnaar, Phillip & Minnaar, Maria. The Emu Farmer's Handbook. (Illus.). 178p. (C). 1992. 40.00 (*0-9643741-1-0*) Nyoni Pubng.**

M

happy. Publisher: Nyoni Publishing Co. (formerly Induna Co.), (C) 1992 Phillip & Maria Minnaar. Retail price: $40 (12.5% bookseller's discount available on single copies). Bulk price (17 or more copies): $30. Bulk orders: Nyoni Co., Box 25, Groveton, TX 75845; tel./FAX 409- 642-2361. All other orders handled by our distributors: Ratite Buyers Service (TX) 800-722-9353; Ratite Supply Co. (TX) 800-392- 1923; Nest Egg (TN) 800-252-4062; Smith Poultry Supply (KS) 913- 879-2587; Feathered Nest (AR) 501-332-3563; Feather Farm (CA) 707- 255-8833; Cutler's Supply (MI) 810-657-9450; Dueitt's Farm (MS) 601-525-3702.
Publisher Provided Annotation.

Minnaert, M. Light & Colour of the Outdoors. rev. ed. Seymour, L., tr. LC 92-33748. 416p. 1995. 49.95 (*0-387-97935-2*) Spr-Verlag.
— Nature of Light & Colour in the Open Air. 1948. pap. text ed. 7.95 (*0-486-20196-1*) Dover.
***Minnaert, M. G.** Light & Color in the Outdoors. 1994. pap. 24.00 (*0-387-84413-9*) Spr-Verlag.
— Light & Color in the Outdoors. (Illus.). xviii, 450p. 1995. 24.00 (*0-387-94413-3*) Spr-Verlag.
Minnaert, M. J. Practical Work in Elementary Astronomy. 247p. 1969. lib. bdg. 51.50 (*90-277-0133-4*) Kluwer Ac.
Minneapolis Institute of Arts Staff. Leger's Le Grand Dejeuner. LC 80-80235. (Illus.). 1980. 8.00 (*0-912964-11-1*) Minneapolis Inst Arts.
Minnella, Thomas A. The Copier Productivity Primer. 92p. 1991. pap. 10.95 (*0-9629936-0-3*) Minnella Ent.
Minnella, Thomas A., ed. see Kasper, Juneann.
Minnelli, Vincente & Arce, Hector. I Remember It Well. LC 90-3330. 391p. 1990. reprint ed. pap. 15.95 (*0-573-60607-2*) S French Trade.
Minneman, Paul G. Large Land Holdings in Ohio & Their Operation. Bruchey, Stuart, ed. LC 78-56664. (Management of Public Lands in the U. S. Ser.). 1979. lib. bdg. 18.95 (*0-405-11344-7*) Ayer.
Minner, R., jt. auth. see McCrea, Steve.
Minnerly, William L., jt. auth. see Heldman, Donald P.
Minnery, John. CIA Catalog of Clandestine Weapons, Tools, & Gadgets. (Illus.). 128p. 1990. pap. 14.95 (*0-87364-576-6*) Paladin Pr.
— The CIA Catalog of Clandestine Weapons, Tools, & Gadgets. LC 92-15887. 1992. pap. 10.00 (*0-942637-69-0*) Barricade Bks.
— Conflict Management in Urban Planning. 250p. 1985. text ed. 68.95 (*0-566-05001-3*) Ashgate Pub Co.
— Fingertip Firepower: Pen Guns, Knives & Bombs. (Illus.). 120p. 1990. pap. 14.00 (*0-87364-560-X*) Paladin Pr.
— Pick Guns: Lock Picking for Spies, Cops & Locksmiths. (Illus.). 128p. 1989. pap. 14.00 (*0-87364-510-3*) Paladin Pr.
Minnesota Advocates for Human Rights, International Service for Human Rights Staff. The U. N. Commission on Human Rights Orientation Manual for Nongovernmental Organizations: An Orientation Manual. 100p. 1993. pap. 7.50 (*0-929293-14-2*) MN Advocates.
Minnesota Advocates for Human Rights Staff. Civilians at Risk: Military & Police Abuses in the Mexican Countryside. Date not set. pap. 5.00 (*0-929293-16-9*) MN Advocates.
— Conquest Continued: Disregard for Human & Indigenous Rights in the Mexican State of Chiapas. 93p. 1992. pap. 10.00 (*0-929293-13-4*) MN Advocates.
— No Double Standards in International Law: Linkage of NAFTA with Hemisphere System of Human Rights Enforcement Is Needed - Canada, Mexico & the United States Must Become Full Partners. 22p. (Orig.). 1992. pap. 5.00 (*0-929293-15-0*) MN Advocates.
Minnesota Council on Foundations Staff. Guide to Minnesota Foundations & Corporate Giving Programs, 1989-90. Bill, Patricia, ed. (Orig.). 1990. 30.00 (*0-9616378-0-3*) MN Coun Found.
— Guide to Minnesota Foundations & Corporate Giving Programs, 1991-92. Bill, Patricia, ed. 220p. 1991. per. 30.00 (*0-9616378-1-1*) MN Coun Found.
Minnesota District Judges Association, Committee on Criminal Jury Instruction Guides. Minnesota Jury Instruction Guides, Criminal (CRIMJIG), Vol. 10. 2nd ed. LC 85-51063. (Minnesota Practice Ser.). 510p. 1985. 59.50 (*0-685-13436-9*) West Pub.
Minnesota Fats. Minnesota Fats on Pool. 1976. 15.95 (*0-8488-1555-6*) Amereon Ltd.
Minnesota Heart Association Staff. Rheumatic Fever: A Symposium Held at the University of Minnesota on November 29, 30, & December 1, 1951. Thomas, Lewis, ed. LC 52-11108. 359p. reprint ed. pap. 102.40 (*0-317-29474-1*, 2055922) Bks Demand.
Minnesota Historical Society Staff, et al. Manuscripts Collections of the Minnesota Historical Society, No. 2: Guide. LC 35-27911. (Publications of the Minnesota Historical Society). 228p. reprint ed. pap. 65.00 (*0-8357-3315-7*, 2039539) Bks Demand.
Minnesota Humanities Commission Staff, ed. Braided Lives: An Anthology of Multicultural American Writing. 288p. (YA). (gr. 9-12). 1991. pap. text ed. 13.00 (*0-9629298-0-8*) MN Humanities.
Minnesota Lawyers Human Rights Committee Staff. The Homicide of Dr. Victor Manuel Oropeza Contreras: A Case Study of Human Rights Reforms in Mexico. 40p. (Orig.). 1991. pap. 5.00 (*0-929293-11-8*) MN Advocates.
— Trimming the Cat's Claws: The Politics of Impunity in Albania. (Minnesota International Human Rights Committee Ser.). 44p. (Orig.). 1992. pap. text ed. 8.50 (*0-685-70374-6*) MN Advocates.
Minnesota Lawyers International Human Rights Committee Staff. Children's Rights in Haiti. 27p. (Orig.). 1989. pap. 5.00 (*0-929293-04-5*) MN Advocates.
— Hidden from View: Human Rights Conditions in the Krome Detention Center. 81p. (Orig.). 1991. pap. 7.00 (*0-929293-10-X*) MN Advocates.
— Oakdale Detention Center: The First Year of Operation. 55p. 1987. pap. 3.00 (*0-929293-17-7*) MN Advocates.
— Shame in the House of Saud: Contempt for Human Rights in the Kingdom of Saudi Arabia. 170p. (Orig.). 1992. pap. 15.00 (*0-929293-12-6*) MN Advocates.
Minnesota Lawyers International Human Rights Committee Staff, ed. see McGuinnes, Celia & Whelan, Leo.
Minnesota State Bar Association Staff & Daly, Joseph L. The Student Lawyer: A Guide to Minnesota's Legal System. 217p. 1987. reprint ed. pap. text ed. 23.25 (*0-314-23039-4*) West Pub.
Minnesota University, Graduate School Staff. Social Sciences at Mid-Century. LC 68-55852. (Essay Index Reprint Ser.). 1977. 17.95 (*0-8369-0710-8*) Ayer.
Minney, R. J. The Private Papers of Hore-Belisha. (Modern Revivals in Military History Ser.). 320p. 1992. 61.95 (*0-7512-0042-5*, Pub. by Gregg Revivals UK) Ashgate Pub Co.
Minnich, Elizabeth, et al. Reconstructing the Academy: Women's Education & Women's Studies. 320p. 1988. lib. bdg. 27.50 (*0-226-53013-2*); pap. text ed. 12.95 (*0-226-53014-0*) U Ch Pr.
Minnich, Elizabeth K. Transforming Knowledge. 240p. 1990. 44.95 (*0-87722-695-4*); pap. 19.95 (*0-87722-880-9*) Temple U Pr.
Minnich, Jerry. Jerry Minnich's Guide to Eating Well in Wisconsin. LC 93-31125. 1993. 8.95 (*1-879483-15-7*) Prairie Oak Pr.
— The Ohio Gardening Guide. (Illus.). 330p. (Orig.). 1995. pap. 18.95 (*0-8214-1118-7*) Ohio U Pr.
— Wisconsin Garden Guide. (Illus.). 326p. 1989. pap. 12.95 (*1-55971-010-1*, 0158, Heartlnd Pr) NorthWord.
— The Wisconsin Garden Guide. 3rd ed. LC 95-2342. 1995. pap. 18.95 (*1-879483-24-6*) Prairie Oak Pr.
Minnich, Jerry, ed. The Wisconsin Almanac. 272p. (Orig.). 1989. pap. 9.95 (*0-944133-06-1*) Nrth Cntry Pr.
Minnich, Jerry, jt. auth. see Visser, Kristin.
Minnich, Michelle. Vanishing Species: The Wildlife Art of Laura Regan. (Illus.). 1993. pap. 19.95 (*1-55912-377-X*) CEDCO Pub.
Minnich, Nelson H. The Catholic Reformation: Council, Churchmen, Controversies. (Collected Studies: No. CS 403). 328p. 1993. 89.95 (*0-86078-350-2*, Pub. by Variorum UK) Ashgate Pub Co.
— The Fifth Lateran Council, 1512-1517: Studies on its Membership, Diplomacy & Proposals for Reform. (Collected Studies: No. CS 392). 352p. 1993. 89.95 (*0-86078-349-9*, Pub. by Variorum UK) Ashgate Pub Co.
***Minnich, Richard A.** The Biogeography of Fire in the San Bernardino Mountains of California: A Historical Study. LC 88-9997. (University of California Publications in Entomology: No. 28). 170p. 1988. pap. 48.50 (*0-7837-7494-X*, 2049216) Bks Demand.
Minnich, Robert G. The Homemade World of Zagaj. (Bergen Studies in Social Anthropology, University of Bergen, Norway: No. 18). 248p. 1985. pap. text ed. 11.95 (*0-936508-56-6*, Pub. by Bergen Univ Dept Social Anthro NO) Barber Pr.
Minnicic, Roy, ed. see Government Land Office Staff.
Minnick, Dale L. How to Get up in Front Without Getting Down. LC 91-76666. 200p. reprint ed. pap. 15.00 (*0-9633476-0-8*) Desert Rain.
— Speaking Without Fear. rev. ed. 194p. 1995. pap. 14.95 (*0-9633476-8-3*) Desert Rain.
Minnick, Dan R. Entomology Laboratory Textbook. (Illus.). 75p. (C). 1981. pap. text ed. 21.95 (*0-89892-038-8*) Contemp Pub Co of Raleigh.
Minnick, Daniel J., ed. A Comprehensive Guide for Third Class Mailers. 162p. 1992. 80.00 (*0-933505-16-7*) Graph Comm Assn.
Minnick, Karla. Divorce, Humor Me. 66p. 1993. pap. 6.50 (*1-880365-16-2*) Prof Pr NC.
Minnick, Kathleen. Kwanzaa: How to Celebrate It in Your Home. Taylor, Charles, ed. (Big Book African American (In Home) Celebration Ser.). (Illus.). 24p. 1994. lib. bdg. 21.95 (*0-935483-19-5*) Praxis Madison.
Minnick, Molly A. Divorce Illustrated. (Illus.). 50p. (Orig.). (C). 1990. 15.00 (*1-878526-02-2*) Pineapple MI.
— Divorce Illustrated: Workbook. (Illus.). 60p. (Orig.). (J). (gr. 4). 1990. pap. 5.00 (*1-878526-03-0*) Pineapple MI.
— Group Work with Children of Divorce. rev. ed. (Illus.). 80p. (C). 1990. 18.00 (*1-878526-01-4*) Pineapple MI.
— A Time to Decide, a Time to Heal. 4th ed. LC 90-91478. 118p. 1994. 6.95 (*1-878526-39-1*) Pineapple MI.
— Yellow Ribbons, Worried Hearts. (Illus.). 65p. (C). 1991. 20.00 (*1-878526-33-2*) Pineapple MI.
— Yesterday I Dreamed of Dreams. 25p. 1991. 1.00 (*1-878526-10-3*) Pineapple MI.
Minnick, Roy. Land Surveyor Test Training Manual. (Illus.). 287p. 1983. pap. 35.00 (*0-910845-17-4*, 801) Landmark Ent.
Minnick, Roy, ed. Laws for the California Surveyor. 210p. 1993. 35.00 (*0-910845-10-7*, 708) Landmark Ent.
— Plotters & Patterns of American Land Surveying. 232p. (Orig.). 1986. pap. 16.00 (*0-910845-28-X*, 974) Landmark Ent.
Minnick, Roy, jt. ed. see Brinker, Russell.
Minnick, Roy, jt. auth. see Cuomo, Paul.
Minnick, Roy, ed. see Schmitz, Michael J.
Minnick, Sylvia S. SamFow: The San Joaquin Chinese Lagacy. LC 87-63495. (Illus.). 320p. (C). 1988. 25.00 (*0-944194-09-5*); pap. 14.95 (*0-944194-10-9*) Heritage West.
Minnick, Wayne C. Public Speaking. 2nd ed. (C). Date not set. pap. 26.50 (*0-8191-9003-9*) U Pr of Amer.
Minnick, Wendell. Spies & Provocateurs: A Worldwide Encyclopedia of Persons Conducting Espionage & Covert Action, 1946-1991. LC 92-50312. 320p. 1992. lib. bdg. 49.95x (*0-89950-746-8*) McFarland & Co.
Minnick, William H. Flux Cored Arc Welding Handbook. LC 93-39708. (Illus.). 160p. (C). 1995. text ed. 22.40 (*1-56637-024-8*) Goodheart.
— Gas Metal Arc Welding Handbook. LC 95-10563. 1995. write for info. (*1-56637-204-6*) Goodheart.
— Gas Tungsten Arc Welding Handbook. LC 95-10564. 1995. write for info. (*1-56637-206-2*) Goodheart.
Minnigerode, Meade. Certain Rich Men. LC 71-121489. (Essay Index Reprint Ser.). 1977. 20.95 (*0-8369-1714-6*) Ayer.
— Lives & Times. LC 76-121490. (Essay Index Reprint Ser.). 1977. 20.95 (*0-8369-1765-0*) Ayer.
— Some American Ladies. LC 70-93361. (Essay Index Reprint Ser.). 1977. 23.95 (*0-8369-1362-0*) Ayer.
— Some Personal Letters of Herman Melville & a Bibliography. LC 78-75511. (Select Bibliographies Reprint Ser.). 1977. 18.95 (*0-8369-5013-5*) Ayer.
Minnikin, David E., jt. ed. see Goodfellow, Michael.
Minninger, Joan. Free Yourself to Read Faster. (Illus.). x, 292p. (Orig.). 1982. pap. 14.95 (*0-9604042-3-6*) Wkshops Innovative Teach.
— Free Yourself to Remember. (Illus.). 60p. 1983. pap. 6.50 (*0-9604042-4-4*) Wkshops Innovative Teach.
— Free Yourself to Write. LC 80-50165. (Illus.). vii, 180p. (Orig.). 1980. pap. 9.95 (*0-9604042-1-X*) Wkshops Innovative Teach.
— Perfect Letter. 1992. pap. 11.00 (*0-385-41998-8*) Doubleday.
— Rapid Memory in Seven Days: The Quick & Easy Guide to Better Remembering. Dugan, Eleanor, ed. LC 94-6937. 208p. (Orig.). 1994. pap. 9.95 (*0-399-52130-5*, Perigree Bks) Berkley Pub.
— Rapid Reading in Five Days: The Quick & Easy Program to Master Faster Reading. LC 94-16092. 240p. (Orig.). 1994. pap. 9.95 (*0-399-52131-3*, Perigree Bks) Berkley Pub.
— Total Recall. 1994. 7.98 (*1-56731-011-7*, MJF Bks) Fine Comms.
— Total Recall. 1989. mass mkt. 5.99 (*0-671-69134-1*) PB.
Minninger, Joan & Dugan, Eleanor. Make Your Mind Work for You. Peters, Sally, ed. 256p. 1990. reprint ed. mass mkt. 4.95 (*0-671-68474-4*) PB.
Minninger, Joan & Putz, C. Delos, Jr. Writing Letters, Memos & Reports. (Illus.). 162p. (Orig.). 1981. pap. 11.95 (*0-9604042-2-8*) Wkshops Innovative Teach.
Minninger, Joan, jt. auth. see Goulter, Barbara.
Minnis, A. J. Medieval Theory of Authorship. 2nd ed. 323p. 1986. 55.00 (*0-85967-741-9*, Pub. by Scolar Pr UK) Ashgate Pub Co.
— The Shorter Poems. (Oxford Guides to Chaucer Ser.: Vol. 3). 580p. 1995. 72.00 (*0-19-811193-2*) OUP.
Minnis, A. J., ed. Latin & Vernacular: Studies in Late-Medieval Manuscripts. (University of York: Centre for Medieval Studies Manuscripts Conference Proceedings: No. 1). 176p. (C). 1989. 79.00 (*0-85991-286-8*) Boydell & Brewer.
— The Medieval Boethius: Studies in the Vernacular Translation of De Consolatione Philosophiae. 196p. 1987. 79.00 (*0-85991-234-5*) Boydell & Brewer.
Minnis, A. J. & Brewer, Charlotte, eds. Crux & Controversy in Middle English Textual Criticism. 224p. (C). 1992. text ed. 63.00 (*0-85991-321-X*, DS Brewer) Boydell & Brewer.
Minnis, A. J. & Scott, A. B., eds. Medieval Literary Theory & Criticism 1100-1375: The Commentary-Tradition. 560p. 1992. reprint ed. pap. 32.00 (*0-19-811274-2*, 8526) OUP.
Minnis, A. J. & Yeager, R. F., eds. John Gower's Poetic: The Search for a New Arion. (Publications of the John Gower Society: No. 2). 286p. 1990. 70.00 (*0-85991-280-9*) Boydell & Brewer.
Minnis, A. J., ed. see Boethius.
Minnis, Alastair. Chaucer & Pagan Antiquity. (Chaucer Studies: No. VIII). 168p. 1982. 79.00 (*0-85991-098-9*) Boydell & Brewer.
Minnis, Alastair, intro. Late-Medieval Religious Texts & Their Transmission. (York Manuscripts Conferences: No. 3). (Illus.). 256p. (C). 1993. text ed. 63.00 (*0-85991-386-4*) Boydell & Brewer.
Minnis, Alistair J. Medieval Theory of Authorship: Scholastic Literary Attitudes in the Later Middle Ages. LC 87-5997. (Middle Ages Ser.). (Illus.). 340p. (C). 1987. reprint ed. pap. text ed. 19.95 (*0-8122-1257-6*) U of Pa Pr.
Minnis, Mary M., jt. auth. see Burks, Bennette D.
Minnis, Paul E. Social Adaptation to Food Stress: A Prehistoric Southwestern Example. LC 84-28103. (Prehistoric Archeology & Ecology Ser.). (Illus.). 256p. 1985. pap. text ed. 8.00 (*0-226-53024-8*) U Ch Pr.
Minnis, Paul E. & Redman, Charles L., eds. Perspectives on Southwestern Prehistory. 434p. (C). 1990. pap. text ed. 72.50 (*0-8133-7930-X*) Westview.
***Minnis, Whitney.** How to Get an Athletic Scholarship: A Student-Athlete's Guide to Collegiate Athletics. 116p. (YA). (gr. 8-12). 1995. pap. 12.95 (*0-9645153-0-X*) ASI Publ.
Minnix, Kathleen. Laughter in the Amen Corner: The Life of Evangelist Sam Jones. LC 92-37645. (Illus.). 328p. 1993. 35.00 (*0-8203-1539-7*) U of Ga Pr.
Minno, Marc C. & Emmel, Thomas C. Butterflies of the Florida Keys. (Illus.). 168p. (Orig.). 1993. 31.50 (*0-945417-88-8*); pap. 18.95 (*0-945417-87-X*) Sci Pubs.
Minnoch, James E. Aground. 1985. 12.95 (*0-07-155319-3*) McGraw.
— Aground: Coping with Emergency Groundings. LC 85-71609. (Illus.). 160p. 1985. 12.95 (*0-8286-0098-8*) J De Graff.
Minns, Amina & Hijab, Nadia. Citizens Apart: A Portrait of Palestinians of Israel. 250p. 1990. 34.50 (*0-685-38700-3*, Pub. by I B Tauris UK) St Martin.
— Citizens Apart: A Portrait of the Palestinians in Israel. 1991. 34.50 (*0-685-48183-2*, Pub. by I B Tauris UK) St Martin.
Minns, Denis. Irenaeus. LC 93-36686. 1994. 35.00 (*0-87840-553-4*) Georgetown U Pr.
Minns, Ellis H. Scythians & Greeks. LC 65-15248. (Illus.). 1913. 50.00 (*0-8196-0277-9*) Biblo.
— Scythians & Greeks: A Survey of Ancient History & Archaeology on the North Coast of the Euxine from the Danube to the Caucasus. 1976. lib. bdg. 59.95 (*0-8490-2578-8*) Gordon Pr.
Minns, F. John, ed. Wealth Well-Given: The Enterprise & Benevolence of Lord Nuffield. (Illus.). 336p. 1994. 28.00 (*0-7509-0656-1*) A Sutton Pub.
Minns, Michael L. The Underground Lawyer. Robertson, L. R. & Nail, Gene, eds. (Illus.). 625p. (C). 1989. 29.95 (*0-929801-00-8*) Gopher Pubns.
Minns, Robert A., ed. Problems of Intracranial Pressure in Childhood. (Clinics in Developmental Medicine Ser.: Nos. 113-114). (Illus.). 458p. (C). 1991. 85.00 (*0-521-41272-2*, Pub. by Mc Keith Pr UK) Cambridge U Pr.
Mino, M., jt. ed. see Hayaishi, Osamu.
Mino, M., et al, eds. Vitamin E: Its Usefulness in Health & in Curing Diseases. (Illus.). xiv, 368p. 1993. 198.50 (*3-8055-5753-1*) S Karger.
Mino, Rose S. El Cono Sur: Dinamica y Dimensiones de Su Literatura. 243p. (Orig.). 1985. pap. 12.00 (*0-933559-00-3*) Montclair State.
Mino, Yutaka & Robinson, James. Beauty & Tranquility: The Eli Lilly Collection of Chinese Art. LC 82-84077. (Indianapolis Museum of Art: Centennial Catalogue Ser.). (Illus.). 268p. (Orig.). 1984. pap. 35.00 (*0-936260-14-9*) Ind Mus Art.
Mino, Yutaka, jt. auth. see Robinson, James.
Minocha, Vivek S. The Problem in Punjab: A Plea for Introspection. (C). 1989. pap. 2.50 (*81-202-0240-6*, Pub. by Ajanta II) S Asia.
***Minock, Mary.** Love in the Upstairs Flat. LC 95-8692. 92p. 1995. pap. 14.95 (*0-7734-2729-5*, Mellen Poetry Pr) E Mellen.
***Minoff, Howard L., et al, eds.** Infections in Women. LC 94-26754. 352p. 1995. 98.00 (*0-7817-0236-4*) Raven.
Minogin, V. G. & Letokhov, V. S. Laser Light Pressure on Atoms. 260p. 1987. text ed. 141.00 (*2-88124-080-1*) Gordon & Breach.
***Minogue, Brendan.** Bioethics: A Committee Approach. (Philosophy Ser.). 420p. 1995. pap. 26.25 (*0-86720-967-4*) Jones & Bartlett.
Minogue, Colette M., jt. auth. see Quinlin, Michael P.
Minogue, Ethel. Irish Cooking: Classic & Modern Recipes. 1988. 10.99 (*0-517-67378-9*) Random Hse Value.
Minogue, Kenneth. Alien Powers: The Pure Theory of Ideology. LC 84-22340. 288p. 1985. pap. 12.95 (*0-312-01860-6*) St Martin.
— A Very Short Introduction to Politics. (Very Short Introductions Ser.). 112p. 1995. pap. 7.95 (*0-19-285309-0*) OUP.
Minogue, Kenneth R. The Concept of a University. LC 72-95301. 239p. reprint ed. pap. 68.20 (*0-685-23494-0*, 2029054) Bks Demand.
Minogue, M. M., jt. ed. see Leeson, P. F.
Minogue, Martin, ed. Local Government in Britain. LC 76-43105. (Documents on Contemporary British Government Ser.: No. 2). 482p. reprint ed. pap. 137.40 (*0-318-34825-X*, 2031694) Bks Demand.
Minogue, Sally, ed. Problems for Feminist Criticism. 256p. 1990. 55.00 (*0-415-02077-8*, A4743); pap. 18.95 (*0-415-05029-4*, A4747) Routledge.
Minogue, Valerie. Nathalie Sarraute: The War of the Words. 230p. 1981. 24.00 (*0-85224-405-3*, Pub. by Edinburgh U Pr UK) Col U Pr.
Minogue, William F., ed. Managing in an Academic Health Care Environment. 213p. (C). 1993. text ed. 50.00 (*0-924674-18-0*) Am Coll Phys Execs.
Minoia, C. & Caroli, S., eds. Applications of Zeeman Graphite Furnace Atomic Absorption Spectroscopy in the Chemical Laboratory & in Toxicology. LC 92-20198. 1992. 285.00 (*0-08-041019-7*, Pergamon Pr) Elsevier.
Minois, Georges. History of Old Age: From Antiquity to the Renaissance. Tenison, Sarah H., tr. LC 89-5221. x, 350p. 1990. 29.95 (*0-226-53031-0*) U Ch Pr.
***Minokur.** True Confessions. 3.99 (*0-517-13576-0*) Random Hse Value.
***Minoli, Daniel.** Analyzing Outsourcing: Reengineering Information & Communication Systems. LC 94-22273. 1994. write for info. (*0-07-042593-0*) McGraw.
— Broadband Network Analysis & Design. LC 93-12353. 1993. write for info. (*0-89006-675-2*) Artech Hse.
— Enterprise Networking: Fractional T1 to Sonet - Frame Relay to BISDN. LC 92-18854. (Telecommunications Ser.). 734p. 1992. text ed. 88.00 (*0-89006-621-3*) Artech Hse.
— First, Second, & Next Generation LANs. (Computer Communications Ser.). 1993. text ed. 45.00 (*0-07-042586-8*) McGraw.
— Imaging in Corporate Environments: Technology & Communication. LC 93-46727. 1994. text ed. 40.00 (*0-07-042588-4*) McGraw.

An Asterisk (*) at the beginning of an entry indicates that the title is appearing in BIP for the first time.

— Practical LAN Interconnection: Featuring FDDI. 1993. text ed. 40.00 (*0-07-042524-8*) McGraw.

— Telecommunications Technology Handbook. (Artech House Telecommunications Library). 680p. 1991. 89.00 (*0-89006-425-3*, C1425) Artech Hse.

— Video Dialtone Technology: Digital Video Services over ADSL, HFC, FTTC, & ATM. LC 94-49661. 1995. text ed. 60.00 (*0-07-042724-0*) McGraw.

Minoli, Daniel & Dobrowski, George. Principles of Signaling for Cell Relay & Frame Relay. LC 94-11381. 1994. 77.00 (*0-89006-708-2*) Artech Hse.

Minoli, Daniel & Keinath, Robert. Distributed Multimedia Through Broadband Communication Services. LC 93-31143. 1993. 69.00 (*0-89006-689-2*) Artech Hse.

Minoli, Daniel & Vitella, Michael. ATM & Cell Relay Service for Corporate Environments. 1994. text ed. 44.00 (*0-07-042591-4*) McGraw.

Minoli, Daniel, jt. auth. see Eldib, Osman.

Minomura, S., ed. Solid State Physics under Pressure. 1985. lib. bdg. 164.00 (*90-277-1897-0*) Kluwer Ac.

Minoprio, John. The Blue & Buff: Portrait of an English Hunt. (Illus.). 144p. 1992. 55.00 (*1-85310-264-4*, Pub. by Airlife Pub Ltd UK) Voyageur Pr.

Minor, Barbara B. Trends in School Library Media Research as Reflected in the ERIC Database. 44p. 1986. 6.00 (*0-937597-11-2*, IR-70) ERIC Clear.

Minor, Barbara B., jt. auth. see Ely, Donald P.

Minor, Barbara B., jt. ed. see Ely, Donald P.

Minor, Carole W., jt. ed. see Brown, Duane.

Minor, Clorinda. Meshullam! or, Tidings from Jersusalem: Journal of a Believer Recently Returned from the Holy Land. Davis, Moshe, ed. LC 77-70755. (America & the Holy Land Ser.). 1977. reprint ed. lib. bdg. 19.95 (*0-405-10302-6*) Ayer.

Minor, Florence F., jt. ed. see Minor, Wendell.

Minor, Herman, IV. The Seven Habits of Highly Ineffective People: Low-Effort Lessons in Mismanaging for Success. LC 94-20355. 1994. pap. 8.95 (*0-8065-1582-1*, Citadel Pr) Carol Pub Group.

Minor, Hinda R. Penny Candy, a Memoir. 300p. 1989. write for info. (*0-318-65425-3*) R Minor Graph Arts.

Minor, Hinda R., ed. see Chadwick, James M.

Minor, Jacqueline K. & Minor, Vern B. Risk Management in Schools: A Guide to Minimizing Liability. 96p. 1991. ring bd. 49.95 (*0-8039-6006-9*, D1478) Corwin Pr.

Minor, Kevin I., jt. auth. see Carlie, Michael K.

Minor, Lee. Table in the Sky. LC 88-51386. 53p. (J). (gr. k-3). 1989. 5.95 (*1-55523-197-7*) Winston-Derek.

Minor, Lucian. The Militant Hack Writer: French Popular Literature 1800-1848 - Its Influence, Artistic & Political. 1975. 11.95 (*0-87972-105-7*); pap. 6.95 (*0-87972-106-5*) Bowling Green Univ.

Minor, Marianne. Coaching & Counseling. Crisp, Michael G., ed. LC 88-72253. (Fifty Minute Ser.). (Illus.). 96p. (Orig.). 1989. pap. 9.95 (*0-931961-68-8*) Crisp Pubns.

— Coaching for Development. Gerould, Philip, ed. (Fifty-Minute Ser.). (Illus.). 100p. (Orig.). 1995. pap. 9.95 (*1-56052-319-0*) Crisp Pubns.

— Preventing Workplace Violence. Gerould, W. Philip, ed. LC 93-73145. (Fifty-Minute Ser.). (Illus.). 100p. (Orig.). 1994. pap. 9.95 (*1-56052-258-5*) Crisp Pubns.

Minor, Mark. Literary-Critical Approaches to the Bible: An Annotated Bibliography. LC 92-7469. 520p. 1992. lib. bdg. 50.00 (*0-933951-48-5*) Locust Hill Pr.

Minor, Mary A. & Minor, Scott D. Patient Care Skills. 3rd ed. (C). 1994. pap. text ed. 34.95 (*0-8385-7709-1*) Appleton & Lange.

Minor, Mary E., ed. see Perry, Katy.

Minor, Marz & Minor, Nono. The American Indian Craft Book. LC 77-14075. (Illus.). 416p. 1978. pap. 10.95 (*0-8032-5891-7*) U of Nebr Pr.

Minor, Michael, jt. auth. see Vrzalik, Larry F.

Minor, Nancy & Bradley, Patricia. Coping with School-Age Motherhood. rev. ed. (J). (gr. 7-12). 1988. lib. bdg. 15.95 (*0-8239-0923-9*) Rosen Group.

Minor, Nono, jt. auth. see Minor, Marz.

Minor, Plinius. Plinius: Concordantiae in C. Plinii Caecilii Secundi Opera, 4 vols., Set. Heberlein, Friedrich & Slaby, Wolfgang, eds. (Alpha-Omega, Reihe A Ser.: Bd. CXIV-2). 3128p. (GER.). 1991. write for info. (*3-487-09403-7*, Pub. by Georg Olms GW) Lubrecht & Cramer.

Minor, Raleigh C. Conflict of Laws; or, Private International Law. iii, 575p. 1985. reprint ed. lib. bdg. 47.50 (*0-8377-0852-4*) Rothman.

Minor, Rick. Prehistoric Settlement & Subsistence in the Upper South Umpqua River Drainage, Southwestern Oregon. (Illus.). 140p. 1989. write for info. (*0-318-64857-1*) NW Herit Pr.

Minor, Rick, ed. Contributions to the Archaeology of Oregon: 1987-1988. (Association of Oregon Archaeologists Occasional Papers). (Illus.). 221p. (Orig.). (C). 1989. pap. text ed. 14.50 (*0-685-40132-4*) Assn Oregon Arch.

Minor, Rick, et al. The Cape Perpetua Shell Middens: Late Prehistoric Subsistence on the Central Oregon Coast. (Illus.). 115p. 1989. write for info. (*0-318-64856-3*) NW Herit Pr.

Minor, Robert. Bhagavad Gita: An Exegetical Commentary. 1982. 38.00 (*0-8364-0817-9*); text ed. 18.50 (*0-8364-0862-4*) S Asia.

Minor, Robert N. Modern Indian Interpreters of the Bhagavadgita. LC 86-14386. (SUNY Series in Religious Studies). 273p. (C). 1986. 59.50 (*0-88706-297-0*); pap. 19.95 (*0-88706-298-9*) State U NY Pr.

— Radhakrishnan: A Religious Biography. LC 86-30191. 189p. 1987. 59.50 (*0-88706-554-6*); pap. 19.95 (*0-88706-555-4*) State U NY Pr.

***Minor, Sandy.** Holiday Mind Joggers. (Illus.). 55p. (Orig.). 1994. pap. 8.95 (*1-879633-19-1*) Eldersong.

— Mind Joggers. 88p. (Orig.). 1993. pap. 12.95 (*1-879633-13-2*) Eldersong.

— Mind Joggers, Vol. 2. 91p. (Orig.). 1995. pap. 12.95 (*1-879633-21-3*) Eldersong.

Minor, Scott D., jt. auth. see Minor, Mary A.

Minor, T. & Marth, E. H. Staphylococci & Their Significance in Foods. 298p. 1976. 102.75 (*0-444-41339-1*) Elsevier.

***Minor, Terry.** My Dream Slipped Away: Inside Football - Clemson University, NCAA, Other Colleges & the Cleveland Browns. 47p. Date not set. pap. write for info. (*1-882194-13-6*) TN Valley Pub.

Minor, Theodore E. Management of Church Music Programs. 83p. 1991. spiral bd. 14.95 (*0-9630146-0-9*) T Minor Keybd.

Minor, Vern B., jt. auth. see Minor, Jacqueline K.

Minor, Vernon H. Art History's History. 1994. 29.95 (*0-8109-1944-3*) Abrams.

— Critical Theory of Art History. 250p. 1993. pap. text ed. write for info. (*0-13-194606-4*) P-H.

***Minor, Wendell & Minor, Florence F., eds.** Wendell Minor: Art for the Written Word: Twenty-Five Years of Book Cover Art. 1995. write for info. (*0-15-195614-6*); pap. write for info. (*0-15-600212-4*) HarBrace.

Minor, William. Goat Pan. (Illus.). 44p. (Orig.). 1984. pap. 5.95 (*0-9612914-0-0*) Betty's Soup.

— Unzipped Souls: A Jazz Journey Through the Soviet Union. LC 94-37345. (Illus.). 256p. (C). 1995. 24.95 (*1-56639-324-8*) Temple U Pr.

Minor, William, jt. auth. see Oehler, Paul.

Minor, William S., jt. ed. see Broyer, John A.

***Minority Rights Group, ed.** No Longer Invisible: Afro-Latin Americans Today. 336p. 1995. 34.95 (*1-873194-80-3*); pap. 21.95 (*1-873194-85-4*) Paul & Co Pubs.

Minority Rights Group Staff. World Directory of Minorities. 427p. 1990. lib. bdg. 85.00 (*1-55862-016-8*) St James Pr.

Minorsky, ed. see Tadhkirat, Al-Muluk.

Minorsky, Nicholas. Non Linear Oscillation. LC 74-8918. 734p. 1974. reprint ed. 69.50 (*0-88275-186-7*) Krieger.

Minorsky, V., tr. Calligraphers & Painters: A Treatise by Qadi Ahmad, Son of Mir-Munshi. (Occasional Papers Ser.: Vol. 3, No. 2). (Illus.). 1959. pap. 6.00 (*0-934686-06-8*) Freer.

Minorsky, Vladimir. Medieval Iran & Its Neighbors. (Collected Studies: No. CS166). (Illus.). 336p. (C). 1982. reprint ed. lib. bdg. 99.50 (*0-86078-114-3*, Pub. by Variorum UK) Ashgate Pub Co.

Minoru, Yoshioka. Celebration in Darkness. Tadayoshi, Onuma, tr. Bd. with Strangers' Sky. LC 84-23423. LC 84-23423. (Asian Poetry in Translation Ser: Japan: No. 6). 206p. (Orig.). 1985. Set pap. 10.95 (*0-295-96360-3*) U of Wash Pr.

Minoso, Minnie & Fagen, Herb. Just Call Me Minnie: My Six Decades in Baseball. (Illus.). 205p. 1994. 19.95 (*0-915611-90-2*) Sagamore Pub.

Minot, Charles S. The Problem of Age, Growth, & Death. Kastenbaum, Robert, ed. LC 78-22211. (Aging & Old Age Ser.). (Illus.). 1979. reprint ed. lib. bdg. 25.95 (*0-405-11824-4*) Ayer.

Minot, George R. History of the Insurrections in Massachusetts in the Year 1786 & the Rebellion Consequent Thereon. 2nd ed. LC 70-107823. (Select Bibliographies Reprint Ser.). 1977. 21.95 (*0-8369-5218-9*) Ayer.

— History of the Insurrections in Massachusetts in 1786. LC 76-148912. (Era of the American Revolution Ser.). 1971. reprint ed. lib. bdg. 27.50 (*0-306-70100-6*) Da Capo.

Minot, John. Notes on the Classification of Mushrooms. LC 88-63668. 210p. 1989. 35.00 (*0-88000-145-3*) Quarterman.

Minot, John C. The Best Stories of Heroism I Know. 1977. 20.95 (*0-8369-4231-0*, 6042) Ayer.

Minot, Marcia. Eclipse: Poems. 64p. (Orig.). 1992. pap. 9.95 (*1-55605-234-0*) Wyndhall Pr.

Minot, Stephen. Surviving the Flood. LC 85-63551. (Illus.). 306p. 1986. reprint ed. 22.00 (*0-933256-62-0*) Second Chance.

— Three Genres: The Writing of Poetry, Fiction, & Drama. 5th ed. LC 92-20807. 384p. (C). 1993. pap. text ed. write for info. (*0-13-918467-8*) P-H.

Minot, Susan. Folly. LC 92-21035. 256p. 1992. 19.95 (*0-395-60339-0*, Seymour Lawrence) HM.

— Folly. large type ed. LC 92-38329. 1993. 21.95 (*0-7927-1566-7*, Curley Lrg Print) Chivers N Amer.

— Folly. Rosenman, Jane, ed. 288p. 1994. reprint ed. pap. 10.00 (*0-671-74951-X*, WSP) PB.

— Lust & Other Stories. 160p. 1990. pap. 10.00 (*0-671-70455-9*, WSP) PB.

— Monkeys. 1989. pap. 10.00 (*0-671-70361-7*, WSP) PB.

***Minott, Jan.** Skirts & Pants Patterns: Minott Method. 4th ed. 183p. 1992. pap. 17.00 (*0-614-04516-9*) Minott Method.

— Total Pattern Fit Minott Method. (Illus.). 221p. (C). 1991. pap. text ed. 17.00 (*0-9633880-4-5*) Minott Method.

Minoux, Michel, jt. auth. see Gondran, Michel.

Minow, Martha. Making All the Difference: Inclusion, Exclusion & American Law. LC 90-1754. 424p. 1990. 36.95 (*0-8014-2446-1*) Cornell U Pr.

— Making All the Difference: Inclusion, Exclusion & American Law. LC 90-1754. 424p. 1991. reprint ed. pap. 15.95 (*0-8014-9977-1*) Cornell U Pr.

Minow, Martha, ed. Family Matters: Readings on Family Lives & the Law. LC 92-53737. 432p. 1993. 40.00 (*1-56584-017-8*); pap. 24.95 (*1-56584-042-9*) New Press NY.

Minow, Martha, et al, eds. Narrative, Violence, & the Law: The Essays of Robert Cover. (Law, Meaning, & Violence Ser.). 180p. (C). 1992. text ed. 44.50 (*0-472-09495-5*) U of Mich Pr.

Minow, Martin, tr. see Sjoman, Vilgot.

Minow, Nell, jt. auth. see Monks, Robert.

***Minow, Newton & Lamay, Craig.** Abandoned in the Wasteland: Children, Television, & the First Amendment. 224p. 1995. 20.00 (*0-8090-2311-3*) Hill & Wang.

Minow, Newton N. & Sloan, Clifford M. For Great Debates: A New Plan for Future Presidential TV Debates - A Twentieth Century Fund Paper. 71p. (Orig.). (C). 1987. pap. text ed. 10.00 (*0-87078-212-6*) TCFP-PPP.

Minow-Pinkney, Makiko. Virginia Woolf & the Problem of the Subject: Feminine Writing in the Major Novels. (Douglass Series on Women's Lives & the Meaning of Gender). 300p. (C). 1987. text ed. 40.00 (*0-8135-1226-3*) Rutgers U Pr.

Minowa, Shigeo. Book Publishing in a Societal Context: Japan & the West. 155p. (C). 1991. 36.95x (*0-87975-640-3*) Prometheus Bks.

Minowitz, Peter. Profits, Priests, & Princes: Adam Smith's Emancipation of Economics from Politics & Religion. LC 93-18798. 364p. (C). 1993. 45.00 (*0-8047-2166-1*) Stanford U Pr.

Minsberg, David. The Bookmonster. (Illus.). 32p. (J). (ps-00). 1981. 7.50 (*0-940674-00-9*); 27.95 (*0-685-03087-3*) Littlebee.

Minshall, Bert. On Board with the Duke: John Wayne & the Wild Goose. LC 92-27938. 168p. 1992. text ed. 39.95 (*0-929765-13-3*) Seven Locks Pr.

***Minshall, Britt.** Renaissance or Ruin: The Final Saga of a Once Great Church. 426p. 1994. pap. 14.95 (*0-9642773-0-1*) Renaissance Inst.

***Minshall, Sharlene G.** RVing North America: Silver, Single, & Solo. LC 94-96691. (Illus.). 288p. (Orig.). 1995. pap. 12.95 (*0-9643970-0-5*) Gypsy Press.

Minsheu, John. Ductor in Linguas: The Guide into Tongues. LC 78-14754. (ENG & SPA.). 1978. reprint ed. lib. bdg. 150.00 (*0-8201-1321-2*) Schol Facsimiles.

Minshull, Evelyn. Abingdon's Christmas Pageants & Plays. 64p. 1990. pap. 5.25 (*0-687-00425-X*) Abingdon.

— Abingdon's Mother's Day Recitations. 56p. 1989. pap. 4.75 (*0-687-00486-1*) Abingdon.

— Familiar Darknesses: A Novel. LC 93-51260. 192p. (Orig.). 1994. pap. 9.99 (*0-8010-6311-6*) Baker Bk.

Minshull, Evelyn W. But I Thought You Really Loved Me. LC 76-14992. 150p. (YA). (gr. 7 up). 1976. 8.00 (*0-664-32600-5*, Westminster) Westminster John Knox.

Minshull, G. N. The New Europe into the 1990s. 4th rev. ed. (Illus.). 348p. 1990. pap. text ed. 27.50 (*0-340-50512-5*, Pub. by Hodder & Stoughton Ltd UK) Lubrecht & Cramer.

Minsker, K. S., et al. Degradation & Stabilization of Vinylchloride Based Polymers. LC 87-36029. 520p. 1988. 216.00 (*0-08-034857-2*, Pub. by Pergamon Repr UK) Franklin.

Minski, Lawrence, jt. auth. see Calvo, Emily.

***Minskoff, Alan.** Blue Ink Runs Out on a Partly Cloudy Day. 36p. (Orig.). 1994. pap. 12.00 (*0-931659-16-7*) Limberlost Pr.

— Blue Ink Runs Out on a Partly Cloudy Day. deluxe limited ed. 36p. (Orig.). 1994. 25.00 (*0-931659-17-5*) Limberlost Pr.

***Minsky, Alan.** Home Run Kings. LC 94-27731. 1995. write for info. (*1-56799-142-4*, MetroBooks) M Friedman Pub Grp Inc.

Minsky, Hyman P. Can "IT" Happen Again? Essays on Instability & Finance. LC 82-10789. 320p. 1984. pap. text ed. 25.95 (*0-87332-305-X*) M E Sharpe.

— John Maynard Keynes. LC 75-17900. (Essays on the Great Economists Ser.). 181p. 1975. text ed. 42.00 (*0-231-03616-7*) Col U Pr.

— Stabilizing & Unstable Economy. LC 85-22737. 354p. 1986. 42.00 (*0-300-03386-9*) Yale U Pr.

Minsky, Marvin. The Society of Mind. 1988. pap. 14.95 (*0-671-65713-5*, Touchstone Bks) S&S Trade.

Minsky, Marvin, jt. auth. see Harrison, Harry.

Minsky, Marvin L., ed. Semantic Information Processing. LC 68-18239. 440p. 1969. 42.50 (*0-262-13044-0*) MIT Pr.

Minsky, Marvin L. & Papert, Seymour A. Perceptrons: An Introduction to Computational Geometry, Expanded Edition. 275p. 1987. pap. 17.50 (*0-262-63111-3*) MIT Pr.

***Minsky, Rosalind.** Psychoanalysis & Gender: An Introductory Reader. LC 95-16457. (Critical Readers in Theory & Practice). 1995. write for info. (*0-415-09220-5*) Routledge.

Minson, A. C., et al, eds. Viruses & Cancer: Fifty-First Symposium for the Society for General Microbiology, Held at the University of Cambridge, March 1994. LC 93-46636. (Society for General Microbiology Symposium Ser.: No. 51). (Illus.). 330p. (C). 1994. 110.00 (*0-521-45472-7*) Cambridge U Pr.

Minson, Dennis J. Forage in Ruminant Nutrition. (Animal Feeding & Nutrition Ser.). 483p. 1990. text ed. 116.00 (*0-12-498310-3*) Acad Pr.

Minson, Jeffrey. Questions of Conduct: Sexual Harassment, Citizenship, Government. LC 92-30625. 254p. 1993. text ed. 39.95 (*0-312-09121-4*) St Martin.

Minson, Maxine. Angel in the Park. 1983. pap. 1.75 (*0-686-38379-6*) Eldridge Pub.

Minster, Margaret, ed. Herbs: From Cultivation to Cooking. LC 82-13229. (Illus.). 228p. 1981. reprint ed. 16.95 (*0-88289-685-7*) Pelican.

Minstrel of Reims. A Thirteenth-Century Minstrel's Chronicle (Recits d'un Menestrel de Reims) A Translation & Introduction. Levine, Robert, tr. (Studies in French Civilization: Vol. 4). 256p. 1990. lib. bdg. 89.95 (*0-88946-623-8*) E Mellen.

Minta, Stephen. Aguirre. 256p. 1995. pap. 11.95 (*0-8050-3104-9*) H Holt & Co.

— Aguirre: The Re-Creation of a Sixteenth-Century Journey Across South America. LC 93-11679. 208p. 1994. 20.00 (*0-8050-3103-0*) H Holt & Co.

Minta, Steven C., jt. auth. see Clark, Tim W.

Minteer, Catherine. Words & What They Do To You. 128p. 1965. 8.00 (*0-910780-06-4*) Inst Gen Seman.

Mintel, Judith K. Insurance Rate Litigation: A Survey of Judicial Treatment of Insurance Ratemaking & Insurance Rate Regulation. (S. S. Huebner International Ser.). 1983. lib. bdg. 71.00 (*0-89838-139-8*) Huebner Foun Insur.

Minter, ed. see Tirso De Molina.

Minter, D. W., jt. ed. see Cannon, P. F.

Minter, D. W., jt. auth. see Hall, G. S.

Minter, David. A Cultural History of the American Novel: Henry James to William Faulkner. 304p. (C). 1994. 47.95 (*0-521-45285-6*) Cambridge U Pr.

— William Faulkner: His Life & Work. LC 80-13089. 344p. 1982. pap. 15.95 (*0-8018-2463-X*) Johns Hopkins.

Minter, David, ed. see Faulkner, William.

Minter-Dowd, Christine. Finders' Guide to Decorative Arts in the Smithsonian Institution. LC 82-600320. (Finders' Guides Ser.: Vol. 2). (Illus.). 212p. 1983. pap. text ed. 18.50 (*0-87474-637-X*, MIFDP) Smithsonian.

Minter, James F. Big Book of Pencil Pastimes: The Best Word Games, Quizzes & Brain Ticklers. 1991. pap. 6.95 (*0-88486-039-6*) Arrowood Pr.

— Second Big Book of Pencil Pastimes. 1993. pap. 6.95 (*0-88486-075-2*, Bristol Park Bks) Arrowood Pr.

Minter, John, ed. & intro. Enrollment Management Ratios: American Four-Year Colleges & Universities, No. 1. (Financial Management Ratios Ser.). 1052p. 1986. lib. bdg. 139.50 (*0-937767-02-6*) Nat Data Service.

— Enrollment Statistics & Ratios: Private Colleges & Universities Awarding the Master's As the Highest Degree. (Institutional Research Reports). 70p. 1986. lib. bdg. write for info. (*0-937767-12-3*) Nat Data Service.

— Enrollment Statistics & Ratios: Private Colleges Awarding the Bachelor's As the Highest Degree. (Institutional Research Reports). 79p. 1986. lib. bdg. write for info. (*0-937767-06-9*) Nat Data Service.

— Enrollment Statistics & Ratios: Private Universities Awarding the Doctoral's As the Highest Degree. (Institutional Research Reports). 50p. 1987. lib. bdg. write for info. (*0-937767-18-2*) Nat Data Service.

— Enrollment Statistics & Ratios: Public Colleges Awarding the Bachelor's As the Highest Degree. (Institutional Research Reports). 50p. 1986. lib. bdg. write for info. (*0-937767-39-5*) Nat Data Service.

— Enrollment Statistics & Ratios: Public Colleges Awarding the Comprehensive As the Highest Degree. (Institutional Research Reports). 95p. 1986. lib. bdg. write for info. (*0-937767-45-X*) Nat Data Service.

— Enrollment Statistics & Ratios: Public Universities Awarding the Doctoral's As the Highest Degree. (Institutional Research Reports). 55p. 1987. lib. bdg. write for info. (*0-937767-48-4*) Nat Data Service.

— Faculty Compensation Index, 1985-1986: Private Colleges & Universities Awarding the Comprehensive As the Highest Degree. (Institutional Research Reports). 85p. 1987. lib. bdg. write for info. (*0-937767-32-8*) Nat Data Service.

— Faculty Compensation Index, 1985-1986: Private Universities Awarding the Doctoral's As the Highest Degree. (Institutional Research Reports). 60p. 1987. lib. bdg. write for info. (*0-937767-34-4*) Nat Data Service.

— Faculty Compensation Index, 1985-1986: Public Colleges Awarding the Bachelor's As the Highest Degree. (Institutional Research Reports). 65p. 1986. lib. bdg. write for info. (*0-937767-40-9*) Nat Data Service.

— Faculty Compensation Index, 85-86: Private Colleges Awarding the Bachelor's As the Highest Degree. (Institutional Research Reports). 344p. 1986. lib. bdg. write for info. (*0-937767-07-7*) Nat Data Service.

— Faculty Compensation Index, 85-86: Public Colleges & Universities Awarding the Master's As the Highest Degree. (Institutional Research Reports). 171p. 1986. lib. bdg. write for info. (*0-937767-13-1*) Nat Data Service.

Minter, John, ed. Financial Statistics & Ratios: Private Universities Awarding the Doctoral's As the Highest Degree. (Institutional Research Reports). 70p. 1987. lib. bdg. write for info. (*0-937767-17-4*) Nat Data Service.

Minter, John, ed. & intro. Financial Statistics & Ratios: Private Colleges Awarding the Bachelor's As the Highest Degree. (Institutional Research Reports). 50p. 1986. lib. bdg. write for info. (*0-937767-05-0*) Nat Data Service.

— Financial Statistics & Ratios: Public Colleges & Universities Awarding the Comprehensive As the Highest Degree. (Institutional Research Reports). 165p. 1986. lib. bdg. write for info. (*0-937767-44-1*) Nat Data Service.

— Financial Statistics & Ratios: Public Colleges Awarding the Bachelor's As the Highest Degree. (Institutional Research Reports). 95p. 1986. lib. bdg. write for info. (*0-937767-38-7*) Nat Data Service.

— Financial Statistics & Ratios: Public Universities Awarding the Doctoral's As the Highest Degree. (Institutional Research Reports). 100p. 1987. lib. bdg. write for info. (*0-937767-36-0*) Nat Data Service.

— Freshman Class Statistics & Ratios: Private Universities Awarding the Doctoral's As the Highest Degree. (Institutional Research Reports). 50p. 1987. lib. bdg. write for info. (*0-937767-20-4*) Nat Data Service.

M

— Freshman Class Statistics & Ratios: Public Colleges & Universities Awarding the Comprehensive As the Highest Degree. (Institutional Research Reports). 50p. 1986. lib. bdg. write for info. (*0-937767-46-8*) Nat Data Service.

— Freshman Class Statistics & Ratios: Public Colleges Awarding the Bachelor's As the Highest Degree. (Institutional Research Reports). 25p. 1987. lib. bdg. write for info. (*0-937767-41-7*) Nat Data Service.

— Fund Raising Management Ratios One. (Financial Management Ratios Ser.: No. 1). 450p. 1987. lib. bdg. 95.00 (*0-937767-28-X*) Nat Data Service.

— Fund Raising Statistics & Ratios: Private Colleges & Universities Awarding the Master's As the Highest Degree. (Institutional Research Reports). 50p. 1986. lib. bdg. write for info. (*0-937767-10-7*) Nat Data Service.

— Fund Raising Statistics & Ratios: Private Colleges Awarding the Bachelor's As the Highest Degree. (Institutional Research Reports). 50p. 1986. lib. bdg. write for info. (*0-937767-04-2*) Nat Data Service.

— Fund Raising Statistics & Ratios: Public Colleges & Universities Awarding the Comprehensive As the Highest Degree. (Institutional Research Reports). 50p. 1987. lib. bdg. write for info. (*0-937767-43-3*) Nat Data Service.

— Fund Raising Statistics & Ratios: Public Colleges Awarding the Bachelor's As the Highest Degree. (Institutional Research Reports). 50p. lib. bdg. 85.00 (*0-937767-37-9*) Nat Data Service.

— Fund Raising Statistics & Ratios: Public or Private Universities Awarding the Doctoral's As the Highest Degree. 50p. 1987. lib. bdg. write for info. (*0-937767-16-6*) Nat Data Service.

— Fund Raising Statistics & Ratios: Public Universities Awarding the Doctoral's As the Highest Degree. (Institutional Research Reports). 50p. 1987. lib. bdg. write for info. (*0-937767-33-6*) Nat Data Service.

— Management Ratios for Colleges & Universities. (Financial Management Ratios Ser.: No. 3). 550p. (C). 1987. lib. bdg. 125.00 (*0-937767-30-1*) Nat Data Service.

— Management Ratios Number Two for Colleges & Universities. (Financial Management Ratios Ser.: No. 2). 500p. 1986. lib. bdg. write for info. (*0-937767-03-4*) Nat Data Service.

— Tuition-Fees, Financial Aid Statistics: Public Colleges & Universities Awarding the Comprehensive As the Highest Degree. (Institutional Research Reports). 50p. 1987. lib. bdg. write for info. (*0-937767-47-6*) Nat Data Service.

— Tuition-Fees, Financial Aid Statistics: Public Colleges Awarding the Bachelor's As the Highest Degree. (Institutional Research Reports). 50p. 1987. lib. bdg. write for info. (*0-937767-42-5*) Nat Data Service.

— Undergraduate Tuition & Fees: Trends 1977 to 1986. 250p. 1987. lib. bdg. 95.00 (*0-937767-31-X*) Nat Data Service.

Minter, John, intro. Financial Statistics & Ratios: Private Colleges & Universities Awarding the Master's As the Highest Degree. (Institutional Research Reports). 120p. 1986. lib. bdg. write for info. (*0-937767-11-5*) Nat Data Service.

— Freshman Class Statistics & Ratios: Private Colleges Awarding the Bachelor's As the Highest Degree. (Institutional Research Reports). 50p. 1986. lib. bdg. write for info. (*0-937767-08-5*) Nat Data Service.

— Tuition-Fees, Financial Aid Statistics: Private Colleges & Universities Awarding the Master's As the Highest Degree. (Institutional Research Reports). 50p. 1986. lib. bdg. write for info. (*0-937767-15-8*) Nat Data Service.

— Tuition-Fees, Financial Aid Statistics: Private Colleges Awarding the Bachelor's As the Highest Degree. (Institutional Research Reports). 50p. 1986. lib. bdg. write for info. (*0-937767-09-3*) Nat Data Service.

— Tuition-Fees, Financial Aid Statistics: Private Universities Awarding the Doctoral's As the Highest Degree. (Institutional Research Reports). 50p. 1987. lib. bdg. write for info. (*0-937767-21-2*) Nat Data Service.

Minter, Roy. The White Pass: Gateway to the Klondike. (Illus.). 394p. 1987. 24.95 (*0-912006-26-9*); pap. 15.95 (*0-912006-33-1*) U of Alaska Pr.

Minter, Sue. The Healing Garden: Flowers & Plants to Nurture the Body, Senses & Spirit. (Illus.). 160p. 1993. 24.95 (*0-8048-1975-0*) C E Tuttle.

Minter, Tinch, tr. see Karge, Manfred.

Minter, William. Apartheid's Contras: An Inquiry into the Roots of War in Angola & Mozambique. LC 95-41587. 320p. (C). 1994. text ed. 69.95 (*1-85649-265-6*, Pub. by Zed Books UK); pap. 29.95 (*1-85649-266-4*, Pub. by Zed Books UK) Humanities.

— Operation Timber: Pages from the Savimbi Dossier. LC 88-71419. 200p. (C). 1988. 19.95 (*0-86543-103-5*); pap. 6.95 (*0-86543-104-3*) Africa World.

— Portuguese Africa & the West. LC 73-8054. 204p. reprint ed. pap. 58.20 (*0-318-34965-5*, 2030763) Bks Demand.

Minter, William, ed. Africa's Problems...African Initiatives. 50p. 1992. pap. 5.00 (*0-9634238-0-0*) Africa Policy Info.

Minters, Frances. Cinder-Elly. LC 93-14533. (Illus.). 32p. (J). (ps-3). 1994. lib. bdg. 13.99 (*0-670-84417-9*) Viking Child Bks.

Minthorn, P. Y., intro. Sapatq'ayn: Twentieth Century Nez Perce Artists. (Orig.). 1991. pap. text ed. 12.95 (*0-914019-27-9*) NW Interpretive.

Minthorn, Philip Y. Vigil of the Wounded. Kenny, Maurice & Gosciak, Josh, eds. (Illus.). 60p. (Orig.). (C). 1987. pap. 5.95 (*0-936556-15-3*) Contact Two.

Minto, Barbara. The Pyramid Principle: The Logic in Writing & Thinking. 3rd ed. (Illus.). 162p. 1991. 67.50x (*0-273-03345-X*, Pub. by Pitman Pub Ltd UK) Trans-Atl Phila.

Minto, W., ed. see Scott, William B.

Minto, William. Daniel Defoe. Morley, John, ed. LC 68-58386. (English Men of Letters Ser.). reprint ed. lib. bdg. 27.50 (*0-404-51718-8*) AMS Pr.

— Logic, Inductive & Deductive. 1977. 19.95 (*0-8369-6997-9*, 7814) Ayer.

Minton, Arthur J. & Shipka, Thomas A. Philosophy: Paradox & Discovery. 3rd ed. 526p. (C). 1990. pap. text ed. write for info. (*0-07-042432-2*) McGraw.

Minton, Bruce & Stuart, John. Men Who Lead Labor. LC 73-93362. (Essay Index Reprint Ser.). 1977. 21.95 (*0-8369-1309-4*) Ayer.

Minton, David H. Boeing 737. (Aero Ser.: Vol. 37). (Illus.). 112p. (Orig.). 1989. pap. 10.95 (*0-8306-8618-5*, TAB-Aero) TAB Bks.

Minton, Helena. The Canal Bed. LC 84-72463. 1985. 15.95 (*0-914086-52-9*); pap. 9.95 (*0-914086-53-7*) Alicejamesbooks.

Minton, Henry L. Lewis M. Terman: Pioneer in Educational Testing. (American Social Experience Ser.: No. 12). (Illus.). 254p. 1988. 50.00x (*0-8147-5442-2*); pap. 18.50x (*0-8147-5452-X*) NYU Pr.

Minton, Henry L., ed. Gay & Lesbian Studies. LC 92-23738. (Journal of Homosexuality: Vol. 24, Nos. 1-2). (Illus.). 205p. 1993. lib. bdg. 29.95 (*1-56024-307-4*); pap. 12.95 (*1-56023-021-5*) Haworth Pr.

Minton, Henry L. & Schneider, Frank W. Differential Psychology. (Illus.). 514p. (C). 1985. reprint ed. text ed. 32.95x (*0-88133-152-X*) Waveland Pr.

Minton, Janis. Basic Skills Map Workbook. (Basic Skills Workbooks). 32p. (J). (gr. 4-7). 1983. 1.98 (*0-8209-0540-2*, SSW-4) ESP.

— Basic Skills Understanding Instructions Workbook. (Basic Skills Workbooks). 32p. (gr. 4-7). 1983. 1.98 (*0-8209-0580-1*, IW-1) ESP.

— Understanding Instructions. (Language Arts Ser.). 24p. (gr. 3-6). 1979. student ed 5.00 (*0-8209-0322-1*, LA-8) ESP.

— Understanding Maps. (Social Studies Ser.). 24p. (gr. 4-7). 1979. student ed 5.00 (*0-8209-0257-8*, SS-24) ESP.

Minton, M. A., jt. auth. see Whitesell, J. A.

Minton, Mary. Flamenco Love Song. large type ed. 299p. 1994. pap. 16.95 (*1-85389-438-9*, Medcom-Trainex) Ulverscroft.

— The House of Destiny. large type ed. 647p. 1994. 26.95 (*0-7505-0677-6*) Ulverscroft.

— Signposts of Love. large type ed. (Dales Large Print Ser.). 1994. pap. 16.95 (*1-85389-469-9*) Ulverscroft.

— Wheel of Love. large type ed. (Dales Ser.). 284p. 1994. pap. 16.95 (*1-85389-436-2*, Dales) Ulverscroft.

Minton, N. P. & Clarke, D. J., eds. Clostridia. (Biotechnology Handbooks Ser.: Vol. 3). (Illus.). 318p. 1989. 65.00 (*0-306-43261-7*, Plenum Pr) Plenum.

Minton, Paul E. Handbook of Evaporation Technology. LC 86-17978. (Illus.). 390p. 1987. 64.00 (*0-8155-1097-7*) Noyes.

Minton, Robert, jt. auth. see Greene, Howard.

Minton, Roland B., jt. auth. see Smith, Robert T.

Minton, Sandra. Modern Dance: Body & Mind. 2nd ed. (Illus.). 144p. (C). 1992. pap. text ed. 14.95x (*0-89582-233-4*) Morton Pub.

Minton, Sandra C. Choreography: A Basic Approach Using Improvisation. LC 86-10422. (Illus.). 144p. (Orig.). (C). 1986. pap. text ed. 20.00 (*0-87322-071-4*, BMIN0071) Human Kinetics.

Minton, Sandra Cerny. Body & Self: Partners in Movement. LC 88-30383. (Illus.). 196p. 1989. pap. text ed. 20.95 (*0-87322-219-9*, BMIN0219) Human Kinetics.

Minton, Steven. Learning Search Control Knowledge: An Explanation-Based Approach. (C). 1988. lib. bdg. 67.00 (*0-89838-294-7*) Kluwer Ac.

Minton, Steven, ed. Machine Learning Methods for Planning. LC 92-19279. (Series in Machine Learning). 550p. 1993. 44.95 (*1-55860-248-8*) Morgan Kaufmann.

Minton, T. M. Offerings. 400p. 1989. pap. 3.95 (*0-8439-2859-X*) Dorchester Pub Co.

Minton, Wilson P. A Tour of Japan in 1920: An American Missionary's Diary with 129 Photographs. Carstetter, David W., ed. LC 90-53511. (Illus.). 328p. 1992. lib. bdg. 45.00 (*0-89950-593-7*) McFarland & Co.

Mints, Grigori. A Short Introduction to Modal Logic. LC 92-2924. (Center for the Study of Language & Information-Lecture Notes Ser.: No. 30). 112p. (Orig.). (C). 1992. text ed. 34.95 (*0-937073-76-8*); pap. text ed. 14.95 (*0-937073-75-X*) Ctr Study Language.

Mints, Lloyd W. A History of Banking Theory in Great Britain & the United States. LC 45-4815. 319p. reprint ed. pap. 91.00 (*0-8357-8906-3*, 2056779) Bks Demand.

Mintu-Wimsatt, Alma T., jt. auth. see Polonsky, Michael J.

Minturn, Leigh & Kapor, Swaran. Sita's Daughters: Coming Out of Purdah. LC 92-22147. (C). 1993. 45.00 (*0-19-507823-3*); pap. 19.95 (*0-19-508035-1*) OUP.

Minty, Brian & Ashcroft, Colin. Child Care & Adult Crime. 224p. 1988. text ed. 75.00 (*0-7190-2469-2*) St Martin.

Minty, Judith. Dancing the Fault. (University of Central Florida Contemporary Poetry Ser.). 86p. 1991. lib. bdg. 18.95 (*0-8130-1079-9*); pap. 10.95 (*0-8130-1080-2*) U Press Fla.

— Letters to My Daughters. 24p. (Orig.). 1981. pap. 5.00 (*0-932412-03-3*) Mayapple Pr.

— Yellow Dog Journal. 1991. pap. 8.00 (*0-938077-85-6*) Parallax Pr.

Mintyre, David. Hidden Life of Prayer. 1993. pap. 5.99 (*1-55661-365-2*) Bethany Hse.

Mintz, jt. auth. see Leon.

Mintz, Alan. Banished from Their Father's Table: Loss of Faith & Hebrew Autobiography. LC 88-45755. (Jewish Literature & Culture Ser.). 240p. 1989. 39.95 (*0-253-33857-3*) Ind U Pr.

— George Eliot & the Novel of Vocation. LC 77-15510. 224p. 1978. 25.00 (*0-674-34873-7*) HUP.

— Hurban: Responses to Catastrophe in Hebrew Literature. LC 83-23979. 288p. 1984. text ed. 42.00 (*0-231-05634-6*) Col U Pr.

Mintz, Alan, ed. Hebrew in America: Perspectives & Prospects. LC 92-13602. (American Jewish Civilization Ser.). 337p. (C). 1992. 24.95 (*0-8143-2351-0*) Wayne St U Pr.

Mintz, Alan, ed. see Agnon, S. Y.

Mintz, Alex, ed. The Political Economy of Military Spending in the United States. 320p. 1991. 59.95 (*0-415-07595-5*, A8200) Routledge Chapman & Hall.

Mintz, Alex, jt. ed. see Chan, Steve.

Mintz, Alex, jt. ed. see Doron, Gideon.

Mintz, Anne & Varlejs, Jana, eds. Information Ethics: Concerns for Librarianship & the Information Industry. LC 89-43634. 96p. 1990. pap. 13.95 (*0-89950-514-7*) McFarland & Co.

Mintz, Barbara, jt. auth. see Katan, Norma J.

Mintz, Benjamin W. OSHA: History, Law, & Policy. LC 84-11333. 800p. reprint ed. pap. 180.00 (*0-7837-4593-1*, 2044312) Bks Demand.

Mintz, Beth & Schwartz, Michael. The Power Structure of American Business. LC 84-8841. (Illus.). 352p. 1985. 27.50 (*0-226-53108-2*) U Ch Pr.

— The Power Structure of American Business. LC 84-8841. (Illus.). 352p. 1987. pap. text ed. 13.95 (*0-226-53109-0*) U Ch Pr.

Mintz, Bill. Different Drummers. (Illus.). 96p. 1975. pap. 11.95 (*0-8256-2660-9*, AM38035) Music Sales.

Mintz, Elizabeth & Schmeidler, G. The Psychic Thread: Paranormal & Transpersonal Aspects of Psychotherapy. 232p. 1983. 35.95 (*0-89885-139-4*) Human Sci Pr.

***Mintz, Ethan.** Cracking the SAT II: Math Subject Tests, 1996 Edition. (Princeton Review Ser.). 1995. student ed, pap. 17.00 (*0-679-75918-2*) Random.

— Princeton Review Cracking the SAT II: Math 1995 Edition. 1994. pap. 16.00 (*0-679-75353-2*, Villard Bks) Random.

Mintz, Frank P. The Liberty Lobby & the American Right: Race, Conspiracy & Culture. LC 84-10761. (Contributions in Political Science Ser.: No. 121). viii, 251p. 1985. text ed. 59.95 (*0-313-24393-X*, MIL/, Greenwood Pr) Greenwood.

Mintz, Grafton K., ed. see Han, Woo-Keun.

Mintz, Harold K., jt. auth. see Vasile, Albert J.

Mintz, Ilse. American Exports During Business Cycles, 1879-1958. (Occasional Papers: No. 76). 106p. 1961. reprint ed. 27.60 (*0-87014-390-5*) Natl Bur Econ Res.

— Cyclical Fluctuations in the Exports of the United States since 1879. (Studies in Business Cycles: No. 15). 352p. 1967. reprint ed. 91.60 (*0-685-61338-0*); reprint ed. mic. film 44.00 (*0-685-61339-9*) Natl Bur Econ Res.

— Dating Postwar Business Cycles: Methods & Their Application to Western Germany, 1950-67. (Occasional Papers: No. 107). 125p. 1970. reprint ed. 32.50 (*0-87014-212-7*) Natl Bur Econ Res.

— Dating United States Growth Cycles. (Explorations in Economic Research One Ser.: No. 1). 113p. 1974. reprint ed. 35.00 (*0-685-61369-0*) Natl Bur Econ Res.

— Deterioration in the Quality of Foreign Bonds Issued in the United States, 1920-1930. Wilkins, Mira, ed. LC 78-3939. (International Finance Ser.). (Illus.). 1979. reprint ed. lib. bdg. 17.95 (*0-405-11240-8*) Ayer.

— Deterioration in the Quality of Foreign Bonds Issued in the United States, 1920-1930. (General Ser.: No. 52). 112p. 1951. reprint ed. 29.20 (*0-87014-051-5*) Natl Bur Econ Res.

— Trade Balances During Business Cycles: U. S. & Britain since 1880. (Occasional Papers: No. 67). 111p. 1959. reprint ed. 28.90 (*0-87014-381-6*); reprint ed. mic. film 20.00 (*0-685-61322-4*) Natl Bur Econ Res.

Mintz, Ira L., jt. ed. see Wilson, C. Philip.

Mintz, Jack M. & Tsiopoulos, Thomas. Corporate Income Taxation & Foreign Direct Investment in Central & Eastern Europe. LC 92-37602. (FIAS Occasional Paper Ser.: No. 4). 28p. 1992. 6.95 (*0-8213-2301-6*, 12301) World Bank.

Mintz, James W. Jesse. LC 84-80352. (Illus.). 329p. 1984. 14.95 (*0-932807-00-3*) Overmountain Pr.

Mintz, James W., ed. see Ball, Bonnie.

Mintz, James W., ed. see Lonon, James L.

Mintz, Jerome R. The Anarchists of Casas Viejas. LC 93-2425. 1994. pap. 14.95 (*0-253-20854-8*) Ind U Pr.

— Hasidic People: A Place in the New World. 434p. 1992. 50.00 (*0-674-38115-7*) HUP.

— Hasidic People: A Place in the New World. 434p. 1994. pap. text ed. 16.95 (*0-674-38116-5*, MINHAX) HUP.

— Legends of the Hasidim: An Introduction to Hasidic Culture & Oral Tradition in the New World. LC 95-6046. 1995. pap. 30.00 (*1-56821-530-4*) Aronson.

Mintz, Jerome R., jt. ed. see Ben-Amos, Dan.

Mintz, Jerry, et al, eds. The Handbook of Alternative Education. LC 94-13903. 448p. 1994. text ed. 75.00 (*0-02-897303-8*) Macmillan.

***Mintz, Joel A.** Enforcement at the EPA: High Stakes & Hard Choices. LC 95-13922. 1996. write for info. (*0-292-75187-7*) U of Tex Pr.

— State & Local Government Environmental Liability. (Liability Prevention Ser.). 1994. write for info. (*0-615-00167-X*) Clark Boardman Callaghan.

Mintz, Lannon. Wise Hombre Quizzes for Westerners. LC 88-29437. (Illus.). 48p. (Orig.). 1989. pap. 3.95 (*0-86534-128-1*) Sunstone Pr.

Mintz, Lawrence E., ed. Humor in America: A Research Guide to Genres & Topics. LC 87-17600. 256p. 1988. text ed. 55.00 (*0-313-24551-7*, MZH/, Greenwood Pr) Greenwood.

Mintz, Malcolm W. Bikol Dictionary. LC 72-152466. (Hawaii University, Honolulu, Pacific & Asian Linguistics Institute Ser.). 1022p. reprint ed. pap. 180.00 (*0-8357-3602-4*, 2007979) Bks Demand.

— Bikol Grammar Notes. LC 76-152467. (Hawaii University, Honolulu, Pacific & Asian Linguistics Institute Ser.). 287p. reprint ed. pap. 81.80 (*0-8357-7208-X*, 2007980) Bks Demand.

— Bikol Text. LC 73-148650. (Hawaii University, Honolulu, Pacific & Asian Linguistics Institute Ser.). 762p. reprint ed. pap. 180.00 (*0-8357-7209-8*, 2016114) Bks Demand.

Mintz, Malcom W. & Britanico, Jose D. Bikol-English Dictionary. viii, 555p. (Orig.). 1985. pap. 27.50 (*971-10-0212-4*, Pub. by New Day Pub PH) Cellar.

Mintz, Max M. The Generals of Saratoga: John Burgoyne & Horatio Gates. 292p. (C). 1990. 30.00 (*0-300-04778-9*) Yale U Pr.

— The Generals of Saratoga: John Burgoyne & Horatio Gates. (Illus.). 296p. (C). 1992. reprint ed. pap. text ed. 17.00 (*0-300-05261-8*) Yale U Pr.

Mintz, Patricia. Dictionary of Graphic Arts Terms: A Communication Tool for People Who Buy Type & Printing. 328p. 1981. text ed. 32.95 (*0-442-26711-8*) Van Nos Reinhold.

Mintz, Penny. The Complete Cholesterol Counter. (Heart Care Titles Ser.). 256p. 1990. mass mkt. 4.95 (*0-345-36321-3*) Ballantine.

— Thomas Edison: Inventing the Future. ("Great Lives" Biography Ser.). (Illus.). 128p. 1989. pap. 3.95 (*0-449-90378-8*, Columbine) Fawcett.

Mintz, Robert J. & Rubens, James J. Lawsuit Proof. 288p. 1994. pap. 16.95 (*0-9639971-0-6*) F OBrien & Sons.

— Lawsuit Proof: Protecting Your Assets from Lawsuits & Claims. LC 94-79491. (Illus.). (Orig.). 1994. pap. text ed. 19.95 (*0-915905-37-X*) Qwik-Code Pubns.

Mintz, Ruth F., ed. Modern Hebrew Poetry: A Billingual Anthology. 425p. 1966. pap. 14.00 (*0-520-04781-8*) U CA Pr.

Mintz, S., et al. On Marxian Perspectives in Anthropology: Essays in Honor of H. Hoijer, 1981. Maquet, Jaques P. & Daniels, N. C., eds. LC 84-52206. (Other Realities Ser.: Vol. 5). 98p. 1985. 26.25 (*0-89003-178-9*); pap. 16.25 (*0-89003-179-7*) Undena Pubns.

Mintz, Samuel. The Hunting of Leviathan: Seventeenth-Century Reactions to the Materialism & Moral Philosophy of Thomas Hobbes. 199p. reprint ed. pap. 56.80 (*0-318-34826-8*, 2031695) Bks Demand.

Mintz, Samuel I., et al, eds. From Smollett to James: Studies in the Novel & Other Essays Presented to Edgar Johnson. LC 79-25865. 317p. reprint ed. pap. 90.40 (*0-685-15928-0*, 2027068) Bks Demand.

Mintz, Sidney. Caribbean Transformations. 384p. 1989. text ed. 57.00 (*0-231-07114-0*); pap. text ed. 17.00 (*0-231-07115-9*) Col U Pr.

Mintz, Sidney W. Caribbean Transformations. LC 83-19997. 367p. reprint ed. pap. 104.60 (*0-8357-8057-0*, 2034113) Bks Demand.

— Sweetness & Power: The Place of Sugar in Modern History. 1986. pap. 12.95 (*0-14-009233-1*, Penguin Bks) Viking Penguin.

— Taso: Trabajador de la Cana. LC 88-82494. 321p. 1988. pap. 11.50 (*0-940238-73-X*) Ediciones Huracan.

— Worker in the Cane: A Puerto Rican Life History. (Illus.). 320p. 1974. reprint ed. pap. 12.95 (*0-393-00731-6*) Norton.

Mintz, Sidney W., comp. Papers in Caribbean Anthropology. LC 74-123185. (Yale University Publications in Anthropology Reprints Ser.: Nos. 57-64). 252p. 1970. pap. 20.00x (*0-87536-524-8*) HRAFP.

Mintz, Sidney W. & Price, Richard. The Birth of African-American Culture: An Anthropological Perspective. LC 91-41020. 144p. 1992. 25.00 (*0-8070-0916-4*); pap. 12.00 (*0-8070-0917-2*) Beacon Pr.

***Mintz, Steven.** Moralists & Modernizers: America's Pre-Civil War Reformers. LC 94-43690. (American Moment Ser.). 208p. 1995. text ed. 38.95x (*0-8018-5080-0*); pap. text ed. 13.95x (*0-8018-5081-9*) Johns Hopkins.

Mintz, Steven, ed. Hollywood's America: Reflections on the Silver Screen. 256p. (Orig.). (C). 1993. pap. text ed. 13.96 (*1-881089-10-X*) Brandywine Press.

— Native American Voices. (Illus.). 270p. (Orig.). (C). 1994. pap. text ed. 13.96 (*1-881089-25-8*) Brandywine Press.

Mintz, Steven, intro. African American Voices: The Life Cycle of Slavery. 202p. (Orig.). (C). 1993. Net. pap. text ed. 10.96 (*1-881089-11-8*) Brandywine Press.

Mintz, Steven & Kellogg, Susan M. Domestic Revolutions: A Social History of American Family Life. 316p. 1989. pap. 12.95 (*0-02-921291-X*) Free Pr.

***Mintz, Steven L.** Five Eminent Contrarians: Careers, Perspectives, & Investment Tactics. LC 94-72582. 129p. (Orig.). pap. 14.00 (*0-87034-115-4*) Fraser Pub Co.

Mintz, Steven M. Cases in Accounting Ethics & Professionalism. 2nd ed. 1992. text ed. write for info. (*0-07-042504-3*) McGraw.

Mintz, Susan L. Safe Sex Never Tasted So Good. LC 90-188642. (Illus.). 144p. 1990. pap. write for info. (*0-9636037-0-1*) Boner Pubns.

Mintz, Susannah B. Progressive Puzzler: A Crossword Book. 1993. pap. 9.00 (*0-88001-340-0*) Ecco Pr.

Mintzberg, Henry. Mintzberg on Management: Inside the Strange World of Organizations. 256p. 1989. text ed. 35.00 (*0-02-921371-1*) Free Pr.

— The Nature of Managerial Work. (Illus.). (C). 1990. pap. text ed. 43.00 (*0-06-044556-4*) HarpCollege.

— Power in & Around Organizations. (Illus.). 704p. 1983. text ed. 76.00 (*0-13-686857-6*) P-H.

— The Rise & Fall of Strategic Planning. 288p. 1994. text ed. 29.95 (*0-02-921605-2*) Free Pr.

— The Rise & Fall of Strategic Planning. LC 93-39492. 1993. pap. write for info. (*0-13-781824-6*) P-H Gen Ref & Trav.

— Structure in Fives: Designing Effective Organizations. 2nd ed. 320p. 1992. pap. text ed. 31.40 (*0-13-855479-X*) P-H.

An Asterisk (*) at the beginning of an entry indicates that the title is appearing in BIP for the first time.

— Structuring of Organizations. (Theory of Management Policy Ser.). (Illus.). 1978. text ed. 70.00 (*0-13-855270-3*) P-H.

Mintzberg, Henry & Quinn, James B. The Strategy Process: Concepts & Contexts. 2nd ed. 454p. 1992. pap. text ed. 32.00 (*0-13-855370-X*) P-H.

— The Strategy Process: Concepts, Contexts, Cases. 2nd ed. 1104p. 1991. text ed. 46.00 (*0-13-851916-1*) P-H.

Mintzberg, Henry, jt. auth. see Quinn, James B.

Mintzberg, Henry, et al. The Strategy Process. LC 94-19998. 1994. text ed. write for info. (*0-13-556557-X*) P-H.

— The Strategy Process: European Edition. LC 95-1818. 1995. write for info. (*0-13-149626-3*) P-H.

Mintzer, Irving, ed. Confronting Climate Change: Risks, Implications & Responses. (Illus.). 324p. (C). 1992. 84.95 (*0-521-42091-1*); pap. 34.95 (*0-521-42109-8*) Cambridge U Pr.

Mintzer, Irving & Leonard, J. A., eds. Negotiating Climate Change: The Inside Story of the Rio Convention. 300p. (C). 1994. 59.95 (*0-521-47355-1*); pap. 22.95 (*0-521-47914-2*) Cambridge U Pr.

Mintzer, Irving & Shopley, Jonathan. A Matter of Degrees: The Potential for Controlling the Greenhouse Effect. LC 87-50417. 72p. (Orig.). 1987. pap. 10.00 (*0-915825-27-9*) World Resources Inst.

***Mintzer, Irving M.** Implementing the Framework Convention on Climate Change: Incremental Costs & the Role of the GEF. (Global Environmental Facility Working Paper Ser.: No. 4). 44p. 1994. write for info. (*1-884122-03-5*, 72035); 6.95 (*0-88412-203-4*, 72035) World Bank.

Mintzer, Irving M., jt. auth. see Moomaw, William R.

Mintzer, Irving M., et al. Protecting the Ozone Shield: Strategies for Phasing Out CFCs During the 1990s. 30p. (Orig.). 1989. pap. 5.00 (*0-915825-43-0*) World Resources Inst.

Mintzer, Richard. The Longest Aisle: An Offbeat Guide to Wedding Planning. LC 94-20506. 1994. pap. 9.95 (*0-8065-1575-9*) Carol Pub Group.

— The Unofficial Secretary's Handbook. (Illus.). 112p. 1991. mass mkt. 6.95 (*0-452-25180-X*, Plume) NAL-Dutton.

Minucci, Mary B. The World Around Me: Exploring Home, Friends, Family, Transportation, & Community. Hayes, Martha, ed. (Creative Concept Ser.). (Illus.). 48p. 1990. pap. 6.95 (*1-878727-04-4*) First Teacher.

Minucci, Mary B., ed. see Pfeffer, Wendy.

Minuchin, Salvador. Families & Family Therapy. LC 73-89710. 268p. 1974. 26.50 (*0-674-29236-7*) HUP.

— Family Healing: Tales of Hope & Renewal from Family Therapy. 1994. pap. 12.00 (*0-671-88099-3*, Touchstone Bks) S&S Trade.

— Family Kaleidoscope. 248p. 1984. 22.00 (*0-674-29230-8*) HUP.

— Family Kaleidoscope: Images of Violence & Healing. 303p. 1981. pap. text ed. 14.95 (*0-674-29231-6*) HUP.

Minuchin, Salvador & Fishman, H. Charles. Family Therapy Techniques. LC 80-25392. (Illus.). 352p. 1990. 26.50 (*0-674-29410-6*) HUP.

Minuchin, Salvador & Nichols, Michael P. Family Healing: Tales of Hope & Renewal from Family Therapy. LC 92-23854. 1992. 24.95 (*0-02-921295-2*) Free Pr.

Minuchin, Salvador, jt. auth. see Elizur, Joel.

Minuchin, Salvador, et al. Psychosomatic Families: Anorexia Nervosa in Context. 351p. 1978. 29.95 (*0-674-72220-5*) HUP.

Minugh, jt. auth. see Hirsch.

Minus, Paul M., ed. The Ethics of Business in a Global Economy. LC 93-7110. (Issues in Business Ethics Ser.: Vol. 4). 160p. 1993. lib. bdg. 59.00 (*0-7923-9334-1*) Kluwer Ac.

Minutoli, Armando. Medjugorje, A Pilgrims Journey. 224p. (Orig.). 1991. pap. 9.95 (*0-9630544-0-6*) Mrng Star NY.

Minyard, John D. Mode & Value in the De Rerum Natura: A Study in Lucretius' Metrical Language. 199p. (Orig.). 1978. pap. text ed. 44.00 (*3-515-02569-3*) Coronet Bks.

Minzer, Marilyn K., et al. Damages in Tort Actions, 10 vols., Set. Updates. 1982. ring bd. write for info. (*0-8205-1309-1*) Bender.

Minzhu, Han, ed. Cries for Democracy: Writings & Speeches from the 1989 Chinese Democracy Movement. (Illus.). 300p. (Orig.). 1990. text ed. 55.00 (*0-691-03146-0*); pap. text ed. 16.95 (*0-691-00857-4*) Princeton U Pr.

Minzner, Pamela B., jt. auth. see Laurence, Robert.

Mioduski, T. & Salomon, M., eds. Scandium, Yttrium, Lanthanum & Lanthanide Halides in Nonaqueous Solvents. (Illus.). 418p. 1985. 155.00 (*0-08-030709-4*, Pub. by PPL UK) Elsevier.

Miola, A., et al, eds. Design & Implementation of Symbolic Computation Systems: International Symposium DISCO '90 Capri, Italy, April 10-12, 1990 Proceedings. (Lecture Notes in Computer Science Ser.: Vol. 429). xii, 284p. 1990. pap. 32.70 (*0-387-52531-9*) Spr-Verlag.

Miola, Alfonso. Computing Tools for Scientific Problem Solving. 181p. 1990. text ed. 55.00 (*0-12-498325-1*) Acad Pr.

Miola, Alfonso, ed. Design & Implementation of Symbolic Computation Systems: International Symposium, DISCO '93, Gmunden, Austria, September 1993: Proceedings. LC 93-21040. (Lecture Notes in Computer Science Ser.: Vol. 722). 1993. 54.00 (*0-387-57235-X*) Spr-Verlag.

Miola, Robert S. Shakespeare & Classical Comedy: The Influence of Plautus & Terence. 240p. 1995. 45.00 (*0-19-818269-4*) OUP.

— Shakespeare & Classical Tragedy: The Influence of Seneca. 240p. 1992. 49.95 (*0-19-811264-5*) OUP.

— Shakespeare's Rome. LC 83-1777. 244p. 1983. 44.95 (*0-521-25307-1*) Cambridge U Pr.

Mioli, V. A., ed. Virus Hepatitis & Kidney. (Journal: Nephron: Vol. 61, No. 3, 1992). (Illus.). 128p. 1992. pap. 52.00 (*3-8055-5621-7*) S Karger.

Mionczynski, John. The Pack Goat. LC 92-16298. (Illus.). 147p. 1992. pap. 15.95 (*0-87108-828-2*) Pruett.

Miotto, Enrico. The Universe: Origin & Evolution. LC 94-3839. (J). 1994. lib. bdg. 22.80 (*0-8114-3334-X*) Raintree Steck-V.

Miour, Michael, ed. see Hobbs, Christopher.

Miovic, Michael, ed. see Hobbs, Christopher.

Miquel, F. A. Illustration de la Flora de la Archipol Indian. (Illus.). 114p. (C). 1983. 60.00 (*0-685-22302-7*, Scientific) St Mut.

— Illustration de la Flore de l'Archipel Indian. (C). 1988. text ed. 60.00 (*0-685-44242-X*, Scientific) St Mut.

Miquel, Friedrich A. Illustrations de la Flore de l'Archipel Indien. (Illus.). x, 112p. 1983. reprint ed. 58.50 (*0-685-38723-2*, 000159) Koeltz Sci Bks.

Miquel I Verges, Jose Maria. Diccionario de Insurgentes. (SPA.). 29.95 (*0-7859-0934-6*, S-12335) Fr & Eur.

Miquel, Jaime, et al, eds. Handbook of Free Radicals & Antioxidants in Biomedicine, Vol. I. 352p. 1988. 185.95 (*0-8493-3268-0*, RB170) CRC Pr.

— Handbook of Free Radicals & Antioxidants in Biomedicine, Vol. II. 384p. 1988. 185.95 (*0-8493-3269-9*, RB170) CRC Pr.

— Handbook of Free Radicals & Antioxidants in Biomedicine, Vol. III. 328p. 1988. 185.95 (*0-8493-3270-2*, RB170) CRC Pr.

— Handbook of Free Radicals & Antioxidants in Biomedicine, Vols. I-III. 1988. write for info. (*0-318-63782-0*, RB170) CRC Pr.

Miquel, Jean. Vocabulaire Pratique de la Philosophie: Practical Vocabulary of Philosophy. 260p. (FRE.). 1974. pap. 12.95 (*0-8288-6220-6*, M-6412) Fr & Eur.

***Miquel, Pierre.** Dictionnaire Symbolique des Animaux. 1991. write for info. (*0-7859-8660-X*, 286377106X) Fr & Eur.

Miquelon, Dale B. Dugard of Rouen, French Trace to Canada & the West Indies, 1729-1770. LC 79-345926. (Illus.). 294p. reprint ed. pap. 83.80 (*0-7837-1150-6*, 2041679) Bks Demand.

Mir, Afzal, et al. An Aid to the MRCP VIVA. (Illus.). 332p. (Orig.). 1992. pap. text ed. 36.00 (*0-443-04659-X*) Churchill.

Mir Ahmed Ali, S. V., tr. The Qur'an. 520p. 1991. pap. 5.95 (*0-9630687-0-9*) Quran Soc.

Mir, Mustansir. Coherence in the Qur'an. American Trust Publications, ed. 125p. 1987. pap. 7.00 (*0-89259-065-3*) Am Trust Pubns.

— Verbal Idioms of the Qur'an. (Michigan Series on the Middle East: No. 1). 378p. (Orig.). 1989. pap. 21.95 (*0-932098-21-5*) UM Ctr MENAS.

Mir, Mustansir & Fossum, Jarl E., eds. Literary Heritage of Classical Islam: Arabic & Islamic Studies in Honor of James A. Bellamy. LC 93-785. 288p. 1993. 35.00 (*0-87850-099-5*) Darwin Pr.

Mir, Mustsir. Verbal Patterns of the Qur'an. 1989. 21.95 (*0-86685-471-1*) Intl Bk Ctr.

Mir, Pedro. Countersong to Walt Whitman & Other Poems. Walsh, Donald D., tr. LC 92-74943. 164p. (Orig.). 1993. pap. 12.95 (*0-9632363-3-4*) Azul Edits.

MIR Publishers, tr. see Agronomov, A., et al.

MIR Publishers, tr. see Alexeyev, Vladimir.

MIR Publishers, tr. see Kireev, V.

MIR Publishers, tr. see Kurlyandsky, V.

MIR Publishers, tr. see Molchanov, V., et al.

MIR Publishers, tr. see Pavlov, Boris & Terentyev, Alexander.

MIR Publishers, tr. see Petrovsky, Boris, et al.

MIR Publishers, tr. see Reutov, O.

MIR Publishers, tr. see Zeueke, G., et al, eds.

MIR Publishers Staff, ed. Lenin & Gorky: Letters, Reminiscences, Articles. (Illus.). 429p. 1973. 25.00 (*0-8464-0555-5*) Beekman Pubs.

Mir Valiuddin. Love of God: A Sufic Approach. LC 85-27481. ix, 205p. 1985. reprint ed. lib. bdg. 27.00x (*0-89370-577-2*) Borgo Pr.

Mira, C. Chaotic Dynamics: From the One-Dimensional Endomorphism to the Two-Dimensional Diffeomorphism. 472p. (C). 1987. text ed. 87.00 (*9971-5-0324-7*) World Scientific Pub.

Mira, C., jt. auth. see Gardini, L.

Mira, C., jt. auth. see Gumowski, Igor.

Mira, C., et al, eds. Iteration Theory. 400p. (C). 1991. text ed. 118.00 (*981-02-0611-9*) World Scientific Pub.

Mira, J., et al, eds. New Trends in Neural Computation: Proceedings of the International Workshop on Artificial Neural Networks IWANN '93, Sitges, Spain, June 9 - 11, 1993. (Lecture Notes in Computer Science Ser.: Vol. 686). xvi, 746p. 1993. pap. 107.00 (*0-387-56798-4*) Spr-Verlag.

Mira, K. K. Police Administration in Ancient India. (C). 1987. 20.00 (*81-7099-005-X*, Pub. by Mittal II) S Asia.

Mira, Mary P., et al. Traumatic Brain Injury in Children & Adolescents: A Sourcebook for Teachers & Other School Personnel. LC 92-3454. 152p. (Orig.). 1992. pap. text ed. 17.00 (*0-89079-531-2*, 4037) PRO-ED.

***Mira T.** A Sponsorship Guide for All Twelve Step Programs: Advice for Recovery Related Problems. 176p. 1995. pap. 16.95 (*0-945456-18-2*) PT Pubns.

***Mirabach & Company Staff.** The Official Guide to One-Write Plus. 1995. 24.99 (*0-7821-1734-1*) Sybex.

***Mirabal, Robert.** Skeleton of a Bridge. 116p. (Orig.). 1994. pap. 10.00 (*1-883968-02-X*) Blinking Yellow.

Mirabeau, Honore. Discours. (FRE.). 1973. pap. 10.95 (*0-7859-4005-7*) Fr & Eur.

Mirabeau, Honore G. Erotika Biblion. rev. ed. LC 78-22290. reprint ed. 47.50 (*0-404-61527-9*) AMS Pr.

— Oeuvres de Mirabeau, 8 Vols, Set. LC 79-172736. reprint ed. 160.00 (*0-404-07360-3*) AMS Pr.

Mirabehn. The Spirit's Pilgrimage. LC 84-6071. (Illus.). 336p. 1984. reprint ed. 16.95 (*0-915556-12-X*); reprint ed. pap. 9.95 (*0-915556-13-8*) Great Ocean.

***Mirabella.** In & Out of Vogue: A Memoir. 1995. (*0-385-42613-5*) Doubleday.

— Internal Reflection Spectroscopy: Methods & Techniques. LC 92-26050. (Practical Spectroscopy Ser.: Vol. 15). 384p. 1992. 160.00 (*0-8247-8730-7*) Dekker.

Mirabella, M. Bella, jt. ed. see Davis, Lennard J.

Mirabelli, Eugene. The World at Noon. 386p. 1994. pap. 13.00 (*1-55071-000-1*) Guernica Editions.

Mirabelli, Margaret, ed. see Boyd, Shylah.

Mirabelli, Margaret, ed. see Collier, Zena.

Mirabelli, Margaret, ed. see Nelson, Shirley.

Mirabelli, Margaret, ed. see Swift, Edward.

Mirabello, Mark L. The Odin Brotherhood. (Orig.). 1992. pap. text ed. 9.95 (*1-55818-198-9*, Sure Fire) Holmes Pub.

Mirabi, Mohsen. The Chronically Mentally Ill: Research & Services. LC 84-6799. 352p. 1984. text ed. 37.50 (*0-88331-118-6*) Luce.

Mirabile, Lisa, ed. International Directory of Company Histories, Vol. II. 1990. text ed. 135.00 (*1-55862-012-5*) St James Pr.

Mirabile, M. Analytical & Experimental Fracture Mechanics. Sih, G. C., ed. 970p. (C). 1981. lib. bdg. 183.00 (*90-286-0890-7*) Kluwer Ac.

Mirabito, Michael M. The New Communications Technologies. 2nd ed. (Illus.). 272p. 1993. pap. 29.95 (*0-240-80180-6*, Focal) Buttrwrth-Heinemann.

— The Radio GM New Communication Technologies. 2nd ed. LC 93-35387. 1993. write for info. (*0-240-80163-6*, Focal) Buttrwrth-Heinemann.

Mirabito, Michael M. & Morgenstern, Barbara L. New Communication Technologies. (Illus.). 244p. 1989. pap. 28.95 (*0-240-80012-5*, Focal) Buttrwrth-Heinemann.

Mirable, Lisa. The Berlin Wall. (Turning Points in World History Ser.). (Illus.). 64p. (YA). (gr. 7 up). 1991. lib. bdg. 14.95 (*0-382-24133-9*); pap. 7.95 (*0-382-24140-1*) Silver Burdett Pr.

Mirachandani, G. G. Massive Mandate for Rajiv Gandhi. 1985. 24.95 (*0-318-36588-X*) Asia Bk Corp.

Miracle, Andrew, jt. ed. see Suggs, David.

Miracle, Andrew W., Jr. & Rees, C. Roger. Lessons of the Locker Room: The Myth of School Sports. 243p. (C). 1994. 25.95 (*0-87975-879-1*) Prometheus Bks.

Miracle, Andrew W., jt. ed. see Rees, C. Roger.

Miracle, Berniece B. & Miracle, Mona R. My Sister Marilyn: A Memoir of Marilyn Monroe. 1994. 19.95 (*1-56512-070-1*) Algonquin Bks.

— My Sister Marilyn: A Memoir of Marilyn Monroe. 256p. Date not set. pap. 12.00 (*1-57297-026-X*, Berkley Trade) Berkley Pub.

Miracle, D., et al, eds. Intermetallic Matrix Composites II. (Materials Research Society Symposium Proceedings Ser.: Vol. 273). 1992. text ed. 62.00 (*1-55899-168-9*) Materials Res.

Miracle Distribution Center Staff. An Introduction to "A Course in Miracles" 43p. (Orig.). 1987. pap. 1.95 (*0-9618309-0-5*) Miracle Dist.

Miracle, G. E., jt. auth. see Rijkens, R.

Miracle, Gordon E. & Nevett, T. R. Voluntary Regulation of Advertising in the United Kingdom & the United States. 352p. 1987. text ed. 45.00 (*0-669-13135-0*) Free Pr.

Miracle, Marvin P. Maize in Tropical Africa. (Illus.). 346p. 1966. 25.00 (*0-299-03850-5*) U of Wis Pr.

Miracle, Mona R., jt. auth. see Miracle, Berniece B.

Miraftabi, Morteza. Mystical Realities: Iranian Short Stories. Azarmsa, Reza, tr. 138p. 1993. pap. 10.95 (*0-9636288-0-1*) Favor Pub.

Miraglia, Luigi. Comparative Legal Philosophies Applied to Legal Institutions. 1977. lib. bdg. 59.95 (*0-8490-1653-3*) Gordon Pr.

— Comparative Legal Philosophy Applied to Legal Institutions. (Modern Legal Philosophy Ser.: Vol. 3). xl, 793p. 1969. reprint ed. 37.50 (*0-8377-2427-9*) Rothman.

Mirak, M. L., jt. auth. see Calasso, M. G.

Mirak, Robert. Torn Between Two Lands: Armenians in America, 1890 to World War I. (Armenian Texts & Studies: No. 7). (Illus.). 378p. 1984. reprint ed. pap. 12.95 (*0-674-89541-X*) HUP.

Mirakhor, Abbas, jt. auth. see Iqbal, Zubair.

Mirakhor, Abbas, jt. ed. see Khan, Muhsin S.

Miraldi, Robert. Muckraking & Objectivity: Journalism's Colliding Traditions. LC 89-26010. (Contributions to the Study of Mass Media & Communications Ser.: No. 18). 200p. 1990. text ed. 45.00 (*0-313-27298-0*, MMQ/, Greenwood Pr) Greenwood.

Miralejos, Carlos. Rabid Beasts. LC 93-61697. 216p. (Orig.). 1994. pap. 14.95 (*0-9625266-3-0*) Outer Space Pr.

Miralles, Ana & Segura, Antonio. Eva Medusa. Simmons, Julie, ed. Nonis, Michela, tr. (Illus.). 48p. 1993. reprint ed. text ed. 14.95 (*1-56862-016-0*) Tundra MA.

***Miralles, Francesc.** Llorens Artigas: Catalogo de Obra. (Grandes Monografias). (Illus.). 432p. (ENG & SPA.). 1993. 600.00 (*84-343-0701-4*) Elliots Bks.

Miralles, Francesc & Alzueta, Miquel. Alvar. (Illus.). 359p. (ENG, FRE & JPN.). 1993. 75.00 (*0-9636243-0-X*) E Newman.

Miralles, Francesc, jt. auth. see Fontbona, Francesc.

Miralles, Maria A. A Matter of Life & Death: Health-seeking Behavior of Guatemalan Refugees in South Florida. LC 88-36497. (Immigrant Communities & Ethnic Minorities in the U. S. & Canada Ser.: No. 52). 1989. 42.50 (*0-404-19462-1*) AMS Pr.

Mirambel, Andre. Petit Dictionnaire Francais-Grec Moderne et Grec Moderne-Francais: Small Modern Greek - French, French - Modern Greek Dictionary. 486p. (FRE & GRE.). 1969. 49.95 (*0-8288-6610-4*, M-6413) Fr & Eur.

Miramontes, David J. How to Deal with Sexual Harassment. LC 85-117560. 110p. (Orig.). 1982. pap. text ed. 16.95 (*0-934913-00-5*) Network CA Comm.

Miramontes, Eduardo Z., jt. ed. see Clement, Norris C.

Miramontes, Ofelia, jt. auth. see Howe, Kenneth R.

Mirams, Mike & McElherton, Paul. The Quality Tool Kit: Gaining & Maintaining BS5750 & ISO 9000. (Financial Times Management Ser.). 224p. 1994. pap. 77.50x (*0-273-60616-6*, Pub. by Pitman Pub Ltd UK) Trans-Atl Phila.

Miran-Khan, Karim, jt. auth. see Brukner, Peter.

***Miranda.** Magic Drum: Stories from Africa's Savannah, Sea, & Skies. 1995. 12.95 (*9966-884-05-X*) Nocturnal Sun.

Miranda, Altina. Love on an Animal Farm. (Illus.). 32p. (Orig.). (J). 1993. pap. 8.95 (*0-86534-202-4*) Sunstone Pr.

Miranda, Anne. Baby-Sit, Vol. 1. (J). (ps). 1990. 9.95 (*0-316-57454-6*, Joy St Bks) Little.

— Baby Talk. (Lift-&-Look Flap Bks.). (Illus.). 16p. (J). (ps). 1987. 9.95 (*0-525-44319-3*, 0772-230, DCB) Dutton Child Bks.

— Baby Walk. (Lift-&-Look Flap Bks.). (Illus.). 14p. (J). (ps). 1988. 8.95 (*0-525-44421-1*, DCB) Dutton Child Bks.

— The Elephant at the Waldorf. LC 93-33804. (Illus.). 32p. (J). (gr. k-3). 1995. lib. bdg. 14.95 (*0-8167-3452-6*) BrdgeWater.

— Night Songs. LC 92-251. (Illus.). 32p. (J). (ps-1). 1993. text ed. 13.95 (*0-02-767250-6*, Bradbury S&S) S&S Childrens.

***Miranda, Anne M.** Counting: A Book about Counting. Crawford, Jean, ed. (Snugglebug Bks.). (Illus.). 24p. (J). (ps). 1994. lib. bdg. write for info. (*0-7835-4502-9*) Time-Life.

— Does a Mouse Have a House? LC 93-20587. (Illus.). 32p. (J). (ps-1). 1994. write for info. (*0-02-767251-4*, Bradbury S&S) S&S Childrens.

— What Do You Hear? A Book about Animal Sounds. Crawford, Jean, ed. (Snugglebug Bks.). (Illus.). 24p. (J). (ps). 1994. write for info. (*0-7835-4500-2*) Time-Life.

Miranda, C. Partial Differential Equations of Elliptic Type. 2nd rev. ed. LC 71-75930. (Ergebnisse der Mathematik und Ihrer Grenzgebiete Ser.: Vol. 2). 1970. 49.00 (*0-387-04804-9*) Spr-Verlag.

Miranda, Carlos R. The Stroessner Era: Authoritarian Rule in Paraguay. 177p. (C). 1990. text ed. 52.00 (*0-8133-0995-6*) Westview.

Miranda, D. R. & Langrehr, D., eds. The ICU -- A Cost Benefit Analysis. 236p. 1987. 106.25 (*0-444-80823-X*, Excerpta Medica) Elsevier.

Miranda, D. Reis, et al, eds. Management of Intensive Care. (Developments in Critical Care, Medicine, & Anesthesiology Ser.). (C). 1990. lib. bdg. 112.50 (*0-7923-0754-2*) Kluwer Ac.

Miranda, Elizabeth, jt. ed. see Brothers, Theresa.

Miranda, Eve. Fragrant Flowers of the South. LC 91-19270. (Illus.). 126p. 1991. 19.95 (*1-56164-000-X*); pap. 14.95 (*1-56164-002-6*) Pineapple Pr.

Miranda, Evelina O. & Magsino, Romula, eds. Teaching, Schools & Society. 444p. 1990. 100.00 (*1-85000-687-3*, Falmer Pr); pap. 38.00 (*1-85000-688-1*, Falmer Pr) Taylor & Francis.

Miranda, Fausto C. & Lacy, John C. Mining Law & Regulations of Mexico 1992-1993. 263p. 1993. student ed, disk 125.00 (*0-929047-37-0*, MEX2) Rocky Mtn Mineral Law Found.

Miranda-Feliciano, Evelyn, ed. All Things to All Men: An Introduction to Missions in Filipino Culture. 63p. (Orig.). (C). 1989. pap. 5.00 (*971-10-0387-2*, Pub. by New Day Pub PH) Cellar.

Miranda, Gary. Following a River: Portland's Congregation Neveh Shalom 1869-1989. (Illus.). 170p. 1989. 15.00 (*0-685-29868-X*) Congregation Neveh Shalom.

— Grace Period. LC 82-61373. (Contemporary Poets Ser.). 72p. 1983. pap. 8.95 (*0-691-01406-X*) Princeton U Pr.

— Listeners at the Breathing Place. LC 78-54153. (Contemporary Poets Ser.). 80p. 1978. pap. 8.95 (*0-691-01353-5*) Princeton U Pr.

Miranda, J. B., jt. auth. see Hallauer, Arnel R.

Miranda, James. Wasting My Life. Crowder, R., ed. LC 93-72729. (Illus.). 132p. (C). 1993. 21.95 (*0-935763-02-3*); pap. 9.95 (*0-935763-03-1*) Chester Hse Pubs.

Miranda, Jeanne, ed. Mental Disorders in Primary Care. (Health Ser.). 490p. 1994. 49.95 (*1-55542-660-3*) Jossey-Bass.

Miranda, Jose P. Being & the Messiah: The Message of St. John. LC 77-5388. Orig. Title: El Ser y el Mesias. 255p. (Orig.). reprint ed. pap. 72.70 (*0-8357-8816-4*, 2033467) Bks Demand.

— Communism in the Bible. Barr, Robert R., tr. LC 81-16936. Orig. Title: Comunismo En la Biblia. 95p. (Orig.). reprint ed. pap. 27.10 (*0-7837-5500-7*, 2045270) Bks Demand.

— Marx Against the Marxists: The Christian Humanism of Karl Marx. Drury, John, tr. LC 80-14415. Orig. Title: El Christianism de Marx. 332p. (Orig.). reprint ed. pap. 94.70 (*0-7837-5517-1*, 2045287) Bks Demand.

Miranda, Juan C. Church Growth Manual. Lamigueiro, Fernando, ed. Orig. Title: Manual De Iglecrecimiento. 192p. 1985. 5.95 (*0-8297-0707-7*) Life Pubs Intl.

Miranda, Julia & Lopez, Maria J. Entrelazos. LC 91-73978. (Coleccion Caniqui Ser.). 220p. (Orig.). (SPA.). 1992. pap. 19.95 (*0-89729-616-8*) Ediciones.

Miranda, Lourdes R. Hispanic Women in the United States: A Puerto Rican Woman's Perspective. LC 86-62281. 42p. (Orig.). 1986. pap. 3.00 (*0-9617524-0-8*) Miranda Assocs.

Miranda, M., jt. auth. see Massari, U.

M

Miranda, M., et al, eds. Calculus of Variations & Partial Differential Equations. (Lecture Notes in Mathematics Ser.: Vol. 1340). x, 301p. 1988. pap. 28.60 (*0-685-21872-4*) Spr-Verlag.

Miranda, Maio, tr. see Kaplan, Stuart R.

Miranda, Prashant. Avatar & Incarnation: A Comparative Analysis. 1990. 19.50 (*81-85151-42-3*, Pub. by Harman Pub Hse II) S Asia.

***Miranda, Rick.** Algebraic Curves & Riemann Surfaces. LC 95-1947. (Graduate Studies in Mathematics: Vol. 5). 1995. write for info. (*0-8218-0268-2*) Am Math.

Miranda, Roger & Ratliff, William. The Civil War in Nicaragua: Inside the Sandinistas. 298p. (C). 1992. 34.95 (*1-56000-064-3*) Transaction Pubs.

— The Civil War in Nicaragua: Inside the Sandinistas. 298p. (C). 1994. pap. 21.95 (*1-56000-761-3*) Transaction Pubs.

***Miranda, Rosalind, ed.** The Book of Cruising: Cruising Around the World West to East, Vol. 2. (Illus.). 464p. (Orig.). 1993. pap. text ed. 29.95 (*1-880465-03-5*) Chiodi Advert.

— The Book of Cruising: Introduction to Cruising, Vol. 1. (Illus.). 148p. (Orig.). 1991. pap. text ed. 12.95 (*1-880465-02-7*) Chiodi Advert.

Miranda, Tom, jt. auth. see Barringer, Bernie.

Miranda, Veronica. Esa Antigua Constancia: That Ancient Devotion. McEwan, Angela, tr. LC 93-78776. (Coleccion Luz Bilingue Ser.). (Illus.). 80p. (ENG & SPA.). 1993. 12.50 (*0-9634009-1-6*) Luz Bilingual.

Miranda, Victoria & Fenini, Camilo. Al Filo de un Cansancio Apatrida: Poemas; On the Edge of a Countryless Weariness: Poems. Fogel, Daniel et al, trs. LC 86-21022. 56p. (Orig.). (ENG & SPA.). 1986. Bilingual ed. pap. 5.00 (*0-910383-24-3*) Ism Pr.

Miranda, Yolanda O. The Sleepwalkers' Ballad: Balada Sonambula De los Desterrados Del Sueno: un Punto Que Se Pierde En la Distancia. Cerosaletti, Mark & Smith, Denise, trs. 223p. (Orig.). (ENG & SPA.). 1991. pap. text ed. 13.00 (*0-918454-89-1*) Senda Nueva.

Mirande, Alfredo. The Chicano Experience: An Alternative Perspective. LC 84-40292. 281p. (C). 1985. pap. text ed. 11.95 (*0-268-00749-7*) U of Notre Dame Pr.

— Gringo Justice. LC 86-40580. 272p. 1987. text ed. 29.95 (*0-268-01012-9*) U of Notre Dame Pr.

— Gringo Justice. LC 86-40580. 261p. (C). 1990. pap. text ed. 13.95x (*0-268-01023-4*) U of Notre Dame Pr.

Mirande, Alfredo & Enriquez, Evangelina. La Chicana: The Mexican-American Woman. LC 79-13536. (Illus.). x, 284p. (C). 1981. reprint ed. pap. text ed. 13.95 (*0-226-53160-0*) U Ch Pr.

***Mirandola, Pico D.** Kabbalistic Conclusions. 1993. pap. 3.95 (*1-55818-232-2*) Holmes Pub.

Mirandola, Pico D. & Francesco, Giovanni. Here Is Coteyned the Lyfe of Joan Picus Erle of Myrandula. More, T., tr. LC 77-7421. (English Experience Ser.: No. 884). 1977. reprint ed. lib. bdg. 35.00 (*90-221-0884-8*) Walter J Johnson.

***Miranker, Cathy & Elliot, Alison.** The Computer Museum Guide to the Best Software for Kids. 1995. pap. 15.00 (*0-06-273376-1*) HarpC.

Miranker, Daniel. TREAT: A New & Efficient Match Algorithm for AI Production Systems. (Research Notes in Artificial Intelligence Ser.). 140p. 1989. 29.95 (*0-934613-71-0*) Morgan Kaufmann.

— Treat: A New & Efficient Match Algorithm for AI Production Systems. 144p. (C). 1989. pap. text ed. 200.00 (*0-273-08793-2*, Pub. by Pitman Pubng UK) St Mut.

Miranker, W. L. & Toupin, R. A., eds. Accurate Scientific Computations. (Lecture Notes in Computer Science Ser.: Vol. 235). xiii, 205p. 1986. pap. 33.00 (*0-387-16798-6*) Spr-Verlag.

Miranker, Willard L. Numerical Methods for Stiff Equations & Singular Perturbation Problems. (Mathematics & Its Applications Ser.: No. 5). 216p. 1980. lib. bdg. 69.00 (*90-277-1107-0*) Kluwer Ac.

Miranker, Willard L., jt. auth. see Kulisch, Ulrich W.

Miransky, V. A. Dynamical Symmetry Breaking in Quantum Field Theories. 500p. 1994. text ed. 99.00 (*981-02-1558-4*) World Scientific Pub.

Mirante, Edith T. Burmese Looking Glass: A Human Rights Adventure & a Jungle Revolution. 352p. 1994. pap. 11.00 (*0-87113-570-1*) Grove-Atltic.

Miranti, Judith, jt. auth. see Burke, Mary T.

Miranti, Judith G., jt. auth. see Burke, Mary T.

Miranti, Paul J., Jr. Accountancy Comes of Age: The Development of an American Profession, 1886-1940. LC 89-27925. xii, 276p. (C). 1990. 34.95 (*0-8078-1893-3*) U of NC Pr.

Miranti, Paul J., Jr., ed. Commerce, Accounts, & Finance, 2 vols., Set. (New Works in Accounting History). 1106p. 1993. reprint ed. 223.00 (*0-8153-1214-8*) Garland.

Miras, Domingo. Las Brujas de Barahona. Serrano, Virtudes, ed. (Nueva Austral Ser.: Vol. 273). (SPA.). 1993. pap. text ed. 24.95x (*84-239-7273-9*) Elliots Bks.

Miras-Portugal, M. T., jt. ed. see Municio, A. M.

Mirassou, Jean B., et al. The Power of Jude. 64p. (Orig.). 1993. pap. 5.95 (*0-9637572-0-2*) Deux Goudez.

***Mirat-Ul-Istilah.** Encyclopaedic Dictionary of Medieval India. Ahmad, Tasneem, tr. (C). 1993. 62.00 (*81-85067-86-4*, Pub. by Sundeep Prakashan II) S Asia.

Mirault, Don. Dancing ... for a Living. LC 93-85551. 190p. 1994. pap. 15.95 (*0-9637864-4-X*) Rafter Pub.

Miravalle, Mark. Heart of the Message of Medugorje. (Illus.). 144p. 1988. pap. 6.95 (*0-940535-08-4*, UP108) Franciscan U Pr.

— Medjugorje & the Family. 174p. 1990. pap. 6.95 (*0-940535-33-5*, UP133) Franciscan U Pr.

Miravalle, Mark I. Mary: Coredemptrix Mediatrix Advocate. Hatzel, Garte, tr. 96p. (GER.). 1993. pap. 1.00 (*1-882972-19-8*) Queenship Pub.

— Mary: Coredemptrix Mediatrix Advocate. Rota, Maria, tr. 96p. (ITA.). 1993. pap. 1.00 (*1-882972-16-3*) Queenship Pub.

— Mary: Coredemptrix Mediatrix Advocate. Pavisich-Ryan, Olga, tr. 96p. (SPA.). 1993. pap. 1.00 (*1-882972-12-0*) Queenship Pub.

— Mary: Coredemptrix Mediatrix Advocate. Hamadi, Salwa, tr. 96p. (FRE.). 1993. pap. 1.00 (*1-882972-18-X*) Queenship Pub.

— Mary: Coredemptrix Mediatrix Advocate. Hooker, Bridget, tr. 96p. (POL.). 1994. pap. 1.00 (*1-882972-17-1*) Queenship Pub.

— Mary, Coredemptrix, Mediatrix Advocate. Hooker, Bridget, tr. 96p. (RUS.). 1994. pap. 1.00 (*1-882972-38-4*) Queenship Pub.

— The Message of Medjugorje: The Marian Message to the Modern World. LC 86-1588. 168p. 1986. pap. 19.50 (*0-8191-5289-7*) U Pr of Amer.

Miravalle, Mark I., ed. The Apostolate of Holy Motherhood. LC 91-62526. 144p. (Orig.). 1991. pap. 3.00 (*1-877678-18-X*) Riehle Found.

Mirbeau, Octave. Le Calvaire. Donougher, Christine, tr. (Dedalus European Classics Ser.). 268p. (Orig.). 1994. pap. 12.95 (*0-7818-0106-0*) Hippocrene Bks.

— The Diary of a Chambermaid. (Dedalus European Fiction Classics Ser.). 356p. 1992. pap. 14.95 (*0-7818-0008-0*, Pub. by Dedalus Bks UK) Hippocrene Bks.

— Diary of a Chambermaid. 1992. pap. 14.95 (*0-946626-82-0*, Pub. by Dedalus Bks UK) Hippocrene Bks.

— Pierre Bonnard: Sketches of a Journey. (Illus.). 176p. 1989. 35.00 (*0-85667-364-1*) Sothebys Pubns.

— The Torture Garden. Juno, Andrea et al, eds. Bessie, Alvah C., tr. (Illus.). 124p. 1989. pap. text ed. 13.99 (*0-940642-13-1*) Re Search Pubns.

— The Torture Garden. Bessie, Alvah, tr. (Illus.). 120p. 1989. 30.00 (*0-940642-15-8*) Re Search Pubns.

***Mircea.** Encyclopedia of Religion. 1994. cd-rom 300.00 (*0-02-897124-8*) Macmillan.

Mircev, Dimitar, et al. The Role of Public Enterprises in the Advancement of Women in Yugoslavia. (ICPE Monograph: No. 11). 95p. 1983. pap. 10.00 (*92-9038-910-9*, Pub. by Intl Ctr Pub Ent XV) Kumarian Pr.

Mirchandani, G. G. Subverting the Constitution, India. 1977. 12.50 (*0-8364-0030-5*) S Asia.

— Thirty Two Million Judges: Analysis of 1977 Lok Sabha & State Elections in India. 1977. 12.00 (*0-8364-0052-6*) S Asia.

Mirchandani, G. G. & Namboodiri, P. K. Nuclear India. 221p. 1981. 19.95 (*0-86578-139-7*) Ind-US Inc.

Mirchandani, Jyoti, jt. auth. see Vaswani, J. P.

Mirchandani, Pitu B. & Francis, Richard L., eds. Discrete Location Theory. 576p. 1990. text ed. 105.00 (*0-471-89233-5*) Wiley.

Mirchandani, Sonu & Khanna, Raman. Fiber Distributed Data Interface (FDDI) Technology & Applications. 384p. 1992. text ed. 54.95 (*0-471-55896-6*) Wiley.

Mircovich, Rhonda. Palatable Pantries & Lavish Larders. LC 92-30475. (Illus.). 208p. 1993. pap. 14.95 (*0-942963-33-4*) Distinctive Pub.

Mire, Betty. It's Funny How Things Change. LC 84-1164. 155p. (YA). (gr. 5-10). 1985. 12.95 (*0-88289-431-5*) Pelican.

— T-Pierre Frog & T-Felix Frog Go to School. LC 93-74275. (Illus.). 32p. (Orig.). (J). (gr. 1-3). 1994. lib. bdg. 6.95 (*0-9639378-0-4*) Cajun Bay Pr.

— Take God's Hand. 64p. 1990. per. write for info. (*0-8187-0128-5*) Harlo Press.

Mireault, Bernie, jt. auth. see Allred, Michael.

Mirecki, Paul A. Understanding the Bible: Workbook. 144p. (C). 1993. spiral bd. 25.95 (*0-8403-9247-8*) Kendall-Hunt.

Mirel, Elizabeth P. Plum Crazy, a Book about Beach Plums. 160p. 1986. reprint ed. pap. 6.95 (*0-940160-34-X*) Parnassus Imprints.

Mirel, Jeffrey. The Rise & Fall of an Urban School System: Detroit, 1907-81. 450p. (C). 1992. text ed. 42.50 (*0-472-10118-8*) U of Mich Pr.

Mireles, Sandra. Lady Nell. large type ed. 1990. pap. 10.95 (*0-7927-0340-5*, C0402, Curley Lrg Print) Chivers N Amer.

Mirelli, V., jt. ed. see Baras, J. S.

Mirelman, Victor A. Jewish Buenos Aires, Eighteen Ninety to Nineteen Thirty: In Search of an Identity. LC 89-16739. (Illus.). 301p. (C). 1990. text ed. 39.95 (*0-8143-2233-6*) Wayne St U Pr.

Mirels, Herbert, jt. ed. see Weary, Gifford.

Mirenda, Pat, jt. auth. see Beukelman, David R.

Mirengoff, William, et al. CETA: Accomplishments, Problems, Solutions. LC 82-2856. 321p. 1982. pap. 7.00 (*0-911558-96-9*) W E Upjohn.

Mirenkov, N., ed. Parallel Computing Technologies. 450p. (C). 1991. text ed. 118.00 (*981-02-0698-4*) World Scientific Pub.

Mirer, Thad W. Economic Statistics & Econometrics. 2nd ed. (Illus.). 416p. (C). 1988. write for info. (*0-02-381821-2*) Macmillan.

— Economic Statistics & Econometrics. 3rd ed. (Illus.). 448p. 1994. write for info. (*0-02-381831-X*, Merrill Pub Co) Macmillan.

Mirew, Gregory. Deltic Designs Giftwrap Paper. Date not set. 2.95 (*0-486-27502-7*) Dover.

Mirfeld, John. Sinonoma Bartholomei. Mowat, J. L., ed. (Anecdota Oxoniensia Ser.: No. 1). 1988. reprint ed. 37.50 (*0-404-63951-8*) AMS Pr.

Mirgon, Barbara B., jt. auth. see Avillion, Adrianne E.

Mirgon, John, et al. Ornamental Water Gardening: How & What to Grow. Weinstein, Gayle, ed. (Illus.). 33p. (Orig.). 1991. pap. 7.95 (*0-9629743-0-7*) Shereth Grp.

Mirhady, David C., jt. ed. see Fortenbaugh, William W.

Mirho, Charles. Multimedia Systems Programming. 1994. pap. text ed. 22.50 (*0-13-100199-X*) P-H.

***Mirho, Charles A. & Terrisse, Andre.** Communications Programming for Windows 95. 1995. disk 39.95 (*1-55615-668-5*) Microsoft.

Miriam. Love Is Enough. 1962. 6.50 (*0-8159-6112-X*) Devin.

Miriani, Patricia. Using Math Manipulatives for Cooperative Problem Solving: Money. (Illus.). 48p. (Orig.). 1992. student ed, bds. 7.95 (*1-55734-185-0*) Tchr Create Mat.

Miriani, Patricia, ed. see Jasmine, Grace, et al.

Miriani, Patricia, ed. see Nakajima, Caroline.

Miriani, Patricia, ed. see Shepherd, Michael.

Miriani, Patricia, ed. see Williams, Diane.

Miriani, Patricia L. & Goldfluss, Karen J. Big Book of Science Charts: Dinosaurs. (Illus.). 26p. (Orig.). 1992. student ed 14.95 (*1-55734-571-6*) Tchr Create Mat.

Miriani, Patricia L., ed. see Thomas, Jennifer.

Mirical, Martin J. Seventeen Little Miricals: Fun & Success in a Family with 17 Children! LC 91-67483. (Illus.). 228p. (Orig.). 1992. pap. 9.95 (*0-9631593-6-4*) Wydaily Pub.

Mirick, Benjamin L. History of Haverhill, Massachusetts. 228p. 1990. reprint ed. text ed. 20.00 (*1-878651-10-2*) HPL Pr.

— The History of Haverhill, Massachusetts. 239p. 1991. reprint ed. pap. 23.00 (*1-55613-497-5*) Heritage Bk.

Mirick, Benjamin L., jt. auth. see Saltonstall, Leverett.

Mirikitani, Janice. Shedding Silence. 176p. 1987. 14.95 (*0-89087-496-4*); pap. 9.95 (*0-89087-493-X*) Celestial Arts.

Mirikitani, Janice, jt. ed. see Williams, Cecil.

Mirikitani, Janice, et al, intros. Watch Out! We're Talking: Speaking Out about Incest & Abuse. 206p. (Orig.). 1993. pap. 12.95 (*0-9622574-2-7*) Glide Word.

Mirikitani, Leatrice T. Speaking Kapampangan. McKaughan, Howard P., ed. LC 70-152468. (PALI Language Texts Philippines). 1011p. (C). reprint ed. 180.00 (*0-8357-9827-5*, 2017219) Bks Demand.

Mirimanov, R. G. Multilingual Electronics Dictionary. 544p. (DUT, ENG, FRE, GER & RUS.). 1986. 150.00 (*0-8288-0313-7*, F1927) Fr & Eur.

Mirimanov, R. G., et al, eds. Dictionary of Electronics: English, German, French, Dutch, Russian. 1985. lib. bdg. 105.50 (*90-201-1788-2*) Kluwer Ac.

Mirin, Steven M., ed. Substance Abuse & Psychopathology. LC 84-6291. (Clinical Insights Ser.). 167p. reprint ed. pap. 47.60 (*0-8357-7819-3*, 2036191) Bks Demand.

Mirin, Steven M., jt. auth. see Weiss, Roger D.

Mirin, Steven M., et al, eds. Psychiatric Treatment: Advances in Outcome Research. LC 91-4535. 375p. 1991. text ed. 28.50 (*0-88048-500-0*) Am Psychiatric.

Miringoff, Lee M. & Carvalho, Barbara L. The Cuomo Factor: Assessing the Political Appeal of New York's Governor. LC 86-62229. 126p. (Orig.). 1987. pap. 12.95 (*0-939319-00-4*) Marist Inst.

Miringoff, Marque-Luisa. The Social Costs of Genetic Welfare. 200p. (C). 1991. text ed. 35.00 (*0-8135-1706-0*); pap. text ed. 15.00 (*0-8135-1707-9*) Rutgers U Pr.

***Mirisztai, E.** Hearing Impairment & the Labyrinthine Perilymphatic System. 134p. (C). 1983. 30.00x (*963-05-3153-4*) St Mut.

Mirkin, B. G., tr. see Rodin, S. N.

Mirkin, Gabe. Consultation with Your Sports Doctor. (Orig.). 1985. pap. 6.95 (*0-671-50491-6*) PB.

— Fat Free, Flavor Full: Dr. Gabe Mirkin's Guide to Losing Weight & Gaining Life, Vol. 1. 1995. 19.95 (*0-316-57440-6*) Little.

— Getting Thin: All about Fat - How You Get It, How You Lose It, How You Keep It off for Good. 1986. pap. 12.95 (*0-316-57439-2*) Little.

— The 20 Gram Diet: Fat Counter. LC 94-77443. 96p. (Orig.). 1994. pap. text ed. 4.99 (*0-9642386-0-8*) Linx Corp.

Mirkin, Gabe & Hoffman, Marshall. The Sportsmedicine Book. LC 78-14908. 1978. 24.95 (*0-316-57434-1*) Little.

Mirkin, Gabe, jt. ed. see Shangold, Mona M.

Mirkin, Gabe, jt. auth. see Shangold, Mona.

Mirkin, Marsha P. The Social & Political Contexts of Family Therapy. 407p. 1990. text ed. 60.00 (*0-205-12455-0*, H24557) Allyn.

Mirkin, Marsha P., ed. Women in Context: Towards a Feminist Reconstructions of Psychotherapy. LC 94-5534. 502p. 1994. lib. bdg. 44.95 (*0-89862-095-3*, C2095) Guilford Pr.

Mirko, Vincent W. Grandpa Says. 300p. (Orig.). (YA). (gr. 10). 1989. pap. 25.00 (*0-9623257-0-8*) Millsmont Pub.

Mirkowicz, Tomasz, tr. see Hlasko, Marek.

Mirkowska, C. & Salwicki, Andrzej. Algorithmic Logic. 1987. lib. bdg. 136.50 (*90-277-1928-4*) Kluwer Ac.

Mirkowska, G., jt. ed. see Kreczmar, A.

Mirman, L. J. & Spulber, Daniel F., eds. Essays in the Economics of Renewable Resources. (Contributions to Economic Analysis Ser.: Vol. 143). 288p. 1982. 95.00 (*0-444-86340-0*, I-120-82, North Holland) Elsevier.

Miro. Miro. (Masterworks Ser.). (Illus.). 144p. 1989. 19.99 (*0-517-65256-0*) Random Hse Value.

Miro, Carmen & Potter, Joseph. Population Policy: Directions for the Future. 1981. text ed. 24.95 (*0-312-63158-8*) St Martin.

Miro, Gabriel. Nuestro Padre San Daniel. El Obispo Leproso. Lozano Marcos, Miguel A., ed. (Nueva Austral Ser.: Vol. 224). (SPA.). 1991. pap. text ed. 34.95x (*84-239-7224-0*) Elliots Bks.

***Miro, Joan.** Els Tres Joans. deluxe limited ed. Brossa, Joan, ed. (Ediciones Especiales y de Bibliofilo Ser.). (Illus.). 104p. (CAT.). 1993. 17,500.00 (*84-343-0272-1*) Elliots Bks.

— Joan Miro: Selected Writings & Interviews. Auster, Paul & Mathews, Patricia, trs. (Illus.). 364p. 1992. reprint ed. pap. 14.95 (*0-306-80485-9*) Da Capo.

— Joan Miro, Litografo, 6 vols. Leiris, M. et al, eds. (Illus.). 1410p. (SPA.). 1993. 3,300.00 (*0-614-00252-4*) Elliots Bks.

— Joan Miro, Litografo, Vol. I. Leiris, Michel, ed. (Illus.). 240p. (SPA.). 1993. 750.00 (*84-343-0886-X*) Elliots Bks.

— Joan Miro, Litografo, Vol. II: 1953-1963. Queneau, Joan, ed. (Illus.). 254p. (SPA.). 1993. 750.00 (*84-343-0221-7*) Elliots Bks.

— Joan Miro, Litografo, Vol. III: 1964-1970. Teixidor, Joan, ed. (Illus.). 220p. (SPA.). 1993. 650.00 (*84-343-0263-2*) Elliots Bks.

— Joan Miro, Litografo, Vol. IV: 1969-1972. Calas, Nicolas & Calas, Elena, eds. (Illus.). 212p. (SPA.). 1993. 650.00 (*84-343-0349-3*) Elliots Bks.

— Joan Miro, Litografo, Vol. V: 1972-1975. Cramer, Patrick, ed. (Illus.). 192p. (SPA.). 1993. 275.00 (*2-86941-188-X*) Elliots Bks.

— Joan Miro, Litografo, Vol. VI: 1976-1981. Cramer, Patrick, ed. (Illus.). 292p. (SPA.). 1993. 275.00 (*2-86941-189-8*) Elliots Bks.

— Miro Lithographs. (Art Library). (Illus.). 48p. (Orig.). 1983. pap. 3.50 (*0-486-24437-7*) Dover.

***Miro, Joan, illus.** Miro, les Essencies de la Terra. (CAT.). 1993. 7,500.00 (*0-614-00037-8*) Elliots Bks.

— Miro, les Essencies de la Terra. limited ed. (CAT.). 1993. 7,500.00 (*0-614-00143-9*) Elliots Bks.

Miro, Joan & Eluard, Paul. Miro: A Toute Epreuve. 104p. 1993. pap. 29.50 (*0-8076-1330-4*) Braziller.

Miro, Joan, Foundation Staff. Joan Miro, 1893-1993. 1993. 85.00 (*0-8212-2024-1*) Bulfinch Pr.

Miro, Norma S., tr. see Elliott, Dan.

***Mirocha.** Awesome Animal Actions. 1994. pap. 2.99 (*0-517-13272-9*) Random Hse Value.

— Baffling Bird Behavior. 1994. pap. 2.99 (*0-517-13276-1*) Random Hse Value.

— Freaky Fish Facts. 1994. pap. 2.99 (*0-517-13277-X*) Random Hse Value.

— Incredible Insect Instincts. Date not set. pap. 2.99 (*0-517-13279-6*) Random.

Mirocha, Paul & Lauffer, Rhod. Back Off! Animal Defense Behavior: A Real Life Pop-Up Book. LC 94-4144. (Illus.). (J). (gr. 3 up). 1995. text ed. 10.95 (*0-7167-6534-9*, Sci Am Yng Rdrs) W H Freeman.

— Look Again! Animal Camouflage & Disguise: A Real Life Pop-Up Book. LC 94-6224. (Illus.). (J). (gr. 3 up). 1994. text ed. 10.95 (*0-7167-6535-7*, Sci Am Yng Rdrs) W H Freeman.

Mirodan, Vladimir. The Balkan Cookbook. LC 89-35639. 208p. 1989. reprint ed. 17.95 (*0-88289-738-1*) Pelican.

Miroff, Bruce. Icons of Democracy: American Leaders as Heroes, Aristocrats, Dissenters, & Democrats. 432p. 1994. pap. 15.00 (*0-465-03261-3*) Basic.

Miroff, Franklin, jt. auth. see Smith, Jerome.

Miroglio, Abel & Miroglio, Yvonne-Delphie. L' Europe et Ses Populations. 1978. lib. bdg. 164.50 (*90-247-2082-6*) Kluwer Ac.

Miroglio, Yvonne-Delphie, jt. auth. see Miroglio, Abel.

Miroiu, Mihai. English-Romanian Conversation Book. 188p. (ENG & RUM.). 1976. 40.00 (*0-317-59448-6*, Pub. by Collets UK) Pro-Am Music.

— Romanian Conversation Guide. (Language Bks.). 199p. (C). 1989. pap. 9.95 (*0-87052-803-3*) Hippocrene Bks.

Mirolubova, G. Portrait of Czarist Russia. 1989. 40.00 (*0-394-58031-1*) Pantheon.

Mirolyubev, E. N., jt. ed. see Tomashov, N. D.

***Miron, Dan.** A Traveler Disguised: The Rise of Modern Yiddish Fiction in the Nineteenth Century. 373p. 1995. pap. 16.95 (*0-8156-0330-4*) Syracuse U Pr.

Miron, Douglas B. Design of Feedback Control Systems. 448p. (C). 1990. text ed. 49.25 (*0-15-517368-5*); Instr.'s manual. teacher ed, pap. text ed. 2.75 (*0-15-517370-7*) SCP.

***Miron, Gaston.** Counterpanes. Egan, Dennis, tr. (Essential Poets Ser.: No. 50). 73p. 1994. pap. 8.00 (*0-920717-60-8*) Guernica Editions.

Miron, Issachar. Eighteen Gates of Jewish Holidays & Festivals. LC 92-41081. (Illus.). 280p. 1993. 50.00 (*0-87668-563-7*) Aronson.

Miron, J. La Amargura (Bitterness) El Pecado Mas Contagioso (The Most Contagious Sin) (SPA.). Date not set. 1.79 (*1-56063-539-8*, 498026) Editorial Unilit.

— Mi Esposo No Es Cristiano (My Husband Is Not a Christian) (SPA.). Date not set. 1.79 (*1-56063-044-2*, 498010) Editorial Unilit.

Miron, John R. Housing in Postwar Canada: Demographic Change, Household Formation, & Housing Demand. 416p. 1988. 49.95 (*0-7735-0614-4*, Pub. by McGill CN) U of Toronto Pr.

Miron, John R., ed. House, Home, & Community: Progress in Housing Canadians, 1945-1986. 416p. 1993. 55.00 (*0-7735-0995-X*, Pub. by McGill CN) U of Toronto Pr.

Miron, Murray S. & Goldstein, Arnold P. Hostage. rev. ed. LC 77-16554. (General Psychology Ser.: No. 79). 170p. 1979. text ed. 49.50 (*0-08-023875-0*, Pergamon Pr) Elsevier.

Miron, Nathan B. Winning the Games People Play: How to Master the Art of Changing People's Behavior. LC 76-52149. (Illus.). 1977. 12.95 (*0-918418-01-1*); pap. 7.95 (*0-918418-02-X*) Mission Pr CA.

Miron, Radu. The Geometry of Lagrange Spaces: Theory & Applications. (Fundamental Theories of Physics Ser.). 304p. (C). 1993. lib. bdg. 134.00 (*0-7923-2591-5*) Kluwer Ac.

Miron, Yael. Pyrite Problems in the Coal Mining Industry. 1994. write for info. (*0-318-72294-1*) US Interior.

An Asterisk (*) at the beginning of an entry indicates that the title is appearing in BIP for the first time.

Mironov, K. E. & Chernikova, L. A. Bibliography on Rare Earth Elements: Including Scandium & Yttrium. 440p. 1970. text ed. 106.50 (*0-685-13629-9*, Pub. by Keter Pub IS) Coronet Bks.

Mironov, V. F. Chemistry Reviews: Synthetic Studies in the Field of Organic Germanium Compounds, Vol. 12. Vol'pin, M. E., ed. (Soviet Scientific Reviews Ser.: Vol. 12, Pt. 6). ii, 78p. 1989. pap. text ed. 46.00 (*3-7186-4855-5*) Gordon & Breach.

Mironov, V. L., jt. auth. see Banakh, V. A.

Mironovitch, Serge G. The Kiev Encounter. 1976. 15.95 (*0-8283-1693-7*) Branden Pub Co.

Miropolsky, Z. L. & Soziev, R. I. Fluid Dynamics & Heat Transfer in Superconducting Equipment. 290p. 1990. 178.00 (*0-89116-852-4*) Hemisp Pub.

***Mirosevich, Toni, et al.** Trio. LC 94-12045. 76p. 1995. pap. 10.00 (*0-9645026-0-7*) Specter Pr.

Mirotvorsky, S., jt. auth. see Dyachenko, P.

Mirouze, Laurant. World War Two Infantry. (Europa Militaria Ser.: No. 2). (Illus.). 64p. 1990. pap. 15.95 (*1-872004-15-6*) Motorbooks Intl.

Mirouze, Laurent. World War One Infantry. (Europa Militaria Ser.: No. 3). 64p. 1990. pap. 15.95 (*1-872004-25-3*) Motorbooks Intl.

Mirov, S. B., jt. auth. see Basiev, T. T.

Mirow, Gregory. Paisley Designs: 44 Original Plates. (Illus.). 48p. 1989. pap. 3.95 (*0-486-25987-0*) Dover.

— Treasury of Design for Artists & Craftsmen. LC 69-18877. (Pictorial Archive Ser.). 1969. reprint ed. pap. 5.95 (*0-486-22002-8*) Dover.

Mirowicz & Stypula, R. Wielki Slownik Polsko-Rosyjski, 2 vols., Set. 1331p. (POL & RUS.). 1980. 150.00 (*0-8288-1037-0*, M9131) Fr & Eur.

Mirowski, Philip. Against Mechanism: Protecting Economics from Science. 264p. 1988. pap. 18.95 (*0-8476-7695-1*) Rowman.

— Against Mechanism: Why Economics Needs Protection from Science. 264p. (C). 1988. 57.00 (*0-8476-7436-3*) Rowman.

— More Heat Than Light: Economics as Social Physics, Physics as Nature's Economics. (Historical Perspectives on Modern Economics Ser.). (Illus.). 456p. (C). 1991. pap. 21.95 (*0-521-42689-8*) Cambridge U Pr.

Mirowski, Philip, ed. Natural Images in Economic Thought: Markets Read in Tooth & Claw. (Historical Perspectives on Modern Economics Ser.). (Illus.). 624p. (C). 1994. 79.95 (*0-521-44321-0*); pap. 29.95 (*0-521-47877-4*) Cambridge U Pr.

— The Reconstruction of Economic Theory. 1986. lib. bdg. 66.00 (*0-89838-211-4*) Kluwer Ac.

Mirowski, Philip J., ed. Edgeworth's Writings on Chance, Probability & Statistics. (Worldly Philosophy Series: Studies at the Intersection of Philosophy & Economics). 224p. (C). 1993. lib. bdg. 45.00 (*0-8476-7751-6*) Rowman.

Mirowsky, John & Ross, Catherine E. Social Causes of Psychological Distress. (Social Institutions & Social Change Ser.). 224p. (Orig.). (C). 1989. lib. bdg. 41.95 (*0-202-30354-3*); pap. text ed. 22.95 (*0-202-30355-1*) Aldine de Gruyter.

Mirowtiz. Atlas of MRI Artifacts & Variants. 1994. 115.00 (*0-8016-7670-3*) Mosby Yr Bk.

Mirpuri, Gouri. Indonesia. LC 89-25457. (Cultures of the World Ser.: Group 1: Asia). (Illus.). 128p. (YA). (gr. 5-9). 1991. lib. bdg. 21.95 (*1-85435-294-6*) Marshall Cavendish.

Mirr, Michaelene, jt. ed. see Snyder, Mariah.

Mirra, Joseph M., et al, eds. Bone Tumors: Clinical, Radiologic & Pathologic Correlations, 2 vols. LC 88-3019. (Illus.). 1857p. 1989. 295.00 (*0-8121-1156-7*) Williams & Wilkins.

Mirrer, Louise. Upon My Husband's Death: Widows in the Literature & Histories of Medieval Europe. (Illus.). 350p. (C). 1992. text ed. 47.50 (*0-472-10257-5*) U of Mich Pr.

Mirrer-Singer, Louise. The Language of Evaluation: A Sociolinguistic Approach to the Story of Pedro el Cruel in Ballad & Chronicle. LC 86-9620. (Purdue University Monographs in Romance Languages: No. 20). xi, 130p. (Orig.). 1986. pap. 35.00x (*0-915027-69-0*) Benjamins North Am.

Mirriam, Joan. Little Girl Lost. 1992. mass mkt. 4.99 (*1-55817-593-8*, Pinnacle NY) Windsor NY.

Mirrielees, Edith R. Story Writing. LC 72-6277. 1988. pap. 8.95 (*0-87116-137-0*) Writer.

Mirrlees-Black, C., jt. auth. see Southgate, P.

Mirschhorn, Robert B., jt. auth. see Bennett, Cathy E.

Mirshekar-Syahkal, D. Spectral Domain Method for Microwave Integrated Circuits. 243p. 1990. text ed. 155.00 (*0-471-92684-1*) Wiley.

Mirsky, A. E., jt. ed. see Brachet, Jean.

Mirsky, Allan F., jt. ed. see Myslobodsky, Michael S.

Mirsky, D. Russia: A Social History. Seligman, C. G., ed. LC 83-26517. (Illus.). 312p. 1984. text ed. 69.50 (*0-313-24296-8*, MRUS, Greenwood Pr) Greenwood.

Mirsky, D. S. Modern Russian Literature. LC 74-6485. (Studies in Russian Literature & Life: No. 100). 1974. lib. bdg. 75.00 (*0-8383-1941-6*) M S G Haskell Hse.

— Pushkin. LC 74-34587. (Studies in Russian Literature & Life: No. 100). 1974. lib. bdg. 75.00 (*0-8383-1998-X*) M S G Haskell Hse.

— Uncollected Writings on Russian Literature. (Modern Russian Literature & Culture, Studies & Texts: Vol. 13). (Illus.). 406p. (Orig.). (ENG & RUS.). (C). 1989. pap. 24.00 (*0-933884-68-0*) Berkeley Slavic.

Mirsky, D. S., tr. see Vladimirtsov, Boris.

Mirsky, David. The Life & Work of Ephraim Luzzatto. 1987. 25.00 (*0-88125-139-9*) Ktav.

Mirsky, Dimitry S. History of Russian Literature: From Its Beginnings to 1900. Whitfield, Francis J., ed. 1958. pap. 7.96 (*0-394-70720-6*, Vin) Random.

***Mirsky, Judith & Radlett, Marty, eds.** Private Decisions, Public Debate: Women, Reproduction & Population. (Illus.). 185p. 1995. pap. 14.95 (*1-870670-34-5*, Pub. by Panos Bks UK) Paul & Co Pubs.

Mirsky, L. Introduction to Linear Algebra. 1990. pap. 10.95 (*0-486-66434-1*) Dover.

***Mirsky, Lawrence & Tropea, Silvana, eds.** The News Aesthetic. (Illus.). (Orig.). 1995. pap. 19.95 (*1-56898-051-5*) Princeton Arch.

Mirsky, Mark. The Red Adam. (New American Fiction Ser.: No. 19). (Illus.). 165p. (Orig.). 1990. pap. 10.95 (*0-940650-92-4*) Sun & Moon CA.

— The Secret Table. LC 74-24914. 167p. 1975. 15.95 (*0-914590-10-3*); pap. 6.95 (*0-914590-11-1*) Fiction Coll.

Mirsky, Mark J. The Absent Shakespeare. LC 92-55118. (C). 1994. write for info. (*0-8386-3511-3*) Fairleigh Dickinson.

Mirsky, Mark J., jt. ed. see Stern, David.

Mirsky, Norman B. Unorthodox Judaism. LC 78-8683. 227p. 1978. 44.50 (*0-8142-0283-7*) Ohio St U Pr.

***Mirsky, Peter H.** Lactose-Free Foods: A Shoppers Guide. (Illus.). 70p. Date not set. write for info. (*0-9644787-0-6*) Bullseye Info Servs.

Mirsky, Stanley & Hellman, Joan R. Controlling Diabetes the Easy Way. 1985. pap. 12.95 (*0-394-72674-X*) Random.

Mirsky, Yehudah & Ahrens, Matt, eds. Democracy in the Middle East: Defining the Challenges. LC 93-28820. 1993. write for info. (*0-944029-53-1*) Wash Inst NEP.

Mirta, Sanjit K. & Kaiser, James F. The Handbook for Digital Signal Processing. 1312p. 1993. text ed. 125.00 (*0-471-61995-7*) Wiley.

Mirth, Karlo. Mestrovic in America: Living from the Clod of Croatian Soil Attached to His Roots' from My Memories of Mestrovic. (Illus.). 80p. 1985. reprint ed. pap. 12.00 (*0-9615737-0-8*) K Mirth.

Mirtle, Jack, comp. Thank You Music Lovers: A Bio-Discography of Spike Jones & His City Slickers, 1941-1965. LC 85-27128. (Discographies Ser.: No. 20). 448p. 1986. text ed. 69.50 (*0-313-24814-1*, MSN/, Greenwood Pr) Greenwood.

Mirtov, B. A. Gaseous Composition of the Atmosphere & Its Analysis. 216p. 1964. text ed. 55.50 (*0-685-43575-X*, Pub. by Keter Pub IS) Coronet Bks.

Mirtschin, Peter & Davis, Richard. Snakes of Australia: Dangerous & Harmless. (Illus.). 216p. (Orig.). 1994. pap. 13.95 (*0-85572-209-6*, Pub. by Hill Content Pubng AT) Seven Hills Bk.

Mirtskhulava, T. E. Reliability of Hydro-Reclamation Installations. (C). 1987. 33.00 (*81-204-0196-4*, Pub. by Oxford IBH II) S Asia.

Mirtskhulava, Te E. Reliability of Hydro-Reclamation Installations. Kothekar, V. S., tr. 308p. (C). 1987. text ed. 90.00 (*90-6191-491-4*, Pub. by A A Balkema NE) Ashgate Pub Co.

Mirvis. Cardiac Electrophysiology: A Physiologic Approach to ECG & Cardiac Arrhythmias. 544p. 1993. pap. 33.95 (*0-8016-7479-4*) Mosby Yr Bk.

Mirvis, David M., ed. Body Surface Electrocardiographic Mapping. (Developments in Cardiovascular Medicine Ser.). (C). 1988. lib. bdg. 100.00 (*0-89838-983-6*) Kluwer Ac.

Mirvis, Philip. Building the Competitive Workforce: Investing in Human Capital for Corporate Success. 272p. 1993. text ed. 34.95 (*0-471-59257-9*) Wiley.

Mirvis, Philip H. Managing the Merger: Making It Work. 1991. 22.95 (*0-13-544636-8*, Busn) P-H.

Mirvis, Philip H., jt. auth. see Kanter, Donald L.

Mirvis, Stuart E. & Young, Jeremy W. Imaging in Trauma & Critical Care. (Illus.). 592p. 1992. 140.00 (*0-683-06075-9*) Williams & Wilkins.

***Mirviss, Joan B. & Carpenter, John T.** The Frank Lloyd Wright Collection of Surimono. LC 94-41903. (Illus.). 336p. 1995. 70.00 (*0-8348-0327-5*) Weatherhill.

***Mirza & Lemmons.** Passport. 300p. 1995. pap. 9.99 (*1-56476-390-0*, 6-3390, Victor Books) SP Pubns.

Mirza, A. I., tr. Modern Urdu Stories. (Writers Workshop Saffronbird Ser.). 1977. 4.80 (*0-89253-643-8*); text ed. 10.00 (*0-89253-642-X*) Ind-US Inc.

Mirza, Heidi S. Young, Female & Black. LC 91-30180. 224p. (Orig.). 1992. 65.00 (*0-415-06704-9*, A6788); pap. 16.95 (*0-415-06705-7*, A6792) Routledge.

Mirza, Iraj. Iraj Mirza's Poetry. LC 92-70487. 328p. (Orig.). (PER.). 1992. pap. 8.95 (*0-936347-25-2*) Iran Bks.

Mirza, Jerome. Illinois Tort Law & Practice. 2nd ed. LC 88-82172. 1991. 105.00 (*0-318-43158-0*) Lawyers Cooperative.

— Illinois Tort Law & Practice, Suppl. 1991. 2nd ed. LC 88-82172. 1991. 40.00 (*0-317-03344-1*) Lawyers Cooperative.

— Illinois Tort Law & Practice, Suppl. 1993. 2nd ed. LC 88-82172. 1991. 55.00 (*0-317-01748-9*) Lawyers Cooperative.

— Winning Litigation the Mirza Way. LC 91-77445. 1992. 135.00 (*0-685-59886-1*) Clark Boardman Callaghan.

Mirza, Rocky & Willis, James. Explorations in Macroeconomics: First Canadian Edition Study Guide. 1992. pap. 22.60 (*1-56226-120-7*) CT Pub.

Mirza, Rocky, et al. Explorations in Macro: First Canadian Edition. 1992. pap. 46.35 (*1-56226-097-9*) CT Pub.

— Explorations in Microeconomics, First Canadian. 645p. (C). 1991. pap. text ed. 47.30 (*1-56226-014-6*) CT Pub.

— Explorations in Microeconomics, First Canadian Study Guide. 125p. (C). 1991. pap. text ed. 22.60 (*1-56226-058-8*) CT Pub.

Mirza, Sarah & Strobel, Margaret, eds. Three Swahili Women: Life Histories from Mombasa, Kenya. LC 88-45093. (Illus.). 176p. 1989. 25.00 (*0-253-36012-9*); pap. 9.95 (*0-253-28854-1*) Ind U Pr.

— Wanawake Watatu Wa Kiswahili: Hadithi za Maisha Kutoka Mombasa, Kenya. Strobel, Margaret, tr. LC 90-84389. (Illus.). 104p. 1991. 19.95 (*0-253-36336-5*); pap. 9.95 (*0-253-28855-X*) Ind U Pr.

Mirza, Sarah M, jt. auth. see Hinnebusch, Thomas J.

Mirza, Youel B. When I Was a Boy in Persia. LC 77-87650. (Illus.). reprint ed. 20.00 (*0-404-16419-6*) AMS Pr.

Mirzabekian, Z. M. Russian-Persian Polytechnical Dictionary. 2nd ed. 720p. (PER & RUS.). 1983. 95.00 (*0-8288-2160-7*, M8890) Fr & Eur.

Mirzabekian, Zh. Russian-Persian Polytechnical Dictionary. 2nd ed. 720p. (C). 1983. 140.00 (*0-685-46895-X*, Pub. by Collets) St Mut.

Mirzai, jt. auth. see Lawson.

Mirzai, A. R., ed. Artificial Intelligence: Concepts & Applications. (Artificial Intelligence Ser.). 320p. 1990. pap. 42.00 (*0-262-13256-7*) MIT Pr.

Mirzkirch, W. Flow Visualization Two. 1982. text ed. 90.00 (*0-07-041530-7*) McGraw.

***Mirzoeff, Nicholas.** Body Power Vision. LC 95-6735. (Visual Cultures Ser.). 1995. write for info. (*0-415-09800-9*); pap. write for info. (*0-415-09801-7*) Routledge.

Mirzoyan, L. V., et al, eds. Flare Stars in Star Clusters, Associations & the Solar Vicinity. (C). 1990. lib. bdg. 133.00 (*0-7923-0770-4*); pap. text ed. 55.00 (*0-7923-0771-2*) Kluwer Ac.

MIS Press Staff. Concepts in Computer Art. (Welcome to... Ser.). (Illus.). 1993. pap. 19.95 (*1-55828-240-8*) MIS Press.

— Power of Framemaker 4.0 for Windows. 1993. pap. 27.95 (*1-55828-314-5*) MIS Press.

— Teach Yourself Word 6.0 for DOS. 1993. pap. 21.95 (*1-55828-312-9*) MIS Press.

— Teach Yourself Works for DOS. 1993. pap. 21.95 (*1-55828-311-0*) MIS Press.

— Welcome to Multimedia. 1992. pap. 24.95 (*1-55828-242-4*) MIS Press.

— Welcome to Programming. 1993. pap. 19.95 (*1-55828-309-9*) MIS Press.

***Misa, Thomas J.** A Nation of Steel: The Making of Modern America. LC 94-38681. (Studies in the History of Technology). (Illus.). 392p. 1994. text ed. 49.95x (*0-8018-4967-5*) Johns Hopkins.

***Misaelides, P., ed.** Application of Particle & Laser Beams in Materials Technology. LC 94-46545. (NATO ASI Ser.: Series E, Applied Sciences: Vol. 283). 1995. lib. bdg. 280.00 (*0-7923-3324-1*) Kluwer Ac.

Misaghi, I. J. Physiology & Biochemistry of Plant-Pathogen Interactions. LC 82-18594. 304p. (C). 1982. 65.00 (*0-306-41059-1*, Plenum Pr) Plenum.

Misak, C. J. Truth & the End of Inquiry: A Peircean Account of Truth. (Oxford Philosophical Monographs). 200p. 1991. 55.00 (*0-19-824231-X*) OUP.

— Verificationism: Its History & Prospects. LC 95-7728. (Philosophical Issues in Science Ser.). 1995. write for info. (*0-415-12597-9*, Routledge NY); pap. write for info. (*0-415-12598-7*, Routledge NY) Routledge.

Misanchuk, Earl R. Preparing Instructional Text: Document Design Using Desktop Publishing. LC 91-32872. (Illus.). 327p. (Orig.). 1992. pap. 32.95 (*0-87778-241-5*) Educ Tech Pubns.

Misanchuk, Earl R., jt. auth. see Schwier, Richard A.

Misanin & Hinderliter. Fundamentals of Statistics for Psychology. (C). 1990. text ed. 61.00 (*0-673-38877-8*) HarpCollege.

— Fundamentals of Statistics for Psychology. (C). 1991. 21.50 (*0-673-46526-8*) HarpCollege.

Misawa, E. A., ed. Advances in Robust & Nonlinear Control Systems. LC 93-73654. 131p. Date not set. pap. 45.00 (*0-7918-1259-6*) ASME.

— Advances in Robust & Nonlinear Control Systems. (DSC Ser.: Vol. 43). 96p. 1992. 30.00 (*0-7918-1114-X*, G00758) ASME.

Misawa, Hiroshi. Introduction to Pencil Techniques. (Easy Start Guide Ser.). (Illus.). 112p. 1994. 36.95 (*4-7661-0714-4*, Pub. by Graphic Sha JA) Bks Nippan.

Misbah, Mohammed. Al-Azhar: A University Between Two Ages. (TWEC World Education Monographs). 1983. 2.50 (*0-685-09456-1*) I N Thut World Educ Ctr.

— The Egyptian Experience in Education. (TWEC World Education Monographs). 18p. 1983. 2.00 (*0-685-09457-X*) I N Thut World Educ Ctr.

Misbah, Muhammad T. World View: Its Importance & Problems. Saadat, Shahyar, tr. 24p. (Orig.). 1989. pap. text ed. 1.70 (*1-871031-21-4*) Abjad Bk.

Misbin, Robert I., ed. Euthanasia: The Good of the Patient, the Good of Society. 245p. 1992. 35.00 (*1-55572-017-X*) Univ Pub Group.

Miscall, Peter D. One Samuel: A Literary Reading. LC 85-42948. (Indiana Studies in Biblical Literature). 224p. (C). 1986. 34.95 (*0-253-34247-3*); pap. 9.95 (*0-253-20365-1*, MB-365) Ind U Pr.

— The Workings of Old Testament Narrative. LC 82-5993. (Society of Biblical Literature Semeia Studies). 158p. (C). 1983. pap. 14.95 (*0-89130-584-X*, 06-06-12) Scholars Pr GA.

Miscamble, Wilson D. George F. Kennan & the Making of American Foreign Policy, 1947-1950. (Illus.). 432p. 1992. text ed. 49.50 (*0-691-08620-6*) Princeton U Pr.

— George F. Kennan & the Making of American Foreign Policy, 1947-1950. (Studies in International History & Politics). (Illus.). 436p. 1993. pap. text ed. 17.95 (*0-691-02483-9*) Princeton U Pr.

***Miscevic, Nikola.** Necropolis & Songs of Hope: Bilingual Poetry. 128p. 1995. lib. bdg. 33.00 (*0-8095-4806-2*) Borgo Pr.

Misch. Contemporary Implant Dentistry. (Illus.). 688p. 1993. 110.00 (*0-8016-6073-4*) Mosby Yr Bk.

Misch, Georg. A History of Autobiography in Antiquity, 2 vols., 1. LC 73-13406. 1974. reprint ed. text ed. 45.00 (*0-8371-7178-4*, MIAB) Greenwood.

— A History of Autobiography in Antiquity, 2 vols., Set. LC 73-13406. 1974. reprint ed. text ed. 65.00 (*0-8371-7053-2*, MIAA) Greenwood.

— A History of Autobiography in Antiquity, 2 vols., Vol. 2. LC 73-13406. 1974. reprint ed. text ed. 45.00 (*0-8371-7179-2*, MIAC) Greenwood.

Mischakoff, Anne. Khandoshkin & the Beginning of Russian String Music. LC 83-17847. (Russian Music Studies: No. 9). 217p. reprint ed. pap. 61.90 (*0-8357-1428-4*, 2070513) Bks Demand.

Mischakoff, Anne, ed. see American String Teachers Association Staff.

Mische, Michael, jt. auth. see Bennis, Warren.

Mischel, Jim. The Developer's Guide to WinHelp.Exe. Duntemann, Jeff, ed. LC 93-47572. 1994. pap. 49.95 (*0-471-30326-7*); pap. text ed. 39.95 (*0-471-30325-9*) Wiley.

— Macro Magic with Turbo Assembler. Duntemann, Jeff, ed. 368p. 1992. pap. 39.95 (*0-471-57815-0*) Wiley.

Mischel, Walter. Introduction to Personality: A New Look. 4th ed. 624p. (C). 1986. text ed. 46.75 (*0-03-005243-2*) HB Coll Pubs.

Mischitelli, Vincent. Your New Restaurant: All the Necessary Ingredients for Success. 190p. 1990. pap. 9.95 (*1-55850-857-0*) Adams Pubng.

Mischka, Joseph. The Percheron Horse in America. (Illus.). 179p. 1991. 19.95 (*0-9622663-5-3*) Heart Prairie Pr.

***Mischka, Robert A.** Draft Horse Images. (Illus.). 160p. 1995. pap. 24.00 (*1-882199-03-0*) Heart Prairie Pr.

— Draft Horses Today: Work Horses & Mules Find Their Way into the 21st Century. (Illus.). 176p. 1992. 29.50 (*0-9622663-6-1*) Heart Prairie Pr.

Mischke, Bernard C. & Mischke, Fritz. Pray Today's Gospel: Reflections on the Day's Good News. LC 80-14186. 358p. (Orig.). 1980. pap. 12.95 (*0-8189-0403-8*) Alba.

Mischke, Charles R., jt. auth. see Shigley, Joseph E.

Mischke, Fritz, jt. auth. see Mischke, Bernard C.

Mischke, James A. Circles, Consciousness, & Culture. 1984. pap. 2.50 (*0-912586-57-5*) Navajo Coll Pr.

Mischke, Richard E. Intersections Between Particle & Nuclear Physics (Steamboat Springs, 1984) Proceedings of AIP Conference, No. 123. LC 84-72790. 1162p. 1984. lib. bdg. 65.00 (*0-88318-322-6*) Am Inst Physics.

Miscimarra, Philip A. The NLRB & Managerial Discretion: Plant Closings, Relocations, Subcontracting, & Automation. LC 83-81557. (Labor Relations & Public Policy Ser.: No. 24). (Illus.). 400p. (Orig.). 1983. pap. 25.00 (*0-89546-038-6*) U PA Wharton Ctr Human Resc.

Misckhe, Charles R., jt. auth. see Shigley, Joseph E.

Miscovich, Gina & Simons, David. Sco Performance Tuning Handbook. 640p. 1994. Incl. Disk. pap. text ed. 45.00 (*0-13-102690-9*) P-H.

Misczynski, Dean J., jt. auth. see Hagman, Donald G.

Misczynski, Dean J., jt. ed. see Hagman, Donald G.

***Misdary, Chris A.** Life, Romance & Poetry. 128p. Date not set. write for info. (*1-56167-201-7*) Noble Hse MD.

Mise, Raymond W. The Gothic Heroine & the Nature of the Gothic Novel. Varma, Devendra P., ed. LC 79-8465. (Gothic Studies & Dissertations). 1980. lib. bdg. 31.95 (*0-405-12675-1*) Ayer.

Misel, Lory. Happy & Alive. 96p. (Orig.). 1986. pap. 6.95 (*0-9615902-1-1*) Paragon Group.

— Heavensong. 81p. (Orig.). 1985. pap. 7.00 (*0-9615902-0-3*) Paragon Group.

Misell, D. L. Image Analysis, Enhancement & Interpretation. (Practical Methods in Electron Microscopy Ser.: Vol. 7). 1979. pap. 35.50 (*0-7204-0666-8*, North Holland) Elsevier.

Misell, D. L. & Brown, E. D. Electron Diffraction: An Introduction for Biologists. (Practical Mehtods in Electron Microscopy Ser.: Vol. 12). 288p. 1988. 130.25 (*0-444-80916-3*); pap. 46.50 (*0-444-80917-1*) Elsevier.

Misell, D. L., jt. auth. see Haratley, J. R.

Misell, D. L., jt. auth. see Hartley, J. R.

Misell, I. D., jt. auth. see Hartley, J. R.

Misenheimer, Barry, jt. auth. see McGurn, Patrick.

***Misenheimer, David.** We, the Church: Eight Small Group Studies. 1993. pap. 12.95 (*0-933173-61-X*) Prince Peace Pub.

Misenheimer, Luther, III. Basic Skills Memory Development Workbook. (Basic Skills Workbooks). 32p. (gr. 5-9). 1983. 1.98 (*0-8209-0582-8*, MDW-1) ESP.

— Basic Skills Speed Reading Workbook. (Basic Skills Workbooks). 32p. (gr. 5-9). 1983. 1.98 (*0-8209-0583-6*, SRW-1) ESP.

— Speed Reading. (Language Arts Ser.). 24p. (gr. 6-10). 1979. student ed 5.00 (*0-8209-0324-8*, LA-10) ESP.

Misenhimer, Deborah. Pilgrim Soul. 215p. 1993. pap. 12.00 (*0-9636313-0-6*) D Misenhimer.

Miser, A., pseud. & Pennypincher, A., pseud. Outlet Guide: West Coast. LC 93-19335. (Voyager Book Ser.). 256p. (Orig.). 1993. pap. 9.95 (*1-56440-235-5*) Globe Pequot.

— Outlet Guide to New England. 9th ed. LC 94-43254. (Outlet Guides Ser.). 272p. 1995. pap. 9.95 (*1-56440-639-3*) Globe Pequot.

Miser, A. & Pennypincher, A. Outlet Guide to the South: Save 25% to 80% on Thousands of Brand-Name Items. 3rd rev. ed. LC 93-47496. Orig. Title: Factory Outlet Guide to the South. (Illus.). 288p. 1994. pap. 10.95 (*1-56440-387-4*) Globe Pequot.

— Outlet Guide to the Southwest: Outlet Malls, Factory Outlets, Deep Discounters. LC 93-8577. (Illus.). 192p. (Orig.). 1994. pap. 9.95 (*1-56440-276-2*) Globe Pequot.

Miser, Hugh & Quade, Edward S. Handbook of Systems Analysis: Craft Issues & Procedural Choices, Vol. 2. 681p. 1989. text ed. 249.00 (*0-471-92020-7*) Wiley.

M

An Asterisk (*) at the beginning of an entry indicates that the title is appearing in BIP for the first time.

*Miser, Hugh J. & Quade, Edward S., eds. Handbook of Systems Analysis Vol. 3: Cases, Vol. 3. Date not set. text ed. 85.00 (0-471-95357-1) Wiley.

Miserendino, Annette, ed. Catholic Telephone Guide. 296p. 1986. 22.00 (0-910635-54-4) Cath News Pub Co.

— Catholic Telephone Guide. 304p. 1987. 25.00 (0-910635-60-9) Cath News Pub Co.

*Miserendino, Leo J. & Pick, Robert M., eds. Lasers in Dentistry. LC 94-41152. 1995. text ed. 98.00 (0-86715-282-6) Quint Pub Co.

Miserez, D., ed. Refugees: The Trauma of Exile. (C). 1989. lib. bdg. 115.50 (0-7923-0112-9) Kluwer Ac.

Mises, Ludwig Von. Economic Freedom & Interventionism: An Anthology of Articles & Essays by Ludwig Von Mises. (Illus.). xiii, 250p. (Orig.). 1990. pap. 14.95 (0-910614-76-8) Foun Econ Ed.

Misev, Tosko A. Powder Coatings: Chemistry & Technology. 379p. 1991. text ed. 185.00 (0-471-92821-6) Wiley.

Misey, Johanna L., ed. National Directory of Multi-Cultural Arts Organizations 1990. 190p. 1990. pap. 15.00 (0-317-04286-6, 5710) Natl Assem State.

Misfeldt, Willard E. The Albums of James Tissot. (Illus.). 134p. 1982. 25.95 (0-87972-209-6); pap. 13.95 (0-87972-210-X) Bowling Green Univ.

Misgeld, Dieter & Nicholson, Graeme, eds. Hans-Georg Gadamer on Education, Poetry, & History: Applied Hermeneutics. Reuss, Monica & Schmidt, Lawrence, trs. LC 91-15119. (SUNY Series in Contemporary Continental Philosophy). 238p. (C). 1992. 59.50 (0-7914-0919-8); pap. 19.95 (0-7914-0920-1) State U NY Pr.

Misgeld, Dieter & Stehr, Nico, eds. Modern German Sociology. (European Perspectives Ser.). 488p. 1990. pap. text ed. 24.50 (0-231-05855-1) Col U Pr.

Misgeld, Klaus, et al, eds. Creating Social Democracy: A Century of the Social Democratic Labor Party in Sweden. (Illus.). 520p. (C). 1993. 65.00 (0-271-00868-7); pap. 16.95 (0-271-00931-4) Pa St U Pr.

Misgeld, Ulrich, jt. auth. see Frotscher, Michael.

Misguich, J., et al, eds. Statistical Description of Transport in Plasma, Astro & Nuclear Physics. (Houches Ser.). (Illus.). 437p. (C). 1993. lib. bdg. 137.00 (1-56072-152-9) Nova Sci Pubs.

Mish, Charles C. English Prose Fiction, Sixteen Hundred to Seventeen Hundred: A Chronological Checklist. LC 68-9322. 110p. reprint ed. pap. 31.40 (0-317-10847-6, 2007188) Bks Demand.

Mish, Charles C., ed. Restoration Prose Fiction, 1666-1700: An Anthology of Representative Pieces. LC 76-98095. 305p. reprint ed. pap. 87.00 (0-685-15680-X, 2027338) Bks Demand.

Mishal, Shaul. The PLO under Arafat: Between Gun & Olive Branch. LC 86-9140. 206p. reprint ed. pap. 58.80 (0-7837-4541-9, 2080310) Bks Demand.

— Speaking Stones: Communiques from the Intifada Underground. (Contemporary Issues in the Middle East Ser.). 272p. 1994. text ed. 45.00 (0-8156-2606-1); pap. text ed. 19.95 (0-8156-2607-X) Syracuse U Pr.

Mishan, E. J. Cost Benefit Analysis. 4th ed. 384p. 1988. pap. text ed. 24.95 (0-04-445092-3) Routledge Chapman & Hall.

— The Costs of Economic Growth. 2nd rev. ed. LC 93-19231. 320p. 1993. text ed. 57.95 (0-275-94703-3, Praeger Pubs) Greenwood.

Mishan, Ezra. What Political Economy Is All About: An Exposition & Critique. LC 82-12880. 256p. 1982. 59.95 (0-521-25072-2); pap. 16.95 (0-521-27195-9) Cambridge U Pr.

Mishanie, Mark E. & Sassoon, Penname E. Jewish Days. LC 88-51225. 116p. (Orig.). 1989. pap. 7.00 (0-916383-77-6, Univ Edtns) Aegina Pr.

*Mishara, Brian L., ed. The Impact of Suicide. LC 95-7293. (Springer Series on Death & Suicide). (Illus.). 304p. 1995. write for info. (0-8261-8870-2) Springer Pub.

Mishark, John W. Road to Revolution, German Marxism & World War 1. 15.00 (0-685-16805-0) Moira.

Mishchenko, A. S., et al. Topology of Lagrangian Manifolds. (Illus.). 320p. 1990. 79.00 (0-387-13613-4) Spr-Verlag.

Mishchenko, E., ed. Topology, Ordinary Differential Equations, Dynamical Systems: A Collection of Survey Articles, Pt. II. LC 87-959. (Proceedings of the Steklov Institute of Mathematics Ser.: Vol. 169). 260p. 1987. pap. text ed. 129.00 (0-8218-3100-3, STEKLO-169) Am Math.

*Mishel, Kristi L. & Thomas, John J. Profitable Personnel Services: Start & Run a Money-Making Business. 1995. pap. text ed. 18.95 (0-07-042369-5) TAB Bks.

Mishel, Lawrence. Better Jobs or Working Longer for Less. (Working Paper Ser.: No. 101). 1990. 10.00 (0-944826-25-3) Economic Policy Inst.

— Manufacturing Numbers: How Inaccurate Statistics Conceal U. S. Industrial Decline. LC 88-81375. 103p. (Orig.). 1988. per., pap. 12.00 (0-944826-03-2) Economic Policy Inst.

Mishel, Lawrence & Bernstein, Jared. The State of Working America, 1992-1993. LC 91-641696. (Economic Policy Institute Ser.). 550p. 1993. 51.95 (1-56324-211-7); pap. text ed. 25.95 (1-56324-212-5) M E Sharpe.

— The State of Working America 1994-95. (Economic Policy Institute Ser.). (Illus.). 426p. (C). 1994. text ed. 55.00 (1-56324-532-9); pap. text ed. 24.95 (1-56324-533-7) M E Sharpe.

Mishel, Lawrence & Frankel, David M. Unions & Economic Competitiveness: 1990-91 Edition. Voos, Paula, ed. (Economic Policy Institute Ser.). 550p. 1991. 46.95 (0-87332-812-4); pap. 20.95 (0-87332-813-2) M E Sharpe.

Mishel, Lawrence & Simon, Jacqueline. The State of Working America. LC 88-82263. 53p. 1988. 12.00 (0-944826-04-0) Economic Policy Inst.

Mishel, Lawrence & Teixeira, Ruy A. The Myth of the Coming Labor Shortage: Jobs, Skills, & Incomes of America's Workforce 2000. 1991. 12.00 (0-944826-33-4) Economic Policy Inst.

Mishel, Lawrence R. & Voos, Paula, eds. Unions & Economic Competitiveness. LC 91-21335. (Economic Policy Institute Ser.). 368p. 1992. 46.95 (0-87332-827-2); pap. text ed. 20.95 (0-87332-828-0) M E Sharpe.

Mishell. Year Book Obstetrics & Gynecology, 1994. 525p. 1994. 64.95 (0-8151-6016-X, Yr Bk Med Pubs) Mosby Yr Bk.

— Year Book Obstetrics & Gynecology, 1996. 525p. 1996. 64.95 (0-8151-6018-6, Yr Bk Med Pubs) Mosby Yr Bk.

— Year Book of Infertility, 1993. 255p. 1993. 64.95 (0-8151-6024-0, Yr Bk Med Pubs) Mosby Yr Bk.

— Year Book of Infertility, 1994. 285p. 1994. 64.95 (0-8151-6005-4, Yr Bk Med Pubs) Mosby Yr Bk.

— Year Book of Infertility, 1995. 285p. 1995. 64.95 (0-8151-6006-2, Yr Bk Med Pubs) Mosby Yr Bk.

— Year Book of Infertility, 1996. 285p. 1996. 64.95 (0-8151-6007-0, Yr Bk Med Pubs) Mosby Yr Bk.

— Year Book of Obstetrics & Gynecology, 1995. 525p. 1995. 64.95 (0-8151-6017-8, Yr Bk Med Pubs) Mosby Yr Bk.

— Yearbook of Infertility, 1990. 264p. 1990. 54.95 (0-8151-6021-6, Yr Bk Med Pubs) Mosby Yr Bk.

— Yearbook of Infertility, 1991. 287p. 1991. 57.95 (0-8151-6022-4) Mosby Yr Bk.

— Yearbook of Infertility, 1992. 271p. 1992. 59.95 (0-8151-6023-2) Mosby Yr Bk.

— Yearbook of Obstetrics & Gynecology, 1991. 570p. 1991. 57.95 (0-8151-6013-5) Mosby Yr Bk.

— Yearbook of Obstetrics & Gynecology, 1992. 525p. 1992. 59.95 (0-8151-6014-3) Mosby Yr Bk.

— Yearbook of Obstetrics & Gynecology, 1993. 576p. 1993. 64.95 (0-8151-6015-1) Mosby Yr Bk.

— Yearbook of Obstetrics, 1990. 536p. 1990. 57.95 (0-8151-6012-7, Yr Bk Med Pubs) Mosby Yr Bk.

Mishell, et al. Year Book of Obstetrics & Gynecology, 1997. 520p. 1997. 64.95 (0-8151-6019-4, Yr Bk Med Pubs) Mosby Yr Bk.

Mishell, D. R., et al. Infertility, Contraception & Reproductive Endocrinology. 3rd ed. 688p. 1991. 125.00 (0-86542-157-9) Blackwell Sci.

Mishell, Daniel R., Jr., ed. Long-Acting Steroid Contraception. (Advances in Human Fertility & Reproductive Endocrinology Ser.: Vol. 2). 216p. 1983. text ed. 74.50 (0-89004-932-7) Raven.

— Long Acting Steroid Contraeption. LC 83-43027. (Advances in Human Fertility & Reproductive Endocrinology Ser.: No. 2). (Illus.). Date not set. reprint ed. pap. 61.60 (0-7837-9558-0, 2060307) Bks Demand.

Mishell, Daniel R. & Brenner, Paul F., eds. Management of Common Problems in Ob-Gyn. 2nd ed. 720p. 1988. pap. 52.95 (0-87489-482-4) Med Economics.

Mishell, Daniel R., Jr. & Brenner, Paul F., eds. Management of Common Problems in OB-GYN. 3rd ed. LC 93-28312. 1994. write for info. (0-86542-269-9) Blackwell Sci.

Mishell, Daniel R. & Davajan, Val. Infertility, Contraception & Reproductive Endocrinology. 2nd ed. 704p. 1986. 72.95 (0-87489-352-6) Med Economics.

Mishell, Daniel R., et al, eds. Infertility, Contraception & Reproductive Endocrinology. 3rd ed. 688p. 1991. text ed. 79.95 (0-87489-439-5) Med Economics.

Mishell, Judith & Serebrenik. The Choice Is Yours. 300p. (C). 1991. 15.95 (1-56062-055-2) CIS Comm.

Mishell, Judith & Srebrenick, S. Beyond the Ego. 420p. (C). 1993. 24.95 (1-56062-083-8) CIS Comm.

Mishetski, Dmitry. The Wheat of Christ. (Orig.). 1988. pap. 3.00 (0-913026-68-9) St Nectarios.

Mishev, D. P., jt. auth. see Bainov, D. D.

Mishew, D. Bulgarians in the Past: Pages from the Bulgarian Cultural History. LC 74-135823. (Eastern Europe Collection Ser.). 1971. reprint ed. 29.95 (0-405-02766-4) Ayer.

Mishica, Clare. Billions of Bugs. (Little Deer Bks.). (Illus.). 28p. (J). (ps). 1993. 5.49 (0-7847-0039-7, 24-03829) Standard Pub.

— Charlie the Champ. (Really Reading! Bks.). (Illus.). 48p. (J). (gr. k-3). 1994. pap. 4.49 (0-7847-0138-5, 24-03958) Standard Pub.

— Fraidy Cat Finds a Friend. Stortz, Diane, ed. (Little Deer Bks.). (Illus.). 28p. (J). (ps). 1994. 5.49 (0-7847-0202-0, 24-03888) Standard Pub.

— Max's Answer. Stortz, Diane, ed. LC 94-2100. (Really Reading! Bks.). (Illus.). 48p. (Orig.). (J). (ps-3). 1994. pap. 4.49 (0-7847-0177-6, 24-03937) Standard Pub.

— The Penquin's Big Win. (Really Reading! Bks.). (Illus.). 48p. (Orig.). (J). (gr. k-3). 1994. pap. 4.49 (0-7847-0139-3, 24-03959) Standard Pub.

Mishima. Golden Pavilion. 1995. pap. 17.00 (0-679-43315-5) Random.

Mishima & Seidensticke. Decay of the Angel. LC 89-40554. (Vintage International Ser.). 256p. 1990. pap. 13.00 (0-679-72243-2, Vin) Random.

Mishima, Akio. Bitter Sea: The Human Cost of Minamata Disease. 248p. 1992. pap. 10.95 (4-333-01479-4, Pub. by Kosei Pub Co JA) C E Tuttle.

Mishima, S., ed. Diseases of the Retina & Uvea. (Journal: Ophthalmologica: Vol. 185, No. 3). (Illus.). 72p. 1982. pap. 38.50 (3-8055-3563-5) S Karger.

Mishima, Sumie. My Narrow Isle: The Story of a Modern Woman in Japan. LC 79-2945. (Illus.). 280p. 1991. reprint ed. 30.00 (0-8305-0109-6) Hyperion Conn.

Mishima, Sumio. The Broader Way: A Woman's Life in the New Japan. LC 74-138596. vi, 247p. 1970. reprint ed. text ed. 35.00 (0-8371-5797-8, MIBW, Greenwood Pr) Greenwood.

Mishima, Yasua. Industrial Development & the Social Fabric, Vol. 11: The Mitsubishi: Its Challenge & Strategy. 350p. 1990. 73.25 (1-55938-031-4) Jai Pr.

Mishima, Yukio. Acts of Worship: Seven Stories. 196p. (C). 1989. 17.95 (0-87011-937-0) Kodansha.

— After the Banquet. Keene, Donald, tr. (Perigee Japanese Library). 288p. 1981. pap. 10.50 (0-399-50486-9, Perigree Bks) Berkley Pub.

— Apres le Banquet. (FRE.). 1979. pap. 10.95 (0-7859-4117-7) Fr & Eur.

— Chevaux Echappes (La Mer de la Fertilite II) 499p. (FRE.). 1981. pap. 15.95 (0-7859-4351-X, 2070383318) Fr & Eur.

— Confession d'un Masque. (FRE.). 1983. pap. 11.95 (0-7859-4183-5) Fr & Eur.

— Confessions of a Mask. Weatherby, Meredith, tr. LC 58-12637. 1968. reprint ed. pap. 9.95 (0-8112-0118-X, NDP253) New Directions.

— Death in Midsummer & Other Stories. LC 66-17819. (Orig.). 1966. pap. 9.95 (0-8112-0117-1, NDP215) New Directions.

— Five Modern No Plays. Keene, Donald, tr. (Illus.). 206p. 1957. pap. 12.95 (0-8048-1380-9) C E Tuttle.

— Forbidden Colors. Marks, Alfred H., tr. (Perigee Japanese Library). 416p. 1981. pap. 10.95 (0-399-50490-7, Perigree Bks) Berkley Pub.

— Le Marin Rejete par la Mer. (FRE.). 1979. pap. 10.95 (0-7859-4122-3) Fr & Eur.

— Patriotism. Sargent, Geoffrey W., tr. (New Directions Bibelot Ser.). 64p. 1995. reprint ed. pap. 6.00 (0-8112-1312-9, NDP814) New Directions.

— Le Pavillion d'Or. (FRE.). 1975. pap. 11.95 (0-7859-4039-1) Fr & Eur.

— The Sailor Who Fell from Grace with the Sea. 1994. pap. 10.00 (0-679-75015-0, Vin) Random.

— The Sound of Waves. Weatherby, Meredith, tr. (Perigee Japanese Library). 192p. 1981. pap. 7.95 (0-399-50487-7, Perigree Bks) Berkley Pub.

— The Sound of Waves. 1994. pap. 10.00 (0-679-75268-4) Random.

— Spring Snow. LC 89-40565. (Vintage International Ser.). 400p. 1990. pap. 12.00 (0-679-72241-6, Vin) Random.

— Sun & Steel. Bester, John, tr. LC 76-100628. 1990. pap. 7.00 (0-87011-425-5) Kodansha.

— Temple of Dawn. LC 89-40557. 1990. pap. 14.00 (0-679-72242-4, Vin) Random.

— The Temple of the Golden Pavilion. Morris, Ivan, tr. (Perigee Japanese Library). (Illus.). 288p. 1981. pap. 9.95 (0-399-50488-5, Perigree Bks) Berkley Pub.

— Temple of the Golden Pavilion. 1994. pap. 11.00 (0-679-75270-6) Random.

— Thirst for Love. Marks, Alfred H., tr. (Perigee Japanese Library). 224p. 1981. pap. 8.95 (0-399-50494-X, Perigree Bks) Berkley Pub.

— Le Tumulte des Flots. (FRE.). 1978. pap. 10.95 (0-7859-4095-2) Fr & Eur.

Mishima, Yukio & Gallagher. Runaway Horses. LC 89-40560. (Vintage International Ser.). 1990. pap. 13.00 (0-679-72240-8, Vin) Random.

Mishina, Hitoshi, jt. auth. see Okuyama, Shinichi.

Mishk, O. L. Treasure Island & Kidnapped Notes. 73p. (Orig.). (C). 1974. pap. text ed. 3.95 (0-8220-1306-1) Cliffs.

Mishkin. Economic Money Banking & Financial Markets. (C). 1991. 15.25 (0-673-52176-1) HarpCollege.

— Economic Money Banking & Financial Markets. 3rd ed. (C). 1991. text ed. 43.00 (0-673-52141-9) HarpCollege.

Mishkin & Morris. On Laws in Courts. 1965. text ed. 26.00 (0-88277-360-7) Foundation Pr.

Mishkin, jt. auth. see Easton.

Mishkin, jt. auth. see Eaton.

Mishkin, Bernard. Rank & Warfare among the Plains Indians. LC 84-45510. (American Ethnological Society Monographs: No. 3). 1988. reprint ed. 20.00 (0-404-62903-2) AMS Pr.

— Rank & Warfare among the Plains Indians. LC 92-15035. 90p. 1992. reprint ed. pap. 6.95 (0-8032-8185-4, Bison Books) U of Nebr Pr.

Mishkin, David J. The American Colonial Wine Industry: An Economic Interpretation, 2 vols., 1. (Dissertations in American Economic History Ser.). (Illus.). 1975. 26.95 (0-405-07209-0) Ayer.

— The American Colonial Wine Industry: An Economic Interpretation, 2 vols., 2. (Dissertations in American Economic History Ser.). (Illus.). 1975. 60.95 (0-405-07210-4) Ayer.

— The American Colonial Wine Industry: An Economic Interpretation, 2 vols., Set. (Dissertations in American Economic History Ser.). (Illus.). 1975. 87.95 (0-405-07208-2) Ayer.

Mishkin, Fred S., jt. auth. see Alazraki, Naomi P.

Mishkin, Frederic S. The Economics of Money, Banking & Financial Markets. (C). 1986. teacher ed write for info. (0-318-60360-8); text ed. 31.95 (0-316-57476-7); student ed write for info. (0-316-57477-5) Little.

— The Economics of Money, Banking & Financial Markets. 4th ed. LC 94-20223. (Series in Economics). (C). 1994. 45.00 (0-673-52378-0) HarpCollege.

— Financial Markets, Institutions & Money. LC 94-25039. (C). 1994. 45.00 (0-673-46997-2) HarpC.

— Money, Interest Rates & Inflation. LC 93-2700. (Economists of the Twentieth Century Ser.). 368p. 1993. 59.95 (1-85278-850-X, Pub. by E Elgar Pub UK) Ashgate Pub Co.

— A Rational Expectations Approach to Macroeconomics: Testing Policy Ineffectiveness & Efficient-Markets Models. LC 82-20049. (National Bureau of Economic Research Monograph Ser.). 192p. (C). 1984. pap. text ed. 10.95 (0-226-53187-2) U Ch Pr.

*Mishkin, Julia. Cruel Duet. (QRL Poetry Book Ser.: Vol. XXVI). 20.00 (0-614-06416-3) Quarterly Rev.

Mishkin, M., jt. ed. see Iwai, E.

Mishler, Clayton. Sampan Sailor: A Navy Man's Adventures in WWII China. (World War II Commemorative Ser.). 240p. 1994. 23.95 (0-02-881073-2) Brasseys Inc.

Mishler, Clifford, jt. auth. see Krause, Chester L.

Mishler, Clifford, jt. auth. see Krause, Chester.

Mishler, Craig. The Crooked Stovepipe: Athapaskan Fiddle Music & Square Dancing in Northeast Alaska & Northwest Canada. LC 92-36827. (Music in American Life Ser.). (Illus.). 248p. 1993. 29.95 (0-252-01996-2) U of Ill Pr.

Mishler, Elliot G. The Discourse of Medicine. Wallat, Cynthia & Green, Judith, eds. LC 84-16832. (Language & Learning for Human Service Professions Ser.: Vol. 3). 224p. 1985. text ed. 35.00 (0-89391-276-X); pap. text ed. 27.50 (0-89391-277-8) Ablex Pub.

— Research Interviewing: Context & Narrative. 208p. 1991. pap. 15.95 (0-674-76461-7, MISREX) HUP.

Mishler, Elliot G. & Waxler, Nancy E., eds. Family Processes & Schizophrenia. LC 84-45085. 336p. 1983. 40.00 (0-87668-711-7) Aronson.

Mishler, Lon L., jt. auth. see Cole, Robert H.

Mishler, William, tr. see Haugen, Paal-Helge.

Mishlove, Jeffrey. The Roots of Consciousness. rev. ed. LC 92-72319. (Illus.). 416p. 1992. pap. 24.95 (0-933031-70-X) Coun Oak Bks.

— Thinking Allowed: Conversations on the Leading Edge of Knowledge & Discovery. LC 91-77972. 372p. 1992. pap. 16.95 (0-933031-64-5) Coun Oak Bks.

Mishne, Judith M. Clinical Work with Adolescents. 320p. 1986. text ed. 29.95 (0-02-921260-X) Free Pr.

— Clinical Work with Children. 1983. text ed. 29.95 (0-02-921630-3) Free Pr.

— The Evolution & Application of Clinical Theory: Perspective from Four Psychologies. LC 92-39586. 1993. text ed. 35.00 (0-02-921635-4) Free Pr.

— The Learning Curve: Elevating Children's Academic & Social Competence. 1996. 30.00 (1-56821-568-1) Aronson.

Mishne, Judith M., jt. ed. see Buchholz, Ester S.

Mishoe, S. & Kelsey, N. Ventilator Concepts. 2nd ed. 497p. (C). 1987. pap. text ed. 35.95 (0-933195-15-X) Allied Hlth Pubns.

Mishr, R. P. Hinduism: The Faith of the Future. 131p. 1981. 16.95 (0-940500-17-5) Asia Bk Corp.

Mishra, B. K. Breast Feeding & Child Development. viii, 178p. 1993. 20.00 (81-7024-567-2, Pub. by Ashish Pub Hse II) Nataraj Bks.

Mishra, B. N. Ecology of Poverty in India. 1990. 39.50 (0-8364-2595-2, Pub. by Chugh Pubns II) S Asia.

Mishra, Bhagabat. Economics of Public Distribution in Foodgrains (India) 1985. 32.00 (0-8364-1467-5, Pub. by Ashish II) S Asia.

Mishra, Bhawani. Numerology for All. (Illus.). 200p. (Orig.). 1973. pap. 2.95 (0-88253-299-5) Ind-US Inc.

Mishra, Bhubaneswar. Algorithmic Algebra. LC 93-14094. (Texts & Monographs in Computer Science). 416p. 1993. 39.95 (0-387-94090-1) Spr-Verlag.

— Algorithmic Algebra. (Texts & Monographs in Computer Science). (Illus.). xiv, 425p. 1993. write for info. (3-540-94090-1) Spr-Verlag.

Mishra, Brajendra & Averill, William A., eds. Actinide Processing: Methods & Materials. LC 94-75038. 394p. 1994. 140.00 (0-87339-265-5) Minerals Metals.

Mishra, C. B. Hindi-English Dictionary: Modern. 561p. 1991. 25.00 (0-88431-098-1) IBD Ltd.

Mishra, D. K. Public Debt & Economic Development in India. 552p. (C). 1984. 225.00 (81-85009-07-4, Pub. by Print Hse II) St Mut.

Mishra, D. N. RSS: Myth & Reality. 218p. 1980. 19.95 (0-7069-1020-6) Asia Bk Corp.

Mishra, G. P. & Joshi, A., eds. Regional Structure of Development & Growth in India, 2 vols., 1. 1985. 38.00 (0-8364-1446-2, Pub. by Ashish II) S Asia.

— Regional Structure of Development & Growth in India, 2 vols., 2. 1985. 38.00 (0-8364-1445-4, Pub. by Ashish II) S Asia.

— Regional Structure of Development & Growth in India, 2 vols., Set. 1985. 76.00 (0-317-38615-8, Pub. by Ashish II) S Asia.

Mishra, G. P., et al. Village Industries & Agriculture in Changing Agrarian Situation. 1985. 18.50 (0-317-40626-4, Pub. by Ashish II) S Asia.

Mishra, Ganeswar & Satapathy, Sarat C., eds. A Modern Seer: Selections from Nehru. ix, 118p. 1990. text ed. 15. 95 (0-86311-106-8, Pub. by Orient Longman Ltd II) Apt Bks.

Mishra, Girish. Nehru & the Congress Economic Policies. vi, 163p. 1988. text ed. 25.00 (81-207-0819-9, Pub. by Sterling Pubs II) Apt Bks.

Mishra, Girish, ed. Economic Effects of Militarism. 108p. 1984. 12.95 (0-318-37234-7) Asia Bk Corp.

Mishra, H. K. Famines & Poverty in India. (C). 1990. 59.00 (81-7024-374-2, Pub. by Ashish II) S Asia.

Mishra, Hemanta R. & Jefferies, Margaret. The Royal Chitwan National Park: Wildlife Sanctuary of Nepal. (Illus.). 192p. 1991. pap. 18.95 (0-89886-266-3) Mountaineers.

Mishra, Jayashri. Social & Economic Conditions under the Imperial Rashtrakutas. (C). 1992. 28.50 (81-7169-171-4, Pub. by Commonwealth II) S Asia.

Mishra, Kamalakar. Kashmir Saivism: The Central Philosophy of Tantrism. LC 93-13103. 1993. 26.95 (0-915801-32-9) Rudra Pr.

Mishra, Kiran. Women in a Tribal Community: A Study of Arunachal Pradesh. 1991. text ed. 15.95 (0-7069-5836-5, Pub. by Vikas II) S Asia.

Mishra, Madhusudan. Critical Study of Amrtacandra's Purusarthasiddhupayah. 1992. 14.00 (81-85094-55-1, Pub. by Punthi Pus II) S Asia.

M

An Asterisk (*) at the beginning of an entry indicates that the title is appearing in BIP for the first time.

Mishra, Munmaya K., ed. Macromolecular Design: Concept & Practice: Macromonomers, Macroinitiator, Macroiniferter, Macroinifer - Macroiniter. (Advanced Polymers Via Macromolecular Engineering Ser.). 500p. 1994. 125.00 (*0-9639138-0-8*) Polymer Frontiers.

***Mishra, Nawin C.** Molecular Biology of Nucleases. 304p. 1995. 189.95 (*0-8493-7658-0*, 7658) CRC Pr.

Mishra, Neelam. The Socialist Orientation of Jawaharlal Nehru. 200p. 1989. 13.00 (*81-212-0285-X*, Pub. by Gian Publng Hse II) S Asia.

Mishra, P. C. Fundamentals of Air & Water Pollution. 1990. 22.00 (*81-7024-306-8*, Pub. by Ashish II) S Asia.

— Soil Pollution & Soil Organisms. (C). 1989. 39.00 (*81-7024-258-4*, Pub. by Ashish II) S Asia.

Mishra, P. K. South Asia in International Politics. 498p. 1986. 49.95 (*0-317-39867-9*) Asia Bk Corp.

Mishra, P. K., ed. The Bhagavata Purana: An Illustrated Oriya Palmleaf Manuscript. (Illus.). 60p. 1987. 32.50 (*81-7017-219-5*, Pub. by Abhinav II) S Asia.

***MIshra, P. K. & Sullerey, S. K.** Heritage of India: Past & Present (Essays in Honour of Prof. R. K. Sharma) (C). 1994. text ed. 185.00 (*81-7320-008-4*) S Asia.

Mishra, Pramod K. Dhaka Summit an SAARC. (C). 1986. 9.50 (*81-7074-000-2*, Pub. by KP Bagchi IA) S Asia.

Mishra, R., et al, eds. Progress in Ecology, Vol. I: Progress of Plant Ecology in India. (Illus.). 162p. 1973. 20.00 (*0-88065-160-1*, Messers Today & Tomorrow) Scholarly Pubns.

Mishra, R. B. Caste & Caste Conflict in Rural Society. 1989. 31.00 (*81-7169-013-0*, Pub. by Commonwealth II) S Asia.

Mishra, R. K., ed. Knowledge, Reality & Happiness. (C). 1991. 25.00 (*0-685-50023-3*, Pub. by Munshiram Manoharial II) S Asia.

— Living State II. 712p. 1985. 121.00 (*9971-978-26-1*) World Scientific Pub.

— Molecular & Biological Physics of Living Systems. (C). 1990. lib. bdg. 109.50 (*0-7923-0470-5*) Kluwer Ac.

Mishra, R. K., tr. see Rossinski, I. I., ed.

Mishra, R. K., tr. see Sokolenko, E. A., ed.

Mishra, R. K., et al. On Self-Organization: An Interdisciplinary Search for a Unifying Principle. LC 93-38258. 1994. 67.00 (*0-387-56485-3*) Spr-Verlag.

Mishra, R. N. Regionalism & State Politics in India. 1985. 27.50 (*0-8364-1370-9*, Pub. by Ashish II) S Asia.

Mishra, R. R., ed. Current Trends in Environmental Biology. (C). 1990. 18.00 (*81-224-0184-8*, Pub. by Wiley Eastern II) S Asia.

Mishra, Rajendra N. Practical English Grammar: Composition & Exercises. 88p. 1991. pap. text ed. 3.95 (*81-207-1319-2*, Pub. by Sterling Pubs II) Apt Bks.

— Search for Belief in the Poetry of Robert Frost. (C). 1992. 18.00 (*81-7017-291-8*, Pub. by Abhinav II) S Asia.

Mishra, Ramesh. The Welfare State in Capitalist Society: Policies of Retrenchment & Maintenance in Europe, North America, & Australia. 208p. 1990. text ed. 60.00 (*0-8020-5895-7*); pap. text ed. 19.95 (*0-8020-6829-4*) U of Toronto Pr.

Mishra, Rammurti S. Fundamentals of Yoga: A Handbook of Theory, Practice, & Application. (Illus.). 256p. 1987. pap. 13.95 (*0-517-56422-X*, Harmony) Crown Pub Group.

— The Textbook of Yoga Psychology. 464p. 1987. pap. 10.95 (*0-517-56434-3*, Harmony) Crown Pub Group.

Mishra, Ramprasad. Sahajayana: A Study of Tantric Buddhism. (C). 1991. 45.00 (*81-85094-45-4*, Pub. by Punthi Pus II) S Asia.

Mishra, Rashmi & Mohanty, Samarendra. Police & Social Change in India. xiv, 229p. 1992. 22.95 (*1-881338-32-0*) Nataraj Bks.

Mishra, Ratan L. The Mortuary Monuments in Ancient & Medieval India. 1991. 18.00 (*81-7018-622-6*, Pub. by BR Pub II) S Asia.

Mishra, S. Fundamental Rights & the Supreme Court Reasonableness of Restrictions. 2nd ed. (C). 1989. 125.00 (*0-685-36530-1*) St Mut.

Mishra, S. G. Legal History of India, 1600-1990. (C). 1992. 22.00 (*81-85565-21-X*, Pub. by Uppal Pub Hse II) S Asia.

***Mishra, S. K.** Sustainable Growth of Agriculture in India. 135p. 1994. 45.00x (*81-85880-30-1*, Pub. by Print Hse II) St Mut.

Mishra, Satya N., jt. auth. see Dudewicz, Edward J.

***Mishra, Shanti.** Voice of Truth: Challenges & Struggles of a Nepalese Woman. (C). 1994. 44.00 (*81-7303-022-7*, Pub. by Book Faith II) S Asia.

Mishra, Shyam M. Yasavarman of Kanauj: Study of Political History, Society & Cultural Life of Northern India. 1978. 15.00 (*0-8364-0105-0*) S Asia.

***Mishra, Srikanta.** Ancient Hindu Marriage Law & Practice. (C). 1994. 26.50x (*81-7100-582-9*, Pub. by Deep) S Asia.

Mishra, Surendra K. & Klimpel, Richard R., eds. Fine Coal Processing. LC 86-3338. (Illus.). 452p. 1987. 48.00 (*0-8155-1123-X*) Noyes.

Mishra, V. B. Supreme Court on Equal Pay for Equal Work. (C). 1989. 110.00 (*0-685-36495-X*) St Mut.

***Mishra, V. D.** Youth Culture: A Comparative Study in the Indon Context. (C). 1993. 18.00x (*81-210-0311-3*, Pub. by Inter-India Pubns) S Asia.

Mishra, Vic, jt. ed. see Singh, Indu B.

Mishra, Vidya B. Refunds under Central Excise & Customs. (C). 1990. 100.00 (*0-89771-225-0*) St Mut.

Mishra, Vijay. The Gothic Sublime. LC 93-147. (SUNY Series on the Sublime). 342p. (C). 1994. 59.50 (*0-7914-1747-6*); pap. 19.95 (*0-7914-1748-4*) State U NY Pr.

Mishra, Vijay, jt. auth. see Hodge, Bob.

***Mishra, Vinod S.** Environment Disasters & the Law. (Illus.). xvi, 146p. 1994. 15.00 (*81-7024-629-6*) Nataraj Bks.

***Mishriky, Salwa E.** Le Misanthrope Ou la Philanthropie de l'Honnete Homme Classique. (Currents in Comparative Romance Languages & Literatures Ser.). 256p. (FRE.). (C). 1995. text ed. 49.95 (*0-8204-2398-X*) P Lang Pubs.

Misiek, Jozef, ed. The Problem of Rationality in Science & Its Philosophy: On Popper vs. Polanyi, the Polish Conferences 1988-89. LC 94-17897. (Boston Studies in Philosophy of Science: Vol. 160). 280p. (C). 1995. lib. bdg. 115.00 (*0-7923-2925-2*) Kluwer Ac.

Misiewicz, J. J. Diseases of the Gut & Pancreas. 2nd ed. (Illus.). 1994. write for info. (*0-632-02783-5*, Pub. by Blckwell Sci Pubns UK) Blackwell Sci.

Misiewicz, J. J., et al. Atlas of Clinical Gastroenterology. LC 87-176795. 294p. 1987. pap. 83.80 (*0-7837-2729-1*, 2043109) Bks Demand.

Misina, A. P. & Skornjakov, L. A. Abelian Groups & Modules. LC 76-22560. (Translations Ser.: No. 2, Vol. 107). 160p. 1976. 50.00 (*0-8218-3057-0*, TRANS 2-107) Am Math.

Misiorowski, Robert, jt. auth. see Lee, Robert.

Misiroglo, Gina, ed. see Chapman, Joyce.

Misiroglo, Gina, ed. see Shadel, Douglas & Ward, Al.

Misiroglu, Gina, ed. see Lawrence, Shirley B.

Misiroglu, Gina, ed. see Robinson, Rita.

Misiroglu, Gina, ed. see Shadel, Douglas P. & T, John.

Misita, Michael. How to Believe in Nothing & Set Yourself Free. 156p. 1994. pap. 9.98 (*0-87554-572-6*) Valley Sun.

Misiunas, Romuald J. & Taagepera, Rein. The Baltic States, Years of Dependence, 1940-1992. LC 92-39806. (C). 1993. 45.00 (*0-520-08227-3*); pap. 17.00 (*0-520-08228-1*) U CA Pr.

***Misiura.** Business Communication (CIM Workbook) 1995. pap. write for info. (*0-7506-1995-3*, Focal) Buttrwrth-Heinemann.

Misiurewicz & Nitecki. Combinatorial Patterns for Maps of the Interval. LC 91-27263. (MEMO Ser.). 112p. 1991. 21.00 (*0-8218-2513-5*, MEMO 94/456) Am Math.

Miska, John. Ethnic & Native Canadian Literature: A Bibliography. 464p. 1990. text ed. 135.00 (*0-8020-5852-3*) U of Toronto Pr.

Miska, Stefan, ed. see Lubinski, Arthur.

Miskal, James F. Buying Trouble? National Security & Reliance on Foreign Industry. LC 92-42182. 1993. 44.50 (*0-8191-9012-8*); pap. 19.50 (*0-8191-9013-6*) U Pr of Amer.

Miskawayh, et al. The Eclipse of the Abbasid Caliphate, 7 vols. Amedroz, H. F. & Margoliouth, D. S., trs. (C). reprint ed. lib. bdg. 500.00 (*0-89241-219-4*) Caratzas.

Miskawayh, Ali. Refinement of Character. Zurayk, Constantine, tr. 1977. pap. 14.00 (*0-8156-6051-0*, Am U Beirut) Syracuse U Pr.

Miskel, Cecil G., jt. auth. see Hoy, Wayne K.

Miskell, Jane R. & Miskell, Vincent. Motivation at Work. LC 93-18112. 96p. 1993. pap. 10.00 (*1-55623-868-1*) -Irwin Prof Pubng.

— Motivation at Work. (AMI How-to Ser.). 100p. 1995. 9.95 (*1-884926-46-0*) Amer Media.

Miskell, Jane R., jt. auth. see Miskell, Vincent.

Miskell, Vincent & Miskell, Jane R. Overcoming Anxiety at Work. LC 93-12077. 128p. 1993. pap. 10.00 (*1-55623-869-X*) Irwin Prof Pubng.

Miskell, Vincent, jt. auth. see Miskell, Jane R.

Miskiel, Lynn W., jt. auth. see Vergara, Kathleen C.

Miskiewicz, Sophia M. & Trehub, Aaron. Social & Economic Rights in the Soviet Union & East Europe. 256p. 1988. 39.95 (*0-88738-186-3*) Transaction Pubs.

Miskimin, Harry A. Cash, Credit & Crisis in Europe, 1300-1600. (Collected Studies: No. CS289). 298p. (C). 1989. lib. bdg. 8,735.00 (*0-86078-237-9*, Pub. by Variorum UK) Ashgate Pub Co.

— Money & Power in Fifteenth-Century France. LC 83-21754. (Economic History Ser.). 320p. 1984. text ed. 40.00 (*0-300-03132-7*) Yale U Pr.

— Money, Prices, & Foreign Exchange in Fourteenth Century France. LC 63-7942. 1999. reprint ed. 15.00 (*0-08-022307-9*, Pergamon Pr) Elsevier.

Miskimin, Harry A., et al, eds. The Medieval City. LC 77-76302. 355p. reprint ed. pap. 101.20 (*0-8357-8218-2*, 2033828) Bks Demand.

Miskimins, R. W. Guide to Floating Whitewater Rivers. (Illus.). 188p. (Orig.). 1987. pap. 8.95 (*0-936608-49-8*) F Amato Pubns.

Miskimins, R. W., jt. auth. see Bonser, Carol.

***Miskimins, Ray.** Lake Tahoe's Top Twenty Bike Rides on Pavement & Dirt. Douglass, Reanne, ed. (Illus.). 48p. (Orig.). Date not set. pap. 6.95 (*0-938665-36-7*) Fine Edge Prods.

— Mountain Biking the Reno-Carson City Area, Guide 13. 1993. 10.95 (*0-938665-22-7*) Fine Edge Prods.

Miskin, Alan S. Full Circle - My Plan for Stimulating a Paradigm Shift in the Structure of Education in America for the 21st Century...with Recommendations for the Future. LC 92-81651. 53p. 1992. pap. text ed. 20.00 (*0-9633223-1-1*) ASM Intl.

Miskin, Val D., jt. auth. see Gmelch, Walter H.

Misko, James A. How to Finance Any Real Estate Any Place Any Time. LC 94-92042. 212p. 1994. pap. 14.95 (*0-9640826-0-8*) NW Ventures.

Miskovitz, Paul & Rochwarger, Arnold. Evae & Treatment of Patients with Diarrhea. (Illus.). 179p. 1992. 45.00 (*1-56372-059-0*, Andover Med Pubs) Buttrwrth-Heinemann.

Miskowiec, Jay, tr. see Aguilar, Eduardo G.

Miskowski, Nick. Hiking Guide to Dealware Water Gap National Recreation Area. rev. ed. Chazin, Daniel D., ed. LC 94-21406. 1994. write for info. (*1-880775-01-8*) NY-NJ Trail Confer.

Miskowski, Mike. Applianoidal Grphcus Birthday Elaps 4-89. (Illus.). 44p. (YA). 1989. pap. text ed. 4.00 (*0-944215-04-1*) Abscond Pubs.

— Suburbreal Drive: A Scattering. 36p. (Orig.). 1987. pap. 3.00 (*0-944215-00-9*) Abscond Pubs.

MisKowski, Mike & Foley, Jack. Artifact Collective - Texts, No. 1. Berry, Jake, ed. 20p. (Orig.). (YA). (gr. 7 up). 1988. pap. 3.00 (*0-944215-02-5*) Abscond Pubs.

Miskowski, Richard L. Tips-to-Top Dollar: A Better Way to Sell Your Car, Truck, Or Van. (Illus.). 32p. (Orig.). Date not set. student ed write for info. (*0-9640051-0-7*) RJC Enter.

Misla, Victor M. Little Anabo from Boriken. (Illus.). 28p. (Orig.). (YA). (gr. 6-7). 1987. pap. 5.00 (*0-9626870-0-6*) NW Monarch Pr.

— The Treasure of Camuy's Cave. (Illus.). 30p. (Orig.). (YA). (gr. 6-7). 1987. pap. 5.00 (*0-9626870-1-4*) NW Monarch Pr.

Misler, Nicoletta & Bowlt, John E. Pavel Filonov: A Hero & His Fate: Collected Writings on Art & Revolution, 1910 - 40. (Institute of Modern Russian Culture Ser.). (Illus.). 378p. 1983. 75.00 (*0-941432-05-X*) R G Landes.

Mislevy, Robert & Bock, R. Darrell. Bilog 3: Item Analysis & Test Scoring with Binary Logistic Models. 2nd ed. 1990. ring bd. 30.00 (*0-89498-026-2*) Sci Ware.

Mislin & Ravera, O. Cadmium in the Environment. (Experientia Supplementa Ser.: Vol. 50). 148p. 1986. 59.00 (*0-8176-1760-4*, Pub. by Birkhauser Vlg SZ) Birkhauser.

Mislin, Guido, ed. The Hilton Symposium 1993. LC 94-16852. (CRM Proceedings & Lecture Notes Ser.: Vol. 6). 1994. write for info. (*0-8218-0273-9*) Am Math.

Mislin, H., jt. ed. see Bachofen, R.

Misnad, Sheikha. Development of Modern Education in the Gulf. 386p. 1985. 40.00 (*0-685-14920-X*, Pub. by Ithaca UK) Evergreen Dist.

Misner, Charles W., et al. Gravitation. LC 78-156043. (Physics Ser.). (Illus.). 1279p. (C). 1995. pap. text ed. write for info. (*0-7167-0344-0*) W H Freeman.

Misner, Frank M. Extra Costs & Incidental Costs in the Erection of School Buildings. LC 71-177075. (Columbia University. Teachers College. Contributions to Education Ser.). reprint ed. 37.50 (*0-404-55624-8*) AMS Pr.

***Misner, Ivan R.** The World's Best Known Marketing Secret: Building Your Business with Word-of-Mouth Marketing. (Illus.). 224p. 1994. 24.95 (*1-885167-05-9*); pap. 14.95 (*1-885167-04-0*) Bard & Stephen.

Misner, Paul. Social Catholicism in Europe Vol. 1: From the Onset of Industrialization to the First World War. 320p. 1991. 29.95x (*0-8245-1097-6*) Crossroad NY.

Misner, Peter, jt. auth. see Glusker, David.

Misono, M., et al, eds. Future Opportunities in Catalytic & Separation Technology. (Studies in Surface Science & Catalysis: Vol. 54). 382p. 1990. 179.50 (*0-444-88592-7*) Elsevier.

Misquitta, L. P. Pressure Groups & Democracy in India. 1991. text ed. 37.50 (*81-207-1105-X*, Pub. by Sterling Pubs II) Apt Bks.

Misra, A. S. Commentaries on U. P. Public Services (Tribunals) (C). 1991. 95.00 (*0-685-39561-8*) St Mut.

— Commentaries on U. P. Public Services (Tribunals) Act, 1976. 277p. 1980. 100.00 (*0-317-54707-0*) St Mut.

— Law & Practice of Character & Integrity Rolls. 348p. 1979. 120.00 (*0-317-54705-4*) St Mut.

— Law of Bias & Malfides. 3rd rev. ed. (C). 1986. 75.00 (*0-685-39794-7*) St Mut.

— Law of Speaking Orders. 1985. 95.00 (*0-317-56717-9*) St Mut.

— Officer's Companion (In Administration & Law) (C). 1988. 225.00 (*0-89771-783-X*, Pub. by Eastern Book II) St Mut.

Misra, A. S., ed. Commentaries on U. P. Public Services (Tribunals) Act, 1980. 2nd rev. ed. (C). 1991. reprint ed. 95.00 (*0-685-39526-X*) St Mut.

Misra, Arun, ed. Virus Taxonomy. 211p. 1985. 25.00 (*1-55528-058-7*, Messers Today & Tomorrow) Scholarly Pubns.

***Misra, Arun, et al.** Astrodynamics 1993. LC 57-43769. (Advances in the Astronautical Sciences Ser.: 85, I, II & III). (Illus.). 2750p. 1994. lib. bdg. 390.00x (*0-87703-380-3*, Pub. by Am Astro Soc) Univelt Inc.

— Plant Tumors. (Illus.). xviii, 222p. 1985. 25.00 (*1-55528-045-5*, Pub. by Today & Tomorrows P & P II) Scholarly Pubns.

— Plant Tumors. (Illus.). xxl, 222p. (C). 1985. lib. bdg. 25.00 (*1-55528-000-5*, Messers Today & Tomorrow) Scholarly Pubns.

Misra, B. Capitalism, Socialism & Planning. (C). 1988. 11.00 (*81-204-0306-1*, Pub. by Oxford IBH II) S Asia.

Misra, B. B. The Unification & Division of India. 456p. 1991. 29.95 (*0-19-562615-X*) OUP.

***Misra, B. D.** Forts & Fortresses of Gwalior & Its Hinterland. (C). 1993. 30.00x (*81-7304-047-8*, Pub. by Manohar Bk Srv II) S Asia.

Misra, B. D., et al. Organization for Change: A Systems Analysis of Family Planning in Rural India. (Michigan Papers on South & Southeast Asia: No. 21). xxiv, 444p. (C). 1982. 5.00 (*0-89148-019-6*) Ctr S&SE Asian.

Misra, Bal G., jt. auth. see Fairbanks, Gordon H.

Misra, Banarsi. Monitoring of Industrial Sickness. (C). 1990. text ed. 30.00 (*81-7100-266-8*, Pub. by Deep) S Asia.

Misra, Bani P. Socioeconomic Adjustments of Tribals: A Case Study of Tripura Jhumias (India) LC 76-903504. 1976. 6.50 (*0-88386-700-1*) S Asia.

Misra, Bhabagrahi. My Mind at Work: Stray Papers. LC 90-50552. vii, 173p. (C). 1990. text ed. 24.95 (*1-55605-178-6*); pap. text ed. 14.95 (*1-55605-177-8*) Wyndhall Pr.

Misra, Bhabagrahi & Preston, James, eds. Community, Self, & Identity. (World Anthropology Ser.). xii, 316p. 1978. 50.80 (*90-279-7650-3*) Mouton.

Misra, Chitranjan. Harold Pinter: The Dramatist. 1993. 25.00 (*81-85231-12-5*, Pub. by Creative Pubs II) Advent Bks Div.

Misra, G. S. Development of Buddhist Ethics. 1984. text ed. 22.00 (*0-685-13698-1*) Coronet Bks.

Misra, Ganeswar. Language, Reality & Analysis: Essays on Indian Philosophy. Mohanty, J. N., ed. LC 90-42506. (Indian Thought & Culture Ser.: Vol. 1). iv, 101p. 1990. 40.00 (*90-04-09305-2*) E J Brill.

Misra, Girish, et al. Block Level Planning. 1987. 35.00 (*0-317-89538-9*, Pub. by Rawat II) S Asia.

Misra, Girishwar, ed. Applied Social Psychology in India. 320p. (C). 1990. 27.50 (*0-8039-9645-4*) Sage.

Misra, H. N. Bhutan: Problems & Policies. 1988. 27.00 (*0-8364-2311-9*, Heritage) S Asia.

— Contributions to Indian Geography: Rural Geography, Vol. 9. 462p. (C). 1987. 54.00 (*0-8364-2100-0*, Pub. by Heritage IA) S Asia.

— Urban System of a Developing Economy. 1988. 32.00 (*0-8364-2312-7*, Heritage) S Asia.

Misra, Jayadev, jt. auth. see Chandy, K. Mani.

Misra, K. C., ed. Volcanogenic Sulfide & Precious Metal Mineralization in the Southern Appalachians. (Studies in Geology). (Illus.). ii, 236p. 1986. pap. 10.00 (*0-910249-15-6*) U of Tenn Geo.

***Misra, K. K.** Tribal Elites & Social Transformation. (C). 1994. 18.00x (*81-210-0319-9*, Pub. by Inter-India Pubns) S Asia.

***Misra, K. N.** Women Education & the Upanishadic System of Education. (C). 1993. 30.00 (*81-85613-76-1*, Pub. by Chugh Pubns II) S Asia.

Misra, K. P. Quest for an International Order in the Indian Ocean. 159p. 1977. 14.95 (*0-318-37255-X*) Asia Bk Corp.

Misra, K. P. & Chopra, V. D. South Asia-Pacific Region: Emerging Trends. 1988. 27.00 (*0-685-21059-6*, Patriot) S Asia.

Misra, K. P. & Gangal, S. C., eds. Gandhi & the Contemporary World: Studies in Peace & War. 1982. 15.00 (*0-8364-0849-7*, Pub. by Chanakya II) S Asia.

Misra, Kashi P. Nonaligned Movement: India's Chairmanship. vii, 248p. (C). 1987. 26.00 (*81-7095-001-5*, Pub. by Lancer II) S Asia.

Misra, Krishna B. Reliability Analysis & Prediction: A Methodology Oriented Treatment. LC 92-13149. (Fundamental Studies in Engineering: No. 15). 1992. write for info. (*0-444-89606-6*) Elsevier.

Misra, Krishna B., ed. New Trends in System Reliability Evaluation. LC 93-38228. (Fundamental Studies in Engineering: Vol. 16). 715p. 1993. 265.75 (*0-444-81660-7*) Elsevier.

Misra, Kula C. Mineral & Energy Resources: Current Status & Future Trends. (Studies in Geology). (Illus.). 276p. (Orig.). (C). 1986. pap. text ed. 15.00 (*0-910249-13-X*) U of Tenn Geo.

Misra, Lakshmi. Womens' Issues: An Indian Perspective. (C). 1992. 22.00 (*81-7211-017-0*, Pub. by Northern Bk Ctr II) S Asia.

Misra, M., jt. ed. see Smith, R. W.

Misra, M. S., jt. ed. see Rath, B. B.

Misra, Mathura P. Trilingual Dictionary Being a Comprehensive Lexicon in English. (C). reprint ed. 49.00 (*0-8364-2639-8*, Pub. by Asian Educ Servs II) S Asia.

***Misra, Neeru.** Succession & Imperial Leadership among the Mughals 1526-1707. (C). 1993. 16.00 (*81-220-0337-0*, Pub. by Konark Pubs II) S Asia.

Misra, O. P. & Lavoine, J. L. Transform Analysis of Generalized Functions. (Mathematical Studies: Vol. 119). 332p. 1986. 74.50 (*0-444-87885-8*, North Holland) Elsevier.

Misra, Porwal. Inflation Accounting in a Developing Economy. 1985. 12.00 (*0-8364-1503-5*, Pub. by Allied II) S Asia.

Misra, R. D. Manual on Irrigation Agronomy. 422p. (C). 1987. 18.00 (*81-204-0184-0*, Pub. by Oxford IBH II) S Asia.

Misra, R. P. Gandhian Model of Development & World Peace. 1990. 32.00 (*81-7022-227-3*, Pub. by Concept II) S Asia.

— Manual for the Production of Anthrax & Blackleg Vaccines. (Animal Production & Health Papers: No. 87). 134p. 1991. pap. 12.00 (*92-5-102920-2*, F9202) UNIPUB.

— Multi-Level Planning & Integrated Rural Development in India. 1980. 15.00 (*0-8364-0576-5*, Pub. by Heritage IA) S Asia.

— Rural Industrialization in Third World Countries. 332p. 1986. text ed. 35.00 (*0-86590-795-1*, Pub. by Sterling Pubs II) Apt Bks.

— Third World Peasantry: A Continuing Saga of Deprivation, 2 vols. 1986. text ed. 75.00 (*81-207-0158-5*, Pub. by Sterling Pubs II) Apt Bks.

Misra, R. P., ed. Contributions to Indian Geography: Vol. 1, Concepts & Approaches. 1983. 34.00 (*0-8364-0947-7*, Pub. by Heritage IA) S Asia.

— District Planning: A Handbook. 1990. 47.50 (*81-7022-313-X*, Pub. by Concept II) S Asia.

Misra, R. P. & Achyutha, R. N. Micro Level Rural Planning: Principles, Methods & Case Studies. (C). 1990. text ed. 40.00 (*0-685-39100-0*, Pub. by Concept II) S Asia.

Misra, R. P. & Bhooshan, B. S. Human Settlements in Asia: Public Policies & Programs. 1979. 17.50 (*0-8364-0541-2*) S Asia.

Misra, R. P. & Ramesh, A. Fundamentals of Cartography. 2nd rev. ed. (C). 1989. 50.00 (*81-7022-222-2*, Pub. by Concept II) S Asia.

Misra, R. P. & Raza, Moonis, eds. Contributions to Indian Geography, Vol. 10: Regional Development. (C). 1988. 76.00 (*81-7026-143-0*, Pub. by Heritage IA) S Asia.

Misra, R. P., jt. ed. see Singh, Tej V.

Misra, R. P., jt. auth. see Subrahmanyam, V. P.
Misra, Renuka, jt. auth. see Dev, Sukh.
Misra, Renuka, jt. ed. see Dev, Sukh.
Misra, S. G. Metallic Pollution. (C). 1992. 20.00 (*81-7024-473-0*, Pub. by Ashish II) S Asia.
Misra, S. G. & Mani, Dinesh. Soil Pollution. (C). 1991. text ed. 22.00 (*81-7024-431-5*, Pub. by Ashish II) S Asia.
Misra, S. G. & Mani, Dinesh, eds. Agricultural Pollution, 2 vols., Set. (Illus.). 1994. 25.00 (*0-685-72742-4*, Pub. by Ashish Pub Hse II) Nataraj Bks.
— Agricultural Pollution, Vol. 1. (Illus.). iv, 98p. 1994. write for info. (*81-7024-574-5*, Pub. by Ashish Pub Hse II) Nataraj Bks.
— Agricultural Pollution, Vol. 2. (Illus.). vi, 188p. 1994. write for info. (*81-7024-601-6*, Pub. by Ashish Pub Hse II) Nataraj Bks.
Misra, S. N. India: The Cold War Years. (C). 1994. 22.50x (*81-7003-154-0*, Pub. by S Asia Pubs II) S Asia.
Misra, S. P. Introduction to Supersymmetry & Supergravity. LC 92-10975. 1992. text ed. 64.95 (*0-470-21862-2*) Halsted Pr.
Misra, Sanjiv. India's Textile Sector: A Policy Analysis. LC 92-46158. (Illus.). 278p. 1993. 36.00 (*0-8039-9474-5*) Sage.
Misra, Satya S. Aryan Problem: A Linguistic Approach. (C). 1992. 14.00 (*81-215-0537-2*, Pub. by Munshiram Manoharlal II) S Asia.
Misra, Shridhar, jt. auth. see Singh, Baljit.
Misra, Sib R. Tea Industry in India. 1986. 24.00 (*81-7024-015-8*, Pub. by Ashish II) S Asia.
Misra, Sibranjan. Fisheries in India. (C). 1987. 13.50 (*81-7024-099-9*, Pub. by Ashish II) S Asia.
Misra, Suchitra K. Taste of Goa: Illustrated Guide to Goan Cooking. (C). 1992. pap. 14.00 (*81-7023-208-2*, Pub. by Allied II) S Asia.
Misra, Suresh. Politico-Peasantry Conflict in India: Dynamics of Agrarian Change. (C). 1991. 15.00 (*81-7099-306-7*, Pub. by Mittal II) S Asia.
Misra, Surya N. Party Politics & Electoral Choice in an Indian State. (C). 1989. 34.00 (*81-202-0247-3*, Pub. by Ajanta II) S Asia.
Misra, Umesh C. Tribal Paintings & Sculptures. (C). 1989. 25.00 (*81-7018-543-2*, Pub. by BR Pub II) S Asia.
Misra, V. B. Evolution of the Constitutional History of India. 1987. 32.00 (*81-7099-010-6*, Pub. by Mittal II) S Asia.
Misra, Vidya N. The Descriptive Technique of Panini: An Introduction. (Janua Linguarum, Series Practica: No. 18). 1966. pap. text ed. 58.50 (*90-279-0637-8*) Mouton.
Misra, Vidya N., ed. Modern Hindi Poetry: An Anthology. (C). 1991. 17.00 (*81-7023-299-6*, Pub. by Allied II) S Asia.
Misrach, Myriam W., jt. auth. see Misrach, Richard.
Misrach, Richard. Richard Misrach. (Min Gallery Series of Contemporary American & Japanese Photography). (Illus.). 88p. 1989. pap. 30.00 (*4-906265-17-0*) Aperture.
— Violent Legacies: Three Cantos. (Illus.). 128p. 1992. 50.00 (*0-89381-519-5*) Aperture.
— Violent Legacies: Three Cantos. 1994. pap. 29.95 (*0-89381-569-1*) Aperture.
Misrach, Richard & Misrach, Myriam W. Bravo Twenty: The Bombing of the American West. LC 90-34150. (Creating the North American Landscape Ser.). (Illus.). 160p. 1990. 49.95 (*0-8018-4064-3*); pap. 29.95 (*0-8018-4065-1*) Johns Hopkins.
Misrahi, Mary M., tr. see Nocent, Adrien.
Misrahi, R. Le Desir et la Reflexion Dans la Philosophie De Spinoza. 382p. 1972. pap. text ed. 45.00 (*0-677-50815-8*) Gordon & Breach.
Misraki, Paul, jt. auth. see Vercors, Jean.
***Misri, Shaila.** Shouldn't I Be Happy? Emotional Problems of Pregnant & Post Partum Women. 1995. 23.00 (*0-02-921405-X*) Free Pr.
Miss Lori. Shapeless & the Magic Box, Bk. 1. White, Lori G., ed. (Illus.). 18p. (Orig.). (J). (ps-1). 1990. pap. 11.99 (*0-9623368-3-1*) Shapeless Enterprises.
— Shapeless & the Magic Box, Bk. 2. White, Lori G., ed. (Illus.). 18p. (Orig.). (J). (ps-1). 1991. pap. 11.99 (*0-9623368-8-2*) Shapeless Enterprises.
Miss Pinnell & the Children of Sapperton School. Village Camera. (Illus.). 128p. 1991. 28.00 (*0-86299-791-7*) A Sutton Pub.
Miss Read. Celebration at Green Thrush. LC 93-22983. 1993. 19.95 (*0-395-65030-5*) HM.
— Changes at Fairacre. large type ed. LC 92-47256. 1993. 20.95 (*0-7927-1593-4*, Eagle Lrg Print) Chivers N Amer.
— Country Cooking. large type ed. 296p. 1993. 21.95 (*0-7505-0217-7*) Ulverscroft.
— Emily Davis. (Illus.). 238p. 1990. pap. 9.00 (*0-89733-340-3*) Academy Chi Pubs.
— The Fairacre Festival. (Illus.). 104p. 1990. reprint ed. pap. 8.00 (*0-89733-333-0*) Academy Chi Pubs.
— Farewell to Fairacre. 192p. 1994. 19.95 (*0-395-68994-5*) HM.
— Farther Afield. (Miss Read Ser.). (Illus.). 235p. 1991. reprint ed. pap. 9.00 (*0-89733-371-3*) Academy Chi Pubs.
— Fresh from the Country. (Illus.). 219p. 1995. reprint ed. pap. 9.00 (*0-89733-417-5*) Academy Chi Pubs.
— Friends at Thrush Green. (Illus.). 256p. 1991. 19.95 (*0-395-57381-5*) HM.
— Friends at Thrush Green. large type ed. LC 92-6847. 355p. 1992. reprint ed. lib. bdg. 17.95 (*1-56054-310-8*) Thorndike Pr.
— Howards of Caxley. 1988. pap. 9.00 (*0-89733-319-5*) Academy Chi Pubs.
— The Market Square. large type ed. 1992. pap. 14.95 (*0-7927-0560-2*, Paragon Lrg Print) Chivers N Amer.
— Miss Clare Remembers. (Illus.). 238p. 1988. reprint ed. pap. 9.00 (*0-89733-308-X*) Academy Chi Pubs.
— Miss Read's Christmas. (Miss Read Ser.). (Illus.). 220p. 1990. 20.00 (*0-89733-352-7*) Academy Chi Pubs.
— Miss Read's Country Cooking. (Illus.). 248p. 1992. 20.00 (*0-89733-373-X*) Academy Chi Pubs.
— News from Thrush Green. (Illus.). 240p. 1989. reprint ed. pap. 9.00 (*0-89733-334-9*) Academy Chi Pubs.
— No Holly for Miss Quinn. (Miss Read Ser.). (Illus.). 148p. 1992. reprint ed. pap. 9.00 (*0-89733-383-7*) Academy Chi Pubs.
— Over the Gate. (Illus.). 238p. 1988. reprint ed. pap. 9.00 (*0-89733-298-9*) Academy Chi Pubs.
— Return to Thrush Green. large type ed. 1993. pap. 15.95 (*0-7927-1266-8*, Paragon Lrg Print) Chivers N Amer.
— Storm in the Village. 247p. 1987. pap. 9.00 (*0-89733-244-X*) Academy Chi Pubs.
— Thrush Green. 1982. reprint ed. lib. bdg. 21.95 (*0-89966-435-0*) Buccaneer Bks.
— Tylers Row. (Illus.). 1990. pap. 9.00 (*0-89733-339-X*) Academy Chi Pubs.
— Tyler's Row. large type ed. LC 92-30416. (General Ser.). 312p. 1993. 19.95 (*0-8161-5509-7*) G K Hall.
— Village Christmas; The Christmas Mouse. large type ed. LC 93-16779. (Large Print Bks.). 1993. 21.95 (*0-8161-5501-1*) Hall.
— Village Christmas; The Christmas Mouse. large type ed. LC 93-16779. (Large Print Bks.). 1994. pap. 15.95 (*0-8161-5502-X*) Hall.
— Village Diary. 255p. 1986. pap. 9.00 (*0-89733-212-1*) Academy Chi Pubs.
— Village Diary. large type ed. LC 92-38332. 1993. 19.95 (*0-7927-1536-5*, Eagle Lrg Print); pap. write for info. (*0-7927-1535-7*, Eagle Lrg Print) Chivers N Amer.
— Village School. large type ed. LC 93-23073. 1994. 18.95 (*0-7927-1763-5*, Paragon Lrg Print); pap. 17.95 (*0-7927-1762-7*, Paragon Lrg Print) Chivers N Amer.
— Winter in Thrush Green. 1982. reprint ed. lib. bdg. 21.95 (*0-89966-436-9*) Buccaneer Bks.
— The Worlds of Thrush Green. large type ed. LC 93-16776. 326p. 1993. 21.95 (*0-8161-5507-0*) Hall.
***Missac, Pierre.** Walter Benjamin's Passages. (Studies in Contemporary German Social Thought). (Illus.). 256p. 1995. 25.00 (*0-262-13305-9*) MIT Pr.
Missair, Alfredo R. & Meyer, Bruce F. The Larue D. Carter Memorial Hospital Case-Study: A Behaviorial Approach to Environmental Normalization in Mental Health Settings. (Illus.). 16p. 1983. pap. 8.00 (*0-912431-03-2*) Ctr Env Des Res.
***Missar, Charles D., ed.** Management of Federally Sponsored Libraries: Case Studies & Analysis. LC 94-48730. (Illus.). 180p. 1995. lib. bdg. 24.95 (*1-56024-395-3*) Haworth Pr.
Misselden, Edward. Circle of Commerce: Or the Ballance of Trade, in Defense of Free Trade. LC 66-21686. (Reprints of Economic Classics Ser.). 145p. 1971. reprint ed. 27.50 (*0-678-00304-1*) Kelley.
— The Circle of Commerce; or The Balance of Trade, in Defence of Free Trade. LC 72-25886. (English Experience Ser.: No. 166). 1969. reprint ed. 35.00 (*90-221-0166-5*) Walter J Johnson.
— Free Trade: Or the Meanes to Make Trade Florish. LC 67-26245. (Reprints of Economic Classics Ser.). 134p. 1971. reprint ed. 27.50 (*0-678-00305-X*) Kelley.
— Free Trade, or, the Means to Make Trade Flourish. LC 70-25644. (English Experience Ser.: No. 267). 136p. 1970. reprint ed. 16.00 (*90-221-0267-X*) Walter J Johnson.
Missen, Ronald W., jt. auth. see Smith, William R.
Missig, James R. & Vance, Robert W., eds. Applications of Cryogenic Technology, Vol. 7. LC 68-57815. (Cryogenic Society of America Applications of Cryogenic Technology Ser.). (Illus.). 1978. text ed. 35.00 (*0-87936-009-7*) Scholium Intl.
Missildine, W. Hugh. Your Inner Child of the Past. 1991. pap. 5.99 (*0-671-74703-7*) S&S Trade.
***Missimer, C. A.** Good Arguments: An Introduction to Critical Thinking. 3rd ed. LC 94-29315. 256p. 1994. pap. text ed. write for info. (*0-13-311804-5*) P-H.
Missimer, Thomas M. Water Supply Development & Concentrate Disposal for Membr. 1994. 75.00 (*0-87371-954-9*) Lewis Pubs.
Missinne, Leo. Reflections on Aging: A Spiritual Guide. LC 89-64247. 112p. (Orig.). 1990. pap. 3.95 (*0-89243-319-1*) Liguori Pubns.
Missinne, Leo E. & Fischer, Ed. All You Could Forget about Older People. LC 81-51459. (Illus.). 150p. (C). 1981. per. 9.95 (*0-88247-600-9*) R & E Pubs.
***Mission Control Staff & Zoev IHO Staff.** E. T. 101: The Cosmic Instruction Manual for Planetary Evolution. 1995. 14.00 (*0-06-251267-6*, HarpT) HarpC.
Missionary Research Library Staff. New York Dictionary Catalog of the Missionary Research Library, 17 vols., Set. 1970. lib. bdg. 1,850.00 (*0-8161-0778-5*, Hall Library) G K Hall.
Missiou, Anna. The Subversive Oratory of Andokides: Politics, Ideology & Decision-Making in Democratic Athens, 410-390 B.C. (Classical Studies). (Illus.). 224p. (C). 1992. 59.95 (*0-521-36009-9*) Cambridge U Pr.
Missirlis, Y. F. & Lemm, W., eds. Modern Aspects of Protein Adsorption on Biomaterials. (C). 1991. lib. bdg. 105.00 (*0-7923-0973-1*) Kluwer Ac.
Missirlis, Y. F. & Wautier, J. L., eds. The Role of Platelets in Blood-Biomaterial Interactions. LC 93-2728. 1993. lib. bdg. 105.00 (*0-7923-2162-6*) Kluwer Ac.
Missiroli, Mario. What Italy Owes to Mussolini. 1976. lib. bdg. 250.00 (*0-8490-2817-5*) Gordon Pr.
Mississippi Cooperative Extension Service, Home Economics Division Staff, ed. The Mississippi Cookbook. LC 74-185345. 476p. 1972. pap. 17.95 (*0-87805-381-6*) U Pr of Miss.
Mississippi Department of Archives & History Staff, ed. The Jefferson Davis Portfolio. (Illus.). 1983. pap. 15.95 (*0-87805-338-7*) U Pr of Miss.
Mississippi Department of Archives and History Staff. Mississippi Provincial Archives: French Dominion, 3 Vols, Set. Rowland, Dunbar & Sanders, A. G., eds. LC 72-172737. reprint ed. 315.00 (*0-404-07370-0*) AMS Pr.
Mississippi Judicial College Staff. Appeals Procedure Deskbook. 1980. write for info. (*0-318-57054-8*) U MS Law Ctr.
Mississippi State University Staff. CO 1053 Fundamentals of Interpersonal Communication. 128p. (C). 1985. per., pap. 18.95 (*0-8403-3733-7*) Kendall-Hunt.
Missler, Chuck, jt. auth. see Young, Woody.
Missotten, L., jt. ed. see Maudgal, P. C.
***Missouri.** World of Plants. 1994. pap. 29.99 (*0-517-13408-X*) Random.
Missouri Association for Criminal Justice Staff. Missouri Crime Survey. LC 68-55778. (Criminology, Law Enforcement, & Social Problems Ser.: No. 10). 1968. reprint ed. 30.00 (*0-87585-010-3*) Patterson Smith.
Missouri Bar Staff. Missouri Juvenile Law. write for info. (*0-318-61044-2*) MO Bar.
Missouri Botanical Garden Staff. Annual Gardening. (American Garden Guides Ser.). (Illus.). 224p. 1995. pap. 25.00 (*0-679-75831-3*) Pantheon.
Missouri Editing Group Staff, ed. see Anderson, Kelly.
Missouri Editing Group Staff, ed. see Broeg, Bob.
Missouri Editing Group Staff, ed. see Hendel, John & Carr, Jim.
Missouri Editing Group Staff, ed. see Hendel, John.
Missouri Editing Group Staff, ed. see McKenzie, Mike.
Missouri General Assembly, Joint Committee of The General Assembly. Report of the Joint Committee of the General Assembly Appointed to Investigate the Police Department of the City of St. Louis. LC 70-154587. (Police in America Ser.). 1971. reprint ed. 24.95 (*0-405-03384-2*) Ayer.
Missouri Historical Society Staff, tr. see Wislizenus, Frederick A.
Missouri River Heritage Association Staff. Heritage of Buchanen County, Missouri, Vol. II. (Illus.). 401p. 1986. 60.00 (*0-88107-061-0*) Curtis Media.
Missouri River Heritage Association Staff, ed. The History of Buchanan County, Missouri, Vol. I. (Illus.). 625p. 1984. 60.00 (*0-88107-014-9*) Curtis Media.
Missri, Jose. Clinical Doppler Echocardiography. 316p. 1990. text ed. 85.00 (*0-07-042436-5*) Hlth Prof Div.
Missri, Jose, ed. Transesophageal Echocardiography: Clinical & Intraoperative Applications. LC 92-23799. (Illus.). 248p. 1993. text ed. 124.95 (*0-443-08852-7*) Churchill.
Misstear, Cecil, et al. The Advanced Airbrush Book. (Illus.). 160p. 1984. text ed. 44.95 (*0-442-28424-1*) Van Nos Reinhold.
Mister Tom. Fuzzy Buzzard. (Illus.). 32p. (J). (gr. 2-4). 1978. write for info. (*0-318-57345-8*) Oddo.
— Gilly the Goose. (Illus.). 32p. (J). (gr. 2-4). 1978. write for info. (*0-318-57343-1*) Oddo.
— The Little Computer. (Illus.). 32p. (J). (gr. 2-4). 1978. write for info. (*0-318-57344-X*) Oddo.
— Queen Fussy. (Illus.). 48p. (J). (gr. 2-4). 1973. Cassette. audio write for info. (*0-318-57347-4*) Oddo.
***Mistlin, I.** How to Win Clients & Interpret Their Needs: A Guide for Hairdressers. (Illus.). 256p. 1994. pap. (*0-632-03891-8*, Pub. by Blckwell Sci Pubns UK) Blackwell Sci.
Mistlin, Ian. How to Win Clients & Interpret Their Needs: A Hairdresser's Guide. 1994. write for info. (*0-318-72927-X*) Blackwell Sci.
Mistral, Frederic. The Memoirs of Frederic Mistral. LC 86-8768. 352p. 1986. 22.95 (*0-8112-0992-X*); pap. 10.95 (*0-8112-1009-X*, NDP632) New Directions.
— Le Tresor de Felibridge: Dictionnaire Provencal-Francais, 2 vols., Set. 2375p. (FRE.). 250.00 (*0-686-56736-6*, M-6414) Fr & Eur.
Mistral, G. Desolacion. 230p. (SPA.). 1972. 10.50 (*0-8288-7130-2*, S8274) Fr & Eur.
Mistree, Farrokh, jt. auth. see Shoup, Terry E.
Mistress Jacqueline. Whips & Kisses: Parting the Leather Curtain. (Illus.). 236p. (C). 1991. 23.95 (*0-87975-656-X*) Prometheus Bks.
Mistretta, Charles. Digital Subtraction Arteriography: An Application of Computerized Fluoroscopy. LC 81-14721. (Illus.). 175p. reprint ed. pap. 49.90 (*0-8357-7623-9*, 2056946) Bks Demand.
Mistretta, Giorgio. The Italian Gourmet. 256p. 1992. 45.00 (*0-696-02379-2*) Meredith Bks.
Mistri, Richard. Mistakes Pharmacists Make - & Why. 184p. (Orig.). 1991. pap. text ed. 8.95 (*0-9631857-0-5*) Tel-All Bks.
Mistry, Freny. Nietzsche & Buddhism. (Monographien und Texte zur Nietzscge-Forschung Ser.: Vol. 6). 211p. 1981. 83.10 (*0-89925-423-3*) De Gruyter.
— Nietzsche & Buddhism. (Monographien und Texte zur Nietzscge-Forschung Ser.: Vol. 6). 211p. 1981. 83.10 (*3-11-008305-1*) De Gruyter.
Mistry, Jim. Letters from the Mandali of Avatar Meher Baba, Vol. II. LC 83-142831. 176p. (Orig.). 1983. pap. 7.95 (*0-913078-46-8*) Sheriar Pr.
Mistry, Jim, comp. Letters from the Mandali of Avatar Meher Baba, Vol. I. LC 83-142831. 152p. (Orig.). 1981. pap. 7.95 (*0-913078-42-5*) Sheriar Pr.
Mistry, Manek, et al. Up Your Score: The Underground Guide to the New SAT & PSAT. rev. ed. LC 93-8931. 272p. 1993. reprint ed. pap. 8.95 (*1-56305-505-8*, 3505) Workman Pub.
Mistry, N. S., et al. Mathematical Model of the Behaviour of Concrete Backfill in an Underground Waste Repository, No. 14090. 140p. 1992. pap. 19.00 (*92-826-3857-X*, CD-NA-14090-EN-C, Pub. by Europ Com) UNIPUB.
Mistry, Rohinton. Such a Long Journey. 1992. pap. 11.00 (*0-679-73871-1*, Vin) Random.
Mistry, Shiavax. Direct Taxes Ready Referencer. (C). 1990. 125.00 (*0-89771-261-7*) St Mut.
Misugi, T. & Shibatomi, A., eds. Compound & Josephson High-Speed Devices. (Microdevices: Physics & Fabrication Technologies Ser.). (Illus.). 340p. (C). 1993. 69.50 (*0-306-44384-8*, Plenum Pr) Plenum.
Misulis, Karl E. Essentials of Clinical Neurophysiology. LC 92-19457. (Illus.). 320p. 1993. 75.00 (*0-7506-9305-3*) Buttrwrth-Heinemann.
Misuraca, Karen. Quick Escapes from San Francisco: 28 Weekend Trips from the Bay Area. LC 93-2744. (Voyager Book Ser.). (Illus.). 352p. (Orig.). 1993. pap. 13.95 (*1-56440-222-3*) Globe Pequot.
Misuraca, Karen, ed. see Paulson, Lynda R. & Watson, Tom.
Misurella, Fred. Understanding Milan Kundera: Public Events, Private Affairs. LC 92-27444. (Understanding Modern European & Latin American Literature Ser.). 231p. (C). 1993. text ed. 34.95 (*0-87249-853-0*) U of SC Pr.
Misyn, R., jt. auth. see Harvey, Ralph.
Miszalok, V. Medtech '89, Vol. 1357: Medical Imaging. 1990. 56.00 (*0-8194-0418-7*) SPIE.
Misztal, Barbara A. & Moss, David, eds. Action on AIDS: National Policies in Comparative Perspective. LC 89-26034. (Contributions in Medical Studies: No. 28). 280p. 1990. text ed. 59.95 (*0-313-26369-8*, MZA/, Greenwood Pr) Greenwood.
Misztal, Bronislaw, ed. Poland After Solidarity: Social Movements versus the State. 1985. 32.95 (*0-88738-049-2*) Transaction Pubs.
Misztal, Bronislaw & Shupe, Anson, eds. Religion & Politics in Comparative Perspective: Revival of Religious Fundamentalism in East & West. LC 92-12120. 240p. 1992. text ed. 45.00 (*0-275-94218-X*, C4218, Praeger Pubs) Greenwood.
Misztal, Goslaw S. Poslanie. 160p. (Orig.). (POL.). 1987. pap. 10.00 (*0-930401-15-8*) Artex Pub.
MIT LNG Research Center Staff. Flameless Vapor Explosions. 62p. 1977. pap. 3.50 (*0-318-12616-8*, M20177) Am Gas Assn.
MIT Staff & Stanford University Staff. Bibliographic Guide to Computer Science, 1989. 250p. 1990. lib. bdg. 150.00 (*0-8161-7130-0*, Hall Reference) Macmillan.
M.I.T. Symposium Staff. Women & the Scientific Professions: Proceedings of the M.I.T. Symposium on American Women in Science & Engineering, 1964. Mattfeld, Jacquelyn & Van Aken, Carol, eds. LC 76-2516. 250p. 1976. reprint ed. text ed. 55.00 (*0-8371-8759-1*, MAWSP) Greenwood.
Mita, Munesuke. Social Psychology of Modern Japan. (Japanese Studies). 535p. 1993. 59.95 (*0-7103-0451-X*, A9864, Pub. by Kegan Paul Intl UK) Routledge Chapman & Hall.
Mita, Randy. ABC Hawaii: A Reference Guide - Everything to Know about the Islands. 208p. 1994. pap. 14.95 (*0-935180-84-2*) Mutual Pub HI.
Mitacek, Lynn, ed. see Murphy, Lyle.
Mital, jt. auth. see Rizvi.
Mital, A. & Anand, S., eds. Handbook of Expert Systems Applications in Manufacturing: Structures & Rules. LC 93-36249. 1993. write for info. (*0-412-46670-8*) Chapman & Hall.
Mital, Anil. Human Strength. (General Engineering Ser.). 1991. text ed. write for info. (*0-442-00602-0*) Van Nos Reinhold.
Mital, Anil, ed. Advances in Ergonomics: Human Factors I. 368p. 1984. 95.00 (*0-444-87659-6*, North Holland) Elsevier.
— Advances in Industrial Ergonomics & Safety, Vol. 2. 100001p. 1990. 220.00 (*0-85066-748-8*) Taylor & Francis.
— Recent Developments in Production Research: Seleceted Papers from the 9th International Conference on Production Research, August 17-20, 1987, Cincinati, Ohio. (Manufacturing Research & Technology Ser.: Vol. 6). 900p. 1988. 192.50 (*0-444-42929-8*) Elsevier.
Mital, Anil & Karwowski, Waldemar. Workspace, Equipment & Tool Design. (Advances in Human Factors-Ergonomics Ser.: Vol. 15). 1991. 128.75 (*0-444-87441-0*) Elsevier.
Mital, Anil, jt. auth. see Ayoub, M. M.
Mital, Anil, jt. auth. see Karwowski, Waldemar.
Mital, Anil, jt. ed. see Karwowski, Waldemar.
Mital, Anil, jt. ed. see Parsaei, H. E.
Mital, Anil, et al. A Guide to Manual Materials Handling. 120p. 1993. pap. 25.00 (*0-85066-801-8*, Pub. by Tay Francis Ltd UK) Taylor & Francis.
Mital, H. C., ed. see Ramalingam, Vimala, et al.
Mital, K. M. Social Responsibilities of Business: Concepts, Areas & Progress. (C). 1988. 32.00 (*81-7001-035-7*, Pub. by Chanakya II) S Asia.
Mital, V. & Johnson, L. Advanced Information Systems for Lawyers. 304p. 1992. 54.95 (*0-442-31591-0*) Chapman & Hall.
Mitamura, Joyce Y., jt. auth. see Mitamura, Yasuko K.
Mitamura, Taisuke. Chinese Eunuchs: The Structure of Intimate Politics. 1992. 14.95 (*0-8048-1881-9*) C E Tuttle.
Mitamura, Yasuko K. Let's Learn Hiragana. LC 84-82275. 72p. (Orig.). 1985. pap. 10.00 (*0-87011-709-2*) Kodansha.
— Let's Learn Katakana. LC 85-40059. (Illus.). 88p. (Orig.). 1986. pap. 10.00 (*0-87011-719-X*) Kodansha.

An Asterisk (*) at the beginning of an entry indicates that the title is appearing in BIP for the first time.

Mitamura, Yasuko K. & Mitamura, Joyce Y. Let's Learn Kanji: Practice Workbook for Learning Basic Japanese Characters. 256p. (Orig.). 1995. pap. 19.95 (*1-880656-13-2*) Stone Bridge Pr.
Mitamura, Yasuo K. Let's Learn Hiragana & Katakana: Two Books of Basic Japanese Writing, Set. 1993. 24.00 (*4-7700-1669-7*) Kodansha.
***Mitani, O. Sam.** Fielding's Malaysia & Singapore. Knoles, Kathy, ed. (Travel Guides Ser.). (Illus.). 352p. (Orig.). 1994. pap. 16.95 (*1-56952-041-0*) Fielding Wrldwide.
Mitch, David F. The Rise of Popular Literacy in Victorian England: The Influence of Private Choice & Public Policy. LC 91-32072. (Illus.). 368p. (C). 1992. text ed. 36.95 (*0-8122-3075-2*) U of Pa Pr.
Mitch, William E. Progressive Nature of Renal Disease. 2nd ed. (Contemporary Issues in Nephrology Ser.: Vol. 26). 288p. 1992. text ed. 71.00 (*0-443-08819-5*) Churchill.
Mitch, William E. & Klahr, Saulo, eds. Nutrition & the Kidney. 2nd ed. (Illus.). 480p. 1993. 93.95 (*0-316-57500-3*) Little.
Mitch, William E., jt. auth. see Alderman, Michael H.
Mitcham, Allison. Grey Owl's Favorite Wilderness. 80p. 1981. 6.95 (*0-920806-17-1*, Pub. by Penumbra Pr CN) U of Toronto Pr.
— The Northern Imagination. 103p. 1983. 17.95 (*0-920806-46-5*, Pub. by Penumbra Pr CN); pap. 7.95 (*0-920806-47-3*, Pub. by Penumbra Pr CN) U of Toronto Pr.
Mitcham, Carl. Thinking Through Technology: The Path Between Engineering & Philosophy. LC 93-44581. 1994. lib. bdg. 49.95 (*0-226-53196-1*); pap. text ed. 17.95 (*0-226-53198-8*) U Ch Pr.
Mitcham, Carl, ed. Philosophy of Technology in Spanish Speaking Countries. LC 93-39783. (Philosophy & Technology Ser.). 356p. (C). 1993. lib. bdg. 142.00 (*0-7923-2567-2*) Kluwer Ac.
Mitcham, Carl & Grote, Jim, eds. Theology & Technology: Essays in Christian Analysis & Exegesis. LC 84-2183. 534p. (Orig.). (C). 1984. lib. bdg. 67.50 (*0-8191-3808-8*) U Pr of Amer.
Mitcham, Carl & Huning, Alois, eds. Philosophy & Technology II. 1986. lib. bdg. 115.50 (*90-277-1975-6*) Kluwer Ac.
Mitcham, Carl & Mackey, Robert. Bibliography of the Philosophy of Technology. LC 74-168204. 288p. reprint ed. pap. 82.10 (*0-8357-7201-2*, 2007277) Bks Demand.
Mitcham, Carl & Mackey, Robert, eds. Philosophy & Technology: Readings in the Philosophical Problems of Technology. LC 82-19818. 416p. (C). 1983. reprint ed. pap. 17.95 (*0-02-921430-0*) Free Pr.
Mitcham, Carl, jt. ed. see Durbin, Paul T.
Mitcham, Carl, jt. ed. see Ferre, Frederick.
Mitcham, Howard. Clams, Mussels, Oysters, Scallops & Snails: A Cookbook & a Memoir. (Illus.). 224p. 1990. pap. 12.50 (*0-940160-47-1*) Parnassus Imprints.
— Creole Gumbo & All That Jazz: A New Orleans Seafood Cookbook. LC 78-8291. (Illus.). 1978. pap. 12.45 (*0-201-05585-6*) Addison-Wesley.
— Creole Gumbo & All that Jazz: A New Orleans Seafood Cookbook. LC 91-26188. (Illus.). 288p. 1992. reprint ed. pap. 14.95 (*0-88289-870-1*) Pelican.
— Provincetown Seafood Cookbook. 288p. 1986. reprint ed. pap. 12.50 (*0-940160-33-1*) Parnassus Imprints.
Mitcham, Judson. Somewhere in Ecclesiastes: Poems. 64p. (Orig.). (C). 1991. text ed. 18.95 (*0-8262-0802-9*); pap. 9.95 (*0-8262-0803-7*) U of Mo Pr.
Mitcham, Samuel. Hitler's Field Marshals. 1993. pap. 17.95 (*0-8128-8542-2*, Scrbrough Hse) Madison Bks UPA.
Mitcham, Samuel W., Jr. & Mueller, Gene. Hitler's Commanders. (Illus.). 384p. 1992. 23.95 (*0-8128-4014-3*, Scrbrough Hse) Madison Bks UPA.
Mitchamore, Pat. Jack Daniel's Hometown Celebration Cookbook, Vol. II. Tolley, Lynne, ed. LC 90-8964. (Illus.). 192p. 1990. 19.95 (*1-55853-085-1*) Rutledge Hill Pr.
— Miss Mary Bobo's Boarding House Cookbook. (Illus.). 256p. 1994. 17.95 (*1-55853-314-1*) Rutledge Hill Pr.
Mitchamore, Pat, jt. auth. see Tolley, Lynne.
Mitchel, Claire. The Third Third: Seeing the World Through Rose-Colored Bifocals. LC 90-19246. 256p. 1991. 16.95 (*0-910155-17-8*) Bartleby Pr.
Mitchel, Fordyce, ed. see Brady, Thomas A.
Mitchel, John J., Jr., ed. Critical Voices in American Catholic Economic Thought. 1989. pap. 10.95 (*0-8091-3029-7*) Paulist Pr.
Mitchel, Larry A. Hesban 7: Hellenistic & Roman Strata: A Study of the Stratigraphy of Tell Hesban from the 2nd Century BC to the 4th Century AD. LC 92-72496. (Heshbon Ser.: Vol. 7). (Illus.). 208p. (C). 1992. text ed. 45.99 (*0-943872-20-0*) Andrews Univ Pr.
— A Student's Vocabulary for Biblical Hebrew & Aramaic. 128p. 1984. 12.99 (*0-310-45461-1*, 11607P) Zondervan.
Mitchel, Ormsby M. The Planetary & Stellar Worlds: A Popular Exposition of the Great Discoveries & Theories of Modern Astronomy. Cohen, I. Bernard, ed. LC 79-7976. (Three Centuries of Science in America Ser.). (Illus.). 1980. reprint ed. lib. bdg. 25.95 (*0-405-12559-3*) Ayer.
Mitchel, Sue A. & Hughes, Barbara A. From the Bridegroom with Love. 144p. (YA). (gr. 8 up). 1992. pap. 6.95 (*0-9634469-0-8*) Chereb Pub.
Mitchelhill, A. Bills of Lading: Law & Practice. 2nd ed. 160p. 1990. pap. 36.95 (*0-412-35750-X*, A4460) Chapman & Hall.
Mitchell. ASR: Physics. 1994. 11.95 (*0-87434-573-1*) Springhouse Pub.
— Bad Design. 1995. pap. write for info. (*0-442-01733-2*) Van Nos Reinhold.
— Microcomputer Systems Using STE Bus. 1989. 20.95 (*0-8493-7144-9*, TK) CRC Pr.
— Nancy Drew & Hardy Boys. Date not set. 22.95 (*0-8057-8822-0*, Twayne); pap. 12.95 (*0-8057-8823-9*, Twayne) Macmillan.
— Nine American Lifestyles. 1983. 19.95 (*0-02-585310-4*) Macmillan.
— Paradise Lost (Milton) (Book Notes Ser.). (C). 1984. pap. 2.50 (*0-8120-3435-X*) Barron.
— The Republic. (Book Notes Ser.). (C). 1985. pap. 2.50 (*0-8120-3436-8*) Barron.
— Trumpet Method, Bk. 1. 1990. 8.95 (*0-685-32178-9*, M304) Hansen Ed Mus.
— Trumpet Method, Bk. 2. 1990. 8.95 (*0-685-32179-7*, M305) Hansen Ed Mus.
— Trumpet Method, Bk. 3. 1990. 8.95 (*0-685-32180-0*, M306) Hansen Ed Mus.
— Trumpet Method, Bk. 4. 1990. 8.95 (*0-685-32181-9*, M307) Hansen Ed Mus.
— Warm-Ups for Brass Instruments. 1990. 8.95 (*0-685-32177-0*, M372) Hansen Ed Mus.
Mitchell & Dyer. Winning Women. 1999. pap. write for info. (*0-14-008091-0*, Penguin Bks) Viking Penguin.
Mitchell & Westerman. Evaluation in the Classroom. 2nd ed. 240p. 1993. per. 27.95 (*0-8403-8499-8*) Kendall-Hunt.
Mitchell, jt. auth. see Bavor.
Mitchell, ed. see Cicero.
Mitchell, jt. auth. see Hendren.
Mitchell, jt. auth. see Sack.
Mitchell, et al. Exeter & Hampton, New Hampshire, Census & Business Directory 1908. LC 79-1145. 1979. reprint ed. 16.00 (*0-917890-15-9*) Heritage Bk.
— I Am! I Can! Vol. 1: Keys to Quality Child Care. LC 91-67111. 217p. (C). 1992. pap. 19.95 (*0-910287-09-0*) TelShare Pub Co.
— Synopsis of Clinical Pulmonary Disease. 4th ed. (Illus.). 384p. 1988. pap. text ed. 28.95 (*0-8016-3908-5*) Mosby Yr Bk.
Mitchell & Gauthier Associates Inc. Staff. ACSL for Windows: Installation & How to Use. 10th ed. 70p. 1991. pap. 10.00 (*0-925649-01-5*) Mitchell & Gauthier.
Mitchell & Gauthier Associates (MGA) Inc., Staff. Advanced Continuous Simulation Language (ACSL) Reference Manual. 10th ed. 384p. 1991. pap. 15.00 (*0-925649-00-7*) Mitchell & Gauthier.
Mitchell, A. The Young Naturalist. (Hobby Guides Ser.). (Illus.). 32p. (J). (gr. 5-10). 1984. lib. bdg. 13.96 (*0-88110-235-0*); pap. 6.95 (*0-86020-653-X*) EDC.
Mitchell, A. & Snodaigh, P. O., eds. Irish Polictical Documents 1869-1916. 192p. 1989. 39.50 (*0-7165-2422-8*, Pub. by Irish Acad Pr IE) Intl Spec Bk.
— Irish Political Documents, 1916-49. 202p. 1985. 35.00 (*0-7165-0588-6*, Pub. by Irish Acad Pr IE) Intl Spec Bk.
Mitchell, A., ed. see American Society for Metals Staff, et al.
Mitchell, A. G. Lady Meed - the Art of Piers Plowman. LC 72-148891. (Select Bibliographies Reprint Ser.). 1977. 15.95 (*0-8369-5679-6*) Ayer.
— Pediatric Bibliography. (SRCD M: Vol. 6, No. 1). 1941. 12.00 (*0-527-01517-2*) Periodicals Srv.
Mitchell, A. H. & Garson, M. S. Mineral Deposits & Global Tectonic Settings. (Earth Science Ser.). 1982. text ed. 126.00 (*0-12-499050-9*) Acad Pr.
Mitchell, A. H. & Leach, T. M. Epithermal Gold in the Philippines: Island Arc Geology & Metallogenesis. (Academic Press Geology Ser.). (Illus.). 457p. 1991. text ed. 140.00 (*0-12-499610-8*) Acad Pr.
Mitchell, A. R. & Griffiths, D. F. The Finite Difference Method in Partial Differential Equations. LC 79-40646. 272p. 1980. text ed. 145.00 (*0-471-27641-3*, Wiley-Interscience) Wiley.
Mitchell, A. R., jt. auth. see Wait, R.
Mitchell, Adrian. Adrian Mitchell's Greatest Hits: His 40 Golden Greats. 96p. 1991. pap. 14.95 (*1-85224-164-0*, Pub. by Bloodaxe Bks UK) Dufour.
— The Patchwork Girl of Oz. Date not set. 4.95 (*0-87129-335-8*, P09) Dramatic Pub.
— The Ugly Duckling. LC 93-39962. (Illus.). 32p. (J). (ps-3). 1994. 14.95 (*1-56458-557-3*) Dorling Kindersley.
Mitchell, Adrian, ed. see Calderon de la Barca, Pedro.
Mitchell, Adrian, ed. see Thomas, Dylan.
Mitchell, Alan. The Gardener's Book of Trees: Over 500 Trees for All. (Illus.). 216p. 1994. pap. 19.95 (*0-460-86085-2*, J M Dent & Sons) Trafalgar.
— The Trees of North America. (Illus.). 208p. 1987. 35.00 (*0-8160-1806-5*) Facts on File.
Mitchell, Alan, jt. ed. see Kocka, Jurgen.
Mitchell, Alan, jt. auth. see Mouchet, Jean-Paul.
Mitchell, Alice, et al. A Systematic Introduction to Improvisation on the Pianoforte: Opus 200. Anderson, Gordon T., ed. LC 82-17225. (Longman Music Ser.). 128p. (C). 1983. text ed. write for info. (*0-582-28329-9*) Macmillan.
Mitchell, Alice M. Children & Movies. LC 70-160240. (Moving Pictures Ser.). xxiv, 181p. 1971. reprint ed. lib. bdg. 24.95 (*0-89198-041-5*) Ozer.
***Mitchell, Alice R.** Interdisciplinary Instruction in Reading Comprehension & Written Communication: A Guide for an Innovative Curriculum. LC 92-41365. 110p. 1993. pap. 15.95 (*0-398-06293-5*) C C Thomas.
— Interdisciplinary Instruction in Reading Comprehension & Written Communication: A Guide for an Innovative Curriculum. LC 92-41365. 110p. (C). 1993. text ed. 29.95 (*0-398-05846-6*) C C Thomas.
Mitchell, Alison E. The New Jersey Highlands: Treasures at Risk. (Illus.). (Orig.). 1992. pap. 9.95 (*0-913234-10-9*) NJ Cons Foun.
Mitchell, Allan. The Divided Path: The German Influence on Social Reform in France after 1870. LC 90-23845. xx, 410p. (C). 1991. 49.95 (*0-8078-1964-6*) U of NC Pr.
— The German Influence in France after 1870: The Formation of the French Republic. LC 78-31677. xviii, 281p. 1979. 34.95 (*0-8078-1357-5*) U of NC Pr.
— The German Influence in France after 1870: The Formation of the French Republic. LC 78-31677. reprint ed. pap. 85.30 (*0-7837-9025-2*, 2049776) Bks Demand.
— Victors & Vanquished: The German Influence on Army & Church in France after 1870. LC 83-25917. xiv, 169p. 1984. 45.00 (*0-8078-1603-5*) U of NC Pr.
Mitchell, Allan, ed. The Nazi Revolution: Hitler's Dictatorship & the German Nation. 3rd ed. LC 89-80515. (Problems in European Civilization Ser.). 188p. (C). 1990. pap. text ed. 8.50 (*0-669-20880-9*) Heath.
Mitchell, Allan & Deak, Istvan. Everyman in Europe, Vol. I. 3rd ed. 240p. (C). 1989. pap. text ed. write for info. (*0-13-293515-5*) P-H.
— Everyman in Europe, Vol. II. 3rd ed. 224p. (C). 1989. pap. text ed. write for info. (*0-13-293523-6*) P-H.
Mitchell, Allan, jt. ed. see Kocka, Jurgen.
Mitchell, Allan C. & Zemansky, Mark W. Resonance Radiation & Excited Atoms. LC 62-5588. 352p. reprint ed. pap. 100.40 (*0-318-34827-6*, 2031696) Bks Demand.
Mitchell, Allen, jt. auth. see Mitchell, Linda.
Mitchell, Alvan. Little Tom & Fats. Bd. with History of Ripley. LC 83-81560. LC 83-81560. (Illus.). 272p. 1983. 14.95 (*0-913507-00-8*) New Forums.
— Little Tom & Fats. Arrington, Veneta B., ed. LC 83-81560. (Illus.). 272p. 1987. reprint ed. 14.95 (*0-9615098-2-1*) Prairie Imp.
***Mitchell, Anastasia, illus.** The Legend of the Magical Lapland Geese: A Christmas Story. 8p. (J). (gr. k-3). 1990. pap. write for info. (*0-943535-03-4*) Primarius Ltd.
Mitchell, Andrew. The Fragile South Pacific: An Ecological Odyssey. (Corrie Herring Hooks Ser.: No. 16). (Illus.). 272p. 1991. 24.95 (*0-292-72466-7*) U of Tex Pr.
Mitchell, Andrew, ed. Advertising Exposure, Memory & Choice. (Advertising & Consumer Psychology Ser.). 352p. 1992. text ed. 69.95 (*0-8058-0685-7*) L Erlbaum Assocs.
***Mitchell, Andrew & Wilcox, David.** Arid Shrubland Plants of Western Australia. Date not set. 55.00 (*1-875560-47-5*, Pub. by Univ of West Aust Pr AT); pap. 45.00 (*1-875560-22-X*, Pub. by Univ of West Aust Pr AT) Intl Spec Bk.
Mitchell, Andrew A., ed. The Effect of Information on Consumer & Market Behavior. LC 77-15505. (American Marketing Association, Proceedings Ser.). 122p. reprint ed. pap. 34.80 (*0-317-20082-8*, 2023363) Bks Demand.
Mitchell, Angela, jt. auth. see Jones, Paul.
Mitchell, Angelina M. Angelina's Favorite Recipes: A Personal Collection of Sicilian Style Italian Recipes. (Illus.). 104p. (Orig.). 1988. pap. text ed. 8.95 (*0-9619750-0-8*) A Mitchell.
Mitchell, Angelyn, ed. Within the Circle: An Anthology of African American Literary Criticism from the Harlem Renaissance to the Present. 544p. 1994. lib. bdg. 49.95 (*0-8223-1536-X*); pap. text ed. 18.95 (*0-8223-1544-0*) Duke.
Mitchell, Anita M., et al, eds. Social Learning & Career Decision Making. LC 78-8930. 1979. 18.50 (*0-910328-21-8*); pap. 14.00 (*0-910328-22-6*) Sulzburger & Graham Pub.
Mitchell, Ann. Children in the Middle: Living Through Divorce. 224p. (Orig.). 1985. 32.00 (*0-422-79260-8*, 9377, Pub. by Tavistock UK); pap. 13.95 (*0-422-79270-5*, 9378, Pub. by Tavistock UK) Routledge Chapman & Hall.
Mitchell, Ann & David, Judy, eds. Explorations with Young Children. 1992. pap. 19.95 (*0-87659-160-8*) Gryphon Hse.
Mitchell, Ann K. Someone to Turn To: Experiences of Help Before Divorce. 136p. 1981. text ed. 22.00 (*0-08-025741-0*, Pergamon Pr) Elsevier.
Mitchell, Ann L. The Dried Flower Garden. (Illus.). 128p. 1992. 34.95 (*0-7134-6221-3*, Pub. by Batsford UK) Trafalgar.
Mitchell, Anne. In the Name of God - Good: A New - Old Philosophy for the 21st Century. 150p. 1993. pap. 7.95 (*0-9636910-0-7*) Liberty Bks.
Mitchell, Anne & King, Eric. Problem Solving with Spreadsheets & Databases. (C). 1993. student ed 25.00 (*1-881592-44-8*) Hayden-McNeil.
Mitchell, Anne, et al. Child Care Choices, Consumer Education, & Low-Income Families. 64p. (Orig.). 1992. pap. text ed. 11.00 (*0-926582-07-0*) NCCP.
— Early Childhood Programs & the Public Schools: Between Promise & Practice. LC 89-31076. 332p. 1989. text ed. 45.00 (*0-86569-193-2*, T193, Auburn Hse); pap. text ed. 17.95 (*0-86569-192-4*, R192, Auburn Hse) Greenwood.
Mitchell, Annie R. Jim Savage & the Tulareno Indians. (Great West & Indian Ser.: Vol. 8). (Illus.). 1990. 19.95 (*0-87026-075-8*) Westernlore.
Mitchell, Arthur. The Past in the Present: What Is Civilisation? LC 77-86453. reprint ed. 28.00 (*0-404-16674-1*) AMS Pr.
Mitchell, Arthur, tr. see Bergson, Henri L.
Mitchell, Austin. The Chase for Labour. LC 82-17162. reprint ed. pap. 57.00 (*0-317-20766-0*, 2025267) Bks Demand.
Mitchell, Austin V. The Case for Labour. LC 82-17162. 228p. reprint ed. pap. 65.00 (*0-317-30099-7*, 2025267) Bks Demand.
Mitchell, B. F., ed. The Physiology & Biochemistry of Human Fetal Membranes. LC 88-19552. (Research in Perinatal Medicine Ser.: No. VI). (Illus.). 215p. 1988. 75.00 (*0-916859-31-2*) Perinatology.
Mitchell, B. J. & Dragoo, M. M. How to See the U. S. on Twelve Dollars a Day: (Per Person, Double Occupancy) LC 82-50779. (Illus.). 112p. (Orig.). 1982. pap. 4.95 (*0-943962-00-5*) Viewpoint Pr.
Mitchell, B. R. British Historical Statistics. 800p. 1988. 165.00 (*0-521-33008-4*) Cambridge U Pr.
— European Statistics: Seventeen Fifty to Nineteen Seventy-Nine. 550p. 1979. pap. text ed. 33.00 (*90-286-0229-1*) Kluwer Ac.
— International Historical Statistics: Africa, Asia & Oceania 1750-1988. 960p. (C). 1995. 295.00 (*1-56159-063-0*, Stockton Pr) Groves Dictionaries.
Mitchell, B. R., ed. International Historical Statistics: Europe 1750-1988. 942p. 1992. 250.00 (*1-56159-038-X*, Stockton Pr) Groves Dictionaries.
— International Historical Statistics: The Americas 1750-1988. 960p. 1993. 250.00 (*1-56159-062-2*, Stockton Pr) Groves Dictionaries.
Mitchell, B. T., jt. auth. see Long, M. B.
Mitchell, Barbara. America, I Hear You: A Story about George Gershwin. (Creative Minds Ser.). (Illus.). 64p. (J). (gr. 3-6). 1987. lib. bdg. 15.95 (*0-87614-309-5*, Carolrhoda) Lerner Group.
— Between Two Worlds: A Story about Pearl Buck. (Creative Minds Ser.). (Illus.). 56p. (J). (gr. 3-6). 1988. lib. bdg. 15.95 (*0-87614-332-X*, Carolrhoda) Lerner Group.
— Click! A Story about George Eastman. (Creative Minds Ser.). (Illus.). 64p. (J). (gr. 3-6). 1986. lib. bdg. 15.95 (*0-87614-289-7*, Carolrhoda) Lerner Group.
— Click! A Story about George Eastman. (Creative Minds Bks.). (Illus.). (J). (gr. 3-6). 1987. reprint ed. pap. 5.95 (*0-87614-472-5*, Lerner Publctns) Lerner Group.
— Down Buttermilk Lane. LC 90-46876. 32p. (J). (ps-3). 1993. 15.00 (*0-688-10114-3*); lib. bdg. 14.93 (*0-688-10115-1*) Lothrop.
— Good Morning Mr. President: A Story about Carl Sandburg. LC 88-7265. (Creative Minds Ser.). (Illus.). 56p. (J). (gr. 3-6). 1988. lib. bdg. 15.95 (*0-87614-329-X*, Carolrhoda) Lerner Group.
— Hush, Puppies. LC 82-4465. (Carolrhoda On My Own Bks.). (Illus.). 48p. (J). (gr. k-4). 1983. lib. bdg. 14.95 (*0-87614-201-3*, Carolrhoda) Lerner Group.
— A Pocketful of Goobers: A Story about George Washington Carver. (Creative Minds Ser.). (Illus.). 64p. (J). (gr. 3-6). 1986. lib. bdg. 15.95 (*0-87614-292-7*, Carolrhoda) Lerner Group.
— A Pocketful of Goobers: A Story about George Washington Carver. (Creative Minds Bks.). (Illus.). (J). (gr. 3-6). 1987. reprint ed. pap. 5.95 (*0-87614-474-1*, Lerner Publctns) Lerner Group.
— The Practical Revolutionaries: A New Interpretation of the French Anarchosyndicalists. LC 86-15028. (Contributions to the Study of World History Ser.: No. 5). 325p. 1987. text ed. 59.95 (*0-313-25289-0*, MLE/, Greenwood Pr) Greenwood.
— Raggin' A Story about Scott Joplin. (Creative Minds Ser.). (Illus.). 64p. (J). (gr. 3-6). 1987. lib. bdg. 15.95 (*0-87614-310-9*, Carolrhoda) Lerner Group.
— Raggin' A Story about Scott Joplin. (J). (gr. 4-7). 1992. pap. 5.95 (*0-87614-589-6*, Carolrhoda) Lerner Group.
— Shoes for Everyone: A Story about Jan Matzeliger. (Creative Minds Ser.). (Illus.). 64p. (J). (gr. 3-6). 1986. lib. bdg. 15.95 (*0-87614-290-0*, Carolrhoda) Lerner Group.
— Shoes for Everyone: A Story about Jan Matzeliger. (Creative Minds Bks.). (Illus.). (J). (gr. 3-6). 1987. reprint ed. pap. 5.95 (*0-87614-473-3*, Lerner Publctns) Lerner Group.
— Waterman's Child. LC 94-40734. (Illus.). (J). 1996. write for info. (*0-688-10861-X*); lib. bdg. write for info. (*0-688-10862-8*) Lothrop.
— We'll Race You, Henry: A Story about Henry Ford. (Creative Minds Ser.). (Illus.). 64p. (J). (gr. 3-6). 1986. lib. bdg. 15.95 (*0-87614-291-9*, Carolrhoda) Lerner Group.
— We'll Race You, Henry: A Story about Henry Ford. (Creative Minds Bks.). (Illus.). (J). (gr. 3-6). 1987. reprint ed. pap. 5.95 (*0-87614-471-7*, Lerner Publctns) Lerner Group.
— The Wizard of Sound: A Story about Thomas Edison. (Creative Minds Ser.). (Illus.). 64p. (J). (gr. 3-6). 1991. lib. bdg. 15.95 (*0-87614-445-8*, Carolrhoda) Lerner Group.
— Wizard of Sound: A Story about Thomas Edison. (J). (gr. 3-6). 1992. pap. 5.95 (*0-87614-563-2*, Carolrhoda) Lerner Group.
Mitchell, Barbara J. & Staats, Cheryl M. Making Children's Choirs Work: Ideas for Developing a Successful Children's Choir. (Illus.). 96p. 1986. pap. 4.99 (*0-87403-076-5*, 3196) Standard Pub.
Mitchell, Barry. Murder & Penal Policy. LC 89-39640. 300p. 1990. text ed. 49.95 (*0-312-03994-8*) St Martin.
— Separable Algebroids. LC 85-15092. (Memoirs of the American Mathematical Society Ser.: No. 333). 96p. 1985. pap. 18.00 (*0-8218-2334-5*) Am Math.
***Mitchell, Basil.** Faith & Criticism. 192p. 1995. text ed. 29.95 (*0-19-826758-4*) OUP.
— The Justification of Religious Belief. (Orig.). 1981. pap. 14.95 (*0-19-520124-8*) OUP.
Mitchell, Basil, ed. Philosophy of Religion. (Oxford Readings in Philosophy Ser.). (Orig.). (C). 1971. pap. text ed. 15.95 (*0-19-875018-8*) OUP.
Mitchell, Beatrice, jt. auth. see Sperry, Paul S.
***Mitchell, Bettie P.** A Need for Understanding: A Handbook of Basic Counseling Information. 190p. (Orig.). 1992. pap. 16.00 (*1-885193-03-3*) Good Samaritan.
— The Power of Conflict & Sacrifice: A Therapy Manual for Christian Marriage. 106p. (Orig.). 1988. pap. 5.00 (*1-885193-01-7*) Good Samaritan.
— Who Is My Neighbor? A Parable. (Illus.). 333p. 1990. pap. 16.00 (*1-885193-00-9*) Good Samaritan.

An Asterisk (*) at the beginning of an entry indicates that the title is appearing in BIP for the first time.

***Mitchell, Betty.** Carbondale: A Pictorial History. (Illinois Pictorial History Ser.). (Illus.). 1992. write for info. (*0-943963-20-6*) G Bradley.

— Delyte Morris of SIU. (Illus.). 256p. 1988. 19.95 (*0-8093-1448-7*) S Ill U Pr.

— Southern Illinois University: A Pictorial History. (Illinois Pictorial History Ser.). (Illus.). 1993. write for info. (*0-943963-32-X*) G Bradley.

Mitchell, Betty J., ed. ALMS: A Budget Based Library Management System. LC 82-81208. (Foundations in Library & Information Science: Vol. 16). 235p. 1983. lib. bdg. 73.25 (*0-89232-246-2*) Jai Pr.

Mitchell, Betty J., et al. Cost Analysis of Library Functions: A Total Systems Approach. Stuwart, Robert D., ed. LC 77-2110. (Foundations in Library & Information Science: Vol. 6). 192p. 1978. lib. bdg. 73.25 (*0-89232-072-9*) Jai Pr.

Mitchell, Betty L. Edmund Ruffin, a Biography. LC 80-8381. 316p. reprint ed. pap. 90.70 (*0-685-44451-1*, 2056711) Bks Demand.

Mitchell, Beverley. Ethel Wilson & Her Works. (Canadian Author Studies). 56p. (C). 1985. pap. 9.95 (*0-920802-63-X*, Pub. by ECW Press CN) Genl Dist Srvs.

Mitchell, Bill. Mitchell's View: Selected Cartoons by Bill Mitchell from 1989-1993. Blanpied, Pam & Blanpied, John, eds. (Illus.). 160p. (Orig.). 1993. pap. 9.95 (*0-9625743-1-7*) Coconut Pr.

Mitchell, Bill, jt. auth. see Canan, Mike.

Mitchell, Bo. You Can Take It with You. LC 89-33093. (Orig.). 1990. pap. 6.99 (*0-8054-5739-9*) Broadman.

Mitchell, Bob. The Heart Has Its Reasons: Reflections on Sports & Life. LC 94-8844. 1994. 18.95 (*0-912083-71-9*) Diamond Communications.

Mitchell, Bonner, ed. Fifteen Ninety-Eight: A Year of Pageantry in Late Renaissance Ferrara. (Renaissance Triumphs & Magnificences, Medieval & Renaissance Texts & Studies: Vol. 71). (Illus.). 176p. 1990. 20.00 (*0-86698-080-6*) MRTS.

Mitchell, Brad & Cunningham, Luvern L., eds. Educational Leadership & Changing Contexts of Families, Communities & Schools. (National Society for the Study of Education Publication Ser.: No. 89, Pt. II). 330p. 1990. 25.95 (*0-226-60153-6*) U Ch Pr.

— Educational Leadership & Changing Contexts of Families, Communities, & Schools. LC 89-63574. (National Society for the Study of Education Publication Ser.). (Illus.). x, 278p. 1992. pap. 13.95 (*0-226-60156-0*) U Ch Pr.

Mitchell, Breon, tr. see Boll, Heinrich.

Mitchell, Breon, tr. see Federspiel, J. F.

Mitchell, Breon, tr. see Grzimek, Martin.

Mitchell, Breon, tr. see Kremer, Rudiger.

Mitchell, Breon, ed. see Lenz, Siegfried.

Mitchell, Breon, tr. see Rothmann, Ralf.

***Mitchell, Brian.** I R I S H Passenger Lists 1803-1806: Lists of Passengers Sailing from Ireland to America. 154p. 1995. 25.00 (*0-8063-1458-3*) Genealog Pub.

— Irish Emigration Lists, 1833-1839: Lists of Emigrants Extracted from the Ordnance Survey Memoirs for Counties Londonderry & Antrim. 128p. 1989. 20.00 (*0-8063-1233-5*, 3854) Genealog Pub.

— A New Genealogical Atlas of Ireland. 123p. 1992. 18.95 (*0-8063-1152-5*, 3853) Genealog Pub.

— Pocket Guide to Irish Genealogy. (Illus.). 63p. (Orig.). 1991. pap. 9.95 (*0-685-60524-8*, 9240) Clearfield Co.

— Running to Keep Fit. 96p. 1980. pap. 2.95 (*0-679-12428-4*) McKay.

— Weak Link: The Feminization of the American Military. LC 88-32539. 160p. 1989. 17.95 (*0-89526-555-9*) Regnery Pub.

Mitchell, Brian, comp. Irish Passenger Lists, Eighteen Forty-Seven to Eighteen Seventy-One. 350p. 1992. 28.50 (*0-8063-1206-8*, 3851) Genealog Pub.

Mitchell, Brian, ed. Parish Maps of Ireland: (Depicting All Townlands in the Four Ulster Counties of Armagh, Donegal, Londonderry & Tyrone) 288p. (Orig.). 1988. pap. text ed. 19.95 (*0-933227-33-7*) Closson Pr.

Mitchell, Brian C. The Paddy Camps: The Irish of Lowell, 1821-61. LC 87-16724. 264p. 1988. 27.50 (*0-252-01371-9*) U of Ill Pr.

Mitchell, Brian R. European Historical Statistics, Seventeen Hundred Fifty to Nineteen Hundred Seventy. 416p. 1979. pap. text ed. 34.50 (*0-231-04569-7*) Col U Pr.

Mitchell, Brian S., comp. Pocket Guide to Irish Genealogy. 103p. (Orig.). 1988. pap. text ed. 7.95 (*1-55856-000-9*) Closson Pr.

Mitchell, Bridget & Vogelsang, Ingo. Telecommunications Pricing: Theory & Practice. (Illus.). 324p. (C). 1991. 64.95 (*0-521-41667-1*); pap. 18.95 (*0-521-42678-2*) Cambridge U Pr.

Mitchell, Brigitte, ed. see Penrose, John.

Mitchell, Broadus. Alexander Hamilton: A Concise Biography. LC 75-16899. (Illus.). 1976. 29.95 (*0-19-501979-2*) OUP.

— The Depression Decade: From New Era Through New Deal, 1929-1941. LC 89-10693. (Economic History of the United States Ser.). 480p. 1977. pap. text ed. 20.95 (*0-87332-097-2*) M E Sharpe.

— Frederick Law Olmsted: A Critic of the Old South. (BCL1 - United States Local History Ser.). 158p. 1991. reprint ed. lib. bdg. 69.00 (*0-7812-6288-7*) Rprt Serv.

— Frederick Law Olmsted, a Critic of the Old South. LC 78-64114. (Johns Hopkins University. Studies in the Social Sciences. Thirtieth Ser. 1912: No. 422). reprint ed. 11.50 (*0-404-61229-6*) AMS Pr.

— The Rise of Cotton Mills in the South. LC 78-63974. (Johns Hopkins University. Studies in the Social Sciences. Thirtieth Ser. 1912: 2). reprint ed. 24.50 (*0-404-61219-9*) AMS Pr.

Mitchell, Broadus, intro. Rise of Cotton Mills in the South. 2nd ed. LC 68-8128. (American Scene Ser.). 1968. reprint ed. lib. bdg. 37.50 (*0-306-71141-9*) Da Capo.

Mitchell, Broadus & Mitchell, George. Industrial Revolution in the South. LC 75-100818. reprint ed. 29.50 (*0-404-00201-3*) AMS Pr.

Mitchell, Brooks. Bet on Cowboys, Not Horses: A Technological Breakthrough for Employee Selection. Ross, T. J. & Ross, Mary, eds. LC 93-60890. (Illus.). 181p. 1994. 19.95 (*0-9634940-2-3*) York Pub.

Mitchell, Bruce. An Invitation to Old English & Anglo-Saxon England. (Illus.). 352p. 1994. 54.95 (*0-631-17435-4*); pap. 24.95 (*0-631-17436-2*) Blackwell Pubs.

— A Man's Kitchen: North Georgia's Favorite Recipes. (Illus.). 392p. (Orig.). 1987. pap. 9.95 (*0-9619975-0-8*) Cooking Angles.

— Old English Syntax, 2 vols., II. 1900p. 1985. 175.00 (*0-19-811944-5*) OUP.

Mitchell, Bruce, ed. Integrated Water Management. 224p. 1992. 41.95 (*1-85293-026-8*, Pub. by Pinter Pubs Ltd UK) CRC Pr.

Mitchell, Bruce & Robinson, Fred C. A Guide to Old English. rev. ed. 416p. 1992. pap. 22.95 (*0-631-16657-2*) Blackwell Pubs.

— A Guide to Old English. 5th rev. ed. 416p. 1992. 54.95 (*0-631-16656-4*) Blackwell Pubs.

— A Guide to Old English. LC 83-101023. 283p. reprint ed. pap. 80.70 (*0-8357-3661-X*, 2036388) Bks Demand.

***Mitchell, Bruce, et al.** Dynamic Classroom. 256p. (C). 1995. per., pap. text ed. 25.95 (*0-7872-0587-7*) Kendall-Hunt.

Mitchell, Bruce M., jt. auth. see Williams, William G.

Mitchell, Bruce M., et al. Dynamic Classroom. 256p. 1990. per. 19.95 (*0-8403-6261-7*) Kendall-Hunt.

Mitchell, C. B. Mitchell: The Mitchell Record. (Illus.). 183p. 1992. reprint ed. lib. bdg. 37.00 (*0-8328-2287-6*); reprint ed. pap. 27.00 (*0-8328-2288-4*) Higginson Bk Co.

Mitchell, C. Bradford. Paddlewheel Inboard. LC 83-50816. (Illus.). 66p. 1984. pap. 12.00 (*0-913423-06-8*) Steamship Hist Soc.

Mitchell, C. Bradford, ed. Merchant Steam Vessels of the United States, 1790-1868: The "Lytle-Holdcamper List" LC 75-18930. 322p. 1975. 26.00 (*0-913423-02-5*) Steamship Hist Soc.

Mitchell, C. M. The Shakespeare Circle. LC 76-30693. (Studies in Shakespeare: No. 24). 1977. lib. bdg. 46.95 (*0-8383-2166-6*) M S G Haskell Hse.

Mitchell, C. P., et al, eds. Ecophysiology of Short Rotation Forest Crops. LC 92-35318. xviii, 308p. 1992. 120.00 (*1-85166-848-9*, Pub. by Elsevier Applied Sci UK) Elsevier.

— Forestry, Forest Biomass, & Biomass Conversion: The IEA Bioenergy Agreement (1986-1989) Summary Reports. 352p. 1990. 88.25 (*1-85166-443-2*) Elsevier.

Mitchell, C. R. The Structure of International Conflict. LC 79-25423. 368p. 1989. pap. 12.95 (*0-312-02414-2*) St Martin.

Mitchell, C. R. & Webb, K., eds. New Approaches in International Mediation. LC 88-10252. (Contributions in Political Science Ser.: No. 223). 268p. 1988. text ed. 59.95 (*0-313-25974-7*, MNA/, Greenwood Pr) Greenwood.

Mitchell, C. R., ed. see McGarvey, Carol & McCartan, Marie.

Mitchell, C. Thomas. Redefining Designing: From Form to Experience. 1993. pap. 34.95 (*0-442-00987-9*) Van Nos Reinhold.

Mitchell, Candace & Weiler, Kathleen, eds. Rewriting Literacy: Culture & the Discourse of the Other. LC 91-15503. (Critical Studies in Education & Culture). 312p. 1991. text ed. 57.95 (*0-89789-225-9*, H225, Quorum Bks); pap. text ed. 17.95 (*0-89789-228-3*, G228, Quorum Bks) Greenwood.

Mitchell, Candace, jt. ed. see Weiler, Kathleen.

Mitchell, Caraveth. Sign in the Subway. (Orig.). 1988. pap. 5.80 (*1-55673-056-X*, 8853) CSS OH.

Mitchell, Carlton, et al, eds. Images of Man. LC 84-14687. (Luce Program on Religion & the Social Crisis Ser.: No. 1). ix, 142p. 1984. 13.95 (*0-86554-124-8*, MUP-H115) Mercer Univ Pr.

Mitchell, Carlton T., ed. Values in Teaching & Professional Ethics. LC 89-29914. (Luce Program on Religion & the Social Crisis Ser.: No. IV). 176p. (C). 1990. 24.95 (*0-86554-362-3*, MUP-H300) Mercer Univ Pr.

Mitchell, Carlton T., ed. see Moltmann, Jurgen, et al.

Mitchell, Carol A. Machine Transcription: A Comprehensive Approach for Today's Office Specialist. 176p. (Orig.). (C). 1983. teacher ed write for info. (*0-672-97987-X*); pap. text ed. write for info. (*0-672-97986-1*); audio write for info. (*0-672-97989-6*); write for info. (*0-672-97988-8*) Macmillan.

— Machine Transcription: A Comprehensive Approach for Today's Office Specialist. 3rd ed. LC 94-36538. 1995. write for info. (*0-02-802221-1*) Glencoe.

— Machine Transcription: A Comprehensive Approach for Today's Office Specialist, Short Course, Student Text. 3rd ed. LC 94-24755. 1995. write for info. (*0-02-802220-3*) Glencoe.

Mitchell, Carol E. Paths of Blessings. 48p. 1991. pap. write for info. (*0-9631852-0-9*) Sparrow Hse.

Mitchell, Carolyn. A Touch of Beauty, a Touch of Sadness. (Collection of Poetry Ser.). (Illus.). 44p. (Orig.). 1992. pap. text ed. 5.95 (*1-882362-02-0*) Caro-Lynn Pubn.

Mitchell, Carolyn & Alden, Richard. College English Fundamentals. rev. ed. (C). 1990. pap. text ed. 25.15 (*1-56226-006-5*) CT Pub.

Mitchell, Carolyn, ed. see Dorsey, James M.

Mitchell, Carolyn, jt. auth. see King, Joyce K.

Mitchell, Carolyn, ed. see Von Meter, Mary L.

Mitchell, Carolynn, ed. see Leiper, Esther.

***Mitchell, Catherine C., ed.** Margaret Fuller's New York Journalism: A Biographical Essay & Key Writings. LC 94-18710. (Illus.). 240p. (C). 1995. text ed. 32.50x (*0-87049-870-3*) U of Tenn Pr.

***Mitchell, Cecily.** Cecily Small & the Rainy Day Adventure. (Illus.). 48p. 1995. 14.95 (*0-8362-0747-5*) Andrews & McMeel.

Mitchell, Charity. Speech Index: An Index to Collections of World Famous Orations & Speeches for Various Occasions-Supplement, 1966-1980. 4th ed. LC 81-23282. 484p. 1982. 45.00 (*0-8108-1518-4*) Scarecrow.

Mitchell, Charlene. Fight to Free Angela Davis: Its Importance for the Working Class. 12p. 1972. pap. 0.25 (*0-87898-085-7*) New Outlook.

***Mitchell, Charles.** The Law of Subrogation. 224p. 1995. 90.00 (*0-19-825938-7*) OUP.

Mitchell, Charles & Jacobson, Michael. Tainted Booze: The Consumer's Guide to Urethane in Alcoholic Beverages. 65p. (Orig.). 1987. pap. 3.95 (*0-89329-017-3*) Ctr Sci Public.

Mitchell, Charlie, et al. Career Exploration: A Self-Paced Approach. 2nd ed. 128p. (C). 1992. spiral bd. 14.95 (*0-8403-8105-0*) Kendall-Hunt.

Mitchell, Charlie R. Math Anxiety: What It Is & What to Do about It. rev. ed. 1987. pap. 8.95 (*0-9610794-3-6*) Action Pr.

Mitchell, Charlie R. & Collins, Lauren F. Job Hunting: A Self-Directed Guide. 1982. pap. 8.95 (*0-9610794-0-1*) Action Pr.

Mitchell, Cheryl C. & Mitchell, F. H., Jr. Developing & Managing an Effective Elder Law Practice. 220p. 1991. pap. text ed. 50.00 (*1-879909-01-4*) Mitchell WA.

— Paying for Long Term In-Home & Nursing Home Care: Washington State, 1991 Edition. 120p. 1991. pap. text ed. 25.00 (*1-879909-00-6*) Mitchell WA.

Mitchell, Chris, ed. Cryptography & Coding, No. 2. (Institute of Mathematics & Its Applications Conference Series, New Ser.: New Series 33). (Illus.). 320p. 1992. 87.00 (*0-19-853393-4*) OUP.

Mitchell, Christopher, ed. Changing Perspectives in Latin American Studies: Insights from Six Disciplines. 256p. 1988. 32.50 (*0-8047-1493-2*) Stanford U Pr.

— Western Hemisphere Immigration & United States Foreign Policy. 384p. 1992. text ed. 45.00 (*0-271-00789-3*); pap. text ed. 14.95 (*0-271-00791-5*) Pa St U Pr.

***Mitchell, Christopher J. & Stavridou, Victoria, eds.** Mathematics of Dependable Systems. (Institute of Mathematics & Its Applications Conference Ser.: No. 55). (Illus.). 308p. 1995. 96.00 (*0-19-853491-4*) OUP.

Mitchell, Christopher W. The Meaning of BRK "To Bless" in the Old Testament. LC 86-4001. (Society of Biblical Literature Dissertation Ser.). 221p. 1987. pap. 18.95 (*1-55540-003-5*, 06-01-95) Scholars Pr GA.

Mitchell, Cindy. Happy Hands & Feet. LC 88-82903. (Illus.). 80p. (J). (ps-3). 1989. pap. text ed. 7.95 (*0-86530-062-3*, IP 166-0) Incentive Pubns.

Mitchell, Claire, jt. auth. see McEwen, Douglas.

Mitchell, Clarence. River Hill Soliloquy. large type ed. (Illus.). 379p. 1989. 17.95 (*0-7089-1946-4*) Ulverscroft.

Mitchell, Claudia, jt. auth. see Weber, Sandra J.

Mitchell, Clifford L., jt. auth. see Tilson, Hugh A.

Mitchell, Colin W. Terrain Evaluation: An Introductory Handbook to the History, Principles, & Methods of Practical Terrain Assessment. 2nd ed. (World's Landscapes Ser.: No. 1785). 441p. 1991. pap. text ed. 52.95 (*0-470-21697-2*) Halsted Pr.

Mitchell-Collins. Math Anxiety: What It Is & What to Do about It. 128p. (C). 1991. pap. text ed. 12.95 (*0-8403-6864-X*) Kendall-Hunt.

Mitchell, Curtis, jt. auth. see Bolton, Iris.

***Mitchell, D. C.** Steamboats on the Fox River: A Pictorial History of Navigation in Northeastern Wisconsin. (Illus.). 208p. 1986. 29.95 (*0-9640937-1-5*) Steamboat Pr.

Mitchell, D. H. & Johnson, T. E. Invertebrate Models in Aging Research. 208p. 1984. 155.00 (*0-8493-5823-X*, QP86, CRC Reprint) Franklin.

Mitchell, D. M., jt. auth. see Ellis, R.

Mitchell, Dale, jt. auth. see Braddock, David.

Mitchell, Daniel F. The Dying Time. 1994. 16.95 (*0-533-10944-2*) Vantage.

Mitchell, Daniel J. Essays on Labor & International Trade. (Monograph & Research Ser.: No. 15). 109p. 1970. 6.00 (*0-89215-016-5*) U Cal LA Indus Rel.

— The Future of Industrial Relations. (Monograph & Research Ser.: No. 47). 181p. 1987. 10.00 (*0-89215-136-6*) U Cal LA Indus Rel.

— Human Resource Management: An Economic Approach. 748p. (C). 1989. text ed. 60.95 (*0-534-91870-0*) Intl Thomson.

— Unions, Wages & Inflation. LC 79-3776. 304p. 1980. pap. 14.95 (*0-8157-5751-4*) Brookings.

Mitchell, Daniel J. & Azevedo, Ross E. Wage-Price Controls & Labor Market Distortions. (Monograph & Research Ser.: No. 16). 174p. 1976. 6.00 (*0-89215-056-4*) U Cal LA Indus Rel.

Mitchell, Daniel J. & Wildhorn, Jane, eds. Can California Be Competitive & Caring? LC 89-11126. (Monograph & Research Ser.: No. 49). 389p. 1989. pap. 17.00 (*0-89215-152-8*) U Cal LA Indus Rel.

— The Effective Use of Human Resources: A Symposium on New Research Approaches. (Monograph & Research Ser.: No. 52). 81p. (Orig.). 1990. pap. 9.50 (*0-89215-160-9*) U Cal LA Indus Rel.

Mitchell, Daniel J., jt. auth. see Lewin, David.

Mitchell, Daniel J., jt. auth. see Way-Smith, Susan.

Mitchell, Daniel J., jt. auth. see Weber, Arnold.

Mitchell, Darby. Blue Eye of a Pond. (Illus.). 10p. (J). (ps-5). 1991. 8.00 (*0-9631809-0-8*) Castle MI.

Mitchell, David. The Overlook Martial Arts Handbook. LC 87-22087. (Illus.). 192p. 1987. 17.95 (*0-87951-285-7*) Overlook Pr.

— Winning Karate Competition. (Illus.). 128p. 1991. pap. 19.95 (*0-7136-3402-2*, Pub. by A&C Black UK) Talman.

— The Young Martial Artist. (Illus.). 128p. (J). 1992. 19.95 (*0-87951-422-1*) Overlook Pr.

— The Young Martial Artist. (Illus.). 128p. (J). 1995. pap. 13.95 (*0-87951-582-1*) Overlook Pr.

Mitchell, David, ed. Recent Advances in Respiratory Medicine 5. (Illus.). 294p. 1991. text ed. 59.00 (*0-443-04467-8*) Churchill.

Mitchell, David & Brown, Roy I., eds. Early Intervention for Young Children with Special Needs. (Rehabilitation Education Ser.: No. 4). 320p. 1990. 59.50 (*0-412-31530-0*, A4418) Chapman & Hall.

Mitchell, David, jt. ed. see Crowley, David.

***Mitchell, David A. & Mitchell, Laura.** Oxford Handbook of Clinical Dentistry. 2nd ed. (Illus.). 800p. 1995. pap. 35.00 (*0-19-262602-7*) OUP.

Mitchell, David A., jt. auth. see Mitchell, Laura.

Mitchell, David M. AIDS & the Lung. Woodcock, Ashley A. et al, eds. (Illus.). 110p. 1990. pap. text ed. 26.00 (*0-7279-0289-X*, Pub. by British Med Jrnl UK) Amer Coll Phys.

Mitchell, Debbie. Diary of a First Class Jerk. LC 87-50267. 96p. (YA). (gr. 6-8). 1987. 8.95 (*1-55523-079-2*) Winston-Derek.

Mitchell, Deborah L., jt. ed. see Dion-Marovitz, Margaret.

***Mitchell, Deborah S.** Debbie Mitchell's Cozy Cubby Collection We're Back: Featuring All Those Lil' "Celebearties" 1995. 10.95 (*0-9647429-0-X*) D Mitchells Pubng.

— Keep on Stipplin! Date not set. reprint ed. 6.95 (*0-9647429-1-8*) D Mitchells Pubng.

Mitchell, Denis, jt. auth. see Collins, Michael P.

Mitchell, Dennis J. Cross & Tory Democracy: A Political Biography of Richard Assheton Cross. LC 91-12409. (Modern European History Ser.). 335p. 1991. 68.00 (*0-8240-2541-5*) Garland.

Mitchell, Diana D., jt. auth. see Tchudi, Stephen N.

***Mitchell, Dick.** Commonsense Betting. LC 94-44882. 1995. write for info. (*0-688-13396-7*) Morrow.

— Commonsense Handicapping. LC 92-38721. 1993. 23.00 (*0-688-11362-1*) Morrow.

— Myths That Destroy a Horseplayer's Bankroll. (Illus.). 110p. (Orig.). 1985. pap. 24.95 (*0-9614168-2-3*) Cynthia Pub Co.

— Thoroughbred Handicapping As an Investment. 300p. 1986. text ed. 39.95 (*0-9614168-3-1*) Cynthia Pub Co.

— Winning Thoroughbred Strategies. LC 88-63277. 324p. 1989. 22.95 (*0-688-07913-X*) Morrow.

— A Winning Thoroughbred Strategy. (Illus.). 118p. (Orig.). 1985. pap. 29.95 (*0-9614168-0-7*) Cynthia Pub Co.

Mitchell, Don. Walkaround Model Railroad Track Plans. Hayden, Bob, ed. (Illus.). 72p. (Orig.). 1989. pap. 12.95 (*0-89024-081-7*) Kalmbach.

Mitchell, Don, jt. auth. see Grimm, Gary.

Mitchell, Don C. The Process of Reading: A Cognitive Analysis of Fluent Reading & Learning to Read. LC 81-21912. 258p. reprint ed. pap. 73.60 (*0-7837-0126-8*, 2040409) Bks Demand.

Mitchell, Donald. Britten & Auden in the Thirties: The Year 1936. LC 80-25980. (Illus.). 176p. 1981. 25.00 (*0-295-95814-6*) U of Wash Pr.

— Gustav Mahler: Songs & Symphonies of Life & Death, Vol. 3. LC 85-40494. (Illus.). 659p. 1985. 50.00 (*0-520-05578-0*) U CA Pr.

— Gustav Mahler: The Early Years. Banks, Paul & Mathews, David, eds. LC 79-9694. 1980. 50.00 (*0-520-04141-0*) U CA Pr.

— Gustav Mahler: The Early Years. Banks, Paul & Mathews, David, eds. LC 79-9694. 1995. pap. 18.00 (*0-520-20214-7*) U CA Pr.

— The Language of Modern Music. LC 94-6523. 192p. (C). 1994. pap. text ed. 10.95 (*0-8122-1543-5*) U of Pa Pr.

Mitchell, Donald, ed. Benjamin Britten: A Commentary on His Works from a Group of Specialists. LC 70-138166. (Illus.). xi, 410p. 1972. reprint ed. text ed. 38.50 (*0-8371-5623-8*, MIBB, Greenwood Pr) Greenwood.

Mitchell, Donald & Reed, Philip, eds. Letters from a Life: Selected Letters & Diaries of Benjamin Britten, 2 vols., Set. LC 90-42998. (Illus.). 1403p. 1991. boxed 175.00 (*0-520-06520-4*) U CA Pr.

— Letters from a Life: Selected Letters & Diaries of Benjamin Britten, 2 vols., Vol. 1: 1923-1939. (Illus.). 1403p. 1991. write for info. (*0-318-68221-4*) U CA Pr.

— Letters from a Life: Selected Letters & Diaries of Benjamin Britten, 2 vols., Vol. 2: 1939-1945. (Illus.). 1403p. 1991. write for info. (*0-318-68222-2*) U CA Pr.

Mitchell, Donald, jt. ed. see Landon, Howard C.

***Mitchell, Donald D.** Ku Kilakila 'O Kamehameha. (Illus.). 160p. (Orig.). 1993. pap. 29.95 (*0-87336-017-6*) Kamehameha Schools.

— Resource Units in Hawaiian Culture. rev. ed. Middlesworth, Nancy, tr. (Illus.). 303p. 1992. pap. text ed. 21.95 (*0-87336-016-8*) Kamehameha Schools.

Mitchell, Donald G. Reveries of a Bachelor. 1972. 59.95 (*0-8490-0951-0*) Gordon Pr.

— Seven Stories with Basement & Attic. 1972. reprint ed. lib. bdg. 29.50 (*0-8422-8096-0*); reprint ed. pap. text ed. 8.95 (*0-8290-0672-9*) Irvington.

Mitchell, Donald G. & Stark, David D. Hepatobiliary Magnetic Resonance Imaging: A Text-Atlas at Mid & High Field. LC 92-8554. 304p. 1992. 99.00 (*0-8016-6804-2*) Mosby Yr Bk.

Mitchell, Donald W. Spirituality & Emptiness: The Dynamics of Spiritual Life in Buddhism & Christianity. 240p. 1991. pap. 12.95 (*0-8091-3266-4*) Paulist Pr.

Mitchell, Douglas, jt. auth. see Goertz, Margaret E.

Mitchell, Douglas, jt. auth. see Kerchner, Charles T.

An Asterisk (*) at the beginning of an entry indicates that the title is appearing in BIP for the first time.

Mitchell, Douglas E., et al. Work Orientation & Job Performance: The Cultural Basis of Teaching Rewards & Incentives. LC 87-1905. (SUNY Series in Educational Leadership). 245p. 1987. 64.50 (*0-88706-567-8*); pap. 21.95 (*0-88706-568-6*) State U NY Pr.

Mitchell, Dugald, ed. The Book of Highland Verse. LC 79-144528. reprint ed. 52.50 (*0-404-08673-X*) AMS Pr.

***Mitchell-Durland, Mary.** Mr. Thank You So Muchly. (Illus.). 32p. (J). (gr. k-2). 1994. 8.95 (*0-9643013-0-X*) Hidden Brook Pr.

Mitchell, E. Employer's & Personnel Manager's Handbook of Draft Letters of Employment Law. 1977. reprint ed. 45.00 (*0-8464-0373-0*) Beekman Pubs.

Mitchell, E., jt. auth. see Leinster, P.

Mitchell, E. Douglas, jt. ed. see Lamb, Sydney M.

***Mitchell, Ed.** Fly Rodding the Coast. (Illus.). 320p. 1995. 29.95 (*0-8117-0628-1*) Stackpole.

— Object-Oriented Programming from Square One. (Illus.). 600p. (Orig.). 1993. pap. 26.95 (*1-56529-160-3*) Que.

— Secrets of the Borland C Plus Plus Masters. (Illus.). (Orig.). 1992. pap. 44.95 (*0-672-30137-7*) Sams.

— Secrets of the Visual C - C Plus Plus Masters. 1993. disk 34.95 (*0-672-30284-5*) Sams.

Mitchell, Edith A. To Feed Thy Soul. Blakely, Romaine & Whitman, Virginia, eds. LC 85-63084. (Illus.). 50p. (Orig.). 1985. pap. 9.95 (*0-88100-051-5*) Natl Writ Pr.

Mitchell, Edna H. Oh! for the Life of a Country Girl. 2nd ed. (Illus.). 253p. (Orig.). 1985. 15.00 (*0-9614640-4-6*); pap. 12.00 (*0-9614640-5-4*) Broadblade Pr.

Mitchell, Edward. Borland Pascal Developer's Guide. (Illus.). 1000p. (Orig.). 1992. pap. 39.95 (*0-88022-862-8*) Que.

Mitchell, Edward & Schulte, Rainer, eds. Continental Short Stories. (C). 1969. pap. text ed. 13.95 (*0-393-09797-8*) Norton.

Mitchell, Edward C., ed. see Furst, Gesenius.

Mitchell, Edward C., jt. auth. see Mitchell, Nahum.

Mitchell, Edward J., ed. The Deregulation of Natural Gas. LC 83-9989. (AEI Symposia Ser.: No. 83B). 176p. reprint ed. pap. 50.20 (*0-8357-4463-9*, 2037307) Bks Demand.

— Question of Offshore Oil. LC 76-16665. 171p. reprint ed. pap. 48.80 (*0-317-29838-0*, 2017492) Bks Demand.

— Vertical Integration in the Oil Industry. LC 76-20267. (National Energy Study Ser.: No. 11). 220p. reprint ed. pap. 62.70 (*0-8357-4542-2*, 2037438) Bks Demand.

Mitchell, Edward J., jt. ed. see Horwich, George.

Mitchell, Edwin V., ed. The Art of Walking. LC 77-92512. (Essay Index in Reprint Ser.). (Illus.). 1978. reprint ed. 16.75 (*0-8486-3009-2*) Roth Pub Inc.

Mitchell, Eleanor & Walters, Sheila. Document Delivery Services: Issues & Answers. 175p. 1994. lib. bdg. 42.50 (*0-88736-913-8*) Learned Info.

Mitchell, Eli. After Hard Guns. 272p. (Orig.). 1980. pap. 1.95 (*0-89083-699-X*) Zebra.

Mitchell, Ella P. Women: To Preach or Not to Preach? 145p. 1991. pap. 11.00 (*0-8170-1169-2*) Judson.

Mitchell, Ella P., ed. Those Preachin' Women. 128p. 1985. pap. 10.00 (*0-8170-1073-4*) Judson.

— Those Preaching Women, Vol 2: More Sermons by Black Women Preachers. 112p. 1988. pap. 10.00 (*0-8170-1131-5*) Judson.

***Mitchell, Ellinor R.** Fighting Drug Abuse with Acupuncture: The Treatment That Works. (Illus.). 220p. (Orig.). 1995. pap. 17.95 (*1-881896-12-9*) Pacific View Pr.

— Plain Talk about Acupuncture. (Illus.). 123p. (Orig.). 1987. pap. 10.95 (*0-9617918-0-2*) Whalehall Inc.

Mitchell, Elsie P. The Lion-Dog of Buddhist Asia. LC 91-70174. (Illus.). 192p. 1991. 50.00 (*0-9628495-0-2*); pap. 27.50 (*0-9628495-1-0*) Fugaisha US.

Mitchell, Elvis, et al. The Motown Album: The Sound of Young America. 1990. 50.00 (*0-312-04517-4*) St Martin.

Mitchell, Eric A. Power: The Power to Create the Future. LC 89-13824. (New Age Ser.). (Illus.). 192p. (Orig.). 1990. pap. 3.95 (*0-87542-499-6*) Llewellyn Pubns.

Mitchell, F. Tank Warfare. (Illus.). 336p. 1989. 30.00 (*0-907590-22-5*, Pub. by SPA Bks Ltd UK) Seven Hills Bk.

***Mitchell, F., ed.** Proceedings of the Conference on Low-Level Exposure to Chemicals & Neurobiological Sensitivity. (Illus.). 252p. 1994. 65.00 (*0-911131-32-9*) Princeton Sci Pubs.

Mitchell, F. H., Jr., jt. auth. see Mitchell, Cheryl C.

Mitchell, F. H., Sr., jt. auth. see Mitchell, Fred H.

Mitchell, Falconer, jt. auth. see Innes, John.

Mitchell, Fannie M., ed. see Stoops, Martha.

***Mitchell, Felicia, ed.** Words & Quilts: A Selection of Quilt Poems. LC 94-36873. 1994. 16.95 (*0-913327-46-8*) Quilt Digest Pr.

Mitchell, Finis. Wind River Trails. Davis, Mel, ed. (Illus.). 144p. 1975. pap. 5.00 (*0-915272-03-2*) Wasatch Pubs.

Mitchell, Flint, ed. The Complete LISFAN. 100p. 1991. pap. 19.95 (*1-880417-05-7*) Star Tech.

Mitchell, Flint & Anchors, William E., Jr. The Lost in Space Twenty-Fifth Anniversary Celebration. 94p. 1991. pap. 11.95 (*1-880417-03-0*) Star Tech.

Mitchell, Frances R. Experiencing the Great Depression & World War II: A Look Back to an Unforgettable Period. LC 89-81426. (Illus.). 144p. (Orig.). 1990. pap. 15.00 (*0-9625408-1-1*) Bears Paw Pr.

—Experiencing the Great Depression & World War II: A Look Back to an Unforgettable Period. LC 89-81426. (Illus.). 144p. (Orig.). 1990. 23.00 (*0-9625408-0-3*) Bears Paw Pr.

***Mitchell, Frank.** A Guide to the Landscape of Ireland. rev. ed. (Illus.). 244p. (C). 1995. pap. 18.95 (*1-57098-032-2*) R Rinehart.

— Navajo Blessingway Singer: The Autobiography of Frank Mitchell, 1881-1967. Frisbie, Charlotte J. & McAllester, David P., eds. LC 77-75661. (Illus.). 456p. reprint ed. pap. 130.00 (*0-7837-5047-1*, 2044725) Bks Demand.

— Redruth Parish Church - St. Euny's. (C). 1989. 30.00 (*1-85022-036-0*, Pub. by Dyllansow Truran UK) St Mut.

Mitchell, Fred H. CIM Systems: An Introduction to Computer Integrated Manufacturing. 752p. 1990. text ed. 79.00 (*0-13-133299-6*) P-H.

Mitchell, Fred H. & Mitchell, F. H., Sr. Introduction to Electronics Design. 2nd ed. 848p. 1991. text ed. 81.00 (*0-13-481748-6*) P-H.

Mitchell, G. Welcoming the French. 1993. 32.00 (*1-85594-054-X*, Pub. by Attic Pr IE) St Mut.

Mitchell, G. & Erwin, J., eds. Comparative Primate Biology, 2 pts., Vol. 2. 1987. Pt. A: Behavior, Conservation & Ecology. text ed. 190.00 (*0-471-62521-3*) Wiley.

Mitchell, G., jt. auth. see Hepburn, H. R.

Mitchell, G. Duncan, ed. A New Dictionary of the Social Sciences. 244p. 1979. lib. bdg. 47.95 (*0-202-30285-7*) Aldine de Gruyter.

Mitchell, Garry. The Heart of the Sale: Making the Customer's Need to Buy the Key to Sales Success. 200p. 1991. 22.95 (*0-8144-5991-9*) AMACOM.

— The Trainer's Handbook: The AMA Guide to Effective Training. 2nd ed. LC 92-27379. 432p. 1992. 75.00 (*0-8144-5062-8*) AMACOM.

— The Trainer's Handbook: The AMA Guide to Effective Training. LC 86-47819. 361p. reprint ed. pap. 102.90 (*0-7837-4238-X*, 2043927) Bks Demand.

Mitchell, Gayle F., jt. ed. see Sargand, Shad M.

Mitchell, George. Blow My Blues Away. LC 82-7266. (Roots of Jazz Ser.). (Illus.). xiii, 208p. 1983. reprint ed. lib. bdg. 29.50 (*0-306-76173-4*) Da Capo.

— I'm Somebody Important: Young Black Voices from Rural Georgia. LC 72-75489. (Illus.). 256p. reprint ed. pap. 73.00 (*0-8357-6150-9*, 2034453) Bks Demand.

— In Celebration of a Legacy: The Traditional Arts of the Lower Chattahoochee Valley. 130p. 1981. pap. 10.00 (*1-882650-03-4*) Colmbs Mus GA.

— Ponce De Leon: An Intimate Portrait of Atlanta's Most Famous Avenue. (Illus.). 160p. (Orig.). 1983. pap. 12.95 (*0-915063-01-8*) Argonne Bks.

— The Practice of Operational Research. 235p. 1993. text ed. 48.95 (*0-471-93982-X*) Wiley.

Mitchell, George, jt. auth. see Mitchell, Broadus.

Mitchell, George J. World on Fire: Saving an Endangered Earth. 320p. 1991. text ed. 22.50 (*0-684-19231-4*, Scribners) S&S Trade.

Mitchell, George S., jt. auth. see Cayton, Horace R.

Mitchell, George T. Dr. George: An Account of the Life of a Country Doctor. LC 93-16589. (Illus.). 400p. 1994. 39.95 (*0-8093-1915-2*); pap. 19.95 (*0-8093-1916-0*) S Ill U Pr.

Mitchell, George W. The Female Breast & Its Disorders: Essentials of Diagnosis & Management. (Illus.). 384p. 1990. 75.00 (*0-683-06100-3*) Williams & Wilkins.

Mitchell, Georgia. Molly Molasses & Me: A Collection of Living Adventures. 3rd ed. (Illus.). 73p. 1994. pap. 9.00 (*1-883957-00-1*) R Hood Little.

Mitchell, Gerald & Mitchell, Kath. Akita. (Illus.). 160p. 1993. 22.95 (*0-948955-11-2*, Pub. by Ringpr Bks UK) Seven Hills Bk.

Mitchell, Gerald E. How to Be a Cruise Consultant. 250p. (C). 1992. student ed 49.95 (*0-685-59463-7*) G E Mitchell & Assocs.

— How to Be a Destination Manager. 240p. (C). 1992. student ed 49.95 (*0-945439-11-3*) G E Mitchell & Assocs.

— How to Be a International Tour Director. 225p. (C). 1992. student ed 49.95 (*0-945439-09-1*) G E Mitchell & Assocs.

— How to Be a Tour Guide. 230p. (C). 1992. student ed 49.95 (*0-945439-10-5*) G E Mitchell & Assocs.

— How to Design & Package Tours. 230p. (C). 1992. student ed 49.95 (*0-945439-12-1*) G E Mitchell & Assocs.

— The Travel Consultant's On-Site Inspection Journal. Morello, Jo, Inc. Staff, ed. (Illus.). 192p. 1990. student ed 30.00 (*0-945439-00-8*) G E Mitchell & Assocs.

— Travel the World Free as an International Tour Director: How to Be an International Tour Director, 5, 1. 300p. 1995. 59.95 (*0-945439-13-X*) G E Mitchell & Assocs.

***Mitchell, Geraldine.** Escape to the West. (Bright Sparks Ser.). 144p. 1994. pap. 9.99 (*1-85594-085-X*, Pub. by Attic IE) InBook.

Mitchell, Gina, jt. auth. see Heaton, Pat.

Mitchell, Ginger, jt. auth. see Richardson, Joseph R.

Mitchell, Ginger, jt. auth. see Tompkins, Patsy.

***Mitchell, Glenn.** The Laurel & Hardy Encyclopedia. (Illus.). 256p. 1995. pap. 22.95 (*0-7134-7711-3*, Pub. by Batsford UK) Trafalgar.

Mitchell, Grace. Help! What to Do About... 1994. pap. 9.95 (*0-590-49604-2*) Scholastic Inc.

— A Very Practical Guide to Discipline with Young Children. LC 82-16951. 160p. (Orig.). (C). 1982. pap. 12.95 (*0-910287-00-7*, HQ770.4.M57) TelShare Pub Co.

***Mitchell, Grace & Dewsnap, Lois.** Common Sense Discipline: Building Self-Esteem in Young Children: Stories from Life. LC 95-11901. (Orig.). (J). (ps-4). 1995. pap. 14.95 (*0-910287-11-2*) TelShare Pub Co.

Mitchell, Grace L. & Chmela, Harriet. I Am, I Can: A Preschool Curriculum. (Illus.). 376p. 1987. pap. 23.95 (*0-89223-039-8*) TelShare Pub Co.

Mitchell, Graham. Medical Physiology: Objectives & Multiple Choice Questions. 2nd ed. 153p. (C). 1986. pap. text ed. 18.95 (*0-409-10727-1*) Buttrwrth-Heinemann.

Mitchell, Greg. The Campaign of the Century: Upton Sinclair's Race for Governor of California & the Birth of Media. 1993. pap. 14.00 (*0-679-74854-7*) Random.

— Going Fishing. LC 92-14449. (Voyages Ser.). (Illus.). (J). 1993. 3.75 (*0-383-03625-9*) SRA Schl Grp.

— Our Playhouse. LC 92-21451. (Voyages Ser.). (Illus.). (J). 1993. 3.75 (*0-383-03647-X*) SRA Schl Grp.

— Simply Sam. LC 92-21452. (Voyages Ser.). (Illus.). (J). 1993. 3.75 (*0-383-03652-6*) SRA Schl Grp.

— Very Seventies. 1995. pap. 14.00 (*0-02-022005-7*, Fireside) S&S Trade.

Mitchell, Greg, jt. auth. see Lifton, Robert J.

Mitchell, H. B. The Theosophical Society & Theosophy. 1988. pap. 3.00 (*0-936072-18-0*) Soc New Lang Study.

Mitchell, H. G., et al. Haggai, Zechariah, Malachi & Jonah: Critical & Exegetical Commentary. (International Critical Commentary Ser.). 544p. 1912. 39.95 (*0-567-05020-3*, Pub. by T & T Clark UK) Bks Intl VA.

Mitchell, H. J., ed. Thirty-Two Bit Microprocessors. 2nd ed. (Illus.). 259p. 1993. pap. 33.50 (*0-7506-1629-6*) Buttrwrth-Heinemann.

Mitchell, H. L. Mean Things Happening in This Land: The Life & Times of H. L. Mitchell, Cofounder of the Southern Tenant Farmer's Union. LC 78-65660. 372p. 1979. text ed. 17.50 (*0-916672-25-5*) Rowman.

— Roll the Union On: A Pictorial History of the Southern Tenant Farmers' Union. (Illus.). 96p. (Orig.). 1987. pap. 12.00 (*0-88286-159-X*) C H Kerr.

Mitchell, Hannah, tr. see Lukacs, George.

Mitchell, Harris. First Aid for Your Home: Five Hundred Household Hints You Need to Know. 124p. (Orig.). 1991. pap. 6.95 (*0-919005-02-0*) Firefly Bks Ltd.

Mitchell-Hatton, Sara L. The Davis Book of Medical Abbreviations: A Deciphering Guide. 1028p. 1991. pap. text ed. 32.95 (*0-8036-6268-8*) Davis Co.

***Mitchell, Henry.** The Essential Earthman. 1995. 21.00 (*0-8446-6863-X*) Peter Smith.

— The Essential Earthman: Henry Mitchell on Gardening. (Illus.). 240p. 1994. pap. 11.95 (*0-395-68632-6*) HM.

— The Evolution of Sinn Fein. 1976. lib. bdg. 59.95 (*0-8490-1795-5*) Gordon Pr.

— One Man's Garden. (Illus.). 262p. 1994. pap. 10.95 (*0-395-70937-7*) HM.

Mitchell, Henry H. Black Preaching: The Recovery of a Powerful Art. LC 90-38642. 1990. pap. 12.95 (*0-687-03614-3*) Abingdon.

— Celebration & Experience in Preaching. LC 90-35024. 1990. pap. 11.95 (*0-687-04744-7*) Abingdon.

Mitchell, Henry H. & Lewter, Nicholas C. Soul Theology: The Heart of American Black Culture. 176p. 1991. reprint ed. pap. 13.95 (*0-687-39125-3*) Abingdon.

Mitchell, Henry H. & Thomas, Emil M. Preaching for Black Self-Esteem. LC 94-12500. 192p. (Orig.). 1994. pap. 14.95 (*0-687-33843-3*) Abingdon.

Mitchell, Herb. Design with Flowers. 240p. 1991. 49.95 (*0-9627922-1-7*) CRB Pub.

Mitchell, Herb, jt. auth. see Hunter, Norah T.

Mitchell, Herbert. The Fundamentals of Profitable Visual Presentation. 208p. 1987. 125.00 (*0-944074-00-6*) AFS Education.

Mitchell, Hobart. We Would Not Kill. LC 83-81893. 300p. (Orig.). 1983. pap. 13.95 (*0-913408-63-8*) Friends United.

Mitchell, Howard W. The Hammered Dulcimer. 3rd ed. 57p. 1971. pap. 3.95 (*0-938702-02-5*, FSI-43) Folk-Legacy.

— The Mountain Dulcimer: How to Make It & Play It - After a Fashion. 50p. 1965. pap. 3.95 (*0-938702-01-7*, FSI-29) Folk-Legacy.

Mitchell, I. A. & Teale, G. R. The Practical House Officer. 3rd ed. (Illus.). 272p. 1992. pap. 20.95 (*0-632-03309-6*) Blackwell Sci.

Mitchell, I. V., ed. Nd-Fe Permanent Magnets: Their Present Use & Future Applications. 292p. 1986. 72.00 (*0-85334-405-1*, Pub. by Elsevier Applied Sci UK) Elsevier.

— Pillared Layered Structures: Current Trends & Applications: Proceedings of a Workshop Organized by the Commission of the European Communities, Directorate-General for Science, Research & Development, under the Brite-Euram Industrial Technologies R & D Program (1989-1992), Brussels, Belgium, 7-8 December, 1989. 252p. 1990. 64.75 (*1-85166-499-8*) Elsevier.

Mitchell, I. V. & Barfoot, K. M. Particle-Induced X-Ray Emission Analysis: Application to Analytical Problems. (Nuclear Science Applications Ser.). 63p. 1981. text ed. 45.00 (*3-7186-0085-4*) Gordon & Breach.

Mitchell, I. V. & Nosbusch, N., eds. European Research on Materials Substitution: Proceedings of the Final Contractor's Meeting Organized by the Commision of the European Communities, Held in Brussels, 9-11th December 1986. 650p. 1988. 137.00 (*1-85166-224-3*) Elsevier.

Mitchell, I. V., jt. ed. see Nosbusch, H.

Mitchell, I. V., et al, eds. Concerted European Action on Magnetics. 928p. 1989. 171.00 (*1-85166-383-5*) Elsevier.

Mitchell, Ian, jt. auth. see Brown, Dave.

Mitchell, Ian, tr. see Canetti, Veza.

Mitchell International Inc. Staff. Mitchell Automatic Transmissions & Transaxles: Fundamentals & Systems. 192p. 1989. text ed. 52.00 (*0-13-587015-1*) P-H.

— Mitchell Automechanics. (C). 1985. text ed. 42.00 (*0-13-586124-1*) P-H.

— Mitchell Automechanics. 2nd ed. 832p. 1991. text ed. 40.00 (*0-13-583782-0*) P-H.

— Mitchell Automotive Braking Systems. 208p. 1989. pap. 28.00 (*0-13-585480-6*) P-H.

— Mitchell Automotive Engines. 368p. 1989. text ed. 58.00 (*0-13-586983-8*) P-H.

— Mitchell Automotive Fuel & Emissions Systems. 304p. 1990. pap. text ed. 51.00 (*0-13-584103-8*) P-H.

— Mitchell Automotive Technology Today. 672p. 1989. text ed. 67.00 (*0-13-585688-4*) P-H.

Mitchell, Irene M. Beatrice Cenci. LC 90-22598. (American University Studies: History: Ser. IX, Vol. 104). 236p. (C). 1991. text ed. 46.95 (*0-8204-1525-1*) P Lang Pubs.

Mitchell, Isaac. The Asylum; or, Alonso & Melissa, 2 vols., Set. LC 78-64080. reprint ed. 75.00 (*0-404-17280-6*) AMS Pr.

Mitchell, J. & Mori, S. A. The Cashew & Its Relatives: Anacardium, Anacardiaceae. LC 87-11292. (Memoirs Ser.: Vol. 42). (Illus.). 76p. 1987. pap. 17.50 (*0-89327-313-9*) NY Botanical.

Mitchell, J. A., ed. see Craighead, J. J., et al.

Mitchell, J. Clyde, jt. ed. see Boissevain, Jeremy.

Mitchell, J. G. Descubriendo la Palabra De Dios (Discovering God's Word) (SPA.). Date not set. 1.79 (*1-56063-361-1*, 498224) Editorial Unilit.

Mitchell, J. M. International Cultural Relations. (Key Concepts in International Relations Ser.: No. 3). 256p. (C). 1986. International & Comparative Industrial Relations - See attached. text ed. 55.00 (*0-04-327082-4*); pap. text ed. 21.95 (*0-04-327083-2*) Routledge Chapman & Hall.

Mitchell, J. M., jt. ed. see Burland, J. B.

Mitchell, J. Murray, Jr., ed. Causes of Climatic Change: A Collection of Papers Derived from the INQUA-NCAR Symposium on Causes of Climate Change, August 30-31, 1968. (Meteorological Monograph Ser.: Vol. 8, No. 30). (Illus.). 159p. 1968. 25.00 (*0-933876-28-9*) Am Meteorological.

Mitchell, J. P. Endoscopic Operative Urology. 466p. 1981. 130.00 (*0-7236-0532-7*, Pub. by John Wright UK) Buttrwrth-Heinemann.

Mitchell, J. Paul, ed. Federal Housing Policies & Programs: Past & Present. LC 85-5737. 413p. 1985. pap. 17.95 (*0-88285-107-1*) Ctr Urban Pol Res.

Mitchell, J. R. & Ledwards, D. A., eds. Functional Properties of Food Macromolecules. 440p. 1986. 119.00 (*0-85334-373-X*, Pub. by Elsevier Applied Sci UK) Elsevier.

Mitchell, J. R., jt. auth. see Blanshard, J. M.

Mitchell, Jack. Alvin Ailey American Dance Theater: Jack Mitchell Photographs. LC 93-13582. (Illus.). 144p. (Orig.). 1993. 29.95 (*0-8362-4509-1*); pap. 19.95 (*0-8362-4508-3*) Andrews & McMeel.

— The Essential O'Casey. LC 80-13284. 400p. (Orig.). 1981. pap. 2.95 (*0-7178-0557-3*) Intl Pubs Co.

— Gun Digest Book of Pistolsmithing. LC 80-66470. (Illus.). 288p. (Orig.). 1980. pap. 15.95 (*0-910676-18-6*) DBI.

— The Gun Digest Book of Riflesmithing. LC 82-72293. (Illus.). 256p. (Orig.). 1982. pap. 15.95 (*0-910676-47-X*) DBI.

Mitchell, Jack, jt. auth. see Morrissey, Maria.

Mitchell, Jack D. The Back Page. Shelsby, Earl, ed. (Illus.). 144p. (Orig.). text ed. 20.00 (*0-686-82338-9*); pap. text ed. 9.95 (*0-935998-44-6*) Natl Rifle Assn.

Mitchell, Jack N. Social Exchange, Dramaturgy & Ethnomethodology: Toward a Paradigmatic Synthesis. LC 78-13198. 187p. 1981. text ed. 35.00 (*0-444-99057-7*, MSX/) Greenwood.

Mitchell, James. Bulimia Nervosa. 188p. (C). 1989. text ed. 24.95 (*0-8166-1626-4*) U of Minn Pr.

— Conservatives & the Union. 224p. 1989. 45.00 (*0-7486-0123-6*, Pub. by Edinburgh U Pr UK) Col U Pr.

— Conservatives & the Union: A Study of Conservative Party Attitudes to Scotland. 192p. 1991. pap. text ed. 29.00 (*0-7486-0176-7*, Pub. by Edinburgh U Pr UK) Col U Pr.

— Fifty Hikes in Arizona. LC 91-70049. (Illus.). 96p. 1991. pap. 6.95 (*0-935182-47-0*) Gem Guides Bk.

— Gem Trails of California. LC 78-187288. (Illus.). 159p. 1989. pap. 7.95 (*0-935182-22-5*) Gem Guides Bk.

— Gem Trails of Nevada. Shepherd, Robin, ed. LC 91-77395. (Illus.). 120p. (Orig.). 1991. pap. 6.95 (*0-935182-53-5*) Gem Guides Bk.

— Gem Trails of New Mexico. LC 87-81646. (Illus.). 110p. 1987. pap. 6.95 (*0-935182-24-1*) Gem Guides Bk.

— Gem Trails of Northern California. Nordhues, Robin, ed. LC 94-78603. (Illus.). 160p. (Orig.). 1994. pap. 9.95 (*0-935182-67-5*) Gem Guides Bk.

— Gem Trails of Oregon. LC 88-82011. (Illus.). 119p. 1989. pap. 7.95 (*0-935182-41-1*) Gem Guides Bk.

— Gem Trails of Texas. LC 87-83524. (Illus.). 104p. 1988. pap. 6.95 (*0-935182-34-9*) Gem Guides Bk.

— Gem Trails of Utah. LC 87-81645. (Illus.). 111p. 1987. pap. 7.95 (*0-935182-25-X*) Gem Guides Bk.

— KGB Kill. large type ed. 416p. 1988. 15.95 (*0-7089-1883-2*) Ulverscroft.

— Short Log & Timber Building Book: A Handbook for Traditional & Modern Post & Beam Houses. (Illus.). 240p. 1985. pap. 14.95 (*0-88179-010-9*) Hartley & Marks.

Mitchell, James, ed. Random House Encyclopedia. rev. ed. LC 83-9596. (Illus.). 2920p. 1983. 99.95 (*0-394-52883-2*) Random.

Mitchell, James E. Anorexia Nervosa & Bulimia: Diagnosis & Treatment. LC 84-26933. (Continuing Medical Education Ser.: Vol. 3). 222p. 1985. text ed. 29.95 (*0-8166-1388-5*) U of Minn Pr.

— Maine Probate Procedure. 2nd rev. ed. 650p. 1994. ring bd. 115.00 (*1-56257-303-9*) Michie Butterworth.

Mitchell, James F. Caribbean Crusade. Bobrow, Jill, ed. (Orig.). 1989. pap. write for info. (*0-9611712-0-0*) Concepts Pub.

Mitchell, James H., jt. auth. see Smith, Roger F.

Mitchell, James K. Community Response to Coastal Erosion: Individual & Collective Adjustments to Hazard on the Atlantic Shore. LC 73-92652. (Research Papers Ser.: No. 156). (Illus.). 209p. 1974. 12.00 (0-89065-063-2) U Chicago Comm Geo.
— Fundamentals of Soil Behavior. 2nd ed. LC 92-21521. (Series in Geotechnical Engineering). 456p. 1993. text ed. 74.95 (0-471-85640-1) Wiley.
***Mitchell, James R.** Gem Trails of Arizona. 3rd ed. Nordhues, Robin, ed. LC 94-74211. (Illus.). 184p. 1995. pap. 9.95 (0-935182-82-9) Gem Guides Bk.
— Gem Trails of Colorado. Shepherd, Robin, ed. LC 92-73590. (Illus.). 120p. (Orig.). 1992. pap. 7.95 (0-935182-57-8) Gem Guides Bk.
— Let Us Pray. 1991. pap. 4.95 (1-55673-291-0, 9124) CSS OH.
Mitchell, James T., comp. The Statutes at Large of Pennsylvania from 1682-1801, 17 vols. reprint ed. 51.50 (0-318-50722-6) AMS Pr.
— The Statutes at Large of Pennsylvania from 1682-1801, 17 vols., Set. LC 74-19615. reprint ed. 875.00 (0-404-12413-5) AMS Pr.
Mitchell, James V., Jr., ed. The Ninth Mental Measurements Yearbook. LC 39-3422. xxx, 2002p. 1985. 175.00 (0-910674-29-9) Buros Inst Mental.
— Tests in Print III. LC 83-18866. xxxii, 714p. 1983. 150.00 (0-910674-52-3) U of Nebr Pr.
Mitchell, James W., jt. auth. see Zief, Morris.
Mitchell, Jane F., tr. see Caesar, Julius.
Mitchell, Jane T. A Thematic Analysis of Mme. D'Aulnoy's "Contes De Fees" LC 78-6947. (Romance Monographs: No. 30). 1978. 24.00 (84-399-8448-0) Romance.
Mitchell, Janet. Arizona, University of: Bear Down: A Chronicle of Athletics at the University of Arizona. 176p. 1992. 29.95 (0-89781-428-2) Preferred Mktg.
— Faith Counts, Vol. 1. (Faith Counts Ser.). (Illus.). 4p. (Orig.). 1995. pap. text ed. 4.50 (0-9644012-2-3) Heavenly Express.
— Faith Counts, Vol. 2. (Faith Counts Ser.). (Illus.). 8p. (Orig.). 1995. pap. text ed. 6.00 (0-9644012-3-1) Heavenly Express.
— Faith Counts, Vol. 3. (Faith Counts Ser.). (Illus.). 8p. (Orig.). 1995. pap. text ed. 6.00 (0-9644012-4-X) Heavenly Express.
Mitchell, Janet L. Out-of-Body Experiences. LC 81-8145. 140p. 1981. lib. bdg. 21.95x (0-89950-031-5) McFarland & Co.
— Out-of-Body Experiences: A Handbook. 208p. 1987. pap. 3.50 (0-345-34119-8) Ballantine.
Mitchell, Janis, illus. The Hamster Opera Company. LC 87-51152. 64p. 1988. 12.95 (0-500-01434-5) Thames Hudson.
Mitchell, Jann. Anorexia. 28p. (Orig.). 1985. pap. 1.55 (0-89486-337-1, 5232B) Hazelden.
— Codependent for Sure! An Original Jokebook. 104p. 1992. pap. 6.95 (0-8362-7998-0) Andrews & McMeel.
— Organized Serenity: How to Manage Your Time & Life in Recovery. 100p. (Orig.). 1992. pap. 6.95 (1-55874-148-8) Health Comm.
Mitchell, Jay P. Runwaway from Innocence. LC 92-60807. 256p. 1993. 10.95 (1-55523-536-0) Winston-Derek.
Mitchell, Jean B. Great Britain: Geographical Essays. 1962. pap. 21.95 (0-521-09986-2) Cambridge U Pr.
Mitchell, Jeffrey & Resnik, H. L. Emergency Response to Crisis. (Illus.). 256p. (C). 1981. text ed. 24.95 (0-87619-856-6); pap. 14.95 (0-87619-828-0) P-H.
***Mitchell, Jeffrey T. & Everly, George S., Jr.** Critical Incident Stress Debriefing: An Operations Manual for the Prevention of Traumatic Stress among Emergency Services & Disaster Workers. 2nd ed. (Illus.). 304p. (Orig.). 1995. pap. text ed. 30.00 (1-883581-02-8) Chevron Pub.
— Critical Incident Stress Debriefing: The Basic Course Workbook. (Illus.). 78p. 1995. 7.00 (0-9646356-0-7) ICISF.
***Mitchell, Jeffrey T. & Everly, George S.** Human Elements Training for Emergency Services, Public Safety & Disaster Personnel: An Instructional Guide to Teaching Debriefing, Crisis Intervention & Stress Management Programs. 235p. (Orig.). 1994. pap. text ed. 31.00 (1-883581-01-X) Chevron Pub.
***Mitchell, Jeremy & Maidment, Richard, eds.** Culture. (The U. S. in the Twentieth Century Ser.). 256p. 1994. pap. 14.95 (0-340-59687-2, Pub. by E Arnld UK) St Martin.
Mitchell, Jerome. Scott, Chaucer, & Medieval Romance: A Study in Sir Walter Scott's Indebtedness to the Literature of the Middle Ages. LC 87-8294. 280p. 1987. 31.00 (0-8131-1609-0) U Pr of Ky.
— Thomas Hoccleve: A Study in Early Fifteenth-Century English Poetic. LC 67-21855. (Illus.). 165p. reprint ed. 47.10 (0-685-07757-8, 2014938) Bks Demand.
Mitchell, Jerome, jt. ed. see Helterman, Jeffrey.
Mitchell, Jerry, ed. Public Authorities & Public Policy. (Orig.). 1990. pap. 12.00 (0-944285-15-5) Pol Studies.
— Public Authorities & Public Policy: The Business of Government. LC 91-47972. (Contributions in Political Science Ser.: No. 301). 216p. 1992. text ed. 59.95 (0-313-28503-9, MBT, Greenwood Pr); pap. text ed. 15.95 (0-275-94321-6, B4321, Praeger Pubs) Greenwood.
Mitchell, Jerry, et al. Human Figure Drawing Test, HFDT: An Illustrated Handbook for Clinical Interpretation & Standardized Assessment of Cognitive Impairment. (Illus.). 182p. 1993. pap. 49.50x (0-87424-286-X, W-286A) Western Psych.
***Mitchell, Jet.** Finding Funds for a Free Education. (Illus.). 8p. 1994. pap. 2.25 (1-884241-43-3) Energeia Pub.
Mitchell, Joan. Joan Mitchell: Trees & Other Paintings, 1960-1990. (Illus.). 34p. (Orig.). 1992. pap. 15.00 (1-881138-01-1) Tallgrass Pr.
— Joan Mitchell, 1992. (Illus.). 52p. 1993. 35.00 (0-944680-44-5) R Miller Gal.
Mitchell, Joan, jt. auth. see Kertess, Klauss.
***Mitchell, Joan L., et al.** MPEG Digital Video Compression Standard: Video Compression Standard. (Electrical Engineering Ser.). 408p. 1994. text ed. 69.95 (0-442-01920-3) Van Nos Reinhold.
Mitchell, Joann, jt. auth. see LeBaron, Gaye.
***Mitchell, Joe.** Saturday's Heroes. 128p. (Orig.). 1994. pap. 8.95 (1-898928-05-3) AK Pr Dist.
***Mitchell, John.** Alaska Stories. 96p. 1984. pap. 6.95 (0-614-04356-5) Plover Pr.
— Alaska Stories. LC 84-60667. 75p. 1984. 11.50 (0-917635-00-0); 11.50 (0-917635-01-9) Plover Pr.
Mitchell, John, Jr. Applied Polymer Analysis & Characterization, Vol. 2. 461p. (C). 1991. text ed. 125.00 (1-56990-065-5) Hanser-Gardner.
Mitchell, John. Applied Polymer Analysis & Characterization, Vol. 1: Recent Developments in Techniques, Instrumentation, Problem Solving. 592p. (C). 1987. text ed. 125.00 (1-56990-064-7) Hanser-Gardner.
— Eccentric Lives & Peculiar Notions. (Illus.). 240p. 1987. pap. 7.95 (0-8065-1031-5, Citadel Pr) Carol Pub Group.
— Exile in Alaska. LC 86-30277. 123p. 1987. 13.95 (0-917635-02-7); pap. 7.95 (0-917635-03-5) Plover Pr.
— On the Window Licks the Night: A Nivola. LC 93-48949. (Plover Nivola Ser.). 104p. 1994. pap. 8.95 (0-917635-18-3) Plover Pr.
— Organized Labor: Its Problems, Purposes & Ideals & the Present & Future of American Wage Earners. LC 68-56263. (Library of American Labor History). (Illus.). xii, 436p. 1973. reprint ed. 49.50 (0-678-00733-0) Kelley.
Mitchell, John & Slim, Hugo. Registration in Emergencies. 64p. (C). 1990. pap. text ed. 21.00 (0-85598-128-8, Pub. by Oxfam Pubns UK) St Mut.
Mitchell, John & Smith, Donald M. Aquametry: A Treatise on Methods for the Determination of Water, Pt. 1. LC 77-518. (Chemical Analysis Ser.: Vol. 5). 646p. reprint ed. pap. 180.00 (0-7837-2402-0, 2040087) Bks Demand.
Mitchell, John, jt. auth. see Hartman, Tom.
Mitchell, John, tr. see Huidobro, Matias M.
Mitchell, John, tr. see Molina, Silvia.
Mitchell, John, tr. see Romero, Jose R.
Mitchell, John, tr. see Taibo, Paco I., 2nd.
Mitchell, John A. Drowsy. LC 74-16512. (Science Fiction Ser.). (Illus.). 316p. 1975. reprint ed. 25.95 (0-405-06306-7) Ayer.
— The Last American. LC 75-104529. reprint ed. lib. bdg. 19.75 (0-8398-1262-0) Irvington.
— The Silent War. LC 68-57541. (Muckrakers Ser.). (Illus.). 222p. 1979. reprint ed. lib. bdg. 24.00 (0-8398-1263-9) Irvington.
— The Silent War. (Muckrakers Ser.). (Illus.). 222p. (C). 1986. reprint ed. pap. text ed. 6.95 (0-8290-2004-7) Irvington.
— That First Affair: Other Sketches. LC 77-98587. (Short Story Index Reprint Ser.). 1977. 19.95 (0-8369-3161-0) Ayer.
Mitchell, John C. Great Lakes & Great Ships: An Illustrated History for Children. (Illus.). 52p. (J). (gr. 2-7). 1991. 15.95 (0-9621466-1-7) Suttons Bay Pubns.
— Indians of the Great Lakes: An Illustrated History for Children. (Illus.). 48p. (YA). 1995. 15.95 (0-9621466-2-5) Suttons Bay Pubns.
— Michigan: An Illustrated History for Children. 2nd ed. (Illus.). 52p. (J). (gr. 1-6). 1987. reprint ed. 14.95 (0-9621466-0-9) Suttons Bay Pubns.
Mitchell, John C., jt. ed. see Gunter, Carl A.
Mitchell, John C., jt. ed. see Hagiya, Masami.
Mitchell, John D. The Director-Actor Relationship: Essays & Articles by John D. Mitchell. LC 92-71961. (Illus.). 180p. (Orig.). (C). 1992. pap. 19.95 (1-882763-03-3) IASTA.
— Gift of Apollo: The Autobiography of John D. Mitchell. LC 92-75254. (Illus.). 418p. (Orig.). (C). 1992. pap. 19.95 (1-882763-04-1) IASTA.
— Lost Mines & Buried Treasures along the Old Frontier. LC 77-121730. (Beautiful Rio Grande Classics Ser.). (Illus.). 260p. 1982. reprint ed. pap. 12.00 (0-87380-144-X) Rio Grande.
— Lost Mines of the Great Southwest. LC 70-114964. (Beautiful Rio Grande Classics Ser.). (Illus.). 202p. 1984. reprint ed. pap. 10.00 (0-87380-013-3) Rio Grande.
— Making a Broadway Musical: Making It Run, An Anatomy of Entrepreneurship. (Illus.). 131p. 1989. 25.00 (0-87359-050-3) Northwood Univ.
— Phedre on Stage. LC 87-61041. 294p. 1987. 25.00 (0-87359-047-3); pap. 17.50 (0-685-25024-5) Northwood Univ.
— Staging Chekhov: Cherry Orchard. LC 91-73015. (Illus.). 416p. (Orig.). (ENG & RUS.). (C). 1991. pap. 19.95 (1-882763-00-9) IASTA.
Mitchell, John D. & Sarabhai, Mrinalini. Staging a Sanskrit Drama: Bhasa's Vision of Vasavadatta. LC 92-70319. (Illus.). 240p. (Orig.). (ENG & SAN.). (C). 1992. pap. 19.95 (1-882763-02-5) IASTA.
Mitchell, John D., jt. auth. see Packard, William.
Mitchell, John D., jt. auth. see Royce, Jack.
***Mitchell, John D., et al.** Staging Japanese Theatre: Noh & Kabuki. (Illus.). 245p. (Orig.). (C). 1994. pap. text ed. 24.95 (1-882763-06-8) IASTA.
***Mitchell, John G.** Dispatches from the Deep Woods. LC 90-36842. 318p. 1991. reprint ed. pap. 90.70 (0-7837-8906-8, 2049617) Bks Demand.
— The Man Who Would Dam the Amazon, & Other Accounts from Afield. LC 20-49618. 382p. 1990. reprint ed. pap. 108.90 (0-7837-8907-6, 2049618) Bks Demand.
— Re-Visioning Educational Leadership: A Phenomenological Approach. LC 90-41109. (Studies in Education & Culture: Vol. 1). 328p. 1990. 35.00 (0-8240-7207-3) Garland.
Mitchell, John H. A Field Guide to Your Own Back Yard. (Illus.). 288p. 1986. reprint ed. pap. 11.95 (0-393-30301-2) Norton.
— Walking Towards Walden: A Pilgrimage in Search of Place. 256p. 1995. write for info. (0-201-40672-1) Addison-Wesley.
— Writing for Technical & Professional Journals. LC 67-31374. (Wiley Series on Human Communication). (Illus.). 415p. reprint ed. pap. 118.30 (0-317-10698-8, 2016469) Bks Demand.
***Mitchell, John J.** Adolescent Struggle for Selfhood & Identity. 218p. (Orig.). (C). 1992. pap. text ed. 18.95x (1-55059-050-2) Temeron Bks.
— Human Growth & Development: The Childhood Years. 281p. (Orig.). (C). 1990. pap. text ed. 16.95x (1-55059-002-2) Temeron Bks.
Mitchell, John P. Stanford University, Nineteen Sixteen to Forty-One. LC 58-59714. 120p. reprint ed. pap. 30.00 (0-317-30440-2, 2024927) Bks Demand.
Mitchell, John P., jt. auth. see Smith, William V.
Mitchell, John S. Introduction to Machinery Analysis & Monitoring. 2nd ed. LC 93-30765. 374p. 1993. 84.95 (0-87814-401-3, P4472) PennWell Bks.
***Mitchell, John V.** An Oil Agenda for Europe in the 1990s. 75p. (C). Date not set. pap. 14.95x (0-905031-78-4) Brookings.
Mitchell, John W. Energy Engineering. LC 82-19977. 328p. 1988. 47.50 (0-471-08772-6) Krieger.
Mitchell, Jonathan. Goose Steps to Peace. 1973. 59.95 (0-8490-0250-8) Gordon Pr.
Mitchell, Joni. Both Sides Now. (Illus.). (J). 1992. 14.95 (0-590-45668-7, Scholastic Hardcover) Scholastic Inc.
Mitchell, Joseph. Bottom of the Harbor. 1994. 12.50 (0-679-60093-0, Modern Lib) Random.
— Up in the Old Hotel. LC 91-50835. 736p. 1992. 27.50 (0-679-41263-8) Pantheon.
— Up in the Old Hotel. LC 92-50835. 1993. pap. 14.00 (0-679-74631-5, Publishers Media) Random.
Mitchell, Joseph B. Decisive Battles of the Civil War. 1980. pap. 2.25 (0-449-30745-X) Fawcett.
— Decisive Battles of the Civil War. 1985. mass mkt. 5.99 (0-449-30031-5, Q745, Prem) Fawcett.
— Decisive Battles of the Civil War. (Reprints Ser.). (Illus.). 226p. 1990. 19.95 (0-88029-410-8) Dorset Pr.
— Military Leaders in the American Revolution. LC 89-1225. 223p. 1989. reprint ed. pap. 10.95 (0-939009-20-X) EPM Pubns.
— Military Leaders in the Civil War. LC 88-24681. 251p. 1988. reprint ed. pap. 10.95 (0-939009-13-7) EPM Pubns.
Mitchell, Joseph C. The Reptiles of Virginia. LC 93-42002. 1994. write for info. (1-56098-356-6) Smithsonian.
Mitchell, Joseph S. Studies in Radiotherapeutics. LC 60-3368. (Illus.). 281p. 1960. 23.95 (0-674-84930-2) HUP.
***Mitchell, Joshua.** The Fragility of Freedom: Tocqueville on Religion, Democracy, & the American Future. LC 94-48763. 1995. 34.95 (0-226-53208-9) U Ch Pr.
— Not By Reason Alone: Religion, History, & Identity in Early Modern Political Thought. LC 93-3048. 272p. 1993. Alk. paper. 34.95 (0-226-53221-6) U Ch Pr.
Mitchell, Joyce. Other Choices for Becoming a Woman. (YA). (gr. 7 up). 1975. pap. 6.00 (0-912786-34-5) Know Inc.
Mitchell, Joyce, jt. auth. see Blackaby, Henry.
Mitchell, Joyce S. The Best Guide to the Top Colleges: How to Get into the Ivies or Nearly Ivies. LC 90-24012. (Illus.). 111p. (Orig.). (YA). (gr. 11-12). 1991. pap. 10.95 (0-912048-85-9) Garrett Pk.
— College Board Guide to Jobs & Career Planning. 2nd ed. 331p. 1994. pap. 14.00 (0-87447-467-1) College Bd.
— College Smarts: The Official Freshman Handbook. LC 91-23766. (Illus.). 83p. (Orig.). 1991. pap. 10.95 (0-912048-92-1) Garrett Pk.
— Mitchell Express: The Fast Track to the Top Colleges. LC 93-16962. 269p. (Orig.). (YA). 1993. pap. 15.00 (1-880774-03-8) Garrett Pk.
— Stopout! Working Ways to Learn. LC 78-59186. 214p. 1978. pap. 8.95 (0-912048-18-2) Garrett Pk.
— Winning the Chemo Battle. 1991. pap. 11.00 (0-393-30713-1) Norton.
Mitchell, Joyce S., ed. see RVer Annie.
Mitchell, Joyce T., ed. see Traver, Gayle A. & Priestly, Gail F.
Mitchell, Judith. The Stone and the Scorpion: The Female Subject of Desire in the Novels of Charlotte Bronte, George Eliot, & Thomas Hardy. LC 93-43751. (Contributions in Women's Studies: Vol. 42). 240p. 1994. text ed. 49.95 (0-313-29043-1, Greenwood Pr) Greenwood.
Mitchell, Judith A., jt. auth. see Poploff, Michelle.
***Mitchell, Judy, ed.** Cut & Create! For All Seasons: Easy Step-by-Step Projects That Teach Scissor Skills. (Illus.). 80p. (Orig.). 1995. pap. 8.95 (1-57310-020-X) Teachng & Lrning Co.
— Cut & Create! On the Farm: Easy Step-by-Step Projects That Teach Scissor Skills. (Illus.). 80p. (Orig.). 1995. pap. 8.95 (1-57310-019-6) Teachng & Lrning Co.
Mitchell, Judy, ed. see Barden, Cindy.
Mitchell, Judy, ed. see Daniel, Becky.
Mitchell, Judy, ed. see Eagan, Robynne.
Mitchell, Judy, ed. see Fisher, Ann R. & Fisher, Bryce A.
Mitchell, Judy, ed. see Fisher, Ann R. & Fisher, Betsy.
Mitchell, Judy, ed. see Whitacre, Deborah & Radtke, Becky.
Mitchell, Julia P. St. Jean De Crevecoeur. LC 71-181959. reprint ed. 37.50 (0-404-04347-X) AMS Pr.
— St. Jean de Crevecoeur. (BCL1-PS American Literature Ser.). 362p. 1992. reprint ed. lib. bdg. 89.00 (0-7812-6660-2) Rprt Serv.
Mitchell, Julie. Tattoo You! Beautiful Expressions. (J). (gr. 5 up). 1994. pap. 5.95 (0-681-45609-4) Longmeadow Pr.
— Tattoo You! Bold Expressions. (J). (gr. 5 up). 1994. pap. 5.95 (0-681-45610-8) Longmeadow Pr.
Mitchell, Julie, ed. see OKeefe, JoAnna.
Mitchell, Juliet. Psychoanalysis & Feminism. LC 74-19067. 1975. pap. 9.56 (0-394-71442-3, Vin) Random.
Mitchell, Juliet, ed. The Selected Melanie Klein: The Essential Writings. 256p. (Orig.). 1987. text ed. 24.95 (0-02-921482-3); pap. 12.95 (0-02-921481-5) Free Pr.
Mitchell, Juliet & Rose, Jacqueline, eds. Feminine Sexuality: Jacques Lacan & the Ecole Freudienne. 1983. 19.50 (0-393-01633-1) Norton.
— Feminine Sexuality: Jacques Lacan & the Ecole Freudienne. 1985. pap. 10.95 (0-393-30211-3) Norton.
Mitchell, June. Amokura. xi, 204p. (Orig.). (YA). (gr. 10 up). 1978. pap. 10.00 (0-582-71765-5) Three Continents.
Mitchell, K. A Taste of Philippines. (Illus.). 40p. 1979. 5.95 (0-318-36280-5) Asia Bk Corp.
***Mitchell, Karen.** Sleep Song. LC 94-24859. (Illus.). 32p. (J). (ps). 1995. lib. bdg. 14.99 (0-531-08728-X) Orchard Bks Watts.
Mitchell, Karen L. The Eating Hill. LC 89-23631. 96p. 1989. pap. 8.95 (0-933377-04-5) Eighth Mount Pr.
***Mitchell, Karen L., ed.** Classic Horse Stories. LC 94-42092. (J). 1995. write for info. (1-56565-231-2) Lowell Hse Juvenile.
Mitchell, Karyn. Reiki: A Torch in Daylight. 128p. 1994. student ed, pap. 14.95 (0-9640822-1-7) Mind Rivers.
— Reiki: Beyond the Usui System. 128p. (Orig.). 1994. student ed, pap. 14.95 (0-9640822-2-5) Mind Rivers.
Mitchell, Karyn, jt. auth. see Mitchell, Steven.
***Mitchell, Karyn K.** Abductions: Stop Them Now. (Illus.). 96p. (Orig.). 1995. per., pap. text ed. 9.95 (0-9640822-3-3) Mind Rivers.
Mitchell, Kath, jt. auth. see Mitchell, Gerald.
***Mitchell, Kathy.** The Joy of Christmas: Favorites Stories, Poems, & Recipes. LC 95-19113. (Illus.). 96p. (J). (gr. 1-3). 1995. lib. bdg. 11.50 (0-8167-3902-1, Little Rainbow); pap. 2.95 (0-8167-3783-5, Little Rainbow) Troll Assocs.
— Silent Night: A Christmas Book with Lights & Music. (Illus.). 12p. (J). (ps-3). 1989. bds. 10.95 (0-689-71330-4, Aladdin Paperbacks) S&S Childrens.
Mitchell, Kathy, jt. auth. see Jordan, Debbie.
Mitchell, Kay. In Stony Places. 1993. mass mkt. 3.99 (0-373-26126-8, 1-26126-2) Harlequin Bks.
— In Stony Places. large type ed. 336p. 1994. 21.95 (0-7089-3115-4) Ulverscroft.
— A Lively Form of Death. large type ed. (General Ser.). 336p. 1993. 21.95 (0-7089-2864-1) Ulverscroft.
— Roots of Evil. (WWL Mystery Ser.). 1995. pap. 3.99 (0-373-26162-4, 1-26162-7) Harlequin Bks.
— Roots of Evil. LC 93-478. (Chief Inspector Morrissey Mystery Ser.). 176p. 1993. 17.95 (0-312-09374-8) St Martin.
— A Strange Desire. large type ed. 432p. 1995. 23.95 (0-7089-3244-4) Ulverscroft.
Mitchell, Ken. Stones of the Dalai Lama. LC 92-42445. 328p. 1993. 22.00 (0-939149-79-6) Soho Press.
Mitchell, Kenneth D., ed. Political Pluralism in Hungary & Poland: Perspectives on the Reforms. 1992. write for info. (0-275-93744-5, C3744, Praeger Pubs) Greenwood.
Mitchell, Kenneth R. Multiple Staff Ministries. LC 88-10049. 164p. 1988. pap. 13.99 (0-664-25027-0, Westminster) Westminster John Knox.
Mitchell, Kenneth R. & Anderson, Herbert. All Our Losses, All Our Griefs: Resources for Pastoral Care. LC 83-19851. 180p. (Orig.). (C). 1983. pap. 10.99 (0-664-24493-9, Westminster) Westminster John Knox.
Mitchell, Kenneth R., jt. auth. see Anderson, Herbert.
Mitchell, Kent, jt. auth. see Vitali, Keith.
Mitchell-Kernan, C., jt. ed. see Berry, Gordon.
Mitchell-Kernan, C., jt. ed. see Ervin-Tripp, S.
Mitchell-Kernan, Claudia, jt. ed. see Tucker, M. Belinda.
Mitchell, Kevin, jt. auth. see Belding, David.
Mitchell, Kieron, ed. Who's Who among Play-by-Mail Gamers, 1990-1991. 167p. (Orig.). 1990. pap. text ed. 12.95 (0-9620846-2-X) K & C Enterp.
Mitchell, Kieron B., ed. The Nineteen Eighty-Eight to Eighty-Nine Who's Who among Play-by-Mail Gamers. 2nd rev. ed. 125p. 1989. per. 9.95 (0-9620846-1-1) K & C Enterp.
Mitchell, Kimi. What on Earth For. 1994. pap. 3.95 (1-55673-929-X) CSS OH.
Mitchell, Kirk. Backdraft. 1991. pap. 4.50 (0-425-12879-2) Berkley Pub.
— Blown Away. 1994. mass mkt. 4.99 (0-380-77844-0) Avon.
— High Desert Malice. 288p. (Orig.). 1995. mass mkt. 4.99 (0-380-77661-8) Avon.
— Shadow on the Valley: A Civil War Thriller. 352p. 1993. 21.95 (0-312-10542-8, Pub. by Thomas Dunne Bks) St Martin.
Mitchell, L. G. Charles James Fox. (Illus.). 356p. 1992. 49.95 (0-19-820104-4) OUP.
Mitchell, L. G., ed. see Burke, Edmund E.
Mitchell, L. G., jt. ed. see Sutherland, Lucy S.
Mitchell, Laisdell. Colonel. LC 72-1512. (Black Heritage Library Collection). 1977. reprint ed. 21.95 (0-8369-9037-4) Ayer.
— Niram: A Dusky Idyl. LC 72-1513. (Black Heritage Library Collection). 1977. reprint ed. 17.95 (0-8369-9038-2) Ayer.
Mitchell, Larry. Zoology. (Illus.). 912p. (C). 1988. teacher ed 19.95 (0-8053-2566-2); text ed. 56.95 (0-8053-2562-X); student ed, spiral bd. 31.25 (0-8053-2563-8) Benjamin-Cummings.
Mitchell, Larry G. Illustrated American Motors Buyer's Guide. (MBI Illustrated Buyer's Guide Ser.). (Illus.). 160p. 1994. pap. 16.95 (0-87938-891-9) Motorbooks Intl.

An Asterisk (*) at the beginning of an entry indicates that the title is appearing in BIP for the first time.

Mitchell, Laura. The Magic of Movement. 96p. (C). 1988. 30.00 (0-86242-076-8, Pub. by Age Concern Eng UK) St Mut.

— Simple Relaxation: The Mitchell Method for Easing Tension. (Illus.). 144p. 1989. pap. 15.95 (0-7195-4388-6, Pub. by John Murray UK) Trafalgar.

Mitchell, Laura & Mitchell, David A. The Oxford Handbook of Clinical Dentistry. (Illus.). 768p. 1991. 35. 00 (0-19-261959-4) OUP.

Mitchell, Laura, jt. auth. see Mitchell, David A.

Mitchell, Lawrence E. & Solomon, Lewis D. Corporate Finance & Governance: Cases, Materials, & Problems for an Advanced Course in Corporations. LC 91-76746. 1140p. 1992. 75.00 (0-89089-469-8) Carolina Acad Pr.

Mitchell, Lee. A Moving Stairway: From Home-Making to Business-Making in Eight Dynamic Steps. 156p. 1991. 10.00 (0-9630693-0-6) Select Mktg.

— Staging Premodern Drama: A Guide to Production Problems. LC 83-5624. xiv, 239p. 1984. text ed. 49.95 (0-313-23685-2, MSD/, Greenwood Pr) Greenwood.

Mitchell, Lee C. Determined Fictions: American Literary Naturalism. 208p. 1989. text ed. 35.00 (0-231-06898-0) Col U Pr.

— Witnesses to a Vanishing America: The Nineteenth-Century Response. LC 80-8567. (Illus.). 344p. 1987. text ed. 47.50x (0-691-06461-X) Princeton U Pr.

— Witnesses to a Vanishing America: The Nineteenth-Century Response. LC 80-8567. 339p. reprint ed. pap. 96.70 (0-7837-1430-0, 2041785) Bks Demand.

Mitchell, Lee C., ed. New Essays on "The Red Badge of Courage" (American Novel Ser.). 176p. 1986. pap. 11.95 (0-521-31512-3) Cambridge U Pr.

Mitchell, Lee C., jt. auth. see Bush, Alfred L.

Mitchell, Lee C., ed. see Dreiser, Theodore.

Mitchell, Lee C., ed. see Grey, Zane.

***Mitchell, Leonard J.** Luchow's German Cookbook. 1994. lib. bdg. 21.95x (1-56849-510-2) Buccaneer Bks.

Mitchell, Leonel L. The Meaning of Ritual. LC 87-28282. 143p. 1991. reprint ed. pap. 7.95 (0-8192-1451-5) Morehouse Pub.

— Planning the Church Year. LC 90-27365. 96p. 1991. pap. 9.95 (0-8192-1554-6) Morehouse Pub.

— Praying Shapes Believing: A Theological Commentary on the Book of Common Prayer. LC 90-28624. 1991. reprint ed. pap. 19.95 (0-8192-1553-8) Morehouse Pub.

— The Way We Pray. 80p. (Orig.). 1984. pap. 1.95 (0-88028-039-5, 759) Forward Movement.

— Worship: Initiation & the Churches. (Orig.). 1991. pap. 12.95 (0-912405-84-8) Pastoral Pr.

Mitchell Library, Sydney, Australia Staff. Dictionary Catalog of Printed Books, 38 Vols, No. 1. suppl. ed. 1970. lib. bdg. 155.00 (0-8161-0848-X, Hall Library) G K Hall.

— Dictionary Catalog of Printed Books, 38 Vols, Set. 1970. lib. bdg. 4,110.00 (0-8161-0790-4, Hall Library) G K Hall.

Mitchell, Lillias. Irish Spinning Dyeing & Weaving. (Illus.). 1978. 16.95 (0-85221-101-5) Dufour.

Mitchell, Linda & Mitchell, Allen. California Parks Access: A Complete Guide to the State & National Parks for Visitors with Limited Mobility. (Illus.). 320p. 1992. pap. 19.95 (0-9630758-3-7) Cougar Pass.

Mitchell, Loften & Le Noire, Rosetta. Bubbling Brown Sugar. 33p. (Orig.). 1985. pap. 4.95 (0-685-22962-9) Broadway Play.

Mitchell, Loren. Beauty of San Diego. LC 89-38291. (Illus.). 1990. 19.95 (0-917630-95-5) LTA Pub.

— Beauty of San Diego. (Illus.). 1991. pap. 9.95 (0-917630-48-3) LTA Pub.

Mitchell, Loretta. Music Teacher's Almanac: Read-to-Use Music Activities for Every Month of the Year. 1992. pap. 27.95 (0-13-605601-6) P-H.

— One, Two, Three...Echo Me! Ready to Use Songs, Games & Activities to Help Children Sing in Tune. 288p. 1991. pap. text ed. 24.95 (0-13-636127-7) P-H.

— Ready to Use Music Reading Activities Kit. 256p. 1991. pap. text ed. 26.95 (0-13-756164-4) P-H.

Mitchell, Lorna. The Revolution of St. Joan. 1993. pap. 8.95 (0-7043-4118-2, Pub. by Womens Pr UK) Interlink Pub.

Mitchell, Lucy S., et al. The Taxi That Hurried. (Little Golden Bks.). (Illus.). 24p. (J). (ps-00). 1992. write for info. (0-307-00144-X, 312-09, Golden Pr) Western Pub.

Mitchell, Lyn, illus. Animals. (Baby Bumper Bks.). 10p. (J). (ps). 1992. 4.95 (0-448-40304-8, G&D) Putnam Pub Group.

— Clothes. (Baby Bumper Bks.). 10p. (J). (ps). 1992. 4.95 (0-448-40307-2, G&D) Putnam Pub Group.

— Eating. (Baby Bumper Bks.). 10p. (J). (ps). 1992. 4.95 (0-448-40305-6, G&D) Putnam Pub Group.

— Playing. (Baby Bumper Bks.). 10p. (J). (ps). 1992. 4.95 (0-448-40306-4, G&D) Putnam Pub Group.

Mitchell, Lynda K., jt. auth. see Hadley, Robert G.

Mitchell, Lynn. Growing up in Smoke. (C). 1990. pap. text ed. 16.00 (0-7453-0446-X, Pub. by Pluto Pr UK) Westview.

Mitchell, Lynn E. The Vision of the New Community: Public Ethics in the Light of Christian Eschatology. (American University Studies: Theology & Religion: Ser. VII, Vol. 29). 213p. (C). 1988. text ed. 37.00 (0-8204-0450-0) P Lang Pubs.

Mitchell, M. Working with French. (C). 1986. student ed 65.00 (0-85950-604-5, Pub. by S Thornes Pubs UK); teacher ed 160.00 (0-85950-605-3, Pub. by S Thornes Pubs UK); audio 100.00 (0-85950-606-1, Pub. by S Thornes Pubs UK) St Mut.

Mitchell, M. B., jt. ed. see Bateson, J. H.

Mitchell, M. M., Jr., jt. ed. see Magee, J. S.

Mitchell, M. R. & Buck, Otto, eds. Cyclic Deformation, Fracture, & Nondestructive Evaluation of Advanced Materials. LC 92-16045. (Special Technical Publication Ser.: No. 1157). (Illus.). 350p. 1992. text ed. 87.00 (0-8031-1444-3, 04-011570-30) ASTM.

— Cyclic Deformation, Fracture, & Nondestructive Evaluation of Advanced Materials, Vol. 2, STP 1184. LC 94-32123. (Special Technical Publication Ser.: Vol. 1184). (Illus.). 400p. 1994. text ed. 115.00 (0-8031-1989-5, 04-011840-30) ASTM.

Mitchell, M. R. & Landgraf, R., eds. Advances in Fatigue Lifetime Predictive Technique, Vol. 2: STP 1211. (Special Technical Publication Ser.). (Illus.). 1993. text ed. 71.00 (0-685-70545-5, 04-012110-30) ASTM.

Mitchell, M. R. & Landgraf, R. W., eds. Advances in Fatigue Lifetime Predictive Techniques. LC 91-36055. (Special Technical Publication Ser.: No. 1122). (Illus.). 500p. 1992. text ed. 104.00 (0-8031-1423-0, 04-011220-30) ASTM.

Mitchell, M. R., jt. ed. see Schroeder, Scott A.

Mitchell, M. S., ed. The Modulation of Immunity. (International Encyclopedia of Pharmacology & Therapeutics Ser.: No. 115). (Illus.). 490p. 1985. 208.00 (0-08-031977-7, Pub. by Pergamon Repr UK) Franklin.

Mitchell, Mairin. Maritime History of Russia, Eight Forty-Eight to Nineteen Forty-Eight. LC 75-94278. (Select Bibliographies Reprint Ser.). 1977. 46.95 (0-8369-5052-6) Ayer.

Mitchell, Malcolm S. Biological Approaches to Cancer Treatment: Biomodulation. (Illus.). 608p. 1992. text ed. 95.00 (0-07-105397-2) Hlth Prof Div.

Mitchell, Malcolm S. & Oettgen, Herbert F., eds. Hybridomas in Cancer Diagnosis & Treatment. (Progress in Cancer Research & Therapy Ser.: Vol. 21). 282p. 1982. text ed. 78.50 (0-89004-768-5) Raven.

Mitchell, Marcia. Becoming Holy Women. 131p. 1992. pap. 7.95 (0-8341-1422-4) Beacon Hill.

— Giftedness: Discovering Your Areas of Strength. LC 88-1211. 192p. (Orig.). 1988. pap. 7.99 (0-87123-995-7) Bethany Hse.

— Jenny: Springsong. (YA). 1994. pap. 3.99 (1-55661-525-6) Bethany Hse.

— Spiritually Single. LC 83-15754. 112p. 1983. pap. 6.99 (0-87123-591-9) Bethany Hse.

Mitchell, Margaree K. Uncle Jed's Barbershop. 40p. (J). (ps-6). 1993. pap. 15.00 (0-671-76969-3, S&S Bks Young Read) S&S Childrens.

Mitchell, Margaret. Autant en Emporte le Vent, 3 vols., Tome I. (FRE.). 1976. pap. 13.95 (0-7859-4054-5) Fr & Eur.

— Autant en Emporte le Vent, 3 vols., Tome III. (FRE.). 1976. pap. 13.95 (0-7859-4055-3) Fr & Eur.

— Gone with the Wind. LC 36-27334. 1037p. 1936. text ed. 21.95 (0-02-585390-2) Macmillan.

— Gone with the Wind. LC 36-27334. 1037p. 1975. text ed. 37.50 (0-02-585350-3) Macmillan.

— Gone With the Wind. 1024p. 1993. mass mkt. 6.99 (0-446-36538-6) Warner Bks.

— Gone with the Wind. 1024p. 1976. reprint ed. mass mkt. 6.50 (0-380-00109-8) Avon.

— Gone with the Wind, 2 vols., Set. large type ed. (General Ser.). 1992. 35.90 (0-8161-5529-1, Large Print Bks); pap. 25.90 (0-8161-5530-5, Large Print Bks) Hall.

Mitchell, Margaret K. Observations on Birds of Southeastern Brazil. LC 57-58538. 280p. reprint ed. pap. 79.80 (0-685-15416-5, 2026538) Bks Demand.

Mitchell, Margaret M. The Bar-Bat Mitzvah Organizer. 50p. 1994. student ed 14.00 (0-9641090-1-8) Wedding Organizer.

— Paul & the Rhetoric of Reconciliation: An Exegetical Investigation of the Language & Composition of 1 Corinthians. LC 92-30364. 400p. 1993. text ed. 24.00 (0-664-21992-6) Westminster John Knox.

— The Wedding Organizer: The Bar - Bat Mitzvah Organizer. 50p. 1990. student ed 14.00 (0-9641090-0-X) Wedding Organizer.

Mitchell, Marge & Sedgwick, Joan. Bakery Lane Soup Bowl Cookbook. rev. ed. (Illus.). 128p. 1993. reprint ed. pap. 14.95 (0-8397-1005-4) Eriksson.

Mitchell, Maria. Life, Letters & Journals. LC 79-152989. (Select Bibliographies Reprint Ser.). 1977. reprint ed. 23. 95 (0-8369-5741-5) Ayer.

— Maria Mitchel, Life, Letters & Journals. (American Biography Ser.). 293p. 1991. reprint ed. lib. bdg. 69.00 (0-7812-8285-3) Rprt Serv.

***Mitchell, Marianne.** Maya Moon. (J). (gr. k-2). 1995. audio 8.95 (0-7608-0494-X); 21.95 (1-56801-793-6); audio 8.95 (0-7608-0499-0); 21.95 (1-56801-335-3); pap. 4.95 (1-56801-794-4); pap. 4.95 (1-56801-358-2) Sundance Pub.

Mitchell, Marianne H., jt. auth. see Gibson, Robert L.

Mitchell, Marilyn H., jt. auth. see Snider, Lawrence K.

Mitchell, Mark. The Mustang Professor: The Story of J. Frank Dobie. 96p. (J). (gr. 4-7). 1993. 12.95 (0-89015-823-1) Sunbelt Media.

Mitchell, Mark, ed. The Penguin Book of Gay Short Fiction. 688p. 1994. 27.50 (0-670-85468-9, Viking) Viking Penguin.

— The Penguin Book of International Gay Writing. 592p. 1995. 27.95 (0-670-85369-0, Viking) Viking Penguin.

Mitchell, Mark & Jolley, Janina. Research Design Explained. 2nd ed. 450p. (C). 1992. text ed. 45.25 (0-03-055972-3) HB Coll Pubs.

Mitchell, Mark, jt. ed. see Leavitt, David.

Mitchell, Mark L., jt. auth. see Jolley, Janina M.

Mitchell, Mary. Dear Ms. Demeanor: A Parent's Guide to Manners for Young People. 240p. 1994. 12.95 (0-8092-3630-3) Contemp Bks.

Mitchell, Mary, jt. auth. see Crowe, Sylvia.

Mitchell, Mary H. Hollywood Cemetery: The Story of a Southern Shrine. (Illus.). xiv, 194p. 1985. 25.00 (0-88490-109-2) VA State Lib.

Mitchell, Melanie. Analogy-Making As Perception: A Computer Model. LC 92-38045. (Neural Network Modeling & Connectionism Ser.). 1993. 45.00 (0-262-13289-3, Bradford Bks) MIT Pr.

— An Introduction to Genetic Algorithms. (Complex Adaptive Systems Ser.). (Illus.). 270p. 1995. 30.00x (0-262-13316-4, Bradford Bks) MIT Pr.

Mitchell, Memory F. North Carolina's Signers: Brief Sketches of the Men Who Signed the Declaration of Independence & the Constitution. (Illus.). viii, 56p. 1980. reprint ed. pap. 3.00 (0-86526-097-4) NC Archives.

Mitchell, Memory F., ed. Addresses & Public Papers of James Baxter Hunt, Jr., Governor of North Carolina, Vol. One Vol. 1, 1977-1981. (Illus.). xxxii, 881p. 1982. 3.00 (0-86526-178-4) NC Archives.

Mitchell, Meredith B. Hero or Victim? 306p. 1994. pap. 19. 95 (0-9639405-0-3) M B Mitchell.

Mitchell, Merle. Mathematical History: Activities, Puzzles, Stories & Games. LC 78-26206. (Illus.). 74p. 1978. pap. 10.00 (0-87353-138-8) NCTM.

Mitchell, Michael, tr. see Mander, Matthias.

Mitchell, Michael, tr. see Meyrick, Gustav.

Mitchell, Michael, tr. see Meyrink, Gustav.

Mitchell, Michael, tr. see Sebestyen, Gyorgy.

Mitchell, Mike, ed. & tr. Dedalus - Ariadne Book of Austrian Fantasy: The Meyrink Years 1890-1930. 416p. 1993. pap. 17.95 (0-929497-63-5) Ariadne CA.

Mitchell, Mike, tr. see Meyrink, Gustav.

Mitchell, Mike, tr. see Rosendorfer, Herbert.

Mitchell-Miller, Judy. Biryani & Plum Pudding. (Passages to India Ser.). (C). 1989. spiral bd. 20.00 (1-56709-010-9) Indep Broadcast.

— Vedas, Ragas & Storytellers. (Passages to India Ser.). (C). 1989. spiral bd. 20.00 (1-56709-012-5) Indep Broadcast.

Mitchell, Mitch & Platt, John. Jimi Hendrix: Inside the Experience. LC 93-35860. 1993. pap. 14.95 (0-312-10098-1) St Martin.

Mitchell, Mozella. New Africa in America Vol. 5: The Blending of African & American Religious & Social Traditions Among Black People in Meridian, Mississippi & Surrounding Counties. LC 93-42526. (Martin Luther King, Jr. Memorial Studies in Religion, Culture, & Social Development: Vol. 5). 245p. (C). 1994. text ed. 39.95 (0-8204-2425-0) P Lang Pubs.

Mitchell, Mozella G., ed. The Human Search: Howard Thurman & the Quest for Freedom: Proceedings of the Second Annual Thurman Convacation. LC 91-13995. 246p. 1991. 47.95 (0-8204-1466-2) P Lang Pubs.

Mitchell, Murray D., ed. Eicosanoids in Reproduction. 304p. 1990. 213.00 (0-8493-6464-7, QP251) CRC Pr.

***Mitchell, Mychal.** Backbone. 1994. 12.95 (0-533-10852-7) Vantage.

Mitchell, Myron J. & Nakas, James P., eds. Microfloral & Faunal Interactions in Natural & Agro-Ecosystems. (Developments in Biogeochemistry Ser.). 1985. lib. bdg. 145.50 (90-247-3246-8) Kluwer Ac.

Mitchell, Nahum. History of Bridgewater, Massachusetts. 456p. 1983. reprint ed. 35.00 (0-917890-36-1) Heritage Bk.

Mitchell, Nancy S. Quality Performance: How to Implement: Quality Awareness; Statistical Process Control; Task Teams; & Statistical Quality Control for Continuous Improvement in Your Organization. LC 90-91657. (Illus.). 184p. 1991. 39.95 (0-9626692-5-3) QP Pub PA.

Mitchell, Naomi. Corn King & Spring Queen. 1988. reprint ed. lib. bdg. 89.00 (0-7812-0167-5) Rprt Serv.

Mitchell, Nathan. Cult & Controversy: The Worship of the Eucharist Outside Mass. 460p. 1992. pap. 19.95 (0-8146-6050-9, Pueblo Bks) Liturgical Pr.

— Mission & Ministry: History & Theology in the Sacrament of Order. LC 82-83722. (Message of the Sacraments Ser.: Vol. 6). 317p. 1982. pap. 14.95 (0-8146-5292-1) Liturgical Pr.

***Mitchell, Nathan D.** Eucharist As Sacrament of Initiation. LC 93-46859. (Forum Essays Ser.). 154p. (Orig.). 1994. pap. 6.00 (0-929650-81-6, EUCHIN) Liturgy Tr Pubns.

***Mitchell, Nathan D. & Leonard, John.** The Postures of Assembly During Eucharistic Prayer. LC 94-31581. 1994. 11.95 (0-929650-64-6) Liturgy Tr Pubns.

Mitchell, Neil J. The Generous Corporation: A Political Analysis of Economic Power. LC 88-14417. 160p. (C). 1989. 22.00 (0-300-04413-5) Yale U Pr.

Mitchell, Nelson S., jt. ed. see Cruess, Richard L.

Mitchell, Nora. Deli Trays Around the World with Nora Mitchell. (Illus.). 112p. 1990. 29.95 (0-9626113-0-1) N Mitchell.

— The Indian Hill-Station: Kodaikanal. LC 72-78250. (Research Papers Ser.: No. 141). (Orig.). 1972. pap. 12. 00 (0-89065-048-9) U Chicago Comm Geo.

— Your Skin Is a Country. LC 88-14632. 72p. (Orig.). (C). 1988. 15.95 (0-914086-82-0); pap. 9.95 (0-914086-83-9) Alicejamesbooks.

Mitchell, Norma T. Francis E. Willard: Yours for Home Protection. 36p. 1976. pap. 0.75 (1-880927-09-8) Gen Comm Arch.

Mitchell, Olivia S., ed. As the Workforce Ages: Costs, Benefits, & Policy Challenges. LC 92-31402. (Frank W. Pierce Memorial Lectureship & Conference Ser.: No. 9). 304p. 1993. 42.00 (0-87546-195-6); pap. 18.95 (0-87546-196-4) ILR Pr.

Mitchell, Olivia S., jt. auth. see Fields, Gary S.

Mitchell, Otis C. Hitler's Nazi State: The Years of Dictatorial Rule (1939-1945) (University of Cincinnati Studies in Historical & Contemporary Europe: Vol. 1). 271p. (C). 1988. text ed. 60.00 (0-8204-0368-7) P Lang Pubs.

— Two German Crowns: Monarchy & Empire in Medieval German. LC 85-51753. 97p. (Orig.). 1985. pap. text ed. 14.95 (0-932269-66-4) Wyndhall Pr.

Mitchell, P. Concepts Basic to Nursing. 3rd ed. (Illus.). 720p. 1981. text ed. 36.95 (0-07-042582-5) McGraw.

— Control Applications of Microcomputers. (Illus.). 160p. (C). 1988. pap. text ed. 19.95 (0-7131-3583-2, Pub. by E Arnold UK) Routledge Chapman & Hall.

Mitchell, P. Chalmers, tr. see Metchnikoff, Elie.

Mitchell, P. J., ed. Electrochemical Engineering & the Environment '92. LC 92-14500. (EFCE Publication: No. 89). 1992. 85.00 (1-56032-256-X) Hemisp Pub.

Mitchell, P. M. Halldor Hermannsson. LC 77-14665. (Islandica Ser.: Vol. XLI). (Illus.). 160p. 1978. 39.95 (0-8014-1085-1) Cornell U Pr.

— History of Danish Literature. LC 71-181092. 1971. 17.50 (0-89067-034-X) Am Scandinavian.

— Johann Christoph Gottsched (1700-1766) Harbinger of German Classicism. (Studies in German Literature, Linguistics, & Culture). 155p. 1995. 54.95 (1-57113-063-2) Camden Hse.

Mitchell, P. M., ed. Johann Christoph Gottsched. Ausgewaehlte Werke, Vol. 7: Ausfuehrliche Redekunst; Pt. 3, Anhang und Variantenverzeichnis. (Ausgaben Deutscher Literatur des XV bis XVIII Jahrhunderts Ser.). (C). 1975. 176.95 (3-11-005926-6) De Gruyter.

Mitchell, P. M. & Ober, Kenneth H., comps. Bibliography of Modern Icelandic Literature in Translation: Including Works Written by Icelanders in Other Languages. LC 74-19751. (Islandica Ser.: Vol. XL). 324p. 1975. 69.50 (0-8014-0897-0) Cornell U Pr.

Mitchell, P. M., jt. ed. see Billeskov-Jansen, F. J.

Mitchell, P. M., tr. see Dinesen, Isak.

Mitchell, P. M., ed. see Gottsched, Johann C.

Mitchell, P. M., tr. see Holberg, Ludvig.

Mitchell, P. M., jt. comp. see Kalinke, Marianne E.

Mitchell, Paige. Wild Seed. 1984. pap. 3.95 (0-8217-1468-6) Zebra.

Mitchell, Pamela H., et al. Differentiating Nursing Practice: Into the Twenty-First Century. 452p. (Orig.). (C). 1991. pap. 25.00 (1-55810-065-2, G182, Am Acad Nursing) Am Nurses Pub.

Mitchell, Patricia B. Apple Country Cooking. 3rd ed. 1991. pap. 4.00 (0-925117-47-1) Mitchells.

— A Bowl of Soup, a Crust of Bread, & Thou. 1995. pap. 4.00 (0-925117-78-1) Mitchells.

— Butter 'em While They're Hot. 3rd ed. 1991. pap. 4.00 (0-925117-50-1) Mitchells.

— Christmas: How Sweet It Is! rev. ed. 1991. pap. 4.00 (0-925117-48-X) Mitchells.

— Colonial Christmas Cooking. rev. ed. 1991. pap. 4.00 (0-925117-43-9) Mitchells.

— Coming Home for Christmas Cookbook. rev. ed. 1991. pap. 4.00 (0-925117-49-8) Mitchells.

— Confederate Camp Cooking. rev. ed. 1991. pap. 4.00 (0-925117-46-3) Mitchells.

— Confederate Home Cooking. rev. ed. 1991. pap. 4.00 (0-925117-45-5) Mitchells.

— Cooking for the Cause: Confederate Recipes, Documented Quotations, Commemorative Recipes. 38p. 1988. pap. 4.00 (0-925117-06-4) Mitchells.

— Cooking in the Young Republic, 1780-1850. 1992. pap. 4.00 (0-925117-57-9) Mitchells.

— Crumbs Between the Covers: Homemade Bread for In & Out of Bed. 1994. pap. 4.00 (0-925117-73-0) Mitchells.

— La Cuisine Francaise des Premieres Annees de l'Amerique du Nord. Black, Mary L., tr. 1992. pap. 4.00 (0-925117-59-5) Mitchells.

— Delightful Dreams of Dixie Dinners. rev. ed. 1992. pap. 4.00 (0-925117-63-3) Mitchells.

— Dining Cars & Depots. 1992. pap. 4.00 (0-925117-55-2) Mitchells.

— Four Centuries of American Herbs. 1993. pap. 4.00 (0-925117-68-4) Mitchells.

— French Cooking in Early America. 1991. pap. 4.00 (0-925117-35-8) Mitchells.

— Girth of the Nation: Pleasures of the Palate in Early America. 1994. pap. 4.00 (0-925117-76-5) Mitchells.

— The Good Land: Native American & Early Colonial Food. 1992. pap. 4.00 (0-925117-60-9) Mitchells.

— Grist Mill Quick Loaf Breads. 1991. pap. 4.00 (0-925117-37-4) Mitchells.

— Hit the Road, Jacques: An Introductory Guide to South Louisiana's Creole & Cajun Restaurants. rev. ed. 1995. pap. 4.00 (0-925117-77-3) Mitchells.

— Just Naturally Sweet: Honey, Sorghum, & Maple Syrup. rev. ed. 1993. pap. 4.00 (0-925117-66-8) Mitchells.

— A Lick & a Promise: Relaxing Recipes & Wise Words. 1994. pap. 4.00 (0-925117-74-9) Mitchells.

— Loaves of Love. rev. ed. 1991. pap. 4.00 (0-925117-52-8) Mitchells.

— Mrs. Billy Yank's Receipt Book: Cooking on the Home Front 1861-1865. rev. ed. 1994. pap. text ed. 4.00 (0-925117-75-7) Mitchells.

— My Heart's in Louisiana but My Supermarket Isn't. 1991. pap. 4.00 (0-925117-40-4) Mitchells.

— Refreshments Now & Then: Colonial, Victorian, & Contemporary Sweets. 1995. pap. 4.00 (0-925117-79-X) Mitchells.

— Revolutionary Recipes. rev. ed. 1991. pap. 4.00 (0-925117-42-0) Mitchells.

— Salad Days: Super Salads & Delicious Dressings. 1993. pap. 4.00 (0-925117-71-4) Mitchells.

— Simply Scrumptious Southern Sweets. rev. ed. 1991. pap. 4.00 (0-925117-39-0) Mitchells.

— Soul on Rice: African Influences on American Cooking. 1993. pap. 4.00 (0-925117-69-2) Mitchells.

— Southern Born & Bread. 4th ed. 1992. pap. 4.00 (0-925117-54-4) Mitchells.

— Southern Specialty Vegetables. 1992. pap. 4.00 (0-925117-61-7) Mitchells.

— Suited to a Tea. 1995. pap. 4.00 (*0-925117-80-3*) Mitchells.

— Sweet 'n' Slow. 3rd ed. 1992. pap. 4.00 (*0-925117-62-5*) Mitchells.

— The Take-It-Easy Good-Times Cookbook. 1991. pap. 4.00 (*0-925117-51-X*) Mitchells.

— True Grist. 3rd ed. 1992. pap. 4.00 (*0-925117-53-6*) Mitchells.

— Union Army Camp Cooking. rev. ed. 1991. pap. 4.00 (*0-925117-41-2*) Mitchells.

— Victorian Christmas Celebration Cookbook. rev. ed. 1991. pap. 4.00 (*0-925117-44-7*) Mitchells.

— Victorian Parlors & Tea Parties. 1991. pap. 4.00 (*0-925117-36-6*) Mitchells.

— Victorian Vacation Recipe Book. 1992. pap. 4.00 (*0-925117-67-6*) Mitchells.

— Waking up Down South. 1992. pap. 4.00 (*0-925117-65-X*) Mitchells.

— Well, Bless Your Heart: High Fiber, Low Fat, Low Cholesterol Recipes, 2 vols. Incl. Vol. II: Dinners. Dinners. 38p. 1992. pap. 4.00 (*0-925117-56-0*); Vol. I. Breakfasts & Lunches. (Illus.). 37p. 1992. pap. 4.00 (*0-615-00342-7*); 8.00 (*0-925117-64-1*) Mitchells.

— Well, Bless Your Heart Vol. I: High Fiber, Low Fat, Low Cholesterol Recipes: Breakfasts & Lunches, 2 vols. 37p. 1989. Vol. I: Breakfasts & Lunches, 37p. pap. 4.00 (*0-925117-13-7*) Mitchells.

— Yanks, Rebels, Rats, & Rations: Scratching for Food in Civil War Prison Camps. 1993. pap. 4.00 (*0-925117-70-6*) Mitchells.

Mitchell, Paula. Given the Opportunity Employee Handbook. (Illus.). (Orig.). 1992. pap. 3.50 (*1-56191-197-6*); write for info. (*1-56191-199-2*) Meridian Educ.

Mitchell, Paula R. & Grippando, Gloria M. Nursing Perspectives & Issues. 5th ed. 1993. pap. text ed. 26.95 (*0-8273-4983-1*) Delmar.

— Nursing Perspectives & Issues: Instructor's Guide. 5th ed. 1993. teacher ed 14.00 (*0-8273-4985-8*) Delmar.

Mitchell, Paulette. The Fifteen-Minute Single Gourmet. LC 93-38178. 224p. 1994. text ed. 23.00 (*0-02-585355-4*) Macmillan.

— The Fifteen-Minute Vegetarian Gourmet. (Illus.). 160p. 1992. pap. 9.00 (*0-02-009815-4*, Pub. by Gebrueder Borntraeger GW) Macmillan.

***Mitchell, Pearline W.** Their Misty Years: Childhood Entanglement - The Magic Raindrop - Sammy Crow Saves the Day - Smoky's Friend "The Thief" Brinson, Rebecca, tr. (Illus.). 32p. (J). 1994. text ed. 12.50 (*0-930329-85-6*) KABEL Pubs.

***Mitchell, Peter.** The Complete Golfer Peter Thomson: A Biography. (Illus.). 287p. 1995. 34.95 (*0-85091-474-4*, Pub. by Lothian Pub AT) Seven Hills Bk.

— The Psychology of Childhood. (Contemporary Psychology Ser.). 224p. 1992. 75.00 (*1-85000-954-6*, Falmer Pr); pap. 27.00 (*1-85000-950-3*, Falmer Pr) Taylor & Francis.

Mitchell, Philip, ed. Tool & Manufacturing Engineers Handbook: Design for Manufacturability, Vol. 6. LC 91-60347. (Illus.). 675p. 1992. 120.00 (*0-87263-402-7*) SME.

— Tool & Manufacturing Engineers Handbook Vol. VIII: Plastic Part Manufacturing. 650p. 1995. 120.00 (*0-87263-456-6*) SME.

Mitchell, Philip L., et al, eds. Butterworths Company Law Service, 2 vols., Set. 1991. ring bd. 440.00 (*0-406-19570-6*, U.K.) Butterworth Legal Pubs.

Mitchell, Pratima. Dance of Shiva. (Way We Live Ser.). (Illus.). 25p. (J). (gr. 2-4). 1991. 13.95 (*0-237-60148-6*, Pub. by Evans Bros Ltd UK) Trafalgar.

Mitchell, R. & Forbes, Nevill, trs. Chronicle of Novgorod, 1016-1471. reprint ed. 32.50 (*0-404-04799-8*) AMS Pr.

Mitchell, R. A. The Buddha: His Life Retold. 274p. (C). 1991. reprint ed. pap. 14.95 (*1-55778-442-6*) Paragon Hse.

Mitchell, R. G. Goulds of Rhode Island. 99p. 1991. reprint ed. lib. bdg. 28.00 (*0-8328-1747-3*); reprint ed. pap. 18.00 (*0-8328-1748-1*) Higginson Bk Co.

***Mitchell, R. J.** C++ Object-Oriented Programming. (Illus.). 268p. 1995. 29.95 (*0-387-91490-0*) Spr-Verlag.

— Modula-2 Applied. Sumner, F. H., ed. (Computer Science Ser.). (Illus.). 284p. (Orig.). (C). 1991. pap. text ed. 35.00 (*0-333-55453-1*, Pub. by Macmill Educ UK) Scholium Intl.

Mitchell, R. Judson. Getting to the Top in the U. S. S. R. Cyclical Patterns in the Leadership Succession Process. 284p. (C). 1990. text ed. 31.95 (*0-8179-8921-8*, P 392); pap. text ed. 23.95 (*0-8179-8922-6*, P 392) Hoover Inst Pr.

Mitchell, Ralph. Environmental Microbiology. (Series in Ecological & Applied Microbiology: No. 1675). 434p. 1992. text ed. 134.95 (*0-471-50647-8*, Wiley-Liss) Wiley.

Mitchell, Ralph, ed. Environmental Microbiology. (Series in Ecological & Applied Microbiology). 434p. 1993. pap. text ed. 64.95 (*0-471-59587-X*) Wiley.

— Water Pollution Microbiology, Vol. 1. LC 73-168641. 428p. reprint ed. pap. 122.00 (*0-317-26263-7*, 2055711) Bks Demand.

Mitchell, Ralph & Shafer, Neil. Standard Catalog of Depression Scrip of U. S. LC 85-52834. (Illus.). 320p. 1985. pap. 27.50 (*0-87341-047-5*) Krause Pubns.

***Mitchell, Randyl B.** Growing Beyond: By Identifying & Understanding the Influences in Your Life. (Illus.). 192p. (Orig.). Date not set. pap. write for info. (*1-884819-00-1*) Red-Giant Pubns.

Mitchell, Ray. Foodservice Operators Guide. 800p. 1993. write for info. (*0-929615-09-3*) FDCI.

Mitchell, Raymond. Foodservice Operators Guide. LC 88-90867. 550p. 1988. pap. 149.00 (*0-929615-00-X*) FDCI.

— Foodservice Operators Guide. 600p. 1990. 149.00 (*0-929615-03-4*) FDCI.

— Foodservice Operators Guide: Update. 220p. 1989. write for info. (*0-929615-01-8*) FDCI.

***Mitchell, Reid.** All on a Mardi Gras Day: Episodes in the History of New Orleans Carnival. LC 94-28098. (Illus.). 255p. 1995. text ed. 29.95 (*0-674-01622-X*, MITALL) HUP.

— Civil War Soldiers. 1989. pap. 9.95 (*0-671-68641-0*, Touchstone Bks) S&S Trade.

— The Vacant Chair: The Northern Soldier Leaves Home. LC 92-36921. 1993. 25.00 (*0-19-507893-4*) OUP.

— The Vacant Chair: The Northern Soldier Leaves Home. (Illus.). 240p. 1995. pap. 12.95 (*0-19-509643-6*) OUP.

***Mitchell, Rhonda, illus.** Sleep Song. LC 94-24859. 32p. (J). (ps). 1995. 14.95 (*0-531-06878-1*) Orchard Bks Watts.

Mitchell, Richard. Abstract Data Types & Ada. 400p. 1992. pap. text ed. 47.00 (*0-13-006099-2*) P-H.

— Abstract Data Types & Modula-2. 400p. 1991. pap. text ed. 47.00 (*0-13-006081-X*) P-H.

— Crisis Intervention in Practice: The Multidisciplinary Team & the Mental Health Social Worker. (Studies of Care in the Community). 150p. 1993. 58.95 (*1-85628-452-2*, Pub. by Avebury Pub UK) Ashgate Pub Co.

— Less Than Words Can Say. LC 79-15484. 1981. pap. 9.95 (*0-316-57507-0*) Little.

Mitchell, Richard E. Patricians & Plebeians: The Origin of the Roman State. LC 90-1680. 288p. 1990. 33.95 (*0-8014-2496-8*) Cornell U Pr.

Mitchell, Richard G., Jr. Mountain Experience: The Psychology & Sociology of Adventure. LC 83-6454. xvi, 272p. 1983. lib. bdg. 14.95 (*0-226-53224-0*) U Ch Pr.

— Secrecy & Fieldwork. (Qualitative Research Methods Ser.: Vol. 29). (Illus.). 96p. (C). 1993. text ed. 21.50 (*0-8039-4384-9*); pap. text ed. 9.50 (*0-8039-4385-7*) Sage.

Mitchell, Richard H. Censorship in Imperial Japan. LC 82-61440. 432p. 1983. 65.00 (*0-691-05384-7*) Princeton U Pr.

— Censorship in Imperial Japan. LC 83-3056. Date not set. reprint ed. pap. 124.60 (*0-7837-9391-X*, 2060136) Bks Demand.

— Janus-Faced Justice: Political Criminals in Imperial Japan. LC 91-41623. 264p. (C). 1992. text ed. 30.00 (*0-8248-1410-X*) UH Pr.

Mitchell, Richard L. The History of Tae Kwon-Do Patterns: The Chang-Hon Pattern Set: Chon-ji Through Choong-Moo. Reece, Nancy S., ed. (Illus.). 100p. (Orig.). pap. 7.95 (*0-317-93102-4*) Lilley Gulch.

— The History of Taekwon-Do Patterns: The Choong-Hon Pattern Set Chon-Ji Through Choong-Moo. 3rd ed. Reece, Nancy S., ed. (Illus.). 100p. 1993. pap. 7.95 (*0-9622129-9-7*) Lilley Gulch.

— The History of Taekwon-Do Patters: The Chang-Hon Pattern Set Con-Ji Through Choong Moo. (Illus.). 100p. 1989. pap. 7.95 (*0-9622129-0-3*) Lilley Gulch.

— Radar Signal Simulation. LC 75-31380. (Artech Radar Library). 224p. reprint ed. pap. 63.90 (*0-317-27681-6*, 2025054) Bks Demand.

— Radar Signal Simulation. LC 75-31380. 200p. 1985. reprint ed. 44.95 (*0-9615109-0-0*) Peninsula CA.

— United States Taekwon-Do Federation Patterns Workout Book. Akard, Freddie C. & Sereff, Charles E., eds. 139p. (Orig.). 1992. pap. text ed. 6.00 (*0-9622129-4-6*) Lilley Gulch.

Mitchell, Richard L. & Akard, Freddie C. United States Taekwon-Do Federation Step-Sparring Handbook: 9th Gup White Belt Through 2nd Dan Black Belt. Sereff, Charles E., ed. 69p. (Orig.). 1992. pap. 5.00 (*0-9622129-2-X*) Lilley Gulch.

— United States Taekwon-Do Federation Testing Requirements: 1st Dan Black Belt Through 4th Dan Black Belt. Sereff, Charles E. & Winegar, Mike D., eds. 50p. (Orig.). 1992. pap. text ed. 4.50 (*0-9622129-3-8*) Lilley Gulch.

— United States Taekwon-Do Federation Testing Requirements: 9th Gup White Belt Through 1st Dan Black Belt. Sereff, Charles E. & Winegar, Mike D., eds. 59p. (Orig.). 1992. pap. text ed. 4.50 (*0-9622129-1-1*) Lilley Gulch.

Mitchell, Richard L., et al. United States Taekwon-Do Federation Testing: 9th Gup White Belt Through 1st Dan Black Belt. 60p. (Orig.). 1993. pap. 4.50 (*0-9622129-8-9*) Lilley Gulch.

— United States Taekwon-Do Federation Testing Requirements: 1st Dan Black Belt Through 4th Dan Black Belt. 52p. (Orig.). 1993. pap. 4.50 (*0-9622129-7-0*) Lilley Gulch.

Mitchell, Richard M. The Steam Launch. Spurlock, Pat, ed. & intro. by. (Classics Ser.). (Illus.). 350p. 1994. 49.95 (*0-9641204-0-2*) Elliott Bay.

Mitchell, Richard P. The Society of the Muslim Brothers. 384p. 1993. pap. 17.95 (*0-19-508437-3*) OUP.

Mitchell, Richard S. Atlas of New York State Ferns: Contribution to a Flora of New York State, Checklist II. (Bulletin Ser.: No. 456). 1984. pap. 2.50 (*1-55557-002-X*) NYS Museum.

— A Checklist of New York State Plants. (Bulletin Ser.: No. 458). 272p. 1986. 12.50 (*1-55557-004-6*) NYS Museum.

— Portulacaceae Through Caryophyllaceae of New York State. (New York State Museum Bulletin Ser.: No. 486). (Illus.). 124p. (Orig.). 1993. pap. 10.00 (*1-55557-228-6*) NYS Museum.

— Using Volumetric Glassware to Measure, Dilute, & Titrate an Acid Solution. Neidig, H. A., ed. (Modular Laboratory Program in Chemistry Ser.). 11p. (C). 1992. pap. text ed. 1.25x (*0-87540-417-0*) Chem Educ Res.

Mitchell, Richard S., jt. auth. see Furlow, John J.

Mitchell, Richard S., jt. auth. see Lloyd, Robert M.

Mitchell, Richard S., jt. auth. see Ogden, Eugene C.

Mitchell, Richard S., et al, eds. Ecosystem Management: Rare Species & Significant Habitats. (Bulletin Ser.: No. 471). (Illus.). 314p. (Orig.). (C). 1990. pap. text ed. 24.95 (*1-55557-192-1*) NYS Museum.

Mitchell, Rick. Airacobra Advantage: The Flying Cannon: The Complete Story of Bell Aircraft Corporation's P-39 Pursuit Fighter Plane. LC 92-80004. (Illus.). 128p. (Orig.). 1992. pap. 11.95 (*0-929521-62-5*) Pictorial Hist.

— Garth Brooks: One of a Kind, Workin' on a Full House. (Illus.). 128p. (Orig.). 1993. pap. 12.00 (*0-671-79688-7*, Fireside) S&S Trade.

Mitchell, Rie Rogers & Friedman, Harriet S. Sandplay: Past, Present, & Future. LC 93-8079. 1993. write for info. (*0-415-10136-0*); pap. write for info. (*0-415-10137-9*) Routledge.

Mitchell, Rita K. Please Take Your Dead Bird Home Today: Portrait of an Alternative School. LC 77-79578. 1978. 15.00 (*0-87212-094-5*) Libra.

Mitchell, Rita P. Hue Boy. LC 92-18560. (Illus.). 32p. (J). (ps-3). 1993. 13.99 (*0-8037-1448-3*) Dial Bks Young.

Mitchell, Robert. Abraham, Sarah & the Promised Son. (Arch Bks.: No. 21). 1984. pap. 1.99 (*0-317-00725-4*, 59-1284) Concordia.

— Forsaken? Two Tenebrae Services. 1992. pap. 4.75 (*1-55673-565-0*) CSS OH.

— GED Test Three: Science. LC 93-49744. 1994. pap. 10.60 (*0-8092-3780-6*) Contemp Bks.

— I Don't Like That Music. Schrader, Jack, ed. LC 92-74589. 144p. (Orig.). (C). 1992. pap. 11.95 (*0-916642-49-6*) Hope Pub.

— Lucinda Legacy. 281p. (C). 1990. pap. 51.00 (*0-646-03980-6*, Pub. by Boolarong Pubns AT) St Mut.

— The Multicultural Student's Guide to Colleges. 1993. 25.00 (*0-374-52362-2*, Noonday) FS&G.

— Number Power Review. LC 93-8627. 1993. pap. 9.20 (*0-8092-3805-5*) Contemp Bks.

Mitchell, Robert & Prickel, Donald. Number Power Four: Geometry. (Number Power Ser.). 176p. (Orig.). 1983. pap. 5.95 (*0-8092-5517-0*) Contemp Bks.

Mitchell, Robert & Zim, Herbert S. Butterflies & Moths. (Golden Guide Ser.). (Illus.). (J). (gr. 5 up). 1964. lib. bdg. write for info. (*0-307-24052-5*) Western Pub.

Mitchell, Robert, jt. auth. see Joseph, Jenny.

Mitchell, Robert B. Heritage & Horizons: A History of the Open Bible Standard Churches. LC 81-18884. (Illus.). (Orig.). (C). 1982. pap. 4.95 (*0-9608160-1-1*) Open Bible.

— Syphilis As AIDS. 152p. (Orig.). 1990. pap. 8.95 (*0-934411-35-2*, Banned Bks) Edward-William Austin.

Mitchell, Robert B., jt. auth. see Tedesco, Eleanor H.

Mitchell, Robert B., et al. Jennie & the Song of the Meadowlark. Vesta Publishing Services Staff & Rhoads, Gwen, eds. (Illus.). 208p. (Orig.). 1988. pap. 6.95 (*0-9608160-2-X*) Open Bible.

Mitchell, Robert C. & Carson, Richard T. Using Surveys to Value Public Goods: The Contingent Valuation Method. LC 87-28633. 463p. 1988. 45.00 (*0-915707-32-2*) Resources Future.

Mitchell, Robert D. Commercialism & Frontier: Perspectives on the Early Shenandoah Valley. LC 76-26610. (Illus.). 267p. reprint ed. pap. 76.10 (*0-7837-4358-0*, 2044068) Bks Demand.

Mitchell, Robert D., ed. Appalachian Frontiers: Settlement, Society, & Development in the Pre-Industrial Era. LC 90-42857. 360p. 1991. text ed. 43.00 (*0-8131-1733-X*) U Pr of Ky.

Mitchell, Robert D. & Groves, Paul A., eds. North America: The Historical Geography of a Changing Continent. (Illus.). 512p. (C). 1987. 83.00 (*0-8476-7347-2*, R7347); pap. 44.00 (*0-8476-7549-1*, R7549) Rowman.

Mitchell, Robert E. Jesus the Good Shepherd. (Arch Bks.). (Illus.). 24p. (J). (ps-2). 1989. pap. 1.99 (*0-570-09018-0*, 59-1441) Concordia.

— Pupil, Parent & School: A Hong Kong Study. (Asian Folklore & Social Life Monographs: No. 26). 1972. 18.00 (*0-89986-027-3*) Oriental Bk Store.

Mitchell, Robert H. Ministry & Music. LC 77-20815. 164p. 1978. pap. 10.99 (*0-664-24186-7*, Westminster) Westminster John Knox.

Mitchell, Robert H. & Putney, James W., Jr., eds. Inositol Lipids in Cellular Signaling. (Current Communications in Molecular Biology Ser.). (Illus.). 165p. (C). 1987. pap. text ed. 32.00 (*0-87969-304-5*) Cold Spring Harbor.

Mitchell, Robert L. Corbiere, Mallarme, Valery: Preservations & Commentary. (Stanford French & Italian Studies: Vol. 23). viii, 149p. 1981. pap. 46.50 (*0-915838-16-8*) Anma Libri.

— Engineering Economics. LC 79-40647. (Illus.). 182p. reprint ed. pap. 51.90 (*0-7837-5203-2*, 2044931) Bks Demand.

— The Hymn to Eros: A Reading of Plato's Symposium. 248p. (Orig.). (C). 1993. lib. bdg. 46.50 (*0-8191-9117-5*); pap. text ed. 27.50 (*0-8191-9118-3*) U Pr of Amer.

— The Poetic Voice of Charles Cros: A Centennial Study of His Songs. LC 76-24891. (Romance Monographs: No. 21). 1976. 26.00 (*84-399-5835-8*) Romance.

Mitchell, Robert L., jt. ed. see Jacobson, John R.

Mitchell, Robert P., ed. see Bain, John A.

Mitchell, Robert W. ACA Legal Series, Vol. 2: Documentation in Counseling Records. Remley, Theodore P., Jr., ed. 75p. (C). 1992. pap. text ed. 12.95 (*1-55620-084-6*) Am Coun Assn.

Mitchell, Robert W. & Thompson, Nicholas S., eds. Deception: Perspectives on Human & Nonhuman Deceit. LC 85-2703. (SUNY Series on Animal Behavior). 388p. 1985. 64.50 (*0-88706-107-9*); pap. 24.95 (*0-88706-108-7*) State U NY Pr.

Mitchell, Robert W., jt. auth. see Pittard, Kay.

Mitchell, Robert W., et al. Mexican Eyeless Characin Fishes, Genus Astyanax: Environment, Distribution, & Evolution. (Special Publications: No. 12). (Illus.). 89p. (Orig.). 1977. pap. 10.00 (*0-89672-038-1*) Tex Tech Univ Pr.

Mitchell, Roger. Clear Pond: The Reconstruction of a Life. (Illus.). 201p. 1991. 19.95 (*0-8156-0257-X*) Syracuse U Pr.

— Clear Space on a Cold Day. (CSU Poetry Ser.: No. XIX). 80p. (Orig.). 1986. 12.00 (*0-914946-65-X*); pap. 6.00 (*0-914946-55-2*) Cleveland St Univ Poetry Ctr.

— Death Valley Jeep Trails. rev. ed. (Illus.). 36p. 1991. 2.50 (*0-910856-30-3*) La Siesta.

— Eastern Sierra Jeep Trails. (Illus.). 36p. 1992. 1.95 (*0-910856-39-7*) La Siesta.

— Exploring Joshua Tree. rev. ed. (Illus.). 48p. 1990. 2.95 (*0-910856-12-5*) La Siesta.

— Grand Canyon Jeep Trails. (Jeep Trails Ser.). (Illus.). 1977. pap. 1.95 (*0-910856-65-6*) La Siesta.

— Inyo-Mono Jeep Trails. (Illus.). 1991. 2.50 (*0-910856-33-8*) La Siesta.

— Moving. 1976. pap. 3.00 (*0-912284-79-X*) New Rivers Pr.

— Western Nevada Jeep Trails. (Illus.). 1990. 1.95 (*0-910856-50-8*) La Siesta.

— Western Sierra Jeep Trails. (Jeep Trails Ser.). (Illus.). 1983. pap. 3.95 (*0-910856-63-X*) La Siesta.

***Mitchell, Roger H.** Kimberelites, Orangeites, & Related Rocks. 425p. 1995. 89.50 (*0-306-45022-4*) Plenum.

— Kimberlites: Mineralogy, Geochemistry, & Petrology. 460p. 1986. 95.00 (*0-306-42173-9*, Plenum Pr) Plenum.

Mitchell, Roger H. & Bergman, S. C. Petrology of Lamproites. (Illus.). 465p. 1991. 85.00 (*0-306-43556-X*, Plenum Pr) Plenum.

Mitchell, Ronald. Opera - Dead or Alive: Production, Performance, & Enjoyment of Musical Theatre. LC 73-121772. (Illus.). 334p. 1972. pap. 14.95 (*0-299-05814-X*) U of Wis Pr.

— Opera-Dead or Alive: Production, Performance, & Enjoyment of Musical Theatre. LC 73-121772. (Illus.). 334p. 1970. 30.00 (*0-299-05811-5*) U of Wis Pr.

Mitchell, Ronald B. Intentional Oil Pollution at Sea: Environmental Policies and Treaty Compliance. (Global Environmental Accords Ser.). 260p. 1994. 34.95 (*0-262-13303-2*) MIT Pr.

Mitchell, Ronald E. America: A Practical Handbook. LC 73-13144. (Foreign Travelers in America, 1810-1935 Ser.). 318p. 1974. reprint ed. 26.95 (*0-405-05467-X*) Ayer.

Mitchell, Roosevelt. Life Is a Merry-Go-Round. 255p. 1993. pap. 12.95 (*0-9636020-0-4*) Mitchell NY.

Mitchell, Rosemary C. & Ricciuti, Gail A. Birthings & Blessings: Liberating Worship Services for the Inclusive Church. 192p. (Orig.). 1991. pap. 12.95 (*0-8245-1126-3*) Crossroad NY.

Mitchell, Rosemary C., jt. auth. see Ricciuti, Gail A.

Mitchell, Roy. The Exile of the Soul. Davenport, John L., ed. LC 83-62528. 338p. 1984. pap. 19.95 (*0-87975-233-5*) Prometheus Bks.

— God Is ... Cartoons Showing the Character of God (And How We Respond to Him) (REPRObooks Ser.). (Illus.). 128p. (Orig.). 1992. pap. 5.99 (*0-8010-6284-5*) Baker Bk.

Mitchell, Roy, jt. auth. see Mills, Jerry.

Mitchell, Ruby D. Virgin of the Sun. LC 84-52477. 1986. 13.95 (*0-87212-189-5*) Libra.

Mitchell, Ruth. Arkansas Heritage: Fifth Grade History Textbook. LC 85-63310. (Illus.). 192p. 1986. 18.00 (*0-914546-62-7*) Rose Pub.

— Testing for Learning: How New Approaches to Evaluation Can Improve American Schools. 165p. 1992. text ed. 24.95 (*0-02-921465-3*) Free Pr.

***Mitchell, Ruth, ed.** Measuring up to the Challenge: What Standards & Assessment Can Do for Arts Education. LC 94-31023. 1994. 16.95 (*1-879903-20-2*) Am Council Arts.

Mitchell, Ruth, jt. auth. see Barth, Patte.

Mitchell, Ruth C. Of Human Kindness. LC 74-22798. (Labor Movement in Fiction & Non-Fiction Ser.). reprint ed. 45.00 (*0-404-58454-3*) AMS Pr.

Mitchell, Ruth K. Information Science & Computer Basics: An Introduction. LC 70-142595. 114p. reprint ed. pap. 32.50 (*0-317-08826-2*, 2021001) Bks Demand.

Mitchell, S. A Bestiary. Date not set. 25.00 (*0-06-016918-4*, HarpT) HarpC.

— Jane's Aircraft Upgrades, 1995-96. 1995. text ed. 265.00 (*0-7106-1281-8*) Janes Info Group.

— Tao Te Ching. 1991. pap. 79.50 (*0-06-092133-1*, PL) HarpC.

Mitchell, S., ed. Poetry Collection. Date not set. pap. 12.00 (*0-06-095049-8*) HarpC.

Mitchell, S. J. D. Perse: A History of the Perse School 1615-1976. (Cambridge Town, Gown & County Ser.: Vol. 7). (Illus.). 1976. 25.00 (*0-902675-71-0*) Oleander Pr.

Mitchell, S. Weir, et al. Gunshot Wounds & Other Injuries of Nerves. (American Civil War Surgery Ser.: No. 3). 164p. 1989. reprint ed. 75.00 (*0-930405-13-7*) Norman SF.

Mitchell, S. Wier. In War Time. Weigand, William, ed. (Masterworks of Literature Ser.). 1991. 15.95 (*0-8084-0420-2*) NCUP.

Mitchell, Sally. The Dictionary of British Equestrian Artists. (Illus.). 518p. 1985. 89.50 (*0-907462-42-1*) Antique Collect.

— The Fallen Angel. LC 79-92711. 1981. 16.95 (*0-87972-155-3*); pap. 9.95 (*0-87972-156-1*) Bowling Green Univ.

Mitchell, Sally, ed. East Lynne: Mrs. Henry Wood. 545p. 1984. reprint ed. 50.00 (*0-8135-1041-4*); reprint ed. pap. 17.00 (*0-8135-1042-2*) Rutgers U Pr.

An Asterisk (*) at the beginning of an entry indicates that the title is appearing in BIP for the first time.

— Victorian Britain: An Encyclopedia. LC 87-29947. (Illus.). 1010p. 1988. lib. bdg. 125.00 (*0-8240-1513-4*, SS438) Garland.

— Victorian Britain: An Encyclopedia. LC 87-29947. 1010p. 1991. pap. 32.50 (*0-8153-0803-5*, SS438) Garland.

Mitchell, Sally, jt. ed. see Costello, Patrick J.

***Mitchell, Sam.** Pura Vida - Waterfalls & Hot Springs of Costa Rica. (Illus.). 1995. pap. 9.95 (*0-89732-172-3*) Menasha Ridge.

Mitchell, Sara. A Deadly Snare. LC 89-81809. 1990. pap. 6.99 (*0-89636-263-9*, AC 214, LifeJourney) Chariot Family.

— Walk in Deep Shadows. LC 88-83752. 192p. 1989. pap. 6.99 (*0-89636-252-3*, LifeJourney) Chariot Family.

Mitchell, Sarah, ed. see Dugas-Bonds, Pat.

Mitchell, Sharon B., jt. auth. see Smith, Laura J.

Mitchell, Shayne, tr. see Fumagalli, Vito.

Mitchell, Shirley, jt. ed. see Heig, James.

Mitchell, Silas W. The Autobiography of a Quack & the Case of George Dedlow. LC 68-57542. (Muckrakers Ser.). (Illus.). reprint ed. lib. bdg. 14.00 (*0-8398-1264-7*) Irvington.

— Complete Poems. (BCL1-PS American Literature Ser.). 447p. 1992. reprint ed. lib. bdg. 99.00 (*0-7812-6799-4*) Rprt Serv.

— Doctor & Patient. LC 71-180584. (Medicine & Society in America Ser.). 182p. 1972. reprint ed. 18.95 (*0-405-03961-1*) Ayer.

— Hephzibah Guinness. LC 74-178448. (Short Story Index Reprint Ser.). 1977. reprint ed. 18.95 (*0-8369-4049-0*) Ayer.

— Hugh Wynne: Free Quaker, 2 vols., Set. LC 17-490. 1969. reprint ed. 15.00 (*0-403-00073-4*) Scholarly.

— Hugh Wynne, Free Quaker, 2 vols in 1. LC 67-29274. (Americans in Fiction Ser.). 573p. reprint ed. lib. bdg. 14.00 (*0-8398-1265-5*) Irvington.

— Hugh Wynne, Free Quaker. 1993. reprint ed. lib. bdg. 89.00 (*0-7812-5491-4*) Rprt Serv.

— Hugh Wynne, Free Quaker, 2 vols., Set. (BCL1-PS American Literature Ser.). 1992. reprint ed. lib. bdg. 150.00 (*0-7812-6800-1*) Rprt Serv.

— Little Stories. LC 76-85691. (Short Story Index Reprint Ser.). 1977. 17.95 (*0-8369-3034-7*) Ayer.

— Wear & Tear; or, Hints for the Overworked. 5th ed. LC 73-2407. (Mental Illness & Social Policy; the American Experience Ser.). 1973. reprint ed. 16.95 (*0-405-05217-0*) Ayer.

Mitchell, Smoot C., jt. auth. see Quarterman, John S.

Mitchell, Stanley, tr. see Lukacs, Georg.

Mitchell, Stanley, tr. see Lukacs, George.

***Mitchell, Stephen.** Anatolia: Land, Men & Gods in Asia Minor, 2 vols. Incl. Vol. 1. Celts in Anatolia & the Impact of Roman Rule. 296p. 1995. pap. 39.95 (*0-19-815029-6*); Vol. 2. Rise of the Church. 216p. 1995. pap. 32.00 (*0-19-815030-X*); write for info. (*0-615-00594-2*) OUP.

— Anatolia: Land, Men, & Gods in Asia Minor: The Celts in Anatolia & the Impact of Roman Rule, 2 vols., Vol. 1. 1994. 69.00 (*0-19-814080-0*) OUP.

— Anatolia: Land, Men, & Gods in Asia Minor: The Rise of the Church, 2 vols., Vol. 2. 1994. 60.00 (*0-19-814933-6*) OUP.

— A Book of Psalms. 112p. 1994. reprint ed. pap. 10.00 (*0-06-092470-5*, PL) HarpC.

— Creation. LC 89-39726. (Illus.). 40p. (J). 1990. 15.95 (*0-8037-0617-0*) Dial Bks Young.

— The Gospel According to Jesus: A New Translation & Guide to His Essential Teachings for Believers & Unbelievers. LC 90-56390. 320p. 1993. pap. 13.00 (*0-06-092321-0*, PL) HarpC.

— Jo Mora: Renaissance Man of the West. (Illus.). 56p. (Orig.). 1994. pap. 9.95 (*0-922029-20-2*) D Stoecklein Photo.

— Parables & Portraits. 96p. 1994. reprint ed. pap. 12.00 (*0-06-092532-9*, PL) HarpC.

— Tao Ching. pap. 8.00 (*0-685-51784-5*, PL) HarpC.

— Tao Te Ching. 1994. 15.00 (*0-06-017154-5*) HarpC.

— Tao Te Ching: A New English Version. 144p. 1992. mass mkt. 6.00 (*0-06-081245-1*, PL) HarpC.

— Tao Te Ching: A New English Version. LC 88-45123. 144p. 1991. reprint ed. pap. 10.00 (*0-06-091608-7*, PL) HarpC.

Mitchell, Stephen, ed. & tr. Dropping Ashes on the Buddha: The Teachings of Zen Master Seung Sahn. 256p. (Orig.). 1987. pap. 12.00 (*0-8021-3052-6*) Grove-Atltic.

Mitchell, Stephen, ed. The Enlightened Heart: An Anthology of Sacred Poetry. LC 89-45320. 192p. 1993. reprint ed. pap. 10.00 (*0-06-092053-X*, PL) HarpC.

— The Enlightened Mind: An Anthology of Sacred Prose. LC 90-55936. 256p. 1993. pap. 12.00 (*0-06-092320-2*, PL) HarpC.

— Tao Ching. 1989. boxed write for info. (*0-318-66674-X*, HarpT) HarpC.

Mitchell, Stephen, frwd. The Enlightened Mind: An Anthology of Sacred Prose. LC 90-55936. 256p. 1991. 20.00 (*0-06-016528-6*, HarpT) HarpC.

Mitchell, Stephen, intro. The Poetry of the Enlightened Heart: An Anthology. LC 89-45320. 192p. 1989. 20.00 (*0-06-016208-2*, HarpT) HarpC.

Mitchell, Stephen, tr. & intro. The Book of Job. LC 92-52637. 1992. pap. 10.00 (*0-06-096959-8*, PL) HarpC.

Mitchell, Stephen, tr. Tao Te Ching: A New English Version. LC 88-45123. 128p. 1988. 15.95 (*0-318-35603-1*, HarpT) HarpC.

— Tao Te Ching: A New English Version. LC 88-45123. 128p. 1989. Slip case edition. 27.50 (*0-06-016169-8*, HarpT) HarpC.

***Mitchell, Stephen & Reeds, Brian, eds.** Seaby Standard Catalogue of British Coins 1996. 31th ed. (Illus.). 366p. 1995. 24.95 (*0-7134-7677-X*, Pub. by Seaby UK) Trafalgar.

Mitchell, Stephen, jt. auth. see Hass, Robert.

Mitchell, Stephen, jt. auth. see Reeds, Brian.

Mitchell, Stephen, tr. see Rilke, Rainer M.

Mitchell, Stephen, ed. see Rilke, Rainer M.

Mitchell, Stephen, tr. see Rilke, Rainer M.

Mitchell, Stephen, ed. see Whitman, Walt.

Mitchell, Stephen A. Heroic Sagas & Ballads. LC 91-9899. (Myth & Poetics Ser.). 256p. 1991. 29.95 (*0-8014-2587-5*) Cornell U Pr.

— Hope & Dread in Psychoanalysis. LC 92-56176. 288p. 1993. 30.00 (*0-465-03059-9*) Basic.

— Hope & Dread in Psychoanalysis. 304p. 1995. pap. 14.00 (*0-465-03062-9*) Basic.

— Relational Concepts in Psychoanalysis: An Integration. LC 88-11168. 312p. 1988. 39.95 (*0-674-75411-5*) HUP.

Mitchell, Stephen A., jt. auth. see Greenberg, Jay R.

Mitchell, Steve. How to Speak Southern. 1984. mass mkt. 4.50 (*0-553-27519-4*) Bantam.

— More Speak Southern. 1983. mass mkt. 4.50 (*0-553-27392-2*) Bantam.

***Mitchell, Steve, ed.** Dramatherapy: Clinical Studies. 250p. 1995. pap. 24.95 (*1-85302-304-3*, Pub. by J Kingsley Pubs UK) Taylor & Francis.

— The Theatre of Self-Expression: Dramatherapy & Its Application in the Clinical Setting. 180p. 1996. pap. 27.00 (*1-85302-283-7*, Pub. by J Kingsley Pubs UK) Taylor & Francis.

Mitchell, Steve, ed. see Mora, Jo.

Mitchell, Steve, ed. see Morgan, Clay.

Mitchell, Steven & Bainbridge, David. Sustainable Agriculture in California: A Guide to Information. 198p. (Orig.). 1991. pap. 15.00 (*1-879906-01-5*, 3348) ANR Pubns CA.

Mitchell, Steven & Mitchell, Karyn. Hypnotherapy for Healing the Mind & Body. 128p. (Orig.). 1994. student ed, pap. 14.95 (*0-9640822-0-9*) Mind Rivers.

Mitchell, Steven D., ed. Space: Countdown to the Future: A Report on Third National Space. 314p. 1987. 50.00 (*0-9616962-1-4*, US Space Found) Univelt Inc.

***Mitchell, Steven P.** Healing Our Schools: A Parent's Guide for Improving Education. LC 94-44297. 1995. 11.95 (*1-885003-08-0*) R D Reed Pubs.

Mitchell, Stewart. HE: Massage: A Practical Introduction. 1993. pap. 9.95 (*1-85230-386-7*) Element MA.

— Horatio Seymour of New York. LC 69-19475. (American Scene Ser.). 1970. reprint ed. lib. bdg. 75.00 (*0-306-71252-0*) Da Capo.

***Mitchell, Susan.** The Official Guide to the Generations. 300p. 1995. 69.95 (*0-9628092-8-4*) New Strategist.

— Rapture: Poems. LC 91-50517. 96p. 1992. pap. 11.00 (*0-06-096906-7*, PL) HarpC.

— The Water Inside the Water. 96p. 1994. reprint ed. pap. 12.00 (*0-06-097591-1*, PL) HarpC.

Mitchell, Susan, ed. see Junior League of Columbus, Georgia, Inc. Staff.

Mitchell, Susan E. Thirty-Minute Meals from the Academy. LC 93-37118. (California Culinary Academy Ser.). Orig. Title: Thirty-Minute Meals. 128p. 1993. reprint ed. pap. 11.95 (*1-56426-043-7*, Calif Culinary Acad) Cole Group.

Mitchell, Susan L. The Hewitts of Athens County, Ohio. LC 88-60196. (Illus.). 456p. (C). 1989. 48.00 (*0-9620263-0-1*) S L Mitchell.

Mitchell, Suzanne. Common Stock DRP Report. 2nd ed. 30p. 1989. lib. bdg. 12.50 (*0-685-27871-9*); pap. 12.50 (*0-685-27872-7*) SAM Designs.

— Common Stock DRP Report. 6th ed. 60p. (C). 1991. spiral bd. 19.50 (*0-9623179-6-9*) SAM Designs.

Mitchell, Sydney B. Gardening in California. 1992. reprint ed. lib. bdg. 75.00 (*0-7812-5065-X*) Rprt Serv.

Mitchell, T. B. Bees of the Eastern United States, 2 vols., Set. 1960. 20.00 (*0-910914-05-2*) J Johnson.

Mitchell, T. Crichton. Charles Wesley: Man with the Dancing Heart. 279p. (Orig.). 1994. pap. 16.95 (*0-8341-1449-6*, 54741) Beacon Hill.

— Great Holiness Classics: The Wesley Century, Vol. 2. 505p. 1984. 24.95 (*0-8341-0910-7*) Beacon Hill.

Mitchell, T. F. Pronouncing Arabic Two. (Illus.). 328p. 1993. 59.00 (*0-19-823989-0*) OUP.

— Teach Yourself Colloquial Arabic. (Teach Yourself Ser.). 1979. 6.95 (*0-679-10165-9*) McKay.

— Writing Arabic: A Practical Introduction to Ruq'ah Script. 1979. pap. 19.95 (*0-19-815150-0*) OUP.

Mitchell, Terence F. & El-Hassan, Shahir. Modality, Mood & Aspect in Spoken Arabic: With Special Reference to Egypt & the Levant. 320p. (C). 1994. text ed. 93.50 (*0-7103-0405-6*, A5603, Pub. by Kegan Paul Intl UK) Routledge Chapman & Hall.

Mitchell, Terence R. & Larson, J. R. People in Organizations: An Introduction to Organizational Behavior. 3rd ed. 624p. 1987. text ed. write for info. (*0-07-042534-5*) McGraw.

Mitchell, Teri K., ed. Bride's Cookbook. LC 90-33673. 1990. ring bd. 19.95 (*1-55853-079-7*) Rutledge Hill Pr.

Mitchell, Theodore. Political Education in the Southern Farmers Alliance, 1887-1900. LC 87-40141. (Illus.). 192p. 1987. pap. text ed. 16.50 (*0-299-11474-0*) U of Wis Pr.

— Political Education in the Southern Farmers Alliance, 1887-1900. LC 87-40141. (Illus.). 192p. (C). 1988. text ed. 39.50 (*0-299-11470-8*) U of Wis Pr.

Mitchell, Theresa. Strensall, Near York, in the Mid-Nineteenth Century. (C). 1988. 80.00 (*1-85072-055-X*, Pub. by W Sessions UK) St Mut.

Mitchell, Thomas G. The Commercial Lease Guidebook: Learn How to Win the Leasing Game! Jessop, Warren, ed. LC 92-80954. (Illus.). 224p. (Orig.). 1992. pap. text ed. 19.95 (*0-9632982-0-8*) Macore Intl.

Mitchell, Thomas N. Cicero, the Senior Statesman. 360p. (C). 1991. text ed. 37.50 (*0-300-04779-7*) Yale U Pr.

Mitchell, Thomas O., jt. ed. see Davis, Keith E.

Mitchell-Thome, Raoul C. Geology of the Middle Atlantic Islands. (Beitraege Zur Regionalen Geologie der Erde Ser.: Vol. 12). (Illus.). 1976. lib. bdg. 138.60 (*3-443-11012-6*) Lubrecht & Cramer.

— Geology of the South Atlantic Islands. (Beitraege Zur Regionalen Geologie der Erde Ser.: Vol. 10). (Illus.). 366p. 1970. lib. bdg. 105.00 (*3-443-11010-X*, Pub. by Gebruder Borntraeger GW) Lubrecht & Cramer.

Mitchell, Thornton W. North Carolina Wills: A Testator Index, 1665-1900. rev. ed. 630p. 1992. 49.50 (*0-8063-1361-7*, 3858) Genealog Pub.

— North Carolina Wills: A Testator Index, 1665-1900, Set. LC 86-51348. 1987. 65.00 (*0-9617343-0-2*) Thornton Mitchell.

Mitchell, Timothy. Blood Sport: A Social History of Spanish Bullfighting. LC 91-7231. (Illus.). 288p. (C). 1991. text ed. 28.95x (*0-8122-3129-5*); pap. text ed. 14.95x (*0-8122-1346-7*) U of Pa Pr.

— Colonising Egypt. (Illus.). 230p. 1991. reprint ed. pap. 14.00 (*0-520-07568-4*, MITCOX) U CA Pr.

— Flamenco Deep Song. LC 94-10659. 256p. 1995. 28.50 (*0-300-06001-7*) Yale U Pr.

— Passional Culture: Emotion, Religion, & Society in Southern Spain. LC 89-40398. (Illus.). 206p. (C). 1990. text ed. 24.95x (*0-8122-8202-7*) U of Pa Pr.

Mitchell, Timothy F. Art & Science in German Landscape Painting 1770-1840. (Clarendon Studies in the History of Art: No. 11). (Illus.). 256p. 1994. 105.00 (*0-19-817507-8*) OUP.

Mitchell, Tom. The Audio Designer's Tube Register. (Common Low-Power Triodes Ser.: Vol. 1). (Illus.). 144p. 1993. 18.00 (*0-9628170-1-5*) Media Cncpt.

Mitchell, Tom, jt. ed. see Steier, David M.

Mitchell, Tony. Dario Fo: People's Court Jester. 2nd ed. 1988. pap. 9.95 (*0-413-60250-8*, A0070, Pub. by Methuen UK) Heinemann.

Mitchell, Tony, ed. File on Brenton. (Methuen Writer-Files Ser.). 96p. 1988. pap. 9.95 (*0-413-14540-9*, A0091, Pub. by Methuen UK) Heinemann.

Mitchell, Tracey, ed. see Eliot, Mike, et al.

Mitchell, Tucker. The Crystal Whizzard. Graves, Helen, ed. LC 88-50120. 64p. (J). (gr. 2-5). 1988. 12.00 (*1-55523-146-2*) Winston-Derek.

— You're Not Alone When You're Alone. LC 92-70981. (Illus.). 130p. (J). 1992. 12.95 (*1-55523-522-0*) Winston-Derek.

Mitchell, V. E. Atlantis Station. (Star Trek: The Next Generation, Starfleet Academy Ser.). (YA). 1994. mass mkt. 3.99 (*0-671-88449-2*, Minstrel Bks) PB.

— Enemy Unseen. Stern, David, ed. (Star Trek Ser.: No. 51). 288p. (Orig.). 1990. mass mkt. 4.99 (*0-671-68403-5*) PB.

— Imbalance. Stern, Dave, ed. (Star Trek: The Next Generation Ser.: No. 22). 288p. (Orig.). 1992. mass mkt. 5.50 (*0-671-77571-5*) PB.

Mitchell, Vance, & Co. Staff. Picture Book of Authentic Mid-Victorian Gas-Lighting Fixtures. (Antiques Ser.). 96p. 1984. reprint ed. pap. 8.95 (*0-486-24640-X*) Dover.

Mitchell, Victor. Birds. (Coloring Bks.). (Illus.). 16p. (J). (gr. k up). 1988. pap. 1.99 (*0-7459-1467-5*) Lion USA.

— Butterflies. (Coloring Bks.). (Illus.). 16p. (J). (gr. k up). 1988. pap. 1.99 (*0-7459-1466-7*) Lion USA.

— Fish. (Coloring Bks.). (Illus.). 16p. (J). (gr. k up). 1988. pap. 1.99 (*0-7459-1468-3*) Lion USA.

— Flowers. (Coloring Bks.). (Illus.). 16p. (J). (gr. k up). 1988. pap. 1.99 (*0-7459-1470-5*) Lion USA.

— Jungles. (Coloring Bks.). (Illus.). 16p. (J). (gr. k up). 1988. pap. 1.99 (*0-7459-1473-X*) Lion USA.

— Pets. (Coloring Bks.). (Illus.). 16p. (J). (gr. k up). 1988. pap. 1.99 (*0-7459-1469-1*) Lion USA.

— Seashore. (Coloring Bks.). (Illus.). 16p. (J). (gr. k up). 1988. pap. 1.99 (*0-7459-1471-3*) Lion USA.

— Woodlands. (Coloring Bks.). (Illus.). 16p. (J). (gr. k up). 1988. pap. 1.99 (*0-7459-1472-1*) Lion USA.

Mitchell, Viola, jt. auth. see Meier, Joel F.

Mitchell, W. & Lemley, Brad. The Man Who Would Not Be Defeated: It's Not What Happens to You, It's What You Do about It. LC 93-30632. (Illus.). 272p. 1993. 17.95 (*1-56796-026-X*) WRS Group.

***Mitchell, W. C.** The Cult of the Big Bang. LC 94-78655. 240p. 1994. write for info. (*0-9643188-0-6*) W C Mitchell.

Mitchell, W. H. & Sawyer, L. A. The Cape Run. 214p. (C). 1988. 150.00 (*0-86138-030-4*, Pub. by T Dalton UK) St Mut.

— Sailing Ship to Supertanker. 1994. 54.00 (*0-86138-055-X*, Pub. by T Dalton UK) St Mut.

Mitchell, W. H., jt. auth. see Sawyer, L. A.

Mitchell, W. J. Blake's Composite Art: A Study of the Illuminated Poetry. LC 77-7116. 1978. 52.50x (*0-691-06348-6*); pap. 14.95x (*0-691-01402-7*) Princeton U Pr.

— Iconology: Image, Text, Ideology. LC 85-1177. x, 226p. (C). 1987. pap. text ed. 9.95 (*0-226-53229-1*) U Ch Pr.

— Image & Text in Arts. (C). 1994. 34.95 (*0-226-53231-3*) U Ch Pr.

— On Narrative. LC 80-53137. 304p. (C). 1981. pap. text ed. 14.95 (*0-226-53217-8*) U Ch Pr.

— Picture Theory: Essays on Verbal & Visual Representation. (Illus.). xvi, 446p. 1995. pap. 16.95x (*0-226-53232-1*) U Ch Pr.

Mitchell, W. J., ed. Against Theory: Literary Studies & the New Pragmatism. LC 84-29127. vi, 146p. 1985. pap. text ed. 9.95 (*0-226-53227-5*) U Ch Pr.

— Art & the Public Sphere. (Illus.). 300p. 1992. lib. bdg. 41.95 (*0-226-53210-0*); pap. 19.95 (*0-226-53211-9*) U Ch Pr.

— Landscape & Power. LC 93-4907. 1994. lib. bdg. 42.50 (*0-226-53206-2*); pap. text ed. 13.95 (*0-226-53207-0*) U Ch Pr.

— The Language of Images. LC 80-5225. 1980. pap. text ed. 17.95 (*0-226-53215-1*, P887) U Ch Pr.

***Mitchell, W. O.** According to Jake & the Kid. 1995. pap. 9.95 (*0-7710-6071-8*, Pub. by McClelland & Stewart CN) Firefly Bks Ltd.

Mitchell, Waddie. Cowboys Night Before Christmas. (Illus.). 60p. 1992. 5.95 (*0-87905-486-7*, Peregrine Smith) Gibbs Smith Pub.

— Waddie's Whole Load, Set, incl. audio tape. LC 94-16502. (Illus.). 144p. 1994. audio, pap. 17.95 (*0-87905-608-8*) Gibbs Smith Pub.

Mitchell, Waldo F. The Uses of Bank Funds. Bruchey, Stuart, ed. LC 80-1162. (Rise of Commercial Banking Ser.). (Illus.). 1981. reprint ed. lib. bdg. 18.95 (*0-405-13669-2*) Ayer.

Mitchell, Walter, tr. see Danielou, Jean.

Mitchell, Wesley C. Backward Art of Spending Money & Other Essays. vii, 421p. 1964. reprint ed. 39.50 (*0-678-00026-3*) Kelley.

— Business Cycles: The Problem & Its Setting. LC 75-19730. (National Bureau of Economic Research Ser.). (Illus.). 1975. reprint ed. 41.95 (*0-405-07608-8*) Ayer.

— Business Cycles: The Problem & Its Setting. (Studies in Business Cycles: No. 1). 519p. 1927. reprint ed. 135.00 (*0-87014-084-1*) Natl Bur Econ Res.

— Business Cycles & Their Causes. LC 86-8182. (Illus.). xii, 226p. 1989. reprint ed. pap. text ed. 12.95 (*0-87991-262-6*) Porcupine Pr.

— Economic Essays in Honor of Wesley Clair Mitchell Presented to Him by His Former Students on the Occasion of His Sixtieth Birthday. LC 68-16928. (Essay Index Reprint Ser.). 1977. 23.95 (*0-8369-0402-8*) Ayer.

— Gold, Prices, & Wages under the Greenback Standard. LC 66-21688. (Library of Money & Banking History). xv, 627p. 1966. reprint ed. 57.50 (*0-678-00200-2*) Kelley.

— Making & Using of Index Numbers. LC 65-19653. (Reprints of Economic Classics Ser.). 114p. 1965. reprint ed. 25.00 (*0-678-00098-0*) Kelley.

— Wartime "Prosperity" & the Future. (Occasional Papers: No. 9). 48p. 1943. reprint ed. 20.00 (*0-87014-324-7*); reprint ed. mic. film 20.00 (*0-685-61241-4*) Natl Bur Econ Res.

— What Happens During Business Cycles? A Progress Report. (Studies in Business Cycles: No. 5). 427p. 1951. reprint ed. 111.10 (*0-87014-088-4*) Natl Bur Econ Res.

Mitchell, Wesley C. & Burns, Arthur F. The National Bureau's Measures of Cyclical Behavior. (NBER Bulletin Ser.: No. 57). 1935. reprint ed. 20.00 (*0-685-61172-8*) Natl Bur Econ Res.

— Production During the American Business Cycle of 1927-1933. (NBER Bulletin Ser.: No. 61). 1936. reprint ed. 20.00 (*0-685-61177-9*) Natl Bur Econ Res.

— Statistical Indicators of Cyclical Revivals. (NBER Bulletin Ser.: No. 69). 1938. reprint ed. 20.00 (*0-685-61191-4*) Natl Bur Econ Res.

Mitchell, Wesley C. & Dorfman, J., eds. Types of Economic Theory: From Mercantilism to Institutionalism, 2 vols., Set. LC 67-16418. 1969. 75.00 (*0-678-00234-7*) Kelley.

— Types of Economic Theory: From Mercantilism to Institutionalism, Vol. 2. LC 67-16418. xii, 875p. 1969. 45.00 (*0-678-04027-3*) Kelley.

Mitchell, Wesley C., jt. auth. see Burns, Arthur F.

Mitchell, Wesley C., ed. see King, Willford I., et al.

Mitchell, Wesley C., et al. Income in the United States: Its Amount & Distribution 1909-1919, Vol. 1. Incl. Vol. 2. LC 75-19731. 1975. 32.00 (*0-405-07610-X*); LC 75-19731. (National Bureau of Economic Research Ser.). (Illus.). 1975. reprint ed. 16.95 (*0-405-07609-6*) Ayer.

Mitchell, Willa. Black American Cookbook, 1. 400p. lib. bdg. 5.95 (*0-9603014-0-2*) Evang Assn.

— Black American Cookbook, 2. 400p. lib. bdg. 6.95 (*0-9603014-1-0*) Evang Assn.

— Black Heritage Recipes to Treasure. LC 77-94215. (Black American Cookbook Ser.: Vol. 3). (Illus.). 200p. 1984. lib. bdg. 8.95 (*0-9603014-2-9*) Evang Assn.

Mitchell, William. A New & Complete System of Book-Keeping by an Improved Method of Double Entry. Brief, Richard P., ed. LC 77-87279. (Development of Contemporary Accounting Thought Ser.). 1978. reprint ed. lib. bdg. 39.95 (*0-405-10907-5*) Ayer.

— The Place of Minds in the World. LC 77-27201. (Gifford Lectures: 1924-26). 400p. reprint ed. 45.00 (*0-404-60477-3*) AMS Pr.

— Prelude to Programming: Problem Solving & Algorithms. (C). 1984. text ed. 30.00 (*0-8359-5614-8*, Reston); pap. text ed. write for info. (*0-8359-5627-X*, Reston) P-H.

— Winged Defense: The Development & Possibilities of Modern Air Power - Economic & Military. 320p. 1988. pap. 7.95 (*0-486-25771-1*) Dover.

Mitchell, William, ed. The Music Forum, Vol. 5. LC 67-47267. 384p. 1980. text ed. 50.00 (*0-231-04720-7*) Col U Pr.

Mitchell, William & Conn, Charles P. The Power of Positive Parenting. 192p. 1994. reprint ed. pap. 4.99 (*0-8007-8617-3*) Revell.

Mitchell, William & LaBarre, James. Producing Business Documents: Integrated Projects & In-Basket Exercises. 1992. 14.50 (*1-56118-361-X*); teacher ed 5.80 (*1-56118-362-8*) Paradigm MN.

Mitchell, William, jt. auth. see Canan, Michael J.

Mitchell, William, jt. ed. see Salzer, Felix.

Mitchell, William, et al. Paradigm Keyboarding & Applications: A Mastery Approach for Microcomputers & Typewriters. 3rd ed. (C). 1990. teacher ed 14.00 (*1-56118-151-X*); 13.25 (*1-56118-156-0*); pap. text ed. 26.50 (*1-56118-160-9*); trans. 7.25 (*1-56118-172-2*); 10.45 (*1-56118-159-5*) Paradigm MN.

— Paradigm Keyboarding Skills: A Mastery Approach for Microcomputers & Typewriters. (C). 1990. pap. text ed. 14.50 (*1-56118-150-1*) Paradigm MN.

Mitchell, William A. Linn County, Kansas: A History. 404p. 1994. reprint ed. lib. bdg. 40.00 (*0-8328-4001-7*) Higginson Bk Co.

Mitchell, William A., jt. auth. see Kolars, John F.

Mitchell, William B. Geography & Resource Analysis. 2nd ed. (Illus.). 386p. 1989. pap. text ed. 59.95 (*0-470-21190-3*) Halsted Pr.

***Mitchell, William C.** Beyond Politics: Markets, Welfare, & the Failure of Bureaucracy. (C). 1994. pap. text ed. 19. 95 (*0-8133-2208-1*) Westview.

— Beyond Politics: Markets, Welfare, & the Failure of Bureaucracy. (C). 1994. text ed. 55.00 (*0-8133-2207-3*) Westview.

Mitchell, William D. Contractor's Survival Manual. LC 86-16620. 160p. (Orig.). 1986. pap. 16.75 (*0-910460-42-6*) Craftsman.

— Estate & Retirement Planning Answer Book. 1994. 96.00 (*1-56706-135-4*) Panel Pubs.

Mitchell, William D., jt. auth. see Canan, Michael J.

Mitchell, William E. The Bamboo Fire: Field Work with the New Guinea Wape. 2nd ed. 256p. (Orig.). (C). 1987. pap. text ed. 9.95 (*0-88133-248-8*) Waveland Pr.

— Mishpokhe: A Study of New York City Jewish Family Clubs. (New Babylon Studies in the Social Sciences: No. 30). (Illus.). 1978. 41.55 (*3-10-800287-2*) Mouton.

Mitchell, William E., ed. Clowning As Critical Practice: Performance Humor in the South Pacific. LC 92-50195. (Association for Social Anthropology in Oceania Monographs). 272p. (C). 1993. text ed. 49.95 (*0-8229-3734-4*); pap. text ed. 19.95 (*0-8229-5487-7*) U of Pittsburgh Pr.

Mitchell, William E. & Walter, Ingo, eds. State & Local Finance. LC 77-110554. 380p. reprint ed. pap. 108.30 (*0-317-09323-1*, 2012396) Bks Demand.

Mitchell, William E., jt. auth. see Leichter, Hope J.

***Mitchell, William J.** City of Bits: Space, Place & the Infobahn. (Illus.). 170p. 1995. 20.00 (*0-262-13309-1*) MIT Pr.

— The Logic of Architecture: Design, Computation, & Cognition. (Illus.). 200p. (Orig.). 1989. pap. 19.95 (*0-262-63116-4*) MIT Pr.

— The Reconfigured Eye: Visual Truth in the Post-Photographic Era. (Illus.). 275p. 1994. pap. 24.95 (*0-262-63160-1*) MIT Pr.

***Mitchell, William J. & McCullough, Malcolm.** Digital Design Media. 2nd ed. LC 94-38689. (Architecture Ser.). 512p. 1995. pap. 29.95 (*0-442-01934-3*) Van Nos Reinhold.

— Digital Design Media: A Guide for the 21st Century. (Illus.). 320p. 1991. text ed. 49.95 (*0-442-26069-5*) Van Nos Reinhold.

Mitchell, William J. & Steel, John R. Fine Structures & Iteration Trees. LC 94-888. (Lecture Notes in Logic Ser.: Vol. 3). vi, 130p. 1994. pap. 32.00 (*0-387-57494-8*) Spr-Verlag.

Mitchell, William J., ed. see Bach, Carl P.

Mitchell, William L. Opening of Alaska, 1901-1903. Woodman, Lyman, ed. LC 82-71848. (Illus.). 124p. 1988. reprint ed. pap. 8.95 (*0-933126-93-X*) Pictorial Hist.

Mitchell, William M., et al. Keyboarding with WordPerfect. LC 92-25693. 400p. 1993. 22.95 (*1-56118-569-8*) Paradigm MN.

— Keyboarding with WordPerfect: A Computer Managed Approach. LC 93-19772. 440p. 1994. teacher ed 8.00 (*1-56118-572-8*); text ed. 25.95 (*1-56118-599-X*); student ed, teacher ed 340.00 (*1-56118-574-4*); student ed, teacher ed 340.00 (*1-56118-573-6*) Paradigm MN.

— Keyboarding with WordPerfect: A Computer Managed Approach: Intermediate Course. 424p. 1994. text ed. 25. 95 (*1-56118-509-4*) Paradigm MN.

— Keyboarding with WordPerfect: A Computer Managed Approach: Intermediate Course. 1994. teacher ed, text ed. 14.00 (*1-56118-693-7*); student ed, teacher ed 340.00 (*1-56118-696-1*); student ed, teacher ed 340.00 (*1-56118-697-X*) Paradigm MN.

— Keyboarding with WordPerfect Version 6.0. LC 94-31079. 1994. write for info. (*1-56118-664-3*) Paradigm MN.

— Paradigm Keyboarding with WordPerfect: Version 5.1: Sessons 1-30. LC 93-27499. 1994. 17.50 (*1-56118-508-6*) Paradigm MN.

Mitchell, William P. Peasants on the Edge: Crop, Cult, & Crisis in the Andes. (Illus.). 278p. 1991. text ed. 35.00 (*0-292-77637-3*) U of Tex Pr.

Mitchell, William P. & Guillet, David, eds. Irrigation at High Altitudes: The Social Organization of Water Control Systems in the Andes. LC 94-20688. (Society for Latin American Anthropology Publication Ser.: Vol. 12). 1994. write for info. (*0-913167-66-5*) Am Anthro Assn.

Mitchell, William R., Jr. Classic Atlanta: Landmarks of the Atlanta Spirit. (Illus.). 208p. 1991. 60.00 (*0-932958-12-5*) Golden Coast.

— Classic Atlanta: Landmarks of the Atlanta Spirit. LC 91-71487. (Golden Coast Book Ser.). (Illus.). 224p. (C). 1991. 60.00 (*0-8203-1549-4*) U of Ga Pr.

— Classic New Orleans. LC 93-77933. (Golden Coast Book Ser.). (Illus.). 224p. 1993. 50.00 (*0-8203-1576-1*) U of Ga Pr.

— Classic Savannah: History, Homes, & Gardens. LC 87-80408. (Golden Coast Book Ser.). (Illus.). 144p. (C). 1991. 35.00 (*0-8203-1550-8*) U of Ga Pr.

Mitchell, William R. Lewis Edmund Crook Jr. Architect, 1898-1967: A Twentieth-Century Traditionalist in the Deep South. LC 84-6240. (Illus.). 144p. 1984. 40.00 (*0-9614203-0-8*) Hist Bus Inc.

Mitchell, William R., Jr. The Residential Architecture of Henry Sprott Long & Associates. 104p. 1992. 40.00 (*0-932958-13-3*) Golden Coast.

— The Residential Architecture of Henry Sprott Long & Associates. LC 91-73919. (Golden Coast Book Ser.). (Illus.). 103p. 1991. 45.00 (*0-8203-1584-2*) U of Ga Pr.

— William Frank McCall, Jr. 1914-1991: A Continuing Tradition. LC 92-74377. (Golden Coast Book Ser.). (Illus.). 136p. 1992. 45.00 (*0-8203-1583-4*) U of Ga Pr.

Mitchell, William R., Jr. & Martin, Van J. Classic Savannah. 144p. 1987. 35.00 (*0-932958-07-9*) Golden Coast.

***Mitchell, William R. & Martin, Van J.** Edward Vason: Architect, Connoisseur, & Collector in the Classical Tradition. (Illus.). 208p. 1995. 50.00 (*0-8203-1744-6*) U of Ga Pr.

Mitchell, Williams M. The Rise of the Revolutionary Party in the English House of Commons, 1603-1629. LC 75-31471. 209p. 1976. reprint ed. text ed. 55.00 (*0-8371-8535-1*, MIRR, Greenwood Pr) Greenwood.

Mitchell, Wilmot B., ed. School & College Speaker. LC 78-74820. (Granger Poetry Library). 1979. reprint ed. 29.50 (*0-89609-139-2*) Roth Pub Inc.

Mitchels, Barbara. Family Law. (C). 1990. 110.00 (*1-85431-084-4*, Pub. by Blackstone Pr UK) St Mut.

— Family Law. (C). 1991. text ed. 22.00 (*1-85431-129-8*, Pub. by Blackstone Pr UK) W W Gaunt.

Mitchelson, Austin. The Baker Street Irregular: The Unauthorized Biography of Sherlock Holmes. 1994. 35. 00 (*0-88734-905-6*) Players Pr.

Mitchelson, Austin & Utechin, Nicholas. Sherlock Holmes & the Earthquake Machine. 1994. 25.00 (*0-86025-283-3*, Pub. by Ian Henry Pubns UK) Empire Pub Srvs.

— Sherlock Holmes & the Earthquake Machine. 1994. 25.00 (*0-88734-903-X*) Players Pr.

— Sherlock Holmes & the Hellbirds. LC 95-13261. 1995. write for info. (*0-88734-916-1*) Players Pr.

Mitchener, C. H. Ohio Annals: Historic Events in the Tuscarawas & Muskingum Valleys. 390p. 1993. reprint ed. pap. text ed. 27.00 (*1-55613-888-1*) Heritage Bk.

***Mitchener, C. H., ed.** Tuscarawas & Muskingum Valley, Ohio: History 1775-1840. 392p. Date not set. 17.00 (*1-885463-27-8*) Ohio Genealogy.

Mitchener, Charles D., jt. ed. see Fletcher, David J.

Mitchener, Tony, ed. The Hampshire Handbook, 1990: Official H. C. C. C. Yearbook. (C). 1989. 39.00 (*1-85455-059-4*, Pub. by Ensign Pubns & Print UK) St Mut.

— The Hampshire Handbook, 1991: Official H. C. C. C. Yearbook. (C). 1989. 45.00 (*1-85455-069-1*, Pub. by Ensign Pubns & Print UK) St Mut.

— The Hampshire Handbook, 1992: Official H. C. C. C. Yearbook. (C). 1989. 39.00 (*0-685-52529-5*, Pub. by Ensign Pubns & Print UK) St Mut.

Mitchenson, Joe, jt. auth. see Mander, Raymond.

Mitcheson, A., jt. auth. see Ulukoy, K.

Mitchetz, Marc. The Bloody Lotus. Hansom, Dick, tr. (Kogaratsu Ser.). (Illus.). 49p. (Orig.). (YA). (gr. 12 up). 1990. pap. 7.95 (*0-87416-103-7*, Comcat Comics) Catalan Communs.

***Mitchie, A.** Computational Analysis of Visual Motion. (Advances in Computer Vision & Machine Intelligence Ser.). (Illus.). 220p. (C). 1994. 65.00 (*0-306-44786-X*, Plenum Pr) Plenum.

Mitchie Company & Harriman, D. P. Wyoming Court Rules Annotated. 973p. 1991. ring bd. 80.00 (*0-87215-487-4*) Michie Butterworth.

Mitchie, James, tr. see De la Fountaine, Jean.

Mitchiner, Michael. Indo-Greek & Indo-Scythian Coinage, 9 vols. Incl. Vol. V. Establishment of the Scythian in Afghanistan & Pakistan, C. 130-40 B.C. 1976. (*0-904173-10-0*); Vol. VI. Dynasties of Azes, C. 60-1 B.C. 1976. (*0-904173-11-9*); Vol. VII. Decline of the Indo-Cythians, Contemporaries of the Indo-Scythians. 1976. (*0-904173-12-7*); Vol. VIII. Indo-Parthians. 1976. (*0-904173-13-5*); Vol. IX. Greeks, Sakas & Their Contemporaries in Central & Southern India. 1976. (*0-904173-14-3*); 35.00 (*0-318-60468-X*, Pub. by Seaby UK) Trafalgar.

— Jetons, Medalets & Tokens, Vol. I: The Medieval Period & Nuremberg. (Illus.). 704p. 1988. 150.00 (*1-85264-036-7*, Pub. by Seaby UK) Trafalgar.

— Oriental Coins & Their Values: Non-Islamic Coins & Western Colonies A.D. 600-1979. 1979. 100.00 (*0-904173-18-6*) Numismatic Fine Arts.

Mitchinson, J., jt. auth. see Mander, R.

Mitchinson, J. M. Biology of the Cell Cycle. LC 72-160100. (Illus.). 1972. 55.00 (*0-521-08251-X*) Cambridge U Pr.

***Mitchinson, M. J., et al.** Essentials of Pathology. LC 95-14348. 1995. text ed. write for info. (*0-632-02944-7*) Blackwell Sci.

Mitchinson, Naomi. Corn King & the Spring Queen. LC 73-145186. 1971. reprint ed. 69.00 (*0-403-01111-6*) Scholarly.

Mitchinson, Rosalind. Why Scottish History Matters. (C). 1989. 39.00 (*0-85411-048-8*, Pub. by Saltire Soc) St Mut.

Mitchinson, Wendy. The Nature of Their Bodies: Women & Their Doctors in Victorian Canada. 512p. 1991. text ed. 60.00 (*0-8020-5901-5*); pap. text ed. 22.95 (*0-8020-6840-5*) U of Toronto Pr.

Mitchison, David & Stallabrass, Julian. Henry Moore. LC 91-40059. (Illus.). 128p. 1992. 24.95 (*0-8478-1559-5*) Rizzoli Intl.

Mitchison, N. A., jt. ed. see Feldmann, Marc.

Mitchison, Naomi. Blood of the Martyrs. Bell, James S., Jr., ed. (Christian Epics Ser.). 325p. 1994. pap. 9.99 (*0-8024-7107-2*) Moody.

— The Corn King & Spring Queen. 720p. 1990. 24.95 (*0-87951-377-2*) Overlook Pr.

— The Corn King & the Spring Queen. LC 93-17897. (Hera Ser.). 721p. 1994. pap. 17.00 (*0-939149-99-0*) Soho Press.

— Life for Africa: The Story of Bram Fischer. (C). 1973. text ed. 29.95 (*0-85036-170-2*, Pub. by Merlin Pr UK) Humanities.

— Solution Three. (Orig.). 1995. text ed. 29.95 (*1-55861-097-9*); pap. 10.95 (*1-55861-096-0*) Feminist Pr.

— Travel Light. (Virago Modern Classic Ser.). 147p. 1992. pap. 9.95 (*0-86068-562-4*, Pub. by Virago Pr UK) Trafalgar.

Mitchison, Naomi M. Barbarian Stories. LC 77-134970. (Short Story Index Reprint Ser.). 1977. 18.95 (*0-8369-3701-5*) Ayer.

— Delicate Fire: Short Stories & Poems. LC 79-145403. (Short Story Index Reprint Ser.). 1977. reprint ed. 23.95 (*0-8369-3778-3*) Ayer.

— When the Bough Breaks, & Other Stories. LC 71-160944. (Short Story Index Reprint Ser.). 1977. reprint ed. 20.95 (*0-8369-3923-9*) Ayer.

Mitchison, Rosalind. Coping with Destitution: Poverty & Relief in Western Europe. (Joanne Goodman Lectures). 96p. 1991. text ed. 30.00 (*0-8020-5912-0*); pap. text ed. 13.95 (*0-8020-6859-6*) U of Toronto Pr.

— Lordship to Patronage. 1991. pap. text ed. 17.00 (*0-7486-0233-X*, Pub. by Edinburgh U Pr UK) Col U Pr.

Mitchison, Rosalind & Leneman, Leah. Illegitimacy: Sexuality & Social Control, 1660-1780. (Family, Sexuality & Social Relations in Past Times Ser.). (Illus.). 256p. (C). 1989. text ed. 39.95 (*0-631-15028-5*) Blackwell Pubs.

Mitchley, Jack & Spalding, Peter. Five Thousand Years of the Theatre. LC 81-20156. (Illus.). 138p. (C). 1982. 18. 95 (*0-8419-0783-8*) Holmes & Meier.

Mitchner, Clarice J. Senator John Sherman Cooper: Consummate Statesman. 1981. 38.95 (*0-405-14099-1*) Ayer.

Mitchner, Morton & Kruger, Charles H., Jr. Partially Ionized Gases. (Illus.). 518p. (C). reprint ed. pap. text ed. write for info. (*0-9635646-0-9*) C H Kruger.

Mitchner, Morton, ed. see Lockheed Symposium on Magnetohydrodynamics Staff.

Mitchum, Hank. Devils Canyon. large type ed. LC 92-18451. (General Ser.). 312p. 1992. pap. 14.95 (*0-8161-5595-X*) G K Hall.

— El Dorado. large type ed. (Nightingale Ser.). 317p. 1991. pap. 14.95 (*0-8161-4948-8*, Nightingale) Hall.

— Mesa Verde. large type ed. (General Ser.). 332p. 1991. lib. bdg. 18.95 (*0-8161-5075-3*, Large Print Bks) Hall.

— Red Buffalo. large type ed. (Nightingale Series Large Print Bks.). 300p. 1992. pap. 14.95 (*0-8161-5322-1*, Nightingale) Hall.

— Royal Coach. large type ed. (General Ser.). 418p. 1990. lib. bdg. 19.95 (*0-8161-4974-7*) G K Hall.

— Stagecoach Station One: Dodge City. 1992. 13.95 (*0-7451-4540-X*, Gunsmoke) Chivers N Amer.

— Stagecoach Station 17: Durango. large type ed. (General Ser.). 274p. 1992. text ed. 19.95 (*0-8161-5332-9*) G K Hall.

Mitchum, John. Them Ornery Mitchum Boys: The Adventures of Robert & John Mitchum. Stanley, John, ed. LC 88-92904. (Illus.). 400p. (Orig.). 1989. pap. 11.95 (*0-940064-06-5*) Creatures at Large.

Mitchum, William. Blues for Mr. Baldwin. (Illus.). 134p. (Orig.). 1985. 9.95 (*0-9612120-2-0*); pap. 5.95 (*0-9612120-3-9*) Para-Bk-Pr.

— The Devil's Bestseller. (Illus.). 151p. 1983. 9.95 (*0-9612120-0-4*); pap. 3.50 (*0-9612120-1-2*) Para-Bk-Pr.

— How to Exorcise or Delete Race Riots & Rodney King Beatings. (Illus.). 235p. Date not set. 19.95 (*0-685-72062-4*); pap. 11.95 (*0-9612120-6-3*) Para-Bk-Pr.

— The Power of Raceless Thinking. (Illus.). 189p. 1988. 9.95 (*0-9612120-4-7*); pap. 5.95 (*0-9612120-5-5*) Para-Bk-Pr.

***Mitchusson, Don.** Introduction to File Processing. 3rd ed. 140p. 1994. pap. text ed. 32.00 (*0-9631748-2-7*) Mitcon.

Mitelman, jt. ed. see Heim.

Mitelman, F. Catalogue of Chromosome Aberrations in Cancer. (Journal: Cytogenetics & Cell Genetics: Vol. 36, No. 1-2). (Illus.). 516p. 1983. pap. 105.75 (*3-8055-3813-8*) S Karger.

Mitelman, F., ed. ISCN Guidelines for Cancer Cytogenetics, 1991: Supplement to an International System for Human Cytogenetic Nomenclature. vi, 58p. 1992. pap. 35.00 (*3-8055-5567-9*) S Karger.

***Mitelman, Felix.** Catalog of Chromosome Aberrations in Cancer. 5th ed. Johansson, Bertil & Mertens, Fredrik, eds. LC 94-30796. 1994. text ed. 450.00 (*0-471-11183-X*) Wiley.

— Catalog of Chromosome Aberrations in Cancer: Chromosomes 1 through 12 & Chromosomes 13 through 22, 2 vols., Set. 4th ed. 2022p. 1991. text ed. 325.00 (*0-471-56087-1*) Wiley.

Mitelman, Felix, jt. ed. see Heim, Sverre.

Mitford, A. B. Tales of Old Japan. LC 66-25436. (Illus.). 430p. 1966. reprint ed. pap. 14.95 (*0-8048-1160-1*) C E Tuttle.

Mitford, Bertram. Through the Zulu Country: Its Battlefields & People. 288p. 1992. 37.50 (*1-85367-116-9*) Stackpole.

Mitford, Jessica. The American Way of Birth. 320p. 1993. pap. 12.00 (*0-452-27068-5*, Dutton-W Abrahams Bk) NAL-Dutton.

— American Way of Death. 1987. pap. 3.95 (*0-449-21506-7*) Fawcett.

— The American Way of Death. 1993. reprint ed. lib. bdg. 25.95x (*1-56849-159-X*) Buccaneer Bks.

— Daughters & Rebels: An Autobiography. LC 81-47450. 304p. 1981. pap. 9.95 (*0-8050-1172-2*, Owl) H Holt & Co.

— Hons & Rebels. large type ed. 356p. 1991. 10.97 (*1-85089-441-8*, Pub. by ISIS UK) Transaction Pubs.

— Kind & Unusual Punishment: The Prison Business. LC 74-3262. 1974. pap. 8.76 (*0-394-71093-2*, Vin) Random.

Mitford, John, ed. see Parnell, Thomas.

Mitford, Mary R. Belford Regis; or, Sketches of a Country Town, 3 vols, Vol. 1. LC 72-4457. (Short Story Index Reprint Ser.). 1977. reprint ed. 66.95 (*0-8369-4185-3*) Ayer.

— Country Stories. LC 70-110208. (Short Story Index Reprint Ser.). 1977. 20.95 (*0-8369-3359-1*) Ayer.

— Our Village. large type ed. (Isis Clear Type Classic Ser.). 170p. 1992. 23.95 (*1-85089-489-2*, Pub. by ISIS UK) Transaction Pubs.

— Recollections of a Literary Life. LC 74-178342. reprint ed. 67.50 (*0-404-56789-4*) AMS Pr.

Mitford, Mary R., ed. Lights & Shadows of American Life, 3 vols. 1972. reprint ed. lib. bdg. 96.00 (*0-8422-8098-7*) Irvington.

Mitford, Nancy. The Blessing. 222p. 1989. pap. 4.95 (*0-88184-498-5*) Carroll & Graf.

— Christmas Pudding. 1987. pap. 4.95 (*0-88184-342-3*) Carroll & Graf.

— Christmas Pudding. braille ed. 338p. 1992. vinyl bd. 27.04 (*1-56956-046-3*, BR8647) W A T Braille.

— Don't Tell Alfred. 223p. 1990. pap. 7.95 (*0-88184-597-3*) Carroll & Graf.

— Frederick the Great. (Illus.). 224p. 1995. pap. 11.95 (*0-14-003653-9*, Penguin Bks) Viking Penguin.

— Highland Fling. 192p. 1988. pap. 3.95 (*0-88184-390-3*) Carroll & Graf.

— Pigeon Pie. 186p. 1987. pap. 4.95 (*0-88184-332-6*) Carroll & Graf.

— The Pursuit of Love & Love in a Cold Climate. LC 83-42953. 1979. 15.00 (*0-394-60481-4*, Modern Lib) Random.

— The Pursuit of Love, & Love in a Cold Climate. 1994. 17. 50 (*0-679-60090-6*) Random.

— The Sun King. (Illus.). 312p. 1995. pap. 19.95 (*0-14-023967-7*, Penguin Bks) Viking Penguin.

Mitford, Nancy, ed. Noblesse Oblige. LC 74-1516. (Illus.). 156p. 1974. reprint ed. text ed. 39.75 (*0-8371-7387-6*, MINO, Greenwood Pr) Greenwood.

Mitford, Nancy & Roussin, Andre. The Little Hut: Manuscript Edition. 1957. pap. 13.00 (*0-8222-0678-1*) Dramatists Play.

Mitford, T. B. Inscriptions of Kourion. LC 78-121295. (Memoirs Ser.: Vol. 83). (Illus.). 1971. 30.00 (*0-87169-083-7*, M083-MIT) Am Philos.

Mitgang, Herbert. Dangerous Dossiers: Exposing the Secret War Against America's Greatest Authors. LC 87-46257. 1988. 18.95 (*1-55611-077-4*) D I Fine.

— Get These Men out of the Hot Sun. LC 86-46389. 204p. 1987. pap. 7.95 (*1-55611-029-4*, Primus Lib Contemp) D I Fine.

— Mister Lincoln: A Drama in Two Acts. LC 81-8895. 67p. 1982. 9.95 (*0-8093-1034-1*) S Ill U Pr.

— Words Still Count with Me: A Chronicle of Literary Conversations. LC 95-5392. 1995. 25.00 (*0-393-03880-7*) Norton.

Mitgang, Herbert, ed. Abraham Lincoln: A Press Portrait. LC 88-33072. 552p. 1989. reprint ed. pap. 17.95 (*0-8203-1137-5*) U of Ga Pr.

— Letters of Carl Sandburg. LC 68-12588. 1968. 18.95 (*0-15-150695-7*) HarBrace.

Mitgang, Herbert, ed. see Brooks, Noah.

Mitgang, Herbert, ed. see Dicey, Edward.

Mitgutsch. Jakob. 1991. 22.95 (*0-15-145978-9*) HarBrace.

Mitgutsch, Ali. From Blossom to Honey. (Carolrhoda Start to Finish Bks.). (Illus.). 24p. (J). (ps-3). 1981. lib. bdg. 13.50 (*0-87614-146-7*, Carolrhoda) Lerner Group.

— From Cacao Bean to Chocolate: Translation of Vom Kakao Zur Schokolade. LC 80-29588. (Carolrhoda Start to Finish Bks.). (Illus.). 24p. (J). (ps-3). 1981. lib. bdg. 13.50 (*0-87614-147-5*, Carolrhoda) Lerner Group.

— From Cement to Bridge. LC 81-334. (Carolrhoda Start to Finish Bks.). Orig. Title: Von Zement Zur Brucke. (Illus.). 24p. (J). (ps-3). 1981. lib. bdg. 13.50 (*0-87614-148-3*, Carolrhoda) Lerner Group.

— From Clay to Bricks. LC 80-29567. (Carolrhoda Start to Finish Bks.). Orig. Title: Vom Lehm Zum Ziegel. (Illus.). 24p. (J). (ps-3). 1981. lib. bdg. 13.50 (*0-87614-149-1*, Carolrhoda) Lerner Group.

— From Cotton to Pants. LC 80-29552. (Carolrhoda Start to Finish Bks.). Orig. Title: Von der Baumwolle Zur Hose. (Illus.). 24p. (J). (ps-3). 1981. lib. bdg. 13.50 (*0-87614-150-5*, Carolrhoda) Lerner Group.

— From Fruit to Jam. LC 81-58. (Carolrhoda Start to Finish Bks.). Orig. Title: Vom Obst Zur Marmelade. (Illus.). 24p. (J). (ps-3). 1981. lib. bdg. 13.50 (*0-87614-154-8*, Carolrhoda) Lerner Group.

— From Gold to Money. LC 84-17488. (Carolrhoda Start-to-Finish Bks.). (Illus.). 24p. (J). (ps-3). 1985. lib. bdg. 13.50 (*0-87614-230-7*, Carolrhoda) Lerner Group.

— From Grain to Bread. LC 80-28592. (Carolrhoda Start to Finish Bks.). Orig. Title: Vom Korn Zum Brot. (Illus.). 24p. (J). (ps-3). 1981. lib. bdg. 13.50 (*0-87614-155-6*, Carolrhoda) Lerner Group.

— From Graphite to Pencil. LC 84-17469. (Carolrhoda Start-to-Finish Bks.). (Illus.). 24p. (J). (ps-3). 1985. lib. bdg. 13.50 (*0-87614-231-5*, Carolrhoda) Lerner Group.

— From Grass to Butter. LC 80-28588. (Carolrhoda Start to Finish Bks.). Orig. Title: Vom Gras Zur Butter. (Illus.). 24p. (J). (ps-3). 1981. lib. bdg. 13.50 (*0-87614-156-4*, Carolrhoda) Lerner Group.

— From Idea to Toy. (Carolrhoda Start to Finish Bks.). (Illus.). 24p. (J). (ps-3). 1988. lib. bdg. 13.50 (*0-87614-352-4*, Carolrhoda) Lerner Group.

— From Milk to Ice Cream. LC 81-81. (Carolrhoda Start to Finish Bks.). Orig. Title: Von der Milch zum Speiseeis. (Illus.). 24p. (J). (ps-3). 1981. lib. bdg. 13.50 (*0-87614-158-0*, Carolrhoda) Lerner Group.

An Asterisk (*) at the beginning of an entry indicates that the title is appearing in BIP for the first time.

— From Oil to Gasoline. LC 80-29562. (Carolrhoda Start to Finish Bks.). Orig. Title: Vom Erdol Zum Benzin. (Illus.). 24p. (J). (ps-3). 1981. lib. bdg. 13.50 (*0-87614-160-2*, Carolrhoda) Lerner Group.

— From Ore to Spoon. LC 80-28862. (Carolrhoda Start to Finish Bks.). Orig. Title: Vom Erz Zum Loffel. (Illus.). 24p. (J). (ps-3). 1981. lib. bdg. 13.50 (*0-87614-161-0*, Carolrhoda) Lerner Group.

— From Picture to Picture Book. (Carolrhoda Start to Finish Bks.). (Illus.). 24p. (J). (ps-3). 1988. lib. bdg. 13.50 (*0-87614-353-2*, Carolrhoda) Lerner Group.

— From Rubber Tree to Tire. Lerner, Mark, tr. (Carolrhoda Start to Finish Bks.). (Illus.). 24p. (J). (ps-3). 1986. lib. bdg. 13.50 (*0-87614-297-8*, Carolrhoda) Lerner Group.

— From Sand to Glass. LC 80-29572. (Carolrhoda Start to Finish Bks.). Orig. Title: Vom Sand Zum Glas. (Illus.). 24p. (J). (ps-3). 1981. lib. bdg. 13.50 (*0-87614-162-9*, Carolrhoda) Lerner Group.

— From Sea to Salt. LC 84-17466. (Carolrhoda Start to Finish Bks.). (Illus.). 24p. (J). (ps-3). 1985. lib. bdg. 13. 50 (*0-87614-232-3*, Carolrhoda) Lerner Group.

— From Seed to Pear. LC 81-83. (Carolrhoda Start to Finish Bks.). Orig. Title: Vom Kern Zur Birne. (Illus.). 24p. (J). (ps-3). 1981. lib. bdg. 13.50 (*0-87614-163-7*, Carolrhoda) Lerner Group.

— From Sheep to Scarf. LC 80-29557. (Carolrhoda Start to Finish Bks.). Orig. Title: Vom Schaf Zum Schal. (Illus.). 24p. (J). (ps-3). 1981. lib. bdg. 13.50 (*0-87614-164-5*, Carolrhoda) Lerner Group.

— From Swamp to Coal. LC 84-17465. (Carolrhoda Start-to-Finish Bks.). (Illus.). 24p. (J). (ps-3). 1985. lib. bdg. 13. 50 (*0-87614-233-1*, Carolrhoda) Lerner Group.

— From Tree to Table. LC 81-672. (Carolrhoda Start to Finish Bks.). Orig. Title: Vom Baum Zum Tisch. (Illus.). 24p. (J). (ps-3). 1981. lib. bdg. 13.50 (*0-87614-165-3*, Carolrhoda) Lerner Group.

— From Wood to Paper. Lerner, Mark, tr. (Carolrhoda Start to Finish Bks.). (Illus.). 24p. (J). (ps-3). 1986. lib. bdg. 13.50 (*0-87614-296-X*, Carolrhoda) Lerner Group.

Mitgutsch, Anna. In Foreign Cities. Bangerter, Lowell A., tr. LC 94-6441. (Studies in Austrian Literature, Culture, & Thought. Translation Ser.). 1995. pap. write for info. (*0-929497-90-2*) Ariadne CA.

Mithal, M. Textbook of Forensic Pharmacy. 8th ed. (C). 1988. 80.00 (*0-685-36221-3*, Current Dist) St Mut.

Mithaug, Dennis E. How to Teach Prevocational Skills to Severely Handicapped Persons. (Teaching the Autistic Ser.). 62p. 1981. pap. 8.00 (*0-89079-056-6*, 1037) PRO-ED.

— Self-Determine Kids: Helping Children Succeed. 288p. 1991. text ed. 24.95 (*0-669-27140-3*) Free Pr.

— Self-Regulation Theory: How Optimal Adjustment Maximizes Gain. LC 92-17812. 256p. 1993. text ed. 49. 95 (*0-275-94422-0*, C4422, Praeger Pubs) Greenwood.

Mitchell, Nahum & Mitchell, Edward C. History of the Early Settlement of Bridgewater, in Plymouth County, Massachusetts, Including an Extensive Family Register. (Illus.). 424p. 1992. reprint ed. lib. bdg. 44.50 (*0-8328-2376-7*) Higginson Bk Co.

Mithcell, V. E. Windows on a Lost World. Stern, Dave, ed. (Star Trek Ser.: No. 65). 288p. (Orig.). 1993. mass mkt. 5.99 (*0-671-79512-0*) PB.

Mithell, Mike, tr. see Furness, Ray, ed. & tr.

Mithen, Steven. Thoughtful Foragers: A Study of Prehistoric Decision Making. (New Studies in Archaeology). (Illus.). 220p. (C). 1990. 79.95 (*0-521-35570-2*) Cambridge U Pr.

Mithers, Carol L. Reasonable Insanity: A True Story of the Seventies. LC 93-30571. 1994. 22.12 (*0-201-57071-8*) Addison-Wesley.

Mithun, Marianne, jt. ed. see Davis, Steven.

Miti, Katabaro, jt. auth. see Chipasula, James C.

Mitias, M. H., ed. Possibility of the Aesthetic Experience. 1986. lib. bdg. 80.50 (*90-247-3278-6*) Kluwer Ac.

Mitias, Michael H., ed. Moral Education & the Liberal Arts. LC 91-22369. (Contributions to the Study of Education Ser.: No. 50). 192p. 1992. text ed. 49.95 (*0-313-27236-0*, MMB, Greenwood Pr) Greenwood.

***Mitic, P. & Keranen, V., eds.** Applications of Mathematics in Science, Mathematics, Technology, Business & Education. 450p. 1995. 135.00 (*1-56252-310-4*) Computational Mech MA.

***Mitideri, Dario, et al, photos.** Children of Bombay. (Illus.). 160p. Date not set. 45.00 (*1-899235-00-0*) Dist Art Pubs.

Mitiguy, Nancy. The Rich Get Richer & the Poor Write Proposals. LC 79-624731. (Illus.). (Orig.). (C). 1978. pap. 7.00 (*0-934210-02-0*) Devlp Commy.

Mitiguy, Nancy, jt. auth. see Dale, Duane.

Mitilieri, Robert, ed. see Schwartz, Karl.

Mitlehner, W., et al, eds. First Lox Workshop Symposium - Rationale & Study Design: Proceedings of the First Lox Workshop on Long Term Portable Oxygen Treatment in Severe Disabled COPD, Germany, Berlin, November 1990. (Journal: Respiration: Vol. 59, Suppl. 2, 1992). (Illus.). vi, 46p. 1992. pap. 21.00 (*3-8055-5645-4*) S Karger.

Mitler, Louis. Contemporary Turkish Writers: A Critical Bio-Bibliography of Leading Writers in the Turkish Republican Period, up to 1980. LC 85-60918. (Uralic & Altaic Ser.: Vol. 146). 1988. 29.50 (*0-933070-14-4*) Res Inst Inner Asian Studies.

— Ottoman Turkish Writers: A Biographical Dictionary of Significant Ottoman Literature. (American University Studies: General Literature: Ser. XIX, Vol. 15). 203p. (C). 1988. text ed. 31.50 (*0-8204-0633-3*) P Lang Pubs.

Mitler, Louis, tr. see Nesin, Aziz.

Mitlin, Vladimir S. Nonlinear Dynamics of Reservoir Mixtures. 1993. 89.95 (*0-8493-4416-6*, TN871) CRC Pr.

Mitman, Gregg. State of Nature: Ecology, Community & American Social Thought, 1900-1950. (Science & Its Conceptual Foundations Ser.). (Illus.). 304p. (C). 1992. pap. text ed. 23.50 (*0-226-53237-2*) U Ch Pr.

— State of Nature: Ecology, Community & American Social Thought, 1900-1950. (Science & Its Conceptual Foundations Ser.). (Illus.). 304p. (C). 1992. lib. bdg. 58. 00 (*0-226-53236-4*) U Ch Pr.

Mitnick, Barbara J. The Changing Image of George Washington. (Illus.). 51p. (Orig.). 1989. pap. 5.00 (*0-9616415-7-6*) Fraunces Tavern.

— Harry Devlin: A Retrospective. Mitnick, John M., ed. 70p. (C). 1991. 4.50 (*0-9613046-4-2*) Morris Mus.

Mitnick, Barbara J. & Mitnick, John M. The Realist Vision of Adolf Konrad: A Retrospective. 63p. 1992. 9.00 (*0-9613046-7-7*) Morris Mus.

Mitnick, Barbara J. & Pennington, Estill C. Jean Leon Gerome Ferris, 1863-1930: American Painter Historian. LC 85-81442. (Illus.). 205p. (Orig.). 1985. pap. 15.00 (*0-935903-01-1*) Lauren Rogers.

Mitnick, Barry M., ed. Corporate Political Activity. (Focus Editions Ser.: Vol. 163). (Illus.). 312p. 1993. 49.95 (*0-8039-4348-2*); pap. 24.95 (*0-8039-4349-0*) Sage.

Mitnick, Harold. How to Handle Your Divorce Step by Step. LC 80-80875. 177p. 1981. 21.95 (*0-685-03094-6*); pap. 14.95 (*0-936550-00-7*) Lone Oak.

Mitnick, John M., ed. see Mitnick, Barbara J.

Mitnick, John M., jt. auth. see Mitnick, Barbara J.

Mitnick, Leonard L., jt. auth. see Lipsitt, Lewis P.

Mitnik, Mark. Was It a Classical Triangle? (Illus.). 192p. (Orig.). (RUS.). 1988. pap. 12.00 (*0-9622027-0-3*) M Mitnik.

Mito, Setsuo. The Honda Book of Management: A Leadership Philosophy for High Industrial Success. LC 89-77751. 224p. (C). 1990. text ed. 45.00 (*0-485-11317-1*, Pub. by Athlone Pr UK) Humanities.

Mito, Setsuo, jt. auth. see Ohno, Taiichi.

Mitofsky, Warren J. & Plissner, Martin. Campaign Seventy Eight: A Comprehensive Political Handbook to the Vote Returns & Candidates. 1980. 51.95 (*0-405-12517-8*) Ayer.

Mitra. Ophthalmic Drug Delivery Systems. (Drugs & the Pharmaceutical Sciences Ser.: Vol. 58). 536p. 1993. 180. 00 (*0-8247-8806-0*) Dekker.

Mitra, A. The Status of Women: Household & Non-Household Economic Activity. 78p. 1979. 6.95 (*0-318-37312-2*) Asia Bk Corp.

— The Status of Women: Literacy & Employment. (Illus.). 74p. 1979. 6.95 (*0-318-37313-0*) Asia Bk Corp.

***Mitra, A. K. & Sahoo, B.** Agricultural Planning & Technology in Rural Development. 266p. (C). 1994. 75. 00x (*81-85880-49-2*, Pub. by Print Hse II) St Mut.

Mitra, A. P. Ionospheric Effects of Solar Flares. LC 74-76480. (Astrophysics & Space Science Library: No. 46). 200p. 1974. lib. bdg. 103.00 (*90-277-0467-8*) Kluwer Ac.

Mitra, A. P., ed. see COSPAR, Twenty-Second Plenary Meeting Staff.

Mitra, Amitava. Fundamentals of Quality Control & Improvement. LC 92-41164. 688p. (C). 1993. text ed. write for info. (*0-02-381791-7*) Macmillan.

Mitra, Ananda. Beyond the Superconscious Mind. (Illus.). 96p. (Orig.). 1991. reprint ed. pap. 6.00 (*0-945934-06-8*) New Wrld Lib.

— Food for Thought: The Vegetarian Philosophy. 112p. 1991. reprint ed. pap. 7.00 (*0-945934-07-6*) New Wrld Lib.

— Television & Popular Culture in India: A Study of the Mahabharat. LC 93-27379. 1993. 28.50 (*0-8039-9134-7*) Sage.

Mitra, Annie, illus. The Christmas Witch. LC 92-562. (J). 1993. mass mkt. 3.99 (*0-553-37187-8*, Little Rooster) Bantam.

Mitra, Ashok. Calcutta Diary. 206p. 1977. 32.50 (*0-7146-3082-9*, Pub. by F Cass Pubs UK) Intl Spec Bk.

Mitra, Ashok, tr. see Tagore, Rabindranath.

Mitra, Asok. Calcutta on the Eve of Her Tercentenary. 1990. 23.00 (*81-7017-270-5*, Pub. by Abhinav II) S Asia.

— The New India, 1948-1955. (C). 1991. 22.50 (*81-7154-691-9*, Pub. by Popular Prakashan II) S Asia.

Mitra, Asok, ed. Functional Classification of India's Urban Areas by Factor-Cluster Method, 1961-1971. 1981. 38. 50 (*0-8364-0806-3*, Pub. by Abhinav II) S Asia.

Mitra, Asok, et al. Shifts in the Functions of Cities & Towns of India, Nineteen Sixty-One to Nineteen Seventy-One. 1981. 47.50 (*0-8364-0719-9*, Pub. by Abhinav II) S Asia.

Mitra, B. B. Criminal Procedure Code, 2 vols. (C). 1988. 480.00 (*0-685-25692-8*) St Mut.

— Guardians & Wards Act, 1890. 13th ed. (C). 1988. 200.00 (*0-685-27910-3*) St Mut.

Mitra, Debala. Bronzes from Achutrajpur Orissa. 1978. 50. 00 (*0-8364-0136-0*) S Asia.

Mitra, Debendra B. Monetary System in the Bengal Presidency. (C). 1991. 20.00 (*81-7074-100-9*) S Asia.

Mitra, G., ed. Computer Assisted Decision Making: Expert Systems, Decision Analysis, Mathematical Programming. 282p. 1986. 87.25 (*0-444-87887-4*, North Holland) Elsevier.

Mitra, G. & Wojtal, S., eds. Geometries & Mechanisms of Thrusting, with Special Reference to the Appalachians. (Special Paper Ser.: No. 222). (Illus.). 230p. 1988. pap. 22.00 (*0-8137-2222-5*) Geol Soc.

Mitra, G., et al, eds. Mathematical Models for Decision Support. (NATO Asi Series F: Vol. 48). ix, 756p. 1988. 153.00 (*0-387-50084-7*) Spr-Verlag.

Mitra, Gautam, jt. auth. see Marshak, Stephen.

Mitra, M. Legal & Commercial Dictionary. (C). 1990. 160. 00 (*0-89771-130-0*) St Mut.

Mitra, Manimanjari. Calcutta in the Twentieth Century: An Urban Disaster. 1990. 27.50 (*0-8364-2627-4*, Pub. by Asiatic Bk Agency JA) S Asia.

Mitra, Manoshi. Agrarian Social Structure: Continuity & Change in Bihar, 1786-1920. 1986. 27.00 (*0-8364-1622-8*, Pub. by Manohar II) S Asia.

Mitra, Mary A. A Book of Inspirational Verse. (C). 1989. 40.00 (*0-7223-2360-3*, Pub. by A H S Ltd UK) St Mut.

Mitra, Parimal C. Santhali: The Base of World Languages. (C). 1988. 15.00 (*0-8364-2379-8*, Pub. by Firma KLM) S Asia.

Mitra, Pradeep K. Adjustment in Oil-Importing Developing Countries: A Comparative Economic Analysis. LC 92-36214. (Illus.). 375p. (C). 1994. 54.95 (*0-521-44316-4*) Cambridge U Pr.

Mitra, Pramada D., jt. tr. see Ballantyne, J. R.

Mitra, Premendra. Snake & Other Stories. 1990. 17.50 (*81-7046-073-5*, Pub. by Seagull Bks II) S Asia.

Mitra, R. B., et al, eds. New Trends in Heterocyclic Chemistry. (Studies in Organic Chemistry: Vol. 3). 408p. 1979. 120.50 (*0-444-41816-4*) Elsevier.

Mitra, Rajendra L. Antiquities of Orissa, Vol. 2. 269p. 1984. 27.50 (*1-55528-086-2*, Pub. by Today & Tomorrows P & P II) Scholarly Pubns.

Mitra, Rajendralal L. Antiquities of Orissa, 2 vols., Set. (Illus.). 600p. 1990. reprint ed. 27.50 (*1-55528-203-2*, Messers Today & Tomorrow) Scholarly Pubns.

Mitra, S. Applied Mossbauer Spectroscopy: Theory & Practice for Geochemists & Archeologists. (Physics & Chemistry of the Earth Ser.: Vol. 18). 400p. 1993. 500. 00 (*0-08-042199-7*, Pergamon Pr) Elsevier.

— Mercury in the Ecosyptem. (Illus.). 270p. 1985. 80.00 (*0-87849-529-0*, Pub. by Trans Tech GW) LPS Dist Ctr.

Mitra, S. K., jt. auth. see Bose, T. K.

Mitra, Sanjit K. & Kurth, Carl F. Miniaturized & Integrated Filters. 422p. 1989. text ed. 104.00 (*0-471-84496-9*) Wiley.

Mitra, Shankar & Fisher, George W., eds. Structural Geology of Fold & Thrust Belts. (Studies in Earth & Space Sciences). (Illus.). 296p. 1992. text ed. 55.00 (*0-8018-4350-2*) Johns Hopkins.

Mitra, Sisirkumar. India: Vision & Fulfillment. (Illus.). vi, 290p. (C). 1981. text ed. 13.95 (*0-86590-044-2*, Pub. by Taraporevala II) Apt Bks.

Mitra, Sourindra. T. S. Eliot - The Critic: A Study in Critical Ideology & Method. xx, 279p. 1985. 16.00 (*0-685-67631-5*, Pub. by Mittal Pubs Dist II) Nataraj Bks.

Mitra, Subrata, ed. Subnational Movements in South Asia. 224p. (C). 1995. pap. text ed. 49.95 (*0-8133-2093-3*) Westview.

Mitra, Subrata K. Power, Protest & Participation: Local Elites & Development in India. LC 92-4000. 240p. 1992. 69.95 (*0-415-07840-7*, A7589) Routledge.

Mitra, Sunanda, et al, eds. Neural Fuzzy Systems: The Emerging Science of Intelligent Computing. LC 94-1640. 1994. write for info. (*0-8194-1566-9*); pap. write for info. (*0-8194-1565-0*) SPIE.

Mitra, Sunil K. Law of Apartment Ownership in West Bengal. (C). 1989. 180.00 (*0-685-36470-4*) St Mut.

Mitrakos, Alexander S. France in Greece in World War I. 1982. text ed. 42.00 (*0-914710-95-8*, 101) Col U Pr.

Mitrani, I., jt. auth. see Gelenbe, Erol.

Mitrani, Jose D. The Critical Path Method: A Self-Study Text. 74p. 1977. pap. 7.00 (*0-935715-07-X*, 0185) Construct Bkstore.

Mitrany, David. Effect of the War in Southeastern Europe. LC 75-114590. 1973. reprint ed. 45.00 (*0-86527-055-4*) Fertig.

Mitrea, Marius. Clifford Wavelets, Singular Integrals, & Hardy Spaces. LC 94-9648. (Lecture Notes in Mathematics: Vol. 1575). 1994. 23.00 (*0-387-57884-6*) Spr-Verlag.

Mitrinovic, D. S. Classical & New Inequalities in Analysis. (Mathematics & Its Applications East European Ser.). 760p. (C). 1992. lib. bdg. 285.00 (*0-7923-2064-6*) Kluwer Ac.

Mitrinovic, D. S., et al. Inequalities Involving Functions & Their Integrals & Derivatives. (C). 1991. lib. bdg. 180.00 (*0-7923-1330-5*) Kluwer Ac.

Mitrinovic, Dragoslav S. The Cauchy Method of Residues, Vol. 2: Theory & Applications. (Mathematics & Its Applications Ser.). 208p. (C). 1993. lib. bdg. 86.50 (*0-7923-2311-4*) Kluwer Ac.

Mitrinovic, Dragoslav S., jt. auth. see Keckic, Jovan D.

***Mitrione, Dan.** Suddenly Gone: The Kansas Murders of Serial Killer Richard Grissom. McFarland, Tom & Colvin, Rod, eds. 300p. 1995. pap. 14.95 (*1-886039-23-2*) Addicus Bks.

Mitripolsky, Yu A., et al. Systems of Evolution Equations. 1992. lib. bdg. 126.00 (*0-7923-2054-9*) Kluwer Ac.

Mitro, A. & Palkovits, M. Morphology of the Rat Brain Ventricles, Ependyma & Periventricular Structures. (Bibliotheca Anatomica Ser.: No. 21). (Illus.). x, 110p. 1981. pap. 78.50 (*3-8055-2546-X*) S Karger.

Mitrofanov, F. P., jt. ed. see Rundqvist, D. V.

Mitroff, Alan I. Business NOT As Usual: Rethinking Our Individual, Corporate, & Industrial Strategies for Global Competition. LC 86-46333. (Management Ser.). 215p. 1987. 26.95 (*1-55542-030-3*) Jossey-Bass.

Mitroff, Alan I. & Pearson, Christine. Crisis Management: A Diagnostic Guide for Improving Your Organization's Crisis-Preparedness. LC 96-16039. (Management Ser.). 160p. 1993. 24.95 (*1-55542-563-1*) Jossey-Bass.

Mitroff, Ian. The Subjective Side of Science. (Systems Inquiry Ser.). 328p. 1983. reprint ed. pap. 15.95 (*0-914105-21-3*) Intersystems Pubns.

Mitroff, Ian & Kilmann, Ralph H. Corporate Tragedies: Product Tampering, Sabotage & Other Catastrophes. LC 84-6764. 156p. 1984. text ed. 45.00 (*0-275-91742-8*, C1742, Praeger Pubs) Greenwood.

Mitroff, Ian I. We're So Big & Powerful That Nothing Bad Can Happen to Us. 1990. 19.95 (*1-55972-051-4*, Birch Ln Pr) Carol Pub Group.

Mitroff, Ian I. & Bennis, Warren. The Unreality Industry. Richardson, Stewart, ed. 292p. 1989. 17.95 (*1-55972-014-X*, Birch Ln Pr) Carol Pub Group.

Mitroff, Ian I. & Bennis, Warren G. The Unreality Industry: The Deliberate Manufacturing of Falsehood & What It Is Doing to Our Lives. LC 92-44601. (C). 1993. pap. 10. 95 (*0-19-508398-9*) OUP.

***Mitroff, Ian I. & Linstone, Harold A.** The Unbounded Mind: Breaking the Chains of Traditional Business Thinking. (Illus.). 190p. 1995. pap. 10.95 (*0-19-510288-6*) OUP.

— The Unbounded Mind: Breaking the Chairs of Traditional Business Thinking. LC 92-15708. (Illus.). 256p. 1993. 25.00 (*0-19-507783-0*) OUP.

Mitroff, Ian I., jt. auth. see Linstone, Harold A.

Mitroff, Ian I., jt. auth. see Pauchant, Thierry C.

Mitroff, Ian J. Stakeholders of the Organizational Mind: Toward a New View of Organizational Policy Making. LC 83-48161. (Management Ser.). 203p. 1983. 28.95 (*0-87589-580-8*) Jossey-Bass.

Mitroff, Ian J., et al. Framebreak: The Radical Redesign of American Business. LC 93-42749. (Business-Management Ser.). 180p. 1994. 24.00 (*1-55542-606-9*) Jossey-Bass.

***Mitroiescu, Ilie.** The Smarandache Class of Paradoxes. Muller, R., ed. (Illus.). 75p. (C). Date not set. pap. 9.99 (*1-879585-46-4*) Xiquan Pubng.

Mitrokhin, L. Failure of Three Missions. 220p. (C). 1987. 40.00 (*0-685-31485-5*, Pub. by Collets UK) Pro-Am Music.

Mitrokhina, V. I. & Motovilova. Russian for Scientists: General Scientific Terminology. 343p. (GER & RUS.). 1981. 49.95 (*0-8288-1561-5*, M13015) Fr & Eur.

Mitronowa, I. Polish-Russian, Russian-Polish Dictionary. deluxe ed. 575p. (POL & RUS.). 1980. 14.95 (*0-8288-4712-6*, M9102) Fr & Eur.

— Russian-Polish-Russian Pocket Dictionary. 19th ed. 575p. (POL & RUS.). 1980. 9.95 (*0-8288-1632-8*, M9102) Fr & Eur.

***Mitropolaky, Yu. A. & Lopatin, A. K.** Nonlinear Mechanics, Groups & Symmetry. LC 94-48068. (Mathematics & Its Applications Ser.: Vol. 319). 377p. 1995. lib. bdg. 163.50 (*0-7923-3339-X*) Kluwer Ac.

Mitropol'skii, Aristarkh K. Correlation Equations for Statistical Computations. LC 65-25246. 111p. reprint ed. pap. 31.70 (*0-317-30339-2*, 2024712) Bks Demand.

Mitropol'skii, y. A. Problems of the Asymptotic Theory of Nonstationary Vibrations. 392p. 1965. text ed. 95.50 (*0-7065-0579-4*, Pub. by Keter Pub IS) Coronet Bks.

Mitropolsky, S. Kratkaja Grammatika Tserkovno-Slavjanskago Jazika. 92p. 1980. pap. 5.00 (*0-317-30307-4*) Holy Trinity.

Mitropolsky, Y. A., jt. auth. see Bogoliubov, N. N.

Mitros, Joseph F. Religions: A Select, Classified Bibliography. LC 77-183042. (Philosophical Questions Ser.: No. 8). 350p. 1973. 55.00 (*0-912116-08-0*) Learned Pubns.

Mitrou, P. S., jt. ed. see Bergmann, L.

Mitrovich, Marta. Collected Poems: From the Personal to the Universal. 80p. (Orig.). 1990. pap. 6.00 (*0-9624205-1-4*) Inevitable Pr.

Mitruka, B. & Bonner, M. Methods of Detection & Identification of Bacteria. LC 76-28809. 1977. 91.00 (*0-8493-5116-2*) CRC Pr.

Mitruka, Brij M. & Rawnsley, Howard M. Clinical Biochemical & Hematological Reference Values in Normal Experimental Animals & Normal Humans. 2nd exp. ed. LC 81-17157. (Illus.). 432p. 1981. lib. bdg. 68. 50 (*0-89352-163-9*, Yr Bk Med Pubs) Mosby Yr Bk.

Mitruka, Brij M., ed. Animals for Medical Research: Models for the Study of Human Disease. LC 80-11455. 608p. 1982. reprint ed. lib. bdg. 49.50 (*0-89874-156-4*) Krieger.

***Mitsch, Erwin.** Egon Schiele. (Illus.). 270p. 1995. pap. 29. 95 (*0-7148-2862-9*, Pub. by Phaidon Press UK) Chronicle Bks.

Mitsch, Raymond. Nurturing Your Child's Potential. 250p. 1994. pap. 10.99 (*0-89283-821-3*, Vine Bks) Servant.

Mitsch, Raymond R. Grieving the Loss of Someone You Love. 200p. (Orig.). 1993. pap. 7.99 (*0-89283-822-1*, Vine Bks) Servant.

Mitsch, W. Wetlands. 2nd ed. 1993. text ed. 59.95 (*0-442-00805-8*) Van Nos Reinhold.

***Mitsch, W. J., ed.** Global Wetlands: Old World & New. 992p. 1994. 285.50 (*0-444-81478-7*) Elsevier.

Mitsch, W. J., jt. ed. see Jorgensen, Sven E.

Mitsch, W. J., et al. Energy & Ecological Modelling: Proceedings of the International Symposium, Louisville, Ky, April 20-23, 1981. (Developments in Environmental Modelling Ser.: Vol. 1). 848p. 1982. 184.75 (*0-444-99731-8*) Elsevier.

Mitsch, W. J., et al, eds. Wetland Modelling. (Developments in Environmental Modelling Ser.: Vol. 12). 238p. 1988. 95.00 (*0-444-42936-0*) Elsevier.

Mitsch, William J. & Jorgensen, Sven E., eds. Ecological Engineering: An Introduction to Ecotechnology. LC 08-823576. (Environmental Science & Technology Ser.). 472p. 1989. text ed. 79.95 (*0-471-62559-0*) Wiley.

Mitsch, Wolfgang, et al. Hochschule in der Demokratie: Kritische Beitrage zur Erbschaft und Reform der Deutschen Universitat. Metzger, Walter P., ed. LC 76-55204. (Academic Profession Ser.). (Illus.). (GER.). 1977. reprint ed. lib. bdg. 41.95 (*0-405-10034-5*) Ayer.

Mitscher, L. A. The Chemistry of the Tetracycline Antibiotics. (Medicinal Research Ser.: Vol. 9). 352p. 1978. 170.00 (*0-8247-6716-0*) Dekker.

Mitscher, Lester A., jt. auth. see Lednicer, Daniel.

Mitsios, Helen, ed. New Japanese Voices: The Best Contemporary Fiction from Japan. 224p. 1992. pap. 10. 95 (*0-87113-522-1*) Grove-Atltic.

Mitsis, Phillip. Epicurus' Ethical Theory: The Pleasures of Invulnerability. LC 88-47746. (Cornell Studies in Classical Philology). 224p. 1988. 28.95 (*0-8014-2187-X*) Cornell U Pr.
Mitson, R. B., jt. ed. see Cheeseman, C. L.
***Mitsubishi Corp. Staff.** Japanese Business Language: An Essential Dictionary. 230p. 1987. 31.00 (*0-7103-0199-5*, Pub. by Kegan Paul Intl UK) Routledge Chapman & Hall.
Mitsubishi Corporation Staff. Tatemae & Honne: Good Form & Real Intention in Japanese Business Culture. 225p. 1988. 24.95 (*0-02-921591-9*) Free Pr.
Mitsuhashi, Jun, ed. Invertebrate Cell System Applications, 2 Vols., Vol. I. (Studies in Christian Ethics Journal). 288p. 1989. 179.00 (*0-8493-4373-9*, QL362) CRC Pr.
— Invertebrate Cell System Applications, 2 Vols., Vol. II. (Studies in Christian Ethics Journal). 288p. 1989. 217.00 (*0-8493-4374-7*, QL362) CRC Pr.
Mitsuhashi, S. & Franceschi, G., eds. Penem Antibiotics. (Illus.). 180p. 1991. 64.00 (*0-387-53142-4*) Spr-Verlag.
Mitsuhashi, S., et al, eds. Antibiotic Resistance: Proceedings. (Illus.). 410p. 1981. 69.00 (*0-387-10322-8*) Spr-Verlag.
Mitsuhashi, Setsuko. Japanese Commodity Flows. LC 78-8319. (Research Papers Ser.: No. 187). (Illus.). 1978. pap. 12.00 (*0-89065-094-2*) U Chicago Comm Geo.
Mitsui, James M. After the Long Train. (Illus.). (Orig.). 1986. pap. 50.00 (*0-931460-22-0*) Bieler.
Mitsui, T. An Introduction to the Physics of Ferroelectrics. (Ferroelectricity & Related Phenomena Ser.). 460p. 1976. text ed. 233.00 (*0-677-30600-8*) Gordon & Breach.
Mitsui, T., et al, eds. Electricity & Biophysics: A Special Issue of the Journal Ferroelectrics. iv, 356p. 1988. pap. text ed. 507.00 (*2-88124-336-3*) Gordon & Breach.
Mitsui, Y. MMIC-Monolithic Microwave Integrated Circuits. 168p. 1989. 57.00 (*0-318-39931-8*) Gordon & Breach.
— Strabismus & the Sensorimotor Reflex. 228p. 1986. 100.00 (*4-900392-74-X*) Elsevier.
Mitsui, Yasuo. MMIC - Monolithic Microwave Integrated Circuits. (Japanese Technology Reviews Ser.: Vol. 2). 144p. 1989. text ed. 64.00 (*2-88124-286-3*) Gordon & Breach.
Mitsumoto. Amyotrophic Lateral Sclerosis: A Comprehensive Guide to Management. 1994. 39.95 (*0-939957-58-2*) Demos Vermande.
Mitsuo, Shimizu, jt. auth. see Stubel, Hans.
Mitsutani, Magaret, tr. see Oe, Kenzaburo.
Mitsuyasu, H., jt. auth. see Toba, Yoshiaki.
Mitsuyasu, H., jt. ed. see Toba, Yoshiaki.
Mittag, M. Building Construction Practice: Pratique de la Construction des Batiments. 11th ed. 352p. (FRE.). 1983. write for info. (*0-7859-4923-2*) Fr & Eur.
***Mittal, Ashok.** Cinema Industry in India: Pricing & Taxation. (C). 1995. 28.00x (*81-7387-023-3*, Pub. by Indus Pub II) S Asia.
Mittal, B. L., ed. Supreme Court on Sales Tax Nineteen Fifty to Nineteen Eighty-Eight. (C). 1988. 150.00 (*0-685-36452-6*) St Mut.
Mittal, D. P. Double Taxation Agreements & Taxation of Foreign Investments in India. (C). 1989. 350.00 (*0-685-27886-7*) St Mut.
Mittal, Gauri. Food Biotechnology: Techniques & Applications. LC 92-60559. 390p. 1992. text ed. 95.00 (*0-87762-888-2*) Technomic.
Mittal, K., jt. ed. see Pizzi, A.
Mittal, K. L. Materialism in Indian Thought. 336p. 1974. 24.95 (*0-318-37022-0*) Asia Bk Corp.
— Surface & Colloid Science in Computer Technology. LC 87-12273. (Illus.). 456p. 1987. 95.00 (*0-306-42602-1*, Plenum Pr) Plenum.
Mittal, K. L., ed. Adhesion Aspects of Polymeric Coatings. LC 82-24870. 670p. 1983. 145.00 (*0-306-41250-0*, Plenum Pr) Plenum.
***MIttal, K. L., ed.** Adhesion Measurement of Films & Coatings. 444p. 1994. 147.50 (*90-6764-182-0*, Pub. by VSP NE) Coronet Bks.
Mittal, K. L., ed. Adhesion Measurement of Thin Films, Thick Films & Bulk Coatings - STP 640. 410p. 1978. 39.25 (*0-8031-0272-0*, 04-640000-25) ASTM.
— Adsorption at Interface: Papers from a Symposium Honoring Robert D. Vold & Majorie J. Vold. LC 74-32040. (American Chemical Society Symposium Ser.: No. 8). 304p. reprint ed. pap. 86.70 (*0-8357-5118-X*, 2015232) Bks Demand.
— Colloidal Dispersions & Micellar Behavior: Papers from A Symposium Honoring Robert D. Vold & Marjorie J. Vold. LC 74-34072. (American Chemical Society ACS Symposium Ser.: No. 9). (Illus.). 362p. reprint ed. pap. 103.20 (*0-317-09351-7*, 2015233) Bks Demand.
— Contact Angle, Wettability & Adhesion: In Honor of Professor Robert J. Good. xxiv, 972p. 1993. 247.50 (*90-6764-157-X*) Coronet Bks.
— Metalized Plastics, Vol. 2: Fundamental & Applied Aspects. (Illus.). 464p. 1992. 115.00 (*0-306-44107-1*, Plenum Pr) Plenum.
— Metallized Plastics, Vol. 3. (Illus.). 400p. (C). 1993. 110.00 (*0-306-44341-4*, Plenum Pr) Plenum.
— Metallized Plastics, Vol. 1: Fundamental & Applied Aspects. LC 89-28395. (Illus.). 292p. 1989. 75.00 (*0-306-43389-3*, Plenum Pr) Plenum.
— Particles in Gases & Liquids, No. 1: Detection, Characterization, & Control. (Illus.). 312p. 1989. 79.50 (*0-306-43151-3*, Plenum Pr) Plenum.
— Particles in Gases & Liquids, No. 2: Detection, Characterization, & Control. (Illus.). 400p. 1991. 89.50 (*0-306-43809-7*, Plenum Pr) Plenum.
— Particles in Gases & Liquids 3: Detection, Characterization, & Control. LC 93-17795. (Illus.). 292p. 1993. 85.00 (*0-306-44485-2*, Plenum Pr) Plenum.
— Particles on Surfaces: Detection, Adhesion, & Removal, Vol. 1. LC 88-28841. (Illus.). 394p. 1988. 95.00 (*0-306-43030-4*, Plenum Pr) Plenum.
— Particles on Surfaces: Detection Adhesion & Removal, Vol. 2. (Illus.). 336p. 1989. 89.50 (*0-306-43367-2*, Plenum Pr) Plenum.
— Particles on Surfaces: Detection, Adhesion, & Removal, Vol. 3. (Illus.). 324p. (C). 1992. 89.50 (*0-306-44180-2*, Plenum Pr) Plenum.
— Physicochemical Aspects of Polymer Surfaces, Vol. 1. 610p. 1983. 115.00 (*0-306-41189-X*, Plenum Pr) Plenum.
— Physicochemical Aspects of Polymer Surfaces, Vol. 2. 652p. 1983. 115.00 (*0-306-41190-3*, Plenum Pr) Plenum.
— Polyimides: Synthesis, Characterization & Applications, 2 vols., Vol. 1. 586p. 1984. 125.00 (*0-306-41670-0*, Plenum Pr) Plenum.
— Polyimides: Synthesis, Characterization & Applications, 2 vols., Vol. 2. 564p. 1984. 125.00 (*0-306-41673-5*, Plenum Pr) Plenum.
— Silanes & Other Coupling Agents. 588p. 1992. 147.50 (*90-6764-142-1*) Coronet Bks.
— Solution Chemistry of Surfactants, 2 vols., Vol. 1. LC 79-15067. 542p. 1979. 105.00 (*0-306-40174-6*, Plenum Pr) Plenum.
— Solution Chemistry of Surfactants, 2 vols., Vol. 2. LC 79-15067. 460p. 1979. 105.00 (*0-306-40175-4*, Plenum Pr) Plenum.
— Surfactants in Solution, 3 Vols., Set. LC 83-19170. 712p. 1984. 325.00 (*0-685-07795-0*, Plenum Pr) Plenum.
— Surfactants in Solution, Set, Vols. 7-10. (Illus.). 2107p. 1990. Set. 395.00 (*0-685-51856-6*, Plenum Pr) Plenum.
— Surfactants in Solution, 3 Vols., Vol. 1. LC 83-19170. 712p. 1984. 125.00 (*0-306-41483-X*, Plenum Pr) Plenum.
— Surfactants in Solution, 3 Vols., Vol. 2. LC 83-19170. 718p. 1984. 125.00 (*0-306-41484-8*, Plenum Pr) Plenum.
— Surfactants in Solution, 3 Vols., Vol. 3. LC 83-19170. 740p. 1984. 125.00 (*0-306-41485-6*, Plenum Pr) Plenum.
— Surfactants in Solution, Vol. 7. (Illus.). 535p. 1989. 125.00 (*0-306-43332-X*, Plenum Pr) Plenum.
— Surfactants in Solution, Vol. 8. LC 83-19170. (Illus.). 476p. 1990. 125.00 (*0-306-43333-8*, Plenum Pr) Plenum.
— Surfactants in Solution, Vol. 9. (Illus.). 548p. 1989. 125.00 (*0-306-43334-6*, Plenum Pr) Plenum.
— Surfactants in Solution, Vol. 10. (Illus.). 548p. 1989. 125.00 (*0-306-43335-4*, Plenum Pr) Plenum.
— Surfactants in Solution, Vol. 4. 550p. 1987. 135.00 (*0-306-42468-1*, Plenum Pr) Plenum.
— Surfactants in Solution, Vol. 4, Set, Vols. 5 & 6. 550p. 1987. Set with Vol. 5 & 6. 325.00 (*0-685-18004-2*, Plenum Pr) Plenum.
— Surfactants in Solution, Vol. 5. 575p. 1987. 135.00 (*0-306-42469-X*, Plenum Pr) Plenum.
— Surfactants in Solution, Vol. 5, Set, Vols. 4 & 6. 575p. 1987. Set with Vol. 4 & 6. 325.00 (*0-685-18005-0*, Plenum Pr) Plenum.
— Surfactants in Solution, Vol. 6. 600p. 1987. 135.00 (*0-306-42470-3*, Plenum Pr) Plenum.
— Surfactants in Solution, Vol. 6, Set, Vols. 4 & 5. 600p. 1987. Set with Vol.4 & 5. 325.00 (*0-685-18006-9*, Plenum Pr) Plenum.
— Treatise on Clean Surface Technology, Vol. 1. 326p. 1987. 89.50 (*0-306-42420-7*, Plenum Pr) Plenum.
Mittal, K. L. & Shah, D. O., eds. Surfactants in Solution, Vol. 11. (Illus.). 658p. (C). 1992. 149.50 (*0-306-44186-1*, Plenum Pr) Plenum.
Mittal, K. L., et al, eds. Solution Behavior of Surfactants: Theoretical & Applied Aspects, 2 vols., Vol. 1. LC 82-10120. 770p. 1982. 125.00 (*0-306-41025-7*, Plenum Pr) Plenum.
— Solution Behavior of Surfactants: Theoretical & Applied Aspects, 2 vols., Vol. 2. LC 82-10120. 822p. 1982. 125.00 (*0-306-41026-5*, Plenum Pr) Plenum.
Mittal, Kamala. History of Bhopal State: Development of Constitution, Administration & National Awakening, 1901-1949. 232p. 1990. reprint ed. 28.50 (*81-215-0474-0*, Pub. by M Manoharial II) Coronet Bks.
Mittal, Kamla. History of Bhopal State: Development of Constitution, Administration & National Awakening, 1901-1949. 1990. 25.00 (*0-685-37832-2*, Pub. by Munshiram Manoharial II) S Asia.
Mittal, M. Supreme Court on Sales Tax (1950-1988) (C). 1988. 150.00 (*0-685-27885-9*) St Mut.
Mittal, M., jt. auth. see Gupta, A.
Mittal, M. M. Law Relating to Highways. (C). 1968. 45.00 (*0-685-39687-8*) St Mut.
***Mittal, Mukta, ed.** Women in India: Today & Tomorrow. (C). 1995. 40.00x (*81-7488-035-6*, Pub. by Anmol II) S Asia.
Mittal, S. C., jt. ed. see Datta, V. N.
Mittal, S. N. Taxation Policies & Financial Decisions. (C). 1988. 200.00 (*0-685-36451-8*) St Mut.
Mittal, S. P., jt. auth. see Goel, D. P.
Mitteis, Ludwig. Reichsrecht und Volksrecht in Den Ostlichen Provinzen Des Romiscshen Kaiserreichs. xiv, 562p. 1984. reprint ed. write for info. (*3-487-00502-6*, Pub. by Georg Olms GW) Lubrecht & Cramer.
Mitteis, Ludwig & Wilcken, Ulrich. Grundzuge und Chrestomathie der Papyruskunde, 4 vols., Set. cix, 1744p. 1978. reprint ed. write for info. (*0-318-70787-X*, Pub. by Georg Olms GW) Lubrecht & Cramer.
Mittelbach, H. R. The Injured Hand: A Handbook for General & Clinical Practice. (Illus.). 1979. 63.00 (*0-387-90365-8*) Spr-Verlag.
Mittelberg, David. Strangers in Paradise: The Israel Kibbutz Experience. 308p. 1988. 34.95 (*0-88738-183-9*) Transaction Pubs.
Mittelberg, Mark, jt. auth. see Hybels, Bill.
Mittelberger, Ernest. The Wine Cellar Record. Sullivan, Maurice & Roux, Henry, eds. (Illus.). 1979. 32.50 (*0-932664-06-7*) Wine Appreciation.
Mittelberger, Ernest, jt. auth. see Lamb, Richard.
Mittelberger, Gottlieb. Journey to Pennsylvania. Handlin, Oscar & Clive, John, eds. LC 60-11555. (John Harvard Library Ser.). 122p. reprint ed. pap. 34.80 (*0-317-30006-7*, 2051866) Bks Demand.
Mittelbrunn, Juan R., et al, eds. Strings & Superstrings: Proceedings of the XVIII International Gift Seminar on Theoretical Physics. 300p. (C). 1988. pap. 46.00 (*9971-5-0524-X*) World Scientific Pub.
Mittell, P., ed. see Paganini, N.
Mittelman, James H. Ideology & Politics in Uganda: From Obote to Amin. LC 75-14712. (Illus.). 304p. 1975. 36.95 (*0-8014-0946-2*) Cornell U Pr.
— Out from Underdevelopment: Prospects for the Third World. 250p. 1988. text ed. 39.95 (*0-312-01188-1*); pap. 12.95 (*0-312-01189-X*) St Martin.
Mittelstadt, Jennifer. Baby Kermit Toes to Noes. (Golden Sturdy Shape Bks.). (Illus.). 14p. (J). 1994. write for info. (*0-307-12496-7*, Golden Bks) Western Pub.
— Muppet Babies Busy Baby Kermit! (Golden Cozy Bks.). (Illus.). 8p. (J). 1994. write for info. (*0-307-13352-4*, Golden Bks) Western Pub.
— What Does Baby Fozzie Hear? (Baby's First Bks.). (Illus.). 12p. (J). 1994. write for info. (*0-307-06033-0*, Golden Bks) Western Pub.
Mittelstaedt, Carol A. Abdominal Ultrasound. LC 86-17143. (Illus.). 734p. reprint ed. pap. 180.00 (*0-7837-6264-X*, 2045976) Bks Demand.
Mittelstaedt, Carol A., ed. General Ultrasound. (Illus.). 1231p. 1992. text ed. 225.00 (*0-443-08735-0*) Churchill.
Mittelstaedt, P., jt. ed. see Lahti, P. J.
Mittelstaedt, Peter. Philosophical Problems of Modern Physics. Cohen, R. S., ed. LC 72-92534. (Boston Studies in the Philosophy of Science: No. 18). 211p. 1975. pap. 17.50 (*0-685-02827-5*) Kluwer Ac.
Mittelstrass, Juergen & Manfred, Riedel, eds. Vernuenftiges Denken. (C). 1978. 119.25 (*3-11-006956-3*) De Gruyter.
Mittelstrass, Jurgen. Zukunft Des Alterns und Gesellschaftliche Entwicklung. Baltes, Paul B., ed. (Akademie der Wissenschaften zu Berlin, Forschungsbericht Ser.: No. 5). xvi, 814p. (GER.). (C). 1992. pap. text ed. 113.85 (*3-11-013248-6*) De Gruyter.
Mittelstrass, Jurgen, jt. ed. see Brown, James R.
Mittelstrass, Jurgen, jt. auth. see Carrier, Martin.
Mittelstrass, Muriel. Creative Giftwrapping for Busy People. Pickens, Judy, ed. (Illus.). 98p. (Orig.). 1990. pap. text ed. 8.95 (*0-9626345-0-6*) Gem Investment.
Mittemeijer, E. J., ed. ASM Heat Treatment & Surface Engineering Conference. 932p. 1992. 220.00 (*0-87849-642-4*, Pub. by Trans Tech GW) LPS Dist Ctr.
— ASM Heat Treatment & Surface Engineering Conference II. (Materials Science Forum Ser.: Vols. 163-5). (Illus.). 800p. (C). 1994. text ed. 200.00 (*0-87849-678-5*, Pub. by Trans Tech SZ) LPS Dist Ctr.
Mittemeijer, E. J., jt. ed. see Delhez, R.
Mitten, David G., jt. auth. see Kozloff, Arielle P.
Mitten, Richard H. The Politics of Antisemitic Prejudice: The Waldheim Phenomenon in Austria. (Special Studies in West European Politics & Society). 261p. 1992. text ed. 52.00 (*0-8133-7630-0*) Westview.
Mittenthal, Jay E. & Baskin, Arthur B., eds. Principles of Organization in Organisms: Proceeding of the Workshop on Principles of Organization in Organisms Held June 1990 in Santa Fe, New Mexico. LC 92-17985. (Santa Fe Institute Studies in the Sciences of Complexity: Vol. 13). (C). 1992. 54.95 (*0-201-52765-0*) Addison-Wesley.
Mittenthal, Suzanne M. The Baltimore Trail Book. rev. ed. Poultney, James W., ed. LC 82-21216. (Illus.). 176p. (Orig.). 1983. pap. 11.95 (*0-8018-2943-7*) Johns Hopkins.
Mitter. Hindu Festivals, Reading Level 4. (Holidays & Festivals Ser.: Set II). (Illus.). 48p. (J). (gr. 3-8). 1989. lib. bdg. 14.60 (*0-86592-986-6*) Rourke Corp.
Mitter, H. & Lang, C. B., eds. Recent Developments in High Energy Physics. (Acta Physica Austriaca Ser.: Suppl. 25). (Illus.). 547p. 1983. 93.00 (*0-387-81771-9*) Spr-Verlag.
Mitter, H. & Pittner, L., eds. Stochastic Methods & Computer Techniques in Quantum Dynamics. (Acta Physica Austriaca Ser.: Supplementum 26). (Illus.). vi, 452p. 1984. 82.00 (*0-387-81835-9*) Spr-Verlag.
Mitter, H. & Plessas, W., eds. Nucleon-Nucleon & Nucleon-Antinucleon Interactions. (Acta Physica Austriaca Ser.: Suppl. 27). (Illus.). 724p. 1986. 114.00 (*0-387-81900-2*) Spr-Verlag.
Mitter, H. & Schweiger, W., eds. Fields & Particles: Proceedings of the XXIX Int. Universitatswochen fur Kernphysik, Schladming, Austria, March 1990. (Illus.). 304p. 1991. 62.00 (*0-387-53178-5*) Spr-Verlag.
Mitter, H., jt. ed. see Latal, H.
Mitter, H., et al, eds. Recent Aspects of Quantum Fields: Proceedings of the XXX Int. Universitatswochen fur Kernphysik, Schladming, Austria February & March 1991. (Lecture Notes in Physics Ser.: Vol. 396). xiii, 332p. 1992. 55.00 (*0-685-54830-9*) Spr-Verlag.
Mitter, P., jt. ed. see Diekmann, A.
Mitter, Partha. Art & Nationalism in Colonial India: Occidental Orientations. (Illus.). 512p. (C). 1995. 89.95 (*0-521-44354-7*) Cambridge U Pr.
— Much Maligned Monsters: A History of European Reactions to Indian Art. (Illus.). 376p. 1992. pap. text ed. 17.95 (*0-226-53239-9*) U Ch Pr.
Mitter, Partha & Herwitz, Daniel A. Indian Art Today: Four Artists from the Chester & Davida Herwitz Family Collection. LC 85-32106. (Illus.). 56p. 1986. pap. 10.00 (*0-943044-07-3*) Phillips Coll.
Mitter, S. & Gill, K. S., eds. Computer-Aided Manufacturing & Women's Employment: The Clothing Industry in Four EC Countries. (Artificial Intelligence & Society Ser.). (Illus.). 192p. 1991. pap. 70.00 (*0-387-19656-0*) Spr-Verlag.
Mitter, S. K., tr. see Lions, J. L.
Mitter, Sara S. Dharma's Daughters: Contemporary Indian Women & Hindu Culture. LC 90-19387. (Illus.). 250p. (C). 1991. text ed. 40.00 (*0-8135-1677-3*); pap. 12.95 (*0-8135-1678-1*) Rutgers U Pr.
Mitter, Shomit. Systems of Rehearsal: Stanislavsky, Brecht, Grotowski & Peter Brook. LC 92-43. 224p. 1992. 59.95 (*0-415-06783-9*, A7097); pap. 15.95 (*0-415-06784-7*, A7101) Routledge.
Mitter Swasti. Common Fate, Common Bond. (C). 1986. pap. text ed. 17.50 (*0-7453-0026-X*) Westview.
Mitter, Swasti, jt. auth. see Rowbotham, Sheila.
Mitter, Wolfgang. Secondary School Graduation: University Entrance Qualification in Socialist Countries. LC 77-30471. 1979. 57.00 (*0-08-022237-4*, Pub. by Pergamon Repr UK) Franklin.
Mitterand, ed. see Zola, Emile.
Mitterand, Francois. The Fist & the Rose. LC 74-82724. write for info. (*0-89388-183-X*) Okpaku Communications.
Mitterand, Frederic. Monte Carlo: A Living Legend. LC 94-16537. (Illus.). 176p. 1994. 45.00 (*0-86565-953-2*) Vendome.
Mitterand, Henri. Mots Francais. 128p. 1968. 9.95 (*0-8288-7461-1*) Fr & Eur.
Mitterand, Henri, jt. auth. see DuBois, Jean M.
Mitterand, Henri, ed. see Zola, Emile.
Mitterauer, Michael. A History of Youth. Dunphy, Graeme, tr. LC 92-15432. (Family, Sexuality & Social Relations in Past Times Ser.). 1992. 49.95 (*0-631-17983-6*); pap. 19.95 (*0-631-17984-4*) Blackwell Pubs.
Mitterauer, Michael & Sieder, Reinhard. The European Family: Patriarchy to Partnership from the Middle Ages to the Present. Oosterveen, Karla & Horzinger, Reinhard, trs. LC 81-21954. xvi, 236p. (C). 1984. pap. text ed. 13.95 (*0-226-53241-0*) U Ch Pr.
Mitterer, Felix. Siberia & Other Plays. (Studies in Austrian Literature, Culture, & Thought. Translation Ser.). 1994. pap. 33.50 (*0-929497-68-6*) Ariadne CA.

—The Wild Woman & Other Plays. Hanlin, Todd C. & Hutchinson, Heidi, trs. LC 94-43185. (Studies in Austrian Literature, Culture, & Thought: Translation). 1995. pap. 28.00 (*1-57241-002-7*) Ariadne CA.

Mitterer, Franz, ed. see Byrn, Anne.
Mittermaier, Karl. The Hand Behind the Invisible Hand. 288p. (C). 1929. text ed. 65.00 (*0-8133-8106-1*) Westview.
Mittermann, Harald & Schendl, Herbert, eds. A Concordance to the Novels of John Lyly. (Elizabethan Concordance Ser.: Vol. 2). 904p. 1984. lib. bdg. 245.70 (*3-487-07564-4*, Pub. by Georg Olms GW) Lubrecht & Cramer.
Mittermann, Lauren. Different Paths: Poems by Lauren Mittermann. 52p. 1994. pap. 6.95 (*0-9638558-0-8*) Maple Grove.
***Mittermeier, Russell A., et al.** Lemurs of Madagascar. LC 94-72352. (Illus.). 360p. 1994. pap. 25.00 (*1-881173-08-9*) Conser Intl.
Mittermeijer, E. J., jt. ed. see Delhez, R.
Mittermeir, R., ed. Shifting Paradigms in Software Engineering: Proceedings of the 7th Joint Conference of the Austrian Computer Society (OCG) & the John Von Neumann Society for Computing Sciences (NJSZT) in Klagenfurt, Austria, 1992. (Illus.). x, 252p. 1992. pap. 38.00 (*0-387-82408-1*) Spr-Verlag.
Mittermeyer, Helen. Til We Meet Again. (Loveswept Ser.: No. 621). 1993. pap. 3.50 (*0-553-44243-0*, Loveswept) Bantam.
— The Veil. 416p. (Orig.). 1996. mass mkt. 5.99 (*0-446-60263-9*) Warner Bks.
***Mitterrand, Francois.** The Wheat & the Chaff. LC 82-3156. 284p. 1982. 16.95 (*0-86579-022-1*) Seaver Bks.
— The Wheat & the Chaff. LC 82-3156. 284p. 1982. pap. 7.95 (*0-86579-026-4*) Seaver Bks.
Mittet, A. Norway Pictures. (Illus.). 88p. (ENG, FRE, GER & NOR.). 1989. 45.00 (*82-7182-069-9*, N437) Vanous.
Mittiga, Linda, jt. auth. see Berger, E. Roy.
Mittins, Bill. Language Awareness for Teachers. (English, Language & Education Ser.). 160p. 1990. pap. 27.00 (*0-335-09559-3*, Open Univ Pr) Taylor & Francis.
Mittl, John. Astral Projection (Modus Operandi) 8p. 1993. reprint ed. spiral bd. 3.30 (*0-7873-0620-7*) Mokelumne.
Mittlebeeler, Emmet V. African Custom & Western Law: The Development of the Rhodesian Criminal Law for Africans. LC 73-86268. 250p. (C). 1976. 49.50 (*0-8419-0107-4*, Africana) Holmes & Meier.
Mittleholzer, Edgar. Corentyne Thunder. (Caribbean Writers Ser.). 229p. 1970. pap. 8.95 (*0-435-98593-0*) Heinemann.
Mittleider, Jacob R. Grow-Bed Gardening. LC 85-31475. (Illus.). 200p. (Orig.). 1986. pap. 14.95 (*0-88007-144-3*) Woodbridge Pr.
— More Food from Your Garden: The Mittleider Method of Grow Box-Greenhouse Gardening. LC 82-704759. (Illus.). 196p. 1982. pap. 11.95 (*0-912800-72-0*) Woodbridge Pr.
— 6 Steps to Successful Gardening. Hall, Leo D., ed. (Illus.). 80p. 1995. pap. 8.95 (*0-914107-04-6*) Lion House Pr.

An Asterisk (*) at the beginning of an entry indicates that the title is appearing in BIP for the first time.

Mittleman, Alan L. Between Kant & Kabbalah: An Introduction to Isaac Breuer's Philosophy of Judaism. LC 89-34101. (SUNY Series in Judaica Hermeneutics, Mysticism, & Religion). 227p. 1990. 59.50 (*0-7914-0239-8*); pap. 19.95 (*0-7914-0240-1*) State U NY Pr.

Mittleman, Don. BASIC Computing. 430p. (C). 1982. pap. text ed. 19.00 (*0-15-504910-0*) HB Coll Pubs.

Mittleman, M. H., ed. Introduction to the Theory of Laser-Atom Interactions: Physics of Atoms & Molecules Ser. 2nd ed. (Illus.). 260p. (C). 1993. 59.50 (*0-306-44432-1*, Plenum Pr) Plenum.

Mittlemann, Hans D. & Roose, Dirk, eds. Continuation Techniques & Bifurcation Problems. (International Series of Numerical Mathematics: No. 92). 225p. 1990. 64.00 (*0-8176-2397-3*) Birkhauser.

***Mittler.** Innovations in Family Support for People with Learning Disabilities. 288p. 1995. pap. 26.00 (*1-870335-15-5*) P H Brookes.

Mittler-Battipaglia, Diana. Franz Mittler: Austro-American Composer, Musician, & Humorous Poet. LC 93-25240. (Austrian Culture Ser.: Vol. 8). 178p. (C). 1994. text ed. 42.95 (*0-8204-2063-8*) P Lang Pubs.

Mittler, Elliott. Natural Hazard Policy Setting: Identifying Supporters & Opponents of Nonstructural Hazard Mitigation. (Program on Environment & Behavior Monograph Ser.: No. 48). 282p. (Orig.). (C). 1989. pap. 10.00 (*0-685-28122-1*) Natural Hazards.

— Natural Hazards Policy Setting: Identifying Supporters & Opponents of Nonstructural Hazard Mitigation. (Program on Environment & Behavior Monograph Ser.: No. 48). 282p. 1989. 10.00 (*0-685-62420-X*) Natural Hazards.

***Mittler, Helle & Mittler, Peter.** Families Speak Out: International Perspectives on Families' Experiences of Disability. LC 94-38388. 1994. pap. 10.95 (*1-57129-001-X*) Brookline Bks.

Mittler, Mary L., jt. ed. see Bers, Trudy H.

Mittler, P. J., jt. ed. see Hogg, J.

Mittler, P. J., jt. ed. see Hogg, James.

Mittler, Peter, ed. Psychological Assessment of Mental & Physical Handicaps. 886p. 1974. pap. 33.00 (*0-422-75600-8*, NO. 2819, Pub. by Tavistock UK) Routledge Chapman & Hall.

Mittler, Peter & McConachie, Helen, eds. Parents, Professionals & Mentally Handicapped People: Approaches to Partnership. LC 84-23751. 243p. 1984. reprint ed. pap. text ed. 17.95 (*0-914797-12-3*) Brookline Bks.

Mittler, Peter, ed. see Hart, S. & Mongon, D.

Mittler, Peter, jt. ed. see Hogg, James.

Mittler, Peter, ed. see Lowe, P.

Mittler, Peter, jt. auth. see Mittler, Helle.

Mittler, Peter, ed. see Montgomery, D.

Mittler, Peter, ed. see Norwich, Brahm.

Mittler, Peter, ed. see Robson, B.

Mittler, Peter, et al, eds. World Yearbook of Education, 1993: Special Needs Education. 304p. 1993. 65.00 (*0-7494-0854-5*, Pub. by Kogan Page Educ UK) Taylor & Francis.

***Mittler, Thomas E., et al, eds.** Annual Review of Entomology, Vol. 40. 1995. lib. bdg. 47.00 (*0-8243-0140-4*) Annual Reviews.

Mittler, Thomas E., jt. ed. see Smith, Ray F.

Mittler, Thomas E., et al, eds. Annual Review of Entomology, Vol. 22. LC 56-5750. (Illus.). 1977. 40.00 (*0-8243-0122-6*) Annual Reviews.

— Annual Review of Entomology, Vol. 23. LC 56-5750. (Illus.). 1978. 40.00 (*0-8243-0123-4*) Annual Reviews.

— Annual Review of Entomology, Vol. 24. LC 56-5750. (Illus.). 1979. 40.00 (*0-8243-0124-2*) Annual Reviews.

— Annual Review of Entomology, Vol. 25. LC 56-5750. (Illus.). 1980. 40.00 (*0-8243-0125-0*) Annual Reviews.

— Annual Review of Entomology, Vol. 26. LC 56-5750. (Illus.). 1981. 40.00 (*0-8243-0126-9*) Annual Reviews.

— Annual Review of Entomology, Vol. 27. LC 56-5750. (Illus.). 1982. 40.00 (*0-8243-0127-7*) Annual Reviews.

— Annual Review of Entomology, Vol. 28. LC 56-5750. (Illus.). 1983. 40.00 (*0-8243-0128-5*) Annual Reviews.

— Annual Review of Entomology, Vol. 29. LC 56-5750. (Illus.). 1984. 40.00 (*0-8243-0129-3*) Annual Reviews.

— Annual Review of Entomology, Vol. 30. LC 56-5750. (Illus.). 1985. 40.00 (*0-8243-0130-7*) Annual Reviews.

— Annual Review of Entomology, Vol. 31. LC 56-5750. (Illus.). 1986. text ed. 40.00 (*0-8243-0131-5*) Annual Reviews.

— Annual Review of Entomology, Vol. 32. LC 56-5750. (Illus.). 1987. text ed. 40.00 (*0-8243-0132-3*) Annual Reviews.

— Annual Review of Entomology, Vol. 33. (Illus.). 1988. text ed. 40.00 (*0-8243-0133-1*) Annual Reviews.

— Annual Review of Entomology, Vol. 34. (Illus.). 1989. text ed. 40.00 (*0-8243-0134-X*) Annual Reviews.

— Annual Review of Entomology, Vol. 35. 1990. text ed. 40.00 (*0-8243-0135-8*) Annual Reviews.

— Annual Review of Entomology, Vol. 36. 1991. text ed. 40.00 (*0-8243-0136-6*) Annual Reviews.

— Annual Review of Entomology, Vol. 37. 1992. text ed. 44.00 (*0-8243-0137-4*) Annual Reviews.

— Annual Review of Entomology, Vol. 38. (Illus.). 1993. text ed. 44.00 (*0-8243-0138-2*) Annual Reviews.

— Annual Review of Entomology, Vol. 39. (Illus.). 1994. text ed. 47.00 (*0-8243-0139-0*) Annual Reviews.

Mittlestaedt, P., jt. ed. see Lahti, P. J.

***Mittman.** Bridge to Yesterday. 1995. mass mkt. 4.50 (*0-06-108364-X*, Harp PBks) HarpC.

Mittman, Barbara G. Spectators on the Paris Stage in the Seventeenth & Eighteenth Centuries. LC 84-16339. (Theater & Dramatic Studies: No. 25). (Illus.). 170p. reprint ed. pap. 48.50 (*0-8357-1610-4*, 2070484) Bks Demand.

Mittman, Elizabeth, jt. ed. see Joeres, Ruth-Ellen B.

Mittman, Karin & Ihsan, Zatar, eds. Culture Shock Pakistan. (Illus.). 1991. pap. 10.95 (*1-55868-059-4*) Gr Arts Ctr Pub.

Mittnik, S., ed. System-Theoretic Methods in Economic Modelling, No. II. (International Series in Modern Applied Mathematics & Computer Science: No. 22). 209p. 1989. 44.00 (*0-08-037932-X*, Pergamon Pr) Elsevier.

— System-Theoretic Methods in Economic Modelling I. (International Series in Modern Applied Mathematics & Computer Science). 184p. 1989. 44.00 (*0-08-037228-7*, Pergamon Pr) Elsevier.

Mitton. Histoire de la Presse Francaise, 2 vols., Set. (FRE.). write for info. (*0-8288-7903-6*) Fr & Eur.

— Histoire de la Presse Francaise, 2 vols., Set. Incl. Tome I. Des Origines a la Revolution. (*0-318-52020-6*); Tome II. Sous la Revolution, le Consulat, l'Empire. (*0-318-52021-4*); 11.90 (*0-685-34002-3*) Fr & Eur.

Mitton, C. Leslie. Ephesians. Black, Matthew, ed. (New Century Bible Commentary Ser.). 256p. 1981. pap. 15.99 (*0-8028-1907-9*) Eerdmans.

Mitton, David & Permane, Terry, photos. Edward's Exploit. LC 92-23189. (Thomas the Tank Engine Picturebacks Ser.). (Illus.). 32p. (J). (ps-3). 1993. pap. 2.25 (*0-679-83896-1*) Random Bks Yng Read.

— Thomas the Tank Engine Storybook. LC 92-35915. (Illus.). (J). 1993. 8.00 (*0-679-84465-1*) Random Bks Yng Read.

Mitton, David, et al, photos. James in a Mess & Other Thomas the Tank Engine Stories. LC 92-25654. (Pictureback Ser.). (Illus.). 32p. (J). (ps-3). 1993. pap. 2.50 (*0-679-83895-3*) Random Bks Yng Read.

Mitton, G. E., ed. see Scott, James G.

Mitton, Jacqueline. Discovering the Planets. LC 90-11020. (Exploring the Universe Ser.). (Illus.). 32p. (J). (gr. 4-6). 1991. lib. bdg. 11.89 (*0-8167-2130-0*); pap. text ed. 3.95 (*0-8167-2131-9*) Troll Assocs.

— Key Definitions in Astronomy. LC 82-183. (Quality Paperback Ser.: No. 375). 174p. (Orig.). (C). 1982. pap. text ed. 13.00 (*0-8226-0375-6*) Littlefield.

— The Penguin Dictionary of Astronomy. (Illus.). 432p. 1993. pap. 12.95 (*0-14-051226-8*, Penguin Bks) Viking Penguin.

Mitton, Jacqueline, ed. A Concise Dictionary of Astronomy. 284p. 1992. 24.95 (*0-19-853967-3*) OUP.

Mitton, Jacqueline, ed. see Spencer, John G.

***Mitton, Jay.** Cover Your Assets. 1995. pap. 14.00 (*0-517-88518-2*, Crown) Crown Pub Group.

Mitton, Jeffry B. & Sturgeon, Kareen B., eds. Bark Beetles in North American Conifers: A System for the Study of Evolutionary Biology. (Corrie Herring Hooks Ser.: No. 6). (Illus.). 539p. (C). 1982. text ed. 30.00 (*0-292-70735-5*); pap. 17.50 (*0-292-70744-4*) U of Tex Pr.

***Mitton, Jennifer.** Fadimatu. Date not set. pap. 14.95 (*0-86492-121-7*, Pub. by Goose Ln Edits CN) InBook.

***Mitton, Michael.** The Soul of Celtic Spirituality: In the Lives of Its Saints. 160p. (Orig.). 1996. pap. 9.95 (*0-89622-662-X*) Twenty-Third.

Mitton, Simon, tr. see Heidmann, Jean.

***Mittoo-Walker, Dorothy E.** The Magical Fountain of Love. (Illus.). 48p. 1994. 10.00 (*0-912444-33-9*) DARE Bks.

Mittra, R. A., ed. Computer Techniques for Electromagnetics. 416p. (C). 1973. 175.00 (*0-08-016888-4*, Pub. by Pergamon Repr UK) Franklin.

Mittra, Raj, ed. Computer Techniques For Electromagnetics. (Summa Bks.). 403p. 1973. reprint ed. 172.00 (*0-89116-748-X*); reprint ed. pap. 67.00 (*0-89116-820-6*) Hemisp Pub.

Mittra, Sid. Practicing Financial Planning: A Complete Guide for Professionals. (Illus.). 658p. (C). 1993. pap. 29.95 (*0-9636527-0-2*) Mittra & Assocs.

Mittra, Sitansu S. Principles of Relational Database Design. 336p. 1990. text ed. 65.00 (*0-13-716796-2*) P-H.

Mittring, Karl E., tr. see Ridderbos, N. H.

Mittwede, S. K. & Stoddard, E. F., eds. Ultramafic Rocks of the Appalachian Piedmont. (Special Paper Ser.: No. 231). 110p. 1989. pap. 14.00 (*0-8137-2231-4*) Geol Soc.

Mittwer, Henry. Zen Flowers: Chabana for the Tea Ceremony. 142p. 1992. 14.95 (*0-8048-1882-7*) C E Tuttle.

Mitty, Ethel L., ed. Mechanisms of Quality in Long-Term Care: Education. LC 93-30194. 1993. 25.95 (*0-88737-602-9*) Natl League Nurse.

— Quality Imperatives in Long-Term Care: The Elusive Agenda. (NLN-Ross Laboratories Long-Term Care Conferences Ser.). 128p. (Orig.). (C). 1992. pap. text ed. 22.95 (*0-88737-536-7*, 41-2440) Natl League Nurse.

Mitty, Harold A., et al. Genitourinary Tract Disease Test & Syllabus. LC 92-21930. (Professional Self-Evaluation & Continuing Education Program Ser.: Vol. 33). (Illus.). 650p. 1992. 175.00 (*1-55903-033-X*) Am Coll Radiology.

Mitwirkung. Dictionary of Modern Written Arabic: Arabisches Woerterbuch fuer die Schriftsprache der Gegenwart. 5th ed. (ARA & GER.). 1984. 295.00 (*0-8288-0193-2*, F57980) Fr & Eur.

Mitzel, David P., ed. Resource Development in the Two-Year College. (C). 1988. text ed. 27.95 (*0-9619545-0-7*); pap. text ed. 17.95 (*0-9619545-1-5*) Natl Coun Res Dev.

Mitzel, Harold, ed. Encyclopedia of Educational Research, 4 vols., Set. 5th ed. LC 82-2332. 1982. lib. bdg. 400.00 (*0-02-900450-0*) Macmillan.

Mitzel, John. Sports & the Macho Male. 2nd ed. 1976. pap. 2.50 (*0-915480-06-9*) Fag Rag.

Mitzel, Joseph P., ed. see American Research Corporation Staff.

Mitzlaff, Klaus von. Engines for Biogas: Theory, Modification, Economic Operation. Deutsches Zentrum fur Entwicklungs-technologien-GATE, ed. (GATE Ser.). (Illus.). 134p. 1988. pap. 17.50 (*3-528-02032-6*, Pub. by Vieweg & Sohn GW) Ballen Bkslr.

Mitzman, Arthur. The Iron Cage: An Historical Interpretation of Max Weber. 340p. (C). 1984. pap. 19.95 (*0-87855-984-1*) Transaction Pubs.

— Michelet, Historia: Rebirth & Romanticism in Nineteenth-Century France. LC 89-27244. 368p. (C). 1990. text ed. 40.00 (*0-300-04551-4*) Yale U Pr.

— Sociology & Estrangement: Three Sociologists of Imperial Germany. 370p. (C). 1986. pap. 21.95 (*0-88738-605-9*) Transaction Pubs.

Mitzman, D. Integral Bases for Affine Lie Algebras & Their Universal Enveloping Algebras. LC 85-1374. (Contemporary Mathematics Ser.: Vol. 40). 159p. 1985. pap. text ed. 27.00 (*0-8218-5043-1*, CONM-40) Am Math.

Mitzner, D. T., et al. Constitutional Problems in Church-State Relations: A Symposium. LC 75-155825. (Symposia on Law & Society Ser.). 1971. reprint ed. lib. bdg. 19.50 (*0-306-70131-6*) Da Capo.

Mitzner, Ira R. ERISA Litigation: A Basic Guide. Brennan, Mary E., ed. LC 93-78910. 186p. (Orig.). 1993. pap. 39.00 (*0-89154-466-6*) Intl Found Employ.

Miu, Denny K. Mechatronics: Electromechanics & Contromechanics. Ling, Frederick F., ed. LC 92-1604. (Mechanical Engineering Ser.). (Illus.). 264p. 1993. 59.00 (*0-387-97893-3*) Spr-Verlag.

Miu, Florea, ed. see Smarandache, Florentin.

Miura, jt. auth. see Dangman.

Miura, Akira. English in Japanese. 203p. (Orig.). (C). 1992. pap. 12.95 (*4-89684-701-6*, Pub. by Yohan Pubns JA) Weatherhill.

— English Loanwords in Japanese: A Selection. LC 78-65031. 192p. (ENG & JPN.). 1979. 14.95 (*0-8048-1248-9*) C E Tuttle.

— Japanese Words & Their Uses. LC 82-51099. 240p. 1983. pap. 12.95 (*0-8048-1639-5*) C E Tuttle.

Miura, Akira, tr. see Suzuki, Takao.

Miura, Akira, tr. see Tsuboi, Sakae.

Miura, Ayako. Freezing Point. Shimizu, H. & Terry, J., trs. (Illus.). 250p. 1987. pap. 11.95 (*0-933704-29-1*) Dawn Pr.

— A Heart of Winter. Caprio, Mark & Moneyhun, Clyde, trs. 168p. (Orig.). 1991. pap. 4.95 (*981-3009-36-5*) OMF Bks.

Miura, Einen. The Art of Marbled Paper: Marbled Papers & How to Make Them. (Illus.). 160p. 1991. 45.00 (*4-7700-1548-8*) Kodansha.

Miura, Hirofumi & Arimoto, Suguru. Robotics Research: The Fifth International Symposium. Brady et al, eds. (Artificial Intelligence Ser.). 500p. 1990. 70.00 (*0-262-13253-2*) MIT Pr.

Miura, Isshu & Sasaki, Ruth F. The Zen Koan. LC 65-19104. (Illus.). 156p. 1966. pap. 8.00 (*0-15-699981-1*, Harvest Bks) HarBrace.

Miura-Mattausch, M., jt. ed. see Treitinger, L.

***Miura, N., et al, eds.** Lowlands: Development & Management. (Illus.). 498p. (C). 1994. text ed. 99.00 (*90-5410-603-4*, Pub. by A A Balkema NE) Ashgate Pub Co.

Miura, R., ed. Some Mathematical Questions in Biology: DNA Sequence Analysis. LC 80-646696. (Lectures in Mathematics in the Life Sciences: Vol. 17). 124p. 1990. reprint ed. pap. text ed. 37.00 (*0-8218-1167-3*, LLSCI-17) Am Math.

— Some Mathematical Questions in Biology: Muscle Physiology. LC 85-28613. (Lectures in Mathematics in the Life Sciences: Vol. 16). 234p. 1986. pap. text ed. 45.00 (*0-8218-1166-5*, LLSCI-16) Am Math.

Miura, R., jt. auth. see Gross, L.

Miura, Toru, jt. ed. see Haneda, Masashi.

Miura, Yuzuru, sel. Classic Haiku: A Master's Selection. (Illus.). 120p. (Orig.). 1992. pap. 12.95 (*0-8048-1682-4*) C E Tuttle.

Miwa, Kimitada, jt. ed. see Schultz, John.

Miwa, M., et al, eds. ADP-Ribosylation, DNA Repair & Cancer: Proceedings of the 13th International Symposium of the Princess Takamatsu Cancer Research Fund, Japan, 1982. 354p. 1983. lib. bdg. 132.25 (*90-6764-003-4*, Pub. by VSP NE) Coronet Bks.

— Retroviruses in Human Lymphoma-Leukemia: Proceedings of the 15th International Symposium of the Princess Takamatsu Cancer Research Fund, Japan, 1984. 352p. 1985. lib. bdg. 142.00 (*90-6764-057-3*, Pub. by VSP NE) Coronet Bks.

Miwa, Nobuya, et al. Water & Survival in an Island Environment: Challenge of Okinawa. LC 87-50463. 176p. 1988. text ed. 25.00 (*0-8248-1174-7*, UH WRRC) UH Pr.

Miwa, Tetsuji, jt. auth. see Jimbo, Michio.

Miwa, Tetsuji, ed. see Kashiwara, M.

Miwatani, T., jt. auth. see Takeda, Yoshihiko.

Mix, et al. Biology. (C). 1992. text ed. 69.00 (*0-673-39869-2*) HarpCollege.

— Biology. (C). 1992. student ed 23.00 (*0-673-52139-7*) HarpCollege.

— Biology. (C). 1992. student ed 30.50 (*0-673-52227-X*) HarpCollege.

Mix, A. J. A Monograph of the Genus Taphrina. (Bibliotheca Mycologica Ser.: Vol.18). 1969. reprint ed. 36.00 (*3-7682-0583-5*) Lubrecht & Cramer.

Mix, Don. Stalking Big Ideas in the Advertising Jungle. LC 85-81845. (Illus.). 144p. (Orig.). 1986. 16.50 (*0-937884-11-1*, Bennington Bks) Hystry Mystry.

Mix, Dwight F. Random Signal Processing. LC 94-15146. 608p. (C). 1994. write for info. (*0-02-381852-2*) Macmillan.

Mix Editors. Sound for Picture: An Insider's Look at Audio Production in Film & Television. 144p. 1993. pap. 17.95 (*0-7935-2002-9*, 00183014) H Leonard.

Mix, Floyd M. House Wiring Simplified. rev. ed. (Illus.). 176p. 1991. text ed. 17.00 (*0-87006-869-5*) Goodheart.

Mix, James B., ed. see Sutton, Charles.

Mix, Lisa A., jt. ed. see McCall, Nancy.

Mix Magazine Staff. Music Producers: Today's Top Record Makers Discuss Their Art & Technology. 128p. 1992. pap. 17.95 (*0-7935-1418-5*, 00183004) H Leonard.

Mix, Oberst-Ing. The Development of German Aircraft Armament to 1945. 107p. reprint ed. pap. 20.95 (*0-89126-154-0*) MA-AH Pub.

Mix, Paul E. The Design & Application of Process Analysis. LC 83-21915. (Chemical Analysis Ser.: No. 1-075). 328p. 1989. 68.00 (*0-471-86518-4*) Krieger.

— Introduction to Nondestructive Testing: A Training Guide. 406p. 1987. text ed. 89.95 (*0-471-83126-3*) Wiley.

— Tom Mix: A Heavily-Illustrated Biography of the Western Star, with a Filmography. (Illus.). 304p. 1995. lib. bdg. 35.00x (*0-89950-964-9*) McFarland & Co.

Mix Software Staff. Using Multi-C: A Portable Multithreaded C Programming Library. 1993. Incl. disk. disk 29.95 (*0-13-606195-8*) P-H.

Mixco, Mauricio, tr. see Nicolau D'Olwer, Luis.

Mixco, Mauricio J. Cochimi & Proto-Yuman: Lexical & Syntactic Evidence for a New Language Family in Lower Calif. (Anthropological Papers: No. 101). 1979. pap. text ed. 15.00 (*0-87480-150-8*) U of Utah Pr.

— Kiliwa Dictionary. (Anthropological Papers: No. 109). 207p. (Orig.). 1985. pap. 27.50 (*0-87480-168-0*) U of Utah Pr.

— Kiliwa Texts: "When I Have Donned My Crest of Stars". (Anthropological Papers: No. 107). (Illus.). xvi, 307p. (Orig.). 1983. pap. 25.00 (*0-87480-219-9*) U of Utah Pr.

Mixdorf, Marcia, jt. auth. see Reynolds, Ed.

Mixer, Jennifer, jt. auth. see Miller, Regina.

Mixer, Joseph R. Principles of Professional Fundraising: Useful Foundations for Successful Practice. LC 93-14551. (Nonprofit Sector-Public Administration Ser.). 255p. 1993. 29.95 (*1-55542-590-9*) Jossey-Bass.

Mixie, Joseph R. The Athiest Trap. 56p. (C). 1994. pap. text ed. 12.75 (*0-8191-9548-0*) U Pr of Amer.

Mixon, Don. Obedience & Civilization: The Origins of Authorized Crime. 208p. 1989. text ed. 34.95 (*0-7453-0331-5*) Routledge Chapman & Hall.

Mixon, John. Texas Municipal Zoning Law. 2nd ed. 500p. 1994. ring bd. 115.00 (*0-409-25656-0*) Michie Butterworth.

— Texas Municipal Zoning Law. 2nd suppl. ed. 500p. 1993. 55.00 (*0-685-74604-6*) Butterworth Legal Pubs.

***Mixon, Myrtis.** Americana: Historical Sportlights in Story & Song. (Illus.). 112p. (Orig.). 1995. pap. 12.95 (*0-943327-13-X*) JAG Pubns.

— Americana: Historical Spotlights in Story & Song. (Illus.). 112p. (Orig.). 1995. audio, pap. 16.95 (*0-943327-15-6*) JAG Pubns.

Mixon, Roy D. The Truth about the Trinity. 43p. (Orig.). 1986. pap. 2.25 (*0-934942-64-1*, 3874) White Wing Pub.

Mixon, Shirley R. Handbook of Data Processing Administration, Operations & Procedures. LC 75-38914. 405p. reprint ed. pap. 115.50 (*0-317-20748-2*, 2023901) Bks Demand.

***Mixon, Wayne.** The People's Writer: Erskine Caldwell & the South. LC 95-8291. (Minds of the New South Ser.). (Illus.). 256p. (C). 1995. 27.50 (*0-8139-1627-5*) U Pr of Va.

Mixson, Wayne, intro. Florida Golf Directory, Nineteen Eighty-Five. 194p. (Orig.). 1985. pap. 8.95 (*0-913041-01-7*) Golfweek Ltd.

— Florida Golf Directory, Nineteen Eighty-Six. 110p. (Orig.). 1986. pap. 8.95 (*0-913041-02-5*) Golfweek Ltd.

Mixter, ed. see Bronson, Gary.

Mixter, ed. see Bronson, Gary & Menconi, Steve.

Mixter, ed. see Bronson, Gary & Menconi, Stephen J.

Mixter, ed. see Dewey, Fred M.

Mixter, ed. see Driver, George N.

Mixter, ed. see Hahn, Cynthia.

Mixter, ed. see Hodes, Elizabeth, et al.

Mixter, ed. see Kumar, Ram & Agrawal, Rakesh.

Mixter, ed. see Nagler, Eric P.

Mixter, ed. see Umland, Jean.

Mixter, ed. see Venit, Stewart M.

Mixter, ed. see Venit, Stewart M. & Schleiffers, Sandra M.

Mixter, ed. see Venit, Stewart M. & Subramanian, P. K.

Mixter, ed. see Walter, Kenneth.

Mixter, ed. see Wen, David Y. & Whipple, Grey G.

Mixter, George W. & Headley, Herrold, eds. Primer of Navigation. 632p. 1994. 35.00 (*0-393-03508-5*) Norton.

Mixter, Timothy, jt. ed. see Kingston-Mann, Esther.

Miya, K. Magnetomechanics in Magnetic Fusion Reactor Technology. (Series in Theoretical & Applied Mechanics: Vol. 7). 400p. (C). 1993. text ed. 64.00 (*9971-5-0726-9*) World Scientific Pub.

Miya, K., jt. ed. see Yamamoto, Y.

Miyadera, Isao. Nonlinear Semigroups. Cho, Choong Y., tr. LC 92-11318. (Translations of Mathematical Monographs: Vol. 109). 230p. 1992. 99.00 (*0-8218-4565-9*) Am Math.

Miyagawa, Shigeru. Elementary Japanese 1. (Illus.). 50p. (Orig.). (JPN.). (C). 1990. teacher ed, pap. 5.00 (*0-87415-162-7*, 67A); student ed, pap. text ed. 25.00 (*0-87415-161-9*, 67) OSU Foreign Lang.

— Elementary Japanese 1, 2 cass., Set. (Orig.). (JPN.). (C). 1990. audio 10.00 (*0-87415-163-5*, 67B) OSU Foreign Lang.

— Elementary Japanese 2. 45p. (Orig.). (JPN.). (C). 1990. teacher ed, pap. 5.00 (*0-87415-165-1*, 68A); student ed, pap. text ed. 20.00 (*0-87415-164-3*, 68) OSU Foreign Lang.

— Elementary Japanese 2, 2 cass., Set. (Orig.). (JPN.). (C). 1990. audio 10.00 (*0-87415-166-X*, 68B) OSU Foreign Lang.

Miyagawa, Shigeru & Anderson, Stephen, eds. Syntax & Semantics, Vol. 22: Structure & Case Marking in Japanese. 259p. 1989. text ed. 108.00 (*0-12-613522-3*); pap. text ed. 55.00 (*0-12-606103-3*) Acad Pr.

Miyagawa, Torao, et al. Chinese Painting. Birnbaum, Alfred T., tr. LC 83-3505. (History of the Art of China Ser.). (Illus.). 232p. 1984. 65.00 (*0-8348-1527-3*) Weatherhill.

Miyagiwa, Kaz. International Capital Mobility. LC 90-3511. (Foreign Economic Policy of the United States Ser.). 105p. 1990. reprint ed. 15.00 (*0-8240-7470-X*) Garland.

Miyaji, ed. Animal Models in Medical Mycology. 1987. 99.00 (*0-8493-5844-2*, RC117, CRC Reprint) Franklin.

***Miyakada, ed.** Process Architecture No. 120: EDAW: The Integrated World. (Illus.). 144p. 1995. pap. 36.95 (*4-89311-120-5*, Pub. by Process Archit JA) Bks Nippan.

Miyakawa, Edward T. Tule Lake. Van Strum, Carol S., ed. (Orig.). 1979. 12.95 (*0-686-25250-0*); pap. 7.95 (*0-686-25251-9*) Hse by the Sea.

***Miyake, A. & Suginami, H., eds.** Endocrine Regulation of Early Embryonic Development & Implantation: Tokyo Conference of Reproductive Physiology II, Tokyo, August 1994. (Journal: Hormone Research Ser.: Vol. 44, Suppl. 2, 1995). (Illus.). iv, 50p. 1995. pap. 26.25 (*3-8055-6169-5*) S Karger.

Miyake, A., jt. ed. see Mori, H.

Miyake, Akiko. Ezra Pound & the Mysteries of Love: A Plan for The Cantos. LC 90-47376. 308p. 1991. text ed. 31.95 (*0-8223-1105-4*) Duke.

***Miyake, Akiko, et al, eds.** A Guide to Ezra Pound & Ernest Fenollosa's Classic Noh Theatre of Japan. (Ezra Pound Scholarship Ser.). 453p. 1994. 47.50 (*0-943373-30-1*) Natl Poet Foun.

— A Guide to Ezra Pound & Ernest Fenollosa's Classic Noh Theatre of Japan. (Ezra Pound Scholarship Ser.). 453p. 1994. pap. 25.00 (*0-943373-31-X*) Natl Poet Foun.

Miyake, T. Modular Forms. (Illus.). 310p. 1989. 79.00 (*0-387-50268-8*) Spr-Verlag.

Miyake, T., et al, eds. Cytoprotection & Biology: Proceedings of the Symposium on Cytoprotection & Biology, 1st, Kyoto, Japan, February 26, 1983. (Current Clinical Practice Ser.: Vol. 24). 200p. 1985. 94.75 (*0-444-90388-7*) Elsevier.

Miyamori, I., jt. ed. see Takeda, R.

Miyamoto, A. S. Silver, Copper & Gold Halates. 1990. 120.00 (*0-08-029208-9*, Pergamon Pr) Elsevier.

Miyamoto, A. S. & Salamon, M. Alkali Metal Halates, Ammonium Iodate & Iodic Acid. (Solubility Data Ser.: No. 30). 1987. 170.00 (*0-08-029210-0*, Pergamon Pr) Elsevier.

— Alkali Metal Halates, Ammonium Iodate & Iodic Acid. (Solubility Data Ser.: No. 30). 1999. Japanese ed. 130.00 (*0-08-029211-9*, Pergamon Pr) Elsevier.

Miyamoto, Akito, tr. see Okawa, Naomi.

Miyamoto, H., et al, eds. Alkaline Earth Metal Halates. 352p. 1983. 130.00 (*0-08-029213-5*, Pergamon Pr) Elsevier.

Miyamoto, Hiroshi, ed. Recent Research on Mechanical Behavior of Solids. 427p. 1979. 67.50 (*0-86008-247-4*, Pub. by U of Tokyo JA) Col U Pr.

Miyamoto, J., ed. Pesticide Chemistry: Human Welfare & the Environment, Vol. 2. (IUPAC Symposium Ser.). 1983. 161.00 (*0-08-029223-2*, Pub. by Pergamon Repr UK); 20.00 (*0-08-029227-5*, Pub. by Pergamon Repr UK) Franklin.

Miyamoto, J. & Kearney, P. C., eds. Pesticide Chemistry - Human Welfare & the Environment: Mode of Action, Metabolism & Toxicology, Vol. 3. (IUPAC Symposium Ser.). (Illus.). 1983. 240.00 (*0-08-029224-0*, Pub. by Pergamon Repr UK); 20.00 (*0-08-029228-3*, Pub. by Pergamon Repr UK) Franklin.

— Pesticide Chemistry - Human Welfare & the Environment: Pesticide Residues & Formulation Chemistry, Vol. 4. (IUPAC Symposium Ser.). 1983. 184.00 (*0-08-029225-9*, Pub. by Pergamon Repr UK); 20.00 (*0-08-029229-1*, Pub. by Pergamon Repr UK) Franklin.

— Pesticide Chemistry - Human Welfare & the Environment: Synthesis & Structure Activity Relationships, Vol. 1. (IUPAC Symposium Ser.). 1983. 165.00 (*0-08-029222-4*, Pub. by Pergamon Repr UK); 20.00 (*0-08-029226-7*, Pub. by Pergamon Repr UK) Franklin.

Miyamoto, Kazuo. Hawaii: The End of the Rainbow. LC 63-20213. 509p. 1964. pap. 12.95 (*0-8048-0233-5*) C E Tuttle.

Miyamoto, Kazuo, ed. One Man's Journey. LC 81-21572. 120p. (Orig.). 1981. pap. 7.95 (*0-938474-01-4*) Buddhist Study.

Miyamoto, Kenro. Plasma Physics for Nuclear Fusion. rev. ed. 640p. 1989. 60.00 (*0-262-13237-0*); pap. 32.50 (*0-262-63117-2*) MIT Pr.

Miyamoto, Masao. The Straitjacket Society: A Rebel Bureaucrat Tells All. Carpenter, Juliet W., tr. 208p. 1994. 22.00 (*4-7700-1848-7*) Kodansha.

Miyamoto, Matao, jt. ed. see Yamazaki, Hiroaki.

Miyamoto, Michael M. & Cracraft, Joel, eds. Phylogenetic Analysis of DNA Sequences. (Illus.). 368p. 1991. 45.00 (*0-19-506698-7*) OUP.

Miyamoto, Naoki. Test Your Go Strength: Fifty Whole Board Problems. Bozulich, Richard, tr. (Illus.). 216p. 1991. reprint ed. pap. 12.95 (*4-87187-018-9*, G18) Ishi Pr Intl.

Miyamoto, Sadaski. Fuzzy Sets in Information Retrieval & Cluster Analysis. (C). 1990. lib. bdg. 120.00 (*0-7923-0721-6*) Kluwer Ac.

Miyamoto, T., jt. ed. see De Weck, Alain L.

Miyamoto, Tadao. Papa & Me. LC 94-1563. (J). (ps-3). 1994. 18.95 (*0-87614-843-7*, Carolrhoda) Lerner Group.

Miyamoto, Tadao, jt. auth. see Kess, Joseph F.

Miyamoto, Terumasa, ed. see Okuda, Minoru.

Miyamoto, Wayne, jt. auth. see Chesney, Lee.

Miyamoto, Y., tr. see Hyde, J. Peters, ed.

Miyamura, O., et al, eds. High Energy Nuclear Collisions & Quark Gluon Plasma. 350p. (C). 1991. text ed. 89.00 (*981-02-0806-5*) World Scientific Pub.

Miyanaga, Kuniko. The Creative Edge: Emerging Individualism in Japan. 145p. (C). 1993. 29.95 (*0-88738-407-2*); pap. 19.95 (*1-56000-701-X*) Transaction Pubs.

Miyanishi, M. Lectures on Curves on Rational & Unirational Surfaces. (Tata Institute Lecture Notes Ser.). 1979. pap. 29.00 (*0-387-08943-8*) Spr-Verlag.

Miyanishi, Masayoshi. Algebraic Geometry. LC 94-2018. (Translations of Mathematical Monographs: Vol. 135). 1994. write for info. (*0-8218-4615-9*) Am Math.

Miyao, Takahiro & Kanemoto, Yoshitsugu. Urban Dynamics & Urban Externalities. (In the Fundamentals of Pure & Applied Economics Ser.: Volume 11). 116p. 1987. pap. text ed. 32.00 (*3-7186-0333-0*) Gordon & Breach.

Miyares, Alina. Apuntes: Reflexiones Acerca de las Interrogantes Que Agobian Al Pueblo Latinoamericano. LC 92-62950. 80p. (Orig.). (SPA.). 1993. pap. 8.00 (*1-882573-01-3*) Serena Bay.

Miyares, Marcelino. Models of Political Participation of Hispanic-Americans. Cortes, Carlos E., ed. LC 79-6216. (Hispanics in the United States Ser.). (Illus.). 1981. lib. bdg. 21.95 (*0-405-13164-X*) Ayer.

Miyasaka & Trnka. Differentiation Antigens in Lymphopoietic Tissues. (Immunology Ser.: Vol. 38). 624p. 1988. 199.00 (*0-8247-7805-7*) Dekker.

Miyasaka, Kojiro, tr. see Niwano, Nikkyo.

Miyashiro, Akiho. Metamorphic Petrology. (Illus.). 416p. (C). 1994. text ed. 59.95 (*0-19-521026-3*) OUP.

Miyashita, Kenichi & Russell, David. Keiretsu: Inside the Hidden Japanese Conglomerates. 256p. 1993. text ed. 22.95 (*0-07-042583-3*) McGraw.

Miyashita, M. Imada & Takayama, H., eds. Computational Approaches in Condensed Matter Physics: Proceedings of the 6th Nishinomiya-Yukawa Memorial Symposium, Nishinomiya, Japan, October 24 & 25, 1991. LC 92-28269. (Proceedings in Physics Ser.: Vol. 70). 1992. 89.00 (*0-387-55799-7*) Spr-Verlag.

Miyashita, Tadao. The Currency & Financial System of Mainland China. (China in the 20th Century Ser.). 1976. reprint ed. lib. bdg. 32.50 (*0-306-70758-6*) Da Capo.

Miyata, Ken, jt. auth. see Forsyth, Adrian.

Miyata, Seizo, ed. Nonlinear Optics: Fundamentals, Materials, & Devices: Proceedings of the Fifth Toyota Conference on Nonlinear, Optical Materials, Aichi-Ken, Japan, 6-9 October 1991. LC 92-8500. 1992. write for info. (*0-444-89304-0*) Elsevier.

Miyatake, T., et al, eds. Molecular Biology & Genetics of Alzheimer's Disease: Proceedings of the International Symposium on Dementia, Nigata, Japan, 11-14 November, 1989. (International Congress Ser.: No. 884). 288p. 1990. 92.50 (*0-444-81112-5*, Excerpta Medica) Elsevier.

***Miyawaki, Akira, et al.** Vegetation in Eastern North America: Vegetation System & Dynamics under Human Activity in the Eastern North American Cultural Region in Comparison with Japan. 515p. 1994. 250.00 (*0-86008-494-9*, Pub. by U of Tokyo JA) Col U Pr.

Miyawaki, N., ed. Problems of Advanced Economics. (Studies in Contemporary Economics: Vol. 10). vi, 319p. 1984. pap. 45.00 (*0-387-13740-8*) Spr-Verlag.

Miyayama, H., et al. A Glossary of Agricultural Terms. 261p. (ENG & JPN.). 1975. 125.00 (*0-8288-5891-8*, M9345) Fr & Eur.

Miyazaki. Water Flow in Soils. (Books in Soils, Plants, & the Environment: Vol. 28). 312p. 1993. 140.00 (*0-8247-8982-2*) Dekker.

Miyazaki, F., jt. ed. see Yoshikawa, T.

Miyazaki, Hayao. Kiki's Delivery Service. Zimmerman, Maureen, ed. Saburi, Eugene, tr. (Magical Adventure Ser.). 14.95 (*4-19-086972-4*) Tokuma Pub.

— Laputa, the Castle in the Sky. Zimmerman, Maureen, ed. Saburi, Eugene, tr. (Magical Adventure Ser.). 14.95 (*4-19-086973-2*) Tokuma Pub.

— My Neighbor Totoro. Zimmerman, Maureen, ed. Saburi, Eugene, tr. (Magical Adventure Ser.). 14.95 (*4-19-086971-6*) Tokuma Pub.

— Nausicaa of the Valley of the Wind, 1. (Illus.). (YA). (gr. 7-12). 1993. 19.95 (*4-19-086975-9*) Tokuma Pub.

— Nausicaa of the Valley of the Wind, 2. (Illus.). (YA). (gr. 7-12). 1993. 19.95 (*4-19-086976-7*) Tokuma Pub.

— Nausicaa of the Valley of Wind, Pt. 2, Bk. 1. Horibuchi, Seiji, ed. Lewis, David & Smith, Toren, trs. (Illus.). 56p. (Orig.). 1989. pap. 2.95 (*0-929279-07-7*) Viz Commns Inc.

— Nausicaa of the Valley of Wind, Pt. 2, Bk. 2. Horibuchi, Seiji, ed. Lewis, David & Smith, Toren, trs. (Illus.). 56p. (Orig.). 1989. pap. 2.95 (*0-929279-08-5*) Viz Commns Inc.

— Nausicaa of the Valley of Wind, Pt. 2, Bk. 3. Horibuchi, Seiji, ed. Lewis, David & Smith, Toren, trs. (Illus.). 56p. (Orig.). 1989. pap. 2.95 (*0-929279-09-3*) Viz Commns Inc.

— Nausicaa of the Valley of Wind, Pt. 2, Bk. 4. Horibuchi, Seiji, ed. Lewis, David & Smith, Toren, trs. (Illus.). 56p. (Orig.). 1989. pap. 2.95 (*0-929279-10-7*) Viz Commns Inc.

— Nausicaa of the Valley of Wind, Vol. 1. Horibuchi, Seiji, ed. Lewis, David & Smith, Toren, trs. (Illus.). 56p. (Orig.). 1988. pap. 2.50 (*0-929279-00-X*) Viz Commns Inc.

— Nausicaa of the Valley of Wind, Vol. 2. Horibuchi, Seiji, ed. Lewis, David & Smith, Toren, trs. (Illus.). 56p. (Orig.). 1988. pap. 2.50 (*0-929279-01-8*) Viz Commns Inc.

— Nausicaa of the Valley of Wind, Vol. 3. Horibuchi, Seiji, ed. Lewis, David & Smith, Toren, trs. (Illus.). 56p. (Orig.). 1989. pap. 2.50 (*0-929279-02-6*) Viz Commns Inc.

— Nausicaa of the Valley of Wind, Vol. 4. Horibuchi, Seiji, ed. Lewis, David & Smith, Toren, trs. (Illus.). 56p. (Orig.). 1989. pap. 2.50 (*0-929279-03-4*) Viz Commns Inc.

— Nausicaa of the Valley of Wind, Vol. 5. Horibuchi, Seiji, ed. Lewis, David & Smith, Toren, trs. (Illus.). 56p. (Orig.). 1989. pap. 2.50 (*0-929279-04-2*) Viz Commns Inc.

— Nausicaa of the Valley of Wind, Vol. 6. Horibuchi, Seiji, ed. Lewis, David & Smith, Toren, trs. (Illus.). 56p. (Orig.). 1989. pap. 2.95 (*0-929279-05-0*) Viz Commns Inc.

— Nausicaa of the Valley of Wind, Vol. 7. Horibuchi, Seiji, ed. Lewis, David & Smith, Toren, trs. (Illus.). 56p. (Orig.). 1989. pap. 2.95 (*0-929279-06-9*) Viz Commns Inc.

— Nausicaa of the Valley of Wind, Graphic Novel, Vol. 1. Horibuchi, Seiji, ed. Lewis, David & Smith, Toren, trs. (Illus.). 138p. (Orig.). 1989. pap. text ed. 13.95 (*0-929279-58-1*) Viz Commns Inc.

— Nausicaa of the Valley of Wind, Graphic Novel, Vol. 2. Horibuchi, Seiji, ed. Lewis, David & Smith, Toren, trs. (Illus.). 138p. (Orig.). 1990. pap. text ed. 13.95 (*0-929279-59-X*) Viz Commns Inc.

— Nausicaa of the Valley of Wind, Graphic Novel, Vol. 3. Horibuchi, Seiji, ed. Lewis, David & Smith, Toren, trs. (Illus.). 138p. (Orig.). 1990. pap. text ed. 13.95 (*0-929279-60-3*) Viz Commns Inc.

— Nausicaa of the Valley of Wind, Graphic Novel, Vol. 4. Horibuchi, Seiji, ed. Lewis, David & Smith, Toren, trs. (Illus.). 138p. (Orig.). 1990. pap. text ed. 13.95 (*0-929279-61-1*) Viz Commns Inc.

— Tokuma's Magical Adventure Series. Zimmerman, Maureen, ed. Saburi, Eugene, tr. (Illus.). 112p. (J). (gr. 3-6). 1992. lib. bdg. 44.85 (*4-19-086974-0*) Tokuma Pub.

Miyazaki, Hayhao. Nausicaa of the Valley of Wind, Vol. 5. (Illus.). 152p. (Orig.). 1993. pap. 15.95 (*0-929279-98-0*) Viz Commns Inc.

Miyazaki, Ichisada. China's Examination Hell: The Civil Service Examinations of Imperial China. Schirokauer, Conrad, tr. LC 80-54223. Orig. Title: Kakyo-Chugoku No Shikenjigoku. 142p. 1981. reprint ed. pap. 12.00 (*0-300-02639-0*, Y-398) Yale U Pr.

Miyazaki, Koji. An Adventure in Multidimensional Space: The Art & Geometry of Polygons, Polyhedra & Polytopes. LC 84-22595. 120p. 1986. text ed. 125.00 (*0-471-81648-5*) Wiley.

Miyazaki, Kumiko. Building Competences in the Firm: Lessons from Japanese & European Optoelectronics. LC 94-20757. 1994. write for info. (*0-312-12314-0*) St Martin.

Miyazaki, T., jt. ed. see Yagi, Kunio.

Miyazaki, Tamotsu, et al, eds. The Mechanism & New Approach on Drug Resistance of Cancer Cells: Proceedings of the International Symposium on the Mechanism & New Approach on Drug Resistance of Cancer Cells, Sapporo, 15-17 October 1992. LC 93-15706. (International Congress Ser.: No. 1026). 335p. 1993. 140.00 (*0-444-81480-9*, Excerpta Medica) Elsevier.

***Miyazaki, Toten.** My Twenty-Three Years' Dream: The Autobiography of Miyazaki Toten. Shinkichi, Eto & Jansen, Marius B., trs. LC 81-47925. (Princeton Library of Asian Translations). (Illus.). Date not set. reprint ed. pap. 93.20 (*0-7837-9444-4*, 2060186) Bks Demand.

Miyazawa, Kenji. Once & Forever: The Tales of Kenji Miyazawa. Shaw, ed. Bester, John, tr. (Illus.). 270p. 1994. 25.00 (*4-7700-1780-4*) Kodansha.

Miyazawa, Masanori, jt. auth. see Goodman, David G.

Miyazawa, S., jt. ed. see Kukimoto, H.

Miyazawa, Setsuo. Policing in Japan: A Study on Making Crime. LC 91-8617. (Critical Issues in Criminal Justice Ser.). 267p. 1992. 64.50 (*0-7914-0891-4*); pap. 21.95 (*0-7914-0892-2*) State U NY Pr.

Miyazawa, T., jt. auth. see Emsley.

Miyazima, Yasuhiko. Children of the World: China. LC 87-42576. (Illus.). 64p. (J). (gr. 5-6). 1988. lib. bdg. 21.26 (*1-55532-207-7*) Gareth Stevens Inc.

Miyoshi, K. & Chung, Y. W. Surface Diagnostics in Tribology - Fundamental Principles & Applications. LC 93-36748. (Series on Modern Tribology: Vol. 1). 352p. 1993. text ed. 121.00 (*981-02-1516-9*) World Scientific Pub.

Miyoshi, Masahiro. Considerations of Equity in the Settlement of Territorial & Boundary Disputes. LC 93-22109. (International Law in Japanese Perspectives Ser.: Vol. 2). 296p. (C). 1993. lib. bdg. 115.00 (*0-7923-2217-7*) Kluwer Ac.

Miyoshi, Masao. As We Saw Them: The First Japanese Embassy to the United States (1860) Urda, John, ed. (Illus.). 232p. 1994. pap. 13.00 (*1-56836-028-2*) Kodansha.

— As We Saw Them: The First Japanese Embassy to the United States (1860) LC 78-62851. (Illus.). 244p. reprint ed. pap. 69.60 (*0-7837-4841-8*, 2044488) Bks Demand.

— Off Center: Power & Culture Relations Between Japan & the United States. (Convergences: Inventories of the Present Ser.). 289p. 1994. pap. text ed. 15.95 (*0-674-63176-5*, MIYOFX) HUP.

Miyoshi, Masao & Harootunian, H. D., eds. Japan in the World. LC 93-2399. 368p. 1993. lib. bdg. 42.50 (*0-8223-1350-2*); pap. text ed. 18.95 (*0-8223-1368-5*) Duke.

— Postmodernism & Japan. LC 89-7709. 322p. 1989. 32.00 (*0-8223-0779-0*); pap. 15.95 (*0-8223-0896-7*) Duke.

Miyoshi, T. Foundations of the Numerical Analysis of Plasticity: Lecture Notes in Numerical & Applied Analysis, Vol. 7. (Mathematics Studies: Vol. 107). 250p. 1987. pap. 79.50 (*0-444-87671-5*, North Holland) Elsevier.

Miyuki, Mokusen, jt. auth. see Spiegelman, J. Marvin.

Mizan Press, tr. see Qutb, Sayyid.

Mize, et al. Understanding MS Project. 1994. pap. 26.99 (*0-7821-1634-5*) Sybex.

Mize, Barbara F. Creative Encounters. (gr. 4-8). 1988. pap. 6.00 (*0-89824-248-7*) Trillium Pr.

Mize, Jack P., jt. auth. see Kuester.

Mize, Jackie & Salts, Connie, eds. Contemporary Readings in Family & Human Development. 200p. (C). 1988. pap. text ed. 15.95 (*0-89892-075-2*) Contemp Pub Co of Raleigh.

***Mize, Jim.** The Winter of Our Discount Tent: A Humorous Look at Flora, Fauna, & Foolishness Outdoors. LC 94-18752. 1995. write for info. (*1-57003-049-9*) U of SC Pr.

Mize, Joe, ed. Guide to Systems Integration. 1993. 35.00 (*0-89806-111-3*) Ind Eng Mgmt Pr.

Mize, Joe H., et al. Operations Planning & Control. (Illus.). 1971. 46.00 (*0-13-637892-7*) P-H.

Mize, Terry. God's Opinion of You. 32p. 1983. pap. 0.98 (*0-89274-178-3*) Harrison Hse.

— More Than Conquerors. rev. ed. 128p. 1990. pap. 5.95 (*0-89274-724-2*, HH724) Harrison Hse.

Mize, Traci. The Church Without Spot or Wrinkle. 1993. pap. 6.95 (*0-933025-26-2*) Blue Bird Pub.

Mizejewski, Gerald J. & Jacobson, Herbert I., eds. Biological Activities of Alpha-Fetoprotein, I. 256p. 1989. 155.00 (*0-8493-5637-7*, QP552, CRC Reprint) Franklin.

— Biological Activities of Alpha-Fetoprotein, II. 256p. 1989. 174.00 (*0-8493-5638-5*, CRC Reprint) Franklin.

— Biological Activities of Alpha-Fetoprotein, Set. 256p. 1989. 110.00 (*0-8493-5636-9*, QP552) CRC Pr.

Mizejewski, Linda. Divine Decadence: Fascism, Female Spectacle, & the Makings of Sally Bowles. LC 92-11858. 272p. (C). 1992. 45.00 (*0-691-07896-3*); pap. 14.95 (*0-691-02346-8*) Princeton U Pr.

Mizel, Mark & Pfeffer, Glen, eds. Selected Bibliography of the Foot & Ankle with Commentary. 325p. 1992. 25.00 (*0-89203-061-5*) Amer Acad Ortho Surg.

Mizel, V., et al, eds. Mechanics & Thermodynamics of Continua: A Collection of Papers Dedicated to B.D. Coleman on His Sixtieth Birthday. (Illus.). xii, 578p. 1991. pap. 110.00 (*0-387-52999-3*) Spr-Verlag.

Mizel, Victor, jt. auth. see Marcus, Moshe.

***Mizell, Hubert.** 95th U. S. Open. Norwood, Bev, ed. (Illus.). 64p. 1995. 20.00 (*1-878843-13-3*) Intl Merc OH.

— Ninety-Fourth U. S. Open. Norwood, Bev, ed. (Illus.). 64p. 1994. 20.00 (*1-878843-10-9*) Intl Merc OH.

Mizell, Linda. Racism. (Think Ser.). 160p. (YA). (gr. 7 up). 1992. lib. bdg. 15.85 (*0-8027-8113-6*); pap. 9.95 (*0-8027-7365-6*) Walker & Co.

***Mizell, Louis R., Jr.** Street Sense for Parents. 176p. (Orig.). 1995. pap. text ed. 4.99 (*0-425-14947-1*) Berkley Pub.

— Street Sense for Seniors. 224p. (Orig.). 1994. pap. text ed. 4.99 (*0-425-14364-3*) Berkley Pub.

— Street Sense for Women. 160p. (Orig.). 1993. pap. 4.99 (*0-425-13971-9*) Berkley Pub.

***Mizen, Paul.** Buffer Stock Models & the Demand for Money. LC 94-20722. 1994. write for info. (*0-312-12318-3*) Macmillan.

Mizener, Arthur. F. Scott Fitzgerald. LC 86-51196. (Literary Lives Ser.). (Illus.). 128p. 1987. reprint ed. pap. 9.95 (*0-500-26024-9*) Thames Hudson.

— Fitzgerald Reader. 1985. pap. 15.95 (*0-684-15871-X*, Scribners) S&S Trade.

Mizener, Arthur, ed. Modern Short Stories. (C). 1979. pap. text ed. 2.95 (*0-393-95032-8*) Norton.

— Modern Short Stories. 4th ed. (C). 1979. pap. text ed. 26.95 (*0-393-95025-5*) Norton.

Mizener, Arthur, ed. see Trollope, Anthony.

Mizer, David, et al. Food Preparation for the Professional. 2nd ed. 526p. 1987. Net. text ed. write for info. (*0-471-88303-4*) Wiley.

Mizer, Ray. Midwest Mosaics. LC 90-71996. 59p. (Orig.). 1992. pap. 8.00 (*1-56002-092-X*) Aegina Pr.

Mizerak, Steve & Cohen, Joel. Steve Mizerak's Pocket Billiards Tips & Trick Shots. (Illus.). 192p. 1982. 15.50 (*0-8092-5780-7*); pap. 10.95 (*0-8092-5779-3*) Contemp Bks.

***Mizerak, Steve & Cohen, Joel H.** Steve Mizerak's Pocket Billiards, Tips, & Trick Shots. 1995. write for info. (*0-517-12332-0*) Wings Bks.

Mizerak, Steve & Panozzo, Michael E. Steve Mizerak's Complete Book of Pool. (Illus.). 208p. (Orig.). 1990. pap. 13.95 (*0-8092-4255-9*) Contemp Bks.

— Steve Mizerak's Winning Pool Tips. (Illus.). 112p. 1995. pap. 6.95 (*0-8092-3428-9*) Contemp Bks.

Mizerski, J. & Fiutak, J., eds. Quantum Optics: Proceedings of the Summer School on Quantum Optics, Sept. 2-8, 1985, Gdansk, Poland. 410p. 1986. pap. 64.00 (*9971-5-0098-1*) World Scientific Pub.

Mizin, I., jt. ed. see Schwartzel, Heinz.

Mizio, Emelicia & Delaney, Anita J., eds. Training for Service Delivery to Minority Clients. LC 80-23468. 208p. reprint ed. pap. 59.30 (*0-8357-8513-0*, 2034810) Bks Demand.

Mizio, Emelicia & Valiente-Barksdale, Clara. Hispanic Community-Based Organizations: Issues of Survival & Non-Survival a Report to Community Service Society. 52p. 1985. 6.00 (*0-88156-045-6*) Comm Serv Soc NY.

Mizner, Addison. Florida Architecture of Addison Mizner. unabridged ed. LC 92-22830. (Illus.). 224p. 1992. reprint ed. pap. text ed. 14.94 (*0-486-27327-X*) Dover.

Mizoguchi, Fumio, ed. AI Technology. x, 187p. 1991. 80.00 (*90-5199-050-2*, Pub. by IOS Pr NE) IOS Press.

An Asterisk (*) at the beginning of an entry indicates that the title is appearing in BIP for the first time.

Mizoguchi, Noriaki. Retail Shops in New York: Interior & Display. (Illus.). 232p. 1994. 98.00 (4-7661-0791-8, Pub. by Graphic Sha JA) Bks Nippan.

Mizoguti, H. A Fifteen-Somite Human Embryo. (Advances in Anatomy, Embryology & Cell Biology Ser.: Vol. 116). (Illus.). 95p. 1989. pap. 113.00 (0-387-50565-2) Spr-Verlag.

Mizohata, Sigeru. On the Cauchy Problem. 180p. 1986. pap. text ed. 65.00 (0-12-501660-3) Acad Pr.

— The Theory of Partial Differential Equations. LC 72-83593. 350p. 1973. 79.95 (0-521-08727-9) Cambridge U Pr.

Mizohata, Sigeru, ed. Hyperbolic Equations & Related Topics. 423p. 1987. text ed. 121.00 (0-12-501658-1) Acad Pr.

Mizokawa, Donald T. Everyday Computing in Academe: A Guide for Scholars, Researchers, Students, & Other Academic Users of Personal Computers. LC 94-2002. 350p. 1994. 37.95 (0-87778-276-8) Educ Tech Pubns.

***Mizrahi & Sullivan.** Finite Mathematics with Applications & Student Solutions Manual Set. 6th ed. 1995. text ed. write for info. (0-471-12316-1) Wiley.

Mizrahi, Abe & Sullivan, Michael. Finite Mathematics with Application for Business & Social Sciences. 6th ed. 768p. (C). 1991. Net. text ed. write for info. (0-471-54744-1) Wiley.

— Finite Mathematics with Applications for Business & Social Sciences. 4th ed. LC 87-31756. 229p. 1988. teacher ed 18.50 (0-471-62238-9); 19.50 (0-471-63435-2); write for info. (0-471-53883-3); write for info. (0-471-53879-5); write for info. (0-471-53882-5) Wiley.

— Finite Mathematics with Applications for Business & Social Sciences. 6th ed. 1993. pap. text ed. 25.00 (0-471-59783-X); pap. text ed. 25.00 (0-471-59784-8) Wiley.

Mizrahi, Abshalom & Sullivan, Michael. Mathematics: For Business, Life Sciences, & Social Sciences. 5th ed. 992p. 1993. Net. text ed. write for info. (0-471-54846-4) Wiley.

Mizrahi, Judith. Seven Hundred Three American Sephardim: Diversity Within Cohesiveness. 100p. 1992. 12.50 (0-9635425-0-8) Gemini Books.

Mizrahi, Terry. Getting Rid of Patients: Contradictions in the Socialization of Physicians. LC 85-2284. 230p. (C). 1986. text ed. 40.00 (0-8135-1128-3) Rutgers U Pr.

***Mizrahi, Terry & Morrison, John, eds.** Community Organization & Social Administration: Advances, Trends, & Emerging Principles. LC 92-47278. (Illus.). 254p. 1992. pap. 17.95 (1-56024-277-9) Haworth Pr.

— Community Organization & Social Administration: Advances, Trends, & Emerging Principles. LC 92-8960. (Illus.). 254p. 1992. lib. bdg. 49.95 (1-56024-257-4) Haworth Pr.

Mizruchi. The Structure of Corporate Political Action: Interfirm Relations & Their Consequences. (Illus.). 299p. 1992. 42.50 (0-674-84377-0) HUP.

Mizruchi, Ephraim H. Regulating Society: Marginality & Social Control in Historical Perspective. 224p. 1983. text ed. 35.00 (0-02-921660-5) Free Pr.

Mizruchi, Mark S. & Schwartz, Michael, eds. Intercorporate Relations: The Structural Analysis of Business. (Structural Analysis in the Social Sciences Ser.: No. 1). (Illus.). 320p. 1988. 49.95 (0-521-33503-5) Cambridge U Pr.

— Intercorporate Relations: The Structural Analysis of Business. (Structural Analysis in the Social Sciences Ser.: No. 1). (Illus.). 344p. (C). 1992. pap. 19.95 (0-521-43794-6) Cambridge U Pr.

Mizruchi, Susan L. Culture of Vigilance. (C). 1992. 39.95 (0-691-06892-5) Princeton U Pr.

— Culture Vigilance. (C). 1992. pap. 14.00 (0-691-01506-6) Princeton U Pr.

— The Power of Historical Knowledge: Narrating the Past in Hawthorne, James, & Dreiser. 336p. 1988. text ed. 42.50 (0-691-06725-2) Princeton U Pr.

Mizsei, Kalman, ed. Public Finance Development. LC 93-23606. 1994. pap. text ed. 23.85 (0-8133-2198-0) Westview.

Mizuike, A. Enrichment Techniques for Inorganic Trace Analysis. (Chemical Laboratory Practice Ser.). (Illus.). 144p. 1983. 87.00 (0-387-12051-3) Spr-Verlag.

Mizukami, K., jt. ed. see Malanowski, K.

Mizukami, Masahiro, et al, eds. Hypertensive Intracerebral Hemorrhage. 272p. 1983. text ed. 93.50 (0-89004-812-6) Raven.

***Mizumori.** Administrator's Guide to X.400 Addressing. (Communications Ser.). 1995. (0-442-02060-0) Van Nos Reinhold.

Mizumura, Kazue, jt. auth. see Stamm, Claus.

Mizuno, D., et al. Self-Defense Mechanisms: Role of Macrophage. 344p. 1983. 137.50 (0-444-80460-9) Elsevier.

Mizuno, E., jt. auth. see Chen, W. F.

Mizuno, K., ed. Ophthalmology: Proceedings of the Eighty Eighth Annual Meeting of the Japanese Ophthalmology Society in Sendai, Japan, May 17-19, 1984. (International Congress Ser.: No. 671). 295p. 1985. 122.75 (0-444-80676-8, Excerpta Medica) Elsevier.

Mizuno, Kogen. Basic Buddhist Concepts. 176p. (Orig.). 1987. pap. 9.95 (4-333-01203-1, Pub. by Kosei Pub Co JA) C E Tuttle.

— The Beginnings of Buddhism. Gage, Richard L., tr. Orig. Title: Bukkyo No Genten. (Illus.). 220p. 1980. pap. 10.95 (4-333-00383-0, Pub. by Kosei Pub Co JA) C E Tuttle.

— Buddhist Sutras: Origin, Development, Transmission. (Illus.). 220p. 1982. pap. 10.95 (4-333-01028-4, Pub. by Kosei Pub Co JA) C E Tuttle.

Mizuno, M., et al, eds. Role of Prolactin in Human Reproduction. (Illus.). x, 314p. 1988. 207.25 (3-8055-4786-2) S Karger.

Mizuno, Seiichi. Asuka Buddhist Art: Horyu-Ji. Gage, Richard L., tr. LC 73-88473. (Heibonsha Survey of Japanese Art Ser.: Vol. 4). (Illus.). 174p. 1974. 20.00 (0-8348-1020-4) Weatherhill.

Mizuno, Shigeru. Company-Wide Total Quality Control. 1987. pap. text ed. 26.50 (92-833-1100-0, Pub. by APO JA) Qual Resc.

— Company-Wide Total Quality Control. 313p. 1988. text ed. 32.50 (92-833-1099-3, Pub. by APO JA) Qual Resc.

Mizuno, Shigeru, ed. Management for Quality Improvement: The Seven New QC Tools. LC 88-42625. (Illus.). 323p. 1988. 65.00 (0-915299-29-1) Prod Press.

***Mizuno, Shigeru & Akao, Yoji, eds.** QFD: The Customer-Driven Approach to Quality Planning & Deployment. (Illus.). 365p. 1994. pap. text ed. 49.95 (92-833-1122-1, Pub. by APO JA) Qual Resc.

— QFD: The Customer-Driven Approach to Quality Planning & Deployment. (Illus.). 365p. 1994. text ed. 59.95 (92-833-1121-3, Pub. by APO JA) Qual Resc.

Mizuno, Y. The Organic Chemistry of Nucleic Acids. (Studies in Organic Chemistry: No. 24). 505p. 1986. 133.50 (0-444-99521-8) Elsevier.

Mizuno, Y., ed. First Sandoz Symposium on the Treatment of Parkinson's Disease, Tokyo, October 1992. (Journal: European Neurology: Vol. 33, Suppl. 1, 1993). (Illus.). vi, 70p. 1993. pap. 30.50 (3-8055-5829-5) S Karger.

***Mizuno, Y., et al, eds.** Advances in Research on Neurodegeneration Vol. II: Etiopathogenesis. (Illus.). xiii, 221p. 1994. text ed. 95.00 (0-8176-3762-1) Birkhauser.

Mizuo, Hiroshi. Edo Painting: Sotatsu & Korin. LC 72-79122. (Heibonsha Survey of Japanese Art Ser.: Vol. 18). (Illus.). 164p. 1973. 20.00 (0-8348-1011-5) Weatherhill.

Mizushima & Amor. Autoimmunity, Rheumatoid Arthritis & Cyclosporin A (Sandimmun) 104p. (C). 1991. 35.00 (1-85070-305-1) Prthnon Pub.

Mizushima, Masataka. The Theory of Rotating Diatomic Molecules. LC 74-34080. 543p. 1975. 42.50 (0-471-61187-5, Wiley) Krieger.

Mizushina, S. Noninvasive Temperature Measurement: In Aspects of Medical Technology, Vol. 1. 160p. 1989. text ed. 96.00 (0-677-25750-3) Gordon & Breach.

Mizuta, Hiroshi & Sugiyama, Chuhei. Adam Smith: International Perspectives. LC 92-25575. 1993. text ed. 75.00 (0-312-08937-6) St Martin.

***Mizuta, Hiroshi & Tanoue, Tomonori.** The Physics & Applications of Resonant Tunnelling Diodes. (Studies in Semiconductor Physics & Microelectronic Engineering: No. 2). (Illus.). 224p. (C). 1995. write for info. (0-521-43218-9) Cambridge U Pr.

Mizuta, Kazuo. The Structures of Everyday Life in Japan in the Last Decade of the Twentieth Century. LC 93-1751. 400p. 1993. text ed. 99.95 (0-7734-9320-4) E Mellen.

Mizuta, Tamae, jt. auth. see Roberts, Marie M.

Mizuta, Tamae, jt. ed. see Roberts, Marie M.

Mizutani, N., ed. see IUMRS International Conference on Advanced Materials Staff.

Mizutani, Nobuko, jt. auth. see NHK Overseas Broadcasting Department Staff.

Mizutani, Shinjiro, jt. ed. see Uemura, Takeshi.

***Mizutani, T., et al.** Geometric Study of Foliations. 512p. 1994. text ed. 109.00 (981-02-1898-2) World Scientific Pub.

Mizutani, T. & Shiraki, H., eds. Clinicopathological Aspects of Creutzfeld-Jacob Disease. 325p. 1986. 147.25 (0-444-80694-6) Elsevier.

Mizutani, T., jt. auth. see Garcilazo, H.

Mizwa, Stephen P. Frederic Chopin, 1810-1849: Music Book Index. 108p. 1993. reprint ed. lib. bdg. 69.00 (0-7812-9590-4) Rprt Serv.

Mizwa, Stephen P., ed. Frederic Chopin, Eighteen Ten to Eighteen Forty-Nine. LC 83-10836. (Illus.). xviii, 108p. 1983. reprint ed. text ed. 45.00 (0-313-24116-3, MIFR, Greenwood Pr) Greenwood.

Mjagkij, Nina. Light in the Darkness: African Americans & the YMCA. 1852-1946. LC 93-19857. (Illus.). 216p. 1993. 23.00 (0-8131-1852-2) U Pr of Ky.

Mjelde, K. M. Methods of the Allocation of Limited Resources. LC 82-16002. 96p. reprint ed. pap. 27.40 (0-8357-4602-X, 2037535) Bks Demand.

Mjelde, Michael J. Glory of the Seas. LC 77-105505. (American Maritime Library: No. 1). 315p. reprint ed. pap. 89.80 (0-8357-2788-2, 2039914) Bks Demand.

Mjor, Ivar A. Reaction Patterns in Human Teeth. 248p. 1983. 143.00 (0-8493-6645-3, RK280) CRC Pr.

Mjor, Ivar A., ed. Dental Materials: Biological Properties & Clinical Evaluation. 224p. 1985. 168.00 (0-8493-6644-5, RK652, CRC Reprint) Franklin.

Mkangi, C. C. The Social Cost of Small Families & Land Reform: A Case Study of the Wataita of Kenya. (International Population Ser.: Vol. 2). (Illus.). 180p. 1983. text ed. 46.00 (0-08-028952-5, Pub. by Pergamon Repr UK) Franklin.

M'Kee, et al. M'Kee Brothers' Victorian Glass: Five Complete Glass Catalogs from 1859-60 to 1871. 16.50 (0-8446-5907-X) Peter Smith.

M'Kee, John R., tr. see Kirsch, J. P.

M'Kerlie, P. H. History of the Lands & Their Owners in Galloway (Scotland), 2 vols., Vols. I & II. 1232p. 1992. reprint ed. pap. 70.00 (1-55613-580-7) Heritage Bk.

Mkhitaryan, A. M. Hydraulics & Fundamentals of Gas Dynamics. 240p. 1964. text ed. 61.00 (0-7065-0281-7, Pub. by Keter Pub IS) Coronet Bks.

Mkhondo, Rich. Reporting South Africa. LC 93-32149. (C). 1993. 21.95 (0-435-08096-2); pap. 13.95 (0-435-08089-X) Heinemann.

Mkrtchian, G. A., jt. auth. see Levinskii, N. N.

Mladenka, Kenneth, jt. auth. see Hill, Kim.

Mladenka, Kenneth R., jt. auth. see Hill, Kim Q.

Mladenovic, Jeanette, ed. Primary Care Secrets: Questions You Will Be Asked on Rounds, in the Clinic, on Oral Exams. (Secrets Ser.). 500p. (Orig.). 1994. pap. text ed. 33.95 (1-56053-105-3) Hanley & Belfus.

Mladenovic, Petr. John Hus at the Council of Constance. Spinka, Matthew, tr. & intro. by. LC 65-11019. (Records of Civilization: Sources & Studies: No. 73). 341p. reprint ed. pap. 97.20 (0-685-20377-8, 2029832) Bks Demand.

Mladjenovic, Milorad. History of Early Nuclear Physics: Radioactivity & Its Radiations, 1896-1931, Vol. 1. LC 92-32997. 260p. (C). 1992. text ed. 61.00 (981-02-0807-3) World Scientific Pub.

Mlak, W. Hilbert Space & Operator Theory. (C). 1900. lib. bdg. 151.50 (0-7923-1042-X) Kluwer Ac.

Mlawer, Teresa, tr. see Adler, David A.

Mlawer, Teresa, tr. see Aliki.

Mlawer, Teresa, tr. see Brown, Marcia.

Mlawer, Teresa, tr. see Eastman, P. D.

Mlawer, Teresa, tr. see Estes, Eleanor.

Mlawer, Teresa, tr. see Ets, Marie H.

Mlawer, Teresa, tr. see Grunsell, Angela.

Mlawer, Teresa, tr. see Hoff, Syd.

Mlawer, Teresa, tr. see Johnson, Crockett.

Mlawer, Teresa, tr. see Jonas, Ann.

Mlawer, Teresa, tr. see Levy, Janice.

Mlawer, Teresa, tr. see Nodar, Carmen M.

Mlawer, Teresa, tr. see Slobodkina, Esphyr.

Mlawer, Teresa, tr. see Steig, William.

Mlawrer, Teresa, tr. see Most, Bernard.

Mlejnek, H. P., jt. ed. see Argyris, J. H.

M'Leod, D. A Brief Review of the Settlement of Upper Canada. 300p. 1992. reprint ed. pap. 21.50 (1-55613-727-3) Heritage Bk.

Mlicki, Marek K., jt. ed. see Gasparski, Wojciech W.

MLIHRC Delegate Staff, et al. Justice Suspended: The Failure of the Habeas Corpus System in Guatemala. 131p. (Orig.). (C). 1990. pap. 7.00 (0-929293-08-8) MN Advocates.

MLIHRC Staff & Gerdtz, Daniel. Paper Protection: Human Rights Violations & the Mexican Criminal Justice System: A Report of the MLIHRC. 65p. (Orig.). (C). 1990. pap. 7.00 (0-929293-07-X) MN Advocates.

MLIHRC Staff, et al. Restavek: Child Labor in Haiti: A Report by the MLIHRC. 51p. (Orig.). 1990. pap. 7.00 (0-929293-06-1) MN Advocates.

Mlikotin, Anthony M. Nietzsche: The Mind's Greatest Storyteller. (Series in Avant-Garde Thought & the Arts). 303p. 1991. pap. write for info. (0-9629448-0-7) New Dimens Pr.

Mlinar, Adravko, ed. Globalization & Territorial Identities. 140p. 1992. 68.95 (1-85628-426-3, Pub. by Avebury Pub UK) Ashgate Pub Co.

Mlinar, Zdravko, jt. auth. see Teune, Henry.

Mlitz, R., ed. General Algebra 1988: Proceedings of the International Conference Held in Memory of Wilfried Nobauer, Krems, Austria, 21-27 Aug., 1988. 266p. 1990. 84.75 (0-444-88617-6, North Holland) Elsevier.

MLJ. General Index & Table of Cases Reported, 1932-1988. 1991. 100.00 (0-409-99595-9) Butterworth Legal Pubs.

Mlodozeniec, Juventyn. I Knew St. Maximilian. 116p. 1982. pap. 2.95 (0-911988-48-3) AMI Pr.

Mloszewski, M. J. The Behavior & Ecology of the African Buffalo. LC 82-1153. (Illus.). 280p. 1983. 64.95 (0-521-24478-1) Cambridge U Pr.

Mlotek, jt. auth. see Gottlieb.

Mlotek, Eleanor G. Mir Trogn A Gezang Yiddish Songbook. 239p. 1977. pap. 10.00 (0-685-05910-3) Workmen's Circle.

Mlotek, Eleanor G. & Gottlieb, Malke. We Are Here: Songs of the Holocaust in Yiddish & Singable English Translation. 104p. 1983. 10.00 (0-686-40805-5) Workmen's Circle.

Mlotek, Eleanor G. & Mlotek, Joseph. Pearls of Yiddish Song. 286p. 1988. pap. 15.00 (1-877909-64-5) Workmen's Circle.

— Pearls of Yiddish Song: Favorite Folk, Art & Theatre Songs. Mlotek, Zalmen, ed. Klepfisz, Irena, tr. 286p. (Orig.). 1989. write for info. (0-318-65126-2) Workmen's Circle.

Mlotek, Joseph. Yiddishe Kinder Alef. 3rd ed. 128p. 1985. pap. 5.00 (0-318-22116-0) Workmen's Circle.

Mlotek, Joseph & Olitsky, Matis. Yiddishe Kinder Beyz. 120p. 1975. pap. 5.00 (0-318-22117-9) Workmen's Circle.

Mlotek, Joseph, jt. auth. see Mlotek, Eleanor G.

Mlotek, Zalmen, ed. see Mlotek, Eleanor G. & Mlotek, Joseph.

Mlyn, Eric. The State, Society, & Limited Nuclear War. LC 94-10966. (SUNY Series in the Making of Foreign Policy). 255p. (C). 1995. pap. 19.95x (0-7914-2348-4) State U NY Pr.

— The State, Society, & Limited Nuclear War. LC 94-10966. (SUNY Series in the Making of Foreign Policy). 255p. (C). 1995. 59.50 (0-7914-2347-6) State U NY Pr.

M'Mahon, Bernard. The American Gardener's Calendar: Adapted to the Climates & Seasons of the United States. 1977. reprint ed. 25.00 (0-913728-25-X) Theophrastus.

Mmari, Geoffrey, jt. ed. see Legum, Colin.

Mmeje. Wastewater Treatment Plant Safety: A Practical Guide. 1994. write for info. (0-87371-492-X) Lewis Pubs.

M'Millan, Samuel, ed. see Boston, Thomas.

Mnarchuk, G. I. Mathematical Models in Immunology. (Illus.). xxv, 351p. 1983. pap. 89.00 (0-387-90901-X) Spr-Verlag.

Mncwabe, Mandla P. Post-Apartheid Education: Towards Non-Racial, Unitary & Democratic Socialisation in the New South Africa. 276p. (C). 1993. lib. bdg. 46.50 (0-8191-8969-3) U Pr of Amer.

Mnemosyne. Rutilius Lupus, No. 11: De Figuris Sententiarum et Elocutionis. 1970. 39.50 (90-04-01474-8) E J Brill.

Mnookin, Robert H. Child, Family & State: Cases & Materials on Children & the Law. 857p. 1978. 32.00 (0-316-57650-6) Little.

— Children & the Law. 2nd ed. 1989. 48.00 (0-316-57651-4) Little.

Mnookin, Robert H., jt. auth. see Maccoby, Eleanor E.

Mnookin, Wendy. Guenever Speaks. 50p. 1991. pap. 10.00 (0-9630918-0-8) Round Table.

Mnyampala, Mathias. The Gogo: History, Customs, & Traditions. Maddox, Gregory, ed. & tr. by. (Sources & Studies in World History Ser.). (Illus.). 160p. 1995. 40.00 (1-56324-405-5); pap. 17.95 (1-56324-406-3) M E Sharpe.

Mo, Jongryn & Myers, Ramon H., eds. Shaping a New Economic Relationship: The Republic of Korea & the United States. LC 93-24019. (Publication Ser.: No. 417). 216p. 1993. text ed. 32.95 (0-8179-9251-0); pap. 19.95 (0-8179-9252-9) Hoover Inst Pr.

Mo, Rosa A., jt. auth. see Lapchick, J. Michael.

Mo Ti. The Ethical & Political Works of Motse. Mei, Yi-pao, tr. LC 73-893. (China Studies: from Confucius to Mao Ser.). xiv, 275p. 1993. reprint ed. 30.00 (0-88355-085-7) Hyperion Conn.

Mo, Tianpei. Anatomy & Systematics of Bagridae (Teleostei), & Siluroid Phylogeny. Fricke, Ronald, ed. (Theses Zoologicae Ser.: Vol. 17). (Illus.). vii, 216p. 1991. 135.00 (1-878762-27-3) Koeltz Sci Bks.

Mo, Timothy. The Monkey King. 275p. 1988. reprint ed. pap. 10.95 (0-571-12966-8) Faber & Faber.

— Sour Sweet. LC 84-40702. (Aventura Ser.). (Orig.). 1985. pap. 9.95 (0-394-73680-X, Vin) Random.

Mo Tzu. Mo Tzu: Basic Writings. Watson, Burton, tr. LC 63-20339. (Translations from the Oriental Classics Ser.). 140p. (Orig.). 1963. pap. text ed. 14.00 (0-231-08608-3) Col U Pr.

Mo, Y. L. Dynamic Behavior of Concrete Structures. LC 94-17073. (Developments in Civil Engineering Ser.: Vol. 44). 1994. write for info. (0-444-81885-5) Elsevier.

Mo Yan. Explosions & Other Stories. 224p. 1991. pap. 10.50 (0-685-56989-6) SPD-Small Pr Dist.

— Explosions & Other Stories. Wickeri, Janice, ed. & tr. by. Hewitt, Duncan, tr. xii, 213p. 1991. pap. 10.50 (0-685-62360-2, Pub. by Renditions Papbk HK) SPD-Small Pr Dist.

— The Garlic Ballads. Goldblatt, Howard, tr. LC 94-34220. 1995. 23.95 (0-670-85401-8, Viking) Viking Penguin.

Moab, Ranne, ed. see Grossman, Leonid P.

Moacanin, Radmila. Jung's Psychology & Tibetan Buddhism: Western & Eastern Paths to the Heart. LC 88-51647. (East-West Book - Grey Ser.). 128p. 1994. pap. 12.95 (0-86171-042-8) Wisdom MA.

Moad, Graeme & Solomon, David H. The Chemistry of Radical Polymerization. LC 94-19382. 1994. text ed. write for info. (0-08-042078-8, Pergamon Pr) Elsevier.

Moaddel, Mansoor. Class, Politics, & Ideology in the Iranian Revolution. 300p. 1992. text ed. 37.50 (0-231-07866-8) Col U Pr.

Moag, Rodney F. Malayalam: A University Course & Reference Grammar. 3rd rev. ed. 625p. 1994. pap. text ed. 33.60 (0-89148-046-3) Ctr S&SE Asian.

Moak, Allen. A Big City ABC. (Illus.). 32p. (J). (ps up). 1989. text ed. 14.95 (0-88776-161-5, U of Toronto Pr); pap. 6.95 (0-88776-238-7, U of Toronto Pr) Tundra Bks.

Moak, D. Michael, jt. auth. see Spear, Robert K.

Moak, Jefferson M., jt. ed. see Lloyd, Mark F.

Moak, Lennox L. Municipal Bonds: Planning, Sale, & Administration. (Debt Administration Ser.). (Illus.). 400p. 37.00 (0-686-84287-1) Municipal.

Moak, Lennox L. & Cowan, Frank, Jr. Manual of Suggested Practice for Administration of Local Sales & Use Taxes. LC 61-18038. (Illus.). 311p. 1961. 8.00 (0-317-34948-1) Municipal.

Moak, Lennox L. & Killian, Kathryn W. Operating Budget Manual. LC 64-12365. (Illus.). 347p. 1963. 12.00 (0-686-84284-7) Municipal.

Moakley, Maureen, ed. Party Realignment & State Politics. 320p. 1992. lib. bdg. 49.50 (0-8142-0571-2); pap. 18.95 (0-8142-0574-7) Ohio St U Pr.

Moallem, Minoo, jt. auth. see Krooth, Richard.

Moan, T., et al. Structural Dynamics: Proceedings, 2nd European Conference, Eurodyn 93, Trondheim, Norway, June 1993. Larsen, P. K. et al, eds. (Illus.). 1300p. 1993. text ed. 170.00 (90-5410-336-1, Pub. by A A Balkema NE) Ashgate Pub Co.

Moat, Albert G. & Foster, John W. Microbial Physiology. 2nd ed. LC 87-28024. 597p. 1988. text ed. 89.95 (0-471-81251-X) Wiley.

— Microbial Physiology. 3rd ed. Date not set. text ed. 124.95 (0-471-01295-5); pap. text ed. 59.95 (0-471-01452-4) Wiley.

Moat, John. Firewater & the Miraculous Mandarin. 1990. pap. 14.95 (1-870612-70-1, Pub. by Enitha Pr UK) Dufour.

— Missing Moon. 288p. (Orig.). 1991. pap. 9.95 (1-870098-13-7, Pub. by Green Bks UK) Seven Hills Bk.

— Three Stories: Snow, Smoke, The Missing Piece. (Illus.). 60p. 1995. 40.00x (0-930126-47-5) Typographeum.

— Three Stories: Snow, Smoke, The Missing Piece. deluxe ed. (Illus.). 60p. 1995. 70.00x (0-614-05577-6) Typographeum.

Moats, Lillian S. The Gate of Dreams. 116p. (J). 1993. 21.95 (0-9636492-0-5) Cranbrook Educ.

Moats, Louisa C., jt. auth. see Bailet, Laura L.

Moats, Tamara, ed. Breaking Down the Boundaries: Artists & Museums. LC 89-24501. (Illus.). 32p. 1989. pap. 7.95 (0-935558-24-1) Henry Art.

Moats, William A., ed. Agricultural Uses of Antibiotics. LC 86-20614. (ACS Symposium Ser.: No. 320). (Illus.). ix, 200p. 1986. 43.95 (*0-8412-0996-0*) Am Chemical.

Moatti, Claude. The Search for Ancient Rome. Zielonka, Anthony, tr. (Discoveries Ser.). (Illus.). 208p. 1993. pap. 12.95 (*0-8109-2839-6*) Abrams.

Moatti, Claude, jt. auth. see Bombarde, Odile.

Moavenzadeh, F. & Geltner, D. Transportation, Energy & Economic Development: A Dilemma in the Developing World. (Energy Research Ser.: Vol. 5). 530p. 1984. 156. 50 (*0-444-42338-9*, I-247-84) Elsevier.

Moavenzadeh, Fred. Global Construction & the Environment: Strategies & Opportunities. LC 93-6346. 1994. text ed. 44.95 (*0-471-01289-0*) Wiley.

Moavenzadeh, Fred, ed. Concise Encyclopedia of Building & Construction Materials. (Advances in Materials Science & Engineering Ser.: No. 4). (Illus.). 650p. 1990. 230.00 (*0-08-034728-2*, Pergamon Pr) Elsevier.

— Concise Encyclopedia of Building & Construction Materials. (Advances in Materials Science & Engineering Ser.). 562p. 1990. 175.00 (*0-262-13248-6*) MIT Pr.

Moawad, Karen & Costain, Lynne R. Managing Medical Office Personnel. (Practice Management Ser.). (Illus.). 325p. 1990. text ed. 49.95 (*0-87489-583-9*) Med Economics.

— New Manual for Managing Dental Office Personnel: A Management Tool for Structuring & Administering Personnel Policies in the Dental Practice. 368p. 1992. 74.95 (*0-685-71295-8*, D4293) PennWell Bks.

Moawad, Karen, jt. auth. see Costain, Lynne R.

Moawad, Karen, et al. The Business of Orthodontics: Management & Administration of Your Orthodontic Practice. 550p. 1991. pap. write for info. (*0-9631446-0-X*) Hummingbrd WA.

Moayeri, Rahi. Sayeh-ye Omr (The Shadow of Life) 244p. (PER.). 1985. pap. 10.00 (*0-936347-44-9*) Iran Bks.

— Sayeh yi Omr: (Shadow of Life) (Illus.). 246p. (Orig.). (PER.). 1988. pap. 10.00 (*0-317-90548-1*) Iran Bks.

Moayyad, Heshmat, intro. Once a Dewdrop: Essays on the Poetry of Parvin E'Tesami. (Bibliotheca Iranica: Literature Ser.: No. 2). (Illus.). 282p. 1994. lib. bdg. 19. 95 (*1-56859-016-4*) Mazda Pubs.

Moayyad, Heshmat & Madelung, Margaret A. A Nightingale's Lament: Selections from the Poems & Fables of Parvin Etesami (1907-41) LC 84-60071. (Iran-e NO Literary Collection Ser.). 289p. 1985. pap. 11.95 (*0-939214-20-2*) Mazda Pubs.

Moayyad, Heshmat, ed. see Alavi, Bozorg, et al.

Moayyad, Heshmat, tr. see Jamalzadeh, Mohammad A.

Mobarg, Mats. English "Standard" Pronounciations: A Study of Attitudes. (Gothenburg Studies in English: No. 62). 380p. (Orig.). 1989. pap. 79.50x (*91-7346-214-4*, Pub. by Almqv & Wiksell SW) Coronet Bks.

Mobasser, Nilou, tr. see Naraghi, Ehsan.

Mobberley, David G. Basic Bible Commentary, Vol. 10: Psalms. Deming, Lynne M., ed. LC 94-10965. 160p. (Orig.). 1994. pap. 4.95 (*0-687-02629-6*) Abingdon.

Mobberley, James, jt. auth. see Henry, Earl.

Mobberley, Marjorie G. Rx: Take One Daily at Bedtime. 64p. (Orig.). 1989. pap. 4.95 (*1-877759-04-X*) Exodus Pr.

Mobbs, Anne, jt. auth. see Silvester, John.

Mobbs, S. D. & King, J. C., eds. Waves & Turbulence in Stably Stratified Flows. LC 92-32076. (Institute of Mathematics & Its Applications Conference Series, New Ser.: New Series 40). (Illus.). 480p. (C). 1993. 115.00 (*0-19-853661-5*, Clarendon Pr) OUP.

*__Moberg & Caldwell.__ Interactive Cases in Organizational Behavior. 2nd ed. (C). 1994. text ed. 20.00 (*0-673-99372-8*) HarpCollege.

*__Moberg, David O.__ Wholistic Christianity. fac. ed. LC 84-29216. 243p. 1985. pap. 69.30 (*0-7837-7348-X*, 2047301) Bks Demand.

Moberg, Dennis J. & Caldwell, David F. Interactive Cases in Management. (C). 1989. pap. text ed. 34.50 (*0-673-38420-9*) HarpCollege.

— Interactive Cases in Organizational Behavior. (C). 1987. pap. text ed. 31.00 (*0-673-38040-8*) HarpCollege.

Moberg, Gary P., ed. Animal Stress. (American Physiological Society Book). (Illus.). 332p. 1988. 42.50 (*0-19-520696-7*) OUP.

Moberg, George, ed. see Danna, Jo.

Moberg, Goran, jt. auth. see Whitney, Robert.

Moberg, Goran G. Writing in Groups: New Techniques for Good Writing Without Drills. 4th ed. 200p. 1994. spiral bd. 21.95 (*0-8403-9342-3*) Kendall-Hunt.

— Writing on Computers in English Composition. 160p. 1990. spiral bd. 20.95 (*0-8403-5753-2*) Kendall-Hunt.

Moberg, John, jt. auth. see Lee, Kaiman.

Moberg, Mark. Citrus, Strategy, & Class: The Politics of Development in Southern Belize. LC 91-45123. (Illus.). 228p. 1992. 29.95 (*0-87745-367-5*) U of Iowa Pr.

Moberg, Randy. TNT Teaching: Over 200 Dynamite Ways to Make Your Classroom Come Alive. Espeland, Pamela, ed. LC 93-37991. (Free Spirited Classroom Ser.). (Illus.). 160p. (Orig.). 1994. pap. 19.95 (*0-915793-64-4*) Free Spirit Pub.

Moberg, Ulf T., ed. Gunnar Ekelof: Dadaist-Constructivist. (Illus.). 60p. 1987. pap. 42.50x (*0-317-65671-6*) Coronet Bks.

Moberg, V. When I Was a Child. 1976. 24.95 (*0-8488-0302-7*) Amereon Ltd.

*__Moberg, Vilhelm.__ The Emigrants. LC 95-15848. (Vilhelm Moberg, Emigrant Novels Ser.: Bk. 1). 1995. pap. write for info. (*0-87351-319-3*, Borealis Book) Minn Hist.

— Emigrants. 1994. reprint ed. lib. bdg. 32.95x (*1-56849-312-6*) Buccaneer Bks.

— The Last Letter Home. LC 95-15845. (Vilhelm Moberg, Emigrant Novels Ser.: Bk. 4). 1995. pap. write for info. (*0-87351-322-3*, Borealis Book) Minn Hist.

— The Settlers. LC 95-15948. (Vilhelm Moberg, Emigrant Novels Ser.: Bk. 3). 1995. pap. write for info. (*0-87351-321-5*, Borealis Book) Minn Hist.

— A Time on Earth. 1994. reprint ed. lib. bdg. 29.95 (*1-56849-314-2*) Buccaneer Bks.

— The Unknown Swedes: A Book about Swedes & America, Past & Present. McKnight, Roger, ed. & tr. by. LC 88-1731. 210p. (C). 1988. text ed. 24.50 (*0-8093-1486-X*) S Ill U Pr.

— Unto a Good Land. LC 95-15847. (Vilhelm Moberg, Emigrant Novels Ser.: Bk. 2). 1995. pap. write for info. (*0-87351-320-7*, Borealis Book) Minn Hist.

— Unto a Good Land. 1994. reprint ed. lib. bdg. 29.95 (*1-56849-313-4*) Buccaneer Bks.

Moberg, Wilhelm. A History of the Swedish People: From Prehistory to the Renaissance, Vol. I. (Reprints Ser.). 210p. 1989. reprint ed. 24.95 (*0-88029-312-8*) Dorset Pr.

— A History of the Swedish People, Vol. 2: From Renaissance to Revolution. (Reprints Ser.). 268p. 1989. reprint ed. 24.95 (*0-88029-313-6*) Dorset Pr.

Moberly, Elizabeth. The Psychology of Self & Other. 112p. 1985. 18.95 (*0-422-79740-5*, 9417, Pub. by Tavistock UK) Routledge Chapman & Hall.

Moberly, Elizabeth R. Psychogenesis: The Early Development of Gender Identity. 120p. 1983. 29.95 (*0-7100-9271-7*, RKP) Routledge.

Moberly, Peter R. A City by Design. LC 93-93802. 144p. (Orig.). 1994. pap. 9.50 (*1-56002-326-0*, Univ Edtns) Aegina Pr.

Moberly, R. W. From Eden to Golgotha: Essays in Biblical Theology. LC 92-32008. (USF Studies in the History of Judaism: No. 52). 157p. 1992. 59.95 (*1-55540-749-8*, 240052) Scholars Pr GA.

— Genesis, 12-50. (Old Testament Guides Ser.). 110p. 1992. pap. 5.95 (*1-85075-371-7*, Pub. by Sheffield Acad UK) CUP Services.

— The Old Testament of the Old Testament: Patriarchal Narratives & Mosaic Yahwism. LC 91-4566. 240p. (Orig.). 1991. pap. 16.00 (*0-8006-1561-1*, 1-1561, Fortress Pr) Augsburg Fortress.

Moberly, William. Partnership Management. 250p. (C). 1983. 110.00 (*0-906322-28-6*, Pub. by Blackstone Pr UK) St Mut.

Mobil Oil Corporation Staff. Mobil Highway Atlas. 1993. pap. 4.95 (*0-671-86427-0*, P-H Travel) P-H Gen Ref & Trav.

— Mobil Pocket Atlas, 1994. 1993. pap. 2.50 (*0-671-79987-8*, P-H Travel) P-H Gen Ref & Trav.

— Mobil Road Atlas Trip Planning Guide. 1993. pap. 7.95 (*0-671-79986-X*, P-H Travel) P-H Gen Ref & Trav.

Mobil Travel Guides Staff, ed. The Northeast, 1994. (Mobil Travel Guide Ser.). (Illus.). 1994. pap. 13.95 (*0-671-87445-4*, P-H Travel) P-H Gen Ref & Trav.

*__Mobile Museum of Art Staff & Huntsville Museum of Art Staff.__ Alabama Impact: Contemporary Artists with Alabama Ties. (Illus.). 84p. (Orig.). (YA). 1995. pap. text ed. 20.00 (*1-885820-01-1*) Huntsville.

Mobilia, Wendy, et al. The Critical Skills Classroom. 1994. pap. text ed. 50.00 (*1-881245-02-0*) Antioch New Eng.

*__Mobilio, Albert, abr.__ The Geographics. (House of Outside Ser.: Vol. 2). 95p. 1995. pap. 10.00 (*0-9638433-2-X*) Hard Pr MA.

Mobium Corporation Staff, ed. see McCausland, Clare.

Mobium Corporation Staff, jt. auth. see National Park Service Staff.

Mobius, D., ed. Langmuir-Blodgett Films - Three: Proceedings of the 3rd International Conference, Gottingen, Federal Republic of Germany, 26-31 July 1987. 994p. 1988. 315.00 (*1-85166-977-9*) Elsevier.

*__Mobius, Mark.__ Investor's Guide to Emerging Markets. 192p. 1994. text ed. 45.00 (*0-7863-0320-4*) Irwin Prof Pubng.

Mobius, Mark, ed. The Investor's Guide to Emerging Markets: Profit from the World's Fastest Growing Markets. (Financial Times Management Ser.). 224p. 1993. 135.00x (*0-273-60327-2*, Pub. by Pitman Pubng UK) St Mut.

Moble, Thomas F. & Head, Thomas, eds. Soldiers of Christ: Saints & Saint's Lives from Late Antiquity & the Early Middle Ages. LC 94-6757. 416p. 1995. 50.00 (*0-271-01344-3*); pap. 18.95 (*0-271-01345-1*) Pa St U Pr.

Mobley, Andrea, jt. auth. see Mobley, Chuck.

Mobley, Carla. The Mysterious Powell Lake. (Illus.). 96p. 1984. 7.95 (*0-88839-983-9*) Hancock House.

Mobley, Charles D. Light & Water: Radiative Transfer in Natural Waters. (Illus.). 592p. 1994. text ed. 79.95 (*0-12-502750-8*) Acad Pr.

Mobley, Charles M. The Campus Site: A Prehistoric Site at Fairbanks, Alaska. LC 90-29894. (Illus.). xx, 104p. 1991. 30.00 (*0-912006-48-X*); pap. 20.00 (*0-912006-52-8*) U of Alaska Pr.

*__Mobley, Christine & Deutsch, Sheryl, eds.__ Medical Staff Management Forms, Policies, & Procedures for Health Care Providers. LC 94-49233. 1995. 179.00 (*0-8342-0539-4*) Aspen Pub.

Mobley, Chuck & Mobley, Andrea. Navajo Rugs & Blankets Coloring Book. Mahan, Nancie, ed. (Illus.). 32p. (Orig.). (J). (ps up). 1994. pap. 2.95 (*0-918080-76-2*) Treas Chest Bks.

*__Mobley, David F. & Wilson, Steven K.__ Impotence Is Reversible - Forever. Pepe, John & Billac, Pete, eds. (Illus.). 100p. Date not set. pap. 9.95 (*0-943629-16-0*) Swan Pub.

Mobley, David P. Plastics From Microbes: Microbial Synthesis of Polymers & Polymer Precursors. 280p. (C). 1994. write for info. (*1-56990-128-7*) Hanser-Gardner.

Mobley, Emily R., jt. auth. see Ferguson, Elizabeth.

Mobley-Fields, Marcy, ed. see Wold, Barbara.

Mobley, Jane & Harris, Nancy W. A City Within a Park: One Hundred Years of Parks & Boulevards in Kansas City Missouri. (Illus.). 108p. 1991. 25.00 (*0-932845-52-5*) Lowell Pr.

*__Mobley, Jane & Stein, Shifra.__ Kansas City: Heart of America. Hughes, Mary Shaw & Turner, James, eds. LC 94-30113. (Illus.). 376p. 1994. 45.00 (*0-9630029-7-X*); per., pap. 24.95 (*0-9630029-8-8*) Community Comm.

Mobley, Joe A. James City: A Black Community in North Carolina, 1863-1900. (Illus.). xiv, 113p. 1994. pap. 5.00 (*0-86526-190-3*) NC Archives.

— Pamlico County: A Brief History. (Illus.). xiv, 144p. (Orig.). 1991. pap. 8.00 (*0-86526-252-7*) NC Archives.

— Ship Ashore! The U. S. Lifesavers of Coastal North Carolina. (Illus.). 197p. (Orig.). (YA). (gr. 8-12). 1994. pap. 10.00 (*0-86526-260-8*) NC Archives.

— The USS North Carolina: Symbol of a Vanished Age. (Illus.). 16p. 1992. reprint ed. pap. 2.00 (*0-86526-219-5*) NC Archives.

*__Mobley, Joe A., ed. & intro.__ The Papers of Zebulon Baird Vance Vol. 2: 1863. (Papers of Zebulon Baird Vance). (Illus.). xxxix, 436p. (C). 1995. 35.00x (*0-86526-262-4*) NC Archives.

Mobley, Jonnie P. NTC's Dictionary of Theatre & Drama Terms. 224p. 1993. 19.95 (*0-8442-5345-6*, Natl Textbk); pap. 14.95 (*0-8442-5333-2*, Natl Textbk) NTC Pub Grp.

Mobley, Julia, jt. auth. see Schwarz, Peter.

Mobley, Lou & McKeown, Kate. Beyond IBM: Leadership, Marketing & Finance for the 1990s. (Illus.). 253p. 1989. reprint ed. 18.95 (*0-9622957-0-1*) Enter Publishing.

Mobley, Marilyn S. Folk Roots & Mythic Wings in Sarah Orne Jewett & Toni Morrison: The Cultural Function of Narrative. LC 91-15031. (Illus.). 193p. 1994. pap. 11.95 (*0-8071-1964-4*) La State U Pr.

Mobley, Mona. Joyful Hospitality. 1983. pap. 6.25 (*0-89137-431-0*) Quality Pubns.

Mobley, R. Keith. Introduction to Predictive Maintenance. 1990. text ed. 49.95 (*0-442-31828-6*) Van Nos Reinhold.

Mobley, Robert P. The Hatchery. 430p. 1994. pap. 12.95 (*1-56901-227-X*) NW Pub.

Mobley, William H. Employee Turnover: Causes, Consequences & Control. LC 81-20485. (Managing Human Resources: Wanous Ser.). 224p. (C). 1982. pap. text ed. write for info. (*0-201-04673-3*) Addison-Wesley.

Moboguunje, Akin L., jt. auth. see Ayeni, Bola.

Mobr, Richard D. Gays-Justice: A Study of Ethics, Society & Law. pap. 13.00 (*0-685-45033-3*) Col U Pr.

Mobray, M. Vincent, comp. R. R. A. S. Field List of the Birds of Nevada. 8p. 1989. pap. 2.00 (*0-9635550-1-4*) Red Rock Audubon.

Mocanu, Constantin. Hertzian Relativistic Electrodynamics & Its Associated Mechanics, 2 vols., Set. (Monographs in Physics: No. V). 439p. 1990. pap. text ed. 100.00 (*0-911767-50-9*) Hadronic Pr Inc.

Mocarski, Stanley, ed. see National Powder Metallurgy Conference Staff.

Mocatta, Moses, tr. see Troki, Isaac.

Moccero, Joyce, jt. auth. see Sanfacon, Cheryl.

Moccia, Patricia, ed. New Approaches to Theory Development. 122p. (Orig.). 1986. pap. text ed. 15.95 (*0-88737-218-X*, 15-1992) Natl League Nurse.

Moccia, Patricia, jt. ed. see Styles, Margretta M.

Mocciola, M. R. & Karantzas, K. Introduction to Expert Systems Using 1st-Class. 1990. pap. write for info. (*0-07-042626-0*) McGraw.

Mocciola, Michael & Karantzas, Constantinos P. A Mastery Approach to Paradox 4.0. 416p. 1993. teacher ed 8.00 (*1-56118-675-9*); text ed., 5.25 hd 25.95 (*1-56118-606-6*); text ed., 3.5 hd 25.95 (*1-56118-609-0*) Paradigm MN.

Mocete, Melissa, jt. ed. see Macy, Harry, Jr.

*__Moch, Cheryl, ed.__ Feels Like Home: An Evocation in Words & Pictures. LC 95-3194. (Illus.). 128p. 1995. 19. 95 (*1-56512-082-5*) Algonquin Bks.

*__Moch, Joseph, et al.__ Pharmacy Law: Litigating Pharmaceutical Cases. 625p. 1995. text ed. 125.00 (*0-913875-09-0*, 5090) Lawyers & Judges.

Moch, Joseph W. Winning Motor Vehicle Accident Cases. 1986. text ed. 75.00 (*0-934547-01-7*, 5080) CRI-Comm Res.

Moch, Joseph W. & Belli, Melvin M. Winning ATV Cases, 2 vols. 1986. ring bd. 149.00 (*0-934547-03-3*) CRI-Comm Res.

Moch, Joseph W. & Borja, Arthur. Litigating Child Restraint Cases. (Illus.). 576p. 1993. text ed. 85.00 (*0-88450-094-2*, 0942) Lawyers & Judges.

Moch, Leslie P. Moving Europeans: Migration in Western Europe since 1650. LC 92-6678. (Interdisciplinary Studies in History). 320p. 1992. 35.00 (*0-253-33859-X*) Ind U Pr.

— Paths to the City: Regional Migration in Nineteenth Century France. LC 83-2955. (New Approaches to Social Science History Ser.: No. 2). (Illus.). 261p. reprint ed. pap. 74.40 (*0-8357-8498-3*, 2034774) Bks Demand.

Moch, Leslie P. & Stark, Gary D., eds. Essays on the Family & Historical Change. LC 82-45900. (Walter Prescott Webb Memorial Lectures: No. 17). 160p. 1983. 17.50 (*0-89096-151-4*) Tex A&M Univ Pr.

Moch, Leslie P., jt. ed. see Hoerder, Dirk.

*__Moch, Susan D., ed.__ Breast Cancer: Twenty Women's Stories. 1995. pap. write for info. (*0-88737-654-1*) Natl League Nurse.

Moche, Dinah. The Astronauts. LC 78-54955. (Pictureback Ser.). (Illus.). (J). (ps-3). 1979. pap. 2.25 (*0-394-83901-3*) Random Bks Yng Read.

— Astronomy Today: Planets, Stars, Space Exploration. LC 82-5211. (Library of Knowledge). (Illus.). 96p. (J). (gr. 5 up). 1982. pap. 13.00 (*0-394-84423-8*) Random Bks Yng Read.

— If You Were an Astronaut. (Golden Look-Look Bks.). (Illus.). 24p. (J). (ps-3). 1992. pap. write for info. (*0-307-11896-7*, 11896-02, Golden Pr) Western Pub.

Moche, Dinah L. Astronomy: A Self Teaching Guide. 4th ed. 368p. 1993. pap. text ed. 17.95 (*0-471-53001-8*) Wiley.

Moche, Dinah L., jt. auth. see Zeilik, Michael.

Mochel, Etta. Residential Care for Business Profit. Date not set. 89.95 (*0-685-74751-4*) E M Vid.

Mochel, Gerhard. Russian-German Economics Dictionaries: Grosses Oekonomisches Woerterbuch Russisch-Deutsch. 3rd ed. 576p. (GER & RUS.). 1983. 95.00 (*0-8288-0821-X*, M7575) Fr & Eur.

Mochizuki, Ken. Baseball Saved Us. LC 92-73215. (Illus.). 32p. (J). (gr. k up). 1993. 14.95 (*1-880000-01-6*) Lee & Low Bks.

— Baseball Saved Us. (Illus.). 32p. (J). (gr. k up). 1995. pap. 5.95 (*1-880000-19-9*) Lee & Low Bks.

— El Beisbol Nos Salvo. Gonzalez, Tomas, tr. LC 94-32517. (Illus.). 32p. (SPA.). (J). (gr. k up). 1995. 14.95 (*1-880000-21-0*); pap. 5.95 (*1-880000-22-9*) Lee & Low Bks.

— Heroes. LC 94-26541. (Illus.). 32p. (J). (gr. k up). 1995. 14.95 (*1-880000-16-4*) Lee & Low Bks.

Mochizuki, M. & Hussa, R., eds. Placental Protein Hormones: Proceedings of the Satellite Symposium, 14-15 July, 1988, Kobe, Japan. (International Congress Ser.: No. 798). 336p. 1989. 102.75 (*0-444-81048-X*, Excerpta Medica) Elsevier.

Mochizuki, M., et al. Japan & the United States: Troubled Partners in a Changing World. 156p. (C). 1991. pap. 11. 95 (*0-08-041074-X*) Brasseys Inc.

Mochizuki, M., et al, eds. Oxygen Transport to Tissue, No. X. LC 87-32879. (Advances in Experimental Medicine & Biology Ser.: Vol. 222). (Illus.). 784p. 1988. 145.00 (*0-306-42795-8*, Plenum Pr) Plenum.

*__Mochizuki, Mike M., et al.__ The Strategic Quadrangle: Japan, China, Russia, & the United States in East Asia. Mandelbaum, Michael, ed. 150p. 1994. pap. text ed. 16. 95 (*0-87609-168-0*) Coun Foreign.

Mochizuki, Selbu, jt. ed. see Yazaki, Yoshio.

Mochmann, E., jt. ed. see De Guchteneire, P. F.

Mochmann, Ekkehard & Muller, Paul J. Data Protection & Social Science Research. 229p. (C). 1982. text ed. 39.50 (*3-593-32604-3*) Irvington.

Mochnick, Beth R. New Holiday Songs for Children: A Creative Approach. Davis, Barbara, ed. (Illus.). iv, 44p. (J). 1988. pap. text ed. 14.95 (*0-916656-25-X*, MFBK 25) Mark Foster Mus.

Mochon, Anne, jt. auth. see Barter, Judith.

Mochslinska, Ania, ed. Angels in the Air. 1994. pap. 14.95 (*0-671-51013-4*, Fireside) S&S Trade.

Mochulsky, Konstantin. Aleksandr Blok. Johnson, Doris V., tr. LC 82-20212. 453p. reprint ed. pap. 129.20 (*0-7837-3633-9*, 2043500) Bks Demand.

— Dostoevsky: His Life & Work. Minihan, Michael A., tr. 1967. pap. 24.95 (*0-691-01299-7*) Princeton U Pr.

Mock, Alfred R., jt. auth. see Gregoire, Christopher P.

Mock, David B. History & Public Policy. 228p. (C). 1991. 24.50 (*0-89464-288-X*) Krieger.

*__Mock, David B., ed.__ Legacy of the West: Readings in the History of Western Civilization, 2, 1. LC 94-26316. (C). 1994. 21.50 (*0-673-46999-9*) HarpCollege.

— Legacy of the West: Readings in the History of Western Civilization, 2, 2. LC 94-26316. (C). 1994. 21.50 (*0-673-99000-1*) HarpCollege.

— Legacy of the West Vol. 1: To the Reformation. (Readings in the History of Western Civilization Ser.). 288p. 1995. reprint ed. pap. 26.95 (*1-886746-14-1*) Talman Pub.

— Legacy of the West Vol. 2: Age of Reason to the Present. (Readings in the History of Western Civilization Ser.). 288p. 1995. reprint ed. pap. 26.95 (*1-886746-15-X*) Talman Pub.

Mock, Dorothy. Aqua Kid Saves the Day: The Good News Kids Learn about Peace. (Good News Kids Ser.). (Illus.). 32p. (Orig.). (J). (ps-2). 1992. pap. 3.99 (*0-570-04718-8*) Concordia.

— Fire Truck Friends: The Good News Kids Learn about Joy. (Good News Kids Ser.). (Illus.). 32p. (Orig.). (J). (ps-2). 1992. pap. 3.99 (*0-570-04717-X*) Concordia.

— One Big Family: The Good News Kids Learn about Kindness. LC 92-27012. (Good News Kids Ser.). (Illus.). 32p. (Orig.). (J). (ps-2). 1993. pap. 3.99 (*0-570-04737-4*) Concordia.

— Springtime Special: The Good News Kids Learn about Patience. LC 92-27010. (Good News Kids Ser.). (Illus.). 32p. (Orig.). (J). (ps-2). 1993. pap. 5.99 (*0-570-04736-6*) Concordia.

— The Trouble with Trevor: The Good News Kids Learn about Goodness. LC 92-27013. (Good News Kids Ser.). (Illus.). 32p. (Orig.). (J). (ps-2). 1993. pap. 3.99 (*0-570-04738-2*) Concordia.

— Worms for Winston: The Good News Kids Learn about Love. (Good News Kids Ser.). (Illus.). 32p. (Orig.). (J). (ps-2). 1992. pap. 5.99 (*0-570-04716-1*) Concordia.

Mock, Dorothy K. The Big Secret: The Good News Kids Learn about Gentleness. LC 93-6865. (Good News Kids Ser.). (Illus.). 32p. (Orig.). (J). (ps-2). 1993. pap. 3.99 (*0-570-04744-7*) Concordia.

— God Is Everywhere: The Good News Kids Learn about Self-Control. LC 93-22311. (Good News Kids Ser.). (Illus.). 32p. (Orig.). (J). (ps-2). 1993. pap. 3.99 (*0-570-04745-5*) Concordia.

— The Thanksgiving Parade: The Good News Kids Learn about Faithfulness. LC 93-2988. (Good News Kids Ser.). (Illus.). 32p. (Orig.). (J). (ps-2). 1993. pap. 3.99 (*0-570-04743-9*) Concordia.

Mock, Douglas. Behavior & Evolution of Birds. (C). 1995. text ed. write for info. (*0-7167-2237-2*) W H Freeman.

Mock, Edward J., jt. auth. see Schuckett, Donald H.

An Asterisk (*) at the beginning of an entry indicates that the title is appearing in BIP for the first time.

Mock, Elizabeth B. The Architecture of Bridges. LC 70-169309. (Museum of Modern Art Publications in Reprint). (Illus.). 128p. 1972. reprint ed. 24.95 (*0-405-01568-2*) Ayer.

Mock, Elizabeth B., et al, eds. Built in U. S. A. Nineteen Thirty-Two to Nineteen Forty-Four. Bd. with Post-War Architecture. LC 68-57299. LC 68-57299. (Museum of Modern Art Publications in Reprint). (Illus.). 260p. 1969. reprint ed. 24.95 (*0-405-01526-7*) Ayer.

Mock, Esther. Four on the Rocks. Van Treese, James B., ed. 250p. 1994. pap. 8.95 (*1-56901-207-5*) NW Pub.

— Taken by Surprise: Travel After Fifty. Parker, Diane, ed. LC 90-50899. 130p. 1991. pap. 5.95 (*0-88247-860-5*) R & E Pubs.

— Taken by Surprise: Travel after Sixty. LC 91-61315. 128p. 1991. pap. 6.95 (*0-88247-880-X*) R & E Pubs.

Mock, Esther G. Roots in Concrete. LC 90-84996. 1992. 15.95 (*0-8158-0466-0*) Chris Mass.

Mock, Gary N., jt. ed. see Grady, Perry L.

Mock, Greg. Virginia's Shenandoah Valley. (Illus.). 104p. (Orig.). 1990. pap. 15.95 (*0-938314-83-1*) Am Wrld Geog.

***Mock, J. Dennis.** Accounts Receivable Management for the Medical Practice. (Orig.). 1995. pap. 39.95 (*0-07-600714-6*) Hlthcare Mgmt Grp.

Mock, James R. Censorship Nineteen Seventeen. LC 74-37864. (Civil Liberties in American History Ser.). 250p. 1972. reprint ed. lib. bdg. 29.50 (*0-306-70436-6*) Da Capo.

Mock, James R. & Larson, Cedric. Words That Won the War: The Mobilization of Mass Hatred. 1985. lib. bdg. 79.95 (*0-87700-652-0*) Revisionist Pr.

Mock, Jeffery I. Preview II: An Introduction to Applications Software. 1987. IBM Version. pap. text ed. 11.95 (*0-8053-2405-4*); disk 11.95 (*0-8053-2334-1*); disk 11.95 (*0-8053-2407-0*); write for info. (*0-8053-2335-X*) Benjamin-Cummings.

Mock, Jerrie. First Woman to Fly Solo Around the World: To Finish What Amelia Began. rev. ed. (Illus.). 300p. 1985. pap. write for info. (*0-931515-04-1*) Triumph Pr.

Mock, Jess, et al, eds. The Engineer's Responsibility to Society. LC 78-102888. 76p. reprint ed. pap. 25.00 (*0-317-08067-9*, 2016823) Bks Demand.

Mock, Lonnie. Excel in Chinese Cooking. Haggerty, Nancy, ed. LC 81-70318. (Illus.). 208p. (Orig.). 1982. pap. 7.95 (*0-941716-00-7*) Alpha Gamma.

— Favorite Dim Sum. Haggerty, Nancy, ed. (Illus.). 130p. (Orig.). 1979. pap. 4.95 (*0-941716-03-1*) Alpha Gamma.

— One Hundred Forty-One & One-Half Chinese-Style Chicken Recipes. Haggerty, Nancy, ed. (Illus.). 208p. (Orig.). 1980. pap. 6.95 (*0-941716-04-X*) Alpha Gamma.

Mock, Nancy. Play-Likes for Preschoolers. Gross, Karen, ed. 8p. (Orig.). 1991. pap. text ed. 5.95 (*1-56309-009-0*, New Hope AL) Womans Mission Union.

Mock, Patricia, jt. auth. see Luder, Ian.

***Mock, Randall D.** Oklahoma Corporate Forms. 1120p. 1993. disk, ring bd. 239.00 (*0-87189-975-2*) Michie Butterworth.

Mock, Theodore J. Measurement & Accounting Information Criteria. (Studies in Accounting Research: Vol. 13). 116p. 1976. 12.00 (*0-86539-025-8*) Am Accounting.

Mock, Theodore J. & Grove, Hugh D. Measurement, Accounting, & Organizational Information. LC 78-10536. (Wiley Series in Accounting & Information Systems). (Illus.). 255p. reprint ed. pap. 73.00 (*0-7837-3458-1*, 2057784) Bks Demand.

Mock, Theodore J. & Turner, Jerry. Internal Accounting Control Evaluation & Auditor Judgment. LC 81-131494. (Auditing Research Monograph Ser.: No. 3). (Illus.). 172p. reprint ed. pap. 49.10 (*0-8357-2811-0*, 2037599) Bks Demand.

Mock, Valerie E. A.S.M.D. Multi-Graded Arithmetic Practice & Drill Sheets. (Makemaster Bk.). (J). (gr. 1-6). 1977. pap. 20.99 (*0-8224-0462-1*) Fearon Teach Aids.

Mock, Valerie E., jt. ed. see Burden, Charles A.

Mockaitis, Thomas. Easy Business English. 200p. (C). 1991. teacher ed 5.45 (*1-56118-015-7*); pap. text ed. 11.95 (*1-56118-016-5*) Paradigm MN.

***Mockaitis, Thomas R.** British Counterinsurgency in the Post-Imperial Era. LC 94-29769. (War, Armed Forces, & Society Ser.). 1995. text ed. write for info. (*0-7190-3919-3*) St Martin.

— British Counterinsurgency, Nineteen Nineteen to Nineteen Sixty. LC 90-30357. 192p. 1990. text ed. 49.95 (*0-312-04618-9*) St Martin.

Mockapetris, Paul. Internet Technology Series: Domain Name System. 1994. text ed. 36.00 (*0-13-106865-2*) P-H.

Mocker, Donald W. & Spear, George E., eds. Urban Education: A Guide to Information Sources. LC 78-13627. (Urban Studies Information Guide Ser.: Vol. 3). 216p. 1978. 68.00 (*0-8103-1431-2*) Gale.

***Mocker, Roger M.** Medical, Mental & Emotional Factors in Human Personality Disorders: Index of New Information with Authors, Subjects & Bibliography. LC 95-16127. 1995. write for info. (*0-7883-0708-8*); pap. write for info. (*0-7883-0709-6*) ABBE Pubs Assn.

— Medical, Mental & Emotional Factors in Human Personality Disorders: Index of New Information with Authors, Subjects & Bibliography. rev. ed. 155p. 1994. 49.50 (*0-7883-0406-2*); pap. 39.50 (*0-7883-0407-0*) ABBE Pubs Assn.

Mockerie, Parmenas G. An African Speaks for His People. LC 74-15068. reprint ed. 27.50 (*0-404-12110-1*) AMS Pr.

***Mocket, Richard.** Doctrina et Politia Ecclesiae Anglicanae: An Anglican Summa : Facsimile with Variants of the Text of 1617. Screech, M. A., ed. & intro. by. LC 94-40063. (Studies in the History of Christian Thought: Vol. 62). 1994. text ed. 125.75 (*90-04-10040-7*) E J Brill.

Mockford, Edward L. North American Psocoptera (Insecta) Arnett, Ross H., Jr., ed. (Flora & Fauna Handbook Ser.: No. 10). (Illus.). xii, 455p. 1993. 69.95 (*1-877743-12-7*) Sandhill Crane.

Mockford, H. God Willing. 1981. pap. 3.99 (*0-9505476-6-2*, Pub. by Evangel Pr UK) Presby & Reformed.

***Mockle, J. Auguste.** A New Generation of Phytomedicines (High Quality Standardized Galenical Prepatations) Ginkgo, Bilberry, Ginseng, Garlic & Their Extraordinary Therapeutic Properties. 50p. (Orig.). 1994. pap. 3.50 (*0-87983-676-8*) Keats.

Mockler, Anthony. King Arthur & His Knights. (Oxford Illustrated Classics Ser.). (Illus.). 308p. (J). 1987. 18.95 (*0-19-274531-X*) OUP.

Mockler, R. J. Knowledge-Based Systems for Management Decisions. 512p. 1988. text ed. 57.00 (*0-13-516907-0*) P-H.

Mockler, Robert, jt. auth. see Dologite, Dorothy G.

Mockler, Robert J. Strategic Management: An Integrative Context Specific Process. 928p. 1993. 84.95 (*1-878289-19-5*) Idea Group Pub.

Mockler, Robert J., ed. Strategic Management Cases. 1993. 30.00 (*0-536-58303-X*) Ginn Pr.

Mockler, Robert J. & Dologite, D. G. Knowledge-Based Systems for Strategic Corporate Planning. 1987. 29.95 (*0-912841-24-9*) Planning Forum.

Mockler, Robert J. & Easop, Harrison. Guidelines for More Effective Planning & Management of Franchise Systems. LC 68-66049. (Research Monograph: No. 42). 1968. spiral bd. 19.95 (*0-88406-056-X*) GA St U Busn Pr.

Mocko, George P. Lord, Empower Us! Sherer, Michael L., ed. (Orig.). 1987. pap. 2.90 (*0-89536-851-X*, 7810) CSS OH.

Mockor, Jiri. Groups of Divisibility. 1983. lib. bdg. 90.00 (*90-277-1539-4*) Kluwer Ac.

Mockor, Jiri, jt. auth. see Alajbegovic, Jusuf H.

Mockridge, Patricia & Mockridge, Philip. Weathervanes. 1989. pap. 25.00 (*0-7478-0191-6*, Pub. by Shire UK) St Mut.

Mockridge, Philip, jt. auth. see Mockridge, Patricia.

Mockrin, Ida. The Big Parade. (Illus.). 16p. (J). (ps-1). 1983. pap. 2.00 (*0-9612244-0-1*) Honeycomb Pr.

Mockus, Jonas. Bayesian Approach to Global Optimization: Theory & Applications. (C). 1989. lib. bdg. 134.00 (*0-7923-0115-3*) Kluwer Ac.

Mocquereau, Andre. Le Nombre Musical Gregorien ou Rythmique Gregorienne - Theorie et Pratique, Vol. 1. 430p. (FRE.). (C). 1908. pap. 36.95 (*1-55725-131-2*, 4071, Pub. by Abbey St Peter Solesmes FR) Paraclete MA.

— Le Nombre Musical Gregorien ou Rythmique Gregorienne - Theorie et Pratique, Vol. 2. 856p. (FRE.). (C). 1927. pap. 32.95 (*1-55725-130-4*, 4072, Pub. by Abbey St Peter Solesmes FR) Paraclete MA.

Mocsny, Daniel, jt. auth. see Govind, Rakesh.

Mocsy, Istvan I. The Uprooted. 1983. text ed. 42.00 (*0-88033-039-2*, 147) Col U Pr.

Moctezuma, Eduardo M. The Great Temple of the Aztecs: Treasures of Tenochtitlan. LC 87-50201. (Illus.). 360p. 1994. pap. 19.95 (*0-500-27752-4*) Thames Hudson.

— Life & Death in the Templo Mayor. Ortiz De Montellano, Bernard R. & Ortiz De Montellano, Thelma, trs. (Illus.). 160p. 1995. pap. 14.95 (*0-87081-400-1*) Univ Pr Colo.

— Teotihuacan. LC 89-43584. 240p. 1990. 75.00 (*0-8478-1198-0*) Rizzoli Intl.

— Treasures of the Great Temple. (Illus.). 180p. 1990. 39.95 (*0-9625399-6-1*) ALTI Pub.

Moctezuma, Eduardo M., jt. auth. see Carrasco, David.

Moctezuma, Eduardo M., jt. auth. see Day, Jane S.

Mocton, D. E., jt. ed. see Brown, G.

Moczar, L., jt. auth. see Gordh, Gordon.

Moczar, Louis J. Balance of Payments of the United States: Concepts, Data Sources, & Estimating Procedures. 160p. 1990. per., pap. 8.50 (*0-16-025051-X*, S/N 003-010-002) USGPO.

Moczydlowski, Pawel. The Hidden Life of Polish Prisons. LC 91-47660. 176p. 1992. 35.00 (*0-253-33861-1*) Ind U Pr.

Modak, B. R. The Ancillary Literature of the Atharva-Veda: A Study with Special Reference to the Parisistas. 570p. 1993. 53.50 (*81-215-0607-7*, Pub. by M Manoharial II) Coronet Bks.

Modan, Shula. Why Jonathan Doesn't Cry. (Illus.). (J). (ps-2). 1988. 7.95 (*1-55774-022-4*, Watts) Modan-Adama Bks.

Modarres, Mohammed. WEESKA Reliability & Risk Analysis. LC 92-32998. (What Every Engineer Should Know Ser.: Vol. 30). 360p. 1992. 55.00 (*0-8247-8958-X*) Dekker.

Modarressi, Hossein. Crisis & Consolidation in the Formative Period of Shi'ite Islam: Abu Ja'far ibn Qiba Al-Razi & His Contribution to Imamite Shi'ite Thought. LC 92-41266. 296p. 1993. 35.00 (*0-87850-095-2*) Darwin Pr.

Modarressi, Mitra. The Dream Pillow. LC 93-49400. (Illus.). 32p. (J). (ps-2). 1994. 14.95 (*0-531-06855-2*); lib. bdg. 14.99 (*0-531-08705-0*) Orchard Bks Watts.

— The Parent Thief. LC 94-45916. (Illus.). 32p. (J). (ps-3). 1995. 15.95 (*0-531-09476-6*); lib. bdg. 15.99 (*0-531-08776-X*) Orchard Bks Watts.

Modayil, Sujatha. Crucifixions. (Redbird Ser.). 1975. 8.00 (*0-88253-725-3*); 4.80 (*0-89253-543-1*) Ind-US Inc.

— We the Unreconciled. (Redbird Ser.). 52p. 1975. 10.00 (*0-88253-672-9*); pap. text ed. 4.80 (*0-88253-671-0*) Ind-US Inc.

Moddel, Cantor P. Max Helfman: A Biographical Tribute. 1974. 10.00 (*0-943376-04-1*) Magnes Mus.

Moddelmog, Debra, jt. comp. see Secor, Robert.

Moddelmog, Debra A. Readers & Mythic Signs: The Oedipus Myth in Twentieth-Century Fiction. LC 92-34304. (Illus.). 208p. (C). 1993. 24.95 (*0-8093-1846-6*) S Ill U Pr.

Modder, U., jt. auth. see Beyer, D.

Modderno, Francine, jt. auth. see Cantrell, Will.

Moddie, A. D., ed. The Concept of Work in Indian Society. 1990. 29.00 (*81-85425-16-7*, Pub. by Manohar II) S Asia.

Moddy, Frank, jt. auth. see Schoenfield, Leslie J.

Mode, C. J. Stochastic Processes in Demography & Their Computer Implementation. (Biomathematics Ser.: Vol. 14). (Illus.). 430p. 1985. 98.00 (*0-387-13622-3*) Spr-Verlag.

Mode, P. G. The Frontier Spirit in American Christianity. 1977. lib. bdg. 59.95 (*0-8490-1870-6*) Gordon Pr.

Mode, Paul J., jt. auth. see Johnson, David R.

Mode, Peter G. Source Book & Bibliographical Guide to American Church History. 1964. reprint ed. 17.50 (*0-910324-06-9*) Canner.

***Model Airplane News Editors Staff.** Radio Control Airplane How-To's, Vol. 2. Masi, Frank, ed. (Illus.). 160p. (Orig.). 1995. pap. 14.95 (*0-911295-33-X*) Air Age.

Model Airplane News Staff. Scale Aircraft Drawings, Vol. 1, WW I. 154p. 1986. pap. 14.95 (*0-911295-02-X*) Air Age.

Model, F. Peter, jt. auth. see Pedersen, Laura.

Model Jury Instructions Committee. Manual of Model Civil Jury Instructions for the Ninth Circuit. 303p. (C). 1993. pap. text ed. write for info. (*0-314-02583-9*) West Pub.

***Model Jury Instructions Committee Staff.** Virginia Model Jury Instructions - Civil, 1993 Edition, 2 vols., Set. 1993. ring bd. 190.00 (*1-55834-145-5*) Michie Butterworth.

— Virginia Model Jury Instructions - Criminal, 1989 Replacement Edition with 1991 Supplements, 2 vols., Set. rev. ed. 1989. 180.00 (*0-87473-482-7*) Michie Butterworth.

— Virginia Model Jury Instructions - Criminal, 1993 Edition, 2 vols., Set. 1993. ring bd. 190.00 (*1-55834-137-4*) Michie Butterworth.

Model, Mitchell L. Data Structures, Data Abstractions: A Contemporary Introduction Using C Plus Plus. LC 93-33118. 1993. text ed. 59.00 (*0-13-088782-X*) P-H.

Model Railroad Magazine Staff, jt. auth. see Drury, George.

Model Railroader Magazine Staff. Building the Burlington Northern RR in N Scale. Emmerich, Michael, ed. (Illus.). 56p. (Orig.). 1990. pap. 8.95 (*0-89024-119-8*) Kalmbach.

— Forty-Eight Top-Notch Track Plans. LC 93-30051. (Model Railroad Handbook Ser.: No. 39). 1993. 14.95 (*0-89024-190-2*) Kalmbach.

— MR Plan Index. Drury, George, ed. 60p. 1993. pap. 11.95 (*0-89024-186-4*) Kalmbach.

— Scenery Tips & Techniques from Model Railroader Magazine. Emmerich, Michael, ed. (Illus.). 116p. (Orig.). 1989. pap. 12.95 (*0-89024-095-7*) Kalmbach.

— Six HO Railroads You Can Build. LC 93-28560. (Model Railroad Handbook Ser.: No. 38). (Illus.). 144p. 1993. 16.95 (*0-89024-189-9*) Kalmbach.

Model Railroader Staff. Model Railroad Bridges & Trestles. Emmerich, Michael, ed. (Illus.). 152p. (Orig.). 1992. pap. 17.95 (*0-89024-128-7*) Kalmbach.

Model Railroader Staff & Dolzall, Donnette, eds. ABCs of Model Railroading. LC 78-55680. 1978. pap. 7.95 (*0-89024-536-3*) Kalmbach.

Modell, Arnold. Psychoanalysis in a New Context. LC 84-12965. xii, 294p. 1985. text ed. 40.00x (*0-8236-5212-2*, 05212) Intl Univs Pr.

Modell, Arnold H. Object Love & Reality: An Introduction to a Psychoanalytic Theory of Object Relations. LC 68-24219. 181p. 1968. text ed. 27.50x (*0-8236-3720-4*) Intl Univs Pr.

— Other Times, Other Realities: Toward a Theory of Psychoanalytic Treatment. 208p. 1990. text ed. 27.50 (*0-685-32245-9*) HUP.

— Other Times, Other Realities: Toward a Theory of Psychoanalytic Treatment. 208p. (C). 1990. 36.00 (*0-674-64498-0*) HUP.

— The Private Self. LC 93-14974. 262p. 1993. 29.95 (*0-674-70752-4*) HUP.

Modell, Bernadette & Modell, Michael. Towards a Healthy Baby: Congenital Disorders & the New Genetics in Primary Health Care. (Illus.). 430p. 1992. 95.00 (*0-19-262234-X*); pap. 49.95 (*0-19-261486-X*) OUP.

Modell, Frank. Ice Cream Soup. LC 87-21097. (Illus.). 24p. (J). (ps-3). 1988. 11.95 (*0-688-07770-6*); lib. bdg. 11.88 (*0-688-07771-4*) Greenwillow.

— Look Out, It's April Fools' Day. LC 84-4138. (Illus.). 24p. (J). (ps up). 1985. 13.00 (*0-688-04016-0*); lib. bdg. 12.88 (*0-688-04017-9*) Greenwillow.

— One Zillion Valentines. LC 81-2215. (Illus.). 32p. (J). (gr. k-3). 1981. 12.93 (*0-688-00565-9*); lib. bdg. 11.88 (*0-688-00569-1*) Greenwillow.

— One Zillion Valentines. LC 81-2215. 32p. (J). (ps up). 1987. reprint ed. pap. 3.95 (*0-688-07329-8*, Mulberry) Morrow.

— Skeeter & the Computer. LC 84-1585. (Illus.). 24p. (J). (ps-3). 1988. 11.95 (*0-688-03703-8*); lib. bdg. 11.88 (*0-688-03706-2*) Greenwillow.

Modell, Harold I. & Michael, Joel A., eds. Promoting Active Learning in the Life Science Classroom. LC 94-3002. (Annals Ser.: Vol. 701). 1994. 25.00 (*0-89766-829-4*); pap. write for info. (*0-89766-830-8*) NY Acad Sci.

Modell, John. Into One's Own: From Youth to Adulthood in the United States, 1920-1975. 1989. 40.00 (*0-520-04136-4*) U CA Pr.

— Into One's Own: From Youth to Adulthood in the United States, 1920-1975. (Illus.). 428p. 1991. reprint ed. pap. 15.00 (*0-520-07641-9*) U CA Pr.

Modell, John, jt. auth. see Bonacich, Edna.

Modell, John, jt. ed. see Karsten, Peter.

Modell, John, ed. see Kikuchi, Charles.

Modell, Joseph D., et al. Transmitter Hunting: Radio Direction Finding Simplified. (Illus.). 336p. (Orig.). 1987. pap. 19.95 (*0-8306-2701-4*) TAB Bks.

Modell, Judith. Kinship with Strangers: Adoption & Interpretations of Kinship in American Culture. LC 92-37617. 230p. 1994. 35.00 (*0-520-08118-8*) U CA Pr.

Modell, Martin E. Data Analysis, Data Modeling, & Classification. 1992. text ed. 43.00 (*0-07-042634-1*) McGraw.

— Data-Directed Systems Design: A Professional's Guide. 1990. text ed. 43.00 (*0-07-042633-3*) McGraw.

— A Professional's Guide to Systems Analysis. 336p. 1988. text ed. 43.00 (*0-07-042632-5*) McGraw.

Modell, Michael & Boyd, Robert. Paediatric Problems in General Practice. 2nd ed. (Oxford General Practice Ser.: No. 13). (Illus.). 336p. 1988. pap. 31.50 (*0-19-261736-2*) OUP.

Modell, Michael & Reid, Robert C. Thermodynamics & Its Applications. 2nd ed. (Illus.). 512p. 1983. text ed. 91.00 (*0-13-915017-X*) P-H.

Modell, Michael, jt. auth. see Modell, Bernadette.

Modelski, Andrew M. Railroad Maps of North America: The First Hundred Years. LC 82-675134. 186p. 1984. 28.00 (*0-8444-0396-2*, 030-004-00021-3) Lib Congress.

— Railroad Maps of North America: The First Hundred Years. LC 82-675134. (Illus.). 207p. 1984. 28.00 (*0-16-004053-1*, S/N 030-004-00021-3) USGPO.

Modelski, George. Long Cycles in World Politics. LC 86-15731. 256p. 1986. 30.00 (*0-295-96430-8*) U of Wash Pr.

***Modelski, George & Thompson, William R.** Leading Sectors & World Powers: The Coevolution of Global Economics & Politics. LC 95-4372. (Studies in International Relations). 1995. write for info. (*1-57003-054-5*) U of SC Pr.

— Seapower in Global Politics: 1494-1993. LC 87-10472. (Illus.). 384p. 1987. 35.00 (*0-295-96502-9*) U of Wash Pr.

Modelski, Sylvia, tr. see Levi-Strauss, Claude.

Moden, Karl-Markus. Tax Incentives of Corporate Mergers & Foreign Direct Investments. (IUI Dissertation Ser.: No. 7). 195p. (Orig.). 1993. pap. 52.50x (*91-7204-442-X*, Pub. by Almqv & Wiksell SW) Coronet Bks.

***Moder, Joseph J., et al.** Project Management with CPM, Pert & Precedence Diagramming. 3rd ed. (Illus.). 389p. (C). 1995. pap. text ed. 40.00 (*0-9606344-8-7*) Blitz Pub Co.

Modern Bride Editors & Dahl, Stephanie H. The Modern Bride Guide to Your Wedding & Marriage. (Illus.). 160p. 1987. pap. 8.95 (*0-345-34792-7*, Ballantine Trade) Ballantine.

Modern Engineering Practice Staff. Pattern Making for Metal Castings. 138p. 1991. reprint ed. 22.00 (*1-877767-45-X*); reprint ed. pap. text ed. 12.00 (*1-877767-46-8*) Univ Publng Hse.

***Modern Language Association of America Staff.** Directory of Undergraduate Internships in the Humanities. fac. ed. LC 84-25486. 154p. 1984. reprint ed. pap. 43.90 (*0-7837-8037-0*, 2047793) Bks Demand.

— Proceedings of the Neo-Classicism Conferences, 1967-1968. Korshin, Paul J., ed. (Studies in the Eighteenth Century: No. 1). reprint ed. 34.50 (*0-404-07949-0*) AMS Pr.

— Profession Eighty: Selected Articles from the Bulletins of the Association of Departments of English & the Association of Foreign Languages. fac. ed. (Illus.). 50p. 1980. reprint ed. pap. 25.00 (*0-7837-8023-0*, 2047779) Bks Demand.

— Profession Eighty-Eight. fac. ed. Zuses, Carol & FRanklin, Phyllis, eds. 83p. 1988. reprint ed. pap. 25.00 (*0-7837-8029-X*, 2047785) Bks Demand.

— Profession Eighty-One: Selected Articles from the Bulletins of the Association of Departments of English & the Association of Departments of Foreign Languages. fac. ed. (Illus.). 49p. 1981. reprint ed. pap. 25.00 (*0-7837-8024-9*, 2047780) Bks Demand.

— Profession Eighty-Two: Selected Articles from the Bulletins of the Association of Departments of English & the Association of Departments of Foreign Languages. fac. ed. 56p. 1982. reprint ed. pap. 25.00 (*0-7837-8025-7*, 2047781) Bks Demand.

— Profession 79: Selected Articles from the Bulletins of the Association of Departments of English & the Association of Departments of Foreign Languages. fac. ed. Neel, Jasper P. & Brod, Richard I., eds. 65p. 1979. reprint ed. pap. 25.00 (*0-7837-8022-2*, 2047778) Bks Demand.

— Sexual & Gender Harassment in the Academy: A Guide for Faculty, Students, & Administrators. fac. ed. LC 81-14059. 79p. 1981. reprint ed. pap. 25.00 (*0-7837-8030-3*, 2047786) Bks Demand.

Modern Language Association Staff. Modern Spanish. 3rd ed. 442p. (C). 1973. text ed. 45.25 (*0-15-563974-9*); teacher ed, pap. text ed. 14.50 (*0-15-563975-7*); Writing Modern Spanish. student ed 19.50 (*0-15-563976-5*) HB Coll Pubs.

Modern Language Association Staff, ed. Directory of Master's Programs in Foreign Languages, Foreign Literatures, & Linguistics. LC 87-11254. ix, 173p. (Orig.). 1987. pap. 15.00 (*0-87352-169-2*, D312P) Modern Lang.

Modern Machine Shop Staff. Electrical Discharge Machining Conference Proceedings, 1991. 221p. (C). 1991. pap. text ed. 45.00 (*1-56990-066-3*) Hanser-Gardner.

M

— Electrical Discharge Machining Conference Proceedings, 1993. 250p. (C). 1993. pap. text ed. 65.00 (*1-56990-124-4*) Hanser-Gardner.

*__Modern Plastics Magazine Staff.__ Plastics Handbook. LC 94-31859. 1995. text ed. 55.50 (*0-07-042805-0*) McGraw.

Modersohn-Becker, Paula. The Letters & Journals of Paula Modersohn-Becker. LC 80-18993. 370p. 1980. 29.50 (*0-8108-1344-0*) Scarecrow.

Modert, Jo. Jane Austen's Manuscript Letters in Facsimile: Reproductions of Every Known Extant Letter, Fragment, & Autograph Copy, with an Annotated List of All Known Letters. LC 88-39599. (Illus.). 572p. (C). 1989. 50.00 (*0-8093-1403-7*) S Ill U Pr.

Moderwell, Hiram K. Theatre of To-Day. LC 72-7078. (Select Bibliographies Reprint Ser.). 1977. reprint ed. 40.95 (*0-8369-6950-2*) Ayer.

Modesitt, Jeanne. Lunch with Milly. LC 93-33808. (Illus.). 32p. (J). (gr. k-3). 1995. lib. bdg. 13.95 (*0-8167-3388-0*) BrdgeWater.

— Mama, If You Had a Wish. LC 91-31354. (Illus.). 40p. (J). (ps-1). 1993. 14.00 (*0-671-75437-8*, Green Tiger S&S) S&S Childrens.

— Night Call. (J). (ps). 1991. pap. 3.95 (*0-14-050944-5*, Puffin) Puffin Bks.

— Sometimes I Feel Like a Mouse. (Illus.). (J). 1992. 14.95 (*0-590-44835-8*, Scholastic Hardcover) Scholastic Inc.

— Songs of Chanukah. (J). (ps-3). 1992. 15.95 (*0-316-57739-1*) Little.

— The Story of Z. LC 89-3923. (Illus.). 28p. (J). (ps up). 1991. pap. 14.95 (*0-88708-105-3*, Picture Book Studio) S&S Childrens.

— The Story of Z. LC 92-6626. (Illus.). 28p. (J). 1992. pap. 4.95 (*0-88708-278-5*, Picture Book Studio) S&S Childrens.

— Vegetable Soup. LC 87-11169. (Illus.). 32p. (J). (ps-1). 1988. text ed. 13.95 (*0-02-767630-7*, Mac Bks Young Read) S&S Childrens.

— Vegetable Soup. LC 91-247. (Illus.). 32p. (J). (ps-3). 1991. reprint ed. pap. 4.50 (*0-689-71523-4*, Aladdin Paperbacks) S&S Childrens.

*__Modesitt, L. E., Jr.__ The Death of Chaos. 1995. 24.95 (*0-312-85721-7*) Tor Bks.

— Hammer of Darkness. 1996. pap. write for info. (*0-614-05535-0*) Tor Bks.

— The Magic Engineer. 624p. 1995. mass mkt. 5.99 (*0-8125-3405-0*) Tor Bks.

— Of Tangible Ghosts. 384p. 1994. 22.95 (*0-312-85720-9*) Tor Bks.

— Of Tangible Ghosts. 1995. mass mkt. 5.99 (*0-8125-4822-1*) Tor Bks.

— The Order War. 480p. 1995. 23.95 (*0-312-85569-9*) Tor Bks.

— The Order War. 480p. 1996. pap. 4.99 (*0-614-05524-5*) Tor Bks.

— The Parafaith War. 1996. write for info. (*0-312-85904-X*) Tor Bks.

Modesitt, Lee E., Jr. The Magic Engineer. 512p. 1994. 23.95 (*0-312-85570-2*) Tor Bks.

— The Magic of Recluce. 512p. 1992. mass mkt. 4.99 (*0-8125-0518-2*) Tor Bks.

— Towers of the Sunset. 368p. 1992. 21.95 (*0-312-85297-5*) Tor Bks.

— The Towers of the Sunset. 576p. 1993. mass mkt. 5.99 (*0-8125-1967-1*) Tor Bks.

Modesitt, Lee E., Jr. & Levins, Bruce S. The Green Progression. 320p. 1995. mass mkt. 4.99 (*0-8125-1641-9*) Tor Bks.

Modest, Diane & Cymerman, Sandra. SAGE: Implementation Manual. 1986. teacher ed 39.00 (*0-944584-05-5*) Sopris.

— Sage: Mini-Study Units. (Illus.). 652p. 1992. teacher ed 50.00 (*0-944584-45-4*) Sopris.

Modest, M. F., et al. General Papers on Convection. LC 93-73714. 71p. 1993. pap. 35.00 (*0-7918-1001-1*) ASME.

Modest, M. F., et al, eds. General Papers in Heat Transfer: Natural & Forced Convection. (HTD Ser.: Vol. 237). 124p. 1993. 37.50 (*0-7918-1150-6*, G00794) ASME.

— General Papers in Radiative Heat Transfer. LC 93-73715. 61p. 1993. pap. 30.00 (*0-7918-1002-X*) ASME.

Modest, Michael F. Radiative Heat Transfer. LC 92-24671. (Mechanical Engineering Ser.). 1992. text ed. write for info. (*0-07-042675-9*) McGraw.

Modesto, Robert, ed. see Ponce, Mario.

Modesto, Ruby & Mount, Guy. Not for Innocent Ears: Spiritual Traditions of a Desert Cahuilla Medicine Woman. rev. ed. (Illus.). 128p. 1986. pap. 9.95 (*0-9604462-0-6*) Sweetlight.

Modestov, V. K., ed. The Use of Radioisotopes in Clinical & Experimental Research. 224p. 1961. text ed. 58.00 (*0-7065-0162-4*, Pub. by Keter Pub IS) Coronet Bks.

Modgil, Celia, jt. auth. see Clark.

Modgil, Celia, jt. auth. see Modgil, Sohan.

Modgil, Celia, jt. ed. see Modgil, Sohan.

Modgil, Sohan, ed. B. F. Skinner: Controversy & Consensus. LC 86-13518. (International Master Minds Challenged Ser.). 400p. 1987. 125.00 (*1-85000-026-3*, Falmer Pr) Taylor & Francis.

— Lawrence Kholberg: Consensus & Controversy. LC 86-6361. (International Master Minds Challenged Ser.). 550p. 1986. 125.00 (*1-85000-025-5*, Falmer Pr) Taylor & Francis.

Modgil, Sohan & Modgil, Celia. Jean Piaget: Consensus & Controversy. LC 81-84205. 500p. 1982. text ed. 55.00 (*0-275-90862-3*, C0862, Praeger Pubs) Greenwood.

Modgil, Sohan & Modgil, Celia, eds. Arthur Jensen: Consensus & Controversy. (International Master Minds Challenged Ser.). 410p. 1987. 125.00 (*1-85000-093-X*, Falmer Pr) Taylor & Francis.

— Hans Eysenck: Consensus & Controversy. LC 86-11473. (International Master Minds Challenged Ser.: Vol. 2). 400p. 1986. 125.00 (*1-85000-021-2*, Falmer Pr) Taylor & Francis.

— Noam Chomsky: Consensus & Controversy. (International Master Minds Challenged Ser.: Vol. 4). 304p. 1987. 125.00 (*1-85000-022-0*, Falmer Pr) Taylor & Francis.

Modgil, Sohan, et al, eds. Multicultural Education: The Interminable Debate. 350p. 1986. pap. 33.00 (*1-85000-055-7*, Falmer Pr) Taylor & Francis.

Modi, Gauri, tr. see Kripalvananda, Svami.

Modi, Ishwar, ed. Emerging Trends in Indian Sociology, 3 vols., 1. 320p. 1986. 40.00 (*0-8364-1883-2*, Pub. by Rawat II) S Asia.

— Emerging Trends in Indian Sociology, 3 vols., 2. 320p. 1986. 40.00 (*0-8364-1884-0*, Pub. by Rawat II) S Asia.

— Emerging Trends in Indian Sociology, 3 vols., 3. 320p. 1986. 40.00 (*0-8364-1885-9*, Pub. by Rawat II) S Asia.

Modi, Jagdish J. Parallel Algorithms & Matrix Computation. (Oxford Applied Mathematics & Computing Science Ser.). (Illus.). 272p. 1989. pap. 35.00 (*0-19-859670-7*) OUP.

Modi, P. M. Aksara: A Forgotten Chapter in the History of Indian Philosophy. 2nd ed. 187p. 1985. reprint ed. 18.50 (*81-7030-041-X*, Pub. by Sri Satguru Pubns II) S Asia.

Modiano, Marko. Domestic Disharmony & Industrialization in D.H. Lawrence's Early Fiction. (Studia Anglistica Upsaliensia Ser.: No. 62). 124p. (Orig.). 1987. pap. 34.00x (*91-554-2084-2*, Pub. by Uppsala Univ Acta Univ Uppsaliensis SW) Coronet Bks.

Modiano, Patrick. Les Boulevards de Ceintures. (FRE.). 1978. pap. 10.95 (*0-7859-3390-5*) Fr & Eur.

— Les Boulevards de Ceintures. (Folio Ser.: No. 1033). (FRE.). pap. 8.95 (*2-07-037033-X*) Schoenhof.

— Catherine Certitude. Rodarmor, William, tr. (Illus.). 64p. (J). (gr. 4-9). 1995. 17.95 (*0-87923-959-X*) Godine.

— De Si Brave Garcons. (FRE.). 1987. pap. 8.95 (*0-7859-3393-X*, 2070378l1X) Fr & Eur.

— De Si Braves Garcons. (Folio Ser.: No. 1811). (FRE.). pap. 6.95 (*2-07-037811-X*) Schoenhof.

— Dimanches d'Aout. (FRE.). 1989. pap. 10.95 (*0-7859-2918-5*) Fr & Eur.

— Dimanches d'Aout. (Folio Ser.: No. 2042). (FRE.). 1989. pap. 8.95 (*2-07-038130-7*) Schoenhof.

— Fleurs de Ruine. (FRE.). 1992. pap. 10.95 (*0-7859-2731-X*, 2020177161) Fr & Eur.

— Honeymoon. Wright, Barbara, tr. (Verba Mundi Ser.). 128p. 1994. 19.95 (*0-87923-947-6*) Godine.

— Jeunesse. (Folio Ser.: No. 1629). (FRE.). pap. 8.95 (*2-07-037629-X*) Schoenhof.

— Une Jeunesse. (FRE.). 1985. pap. 10.95 (*0-7859-3391-3*) Fr & Eur.

— Livret de Famille. (FRE.). 1981. pap. 10.95 (*0-7859-2897-9*) Fr & Eur.

— Livret de Famille. (Folio Ser.: No. 1293). (FRE.). 1981. pap. 8.95 (*2-07-037293-6*) Schoenhof.

— Memory Lane. 1983. pap. 10.95 (*0-7859-2692-5*) Fr & Eur.

— Place de l'Etoile. (Folio Ser.: No. 698). (FRE.). pap. 8.95 (*2-07-036698-7*) Schoenhof.

— La Place de l'Etoile. (FRE.). 1975. pap. 10.95 (*0-7859-2882-0*) Fr & Eur.

— Poupee Blonde. (FRE.). 1992. pap. 14.95 (*0-7859-2723-9*) Fr & Eur.

— Quartier Perdu. (FRE.). 1988. pap. 10.95 (*0-7859-2916-9*) Fr & Eur.

— Quartier Perdu. (Folio Ser.: No. 1942). (FRE.). pap. 8.95 (*2-07-037942-6*) Schoenhof.

— Remise de Peine. (FRE.). 1989. pap. 10.95 (*0-7859-2712-3*) Fr & Eur.

— Ronde de Nuit. (Folio Ser.: No. 835). 152p. (FRE.). 1976. pap. 6.95 (*2-07-036835-1*) Schoenhof.

— La Ronde de Nuit. (FRE.). 1976. pap. 8.95 (*0-7859-2887-1*) Fr & Eur.

— Rue des Boutiques Obscures. (FRE.). 1982. pap. 10.95 (*0-7859-2899-5*) Fr & Eur.

— Rue des Boutiques Obscures. (Folio Ser.: No. 1358). 250p. (FRE.). 1982. pap. 8.95 (*2-07-037358-4*) Schoenhof.

— Vestiaire de l'Enfance. (FRE.). 1991. pap. 10.95 (*0-7859-2925-8*) Fr & Eur.

— Vestiaire de l'Enfance. (Folio Ser.: No. 2253). (FRE.). pap. 8.95 (*2-07-038364-4*) Schoenhof.

— Villa Triste. (FRE.). 1977. pap. 10.95 (*0-7859-2890-1*) Fr & Eur.

— Villa Triste. (Folio Ser.: No. 953). (FRE.). pap. 8.95 (*2-07-036953-6*) Schoenhof.

— Voyage de Noces. (Folio Ser.: No. 2330). (FRE.). pap. 8.95 (*2-07-038454-3*) Schoenhof.

Modiano, Patrick & Sempe, J. J. Catherine Certitude. (Folio - Junior Ser.: No. 600). 95p. (FRE.). (J). (gr. 5-10). 1988. pap. 9.95 (*2-07-033600-X*) Schoenhof.

Modiano, Raimonda. Coleridge & the Concept of Nature. LC 84-8043. xiv, 270p. 1985. 34.95 (*0-8130-0808-5*) U Press Fla.

Modic. Magnetic Resonance Imaging of the Spine. 296p. 1988. 125.00 (*0-8151-5956-0*, Yr Bk Med Pubs) Mosby Yr Bk.

— Magnetic Resonance Imaging of the Spine. 2nd ed. 355p. 1993. 129.00 (*0-8016-6838-7*) Mosby Yr Bk.

Modica, Terry A. The Dark Secret of the Ouija. (Young Reader's Christian Library). (Illus.). 224p. (YA). (gr. 9-12). 1990. reprint ed. pap. text ed. 2.50 (*1-55748-138-5*) Barbour & Co.

— How to Get Free Publicity, Level 1: A Home Study Course. (Home Study Ser.). 40p. 1987. student ed 30.00 (*0-939926-34-2*); audio (*0-939926-33-4*) Fruition Pubns.

— How to Get Free Publicity, Level 2: A Home Study Course. (Home Study Ser.). 36p. 1988. 30.00 (*0-939926-42-3*); audio (*0-939926-41-5*) Fruition Pubns.

Modif, Kamran. The Economic Consequences of the Gulf War. 192p. 1990. 72.50 (*0-415-05295-5*, A4707) Routledge.

*__Modigh, Kjell, et al, eds.__ Anticonvulsants in Psychiatry. LC 94-28069. 176p. 1994. 49.00x (*1-871816-25-4*, Pub. by Wrightson Biomed UK) Taylor & Francis.

Modigliani. Drawings of Modigliani. Longstreet, Stephen, ed. (Master Draughtsman Ser.). 1972. 10.95 (*0-87505-024-7*); pap. 4.95 (*0-87505-177-4*) Borden.

Modigliani, Franco. Collected Papers of Franco Modigliani, 3 vols., Vol. 1: Essays in Macroeconomics. Abel, Andrew, ed. 1980. Vol. 1, Essays In Macroeconomics. 52.50x (*0-262-13150-1*) MIT Pr.

— The Collected Papers of Franco Modigliani, Vol. 4: Monetary Theory & Stabilization Policies. Johnson, Simon, ed. 350p. 1989. 47.50 (*0-262-13244-3*) MIT Pr.

— The Collected Papers of Franco Modigliani, Vol. 5: Saving, Deficits, Inflation, & Financial Theory. Johnson, Simon, ed. 450p. 1989. 52.50 (*0-262-13245-1*) MIT Pr.

Modigliani, Franco, jt. ed. see Baldassarri, Mario.

Modigliani, Franco, jt. auth. see Fabozzi, Frank J.

Modigliani, Kathy, et al. Opening Your Door to Children: How to Start a Family Day Care Program. LC 87-60747. 69p. 1987. pap. 3.50 (*0-935989-06-4*, NAEYC #203) Natl Assn Child Ed.

*__Modin, Yuri.__ My Five Cambridge Friends. 1994. 23.00 (*0-374-21698-3*) FS&G.

Modinos, A. Field, Thermionic, & Secondary Electron Emission Spectroscopy. LC 83-21311. 384p. 1984. 95.00 (*0-306-41321-3*, Plenum Pr) Plenum.

Modis. Organization - The Extracellular Matrix: A Polarz Microsc Appr. 1990. 217.00 (*0-8493-5786-1*, QM563) CRC Pr.

Modis, Theodore. Predictions: Society's Telltale Signature Reveals the Past & Forecasts the Future. 288p. 1992. 21.00 (*0-671-75917-5*) S&S Trade.

Modisett, Noah F. & Luter, James, Jr. Speaking Clearly: The Basics of Voice & Articulation. 3rd rev. ed. (Illus.). 304p. 1988. pap. text ed. write for info. (*0-8087-3295-1*) Burgess MN Intl.

Modjeska, Abigail C., jt. auth. see Modjeska, Lee.

Modjeska, Drusilla, ed. see Mears, Gillian, et al.

Modjeska, Helena. Memories & Impressions of Helena Modjeska. LC 75-81212. (Illus.). 1972. reprint ed. 24.95 (*0-405-08791-8*, Pub. by Blom Pubns UK) Ayer.

Modjeska, Helena O. Memories & Impressions: An Autobiography. (American Biography Ser.). 571p. 1991. reprint ed. lib. bdg. 99.00 (*0-7812-8286-1*) Rprt Serv.

Modjeska, Lee. Administrative Law: Practice & Procedure. LC 82-80575. 1982. 95.00 (*0-686-35770-1*) Lawyers Cooperative.

— Administrative Law: Practice & Procedure. suppl. ed. LC 82-80575. 1993. Suppl. 1993. 54.00 (*0-317-03153-8*) Lawyers Cooperative.

— Keeper of the Night: A Portrait of Life in the Shadow of Death. Geiger, Lura J., ed. 128p. (Orig.). 1995. pap. 14.95 (*1-880913-15-1*) LuraMedia.

*__Modjeska, Lee & Modjeska, Abigail C.__ Federal Labor Law: NLRB Practice. rev. ed. LC 94-48176. 1994. write for info. (*0-615-00454-7*) Clark Boardman Callaghan.

Modleski. Women Who Knew Too Much. 1987. pap. 10.95 (*0-416-01711-8*) Routledge Chapman & Hall.

Modleski, Tania. Feminism Without Women: Culture & Criticism in a "Postfeminist" Age. 160p. 1991. 39.95 (*0-415-90416-1*, A5338, Routledge NY); pap. 113.95 (*0-415-90417-X*, A5342, Routledge NY) Routledge.

— Loving with a Vengance: Mass-Produced Fantasies for Women. 225p. 1984. pap. 9.95 (*0-415-90136-7*, NO. 9176, Routledge NY) Routledge.

— The Women Who Knew Too Much. 200p. 1987. 35.00 (*0-416-01701-0*, A0412, Routledge NY); pap. 12.95 (*0-415-90176-6*, Routledge NY) Routledge.

Modleski, Tania, ed. Studies in Entertainment: Critical Approaches to Mass Culture. LC 85-45980. (Theories of Contemporary Culture Ser.). (Illus.). 228p. 1986. 29.95 (*0-253-35566-4*); pap. 9.95 (*0-253-20395-3*, MB-395) Ind U Pr.

Modley, Rudol F. & Myers, William R. Handbook of Pictorial Symbols: 3,250 Examples from International Sources. 21.00 (*0-8446-5516-3*) Peter Smith.

Modley, Rudolf & Myers, William R. Handbook of Pictorial Symbols. 1976. pap. 6.95 (*0-486-23357-X*) Dover.

Modlin, Charles E., ed. Sherwood Anderson's Love Letters to Eleanor Copenhaver Anderson. LC 89-4895. (Illus.). 352p. 1990. 35.00 (*0-8203-1150-2*) U of Ga Pr.

*__Modlin, Charles E. & Norton, W. W., eds.__ Winesburg, Ohio: An Authoritative Text, Backgrounds & Contexts, Criticism. LC 95-10378. (Critical Editions Ser.). 1995. pap. write for info. (*0-393-96795-6*) Norton.

Modlin, Charles E., ed. see Anderson, Sherwood.

Modlin, Dan & Martin, Harry. Farming Talk. LC 85-71902. 221p. 1985. pap. 7.95 (*0-9611416-1-1*) RRN Bks.

Modlin, I. M., jt. ed. see Scarpignato, C.

Modlin, Marilyn J., jt. auth. see Fitzpatrick, Gary L.

Modlin, Rick, ed. see Frolick, Jeanne C.

*__Modly, Doris, et al, eds.__ Advancing Nursing Education Worldwide. LC 94-35282. (Illus.). 192p. 1995. 33.95 (*0-8261-8650-5*) Springer Pub.

*__Modnar, Les.__ Power Gin Rummy: A Simple Guide to Odds & Winning Plays. 122p. 1994. pap. 12.95 (*0-9643734-0-8*) Wisedge.

Modoc Press Editors. The Macmillan Guide to Correspondence Study. LC 83-9854. 497p. 1983. 65.00 (*0-02-921550-1*) Macmillan.

Modoc Press, Inc. Staff. Guide to Schools & Departments of Religion & Seminaries in the U. S. & Canada. 736p. 1987. 100.00 (*0-02-921650-8*) Macmillan.

Modoc Press, Inc. Staff, ed. Special Collections in College & University Libraries. 650p. 1989. text ed. 110.00 (*0-02-921651-6*) Macmillan.

Modoc Press Staff, ed. The Oryx Guide to Distance Learning. 384p. 1994. pap. 98.50 (*0-89774-823-9*) Oryx Pr.

Modrak, Deborah K. Aristotle: The Power of Perception. LC 86-19208. x, 250p. (C). 1987. 29.95 (*0-226-53338-7*) U Ch Pr.

— Aristotle: The Power of Perception. LC 86-19208. x, 250p. (C). 1989. pap. text ed. 13.95 (*0-226-53339-5*) U Ch Pr.

Modrak, Nancy, jt. ed. see Brandt, Ronald S.

Modrak, Nancy, ed. see Wiles, Jon & Bondi, Joseph.

Modrak, Nancy C., ed. see Benson, Carolyn V.

Modras, Ronald. Paul Tillich's Theology of the Church: A Catholic Appraisal. LC 76-6082. 314p. reprint ed. pap. 89.50 (*0-7837-3605-3*, 2043470) Bks Demand.

Modrezejewsci, Joseph M. Droit Imperial et Traditions Locales dans l'Egypte Romaine. (Collected Studies: No. 321). 336p. 1990. text ed. 95.00 (*0-86078-270-0*, Pub. by Variorum UK) Ashgate Pub Co.

*__Modro, Margie.__ Safekeeping: Adult Responsibility - Children's Right. 70p. Date not set. pap. text ed. 19.95 (*1-884937-24-1*) Manisses Communs.

Modrow, John. How to Become a Schizophrenic: The Case Against Biological Psychiatry. LC 92-71410. 291p. (Orig.). 1992. pap. 14.95 (*0-9632626-2-9*) Apollyon Pr.

*__Modrzejewski, Joseph M.__ Jews of Egypt, from Rameses II to Emperor Hadrian. 1995. 30.00 (*0-8276-0522-6*) JPS Phila.

Modrzhinskaya, Y. D., et al. Future of Society: A Soviet View. 375p. 1973. 22.00 (*0-8464-0442-7*) Beekman Pubs.

*__Modrzyk, Stanley J.__ Celebrating Times of Change: A Wiccan Book of Shadows for Family & Coven Growth. (Illus.). 176p. (Orig.). 1995. pap. 12.95 (*0-87728-820-8*) Weiser.

— Turning of the Wheel: A Wiccan Book of Shadows for Moons & Festivals. (Illus.). 280p. (Orig.). 1993. pap. 12.95 (*0-87728-767-8*) Weiser.

— Wedding Videographer's Handbook. 82p. (Orig.). 1986. pap. 4.50 (*0-939751-00-3*) Seeing Is Believing Video.

Modrzynski, Mike. Great Lakes Steelhead Guide. (Illus.). 80p. 1992. 34.95 (*1-878175-16-5*); pap. 19.95 (*1-878175-15-7*) F Amato Pubns.

— Michigan Steelheading. (Illus.). (Orig.). 1987. 5.95 (*0-685-17236-8*) Mich United Conserv.

*__Modugno, Carolyn & McDermott, Rosalie.__ Envirolearn Four. (Illus.). 96p. 1995. teacher ed, pap. write for info. (*1-57022-042-5*) ECS Lrn Systs.

— Envirolearn K-1. (Illus.). 96p. (Orig.). 1995. teacher ed, pap. write for info. (*1-57022-039-5*) ECS Lrn Systs.

— Envirolearn Three. (Illus.). 96p. (Orig.). 1995. teacher ed, pap. write for info. (*1-57022-041-7*) ECS Lrn Systs.

— Envirolearn Two. (Illus.). 96p. (Orig.). 1995. teacher ed, pap. write for info. (*1-57022-040-9*) ECS Lrn Systs.

— Environlearn Five. (Illus.). 96p. (Orig.). 1995. teacher ed, pap. write for info. (*1-57022-043-3*) ECS Lrn Systs.

Modupe' Bode'-Thomas, tr. see Mariama Ba.

Mody, Ashoka. Staying in the Loop: International Alliances for Sharing Technology, No. 61. (Discussion Paper Ser.). 22p. 1989. 6.95 (*0-8213-1344-4*, 11344) World Bank.

Mody, Bella. Designing Messages for Development Communication: An Audience Participation-Based Approach. 216p. (C). 1992. 49.95 (*0-8039-9105-3*); pap. 24.00 (*0-8039-9106-1*) Sage.

*__Mody, Bella, et al, eds.__ Telecommunications Politics: Ownership & Control of the Information Highway in Developing Countries. (LEA's Telecommunications Ser.). 432p. 1995. 55.00 (*0-8058-1752-2*) L Erlbaum Assocs.

— Telecommunications Politics: Ownership & Control of the Information Highway in Developing Countries. (LEA's Telecommunications Ser.). 432p. 1995. pap. 30.00 (*0-8058-1753-0*) L Erlbaum Assocs.

Mody, Istvan, jt. ed. see Gutnick, Michael J.

*__Mody, Monica.__ Zoomba in Toyland. (Illus.). 24p. (J). (ps-3). 1995. 4.95 (*1-57064-045-9*) Barney Pub.

Mody, Nawaz. Indonesia under Suharto: A Study in the Concentration of Power. LC 87-70631. 325p. 1987. text ed. 40.00 (*0-86590-792-7*) Apt Bks.

Mody, V. & Jakhete, R. Dust Control Handbook. LC 88-19061. (Pollution Technology Review Ser.: No. 161). (Illus.). 203p. 1989. 39.00 (*0-8155-1182-5*) Noyes.

Modzelewski, Jozef. Das Pandamonium der Achtziger Jahre: Kurzprosa des Jahres 1983. LC 90-33820. (Studies in Modern German Literature: Vol. 37). 313p. (GER.). (C). 1990. text ed. 66.95 (*0-8204-1226-0*) P Lang Pubs.

Modzelewski, Zygmunt. Hiding in Plain Sight. (Illus.). 142p. 1994. 20.00 (*1-885103-00-X*) Capstone NY.

Moe, jt. auth. see Asbjornsen.

Moe, Alden J., jt. auth. see Wood, Mary L.

Moe, Alden J., jt. auth. see Woods, Mary L.

Moe, Barbara. Coping When You Are the Survivor of a Violent Crime. LC 94-14117. (YA). 1994. 15.95 (*0-8239-1882-3*) Rosen Group.

— Coping with Chronic Illness. Rosen, Ruth, ed. LC 92-15377. (Coping Ser.). (YA). (gr. 7-12). 1992. 15.95 (*0-8239-1464-X*) Rosen Group.

— Coping with Eating Disorders. (Coping Ser.). (YA). (gr. 7-12). 1991. lib. bdg. 15.95 (*0-8239-1343-0*) Rosen Group.

— Dog Days for Dudley. (J). 1994. pap. 13.95 (*0-02-767260-3*, Bradbury S&S) S&S Childrens.

— Everything You Need to Know about PMS. LC 94-25640. (Need to Know Library). (Illus.). 64p. (YA). (gr. 7-12). 1995. 15.95 (*0-8239-1877-7*) Rosen Group.

— Gt Los Angeles Garment Distric. 1987. pap. 5.99 (*0-916811-04-2*) C Taylor Pub.

— Guide to the Los Angeles Garment District. 15th ed. (Illus.). 144p. 1990. pap. 7.95 (*0-916811-08-5*) C Taylor Pub.

Moe, Christian, ed. see Lash, James.

An Asterisk (*) at the beginning of an entry indicates that the title is appearing in BIP for the first time.

Moe, Christian H. & Eugene, R. Jackson, eds. Eight Plays for Youth: Varied Theatrical Experiences for Stage & Study. LC 91-18425. (American University Studies: Theatre Arts: Ser. XXVI, Vol. 8). 369p. 1991. 59.95 (*0-8204-1554-5*) P Lang Pubs.

Moe, Daniel. Basic Choral Concepts. 32p. 1986. pap. 5.25 (*0-8066-1216-9*, 11-9080, Augsburg) Augsburg Fortress.

— Problems in Conducting. rev. ed. 20p. 1968. pap. 5.00 (*0-8066-0834-X*, 11-9369, Augsburg) Augsburg Fortress.

Moe, David. Collected Poems Nineteen Eighty-Nineteen Ninety. Caroland, Mary, ed. LC 90-70974. 94p. 1990. pap. 5.95 (*1-55523-362-7*) Winston-Derek.

Moe, David E. The Making of a Winner. (Illus.). 110p. (Orig.). 1987. lib. bdg. 12.95 (*0-9615797-2-2*); pap. 6.95 (*0-9615797-1-4*) Moe-Tavation.

— Opening Hearts & Minds: The Joy of Teaching. (Illus.). (Orig.). 1985. pap. 6.95 (*0-9615797-0-6*) Moe-Tavation.

Moe, Dean L. Christian Symbols Handbook: Commentary & Patterns for Traditional & Contemporary Symbols. 96p. (Orig.). 1985. pap. 13.99 (*0-8066-2153-2*, 10-1180, Augsburg) Augsburg Fortress.

Moe, Doug. Madison: Meeting the 21st Century. 1990. 29.95 (*0-89781-313-8*) Preferred Mktg.

***Moe, Erik.** Couches from the Underworld: Cartoons & Stories from Moe's Notebook. 128p. 1994. pap. 9.95 (*0-9644905-0-1*) E Moe.

Moe, Harold. Make Your Paycheck Last: The Complete Step by Step Guide to Personal & Family Financial Success. 2nd ed. (Illus.). 128p. 1993. reprint ed. pap. 8.95 (*1-56414-058-X*) Career Pr Inc.

Moe, Harold R. Make Your Paycheck Last: The Complete Step by Step Guide to Financial Success. expanded rev. ed. Choutka, Jeanne, ed. (Illus.). 116p. 1994. student ed 14.95 (*0-9612310-5-X*) Harsand Pr.

— Make Your Paycheck Last: The Complete Step by Step Guide to Financial Success. 2nd rev. ed. Choutka, Jeanne, ed. (Illus.). 120p. 1994. pap. 7.95 (*0-9612310-2-5*) Harsand Pr.

Moe, J. E., jt. auth. see Asbjornsen, P. C.

Moe, J. E., jt. auth. see Asbjornsen, Peter C.

Moe, Jerry. Discovery: Finding the Buried Treasure. 1994. pap. 14.95 (*0-922641-93-5*) Stem Pubns.

Moe, Jerry & Pohlman, Don. Kids' Power: Healing Games for Children of Alcoholics. 108p. 1989. 7.95 (*1-55874-022-8*) Health Comm.

Moe, Jorgen, jt. auth. see Asbjornsen, Peter C.

Moe, Lawrence H., jt. ed. see Wallmann, James L.

Moe, Louisa, ed. Female Artists Past & Present: International Women's Year 1975 Supplement. 1975. pap. 4.00 (*0-685-70574-9*) Women's Hist.

***Moe, Marilynn M.** Creative Chords. 88p. 1994. student ed 15.50 (*1-884816-00-2*) M M Moe.

— Creative Chords Answer Key. 88p. 1994. pap. text ed. 7.95 (*1-884816-01-0*) M M Moe.

— Patterns & Pathways. 88p. 1994. 11.95 (*1-884816-02-9*) M M Moe.

Moe, Martin A., Jr. Lobsters: Florida, Bahamas, & the Caribbean. LC 91-23948. (Illus.). 512p. (Orig.). 1991. pap. 22.95 (*0-939960-06-0*) Green Turtle Pubns.

— The Marine Aquarium Handbook: Beginner to Breeder. 2nd ed. LC 92-4908. (Illus.). 320p. (Orig.). 1992. pap. 16.95 (*0-939960-07-9*) Green Turtle Pubns.

— The Marine Aquarium Reference: Systems & Invertebrates. (Illus.). 512p. (Orig.). (C). 1989. pap. 21.95 (*0-939960-05-2*) Green Turtle Pubns.

— The Marine Aquarium Reference: Systems & Invertebrates. (Illus.). 512p. (Orig.). (C). 1989. lib. bdg. 39.95 (*0-939960-08-7*) Green Turtle Pubns.

— Project Phoenix: A Concept for Future Existence. 96p. (Orig.). 1981. pap. 4.50 (*0-939960-00-1*) Green Turtle Pubns.

Moe, Mary, ed. see Sullivan, Mick.

Moe, Michael C. The Words of Jesus Christ. 128p. 1994. pap. 5.95 (*0-9638982-0-5*) M C Moe.

Moe, Nelson, tr. see Rella, Franco.

Moe, Paul V., et al, eds. Energy Metabolism of Farm Animals: Proceedings of the Symposium of the European Association for Animal Production, 10th. 381p. 1987. 89.50 (*0-8476-7531-9*) Rowman.

Moe, Richard. The Last Full Measure: The Life & Death of the First Minnesota Volunteers. LC 92-32687. (Illus.). 368p. 1993. 29.95 (*0-8050-2309-7*) H Holt & Co.

— The Last Full Measure: The Life & Death of the First Minnesota Volunteers. 376p. 1994. reprint ed. pap. 15.00 (*0-380-72322-0*) Avon.

Moe, Terry M. The Organization of Interests: Incentives & the Internal Dynamics of Political Interests Groups. 292p. 1988. pap. text ed. 19.95 (*0-226-53353-0*, Midway Reprint) U Ch Pr.

Moe, Terry M., jt. auth. see Chubb, John E.

Moe, Thorvald. Demographic Developments & Economic Growth in Norway 1740-1940: An Econometric Study. Bruchey, Stuart, ed. LC 77-77190. (Dissertations in European Economic History Ser.). 1978. lib. bdg. 29.95 (*0-405-10802-8*) Ayer.

Moebius. Art of Moebius. (Illus.). 96p. 1989. 14.95 (*0-87135-610-4*) Marvel Entmnt.

— Chaos (Moebius Artbook) 96p. 1991. 18.95 (*0-87135-833-6*) Marvel Entmnt.

— Metallic Memories: Moebius Artbook. (Illus.). 1992. 18.95 (*0-87135-834-4*) Marvel Entmnt.

— Moebius, Vol. 2: Arzach. 72p. 1987. 9.95 (*0-87135-279-6*) Marvel Entmnt.

— Moebius, Vol. 3: Airtight Garage. 96p. 1987. 12.95 (*0-87135-280-X*) Marvel Entmnt.

— Moebius, Vol. 4: Long Tomorrow. 64p. 1987. 9.95 (*0-87135-281-8*) Marvel Entmnt.

— Moebius, Vol. 5: Gardens Aedena. 64p. 1988. 9.95 (*0-87135-282-6*) Marvel Entmnt.

— Moebius, Vol. 6: Pharagonesia. 64p. 1988. 9.95 (*0-87135-283-4*) Marvel Entmnt.

— Moebius, Vol. 7: The Goddess. 88p. 1990. 12.95 (*0-87135-714-3*) Marvel Entmnt.

— Moebius, Vol. 8: Mississippi River. 64p. 1990. 9.95 (*0-87135-715-1*) Marvel Entmnt.

Moebius & Lofficier, R. J. Moebius: Stel. 80p. 1994. 14.95 (*0-7851-0020-2*) Marvel Entmnt.

Moebius, jt. auth. see Charlier.

Moebius, jt. auth. see Jodorowsky, Alexandro.

Moebius, jt. auth. see Lee, Stan.

Moebs, Betty R. Gilchrist Revisited: For Hers Is the Kingdom. LC 89-91672. 200p. (Orig.). 1989. pap. 8.95 (*0-9623016-0-4*) B R Moebs.

Moebs, G. Michael, et al. The Home Equity Survival Guide. 160p. 1988. pap. 14.95 (*0-88462-735-7*, 5606-25) Dearborn Finan.

Moebs, William & Sanny, Jeff. University Physics. 350p. 1995. student ed, pap. text ed. write for info. (*0-697-05886-7*); student ed, pap. text ed. write for info. (*0-697-23258-1*) Wm C Brown Pubs.

— University Physics. 1072p. (C). 1995. text ed. write for info. (*0-697-05884-0*) Wm C Brown Pubs.

Moeck, Arthur H. Geographic Variability in Speyeria: Comments, Records & Description of a New Subspecies (Nymphalidae) LC 75-4525. (Illus.). 48p. 1975. reprint ed. pap. 3.50 (*0-911836-08-X*) Entomological Repr.

Moeckel, Fred. None But a Child May Enter: Poetry. 80p. 1982. pap. 2.95 (*0-910452-49-0*) Covenant.

Moeckli, Peter. Residual Stresses in CBN & Corundum Ground Gear Tooth Flanks As the Determining Factor in Abrasive Wheel Selections. (Fall Technical Meeting Papers). (Illus.). 14p. 1986. pap. 30.00 (*1-55589-475-5*, 86FTM11) AGMA.

Moede, Paul, jt. auth. see Reynolds, Randy.

Moeglin, C. & Waldspurger, J. L. Decomposition Spectrale et Series d'Eisenstein: Une Paraphase de L'Ecriture. (Progress in Mathematics Ser.: Vol. 113). 1994. 98.00 (*0-8176-2938-6*) Spr-Verlag.

— Spectral Decomposition & Eisenstein Series: A Paraphrase of the Scriptures. (Cambridge Tracts in Mathematics Ser.: No. 113). (Illus.). 350p. (C). 1992. write for info. (*0-521-41893-3*) Cambridge U Pr.

Moeglin, C., et al. Correspondances de Howe sur un Corps P-adique. (Lecture Notes in Mathematics Ser.: Vol. 1291). vii, 163p. 1987. pap. 35.30 (*0-387-18699-9*) Spr-Verlag.

Moehing, Walter G., IV, jt. auth. see Stallings, Ronald.

Moehle, Natalia R. From Myth to Philosophy: Philosophical Implications of the Mythic Understanding of Transtemporal Identity. LC 87-8212. (Illus.). 156p. (Orig.). (C). 1987. lib. bdg. 43.50 (*0-8191-6356-2*) U Pr of Amer.

Moehlenpah, Arlo & Moehlenpah, Jane. Teaching with Variety. LC 90-43007. (Illus.). 184p. (Orig.). 1990. pap. 7.99 (*0-932581-67-6*) Word Aflame.

Moehlenpah, Jane, jt. auth. see Moehlenpah, Arlo.

Moehling, Vohny, jt. auth. see Wilmes, Liz.

Moehlman, Arthur B. Public Education in Detroit. LC 73-11930. (Metropolitan America Ser.). (Illus.). 268p. 1974. reprint ed. 23.95 (*0-405-05404-1*) Ayer.

Moehlmann, John F. A Concordance to the Complete Poems of John Wilmot, Earl of Rochester. LC 78-69872. 1979. 20.00 (*0-87875-164-5*) Whitston Pub.

Moehn, Edwin. System und Phylogenie der Lebewesen. Physikalische, chemische und biologische Evolution., Vol. 1. (Illus.). 884p. 1984. lib. bdg. 198.00 (*3-510-65117-0*) Lubrecht & Cramer.

Moehring, Eugene P. Public Works & the Patterns of Urban Real Estate Growth in Manhattan, 1835-1849. 28.00 (*0-317-19169-1*, 19819) Ayer.

— Public Works & Urban Real Estate Growth. 1981. write for info. (*0-318-50874-5*) Ayer.

— Resort City in the Sunbelt: Las Vegas, 1930-1970. LC 89-9130. (Illus.). 360p. 1989. 29.95 (*0-87417-147-4*) U of Nev Pr.

— Resort City in the Sunbelt: Las Vegas, 1930-1970. LC 89-9130. (Illus.). 360p. 1995. pap. 17.95 (*0-87417-267-5*) U of Nev Pr.

— Urban America & the Foreign Traveler, 1815-1855. LC 73-13465. (Foreign Travelers in America, 1810-1935 Ser.). 334p. 1974. reprint ed. 25.95 (*0-405-05468-8*) Ayer.

Moehring, Eugene P., ed. see Charleston Mercury Staff & The, New York Times Staff.

Moehring, Eugene P., jt. ed. see Schlesinger, Arthur M., Jr.

Moehs, Teta E., tr. The Gospel of Jesus Christ According to Mistress Ava. (Senda de Estudios y Ensayos Ser.). (Illus.). 176p. (Orig.). (ENG & GER.). 1986. pap. 12.95 (*0-918454-53-0*) Senda Nueva.

Moell, Joseph D., jt. auth. see Curlee, Thomas N.

Moellendorff, U., jt. auth. see Wilamowitz.

Moeller. Shattering an American Myth. 1976. 23.95 (*0-8488-1551-3*) Amereon Ltd.

Moeller, Adeidine K. The Women As Survivor: The Evolution of the Female Figure in the Works of Heinrich Boll. LC 91-17714. (American University Studies: Germanic Languages & Literature: Ser. I, Vol. 85). 171p. (C). 1992. text ed. 35.95 (*0-8204-1131-0*) P Lang Pubs.

Moeller, Alice M., see Rose Anna, pseud..

Moeller, Bernard. Imperial Cities & the Reformation. Midelfort, H. C. Erik & Edwards, Mark U., Jr., eds. LC 82-6600. 128p. (C). 1982. reprint ed. pap. text ed. 6.95 (*0-939464-04-7*) Labyrinth Pr.

Moeller, Beverly B. Phil Swing & Boulder Dam. LC 71-633550. (Illus.). 217p. reprint ed. pap. 61.90 (*0-685-44493-7*, 2031508) Bks Demand.

***Moeller, Bill & Moeller, Jan.** Chief Joseph & the Nez Perces. Greer, Dan, ed. (Illus.). 144p. (Orig.). 1995. pap. 15.00 (*0-87842-319-2*) Mountain Pr.

— Full-Time RVing: A Complete Guide to Life on the Open Road. 2nd ed. LC 93-3006. 488p. 1993. pap. 29.95 (*0-934798-34-6*) TL Enterprises.

— Intracoastal Waterway. 2nd ed. LC 82-10632. (Cruising Navigator Ser.: Vol. 1). 160p. 1986. 14.95 (*0-915160-23-4*) Seven Seas.

— RV Electrical Systems: Basic Troubleshooting, Repair & Improvement. LC 94-30072. 1994. 19.95 (*0-07-042778-X*) McGraw.

Moeller, Bill, jt. auth. see Moeller, Jan.

***Moeller, Bob.** To Have & to Hold: Achieving Lifelong Sexual Intimacy & Satisfaction. 1995. pap. 8.99 (*0-88070-679-1*) Questar Pubs.

Moeller, Carol, jt. auth. see Otero, George G., Jr.

Moeller, Dade. Environmental Health. (Illus.). 332p. (C). 1992. 47.50 (*0-674-25858-4*) HUP.

Moeller, Dietmar P., ed. System Analysis of Biological Processes: Erwin-Riesch-Workshop, Second Ebernburger Working Conference, Bad Munster am Stein-Eberburg, April 9-11, 1987. (Advances in System Analysis Ser.: Vol. 2). viii, 223p. 1987. pap. 50.00 (*3-528-08983-0*, Pub. by Vieweg & Sohn GW) Ballen Bkslr.

Moeller, Doris. Dear God, When Is It My Turn? 1991. pap. 9.95 (*0-9629058-0-1*) Scandia Pr.

Moeller, Jack, et al. Kaleidoskop: Kultur, Literatur und Grammatik. 3rd ed. (C). 1991. write for info. (*0-395-43224-3*) HM Soft Schl Col Div.

Moeller, Jack R. Blickpunkt Deutschland. 2nd ed. (C). 1982. teacher ed, pap. 13.88 (*0-395-32894-2*) HM.

— Blickpunkt Deutschland. 2nd ed. (C). 1982. text ed. 44.12 (*0-395-32689-3*); student ed, pap. 12.76 (*0-395-32691-5*); audio 132.16 (*0-395-32692-3*) HM.

Moeller, Jack R. & Liedloff, Helmut. Deutsch Heute. 3rd ed. LC 83-81521. 480p. (GER.). 1984. audio 2.75 (*0-685-08252-0*) HM.

Moeller, Jack R., jt. auth. see Drath, Viola.

Moeller, Jack R., et al. Deutsch Heute, 5 Vols. 5th ed. (C). 1992. text ed. 51.56 (*0-395-47299-7*) HM.

— Kaleidoskop: Kultur, Literatur und Grammatik, 2 Vols. 2nd ed. LC 86-81691. 384p. (C). 1986. pap. 40.76 (*0-395-35949-X*) HM.

— Kaleidoskop: Kultur, Literatur und Grammatik, 2 Vols. 2nd ed. LC 86-81691. 384p. (C). 1987. student ed, pap. 23.96 (*0-395-42418-6*) HM.

— Kaleidoskop: Kultur, Literatur und Grammatik, 2 Vols. 2nd ed. LC 86-81691. 384p. (C). 1987. reel tape 223.96 (*0-395-42433-X*) HM.

— Kaleidoskop: Kultur, Literatur und Grammatik, 2 Vols. 2nd ed. LC 86-81691. 384p. (C). 1990. pap. 4.76 (*0-395-42432-1*) HM.

— Kaleidoskop: Kultur, Literatur und Grammatik, 2 Vols., Pt. 1. 2nd ed. LC 86-81691. 384p. (C). 1987. audio 24.76 (*0-395-42434-8*) HM.

— Kaleidoskop: Kultur, Literatur und Grammatik, 2 Vols., Pt. 2. 2nd ed. LC 86-81691. 384p. (C). 1987. audio 24.76 (*0-395-42435-6*) HM.

***Moeller, Jan.** RVing Basics. 1995. pap. text ed. 14.95 (*0-07-042779-8*) McGraw.

Moeller, Jan & Moeller, Bill. The Intracoastal Waterway. LC 79-66981. (Illus.). 1987. pap. text ed. 14.60 (*0-915160-88-9*) Seven Seas.

— The Intracoastal Waterway, Norfolk to Miami: A Cockpit Cruising Handbook. 3rd ed. 1991. 17.95 (*0-07-158021-2*) McGraw.

— The Intracoastal Waterway, Norfolk to Miami: A Cockpit Cruising Handbook. 3rd ed. 160p. 1991. pap. 16.95 (*0-915160-36-6*, 0306) Seven Seas.

Moeller, Jan, jt. auth. see Moeller, Bill.

Moeller, Jim, ed. see Zhou, Peter.

***Moeller, Mark.** Karate-Do Foundations. (Illus.). (Orig.). 1995. pap. 17.95 (*1-57028-026-6*) Masters Pr IN.

Moeller, Misse. Favorite Charted Designs. 48p. (Orig.). 1986. pap. 2.95 (*0-486-25091-1*) Dover.

Moeller, Misse, illus. Charted Decorative Initials. (Embroidery, Needlepoint, Charted Designs Ser.). 32p. 1984. pap. 2.50 (*0-486-24646-9*) Dover.

Moeller, P., ed. Magnesite: Geology, Mineralogy, Geochemistry Formation of Mg-Carbonates. (Monograph Series on Mineral Deposits: No. 28). (Illus.). 300p. 1989. pap. text ed. 60.00 (*3-443-12028-8*, Pub. by Gebruder Borntraeger GW) Lubrecht & Cramer.

***Moeller, P. & Lueders, V., eds.** Formation of Hydrothermal Vein Deposits: A Case Study of the Pb-Zn, Beriteand Fluoritedeposits in the Harz Mountains. (Monograph Series on Mineral Deposits: No. 30). (Illus.). 291p. 1993. pap. 88.90 (*3-443-12030-X*, Pub. by Cramer-Borntraeger GW) Lubrecht & Cramer.

Moeller, Pamela A. A Kinesthetic Homiletic: Embodying Gospel in Preaching. LC 92-31711. 112p. 1993. pap. 11.00 (*0-8006-2650-8*, 1-2650) Augsburg Fortress.

Moeller, Robert. For Better, For Worse, For Keeps: Getting & Keeping Your Marriage on Track. 224p. 1994. pap. 8.99 (*0-88070-624-4*, Multnomah Bks) Questar Pubs.

— Love in Action. 220p. 1994. pap. 8.99 (*0-88070-672-4*, Multnomah Bks) Questar Pubs.

Moeller, Robert G. German Peasants & Agrarian Politics, 1914-1924: The Rhineland & Westphalia. LC 85-14120. xv, 286p. (C). 1986. 37.50 (*0-8078-1676-0*) U of NC Pr.

— Protecting Motherhood: Women & the Family in the Politics of Postwar West Germany. (C). 1992. 42.00 (*0-520-07903-5*) U CA Pr.

Moeller, Robert G., ed. Peasants & Lords in Modern Germany: Recent Studies in Agricultural History. LC 85-6113. 256p. 1986. text ed. 60.00 (*0-04-943037-8*) Routledge Chapman & Hall.

Moeller, Robert R. Artificial Intelligence: A Primer. (IIA Monograph). 35p. 1987. pap. text ed. 15.00 (*0-89413-172-9*) Inst Inter Aud.

— Computer Audit Control & Security. 598p. 1989. text ed. 135.00 (*0-471-85310-0*) Wiley.

Moeller, Roger, ed. see Davis, Henry K.

Moeller, Roger W. Guide to Indian Artifacts of the North East. (Illus.). 32p. 1984. pap. 3.95 (*0-88839-127-7*) Hancock House.

— Practicing Environmental Archaeology: Methods & Interpretations. LC 82-73087. (Occasional Papers: No. 3). (Illus.). 112p. 1982. pap. text ed. 10.00 (*0-936322-00-4*) Am Indian Arch.

— Six LF 21: A Paleo-Indian Site in Western Ct. LC 80-65186. (Occasional Papers: No. 2). (Illus.). 160p. 1980. pap. 12.50 (*0-89488-010-1*) Am Indian Arch.

Moeller, Roger W., ed. Archaeological Bibliography for Eastern North America. 198p. 1977. pap. 7.00 (*0-936322-03-9*) Am Indian Arch.

— Experiments & Observations on the Terminal Archave of the Middle Atlantic Region. (Illus.). iv, 130p. (Orig.). 1990. pap. text ed. 15.00 (*0-9622320-1-7*) Archaeol Servs.

Moeller, Roger W., jt. ed. see Kinsey, W. Fred, III.

Moeller, Susan E., jt. auth. see Ramaswami, Murali.

Moeller, Therald, et al. Chemistry with Inorganic Qualitative Analysis. 3rd ed. 964p. (C). 1989. text ed. 64.00 (*0-15-506492-4*) HB Coll Pubs.

Moeller, Uwe, tr. see Von Sacher-Masoch, Leopold.

Moeller Van Den Bruck, Arthur. Germany's Third Empire. 1972. 45.00 (*0-86527-085-6*) Fertig.

Moeller, Walter O., tr. see Makhlouf, Georgia.

Moellering, H., ed. Spatial Database Transfer Standards: Current International Status. 248p. 1991. 115.00 (*1-85166-677-X*) Elsevier.

***Moellering, Robert C., Jr.** Oral Cepahlosporins. (Antibiotics & Chemotherapy: Vol. 47). (Illus.). viii, 200p. 1995. 168.00 (*3-8055-6163-6*) S Karger.

Moellering, Robert C., Jr., ed. Frontiers in Antimicrobial Chemotherapy: A Collection of Minireviews from Antimicrobial Agents & Chemotherapy. LC 93-10196. 150p. 1993. pap. 11.95 (*1-55581-061-6*) Am Soc Microbio.

Moellerke, George. Concise Electronics Dictionary, Vol. I. 5th ed. 174p. (ENG & GER.). 0198. pap. 29.95 (*0-8288-4407-0*, M15120) Fr & Eur.

— Concise Electronics Dictionary, Vol. 2: German-English. 2nd ed. 160p. (ENG & GER.). 1985. pap. 29.95 (*0-8288-0291-2*, M15119) Fr & Eur.

— Engineering Reader. 101p. (ENG & GER.). 1980. 55.00 (*0-8288-1545-3*, M15072) Fr & Eur.

Moellman, Carol. Effective State Councils on Vocational Education: A Guide for Staff. 1987. 11.50 (*0-317-03878-8*, SN55) Ctr Educ Trng Employ.

***Moeloek, F. A., et al, eds.** Advances in Human Reproduction: Proceedings of the 8th World Congress on Human Reproduction Jointly with the 4th World Conference on Fallopian Tube in Health & Disease, Bali, Indonesia, April 1993. LC 94-21471. (International Congress, Symposium, & Seminar Ser.). 1994. 88.00 (*1-85070-521-6*) Prthnon Pub.

Moelwyn-Hughes, E. A. Physical Chemistry. 2nd rev. ed. 1961. text ed. 546.00 (*0-08-010846-6*, Pub. by Pergamon Repr UK) Franklin.

Moemeka, Andrew A., ed. Communicating for Development: A New Pan-Disciplinary Perspective. LC 93-3456. (SUNY Series, Human Communication Processes). 280p. 1994. 59.50 (*0-7914-1833-2*); pap. 19.95 (*0-7914-1834-0*) State U NY Pr.

Moen, Arthur J., comp. Selected Summaries of Court Decisions Relating to the Provision of Library Services in Institutions. 46p. 10.00 (*0-8389-6539-3*); 9.00 (*0-318-13354-7*) ASCLA.

Moen, Daryl R. Newspaper Layout & Design: A Team Approach. 3rd ed. LC 94-15567. (Illus.). 304p. 1995. pap. 31.95 (*0-8138-1225-9*) Iowa St U Pr.

Moen, Elizabeth B., tr. see Borgen, Johan.

Moen, Larry. Guided Imagery, Vol. 1. 250p. (Orig.). 1992. pap. text ed. 11.95 (*1-880698-01-3*) US Pub FL.

— Guided Imagery, Vol. 2. 252p. (Orig.). 1992. pap. text ed. 11.95 (*1-880698-02-1*) US Pub FL.

Moen, Larry & Smith, Patty. Meditations for Awakening. rev. ed. LC 93-37569. (Illus.). 264p. 1994. reprint ed. pap. 11.95 (*1-880698-77-3*) US Pub FL.

— Meditations for Healing. rev. ed. LC 93-34926. (Illus.). 264p. 1994. reprint ed. pap. 11.95 (*1-880698-69-2*) US Pub FL.

— Meditations for Transformation. rev. ed. LC 93-34925. (Illus.). 264p. 1994. reprint ed. pap. 11.95 (*1-880698-33-1*) US Pub FL.

Moen, Marcia, jt. ed. see Den Ouden, Bernard.

Moen, Matthew C. The Christian Right & Congress. LC 88-34010. 248p. (C). 1989. pap. 19.95 (*0-685-67698-6*) U of Ala Pr.

— The Transformation of the Christian Right. 224p. 1992. 26.95 (*0-8173-0574-2*) U of Ala Pr.

Moen, Matthew C. & Gustafson, Lowell S., eds. The Religious Challenge to the State. (C). 1991. 44.95 (*0-87722-856-6*) Temple U Pr.

Moen, Phyllis. Women's Two Roles: A Contemporary Dilemma. LC 91-36728. 192p. 1992. text ed. 45.00 (*0-86569-198-3*, T198, Auburn Hse); pap. text ed. 16.95 (*0-86569-199-1*, R199, Auburn Hse) Greenwood.

— Working Parents: Transformations in Gender Roles & Public Policies in Sweden. LC 88-40439. (Life Course Studies). 192p. (Orig.). (C). 1989. pap. text ed. 15.75 (*0-299-12104-6*) U of Wis Pr.

***Moen, Phyllis, et al, eds.** Examining Lives in Context: Perspectives on the Ecology of Human Development. (Science Ser.). 624p. 1995. text ed. 40.00 (*1-55798-293-7*) Am Psychol.

Moen, Ronald D., et al. Improving Quality Through Planned Experimentation. 432p. 1991. text ed. write for info. (*0-07-042673-2*) McGraw.

M

Moen, Ronald S., ed. Accreditation Handbook for Ambulatory Health Care: 1989-90 Edition. rev. ed. 73p. 1989. pap. 30.00 (0-685-18876-0) Accredit Assn Ambulatory.

Moen, Ruth R. Deadly Deceptions. 183p. (Orig.). 1994. pap. 7.95 (0-9635653-1-1) R R Moen.

— Hayseeds in My Hair. 150p. (Orig.). 1992. pap. 12.95 (0-9635653-0-3) R R Moen.

— Only One Way Out. (Kathleen O'Shaugnessey Ser.). (Orig.). (C). 1995. pap. 7.95 (0-9635653-2-X) Flying Swan.

— Self-Publishing Can Be Profitable & Immensely Rewarding. (Orig.). (C). 1995. pap. text ed. 17.49 (0-9635653-4-6) R R Moen.

***Moen, William E., ed.** Scholarly Information & Standardization: Proceedings of the 12th Open Forum on the Study of the International Exchange of Japanese Information... (National Information Standards Ser.). 123p. 1994. 40.00 (1-880124-06-8) NISO.

Moench, ed. Northern Appalachian Transect: Southeastern Quebec, Canada, Through Western Maine, U. S. A. (IGC Field Trip Guidebooks Ser.). 56p. 1989. 21.00 (0-87590-559-5, T358) Am Geophysical.

Moench & Gulacy. Six from Sirius. 128p. 1988. pap. 8.95 (0-87135-334-2) Marvel Entmnt.

***Moench, et al.** Batman: KnightsEnd. Kahan, ed. (Illus.). 320p. 1995. pap. 14.95 (1-56389-191-3) DC Comics.

— Conan: Skull of Set. 64p. 1989. 8.95 (0-87135-579-5) Marvel Entmnt.

Moench, Cynthia. Binding up the Brokenhearted. 132p. (Orig.). 1991. pap. text ed. 6.99 (0-89900-399-0) College Pr Pub.

***Moench, D.** Batman: Bloodstorm. O'Neil, Denny, ed. (Illus.). 96p. Date not set. pap. 12.95 (1-56389-185-9) DC Comics.

— Batman: Bloodstorm. O'Neil, Denny, ed. (Illus.). 96p. 1994. 24.95 (1-56389-177-8) DC Comics.

— Batman: Dark Joker - the Wild. O'Neil, D., ed. (Illus.). 96p. (Orig.). 1993. 24.95 (1-56389-111-5) DC Comics.

— Batman: Dark Joker - the Wild. O'Neil, D., ed. (Illus.). 96p. (Orig.). 1994. pap. 9.95 (1-56389-140-9) DC Comics.

— Big Book of Conspiracies. Taggart, ed. (Illus.). 224p. 1995. pap. 12.95 (1-56389-186-7, Paradox) DC Comics.

Moench, D. & Dixon, C. Batman: Knightfall, Pt. 1: Broken Bat. Kahan, Bob, ed. (Illus.). 288p. (YA). 1993. pap. 12.95 (1-56389-142-5) DC Comics.

— Batman: Knightfall, Pt. 2: Who Rules the Night. Kahan, Bob, ed. (Illus.). 296p. (YA). 1993. pap. 12.95 (1-56389-148-4) DC Comics.

Moench, D., et al. Batman - Spawn: War Devil. O'Neil, D., ed. (Illus.). 48p. 1994. pap. 4.95 (1-56389-144-1) DC Comics.

Moench, Dag. Escape from the Planet of the Apes: Feature Film Adaption. 133p. (Orig.). 1991. pap. 9.95 (0-944735-07-X) Malibu Graphics.

Moench, Doug. Batman: Prey. Kahan, Bob, ed. 136p. 1992. pap. 12.95 (0-930289-68-4) DC Comics.

— Batman - Dracula: Red Rain. O'Neil, Dennis, ed. 96p. 1992. pap. 9.95 (1-56389-036-4) DC Comics.

— James Bond 007 Bk. 1: Serpent's Tooth. (Illus.). 160p. 1995. pap. 15.95 (1-878574-78-7) Dark Horse Comics.

Moench, Doug & Gulacy, Paul. James Bond 007: Serpent's Tooth, Vol. 2. Prosser, Jerry, ed. (Illus.). 48p. (Orig.). 1992. pap. 4.95 (1-878574-39-6) Dark Horse Comics.

— James Bond 007: Serpent's Tooth, Vol. 3. Prosser, Jerry, ed. (Illus.). 48p. (Orig.). 1992. pap. 4.95 (1-878574-40-X) Dark Horse Comics.

— James Bond 007, Vol. 1: Serpent's Tooth. Prosser, Jerry, ed. (Illus.). 48p. (Orig.). 1992. pap. 4.95 (1-878574-38-8) Dark Horse Comics.

Moench, Doug, et al. Batman: Prey. 136p. 1993. 12.99 (0-446-39521-8) Warner Bks.

— Batman & Dracula: Red Rain. 96p. 1992. pap. 9.99 (0-446-39465-3) Warner Bks.

Moench, John O. Marauder Men: An Account of the Martin B-26 Marauder. (Illus.). 400p. 1989. write for info. (0-318-64885-7) Malia Enterprises.

— The Stone with Seven Eyes: A Book of Knowledge. (Illus.). 300p. 1989. write for info. (0-318-64886-5) Malia Enterprises.

Moench, John O., ed. The Martin B-26 Marauder: A Bibliography & Guide to Research Sources. 200p. 1992. pap. text ed. 7.95 (1-877597-03-1) Malia Enterprises.

Moench, John O. & Oyster, Esther M. The Martin B-26 Marauder: A Bibliography, 1990. 43p. (Orig.). 1990. pap. 6.50 (1-877597-02-3) Malia Enterprises.

Moene, Karl O., jt. ed. see Andersen, Toben M.

Moene, Karl O., jt. ed. see Elster, Jon.

***Moeng, Sao T.** Shan-English Dictionary. 1995. write for info. (0-931745-92-6) Dunwoody Pr.

Moeng, Sao T., jt. auth. see Scott, Eileen M.

Moenich, David. Lizards. 1990. 9.95 (0-86622-823-3) TFH Pubns.

Moenke-Blankenburg, Lieselotte. Laser Microanalysis. (Chemical Analysis: a Series of Monographs on Analytical Chemistry & Its Applications). 304p. 1989. text ed. 120.00 (0-471-63707-6) Wiley.

Moenkemeyer, Heinz. Francois Hemsterhuis. LC 74-13651. (Twayne's World Authors Ser.). 206p. (C). 1975. lib. bdg. 17.95 (0-8057-2419-2) Irvington.

Moenkemeyer, W. Andreaeales-Bryales. 226p. 1991. reprint ed. 264.00 (3-87429-296-7) Koeltz Sci Bks.

Moenne-Loccoz, P. & Reumaux, P. Fungorum Rariorum Icones Coloratae, Pars 18: Cortinaires Recents, Nouveaux ou Fantomes. (Illus.). 59p. (FRE.). 1989. pap. text ed. 36.00 (3-443-69004-1, Pub. by Gebruder Borntraeger GW) Lubrecht & Cramer.

Moenne-Loccoz, P., et al. Fungorum Rariorum Icones Coloratae, Pars 19: Inocybes Criticables et Critiques. (Illus.). 55p. (FRE.). 1990. pap. text ed. 36.00 (3-443-69005-X, Pub. by Gebruder Borntraeger GW) Lubrecht & Cramer.

***Moens, Alexander & Anstis, Christopher.** Disconcerted Europe: The Search for a New Security Architecture. LC 94-21959. (C). 1994. text ed. 56.95 (0-8133-2324-X) Westview.

Moens, Peter B. Meiosis. (Cell Biology Ser.). 1987. text ed. 106.00 (0-12-503365-6) Acad Pr.

***Moens, W. J.** Register of the Baptisms in the Dutch Church at Colchester from 1645 to 1728: Edited for the Huguenot Society of London. 177p. 1994. pap. text ed. 30.00 (1-55613-998-5) Heritage Bk.

Moenssens, Andre A., et al. Scientific Evidence in Criminal Cases. 3rd ed. (University Textbook Ser.). 805p. 1986. text ed. 38.95 (0-88277-281-3) Foundation Pr.

— Criminal Law, Instructor's Manual for Cases & Comments. 5th ed. (University Casebook Ser.). 201p. 1992. pap. text ed. write for info. (0-88277-989-3) Foundation Pr.

— Criminal Procedure: Cases & Comments. 2nd ed. (Contemporary Legal Education Ser.). 941p. 1987. 32.50 (0-87473-294-8) Michie Butterworth.

— Scientific Evidence in Civil & Criminal Cases. 4th ed. 1230p. 1994. text ed. 48.95 (1-56662-233-6) Foundation Pr.

Moeran, Brian. Lost Innocence: Folk Craft Potters of Onta, Japan. LC 82-23840. (Illus.). 210p. 1984. 45.00 (0-520-04692-7) U CA Pr.

— Okubo Diary: Portrait of a Japanese Valley. 272p. 1985. 35.00 (0-8047-1296-4); pap. 11.95 (0-8047-1521-1) Stanford U Pr.

Moeran, Brian, jt. auth. see Kalland, Arne.

Moerbeek, Kees. All Mixed Up. LC 93-87684. (Illus.). 10p. (J). (ps-3). 1994. 9.95 (0-8431-3761-4) Price Stern.

— Boo Whoo? (Mix & Match Ser.). (Illus.). 10p. (J). (ps up). 1993. 9.99 (0-8431-3623-5) Price Stern.

— Can't Sleep. (Pop-up Ser.). (Illus.). 12p. (J). (ps-3). 1994. 9.95 (0-8431-3689-8) Price Stern.

— Fancy That! LC 91-39451. (J). 1992. 9.95 (0-85953-543-6) Childs Play.

— Four Courageous Climbers. (Triangle Pop-up Ser.). (Illus.). 12p. (J). (ps up). 1991. 9.95 (0-8431-2915-8) Price Stern.

— Have You Seen a Pog? (Mix & Match Pop-up Ser.). (Illus.). 10p. (J). (ps up). 1988. 9.95 (0-8431-2261-7) Price Stern.

— Let's Go. LC 91-38117. (J). 1992. 9.95 (0-85953-542-8) Childs Play.

— New at the Zoo: A Mix-&-Match Pop-up Book. LC 89-60077. (Illus.). 10p. (J). (ps-1). 1989. bds. 8.99 (0-679-80076-5) Random Bks Yng Read.

— New at the Zoo Two: A Mix-&-Match Pop-up Book. LC 92-60763. (Illus.). 10p. (J). (ps-1). 1993. 8.99 (0-679-83711-6) Random Bks Yng Read.

— Night Before Christmas. (Triangle Pop-up Ser.). 12p. (J). (ps up). 1992. 10.99 (0-8431-3445-3) Price Stern.

— Oh No, Santa! (Triangle Pop-up Ser.). (Illus.). 12p. (J). (ps up). 1991. 9.95 (0-8431-2984-0) Price Stern.

— Penguins Slide. LC 91-42040. (J). 1992. 9.95 (0-85953-544-4) Childs Play.

Moerbeek, Kees & Dijs, Carla. Six Brave Explorers. (Triangle Pop-up Ser.). (Illus.). 12p. (J). (ps up). 1988. 9.95 (0-8431-2253-6) Price Stern.

Moerbeek, Kees, jt. auth. see Dijs, Carla.

***Moerdijk, I. & Joyal, A.** Algebraic Set Theory. (Studies in Publishing & Printing: No. 220). (Illus.). 200p. (C). Date not set. pap. write for info. (0-521-55830-1) Cambridge U Pr.

Moerdijk, I. & Reyes, G. E. Models for Smooth Infinitesimal Analysis. (Illus.). x, 399p. 1990. 79.00 (0-387-97489-X) Spr-Verlag.

Moerdijk, I., jt. auth. see Mac Lane, S.

Moerenhout, J. A. Travels to the Islands of the Pacific Ocean. Borden, Arthur R., Jr., tr. LC 92-26842. 564p. (Orig.). (C). lib. bdg. 59.50 (0-8191-8898-0); pap. text ed. 32.50 (0-8191-8899-9) U Pr of Amer.

Moeri, Louise. Forty-Third War. (YA). 1993. pap. 4.95 (0-395-66955-3) HM.

— Save Queen of Sheba. 112p. 1982. pap. 2.95 (0-380-58529-4, Flare) Avon.

— Save Queen of Sheba. 112p. (J). 1990. pap. 3.50 (0-380-71154-0, Camelot) Avon.

— Save Queen of Sheba. 128p. (J). (gr. 3-7). 1994. pap. 3.99 (0-14-037148-6) Puffin Bks.

— Star Mother's Youngest Child. (Illus.). 48p. (J). (ps-2). 1975. 14.95 (0-395-21406-8, Sandpiper) HM.

— Star Mother's Youngest Child. (Illus.). 48p. (J). (ps-2). 1980. pap. 5.95 (0-395-29929-2, Sandpiper) HM.

Moerings, Martin, jt. auth. see Thomas, Philip A.

Moerk, Ernst. A First Language Taught & Learned. 272p. (C). 1992. 37.00 (1-55766-081-6, 0816) P H Brookes.

Moerk, Ernst L. The Mother of Eve-As a First Language Teacher. Lipsitt, Lewis P., ed. LC 82-16358. (Monographs on Infancy: Vol. 3). 160p. 1984. text ed. 39.50 (0-89391-162-3) Ablex Pub.

Moerkotte, Guido, jt. auth. see Kemper, Alfons.

Moerman, Daniel E. Geraniums for the Iroquois: A Field Guide to American Indian Medicinal Plants. Irvine, Keith, ed. LC 81-52514. (Illus.). 1982. 24.95 (0-917256-15-8) Ref Pubns.

Moerman, Michael. Talking Culture: Ethnography & Conversational Analysis. LC 87-14973. (Conduct & Communication Ser.). 212p. (C). 1987. pap. text ed. 19.95 (0-8122-1246-0) U of Pa Pr.

Moermond, Kim I. & Snyder, Jack. The Second Berlin Crisis, 1958-1959. (Pew Case Studies in International Affairs). 50p. (C). 1988. pap. text ed. 2.50 (1-56927-441-X) Geo U Inst Dplmcy.

Moerner, W. E., ed. Persistent Spectral Hole-Burning: Science & Applications. (Topics in Current Physics Ser.: Vol. 44). (Illus.). 325p. 1988. 62.00 (0-387-18607-7) Spr-Verlag.

Moers, Ellen. Harriet Beecher Stowe & American Literature. LC 78-4149. (Illus.). 1978. pap. text ed. 5.00 (0-917482-15-8) Stowe-Day.

— Literary Women. (Illus.). 384p. 1985. pap. 13.95 (0-19-503582-8) OUP.

Moers, Gigi. How & Why Lovers Cheat: And What You Can Do About It. 1991. 19.95 (0-944007-18-X) Sure Sellers.

***Moers, Herman.** Katie & the Big, Brave Bear. Martens, Marianne, tr. LC 94-45208. (Illus.). 32p. (ENG & GER.). (J). (ps-3). 1995. 14.95 (1-55858-397-1); lib. bdg. 14.88 (1-55858-398-X) North-South Bks NYC.

Moersch, Martha M., jt. ed. see Schafer, D. Sue.

Moersch, Martha S., jt. ed. see D'Eugenio, Diane B.

Moertono, Soemarsaid. State & Statecraft in Old Java: A Study of the Later Mataram Period, 16th to 19th Century. rev. ed. (Monograph Ser.: No. 43). 181p. 1981. 9.00 (0-87763-017-8) Cornell Mod Indo.

Moes, Robert. Southeast Asian Ceramics. (Illus.). 16p. 1975. pap. 1.00 (0-87273-051-4) Bklyn Mus.

Moes, Robert, jt. auth. see Baekeland, Frederick.

Moeschberger, M. L., jt. auth. see David, H. A.

Moeschberger, Melvin L., jt. auth. see Madsen, Richard W.

Moeschl, Richard. Exploring the Sky: Projects for Beginning Astronomers. rev. ed. LC 92-18863. (Illus.). 320p. (YA). (gr. 9-12). 1992. pap. 14.95 (1-55652-160-X) Chicago Review.

Moeschlin, O., jt. ed. see Hehn, R.

Moeser, John V. & Dennis, Rutledge M. The Politics of Annexation: Oligarchic Power in a Southern City. 232p. 1982. 22.95 (0-87073-501-2); pap. 13.95 (0-87073-502-0) Schenkman Bks Inc.

Moeser, John V., jt. auth. see Silver, Christopher.

Moeser, June. Four Sentinels: The Story of San Diego's Lighthouses. LC 91-66002. (Illus.). 70p. (Orig.). 1991. pap. 5.95 (0-938711-10-5) Tecolote Pubns.

Moeskops, J., jt. auth. see Leeuwen, M.

Moesli, Annitta. Know Austria by Cooking: A Cook Book with a Difference. 171p. (C). 1988. 75.00 (0-947621-01-6, Pub. by Stuart Titles Ltd UK) St Mut.

Moessinger, Pierre. Socrates. LC 92-44060. (J). 1993. 14.95 (0-88682-606-3) Creative Ed.

Moessner, Jeanne S., jt. ed. see Glaz, Maxine.

Moessner, V. J., tr. see Black, J. L. & Buse, D. K.

Moessner, Victoria J., tr. see Von Langsdorff, Georg H.

Moesta, Rebecca, jt. auth. see Anderson, Kevin J.

Moestra, Rebecca, jt. auth. see Anderson, Kevin J.

Moestrup, Jorn. The Structural Patterns of Pirandello's Work. (Etudes Romanes: No. 2). 294p. (Orig.). 1972. pap. 32.50 (87-7492-056-1, Pub. by Odense Universitets Forlag DK) Coronet Bks.

Moet, A., jt. auth. see Akelah, A.

Moet, Abdelsamie, jt. auth. see Baer, Eric.

Moevs, Christian, tr. see Mazzoleni, Mario.

Moews, Daniel. Keaton: The Silent Features Close up. 1977. pap. 11.00 (0-520-03155-5) U CA Pr.

***Moews, Paul C., Jr., et al.** Kinetic Study of a Chemical Reaction. Neidig, H. A., ed. (Modular Laboratory Program in Chemistry Ser.). 16p. (C). 1987. pap. text ed. 1.25x (0-87540-340-9) Chem Educ Res.

Moeykens, Theresa, jt. auth. see Canter, Patricia.

Moffa, Peter E., et al. Control & Treatment of Combined Sewer Overflows. (Illus.). 150p. 1990. text ed. 54.95 (0-442-26491-7) Van Nos Reinhold.

Moffat. Clarke's Isolation & Identification of Drugs. 2nd ed. 1992. 218.50 (0-85369-166-5, Pub. by Pharmaceutical Pr UK) Rittenhouse.

Moffat, A. J., jt. auth. see Dobson, M. C.

***Moffat, Alexander & Francis, Mark, eds.** Johnston, Alan. 1978. pap. 20.00 (0-905836-08-1, Pub. by Museum Modern Art UK) St Mut.

***Moffat, Anthony F., ed.** Instability & Variability of Hot-Star Winds: Proceedings of an International Workshop Held at Isle-Aux-Coudres. LC 94-45298. 1995. lib. bdg. 129.00 (0-7923-3331-4) Kluwer Ac.

Moffat, Bettyclare. SoulWork: Clearing the Mind, Opening the Heart & Replenishing the Spirit. 150p. (Orig.). 1994. pap. 9.95 (1-885171-01-3) Wldcat Canyon.

Moffat, Bobby. The Basic Soccer Guide. LC 75-16004. (Illus.). 144p. (Orig.). 1978. pap. 4.95 (0-89037-060-5) Anderson World.

— The Basic Soccer Guide. LC 85-4213. (Orig.). 1985. pap. 8.95 (0-02-028780-1, Collier S&S) S&S Trade.

— Intermediate Soccer Guide. (Illus.). 170p. (Orig.). 1982. pap. 12.95 (0-89037-181-4) Anderson World.

***Moffat, Bruce G.** The "L" (Central Electric Railfans' Association Bulletin Ser.: No. 131). (Illus.). 306p. 1995. 55.00 (0-915348-30-6) Central Electric.

Moffat, Charles H. A History of the Cabell County Medical Society in West Virginia 1890-1985. 336p. 1986. 76.00 (0-9616839-0-2) Cabell Cty Med Soc.

Moffat, D., jt. auth. see Asscher, A. W.

Moffat, D. W. Economics Dictionary. 331p. 1985. 85.00 (0-7859-0581-2, M7905) Fr & Eur.

Moffat, David V. UCSD Pascal Examples & Exercises. (Illus.). 224p. 1986. pap. text ed. 16.00 (0-13-935396-8) P-H.

Moffat, Donald W. Concise Desk Book of Business Finance. 2nd ed. 385p. 1984. text ed. 44.95 (0-13-166851-X, Busn) P-H.

— Economics Dictionary. 2nd ed. 331p. 1984. 43.50 (0-444-00798-9) P-H.

— Elementary Statistics for IBM PC's. 192p. 1987. 27.95 (0-13-260050-1) P-H.

— Elementary Statistics for the IBM PC's. (Illus.). 160p. 1988. pap. 23.95 (0-317-62510-1) P-H.

— Handbook of Manufacturing & Production Management Formulas, Charts, & Tables. 320p. 1987. text ed. 59.95 (0-13-379256-0) P-H.

— Handbook of Plant Monitoring & Inspection. 1995. text ed. 79.95 (0-13-124298-9) P-H.

— Manual de Formulas, Graficos y Tablas del Ingeniero de Plantas. Loinaz, Jorge, tr. LC 85-80464. (Illus.). 328p. (SPA.). 1985. 70.00 (0-9612412-1-7) Lineal Pub Co.

— Plant Engineer's Handbook of Formulas, Charts & Tables. 2nd ed. LC 81-15811. 397p. 1982. 57.95 (0-13-680298-2, Busn) P-H.

— Plant Engineer's Handbook of Formulas, Charts, & Tables. 3rd ed. 576p. 1991. 69.95 (0-13-680901-4, 350501) P-H.

— Plant Engineer's Portable Problem-Solver. LC 92-30290. 1993. write for info. (0-13-678921-8) P-H.

— The Plant Manager's Daily Planner, 1988. 448p. 1988. text ed. 32.50 (0-13-680257-5, Busn) P-H.

— Plant Manager's Handbook of Model Reports & Formats. 432p. 1990. text ed. 59.95 (0-13-679630-3) P-H.

Moffat, Donald W. & Poage, Greg A. The Plant Manager's Practical Guide to Accounting & Finance. LC 93-8923. 1993. write for info. (0-13-676966-7) P-H Gen Ref & Trav.

Moffat, Douglas. Old English "Soul & Body" An Edition. 160p. (C). 1990. 71.00 (0-85991-232-9) Boydell & Brewer.

Moffat, Douglas, ed. The Soul's Address to the Body: The Worcester Fragments. LC 86-72187. (Medieval Texts & Studies: No. 1). 142p. 1987. 28.00 (0-937191-01-9) Colleagues Pr Inc.

Moffat, Douglas, jt. ed. see Frantzen, Allen J.

Moffat, Frederick L. Breast Conservation in the Treatment of Early Breast Cancer. (Medical Intelligence Unit Ser.). 115p. 1994. 89.95 (1-57059-087-7, LN9087) R G Landes.

Moffat, Geoffrey, jt. auth. see Hotaling, Robert B.

***Moffat, Graham & Chesterman, Michael.** Trust Law: Texts & Materials. 2nd ed. 1994. pap. text ed. 64.00 (0-406-04537-2, UK) Butterworth Legal Pubs.

Moffat, Gwen. The Corpse Road. large type ed. (Mystery Ser.). 400p. 1993. 21.95 (0-7089-2990-7) Ulverscroft.

— Die Like a Dog. large type ed. (Linford Mystery Library). 304p. 1988. pap. 11.95 (0-7089-6627-6, Linford) Ulverscroft.

— Grizzly Trail. large type ed. (Linford Mystery Library). 336p. 1987. pap. 11.95 (0-7089-6357-9, Linford) Ulverscroft.

— Hard Road West. large type ed. 448p. 1983. 21.95 (0-7089-0908-6) Ulverscroft.

— Over the Sea to Death. large type ed. 368p. 1994. 23.95 (0-7089-3137-5) Ulverscroft.

— Rage. large type ed. 400p. 1995. 23.95 (0-7089-2901-X) Ulverscroft.

— The Raptor Zone. large type ed. (General Ser.). 416p. 1993. 21.95 (0-7089-2881-1) Ulverscroft.

— Snare. large type ed. 1990. 21.95 (0-7089-2128-0) Ulverscroft.

— Veronica's Sisters. large type ed. LC 93-11684. 1993. 21.95 (0-7927-1801-1, Curley Lrg Print); pap. 19.95 (0-7927-1800-3, Curley Lrg Print) Chivers N Amer.

Moffat, Hugh. East Anglia's First Railways. 1994. 48.00 (0-86138-038-X, Pub. by T Dalton UK) St Mut.

Moffat, Mary J. In the Midst of Winter: Selections from the Literature of Mourning. LC 81-52920. 1982. pap. 7.95 (0-394-75327-5, Vin) Random.

— The Times of Our Lives: A Guide to Writing Autobiography & Memoir. rev. ed. LC 89-1529. 64p. (Orig.). 1989. reprint ed. pap. 7.95 (0-936784-75-X) J Daniel.

Moffat, Mary J., ed. In the Midst of Winter: Selections from the Literature of Mourning. 1992. 12.00 (0-679-73827-4, Vin) Random.

Moffat, Mary J. & Painter, Charlotte, eds. Revelations: Diaries of Women. 1975. pap. 10.00 (0-394-71151-3, Vin) Random.

Moffat, Pelham. Twenty-One Plays for Children. 224p. 1990. 29.50 (0-86315-094-2, 1287, Pub. by Floris Books UK) Anthroposophic.

Moffat, R. Burnham. The Barclays of New York: Who They Are & Who They Are Not, & Some Other Barclays. 481p. 1988. reprint ed. lib. bdg. 85.00 (0-8328-0184-4); reprint ed. pap. 75.00 (0-8328-0185-2) Higginson Bk Co.

Moffat, Riley. Population History of Eastern U. S. Cities & Towns, 1790-1870. LC 92-6364. 242p. 1992. 42.50 (0-8108-2553-8) Scarecrow.

— Population History of Western U. S. Cities & Towns, 1850-1990. LC 95-14583. 1995. write for info. (0-8108-3033-7) Scarecrow.

Moffat, Riley, jt. auth. see Fitzpatrick, Gary.

Moffat, Riley M. Map Index to Topographic Quadrangles of the United States, 1882-1940. LC 84-21984. (Occasional Papers: No. 10). (Illus.). 238p. (Orig.). 1986. 32.50 (0-939112-12-4) Western Assn Map.

— Printed Maps of Utah to 1900: An Annotated Cartobibliography. LC 81-659. (Occasional Papers: No. 8). (Illus.). 193p. (Orig.). 1981. pap. 10.00 (0-939112-09-4) Western Assn Map.

Moffat, Robert. Adventures of a Missionary: Or, Rivers of Water in a Dry Place. LC 70-89387. (Black Heritage Library Collection). 1977. 17.95 (0-8369-8635-0) Ayer.

Moffat, Robert C., et al, eds. Perspectives on the Family. LC 90-6472. (Studies in Social & Political Theory: Vol. 8). 400p. 1990. lib. bdg. 109.95 (0-88946-685-8) E Mellen.

Moffat, Susan D. Kids Explore Boston: The Very Best Kids' Activities Within an Easy Drive of Boston. (J). (gr. 4 up). 1994. pap. 10.95 (1-55850-392-7) Adams Pubng.

An Asterisk (*) at the beginning of an entry indicates that the title is appearing in BIP for the first time.

— Kids Explore Chicago: The Very Best Kid's Activities Within an Easy Drive of Chicago. (Kids Explore Ser.). (Illus.). 176p. (Orig.). (J). 1995. pap. 10.95 (*1-55850-499-0*) Adams Pubng.

— Kids Explore Florida. (Illus.). 176p. (J). 1994. pap. 10.95 (*1-55850-427-3*) Adams Pubng.

*__Moffatt, Bettyclare.__ Journey Toward Forgiveness: Finding Your Way Home. 176p. 1995. pap. 11.95 (*1-57101-050-5*) MasterMedia Ltd.

— Looking Good: A Woman's Guide to Personal Unfoldment. LC 87-1687. 136p. 1987. reprint ed. lib. bdg. 25.00x (*0-8095-6550-1*) Borgo Pr.

— Opening to Miracles: True Stories of Blessings & Renewal. (Orig.). 1995. pap. 11.95 (*1-885171-04-8*) Wldcat Canyon.

— Opening to Miracles: True Stories of Blessings & Renewal. LC 95-3396. 1995. 11.95 (*1-885171-29-3*) Wldcat Canyon.

— When Someone You Love Has AIDS: A Book of Hope for Family & Friends. LC 87-721. 154p. (Orig.). 1986. reprint ed. lib. bdg. 27.00x (*0-8095-6551-X*) Borgo Pr.

Moffatt, Charles. Ken Hechler Maverick Public. 1987. 20.00 (*0-941092-18-6*) Mtn St Pr.

Moffatt, Charles C., ed. see American Society of Mechanical Engineers Staff.

*__Moffatt, David.__ Explorations in the Ordinary: A Backyard Naturalist's View of Minnesota. (Illus.). 144p. (Orig.). 1995. 12.95 (*0-87839-099-5*) North Star.

Moffatt, Dorothy H. Time for Remembrance: Poems. LC 94-15047. 1994. write for info. (*0-87233-115-6*) Bauhan.

Moffatt, Edward A., ed. see American Society of Mechanical Engineers Staff.

*__Moffatt, Emma L.__ The Silent One & Other Poems. 16p. (Orig.). 1995. pap. write for info. (*1-885206-10-0*, Iliad Pr) Cader Pubng.

— Worthwhile. 14p. (Orig.). 1995. pap. write for info. (*1-885206-24-0*, Iliad Pr) Cader Pubng.

*__Moffatt, Emmo.__ The Primordial Lure. 20p. (Orig.). 1994. pap. write for info. (*1-885206-06-2*, Iliad Pr) Cader Pubng.

*__Moffatt, Frank.__ Grandma Ollie. (Jam Roll Picture Bks.). 32p. (J). 1995. pap. 12.95 (*0-7022-2850-8*, Pub. by Univ Queensland Pr AT) Intl Spec Bk.

Moffatt, Graham & Chesterman, Michael. Trusts Law: Text & Materials. (Law in Context Ser.). xlii, 746p. 1988. 75.00 (*0-297-79402-7*) Rothman.

Moffatt, H. K., ed. Topological Aspects of the Dynamics of Fluids & Plasmas. (NATO Advanced Science Institutes Series C: Mathematical & Physical Sciences). 624p. (C). 1992. lib. bdg. 200.00 (*0-7923-1900-1*) Kluwer Ac.

Moffatt, H. K. & Tsinober, A., eds. Topical Fluid Mechanics: Proceedings of the IUTAM Symposium. 800p. (C). 1990. 135.00 (*0-521-38145-2*) Cambridge U Pr.

Moffatt, James. The Approach to the New Testament. LC 77-27150. (Hibbert Lectures: 1921). reprint ed. 35.00 (*0-404-60420-X*) AMS Pr.

— The Bible - James Moffatt Translation. 1536p. 1994. 44.99 (*0-8254-3264-2*) Kregel.

— Hebrews: Critical & Exegetical Commentary. Driver, Samuel R. et al, eds. LC 24-21703. (International Critical Commentary Ser.). 336p. 1924. 36.95 (*0-567-05034-3*, Pub. by T & T Clark UK) Bks Intl VA.

— The Moffatt Bible. 1976. 32.00 (*0-06-065778-2*) Harper SF.

Moffatt, James, tr. see Harnack, Adolf.

Moffatt, James, ed. see Harnack, Adolf.

Moffatt, Laurie N., ed. Norman Rockwell: A Definitive Catalogue, 2 vols. LC 85-18881. (Illus.). 1197p. 1986. Boxed. boxed 195.00 (*0-9615273-1-5*) U Pr of New Eng.

Moffatt, Marjorie. Children's Word Liturgies, Vol. 1. 120p. 1986. pap. 9.95 (*0-8146-1537-6*) Liturgical Pr.

Moffatt, Michael. Coming of Age in New Jersey: College & American Culture. 345p. 1989. text ed. 35.00 (*0-8135-1358-8*); pap. 12.95 (*0-8135-1359-6*) Rutgers U Pr.

— The Rutgers Picture Book: An Illustrated History of Student Life in the Changing College & University. (Illus.). 250p. 1985. text ed. 12.50 (*0-8135-1091-0*) Rutgers U Pr.

— An Untouchable Community in South India: Structure & Consensus. LC 78-51183. 1979. 55.00x (*0-691-09377-6*) Princeton U Pr.

— An Untouchable Community in South India: Structure & Consensus. LC 78-51183. Date not set. reprint ed. pap. 104.90 (*0-7837-9392-8*, 2060137) Bks Demand.

Moffatt, Michael, ed. see Dumont, Louis.

Moffatt, William D. Your Traffic Ticket Adventure. 270p. 1992. pap. text ed. 23.95 (*0-9634069-0-6*) W D Moffatt.

Moffatt, William G. Handbook of Binary Phase Diagrams, 5 vols. (Illus.). 1500p. 1981. 339.00 (*0-931690-00-5*) Genium Pub.

Moffeit, Tony. Boogie Alley: Kangaroo Court No. 6. Lopez, Rick & Sherman, Lonnie, eds. (Illus.). (Orig.). 1989. pap. 7.00 (*0-940381-11-7*) Kangaroo Ct Pub.

— Boogie Alley: Kangaroo Court No. 6. limited ed. Lopez, Rick & Sherman, Lonnie, eds. (Illus.). (Orig.). 1989. 50.00 (*0-940381-12-5*) Kangaroo Ct Pub.

— Luminous Animal. 56p. (Orig.). 1989. pap. 6.00 (*0-916156-86-9*) Cherry Valley.

— Neon Peppers. LC 92-36466. 64p. (Orig.). 1992. pap. 7.00 (*0-916156-90-7*) Cherry Valley.

— Poetry Is Dangerous: The Poet Is an Outlaw. (Illus.). 104p. (Orig.). 1995. 10.00 (*0-912449-44-6*) Floating Island.

— The Spider Who Walked Underground. 2nd ed. Sherman, Lonnie & Lopez, Rick, eds. (Kangaroo Court Ser.: No. 4). (Illus.). 32p. 1986. 3.00 (*0-940381-03-6*) Kangaroo Ct Pub.

Moffet, Charles S. & Wood, James N., intros. Monet's Years at Giverny: Beyond Impressionism. LC 78-328. (Illus.). 1978. 29.95 (*0-87099-175-2*); pap. 14.95 (*0-87099-174-4*) Metro Mus Art.

Moffet, Glendon L. Down to the River by Trolley: The History of the New Paltz-Highland Trolley Line. LC 93-38796. (Illus.). 94p. (Orig.). 1993. pap. 10.00 (*0-935796-46-0*) Purple Mnt Pr.

Moffet, Hugh L. Pediatric Infectious Diseases: A Problem Oriented Approach. 3rd ed. LC 65-10986. (Illus.). 640p. 1988. text ed. 52.00 (*0-397-50933-2*, Lippincott Medical) Lippincott.

*__Moffet, Jim.__ American Corn Huskers: A Patent History. LC 94-74980. 1994. pap. 7.00 (*0-9641243-1-9*) Off Beat Bks.

Moffet, Judith. The Ragged World. 1992. mass mkt. 3.99 (*0-345-37500-9*, Del Rey) Ballantine.

Moffet, Kenworth, jt. auth. see Department of Contemporary Art.

Moffet, Promise K., jt. auth. see Kloss, Jethro.

Moffet, Ruth. Du'A, on Wings of Prayer. rev. ed. Brown, Keven, ed. 96p. 1984. 14.95 (*0-87961-142-1*); pap. 6.95 (*0-87961-143-X*) Naturegraph.

Moffet, Stanley N. & Ritzman, Marlene. Homeplace: A True Saga of the Midwest. LC 85-128222. (Illus.). 257p. (Orig.). 1984. pap. 22.50 (*0-9614613-8-1*) SNM Pub.

Moffett, jt. auth. see Schauf.

Moffett, Berdell, ed. see Chaney, Casey.

Moffett, Blair A., tr. see Girard, Raphael.

Moffett, Carol G. & Strydesky, Rebecca. The Receiving-Checking-Marking-Stocking Clerk. 2nd ed. (Illus.). 160p. (YA). (gr. 10-12). 1979. text ed. 13.32 (*0-07-042667-8*) McGraw.

Moffett, Charles S. Impressionist & Post-Impressionist Paintings in the Metropolitan Museum of Art. 1991. pap. 29.98 (*0-8109-8108-4*) Abrams.

— The New Painting: Impressionism 1874-1886. (Illus.). 510p. (Orig.). 1989. 29.95 (*0-295-96883-4*) U of Wash Pr.

Moffett, Charles S., et al. The New Painting: Impressionism 1874-1886. LC 85-24537. (Illus.). 510p. (Orig.). 1986. pap. 29.95 (*0-88401-047-3*) Fine Arts Mus.

Moffett, Cleveland. Through the Wall. 1,909th ed. LC 75-32768. (Literature of Mystery & Detection Ser.). (Illus.). 1976. reprint ed. 34.95 (*0-405-07887-0*) Ayer.

Moffett, Eileen. Korean Ways. (Illus.). 56p. (J). (gr. k up). 1986. 12.95 (*0-8048-7013-6*, Pub. by Seoul Intl Tourist KO) C E Tuttle.

*__Moffett, George D.__ Critical Masses: The Global Population Challenge. 368p. 1995. pap. 12.95 (*0-14-023226-5*, Penguin Bks) Viking Penguin.

Moffett, George D., III. Critical Masses: The Global Population Crisis into the 21st Century. 224p. 1994. 26.95 (*0-670-85235-X*, Viking) Viking Penguin.

*__Moffett, George D.__ Global Population Growth: Twenty-First Century Challenges. Hoepli, Nancy L., ed. LC 94-71669. (Headline Ser.). (Illus.). 72p. (Orig.). 1994. pap. 5.95 (*0-87124-158-7*) Foreign Policy.

— The Limits of Victory: The Ratification of the Panama Canal Treaties. LC 84-14920. 265p. 1985. 34.00 (*0-8014-1737-6*) Cornell U Pr.

*__Moffett, Glendon L.__ To Poughkeepsie & Back: The Story of the Poughkeepsie-Highland Ferry. 1994. 10.00 (*0-935796-56-8*) Purple Mnt Pr.

Moffett, James. Active Voice: A Writing Program Across the Curriculum. LC 81-6156. 160p. (Orig.). (C). 1981. pap. text ed. 14.00 (*0-86709-001-4*) Boynton Cook Pubs.

— Active Voice: A Writing Program Across the Curriculum. 2nd ed. 203p. (Orig.). 1992. pap. text ed. 17.00 (*0-86709-289-0*, 0289) Boynton Cook Pubs.

— Coming on Center: Essays in English Education. 2nd rev. ed. LC 87-27774. 208p. 1988. pap. text ed. 17.00 (*0-86709-219-X*) Boynton Cook Pubs.

— Detecting Growth in Language. LC 92-18851. 70p. 1992. pap. text ed. 14.00 (*0-86709-311-0*) Boynton Cook Pubs.

— Harmonic Learning: Keynoting School Reform. LC 92-23576. 1992. pap. text ed. 17.50 (*0-86709-312-9*, 0312) Boynton Cook Pubs.

— Storm in the Mountains: A Case Study of Censorship, Conflict, & Consciousness. LC 87-20614. 280p. (C). 1989. pap. 15.95 (*0-8093-1584-X*) S Ill U Pr.

— Teaching the Universe of Discourse. LC 87-27816. xviii, 215p. (C). 1983. reprint ed. pap. text ed. 17.50 (*0-86709-181-9*) Boynton Cook Pubs.

— The Universal Schoolhouse: Spiritual Awakening Through Education. LC 93-40694. (Education-Higher Education Ser.). 391p. 1994. 27.00 (*1-55542-607-7*) Jossey-Bass.

Moffett, James, ed. Points of Departure: An Anthology of Nonfiction. 1985. pap. 4.95 (*0-451-62380-0*, Ment); pap. 6.99 (*0-451-62728-8*) NAL-Dutton.

*__Moffett, James & McElheny, Kenneth R., eds.__ Points of View. rev. ed. 608p. 1995. mass mkt. 5.99 (*0-451-62872-1*, Sig) NAL-Dutton.

— Points of View: An Anthology of Short Stories. 1968. pap. 5.99 (*0-451-62722-9*, Ment) NAL-Dutton.

Moffett, James & Tashlik, Phyllis. Active Voices, II: A Writer's Reader. 317p. (J). (gr. 7-9). 1987. teacher ed 1.75 (*0-86709-182-7*) Boynton Cook Pubs.

— Active Voices, II: A Writer's Reader. 317p. (YA). (gr. 7-9). 1987. pap. text ed. 16.50 (*0-86709-111-8*) Boynton Cook Pubs.

Moffett, James & Wagner, Betty J. Student-Centered Language Arts, K-12. 4th ed. 437p. 1991. pap. text ed. 29.50 (*0-86709-292-0*, 0292) Boynton Cook Pubs.

Moffett, James, et al. Active Voices, I: A Writer's Reader. 265p. (J). (gr. 4-6). 1987. teacher ed 1.75 (*0-86709-184-3*) Boynton Cook Pubs.

— Active Voices, I: A Writer's Reader. 265p. (J). (gr. 4-6). 1987. text ed. 16.50 (*0-86709-091-X*) Boynton Cook Pubs.

— Active Voices, III: A Writer's Reader. 414p. (YA). (gr. 10-12). 1987. pap. text ed. 17.50 (*0-86709-113-4*) Boynton Cook Pubs.

— Active Voices, III: A Writer's Reader. 414p. (YA). (gr. 10-12). 1987. teacher ed 1.75 (*0-86709-180-0*) Boynton Cook Pubs.

— Active Voices IV. LC 85-27996. 344p. (Orig.). (C). 1985. pap. text ed. 18.50 (*0-86709-115-0*) Boynton Cook Pubs.

— Active Voices IV. LC 85-27996. 344p. (Orig.). (C). 1986. teacher ed 1.75 (*0-86709-179-7*) Boynton Cook Pubs.

*__Moffett, Jerry E.__ The Computer Buyer Survival Kit: How to Select & Buy a Personal Computer. LC 94-96308. (Illus.). 115p. (Orig.). 1995. pap. 9.95 (*0-9642508-0-2*) Jerett Pubng.

— Self-Publishing: The Art of Turning Words into Cash. LC 94-96309. 150p. (Orig.). Date not set. pap. 19.95 (*0-9642508-1-0*) Jerett Pubng.

Moffett, Joseph O. Some Beekeepers & Associates, Pt. I. (Illus.). 140p. lib. bdg. 19.90 (*0-686-31814-5*); pap. 9.90 (*0-686-28741-X*) Moffett.

Moffett, Joyce, ed. see Manassah, Sallie M., et al.

Moffett, Joyce L., ed. Mid-Michigan First: A Capital Choice for Future Growth. (Illus.). 184p. 1993. 29.95 (*0-9616743-4-2*) Contemp Image.

*__Moffett, Judith.__ Homestead Year. 320p. 1995. 22.95 (*1-55821-352-X*) Lyons & Burford.

— James Merrill: An Introduction to the Poetry. LC 83-15022. (Introduction to Twentieth Century American Poetry Ser.). 247p. 1984. text ed. 34.00 (*0-231-05210-3*) Col U Pr.

— Keeping Time: Poems. fac. ed. LC 76-28256. 87p. 1976. reprint ed. pap. 25.00 (*0-7837-7809-0*, 2047565) Bks Demand.

— Pennterra. 1993. mass mkt. 5.50 (*0-345-37824-5*, Del Rey Discovery) Ballantine.

— Time, Like an Ever-Rolling Stream. 1993. mass mkt. 5.50 (*0-345-38275-7*, Del Rey) Ballantine.

— Whinny Moor Crossing. LC 83-43055. (Contemporary Poets Ser.). 100p. 1984. 21.95 (*0-691-06591-8*); pap. 9.95 (*0-691-01410-8*) Princeton U Pr.

Moffett, Julie. Fleeting Splendor. 368p. (Orig.). 1993. pap. 4.50 (*0-8439-3434-4*) Dorchester Pub Co.

— A Touch of Fire. 368p. (Orig.). 1994. mass mkt., pap. text ed. 4.50 (*0-8439-3633-9*) Dorchester Pub Co.

Moffett, Kathleen. Designs for Dreamers. (Illus.). 52p. 1990. 10.95 (*0-936459-14-X*) Stained Glass.

— Dreamin' On. Stained Glass Images Staff, ed. (Illus.). 52p. 1991. 10.95 (*0-936459-15-8*) Stained Glass.

Moffett, Kenworth. Larry Poons: Paintings 1971-1981. (Illus.). 32p. (Orig.). 1981. pap. 5.95 (*0-87846-206-6*) Mus Fine Arts Boston.

— Morris Louis in the Museum of Fine Arts, Boston. LC 79-6360. (Illus.). 40p. 1979. pap. 7.95 (*0-87846-135-3*) Mus Fine Arts Boston.

Moffett, Lorraine J. Sex Life of Slugs. (All Life Speaks Out Ser.). 10p. 1992. pap. write for info. (*0-9633997-0-5*) Rolaine Pub.

Moffett, Marian & Wodehouse, Lawrence. East Tennessee Cantilever Barns. LC 92-42651. (Illus.). 160p. (C). 1993. text ed. 29.95 (*0-87049-798-7*) U of Tenn Pr.

Moffett, Marian, jt. auth. see Wodehouse, Lawrence.

Moffett, Mark W. High Frontier: Exploring the Tropical Rainforest Canopy. 192p. (C). 1994. text ed. 39.95 (*0-674-39038-5*); pap. text ed. 24.95 (*0-674-39039-3*) HUP.

Moffett, M'Ledge. The Social Background & Activities of Teachers College Students. LC 79-177077. (Columbia University. Teachers College. Contributions to Education Ser.: No. 375). reprint ed. 37.50 (*0-404-55375-3*) AMS Pr.

Moffett, Noel. The Best of British Architecture, 1980-2000. LC 92-40841. 1992. write for info. (*0-419-17240-8*, E & FN Spon); write for info. (*0-442-31640-2*, E & FN Spon) Routledge Chapman & Hall.

Moffett, Ross. Art in Narrow Streets. LC 89-62403. (Provincetown Classics in History, Literature, & Art Ser.: No. 3). (Illus.). 110p. 1989. reprint ed. pap. 6.95 (*0-945135-02-5*) Cape Cod Pilgrim.

Moffett, Ross, jt. auth. see Del Deo, Josephine C.

Moffett, Russell E. Macor-Economic Primer. 240p. (C). 1993. per., pap. text ed. 19.95 (*0-8403-8526-9*) Kendall-Hunt.

Moffett, Samuel H. A History of Christianity in Asia: Vol. I, Beginnings to 1500. LC 91-55085. 560p. 1992. 45.00 (*0-06-065779-0*) Harper SF.

Moffett, Toby. Nobody's Business: The Political Intruder's Guide to Everyone's State Legislature. LC 73-83355. (Illus.). 196p. 1973. 9.50 (*0-85699-080-9*); pap. 3.95 (*0-85699-081-7*) Chatham Pr.

Moffi, Larry. Citizen's Handbook. LC 89-8626. 48p. (Orig.). 1989. pap. 6.95 (*0-914061-10-0*) Orchises Pr.

— This Side of Cooperstown: An Oral History of Major League Baseball in the 1950s. (Illus.). 288p. 1996. 24.95 (*0-87745-521-X*) U of Iowa Pr.

Moffi, Larry & Kronstadt, Jonathan. Crossing the Line: Black Major Leaguers, 1947-1959. 251p. 1994. lib. bdg. 35.00 (*0-89950-930-4*) McFarland & Co.

Moffic, H. Steven, et al. Mental Health Care for Allied Health & Nursing Professionals. 240p. 1989. 27.50 (*0-87527-344-0*) Green.

Moffill, G. E. & Scholer, M., eds. Physical Processes in Interstellar Clouds. (C). 1987. lib. bdg. 169.50 (*90-277-2563-2*) Kluwer Ac.

Moffit, Donald. Second Genesis. 1986. pap. 3.50 (*0-345-33804-9*, Del Rey) Ballantine.

Moffit, Gisela. Bonds & Bondage: Daughter-Father Relationships in the Father Memoirs of German-Speaking Women Writers of the 1970s. LC 92-35430. (Studies in Modern German Literature: Vol. 53). 284p. 1993. 56.95 (*0-8204-2014-X*) P Lang Pubs.

Moffit, L. W. England on Eve of Industrial Revolution. 312p. 1963. reprint ed. 32.00 (*0-7146-1345-2*, BHA-01345, Pub. by F Cass Pubs UK) Intl Spec Bk.

Moffit, Linda L. The Magic Mirror. LC 89-50125. (Illus.). 80p. (Orig.). (J). (gr. k-7). 1989. pap. 8.95 (*0-87516-615-6*) DeVorss.

Moffitt, Alan, et al, eds. The Functions of Dreaming. (SUNY Series in Dream Studies). 610p. (C). 1993. 74.50 (*0-7914-1297-0*); pap. 24.95 (*0-7914-1298-9*) State U NY Pr.

Moffitt, Donald, ed. The Wall Street Journal Views America Tomorrow. LC 76-52501. 190p. reprint ed. pap. 54.20 (*0-317-27197-0*, 2023931) Bks Demand.

Moffitt, Francis H. & Bouchard, Harry. Surveying. 8th ed. (C). 1989. text ed. 50.00 (*0-06-044554-8*) HarpCollege.

— Surveying. 9th ed. (C). 1991. text ed. 79.00 (*0-06-500059-5*) HarpCollege.

Moffitt, James, jt. auth. see Orr, Robert T.

*__Moffitt, John F.__ Art Forgery: The Case of the Lady of Elche. LC 94-29181. (Illus.). 354p. 1995. lib. bdg. 39.95 (*0-8130-1330-5*) U Press Fla.

— Occultism in Avant-Garde Art: The Case of Joseph Beuys. Foster, Stephen, ed. LC 88-5774. (Studies in the Fine Arts: The Avant-Garde: No. 63). 238p. reprint ed. 67.90 (*0-8357-1881-6*, 2070674) Bks Demand.

*__Moffitt, John F. & Sebastian, Santiago.__ O Brave New People: The European Image of Native Americans. LC 94-48680. (Illus.). 296p. 1995. 45.00x (*0-8263-1639-5*) U of NM Pr.

Moffitt, Leonard C. Global Positioning for the Twenty-First Century: Rethinking Strategic Planning. LC 89-42581. 230p. (C). 1990. text ed. 24.95 (*0-87013-272-5*) Mich St U Pr.

— Strategic Management: Public Planning at the Local Level. (Contemporary Studies in Economic & Financial Analysis: Vol. 45). 1984. 73.25 (*0-89232-428-7*) Jai Pr.

Moffitt, Peggy, et al. The Rudi Gernreich Book. LC 91-2981. (Illus.). 224p. 1991. 50.00 (*0-8478-1422-X*) Rizzoli Intl.

Moffitt, Phillip & Smolan, Rick. Worth a Thousand Words: Scanning to Communicate. 80p. 1991. pap. 7.95 (*0-9630008-0-2*) Light Source.

Moffitt, Phillip, jt. auth. see Smolan, Rick.

Moffitt, Terrie E. & Mednick, Sarnoff A., eds. Biological Contributions to Crime Causation. 1988. lib. bdg. 125.50 (*90-247-3655-2*) Kluwer Ac.

*__Mofford, Juliet, intro.__ Cry "Witch" - Salem 1692. LC 95-68765. (Perspectives on History Ser.). (Illus.). 68p. (Orig.). (YA). (gr. 5-12). 1995. pap. text ed. 4.95 (*1-878668-52-8*) Disc Enter Ltd.

Mofford, Juliet H., ed. Greater Lawrence: A Bibliography. LC 78-71920. 1978. 15.00 (*0-937474-01-0*) Mus Am Textile Hist.

Mofid, Bijan. The Butterfly. (J). 1974. 5.00 (*0-87602-111-9*) Anchorage.

Mofolo, Thomas. Chaka. Kunene, Daniel, tr. (African Writers Ser.). (Orig.). (C). 1981. pap. 9.95 (*0-435-90229-6*) Heinemann.

— The Traveller of the East. Ashton, H., tr. (B. E. Ser.: No. 100). 1934. 18.00 (*0-8115-3032-9*) Periodicals Srv.

Moga, Thomas T. Patent Practice & Policy in the Pacific Rim. 1995. ring bd. 160.00 (*0-379-01263-4*) Oceana.

Mogab, C. J., jt. ed. see Frieser, R. G.

Mogadam, Michael. Choosing Foods for a Healthy Heart: Introducing the CEF Index. LC 92-39213. 192p. 1993. 19.95 (*0-89043-633-9*) Consumer Reports.

*__Mogan, Jewel.__ Beyond Telling. LC 94-39166. 173p. 1995. 19.95 (*0-86538-082-1*) Ontario Rev NJ.

Mogano, Mike C. How to Make Bigger Profits. (C). 1991. lib. bdg. 40.00 (*1-85333-603-3*, Pub. by Graham & Trotman UK) Kluwer Ac.

— How to Start & Run Your Own Business. 160p. 1989. pap. text ed. 14.00 (*0-86010-577-6*); pap. text ed. 15.00 (*1-85333-288-7*) G & T Inc.

— How to Start & Run Your Own Business. (C). 1988. pap. text ed. 14.00 (*1-85333-093-0*, Pub. by Graham & Trotman UK) Kluwer Ac.

— How to Start & Run Your Own Business. 7th ed. 1989. lib. bdg. 27.50 (*1-85333-190-2*, Pub. by Graham & Trotman UK); pap. text ed. 13.50 (*1-85333-191-0*, Pub. by Graham & Trotman UK) Kluwer Ac.

— How to Win Promotion. (Better Business Ser.). 128p. 1990. pap. text ed. 15.00 (*1-85333-381-6*, Pub. by Graham & Trotman UK) Kluwer Ac.

Mogard, Sue & McDonnell, Ginny. Gobble up Math. LC 94-75876. (Primary Math Ser.). 136p. (J). (gr. k-3). 1994. 9.95 (*0-88160-262-0*, LW105) Learning Wks.

Mogavero & Shane. WEESKA Technology Transfer & Innovation. (What Every Engineer Should Know Ser.: Vol. 8). 168p. 1982. 55.00 (*0-8247-1863-1*) Dekker.

Mogee, Mary E. Technology Policy & Critical Technologies: A Summary of Recent Reports. 50p. (Orig.). (C). 1993. pap. text ed. 29.95 (*0-7881-0031-9*) Diane Pub.

Mogel, jt. auth. see Mulchow.

Mogel, Leonard. The Magazine: Everything You Need to Know to Make It in the Magazine Business. 3rd ed. 240p. (C). 1992. pap. 19.95 (*1-56440-086-7*) Globe Pequot.

— Making It in Advertising: An Inside's Guide to Career Opportunities. LC 92-32051. 193p. 1993. pap. 10.00 (*0-02-034552-6*, Collier S&S) S&S Trade.

— Making it in Broadcasting: An Insider's Guide to Career Opportunities. 320p. 1994. pap. 14.00 (*0-02-034553-4*, Collier S&S) S&S Trade.

— Making It in Public Relations. LC 92-27334. 191p. 1993. pap. 10.00 (*0-02-070180-2*, Collier S&S) S&S Trade.

— Making It in Publishing: An Insider's Guide to Career Opportunities. LC 93-9012. 1994. write for info. (*0-02-034533-X*, Collier S&S) S&S Trade.

Mogelever, Diane, ed. see Family Circle Editors.

Mogelon, Alex & Laliberte, Norman. Art in Boxes. LC 74-5947. (Illus.). 240p. reprint ed. pap. 68.40 (*0-8357-5759-5*, 2005810) Bks Demand.

Mogelonsky, Marcia. Everybody Eats: Supermarket Consumers in the 1990s. 229p. (C). 1995. 42.50 (*0-936889-31-4*); pap. 29.95 (*0-936889-32-2*) American Demo.

Mogen, David. Ray Bradbury. (Twayne's United States Authors Ser.: No. 504). 184p. 1986. text ed. 20.95 (*0-8057-7464-5*, Twayne) Macmillan.

— Wilderness Visions: The Western Theme in Science Fiction Literature. 2nd ed. LC 92-46389. (I. O. Evans Studies in the Philosophy & Criticism of Literature: No. 1). 128p. 1993. lib. bdg. 27.00x (*0-89370-300-1*); pap. 17.00x (*0-89370-400-8*) Borgo Pr.

Mogen, David, et al, eds. The Frontier Experience & the American Dream: Essays on American Literature. LC 88-35474. 288p. 1989. 29.50 (*0-89096-398-3*); pap. 14.95 (*0-89096-417-3*) Tex A&M Univ Pr.

Mogendovich, Eugene. Hydropulse Systems & Technology in the U. S. S. R. Jones, Steven, ed. 105p. (Orig.). 1985. pap. text ed. 75.00 (*1-55831-030-4*) Delphic Associates.

Mogenet, Joseph, et al. Nicephore Gregoras Calcul de l'eclipse de soleil du 16 Juillet 1330. (Corpus des Astronomes Byzantins Ser.: Vol. I). 222p. (Orig.). (FRE.). (C). 1983. pap. 46.00 (*90-70265-34-6*, Pub. by Gieben NE) Benjamins North Am.

Mogens, Jul. The Quality of Frozen Food. 1984. text ed. 80.00 (*0-12-391980-0*) Acad Pr.

Mogensen, Allan H. & Rausa, Rosario. Mogy; An Autobiography: Father of Work Simplification. 2nd ed. Denyes, Jim, ed. 204p. 1990. pap. text ed. 9.95 (*0-9623050-0-6*) Idea Assocs VA.

Mogensen, C. E., ed. The Kidney & Hypertensions in Diabetes Mellitus. (Topics in Renal Medicine Ser.). (C). 1988. lib. bdg. 157.00 (*0-89838-958-5*) Kluwer Ac.

Mogensen, C. E. & Standl, E., eds. Concepts for the Ideal Diabetes Clinic. LC 92-49365. xiv, 402p. (C). 1993. pap. text ed. 113.85 (*3-11-013231-1*) De Gruyter.

— Pharmacology of Diabetes: Present Practice & Future Perspectives. (Illus.). xii, 374p. (C). 1991. pap. text ed. 98.50 (*3-11-012636-2*) De Gruyter.

— Prevention & Treatment of Diabetic Late Complications. x, 226p. (C). 1989. pap. 69.25x (*0-89925-637-6*) De Gruyter.

— Prevention & Treatment of Diabetic Late Complications. x, 226p. (C). 1989. pap. 69.25 (*3-11-012297-9*) De Gruyter.

— Research Methodologies in Human Diabetes. LC 93-50659. 470p. 1994. 129.25 (*3-11-014248-1*) De Gruyter.

Mogensen, Carl E., ed. The Kidney & Hypertension in Diabetes Mellitus. 2nd ed. 576p. 1994. lib. bdg. 165.00 (*0-7923-2829-9*) Kluwer Ac.

Mogensen, Jan. The Forty-Six Little Men. LC 90-36470. (Illus.). 28p. (J). (ps up). 1991. 13.95 (*0-688-09283-7*); lib. bdg. 13.88 (*0-688-09284-5*) Greenwillow.

— The Forty-Six Little Men. LC 92-25329. (Illus.). (J). 1993. pap. 4.99 (*0-14-054831-9*) Puffin Bks.

— The Land of the Big. LC 92-18302. (Illus.). 32p. (J). (ps-3). 1993. 14.95 (*1-56656-111-6*, Crocodile Bks) Interlink Pub.

— The Tiger's Breakfast. LC 91-3606. (Illus.). 32p. (J). (ps-3). 1991. 14.95 (*0-940793-83-0*, Crocodile Bks) Interlink Pub.

Mogensen, Jan, illus. & ret. Kakalambalala: An African Tale. LC 93-2910. 1993. 14.95 (*1-56656-136-1*, Crocodile Bks) Interlink Pub.

Mogensen, Sandra & Magarian-Gold, Judi. Exploring with Color Tiles. 96p. (J). (gr. k-3). 1990. pap. text ed. 8.95 (*0-938587-17-X*) Cuisenaire.

Mogensen, Sandra & Magarian-Gold, Judy. Pattern Animals Book. (Illus.). 48p. (J). (gr. 1-4). 1986. pap. text ed. 8.50 (*0-914040-46-4*) Cuisenaire.

Mogenson, Greg. God Is a Trauma: Vicarious Religion & Soul-Making. LC 89-5998. 167p. (Orig.). 1989. pap. 13.50 (*0-88214-339-5*) Spring Pubns.

— Greeting the Angels: An Imaginal View of the Mourning Process. (Death, Value, & Meaning Ser.). 171p. 1992. text ed. 21.95 (*0-89503-097-7*); pap. text ed. 16.95 (*0-89503-096-9*) Baywood Pub.

Moger, Allen W. Virginia: Bourbonism to Byrd, 1870-1925. LC 68-8538. (Illus.). 414p. reprint ed. pap. 118.00 (*0-7837-4349-1*, 2044059) Bks Demand.

Moger, Art. The Best Book of Puns. 192p. 1988. pap. 7.95 (*0-8065-1097-8*, Citadel Pr) Carol Pub Group.

— The Complete Pun Book. 256p. 1981. pap. 5.95 (*0-8065-0776-4*, Citadel Pr) Carol Pub Group.

— Hello, My Real Name Is.... (Illus.). 160p. 1983. pap. 6.95 (*0-8065-0802-7*, Citadel Pr) Carol Pub Group.

Moger, Byron J. How to Buy a House. LC 69-10635. 1969. 4.95 (*0-8184-0040-4*) Carol Pub Group.

Mogey, John H., ed. Aiding & Aging: The Coming Crisis in Support for the Elderly by Kin & State. LC 89-25670. (Contributions to the Study of Aging Ser.: No. 17). 312p. 1990. text ed. 59.95 (*0-313-27315-4*, MOD/, Greenwood Pr) Greenwood.

Mogey, John H., ed. see Howard, Ronald L.

Mogey, John M. Rural Life in Northern Ireland: Five Regional Studies Made for the Northern Ireland Council of Social Service, Inc. LC 77-87692. reprint ed. 38.00 (*0-404-16488-9*) AMS Pr.

Mogford-Bevan, Kay & Sadler, Jane, eds. Child Language Disability, Vol. 2: Semantic & Pragmatic Difficulties. 114p. 1991. 59.00 (*1-85359-128-9*, Pub. by Multilingual Matters UK); pap. 19.50 (*1-85359-127-0*, Pub. by Multilingual Matters UK) Taylor & Francis.

— Child Language Disability, Vol. 3: Hearing Impairment. 120p. 1992. 59.00 (*1-85359-169-6*, Pub. by Multilingual Matters UK); pap. 19.50 (*1-85359-168-8*, Pub. by Multilingual Matters UK) Taylor & Francis.

Mogford, Kay & Sadler, Jane, eds. Child Language Disability: Implications in an Educational Setting. 104p. 1989. 49.00 (*1-85359-052-5*, Pub. by Multilingual Matters UK); pap. 17.00 (*1-85359-051-7*, Pub. by Multilingual Matters UK) Taylor & Francis.

Mogford, Kay, jt. ed. see Bishop, Dorothy.

Moggach, Deborah. Stand-In. 400p. 1991. 19.95 (*0-316-57751-0*) Little.

— The Stand-In. 400p. 1994. reprint ed. pap. text ed. 5.99 (*0-425-14289-2*) Berkley Pub.

Moggeridge, Donald, jt. ed. see Howson, Susan.

Moggi, Guido, et al. Simon & Schuster's Guide to Garden Flowers. Schuler, Stanley, ed. (Illus.). 1983. pap. 15.00 (*0-671-46678-X*) S&S Trade.

Moggridge, D. E. British Monetary Policy, 1924-1931: The Norman Conquest of Four Dollars & Eighty-Six Cents. (Modern Revivals in Economic & Social History Ser.). 302p. 1992. 59.95 (*0-7512-0092-1*, Pub. by Gregg Revivals UK) Ashgate Pub Co.

— Keynes. 3rd ed. 200p. 1993. 45.00 (*0-8020-0515-2*); pap. 19.95 (*0-8020-6951-7*) U of Toronto Pr.

Moggridge, D. E., ed. Editing Modern Economists: Papers Given at the Twenty-Second Annual Conference on Editorial Problems, University of Toronto, 7-8 November, 1986. LC 87-45817. (Conference on Editorial Problems Ser.: No. 22). 1988. 37.50 (*0-404-63672-1*) AMS Pr.

Moggridge, D. E., jt. ed. see Howson, Susan.

***Moggridge, Don.** Maynard Keynes: An Economists' Biography. (Illus.). 968p. 1995. pap. 19.95 (*0-415-12676-2*, C0539) Routledge.

Moggridge, Donald, ed. see Keynes, John Maynard.

Moggridge, Donald E. John Maynard Keynes: An Economist's Biography. 1992. 37.50 (*0-415-05141-X*, A5993) Routledge.

Moggridge, Donald E., ed. Perspectives in the History of Economic Thought, Vol. III: Classicals, Marzians & Neo-Classicals. 224p. 1990. text ed. 64.95 (*1-85278-293-5*, Pub. by E Elgar Pub UK) Ashgate Pub Co.

— Perspectives on the History of Economic Thought, Vol. IV: Keynes, Macroeconomics & Method. (Illus.). 288p. 1990. text ed. 64.95 (*1-85278-294-3*, Pub. by E Elgar Pub UK) Ashgate Pub Co.

Mogha, V. Indian Conveyancer. (C). 1987. 80.00 (*0-685-25709-6*) St Mut.

— Law of Pleadings. (C). 1987. 90.00 (*0-685-25708-8*) St Mut.

Moghadam, A. A. The North-South Science & Technology Gap. LC 91-18135. (Developing Economies of the Third World Ser.). 342p. 1991. 70.00 (*0-8153-0634-2*) Garland.

***Moghadam, H. & Fagan, Joel.** Attention Deficit Disorder: A Concise Source of Information for Parents & Teachers. 2nd rev. ed. 112p. 1994. pap. 12.95 (*1-55059-082-0*) Temeron Bks.

Moghadam, Valentine, ed. Democratic Reform & the Position of Women in Transitional Economies. (WIDER Studies in Development Economics). (Illus.). 376p. 1994. 60.00 (*0-19-828820-4*) OUP.

Moghadam, Valentine M. Modernizing Women: Gender & Social Change in the Middle East. LC 92-37454. (Women & Change in the Developing World Ser.). 312p. 1993. pap. text ed. 17.95 (*1-55587-354-5*) Lynne Rienner.

— Politics & Ideology in Contemporary Iran: The Social Bases of Conflict. (C). 1929. text ed. 34.00 (*0-8133-7766-8*) Westview.

Moghadam, Valentine M., ed. Gender & National Identity: Women & Politics in Muslim Society. LC 94-10887. 192p. (C). 1994. text ed. 55.00 (*1-85649-245-1*, Pub. by Zed Books UK); pap. 19.95 (*1-85649-246-X*, Pub. by Zed Books UK) Humanities.

— Identity Politics & Women: Cultural Reassertions & Feminisms in International Perspective. LC 93-28018. 458p. (C). 1993. pap. text ed. 21.50 (*0-8133-8692-6*) Westview.

— Identity Politics & Women: Cultural Reassertions & Feminisms in International Perspective. LC 93-28018. 458p. (C). 1993. text ed. 62.00 (*0-8133-8691-8*) Westview.

Moghadam, Valentine M., jt. ed. see Khoury, Nabil F.

Moghaddam, Fathali M., jt. auth. see Taylor, Donald M.

Moghaddam, Fathali M., et al. Social Psychology in Cross-Cultural Perspective. LC 92-23851. (C). 1995. text ed. write for info. (*0-7167-2354-9*); pap. text ed. write for info. (*0-7167-2355-7*) W H Freeman.

Moghdam, Dineh. Computers in Newspaper Publishing: User-Oriented Systems. LC 77-17887. (Books in Library & Information Science: No. 22). (Illus.). 221p. reprint ed. pap. 63.00 (*0-7837-3387-9*, 2043345) Bks Demand.

***Moghe, S. G.** Sraddha-Sagara of Kullukabhatta: With a Critical Exposition & Introduction. 1994. 29.00 (*81-246-0016-3*, Pub. by DK Pubs Dist II) S Asia.

Moghimi, Sasha, ed. see Kian, Fereydoun.

Moghissi, A. A., ed. Oil Spills. 80p. 1980. pap. 15.50 (*0-08-026237-6*, Pergamon Pr) Elsevier.

Moghissi, Haideh. Populism & Feminism in Iran: Women's Struggle in a Male-Defined Revolutionary Movement. LC 93-47024. 1994. 59.95 (*0-312-12068-0*) St Martin.

Moghissi, Kamran, jt. ed. see Blandau, Richard J.

Moghissi, Kamran S., ed. Controversies in Contraception. LC 78-15812. 249p. reprint ed. pap. 71.00 (*0-317-42397-5*, 2056070) Bks Demand.

Moghissi, Kamran S., ed. see Harold C. Mack Symposium on the Physiology & Pathology of Reproduction Staff.

***Mogi, Goro, et al, eds.** Immunobiology in Otorhinolaryngology: Progress of a Decade. (Illus.). xliv, 674p. 1994. 190.00 (*90-6299-114-9*) Kugler Pubns.

— Recent Advances in Otitis Media. LC 93-41768. (Illus.). xxxvi, 875p. 1994. 243.00 (*90-6299-101-7*, Pub. by Kugler NE) Kugler Pubns.

Mogie, Michael. The Evolution of Asexual Reproduction in Plants. (Illus.). 288p. 1992. 79.95 (*0-412-44220-5*, A7549) Chapman & Hall.

Mogil, Christopher & Slepian, Anne. We Gave Away a Fortune. 256p. 1992. pap. 14.95 (*0-86571-221-2*) New Soc Pubs.

— We Gave Away a Fortune. 256p. 1992. lib. bdg. 39.95 (*0-86571-220-4*) New Soc Pubs.

Mogil, H. Michael & Hirsch, Sol. The Cloud Chart One, Two, Three. (NWA Publication Ser.: No. 1-88). (Illus.). 3p. 1988. pap. text ed. 9.50 (*1-883563-05-4*) Natl Weather.

Mogil, H. Michael & Levine, Barbara G. The Amateur Meteorologist: Explorations & Investigations. LC 93-17506. (Amateur Science Ser.). (Illus.). 144p. (J). (gr. 6-9). 1993. lib. bdg. 13.93 (*0-531-11045-1*) Watts.

— The Amateur Meteorologist: Explorations & Investigations. (Amateur Science Ser.). (Illus.). (J). (gr. 5-8). 1994. pap. 6.95 (*0-531-15696-6*) Watts.

Mogil, Holly M., ed. In-Plant Networking Source Guide, 1994-95. 600p. 1994. pap. 278.00 (*0-912920-87-4*) North Am Pub Co.

Mogilanski, Roman, ed. The Ghetto Anthology. (Illus.). 508p. 1986. 18.00 (*0-318-20028-7*) ACJPSCC.

Mogilner, A. I. Few-Particle Schrodinger Operators on a Lattice: Applications in Condensed Matter Physics. 300p. (C). 1995. text ed. 40.00 (*981-02-0735-2*) World Scientific Pub.

Mogle, Dawn, jt. auth. see Scholtz, Jim.

Moglen, Helene. Charlotte Bronte: The Self Conceived. LC 76-16010. 256p. 1984. reprint ed. text ed. 27.50 (*0-299-10140-1*); reprint ed. pap. 13.95 (*0-299-10144-4*) U of Wis Pr.

— The Philosophical Irony of Laurence Sterne. LC 75-4574. 1975. 18.95 (*0-8130-0363-6*) U Press Fla.

Moglestue, C. Monte Carlo Simulation of Semiconductor Devices. LC 92-47359. 326p. 1993. 99.95 (*0-412-47770-X*) Chapman & Hall.

Mogliner, Alijandra. The Children's Writer's Word Book. 352p. 1992. 19.99 (*0-89879-511-7*) Writers Digest.

***Mogotsi, Isaac.** The Alexandra Tales. 172p. (Orig.). 1994. pap. text ed. 14.95x (*0-86975-446-7*, Pub. by Ravan Pr ZA) Ohio U Pr.

Mogstad, T. E., ed. see International Congress of Psychotherapy Staff.

Moguet, Pamela J., jt. auth. see Belchez, Chito.

***Mogul, Kathleen M. & Dickstein, Leah J., eds.** Career Planning for Psychiatrists. (Issues in Psychiatry Ser.). 327p. 1995. text ed. 28.50 (*0-88048-197-8*, 8197) Am Psychiatric.

Mogwe, Gaele. The Magic Pool. (Junior African Writers Ser.). (Illus.). (J). (gr. 4-5). 1992. pap. 2.95 (*0-7910-2910-7*) Chelsea Hse.

Mogyorodi, J., ed. Statistics & Probability. 1984. lib. bdg. 152.50 (*90-277-1675-7*) Kluwer Ac.

Mohaddessin, Mohammad. Islamic Fundamentalism: The New Global Threat. LC 92-43002. 224p. 1993. pap. 14.95 (*0-929765-22-2*) Seven Locks Pr.

— Islamic Fundamentalism: The New Global Threat. LC 92-43002. 224p. 1993. 18.95 (*0-929765-32-X*) Seven Locks Pr.

Mohaghegh, Mehdi, tr. see Sabzavari, Hadi Ibn Mahdi.

Mohai, Paul, jt. ed. see Bryant, Bunyan.

***Moham, Chilukuri D., et al.** Advances in Logic Programming & Automated Reasoning Vol. 2. 240p. 1995. 55.00 (*0-89391-841-5*) Ablex Pub.

Mohamad, Dost. International Liquidity. 1987. text ed. 25.00 (*81-207-0639-0*, Pub. by Sterling Pubs II) Apt Bks.

Mohamed, Abbas A. White Nile Arabs: Political Leadership & Economic Change. (London School of Economics Monographs on Social Anthropology: No. 53). (Illus.). 193p. (C). 1980. text ed. 42.50 (*0-485-19553-4*, Pub. by Athlone Pr UK) Humanities.

Mohamed Abdel Magid, Isam, jt. auth. see Rowe, Donald R.

Mohamed El-Khawas. Qaddafi: His Ideology in Theory & Practice. 1987. lib. bdg. 79.95 (*0-8490-3940-1*) Gordon Pr.

Mohamed, Haji & Robinson, Harold. A Taxonomic Revision of the Moss Families Hookeriaceae & Hypopterygiaceae in Malaya. LC 91-4223. (Smithsonian Contributions to Botany Ser.: No. 80). (Illus.). 48p. reprint ed. pap. 25.00 (*0-7837-1890-X*, 2042094) Bks Demand.

Mohamed, Hawa, tr. see Hosken, Fran P.

Mohamed, J. L., jt. auth. see Delves, L. M.

Mohamed, M. K. How to Spend Less Time, Money, & Effort in the Kitchen. 1992. 7.95 (*0-533-09587-5*) Vantage.

Mohamed, N. P. Driftwood-The Bull. LC 76-902191. 1976. lib. bdg. 3.75 (*0-88386-810-5*) S Asia.

Mohamed, O., ed. Formulating a National Policy for Library & Information Services: The Malaysian Experience. 144p. 1988. text ed. 80.00 (*0-7201-1951-0*, Mansell Pub) Cassell.

Mohamed, Ramzan, jt. ed. see Gray, Phil D.

Mohamed, Saad M. & Muller, Bruno J. Continuous & Discrete Modules. (London Mathematical Society Lecture Note Ser.: No. 147). 126p. (C). 1990. pap. 27.95 (*0-521-39975-0*) Cambridge U Pr.

Mohamed, Tarek & Sakr, Refaat. Early Twentieth-Century Islamic Architecture in Cairo. (Illus.). 256p. (C). 1993. 35.00 (*977-424-300-5*, Pub. by Am Univ Cairo Pr UA) Col U Pr.

Mohamed Yusoff Ismail. Buddhism & Ethnicity: Social Organization of a Buddhist Temple in Kelantan. 165p. 1993. 32.50 (*981-3016-26-4*, Pub. by Inst SE Asian Studies SI) Ashgate Pub Co.

Mohamed, Zubair M. Flexible Manufacturing Systems: Planning Issues & Solutions. rev. ed. LC 94-484. (Studies on Industrial Productivity). (Illus.). 192p. 1994. 48.00 (*0-8153-1630-5*) Garland.

— Studies on Industrial Productivity, Set. LC 94-484. 192p. 1994. 783.00 (*0-8153-1529-5*) Garland.

Mohammad-Djafari, Ali, ed. Maximum Entropy & Bayesian Methods in Paris, France, 1992: Proceedings of the Twelfth International Workshop on Maximum Entropy & Bayesian Methods. LC 93-3024. (Fundamental Theories of Physics Ser.). 452p. (C). 1993. lib. bdg. 180.00 (*0-7923-2280-0*) Kluwer Ac.

Mohammad Hashim Kamali. Principles of Islamic Jurisprudence. rev. ed. 417p. 1995. pap. 22.95 (*0-946621-24-1*, Pub. by Islamic Texts UK) Atrium Pubs.

Mohammad, Noor. Caste & Primary Occupations: A Geographical Analysis. 1988. 32.00 (*81-7022-038-6*, Pub. by Concept II) S Asia.

Mohammad Yusuf Khan. Generation Gap: Its Causes & Consequences. (Orig.). 1985. pap. 3.00 (*1-56744-278-1*) Kazi Pubns.

Mohammadi, Ali, jt. auth. see Sreberny-Mohammadi, Annabelle.

Mohammadioun, Mina, jt. ed. see McDonald, Stephen L.

Mohammed, Aisha. West of Sheba. LC 91-66858. 527p. 1991. pap. 11.95 (*1-55523-477-1*) Winston-Derek.

Mohammed-Ali, Abbas, jt. ed. see Marks, Anthony E.

Mohammed, Azizali F., jt. auth. see Andrus, J. Russell.

***Mohammed, B., et al.** Analysis of the K-Epsilon Turbulence Model. (Applied Mathematics Ser.). 1994. pap. text ed. 47.95 (*0-471-94460-2*) Wiley.

Mohammed, Imam W. Al-Islam: Unity & Leadership. LC 91-61449. (Illus.). 176p. (Orig.). 1992. pap. 7.95 (*1-879698-00-5*) Sense Maker.

Mohammed, Imam W. D. Islam's Climate for Business Success. 200p. 1992. pap. 7.95 (*1-879698-01-3*) Sense Maker.

Mohammed Khaliq Ma'aroof. United Nations & Afghanistan Crisis. 1990. 40.00 (*81-7169-044-0*, Commonwealth) S Asia.

Mohammed Second. The Turkes Secretarie, Conteining His Sundrie Letters to Divers Emperours. LC 72-217. (English Experience Ser.: No. 263). 34p. 1970. reprint ed. 20.00 (*90-221-0263-7*) Walter J Johnson.

***Mohan, A. G.** Yoga for Body, Breath, & Mind: A Guide to Personal Reintegration. rev. ed. Miller, Kathaleen, ed. LC 92-32175. (Illus.). 219p. 1995. pap. 16.95 (*0-915801-51-5*) Rudra Pr.

Mohan, Anand, jt. ed. see SarDesai, D. R.

Mohan, Anil & Kripavikshu. Miracles Still Happen in Brindavan. (Illus.). vi, 240p. 1991. 21.00 (*81-85318-55-7*, H K Pubs & Dist) Nataraj Bks.

Mohan, B. M., jt. auth. see Datta, K. B.

Mohan, Bernard. Language & Content. (A-W Second Language Professional Library). (C). 1986. pap. text ed. 26.40 (*0-201-05288-1*) Addison-Wesley.

Mohan, Brij. Eclipse of Freedom: The World of Oppression. LC 92-37529. 200p. 1993. text ed. 49.95 (*0-275-94373-9*, C4373, Praeger Pubs) Greenwood.

— Global Development: Post-Material Values & Social Praxis. LC 91-32923. 152p. 1992. text ed. 45.00 (*0-275-93946-4*, C3946, Praeger Pubs) Greenwood.

— The Logic of Social Welfare: Conjectures & Formulations. LC 87-36073. 292p. 1988. text ed. 45.00 (*0-312-01982-3*) St Martin.

Mohan, Brij, ed. New Horizons of Social Welfare & Policy. (Illus.). 140p. (Orig.). 1985. 18.95 (*0-87073-158-0*); pap. 11.95 (*0-87073-159-9*) Schenkman Bks Inc.

— Toward Comparative Social Welfare. (Illus.). 192p. (Orig.). (C). 1986. 18.95 (*0-87047-025-6*); pap. 11.95 (*0-87047-026-4*) Schenkman Bks Inc.

Mohan, C. Raja, et al. Indian Ocean & U.S.-Soviet Detente. 1991. 22.50 (*81-7050-131-8*, Patriot) S Asia.

Mohan, Chandra, ed. Aspects of Comparative Literature: Current Approaches. xviii, 300p. 1990. text ed. 35.00 (*81-85214-04-2*, Pub. by Reliance Pub Hse II) Apt Bks.

Mohan, Claire J. Kaze's True Home: The Young Life of a Modern Day Saint, Mother Maria Kaupas. LC 91-66722. (Christian Hero Ser.). (Illus.). 64p. (J). (gr. 4-9). 1992. 8.95 (*0-9621500-5-3*) Young Sparrow Pr.

— Mother Teresa's Someday: The Young Life of Mother Teresa of Calcutta. Gallagher, Patricia C., ed. (Contemporary Heroes Ser.). (Illus.). 60p. (Orig.). (J). (gr. k-6). 1990. lib. bdg. 14.95 (*0-9621500-6-1*); pap. 6.95 (*0-9621500-7-X*) Young Sparrow Pr.

— A Red Rose for Francis: A Story of the Young Life of Francis Siedlisha. 2nd ed. (Illus.). (J). (gr. 4-7). 1990. lib. bdg. write for info. (*0-9621500-9-6*) Young Sparrow Pr.

— A Red Rose for Frania: A Story of the Young Life of Francis Siedliska. (Illus.). (J). (gr. 4-7). 1989. lib. bdg. 5.95 (*0-9621500-8-8*) Young Sparrow Pr.

— The Young Life of Pope John Paul II. (Illus.). 64p. (Orig.). (J). (gr. 4-8). 1995. text ed. 14.95 (*0-943135-11-7*); pap. 7.95 (*0-943135-12-5*) Young Sparrow Pr.

Mohan, Dinesh. Pile Foundations. 178p. (C). 1988. text ed. 46.00 (*90-6191-918-5*, Pub. by A A Balkema NE) Ashgate Pub Co.

— Pile Foundations. (C). 1988. 28.00 (*81-204-0324-X*, Pub. by Oxford IBH II) S Asia.

Mohan, I. Environment & Habitat. (C). 1989. 44.00 (*81-7024-240-1*, Pub. by Ashish II) S Asia.

— Environmental Awareness & Urban Development: A Global Study of Environmental Constraints, Pollution, City Planning, Wasteland Development, Social Forestry. (C). 1988. 36.00 (*81-7024-194-4*, Pub. by Ashish II) S Asia.

— Environmental Issues & Urban Development of Walled Cities. (C). 1992. text ed. 22.00 (*81-7099-319-9*, Pub. by Mittal II) S Asia.

— Environmental Pollution & Management. (C). 1989. 50.00 (*81-7024-242-8*, Pub. by Ashish II) S Asia.
— The Fragile Environment. (C). 1990. 48.00 (*81-7024-365-3*, Pub. by Ashish II) S Asia.
Mohan, I., ed. Environmental Issues & Programmes. (New World Environment Ser.). 1989. 48.50 (*81-7024-256-8*, Pub. by Ashish II) S Asia.
***Mohan, John.** A National Health Service? The Restructuring of Health Care in Britain since 1979. LC 94-22962. 1995. write for info. (*0-312-12410-4*) St Martin.
Mohan, Kamlesh. Militant Nationalism in the Punjab 1919-1935. 447p. 1986. 40.00 (*0-8364-1956-1*, Pub. by Manohar II) S Asia.
***Mohan, Kim, ed.** Amazing Stories: The Anthology. 320p. 1995. pap. 13.95 (*0-312-89048-6*) Tor Bks.
Mohan, Madan & Hull, Ronald E., eds. Teaching Effectiveness: Its Meaning, Assessment & Improvement. LC 75-14090. 326p. 1975. 34.95 (*0-87778-084-6*) Educ Tech Pubns.
Mohan, Madan & Laspada, Sebastian. Mind-Stimulating Activities. (Illus.). 88p. (Orig.). 1979. pap. text ed. 3.95 (*0-914634-63-1*, 7906) DOK Pubs.
Mohan, Maden & Risko, Victoria. More Mind Stimulating Activities. (Illus.). 64p. (Orig.). 1980. teacher ed 3.95 (*0-914634-80-1*, 6932) DOK Pubs.
Mohan, Mary L. Organizational Communication & Cultural Vision: Approaches for Analysis. LC 92-30247. (Series in Human Communication Processes). 202p. (C). 1993. 59.50 (*0-7914-1537-6*); pap. 19.95 (*0-7914-1538-4*) State U NY Pr.
Mohan, N. Shantha. Returns from Education to Employed Women in India. (C). 1989. 30.00 (*81-85024-63-4*, Pub. by Uppal Pub Hse II) S Asia.
Mohan, Nancy, jt. auth. see Campbell, Jane E.
Mohan, Ned, et al. Power Electronics: Converters, Applications & Design. 667p. 1989. Net. text ed. write for info. (*0-471-61342-8*); teacher ed 18.00 (*0-471-62213-3*) Wiley.
— Power Electronics: Converters, Applications, & Design. 2nd ed. 1995. text ed. write for info. (*0-471-58408-8*) Wiley.
***Mohan, P. C., ed.** Bibliography of Publications: Technical Department, Africa Region, July 1987 to April 1994. (Technical Paper Ser.: No. 255). 54p. 1994. 6.95 (*0-8213-2972-3*, 12972) World Bank.
— Bibliography of Publications: Technical Department, Africa Region, July 1987 to December 1992. (Technical Paper Ser.: No. 218). 48p. 1993. 6.95 (*0-8213-2513-2*, 12513) World Bank.
Mohan, P. E. Scheduled Castes: History of Elevation, Tamil Nadu, 1900-1955. 1993. 19.00 (*0-8364-2875-7*, Pub. by New Era) S Asia.
Mohan, R. Vasundhara. Identity Crises of Muslims in Sri Lanka. 163p. 1987. 15.00 (*0-8364-2077-2*, Pub. by Mittal II) S Asia.
Mohan, Raj P., ed. Management & Complex Organizations in Comparative Perspective. LC 78-22133. (Contributions in Sociology Ser.: No. 36). (Illus.). 273p. 1979. text ed. 65.00 (*0-313-20752-6*, MMA/, Greenwood Pr) Greenwood.
— The Mythmakers: Intellectuals & the Intelligentsia in Perspective. LC 86-29597. (Contributions in Sociology Ser.: No. 63). 160p. 1987. text ed. 45.00 (*0-313-25836-8*, MMY/, Greenwood Pr) Greenwood.
Mohan, Raj P. & Martindale, Don, eds. Handbook of Contemporary Developments in World Sociology. LC 75-70. (Contributions in Sociology Ser.: No. 17). 493p. 1975. text ed. 125.00 (*0-8371-7961-0*, MWS/, Greenwood Pr) Greenwood.
Mohan, Raj P. & Wilkie, Arthur S., eds. International Handbook of Contemporary Developments in Sociology. LC 93-37504. 856p. 1994. text ed. 145.00 (*0-313-26719-7*, Greenwood Pr) Greenwood.
***Mohan, Rakesh.** Understanding the Developing Metropolis: Lessons from the City Study of Bogota & Cali, Colombia. (World Bank Publication). 344p. 1994. text ed. 32.95 (*0-19-520882-X*) OUP.
— Work, Wages & Welfare in a Developing Metropolis: Consequences of Growth in Bogota, Columbia. (World Bank Publication Papers). 400p. 1987. 29.95 (*0-19-520540-5*) OUP.
Mohan, Rakesh, ed. see Bolle, Ruud M., et al.
Mohan, Robert, tr. see Scupoli, Dom L.
Mohan, S. Krishna, jt. ed. see Schwartz, Howard F.
Mohan, Vasundhara R. Identity Crisis of Sri Lankan Muslims. xv, 183p. (C). 1987. 14.00 (*0-8364-2168-X*, Pub. by Mittal II) S Asia.
Mohanakumar, T. The Role of MHC & Non-MHC Antigens in Allograft Immunity. (Medical Intelligence Unit Ser.). 1993. 89.95 (*1-879702-87-8*) R G Landes.
Mohanan, K. P. The Theory of Lexical Phonology. 1987. lib. bdg. 63.00 (*0-317-56506-0*); pap. text ed. 23.00 (*0-317-56507-9*) Kluwer Ac.
Mohanan, K. P., ed. & pref. Experiencer Subjects in South Asian Languages. LC 90-84176. 365p. (Orig.). 1991. 45.00 (*0-937073-60-1*); pap. 18.95 (*0-937073-61-X*) Ctr Study Language.
Mohanan, Tara. Argument Structure in Hindi. LC 94-12973. (Dissertations in Linguistics Ser.). 1994. 45.00 (*1-881526-44-5*); pap. 22.95 (*1-881526-43-7*) Ctr Study Language.
Mohanan, V. K. Crime, Community & Police. 1987. 27.50 (*81-212-0107-1*, Pub. by Gian Publng Hse II) S Asia.
— Crime, Community & Police. (C). 1990. 90.00 (*0-89771-159-9*) St Mut.
Mohandas, Narla, jt. ed. see Shohet, Stephen B.
Mohanna, Tim, ed. see Medley, Wes.
Mohanram, Radhika, jt. ed. see Rajan, Gita.
***Mohanti, K. K.** Social Mobility & Caste Dynamics. (C). 1993. 18.00x (*81-7033-211-7*, Pub. by Rawat II) S Asia.
Mohanty, Amarendra. Indian Prison System. 1990. 30.00 (*81-7024-308-4*, Pub. by Ashish II) S Asia.
Mohanty, B. Pata-Paintings of Orissa. 52p. 1984. 49.95 (*0-318-36346-1*) Asia Bk Corp.
Mohanty, Bedabati. Economics of Small Scale Industry, India. 218p. 1986. 28.00 (*81-7024-049-2*, Pub. by Ashish II) S Asia.
Mohanty, Bijoyini. Municipal System in India: Citizens' Involvement. (Illus.). vi, 245p. 1993. 20.00 (*81-7024-530-3*, Pub. by Ashish Pub Hse II) Nataraj Bks.
Mohanty, Chandra T., et al, eds. Third World Women & the Politics of Feminism. LC 90-43510. (Illus.). 352p. 1991. 39.95 (*0-253-33873-5*); pap. 14.95 (*0-253-20632-4*, MB-632) Ind U Pr.
Mohanty, Gopinath. Paraja. Das, Bikram K., tr. (India Paperbacks Ser.). 384p. 1993. pap. 9.95 (*0-19-562391-6*) OUP.
Mohanty, J. Educational Broadcasting: Radio & Television in Education. 1984. text ed. 22.50 (*0-86590-261-5*, Pub. by Sterling Pubs II) Apt Bks.
Mohanty, J. B., tr. see Satpathi, Nandini.
Mohanty, J. N. J. N. Mohanty: Essays on Indian Philosophy, Traditional & Modern. Bilimoria, Purushottama, ed. 360p. 1994. 35.00 (*0-19-563142-0*) OUP.
Mohanty, J. N. & McKenna, William R., eds. Husserl's Phenomenology: A Textbook. LC 89-36108. (Current Continental Research Ser.: No. 551). 504p. (Orig.). (C). 1989. lib. bdg. 65.00 (*0-8191-7530-7*, Ctr Adv Res); pap. text ed. 38.50 (*0-8191-7531-5*, Ctr Adv Res) U Pr of Amer.
Mohanty, J. N. & Shahan, Robert W. Essays on Kant's Critique of Pure Reason. LC 81-40295. 208p. 1982. 28.95 (*0-8061-1782-6*) U of Okla Pr.
Mohanty, J. N., ed. see Misra, Ganeswar.
Mohanty, J. N., jt. auth. see Shahan, Robert W.
Mohanty, Jagganath. Indian Education in the Emerging Society. 205p. 1982. 24.95 (*0-940500-52-3*, Pub. by Sterling II) Asia Bk Corp.
Mohanty, Jitendra N. The Concept of Intentionality. LC 70-176186. (Illus.). 224p. 1971. 10.60 (*0-87527-115-4*) Green.
— Edmund Husserl's Theory of Meaning. 3rd enl. ed. (Phaenomenologica Ser.: No. 14). 1976. lib. bdg. 47.00 (*90-247-0247-X*) Kluwer Ac.
— Husserl & Frege. LC 81-48554. (Studies in Phenomenology & Existential Philosophy). 160p. 1982. 24.95 (*0-253-32878-0*) Ind U Pr.
— Phenomenology & Ontology. (Phaenomenologica Ser.: No. 37). 1970. lib. bdg. 47.00 (*90-247-5053-9*) Kluwer Ac.
Mohanty, Jitendra N., ed. Phenomenology & the Human Sciences. 242p. 1984. pap. text ed. 85.50 (*90-247-3126-7*) Kluwer Ac.
— Readings on Edmund Husserl's Logical Investigations. 1977. pap. text ed. 70.00 (*90-247-1928-3*) Kluwer Ac.
Mohanty, Jitendranath. Gangesa's Theory of Truth Containing the Text of Gangesa's Pramanya Vada. (C). 1989. 26.00 (*81-208-0618-2*, Pub. by Motilal Banarsidass II) S Asia.
Mohanty, Nirode C. Random Signals Estimation & Identification: Analysis & Applications. 640p. 1986. text ed. 89.95 (*0-442-26396-1*) Van Nos Reinhold.
— Signal Processing Signals, Filtering & Detection. 1987. text ed. 99.95 (*0-442-26476-3*) Van Nos Reinhold.
— Space Communication & Nuclear Scintillation. 1991. text ed. 84.95 (*0-442-23696-4*) Van Nos Reinhold.
Mohanty, Nivedita. Oriya Nationalism: Quest for a United Orissa. 1983. 21.00 (*0-8364-0954-X*, Pub. by Manohar II) S Asia.
Mohanty, O. N. & Sivaramakrishnan, C. S., eds. Rapid Solidification Processing & Technology. 436p. 1990. text ed. 128.00 (*0-87849-599-1*, Pub. by Trans Tech GW) LPS Dist Ctr.
Mohanty, O. N., ed. see Indo-U. S. Workshop LCFA Staff.
Mohanty, Prafulla K. Stories from Sarala's Mahabharat. 205p. 1990. text ed. 27.50 (*0-7069-4589-1*, Pub. by Vikas II) S Asia.
Mohanty, Pragati. Hotel Industry & Tourism in India. (Illus.). xiv, 262p. 1992. 25.00 (*81-7024-507-9*, Pub. by Ashish Pub Hse II) Nataraj Bks.
Mohanty, Samarendra. Crimes & Criminals: A Socio-Economic Survey. 1990. 24.00 (*81-7024-326-2*, Pub. by Ashish II) S Asia.
Mohanty, Samarendra, jt. auth. see Mishra, Rashmi.
Mohanty, Saroj K. Concept of Action: An Analytical Study. (C). 1992. 18.00 (*81-85182-67-1*, Pub. by Indus Pub II) S Asia.
Mohanty, Sashi B. & Dutta, Sukanta K. Veterinary Virology. LC 80-26157. 381p. reprint ed. pap. 108.60 (*0-7837-2849-2*, 2057623) Bks Demand.
Mohanty, Susama. Political Development & Ethnic Identity in Africa: A Study of Angola since 1960. vii, 246p. (C). 1992. text ed. 27.95 (*0-685-55354-X*, Pub. by Radiant Pubs II) S Asia.
Mohapatra, A. R. Philosophy of Religion. 1985. 24.95 (*0-318-37030-1*) Asia Bk Corp.
— Philosophy of Religion: An Approach to World Religions. 2nd ed. 1990. reprint ed. text ed. 27.50 (*81-207-1221-8*, Pub. by Sterling Pubs II) Apt Bks.
***Mohapatra, Amulya.** Hinduism: Analytical Study. (C). 1993. 15.00x (*81-7099-388-1*, Pub. by Mittal II) S Asia.
Mohapatra, R. N. Unification & Supersymmetry. (Contemporary Physics Ser.). (Illus.). xiv, 328p. 1986. 44.00 (*0-387-96285-9*) Spr-Verlag.
— Unification & Supersymmetry: The Frontiers of Quark-Lepton Physics. 2nd ed. (Graduate Texts in Contemporary Physics Ser.). (Illus.). 424p. 1991. 49.95 (*0-387-97646-9*) Spr-Verlag.
Mohapatra, R. N. & Lai, C. H., eds. Gauge Theories of Fundamental Interactions. 702p. 1981. text ed. 70.00 (*9971-83-013-2*); pap. text ed. 41.00 (*9971-83-014-0*) World Scientific Pub.
Mohapatra, R. N. & Pal, Palash B. Massive Neutrinos in Physics & Astrophysics. 336p. 1991. text ed. 78.00 (*981-02-0434-5*); pap. text ed. 41.00 (*981-02-0435-3*) World Scientific Pub.
Mohapatra, R. P. Fashion Styles of Ancient India: A Study of Kalinga from Earliest Times to Sixteenth Century AD. (C). 1992. 88.00 (*81-7018-723-0*, Pub. by BR Pub II) S Asia.
Mohapatra, S., jt. auth. see Das, Hari H.
***Mohapatra, Shyam S. & Knox, R. Bruce, eds.** Pollen Biotechnology: Gene Expression & Allergen Characterization. LC 94-42327. 1995. write for info. (*0-412-03521-9*) Chapman & Hall.
Moharir, P. S. Pattern-Recognition Transforms. LC 92-20310. (Electronic Circuits & Systems Ser.: No. 4). 272p. 1992. text ed. 144.00 (*0-471-93633-2*) Wiley.
Mohassess, Ardeshir. Life in Iran: The Library of Congress Drawings. LC 93-40224. 1993. 20.00 (*0-934211-39-6*) Mage Pubs Inc.
***Mohay, A.** Modern Greek-Hungarian Concise Dictionary. 773p. (C). 1988. 45.00x (*963-05-4387-7*, Pub. by Akad Kiado HU) St Mut.
Mohay, George, jt. auth. see Gough, John.
Mohbat, Joseph, ed. see Wiener, Daniel P., et al.
Mohd, Anis M. Zapin, Folk Dance of the Malay World. LC 92-20381. (South-East Asian Social Science Monographs). (Illus.). 224p. 1993. 39.95 (*0-19-588598-8*) OUP.
Mohd, N. Wan. The Concept of Knowledge in Islam: And Its Implications for Education in a Developing Country. 224p. 1989. text ed. 80.00 (*0-7201-2002-0*, Mansell Pub) Cassell.
***Mohdx, Nilavu, et al.** New Place, Old Ways: Essays on Indian Society & Culture in Modern Singapore. Walker, Anthony E., ed. (C). 1994. 36.00 (*81-7075-027-X*, Pub. by Hindustan IA) S Asia.
Mohen, Jean-Pierre. The World of Megaliths. LC 89-16972. (Illus.). 318p. reprint ed. pap. 90.70 (*0-7837-6689-0*, 2046305) Bks Demand.
Mohiaddin, R. H. & Longmore, D. B. Atlas of Whole Body MRI. (Series in Radiology). (C). 1992. lib. bdg. 129.00 (*0-7923-8974-3*) Kluwer Ac.
Mohilio, Albert. Bendable Siege Poems. 14p. 1991. 3.00 (*0-87376-068-9*) Red Dust.
Mohilla, R. & Ferencz, B. Chemical Process Dynamics. (Fundamental Studies in Engineering: Vol. 4). 300p. 1982. 95.00 (*0-444-99730-X*) Elsevier.
Mohindra, Raj, jt. auth. see Slade, Bernard N.
Mohindra, S. The Japanese Economic Miracle. (C). 1987. 15.00 (*0-317-89478-1*, Pub. by Lancer II) S Asia.
Mohiuddin, Abid. Echoes of My Mind. LC 93-93777. 80p. (Orig.). 1994. pap. 9.00 (*1-56002-312-0*, Univ Edtns) Aegina Pr.
Mohl, et al, eds. A Textbook of Occlusion. (Illus.). 408p. 1988. text ed. 52.00 (*0-86715-167-6*, 1676) Quint Pub Co.
Mohl, F. George. Introduction a la Chronologie du Latin Vulgaire. xii, 339p. 1974. reprint ed. write for info. (*3-487-05222-9*, Pub. by Georg Olms GW) Lubrecht & Cramer.
Mohl, Raymond A. The New City: Urban America in the Industrial Age, 1860-1920. Franklin, John H. & Eisenstadt, Abraham, eds. LC 84-214170. (American History Ser.). 256p. (C). 1985. pap. text ed. write for info. (*0-88295-830-5*) Harlan Davidson.
Mohl, Raymond A., ed. The Making of Urban America. (C). 1988. 40.00 (*0-8420-2270-8*); pap. text ed. 15.95 (*0-8420-2271-6*) Scholarly Res Inc.
— Searching for the Sunbelt: Historical Perspectives on a Region. LC 89-77169. 288p. 1990. text ed. 36.00x (*0-87049-640-9*) U of Tenn Pr.
— Searching for the Sunbelt: Historical Perspectives on a Region. LC 89-77169. 272p. 1993. reprint ed. pap. 14.95 (*0-8203-1579-6*) U of Ga Pr.
Mohl, Raymond A. & Betten, Neil. Steel City: Urban & Ethnic Patterns in Gary, Indiana, 1906-1950. LC 85-963. (Illus.). 227p. 1986. 34.95 (*0-8419-1010-3*); pap. 23.50 (*0-8419-1077-4*) Holmes & Meier.
Mohl, Raymond A., jt. ed. see Hirsch, Arnold R.
Mohl, Werner, ed. Coronary Sinus Intervention in Cardiac Surgery. LC 93-23284. (Medical Intelligence Unit Ser.). 1993. 89.95 (*1-879702-73-8*) R G Landes.
Mohle, Helmut, jt. auth. see Meinck, Fritz.
Mohle, K., jt. auth. see Meinck, Fritz.
Mohle, R. Henry, jt. auth. see Murthy, A. S.
Mohlebach, Richard F., jt. auth. see Alexander, Alan A.
Mohlenbrock. You Can Grow Tropical Fruit Trees. (Illus.). 1979. pap. 3.95 (*0-8200-0409-X*) Great Outdoors.
Mohlenbrock, Robert H. Flowering Plants: Basswoods to Spurges. LC 81-8585. (Illustrated Flora of Illinois Ser.). (Illus.). 256p. 1982. 24.95 (*0-8093-1025-2*) S Ill U Pr.
— Flowering Plants: Flowering Rush to Rushes. LC 69-16117. (Illustrated Flora of Illinois Ser.). (Illus.). 286p. 1970. 24.95 (*0-8093-0407-4*) S Ill U Pr.
— Flowering Plants: Hollies to Loasas. LC 77-28934. (Illustrated Flora of Illinois Ser.). (Illus.). 320p. 1978. 24.95 (*0-8093-0845-2*) S Ill U Pr.
— Flowering Plants: Lilies to Orchids. LC 69-16118. (Illustrated Flora of Illinois Ser.). (Illus.). 304p. 1970. 30.00 (*0-8093-0408-2*) S Ill U Pr.
— Flowering Plants: Magnolias to Pitcher Plants. LC 80-18529. (Illustrated Flora of Illinois Ser.). (Illus.). 276p. 1981. 29.95 (*0-8093-0920-3*) S Ill U Pr.
— Flowering Plants: Willows to Mustards. LC 79-10981. (Illustrated Flora of Illinois Ser.). (Illus.). 302p. 1980. 24.95 (*0-8093-0922-X*) S Ill U Pr.
— Grasses: Panicum to Danthonia. LC 73-6807. (Illustrated Flora of Illinois Ser.). (Illus.). 398p. 1973. 29.95 (*0-8093-0521-6*) S Ill U Pr.
— Guide to the Vascular Flora of Illinois. rev. ed. LC 85-26259. 512p. (Orig.). 1986. 45.00 (*0-8093-1272-7*) S Ill U Pr.
— The Illustrated Flora of Illinois: Flowering Plants: Nightshades to Mistletoe. LC 89-8353. (Illus.). 256p. (C). 1990. text ed. 40.00 (*0-8093-1567-X*) S Ill U Pr.
— Macmillan Field Guide to Trees & Shrubs. 1987. pap. 12.95 (*0-02-063430-7*, Collier S&S) S&S Trade.
— Macmillan Field Guide: Wildflower. 1987. 9.95 (*0-685-46248-X*, Collier S&S) S&S Trade.
— Sedges: Cyperus to Scleria. LC 76-15267. (Illustrated Flora of Illinois Ser.). (Illus.). 208p. 1976. 24.95 (*0-8093-0604-2*) S Ill U Pr.
Mohlenbrock, Robert H. & Ladd, Douglas M. Distribution of Illinois Vascular Plants. LC 77-15987. (Illus.). 289p. (Orig.). 1978. pap. 12.95 (*0-8093-0848-7*) S Ill U Pr.
Mohlenbrock, Robert H. & Thomson, Paul M., Jr. The Illustrated Flora of Illinois: Flowering Plants: Smartweeds to Hazelnuts. LC 86-6698. (Illus.). 256p. 1986. text ed. 40.00 (*0-8093-1104-6*) S Ill U Pr.
Mohlenbrock, Robert H. & Voigt, John W. Flora of Southern Illinois. LC 73-12984. (Arcturus Books Paperbacks). 399p. 1974. 8.95 (*0-8093-0026-5*); pap. 4.95 (*0-8093-0662-X*) S Ill U Pr.
Mohlenbrock, Robert H., jt. auth. see Voigt, John W.
Mohler, Dorothy A., jt. ed. see Dunn, Catherine.
Mohler, J. Electroplating & Related Processes. 1969. 53.50 (*0-8206-0037-7*) Chem Pub.
Mohler, James A. Dimensions of Faith: Yesterday & Today. LC 69-13120. 228p. reprint ed. pap. 65.30 (*0-8357-8569-6*, 2034935) Bks Demand.
— Heresy of Monasticism. LC 76-148683. 1971. 5.95 (*0-8189-0183-7*) Alba.
— Love, Marriage & the Family: Yesterday & Today. LC 82-8699. 224p. (Orig.). 1982. pap. 7.95 (*0-8189-0434-8*) Alba.
— School of Jesus. LC 72-11835. 280p. 1973. 5.95 (*0-8189-0262-0*) Alba.
— A Speechless Child Is the Word of God: An Interpretation of St. Augustine. 176p. (Orig.). 1992. pap. 9.95 (*1-56548-009-0*) New City.
***Mohler, Johann A.** Unity in the Church: The Principles of Catholicism As Portrayed in the Spirit of the Church Fathers of the First Three Centuries. Erb, Peter, tr. LC 95-7264. (YA). 1995. 59.95x (*0-8132-0621-9*) Cath U Pr.
Mohler, M. Teresa. COTA Examination Review Manual: A Practical Guide to Receiving Professional Certification. LC 93-7930. 1993. pap. 20.00 (*1-55642-228-8*) SLACK Inc.
Mohler, Peter, jt. ed. see Borg, Ingwer.
Mohler, Ronald R. Nonlinear Systems, Vol. 1: Dynamics & Control. 288p. 1990. text ed. 73.00 (*0-13-623489-5*) P-H.
— Nonlinear Systems, Vol. 2: Applications to Bilinear Control. 224p. 1990. text ed. 64.00 (*0-13-623521-2*) P-H.
Mohler, Rudy. Practical Welding Technology. LC 83-23298. 216p. (C). 1983. 29.95 (*0-8311-1143-7*) Indus Pr.
Mohlhenrich, Janice, ed. Preservation of Electronic Formats & Electronic Formats for Preservation. LC 92-38498. 128p. 1993. pap. text ed. 25.00 (*0-917846-17-6*, 95522) Highsmith Pr.
Mohlie, Steven, jt. ed. see Bloomberg, Mark.
Mohline, L. Jane. A Woman of Excellence: Developing Your Special Female Self. 1991. 13.99 (*0-8054-6034-9*, 4260-34) Broadman.
***Mohn, Caroline & Bays, Kathryn, eds.** Dual Diagnosis Bibliography: 1995 Edition. 101p. (C). 1995. pap. 18.00 (*1-884442-13-7*) Vida Pubng.
Mohn, G., jt. ed. see Van Hof, M. W.
Mohn, J. F., ed. see International Convocation on Immunology Staff.
Mohn, Michael. Preparing Tradtitional Music Manuscript: Including a Handbook of Instrumentation, Theory, & Musical Terms. 2nd rev. ed. (Illus.). 176p. (C). 1990. pap. 22.50 (*0-9624986-0-2*) M Mohn Pub.
— Use DOS! (Illus.). 48p. (Orig.). (C). 1991. pap. 3.95 (*0-9624986-1-0*) M Mohn Pub.
Mohn, Paul O., jt. auth. see Garoyan, Leon.
Mohn, Reinhard. Success Through Partnership. 1988. 16.95 (*0-385-24789-3*) Doubleday.
***Mohn, Richard D.** A More Perfect Union: Why Straight America Must Stand up for Gay Rights. 144p. 1995. pap. 9.00 (*0-8070-7933-2*) Beacon Pr.
Mohn, Ronald D. Shortcuts in Gun Dog Training. (Illus.). 112p. (Orig.). 1991. pap. 9.95 (*0-9629840-9-4*) RDM Enter.
Mohney, David & Easterling, Keller. Seaside: Making a Town in America. (Illus.). 272p. (Orig.). 1991. 39.95 (*1-878271-44-X*); pap. 29.95 (*0-910413-26-6*) Princeton Arch.
Mohney, Nell W. Don't Put a Period Where God Put a Comma: Self-Esteem for Christians. LC 93-359. 104p. (Orig.). 1993. pap. 7.50 (*0-687-11061-0*) Dimen for Liv.
Mohney, Ralph W., jt. auth. see Harding, Joe A.
Mohnot, S. M., jt. auth. see Roonwal, Mithan L.
Mohns, Judith, jt. auth. see Deschamps, Francois.
Mohnsen, Bonnie S. Using Technology in Physical Education. LC 94-4550. (Illus.). 168p. 1995. pap. text ed. 14.00x (*0-87322-661-5*, BMOH0661) Human Kinetics.
Moholt, Ray, jt. auth. see Landis, Michael.
Moholy-Nagy & Kassak. Moholy-Nagy - Kassak: Buch Neuer Kunstler (Book of New Artists) (Illus.). 92p. 1991. pap. 35.00 (*3-906700-37-2*, Pub. by Lars Muller SZ) Dist Art Pubs.

Moholy-Nagy, L. & Benedetta, Mary. The Street Markets of London. LC 72-84542. (Illus.). 1972. reprint ed. 19.95 (*0-405-08792-6*, Pub. by Blom Pubns UK) Ayer.

***Moholy-Nagy, Laszlo.** In Focus: Laszlo Moholy-Nagy: Photographs from the J. Paul Getty Museum. LC 94-42443. (In Focus Ser.). (Illus.). 128p. (Orig.). 1995. pap. 15.95 (*0-89236-324-X*, J P Getty Museum) J P Getty Trust.

— Painting, Photography, & Film. (Paperback Ser.). 150p. 1969. pap. 11.95 (*0-262-63046-X*, 220) MIT Pr.

Moholy-Nagy, Laszlo, et al. Moholy-Nagy: An Anthology. (Quality Paperbacks Ser.). (Illus.). 238p. 1991. reprint ed. pap. 15.95 (*0-306-80455-7*) Da Capo.

Mohor, Arthur B., Jr. Basic Budget Guide for Small Cities & Counties. rev. ed. 49p. 1985. pap. 6.00 (*0-89854-112-3*) U of GA Inst Govt.

***Mohos, M.** Budapest & Seine Geschichte. (Illus.). 32p. (ENG, GER & HUN.). 1993. pap. 18.00 (*963-05-6624-9*, Pub. by A K HU) Intl Spec Bk.

Mohowski, Robert. New York, Ontario & Western in the Diesel Age. 96p. (Orig.). 1994. pap. 29.95 (*0-944119-15-8*) Andover Junction.

Mohr. Manual of Neurology ISE. 2nd ed. 1989. 15.95 (*0-316-57749-7*) Little.

Mohr & Pomerening. Affinity Chromatography: Practical & Theoretical Aspects. (Chromatographic Science Ser.: Vol. 33). 320p. 1985. 150.00 (*0-8247-7468-X*) Dekker.

Mohr, Anton. The Oil War. LC 75-6482. (History & Politics of Oil Ser.). vii, 267p. 1976. reprint ed. 21.50 (*0-88355-299-X*) Hyperion Conn.

Mohr, Bernard, jt. ed. see Porter, Lawrence.

Mohr, Brigitte, jt. ed. see Ebel, Arnold.

Mohr, C. Plant Life of Alabama. (Illus.). 1969. reprint ed. 48.00 (*3-7682-0622-X*) Lubrecht & Cramer.

Mohr, Carole, jt. auth. see Goodman, Donald J.

Mohr, Carole, jt. auth. see Nist, Sherrie L.

Mohr, Carole, jt. auth. see Smith, Kent.

Mohr, Caroline & Bays, Kathryn. Dual Diagnosis Bibliography: 1993 Edition. 88p. 1993. pap. 15.00 (*1-884442-09-9*) Vida Pubng.

Mohr, Carolyn, et al. Books That Heal: A Whole Language Approach. 283p. 1991. pap. 23.50 (*0-87287-829-5*) Teacher Ideas Pr.

Mohr-Catalano, Ellen, et al. The Chronic Pain Control Workbook. (Illus.). 216p. 1987. 24.95 (*0-934986-46-0*); pap. 13.95 (*0-934986-45-2*) New Harbinger.

Mohr, Charles M., et al. Membrane Applications & Research in Food Processing. LC 89-16036. (Illus.). 305p. 1990. 45.00 (*0-8155-1216-3*) Noyes.

Mohr, Clarence L. On the Threshold of Freedom: Masters & Slaves in Civil War Georgia. LC 85-5796. (Illus.). 424p. 1986. 35.00 (*0-8203-0793-9*) U of Ga Pr.

— On the Threshold of Freedom: Masters & Slaves in Civil War Georgia. LC 85-5796. (Illus.). 424p. 1987. pap. 16. 50 (*0-8203-0941-9*) U of Ga Pr.

Mohr, D. V., et al, eds. Advances in Controlled Clinical Inhalation Studies. (ILSI Monographs). (Illus.). 384p. 1993. 175.00 (*0-387-54958-7*) Spr-Verlag.

Mohr, David & Schwartz, Faye. From Birth to Death. 1983. 2.90 (*0-89536-599-5*, 0604) CSS OH.

Mohr, David, jt. auth. see Schwartz, Faye.

Mohr, E. & Brouwers, P., eds. Handbook of Clinical Trials: The Neurobehavioral Approach. 1991. 70.00 (*90-265-1028-4*, Pub. by Swets Pub Serv NE) Taylor & Francis.

Mohr, Ernst. Economic Theory & Sovereign International Debt. (Illus.). 231p. 1991. pap. text ed. 50.00 (*0-12-504165-9*) Acad Pr.

Mohr, Eugene V. The Nuyorican Experience: Literature of the Puerto Rican Minority. LC 82-9282. (Contributions in American Studies: No. 62). xv, 137p. 1982. text ed. 45.00 (*0-313-23334-9*, MNE/, Greenwood Pr) Greenwood.

Mohr, Franz & Schaeffer, Edith. My Life with the Great Pianists. 1992. 16.99 (*0-8010-6296-9*) Baker Bk.

Mohr, Georg. Stammverbesserung Biotechnologisch Relevanter Hyphenpilze durch Gentechnik: Integrative Transformation von Aspergillus Niger. (Dissertationes Botanicae Ser.: Vol. 131). (Illus.). 116p. (GER.). 1989. spiral bd. 40.00 (*3-443-64043-5*, Pub. by Cramer GW) Lubrecht & Cramer.

Mohr, Gilbert J., et al. SPI Handbook of Technology & Engineering of Reinforced Plastics-Composites. 2nd ed. LC 80-26338. 416p. 1981. reprint ed. 35.50 (*0-89874-295-1*) Krieger.

Mohr, H. Photomorphogenesis. Shropshire, Walter, Jr., ed. (Encyclopedia of Plant Physiology Ser.: Vol. 16, Pts. A & B). (Illus.). 900p. 1983. 322.00 (*0-387-12143-9*) Spr-Verlag.

***Mohr, Hans & Schopfer, Peter.** Plant Physiology. Lawlor, Gudron & Lawlor, David W., trs. LC 94-21765. Orig. Title: Lehrbuch der Pflanzenphysiologie. 1994. write for info. (*0-387-58016-6*) Spr-Verlag.

***Mohr, Harriet.** What the Soul Teaches. 170p. 1994. pap. 6.95 (*0-9629467-1-0*) New Focus Pr.

Mohr, Harriet, jt. auth. see Mohr, William L.

Mohr, Howard. How to Talk Minnesotan. 224p. 1987. pap. 10.95 (*0-14-009284-6*, Penguin Bks) Viking Penguin.

Mohr, J. A., jt. ed. see Lighthart, Bruce.

Mohr, J. P. Manual of Clinical Problems in Neurology: With Annotated Key References. (Spiral Manual Ser.). 1984. spiral bd. 21.00 (*0-316-57747-2*) Little.

— Manual of Neurology. 2nd ed. 1989. 32.95 (*0-316-57748-0*) Little.

***Mohr, J. P. & Gautier, J. C., eds.** Guide to Clinical Neurology. LC 95-8195. (Illus.). 1995. write for info. (*0-443-08927-2*) Churchill.

Mohr, James C. Abortion in America: The Origins & Evolution of National Policy, 1800-1900. (Illus.). 1979. reprint ed. pap. 10.95 (*0-19-502616-0*) OUP.

— Doctors & the Law: Medical Jurisprudence in Nineteenth-Century America. LC 92-12876. (Illus.). 336p. 1993. 30.00 (*0-19-505384-2*) OUP.

Mohr, James C., ed. Radical Republicans in the North: State Politics During Reconstruction. LC 75-36939. 219p. reprint ed. pap. 62.50 (*0-7837-3389-5*, 2043347) Bks Demand.

***Mohr, James C. & Winslow, Richard E., 3rd, eds.** The Cormany Diaries: A Northern Family in the Civil War. LC 81-16345. 623p. 1982. pap. 177.60 (*0-7837-8550-X*, 2049365) Bks Demand.

Mohr, Janet L., ed. see Travel Companions International, Inc. Staff.

Mohr, Joseph. Precious Moments Silent Night. (Sounds of the Season Ser.). (Illus.). 10p. (J). 1994. write for info. (*0-307-17452-2*) Western Pub.

— Silent Night. LC 84-8113. (J). 1988. pap. 4.95 (*0-685-57131-9*, DCB) Dutton Child Bks.

Mohr, Lawrence B. Explaining Organizational Behavior. LC 81-20747. (Jossey-Bass Social & Behavioral Science Ser.). 280p. reprint ed. pap. 79.80 (*0-8357-4999-1*, 2037932) Bks Demand.

— Impact Analysis for Program Evaluation. 1992. pap. 21.95 (*0-8039-4981-2*) Sage.

— Understanding Significance Testing. (Quantitative Applications in the Social Sciences Ser.: Vol. 73). (Illus.). 96p. (C). 1990. pap. text ed. 9.95 (*0-8039-3568-4*) Sage.

Mohr, M., jt. auth. see Moores, T.

Mohr, Marian M. Revision: The Rhythm of Meaning. 248p. (Orig.). 1984. pap. text ed. 17.50 (*0-86709-087-1*) Boynton Cook Pubs.

Mohr, Marie H. St. Philomena: Powerful with God. LC 88-50160. 136p. 1988. reprint ed. pap. 7.00 (*0-89555-332-5*) TAN Bks Pubs.

Mohr, Marilyn. Satchel. Barkan, Stanley H., ed. (Review Jewish Writers Chapbook Ser.: No. 8). 48p. 1992. 15.00 (*0-89304-312-5*); 15.00 (*0-89304-314-1*); pap. 5.00 (*0-89304-313-3*); pap. 5.00 (*0-89304-315-X*) Cross-Cultrl NY.

Mohr, Merilyn. Art of Soapmaking. 128p. 1989. pap. 9.95 (*0-920656-03-X*, Pub. by Camden Hse CN) Firefly Bks Ltd.

— Chronicle of Our House: Important Details about. 128p. 1988. 19.95 (*0-920656-75-7*, Pub. by Camden Hse CN) Firefly Bks Ltd.

— Home Playgrounds. 1988. 22.50 (*0-8446-6316-6*) Peter Smith.

— Home Playgrounds, Building Backyard Play Structure. (Illus.). 160p. 1987. pap. 15.95 (*0-920656-62-5*, Pub. by Camden Hse CN) Firefly Bks Ltd.

— Our House: A History. 1994. 12.95 (*0-921820-92-5*, Pub. by Camden Hse CN) Firefly Bks Ltd.

— Sunwings Harrowsmith Guide to Solar Addition Architecture. (Illus.). 148p. 1985. pap. 14.95 (*0-920656-37-4*, Pub. by Camden Hse CN) Firefly Bks Ltd.

Mohr, Merilyn, ed. see Buckingham, Sandra.

Mohr, Merilyn S. The Games Treasury: More Than Three Hundred Indoor & Outdoor Favorites with Strategies, Rules & Traditions. LC 93-3635. (Illus.). 352p. (Orig.). (J). 1993. 29.95 (*1-881527-24-7*); pap. 19.95 (*1-881527-23-9*) Chapters Pub.

Mohr, Merilyn S., jt. auth. see Forsyth, Turid.

Mohr, Nicholas. Jaime & the Conch Shell. LC 93-30403. (J). 1995. 12.95 (*0-590-47110-4*) Scholastic Inc.

Mohr, Nicholasa. All for the Better: A Story of el Barrio. LC 92-23639. (Stories of America Ser.). (Illus.). 56p. (J). (gr. 2-5). 1992. lib. bdg. 21.36 (*0-8114-7220-5*) Raintree Steck-V.

— El Bronx Remembered. LC 75-6306. (Trophy Keypoint Bk.). 288p. (YA). (gr. 7 up). 1993. pap. 4.95 (*0-06-447100-4*, Trophy) HarpC Child Bks.

— El Bronx Remembered. (J). 1994. 17.75 (*0-8446-6779-X*) Peter Smith.

— Felita. 1990. pap. 3.50 (*0-553-15792-2*) Bantam.

— Going Home. (J). (gr. 4-7). 1989. mass mkt. 3.99 (*0-553-15699-3*, Skylark) Bantam.

— Going Home. LC 85-20621. 176p. (YA). (gr. 5-8). 1986. lib. bdg. 13.89 (*0-8037-0338-4*) Dial Bks Young.

— In Nueva York. LC 87-18745. 196p. 1988. reprint ed. pap. 9.50 (*0-934770-78-6*) Arte Publico.

— Nilda. 2nd ed. LC 87-70274. 292p. 1986. pap. 10.50 (*0-934770-61-1*) Arte Publico.

— Rituals of Survival: A Woman's Portfolio. LC 84-72300. 120p. (Orig.). (C). 1985. pap. 8.50 (*0-934770-39-5*) Arte Publico.

— The Song of el Coqui & Other Tales of Puerto Rico. LC 94-43075. (Illus.). (J). 1995. 15.99 (*0-670-85837-4*, Viking) Viking Penguin.

Mohr, Peter, et al. Immunosorption Techniques: Fundamentals & Applications. 173p. 1993. 75.00 (*0-685-67327-8*, Pub. by Akademie GW) VCH Pubs.

Mohr, R., et al. Structural Pattern Analysis. (Series in Computer Science: Vol. 19). 268p. (C). 1990. pap. 18.00 (*981-02-0147-8*) World Scientific Pub.

Mohr, Renate M., jt. ed. see Roberts, Julian V.

Mohr, Richard D. Between Men-Between Women: Lesbian & Gay Cultures. 1988. 39.00 (*0-685-41314-4*) Col U Pr.

— Gay Ideas: Outing & Other Controversies. LC 92-4686. (Illus.). 324p. 1992. 25.00 (*0-8070-7920-0*) Beacon Pr.

— Gay Ideas: Outing & Other Controversies. (Illus.). 336p. 1994. pap. 15.00 (*0-8070-7921-9*) Beacon Pr.

— Gays - Justice: A Study of Ethics, Society, & Law. 357p. 1989. pap. text ed. 14.00 (*0-231-06735-6*) Col U Pr.

— A More Perfect Union: Why Straight America Must Stand up for Gay Rights. LC 93-37529. 128p. 1994. 15. 00 (*0-8070-7932-4*) Beacon Pr.

Mohr, Sabine. Einfluss von Kern & Zytoplasma auf die Organisation & Expression Mitochondrialer Gene bei Triticum, Triticale & Secale. (Dissertationes Botanicae Ser.: Vol. 180). (Illus.). 124p. (GER.). 1991. pap. 52.00 (*3-443-64092-3*, Pub. by Gebrueder Borntraeger GW) Lubrecht & Cramer.

Mohr-Stephens, Judy. Fence Me In...with Understanding, Vol. 28, Bk. 7. Riegert, Evelyn, ed. (Please Understand Us Ser.). (Illus.). 1990. write for info. (*0-935323-28-7*) Barrington Hse.

— Fence Me In...with Understanding, Vol. 29. Riegert, Evelyn, ed. (Please Understand Us Ser.). (Illus.). 1990. teacher ed write for info. (*0-935323-29-5*) Barrington Hse.

— Fence Me In...with Understanding, Vol. 30, Bk. 7. Riegert, Evelyn, ed. (Please Understand Us Ser.). (Illus.). 1990. write for info. (*0-935323-30-9*) Barrington Hse.

— Fence Me In...with Understanding, Vol. 31, Bk. 8. Riegert, Evelyn, ed. (Please Understand Us Ser.). (Illus.). 1990. write for info. (*0-935323-31-7*) Barrington Hse.

— Fence Me In...with Understanding, Vol. 32, Bk. 8. Riegert, Evelyn, ed. (Please Understand Us Ser.). (Illus.). 1990. teacher ed write for info. (*0-935323-32-5*) Barrington Hse.

— Fence Me In...with Understanding, Vol. 33, Bk. 8. Riegert, Evelyn, ed. (Please Understand Us Ser.). (Illus.). 1990. write for info. (*0-935323-33-3*) Barrington Hse.

— Is the World As I See It? Riegert, Evelyn, ed. (Please Understand Us Ser.). (Illus.). 1990. write for info. (*0-935323-01-5*, VOL. 1, BK. 1, STUDENT BK.); Vol. 2, Bk. 1 Teacher's Handbook. write for info. (*0-935323-02-3*); Vol. 16, Bk. 3 Text. write for info. (*0-935323-16-3*); Vol. 17, Bk. 3 Tchr's Tips. write for info. (*0-935323-17-1*); Vol. 18, Bk 3 role plays. write for info. (*0-935323-18-X*); Vol. 19, Bk. 4 text. write for info. (*0-935323-19-8*); Vol. 20, Bk. 4 tchr's tips. write for info. (*0-935323-20-1*); Vol. 21, Bk. 4 role plays. write for info. (*0-935323-21-X*) Barrington Hse.

— Is the World As I See It?, Vol. 3, Bk. 1. Riegert, Evelyn, ed. (Please Understand Us Ser.). (Illus.). 1990. audio write for info. (*0-935323-03-1*) Barrington Hse.

— My Little World Book, Vol. 4. Riegert, Evelyn, ed. (Please Understand Us Ser.). (Illus.). 500p. 1990. student ed write for info. (*0-935323-04-X*) Barrington Hse.

— My Little World Book, Vol. 5. Riegert, Evelyn, ed. (Please Understand Us Ser.). (Illus.). 500p. 1990. teacher ed write for info. (*0-935323-05-8*) Barrington Hse.

— My Little World Book, Vol. 6. Riegert, Evelyn, ed. (Please Understand Us Ser.). (Illus.). 500p. 1990. audio write for info. (*0-935323-06-6*) Barrington Hse.

— My Little World Book, Vol. 7. Riegert, Evelyn, ed. (Please Understand Us Ser.). (Illus.). 500p. 1990. teacher ed write for info. (*0-935323-07-4*) Barrington Hse.

— My Little World Book, Vol. 8. rev. ed. Riegert, Evelyn, ed. (Please Understand Us Ser.). (Illus.). 500p. 1990. teacher ed write for info. (*0-935323-08-2*) Barrington Hse.

— My Little World Book, Vol. 9. rev. ed. Riegert, Evelyn, ed. (Please Understand Us Ser.). (Illus.). 500p. 1990. student ed write for info. (*0-935323-09-0*) Barrington Hse.

— My Little World Book, Vol. 10, Bk. 1: Text. Riegert, Evelyn, ed. (Please Understand Us Ser.). (Illus.). 1990. Vol. 10, Bk. 1 text. write for info. (*0-935323-10-4*) Barrington Hse.

— My Little World Book, Vol. 11: Teacher's Tips. Riegert, Evelyn, ed. (Please Understand Us Ser.). (Illus.). 1990. Vol. 11, Bk. 1 tchr's tips. write for info. (*0-935323-11-2*) Barrington Hse.

— My Little World Book, Vol. 12: Teacher's Tips. Riegert, Evelyn, ed. (Please Understand Us Ser.). (Illus.). 1990. Vol. 12, Bk. 1 tchr's tips. write for info. (*0-935323-12-0*) Barrington Hse.

— My Little World Book, Vol. 13, Bk. 2: Text. Riegert, Evelyn, ed. (Please Understand Us Ser.). (Illus.). 1990. Vol. 13, Bk. 2 text. write for info. (*0-935323-13-9*) Barrington Hse.

— My Little World Book, Vol. 14, Bk. 2: Teacher's Tips. Riegert, Evelyn, ed. (Please Understand Us Ser.). (Illus.). 1990. Vol. 14, Bk. 2 tchr's tips. write for info. (*0-935323-14-7*) Barrington Hse.

— My Little World Book, Vol. 15, Bk. 2: Role Plays. Riegert, Evelyn, ed. (Please Understand Us Ser.). (Illus.). 1990. Vol. 15, Bk. 2 role plays. write for info. (*0-935323-15-5*) Barrington Hse.

— Open Minded Kids!, Vol. 22, Bk. 5. Riegert, Evelyn, ed. (Please Understand Us Ser.). (Illus.). 1990. write for info. (*0-935323-22-8*) Barrington Hse.

— Open Minded Kids!, Vol. 23, Bk. 5. Riegert, Evelyn, ed. (Please Understand Us Ser.). (Illus.). 1990. write for info. (*0-935323-23-6*) Barrington Hse.

— Open Minded Kids!, Vol. 24, Bk. 5. Riegert, Evelyn, ed. (Please Understand Us Ser.). (Illus.). 1990. write for info. (*0-935323-24-4*) Barrington Hse.

— Open Minded Kids!, Vol. 25, Bk. 6. Riegert, Evelyn, ed. (Please Understand Us Ser.). (Illus.). 1990. write for info. (*0-935323-25-2*) Barrington Hse.

— Open Minded Kids!, Vol. 26, Bk. 6. Riegert, Evelyn, ed. (Please Understand Us Ser.). (Illus.). 1990. write for info. (*0-935323-26-0*) Barrington Hse.

— Open Minded Kids!, Vol. 27, Bk. 6. Riegert, Evelyn, ed. (Please Understand Us Ser.). (Illus.). 1990. write for info. (*0-935323-27-9*) Barrington Hse.

— Please Understand Us! Is the World As I See It?; My Little World Book; Open Minded Kids!; Fence Me In... with Understanding, 33 vols., Set. Riegert, Evelyn, ed. (Illus.). 500p. (J). (gr. k-8). 1990. 139.95 (*0-935323-00-7*) Barrington Hse.

Mohr, U., ed. International Classification of Rodent Tumours, Part 1: The Rat, Fascicle No. 6: Endocrine System. (IARC Scientific Publications: Vol. 122). (Illus.). 76p. 1994. pap. 30.00 (*92-832-0126-4*) OUP.

— International Classification of Rodent Tumours, Part 1: The Rat, Fascicle No. 7: Central Nervous System, Heart, Eye, Mesothelium. (IARC Scientific Publications: Vol. 122). (Illus.). 78p. 1994. pap. 30.00 (*92-832-0127-2*) OUP.

Mohr, U., ed. see Hanover International Carcinogenesis Meeting Staff.

Mohr, U., ed. see International Agency for Research on Cancer Staff.

Mohr, U., jt. ed. see Turusov, V. S.

***Mohr, U., et al, eds.** Correlations Between In Vitro & In Vivo Investigations in Inhalation Toxicology. (Illus.). Date not set. write for info. (*0-944398-47-2*) ILSI.

— Pathobiology of the Aging Mouse, Vol. 2. (Illus.). Date not set. write for info. (*0-944398-46-4*) ILSI.

— Pathobiology of the Aging Rat, Vol. 1. LC 92-74194. (Illus.). 485p. 1992. 155.00 (*0-944398-09-X*) ILSI.

— Pathobiology of the Aging Rat, Vol. 2. LC 92-74194. (Illus.). 647p. 1994. 155.00 (*0-944398-20-0*) ILSI.

— Toxic & Carcinogenic Effects of Solid Particles in the Respiratory Tract. LC 94-75676. (Illus.). 652p. 1994. 95. 00 (*0-944398-14-6*) ILSI.

Mohr, Ulrich, ed. International Classification of Rodent Tumours, Pt. 1: The Rat Fascicle No. 2: Soft Tissue & Musculoskeletal System. (IARC Scientific Publications: No. 122). (Illus.). 72p. 1993. Fascicle No. 2: Soft Tissue & Musculoskeletal System. pap. 30.00 (*92-832-0122-1*) OUP.

Mohr, Ulrich, jt. auth. see Turusov, V. S.

Mohr, Ulrich, et al, eds. International Classification of Rodent Tumours, Pt. 1: The Rat Fascicle No. 2: Soft Tissue & Musculoskeletal System, Fascicle No. 1: Respiratory System. (IARC Scientific Publications: No. 122). (Illus.). 68p. 1993. pap. 30.00 (*92-832-0121-3*) OUP.

— International Classifications of Rodent Tumors, Pt. 1: The Rat, Fascicle No. 3: Urinary System. (IARC Scientific Publications: No. 122). (Illus.). 56p. 1993. pap. 30.00 (*92-832-0123-X*) OUP.

— International Classifications of Rodent Tumors, Pt. 1: The Rat, Fascicle No. 4: Haematopoietic System. (IARC Scientific Publications: No. 122). (Illus.). 40p. 1994. pap. 30.00 (*92-832-0124-8*) OUP.

— International Classifications of Rodent Tumors, Pt. 1: The Rat, Fascicle No. 5: Integumentary System. (IARC Scientific Publications: No. 122). (Illus.). 56p. 1994. pap. 30.00 (*92-832-0125-6*) OUP.

Mohr, V. & Lewkowski, J. P. The Effect of Diet on Tumor Development in Animals. LC 88-10680. 144p. 1988. lib. bdg. 100.00 (*0-89573-453-2*) VCH Pubs.

***Mohr, V., et al, eds.** Pathobiology of the Aging Mouse, Vol. 1. (Illus.). Date not set. write for info. (*0-944398-45-6*) ILSI.

Mohr, Walter H. Federal Indian Relations, Seventeen Seventy-Four - Seventeen Eighty-Eight. LC 76-158854. reprint ed. 37.50 (*0-404-07147-3*) AMS Pr.

Mohr, William L. & Mohr, Harriet. Quality Circles: Changing Images of People at Work. LC 83-5970. (Illus.). 256p. 1983. write for info. (*0-201-05207-5*) Addison-Wesley.

Mohraz, Judy J. The Separate Problem: Case Studies of Black Education in the North, 1900-1930. LC 78-4026. (Contributions in Afro-American & African Studies: No. 42). xvi, 165p. 1979. text ed. 49.95 (*0-313-20411-X*, MSP/, Greenwood Pr) Greenwood.

Mohrbacher, Nancy & Stock, Julie. The Breastfeeding Answer Book. LC 91-62087. 455p. 1991. spiral bd. 34.95 (*0-912500-33-6*) La Leche.
During the last decade, the average length of hospital stay following birth has been cut almost in half as the health-care industry strives to keep costs down. As a result, women are often sent home to grapple through common breastfeeding challenges without the information & support they need. This book presents a broad spectrum of information & explores in-depth all types of breastfeeding questions along with a variety of possible approaches & solutions. It is a concise, practical & well-documented guide to not only what to do in virtually any breastfeeding circumstance, but why. Although originally written for lay breastfeeding counselors, the non-medical language & easy to use format make this book an effective resource for anyone interested in obtaining or providing reliable information about breastfeeding. To order contact La Leche League International, 1400 N. Meacham Road, Schaumburg, IL 60173. 708-519-7730. No. 480, $34.95. ***Publisher Provided Annotation.***

Mohrbacher, Nancy & Torgus, Judy, eds. The New La Leche League International Leader's Handbook. LC 89-83709. (Illus.). 223p. 1989. spiral bd. 14.50 (*0-912500-32-8*) La Leche.

Mohrbacher, Nancy, jt. ed. see Halonen, Virginia S.

Mohrbacher, Paul. The Chancellor's Tale. (Orig.). 1992. pap. 5.45 (*0-87129-168-1*, C85) Dramatic Pub.

Mohren, Paul, jt. auth. see Menges, Georg.

Mohrhardt, David. How to Paint Dabbling Ducks. LC 90-38135. (How to Paint Ser.). (Illus.). 128p. (Orig.). 1991. pap. 24.95 (*0-8117-3010-7*) Stackpole.

— How to Paint Diving Ducks. LC 90-38134. (How to Paint Ser.). (Illus.). 128p. (Orig.). 1991. pap. 24.95 (*0-8117-3011-5*) Stackpole.

— How to Paint Songbirds: A Guide to Materials, Tools, & Technique. LC 88-16065. (Illus.). 128p. 1989. pap. 24.95 (*0-8117-2274-0*) Stackpole.

— Songbird Painting Projects. LC 91-29575. (Illus.). 128p. 1992. pap. 24.95 (*0-8117-3012-3*) Stackpole.

Mohrhardt, David & Schinkel, Richard E. Suburban Nature Guide: How to Discover & Identify the Wildlife in Your Backyard. LC 90-10237. (Illus.). 192p. (Orig.). 1991. pap. 16.95 (*0-8117-3080-8*) Stackpole.

Mohri, H. New Horizons in Sperm Cell Research. 516p. 1987. text ed. 224.00 (*2-88124-254-5*) Gordon & Breach.

Mohri, H., et al, eds. Biology of the Germ Line: In Animals & Man. (Illus.). x, 304p. 1993. 157.00 (*3-8055-5773-6*) S Karger.

Mohrig & Child. Chemistry in Perspective. 560p. 1987. teacher ed write for info. (*0-318-61504-5*, H05648); text ed. write for info. (*0-205-10270-0*) P-H.

Mohring, Herbert, ed. The Economics of Transport. LC 93-32024. (International Library of Critical Writings in Business History: Vol. 34). 1056p. 1994. 294.95 (*1-85278-186-6*, Pub. by E Elgar Pub UK) Ashgate Pub Co.

Mohring, R. H., ed. Graph-Theoretic Concepts in Computer Science. (Lecture Notes in Computer Science Ser.). ix, 360p. 1991. pap. 37.00 (*0-387-53832-1*) Spr-Verlag.

Mohrlang, Roger. Matthew & Paul: A Comparison of Ethical Perspectives. LC 83-10147. (Society for New Testament Studies Monographs: No. 48). 220p. 1984. 64.95 (*0-521-25093-5*) Cambridge U Pr.

Mohrle, Johannes. Architecture in Perspective. rev. ed. LC 93-44937. 1994. 45.00 (*0-8230-0237-3*, Whitney Lib) Watsn-Guptill.

Mohrman, Allan M., Jr., et al. Designing Performance Appraisal Systems: Aligning Appraisals & Organizational Realities. LC 88-32894. (Management Ser.). 256p. 1989. 31.95x (*1-55542-149-0*) Jossey-Bass.

— Large-Scale Organizational Change. LC 89-45602. (Management Ser.). 336p. 1989. 31.95 (*1-55542-164-4*) Jossey-Bass.

Mohrman, David E. & Heller, Lois J. Cardiovascular Physiology. 3rd ed. 224p. 1991. pap. text ed. 25.50 (*0-07-027999-3*) Hlth Prof Div.

Mohrman, Kathryn. Adult Students & the Humanities. 48p. 1983. 8.00 (*0-911696-17-2*) Assn Am Coll.

Mohrman, Susan A. & Cummings, Thomas G. Self-Designing Organizations: Learning How to Create High Performance. (Organization Development Ser.). (Illus.). 200p. (C). 1989. pap. text ed. 26.95 (*0-201-14603-7*) Addison-Wesley.

Mohrman, Susan A. & Wohlstetter, Priscilla. School-Based Management: Organizing for High Performance. LC 94-17756. (Education Ser.). 396p. 1994. 34.95 (*0-7879-0035-4*) Jossey-Bass.

Mohrman, Susan A., jt. ed. see Von Glinow, Mary A.

***Mohrman, Susan A., et al.** Designing Team-Based Organizations: New Forms for Knowledge Work. (Management Ser.). 400p. 1995. 29.95 (*0-7879-0080-X*) Jossey-Bass.

***Mohrmann, Gary, illus.** 1001 Rhymes & Fingerplays. (1001 Ser.). 312p. (J). 1995. teacher ed 21.95 (*0-614-06823-1*, WPH 1503) Totline Bks.

— 1001 Teaching Props. (1001 Ser.). 248p. (J). 1995. teacher ed 18.95 (*0-614-06821-5*, WPH 1501) Totline Bks.

— 1001 Teaching Tips. (1001 Ser.). 208p. (J). 1995. teacher ed 16.95 (*0-614-06822-3*, WPH 1502) Totline Bks.

Mohrmann, Gerald, ed. see Stewart, Charles I.

***Mohrmann, Margaret E.** Medicine as Ministry: Reflections on Suffering, Ethics, & Hope. 120p. (Orig.). 1995. pap. 14.95 (*0-8298-1073-0*) Pilgrim OH.

Mohrt, Michel. Le Campagne d'Italie. (FRE.). 1973. pap. 10.95 (*0-7859-4015-4*) Fr & Eur.

— Deux Indiennes a Paris. (FRE.). 1978. pap. 10.95 (*0-7859-4090-1*) Fr & Eur.

— Les Moyens du Bord. (FRE.). 1982. pap. 11.95 (*0-7859-4164-9*) Fr & Eur.

— La Prison Maritime. (FRE.). 1973. pap. 10.95 (*0-7859-4009-X*, 2070364089) Fr & Eur.

Mohs, Bruce B. The Amazing Mr. Mohs. (Illus.). 256p. (Orig.). (C). 1984. pap. 14.95 (*0-931279-00-3*) Mohs Seaplane Co.

— Free Enterprise: A Wisconsin Constitutional Amendment. (Illus.). (Orig.). 1985. reprint ed. pap. 3.50 (*0-317-13759-X*) Mohs Seaplane Co.

Mohs, Frederic E. Chemosurgery: Microscopically Controlled Surgery for Skin Cancer. fac. ed. (Illus.). 400p. 1978. 75.95 (*0-398-03725-6*) C C Thomas.

Mohsen, J. P., ed. see Technical Council on Computer Practice, Committee on Coordination Outside ASCE Staff.

***Mohsen, Shahbazzadeh.** Role of Multinational Companies in Nation's Economy: A Case Study of Iran. (C). 1994. 42.00 (*81-7018-747-8*, Pub. by BR Pub II) S Asia.

Mohseni, Mahmoud, tr. see Shariati, Ali.

Mohsenin, N. N. Physical Properties of Plant & Animal Materials. 758p. 1970. 150.00 (*0-677-02300-6*) Gordon & Breach.

Mohsenin, Nuri N. Electromagnetic Radiation Properties of Foods & Agricultural Products. 650p. 1984. text ed. 194.00 (*0-677-06190-0*) Gordon & Breach.

— Physical Properties of Food & Agricultural Materials: A Teaching Manual. 157p. (C). 1989. text ed. 63.00 (*0-677-05630-3*) Gordon & Breach.

— Physical Properties of Plant & Animal Materials. 2nd ed. 500p. 1986. text ed. 176.00 (*0-677-21370-0*) Gordon & Breach.

— Thermal Properties of Food & Agricultural Materials. 418p. 1980. text ed. 195.00 (*0-677-05450-5*) Gordon & Breach.

***Mohsenipour, I., et al.** Operative Approaches in Neurosurgery: Central & Peripheral Nervous System. LC 94-32117. (Illus.). 200p. 1994. 199.00 (*0-86577-541-9*) Thieme Med Pubs.

Mohsin, Nadeem. Lull after the Storm: Poverty & Integrated Rural Development. 1989. 28.50 (*81-7169-035-1*, Pub. by Commonwealth II) S Asia.

Mohtadi, M. F. Man & His Environment: Proceedings of the Third International Banff Conference, May 1980, Vol. 3. 1980. 68.00 (*0-08-025792-5*, Pub. by Pergamon Repr UK) Franklin.

Mohtadi, M. F., ed. Man & His Environment, Vol. 2: Proceedings of the Second Banff Conference. 216p. 1976. 98.00 (*0-08-019922-4*, Pub. by Pergamon Repr UK) Franklin.

Mohts, Susan B. When God's People Pray: Pastorial Prayers for the Congregation First United Methodist Church, Dallas. Hale, Margaret, ed. 96p. (Orig.). 1989. pap. 4.95 (*0-685-26559-5*) First United Meth Ch.

Mohun, Simon, ed. Debates in Value Theory. LC 93-44298. 1994. text ed. 59.95 (*0-312-12098-2*, Pub. by Macm UK) St Martin.

Mohyla, O., jt. auth. see Ludvik, M.

Moi, Toril. Feminist Theory & Simone De Beauvoir. 128p. 1992. pap. 15.95 (*0-631-17324-2*) Blackwell Pubs.

— Sexual-Textual Politics. 200p. 1985. pap. 13.95 (*0-415-02974-0*, 9451) Routledge Chapman & Hall.

— Simone de Beauvoir: The Making of an Intellectual Woman. 352p. 1994. 54.95 (*0-631-14673-3*); pap. 21.95 (*0-631-19181-X*) Blackwell Pubs.

Moi, Toril, ed. French Feminist Thought: Politics, Patriarchy & Sexual Difference. 240p. (Orig.). 1987. pap. 15.95 (*0-631-14973-2*) Blackwell Pubs.

Moi, Toril & Radway, Janice, eds. Materialist Feminism. 200p. 1994. pap. 10.00 (*0-8223-6421-2*) Duke.

Moi, Toril, ed. see Kristeva, Julia.

Moidel, Steve. Speed Reading. (Business Success Ser.). (Orig.). 1994. pap. 4.95 (*0-8120-1845-1*) Barron.

Moignard, Elizabeth. Corpus Vasorum Antiquorum: Great Britain, Fascicule 16, National Museums of Scotland, Edinburgh. (British Academy Ser.). (Illus.). 128p. 1990. 115.00 (*0-19-726077-2*) OUP.

***Moigno, Yves.** Dictionnaire Pratique de Sexualite. 1991. write for info. (*0-7859-7889-5*, 2-501-01407-3) Fr & Eur.

Moiiere. The School for Husbands & Sganarelle, or the Imaginary Cuckold. Wilbur, Richard, tr. 1994. pap. 12.95 (*0-15-679500-0*) HarBrace.

Moikobu, Josephine M. Blood & Flesh: Black American & African Identifications. LC 80-1706. (Contributions in Afro-American & African Studies: No. 59). (Illus.). xii, 226p. 1981. text ed. 49.95 (*0-313-22549-4*, MBF/, Greenwood Pr) Greenwood.

***Moilanen, Markku & Tiittula, Liisa, eds.** Ueberredung in der Presse: Texte, Strategien, Analysen. (Sprache, Politik, Oeffentlichkeit Ser.: Bd. 3). 249p. (GER.). (C). 1994. lib. bdg. 103.10 (*3-11-014346-1*) De Gruyter.

***Moiles, Steven.** Summer of My First Pediddle. 190p. (Orig.). (YA). (gr. 9-12). 1995. lib. bdg. 15.00 (*0-88092-123-4*); pap. 5.00 (*0-88092-122-6*) Royal Fireworks.

***Mo'in, Mohammad.** Mo'in's: Intermediate Persion Dictionary, 6 vols., Set. (Illus.). 8058p. (PER.). 1994. lib. bdg. 195.00 (*1-56859-031-8*) Mazda Pubs.

Moine, Donald J. & Herd, John H. Modern Persuasion Strategies: The Hidden Advantage in Selling. LC 84-11552. 204p. 1984. 19.95 (*0-13-596099-1*) P-H.

Moine, Donald J. & Lloyd, Kenneth. Unlimited Selling Power: How to Master Hypnotic Skills. 288p. 1990. pap. 12.95 (*0-13-689126-8*) P-H.

Moine, Donald J., jt. auth. see Gschwandtner, Gerhard.

Moinot, Pierre. La Chasse Royale. (FRE.). 1981. pap. 10.95 (*0-7859-4146-0*) Fr & Eur.

— Le Guetteur d'Ombre. (FRE.). 1984. pap. 15.95 (*0-7859-4204-1*) Fr & Eur.

— Le Sable Vif. (FRE.). 1979. pap. 10.95 (*0-7859-4120-7*) Fr & Eur.

Moioli, G. Dictionnaire de Dietique. 364p. (FRE.). 1993. pap. 59.95 (*0-7859-5640-9*, 2732817066) Fr & Eur.

Moir, Alfred. Caravaggio. (Masters of Art Ser.). (Illus.). 128p. 1989. 22.95 (*0-8109-3150-8*) Abrams.

— European Drawings in the Collection of the Santa Barbara Museum of Art. LC 76-4685. (Illus.). 298p. (Orig.). 1976. pap. 12.00 (*0-89951-021-3*) Santa Barb Mus Art.

— The Italian Followers of Caravaggio, 1. LC 66-10315. reprint ed. pap. 68.30 (*0-317-10574-4*, 2006017) Bks Demand.

— The Italian Followers of Caravaggio, 2. LC 66-10315. reprint ed. pap. 65.60 (*0-317-10575-2*) Bks Demand.

— Old Master Drawings from the Feitelson Collection. (Illus.). 167p. (Orig.). 1983. 20.00 (*0-942006-04-6*) U of CA Art.

Moir, Alfred, text. Anthony Van Dyck. LC 94-8419. 1994. write for info. (*0-8109-3917-7*) Abrams.

Moir, Anne. Brain Sex: The Real Difference Between Men & Women. 1991. 17.95 (*0-8184-0543-0*) Carol Pub Group.

Moir, Anne & Jessel, David. Brain Sex. 1992. pap. 12.95 (*0-385-31183-4*, Delta) Dell.

Moir, Donald D. Pain Relief in Labour. 5th ed. LC 85-11702. (Illus.). 196p. 1985. pap. text ed. write for info. (*0-443-03389-7*) Churchill.

Moir, Duncan W., ed. see Candamo, Francisco B.

Moir, Frederick L. After Livingstone: An African Trade Romance. 1977. 17.95 (*0-8369-9212-1*, 9068) Ayer.

Moir, G., ed. Into Television. LC 68-8870. 1969. pap. 50.00 (*0-08-013032-1*, Pub. by Pergamon Repr UK) Franklin.

Moir, George E. Poems From the Heart. (Illus.). 1986. 7.95 (*0-9616974-0-7*) G E Moir.

Moir, Guthrie. Beyond Hatred. LC 74-119326. 183p. reprint ed. pap. 52.20 (*0-8357-7157-1*, 2026963) Bks Demand.

Moir, Hughes, ed. Collected Perspectives: Choosing & Using Books for the Classroom. 2nd ed. 417p. (Orig.). (J). (gr. k-12). 1991. pap. text ed. 38.95 (*0-926842-12-9*) CG Pubs Inc.

Moir, James R. The Antiquity of Man in East Anglia. LC 76-44762. reprint ed. 17.00 (*0-404-15953-2*) AMS Pr.

Moir, John S. A History of Biblical Studies in Canada: A Sense of Proportion. LC 82-5979. (Society of Biblical Literature Biblical Scholarship in North America Ser.: Biblical Scholarship in North America Ser.). 132p. 1982. pap. 20.95 (*0-89130-581-5*, 06 11 07) Scholars Pr GA.

Moir, John S. & McIntire, C. T. Canadian Protestant & Catholic Missions, 1820-1960: Historical Essays in Honor of Webster. (Toronto Studies in Religion: Vol. 3). 266p. 1988. text ed. 39.00 (*0-8204-0465-9*) P Lang Pubs.

Moir, Lance. The ACT Guide to Managing Liquidity. LC 92-20996. 176p. 1992. pap. 24.95 (*0-631-18736-7*) Blackwell Pubs.

Moir, Lindsay, jt. auth. see Dempsey, Hugh A.

Moir, Lyn, tr. see Simenon, Georges.

Moir, May. Flower Sculpture: A Handbook. (Illus.). 1977. pap. 1.95 (*0-914916-25-4*) Ku Paa.

— The Garden Watcher. rev. ed. LC 82-24782. (Illus.). 136p. 1989. pap. text ed. 14.95 (*0-8248-1224-7*) UH Pr.

Moir, May A., jt. auth. see Moir, W. W.

Moir, Sheila, jt. auth. see Smith, LeCain W.

Moir, W. W. & Moir, May A. Creating Oncidinae Intergenerics. LC 81-16182. (Illus.). 120p. 1982. pap. text ed. 12.00 (*0-8248-0784-7*) UH Pr.

— Laeliinae Intergenerics. LC 82-4887. (Illus.). 62p. 1982. pap. text ed. 12.00 (*0-8248-0814-2*) UH Pr.

Moir, William H. Forests of Mount Rainier. (Illus.). 111p. (Orig.). 1989. pap. text ed. 8.95 (*0-914019-24-4*) NW Interpretive.

Moirand. Dictionnaire Technologique, (Ebenisterie-Menuiserie-Scierie-Technologie) Vol. 6. 356p. (FRE.). 1986. pap. 150.00 (*0-7859-3910-5*, 2856080219) Fr & Eur.

Moirant, R., jt. auth. see Cassart, C.

Moirant, T. Technical Dictionary of Woodworking: French Definitions Plus Index with Appendix of Technical Terms in French-German-English-Spanish-Dutch-Italian-Swedish. 350p. 1986. pap. 72.50 (*2-85608-021-9*) IBD Ltd.

Moisan, Ed, ed. see Theberge, Remy.

Moisan, Michel & Pelletier, Jacques, eds. Microwave Excited Plasmas. LC 92-30694. 1992. write for info. (*0-444-88815-2*) Elsevier.

Moisan, Michel, jt. ed. see Ferreira, C. M.

Moisan, R., ed. see Theberge, J. Remy.

Moisan, R., ed. see Theberge, Remy.

Moisar, Erik, jt. ed. see Granzer, Friedrich.

Moise, E. E. Introductory Problem Courses in Analysis & Topology. (Universitext Ser.). 94p. 1982. pap. 28.00 (*0-387-90701-7*) Spr-Verlag.

Moise, Edwin E. Elementary Geometry from an Advanced Standpoint. 2nd ed. LC 73-2347. (C). 1974. text ed. 37.56 (*0-201-04793-4*) Addison-Wesley.

— Land Reform in China & North Vietnam: Consolidating the Revolution at the Village Level. LC 82-15900. xiv, 305p. (C). 1983. 29.95 (*0-8078-1547-0*) U of NC Pr.

— Modern China: A History. (Illus.). 256p. (C). 1986. pap. text ed. 21.95 (*0-582-49077-4*, 73474); boxed 26.95 (*0-582-49076-6*, 73474) Longman.

— Modern China, a History. 2nd ed. LC 93-47289. (Present & the Past Ser.). (C). 1995. pap. text ed. 21.95 (*0-582-07480-0*, 76772, Pub. by Longman UK) Longman.

Moiseev, Yu V. & Zaikov, G. E. Chemical Resistance of Polymers in Aggressive Media. Mosley, R. J., tr. LC 87-9075. (Illus.). 384p. 1987. 110.00 (*0-306-10997-2*, Consultants) Plenum.

Moiseiwitsch, B. L., jt. ed. see Burke, P. G.

Moiseiwitsch, Benjamin L. Variational Principles. LC 66-17233. (Interscience Monographs & Texts in Physics & Astronomy: Vol. 20). 320p. reprint ed. pap. 91.20 (*0-317-11049-7*, 2016148) Bks Demand.

Moiser, C. H. & Philips, V. A. Practice & Procedure in Magistrates Courts. 3rd ed. 268p. 1992. 75.00 (*1-85190-163-9*, Pub. by Tolley Pubng UK) St Mut.

Moiser, Jeremy. Silent Pilgrimage to God: The Spirituality of Charles de Foucauld. LC 74-32516. 100p. reprint ed. pap. 28.50 (*0-8357-4072-2*, 2036762) Bks Demand.

Moiser, Jeremy, tr. see Carretto, Carlo.

Moises, Rosalio, et al. A Yaqui Life: The Personal Chronicle of a Yaqui Indian. LC 76-56789. Orig. Title: The Tall Candle: the Personal Chronicle of a Yaqui Indian. (Illus.). lxviii, 259p. 1977. reprint ed. pap. 10.95 (*0-8032-8175-7*) U of Nebr Pr.

Moiseyev, Ivan V. A Russian Martyr. 1974. 1.95 (*0-89985-107-X*) Christ for the Nations.

Moisil, G. & Sneddon, I. N. Algebraic Theory of Switching Circuits. LC 63-10024. (International Series of Monographs on Pure & Applied Mathematics: Vol. 41). 1969. 292.00 (*0-08-010148-8*, Pub. by Pergamon Repr UK) Franklin.

***Moitessier, Bernard.** The Long Way. (Illus.). 252p. 1995. pap. text ed. 14.95 (*0-924486-84-8*) Sheridan.

— Tamata & the Alliance. Rodarmor, William, tr. (Illus.). 400p. 1995. 30.00 (*0-924486-77-5*) Sheridan.

Moitoza, Joe. The Kibitzer. (Illus.). 96p. 1984. 9.95 (*0-915509-04-0*); pap. 4.95 (*0-915509-03-2*) Argos Pub Co.

***Moiz, Azra.** Taiwan. (Cultures of the World Ser.). 128p. (J). (gr. 3-5). 1995. lib. bdg. 21.95 (*0-7614-0180-6*) Marshall Cavendish.

Moizer, Barbara, jt. auth. see Moizer, Stanley.

Moizer, Stanley & Moizer, Barbara. The Complete Book of Budgerigars. (Illus.). 144p. 1988. 16.95 (*0-8120-6059-8*) Barron.

Mojab, Cynthia A., et al. Innovative Materials Development & Testing, Vol. 5: Partial Depth Spall Repair. 197p. (Orig.). (C). 1993. pap. text ed. 15.00 (*0-309-05613-6*, SHRP-H-356) SHRP.

Mojaiev. English-Russian Dictionary of Forestry & Forest Industries. 670p. (ENG & RUS.). 1983. 49.95 (*0-8288-0331-5*, M14046) Fr & Eur.

Mojares, Resil B., jt. ed. see Kerkvliet, Benedict J.

Mojay, Gabriel, jt. auth. see Jarmey, Chris.

Mojena, Richard. Turbo Pascal. 700p. (C). 1992. pap. 46.95 (*0-534-13050-X*) PWS Pubs.

Mojena, Richard & Ageloff, Roy. FORTRAN 77. 600p. (C). 1990. pap. 48.95 (*0-534-11742-2*) PWS Pubs.

Mojena, Richard, jt. auth. see Ageloff, Roy.

Mojetta, Angelo. Simon & Schuster's Guide to Saltwater Fish & Fishing. (Illus.). 256p. (Orig.). 1992. pap. 14.00 (*0-671-77947-8*, Fireside) S&S Trade.

Moji, Clifton C., jt. auth. see Baratloo, Balch.

Mojica-Sandoz, Luis. Aguedo Mojica: La Luminosa Entrega. LC 83-82447. 336p. 1983. pap. 12.95 (*0-940238-70-5*) Ediciones Huracan.

— La Meditacion Segun la Mas Antigua Tradicion Budista. (UPREX, Manuales Ser.: No. 54). (Illus.). 92p. (SPA.). 1979. pap. text ed. 1.50 (*0-8477-0054-2*) U of PR Pr.

Mojsisch, Burkhard. Sprachphilosophie in Antike und Mittelalter: Bochumer Kolloquim, 2-4, June 1982. (Bochum Studies in Philosophy: No. 3). 448p. (GER.). 1986. 58.00 (*90-6032-233-9*, Pub. by B R Gruener NE) Benjamins North Am.

Mojsisch, Burkhard & Pluta, Olaf, eds. Historia Philosophiae Medii Aevi: Studien zur Geschichte der Philosophie des Mittelalters, zu Seinem 60, Geburtstag, Band I & II, 2 vols., 1. LC 91-47183. (GER.). 1992. write for info. (*90-6032-333-5*, Pub. by Gruner NE) Benjamins North Am.

— Historia Philosophiae Medii Aevi: Studien zur Geschichte der Philosophie des Mittelalters, zu Seinem 60, Geburtstag, Band I & II, 2 vols., 2. LC 91-47183. (GER.). 1992. write for info. (*90-6032-343-2*, Pub. by Gruner NE) Benjamins North Am.

— Historia Philosophiae Medii Aevi: Studien zur Geschichte der Philosophie des Mittelalters, zu Seinem 60, Geburtstag, Band I & II, 2 vols., Set. LC 91-47183. (GER.). 1992. 177.00 (*90-6032-090-5*, Pub. by Gruner NE) Benjamins North Am.

Mojsov, Lazar. Dimensions of Non-Alignment. 282p. 1981. 65.00 (*0-317-53806-3*, Pub. by Collets UK) Pro-Am Music.

Mojtabai, A. G. Called Out. LC 93-32776. 1994. 22.00 (*0-385-47430-X*, N A Talese) Doubleday.

***Mojuetan, B. A.** History & Underdevelopment. (Monographs, International African Institute). (C). 1995. pap. text ed. 58.00 (*3-89473-697-6*) Westview.

Mojumdar, Kanchanmoy. Anglo-Nepalese Relations in the Nineteenth Century. LC 73-906205. vi, 195p. 1973. 9.00 (*0-88386-214-X*) S Asia.

Mojzes, Paul. Yugoslavian Inferno: Ethnoreligious Warfare in the Balkans. LC 94-3737. 248p. (C). 1994. 24.95 (*0-8264-0683-1*) Continuum.

Mojzes, Paul, comp. Church & State in Postwar Eastern Europe: A Bibliographical Survey. LC 87-8358. (Bibliographies & Indexes in Religious Studies: No. 11). 120p. 1987. text ed. 55.00 (*0-313-24002-7*, MOJ/, Greenwood Pr) Greenwood.

Mojzes, Paul, ed. Religious Liberty in Eastern Europe & the U. S. S. R. Before & after the Great Transformation. 400p. 1992. text ed. 56.00 (*0-88033-234-4*) Col U Pr.

— Varieties of Christian-Marxist Dialogue. 210p. (Orig.). 1978. pap. 3.00 (*0-931214-02-5*) Ecumenical Phila.

Mojzes, Paul & Swidler, Leonard, eds. Christian Mission & Interreligious Dialogue. LC 91-2010. (Religions in Dialogue Ser.: Vol. 4). 288p. 1991. lib. bdg. 89.95 (*0-88946-520-7*) E Mellen.

Mojzes, Paul, jt. ed. see Swidler, Leonard.

Mok. Cytokini vs. Chemistry Activity & Function. 1994. 179.95 (*0-8493-6252-0*) CRC Pr.

Mok, Esther. Sumo, the Wrestling Elephant. (Illus.). 24p. (J). (gr. 2-5). 1994. pap. 4.95 (*0-943864-68-2*) Davenport.

***Mok, Jacqueline & Newell, Marie-Louise, eds.** HIV Infection in Children: A Guide to Practical Management. (Illus.). 300p. (C). 1995. write for info. (*0-521-45421-2*) Cambridge U Pr.

Mok, Leo. International Handbook on Pensions Law & Similar Employee Benefits. 352p. 1989. lib. bdg. 180.00 (*0-86010-994-1*) Kluwer Ac.

Mok, N., ed. Metric Rigidity Theorems on Hermitian Locally Symmetric Manifolds. (Series in Pure Mathematics: Vol. 6). 292p. (C). 1989. text ed. 61.00 (*9971-5-0800-1*); pap. text ed. 32.00 (*9971-5-0802-8*) World Scientific Pub.

Mok, Olivia, tr. see Jin Yong.

Mok, Q. I., jt. auth. see Smeets, J. R.

Mokaila, Dingaan M., jt. auth. see Cole, Desmond T.

***Mokakit Indian Education Research Association Staff.** Courageous Spirits: Aboriginal Heroes of Our Children. 76p. (Orig.). 1993. teacher ed, pap. 5.95 (*0-919441-51-3*, Pub. by Theytus Bks Ltd CN) Orca Bk Pubs.

*Mokakit Indian Education Research Association Staff, ed. Courageous Spirits: Aboriginal Heroes of Our Children. 180p. (Orig.). 1993. student ed, pap. 8.95 (0-919441-50-5, Pub. by Theytus Bks Ltd CN) Orca Bk Pubs.

Mokashi, D. B. Palkhi: An Indian Pilgrimage. Engblom, Philip C. & Zelliot, Eleanor, trs. LC 86-30001. 291p. 1987. 59.50 (0-88706-461-2); pap. 19.95 (0-88706-462-0) State U NY Pr.

Mokashi-Punekar, S. An Epistle to Professor David McCutchion. (Writers Workshop Redbird Ser.). 19p. 1975. 4.80 (0-88253-534-X); pap. text ed. 4.00 (0-88253-533-1) Ind-US Inc.

— The Indo-Anglian Creed. (Writers Workshop Greybird Ser.). 72p. 1975. 14.00 (0-88253-566-8); pap. text ed. 4.80 (0-88253-565-X) Ind-US Inc.

— P. Lal: An Appreciation. (Greybird Ser.). 1975. 4.00 (0-89253-790-6) Ind-US Inc.

— The Pretender. 6.75 (0-89253-702-7); 4.00 (0-89253-703-5) Ind-US Inc.

Mokbel, K. M. MCQs in Applied Basic Sciences: For the Primary FRCS. (C). 1992. pap. text ed. 15.50 (0-7923-8994-8) Kluwer Ac.

— MCQs in Applied Basic Sciences for the FRCS. 2nd ed. 96p. (C). 1994. pap. text ed. 14.50 (0-7923-8856-9) Kluwer Ac.

— MCQs in Clinical Neurology. LC 94-11239. 96p. (C). 1994. pap. text ed. 21.50 (0-7923-8857-7) Kluwer Ac.

— Operative Techniques & Surgical Topics for the FRCS: Viva Practice. 128p. (C). 1995. pap. text ed. 21.00 (0-7923-8881-X) Kluwer Ac.

— SAQs in Clinical Surgery-in-General for the FRCS. LC 92-49742. 96p. (C). 1994. pap. text ed. 15.50 (0-7923-8801-1) Kluwer Ac.

Moke, Susan, jt. auth. see Shermis, Michael.

Moked, Gabriel, ed. The Tel Aviv Review, No. 1. 360p. 1988. pap. 21.95 (0-8223-0873-8) Duke.

— The Tel Aviv Review Three. 450p. 1991. pap. 21.95 (0-8223-1120-8) Duke.

— The Tel Aviv Review Two. 450p. (Orig.). (C). 1989. pap. 21.95 (0-685-74190-7) Duke.

Mokeiev, Mikhail, ed. see Dostoyevsky, Fyodor.

Mokhiber, Russell. Corporate Crime & Violence: Big Business Power & the Abuse of the Public Trust. LC 87-4730. 384p. 1989. pap. 16.00 (0-87156-608-7) Sierra.

Mokhtar, G., ed. UNESCO General History of Africa Vol. II: Ancient of Africa. 1980. pap. 12.00 (0-520-06697-9) U CA Pr.

Mokken, R. J. A Theory & Procedure of Scale Analysis with Applications in Political Research. (Methods & Models in the Social Sciences Ser.). 353p. 1971. text ed. 44.00 (90-279-6882-9) Mouton.

Mokken, Robert J. & Roschar, Frans M. Dutch Parliamentary Election Study, 1971. LC 75-32254. 1975. write for info. (0-89138-118-X) ICPSR.

Mokobodzki, G., jt. ed. see Hirsch, F.

Mokoena, Kenneth, ed. South Africa & the United States: The Declassified History. 344p. 1994. 35.00 (1-56584-081-X) New Press NY.

Mokoena, Kenneth, ed. see National Security Archive Staff & Chadwyck-Healey Staff.

Mokoli, Mondonga. State Against Development: The Experience of Post-1965 Zaire. LC 91-47973. (Contributions in Afro-American & African Studies: No. 150). 168p. 1992. text ed. 47.95 (0-313-28213-7, MKD, Greenwood Pr) Greenwood.

Mokosso, Henry E. My First Pair of Shoes & the Little Altar Boy: Two Childhood Memories. LC 91-33536. 90p. (YA). (gr. 6-12). 1992. 7.95 (0-944957-08-0) Rivercross Pub.

*Mokotoff, Gary. How to Document Victims & Locate Survivors of the Holocaust. (Illus.). 208p. (Orig.). 1995. pap. 25.95 (0-9626373-8-6) Avotaynu.

*Mokotoff, Gary, comp. WOWW Companion: A Guide to the Communities Surrounding Central & Eastern European Towns. (Monograph Ser.). 208p. (Orig.). 1995. text ed. 25.95 (0-9626373-6-X) Avotaynu.

Mokotoff, Gary & Sack, Sallyann A. Where Once We Walked: A Guide to the Jewish Communities Destroyed in the Holocaust. LC 91-70405. (Illus.). xxviii, 544p. 1991. 69.50 (0-9626373-1-9) Avotaynu.

Mokri, M. Kurdish-Arabic Dictionary: Al-Hadiyati 'l-Hamidiyah. (ARA.). 1975. 29.95 (0-86685-126-7) Intl Bk Ctr.

Mokrinskaia, Nina. Moia Zhizn' (My Life) Detstvo v Sibiri, junost' v Shankkhaie 1914-1392 gody. Valk, Gabriel, ed. LC 90-85815. (Illus.). 224p. (Orig.). (RUS.). (J). 1991. pap. 16.00 (0-911971-61-0) Effect Pub.

*Mokros, Hartmut B., ed. Interaction & Identity. (Information & Behavior Ser.: Vol. 5). 448p. (C). 1995. 49.95 (1-56000-191-7) Transaction Pubs.

Mokry, Benjamin W. Entrepreneurship & Public Policy: Can Government Stimulate Business Start-Ups? LC 87-24934. 169p. 1988. text ed. 49.95 (0-89930-239-4, MSV/, Quorum Bks) Greenwood.

Mokrzycki, Edmund, jt. ed. see Bryant, Christopher G.

Moktefi, Mokhtar. The Arabs: In the Golden Age. LaRose, Mary K., tr. LC 92-4989. (People of the Past Ser.). (Illus.). 64p. (J). (gr. 4-6). 1992. lib. bdg. 15.90 (1-56294-201-8) Millbrook Pr.

Mokuau, Noreen, ed. Handbook of Social Services for Asian & Pacific Islanders. LC 91-11339. 272p. 1991. text ed. 55.00 (0-313-26116-4, MKH/, Greenwood Pr) Greenwood.

Mokujiki. Mokujiki: Thirteen Tanka. Pendell, Dale & Tanahaski, Kazuaki, trs. 20p. 1988. 6.00 (1-882623-07-X) Exiled-Am Pr.

Mokwa, Michael P., et al. Marketing the Arts: Praeger Series in Public & Nonprofit Sector Marketing. Permut, Steven E., ed. LC 79-26603. (Praeger Special Studies). 304p. 1980. text ed. 55.00 (0-275-90526-8, C0526, Praeger Pubs) Greenwood.

Mokwa, Michael P. & Permut, Steven E., eds. Government Marketing: Theory & Practice. LC 81-308. (Public & Nonprofit Sector Marketing Ser.). 400p. 1981. text ed. 65.00 (0-275-90685-X, C0685, Praeger Pubs) Greenwood.

Mokwunye, A. Uzo, ed. Alleviating Soil Fertility Constraints to Increase Crop Production in West Africa. (Developments in Plant & Soil Sciences Ser.). 264p. (C). 1991. lib. bdg. 129.00 (0-7923-1221-X) Kluwer Ac.

Mokwunye, A. Uzo, jt. ed. see Gerner, Henry.

Mokwunye, Uzo M. & Vlek, Paul L., eds. Management of Nitrogen & Phosphorus Fertilizers in Sub-Saharan Africa. (Developments in Plant & Soil Sciences Ser.). 1986. lib. bdg. 163.00 (90-247-3312-X) Kluwer Ac.

Mokyr, J. Twenty-Five Centuries of Technological Change: An Historical Survey. Lesourne, J. & Sonnenschein, H., eds. (Fundamentals of Pure & Applied Economics Ser.: 35). viii, 148p. 1990. pap. text ed. 51.00 (3-7186-4936-5) Gordon & Breach.

Mokyr, Joel. The Lever of Riches: Technological Creativity & Economic Progress. 368p. 1992. pap. 13.95 (0-19-507477-7) OUP.

— Why Ireland Starved: A Quantitative & Analytical History of the Irish Economy, 1800-1850. (Illus.). 344p. 1985. pap. text ed. 24.95 (0-04-941014-8) Routledge Chapman & Hall.

Mokyr, Joel, ed. The British Industrial Revolution: An Economic Perspective. LC 92-21167. 362p. (C). 1993. text ed. 58.00 (0-8133-8509-1); pap. text ed. 23.50 (0-8133-8510-5) Westview.

— The Economics of the Industrial Revolution. LC 84-17757. 250p. (C). 1985. text ed. 51.25 (0-86598-148-5); pap. text ed. 19.75 (0-86598-154-X) Rowman.

Mol, Andre. Delicious Dutch Cuisine: Exquisite Recipes of the Restaurant Kaatje Bij de Sluis. 160p. 1993. 35.00 (1-55868-156-6) Gr Arts Ctr Pub.

Mol, Dick, et al. Mammoths. 1993. pap. 5.95 (0-9624750-2-5) L Agenbroad.

Mol, Hans, ed. & intro. Western Religion: A Country by Country Sociological Inquiry. (Religion & Reason Ser.: No. 2). (Illus.). 642p. 1972. text ed. 74.70 (90-279-7004-1) Mouton.

Mol, Hendrick. Fundamentals of Phonetics, Vol. 2: Acoustical Models Generating the Formants of the Vowel Phonemes. LC 70-110954. (Janua Linguarum, Ser. Minor: No. 26). (Illus.). (Orig.). 1970. pap. text ed. 22.00 (90-279-0715-3) Mouton.

Mol, Joseph N. & Van der Krol, Alexander R., eds. Antisense Nucleic Acids & Proteins: Fundamentals & Applications. 248p. 1991. pap. 115.00 (0-8247-8516-9) Dekker.

Molak, V., et al, eds. A Comprehensive Approach to Problems with Oil Spills in Marine Environments: The Alaska Story. (Illus.). 165p. (Orig.). 1992. pap. text ed. 48.00 (0-911131-26-4) Princeton Sci Pubs.

Molan, Chris, illus. The First Easter: Retold by Catherine Storr. (People of the Bible Ser.). 32p. (J). (gr. k-4). 1984. 14.65 (0-8172-1987-0) Raintree Steck-V.

— Heroic Stories. LC 93-45413. (Story Library). 256p. (J). (gr. 5-10). 1994. pap. 6.95 (1-85697-983-0, Kingfisher LKC) LKC.

— Joseph the Dream Teller: Retold by Catererine Storr. (People of the Bible Ser.). 32p. (J). (gr. k-4). 1984. 14.65 (0-8172-1989-7) Raintree Steck-V.

Molan, Chris, teller. The Viking Saga. (Legends & Folktales Ser.). (Illus.). 32p. (J). (gr. k-5). 1985. lib. bdg. 19.97 (0-8172-2503-X) Raintree Steck-V.

Molan, Christine, illus. Miracles by the Sea. LC 82-23022. (People of the Bible Ser.). 32p. (J). (gr. k-4). 1983. 14.65 (0-8172-1983-8) Raintree Steck-V.

Molan, Michael T. Criminal Law. 230p. (C). 1991. 65.00 (1-85352-697-5, Pub. by HLT Pubns UK) St Mut.

Molan, Michael T., ed. Constitutional & Administrative Law. 235p. (C). 1991. 60.00 (1-85352-693-2, Pub. by HLT Pubns UK); 60.00 (1-85352-352-6, Pub. by HLT Pubns UK); pap. 60.00 (1-85352-822-6, Pub. by HLT Pubns UK) St Mut.

— Criminal Law. 230p. (C). 1991. pap. 65.00 (1-85352-833-1, Pub. by HLT Pubns UK) St Mut.

Molana-al-Moazam Hazrat Shah & Maghsoud Sadegh-ibn-Mohammad Angha. Al Rasa'El. 146p. (Orig.). 1986. pap. 19.50 (0-8191-5332-X) U Pr of Amer.

Moland, Louis, ed. see Voltaire, Francois-Marie de.

Molander, Chris & Winterton, Jonathan, eds. Managing Human Resources. LC 94-15560. (Elements of Business Ser.). 208p. 1994. 55.00x (0-415-06853-3, B4619); pap. 19.95 (0-415-06854-1, B0190) Routledge.

Molander, D. W., ed. Diseases of the Lymphatic System: Diagnosis & Therapy. (Illus.). 500p. 1983. 152.00 (0-387-90850-1) Spr-Verlag.

*Molander, Per. Society in War: Planning Perspectives. 141p. (Orig.). (C). 1994. pap. text ed. 40.00x (0-7881-1227-9) Diane Pub.

Molander, Roger & Wilson, Peter A. The Nuclear Asymptote: On Containing Nuclear Proliferation. LC 93-28969. 1993. write for info. (0-8330-1435-8, MR-214-CC) Rand Corp.

Molander, Roger C. & Nichols, Robbie. Who Will Stop the Bomb? A Primer on Nuclear Proliferation. LC 85-10362. 160p. reprint ed. pap. 45.60 (0-7837-5341-1, 2045083) Bks Demand.

*Molarsky, Osmond. A Sky Full of Kites. LC 94-49535. (Illus.). 32p. (J). (gr. k-2). 1995. 12.95 (1-883672-26-0) Tricycle Pr.

Molas-Gallart, Jordi. Military Production & Innovation in Spain. LC 92-30353. 1992. text ed. 68.00 (3-7186-5280-3) Gordon & Breach.

Molas Ribalta, Pere. Manual de Historia de Espana Vol. 3: Edad Moderna (1474-1808) 582p. 1989. 125.00x (84-239-5093-X) Elliots Bks.

Molau, U. Scrophulariaceae, Pt. I: Calceolarieae. (Flora Neotropica Monograph Ser.: No. 47). 326p. 1988. 59.00 (0-685-63142-7) NY Botanical.

*Molberg, Andrea. Conflict Resolution: Making It Work in the Medical Group. 32p. (Orig.). 1993. student ed 165.00 (1-56829-002-0) Med Group Mgmt.

Molcan, Poorman W. Good Thinking: Test-Taking, Problem Solving & Study Skills for Nursing Students. (Illus.). 300p. (C). 1994. pap. text ed. 27.00 (0-9640556-0-0) Stat Nursing.

Molchan, Deborah S. Our Secret Feelings: Activities for Children of Alcoholics in Support Groups. 58p. (Orig.). 1989. pap. 10.95 (1-55691-020-7) Learning Pubns.

Molchan, Peter, jt. auth. see McNally, Clayton L., Jr.

Molchan, Peter, jt. auth. see McNally, Clayton L.

Molchan, Peter, jt. auth. see Sayles, Jonathan S.

Molchanov, A. & Zanadvorov, P. Electrical & Radio Engineering for Physicists. (Illus.). 480p. 1975. 30.00 (0-8464-0360-9) Beekman Pubs.

Molchanov, A. A. The Hydrological Role of Forests. 416p. 1963. text ed. 97.50 (0-7065-0253-1, Pub. by Keter Pub IS) Coronet Bks.

Molchanov, Boris. Antichrist. (Illus.). 28p. (Orig.). 1987. pap. 2.50 (0-912927-24-0, X025) St John Kronstadt.

Molchanov, Ilya S. Limit Theorems for Unions of Random Closed Sets. (Lecture Notes in Mathematics Ser.: Vol. 1561). 1993. 29.00 (0-387-57393-3) Spr-Verlag.

Molchanov, S. A., jt. auth. see Carmona, Rene A.

Molchanov, V., et al. Propedeutics of Children's Diseases. MIR Publishers, tr. (Illus.). 392p. (C). 1975. text ed. 29.00 (0-8464-0768-X) Beekman Pubs.

Molchanov, V. A., jt. auth. see Mashkova, E. S.

Molchanov, V. Y., jt. auth. see Magdich, L. N.

Molchanova, I. V., jt. auth. see Kulikov, N. V.

Moldan, Bedrich & Cerny, Jiri, eds. Biogeochemistry of Small Catchments: A Tool for Environmental Research. LC 93-5685. 465p. 1994. text ed. 125.00 (0-471-93723-1) Wiley.

Moldave, Kivie, jt. ed. see Cohen, Waldo E.

Moldave, Kivie, jt. ed. see Cohn, Waldo E.

Moldave, Kivie, jt. ed. see Wu, Ray.

Moldaw, Carol. Taken from the River: Poems. LC 92-74649. (Series of Poetry & Verse Translation). 48p. (Orig.). 1993. pap. 10.00 (1-882509-00-5) Alef Bks.

Molde, B. Danish-Swedish Dictionary: Dansk-Svensk Ordbok. 3rd ed. 722p. (DAN & SWE.). 1980. 125.00 (0-8288-1675-1, M4577) Fr & Eur.

Moldea. The Hunting of Cain. 1988. mass mkt. 4.50 (0-312-91005-3) St Martin.

Moldea, Dan E. The Hoffa Wars: The Rise & Fall of Jimmy Hoffa. 336p. 1992. 5.99 (1-56171-200-0, S P I Bks) Sure Sellers.

— Interference: How Organized Crime Influences Professional Football. 544p. 1995. pap. 15.95 (1-882605-27-6) Natl Pr Bks.

— The Killing of Robert F. Kennedy: An Investigation of Motive, Means, & Opportunity. (Illus.). 416p. 1995. 27.50 (0-393-03791-6) Norton.

Moldenaers, P. & Keunings, R., eds. Theoretical & Applied Rheology: Proceedings of the XIth International Congress on Rheology, Brussels, Belgium August 17-21, 1992. LC 92-21902. 1992. write for info. (0-444-89007-6) Elsevier.

*Moldenhauer, Esther R. From Grandma's Corner: Do You Really See & Hear the Outdoors? LC 95-07296. (Illus.). (J). 1995. pap. 6.95 (0-9643937-4-3) Rutledge Bks.

Moldenhauer, Hans. The Death of Anton Webern. (Music Reprint Ser.). 118p. 1987. reprint ed. lib. bdg. 18.50 (0-306-76196-3) Da Capo.

Moldenhauer, Hans & Irvine, Demar, comps. Anton Von Webern: Perspectives. LC 77-9523. (Music Reprint Ser.: 1978). (Illus.). 1978. reprint ed. lib. bdg. 32.50 (0-306-77518-2) Da Capo.

Moldenhauer, Janice. Developing Dictionary Skills. 64p. (J). (gr. 3-8). 1979. 8.95 (0-916456-48-X, GA120) Good Apple.

Moldenhauer, Joseph J. & Witherell, Elizabeth H., eds. Cape Cod: The Writings of Henry D. Thoreau. 400p. 1988. 49.50 (0-691-06532-2) Princeton U Pr.

Moldenhauer, Joseph J., ed. see Thoreau, Henry David.

Moldenhauer, W. C. & Hudson, N. W., eds. Conservation Farming on Steep Lands. LC 88-26325. 296p. 1988. text ed. 25.00 (0-935734-19-8) Soil & Water Conserv.

Moldenhauer, W. C., et al, eds. Development of Conservation Farming on Hillslopes. 320p. (C). 1991. 36.00 (0-935734-24-4) Soil & Water Conserv.

Moldenhauer, William C., pref. Soil Conservation Policies: An Assessment. LC 80-406. 154p. (Orig.). 1980. pap. 7.50 (0-935734-04-X) Soil & Water Conserv.

Moldenhawer, Julius. Voice of Books. LC 70-121491. (Essay Index Reprint Ser.). 1977. 19.95 (0-8369-1766-9) Ayer.

Moldenke, Alma L., jt. auth. see Moldenke, Harold N.

Moldenke, Charles E. The Tale of Two Brothers. 60p. 1988. pap. 6.95 (0-933121-16-4) Black Classic.

Moldenke, Harold N. A Fifth Summary of the Verbenaceae, Avicenniaceae, Stilbaceae, Dicrastylidaceae, Simphoremaceae, Nyctanthaceae, & Eriocaulaceae of the World As to Valid Taxa, Geographic Distribution & Synonymy, 2 vols. (Illus.). 974p. 1971. pap. text ed. 25.00 (0-934454-65-5) Lubrecht & Cramer.

Moldenke, Harold N. & Moldenke, Alma L. Plants of the Bible. 384p. 1986. reprint ed. pap. 9.95 (0-486-25069-5) Dover.

Moldeven, Meyer. Military-Civilian Teamwork in Suicide Prevention: Armed Forces Strategies, Procedures & Responsibilities to Implement Their Policy That Suicide Prevention Is Everybody's Business. LC 88-90534. 272p. 1994. pap. 10.95 (0-9615092-7-9) M Moldeven.

Moldovan, Dan I. Modern Parallel Processing. (Series in Supercomputing & Artificial Intelligence). (Illus.). 512p. 1992. text ed. write for info. (0-07-042656-2) McGraw.

— Parallel Processing from Applications to Systems. LC 92-44256. 567p. 1993. 64.95 (1-55860-254-2) Morgan Kaufmann.

Moldow, D. Gay & Martinson, Ida M. Home Care for Seriously Ill Children: A Manual for Parents. 2nd ed. 92p. 1984. reprint ed. pap. 9.45 (0-932321-00-3) Child Hospice VA.

Moldow, Gloria. Women Doctors in Gilded-Age Washington: Race, Gender, & Professionalization. LC 86-19251. (Women in American History Ser.). (Illus.). 262p. 1987. 27.50 (0-252-01379-4) U of Ill Pr.

Moldowan, J. M., jt. auth. see Yen, T. F.

Moldowan, J. Michael, jt. auth. see Peters, Kenneth E.

Moldowan, John J., et al. Biological Markers in Sediments & Petroleum. 384p. 1991. text ed. 89.00 (0-13-083742-3) P-H.

Moldvay, Albert & Fabian, Erika. The Ph.D. Guide for Travel Photographers: Professional Techniques - The National Geography Way. (Illus.). 104p. (Orig.). 1995. pap. text ed. 12.95 (0-9638417-2-6) Eriako Assocs. All the essentials of how to take successful travel pictures are in this handy, portable volume. Written by two experts, Albert Moldvay, former staff photographer & Chief of Film Review for the National Geographic Magazine, & Erika Fabian, writer/photographer of photo-illustrated articles & books, this volume is a distillation of a lifetime of practical techniques developed by the authors on countless National Geographic & other assignments around the world. Informative, instructive & entertaining, the book covers the cameras, lenses, flash, & photographic techniques required for all the situations one may encounter on a trip. In addition to the practical applications, the art & aesthetics of photography are discussed, empowering the user with a new way to see & shoot. The text is profusely illustrated with cartoons, charts, & "photo bytes." It also includes a Glossary for reference & extra information. For the accomplished photographer, THE PH.D. GUIDE will provide some new, simplified applications to complex situations in the field. For the amateur, this book is all he or she will need to become both knowledgeable & proficient in travel photography. To order: Eriako Associates, 1380 Morningside Way, Venice, CA 90291, 310-392-9019.** ***Publisher Provided Annotation.

Mole. HE: Acupuncture. 1992. pap. 9.95 (1-85230-319-0) Element MA.

— When in Rome... A Business Guide to Cultures & Customs in 12 European Nations. 200p. 1991. pap. 16.95 (0-8144-7769-0, 040540) AMACOM.

— The Wrongful Dismissal Handbook. 216p. 1990. pap. 36.00 (0-409-88842-7) Butterworth Legal Pubs.

Mole, Annie. What Foods Feed Us & How to Cook Them, with Recipes. 1974. lib. bdg. 69.95 (0-685-51381-5) Revisionist Pr.

Mole, Elsie H. A Christmas Tree from Puddin' Stone Hill. (Illus.). 36p. (J). (ps-8). 1985. 6.95 (0-920806-74-0, Pub. by Penumbra Pr CN) U of Toronto Pr.

Mole, Gary D., tr. see Levinas, Emmanuel.

Mole, S., jt. auth. see Waterman, P.

Mole, Veronica & Elliot, Dave. Enterprising Innovation: Technology for People. 220p. 1992. 47.50 (0-86187-577-X, Pub. by Pinter Pubs UK) St Martin.

Moleah, Alfred T. Namibia: The Struggle for Liberation. 341p. (Orig.). 1983. 22.95 (0-913255-00-9); pap. 12.95 (0-913255-01-7) Disa Press Inc.

— South Africa: Colonialism, Apartheid & African Dispossession. 550p. (Orig.). 1993. 45.00 (0-913255-02-5); text ed. 45.00 (0-685-67439-8); lib. bdg. 45.00 (0-685-67438-X); pap. 35.00 (0-913255-03-3); pap. text ed. 35.00 (0-685-67441-X) Disa Press Inc.

Moleas, Wendy. The Development of the Greek Language. (Studies in Modern Greek). 118p. (Orig.). (C). 1989. lib. bdg. 25.00 (0-89241-485-5); pap. text ed. 16.00 (0-89241-486-3) Caratzas.

Moleck, Fred, et al. Liturgy: Active Participation in the Divine Life. 120p. 1990. 4.95 (0-8146-1967-3) Liturgical Pr.

Molema, Jan. Jan Duiker. (Illus.). 200p. (ENG & SPA.). 1992. pap. 18.95 (84-252-1520-X) Rizzoli Intl.

Molen. Take Two & Hit to Right. 1976. 19.95 (0-8488-1575-0) Amereon Ltd.

An Asterisk (*) at the beginning of an entry indicates that the title is appearing in BIP for the first time.

***Molen, Ron.** Soiled Judgement. 300p. 1995. pap. 9.95 (*0-7610-0040-2*) NW Pub.

Molen, Thor. Thought Splinters: Fiction Today, Reality Tomorrow. (Illus.). 96p. 1994. 25.95 (*0-8059-3525-8*) Dorrance.

Molenaar, Dee. The Challenge of Rainier. LC 79-14923. (Illus.). 1979. pap. 14.95 (*0-916890-70-8*) Mountaineers.

Molenaar, Ivo W., jt. ed. see Fischer, Gerhard H.

Molenda, Michael, ed. Making the Ultimate Demo. 136p. (Orig.). 1994. pap. 17.95 (*0-7935-2770-8*, 00330071) H Leonard.

Moler, Cleve B., jt. auth. see Forsythe, George E.

Moler, Cleve B., ed. see Hill, David R.

Moler, Kenneth L. Jane Austen's Art of Allusion. LC 68-12704. 240p. reprint ed. pap. 68.40 (*0-7837-1470-X*, 2057165) Bks Demand.

— Pride & Prejudice: A Study in Artistic Economy. (Twayne's Masterwork Studies: No. 21). 144p. 1988. text ed. 21.95 (*0-8057-7983-3*, Twayne); pap. 12.95 (*0-8057-8032-7*, Twayne) Macmillan.

Moler, Paul E. & Ashton, Ray E., Jr., eds. Rare & Endangered Biota of Florida Vol. 3: Amphibians & Reptiles. (Illus.). 272p. 1992. lib. bdg. 49.95 (*0-8130-1141-8*) U Press Fla.

— Rare & Endangered Biota of Florida Vol. 3: Amphibians & Reptiles, Vol. 3. (Illus.). 272p. 1992. pap. 23.95 (*0-8130-1142-6*) U Press Fla.

Molera, Antonio M. Diccionario Anadaluz, 4 vols. 2000p. (SPA.). 1980. 175.00 (*0-7859-3708-0*, 8430027696) Fr & Eur.

— Diccionario Anadaluz, Vol. 1. 500p. 1980. 45.00 (*0-7859-6460-6*) Fr & Eur.

— Diccionario Andaluz, Vol. 2. 500p. (SPA.). 1980. 45.00 (*0-7859-5880-0*, 8430027718) Fr & Eur.

— Diccionario Andaluz, Vol. 3. 500p. (SPA.). 1980. 45.00 (*0-7859-5881-9*, 8430027726) Fr & Eur.

— Diccionario Andaluz, Vol. 4. 500p. (SPA.). 1980. 45.00 (*0-7859-5882-7*, 8430027734) Fr & Eur.

Molerus, O. Principles of Flow in Diperse Systems. LC 92-36080. 299p. 1993. 109.00 (*0-412-40630-6*) Chapman & Hall.

Moles, ed. see Plutarch.

Moles, Alistair. Nietzsche's Philosophy of Nature & Cosmology. (American University Studies: Philosophy: Ser. V, Vol. 80). 435p. (C). 1989. text ed. 35.95 (*0-8204-0970-7*) P Lang Pubs.

Moles, E. & Peacock, N. A. The Seventeenth Century: Directions Old & New. 144p. 1993. 49.00 (*0-85261-344-X*, Pub. by Univ of Glasgow UK) St Mut.

***Moles, Marci.** Loving Joseph Smith Out of Hell. LC 94-96578. 188p. 1994. pap. write for info. (*1-886389-02-0*) Inside Job.

Moles, Oliver C. Student Discipline Strategies: Research & Practice. LC 89-4578. (Educational Leadership Ser.). 331p. 1990. 59.50 (*0-7914-0192-8*); pap. 19.95 (*0-7914-0193-6*) State U NY Pr.

Moles, Randall C. Ending Head & Neck Pain: The TMJ Connection. (Illus.). 200p. (Orig.). 1989. pap. 12.95 (*0-925004-02-2*) CGM WI.

Moles, Robert N., ed. see Assn for Legal & Social Philosophy Staff.

Moleski, Joanne E. Mirrors of Fate: A Journey into Past Lives. (Illus.). 158p. (Orig.). 1988. pap. 9.95 (*1-882053-00-1*) Tamaris Pub Hse.

Molesworth, Candy T., jt. auth. see Molesworth, J. T.

Molesworth, Carl. Sharks over China: The 23rd Fighter Group in World War II. (World War II Commemorative Ser.). (Illus.). 252p. 1995. 23.95 (*0-02-881094-5*) Brasseys Inc.

Molesworth, Charles. Common Elegies. (Illus.). 1977. per. 2.50 (*0-912284-85-4*) New Rivers Pr.

— Donald Barthelme's Fiction: The Ironist Saved from Drowning. LC 81-69833. (Literary Frontiers Editions Ser.). 96p. 1982. pap. text ed. 9.95 (*0-8262-0338-8*) U of Mo Pr.

— The Fierce Embrace: A Study of Contemporary American Poetry. LC 79-1561. 224p. 1979. text ed. 27.50 (*0-8262-0278-0*); pap. text ed. 15.00 (*0-8262-0283-7*) U of Mo Pr.

— Gary Snyder's Vision: Poetry & the Real Work. LC 83-6993. (Literary Frontiers Ser.). 136p. 1983. pap. 10.95 (*0-8262-0414-7*) U of Mo Pr.

— Marianne Moore: A Literary Life. 472p. 1991. reprint ed. pap. text ed. 16.95 (*1-55553-115-6*) NE U Pr.

— Words to That Effect. LC 81-13587. 64p. 1981. pap. 5.75 (*0-913282-23-5*) Seven Woods Pr.

Molesworth, J. T. English-Marathi Dictionary. 864p. (ENG & MAR.). 1981. 75.00 (*0-8288-1152-0*, M14469) Fr & Eur.

— English-Marathi Dictionary. 2nd ed. (ENG & MAR.). 1990. 45.00 (*0-7859-8958-7*) Fr & Eur.

— English-Marathi Dictionary. 2nd ed. 974p. 1990. 45.00 (*81-206-0089-4*) IBD Ltd.

— Marathi & English Dictionary. 952p. 1989. 95.00 (*0-8288-8470-6*, F27270) Fr & Eur.

Molesworth, J. T. & Molesworth, Candy T. Marathi English Dictionary. 1986. reprint ed. 50.00 (*0-8364-1702-X*, Pub. by Popular Prakashan II) S Asia.

Molesworth, Ralph. Introduction to Assembly Language for the TI Home Computer. Davis, Steve, ed. 140p. 16.95 (*0-317-13069-2*) P-H.

Molesworth, William, ed. Thomas Hobbes Collected Works, 12 vols., Set. 5423p. 1993. 895.00 (*0-415-08811-9*, B0740, Pub. by Thoemmes Pr UK) Routledge.

Molesworth, William N. The History of the Reform Bill of 1832. LC 68-30533. xii, 354p. 1972. reprint ed. lib. bdg. 45.00 (*0-678-00893-0*) Kelley.

Moleta, Vincent. From Francis to Giotto. 1983. 25.00 (*0-8199-0853-3*, Frncscn Herld) Franciscan Pr.

Molette, Barbara, jt. auth. see Molette, Carlton.

Molette, Barbara J., jt. auth. see Molette, Carlton W.

Molette, Carlton & Molette, Barbara. Rosalee Pritchett. 1972. pap. 2.75 (*0-8222-0968-3*) Dramatists Play.

Molette, Carlton W. & Molette, Barbara J. Black Theatre: Premise & Presentation. rev. ed. LC 86-50584. 266p. (C). 1992. pap. text ed. 19.95 (*0-932269-94-X*) Wyndhall Pr.

— Black Theatre: Premise & Presentation. 2nd rev. ed. LC 86-50584. 266p. (C). 1992. text ed. 29.95 (*1-55605-212-X*) Wyndhall Pr.

Moley, J. F. Molecular Genetics in Surgical Oncology. (Medical Intelligence Unit Ser.). 115p. 1994. 89.95 (*1-879702-18-5*) R G Landes.

Moley, Raymond. After Seven Years. LC 71-168390. (FDR & the Era of the New Deal Ser.). 446p. 1972. reprint ed. lib. bdg. 55.00 (*0-306-70327-0*) Da Capo.

— Daniel O'Connell: Nationalism Without Violence. LC 73-93142. xxiv, 246p. 1974. 30.00 (*0-8232-0977-6*) Fordham.

— The Hays Office. LC 73-160241. (Moving Pictures Ser.). 266p. 1971. reprint ed. lib. bdg. 29.95 (*0-89198-042-3*) Ozer.

— Our Criminal Courts. LC 74-3835. (Criminal Justice in America Ser.). 1974. reprint ed. 25.95 (*0-405-06181-1*) Ayer.

— Politics & Criminal Prosecution. LC 73-19161. (Politics & People Ser.). 256p. 1974. reprint ed. 20.95 (*0-405-05883-7*) Ayer.

— Twenty-Seven Masters of Politics, in a Personal Perspective. (History - United States Ser.). 276p. 1993. reprint ed. lib. bdg. 79.00 (*0-7812-4812-4*) Rprt Serv.

Molfese, Dennis L. & Segalowitz, Sidney J., eds. Brain Lateralization in Children: Developmental Implications. LC 88-11269. 612p. 1988. lib. bdg. 65.00 (*0-89862-719-2*) Guilford Pr.

Molfese, Victoria J. Perinatal Risk & Infant Development: Assessment & Prediction. LC 88-24326. 199p. 1989. lib. bdg. 35.00 (*0-89862-728-1*) Guilford Pr.

Molgaard, Craig, ed. Neuroepidemiology: Theory & Method. (Illus.). 381p. 1993. text ed. 55.00 (*0-12-504220-5*) Acad Pr.

Molgaard, J. & Waldschmidt, K., eds. Microarchitectures, Developments & Applications. 694p. 1986. 120.50 (*0-444-70096-X*, North Holland) Elsevier.

Molgaard, J., jt. ed. see Schumny, H.

Molgaard, jt. auth. see Burgess.

Molgard, Bette. Best Baptism Ever: Jake's Story. 1993. pap. 4.95 (*0-88494-880-3*) Bookcraft Inc.

— The Best Baptism Ever: Jenny's Story. 1993. pap. 4.95 (*0-88494-868-4*) Bookcraft Inc.

Molgard, Max. Inviting the Spirit into Our Lives. 1993. pap. 6.95 (*0-88494-871-4*) Bookcraft Inc.

Molgard, Max, jt. auth. see Burgess, Allan.

Molgard, Max H., jt. auth. see Burgess, Allan K.

Molhan, Sue, jt. auth. see Kavanagh, Jack.

Molho. Semantique et Poetique. (Coll. Ducros, Ser.). 9.95 (*0-685-36656-1*) Fr & Eur.

Molho, Anthony. Florentine Public Finances in the Early Renaissance, 1400-1433. LC 70-168431. (Historical Monographs: No. 65). 224p. 1971. 20.00 (*0-674-30665-1*) HUP.

— Marriage Alliance in Late Medieval Florence. LC 93-8470. (Harvard Historical Studies: Vol. No. 117). 478p. 1994. text ed. 59.00 (*0-674-55070-6*) HUP.

Molho, Anthony, et al, eds. City-States in Classical Antiquity & Medieval Italy. (Illus.). 500p. 1992. text ed. 62.50 (*0-472-10286-9*) U of Mich Pr.

Molho, Emanuel. The Dictionary Catalogue. LC 80-67876. 250p. 1988. 14.95 (*0-8288-0150-9*) Fr & Eur.

Molho, M., ed. see Molho, Maurice.

Molho, Maurice. Romans Picaresques Espagnols. Molho, M., ed. 1120p. (FRE.). 1968. lib. bdg. 95.00 (*0-7859-3786-2*, 2070104842) Fr & Eur.

***Molholm, Kurt, et al, eds.** Government Information & Policy: Changing Roles in a New Administration. (1994 NFAIS Report Ser.). 125p. (Orig.). 1994. pap. 60.00 (*0-942308-44-1*) NFAIS.

Molholt, Pat, jt. ed. see Petersen, Toni.

Molier. The Misanthrope. Wilbur, Richard, tr. 1965. pap. 4.75 (*0-8222-1389-3*) Dramatists Play.

Moliere. L' Amour Medecin. 128p. (FRE.). 1992. reprint ed. pap. 8.95 (*0-685-73252-5*) Fr & Eur.

— Amphitryon. Wilbur, Richard, tr. 1995. pap. 4.75 (*0-8222-1439-3*) Dramatists Play.

— Amphitryon. (FRE.). 1973. 7.95 (*0-8288-9933-9*, F39870) Fr & Eur.

— Amphitryon: George Dandin. L'Avare. (Folio Ser.: No. 333). (FRE.). 1973. pap. 9.95 (*2-07-036333-3*) Schoenhof.

— Amphitryon; George Dandin; L'Avare. (FRE.). 1973. pap. 12.95 (*0-7859-2873-1*) Fr & Eur.

— Amphytrion. Mandel, Oscar, tr. LC 76-41934. (Illus.). 1977. 7.50 (*0-914502-03-4*) Spectrum Prods.

— L' Avare. (FRE.). 1986. pap. 10.95 (*0-7859-3130-9*) Fr & Eur.

Moliere, pseud. L' Avare. 1966. pap. 2.95 (*0-685-11020-6*) Fr & Eur.

— L' Avare. 210p. 1969. write for info. (*0-7859-5278-0*) Fr & Eur.

Moliere. Le Bourgeois Gentilhomme. Thoraval, Jean, ed. 64p. (FRE.). 1975. 7.95 (*0-7859-0050-0*, FC1413) Fr & Eur.

— Bourgeois Gentilhomme. Les Femmes Savantes. Le Malade Imaginaire. (Folio Ser.: No. 334). 448p. (FRE.). 1973. pap. 10.95 (*2-07-036334-1*) Schoenhof.

— Le Bourgeois Gentilhomme. Les Femmes Savantes. Le Malade Imaginaire. (FRE.). 1973. pap. 12.95 (*0-7859-2874-X*, 2070363341) Fr & Eur.

— La Critique de l'Ecole des Femmes. (FRE.). 1985. pap. 8.95 (*0-7859-4648-9*) Fr & Eur.

— The Doctor in Spite of Himself & the Bourgeois Gentleman. Bermel, Albert, tr. (Actor's Moliere Ser.: Vol. 2). 128p. (Orig.). 1987. pap. 6.95 (*0-936839-77-5*) Applause Theatre Bk Pubs.

Moliere, pseud. Dom Juan. (Class. Ill. Hachette Ser.). (FRE.). pap. 7.95 (*0-8288-9936-3*, F39936) Fr & Eur.

Moliere. Don Juan. 1973. pap. 4.75 (*0-8222-0323-5*) Dramatists Play.

— Don Juan & Other Plays. Maclean, Ian, ed. & tr. by. Gravely, George, tr. (World's Classics Ser.). 416p. 1989. pap. 6.95 (*0-19-282130-X*) OUP.

— L' Ecole des Femmes. (FRE.). 1986. pap. 10.95 (*0-7859-3131-7*) Fr & Eur.

Moliere, pseud. Ecole des Femmes. (Coll. Class. du Theatre). (FRE.). 1964. pap. 7.95 (*0-8288-9937-1*, F39942) Fr & Eur.

Moliere. L' Ecole des Femmes; L'Ecole des Maris; La Critique de l'Ecole des Femmes. (FRE.). 1985. pap. 16.95 (*0-7859-2911-8*) Fr & Eur.

— Ecole des Maris. L'Ecole des Femmes. La Critique de l'Ecole des Femmes. L'Impromptu de Versailles. (Folio Ser.: No. 1688). (FRE.). 1985. pap. 12.95 (*2-07-037688-5*) Schoenhof.

— Eight Plays by Moliere. 25.95 (*0-88411-448-1*, Aeonian Pr) Amereon Ltd.

— Les Facheux. Bd. with Facheux de Georges Braque. (Coll. Le Theatre et les Peintres). 595.00 (*0-685-34235-2*) Fr & Eur.

— Les Femmes Savantes. Williamson, Richard, ed. Wilbur, Richard, tr. (Hippocrene Mastering Language Through Literature Ser.). 150p. 1995. 11.95 (*0-7818-0398-5*) Hippocrene Bks.

Moliere, pseud. Les Femmes Savantes. (ENG & FRE.). pap. 7.95 (*0-8288-9938-X*, F39956) Fr & Eur.

— Les Fourberies de Scapin. (Illus.). (FRE.). 1965. pap. 7.95 (*0-8288-9939-8*, F39974) Fr & Eur.

— Les Fourberies de Scapin; L'Amour Medicin; Le Medicin Malgre Lui. (FRE.). 1978. pap. 12.95 (*0-7859-3389-1*) Fr & Eur.

Moliere. George Dandin. Bd. with Grand Divertissement Royal de Versailles. (Coll. Petits Class. Bordas). (FRE.). Set pap. 7.95 (*0-8288-9940-1*, F39980) Fr & Eur.

— George Dandin; Amphitryon. 1987. pap. 10.95 (*0-7859-3140-6*, 2253042862) Fr & Eur.

— The Imaginary Cuckold. Wilbur, Richard, tr. 1993. 4.75 (*0-8222-1331-1*) Dramatists Play.

— Les Incompatibles: Montpellier, Sixteen Fifty-Five. 32p. (FRE.). 1969. pap. 19.95 (*0-7859-5386-8*) Fr & Eur.

— La Jalousie du Barbouille. 5.95 (*0-686-54770-5*) Fr & Eur.

— Joguenet ou les Viellards Dupes: Geneve, 1868. 150p. 1968. 24.00 (*0-686-54771-3*) Fr & Eur.

— Kiltartan Moliere. Gregory, Augusta, tr. LC 70-175879. 1972. reprint ed. 15.95 (*0-405-08793-4*, Pub. by Blom Pubns UK) Ayer.

Moliere, pseud. The Learned Ladies. Wilbur, Richard, tr. 1977. pap. 4.75 (*0-8222-0648-X*) Dramatists Play.

— Le Malade Imaginaire. (Coll. Class. du Theatre). (Illus.). (FRE.). 1964. pap. 7.95 (*0-8288-9941-X*, F39998) Fr & Eur.

Moliere. Le Medecin Malgre Lui. Bd. with Medecin Volant. (Univers des Lettres Bordas Ser.). (FRE.). 1964. Set pap. 7.95 (*0-8288-9942-8*, F10008) Fr & Eur.

— Le Misanthrope. Two cassettes plus text. audio 49.95 (*0-685-21217-3*) Fr & Eur.

— The Misanthrope. (Thrift Editions Ser.). 64p. 1992. reprint ed. pap. 1.00 (*0-486-27065-3*) Dover.

Moliere, pseud. Le Misanthrope. (ENG & FRE.). pap. 7.95 (*0-685-34239-5*) Fr & Eur.

— Le Misanthrope. (Coll. Class. du Theatre). (Illus.). (FRE.). 1965. pap. 7.95 (*0-8288-9943-6*, F40016) Fr & Eur.

— The Misanthrope. Wall, Charles H., tr. LC 93-16948. 1993. pap. 6.00 (*0-88734-267-1*) Players Pr.

Moliere. The Misanthrope & Other Plays. 1989. pap. 3.50 (*0-451-51721-0*) NAL-Dutton.

Moliere, pseud. Misanthrope & Other Plays. Frame, Donald M., tr. (Orig.). 1968. pap. 5.95 (*0-451-52415-2*, CE1721, Sig Classics) NAL-Dutton.

Moliere. The Misanthrope & Tartuffe. Wilbur, Richard, ed. Bd. with Tartuffe. LC 65-29707. LC 65-29707. (Illus.). 326p. 1965. Set pap. 9.95 (*0-15-660517-1*, Harvest Bks) HarBrace.

— The Miser. 1993. 4.75 (*0-8222-1341-9*) Dramatists Play.

— The Miser. 1942. 5.00 (*0-87129-454-0*, M28) Dramatic Pub.

— The Miser & George Dandin: Two Plays. Bermel, Albert, tr. (Actor's Moliere Ser.: Vol. 1). 176p. (Orig.). 1987. pap. 6.95 (*0-936839-75-9*) Applause Theatre Bk Pubs.

— Miser & Other Plays. Wood, John, tr. Incl. Would-Be Gentleman. 1953. (*0-318-55056-3*); That Scoundrel Scapin. 1953. (*0-318-55057-1*); Don Juan. 1953. (*0-318-55058-X*); Love's the Best Doctor. 1953. (*0-318-55059-8*); (Classics Ser.). (Orig.). (YA). (gr. 9 up). 1953. Set mass mkt. 7.95 (*0-14-044036-4*, Penguin Classics) Viking Penguin.

Moliere, pseud. Moliere: Don Juan. Howarth, W., ed. (Bristol French Texts Ser.). 142p. (FRE.). 1992. reprint ed. 11.95 (*0-631-00580-3*, Pub. by Brstl Class Pr UK) Focus Info Gr.

— Moliere: Le Misanthrope. Rudler, G., ed. (Bristol French Texts Ser.). 192p. (FRE.). 1992. reprint ed. 12.95 (*0-631-00520-X*, Pub. by Brstl Class Pr UK) Focus Info Gr.

Moliere. Oeuvres Completes, 11 tomes, Set. Meyer, ed. (Illus.). 850.00 (*0-685-34234-4*) Fr & Eur.

— Oeuvres Completes, Vol. 1. deluxe ed. Couton, Georges, ed. 1488p. (FRE.). 1972. 115.00 (*0-7859-3765-X*, 2070103609) Fr & Eur.

— Oeuvres Completes, 2 tomes, Vol. 2. deluxe ed. Courton, ed. (Pleiade Ser.). (FRE.). 1933. 72.95 (*2-07-010361-7*) Schoenhof.

Moliere, pseud. Oeuvres Completes, Vol. 2. Couton, Georges, ed. 1584p. (FRE.). 1988. lib. bdg. 110.00 (*0-7859-3766-8*, 2070103617) Fr & Eur.

Moliere. One-Act Comedies of Moliere: Seven Plays. Bermel, Albert, tr. & intro. by. 192p. 1991. reprint ed. pap. 8.95 (*1-55783-109-2*) Applause Theatre Bk Pubs.

Moliere, pseud. Precieuses Ridicules. (FRE.). 1965. pap. 7.95 (*0-8288-9944-4*, F40042) Fr & Eur.

Moliere. Scapin & Don Juan. Bermel, Albert, tr. & adapt. by. (Actor's Moliere Ser.: Vol. 3). 1987. pap. 6.95 (*0-936839-80-5*) Applause Theatre Bk Pubs.

— School for Husbands. (Illus.). 43p. 1966. pap. 10.00 (*0-88680-170-2*); pap. 2.00 (*0-88680-169-9*) I E Clark.

— The School for Husbands. Wilbur, Richard, tr. 1991. pap. 4.75 (*0-8222-0998-5*) Dramatists Play.

— The School for Wives. Wilbur, Richard, tr. 1991. pap. 4.75 (*0-8222-0999-3*) Dramatists Play.

Moliere, pseud. The School for Wives. Wilbur, Richard, ed. LC 70-153693. 1972. reprint ed. pap. 6.95 (*0-15-679501-9*, HB228, Harvest Bks) HarBrace.

— School for Wives: An Adaptation in Rhymed Verse. Steel, Eric M., tr. LC 75-154426. 1977. pap. 4.95 (*0-8120-0436-1*) Barron.

— Le Tartuffe. (ENG & FRE.). 1992. pap. 10.95 (*0-7859-3240-2*, 2266043218) Fr & Eur.

— Tartuffe. Block, Haskell M., ed. & tr. by. (Crofts Classics Ser.). 96p. 1958. pap. text ed. write for info. (*0-88295-059-2*) Harlan Davidson.

— Tartuffe. Wilbur, Richard, tr. LC 63-17778. 164p. 1968. reprint ed. pap. 5.95 (*0-15-688180-2*, Harvest Bks) HarBrace.

— Tartuffe & Other Plays: Ridiculous Precieuses, School for Husbands, School for Wives, Critique for the School for Wives, Versailles Impromptu, Don Juan. Frame, Donald M., tr. 1960. pap. 3.50 (*0-451-52011-4*, CE1566, Sig Classics) NAL-Dutton.

Moliere. Tartuffe. Dom Juan. Le Misanthrope. (Folio Ser.: No. 332). (FRE.). pap. 9.95 (*2-07-036332-5*) Schoenhof.

— Le Tartuffe; Don Juan; Le Misanthrope. (FRE.). 1973. pap. 11.95 (*0-7859-2872-3*) Fr & Eur.

— Le Tartuffe ou L'Imposteur. Martin, Daniel R., ed. (Illus.). 141p. 1989. 10.95 (*1-878417-21-5*) Hestia Pr.

— The Trickeries of Scapin. Yalman, Tunc, tr. 1989. pap. 4.75 (*0-8222-1173-4*) Dramatists Play.

Molin, Donald H. Actor's Encyclopedia of Dialects. 2nd rev. ed. (Illus.). 256p. 1991. pap. 16.95 (*0-9628545-0-6*) Bragi Pr.

Molin, Paulette, jt. auth. see Hirschfelder, Arlene.

Molin, S. E. & Goodefellowe, R. Dion Boucicault, the Shaughraun, Pt. 2: Up & down in Paris & London. 1982. pap. 3.95 (*0-912262-78-8*) Proscenium.

— Dion Boucicault, the Shaughraun, Pt. 3: Three Early Plays. 1985. pap. 4.95 (*0-912262-85-0*) Proscenium.

— Dion Boucicault, the Shaughraun, Pt. 4: Three Early Potboilers. 1989. pap. 4.95 (*0-912262-89-3*) Proscenium.

— Dion Boucicault, the Shaughraun, Pt. 5: The American Debut. 1991. pap. 4.95 (*0-912262-90-7*) Proscenium.

Molin, Yu N. Spin Polarizarion & Magnetic Effects in Radical Reactions. (Studies in Physical & Theoretical Chemistry: Vol. 22). 1984. 128.25 (*0-444-99677-X*) Elsevier.

Molina, A., et al, eds. Rehabilitation Medicine: Proceedings of the Sixth International Rehabilitation Medicine Association Congress, Madrid, 17-22 June, 1990. (International Congress Ser.: No. 928). 312p. 1991. 100.00 (*0-444-81133-8*, Excerpta Medica) Elsevier.

Molina, Alfonso H. The Social Basis of the Microelectronics Revolution. 176p. 1989. 30.00 (*0-85224-594-7*, Pub. by Edinburgh U Pr UK) Col U Pr.

— The Social Basis of the Microelectronics Revolution. 1990. pap. text ed. 15.00 (*0-85224-605-6*, Pub. by Edinburgh U Pr UK) Col U Pr.

Molina Aranda, Fernando. Diccionario Tecnico Hostelero. 245p. (SPA.). 1972. pap. 19.95 (*0-8288-6365-2*, S-50021) Fr & Eur.

Molina, Armando M. Almuerzo Entre Dioses y Otros Relatos. Solaris Staff, ed. Borja, Lalo, tr. 110p. (SPA.). 1989. write for info. (*0-318-65310-9*) Ed Solaris.

— El Amanecer de los Tontos. Solaris Staff, ed. Borja, Lalo, tr. 220p. (SPA.). 1989. write for info. (*0-318-65311-7*) Ed Solaris.

Molina, Bruce. Alaska's Glaciers. (Alaska Geographic Ser.: Vol. 9, No. 1). (Illus.). 144p. 1993. lib. bdg. 26.95 (*1-56661-017-6*); pap. 19.95 (*1-56661-016-8*) Alaska Geog Soc.

***Molina, Carlos W. & Aguirre-Molina, Marilyn, eds. Latino Health in the U. S.: A Growing Challenge. 513p. 1994. pap. 42.50 (*0-87553-215-2*) Am Pub Health.**

Although Latinos are the fastest growing ethnic/racial population in the U. S. & are projected to be the largest by the turn of the century, little has been published until now about the health status of this important segment of the population. This text fills an information void, written for Latinos & for those with an investment in the health & well-being of Latinos. The book reflects the research, knowledge, & expertise of nationally recognized Latino researchers, scholars, educators, & activists. Public health workers, social workers, professors, & others will find this an indispensable reference. Sections of the book address a profile of

An Asterisk (*) at the beginning of an entry indicates that the title is appearing in BIP for the first time.

Latinos; Latinos in the health care system; life cycle & family health; patterns of chronic disease; occupational health; & alcohol, drug, & mental health issues among Latinos. Nonmembers: $42.50 APHA Members $29.75. ***Publisher Provided Annotation.***

Molina, Cesar A., tr. see Dieste, Rafael.

***Molina, David.** Graphing Power High School Activities for the TI-81 & TI-82. Aguirre, Alma, ed. (Illus.). 208p. 1994. pap. 19.95 (*0-86651-827-4*) Seymour Pubns.

Molina, E. C. Poisson's Exponential Binomial Limit. 56p. 1973. reprint ed. pap. 9.50 (*0-88275-107-7*) Krieger.

Molina, Felipe S., ed. Coyote Songs - Wo'i Bwikam: Songs from the Yaqui Bow Leaders' Society. Miller, Cynthia, tr. & illus. by. LC 89-680. 44p. (Orig.). (C). 1989. Hand-printed on homemade paper. 200.00 (*0-925904-01-5*) Chax Pr.

— Coyote Songs - Wo'i Bwikam: Songs from the Yaqui Bow Leaders' Society. Evers, Larry & Molina, Felipe S., trs. LC 89-680. (Illus.). 44p. (Orig.). (C). 1989. pap. 8.00 (*0-925904-02-3*) Chax Pr.

Molina, Felipe S., jt. auth. see Evers, Larry.

Molina, Felipe S., tr. see Molina, Felipe S., ed.

Molina, Fidel. Consejos a la Familia: Advice for the Family. (SPA.). 3.95 (*84-7645-384-1*, 223495, Pub. by Edit Clie SP) TSELF.

Molina, Janet. Helping Our Peers Effectively: A Skills Development Manual. 220p. 1992. pap. text ed. 19.95 (*0-9634612-0-6*) Metamorphic.

Molina, Juan I. Geographical, Natural & Civil History of Chili, 2 Vols, Set. LC 76-172738. reprint ed. 115.00 (*0-404-04354-2*) AMS Pr.

***Molina, Louis & DeBenedictis, Michel.** Picture Yourself: A Casebook for Reading & Writing. 224p. (C). 1994. per., pap. text ed. 25.95 (*0-8403-9613-9*) Kendall-Hunt.

Molina, Miguel E. Inscriptiones Corinthi - Index Erborum in Inscriptiones Corinthi et Coloniarum. (Alpha-Omega, Reihe A Ser.: Bd. CXVII). xii, 173p. (GER.). 1990. write for info. (*3-487-09364-2*, Pub. by Georg Olms GW) Lubrecht & Cramer.

— Inscriptiones Megarae: Index Verborum in Inscriptiones Megarae et Coloniarum. (Alpha-Omega, Reihe A Ser.: Bd. CXXI). xiii, 398p. (GER.). 1991. write for info. (*3-487-09401-0*, Pub. by Georg Olms GW) Lubrecht & Cramer.

Molina-Negro, P., ed. Vestibular Neurotology. (Advances in Oto-Rhino-Laryngology Ser.: Vol. 28). (Illus.). viii, 148p. 1982. 92.00 (*3-8055-3490-6*) S Karger.

Molina, Rodolfo A. Medical Guide for Travelers. 180p. 1989. per. 9.95 (*0-943289-00-9*) Passport Adventure.

Molina, S. P., tr. see Dobbins, G. S.

Molina, Sara P., tr. see Edge, Findley B.

Molina, Silvia. Gray Skies Tomorrow: A Nivola. Mitchell, John & de Aguilar, Ruth M., trs. LC 92-42497. 104p. 1995. 17.95 (*0-917635-14-0*); pap. 8.95 (*0-917635-15-9*) Plover Pr.

***Molina, Tarea.** Your Life Depends on It: Four Easy Steps to Food Storage, Vol. 1. Lamb, Toni, ed. (Illus.). 33p. (Orig.). 1993. student ed, pap. 7.99 (*0-9642779-6-4*) T Molina Ent.

— Your Life Depends on It Vol. II: A Complete Emergency Workbook. Lamb, Toni, ed. (Illus.). 70p. 1994. 11.99 (*0-9642779-1-3*) T Molina Ent.

Molina, Tarea, ed. see Longfellow, Henry Wadsworth.

Molina, Tirso de. El Burlador de Sevilla. Arellano, Ignacio, ed. (Nueva Austral Ser.: Vol. 86). (SPA.). 1991. pap. text ed. 13.95x (*84-239-1886-6*) Elliots Bks.

— El Condenado Por Desconfiado. Fernandez, Angel R., ed. (Nueva Austral Ser.: Vol. 139). (SPA.). 1991. pap. text ed. 24.95x (*84-239-1939-0*) Elliots Bks.

Molinar, G., jt. ed. see Pavese, F.

Molinari, A. & Ricci, R., eds. From Nuclei to Stars. (Summer School of Physics Ser.: Vol. 91). 325p. 1986. 105.25 (*0-444-86988-3*, North Holland) Elsevier.

Molinari, Carol, et al. Out of Nowhere. 100p. 1993. pap. 7.00 (*0-8059-3324-7*) Dorrance.

Molinari, Dave. Best in the Game: The Turbulent Story of the Pittsburgh Penguins' Rise to Stanley Cup Champions. LC 92-82548. (Illus.). 250p. 1992. 19.95 (*0-915611-66-X*) Sagamore Pub.

Molinari, Joseph, jt. auth. see Langman, Larry.

Molinaro, Angelo A. The Two State Universe. (C). 1988. pap. 14.95 (*0-8283-1997-9*) Branden Pub Co.

Molinaro, J. A., jt. ed. see Chandler, Stanley B.

Molinaro, Julius A. Matteo Maria Boiardo: A Bibliography of Works & Criticism from 1487-1980. (CFH-FCEH Ser.: No. 5). (Illus.). 100p. (Orig.). (C). 1984. pap. 10.00 (*0-920050-94-8*, Pub. by Can Fed Human CN) Speedimpex.

Molinaro, Julius A., ed. Petrarch to Pirandello: Studies in Italian Literature in Honour of Beatrice Corrigan. LC 72-185725. 276p. reprint ed. pap. 78.70 (*0-317-28773-7*, 2020509) Bks Demand.

Molinaro, Julius A., tr. see Alfieri, Vittorio.

***Molinaro, Larry.** A Roadmap to Resolution. 20p. 1995. pap. text ed. write for info. (*0-9646852-6-4*) Wildlife Habitat.

***Molinaro, Larry, et al.** Agenda for Action. 24p. 1994. pap. text ed. write for info. (*0-9646852-0-5*) Wildlife Habitat.

Molinaro, Nina. Foucault, Feminism, & Power: Reading Esther Tusquets. LC 90-55653. 128p. 1991. 27.50 (*0-8387-5200-4*) Bucknell U Pr.

Molinaro, Ursule. Analects of Self-Contempt: Sweet Cheat of Freedom. 24p. (Orig.). 1983. pap. 3.00 (*0-917061-16-0*) Top Stories.

— The Autobiography of Cassandra, Princess & Prophetess of Troy. 2nd ed. LC 92-17468. 112p. 1992. pap. 9.00 (*0-929701-24-0*) McPherson & Co.

— Bastards: Footnotes to History. deluxe ed. (Treacle Story Ser.: No. 7). (Illus.). 48p. 1979. 8.00 (*0-914232-27-4*) McPherson & Co.

— Encores for a Dilettante. LC 77-81003. 1977. 10.95 (*0-914590-44-8*); pap. 6.95 (*0-914590-45-6*) Fiction Coll.

— Fat Skeletons. 1994. per. 11.95 (*1-897959-02-8*) InBook.

— A Full Moon of Women: Twenty-Nine Word Portraits of Notable Women from Different Times & Places Plus One Void of Course. LC 90-30077. 149p. 1993. reprint ed. pap. 10.00 (*0-929701-32-1*) McPherson & Co.

— Needlepoint: A Dialogue. LC 87-42543. 24p. 1987. pap. 3.00 (*0-87376-055-7*) Red Dust.

— The New Moon with the Old Moon in Her Arms. 119p. (Orig.). 1993. 22.00 (*0-7043-5057-2*); pap. 10.00 (*0-929701-29-1*) McPherson & Co.

— Nightschool for Saints. 128p. 1981. 10.95 (*0-89097-021-1*); pap. 6.95 (*0-89097-022-X*) Archer Edns.

— Positions with White Roses. limited ed. LC 82-24916. 104p. 1989. 25.00 (*0-914232-59-2*) McPherson & Co.

— Positions with White Roses. LC 82-24916. 104p. 1989. reprint ed. 12.95 (*0-914232-58-4*); reprint ed. pap. 8.00 (*0-929701-00-3*) McPherson & Co.

— Power Dreamers: The Jocasta Complex. 128p. 1995. 16.00 (*0-929701-44-5*) McPherson & Co.

— Thirteen. LC 89-31186. 128p. 1989. 16.00 (*0-929701-02-X*); pap. 9.00 (*0-929701-01-1*) McPherson & Co.

Molinaro, Ursule, jt. auth. see Evans, John.

Molinaro, Ursule, tr. see Hesse, Hermann.

Molinaro, Ursule, tr. see Johnson, Uwe.

Molinaro, Ursule, tr. see Mercier, Jacques.

Molinaro, Ursule, tr. see Ollier, Claude.

Molinaro, Ursule, tr. see Sollers, Philippe.

Molinaro, Ursule, tr. see Wolf, Christa.

Molinary, Paul & Hennessy, Anne. The Vocation & Mission of Joseph & Mary. 60p. 1992. 5.95 (*1-85390-149-0*) Ignatius Pr.

Molinatti, G. M. & Martini, Luciano, eds. Endocrinology '85. (International Congress Ser.: No. 683). 496p. 1986. 162.00 (*0-444-80811-6*) Elsevier.

Molinatti, G. M., et al, eds. Endothelial Cell Function in Diabetic Microangiopathy: Problems in Methodology & Clinical Aspects. (Frontiers in Diabetes Ser.: Vol. 9). (Illus.). 212p. 1990. pap. 155.25 (*3-8055-5052-9*) S Karger.

***Molinatti, Gian M., et al, eds.** Androgenization in Women: Pathophysiology & Clinical Aspects. fac. ed. LC 81-48338. (Illus.). 216p. Date not set. pap. 61.60 (*0-7837-7216-5*, 2047082) Bks Demand.

Moline, Jack. Growing up Jewish: Or, Why Is This Book Different from All Other Books? (Illus.). 96p. 1987. mass mkt. 6.50 (*0-14-009836-4*, Penguin Bks) Viking Penguin.

***Moline, Johanna C.** The Server's Art I: A Guide for the Serving Professional. (Illus.). 50p. (Orig.). (C). 1994. pap. text ed. 8.95 (*0-9644063-0-6*) Anvilcross.

— The Server's Art II: A Short Course for the Serving Professional. abr. ed. (Illus.). 16p. (C). 1995. pap. text ed. 3.75 (*0-9644063-1-4*) Anvilcross.

Moline, Jon. Plato's Theory of Understanding. 272p. 1981. 27.50 (*0-299-08660-7*) U of Wis Pr.

Moline, Karen. Lunch. LC 94-9496. 1994. 22.00 (*0-688-13320-7*) Morrow.

Moline, Margaret L., jt. auth. see Severino, Sally K.

Moline, Mary. The Eagle & the Butterfly. (Illus.). 57p. (Orig.). 1986. pap. 8.00 (*0-913444-10-3*) Green Val World.

— Model A Miseries & Cures. 1988. pap. 15.00 (*0-317-89793-4*) Green Val World.

— Norman Rockwell Collectibles Value Guide. 6th ed. 1988. pap. 15.00 (*0-317-89792-6*) Green Val World.

Moline, Norman T. Mobility & the Small Town, Nineteen Hundred to Nineteen Thirty. LC 79-133029. (Research Papers Ser.: No. 132). (Illus.). 1971. pap. 12.00 (*0-89065-039-X*, 132) U Chicago Comm Geo.

Moline, Peg, jt. auth. see Dworkis, Sam.

Moliner, M. Diccionario de Uso del Espagnol, 2 vols., Set. 1991. 170.00 (*84-249-1344-2*) IBD Ltd.

— Diccionario de Uso del Espagnol, Vol. 1. 1446p. 1991. write for info. (*0-318-72431-6*) IBD Ltd.

— Diccionario de Uso del Espagnol, Vol. 2. 1585p. 1991. write for info. (*0-318-72432-4*) IBD Ltd.

Moliner, Maria. Diccionario de Uso del Espanol, 2 vols. 4th ed. 3088p. 1993. 239.50 (*0-685-75413-8*) Elliots Bks.

— Diccionario de Uso del Espanol, 1. 1991. write for info. (*0-7859-5791-X*) Fr & Eur.

— Diccionario de Uso del Espanol, 2. 1991. 150.00 (*0-7859-5792-8*) Fr & Eur.

— Diccionario de Uso del Espanol, Set. 1991. 295.00 (*0-7859-5790-1*) Fr & Eur.

Moliner, Maria D., tr. I Can Read Spanish. (Illus.). 96p. (J). (gr. 2-5). 1994. pap. 9.95 (*1-56294-755-9*) Millbrook Pr.

— I Can Read Spanish: My First English-Spanish Word Book. (Illus.). 96p. (ENG & SPA.). (J). (gr. 2-4). 1994. lib. bdg. 13.90 (*1-56294-547-5*) Millbrook Pr.

Molinero, Leticia, tr. see Zuckerman, Martin M.

Molineux, G., jt. ed. see Testa, N. G.

Molineux, Marie A. A Phrase Book from the Poetic & Dramatic Works of Robert Browning. 1972. 59.95 (*0-8490-0831-X*) Gordon Pr.

Molini, Cindy & Garlock, Diane, eds. Faith Moments: A Reproducible Book of Weekly Reflections on Christian Spirituality. 120p. (Orig.). 1990. pap. 69.95 (*1-55612-301-9*) Sheed & Ward MO.

***Molinie, Georges.** Dictionnaire de Rhetorique. 352p. (FRE.). 1992. pap. 22.95 (*0-7859-8635-9*, 225306257x) Fr & Eur.

Molino, Anthony, tr. see De Filippo, Eduardo.

Molino, Anthony, tr. see Magrelli, Valerio.

Molino, Anthony, tr. see Porta, Antonio.

Molino, Michael R. Questioning Tradition, Language, & Myth: The Poetry of Seamus Heaney. LC 93-42712. 240p. 1994. 29.95 (*0-8132-0796-7*) Cath U Pr.

Molino, Pierre. Riemannian Foliations. (Progress in Mathematics Ser.: No. 73). 360p. 1987. 49.50 (*0-8176-3370-7*) Birkhauser.

Molinoff, Henry. Let's Go See By Bicycle. 2nd ed. (Illus.). 120p. 1986. reprint ed. pap. 8.95 (*0-9616983-0-6*) H C Molinoff.

Molinoff, Perry, ed. see Frazer, Alan, et al.

Molinos, Michael. The Spiritual Guide. Edwards, Gene, ed. 110p. 1982. pap. 8.95 (*0-940232-08-1*) Seedsowers.

Molins, ed. Phosphates in Food. 1990. 190.00 (*0-8493-4588-X*, TX553) CRC Pr.

Molins, Victoria. Henry de Osso: Priest & Teacher. 108p. 1993. pap. 6.95 (*0-9638041-0-3*) Soc St Teresa.

Molinsky, Steven & Bliss, Bill. Communicator I. 192p. 1994. pap. text ed. 10.75 (*0-13-301649-8*) P-H.

— Full Set Voc. Game Cards. 1994. 15.95 (*0-13-121161-7*) P-H.

— Full Set Wall Charts. 1994. pap. text ed. 210.00 (*0-13-121120-X*) P-H.

— Pictoral Dictionary Chinese-English Edition. 1995. pap. text ed. 8.50 (*0-13-125824-9*) P-H.

— Pictoral Dictionary Japanese-English Edition. 1995. pap. text ed. 8.50 (*0-13-125832-X*) P-H.

— Pictoral Dictionary Korean-English Edition. 1995. pap. text ed. 8.50 (*0-13-125840-0*) P-H.

— Pictoral Dictionary Portugal-English Edition. 1995. pap. text ed. 8.50 (*0-13-128018-X*) P-H.

— Pictoral Dictionary Russian-English Edition. 1995. pap. text ed. 8.50 (*0-13-125857-5*) P-H.

— Pictoral Dictionary Spanish-English Edition. 1995. pap. text ed. 8.50 (*0-13-125865-6*) P-H.

— Set Three Voc. Game Cards. 1994. 6.50 (*0-13-121153-6*) P-H.

— Set Three Wall Charts. 1994. pap. text ed. 74.25 (*0-13-121112-9*) P-H.

— Set 1 Voc. Game Cards. 1994. 6.50 (*0-13-121138-2*) P-H.

— Set 2 Voc. Game Cards. 1994. 6.50 (*0-13-121146-3*) P-H.

***Molinsky, Steven H. & Bliss, Bill.** Communicator II: The Comprehensive Course in Functional English. LC 94-23686. (Illus.). 1995. pap. text ed. 10.00 (*0-13-340688-1*) P-H.

Molinsky, Steven J. Patterns of Ellipsis in Russian Compound Noun Formations. LC 72-94527. (Slavistic Printings & Reprintings Ser.: No. 278). 1973. text ed. 56.70 (*90-279-2474-0*) Mouton.

— A Russian Course: Teacher's Manual. (Illus.). 222p. (Orig.). 1981. pap. 12.95 (*0-89357-083-4*) Slavica.

— Side by Side, Bk. 3. 2nd ed. 1989. pap. text ed. 9.00 (*0-13-811761-6*) P-H.

— Side by Side, Bk. 4. 2nd ed. 1989. pap. text ed. 9.00 (*0-13-811811-6*) P-H.

Molinsky, Steven J. & Blass, Bill. Side by Side: English Grammar Through Guided Conversations Bk. II. 1980. pap. text ed. 15.95 (*0-13-809855-7*) P-H.

— Word by Word: Teachers Resource Book & Activity Masters. LC 94-231. 1994. pap. text ed. 26.50 (*0-13-124264-4*) P-H.

Molinsky, Steven J. & Bliss, Bill. Access: Fundamentals of Literacy & Communication. 128p. (C). 1990. pap. text ed. 10.25 (*0-13-004235-8*) P-H.

— Core Conversation Course: Beginning Text. 2nd ed. 208p. (C). 1989. pap. text ed. 15.95 (*0-13-811860-4*) P-H.

— Day by Day: English for Employment Communication. LC 93-44412. 1993. pap. 10.67 (*0-13-328238-4*) P-H Intl.

— English Word by Word: A Talking Picture Dictionary English. 1993. pap. text ed. 9.00 (*0-13-278235-9*) P-H.

— English Word by Word: A Talking Picture Dictionary English. 1993. text ed. 12.25 (*0-13-278319-3*) P-H.

— Express Ways: English for Communication, Bk. I. (Illus.). 224p. (C). 1988. pap. text ed. 16.95 (*0-13-298423-7*) P-H.

— Express Ways-Book II (Advanced) 224p. (C). 1986. pap. text ed. 16.95 (*0-13-298274-9*) P-H.

— Express Ways-Book IIA (Advanced) 112p. (C). 1986. pap. text ed. 8.50 (*0-13-298282-X*) P-H.

— Express Ways-Book IIB (Advanced) 112p. 1986. pap. text ed. 8.50 (*0-13-298316-8*) P-H.

— Expressways: English for Communication, Bk. 2. (Illus.). 240p. (C). 1987. pap. text ed. 16.95 (*0-13-298365-6*) P-H.

— Expressways: English for Communication, Bk. 2A. (Illus.). 120p. (C). 1987. pap. text ed. 8.50 (*0-13-298373-7*) P-H.

— Expressways: English for Communication, Bk. 2B. (Illus.). 120p. (C). 1987. pap. text ed. 8.50 (*0-13-298381-8*) P-H.

— Expressways: English for Communication, Bk. 3A. 224p. (C). 1987. Guide book. student ed, pap. text ed. 15.50 (*0-13-298399-0*) P-H.

— Expressways: English for Communication, Bk. 3B. 224p. (C). 1987. Guide book. student ed, pap. text ed. 15.50 (*0-13-298407-5*) P-H.

— Expressways: English for Communication, 2 bks., Bk. IA. (Illus.). 112p. (C). 1987. pap. text ed. 8.50 (*0-13-298431-8*) P-H.

— Expressways: English for Communication, 2 bks., Bk. IB. (Illus.). 112p. (C). 1988. pap. text ed. write for info. (*0-318-62137-1*) P-H.

— Expressways: English for Communication Foundations, 3 pts., Pt. A. (Illus.). 112p. (C). 1988. pap. text ed. 8.25 (*0-13-297730-3*) P-H.

— Expressways: English for Communication Foundations, 3 pts., Pt. B. (Illus.). 112p. (C). 1988. pap. text ed. write for info. (*0-318-62294-7*) P-H.

— Expressways: English for Communication Foundations, 3 pts., Set. (Illus.). 224p. (C). 1988. Full Bk., 224 pgs. pap. text ed. write for info. (*0-318-62295-5*) P-H.

— Expressways-Book IB. 112p. (C). 1988. pap. text ed. 8.50 (*0-13-298449-0*) P-H.

— International Expressways. 1991. pap. text ed. write for info. (*0-13-472887-4*) P-H.

— Line by Line: English Through Grammar Stories, Bk. 1A. (Illus.). 128p. (C). 1983. pap. text ed. 6.50 (*0-13-537092-2*) P-H.

— Line by Line: English Through Grammar Stories, Bk. 2. (Illus.). 224p. (C). 1983. pap. text ed. 10.75 (*0-13-537233-X*) P-H.

— Line by Line: English Through Grammar Stories, Bk. 2A. (Illus.). 112p. (C). 1983. pap. text ed. 6.50 (*0-13-537241-0*) P-H.

— Line by Line: English Through Grammar Stories, Bk. 2B. (Illus.). 124p. (C). 1983. pap. text ed. 6.50 (*0-13-537258-5*) P-H.

— Line by Line: English Through Grammar Stories, Bk.1B. (Illus.). 112p. (C). 1983. pap. text ed. 6.50 (*0-13-537175-9*) P-H.

— Line by Line: Intermediate Text. 2nd ed. (C). 1991. pap. text ed. 12.75 (*0-13-536889-8*) P-H.

— Line by Line: Reading English Through Grammar Stories, Bk. I. (Illus.). 208p. 1983. pap. text ed. write for info. (*0-13-537076-0*) P-H.

— Placement Test. (C). 1989. text ed. write for info. (*0-318-65462-8*) P-H.

— Side by Side, Bk. 1. 2nd ed. 1988. pap. text ed. 9.00 (*0-13-811076-X*) P-H.

— Side by Side: English Grammar Through Guided Conversation 1A. 128p. (C). 1982. pap. text ed. 8.50 (*0-13-809715-1*); pap. text ed. 6.50 (*0-13-809525-6*) P-H.

— Side by Side: English Grammar through Guided Conversation 1B. 128p. (C). 1982. pap. text ed. 8.50 (*0-13-809723-2*) P-H.

— Side by Side: English Grammar through Guided Conversation 1B. 128p. (C). 1983. Study guide. student ed, pap. text ed. 6.50 (*0-13-809582-5*) P-H.

— Side by Side: English Grammar Through Guided Conversation 2A. 128p. (C). 1982. pap. text ed. 8.50 (*0-13-809772-0*) P-H.

— Side by Side: English Grammar Through Guided Conversation 2A. 128p. (C). 1983. pap. text ed. 6.50 (*0-13-809640-6*) P-H.

— Side by Side: English Grammar Through Guided Conversation 2B. 128p. (C). 1982. pap. text ed. 8.50 (*0-13-809798-4*) P-H.

— Side by Side: English Grammar Through Guided Conversation 2B. 128p. (C). 1983. Wkbk. student ed, pap. text ed. 6.50 (*0-13-809699-6*) P-H.

— Side by Side: English Grammar Through Guided Conversations, Bk. I. 1980. pap. text ed. 15.95 (*0-13-809848-4*) P-H.

— Side by Side: English Grammar Through Guided Conversations, Bk. I. 1980. write for info. (*0-13-809830-1*) P-H.

— Side by Side Core Conversation, Intermediate Text. 2nd ed. (C). 1991. pap. text ed. 15.95 (*0-13-811878-7*) P-H.

— Word by Word Basic Picture Dictionary. LC 95-717. 1995. pap. text ed. 8.50 (*0-13-278565-X*) P-H.

Molinsky, Steven J., jt. auth. see Bliss, Bill.

Molinsky, Steven J., et al. Handbook of Vocabulary Teaching Strategies: Communication Activities with the Word by Word Picture Dictionary. LC 93-49401. 1994. pap. text ed. 10.75 (*0-13-278441-6*) P-H.

Molis, Petra, et al. Lithuanian Scouting. 2nd rev. ed. Vitas, Robertas, ed. (Illus.). 40p. 1983. reprint ed. pap. write for info. (*0-9611488-0-2*) Lith Scouts.

Molitch, Mark E. Management of Medical Problems in Surgical Patients. LC 81-9831. 795p. 1982. 50.00 (*0-8036-6286-6*) Davis Co.

Moliterno, James E. Ethics of Lawyer's Work. Levy, John M., ed. (American Casebook Ser.). 320p. (C). 1993. pap. text ed. 18.50 (*0-314-02395-X*); pap. text ed. write for info. (*0-314-02414-X*) West Pub.

Moliterno, James E. & Lederer, Frederic. An Introduction to Law, Law Study & the Lawyer's Role. LC 91-70489. 206p. 1991. 22.95 (*0-89089-453-1*); pap. 12.50 (*0-89089-452-3*) Carolina Acad Pr.

Moliterno, Steven, ed. see American Institute of Certified Public Accountants Staff.

Moliterno, Steven, ed. see BEFEC Mulguin & Associates Staff & Seidman & Seidman Staff.

Molitero, Steven, ed. see American Institute of Certified Public Accountants Staff.

Molitor, Michael R., ed. International Environmental Law. 580p. 1991. 85.00 (*90-6544-527-7*) Kluwer Law Tax Pubs.

Molitoris, Milo, intro. The International Concordance of Inspired Writings: 1989 Edition. 676p. (Orig.). 1989. pap. 20.00 (*0-9624058-0-9*); disk 20.00 (*0-9624058-1-7*) Milo Molitoris.

Molk, Jules, jt. auth. see Tannery, Jules.

Molk, Ulrich, ed. see Spanke, Hans.

Molk, Yuda. Common Sense about Abortion. 112p. 1992. pap. 9.95 (*0-9633910-5-4*) Comm Sense.

— Common Sense Society: A Logical Analysis of Basic Social Issues, a Guide to Prejudice-Free Society. 294p. (Orig.). 1995. pap. write for info. (*0-9633910-6-2*) Comm Sense.

— Common-Sense Society: A Logical Analysis of Basic Social Issues, a Guide to Prejudice-Free Society. 298p. 1995. pap. write for info. (*0-614-07414-2*) Comm Sense.

Molkenthin, A. Influence Surfaces of Two-Span Continuous Plates with Free Longitudinal Edges: Bilingual Edition. (Illus.). 220p. (ENG & GER.). 1971. 86.00 (*0-387-05212-7*) Spr-Verlag.

Moll, Albert. Hypnotism. (Hypnosis & Altered States of Consciousness Ser.). 626p. 1982. reprint ed. lib. bdg. 49.50 (*0-306-76079-7*) Da Capo.

An Asterisk (*) at the beginning of an entry indicates that the title is appearing in BIP for the first time.

— Libido Sexualis: Studies in the Psychosexual Laws of Love Verified by Clinical Sexual Case Histories. Berger, David, tr. LC 72-11288. reprint ed. 36.00 (*0-404-57481-5*) AMS Pr.

— Perversions of the Sex Instinct. LC 72-11289. (ENG.). reprint ed. 38.50 (*0-404-57482-3*) AMS Pr.

— The Sexual Life of the Child. Paul, Eden, tr. LC 72-11290. reprint ed. 39.00 (*0-404-57483-1*) AMS Pr.

Moll, Aristides A. Aesculapius in Latin America. LC 76-101589. (Illus.). 1969. reprint ed. 25.00 (*0-87266-022-2*) Argosy.

Moll, Ernest G. The View from a Ninetieth Birthday: Lyrical Poems of Old Age. Iddings, Kathleen, ed. LC 91-77893. 71p. (Orig.). 1992. per. 10.00 (*0-931721-12-1*) La Jolla Poets.

Moll, Gary & Young, Stanley. Growing Greener Cities: A Tree-Planting Handbook. Berland, Dinah, ed. LC 91-78089. (Illus.). 126p. (Orig.). 1992. pap. 7.95 (*1-879326-13-2*) Living Planet Pr.

Moll, H. A. The Economics of Oil Palm. (C). 1991. text ed. 395.00 (*0-89771-598-5*, Pub. by Intl Bk Distr II) St Mut.

Moll, Hans G., jt. auth. see Cumming, James T.

Moll, Harold W., ed. see Baierlein, E. R.

***Moll, Heidrun.** The Immune Functions of Epidermal Langerhans Cells. (Medical Intelligence Unit Ser.). 175p. 1995. write for info. (*1-57059-234-9*) R G Landes.

Moll, J. M. Management of Rheumatic Disorders. 450p. 1984. text ed. 81.50 (*0-89004-321-3*) Raven.

— Rheumatology. (Colour Guide Ser.). (Illus.). 154p. (Orig.). 1992. pap. text ed. 19.95 (*0-443-04614-X*) Churchill.

Moll, J. M., et al, eds. Therapeutics in Rheumatology. 606p. 1986. text ed. 79.00 (*0-88167-258-0*) Raven.

Moll, J. R., jt. ed. see Kraijenhoff, D. A.

Moll, Joy K., jt. auth. see Flood, Barbara J.

***Moll, Linda J. A Poison Tree: A Children's Fairy Tale. (Illus.). 40p. (J). (gr. 1). 1994. 12.95 (*0-9641641-1-6*) Punking Pr.**
A POISON TREE is a children's fairy tale set in Ireland's countryside. Ian McGonagle feels rage for his wee brother, Malachy, after discovering his younger sibling ruined his birthday surprise. Ian vows revenge & calls on the evil fairies for help. Indeed, the evil fairies come with a black seed from which a poison tree will grow. But what happens next is not what Ian expected. Find out how sibling anger turns into forgiveness & how brotherly love prevails in this enchanting Irish fairy tale. A POISON TREE is a charming story for any child learning the sometimes difficult skill of getting along with others. Parents, caregivers & teachers will find A POISON TREE a valuable social tool in the family, neighborhood or classroom. Children love the comical antics of the fairies & SIT in anticipation of A POISON TREE's climactic ending. Teachers will find A POISON TREE a wonderful source for introducing literary devices & techniques to young scholars. A POISON TREE is rich in simile, metaphor, alliteration, rhyming verse,... Illustrations include quaint silhouettes & the text which is scripted in modified 4th-century Celtic lettering. A Celtic knotwork border frames the page & completes the beauty of the book. To order A POISON TREE, contact Christopher Moll, P.O. Box 25, Williamson, NY 14589; 315-589-5119. ***Publisher Provided Annotation.***

Moll, Louise B. Clever Cryptograms. LC 94-17397. (Illus.). 128p. 1994. pap. 5.95 (*0-8069-0756-8*) Sterling.

— Great Book of Cryptograms. LC 92-39447. (Illus.). 128p. (YA). (gr. 10-12). 1993. pap. 5.95 (*0-8069-8784-7*) Sterling.

Moll, Luis C., ed. Vygotsky & Education: Instructional Implications & Applications of Socio-Historical Psychology. (Illus.). 432p. (C). 1990. 69.95 (*0-521-36051-X*) Cambridge U Pr.

— Vygotsky & Education: Instructional Implications & Applications of Socio-Historical Psychology. (Illus.). 456p. (C). 1992. pap. 22.95 (*0-521-38579-2*) Cambridge U Pr.

***Moll, Manfred.** Beers & Coolers. Date not set. 155.00 (*1-898298-09-2*) Spr-Verlag.

***Moll, Patricia B.** Children & Books I: African American Story Books & Activities for All Children. (Children &... Ser.). (Illus.). 250p. 1994. spiral bd. 14.95 (*0-9616511-5-6*) Hampton Mae.

— Children & Books I: African American Story Books & Activities for All Children. 2nd ed. (Children &... Ser.). (Illus.). 250p. 1994. pap. 14.95 (*0-9616511-4-8*) Hampton Mae.

— Children & Books I: African American Storybooks & Activities for All Children. 218p. (J). (ps-3). 1991. pap. 14.95 (*0-9616511-2-1*); spiral bd. 14.95 (*0-9616511-3-X*) Hampton Mae.

— Children & Scissors. (Illus.). 153p. 1985. spiral bd. 7.75 (*0-9616511-1-3*); per. 7.75 (*0-9616511-0-5*) Hampton Mae.

Moll, R. N., et al. An Introduction to Formal Language Theory. (Texts & Monographs in Computer Science). (Illus.). 232p. 1988. 54.00 (*0-387-96698-6*) Spr-Verlag.

Moll, Richard. Playing the Private College Admissions Game. rev. ed. 260p. 1986. pap. 7.95 (*0-14-009385-0*, Penguin Bks) Viking Penguin.

— Playing the Selective College Admissions Game. 256p. (Orig.). 1994. pap. 9.95 (*0-14-051303-5*, Penguin Bks) Viking Penguin.

Moll, Richard W. The Lure of the Law: Why People Become Lawyers & What the Profession Does to Them. 256p. 1991. pap. 11.95 (*0-14-010556-5*, Penguin Bks) Viking Penguin.

Moll, V. Virgin Islands. (World Bibliographical Ser.). 1992. lib. bdg. 78.00 (*1-85109-165-3*) ABC-CLIO.

Moll, Walter L., tr. see Ehrlich, Eugen.

Molla, Juan. Teatro Espanol E Iberoamericano En Madrid: (1962-1991) 300p. 1993. pap. 40.00 (*0-89295-070-6*) Society Sp & Sp-Am.

Molla, Rafiqul K. Electronic Color Separation. (Illus.). 288p. (C). 1988. 59.95 (*0-9620453-0-6*) RK Printing & Pub.

Mollan-Masters, Renee. You Are Smarter Than You Think! A Practical Guide to Academic Success Using Your Personal Learning Style. LC 92-60578. (Illus.). 146p. (Orig.). (C). 1992. pap. text ed. 20.00 (*0-9608622-1-8*) Reality Prods.
ARE YOU A STUDENT OR DO YOU KNOW OF A STUDENT WHO: Studies for hours & then performs poorly on tests? Forgets material learned shortly after the test is over? Works very hard for A's & B's? Students who answer yes to these questions are probably a lot smarter than they think. For over 10 years nationally, the YOU ARE SMARTER THAN YOU THINK Learning program has been turning mediocre learners into classroom successes. This book helps the reader discover their unique learning style, & then shows them step-by- step how to apply this information to enhance classroom performance. Students & teachers report to us that after using the YOU ARE SMARTER THAN YOU THINK Program, grades improve, critical thinking becomes easier, student attrition decreases, learning retention increases & teacher frustration is reduced. ***Publisher Provided Annotation.***

— You Are Smarter Than You Think! A Practical Guide to Academic Success Using Your Personal Learning Style. (Orig.). (C). 1992. audio 10.00 (*0-614-05019-7*); vhs 30.00 (*0-614-05020-0*) Reality Prods.

Mollan, R. C., jt. ed. see Robinson, D. W.

Molland, Einar. Church Life in Norway: 1800-1950. Harris, Kaasa, tr. LC 78-2711. 120p. 1978. reprint ed. text ed. 45.00 (*0-313-20342-3*, MOCL, Greenwood Pr) Greenwood.

***Molland, George.** Mathematics & the Medieval Ancestry of Physics. (Collected Studies: Vol. CS481). 350p. 1995. 84.95 (*0-86078-470-3*, Pub. by Variorum UK) Ashgate Pub Co.

Mollard, F. R., jt. ed. see Murty, Y. V.

Mollat du Jourdin, Michel. Europe & the Sea. Fagan, Teresa L., tr. LC 92-37706. (Making of Europe Ser.). (FRE.). 1993. 24.95 (*0-631-17227-0*) Blackwell Pubs.

Mollat, G., ed. see Bernardus Guidonis.

Mollat, Michel. The Poor in the Middle Ages: An Essay in Social History. Goldhammer, Arthur, tr. LC 86-1686. 336p. 1986. text ed. 42.00 (*0-300-02789-3*) Yale U Pr.

— The Poor in the Middle Ages: An Essay in Social History. (FRE.). 1990. pap. 18.00 (*0-300-04605-7*) Yale U Pr.

Mollat, Michel, jt. auth. see Devisse, Jean.

Molle, Willem. The Economics of European Integration: Theory, Practice, Policy. rev. ed. LC 94-11914. 576p. 1994. pap. 26.95 (*1-85521-506-3*) Ashgate Pub Co.

— The Economics of European Integration: Theory, Practice, Policy. 2nd rev. ed. LC 94-11914. 576p. 1994. 69.95 (*1-85521-498-9*, Pub. by Dartmth Pub UK) Ashgate Pub Co.

Molle, Willem & Cappellin, Riccardo. Regional Impact of Community Policies in Europe. 210p. 1988. text ed. 76.95 (*0-566-05587-2*, Pub. by Avebury Pub UK) Ashgate Pub Co.

Molle, Willem & Van Mourik, Aad. Wage Differentials in the European Community: Convergence or Divergence? (Illus.). 203p. 1989. text ed. 72.95 (*0-566-07098-7*, Pub. by Gower UK) Ashgate Pub Co.

Mollel, Tololwa M. Big Boy. (Illus.). (J). 1995. write for info. (*0-318-72305-0*, Clarion Bks) HM.

— The King & the Tortoise. LC 92-12485. (Illus.). 32p. (J). (gr. k-3). 1993. 14.95 (*0-395-64480-1*, Clarion Bks) HM.

— Orphan Boy. (Illus.). 32p. (J). (gr. k-3). 1991. 15.95 (*0-89919-985-2*) HM.

— Orphan Boy. LC 90-2358. (J). (ps-3). 1995. pap. 5.95 (*0-395-72079-6*, Clarion Bks) HM.

— The Orphan Boy. (Illus.). (J). 1991. 14.95 (*0-685-53587-8*, Clarion Bks) HM.

— A Promise to the Sun: A Story of Africa. (Illus.). 32p. (J). (ps-3). 1992. 15.95 (*0-316-57813-4*, Joy St Bks) Little.

— Rhinos for Lunch & Elephants for Supper! (Illus.). 32p. (J). (ps-3). 1992. 15.95 (*0-395-60734-5*, Clarion Bks) HM.

***Mollel, Tolowa M.** Big Boy. (J). (ps-3). 1994. 14.95 (*0-395-67403-4*, Clarion Bks) HM.

Mollenauer, L. F. & White, J. C., eds. Tunable Lasers. (Topics in Applied Physics Ser.: Vol. 59). (Illus.). 425p. 1987. 97.00 (*0-387-16921-0*) Spr-Verlag.

Mollenauer, L. F., et al, eds. Tunable Lasers. 2nd ed. LC 92-19149. (Topics in Applied Physics Ser.: Vol. 59). (Illus.). 440p. 1992. pap. 69.00 (*0-387-55571-4*) Spr-Verlag.

Mollenauer, Robert. Introduction to Modernity: A Symposium on Eighteenth Century Thought. LC 65-16473. 181p. reprint ed. pap. 51.60 (*0-317-08970-6*, 2004694) Bks Demand.

Mollenauer, Sandra, jt. auth. see Plotnik, Rodney.

Mollenhauer, Peter. Friedrich Nicolais Satiren: Ein Beitrag Zur Kulturgeschichte Des 18. Jahrhunderts. (German Language & Literature Monographs: No. 2). viii, 267p. 1977. 59.00x (*90-272-4006-X*) Benjamins North Am.

Mollenhauer, Peter, tr. see Steiner, Rudolf.

Mollenhauer, Peter, ed. see Steiner, Rudolf.

Mollenhauer, Peter, tr. see Steiner, Rudolf.

Mollenhoff, Clark. Ballad to an Iowa Farmer & Other Reflections by Clark Mollenhoff. LC 91-11279. (Illus.). 116p. 1991. 17.95 (*0-8138-1458-8*) Iowa St U Pr.

Mollenkamp, Robert A. Introduction to Automatic Process Control: Student Text. LC 84-170349. (Instructional Resource Package Ser.). 177p. 1984. reprint ed. pap. 50.50 (*0-7837-5133-8*, 2044861) Bks Demand.

Mollenkopf, John H. The Contested City. LC 83-42568. 350p. 1983. 49.50 (*0-691-07659-6*); pap. 13.95x (*0-691-02220-8*) Princeton U Pr.

— A Phoenix in the Ashes: The Rise & Fall of Koch Coalition in New York City Politics. (Illus.). 280p. 1992. text ed. 39.50 (*0-691-07854-8*) Princeton U Pr.

— Phoenix in the Ashes: The Rise & Fall of the Coalition in New York City Politics. (C). 1994. pap. 14.95 (*0-691-03673-X*) Princeton U Pr.

Mollenkopf, John H., ed. Power, Culture & Place: Essays on New York City. LC 88-39077. 320p. 1989. 40.00 (*0-87154-603-5*) Russell Sage.

Mollenkopf, John H. & Castells, Manuel. Dual City: The Restructuring of New York. LC 90-45448. 256p. 1991. 45.00 (*0-87154-606-X*) Russell Sage.

Mollenkopf, John H. & Castells, Manuel, eds. Dual City: The Restructuring of New York. (Illus.). 496p. 1992. pap. 16.95 (*0-87154-608-6*) Russell Sage.

Mollenkott, Virginia. Women, Men & the Bible. 160p. 1988. pap. 10.95 (*0-8245-0893-9*) Crossroad NY.

Mollenkott, Virginia R. The Divine Feminine: The Biblical Imagery of God As Female. 128p. 1984. pap. 10.95 (*0-8245-0669-3*) Crossroad NY.

— Godding: Human Responsibility & the Bible. 144p. 1988. 13.95 (*0-8245-0824-6*); pap. 8.95 (*0-8245-0948-X*) Crossroad NY.

— Sensuous Spirituality: Out from Fundamentalism. 192p. 1992. pap. 12.95 (*0-8245-1168-9*) Crossroad NY.

— Women of Faith in Dialogue. 144p. (Orig.). 1987. pap. 9.95 (*0-8245-0823-8*) Crossroad NY.

Mollenkott, Virginia R., jt. auth. see Scanzoni, Letha D.

Moller & Horton. Connecticut Practice Book Annotated - Supreme Court & Appellate Court Rules & Forms. 336p. 1985. pap. 28.50 (*0-317-52100-4*) West Pub.

Moller, jt. auth. see Sherlock.

Moller, A. P., jt. auth. see Birkhead, Tim R.

Moller, A. R., jt. ed. see Schramm, J.

Moller, Aage R. Auditory Physiology. 279p. 1982. text ed. 84.00 (*0-12-503450-4*) Acad Pr.

Moller, Aage R., jt. ed. see Vernon, Jack A.

Moller, Anders P. Sexual Selection & the Barn Swallow. LC 93-37324. (Series in Ecology & Evolution). (Illus.). 376p. (C). 1994. 49.95 (*0-19-854029-9*); pap. 24.95 (*0-19-854028-0*) OUP.

Moller, Bernhard, et al. Formal Program Development: IFIP TC 2-WG 2.1 State of the Art Report. LC 93-41255. 1993. 54.00 (*0-387-57499-9*) Spr-Verlag.

Moller, Bjorn. Common Security & Nonoffensive Defense: A Neorealist Perspective. LC 91-28864. 285p. 1992. lib. bdg. 40.00 (*1-55587-259-X*) Lynne Rienner.

— The Dictionary of Alternative Defense. LC 92-27347. 540p. 1995. lib. bdg. 79.95 (*1-55587-386-3*) Lynne Rienner.

— Resolving the Security Dilemma in Europe: The German Debate on Non-Offensive Defence. 339p. 1991. 56.00 (*0-08-041315-3*, Pub. by Brasseys UK) Brasseys Inc.

Moller, Chris. Evolution, Civilisation & the Horse! 128p. 1990. pap. 21.00 (*0-85131-564-X*, Pub. by J A Allen & Co UK) St Mut.

Moller, D. P., ed. Advanced Simulation in Biomedicine. (Advances in Simulation Ser.: Vol. 3). (Illus.). xi, 203p. 1989. pap. 49.00 (*0-387-97184-X*) Spr-Verlag.

Moller, David, ed. Insulin Resistance. LC 93-18929. 425p. 1993. text ed. 159.00 (*0-471-93977-3*) Wiley.

Moller, David W. Death & Dying: Values, Institutions, & Human Mortality. (Illus.). 304p. (C). 1995. pap. text ed. 16.95 (*0-19-504296-4*) OUP.

— Death & Dying: Values, Institutions, & Human Mortality. (Illus.). 304p. (C). 1995. 45.00 (*0-19-504295-6*) OUP.

— On Death Without Dignity: The Human Impact of Technological Dying. (Perspectives on Death & Dying Ser.). 134p. 1990. text ed. 23.95 (*0-89503-067-5*) Baywood Pub.

Moller, Deanna. Line upon Line: Challenging Crossword Classics for Latter-Day Saints. 56p. 1993. 7.98 (*0-88290-480-9*, 2061) Horizon Utah.

Moller, Doris. How to Color Your Hair Just Like a Professional. (Illus.). 104p. 1992. pap. 5.95 (*0-9694965-0-8*) Firefly Bks Ltd.

Moller, Erik, jt. auth. see Rolph, Elizabeth.

Moller, Erik, et al. Private Dispute Resolution in the Banking Industry. LC 93-33574. 1993. 13.00 (*0-8330-1469-2*, MR-259) Rand Corp.

Moller, George D. American Military Shoulder Arms, Vol. II: From the 1790s to the End of the Flintlock Period. (Illus.). 496p. 1993. 75.00 (*0-87081-308-0*) Univ Pr Colo.

— American Military Shoulder Arms, 1492-1992, Vol. I. (Illus.). 528p. 1993. 75.00 (*0-87081-286-6*) Univ Pr Colo.

— Massachusetts Military Shoulder Arms, 1784-1877. LC 88-60020. (Illus.). 124p. 1988. 24.00 (*0-917218-34-5*) A Mowbray.

Moller, H. J., et al. Polycrystalline Semiconductors Grain Boundaries & Interfaces. (Proceedings in Physics Ser.: Vol. 35). (Illus.). 380p. 1989. 78.00 (*0-387-50887-2*) Spr-Verlag.

Moller, Hans J. Semiconductors for Solar Cells. LC 92-40718. (Optoelectronics Ser.). 275p. 1993. text ed. 88.00 (*0-89006-574-8*) Artech Hse.

Moller, I. M., jt. ed. see Larsson, C.

Moller, J. Orstrom. The Future European Model: Economic Internationalization & Cultural Decentralization. LC 94-21688. 152p. 1995. text ed. 55.00 (*0-275-95012-3*, Praeger Pubs) Greenwood.

Moller, James H. & Neal, William A. Fetal, Neonatal & Infant Cardiac Disease. (Illus.). 1061p. 1990. boxed 180.00 (*0-8385-2575-X*, A2575-7) Appleton & Lange.

Moller, James H., et al. A Parent's Guide to Heart Disorders. LC 87-19225. (Guides to Birth & Childhood Disorders Ser.). (Illus.). 160p. 1988. 14.95 (*0-8166-1478-4*) U of Minn Pr.

Moller, Jarub. Theme of Identity in the Essays of James Baldwin. 196p. (Orig.). 1975. pap. text ed. 40.00x (*91-7346-008-7*, Pub. by Almqv & Wiksell SW) Coronet Bks.

Moller, Jeanne, ed. International Directory of Solid Waste Management 1993-94: The ISWA Yearbook. (Illus.). 350p. (Orig.). (C). 1993. 75.00 (*1-873936-15-X*, Pub. by J & J Sci Pubs UK) Bks Intl VA.

— The International Directory of Solid Waste Management 1994-1995: The ISWA Yearbook. (Illus.). 350p. (Orig.). 1994. pap. text ed. 75.00 (*1-873936-28-1*, Pub. by Ponte Pr GW) Bks Intl VA.

Moller, Jeanne, jt. ed. see Andersen, Lizzi.

Moller, Jeanne, jt. ed. see Anderson, Lizzi.

Moller, Jesper. Lectures on Random Voronoi Tesselations. LC 94-248. (Lecture Notes in Statistics Ser.: Vol. 87). (Illus.). 144p. 1994. pap. 29.00 (*0-387-94264-5*) Spr-Verlag.

Moller, Jonathan R. The Protocol Advantage. LC 93-93668. (Illus.). 408p. (Orig.). 1993. pap. 110.00 (*1-884045-00-6*) Protocol Res.

Moller, Jonathan R., jt. ed. see Margolis, Barbara A.

Moller, K. D. Optics. (Illus.). 525p. (C). 1988. text ed. 52.00 (*0-935702-20-2*) Univ Sci Bks.

— Optics Solutions Manual. 237p. 1988. 22.00 (*0-935702-55-5*) Univ Sci Bks.

Moller, Karlind, et al. A Parent's Guide to Cleft Lip & Palate. 137p. 1989. 14.95 (*0-8166-1491-1*) U of Minn Pr.

Moller, Karlind T. & Starr, Clark D., eds. Cleft Palate: Interdisciplinary Issues & Treatment. LC 92-12022. (For Clinicians by Clinicians Ser.). 399p. 1992. pap. text ed. 33.00 (*0-89079-567-3*, 4046) PRO-ED.

***Moller, Kristian & Wilson, David T., eds.** Business Marketing: An Interaction & Network Perspective. LC 94-29887. 1995. lib. bdg. write for info. (*0-7923-9504-2*) Kluwer Ac.

Moller, Linda. The Great Pig Escape: A Green Story - A Wild Adventure. (Illus.). 111p. (Orig.). (J). (gr. 2-6). 1990. pap. 8.95 (*0-86278-213-9*, Pub. by OBrien Pr IE) Dufour.

Moller, Lis. The Freudian Reading: Analytical & Fictional Constructions. LC 91-22539. 184p. (Orig.). (C). 1991. text ed. 28.95 (*0-8122-3126-0*); pap. text ed. 14.95 (*0-8122-1381-5*) U of Pa Pr.

Moller, Lisa, ed. see Billstein, Rick, et al.

Moller, Lisa, ed. see Nagle & Staff.

Moller, Lisa, ed. see Triola, Mario F.

Moller, Lisa, ed. see Washington, Allyn J.

Moller, Mary E. Thoreau in the Human Community. LC 79-22549. 224p. 1980. lib. bdg. 27.50 (*0-87023-293-2*) U of Mass Pr.

***Moller, Ostrom J.** The Future European Model: Economic Internationalization & Cultural Decentralization. LC 94-21688. (Studies on the 21st Centuries). 144p. 1995. pap. text ed. 18.95 (*0-275-95187-1*) Greenwood.

Moller, Peter, jt. auth. see Breyer, Richard.

Moller, Susann. I Dance in Your Light That Is Also My Own. LC 93-32605. 64p. 1993. pap. 12.95 (*0-7734-2793-7*, Mellen Poetry Pr) E Mellen.

Moller, Torsten, et al. Pocket Atlas of Cross-Sectional Anatomy: Computer Tomography & Magnetic Resonance Imaging. Bergman, Clifford, tr. LC 93-43883. 1993. pap. 27.00 (*0-86577-510-9*) Thieme Med Pubs.

Moller, Torsten B. & Reif, Emil. MRI Atlas of the Musculo-Skeletal System. LC 93-2493. 1993. 135.00 (*0-86542-291-5*) Blackwell Sci.

— Pocket Atlas of Cross-Sectional Anatomy: Computer Tomography & Magnetic Resonance Imaging. LC 93-43883. 246p. 1994. pap. 27.00 (*0-86577-511-7*) Thieme Med Pubs.

Moller, Torsten B., et al. Pocket Atlas of Radiographic Anatomy. Reif, Emil, ed. Robertson, Michael, tr. LC 92-49310. 356p. 1993. pap. 27.00 (*0-86577-459-5*) Thieme Med Pubs.

Molleson, Diane. Easy Science Experiments. (J). (ps-3). 1993. pap. 3.95 (*0-590-45304-1*) Scholastic Inc.
— How Ducklings Grow. (Read with Me Paperback Ser.). 32p. (J). (ps-2). 1993. pap. 2.50 (*0-590-45201-0*) Scholastic Inc.
— Secret Garden, with Charm, Key-Shaped. (Illus.). (J). (ps-3). 1993. pap. 12.95 (*0-590-47173-2*) Scholastic Inc.
Mollet, P. Optics in Metrology: Colloqui International Committee on Optics, May, 1958. LC 59-6847. 1960. 232.00 (*0-08-009269-1*, Pub. by Pergamon Repr UK) Franklin.
Mollett, J. A. Planning for Agricultural Development. 2nd ed. 220p. 1990. text ed. 75.00 (*0-566-07142-8*, Pub. by Avebury Pub UK) Ashgate Pub Co.
Mollett, J. A., ed. Migrants in Agricultural Development. 260p. 1991. text ed. 80.00x (*0-8147-5459-7*) NYU Pr.
Mollhausen, Baldwin. Diary of a Journey from the Mississippi to the Coasts of the Pacific: With a United States Government Expedition, 2 vols., Set. (American Biography Ser.). 1991. reprint ed. lib. bdg. 148.00 (*0-7812-8287-X*) Rprt Serv.
Molli, Jeanne, jt. auth. see Grabriel, Vernice.
Mollica, Anthony & Northup, Bill. Those Wonderful Chriscraft Speedboats. (Coloring the Classics Ser.). (Illus.). 28p. (J). 1992. student ed 3.95 (*1-883029-02-3*) CHP NY.
Mollica, Peter. Stained Glass Primer, Vol. 1. 1971. pap. 6.95 (*0-9601306-1-6*) Mollica Stained Glass.
Mollica, Tony & Northup, Bill. Those Wonderful Garwood Speedboats. (Coloring the Classics Ser.). (Illus.). 28p. (J). 1992. student ed 3.95 (*1-883029-01-5*) CHP NY.
— Those Wonderful Old Racing Boats. (Coloring the Classics Ser.). (Illus.). 28p. (J). 1992. student ed 3.95 (*1-883029-00-7*) CHP NY.
— Touring the One Thousand Islands. (Coloring America Ser.). (Illus.). 28p. (J). 1993. student ed 3.95 (*1-883029-03-1*) CHP NY.
Mollica, V., ed. see Fellini, Federico.
Mollien, G. Travels in the Interior of Africa. Bowdich, T. E., ed. (Illus.). 408p. 1967. 45.00 (*0-7146-1077-1*, Pub. by F Cass Pubs UK) Intl Spec Bk.
***Mollin, Richard A.** Quadratics. 375p. 1995. write for info. (*0-8493-3983-9*, 3983) CRC Pr.
Mollin, Richard A., ed. Number Theory: Proceedings of the First Conference of the Canadian Number Theory Association Held at the Banff Center, Banff, Alberta, April 17-27, 1988. xiv, 659p. (C). 1990. lib. bdg. 129.95 (*0-89925-570-1*) De Gruyter.
— Number Theory: Proceedings of the First Conference of the Canadian Number Theory Association Held at the Banff Center, Banff, Alberta, April 17-27, 1988. xiv, 659p. (C). 1990. lib. bdg. 129.95 (*3-11-011723-1*) De Gruyter.
— Number Theory & Applications. (C). 1989. lib. bdg. 196. 50 (*0-7923-0149-8*) Kluwer Ac.
Mollinger, Robert N. Psychoanalysis & Literature: An Introduction. LC 80-26256. 192p. 1981. 29.95 (*0-88229-363-X*) Nelson-Hall.
Mollison, Bill. Permaculture: A Designer's Manual. 575p. 1993. 55.00 (*0-908228-01-5*, Pub. by Tagari Pubns AT) Permaculture.
— The Permaculture Book of Ferment & Human Nutrition. 280p. 1993. pap. text ed. 25.00 (*0-908228-06-6*) Permaculture.
***Mollison, Bill & Slay, Reny M.** Introduccion A la Permacultura. 202p. 1994. pap. text ed. 25.00 (*0-908228-09-0*) Permaculture.
— Introduction to Permaculture. 198p. (Orig.). 1994. pap. text ed. 29.95 (*0-908228-05-8*, Pub. by Tagari Pubns AT) Permaculture.
***Mollison, Denis, ed.** Epidemic Models: Their Structure & Relation to Data. (Publications of the Newton Institute: No. 5). (Illus.). 400p. (C). Date not set. write for info. (*0-521-47536-8*) Cambridge U Pr.
Mollison, Jim, jt. auth. see Stegmaier, Harry.
Mollison, P. L. Blood Transfusion. 9th ed. (Illus.). 1056p. 1992. 135.00 (*0-632-02584-0*) Blackwell Sci.
Mollman, Sarah C., ed. see Janis, Eugenia P.
Mollmann, Gerd. C-128 Programming in Machine Language. Dorn, Susan, ed. Prazak, Ludwig J., tr. 250p. (Orig.). 1987. pap. 19.95 (*0-941689-02-6*) Prog Peripherals.
Mollmann, H. Introduction to the Theory of Thin Shells. LC 82-123910. (Illus.). 191p. reprint ed. pap. 54.50 (*0-8357-4621-6*, 2037553) Bks Demand.
Mollnes, T. E., ed. Antigenic Changes Associated with Complement Activation: Journal: Complement & Inflammation, Vol. 6, No. 3, 1989. (Illus.). 120p. 1989. pap. 33.75 (*3-8055-5048-0*) S Karger.
***Mollo.** Army Uniforms of World War 2. 1980. (*0-7137-0611-2*, Pub. by Blandford Pr UK) Sterling.
— Uniforms of Seven Years War. 1977. 7.95 (*0-88254-444-6*) Hippocrene Bks.
Mollo, et al. Uniforms of the SS, Vol. 3. (Illus.). 64p. 1991. 29.95 (*1-872004-51-2*, Pub. by Windrow & Green UK) Motorbooks Intl.
Mollo, Andrew. Uniforms of the SS, Vol. 4. (Illus.). 64p. 1991. 29.95 (*1-872004-66-0*, Pub. by Windrow & Green UK) Motorbooks Intl.
— Uniforms of the SS, Vol. 5: Sicherheitsdienst U. Sicherheitspolzel. (Illus.). 64p. 1992. 29.95 (*1-872004-62-8*, Pub. by Windrow & Green UK) Motorbooks Intl.
— Uniforms of the SS, Vol. 6: Waffen SS Clothing & Equipment. (Illus.). 144p. 1992. 29.95 (*1-872004-67-9*, Pub. by Windrow & Green UK) Motorbooks Intl.
Mollo, Andrew & Shalito, Anton. Red Army Uniforms of World War II in Color Photographs. (Europa Militaria Ser.: No. 14). (Illus.). 64p. 1993. pap. 15.95 (*1-872004-59-8*, Pub. by Windrow & Green UK) Motorbooks Intl.
Mollo, Andrew & Taylor, Hugh. Uniforms of the SS, Vol. 1. (Illus.). 80p. 1991. 29.95 (*1-872004-90-3*, Pub. by Windrow & Green UK) Motorbooks Intl.
— Uniforms of the SS, Vol. 2. (Illus.). 80p. 1991. 29.95 (*1-872004-95-4*, Pub. by Windrow & Green UK) Motorbooks Intl.
Mollo-Christensen, E., jt. auth. see Landahl, M. T.
Mollo, John. Uniforms of the American Revolution. LC 90-23671. (Illus.). 232p. 1991. pap. 12.95 (*0-8069-8240-3*) Sterling.
Mollo, Victor. Bridge in the Menagerie. 152p. 1977. reprint ed. pap. 8.95 (*0-571-11439-3*) Faber & Faber.
Mollo, Victor & Gardener, Nico. Card Play Technique. rev. ed. 384p. 1981. pap. 12.95 (*0-571-11759-7*) Faber & Faber.
***Mollon.** The Fragile Self: The Structure of Narcissistic Disturbance. 220p. 1993. pap. 48.00 (*1-56593-245-5*, 0316) Singular Publishing.
Mollon, J. D., jt. ed. see Barlow, H. B.
Mollon, John & Sharpe, L. Ted, eds. Colour Vision: Physiology & Psychophysics. 1983. text ed. 115.00 (*0-12-504280-9*) Acad Pr.
Mollon, Phil. The Fragile Self: The Structure of Narcissistic Disturbance & Its Therapy. LC 94-4248. 220p. 1994. 30. 00 (*1-56821-234-8*) Aronson.
Molloy, Bernard, tr. see Mendoza, Eduardo.
Molloy, Bruce. Before the Interval: Australian Film 1930-1960. 1990. pap. 29.95 (*0-7022-2269-0*, Pub. by Univ Queensland Pr AT) Intl Spec Bk.
Molloy, Catherine, jt. auth. see Bernstine, Richard L.
***Molloy, David J.** The First Landfall: Historic Lighthouses of Newfoundland & Labrador. (Illus.). 172p. 1994. pap. 24.95 (*1-55081-096-0*) Paul & Co Pubs.
Molloy, Edward, ed. Small Motors & Transformers: Design & Construction. LC 54-32875. 176p. reprint ed. pap. 50. 20 (*0-317-10064-5*, 2051335) Bks Demand.
Molloy, Frances. No Mate for the Magpie. 1986. pap. 8.95 (*0-89255-105-4*) Persea Bks.
Molloy, J. Paul. Self-Run, Self-Supported Houses for More Effective Recovery from Alcohol & Drug Addiction: A Technical Assistance Manual. (Illus.). 124p. (Orig.). (C). 1994. pap. text ed. 35.00 (*0-7881-0307-5*) Diane Pub.
Molloy, Janice, tr. see Agosin, Marjorie.
Molloy, John T. John T. Molloy's New Dress for Success. 400p. 1988. pap. 12.99 (*0-446-38552-2*) Warner Bks.
— The Woman's Dress for Success Book. (Illus.). 1987. pap. 10.99 (*0-446-38586-7*) Warner Bks.
Molloy, John W., Jr. & Adams, Richard C., eds. The Spirit of Sport: Essays about Sport & Values. LC 87-50692. 150p. (C). 1987. text ed. 27.95 (*0-317-67979-1*); pap. text ed. 16.95 (*1-55605-012-7*) Wyndhall Pr.
Molloy, Karen. System One Thousand & Thirty-Two: Reference Booklet. rev. ed. 91p. 1987. spiral bd. 12.00 (*0-317-63455-0*) CompuServe Data Tech.
— System 1032 Reference Booklet. rev. ed. Stone, Shirley, ed. 91p. 1987. spiral bd. 12.00 (*0-912055-23-5*) CompuServe Data Tech.
— Systems One Thousand & Thirty-Two Reference Booklet. rev. ed. 91p. 1987. spiral bd. 12.00 (*0-317-61662-5*) CompuServe Data Tech.
Molloy, M. J. Petticoat Loose. (Irish Play Ser.). 1982. pap. 3.95 (*0-912262-76-1*) Proscenium.
— Three Plays. 1975. 10.00 (*0-912262-30-3*) Proscenium.
***Molloy, Molly, et al.** For S. K. In Celebration of the Life & Career of Simon Karlinsky. Flier, Michael S. & Hughes, Robert P., eds. (Modern Russian Literature & Culture, Studies & Texts: Vol. 33). (Illus.). xi, 319p. (Orig.). (C). 1994. pap. 20.00 (*1-57201-002-9*) Berkeley Slavic.
Molloy, Nancy H., jt. auth. see Lewis, William A.
Molloy-Olund, Barbara. In Favor of Lightning. LC 86-32441. (Wesleyan New Poets Ser.). 63p. 1987. pap. 10. 95 (*0-8195-1133-1*, Wesleyan Univ Pr) U Pr of New Eng.
Molloy, Pat. And They Blessed Rebecca. 352p. (C). 1987. text ed. 55.00 (*0-86383-187-7*, Pub. by Gomer Pr UK) St Mut.
— Four Cheers for Carmarthen. 218p. (C). 1989. text ed. 42. 00 (*0-85088-925-1*, Pub. by Gomer Pr UK) St Mut.
— A Legacy of Demons. 214p. (C). 1989. pap. 27.00x (*0-86383-615-1*, Pub. by Gomer Pr UK) St Mut.
— Operation Seal Bay. 274p. (C). 1989. text ed. 50.00 (*0-86383-542-2*, Pub. by Gomer Pr UK) St Mut.
— A Shilling for Carmarthen...the Town They Nearly Tamed. 201p. (C). 1993. pap. 22.00x (*0-86383-182-6*, Pub. by Gomer Pr UK) St Mut.
Molloy, Pat, ed. Not the Moors Murders: A Detective's Story of the Biggest Child-Killer Hunt in History. 266p. (C). 1988. 24.00x (*0-86383-473-6*, Pub. by Gomer Pr UK) St Mut.
Molloy, Peter M. The History of Metal Mining & Metallurgy: An Annotated Bibliography. LC 83-48278. (Bibliographies of the History of Science & Technology Ser.). 336p. 1986. lib. bdg. 65.00 (*0-8240-9065-9*) Garland.
Molloy, Robert A. Plastic Part Design for Injection Molding: An Introduction. 450p. (C). 1994. write for info. (*1-56990-129-5*) Hanser-Gardner.
Molloy, Sylvia. At Face Value: Autobiographical Writing in Spanish America. (Studies in Latin American & Iberian Literature: No. 4). 320p. (C). 1991. 49.95 (*0-521-33195-1*) Cambridge U Pr.
— Certificate of Absence. Balderston, Daniel, tr. (Texas Pan American Ser.). 131p. 1989. text ed. 18.95 (*0-292-71122-0*); pap. 8.95 (*0-292-71124-7*) U of Tex Pr.
— Signs of Borges. Montero, Oscar, tr. LC 93-11260. (Post-Contemporary Interventions Ser.). 160p. 1994. lib. bdg. 32.50 (*0-8223-1406-1*); pap. text ed. 15.95 (*0-8223-1420-7*) Duke.
Molloy, Sylvia & Cifuentes, Luis F., eds. Essays on Hispanic Literature in Honor of Edmund L. King: Spanish & English Essays. (Serie A: Monagrafias, XCVIII). 269p. (C). 1983. 63.00 (*0-7293-0162-1*, Pub. by Tamesis Bks Ltd UK) Boydell & Brewer.
Molloy, Tom. The Green Line. 205p. 1982. 12.95 (*0-89182-052-3*) Charles River Bks.
— The Vandal. LC 89-62513. 220p. 1990. 22.00 (*0-932966-98-5*) Permanent Pr.
***Molloy, William & Mepham, Virginia.** Let Me Decide: The Health Care Directive That Speaks for You When You Can't. LC 94-61128. 72p. 1994. 4.95 (*0-934104-09-3*) Woodland.
***Molloy, William J.** The Complete Home Buyer's Bible: Everything You Need to Know to Buy a Resale Home, a New Construction Home, a Building Lot. LC 95-17416. 1996. write for info. (*0-471-13110-5*); pap. write for info. (*0-471-13111-3*) Wiley.
Molluso, Christine E., ed. see Gannon, Maureen, et al.
***Molluzzo, John C.** C for Business Programming. LC 94-40848. 1995. pap. text ed. 44.00 (*0-13-482282-X*) P-H.
Molluzzo, John C. & Buckley, Fred. A First Course in Discrete Mathematics. 507p. (C). 1986. text ed. 65.95 (*0-534-05310-6*) PWS Pubs.
Molmenti, P. Venice: From the Earliest Beginnings to the Fall of the Republic, 2 vols. 1977. lib. bdg. 250.00 (*0-8490-2795-0*) Gordon Pr.
Molnar, Alex, ed. Social Issues & Education: Challenge & Responsibility. LC 86-72697. 138p. 1987. pap. text ed. 9.75 (*0-87120-141-0*, 611-86048) Assn Supervision.
Molnar, Alex & Lindquist, Barbara. Changing Problem Behavior in Schools. LC 88-31388. (Social & Behavioral Science - Education Ser.). 224p. 1989. 24.95 (*1-55542-134-2*) Jossey-Bass.
Molnar, Arpad, jt. auth. see Olah, George A.
Molnar, Donald & Rutledge, Albert. Anatomy of a Park: The Essentials of Recreation Area Planning & Design. 2nd ed. (Illus.). 189p. (C). 1992. reprint ed. text ed. 28. 95x (*0-88133-699-8*) Waveland Pr.
Molnar, Dorothy E. & Fenton, Stephen H. Who Will Pick Me up When I Fall? Mathews, Judith, ed. LC 90-28250. (Illus.). 32p. (J). (ps-2). 1991. 13.95 (*0-8075-9072-X*) A Whitman.
Molnar, E. Michael. Forever Young: The Practical Handbook of Youth Extension. LC 85-51236. (Illus.). 348p. (Orig.). 1985. pap. 9.95 (*0-317-27109-1*) Witkower.
Molnar, Ferenc A. On the History of Word-Final Vowels in the Permian Languages. (Studia Uralo-altaica Ser.: No. 5). 87p. 1974. pap. 26.00 (*0-686-31504-9*) Benjamins North Am.
Molnar, Gabriella E. Pediatric Rehabilitation. 2nd ed. (Illus.). 562p. 1992. 69.00 (*0-683-06118-6*) Williams & Wilkins.
Molnar, J. J. & Banks, Theodore R. How to Read Music: A Programmed Book. (Illus.). 1966. pap. text ed. 5.00 (*0-931924-00-6*) E-Z Learning.
***Molnar, James.** Alex & Alexa Try to Touch a Star. (Kids Safe Ser.). (Illus.). 24p. (Orig.). (J). (gr. k-3). 1995. pap. 5.00 (*0-9644142-3-6*) Open Book Pubng.
— Otto's Box of Bad Feelings. (Kid Safe Ser.). (Illus.). (Orig.). (J). (ps-3). 1995. pap. 5.00 (*0-9644142-1-X*) Open Book Pubng.
— Some Touch Is Good, Some Touch Is Bad. (Illus.). 16p. (Orig.). (J). (ps-1). 1994. pap. 5.00 (*0-9644142-0-1*) Open Book Pubng.
— Some Touch Is Good, Some Touch Is Bad - The Coloring Book. (Illus.). 8p. (Orig.). (J). (ps-k). 1995. pap. 1.25 (*0-9644142-4-4*) Open Book Pubng.
Molnar, John. Facilities Management Handbook. 256p. 1983. text ed. 57.95 (*0-442-26347-3*) Chapman & Hall.
Molnar, Julie A. Out from under the Artist's Brush: A Lacanian Approach to Painting & Naturalism. LC 91-3967. (American University Studies, II, Romance Language & Literature: Vol. 176). 173p. (C). 1994. text ed. 43.95 (*0-8204-1642-8*) P Lang Pubs.
Molnar, Michael, tr. see Shvarts, Elena.
Molnar, Miklos. Egy Vereseg Diadala. Kis, Janos, ed. (Adalekok az Ujabbikori Magyar Tortenelemhe Ser.). (Illus.). 221p. (Orig.). (HUN.). 1988. reprint ed. pap. 16. 00 (*0-929322-00-2*) Atl Rsch & Pubns.
— From Bela Kun to Janos Kadar: Seventy Years of Hungarian Communism. Pomerans, Arnold J., tr. LC 89-28943. 305p. 1990. 65.00 (*0-85496-599-8*) Berg Pubs.
Molnar, Miklos & Nagy, Laszlo. In Defense of the Hungarian People. 250p. (Orig.). (HUN.). 1984. pap. 13. 00 (*0-930888-23-5*) Brooklyn Coll Pr.
Molnar, Niklos & Nagy, Laszlo. Reformer Vagy Forradalmar Volt-e Nagy Imre? LC 83-61981. 160p. (HUN.). 1983. pap. 10.00 (*0-930888-22-7*) Brooklyn Coll Pr.
Molnar, P., jt. auth. see Burtman, V. S.
Molnar, P., jt. ed. see Grastyan, E.
Molnar, P., jt. auth. see Lissak, K.
Molnar, Ralph E., jt. auth. see Farlow, James O.
Molnar, Stephen. Human Variation: Races, Types, & Ethnic Groups. 3rd ed. 368p. (C). 1991. pap. text ed. write for info. (*0-13-446162-2*) P-H.
***Molnar, Thomas.** Authority & Its Enemies. rev. ed. LC 94-21409. 162p. (C). 1994. pap. 19.95 (*1-56000-777-X*) Transaction Pubs.
— Christian Humanism, a Critique of the Secular City & Its Ideology. 1978. 8.95 (*0-8199-0694-8*, Frncscn Herld) Franciscan Pr.
— The Decline of the Intellectual. rev. ed. LC 94-14112. 380p. (C). 1994. pap. 24.95 (*1-56000-743-5*) Transaction Pubs.
— Dialogues & Ideologues. 1977. reprint ed. 4.95 (*0-8199-0679-4*, Frncscn Herld) Franciscan Pr.
— The Emerging Atlantic Culture. LC 93-11170. 120p. (C). 1993. text ed. 29.95 (*1-56000-124-0*) Transaction Pubs.
— God & the Knowledge of Reality. LC 92-32934. 263p. (C). 1993. pap. text ed. 21.95 (*1-56000-665-X*) Transaction Pubs.
— Philosophical Grounds. LC 91-10918. (American University Studies: Philosophy: Ser. V, Vol. 114). 162p. (C). 1991. text ed. 32.95 (*0-8204-1485-9*) P Lang Pubs.
— Theist & Atheist: A Typology of Non-Belief. 1979. text ed. 44.75 (*90-279-7788-7*) Mouton.
— Utopia, the Perennial Heresy. rev. ed. 260p. (C). 1990. reprint ed. text ed. 43.00 (*0-8191-7667-2*); reprint ed. pap. text ed. 24.00 (*0-8191-7668-0*) U Pr of Amer.
***Molnar, Thomas S.** The Church, Pilgrim of Centuries. fac. ed. LC 90-41597. 192p. 1990. reprint ed. pap. 54.80 (*0-7837-7965-8*, 2047721) Bks Demand.
— The Pagan Temptation. LC 87-8898. 205p. (Orig.). reprint ed. pap. 58.50 (*0-7837-0519-0*, 2040843) Bks Demand.
— Twin Powers: Politics & the Sacred. LC 88-10204. 157p. reprint ed. pap. 44.80 (*0-7837-0520-4*, 2040844) Bks Demand.
***Molner, Leo J.** Recollections in Verse. 1995. 10.95 (*0-533-11291-5*) Vantage.
Molnia, B. F., jt. ed. see Anderson, J. B.
Molnia, Bruce F., ed. Glacial-Marine Sedimentation. LC 83-19104. 854p. 1984. 145.00 (*0-306-41497-X*, Plenum Pr) Plenum.
Molnos, Angela. Our Responses to a Deadly Virus: The Group-Analytic Approach to AIDS. 248p. 1990. pap. 30.95 (*0-946439-80-X*, Pub. by Karnac Bks UK) Brunner-Mazel.
— A Question of Time: Essentials of Brief Dynamic Psychotherapy. 152p. 1995. pap. 27.50 (*1-85575-107-0*) Brunner-Mazel.
Molodenskii, M. S., et al. Methods for Study of the External Gravitational Field & Figure of the Earth. LC 62-61244. 254p. reprint ed. pap. 72.40 (*0-317-07809-7*, 2002332) Bks Demand.
Molodyi, Boris, tr. see Lingenfelter, Scott, ed.
Molodyi, Vadim, tr. see Lingenfelter, Scott, ed.
Moloff, Ronald L. & Stein, Stephen D. Realities of Dental Therapy: A Detailed Review of Periodontal Prosthetic Treatment. (Illus.). 456p. 1982. text ed. 98.00 (*0-931386-42-X*) Quint Pub Co.
Molokhovets, Elena. Classic Russian Cooking: Elena Molokhovets' a Gift to Young Housewives. Toomre, Joyce, tr. & anno. by. LC 91-46254. (Indiana-Michigan Series in Russian & East European Studies). (Illus.). 704p. 1992. 39.95 (*0-253-36026-9*) Ind U Pr.
Moloney, Brian. Italo Svevo. 139p. 1974. 18.00 (*0-85224-248-4*, Pub. by Edinburgh U Pr UK) Col U Pr.
Moloney, Brian, intro. Novelle del Novecento. (Italian Texts Ser.). 150p. (Orig.). (ITA.). 1988. reprint ed. text ed. 14.95 (*0-7190-0200-1*, Pub. by Manchester Univ Pr UK) St Martin.
Moloney, Ed & Pollak, Andy. Paisley. (Illus.). 464p. 1986. pap. 13.95 (*0-905169-75-1*, Pub. by Poolbeg Pr IE) Dufour.
***Moloney, Francis J.** Beginning the Good News: A Narrative Approach. 176p. (Orig.). 1995. pap. text ed. 9.95 (*0-8146-2265-8*, Liturg Pr Bks) Liturgical Pr.
— Belief in the Word: Reading John 1-4. LC 92-21757. 336p. 1993. pap. 19.00 (*0-8006-2584-6*, 1-2584) Augsburg Fortress.
— Gospel of the Lord: Reflections on the Gospel Readings, Year C. LC 94-6110. 208p. 1994. 11.95 (*0-8146-2270-4*) Liturgical Pr.
— The Gospel of the Lord Year C: Reflections on the Gospel Readings. LC 95-7431. 1995. write for info. (*0-8146-2268-2*) Liturgical Pr.
— Mary: Woman & Mother. 72p. 1989. pap. 4.95 (*0-8146-1845-6*) Liturgical Pr.
Moloney, G. E. A Doctor in Saudi Arabia. (Arabia Past & Present Ser.: Vol. 23). (Illus.). 356p. 1985. 32.50 (*0-906672-81-3*) Oleander Pr.
Moloney-Harmon, Pat. Managing Pediatric Emergencies. (Cardiopulmonary Arrest Ser.). (Illus.). 104p. (Orig.). 1984. pap. text ed. 9.50 (*0-932491-03-0*) Res Appl Inc.
Moloney, James. Dougy. (YA). 1993. pap. 10.95 (*0-7022-2499-5*, Pub. by Univ Queensland Pr AT) Intl Spec Bk.
— The House on River Terrace. (YA). 1995. pap. 11.95 (*0-7022-2742-0*, Pub. by Univ Queensland Pr AT) Intl Spec Bk.
— Swashbuckler. (Storybridge Ser.). 96p. (J). (gr. 4-7). 1995. pap. 9.95 (*0-7022-2825-7*, Pub. by Univ Queensland Pr AT) Intl Spec Bk.
Moloney, James C. Understanding the Japanese Mind. LC 68-23316. 252p. 1968. reprint ed. text ed. 35.00 (*0-8371-0172-7*, MOJM, Greenwood Pr) Greenwood.
Moloney, Jerome V. & Newell, Alan C. Nonlinear Optics. (ATIMS Ser.). 320p. (C). 1992. 46.95 (*0-201-51014-6*, Adv Bk Prog) Addison-Wesley.
Moloney, Kathleen, jt. auth. see Ritchard, Dan.
Moloney, Margaret. Professionalization of Nursing: Current Issues & Trends. 2nd ed. (Illus.). 352p. 1991. pap. 25.95 (*0-397-54842-7*) Lippincott.
Moloney, Neil W. Cops, Crooks, & Politicians. 340p. pap. write for info. (*0-318-72640-8*) Peanut Butter.
— Cops, Crooks & Politicians. Date not set. pap. 17.95 (*0-89716-467-9*) Peanut Butter.
— Cops, Crooks & Politicians: A Bank Heist Exposed a Major Political Scandal. (Illus.). 340p. 1994. pap. text ed. 17.95 (*0-89716-510-1*) P B Pubng.
Moloney, Thomas, ed. Westminster, Whitehall & the Vatican: The Role of Cardinal Hinsley 1935-43. 264p. 1990. 39.00 (*0-86012-138-0*, Pub. by Srch Pr UK) St Mut.
Molony, Barbara. Technology & Investment: The Prewar Japanese Chemical Industry. LC 89-48815. (East Asian Monographs: No. 145). 396p. 1990. 32.00 (*0-674-87260-6*) HUP.

An Asterisk (*) at the beginning of an entry indicates that the title is appearing in BIP for the first time.

Molony, John C. Ireland's Tragic Comedians. LC 73-134117. (Essay Index Reprint Ser.). 1977. 21.95 (*0-8369-1933-5*) Ayer.

Molot, Maureen A., jt. auth. see Laux, Jeanne K.

Molotch, Harvey L., jt. ed. see Logan, John R.

Molotova, L. N. Folk Art of the Russian Federation. 204p. 1981. 143.00 (*0-317-61264-6*, Pub. by Collets UK) Pro-Am Music.

Molotova, L. N. & Sosnina, N. N. Russian Folk Clothing. 222p. 1984. 160.00 (*0-317-61374-X*, Pub. by Collets UK) Pro-Am Music.

Molotskii, M. I. Chemistry Reviews: Electronic Excitation During the Plastic Deformation & Fracture of Crystals, Vol. 13. Vol'pin, M. E., ed. (Soviet Scientific Reviews Ser.: Vol. 13, Pt. 3). ii, 94p. 1989. pap. text ed. 44.00 (*3-7186-4949-7*) Gordon & Breach.

Moloy, Peter & Nicolson, Garth L., eds. Cellular Oncology: New Approaches in Biology, Diagnosis & Treatment, Vol. 1. LC 83-11222. (Cancer Research Monographs). 320p. 1983. text ed. 65.00 (*0-275-91405-4*, C1405, Praeger Pubs) Greenwood.

— Occult Nodal Metastasis in Solid Carcinomata: Second International Symposium on Celluar Oncology. LC 87-15764. 267p. 1987. text ed. 75.00 (*0-275-92665-6*, C2665, Praeger Pubs) Greenwood.

Molpus, Ann R. The Expert Editor. 100p. 1990. pap. 12.00 (*0-935012-13-3*) Edit Experts.

Molrine, Charlotte N. & Molrine, Ronald C. Encountering Christ in the Episcopal Church: A Youth - Intergenerational Faith Experience Leading to a Renewal & Reaffirmation of the Baptismal Covenant. 150p. 1992. teacher ed. pap. 20.00 (*0-8192-4111-3*); pap. 9.95 (*0-8192-4112-1*) Morehouse Pub.

Molrine, Ronald C., jt. auth. see Molrine, Charlotte N.

Molseed, Elwood. The Genus Tigridia (Iridaceae) of Mexico & Central America. LC 70-626142. (University of California Publications in Social Welfare: Vol. 54). (Illus.). 139p. reprint ed. pap. 39.70 (*0-685-23552-1*, 2014699) Bks Demand.

Molson-Chesaw-Knob Hill Community Development Staff & Loe, Mary L. Okanogan Highland Album. (Illus.). 510p. (Orig.). 1988. pap. 19.95 (*0-940151-05-7*) Statesman Exam.

***Molson, K. M. & Shortt, A. J.** The Curtiss HS Flying Boats. (Illus.). 156p. 1995. pap. 29.95 (*1-55750-142-4*) Naval Inst Pr.

Molt, Cynthia M. Gone with the Wind on Film: A Complete Reference. LC 89-42736. 526p. 1990. lib. bdg. 49.95x (*0-89950-439-6*) McFarland & Co.

— Vivien Leigh: A Bio-Bibliography. LC 92-23785. (Bio-Bibliographies in the Performing Arts Ser.: No. 35). 352p. 1992. text ed. 45.00 (*0-313-27578-5*, MVL, Greenwood Pr) Greenwood.

Molt, Mary, jt. auth. see Shugart, Grace.

Molter, Gunther. Ferry Porsche. (Illus.). 316p. 1989. 39.95 (*1-85260-259-7*, Pub. by Thorsons UK) Motorbooks Intl.

Moltke-Hansen, David, jt. ed. see O'Brien, Michael.

***Moltmann, Johann F. & Rombke, Jorg, eds.** Applied Ecotoxicology. 272p. 1995. 59.95 (*1-56670-070-1*, L1070) Lewis Pubs.

Moltmann, Jurgen. The Church in the Power of the Spirit: A Contribution to Messianic Ecclesiology. Kohl, Margaret, tr. LC 93-29951. 1993. 16.00 (*0-8006-2821-7*, Fortress Pr) Augsburg Fortress.

— The Crucified God: The Cross of Christ as the Foundation & Criticism of Christian Theology. Wilson, R. A. & Bowden, John, trs. LC 93-29953. 1993. 16.00 (*0-8006-2822-5*, Fortress Pr) Augsburg Fortress.

— God in Creation: A New Theology of Creation & the Spirit of God. LC 93-26365. 1993. 16.00 (*0-8006-2823-3*, Fortress Pr) Augsburg Fortress.

— The History & the Triune God. 256p. 1992. 27.50 (*0-8245-1127-1*) Crossroad NY.

— Jesus Christ for Today's World. Kohl, Margaret, tr. LC 94-13407. 1994. pap. 12.00 (*0-8006-2817-9*, 1-2817, Fortress Pr) Augsburg Fortress.

— Man: Christian Anthropology in the Conflicts of the Present. LC 73-88350. 136p. reprint ed. pap. 38.80 (*0-685-15399-1*, 2026872) Bks Demand.

— The Spirit of Life: A Universal Affirmation. Kohl, Margaret, tr. LC 92-18513. 360p. 1992. 25.00 (*0-8006-2737-7*, 1-2737) Augsburg Fortress.

— Theology of Hope: On the Ground & the Implications of a Christian Eschatology. Leitch, James W., tr. LC 93-29966. 1993. pap. 16.00 (*0-8006-2824-1*, 1-2824, Fortress Pr) Augsburg Fortress.

— The Trinity & the Kingdom: The Doctrine of God. Kohl, Margaret, tr. LC 93-29952. (ENG.). 1993. reprint ed. 16.00 (*0-8006-2825-X*) Augsburg Fortress.

— The Way of Jesus Christ: Christology in Messianic Dimensions. Kohl, Margaret, tr. LC 93-29961. 1993. 19.00 (*0-8006-2826-8*, Fortress Pr) Augsburg Fortress.

Moltmann, Jurgen, jt. ed. see Kung, Hans.

Moltmann, Jurgen, jt. auth. see Lapide, Phinn E.

Moltmann, Jurgen, jt. auth. see Metz, Johann-Baptist.

Moltmann, Jurgen, jt. auth. see Moltmann-Wendel, Elisabeth.

Moltmann, Jurgen, et al. Communities of Faith & Radical Discipleship. Mitchell, Carlton T. & Bryan, McLeod G., eds. LC 86-16452. (Luce Program on Religion & the Social Crisis Ser.: No. 2). x, 130p. 1986. 16.95 (*0-86554-216-3*, H195) Mercer Univ Pr.

— Religion & Political Society. LC 73-18424. (Symposium Ser.: Vol. 1). xi, 209p. 1976. reprint ed. 89.95 (*0-88946-953-9*) E Mellen.

***Moltmann-Wendel, Elisabeth.** I am my Body: New Waves of Embodiment. Bowden, John, tr. LC 94-37801. 128p. 1995. pap. text ed. 11.95 (*0-8264-0786-2*) Continuum.

— A Land Flowing with Milk & Honey: Perspectives on Feminist Theology. 224p. 1988. pap. 9.95 (*0-8245-0863-7*) Crossroad NY.

— The Women Around Jesus. LC 82-72478. 160p. 1982. pap. 9.95 (*0-8245-0535-2*) Crossroad NY.

Moltmann-Wendel, Elisabeth & Moltmann, Jurgen. God - His & Hers. 128p. 1991. pap. 9.95 (*0-8245-1128-X*) Crossroad NY.

— Humanity in God. LC 83-4180. (Illus.). 152p. (Orig.). 1993. reprint ed. pap. 12.95 (*0-8298-0670-9*) Pilgrim OH.

Moltmann-Wendel, Elizabeth. Liberty, Equality, Sisterhood: On the Emancipation of Women in Church & Society. Gritsch, Ruth, tr. LC 77-15240. 95p. reprint ed. pap. 27.10 (*0-685-15981-7*, 2026919) Bks Demand.

Moltoft, J. & Jensen, F., eds. Reliability Technology: Theory & Applications. 450p. 1986. 110.25 (*0-444-70039-0*, North Holland) Elsevier.

Molton, Warren L. Friends, Partners & Lovers: Marks of Vital Marriage. rev. ed. LC 93-16196. 192p. 1993. pap. 14.00 (*0-8170-1187-0*) Judson.

Moltrecht, K. H. Machine Shop Practice, Vol. 1. 2nd ed. LC 79-91236. (Illus.). 496p. (C). 1981. 19.95 (*0-8311-1126-7*) Indus Pr.

— Machine Shop Practice, Vol. 2. 2nd ed. LC 79-91236. (Illus.). 517p. (C). 1981. 19.95 (*0-8311-1132-1*) Indus Pr.

Moltz, Howard. Symbiosis In Parent-Offspring Interactions. Rosenblum, Leonard A., ed. 300p. 1983. 65.00 (*0-306-41410-4*, Plenum Pr) Plenum.

Moltz, James C., ed. see Dewing, Martin J.

Moltzan, Antoinette. Open to Light. Cagan, Lisa J., ed. 170p. (Orig.). 1992. pap. text ed. 12.95 (*1-881107-00-0*) Masters Pub.

Moltzer, J. Oelfeld-Fachwoerterbuch. deluxe ed. (DUT, ENG, FRE, GER & SPA.). 1965. 37.50 (*0-7859-0838-2*, M-7576) Fr & Eur.

Molumphy, Henry D. Development Through Health. (Illus.). 16p. 1985. 1.00 (*0-918397-01-4*) Foster Parents.

— For Common Decency: The History of Foster Parents Plan, 1937-1983. LC 84-223205. (Illus.). 380p. (Orig.). 1984. pap. text ed. 10.00 (*0-918397-00-6*) Foster Parents.

— Time, Water & Development. (Illus.). 16p. 1986. 1.00 (*0-918397-02-2*) Foster Parents.

Molund, Stefan. First We Are People: The Koris of Kanpur Between Caste & Class. (Stockholm Studies in Social Anthropology: No. 20). (Illus.). 284p. (Orig.). 1988. pap. 67.00x (*91-7146-701-7*, Pub. by Almqv & Wiksell SW) Coronet Bks.

Molutsi, Patrick P., jt. ed. see Holm, John D.

Molvaer, Reidulf K. Environmental Cooperation & Confidence Building in the Horn of Africa. (International Peace Research Institute Ser.). (Illus.). 240p. (C). 1995. text ed. 62.00 (*0-8039-8847-8*) Sage.

Molvar, Eric. Trail Guide to Bob Marshall Country. (Falcon Guides Ser.). (Illus.). 200p. (Orig.). 1994. pap. 19.95 (*1-56044-254-9*) Falcon Pr MT.

Molvar, Erik. Trail Guide to Glacier & Waterton National Parks. (FalconGuide Ser.). (Illus.). 160p. 1994. reprint ed. pap. 10.95 (*1-56044-245-X*) Falcon Pr MT.

— The Trail Guide to Olympic National Park. LC 95-12211. (Falcon Guide Ser.). (Illus.). 232p. 1995. pap. 14.95 (*1-56044-333-2*) Falcon Pr MT.

Molver, Eileen. Lindiwi Finds a Way. (Junior African Writers Ser.). (Illus.). (J). (gr. 5-6). 1992. pap. 4.95 (*0-7910-2915-8*) Chelsea Hse.

Molyneaux, B. L., jt. auth. see Stone, P. G.

***Molyneaux, Brian.** The Sacred Earth. 1995. pap. 14.95 (*0-316-90303-5*) Little.

Molyneaux, David G. & Sackman, Sue, eds. Seventy-Five Years, an Informal History of Shaker Heights. (Illus.). (Orig.). 1987. pap. text ed. 8.50 (*0-9619188-0-2*) Shaker Hgts Pub Lib.

Molyneaux, Dorothy & Lane, Vera W. Successful Interactive Skills for Speech-Language Pathologists & Audiologists. (Excellence in Practice Ser.). 218p. (C). 1989. text ed. 52.00 (*0-8342-0106-2*) Aspen Pub.

Molyneaux, Dorothy, jt. auth. see Lane, Vera W.

Molyneaux, Frank, et al, eds. Learning for Life: Politics & Progress in Recurrent Education. 336p. 1987. lib. bdg. 59.00 (*0-317-64375-4*, Pub. by Croom Helm UK) Routledge Chapman & Hall.

Molyneaux, Gary A., jt. auth. see Altengarten, James S.

***Molyneaux, Gerard.** Gregory Peck: A Bio-Bibliography. LC 95-12419. (Bio-Bibliographies in the Performing Arts Ser.: No. 19). 376p. 1995. text ed. 55.00 (*0-313-28668-X*, Greenwood Pr) Greenwood.

— James Stewart: A Bio-Bibliography. LC 91-36134. (Bio-Bibliographies in the Performing Arts Ser.: No. 24). 320p. 1992. text ed. 45.00 (*0-313-27352-9*, MJT/, Greenwood Pr) Greenwood.

Molyneux, Bill & Forrester, Sue. Choosing & Growing Australian Plants. (Illus.). 192p. (Orig.). 1994. pap. 12.95 (*0-86417-516-7*, Pub. by Kangaroo Pr AT) Seven Hills Bk.

— Native Gardens in Miniature. (Illus.). 136p. (Orig.). 1993. pap. 12.95 (*0-86417-463-2*, Pub. by Kangaroo Pr AT) Seven Hills Bk.

Molyneux, Bill & MacDonald, Ross. Native Gardens: How to Create an Australian Native Landscape. (Illus.). 136p. (Orig.). 1993. pap. 12.95 (*0-86417-462-4*, Pub. by Kangaroo Pr AT) Seven Hills Bk.

Molyneux, D. H., et al. The Biology of Trypansoma & Leishmania: Parasites of Man & Domestic Animals. 274p. 1983. 71.00 (*0-8002-3078-7*) Taylor & Francis.

***Molyneux, Isabel.** The Vietnam Connection. (Illus.). 264p. 1995. pap. 18.95 (*1-85756-134-1*) Paul & Co Pubs.

Molyneux, John. Leon Trotsky's Theory of Revolution. 1981. text ed. 29.95 (*0-312-47994-8*) St Martin.

***Molyneux, Joyce & Grigson, Sophie.** The Carved Angel Cookery Book. 176p. 1994. 28.00 (*0-00-411264-4*, HarpT) HarpC.

Molyneux, K. Gordon. African Christian Theology: The Quest for Self-hood. LC 93-16622. 432p. 1993. pap. 89.95 (*0-7734-1946-2*) E Mellen.

Molyneux, Liz, jt. auth. see Leppard, John.

Molyneux, Lynn. Active Learning for Young Children. (Illus.). 228p. 1989. 19.95 (*0-685-29143-X*) Trellis Bks Inc.

— Get It Together: Group Projects for Creative Bulletin Boards. (Illus.). 160p. (J). (gr. k-4). 1983. per. 9.95 (*0-685-29141-3*) Trellis Bks Inc.

— Lifesavers. (Illus.). 192p. (gr. k-6). 1987. spiral bd. 14.95 (*0-685-29138-3*) Trellis Bks Inc.

— Up the Math Ladder: Activity Based Ideas for Teaching Math to Primary Grades. (Illus.). 160p. (gr. k-4). 1984. per. 9.95 (*0-685-29137-5*) Trellis Bks Inc.

— Up the Science Ladder: Activity Based Ideas for Teaching Science to Primary Grades. (Illus.). 128p. 1988. per. 9.95 (*0-685-29136-7*) Trellis Bks Inc.

— Up the Social Studies Ladder: Activity Based Ideas for Teaching Social Studies to Primary Grades. (Illus.). 128p. 1988. per. 9.95 (*0-685-29135-9*) Trellis Bks Inc.

Molyneux, Lynn & Bucur, Mike. Your Own Thing: Individual Art Projects for Primary Grades. (Illus.). 160p. (J). (gr. k-6). 1983. per. 9.95 (*0-685-29140-5*) Trellis Bks Inc.

Molyneux, Lynn & Gordner, Brad. Act It Out: Original Plays Plus Crafts for Costumes & Scenery. (Illus.). 192p. (J). (gr. 2-6). 1986. spiral bd. 12.95 (*0-685-29139-1*) Trellis Bks Inc.

Molyneux, Lynn & Lipson, Fran. Up the Reading Ladder: Activity Based Ideas for Teaching Reading to Primary Grades. (Illus.). 160p. 1984. per. 9.95 (*0-685-29142-1*) Trellis Bks Inc.

Molyneux, Mary. Lessons for a Fourth Grade Class. (Illus.). 13p. 1982. 7.50 (*0-915124-74-2*, Toothpaste) Coffee Hse.

Molyneux, N. Z. Eaton: History, Genealogical & Biography of the Eaton Family. (Illus.). 782p. 1991. reprint ed. lib. bdg. 109.00 (*0-8328-1903-4*); reprint ed. pap. 99.00 (*0-8328-1904-2*) Higginson Bk Co.

— History, Genealogical & Biographical of the Molyneux Family. (Illus.). 370p. 1989. reprint ed. lib. bdg. 63.50 (*0-8328-0874-1*); reprint ed. pap. 55.50 (*0-8328-0875-X*) Higginson Bk Co.

Molyneux, P. Water Soluble Synthetic Polymers: Properties & Behavior, 2 Vols., Vol. I. 240p. 1984. 168.00 (*0-8493-6135-4*, QD382) CRC Pr.

— Water Soluble Synthetic Polymers: Properties & Behavior, 2 Vols., Vol. II. 280p. 1984. 168.00 (*0-8493-6136-2*, QD382) CRC Pr.

Molyneux, Phil, jt. ed. see Ennals, Richard.

Molyneux, Philip, ed. Directory of European Banking & Financial Associations. 238p. 1990. lib. bdg. 65.00 (*1-55862-077-X*) St James Pr.

Molyneux, Philip, jt. auth. see Gardener, Edward P.

Molyneux, Philip, jt. auth. see Gardner, Edward P.

Molyneux, R. The Gerould Statistics, 1907-08 Through 1961-62. 266p. 1986. 25.00 (*0-918006-11-2*) ARL.

Molyneux, Robert E., comp. ACRL - Historically Black Colleges & Universities Library Statistics, 1988-89. 101p. 1991. 35.95 (*0-8389-7547-X*); 25.95 (*0-685-59355-X*) Assn Coll & Res Libs.

— ACRL University Library Statistics, 1987-88. 79p. 1989. 49.95 (*0-8389-7288-8*); 29.95 (*0-685-58538-7*) Assn Coll & Res Libs.

Molyneuy, J. H. Simonides: A Historical Study. 300p. (Orig.). 1991. 39.00 (*0-86516-222-0*); pap. 24.00 (*0-86516-223-9*) Bolchazy-Carducci.

Molz, Redmond K. Library Planning & Policy Making: The Legacy of the Public & Private Sectors. LC 90-8020. (Library Administration Ser.: No. 2). 233p. 1990. 20.00 (*0-8108-2272-5*) Scarecrow.

Molz, Rick. Privatization & Management Adaptation. 350p. (C). 1929. pap. text ed. 34.95 (*0-8133-7834-6*) Westview.

Momaday, N. Scott. The Ancient Child: A Novel. LC 89-46497. 336p. 1990. reprint ed. pap. 12.00 (*0-06-097345-5*, PL) HarpC.

— Circle of Wonder: A Native American Christmas Story. LC 93-5387. (Illus.). 82p. 1993. 14.95 (*0-940666-32-4*) Clear Light.

— House Made of Dawn. 192p. 1994. lib. bdg. 29.00x (*0-8095-9141-3*) Borgo Pr.

— House Made of Dawn. LC 89-45125. 192p. 1989. reprint ed. pap. 12.00 (*0-06-091633-8*, PL) HarpC.

— In the Presence of the Sun: A Gathering of Shields. deluxe limited ed. (Illus.). 40p. 1991. 300.00 (*0-911292-04-7*) Rydal.

— In the Presence of the Sun: Stories & Poems, 1961-1991. (Illus.). 160p. 1992. 17.95 (*0-312-08222-3*) St Martin.

— In the Presence of the Sun: Stories & Poems, 1961-1991. (Illus.). 176p. 1993. pap. 9.95 (*0-312-09830-8*) St Martin.

— In the Presence of the Sun: Stories & Poems, 1961-1991. deluxe ed. (Illus.). 160p. 1992. 100.00 (*0-312-08506-0*) St Martin.

— The Names. LC 87-18785. (Sun Tracks Ser.: Vol. 16). 170p. 1987. reprint ed. pap. 9.95 (*0-8165-1046-6*) U of Ariz Pr.

— The Way to Rainy Mountain. LC 69-19154. (Illus.). 90p. 1976. reprint ed. pap. 8.95 (*0-8263-0436-2*) U of NM Pr.

Momaday, N. Scott, et al. The Native Americans: Indian Country. 1993. write for info. (*0-318-69805-6*) Turner Pub GA.

Momaday, Natachee S. Owl in the Cedar Tree. LC 91-41866. (Illus.). viii, 117p. (J). 1992. reprint ed. pap. 9.95 (*0-8032-8184-6*, Bison Books) U of Nebr Pr.

Momar-Coumba, Diop & Real, Lavergne, eds. Regional Integration in West Africa: Proceedings of the International Conference. 67p. 1994. pap. 9.95 (*0-88936-712-4*, IDRC7124, Pub. by IDRC CN) UNIPUB.

***Momas, John C.** Public Participation in Public Decisions: New Skills & Strategies for Public Managers. LC 95-13425. (Public Administration Ser.). 1995. 26.95 (*0-7879-0129-6*) Jossey-Bass.

Momatiuk & Eastcott. This Marvellous Terrible Place, Images of Newfoundland & Labrador. 176p. 1988. pap. 19.95 (*0-920656-67-6*, Pub. by Camden Hse CN) Firefly Bks Ltd.

Momatiuk, Yva & Eastcott, John. In a Sea of Wind: Images of the Prairies. (Illus.). 160p. 1991. pap. 22.95 (*0-921820-35-6*, Pub. by Camden Hse CN) Firefly Bks Ltd.

Mombello, Ronald P. The Martial Artist As a Work of Art: A Biography. LC 91-73108. 70p. 1991. pap. 14.95 (*0-9631732-0-0*) Document Wks.

Mombert, J. I. An Authentic History of Lancaster County, Pennsylvania. Iscrupe, William L. & Iscrupe, Shirley G., eds. 760p. 1988. reprint ed. 45.00 (*0-944128-01-7*) SW PA Geneal Servs.

Mombritius, Boninus. Sanctuarium Seu Vitae Sanctorum, 2 vols., Set. 1978. reprint ed. write for info. (*3-487-06527-4*, Pub. by Georg Olms GW) Lubrecht & Cramer.

— Sanctuarium seu Vitae Sanctorum: Editionem Curaverunt Duo Monachi Solesmenses. 680p. (LAT.). 1978. reprint ed. lib. bdg. write for info. (*3-487-06528-2*, Pub. by Georg Olms GW); reprint ed. lib. bdg. write for info. (*3-487-06529-0*, Pub. by Georg Olms GW) Lubrecht & Cramer.

— Sanctuarium seu Vitae Sanctorum: Editionem Curaverunt Duo Monachi Solesmenses, 2 vols., Set. 1513p. (LAT.). 1978. lib. bdg. 338.00x (*0-614-03385-3*, Pub. by Georg Olms GW) Lubrecht & Cramer.

***Momen, Moojan.** Buddhism & the Baha'i Faith: An Introduction to the Baha'i Faith for Theravada Buddhists. 128p. (Orig.). 1995. pap. 11.95 (*0-85398-384-4*) G Ronald Pub.

— Hinduism & the Baha'i Faith. 96p. (Orig.). 1990. pap. 9.25 (*0-85398-299-6*) G Ronald Pub.

— Selections from the Writings of E. G. Browne on the Babi & Baha'i Religions. 528p. 1987. 36.50 (*0-85398-246-5*); pap. 19.95 (*0-85398-247-3*) G Ronald Pub.

Momen, Moojan, ed. Studies in Babi & Baha'i History, Vol. 1. (Illus.). 337p. (C). 1982. text ed. 32.50 (*0-933770-16-2*) Kalimat.

Momen, Moojan, jt. ed. see Cole, Juan R.

Momen, Moojan, tr. see Labib, Muhammad.

Momen, Wendi, ed. A Basic Baha'i Dictionary. (Illus.). 261p. 1989. pap. 21.50 (*0-85398-231-7*) G Ronald Pub.

— Family Worship. 90p. 1989. 11.25 (*0-85398-289-9*) G Ronald Pub.

Momeni, Jamshid A. Demography of Racial & Ethnic Minorities in the United States: An Annotated Bibliography with a Review Essay. LC 84-6724. (Bibliographies & Indexes in Sociology Ser.: No. 2). (Illus.). xxiii, 292p. 1984. text ed. 75.00 (*0-313-23975-4*, MDR/) Greenwood.

— Demography of the Black Population in the United States: An Annotated Bibliography with a Review Essay. LC 83-5544. (Illus.). xxi, 353p. 1983. text ed. 65.00 (*0-313-23812-X*, MDB/, Greenwood Pr) Greenwood.

— Housing & Racial-Ethnic Minority Status in the United States: An Annotated Bibliography with a Review Essay. LC 86-27089. (Bibliographies & Indexes in Sociology Ser.: No. 8). 352p. 1987. text ed. 65.00 (*0-313-24820-6*, MHR/) Greenwood.

Momeni, Jamshid A., ed. Homelessness in the United States, 2 vols. (Contributions in Sociology Ser.). (Illus.). 1989. 110.00 (*0-313-26793-6*, MHL/, Greenwood Pr) Greenwood.

— Homelessness in the United States - State Surveys. LC 90-30385. 283p. 1989. text ed. 55.00 (*0-313-25566-0*, MHL01, Greenwood Pr) Greenwood.

— Homelessness in the United States - State Surveys. LC 90-30385. 283p. 1990. pap. text ed. 16.95 (*0-275-93603-1*, B3603, Praeger Pubs) Greenwood.

— Homelessness in the United States, Vol. II: Data & Issues. LC 88-10964. (Contributions in Sociology Ser.: No. 87). 216p. 1990. pap. text ed. 15.95 (*0-275-93632-5*, B3632, Greenwood Pr) Greenwood.

— Homelessness in the United States, Vol. II: Data & Issues, Vol. 2. LC 88-10964. (Contributions in Sociology Ser.: No. 87). 216p. 1990. text ed. 55.00 (*0-313-26792-8*, MHL02, Greenwood Pr) Greenwood.

— Race, Ethnicity, & Minority Housing in the United States. LC 86-9971. (Contributions in Ethnic Studies: No. 16). (Illus.). 249p. 1986. text ed. 55.00 (*0-313-24848-6*, MRY/, Greenwood Pr) Greenwood.

Moment, Gairdner B. Nutritional Approaches to Aging Research. 280p. 1982. 134.00 (*0-8493-5831-0*, QP86, CRC Reprint) Franklin.

***Momentum Books Staff.** Pocket Guide to Detroit & Michigan Restaurants. 1994. pap. 8.95 (*1-879094-32-0*) Momentum Bks.

Momentum Wave Function Determination in Atomic, Molecular & Nuclear Systems Workshop Staff. Momentum Wave Functions: Proceedings of the Workshop, Indiana Univ., Bloomington, May 31-June 4, 1976. Devins, D. W., ed. LC 77-82145. (AIP Conference Proceedings Ser.: No. 36). (Illus.). 1977. lib. bdg. 17.50 (*0-88318-135-5*) Am Inst Physics.

Momeyer, Richard W. Confronting Death. LC 87-45439. (Medical Ethics Ser.). 204p. 1988. 25.00 (*0-253-31403-8*) Ind U Pr.

Momigliano. Essays on Hebrews. (C). 1994. 24.95 (*0-226-53381-6*) U Ch Pr.

Momigliano, Arnaldo. A.D. Momigliano: Studies on Modern Scholarship. Bowersock, G. W. & Cornell, T. J., eds. Cornell, T. J., tr. LC 93-42827. 1994. 40.00 (*0-520-07001-1*); pap. 17.00 (*0-520-85450-0*) U CA Pr.

An Asterisk (*) at the beginning of an entry indicates that the title is appearing in BIP for the first time.

— Essays in Ancient & Modern Historiography. LC 76-41484. 397p. 1982. pap. 20.00 (*0-8195-6074-X*, Wesleyan Univ Pr) U Pr of New Eng.
— On Pagans, Jews, & Christians. LC 87-24264. 357p. (C). 1989. pap. 18.95 (*0-8195-6218-1*, Wesleyan Univ Pr) U Pr of New Eng.
Momigliano, Arnaldo D. Alien Wisdom: The Limits of Hellenization. LC 75-10237. 140p. 1976. 45.00 (*0-521-20876-9*) Cambridge U Pr.
— Alien Wisdom: The Limits of Hellenization. 184p. (C). 1990. pap. 18.95 (*0-521-38761-2*) Cambridge U Pr.
— The Classical Foundations of Modern Historiography. LC 89-20510. (Sather Classical Lectures: No. 54). 180p. 1990. pap. 12.00 (*0-520-07870-5*) U CA Pr.
— Claudius, the Emperor & His Achievement. rev. ed. Hogarth, W. D., tr. LC 80-26158. xv, 143p. 1981. reprint ed. text ed. 59.75 (*0-313-20813-1*, MOCE, Greenwood Pr) Greenwood.
— The Development of Greek Biography. LC 92-34861. 155p. 1993. pap. 13.95 (*0-674-20041-1*) HUP.
Momigliano, Arnoldo. Sagesses Barbares. (FRE.). 1991. pap. 11.95 (*0-7859-3980-6*) Fr & Eur.
Momigny, J., jt. auth. see Illenberger, E.
Momiyama, Masako S., ed. Seasonality in Human Mortality: A Medico-Geographical Study. 177p. 1977. 29.50 (*0-86008-182-6*, Pub. by U of Tokyo JA) Col U Pr.
Momiyama, Nanae. Sumi-E: An Introduction to Ink Painting. LC 67-15320. (Illus.). 36p. (J). 1967. pap. 6.95 (*0-8048-0554-7*) C E Tuttle.
Momm, Willi, jt. auth. see Harper, Malcolm.
***Mommaers, Paul & van Braegt, Jan.** Mysticism, Buddhist & Christian: Encounters with Jan van Ruusbroec. LC 94-31692. (Nanzan Studies in Religion & Culture). 272p. 1995. 29.95 (*0-8245-1455-6*) Crossroad NY.
Mommen, Andre. The Belgian Economy in the Twentieth Century. LC 93-34914. (Contemporary Economic History of Europe Ser.). 272p. 1994. 75.00x (*0-415-01936-2*, B3913, Routledge NY) Routledge.
Mommsen, A. Athenae Christianae. (Illus.). 177p. 1977. 25.00 (*0-89005-216-6*) Ares.
Mommsen, H. Diccionario Medico Labor para la Familia. (SPA.). 1979. write for info. (*0-8288-4775-4*, S50063) Fr & Eur.
— Diccionario Medico Labor para la Familia. 6th ed. 880p. (SPA.). 1982. 150.00 (*0-7859-5093-1*) Fr & Eur.
Mommsen, Hans. From Weimar to Auschwitz: Essays in German History. O'Connor, Philip, tr. 320p. 1991. 35.00 (*0-691-03198-3*) Princeton U Pr.
Mommsen, Katharina, ed. Goethe, Johann Wolfgang von: Who Is Goethe? Willson, Jeanne & Willson, Leslie, trs. LC 82-10674. (Illus.). 127p. (Orig.). 1983. 10.00 (*3-518-03054-X*, Pub. by Suhr Verlag GW) Intl Bk Import.
Mommsen, Katharina & Koc, Richard A., eds. Goethe, Johann Wolfgang von: Die Leiden des Jungen Werther. LC 85-12554. (Suhrkamp Text Edition Ser.). (Illus.). xviii, 216p. (Orig.). (ENG & GER.). (C). 1987. pap. 14.95 (*3-518-02971-1*, Pub. by Suhr Verlag GW) Intl Bk Import.
Mommsen, Katharina, ed. see Guthke, Karl S.
Mommsen, T. P., jt. ed. see Hochachka, P. W.
Mommsen, T. P., jt. auth. see Hochachka, Peter W.
Mommsen, Theodor. Abriss Des Romischen Staatsrechts. Mayer, J. P., ed. LC 78-67369. (European Political Thought Ser.). (GER.). 1980. reprint ed. lib. bdg. 30.95 (*0-405-11721-3*) Ayer.
— Gesammelt Schriften, Bd. I: Juristische Schriften. viii, 479p. 1965. write for info. (*3-296-14641-5*, Pub. by Georg Olms GW) Lubrecht & Cramer.
— Gesammelt Schriften, Bd. II: Juristische Schriften. viii, 459p. 1965. write for info. (*3-296-14642-3*, Pub. by Georg Olms GW) Lubrecht & Cramer.
— Gesammelt Schriften, Bd. III: Juristische Schriften. xii, 632p. 1965. write for info. (*3-296-14643-1*, Pub. by Georg Olms GW) Lubrecht & Cramer.
— Gesammelt Schriften, Bd. IV: Historische Schriften. viii, 566p. 1965. write for info. (*3-296-14644-X*, Pub. by Georg Olms GW) Lubrecht & Cramer.
— Gesammelt Schriften, Bd. V: Historische Schriften. vi, 617p. 1965. write for info. (*3-296-14645-8*, Pub. by Georg Olms GW) Lubrecht & Cramer.
— Gesammelt Schriften, Bd. VI: Historische Schriften. viii, 695p. 1965. write for info. (*3-296-14646-6*, Pub. by Georg Olms GW) Lubrecht & Cramer.
— Gesammelt Schriften, Bd. VII: Philologische Schriften. xi, 825p. 1965. write for info. (*3-296-14647-4*, Pub. by Georg Olms GW) Lubrecht & Cramer.
— Gesammelt Schriften, Bd. VIII: Epigraphische und Numismatische Schriften. x, 626p. 1965. write for info. (*3-296-14648-2*, Pub. by Georg Olms GW) Lubrecht & Cramer.
— Inscriptiones Regni Neapolitani Latinae. xxiv, 526p. reprint ed. write for info. (*0-318-72105-8*, Pub. by Georg Olms GW) Lubrecht & Cramer.
— The Provinces of the Roman Empire, 2 vols., Set. 756p. 1974. pap. 50.00 (*0-89005-052-X*) Ares.
— Reden und Aufsatze. vi, 479p. 1976. reprint ed. write for info. (*3-487-06043-4*, Pub. by Georg Olms GW) Lubrecht & Cramer.
— Roemische Geschichte, 4. 121p. (GER.). 1966. pap. text ed. 13.95 (*3-487-10124-6*, Pub. by Georg Olms GW) Lubrecht & Cramer.
— Romische Forschungen, 2 vols. viii, 952p. 1962. reprint ed. write for info. (*0-318-71178-8*, Pub. by Georg Olms GW) Lubrecht & Cramer.
— Romissche Geschichte. Vierter Band. Bd. 13. 33p. 1966. reprint ed. write for info. (*0-318-71179-6*, Pub. by Georg Olms GW) Lubrecht & Cramer.
— Die Unteritalischen Dialekte. (Illus.). viii, 368p. reprint ed. write for info. (*0-318-71603-8*, Pub. by Georg Olms GW) Lubrecht & Cramer.
Mommsen, Theodor & Meyer, Paul M., eds. Codex Theodosianus, Vol. I, Pars 1. 1970. write for info. (*3-296-11701-6*, Pub. by Georg Olms GW) Lubrecht & Cramer.
— Codex Theodosianus, Vol. I, Pars 2. iv, 932p. 1971. write for info. (*3-296-11702-4*, Pub. by Georg Olms GW) Lubrecht & Cramer.
— Codex Theodosianus, Vol. II: Novellae. cx, 220p. 1971. write for info. (*3-296-11703-2*, Pub. by Georg Olms GW) Lubrecht & Cramer.
Mommsen, Theodor & Rice, Eugene F., Jr. Medieval & Renaissance Studies. LC 82-2855. (Illus.). 353p. 1982. reprint ed. text ed. 59.75 (*0-313-23482-5*, MOMM, Greenwood Pr) Greenwood.
Mommsen, Theodor, jt. ed. see Kruger, Paul.
Mommsen, Theodor, ed. see Solinus.
Mommsen, Theodorus, ed. see Augustus, Justinianus.
Mommsen, T.P., jt. auth. see Hochachka, P.W.
Mommsen, W. J., ed. The Emergence of the Welfare State in Britain & Germany, 1850-1950. 443p. 1981. 37.50 (*0-7099-1710-4*, Pub. by Croom Helm UK) Routledge Chapman & Hall.
Mommsen, W. J. & De Moor, J. A., eds. European Expansion & Law: The Encounter of European & Indigenous Law in 19th- & 20th-Century Africa & Asia. 352p. 1992. 68.00 (*0-85496-762-1*) Berg Pubs.
Mommsen, W. J. & Hirschfield, Gerhard. Social Protest, Violence & Terror in Nineteenth & Twentieth-Century Europe. LC 81-51615. 320p. 1982. text ed. 32.50 (*0-312-73471-9*) St Martin.
Mommsen, Wolfgang. Long Way to Europe: Historical Observations from a Contemporary View. LC 93-36819. 254p. 1994. 24.95 (*0-86715-270-2*) Edition Q.
Mommsen, Wolfgang J. Max Weber & German Politics: 1890-1920. Steinberg, Michael S., tr. LC 84-16274. 456p. 1985. lib. bdg. 50.00 (*0-226-53397-2*) U Ch Pr.
— Max Weber & German Politics: 1890-1920. Steinberg, Michael S., tr. LC 84-16274. xxii, 498p. 1990. pap. text ed. 19.95 (*0-226-53399-9*) U Ch Pr.
— The Political & Social Theory of Max Weber: Collected Essays. LC 88-36950. 260p. 1989. 39.95 (*0-226-53398-0*) U Ch Pr.
— The Political & Social Theory of Max Weber: Collected Essays. LC 88-36950. xiv, 208p. 1992. pap. text ed. 13.95 (*0-226-53400-6*) U Ch Pr.
— Theories of Imperialism. Falla, P. S., tr. LC 81-16091. (C). 1982. reprint ed. pap. text ed. 10.95 (*0-226-53396-4*) U Ch Pr.
Momo, Taro. Adorable Mini Dolls. (Illus.). 96p. (Orig.). 1988. pap. 12.95 (*0-87040-761-9*) Japan Pubns USA.
***Momorsky, Jeffrey D., ed.** Health Care Guide. LC 94-186078. 1995. 297.00 (*0-7913-1968-7*) Warren Gorham & Lamont.
Momotani, Yoshihide. Flying Bird Origami. (Illus.). 70p. (Orig.). 1993. pap. 12.95 (*0-87040-908-5*) Japan Pubns USA.
— Origami Dinosaurs. Noma, Chikako & Einzig, Barbara, eds. (Illus.). 68p. 1993. pap. 12.00 (*1-56836-008-8*) Kodansha.
— Trick Origami. (Illus.). 69p. 1994. pap. 16.00 (*0-87040-929-8*) Japan Pubns USA.
Momrow, Edward G. Creative Partnership: A Guide for Couples in Serious Relationships. 119p. (Orig.). 1992. pap. text ed. 9.95x (*0-9641321-0-9*) E G Momrow.
Momsen, Janet H. Women & Development in the Third World. (Illus.). 128p. 1991. pap. 15.95 (*0-415-01695-9*, A5479) Routledge.
Momsen, Janet H., ed. Women & Change in the Caribbean. LC 93-422. 1993. 35.00 (*0-253-33897-2*); pap. 16.95 (*0-253-33896-4*) Ind U Pr.
Momsen, Janet H. & Kinnaird, Vivian, eds. Different Places, Different Voices: Gender & Develpment in Africa, Asia, & Latin America. LC 92-18427. (International Studies of Women & Places). (Illus.). 352p. 1993. 55.00 (*0-415-07538-6*, A9887, Routledge NY); pap. 16.95 (*0-415-07563-7*, A9891, Routledge NY) Routledge.
Momson, Ann M., et al, eds. Breaking the Glass Ceiling: Can Women Reach the Top of America's Largest Corporations? 2nd ed. 256p. 1994. pap. 12.50 (*0-201-62702-7*) Addison-Wesley.
Momyer, William W. Air Power in Three Wars: World War Two, Korea & Vietnam. (Illus.). 358p. 1986. reprint ed. pap. write for info. (*0-912799-33-1*) Off Air Force.
— Airpower in Three Wars. Gilbert, James B., ed. LC 79-7287. (Flight: Its First Seventy-Five Years Ser.). (Illus.). 1980. lib. bdg. 27.95 (*0-405-12196-2*) Ayer.
Momyer, William W. & Wilson, Louis L., Jr. The Vietnamese Air Force, Nineteen Fifty-One - Nineteen Seventy-Five: An Analysis of Its Role In Combat & Fourteen Hours At Kohn Tang. (USAF Southeast Asia Monograph Ser.: Vol. 3, Monograph 4 & 5). (Illus.). 161p. 1986. reprint ed. pap. write for info. (*0-912799-28-5*) Off Air Force.
Mon, K. K., jt. ed. see Landau, D. P.
Mon, Susan, jt. auth. see McCullough, Bonnie R.
Monacco, A. P., ed. Transplantation Therapeutics. (Journal: Nephron: Vol. 46, Suppl. 1, 1987). (Illus.). iv, 60p. 1987. pap. 18.50 (*3-8055-4642-4*) S Karger.
Monacelli, Linda. Lacing the Moon. 40p. 1978. pap. 2.50 (*0-914946-11-0*) Cleveland St Univ Poetry Ctr.
Monach, James H. Childless, No Choice: The Experience of Involuntary Childlessness. LC 92-26075. (Illus.). 272p. 1993. 65.00 (*0-415-04090-6*, A9946, Routledge NY) Routledge.
Monachesi, Elio D., jt. auth. see Hathaway, Starke R.
Monaco. Biographical Dictionary of Gifted Education. 1988. pap. 15.00 (*0-89824-183-9*) Trillium Pr.
— Introduction to Microwave Technology. 320p. (C). 1989. write for info. (*0-675-21030-5*, Merrill Pub Co) Macmillan.
— Laboratory Activities in Microwave Technology. 208p. (C). 1989. pap. write for info. (*0-675-21031-3*, Merrill Pub Co) Macmillan.
***Monaco, A. P., ed.** Pulsed Field Gel Electrophoresis: A Practical Approach. (The Practical Approach Ser.: No. 158). (Illus.). 224p. 1995. 79.00 (*0-19-963536-6*); pap. 44.00 (*0-19-963535-8*) OUP.
***Monaco, Carol.** At Last. 257p. (Orig.). 1994. pap. text ed. 10.00 (*0-9645158-0-6*) Designs Extraord.
Monaco, Fabrizio. Thyroid Diseases: Clinical Fundamentals & Therapy. 1993. 249.95 (*0-8493-4821-8*, RC655) CRC Pr.
Monaco, Fabrizio, et al, eds. Thyroid Diseases: Clinical Fundamentals & Therapy. 1993. 249.95 (*0-8439-4821-3*, RC655) CRC Pr.
Monaco, Fred. Essentials of Mathematics for Electronics Technicians. 481p. (C). 1990. write for info. (*0-675-21172-7*, Merrill Pub Co) Macmillan.
— Preparing for the FCC General Radiotelephone Operator Exam. 336p. (C). 1991. pap. write for info. (*0-675-21313-4*, Merrill Pub Co) Macmillan.
Monaco, James. The French Revolutionary Perpetual Calendar. (Illus.). 32p. 1982. pap. 4.95 (*0-918432-43-X*) Baseline Bks.
— How to Read a Film: The Art, Technology, Language, History, & Theory of Film & Media. rev. ed. (Illus.). 1981. 40.00 (*0-19-502802-3*); pap. 17.95 (*0-19-502806-6*) OUP.
— The Movie Guide. Baseline Editors, ed. 1152p. (Orig.). 1992. pap. 24.95 (*0-399-51780-4*, Perigree Bks) Berkley Pub.
— The New Wave: Truffaut, Godard, Chabrol, Rohmer, Rivette. LC 75-38099. (Illus.). 372p. 1977. pap. 11.95 (*0-19-502246-7*) OUP.
— Who's Who in American Film Now. (Illus.). 600p. 1984. 39.95 (*0-918432-63-4*); pap. 19.95 (*0-918432-62-6*) Baseline Bks.
Monaco, James, jt. auth. see Baseline Editors.
Monaco, Lawrence. The Actors Master Log Book. 131p. 1987. student ed 10.95 (*0-9618647-0-2*) Shoreham Dr Pub.
***Monaco, Nora & Hubbs, Juliet.** Angel Reflections: A Personal Journal of Awareness. (Illus.). 112p. 1995. pap. write for info. (*0-9631714-3-7*) AngelStar.
***Monaco, Nora & Hubbs, Juliet J.** Angel Whispers: A Personal Journal of Reflection. (Universal Angels Ser.). (Illus.). 112p. 1994. pap. 9.95 (*0-9631714-2-9*) AngelStar.
Monaco, Nora, jt. auth. see Hubbs, Juliet J.
Monaco, Nora, jt. auth. see Jaffray-Hubbs, Juliet.
Monaco, Paul. Cinema & Society: France & Germany During the Twenties. LC 75-40650. 194p. 1981. text ed. 35.00 (*0-444-99019-4*, MOC/) Greenwood.
— Ribbons in Time: Movies & Society since 1945. LC 86-42996. (Interdisciplinary Studies in History). 170p. reprint ed. pap. 48.50 (*0-7837-3719-X*, 2057897) Bks Demand.
Monaco, Paul, et al. Art Around the Bay: A Guide to Galleries & Art Museums in the San Francisco Bay Area. (Illus.). (Orig.). 1990. pap. 12.95 (*0-9627649-1-4*) Trumpetvine.
Monaco, R. & Preziosi, L. Fluid Dynamic Applications of the Discrete Boltzmann Equation Vol. 3: Advances in Mathematics for Applied Science. 250p. 1991. text ed. 44.00 (*981-02-0466-3*) World Scientific Pub.
Monaco, Richard & Bascom, Lionel. Rubouts: Mob Murders in America. 200p. (Orig.). 1991. mass mkt. 4.50 (*0-380-75938-1*) Avon.
Monaco, Richard & Burt, Bill. The Dracula Syndrome. 184p. (Orig.). 1993. mass mkt. 4.99 (*0-380-77062-8*) Avon.
Monaco, Richard, jt. auth. see Briggs, John.
Monaco, Steve, jt. auth. see Fruzzetti, Mike.
Monaco, Thomas J., jt. auth. see Ashton, Floyd M.
Monafo, William W. & Pappalardo, Carlos. The Treatment of Burns: Principles & Practice. LC 71-138827. (Illus.). 286p. 1971. 19.10 (*0-87527-055-7*) Green.
Monagan. Waterbury: A Region Reborn. 1989. 32.95 (*0-89781-317-0*) Preferred Mktg.
Monagan, John S. The Grand Panjandrum: Mellow Years of Justice Holmes. LC 87-34628. (Illus.). 170p. (Orig.). (C). 1988. lib. bdg. 43.00 (*0-8191-6853-X*) U Pr of Amer.
— Horace: Priest of the Poor. LC 85-10042. (Illus.). 240p. reprint ed. pap. 68.40 (*0-7837-6702-1*, 2046334) Bks Demand.
Monagan, Robert T. The Disappearance of Representative Government: A California Solution. (Illus.). 184p. (Orig.). 1990. pap. 10.95 (*0-933994-10-9*) Comstock Bon.
Monaghan, Andrew. Counselling As a Christian Challenge. 183p. pap. 19.95 (*0-7171-1831-2*, CC-01831) Chr Classics.
— God's People? One Hundred & Ten Characters in the Story of Scottish Religion. 288p. (C). 1992. pap. 59.00 (*0-685-60706-2*, Pub. by St Andrew UK) St Mut.
— God's People? One Hundred & Ten Characters in the Story of Scottish Religion. 288p. 1993. pap. 30.00 (*0-7152-0656-7*, Pub. by St Andrew UK) St Mut.
Monaghan, Claire, jt. auth. see Midwinter, Arthur.
Monaghan, David, ed. Emma. LC 92-2793. (New Casebooks Ser.). 224p. 1992. text ed. 45.00 (*0-312-07908-7*) St Martin.
***Monaghan, E. A.** Whiskey Dan & Me. LC 95-92281. 162p. (Orig.). (YA). (gr. 8-12). 1995. pap. text ed. 7.50 (*0-9622840-1-7*) NEB Pr.
Monaghan, Earl A., ed. Anthology Seven. LC 89-91096. 128p. (Orig.). 1989. pap. text ed. 7.50 (*0-9622840-0-9*) NEB Pr.
Monaghan, Floyd V., jt. auth. see Corcos, Alain F.
Monaghan, Forbes J. Breakthrough to Shakespeare. LC 76-29144. 1979. 12.00 (*0-916620-07-7*) Portals Pr.
Monaghan, Frank. John Jay. LC 74-153339. reprint ed. 45.00 (*0-404-04647-9*) AMS Pr.
— John Jay, Defender of Liberty Against Kings & Peoples. (History - United States Ser.). 497p. 1993. reprint ed. lib. bdg. 99.00 (*0-7812-4879-5*) Rprt Serv.
Monaghan, Frank & Lowenthal, Marvin. This Was New York: The Nation's Capital in 1789. LC 70-117884. (Select Bibliographies Reprint Ser.). 1977. reprint ed. 29.95 (*0-8369-5337-1*) Ayer.
Monaghan, Gail. Perfect Picnics for All Seasons. 1994. 12.95 (*1-55859-802-2*) Abbeville Pr.
Monaghan, J. M., ed. Operative Surgery: Gynecology & Obstetrics. 4th ed. (Rob & Smith's Operative Surgery Ser.). (Illus.). 320p. 1987. text ed. 170.00 (*0-407-00680-X*) Buttrwrth-Heinemann.
Monaghan, J. M., jt. ed. see Shepherd, J. H.
Monaghan, James. The Man Who Elected Lincoln. LC 73-7310. (Illus.). 334p. 1973. reprint ed. text ed. 35.00 (*0-8371-6920-8*, MOMW, Greenwood Pr) Greenwood.
— Overland Trail. LC 73-107726. (Essay Index Reprint Ser.). 1977. 30.95 (*0-8369-1999-8*) Ayer.
Monaghan, James, jt. auth. see Cheepen, Christine.
Monaghan, Jay. Australians & the Gold Rush: California & Down Under, 1849-1854. LC 66-23182. 345p. reprint ed. pap. 98.40 (*0-8357-5895-8*, 2031440) Bks Demand.
— Civil War on the Western Border, 1854-1865. LC 84-11856. viii, 454p. 1984. reprint ed. 40.00 (*0-8032-3091-5*); reprint ed. pap. 11.95 (*0-8032-8126-9*) U of Nebr Pr.
— Custer: The Life of General George Armstrong Custer. LC 59-5937. (Illus.). xii, 479p. 1971. reprint ed. pap. 15.95 (*0-8032-5732-5*) U of Nebr Pr.
— Diplomat in Carpet Slippers: Abraham Lincoln Deals with Foreign Affairs. LC 79-39200. (Select Bibliographies Reprint Ser.). 1977. reprint ed. 34.95 (*0-8369-6802-6*) Ayer.
***Monaghan, Joe & Huffaker, Julie S.** Espresso! Starting & Succeeding with Your Own Specialty Coffee Business. LC 95-17895. 1995. pap. text ed. 14.95 (*0-471-12138-X*) Wiley.
Monaghan, John. Best Places to Stay in the Midwest. 2nd rev. ed. (Best Places to Stay Ser.). (Illus.). 352p. 1994. pap. 16.95 (*0-395-66618-X*) HM.
— The Covenants with Earth & Rain: Exchange, Sacrifice & Revelation in Mixtec Sociality. LC 95-2527. (Civilization of the American Indian Ser.: Vol. 219). 1995. write for info. (*0-8061-2762-7*) U of Okla Pr.
Monaghan, John, jt. auth. see Hill, Robert M., II.
Monaghan, John M. Bonney's Gynaecological Surgery. 9th ed. (Illus.). 605p. 1987. text ed. 73.50 (*0-7020-1019-7*, Bailliere-Tindall) Saunders.
***Monaghan, Kelly.** Air Courier Bargains: How to Travel Worldwide for Next to Nothing. 4th ed. LC 94-73669. Orig. Title: Insiders Guide to Air Courier Bargains. 240p. (Orig.). 1995. pap. 14.95 (*0-9627892-8-3*) Intrepid Trvlr.
— Consolidators: Air Travel's Bargain Basement. 80p. 1995. pap. 6.95 (*0-614-06305-1*) Intrepid Trvlr.
— Part-Time Travel Agent: How to Cash in on the Exciting New World of Travel Marketing. Scanlon, Sally, ed. 256p. (Orig.). 1994. pap. 24.95 (*0-9627892-4-0*) Intrepid Trvlr.
Monaghan, Kelly, jt. auth. see Scanlon, Sally.
Monaghan, M. J., jt. ed. see Chambers, John.
Monaghan, Margaret. Index to Accounting & Auditing Technical Pronouncements, As of October 1, 1989. Wolfteich, Lois, ed. LC 78-648377. 838p. reprint ed. pap. 180.00 (*0-7837-1060-7*, 2041554) Bks Demand.
Monaghan, Margaret, ed. see American Institute of Certified Public Accountants Staff.
Monaghan, Mark J. Practical Echocardiography & Doppler. 142p. 1990. text ed. 99.95 (*0-471-92069-X*) Wiley.
Monaghan, P. & Wood-Gush, D. G., eds. Managing the Behaviour of Animals. (Illus.). 240p. 1990. 82.00 (*0-412-29980-1*, A5004) Chapman & Hall.
Monaghan, P. K., jt. auth. see Puddephatt, Richard J.
Monaghan, Patricia. The Book of Goddesses & Heroines. rev. ed. LC 89-77418. (Illus.). 456p. (C). 1990. reprint ed. pap. 17.95 (*0-87542-573-9*) Llewellyn Pubns.
— Oh Mother Sun! A New View of the Cosmic Feminine. 240p. 1994. pap. 12.95 (*0-89594-722-6*) Crossing Pr.
— Seasons of the Witch. (Illus.). 176p. (Orig.). 1992. pap. 11.95 (*1-878980-09-2*) Delphi IL.
— Winterburning. (New Alaskan Poets Ser.). 78p. (Orig.). 1991. pap. 7.95 (*0-914221-10-8*) Fireweed Pr AK.
— Working Wisdom: A Guide to the Art & Strategy of Success at Work. LC 94-558. 192p. 1994. 12.00 (*0-06-251074-6*) Harper SF.
Monaghan, Patricia, ed. Hunger & Dreams: The Alaskan Women's Anthology. (Illus.). 128p. (Orig.). 1983. pap. 7.95 (*0-914221-00-0*) Fireweed Pr AK.
Monaghan, Patricia, ed. & intro. The Next Parish Over: A Collection of Irish American Writing. LC 93-83973. (Many Minnesotas Project Ser.). 312p. (Orig.). 1993. pap. 15.95 (*0-89823-150-7*) New Rivers Pr.
Monaghan, Patricia, ed. see Gallagher, Tess, et al.
Monaghan, Patrick C. Writing Letters That Sell: You, Your Ideas, Products & Services. LC 68-19911. 205p. reprint ed. pap. 58.50 (*0-317-58163-5*, 2029743) Bks Demand.
Monaghan, Robert P. Greenberg's Guide to Marklin OO - HO: Collector Guide. (Illus.). 166p. 1989. 35.00 (*0-89778-029-9*, 10-6875) Greenberg Bks.
Monaghan, S. F. The Child Within: A Powerful Therapeutic Ally. (Illus.). 245p. 1989. 35.50 (*0-89885-471-7*) Human Sci Pr.
Monaghan, Thomas & Anderson, Robert. Pizza Tiger. LC 86-10131. (Illus.). 336p. 1986. 17.95 (*0-394-55359-4*) Random.
Monagle, John F. Risk Management: A Guide for Health Care Professionals. 250p. 1985. 63.00 (*0-87189-122-0*) Aspen Pub.

An Asterisk (*) at the beginning of an entry indicates that the title is appearing in BIP for the first time.

Monagle, John F. & Thomasma, David C. Health Care Ethics: Critical Issues. 467p. 1994. 59.00 (0-8342-0505-X, 20505) Aspen Pub.

Monagle, John F. & Thomasma, David C., eds. Medical Ethics: Policies, Protocols, Guidelines & Programs. LC 92-21893. 1992. ring bd. 215.00 (0-8342-0349-9) Aspen Pub.

***Monaham, Kevin M. & Society of Photo-Optical Instrumentation Engineers Staff, eds.** Integrated Circuit Metrology & Process Control: Proceedings of a Conference Held 27-29 September 1993, California, Monterey. LC 94-27970. (Critical Reviews of Optical Science Technology Ser.: Vol. CR52). 1994. write for info. (0-8194-1364-X); pap. write for info. (0-8194-1363-1) SPIE.

Monahan, ed. Integrated Circuit Metrology, Inspection & Process Control. 335p. 1987. 50.00 (0-89252-810-9, 775) SPIE.

— Integrated Circuit Metrology, Inspection, & Process Control. 1988. 65.00 (0-89252-956-3, 921) SPIE.

Monahan & Scott. The Puget Sound Region: A Second Portfolio of Topical Maps. (Occasional Papers: No. 8). 1986. pap. 2.95 (0-318-23327-4) WWU CPNS.

Monahan, Arthur, tr. see Aegidius.

Monahan, Arthur P. Consent, Coercion, & Limit: The Medieval Origins of Parliamentary Democracy. xxi, 345p. 1987. 64.75 (90-04-08304-9) E J Brill.

— Consent, Coercion, & Limit: The Medieval Origins of Parliamentary Democracy. 1987. 49.95 (0-7735-1012-5, Pub. by McGill CN) U of Toronto Pr.

— From Personal Duties Towards Personal Rights: Late Medieval & Early Modern Political Thought, 1300-1600. (McGill-Queen's Studies in the History of Religion). 480p. 1994. 65.00 (0-7735-1017-6, Pub. by McGill CN) U of Toronto Pr.

— John of Paris on Royal & Papal Power: A Translation with Introduction of the de Postestate Regia et Papali of John of Paris. LC 73-16302. (Records of Civilization, Sources & Studies). 197p. 1974. text ed. 42.00 (0-231-03690-6) Col U Pr.

Monahan, B. The Problem of the Medical Profession: A Political Primer for Patients & Doctors. 1991. lib. bdg. 69.00 (0-8490-4404-9) Gordon Pr.

Monahan, Barbara. A Dictionary of Russian Gesture. LC 83-26413. (Illus.). 188p. (C). 1984. pap. text ed. 10.50 (0-938920-38-3) Hermitage.

Monahan, Bea, et al. Family Court of the State of Delaware: Survey of Alternatives to Incarceration: Juvenile Case Assignment: Proposed Child Support Brochure. 101p. 1990. 6.00 (0-685-50611-8, SERO061) Natl Ctr St Courts.

— Management Audit of the Alderman's Court, Newark, Delaware. 122p. 1990. 7.00 (0-685-38120-X, SERO-059) Natl Ctr St Courts.

Monahan, Beatrice, et al. Practice & Procedures Manual for South Carolina Clerks of Court. 550p. 1988. write for info. (0-318-66987-0, SERO-047) Natl Ctr St Courts.

Monahan, Brent. The Book of Common Dread: A Novel of the Infernal. 336p. 1993. 19.95 (0-312-09349-7) St Martin.

— Book of Common Dread Vol. 1. 1994. pap. 4.99 (0-312-95359-3) St Martin.

Monahan, Bryan. Introduction to Social Credit. 1982. lib. bdg. 69.00 (0-87700-442-0) Revisionist Pr.

***Monahan, C. C.** Early Fatigue Crack Growth at Welds. (Topics in Engineering Ser.: No. 26). 204p. 1995. 92.00 (1-56252-288-4) Computational Mech MA.

Monahan-Earley, Rita A., jt. auth. see Dvorak, Ann M.

Monahan-Earley, Rita A., jt. ed. see Dvorak, Ann M.

Monahan, Edward C. & Niocaill, Gearoid M., eds. Oceanic Whitecaps & Their Role in Air-Sea Exchange Processes. 1986. lib. bdg. 112.00 (90-277-2251-X) Kluwer Ac.

Monahan, Edward C. & Van Patten, Margaret A., eds. Climate & Health Implications of Bubble-Mediated Sea-Air Exchange. (Illus.). (Orig.). (C). 1989. pap. 12.50 (0-685-29355-6) CT Sea Grant.

Monahan, Edward J. Construction of & on Compacted Fills. LC 85-29644. (Practical Construction Guides Ser.). 200p. 1986. text ed. 64.95 (0-471-87463-9) Wiley.

— Construction of Fills. 2nd ed. LC 93-29806. (Series of Practical Construction Guides). 224p. 1993. text ed. 64.95 (0-471-58523-8) Wiley.

Monahan, Evelyn. Miracle of Metaphysical Healing. 1977. pap. text ed. 8.95 (0-13-585778-3, Reward) P-H.

— Miracle of Metaphysical Healing. 1986. 8.95 (0-13-585752-X, Reward) P-H.

Monahan, Evelyn & Bakken, Terry. Put Your Psychic Powers to Work: A Practical Guide to Parapsychology. LC 73-84208. 151p. 1973. 23.95 (0-88229-132-7) Nelson-Hall.

Monahan, Frances D., et al. Nursing Care of Adults. (Illus.). 2048p. 1994. text ed. 55.00 (0-7216-1644-5) Saunders.

Monahan, Frank J., jt. auth. see Coons, John E.

Monahan, Grace, tr. see Augustine.

Monahan, J. Community Mental Health & the Criminal Justice System. LC 74-28001. (Pergamon General Psychology Ser.). 1976. 140.00 (0-08-018759-5, Pub. by Pergamon Repr UK) Franklin.

Monahan, Jean. Hands. Brock, Geoff & Rogers, Maureen, eds. (Anhinga Prize for Poetry, 1991 Ser.). 64p. (Orig.). (C). 1992. pap. 8.00 (0-938078-34-8) Anhinga Pr.

Monahan, John. Food Poisoning. rev. ed. 125p. 1987. pap. 11.95 (0-317-67410-2) Med-Info Bks.

— Predicting Violent Behavior: An Assessment of Clinical Techniques. LC 81-851. (Sage Library of Social Research: No. 114). 183p. reprint ed. pap. 52.20 (0-8357-8499-1, 2034775) Bks Demand.

Monahan, John & Steadman, Henry J., eds. Mentally Disordered Offenders: Perspectives from Law & Social Science. LC 83-2329. (Perspectives in Law & Psychology Ser.: Vol. 6). 296p. 1983. 54.50 (0-306-41151-2, Plenum Pr) Plenum.

— Violence & Mental Disorder: Developments in Risk Assessment. LC 93-1670. (John D. & Catherine T. MacArthur Foundation Series on Mental Health & Development). (Illus.). 344p. 1993. Acid-free paper. 34.95 (0-226-53405-7) U Ch Pr.

Monahan, John & Walker, Laurens. Social Science in Law: Cases & Materials. 2nd ed. (University Casebook Ser.). 561p. 1991. reprint ed. text ed. 37.00 (0-88277-765-3) Foundation Pr.

— Social Science in Law: Cases & Materials. 3rd ed. LC 93-32890. (University Casebook Ser.). 609p. 1993. text ed. 40.95 (1-56662-121-6) Foundation Pr.

— Social Science in Law: Cases & Materials, Revised Teachers Manual To. 2nd ed. 52p. (C). 1992. text ed. write for info. (0-318-69339-9) Foundation Pr.

Monahan, John P. Food Poisoning. LC 83-63604. 125p. 1984. pap. 11.95 (0-916093-00-X) Med-Info Bks.

Monahan, Joy & Hinson, Bess. New Directions in Reading Instruction. 30p. 1988. pap. 3.95 (0-87207-796-9) Intl Reading.

Monahan, Kevin M., ed. Integrated Circuit Metrology, Inspection, & Process Control III. 545p. 1989. 77.00 (0-8194-0122-6, VOL. 1087) SPIE.

Monahan, Michael. Attic Dreamer. LC 68-20321. (Essay Index Reprint Ser.). 1977. 20.95 (0-8369-0711-6) Ayer.

— Nemesis. LC 68-54362. (Essay Index Reprint Ser.). 1977. 20.95 (0-8369-0712-4) Ayer.

— New Adventures. LC 77-93363. (Essay Index Reprint Ser.). 1977. 26.95 (0-8369-1310-8) Ayer.

— Nova Hibernia, Irish Poets & Dramatists of Today & Yesterday. LC 67-23249. (Essay Index Reprint Ser.). 1977. 21.95 (0-8369-0713-2) Ayer.

Monahan, Michael, et al. California Environmental Law Handbook. 7th ed. (State Environmental Law Ser.). 304p. 1993. pap. text ed. 76.00 (0-86587-342-9) Gov Insts.

Monahan, Patricia. Beginner's Guides: Oil Painting. (Illus.). 96p. (YA). (gr. 10-12). 1992. pap. 17.95 (0-289-80058-7, Pub. by Studio Vista Bks UK) Sterling.

— Beginner's Guides: Painting in Acrylics. (Illus.). 96p. (YA). (gr. 10-12). 1993. pap. 17.95 (0-289-80072-2, Pub. by Cassell UK) Sterling.

— Beginner's Guides: Painting in Gouache. (Illus.). 96p. 1993. pap. 17.95 (0-289-80080-3, Pub. by Studio Vista Bks UK) Sterling.

— Beginner's Guides: Painting Landscape in Watercolour. (Illus.). 96p. 1994. pap. 17.95 (0-289-80082-X) Sterling.

— Step by Step Art School: Watercolor. 1987. 12.98 (0-671-08907-2) S&S Trade.

Monahan, Patrick, jt. ed. see McRoberts, Kenneth.

Monahan, Patrick J. Meech Lake: The Inside Story. 336p. 1991. 50.00 (0-8020-5969-4); pap. 19.95 (0-8020-6896-0) U of Toronto Pr.

***Monahan, Ray E.** Engineering Documentation Control: Practices & Procedures. LC 94-24923. (Mechanical Engineering Ser.: Vol. 94). 265p. 1994. 85.00 (0-8247-9574-1) Dekker.

Monahan, Thomas J., jt. auth. see Margolis, Alan M.

Monahan, W. Gregory. Year of Sorrows: The Great Famine of 1709 in Lyon. LC 92-45193. 256p. 1993. 55.00 (0-8142-0608-5) Ohio St U Pr.

***Monahan, William G. & Smith, Edwin R.** Leading People: What School Leaders Can Learn from Military Leadership Development. 2nd ed. LC 94-34930. (Illus.). 216p. 1995. 24.95x (0-590-49749-9) Scholastic Inc.

***Monahon, Cynthia.** Children & Trauma: A Parent's Guide to Helping Children Heal. 1995. pap. 13.00 (0-02-921666-4) Free Pr.

— Healing the Wounds of Terror: A Parent's Guide for Helping Children Through Trauma. LC 92-46318. 1993. text ed. 19.95 (0-02-921665-6) Free Pr.

Monakhov, V. N. Boundary-Value Problems with Free Boundaries for Elliptic Systems of Equations. McFaden, H. H., tr. LC 83-2754. (Translations of Mathematical Monographs: Vol. 57). 522p. 1983. 149.00 (0-8218-4510-1, MMONO/57C) Am Math.

Monan, Jim. Bangladesh: The Strength to Succeed. (C). 1990. pap. text ed. 21.00 (0-85598-127-X, Pub. by Oxfam Pubns UK) St Mut.

Monane, Tazuko A. Japanese Made Easy. LC 79-6482. 202p. (Orig.). 1979. pap. 8.95 (0-8048-1219-5) C E Tuttle.

***Monarch.** Quick Course Classic American Literature. 1995. pap. 14.95 (0-02-860016-9) Macmillan.

— Quick Course Shakespeare. 1995. pap. 14.95 (0-02-860015-0) Macmillan.

Monardes, Nicolas. Joyfull Newes Out of the Newe Founde Worlde. Frampton, J., tr. LC 74-25786. (English Experience Ser.: No. 251). 110p. 1970. reprint ed. 30.00 (90-221-0251-3) Walter J Johnson.

— Joyfull Newes Out of the Newe Founde Worlde, 2 Vols, 1. Frampton, John, tr. LC 25-20529. (Tudor Translations, Second Ser.: Nos. 9, 10). reprint ed. 57.50 (0-404-51991-1) AMS Pr.

— Joyfull Newes Out of the Newe Founde Worlde, 2 Vols, 2. Frampton, John, tr. LC 25-20529. (Tudor Translations, Second Ser.: Nos. 9, 10). reprint ed. 57.50 (0-404-51992-X) AMS Pr.

— Joyfull Newes Out of the Newe Founde Worlde, 2 Vols, Set. Frampton, John, tr. LC 25-20529. (Tudor Translations, Second Ser.: Nos. 9, 10). reprint ed. 115.00 (0-404-51990-3) AMS Pr.

Monardo, Anna. The Courtyard of Dreams. large type ed. LC 93-40853. 1994. pap. 17.95 (0-7862-0126-6) Thorndike Pr.

Monas, Sidney, tr. see Dostoyevsky, Fyodor.

Monasa, Frank F., ed. Approximate Methods & Verification Procedures of Structural Analysis & Design. LC 91-13417. 96p. 1991. pap. text ed. 17.00 (0-87262-830-2) Am Soc Civil Eng.

Monash. Lumped Parameter Models of Hydrocarbon Reservoirs. 112p. 1983. 18.00 (0-685-66789-8, SS12-1); 36.00 (0-685-66824-X, SS12-1) Soc Computer Sim.

Monash, John. Australian Victories in France in 1918. (Great War Ser.: No. 24). (Illus.). 424p. reprint ed. 39.95 (0-89839-181-4) Battery Pr.

Monash University Staff, jt. auth. see Murray, Sue.

Monasterio, J., et al, eds. Antiphospholipid Antibodies. (Journal: Haemostasis Ser.: Vol. 24, No. 3, 1994). (Illus.). iv, 56p. 1994. pap. 18.50 (3-8055-6027-3) S Karger.

— International Congress on Thrombosis: Plenary Lectures, 13th Congress, Bilbao, 1994. (Journal: Haemostasis Ser.: Vol. 24, No. 2, 1994). (Illus.). 94p. 1994. pap. 18.50 (3-8055-6019-2) S Karger.

Monasterio, Maximina, jt. ed. see Vuilleumier, Francois.

***Monasterio, Pablo O.** La Ultima Ciudad - The Last City. 104p. 1995. 50.00 (0-944092-32-2) Twin Palms Pub.

Monasterio, Xavier O. To Be Human: An Introductory Experiment in Philosophy. LC 92-35826. 250p. (Orig.). (C). 1993. reprint ed. pap. text ed. 21.50 (0-8191-8958-8) U Pr of Amer.

***Monastersky, Glenn M. & Robl, James M., eds.** Strategies in Transgenic Animal Science. LC 95-2396. 1995. write for info. (1-55581-096-9) Am Soc Microbio.

Monastery of Arkashea Staff & Nier, Susan. The Discovery. 580p. 1993. pap. 24.95 (0-9636142-0-7) Gldn Scribe.

Monastier, Antoine. A History of the Vaudois Church from Its Origin & of the Vaudois of Piedmont to the Present Day. LC 80-24096. (Heresies of the Early Christian & Medieval Era Ser.: Second Ser.). reprint ed. 57.50 (0-404-16554-0) AMS Pr.

Monastryrsky, M., jt. ed. see Arnold, V. I.

Monastyrsky, M. Topology of Gauge Fields & Condensed Matter. Efimov, Oleg, tr. LC 92-43571. (Illus.). 372p. (C). 1993. 95.00 (0-306-44336-8, Plenum Pr) Plenum.

Monastyrsky, Michael. Riemann, Topology & Physics. 1986. 39.50 (0-8176-3262-X) Birkhauser.

Monat, Alan & Lazarus, Richard S. Stress & Coping. 3rd ed. 1991. text ed. 52.50 (0-231-07456-5); pap. text ed. 22.50 (0-231-07457-3) Col U Pr.

— Stress & Coping: An Anthology. 2nd ed. LC 77-3264. 560p. 1985. text ed. 61.00 (0-231-05820-9); pap. text ed. 19.50 (0-231-05821-7) Col U Pr.

Monat, Jacques & Sarfati, Hedva, eds. Workers' Particpation: A Voice in Decisions, 1981-1985. 284p. 1986. pap. 24.00 (92-2-105232-X) Intl Labour Office.

***Monat, Robert.** Pro - Engineer Quick Reference. 2nd ed. 300p. 1995. pap. 24.95 (1-56690-066-2, 1911, OnWord Pr) High Mtn.

Monath, Norman. How to Play Popular Guitar in 10 Easy Lessons. 128p. 1994. pap. 9.95 (0-8092-3765-2) Contemp Bks.

— How to Play Popular Piano in Ten Easy Lessons. (Illus.). 160p. (Orig.). 1984. pap. 10.95 (0-671-53067-4, Fireside) S&S Trade.

Monath, Thomas P., ed. Arboviruses: Epidemiology & Ecology, 5 vols. 1988. write for info. (0-318-63026-5, QR201) CRC Pr.

— Arboviruses: Epidemiology & Ecology, 5 vols. 1988. Vol. IV: Oropouche Fever to Venezuelan Equine Encephalitis, 256 pgs. 145.00 (0-8493-4388-7, QR201, CRC Reprint) Franklin.

— Arboviruses: Epidemiology & Ecology, 5 vols., Vol. I: General Principles. 336p. 1988. 191.00 (0-8493-4385-2, QR541, CRC Reprint) Franklin.

— Arboviruses: Epidemiology & Ecology, 5 vols., Vol. II: African Horse Sickness to Dengue. 288p. 1988. 161.00 (0-8493-4386-0, QR201, CRC Reprint) Franklin.

— Arboviruses: Epidemiology & Ecology, 5 vols., Vol. III: Oropouche Fever to Venezuelan Equine Enc. 256p. 1988. Vol. III: Eastern Equine Encephalomyelitis to O'Nyong Nyong, 256 pgs. 140.00 (0-8493-4387-9, QR201, CRC Reprint) Franklin.

— Arboviruses: Epidemiology & Ecology, 5 vols., Vol. V: Wesselsbron Virus Disease to Vesicular Sto. 256p. 1988. 144.00 (0-8493-4389-5, QR201, CRC Reprint) Franklin.

Monato, M., ed. Primary Raw Materials 1986-1989, Vol. 3, No. 13647: Summary of the R&D Programme. 496p. 1992. pap. 70.00 (92-826-3796-4, CD-NC-13647-EN-C, Pub. by Europ Com) UNIPUB.

Monavvar, Mohammad E. The Secrets of God's Mystical Oneness (Asrar al-Towhid) The Spiritual Stations of Shaikh Abu-Sai'd. O'Kane, John, tr. (Persian Heritage Ser.: No. 38). 670p. (C). 1992. lib. bdg. 55.00 (0-939214-87-3); pap. text ed. 28.00 (0-939214-88-1) Mazda Pubs.

Monbeck, Michael E. The Meaning of Blindness: Attitudes Toward Blindness & Blind People. LC 73-77853. 224p. reprint ed. 63.90 (0-8357-9225-0, 2017630) Bks Demand.

Monberg, Torben. Bellona Island Beliefs & Rituals. LC 90-20224. (Pacific Islands Monograph Ser.: No. 9). (Illus.). 480p. 1991. text ed. 42.00 (0-8248-1147-X) UH Pr.

Monbleau, Wayne. Arise & Eat. 20p. (Orig.). 1991. pap. 2.00 (0-944648-08-8) Loving Grace Pubns.

— Grace: The Essence of God. 205p. (Orig.). 1989. reprint ed. pap. 7.00 (0-944648-05-3) Loving Grace Pubns.

Monbleau, Wayne, intro. The Odes of Solomon: An Authentic 1st Century Book of Christian Psalms. 89p. 1989. pap. 7.00 (0-944648-04-5) Loving Grace Pubns.

Monbleau, Wayne F. Friendship with God. 159p. (Orig.). 1982. pap. 7.00 (0-944648-02-9) Loving Grace Pubns.

— Living in Love: Real Values for a Relevant Faith. 158p. (Orig.). 1987. pap. 7.00 (0-944648-00-2) Loving Grace Pubns.

— Love One Another: In Defense of Our Catholic Brothers & Sisters. 47p. (Orig.). 1983. pap. 4.00 (0-944648-03-7) Loving Grace Pubns.

Monboddo, James B. Of the Origin & Progress of Language, 6 vols, Set. LC 76-147982. reprint ed. 895.00 (0-404-08260-2) AMS Pr.

***Monbrun, Estelle.** Murder Chez Proust. Martyn, David, tr. LC 94-39260. 256p. (ENG & FRE.). 1995. 19.95 (1-55970-283-4) Arcade Pub Inc.

***Moncada, Jesus.** The Towpath. Willis, Judith, tr. 256p. 1995. pap. 14.00 (0-00-273005-7, Pub. by HarpC UK) HarpC.

Moncada, S., et al, eds. The Biology of Nitric Oxide Pt. 1: Physiological & Clinical Aspects. (Proceedings Ser.: Vol. 1). 420p. 1992. 160.00 (1-85578-012-7, Pub. by Portland Pr Ltd UK) Ashgate Pub Co.

— The Biology of Nitric Oxide Pt. 2: Enzymology, Biochemistry, & Immunology. (Proceedings Ser.: Vol. 1). 230p. 1993. 110.00 (1-85578-013-5, Pub. by Portland Pr Ltd UK) Ashgate Pub Co.

Moncado, S. & Higgs, E. A., eds. Nitric Oxide from L-Arginine: a Bioregulatory System: Proceedings of the Symposium on Biological Importance of Nitric Oxide, London, 14-15 Sept., 1989. (International Congress Ser.: No. 897). 520p. 1990. 174.50 (0-444-81154-0, Excerpta Medica) Elsevier.

Moncarz, Elisa S. Financial Accounting for Hospital Management Instruction Manual. 1986. pap. 20.95 (0-87055-539-1) Van Nos Reinhold.

Moncarz, Elisa S. & Portocarrero, Nestor de J. Financial Accounting for Hospitality Management. (Illus.). (C). 1986. text ed. 54.95 (0-87055-505-7) AVI.

***Moncarz, Raul, ed.** International Trade & the New Economic Order. LC 95-2526. (Series in International Business & Economics). 1995. text ed. 62.00 (0-08-042574-7, Pergamon Pr) Elsevier.

Moncayo, Helga E., jt. ed. see Moncayo, Roy.

***Moncayo, Roy & Moncayo, Helga E., eds.** Ovarian Autoimmunity: Clinical & Experimental Data. LC 94-42131. (Neuroscience Intelligence Unit Ser.). 120p. 1995. 59.00 (1-57059-219-5) R G Landes.

Monceau, Pierre. Electronic Properties of Inorganic Quasi-One-Dimensional Compounds, Pt. I, Theoretical. 1987. Part I, Theoretical. lib. bdg. 48.00 (0-318-03895-1) Kluwer Ac.

— Electronic Properties of Inorganic Quasi-One-Dimensional Compounds, Pt. I Experimental. 1987. Part I Experimental. lib. bdg. 143.50 (90-277-1801-6) Kluwer Ac.

— Electronic Properties of Inorganic Quasi-One-Dimensional Compounds, Pt. II Experimental. 1985. Part II Experimental. lib. bdg. 134.50 (90-277-1800-8) Kluwer Ac.

Monceaux, Morgan. Jazz. LC 93-38177. (Illus.). (J). 1994. 18.00 (0-679-86518-7) Knopf Bks Yng Read.

— Jazz: My Music, My People. (Illus.). 64p. (J). (gr. 4 up). 1994. 18.00 (0-679-85618-8) Knopf Bks Yng Read.

Monch, D., et al, eds. Japanese Information in Science, Technology & Commerce: Proceedings of the 2nd International Conference, Berlin, F. R. Germany, 1989. 629p. 1990. pap. 97.00 (90-5199-022-7, Pub. by IOS Pr NE) IOS Press.

***Monch, W.** Semiconductor Surfaces & Interfaces. 2nd ed. (Surface Sciences Ser.: Vol. 26). 432p. 1995. pap. 49.95 (3-540-58625-3) Spr-Verlag.

Monch, Winfried. Semiconductor Surfaces & Interfaces. LC 93-9523. (Surface Sciences Ser.: Vol. 26). 1993. 79.00 (0-387-54423-2) Spr-Verlag.

— Semiconductor Surfaces & Interfaces. 2nd ed. LC 95-1412. (Series in Surface Sciences: Vol. 26). 1995. write for info. (0-358-67533-2) Spr-Verlag.

Monch, Winfried, ed. Electronic Structure of Metal-Semiconductor Contacts. (C). 1990. lib. bdg. 164.00 (0-7923-0854-9) Kluwer Ac.

Monchak, Ronald W. The Last White Christmas. (Illus.). 193p. 1994. 16.95 (1-879094-17-7) Momentum Bks.

***Monchan, David M.** All You Need to Know about Copyrights & Trademarks. 105p. 1994. 29.95 (1-57002-035-3); pap. 19.95 (0-614-03065-X) Univ Publng Hse.

Monck, C. S., et al. Science Parks & the Growth of High Technology Firms. 224p. (C). 1988. lib. bdg. 72.50 (0-415-00092-0) Routledge.

Monckton, Charles A. Last Days in New Guinea. LC 75-35142. reprint ed. 25.00 (0-404-14158-7) AMS Pr.

— Taming New Guinea. LC 75-35143. (Illus.). reprint ed. 28.50 (0-404-14159-5) AMS Pr.

Monckton, E. The White Canoe & Other Legends of the Ojibways. 1977. lib. bdg. 59.95 (0-8490-2819-1) Gordon Pr.

***Monckton, Georgiana & Burden, Hilary.** Dear Isobel: Coming to Terms with the Death of a Child. 128p. 1995. pap. 17.95 (0-09-178137-X, Vermillion) Trafalgar.

Monckton, P. L. Construction Technology for Civil Engineering Technicians. LC 82-32466. (Longman Technician Series, Construction & Civil Engineering). (Illus.). 323p. reprint ed. pap. 92.10 (0-8357-6075-8, 2034475) Bks Demand.

Monckton, Shirley. The Complete Book of Wedding Flowers: Stunning Flower Arranging Inspiration for Everyone & Every Location. (Illus.). 96p. 1993. pap. 19.95 (0-304-34201-7, Pub. by Cassell UK) Sterling.

— The Complete Book of Wedding Flowers: Stunning Flower Arranging Inspiration for Everyone & Every Location. (Illus.). 96p. 1995. pap. 12.95 (0-304-34565-2, Pub. by Cassell UK) Sterling.

Monclova, Lidio C. Baldorioty De Castro. (Puerto Rico Ser.). 1979. lib. bdg. 59.95 (0-8490-2870-1) Gordon Pr.

M

An Asterisk (*) at the beginning of an entry indicates that the title is appearing in BIP for the first time.

Moncomble, Gerard. Octave & His Flute. (Finding Out about Music Ser.). (Illus.). 275p. (Orig.). (J). (gr. 1-5). 1994. pap. 19.95 (*0-572-01965-3*, Pub. by W Foulsham UK) Trans-Atl Phila.

— Octave & His Piano. (Finding Out about Instruments Ser.). (Illus.). 275p. (J). (gr. 1-5). 1993. pap. 19.95 (*0-572-01966-1*, Pub. by W Foulsham UK) Trans-Atl Phila.

— Octave & His Violin. (Finding Out about Instruments Ser.). (Illus.). 275p. (Orig.). (J). (gr. 1-5). 1994. pap. 19.95 (*0-572-01967-X*, Pub. by W Foulsham UK) Trans-Atl Phila.

Monconduit, Barbara, ed. see Mac Lean, Alistair & Bowser, Milton.

Moncreiffe, Iain. The Robertsons. 3rd ed. (Johnston & Bacon Clan Histories Ser.). (Illus.). 32p. 1993. reprint ed. pap. 8.95 (*0-685-69991-9*, 9618) Clearfield Co.

Moncrief & Shipp. Sales Management Role Plays. (C). 1993. text ed. 20.75 (*0-673-46904-2*) HarpCollege.

Moncrief, Gary G. & Thompson, Joel A., eds. Changing Patterns in State Legislative Careers. LC 92-26575. (Illus.). 280p. (C). 1992. text ed. 39.50 (*0-472-10344-X*) U of Mich Pr.

Moncrief, Nancy D., et al, eds. Proceedings of the Second Symposium on Southeastern Fox Squirrels. 90p. 1993. pap. 15.00 (*0-9625801-6-3*) VA Mus Natl Hist.

Moncrief, Scott, tr. see Stendhal, pseud.

***Moncrieff, A. R. Hope.** Romance & Legend of Chivalry. LC 94-42279. 1995. 9.99 (*0-517-11862-9*) Random Hse Value.

Moncrieff, C. K. & Kilmartin, Terence, trs. Sodom & Gomorrah. LC 92-27272. (In Search of Lost Time Ser.: Vol. 4). 1993. 18.50 (*0-679-60029-9*, Modern Lib) Random.

Moncrieff, C. K., tr. see Proust, Marcel.

Moncrieff, C. K., tr. see Stendhal.

Moncrieff, C. Scott, tr. see Stendhal.

Moncrieff, J., jt. auth. see Grace, J.

Moncrieff, K. Scott, tr. see De Moncrif, Francois A.

Moncrieff, K. Scott, tr. see De Moncrif, Paradis.

Moncrif, jt. auth. see Brown, Lena.

Moncur, M. W. Floral Development of Subtropical Fruit & Nut Species. 1988. pap. 40.00 (*0-643-04792-1*, Pub. by CSIRO AT) Intl Spec Bk.

Moncur, Susan. They Still Shoot Models My Age. 1993. pap. 12.99 (*1-85242-230-0*) Serpents Tail.

***Moncure.** Apes Find Shapes: Magic Castle Reader. (Magic Castle Ser.). 1993. pap. text ed. 3.95 (*1-56189-347-1*) Amer Educ Pub.

— Here We Go 'Round the Year: Magic Castle Reader. (Magic Castle Ser.). 1993. pap. text ed. 3.95 (*1-56189-378-1*) Amer Educ Pub.

— My "A" Sound Box. (Magic Castle Ser.). 1993. pap. text ed. 3.95 (*1-56189-384-6*) Amer Educ Pub.

— My Sound Parade. (Magic Castle Ser.). 1993. pap. text ed. 3.95 (*1-56189-389-7*) Amer Educ Pub.

— Pocketful of Pets: Magic Castle Reader. (Magic Castle Ser.). 1993. pap. text ed. 3.95 (*1-56189-380-3*) Amer Educ Pub.

— Student Workbook & Laboratory Manual to Accompany Guide. 352p. 1991. pap. 19.95 (*0-8016-3354-0*) Mosby Yr Bk.

— Where Is Baby Bear? Magic Castle Reader. (Magic Castle Ser.). 1993. pap. text ed. 3.95 (*1-56189-381-1*) Amer Educ Pub.

Moncure, James, ed. Research Guide to European Historical Biography, Set, Vols. 1-4. (Illus.). 2240p. 1992. Set. lib. bdg. 299.00 (*0-933833-28-8*) Beacham Pub.

— Research Guide to European Historical Biography, Set, Vols. 5-8. 2995p. 1993. Set. lib. bdg. 299.00 (*0-933833-30-X*) Beacham Pub.

Moncure, Jane. Peter Pan: A Classic Tale. (Illus.). 32p. (J). (gr. k-2). 1988. lib. bdg. 13.95 (*0-89565-469-5*) Childs World.

***Moncure, Jane B.** Apes Find Shapes. LC 87-11747. (Magic Castle Readers Ser.). (Illus.). 32p. (ENG & SPA.). (J). (ps-2). 1987. lib. bdg. 14.95 (*0-89565-917-4*) Childs World.

— Apes Find Shapes. LC 87-11747. (Magic Castle Readers Ser.). (Illus.). 32p. (ENG & SPA.). (J). (ps-2). 1987. lib. bdg. 21.36 (*0-89565-364-8*) Childs World.

— Away Went the Farmer's Hat. LC 87-11742. (Magic Castle Readers Ser.). (Illus.). 32p. (ENG & SPA.). (J). (ps-2). 1987. lib. bdg. 21.36 (*0-89565-909-3*) Childs World.

— Away Went the Farmer's Hat. LC 87-11742. (Magic Castle Readers Ser.). (Illus.). 32p. (ENG & SPA.). (J). (ps-2). 1987. lib. bdg. 21.36 (*0-89565-367-2*) Childs World.

— The Bears Upstairs. LC 87-11715. (Magic Castle Readers Ser.). (Illus.). 32p. (ENG & SPA.). (J). (ps-2). 1987. pap. 14.95 (*0-89565-927-1*) Childs World.

— The Bears Upstairs. LC 87-11715. (Magic Castle Readers Ser.). (Illus.). 32p. (ENG & SPA.). (J). (ps-2). 1987. lib. bdg. 21.36 (*0-89565-373-7*) Childs World.

— Biggest Snowball of All. LC 88-25600. (Magic Castle Readers Ser.). (Illus.). 32p. (ENG & SPA.). (J). (ps-2). 1989. lib. bdg. 21.36 (*0-89565-391-5*) Childs World.

— Biggest Snowball of All. LC 88-25600. (Magic Castle Readers Ser.). (Illus.). 32p. (ENG & SPA.). (J). (ps-2). 1989. pap. 21.36 (*0-89565-918-2*) Childs World.

— Butterfly Express. LC 88-22944. (Magic Castle Readers Ser.). (Illus.). 32p. (ENG & SPA.). (J). (ps-2). 1989. lib. bdg. 21.36 (*0-89565-392-3*) Childs World.

— Caring. rev. ed. LC 80-27506. (Values to Live By Ser.). (Illus.). (ENG & SPA.). (J). (ps-2). 1981. lib. bdg. 21.36 (*0-89565-201-3*) Childs World.

— Caring. rev. ed. LC 80-27506. (Values to Live By Ser.). (Illus.). (ENG & SPA.). (J). (ps-2). 1981. pap. text ed. 21.36 (*0-89565-934-4*) Childs World.

— Caring for My Baby Sister. (Growing Responsible Bks.). (Illus.). 32p. (J). (ps-2). 1990. lib. bdg. 18.50 (*0-89565-669-8*) Childs World.

— Caring for My Body. (Growing Responsible Bks.). (Illus.). 32p. (J). (ps-2). 1990. lib. bdg. 18.50 (*0-89565-668-X*) Childs World.

— Caring for My Home. (Growing Responsible Bks.). (Illus.). 32p. (J). (ps-2). 1990. lib. bdg. 18.50 (*0-89565-667-1*) Childs World.

— Caring for My Kitty. (Growing Responsible Bks.). (Illus.). 32p. (J). (ps-2). 1990. lib. bdg. 18.50 (*0-89565-666-3*) Childs World.

— Caring for My Things. (Growing Responsible Bks.). (Illus.). 32p. (J). (ps-2). 1990. lib. bdg. 18.50 (*0-89565-670-1*) Childs World.

— A Color Clown Comes to Town. LC 87-11605. (Magic Castle Readers Ser.). (Illus.). 32p. (ENG & SPA.). (J). (ps-2). 1987. pap. text ed. 21.36 (*0-89565-926-3*) Childs World.

— A Color Clown Comes to Town. LC 87-11605. (Magic Castle Readers Ser.). (Illus.). 32p. (ENG & SPA.). (J). (ps-2). 1987. lib. bdg. 21.36 (*0-89565-369-9*) Childs World.

— Courage. rev. ed. LC 80-39515. (Values to Live By Ser.). (Illus.). 32p. (ENG & SPA.). (J). (ps-2). 1981. lib. bdg. 21.36 (*0-89565-202-1*) Childs World.

— Courage. rev. ed. LC 80-39515. (Values to Live By Ser.). (Illus.). 32p. (ENG & SPA.). (J). (ps-2). 1981. pap. text ed. 21.36 (*0-89565-935-2*) Childs World.

— Dinosaurs: Back in Time. LC 89-38469. (Discovery World Ser.). (Illus.). 32p. (J). (ps-2). 1990. lib. bdg. 21.36 (*0-89565-550-0*) Childs World.

— A Dragon in a Wagon. LC 87-11755. (Magic Castle Readers Ser.). (Illus.). 32p. (ENG & SPA.). (J). (ps-2). 1987. pap. text ed. 21.36 (*0-89565-907-7*) Childs World.

— A Dragon in a Wagon. LC 87-11755. (Magic Castle Readers Ser.). (Illus.). 32p. (ENG & SPA.). (J). (ps-2). 1987. lib. bdg. 21.36 (*0-89565-400-8*) Childs World.

— The Five Senses: Treasures Outside. LC 90-30635. (Discovery World Ser.). (Illus.). 32p. (J). (ps-2). 1990. lib. bdg. 21.36 (*0-89565-575-6*) Childs World.

— Happy Birthday, Word Bird. LC 83-15256. (Word Bird Readers Ser.). (Illus.). 32p. (J). (ps-2). 1983. lib. bdg. 21.36 (*0-89565-256-0*) Childs World.

— Here We Go 'Round the Year. (Magic Castle Readers Ser.). (Illus.). 32p. (ENG & SPA.). (J). (ps-2). 1987. pap. 21.36 (*0-89565-914-X*) Childs World.

— Here We Go 'Round the Year. LC 87-13257. (Magic Castle Readers Ser.). (Illus.). 32p. (ENG & SPA.). (J). (ps-2). 1987. lib. bdg. 21.36 (*0-89565-402-4*) Childs World.

— Hi, Word Bird. LC 80-15919. (Word Bird Readers Ser.). (Illus.). 32p. (J). (ps-2). 1981. lib. bdg. 21.36 (*0-89565-159-9*) Childs World.

— Hide-&-Seek Word Bird. LC 81-18068. (Word Bird Readers Ser.). (Illus.). (J). (ps-2). 1982. lib. bdg. 21.36 (*0-89565-218-8*) Childs World.

— Honesty. rev. ed. LC 80-39571. (Values to Live By Ser.). (Illus.). 32p. (ENG & SPA.). (J). (ps-2). 1981. lib. bdg. 21.36 (*0-89565-203-X*) Childs World.

— Honesty. rev. ed. LC 80-39571. (Values to Live By Ser.). (Illus.). 32p. (ENG & SPA.). (J). (ps-2). 1981. pap. 21.36 (*0-89565-938-7*) Childs World.

— Hop-Skip-Jump-a-Roo Zoo. LC 87-11743. (Magic Castle Readers Ser.). (Illus.). 32p. (ENG & SPA.). (J). (ps-2). 1987. pap. 21.36 (*0-89565-928-X*) Childs World.

— Hop-Skip-Jump-a-Roo Zoo. LC 87-11743. (Magic Castle Readers Ser.). (Illus.). 32p. (ENG & SPA.). (J). (ps-2). 1987. lib. bdg. 21.36 (*0-89565-371-0*) Childs World.

— How Many Ways Can You Cut a Pie? LC 87-15807. (Magic Castle Readers Ser.). (Illus.). 32p. (ENG & SPA.). (J). (ps-2). 1987. pap. 21.36 (*0-89565-919-0*) Childs World.

— How Many Ways Can You Cut a Pie? LC 87-15807. (Magic Castle Readers Ser.). (Illus.). 32p. (ENG & SPA.). (J). (ps-2). 1987. lib. bdg. 21.36 (*0-89565-408-3*) Childs World.

— How Seeds Travel: Popguns & Parachutes. LC 89-71171. (Discovery World Ser.). (Illus.). 32p. (J). (ps-2). 1990. lib. bdg. 21.36 (*0-89565-569-1*) Childs World.

— I Never Say I'm Thankful, But I Am. LC 78-21577. (Understanding Myself Picture Bks.). (Illus.). (J). (ps-2). 1979. lib. bdg. 21.36 (*0-89565-023-1*) Childs World.

— Ice-Cream Cows & Mitten Sheep. (Magic Castle Readers Ser.). (Illus.). 32p. (ENG & SPA.). (J). (ps-2). 1987. lib. bdg. 21.36 (*0-89565-915-8*) Childs World.

— Ice-Cream Cows & Mitten Sheep. LC 87-14603. (Magic Castle Readers Ser.). (Illus.). 32p. (ENG & SPA.). (J). (ps-2). 1987. lib. bdg. 21.36 (*0-89565-403-2*) Childs World.

— Joy. (Values to Live By Ser.). (Illus.). 32p. (ENG & SPA.). (J). (ps-2). 1980. lib. bdg. 21.36 (*0-89565-224-2*) Childs World.

— Joy. LC 82-1145. (Values to Live By Ser.). (Illus.). 32p. (ENG & SPA.). (J). (ps-2). 1980. lib. bdg. 21.36 (*0-89565-940-9*) Childs World.

— Kindness. rev. ed. LC 80-39535. (Values to Live By Ser.). (Illus.). 32p. (ENG & SPA.). (J). (ps-2). 1981. lib. bdg. 21.36 (*0-89565-204-8*) Childs World.

— Kindness. rev. ed. LC 80-39535. (Values to Live By Ser.). (Illus.). 32p. (ENG & SPA.). (J). (ps-2). 1981. lib. bdg. 21.36 (*0-89565-941-7*) Childs World.

— Kinds of Animals: Flyers, Leapers, Crawlers, Creepers. LC 89-71172. (Discovery World Ser.). (Illus.). 32p. (J). (ps-2). 1990. lib. bdg. 21.36 (*0-89565-567-5*) Childs World.

— Life Cycles: The Singing Mailbox. LC 89-24000. (Discovery World Ser.). (Illus.). 32p. (J). (ps-2). 1990. lib. bdg. 21.36 (*0-89565-552-7*) Childs World.

— Little Too-Tall. LC 87-11632. (Magic Castle Readers Ser.). (Illus.). 32p. (ENG & SPA.). (J). (ps-2). 1987. lib. bdg. 21.36 (*0-89565-374-5*) Childs World.

— Little Too-Tall. LC 87-11632. (Magic Castle Readers Ser.). (Illus.). 32p. (ENG & SPA.). (J). (ps-2). 1987. lib. bdg. 21.36 (*0-89565-930-1*) Childs World.

— The Look Book. LC 82-4517. (Five Senses Ser.). (Illus.). 32p. (J). (ps-3). 1982. pap. 3.95 (*0-516-43251-6*) Childrens.

— Love. rev. ed. LC 80-27479. (Values to Live By Ser.). (Illus.). 32p. (ENG & SPA.). (J). (ps-2). 1981. lib. bdg. 21.36 (*0-89565-205-6*) Childs World.

— The Magic Moon Machine. LC 87-30959. (Magic Castle Readers Ser.). (Illus.). 32p. (ENG & SPA.). (J). (ps-2). 1987. lib. bdg. 21.36 (*0-89565-920-4*) Childs World.

— The Magic Moon Machine. LC 87-30959. (Magic Castle Readers Ser.). (Illus.). 32p. (J). (ps-2). 1987. lib. bdg. 21.36 (*0-89565-410-5*) Childs World.

— Mousekin's Special Day. LC 87-11750. (Magic Castle Readers Ser.). (Illus.). 32p. (ENG & SPA.). (J). (ps-2). 1987. lib. bdg. 21.36 (*0-89565-366-4*) Childs World.

— Mousekin's Special Day. LC 87-11750. (Magic Castle Readers Ser.). (Illus.). 32p. (ENG & SPA.). (J). (ps-2). 1987. lib. bdg. 21.36 (*0-89565-922-0*) Childs World.

— Mr. Doodle Had a Poodle. LC 87-15808. (Magic Castle Readers Ser.). (Illus.). 32p. (ENG & SPA.). (J). (ps-2). 1987. lib. bdg. 21.36 (*0-89565-910-7*) Childs World.

— Mr. Doodle Had a Poodle. LC 87-15808. (Magic Castle Readers Ser.). (Illus.). 32p. (ENG & SPA.). (J). (ps-2). 1987. lib. bdg. 21.36 (*0-89565-409-1*) Childs World.

— My "a" Sound Box. LC 84-17024. (Sound Box Bks.). (Illus.). 32p. (J). (ps-2). 1984. lib. bdg. 21.36 (*0-89565-296-X*) Childs World.

— My "b" Sound Box. LC 77-23588. (Sound Box Bks.). (Illus.). (J). (ps-2). 1977. lib. bdg. 21.36 (*0-913778-92-3*) Childs World.

— My Baby Brother Needs a Friend. LC 78-21935. (Understanding Myself Picture Bks.). (Illus.). (J). (ps-3). 1979. lib. bdg. 21.36 (*0-89565-019-3*) Childs World.

— My "c" Sound Box. LC 78-23638. (Sound Box Bks.). (Illus.). (J). (ps-2). 1979. lib. bdg. 21.36 (*0-89565-052-5*) Childs World.

— My "d" Sound Box. LC 78-8450. (Sound Box Bks.). (Illus.). (J). (ps-2). 1978. lib. bdg. 21.36 (*0-89565-044-4*) Childs World.

— My "e" Sound Box. LC 84-17021. (More Sound Box Bks.). (Illus.). 32p. (J). (ps-2). 1984. lib. bdg. 21.36 (*0-89565-297-8*) Childs World.

— My Eight Book. LC 85-30962. (My Number Books). (Illus.). 32p. (J). (ps-2). 1986. lib. bdg. 21.36 (*0-89565-319-2*) Childs World.

— My "f" Sound Box. LC 77-9377. (Sound Box Bks.). (Illus.). (J). (ps-2). 1977. lib. bdg. 21.36 (*0-913778-93-1*) Childs World.

— My First Book. LC 84-17455. (Sound Box Bks.). (Illus.). 32p. (J). (ps-2). 1984. lib. bdg. 21.36 (*0-89565-271-4*) Childs World.

— My First Presidents' Day Book. LC 87-10309. (My First Holiday Bks.). (Illus.). 32p. (J). (ps-2). 1987. pap. 3.95 (*0-516-42910-8*) Childrens.

— My First Thanksgiving Book. LC 84-9433. (My First Holiday Bks.). (Illus.). 32p. (J). (ps-2). 1984. lib. bdg. 11.55 (*0-516-02903-7*); pap. 3.95 (*0-516-42903-5*) Childrens.

— My Five Book. LC 85-9699. (My Number Bks.). (Illus.). 32p. (J). (ps-2). 1985. lib. bdg. 21.36 (*0-89565-316-8*) Childs World.

— My Four Book. LC 85-9700. (My Number Bks.). (Illus.). 32p. (J). (ps-2). 1985. lib. bdg. 21.36 (*0-89565-315-X*) Childs World.

— My "g" Sound Box. LC 78-22037. (Sound Box Bks.). (Illus.). (J). (ps-2). 1979. lib. bdg. 21.36 (*0-89565-053-3*) Childs World.

— My "h" Sound Box. LC 77-8977. (Sound Box Bks.). (Illus.). (J). (ps-2). 1977. lib. bdg. 21.36 (*0-913778-94-X*) Childs World.

— My "i" Sound Box. LC 84-17022. (More Sound Box Bks.). (Illus.). 32p. (J). (ps-2). 1984. lib. bdg. 21.36 (*0-89565-298-6*) Childs World.

— My "j" Sound Box. LC 78-23178. (Sound Box Bks.). (Illus.). (J). (ps-2). 1979. lib. bdg. 21.36 (*0-89565-049-5*) Childs World.

— My "k" Sound Box. LC 78-22034. (Sound Box Bks.). (Illus.). (J). (ps-2). 1979. lib. bdg. 21.36 (*0-89565-050-9*) Childs World.

— My "l" Sound Box. LC 78-8373. (Sound Box Bks.). (Illus.). (J). (ps-2). 1978. lib. bdg. 21.36 (*0-89565-045-2*) Childs World.

— My "m" Sound Box. LC 78-24458. (Sound Box Bks.). (Illus.). (J). (ps-2). 1979. lib. bdg. 21.36 (*0-89565-051-7*) Childs World.

— My "n" Sound Box. LC 78-22053. (Sound Box Bks.). (Illus.). (J). (ps-2). 1979. lib. bdg. 21.36 (*0-89565-054-1*) Childs World.

— My Nine Book. LC 85-30959. (My Number Bks. - First Steps to Math). (Illus.). 32p. (J). (ps-2). 1986. lib. bdg. 21.36 (*0-89565-320-6*) Childs World.

— My "o" Sound Box. LC 84-17023. (Sound Box Bks.). (Illus.). 32p. (J). (ps-2). 1984. lib. bdg. 21.36 (*0-89565-299-4*) Childs World.

— My One Book. LC 85-5897. (My Number Bks.). (Illus.). 32p. (J). (ps-2). 1985. lib. bdg. 21.36 (*0-89565-312-5*) Childs World.

— My "p" Sound Box. LC 78-7841. (Sound Box Bks.). (Illus.). (J). (ps-2). 1978. lib. bdg. 21.36 (*0-89565-047-9*) Childs World.

— My "q" Sound Box. LC 79-13085. (Sound Box Bks.). (Illus.). (J). (ps-2). 1979. lib. bdg. 21.36 (*0-89565-100-9*) Childs World.

— My "r" Sound Box. LC 78-7842. (Sound Box Bks.). (Illus.). (J). (ps-2). 1978. lib. bdg. 21.36 (*0-89565-048-7*) Childs World.

— My "s" Sound Box. LC 77-8970. (Sound Box Bks.). (Illus.). (J). (ps-2). 1977. lib. bdg. 21.36 (*0-913778-95-8*) Childs World.

— My Seven Book. LC 86-2594. (My Number Bks.). (Illus.). 32p. (J). (ps-2). 1986. lib. bdg. 21.36 (*0-89565-318-4*) Childs World.

— My Six Book. LC 85-30961. (My Number Bks.). (Illus.). 32p. (J). (ps-2). 1986. lib. bdg. 21.36 (*0-89565-317-6*) Childs World.

— My Sound Parade. LC 79-15930. (Sound Box Bks.). (Illus.). (J). (ps-2). 1979. lib. bdg. 21.36 (*0-89565-103-3*) Childs World.

— My "t" Sound Box. LC 77-23587. (Sound Box Bks.). (Illus.). (J). (ps-2). 1977. lib. bdg. 21.36 (*0-913778-96-6*) Childs World.

— My Ten Book. LC 86-2293. (My Number Bks.). (Illus.). 32p. (J). (ps-2). 1986. lib. bdg. 21.36 (*0-89565-321-4*) Childs World.

— My Three Book. LC 85-5898. (My Number Bks.). (Illus.). 32p. (J). (ps-2). 1985. lib. bdg. 21.36 (*0-89565-314-1*) Childs World.

— My Two Book. LC 85-7885. (My Number Bks.). (Illus.). 32p. (J). (ps-2). 1985. lib. bdg. 21.36 (*0-89565-313-3*) Childs World.

— My "u" Sound Box. LC 84-17012. (Sound Box Bks.). (Illus.). 32p. (J). (ps-2). 1984. lib. bdg. 21.36 (*0-89565-300-1*) Childs World.

— My "v" Sound Box. LC 79-13084. (Sound Box Bks.). (Illus.). (J). (ps-2). 1979. lib. bdg. 21.36 (*0-89565-101-7*) Childs World.

— My "w" Sound Box. LC 78-8614. (Sound Box Bks.). (Illus.). (J). (ps-2). 1978. lib. bdg. 21.36 (*0-89565-046-0*) Childs World.

— My "x, y, z" Sound Box. LC 79-13086. (Sound Box Bks.). (Illus.). (J). (ps-2). 1979. lib. bdg. 21.36 (*0-89565-102-5*) Childs World.

— Nanny Goat's Boat. LC 87-12839. (Magic Castle Readers Ser.). (Illus.). 32p. (ENG & SPA.). (J). (ps-2). 1987. lib. bdg. 21.36 (*0-89565-929-8*) Childs World.

— Nanny Goat's Boat. LC 87-12839. (Magic Castle Readers Ser.). (Illus.). 32p. (ENG & SPA.). (J). (ps-2). 1987. lib. bdg. 21.36 (*0-89565-404-0*) Childs World.

— Night Animals: Wake-Up, Little Owl! LC 89-71173. (Discovery World Ser.). (Illus.). 32p. (J). (ps-2). 1990. lib. bdg. 21.36 (*0-89565-568-3*) Childs World.

— Now I Am Five! LC 83-25264. (Now I Am Ser.). (Illus.). 32p. (J). (ps-2). 1984. pap. 3.95 (*0-516-41879-3*) Childrens.

— Now I Am Four! LC 83-25270. (Now I Am Ser.). (Illus.). 32p. (J). (ps-2). 1984. pap. 3.95 (*0-516-41878-5*) Childrens.

— Now I Am Three! LC 83-20892. (Now I Am Ser.). (Illus.). 32p. (J). (ps). 1984. pap. 3.95 (*0-516-41877-7*) Childrens.

— Now I Am Two! LC 83-20891. (Now I Am Ser.). (Illus.). 32p. (J). (ps). 1984. pap. 3.95 (*0-516-41876-9*) Childrens.

— One Tricky Monkey Up on Top. LC 87-11612. (Magic Castle Readers Ser.). (Illus.). 32p. (ENG & SPA.). (J). (ps-2). 1987. lib. bdg. 21.36 (*0-89565-921-2*) Childs World.

— One Tricky Monkey Up on Top. LC 87-11612. (Magic Castle Readers Ser.). (Illus.). 32p. (J). (ps-2). 1987. lib. bdg. 21.36 (*0-89565-365-6*) Childs World.

— Our Birthday Book. LC 86-30976. (Special-Day Bks.). (Illus.). 32p. (J). (ps-3). 1987. lib. bdg. 21.36 (*0-89565-349-4*) Childs World.

— Our Christmas Book. rev. ed. LC 85-29132. (Special-Day Bks.). (Illus.). 32p. (J). (ps-3). 1986. lib. bdg. 21.36 (*0-89565-341-9*) Childs World.

— Our Columbus Day Book. LC 86-6818. (Special-Day Bks.). (Illus.). 32p. (J). (ps-3). 1986. lib. bdg. 21.36 (*0-89565-347-8*) Childs World.

— Our Easter Book. rev. ed. LC 86-29876. (Special-Day Bks.). (Illus.). 32p. (J). (ps-3). 1987. lib. bdg. 21.36 (*0-89565-345-1*) Childs World.

— Our Halloween Book. rev. ed. LC 85-30868. (Special-Day Bks.). (Illus.). 32p. (J). (ps-3). 1986. lib. bdg. 21.36 (*0-89565-348-6*) Childs World.

— Our Mother's Day Book. rev. ed. LC 86-29980. (Special-Day Bks.). (Illus.). (J). (ps-3). 1987. lib. bdg. 21.36 (*0-89565-346-X*) Childs World.

— Our Thanksgiving Book. rev. ed. LC 85-29077. (Special-Day Bks.). (Illus.). 32p. (J). (ps-3). 1986. lib. bdg. 21.36 (*0-89565-340-0*) Childs World.

— Our Valentine's Day Book. rev. ed. LC 86-28387. (Special-Day Bks.). (Illus.). 32p. (J). (ps-3). 1987. lib. bdg. 21.36 (*0-89565-343-5*) Childs World.

— Play with A & T. LC 89-774. (Alphabet Bks.). (Illus.). 32p. (J). (gr. k-2). 1989. lib. bdg. 21.36 (*0-89565-505-5*) Childs World.

— Play with E & D. LC 73-4743. (Alphabet Bks.). (Illus.). 32p. (J). (gr. k-2). 1989. lib. bdg. 21.36 (*0-89565-508-X*) Childs World.

— Play with I & G. LC 73-4739. (Alphabet Bks.). (Illus.). 32p. (J). (gr. k-2). 1989. lib. bdg. 21.36 (*0-89565-507-1*) Childs World.

— Play with O & G. LC 73-4742. (Alphabet Bks.). (Illus.). 32p. (J). (gr. k-2). 1989. lib. bdg. 21.36 (*0-89565-506-3*) Childs World.

— Play with U & G. LC 73-4741. (Alphabet Bks.). (Illus.). 32p. (J). (gr. k-2). 1989. lib. bdg. 21.36 (*0-89565-509-8*) Childs World.

— A Pocketful of Pets. LC 87-11748. (Magic Castle Readers Ser.). (Illus.). 32p. (ENG & SPA.). (J). (ps-2). 1987. lib. bdg. 21.36 (*0-89565-370-2*) Childs World.

— A Pocketful of Pets. LC 87-11748. (Magic Castle Readers Ser.). (Illus.). 32p. (ENG & SPA.). (J). (ps-2). 1987. lib. bdg. 21.36 (*0-89565-912-3*) Childs World.

An Asterisk (*) at the beginning of an entry indicates that the title is appearing in BIP for the first time.

— Polka-Dot Puppy. (Magic Castle Readers Ser.). (Illus.). 32p. (ENG & SPA.). (J). (ps-2). 1987. lib. bdg. 21.36 (*0-89565-911-5*) Childs World.
— Polka-Dot Puppy. LC 87-15813. (Magic Castle Readers Ser.). (Illus.). 32p. (ENG & SPA.). (J). (ps-2). 1987. lib. bdg. 21.36 (*0-89565-407-5*) Childs World.
— Rabbits' Habits. LC 87-12841. (Magic Castle Readers Ser.). (Illus.). 32p. (J). (ps-2). 1987. lib. bdg. 21.36 (*0-89565-406-7*) Childs World.
— Rain: A Great Day for Ducks. LC 89-24010. (Discovery World Ser.). (Illus.). 32p. (J). (ps-2). 1990. lib. bdg. 21.36 (*0-89565-553-5*) Childs World.
— Saying Please. LC 82-19927. (Moods & Emotions Ser.). (Illus.). 32p. (J). (ps-2). 1983. lib. bdg. 21.36 (*0-89565-248-X*) Childs World.
— Short A & Long A Play a Game. LC 79-10300. (Short & Long Vowels Ser.). (Illus.). (J). (gr. k-2). 1979. lib. bdg. 21.36 (*0-89565-089-4*) Childs World.
— Short E & Long E Play a Game. LC 79-10305. (Short & Long Vowels Ser.). (Illus.). (J). (gr. k-2). 1979. lib. bdg. 21.36 (*0-89565-090-8*) Childs World.
— Short I & Long I Play a Game. LC 79-10303. (Short & Long Vowels Ser.). (Illus.). (J). (gr. k-2). 1979. lib. bdg. 21.36 (*0-89565-091-6*) Childs World.
— Short O & Long O Play a Game. LC 79-10304. (Short & Long Vowels Ser.). (Illus.). (J). (gr. k-2). 1979. lib. bdg. 21.36 (*0-89565-092-4*) Childs World.
— Short U & Long U Play a Game. LC 79-10306. (Short & Long Vowels Ser.). (Illus.). (J). (gr. k-2). 1979. lib. bdg. 21.36 (*0-89565-093-2*) Childs World.
— Smile, Says Little Crocodile. LC 87-13833. (Magic Castle Readers Ser.). (Illus.). 32p. (ENG & SPA.). (J). (ps-2). 1987. lib. bdg. 21.36 (*0-89565-932-8*) Childs World.
— Smile, Says Little Crocodile. LC 87-13833. (Magic Castle Readers Ser.). (Illus.). 32p. (J). (ps-2). 1987. lib. bdg. 21.36 (*0-89565-401-6*) Childs World.
— Sounds All Around. LC 82-4516. (Five Senses Ser.). (Illus.). 32p. (J). (ps-3). 1982. pap. 3.95 (*0-516-43252-4*) Childrens.
— Step into Fall: A New Season. LC 90-30637. (Discovery World Ser.). (Illus.). 32p. (J). (ps-2). 1990. lib. bdg. 21.36 (*0-89565-573-X*); lib. bdg. 21.36 (*0-685-56189-5*) Childs World.
— Step into Spring: A New Season. LC 90-30375. (Discovery World Ser.). (Illus.). 32p. (J). (ps-2). 1990. lib. bdg. 21.36 (*0-89565-571-3*) Childs World.
— Step into Summer: A New Season. LC 90-30456. (Discovery World Ser.). (Illus.). 32p. (J). (ps-2). 1990. lib. bdg. 21.36 (*0-89565-572-1*) Childs World.
— Step into Winter: A New Season. LC 90-30636. (Discovery World Ser.). (Illus.). 32p. (J). (ps-2). 1990. lib. bdg. 21.36 (*0-89565-574-8*) Childs World.
— Stop! Go! Word Bird. LC 80-16273. (Word Bird Readers Ser.). (Illus.). 32p. (J). (ps-2). 1981. lib. bdg. 21.36 (*0-89565-160-2*) Childs World.
— The Sun: Our Daytime Star. LC 89-24009. (Discovery World Ser.). (Illus.). 32p. (J). (ps-2). 1990. lib. bdg. 21.36 (*0-89565-551-9*) Childs World.
— A Tasting Party. LC 82-4411. (Five Senses Ser.). (Illus.). 32p. (J). (ps-3). 1982. pap. 3.95 (*0-516-43253-2*) Childrens.
— The Touch Book. LC 82-4154. (Five Senses Ser.). (Illus.). (J). (ps-3). 1982. pap. 3.95 (*0-516-43254-0*) Childrens.
— Watch Out! Word Bird. (Word Bird Readers Ser.). (Illus.). (J). (ps-2). 1982. lib. bdg. 21.36 (*0-89565-219-6*) Childs World.
— What Can We Play Today? LC 87-32565. (Magic Castle Readers Ser.). (Illus.). 32p. (ENG & SPA.). (J). (ps-2). 1987. lib. bdg. 21.36 (*0-89565-412-1*); lib. bdg. 21.36 (*0-89565-923-9*) Childs World.
— What Do You Do with a Grumpy Kangaroo? LC 87-11731. (Magic Castle Readers Ser.). (Illus.). 32p. (ENG & SPA.). (J). (ps-2). 1987. lib. bdg. 21.36 (*0-89565-372-9*) Childs World.
— What Do You Do with a Grumpy Kangaroo? LC 87-11731. (Magic Castle Readers Ser.). (Illus.). 32p. (ENG & SPA.). (J). (ps-2). 1987. lib. bdg. 21.36 (*0-89565-924-7*) Childs World.
— What Do You Say When a Monkey Acts This Way? LC 87-11736. (Magic Castle Readers Ser.). (Illus.). 32p. (ENG & SPA.). (J). (ps-2). 1987. 5.25 hd 21.36 (*0-89565-368-0*) Childs World.
— What Do You Say When a Monkey Acts This Way? LC 87-11736. (Magic Castle Readers Ser.). (Illus.). 32p. (ENG & SPA.). (J). (ps-2). 1987. lib. bdg. 21.36 (*0-89565-925-5*) Childs World.
— What Does Word Bird See? LC 81-21594. (Word Bird Readers Ser.). (Illus.). (J). (ps-2). 1982. lib. bdg. 21.36 (*0-89565-220-X*) Childs World.
— What Plants Need: The Rabbit Who Knew. LC 89-24001. (Discovery World Ser.). (Illus.). 32p. (J). (ps-2). 1990. lib. bdg. 21.36 (*0-89565-559-4*) Childs World.
— What Your Nose Knows! LC 82-9464. (Five Senses Ser.). (Illus.). 32p. (J). (ps-3). 1982. pap. 3.95 (*0-516-43255-9*) Childrens.
— What's So Special about Lauren? She's My Baby Sister. LC 87-21927. (What's So Special Ser.). (Illus.). 32p. (J). (ps-2). 1987. lib. bdg. 21.36 (*0-89565-413-X*) Childs World.
— What's So Special about This Fall? I'm Going to School: I'm Going to School. LC 88-2868. (What's So Special Ser.). (Illus.). 32p. (J). (ps-2). 1988. lib. bdg. 21.36 (*0-89565-420-2*) Childs World.
— What's So Special about Today? It's My Birthday. LC 87-21907. (What's So Special Ser.). (Illus.). 32p. (J). (ps-2). 1987. lib. bdg. 21.36 (*0-89565-414-8*) Childs World.
— Where Is Baby Bear? LC 87-12840. (Magic Castle Readers Ser.). (Illus.). 32p. (ENG & SPA.). (J). (ps-2). 1987. lib. bdg. 21.36 (*0-89565-916-6*) Childs World.
— Where Is Baby Bear? LC 87-12840. (Magic Castle Readers Ser.). (Illus.). 32p. (ENG & SPA.). (J). (ps-2). 1987. lib. bdg. 21.36 (*0-89565-405-9*) Childs World.
— A Wish-for Dinosaur. LC 88-20302. (Dinosaur Bks.). (Illus.). 32p. (ENG & SPA.). (J). (ps-2). 1989. lib. bdg. 21.36 (*0-89565-908-5*) Childs World.
— A Wish-for Dinosaur. LC 88-20302. (Magic Castle Readers Ser.). (Illus.). 32p. (ENG & SPA.). (J). (ps-2). 1989. lib. bdg. 21.36 (*0-89565-393-1*) Childs World.
— Wishes, Whispers & Secrets. LC 78-31295. (Understanding Myself Picture Bks.). (Illus.). (J). (ps-3). 1979. lib. bdg. 21.35 (*0-89565-024-X*) Childs World.
— Word Bird Asks: What? What? What? LC 83-15258. (Word Bird Readers Ser.). (Illus.). 32p. (J). (gr. k-2). 1983. lib. bdg. 21.36 (*0-89565-258-7*) Childs World.
— Word Bird Builds a City. LC 83-15275. (Word Bird Readers Ser.). (Illus.). 32p. (J). (ps-2). 1983. lib. bdg. 21.36 (*0-89565-257-9*) Childs World.
— Word Bird Makes Words with Cat. LC 83-23948. (Short Vowel Adventures Ser.). (Illus.). 32p. (J). (gr. k-2). 1984. lib. bdg. 21.36 (*0-89565-259-5*) Childs World.
— Word Bird Makes Words with Dog. LC 83-23946. (Short Vowel Adventures Ser.). (Illus.). 32p. (J). (gr. k-1). 1984. lib. bdg. 21.36 (*0-89565-263-3*) Childs World.
— Word Bird Makes Words with Duck. LC 83-23943. (Short Vowel Adventures Ser.). (Illus.). 32p. (J). (gr. k-2). 1984. lib. bdg. 21.36 (*0-89565-261-7*) Childs World.
— Word Bird Makes Words with Hen. LC 83-23944. (Short Vowel Adventures Ser.). (Illus.). 32p. (J). (gr. k-2). 1984. lib. bdg. 21.36 (*0-89565-260-9*) Childs World.
— Word Bird Makes Words with Pig. LC 83-23945. (Short Vowel Adventures Ser.). (Illus.). 32p. (J). (gr. k-2). 1984. lib. bdg. 21.36 (*0-89565-262-5*) Childs World.
— Word Bird's Christmas Words. LC 86-31666. (Word House Words Ser.). (Illus.). 32p. (J). (gr. k-2). 1987. lib. bdg. 21.36 (*0-89565-361-3*) Childs World.
— Word Bird's Circus Surprise. LC 80-29528. (Word Bird Readers Ser.). (Illus.). 32p. (J). (gr. k-2). 1981. lib. bdg. 21.36 (*0-89565-162-9*) Childs World.
— Word Bird's Dinosaur Day. (School-Day Bks.). (Illus.). 32p. (J). (ps-2). 1990. lib. bdg. 21.36 (*0-89565-617-5*) Childs World.
— Word Bird's Easter Words. (Word House Words Ser.). (Illus.). 32p. (J). (gr. k-2). 1987. lib. bdg. 21.36 (*0-89565-363-X*) Childs World.
— Word Bird's Fall Words. LC 85-5935. (Word House Words Ser.). (Illus.). 32p. (J). (gr. k-2). 1985. lib. bdg. 21.36 (*0-89565-308-7*) Childs World.
— Word Bird's Halloween Words. LC 86-31024. (Word House Words Ser.). (Illus.). 32p. (J). (gr. k-2). 1987. lib. bdg. 21.36 (*0-89565-359-1*) Childs World.
— Word Bird's Hats. LC 81-18065. (Word Bird Readers Ser.). (Illus.). (J). (ps-2). 1982. lib. bdg. 21.36 (*0-89565-221-8*) Childs World.
— Word Bird's Magic Wand. LC 90-1645. (School-Day Bks.). (Illus.). 32p. (J). (ps-2). 1990. lib. bdg. 21.36 (*0-89565-580-2*) Childs World.
— Word Bird's New Friend. LC 90-37002. (School-Day Bks.). (Illus.). 32p. (J). (ps-2). 1990. lib. bdg. 21.36 (*0-89565-616-7*) Childs World.
— Word Bird's Rainy-Day Dance. LC 90-31693. (School-Day Bks.). (Illus.). 32p. (J). (ps-2). 1990. lib. bdg. 21.36 (*0-89565-579-9*) Childs World.
— Word Bird's School Words. LC 89-7179. (School-Day Bks.). (Illus.). 32p. (J). (ps-2). 1989. lib. bdg. 21.36 (*0-89565-510-1*) Childs World.
— Word Bird's Shapes. LC 83-15255. (Word Bird Readers Ser.). (Illus.). 32p. (J). (gr. k-2). 1983. lib. bdg. 21.36 (*0-89565-255-2*) Childs World.
— Word Bird's Spring Words. LC 85-5902. (Word House Words Ser.). (Illus.). 32p. (J). (gr. k-2). 1985. lib. bdg. 21.36 (*0-89565-310-9*) Childs World.
— Word Bird's Summer Words. LC 85-5930. (Word House Words Ser.). (Illus.). 32p. (J). (gr. k-2). 1985. lib. bdg. 21.36 (*0-89565-311-7*) Childs World.
— Word Bird's Thanksgiving Words. LC 86-32639. (Word House Words Ser.). (Illus.). 32p. (J). (gr. k-2). 1987. lib. bdg. 21.36 (*0-89565-360-5*) Childs World.
— Word Bird's Valentine Day Words. (Word House Words Ser.). (Illus.). 32p. (J). (gr. k-2). 1987. lib. bdg. 21.36 (*0-89565-362-1*) Childs World.
— Word Bird's Winter Words. LC 85-5942. (Word House Words Ser.). (Illus.). 32p. (J). (gr. k-2). 1985. lib. bdg. 21.36 (*0-89565-309-5*) Childs World.
— Yes, No, Little Hippo. LC 87-21211. (Magic Castle Readers Ser.). (Illus.). 32p. (ENG & SPA.). (J). (ps-2). 1987. lib. bdg. 21.36 (*0-89565-411-3*) Childs World.

Moncure, Jane B., tr. Fearless John: A Classic Tale. LC 88-35215. (Illus.). 32p. (J). (gr. 1-4). 1988. lib. bdg. 19.93 (*0-89565-470-9*) Childs World.
Moncure, Jane B., tr. see Andersen, Hans Christian.
Moncure, Jane B., tr. see Collodi, Carlo.
Moncure, Jane B., tr. see Grimm, Jacob & Grimm, Wilhelm K.
Moncure, Jane B., tr. see Jose, Eduard, ed.
Moncure, Jane B., tr. see Perrault, Charles.
Moncure, John. Forging the King's Sword: Military Education Between Tradition & Modernization: the Case of the Royal Prussian Cadet Corps, 1871- 1918. LC 92-18515. (American University Studies: History: Ser. IX, Vol. 132). 323p. 1992. 58.95 (*0-8204-1960-5*) P Lang Pubs.
Moncure-Sime, A. H. Shakespeare: His Music & Song. LC 70-177518. 1972. reprint ed. 15.95 (*0-405-08795-0*, Pub. by Blom Pubns UK) Ayer.
Moncuse, Steve. Fish Police. 1987. pap. 8.95 (*0-446-38739-8*) Warner Bks.
Moncy, Agnes, tr. see Delibes, Miguel.
***Monczka, Robert M. & Trent, Robert J.** Cross-Functional Sourcing Team Effectiveness. Ketchum, Carol, ed. 72p. (Orig.). (C). 1993. pap. text ed. 20.00 (*0-945968-15-9*) Ctr Advanced Purchasing.
Mond, D., jt. ed. see Montaldi, J. A.
Mond, Harry. Cardiac Pacemaker: Function & Malfunction. (Monographs in Clinical Cardiology). 560p. 1983. text ed. 121.00 (*0-8089-1578-9*, 792974, Grune) Saunders.
Mond, James J., et al. Cell Activation: Genetic Approaches. (Advances in Regulation of Cell Growth Ser.: Vol. 2). 352p. 1991. 116.50 (*0-88167-819-8*) Raven.
— Regulation of Cell Growth & Activation. (Advances in Regulation of Cell Growth Ser.: Vol. 1). 304p. 1989. 88.50 (*0-88167-573-3*, 2047) Raven.
***Mond, Robert W.** What Christians & Muslims Should Know about Themselves. 1994. write for info. (*0-9625301-4-X*) Forum Islamic.
Mondadori. English-Italian Business Dictionary. 306p. (ENG & ITA.). 1986. 49.95 (*0-8288-7350-X*, 8804289775) Fr & Eur.
— Italian English - English Italian Dictionary. 1990. pap. 5.99 (*0-671-72721-4*) S&S Trade.
Mondadori, ed. Simon & Schuster's Guide to Dogs. 1980. pap. 14.00 (*0-671-25527-4*) S&S Trade.
— Simon & Schuster's Guide to Rocks & Minerals. 1978. pap. 15.00 (*0-671-24417-5*) S&S Trade.
Mondain, M., jt. ed. see Uziel, A. S.
Mondal, M. S. Pollen Morphology & Systematic Relationships of Families Sabiaceae & Connaraceae. (Advances in Pollen Spore Research Ser.: Vol. 12). (Illus.). 152p. 1990. 65.00 (*1-55528-222-9*, Pub. by Today & Tomorrows P & P II) Scholarly Pubns.
Mondal, S. R., jt. ed. see Bhadra, R. K.
***Mondal, Sekh R.** Dynamics of Muslim Society. (C). 1993. 28.50x (*81-210-0322-9*, Pub. by Inter-India Pubns) S Asia.
Mondale, Clarence, jt. auth. see Steiner, Michael.
Mondanaro, Josette. Chemically Dependent Women: Assessment & Treatment. 192p. 1988. pap. 35.00 (*0-669-17235-9*) Free Pr.
Mondano, Mark R. Divers Guide to Shipwrecks: Cape Canaveral to Jupiter Light. (Illus.). 150p. (Orig.). 1992. pap. 19.00 (*0-9631346-1-2*) Sandman Prods.
***Mondavi, Robert.** America's Rising Star Chefs: At the Robert Mondavi Great Chefs Cooking School in Napa Valley. 1994. pap. 19.95 (*0-9641403-0-6*) Santa Fe Ventures.
Mondavi, Robert, jt. auth. see Shocklely, Bob.
Monday, Jane C., jt. auth. see Prather, Patricia S.
Monday, Lori. Official Guide to the HP-LX: A Desktop Computer That Fits in Your Pocket. 1993. pap. 20.00 (*0-679-74644-7*) Random.
Monday, Lori & Robinson, Tracy. Using Your HP 95LX. (Hewlett-Packard Ser.). 416p. 1991. pap. 24.95 (*0-201-56338-X*) Addison-Wesley.
***Monday, Mark & Stubblefield, Gary.** Killing Zone: A Professional's Guide to Preparing or Preventin Ambushes. 264p. 1994. pap. 25.00 (*0-87364-786-6*) Paladin Pr.
Monday, Paul E. & Dell, Robert W. Including & Involving New People. (Evangelism Study Ser.). 96p. 1992. pap. 4.95 (*0-87178-452-1*) Brethren.
Monday, Stella, ed. see Frank, Cynthia.
Mondejar, Publio L., jt. intro. see Ranney, Edward.
Mondello, Candace. Credits & Collections. Brett, Elaine, ed. LC 90-84234. (Fifty-Minute Ser.). (Illus.). (Orig.). 1991. pap. 8.95 (*1-56052-080-9*) Crisp Pubns.
Mondello, Christopher, jt. auth. see Sandhouse, Mark.
Mondello, Giulio. The Secret of Costa Brava. 120p. pap. 9.95 (*0-9630779-0-2*) PPC Bks.
Mondello, Salvatore. The Private Papers of John Vanderlyn (1775-1852), American Portrait Painter. LC 89-9380. (Studies in American History: Vol. 3). (Illus.). 250p. 1990. lib. bdg. 89.95 (*0-88946-096-5*) E Mellen.
Mondello, Salvatore, jt. auth. see Iorizzo, Luciano J.
Mondello, Salvatore A. The Italian Immigrant in Urban America, 1880-1920, As Reported in the Contemporary Periodical Press. Cordasco, Francesco, ed. LC 80-880. (American Ethnic Groups Ser.). 1981. lib. bdg. 30.95 (*0-405-13441-X*) Ayer.
Monden, Yasuhiro. Cost Management in the New Manufacturing Age: Innovations in the Japanese Automotive Industry. Vitek, Stephen, tr. (Illus.). 198p. 1992. 45.00 (*0-915299-90-9*) Prod Press.
— Cost Reduction System: Target Costing & Kaizen Costing. (Illus.). 400p. (JPN.). 1995. text ed. 50.00 (*1-56327-068-4*) Prod Press.
— The Toyota Management System: Linking the Seven Key Functional Areas. LC 92-27133. 245p. 1993. 45.00 (*1-56327-014-5*) Prod Press.
— Toyota Production System: An Integrated Approach to Just-in-Time. 2nd ed. LC 92-27711. 1993. 53.95 (*0-89806-129-6*) Ind Eng Mgmt Pr.
Monden, Yasuhiro & Sakurai, Michiharu, eds. Japanese Management Accounting: A World Class Approach to Profit Management. LC 88-43585. (Illus.). 568p. 1990. 65.00 (*0-915299-50-X*) Prod Press.
Mondenard, J. P. Dictionary of Doping Substances & Procedures in Sports. 288p. (FRE.). 1991. 125.00 (*0-8288-6959-6*, 2225822905) Fr & Eur.
Monder, Eric. George Sidney: A Bio-Bibliography. LC 94-10853. (Bio-Bibliographies in the Performing Arts Ser.: No. 56). 360p. 1994. text ed. 69.50 (*0-313-28457-1*, Greenwood Pr) Greenwood.
***Mondey, David.** Concise Guide to American Aircraft of WW II. 1994. 10.98 (*0-7858-0147-2*) Bk Sales Inc.
— Concise Guide to British Aircraft of WW II. 1994. 10.98 (*0-7858-0146-4*) Bk Sales Inc.
Mondey, David & Trippe, Juan, eds. The International Encyclopedia of Aviation. (Illus.). 1977. 19.95 (*0-517-53157-7*) Random Hse Value.
Mondey, David, jt. auth. see Taylor, Michael.
Mondfeld, Wolfram Z. Historic Ship Models. LC 89-11380. (Illus.). 352p. 1989. pap. 19.95 (*0-8069-5733-6*) Sterling.
Mondimore, Francis M. Depression: The Mood Disease. rev. ed. LC 92-40513. 248p. 1993. 22.95 (*0-8018-4592-0*) Johns Hopkins.
— Depression, the Mood Disease. (Health Book Ser.). 248p. 1995. reprint ed. pap. 15.95 (*0-8018-5184-X*) Johns Hopkins.
Mondo. Morning of the Bright Bird. (Illus.). 48p. (J). 1993. pap. 8.95 (*0-88378-136-0*) Third World.
Mondol, Raji. Marianne's Michigan. (Illus.). 36p. (C). 1992. pap. text ed. 6.00 (*0-9628611-8-9*) Blue Denim.
Mondolf, Lucio F. & Zmeskal, Otto. Engineering Metallurgy. LC 54-12253. 407p. reprint ed. pap. 116.00 (*0-317-10673-2*, 2003417) Bks Demand.
Mondon, Kathryn T., jt. auth. see Wennergren, Kenneth H.
Mondor, ed. see Mallarme, Stephane.
Mondovi, Bruno, ed. Structure & Functions of Amine Oxidases. 304p. 1986. 179.00 (*0-8493-5869-8*, QP603, CRC Reprint) Franklin.
Mondradon, J. Sanchez & Wolf, K. B., eds. Lie Methods in Optics. (Lecture Notes in Physics Ser.: Vol. 250). xiv, 249p. 1986. 39.00 (*0-387-16471-5*) Spr-Verlag.
Mondragon, J. R., jt. auth. see Abas, J.
***Mondrian, Piet.** Natural Reality & Abstract Reality: An Essay in Trialogue Form (1919-1920) Beekman, E. M., tr. 112p. 1995. write for info. (*0-8076-1372-X*) Braziller.
— Natural Reality & Abstract Reality: An Essay in Trialogue Form (1919-1920) 1995. write for info. (*0-8076-1371-1*) Braziller.
— The New Art - the New Life: The Collected Writings of Piet Mondrian. Holtzman, Harry & James, Martin S., eds. James, Martin S., tr. (Illus.). 440p. 1992. reprint ed. pap. 24.95 (*0-306-80508-1*) Da Capo.
Mondros, Jacqueline B. & Wilson, Scott M. Organizing for Power & Empowerment. LC 93-31676. (Empowering the Powerless Ser.). 279p. 1994. 49.00 (*0-231-06718-6*); pap. 22.50 (*0-231-06719-4*) Col U Pr.
Mondry, Adele. A Shtetl on the Bug River. 1979. 11.95 (*0-87068-657-7*) Ktav.
Monds, F. Business of Electronic Product Development. Montgomerie, G. A., ed. (Management Ser.). 152p. 1986. reprint ed. pap. 54.00 (*0-86341-012-X*, MT002) Inst Elect Eng.
Mondy, R. Wayne & Noe, Robert M., III. Human Resource Management. 4th ed. 650p. 1989. teacher ed write for info. (*0-318-66375-9*, H21223); text ed. 52.00 (*0-205-12121-7*, H21215); student ed 18.00 (*0-685-29836-1*, H20787); trans. write for info. (*0-318-66377-5*, H21249); write for info. (*0-318-66376-7*, H21223) Allyn.
***Mondy, R. Wayne & Premeaux, Shane R.** Management - Concepts, Practice, & Skills. 7th ed. LC 94-41368. 1994. text ed. 65.33 (*0-205-16378-5*) P-H.
— Management - Concepts, Practices, & Skills. 6th ed. LC 92-25673. 1992. text ed. write for info. (*0-205-13854-3*) Allyn.
Mondy, R. Wayne, III, et al. Human Resource Management. 5th ed. LC 92-27718. 1992. text ed. write for info. (*0-205-14218-4*) Allyn.
Mondy, R. Wayne, et al. Management & Organizational Behavior. 720p. 1989. teacher ed write for info. (*0-318-66379-1*, H20571); text ed. 51.00 (*0-205-12056-3*, H20563); student ed 18.00 (*0-685-29837-X*, H20621); trans. write for info. (*0-318-66381-3*, H20605); vhs write for info. (*0-318-66383-X*, H26131); write for info. (*0-318-66380-5*, H20597); write for info. (*0-318-66382-1*, H23948) Allyn.
— Management, Concepts, Practices & Skills. 5th ed. (Illus.). 768p. 1990. text ed. 51.00 (*0-205-12614-6*, H26149) Allyn.
— Personal Selling: Function, Theory, & Practice. 3rd ed. 480p. 1988. teacher ed write for info. (*0-318-63843-6*, H19185) Allyn.
— Supervision. 2nd ed. 520p. 1990. teacher ed write for info. (*0-318-66378-3*, H25067) Allyn.
Mondy, Robert W. Pioneers & Preachers: Stories of the Old Frontier. LC 79-16906. (Illus.). 272p. 1980. 38.95 (*0-88229-619-1*) Nelson-Hall.
Mone, Edward M., jt. auth. see London, Manuel.
Mone, Edward M., jt. ed. see London, Manuel.
Mone, Franz J. Geschichte Des Heidenthums Im Nordlichen Europa, 2 vols., Ser. xl, 1085p. 1990. reprint ed. write for info. (*0-318-70732-2*, Pub. by Georg Olms GW) Lubrecht & Cramer.
Mone, Louis C. Private Practice: A Professional Business. (Illus.). 113p. (Orig.). (C). 1983. pap. 12.95 (*0-9613420-0-5*) Elm Pr.
Monegain, Bernie. Coastal Islands: A Guide to Exploring Maine's Isles. (Maine Geographic Ser.). (Illus.). 48p. 1988. pap. 4.95 (*0-89933-046-0*) DeLorme Map.
— Historic Sites: A Guide to Maine's Museums, Period Homes & Forts. Feller-Roth, Barbara, ed. (Maine Geographic Ser.). (Illus.). 48p. 1992. pap. 4.95 (*0-89933-057-6*) DeLorme Map.
— Natural Sites: A Guide to Maine's Natural Phenomena. Feller-Roth, Barbara, ed. (Maine Geographic Ser.). (Illus.). 48p. 1988. pap. 4.95 (*0-89933-058-4*) DeLorme Map.
Monegain, Bernie, ed. see Feller-Roth, Barbara.
Monegal, Emir R., ed. The Borzoi Anthology of Latin American Literature, 2 vols, 1. 1977. pap. 19.95 (*0-394-73301-0*) Knopf.
— The Borzoi Anthology of Latin American Literature, 2 vols, 2. 1977. pap. 19.95 (*0-394-73366-5*) Knopf.
Monegal, Emir R. & Levine, Suzanne J. Maestros Hispanicos del Siglo Viente. 194p. (Orig.). (C). 1979. pap. text ed. 20.75 (*0-15-551270-6*) HB Coll Pubs.
***Monek, Francis H.** Canes Through the Ages. (Illus.). 320p. 1995. 79.95 (*0-88740-862-1*) Schiffer.

M

Monell, Gary E., jt. auth. see Nasatir, Abraham P.

Monely, Jonathan, jt. auth. see Watling, Tom.

Moner, Fray F. Obras Castellanas Tomo I: Poemas Menores, 2. Cocozeella, Peter, ed. LC 91-20691. (Hispanic Literature Ser.: Vols. 2 & 3). 1991. 99.95 (*0-88946-388-3*) E Mellen.

— Obras Castellanas Tomo I: Poemas Menores, Vol. 3. Cocozeella, Peter, ed. LC 91-20691. (Hispanic Literature Ser.: Vols. 2 & 3). 1991. 99.95 (*0-88946-389-1*) E Mellen.

Moner, John G. The Animal Cell. Head, J. J., ed. LC 83-70597. (Carolina Biology Readers Ser.: No. 147). (Illus.). 32p. (YA). (gr. 10 up). 1987. pap. text ed. 3.00 (*0-89278-347-8*, 45-9747) Carolina Biological.

Mones, illus. Walt Disney's Bambi. (Little Nugget Bks.). 28p. (J). (ps). 1992. bds. write for info. (*0-307-12535-1*, 12535, Golden Pr) Western Pub.

— Walt Disney's Cinderella. (Little Nugget Bks.). 28p. (J). (ps). 1992. bds. write for info. (*0-307-12530-0*, 12530, Golden Pr) Western Pub.

— Walt Disney's One Hundred One Dalmatians. (Little Nugget Bks.). 28p. (J). 1994. write for info. (*0-307-12546-7*, Golden Bks) Western Pub.

— Walt Disney's Snow White & the Seven Dwarfs. (Little Nugget Bks.). 28p. (J). (ps). 1992. bds. write for info. (*0-307-12531-9*, 12531, Golden Pr) Western Pub.

***Mones, Isidre, illus.** Snow White & the Seven Dwarfs: It's Time to Wash! LC 94-71695. (Surprise Lift-the-Flap Ser.). 18p. (J). (ps-k). 1995. 9.95 (*0-7868-3030-1*) Disney Pr.

***Mones, Paul.** Stalking Justice: The Dramatic True Story of the Detective Who First Used DNA Testing to Catch a Serial Killer. Zion, Claire, ed. 320p. 1995. 23.00 (*0-671-70348-X*) PB.

— When a Child Kills. Zion, Claire, ed. 416p. 1992. reprint ed. mass mkt. 5.99 (*0-671-67421-8*) PB.

Monesson, Harry S. The World's Biggest Tummy. LC 92-96830. (Illus.). 40p. (Orig.). (J). (gr. k-3). 1992. pap. 6.95 (*0-9633735-0-1*) H S Monesson.

Monestiere, Martin. Human Oddities. Campbell, Robert, tr. (Illus.). 256p. 1987. pap. 14.95 (*0-8065-1021-8*, Citadel Pr) Carol Pub Group.

Monet, Claude. The Bridge at Argenteuil. (Fine Art Jigsaw Puzzles Ser.). 1989. 9.95 (*0-934967-50-4*) Battle Rd Pr.

Monet, Claude, illus. Monet. (Miniature Art Bks.). 64p. 1992. 4.99 (*0-517-07761-2*, Pub. by Wings Bks) Random Hse Value.

Monet, Don & Wilson, Ardythe. Colonialism on Trial: Indigenous Land Rights & the Gitksan-We'suwet'en Sovereignty Case. 224p. 1991. lib. bdg. 49.95 (*0-86571-218-2*); pap. 17.95 (*0-86571-219-0*) New Soc Pubs.

Monet, Gabriel & Roman, Bruce W. Dynamic Cube Strategy. (Illus.). 134p. (Orig.). 1980. pap. text ed. 50.00 (*0-9608566-0-9*) Advanced Back.

Monet, Jacques. The Last Cannon Shot: A Study of French-Canadian Nationalism, 1837-1850. LC 70-455781. 432p. reprint ed. pap. 123.20 (*0-685-15412-2*, 2026537) Bks Demand.

Moneta, Daniela P., ed. Chas. F. Lummis: The Centennial Exhibition Commemorating His Tramp Across the Continent. LC 84-27589. (Illus.). 80p. (Orig.). 1985. 24.95 (*0-916561-67-4*); pap. 14.95 (*0-916561-01-1*) Southwest Mus.

Moneta, G. C. On Identity. (Phaenomenologica Ser.: No. 71). 1977. pap. text ed. 47.00 (*90-247-1860-0*) Kluwer Ac.

Moneta, Giuseppina, et al, eds. The Collegium Phaenomenologicum. (C). 1988. lib. bdg. 133.00 (*90-247-3709-5*) Kluwer Ac.

Moneti, Annamaria, jt. auth. see Lazzarino, Graziana.

Monette. Becoming a Man: Half a Life Story. 1992. 19.95 (*0-15-111519-2*) HarBrace.

Monette, Clarence J. Delaware, Michigan, Its History. (Copper Country Local History Ser.: Vol. 28). (Illus.). 120p. (Orig.). 1987. pap. 3.00 (*0-942363-27-2*) C J Monette.

— The Gay, Michigan, Story. (Copper Country Local History Ser.: No. 31). (Illus.). 120p. (Orig.). 1988. pap. 2.50 (*0-942363-30-2*) C J Monette.

— Lac La Belle. (Copper Country Local History Ser.: Vol. 28). (Illus.). 120p. 1990. 3.00 (*0-942363-37-X*) C J Monette.

— Lake Linden's Living History - 1985. (Copper Country Local History Ser.: Vol. 29). (Illus.). 112p. (Orig.). 1987. pap. 2.50 (*0-942363-28-0*) C J Monette.

— Some of the Best from C & H News & Views, Vol. II. (Copper Country Local History Ser.: No. 30). (Illus.). 120p. (Orig.). 1987. pap. 2.50 (*0-942363-29-9*) C J Monette.

Monette, Duane R., et al. Applied Social Research: Tool for the Human Services. 2nd ed. 512p. (C). 1990. text ed. 44.75 (*0-03-026293-3*) HB Coll Pubs.

Monette, John W. History of the Discovery & Settlement of the Valley of the Mississippi by the Three Great European Powers Spain, France, & Great Britain, & the Subsequent Occupation Settlement & Extension of Civil Government by the United States Until the Year 1846, 2 Vols. in 1. LC 78-146408. (First American Frontier Ser.). (Illus.). 1971. reprint ed. 74.95 (*0-405-02868-7*) Ayer.

Monette, L. G. The Art of Organ Voicing. LC 92-23871. 1992. 35.00 (*0-932826-25-3*) New Issues MI.

Monette, Louis G. Index to l'Art du Facteur d'Orgues. 62p. 1992. pap. 9.00 (*0-913746-34-7*) Organ Lit.

Monette, Maurice L. Kindred Spirits: Bonding of Laity & Religious. LC 87-61530. 100p. (Orig.). 1987. pap. 6.95 (*1-55612-070-2*) Sheed & Ward MO.

Monette, Maurice L., ed. Partners in Ministry: Priests in Collaboration with Parish Life Coordinators. LC 88-62579. 72p. (Orig.). (C). 1988. pap. 4.95 (*1-55612-243-8*) Sheed & Ward MO.

Monette, Maurice L., jt. ed. see Institute for Pastoral Life Staff.

Monette, Paul. Afterlife. 288p. 1991. pap. 10.00 (*0-380-71197-4*) Avon.

— Afterlife. 1990. 19.95 (*0-517-57339-3*, Crown) Crown Pub Group.

— Afterlife. braille ed. 563p. 1991. vinyl bd. 45.04 (*1-56956-360-8*, BR8410) W A T Braille.

— Becoming a Man: Half a Life Story. LC 92-54661. 288p. 1993. reprint ed. pap. 12.00 (*0-06-250724-9*) Harper SF.

— Borrowed Time: An AIDS Memoir. 1990. pap. 11.00 (*0-380-70779-9*) Avon.

— Borrowed Time: An AIDS Memoir. 400p. 1988. 22.00 (*0-15-113598-3*) HarBrace.

— Borrowed Time: An AIDS Memoir. braille ed. 658p. 1992. vinyl bd. 52.64 (*1-56956-198-2*, BR7469) W A T Braille.

— Halfway Home. 272p. 1992. pap. 11.00 (*0-380-71797-2*) Avon.

— Halfway Home. 1991. 20.00 (*0-517-58329-1*, Crown) Crown Pub Group.

— Havana. 208p. 1991. mass mkt. 4.95 (*0-8041-0734-3*) Ivy Books.

— Last Watch of the Night: Essays. LC 93-47655. 1994. 21.95 (*0-15-100071-9*) HarBrace.

— Last Watch of the Night: Essays Too Personal & Otherwise. 320p. 1995. pap. 12.00 (*0-15-600202-7*) HarBrace.

— The Long Shot. 328p. 1988. reprint ed. pap. 7.95 (*0-8216-2004-5*) Carol Pub Group.

— Love Alone: Eighteen Elegies for Rog. (Stonewall Inn Editions Ser.). 80p. 1988. pap. 8.95 (*0-312-02602-1*) St Martin.

— The Politics of Silence. LC 93-33721. (National Book Week Lectures Ser.). 21p. 1994. write for info. (*0-8444-0808-5*) Lib Congress.

— Selected from Borrowed Time: An AIDS Memoir. abr. ed. Literacy Volunteers of New York City Staff & Fogarty, Patricia, eds. (Writers' Voices Ser.). 64p. (Orig.). 1992. pap. text ed. 3.50 (*0-929631-56-0*, Signal Hill) New Readers.

— Taking Care of Mrs. Carroll. (Stonewall Inn Editions Ser.). 288p. 1988. pap. 8.95 (*0-312-01515-1*) St Martin.

— West of Yesterday, East of Summer: New & Selected Poems, 1973-1993. LC 94-16119. 1994. 17.95 (*0-312-11379-X*) St Martin.

***Monette, Solange.** Dictionnaire Encyclopedique des Aliments. 1991. write for info. (*0-7859-8203-5*, 2-89037-475-0) Fr & Eur.

Monetti-Souple, Marta. A Year-Round Recruitment & Retention Plan. (How to Development Ser.). 53p. (Orig.). 1990. pap. 8.00 (*1-55833-047-X*) Natl Cath Educ.

Money, D. C. China: The Land & the People. (Illus.). 192p. 1992. 34.95 (*0-237-51164-9*, Pub. by Evans Bros Ltd UK); pap. 17.95 (*0-237-51118-5*, Pub. by Evans Bros Ltd UK) Trafalgar.

Money, J. Biographies of Gender & Hermaphroditism in Paired Comparisons: Clinical Supplement to the Handbook of Sexology. 388p. 1991. 262.00 (*0-444-81403-5*); pap. 60.00 (*0-444-89129-3*) Elsevier.

Money, J. & Musaph, H., eds. Handbook of Sexology. 1402p. 1977. 236.50 (*90-219-2104-9*) Elsevier.

Money, J., et al. Handbook of Sexology, Vol. 7: Childhood & Adolescent Sexology. 1991. 253.25 (*0-444-81262-8*) Elsevier.

Money, J. W. To All the Girls I've Loved Before: An AIDS Diary. 188p. (Orig.). 1987. pap. 6.95 (*1-55583-121-4*) Alyson Pubns.

Money, John. The Adam Principle: Genes, Genitals, Hormones & Gender - Selected Readings in Sexology. (New Concepts in Human Sexuality Ser.). 364p. (C). 1993. 39.95 (*0-87975-804-X*) Prometheus Bks.

— The Destroying Angel: Sex, Fitness, & Food in the Legacy of Degeneracy Theory, Graham Crackers, Kellogg's Corn Flakes, & American Health History. LC 84-43104. 213p. 1985. 27.95 (*0-87975-277-7*) Prometheus Bks.

— Gay, Straight, & In-Between: The Sexology of Erotic Orientation. (Illus.). 304p. 1988. 29.95 (*0-19-505407-5*) OUP.

— Gay, Straight, & In-Between: The Sexology of Erotic Orientation. (Illus.). 304p. 1990. reprint ed. pap. 9.95 (*0-19-506331-7*) OUP.

— Gendermaps: Social Constructionism, Feminism & Sexosophical History. 168p. 1995. 22.95 (*0-8264-0852-4*) Continuum.

— The Kaspar Hauser Syndrome of Psychosocial Dwarfism: Deficient Statural, Intellectual, & Social Growth Induced by Child Abuse. 290p. (C). 1992. 25.95 (*0-87975-754-X*) Prometheus Bks.

— Love & Love Sickness: The Science of Sex; Gender. Difference & Pair Bonding. LC 79-3679. 1980. 38.50x (*0-8018-2317-X*); pap. text ed. 14.95x (*0-8018-2318-8*) Johns Hopkins.

— Lovemaps: Clinical Concepts of Sexual-Erotic Health & Pathology, Paraphilia & Gender Transposition in Childhood, Adolescence & Maturity. LC 85-24153. (Illus.). 350p. (C). 1986. 34.50 (*0-8290-1589-2*) Irvington.

— Lovemaps: Clinical Concepts of Sexual-Erotic Health & Pathology, Paraphilia & Gender Transposition in Childhood, Adolescence & Maturity. 331p. 1988. pap. 18.95 (*0-87975-456-7*) Prometheus Bks.

— Lovemaps: Clinical Concepts of Sexual-Erotic Health & Pathology, Paraphilia & Gender Transposition in Childhood, Adolescence & Maturity. LC 85-24153. (Illus.). 350p. (C). 1989. reprint ed. pap. 18.95 (*0-8290-1892-1*) Irvington.

— Reinterpreting the Unspeakable: Human Sexuality 2000. 288p. 1994. 29.95 (*0-8264-0651-3*) Continuum.

— Sex Errors of the Body: Dilemmas, Education, Counseling. LC 68-15447. (Illus.). 160p. reprint ed. pap. 45.60 (*0-7837-3393-3*, 2043351) Bks Demand.

— Sex Errors of the Body & Related Syndromes: A Guide to Counseling Children, Adolescents, & Their Families. 2nd ed. LC 94-14341. 160p. 1994. 25.00 (*1-55766-150-2*) P H Brookes.

— Venuses Penuses. 659p. 1986. 37.95x (*0-87975-327-7*) Prometheus Bks.

Money, John, ed. The Disabled Reader: Education of the Dyslexic Child. LC 66-20713. 441p. reprint ed. pap. 125.70 (*0-8357-9266-8*, 2011900) Bks Demand.

Money, John & Ehrhardt, Anke A. Man & Woman, Boy & Girl: The Differentiation & Dimorphism of Gender Identity from Conception to Maturity. LC 72-4012. (Illus.). 327p. reprint ed. pap. 93.20 (*0-7837-3394-1*, 2043352) Bks Demand.

Money, John & Lamacz, Margaret. Vandalized Lovemaps: Paraphilic Outcome of Seven Cases in Pediatric Sexology. 224p. 1989. 29.95 (*0-87975-513-X*) Prometheus Bks.

Money, John, ed. see Johns Hopkins Conference on Research Needs & Prospects in Dyslexia & Related Aphasic Disorders Staff.

Money, John, jt. auth. see Keyes, Ronald W.

Money, John, jt. ed. see Krivacska, James J.

Money, John, jt. auth. see Williams, Gertrude.

Money, John, jt. ed. see Wolman, Benjamin B.

Money, John, et al. The Breathless Orgasm: A Lovemap Biography of Asphyxiophilia. 178p. (C). 1991. 25.95x (*0-87975-664-0*) Prometheus Bks.

***Money, K.** Fonteyne & Nureyev. 1994. 60.00 (*0-00-271375-6*, Pub. by HarpC UK) HarpC.

Money-Kyrle, R. E. Psychoanalysis & Politics: A Contribution to the Psychology of Politics & Morals. LC 72-12143. 182p. 1973. reprint ed. text ed. 75.00 (*0-8371-6714-0*, MOPS, Greenwood Pr) Greenwood.

Money, Lloyd J. Transportation Energy & the Future. (Illus.). 144p. (C). 1984. text ed. 38.00 (*0-13-930230-1*) P-H.

Money Magazine Editors. Your Best Money Moves Now. 224p. 1993. 19.95 (*0-8487-1157-2*) Oxmoor Hse.

Money Magazine Editors, jt. auth. see Sprouse, Mary L.

Money Magazine Staff. Money Safe Investing. 224p. 1992. pap. 14.99 (*0-8487-1106-8*) Oxmoor Hse.

Money, Mike, ed. Health & Community: Holism in Practice. (Illus.). 212p. (Orig.). 1994. pap. 12.95 (*1-870098-53-6*, Pub. by Green Bks UK) Seven Hills Bk.

Money, Peter. These Are My Shoes. 96p. (Orig.). 1991. pap. 6.95 (*0-9623193-8-4*) Boz Pub.

Money, Randy C., jt. auth. see Hill, Tom H.

Money, Robert E. Christian Marriage: Grace & Work. LC 89-28939. 1991. pap. 7.99 (*0-8054-3004-0*) Broadman.

Money, Royce. Building Stronger Families. LC 83-51300. 156p. 1984. pap. 7.99 (*0-88207-244-7*, Victor Books) SP Pubns.

— Ministering to Families. LC 86-72162. 300p. 1987. pap. 10.95 (*0-915547-92-9*) Abilene Christ U.

Money, S. A. Practical Microprocessor Interfacing. LC 87-23204. 247p. 1987. text ed. 79.95 (*0-471-63788-2*) Wiley.

Money, S. A., ed. Microprocessor Data Book. 2nd ed. 316p. 1990. text ed. 69.00 (*0-12-504445-3*) Acad Pr.

Money, Steve. Commodore 64 Graphics & Sound. 1985. 12.95 (*0-13-152034-2*) P-H.

— Radio Amateur & Listener's Data Handbook. (Illus.). 240p. 1995. pap. 39.95 (*0-7506-2094-3*) Buttrwrth-Heinemann.

Moneyhon, Carl & Roberts, Bobby. Portraits of Conflict: A Photographic History of Louisiana in the Civil War. (Illus.). 370p. 1990. 50.00 (*1-55728-158-0*); pap. 30.00 (*1-55728-159-9*) U of Ark Pr.

Moneyhon, Carl, jt. auth. see Roberts, Bobby.

Moneyhon, Carl H. Impact of the Civil War & Reconstruction on Arkansas: Persistence in the Midst of Ruin. LC 93-26080. (Illus.). 336p. (C). 1993. text ed. 35.00 (*0-8071-1840-0*) La State U Pr.

— Republicanism in Reconstruction Texas. LC 79-14283. (Illus.). 335p. 1980. text ed. 22.50 (*0-292-77553-9*) U of Tex Pr.

Moneyhon, Carl H., jt. auth. see Hanson, Gerald.

Moneyhon, Jack N. Buying Actuals: An Investor's Manual for Evaluating Gold & Silver. (Illus.). 80p. (Orig.). 1984. pap. 16.95 (*0-930907-00-0*) Great & Sm Pubs.

Moneyhun, Clyde, tr. see Miura, Ayako.

Moneyhun, George. The Mill Girls. 304p. 1986. reprint ed. pap. 3.50 (*0-8439-2312-1*) Dorchester Pub Co.

Monfardini, S. & Veronesi, U., eds. The Management of Non-Hodgkin's Lymphomas in Europe. (ESO Intercity Report Ser.). viii, 92p. 1990. pap. 55.00 (*0-387-52297-2*) Spr-Verlag.

Monfardini, S., et al, eds. Manual of Adult & Paediatric Medical Oncology. (Illus.). 420p. 1987. pap. 52.00 (*0-387-15347-0*) Spr-Verlag.

Monfardini, Silvio, jt. ed. see Fentiman, Ian S.

***Monfasani, John.** Byzantine Scholars in Renaissance Italy: Cardinal Bessarion & Other Emigres. (Collected Studies Ser.: Vol. CS485). 1995. 68.95 (*0-86078-477-0*, Pub. by Variorum UK) Ashgate Pub Co.

— Fernando of Cordova: A Biographical & Intellectual Profile. LC 92-72642. (Transactions Ser.: Vol. 82, Pt. 6). 125p. (C). 1992. pap. 18.00 (*0-87169-826-9*, T826-MOJ) Am Philos.

— Language & Learning in Renaissance Italy: Selected Articles. (Collected Studies: CS 460). (Illus.). 336p. 1994. 89.95 (*0-86078-403-7*, Pub. by Variorum UK) Ashgate Pub Co.

Monfasani, John, ed. Collectanea Trapezuntiana: Texts, Documents & Bibliographies of George of Trebizond. LC 83-19366. (Medieval & Renaissance Texts & Studies: Vol. 25). 896p. 1984. 60.00 (*0-86698-060-1*) MRTS.

Monfasani, John & Musto, Ronald G., eds. Renaissance Society & Culture: Essays in Honor of Eugene F. Rice, Jr. LC 90-55872. 328p. 1991. 55.00 (*0-934977-24-0*) Italica Pr.

Monfasani, John, et al, eds. Supplementum Festivum: Studies in Honor of Paul Oskar Kristeller. LC 87-18422. (Medieval & Renaissance Texts & Studies: Vol. 49). (Illus.). 672p. 1987. 50.00 (*0-86698-033-4*) MRTS.

Monfasoni, John, ed. Collectanea Trapezuntiana: Texts, Documents, & Bibliographies of George of Trebizond. (Renaissance Text Ser.: No. 8). xxii, 866p. 1984. 60.00 (*0-685-11970-X*) Renaiss Society Am.

Monfort, Alain, jt. auth. see Gourieroux, Christian.

Monfort, Franklin & Orfield, Gary. Racial Change & Desegregation in Large School Districts: Trends Through the 1986-1987 School Year. 34p. (Orig.). 1988. pap. text ed. 10.00 (*0-88364-172-0*) Natl Sch Boards.

Monfort, Franklin, jt. auth. see Orfield, Gary.

Monforte, J. M., jt. auth. see Casciaro, J. M.

Monforte, Joseph R., ed. Analytical Toxicology of Cannabinoids. 176p. (Orig.). Date not set. pap. write for info. (*0-912474-17-3*) Preston Pubns.

— Analytical Toxicology of Cocaine. 288p. (Orig.). Date not set. pap. write for info. (*0-912474-19-X*) Preston Pubns.

***Monfredo, Miriam G.** Blackwater Spirits. 1995. 21.95 (*0-312-11754-X*, Pub. by Thomas Dunne Bks) St Martin.

— North Star Conspiracy. 368p. 1995. pap. text ed. 4.99 (*0-425-14720-7*, Prime Crime) Berkley Pub.

— North Star Conspiracy. 256p. 1993. 21.95 (*0-312-09355-1*, Pub. by Thomas Dunne Bks) St Martin.

— Seneca Falls Inheritance. 304p. 1994. pap. text ed. 4.99 (*0-425-14465-8*) Berkley Pub.

— Seneca Falls Inheritance. 320p. 1992. 19.95 (*0-312-07082-9*, Pub. by Thomas Dunne Bks) St Martin.

Monfried, Lucia. The Daddies Boat. (Illus.). 32p. (J). (ps-3). 1993. pap. 4.99 (*0-14-054938-2*, Puff Unicorn) Puffin Bks.

— No More Animals! LC 94-47572. (Speedsters Ser.). (Illus.). (J). 1995. 12.99 (*0-525-45390-3*, DCB) Dutton Child Bks.

***Monfries, Marcelle.** Gardening in the Shade. (Illus.). 76p. (Orig.). 1995. pap. 11.95 (*0-86417-623-6*) Seven Hills Bk.

Mong, Lee S. Understanding Jade. 104p. 1992. 11.95 (*9971-65-496-2*) Heian Intl.

Mong, RoseMary. Barefoot Forever. (Illus.). 96p. 1986. 12.95 (*0-941974-07-3*) Baranski Pub Co.

***Monga, G. S. & Sanctis, V. J.** India's Energy Prospects. (C). 1994. 28.50x (*0-7069-7616-9*, Pub. by Vikas II) S Asia.

Monga, Mohinder. Through the Night Raptly. 8.00 (*0-89253-778-7*); 4.80 (*0-89253-779-5*) Ind-US Inc.

Monga, Pradeep, ed. Energy, Environment & Sustainable Development in the Himalayas. (C). 1992. 32.00 (*81-85182-76-0*, Pub. by Indus Pub II) S Asia.

Monga, Pradeep & Lakhanpal, T. N. Rural Energy Alternatives in the Hilly Areas: (Social Forestry & Biogas Systems) (International Bioscience Monographs: Vol. XX). (Illus.). 225p. 1988. 39.00 (*1-55528-155-9*, Messers Today & Tomorrow) Scholarly Pubns.

Mongait, A. L., jt. auth. see Tretiakov, P. N.

Mongan, Agnes. David to Corot: French Drawings in the Fogg Art Museum. 448p. 1993. text ed. 95.00 (*0-674-19320-2*) HUP.

Mongan, Agnes, ed. One Hundred Master Drawings. LC 75-95129. (Illus.). 208p. 1971. reprint ed. text ed. 55.00 (*0-8371-3989-9*, MOMD, Greenwood Pr) Greenwood.

Mongan, Agnes, et al. Timken Art Gallery: European & American Works of Art in the Putnam Foundation Collection. (Illus.). 127p. 1983. 15.00 (*0-9610866-0-2*); pap. 7.50 (*0-9610866-1-0*) Putnam Found.

Mongan, Norman. The History of the Guitar in Jazz. (Illus.). 240p. pap. 24.95 (*0-8256-0255-6*) Music Sales.

Mongar, Thomas M. The Death of Communism & the Rebirth of Original Marxism. LC 94-12459. 400p. 1994. text ed. 99.95 (*0-7734-9074-4*) E Mellen.

Mongault, Henri, jt. auth. see Merimee, Prosper.

Monge, C. Carlos, jt. auth. see Winslow, Robert M.

Monge, Jose T. El Choque de Dos Culturas Juridicas en Puerto Rico: El Caso de la Respons Civil Extracontrac. 470p. 1991. 60.00 (*0-409-25574-2*) Michie Butterworth.

— Historia Constitucional de Puerto Rico, Vol. IV. LC 79-55193. 487p. 1983. 15.00 (*0-8477-0871-3*) U of PR Pr.

— Sociedad, Derecho y Justicia. LC 84-25862. 538p. (SPA.). 1986. lib. bdg. 25.00 (*0-8477-3020-4*) U of PR Pr.

Mongeon, John E., jt. ed. see Ziebold, Thomas O.

***Monger, Christopher.** The Englishman Who Went up a Hill but Came down a Mountain. 256p. 1995. pap. 9.95 (*0-7868-8140-2*) Hyperion.

Monger, J. W. & Francheteau, J., eds. Circum-Pacific Orogenic Belts & Evolution of the Pacific Ocean Basin. (Geodynamics Ser.: Vol. 18). (Illus.). 176p. 1987. 22.00 (*0-87590-519-6*) Am Geophysical.

Monger, Joyce, jt. auth. see Coleman, Diane.

Monger, Rod F. Managerial Decision Making with Technology. (Studies in Productivity: No. 45). 69p. 1986. pap. text ed. 55.00 (*0-08-029517-7*) Work in Amer.

— Mastering Technology: A Management Formula for Getting Results. 330p. 1988. text ed. 35.00 (*0-02-921680-X*) Free Pr.

Monger, Samuel C. HVAC Optimization Handbook. LC 92-10683. 1992. write for info. (*0-13-446493-1*) P-H.

An Asterisk (*) at the beginning of an entry indicates that the title is appearing in BIP for the first time.

— Testing & Balancing HVAC Air & Water Systems. LC 88-45792. 300p. 1989. text ed. 67.00 (0-88173-075-0) Fairmont Pr.

Monges, tr. see Steiner, Rudolf.

Monges, Henry B., tr. see Steiner, Rudolf.

Monges, Lisa D., tr. see Steiner, Rudolf.

Monges, Maud B., tr. see Steiner, Rudolf.

Mongia, J. N. Banking Around the World: A Treatise on Comparative Banking. 583p. 1982. 35.00 (0-318-37331-9) Asia Bk Corp.

Mongia, J. N., ed. India's Economic Development Strategies: 1951-2000 A.D. 1986. lib. bdg. 163.00 (90-277-2200-5) Kluwer Ac.

— India's Economic Policies. 1985. 42.00 (0-8364-1444-6, Pub. by Allied II) S Asia.

Mongiardino, Renzo. Roomscapes: The Decorative Architecture of Renzo Mongiardino. LC 93-10435. (Illus.). 208p. 1993. 60.00 (0-8478-1553-6) Rizzoli Intl.

Mongilla, John F., jt. auth. see Saslow, Joan M.

Mongillo, John F., jt. auth. see Saslow, Joan M.

Mongiore, Angelo L., jt. ed. see Schroer, Melvin E.

Mongiovi, Gary & Ruhl, Christof, eds. Macroeconomic Theory: Diversity & Convergence. 256p. 1993. 69.95 (1-85278-368-0, Pub. by E Elgar Pub UK) Ashgate Pub Co.

Mongis, H. Heidegger et la Critique de la Notion de Valeur. (Phaenomenologica Ser.: No. 74). 1977. lib. bdg. 94.00 (90-247-1904-6) Kluwer Ac.

Mongkolsuk, S., et al, eds. Biotechnology & Environmental Science: Molecular Approaches. (Illus.). 220p. (C). 1993. 75.00 (0-306-44352-X, Plenum Pr) Plenum.

Mongle, Thomas. Dr. Simplespread: Or, How I Learned to Quit Losing & Started Taking Money out of Wall Street. 171p. 1986. pap. 21.95 (0-938063-05-7) Ivers St Lloyd.

Mongolia Society Staff. Bulletin, Vols. 4-6 In 1 Vol. 1966. pap. 5.00 (0-910980-02-0) Mongolia.

— Newsletter, Vols. 1-3. 1964. pap. 5.00 (0-910980-01-2) Mongolia.

Mongolian People's Republic Academy of Sciences Staff, tr. see Pergamon Press Staff, ed.

Mongon, D., jt. auth. see Hart, S.

Mongon, Denis, et al. Improving Classroom Behaviour: New Directions for Teachers & Pupils. 256p. (C). 1989. pap. text ed. 18.95 (0-8077-2995-7) Tchrs Coll.

Mongoven, Anna M., et al. Living Waters Family Matters. Erevia, Hermana A., ed. Serra, Cody, tr. 72p. 1993. pap. text ed. 18.95x (0-7829-0366-5, 88164) Tabor Pub.

Mongredien, Georges & Robert, Jean. Dictionnaire Biographique des Comediens Francais du 17e Siecle. 3rd ed. 330p. (FRE.). 1981. 75.00 (0-7859-4842-2) Fr & Eur.

Mongredien, Jean, ed. see Le Sueur, Jean-Francois & Dercy, Palat dit.

Mongres, Lisa. Eurythmy Exercises. (Illus.). 107p. (Orig.). pap. 3.00 (0-88010-025-7) Anthroposophic.

***Monheit, Herbert.** Beyond Belief: A Guide to Spirituality. 120p. (Orig.). 1995. pap. 9.95 (0-9646841-0-1) Plum Street.

Monhollen, Christine. Razor Moon. 72p. 1993. pap. 7.95 (1-884118-00-3) Triage Pr.

Monhollon, Alice B. High Tide of Courage. LC 93-61294. 332p. 1994. pap. 11.95 (1-55523-666-9) Winston-Derek.

Monhollon, Michael L. Criminal Intent. 288p. (Orig.). 1992. pap. 4.99 (0-451-17330-9, Sig) NAL-Dutton.

***Monicard, Robert P.** Properties of Reservoir Rocks: Core Analysis. (Illus.). 184p. 1980. pap. text ed. 66.00 (2-7108-0387-9) Technip.

Monich, Timothy, jt. auth. see Skinner, Edith.

Monich, Timothy, ed. see Skinner, Edith.

***Monick.** Castration & Male Rage. 1995. pap. 16.00 (0-919123-51-1) Atrium Pubs.

— Phallos. 1995. pap. 16.00 (0-919123-26-0) Atrium Pubs.

Monick, Eugene. Evil, Sexuality, & Disease in Grunewald's Body of Christ. LC 92-46068. (Illus.). 189p. (Orig.). 1993. pap. 18.50 (0-88214-356-5) Spring Pubns.

Monie, Karin, et al. The Library of the Eighties: Swedish Public Library Buildings, 1980-89. (Illus.). 78p. (Orig.). 1990. pap. 65.00x (0-685-41471-X, Pub. by Almqv & Wiksell SW) Coronet Bks.

Monien, B., et al, eds. Data Structures & Efficient Algorithms: Final Report on the DFG Special Joint Initiative. LC 92-10725. (Lecture Notes in Computer Science Ser.: Vol. 594). vii, 389p. 1992. write for info. (3-540-55488-2); pap. 52.00 (0-387-55488-2) Spr-Verlag.

Monien, B. & Cori, R., eds. STACS, 89. (Lecture Notes in Computer Science Ser.: Vol. 349). 544p. 1989. pap. 55.00 (0-387-50840-6) Spr-Verlag.

Monien, B. & Vidal-Naquet, G., eds. Stacs 86. (Lecture Notes in Computer Science Ser.: Vol. 210). ix, 368p. 1986. pap. 42.00 (0-387-16078-7) Spr-Verlag.

Monier, Stephen R., jt. auth. see Ahlgren, Greg.

Monier-Williams. Buddhism, in Its Connection with Brahmanism & Hinduism, & in Contrast with Christianity. 2nd ed. LC 78-70101. reprint ed. 57.50 (0-404-17349-7) AMS Pr.

Monier-Williams, M. Hinduism: Non-Christian Religious Systems. 1972. lib. bdg. 79.95 (0-87968-546-8) Krishna Pr.

— Indian Epic Poetry: An Analysis of Ramayana. 1972. lib. bdg. 79.95 (0-87968-547-6) Krishna Pr.

— Kalidasa-Sakoontala: or The Lost Ring. 238p. 1979. 16.95 (0-318-36909-5) Asia Bk Corp.

Monier-Williams, Monier. English Sanskrit Dictionary. (ENG & SAN.). 1979. 65.00 (0-89744-966-5) Auromere.

— English-Sanskrit Dictionary. 4th ed. 858p. 1986. 95.00 (0-8288-1783-9, M14103) Fr & Eur.

— Sanskrit-English Dictionary. 4th ed. 1333p. 1986. 125.00 (0-8288-4403-8, M14103) Fr & Eur.

Monier-Williams, Monier, et al. Sanskrit-English Dictionary. rev. ed. 1369p. (ENG & SAN.). 1920. 139.00 (0-19-864308-X) OUP.

***Monif, Gilles R.** Interpretation of Wet Mount Preparation. (Illus.). 40p. 1995. 11.95 (1-880906-44-9) IDI Pubns.

— A Physician's Guide for the Collection of Bacteriogical & Viral Specimens. 55p. Date not set. 7.95 (1-880906-73-2) IDI Pubns.

— Torch Syndrome: Infections of the Human Fetus. (Illus.). 171p. (C). 1993. text ed. 34.95 (1-880906-02-3) IDI Pubns.

Monif, Gilles R., ed. Infectious Diseases in Obstetrics & Gynecology. 3rd ed. (Illus.). 450p. (C). 1993. 89.95 (1-880906-04-X) IDI Pubns.

Monig, J., et al. HAW Project Test Disposal of High Level Waste in the Asse Salt Mine International, No. EUR 12946. 88p. 1990. pap. 11.00 (92-826-1686-X, CD-NA-12946-E-N-C) UNIPUB.

Monighan-Nourot, Patricia M., et al. Looking at Children's Play: The Bridge from Theory to Practice. (Early Childhood Education Ser.). 176p. (C). 1987. pap. text ed. 14.95 (0-8077-2872-1) Tchrs Coll.

Monigle, Martha. Mother, Love Me. LC 87-61308. (Orig.). 1986. pap. 5.00 (0-88734-313-9) Players Pr.

Monin, A. S. Fundamentals of Geophysical Fluid Dynamics. (C). 1990. lib. bdg. 197.50 (0-7923-0426-8) Kluwer Ac.

— An Introduction to the Theory of Climate. 1986. lib. bdg. 127.00 (90-277-1935-7) Kluwer Ac.

Monin, A. S. & Ozmidov, R. V. Turbulence in the Ocean. 1985. lib. bdg. 97.50 (90-277-1735-4) Kluwer Ac.

Monin, A. S., et al. Synoptic Eddies in the Ocean. 1986. lib. bdg. 154.50 (90-277-1925-X) Kluwer Ac.

Monin, Hippolyte. L' Etat De Paris En 1789: Etudes et Documents Sur L'ancien Regime a Paris. LC 70-172739. reprint ed. 96.50 (0-404-52556-3) AMS Pr.

Monin, J. P., et al. Initiation to the Mathematics of the Processes of Diffusion, Contagion & Propagation. Brandon, M., tr. (Methods & Models in the Social Sciences Ser.: No. 4). 1976. pap. text ed. 19.25 (90-279-7611-2) Mouton.

Moning. Veterinary Helmenthology & Entomology. 1987. 460.00 (81-7089-041-1, Pub. by Intl Bk Distr II) St Mut.

Monique-Kersey, Tanya & Hawkins, Bruce. Black State of the Arts: A Guide to Developing a Successful Career As a Black Performing Artist. LC 90-91817. (Illus.). 352p. 1995. pap. 19.95 (0-9627515-0-2) Love Child.

Monir, M. Law of Evidence. (C). 1990. 163.00 (0-89771-177-7) St Mut.

— Law of Evidence with Medico-Legal Guide. (C). 1988. 275.00 (0-685-27906-5) St Mut.

— Principles & Digest of Law of Evidence. (C). 1988. 550.00 (0-685-27907-3) St Mut.

— Principles & Digest of the Law of Evidence, 2 vols., Set. Nandan, Deoki, ed. (C). 1990. 325.00 (0-89771-178-5) St Mut.

Monir, V. Law of Evidence & Field's Medico Legal Guide. (C). 1988. 175.00 (0-685-25690-1) St Mut.

Monismith, Carl L. TRB Distinguished Lecture, 1992. LC 92-29494. 100p. 1992. 21.00 (0-309-05218-1, R1354) Transport Res Bd.

Monismith, Samuel W., et al. An Introduction to Health & Disease. 2nd ed. 160p. 1993. per. 17.95 (0-8403-8824-1) Kendall-Hunt.

Monit, P. L. Diccionario Enciclopedica Informatica. 275p. 1989. 39.95 (0-7859-6257-3, 8476761166) Fr & Eur.

Monition, L., et al. Micro Hydro-Electric Power Stations. LC 84-7454. 185p. 1985. text ed. 135.00 (0-471-90255-1, Wiley-Interscience) Wiley.

***Monition, Lucien, et al.** Micro Hydroelectric Power Stations. fac. ed. McMullan, Joan, tr. LC 84-7454. 187p. Date not set. pap. 53.30 (0-7837-7377-3, 2047187) Bks Demand.

Monito, Lisa. Access for Windows Quick Reference. (Quick Reference Ser.). (Illus.). 192p. (Orig.). 1993. pap. 9.95 (1-56529-233-2) Que.

Monitor. Enciclopedia Salvat para Todos, 13 vols., Set. 6760p. (SPA.). 1965. 995.00 (0-8288-6752-6, S-12311) Fr & Eur.

Monitto, Lisa, jt. auth. see Veale, David.

Moniz, B. J. Metallurgy. 2nd ed. LC 92-17869. (Illus.). 538p. 1994. 38.96 (0-8269-3509-5) Am Technical.

Moniz, B. J. & Pollock, W. I., eds. Process Industries Corrosion: The Theory & Practice. LC 86-62318. (Illus.). 858p. 1986. 125.00 (0-915567-46-6) NACE Intl.

Moniz, E., jt. ed. see Brodsky, S.

Monji, Michael A. Does It Pay to Die? How to Pick a Dead Man's Pocket! rev. ed. 224p. 1994. reprint ed. student ed 9.99 (0-9627839-1-9) M Monji Assocs.

Monjo, F. N. The Drinking Gourd. LC 92-10823. (I Can Read Bk.). (Illus.). 64p. (J). (gr. k-3). 1970. 14.95 (0-06-024329-5); lib. bdg. 14.89 (0-06-024330-9) HarpC Child Bks.

— The Drinking Gourd. LC 92-10823. (Trophy I Can Read Bk.). (Illus.). 64p. (J). (gr. k-3). 1983. pap. 3.50 (0-06-444042-7, Trophy) HarpC Child Bks.

— The One Bad Thing about Father. LC 71-85036. (Trophy I Can Read Bk.). (Illus.). 64p. (J). (gr. k-3). 1987. pap. 3.50 (0-06-444110-5, Trophy) HarpC Child Bks.

Monk. Fundamentals of Human-Computer Interaction. 1984. text ed. 73.00 (0-12-504580-8) Acad Pr.

— Fundamentals of Human-Computer Interaction. 1985. pap. text ed. 42.00 (0-12-504582-4) Acad Pr.

Monk, et al. Business One Irwin Banker's Guide to Online Databases. 300p. 1988. text ed. 60.00 (0-87094-749-4) Irwin Prof Pubng.

Monk, A. F., et al, eds. People & Computers VII. (British Computer Society Conference Ser.). (Illus.). 544p. (C). 1992. pap. 79.95 (0-521-44591-4) Cambridge U Pr.

Monk, Abraham, ed. The Age of Aging: A Reader in Social Gerontology. LC 79-2727. 367p. (C). 1979. 22.95 (0-87975-111-8); pap. 12.95 (0-87975-114-2) Prometheus Bks.

— The Columbia Retirement Handbook. LC 92-35740. 605p. 1994. 60.00 (0-231-07626-6) Col U Pr.

— Handbook of Gerontological Services. 2nd ed. 656p. 1990. text ed. 60.00 (0-231-06902-2) Col U Pr.

— Health Care of the Aged: Needs, Policies & Services. LC 90-4941. (Journal of Gerontological Social Work: Vol. 15, Nos. 3-4). 185p. 1990. text ed. 29.95 (1-56024-065-2) Haworth Pr.

Monk, Abraham & Cox, Carole. Home Care for the Elderly: An International Perspective. LC 90-1280. 184p. 1991. text ed. 42.95 (0-86569-005-7, T005, Auburn Hse) Greenwood.

Monk, Abraham, ed. see Foner, Nancy.

Monk, Abraham, jt. ed. see Kaye, Lenard W.

Monk, Abraham, ed. see Moody, Harry R.

Monk, Abraham, ed. see Sherman, Susan R. & Newman, Evelyn S.

Monk, Abraham, ed. see Streib, Gordon.

Monk, Abraham, ed. see Wolf, Rosalie S. & Pillemer, Karl A.

Monk, Abraham, et al. Resolving Grievances in the Nursing Home: A Study of the Ombudsman Program. (Social Work & Social Issue, Columbia Studies of Social Gerontology & Aging). 1984. text ed. 46.00 (0-231-05702-4) Col U Pr.

Monk, Andrew. Exploring Statistics with Minitab, a Workbook for the Behavioural Sciences. 247p. 1991. pap. text ed. 34.95 (0-471-92391-5) Wiley.

***Monk, Andrew & Gilbert, Nigel, eds.** Perspectives on HCI: Diverse Approaches. (Computers & People Ser.). (Illus.). 300p. 1995. text ed. 59.95 (0-12-504575-1) Acad Pr.

Monk, Arlene & Franz, Marion. Convenience Food Facts: Help for the Healthy Meal Planner. enl. rev. ed. LC 91-40471. 472p. 1991. reprint ed. pap. 10.95 (0-937721-77-8) Chronimed.

Monk, Arlene, et al. Managing Type Two Diabetes. 2nd rev. ed. 192p. 1995. 10.95 (1-56561-060-1) Chronimed.

Monk, Betty J., jt. auth. see Harris, Ben M.

***Monk, Connie.** Flame of Courage. large type ed. 1994. 23.95 (0-7089-3190-1) Ulverscroft.

— Jessica. large type ed. 528p. 1988. 15.95 (0-7089-1803-4) Ulverscroft.

— Rachel's Way. large type ed. 1991. 21.95 (0-7089-2521-9) Ulverscroft.

Monk, Donny, jt. auth. see Hernandez, Betsy.

Monk, Edwin. How to Build Wooden Boats: With Sixteen Small-Boat Designs. unabridged ed. LC 92-20138. Orig. Title: Small Boat Building. (Illus.). 96p. 1993. reprint ed. pap. text ed. 7.95 (0-486-27313-X) Dover.

Monk, Eric. Keys - Their History & Collection. 64p. 1989. pap. 25.00 (0-85263-254-1, Pub. by Shire UK) St Mut.

***Monk, Harold L., Jr., et al.** Guide to Preparing Nonprofit Financial Statements Vol. 2. 1994. ring bd. write for info. (1-56433-508-9) Prctnrs Pub Co.

— Guide to Preparing Nonprofit Financial Statements Vol. 2, 2 vols., Set. 1994. ring bd. 125.00 (1-56433-506-2) Prctnrs Pub Co.

— Guide to Preparing Nonprofit Financial Statements Vol. 2, Vol. 1. 1994. ring bd. write for info. (1-56433-507-0) Prctnrs Pub Co.

Monk, J. D. Cardinal Functions on Boolean Algebras. (Lectures in Mathematics ETH Zurich). 164p. 1990. pap. 24.50 (0-8176-2495-3) Birkhauser.

Monk, J. D., ed. Handbook of Boolean Algebras, 3 vols. 1440p. 1989. 118.00 (0-444-87152-7) Elsevier.

— Handbook of Boolean Algebras, 3 vols., 1. 1440p. 1989. 72.00 (0-444-70261-X) Elsevier.

Monk, J. D., et al. Cylindric Algebras, Pt. II. (Studies in Logic & the Foundations of Mathematics: Vol. 115). 302p. 1985. 66.75 (0-444-87679-0, North Holland) Elsevier.

Monk, Janice, jt. ed. see Katz, Cindi.

Monk, Janice, jt. auth. see Norwood, Vera.

Monk, John S., jt. auth. see Keefe, James W.

***Monk, Karyn.** Surrender to a Stranger. 1995. mass mkt. 5.50 (0-553-56909-0) Bantam.

Monk, Keith. Go International: Your Guide to Marketing & Business Development. 208p. 1989. pap. text ed. 13.95 (0-07-707096-8) McGraw.

Monk, Leland. Standard Deviations: Change & the Modern British Novel. LC 92-38358. 216p. (C). 1993. 32.50 (0-8047-2174-2) Stanford U Pr.

Monk, Lenore, ed. see Pelzel, Vernise E.

Monk, Linda. The Bill of Rights: A User's Guide. (Illus.). 248p. (Orig.). 1991. pap. text ed. 12.95 (0-932765-38-6, 996-920) Close Up.

— The Bill of Rights: A User's Guide. suppl. ed. Zack, David, ed. (Illus.). 248p. (Orig.). 1991. teacher ed 9.95 (0-685-57437-7) Close Up.

Monk, Linda, ed. Ordinary Americans: U. S. History Through the Eyes of Everyday People. LC 93-33401. 320p. 1994. teacher ed 15.95 (0-685-71171-4, 1380-94); pap. 16.95 (0-932765-47-5, 1304-94) Close Up.

Monk, Linda, ed. see Close Up Staff.

***Monk, Linda R.** The First Amendment: America's Blueprint for Tolerance. 100p. 1994. teacher ed 14.95 (0-614-07115-1) Close Up.

— The First Amendment: America's Blueprint for Tolerance. LC 94-35273. (J). 1994. 7.95 (0-932765-54-8) Close Up.

Monk, Lorraine. Canada with Love - Canada Avec Amour. 1993. pap. 19.95 (1-895565-27-8) Firefly Bks Ltd.

Monk, Lorraine, prod. Canada with Love: Canada Avec Amour. (Illus.). 112p. 1992. 29.95 (1-895565-00-6) Firefly Bks Ltd.

Monk, M., ed. Mammalian Development: A Practical Approach. (Practical Approach Ser.). 340p. 1987. pap. 39.00 (1-85221-029-X, IRL Pr) OUP.

Monk, Maria & Grob, Gerald. Awful Disclosures by Marcia Monk of the Hotel Dieu Nunnery of Montreal. LC 76-46089. (Anti-Movements in America Ser.). 1977. lib. bdg. 35.95 (0-405-09962-2) Ayer.

Monk, Marion, jt. auth. see Soltes, Ori Z.

***Monk, Martin & Dillon, Justin, eds.** Learning to Teach Science: Activities for Student Teachers & Mentors. LC 94-39748. 224p. 1995. 80.00x (0-7507-0385-7, Falmer Pr); pap. 27.00x (0-7507-0386-5, Falmer Pr) Taylor & Francis.

Monk, Noel E. & Guterman, Jimmy. Twelve Days on the Road: The Sex Pistols & America. LC 92-11416. 1992. 8.00 (0-688-11274-9, Quill) Morrow.

Monk of Farne. Christ Crucified: Meditations of a Benedictine Monk. Farmer, Hugh, ed. LC 93-74850. Orig. Title: Monk of Farne. 164p. 1994. reprint ed. pap. 12.95 (0-87061-202-6) Chr Classics.

Monk of the Eastern Church. Orthodox Spirituality: An Outline of the Orthodox Ascetical & Mystical Tradition. 111p. 1978. pap. 7.95 (0-913836-51-6) St Vladimirs.

Monk of the Eastern Church Staff, pseud. Serve the Lord with Gladness. Breck, John, tr. LC 90-20916. 112p. (Orig.). 1990. pap. 7.95 (0-88141-085-3) St Vladimirs.

Monk, Patricia. The Gilded Beaver: An Introduction to the Life & Works of James De Mille. 293p. (C). 1991. pap. text ed. 26.00 (1-55022-106-X, Pub. by ECW Press CN) Genl Dist Srvs.

— Mud & Magic Shows: Robertson Davies' Fifth Business. (Canadian Fiction Studies: No. 13). 88p. (C). 1992. pap. text ed. 14.95 (1-55022-128-0, Pub. by ECW Press CN) Genl Dist Srvs.

Monk, Peter. Technological Change in the Information Economy. 256p. 1992. 54.00 (0-86187-713-6, Pub. by Pinter Pubs UK) St Martin.

Monk, Ray. Ludwig Wittgenstein: The Duty of Genius. (Illus.). 654p. 1990. text ed. 35.00 (0-02-921670-2) Free Pr.

— Ludwig Wittgenstein: The Duty of Genius. (Illus.). 672p. 1991. reprint ed. pap. 15.95 (0-14-015995-9, Penguin Bks) Viking Penguin.

Monk, Raymond, ed. Edward Elgar: Music & Literature. 300p. 1993. 69.95 (0-85967-937-3, Pub. by Scolar Pr UK) Ashgate Pub Co.

— Elgar Studies. (Illus.). 320p. 1990. text ed. 69.95 (0-85967-810-5, Pub. by Scolar Pr UK) Ashgate Pub Co.

Monk, Rich, ed. Wisdom: One Hundred One of the Wisest Human Perceptions of All Time. 20p. 1992. 1.99 (1-882342-00-3) Panther WI.

***Monk, Richard.** The MG Collection Vol. 1: Pre-War Models, Vol. 1. (Illus.). 192p. 1994. 39.95 (1-85260-496-4, Pub. by J H Haynes & Co UK) Motorbooks Intl.

Monk, Richard, ed. Taking Sides: Clashing Views on Controversial Issues in Race & Ethnicity. (Illus.). 324p. 1994. pap. text ed. 13.95 (1-56134-127-4) Dushkin Pub.

Monk, Richard C., ed. Taking Sides: Clashing Views on Controversial Issues in Crime & Criminology. 3rd ed. LC 92-74289. (Illus.). 372p. 1993. pap. text ed. 13.95 (1-56134-126-6) Dushkin Pub.

Monk, Robert C. & Stamey, Joseph D. Exploring Christianity: An Introduction. 2nd ed. 256p. (C). 1989. pap. text ed. write for info. (0-13-296153-9) P-H.

Monk, Robert C., et al. Exploring Religious Meaning. 4th ed. LC 93-25757. 1993. pap. text ed. 21.00 (0-13-299660-X) P-H.

Monk, Samuel H., jt. auth. see Latt, David J.

Monk, Tim. Windows Programmer's Guide to Serial Communications. (Illus.). (Orig.). 1992. pap. 39.95 (0-672-30030-3) Sams.

Monk, Timothy. How to Make Shift Work Safe & Effective. 58p. 1988. 23.00 (0-939874-84-9) ASSE.

Monk, Timothy H., ed. Sleep, Sleepiness & Performance. (Series on Studies in Human Performance & Cognition: No. 1507). 325p. 1991. text ed. 96.50 (0-471-93002-4) Wiley.

Monk, Timothy H. & Folkard, Simon. Making Shiftwork Tolerable. 101p. 1992. pap. 25.00 (0-85066-822-0, Pub. by Tay Francis Ltd UK) Taylor & Francis.

Monk, Timothy H., jt. auth. see Alward, Ruth R.

Monk, Timothy H., jt. ed. see Folkard, Simon.

Monk, Val. Abuse. Schulz, William, ed. (Options Ser.). 100p. (Orig.). (gr. 1-8). 1989. teacher ed, pap. 8.95 (0-920541-63-1) Peguis Pubs Ltd.

Monk, William E. Theodore & Alice: A Love Story: The Life & Death of Alice Lee Roosevelt. 80p. 1994. lib. bdg. 20.00 (1-55787-117-5, NY71061, Empire State Bks) Hrt of the Lakes.

Monkcom, Stephen, jt. ed. see Smith, Colin.

Monke, Eric & Pearson, Scott. Policy Analysis Matrix for Agricultural Development. LC 88-47938. 312p. 1989. 39.95 (0-8014-1953-0); pap. 16.95 (0-8014-9551-2) Cornell U Pr.

Monke, Eric, et al. Structural Change & Small-Farm Agriculture in Northwest Portugal. LC 92-54973. (Food Systems & Agrarian Change Ser.). 240p. (C). 1993. 39.95 (0-8014-2640-5) Cornell U Pr.

Monke, Ingrid. Boston. LC 88-20202. (Downtown America Bks.). (Illus.). 60p. (J). (gr. 3 up). 1988. text ed. 13.95 (0-87518-382-4, Dillon Silver Burdett) Silver Burdett Pr.

Monkhouse, Allan. Books & Plays. LC 72-292. (Essay Index Reprint Ser.). 1977. reprint ed. 19.95 (0-8369-2807-5) Ayer.

— Mary Broome: A Comedy in Four Acts. LC 83-45818. reprint ed. 16.00 (0-404-20181-4) AMS Pr.

— Moscow, Nineteen Eleven to Nineteen Thirty-Three. LC 76-115566. (Russia Observed Ser., No. 1). 1970. reprint ed. 23.95 (0-405-03051-7) Ayer.

Monkhouse, Bob. Just Say a Few Words: The Complete Speaker's Handbook. 1991. 18.95 (0-87131-661-7) M Evans.

M

An Asterisk (*) at the beginning of an entry indicates that the title is appearing in BIP for the first time.

Monkhouse, Christopher P. American Furniture in Pendleton House. (Illus.). 228p. (C). 1986. pap. 25.00 (*0-685-18008-5*) Mus of Art RI.

Monkhouse, Elaine, jt. auth. see Clarke, Thomas.

Monkhouse, F. J. Diccionario de Terminos Geograficos: Dictionary of Geographical Terms. 560p. (SPA.). 1978. 150.00 (*0-8288-4894-7*, S50017) Fr & Eur.

Monkhouse, George. Mercedes Benz Grand Prix Racing, Nineteen Thirty-Four to Nineteen Fifty-Five. Posthumus, Cyril, ed. (Illus.). 208p. 1984. 45.00 (*0-88740-009-4*, Pub. by New Cavendish UK) Pincushion Pr.

Monkhouse, George C. Mercedes-Benz Grand Prix Racing, 1934-1955. 1992. 75.00 (*0-904568-42-3*) Schiffer.

Monkkonen, Eric H. America Becomes Urban: The Development of U. S. Cities & Towns, 1780-1980. 336p. (C). 1988. 38.00 (*0-520-06191-8*); pap. 14.00 (*0-520-06972-2*) U CA Pr.

— The Local State: Public Money & American Cities. LC 95-1074. (Stanford Studies in the New Political History). 214p. 1995. 39.50x (*0-8047-2412-1*) Stanford U Pr.

Monkkonen, Eric H., ed. Crime & Justice in American History, 11 vols., Set. Incl. Vol. 1, Pt. 1. Colonies & Early Republic. 450p. 1991. 240.00 (*3-598-41408-0*); Vol. 1, Pt. 2. Colonies & Early Republic. 450p. 1991. 240.00 (*3-598-41409-9*); Vol. 2. Courts & the Criminal Procedure. 560p. 1991. 120.00 (*3-598-41410-2*); Vol. 3. Delinquency & Disorderly Behavior. 325p. 1991. 120.00 (*3-598-41411-0*); Vol. 4, Pt. 1. Frontier. 450p. 1991. 120.00 (*3-598-41412-9*); Vol. 5, Pt. 1. Policing & Crime Control. 550p. 1992. 120.00 (*3-598-41413-7*); Vol. 5, Pt. 2. Policing & Crime Control. 550p. 1992. 120.00 (*3-598-41414-5*); Vol. 5, Pt. 3. Policing & Crime Control. 550p. 1992. 120.00 (*3-598-41680-6*); Vol. 6, Pt. 1. Prison & Jails. 360p. 1992. 120.00 (*3-598-41415-3*); Vol. 6, Pt. 2. Prison & Jails. 360p. 1992. 120.00 (*3-598-41416-1*); Vol. 7, Pt. 1. South. 336p. 1992. 120.00 (*3-598-41417-X*); Vol. 7, Pt. 2. South. 336p. 1992. 120.00 (*3-598-41681-4*); Vol. 8, Pt. 1. Prostitution, Drugs, Gambling & Organized Crime. 360p. 1992. 120.00 (*3-598-41418-8*); Vol. 8, Pt. 2. Prostitution, Drugs, Gambling & Organized Crime. 360p. 1992. 120.00 (*3-598-41419-6*); Vol. 9, Pt. 1. Violence & Theft. 525p. 1992. 120.00 (*3-598-41420-X*); Vol. 9, Pt. 2. Violence & Theft. 525p. 1992. 120.00 (*3-598-41421-8*); Vol. 9, Pt. 3. Violence & Theft. 525p. 1992. 120.00 (*3-598-41682-2*); Vol. 10. Reform. 425p. 1992. 120.00 (*3-598-41422-6*); Vol. 11, Pt. 1. Theory & Methods in Criminal Justice History. 550p. 1992. 120.00 (*3-598-41423-4*); Vol. 11, Pt. 2. Theory & Methods in Criminal Justice History. 550p. 1992. 120.00 (*3-598-41424-2*); 2,175.00 (*3-598-41407-2*) U Pubns Amer.

— Engaging the Past: The Uses of History across the Social Sciences. LC 93-37086. 208p. 1994. lib. bdg. 39.95 (*0-8223-1440-1*); pap. text ed. 15.95 (*0-8223-1431-2*) Duke.

— Walking to Work: Tramps in America, 1790-1935. LC 83-21807. 259p. reprint ed. pap. 73.90 (*0-7837-1844-6*, 2042044) Bks Demand.

Monkman, Leslie. A Native Heritage: Images of the Indian in English-Canadian Literature. 208p. 1981. 35.00 (*0-8020-5537-0*) U of Toronto Pr.

Monkman, Roberta, jt. ed. see Kupfersmid, Joel.

***Monkres, Peter R. & Ostermiller, R. Kenneth.** The Rite of Confirmation: Moments When Faith Is Strengthened. 96p. (Orig.). 1995. pap. 8.95 (*0-8298-1020-X*) Pilgrim OH.

Monks, Alfred L. The Soviet Intervention in Afghanistan. LC 81-2003. (Studies in Defense Policy: Vol. 314). 64p. reprint ed. 25.00 (*0-685-15977-9*, 2027554) Bks Demand.

Monks, Franz J., et al, eds. Education of the Gifted in Europe: Theoretical & Research Issues Report of the Educational Research Workshop Held in Nijmegen, The Netherlands, July 23-26, 1991. LC 92-5639. (European Meetings on Educational Research Ser.: Vol. 28, Pt. A). 1992. 52.00 (*90-265-1262-7*, Pub. by Swets Pub Serv NE) Taylor & Francis.

Monks, J. G. Operations Management. 3rd ed. (Management Ser.). 800p. 1987. pap. text ed. write for info. (*0-07-042727-5*); Study guide. student ed, pap. text ed. write for info. (*0-07-042729-1*) McGraw.

— Schaum's Outline of Theory & Problems of Operations Management. 38p. 1985. pap. text ed. 13.95 (*0-07-042726-7*) McGraw.

Monks, John, Jr. Ribbon & a Star: The Third Marines at Bougainville. LC 79-19749. (Illus.). reprint ed. 25.00 (*0-89201-077-0*) Zenger Pub.

Monks, Joseph. Schaum's Outline of Operations Management. 2nd ed. (Schaum's Outline Ser.). 1995. pap. text ed. write for info. (*0-07-042764-X*) McGraw.

Monks, Joseph G., jt. auth. see Ingram, John A.

Monks of New Skete. Dormition of the Theotokos. Mancuso, Laurence, tr. (Liturgical Music Series I: Great Feasts: Vol. 2). 40p. 1986. pap. text ed. 12.00 (*0-935129-03-0*) Monks of New Skete.

— Entry of the Theotokos. Mancuso, Laurence, tr. (Liturgical Music Series I: Great Feasts: Vol. 5). 40p. 1986. pap. text ed. 12.00 (*0-935129-06-5*) Monks of New Skete.

— Transfiguration of Christ. Mancuso, Laurence, tr. (Liturgical Music Series I: Great Feasts: Vol. 1). 40p. 1986. pap. text ed. 12.00 (*0-935129-02-2*) Monks of New Skete.

Monks of New Skete, tr. The Psalter. 286p. 1984. 39.50x (*0-9607924-5-7*) Monks of New Skete.

***Monks of New Skete Staff.** Annunciation of the Theotokos, Vol. 10. Mancuso, Laurence, tr. (Liturgical Music Ser.: Vol. I). 35p. (Orig.). 1995. pap. 15.00 (*0-935129-33-2*) Monks of New Skete.

— A Book of Prayers: Horologion, Casoslov. Mancuso, Laurence, tr. 628p. 1988. 69.00 (*0-935129-12-X*) Monks of New Skete.

— The Christmas Season. Mancuso, Laurence, tr. (Liturgical Music Series I: Great Feasts: Vol. 7). viii, 221p. (Orig.). 1990. pap. text ed. 50.00 (*0-935129-16-2*) Monks of New Skete.

— The Divine Liturgy. Mancuso, Laurence, tr. 306p. 1988. 50.00 (*0-935129-11-1*) Monks of New Skete.

— The Divine Liturgy of St. John Chrysostom. Mancuso, Laurence, tr. 190p. (Orig.). 1994. pap. 25.00 (*0-935129-24-3*) Monks of New Skete.

— Encounter of Christ, Vol. 9. Mancuso, Laurence, tr. (Liturgical Music Ser.: Vol. I). 45p. (Orig.). 1995. pap. 15.00x (*0-935129-32-4*) Monks of New Skete.

— Great & Holy Pascha. Reverend Laurence Mancuso, tr. (Liturgical Music Series I: Great Feasts: Vol. 6). 60p. (Orig.). 1986. pap. text ed. 15.00 (*0-935129-07-3*) Monks of New Skete.

— How to Be Your Dog's Best Friend: A Training Manual for Dog Owners. LC 78-8553. (Illus.). 1978. 21.95 (*0-316-60491-7*) Little.

— Hymns of Entreaty: Selections from the Octoechos or Book of Eight Tones. Mancuso, Laurence, ed. (Monastic Offices at New Skete Ser.). 450p. 1987. text ed. 49.50 (*0-935129-09-X*) Monks of New Skete.

— Monastic Typicon. 2nd rev. ed. viii, 59p. 1988. reprint ed. pap. 10.00 (*0-935129-13-8*) Monks of New Skete.

— New Skete Communities. 32p. 1985. pap. 2.00 (*0-9607924-9-X*) Monks of New Skete.

— Pannychis: The Office of Christian Burial. Mancuso, Laurence, tr. (Liturgical Music Series II: Divine Services: Vol. I). 40p. 1987. pap. text ed. 15.00 (*0-935129-08-1*) Monks of New Skete.

— Passion & Resurrection: Lazarus Saturday, Entry into Jerusalem, Holy & Great Week, the Pasch of the Lord. Mancuso, Laurence, ed. 332p. Date not set. 65.00x (*0-935129-25-1*) Monks of New Skete.

— Theophany of Christ, Vol. 8. Mancuso, Laurence, tr. (Liturgical Music Ser.: Vol. I). 100p. (Orig.). 1995. pap. 25.00x (*0-935129-17-0*) Monks of New Skete.

— Vespers & Matins. Mancuso, Laurence, tr. (Liturgical Music Series II: Divine Services: Vol. 2). 220p. (Orig.). 1988. pap. 45.00 (*0-935129-10-3*) Monks of New Skete.

— Vespers & Matins. Mancuso, Laurence, tr. 154p. (Orig.). 1994. pap. 20.00 (*0-935129-23-5*) Monks of New Skete.

Monks of the Abbey of St. Peter of Solesmes Staff. Benedictiones Mensae. 16p. (LAT.). pap. 3.95 (*2-85274-058-3*, 3018, Pub. by Abbey St Peter Solesmes FR) Paraclete MA.

— Liber Cantualis. 120p. (LAT.). (C). text ed. 11.95 (*2-85274-040-0*, 3009, Pub. by Abbey St Peter Solesmes FR) Paraclete MA.

— Litaniae in Cantu. 64p. (LAT.). pap. 7.95 (*1-55725-034-0*, 3016, Pub. by Abbey St Peter Solesmes FR) Paraclete MA.

***Monks of the Ramakrishna Order.** Meditation. 161p. Date not set. pap. 15.00 (*0-7025-0073-9*) Vedanta Ctr.

Monks of the Ramakrishna Order Staff. Meditation. Bhavyananda, Swami, ed. 1977. pap. 12.00 (*0-7025-0019-4*) Vedanta Pr.

Monks, Peter R. The Brussels Horloge de Sapience: Iconography & Text of Brussels, Bibliotheque Royale, MS. IV 111. LC 90-2215. (Litterae Textuales Ser.). (Illus.). viii, 223p. (ENG & FRE.). 1990. pap. 48.75 (*90-04-09088-6*) E J Brill.

Monks, Peter R. & Owen, D. D. R., eds. Medieval Codicology, Iconography, Literature, & Translation: Studies for Deith Val Sinclair. LC 94-2818. (Litterae Textuales Ser.). 1994. 125.75 (*90-04-09958-1*) E J Brill.

Monks, Pieta, tr. see Baranskaya, Natalya.

***Monks, Robert & Minow, Nell.** Corporate Governance. (Illus.). 400p. 1994. pap. 34.95 (*1-55786-490-X*) Blackwell Pubs.

Monks, Robert L. & Proulx, Ernest I. Legal Basics for Teachers. LC 85-63690. (Fastback Ser.: No. 235). 50p. (Orig.). 1986. pap. 1.25 (*0-87367-235-6*) Phi Delta Kappa.

Monkshood, G., tr. see De Goncourt, Edmond L.

Monleon, Jose B. A Specter Is Haunting Europe: A Sociohistorical Approach to the Fantastic. 199p. (C). 1990. text ed. 29.95 (*0-691-06862-3*) Princeton U Pr.

Monloubou, Louis. Diccionario Biblico Compendiado. 300p. 1991. pap. 39.95 (*0-7859-6086-4*, 8470502689) Fr & Eur.

— Dictionnaire Biblique Abrege. 1989. 59.95 (*0-7859-7959-X*, 2-7189-0399-6) Fr & Eur.

— Universal Bible Dictionary: Dictionnaire Biblique Universel. 772p. (FRE.). 1985. 150.00 (*0-8288-1203-9*, F10644) Fr & Eur.

Monluc. Commentaires. (FRE.). 1964. lib. bdg. 99.50 (*0-8288-3567-5*, F30400) Fr & Eur.

— Vine & Branches: Chronique des Guerres de Religion, Vol. 2. 1640p. 42.95 (*0-686-56543-6*) Fr & Eur.

Monmonier, Mark. Drawing the Line: Tales of Maps & Cartocontroversy. LC 94-16945. 1994. 27.50 (*0-8050-2581-2*) H Holt & Co.

— How to Lie with Maps. LC 90-40687. (Illus.). 168p. 1991. pap. 12.95 (*0-226-53415-4*) U Ch Pr.

— Mapping It Out: Expository Cartography for the Humanities & Social Sciences. LC 92-39894. (Chicago Guides to Writing, Editing, & Publishing Ser.). (Illus.). 352p. (C). 1993. lib. bdg. 37.00 (*0-226-53416-2*); pap. 15.95 (*0-226-53417-0*) U Ch Pr.

— Maps with the News: The Development of American Journalistic Cartography. LC 88-23829. (Illus.). 352p. 1989. 24.95 (*0-226-53411-1*) U Ch Pr.

***Monmonier, Mark & MacEachren, Alan M., eds.** Geographic Visualization. (Cartography & Geographic Information Systems Journal Ser.: Vol. 19, No. 4). 76p. 1992. 20.00 (*0-614-06093-1*, AC194) Am Congrs Survey.

Monmonier, Mark S. Technological Transistion in Cartography. LC 84-40499. (Illus.). 304p. 1985. text ed. 25.00 (*0-299-10070-7*) U of Wis Pr.

Monn, David E. Three Hundred Sixty-Five Ways to Prepare for Christmas. LC 92-56214. (Three Hundred Sixty-Five Ways Ser.). 288p. 1993. 16.95 (*0-06-017048-4*, HarpT) HarpC.

***Monne, Miguel A. & Giesbert, Edmund F.** Checklist of the Cerambycidae & Disteniidae (Coleoptera) of the Western Hemisphere. (C). 1994. write for info. (*0-614-01928-1*); lib. bdg. 74.60 (*1-885850-00-X*) Wolfsgarden.

***Monneret.** Renoir. Date not set. 19.99 (*0-7126-3738-9*) Random Hse Value.

***Monneret, Sophie.** L' Impressionisme et son Epoque Dictionnaire International Vol. 1: Noms Propres A-T. 1040p. (FRE.). 1987. pap. 49.95 (*0-7859-7804-6*, 2221054121) Fr & Eur.

— L' Impressionisme et son Epoque Dictionnaire International Vol. 2: Noms Propres U-Z, Noms Communs A-Z. 1200p. (FRE.). 1987. pap. 49.95 (*0-7859-8632-4*, 222105413x) Fr & Eur.

— Renoir. (Illus.). 160p. 1990. 29.95 (*0-8050-1359-8*) H Holt & Co.

Monnerie, A., ed. Le Nouvel Observateur: Arts, Idees, Spectacles. 112p. (FRE.). 1989. pap. 17.25 (*0-8442-1786-7*, Natl Textbk) NTC Pub Grp.

***Monnerie, L. & Suter, U. W., eds.** Advances in Polymer Science: Atomitic Modeling Physical Properties of Polymers, Vol. 116. 398p. 1994. 175.00 (*0-387-57827-7*) Spr-Verlag.

Monnerot, Jules. Sociology of Communism. Degras, Jane & Rees, Richard, trs. LC 76-46469. 1977. reprint ed. text ed. 55.00 (*0-8371-9309-5*, MOSO, Greenwood Pr) Greenwood.

***Monnery.** Corporate Value Creation. 1995. 35.00 (*0-273-61114-3*, Pub. by Pitman Publishing UK) Krieger.

Monnet, John H. The Battle of Beecher Island & the Indian War of 1867-1869. (Illus.). 248p. pap. 17.50 (*0-87081-347-1*) Univ Pr Colo.

Monnett, H. N., jt. auth. see Vanderslice, H.

***Monnett, Howard N.** Action Before Westport. Monnett, John H., ed. & intro. by. (Illus.). 240p. (Orig.). 1995. reprint ed. pap. 19.95 (*0-614-06699-9*) Univ Pr Colo.

Monnett, John H. A Rocky Mountain Christmas: Yuletide Stories of the West. 2nd ed. (Illus.). 125p. 1992. pap. 12.95 (*0-87108-830-4*) Pruett.

Monnett, John H. & McCarthy, Michael. Colorado Profiles: Men & Women Who Shaped the Centennial State. (Illus.). 350p. (Orig.). 1987. pap. 14.95 (*0-917895-19-3*) Cordillera CO.

Monnett, John H., ed. see Monnett, Howard N.

Monnette, Barbara, jt. auth. see Steen, Charlene.

Monney, Neil T., ed. Ocean Energy Resources: Presented at the Energy Technology Conference, Houston, Texas, Sept. 18-23, 1977. LC 77-82206. (American Society of Mechanical Engineers Handbook: Vol. 4). (Illus.). 110p. reprint ed. pap. 31.40 (*0-317-09776-8*, 2016806) Bks Demand.

Monney, Paul-Andre, jt. auth. see Kohlas, Jurg.

***Monnich, Michael G.** Footprints in the Snow. 1995. 24.95 (*0-533-10958-2*) Vantage.

Monnich, Uwe, ed. Aspects of Philosophical Logic. 296p. 1981. lib. bdg. 99.00 (*90-277-1201-8*) Kluwer Ac.

Monnier-Clay, Simone, tr. see Berard, Guy.

Monnier, Eric, et al, eds. Consumer Behavior & Energy Policy: An International Perspective. LC 86-9295. 357p. 1986. text ed. 65.00 (*0-275-92179-4*, C2179, Praeger Pubs) Greenwood.

Monnier, G. & Goss, M. J., eds. Soil Compaction & Regeneration: Proceedings of the Workshop on "Soil Compaction: Consequences; Structural Regeneration Processes", Avignon, 17-18 September 1985. 160p. (C). 1987. text ed. 70.00 (*90-6191-780-8*, Pub. by A A Balkema NE) Ashgate Pub Co.

Monnier, Henry. Etudes de Droit Byzantin. (Collected Studies: No. CS33). 672p. (C). 1974. reprint ed. lib. bdg. 124.95 (*0-902089-69-2*, Pub. by Variorum UK) Ashgate Pub Co.

Monnier, Marcel. Functions of the Nervous System: Sensory & Perceptual Functions, Vol. 3. 1975. 280.50 (*0-444-41231-X*) Elsevier.

Monnier, Richard. Richard Monnier. (Illus.). 108p. (Orig.). 1993. pap. 25.00 (*2-908257-07-6*, Pub. by F R A C FR) Dist Art Pubs.

Monnier, Vincent M., jt. ed. see Baynes, John W.

Monnig, Judith, jt. auth. see Carter, Sharon.

Monniger, jt. auth. see Taigen.

Monninger, Joe. Incident at Potter's Bridge. LC 91-55180. 272p. 1992. 21.00 (*1-55611-307-2*) D I Fine.

— Razor's Song. 256p. 1993. mass mkt. 4.99 (*0-380-71874-X*) Avon.

Monnot, G., et al. Principles of Turbulent Fired Heat. LC 84-73311. (Illus.). 298p. 1985. 79.00 (*0-87201-724-9*) Gulf Pub.

***Monnot, Georges.** Principles of Turbulent Fired Heat. (Illus.). 320p. (C). 1985. text ed. 118.00 (*2-7108-0457-3*) Technip.

Monnot, Michel. From Rage to Courage: The Road to Dignity Walk. (Illus.). 350p. (Orig.). 1988. pap. 10.00 (*0-9621309-0-7*) St Denis Pr.

Monobe, David. The Snow Woman. 165p. 1984. 7.95 (*0-89697-167-8*) Intl Univ Pr.

Monod, Adolphe. A Dying Man's Regrets. rev. ed. 32p. 1992. pap. 2.00 (*1-879737-07-8*) Calvary Press.

Monod-Fontaine, Isabelle, jt. ed. see Tabart, Marielle.

Monod, Jacques & Borek, Ernest, eds. Of Microbes & Life. LC 71-133382. (Molecular Biology Ser.). (Illus.). 312p. 1971. text ed. 52.50 (*0-231-03431-8*) Col U Pr.

Monod, Lucien. Aide-Memoire de l'Amateur et du Professionnel. 1972. 342.00 (*0-8115-0045-4*) Periodicals Srv.

Monod, Maurice, ed. see Conrad, Joseph.

Monod, Paul K. Jacobitism & the English People, 1688-1788. (Illus.). (C). 1990. 69.95 (*0-521-33534-5*) Cambridge U Pr.

— Jacobitism & the English People, 1688-1788. (Illus.). 412p. (C). 1993. pap. 24.95 (*0-521-44793-3*) Cambridge U Pr.

Monod, Sylvere, ed. see Dickens, Charles.

Monopoli, Richard, jt. ed. see Narendra, Kumpati S.

Monopolies & Mergers Commission Staff. British United Provident Association Ltd & HCA United Kingdom Ltd. (Monopolies & Mergers Commission Report Ser.). 92p. 1990. pap. 17.50 (*0-10-109962-2*, HM9622) UNIPUB.

Monos, Dimitri. The Greek Americans. (Peoples of North America Ser.). 112p. (Orig.). (YA). (gr. 5 up). 1988. 17.95 (*0-87754-880-3*); pap. 9.95 (*0-7910-0266-7*) Chelsea Hse.

***Monos, Dimitris.** The Greek Americans. Stotsky, Sandra, ed. LC 95-716. (Immigrant Experience Ser.). (J). 1995. write for info. (*0-7910-3356-2*); pap. write for info. (*0-7910-3378-3*) Chelsea Hse.

Monostory, Denes, jt. ed. see Ryan, Thomas E.

Monrad, Jean. How Many Kisses Goodnight: Just Right for 2's & 3's. LC 88-6453. (Just Right Bks.). (Illus.). 24p. (J). (ps). 1986. 6.00 (*0-394-88253-9*) Random Bks Yng Read.

Monreal, David. Cinco de Mayo: An Epic Novel. 180p. 1990. 25.00 (*0-685-38354-7*) Floricanto Pr.

Monreal, David N. The New Neighbor & Other Stories. LC 87-63154. 173p. 1987. pap. 9.95 (*0-944870-00-7*) Pacific Writers Pr.

Monreal, M., jt. ed. see Latorre, J.

Monreal-Wickert, Irene. Die Sprachforschung der Aufklaerung Im Spiegel der Grossen Franzoesischen Enzyklopaedie. 210p. (GER.). 1977. 59.95 (*0-8288-5518-8*, M7054) Fr & Eur.

Monreal y Tejada, Luis & Haggar, R. G. Diccionario De Terminos De Arte. 426p. 1992. pap. 28.00 (*84-261-2701-0*) IBD Ltd.

Monro, Alida, jt. auth. see Bowring, Clara.

Monro, C. H., ed. & tr. Digest, No. IX, 2: Lex Aquilia. LC 93-79700. 106p. 1994. reprint ed. 30.00 (*1-56169-058-9*) W W Gaunt.

Monro, Cecil, ed. Letters of Queen Margaret of Anjou & Bishop Beckington & Others. LC 17-1255. (Camden Society, London. Publications, First Ser.: No. 86). reprint ed. 45.00 (*0-404-50186-9*) AMS Pr.

Monro, Chris. Surfer Tools. LC 92-36130. 1993. pap. 45.00 (*0-442-01506-2*) Van Nos Reinhold.

Monro, Christopher. Networking NT: Using Windows NT in the Corporate LAN Environment. LC 93-49069. 1994. pap. 29.95 (*0-442-01829-0*) Van Nos Reinhold.

Monro, David B. A Grammar of the Homeric Dialect. 2nd ed. xxiv, 436p. 1986. reprint ed. 76.70 (*3-487-05307-1*, Pub. by Georg Olms GW) Lubrecht & Cramer.

— A Grammar of the Homeric Dialect. 2nd enl. rev. ed. 436p. 1993. 25.00 (*0-9637069-0-X*) W H Allen Bksell.

Monro, David H. Empiricism & Ethics. LC 67-12143. 244p. reprint ed. pap. 69.60 (*0-317-28409-6*, 2022462) Bks Demand.

Monro, Harold. The Collected Poems of Harold Monro. 217p. 1933. reprint ed. 39.00 (*0-403-08943-3*) Somerset Pub.

— Collected Poems of Harold Monro. 1988. reprint ed. lib. bdg. 59.00 (*0-7812-0007-5*) Rprt Serv.

— Collected Poems of Harold Monro. 1971. reprint ed. 49.00 (*0-403-03562-7*) Scholarly.

Monro, Harold, ed. Twentieth Century Poetry, an Anthology. reprint ed. 29.00 (*0-403-03062-5*) Somerset Pub.

Monro, Kate M., jt. auth. see Taintor, Sarah A.

Monro, Margaret T. Book of Unlikely Saints. LC 77-107727. (Essay Index Reprint Ser.). 1977. 21.95 (*0-8369-1528-3*) Ayer.

Monro, R., et al. Mind-Body Therapies: A Select Bibliography of Books in English. 176p. 1987. text ed. 70.00 (*0-7201-1811-5*, Mansell Pub) Cassell.

Monro, Susan, et al. The Next Step Forward: Music Therapy for the Terminally Ill. 100p. 1989. pap. 16.95 (*0-930194-46-2*) Ctr Thanatology.

Monrobey, Hank. Bear Fruit in Plenty: Economic Lessons of the Supreme Economist. (Illus.). 200p. (Orig.). 1990. write for info. (*0-9623564-4-1*); pap. text ed. write for info. (*0-9623564-3-3*) H Monrobey & Assocs.

— Financial Economic Freedom on the Electronic Super Highway. (Illus.). 74p. (Orig.). 1994. 15.00 (*0-9623564-5-X*) H Monrobey & Assocs.

— Good Bye Recessions: Removing Economic Pollution. LC 90-92304. (Illus.). 250p. (Orig.). 1990. pap. text ed. write for info. (*0-9623564-1-7*) H Monrobey & Assocs.

— The Monrobey Report: An Economic Detective Story Solving the Mysteries of Inflations & Recessions. LC 89-174366. (Illus.). 362p. 1989. 42.50 (*0-9623564-2-5*); pap. 29.90 (*0-9623564-0-9*) H Monrobey & Assocs.

Monroe. Economic Approach to Politics. (C). 1991. pap. text ed. 28.50 (*0-673-46426-1*) HarpCollege.

— Long Road Home. 1995. mass mkt. 4.50 (*0-06-108275-9*, Harp PBks) HarpC.

Monroe, jt. ed. see Roberts.

Monroe, Anne S. Happy Valley. LC 90-7167. (Northwest Reprints Ser.). 392p. 1991. reprint ed. text ed. 24.95 (*0-87071-506-2*); reprint ed. pap. 13.95 (*0-87071-507-0*) Oreg St U Pr.

Monroe, Arthur E. Early Economic Thought. 1975. 300.00 (*0-87968-251-5*) Gordon Pr.

An Asterisk (*) at the beginning of an entry indicates that the title is appearing in BIP for the first time.

— Monetary Theory Before Adam Smith. LC 64-66154. xi, 312p. 1966. reprint ed. 37.50 (*0-678-00134-0*) Kelley.

Monroe, Betsy. My Visit to My Doctor: A Coloring Book for Kids. (Medical Ser.: No. 4). (Illus.). 24p. (Orig.). (J). (gr. k-4). 1989. pap. write for info. (*1-878083-01-5*) Color Me Well.

— My Visit to the Emergency Room: A Coloring Book for Kids. (Medical Ser.: No. 1). (Illus.). 32p. (SPA.). (J). (gr. k-4). 1990. reprint ed. pap. write for info. (*1-878083-03-1*) Color Me Well.

— My Visit to the Hospital: A Coloring Book for Kids. (Medical Ser.: No. 2). (Illus.). 32p. (Orig.). (J). (gr. k-4). 1986. pap. write for info. (*1-878083-02-3*) Color Me Well.

— My Visit to the Outpatient Department: A Coloring Book for Kids. (Medical Ser.: No. 3). (Illus.). 24p. (J). (gr. k-4). 1986. pap. write for info. (*1-878083-04-X*) Color Me Well.

— Sibling Scrapbook: An Activity Book for the New Big Brother & Big Sister. (Medical Ser.: No. 5). (Illus.). 24p. (Orig.). (J). (gr. k-4). 1989. pap. write for info. (*1-878083-00-7*) Color Me Well.

Monroe, Betty, illus. Huntsville Heritage Cookbook. LC 67-30090. 387p. 1986. reprint ed. 12.95 (*0-9618113-0-7*) J L Huntsville.

Monroe, Bill. Bill Monroe's Grande Ole Opry USM Song Folio No. 1. pap. 8.95 (*0-686-09065-9*, Peer-Southern) CPP Belwin.

Monroe, Burt L., Jr. The Birds of Kentucky. LC 93-44364. (C). 1994. 49.95 (*0-253-33892-1*) Ind U Pr.

— Distributional Survey of the Birds of Honduras. 458p. 1968. 14.00 (*0-943610-07-9*) Am Ornithologists.

Monroe, Burt L., Jr. & Sibley, Charles G. A World Checklist of Birds. 400p. 1993. 45.00 (*0-300-05547-1*) Yale U Pr.

Monroe, Burt L., Jr., jt. auth. see Sibley, Charles G.

Monroe, Bury L., Jr., jt. auth. see Sibley, Charles G.

Monroe, Carolyn. Help Wanted: Daddy Fabulous Father. (Silhouette Romance Ser.). 1993. pap. 2.75 (*0-373-08970-8*, 5-08970-1) Silhouette.

***Monroe, Charles E.** World Religions: An Introduction. 400p. (C). 1995. 29.95x (*0-87975-932-1*) Prometheus Bks.

— World Religions: An Introduction. (C). 1995. pap. 15.95 (*0-87975-942-9*) Prometheus Bks.

Monroe, Charles E., tr. see Brunswig, Heinrich.

***Monroe, Charles R.** Motoring to Yellowstone in Slim's Model T 1927. (Illus.). 64p. (Orig.). 1994. pap. 7.95 (*0-9615125-1-2*) Merryleaf.

Monroe County Genealogical Society Staff, ed. Marriage Records of Monroe County, Michigan, Vol. V. 354p. 1993. pap. text ed. 19.50 (*0-940696-37-1*) Monroe County Lib.

Monroe County Library System. To Share a Moment. (Community Anthology Ser.). 144p. (Orig.). 1987. pap. 4.00 (*0-940696-15-0*) Monroe County Lib.

Monroe County Library System, ed. see Community Anthology.

Monroe County Library System Staff, ed. Faces of Carleton: Pictures of the Past. 110p. 1992. pap. text ed. 10.00 (*0-940696-33-9*) Monroe County Lib.

Monroe County Sesquicentennial Staff. Monroe County, Mississippi. (Illus.). 971p. 1989. 60.00 (*0-88107-132-3*) Curtis Media.

Monroe, Day. Chicago Families: A Study of Unpublished Census Data. LC 70-169395. (Family in America Ser.). 370p. 1972. reprint ed. 20.95 (*0-405-03872-0*) Ayer.

Monroe, Debbie & Sweeney, Marci. Exploring Memphis. 1992. pap. 12.95 (*0-9628349-1-2*) Sigma Pubns.

Monroe, Deborah, ed. see Johnson, Denny.

Monroe, Debra. The Source of Trouble. LC 90-31189. (Flannery O'Connor Award for Short Fiction Ser.). 184p. 1990. 17.95 (*0-8203-1246-0*) U of Ga Pr.

— Source of Trouble. 1995. pap. 10.00 (*0-671-89716-0*) S&S Trade.

— A Wild Cold State. 272p. 1995. 21.00 (*0-671-89717-9*) S&S Trade.

Monroe, Douglas. The Twenty-One Lessons of Merlyn: Adventures in Druid Magic & Lore. LC 92-20033. (Illus.). 448p. 1992. pap. 12.95 (*0-87542-496-1*) Llewellyn Pubns.

Monroe, Elizabeth. Philby of Arabia. 7.95 (*0-7043-3346-5*, Pub. by Quartet UK) Charles River Bks.

Monroe, Elizabeth B. The Wheeling Bridge Case: Its Significance in American Law & Technology. 256p. 1992. text ed. 45.00 (*1-55553-130-X*) NE U Pr.

Monroe, Elvira. A Guide to Places of Worship in & Around San Francisco. 186p. (Orig.). 1984. pap. 6.95 (*0-933174-24-1*) Wide World-Tetra.

— Say Cheesecake & Smile. 2nd rev. ed. LC 80-54453. (Illus.). 176p. 1983. pap. 6.95 (*0-933174-17-9*) Wide World-Tetra.

— Walk Don't Run. LC 79-63351. 1979. pap. 3.95 (*0-933174-04-7*) Wide World-Tetra.

***Monroe, Elvira & Margah, Irish.** Hawaii: Cooking with Aloha. 6th ed. LC 87-51516. (Illus.). 220p. 1990. pap. 9.95 (*0-933174-95-0*) Wide World-Tetra.

Monroe, Elvira & Monroe, Mia, eds. Hawaii: Island Paradise. LC 86-51426. (Illus.). 150p. (Orig.). 1987. pap. 9.95 (*0-933174-42-X*) Wide World-Tetra.

Monroe, Elvira, jt. auth. see Arnot, Phil.

Monroe, Elvira, jt. auth. see Pappas, Theoni.

Monroe, Gary. Haiti: Photographs by Gary Monroe. (Illus.). 56p. 1992. pap. 15.00 (*0-9618986-2-3*) Forest & Trees.

— Life in South Beach. (Illus.). 52p. 1989. 35.00 (*0-9618986-0-7*); pap. 20.00 (*0-685-61670-3*) Forest & Trees.

Monroe, Gary & Sweet, Andy. Miami Beach. (Illus.). 60p. 1989. pap. write for info. (*0-9618986-1-5*) Forest & Trees.

Monroe, Gary L. A Handbook for the Traveling Free-Lance Physician: A Guide for Free-Lancers, Part-time Physicians, & Moonlighters. Streetman, James, ed. LC 90-92170. 154p. 1990. 75.00 (*0-9628241-0-0*) Magellan Pub.

Monroe, Gregory. Colorado's Modern Narrow Gauge Circle. (Illus.). 96p. 1994. 37.95 (*0-9604122-8-X*) Fox Pubns.

Monroe, Harriet. The New Poetry: An Anthology. LC 78-64048. (Des Imagistes: Literature of the Imagist Movement Ser.). reprint ed. 49.50 (*0-404-17080-3*) AMS Pr.

— Poets & Their Art. (BCL1-PS American Literature Ser.). 300p. 1992. reprint ed. lib. bdg. 79.00 (*0-7812-6630-0*) Rprt Serv.

— Poet's Life. LC 71-93777. reprint ed. 22.50 (*0-404-04349-6*) AMS Pr.

— A Poet's Life: Seventy Years in a Changing World. (American Biography Ser.). 488p. 1991. reprint ed. lib. bdg. 89.00 (*0-7812-8288-8*) Rprt Serv.

— Poet's Life: Seventy Years in a Changing World. (BCL1-PS American Literature Ser.). 488p. 1993. reprint ed. lib. bdg. 99.00 (*0-7812-6995-4*) Rprt Serv.

***Monroe, Hary.** Time & Time Again: Two Immigrant Groups. (Illus.). 1985. 3.00 (*0-615-00718-X*) Balch IES Pr.

Monroe, Haskell M., Jr., ed. see Davis, Jefferson.

***Monroe Historical Society Staff.** The Village of Monroe: The Celebration of a Century. limited ed. (Illus.). 400p. 1994. pap. 20.00 (*0-88092-185-4*) Royal Fireworks.

— The Village of Monroe: The Celebration of a Century. limited ed. (Illus.). 400p. 1994. 30.00 (*0-88092-186-2*) Royal Fireworks.

Monroe, Howard, jt. auth. see Williams, John C.

Monroe, James. Writings, 7 Vols, Set. Hamilton, Stanislaus M., ed. LC 69-18218. reprint ed. 270.00 (*0-404-04400-X*) AMS Pr.

— The Writings of James Monroe, Including a Collection of His Public & Private Papers & Correspondence, Now for the First Time Printed, 7 vols., Set. (American Biography Ser.). 1991. reprint ed. lib. bdg. 630.00 (*0-7812-8289-6*) Rprt Serv.

Monroe, James & Jackson, Bonnie. Physical Science: An Inquiry Approach. LC 76-51749. 623p. reprint ed. pap. 177.60 (*0-317-28117-8*, 2022507) Bks Demand.

Monroe, James S. & Wicander, Reed. The Changing Earth: Exploring Geology & Evolution. Westby, ed. LC 93-43307. 650p. (C). 1994. pap. text ed. 55.50 (*0-314-02833-1*) West Pub.

— Physical Geology: Exploring the Earth. Westby, ed. 639p. (C). 1992. text ed. 58.75 (*0-314-92195-8*) West Pub.

Monroe, James S., jt. auth. see Wicander, Reed.

Monroe, James T. The Art of Badi az-Zaman Al Hamadhani: As Picaresque Narrative. 175p. (Orig.). 1984. pap. text ed. 15.00 (*0-8156-6070-7*, Am U Beirut) Syracuse U Pr.

— The Shu'ubiyya in Al-Andalus: The Risala of Ibn Garcia & Five Refutations. LC 77-627464. (University of California Publications, Near Eastern Studies: No. 13). (Illus.). 113p. reprint ed. pap. 32.30 (*0-685-20581-9*, 2030679) Bks Demand.

Monroe, James T., jt. auth. see Liu, Benjamin M.

Monroe, Jean G., jt. auth. see Williamson, Ray A.

Monroe, John B., ed. Blood Brothers: B-Movie Monsters & Adventures. (Call of Cthulhu Roleplaying Game System Ser.). (Illus.). 128p. (Orig.). (YA). (gr. 12 up). 1990. pap. 18.95 (*0-933635-69-9*, 2329) Chaosium.

Monroe, John B., ed. see St. Andre, Ken & Perrin, Steve.

Monroe, John B., ed. see Stafford, Greg.

Monroe, John G., jt. auth. see McDonnell, Denis L.

Monroe, Jonathan. A Poverty of Objects: The Prose Poem & the Politics of Genre. LC 86-24026. 352p. 1987. 39.95 (*0-8014-1967-0*) Cornell U Pr.

Monroe, Joseph G. Winning in High-Tech Markets: The Role of General Management. 1993. text ed. 29.95 (*0-07-103386-6*) McGraw.

Monroe, Judith W. Widdershins. (Illus.). 264p. (Orig.). 1989. pap. 9.95 (*0-9615216-5-1*) Crones Own Pr.

Monroe, Judy. Alcohol. LC 93-28607. (Drug Library Ser.). (Illus.). 128p. (YA). (gr. 6 up). 1994. lib. bdg. 17.95 (*0-89490-470-1*) Enslow Pubs.

— Censorship. LC 89-25407. (Facts About Ser.). (Illus.). 48p. (J). (gr. 5-6). 1990. text ed. 4.95 (*0-89686-490-1*, Crstwood Hse) Silver Burdett Pr.

— Dave Winfield. LC 87-30503. (Sports Close-Ups 2 Ser.). (Illus.). 48p. (J). (gr. 5-6). 1988. lib. bdg. 11.95 (*0-89686-370-0*, Crstwood Hse) Silver Burdett Pr.

— Drug Testing. LC 89-25425. (Facts About Ser.). (Illus.). 48p. (J). (gr. 5-6). 1990. text ed. 12.95 (*0-89686-492-8*, Crstwood Hse) Silver Burdett Pr.

— John Elway. LC 87-27430. (Sports Close-Ups 2 Ser.). (Illus.). 48p. (J). (gr. 5-6). 1988. text ed. 11.95 (*0-89686-367-0*, Crstwood Hse) Silver Burdett Pr.

— Latchkey Children. LC 89-1383. (Facts About Ser.). (Illus.). 48p. (J). (gr. 5-6). 1989. text ed. 12.95 (*0-89686-438-3*, Crstwood Hse) Silver Burdett Pr.

— Leukemia. LC 90-33663. (Facts About Ser.). (Illus.). 48p. (J). (gr. 5-6). 1990. text ed. 12.95 (*0-89686-532-0*, Crstwood Hse) Silver Burdett Pr.

— Nicotine. LC 94-47280. (Drug Library). (Illus.). 128p. (YA). (gr. 6 up). 1995. lib. bdg. 17.95 (*0-89490-505-8*) Enslow Pubs.

— Prescription Drugs. LC 88-22911. (Facts About Ser.). (Illus.). 48p. (J). (gr. 5-6). 1988. text ed. 12.95 (*0-89686-414-6*, Crstwood Hse) Silver Burdett Pr.

— Steffi Graf. LC 87-30115. (Sports Close-Ups 2 Ser.). (Illus.). 48p. (J). (gr. 5-6). 1988. text ed. 11.95 (*0-89686-368-9*, Crstwood Hse) Silver Burdett Pr.

— Stimulants & Hallucinogens. LC 88-20350. (Facts About Ser.). (Illus.). 48p. (J). (gr. 5-6). 1988. text ed. 12.95 (*0-89686-415-4*, Crstwood Hse) Silver Burdett Pr.

Monroe, Judy, jt. auth. see Chung, Okwha.

Monroe, Judy, jt. auth. see Harrison, Supenn.

Monroe, Judy M., jt. auth. see Nguyen, Chi.

Monroe, Kelly. Finding God at Harvard: Thirty Ivy League Christians Shape Their Journeys of Faith. 224p. 1994. 17.99 (*0-310-40560-2*) Zondervan.

Monroe, Kent, ed. see Paul D. Converse Symposium Staff.

Monroe, Kent B. Pricing: Making Profitable Decisions. 2nd ed. 1990. text ed. write for info. (*0-07-042782-8*) McGraw.

Monroe, Kristen. Presidential Popularity & the Economy. LC 83-13943. 224p. 1984. text ed. 49.95 (*0-275-91231-0*, C1231, Praeger Pubs) Greenwood.

Monroe, Kristen R., ed. The Political Process & Economic Change. LC 83-11866. 250p. 1983. 42.00 (*0-87586-063-X*); pap. 18.00 (*0-87586-062-1*) Agathon.

Monroe, Laura, ed. see Long, Jeanne, et al.

Monroe, Lee S., jt. auth. see Spencer, Francis M.

Monroe, Lewis B., ed. Dialogues & Dramas. LC 78-38602. (Granger Index Reprint Ser.). 1977. reprint ed. 19.95 (*0-8369-6334-2*) Ayer.

— Humorous Readings. LC 70-121932. (Granger Index Reprint Ser.). 1977. 21.95 (*0-8369-6173-0*) Ayer.

— Miscellaneous Readings. LC 71-38603. (Granger Index Reprint Ser.). 1977. 23.95 (*0-8369-6335-0*) Ayer.

Monroe, Lucy. Creepy Cuisine. LC 92-41654. (Illus.). 80p. (J). (gr. 4-7). 1993. pap. 4.99 (*0-679-84402-3*) Random Bks Yng Read.

— Fifty Nifty Ways to Paint Your Face. LC 92-549. (Illus.). (J). 1992. pap. 3.95 (*1-56565-029-8*) Lowell Hse.

Monroe, Lynn L. Sonnenberg Gardens: A Splendid Collection of Gardens. (Illus.). 32p. (Orig.). 1985. pap. 4.98 (*0-9615125-0-4*) Merryleaf.

Monroe, Manus & Abrams, Karl. Experimental Chemistry: A Laboratory Course. 2nd ed. (Illus.). 400p. (C). 1991. text ed. 28.95 (*0-89863-151-3*) Star Pub CA.

Monroe, Margaret E., ed. Seminar on Bibliotherapy: Proceedings of Sessions on Bibliotherapy Madison, Wisconsin, June 21-23, 1978. 180p. 1978. pap. 6.00 (*0-936442-07-7*) U Wis Sch Lib.

Monroe, Marion. Growing into Reading: How Readiness for Reading Develops at Home & at School. LC 70-95130. 274p. 1970. reprint ed. text ed. 59.75 (*0-8371-2533-2*, MOGR, Greenwood Pr) Greenwood.

Monroe, Mark. An Indian in White America. Reyer, Carolyn, ed. (Illus.). 256p. (C). 1994. text ed. 49.95 (*1-56639-234-9*); pap. text ed. 19.95 (*1-56639-235-7*) Temple U Pr.

***Monroe, Martha C. & Cappaert, David.** Integrating Environmental Education into the School Curriculum. (EEToolbox-Workshop Resource Manual Ser.). (Illus.). 56p. 1994. 8.00 (*1-884782-04-3*) Natl Consort EET.

Monroe, Martha C., jt. auth. see Braus, Judy A.

Monroe, Martha C., jt. auth. see Disinger, John F.

Monroe, Martha C., ed. see Osborn, Nancy A.

Monroe, Martha C., ed. see Pennock, Margaret T. & Bardwell, Lisa V.

Monroe, Mia, jt. ed. see Monroe, Elvira.

***Monroe, Michael & Diamonstein, Barbaralee.** The White House Collection of American Crafts. (Illus.). 128p. 1995. 35.00 (*0-8109-4035-3*) Abrams.

***Monroe, Mike.** Hardwood Gold: The Rise & Fall...& Rise of the Denver Nuggets. 1994. 29.95 (*0-87833-105-0*) Taylor Pub.

Monroe, Paul. The Lost in Space Handbook. 174p. 1991. pap. 19.95 (*1-880417-02-2*) Star Tech.

— Textbook in the History of Education. LC 77-109914. reprint ed. 49.50 (*0-404-04357-7*) AMS Pr.

Monroe, Paul, ed. Cyclopedia of Education, 5 vols., Set. (Illus.). 1968. reprint ed. 425.00 (*1-55888-953-1*) Omnigraphics Inc.

***Monroe, Paula A.** Left-Brain Finance for Right-Brain People: A Money Guide for the Creatively Inclined. 320p. 1995. 29.95 (*1-57071-057-0*); pap. 18.95 (*1-57071-056-2*) Sourcebks.

— Money 101 for the Creatively Inclined: Left-Brain Finance for Right-Brained People. LC 94-25515. 1995. 28.95 (*1-57071-018-X*); pap. 17.95 (*1-57071-017-1*) Sourcebks.

Monroe, Rick. Writing & Thinking with Computers: A Practical & Progressive Approach. (Illus.). 121p. (Orig.). 1993. pap. 16.95 (*0-8141-5893-5*) NCTE.

Monroe, Robert A. Far Journeys. 312p. 1987. pap. 12.00 (*0-385-23182-2*, Dolp) Doubleday.

— Journeys out of the Body. LC 72-15761. 288p. 1973. reprint ed. pap. 11.00 (*0-385-00861-9*, Anchor NY) Doubleday.

— Ultimate Journey. LC 93-32139. 1994. 22.95 (*0-385-47207-2*) Doubleday.

Monroe, Robin P. In This Very Hour: Devotions in Your Time of Need: Loss of a Dream. LC 94-5002. 48p. 1994. pap. 4.99 (*0-8054-5377-6*, 4253-77) Broadman.

— In This Very Hour: Devotions in Your Time of Need: Loss of A Loved One. LC 94-5001. 48p. 1994. pap. 4.99 (*0-8054-5381-4*, 4253-81) Broadman.

Monroe, Ruseell R. Creative Brainstorms: The Relationship Between Madness & Genius. (Frontiers of Consciousness Ser.). 312p. 1992. 27.95 (*0-8290-1769-0*) Irvington.

Monroe, Russell R. Episodic Behavioral Disorders: A Psychodynamic & Neurophysiologic Analysis. LC 72-95916. (Illus.). 536p. reprint ed. pap. 152.80 (*0-7837-1719-9*, 2057248) Bks Demand.

Monroe, Sylvester & Goldman, Peter. Brothers: Black & Poor: A True Story of Courage & Survival. 288p. 1989. mass mkt. 4.95 (*0-345-36156-3*) Ballantine.

Monroe-Terrance, Heidi R. You've Got to Read This Book!! Answers to Those Questions That Have Been Bothering You for Years! LC 95-94504. (Illus.). 80p. (Orig.). 1995. pap. 4.95 (*0-9646797-0-1*) H Monroe-Terrance. Powerful, uncompromising explanation of the central theme of the Bible: the penalty for breaking any of the 10 Commandments is eternal damnation, but if one meets all of God's 11 requirements, his/her destiny can be changed into one to be forever enjoyed in Heaven. Answers are given to many of the most common theological questions that people have. Can you even prove that God exists? Why does God allow such terrible things to happen in the world? Doesn't evolution disprove the Bible? What about reincarnation? Won't I have another chance in Limbo or Purgatory? & many more. Easy to understand. Hard to put down! Great evangelism tool!! Over 120 illustrations. Order from Heidi R. Monroe-Terrance, 278 McIntyre Road, Ogdensburg, NY 13669. $4.95 plus shipping ($1.50 for one book plus $.20 for each additional book.) 40% discount on 10 or more books.** ***Publisher Provided Annotation.

Monroe, Tom. Clutch & Flywheel Handbook. rev. ed. 184p. 1991. reprint ed. pap. 14.95 (*1-55788-030-1*) Price Stern.

— How to Rebuild Your Ford V-8. LC 80-80171. (Orig.). 1980. pap. 14.95 (*0-89586-036-8*) Price Stern.

— How to Rebuild Your Small-Block Ford. LC 78-74545. (Illus.). 1979. pap. 14.95 (*0-912656-89-1*) Price Stern.

Monroe, Tom, jt. auth. see Finch, Richard.

Monroe, Tom, ed. see Gabbard, Alex.

Monroe, Valerie, jt. auth. see Haven, Susan P.

Monroe, W. S. Turkey & the Turks. 448p. 1985. 280.00 (*1-85077-061-1*, Darf Pubs Ltd) St Mut.

Monroe, Watson H. Memories of a Long & Happy Life. 1993. 19.95 (*0-533-10370-3*) Vantage.

Monroe, Will S. Comenius & the Beginnings of Educational Reform. LC 78-135824. (Eastern Europe Collection Ser.). 1971. reprint ed. 16.95 (*0-405-02765-6*) Ayer.

— History of the Pestalozzian Movement in the United States. LC 70-89206. (American Education: Its Men, Institutions & Ideas, Ser. 1). 1971. reprint ed. 21.95 (*0-405-01444-9*) Ayer.

Monroy, A., jt. ed. see Le Douarin, Nicole.

Monroy, Alberto & Moscona, Aron A., eds. Current Topics in Developmental Biology, Vols. 1-12. Incl. Vol. 3. 1968. 65.00 (*0-12-153103-1*); write for info. (*0-318-50254-2*) Acad Pr.

Monroy, Alberto, jt. auth. see Metz, Charles B.

Monroy, Alberto, jt. ed. see Metz, Charles B.

Monroy, Alberto, tr. see Moscona, Aron A., ed.

Monroy, Alberto, jt. ed. see Nielsen-Hamilton, Marit.

Monroy, C., jt. auth. see Perales, T.

Monroy, Douglas. Thrown among Strangers: The Making of Mexican Culture in Frontier California. LC 89-49035. (Illus.). 288p. 1990. 30.00 (*0-520-06914-5*) U CA Pr.

— Thrown Among Strangers: The Making of Mexican Culture in Frontier California. 1993. pap. 15.00 (*0-520-08275-3*) U CA Pr.

***Monroy, Elizabeth.** the Magical Mist. LC 93-91857. 52p. (J). (ps-6). 1994. 15.95 (*0-9639760-0-1*) Going Home.

Monroy, Josue G. Familia Feliz. Orig. Title: La Familia Feliz. 29p. (Orig.). (SPA.). 1987. pap. 1.25 (*0-939125-54-4*) Evangelical Lit.

Monroy, Juan A. Angustia, Depresion y Esperanza: Anguish, Depression & Hope. (SPA.). 3.95 (*84-7645-389-2*, 223516, Pub. by Edit Clie SP) TSELF.

— Apuntando A la Torre: Aiming at the Watch Tower. (SPA.). 7.25 (*84-7645-225-X*, 223314, Pub. by Edit Clie SP) TSELF.

— La Biblia En el Quijote: The Bible in Quijote. (SPA.). 4.95 (*84-7228-468-9*, 220099, Pub. by Edit Clie SP) TSELF.

— Como Vencer Al Diablo: How to Win over Satan. (SPA.). 4.25 (*84-7645-372-8*, 223491, Pub. by Edit Clie SP) TSELF.

— Enfoque Evangelico a la Teologia de la Liberacion: Christian Approach to... (SPA.). 4.25 (*84-7645-474-0*, 223551, Pub. by Edit Clie SP) TSELF.

— Hombres De Fuego: Men of Fire. (SPA.). 4.95 (*84-7228-473-5*, 220467, Pub. by Edit Clie SP) TSELF.

— Misterio de Dios: Mystery of God: An Apologetic View. (SPA.). 3.95 (*84-7228-776-9*, 222339, Pub. by Edit Clie SP) TSELF.

Monrrow, James. The Pro-Life Prayer Book. 1988. 5.00 (*0-9513351-0-3*, 606) Human Life Intl.

Mons, W. E. Beyond Mind. LC 84-52292. 256p. (Orig.). 1985. pap. 8.95 (*0-87728-633-7*) Weiser.

Monsaingeon, Bruno, ed. Mademoiselle: Conversations with Nadia Boulanger. Marsack, Robyn, tr. 141p. 1988. reprint ed. pap. 9.95 (*1-55553-026-5*) NE U Pr.

Monsanto, J. M., tr. see Zwickel, Jean W.

Monsarrat, John. Angel on the Yardarm: The Beginnings of Fleet Radar Defense & the Kamikaze Threat. LC 85-13850. (Historical Monograph: No. 6). (Illus.). 188p. (C). 1985. pap. 4.25 (*0-9637973-7-9*) Naval War Coll.

— Angel on the Yardarm: The Beginnings of Fleet Radar Defense & the Kamikaze Threat. LC 85-13850. (Naval War College Historical Monograph: No. 6). (Illus.). 196p. 1985. pap. 4.25 (*0-16-002043-3*, S/N 008-046-001) USGPO.

M

— Angel on the Yardarm: The Beginnings of Fleet Radar Defense & the Kamikaze Threat. (Illus.). 188p. 1994. reprint ed. pap. text ed. 29.95x (0-7881-1453-0) Diane Pub.

Monsarrat, Nicholas. Cruel Sea. 1951. 25.00 (0-394-42090-X) Knopf.

— The Cruel Sea. Sweetman, Jack, ed. LC 88-15126. (Classics of Naval Literature Ser.). (Illus.). 400p. 1988. 32.95 (0-87021-055-6) Naval Inst Pr.

— The Kappillan of Malta. large type ed. 1976. 16.95 (0-85456-564-7) Ulverscroft.

— The Ship That Died of Shame, & Other Stories. LC 70-163044. (Short Story Index Reprint Ser.). 1977. reprint ed. 18.95 (0-8369-3958-1) Ayer.

— Smith & Jones. 18.95 (0-89190-349-6, Am Repr) Amereon Ltd.

— Three Corvettes. 223p. 1982. reprint ed. pap. 6.00 (0-583-12085-7, Pub. by Granada UK) Academy Chi Pubs.

Monse, Keith, jt. auth. see Weissman, Martin.

***Monseau, Virginia.** Presenting Ouida Sebestyen. (Twayne's Young Adult Author Ser.). 152p. 1994. text ed. 20.95x (0-8057-8224-9, Twayne) Macmillan.

Monseau, Virginia R. & Salvner, Gary M., eds. Reading Their World: The Young Adult Novel in the Classroom. LC 92-22108. 185p. 1992. pap. text ed. 17.50 (0-86709-306-4) Boynton Cook Pubs.

Monsees, J. E., jt. ed. see Bowerman, L. D.

Monsees, Laurie. Building the Temple: A Selection of Herald Articles. 100p. (Orig.). 1992. pap. text ed. 10.00 (0-8309-0607-X) Herald Hse.

— A Week in the Life of the Church. 1992. 5.00 (0-8309-0606-1) Herald Hse.

Monsees, Laurie S. The Temple. LC 93-20854. 1994. 60.00 (0-8309-0648-7) Herald Hse.

Monselise, Shaul P. Handbook of Fruit Set & Development. 624p. 1986. 295.00 (0-8493-3260-5, SB357, CRC Reprint) Franklin.

Monsell, Helen A. Robert E. Lee: Young Confederate. LC 86-10736. (Childhood of Famous Americans Ser.). (Illus.). 192p. (J). (gr. 2-6). 1986. reprint ed. pap. 3.95 (0-02-042020-X, Mac Bks Young Read) S&S Childrens.

— Susan B. Anthony: Champion of Women's Rights. LC 86-10716. (Childhood of Famous Americans Ser.). (Illus.). 192p. (J). (gr. 2-6). 1986. reprint ed. pap. 3.95 (0-02-041800-0, Mac Bks Young Read) S&S Childrens.

— Tom Jefferson: The Third President of the United States. LC 89-37841. (Childhood of Famous Americans Ser.). (Illus.). 192p. (J). (gr. 2-6). 1989. reprint ed. pap. 3.95 (0-689-71347-9, Aladdin Paperbacks) S&S Childrens.

Monsell, Mary E. Armadillo. LC 90-19135. (Illus.). 32p. (J). (ps-1). 1991. text ed. 13.95 (0-689-31676-3, Atheneum Bks Young) S&S Childrens.

— Crackle Creek. LC 89-15105. (Illus.). 64p. (J). (gr. 2-4). 1990. text ed. 12.95 (0-689-31564-3, Atheneum Bks Young) S&S Childrens.

— A Fish Named Yum: Mr. Spin, Vol. 4. LC 93-25731. (Illus.). 64p. (J). (gr. 1-4). 1994. text ed. 13.95 (0-689-31882-0, Atheneum Bks Young) S&S Childrens.

— Mr. Pin: The Chocolate Files. LC 89-78228. (Illus.). 64p. (J). (gr. 2-5). 1990. text ed. 12.95 (0-689-31639-9, Atheneum Bks Young) S&S Childrens.

— Mr. Pin: The Chocolate Files. MacDonald, Patricia, ed. (Illus.). 64p. (J). 1992. reprint ed. pap. 2.99 (0-671-74085-7, Minstrel Bks) PB.

— The Mysterious Cases of Mr. Pin. MacDonald, Patricia, ed. (Illus.). 64p. (J). 1992. pap. 3.50 (0-671-74084-9, Minstrel Bks) PB.

— The Mysterious Cases of Mr. Pin. LC 88-8102. (Illus.). 64p. (J). (gr. 2-5). 1989. text ed. 12.95 (0-689-31435-3, Atheneum Bks Young) S&S Childrens.

— The Spy Who Came North from the Pole. Childs, Alexandria, ed. (Mr. Rogers' First Experience Bks.: Vol. III). 64p. (J). 1995. pap. 3.50 (0-671-88399-2, Minstrel Bks) PB.

— The Spy Who Came North from the Pole: Mr. Pin, Vol. 3. LC 92-24646. (Mr. Pin Ser.: Vol. III). (Illus.). 64p. (J). (gr. 1-4). 1993. text ed. 12.95 (0-689-31754-9, Atheneum Bks Young) S&S Childrens.

— Toohy & Wood. LC 91-38217. (Illus.). 80p. (J). (gr. 2-5). 1992. lib. bdg. 12.95 (0-689-31721-2, Atheneum Bks Young) S&S Childrens.

— Underwear! Levine, Abby, ed. LC 87-25419. (Illus.). 24p. (J). (ps-2). 1988. lib. bdg. 11.95 (0-8075-8308-1) A Whitman.

— Underwear! (J). (ps-3). 1993. pap. 4.95 (0-8075-8309-X) A Whitman.

Monsen & Baer Staff. Perfume Bottle Auction Three: May 1, 1993. (Illus.). 80p. 1993. pap. 28.00 (0-9636102-0-1) Monsen & Baer.

***Monsen, Christine T. & Zenk, Stan.** Guide Me to Eternity. LC 94-24151. 206p. 1994. 11.95 (1-56236-215-1) Aspen Bks.

Monsen, Elaine R. Research: Successful Approaches. LC 91-31303. 1991. pap. 29.95 (0-88091-092-5, 0180) Am Dietetic Assn.

Monsen, Harry. Handbook of Anatomy. (Illus.). 140p. Date not set. pap. text ed. 36.00 (0-8385-3598-4, A3598-8) Appleton & Lange.

Monsen, Harry, tr. see Pernkopf, Eduard.

***Monsen, Randall B.** Collectors' Compendium of Roseville Pottery, Vol. 1. (Illus.). 128p. 1995. 35.00 (0-9636102-2-8) Monsen & Baer.

***Monsen, Randall B., ed.** Perfume Bottle Auction Five Vol. V: May 6, 1995. (Illus.). 96p. (FRE & GER.). 1995. pap. 35.00 (0-9636102-3-6) Monsen & Baer.

— Perfume Bottle Auction Four Vol. IV: May 14, 1994. (Illus.). 80p. 1994. pap. 29.00 (0-9636102-1-X) Monsen & Baer.

Monserrat, Catherine, jt. auth. see Barr, Linda.

Monserrat, Catherine P., jt. auth. see Lindsay, Jeanne W.

Monserrat, Ileana G. La Habana, Nineteen Ninety-Five. LC 90-84647. (Coleccion Caniqui Ser.). 80p. (Orig.). (SPA.). 1991. pap. 9.95 (0-89729-565-X) Ediciones.

Monset-Couchard, M., jt. ed. see Minkowski, A.

***Monsey, Barbara, et al.** What Works in Preventing Rural Violence: Strategies, Risk Factors, & Assessment Tools. LC 94-49041. 1995. pap. write for info. (0-940069-04-0) A H Wilder.

Monsey, Barbara R., jt. auth. see Mattessich, Paul W.

Monshau, Michael. Praying with Dominic. Koch, Carl, ed. (Companions for the Journey Ser.). (Illus.). 119p. (Orig.). 1993. pap. 5.95 (0-88489-288-3) St Marys.

***Monshipouri, Mahmood.** Democratization, Liberalization, & Human Rights in the Third World. LC 94-31377. 200p. 1995. lib. bdg. 42.00 (1-55587-529-7); pap. text ed. 17.95 (1-55587-550-5) Lynne Rienner.

Monsi, M. & Saeki, T., eds. Ecophysiology of Photosynthetic Productivity, Vol. 19. (Japan International Biological Program Synthesis Ser.). 272p. 1978. pap. 62.50 (0-86008-229-6, Pub. by U of Tokyo JA) Col U Pr.

***Monske, Ken & Moore, Diana.** Travelers Guide to the Historic Columbia River Highway. (Illus.). 52p. Date not set. pap. 2.95 (1-883606-26-8) Intl Lov Touch.

Monsma, Hester. Devotions for Graduates. 25p. (Orig.). 1984. pap. 2.49 (0-8010-2939-2) Baker Bk.

— Devotions for Mothers. 30p. 1984. pap. 1.99 (0-8010-2942-2) Baker Bk.

***Monsma, Stephen V.** Positive Neutrality: Letting Religious Freedom Ring. LC 95-10811. 302p. 1995. reprint ed. pap. 15.99 (0-8010-2047-6) Baker Bk.

— Positive Neutrality: Letting Religious Freedom Ring, Vol. 69. LC 92-25738. (Contributions in Legal Studies: No. 69). 304p. 1992. text ed. 55.00 (0-313-27963-2, MUY, Greenwood Pr) Greenwood.

Monsma, Timothy M., jt. auth. see Greenway, Roger S.

Monsman, Gerald. Confessions of a Prosaic Dreamer: Charles Lamb's Art of Autobiography. LC 84-4021. vii, 165p. 1984. text ed. 31.95 (0-8223-0596-8) Duke.

— Olive Schreiner's Fiction: Landscape & Power. LC 91-9431. 220p. (C). 1991. text ed. 45.00 (0-8135-1724-9) Rutgers U Pr.

Monsman, Gerald, ed. see Pater, Walter.

Monsman, Gerald C. Walter Pater. LC 76-58511. (Twayne's English Authors Ser.). 213p. (C). 1977. lib. bdg. 17.95 (0-8057-6676-6) Irvington.

— Walter Pater's Art of Autobiography. LC 80-11941. 184p. reprint ed. pap. 52.50 (0-8357-3753-5, 2036479) Bks Demand.

Monson, A. M. The Deer Stand. LC 91-32122. 160p. (J). (gr. 4 up). 1992. 14.00 (0-688-11057-6) Lothrop.

— The Deer Stand. Cohn, Amy, ed. LC 91-32122. 176p. (J). (gr. 7 up). 1994. reprint ed. pap. 4.95 (0-688-13623-0, Pub. by Beech Tree Bks) Morrow.

— The Secret of Sanctuary Island. LC 90-6479. 128p. (J). (gr. 4-7). 1991. 12.95 (0-688-10111-9) Lothrop.

— The Secret of Sanctuary Island. ALC Staff, ed. LC 90-6479. 176p. (J). (gr. 5 up). 1992. pap. 3.95 (0-688-11693-0, Pub. by Beech Tree Bks) Morrow.

***Monson, Brad R.** Make Your Own Steel Framed House & Save Money! (Illus.). 131p. 1994. 29.95 (1-57002-032-9); pap. 19.95 (1-57002-007-8) Univ Publng Hse.

Monson, Christine. A Flame Run Wild. 400p. 1988. pap. 3.95 (0-380-89976-0) Avon.

— Stormfire. 592p. 1984. pap. 3.95 (0-380-87668-X) Avon.

— Surrender the Night. 400p. 1987. pap. 3.95 (0-380-89969-8) Avon.

***Monson, Craig A.** Disembodied Voices: Music & Culture in an Early Modern Italian Convent. LC 94-28823. 1995. 38.00 (0-520-08875-1) U CA Pr.

Monson, Craig A., ed. The Crannied Wall: Women, Religion, & the Arts in Early Modern Europe. (Studies in Medieval & Early Modern Civilization). (Illus.). 300p. (C). 1992. text ed. 42.50 (0-472-10271-0) U of Mich Pr.

Monson, Dale, ed. Adriano in Siria. LC 86-750172. (Giovanni Battista Pergolesi Complete Works: No. 1, Vol. III). (Illus.). 1987. lib. bdg. 187.00 (0-918728-32-0) Pendragon NY.

Monson, Dianne L. & McClenathan, DayAnn K., eds. Developing Active Readers: Ideas for Parents, Teachers, & Librarians. LC 79-9058. 112p. reprint ed. pap. 32.00 (0-8357-4308-X, 2037105) Bks Demand.

Monson, Dianne L., jt. auth. see Purves, Alan C.

Monson, Gale & Phillips, Allan. Annotated Checklist of the Birds of Arizona. 2nd rev. ed. LC 81-11687. 240p. 1981. pap. 12.95 (0-8165-0753-8) U of Ariz Pr.

Monson, Gale & Sumner, Lowell, eds. The Desert Bighorn: Its Life History, Ecology, & Management. LC 80-18889. 370p. 1980. pap. 17.95 (0-8165-0713-9) U of Ariz Pr.

Monson, Harry, tr. see Pernkopf, Eduard.

Monson, J. Bruce. All the Marbles: A Novel. LC 91-11721. 288p. (Orig.). 1991. pap. 10.95 (0-931832-91-8) Fithian Pr.

— Crimson Ice, Sugar & Spice: A Novel of Suspense. 224p. (Orig.). 1994. pap. 10.95 (1-56474-083-8) Fithian Pr.

— The Scorpion Sapphire: A Novel of Suspense. LC 89-38510. 256p. 1990. 17.95 (0-931832-40-3) Fithian Pr.

Monson, James E., jt. auth. see Hoagland, Al.

Monson, Luetta, jt. auth. see Myers, John.

Monson, Mavis K., jt. auth. see Parker, Lorne A.

Monson, Michele P. & Monson, Robert J., eds. Literacy in the Content Areas. 48p. 1994. pap. 7.00 (0-87207-398-X) Intl Reading.

Monson, Rela G. Jewish Campus Life: A Survey of Student Attitudes Toward Marriage & Family. LC 84-70026. 52p. 1984. pap. 3.00 (0-87495-060-0) Am Jewish Comm.

Monson, Rela G., ed. Jewish Women on the Way Up: The Challenge of Family, Career & Community. LC 87-73347. 36p. (Orig.). 1987. pap. 5.00 (0-87495-097-X) Am Jewish Comm.

Monson, Rela G., jt. auth. see Crawford, Albert G.

Monson, Richard R. Occupational Epidemiology. 232p. 1986. 125.00 (0-8493-5793-4, RC964, CRC Reprint) Franklin.

— Occupational Epidemiology. 2nd ed. 232p. 1990. 104.00 (0-8493-4927-3, RC964) CRC Pr.

Monson, Robert J., jt. ed. see Monson, Michele P.

Monson, Terri, ed. see Dewazien, Karl.

Monson, Thomas S. Be Your Best Self. LC 79-54782. 209p. 1979. 9.95 (0-87747-787-6) Deseret Bk.

— Inspiring Experiences That Build Faith: From the Life & Ministry of Thomas S. Monson. LC 94-28433. 1994. 14.95 (0-87579-901-9) Deseret Bk.

— Live the Good Life. LC 88-71770. 135p. 1988. 8.95 (0-87579-192-1) Deseret Bk.

— Pathways to Perfection. LC 73-88634. xiv, 302p. 1973. 10.95 (0-87747-511-3) Deseret Bk.

Monson, Thomas S., comp. Favorite Quotations from the Collection of Thomas S. Monson. LC 85-16279. viii, 296p. 1985. 11.95 (0-87747-749-3) Deseret Bk.

Monsour, Leslie. Gringuita Poems. LC 90-91893. (Illus.). 50p. (Orig.). 1990. pap. text ed. write for info. (0-9627316-0-9) L Monsour.

Monsour, Margaret, ed. Senior Services Resource Directory. 53p. (Orig.). 1989. spiral bd. (0-9623088-0-3) Eureka St Pubns.

Monsour, Margaret & Talan, Carole. Library-Based Family Literacy Projects. LC 92-41088. 74p. (C). 1993. pap. text ed. 15.00 (0-8389-0610-9) ALA.

***Monssen, Franz.** Use of Pspice in Circuit Analysis. 1994. pap. 36.00 (0-675-21376-2, Merrill Pub Co) Macmillan.

Monsted, Mette & Parveen, Walji. A Demographic Analysis of East Africa: A Sociological Interpretation. 212p. (Orig.). 1978. pap. 21.50x (91-7106-126-6, Pub. by Nordisk Afrikainstitutet SW) Coronet Bks.

Monster, Ann. I Love You: Letters from a Loving Friend. LC 90-26324. (Orig.). 1990. pap. 4.00 (0-915541-64-5) Star Bks Inc.

Mont-Joy, Marc D. The New American Challenge. LC 85-1445. 1988. pap. 13.95 (0-87949-263-5) Ashley Bks.

Mont-Laurier Benedictine Nuns Staff. Goat Cheese Small-Scale Production. 2nd ed. Inksetter, Eveline, tr. Orig. Title: Fromages De Chevre Fabrication Artisinale. (Illus.). 96p. 1983. pap. 4.95 (0-9607404-1-4) Cheesemakers Jrnl.

Montabue, Shillaber. Beyond Beyond Beyond: The Morrow of Life. 90p. (Orig.). 1990. pap. 9.95 (0-9623473-1-0) Wide-Awake Bks.

Montacute, Charles M. Administration of Health Service. (C). 1987. pap. 120.00 (0-685-28612-6) St Mut.

Montada, L. & Bierhoff, H. W., eds. Altruism in Social Systems. (Illus.). 268p. 1991. text ed. 43.00 (0-88937-045-1) Hogrefe & Huber Pubs.

Montada, Leo, et al, eds. Life Crises & Experiences of Loss in Adulthood. 560p. 1992. text ed. 99.95 (0-8058-1001-3) L Erlbaum Assocs.

Montag, Bill. Best Resumes for Seventy-Five Thousand Dollar Plus Executive Jobs. 240p. 1992. pap. text ed. 14.95 (0-471-57789-8) Wiley.

— Best Resumes for Seventy-Five Thousand Dollar Plus Executive Jobs. 240p. 1992. text ed. 39.95 (0-471-57791-X) Wiley.

Montag, Carol, jt. ed. see Jervis, Kathe.

Montag, Horst & Reigber, Christoph, eds. Geodesy & Physics of the Earth: Geodetic Contributions to Geodynamics, 7th International Symposium Geodesy & Physics of the Earth, Potsdam, October 5-10, 1992. LC 93-33122. (International Association of Geodesy Symposia Ser.: No. 112). 1993. 144.00 (0-387-56572-8) Spr-Verlag.

***Montag, Leona.** Mitchell County, Iowa. (Illus.). 484p. 1989. 55.00 (0-88107-151-X) Curtis Media.

***Montag, Thomas W.** The Women's Cancer Book: A Comprehensive Guide for Patients & Their Families. (Illus.). 400p. 1995. 24.95 (1-883955-06-8) Penmarin Bks.

Montag, Tom. The Essential Ben Zen. (Chickadee Ser.: No. 6). 1992. 10.00 (1-55780-124-X); pap. 6.00 (1-55780-123-1) Juniper Pr WI.

— Learning to Read Again. 1976. 1.00 (0-916866-01-7) Cats Pajamas.

Montag, Ulrich, ed. Will the Chain Break? Differential Pricing As Part of a New Pricing Structure for Research Literature & Its Consequences for the Future of Scholarly Communication. (IFLA Publication Ser.: Vol. 61). 95p. 1992. lib. bdg. 45.00 (3-598-21789-7) K G Saur.

***Montag, Warren.** The Unthinkable Swift: Jonathan Swift & the Ideological Crisis of Church & State, 1688-1730. 1994. 59.95 (1-85984-900-8, B4687, Pub. by Verso UK) Routledge Chapman & Hall.

Montage Staff, ed. Montage. (Illus.). 72p. (Orig.). 1989. pap. 5.95 (0-9623452-1-0) Oregon Coast Cmnty Col.

Montagna, F. Joseph. The Herbal Desk Reference. 1280p. 1990. boxed 79.95 (0-8403-5813-X) Kendall-Hunt.

Montagna, Paul D. Certified Public Accounting: A Sociological View of a Profession in Change. LC 73-90140. 1975. text ed. 20.00 (0-914348-14-0) Scholars Bk.

Montagna, W. Aging: Proceedings Symposium, University of Oregon Medical School, 1964. LC 60-10839. (Advances in Biology of Skin Ser.: Vol. 6). 1965. 120.00 (0-08-011387-7, Pub. by Pergamon Repr UK) Franklin.

— Cutaneous Innervation: Proceedings of the Brown University Symposium on the Biology of Skin, 1959. LC 60-10839. (Advances in Biology of Skin Ser.: Vol. 1). 1960. 96.00 (0-08-009385-X, Pub. by Pergamon Repr UK) Franklin.

Montagna, W. & Billingham, R. Wound Healing: Proceedings, Brown University Symposium Biology of Skin, 1963. LC 60-10839. (Advances in Biology of Skin Ser.: Vol. 5). 1964. 106.00 (0-08-010682-X, Pub. by Pergamon Repr UK) Franklin.

Montagna, W. & Dobson, R. Carcinogenesis: Proceedings of the Symposium Biology of Skin, University of Oregon Medical School, 1965. LC 60-10839. (Advances in Biology of Skin Ser.: Vol. 7). 1966. 153.00 (0-08-011576-4, Pub. by Pergamon Repr UK) Franklin.

— Hair Growth: Proceedings of University of Oregon Medical School Symposium on Biology of Skin 1967. LC 60-10839. (Advances in Biology of Skin Ser.: Vol. 9). 1969. 247.00 (0-08-012967-6, Pub. by Pergamon Repr UK) Franklin.

Montagna, W. & Ellis, R. Blood Vessels & Circulation: Proceedings of the Brown University Symposium on Biology of Skin, 1960. LC 60-10839. (Advances in Biology of Skin Ser.: Vol. 2). 1961. 69.00 (0-08-009345-0, Pub. by Pergamon Repr UK) Franklin.

— Eccrine Sweat Glands & Eccrine Sweating: Proceedings of the Brown University Symposium on Biology of Skin, 1961. LC 60-10839. (Advances in Biology of Skin Ser.: Vol. 3). 1962. 116.00 (0-08-009695-6, Pub. by Pergamon Repr UK) Franklin.

Montagna, W. & Funan, H. Pigmentary System: Proceedings of the Symposium on Biology of Skin, University of Oregon Medical School, 1966. LC 60-10839. (Advances in Biology of Skin Ser.: Vol. 8). 1967. 278.00 (0-08-012411-9, Pub. by Pergamon Repr UK) Franklin.

Montagna, W., jt. ed. see Morganti, P.

Montagna, W., jt. ed. see Noback, C. R.

Montagna, W., et al. Advances in Biology of Skin, Vols. 3 & 4. Incl. Vol. 4. Sebaceous Glands. 1963. 116.00 (0-08-009945-9); write for info. (0-318-55120-9, Pub. by Pergamon Repr UK) Franklin.

— Atlas of Normal Human Skin. (Illus.). 384p. 1994. 125.00 (0-387-97769-4) Spr-Verlag.

Montagna, William. Human Skin. Head, J. J., ed. LC 84-45831. (Carolina Biology Readers Ser.: No. 159). (Illus.). 16p. (Orig.). (YA). (gr. 10 up). 1986. pap. text ed. 2.75 (0-89278-159-9, 45-9759) Carolina Biological.

— Nonhuman Primates in Biomedical Research. LC 76-7881. (Wesley W. Spink Lectures on Comparative Medicine: No. 3). (Illus.). 161p. reprint ed. pap. 45.90 (0-8357-8972-1, 2033273) Bks Demand.

Montagna, William & Parakkal, P. F. The Structure & Function of the Skin. 3rd ed. 1974. text ed. 148.00 (0-12-505263-4) Acad Pr.

Montagna, William, et al. Skin: Your Owner's Manual. (Illus.). xiii, 187p. 1990. 33.00 (88-7810-049-8) Micelle Pr.

Montagna, William, et al, eds. Black Skin: Structure & Function. LC 93-14784. 158p. 1993. text ed. 49.95 (0-12-505260-X) Acad Pr.

Montagne. Atlas of Foot Radiology. 1981. 81.50 (0-89352-097-7) Mosby Yr Bk.

***Montagne, Anne & Prinz, Noelle.** Goldilocks & the Three Bears. LC 94-48720. (J). 1995. 9.95 (1-85697-622-X, Kingfisher LKC) LKC.

Montagne, Mary. Staying Straight: Adolescent Recovery. 32p. (Orig.). 1987. pap. 3.95 (0-9613416-6-1) Comm Intervention.

Montagne, Michael, jt. auth. see Basara, Lisa R.

Montagne, Rogelio S., jt. auth. see Casad, Robert C.

Montagnes, Ian, jt. ed. see Harman, Eleanor.

Montagnier. AIDS & HIV Diseases. 1990. 51.95 (0-8151-6008-9, Yr Bk Med Pubs) Mosby Yr Bk.

Montagnier, Luc & Gougeon, Marie-Lise. New Concepts in AIDS Pathogenesis. LC 93-4765. 344p. 1993. 115.00 (0-8247-9127-4) Dekker.

Montagnon. European Competition Policy. (Chatham House Papers). 128p. (Orig.). 1990. pap. 14.95 (0-87609-090-0) Coun Foreign.

Montagnon, Philip. Foundations of Statistics: A Survey for Managers. 152p. (C). 1980. 52.00 (0-85950-456-5, Pub. by S Thornes Pubs UK) St Mut.

Montagu, Ashley. Coming into Being among the Australian Aborigines. LC 75-41195. (Illus.). reprint ed. 55.00 (0-404-14573-6) AMS Pr.

— The Elephant Man. rev. ed. Angers, Trent, ed. (Illus.). 120p. 1995. pap. 11.95 (0-925417-18-1) Acadian Hse Pub.

Montagu Butler, J. H., ed. Interactive Projects: Teacher's Book & Key. (C). 1984. 65.00 (0-7175-1250-9, Pub. by S Thornes Pubs UK) St Mut.

Montagu, Elizabeth. Essay on the Writings & Genius of Shakespeare Compared with the Greek & French Dramatic Poets. 6th ed. LC 17-29281. reprint ed. 45.00 (0-404-04358-5) AMS Pr.

— Essay on the Writings & Genius of Shakespeare Compared with the Greek & French Dramatic Poets: 1785-1839. 292p. 1970. reprint ed. 28.50 (0-7146-2515-9, Pub. by F Cass Pubs UK) Intl Spec Bk.

— The Letters of Mrs. Elizabeth Montagu, with Some of the Letters of Her Correspondents, 4 vols, Set. LC 72-37704. 1813. reprint ed. 295.00 (0-404-56800-9) AMS Pr.

Montagu, Elizabeth R. Essay on the Writings & Genius of Shakespeare: Compared with the Greek & French Dramatic Poets. LC 73-96372. (Eighteenth Century Shakespeare Ser.: No. 12). 288p. 1970. reprint ed. lib. bdg. 37.50 (0-678-05139-9) Kelley.

Montagu, Henry. Contemplatio Mortis et Immortalitatis. LC 72-218. (English Experience Ser.: No. 337). 148p. 1971. reprint ed. 20.00 (90-221-0337-4) Walter J Johnson.

Montagu, Ivor. With Eisenstein in Hollywood. 356p. 1969. pap. 1.95 (0-7178-0220-5) Intl Pubs Co.

Montagu, Ivor, tr. see Babel, Isaak E.

Montagu, Ivor, tr. see Briusov, Valerii I.

Montagu, Ivor, tr. see Eisenstein, Sergei.

An Asterisk (*) at the beginning of an entry indicates that the title is appearing in BIP for the first time.

Montagu, Ivor, tr. see Leonov, Leonid M.
Montagu, Jennifer. Alessandro Algradi. LC 84-53344. (Illus.). 762p. 1985. 130.00 (*0-300-03173-4*) Yale U Pr.
— The Expression of the Passions: The Origin & the Influence of Charles Le Brun's "Conference Sur l'Expression Generale et Particuliere" LC 94-130. (Illus.). 256p. 1994. 45.00x (*0-300-05891-8*) Yale U Pr.
— Gold, Silver & Bronze: Metal Sculpture of the Roman Baroque. LC 95-15892. 1996. write for info. (*0-300-06336-9*) Yale U Pr.
— Roman Baroque Sculpture: The Industry of Art. LC 88-30482. (C). 1989. text ed. 50.00 (*0-300-04392-9*) Yale U Pr.
— Roman Baroque Sculpture: The Industry of Art. (Illus.). 256p. (C). 1993. reprint ed. pap. text ed. 26.50 (*0-300-05366-5*) Yale U Pr.
Montagu, Jeremy. The Flute. 1989. pap. 25.00 (*0-685-71519-1*, Pub. by Shire UK) St Mut.
— The French Horn. 1989. pap. 25.00 (*0-7478-0086-3*, Pub. by Shire UK) St Mut.
— The World of Baroque & Classical Musical Instruments. LC 78-65227. (Illus.). 136p. 1979. 39.95 (*0-87951-089-7*) Overlook Pr.
— The World of Medieval & Renaissance Musical Instruments. LC 76-5987. (Illus.). 136p. 1976. 39.95 (*0-87951-045-5*) Overlook Pr.
— The World of Romantic & Modern Musical Instruments. LC 80-26106. (Illus.). 136p. 1981. 39.95 (*0-87951-126-5*) Overlook Pr.
Montagu, Lord. The Blue Plaque Guide. (Illus.). 132p. (Orig.). (C). 1991. pap. text ed. 18.00 (*1-85172-005-7*, Pub. by Journeyman Pr UK) Westview.
Montagu, Mary. Letters from the Right Honourable Lady Mary Wortley Montagu, 1709-1762. (BCL1-PR English Literature Ser.). 551p. 1992. reprint ed. lib. bdg. 99.00 (*0-7812-7391-9*) Rprt Serv.
Montagu, Mary W. Embassy to Constantinople. (Illus.). 224p. (C). 1988. 30.00 (*0-941533-41-7*) New Amsterdam Bks.
— Essays & Poems & Simplicity, a Comedy. Halsband, Robert & Grundy, Isobel, eds. 456p. 1993. reprint ed. pap. 19.95 (*0-19-812288-8*) OUP.
— Letters. LC 92-52913. 592p. 1992. 20.00 (*0-679-41747-8*, Everymans Lib) Knopf.
— Letters & Works of Lady Mary Wortley Montagu, 2 vols., Set. Lord Wharncliffe, ed. LC 70-115358. reprint ed. 125.00 (*0-404-04378-X*) AMS Pr.
— Letters from the Levant: During the Embassy to Constantinople, 1716-18. LC 71-135825. (Eastern Europe Collection Ser.). 1971. reprint ed. 32.95 (*0-405-02767-2*) Ayer.
— Nonsense of Common Sense, 1737-1738. Halsband, Robert, ed. LC 71-129373. (Northwestern University. Humanities Ser.: No. 17). reprint ed. 19.00 (*0-404-50717-4*) AMS Pr.
— Turkish Embassy Letters. 256p. 1995. pap. 13.95 (*1-85381-679-5*, Pub. by Virago Pr UK) Trafalgar.
— Turkish Embassy Letters: Lady Mary Wortley Montagu. LC 93-928. 200p. (C). 1993. 35.00 (*0-8203-1580-X*) U of Ga Pr.
Montagu-Nathan, Montagu. Contemporary Russian Composers. LC 72-109795. 329p. 1970. reprint ed. text ed. 65.00 (*0-8371-4285-7*, MORC, Greenwood Pr) Greenwood.
— Contemporary Russian Composers. 329p. 1990. reprint ed. lib. bdg. 79.00 (*0-7812-9041-4*) Rprt Serv.
— Glinka. LC 74-24156. reprint ed. 29.50 (*0-404-13049-6*) AMS Pr.
— A History of Russian Music. LC 76-82815. 1918. 24.00 (*0-8196-0251-5*) Biblo.
— A History of Russian Music: Being an Account of the Rise & Progress of the Russian School of Composers, with a Survey of Their Lives & a Description of Their Works. 346p. 1990. reprint ed. lib. bdg. 79.00 (*0-7812-9034-1*) Rprt Serv.
— Moussorgsky. LC 74-24157. reprint ed. 29.50 (*0-404-13050-X*) AMS Pr.
— Rimsky-Korsakov. LC 74-24158. reprint ed. 29.50 (*0-404-13051-8*) AMS Pr.
Montagu, Richard. Appello Caesarem: A Just Appeale from Two Unjust Informers. LC 75-38210. (English Experience Ser.: No. 475). 348p. 1972. reprint ed. 49.00 (*90-221-0475-3*) Walter J Johnson.
— A Gagg for the New Gospell? No: A New Gagg for an Old Goose. LC 74-28872. (English Experience Ser.: No. 751). 1975. reprint ed. 26.00 (*90-221-0751-5*) Walter J Johnson.
Montague. Abstracts & Recursion Theory. (Studies in Logic). write for info. (*0-444-86159-9*, North Holland) Elsevier.
— Dread Culture. 1994. per. 12.95 (*0-920813-53-4*, Pub. by Sister Vision CN) InBook.
Montague, Ann, jt. auth. see Alibhai-Brown, Yasmin.
***Montague, Bill.** Concord Guidebook: Tourist Information for Concord, Mass. Roof, Christopher, ed. LC 95-67744. (Illus.). 56p. 1995. pap. text ed. 15.95 (*0-9638644-4-0*) Concord MouseTrap.
— Little Mouse: The Mouse Who Lived with Henry David Thoreau at Walden Pond. Roof, Christopher, ed. LC 93-73231. (Illus.). 56p. (Orig.). (J). (gr. 2-4). 1993. pap. text ed. 7.95 (*0-9638644-0-8*) Concord MouseTrap.
Montague, C. J. Sixty Years in Waifdom: The Ragged School Movement in English History. LC 79-5721. (Social History of Education 1st Ser.: No. 7). (Illus.). xv, 459p. 1969. reprint ed. 45.00 (*0-678-08450-5*) Kelley.
— Sixty Years in Waifdom or, the Ragged School Movement in English History. LC 70-108225. (Criminology, Law Enforcement, & Social Problems Ser.: No. 108). 1970. reprint ed. 18.00 (*0-87585-108-8*) Patterson Smith.
Montague, Charles E. Action & Other Stories. LC 70-134971. (Short Story Index Reprint Ser.). 1977. 19.95 (*0-8369-3702-3*) Ayer.
— Dramatic Values. (BCL1-PR English Literature Ser.). 274p. 1992. reprint ed. lib. bdg. 79.00 (*0-7812-7095-2*) Rprt Serv.
— Dramatic Values. reprint ed. 14.00 (*0-403-01112-4*) Scholarly.
— Fiery Particles. LC 79-131781. 1971. 29.00 (*0-403-00668-6*) Scholarly.
— Tales of a Nomad; Or, Sport & Strife. LC 72-5559. (Black Heritage Library Collection). 1977. reprint ed. 21.95 (*0-8369-9144-3*) Ayer.
Montague, Clifford. Farewell, Goodbye, the End? The Secret History of a Literary Era. 96p. (Orig.). 1993. pap. 8.95 (*1-56474-050-1*) Fithian Pr.
Montague, Diana M., ed. see Rayle, James F.
Montague, Drogo K., ed. Disorders of Male Sexual Function. (Illus.). 280p. 1987. 75.00 (*0-8151-5939-0*, MSF-1, Yr Bk Med Pubs) Mosby Yr Bk.
Montague, Earl J. Fundamentals of Secondary Classroom Instruction. 320p. (C). 1987. pap. write for info. (*0-675-20555-7*, Merrill Pub Co) Macmillan.
Montague, Earl J., et al. Fundamentals of Elementary & Middle School Classroom Instruction. 384p. (C). 1989. pap. write for info. (*0-675-20851-3*, Merrill Pub Co) Macmillan.
Montague, Francis C. History of England from the Accession of James First to the Restoration: Sixteen Hundred-Three to Sixteen Sixty. (Political History of English Ser.). 1969. reprint ed. 45.00 (*0-527-00852-4*) Periodicals Srv.
— History of England from the Accession of James First to the Restoration, 1603-1660. LC 78-5631. (Political History of England Ser.: No. 7). reprint ed. 22.50 (*0-404-50777-8*) AMS Pr.
Montague, Francis C., ed. see Bentham, Jeremy.
Montague, G. W. History & Genealogy of Peter Montague, of Nansemond & Lancaster County, Virgina & His Descendants, 1621-1894. (Illus.). 494p. 1989. reprint ed. lib. bdg. 82.00 (*0-8328-0878-4*); reprint ed. pap. 74.00 (*0-8328-0879-2*) Higginson Bk Co.
Montague, G. W. & Montague, W. L. History & Genealogy of the Montague Family of America, Descended from Richard Montague of Hadley, Mass., & Peter of Lancaster County, Virginia, with Genealogical Notes of Other Families by the Name of Montague. (Illus.). 785p. 1989. reprint ed. lib. bdg. 125.50 (*0-8328-0876-8*); reprint ed. pap. 117.50 (*0-8328-0877-6*) Higginson Bk Co.
Montague, George. The Apocalypse. 248p. (Orig.). 1992. pap. 8.99 (*0-89283-746-2*) Servant.
— Holy Spirit: Growth of a Biblical Tradition. 374p. 1994. pap. 16.95 (*1-56563-056-4*) Hendrickson MA.
— Still Riding the Wind: Learning the Ways of the Spirit. rev. ed. LC 94-66742. 112p. 1994. pap. 7.95 (*1-878718-22-3*) Resurrection.
Montague, George T. Mark: Good News for Hard Times - A Popular Commentary on the Earliest Gospel. 197p. 1992. 6.95 (*0-940535-53-X*, UP 153) Franciscan U Pr.
— Our Father, Our Mother: Mary & the Faces of God. 175p. 1990. pap. 6.95 (*0-940535-28-9*, UP128) Franciscan U Pr.
— The Woman & the Way: A Marian Path to Jesus. 230p. 1994. pap. 8.99 (*0-89283-856-6*, Charis) Servant.
Montague, George T., jt. auth. see McDonnell, Kilian.
Montague, Gert. Sago Saga. LC 88-84093. (Illus.). 107p. (Orig.). reprint ed. 12.95 (*0-9623565-0-6*); reprint ed. pap. 9.95 (*0-9623565-1-4*) G Montague.
Montague, Gilbert H. The Rise & Progress of the Standard Oil Company. LC 73-2525. (Big Business; Economic Power in a Free Society Ser.). 1973. reprint ed. 15.95 (*0-405-05104-2*) Ayer.
Montague, H. Patrick. The Saints & Martyrs of Ireland: Feast Days Calendar. (Illus.). 138p. 1981. 18.95 (*0-86140-106-9*, Pub. by Colin Smythe Ltd UK); pap. 7.95 (*0-86140-107-7*, Pub. by Colin Smythe Ltd UK) Dufour.
Montague, J. Franklin. The Why of Albert Schweitzer. large type ed. 1967. 15.95 (*0-85456-575-2*) Ulverscroft.
Montague, Jeanne. Courtney's Wench. large type ed. 390p. 1994. pap. 16.95 (*1-85389-485-0*, Medcom-Trainex) Ulverscroft.
— Wild Bride. 416p. 1994. mass mkt. 4.50 (*0-8217-4510-7*) Zebra.
Montague, Joel B., Jr. Class & Nationality: English & American Studies. 1963. pap. 16.95 (*0-8084-0080-0*) NCUP.
Montague, John. About Love. LC 93-14670. 176p. (Orig.). 1993. pap. 13.95 (*1-878818-23-6*) Sheep Meadow.
— Basic Perspective Drawing. (Illus.). 176p. 1985. pap. 19.95 (*0-442-26653-7*) Van Nos Reinhold.
— Basic Perspective Drawing. 2nd ed. LC 92-36128. 1993. pap. 24.95 (*0-442-01263-2*) Van Nos Reinhold.
— Bitter Harvest. 128p. 1989. text ed. 22.50 (*0-684-19032-X*, Scribners) S&S Trade.
— Book of Irish Verse: Irish Poetry from the Sixth Century to the Present. 1995. 9.98 (*0-88365-881-X*) Galahad Bks.
— Born in Brooklyn. 128p. 1991. pap. 10.00 (*1-877727-13-X*) White Pine.
— Collected Poems. 300p. (C). 1995. text ed. 16.95 (*0-916390-68-3*) Wake Forest.
— Collected Poems. 300p. (C). 1995. 24.95 (*0-916390-69-1*) Wake Forest.
— The Figure in the Cave & Other Essays. LC 89-4635. (Irish Studies). 240p. (Orig.). 1989. text ed. 35.00x (*0-8156-2478-6*); pap. 14.95 (*0-8156-0240-5*) Syracuse U Pr.
— The Great Cloak. 63p. 1978. pap. 6.95 (*0-916390-07-1*) Wake Forest.
— Lost Notebook. 96p. 1987. pap. 16.95 (*0-85342-832-8*, Pub. by Mercier Pr IE) Dufour.
— Mount Eagle. LC 88-40663. 75p. 1989. 11.95 (*0-916390-34-9*); pap. 6.95 (*0-916390-33-0*) Wake Forest.
— An Occasion of Sin. 1992. pap. 12.00 (*1-877727-21-0*) White Pine.
— The Rough Field. 5th rev. ed. LC 89-40526. (Illus.). 100p. 1989. pap. 7.95 (*0-916390-42-X*) Wake Forest.
— Selected Poems. LC 81-71131. 189p. 1982. pap. 9.95 (*0-916390-15-2*) Wake Forest.
Montague, Ludwell L. General Walter Bedell Smith as Director of Central Intelligence, October 1950 - February 1953. 500p. 1992. 45.00 (*0-271-00750-8*); pap. 14.95 (*0-271-00751-6*) Pa St U Pr.
Montague, Margaret P. Up Eel River. LC 77-150552. (Short Story Index Reprint Ser.). (Illus.). 1977. reprint ed. 19.95 (*0-8369-3849-6*) Ayer.
Montague, Marjorie. Computers, Cognition, & Writing Instruction. LC 89-27033. (Computers in Education Ser.). (Illus.). 205p. 1990. 64.50 (*0-7914-0335-1*); pap. 21.95 (*0-7914-0336-X*) State U NY Pr.
Montague, Owen, jt. ed. see Fraser, George C.
Montague, Phillip. In the Interests of Others: An Essay in Moral Philosophy. LC 92-20029. (Philosophical Studies in Philosophy Ser.: Vol. 55). 160p. (C). 1992. lib. bdg. 75.00 (*0-7923-1856-0*) Kluwer Ac.
— Punishment As Societal Defense. (Studies in Social & Political Philosophy). 224p. (C). 1995. text ed. 56.50 (*0-8476-8071-1*); pap. text ed. 22.95 (*0-8476-8072-X*) Rowman.
Montague, Richard. Formal Philosophy: Selected Papers of Richard Montague. LC 73-77159. 375p. reprint ed. pap. 106.90 (*0-8357-8134-8*, 2033829) Bks Demand.
Montague, Richard & Goldstein, Joel. Lotus 1-2-3 the Easy Way. (Illus.). 53p. (Orig.). (C). 1990. pap. text ed. 9.00 (*0-936285-09-5*) U New Haven Pr.
Montague, Rosie. Brazilian Three-Dimensional Embroidery: Instructions & 60 Transfer Patterns. (Embroidery, Needlework Designs Ser.). (Illus.). 64p. (Orig.). 1983. pap. 3.95 (*0-486-24384-2*) Dover.
Montague-Smith, Patrick, comp. Debrett's Correct Form: Standard Styles of Address for Everyone from Peers to Presidents. (Illus.). 432p. 1993. 45.00 (*0-7472-0658-9*, Pub. by Headline UK); pap. 17.95 (*0-7472-3926-6*, Pub. by Headline UK) Trafalgar.
Montague, Terry. Fireweed. LC 92-72487. 1992. pap. 9.95 (*1-55503-407-1*, 01111078) Covenant Comms.
Montague, Terry B. Mine Angels Round About: Mormon Missionary Evacuation from Western Germany - 1939. 13.50 (*0-685-30414-0*) Roylance Pub.
Montague, W. L., jt. auth. see Montague, G. W.
Montague, William P. Belief Unbound. LC 72-109630. (Select Bibliographies Reprint Ser.). 1977. 18.95 (*0-8369-5239-1*) Ayer.
— The Way of Things: A Philosophy of Knowledge, Nature & Value. LC 75-3283. reprint ed. 49.50 (*0-404-59271-6*) AMS Pr.
Montaigne, Bill. How to Begin & Operate a Successful Commercial Photography Business. (Illus.). 1979. pap. 10.00 (*0-912256-14-1*) Halls of Ivy.
Montaigne, Fen, jt. auth. see Kalugin, Oleg.
Montaigne, Erle. Advanced Dim-Mak. (Illus.). 328p. 1994. pap. 35.00 (*0-87364-779-3*) Paladin Pr.
— Dim-Mak: Death-Point Striking. (Illus.). 240p. 1993. pap. 25.00 (*0-87364-718-1*) Paladin Pr.
Montalban, Manuel V. The Angst-Ridden Executive. Emery, Ed, tr. (Mask Noir Ser.). 240p. (Orig.). 1990. pap. 9.95 (*1-85242-159-2*) Serpents Tail.
— Barcelonas. Robinson, Andrew, tr. (Illus.). 280p. 1991. 34.95 (*0-86091-353-8*, A6395, Pub. by Verso UK) Routledge Chapman & Hall.
— Galindez. Christensen, Carol & Christensen, Thomas, trs. 320p. 1992. text ed. 21.00 (*0-689-12121-0*, Pub. by Ctrl Bur voor Schimmel NE) Macmillan.
— Southern Seas. Camiller, Patrick, tr. 224p. (Orig.). 1990. pap. 9.95 (*1-85242-132-0*) Serpents Tail.
Montalbetti, Rocio, ed. see Carlson, Daniel J.
***Montalbo, Thomas.** Public Speaking Made Easy. 1994. pap. 10.00 (*0-87980-434-3*) Wilshire.
Montaldi, J., tr. see Sernesi, Edoardo.
Montaldi, J. A. & Mond, D., eds. Singularity Theory & Its Applications: Warwick 1989, Vol. I: Symposium Held at the University of Warwick 1988-1989. (Lecture Notes in Mathematics Ser.: Vol. 1462). viii, 428p. 1991. pap. 52.00 (*0-387-53737-6*) Spr-Verlag.
Montale. Quarterly Review of Literature: The 1960s, Special Issue, Vol. XI, No. 4. 1960. pap. 35.00 (*0-317-05306-X*) Quarterly Rev.
***Montale, Eugenio.** The Bones of Cuttlefish. Mazza, Antonino, tr. 96p. 1995. lib. bdg. 27.00 (*0-8095-4908-5*) Borgo Pr.
— The Butterfly of Dinard. Singh, G., tr. LC 72-160048. reprint ed. pap. 53.10 (*0-7837-9584-X*, 2060333) Bks Demand.
— Cuttlefish Bones. Arrowsmith, William, tr. 192p. 1993. 25.00 (*0-393-02803-8*) Norton.
— Cuttlefish Bones. 1994. pap. 10.95 (*0-393-31171-6*) Norton.
— It Depends: A Poet's Notebook. Singh, G., tr. LC 80-16629. 192p. 1980. 12.95 (*0-8112-0773-0*); pap. 4.95 (*0-8112-0774-9*, NDP507) New Directions.
— Mottetti: Poems of Love: The Motets of Eugenio Montale. Gioia, Dana, tr. & aft. by. LC 89-25957. 80p. 1990. 14.95 (*1-55597-123-7*) Graywolf.
— New Poems. Singh, G., tr. LC 75-31600. 169p. 1976. 7.95 (*0-8112-0598-3*); pap. 2.95 (*0-8112-0599-1*, NDP410) New Directions.
— The Occasions. Arrowsmith, William, tr. LC 86-16269. 1987. pap. 9.95 (*0-393-30324-1*) Norton.
— The Second Life of Art: Selected Essays. Galassi, Jonathan, ed. LC 81-9861. 375p. 1982. 17.50 (*0-912946-84-9*) Ecco Pr.
— The Second Life of Art: Selected Essays. Galassi, Jonathan, ed. LC 81-9861. 350p. 1985. pap. 9.50 (*0-912946-85-7*) Ecco Pr.
— Selected Poems. Cambon, Glauco, ed. LC 65-15669. (Orig.). (ENG & ITA.). 1966. pap. 8.95 (*0-8112-0119-8*, NDP193) New Directions.
— The Storm & Other Poems. Wright, Charles, tr. (Field Translation Ser.: No. 1). (Orig.). 1978. 8.95 (*0-932440-00-2*) Oberlin Coll Pr.
Montale, Eugenio & Reed, Jeremy. Coast Guard's House. 224p. 1990. pap. 18.95 (*1-85224-100-4*, Pub. by Bloodaxe Bks UK) Dufour.
Montalembert, Charles, pseud. The Monks of the West from St. Benedict to St. Bernard, 6 vols., 1. LC 03-11386. reprint ed. write for info. (*0-404-04411-5*) AMS Pr.
— The Monks of the West from St. Benedict to St. Bernard, 6 vols., 2. LC 03-11386. reprint ed. write for info. (*0-404-04412-3*) AMS Pr.
— The Monks of the West from St. Benedict to St. Bernard, 6 vols., 3. LC 03-11386. reprint ed. write for info. (*0-404-04413-1*) AMS Pr.
— The Monks of the West from St. Benedict to St. Bernard, 6 vols., 4. LC 03-11386. reprint ed. write for info. (*0-404-04414-X*) AMS Pr.
— The Monks of the West from St. Benedict to St. Bernard, 6 vols., 5. LC 03-11386. reprint ed. write for info. (*0-404-04415-8*) AMS Pr.
— The Monks of the West from St. Benedict to St. Bernard, 6 vols., 6. LC 03-11386. reprint ed. write for info. (*0-404-04416-6*) AMS Pr.
— The Monks of the West from St. Benedict to St. Bernard, 6 vols., Set. LC 03-11386. reprint ed. 410.00 (*0-404-04410-7*) AMS Pr.
Montali, Richard J., ed. Mycobacterial Infections of Zoo Animals. LC 77-60860. (National Zoological Park Symposia for the Public Ser.: No. 1). (Illus.). 276p. 1979. pap. text ed. 18.95 (*0-87474-645-0*, MOMIP) Smithsonian.
Montali, Richard J. & Migaki, George, eds. The Comparative Pathology of Zoo Animals. LC 79-24354. (National Zoological Park Symposia for the Public Ser.: No. 6). (Illus.). 684p. 1980. pap. text ed. 29.95 (*0-87474-643-4*, MOCCP) Smithsonian.
Montalto, Karen, ed. Proceedings of the National Association of Insurance Commissioners, 1991, Vol. II. 1343p. (C). 1992. 125.00 (*0-89382-176-4*) Nat Assn Insu Comm.
Montalto, Nicholas V., ed. The International Institute Movement: A Guide to Records of Immigrant Service Agencies in the United States. (Illus.). xx, 74p. 1978. pap. text ed. write for info. (*0-932833-01-2*) Immig His Res.
Montalvao e Silva, J. M. & Pina da Silva, F. A., eds. Vibration & Wear in High Speed Rotating Machinery: Proceedings of the NATO Advanced Study Institute on Vibration & Wear Damage in High Speed Rotating Machinery, Troia, Sebutal, April 10-22, 1989. (C). 1990. lib. bdg. 259.50 (*0-7923-0533-7*) Kluwer Ac.
Montalvo, Berta. Miniaturas. LC 88-84023. (Coleccion Espejo de Paciencia Ser.). (Illus.). 38p. (Orig.). (SPA.). 1991. pap. 6.00 (*0-89729-522-6*) Ediciones.
— Para Mi Gaveta. LC 88-84022. (Coleccion Espejo de Paciencia Ser.). 139p. (Orig.). (SPA.). 1990. pap. 12.00 (*0-89729-523-4*) Ediciones.
Montalvo, Joseph G., Jr., ed. Cotton Dust: Controlling an Occupational Health Hazard. LC 82-6857. (ACS Symposium Ser.: No. 189). 1982. 49.95 (*0-8412-0716-X*) Am Chemical.
Montalvo, Juan. Montalvo en Su Epistolario. LC 78-9810. (Illus.). 456p. 1982. pap. 10.00 (*0-8477-0856-X*) U of PR Pr.
Montalvo, Margarita B., tr. see Anaya, R., et al.
Montana. Management. (Barron's E Z 101 Study Keys Ser.). 144p. 1991. pap. 5.95 (*0-8120-4606-4*) Barron.
Montana, Bruce, jt. auth. see Ulferts, Stuart.
***Montana, Denby.** Orion's Belt. Mould, Owen, ed. 85p. (Orig.). 1994. pap. 8.00 (*0-9644856-9-9*, Celtic Butterfly) Spellman-Tris.
Montana Department of Fish, Wildlife & Parks Staff. Savoring the Wild. (Illus.). 96p. (Orig.). 1989. pap. 7.95 (*0-937959-76-6*) Falcon Pr MT.
Montana, Eduardo. How to Get the Most Out of Your Visits to the Pediatrician. (Illus.). 232p. (Orig.). 1992. pap. 9.95 (*0-933701-59-4*) Westport Pubs.
Montana, Gladiola. Never Ask a Man the Size of His Spread: A Cowgirl's Guide to Life. LC 92-43920. (Illus.). 144p. 1993. pap. 5.95 (*0-87905-554-5*, Peregrine Smith) Gibbs Smith Pub.
Montana, Gladiola, jt. auth. see Bender, Texas B.
Montana Historical Society Staff. F. Jay Haynes: Fifty Views: Photos from the Haynes Collection. (Illus.). 32p. (Orig.). 1981. pap. 4.95 (*0-917298-05-5*) MT Hist Soc.
— F. Jay Haynes, Photographer. LC 81-6712. 192p. 1981. pap. 14.95 (*0-917298-04-7*) MT Hist Soc.
Montana, Hunter & Montana, Shelkie. Cowboy Ties. LC 94-17387. (Illus.). 64p. 1994. 17.95 (*0-87905-623-1*) Gibbs Smith Pub.
Montana, Joe & Raissman, Bob. Audibles: My Life in Football. 1990. pap. 3.95 (*0-380-71326-8*, Flare) Avon.
***Montana, Joe & Schaap, Dick.** Montana. (Illus.). 144p. 1995. 25.00 (*1-57036-236-X*) Turner Pub GA.
Montana, Joe & Steinberg, Alan. Cool under Fire: Reflections on the San Francisco 49ers-How We Came of Age in the 1980's. 1989. 17.95 (*0-316-57847-9*) Little.
Montana Land Reliance Staff & Land Trust Exchange Staff. Private Options: Tools & Concepts for Land Conservation. LC 82-13070. 292p. (Orig.). 1982. pap. 25.00 (*0-933280-15-7*) Island Pr.

M

An Asterisk (*) at the beginning of an entry indicates that the title is appearing in BIP for the first time.

Montana, LeRoy & Waldron, Linda. The Crystal Oracle. 128p. 1993. pap. 29.95 (*1-883783-01-1*) Crystal Oracle.
Montana, LeRoy, jt. auth. see Waldron, Linda.
Montana Magazine Staff. My Montana: The Best of Montana Magazine. (Illus.). 120p. 1992. 29.95 (*1-56037-017-3*); pap. 21.95 (*1-56037-015-7*) Am Wrld Geog.
Montana, Montie. Montie Montana: (Not Without My Horse!) (Illus.). 350p. 1993. pap. 19.95 (*1-883472-55-5*) Double M CA.
Montana Palaez, Servando, ed. see Canales, Nemesio.
***Montana, Pat.** Babies Inc. (Bundles of Joy) (Sil Romance Ser.). 1995. mass mkt. 2.99 (*0-373-19076-X*, 1-19076-8) Silhouette.
— One Unbelievable Man. (Silhouette Romance Ser.). 1994. pap. 2.75 (*0-373-08993-7*, 5-08993-3) Silhouette.
— Storybook Cowboy. 1995. mass mkt. 2.99 (*0-373-19111-1*, 1-19111-3) Silhouette.
Montana, Patrick. Management. 1987. pap. 11.95 (*0-8120-3559-3*) Barron.
Montana, Patrick & Charnov, Bruce. Management. 2nd ed. LC 92-27960. (Barron's Business Review Ser.). 492p. 1993. pap. 11.95 (*0-8120-1549-5*) Barron.
Montana, Patrick J. Preretirement Planning: A Plan Sponsor's Guide. 128p. (Orig.). 1988. pap. 25.00 (*0-89154-364-3*) Intl Found Employ.
Montana, Patrick J., ed. Marketing in Nonprofit Organizations. LC 78-18322. 316p. reprint ed. pap. 90.10 (*0-317-26847-3*, 2023547) Bks Demand.
Montana, Patrick J. & Roukis, George S., eds. Managing Terrorism: Strategies for the Corporate Executive. LC 82-11224. 182p. 1983. text ed. 49.95 (*0-89930-013-8*, MTE/, Quorum Bks) Greenwood.
Montana, Patrick J., jt. ed. see Roukis, George S.
Montana, Ron. The Cathedral Option. (Orig.). 1978. pap. 2.25 (*0-89083-404-0*) Zebra.
Montana, Shelkie, jt. auth. see Montana, Hunter.
Montanari, Armando, et al, eds. Urban Landscape Dynamics: A Multi-Level Innovation Process. (Urban Europe Ser.). 395p. 1993. 68.95 (*1-85628-203-1*, Pub. by Avebury Technical UK) Ashgate Pub Co.
Montanari, D. Dizionario Delle Attivita Sementiere E Vivais Tiche. 270p. (DUT, ENG, FRE, GER & ITA.). 1981. 35.00 (*0-8288-0038-3*, M15642) Fr & Eur.
Montanari, Donata, illus. Shadow Magic! (J). (ps up). 1994. bds. 6.95 (*1-55550-991-6*) Universe.
Montanari, F. & Casella, L., eds. Metalloporphyrins Catalyzed Oxidations. LC 93-43396. (Catalysis by Metal Complexes Ser.: Vol. 17). 368p. (C). 1994. lib. bdg. 145.50 (*0-7923-2657-1*) Kluwer Ac.
Montanari, Franco. I Frammenti Dei Grammatici Agathokles, Hellanikos, Ptolemaios Epithetes: In Appendice I Grammatici Theophilos, Anaxagoras, Xenon. (Sammlun Griechischer und Lateinisher Grammatik Ser.: Vol. 7). vi, 265p. (C). 1988. lib. bdg. 173.10 (*0-89925-538-8*) De Gruyter.
— I Frammenti Dei Grammatici Agathokles, Hellanikos, Ptolemaios Epithetes: In Appendice I Grammatici Theophilos, Anaxagoras, Xenon. (Sammlun Griechischer und Lateinisher Grammatik Ser.: Vol. 7). vi, 265p. (C). 1988. lib. bdg. 173.10 (*3-11-010721-X*) De Gruyter.
Montanari, Massimo. The Culture of Food. Ipsen, Carl, tr. (Making of Europe Ser.). 224p. 1994. 24.95 (*0-631-18265-9*) Blackwell Pubs.
***Montanari, Richard.** Deviant Way. 288p. 1995. 22.00 (*0-684-80357-7*) S&S Trade.
Montanari, Richard, et al. Strategic Management: A Choice Approch. 1216p. (C). 1990. text ed. 54.00 (*0-03-008857-7*) Dryden Pr.
Montanari, Sally. Look Again! Clues to Modern Paintings. (Illus.). 68p. (Orig.). 1989. pap. 8.95 (*0-913515-36-1*, Starrhill) Elliott & Clark.
Montanari, U., jt. ed. see Habermann, A. Nico.
Montanaro. Getting by in Chinese. (Getting by Language Ser.). 90p. 1983. pap. 4.95 (*0-8120-2665-9*) Barron.
— Getting by in Chinese, Set. (Getting by Language Ser.). 90p. 1983. Book & cassette set. audio 18.95 (*0-8120-7152-2*) Barron.
Montanaro, Ann R. Pop-up & Movable Books: A Bibliography. (Illus.). 588p. 1992. 59.50 (*0-8108-2650-X*) Scarecrow.
Montanaro, John. Complex & Simplified Forms of Chinese Characters with Conversion Tables. rev. ed. (Mirror Ser. C-16: No. C-16). 88p. (CHI.). 1985. 4.95 (*0-88710-142-9*) Yale Far Eastern Pubns.
Montanaro, John S., ed. Chinese Vocabulary Cards. rev. ed. (CHI & ENG.). 1987. 13.95 (*0-88710-126-7*) Yale Far Eastern Pubns.
Montanaro, Karen H., jt. auth. see Montanaro, Tony.
Montanaro, Silvana Q. Understanding the Human Being: The Importance of the First Three Years of Life. (Illus.). 166p. (Orig.). (C). 1991. pap. text ed. 14.95 (*1-879341-00-X*) N Montessori.
***Montanaro, Tony & Montanaro, Karen H.** Mime Spoken Here: A Practical Guide to the Art of Performing. 1995. 34.95 (*0-88448-178-6*); pap. 19.95 (*0-88448-177-8*) Tilbury Hse.
Montand, Y. Biography of Fr. Alexander Menn: A Modern Saint of Russia. Bigham, Steven, tr. 150p. 1995. write for info. (*1-879038-12-9*) Oakwood Pubns.
Montand, Yves. Tu Vois, Je N'ai Pas Oublie. 1992. pap. 24.50 (*0-679-41012-0*) McKay.
Montandon, Denys, et al. Plastic & Reconstructive Surgery of the Orbitopalpebral Region. (Illus.). 360p. 1990. text ed. 98.00 (*0-443-04486-4*) Churchill.
Montaner, Carlos. The Witches' Poker Game & Other Stories. Robinson, Robert, tr. LC 73-84203. 171p. 1973. pap. 1.95 (*0-913480-18-5*) Inter Am U Pr.
Montaner, Carlos A. Cuba: Claves para una Conciensa en Crisis. 154p. 1982. pap. text ed. 18.95 (*84-359-0286-2*) Transaction Pubs.
— Fidel Castro: Y la Revolucion Cubana. 255p. 1983. pap. text ed. 24.95 (*84-359-0344-3*) Transaction Pubs.
— Fidel Castro & the Cuban Revolution: Age, Position, Character, Destiny, Personality, & Ambition. 244p. 1989. 32.95 (*0-88738-235-5*) Transaction Pubs.
— Two Hundred Years of Gringos. Fernandez de la Torriente, Gaston & Horton, James F., trs. 142p. (Orig.). (C). 1983. lib. bdg. 45.00 (*0-8191-3374-4*); pap. text ed. 19.50 (*0-8191-3375-2*) U Pr of Amer.
***Montaner, Josep M.** Museums for the New Century. (Illus.). 192p. (ENG & SPA.). 1995. pap. 55.00 (*84-252-1631-1*, Pub. by Gustavo Gili SP) Rizzoli Intl.
— New Museums. (Illus.). 192p. 1990. 22.50 (*0-910413-84-3*) Princeton Arch.
Montanez-Cartaxo, Luis E., jt. ed. see Vieitez-Utesa, Luis.
***Montanez, Jose A.** Medical Device Quality Assurance Manual. (Illus.). 300p. 1995. ring bd. 225.00 (*0-935184-84-8*) Interpharm.
Montange, Charles H. Preserving Abandoned Railroad Rights-of-Way for Public Use: A Legal Manual. 178p. (Orig.). (C). 1989. pap. text ed. 42.50 (*0-925794-00-7*) Rails Trails.
Montano, Judith. The Crazy Quilt Handbook. LC 86-71560. (Illus.). 80p. (Orig.). 1986. pap. 18.95 (*0-914881-05-1*) C & T Pub.
— Crazy Quilt Odyssey: Adventures in Victorian Needlework. Frankel, Candie, ed. LC 90-86060. (Illus.). 128p. (Orig.). 1991. pap. 21.95 (*0-914881-41-8*) C & T Pub.
Montano, Judith B. The Art of Silk Ribbon Embroidery. Townsend, Louise O., ed. LC 92-53801. (Illus.). 80p. 1993. pap. 21.95 (*0-914881-55-8*) C & T Pub.
— Elegant Stitches: An Illustrated Stitch Guide & Source Book of Inspiration. Konzak-Kuhn, Barbara, ed. (Illus.). 176p. 1995. pap. 24.95 (*0-914881-85-X*, 10106) C & T Pub.
— Recollections. Nadel, Harold, ed. LC 92-44544. (Illus.). 152p. 1993. 16.95 (*0-914881-59-0*, 10071) C & T Pub.
Montano, Linda. Art in Everyday Life. LC 81-65318. (Illus.). 152p. (Orig.). 1981. pap. 10.00 (*0-937122-05-X*) Astro Artz.
Montano, Macrina C., ed. see Zollars, Jean A.
***Montano, Mary.** Loving Mozart: A Past Life Memory of the Composer's Final Years. 239p. 1995. pap. 12.95 (*0-9642577-0-X*) Cantus Verus.
Montano, Rocco. Dante's Thought & Poetry. (Orig.). 1988. pap. 14.95 (*0-89526-771-3*) Regnery Pub.
— Shakespeare's Concept of Tragedy: The Bard As Anti-Elizabethan. LC 85-4536. 288p. 1986. pap. 12.00 (*0-89526-810-8*) Regnery Pub.
Montano, Severino. Selected Plays of Severino Montano, Vol. 1. (Illus.). 234p. (Orig.). 1982. pap. 7.50 (*0-686-37565-3*, Pub. by New Day Pub PH) Cellar.
— Selected Plays of Severino Montano, Vol. 2. (Illus.). 319p. (Orig.). 1982. pap. 8.50 (*0-686-37566-1*, Pub. by New Day Pub PH) Cellar.
— Selected Plays of Severino Montano, Vol. 3. (Illus.). 64p. (Orig.). 1983. pap. 5.00 (*971-10-0046-6*, Pub. by New Day Pub PH) Cellar.
Montante, Joseph C. Life...A Competitive Nightmare: How to Target Yourself for Success. Allen, Eunice M., ed. LC 90-83997. (Illus.). 220p. (Orig.). 1991. pap. 12.95 (*0-9625822-3-9*) Apex MI.
Montanus. Lotus 1-2-3: Self-Paced. 208p. (C). 1990. spiral bd. 19.95 (*0-8403-5876-8*) Kendall-Hunt.
Montanus, Charlotte, jt. auth. see Montanus, Mark.
Montanus, Charlotte, et al. Micro Skills Lab: Beginning WordPerfect Works for DOS. 244p. 1994. pap. 15.95 (*0-534-24108-5*) Boyd & Fraser.
— Micro Skills Lab: Intermediate WordPerfect Works for DOS. 255p. 1994. pap. 15.95 (*0-534-24109-3*) Boyd & Fraser.
— Micro Skills Lab: Microsoft Excel for the Macintosh, Version 4.0. 226p. 1995. pap. 16.95 (*0-534-24111-5*) Boyd & Fraser.
— Micro Skills Lab: Microsoft Excel 5.0. 267p. 1994. pap. text ed., spiral bd. 14.95 (*0-534-24112-3*) Intl Thomson.
— Micro Skills Lab: Microsoft Word for the Macintosh, Version 5.0, 5.1. 204p. 1994. pap. 15.95 (*0-534-24110-7*) Boyd & Fraser.
— Micro Skills Lab: WordPerfect 6.0 & 6.0e for Windows. 399p. 1994. spiral bd. 14.95 (*0-534-24113-1*) Intl Thomson.
Montanus, Mark & Montanus, Charlotte. Microsoft Works for Macintosh: A Beginning Computer Literacy Manual Using Software Version 2.X. 224p. 1992. spiral bd. 22.95 (*0-8403-7387-2*) Kendall-Hunt.
— Microsoft Works for the Macintosh: An Intermediate Computer Literacy Manual Using Software Version 2.X. 196p. 1992. 3.5 hd, spiral bd. 22.95 (*0-8403-7884-X*) Kendall-Hunt.
Montanus, Mark, et al. Essentials of WordPerfect 5: Perfect Mastery Step by Step. 368p. 1992. disk, spiral bd. 24.95 (*0-8403-7211-6*) Kendall-Hunt.
— Essentials of WordPerfect 5.1: Perfect Mastery Step by Step. 368p. 1991. disk, spiral bd. 24.95 (*0-8403-7376-7*) Kendall-Hunt.
— Essentials of WordPerfect 5.1: Perfect Mastery Step by Step. 2nd ed. 368p. 1992. disk, spiral bd. 24.95 (*0-8403-8115-8*) Kendall-Hunt.
Montapert, Alfred A. Distilled Wisdom. 10th ed. LC 64-8181. 1977. 8.95 (*0-9603174-0-6*, 21618) Bks of Value.
— Inspiration & Motivation: Noblest & Finest Ideas for Successful Living. 1982. 9.95 (*0-13-467605-X*) Borden.
— Laws of Life: Nature's Laws to Successful Living. 1992. per. 10.00 (*0-614-04219-4*) Bks of Value.
— Personal Planning Manual. LC 67-12652. 1967. 4.95 (*0-9603174-1-4*, 85920) Bks of Value.
— Personal Planning Manual. 1977. pap. 6.95 (*0-87505-364-5*) Borden.
— Pray to Win! A Blueprint for Success. LC 86-73037. 235p. 1986. per. 4.95 (*0-9603174-4-9*) Bks of Value.
— The Supreme Philosophy of Man. 7th ed. LC 70-119515. 1977. 2.95 (*0-9603174-2-2*) Bks of Value.
— Supreme Philosophy of Man: The Laws of Life. 1977. pap. 4.95 (*0-686-85728-3*) Borden.
— The Way to Happiness. LC 77-13678. 1978. pap. 2.95 (*0-9603174-3-0*) Bks of Value.
— The Way to Happiness. (Eternal Quest of Mankind Ser.). 1978. pap. 2.95 (*0-13-946228-7*) Borden.
— Words of Wisdom to Live By: An Encyclopedia of Wisdom in Condensed Form. LC 86-73036. 280p. 1986. per. 4.95 (*0-9603174-5-7*) Bks of Value.
Montaser, Akbar & Golightly, D. W., eds. Inductively Coupled Plasmas in Analytical Atomic Spectrometry. 2nd ed. LC 92-25254. 1017p. 1992. 195.00 (*1-56081-514-0*) VCH Pubs.
***Montasser, Thomas.** Lexikon der Rechtsbegriffe. 512p. (GER.). 1991. 29.95 (*0-7859-8566-2*, 3927117692) Fr & Eur.
Montauk, Susan L. & Grasha, Anthony. Adult HIV Outpatient Care: A Handbook for Clinical Teaching. 754p. (C). 1993. write for info. (*0-9639194-0-7*) U Cinn CMFM.
Montavon, Jay. A History Mystery: The Curse of King Tut's Tomb. 96p. (Orig.). (J). 1991. pap. 3.50 (*0-380-76220-X*, Camelot) Avon.
Montazedi, Bob. Beginner's Guide to Safe & Easy RC Flying. Emmerich, Michael, ed. (Illus.). 72p. (Orig.). 1992. pap. 9.95 (*0-89024-114-7*, 12104) Kalmbach.
Montbayet, Jean P. Carriers. 1990. 12.99 (*0-517-01219-7*) Random Hse Value.
***Montcrieff, Ascott R.** Myths & Legends of Ancient Greece. LC 94-39818. 1995. 9.99 (*0-517-11861-0*) Random Hse Value.
***Monte, Christopher F.** Beneath the Mask: An Introduction to the Theories of Personality. 5th ed. LC 94-30056. (C). 1994. text ed. 56.00 (*0-15-501541-9*) HB Coll Pubs.
— Beneath the Mask: An Introduction to Theories of Personality. 4th ed. 700p. (C). 1991. text ed. 46.75 (*0-03-033708-9*) HB Coll Pubs.
— Merlin: The Sorcerer's Guide to Survival in College. 130p. (C). 1990. pap. 10.95 (*0-534-13482-3*) Intl Thomson.
— Still, Life: Clinical Portraits in Psychopathology. LC 92-49802. 240p. 1992. pap. text ed. 21.00 (*0-13-137217-3*) P-H.
Monte, Evelyn, jt. ed. see Pisano, Beverly.
Monte, J. Fred Astaire Dance Book. (Ballroom Dance Ser.). 1986. lib. bdg. 250.00 (*0-8490-3363-2*) Gordon Pr.
— Fred Astaire Dance Book. (Ballroom Dance Ser.). 1985. lib. bdg. 250.00 (*0-87700-701-2*) Revisionist Pr.
Monte, Providencia C., ed. Learning Modules for the Basic Course in English, Vol. 1. LC 79-22332. 304p. 1980. pap. 7.00 (*0-8477-3423-4*) U of PR Pr.
Monte, Rudeen. Working Together. (Illus.). 240p. 1985. teacher ed 34.95 (*0-915950-70-7*) Bull Pub.
Monte, Tom. The Way of Hope: Michio Kushi's Anti-AIDS Program. 1990. pap. 12.95 (*0-446-39174-3*) Warner Bks.
Monte, Tom, jt. auth. see Decoz, Hans.
Monte, Tom, jt. auth. see EastWest Natural Health Editors.
Monte, Tom, jt. auth. see Lawson, Margaret.
Monte, Tom, jt. auth. see Ohashi, Watari.
Monte, Tom, jt. auth. see Prevention Magazine Health Books Editors.
Monte, Tom, jt. auth. see Sattilaro, Anthony J.
Monteath, C. D. Applications of the Electromagnetic Reciprocity Principle. 1973. 72.00 (*0-08-016895-7*, Pub. by Pergamon Repr UK) Franklin.
Monteath, Peter. The Spanish Civil War in Literature, Film & Art: An International Bibliography of Secondary Literature. LC 94-16070. (Bibliographies & Indexes in World Literature Ser.: No. 43). 160p. 1994. text ed. 55.00 (*0-313-29262-0*, Greenwood Pr) Greenwood.
— Writing the Good Fight: Political Commitment in the International Literature of the Spanish Civil. LC 93-21130. (Contributions to the Study of World Literature Ser.: No. 52). 240p. 1994. text ed. 55.00 (*0-313-28766-X*, Greenwood Pr) Greenwood.
Montebello, Anthony R. Work Teams That Work: Skills for Managing Across the Organization. 1994. 24.95 (*0-9636268-1-7*) Best Sell Pub.
Montecel, Maria R., et al. Hispanic Families As Valued Partners: An Educator's Guide. (Illus.). 90p. (Orig.). 1993. pap. 19.95 (*1-878550-47-0*) Inter Dev Res Assn.
Montecino, Marcel. Big Time. Rubenstein, Julie, ed. 544p. 1991. reprint ed. mass mkt. 5.99 (*0-671-70971-2*, Pocket Star Bks) PB.
— Crosskiller. 1989. mass mkt. 5.99 (*0-671-67894-9*) PB.
Montefiore, Alan, ed. Neutrality & Impartiality. 320p. 1975. pap. 10.95 (*0-521-09923-4*) Cambridge U Pr.
— Philosophy in France Today. LC 82-9730. 200p. 1983. 69.95 (*0-521-22838-7*); pap. 19.95 (*0-521-29673-0*) Cambridge U Pr.
Montefiore, C. G. Ancient Jewish & Greek Consolation. LC 75-184052. 86p. (C). 1973. text ed. 7.95 (*0-87677-045-6*) Hartmore.
Montefiore, Claude G. Judaism & St. Paul. LC 73-2222. (Jewish People; History, Religion, Literature Ser.). 1978. reprint ed. 25.95 (*0-405-05284-7*) Ayer.
— Some Elements of the Religious Teaching of Jesus According to the Synoptic Gospels. LC 73-2223. (Jewish People; History, Religion, Literature Ser.). 1973. reprint ed. 19.95 (*0-405-05285-5*) Ayer.
Montefiore, Claude J. Lectures on the Origin & Growth of Religion As Illustrated by the Religion of the Ancient Hebrews. 3rd ed. LC 77-27162. (Hibbert Lectures: 1892). reprint ed. 59.50 (*0-404-60410-2*) AMS Pr.
Montefiore, Hugh. Communicating the Gospel in a Scientific Age. 76p. (C). 1988. pap. text ed. 24.00 (*0-7152-0631-1*) St Mut.
— Credible Christianity: The Gospel in Contemporary Society. LC 94-16689. xii, 287p. 1994. 19.99 (*0-8028-3768-9*) Eerdmans.
— Reclaiming the High Ground: A Christian Response to Secularism. 155p. 1990. text ed. 45.00 (*0-312-04247-7*) St Martin.
— So Near & Yet So Far: Rome, Canterbury & ARCIC. 160p. (C). 1986. pap. text ed. 11.95 (*0-334-01517-0*, SCM Pr) TPI PA.
Montefiore, Hugh, ed. Communicating the Gospel in a Scientific Age. 76p. (C). 1989. pap. 20.00 (*0-685-60689-9*, Pub. by St Andrew UK) St Mut.
Montefiore, Hugh, jt. auth. see Dominian, Jack.
Montefiore, Jan. Feminism & Poetry: Language, Experience, Identity in Women's Writing. 224p. 1994. pap. 13.00 (*0-04-440893-5*, Pub. by Pandora UK) Harper SF.
Montegna, Donna. Prisoner of Innocence. LC 89-12775. 120p. (Orig.). 1989. pap. 8.95 (*0-9613205-7-5*) Launch Pr.
Monteil, C. Soudan Francais. LC 78-20138. (Collection de contes et de chansons populaires: Vol. 28). reprint ed. 21.50 (*0-404-60378-5*) AMS Pr.
Monteil, Charles. Les Khassonke: Monographie d'Une Peuplade du Soudan Francais. (B. E. Ser.: No. 137). (FRE.). 1915. 39.00 (*0-8115-3060-4*) Periodicals Srv.
— Soudan Francais: Contes Soudanaises. (B. E. Ser.: No. 119). (FRE.). 1905. 20.00 (*0-8115-3048-5*) Periodicals Srv.
Monteilhet, Hubert. Sophie ou les Galanteries Exemplaires. (FRE.). 1978. pap. 10.95 (*0-7859-4097-9*) Fr & Eur.
Monteiro, Anthony, jt. auth. see Perlo, Victor.
Monteiro, Barry E. Airline Career Opportunities. 52p. 1994. pap. 12.95 (*0-9639973-0-0*) Airline Career.
Monteiro, Cynthia B. Paralegal Preparation of Pleadings. (Paralegal Law Library: No. 1977). 456p. 1991. ring bd. 95.00 (*0-471-58774-5*) Wiley.
— Paralegal Preparation of Pleadings. suppl. ed. (Paralegal Law Library: No. 1977). 200p. 1993. 45.00 (*0-471-58705-2*) Wiley.
— Paralegal Preparation of Pleadings Supplement, No. 3. 176p. 1991. pap. text ed. 35.00 (*0-471-58778-8*) Wiley.
Monteiro, George. The Coffee Exchange. LC 82-81571. (Illus.). 77p. (Orig.). (C). 1982. pap. 3.50 (*0-943722-02-0*) Gavea-Brown.
— Critical Essays on Hemingway's Farewell to Arms. LC 94-19102. (Critical Essays on American Literature Ser.). 208p. 1994. text ed. 45.00x (*0-7838-0011-8*, Twayne) Macmillan.
— Henry James & John Hay: The Record of a Friendship. LC 65-24094. 219p. reprint ed. 62.50 (*0-685-15757-1*, 2027519) Bks Demand.
— Robert Frost & the New England Renaissance. LC 88-5479. 192p. 1988. 21.00 (*0-8131-1649-X*) U Pr of Ky.
Monteiro, George, ed. Correspondence of Henry James & Henry Adams, 1877-1914. LC 91-5175. (Illus.). 128p. (C). 1992. text ed. 22.50 (*0-8071-1729-3*) La State U Pr.
Monteiro, George, tr. Fernando Pessoa: Self-Analysis & Thirty Other Poems. LC 88-82009. 89p. 1988. 10.00 (*0-943722-14-4*) Gavea-Brown.
Monteiro, George, tr. see Almeida, Onesimo T., ed.
Monteiro, George, tr. see Jorge de Sena.
Monteiro, George, tr. see Migueis, Jose R.
Monteiro, J. J. Angola & the River Congo, 2 vols., Set. 1968. reprint ed. 85.00 (*0-7146-1838-1*, BHA-01838, Pub. by F Cass Pubs UK) Intl Spec Bk.
***Monteiro, Kenneth.** Pak: Ethnicity & Psychology. (C). 1994. student ed write for info. (*0-7872-0470-6*); 32.94 (*0-7872-0471-4*); pap. text ed. write for info. (*0-7872-0425-0*) Kendall-Hunt.
Monteiro, Mariana. Legends & Popular Tales of the Basque People. 1976. lib. bdg. 59.95 (*0-8490-2143-X*) Gordon Pr.
— Legends & Popular Tales of the Basque People. LC 72-173115. 1972. reprint ed. 18.95 (*0-405-08796-9*, Pub. by Blom Pubns UK) Ayer.
Monteiro, Mario. Aleixo Garcia: Descobridor Portuguez do Paraguay & da Bolivia em 1524-1525. LC 24-20323. 69p. 1983. reprint ed. lib. bdg. 20.00x (*0-89370-795-3*) Borgo Pr.
Monteiro Marques, Manuel D. Differential Inclusions in Nonsmooth Mechanical Problems: Shocks & Dry Friction. LC 93-17931. (Progress in Nonlinear Differential Equations & Their Applications Ser.: Vol. 9). 179p. 1993. 69.00 (*0-8176-2900-9*) Birkhauser.
Monteiro, Palmyra V. A Catalogue of Latin American Flat Maps, 1926-1964, Vols. 1 & 2, 1. LC 67-64686. (Guides & Bibliographies Ser.: No. 2). reprint ed. pap. 102.80 (*0-685-17114-0*, 2027325) Bks Demand.
— A Catalogue of Latin American Flat Maps, 1926-1964, Vols. 1 & 2, 2. LC 67-64686. (Guides & Bibliographies Ser.: No. 2). reprint ed. pap. 110.50 (*0-685-17115-9*) Bks Demand.
Monteiro, Paulo, jt. auth. see Mehta, P. Kumar.
Monteith, J. L. & Unsworth, M. Principles of Environmental Physics. 2nd ed. (Illus.). 228p. 1989. 60.00 (*0-7131-2981-6*, Pub. by E Arnold UK); pap. 29.95 (*0-7131-2931-X*, Pub. by E Arnold UK) Routledge Chapman & Hall.
Monteith, J. L., ed. see Easter School of Agricultural Science (20th: 1973: University of Nottingham) Staff.
Monteith, Jay. ABCs African Art Coloring Book. (Illus.). 32p. (J). (ps-3). 1992. pap. text ed. 6.95 (*0-9627366-3-5*) Arts & Comns NY.
— African Art: Activity Workbook. (Illus.). 24p. (Orig.). (J). 1993. pap. text ed. 8.75 (*0-9627366-4-3*) Arts & Comns NY.

An Asterisk (*) at the beginning of an entry indicates that the title is appearing in BIP for the first time.

— A Multicultural Activity Workbook: Africa, Asia & the Americas. (Illus.). 72p. (Orig.). (J). (gr. 1 up). 1991. pap. text ed. 7.95 (*0-9627366-1-9*) Arts & Comns NY.

Monteith, John & Webb, Colin. Soil-Water & Nitrogen: In Mediterranean-Type Environments. 1981. lib. bdg. 121.50 (*90-247-2406-6*) Kluwer Ac.

Monteith, Marcy, ed. Taste California: A Sampling of the Golden State. (Illus.). 150p. (Orig.). 1993. pap. text ed. 11.95 (*0-9638619-0-5*) CA Dietetic.

Monteith, Moira. Computers & Language. 160p. (Orig.). 1993. pap. text ed. 22.95 (*1-871516-27-7*, Pub. by Intellect Bks UK) Cromland.

Monteith, Moira, ed. Women's Writing: A Challenge to Theory. LC 86-10056. 192p. 1986. text ed. 35.00 (*0-312-88798-1*) St Martin.

Monteith, Moira & Miles, Robert, eds. Teaching Creative Writing: Theory & Practice. 192p. 1992. 90.00 (*0-335-15685-1*, Open Univ Pr); pap. 32.00 (*0-335-15684-3*, Open Univ Pr) Taylor & Francis.

Monteith, Stanley. AIDS, the Unnecessary Epidemic: America under Seige. 392p. 1991. pap. 14.95 (*0-925591-17-3*) Covenant Hse Bks.

Monteith, W. Graham. Disability: Faith & Acceptance. 126p. (C). 1988. pap. text ed. 35.00 (*0-7152-0614-1*) St Mut.

Montejano, David. Anglos & Mexicans in the Making of Texas, 1836-1986. (Illus.). 397p. 1987. pap. 14.95 (*0-292-77596-2*) U of Tex Pr.

Montejano, Luis, et al. Beta-Homotopy Equivalences Have Alpha Cross Sections. LC 82-20616. (Memoirs Ser.: No. 41/274). 37p. 1982. pap. 16.00 (*0-8218-2274-8*, MEMO 41/274) Am Math.

Montejo, Victor. The Bird Who Cleans the World: And Other Mayan Fables. Kaufman, Wallace, tr. LC 90-52757. (Illus.). 128p. (Orig.). (J). 1991. 22.95 (*0-915306-93-X*); pap. 13.95 (*1-880684-03-9*) Curbstone.

— Sculpted Stones. Perera, Victor, tr. 128p. 1995. pap. 12.95 (*1-880684-14-4*) Curbstone.

— Testimony: Death of a Guatemalan Village. Perera, Victor, tr. LC 86-71063. 144p. 1987. pap. 9.95 (*0-915306-65-4*) Curbstone.

Montejo, Victor D. El Kanil: Man of Lightning. 61p. (ENG & SPA.). 1984. 6.95 (*0-930095-01-4*) Signal Bks.

Montel, Edmee, tr. see Mhire, Herman.

Montel, Edmee, tr. see Tucker, Mary L., et al.

Montel, Paul. Familles Normales. LC 73-14649. xiii, 301p. 1974. text ed. 19.95 (*0-8284-0271-X*) Chelsea Pub.

Montel, Pierre. Enciclopedia De la Fotografria. 464p. (SPA.). 1975. 49.95 (*0-8288-5864-0*, S50554) Fr & Eur.

Monteleone, James A. Recognition of Child Abuse for the Mandated Reporter. 252p. (C). 1994. per. 32.00 (*1-878060-14-7*) GW Medical. PEDIATRICIANS AREN'T THE ONLY ONES WHO NEED ADVICE ON REPORTING CHILD ABUSE, YET MOST PERTINENT REFERENCES ARE FOR THEIR EYES ONLY. THIS BOOK IS A BREAKTHROUGH. IT ADVISES THE BROAD RANGE OF ADULTS WORKING WITH CHILDREN ON HOW TO IDENTIFY CHILD ABUSE WHEN THEY HAVE "REASON TO SUSPECT" IT & EMPOWERS THEM TO REPORT IT. This book is a must for TEACHERS, NURSES, SOCIAL WORKERS, DAY-CARE WORKERS, LAW ENFORCEMENT AGENCIES & others who work with children & are lawfully or morally expected to recognize & report abused children to state social services. Included is revealing information about how the legal & social systems process a child abuse case. Table of Contents: Identifying physical abuse; Burns, Sexual abuse; Multiple personalities & dissociative disorders; Munchausen syndrome by proxy; Neglect & abandonment; Emotional abuse; The cycle of abuse; Legal issues; Working with child abuse victims in the classrooms; Abuse, schools & the law; Prevention. ***Publisher Provided Annotation.***

Monteleone, John. A Day in the Life of a Major League Baseball Player. LC 90-36052. (Day in the Life of...Ser.). (Illus.). 32p. (J). (gr. 4-8). 1991. lib. bdg. 11.79 (*0-8167-2216-1*); pap. text ed. 2.95 (*0-8167-2217-X*) Troll Assocs.

***Monteleone, John J., ed.** Branch Rickey's Little Blue Book: Wit & Strategy from Baseball's Last Wise Man. LC 95-4146. 1995. write for info. (*0-02-860400-8*) Macmillan.

Monteleone, Joseph P., jt. auth. see Cottrell, Paul.

Monteleone, Sue A., comp. Data Recovery at Prehistoric Localities at U19af, Pahute Mesa, Nye County, Nevada. (Illus.). 31p. 1991. 4.00 (*0-945920-63-6*) Desert Rsch Inst.

Monteleone, Thomas F. Blood of the Lamb. 448p. 1993. mass mkt. 5.99 (*0-8125-2222-2*) Tor Bks.

— Borderlands. 1990. pap. 3.95 (*0-380-75924-1*) Avon.

— The Resurrectionist. 1995. 19.95 (*0-446-51906-5*, Aspect) Warner Bks.

Monteleone, Thomas F., ed. Borderlands Two. 304p. (Orig.). 1991. mass mkt. 4.99 (*0-380-76517-9*) Avon.

Monteleone, Tom. Borderlands 2. 1994. pap. 4.99 (*1-56504-108-9*, 11802) White Wolf.

— Necropolis Atlanta. 1994. per., pap. 4.99 (*1-56504-164-X*, 6200) White Wolf.

Montelius, O. Civilization of Sweden in Heathen Times. LC 68-25251. (World History Ser.: No. 48). (Illus.). 1969. reprint ed. lib. bdg. 75.00 (*0-8383-0216-5*) M S G Haskell Hse.

Montelius, Oscar. Dating in the Bronze Age with Special Reference to Scandinavia. 148p. (Orig.). 1986. pap. 37.50x (*91-7402-182-6*) Coronet Bks.

Montell, Lynwood, ed. see Ancelet, Barry J., et al.

Montell, William L. Don't Go up Kettle Creek: Verbal Legacy of the Upper Cumberland. LC 82-8566. (Illus.). 264p. 1983. text ed. 31.00x (*0-87049-365-5*) U of Tenn Pr.

— Ghosts along the Cumberland: Deathlore in the Kentucky Foothills. LC 74-32241. (Illus.). 272p. 1975. pap. 16.95 (*0-87049-535-6*) U of Tenn Pr.

— Kentucky Ghosts. LC 93-37211. (New Books for New Readers Ser.). 64p. (C). 1993. pap. 4.50 (*0-8131-0909-4*) U Pr of Ky.

— Killings: Folk Justice in the Upper South. 216p. 1994. pap. 17.00 (*0-8131-0824-1*) U Pr of Ky.

— Saga of Coe Ridge: A Study in Oral History. LC 74-77846. (Illus.). 256p. 1970. 31.00x (*0-87049-096-6*); pap. 16.00x (*0-87049-315-9*) U of Tenn Pr.

— Singing the Glory Down: Amateur Gospel Music in South Central Kentucky, 1900-1991. LC 91-8688. (Illus.). 264p. 1991. text ed. 27.00 (*0-8131-1757-7*) U Pr of Ky.

— Upper Cumberland. LC 93-6972. (Folklife in the South Ser.). (Illus.). 256p. 1993. text ed. 37.50 (*0-87805-630-0*); pap. 16.95 (*0-87805-631-9*) U Pr of Miss.

Montell, William L. & Morse, Michael L. Kentucky Folk Architecture. LC 76-4437. (Kentucky Bicentennial Bookshelf Ser.). (Illus.). 120p. 1976. 10.00 (*0-8131-0230-8*) U Pr of Ky.

— Kentucky Folk Architecture. (Illus.). 120p. 1995. pap. 9.95 (*0-8131-0843-8*) U Pr of Ky.

Montella, Ralph. Plastics in Architecture: A Guide to Acrylic & Polycarbonate. LC 85-1645. (Plastics Engineering Ser.: No. 10). (Illus.). 231p. reprint ed. pap. 65.90 (*0-7837-0868-8*, 2041176) Bks Demand.

Montellano, Marisol. Mammalian Fauna of the Judith River Formation, Late Cretaceous, Judithian, Northcentral Montana. (Publications in Geological Sciences: Vol. 136). (C). 1992. pap. 17.00 (*0-520-09768-8*) U CA Pr.

Montemagno, U., et al, eds. Neuroendocrinology of Female Reproductive Function: Proceedings of the 2nd International Capri Conference on Neuroendocrine & Peripheral Disorders of Female Reproductive System--Pathophysiology & Therapies, Capri, May 1992. LC 93-5174. (International Congress, Symposium & Seminar Ser.: No. 4). (Illus.). 450p. 1993. 75.00 (*1-85070-509-7*) Prthnon Pub.

Montemayer, Raymond, et al, eds. Personal Relationships During Adolescence. (Advances in Adolescent Development Ser.: Vol. 6). (C). 1994. text ed. 52.00 (*0-8039-5680-0*); pap. text ed. 24.00 (*0-8039-5681-9*) Sage.

Montemayor, Aurelio M. Workshops on Workshops. (Illus.). 106p. (Orig.). 1988. pap. text ed. 16.95 (*1-878550-09-8*) Inter Dev Res Assn.

Montemayor, Aurelio M. & Cavazos, Charles, eds. Valued Youth Anthology: Articles on Dropout Prevention. 118p. (Orig.). 1989. pap. text ed. 14.95 (*1-878550-27-6*) Inter Dev Res Assn.

***Montemayor, Carlos.** Blood Relations. Carter, Dale & Gonzalez, Alfonso, trs. LC 95-1265. (Contemporary Latin-American Classics in English Translation Ser.). 111p. 1995. 17.95 (*0-917635-16-7*) Plover Pr.

Montemayor, Carlos, ed. see Rulfo, Juan.

***Montemayor, Jorge de.** Siete Libros de Diana. Moreno Baez, Enrique, ed. 239p. (SPA.). 1968. pap. 100.00 (*0-614-00109-9*) Elliots Bks.

— Siete Libros de Diana. Moreno Baez, Enrique, ed. 239p. (SPA.). 1968. pap. 100.00 (*0-614-00214-1*) Elliots Bks.

Montemayor, Raymond, et al, eds. From Childhood to Adolescence: A Transitional Period? (Advances in Adolescent Development Ser.: Vol. 2). (Illus.). 300p. (C). 1990. 52.00 (*0-8039-3725-3*); pap. 24.00 (*0-8039-3726-1*) Sage.

Montemurro, Donald G. & Bruni, J. Edward. The Human Brain in Dissection. 2nd ed. (Illus.). 208p. 1988. pap. 27.50 (*0-19-504926-8*) OUP.

Montenari, F. W., et al, eds. Resource Mobilization for Drinking Water & Sanitation in Developing Nations. 768p. 1987. 62.00 (*0-87262-629-6*) Am Soc Civil Eng.

Montenat, C. & Plateaux, L. How to Read the World: Creation & Evolution. (How-to Ser.). (Illus.). 144p. 1985. pap. 10.95 (*0-8245-0721-5*) Crossroad NY.

Montenbruck, O. Astronomy on the Personal Computer. 2nd ed. 1994. disk 59.00 (*0-387-57700-9*) Spr-Verlag.

Montenbruck, O. & Pfleger, T. Astronomy on the Personal Computer. Dunlop, S., tr. (Illus.). 272p. 1991. disk 51.00 (*0-387-52754-0*) Spr-Verlag.

Montenegro Duque, Angel, et al. Historia de Espana: 2. Espana Romana, Vol. I: La Conquista y la Explotacion Economica. 762p. 1992. 189.50x (*84-239-4983-4*) Elliots Bks.

Montenegro, Hugo D., jt. ed. see Nochomovitz, Micheal L.

Montenegro, Laura. Sweet Tooth. LC 93-49643. (J). 1995. 14.95 (*0-395-68078-6*) HM.

Montenegro, Laura N. One Stuck Drawer. LC 90-46139. (Illus.). 32p. (J). (gr. k-3). 1991. 14.95 (*0-395-57319-X*) HM.

Montenegro, M. Irene, et al, eds. Microelectrodes: Theory & Applications. (C). 1991. lib. bdg. 164.00 (*0-7923-1229-5*) Kluwer Ac.

Montenegro, Omar L. El Desierto que Canta: Poesia Underground Cubana. 85p. (SPA.). (C). 1993. pap. 8.00 (*1-884619-01-0*) Endowment CAS.

Montenegro, Xenia. Women & Racial Minority Representation in School Administration, 1993. 20p. 1993. pap. 11.00 (*0-87652-203-7*, 21-00417) Am Assn Sch Admin.

Monteon, Michael. Chile in the Nitrate Era: The Evolution of Economic Dependence, 1880-1930. LC 81-70009. 284p. 1982. 35.00 (*0-299-08820-0*) U of Wis Pr.

Monter, E. William. European Witchcraft. 177p. (C). 1969. pap. text ed. write for info. (*0-394-34197-X*) Random.

Monter, William. Frontiers of Heresy: The Spanish Inquisition from the Basque Lands to Sicily. (Studies in Early Modern History). (Illus.). 360p. (C). 1990. 59.95 (*0-521-37468-5*) Cambridge U Pr.

Monterde, Francisco, ed. see Raluy Poudevila, Antonio.

***Monterey Bay Aquarium Foundation Staff.** Mating Games, Nineteen Ninety-Three. (Illus.). 32p. (Orig.). 1993. pap. 5.95 (*1-878244-09-4*) Monterey Bay Aquarium.

Monterey History & Art Association Staff. Old Capital Cookbook. 316p. 1989. 17.95 (*0-9627008-0-0*) Monterey Hist & Art.

***Montero, Gloria.** The Summer the Whales Sang. (YA). (gr. 5 up). 1995. 16.95 (*0-88862-904-4*); pap. 6.95 (*0-88862-903-6*) Formac Dist Ltd.

Montero, Jaime A. Gatan & Talaw. (Sagada Folk Tales Ser.: No. 1). (Illus.). (Orig.). (J). (gr. 1-3). 1984. pap. 3.50 (*971-10-0164-0*, Pub. by New Day Pub PH) Cellar.

Montero, Julio, ed. see Blanc, Iris & Hildebrandt, Elinore J.

Montero, Lidia D., tr. see Goetz, Joan.

Montero, Luis A. & Smeyers, Yves G. Trends in Applied Theoretical Chemistry. LC 92-12289. (Topics in Molecular Organization & Engineering Ser.: Vol. 9). 224p. (C). 1992. lib. bdg. 109.50 (*0-7923-1745-9*) Kluwer Ac.

Montero, Miguel, tr. see Ronnholm, Ursula O.

Montero, Oscar. The Name Game: The Semiotic Intertext of De donde son los cantantes. (Studies in the Romance Languages & Literatures: No. 231). 160p. (C). 1988. pap. 22.50 (*0-8078-9236-X*) U of NC Pr.

Montero, Oscar, tr. see Molloy, Sylvia.

Montero, Rosa. Absent Love: A Chronicle. De la Torre, Cristina & Glad, Diana, trs. LC 90-28657. xxiv, 188p. 1991. 30.00 (*0-8032-3141-5*); pap. 9.95 (*0-8032-8176-5*) U of Nebr Pr.

— The Delta Function. Easton, Kari & Gavilan, Yolanda M., trs. LC 91-16576. (European Women Writers Ser.). viii, 267p. 1992. 35.00 (*0-8032-3152-0*); pap. 14.95 (*0-8032-8183-8*) U of Nebr Pr.

Monterrosa, Ricardo, tr. see Quain, Bill.

***Monterroso.** Los Buscadores de Oro: The Gold Searchers. 1995. pap. 12.50 (*0-679-76098-9*, Villard Bks) Random.

***Monterroso, Augusto.** Complete Works (And Other Stories) Grossman, Edith, tr. LC 95-14550. (Texas Pan American Ser.). 1995. write for info. (*0-292-75183-4*); pap. write for info. (*0-292-75184-2*) U of Tex Pr.

***Montes.** Using Microsoft Works 4 for MacIntosh. 1994. pap. 27.99 (*1-56529-920-5*) Que.

Montes, Al. Robots & Gardens: Science Fantasy Poems. 48p. 1985. 4.00 (*0-918476-14-3*) Cornerstone Pr.

***Montes, Alfredo & Holle, M.** El Cultivo de las Amarilidaceas: Cebolla, Ajo y Puerro. 47p. (C). 1987. pap. 4.00 (*1-885995-00-8*) Escuela Agricola.

— Guia Practica para el Cultivo de Hortalizas. 47p. (C). 1993. pap. text ed. 5.00 (*1-885995-07-5*) Escuela Agricola.

***Montes, Alfredo & O., M. Holle.** El Oultivo Del Esparrago En el Tropico. 90p. (SPA.). (C). 1994. pap. 8.00 (*1-885995-15-6*) Escuela Agricola.

Montes, Carmel. Computer Shorthand: Dictionary. 151p. (C). 1987. pap. 13.99 (*0-9618340-0-5*) Prof Educ Dist.

Montes De Oca, Marco A. Twenty-One Poems. Miller, Yvette E., ed. Villasenor, Laura, tr. LC 82-20833. 80p. (ENG & SPA.). 1982. pap. 9.00 (*0-935480-09-9*) Lat Am Lit Rev Pr.

Montes, Elizabeth & Hart, Corinne. Baby's Baptism: Sacrament of Welcome. (Illus.). 32p. 1990. reprint ed. pap. text ed. 3.60 (*1-55944-019-8*, 9444) Franciscan Comns.

Montes, Elizabeth, jt. auth. see Aisenberg, Gino.

Montes, Fernando. Enciclopedia de la Sexualidad. 944p. 1975. 44.95 (*0-8288-5865-9*, S32223) Fr & Eur.

Montes-Huidobro, Matias. Funeral en Teruel. (Teatro Ser.). 96p. (SPA.). 1989. pap. 15.00 (*0-945791-05-4*) Editorial Persona.

— Obras en un Acto. (Teatro Ser.). (Illus.). 128p. (Orig.). (SPA.). 1989. pap. 15.00 (*0-945791-06-2*) Editorial Persona.

— Ojos para No Ver. LC 79-52160. (Coleccion Teatro). (Illus.). 59p. (SPA.). 1980. pap. 6.00 (*0-89729-229-4*) Ediciones.

— Persona: Vida y Mascara en el Teatro Puertorriqueno. LC 84-19721. (Illus.). 560p. (SPA.). (C). 1984. pap. 15.00 (*0-913480-61-4*) Inter Am U Pr.

Montes-Huidobro, Matias, ed. see Hernandez, Guillermo.

Montes, Manuel Velez. Public Policy for Developing Market Economies. 119p. 1969. pap. 2.50 (*0-8477-2425-5*) U of PR Pr.

Montesano, R., ed. see International Agency for Research on Cancer Staff & Catholic University of Louvain Staff.

Montesano, R., ed. see International Agency for Research on Cancer Staff.

Montesano, R., ed. see International Agency for Research on Cancer Staff & Commission of the European Communities.

Montesano, R., et al, eds. Long-term & Short-term Assays for Carcinogens: A Critical Appraisal. (IARC Scientific Publications: No. 83). (Illus.). 580p. 1987. pap. 70.00 (*92-832-1183-9*) OUP.

— Molecular & Cellular Aspects of Carcinogen Screening Tests. (IARC Scientific Publications: No. 27). (Illus.). 372p. 1986. 43.00 (*0-19-723027-X*) OUP.

Montesi, Al. Peter Bently: The Super Sleuth Cat. 60p. 1987. pap. 5.00 (*0-918476-15-1*) Cornerstone Pr.

— Windows & Mirrors. LC 77-89821. 1977. 3.95 (*0-918476-00-3*) Cornerstone Pr.

Montesinos, Jose M. Classical Tesselations & Three Manifolds. (Universitext Ser.). (Illus.). xvii, 230p. 1987. pap. text ed. 44.00 (*0-387-15291-1*) Spr-Verlag.

Montesinos, L. Fernando. Memorias Antiguas Historiales del Peru. Means, Philip A., ed. (Hakluyt Society Works Ser.: No. 2, Vol. 48). (Illus.). 1974. reprint ed. 35.00 (*0-8115-0354-2*) Periodicals Srv.

Montesquieu. Lettres Persanes. (Folio Ser.: No. 475). (FRE.). pap. 9.95 (*2-07-036475-5*) Schoenhof.

— Selected Political Writings. rev. ed. Richter, Melvin, tr. & intro. by. LC 89-29578. 299p. (C). 1990. reprint ed. lib. bdg. 32.50 (*0-87220-091-4*); reprint ed. pap. text ed. 9.95 (*0-87220-090-6*) Hackett Pub.

Montesquieu, Charles D. The Persian Letters. Healy, George R., tr. LC 62-21265. 1964. 29.50 (*0-672-51053-7*) Irvington.

Montesquieu, Charles-Louis de. De l'Espirit des Lois: Les Grands Themes. 1970. 9.95 (*0-686-54781-0*) Fr & Eur.

— De l'Esprit des Lois, 2 vols. 566p. 1973. Vol. 1, 566p. 19.95 (*0-8288-7485-9*); Vol. 2, 753p. 19.95 (*0-8288-7486-7*); write for info. (*0-685-74480-9*) Fr & Eur.

— Oeuvres Completes, 2 tomes, 1. deluxe ed. Caillois, ed. (Pleiade Ser.). (FRE.). 84.95 (*2-07-010365-X*) Schoenhof.

— Oeuvres Completes, 2 tomes, 2. deluxe ed. Caillois, ed. (Pleiade Ser.). (FRE.). 88.95 (*2-07-010366-8*) Schoenhof.

— Persian Letters. Betts, C. J., tr. (Classics Ser.). 1973. pap. 10.95 (*0-14-044281-2*, Penguin Classics) Viking Penguin.

— The Spirit of the Laws. 1969. pap. 13.95 (*0-317-30542-5*) Free Pr.

— The Spirit of the Laws: A Compendium of the First English Editon with an English Translation of "An Essay on Causes Affecting Mind & Characters", 1737-1743. Carrithers, David W., ed. 1978. 50.00 (*0-520-02566-0*); pap. 16.00 (*0-520-03455-4*) U CA Pr.

Montesquiou-Fezensac, Raymond. The Russian Campaign, Eighteen Hundred Twelve. LC 70-90563. 159p. reprint ed. pap. 45.40 (*0-318-34879-9*, 2031091) Bks Demand.

Montessori. Pedagogie Scientifique, 3 tomes, Set. 99.95 (*0-685-33998-X*) Fr & Eur.

***Montessori, Maria.** The Absorbent Mind. LC 95-18404. 1995. pap. write for info. (*0-8050-4156-7*, Owl) H Holt & Co.

— The Absorbent Mind. 1993. reprint ed. lib. bdg. 25.95x (*1-56849-212-X*) Buccaneer Bks.

— Collected Works. 1973. 500.00 (*0-87968-894-7*) Gordon Pr.

— The Discovery of the Child. 1986. mass mkt. 5.95 (*0-345-33656-9*) Ballantine.

— Discovery of the Child. 1976. 23.95 (*0-8488-0583-6*) Amereon Ltd.

— Dr. Montessori's Own Handbook. LC 65-14827. (Illus.). 192p. (C). 1988. pap. 11.00 (*0-8052-0921-2*) Schocken.

— Dr. Montessori's Own Handbook. (Basic Montessori Library Ser.). (Illus.). 170p. reprint ed. pap. text ed. 8.50 (*0-916011-01-1*) Ed Sys Pub.

— The Montessori Elementary Materials. Livingston, Arthur, tr. (Basic Montessori Library Ser.). (Illus.). 166p. pap. text ed. 14.95 (*0-916011-03-8*) Ed Sys Pub.

— The Montessori Method. LC 64-24014. 416p. (C). 1988. pap. 14.00 (*0-8052-0922-0*) Schocken.

— Montessori Method. 1976. 24.95 (*0-8488-0303-5*) Amereon Ltd.

— The Secret of Childhood. 1982. mass mkt. 4.95 (*0-345-30583-3*) Ballantine.

— The Secret of Childhood: A Book for All Parents & Teachers. Carter, Barbara B., tr. viii, 239p. (C). 1983. text ed. 14.95 (*0-86131-375-5*, Pub. by Kalakshetra Pubns II) N Montessori.

— Spontaneous Activity in Education. (Basic Montessori Library Ser.). (Illus.). 384p. 1984. pap. 12.95 (*0-916011-02-X*) Ed Sys Pub.

Montet, Pierre. Everyday Life in Egypt in the Days of Ramesses the Great. LC 80-26390. 400p. 1981. pap. 21.95 (*0-8122-1113-8*) U of Pa Pr.

— Everyday Life in Egypt in the Days of Ramesses the Great. Maxwell-Hyslop, A. R. & Drower, Margaret S., trs. LC 74-3625. (Illus.). 365p. 1974. reprint ed. text ed. 65.00 (*0-8371-7446-5*, MOLE, Greenwood Pr) Greenwood.

Montet-White, Anta, jt. ed. see Dibble, Harold L.

Montevecchi, William A. & Tuck, Leslie M. Newfoundland Birds: Exploitation, Study, Conservation. (Publications of the Nuttall Ornithological Club: No. 21). (Illus.). 273p. 1987. 10.50 (*1-877973-31-9*) Nuttall Ornith.

Monteverde, Alonso A. Pan-Americanism from Monroe to the Present: A View from the Other Side. rev. ed. Zatz, Asa, tr. LC 68-13659. 192p. reprint ed. pap. 54.80 (*0-7837-3914-1*, 2043762) Bks Demand.

Monteverdi, Claudio. Madrigals, Bk. 8. 1991. pap. 13.95 (*0-486-26739-3*) Dover.

— Madrigals, Bks. 4-5. 1991. pap. 12.95 (*0-486-25102-0*) Dover.

— Ten Madrigals. Stevens, Denis, ed. 1979. pap. 22.95 (*0-19-343676-0*) OUP.

***Montey, Sharon.** Looking Out for Ollie. (Storybridge Ser.). 80p. (J). (gr. 3-7). 1995. pap. 9.95 (*0-7022-2734-X*, Pub. by Univ Queensland Pr AT) Intl Spec Bk.

An Asterisk (*) at the beginning of an entry indicates that the title is appearing in BIP for the first time.

Montez, Lola. The Arts of Beauty: Or, Secrets of a Lady's Toilet, with Hints to Gentlemen on the Art of Fascinating. LC 77-19081. 1978. reprint ed. 4.95 (0-912946-52-0) Ecco Pr.
— The Arts of Beauty: Or, Secrets of a Lady's Toilet with Hints to Gentlemen on the Art of Fascination. 125p. 1986. reprint ed. pap. 14.95 (0-933883-01-3) Aquarius Rising Pr.
Montez, Susan. Radio-Free Queens. LC 93-39304. 80p. 1994. pap. 10.95 (0-8076-1345-2) Braziller.
Montfiro, H., tr. see Consigleri, Pederoso.
***Montford.** Contraceptive Care: Meeting Individual Needs. 256p. 1993. pap. 47.75 (1-56593-213-7, 0554) Singular Publishing.
Montford, John T., et al. A Guide to Texas Workers' Compensation Reform, 2 vols., Set. 1000p. 1991. ring bd. 250.00 (0-409-25480-0) Michie Butterworth.
***Montfort, Alain & Van Dijk, Herman K., eds.** Econometric Inference Using Simulation Techniques. LC 95-7779. 1995. text ed. 65.00 (0-471-95623-6) Wiley.
***Montfort, Catherine R., ed.** Literature Women & the French Revolution of 1789. LC 94-69023. (Illus.). 318p. 1995. lib. bdg. 45.95 (1-883479-07-X) Summa Pubns.
Montfort, Elizabeth S. That Special Magic. LC 87-71719. (Illus.). 53p. (Orig.). (J). (gr. 2-3). 1988. pap. 5.00 (0-916383-37-7) Aegina Pr.
Montfort, Matthew C. Ancient Traditions-Future Possibilities: Rhythmic Training Through the Traditions of Africa, Bali & India. Delma, Adriana, ed. LC 86-60024. 141p. (C). 1987. pap. text ed. 24.95 (0-937879-00-2) Panoramic Pr CA.
Montgomerie, G. A., ed. see Bayliss, J. S.
Montgomerie, G. A., ed. see Monds, F.
Montgomerie, G. A., ed. see Ryan, C. G.
Montgomerie, G. A., ed. see Verschuur, J. J.
Montgomerie, G. A., ed. see Williams, L. A.
Montgomery. Animal Biology Lab Manual. 96p. (C). 1992. spiral bd. 9.95 (0-8403-8178-6) Kendall-Hunt.
— At the Alter: Matrimonial Tales. 1995. mass mkt. 4.99 (0-553-56748-9) Bantam.
— Carpal Tunnel Syndrome. 1995. 10.95 (1-880688-03-4) New Life Opt.
— Castle of Doom. (Choose Your Own Nightmare Ser.: No. 04). 1995. pap. (0-553-48232-7) Bantam.
— Possessed. (Choose Your Own Adventure Ser.: No. 161). (J). 1995. mass mkt. 3.50 (0-553-56723-3) Bantam.
— Tattoo of Death. (Choose Your Own Adventure Ser.: No. 159). (J). 1995. mass mkt. 3.50 (0-553-56616-4) Bantam.
Montgomery & Atkins. Decision Making in Cardiac Life Support, No. 1. 1991. 49.00 (0-941158-50-0) Mosby Yr Bk.
— Decision Making in Emergency Cardiology. 1991. 40.00 (0-8016-3486-5) Mosby Yr Bk.
Montgomery, jt. auth. see Keats.
Montgomery, jt. auth. see Mandelker, Daniel R.
Montgomery, et al. Biochemistry: A Case-Oriented Approach. 5th ed. (Illus.). 896p. 1990. pap. text ed. 44.95 (0-8016-3549-7); International ed. pap. text ed. 20.95 (0-8016-5495-5) Mosby Yr Bk.
Montgomery, Albert A. Washington Municipal Expenditures, 1941-1957: An Economic Analysis. LC 63-63374. (Illus.). 179p. reprint ed. pap. 51.10 (0-8357-8370-7, 2034104) Bks Demand.
Montgomery, Alexander. The Cherrie & the Slaye. Composed in Scottis Meeter. LC 72-219. (English Experience Ser.: No. 338). 32p. 1971. reprint ed. 20.00 (90-221-0338-2) Walter J Johnson.
Montgomery, Anne, ed. BioPharm Conference Proceedings '93. 133p. 1993. pap. text ed. 45.00 (0-943330-39-4) Advanstar Commns.
Montgomery, Austin, jt. auth. see Riley, William B.
Montgomery, Barbara M. & Duck, Steve, eds. Studying Interpersonal Interaction. LC 90-20933. (Communication Ser.). 346p. 1993. lib. bdg. 37.95 (0-89862-312-X); pap. text ed. 18.95 (0-89862-290-5) Guilford Pr.
Montgomery, Becky, jt. auth. see Grimm, Carol.
Montgomery, Bernard. Approach to Sanity: A Study of East-West Relations. LC 74-156696. (Essay Index Reprint Ser.). 1977. reprint ed. 17.95 (0-8369-2779-6) Ayer.
— The Memoirs of Field Marshal Montgomery. (Quality Paperbacks Ser.). (Illus.). 508p. 1982. reprint ed. pap. 10.95 (0-306-80173-6) Da Capo.
Montgomery, Bertha & Nabwire, Constance. Cooking the African Way. (Easy Menu Ethnic Cookbooks Ser.). (Illus.). 48p. (J). (gr. 5 up). 1988. lib. bdg. 14.95 (0-8225-0919-9, Lerner Publctns) Lerner Group.
Montgomery, Bill. Senior Citizen Alert. 1991. pap. 9.95 (0-9630975-0-4) Mont Assocs.
***Montgomery, Bob.** The Truth about Success & Motivation: Plain Advice on How to be One of Life's Real Winners. 170p. (Orig.). 1995. pap. 12.95 (0-85091-284-9, Pub. by Lothian Pub AT) Seven Hills Bk.
Montgomery, Bob & Hill, Willie. Learning to Sight Read Jazz, Rock, Latin, & Classical Styles. (Illus.). (C). 1994. pap. text ed. 27.95 (1-880157-16-0) Ardsley.
***Montgomery, Bob & Morris, Laurel.** Living with Anxiety: A Practical Research-Based Plan for Managing Anxiety Problems. 232p. (Orig.). 1995. pap. 14.95 (0-85091-425-6, Pub. by Lothian Pub AT); digital audio, pap. 24.95 (0-85091-540-6, Pub. by Lothian Pub AT); digital audio 11.95 (0-85091-539-2, Pub. by Lothian Pub AT) Seven Hills Bk.
— Surviving: Coping with a Life Crisis. 210p. (Orig.). 1995. pap. 14.95 (0-85091-370-5, Pub. by Lothian Pub AT) Seven Hills Bk.
— Your Good Health: A Whole Health Program to Live Healthier, Live Happier, & Live Longer. 264p. (Orig.). 1995. pap. 14.95 (0-85091-411-6, Pub. by Lothian Pub AT) Seven Hills Bk.
Montgomery, Bryan, jt. auth. see Allwood, John.
***Montgomery, Bucky.** The Stonebearer. (Orig.). (YA). (gr. 6 up). 1995. pap. 5.00 (0-88092-258-3) Royal Fireworks.
Montgomery, Carla W. Environmental Geology. 3rd ed. 480p. (C). 1991. pap. write for info. (0-697-14553-0) Wm C Brown Pubs.
— Environmental Geology. 4th ed. 512p. (C). 1994. pap. text ed. 45.00 (0-697-15811-X) Wm C Brown Pubs.
— Fundamentals of Geology. 160p. (C). 1990. student ed write for info. (0-697-10795-7) Wm C Brown Pubs.
— Fundamentals of Geology. (C). 1991. pap. write for info. (0-697-04297-9) Wm C Brown Pubs.
— Fundamentals of Geology. 2nd ed. 352p. (C). 1992. pap. text ed. write for info. (0-697-09806-0) Wm C Brown Pubs.
— Physical Geology. 3rd ed. 560p. (C). 1992. pap. text ed. write for info. (0-697-16555-8) Wm C Brown Pubs.
— Student Study Guide to Accompany Environmental Geology. 4th ed. 160p. (C). 1994. spiral bd. write for info. (0-697-15813-6) Wm C Brown Pubs.
Montgomery, Carla W. & Dathe, David. Earth: Then & Now. 640p. (C). 1991. pap. write for info. (0-697-11519-4) Wm C Brown Pubs.
— Earth: Then & Now. 2nd ed. 592p. (C). 1993. pap. text ed. write for info. (0-697-13622-1) Wm C Brown Pubs.
— Earth: Then & Now. 2nd ed. 592p. (C). 1993. Study guide. student ed write for info. (0-697-17232-5) Wm C Brown Pubs.
Montgomery, Carla W., jt. ed. see Perry, Eugene C., Jr.
Montgomery, Carol. Outlines. (Illus.). 32p. 1990. 35.00 (0-934714-21-5); pap. 3.00 (0-934714-20-7) Swamp Pr.
— Starting Something. LC 91-73630. 90p. (Orig.). 1992. pap. 6.95 (1-879603-01-2) Los Hombres.
Montgomery, Carol L. Healing Through Communication: The Practice of Caring. (Illus.). 180p. (C). 1993. text ed. 39.95 (0-8039-5120-5); pap. text ed. 17.95 (0-8039-5121-3) Sage.
Montgomery, Charles. The Choir Director's Handbook. Montgomery, Jane, ed. (Illus.). 44p. (Orig.). 1984. pap. 3.95 (0-916043-01-0) Light Hearted Pub Co.
Montgomery, Charles, ed. see Miller, Sarah W. & Madaris, Don L.
Montgomery, Charles, ed. see Montgomery, Jane.
Montgomery, Charlotte B. Como Darle una Mano a los Perros y los Gatos: (How to Be a Helping Hand for Dogs & Cats) (Illus.). 32p. (Orig.). (ENG & SPA.). (J). (gr. k). Date not set. pap. 3.00 (0-941246-07-8) NAHEE.
***Montgomery Co. Vocational Education Planning Dist, Center Career Development Program Staff.** Tuning into My Future: A Middle School Career Guidance Program. 36p. (J). (gr. 6-10). 1992. student ed, pap. write for info. (1-57515-038-7); teacher ed, pap. write for info. (1-57515-039-5) PPI Pubng.
Montgomery County Historical Society, Genealogy Section Staff. Family Histories, Montgomery County, Indiana. LC 89-51787. 416p. 1989. 49.95 (0-938021-74-5) Turner Pub KY.
***Montgomery, Cynthia A.** Resource-Based & Evolutionary Theories of the Firm: Towards a Synthesis. LC 95-3537. 288p. (C). 1995. lib. bdg. 87.50 (0-7923-9562-X) Kluwer Ac.
Montgomery, Cynthia A. & Porter, Michael E., eds. Strategy: Seeking & Securing Competitive Advantage. (Harvard Business Review Book Ser.). 512p. 1991. 29.95 (0-87584-243-7) Harvard Busn.
— Strategy: Seeking & Securing Competitive Advantage. 1991. text ed. 29.95 (0-07-103295-9) McGraw.
Montgomery, D. Children with Learning Difficulties. Mittler, Peter, ed. (Special Needs in Ordinary Schools Ser.). 304p. 1990. pap. text ed. 22.50 (0-304-31472-2) Cassell.
Montgomery, D. B. Montgomery: A Genealogy History of the Montgomerys & Their Descendants. (Illus.). 436p. 1991. reprint ed. lib. bdg. 77.50 (0-8328-1711-2); reprint ed. pap. 67.50 (0-8328-1712-0) Higginson Bk Co.
Montgomery, D. Bruce. Solenoid Magnet Design: The Magnetic & Mechanical Aspects of Resistive & Superconducting Systems. LC 79-13585. 328p. 1980. reprint ed. lib. bdg. 35.50 (0-88275-993-0) Krieger.
Montgomery, D. H., ed. Heroic Ballads. LC 68-58820. (Granger Index Reprint Ser.). 1977. 20.95 (0-8369-6031-9) Ayer.
***Montgomery, Dan.** God & Your Personality. LC 95-3256. 175p. 1995. reprint ed. pap. 9.95 (0-8198-3075-5, St Paul Editions) Pauline Bks.
— How to Survive Practically Anything. 221p. 1993. pap. 8.99 (0-89283-816-7, Vine Bks) Servant.
Montgomery, David. Beyond Equality: Labor & the Radical Republicans, 1862-1872. LC 80-24434. 552p. 1981. reprint ed. pap. 15.95 (0-252-00869-3) U of Ill Pr.
— Citizen Worker: The Experience of Workers in the United States with Democracy & the Free Market During the Nineteenth Century. 224p. (C). 1994. 22.95 (0-521-42057-1) Cambridge U Pr.
— Citizen Worker: The Experience of Workers in the United States with Democracy & the Free Market During the Nineteenth Century. 1995. pap. 13.95 (0-521-48380-8) Cambridge U Pr.
— The Fall of the House of Labor: The Workplace, the State, & American Labor Activism, 1865-1925. (Illus.). 464p. 1987. 44.95 (0-521-22579-5) Cambridge U Pr.
— The Fall of the House of Labor: The Workplace, the State, & American Labor Activism, 1865-1925. (Illus.). 464p. 1989. pap. 16.95 (0-521-37982-2) Cambridge U Pr.
— Mountain Man Crafts & Skills: An Illustrated Guide to Clothing, Shelter, Equipment & Wilderness Living. LC 80-82706. (Illus.). 1981. 16.98 (0-88290-156-7, 4024) Horizon Utah.
— Workers' Control in America: Studies in the History of Work, Technology, & Labor Struggles. 1980. pap. 15.95 (0-521-28006-0) Cambridge U Pr.
Montgomery, David, jt. auth. see Horne, Alistair.
Montgomery, David, jt. auth. see Horne, Alistaire.
Montgomery, David C. Mongolian Newspaper Reader. LC 78-627747. (Uralic & Altaic Ser.: Vol. 102). 203p. (Orig.). 1969. pap. text ed. 13.00 (0-87750-083-5) Res Inst Inner Asian Studies.
— Theory of the Unmagnetized Plasma. (Illus.). 412p. 1971. 169.00 (0-677-03350-8) Gordon & Breach.
Montgomery, David R. Indian Crafts & Skills: An Illustrated Guide for Making Authentic Indian Clothing, Shelters & Ornaments. LC 85-60510. 224p. 1985. 16.98 (0-88290-300-4) Horizon Utah.
Montgomery, Deane & Zippin, Leo. Topological Transformation Groups. LC 74-265. 302p. 1974. reprint ed. 26.00 (0-88275-169-7) Krieger.
Montgomery, Diana. Children with Learning Difficulties. 224p. 1990. pap. 29.95 (0-89397-351-3) Nichols Pub.
Montgomery, Diane. Educating the Able. 160p. 1995. pap. text ed. 22.50 (0-304-32587-2) Cassell.
***Montgomery, Don.** Authentic Hot Rods: The Real "Good Old Days" (Illus.). 208p. 1994. 32.95 (0-9626454-4-3) D Montgomery.
— Hot Rod Memories: Relived Again. (Illus.). 176p. 1991. 28.95 (0-9626454-2-7) D Montgomery.
— Supercharged Gas Coupes: Remembering the "Sixties" (Illus.). 192p. 1992. 30.95 (0-9626454-3-5) D Montgomery.
Montgomery, Don, ed. see Uarlamoff, Susan.
Montgomery, Donald R. Hot Rods As They Were: Another Blast from the Past. LC 90-164762. (Illus.). 160p. 1989. 26.95 (0-9626454-1-9) D Montgomery.
— Hot Rods in the Forties: A Blast from the Past. LC 90-164756. (Illus.). 144p. 1988. 26.95 (0-9626454-0-0) D Montgomery.
Montgomery, Donna, ed. see Tamler, Julie.
***Montgomery, Donna L.** Coffee Talk. (Illus.). 204p. (Orig.). 1995. pap. 12.95 (0-938577-09-3) St Johns Pub.
— Kids Plus Modeling Equal Money: How to Help Your Children Succeed in Modeling. 178p. 1984. 9.95 (0-13-515172-4) P-H.
— Love, Life & Chocolate Chip Cookies. 128p. (Orig.). 1995. pap. 6.95 (0-938577-10-7) St Johns Pub.
— Parenting a Business. LC 88-63423. (Illus.). (Orig.). 1989. pap. 14.95 (0-938577-04-2) St Johns Pub.
— Surviving Motherhood. (Illus.). 200p. (Orig.). 1986. pap. 6.95 (0-938577-00-X) St Johns Pub.
Montgomery, Dorothy. Countdown. (Illus.). (J). (gr. k-6). 1966. 4.50 (3-901170-10-3) CEF Press.
— Knowing Christ Song. (Illus.). 19p. (J). (gr. k-6). 1981. 2.99 (3-901170-25-1) CEF Press.
Montgomery, Dorothy B. Angling for Words: The Teacher's Line. 1975. pap. 10.00 (0-87879-105-1) Acad Therapy.
Montgomery, Dorothy B. & Gipson, Linda M. Basic Angling. (Angling for Words Ser.). 48p. teacher ed 8.00 (0-87879-519-7); student ed 10.00 (0-87879-518-9) Acad Therapy.
Montgomery, Douglas C. Design & Analysis of Experiments. 3rd ed. 649p. 1991. Net. text ed. write for info. (0-471-52000-4); write for info. (0-318-67349-5) Wiley.
— Introduction to Statistical Quality Control. 2nd ed. 744p. 1991. Net. text ed. write for info. (0-471-51988-X); teacher ed 20.00 (0-471-53523-0) Wiley.
***Montgomery, Douglas C. & Myers, Raymond H.** Response Surface Methodology: Process & Product in Optimization Using Designed Experiments. LC 94-45548. (Series in Probability & Mathematical Statistics). 1995. text ed. 59.95 (0-471-58100-3) Wiley.
Montgomery, Douglas C. & Peck, Elizabeth A. Introduction to Linear Regression Analysis. 2nd ed. (Probability & Mathematical Statistics: Applied Probability & Statistics Section Ser.: No. 1346). 544p. 1992. text ed. 64.95 (0-471-53387-4) Wiley.
Montgomery, Douglas C. & Runger, George C. Applied Statistics & Probability for Engineers. LC 93-29954. 896p. 1994. text ed. write for info. (0-471-54041-2) Wiley.
Montgomery, Douglas C., jt. auth. see Hines, William W.
Montgomery, Douglas C., jt. auth. see Johnson, Lynwood A.
Montgomery, Douglas C., et al. Forecasting & Time Series Analysis. 2nd ed. (Illus.). 400p. 1990. text ed. 55.00 (0-07-042858-1) McGraw.
Montgomery, Ed. Breaking the Spirit of Poverty. 154p. (Orig.). 1988. pap. 8.99 (0-914903-57-8) Destiny Image.
— What to Do When It Hurts So Bad. 240p. 1993. text ed. 14.99 (1-56043-770-7); pap. 12.99 (1-56043-124-5) Destiny Image.
Montgomery, Elizabeth. The Builder Also Grows. Ashton, Sylvia, ed. LC 77-82653. 1979. 19.95 (0-87949-099-3) Ashley Bks.
Montgomery, Elizabeth M. Best of MGM. 1993. 15.98 (1-55521-953-5) Bk Sales Inc.
Montgomery, Elizabeth M. & Rockwell, Norman. Norman Rockwell. (Gallery of Art Ser.). (Illus.). 176p. 1995. 19.98 (0-8317-6409-0) Smithmark.
Montgomery, Evelyn I. Giant on the Wall. rev. ed. LC 93-74248. (Illus.). 240p. 1993. lib. bdg. 17.95 (0-923687-30-0) Celo Valley Bks.
Montgomery, Florence M. Textiles in America, Sixteen Fifty to Eighteen Seventy. LC 83-42682. (Winterthur Museum Book Ser.). (Illus.). 412p. 1984. 45.00 (0-393-01703-6) Norton.
Montgomery, Frances T. Billy Whiskers: Autobiography of a Goat. (Illus.). 159p. (J). (gr. 2 up). 1985. reprint ed. pap. 4.50 (0-486-22345-0) Dover.
Montgomery, G. Gene, ed. The Evolution & Ecology of Armadillos, Sloths & Vermilinguas. LC 84-600292. (Illus.). 462p. (Orig.). 1986. pap. 49.95 (0-87474-649-3, MOESP) Smithsonian.
Montgomery, George. The Shadow Knew. Walsh, Joy, ed. (Esprit Critique Ser.). 30p. (Orig.). 1988. pap. 9.95 (0-938838-50-4) Textile Bridge.
***Montgomery, George A.** The Eye of the Eagle. 210p. Date not set. pap. 8.95 (0-7610-0431-9) NW Pub.
— Pillow of Gold. 256p. 1985. pap. 3.95 (0-939332-13-2) J Pohl Assocs.
Montgomery, Glenn E. & Schuch, Harold C. GIS Data Conversion Handbook. (Illus.). 319p. (Orig.). (C). 1993. text ed. 44.95 (0-9625063-4-6) GIS World Bks.
Montgomery, H. Mongoose Magoo. LC 68-56822. (Illus.). 64p. (J). (gr. 2-5). 1968. lib. bdg. 10.95 (0-87783-026-6) Oddo.
— Mongoose Magoo. deluxe ed. LC 68-56822. (Illus.). 64p. (J). (gr. 2-5). 1968. pap. 3.94 (0-87783-100-9) Oddo.
Montgomery, H. R. Memoirs of Sir Richard Steele, 2 vols., Set. LC 76-128570. (English Biography Ser.: No. 31). 1970. reprint ed. lib. bdg. 79.95 (0-8383-0903-8) M S G Haskell Hse.
Montgomery, Harry H., Jr. Personal Affairs: Family & Estate Records Organizer. LC 94-90049. (Illus.). 139p. 1994. ring bd. 34.95 (0-9640265-0-3) Windmark Pubns.
Montgomery, Henry & Svenson, Olga, eds. Process & Structure in Human Decision Making. 321p. 1989. text ed. 124.95 (0-471-91977-2) Wiley.
Montgomery, Herb & Montgomery, Mary. Splendor of the Psalms: A Photographic Meditation. LC 77-78261. (Books to Encourage & Inspire). (Illus.). 1977. pap. 6.95 (0-03-022956-1) Harper SF.
Montgomery, Herb, jt. auth. see Delbene, Ron.
Montgomery, Herb, jt. auth. see Montgomery, Mary.
Montgomery, Hugh. A Dictionary of Political Phrases & Allusions. 1972. 75.00 (0-8490-0044-0) Gordon Pr.
***Montgomery, Hugh L.** Ten Lectures on the Interface Between Analytic Number Theory & Harmonic Analysis. LC 94-26864. (Regional Conference Mathematics Ser.: No. 84). 1994. pap. 44.00 (0-8218-0737-4) Am Math.
Montgomery, Ian. London. (C). 1988. 30.00 (1-85368-028-1, Pub. by New Holland Pubs UK) St Mut.
Montgomery, J. P., ed. see Kreis, E. J.
Montgomery, Jacqueline. Physical Therapy for Traumatic Head Injury. 1994. 59.95 (0-443-08908-6) Churchill.
Montgomery, Jacqueline, jt. auth. see Hislop, Helen J.
Montgomery, James. Isaiah, 2 vols, 1. 1967. 2.50 (0-89315-125-4) Lambert Bk.
— Isaiah, 2 vols, 2. 1967. 2.50 (0-89315-126-2) Lambert Bk.
— Practical Detail of the Cotton Manufacture of the United States of America. LC 68-56266. (Library of Early American Business & Industry: No. 32). (Illus.). 219p. 1969. reprint ed. 35.00 (0-678-00572-9) Kelley.
Montgomery, James, et al. Poems on the Abolition of the Slave Trade. LC 79-149871. (Black Heritage Library Collection). 1977. 24.95 (0-8369-8751-9) Ayer.
Montgomery, James A. Arabia & the Bible. rev. ed. (Library of Biblical Studies). 1969. 25.00 (0-87068-090-0) Ktav.
— Daniel: Critical & Exegetical Commentary. Driver, Samuel R. et al, eds. LC 27-14200. (International Critical Commentary Ser.). 520p. 1926. 39.95 (0-567-05017-3, Pub. by T & T Clark UK) Bks Intl VA.
— Kings I & II: Critical & Exegetical Commentary. Driver, Samuel R. et al, eds. LC 52-8522. (International Critical Commentary Ser.). 624p. 1951. 39.95 (0-567-05006-8, Pub. by T & T Clark UK) Bks Intl VA.
Montgomery, James A. & Harris, Zellig S. The Ras Shamra Mythological Texts. LC 36-2726. (American Philosophical Society, Philadelphia. Memoirs Ser.: Vol. 4). 139p. reprint ed. pap. 39.70 (0-317-09878-0, 2000354) Bks Demand.
Montgomery, James D. & Fairbrothers, David E. New Jersey Ferns & Fern-Allies. LC 91-40920. (Illus.). 300p. (C). 1992. text ed. 45.00 (0-8135-1817-2) Rutgers U Pr.
Montgomery, James H. Dawn Two Thousand: Seven Million Churches to Go. LC 89-61042. 200p. (C). 1989. pap. 8.95 (0-87808-220-4) William Carey Lib.
Montgomery, James H. & McGavran, Donald A. The Discipling of a Nation. LC 80-17255. 1980. 4.80 (0-318-17874-5) Overseas Crusade.
Montgomery, James M. Water Treatment Principles & Design. LC 85-5344. 696p. 1985. text ed. 95.00 (0-471-04384-2, Wiley-Interscience) Wiley.
Montgomery, James R., et al. To Foster Knowledge: A History of the University of Tennessee, 1794-1970. LC 83-1050. (Illus.). 506p. 1983. text ed. 40.00x (0-87049-391-4) U of Tenn Pr.
Montgomery, James W. Liberated Woman: A Life of May Arkwright Hutton. LC 85-8401. (Illus.). 407p. 1985. reprint ed. 14.95 (0-87770-353-1); reprint ed. pap. 9.95 (0-87770-354-X) Ye Galleon.
Montgomery, Jane. The Handbook for the Ultimate Church Musician. Montgomery, Charles, ed. 1985. pap. 3.95 (0-916043-04-5) Light Hearted Pub Co.
— Old Songs, Fellowships & a Few Skits for Younger Senior Adults. Montgomery, Charles, ed. 1985. write for info. (0-916043-03-7) Light Hearted Pub Co.
Montgomery, Jane, ed. see Montgomery, Charles.
Montgomery, Jason & Fewer, Willard. Family Systems & Beyond. 174p. (C). 1988. 30.95 (0-89885-386-9) Human Sci Pr.
Montgomery, Jaye L. Sell Your Short Stories & Poetry. 88p. 1988. pap. 12.95 (0-86617-038-3) Multi Media TX.
Montgomery, Jill D. & Greif, Ann C., eds. Masochism: The Treatment of Self-Inflicted Suffering. 1989. 37.50x (0-8236-3145-1, BN#03145) Intl Univs Pr.
Montgomery, John. Brighton Past & Present. 96p. 1987. 30.00 (0-905392-70-1) St Mut.
— Fifties. 368p. 1965. 69.50 (0-614-00066-1) Elliots Bks.
— Fifties. 368p. 1965. 69.50 (0-614-00277-X) Elliots Bks.
— Troubleshooting Your Multimedia PC. LC 95-1577. 1995. pap. 19.95 (0-201-48347-5) Addison-Wesley.

— Underground Guide to Unix: Slightly Askew Advice from a Unix Wizard. 1995. pap. 24.95 (*0-201-40653-5*) Addison-Wesley.

Montgomery, John, comp. Kerouac at the "Wild Boar" & Other Skirmishes. LC 86-81178. 159p. 1986. 30.00 (*0-685-19183-4*); 48.00 (*0-918704-07-3*); pap. 16.95 (*0-918704-06-5*) Fels & Firn.

Montgomery, John, ed. The Kerouac We Knew: Unposed Portraits, Action Shots. rev. ed. LC 87-80922. 48p. 1987. kivar 5.25 (*0-918704-04-9*) Fels & Firn.

Montgomery, John, ed. see Kerouac, Jack.

Montgomery, John, tr. see Muston, Alexis.

Montgomery, John, jt. auth. see Thornley, Andy.

***Montgomery, John A.** Columbia: South Carolina: History. 1979. 17.95 (*0-89781-006-6*) Preferred Mktg.

Montgomery, John D. Bureaucrats & People: Grassroots Participation in Third World Development. LC 87-15344. (Studies in Development). 160p. 1988. text ed. 28.00 (*0-8018-3541-0*) Johns Hopkins.

Montgomery, John D. & Sullivan, William, frwds. Aftermath: Tarnished Outcomes of American Foreign Policy. LC 85-11176. 200p. (C). 1985. text ed. 45.00 (*0-86569-126-6*, Auburn Hse) Greenwood.

Montgomery, John D., jt. ed. see Carroll, Thomas F.

***Montgomery, John D., et al, eds.** Great Policies: Strategic Innovations in Asia & the Pacific Basin. LC 95-13915. 1995. text ed. write for info. (*0-275-95050-6*, Praeger Pubs) Greenwood.

— Patterns of Policy: Comparative & Longitudinal Studies of Population Events. LC 77-94305. 300p. 1979. 39.95 (*0-87855-269-3*) Transaction Pubs.

Montgomery, John F. History of Old Stone Presbyterian Church. 1983. write for info. (*0-9611706-0-3*) Old Stone Pres Church.

Montgomery, John H. Agrochemicals Desk Reference. 1993. 89.95 (*0-87371-738-4*, TD427) Lewis Pubs.

— Groundwater Chemicals Desk Reference, Vol. 2. 981p. 1991. 49.95 (*0-87371-554-3*, RA591) Lewis Pubs.

Montgomery, John H. & Welkom, Linda M. Ground Water Chemicals Desk Reference, Vol. I. (Illus.). 600p. 1989. 89.95 (*0-87371-286-2*, TD426) Lewis Pubs.

Montgomery, John W. Demon Possession. LC 75-19313. 1976. pap. 13.99 (*0-87123-102-6*) Bethany Hse.

— Faith Founded on Fact: Essays in Evidential Apologetics. 240p. (C). 1994. pap. text ed. 12.95 (*1-885914-01-6*) Trinity Bible Coll.

— History & Christianity. LC 83-47517. 128p. 1986. reprint ed. pap. 6.99 (*0-87123-890-X*) Bethany Hse.

— In Defense of Martin Luther. (Illus.). 1970. 2.50 (*0-8100-0026-1*, 12N0339) Northwest Pub.

— Principalities & Powers. LC 74-29081. 256p. 1981. pap. 10.99 (*0-87123-470-X*) Bethany Hse.

— The Suicide of Christian Theology. 528p. (C). 1993. pap. text ed. 21.95 (*1-885914-04-0*) Trinity Bible Coll.

***Montgomery, John W., ed.** Christianity for the Tough Minded: Essays in Support of an Intellectually Defensible Religious Commitment. 296p. (C). 1994. pap. text ed. 14.95 (*1-885914-00-8*) Trinity Bible Coll.

— Demon Possession: A Medical, Historical, Anthropological & Theological Symposium. 384p. (C). 1994. pap. text ed. 14.95 (*1-885914-05-9*) Trinity Bible Coll.

— Evidence for Faith: Deciding the God Question. LC 91-8917. 366p. (Orig.). (C). 1991. pap. 14.99 (*0-945241-15-1*) Probe Bks.

— God's Inerrant Word: A International Symposium on the Trustworthiness of Scripture. (C). 1994. pap. text ed. 14.95 (*1-885914-02-4*) Trinity Bible Coll.

Montgomery, John W., ed. see Fuller, Edmund, et al.

***Montgomery, Jonathan.** Health Care Law. 500p. 1995. pap. 17.95 (*0-19-876259-3*) OUP.

— Health Care Law. 500p. 1995. 49.95 (*0-19-876260-7*) OUP.

Montgomery, K. C., jt. auth. see Holmes, Frank, Jr.

Montgomery, K. Leon. Document Retrieval Systems: Factors Affecting Search Time. LC 75-18692. (Books in Library & Information Science: No. 14). 156p. reprint ed. pap. 44.50 (*0-7837-0928-5*, 2041233) Bks Demand.

Montgomery, Kate. Carpal Tunnel Syndrome: Prevention & Treatment. Gage, Diane, ed. (Illus.). 80p. (Orig.). 1992. Wkbk. student ed 14.95 (*1-878069-03-9*) Sports Touch.

— Carpal Tunnel Syndrome: Prevention & Treatment. 3rd rev. ed. Gage, Diane, ed. (Illus.). 80p. (Orig.). 1994. pap. 16.95 (*1-878069-35-7*) Sports Touch. CARPAL TUNNEL SYNDROME/ PREVENTION & TREATMENT. Fully illustrated with graphics & photographs...easy to read & follow! This book introduces a series of quick & easy techniques to correct, strengthen & prevent Carpal Tunnel Syndrome. Using these simple steps, you can change the structural misalignment that causes the entrapment & compression of the median nerve in the elbow & wrist. The program consists of correct posture, acupressure, self-massage, stretching & strengthening exercises to restore over-worked, over- strained & sore muscles to their original pain-free state. Alleviating stress & tension on the elbow & wrist joints. The only self-help manual of its kind that teaches specific corrective exercises. This is a NON-SURGICAL, DRUG-FREE APPROACH! "I found her method safe, cost effective & eliminates the need for surgical intervention in most cases. The exercises are simple & easy-to-do, with minimal amount of instruction. The corrective techniques are designed to be done anywhere. It is an answer to decreasing the workers compensation problem & getting employees back to work with minimal or no work time lost. I highly recommend this program."-- Warren Jacobs, MD. Sports Touch (R) Publishing, P.O. Box 221074, San Diego, CA 92192-1074. FAX: (619) 455-5039. ***Publisher Provided Annotation.***

— Sports Touch: The Athletic Ritual. Trainer, Beverly, ed. (Illus.). 162p. (Orig.). 1990. Wkbk. student ed 24.95 (*1-878069-00-4*) Sports Touch.

Montgomery, Kathryn C. Target: Prime Time: Advocacy Groups & Entertainment TV. (Communication & Society Ser.). (Illus.). 288p. 1989. 25.00 (*0-19-504964-0*) OUP.

— Target: Prime Time: Advocacy Groups & the Struggle over Entertainment Television. (Communication & Society Ser.). (Illus.). 288p. 1990. reprint ed. pap. 9.95 (*0-19-506320-1*) OUP.

Montgomery, L. June. Young Adults: A Call to Dialogue. LC 79-92088. 1980. 12.00 (*0-87212-112-7*) Libra.

Montgomery, L. M. Against the Odds. (YA). 1994. mass mkt. 4.50 (*0-553-56592-3*) Bantam.

— Anne of Avonlea. (Airmont Classics Ser.). (YA). (gr. 8 up). 1984. pap. 0.75 (*0-8049-0219-4*) Airmont.

— Anne of Avonlea. 304p. (YA). 1995. mass mkt. 2.99 (*0-8125-5196-6*) Tor Bks.

— Anne of Green Gables. (Airmont Classics Ser.). (YA). (gr. 7 up). 1984. pap. 1.95 (*0-8049-0218-6*) Airmont.

— Anne of Green Gables. (J). (gr. 1-7). 1994. pap. 12.95 (*0-7704-2589-5*, Little Rooster) Bantam.

— Anne of Green Gables. 1989. 4.95 (*0-87129-242-4*, A41) Dramatic Pub.

— Anne of Green Gables. (Illustrated Junior Library). (Illus.). (J). (gr. 4 up). 1983. 13.95 (*0-448-06030-2*, G&D) Putnam Pub Group.

— Anne of Green Gables. LC 93-36331. (Bullseye Step into Classics Ser.). 108p. (J). (gr. 2-6). 1994. pap. 2.99 (*0-679-85467-3*) Random Bks Yng Read.

— Anne of Green Gables. (YA). 1995. pap. 2.99 (*0-8125-5152-4*) Tor Bks.

— Anne of Green Gables. (Dover Children's Thrift Classics Ser.). (Illus.). 96p. (J). 1994. pap. text ed. 1.00 (*0-486-28366-6*) Dover.

— Anne of Green Gables. 429p. 1977. reprint ed. lib. bdg. 21.95 (*0-89966-262-5*) Buccaneer Bks.

— Anne of the Island. large type ed. LC 94-1765. 377p. (J). 1994. pap. 17.95 (*0-7862-0205-X*) Thorndike Pr.

— Emily of New Moon. large type ed. (Orig.). 1980. 12.00 (*0-7089-0401-7*) Ulverscroft.

— Emily's Quest. 1982. reprint ed. lib. bdg. 16.95 (*0-89966-418-0*) Buccaneer Bks.

— Rainbow Valley. braille ed. 422p. (J). 1992. vinyl bd. 33.76 (*1-56956-121-4*, BR8662) W A T Braille.

Montgomery, Lacy M. Among the Shadows. 1976. 21.95 (*0-8488-1433-9*) Amereon Ltd.

— Anne of Avonlea. 1976. 20.95 (*0-89190-155-8*, Am Repr) Amereon Ltd.

— Anne of Green Gables. 1976. 21.95 (*0-8488-0584-4*) Amereon Ltd.

— Anne of Ingleside. 1976. 21.95 (*0-8488-1101-1*) Amereon Ltd.

— Anne of the Island. 1976. 20.95 (*0-8488-0585-2*) Amereon Ltd.

— Anne of Windy Poplars. 1976. 20.95 (*0-8488-0586-0*) Amereon Ltd.

— Anne's House of Dreams. 1976. 18.95 (*0-8488-0587-9*) Amereon Ltd.

— Chronicles of Avonlea. 1976. 22.95 (*0-8488-0719-7*) Amereon Ltd.

— A Tangled Web. 1976. 23.95 (*0-8488-0722-7*) Amereon Ltd.

Montgomery, Lee, et al, eds. Transgressions: The Iowa Anthology of Innovative Fiction. LC 94-60574. 274p. (Orig.). 1994. pap. 19.95 (*0-87745-474-4*) U of Iowa Pr.

Montgomery, Linda J. Silent Strength. Alicino, Nick & Zopf, Jane, eds. LC 89-81213. (Illus.). 48p. (Orig.). 1989. pap. 16.95 (*0-9624768-0-3*) Divine Designs.

Montgomery, Lizzie W. Sketches of Old Warrenton, North Carolina: Traditions & Reminiscences of the Town & People Who Made It. (Illus.). 488p. 1984. reprint ed. 27.50 (*0-87152-393-0*, 83-23120) Reprint.

Montgomery, Louise. Mrs. Mahoney of the Tenement. LC 74-128741. (Short Story Index Reprint Ser.). (Illus.). 1977. 17.95 (*0-8369-3632-9*) Ayer.

Montgomery, Low, jt. auth. see Strider, Errol.

Montgomery, Lucy M. After Many Days. 1992. mass mkt. 3.99 (*0-553-29184-X*) Bantam.

— Akin to Anne: Tales of Other Orphans. 1990. mass mkt. 3.99 (*0-553-28387-1*) Bantam.

— Along the Shore: Tales by the Sea. 1990. mass mkt. 3.99 (*0-553-28589-0*) Bantam.

— Among the Shadows. (YA). 1991. mass mkt. 4.50 (*0-553-28959-4*) Bantam.

— Anne of Avonlea. (J). 1992. pap. 3.25 (*0-553-15114-2*) Bantam.

— Anne of Avonlea. LC 93-85541. (Courage Literary Classics Ser.). 256p. 1994. 5.98 (*1-56138-368-6*) Courage Bks.

— Anne of Avonlea. 288p. 1987. pap. 3.95 (*0-451-52113-7*, Sig Classics) NAL-Dutton.

— Anne of Avonlea. LC 92-10199. (Children's Classics Ser.). (Illus.). (YA). 1992. 12.99 (*0-517-08127-X*, Child Classics) Random Hse Value.

— Anne of Avonlea. (J). (gr. 4-7). 1991. pap. 3.25 (*0-590-44556-1*, Apple Classics) Scholastic Inc.

— Anne of Avonlea. large type ed. (Large Print Ser.). 435p. 1993. reprint ed. lib. bdg. 22.00 (*0-939495-26-0*) North Bks.

— Anne of Avonlea. large type ed. LC 93-22574. (YA). 1993. 15.95 (*1-56054-780-4*) Thorndike Pr.

— Anne of Avonlea, No. 2. 1984. pap. 2.95 (*0-553-21314-8*) Bantam.

— Anne of Avonlea: An Anne of Green Gables Story. (Illustrated Junior Library). (Illus.). 320p. (YA). 1990. 13.95 (*0-448-40063-4*, G&D) Putnam Pub Group.

— Anne of Green Gables. (J). 1982. 2.95 (*0-553-21313-X*, Bantam Classics) Bantam.

— Anne of Green Gables. (J). 1987. Boxed set. boxed 8.95 (*0-553-33306-2*) Bantam.

— Anne of Green Gables, 3 vols. (YA). (gr. 7-12). 1987. Boxed Set. boxed 8.85 (*0-553-33307-0*) Bantam.

— Anne of Green Gables. LC 93-70551. (Literary Classics Ser.). 240p. (J). (gr. 4 up). 1993. 5.98 (*1-56138-324-4*) Courage Bks.

— Anne of Green Gables. 338p. (YA). 1993. pap. 4.95 (*0-7710-9883-9*) Firefly Bks Ltd.

— Anne of Green Gables. (Illus.). 256p. (J). 1994. 25.00 (*0-88363-994-7*) H L Levin.

— Anne of Green Gables. 320p. 1987. pap. 3.95 (*0-451-52112-9*, Sig Classics) NAL-Dutton.

— Anne of Green Gables. 256p. (J). (gr. 5 up). 1994. pap. 2.99 (*0-14-035148-5*) Puffin Bks.

— Anne of Green Gables, 3 vols. in 1. 1988. 11.99 (*0-517-60517-1*) Random Hse Value.

— Anne of Green Gables. LC 87-31868. (Children's Classics Ser.). (J). 1988. 12.99 (*0-517-65958-1*) Random Hse Value.

— Anne of Green Gables. 384p. (J). (gr. 4-7). 1989. pap. 2.95 (*0-590-42243-X*, Apple Classics) Scholastic Inc.

— Anne of Green Gables. Mattern, Joanne, ed. LC 92-12703. (Illustrated Classics Ser.). (Illus.). 48p. (J). (gr. 3-6). 1992. lib. bdg. 12.89 (*0-8167-2866-6*); pap. text ed. 3.95 (*0-8167-2867-4*) Troll Assocs.

— Anne of Green Gables. large type ed. 448p. 1993. reprint ed. lib. bdg. 22.00 (*0-939495-25-2*) North Bks.

— Anne of Green Gables. large type ed. LC 92-43772. 484p. (YA). 1993. reprint ed. lib. bdg. 15.95 (*1-56054-643-3*) Thorndike Pr.

— Anne of Green Gables. 352p. (J). 1992. reprint ed. 16.95 (*1-55109-013-9*, Pub. by Nimbus Publishing Ltd CN) Chelsea Green Pub.

— Anne of Green Gables, Vol. 1. (J). (gr. 4-7). 1984. pap. 3.50 (*0-553-15327-7*) Bantam.

— Anne of Green Gables Birthday Book. (Illus.). (J). 1990. 8.95 (*0-7704-2362-0*) Bantam.

— Anne of Green Gables Storybook. (Illus.). 80p. (J). (gr. 3 up). 1987. 16.95 (*0-920668-43-7*); pap. 9.95 (*0-920668-42-9*) Firefly Bks Ltd.

— Anne of Ingleside, No. 6. (J). 1984. 2.95 (*0-553-21315-6*, Bantam Classics) Bantam.

— Anne of the Island. (J). 1983. pap. 2.95 (*0-553-21317-2*, Bantam Classics) Bantam.

— Anne of the Island. (J). (gr. 3-7). 1992. pap. 3.50 (*0-553-48066-9*) Bantam.

— Anne of the Island. LC 93-85542. (Courage Literary Classics Ser.). 240p. 1994. 5.98 (*1-56138-369-4*) Courage Bks.

— Anne of the Island. (Illustrated Junior Library). (Illus.). 288p. (J). (gr. 4 up). 1992. 14.95 (*0-448-40311-0*, G&D) Putnam Pub Group.

— Anne of the Island. (J). (gr. 4-7). 1993. pap. 3.25 (*0-590-46163-X*) Scholastic Inc.

— Anne of the Island. large type ed. 1991. pap. 2.95 (*0-451-52534-5*, Sig Classics) NAL-Dutton.

— Anne of the Island & Other Tales of Avonlea. (J). 1991. 10.99 (*0-517-03705-X*) Random Hse Value.

— Anne of Windy Poplars. (J). (gr. 3-7). 1992. pap. 3.50 (*0-553-48065-0*) Bantam.

— Anne of Windy Poplars, No. 4. (J). 1984. pap. 2.95 (*0-553-21316-4*, Bantam Classics) Bantam.

— Anne's House of Dreams. (J). 1983. 2.95 (*0-553-21318-0*, Bantam Classics) Bantam.

— Anne's House of Dreams. (Courage Literary Classics Ser.). 304p. 1994. 5.98 (*1-56138-430-5*) Running Pr.

— The Blue Castle. (YA). (gr. 7 up). 1989. pap. 3.50 (*0-553-28051-1*, Starfire) Bantam.

— Chronicles of Avonlea. (J). 1988. 2.95 (*0-553-21378-4*, Bantam Classics) Bantam.

— Chronicles of Avonlea. 224p. (YA). 1988. pap. 3.95 (*0-451-52233-8*, Sig Classics) NAL-Dutton.

— Days of Dreams & Laughter: The Story Girl & Other Tales. (J). 1990. 10.99 (*0-517-05137-0*) Random Hse Value.

— Doctor's Sweetheart. (YA). 1993. mass mkt. 4.50 (*0-553-56330-0*) Bantam.

— Emily, 3 vols., Set. (YA). (gr. 9-12). 1990. Boxed set. boxed 10.50 (*0-553-33308-9*) Bantam.

— Emily Climbs. (Orig.). (J). 1976. 23.95 (*0-8488-0588-7*) Amereon Ltd.

— Emily Climbs. 336p. (Orig.). (YA). 1983. mass mkt. 3.99 (*0-553-26214-9*, Starfire) Bantam.

— Emily of New Moon. (Orig.). (J). 1976. 23.95 (*0-8488-0589-5*) Amereon Ltd.

— Emily of New Moon. (Orig.). 1983. mass mkt. 3.99 (*0-553-23370-X*) Bantam.

— Emily's Quest. (J). 1976. 19.95 (*0-8488-0590-9*) Amereon Ltd.

— Emily's Quest. 240p. 1983. pap. 3.50 (*0-553-26493-1*) Bantam.

— Further Chronicles of Avonlea. 208p. (Orig.). (YA). 1989. 2.95 (*0-553-21381-4*, Starfire) Bantam.

— Golden Road. (J). 1976. 21.95 (*0-8488-0720-0*) Amereon Ltd.

— Golden Road. 1989. pap. 2.95 (*0-553-21367-9*, Bantam Classics) Bantam.

— Jane of Lantern Hill. (J). 1976. 19.95 (*0-8488-1434-7*) Amereon Ltd.

— Kilmeny of the Orchard. (J). 1976. 20.95 (*0-8488-0721-9*) Amereon Ltd.

— Kilmeny of the Orchard. 1989. pap. 2.95 (*0-553-21377-6*) Bantam.

— Magic for Marigold. (J). 1976. 21.95 (*0-8488-1102-X*) Amereon Ltd.

— Magic for Marigold. 1989. pap. 3.50 (*0-553-28046-5*) Bantam.

— Mistress Pat. (J). 1976. 21.95 (*0-8488-1103-8*) Amereon Ltd.

— Pat of Silver Bush. 1989. pap. 3.50 (*0-553-28047-3*) Bantam.

— Rainbow Valley. (J). 1976. 19.95 (*0-8488-0591-7*) Amereon Ltd.

— Rainbow Valley. (J). 1985. mass mkt. 3.99 (*0-553-26921-6*) Bantam.

— Rainbow Valley. LC 94-23683. (Illus.). (J). 1995. 7.99 (*0-517-10192-0*) Random Hse Value.

— Rilla of Ingleside. (J). 1976. 21.95 (*0-8488-0592-5*) Amereon Ltd.

— Rilla of Ingleside. (J). 1985. pap. 3.50 (*0-553-26922-4*) Bantam.

— Road to Yesterday. (YA). 1993. mass mkt. 3.99 (*0-553-56068-9*) Bantam.

— The Selected Journals of L. M. Montgomery: 1921-1929, Vol. 3. Rubio, Mary & Waterston, Elizabeth, eds. (Illus.). 464p. 1993. 30.00 (*0-19-540936-1*) OUP.

— The Story Girl. (J). 1989. pap. 2.95 (*0-553-21366-0*, Bantam Classics) Bantam.

— The Story Girl. 1991. pap. 2.95 (*0-451-52532-9*, Sig Classics) NAL-Dutton.

Montgomery, Lucy M., text. The Avonlea Album. (Illus.). 72p. (J). 1991. lib. bdg. 16.95 (*0-920668-96-8*); pap. 9.95 (*0-920668-97-6*) Firefly Bks Ltd.

Montgomery, Lucy M., et al, eds. The Selected Journals of L. M. Montgomery: 1889-1910, Vol. 1. (Illus.). 424p. 1986. 35.00 (*0-19-540503-X*) OUP.

Montgomery, Lynn. Health & Safety Guidelines for the Laboratory. LC 94-8501. 1994. 35.00 (*0-89189-382-2*) Am Soc Clinical.

***Montgomery, M.** Telling the Beads. 80p. 1994. write for info. (*0-932616-50-X*) New Poets Chestnut Hills.

Montgomery, M. L. History of Berks County, Pennsylvania. (Illus.). 1204p. 1989. reprint ed. lib. bdg. 129.50 (*0-8328-1431-8*) Higginson Bk Co.

Montgomery, M. R. A Field Guide to Airplanes of North America. LC 83-26438. (Illus.). 1984. ring bd. 12.95 (*0-685-09372-7*) HM.

— Many Rivers to Cross. 1995. 22.00 (*0-671-79286-5*) S&S Trade.

— Way of the Trout: An Essay on Anglers, Wild Fish & Running Water. 1991. 22.00 (*0-394-58063-X*) Knopf.

— The Way of the Trout: Anglers, Wild Fish & Running Water. 288p. 1993. reprint ed. pap. 11.00 (*0-380-71884-7*) Avon.

Montgomery, M. R. & Foster, Gerald L. A Field Guide to Airplanes. rev. ed. (Illus.). 256p. 1992. pap. 13.95 (*0-395-62888-1*) HM.

Montgomery, Mabel G. & Pettem, Silvia. A Story of Gold Hill Colorado: Seventy-Odd Years in the Heart of the Rockies. rev. ed. (Illus.). 37p. 1987. reprint ed. pap. 4.50 (*0-9617799-1-8*) Book Lode.

Montgomery, Margaret, ed. see Daitz, Myrna.

Montgomery, Margaret, ed. see Daitz, Myrna & Williams, Shirley.

Montgomery, Margaret, ed. see Daitz, Myrna.

Montgomery, Marion. Eliot's Reflective Journey to the Garden. LC 78-57220. 170p. 1979. 12.00 (*0-87875-142-4*) Whitston Pub.

— Liberal Arts & Community: The Feeding of the Larger Body. LC 89-12792. 184p. 1990. text ed. 30.00 (*0-8071-1558-4*) La State U Pr.

— The Men I Have Chosen for Fathers: Literary & Philosophical Passages. LC 90-10854. 264p. 1990. 24.95 (*0-8262-0740-5*) U of Mo Pr.

— Virtue & Modern Shadows of Turning: Preliminary Agitations. 186p. (C). 1989. lib. bdg. 45.00 (*0-8191-7655-9*); pap. text ed. 22.50 (*0-8191-7656-7*) U Pr of Amer.

— Why Flannery O'Connor Stayed Home. (Prophetic Poet & the Spirit of the Age Ser.: Vol. I). 486p. 1981. pap. 14.95 (*0-89385-033-0*) Sugden.

— Why Hawthorne Was Melancholy. (Prophetic Poet & the Spirit of the Age Ser.: Vol. III). 576p. (Orig.). 1984. 26.95 (*0-89385-027-6*) Sugden.

— Why Poe Drank Liquor. (Prophetic Poet & the Spirit of the Age Ser.: Vol. II). 442p. 1982. pap. 14.95 (*0-89385-036-5*) Sugden.

***Montgomery, Mark, et al.** The Tradeoff Between Number of Children & Child Schooling: Evidence from Cote d'Ivoire & Ghana. LC 94-23764. (LSMS Working Paper Ser.: Vol. 112). 1994. write for info. (*0-8213-3123-X*) World Bank.

Montgomery, Martin. An Introduction to Language & Society. 220p. 1986. text ed. 25.00 (*0-416-34620-0*, 9789); pap. text ed. 10.95 (*0-416-34630-8*, 9803) Routledge Chapman & Hall.

Montgomery, Martin & Coulthard, Malcolm, eds. Studies in Discourse Analysis. 1981. pap. 15.95 (*0-7100-0510-5*, RKP) Routledge.

Montgomery, Martin, et al. Ways of Reading: Advanced Reading Skills for Students of English Literature. LC 91-39237. 256p. 1992. 59.95 (*0-415-05319-6*, A7138); pap. 16.95 (*0-415-05320-X*, A7142) Routledge.

Montgomery, Mary, ed. Joy Beginning. (Joy Ser.). (ps-00). 1985. teacher ed 8.95 (*0-03-017646-8*) Harper SF.

Montgomery, Mary & Baraldi, Severino. Marie Curie. (What Made Them Great Ser.). (Illus.). 104p. (J). (gr. 5-8). 1990. lib. bdg. 12.95 (*0-382-09981-8*) Silver Burdett Pr.

Montgomery, Mary & Clawson, Marion. History of Legislation & Policy Formation of the Central Valley Project. Bruchey, Stuart, ed. LC 78-53558. (Development of Public Land Law in the U. S. Ser.). 1979. reprint ed. lib. bdg. 23.95 (*0-405-11381-1*) Ayer.

Montgomery, Mary & Montgomery, Herb. The Jesus Story. 1974. student ed 5.55 (*0-03-012951-6*, 125); teacher ed 8.95 (*0-03-012956-7*, 126) Harper SF.

— Live This Gift: A Program for Confirmation Preparation. 1981. student ed 3.25 (*0-03-014266-0*, 127) Harper SF.

— Together at the Lord's Supper: Preparation for Holy Communion. (Illus.). (gr. 5 up). 1977. 2.25 (*0-03-021286-3*, 192); pap. text ed. 3.25 (*0-03-021291-X*, 141) Harper SF.

Montgomery, Mary, jt. auth. see Montgomery, Herb.

Montgomery-Massingberd, Hugh. Great Houses of England & Wales. LC 94-6987. (Illus.). 424p. 1994. 75.00 (*0-8478-1824-1*) Rizzoli Intl.

Montgomery, Maureen. Gilded Prostitution. 332p. 1989. 37.50 (*0-415-00626-0*) Routledge.

Montgomery, Maxine. A Zora Neale Hurston Reader. Date not set. 19.95 (*1-56164-019-0*) Pineapple Pr.

***Montgomery, Michael.** Fifth Men. 256p. 1995. 24.95 (*1-85158-678-4*, Pub. by Mnstream UK) Trafalgar.

— An Introduction to Language & Society. 2nd rev. ed. LC 95-7513. (Studies in Culture & Communication). 1995. pap. write for info. (*0-415-07238-7*) Routledge.

Montgomery, Michael, ed. Crucible of Carolina: Essays on the Development of Gullah Language & Culture. LC 93-32145. (Illus.). 256p. 1994. 50.00 (*0-8203-1623-7*) U of Ga Pr.

***Montgomery, Michael B.** Centennial Usage Studies: Publication of the American Dialect Society 78. Little, Greta D., ed. LC 94-31291. (Publication of the American Dialect Society: Vol. 78). 1994. pap. 16.00 (*0-8173-0739-7*) U of Ala Pr.

Montgomery, Michael B. & Bailey, Guy, eds. Language Variety in the South: Perspectives in Black & White. LC 84-16396. (Illus.). 448p. 1986. 34.50 (*0-8173-0244-1*) U of Ala Pr.

Montgomery, Michael B., jt. auth. see McMillan, James B.

Montgomery, Michael S. Networking with LANtastic. 1992. 34.95 (*0-07-042906-5*); pap. 22.95 (*0-07-042907-3*) McGraw.

— Networking with LANtastic. 632p. 1992. 34.95 (*0-8306-4223-4*, 4273, Windcrest); pap. 22.95 (*0-8306-4222-6*, 4273, Windcrest) TAB Bks.

— Running Windows on LANtastic. 1993. text ed. 34.95 (*0-07-042911-1*); pap. text ed. 22.95 (*0-07-042912-X*) McGraw.

— Running Windows on LANtastic. 1993. pap. 22.95 (*0-8306-4447-4*, Windcrest) TAB Bks.

Montgomery, Michael S., comp. American Puritan Studies: An Annotated Bibliography of Dissertations, 1882-1981. LC 84-6553. (Bibliographies & Indexes in American History Ser.: No. 1). xxii, 419p. 1984. text ed. 89.50 (*0-313-24237-2*, MON/) Greenwood.

Montgomery, Michael S. & Stratton, John. The Writer's Hotline Handbook: A Guide to Good Usage & Effective Writing. 384p. 1981. pap. 4.95 (*0-451-62225-1*, ME2225, Ment) NAL-Dutton.

Montgomery, Michael T., jt. ed. see Redding, Spencer W.

Montgomery, Michael V. Carnivals & Commonplaces: Bakhtin's Chronotope, Cultural Studies & Film. LC 93-8772. (American University Studies, IV: English Language & Literature: Vol. 173). 142p. (C). 1994. text ed. 43.95 (*0-8204-2194-4*) P Lang Pubs.

Montgomery, Michelle. Imperialist Japan. 534p. 1988. text ed. 39.95 (*0-312-01557-7*) St Martin.

Montgomery, Monty. The One & Only Original Sanibel-Captiva Alphabet Coloring Book. (Illus.). 32p. (Orig.). (J). (gr. 7 up). 1988. pap. 6.95 (*0-945026-00-5*) SME Pr.

Montgomery Museum of Fine Arts Staff. Art Inc: American Paintings from Corporate Collections. Kahan, Mitchell D., ed. LC 78-65838. (Illus.). (ps-12). 1979. 15.00 (*0-89616-008-4*); pap. 15.00 (*0-89616-009-2*) Montgomery Mus.

— Art of the Eighties: Selections from the Permanent Collection of the Whitney Museum of American Art. Ausfeld, Margaret L., ed. LC 90-13475. (Illus.). 42p. (J). (ps-12). 1990. pap. text ed. 9.00 (*0-89280-026-7*) Montgomery Mus.

— The Grand Tour: The Tradition of Patronage in Southern Art Museums. LC 88-19929. (Illus.). 80p. (ps-12). 1988. pap. 12.00 (*0-89280-025-9*) Montgomery Mus.

— Italian Masterpieces of the 18th Century: Selections from the Collection of Mr. & Mrs. Adolf Weil Jr. LC 84-18876. (Illus.). 50p. (Orig.). (ps-12). 1984. pap. 8.00 (*0-89280-022-4*) Montgomery Mus.

— Palladio in Alabama: An Architectural Legacy. Joyner, Louise, ed. LC 91-33515. (Illus.). 80p. 1991. pap. 10.00 (*0-89280-029-1*) Montgomery Mus.

— A Sense of Place: Seven Contemporary Southern Artists. Neal, Christine C., ed. LC 90-49675. (Illus.). 16p. (ps-12). 1990. pap. 2.50 (*0-89280-027-5*) Montgomery Mus.

— A Symphony of Color: The World of Kelly Fitzpatrick. Ausfeld, Margaret L., ed. LC 90-25173. (Illus.). 72p. (ps-12). 1991. pap. 18.00 (*0-89280-028-3*) Montgomery Mus.

Montgomery, Myles. Best Choices in Ohio. LC 88-83473. 700p. 1989. pap. 14.95 (*1-877912-06-9*) Monongahela PA.

Montgomery, N. L., jt. auth. see Montgomery, W. H.

Montgomery, Patricia. CityGuide Locator of Denver. rev. ed. 64p. 1993. pap. text ed. 7.95 (*0-9631668-2-4*) CtyGuide Loc.

— Mythmaking: Heal Your Past, Claim Your Future. 224p. (Orig.). 1994. pap. 14.95 (*0-9638327-3-5*) Sibyl Pubns.

Montgomery, Patricia & Richter, Eileen. Sensorimotor Integration for Developmentally Disabled Children: A Handbook. 2nd ed. LC 76-62660. 100p. 1991. pap. 65.00 (*0-87424-142-1*, W-142A) Western Psych.

Montgomery, Patricia C. & Connolly, Barbara, eds. Motor Control & Physical Therapy: Theoretical Framework & Practical Applications. 240p. (Orig.). (C). 1991. pap. text ed. 34.95 (*1-879971-00-3*) Chattanga Grp.

— Therapeutic Exercise in Developmental Disabilities. 2nd ed. (Illus.). 244p. (Orig.). (C). 1993. pap. text ed. 34.95 (*1-879971-01-1*) Chattanga Grp.

Montgomery, Patricia C., jt. auth. see Richter, Eileen W.

Montgomery, Paul. Monarch Notes on Goethe's Faust. (Orig.). (C). 1989. pap. 3.95 (*0-671-00521-9*, Arco Test) P-H Gen Ref & Trav.

Montgomery, Paul J. Nutritional Analysis of Ready-to-Eat Cereal. rev. ed. 274p. (YA). (gr. 7 up). 1989. pap. text ed. 19.95 (*0-9621865-0-3*) Prod Info Analysis.

— Nutritional Cereal Counter. (Illus.). 92p. (Orig.). (YA). (gr. 9 up). 1989. pap. 2.95 (*0-9621865-1-1*) Prod Info Analysis.

— The Nutritional Microwave Food Counter. 410p. (Orig.). 1991. pap. 24.95 (*0-9621865-2-X*) Prod Info Analysis.

— The Nutritional Sweets & Snacks Counter. 450p. (Orig.). 1993. pap. 24.95 (*0-9621865-3-8*) Prod Info Analysis.

Montgomery, Paul K. Approaches to Literature Through Literary Form. (Reading Motivation Ser.). 184p. 1995. pap. 29.95 (*0-89774-775-5*) Oryx Pr.

Montgomery, Paula. How to Believe When You Hurt. 96p. 1991. pap. 0.79 (*0-8163-1024-6*) Pacific Pr Pub Assn.

Montgomery, Paula K. Approaches to Literature Through Subject. LC 93-967. (Reading Motivation Ser.). 256p. 1993. pap. 29.95 (*0-89774-774-7*) Oryx Pr.

— Approaches to Literature Through Theme. LC 92-13072. (Reading Motivation Ser.). 132p. 1992. pap. 29.95 (*0-89774-772-0*) Oryx Pr.

Montgomery, Paula K., ed. see Hackman, Mary.

Montgomery, Paula K., ed. see Krimmelbein, Cindy J.

Montgomery, Paula K., ed. see Leonard, Phyllis.

Montgomery, Paula K., ed. see Seaver, Alice R.

Montgomery, Paula K., ed. see Winn, Patricia.

Montgomery, R. A. Everest Attempt. (Young Readers Ser.: No. 145). (J). 1994. pap. 3.50 (*0-553-56005-0*) Bantam.

— Last Run. (Choose Your Own Adventure Ser.: No. 153). (YA). 1994. pap. 3.50 (*0-553-56394-7*) Bantam.

Montgomery, R. G., et al. Franciscan Awatovi: The Excavation & Conjectural Reconstruction of a Seventeenth Century Spanish Mission. (Harvard University Peabody Museum of Archaeology & Ethnology Papers: Vol. 36). 1949. 26.00 (*0-527-01292-0*) Periodicals Srv.

Montgomery, R. H. The Solar Decision Book: Your Guide to Making a Sound Investment. LC 79-762. 1976. pap. text ed. 25.95 (*0-685-05406-3*) Wiley.

Montgomery, Ramsey. Outlaw Gulch. (Choose Your Own Adventure Ser.: No. 125). (J). (gr. 4-7). 1992. pap. 3.50 (*0-553-29295-1*) Bantam.

— U. N. Adventure. (Choose Your Own Adventure Ser.: No. 157). (YA). 1995. pap. 3.50 (*0-553-56396-3*) Bantam.

Montgomery, Raymond A. The Abominable Snowman. large type ed. (Choose Your Own Adventure Ser.). (Illus.). 116p. (J). (gr. 2-7). 1987. 8.95 (*0-942545-02-8*); lib. bdg. 9.95 (*0-942545-08-7*) Grey Castle.

— Behind the Wheel. (J). 1992. pap. 3.25 (*0-553-29401-6*) Bantam.

— The Haunted House. (J). 1983. 2.99 (*0-553-15679-9*) Bantam.

— The Island of Time. (Choose Your Own Adventure Ser.: No. 115). (YA). 1991. pap. 3.50 (*0-553-29057-6*) Bantam.

— Journey to the Sea. (Choose Your Own Adventure Ser.: No. 2). (J). 1982. pap. 3.50 (*0-553-27393-0*) Bantam.

— Journey under the Sea. large type ed. (Choose Your Own Adventure Ser.). (Illus.). 117p. (J). (gr. 3-7). 1987. reprint ed. 8.95 (*0-942545-04-4*); reprint ed. lib. bdg. 9.95 (*0-942545-10-9*) Grey Castle.

— Motocross Mania. (Choose Your Own Adventure Ser.: No. 139). (J). (gr. 4-6). 1993. pap. 3.50 (*0-553-56002-6*) Bantam.

— Mystery of the Maya. large type ed. (Choose Your Own Adventure Ser.). (Illus.). 134p. (J). (gr. 3-7). 1987. reprint ed. 8.95 (*0-942545-00-1*); reprint ed. lib. bdg. 9.95 (*0-942545-06-0*) Grey Castle.

— The Race Forever. large type ed. (Choose Your Own Adventure Ser.). 116p. (J). (gr. 3-7). 1987. reprint ed. 8.95 (*0-942545-12-5*); reprint ed. lib. bdg. 9.95 (*0-942545-17-6*) Grey Castle.

— Secret of Ninja, No. 66. (J). 1987. pap. 3.50 (*0-553-27565-8*) Bantam.

— Silver Wings. (J). 1992. pap. 3.25 (*0-553-29293-5*) Bantam.

— Space & Beyond. (Choose Your Own Adventure Ser.: No. 4). (J). (ps-7). 1982. pap. 3.50 (*0-553-27453-8*) Bantam.

— Space & Beyond. large type ed. (Choose Your Own Adventure Ser.). 117p. (J). (gr. 3-7). 1987. reprint ed. 8.95 (*0-942545-11-7*); reprint ed. lib. bdg. 9.95 (*0-942545-16-8*) Grey Castle.

Montgomery, Reid H., Jr. & Dillingham, Steven D. Probation & Parole in Practice. LC 84-105982. 188p. 1983. pap. 12.95 (*0-932930-61-1*) Pilgrimage Inc.

Montgomery, Rhonda J., ed. Family Seminars for Caregiving: Helping Families Help (Facilitator's Manual) 223p. 1985. Incls. It's the Little Things, 69 35-mm color slides in carousel & 20-min. audiocass. audio, sl. 135.00 (*0-295-72509-5*); student ed 45.00 (*0-295-96316-6*); ring bd. 50.00 (*0-295-96286-0*) U of Wash Pr.

Montgomery, Rhonda J. & Prothero, Joyce, eds. Developing Respite Services for the Elderly. LC 85-40980. (Illus.). 82p. (Orig.). (C). 1986. 25.00 (*0-295-96386-7*); pap. 10.00 (*0-295-96347-6*) U of Wash Pr.

Montgomery, Richard G. The White-Headed Eagle: John McLoughlin, Builder of an Empire. LC 76-164616. (Select Bibliographies Reprint Ser.). 1977. reprint ed. 26.95 (*0-8369-5900-0*) Ayer.

Montgomery, Richard H. Build the Market Offering: How to Take Your Products to Market. (Illus.). 200p. 1989. ring bd. 34.95 (*0-915991-13-6*); ring bd. 39.95 (*0-915991-14-4*) R H Mont Assocs.

— The Computer Store: A Guide to Retail Success. (Illus.). 212p. (Orig.). 1984. pap. 16.95 (*0-915991-02-0*); ring bd. 26.95 (*0-915991-00-4*) R H Mont Assocs.

— Disciplined Creative Innovation: How to Turn New Ideas into Profitable Sales. (Illus.). 260p. 1987. pap. 44.95 (*0-915991-11-X*); ring bd. 59.95 (*0-915991-05-5*) R H Mont Assocs.

— Investigate Before You Invest: How to Market in a Small Business. (Illus.). 182p. 1989. ring bd. 39.95 (*0-915991-10-1*) R H Mont Assocs.

— Turn Your Ideas into Dollars: How to Commercialize Your Invention. 200p. 1989. ring bd. 29.95 (*0-318-41710-3*) R H Mont Assocs.

— Workbook & Study Guide for Disciplined Creative Innovation. (Illus.). 1987. ring bd. 13.95 (*0-915991-07-1*) R H Mont Assocs.

Montgomery, Richard H. & Miles, Walter F. The Solar Decision Book of Homes: A Guide to Designing & Remodeling for Solar Heat. (Illus.). 332p. 1988. reprint ed. ring bd. 54.95 (*0-915991-12-8*); reprint ed. ring bd. 59.95 (*0-915991-08-X*) R H Mont Assocs.

Montgomery, Richard J & Elliott, William D. Investigations in Biology. 413p. (C). 1991. 17.50 (*0-669-12010-3*); Instr.'s guide. teacher ed 2.00 (*0-669-24447-3*) Heath.

— Investigations in Biology. 2nd ed. 405p. 1994. text ed. write for info. (*0-669-34084-7*) Heath.

Montgomery, Robert. Grand Slam. LC 89-5198. (Gary Carter's Iron Mask Ser.). (Illus.). 176p. (J). (gr. 5-8). 1991. lib. bdg. 9.89 (*0-8167-1988-8*); pap. text ed. 2.95 (*0-8167-1989-6*) Troll Assocs.

— Hitting Streak. LC 90-10968. (Gary Carter's Iron Mask Ser.). (Illus.). 176p. (J). (gr. 5-8). 1991. lib. bdg. 9.89 (*0-8167-1982-9*); pap. text ed. 2.95 (*0-8167-1983-7*) Troll Assocs.

— Home Run! LC 89-5190. (Gary Carter's Iron Mask Ser.). (Illus.). 176p. (J). (gr. 5-8). 1991. lib. bdg. 9.89 (*0-8167-1986-1*); pap. text ed. 2.95 (*0-8167-1987-X*) Troll Assocs.

— Listen Your Way to Success. 35p. 1984. audio 39.95 (*1-55678-009-5*) Learn Inc.

— MVP. LC 89-20180. (Gary Carter's Iron Mask Ser.). (Illus.). 176p. (J). (gr. 5-8). 1991. lib. bdg. 9.89 (*0-8167-1992-6*); pap. text ed. 2.95 (*0-8167-1993-4*) Troll Assocs.

— The Show! LC 90-20586. (Gary Carter's Iron Mask Ser.). (Illus.). 176p. (J). (gr. 5-8). 1991. lib. bdg. 9.89 (*0-8167-1984-5*); pap. text ed. 2.95 (*0-8167-1985-3*) Troll Assocs.

— Smart Tapes: A Great Memory. 36p. 1984. audio, pap. text ed. 19.95 (*1-55678-051-6*) Learn Inc.

— Smart Tapes: Listen Up. 28p. 1994. audio, pap. text ed. 19.95 (*1-55678-053-2*) Learn Inc.

— Smart Tapes: Speak for Yourself. 36p. 1994. audio, pap. text ed. 19.95 (*1-55678-052-4*) Learn Inc.

— Triple Play. LC 89-20179. (Gary Carter's Iron Mask Ser.). (Illus.). 176p. (J). (gr. 5-8). 1991. lib. bdg. 9.89 (*0-8167-1990-X*); pap. text ed. 2.95 (*0-8167-1991-8*) Troll Assocs.

Montgomery, Robert & Barnwell, John. Most Delightful Golden Islands. LC 77-76733. 88p. 1969. reprint ed. bds. 12.95 (*0-87797-007-6*) Cherokee.

Montgomery, Robert, ed. see Brown, Douglas R.

Montgomery, Robert, jt. auth. see Shackleford, Lee E.

Montgomery, Robert E. The Visionary D. H. Lawrence: Beyond Philosophy & Art. 256p. (C). 1994. 54.95 (*0-521-45213-9*) Cambridge U Pr.

Montgomery, Robert H. Auditing Theory & Practice. LC 75-18477. (History of Accounting Ser.). (Illus.). 1979. reprint ed. 53.95 (*0-405-07559-6*) Ayer.

— Fifty Years of Accountancy. Brief, Richard P., ed. LC 77-87280. (Development of Contemporary Accounting Thought Ser.). 1978. reprint ed. lib. bdg. 58.95 (*0-405-10908-3*) Ayer.

Montgomery, Robert H., ed. see Dicksee, Lawrence R.

Montgomery, Robert L. Effective Speaking for Managers, Set 4. 49p. 1984. audio 49.95 (*1-55678-026-5*) Learn Inc.

— The Future Machine. 291p. (C). 1993. pap. 15.95 (*0-9637081-0-4*) Mtgmry Zuk Davis.

— Memory Made Easy: The Complete Book of Memory Training. LC 79-10889. 122p. reprint ed. pap. 34.80 (*0-317-08115-2*, 2022623) Bks Demand.

— The Quick & Easy Way to Top Selling. 51p. 1985. audio 39.95 (*1-55678-023-0*) Learn Inc.

— Terms of Response: Language & the Audience in Seventeenth- & Eighteenth-Century Theory. 208p. 1991. 30.00 (*0-271-00764-8*) Pa St U Pr.

Montgomery, Robert L. & Giffen, Debra. Memory Made Easy. 32p. 1994. audio, pap. 59.95 (*1-55678-048-6*) Learn Inc.

***Montgomery, Roger.** Twenty Count: Secret Mathematical System of the Aztec-Maya. (Illus.). 1995. pap. 15.00 (*1-879181-26-6*) Bear & Co.

Montgomery, Roger, jt. ed. see Marshall, Dale.

Montgomery, Roger, jt. auth. see Woodbridge, Sally B.

Montgomery, Royal E. Industrial Relations in the Chicago Building Trades. LC 77-156434. (American Labor Ser., No. 2). 1971. reprint ed. 23.95 (*0-405-02934-9*) Ayer.

Montgomery, Royce L., et al. Appleton & Lange's Review of Anatomy. 4th ed. (Illus.). 207p. 1989. pap. text ed. 25.95 (*0-8385-0213-X*, A0213-7) Appleton & Lange.

— Appleton & Lange's Review of Anatomy. 5th ed. LC 94-31509. 1995. pap. text ed. 25.95 (*0-8385-0246-6*, A0246-6) Appleton & Lange.

Montgomery, Ruth. Aliens among Us. 1986. mass mkt. 4.95 (*0-449-20809-5*, Crest) Fawcett.

— Born to Heal. 1985. pap. 3.50 (*0-449-21111-8*) Fawcett.

— Companions along the Way. 1985. mass mkt. 5.99 (*0-449-21221-1*) Fawcett.

— Here & Hereafter. 176p. 1985. mass mkt. 5.99 (*0-449-20830-3*, Crest) Fawcett.

— A Search for the Truth. 256p. (Orig.). 1985. mass mkt. 4.95 (*0-449-21085-5*, Crest) Fawcett.

— Strangers Among Us. 256p. 1984. mass mkt. 4.99 (*0-449-20801-X*, Crest) Fawcett.

— Threshold to Tomorrow. 1985. mass mkt. 4.95 (*0-449-20847-8*) Fawcett.

— The World Before. 1985. mass mkt. 4.95 (*0-449-20923-7*, Crest) Fawcett.

— World Beyond. 1985. mass mkt. 4.95 (*0-449-20832-X*) Fawcett.

Montgomery, Ruth & Garland, Joanne. Ruth Montgomery: Herald of the New Age. 288p. 1987. mass mkt. 5.99 (*0-449-21252-1*, Crest) Fawcett.

Montgomery, Rutherford. Kildee House. (Newbery Honor Roll Ser.). (Illus.). 224p. (J). (gr. 3-7). 1993. reprint ed. pap. 7.95 (*0-8027-7388-5*) Walker & Co.

Montgomery, Rutherford G. The Capture of the Golden Stallion. 20.95 (*0-8488-0132-6*, Amereon Hse) Amereon Ltd.

— Carcajou. LC 36-6665. (Illus.). (J). (gr. 6-8). 1936. 4.95 (*0-87004-105-3*) Caxton.

— The Golden Stallion's Victory. 18.95 (*0-8488-0133-4*, Amereon Hse) Amereon Ltd.

— High Country. (Fifty Greatest Bks.). (Illus.). 248p. (YA). (gr. 10 up). 1993. reprint ed. 40.00 (*1-56416-043-2*) Derrydale Pr.

— A Kinkajou on the Town. 1976. 16.95 (*0-8488-0835-5*) Amereon Ltd.

— Pekan the Shadow. LC 78-84779. (Illus.). (J). (gr. 8-12). 1970. 3.95 (*0-87004-132-0*) Caxton.

— Rufus. LC 78-150819. (Illus.). (Orig.). (J). (gr. 4-8). 1973. 4.95 (*0-87004-227-0*) Caxton.

Montgomery, S., ed. Group Actions on Rings. LC 85-11242. (Contemporary Mathematics Ser.: Vol. 43). 277p. 1990. reprint ed. pap. text ed. 38.00 (*0-8218-5046-6*, CONM-43) Am Math.

Montgomery, S., et al, eds. Noncommutative Rings. (Mathematical Sciences Research Institute Publications: Vol. 24). 200p. 1991. 43.00 (*0-387-97704-X*) Spr-Verlag.

Montgomery, S. A. & Rouillon, F. Prospectives in Psychiatry Long Term Treatment of Depression, Vol. 3. (Perspectives in Psychiatry Ser.: No. 1951). 275p. 1992. text ed. 84.95 (*0-471-92892-5*, Wiley-Liss) Wiley.

Montgomery, S. L. Profitable Pricing Strategies. 192p. 1988. text ed. 29.95 (*0-07-042860-3*) McGraw.

Montgomery, Sarah, jt. auth. see Oster, Gerald D.

Montgomery, Scott L. Minds for the Making: The Role of Science in American Education, 1750-1990. LC 93-38389. 316p. 1994. lib. bdg. 39.95 (*0-89862-189-5*); pap. text ed. 18.95 (*0-89862-188-7*) Guilford Pr.

Montgomery, Scott M. A Theology for Youth: God 101. 128p. (YA). (gr. 9-12). 1994. pap. 7.95 (*0-9641817-0-3*) S M Montgomery.

Montgomery, Stephen. The Pygmalion Project: The Artisans. 178p. (Orig.). 1989. pap. 9.95 (*0-9606954-2-7*) Prometheus Nemesis.

— The Pygmalion Project, Vol. II: The Guardian. (Love & Coercion among the Types Ser.). 255p. (Orig.). (C). 1990. pap. 9.95 (*0-9606954-5-1*) Prometheus Nemesis.

Montgomery, Stephen, ed. see Choiniere, Ray & Keirsey, David.

Montgomery, Stephen, ed. see Keirsey, David W.

Montgomery, Stephen E. The Pygmalion Project Vol. III: The Idealist, Vol. 3. 297p. (Orig.). (C). 1993. pap. 9.95 (*0-9606954-9-4*) Prometheus Nemesis.

Montgomery, Stephen L. ADIcycle: IBM Framework for Application. (Illus.). 250p. 1991. text ed. 49.95 (*0-442-30825-6*) Van Nos Reinhold.

— Object-Oriented Information Engineering: Analysis, Design, & Implementation. LC 93-43044. (Illus.). 324p. 1994. pap. 39.95 (*0-12-505040-2*, AP Prof) Acad Pr.

— Relational Database Design & Implementation Using Db2. 1990. text ed. 44.95 (*0-442-00134-7*) Van Nos Reinhold.

***Montgomery, Steven J.** Build Your Own Intelligent Mobile Space Robot. 1995. disk, pap. text ed. 29.95 (*0-07-042946-4*) McGraw.

Montgomery, Stuart, jt. ed. see Horobin, Gordon.

Montgomery, Stuart A., ed. Psychopharmacology of Panic. LC 92-16486. (British Association for Psychopharmacology Monographs: No. 12). 1993. 43.50 (*0-19-262087-8*) OUP.

Montgomery, Stuart A. & Corn, Tim H., eds. The Psychopharmacology of Depression. LC 93-44896. (British Association for Psychopharmacology Monographs: No. 13). 272p. (C). 1994. 75.00 (*0-19-262278-1*) OUP.

Montgomery, Susan. Hopf Algebras & Their Actions on Rings. LC 93-25786. (Regional Conference Mathematics Ser.). 238p. 1993. pap. 34.00 (*0-8218-0738-2*) Am Math.

Montgomery, Susan & Ralston, Elizabeth W., eds. Selected Papers on Algebra. LC 77-79280. (Raymond W. Brink Selected Mathematical Papers: Vol. 3). 537p. 1977. 10.00 (0-88385-203-9) Math Assn.

Montgomery, Susan, jt. ed. see Bergen, Jeffrey.

Montgomery, Susan J. The Ceramics of William H. Grueby: The Spirit of New Idea in Artistic Handicraft. Rago, David & Schoen, Michelle S., eds. (Illus.). 165p. 1993. 55.00 (0-9637896-0-0); pap. 40.00 (0-9637896-3-5) Arts & Crafts.

Montgomery, Susan J., et al. Healthy Living in Wisconsin. (Orig.). 1988. pap. 12.95 (0-929807-00-6) Montgomery Media.

Montgomery, Sy. Nature's Everyday Mysteries: A Field Guide to the World in Your Backyard. LC 92-36189. (Curious Naturalist Ser.). (Illus.). 152p. (Orig.). 1993. pap. 9.95 (0-9631591-9-4) Chapters Pub.

— Seasons of the Wild: A Year of Nature's Magic & Mysteries. Taylor, Sandy, ed. (Curious Naturalist Ser.). (Illus.). 160p. 1995. pap. 10.95 (1-881527-90-5) Chapters Pub.

— Spell of the Tiger: Man-Eaters of the Sundarbans. (Peter Davidson Book). 256p. 1995. 22.95 (0-395-64169-1) HM.

— Walking with the Great Apes: Jane Goodall, Dian Fossey, Birute Galdikas. 1992. pap. 12.95 (0-395-61156-3) HM.

Montgomery, Tommie S. Revolution in El Salvador: Origins & Evolution. 2nd rev. ed. 344p. 1994. text ed. 69.00 (0-8133-0070-3) Westview.

— Revolution in El Salvador: Origins & Evolution. 2nd rev. ed. 344p. (C). 1994. pap. text ed. 19.95 (0-8133-0071-1) Westview.

Montgomery, Tracy T., jt. auth. see Kennedy, George E.

Montgomery, Vickie. Smart Woman's Guide to Starting a Business. 216p. (Orig.). 1994. pap. 14.95 (1-56414-129-2) Career Pr Inc.

Montgomery, W. St. Augustine: Aspects of His Life & Thought. 1977. lib. bdg. 34.95 (0-8490-2556-7) Gordon Pr.

Montgomery, W., tr. see Pfleiderer, Otto.

Montgomery, W. David, jt. auth. see Bohi, Douglas R.

Montgomery, W. H. & Montgomery, N. L. Dare Family History. (Illus.). 340p. 1991. reprint ed. lib. bdg. 64.00 (0-8328-1809-7); reprint ed. pap. 54.00 (0-685-38991-X) Higginson Bk Co.

Montgomery Ward Staff. Catalogue & Buyers Guide Summer & Spring 1895: No. 57. 1969. reprint ed. pap. 19.95 (0-486-22377-9) Dover.

Montgomery, William A. Tying Arrangements. (Corporate Practice Ser.: No. 39). 1984. 92.00 (1-55871-248-8) BNA.

Montgomery, William E. Under Their Own Vine & Fig Tree: The African-American Church in the South, 1865-1900. LC 92-21041. 358p. (C). 1994. pap. 14.95 (0-8071-1965-2) La State U Pr.

***Montgomery, William L.** Power-up Teams & Tools: For Process Improvement & Problem Solving. 223p. 1995. pap. write for info. (0-9641124-0-X) Montgomery.

***Montgomery, William W.** The Mustache That Walks Like a Man. LC 95-75082. 228p. 1995. 19.95 (0-8338-0216-X) M Jones.

— Surgery of the Upper Respiratory System, Vol. 2. 2nd ed. LC 78-9004. (Illus.). 760p. 1989. text ed. 110.00 (0-8121-1142-7) Williams & Wilkins.

Montgomery, Yvonne. Obstacle Course. 192p. (Orig.). 1990. pap. 3.50 (0-380-75992-6) Avon.

— Scavengers. 256p. 1990. pap. 3.50 (0-380-71002-1) Avon.

Montgomery, Zach. Poison Drops in the Federal Senate: The School Question from a Parental & Non-Sectarian Standpoint. 138p. 1983. reprint ed. pap. 4.95 (0-685-04742-3) St Thomas.

Montgomery, Zach, ed. Poison Drops in the Federal Senate. LC 72-172221. (Right Wing Individualist Tradition in America Ser.). 1972. reprint ed. 19.95 (0-405-00430-3) Ayer.

Month, M. & Herrera, J. C., eds. Nonlinear Dynamics & the Beam-Beam Interaction. LC 79-57341. (AIP Conference Proceedings Ser.: No. 57). (Illus.). 340p. lib. bdg. 20.50 (0-88318-156-8) Am Inst Physics.

Month, M. & Turner, S., eds. Frontiers of Particle Beams. (Lecture Notes in Physics Ser.: Vol. 296). xii, 700p. 1988. 85.00 (0-387-19022-8) Spr-Verlag.

— Frontiers of Particle Beams, Observation, Diagnosis & Correction. (Lecture Notes in Physics Ser.: Vol. 343). ix, 509p. 1989. 73.00 (0-387-51616-6) Spr-Verlag.

Month, Melvin. Physics of High Energy Particle Accelerators: SLAC Summer School, 1982, No. 105. LC 83-72986. (AIP Conference Proceedings Ser.: No. 105). 1102p. 1983. lib. bdg. 55.50 (0-88318-304-8) Am Inst Physics.

Month, Melvin & Dienes, Margaret. Physics of Particle Accelerators, 2 vols., Set. LC 87-70103. (AIP Conference Proceedings Ser.: No. 153). 1748p. 1987. lib. bdg. 175.00 (0-88318-353-6) Am Inst Physics.

Month, Melvin & Dienes, Margaret, eds. Physics of Particle Accelerators. LC 89-83575. (AIP Conference Proceedings Ser.: No. 184). 2376p. 1989. lib. bdg. 199.00 (0-88318-384-6) Am Inst Physics.

Month, Melvin, et al, eds. AIP Conference Proceedings, No. 134. LC 85-73170. 382p. 1985. lib. bdg. 46.00 (0-88318-333-1) Am Inst Physics.

— Physics of High Energy Particle Accelerators: BNL-SUNY Summer School. LC 85-70057. (AIP Conference Proceedings Ser.: No. 127). 970p. 1985. lib. bdg. 65.00 (0-88318-326-9) Am Inst Physics.

— The Physics of Particle Accelerators, Vol. 1 & 2: AIP Conference Proceedings, 2 vols., Set. LC 92-52843. (AIP Conference Proceedings Ser.). (Illus.). 220p. (C). 1992. 245.00 (0-88318-789-2) Am Inst Physics.

Monthan, Doris. R. C. Gorman: A Retrospective. LC 90-53286. (Illus.). 208p. 1990. 35.00 (0-87358-505-4) Northland AZ.

Monthan, Doris, ed. see Harmsen, Dorothy.

Montherlant, Henri de. Theatre. Laprade, Armand, ed. 1472p. (FRE.). 1955. lib. bdg. 115.00 (0-7859-3768-4, 2070103749) Fr & Eur.

Montherlant, Henry de. Aux Fontaines du Desir. 248p. 1954. 4.95 (0-686-54803-5) Fr & Eur.

— Les Bestaires. (FRE.). 1972. pap. 10.95 (0-8288-3714-7, F115680) Fr & Eur.

— Broceliande. 192p. (FRE.). 1956. pap. 10.95 (0-7859-1289-4, 2070245861) Fr & Eur.

— Le Cardinal D'Espagne. (FRE.). 1974. pap. 10.95 (0-8288-3715-5, M3784) Fr & Eur.

— Les Celibataires. (FRE.). 1972. pap. 10.95 (0-8288-3716-3, F115690) Fr & Eur.

— Celles Qu'on Prend dans Ses Bras. (FRE.). 1983. pap. 10.95 (0-8288-3717-1, F115290) Fr & Eur.

— Le Chaos et la Nuit. (FRE.). 1973. pap. 10.95 (0-8288-3718-X, M3786) Fr & Eur.

— Coups de Soleil: Textes. 344p. (FRE.). 1976. pap. 19.95 (0-7859-1346-7, 2070293637) Fr & Eur.

— Le Demon du Bien. (Jeunes Filles Ser.: Vol. 3). (FRE.). 1972. pap. 10.95 (0-8288-3719-8, F115710) Fr & Eur.

— Le Fichler Parisien. 184p. (FRE.). 1974. pap. 16.95 (0-7859-1342-4, 2070289842) Fr & Eur.

— Les Jeunes Filles, Vol. 1. (FRE.). 1978. pap. 10.95 (0-8288-3720-1, F115730) Fr & Eur.

— Les Lepreuses, Les Jeunes Filles. (Jeunes Filles Ser.: Vol. 4). (FRE.). 1972. pap. 10.95 (0-8288-3721-X, F115740) Fr & Eur.

— Le Maitre de Santiago. (FRE.). 1972. pap. 10.95 (0-8288-3722-8, F115750) Fr & Eur.

— Le Maitre de Santiago. (Folio Ser.: No. 142). 160p. (FRE.). 1972. 6.95 (2-07-036142-X) Schoenhof.

— Malatesta. (FRE.). 1973. pap. 10.95 (0-8288-3723-6, M3790) Fr & Eur.

— La Mort Qui Fait le Trottoir: Don Juan. (FRE.). 1991. pap. 10.95 (0-8288-3724-4, F115760) Fr & Eur.

— Les Olympiques. (FRE.). 1973. pap. 10.95 (0-8288-3750-3, M3791) Fr & Eur.

— La Petite Infante de Castille. (FRE.). 1973. pap. 10.95 (0-8288-3751-1, M3792) Fr & Eur.

— Pitie pour les Femmes. (Folio Ser.: No. 156). 224p. (FRE.). 1972. 8.95 (2-07-036156-X) Schoenhof.

— Pitie Pour les Femmes. (Jeunes Filles Ser.: Vol. 2). (FRE.). 1972. pap. 10.95 (0-8288-3752-X, F115780) Fr & Eur.

— Port Royal. (FRE.). 1972. pap. 10.95 (0-8288-3753-8, F115790) Fr & Eur.

— Port Royal & Notes de Theatre sur le Maitre de Santiago et Port-Royal. (Folio Ser.: No. 253). 192p. (FRE.). 1972. pap. 6.95 (2-07-036253-1) Schoenhof.

— La Reine Morte. (FRE.). 1972. pap. 10.95 (0-8288-3754-6, F115800) Fr & Eur.

— La Releve du Matin. (FRE.). 1972. pap. 10.95 (0-8288-3755-4, F115810) Fr & Eur.

— Romans, Vol. 1. (FRE.). 1960. lib. bdg. 110.00 (0-8288-3568-3, F115180) Fr & Eur.

— Romans, Vol. 2. (FRE.). 1982. lib. bdg. 125.00 (0-8288-3569-1, M12083) Fr & Eur.

— Romans et Oeuvres De Fiction Non Theatrales, 1. (Pleiade Ser.). 1960. 72.95 (0-685-11538-0) Fr & Eur.

— Romans et Oeuvres De Fiction Non Theatrales, 2. (Pleiade Ser.). 1960. 64.95 (0-685-01762-1) Fr & Eur.

— Le Songe. (FRE.). 1982. pap. 13.95 (0-8288-3756-2, F115510) Fr & Eur.

— Tous Feux Eteints: Carnets 1965, 1966, 1697, Carnets sans Dates et Carnets 1972. 192p. (FRE.). 1975. pap. 19.95 (0-7859-1343-2, 2070293025) Fr & Eur.

— Le Treizieme Cesar. 200p. (FRE.). 1970. pap. 14.95 (0-7859-1335-1, 2070272222) Fr & Eur.

— La Ville Dont le Prince Est un Enfant. (FRE.). 1973. pap. 11.95 (0-8288-3757-0, M3794) Fr & Eur.

Montherlant, Henry De & Kilmartin, Terence. The Bachelors. LC 77-10926. 189p. 1977. reprint ed. text ed. 49.75 (0-8371-9811-9, MOTB, Greenwood Pr) Greenwood.

***Monthule, Pierre.** Relais et Chateaux 1994. (ENG, FRE & GER.). 1994. pap. 9.95 (0-7859-7428-8) Fr & Eur.

— Silencehotels: Relais du Silence. 192p. (ENG, FRE & GER.). 1994. pap. 9.95 (0-7859-7426-1) Fr & Eur.

Monti-Belkaoui, Janice, jt. auth. see Riahi-Belkaoui, Ahmed.

Monti, Daniel J. Race, Redevelopment & the New Company Town. LC 89-21829. (SUNY Series in Urban Public Policy). 250p. 1990. 64.50 (0-7914-0325-4); pap. 21.95 (0-7914-0326-2) State U NY Pr.

— A Semblance of Justice: St. Louis School Desegregation & Order in Urban America. LC 85-1008. 240p. 1985. text ed. 26.00 (0-8262-0476-7) U of Mo Pr.

— Wannabe. Orig. Title: America's Suburban Gangs. 240p. (Orig.). 1994. 49.95 (1-55786-614-7); pap. 16.95 (1-55786-615-5) Blackwell Pubs.

Monti, Daniel J., jt. ed. see Cummings, Scott.

Monti, James. The Week of Salvation: History & Traditons of Holy Week. LC 93-83256. 400p. (Orig.). 1993. pap. 19.95 (0-87973-532-5, 532) Our Sunday Visitor.

***Monti, Joseph.** Arguing about Sex: The Rhetoric of Chistian Sexual Morality. LC 94-26956. 272p. (C). 1995. text ed. 59.50x (0-7914-2479-0); pap. text ed. 19.95x (0-7914-2480-4) State U NY Pr.

Monti, Laura V. A Calendar of Rochambeau Papers at the University of Florida Libraries. LC 72-91130. (Illus.). 341p. reprint ed. pap. 97.20 (0-7837-4931-7, 2044597) Bks Demand.

— French Revolutionary Pamphlets at the University of Florida. LC 74-182319. 174p. reprint ed. pap. 49.60 (0-7837-4929-5, 2044595) Bks Demand.

Monti, Lisa, jt. auth. see Higginbotham, Sylvia.

Monti, Mario, ed. Fiscal Policy, Economic Adjustment, & Financial Markets. x, 283p. 1989. pap. 16.00 (1-55775-118-8) Intl Monetary.

— Fiscal Policy, Economic Adjustment & Financial Markets. LC 89-19934. 294p. reprint ed. pap. 83.80 (0-7837-1260-X, 2041397) Bks Demand.

Monti, Nicolas, jt. auth. see Albera, Giovanni.

Monti, Peter M., jt. ed. see Curran, James P.

Monti, Peter M., jt. ed. see Curran, James.

Monti, Peter M., et al. Treating Alcohol Dependence: A Coping Skills Training Guide. LC 88-36838. (Treatment Manuals for Practitioners Ser.). 240p. 1989. lib. bdg. 45.00 (0-89862-204-2); pap. text ed. 19.95 (0-89862-215-8) Guilford Pr.

***Monti, R. George & Barile, Andrew.** Practical Guide to Finite Risk Insurance & Reinsurance. 1994. text ed. 135.00 (0-471-11289-5) Wiley.

Monti, Ralph. Bet on Your Golf Game! An Indispensable Guide for Betting on the Golf Course. LC 93-74488. (Illus.). 160p. 1994. pap. 7.95 (1-884490-20-4) Fortune Media.

— I Remember Brooklyn: Memories of Favorite Sons & Daughters. (Illus.). 224p. 1991. 22.95 (1-55972-093-X, Birch Ln Pr) Carol Pub Group.

Monti, Richard C. Terence Andria. (Latin Commentaries Ser.). 153p. (Orig.). (C). 1986. pap. text ed. 8.00 (0-929524-58-6) Bryn Mawr Commentaries.

Montias, John M. Artists & Artisans in Delft: A Socio-Economic Study of the Seventeenth Century. LC 81-11953. (Illus.). 445p. reprint ed. pap. 126.90 (0-8357-2920-6, 2039160) Bks Demand.

— Central Planning in Poland. LC 74-6785. (Yale Studies in Economics: No. 13). (Illus.). 410p. 1974. reprint ed. text ed. 75.00 (0-8371-7560-7, MOCP, Greenwood Pr) Greenwood.

— The Structure of Economic Systems. LC 75-43327. 336p. reprint ed. pap. 95.80 (0-8357-8335-9, 2033830) Bks Demand.

— Vermeer & His Milieu: A Web of Social History. (Illus.). 427p. 1991. text ed. 70.00 (0-691-04051-6); pap. text ed. 21.95 (0-691-00289-4) Princeton U Pr.

Montias, John M., jt. ed. see Marer, Paul.

Montias, John M., et al. Comparative Economics. LC 93-38882. 1994. pap. text ed. 32.00 (3-7186-5451-2) Gordon & Breach.

Montice, Jim. The Dartnell Guide to Cost Conscious Advertising. 209p. 1991. ring bd. 91.50 (0-85013-175-8) Dartnell Corp.

Monticelli, Barbara S. Fun Sculpting: A Humorous Approach to the Three-Dimensional Cartooning in Clay. LC 84-51804. (Illus.). 52p. (Orig.). 1984. pap. text ed. 2.98 (0-916809-11-0) Scott Pubns MI.

Monticone, Diane K. Montesquieu & His Reader: A Study of the Esprit Des Lois. LC 89-38370. (Illus.). 168p. (C). 1989. lib. bdg. 41.00 (0-8191-7596-X) U Pr of Amer.

Monticone, Ronald C. The Catholic Church in Communist Poland, 1945-1985: Forty Years of Church-State Relations. (East European Monographs: No. 205). 256p. 1986. text ed. 36.00 (0-88033-102-X) East Eur Quarterly.

Montie, James E., et al. Clinical Management of Renal Cell Cancer. (Illus.). 200p. 1990. 55.00 (0-8151-5942-0, Yr Bk Med Pubs) Mosby Yr Bk.

Montiel, Francisco-Felix. El Tercer Ejercito de la U. R. S. S. LC 88-81600. 116p. (Orig.). (SPA.). 1989. pap. 12.00 (0-89729-497-1) Ediciones.

Montiel, Peter J., jt. auth. see Agenor, Pierre-Richard.

Montiel, Peter J., et al. Informal Financial Markets in Developing Countries: Macroeconomic Analysis. LC 92-26400. (Advances in Theoretical & Applied Economics Ser.). 1993. 49.95 (1-55786-357-1) Blackwell Pubs.

Montiero & Associates Staff, tr. see Makana, Carol.

Montiero, Aristides. War Reminiscences. 1976. 20.95 (0-8488-1104-6) Amereon Ltd.

Montignac, Michel. Dine Out & Lose Weight. 1991. pap. 19.95 (2-906236-17-9, Pub. by Editions Artulen) Montignac USA.

***Montijo, Yolanda.** How Creator & Coyote Made the World: Traditional Myths of the Concow Indians of California. (Illus.). 64p. 1995. pap. 6.95 (0-930588-74-6) Heyday Bks.

Montijo, Yolanda, jt. auth. see Hinton, Leanne.

Montijo, Yolanda, jt. auth. see Margolin, Malcolm.

Montilus, Guerin. Dompim: The Spirituality of African Peoples. LC 89-50459. 1990. pap. 9.95 (1-55523-227-2) Winston-Derek.

Montin, Karin, tr. see Irigaray, Luce.

Montinari, M., jt. ed. see Colli, C.

Montinari, M., jt. ed. see Colli, G.

Montinari, M., ed. see Nietzsche, Friedrich.

Montinari, Mazzino. Friedrich Neitzsche: Eine Einfuhrung. xv, 146p. (GER.). (C). 1991. pap. text ed. 24.65 (3-11-012213-8) De Gruyter.

Montinari, Mazzino, ed. see Nietzsche, Friedrich.

Montiwalla, Luvai. A Primer on EXSYS for DOS. LC 94-145. 128p. (C). 1995. pap. text ed. 23.95 (0-256-16336-7) Irwin Prof Pubng.

***Montjoy, Robert S.** Innovations in Election Administration: Mail Voter Registration Programs. (Illus.). 55p. (Orig.). (C). 1994. pap. text ed. 45.00x (0-7881-1254-6) Diane Pub.

Montjoy, Robert S., jt. auth. see O'Toole, Laurence J.

Montler, Timothy. An Outline of the Morphology & Phonology of Saanich, North Straits Salish. (Occasional Papers in Linguistics). xiv, 264p. 1986. pap. 11.00 (1-879763-04-4) U MT UMOPL.

— Saanich, North Straits Salish: Classified Word List. (Canadian Museum of Civilization Mercury Ser.). x, 170p. 1992. pap. 17.95 (0-660-12908-6) U Ch Pr.

Montler, Timothy, jt. ed. see Mattina, Anthony.

Montmarquet, James A. Idea of Agrarianism: From Hunter-Gatherer to Agrarian Radical in Western Culture. LC 88-39514. 266p. (C). 1989. pap. 14.95 (0-89301-130-4) U of Idaho Pr.

Montney. Directories in Print, 2 vols. 11th ed. 1993. 290.00 (0-8103-8197-4) Gale.

— Directories in Print, 2 Vols., Vol. 1. 12th ed. 1994. 315.00 (0-8103-8502-3) Gale.

— Directories in Print, Vol. 1, Sect. 1-11. 11th ed. 1993. write for info. (0-8103-8198-2) Gale.

— Directories in Print, Vol. 1, Sect. 1-11. 12th ed. 1994. write for info. (0-8103-8503-1) Gale.

— Directories in Print, Vol. 2. 12th ed. 1994. write for info. (0-8103-8504-X) Gale.

— Directories in Print, Vol. 2, Sect. 12-16. 11th ed. 1993. write for info. (0-8103-8199-0) Gale.

— Senior Citizen Services, 4 Vols., Vol. 4. 1992. 100.00 (0-8103-8319-5) Gale.

— Senior Citizen Services: Midwest, Vol. 3. 1992. 40.00 (0-8103-8322-5) Gale.

— Senior Citizen Services: Northeast, Vol. 1. 1992. 40.00 (0-8103-8320-9) Gale.

— Senior Citizen Services: Southeast, Vol. 2. 1992. 40.00 (0-8103-8321-7) Gale.

— Senior Citizen Services: West, Vol. 4. 1992. 40.00 (0-8103-8323-3) Gale.

Montney, jt. ed. see Towell, Julie E.

Monto, Alexander. The Roots of Mexican Labor Migration. LC 93-25058. 272p. 1994. text ed. 59.95 (0-275-94630-4, C4630, Praeger Pubs) Greenwood.

Monton, Dennis, jt. auth. see Maris, Michael.

Montonati, Angelo. A Journalist Looks at the Parables. 144p. (C). 1992. pap. 24.95 (0-85439-385-4, Pub. by St Paul Pubns UK) St Mut.

Montone, Wayne V., jt. auth. see Miller, Richard K.

Montonen, C., jt. auth. see Laurikainen, K. V.

Montor, Karel. Naval Leadership: Voices of Experience. LC 87-10986. (Illus.). 504p. (C). 1987. text ed. 26.95 (0-87021-325-3) Naval Inst Pr.

Montor, Karel, comp. Ethics for the Junior Officer: Selected Cases from Current Military Experience. LC 93-42085. 301p. 1994. 25.00 (1-55750-591-8) Naval Inst Pr.

Montoro-Blanch, M. Premio, Stage 1. (C). 1988. student ed 45.00 (0-85950-750-5, Pub. by S Thornes Pubs UK); teacher ed 225.00 (0-85950-751-3, Pub. by S Thornes Pubs UK); audio 220.00 (0-85950-753-X, Pub. by S Thornes Pubs UK); 300.00 (0-85950-752-1, Pub. by S Thornes Pubs UK); Bulk cassette pack (minimum order 10 sets). 55.00 (0-85950-915-X, Pub. by S Thornes Pubs UK) St Mut.

— Premio, Stage 2. (C). 1990. student ed 45.00 (0-7487-0134-6, Pub. by S Thornes Pubs UK); teacher ed 175.00 (0-7487-0135-4, Pub. by S Thornes Pubs UK); audio 220.00 (0-7487-0137-0, Pub. by S Thornes Pubs UK); 220.00 (0-7487-0136-2, Pub. by S Thornes Pubs UK); Bulk cassette pack (minimum order 10 sets). 55.00 (0-7487-0138-9, Pub. by S Thornes Pubs UK) St Mut.

Montorsi, A., ed. The Hubbard Model. 300p. (C). 1992. reprint ed. text ed. 86.00 (981-02-0585-6); reprint ed. pap. text ed. 40.00 (981-02-0586-4) World Scientific Pub.

Montorsi, A., jt. ed. see Rasetti, M.

Montoto, M., et al. Natural Analogue & Microstructural Studies in Relation to Radionuclide Retardation, No. EUR 14352. (Nuclear Science & Technology Ser.). 129p. 1993. pap. 19.00 (92-826-4961-X, CD-NA-14352-EN-C, Pub. by Europ Com) UNIPUB.

Montouri, Alfonso A. Evolutionary Competence: Creating the Future. x, 378p. 1990. pap. 31.00 (90-5063-047-2, Pub. by Gieben NE) Benjamins North Am.

Montousse, Juan L. & Perez, Candi. First Two Hundred Words in Spanish. LC 93-29561. (Little Library). (Illus.). 32p. (ENG & SPA.). (J). (gr. 1-4). 1994. 3.95 (1-85697-957-1, Kingfisher LKC) LKC.

Montoya, Ana M., tr. see Pena, Betty W.

Montoya, Candace G. & Roxberg, Joan M. Composition as Communication. 496p. (C). 1994. pap. write for info. (0-02-382431-X) Macmillan.

***Montoya, Jose.** In Formation: 20 Years of Joda. 254p. 1992. pap. 17.95 (0-9624536-1-7) Chusma Hse.

— El Sol y Los De Abajo. (Illus.). 13p. (ENG & SPA.). 1992. 90.00 (0-9614597-8-6) Ninja Pr.

Montoya, Maria, ed. see Keller, John E.

Montoya-Ramirez, Maria I., ed. Texto y Concordancias de la Defenssa de Virtuossas Mugeres de Mosen Diego de Valera, MS. 1341 de la Biblioteca Nacional. (Spanish Ser.: No. 72). 8p. 1992. 10.00 (0-940639-73-4) Hispanic Seminary.

Montoya-Welsh, Sharon & Speare-Yerxa, Marjorie. Oyster Cookery. 2nd ed. (Illus.). 168p. 1984. reprint ed. pap. 9.95 (0-9613895-0-8) Shoalwater Kitch.

Montoye, Henry, et al. Living Fit. 300p. (Orig.). (C). 1988. pap. text ed. 23.75 (0-8053-8180-5); 10.75 (0-8053-8181-3) Benjamin-Cummings.

Montoye, Henry J., jt. ed. see Eckert, Helen M.

***Montoye, Henry J., et al.** Measuring Physical Activity & Energy Expenditure. LC 94-38604. (Illus.). 200p. 1995. text ed. write for info. (0-87322-500-7, BMON0500) Human Kinetics.

Montparker, Carol. The Anatomy of a New York Debut Recital: A Chronicle. (Illus.). 94p. 1989. reprint ed. 12.95 (0-912483-48-2) Pro-Am Music.

Montplaisir, Jacques & Godbout, Roger, eds. Sleep & Biological Rhythms: Basic Mechanisms & Applications to Psychiatry. (Illus.). 256p. 1990. 49.95 (0-19-505825-9) OUP.

Montreal Health Press Staff. Menopause: A Well-Woman Book. (NFS Canada Ser.). Date not set. pap. 14.95 (0-929005-10-4, Pub. by Second Story Pr CN) InBook.

M

Montresor, Jaye B., ed. The Critical Response to Ann Beattie. LC 92-46531. (Critical Responses in Arts & Letters Ser.: No. 4). 296p. 1993. text ed. 49.95 (*0-313-28358-3*, MTW, Greenwood Pr) Greenwood.

Montreynaud, Florence. Diccionario de Citas Literarias. 640p. 1990. 59.95 (*0-7859-5771-5*) Fr & Eur.

— Robert Dictionnaire de Proverbes et Dictions. 750p. (FRE.). 1989. pap. 28.95 (*0-7859-8059-8*, 2850361046) Fr & Eur.

Montreynaud, Florence & Matignon, Jeanne. Robert Dictionnaire de Citations du Monde Entier. 794p. (FRE.). 1989. 75.00 (*0-8288-9466-3*) Fr & Eur.

***Montreynuad, Florence.** Dictionnaire des Citations Francaises et Etrangeres. 544p. (FRE.). 1985. 69.95 (*0-7859-7727-9*, 2092910612) Fr & Eur.

Montroll, Andrew, ed. see Montroll, John.

Montroll, Andrew, ed. see Montroll, John & Lang, Robert.

Montroll, E. W. & Badger, L. W. Introduction to Quantitative Aspects of Social Phenomena. 360p. 1975. text ed. 77.00 (*0-677-04070-9*) Gordon & Breach.

Montroll, E. W. & Lebowitz, Joel L., eds. Fluctuation Phenomena. (North-Holland Personal Library). 340p. 1987. reprint ed. pap. 32.50 (*0-444-87038-5*, North Holland) Elsevier.

Montroll, E. W., jt. ed. see Lebowitz, J. L.

Montroll, E. W., jt. ed. see Lebowitz, Joel L.

Montroll, E. W., ed. see Vanier, Jacques.

Montroll, John. African Animals in Origami. LC 91-76400. (Illus.). 160p. (Orig.). (YA). 1993. pap. 9.95 (*1-877656-09-7*) Antroll Pub.

— African Animals in Origami. (Illus.). 160p. (Orig.). pap. 9.95 (*0-486-26977-9*) Dover.

— Animal Origami for the Enthusiast: Step-by-Step Instructions in over 900 Diagrams. 1985. pap. 6.95 (*0-486-24792-9*) Dover.

— Birds in Origami. LC 94-40618. 1994. pap. write for info. (*0-486-28341-0*) Dover.

— Easy Origami. LC 92-16933. 1992. pap. write for info. (*0-486-27298-2*) Dover.

— North American Animals in Origami. LC 94-96743. (Illus.). 120p. (Orig.). (YA). 1995. pap. text ed. 9.95 (*1-877656-10-0*) Antroll Pub.

— North American Animals in Origami. LC 94-49013. (Orig.). 1995. pap. write for info. (*0-486-28667-3*) Dover.

— Origami American Style. 32p. (J). (gr. 2 up). 1990. pap. 6.00 (*0-9627254-0-4*) Zenagraf.

— Origami Inside-Out. LC 95-90214. (Illus.). 120p. (YA). 1993. pap. 9.95 (*1-877656-08-9*) Antroll Pub.

— Origami Inside-Out. LC 93-4147. 1993. reprint ed. pap. write for info. (*0-486-27674-0*) Dover.

— Origami Sculptures. 2nd ed. Montroll, Andrew, ed. LC 89-81888. (Illus.). 120p. (Orig.). (YA). 1990. pap. text ed. 9.95 (*1-877656-02-X*) Antroll Pub.

— Origami Sculptures. 2nd ed. (Orig.). 1991. pap. 9.95 (*0-486-26587-0*) Dover.

— Origami Sea Life. 1991. pap. 10.95 (*0-486-26765-2*) Dover.

— Prehistoric Origami: Dinosaurs & Other Creatures. LC 88-84160. (Illus.). 120p. (Orig.). 1989. pap. text ed. 9.95 (*1-877656-01-1*) Antroll Pub.

— Prehistoric Origami Dinosaurs & Other Creatures. 1991. pap. 9.95 (*0-486-26588-9*) Dover.

Montroll, John & Lang, Robert. Origami Sea Life. 2nd ed. Montroll, Andrew, ed. LC 90-80778. (Illus.). 192p. 1991. pap. text ed. 10.95 (*1-877656-05-4*) Antroll Pub.

Montroll, John & Oppenheimer, Lillian. Origami for the Enthusiast: Step-by-Step Instructions in Over 700 Diagrams. (Illus.). 1980. pap. 5.95 (*0-486-23799-0*) Dover.

Montrond, Julia L., tr. see Seely, Contee & Romijn, Elizabeth.

Montrose, Anne. The Love Quadrangle. (Home Video Producer Ser.). (Illus.). 96p. (Orig.). 1987. pap. 14.95 (*0-931145-12-0*) Sandlight Pubns.

Montrose, Catherine. The Wendigo Border. 288p. (Orig.). 1995. pap. 4.99 (*0-8125-2432-2*) Tor Bks.

Montrose, Donald W. Guerra Espiritual: El Ocultismo Tiene Influencia Demoniaca. 1991. 0.50 (*1-56036-016-X*) AMI Pr.

— Spiritual Warfare: The Occult Has Demonic Influence. 1991. 0.50 (*1-56036-014-3*) AMI Pr.

Montross & Canzona. U. S. Marine Operations in Korea, Vol. I: The Pusan Perimeter. (Illus.). 279p. (C). 1992. reprint ed. lib. bdg. 25.00 (*0-944495-01-X*) R J Speights.

— U. S. Marine Operations in Korea, Vol. II: The Inchon-Seoul Operation. (Illus.). 373p. (C). 1992. reprint ed. lib. bdg. 25.00 (*0-944495-02-8*) R J Speights.

— U. S. Marine Operations in Korea, Vol. III: The Chosin Reservoir Campaign. (Illus.). 444p. (C). 1992. reprint ed. lib. bdg. 25.00 (*0-944495-03-6*) R J Speights.

— U. S. Marine Operations in Korea, Vol. IV: The East Central Front. (Illus.). 352p. (C). 1992. reprint ed. lib. bdg. 25.00 (*0-944495-04-4*) R J Speights.

***Montross & Levine.** Vistas: Voces del Mundo Hispanico. 2nd ed. (Illus.). 224p. (C). 1994. pap. text ed. write for info. (*0-13-181686-1*) P-H.

Montross, Ca, jt. auth. see Montross, Lynn.

Montross, David H. & Shinkman, Christopher J., eds. Career Development: Theory & Practice. (Illus.). 442p. (C). 1992. text ed. 67.95x (*0-398-05764-8*) C C Thomas.

— Career Development: Theory & Practice. (Illus.). 442p. 1992. pap. 37.95 (*0-398-06294-3*) C C Thomas.

***Montross, David H., et al.** Real People, Real Jobs: Reflecting Your Interests in the World of Work 40 People Tell You How. LC 95-8818. 250p. (Orig.). 1995. pap. 15.95 (*0-89106-077-4*, 7115) Davies-Black.

Montross, Lois S. Among Those Present. LC 77-132121. (Short Story Index Reprint Ser.). 1977. 19.95 (*0-8369-3678-7*) Ayer.

Montross, Lois S., jt. auth. see Montross, Lynn.

Montross, Lynn & Canzona, Nicholas A. The Chosin Reservoir Campaign. 7th ed. (Elite Unit Ser.). 432p. 1986. reprint ed. 24.95 (*0-89839-098-2*) Battery Pr.

— U. S. Marine Operations in Korea, 1950-53, 4 vols., Ea. 1971. reprint ed. 50.00 (*0-318-68145-5*) Scholarly.

— U. S. Marine Operations in Korea, 1950-53, 4 vols., Set. 1971. reprint ed. 250.00 (*0-403-00030-0*) Scholarly.

Montross, Lynn & Montross, Ca. U. S. Marine Operations in Korea, 1950-53, 4 vols., Set. 1988. reprint ed. lib. bdg. 295.00 (*0-7812-0421-6*) Rprt Serv.

Montross, Lynn & Montross, Lois S. Town & Gown. LC 70-132122. (Short Story Index Reprint Ser.). 1977. 19.95 (*0-8369-3679-5*) Ayer.

Montseny, E. & Frau, J., eds. Specialized Processors for Real-Time Image Analysis: Workshop Proceedings. (ESPRIT Basic Research Ser.). xi, 220p. 1994. 59.00 (*0-387-57016-0*) Spr-Verlag.

Montserrat, Joseph M. Diccionari Manual de la Llengua Catalana. 1401p. (CAT.). 1975. 65.00 (*0-8288-5800-4*, S31550) Fr & Eur.

Montt, Luis, jt. auth. see Mayorga, Roberto.

Montuori, Mario. De Socrate Iuste Damnato: The Rise of the Socratic Problem in the Eighteenth Century. (London Studies in Classical Philology: Vol. 7). 153p. (Orig.). (C). 1981. pap. 27.00 (*90-70265-73-7*, Pub. by Gieben NE) Benjamins North Am.

— John Locke on Toleration & the Unity of God. l, 235p. (C). 1983. 55.00 (*90-70265-25-7*, Pub. by Gieben NE) Benjamins North Am.

— Socrates - An Approach. (Philosphica Ser.: Vol. 2). 235p. (C). 1988. 50.00 (*90-70265-89-3*, Pub. by Gieben NE) Benjamins North Am.

— Socrates Physiology of a Myth. (London Studies in Classical Philology: Vol. 6). viii, 246p. (Orig.). (C). 1981. pap. 41.00 (*90-70265-23-0*, Pub. by Gieben NE) Benjamins North Am.

— The Socratic Problem: The History - Solutions. (Philosophica Ser.: Vol. IV). ix, 475p. 1992. 93.00 (*90-5063-048-0*, Pub. by Gieben NE) Benjamins North Am.

Monture, Joel. The Native American Guide to Traditional Beadwork. LC 93-12101. (Illus.). 112p. 1993. pap. 14.00 (*0-02-066430-3*, Collier S&S) S&S Trade.

Montvay, Istvan & Munster, Gernot. Quantum Fields on a Lattice. (Monographs on Mathematical Physics). (Illus.). 500p. (C). 1994. 100.00 (*0-521-40432-0*) Cambridge U Pr.

Montville, John B. Bulldog: The World's Most Famous Truck. (Illus.). 1979. pap. 19.95 (*0-89404-008-1*) Aztex.

Montville, Joseph V., ed. Conflict & Peacemaking in Multiethnic Societies. 554p. 1989. text ed. 29.95 (*0-669-21453-1*) Free Pr.

Montville, Leigh. Manute: The Center of Two Worlds. (Illus.). 224p. 1993. 20.00 (*0-671-74928-5*) S&S Trade.

Montville, Thomas J. Food Microbiology, 2 vols., Set. 480p. 1987. 289.00 (*0-8493-6474-4*, QR115) CRC Pr.

— Food Microbiology, Vol. I: Concepts in Physiology & Metabolism. 176p. 1987. Vol. I: Concepts in Physiology & Meatbolism, 176pp. write for info. (*0-318-61686-6*) CRC Pr.

— Food Microbiology, Vol. II: New & Emerging Technologies. 232p. 1987. write for info. (*0-318-61687-4*) CRC Pr.

Montville, Vicki, ed. see Houde, Mary J.

Montwieler, Nancy H. The Immigration Reform Law of 1986: Analysis, Text, & Legislative History. LC 87-15784. 571p. reprint ed. pap. 162.80 (*0-7837-6418-9*, 2046398) Bks Demand.

Montwill, Michael A., et al. Public Awareness of the Nebraska Regional Poison Control Center. 14p. (Orig.). 1979. pap. 1.50 (*1-55719-023-2*) U NE CPAR.

***Monty, C. L., et al, eds.** Carbonate Mud-Mounds: Their Origins & Evolution. LC 94-41305. (Special Publications of the International Association of Sedimentologists: No. 23). 1995. write for info. (*0-86542-933-2*) Blackwell Sci.

Monty, Claude, jt. ed. see Bertrand-Sarfati, Janine.

Monty, Margaret. Cumulative Index of First Days Magazine. 350p. 1992. pap. text ed. 14.95 (*1-879390-11-6*) Am First Day.

Montz, G., jt. auth. see Brown, C.

Montzka, Arthur & Timmerman, Craig. Suzuki Images. LC 88-62934. 64p. (Orig.). 1988. pap. text ed. 19.95 (*0-9621416-0-7*) Shar Prods.

Monush, Barry. International Motion Picture Almanac, Vol. 62. 760p. 1991. 77.00 (*0-900610-44-1*) Quigley Pub Co.

— International Television & Video Almanac, 1991, Vol. 36. 752p. 1991. 77.00 (*0-900610-45-X*) Quigley Pub Co.

***Monush, Barry, ed.** International Motion Picture Almanac. 66th ed. 800p. 1995. 91.00x (*0-900610-52-2*) Quigley Pub Co.

— International Motion Picture Almanac 1993. 1993. 85.00 (*0-900610-48-4*) Quigley Pub Co.

— International Motion Picture Almanac, 1994. 800p. 1994. 88.50 (*0-900610-50-6*) Quigley Pub Co.

— International Television & Video Almanac. 40th ed. 800p. 1995. 91.00x (*0-900610-53-0*) Quigley Pub Co.

— International Television & Video Almanac, 1993. 1993. 85.00 (*0-900610-49-2*) Quigley Pub Co.

— International Television & Video Almanac, 1994. 800p. 1994. 88.50 (*0-900610-51-4*) Quigley Pub Co.

Monush, Barry, jt. ed. see Quigley, Martin.

Monville-Burston, Monique, ed. see Jakobson, Roman.

Monz, John, ed. see Fisher, Franklin M.

Monzert. Practical Distiller. 1987. reprint ed. pap. 7.95 (*0-917914-58-9*) Lindsay Pubns.

Monzingo, Robert. Thomas Starr King. (Illus.). 1991. pap. 12.50 (*0-940168-20-0*) Boxwood.

Moo, Douglas. James. Tasker, R. V., ed. (Tyndale New Testament Commentaries Ser.). 176p. (Orig.). 1987. pap. 9.99 (*0-8028-0079-3*) Eerdmans.

— Romans 1-8. (Wycliffe Exegetical Commentary Ser.). 640p. 1991. 29.99 (*0-8024-9263-0*) Moody.

Moo-Sook, Hahn. Encounter: A Novel of Nineteenth-Century Korea. Chang, Ok Y., tr. (Voices from Asia Ser.: No. 5). (C). 1992. 45.00 (*0-520-07380-0*); pap. 15.00 (*0-520-07381-9*) U CA Pr.

Moo-Young, M., ed. Bioreactor Immobilized Enzymes & Cells: Fundamentals & Applications. 328p. 1988. 77.50 (*1-85166-160-3*) Elsevier.

— Comprehensive Biotechnology: The Practice of Biotechnology: Current Comodity Products, Vol. 3. LC 85-6509. (Illus.). 1136p. 1985. 635.00 (*0-08-032511-4*, Pergamon Pr); Incl. 4 vols. 995.00 (*0-317-63020-2*, Pergamon Pr) Elsevier.

— Comprehensive Biotechnology: The Principles, Applications & Regulations of Biotechnology in Industry, Agriculture & Medicine, 4 Vols. (Illus.). 3500p. 1985. 2,015.00 (*0-08-026204-X*, Pergamon Pr); 350.00 (*0-08-032510-6*, Pergamon Pr) Elsevier.

— Comprehensive Biotechnology: The Principles of Biotechnology: Scientific Fundamentals, Vol. 1. LC 85-6509. (Illus.). 688p. 1985. 375.00 (*0-08-032509-2*, Pergamon Pr); Incl. 4 vols. 995.00 (*0-317-63019-9*, Pergamon Pr) Elsevier.

Moo-Young, M. & Gregory, F., eds. Microbial Biomass Proteins. 185p. 1987. 52.25 (*1-85166-085-2*, Pub. by Elsevier Applied Sci UK) Elsevier.

Moo-Young, M. & Robinson, C. W., eds. Comprehensive Biotechnology: The Practice of Biotechnology: Specialty Products & Service Activities, Vol. 4. LC 85-6509. (Illus.). 1308p. 1985. 705.00 (*0-08-032512-2*, Pergamon Pr); Incl. 4 vols. 995.00 (*0-317-63021-0*, Pergamon Pr) Elsevier.

Moo-Young, M., jt. ed. see Alani, D. I.

Moo-Young, M., jt. auth. see United Nations Environment Programme Staff.

Moo-Young, M., et al, eds. Biomass Conversion Technology, Principles & Practice: Symposium on Biomass Conversion Technology 1984. (Illus.). 224p. 1987. 97.00 (*0-08-033174-2*, Pergamon Pr) Elsevier.

— Waste Treatment & Utilization: Theory & Practice of Waste Management Two, Proceedings. (Illus.). 587p. 1982. 238.00 (*0-08-024012-7*, Pub. by Pergamon Repr UK) Franklin.

Mooar, G. The Cummings Memorial: A Genealogical History of the Descendants of Isaac Cummings, an Early Settler of Topsfield, Mass. 535p. 1989. reprint ed. lib. bdg. 77.50 (*0-8328-0442-8*); reprint ed. pap. 67.50 (*0-8328-0443-6*) Higginson Bk Co.

Mooberry, F. M. & Scott, Jane H. Grow Native Shrubs in Your Garden. LC 80-69807. 1980. 4.95 (*0-940540-01-0*) Brandywine Conserv.

Moock, Joyce L. & Moock, Peter R. Higher Education & Rural Development in Africa. 42p. 1977. pap. 1.75 (*0-89192-228-8*) Interbk Inc.

Moock, Joyce L. & Rhoades, Robert E., eds. Diversity, Farmer Knowledge, & Sustainability. LC 92-52768. (Food Systems in Agrarian Change Ser.). 296p. 1992. 49.95 (*0-8014-2682-0*); pap. 18.95 (*0-8014-9968-2*) Cornell U Pr.

Moock, Peter R., jt. auth. see Moock, Joyce L.

Mood, et al. Sports & Recreational Activities for Men & Women. (Illus.). 576p. (C). 1990. pap. 29.95 (*0-8016-6202-8*) Mosby Yr Bk.

Mood, A. M. Introduction to Policy Analysis. 302p. 1982. 49.75 (*0-444-00671-0*, North Holland) Elsevier.

Mood, Alexander M., et al. Introduction to the Theory of Statistics. 3rd ed. (Illus.). 480p. (C). 1974. text ed. write for info. (*0-07-042864-6*) McGraw.

Mood, Dale, et al. Sports & Recreational Activities for Men & Women. 11th ed. LC 94-19503. 1994. write for info. (*0-8151-5955-2*) Mosby Yr Bk.

Mood, Eric W., ed. Housing & Health: APHA-CDC Recommended Minimum Housing Standards. LC 86-10884. 1986. 8.50 (*0-87553-138-5*) Am Pub Health.

— Public Swimming Pools: Recommended Regulations for Design & Construction, Operation & Maintenance. LC 81-68843. 72p. 1981. 6.00 (*0-87553-096-6*, 055) Am Pub Health.

Mood, John J. Rilke on Love & Other Difficulties: Translations & Considerations of Rainer Maria Rilke. 120p. 1994. pap. 8.95 (*0-393-31098-1*) Norton.

Mood, Karen. George Walton: Designer & Architect. (Illus.). 200p. 1994. 55.00 (*1-873487-01-0*, Pub. by White Cockade UK) Paul & Co Pubs.

***Mood, Terry A.** Distance Education: An Annotated Bibliography. 200p. 1995. pap. text ed. 27.50 (*1-56308-160-1*) Libs Unl.

Moodie, C. L., jt. ed. see Nof, Shimon Y.

Moodie, Craig. A Sailor's Valentine. 208p. 1994. 17.95 (*0-312-11053-7*) St Martin.

Moodie, D. C. History of the Battles & Adventures of the British, the Boers & the Zulus, Etc. in Southern Africa, 2 vols., Set. (Illus.). 1968. reprint ed. 95.00 (*0-7146-1776-8*, Pub. by F Cass Pubs UK) Intl Spec Bk.

Moodie, Fiona. Boy & the Giants. (J). (ps-3). 1993. 15.00 (*0-374-30927-2*) FS&G.

— The Sugar Prince. (Illus.). (J). (ps-3). 1987. 12.95 (*1-55774-005-4*) Modan-Adama Bks.

Moodie, G. C. Standards & Criteria in Higher Education: Proceedings of Annual Conference Held December 1986. 170p. 1986. pap. 45.00 (*1-85059-015-X*) Taylor & Francis.

Moodie, John. Hath the Lion Prevailed. (Illus.). (Orig.). Date not set. pap. 6.95 (*1-56411-060-5*) Untd Bros & Sis.

Moodie-Kublalsingh, Sylvia. The Payols of Trinidad: A Vanishing Culture. 272p. 1994. text ed. 55.00 (*1-85043-660-6*, Pub. by I B Tauris UK) St Martin.

Moodie, Michael. Conventional Arms Control & Defense Acquisition: Catching the Caboose? (Significant Issues Ser.). (Orig.). 1990. pap. text ed. 1.00 (*0-89206-148-0*) CSI Studies.

— Defense Implications of Europe 92. (Significant Issues Ser.: Vol. 12, No. 2). 36p. (Orig.). 1990. pap. text ed. 1.00 (*0-89206-151-0*) CSI Studies.

— The Dreadful Fury: Advanced Military Technology and the Atlantic Alliance. LC 88-38059. (CSIS Washington Papers). 190p. 1989. text ed. 45.00 (*0-275-93236-2*, Praeger Pubs); pap. text ed. 10.95 (*0-275-93237-0*, Praeger Pubs) Greenwood.

— The Dreadful Fury: Advanced Military Technology & the Atlantic Alliance. (Washington Papers: No. 136). 155p. 1989. 34.95 (*0-685-47126-8*, C3236, Praeger Pubs); pap. 10.95 (*0-685-47127-6*, B3237, Praeger Pubs) Greenwood.

Moodie, Michael, jt. auth. see Bray, Frank T.

Moodie, Roy L. The Antiquity of Disease. LC 75-23743. reprint ed. 29.50 (*0-404-13298-7*) AMS Pr.

Moodie, Roy Lee. Paleopathology: An Introduction to the Study of Ancient Evidences of Disease. LC 75-23744. reprint ed. 74.50 (*0-404-13350-9*) AMS Pr.

Moodie, Roy Lee, ed. see Ruffer, Marc A.

Moodie, T. B., jt. auth. see Rogers, C. A.

Moodie, T. Dunbar & Ndatshe, Vivienne. Going for Gold: Men, Mines, & Migration. LC 93-28187. 1994. 45.00 (*0-520-08130-7*); pap. 16.00 (*0-520-08644-9*) U CA Pr.

Moodie, William. Hypnosis in Treatment. 1960. 12.95 (*0-87523-121-7*) Emerson.

Moodley, Kogila, jt. auth. see Adam, Heribert.

***Moodley, Kogila A., ed. & intro.** Beyond Multicultural Education: International Perspectives. 318p. (Orig.). (C). 1992. pap. text ed. 18.95x (*1-55059-029-4*) Temeron Bks.

Moodley, Parimala, et al. Patient Management Problems in Psychiatry: For the Mrcpsych Oral Examination. (Illus.). 144p. (Orig.). 1991. pap. text ed. 24.00 (*0-443-04374-4*) Churchill.

Moody. Incontinence. 184p. 1990. pap. text ed. 39.95 (*0-433-00086-4*) Buttrwrth-Heinemann.

— Surgical Treatment of Digestive Diseases. 2nd ed. 960p. 1989. 169.00 (*0-8151-5945-5*, Yr Bk Med Pubs) Mosby Yr Bk.

— What to Do When a Micro Lands on Your Desk. 1990. pap. 34.95 (*0-85384-011-3*) Buttrwrth-Heinemann.

Moody & Spurgeon. El Milagro de la Cruz: The Calvary's Cross. (SPA.). 3.95 (*84-7645-103-2*, 223156, Pub. by Edit Clie SP) TSELF.

***Moody, et al.** Hablaron De la Gracia. Austin, Bobby, ed. Arancibia, Rene, tr. 192p. 1994. pap. text ed. write for info. (*0-9639640-2-X*) Grace Vision.

Moody, A. D. Thomas Stearns Eliot: Poet. 2nd ed. 420p. (C). 1995. pap. 18.95 (*0-521-46750-0*) Cambridge U Pr.

Moody, A. David. Thomas Stearns Eliot: Poet. 2nd ed. 420p. (C). 1995. 59.95 (*0-521-46186-3*) Cambridge U Pr.

Moody, A. David, ed. The Cambridge Companion to T. S. Eliot. LC 93-43558. (Cambridge Companions to Literature Ser.). 300p. (C). 1995. 59.95 (*0-521-42080-6*) Cambridge U Pr.

— The Cambridge Companion to T. S. Eliot. LC 93-43558. (Companions to Literature Ser.). 300p. (C). 1995. pap. 16.95 (*0-521-42127-6*) Cambridge U Pr.

Moody, A. H., jt. auth. see Fleck, S.

Moody, Alice B. Clippings from the Garden. LC 91-67103. 55p. 1992. 6.95 (*1-55523-483-6*) Winston-Derek.

Moody, Allen C. Crisis on the Miracle Planet. LC 92-61967. 152p. 1994. pap. 9.00 (*1-56002-207-8*, Univ Edtns) Aegina Pr.

Moody, Ann B., illus. & intro. U & I. 200p. 1994. pap. 9.95 (*0-9639366-0-3*) A B Moody.

Moody, Anne. Coming of Age in Mississippi. 384p. (gr. 9 up). 1992. mass mkt. 5.99 (*0-440-31488-7*, LE) Dell.

Moody, Bernard J. Comparative Inorganic Chemistry. 3rd ed. (Illus.). 510p. 1990. pap. text ed. 35.00 (*0-7131-3679-0*, A4393, Pub. by E Arnold UK) Routledge Chapman & Hall.

***Moody, Bert.** A Pictorial History of Southampton Docks. 64p. 1994. pap. 15.95 (*0-946184-82-8*) Hallenbook.

***Moody, Bill.** Death of a Tenor Man: An Evan Horne Mystery. Date not set. 19.95 (*0-614-05631-4*) Walker & Co.

— The Jazz Exiles: American Musicians Abroad. LC 92-26936. (Illus.). 168p. 1993. 21.95 (*0-87417-214-4*) U of Nev Pr.

— Solo Hand. 1994. 19.95 (*0-8027-3248-8*) Walker & Co.

Moody, C., ed. Ilya Ehrenburg: Selections from People, Years & Life. LC 73-128339. 312p. 1972. pap. 125.00 (*0-08-006354-3*, Pub. by Pergamon Repr UK) Franklin.

Moody, Charles S. Backwoods Surgery & Medicine. (Shorey Lost Arts Ser.). 1974. reprint ed. pap. 3.95 (*0-8466-6034-2*, U 34) Shorey.

***Moody, Chip.** Moments: The Life & Career of a Texas Newsman. 216p. 1995. 19.95 (*0-87833-895-0*) Taylor Pub.

Moody, Chris J., jt. auth. see Harwood, L. M.

Moody, Christine. Five Minute Hairstylist. 1991. 18.00 (*0-517-58224-4*, Crown) Crown Pub Group.

Moody, Christopher J. & Whitham, Gordon H. Reactive Intermediates. (Oxford Chemistry Primers Ser.: No. 8). (Illus.). 96p. (C). 1992. pap. text ed. 9.95 (*0-19-855672-1*) OUP.

Moody, Christopher L. The Wit & Wisdom of Idi Amin. LC 77-88611. (Illus.). 1977. pap. 2.75 (*0-930830-01-6*) Great Basin.

Moody, D. L. Amor Maravilloso: Wondrous Love. (SPA.). 4.95 (*84-7228-969-9*, 223021, Pub. by Edit Clie SP) TSELF.

— El Camino Hacia el Cielo: Heaven & How to Get There. (SPA.). 3.95 (*84-7228-945-1*, 223019, Pub. by Edit Clie SP) TSELF.

An Asterisk (*) at the beginning of an entry indicates that the title is appearing in BIP for the first time.

— Heaven: How to Get There. 112p. 1982. reprint ed. pap. text ed. 4.99 (*0-88368-115-3*) Whitaker Hse.

— Oracion Que Prevalece: Prevailing Prayer. (SPA.). 3.95 (*84-7228-691-6*, 220638, Pub. by Edit Clie SP) TSELF.

— The Overcoming Life: Moody Press Centennial Edition 1894-1994. 1994. pap. 0.25 (*0-8024-0547-9*) Moody.

— Peregrinos Hacia el Hogar Celestial: The Way Home. (SPA.). 3.25 (*84-7228-946-X*, 223026, Pub. by Edit Clie SP) TSELF.

— Prevailing Prayer. (Moody Classics Ser.). pap. 3.99 (*0-8024-6731-8*) Moody.

— Thoughts for the Quiet Hour. 256p. 1993. pap. 4.99 (*0-88368-247-8*) Whitaker Hse.

— The Way to God. 160p. 1983. pap. text ed. 4.99 (*0-88368-131-5*) Whitaker Hse.

Moody, Dale. Apostasy: A Study in the Epistle to the Hebrews & in Baptist History. 84p. (Orig.). 1991. pap. text ed. 6.95 (*0-9628455-3-1*) Smyth & Helwys.

— The Word of Truth: A Summary of Christian Doctrine Based on Biblical Revelation. fac. ed. LC 80-19103. 640p. 1990. reprint ed. pap. 180.00 (*0-7837-7966-6*, 2047722) Bks Demand.

Moody, Daniel J., jt. auth. see Tolos, Peter C.

***Moody, David.** Scottish Family History. 219p. 1989. pap. 18.95 (*0-614-03821-9*, 3860) Genealog Pub.

— Scottish Local History. 178p. 1994. 18.95 (*0-8063-1269-6*, 3861) Genealog Pub.

Moody, David E., ed. Peroxisome Proliferators: Unique Inducers of Drug-Metabolizing Enzymes. 208p. 1994. 179.95 (*0-8493-8305-6*, 8305) CRC Pr.

Moody, David W., et al, eds. National Water Summary, 1985: Hydrologic Events & Surface-Water Resources. (Geological Survey Water Supply Papers: No. 2300). (Illus.). 516p. 1986. pap. 31.00 (*0-318-21581-0*, S/N 024-001-03549-9) USGPO.

Moody, Debby, jt. auth. see Rettig, Tom.

Moody, Debra L. Youth Training Leadership Program. (Illus.). 92p. (Orig.). (J). (gr. 6-12). 1989. teacher ed, pap. 25.00 (*0-9618164-3-0*) PA Coun Churches.

Moody, Douglas, ed. Patterson's American Education. rev. ed. LC 04-12935. (Nineteen Ninety-Four Edition Ser.: Vol. 90). 850p. 1993. 79.00 (*0-910536-58-9*) Ed Direct.

— Patterson's American Education, Vol. 92, 1996. rev. ed. LC 94-12935. 912p. 1995. 83.00 (*0-910536-61-9*) Ed Direct.

— Patterson's American Education, 1993, Vol. 89. rev. ed. 830p. 1992. 75.00 (*0-910536-55-4*, 4-12935) Ed Direct.

— Patterson's Elementary Education Vol. 7, 1995. rev. ed. LC 89-646629. 992p. 1994. 81.00 (*0-910536-62-7*) Ed Direct.

— Patterson's Elementary Education, 1993, Vol. 5. rev. ed. 870p. 1992. 75.00 (*0-910536-56-2*) Ed Direct.

— Patterson's Elementary Education, 1994. rev. ed. (Nineteen Ninety-Four Edition Ser.: Vol. 6). 870p. 1993. 79.00 (*0-910536-59-7*) Ed Direct.

Moody, Dwight L. The Best of Dwight L. Moody. (Best Ser.). 249p. 1991. pap. 7.99 (*0-8010-6216-0*) Baker Bk.

— El Camino Hacia Dios. Orig. Title: The Way to God. 128p. (SPA.). 1983. pap. 3.99 (*0-8254-1490-3*) Kregel.

— Doscientas Anecdotas e Ilustraciones. Orig. Title: Two Hundred Anecdotes & Illustrations. 128p. (SPA.). 1983. pap. 3.99 (*0-8254-1491-1*) Kregel.

— Moody's Child Stories. (Illus.). 237p. (J). (gr. 1 up). reprint ed. 19.95 (*1-880045-12-5*) Back Home Indust.

— Thoughts for the Quiet Hour: A Daily Devotional. 1994. 12.99 (*1-56507-275-8*) Harvest Hse.

Moody, Dwight L. & Martin, Walter. Secret Power. rev. ed. LC 87-9533. 1987. reprint ed. pap. 7.99 (*0-8307-1219-4*, 5419181) Regal.

Moody, Dwight L., jt. auth. see Drummond, Henry.

***Moody, E. Grant.** Raising Small Animals. 330p. 1990. text ed. 32.95 (*0-85236-228-5*, Pub. by Farming Pr UK) Diamond Farm Bk.

Moody, Elizabeth, et al. Wills & Trusts. (Smith's Review Ser.). 180p. 1993. pap. text ed. 13.95 (*1-56542-181-7*) E Law Outlines.

Moody, Eric N. Flanigan: Anatomy of a Railroad Ghost Town. (Illus.). 121p. (Orig.). 1986. pap. 8.25 (*0-938373-13-7*) Lahontan Images.

Moody, Eric N., ed. see Fitch, Thomas.

Moody, Ernest A. Truth & Consequence in Medieval Logic. LC 76-44307. (Studies in Logic & the Foundations of Mathematics). 113p. 1976. reprint ed. text ed. 38.50 (*0-8371-9053-3*, MOTC, Greenwood Pr) Greenwood.

Moody, Ernest A., ed. see Buridan, Jean.

Moody, F. J. & Shin, Y. W., eds. Advances in Fluid Structure Interaction Dynamics. (PVP Ser.: Vol. 75). 184p. 1983. text ed. 17.00 (*0-317-02546-5*, H00261); pap. text ed. 34.00 (*0-317-02547-3*) ASME.

Moody, F. J. & Wiggert, D. C., eds. Unsteady Flows, 1993. 501p. 1993. pap. 30.00 (*0-7918-1014-3*) ASME.

Moody, F. J., ed. see American Society of Mechanical Engineers Staff.

Moody, F. J., jt. auth. see Lahey, R. T.

***Moody, Fred.** I Sing the Body Electronic. LC 95-1919. 1995. 24.95 (*0-670-84875-1*, Viking) Viking Penguin.

Moody, Frederick J. Introduction to Unsteady Thermofluid Mechanics. 654p. 1990. text ed. 115.00 (*0-471-85705-X*) Wiley.

Moody, G. J. & Thomas, J. D. Chromatographic Separation & Extraction with Foamed Plastics & Rubbers. LC 82-4636. (Chromatographic Science Ser.: No. 21). (Illus.). 151p. reprint ed. pap. 43.10 (*0-7837-0622-7*, 2040966) Bks Demand.

Moody, G. M. & Thomas, J. Noble Gases & Their Compounds. LC 64-17965. 1964. 37.00 (*0-08-010843-1*, Pub. by Pergamon Repr UK) Franklin.

Moody, G. W. & Baker, P. B., eds. Bioreactors & Biotransformations. 406p. 1987. 83.00 (*1-85166-162-X*, Pub. by Elsevier Applied Sci UK) Elsevier.

Moody, Gary A., et al. Device-Based Training of Armor Crewmen. LC 93-13905. 1993. write for info. (*0-8330-1397-1*, MR-119-A) Rand Corp.

***Moody, Glen.** The Internet with Windows. 350p. 1995. pap. 24.95 (*0-7506-9704-0*) Buttrwrth-Heinemann.

***Moody, Glyn.** The Internet: A Practical Companion. 350p. 1995. pap. 47.95 (*0-7506-2099-4*, Focal) Buttrwrth-Heinemann.

— Windows & PCs: A Complete Introduction. 320p. 1993. pap. 29.95 (*0-7506-0956-7*) Buttrwrth-Heinemann.

***Moody, Greg.** Two Wheels: A Cycling Murder Mystery Novel. 142p. 1995. pap. 12.95 (*1-884737-11-0*) VeloPress.

Moody, Harry R. Abundance of Life: Human Development Policies for an Aging Society. Monk, Abraham, ed. (Studies of Social Gerontology & Aging). 320p. 1988. text ed. 41.00 (*0-231-06592-2*) Col U Pr.

Moody, Harry R., Jr. Aging: Concepts & Controversies. 512p. 1994. pap. 31.95 (*0-8039-9013-8*) Pine Forge.

Moody, Harry R. Ethics in an Aging Society. 288p. 1992. text ed. 40.00 (*0-8018-4323-5*) Johns Hopkins.

Moody, Helen, ed. see Thompson, George J. & Stroud, Michael J.

***Moody Institute of Science Staff.** Dust of Destiny. CRM Staff, tr. 15p. (CHI.). 1985. 0.35 (*1-56582-053-3*) Christ Renew Min.

— Empty Cities. CRM Staff, tr. 15p. (CHI.). 1978. 0.35 (*1-56582-062-2*) Christ Renew Min.

— Facts of Faith. CRM Staff, tr. 15p. (CHI.). 1984. 0.35 (*1-56582-059-2*) Christ Renew Min.

— God of Creation. CRM Staff, tr. 15p. (CHI.). 1985. 0.35 (*1-56582-065-7*) Christ Renew Min.

— God of the Atom. CRM Staff, tr. 15p. (CHI.). 1986. 0.35 (*1-56582-054-1*) Christ Renew Min.

— Hidden Treasures. CRM Staff, tr. 15p. (CHI.). 1985. 0.35 (*1-56582-066-5*) Christ Renew Min.

— Of Books & Sloths. CRM Staff, tr. 15p. (CHI.). 1976. 0.35 (*1-56582-057-6*) Christ Renew Min.

— The Prior Claim. CRM Staff, tr. 15p. (CHI.). 1985. 0.35 (*1-56582-067-3*) Christ Renew Min.

— Professor & the Prophets. CRM Staff, tr. 15p. (CHI.). 1982. 0.35 (*1-56582-064-9*) Christ Renew Min.

— Red River of Life. CRM Staff, tr. 15p. (CHI.). 1977. 0.35 (*1-56582-061-4*) Christ Renew Min.

— Signposts Aloft. CRM Staff, tr. 15p. (CHI.). 1985. 0.35 (*1-56582-068-1*) Christ Renew Min.

— Time & Eternity. CRM Staff, tr. 15p. (CHI.). 1977. 0.35 (*1-56582-060-6*) Christ Renew Min.

— The Ultimate Adventure. CRM Staff, tr. 15p. (CHI.). 1986. 0.35 (*1-56582-055-X*) Christ Renew Min.

— Voice of the Deep. CRM Staff, tr. 15p. (CHI.). 1982. 0.35 (*1-56582-063-0*) Christ Renew Min.

— Where the Waters Run. CRM Staff, tr. 15p. (CHI.). 1980. 0.35 (*1-56582-056-8*) Christ Renew Min.

— Window of the Soul. CRM Staff, tr. 15p. (CHI.). 1983. 0.35 (*1-56582-058-4*) Christ Renew Min.

Moody, J. B. My Church. 325p. 1974. reprint ed. 9.50 (*0-87921-030-3*) Attic Pr.

Moody, J. V. & Francke, O. F. The Ants (Hymenoptera, Formicidae) of Western Texas: Part I - Subfamily Myrmicinae. (Graduate Studes: No. 27). 80p. (Orig.). 1982. pap. 12.00 (*0-89672-107-8*) Tex Tech Univ Pr.

Moody, James. Lieutenant James Moody's Narrative of His Exertions & Sufferings in the Cause of Government, Since the Year 1776. LC 67-29040. (Eyewitness Accounts of the American Revolution Ser., No. 1). 1976. reprint ed. 17.95 (*0-405-01138-5*) Ayer.

Moody, James L. Concert Lighting: Techniques, Art, & Business. 240p. 1989. 44.95 (*0-240-80010-9*, Focal) Buttrwrth-Heinemann.

Moody, Jean S., ed. see Moody, Ralph.

Moody, Jennifer, jt. auth. see Rackham, Oliver.

Moody, Jo. Beads. (Keepsake Crafts Ser.). 1995. pap. 9.99 (*0-376-04258-3*) Sunset Menlo Pk.

— Buttons. (Keepsake Crafts Ser.). 1995. pap. 9.99 (*0-376-04257-5*) Sunset Menlo Pk.

Moody, Jo A., jt. auth. see Huey, Susan O.

Moody, Joan, jt. ed. see Wizansky, Richard.

Moody, John. The Art of Wise Investing. 93p. reprint ed. 16.95 (*0-931133-07-6*, Busn Class) Pac Pub Grp.

— Group for Undergraduates. 180p. 1994. text ed. 36.00 (*981-02-1557-6*) World Scientific Pub.

— The Long Road Home: An Autobiography. LC 75-2650. (Wall Street & the Security Market Ser.). 1975. reprint ed. 25.95 (*0-405-06975-8*) Ayer.

— Profitable Investing: Fundamentals of the Science of Investing. LC 75-2651. (Wall Street & the Security Market Ser.). 1975. reprint ed. 28.95 (*0-405-06976-6*) Ayer.

Moody, John, tr. see Bizet, Georges.

Moody, John, jt. ed. see Potts, Ken.

Moody, John E., et al, eds. Advances in Neural Information Processing Systems, Vol. 4. 1993. text ed. 54.95 (*1-55860-222-4*) Morgan Kaufmann.

Moody, Joo. The Book of Jewelry: Create Your Own Jewelry with Beads, Clay, Papier-mache, Fabric & Other Everyday Items. LC 94-1812. 1994. 22.95 (*0-671-89096-4*) S&S Trade.

Moody, Joseph N. French Education since Napoleon. 1978. 39.95x (*0-8156-2193-0*) Syracuse U Pr.

Moody, Joseph N., ed. see Carter, Edward C.

Moody, Karen, ed. see Whetzell, Becky J.

Moody, Kim. An Injury to All. 400p. 1988. text ed. 50.00 (*0-86091-216-7*, Pub. by Verso UK); pap. text ed. 16.95 (*0-86091-929-3*, Pub. by Verso UK) Routledge Chapman & Hall.

Moody, Kim & McGinn, Mary. Unions & Free Trade: Solidarity vs. Competition. LC 92-70092. (Illus.). 84p. (Orig.). 1992. pap. 7.00 (*0-914093-05-3*) Labor Notes.

Moody, Larry, jt. auth. see Boa, Kenneth.

Moody, Linda, ed. see Clayton, Gloria & Broome, Marion.

Moody, Linda, ed. see Diekelmann, Nancy, et al.

Moody, Linda E., ed. Advancing Nursing Science Through Research, Vol. 2. 328p. (C). 1990. text ed. 46.00 (*0-8039-3812-8*) Sage.

— Advancing Theory for Nursing Science Through Research, Vol. 1. (Illus.). 288p. (C). 1990. text ed. 44.00 (*0-8039-3811-X*) Sage.

Moody, Loring. Facts for the People: Showing the Relations of the United States Government to Slavery. LC 72-149872. (Black Heritage Library Collection). 1977. 19.95 (*0-8369-8752-7*) Ayer.

Moody, M., jt. auth. see Bennet, G.

Moody, Marilyn K., jt. auth. see Sears, Jean L.

Moody, Marvin D. A Classification of Noun De Noun Construction in French. 1973. pap. text ed. 73.85 (*90-279-2434-1*) Mouton.

***Moody, Mary.** Folk Art. 1994. 5.99 (*0-517-10254-4*) Random Hse Value.

***Moody, Mary, ed.** 100 Plants for Easy to Maintain Gardens. LC 94-33556. 1995. write for info. (*0-517-12127-1*) Random Hse Value.

— 100 Plants for Pots & Containers. LC 94-33557. 1995. write for info. (*0-517-12125-5*) Random Hse Value.

— 100 Plants for Quick-Growing Gardens. LC 94-33559. 1995. write for info. (*0-517-12134-4*) Random Hse Value.

— 100 Plants for Shady Gardens. LC 94-33554. 1995. write for info. (*0-517-12126-3*) Random Hse Value.

Moody, Mary & Harkness, Peter, eds. Illustrated Encyclopedia of Roses. (Illus.). 304p. 1992. 39.95 (*0-88192-271-4*) Timber.

***Moody, Mary C.** 1890 Caldwell County TX Census Uniquely Reconstructed & Annotated. Date not set. pap. write for info. (*0-614-06214-4*) Blackstone Pub.

— 1890 Cass County, Texas Census Uniquely Reconstructed & Annotated. LC 94-79305. 284p. (Orig.). 1994. pap. 32.50 (*1-884130-02-X*) Blackstone Pub.

— Every Name Index to the Montgomery County, Texas Federal Census, 1880. LC 94-70532. 82p. (Orig.). 1994. pap. 14.95 (*1-884130-01-1*) Blackstone Pub.

— Every Name Index to the 1880 Cass County, Texas Federal Census. LC 95-75182. 155p. (Orig.). 1995. pap. 24.50 (*1-884130-03-8*) Blackstone Pub.

— Every Name Index to the 1880 Cass County TX Census. LC 95-75182. 155p. (Orig.). 1995. pap. 24.50 (*0-614-06213-6*) Blackstone Pub.

— Every Name Index to the 1880 Walker County, Texas Census. LC 93-70268. 94p. 1993. pap. 23.95 (*0-9615836-9-X*) Blackstone Pub.

— Montgomery County, Texas Census Uniquely Reconstructed & Annotated, 1890. LC 93-74229. 211p. (Orig.). 1993. pap. 34.50 (*1-884130-00-3*) Blackstone Pub.

— Walker County, Texas Census Uniquely Reconstructed & Annotated, 1890. 1992. pap. 34.50 (*0-9615836-8-1*) Blackstone Pub.

Moody, Mary C., comp. Every Name Index to the Limestone County, Texas Federal Census, 1880. LC 88-92688. 153p. (Orig.). 1989. pap. 27.95 (*0-9615836-4-9*) Blackstone Pub.

— Every Name Index to the 1880 Travis County, Texas Federal Census. LC 90-81080. (Orig.). 1990. pap. 32.50 (*0-9615836-5-7*) Blackstone Pub.

— Every Name Index to W. W. Sellers, Esq. A History of Marion County, South Carolina. LC 85-72904. 188p. (Orig.). 1985. pap. 24.95 (*0-9615836-1-4*) Blackstone Pub.

— Limestone County 1890, Texas Census: Uniquely Reconstructed & Annotated. LC 87-63560. 272p. (Orig.). 1988. pap. 32.50 (*0-9615836-3-0*) Blackstone Pub.

— A New Index to Bishop Gregg's History of the Old Cheraws: People & Places, Indians, Slaves. LC 86-70106. 100p. (Orig.). 1986. pap. 15.50 (*0-9615836-2-2*) Blackstone Pub.

— Travis County, Texas Census, 1890 Pt. I: Uniquely Reconstructed & Annotated. LC 91-76865. 418p. (Orig.). 1991. Part I. pap. 57.95 (*0-9615836-6-5*) Blackstone Pub.

— Travis County, Texas Census, 1890 Pt. II: Uniquely Reconstructed & Annotated. LC 91-76865. 418p. (Orig.). 1991. Part II. pap. write for info. (*0-9615836-7-3*) Blackstone Pub.

Moody, Mary C. & Moody, Virgil B. The Moodys & Related Families. LC 79-90278. 184p. 1979. 35.00 (*0-9615836-0-6*) Blackstone Pub.

Moody, Michael D. The Shortchanged Review. 1976. pap. 4.75 (*0-8222-1024-X*) Dramatists Play.

Moody, N. R., jt. ed. see Thompson, A. W.

Moody, Nell, tr. see Bizet, Georges.

Moody, Neville R., ed. see International Conference on Effect of Hydrogen on Behavior of Materials Staff.

Moody, O. William, jt. auth. see Seelye, Richard S.

Moody, P., jt. auth. see Smith, B.

Moody, P. C., jt. auth. see Wilkinson, A. J.

Moody, Patricia. Strategic Manufacturing: Dynamic New Directions for the 1990s. 350p. 1989. text ed. 45.00 (*1-55623-193-8*) Irwin Prof Pubng.

Moody, Patricia E. Breakthrough Partnering: Creating a Collective Enterprise Advantage. LC 93-60669. 256p. 1993. 75.00 (*0-939246-39-2*) Oliver Wight.

Moody, Paul D., et al. Religion of Soldier & Sailor. LC 45-3352. 123p. 1945. 13.95 (*0-674-75750-5*) HUP.

Moody, Peter R., Jr. Chinese Politics after Mao: Development & Liberalization, 1976-1983. LC 83-13925. 220p. 1983. text ed. 55.00 (*0-275-91046-6*, C1046, Praeger Pubs) Greenwood.

— Political Change on Taiwan: A Study of Ruling Party Adaptability. LC 91-15311. 224p. 1991. text ed. 55.00 (*0-275-94035-7*, C4035, Praeger Pubs) Greenwood.

— Political Opposition in Post-Confucian Society. LC 88-11759. 296p. 1988. text ed. 55.00 (*0-275-93063-7*, C3063, Praeger Pubs) Greenwood.

Moody, Peter R. Three Hundred Sixty-Seventh Fighter Group in World War Two. (Illus.). 75p. (Orig.). 1979. pap. 19.00 (*0-89126-080-3*) MA-AH Pub.

Moody, Peter R., Jr. Tradition & Modernization in China & Japan. LC 94-16413. 360p. 1995. pap. 19.95 (*0-534-24546-3*) Intl Thomson.

Moody, Peter R., Jr., ed. China Documents Annual, 1989-1990-1991-1992. 1992. 75.00 (*0-87569-160-9*) Academic Intl.

Moody Press Editors. What Christians Believe. (C). 1951. pap. 4.99 (*0-8024-9378-5*) Moody.

Moody Press Staff, ed. see Nave, Orville J.

Moody, R. Principles of Accounts. 384p. (C). 1986. 70.00 (*0-7175-0683-5*, Pub. by S Thornes Pubs UK) St Mut.

Moody, R. V. & Pianzola, A. Lie Algebras with Triangular Decompositions. (Canadian Mathematical Society Series of Mnongraphs & Advanced Texts). 704p. 1995. text ed. 79.95 (*0-471-63304-6*, Interscience) Wiley.

Moody, Ralph. The Dry Divide. Moody, Jean S. & Morales, Edna M., eds. LC 94-14522. (Illus.). 230p. 1994. pap. 8.95 (*0-8032-8216-8*, Bison Books) U of Nebr Pr.

— The Fields of Home. LC 92-37788. 335p. (C). 1993. pap. 10.95 (*0-8032-8194-3*, Bison Books) U of Nebr Pr.

— The Fields of Home. 340p. 1991. reprint ed. lib. bdg. 29.95x (*0-89966-831-3*) Buccaneer Bks.

— The Home Ranch. LC 93-39762. (Illus.). 280p. 1994. write for info. (*0-8032-3179-2*) U of Nebr Pr.

— The Home Ranch. LC 93-39762. (Illus.). 279p. 1994. pap. 10.95 (*0-8032-8210-9*) U of Nebr Pr.

— Horse of a Different Color. (J). 1976. 21.95 (*0-8488-1106-2*) Amereon Ltd.

— A Horse of a Different Color: Reminiscences of a Kansas Drover. Moody, Jean S. & Morales, Edna M., eds. LC 94-14523. 272p. 1994. pap. 9.95 (*0-8032-8217-6*, Bison Books) U of Nebr Pr.

— Little Britches. (J). 1976. 24.95 (*0-8488-1105-4*) Amereon Ltd.

— Little Britches. 262p. 1986. reprint ed. lib. bdg. 25.95 (*0-89966-563-2*) Buccaneer Bks.

— Little Britches: Father & I Were Ranchers. LC 91-4139. (Illus.). 260p. 1991. reprint ed. pap. 9.95 (*0-8032-8178-1*) U of Nebr Pr.

— Man of the Family. (J). 1976. 24.95 (*0-8488-1436-3*) Amereon Ltd.

— Man of the Family. LC 92-37787. 272p. (C). 1993. pap. 9.95 (*0-8032-8195-1*, Bison Books) U of Nebr Pr.

— Man of the Family. 1986. reprint ed. lib. bdg. 25.95 (*0-89966-564-0*) Buccaneer Bks.

— Mary Emma. (J). 1976. 21.95 (*0-8488-1107-0*) Amereon Ltd.

— Mary Emma & Company. (J). 1976. 24.95 (*0-8488-1513-0*) Amereon Ltd.

— Mary Emma & Company. LC 93-43936. (Illus.). 235p. (C). 1994. pap. 9.95 (*0-8032-8211-7*, Bison Books) U of Nebr Pr.

— Mary Emma & Company. 340p. 1991. reprint ed. lib. bdg. 25.95 (*0-89966-830-5*) Buccaneer Bks.

— Shaking the Nickel Bush. (J). 1976. 20.95 (*0-8488-1108-9*) Amereon Ltd.

— Shaking the Nickel Bush. Moody, Jean S. & Morales, Edna M., eds. LC 94-14503. (Illus.). 236p. 1994. reprint ed. pap. 8.95 (*0-8032-8218-4*, Bison Books) U of Nebr Pr.

Moody, Raymond. Reunions: Visionary Encounters with Departed Loved Ones. 1993. 20.00 (*0-679-42570-5*, Villard Bks) Random.

***Moody, Raymond & Perry, Paul.** Reunions: Visionary Encounters with Departed Loved Ones. 1994. mass mkt. 5.99 (*0-8041-1235-5*) Ivy Books.

Moody, Raymond, jt. ed. see Moore, Cornelia N.

Moody, Raymond A., Jr. Coming Back. 1992. 5.99 (*0-553-29398-2*) Bantam.

Moody, Raymond A. Life after Life: The Investigation of a Phenomenon, Survival of Bodily Death. large type ed. 1988. pap. 9.95 (*0-8027-2599-6*) Walker & Co.

Moody, Raymond A., Jr. Life after Life. 1988. mass mkt. 5.99 (*0-553-27484-8*) Bantam.

— Life after Life. 176p. 1981. 14.95 (*0-89176-037-7*, Mckingbird) R Bemis Pub.

— The Light Beyond. 1989. mass mkt. 5.99 (*0-553-27813-4*) Bantam.

— Reflections on Life after Life. 1985. mass mkt. 5.99 (*0-553-25227-5*) Bantam.

***Moody, Raymond A.** Scrying: The Art of Female Divination. 1994. pap. 8.95 (*0-89176-999-4*) R Bemis Pub.

Moody, Raymond A., Jr. Scrying: A Feminine Mode of Divination. 110p. 1994. pap. 7.95 (*0-89176-045-8*, Visionry Pr) R Bemis Pub.

Moody, Raymond A., tr. see Page, Earle C.

***Moody, Regina B.** Coming to Terms: Subject Search Strategies in the School Media Center. LC 94-37893. 1995. write for info. (*1-55570-225-2*) Neal-Schuman.

Moody, Richard. Fossils. (Illus.). 128p. 1979. 8.95 (*0-600-36313-9*) Transatl Arts.

— Fossils: How to Find & Identify over 300 Genera. (Field Guide Ser.). (Illus.). 192p. 1986. pap. 11.95 (*0-02-063370-X*, Collier S&S) S&S Trade.

Moody, Richard T. Over Sixty-Five Million Years Ago: Before the Dinosaurs Died. LC 91-44774. (History Detectives Ser.). (Illus.). 32p. (J). (gr. 6 up). 1992. text ed. 13.95 (*0-02-767270-0*, Mac Bks Young Read) S&S Childrens.

Moody, Rick. Garden State: A Novel. 1992. 18.50 (*0-916366-73-1*) Pushcart Pr.

— Garden State: A Novel. 1993. pap. 11.50 (*0-916366-85-5*) Pushcart Pr.

— The Ice Storm. LC 93-26677. 1994. 19.95 (*0-316-57921-1*) Little.

— The Ice Storm. 288p. 1995. pap. 10.99 (*0-446-67148-7*) Warner Bks.

— The Ring of Brightest Angels Around Heaven: A Novella & Stories. LC 94-45903. 256p. 1995. 21.95 (*0-316-57929-7*) Little.

Moody, Robert E., ed. Papers of Leverett Saltonstall, 1816-1845, Vol. 82. LC 78-70086. (Collections of the Massachusetts Historical Society). (Illus.). 1978. Vol. 1, 1978. 50.00 (*0-934909-21-0*) Mass Hist Soc.

— Papers of Leverett Saltonstall, 1816-1845, Vol. 83. LC 78-70086. (Collections of the Massachusetts Historical Society). (Illus.). 1981. Vol. 2, 1981. 50.00 (*0-934909-22-9*) Mass Hist Soc.

— Papers of Leverett Saltonstall, 1816-1845, Vol. 84. LC 78-70086. (Collections of the Massachusetts Historical Society). (Illus.). 1984. Vol. 3, 1984. 50.00 (*0-934909-23-7*) Mass Hist Soc.

— Papers of Leverett Saltonstall, 1816-1845, Vol. 85. LC 78-70086. (Collections of the Massachusetts Historical Society). (Illus.). 1991. Vol. 4. 50.00 (*0-934909-37-7*) Mass Hist Soc.

— Papers of Leverett Saltonstall, 1816-1845, Vol. 86. (Collections of the Massachusetts Historical Society). (Illus.). 1992. 50.00 (*0-934909-53-9*) Mass Hist Soc.

— The Saltonstall Papers Vol. 1: 1607-1815. (Collections of the Massachusetts Historical Society Ser.: Vols. 80-81). (Illus.). 1974. Vol. 2 1974, 655 pps. 50.00 (*0-934909-24-5*) Mass Hist Soc.

— The Saltonstall Papers Vol. 2: 1607-1815, Vol. 1: 1972. (Collections of the Massachusetts Historical Society Ser.: Vols. 80-81). (Illus.). 574p. 1974. Vol. 1 1972, 574 pps. 50.00 (*0-934909-25-3*) Mass Hist Soc.

— The Saltonstalls of New England: 350 Years in Public Life. LC 78-106214. (Massachusetts Historical Society Picture Books Ser.). 1978. pap. 4.00 (*0-934909-14-8*) Mass Hist Soc.

Moody, Robert E. & Simmons, Richard C., eds. The Glorious Revolution in Massachusetts: Selected Documents, 1689-1692. (Illus.). 760p. (C). 1989. 30.00 (*0-9620737-0-9*) Colonial MA.

Moody, Rodger, ed. see Aruguelles, Ivan.

Moody, Rodger, ed. see Goldman, Judy.

Moody, Rodger, ed. see Henry, Laurie.

Moody, Rodger, ed. see Humes, Harry.

Moody, Rodger, ed. see Rossini, Frank.

Moody, Rodger, ed. see Skloot, Floyd.

Moody, Rodger, ed. see Turco, Lewis.

Moody, Rodger, ed. see Wallace, D. M.

Moody, Roger, ed. Indigenous Voices: Visions & Realities, 2 vols., II. LC 88-17177. (C). 1988. pap. 19.95 (*0-86232-519-6*, Pub. by Zed Books UK) Humanities.

Moody, Shirley. Charmers. LC 87-61416. 65p. (Orig.). 1991. pap. 9.95 (*0-932662-69-2*) St Andrews NC.

Moody, Sidney C. & Associated Press Photographers. War Against Japan. 192p. 1994. 19.95 (*0-89141-495-9*) Presidio Pr.

Moody, Sidney C. & Associated Press Staff. War in Europe: The Unnecessary War. LC 93-23095. (Illus.). 192p. 1993. 19.95 (*0-89141-494-0*) Presidio Pr.

***Moody, Skye K., ed. & illus.** Southern Lights: PEN-South Literary Journal. (PEN-South Literary Ser.). 128p. (Orig.). 1995. pap. 10.00 (*0-9638061-1-4*) M DeLeon Bksmith.

***Moody, Spurgeon, Whitefield, MacKay Staff.** They Spoke of Grace. Austin, Bobby W., ed. & intro. by. 190p. (Orig.). 1994. pap. write for info. (*0-9639640-1-1*) Grace Vision.

***Moody Staff.** Overcoming Life. 1995. pap. 3.99 (*0-8024-5445-3*) Moody.

***Moody, Susan.** Death Takes a Hand. 240p. (Orig.). 1995. pap. text ed. 4.99 (*0-425-14639-1*, Prime Crime) Berkley Pub.

— Death Takes a Hand. large type ed. LC 94-19360. 397p. (Orig.). 1994. pap. 17.95 (*0-7862-0278-5*) Thorndike Pr.

— Death Takes a Hand: A Cassandra Swann Bridge Mystery. 288p. 1994. 20.00 (*1-883402-00-X*) S&S Trade.

— Grand Slam: A Cassandra Swann Bridge Mystery. LC 94-29364. 1995. 21.00 (*1-883402-32-8*) S&S Trade.

— Mosaic. large type ed. (General Ser.). 563p. 1992. text ed. 21.95 (*0-8161-5367-1*, Large Print Bks) Hall.

— Penny Dreadful. large type ed. 416p. 1987. 16.95 (*0-7089-1603-1*) Ulverscroft.

— Penny Pinching. 240p. 1989. pap. 3.50 (*0-449-13237-4*, GM) Fawcett.

— Penny Pinching. large type ed. 1991. 21.95 (*0-7089-2374-7*) Ulverscroft.

— Penny Post. large type ed. 416p. 1987. 16.95 (*0-7089-1703-8*) Ulverscroft.

— Penny Saving. large type ed. (Mystery Ser.). 464p. 1993. 21.95 (*0-7089-2938-9*) Ulverscroft.

Moody, T. W. Davitt & Irish Revolution: Eighteen Forty-Six to Eighteen Eighty-Two. (Illus.). 1984. pap. 32.00 (*0-19-820069-2*) OUP.

— Fenian Movement. 128p. 1985. pap. 7.95 (*0-85342-121-8*, Pub. by Mercier Pr IE) Dufour.

Moody, T. W. & Martin, F. X., eds. Course of Irish History. (Illus.). 479p. 1989. pap. 25.95 (*0-85342-710-0*, Pub. by Mercier Pr IE) Dufour.

— The Course of Irish History. rev. ed. (Illus.). 504p. (C). 1995. pap. 16.95 (*1-57098-015-2*) R Rinehart.

Moody, T. W., et al, eds. A Chronology to Irish History to Nineteen Seventy-Six: A Companion to Irish History, Part 1. (New History of Ireland Ser.: No. 8). (Illus.). 1983. 130.00 (*0-19-821744-7*) OUP.

Moody, Terry W., ed. Neural & Endocrine Peptides & Receptors. LC 86-20462. (GWUMC Department of Biochemistry Annual Spring Symposia Ser.). 734p. 1986. 135.00 (*0-306-42300-6*, Plenum Pr) Plenum.

Moody, Terry W., ed. see International Washington Spring Symposium Staff.

Moody, Thomas E., jt. ed. see Schmitt, Richard.

Moody, Todd G. Philosophy & Artificial Intelligence. 192p. (C). 1992. pap. text ed. write for info. (*0-13-663816-3*) P-H.

Moody, Vernie A. Slavery on Louisiana Sugar Plantations. LC 74-22753. (Labor Movement in Fiction & Non-Fiction Ser.). reprint ed. 2,905.00 (*0-404-58505-1*) AMS Pr.

Moody, Virgil B., jt. auth. see Moody, Mary C.

Moody, Wayne, ed. Patterson's Schools Classified. rev. ed. (Nineteen Ninety-Three Edition Ser.: Vol. 43). 314p. (Orig.). 1993. pap. 15.00 (*0-910536-57-0*) Ed Direct.

— Patterson's Schools Classified, Vol. 45, 1995. rev. ed. LC 59-4567. 306p. 1995. pap. 15.00 (*0-910536-63-5*) Ed Direct.

— Patterson's Schools Classified Vol. 44, 1994. rev. ed. LC 59-4567. 320p. 1994. pap. 15.00 (*0-910536-60-0*) Ed Direct.

— Patterson's Schools Classified, 1992 Edition, Vol. 42. rev. ed. 320p. 1992. pap. 15.00 (*0-910536-54-6*) Ed Direct.

***Moody, William.** Langue des Signes Vol. 3: Dictionnaire Billingue Elementaire. 224p. (FRE.). 1990. pap. 105.00 (*0-7859-8227-2*, 2904641025) Fr & Eur.

Moody, William B. And the Greatest of These. 112p. Date not set. 10.00 (*0-9616499-1-7*) Good Soldier.

— The Good Soldiers. (Illus.). 129p. 1986. 9.95 (*0-9616499-0-9*) Good Soldier.

Moody, William J., ed. Artistic Intelligences: Implications for Education. 240p. (C). 1990. text ed. 20.95 (*0-8077-3050-5*) Tchrs Coll.

Moody, William V. Poems & Plays, 2 vols, Set. LC 70-80719. reprint ed. 97.50 (*0-404-04388-7*) AMS Pr.

— Poems & Plays, 2 vols., Set. (BCL1-PS American Literature Ser.). 1992. reprint ed. lib. bdg. 150.00 (*0-7812-6801-X*) Rprt Serv.

— Some Letters of William Vaughn Moody. Mason, D. G., ed. LC 76-94471. reprint ed. 31.50 (*0-404-04359-3*) AMS Pr.

— Some Letters of William Vaughn Moody. (American Biography Ser.). 170p. 1991. reprint ed. lib. bdg. 59.00 (*0-7812-8290-X*) Rprt Serv.

— Some Letters of William Vaughn Moody. (BCL1-PS American Literature Ser.). 170p. 1992. reprint ed. lib. bdg. 69.00 (*0-7812-6802-8*) Rprt Serv.

Moody, Winfield Scott. Pickwick Ladle, & Other Collector's Stories. LC 70-37556. (Short Story Index Reprint Ser.). 1977. reprint ed. 21.95 (*0-8369-4115-2*) Ayer.

***Moodys Investor Service Staff.** Moody's Handbook of Dividend Achievers 1994. 1994. pap. 19.95 (*1-56429-007-7*) Moodys Invest.

Moody's Investors Service Staff. Moody's Handbook of Dividend Achievers, 1992. 400p. 1992. pap. 19.95 (*1-56429-003-4*) Moodys Invest.

Moody's Staff. Handbook of Common Stocks. 1991. pap. 80.00 (*1-56429-002-6*) Moodys Invest.

— Handbook of NASDAQ Stocks. 1991. pap. 25.00 (*1-56429-001-8*) Moodys Invest.

Mooers. Coastal Ocean Prediction. 1995. write for info. (*0-8493-8954-2*) CRC Pr.

Mooers, C., ed. Baroclinic Processes on Continental Shelves. (Coastal & Estuarine Sciences Ser.: Vol. 3). (Illus.). 144p. 1986. 25.00 (*0-87590-252-9*) Am Geophysical.

Mooers, Colin. The Making of Bourgeois Europe. 192p. 1991. 59.95 (*0-86091-291-4*, A4506, Pub. by Verso UK); pap. 17.95 (*0-86091-507-7*, A4510, Pub. by Verso UK) Routledge Chapman & Hall.

***Mooers, Robert L.** Finding Your Way in the Outdoors: An Outdoor Life Book. 1984. pap. 12.95 (*0-696-11032-6*) Meredith Bks.

Moog, Bob, ed. see Cahill, Kent & Cahill, Kathleen.

Moog, Bob, ed. see Soza, Jan & Soza, Harry.

Moog, Bob, ed. see Stewart, Patricia A. & Maples, Edna H.

Moog, Helmut, jt. ed. see Pratt, Rosalie R.

Moog, John, jt. auth. see Stroschin, Jane.

Moog, Shirleigh. A Guide to the Food Pyramid: Recipes & Information. 300p. 1993. pap. 12.95 (*0-89594-598-3*) Crossing Pr.

Mooij, A. Psychoanalysis & the Concept of a Rule: An Essay in the Philosophy of Psychoanalysis. Firth, S. & Scheffer, J. H., trs. 100p. 1991. pap. 29.00 (*0-387-53573-X*) Spr-Verlag.

Mooij, J. J. Fictional Realities: The Uses of Literary Imagination. LC 93-1452. (Ultrecht Publications in General & Comparative Literature (UPaL): No. 30). xii, 290p. 1993. 67.00x (*1-55619-429-3*) Benjamins North Am.

Mooij, T. Interactional Multi-Level Investigation into Pupil Behaviour, Achievement, Competence & Orientation in Educational Situations. (Selecta Reeks Ser.: Vol. 68). viii, 234p. 1987. 32.00 (*90-6472-112-2*, Pub. by Swets Pub Serv NE) Taylor & Francis.

Mook, jt. auth. see Nayfeh.

Mook, Byron T. The World of the Indian Field Administrator. 272p. 1983. text ed. 25.00 (*0-7069-1960-2*, Pub. by Vikas II) S Asia.

Mook, Dean T., jt. auth. see Nayfeh, Ali H.

Mook, Delo E. & Vargish, Thomas. Inside Relativity. (Illus.). 320p. 1991. text ed. 49.50 (*0-691-08472-6*); pap. text ed. 14.95 (*0-691-02520-7*) Princeton U Pr.

Mook, Douglas. Motivation: The Organization of Animal & Human Action. (C). 1986. text ed. 49.95 (*0-393-95474-9*) Norton.

Mook, Jennifer J. The Secret Room. LC 91-67102. 148p. 1992. pap. 7.95 (*1-55523-487-9*) Winston-Derek.

Mookerjee, Ajay S. Global Electronic Wholesale Banking. (C). 1990. lib. bdg. 74.00 (*1-85333-415-4*, Pub. by Graham & Trotman UK) Kluwer Ac.

Mookerjee, Ajit. Kali: The Feminine Force. 1988. pap. 14.95 (*0-89281-212-5*, Destiny Bks) Inner Tradit.

— Kundalini: The Arousal of the Inner Energy. (Illus.). 112p. (Orig.). 1983. pap. 14.95 (*0-89281-020-3*, Destiny Bks) Inner Tradit.

Mookerjee, Ajit & Khanna, Madhu. The Tantric Way: Art-Science-Ritual. LC 88-51353. (Illus.). 350p. (Orig.). 1989. pap. 16.95 (*0-500-27088-0*) Thames Hudson.

Mookerjee, Amalendu P. Social & Political Ideas of Bipin Chandra Pal. LC 75-901635. 1974. 11.00 (*0-88386-473-8*) S Asia.

Mookerjee, Anjali. Environment - Nursery of Life. 103p. 1985. 9.95 (*0-318-36790-4*) Asia Bk Corp.

Mookerjee, Asutosh. Juvenile Justice: An in-Depth Study on Matters Relating to Children. (C). 1990. 70.00 (*0-89771-174-2*) St Mut.

Mookerjee, Nanda, ed. Sri Ramakrishna in the Eyes of Brahma & Christian Admirers. LC 76-904430. 1976. 6.50 (*0-88386-791-5*) S Asia.

— Sri Sarada Devi: Consort of Sri Ramakrishna. 1978. 6.00 (*0-8364-0173-5*) S Asia.

Mookerjee, Nanda, ed. see Max Mueller, F.

Mookerjee, Sameer C. Role of Comptroller & Auditor General in Indian Democracy. (C). 1989. 64.00 (*81-7024-224-X*, Pub. by Ashish II) S Asia.

Mookerjee, Satkari. The Jaina Philosophy of Non-Absolutism. 289p. 1978. 24.95 (*0-89684-021-2*) Asia Bk Corp.

Mookerjee, Syama P. Leaves from a Diary. (Illus.). 210p. 1993. 24.00 (*0-19-563119-6*) OUP.

Mookerji, Radha K. Chandragupta Maurya & His Times. (C). 1988. reprint ed. 18.00 (*81-208-0405-8*, Pub. by Motilal Banarsidass II) S Asia.

— Gupta Empire. (C). 1989. reprint ed. text ed. 17.50 (*81-208-0089-3*, Pub. by Motilal Banarsidass II) S Asia.

Mookerji, Radhakumud. Local Government in Ancient India. 1989. reprint ed. 11.50 (*81-85395-01-2*, Pub. by Low Price II) S Asia.

Mookherjee, A. & Bhattacharjee, S. B., eds. Aspects of Radiation Biophysics. 120p. (C). 1984. 80.00 (*81-85017-16-6*, Pub. by Interprint II) St Mut.

***Mookherjee, Dilip, ed.** Indian Industry: Policies & Performance. (Oxford in India Readings Ser.). (Illus.). 368p. 1995. 29.95 (*0-19-563666-X*) OUP.

Mookherjee, Dilip & Ray, Debraj. Economic Theory & Practice: Essays in Honour of Dipak Baherjee. Dutta, Bahskar et al, eds. (Illus.). 320p. 1991. 18.95 (*0-19-562545-5*) OUP.

Mookherjee, G. C. Text Book of Medicine. (C). 1989. 150.00 (*0-89771-371-0*, Current Dist) St Mut.

Mookherjee, Surya. Joint Management Councils. (C). 1987. 14.00 (*81-204-0256-1*, Pub. by Oxford IBH II) S Asia.

Mookini, Ester K. The Hawaiian Newspapers. 1974. pap. 1.00 (*0-685-14611-1*) Ku Paa.

Mookini, Esther T. O Na Holoholona Wawae Eha O Ka Lama Hawaii: The Four-Footed Animals of Ka Lama Hawaii. Richards, William, tr. LC 84-72886. (Illus.). 129p. (Orig.). 1985. pap. 6.00 (*0-910043-09-4*) Bamboo Ridge Pr.

Mookini, Esther T. & Nakoa, Sarah, trs. The Wind Gourd of La'amaomao. LC 89-64411. 160p. (Orig.). 1990. pap. text ed. 6.00 (*0-9623102-0-4*) Kalamaku Pr.

Mookini, Esther T., ed. see Gutmanis, June.

Moolenaar, Ruth. Profiles of Outstanding Virgin Islanders, Vol. 2. Advisory Committee to Publication Staff, ed. (Illus.). 1986. text ed. 19.95 (*0-937421-01-4*) VICY.

***Moolenburgh.** Handbook of Angels. 1995. pap. 13.95 (*0-85207-169-8*) Atrium Pubs.

Moolenburgh, H. C. A Handbook of Angels. (Illus.). 256p. (Orig.). Date not set. pap. 20.95 (*0-8464-4223-X*) Beekman Pubs.

— Meetings with Angels. 256p. (Orig.). Date not set. pap. 19.95 (*0-8464-4253-1*) Beekman Pubs.

— Meetings with Angels: A Hundred & One Real-Life Encounters. 1995. pap. 19.95 (*0-85207-260-0*, Pub. by C W Daniel UK) Atrium Pubs.

Moolgavkar, S. Scientific Issues in Quantitative Cancer Risk Assessment. 320p. 1990. 52.50 (*0-8176-3501-7*) Birkhauser.

Moolgavkar, Suresh H. & Prentice, Ross L., eds. Modern Statistical Methods in Chronic Disease Epidemiology: Proceedings of a Conference Sponsored by SIAM Institute for Mathematics & Society & Supported by the Department of Energy. LC 86-1597. 282p. 1986. text ed. 79.95 (*0-471-83904-3*, Wiley-Interscience) Wiley.

Moolten, David N. Plums & Ashes. (Samuel French Morse Poetry Prize Ser.). 64p. 1994. pap. text ed. 9.95 (*1-55553-208-X*) NE U Pr.

Moom, S. C. & Keda, H. I. Database Systems for Advanced. (Advanced Database Research & Development Ser.). 468p. 1993. text ed. 121.00 (*981-02-1380-8*) World Scientific Pub.

***Moomaw, Sally & Hieronymus, Brenda.** More Than Counting: Whole Math Activities for Preschool & Kindergarten. 244p. (Orig.). 1995. pap. 24.95 (*1-934140-82-1*) Redleaf Pr.

— More Than Counting: Whole Math Activities for Preschool & Kindergarten. LC 95-13460. (Orig.). 1995. write for info. (*1-884834-03-5*) Redleaf Pr.

Moomaw, William & Najam, Adil, eds. Papers on International Environmental Negotiation, 1993, Vol. 3. 220p. (Orig.). (C). 1993. pap. 15.00 (*1-880711-06-0*) Prog Negot HLS.

Moomaw, William R. & Mintzer, Irving M. Strategies for Limiting Global Climate Change. 30p. (Orig.). 1989. pap. 5.00 (*0-915825-44-9*) World Resources Inst.

Moomey, Diane. While on the Way Home. LC 87-72319. (Illus.). 64p. 1988. 18.00 (*0-9619714-0-1*) Dayseye Pr.

***Moon.** Constructing Community: Moral Pluralism & Tragic Conflicts. 1995. pap. (*0-691-02550-9*) Princeton U Pr.

— Making School & Community Recreation Fun for Everyone: Places & Ways to Integrate. LC 94-28438. 256p. 1994. pap. 31.00 (*1-55766-155-3*) P H Brookes.

Moon & Micozzi. Nutrition & Cancer Prevention. 608p. 1989. 190.00 (*0-8247-7993-2*) Dekker.

Moon, jt. auth. see Micozzi.

Moon, Arinna, jt. ed. see Weiner, Kayla.

Moon, B. P., jt. ed. see Dardis, G. F.

Moon, Bob. The New Maths Curriculum Controversy: An International Story, Vol. 5. (Studies in Curriculum History Ser.). 220p. 1986. 60.00 (*1-85000-122-7*, Falmer Pr); pap. 33.00 (*1-85000-123-5*) Taylor & Francis.

Moon, Bob, ed. Modular Curriculum. 192p. (C). 1988. 36.00 (*1-85396-008-X*, Pub. by P Chapman Pub UK) St Mut.

Moon, Bob & Mayes, Ann S., eds. Teaching & Learning in the Secondary School. LC 93-25147. 1994. write for info. (*0-415-10250-2*) Routledge.

Moon, Bob, jt. ed. see Galton, Maurice.

Moon, Brenda E., comp. Periodicals for South-East Asian Studies: A Union Catalogue of Holdings in British & Selected European Libraries. 630p. 1979. 140.00 (*0-7201-0730-X*, Mansell Pub) Cassell.

Moon, Bruce E. The Political Economy of Basic Human Needs. LC 91-14912. 336p. 1991. 46.50 (*0-8014-2448-8*); pap. 15.95 (*0-8014-9982-8*) Cornell U Pr.

***Moon, Bruce L.** Essentials of Art Therapy Training & Practice. (Illus.). 188p. 1992. pap. 22.95 (*0-398-06295-1*) C C Thomas.

— Essentials of Art Therapy Training & Practice. (Illus.). 188p. (C). 1992. text ed. 37.95x (*0-398-05794-X*) C C Thomas.

— Existential Art Therapy: The Canvas Mirror. 2nd ed. LC 95-3655. (Illus.). 230p. (C). 1995. text ed. 49.95x (*0-398-05999-3*); pap. text ed. 29.95x (*0-398-06514-4*) C C Thomas.

— Introduction to Art Therapy: Faith in the Product. (Illus.). 222p. 1994. pap. 29.95 (*0-614-02310-6*) C C Thomas.

— Introduction to Art Therapy: Faith in the Product. LC 93-36346. (Illus.). 222p. (C). 1994. text ed. 47.95 (*0-398-05893-8*) C C Thomas.

Moon, Bruce L., ed. Existential Art Therapy: The Canvas Mirror. (Illus.). 184p. (C). 1990. text ed. 38.95 (*0-398-05668-4*) C C Thomas.

— Existential Art Therapy: The Canvas Mirror. (Illus.). 184p. 1990. pap. 24.95 (*0-398-06296-X*) C C Thomas.

Moon, Bucklin. High Cost of Prejudice. LC 70-111584. 168p. 1970. reprint ed. text ed. 52.50 (*0-8371-4608-9*, MCP&, Negro U Pr) Greenwood.

Moon, C., jt. auth. see Moon, G.

***Moon, C. Jean & Schulman, Linda.** Finding the Connections: Linking Assessment, Instruction & Curriculum in Elementary Mathematics. LC 94-46724. 240p. 1995. pap. text ed. 19.50 (*0-435-08370-8*) Heinemann.

***Moon, Christopher.** The Power of the Gift. 144p. (Orig.). 1992. pap. 10.95 (*0-919591-12-4*, Pub. by Polestar Bk Pubs CN) Orca Bk Pubs.

Moon, Chung-in, jt. ed. see Haggard, Stephen.

Moon, Chung-In, et al. Alliance under Tension: The Evolution of South Korean-U. S. Relations. 229p. (C). 1988. text ed. 63.00 (*0-8133-0835-6*) Westview.

Moon, Cliff & Raban, Bridie. A Question of Reading: National Curriculum Edition. 3rd ed. 240p. 1992. pap. 32.50 (*1-85346-146-6*, Pub. by D Fulton UK) Taylor & Francis.

Moon, Cyris H. A Korean Minjung Theology: An Old Testament Perspective. 93p. (Orig.). reprint ed. pap. 26.60 (*0-8357-4064-1*, 2036754) Bks Demand.

Moon, Deak. Dah Ming. (Dah Ming Ser.). (Orig.). pap. write for info. (*0-940560-10-0*) Custom Hse.

Moon, Delia, ed. see King, Una.

Moon, Delia, ed. see Morningstar, Ramon S.

Moon, Delia, ed. see Raye, Don.

Moon, Dolly. My Very First Piano Book of Cowboy Songs: Twenty-Two Favorite Songs Easy in Piano Arrangement. (Illus.). 32p. (J). (gr. 2 up). 1983. pap. 3.50 (*0-486-24311-7*) Dover.

Moon, Dolly M. My First Book of Marches. 1990. pap. 3.50 (*0-486-26338-X*) Dover.

Moon, Don & Moon, Ruth. Collection of Poetry. LC 85-63483. (Illus.). 64p. 7.95 (*0-9615098-0-5*) Prairie Imp.

Moon, Elaine L. Untold Tales, Unsung Heroes: An Oral History of Detroit's African American Community, 1918-1967. LC 93-26073. (African American Life Ser.). (Illus.). 409p. (C). 1994. text ed. 39.95 (*0-8143-2464-9*); pap. text ed. 19.95 (*0-8143-2465-7*) Wayne St U Pr.

Moon, Elizabeth. The Deed of Paksenarrion. 1040p. 1992. pap. 15.00 (*0-671-72104-6*) Baen Bks.

— Divided Allegiance. (Deed of Paksenarrion Ser.: Bk. 2). 528p. (Orig.). 1988. mass mkt. 5.99 (*0-671-69786-2*) Baen Bks.

— Hunting Party. 384p. 1993. mass mkt. 5.99 (*0-671-72176-3*) Baen Bks.

— Liar's Oath. 480p. (Orig.). 1992. mass mkt. 5.99 (*0-671-72117-8*) Baen Bks.

— Lunar Activity. 288p. 1990. pap. 3.50 (*0-671-69870-2*) Baen Bks.

— Oath of Gold. (Deed of Paksenarrion Ser.: Bk. III). 512p. (Orig.). 1989. pap. 3.95 (*0-671-69798-6*) Baen Bks.

— Sheepfarmer's Daughter. (Deed of Paksenarrion Ser.: Bk. 1). 512p. (Orig.). 1988. pap. 5.99 (*0-671-65416-0*) Baen Bks.

— Sporting Chance. 416p. (Orig.). 1994. mass mkt. 5.99 (*0-671-87619-8*) Baen Bks.

— Surrender None: The Legacy of Gird. 544p. 1990. mass mkt. 5.99 (*0-671-69878-8*) Baen Bks.

— Winning Colors. 1995. mass mkt. 5.99 (*0-671-87677-5*) Baen Bks.

Moon, Elizabeth, jt. auth. see McCaffrey, Anne.

Moon, Eric. A Desire to Learn: Selected Writings. LC 93-15146. (Illus.). 458p. 1993. 47.50 (*0-8108-2686-0*) Scarecrow.

Moon, Francis C. Chaotic & Fractal Dynamics: An Introduction for Applied Scientists & Engineers. 528p. 1992. text ed. 64.95 (*0-471-54571-6*) Wiley.
— Magneto-Solid Mechanics. LC 83-23372. (Wiley-Interscience Publication Ser.). 448p. reprint ed. pap. 127.70 (*0-7837-2403-9*, 2040088) Bks Demand.
— Superconducting Levitation: Applications to Bearings & Magnetic Transportation. LC 93-31759. 1994. text ed. 59.95 (*0-471-55925-3*) Wiley.
Moon, Francis C., ed. see American Society of Mechanical Engineers Staff.
Moon, G. & Moon, C. Lost Indian Magic: A Mystery Story of the Red Man As He Lived Before the White Man Came. 1977. lib. bdg. 39.95 (*0-8490-2185-5*) Gordon Pr.
***Moon, Graham & Gillespie, Rosemary, eds.** Society & Health: An Introduction to Social Science for Health Professionals. LC 94-45145. (Illus.). 196p. 1995. 59.95x (*0-415-11021-1*, C0179); pap. 17.95 (*0-415-11022-X*, C0180) Routledge.
Moon, Graham & Jones, Kelvyn. Health, Disease & Society: An Introduction to Medical Geography. (Illus.). 256p. 1988. pap. text ed. 19.95 (*0-7102-1219-4*, RKP) Routledge.
Moon, Graham, jt. auth. see Atkinson, Rob.
Moon, H. Office Procedures & Technology. 1990p. 26.95 (*0-87350-289-2*); teacher ed 12.95 (*0-87350-337-6*); student ed 9.95 (*0-87350-340-6*); teacher ed 9.95 (*0-87350-338-4*); 2.25 (*0-87350-339-2*) Milady Pub.
Moon, Harold, jt. auth. see Ashworth, Peter.
Moon, Harry R. Typing from Rough Drafts. 1984. 19.95 (*0-87350-335-X*); teacher ed 19.50 (*0-87350-288-4*); 9.95 (*0-87350-306-6*) Milady Pub.
Moon, Harry R., ed. see Elia, Lewis M. & Fall, Joseph A.
Moon, Havana. Uno, Dos, Cuatro: A Guide to the Number Stations. 76p. (Orig.). 1987. pap. 13.95 (*0-936653-06-X*) Tiare Pubns.

***Moon, Henry. The Interstate Highway System. Cromley, Robert & Cromley, Ellen, eds. (Resource Publications in Geography). 1995. 10.00 (*0-89291-215-4*) Assn Am Geographers.**
This monograph, part of the Resource Publications in Geography Series of the Association of American Geographers, surveys the development of the Interstate Highway System. The impacts of the system at the national level, in selected metropolitan areas, & on regional economic development are emphasized. Patterns of land use change around key interchanges are described. Tables, figures, & photographs drawn from government documents & other research illustrate the development of the system from the 1950s to the early 1990s. Order from The Association of American Geographers, 1710 16th St. NW, Washington, DC 20009; 202-234-1450. ***Publisher Provided Annotation.***

Moon, Henry L. Balance of Power: The Negro Vote. LC 77-4915. 256p. 1977. reprint ed. text ed. 59.75 (*0-8371-9619-1*, MOBA, Greenwood Pr) Greenwood.
Moon, J. Donald. Constructing Community: Moral Pluralism & Tragic Conflicts. LC 93-12930. 256p. 1993. text ed. 29.95 (*0-691-08642-7*) Princeton U Pr.
Moon, J. E., jt. auth. see Gillett, W. B.
Moon Ja Yoon. Korean Cooking for You. LC 87-81793. (Illus.). 111p. 1987. 17.50 (*0-942091-02-7*) Golden Pond Pr.
Moon, Jaekyun & Carley, L. Richard. Sequence Detection for High-Density Storage Channels. LC 92-2346. (International Series in Engineering & Computer Science, VLSI, Computer Architecture, & Digital Screen Processing: SECS 63). 176p. (C). 1992. lib. bdg. 65.50 (*0-7923-9264-7*) Kluwer Ac.
Moon, James E., jt. auth. see Harris, LeBrone C.
Moon, Jeremiah. Contributions. LC 90-71357. 51p. 1991. pap. 5.95 (*1-55523-386-4*) Winston-Derek.
Moon, Jeremy. European Integration in British Politics, 1950-1963: A Study of Issue Change. 278p. 1985. text ed. 58.00 (*0-566-00786-X*) Ashgate Pub Co.
— Innovative Leadership in Democracy: Policy Change under Thatcher. 170p. 1993. 59.95 (*1-85521-420-2*, Pub. by Dartmth Pub UK) Ashgate Pub Co.
Moon, Jeremy, jt. auth. see Richardson, J.
Moon, Jerry. W. C. White & Ellen G. White. (Andrews University Seminary Doctoral Dissertation Ser.: Vol. 19). 473p. 1993. pap. 16.95 (*1-883925-01-0*) Andrews Univ Pr.
Moon, John C. An Instructor for the Drum. LC 80-29134. (Music of the Fifes & Drums Ser.: Vol. 4). (Illus.). 50p. (Orig.). 1981. pap. 4.95 (*0-87935-059-8*) Colonial Williamsburg.
— An Instructor for the Drum, Set. LC 80-29134. (Music of the Fifes & Drums Ser.: Vol. 4). (Illus.). 50p. (Orig.). 1981. pap. 8.95 (*0-87935-060-1*) Colonial Williamsburg.
— Quick Marches. LC 75-19259. (Music of the Fifes & Drums Ser.: Vol. 1). 24p. 1976. pap. 7.95 (*0-87935-031-8*) Colonial Williamsburg.
Moon, John C., ed. Slow Marches. LC 75-19259. (Music of Fifes & Drums Ser.: Vol. 2). 24p. 1977. pap. 7.95 (*0-87935-046-6*) Colonial Williamsburg.
Moon, John C., et al. Medleys. LC 75-19259. (Music of the Fifes & Drums Ser.: Vol. 3). 23p. 1980. pap. 7.95 (*0-87935-050-4*) Colonial Williamsburg.
Moon, M. Sherrill, et al. Helping Persons with Severe Mental Retardation Get & Keep Employment: Supported Employment Strategies & Outcomes. LC 89-25371. 224p. (Orig.). 1990. pap. text ed. 32.00 (*1-55766-042-5*, 0425) P H Brookes.
Moon, Margaret & Maurine. The Jupiter Experiment. LC 76-3897. 224p. 1976. pap. 1.95 (*0-87542-498-8*) Llewellyn Pubns.
— Wedge: The Extraordinary Communications of an Earthbound Spirit. (Illus.). 136p. 1975. pap. 3.95 (*0-87542-497-X*) Llewellyn Pubns.
Moon, Maria E., tr. see McMeekin, Dorothy.
Moon, Marie. Grandma Moon's Story Poems. York, Sheryl, ed. LC 87-40253. 160p. 1987. 10.95 (*1-55523-109-8*) Winston-Derek.
Moon, Marilyn. Medicare Now & in the Future. LC 92-38302. 260p. (Orig.). (C). 1993. lib. bdg. 57.00 (*0-87766-590-7*); pap. text ed. 24.00 (*0-87766-591-5*) Urban Inst.
***Moon, Marilyn & Mulvey, Janemarie.** Entitlements & the Elderly: Protecting Promises, Recognizing Realities. 200p. (C). 1995. 19.95 (*0-87766-636-9*) Urban Inst.
Moon, Marjorie. Benjamin Tabart's Juvenile Library: A Bibliography of Books for Children, Published, Written, Edited, & Sold by Mr. Tabart 1801-1820. (Illus.). 180p. 1990. lib. bdg. 36.00 (*0-906795-89-3*) Oak Knoll.
— The Children's Books of Mary (Belson) Elliott: Blending Sound Christian Principles with Cheerful Cultivation - A Bibliography. 142p. 1987. 28.00 (*0-906795-44-3*) Oak Knoll.
Moon, Marjorie, ed. A Is for Art. (Illus.). (Orig.). (J). (ps-2). 1988. pap. 10.95 (*0-317-91187-2*) M Moon.
Moon, Marjorie N. A Is for Art, an Alphabetical Tour of the Milwaukee Art Museum. 1988. pap. 10.95 (*0-9620834-0-2*) M Moon.
Moon, Marylin, ed. Economic Transfers in the United States. LC 84-52. (National Bureau of Economic Research Studies in Income & Wealth: Vol. 49). (Illus.). 376p. 1984. lib. bdg. 45.00 (*0-226-53505-3*) U Ch Pr.
Moon, Michael. Disseminating Whitman: Revision & Corporeality in Leaves of Grass. LC 90-35138. 249p. 1991. 40.00 (*0-674-21276-2*, MOODIS) HUP.
— Disseminating Whitman: Revision & Corporeality in Leaves of Grass. 249p. (C). 1993. pap. 18.95 (*0-674-21245-2*) HUP.
***Moon, Michael & Davidson, Cathy N., eds.** Subjects & Citizens: Nation, Race, & Gender from Oroonoko to Anita Hill. 496p. 1995. lib. bdg. 49.95 (*0-8223-1529-7*) Duke.
— Subjects & Citizens: Nation, Race, & Gender from Oroonoko to Anita Hill. 496p. 1995. pap. 17.95 (*0-8223-1539-4*) Duke.
Moon, Michele, ed. see Moon, Scott A., et al.
***Moon, Milton.** The Living Road: A Meditation Sequence. 126p. 1995. pap. 8.95 (*1-86429-008-0*, Pub. by Millennium Bks AT) Seven Hills Bk.
Moon, Modean. Evermore. (Illus.). 352p. 1993. mass mkt. 4.99 (*0-446-36213-1*) Warner Bks.
— The Giving. (Desire Ser.). 1994. mass mkt. 2.99 (*0-373-05868-3*, 1-05868-4) Silhouette.
— Interrupted Honeymoon. (Desire Ser.). 1995. pap. 2.99 (*0-373-05904-3*, 1-05904-7) Silhouette.
Moon, Myra B., ed. see Smith, Duane.
Moon, Nicola. At the Beginning of a Pig. LC 93-41504. (Illus.). 24p. (J). (ps-00). 1994. 8.95 (*1-85697-977-6*, Kingfisher LKC) LKC.
— Jodie's Colours. (Illus.). 32p. (J). (gr. k-2). 1995. 17.95 (*1-85793-128-9*, Pub. by Pavilion UK) Trafalgar.
— Lucy's Pictures. LC 94-11178. (J). (gr. 7-9). 1995. 14.99 (*0-8037-1833-0*) Dial Bks Young.
Moon, P. & Spencer, D. E. Field Theory Handbook: Including Coordinate Systems, Differential Equations & Their Solutions. 2nd ed. LC 77-178288. (Illus.). viii, 236p. 1971. 59.40 (*0-387-02732-7*) Spr-Verlag.
Moon, Parry & Spencer, Domina E. Theory of Holors: A Generalization of Tensors. (Illus.). 330p. 1986. 89.95 (*0-521-24585-0*) Cambridge U Pr.
Moon, Pat. Earth Lines: Poems for the Green Age. LC 92-27570. 64p. (J). (gr. 5 up). 1993. 14.00 (*0-688-11853-4*) Greenwillow.
— This Is the Earth. (Illus.). 32p. (J). 1994. lib. bdg. 14.99 (*0-670-85488-3*) Viking Child Bks.
Moon, Penderel. The British Conquest & Dominion of India. LC 89-2003. 1248p. 1989. 89.95 (*0-253-33836-0*) Ind U Pr.
Moon, Peter, jt. auth. see Nichols, Preston B.
Moon, Peter, jt. auth. see Nichols, Preston.
Moon, Philip. Training for Time Management. 304p. 1994. 149.95 (*0-566-07416-8*, Pub. by Gower UK) Ashgate Pub Co.
Moon, Ralph, ed. see Tulku, Tarthang.
Moon, Robert A. & Davis, Robert D. Elementary Algebra. suppl. ed. 528p. (C). 1980. write for info. (*0-318-54301-X*, Merrill Pub Co) Macmillan.
— Elementary Algebra. 3rd ed. 528p. (C). 1980. pap. write for info. (*0-675-08158-0*, Merrill Pub Co) Macmillan.
Moon, Robert G. Applied Mathematics for Technical Programs: Algebra. LC 73-75638. (C). 1973. pap. write for info. (*0-675-08943-3*, Merrill Pub Co) Macmillan.
— Applied Mathematics for Technical Programs: Arithmetic & Geometry. (C). 1973. pap. write for info. (*0-675-08983-2*, Merrill Pub Co) Macmillan.
Moon, Robert G., Jr., et al. Basic Arithmetic. 3rd ed. 528p. (C). 1984. pap. write for info. (*0-675-20136-5*, Merrill Pub Co) Macmillan.
Moon, Robert O. Hippocrates & His Successors in Relation to the Philosophy of Their Time. LC 75-23745. reprint ed. 37.50 (*0-404-13351-7*) AMS Pr.
***Moon, Rosemary.** CL Cuisine: French. (Illus.). 256p. 1995. 7.98 (*0-8317-1121-3*) Smithmark.
— CL Cuisine: Pasta. (Illus.). 256p. 1995. 7.98 (*0-8317-1123-X*) Smithmark.
— CL Cuisine: Vegetarian. (Illus.). 256p. 1995. 7.98 (*0-8317-1122-1*) Smithmark.
Moon, Ross A. About Islam. Ingram, tr. 1992. pap. 7.95 (*1-880416-19-0*) NW Pub.
Moon, Ruth, jt. auth. see Moon, Don.
Moon, Samuel. Tall Sheep: Harry Goulding, Monument Valley Trader. LC 91-50866. (Illus.). 256p. (C). 1992. 24.95 (*0-8061-2415-6*) U of Okla Pr.
Moon, Samuel, ed. One Act: Eleven Short Plays of the Modern Theatre. 22.00 (*0-8446-2603-1*) Peter Smith.
***Moon, Scott A., et al.** Poems for a Thursday Morning. Moon, Michele, ed. LC 94-65412. (Illus.). 144p. (Orig.). 1994. pap. 12.95 (*0-934426-59-7*) NAPSAC Reprods.
Moon, Sheila. Changing Woman & Her Sisters. LC 84-27901. 233p. (Orig.). 1985. 14.00 (*0-917479-02-5*); pap. 11.50 (*0-917479-03-3*) Guild Psy.
— Deepest Roots. LC 86-19578. (Illus.). 240p. (J). (gr. 8-12). 1986. pap. 8.95 (*0-917479-10-6*) Guild Psy.
— Dreams of a Woman: An Analyst's Inner Journey. LC 83-10826. (Illus.). 207p. 1983. 27.50 (*0-938434-17-9*); pap. 13.95 (*0-938434-14-4*) Sigo Pr.
— Hunt down the Prize. LC 86-19576. (Illus.). 245p. (J). (gr. 8-12). 1986. reprint ed. pap. 8.95 (*0-917479-09-2*) Guild Psy.
— Knee-Deep in Thunder. LC 86-19534. (Illus.). 307p. (J). (gr. 8-12). 1986. reprint ed. pap. 8.95 (*0-917479-08-4*) Guild Psy.
— A Magic Dwells: A Poetic & Psychological Study of the Navaho Emergence Myth. LC 85-12620. 206p. 1985. pap. 7.95 (*0-917479-06-8*) Guild Psy.
Moon, Sheila, jt. auth. see Howes, Elizabeth B.
Moon, Sheila, ed. see Pelgrin, Mark.
Moon, Spencer, jt. auth. see Hill, George.
Moon, Sun M. The Divine Principle. 2nd rev. ed. 536p. 1973. 10.95 (*0-910621-05-5*); pap. 7.95 (*0-685-42755-2*) HSA Pubns.
— The Divine Principle. 2nd rev. ed. 536p. (C). 1973. pap. 7.95 (*0-910621-04-7*) HSA Pubns.
— The Divine Principle. 5th rev. ed. 536p. (C). 1977. pap. 5.95 (*0-910621-03-9*) HSA Pubns.
— Home Church. LC 82-88432. (Illus.). 474p. 1983. 14.95 (*0-318-03061-6*); pap. 11.95 (*0-910621-21-7*) HSA Pubns.
— A Life of Prayer. 142p. Date not set. 14.95 (*0-910621-59-4*); pap. 9.95 (*0-910621-60-8*) HSA Pubns.
— New Hope: Twelve Talks. 2nd ed. 1982. 4.95 (*0-910621-02-0*) HSA Pubns.
— True Love. 266p. Date not set. 15.95 (*0-910621-53-5*); pap. 11.95 (*0-685-61698-3*) HSA Pubns.
— The Way of God's Will. 418p. (Orig.). reprint ed. pap. 6.95 (*0-910621-31-4*) HSA Pubns.
— The Way of Tradition, Vol. 1. 326p. reprint ed. pap. 6.95 (*0-910621-22-5*) HSA Pubns.
— The Way of Tradition, Vol. 2. 295p. reprint ed. pap. 6.95 (*0-910621-23-3*) HSA Pubns.
— The Way of Tradition III. 541p. reprint ed. pap. 6.95 (*0-910621-24-1*) HSA Pubns.
— The Way of Tradition IV. 462p. 1980. pap. 8.00 (*0-910621-35-7*) HSA Pubns.
Moon, Susan. Aunt Marty & Uncle Charlie Go to Giza. (Illus.). 18p. (Orig.). 1987. pap. 5.95 (*0-931416-05-1*) Open Books.
Moon, Susan, jt. auth. see Cabasso, Jackie.
Moon, Sylvia, jt. auth. see Stang, David.
Moon, Teresa, jt. auth. see Davis, Nancy M.
Moon, Terry & Brokmeyer, Ron. Then & Now: On the One Hundreth Anniversary of the First General Strike in the U. S. (Illus.). 50p. 1977. pap. 1.00 (*0-914441-17-5*) News & Letters.
Moon, Tom. This Grim & Savage Game: OSS & the Beginning of U. S. Covert Operations in World War Two. 352p. 1991. 21.95 (*1-878179-01-2*) Burning Gate Pr.
Moon, Van T., jt. auth. see Horstman, James L.
Moon, Vicky. The Official Middleburg Life Cookbook. (Illus.). (Orig.). Date not set. 10.00 (*0-9617683-0-4*) Pink Sheet.
Moon, Warren G., ed. Ancient Greek Art & Iconography. LC 83-47765. (Illus.). 368p. 1983. 50.00 (*0-299-09250-X*) U of Wis Pr.
— Polykleitos, the Doryphoros, & Tradition. LC 94-30288. (Wisconsin Studies in Classics Ser.). (Illus.). 1995. 50.00 (*0-299-14310-4*) U of Wis Pr.
Moonah, Faria. In Infinite Pursuit. 1994. 10.00 (*0-533-10713-X*) Vantage.
Moonan, Lawrence. Divine Power: The Medieval Power Distinction up to Its Adoption by Albert, Bonaventure, & Aquinas. LC 93-30542. 400p. 1994. 59.00 (*0-19-826755-X*, Clarendon Pr) OUP.
Moonbeam, Kathy M. Why? The Road from There to Here was Tough but Now I'm on the Highway. LC 91-76844. (Illus.). 192p. (Orig.). 1992. pap. 9.95 (*1-880601-07-9*) Danon Pub.
Moondance, Wolf. Rainbow Medicine: A Visionary Guide to Native American Shamanism. LC 93-39600. (Illus.). 192p. 1994. pap. 12.95 (*0-8069-0364-3*) Sterling.
Moone, Eric, jt. auth. see Gale, D.
Moonen, J. & Plomp, T., eds. Eurit 86: Developments in Educational Software & Courseware. 762p. 1987. 303.00 (*0-08-032693-5*, Pub. by Pergamon Repr UK); 45.00 (*0-08-035833-0*, Pub. by Pergamon Repr UK) Franklin.
Moonen, Joep, et al. Surinaamse Slangeninkleur: Surinam Snakes in Color. (Illus.). 119p. 1979. pap. 29.95 (*0-88359-016-6*) R Curtis Pubng.
***Moonen, Marc & Catthoor, Francky, eds.** Algorithms & Parallel VLSI Architectures III: Proceedings of The International Workshop, Algorithms & Parallel VLSI Architectures III, Leuven, Belgium, August 29-31, 1994. LC 94-44668. 1995. write for info. (*0-444-82106-6*) Elsevier.
***Moonen, Marc & De Moor, Bart, eds.** SVD & Signaling Processing III: Algorithms, Architectures, & Applications. LC 95-3193. 1995. write for info. (*0-444-82107-4*) Elsevier.
Moonen, Marc S., ed. Linear Algebra for Large-Scale & Real-Time Applications: Proceedings of the NATO Advanced Study Institute, Leuven, Belgium, August 3-14, 1992. (NATO ASI Series E, Applied Sciences). 436p. (C). 1993. lib. bdg. 163.00 (*0-7923-2151-0*) Kluwer Ac.
Mooney. Newsmakers Sub, 1994, Pt. 1. (Newsmakers Ser.). 1994. write for info. (*0-8103-8561-9*, 101350) Gale.
— Newsmakers Sub, 1994, Pt. 2. (Newsmakers Ser.). 1994. write for info. (*0-8103-8562-7*, 101351) Gale.
— Newsmakers Sub, 1994, Vol. 3. 94th ed. (Newsmakers Ser.). 1994. write for info. (*0-8103-8563-5*, 101352) Gale.
— Newsmakers Sub, 1994, Vol. 4. (Newsmakers Ser.). 1994. write for info. (*0-8103-8564-3*, 101353) Gale.
— Newsmakers, 1994. 1994. 95.00 (*0-8103-8560-0*, 001820) Gale.
Mooney, Al, et al. The Recovery Book. LC 92-50284. 1992. pap. 13.95 (*1-56305-084-6*, 3084) Workman Pub.
Mooney, Ann J. The Sock Animals: Tiger's New Friends. LC 91-76359. (Sock Animals Ser.). (Illus.). 32p. (Orig.). (J). (ps-2). 1992. pap. 7.95 (*0-9631035-0-4*) Jamondas Pr.
Mooney, Anne S., ed. see Maguire, Marjorie R. & Maguire, Daniel C.
***Mooney, Barbara J., et al.** Feeling Good about Me. (Illus.). 17p. (J). (gr. 3-8). 1993. pap. 6.00 (*1-57402-302-0*); student ed, teacher ed 6.00 (*1-57402-304-7*) Athena Info Mgt.
— Feelings: Having Them - Sharing Them. (Illus.). 17p. (J). (gr. 3-8). 1993. student ed, pap. 6.00 (*1-57402-301-2*); student ed, teacher ed 6.00 (*1-57402-303-9*) Athena Info Mgt.
Mooney, Bel. From This Day Forward: An Anthology of Marriage. 372p. 1990. 29.95 (*0-7195-4748-2*, Pub. by John Murray UK) Trafalgar.
— Perspectives for Living: Conversations on Bereavement & Love. (Illus.). 208p. 1993. pap. 18.95 (*0-7195-5125-0*, Pub. by John Murray UK) Trafalgar.
Mooney, Belinda T. Leave Me Alone! Helping Your Troubled Teenager. 1992. pap. 9.95 (*0-07-042866-2*) McGraw.
— Leave Me Alone! Helping Your Troubled Teenager. 192p. 1992. write for info. (*0-8306-2538-0*, 3990, TAB-Human Servs Inst); pap. 9.95 (*0-8306-2537-2*, 3990, TAB-Human Servs Inst) TAB Bks.
Mooney, Bill, jt. ed. see Holt, David.
Mooney, Blake. Altitude-Rated Places: A Medical Atlas, Vol. 1. 2nd rev. ed. Landry, Juliette, ed. (Illus.). 225p. (Orig.). 1994. pap. 16.95 (*0-9638226-0-8*) Med-Travel Bks.
Mooney, Bonnie F. Grandma Fraley's Verse Book. LC 88-50926. 44p. (Orig.). 1989. pap. 4.95 (*1-55523-170-5*) Winston-Derek.
Mooney, Carol A., jt. auth. see Shaffer, Thomas L.
***Mooney, Catherine, ed.** Eat, Drink & Sleep Smoke-Free. (Illus.). 258p. (Orig.). 1995. pap. 14.95 (*1-899583-00-9*, Pub. by Jarrold Pub UK) Seven Hills Bk.
— The Good Vegetarian Travel Guide. (Illus.). 162p. (Orig.). 1995. pap. 14.95 (*1-899583-01-7*, Pub. by Jarrold Pub UK) Seven Hills Bk.
Mooney, Charles W. Doctor in Belle Starr Country. LC 74-30947. (Illus.). 291p. 1975. write for info. (*0-685-53674-2*) Century Pr.
Mooney, Charles W., Jr., ed. see Honnold, John O. & Harris, Steven L.
Mooney, Chase. William H. Crawford, Seventeen Seventy-Two to Eighteen Thirty-Four. LC 70-190534. 386p. reprint ed. pap. 110.10 (*0-317-26727-2*, 2024361) Bks Demand.
Mooney, Christopher F. Boundaries Dimly Perceived: Law, Religion, Education, & the Common Good. LC 89-40393. (C). 1990. text ed. 26.95 (*0-268-00682-2*) U of Notre Dame Pr.
— Cybernation, Responsibility & Providential Design. (Teilhard Studies). 1991. 3.50 (*0-89012-063-3*) Anima Pubns.
— Public Virtue: Law & the Social Character of Religion. LC 85-41014. 192p. (C). 1989. text ed. 22.95 (*0-268-01561-9*); pap. text ed. 10.95 (*0-268-01583-X*) U of Notre Dame Pr.
— Theology & Scientific Knowledge: Changing Models of God's Presence in the World. (C). 1996. text ed. 34.95 (*0-614-07369-3*) U of Notre Dame Pr.
Mooney, Christopher F., ed. The Presence & Absence of God. LC 68-8748. (Cardinal Bea Lectures). 190p. reprint ed. pap. 54.20 (*0-7837-0458-5*, 2040781) Bks Demand.
Mooney, Christopher Z. & Duval, Robert D. Bootstrapping: A Nonparamentric Approach to Statistical Inference. (Quantitative Applications in the Social Sciences Ser.: Vol. 95). (Illus.). 96p. (C). 1993. pap. text ed. 9.95 (*0-8039-5381-X*) Sage.
Mooney, Chuck, III. The Recruiting Survival Guide: How to Be a Smart Recruit. Bucheit, Kelly S., ed. (Illus.). 84p. (Orig.). (YA). (gr. 11-12). 1991. pap. 9.95 (*0-9630239-0-X*) C Mooney.
Mooney, Dale. Western Glass Auctions: Auction Catalog, 3 vols., 1. (Illus.). 1991. 16.00 (*1-883192-00-5*) Wstrn Glass.
— Western Glass Auctions: Auction Catalog, 3 vols., 2. (Illus.). 1992. 18.00 (*0-685-63559-7*) Wstrn Glass.

— Western Glass Auctions: Auction Catalog, 3 vols., 3. (Illus.). 1992. 20.00 (0-685-63560-0) Wstrn Glass.

Mooney, E. F. Annual Reports on NMR Spectroscopy, 1982, Vol. 11B. 1982. text ed. 222.00 (0-12-505349-5) Acad Pr.

Mooney, E. F. & Webb, Graham A. Annual Reports on NMR Spectroscopy, Vol. 15. 1984. text ed. 203.00 (0-12-505315-0) Acad Pr.

Mooney, E. F. & Webb, Graham A., eds. Annual Reports on NMR Spectroscopy, 2 Vols., 13. 1983. text ed. 222.00 (0-12-505313-4) Acad Pr.

— Annual Reports on NMR Spectroscopy, Vol. 10A. 1980. text ed. 203.00 (0-12-505310-X) Acad Pr.

— Annual Reports on NMR Spectroscopy, Vol. 10B. 1980. text ed. 222.00 (0-12-505348-7) Acad Pr.

— Annual Reports on NMR Spectroscopy, Vol. 11A. 1981. text ed. 203.00 (0-12-505311-8) Acad Pr.

— Annual Reports on NMR Spectroscopy, Vol. 12. 1982. text ed. 203.00 (0-12-505312-6) Acad Pr.

Mooney, Edward F. Knights of Faith & Resignation: Reading Kierkegaard's "Fear & Trembling" LC 90-36515. (SUNY Series in Philosophy). 205p. (C). 1991. 59.50 (0-7914-0572-9); pap. 19.95 (0-7914-0573-7) State U NY Pr.

Mooney, Edward S. An Analysis of the Supervision of Student Teaching: A Study Based on the New York State Teacher-Education Institutions for the Preparation of Elementary School Teachers. LC 72-177078. (Columbia University. Teachers College. Contributions to Education Ser.: No. 711). 37.50 (0-404-55711-2) AMS Pr.

Mooney, Elizabeth C. Country Adventures in Maryland, Virginia & West Virginia. 164p. (Orig.). 1984. pap. 5.95 (0-915168-01-4) Wash Bk Trad.

Mooney, F. Bentley, Jr. The Artful Use of Offshore Tax Havens. Perry, Lee, ed. 335p. (Orig.). 1988. pap. write for info. (0-943637-01-5) Amer Commerce Pub.

— Going Bare. Perry, Lee, ed. 40p. (Orig.). 1988. pap. write for info. (0-943637-02-3) Amer Commerce Pub.

— Handcuff the Taxman. Perry, Lee, ed. 125p. (Orig.). 1988. pap. write for info. (0-943637-00-7) Amer Commerce Pub.

— Preserving Your Wealth: Expert Advice You Can Use to Protect Your Estate from the Risks of Litigation & the Ravages of Taxes, Inflation & Declining Asset Values. 460p. 1993. reprint ed. pap. 22.95 (1-55738-488-6) Probus Pub Co.

— When Health Is Lost: Providing for Long-Term Nursing Care. Perry, Lee, ed. 183p. 1989. 24.95 (0-943637-04-X) Amer Commerce Pub.

Mooney, Gary, ed. see LaCroix, Richard.

Mooney, Gavin. Economics, Medicine & Health Care. 2nd ed. 170p. (C). 1992. text ed. 58.50 (0-389-20991-0) Rowman.

— Key Issues in Health Economics. 192p. 1994. pap. 39.95 (0-13-302746-5) P-H.

Mooney, Gavin, jt. ed. see Jensen, Uffe J.

Mooney, Gavin H. International Perspectives in Health Economics: Selected Papers from the World Congress in Health Economics, Leiden, the Netherlands, September 1980. (Journal of Social Science & Medicine Ser.: No. 15). 72p. 1981. pap. 18.00 (0-08-028131-1, Pergamon Pr) Elsevier.

Mooney, George W., ed. see Suetonius.

Mooney, H. Supplement to the Botany of Bihar & Orissa. 294p. 1986. reprint ed. 140.00 (0-685-21849-X, Pub. by Intl Bk Distr II) St Mut.

Mooney, H., jt. ed. see Huenneke, L. F.

Mooney, Harold A. & Bernardi, G., eds. Introduction of Genetically-Modified Organisms into the Environment. (Scientific Committee on Problems of the Environment Ser.: No. 44). 201p. 1990. text ed. 165.00 (0-471-92677-9) Wiley.

Mooney, Harold A. & Drake, J. A., eds. Ecology of Biological Invasions of North America & Hawaii. (Ecological Studies, Analysis & Synthesis: Vol. 58). (Illus.). 330p. 1986. 87.00 (0-387-96289-1) Spr-Verlag.

Mooney, Harold A., jt. ed. see Hobbs, R. J.

Mooney, Harold A., jt. ed. see Margaris, N. S.

Mooney, Harold A., jt. ed. see Putz, F. E.

Mooney, Harold A., jt. ed. see Schulze, Ernst-Detlef.

Mooney, Harold A., et al, eds. Earth System Responses to Global Change: Contrasts Between North & South America. (Illus.). 365p. 1993. text ed. 59.95 (0-12-505300-2) Acad Pr.

— Ecosystem Experiments: Scope Forty-Five. (Scientific Committee on Problems of the Environment Ser.: No. 1409). 268p. 1991. text ed. 195.00 (0-471-92926-3) Wiley.

— Response of Plants to Multiple Stresses. (Physiological Ecology Ser.). (Illus.). 422p. 1991. text ed. 79.95 (0-12-505355-X) Acad Pr.

Mooney, Harry J. & Staley, Thomas F., eds. The Shapeless God: Essays on Modern Fiction. LC 68-21630. 232p. reprint ed. pap. 66.20 (0-685-15962-0, 2026314) Bks Demand.

Mooney, Jack. Printers in Appalachia: The International Printing Pressmen & Assistants' Union of North America, 1907-1967. LC 93-70235. 193p. (C). 1993. 39.95 (0-87972-576-1); pap. 16.95 (0-87972-577-X) Bowling Green Univ.

Mooney, James. Calendar History of the Kiowa Indians. LC 78-10789. (Classics of Smithsonian Anthropology Ser.: No. 2). (Illus.). 460p. 1979. reprint ed. pap. text ed. 24.95 (0-87474-655-8, MOCHP) Smithsonian.

— The Ghost-Dance Religion & the Sioux Outbreak of 1890. (Illus.). xxx, 531p. 1991. reprint ed. 65.00 (0-8032-3155-5); reprint ed. pap. 25.00 (0-8032-8177-3) U of Nebr Pr.

— Ghost-Dance, Religion & Wounded Knee. 1991. pap. 12.95 (0-486-26759-8) Dover.

— James Mooney's History, Myths & Sacred Formulas of the Cherokees. LC 91-42830. 768p. 1992. pap. 15.95 (0-914875-19-1, Historical Images) Bright Mtn Bks.

— Myths of the Cherokee. LC 70-108513. (American Indian History Ser.). 1970. reprint ed. 89.00 (0-403-00221-4) Scholarly.

— Myths of the Cherokee & Sacred Formulas of the Cherokees. LC 72-188151. (Illus.). 1982. reprint ed. 20.00 (0-918450-05-5); reprint ed. pap. 16.95 (0-918450-22-5) C Elder.

— Siouan Tribes of the East. LC 73-108504. (American Indian History Ser.). (Illus.). 1970. reprint ed. 39.00 (0-403-00348-2) Scholarly.

— Siouuan Tribes of the East. (Bureau of American Ethnology Bulletins Ser.). 101p. 1995. lib. bdg. 79.00 (0-7812-4022-0) Rprt Serv.

— Swimmer Manuscript: Cherokee Sacred Formulas & Medicinal Prescriptions. (Bureau of American Ethnology Bulletins Ser.). 319p. 1995. lib. bdg. 99.00 (0-7812-4099-9) Rprt Serv.

Mooney, James & Wat, Thomas R. To Redeem a Nation: The American Civil Rights Movement. 271p. (C). 1993. pap. text ed. 13.50 (1-881089-20-7) Brandywine Press.

Mooney, James E., comp. Maps, Globes, Atlases & Geographies Through the Year 1800: The Eleanor Houston & Lawrence M. C. Smith Cartographic Collection. (Illus.). 168p. (C). 1988. 75.00 (0-939561-03-4) Univ South ME.

Mooney, James E., jt. auth. see Shipton, Clifford K.

Mooney, James W. & West, Thomas R., eds. Vietnam: A History & Reader. 250p. (Orig.). (C). 1994. pap. text ed. 13.50 (1-881089-28-2) Brandywine Press.

***Mooney, Linne R., ed.** The Index of Middle English Prose: Handlist XI. Manuscripts in The Library of Trinity College, Cambridge. 73p. (C). 1995. text ed. 63.00 (0-85991-457-7, DS Brewer) Boydell & Brewer.

Mooney, Louise, ed. Annual Obituary, 1995. 850p. 1993. 92.00 (1-55862-339-6, 200267) St James Pr.

Mooney, Margaret. Developing Life-Long Readers. 30p. (C). 1988. reprint ed. pap. text ed. 5.95 (0-478-02701-X) R Owen Pubs.

— A Matter of Balance. LC 93-26222. (Illus.). (J). 1994. 4.25 (0-383-03759-X) SRA Schl Grp.

— Outwitting the Tiger: A Chinese Legend. LC 93-26261. (Illus.). (J). 1994. 4.25 (0-383-03776-X) SRA Schl Grp.

Mooney, Margaret E. Reading to, with, & by Children. LC 90-30678. 104p. (Orig.). (C). 1990. pap. text ed. 10.95 (0-913461-18-0) R Owen Pubs.

Mooney, Margaret L., jt. auth. see Peabody, Kathleen L.

Mooney, Margaret M. & Pratzel, Alan D. Missouri Civil Procedure Forms. 500p. 1994. disk, ring bd. 159.00 (0-87189-066-6) Michie Butterworth.

— Missouri Civil Procedure Forms. suppl. ed. 1994. ring bd. 87.00 (0-685-74598-8) Butterworth Legal Pubs.

Mooney, Martin. The Comanche Indians. (Junior Library of American Indians). (Illus.). 80p. (J). (gr. 3-7). 1993. lib. bdg. 14.95 (0-7910-1653-6) Chelsea Hse.

— Grub. 85p. 1994. pap. 11.95 (0-85640-500-0, Pub. by Blackstaff Pr IE) Dufour.

Mooney, Mary F., tr. see Baudouin-Croix, Marie.

Mooney, Michael. Ancient Voices & Other Stories. (Orig.). 1987. pap. 8.95 (0-935399-04-6) Main St Pub.

— Names. deluxe ed. (Treacle Story Ser.: No. 10). 64p. 1979. 8.00 (0-914232-33-9) McPherson & Co.

— Shakespeare's Dramatic Transactions. LC 90-2770. 243p. (C). 1990. text ed. 34.50 (0-8223-1039-2) Duke.

— Vico in the Tradition of Rhetoric. (Illus.). 318p. (C). 1994. pap. text ed. 16.95 (1-880393-24-7) Hermagoras Pr.

— Vico in the Tradition of Rhetoric. LC 84-42569. 343p. reprint ed. pap. 97.80 (0-8357-2930-3, 2039169) Bks Demand.

Mooney, Michael, ed. see Kristeller, Paul O.

Mooney, Pat, jt. auth. see Fowler, Cary.

Mooney, Patrick H. & Majka, Theo J. Farmers' & Farm Workers' Movements. LC 94-18178. (Twayne's Social Movements Past & Present Ser.). 288p. 1994. text ed. 26.95x (0-8057-3869-X, Twayne); pap. 15.95 (0-8057-3870-3, Twayne) Macmillan.

Mooney, Paula Y. Payroll Accounting. LC 93-35659. 1993. pap. text ed. write for info. (0-13-091308-1) P-H.

Mooney, Peter. Transparent Plastics, No. P-053R: Broadening the Base of Materials & Applications. 204p. 1990. 2,850.00 (0-89336-706-0) BCC.

Mooney, Peter J. Impact of Immigrants on the Growth & Development of the U. S. Economy, 1890-1920. LC 90-3718. (European Immigrants & American Society Ser.). 280p. 1990. reprint ed. 20.00 (0-8240-0300-4) Garland.

Mooney, Philip. Images of Personal Value. 192p. (Orig.). 1994. pap. 10.95 (1-55612-705-7) Sheed & Ward MO.

Mooney, Raymond, jt. ed. see Porter, Bruce.

Mooney, Raymond J. General Explanation-Based Learning Mechanism & Its Applications to Narrative Understanding. (Research Notes in Artificial Intelligence Ser.). 1990. 29.95 (1-55860-091-4) Morgan Kaufmann.

Mooney, Raymond J., ed. A General Explanation-Based Learning Mechanism & Its Application to Narrative Understanding. 240p. (C). 1989. pap. text ed. 200.00 (0-273-08815-7, Pub. by Pitman Pubng UK) St Mut.

Mooney, Rick. Ensembles for Cello, Vol. 3. 40p. 1991. pap. text ed. 6.50 (0-87487-299-5) Summy-Birchard.

Mooney, Rick, des. Ensembles for Cello, Vol. 2. 24p. 1991. pap. text ed. 6.50 (0-87487-298-7) Summy-Birchard.

Mooney, Rick, ed. Cello Ensembles. 87p. 1987. 6.50 (0-87487-296-0) Summy-Birchard.

Mooney, Robert F. Tales of Nantucket: Chronicles & Characters of America's Favorite Island. (Illus.). 184p. (Orig.). 1990. pap. 12.95 (0-9627851-0-5) Wesco Pub MA.

Mooney, Robert F., text. Portrait of Nantucket, 1659-1890: Paintings by Rodney Charman. 45p. Date not set. text ed. 50.00 (0-9638910-3-0); pap. text ed. 20.00 (0-9638910-4-9) Mill Hill Pr.

Mooney, Robert F., jt. auth. see Miller, Richard F.

Mooney, Samantha. A Snowflake in My Hand. 1989. 8.95 (0-385-29721-1, Delta) Dell.

— A Snowflake in My Hand. large type ed. 1995. pap. 19.95 (1-56895-227-9) Wheeler Pub.

Mooney, Sean. Insuring Your Business: What You Need to Know to Get the Best Insurance Coverage for Your Business. LC 91-29128. 200p. 1993. 22.50 (0-932387-29-2) Insur Info.

Mooney, Sean & Cohen, Larry. Basic Concepts of Accounting & Taxation of Property-Casualty Insurance Companies. 1994. lib. bdg. write for info. (0-318-72709-9) Insur Info.

Mooney, Sheila. Strange Kind of Loving. 192p. 1990. pap. 11.95 (1-85371-076-8, Pub. by Poolbeg Pr IE) Dufour.

Mooney, Sheila, ed. see Ramsay, Caroline C.

Mooney, Sheila A., jt. auth. see Ramsay, Caroline C.

Mooney, Shirley, jt. auth. see Davis, Chuck.

Mooney, Stephen. News from the South: Poems. 2nd ed. LC 66-14773. 78p. reprint ed. pap. 25.00 (0-317-29908-5, 2021781) Bks Demand.

Mooney, Steven. In Cellophane of Time. 65p. (Orig.). 1988. pap. 3.00 (0-317-91185-6) MoonDog Pr.

Mooney, Ted. Easy Travel to Other Planets. 240p. 1982. pap. 3.95 (0-345-30547-7) Ballantine.

— Easy Travel to Other Planets. 1992. pap. 10.00 (0-679-73883-5, Vin) Random.

— Traffic & Laughter. 1992. pap. 12.00 (0-679-73884-3, Vin) Random.

Mooney, Thomas O., et al. Sexual Options for Paraplegics & Quadriplegics. (Illus.). 150p. 1975. pap. 29.95 (0-316-57937-8) Little.

Mooney, Tom. The Amoralists. pap. 3.00 (0-317-28509-2) Mooney.

— Black Tuesday: A Story of Nuclear War. pap. 3.00 (0-317-28511-4) Mooney.

— The Boom & Bust Cycle. pap. 3.00 (0-317-28512-2) Mooney.

— The Early History of a Purpose Machine. 1976. 5.95 (0-9601240-1-2); pap. 2.95 (0-9601240-2-0) Mooney.

— Notes on the Nature of Man. pap. 3.00 (0-317-28508-4) Mooney.

— Wally Wooluf & Other Stories: A Young Person's Guide to Humor. pap. 3.00 (0-317-28510-6) Mooney.

— War: Toward a Solution. pap. 2.00 (0-317-28513-0) Mooney.

Mooney, W. D., jt. ed. see Pakiser, L. C.

Mooney, Will C. Chinese Names for Oriental Dogs. LC 74-29656. (Other Dog Bks.). (Illus.). 1975. 12.95 (0-87714-031-6) Denlingers.

Mooney, William. ASAP: The Fastest Way to Create a Memorable Speech. 1992. 14.95 (0-8120-6280-9) Barron.

Moonie, Neil, et al. Human Behaviour in the Caring Context. 128p. (Orig.). 1995. pap. 27.50 (0-7487-1769-2, Pub. by Stanley Thornes UK) Trans-Atl Phila.

Moonitz, Maurice. The Entity Theory of Consolidated Statements. Brief, Richard P., ed. LC 77-87282. (Development of Contemporary Accounting Thought Ser.). 1978. reprint ed. lib. bdg. 19.95 (0-405-10910-5) Ayer.

— Obtaining Agreement on Standards in the Accounting Profession. (Studies in Accounting Research: Vol. 8). 93p. 1974. 12.00 (0-86539-020-7) Am Accounting.

Moonitz, Maurice & Brief, Richard P., eds. Three Contributions to the Development of Accounting Thought. LC 77-87315. (Development of Contemporary Accounting Thought Ser.). 1978. lib. bdg. 37.95 (0-405-10928-8) Ayer.

Moonitz, Maurice, jt. ed. see Zeff, Stephen A.

Moonlight, Rabbi. The Brand New Testament. LC 85-60482. (Illus.). 128p. 1985. pap. 4.95 (0-913483-04-4) Joydeism Pr.

Moonlitz, Maurice. Selected Writings of Maurice Moonlitz, 2 vols., Set. (Accounting History & Thought Ser.). 540p. 1990. reprint ed. 65.00 (0-8240-3322-1) Garland.

Moonman, Eric. British Computers & Industrial Innovation: Implications of the Parliamentary Select Committee. 1971. 22.00 (0-8464-0210-6) Beekman Pubs.

Moonman, Eric, ed. Violent Society. 168p. 1987. 35.00 (0-7146-3309-7, Pub. by F Cass Pubs UK); pap. 12.50 (0-7146-4055-7, Pub. by F Cass Pubs UK) Intl Spec Bk.

Moonsammy, Rita Z., et al, eds. Pinelands Folklife. (Illus.). 234p. 1987. text ed. 38.00 (0-8135-1188-7); pap. 16.95 (0-8135-1189-5) Rutgers U Pr.

Moor, Christine H. From School to Work: Effective Counselling & Guidance. LC 74-31569. (Sage Studies in Social & Educational Change: Vol. 3). 192p. reprint ed. pap. 54.80 (0-317-12983-X, 2021934) Bks Demand.

Moor, Christine H., jt. auth. see King, Edmund J.

Moor, Douglas V., ed. see Leinfelder, Karl F. & Taylor, Duane F.

Moor, Edward. Hindu Pantheon. 29.95 (0-89314-409-6) Philos Res.

Moor, Fred B., et al. Manual of Hydrotherapy & Massage. LC 64-23214. 169p. 1964. 11.95 (0-8163-0023-2, 13160-7) Pacific Pr Pub Assn.

Moor, Gilbert. Rage. 304p. 1993. pap. 10.95 (0-88184-973-1) Carroll & Graf.

Moor, J. H. Notices of the Indian Archipelago & Adjacent Countries. 398p. 1968. reprint ed. 85.00 (0-7146-2020-3, Pub. by F Cass Pubs UK) Intl Spec Bk.

Moor, James. An Essay on Historical Composition: Read, February, 6, 1752 (from Essays Read to a Literary Society) LC 92-25503. (Augustan Reprints Ser.: No. 187 (1978)). reprint ed. 12.00 (0-404-70187-6, D13.M66) AMS Pr.

Moor-Jankowski, J., ed. see Conference on Experimental Medicine & Surgery in Primates, 2nd, New York, 1969.

Moor-Jankowski, J., ed. see Conference on Marmosets in Experimental Medicine, Oak Ridge Tenn., March 16-18, 1977.

Moor, John & Smith, Larry, eds. In Buckeye Country: Photos & Essays of Ohio Life. (Ohio Writers Ser.). (Illus.). 208p. (Orig.). 1994. 9.95 (0-933087-31-4) Bottom Dog Pr.

Moor, Keith. Crims in Grass Castles: The Trimbole Affair. 224p. (C). 1990. 45.00 (0-947087-17-6, Pub. by Pascoe Pub AT) St Mut.

Moor, Lise. Glossary of Psychiatry: Glossaire de Psychiatrie. 196p. (FRE.). 1986. 75.00 (0-8288-1819-3, M6417) Fr & Eur.

— Lexicon of Usual Terms in Psychiatry, Neuropsychiatry & Psychopathology. 3rd ed. 236p. (ENG, FRE & GER.). 1980. 49.95 (0-8288-0584-9, M 15383) Fr & Eur.

Moor, Paul, jt. auth. see Klein, Michael R.

Moor, Paul, ed. see Morgenthaler, Fritz.

Moor, Rosemary. Correct Me If I'm Wrong: A Practical Approach to Improving Written English. 96p. (Orig.). 1988. pap. 11.95 (0-85950-713-0, Pub. by Stanley Thornes UK) Trans-Atl Phila.

Moor, Rosemary, ed. Take It from Here: GCSE & Standard Grade Project Work Through the Short Story. 128p. (C). 1989. 39.00 (0-7487-0064-1, Pub. by S Thornes Pubs UK) St Mut.

Moorachian, Rose, ed. What Is a City: A Multi-Media Guide on Urban Living. 1969. 2.00 (0-89073-016-4) Boston Public Lib.

Mooradian, A., et al, eds. Tunable Lasers & Applications. (Optical Sciences Ser: Vol. 3). 1976. 42.00 (0-387-07968-8) Spr-Verlag.

Moorbeek, Kees, jt. auth. see Morbeek, Kees.

Moorby, Ed. How to Succeed in Employee Development: Moving from Vision to Results. 1991. pap. text ed. 24.95 (0-07-707459-9) McGraw.

Moorby, Jeffrey. Transport Systems in Plants. LC 80-41374. (Integrated Themes in Biology Ser.). (Illus.). 175p. reprint ed. pap. 49.90 (0-8357-3573-7, 2034503) Bks Demand.

Moorby, Philip, jt. auth. see Thomas, Donald E.

Moorcock, Michael. Bane of the Black Sword. 160p. 1987. pap. 4.99 (0-441-04885-4) Ace Bks.

— Behold the Man. 150p. 1987. pap. 2.95 (0-88184-369-5) Carroll & Graf.

— Blood: A Southern Novel. LC 95-15749. 1995. write for info. (0-688-14362-8) Morrow.

— Breakfast in the Ruins. 176p. 1980. pap. 3.50 (0-380-49148-6) Avon.

— Breakfast in the Ruins. 1991. reprint ed. lib. bdg. 21.95 (1-56849-086-0) Buccaneer Bks.

— The Brothel in Rosenstrasse. 191p. 1986. 17.00 (0-931763-02-9) Tigereyes Pr.

— The Brothel in Rosenstrasse. deluxe limited ed. 191p. 1986. 35.00 (0-931763-03-7) Tigereyes Pr.

— The Cornelius Chronicles, Vol. 1. 992p. 1977. mass mkt. 4.95 (0-380-00878-5) Avon.

— The Cornelius Chronicles, Vol. II. 352p. 1986. pap. 3.50 (0-380-75003-1) Avon.

— The Cornelius Chronicles, Vol. III. 352p. 1987. pap. 3.50 (0-380-70255-X) Avon.

— Elric at the End of Time. (Elric of Melnibone Ser.: Vol. 7). 224p. 1985. pap. 4.50 (0-88677-228-1) DAW Bks.

— Elric at the End of Time. (Illus.). 175p. 1986. 20.00 (0-931763-04-5) Tigereyes Pr.

— Elric at the End of Time. deluxe limited ed. (Illus.). 175p. 1986. 35.00 (0-931763-05-3) Tigereyes Pr.

— The Elric Saga Pt. I, 3 vols. in 1. 416p. 1983. 9.98 (1-56865-040-X, GuildAmerica) Dblday Bk Music.

— The Elric Saga Pt. II, 3 vols. in 1. (Illus.). 480p. 1984. 9.98 (1-56865-041-8, GuildAmerica) Dblday Bk Music.

— Elric Saga, Bk. 1: Elric of Melnibone. 1992. pap. 4.50 (0-441-20398-1) Ace Bks.

— Elric Saga, Bk. 2: Sailor on Seas of Fate. 1989. pap. 4.50 (0-441-74863-5) Ace Bks.

— Elric Saga, Bk. 3: Weird of the White Wolf. 1989. mass mkt. 4.99 (0-441-88805-4) Ace Bks.

— Elric Saga, Bk. 7: Fortress of the Pearl. 1990. mass mkt. 4.99 (0-441-24866-7) Ace Bks.

— The Eternal Champion. (The Eternal Champion: Vol. 1). 1994. 19.99 (1-56504-176-3, 12501) White Wolf.

— Hawkmoon. (The Eternal Champion: Vol. 3). 1995. 19.99 (1-56504-178-X, 12504) White Wolf.

— The Land Leviathan. 17.95 (0-89190-153-1, Am Repr) Amereon Ltd.

— Lunching with the AntiChrist. 1994. 25.00 (0-929480-46-5) Mark Ziesing.

— Lunching with the AntiChrist. limited ed. 1994. 60.00 (0-929480-47-3) Mark Ziesing.

— A Nomad of the Time Streams, Vol. 4. (Eternal Champion: Vol. 4). 1995. 19.99 (1-56504-179-8, 12505) White Wolf.

— The Revenge of the Rose. 256p. 1994. pap. text ed. 4.99 (0-441-00106-8) Ace Bks.

— Stormbringer. 1987. pap. 4.50 (0-441-78754-1) Ace Bks.

— Tales from the End of Time. 288p. 1989. 7.98 (1-56865-034-5, GuildAmerica) Dblday Bk Music.

— Vanishing Tower. 176p. 1987. mass mkt. 4.99 (0-441-86039-7) Ace Bks.

— Von Bek. (The Eternal Champion: Vol. 2). 1994. 19.99 (1-56504-177-1, 12503) White Wolf.

— The War Hound & the World's Pain: A Fable. LC 81-9030. 239p. 1981. 25.00 (0-671-43708-9) Ultramarine Pub.

Moorcock, Michael & Cawthorne, James. Fantasy: The One Hundred Best Books. 220p. 1988. 15.95 (0-88184-335-0) Carroll & Graf.

An Asterisk (*) at the beginning of an entry indicates that the title is appearing in BIP for the first time.

Moorcock, Michael & Thomas, Roy. Elric of Melnibone. Oliver, Rick, ed. (Illus.). 176p. 1986. pap. 14.95 (*0-915419-05-X*) First Pub IL.

Moorcock, Michael, jt. auth. see Cawthorne, James.

Moorcock, Michael, jt. auth. see Thomas, Roy.

Moorcock, Michael, ed. see Wells, H. G.

*__Moorcock, Michael.__ Crystal & the Amulet. (Illus.). 100p. (Orig.). 1981. pap. 12.95 (*0-86130-044-0*, Pub. by Savoy Bks UK) AK Pr Dist.

— Sojan. 160p. (Orig.). 1980. pap. 11.95 (*0-86130-000-9*, Pub. by Savoy Bks UK) AK Pr Dist.

*__Moorcraft, Paul.__ What the Hell Am I Doing Here? Travels with an Occasional War Correspondent. LC 95-2658. (Illus.). x, 295p. (C). 1995. 29.95 (*1-85753-121-3*, Pub. by Brasseys UK) Macmillan.

Moorcraft, Paul L. African Nemesis: War & Revolution in Southern Africa, 1945-2010. (Illus.). 540p. 1990. 47.50 (*0-08-036715-1*, Pub. by Brasseys UK) Brasseys Inc.

Moorcroft, Sheila M., ed. Visions for the Twenty-First Century. LC 92-35824. 1993. text ed. 55.00 (*0-275-94571-5*, C4571, Praeger Pubs) Greenwood.

— Visions for the Twenty-First Century. LC 92-35824. 1993. pap. text ed. 17.95 (*0-275-94572-3*, B4572, Praeger Pubs) Greenwood.

Moorcroft, William H. Sleep, Dreaming, & Sleep Disorders: An Introduction. 2nd ed. 508p. (Orig.). (C). 1993. lib. bdg. 59.00 (*0-8191-9250-3*); pap. text ed. 37.50 (*0-8191-9251-1*) U Pr of Amer.

Moore. Ancestor's Footsteps. (Indian Culture Ser.). (Illus.). 1978. 4.95 (*0-89992-073-X*) Coun India Ed.

— Basic Practice of Statistics. (C). 1995. text ed. (*0-7167-2653-X*) W H Freeman.

— Collected Poems: Moore. 1981. 10.95 (*0-02-586170-0*) Macmillan.

— Dreams of Revenge: Dark Moon, Bk. II. 1995. mass mkt. (*0-590-25510-X*) Scholastic Inc.

— Early Care of the Injured Patient. 341p. 1990. 61.00 (*1-55664-054-4*) Mosby Yr Bk.

— Essentials of Embryology. (Illus.). 198p. (C). 1988. 33.95 (*0-941158-97-7*) Mosby Yr Bk.

— IPS & Data Sets. 2nd ed. (C). 1995. text ed. write for info. (*0-7167-2493-6*) W H Freeman.

— Kiss of Death: Dark Moon, Bk. I. 1995. mass mkt. (*0-590-25509-6*) Scholastic Inc.

— Live with It. 1994. per. 10.95 (*0-921368-39-9*, Pub. by Blizzard Pub CN) InBook.

— Modern Amateur Astronomer. 1995. pap. (*0-387-19900-4*) Spr-Verlag.

— Monitoring Building Structures. 1992. text ed. 84.95 (*0-442-31333-0*) Chapman & Hall.

— Native Artists of Africa. 1995. pap. text ed. 9.95 (*1-56261-229-8*) John Muir.

— Native Artists of Europe. 1995. pap. text ed. 9.95 (*1-56261-230-1*) John Muir.

— Native Artists of North America. 1995. pap. text ed. 9.95 (*1-56261-231-X*) John Muir.

— Neurovasc Immun: Vasoactive Neurotrans & Modul-Cell Immun. 1992. 173.00 (*0-8493-6894-4*, QP356) CRC Pr.

— Night Before Christmas. 1994. 4.99 (*0-517-13545-0*) Random Hse Value.

— Observational Amateur Astronomer. 1995. pap. (*0-387-19899-7*) Spr-Verlag.

— PDQ Embryology. 1986. 27.95 (*0-8016-3533-0*) Mosby Yr Bk.

— Soul & Everyday Life. 1995. 19.95 (*1-879323-16-8*) Sound Horizons AV.

— Statistics: Concepts & Controversies. 3rd ed. (C). 1995. pap. text ed. 17.95 (*0-7167-2199-6*) W H Freeman.

— Transforming Communities. 1995. write for info. (*0-89464-899-3*) Krieger.

— Underground. 1995. 24.95 (*0-8057-9113-2*, Twayne) Macmillan.

— Vehicle Rescue & Extrication. 319p. 1989. pap. 29.95 (*0-8016-3351-6*) Mosby Yr Bk.

Moore, ed. Carbonate Rock Sequences from the Cretaceous of Texas, No. T376. (IGC Field Trip Guidebooks Ser.). 56p. 1989. 21.00 (*0-87590-656-7*) Am Geophysical.

— Lesbiot: Isreli Lesbians Talk About Sexuality, Feminism, Judaism. Date not set. 55.00x (*0-304-33156-2*) InBook.

Moore & Chafin. Tennis Everyone. 4th ed. 250p. 1990. pap. text ed. 12.95 (*0-88725-136-6*) Hunter Textbks.

Moore & Couper. Halley's Comet Pop-Up Book. 1985. 9.98 (*0-517-48351-3*) Random Hse Value.

Moore & Eastman. Handbook of Diagnostic Endocrinology. 416p. 1989. 75.00 (*1-55664-079-X*) Mosby Yr Bk.

Moore & McCabe. Data Sets: IPS. (C). 1995. text ed. write for info. (*0-7167-2490-1*) W H Freeman.

— Statistics. (C). 1995. text ed. write for info. (*0-7167-2450-2*) W H Freeman.

Moore & Navaretta, eds. Artists & Their Cats: In Their Own Voices. LC 90-61443. (Illus.). 64p. (Orig.). 1990. pap. text ed. 10.00 (*1-877675-02-4*) Midmarch Arts-WAN.

Moore & Totleben. Miracleman, Bk. 3: Olympus. (Illus.). 1991. 34.95 (*1-56060-079-9*); pap. 12.95 (*1-56060-080-2*) Eclipse Bks.

Moore & Vodopich. General Biology Lab Manual. 424p. 1991. spiral bd. 21.95 (*0-8016-4486-0*) Mosby Yr Bk.

Moore & Yaqub, Adil. First Course Linear Algebra. (C). 1992. 18.00 (*0-673-46288-9*) HarpCollege.

— First Course Linear Algebra. 2nd ed. (C). 1992. text ed. 66.50 (*0-673-38392-X*) HarpCollege.

Moore, jt. auth. see Caviris.

Moore, jt. ed. see Lewis.

Moore, jt. auth. see Sparkes.

Moore, jt. auth. see Stokes.

Moore, jt. auth. see Vodopich.

Moore, jt. auth. see White.

Moore, et al. Manual of Trauma & Critical Care Procedures. 400p. Date not set. spiral bd. 29.00 (*0-8016-7480-8*) Mosby Yr Bk.

— Manual of Trauma & Critical Care Procedures. (Illus.). 400p. 1991. 29.00 (*0-8016-3485-7*) Mosby Yr Bk.

— Pocket Manual of Emergency Trauma Procedures. (Illus.). 300p. 1988. pap. 20.00 (*0-8016-3582-9*) Mosby Yr Bk.

— Secrets of the New Age, 4 vols. in 1. (Illus.). 395p. 1989. 7.99 (*0-517-68020-3*) Random Hse Value.

— Three-Wall Racquetball Everyone. 3rd ed. 150p. 1987. pap. text ed. 12.95 (*0-88725-082-3*) Hunter Textbks.

Moore, A. Questions & Answers on Ballroom Dancing. (Ballroom Dance Ser.). 1984. lib. bdg. 79.95 (*0-87700-511-7*) Revisionist Pr.

Moore, A., jt. auth. see Ball, J.

Moore, A. L. Moore Family History, 1599-1962. 42p. 1994. reprint ed. pap. 8.50 (*0-8328-4127-7*) Higginson Bk Co.

Moore, A. L. & Beechey, R. B., eds. Plant Mitochondria: Structural, Functional, & Physiological Aspects. LC 87-15303. (Illus.). 424p. 1987. 89.50 (*0-306-42572-6*, Plenum Pr) Plenum.

Moore, A. Tuell & Gibson, H. M. ADF: Automatic Direction Finding Computer Instruction Manual. (ENG & SPA.). 1984. teacher ed 3.50 (*0-317-91368-9*) MAG Mfg.

— ADF: Automatic Direction Finding Computer Instruction Manual. rev. ed. (ENG & SPA.). 1984. reprint ed. 5.85 (*0-317-91367-0*); reprint ed. 3.95 (*0-317-91369-7*) MAG Mfg.

Moore, A. W. A History of the Isle of Man, 2 vol. set. 75.00 (*0-89979-020-8*) British Am Bks.

— The Infinite. 320p. 1990. 39.95 (*0-415-03307-1*, A1646) Routledge.

— The Infinite. (Problems of Philosophy: Their Past & Present Ser.). 320p. 1991. pap. 16.95 (*0-415-07048-1*, A6254) Routledge.

Moore, A. W., ed. Meaning & Reference. LC 92-27073. (Oxford Readings in Philosophy Ser.). (Illus.). 312p. 1993. 49.95 (*0-19-875124-9*); pap. 15.95 (*0-19-875125-7*) OUP.

Moore, Aaron. Carpentry Toolmaking: An Instructor's Guide. 208p. (Orig.). 1994. pap. 28.50 (*1-85339-196-4*, Pub. by Intermed Tech UK) Women Ink.

Moore, Adam. Broken Arrow Boy. Thatch, Nancy R., ed. LC 90-5933. (Books for Students by Students Ser.). (Illus.). 26p. (J). (gr. 3-8). 1990. lib. bdg. 14.95 (*0-933849-24-9*) Landmark Edns.

Moore, Adam C. Song from the Starting Tree. 48p. 1986. 9.00 (*0-7223-2034-5*, Pub. by A H S Ltd UK) St Mut.

Moore, Addison W. The Functional Versus the Representational Theories of Knowledge in Locke's Essay. LC 75-3629. reprint ed. 24.50 (*0-404-59002-0*) AMS Pr.

Moore, Adrian, ed. Infinity. (International Research Library of Philosophy). 480p. 1993. 129.95 (*1-85521-260-9*, Pub. by Dartmth Pub UK) Ashgate Pub Co.

Moore, Alan. Batman: The Killing Joke. O'Neil, Dennis, ed. 48p. 1988. pap. 3.95 (*0-930289-45-5*) DC Comics.

— From Hell, Vol. 1. Amara, Phil, ed. (Illus.). 64p. 1994. reprint ed. pap. 4.95 (*0-87816-286-0*) Kitchen Sink.

— From Hell, Vol. 2. Amara, Philip, ed. (Illus.). 64p. 1994. pap. 4.95 (*0-87816-287-9*) Kitchen Sink.

— From Hell, Vol. 3. (Illus.). 80p. 1993. reprint ed. pap. 4.95 (*0-87816-252-6*) Kitchen Sink.

— From Hell, Vol. 4. Vance, James, ed. (Illus.). 48p. 1994. pap. 4.95 (*0-87816-270-4*) Kitchen Sink.

— From Hell, Vol. 5. Amara, Phil & Campbell, Eddie, eds. (Illus.). 60p. 1994. pap. 4.95 (*0-87816-300-X*) Kitchen Sink.

— From Hell: Being a Melodrama in Sixteen Parts, Vol. 6. Amara, Phil, ed. (Illus.). 64p. 1994. pap. 4.95 (*0-87816-308-5*) Kitchen Sink.

— From Hell Vol. 7: Being a Melodrama in Sixteen Parts. Amara, Philip, ed. (Illus.). 48p. (YA). 1995. pap. 4.95 (*0-87816-338-7*) Kitchen Sink.

— Miracleman Bk Two: The Red King Syndrome. (Illus.). 1990. 29.95 (*1-56060-035-7*); pap. 12.95 (*1-56060-036-5*) Eclipse Bks.

— Miracleman, Bk. 1: A Dream of Flying. (Illus.). 80p. 1988. 29.95 (*0-913035-62-9*); pap. 9.95 (*0-913035-61-0*) Eclipse Bks.

— The Saga of Swamp Thing. 184p. (Orig.). 1987. pap. 10.95 (*0-446-38690-1*) Warner Bks.

— Saga of the Swamp Thing. Marx, Barry, ed. 88p. 1987. pap. 12.95 (*0-930289-22-6*, Vertigo) DC Comics.

— Swamp Thing Love & Death. 1990. pap. 17.95 (*0-446-39192-1*) Warner Bks.

— V for Vendetta. Carlson, KC, ed. 288p. 1990. pap. 17.50 (*0-930289-52-8*, Vertigo) DC Comics.

— Watchmen. Marx, Barry, ed. 416p. (Orig.). 1986. pap. 19.95 (*0-930289-23-4*) DC Comics.

Moore, Alan & Gibbons, Dave. Watchmen. 384p. (Orig.). 1987. pap. 14.95 (*0-446-38689-8*) Warner Bks.

Moore, Alan & Gosciak, Josh, eds. Day in the Life: Tales from the Lower East. (Illus.). 192p. (Orig.). (C). 1990. pap. 7.95 (*0-936556-22-6*) Autonomedia.

Moore, Alan & Lloyd, David. V for Vendetta. 288p. 1990. pap. 14.95 (*0-446-39190-5*) Warner Bks.

Moore, Alan & Parkhouse, Steve. The Bojeffries Saga. Leach, Garry & Jenkins, Paul, eds. (Illus.). 80p. 1993. pap. 9.95 (*1-879450-65-8*) Tundra MA.

*__Moore, Alan & Somers, James D.__ Butterworths Ireland Vat Acts 1993-94. 1993. pap. text ed. 99.00 (*1-85475-636-2*, IE) Butterworth Legal Pubs.

Moore, Alan & Zarate, Oscar. A Small Killing. (VG Graphics Ser.). (Illus.). 96p. (Orig.). 1993. pap. 12.95 (*1-878574-45-0*) Dark Horse Comics.

Moore, Alan, ed. see Huncke, Herbert, et al.

Moore, Alan, jt. auth. see Pyle, David R.

Moore, Alan, et al. Brought to Light: Thirty Years of Drug Smuggling, Arms Deals, & Covert Action. (Illus.). 80p. 1989. 29.95 (*0-913035-70-X*); pap. 8.95 (*0-913035-67-X*) Eclipse Bks.

— Butterworths Ireland Capital Tax Acts 1993-94. 1993. pap. text ed. 99.00 (*0-614-05555-5*, IE) Butterworth Legal Pubs.

— Butterworths Ireland Tax Acts 1993-94. 1993. pap. text ed. 126.00 (*1-85475-631-1*, IE) Butterworth Legal Pubs.

Moore, Albert. Gabriel's Odyssey. 210p. (Orig.). (YA). (gr. 12). 1990. pap. 15.95 (*1-85371-081-4*, Pub. by Poolbeg Pr IE) Dufour.

*__Moore, Albert C.__ Arts in the Religions of the Pacific: Symbols of Life. LC 95-6217. (Illus.). 256p. 1995. 45.00 (*0-86187-186-3*, Pub. by Pinter Pubs UK) St Martin.

Moore, Albert M. How Much Price Competition? The Prerequisites of an Effective Canadian Competition Policy. LC 71-135415. 231p. reprint ed. pap. 65.90 (*0-7837-6930-X*, 2046759) Bks Demand.

Moore, Alex. Ballroom Dancing. (Ballroom Dance Ser.). 1986. lib. bdg. 125.00 (*0-8490-3309-8*) Gordon Pr.

— Ballroom Dancing. (Ballroom Dance Ser.). 1984. lib. bdg. 250.00 (*0-87700-499-4*) Revisionist Pr.

— Instructions to Young Dancers. (Ballroom Dance Ser.). 1986. lib. bdg. 79.95 (*0-8490-3340-3*) Gordon Pr.

— Instructions to Young Dancers. (Ballroom Dance Ser.). 1985. lib. bdg. 75.00 (*0-87700-664-4*) Revisionist Pr.

— Popular Variations in Ballroom Dancing. (Ballroom Dance Ser.). 1986. lib. bdg. 79.95 (*0-8490-3310-1*) Gordon Pr.

— Popular Variations in Ballroom Dancing. (Ballroom Dance Ser.). 1984. lib. bdg. 79.95 (*0-87700-508-7*) Revisionist Pr.

— Revised Technique of Ballroom Dancing. (Ballroom Dance Ser.). 1986. lib. bdg. 79.95 (*0-8490-3311-X*) Gordon Pr.

— Revised Technique of Ballroom Dancing. (Ballroom Dance Ser.). 1984. lib. bdg. 79.95 (*0-87700-498-6*) Revisionist Pr.

Moore, Alex & Quickmire, Carolyn, eds. Biographical Directory of the South Carolina House of Representatives, 1816-1828, Vol. V. 384p. 1992. write for info. (*1-880067-07-2*) SC Dept of Arch & Hist.

Moore, Alexander. Cultural Anthropology: The Field Study of Human Beings. (Illus.). 540p. (C). 1992. pap. text ed. 29.75 (*0-939693-23-2*) Collegiate Pr.

Moore, Alexander, ed. see Nairne, Thomas.

Moore, Alexander, jt. auth. see Smith, Henry A.

Moore, Alick, jt. auth. see Howard, Richard.

Moore, Alison. Small Spaces Between Emergencies. LC 91-30614. 1992. 18.95 (*1-56279-022-6*) Mercury Hse Inc.

— Synonym for Love. LC 94-40442. 256p. 1995. text ed. 19.95 (*1-56279-074-9*) Mercury Hse Inc.

Moore, Allan D., jt. auth. see Martin, David G.

Moore, Allan F. Rock, the Primary Text: Developing a Musicology of Rock. LC 92-12471. (Popular Music in Britain Ser.). 1993. 90.00 (*0-335-09787-1*, Open Univ Pr); pap. 29.00 (*0-335-09786-3*, Open Univ Pr) Taylor & Francis.

Moore, Allen B. & Feldt, James A. Facilitating Community & Decision-Making Groups. 168p. (C). 1993. 18.50 (*0-89464-650-8*) Krieger.

Moore, Allen J., ed. Religious Education As Social Transformation. LC 88-36413. 258p. 1989. 18.95 (*0-89135-069-1*) Religious Educ.

Moore, Alvin, Jr., ed. see Coomaraswamy, Ananda K.

Moore, Alvin, Jr., tr. see Guenon, Rene, Jr.

Moore, Alvin, tr. see Lindbom, Tage.

Moore, Alvin E. Border Patrol. LC 87-16004. 128p. (Orig.). 1988. pap. 10.95 (*0-86534-113-3*) Sunstone Pr.

— Red Jewel of the East. 300p. 1989. per. 11.95 (*0-89697-310-7*) Intl Univ Pr.

Moore, Amanda L., jt. auth. see Finch, Edward R., Jr.

Moore, Amy G., ed. see Martin, Thomas M.

*__Moore, Andrew.__ The Right Road: A History of Right Wing Politics in Australia. (Australian Retropective Ser.). 1995. pap. 22.00 (*0-19-553512-X*) OUP.

— The Secret Army & the Premier: Conservative Paramilitary Organizations in NSW 1930-32. 312p. 1990. pap. 24.95 (*0-86840-283-4*, Pub. by New South Wales Univ Pr AT) Intl Spec Bk.

Moore, Andy. Moore's Imaging Dictionary. 1993. 19.95 (*0-936648-37-6*) Telecom Lib.

Moore, Andy & Moore, Susan. The Penny Bank Book. rev. ed. LC 83-51775. (Illus.). 192p. 1994. 49.95 (*0-916838-97-8*) Schiffer.

Moore, Anne. Passion's Glory. 1983. pap. 3.50 (*0-685-07868-X*) Zebra.

Moore, Anne C., ed. see Irving, Washington.

Moore, Anne S. Breeding Purebred Cats. enl. rev. ed. 132p. (Orig.). 1987. pap. 12.95 (*0-318-41068-0*) Abraxas Pub WA.

*__Moore, Annette.__ They Don't Understand. (J). 1995. 8.95 (*0-8062-5297-9*) Carlton.

Moore, Annette C. The Game Finder: A Leader's Guide to Great Activities. LC 92-61287. (Illus.). 200p. (C). 1992. pap. text ed. 18.95 (*0-910251-57-6*) Venture Pub PA.

Moore, Anthony L., ed. see Hall, John I.

Moore, Anthony R. The Missing Medical Text: Humane Patient Care. 1978. 29.95 (*0-522-84139-2*) Intl Spec Bk.

Moore, Anthony T. Introduction to Christology Project Book. 56p. 1987. pap. 5.95 (*0-89505-481-7*) Tabor Pub.

Moore, Antony, jt. auth. see Ogilvie, Gregory K.

Moore, April. The Earth & You: Eating for Two. Stark, Elizabeth, ed. (Illus.). 165p. (Orig.). (YA). (gr. 8-12). 1993. write for info. (*0-938443-05-4*) Potomac Val Pr.

Moore, Archimandrite L. St. Seraphim of Sarov: A Spiritual Biography. 504p. 1994. pap. write for info. (*1-880364-13-1*) New Sarov.

Moore, Arthur. The Kid from Rincon. 1988. mass mkt. 3.99 (*0-449-13425-3*, GM) Fawcett.

— The Proud. (River of Fortune Ser.). 400p. (Orig.). 1980. pap. 2.50 (*0-89083-665-5*) Zebra.

— River of Fortune: The Passion. (Orig.). 1979. pap. 2.50 (*0-89083-561-6*) Zebra.

— The Tapestry. (Orig.). 1979. pap. 2.50 (*0-89083-523-3*) Zebra.

— The Tempest. (Orig.). 1979. pap. 2.50 (*0-89083-521-7*) Zebra.

— The Triumph. (Orig.). 1979. pap. 2.50 (*0-89083-522-5*) Zebra.

— The Turmoil. 2nd ed. 1979. pap. 2.25 (*0-89083-490-3*) Zebra.

Moore, Arthur H. & Elonka, Stephen M. Electrical Systems & Equipment for Industry. LC 77-5640. (Illus.). 368p. 1977. reprint ed. lib. bdg. 31.50 (*0-88275-561-7*) Krieger.

Moore, Arthur K. The Frontier Mind: A Cultural Analysis of the Kentucky Frontiersman. LC 57-11379. 276p. reprint ed. 78.70 (*0-8357-9785-6*, 2016098) Bks Demand.

— Secular Lyric in Middle English. LC 71-100170. 255p. 1970. reprint ed. text ed. 35.00 (*0-8371-2973-7*, MOME, Greenwood Pr) Greenwood.

Moore, Arthur R. A Careless Word... A Needless Sinking. 3rd ed. LC 82-73552. (Illus.). 565p. (Orig.). 1983. 55.00 (*0-317-00663-0*) Granite Hill.

Moore, Arthur W., ed. Manx Ballads & Music. LC 78-72642. (Celtic Language & Literature Ser.: Goidelic & Brythonic). reprint ed. 26.00 (*0-404-17575-9*) AMS Pr.

Moore, B. Keith, jt. auth. see Phillips, Ralph W.

Moore, B. P. & Beal, R. W., eds. Socio-Economic Aspects of Blood Transfusion. (Journal: Vox Sanguinis: Vol. 46, Suppl. 1). (Illus.). iv, 108p. 1984. pap. 32.00 (*3-8055-3880-4*) S Karger.

*__Moore, Ballard & Snow, Randy.__ Wheelchair Tennis: Myth to Reality. 256p. 1994. per., pap. text ed. 21.95 (*0-8403-9581-7*) Kendall-Hunt.

Moore, Barbara. Farewell to the Body. LC 90-71210. 72p. 1990. 10.00 (*0-915380-27-7*) Word Works.

Moore, Barbara & Yellin, David G., eds. Horton Foote's Three Trips to Bountiful. LC 91-52779. 272p. 1993. text ed. 24.95x (*0-87074-326-0*); pap. 14.95 (*0-87074-327-9*) SMU Press.

Moore, Barbara C., jt. auth. see Hewitt, Lonnie B.

Moore, Barbara H., ed. The Entrepreneur in Local Government. LC 83-10806. (Practical Management Ser.). (Illus.). 214p. (Orig.). (C). 1983. pap. 23.95 (*0-87326-039-2*) Intl City-Cnty Mgt.

*__Moore, Barbara W. & Weesner, Gail.__ Back Bay: A Living Portrait. LC 95-67827. (Illus.). 144p. 1995. 35.00 (*0-9632077-2-5*); pap. 25.00 (*0-9632077-3-3*) Centry Hill Pr.

— Beacon Hill: A Living Portrait. 120p. 1992. 30.00 (*0-9632077-0-9*); pap. 20.00 (*0-9632077-1-7*) Centry Hill Pr.

— Hidden Gardens of Beacon Hill. LC 86-72541. (Illus.). 64p. 1991. reprint ed. 18.95 (*0-9628658-1-8*); reprint ed. pap. 11.95 (*0-9628658-0-X*) Beacon MA.

Moore, Barrington, Jr. Authority & Inequality under Capitalism & Socialism: U. S. A., U. S. S. R., & China. 160p. 1987. 35.00 (*0-19-828540-X*) OUP.

— Injustice: The Social Bases of Obedience & Revolt. LC 77-98162. 560p. 1978. 73.95 (*0-87332-114-6*); pap. text ed. 25.95 (*0-87332-145-6*) M E Sharpe.

Moore, Barrington. Privacy: Studies in Social & Cultural History. LC 83-23524. 342p. reprint ed. pap. 97.50 (*0-7837-0041-5*, 2040106) Bks Demand.

Moore, Barrington, Jr. Social Origins of Dictatorship & Democracy: Lord & Peasant in the Making of the Modern World. LC 93-17802. 592p. 1993. pap. 18.00 (*0-8070-5073-3*) Beacon Pr.

— Soviet Politics - The Dilemma of Power: The Role of Ideas in Social Change. LC 76-19137. 518p. 1976. reprint ed. pap. text ed. 41.95 (*0-87332-088-3*) M E Sharpe.

— Terror & Progress U. S. S. R. LC 54-5995. (Russian Research Center Studies: No. 12). 278p. 1954. 29.00 (*0-674-87450-1*) HUP.

Moore, Barry W. Aesthetic Aspects of Recent Experimental Film. Jowett, Garth S., ed. LC 79-6680. (Dissertations on Film, 1980 Ser.). 1980. lib. bdg. 15.95 (*0-405-12913-0*) Ayer.

Moore, Basil, ed. Basil Moore's Lincoln. (Illus.). 100p. 1991. 19.95 (*1-878044-02-8*) Mayhaven Pub.

Moore, Basil J. Horizontalists & Verticalists: The Macroeconomics of Credit Money. (Illus.). 432p. 1988. 79.95 (*0-521-35079-4*) Cambridge U Pr.

— An Introduction to Modern Economic Theory. LC 77-96708. (C). 1973. text ed. 24.95 (*0-02-921960-4*) Free Pr.

Moore, Bert S. & Isen, Alice M. Affect & Social Behavior. (Studies in Emotion & Social Interaction). (Illus.). 288p. (C). 1990. 59.95 (*0-521-32768-7*) Cambridge U Pr.

Moore, Bertha B. As by Fire. 325p. 1977. reprint ed. lib. bdg. 14.95 (*0-89966-277-3*) Buccaneer Bks.

*__Moore, Bette D.__ Redeemed! Readers Theatre for Building the Body. 1995. 8.50 (*0-8341-9271-3*, MP-756) Lillenas.

Moore, Betty, jt. auth. see Moore, Rudy.

Moore-Betty, Maurice, jt. auth. see Travers, Pamela L.

Moore, Betty T. & Wilkinson, Richard, eds. Quality Assurance in Ambulatory Health Care. 2nd ed. LC 90-60417. 88p. 1990. pap. 30.00 (*0-86688-214-6*) Joint Comm Hlthcare.

Moore, Betty T., ed. see Parker, Rosetta E.

Moore, Beverly. Echo's Song. (Illus.). 40p. (J). (gr. k-3). 1993. lib. bdg. 13.95 (*0-9637288-7-3*) River Walker Bks.

Moore, Bibby. Growing with Gardening: A Twelve-Month Guide for Therapy, Recreation, & Education. LC 88-27992. (Illus.). x, 234p. (C). 1989. 19.95 (*0-8078-1830-5*) U of NC Pr.

Moore, Bill. Plays for Holidays. 176p. 1991. pap. 7.99 (*0-87403-853-7*, 14-03353) Standard Pub.

— Quick Reference Guide Quicken Macintosh. 1993. pap. 8.95 (*1-56243-123-4*) DDC Pub.

— Two on the Square. LC 86-20781. (Illus.). 208p. 1986. 14.95 (*0-914875-13-2*) Bright Mtn Bks.

M

Moore, Blaine F. Supreme Court & Unconstitutional Legislation. LC 68-56672. (Columbia University. Studies in the Social Sciences: No. 133). reprint ed. 31.50 (*0-404-51133-3*) AMS Pr.

Moore, Blaine R., jt. ed. see Mankad, Vipul N.

Moore, Bloomfield. Keely & His Discoveries. 373p. 1971. reprint ed. spiral bd. 22.00 (*0-7873-0621-5*) Mokelumne.

Moore-Blunt, J. J. A Commentary on Ovid Metamorphoses Vol. II. viii, 192p. 1977. pap. 39.00x (*90-256-0638-5*, Pub. by A M Hakkert NE) Benjamins North Am.

— A Commentary on Ovid Metamorphoses II. 192p. 1977. pap. text ed. 44.00 (*0-685-43581-4*, Pub. by A M Hakkert SP) Coronet Bks.

Moore, Bob. You Can Be President (or Anything Else) LC 80-36832. 128p. 1980. 12.95 (*0-88289-268-1*) Pelican.

Moore, Bob & Grauwels, Patrick. Route Sixty Six: A Guidebook to the Mother Road. (Illus.). 100p. 1994. 17. 95 (*0-9641457-0-7*) USDC.

Moore, Bob & Moore, Maxine. Up from the Roots: Growing a Vocabulary. 1993. 13.95 (*0-685-63083-8*) New Chapter Pr.

Moore, Bob & Reynolds, R. J., intros. Nascar Yearbook & Press Guide. (Illus.). 110p. (Orig.). 1992. pap. 6.95 (*0-318-17137-6*) Nat Assn Stock.

***Moore, Brenda L.** To Serve My Country, to Serve My Race: The Story of the Only African-American WACs Stationed Overseas During World War II. (Illus.). 296p. 1996. 24.95 (*0-8147-5522-4*) NYU Pr.

Moore, Brian. Black Robe. 224p. 1986. mass mkt. 4.99 (*0-449-20947-4*, Crest) Fawcett.

— Colour of Blood. large type ed. (Mainstream Ser.). 204p. 1988. reprint ed. lib. bdg. 9.97 (*1-85089-248-2*, Pub. by ISIS UK) Transaction Pubs.

— The Gospel Day by Day Through Easter: Gospel Reflections for the Easter Season. 94p. (Orig.). 1991. pap. 6.95 (*0-8146-2003-5*) Liturgical Pr.

— Lies of Silence. 208p. 1991. pap. 9.00 (*0-380-71547-3*) Avon.

— Lies of Silence. large type ed. 1991. 23.95 (*0-7089-8611-0*, Charnwood) Ulverscroft.

— The Lonely Passion of Judith Hearne. 224p. 1988. mass mkt. 9.95 (*0-316-57966-1*) Little.

— The Lonely Passion of Judith Hearne. large type ed. 312p. 1991. 18.95 (*1-85089-273-3*, Pub. by ISIS UK) Transaction Pubs.

— No Other Life. LC 92-41181. 1993. 21.00 (*0-385-41515-X*, N A Talese) Doubleday.

— No Other Life. large type ed. LC 93-33308. 1993. 21.95 (*0-8161-5897-5*) Hall.

— Two Stories. limited ed. (Santa Susana Press Ser.). 1979. 35.00 (*0-937048-22-4*); 60.00 (*0-937048-29-1*) CSUN.

Moore, Brian C. Frequency Selectivity in Hearing. 1986. text ed. 153.00 (*0-12-505625-7*) Acad Pr.

— Introduction to the Psychology of Hearing. 3rd ed. 368p. 1989. text ed. 42.00 (*0-12-505623-0*) Acad Pr.

— Introduction to the Psychology of Hearing. 3rd ed. 368p. 1990. text ed. 42.00 (*0-12-505624-9*) Acad Pr.

***Moore, Brian C., ed.** Hearing. 2nd ed. (Handbook of Perception & Cognition Ser.). (Illus.). 575p. 1995. text ed. write for info. (*0-12-505626-5*) Acad Pr.

Moore, Brian C. & Patterson, Roy D., eds. Auditory Frequency Selectivity. LC 86-22700. (NATO ASI Series A, Life Sciences: Vol. 119). 466p. 1986. 105.00 (*0-306-42462-2*, Plenum Pr) Plenum.

Moore, Brian F. Sharing the Gains of Productivity. (Studies in Productivity: No. 24). 57p. 1982. pap. 55.00 (*0-08-029505-3*) Work in Amer.

Moore, Brian L. Race, Power & Social Segmentation in Colonial Society. 320p. 1987. 48.00 (*2-88124-203-0*) Gordon & Breach.

— Race, Power, & Social Segmentation in Colonial Society: Plantation Guyana After Slavery 1838-1891. (Caribbean Studies: Vol. 4). 315p. 1987. text ed. 41.00 (*0-677-21980-6*) Gordon & Breach.

***Moore, Brooke N.** Making Your Case: Critical Thinking & the Argumentative Essay. LC 94-38160. 246p. (C). 1995. pap. text ed. 16.95 (*1-55934-331-1*) Mayfield Pub.

Moore, Brooke N. & Bruder, Kenneth. Philosophy: The Power of Ideas. LC 92-20142. 624p. (C). 1993. text ed. 45.95 (*1-55934-131-9*) Mayfield Pub.

— Philosophy: The Power of Ideas, Brief. 2nd abr. ed. LC 94-37688. 422p. 1995. pap. text ed. 27.95 (*1-55934-435-0*) Mayfield Pub.

***Moore, Brooke N. & Bruder, Kennith.** Instructor's Manual for Philosophy: The Power of Ideas. (C). 1993. teacher ed, pap. text ed. write for info. (*1-55934-183-1*) Mayfield Pub.

Moore, Brooke N. & Parker, Richard. Critical Thinking. rev. ed. 528p. (C). 1992. teacher ed, pap. text ed. write for info. (*0-318-68888-3*) Mayfield Pub.

— Critical Thinking. 3rd rev. ed. 528p. (C). 1992. pap. text ed. 35.95 (*1-55934-072-X*) Mayfield Pub.

Moore, Brooke N. & Stewart, Robert M. Moral Philosophy: A Comprehensive Introduction. LC 93-11106. 660p. (C). 1993. 44.95 (*1-55934-037-1*) Mayfield Pub.

Moore, Brooke N., jt. auth. see Moore, Ralph J.

***Moore, Brooke N., et al.** Critical Thinking, Testbank. (C). 1994. teacher ed, disk write for info. (*1-55934-340-0*) Mayfield Pub.

— Critical Thinking. 4th ed. LC 94-12647. 544p. (C). 1994. pap. text ed. 34.95 (*1-55934-339-7*) Mayfield Pub.

Moore, Bruce D., jt. auth. see Press, Leonard J.

***Moore, Burness E. & Fine, Bernard D., eds.** Psychoanalysis: The Major Concepts. LC 95-173. 1995. write for info. (*0-300-06329-6*) Yale U Pr.

— Psychoanalytic Terms & Concepts. LC 89-36223. 225p. (C). 1990. pap. 15.00 (*0-300-04701-0*) Yale U Pr.

Moore, Burton M., jt. auth. see Moore, Joan W.

Moore, Byron. The First Five Million Miles. Gilbert, James B., ed. LC 79-7289. (Flight: Its First Seventy-Five Years Ser.). (Illus.). 1980. reprint ed. lib. bdg. 28.95 (*0-405-12197-0*) Ayer.

Moore, C. Pop-up Night Before Christmas. 1967. 9.00 (*0-394-81867-9*) Random.

Moore, C., jt. auth. see Frye, D.

Moore, C. A. Automation in the Food Industry. 1991. text ed. 105.00 (*0-442-31432-9*) Chapman & Hall.

Moore, C. C., ed. Group Representations, Ergodic Theory, Operator Algebras, & Mathematical Physics: Proceedings of a Conference in Honor of George W. Mackey. (Mathematical Sciences Research Institute Publications: Vol. 6). (Illus.). 290p. 1986. 41.00 (*0-387-96471-1*) Spr-Verlag.

Moore, C. C. & Schochet, C. Global Analysis on Foliated Spaces. (Mathematical Sciences Research Institute Publications: Vol. 9). (Illus.). vii, 337p. 1987. 47.00 (*0-387-96664-1*) Spr-Verlag.

Moore, C. C., jt. auth. see Auslander, Louis.

***Moore, C. E.** Amanda: The Untold Story. (Orig.). 1995. pap. 5.99 (*1-57297-056-1*) Blvd Books.

Moore, C. L. The Best of C. L. Moore. 384p. (Orig.). 1980. pap. 2.25 (*0-345-28952-8*) Ballantine.

— The Best of C. L. Moore. (Orig.). 1993. reprint ed. lib. bdg. 18.95 (*0-89968-354-1*, Lghtyr Pr) Buccaneer Bks.

— Scarlet Dream. (Illus.). 1981. 20.00 (*0-937986-42-9*) D M Grant.

Moore, C. Raymond & Laudon, Lowell R. Evolution & Classification of Paleozoic Crinoids: Geological Society of America Special Papers, No. 46. Gould, Stephen J., ed. LC 79-8352. (History of Paleontology Ser.). (Illus.). 1980. reprint ed. lib. bdg. 17.95 (*0-405-12721-9*) Ayer.

Moore, Cairl E. Concrete Form Construction. 1977. pap. text ed. 21.95 (*0-8273-1094-3*); 6.00 (*0-8273-1093-5*) Delmar.

Moore, Calvin C., ed. see Pure Mathematics Symposium Staff.

Moore, Calvin J. Rekindled Lifestyles. 1993. 10.00 (*0-533-10629-X*) Vantage.

Moore, Carey & Moore, Pamela R. If Two Shall Agree: Praying Together As a Couple. LC 92-17189. 1992. pap. 8.99 (*0-8007-9205-X*) Chosen Bks.

Moore, Carey A. Daniel, Esther, & Jeremiah: The Additions. LC 76-42376. (Anchor Bible Ser.: Vol. 44). (Illus.). 1977. 34.00 (*0-385-04702-9*, Anchor NY) Doubleday.

— Judith. LC 83-11694. (Anchor Bible Ser.: Vol. 40). (Illus.). 312p. 1985. pap. 14.00 (*0-385-14424-5*) Doubleday.

— Studies in the Book of Esther. 1982. 79.50 (*0-87068-718-2*) Ktav.

Moore, Carey A., ed. Esther. LC 75-140615. (Anchor Bible Ser.: Vol. 7B). 1971. pap. 29.00 (*0-385-00472-9*, Anchor NY) Doubleday.

Moore, Carl C. & Moore, Dorothy H. Descendants of William Moore. (Illus.). 153p. 1984. 15.00 (*0-87770-322-1*) Ye Galleon.

Moore, Carl H. The Federal Reserve System: A History of the First 75 Years. LC 89-43660. (Illus.). 280p. 1990. lib. bdg. 32.50x (*0-89950-503-1*) McFarland & Co.

Moore, Carl H. & Russell, Alvin E. Money: Its Origin, Development & Modern Use. LC 87-42515. 176p. 1987. lib. bdg. 23.95x (*0-89950-272-5*) McFarland & Co.

Moore, Carl M. Group Processes for Idea Building. 2nd ed. (Applied Social Research Methods Ser.: Vol. 9). 160p. (C). 1994. text ed. 37.00 (*0-8039-5642-8*); pap. text ed. 16.95 (*0-8039-5643-6*) Sage.

Moore, Carlos. Castro, the Blacks, & Africa. (Afro-American Culture & Society Monograph Ser.: Vol. 8). (Illus.). 472p. 1988. pap. 23.50 (*0-934934-33-9*) UCLA CAAS.

— Fela, Fela. (Illus.). 287p. 1992. pap. write for info. (*0-8052-8221-1*) Schocken.

Moore, Carlos W., jt. auth. see Longenecker, Justin G.

Moore, Carman, jt. auth. see Beethoven, Jane.

***Moore, Carol J.** Carol's Kitchen. (Illus.). 421p. (Orig.). 1993. ring bd. 27.00 (*0-9645003-0-2*) C J Moore.

Moore, Carol-Lynne & Yamamoto, Kaoru. Beyond Words: Movement Observation & Analysis. 320p. (C). 1988. text ed. 58.00 (*2-88124-250-2*); pap. text ed. 30.00 (*2-88124-251-0*); teacher ed, pap. text ed. 25.00 (*2-88124-252-9*); vhs 247.00 (*2-88124-313-4*); vhs 257. 00 (*2-88124-315-0*) Gordon & Breach.

Moore, Carolyn, ed. see Calandro, Ed.

Moore, Carolyn, jt. ed. see Cooley, Denton A.

Moore, Carolyn, jt. auth. see Cooley, Denton.

Moore, Carolyn E., et al. Keys to Children's Nutrition. (Parenting Keys Ser.). 160p. 1991. pap. 5.95 (*0-8120-4675-7*) Barron.

— Young Chef's Nutrition Guide & Cookbook. LC 89-18218. 224p. 1990. spiral bd. 11.95 (*0-8120-5789-9*) Barron.

Moore, Carolynne, jt. auth. see Miles, John.

Moore, Casey & Alessi, Bob. The Complete Fantasy Sports Handbook: Comprehensive Rules & Guidelines for Playing Fantasy Versions of All Four Major Sports. 106p. (Orig.). 1994. pap. write for info. (*0-9641982-0-7*) FSF.

Moore, Catherine. The Composer Michelangelo Rossi: A "Diligent Fantasy Maker" in Seventeenth-Century Rome. LC 93-13018. (Outstanding Dissertations in Music from British Universities Ser.). (Illus.). 312p. 1993. 69.00 (*0-8153-0954-6*) Garland.

Moore, Cathy, jt. auth. see Bernstein, Robin F.

Moore, Cathy, et al. Arkansas Basic Skills: Science. 170p. 1992. spiral bd. 19.75 (*0-914546-91-0*) Rose Pub.

Moore, Catriona. Indecent Exposures: Shifts in Feminist Photography 1970-90. (Illus.). 220p. (Orig.). 1994. pap. text ed. 19.95 (*1-86373-162-8*, Pub. by Allen Unwin AT) Paul & Co Pubs.

Moore, Catriona, ed. Dissonance: Feminism & the Arts 1970-90. (Illus.). 240p. 1994. pap. 18.95 (*1-86373-325-6*, Pub. by Allen Unwin AT) Paul & Co Pubs.

Moore, Celia L., jt. auth. see Michel, George F.

Moore, Charles. Beauty & the Beast. LC 90-26307. (Illus.). 32p. (J). 1991. 17.95 (*0-8478-1368-1*) Rizzoli Intl.

— Billy Pridemore. Van Treese, James B., ed. 124p. (Orig.). 1993. pap. 7.95 (*1-880416-45-X*) NW Pub.

— Daniel H. Burnham: Architect Planner of Cities. LC 68-27726. (Architecture & Decorative Art Ser.). (Illus.). 1968. reprint ed. lib. bdg. 75.00 (*0-306-71151-6*) Da Capo.

— The Exercise of Church Leadership. 1976. pap. 2.75 (*0-88027-032-2*) Firm Foun Pub.

— Functioning Leadership in the Church. 1973. pap. 2.75 (*0-88027-034-9*) Firm Foun Pub.

— Life & Times of Charles Follen McKim. LC 70-99857. (Architecture & Decorative Art Ser.). (Illus.). 1970. reprint ed. lib. bdg. 45.00 (*0-306-71324-1*) Da Capo.

Moore, Charles, et al. A Place of Houses. LC 70-182776. (Illus.). 288p. 1979. pap. 19.95 (*0-8050-1044-0*, Owl) H Holt & Co.

Moore, Charles, contrib. Lawrence Halprin. (Illus.). 152p. 1992. pap. 17.50 (*0-918471-06-0*) San Fran MOMA.

Moore, Charles, ed. see Burnham, Daniel H. & Bennett, Edward H.

Moore, Charles A., ed. Chinese Mind: Essentials of Chinese Philosophy & Culture. LC 66-24011. 411p. 1967. pap. text ed. 12.95 (*0-8248-0075-3*) UH Pr.

— The Japanese Mind: Essentials of Japanese Philosophy & Culture. LC 67-16704. 367p. 1967. pap. text ed. 9.95 (*0-8248-0077-X*) UH Pr.

— Philosophy: East & West. LC 72-119008. (Essay Index Reprint Ser.). 1977. 26.95 (*0-8369-1677-8*) Ayer.

Moore, Charles A., ed. see East-West Philosophers Conference (4th: 1964, University of Hawaii).

Moore, Charles A., jt. ed. see Radhakrishnan, Sarvepalli.

Moore, Charles A., ed. see Takakusu, J.

Moore, Charles A., ed. see Takakusu, Junjiro.

Moore, Charles C. Behind the Bars. 2nd ed. 259p. 1990. pap. 7.50 (*0-910309-65-5*, 5332) Am Atheist.

— Dog Fennel in the Orient. (Illus.). 323p. 1984. reprint ed. pap. 9.00 (*0-910309-16-7*, 5336) Am Atheist.

Moore, Charles H. Development & Character of Gothic Architecture. 1977. lib. bdg. 139.95 (*0-8490-1713-0*) Gordon Pr.

— The Mediaeval Church Architecture of England. LC 74-37900. (Select Bibliographies Reprint Ser.). 1977. reprint ed. 21.95 (*0-8369-6738-0*) Ayer.

***Moore, Charles W.** The New Masonic Trestle-Board: Adapted to the Work & Lectures As Practiced in the Lodges, Chapters, Councils, & Encampments of Knight Templars in the U. S. A. (Illus.). 207p. 1994. pap. 16.95 (*1-56459-462-9*) Kessinger Pub.

Moore, Charles W. & Attoe, Wayne, eds. Ah, Mediterranean: Twentieth Century Classicism in America, Vol. 2. (Illus.). 128p. 1986. pap. 15.00 (*0-8478-5414-0*) Ctr Study of Amer Archit.

Moore, Charles W., jt. auth. see Bloomer, Kent C.

Moore, Charles W., jt. auth. see Lyndon, Donlyn.

Moore, Charles W., et al. The Poetics of Gardens. (Illus.). 288p. 1988. 47.50 (*0-262-13231-1*) MIT Pr.

— Poetics of Gardens. 494p. 1993. pap. 19.95 (*0-262-63153-9*) MIT Pr.

***Moore, Charlotte.** Belated Bride. (Romance Ser.). 1995. mass mkt. 2.99 (*0-373-19088-3*, 1-19088-3) Silhouette.

— Not the Marrying Kind. (Silhouette Romance Ser.). 1993. pap. 2.75 (*0-373-08975-9*, 5-08975-0) Silhouette.

Moore, Chauncey O., jt. auth. see Moore, Ethel.

Moore, Chris. The Oceans & the Jungles. (J). 1988. write for info. (*0-318-62377-3*, Puffin) Puffin Bks.

Moore, Chris & Booth, Simon A. Managing Competition: Meso-Corporatism, Pluralism, & the Negotiated Order in Scotland. (Illus.). 184p. 1989. 45.00 (*0-19-827578-1*) OUP.

***Moore, Chris & Dunham, Philip, eds.** Joint Attention: Its Origin & Role in Development. LC 94-40160. 296p. 1995. text ed. 59.95 (*0-8058-1437-X*) L Erlbaum Assocs.

Moore, Christine, jt. auth. see English, Philip T.

***Moore, Christine Palamidessi.** The Virgin Knows. 320p. 1995. 22.95 (*0-312-13203-4*) St Martin.

***Moore, Christopher.** Bloodsucking Friends: A Love Story. LC 95-7463. 1995. 23.50 (*0-684-81097-2*) S&S Trade.

— Coyote Blue. 1994. 21.00 (*0-671-88188-4*) S&S Trade.

— Coyote Blue. 304p. 1995. reprint ed. pap. 10.00 (*0-380-72523-1*) Avon.

— His Lordship's Arsenal. 232p. 1985. 15.95 (*0-88191-033-3*) Freundlich.

— Loyalists: Revolution, Exile, Settlement. 1994. pap. 16.95 (*0-7710-6093-9*, Pub. by McClelland & Stewart CN) Firefly Bks Ltd.

— Practical Demonkeeping. 1991. 113.70 (*0-312-07170-1*) St Martin.

— Practical Demonkeeping. 1993. mass mkt. 4.99 (*0-312-95146-9*) St Martin.

Moore, Christopher, ed. see Glockler, Michaela & Goebel, Wolfgang.

***Moore, Christopher C.** Opening the Clergy Parachute: Soft Landings for Church Leaders Who Are Seeking Change. 160p. (Orig.). 1995. pap. 14.95 (*0-687-08659-0*) Abingdon.

— What I Really Want to Do. 144p. (Orig.). 1989. pap. 10. 99 (*0-8272-4226-3*) Chalice Pr.

Moore, Christopher W. The Mediation Process: Practical Strategies for Resolving Conflict. LC 85-23675. (Social & Behavioral Science Ser.). 370p. 1986. 29.95 (*0-87589-673-1*) Jossey-Bass.

Moore, Cindy. Planning a Wedding with Divorced Parents. 1992. pap. 10.00 (*0-517-58451-4*, Crown) Crown Pub Group.

Moore, Clancy, jt. auth. see Williams, Charles.

Moore, Clara B. Keely & His Discoveries. 1972. 10.00 (*0-8216-0104-0*, Univ Bks) Carol Pub Group.

Moore, Clare, ed. The Visual Dimension: Aspects of the Jewish Art. 184p. 1993. text ed. 29.95 (*0-8133-1259-0*) Westview.

Moore, Clement. The Night Before Christmas. LC 85-40334. 32p. 1985. pap. 12.95 (*0-394-54809-4*) Knopf.

— The Night Before Christmas. (Illus.). (J). (gr. k-3). 1984. audio 22.95 (*0-941078-39-6*) Live Oak Media.

— The Night Before Christmas, 4 bks., Set. (Illus.). (J). (gr. k-3). 1984. audio, pap. 36.95 (*0-941078-38-8*) Live Oak Media.

— Night Before Christmas Pop-Ups. (J). 1991. 4.99 (*0-517-06127-9*) Random Hse Value.

Moore, Clement C. Disney Babies the Night Before Christmas. LC 91-58969. (Disney Babies Ser.). (Illus.). (J). 1992. 11.95 (*1-56282-244-6*) Disney Pr.

— The Grandma Moses Night before Christmas. 2nd ed. LC 90-24145. (Illus.). 32p. (J). 1991. 15.00 (*0-679-81526-0*); lib. bdg. 15.99 (*0-679-91526-5*) Random Bks Yng Read.

— The Night Before Christmas. LC 84-4342. (Illus.). 32p. (J). (ps-5). 1984. 12.00 (*0-394-86863-3*) Knopf Bks Yng Read.

— The Night Before Christmas. (Illus.). 24p. (J). (ps-2). 1984. pap. 2.95 (*0-89542-498-3*, Ideals Child) Hambleton-Hill.

— The Night Before Christmas. (Illus.). 24p. (J). (ps-2). 1994. pap. 7.95 (*1-57102-011-X*, Ideals Child) Hambleton-Hill.

— The Night Before Christmas. LC 80-84842. (Illus.). 12p. (J). (gr. k up). 1981. 12.95 (*0-8050-0900-0*, Bks Young Read) H Holt & Co.

— The Night Before Christmas. LC 80-11758. (Illus.). 32p. (J). (ps up). 1980. 15.95 (*0-8234-0414-5*); pap. 6.95 (*0-8234-0417-X*) Holiday.

— The Night Before Christmas. (Illus.). (J). (gr. k-3). 1984. 27.95 (*0-685-08869-3*) Live Oak Media.

— The Night Before Christmas. (Illus.). 10p. (J). (ps-7). 1989. pap. 3.95 (*0-922589-06-2*) More than Card.

— The Night Before Christmas. LC 89-34789. (Illus.). 32p. (J). 1990. 14.95 (*0-88289-755-1*) Pelican.

— The Night Before Christmas. LC 75-7511. (Pictureback Ser.). (Illus.). 32p. (J). (gr. 2-6). 1975. 2.25 (*0-394-83019-9*) Random Bks Yng Read.

— The Night Before Christmas. LC 82-62171. (Illus.). 32p. (J). 1988. pap. 1.50 (*0-394-81938-1*) Random Bks Yng Read.

— The Night Before Christmas. LC 88-35019. (Illus.). 40p. (J). (ps-8). 1990. 6.99 (*0-394-82698-1*) Random Bks Yng Read.

— The Night Before Christmas. LC 89-42998. (Miniature Editions Ser.). (Illus.). 80p. (J). 1989. 4.95 (*0-89471-754-5*) Running Pr.

— The Night Before Christmas. (Illus.). 28p. (J). 16.95 (*0-9613476-2-7*) Shirlee.

— The Night Before Christmas. (Illus.). 32p. (J). (ps-1). 1986. pap. 5.95 (*0-671-62209-9*, Litl Simon S&S) S&S Childrens.

— The Night Before Christmas. LC 75-8858. (Illus.). 64p. (J). (ps-1). 1990. text ed. 12.95 (*0-02-767643-9*, Mac Bks Young Read) S&S Childrens.

— The Night Before Christmas. (J). 1989. pap. 2.25 (*0-671-68408-6*) S&S Trade.

— The Night Before Christmas. LC 87-15343. (Illus.). 48p. (J). (gr. k-3). 1988. lib. bdg. 12.89 (*0-8167-1209-3*); pap. text ed. 3.95 (*0-8167-1210-7*) Troll Assocs.

— The Night Before Christmas. LC 88-50097. (Rebus Bk.). (Illus.). (J). (ps up). 1988. pap. 11.95 (*0-670-82388-0*) Viking Child Bks.

— The Night Before Christmas. (Golden Story Bks.). (Illus.). (J). (ps up). 1986. write for info. (*0-307-13724-4*) Western Pub.

— Night Before Christmas. (J). (ps-3). 1994. 9.95 (*1-57036-040-5*) Turner Pub GA.

— The Night Before Christmas. LC 95-1775. (Illus.). 1995. lib. bdg. write for info. (*1-55858-466-8*); pap. write for info. (*1-55858-465-X*) North-South Bks NYC.

— The Night Before Christmas. rev. ed. (Illus.). 24p. (J). 1995. 5.95 (*1-57102-082-9*, Ideals Child); pap. 1.99 (*1-57102-076-4*, Ideals Child) Hambleton-Hill.

— The Night Before Christmas. (Illus.). 1971. reprint ed. pap. 2.50 (*0-486-22797-9*) Dover.

— The Night Before Christmas. (Illus.). 16p. (J). (gr. 1-8). 1970. reprint ed. pap. 4.00 (*0-914510-01-0*) Evergreen.

— The Night Before Christmas, Set. (Illus.). (J). (gr. k-3). 1984. audio, pap. 14.95 (*0-941078-37-X*) Live Oak Media.

— The Night Before Christmas, Set. (Illus.). (J). (gr. k-3). 1984. audio 19.95 (*0-317-07112-2*) Live Oak Media.

— The Night Before Christmas, Set. (Pictureback Book & Cassette Library). (Illus.). 32p. (J). (ps-1). 1985. audio 5.95 (*0-394-87658-X*) Random Bks Yng Read.

— The Night Before Christmas: A Pop-Up Book. (Illus.). (J). (ps-1). 1993. 9.95 (*1-56397-003-1*) Boyds Mills Pr.

— The Night Before Christmas: A Reproduction of an Antique Christmas Classic. LC 88-19600. (Illus.). 32p. (J). 1989. 15.95 (*0-399-21614-6*, Philomel Bks) Putnam Pub Group.

— The Night Before Christmas: Or: Account of a Visit from St. Nicholas. Irwin, Colin, ed. (Illus.). 22p. (J). 1984. 150.00 (*0-923980-03-2*) Arundel Pr.

— The Night Before Christmas: Told in Signed English. 64p. 1994. 14.95 (*1-56368-020-3*) Gallaudet Univ Pr.

— The Night Before Christmas Board Book. LC 91-46766. (Illus.). 26p. (J). (ps). 1992. 4.95 (*0-694-00424-3*) HarpC Child Bks.

— Night Before Christmas Coloring Book. (J). 1986. pap. 2.95 (*0-671-62959-X*, Litl Simon S&S) S&S Childrens.

— Night Before Christmas der Fun Lib. 1994. pap. 3.99 (*0-517-32105-X*) Random Hse Value.

An Asterisk (*) at the beginning of an entry indicates that the title is appearing in BIP for the first time.

— The Night Before Christmas Hidden Picture Book. (Illus.). 32p. (J). 1992. bds. 7.95 (*1-56397-116-X*) Boyds Mills Pr.

— Night Before Christmas House. (J). (ps-3). 1994. pap. 7.95 (*0-448-40549-0*, G&D) Putnam Pub Group.

— The Night Before Christmas in Hawaii. (Illus.). 32p. (J). 1991. text ed. write for info. (*0-9627294-2-6*) Hawaiian Resources.

— The Three-D Night Before Christmas. 32p. (J). 1994. pap. text ed. 7.95 (*0-9641811-5-0*) Three-D Revel.

— Twas the Night Before Christmas. (J). 1992. pap. 4.95 (*0-395-64374-0*) HM.

— Twas the Night Before Christmas. (Christmas Fun-to-Read Fairy Tales Ser.). (Illus.). 24p. (J). (gr. k-3). 1992. pap. 2.50 (*1-56144-163-5*, Honey Bear Bks) Modern Pub NYC.

— Twas the Night Before Christmas. LC 92-10726. (Illus.). 1992. 4.99 (*0-517-08136-9*, Derrydale Bks) Random Hse Value.

Moore, Clement C. Twas the Night Before Christmas. LC 93-40243. (Illus.). 32p. (J). (ps up). 1994. text ed. 14.95 (*0-02-767646-3*, Bradbury S&S) S&S Childrens.

Moore, Clement C. Twas the Night Before Christmas: A Visit from St. Nicholas. (Illus.). (J). (ps-2). 1912. 14.95 (*0-395-06952-1*) HM.

— Two Little Christmas Classics. (Illus.). 32p. (J). (ps up). 1989. pap. 4.95 (*0-394-84629-X*) Random Bks Yng Read.

— A Visit from St. Nicholas. LC 93-33703. (Little Activity Bks.). (Illus.). (J). (gr. 2 up). 1994. pap. write for info. (*0-486-27978-2*) Dover.

*__Moore, Clement L.__ The Night Before Christmas. 1994. lib. bdg. 29.95x (*1-56849-423-8*) Buccaneer Bks.

Moore, Clifton A., jt. auth. see Ashford, Norman J.

Moore, Clyde B. Civic Education, Its Objectives & Methods for a Specific Case Group: A Study in Educational Sociology. LC 70-177080. (Columbia University. Teachers College. Contributions to Education Ser.: No. 151). reprint ed. 37.50 (*0-404-55151-3*) AMS Pr.

Moore, Colleen G. Pud's in Practice. LC 85-51488. 94p. 1985. pap. 36.95 (*0-87420-644-8*, P36) Urban Land.

Moore College of Arts & Design Staff. Terry Fox: Articulations. (Labyrinth - Text Works). (Illus.). 46p. 1992. pap. 15.00 (*0-685-67186-0*) Feldman Fine Arts.

Moore-Colyer, Richard J. Man's Proper Study. 182p. (C). 1982. 25.00x (*0-85088-944-8*, Pub. by Gomer Pr UK) St Mut.

Moore-Colyer, Richard J., ed. & intro. A Land of Pure Delight: Selections from the Letters of Thomas Johnes of Hafod 1748 - 1816. 314p. (C). 1992. 50.00x (*0-86383-751-4*, Pub. by Gomer Pr UK) St Mut.

Moore, Connie. Snow Globes. LC 93-70596. (Collector's Library). (Illus.). 80p. 1993. 12.98 (*1-56138-218-3*) Courage Bks.

Moore, Connie, jt. auth. see Grainger, Janette.

Moore, Cornelia, jt. ed. see Wayne, Valerie.

Moore, Cornelia N., ed. Insulinde: Selected Translations from Dutch Writers of Three Centuries on the Indonesian Archipelago. LC 78-139. (Asian Studies at Hawaii: No. 20). 199p. 1978. pap. text ed. 10.50 (*0-8248-0564-X*) UH Pr.

Moore, Cornelia N. & Lower, Lucy B., eds. Translation East & West: A Cross-Cultural Approach. (Literary Studies: East & West: No. 5). 242p. (C). 1992. pap. text ed. 19.95 (*0-8248-1431-2*) UH Pr.

Moore, Cornelia N. & Moody, Raymond, eds. Comparative Literature East & West: Traditions & Trends. (Literary Studies: East & West: Vol. 1). 304p. 1989. pap. text ed. 18.00 (*0-8248-1247-6*, Univ HI Coll Languages) UH Pr.

Moore, Cornelia N., jt. ed. see Rauch, Irmengard.

Moore, Craig, jt. auth. see Stevens, Benjamin H.

Moore, Craig L., et al. The Impact of Banking on the Regional Income Multiplier. (Discussion Paper Ser.: No. 112). 1979. pap. 10.00 (*1-55869-053-0*) Regional Sci Res Inst.

Moore, Curtis & Miller, Alan. Green Gold: Japan, Germany, the United States, & the Race for Environmental Technology. LC 93-49354. 288p. 1994. 25.00 (*0-8070-8530-8*) Beacon Pr.

— Green Gold: Japan, Germany, the United States, & the Race for Environmental Technology. 288p. (C). 1995. pap. 14.95 (*0-8070-8531-6*) Beacon Pr.

Moore, Cynthia. Paraprofessionals in Village-Level Development in Sri Lanka: The Sarvodaya Shramadana Movement. (Special Series on Paraprofessionals: No. 4). 64p. (Orig.). (C). 1981. pap. 6.85 (*0-86731-047-2*) Cornell CIS RDC.

Moore, D. The Zen Gardening Kit. (Illus.). 96p. 1992. 30.00 (*1-56138-148-9*) Running Pr.

Moore, D. A. International Light, Shape & Sound Signals. 2nd ed. (Illus.). 140p. 1982. 36.95 (*0-434-91310-3*) Buttrwrth-Heinemann.

— Marine Chartwork. 2nd ed. (Illus.). 110p. 1981. pap. 17.95 (*0-7136-3438-3*) Sheridan.

Moore, D. F. Elastomer Friction Lubrication. 305p. (C). 1975. text ed. 128.00 (*0-08-016749-7*, Pub. by Pergamon Repr UK) Franklin.

— The Friction of Pneumatic Tyres. 220p. 1975. 74.50 (*0-444-41323-5*) Elsevier.

— Principles & Applications of Tribology. (C). 1975. 168.00 (*0-08-017902-9*, Pub. by Pergamon Repr UK) Franklin.

Moore, D. J. A Metaphysics of the Computer: The Reality Machine & a New Science for the Holistic Age. LC 92-10574. 392p. 1992. lib. bdg. 99.95 (*0-7734-2302-8*) E Mellen.

Moore, D. M., tr. see Martin, Marie-Louise.

Moore, D. R., jt. ed. see Oestreicher, H. L.

Moore, Dahlia. Labor Market Segmentation & Its Implications: Inequality, Deprivation & Entitlement. LC 91-23810. (Library of Sociology: Vol. 21). 356p. 1992. 54.00 (*0-8240-6994-3*, 665) Garland.

Moore, Dalian. Madman on Lakeshore Drive. 32p. 1994. pap. text ed. 9.95 (*1-885206-00-3*, Iliad Pr) Cader Pubng.

Moore, Dana T. Quicksilver & Quills. LC 94-60196. 272p. 1994. 12.95 (*1-884570-06-2*) Research Triangle.

Moore, Daniel, ed. Warrior Wisdom. LC 93-83457. (Illus.). 192p. 1993. 11.95 (*1-56138-312-0*) Running Pr.

Moore, Daniel C. Regional Block: A Handbook for Use in the Clinical Practice of Medicine & Surgery. 4th ed. (Illus.). 532p. 1981. 46.95x (*0-398-01337-3*) C C Thomas.

Moore, Daniel G. Enter Without Knocking. LC 68-22333. (Illus.). 271p. reprint ed. pap. 77.30 (*0-7837-5171-0*, 2044901) Bks Demand.

Moore, Daphna. The Rabbi's Tarot: Spiritual Secrets of the Tarot. LC 89-2489. (New Age Tarot Ser.). (Illus.). 406p. (Orig.). 1989. pap. 12.95 (*0-87542-572-0*) Llewellyn Pubns.

Moore, Daryl, jt. auth. see Cassidy, Helen.

Moore, David. Age of Progress, Or, a Panorama of Time: In Four Visions. LC 76-154453. (Utopian Literature Ser.). (Illus.). 1976. reprint ed. 26.95 (*0-405-03535-7*) Ayer.

— The Lads in Action: Ethnicity, Identity & Social Process Amongst Australian Skinheads. (Popular Cultural Studies). 191p. 1994. 50.95 (*1-85742-203-1*, Pub. by Avebury Pub UK) Ashgate Pub Co.

— Reinventing NASA. (Illus.). 52p. (Orig.). (C). 1994. pap. text ed. 45.00x (*0-7881-1403-4*) Diane Pub.

Moore, David, tr. Curzio Malaparte: The Skin. LC 87-63048. 344p. 1988. pap. 12.95 (*0-685-22436-8*) Marlboro Pr.

Moore, David & Hoaglin, David, eds. Perspectives on Contemporary Statistics. LC 91-62170. (MAA Notes Ser.: Vol. 21). 192p. 1992. pap. 26.00 (*0-88385-075-3*, NTE-21) Math Assn.

Moore, David, tr. see Alfieri, Dino.

Moore, David, ed. see Buscaino, Dale & Daniel, Scott.

Moore, David, tr. see Gatti, Guido M.

Moore, David, tr. see Gilson, Etienne.

Moore, David, et al. Developing Readers & Writers in the Context Areas: K-12. 2nd ed. LC 93-19974. 400p. (C). 1994. pap. text ed. 37.95 (*0-8013-0467-9*, 78297) Longman.

*__Moore, David C.__ Government Contracting: How to Bid, Administer, & Get Paid. LC 94-29852. 1995. text ed. 65.00 (*0-471-11011-6*) Wiley.

— Politics of Deference: A Study of the Mid-Nineteenth Century English Political System. (Modern Revivals in History Ser.). 536p. 1994. 93.95 (*0-7512-0236-3*, Pub. by Gregg Revivals UK) Ashgate Pub Co.

Moore, David D. Choosing a Path. 1990. pap. 4.95 (*0-913543-17-9*) African Am Imag.

*__Moore, David G.__ The Battle for Hell: A Survey & Evaluation of Evangelicals' Growing Attraction to the Doctrine of Annihilationism. LC 95-10744. 1995. write for info. (*0-8191-9955-9*) U Pr of Amer.

— False Idols. (Orig.). Date not set. pap. 15.95 (*0-9639494-0-3*) Jupiter NY.

Moore, David G., ed. see Worthy, James C.

Moore, David J. Job Search for the Technical Professional. 272p. 1991. text ed. 42.50 (*0-471-53136-7*) Wiley.

Moore, David J., jt. auth. see Lewis, Adele B.

Moore, David L. The Liberating Power of Pain. 96p. (Orig.). 1989. pap. 6.99 (*0-8272-2120-7*) Chalice Pr.

Moore, David M. Flora of Tierra del Fuego. (Illus.). 396p. 1983. lib. bdg. 75.00 (*0-904614-05-0*) Lubrecht & Cramer.

— Plant Life. (Illustrated Encyclopedia of World Geography Ser.: Vol. 4). (Illus.). 256p. 1991. 45.00 (*0-19-520863-3*) OUP.

Moore, David M. & Dwyer, Francis M., eds. Visual Literacy: A Spectrum of Visual Learning. LC 93-2437. 450p. 1994. 39.95 (*0-87778-264-4*) Educ Tech Pubns.

Moore, David R. Arts & Crafts of Torres Strait. 1989. pap. 25.00 (*0-7478-0007-3*, Pub. by Shire UK) St Mut.

*__Moore, David S.__ The Basic Practice of Statistics. LC 94-40756. (C). 1995. text ed. write for info. (*0-7167-2628-9*) W H Freeman.

Moore, David S. & McCabe, George P. Introduction to the Practice of Statistics. 2nd ed. LC 92-22880. (C). 1995. text ed. write for info. (*0-7167-2250-X*) W H Freeman.

Moore, David T. America, Where Did You Go, & Why? 64p. (Orig.). 1994. pap. 5.95 (*1-879560-26-7*) Harbor Hse West.

— America, You're Too Young to Die. 64p. (Orig.). 1994. pap. 5.95 (*1-879560-31-3*) Harbor Hse West.

Moore, David T., jt. auth. see Beck, James R.

Moore, David W. The Superpollsters: How They Measure & Manipulate Public Opinion in America. LC 91-30396. 300p. 1992. 21.95 (*0-941423-74-3*) FWEW.

— The Superpollsters: How They Measure & Manipulate Public Opinion in America. (Illus.). 390p. 1995. pap. 14.95 (*1-56858-023-1*) FWEW.

Moore, David W., et al. Prereading Activities for Content Area Reading & Learning. 2nd ed. 88p. (Orig.). 1988. pap. 7.75 (*0-87207-233-9*) Intl Reading.

Moore, Dean. Ohio Studies Program: Teacher's Guide. Combs, Eunice A., ed. (Illus.). 1982. teacher ed 10.00 (*0-943068-44-4*) Graphic Learning.

Moore, Deborah & Kugelmass, Jack, eds. Going Home: YIVO Annual, Vol. 21. (Illus.). 350p. Date not set. 45.95 (*0-8101-0929-8*) Northwestern U Pr.

*__Moore, Deborah & Seckler, David, eds.__ Water Scarcity in Developing Countries: Reconciling Development & Environmental Protection. 80p. (Orig.). (C). 1993. pap. text ed. 9.95x (*0-933595-80-8*) Winrock Intl.

Moore, Deborah D. At Home in America: Second Generation New York Jews. LC 80-18777. (Columbia History of Urban Life Ser.). (Illus.). 280p. 1983. text ed. 40.50 (*0-231-05062-3*); pap. text ed. 18.50 (*0-231-05063-1*) Col U Pr.

— B'nai B'rith & the Challenge of Ethnic Leadership. LC 81-906. (Modern Jewish History Ser.). 288p. 1981. 29.50 (*0-87395-480-7*) State U NY Pr.

— To the Golden Cities: Pursuing the American Jewish Dream in Miami & L. A. 300p. 1994. text ed. 22.95 (*0-02-922111-0*) Free Pr.

Moore, Deborah D., ed. YIVO Annual, Vol. 22. 300p. 1994. 49.95 (*0-8101-0931-X*) Northwestern U Pr.

*__Moore, Debra & Kutter, Jackie.__ Parties for Children: Ideas & Instructions for Invitations, Decorations, Refreshments, Favors, Crafts, Games & Gifts for 19 Theme Parties. (Illus.). 160p. 1995. pap. 23.50 (*0-7864-0104-4*) McFarland & Co.

Moore, Debra K. Set Free from the Prison of Unforgiveness. 1991. pap. write for info. (*1-56588-000-5*) Moore Educ.

*__Moore, Della H.__ Hot Springs of North Carolina. (Illus.). 140p. (Orig.). 1994. write for info. (*0-9642625-0-9*) D H Moore.

— Yesteryears of Hot Springs, North Carolina. (Illus.). 150p. (Orig.). 1995. lib. bdg. write for info. (*0-9642625-1-7*) D H Moore.

Moore, Denise, ed. see McNeil, Edna.

Moore, Dennis D., ed. see St. John de Crevecoeur, J. Hector.

Moore, Dennis W., jt. auth. see Stommel, Henry.

*__Moore, Denton R.__ Alaska's Lost Frontier: Life in the Days of Homesteads, Dog Teams, & Sailboat Fisheries. LC 94-67836. (Illus.). 448p. 1995. pap. 19.95 (*0-9628828-8-7*) Prospector Pr.

— Alaska's Lost Frontier: Life in the Days of Homesteads, Dog Teams, & Sailboat Fisheries. LC 94-67836. (Illus.). 448p. 1995. 27.95 (*0-9628828-9-5*) Prospector Pr.

— Gentlemen Never Sail to Weather: The Story of an Accidental Odyssey. 2nd ed. LC 93-83834. (Illus.). 512p. 1993. pap. 19.95 (*0-9628828-3-6*) Prospector Pr.

Moore, Denton R., ed. see Arnold, Eugene.

Moore, Derry, jt. auth. see Lee-Milne, Avide.

Moore, Desmond F. Thermodynamic Principles of Energy Degrading. (Illus.). 155p. (C). 1981. 40.00 (*0-333-29504-8*, Pub. by Macmill Press UK); pap. 26.50 (*0-333-29506-4*, Pub. by Macmill Press UK) Scholium Intl.

— Viscoelastic Machine Elements: Elastomers & Lubricants in Machine Systems. 341p. 1993. 89.95 (*0-7506-1305-X*) Buttrwrth-Heinemann.

Moore, Dessie. Getting Dressed. (Jump at the Sun Board Bks.). 16p. (J). (ps). 1994. 5.95 (*0-694-00590-8*, Festival) HarpC Child Bks.

— Good Morning. (Jump at the Sun Board Bks.). 16p. (J). (ps). 1994. 5.95 (*0-694-00593-2*, Festival) HarpC Child Bks.

— Good Night. (Jump at the Sun Board Bks.). 16p. (J). (ps). 1994. 5.95 (*0-694-00592-4*, HarpT) HarpC Child Bks.

— Let's Pretend. (Jump at the Sun Board Bks.). 16p. (J). (ps). 1994. 5.95 (*0-694-00591-6*, HarpT) HarpC Child Bks.

Moore, Diana, jt. auth. see Monske, Ken.

Moore, Diane M. Iran: In a Persian Market. LC 79-93424. 118p. (Orig.). 1980. pap. 5.00 (*0-686-61402-X*) D M Moore.

— Martin's Quest. (Illus.). 96p. (YA). (gr. 5-12). 1995. 16.00 (*1-884725-05-8*); pap. 10.00 (*0-614-04818-4*) Blue Heron LA.

Moore, Dianne J. Emotional Child Abuse: Breaking the Cycle. 20p. (Orig.). 1992. pap. 4.00 (*1-880670-02-X*) Write On Servs.

— How Can I Help When Someone Dies: What Do I Say after, I'm Sorry? 17p. 1992. pap. 4.00 (*1-880670-00-3*) Write On Servs.

— It's Not Fair: And Other Parenting Pressures. 38p. 1993. pap. 5.00 (*1-880670-03-8*) Write On Servs.

— Shortcuts to Business Success. 27p. 1992. pap. 4.00 (*1-880670-01-1*) Write On Servs.

Moore, Dick. Opportunities in Acting Careers. LC 92-16078. (Opportunities in...Ser.). 1993. 13.95 (*0-8442-4024-9*, VGM Career Bks); pap. 10.95 (*0-8442-4025-7*, VGM Career Bks) NTC Pub Grp.

— Opportunities in Acting Careers. rev. ed. LC 74-25904. (Illus.). (C). 1985. 13.95 (*0-8442-6229-3*, VGM Career Bks); pap. 10.95 (*0-8442-6230-7*, VGM Career Bks) NTC Pub Grp.

*__Moore, Dinty.__ The Emperor's Virtual Clothes. 266p. 1995. write for info. (*1-56512-096-5*) Algonquin Bks.

Moore, Don. Webster: The Critical Heritage. (Critical Heritage Ser.). 172p. 1981. 69.50 (*0-7100-0773-6*, RKP) Routledge.

Moore, Don, jt. auth. see Fane, Francis D.

*__Moore, Donald.__ All about Composers. Busch, Brian, ed. (All about Crosswords Ser.). 24.95p. (Orig.). (YA). (gr. 10-12). Date not set. pap. text ed. 24.95 (*0-89898-943-4*) CPP Belwin.

— All about Crosswords: Choirs. Busch, Brian, ed. (A.A.C. Ser.). (Illus.). 40p. (Orig.). (YA). 1994. pap. text ed. 24.95 (*0-89898-716-4*) CPP Belwin.

— All about Crosswords: Composers. Busch, Brian, ed. (A. A.C. Ser.). (Illus.). 40p. (Orig.). (YA). 1994. pap. text ed. 24.95 (*0-89898-756-3*) CPP Belwin.

— All about Crosswords: Instruments. Busch, Brian, ed. (A. A.C. Ser.). (Illus.). 40p. (Orig.). (YA). 1994. pap. text ed. 24.95 (*0-89898-715-6*) CPP Belwin.

— All about Crosswords: Rock & Pop. Busch, Brian, ed. (A. A.C. Ser.). (Illus.). 40p. (Orig.). (YA). 1994. pap. text ed. 24.95 (*0-89898-714-8*) CPP Belwin.

— Cavalrymen. (Illus.). 48p. 1983. 20.00 (*0-88014-060-7*) Mosaic Pr OH.

— A Daily Guide to a Better Marriage. 32p. 1984. pap. 0.75 (*0-88144-021-3*) Christian Pub.

— Improving Your Christian Personality. 61p. 1984. pap. 2.25 (*0-88144-037-X*) Christian Pub.

Moore, Donald J. The Human & the Holy: The Spirituality of Abraham Joshua Heschel. LC 89-80461. viii, 215p. 1989. 29.95 (*0-8232-1235-1*) Fordham.

— Youth Try the Impossible. 96p. 1983. pap. 3.95 (*0-942684-03-6*) Camp Guidepts.

Moore, Donald K., jt. ed. see Erdman, David V.

Moore, Donald R., ed. Financial Officers: What They Do - to You & for You. 8th ed. (Illus.). 32p. 1994. 4.00 (*0-945981-88-0*) Octameron Assocs.

Moore, Donna, ed. see Campbell, Stu.

Moore, Donna J. Take Charge of Your Own Career. LC 79-88808. 284p. (Orig.). 1994. pap. 24.95 (*0-911907-16-5*) Psych Assess.

Moore, Dorothy, jt. auth. see Moore, Raymond.

*__Moore, Dorothy D.__ Mischievous Molly. LC 95-60902. (Illus.). 23p. (J). (gr. 1-5). 1995. pap. 9.95 (*1-883650-25-9*) Windswept Hse.

Moore, Dorothy H., jt. auth. see Moore, Carl C.

Moore, Dorothy P., jt. auth. see Moore, Jamie W.

Moore, Douglas. Entertainment: Movies. (All about Language Ser.). (Illus.). 50p. (Orig.). (J). (gr. 7 up). 1986. audio 22.00 (*0-939990-48-2*) Intl Linguistics.

— Guide to Musical Styles: From Madrigal to Modern Music. (Illus.). 1963. pap. 12.95 (*0-393-00200-4*) Norton.

— Post Office. (All about Language Ser.). (Illus.). (Orig.). 1987. audio 22.00 (*0-939990-52-0*) Intl Linguistics.

Moore, Douglas & Winitz, Harris. Dictionary for Spontaneous Descriptions. 120p. (Orig.). 1985. pap. text ed. 15.00 (*0-939990-43-1*) Intl Linguistics.

— Transportation: Basic Terms. (All about Language Ser.). (Illus.). 35p. (Orig.). 1987. pap. text ed. 22.00 (*0-939990-51-2*) Intl Linguistics.

Moore, Douglas, jt. auth. see Lennon, Patricia.

Moore, Douglas, jt. auth. see Winitz, Harris.

Moore, Douglas V., jt. auth. see Miller, Herb.

Moore, Duane M. & Reynolds, Robert C. X-Ray Diffraction & the Identification & Analysis of Clay Minerals. (Illus.). 352p. (C). 1989. text ed. 34.95 (*0-19-505170-X*) OUP.

Moore, Dudley. Off Beat: A Musical Companion. LC 93-10025. Orig. Title: Musical Bumps. (Illus.). 176p. 1993. reprint ed. pap. 10.95 (*0-312-09356-X*) St Martin.

Moore, Dulce D. A Place in Mind. 1992. 18.00 (*0-9627509-9-9*) Baskerville.

— A Place in Mind: A Novel. large type ed. LC 92-33395. 430p. 1993. reprint ed. lib. bdg. 16.95 (*1-56054-587-9*) Thorndike Pr.

Moore, Duncan & Walker, Henry. Yield Simulation for Integrated Circuits. (C). 1987. lib. bdg. 56.00 (*0-89838-244-0*) Kluwer Ac.

Moore, Duncan T., ed. Selected Papers on Gradient-Index Optics. LC 92-34884. (Milestone Ser.: Vol. MS 67). 1992. write for info. (*0-8194-1059-4*); pap. write for info. (*0-8194-1058-6*) SPIE.

— Tutorials in Optics. LC 92-80124. 250p. (Orig.). 1992. pap. 61.00 (*1-55752-038-0*) Optical Soc.

Moore, Dwight. Problem Solving Strategies for Men in Conflict. Leafgren, Fred, ed. 356p. 1990. 17.95 (*1-55620-067-6*) Am Coun Assn.

Moore, E. Dante & His Early Biographers. LC 70-122459. (Studies in Dante: No. 9). (C). 1970. reprint ed. lib. bdg. 59.95 (*0-8383-1002-8*) M S G Haskell Hse.

— Studies in Dante, First Series. LC 68-24955. (Studies in Dante: No. 9). 1969. reprint ed. lib. bdg. 75.00 (*0-8383-0217-3*) M S G Haskell Hse.

— Studies in Dante, Fourth Series: A Textual Criticism of the Convivo & Miscellaneous Essays. LC 68-29737. (Studies in Dante: No. 9). 1968. reprint ed. lib. bdg. 75.00 (*0-8383-0220-3*) M S G Haskell Hse.

— Studies in Dante, Second Series. LC 68-24956. (Studies in Dante: No. 9). 1969. reprint ed. lib. bdg. 75.00 (*0-8383-0218-1*) M S G Haskell Hse.

— Studies in Dante, Third Series. LC 68-24957. (Studies in Dante: No. 9). (Illus.). 1969. reprint ed. lib. bdg. 39.95 (*0-8383-0219-X*) M S G Haskell Hse.

Moore, E. F. Modelbuilder's Notebook: A Guide for Architects & Interior Designers. 1990. pap. text ed. write for info. (*0-07-043026-8*) McGraw.

Moore, E. Hamilton. English Miracle Plays & Moralities. LC 77-100517. reprint ed. 17.25 (*0-404-00598-5*) AMS Pr.

— English Miracle Plays & Moralities. (BCL1-PR English Literature Ser.). 199p. 1992. reprint ed. lib. bdg. 69.00 (*0-7812-7100-2*) Rprt Serv.

Moore, E. L., jt. auth. see Lewis, N. E.

Moore, E. L., jt. ed. see Lewis, N. E.

Moore, E. Neil, jt. auth. see Morganroth, Joel.

Moore, E. Neil, jt. ed. see Morganroth, Joel.

Moore, E. P. Novelist of the Mexican Revolution. 1972. 59.95 (*0-8490-0741-0*) Gordon Pr.

Moore, Earl F. Silent Arrows. 3rd ed. LC 23-939860. 1977. 12.95 (*0-939860-03-1*) Tremaine Graph & Pub.

— Western Echoes. LC 23-939860. (Illus.). 198p. (J). (gr. 4-12). 1980. 12.95 (*0-939860-00-7*) Tremaine Graph & Pub.

Moore, Earl J., jt. auth. see Gysbers, Norman C.

Moore, Earl V. & Heger, Theodore E. The Symphony & the Symphonic Poem. 6th rev. ed. LC 57-63375. (C). 1974. text ed. 15.95 (*0-914004-01-8*) Ulrich.

Moore, Ed. Apocalypse When? (Illus.). 284p. (Orig.). (C). 1990. pap. 10.00 (*0-9624843-0-X*) Christchurch Pubns.

Moore-ede, Martin. Twenty-Four-Hour Society: Understanding Human Limits in a World That Never Stops. 1993. pap. 11.54 (*0-201-62611-X*) Addison-Wesley.

Moore-Ede, Martin C. & Czeisler, Charles A., eds. Mathematical Models of the Circadian Sleep-Wake Cycle. (Illus.). 224p. 1984. text ed. 97.50 (*0-89004-843-6*) Raven.

An Asterisk (*) at the beginning of an entry indicates that the title is appearing in BIP for the first time.

Moore-Ede, Martin C., et al. The Clocks That Time Us: Physiology of the Circadian Timing System. LC 81-6780. (Commonwealth Fund Publications). 464p. 1984. pap. 18.95 (*0-674-13581-4*) HUP.

Moore-Ede, Martin C., et al, eds. Electromagnetic Fields & Circadian Rhythmicity. (Circadian Factors in Human Health & Performance Ser.). vii, 210p. 1993. 49.50 (*0-8176-3552-1*) Birkhauser.

Moore, Edgar, et al. Creative & Critical Thinking, 2 Vols. 2nd ed. LC 84-81047. (Illus.). 384p. (C). 1984. text ed. 59.16 (*0-395-35780-2*) HM.

— Creative & Critical Thinking, 2 Vols. 2nd ed. LC 84-81047. (Illus.). 384p. (C). 1985. teacher ed, pap. 2.36 (*0-395-36459-0*) HM.

***Moore, Edward.** The Foundling: A Comedy & the Gamester: A Tragedy. Amberg, Anthony, ed. & intro. by. LC 94-41277. 1995. write for info. (*0-87413-530-3*) U Delaware Pr.

— Studies in Dante, Second Series: Miscellaneous Essays. LC 68-57628. (Illus.). 386p. 1970. reprint ed. text ed. 65.00 (*0-8371-0908-6*, MOSD, Greenwood Pr) Greenwood.

Moore, Edward A. Story of a Cannoneer Under Stonewall Jackson. LC 77-146866. (Select Bibliographies Reprint Ser.). 1977. reprint ed. 24.95 (*0-8369-5633-8*) Ayer.

Moore, Edward C. American Pragmatism: Peirce, James & Dewey. LC 84-25291. 285p. 1985. reprint ed. text ed. 52.50 (*0-313-24740-4*, MOOA, Greenwood Pr) Greenwood.

— Forty Years of Opera in Chicago. Farkas, Andrew, ed. LC 76-29956. (Opera Biographies Ser.). (Illus.). 1977. reprint ed. lib. bdg. 44.95 (*0-405-09697-6*) Ayer.

Moore, Edward C., ed. Charles S. Pierce & the Philosophy of Science: Papers from the Harvard Sesquicentennial Congress. 512p. (C). 1993. 49.95 (*0-8173-0665-X*) U of Ala Pr.

Moore, Edward C. & Robin, Richard S., eds. From Time & Chance to Consciousness: Studies in the Metaphysics of Charles Peirce - Papers from the Sesquicentennial Harvard Congress. LC 93-18010. 224p. 1994. 49.95 (*0-85496-379-0*) Berg Pubs.

Moore, Edward C., ed. see Clayton, Lawrence A., et al.

Moore, Edward C., ed. see Peirce, Charles S.

Moore, Elaine. Deep River. LC 93-23043. (Illus.). (J). 1994. pap. 14.00 (*0-671-86534-X*, S&S Bks Young Read) S&S Childrens.

— Good Morning, City. LC 94-35458. (Illus.). 32p. (J). (gr. k-3). 1995. lib. bdg. 14.95 (*0-8167-3654-5*) BrdgeWater.

— Grammy, Do You Love Me? 1995. 7.95 (*0-681-00442-8*) Longmeadow Pr.

— Grandma's Garden. LC 90-6052. (J). (ps-3). 1994. 15.00 (*0-688-08693-4*); 14.93 (*0-688-08694-2*) Lothrop.

— Grandma's House. LC 84-11233. (Illus.). 32p. (J). (gr. k up). 1985. 16.00 (*0-688-04115-9*); lib. bdg. 15.93 (*0-688-04116-7*) Lothrop.

— Grandma's Promise. LC 86-33762. (Illus.). (J). (gr. k-3). 1988. 16.00 (*0-688-06740-9*); lib. bdg. 15.93 (*0-688-06741-7*) Lothrop.

— Grandma's Smile. LC 94-23679. (Illus.). (J). 1995. write for info. (*0-688-11075-4*); lib. bdg. write for info. (*0-688-11076-2*) Lothrop.

— I'd Rather Be Eaten by Sharks. (J). (gr. 4-7). 1995. pap. 2.99 (*0-590-47918-0*) Scholastic Inc.

— Jesus Had a Family Just Like Me. (Illus.). 32p. 1987. 5.99 (*0-570-04170-8*, 56-1627) Concordia.

— The Substitute Teacher from Mars. LC 93-37527. (Illus.). 96p. (J). (gr. 2-6). 1993. pap. text ed. 2.95 (*0-8167-3283-3*) Troll Assocs.

— What Is a Family? (Illus.). 32p. 1987. 5.99 (*0-570-04171-6*, 56-1628) Concordia.

— Who Let Girls in the Boys' Locker Room? LC 94-820. (Illus.). 144p. (J). (gr. 3-6). 1994. pap. text ed. 2.95 (*0-8167-3439-9*) Troll Assocs.

Moore, Elaine, jt. auth. see Smart, Lesley.

Moore, Elizabeth, jt. auth. see Couvillon, Alice.

Moore, Elizabeth B. & Couvillon, Alice W. Louisiana Indian Tales. LC 89-71060. 112p. (J). 1990. 11.95 (*0-88289-756-X*) Pelican.

Moore, Ellen. Lead Me to the Exit. LC 77-9949. 1977. 6.95 (*0-918056-01-2*) Ariadne Pr.

— One Snowy Night. 224p. (Orig.). 1992. pap. 2.95 (*1-56597-000-4*, Kismet) Meteor Pub.

Moore, Ellen J. Fossil Mollusks of Coastal Oregon. LC 71-634653. (Oregon State Monographs. Studies in Geology: No. 10). 64p. reprint ed. pap. 25.00 (*0-7837-3943-5*, 2043698) Bks Demand.

— Fossil Shells from Oregon Beach Cliffs. LC 94-94004. (Illus.). 88p. 1994. pap. 9.95 (*0-9640066-0-X*) Chintimini Pr.

Moore, Elsie G., jt. auth. see Bock, R. Darrell.

Moore, Elwood S. American Influence in Canadian Mining. Bruchey, Stuart, ed. LC 80-561. (Multinational Corporations Ser.). (Illus.). 1981. reprint ed. lib. bdg. 19.95 (*0-405-13358-8*) Ayer.

***Moore, Emerson.** The Bluebird of Happiness. (J). 1995. 8.95 (*0-8062-5221-9*) Carlton.

— Two for One: I Wish I Wish & Patty's Newfound Friends. 1995. 9.95 (*0-8062-5328-2*) Carlton.

Moore, Emery L., jt. ed. see Lewis, Norris E.

Moore, Emily. Just My Luck: Meet Olivia & Jeffrey, Canine Detectives. 112p. (J). (gr. 3-7). 1991. pap. 3.99 (*0-14-034790-9*, Puffin) Puffin Bks.

— Something to Count On. 1995. 17.25 (*0-8446-6799-4*) Peter Smith.

— Something to Count On. 112p. (J). (gr. 3-7). 1991. pap. 3.99 (*0-14-034791-7*, Puffin) Puffin Bks.

— Whose Side Are You On? 128p. (J). (gr. 3-7). 1988. 14.00 (*0-374-38409-6*) FS&G.

— Whose Side Are You On? 128p. (J). (gr. 3-7). 1990. pap. 3.95 (*0-374-48373-6*, Sunburst Bks) FS&G.

Moore, Ercelle. Going for the Butter. 32p. 1988. pap. 3.00 (*1-880649-21-7*) Writ Ctr Pr.

Moore, Eric. Gardening in the Middle East. 39.95 (*0-86685-548-3*) Intl Bk Ctr.

Moore, Eric G., jt. ed. see Clark, William A.

Moore, Ernest, ed. Bases of Auditory Brain Stem Evoked Responses. 481p. 1983. text ed. 54.50 (*0-8089-1465-0*, 792976, Grune) Saunders.

Moore, Ernest E., et al. Trauma. 2nd ed. (Illus.). 1059p. (C). 1991. boxed 150.00 (*0-8385-9007-1*, A9007-4) Appleton & Lange.

Moore, Ethel, ed. Letters from Thirty-One Artists. (Gallery Notes Ser.). (Illus.). (Orig.). 1970. pap. 1.50 (*0-685-07682-2*, C214) Buffalo Acad.

Moore, Ethel & Moore, Chauncey O. Ballads & Folksongs of the Southwest: More than 600 Titles, Melodies, & Texts Collected in Oklahoma. 432p. reprint ed. pap. 123.20 (*0-8357-5951-2*, 2007261) Bks Demand.

Moore, Ethel, jt. auth. see Francis, Elisabeth.

Moore, Eugenia. Climb the Waterfall & the Days of Rye. Derman, Elizabeth, ed. LC 86-28061. (Illus.). 216p. 1987. 14.95 (*0-9617284-1-8*); pap. 9.95 (*0-9617284-0-X*) Sand & Silk.

— Dark Moon Rising. Leiper, Esther M., ed. 32p. (Orig.). 1989. pap. 3.95 (*0-9617284-7-7*) Sand & Silk.

— Home Cooking from the Hollow. 32p. 1987. pap. 3.95 (*0-9617284-3-4*) Sand & Silk.

— In a Minute! Leiper, Esther M., ed. 32p. (Orig.). (YA). (gr. 9 up). 1988. pap. 3.95 (*0-9617284-9-3*) Sand & Silk.

— Kidnapped by an Angel. Leiper, Esther M., ed. (Illus.). 32p. (Orig.). (J). (gr. 3-4). 1988. pap. 3.95 (*0-9617284-4-2*) Sand & Silk.

— The Sweet Water River. LC 90-92340. (Illus.). 72p. 1991. pap. 7.95 (*1-878116-05-3*) JVC Bks.

Moore, Eugenia, ed. see Leiper, Esther M.

Moore, Eugenia, ed. see Lindow, Sandra.

***Moore, Eva.** Buddy, the First Seeing Eye Dog. LC 95-6725. (Hello Reader! Ser., Level 4). (Illus.). (J). 1996. write for info. (*0-590-26585-7*) Scholastic Inc.

— The Fairy Tale Life of Hans Christian Andersen. (Illus.). 80p. (J). 1992. pap. 2.75 (*0-590-45225-8*, Apple Paperbacks) Scholastic Inc.

— Johnny Appleseed. (Orig.). (J). (gr. 2-3). pap. 2.95 (*0-590-40297-8*) Scholastic Inc.

— Story of George Washington Carver. (J). 1990. pap. 3.50 (*0-590-42660-5*) Scholastic Inc.

Moore, Eva, et al, eds. Sing a Song of Popcorn: Every Child's Book of Poems. (Illus.). 160p. (J). (gr. k up). 1988. pap. 18.95 (*0-590-43974-X*, Scholastic Hardcover) Scholastic Inc.

***Moore, Eve E.** Guardian. 1994. 12.95 (*0-533-11181-1*) Vantage.

Moore, Evelyn, ed. see Gums, Bonnie L.

Moore, Evelyn, ed. see Jelks, Edward B., et al.

Moore, Evelyn, ed. see Skele, Mikels.

Moore, Evelyn, ed. see Walthall, John A. & Benchley, Elizabeth D.

Moore, Evelyn K. The Passions of Rhetoric: Lessing's Theory of Argument & the German Enlightenment. LC 93-13187. (Library of Rhetorics: Vol. 3). 144p. (C). 1993. lib. bdg. 83.00 (*0-7923-2308-4*) Kluwer Ac.

Moore, F. Descriptions of New Indian Lepidoperous Insects from the Collection of Late Mr. W. S. Atkinson, M.A., F.L.S., Pts. 1-2. 1987. 750.00 (*0-685-21848-1*, Pub. by Intl Bk Distr II) St Mut.

— Descriptions of New Indian Lepidoterous Insects from the Collection of Late Mr. W. S. Atkinson, Pts. 1-2. 1987. 375.00 (*81-7089-889-7*, Pub. by Intl Bk Distr II) St Mut.

— Descsriptions of New Indian Lepidoterous Insects from the Collection of Late Mr. W. S. Atkinson, Pts. 1-2. (C). 1987. text ed. 400.00 (*0-685-52011-0*, Pub. by Intl Bk Distr II) St Mut.

Moore, F., ed. Descriptions of New Indian Lepidoterous Insects from the Collection of Late Mr. W. S. Atkinson, Pts. 1-2. (C). 1987. 600.00 (*0-685-61466-2*, Pub. by Intl Bk Distr II) St Mut.

— Descriptions of New Indian Lepidoterous Insects from the Collection of Late Mr. W. S. Atkinson, Pts. 1 & 2. 1987. 200.00 (*0-685-49626-0*, Pub. by Intl Bk Distr II) St Mut.

Moore, F. Michael. Drag! Male & Female Impersonators on Stage, Screen & Television: An Illustrated World History. 336p. 1994. lib. bdg. 45.00 (*0-89950-996-7*) McFarland & Co.

Moore, F. Richard. Programming in C with a Bit of UNIX. (Illus.). 208p. 1986. 26.95 (*0-13-730094-8*) P-H.

***Moore, Fauzya.** Beyond Development Cooperation: Toward a New Era of Global & Human Security. 78p. 1994. pap. 19.95 (*0-88936-714-0*, IDRC7140, Pub. by IDRC CN) UNIPUB.

Moore, Fionna, jt. auth. see Morris, Francis.

***Moore, Floyd C.** I Gave Thomas Edison My Sandwich. LC 94-22009. (Illus.). (J). 1995. write for info. (*0-8075-3504-4*) A Whitman.

Moore, Francis. Old Moore's Almanack 1994. 79p. 1993. pap. 1.95 (*0-572-01879-7*, Pub. by Foulsham UK) Atrium Pubs.

***Moore, Francis D. & Brigham, Peter B.** A Miracle & a Privilege: Recounting a Half-Century of Surgical Advance. 400p. (Orig.). (C). 1995. 29.95 (*0-309-05188-6*) Natl Acad Pr.

Moore, Francis J., comp. Prayers for All Occasions. large type ed. 96p. 1987. pap. 2.50 (*0-685-28630-4*) Forward Movement.

Moore, Frank. The Civil War in Song & Story, 2 vols., Set. 1980. lib. bdg. 195.75 (*0-8490-3130-3*) Gordon Pr.

— The Magic Moving Alphabet. (Illus.). 32p. 1978. pap. 3.95 (*0-486-23593-9*) Dover.

— Songs & Ballads of the American Revolution. (BCL1 - U. S. History Ser.). 288p. 1991. reprint ed. lib. bdg. 79.00 (*0-7812-6106-6*) Rprt Serv.

Moore, Frank, ed. Rebel Rhymes & Rhapsodies. 1976. lib. bdg. 59.95 (*0-8490-2503-6*) Gordon Pr.

— Rebellion Record: A Diary of American Events, 12 vols., Set. (Illus.). 1976. reprint ed. pap. 300.00 (*0-405-09846-4*) Ayer.

Moore, Frank & Decker, Peter, eds. Diary of the American Revolution: From Newspapers & Original Documents, 2 vols., 1. LC 72-76563. (Eyewitness Accounts of the American Revolution Ser., No. 1). (Illus.). 1969. reprint ed. 23.95 (*0-405-01166-0*) Ayer.

— Diary of the American Revolution: From Newspapers & Original Documents, 2 vols., 2. LC 72-76563. (Eyewitness Accounts of the American Revolution Ser., No. 1). (Illus.). 1969. reprint ed. 23.95 (*0-405-01167-9*) Ayer.

— Diary of the American Revolution: From Newspapers & Original Documents, 2 vols., Set. LC 72-76563. (Eyewitness Accounts of the American Revolution Ser., No. 1). (Illus.). 1969. reprint ed. 46.95 (*0-405-01165-2*) Ayer.

— Songs & Ballads of the American Revolution. LC 79-76562. (Eyewitness Accounts of the American Revolution Ser., No. 1). (Illus.). 1976. reprint ed. 25.95 (*0-405-01164-4*) Ayer.

Moore, Frank & Hynam, John. The Horses Knew the Way: Memories of a Lincolnshire Life. 160p. 1991. 25.00 (*0-86299-989-8*) A Sutton Pub.

Moore, Frank G. The Roman's World. LC 65-23486. (Illus.). 502p. (J). (gr. 7 up). 1936. 25.00 (*0-8196-0155-1*) Biblo.

Moore, Frank J. The Incredible Moving Picture Book. 32p. (J). (gr. 1 up). 1987. pap. 3.95 (*0-486-25374-0*) Dover.

Moore, Frank J., et al. Thailand: Its People, Its Society, Its Culture. LC 74-79218. (Survey of World Cultures Ser.: No. 15). 629p. reprint ed. pap. 179.30 (*0-317-11189-2*, 2010454) Bks Demand.

Moore, Frank L. Crowell's Handbook of World Opera. LC 73-3025. (Illus.). 683p. 1974. reprint ed. text ed. 43.00 (*0-8371-6822-8*, MOCH, Greenwood Pr) Greenwood.

Moore, Frank W., ed. Readings in Cross-Cultural Methodology. LC 66-28127. (Comparative Studies). 350p. 1966. reprint ed. 15.00 (*0-87536-101-3*); reprint ed. pap. 10.00 (*0-87536-102-1*) HRAFP.

Moore, Franklin G., jt. auth. see Hendrick, Thomas.

Moore, Franklin K., ed. Theory of Laminar Flows. (High Speed Aerodynamics & Jet Propulsion Ser.: Vol. 4). 1964. 145.00x (*0-691-08051-8*) Princeton U Pr.

Moore, Franklin L. Agent's Bonding Guide. 24.00 (*0-942326-02-4*, 26080) Rough Notes.

— Property & Casualty Insurance: Study Guide. 1991. 40.00 (*0-942326-25-3*, 26629) Rough Notes.

Moore, Fred, comp. Iraq Speaks: Documents on the Gulf Crisis. 92p. (Orig.). (C). 1993. pap. text ed. 35.00 (*0-7881-0029-7*) Diane Pub.

Moore, Frederick W. Balkan Trial. LC 75-134826. (Eastern Europe Collection Ser.). 1971. reprint ed. 26.95 (*0-405-02768-0*) Ayer.

Moore, Frederick W., tr. see Gumplowicz, Ludwig.

Moore, Fuller. Concepts & Practice of Architectural Daylighting. LC 84-29929. (Illus.). 304p. 1991. pap. 34.95 (*0-442-00679-9*) Van Nos Reinhold.

— Environmental Control Systems: Heating, Cooling, Lighting. 1993. text ed. write for info. (*0-07-042889-1*) McGraw.

Moore, G. Coastal State Requirements for Foreign Fishing. (Legislative Study Ser.: No. 21, Rev. 3). (Illus.). 393p. 1988. pap. 45.00 (*92-5-102750-1*, F7501) UNIPUB.

— Practice of Social Inquiry. 136p. 1984. text ed. 23.00 (*0-08-030369-2*, Pergamon Pr); pap. text ed. 14.50 (*0-08-030370-6*, Pergamon Pr) Elsevier.

Moore, G. Alexander. Life Cycles in Atchalan: The Diverse Careers of Certain Guatemalans. LC 72-93732. 232p. reprint ed. pap. 66.20 (*0-317-26790-6*, 2024329) Bks Demand.

Moore, G. E. The Elements of Ethics. (C). 1991. 54.95 (*0-87722-770-5*) Temple U Pr.

— G. E. Moore: Selected Writings. Baldwin, Thomas, ed. LC 93-16366. (International Library of Philosophy). 256p. 1993. 49.95 (*0-415-09853-X*, B2415); pap. 17.95 (*0-415-09854-8*, B2419) Routledge.

— Principia Ethica. (C). 1903. pap. 19.95 (*0-521-09114-4*) Cambridge U Pr.

— Principia Ethica: With the Preface to the Second Edition & Other Papers. rev. ed. Baldwin, Thomas, ed. LC 93-6493. 360p. (C). 1993. 64.95 (*0-521-44378-4*); pap. 19.95 (*0-521-44848-4*) Cambridge U Pr.

Moore, G. E., jt. auth. see Bennett, P. R.

Moore, G. L., ed. Introduction to Inductively Coupled Plasma Atomic Emission Spectroscopy. (Analytical Spectroscopy Library: No. 3). 340p. 1989. 97.50 (*0-444-43029-6*) Elsevier.

Moore, G. R. & Pettigrew, G. W. Cytochromes C: Evolutionary, Structural & Physicochemical Aspects. Rich, A., ed. (Molecular Biology Ser.). (Illus.). xvi, 478p. 1990. 109.00 (*0-387-50852-X*) Spr-Verlag.

Moore, G. R., jt. auth. see Pettigrew, G. W.

Moore, G. T., jt. ed. see Zube, Ervin H.

Moore, Gail & MacKenzie, Marilyn. The Volunteer Development Tool Box. 1993. pap. 20.00 (*0-911029-41-9*) Heritage Arts.

Moore, Gail, jt. auth. see MacKenzie, Marilyn.

Moore, Gareth. Believing in God: A Philosophical Essay. 300p. 1989. 37.95 (*0-567-09498-7*, Pub. by T & T Clark UK) Bks Intl VA.

***Moore, Gary.** Child Is Born. (J). 1994. 3.99 (*0-517-10273-0*) Random Hse Value.

— Golf, Gambling & Gamesmanship. 1986. 7.95 (*0-89746-054-5*) Gambling Times.

Moore, Gary, jt. auth. see Richardson, William B.

***Moore, Gary D.** The Christian's Guide to Wise Investing. rev. ed. 336p. 1994. pap. 14.99 (*0-310-49261-0*) Zondervan.

***Moore, Gary T.** Early Childhood Physical Environment Observation Schedules & Rating Scales: Preliminary Scales for the Measurement of the Physical Environment of Child Care Centers & Related Environments. vi, 74p. (C). 1995. 12.00 (*0-938744-83-6*, R94-2) U of Wis Ctr Arch-Urban.

***Moore, Gary T., comp.** Comprehensive Bibliography on Child Care & Preschool Design. v, 49p. (C). 1995. 10.00 (*0-938744-84-4*, R94-3) U of Wis Ctr Arch-Urban.

Moore, Gary T., ed. Genesis II: Advanced Lunar Outpost. (Publications in Architecture & Urban Planning: No. R91-2). (Illus.). xvi, 70p. 1991. 10.00 (*0-938744-74-7*) U of Wis Ctr Arch-Urban.

***Moore, Gary T. & Lackney, Jeffery A.** Educational Facilities for the Twenty-First Century: Research Analysis & Design Patterns. (Publications in Architecture & Urban Planning: No. R94-1). (Illus.). 90p. 1994. 18.00 (*0-938744-80-1*) U of Wis Ctr Arch-Urban.

Moore, Gary T., ed. see Baschiera, Dino, et al.

Moore, Gary T., ed. see Burg, Cynthia M., et al.

Moore, Gary T., ed. see Gartz, William F., et al.

Moore, Gary T., ed. see Huebner-Moths, Janis, et al.

Moore, Gary T., ed. see Schnarsky, Anthony, et al.

Moore, Gary T., jt. auth. see University of Wisconsin Ph.D Faculty Staff.

Moore, Gary T., jt. ed. see Zube, Ervin H.

Moore, Gary T., et al. Environmental Design: Research Directions. LC 84-15975. 222p. 1984. text ed. 55.00 (*0-275-91232-9*, C1232, Praeger Pubs) Greenwood.

— Recommendations for Child Care Centers. rev. ed. (Publications in Architecture & Urban Planning: No. R79-2). (Illus.). viii, 450p. 1994. 27.50 (*0-938744-06-2*) U of Wis Ctr Arch-Urban.

Moore, Gary W. Developing & Evaluating Educational Research. (C). 1987. text ed. 38.25 (*0-673-39172-8*) HarpCollege.

Moore, Gary W., jt. ed. see Moore, Hastings.

Moore, Gay M. Seaport in Virginia: George Washington's Alexandria. LC 73-188711. 288p. reprint ed. 82.10 (*0-8357-9817-8*, 2019203) Bks Demand.

Moore, Gene E. Bucco. (Illus.). 64p. 1992. pap. 6.95 (*0-9633267-0-8*) Greenhawk Bks.

— Gossamer: The Green Giraffe. 44p. reprint ed. pap. 4.00 (*0-9633267-1-6*) Greenhawk Bks.

Moore, Gene M., tr. see Amsterdamski, Stefan.

***Moore, Geoff & Higginson, Richard.** Apocalypse! The Business Ethics Game. Date not set. pap. text ed. write for info. (*0-471-95115-3*) Wiley.

Moore, Geoff, jt. auth. see Higginson, Richard.

Moore, Geoffrey. Byron. 1989. 8.95 (*0-517-57482-9*, C P Pubs) Crown Pub Group.

— Crossing the Chasm. 256p. 1995. pap. 13.00 (*0-88730-717-5*) Harper Busn.

— Henry Wadsworth Longfellow. (Great Poets Ser.). 1989. 10.00 (*0-517-57380-6*, Crown) Crown Pub Group.

— John Keats. LC 93-5582. (Great English Poets Ser.). 1994. 10.00 (*0-517-59647-4*, C P Pubs) Crown Pub Group.

Moore, Geoffrey, ed. Edgar Allan Poe. (Great Poets Ser.). (Illus.). 64p. 1986. 10.00 (*0-517-57010-6*, Crown) Crown Pub Group.

— John Donne. (Great Poets Ser.). (Illus.). 64p. 1988. 10.00 (*0-517-57011-4*, Crown) Crown Pub Group.

— Rudyard Kipling. (Great Poets Ser.). (Illus.). 64p. 1992. 10.00 (*0-517-58934-6*, C P Pubs) Crown Pub Group.

Moore, Geoffrey, intro. Walt Whitman. (Great Poets Ser.). (Illus.). 64p. 1988. 10.00 (*0-517-56707-5*, Crown) Crown Pub Group.

Moore, Geoffrey, jt. auth. see Klein, Philip A.

Moore, Geoffrey, jt. intro. see Porter, Peter.

***Moore, Geoffrey A.** Inside the Tornado. 272p. 1995. 25.00 (*0-88730-765-5*) Harper Busn.

Moore, Geoffrey H. Business Cycles: Inflation & Forecasting. 2nd ed. LC 83-3829. (National Bureau of Economic Research, Studies in Business Cycles: No. 24). 499p. reprint ed. pap. 142.30 (*0-8357-6986-0*, 2057069) Bks Demand.

— Leading Indicators for the 1990s. 200p. 1989. text ed. 40.00 (*1-55623-258-6*) Irwin Prof Pubng.

— Measuring Recessions. (Occasional Papers: No. 61). 64p. 1958. reprint ed. 20.00 (*0-87014-375-1*) Natl Bur Econ Res.

— Production of Industrial Materials in World Wars I & II. (Occasional Papers: No. 18). 84p. 1944. reprint ed. 21.90 (*0-87014-333-6*); reprint ed. mic. film 20.00 (*0-685-61253-8*) Natl Bur Econ Res.

— Productivity, Costs, & Prices: New Light from an Old Hypothesis. (Explorations in Economic Research Two Ser.: No. 2). 17p. 1975. reprint ed. 35.00 (*0-685-61378-X*) Natl Bur Econ Res.

— Slowdowns, Recessions, & Inflation: Some Issues & Answers. (Explorations in Economic Research Two Ser.: No. 2). 42p. 1975. reprint ed. 35.00 (*0-685-61382-8*) Natl Bur Econ Res.

— Statistical Indicators of Cyclical Revivals & Recessions. (Occasional Papers: No. 31). 104p. 1950. reprint ed. 27.10 (*0-87014-346-8*) Natl Bur Econ Res.

Moore, Geoffrey H., ed. Business Cycle Indicators, 1. LC 60-14062. (National Bureau of Economic Research Ser.: Vol. 10). 793p. reprint ed. pap. 180.00 (*0-8357-7486-4*, 2005917) Bks Demand.

— Business Cycle Indicators, 2. LC 60-14062. (National Bureau of Economic Research Ser.: Vol. 10). 197p. reprint ed. pap. 56.20 (*0-8357-7487-2*, 2019644) Bks Demand.

Moore, Geoffrey H. & Klein, Philip A. The Quality of Consumer Instalment Credit. (Financial Research Program II: Studies in Consumer Installment Financing: No. 13). 282p. 1967. reprint ed. 73.40 (*0-87014-484-7*) Natl Bur Econ Res.

An Asterisk (*) at the beginning of an entry indicates that the title is appearing in BIP for the first time.

Moore, Geoffrey H. & Moore, Melita H. International Economic Indicators: A Sourcebook. LC 84-19194. (Illus.). ix, 373p. 1985. text ed. 69.50 (*0-313-21989-3*, MII/, Greenwood Pr) Greenwood.

Moore, Geoffrey H. & Shiskin, Julius. Indicators of Business Expansions & Contractions. (Occasional Papers: No. 103). 141p. 1967. reprint ed. 36.70 (*0-87014-444-8*) Natl Bur Econ Res.

Moore, Geoffrey H., jt. auth. see Cagan, Phillip.

Moore, Geoffrey H., jt. ed. see Lahiri, Kajal.

Moore, Geoffrey H., jt. auth. see Shiskin, Julius.

Moore, Geoffrey H., jt. auth. see Wallis, W. Allen.

Moore, Geoffrey H., jt. auth. see Zarnowitz, Victor.

Moore, George. A Communication to My Friends. LC 74-8663. (English Literature Ser.: No. 33). 1974. lib. bdg. 49.95 (*0-8383-1910-6*) M S G Haskell Hse.

— Confessions of a Young Man. (BCL1-PR English Literature Ser.). 301p. 1992. reprint ed. lib. bdg. 89.00 (*0-7812-7601-2*) Rprt Serv.

— Confessions of a Young Man. LC 70-145188. (Literature Ser.). (Illus.). 314p. 1972. reprint ed. 29.00 (*0-403-01113-2*) Scholarly.

— A Drama in Muslin. 330p. 1981. 30.00 (*0-86140-055-0*, Pub. by Colin Smythe Ltd UK); pap. 11.95 (*0-86140-056-9*, Pub. by Colin Smythe Ltd UK) Dufour.

— Flowers of Passion. Fletcher, Ian & Stokes, John, eds. Bd. with Pagan Poems. LC 76-20138. LC 76-20138. (Decadent Consciousness Ser.). 1978. Set lib. bdg. 46.00 (*0-8240-2778-7*) Garland.

— George Moore in Transition: Letters to T. Fisher Unwin & Lena Milman, 1894-1910. Gerber, Helmut E., ed. LC 67-23323. 343p. reprint ed. pap. 97.80 (*0-685-15627-3*, 2027635) Bks Demand.

— Grasville Abbey: A Romance, 3 vols., Set. LC 73-22769. (Gothic Novels II Ser.). 792p. 1979. reprint ed. 94.95 (*0-405-06019-X*) Ayer.

— Hail & Fairewell. (Illus.). 774p. 1976. 60.00 (*0-900675-64-0*, Pub. by Colin Smythe Ltd UK) Dufour.

— Hail & Farewell: Ave, Salve, Vale. Cave, Richard A., ed. LC 85-465. (Illus.). 774p. reprint ed. pap. 180.00 (*0-7837-4633-4*, 2044357) Bks Demand.

— Impressions & Opinions. LC 72-80501. 1972. reprint ed. 26.95 (*0-405-08797-7*, Pub. by Blom Pubns UK) Ayer.

— In Minor Keys: The Uncollected Short Stories of George Moore. Eakin, David B. & Gerber, Helmut E., eds. (Irish Studies). (Illus.). 180p. 1985. text ed. 34.95x (*0-8156-2338-0*) Syracuse U Pr.

— In Single Strictness. LC 73-37557. (Short Story Index Reprint Ser.). 1977. reprint ed. 23.95 (*0-8369-4116-0*) Ayer.

— The Lake. 1980. 30.00 (*0-900675-75-6*, Pub. by Colin Smythe Ltd UK); pap. 14.95 (*0-901072-82-6*, Pub. by Colin Smythe Ltd UK) Dufour.

— Practical Problems in Mathematics for Automotive Technicians. 4th ed. 1991. pap. text ed. 14.95 (*0-8273-4622-0*) Delmar.

— Practical Problems in Mathematics for Automotive Technicians Instructors Guide. 4th ed. 1991. teacher ed 12.00 (*0-8273-4623-9*) Delmar.

— A Story-Teller's Holiday, 2 vols., Set. (BCL1-PR English Literature Ser.). 1992. reprint ed. lib. bdg. 150.00 (*0-7812-7602-0*) Rprt Serv.

— Untilled Field. LC 70-125233. (Short Story Index Reprint Ser.). 1977. 30.95 (*0-8369-3600-0*) Ayer.

— The Use of the Body in Relation to the Mind. LC 78-72812. reprint ed. 32.50 (*0-404-60882-5*) AMS Pr.

Moore, George, ed. & intro. An Anthology of Pure Poetry. 1973. pap. 2.75 (*0-87140-276-9*) Liveright.

Moore, George & Wood, Chris. Social Work & Criminal Law in Scotland. 220p. 1982. text ed. 22.00 (*0-08-025731-3*, Pergamon Pr) Elsevier.

— Social Work & Criminal Law in Scotland. 2nd ed. (Aberdeen University Press Bks.). 250p. 1991. text ed. 25.50 (*0-08-041221-1*, Pub. by Aberdeen U Pr) Macmillan.

— Social Work & Criminal Law in Scotland: An Update. (Aberdeen University Press Bks.). 32p. 1987. pap. text ed. 8.00 (*0-08-035069-0*, Pub. by Aberdeen U Pr) Macmillan.

Moore, George B. And Forgive Us Our Debts: A Guide to Ending Financial Stress in Your Life - Permanently! 160p. 1992. pap. 9.95 (*0-9632783-3-9*) Cleveland Bk.

— The Long Way Around: Poems by George B. Moore. LC 92-73503. 64p. (Orig.). (C). 1992. pap. text ed. 24.95 (*1-55605-214-6*) Wyndhall Pr.

Moore, George E. Esther Waters. Laurie, Hilary, ed. 384p. 1993. pap. 9.95 (*0-460-87326-1*, Everyman's Classic Lib) C E Tuttle.

— Esther Waters. Skilton, David, ed. (World's Classics Paperback Ser.). 1983. pap. 9.95 (*0-19-281578-4*) OUP.

— Esther Waters. large type ed. (Large Print Ser.). 440p. 1993. reprint ed. lib. bdg. 22.00 (*0-939495-29-5*) North Bks.

— Principia Ethica. (Great Books in Philosophy). 225p. (C). 1988. pap. text ed. 8.95 (*0-87975-498-2*) Prometheus Bks.

Moore, George F. History of Religions, 2 vols. write for info. (*0-318-50934-2*, Pub. by T T Clark UK) Bks Intl VA.

— History of Religions, 2 vols., Vol. 1. 654p. 1914. 39.95 (*0-567-07202-9*, Pub. by T & T Clark UK) Bks Intl VA.

— History of Religions, 2 vols., Vol. 2. 568p. 1920. 39.95 (*0-567-07203-7*, Pub. by T & T Clark UK) Bks Intl VA.

— Judges: Critical Exegetical Commentary. Driver, Samuel R. et al, eds. LC 25-19368. (International Critical Commentary Ser.). 528p. 1895. 39.95 (*0-567-05004-1*, Pub. by T & T Clark UK) Bks Intl VA.

Moore, George L. The Moore Family in America: Descendants of Shildes Moore of Wales from 1732 to 1891. Virdin, Donald O., ed. 160p. 1991. reprint ed. pap. 20.00 (*1-55613-508-4*) Heritage Bk.

Moore, George T., jt. auth. see Barron, Eric J.

Moore, George T., jt. ed. see Stanley, Daniel J.

Moore, George W. & Sullivan, G. Nicholas. Speleology: The Study of Caves. LC 77-18176. (Illus.). reprint ed. pap. text ed. 6.95 (*0-939748-00-2*) Cave Bks MO.

Moore, Gerald. Singer & Accompanist: The Performance of Fifty Songs. LC 73-11859. (Illus.). xi, 232p. 1974. reprint ed. text ed. 49.75 (*0-8371-7090-7*, MOSC, Greenwood Pr) Greenwood.

— Tsuen-Wan Township: Study Group Report on Its Development. 47p. reprint ed. pap. 25.00 (*0-317-11282-1*, 2017719) Bks Demand.

Moore, Gerald, jt. ed. see Beier, Ulli.

Moore, Gerald, tr. see Lopes, Henri.

Moore, Gerald, tr. see Pressburger, Giorgio & Pressburger, Nicola.

Moore, Gerald L. The Politics of Management Consulting. LC 83-19231. 176p. 1984. text ed. 45.00 (*0-275-91743-6*, C1743, Praeger Pubs) Greenwood.

Moore, Gerald T. & Scully, Marian O., eds. Frontiers of Nonequilibrium Statistical Physics. LC 85-31171. (NATO ASI Series B, Physics: Vol. 135). 510p. 1986. 110.00 (*0-306-42233-6*, Plenum Pr) Plenum.

Moore, Gilbert. Lorraine As in a Chagall Painting: Lorraine Comme Dans une Toile de Chagall. Livingstone, Harrison E., ed. 96p. (ENG & FRE.). 1990. pap. text ed. 8.95 (*0-941401-03-0*) Conservatory.

Moore-Gilbert, B. J. Kipling & "Orientalism" LC 86-15446. 240p. 1986. text ed. 32.50 (*0-312-45644-1*) St Martin.

Moore-Gilbert, Bart, ed. The Arts in the 1970s: Cultural Closure? LC 93-3712. 1993. write for info. (*0-415-09905-6*); pap. write for info. (*0-415-09906-4*) Routledge.

Moore-Gilbert, Bart & Seed, John, eds. Cultural Revolution? The Challenge of the Arts in the 1960s. 256p. 1992. 69.95 (*0-415-07824-5*, A7455) Routledge.

Moore, Gilbert W., jt. auth. see Irons, Edward D.

***Moore, Giselle & Almadrones, Lois.** Women & Cancer: Gynecologic Nursing Perspectives. (Nursing Ser.). 500p. 1995. 45.00 (*0-86720-714-0*) Jones & Bartlett.

Moore, Glenn. Plan to Win: Success Guide for Young Athletes. LC 93-72102. (Illus.). 176p. (Orig.). 1993. pap. 12.95 (*0-9637345-0-4*) Champ Spts Pr.

Moore, Gloria, jt. auth. see Moore, Ronald.

Moore, Gordon E., ed. see National Academy of Sciences, Committee on Linking Trade & Technology Policies Staff.

Moore, Gordon P., jt. ed. see Rosenberg, Martin.

Moore, Grace. You're Only Human Once. Farkas, Andrew, ed. LC 76-29958. (Opera Biographies Ser.). (Illus.). 1977. reprint ed. lib. bdg. 25.95 (*0-405-09698-4*) Ayer.

Moore, Grant H., et al, trs. Khibaru Fan'yi Mikhie Be: The New Testament in the Soso Language. 1988. spiral bd. write for info. (*0-318-66962-5*) Open Bible.

Moore, Granville M. Poisonous Snakes of the World: Manual for Use by the United States Amphibious Forces. (Illus.). 220p. 1979. reprint ed. boxed 24.00 (*0-16-002014-X*, S/N 008-045-00009-7) USGPO.

Moore, Greg. Rock & Roll Collectibles. LC 93-91812. 112p. 1993. pap. 22.95 (*0-9639495-0-0*) G Moore Pubng.

— Tree Care for the Home Gardener. Patrick, John, ed. (Lothian Australian Garden Ser.). (Illus.). 64p. (Orig.). 1995. pap. 9.95 (*0-85091-321-7*, Pub. by Lothian Pub AT) Seven Hills Bk.

Moore, Greg & McClaran, Don. Idaho Whitewater: The Complete River Guide. Hesselbarth, Woody, ed. LC 89-90989. (Illus.). 224p. (Orig.). 1989. pap. text ed. 19.95 (*0-9623828-0-9*) Class Six.

Moore, Gregory H., ed. see Russell, Bertrand.

Moore, Gwen. Women & Politics: Activism, Attitudes & Office-Holding, Vol. 2. (Research in Politics & Society Ser.). 1986. 73.25 (*0-89232-556-9*) Jai Pr.

Moore, Gwen, ed. Research in Politics & Society, Vol. 3. 1987. 73.25 (*0-89232-714-6*) Jai Pr.

— Studies & the Structure of National Elite of National Elite Groups. (Research in Politics & Society Ser.: Vol. 1). 1985. 73.25 (*0-89232-335-3*) Jai Pr.

Moore, Gwen B. & Serby, Todd. Becoming Whole Through Games. 288p. 1991. pap. 16.95 (*0-915190-70-2*, JP9072-2) Jalmar Pr.

Moore, Gwendolyn, tr. see Paris, Ginette.

Moore, Gwendolyn, tr. see Theriault, Yves.

Moore, H. Miles. Early History of Leavenworth City & County (Kansas) (Illus.). 339p. 1993. reprint ed. lib. bdg. 36.00 (*0-8328-2957-9*) Higginson Bk Co.

Moore, H. P. Moor: The Descendants of Ensign John Moor of Canterbury, N.H., born 1696 - died 1786. (Illus.). 370p. 1992. reprint ed. lib. bdg. 67.00 (*0-8328-2690-1*); reprint ed. pap. 57.00 (*0-8328-2691-X*) Higginson Bk Co.

Moore, H. S., et al, eds. Biotechnology & the Conservation of Genetic Diversity. (Symposia of the Zoological Society of London Ser.: No. 64). (Illus.). 256p. 1992. 98.00 (*0-19-854030-2*) OUP.

Moore, Hagan. Fair by Eleven. (Illus.). 87p. (Orig.). 1987. pap. 6.95 (*0-916930-15-7*) Gardner Oregon.

Moore, Hannah H. Wedgwood & His Imitators. 2nd rev. ed. LC 76-2888. (Illus.). 1978. 29.95 (*0-89344-005-1*) Ars Ceramica.

Moore, Harold G. We Were Soldiers Once...& Young. LC 92-53642. 1992. 25.00 (*0-679-41158-5*) Random.

Moore, Harold G. & Galloway, Joseph. We Were Soldiers Once...& Young: Ia Drang, the Battle That Changed the War in Vietnam. LC 93-15836. (Illus.). 448p. 1993. reprint ed. pap. 13.00 (*0-06-097576-8*, PL) HarpC.

Moore, Harriet L. Soviet Far Eastern Policy, 1931-1945. 40.00 (*0-86527-187-9*) Fertig.

Moore, Harris W. Chip Carving. LC 75-19755. (Illus.). 48p. 1976. reprint ed. pap. 2.95 (*0-486-23256-5*) Dover.

Moore, Harry D., ed. Materials & Processes for NDT Technology. (Illus.). 204p. 1984. reprint ed. 44.50 (*0-931403-06-5*, 2250) Am Soc Nondestructive.

Moore, Harry H., ed. Survival or Suicide. LC 77-134118. (Essay Index Reprint Ser.). 1977. 20.95 (*0-8369-2001-5*) Ayer.

Moore, Harry L. A Geologic Trip Across Tennessee by Interstate 40. LC 93-43322. (Outdoor Tennessee Ser.). (Illus.). 384p. (C). 1994. pap. 19.95 (*0-87049-832-0*) U of Tenn Pr.

Moore, Harry L., Jr. Health Care Strike Manual. 138p. reprint ed. ring bd. 67.75 (*0-911911-00-6*) S Enright.

— Industrial Strike Manual. 208p. 1984. ring bd. 73.75 (*0-911911-02-2*) S Enright.

Moore, Harry L. A Roadside Guide to the Geology of the Great Smoky Mountains National Park. LC 87-18796. (Illus.). 192p. 1988. pap. 11.95 (*0-87049-558-5*) U of Tenn Pr.

Moore, Harry L., Jr., ed. see Clark, James B.

Moore, Harry T. & Parry, Albert. Twentieth-Century Russian Literature. LC 74-13812. (Crosscurrents-Modern Critiques Ser.). 208p. 1974. 7.95 (*0-8093-0703-0*) S Ill U Pr.

Moore, Harry T. & Roberts, Warren. D. H. Lawrence. LC 87-51298. (Literary Lives Ser.). (Illus.). 144p. 1988. pap. 9.95 (*0-500-26030-3*) Thames Hudson.

Moore, Harry T., jt. ed. see Partlow, Robert B., Jr.

Moore, Harvey A. Drug Users & Emergent Organizations. LC 77-9901. (University of Florida Monographs: Social Sciences: No. 60). 144p. reprint ed. pap. 41.10 (*0-7837-5065-X*, 2044760) Bks Demand.

Moore, Hastings & Moore, Gary W., eds. The Neighborhood of IS, Approaches to the Inner Solitude, A Thematic Anthology: Plotinus, Dionysius the Areopagite, The Cloud of Unknowing, The Book of Privy Counseling, Meister Eckhart. 108p. (Orig.). (C). 1984. pap. text ed. 17.00 (*0-8191-3972-6*) U Pr of Amer.

Moore, Helan, jt. auth. see Ollenburger, Jane.

Moore, Henrietta. Feminism & Anthropology. LC 88-22032. (Feminist Perspectives Ser.). ix, 246p. (Orig.). 1989. text ed. 44.95 (*0-8166-1748-1*); pap. text ed. 15.95 (*0-8166-1750-3*) U of Minn Pr.

— Fisherman's Island. 1990. 12.95 (*0-533-08909-3*) Vantage.

— Melissa. 1993. 14.95 (*0-533-10434-3*) Vantage.

— Space, Text & Gender: An Anthropological Study of the Marakwet of Kenya. (Illus.). 220p. 1986. 74.95 (*0-521-30333-8*) Cambridge U Pr.

Moore, Henrietta, jt. auth. see Vaughan, Megan.

***Moore, Henrietta L.** A Passion for Difference: Essays in Anthropology & Gender. LC 94-31477. 1995. 39.95 (*0-253-33858-1*); pap. 14.95 (*0-253-20951-X*) Ind U Pr.

Moore, Henry. Drawings of Henry Moore. (Master Draughtsman Ser.). (Illus.). 1970. 10.95 (*0-87505-025-5*); pap. 4.95 (*0-87505-178-2*) Borden.

Moore, Henry & Scott, Deborah E. Henry Moore: Maquettes & Working Models. Leveton, Deborah, ed. (Illus.). 24p. (Orig.). 1987. pap. 3.00 (*0-942614-11-9*) Nelson-Atkins.

Moore, Henry, jt. auth. see Kaufman, Shirley.

Moore, Henry L. Economic Cycles: Their Law & Cause. LC 67-16342. (Reprints of Economic Classics Ser.). (Illus.). viii, 149p. 1967. reprint ed. 25.00 (*0-678-00229-0*) Kelley.

— Forecasting the Yield & Price of Cotton. LC 67-16343. (Reprints of Economic Classics Ser.). (Illus.). vi, 173p. 1967. reprint ed. 29.50 (*0-678-00230-4*) Kelley.

— Generating Economic Cycles. LC 65-26370. (Reprints of Economic Classics Ser.). (Illus.). xi, 141p. 1967. reprint ed. 25.00 (*0-678-00231-2*) Kelley.

— Law of Wages: An Essay in Statistical Economics. LC 65-26371. (Reprints of Economic Classics Ser.). (Illus.). 196p. 1967. reprint ed. 29.50 (*0-678-00232-0*) Kelley.

— Synthetic Economics. LC 67-18571. (Reprints of Economic Classics Ser.). vii, 186p. 1967. reprint ed. 29.50 (*0-678-00233-9*) Kelley.

Moore, Herb. Axis Correlation: A Modern Guide to Tonal Colors. rev. ed. Moore, Sharon, ed. 72p. (C). (gr. 9-12). 1993. pap. text ed. 15.00 (*0-9635896-0-1*) Moores Music.

Moore, Herbert L., Jr. Rows of Corn: A True Account of a Parris Island Recruit. LC 83-3229. (Illus.). 232p. 1983. 9.95 (*0-87844-048-8*) Sandlapper Pub Co.

Moore, Herff, et al. Language, Customs, & Protocol. LC 90-85486. (Fifty-Minute Ser.). (Illus.). 96p. (Orig.). 1991. pap. 9.95 (*1-56052-097-3*) Crisp Pubns.

Moore, Hillary. Sunburst Guide to Cross Stitch. 1994. 4.98 (*0-7858-0008-5*) Bk Sales Inc.

— Sunburst Guide to Needlepoint. 1994. 4.98 (*0-7858-0012-3*) Bk Sales Inc.

— Sunburst Guide to Patchwork. 1994. 4.98 (*0-7858-0009-3*) Bk Sales Inc.

— Sunburst Guide to Sewing. 1994. 4.98 (*0-7858-0011-5*) Bk Sales Inc.

Moore, Hilmar, jt. auth. see Querido, Rene.

Moore, Honor. Memoir. LC 88-25647. 79p. (Orig.). 1988. pap. 11.95 (*0-9619111-1-5*) Chicory Blue.

Moore, Howard E. Protecting Residences from Wildfires: A Guide for Homeowners, Lawmakers, & Planners. 44p. (Orig.). (C). 1993. pap. text ed. 20.00 (*1-56806-971-5*) Diane Pub.

Moore, Howard W. Plowing My Own Furrow. LC 93-7918. (Studies on Peace & Conflict Resolution). 224p. 1993. reprint ed. pap. 14.95 (*0-8156-0276-6*) Syracuse U Pr.

Moore, Hubert. Rolling Stock. 56p. (Orig.). 1991. pap. 14.95 (*1-870612-51-5*, Pub. by Enitha Pr UK) Dufour.

Moore, Hyatt, jt. auth. see Anderson, Neil.

***Moore, I.** Little Lost Dog. Date not set. pap. 4.99 (*0-517-13330-X*) Random.

Moore, I. D., jt. ed. see Bevin, Keith J.

Moore, Ian & Legner, E. F. An Illustrated Guide to the Genera of the Staphylinidae of America North of Mexico. LC 78-75027. (Illus.). 344p. 1979. pap. 10.00 (*0-931876-31-1*, 4093) ANR Pubns CA.

Moore, Inga. A Big Day for Little Jack. LC 93-6272. (Illus.). 32p. (J). 1994. text ed. 14.95 (*1-56402-418-0*) Candlewick Pr.

— Oh, Little Jack. LC 91-71827. (Illus.). 32p. (J). (ps up). 1992. 14.95 (*1-56402-028-2*) Candlewick Pr.

— Oh, Little Jack. LC 91-71827. 32p. (J). (ps-3). 1994. pap. 4.99 (*1-56402-273-0*) Candlewick Pr.

— Six Dinner Sid. LC 90-42749. (J). (gr. k-3). 1991. pap. 15.00 (*0-671-73199-8*, S&S Bks Young Read) S&S Childrens.

— Six-Dinner Sid. LC 90-42749. (Illus.). 32p. (J). (ps-3). 1993. pap. 5.95 (*0-671-79613-5*, S&S Bks Young Read) S&S Childrens.

— The Truffle Hunter. (Illus.). 32p. (J). (ps-3). 1987. 10.95 (*0-916291-09-X*) Kane-Miller Bk.

Moore, Inga, illus. The Little Book of Prayers. LC 92-30860. (J). 1993. 7.95 (*1-85697-888-5*, Kingfisher LKC) LKC.

— A Spider Bought a Bicycle: And Other Poems for Young Children. 120p. (J). (ps up). 1995. pap. 5.95 (*1-85697-537-1*, Kingfisher LKC) LKC.

Moore, J. & Pizer, R. Moment Methods in Electromagnetics: Techniques & Applications. LC 84-2133. (Antenna Ser.: Nos. 1-641). 398p. 1984. text ed. 260.00 (*0-471-90414-7*) Wiley.

Moore, J. A., jt. auth. see Herb, S. M.

Moore, J. C., jt. auth. see Eilenberg, S.

Moore, J. Casey, ed. Structural Fabrics in Deep Sea Drilling Project Cores from Forearcs. (Memoir Ser.: No. 166). (Illus.). 168p. 1987. 5.00 (*0-8137-1166-5*) Geol Soc.

Moore, J. D. South Africa & Nuclear Proliferation. 260p. 1988. text ed. 39.95 (*0-312-74698-9*) St Martin.

Moore, J. E. Design for Good Acoustics & Noise Control. (Illus.). 1988. reprint ed. pap. text ed. 30.00 (*0-333-24293-9*) Scholium Intl.

Moore, J. F., jt. auth. see Chaykin, H.

Moore, J. G., jt. auth. see Ballard, R. D.

Moore, J. George, jt. auth. see Hacker, Neville.

Moore, J. I. Pharmacology. 3rd ed. (Oklahoma Notes Ser.). (Illus.). 280p. 1992. 17.95 (*0-387-97779-1*) Spr-Verlag.

— Writers on Strategy & Strategic Management: The Theory of Strategy & the Practice of Strategic Management at Enterprise, Corporate, Business & Functional Levels. (Illus.). 336p. 1993. pap. 12.00 (*0-14-013985-0*, Penguin Bks) Viking Penguin.

Moore, J. I., ed. Pharmacology. (Oklahoma Notes Ser.). xi, 247p. (C). 1988. pap. 14.95 (*0-387-96332-4*) Spr-Verlag.

— Pharmacology. (Oklahoma Notes Ser.). xi, 251p. 1991. pap. 15.95 (*0-387-97194-7*) Spr-Verlag.

Moore, J. J. Chemical Metallurgy. 2nd ed. (Illus.). 456p. 1993. pap. 39.95 (*0-7506-1646-6*) Buttrwrth-Heinemann.

Moore, J. J., jt. ed. see Upadhya, K.

Moore, J. Kenneth, ed. see Phillips, Harry R.

***Moore, J. M.** Mechanical Working (Rolling Mills) Dev. of Modal Analysis for Rolling Mills - Final Report. (Technical Steel Research Ser.: No. Eur 14792). 53p. 1994. pap. 12.00 (*92-826-7731-1*, CGNA14792ENC, Pub. by Europ Com) UNIPUB.

Moore, J. M., ed. see Augustus.

Moore, J. M., jt. ed. see Hollier, R.

Moore, J. Michael. Shang Han Lun & Other Traditional Formulas: A Clinical Reference. LC 93-35804. 1993. write for info. (*0-941942-42-2*) Orient Heal Arts.

Moore, J. N. Vida, Herencia y Desarrollo: Life, Inheritance & Development. (SPA.). 4.95 (*84-7645-003-6*, 223062, Pub. by Edit Clie SP) TSELF.

Moore, J. Percy, jt. auth. see Harding, W. A.

Moore, J. R. Principles of Oral Surgery. (Pergamon Series on Dentistry: Vol. 3). 1965. 110.00 (*0-08-011395-8*, Pub. by Pergamon Repr UK) Franklin.

Moore, J. R. & Gillbe, G. V., eds. Principles of Oral Surgery. 3rd ed. 254p. 1988. text ed. 27.95 (*0-7190-0801-8*, Pub. by Manchester Univ Pr UK) St Martin.

Moore, J. R., et al. Intercomparison of Luminous Flux Measurements on High Pressure Sodium, EUR 14076. 106p. 1992. pap. 15.00 (*92-826-3668-2*, CD-NA-14076-EN-C, Pub. by Europ Com) UNIPUB.

Moore, J. Strother, jt. auth. see Boyer, Robert S.

Moore, J. Stuart. Chiropractic in America: The History of a Medical Alternative. LC 92-48232. (Illus.). 240p. (C). 1993. text ed. 34.95 (*0-8018-4539-4*) Johns Hopkins.

Moore, J. T. Introduction to Abstract Algebra. 1975. text ed. 61.00 (*0-12-505750-4*) Acad Pr.

Moore, J. T., jt. auth. see Kruglak, Haym.

Moore, J. Thomas. Night after Christmas. (J). (gr. k up). 1990. pap. 5.95 (*0-925928-07-0*) Tiny Thought.

Moore, J. W. Anasazi. LC 79-56134. (Illus.). 88p. (Orig.). 1980. pap. 8.95 (*0-935800-00-X*) Sunrise Pr IL.

— Balancing the Needs of Water Use. (Environmental Management Ser.). (Illus.). 310p. 1988. 109.00 (*0-387-96709-5*) Spr-Verlag.

— The Changing Environment. (Environmental Management Ser.). (Illus.). x, 240p. 1986. 79.00 (*0-387-96314-6*) Spr-Verlag.

— Inorganic Contaminants of Surface Water: Research & Monitoring Priorities. DeSanto, R. S., ed. (Environmental Management Ser.). (Illus.). 392p. 1990. 89.00 (*0-387-97281-1*) Spr-Verlag.

— Moore's Rules Pamphlet. 1961. write for info. (*0-8205-1415-2*) Bender.

— New & Critical Plants from Raiatea. (BMB Ser.: No. 102). 1974. reprint ed. pap. 15.00 (*0-527-02208-X*) Periodicals Srv.

— Rev. John Moore of Newtown, of Newtown, Long Island, & Some of His Descendants. (Illus.). 541p. 1989. reprint ed. lib. bdg. 89.00 (*0-8328-0880-6*); reprint ed. pap. 81.00 (*0-8328-0881-4*) Higginson Bk Co.

Moore, J. W. & Ramamoorthy, S. Heavy Metals in Natural Waters. (Environmental Management Ser.). (Illus.). 255p. 1983. 80.00 (*0-387-90885-4*) Spr-Verlag.

An Asterisk (*) at the beginning of an entry indicates that the title is appearing in BIP for the first time.

— Organic Chemicals in Natural Water: Applied Monitoring & Impact Assessment. (Environmental Management Ser.). (Illus.). 290p. 1984. 80.00 (*0-387-96034-1*) Spr-Verlag.

Moore, Jack. Power Serve. 210p. (Orig.). 1989. pap. 7.99 (*0-914903-96-9*) Destiny Image.

— Skinheads Shaved for Battle: A Cultural History of American Skinheads. LC 93-70440. (Illus.). 200p. 1993. 37.95 (*0-87972-582-6*); pap. 14.95 (*0-87972-583-4*) Bowling Green Univ.

— Taming Ancient Rivers of Greece. 337p. 1981. 75.00 (*0-9507476-0-2*) St Mut.

Moore, Jack B. Joe DiMaggio: A Bio-Bibliography. LC 85-14665. (Popular Culture Bio-Bibliographies Ser.). (Illus.). 288p. 1986. text ed. 39.95 (*0-313-23917-7*, MJD/, Greenwood Pr) Greenwood.

— Joe DiMaggio: Baseball's Yankee Clipper. LC 87-2369. 263p. 1987. pap. text ed. 9.95 (*0-275-92712-1*, B2712, Praeger Pubs) Greenwood.

Moore, Jack B., jt. auth. see Snyder, Robert E.

Moore, Jack S. The Official Redneck Handbook. Chichester, A. Lee, ed. (Illus.). 146p. (Orig.). 1983. pap. 9.95 (*0-89896-076-2*) Larksdale.

***Moore, Jacob B.** Annals of the Town of Concord, in the County of Merrimack, from Its First Settlement in the Year 1726 to the Year 1823, with Several Biographical Sketches. (Illus.). 112p. 1995. reprint ed. pap. 21.00 (*0-8328-4705-4*) Higginson Bk Co.

Moore, James. Can You Remember to Forget: And 32 Other Questions for Tomorrow's Leaders. 1991. 8.95 (*0-687-04628-9*) Abingdon.

— The Darwin Legend. LC 94-39407. (Illus.). 208p. (Orig.). 1994. 19.99 (*0-8010-6321-3*); pap. 11.99 (*0-8010-6318-3*) Baker Bk.

— Get of Fenris: Werewolf Tribebook. (Werewolf). 72p. 1995. per., pap. 10.00 (*1-56504-326-X*, 3055) White Wolf.

— Gurdjieff: The Anatomy of a Myth. 1991. 27.95 (*1-85230-114-7*, GURDJC) Element MA.

— Gurdjieff: The Anatomy of a Myth-a Biography. (Illus.). 415p. 1993. pap. 19.95 (*1-85230-450-2*) Element MA.

— Self-Image. (Institute of Biblical Counseling Discussion Guides Ser.). 64p. (Orig.). 1992. pap. 5.00 (*0-89109-684-1*) NavPress.

— Standing on the Promises, or Sitting on the Premises. LC 95-8274. 144p. (Orig.). 1995. pap. 9.50 (*0-687-00807-7*) Dimen for Liv.

Moore, James, contrib. Robert M. Ellis - A Painter's Space: Paintings & Works on Paper 1951-1990. (Illus.). 29p. (Orig.). 1990. pap. 10.50 (*0-944282-10-5*) UNM Art Mus.

Moore, James & Micolean, Tyler. Football Techniques Illustrated. LC 62-17402. 96p. reprint ed. pap. 27.40 (*0-317-28590-4*, 2055176) Bks Demand.

***Moore, James & Murphy, Kevin, contribs.** House of Secrets. 1995. pap. 5.99 (*1-56504-843-1*, 11500) White Wolf.

Moore, James, jt. ed. see Baylor, Robert.

Moore, James, jt. auth. see Desmond, Adrian.

Moore, James A. The Chaos Factor. (Mage). 160p. 1994. per., pap. 15.00 (*1-56504-125-9*, 4101) White Wolf.

Moore, James A. & Keene, Arthur S., eds. Archaeological Hammers & Theories. LC 82-11669. 1983. text ed. 59.00 (*0-12-505980-9*) Acad Pr.

Moore, James A., ed. see NATO Advanced Study Institute Staff.

Moore, James A., et al. Experimental Methods in Organic Chemistry. 3rd ed. (C). 1982. text ed. 51.00 (*0-03-056896-X*) SCP.

Moore, James D. WATFIV. 1975. pap. write for info. (*0-87909-876-7*, Reston) P-H.

Moore, James E. Pelican Guide to the Bahamas. 353p. 1988. pap. 12.95 (*0-88289-663-6*) Pelican.

Moore, James F. Christian Theology After the Shoah: A Re-Interpretation of the Passion Narratives. LC 93-2806. (Studies in the Shoah: Vol. VII). 204p. (C). 1993. Alk. paper. lib. bdg. 44.50 (*0-8191-9074-8*) U Pr of Amer.

Moore, James K. Enjoy the Slim Life: The Art of Keeping It Off! 272p. 1991. pap. 9.95 (*0-9629859-0-2*) Pac Coast WA.

Moore, James N. & Janick, Jules, eds. Methods in Fruit Breeding. LC 81-80945. (Illus.). 464p. 1983. 40.00 (*0-911198-63-6*) Purdue U Pr.

Moore, James N., jt. ed. see Janick, Jules.

Moore, James R., ed. History, Humanity & Evolution: Essays for John C. Greene. (Illus.). 464p. (C). 1990. 64. 95 (*0-521-33511-6*) Cambridge U Pr.

— Religion in Victorian Britain, Vol. III: Sources. LC 88-12359. 592p. 1989. text ed. 75.00 (*0-7190-2943-0*, Pub. by Manchester Univ Pr UK); text ed. 24.95 (*0-7190-2944-9*, Pub. by Manchester Univ Pr UK) St Martin.

Moore, James R., Jr., jt. auth. see Moore, Madeleine H.

Moore, James T. Indian & Jesuit: A Seventeenth Century Encounter. 280p. (C). 1982. 12.95 (*0-8294-0395-7*) Loyola Univ Pr.

— Through Fire & Flood: The Catholic Church in Frontier, Texas, 1836-1900. LC 91-34327. (Centennial Series of the Association of Former Students: No. 42). 304p. 1992. 39.50 (*0-89096-504-8*) Tex A&M Univ Pr.

— Two Paths to the New South: The Virginia Debt Controversy, 1870-1883. LC 73-86404. 181p. reprint ed. pap. 51.60 (*0-8357-4296-2*, 2037095) Bks Demand.

Moore, James W. Healing Where It Hurts. LC 92-45706. 144p. (Orig.). 1993. pap. 9.00 (*0-687-16743-4*) Dimen for Liv.

— Is There Life after Stress? LC 91-42390. 144p. (Orig.). 1992. pap. 9.00 (*0-687-19708-2*) Dimen for Liv.

— Moore's Federal Practice, 34 vols. 2nd ed. 1948. Updates. ring bd. write for info. (*0-8205-1410-1*) Bender.

— Moore's Manual: Federal Practice & Procedure, 3 vols. 1962. Updates. ring bd. write for info. (*0-8205-1411-X*) Bender.

— Seizing the Moments. 1992. pap. 9.95 (*0-687-37151-1*) Abingdon.

— Some Things Are Just Too Good Not to Be True. LC 93-44091. 144p. (Orig.). 1994. pap. 9.50 (*0-687-00237-0*) Dimen for Liv.

— When All Else Fails, Read the Instructions. LC 92-24122. 144p. (Orig.). 1993. pap. 9.00 (*0-687-44918-9*) Dimen for Liv.

— Yes, Lord, I Have Sinned but I Have Several Excellent Excuses. LC 90-40832. 112p. 1991. pap. 6.95 (*0-687-46661-X*) Abingdon.

Moore, James W. & Frumer, Louis R. Moore's Manual: Forms, 5 vols. 1964. Updates. ring bd. write for info. (*0-8205-1413-6*) Bender.

Moore, Jamie W. & Moore, Dorothy P. The Army Corps of Engineers & the Evolution of Federal Flood Plain Management Policy. Dane, Sylvia, ed. (Environment & Behavior Program, Special Publication Ser.: No. 20). 200p. (Orig.). (C). 1989. pap. 15.00 (*1-877943-00-2*) Natural Hazards.

Moore, Jane. Cityward Migration: Swedish Data. 1938. 69. 50 (*0-686-51354-1*) Elliots Bks.

Moore, Jane B., jt. ed. see Miller, Ilene.

Moore, Janet B. Pendulum Plus Kit. (Illus.). 32p. 1992. pap. 29.95 (*0-9635665-1-2*) Pendulum Plus.

Moore, Jared S. The Foundations of Psychology. 1977. text ed. 18.95 (*0-8369-8189-8*, 8327) Ayer.

Moore, Jean. ABC of Child Protection Work. 2nd ed. 120p. 1992. pap. 16.95 (*1-85742-027-6*, Pub. by Ashgate UK) Ashgate Pub Co.

— Cat Lover's Yearbook: A Book of Cat Days & Cat Ways. (Illus.). 160p. 1995. 9.98 (*0-8317-5169-X*) Smithmark.

Moore, Jean & Crabb, Richard. Young People's Story of DuPage County. (Illus.). 120p. 1981. 8.95 (*0-916445-03-8*) Crossroads Comm.

Moore, Jean G. The A.B.C. of Child Abuse Work. LC 85-9738. 105p. 1985. pap. 19.95 (*0-566-00860-2*) Ashgate Pub Co.

Moore, Jeanne, tr. see Braun, Otto.

***Moore, Jeanne, et al.** The Faces of Homelessness in London. LC 94-42385. (Illus.). 345p. 1995. text ed. 57. 95 (*1-85521-252-8*, Pub. by Dartmth Pub UK) Ashgate Pub Co.

Moore, Jeff & Carlton, Geoff. The Book of Slugs: A Guide to Slug Fun in the Garden & the Home. (Illus.). 140p. 1982. pap. 4.95 (*0-9606752-1-3*) Sauvie Island.

Moore, Jeffrey A. Crossing the Chasm: Marketing & Selling Smart Products to Apprehensive Customers. LC 17-3183. 224p. 1991. 25.00 (*0-88730-519-9*) Harper Busn.

Moore, Jennifer M., jt. auth. see Hoffman, W. Michael.

Moore, Jeri, jt. ed. see Thorson, Esther.

Moore, Jerold N. Confederate Commissary General: Lucius Bellinger Northrop & the Subsistence Bureau of the Southern Army. (Illus.). 256p. (C). 1995. text ed. 24.95 (*0-942597-75-3*) White Mane Pub.

Moore, Jerrold N. Edward Elgar: A Creative Life. (Illus.). 1984. reprint ed. 98.00 (*0-19-315447-1*) OUP.

— Elgar: A Life in Photographs. (Illus.). 112p. 1988. 35.00 (*0-19-315425-0*) OUP.

— Vaughan Williams: A Life in Photographs. LC 92-15513. (Illus.). 128p. 1992. 39.95 (*0-19-816296-0*, Old Oregon Bk Store) OUP.

Moore, Jerrold N., ed. Elgar & His Publishers: Letters of a Creative Life, 2 vols., Set. (Illus.). 1000p. 1987. 109.00 (*0-19-315446-3*) OUP.

Moore, Jesse T., Jr. A Search for Equality: The National Urban League, 1910-1961. LC 80-24302. (Illus.). 264p. 1981. 30.00 (*0-271-00302-2*) Pa St U Pr.

Moore, Jill. Night of Gold. large type ed. (Linford Romance Library). 288p. 1986. pap. 11.95 (*0-7089-6228-9*, Linford) Ulverscroft.

Moore, Jim. By Way of the Wind. (Illus.). 224p. 1991. 22.95 (*0-924486-09-0*) Sheridan.

— Clinton: Young Man in a Hurry. (Illus.). 290p. 1992. 22. 95 (*1-56530-006-8*) Summit TX.

— Conspiracy of One: The Definite Book on the Kennedy Assassination. 1991. pap. 11.95 (*0-9626219-6-X*) Summit TX.

— Conspiracy of One: The Definitive Book on the Kennedy Assassination. (Illus.). 217p. 1990. 24.95 (*0-9626219-2-7*) Summit TX.

— Conspiracy of One: The Definitive Book on the Kennedy Assassination. Turner, Don, ed. 217p. (C). 1990. 24.95 (*0-9626219-5-1*) Summit TX.

— Flip Line. LC 65-669. 324p. (Orig.). 1981. pap. 3.45 (*0-939662-01-9*) Tuppence.

— The Freedom of History: Poems. LC 88-42975. 104p. (Orig.). 1988. pap. 7.95 (*0-915943-32-8*) Milkweed Ed.

— The Long Experience of Love. LC 94-32531. 100p. (Orig.). 1995. pap. 12.95 (*1-57131-401-6*) Milkweed Ed.

— Rampage: America's Largest Family Murder. (Illus.). 216p. (C). 1991. 19.95 (*1-56530-002-5*) Summit TX.

— Swan - The Second Voyage. (Illus.). 250p. 1994. 22.95 (*0-924486-45-7*) Sheridan.

— UNIX: A Minimal Manual. LC 88-29943. 238p. (C). 1995. pap. text ed. write for info. (*0-7167-8195-6*) W H Freeman.

— When Grief Breaks your Heart. LC 94-19609. 80p. (Orig.). 1994. pap. 4.95 (*0-687-00791-7*) Abingdon.

***Moore, Jim, teller.** How I Got Out of Jail & Ran for Governor of Indiana. LC 95-5818. 120p. (Orig.). (YA). 1994. pap. 9.95 (*0-916147-66-5*) Regent Pr.

— How I Got Out of Jail & Ran for Governor of Indiana: The Jim Moore Story as Told to Claire Burch. LC 95-5818. 1995. write for info. (*0-615-00632-9*) Regent Pr.

Moore, Jim & Vermilyea, Natalie. Ernest Thayer's "Casey at the Bat" Background & Characters of Baseball's Most Famous Poem. 376p. 1994. lib. bdg. 32.50 (*0-89950-997-5*) McFarland & Co.

Moore, Jim & Waterman, Cary, eds. Minnesota Writes: Poetry. LC 87-200754. 240p. (Orig.). 1987. pap. 11.95 (*0-915943-21-2*) Milkweed Ed.

Moore, Jim, et al. In - Sights: Moore Photographs. Leabhart, Thomas, ed. (Mime Journal Ser.). (Illus.). 232p. (Orig.). 1988. pap. text ed. 12.00 (*0-9611066-3-8*) Pomona Coll.

Moore, Jo E. Aesop's Fables: Literature Mini-Unit. (Illus.). 16p. 1989. pap. 5.95 (*1-55799-145-6*, EMC518) Evan-Moor Corp.

— Africa. (Illus.). 16p. 1993. pap. 5.95 (*1-55799-247-9*) Evan-Moor Corp.

— Antarctica. (Illus.). 16p. 1993. pap. 5.95 (*1-55799-246-0*) Evan-Moor Corp.

— Asia. (Illus.). 16p. 1993. pap. 5.95 (*1-55799-244-4*) Evan-Moor Corp.

— Australia. (Illus.). 16p. (J). (gr. 3-6). 1993. pap. 5.95 (*1-55799-243-6*) Evan-Moor Corp.

— Beginning Geography, Vol. 2: Landforms & Bodies of Water. (Illus.). 16p. (J). (gr. k-2). 1993. pap. text ed. 5.95 (*1-55799-253-3*) Evan-Moor Corp.

— Beginning Geography, Vol. 3: Continents & Oceans. (Illus.). 16p. (J). (gr. k-2). 1993. pap. text ed. 5.95 (*1-55799-254-1*) Evan-Moor Corp.

— Big Book of Science Stories, Vol. 2. (Illus.). 64p. 1994. pap. text ed. 11.95 (*1-55799-265-7*) Evan-Moor Corp.

— Children Around the World-Writing Forms. (Illus.). 48p. 1992. pap. 5.95 (*1-55799-239-8*) Evan-Moor Corp.

— Dinosaurs & Other Prehistoric Animals. (Illus.). 48p. 1992. pap. 9.95 (*1-55799-213-4*) Evan-Moor Corp.

— Dragons. (Illus.). 48p. (J). (gr. 2-5). 1990. pap. 5.95 (*1-55799-161-8*) Evan-Moor Corp.

— Endangered Species. (Illus.). 48p. 1992. pap. 5.95 (*1-55799-217-7*) Evan-Moor Corp.

— Europe. (Illus.). 16p. 1993. pap. 5.95 (*1-55799-245-2*) Evan-Moor Corp.

— Families Around the World. (Illus.). 48p. 1992. pap. 9.95 (*1-55799-214-2*) Evan-Moor Corp.

— Forms for Report Writing. (Writing Ser.). (Illus.). 64p. 1994. pap. text ed. 7.95 (*1-55799-286-X*) Evan-Moor Corp.

— How to Write a Story. (Writing Ser.). (Illus.). 48p. 1994. pap. text ed. 5.95 (*1-55799-284-3*, EMC286) Evan-Moor Corp.

— How to Write Nonfiction. (Writing Ser.). (Illus.). 48p. 1994. pap. text ed. 5.95 (*1-55799-285-1*, EMC287) Evan-Moor Corp.

— Learning about the Earth. (Learning About Science Series for PreK-1: Vol. 2). (Illus.). 48p. 1994. pap. text ed. 5.95 (*1-55799-306-8*, EMC845) Evan-Moor Corp.

— Learning about Weather. (Learning About Science Series for PreK-1: Vol. 1). (Illus.). 48p. (J). (ps-1). 1994. pap. text ed. 5.95 (*1-55799-305-X*, EMC844) Evan-Moor Corp.

— Making Books with Beginning Writers. (Illus.). 48p. (J). (gr. k-2). 1992. pap. 6.95 (*1-55799-225-8*, EMC262) Evan-Moor Corp.

— Math & Classroom Pets. (Math Is Everywhere Ser.). (Illus.). 48p. 1994. teacher ed, pap. text ed. 6.45 (*1-55799-322-X*, EMC 094) Evan-Moor Corp.

— Math at Playtime. (Math Is Everywhere Ser.). (Illus.). 48p. 1994. teacher ed, pap. text ed. 6.45 (*1-55799-323-8*, EMC 095) Evan-Moor Corp.

— My Pets. (Illus.). 48p. (J). (ps-1). 1988. pap. 9.95 (*1-55799-131-6*) Evan-Moor Corp.

— North America. (Illus.). 16p. 1993. pap. 5.95 (*1-55799-241-X*) Evan-Moor Corp.

— Science Fun. (Illus.). 48p. 1991. teacher ed, pap. text ed. 4.95 (*1-55799-206-1*, EMC 824) Evan-Moor Corp.

— Science Puzzles. (Illus.). 48p. 1991. teacher ed, pap. text ed. 4.95 (*1-55799-205-3*, EMC 823) Evan-Moor Corp.

— Sharks. (Illus.). 48p. 1992. pap. 5.95 (*1-55799-215-0*) Evan-Moor Corp.

— Shoe Box Centers Writing Activities: Shoe Box Centers. (Illus.). 64p. (J). (gr. 1-3). 1992. pap. 7.95 (*1-55799-224-X*) Evan-Moor Corp.

— Shoebox Center: Math Activities. (Illus.). 64p. (J). (gr. 1-3). 1993. pap. text ed. 7.95 (*1-55799-252-5*) Evan-Moor Corp.

— South America. (Illus.). 16p. 1993. pap. 5.95 (*1-55799-242-8*) Evan-Moor Corp.

— Who Discovered America? (Illus.). 48p. 1992. pap. 5.95 (*1-55799-218-5*) Evan-Moor Corp.

Moore, Jo E. & Camilli, Thomas. Exploring Science Through Literature: Level B. (Illus.). 48p. (J). (gr. 2-3). 1991. pap. 5.95 (*1-55799-203-7*, EMC821) Evan-Moor Corp.

— Exploring Science Through Literature: Level C. (Illus.). 48p. 1991. pap. 5.95 (*1-55799-204-5*, EMC822) Evan-Moor Corp.

Moore, Jo E. & Evans, Joy. El Agua. Ficklin, Dora & Wolfe, Liz, trs. (Science Mini-Units Ser.). (Illus.). 16p. (SPA.). (J). (gr. 1-3). 1992. pap. text ed. 5.95 (*1-55799-234-7*) Evan-Moor Corp.

— Beginning Geography. (Geography Mini-Unit Ser.). (Illus.). 16p. (J). (gr. k-2). 1992. pap. text ed. 5.95 (*1-55799-219-3*) Evan-Moor Corp.

— Categorias. Wolfe, Liz & Ficklin, Dora, trs. (Illus.). 32p. (SPA.). (J). (gr. 1-2). 1990. pap. text ed. 4.95 (*1-55799-180-4*) Evan-Moor Corp.

— Creative Writing Ideas. (Creative Writing Ser.). (Illus.). 80p. (J). (gr. 1-6). 1987. pap. 9.95 (*1-55799-060-3*, EMC206) Evan-Moor Corp.

— Helping Children Learn-Basic Math Skills, Grade 1. (Illus.). 48p. 1994. teacher ed, pap. text ed. 19.45 (*1-55799-333-5*, EMC 089) Evan-Moor Corp.

— Helping Children Learn-Basic Math Skills, Grade 2. (Illus.). 192p. 1994. teacher ed, pap. text ed. 19.45 (*1-55799-334-3*, EMC 090) Evan-Moor Corp.

— Helping Children Learn-Basic Math Skills, Grade 3. (Illus.). 192p. 1994. teacher ed, pap. text ed. 19.45 (*1-55799-335-1*, EMC 091) Evan-Moor Corp.

— How Is It Made? (Illus.). 48p. 1990. pap. 5.95 (*1-55799-162-6*) Evan-Moor Corp.

— How to Make Centers Across the Curriculum. (Illus.). 64p. (J). (gr. k-3). 1992. pap. 11.95 (*1-55799-222-3*, EMC308) Evan-Moor Corp.

— Wolves. (Illus.). 48p. 1990. pap. 5.95 (*1-55799-163-4*) Evan-Moor Corp.

— Write a SUPER Sentence. (Illus.). 32p. (J). (gr. 1-3). 1984. pap. text ed. 4.95 (*1-55799-059-X*) Evan-Moor Corp.

— Writing Poetry with Children. (Illus.). 64p. (J). (gr. 1-6). 1988. pap. 6.95 (*1-55799-129-4*) Evan-Moor Corp.

Moore, Jo E. & Tryon, Leslie. Bears Bears Bears. (Illus.). 48p. (J). (gr. k-1). 1988. pap. 8.95 (*1-55799-130-8*) Evan-Moor Corp.

— The Big Book of Science Rhymes & Chants. (Illus.). 64p. (J). (gr. k-2). 1991. pap. 11.95 (*1-55799-211-8*, EMC306) Evan-Moor Corp.

— The Big Book of Science Stories. (Illus.). 64p. (J). (gr. k-2). 1991. pap. 11.95 (*1-55799-210-X*) Evan-Moor Corp.

— Life Cycles: Science Sequencing Cards. (Illus.). 24p. 1988. pap. 9.95 (*1-55799-132-4*, EMC816) Evan-Moor Corp.

— Paragraph Writing. (Illus.). 32p. (J). (gr. 2-4). 1990. pap. 4.95 (*1-55799-177-4*, EMC246) Evan-Moor Corp.

Moore, Jo E., jt. auth. see DeWeese, Robert.

Moore, Jo E., jt. auth. see Evans, Jo.

Moore, Jo E., jt. auth. see Evans, Joy.

Moore, Jo E., jt. auth. see Evans, Joyy.

Moore, Jo E., et al. A Happy, Healthy Me. (Thematic Resource Unit Ser.). (Illus.). 48p. (J). (ps-1). 1990. pap. text ed. 9.95 (*1-55799-170-7*) Evan-Moor Corp.

— How to Do Plays with Children. (Illus.). 288p. 1994. teacher ed, pap. text ed. 28.80 (*1-55799-332-7*, EMC 110) Evan-Moor Corp.

— Making Seasonal Big Books with Children. (Illus.). 64p. (J). (gr. k-3). 1990. pap. 11.95 (*1-55799-194-4*, EMC304) Evan-Moor Corp.

— Whales. (Illus.). 48p. (J). (gr. 2-5). 1990. pap. 5.95 (*1-55799-164-2*) Evan-Moor Corp.

— Write Every Day. (Illus.). 48p. (J). (gr. 1-6). 1988. pap. 4.95 (*1-55799-128-6*) Evan-Moor Corp.

***Moore, Jo Ellen.** Beginning Reading Bk. 1: Beginning Sounds & Rhymes. (At Home Ser.: Vol. 5). (Illus.). 48p. (J). (gr. k-2). 1995. teacher ed, pap. text ed. 2.95 (*1-55799-342-4*, EMC 617) Evan-Moor Corp.

— Beginning Reading Bk. 2: Short Vowels. (At Home Ser.: Vol. 6). (Illus.). 48p. (J). (gr. k-2). 1995. teacher ed, pap. text ed. 2.95 (*1-55799-343-2*, EMC 618) Evan-Moor Corp.

— Beginning Reading Bk. 3: Long Vowels. (At Home Ser.: Vol. 7). (Illus.). 48p. (J). (gr. k-2). 1995. teacher ed, pap. text ed. 2.95 (*1-55799-344-0*, EMC 619) Evan-Moor Corp.

— Beginning Reading Bk. 4: Word Families. (At Home Ser.: Vol. 8). (Illus.). 48p. (J). (gr. 1-3). 1995. teacher ed, pap. text ed. 2.95 (*1-55799-345-9*, EMC 620) Evan-Moor Corp.

— Getting Ready to Read & Write - Colors & Shapes. (At Home Ser.: Vol. 1). (Illus.). 48p. (J). (ps-1). 1995. teacher ed, pap. text ed. 2.95 (*1-55799-338-6*, EMC 613) Evan-Moor Corp.

— Getting Ready to Read & Write - Draw & Talk. (At Home Ser.: Vol. 4). (Illus.). 48p. (J). (ps-1). 1995. teacher ed, pap. text ed. 2.95 (*1-55799-341-6*, EMC 616) Evan-Moor Corp.

— Getting Ready to Read & Write - Sorting & Sequencing. (At Home Ser.: Vol. 2). (Illus.). 48p. (J). (ps-1). 1995. teacher ed, pap. text ed. 2.95 (*1-55799-339-4*, EMC 614) Evan-Moor Corp.

— Getting Ready to Read & Write - Trace & Write. (At Home Ser.: Vol. 3). (Illus.). 48p. (J). (ps-1). 1995. teacher ed, pap. text ed. 2.95 (*1-55799-340-8*, EMC 615) Evan-Moor Corp.

— Grammar & Punctuation. (At Home Ser.: Vol. 24). (Illus.). 48p. (J). (gr. 4-6). 1995. teacher ed, pap. text ed. 2.95 (*0-614-06232-2*, EMC 636) Evan-Moor Corp.

— Grammar & Punctuation, Bk. 1. (At Home Ser.: Vol. 22). (Illus.). 48p. (J). (ps-1). 1995. teacher ed, pap. text ed. 2.95 (*1-55799-359-9*, EMC 634) Evan-Moor Corp.

— Grammar & Punctuation, Bk. 21. (At Home Ser.: Vol. 23). (Illus.). 48p. (J). (gr. 2-4). 1995. teacher ed, pap. text ed. 2.95 (*1-55799-360-2*, EMC 635) Evan-Moor Corp.

— Handwriting - Cursive. (At Home Ser.: Vol. 16). (Illus.). 48p. (J). (gr. 2-6). 1995. teacher ed, pap. text ed. 2.95 (*1-55799-353-X*, EMC 628) Evan-Moor Corp.

— Handwriting - Manuscript. (At Home Ser.: Vol. 15). (Illus.). 48p. (J). (gr. k-2). 1995. teacher ed, pap. text ed. 2.95 (*1-55799-352-1*, EMC 627) Evan-Moor Corp.

— Series about Children from Many Lands. (Illus.). 64p. (J). (gr. k-2). 1993. teacher ed, pap. 11.95 (*1-55799-248-7*, EMC 310) Evan-Moor Corp.

— Writing - All about Me. (At Home Ser.: Vol. 18). (Illus.). 48p. (J). (gr. k-2). 1995. teacher ed, pap. text ed. 2.95 (*1-55799-355-6*, EMC 630) Evan-Moor Corp.

— Writing - How to Write a Report. (At Home Ser.: Vol. 21). (Illus.). 48p. (J). (gr. 5-6). 1995. teacher ed, pap. text ed. 2.95 (*1-55799-358-0*, EMC 633) Evan-Moor Corp.

— Writing - My Own Stories. (At Home Ser.: Vol. 20). (Illus.). 48p. (J). (gr. 4-6). 1995. teacher ed, pap. text ed. 2.95 (*1-55799-357-2*, EMC 632) Evan-Moor Corp.

— Writing - Paragraphs. (At Home Ser.: Vol. 19). (Illus.). 48p. (J). (gr. 4-6). 1995. teacher ed, pap. text ed. 2.95 (1-55799-356-4, EMC 631) Evan-Moor Corp.

— Writing - Words & Sentences. (At Home Ser.: Vol. 17). (Illus.). 48p. (J). (gr. k-2). 1995. teacher ed, pap. text ed. 2.95 (1-55799-354-8, EMC 629) Evan-Moor Corp.

***Moore, Jo Ellen & Evans, Joy.** How to Plan Your School Year. (Teaching Strategies Ser.). (Illus.). 192p. (J). (gr. k-6). 1994. teacher ed, pap. 14.95 (1-55799-155-3, EMC 992) Evan-Moor Corp.

***Moore, Jo Ellen & Holliman, Linda.** Thematic Teaching. (Teaching Strategies Ser.). (Illus.). 86p. (J). (gr. k-6). 1994. teacher ed, pap. 14.95 (1-55799-197-9, EMC 996) Evan-Moor Corp.

***Moore, Jo Ellen & Shiran, Gary.** The Life of Christopher Columbus - A Timeline. (Illus.). 16p. (Orig.). (J). (gr. 2-6). 1992. teacher ed, pap. 9.95 (1-55799-226-6, EMC 354) Evan-Moor Corp.

***Moore, Jo Ellen & Tryon, Leslie.** Never Too Old for Picture Books. (Illus.). 48p. (J). (gr. 3-6). 1989. teacher ed, pap. 5.95 (1-55799-151-0, EMC 514) Evan-Moor Corp.

Moore, Jo Ellen, jt. auth. see Evans, Joy.

Moore, Joan & Pinderhughes, Raquel, eds. In the Barrios: Latinos & the Underclass Debate. 352p. 1993. 49.95 (0-87154-612-4); pap. 16.95 (0-87154-613-2) Russell Sage.

Moore, Joan, jt. ed. see Glick, Ronald.

Moore, Joan W. Going Down to the Barrio: Homeboys & Homegirls in Change. (C). 1991. 39.95 (0-87722-854-X); pap. 18.95 (0-87722-855-8) Temple U Pr.

Moore, Joan W. & Moore, Burton M. Social Problems. (Illus.). 464p. (C). 1982. text ed. write for info. (0-13-817387-7) P-H.

Moore, Joan W. & Pachon, Harry. Hispanics in the United States. (Illus.). 208p. (C). 1985. pap. text ed. write for info. (0-13-388984-X) P-H.

Moore, Joanna D. Participating in Explanatory Dialogues: Interpreting & Responding to Questions in Context. (ACL-MIT Series in Natural Language Processing). (Illus.). 350p. 1994. 47.50 (0-262-13301-6, Bradford Bks) MIT Pr.

Moore, JoAnne, jt. auth. see Garrett, Linda J.

Moore, JoAnne, jt. auth. see Roach, Catharyn.

***Moore, Joanne I., ed.** Pharmacology. 4th ed. LC 94-43678. (Oklahoma Notes Ser.). 1995. write for info. (0-387-94394-3) Spr-Verlag.

Moore, Joe B. Japanese Workers & the Struggle for Power, 1945-1947. LC 82-70552. (Illus.). 272p. 1983. 23.95 (0-299-09320-4) U of Wis Pr.

***Moore, Joellen.** Getting Ready to Read Vol. 1: Readiness Fundamentals. (Illus.). 48p. (J). (ps-1). 1995. teacher ed, pap. text ed. 19.95 (1-55799-371-8, EMC 389) Evan-Moor Corp.

Moore, Johanna, tr. see Stefan, Verena.

***Moore, Johanna D. & Lehman, Jill F., eds.** Proceedings of the Seventeenth Annual Conference of the Cognitive Science Society. 824p. 1995. pap. 125.00 (0-8058-2159-7) L Erlbaum Assocs.

Moore, John. Colloquial Vietnamese. 1994. pap. 35.00 (0-415-09207-8, Pub. by Tavistock UK) Routledge Chapman & Hall.

— Feel Safe Anywhere: You Can Be Your Own Bodyguard. Ancona, Joe, ed. LC 92-61239. 101p. (Orig.). 1992. pap. 10.00 (0-9633458-0-X) Tiger Ent.

— The First Fleet Marines: Seventeen Eighty-Six to Seventeen Ninety-Two. LC 86-30904. (Illus.). 345p. 1988. text ed. 39.95 (0-7022-2065-5, Pub. by Univ Queensland Pr AT) Intl Spec Bk.

— Ramon de la Cruz. LC 70-153997. (Twayne's World Authors Ser.). 181p. (C). 1972. lib. bdg. 17.95 (0-8290-1746-1) Irvington.

— Sexuality Spirituality: A Study of Feminine-Masculine Relationships. 256p. 1990. pap. 14.95 (0-906540-10-0) Element MA.

— Slay & Rescue. 256p. 1993. mass mkt. 4.99 (0-671-72152-6) Baen Bks.

Moore, John, ed. MIT Marine-Related Research Directory, 1993-1994. Date not set. write for info. (1-56172-008-9) MIT Sea Grant.

Moore, John & Moore, Patricia. Enjoy Arithmetic: Addition. (C). 1988. text ed. 30.00 (1-871044-15-4, Pub. by Hawthorns Pubns UK) St Mut.

— Enjoy Arithmetic: Answers. (C). 1988. text ed. 30.00 (1-871044-30-8, Pub. by Hawthorns Pubns UK) St Mut.

— Enjoy Arithmetic: Division. (C). 1988. text ed. 30.00 (1-871044-10-3, Pub. by Hawthorns Pubns UK) St Mut.

— Enjoy Arithmetic: Multiplication. (C). 1988. text ed. 21.00 (1-871044-05-7, Pub. by Hawthorns Pubns UK) St Mut.

— Enjoy Arithmetic: Revision. (C). 1988. text ed. 21.00 (1-871044-25-1, Pub. by Hawthorns Pubns UK) St Mut.

— Enjoy Arithmetic: Subtraction. (C). 1988. text ed. 21.00 (1-871044-20-0, Pub. by Hawthorns Pubns UK) St Mut.

Moore, John & Morrison, Neil. Someone Else's Problem? Teacher Development to Meet Special Educational Needs. 180p. 1988. 55.00 (1-85000-373-4, Falmer Pr); pap. 30.00 (1-85000-374-2, Falmer Pr) Taylor & Francis.

Moore, John & Rodchue, Soawalak. Colloquial Thai: A Complete Language Course. LC 94-11582. 1994. write for info. (0-415-09574-3); Cassettes. audio write for info. (0-415-09575-1) Routledge.

Moore, John & Vuong, Tuan D. Colloquial Vietnamese. LC 93-33737. 1994. write for info. (0-415-09205-1); audio write for info. (0-415-09206-X) Routledge.

Moore, John, tr. see Agasso, Domenica.

Moore, John, jt. auth. see Gabriel, Michael.

Moore, John, tr. see Lefebvre, Henri.

Moore, John, et al. Voices of the People: The Politics & Life of "La Sociale" at the End of the Second Empire. (History Workshop Ser.). 376p. 1988. text ed. 65.00 (0-7102-1308-5, RKP) Routledge.

Moore, John A. Anabaptist Portraits. LC 84-12769. 256p. (Orig.). 1984. pap. 10.95 (0-8361-3361-7) Herald Pr.

— Baptist Mission Portraits. 180p. (Orig.). 1994. pap. 11.95 (1-880837-79-X) Smyth & Helwys.

Moore, John A., Jr. The Pursuit of Happiness: Government & Politics in America. 5th ed. 416p. (C). 1992. pap. write for info. (0-02-383190-1) Macmillan.

***Moore, John A.** Science As a Way of Knowing: The Foundations of Modern Biology. 1993. text ed. 34.50 (0-674-79481-8) HUP.

— Science As a Way of Knowing: The Foundations of Modern Biology. (Illus.). 544p. (C). 1993. text ed. 29.95 (0-674-79480-X) HUP.

— Write for the Religion Market. LC 80-25607. 128p. 1981. 14.95 (0-88280-084-1) ETC Pubns.

Moore, John A., Jr. & Murphy, John E., eds. A Grand Experiment: The Constitution at 200. LC 87-16754. 192p. 1987. 40.00 (0-8420-2289-9) Scholarly Res Inc.

Moore, John A., Jr., jt. ed. see Englehart, Stephen F.

Moore, John A., jt. ed. see Nicholson, William J.

Moore, John B. Digest of International Law, 8 Vols, Set. LC 77-101908. reprint ed. 1,045.00 (0-404-04420-4) AMS Pr.

— Four Phases of American Development: Federalism, Democracy, Imperialism, Expansion. LC 72-109551. (Law, Politics & History Ser.). 1970. reprint ed. lib. bdg. 32.50 (0-306-71905-3) Da Capo.

— History & Digest of the International Arbitrations to Which the United States Has Been a Party, 6 vols., Set. LC 74-19729. reprint ed. 1,800.00 (0-404-12270-1) AMS Pr.

— International Law & Some Current Illusions & Other Essays. 381p. 1987. reprint ed. lib. bdg. 37.50 (0-8377-2435-X) Rothman.

— Pascal: Text & Reference. 2nd ed. (C). 1984. pap. text ed. 31.00 (0-8359-5440-4, Reston) P-H.

Moore, John B., ed. see Buchanan, James.

Moore, John B., jt. auth. see Kelmke, Uwe.

Moore, John B., Jr., jt. auth. see Magill, Jane M.

Moore, John B., jt. auth. see Simms, Clifford R.

Moore, John C. Country Men. LC 69-17585. (Essay Index Reprint Ser.). 1977. 20.95 (0-8369-0088-X) Ayer.

— Missouri. Evans, Clement A., ed. (Confederate Military History Extended Edition Ser.: Vol. XII). (Illus.). 451p. 1988. reprint ed. 50.00 (1-56837-031-8) Broadfoot.

Moore, John C., jt. ed. see Sheringham, Hugh.

Moore, John E., ed. Jane's Fighting Ships 1975-76. LC 75-15172. 1975. 79.50 (0-531-03251-5) Key Bk Serv.

— Jane's Fighting Ships 1976-77. LC 75-15172. 1976. 79.50 (0-934636-03-6) Key Bk Serv.

Moore, John E. & Jackson, Julia A., eds. Geology, Hydrology & History of the Washington DC Area. LC 89-83680. (Illus.). (Orig.). 1989. pap. text ed. 14.95 (0-922152-00-4) Am Geol.

Moore, John E., jt. ed. see Sergiovanni, Thomas J.

Moore, John F. Superman: "Under a Yellow Sun" A Novel by Clark Kent. Carlin, Mike, ed. (Illus.). 64p. (YA). 1994. pap. 5.95 (1-56389-109-3) DC Comics.

Moore, John H. The Cheyenne Nation: A Social & Demographic History. LC 87-5856. (Illus.). xxvi, 390p. 1987. 40.00 (0-8032-3107-5) U of Nebr Pr.

— Columbia & Richland County: A South Carolina Community, 1740-1990. LC 92-18919. (Illus.). 534p. 1992. text ed. 29.95 (0-87249-827-1) U of SC Pr.

— The Emergence of the Cotton Kingdom in the Old Southwest: Mississippi, 1770-1860. LC 87-2803. (Illus.). 352p. 1988. text ed. 45.00 (0-8071-1382-4); pap. text ed. 17.95 (0-8071-1404-9) La State U Pr.

— The Federal Role in University Research: The Coming Years. Pejovich, Steve & Dethloff, Henry, eds. (Series on Public Issues: No. 20). 9p. 1985. pap. 2.00 (0-86599-056-5) PERC.

— The Political Economy of North American Indians. LC 92-50719. (C). 1993. 32.95 (0-8061-2505-5) U of Okla Pr.

— South Carolina in the Eighteen Eighties: A Gazetteer. 1989. 19.95 (0-87844-069-0) Sandlapper Pub Co.

Moore, John H., ed. Legacies of the Collapse of Marxism. 276p. (C). 1994. 59.50 (0-913969-71-0, G Mason Univ Pr); pap. 24.50 (0-913969-72-9, G Mason Univ Pr) Univ Pub Assocs.

— To Promote Prosperity: U. S. Domestic Policy in the Mid-1980's. (Publication Ser.: No. 295). 464p. 1984. 7.98 (0-8179-7951-4) Hoover Inst Pr.

Moore, John H., ed. see Brevard, Keziah G.

Moore, John H., jt. auth. see Sergiovanni, Thomas J.

Moore, John H., ed. see Vignoles, Charles B.

Moore, John H., ed. see Zaleski, Eugene.

Moore, John H., et al. Building Scientific Apparatus. 1983. text ed. write for info. (0-201-05532-5, Adv Bk Prog) Addison-Wesley.

— Building Scientific Apparatus. 2nd ed. (Illus.). 576p. (C). 1989. 52.95 (0-201-13187-0, Adv Bk Prog); pap. 39.95 (0-201-13189-7, Adv Bk Prog) Addison-Wesley.

Moore, John J. Chemical Metallurgy. 2nd ed. 408p. 1990. text ed. 70.00 (0-408-05369-0) Buttrwrth-Heinemann.

Moore, John L. Letters to Jess. LC 90-31946. 197p. 1990. 14.95 (0-911519-23-8) Richelieu Court.

— Speaking of Washington: Facts, Firsts, Folklore. 288p. 1993. 34.95 (0-87187-762-7); pap. 16.95 (0-87187-741-4) Congr Quarterly.

Moore, John L., jt. ed. see Diller, Daniel C.

Moore, John M. Aristotle & Xenophon on Democracy & Oligarchy. LC 74-16713. 1975. pap. 16.00 (0-520-02909-7) U CA Pr.

— South Today. LC 75-152996. (Select Bibliographies Reprint Ser.). 1977. reprint ed. 25.95 (0-8369-5748-2) Ayer.

— Three Aspects of the Late Alfred Lord Tennyson. LC 79-185968. (Studies in Tennyson: No. 27). vi, 144p. 1972. reprint ed. lib. bdg. 55.95 (0-8383-1387-6) M S G Haskell Hse.

Moore, John M., ed. Friends in the Delaware Valley: Philadelphia Yearly Meeting, 1681-1981. 273p. 1981. 5.00 (0-9609122-0-7); pap. 3.00 (0-9609122-1-5) Friends Hist Assn.

Moore, John N. Crisis in the Gulf: Enforcing the Rule of Law. (Terrorism, Documents of International & Local Control, Second Ser.: Vol. 1). 677p. 1992. 60.00 (0-379-20166-6) Oceana.

— Law & the Indo-China War. LC 73-166383. 704p. 1972. 110.00 (0-691-03089-8); pap. 26.95 (0-691-10004-7) Princeton U Pr.

— The Secret War in Central America: Sandinista Assault on World Order. LC 86-28092. 204p. 1987. text ed. 42.95 (0-313-27041-4, U7041, Greenwood Pr) Greenwood.

Moore, John N., ed. The Arab-Israeli Conflict, Vol. IV: The Difficult Search for Peace, 1975-1988, 2 pts. (American Society of International Law Ser.). 1992. 99.50 (0-691-05672-2) Princeton U Pr.

— The Arab-Israeli Conflict, Vol. IV: The Difficult Search for Peace, 1975-1988, 2 pts., Pt. 2. (American Society of International Law Ser.). 1992. 99.50 (0-691-05678-1) Princeton U Pr.

— Deception & Deterrence: In "Wars of National Liberation," State-Sponsored Terrorism, & Other Forms of Secret Warfare. LC 95-68696. (C). 1995. text ed. write for info. (0-89089-858-8) Carolina Acad Pr.

— International & United States Documents on Oceans Law & Policy, 5 vols., Set. LC 86-83006. 4550p. 1986. lib. bdg. 265.00 (0-89941-529-6, 304640) W S Hein.

— The Vietnam Debate: A Fresh Look at the Arguments. LC 89-30902. 330p. (Orig.). (C). 1990. pap. text ed. 24.50 (0-8191-7417-3, Ctr for Law & Natl Security) U Pr of Amer.

Moore, John N. & Turner, Robert F. International Law & the Brezhnev Doctrine. 144p. (Orig.). (C). 1987. lib. bdg. 40.50 (0-8191-5794-5, Ctr for Law & Natl Security); pap. text ed. 17.00 (0-8191-5795-3, Ctr for Law & Natl Security) U Pr of Amer.

Moore, John N., ed. see Tipson, Frederick, et al.

***Moore, John N., et al.** National Security Law Documents. LC 94-72697. 998p. (C). 1995. lib. bdg. 75.00 (0-89089-854-5) Carolina Acad Pr.

Moore, John R. Defoe's Sources for Robert Drury's Journal. LC 72-6862. (English Literature Ser.: No. 33). 1972. reprint ed. lib. bdg. 46.95 (0-8383-1656-5) M S G Haskell Hse.

— The Impact of Foreign Direct Investment on an Underdeveloped Economy: The Venezuelan Case. Bruchey, Stuart & Bruchey, Eleanor, eds. LC 76-5018. (American Business Abroad Ser.). 1976. lib. bdg. 31.95 (0-405-09285-7) Ayer.

— Senator Josiah William Bailey of North Carolina: A Political Biography. LC 68-24639. 271p. reprint ed. 77.30 (0-8357-9118-1, 2017914) Bks Demand.

Moore, John R., ed. The Economic Impact of TVA. LC 67-12217. 179p. reprint ed. pap. 51.10 (0-317-29307-9, 2022220) Bks Demand.

— Representative Essays: English & American. LC 72-284. (Essay Index Reprint Ser.). 1977. reprint ed. 23.95 (0-8369-2808-3) Ayer.

Moore, John T. The Bishop of Cottontown: A Story of the Southern Cotton Mills. LC 72-4610. (Black Heritage Library Collection). (Illus.). 1977. reprint ed. 35.95 (0-8369-9113-3) Ayer.

— Pepito's Journey. 47p. 1987. pap. 3.95 (92-1-100308-3, E.87.I.4) UN.

— Pepito's World. 1988. 4.95 (92-1-100399-7, E.88.I.14) UN.

— Songs & Stories from Tennessee. LC 70-94739. (Short Story Index Reprint Ser.). 1977. 23.95 (0-8369-3119-X) Ayer.

Moore, John T., jt. ed. see Elliott, Colleen M.

Moore, John T., et al. Christmas Classics for Children. (J). (ps-00). 1981. 14.99 (0-570-04058-2, 56-1351) Concordia.

Moore, John T., et al, eds. Tennessee Civil War Questionnaires, 5 vols., 1. 1985. 30.00 (0-89308-216-3) Southern Hist Pr.

— Tennessee Civil War Questionnaires, 5 vols., 2. 1985. 30.00 (0-89308-217-1) Southern Hist Pr.

— Tennessee Civil War Questionnaires, 5 vols., 3. 1985. 30.00 (0-89308-218-X) Southern Hist Pr.

— Tennessee Civil War Questionnaires, 5 vols., 4. 1985. 30.00 (0-89308-219-8) Southern Hist Pr.

— Tennessee Civil War Questionnaires, 5 vols., 5. 1985. 30.00 (0-89308-220-1) Southern Hist Pr.

— Tennessee Civil War Questionnaires, 5 vols., Set. 1985. 150.00 (0-89308-221-X) Southern Hist Pr.

Moore, John Travers. Poems: On Writing Poetry. LC 79-181366. 1971. 5.00 (0-87212-025-2) Libra.

Moore, John V., Jr. Gwinnett County, Georgia: Eighteen-Sixty Census. 242p. 1986. 15.00 (0-317-56127-8) Gwinnett Hist.

Moore, John W. Complete Encyclopedia of Music. LC 72-1713. reprint ed. 79.50 (0-404-09916-5) AMS Pr.

— A Dictionary of Musical Information. LC 72-1714. reprint ed. 32.50 (0-404-09915-7) AMS Pr.

— Labor Union Elections & Corporate Financial Performance. rev. ed. LC 94-45049. (Studies on Industrial Productivity). 173p. 1995. 44.00 (0-8153-1973-8) Garland.

— Moore's Notes on Printing & Publishing in the United States, 1420-1886. 1973. 59.95 (0-8490-0668-6) Gordon Pr.

Moore, John W., ed. Iterations: Computing in the Journal of Chemical Education. 1981. 20.00 (0-910362-17-3) Chem Educ.

Moore, John W. & Pearson, Ralph G. Kinetics & Mechanism. 3rd ed. LC 81-981. 455p. 1981. text ed. 77.95 (0-471-03558-0) Wiley.

Moore, John W., jt. ed. see Batt, Russell.

Moore, Johnnie N., jt. auth. see Fritz, William J.

Moore, Jonathan, ed. Campaign for President: The Managers Look at '84. LC 85-20070. 320p. 1986. text ed. 49.95 (0-86569-132-0, Auburn Hse); pap. 16.95 (0-86569-136-3, Auburn Hse) Greenwood.

Moore, Joseph. Choice: Confirmation Journal. 96p. 1993. pap. text ed. 3.95 (0-8091-9572-0) Paulist Pr.

— Choice: Leader's Guide, a Confirmation Process for Emerging Young Adults. 160p. 1993. pap. 9.95 (0-8091-9573-9) Paulist Pr.

— Friend for the Journey: A Peer Ministry Training Program for Teens. 1994. teacher ed 12.95 (0-86716-210-4); 5.95 (0-86716-211-2) St Anthony Mess Pr.

— Helping Skills for the Nonprofessional Counselor. 72p. 1992. 3.95 (0-86716-174-4) St Anthony Mess Pr.

— Learning to Serve - Serving to Learn: A Christian Service Program for Students. LC 94-70327. 112p. (Orig.). (YA). (gr. 9-12). 1993. pap. text ed. 3.95 (0-87793-526-2); teacher ed, pap. text ed. 10.95 (0-87793-531-9) Ave Maria.

— Monday Morning Jesus. 96p. (Orig.). 1984. pap. 3.95 (0-8091-2591-9) Paulist Pr.

— Nurturing Young Catholics: A Guide for Confirmation Sponsors, & Other Caring Adults. LC 95-7826. 64p. (Orig.). 1995. pap. 4.95 (0-8091-3575-2) Paulist Pr.

— Prayers for a New Generation. LC 91-21397. 64p. 1991. pap. 4.95 (0-8091-3246-X) Paulist Pr.

— When a Teenager Chooses You - As Friend, Confidante, Confirmation Sponsor: Practical Advice for Any Adult. rev. ed. 82p. 1989. 3.95 (0-86716-139-6) St Anthony Mess Pr.

Moore, Joseph A. Famous Leaders of Industry: Life Stories of Men Who Have Succeeded, Fifth Series. LC 68-8505. (Essay Index Reprints - Famous Leaders Ser). 1977. reprint ed. 28.95 (0-8369-2326-X) Ayer.

Moore, Joseph H., ed. First Families of Henry County, Georgia Vol. I. (Illus.). 766p. 1993. 65.00 (0-9628557-3-1) Genlgcl Socs Henry & Clayton.

Moore, Joseph T. Pride Against Prejudice: The Biography of Larry Doby. LC 87-17743. (Contributions in Afro-American & African Studies: No. 113). 208p. 1988. text ed. 49.95 (0-313-25995-X, MPJ/, Greenwood Pr) Greenwood.

— Pride Against Prejudice: The Biography of Larry Doby. LC 87-17743. 208p. 1988. pap. text ed. 12.95 (0-275-92984-1, B2984, Praeger Pubs) Greenwood.

Moore, Josephine C. Brain Atlas & Functional Systems. (Illus.). 58p. (Orig.). (C). 1993. 22.00 (1-56900-000-X) Am Occup Therapy.

Moore, Joy, ed. see Thurston, Doris.

Moore, Judith. The Appearance of Truth: The Story of Elizabeth Canning & Eighteenth-Century Narrative. LC 93-46260. 1994. write for info. (0-87413-494-3) U Delaware Pr.

— The Left Coast of Paradise: California & the American Heart. LC 87-20481. 256p. 1987. 20.00 (0-939149-03-6) Soho Press.

***Moore, Julia & Johnson, Barbara.** Choosing Losing. 1995. write for info. (0-87397-998-2) Strode.

***Moore, Karen B.** Book Binding Made Easy. (Illus.). 129p. 1994. 29.95 (1-57002-034-5); pap. 19.95 (1-57002-009-4) Univ Publng Hse.

***Moore, Kate.** An Improper Widow. 224p. (Orig.). 1995. mass mkt. 3.99 (0-380-77542-5) Avon.

— The Mercenary Major. 224p. (Orig.). 1994. mass mkt. 3.99 (0-380-77541-7) Avon.

— Sweet Bargain. 224p. (Orig.). 1993. mass mkt. 3.99 (0-380-77056-3) Avon.

— To Kiss a Thief. (Regency Romance Ser.). 224p. (Orig.). 1992. mass mkt. 3.99 (0-380-76473-3) Avon.

Moore, Katharine. Moving House. large type ed. 201p. 1989. reprint ed. lib. bdg. 9.47 (1-85089-263-6, Pub. by ISIS UK) Transaction Pubs.

Moore, Katherine D., jt. auth. see Van Vactor, David.

Moore, Kathleen. Inductive Arguments: Developing Critical Thinking Skills. 176p. (C). 1994. per. 18.95 (0-8403-8475-0) Kendall-Hunt.

Moore, Kathleen D. Pardons: Justice, Mercy, & the Public Interest. 288p. 1989. 27.95 (0-19-505871-2) OUP.

— Reasoning & Writing. LC 92-20965. 384p. (C). 1993. pap. write for info. (0-02-383325-4) Macmillan.

— Riverwalking. 176p. 1995. 19.95 (1-55821-408-9) Lyons & Burford.

***Moore, Kathleen M.** Al-Mughtaribun: American Law & the Transformation of Muslim Life in the United States. (Middle Eastern Studies Ser.). 208p. (C). 1995. text ed. 49.50x (0-7914-2579-7); pap. text ed. 16.95x (0-7941-2580-8) State U NY Pr.

Moore, Kathryn. Manhole Covers of Ft. Wayne, Indiana. (Illus.). 128p. (Orig.). 1989. pap. 10.95 (0-89708-191-9) And Bks.

Moore, Kathryn C. My First Flight. rev. ed. Hutson, Ronald, ed. (Illus.). (J). (ps-4). 1991. lib. bdg. 3.95 (0-9633295-0-2) K Cs Bks N Stuff.

***Moore, Kathryn M. & Amey, Marilyn J.** Making Sense of the Dollars: The Costs & Uses of Faculty Compensation. Fife, Jonathan D., ed. & frwd. by. (ASHE-ERIC Higher Education Report Ser.: No. 5). 111p. (Orig.). 1994. pap. 18.00x (1-878380-26-5) GWU Schl E&HD.

Moore, Kathryn M. & Trow, Jo Anne J. Professional Advancement Kit - What to Do until the Mentor Arrives: Administrative Procedures - A Practice Manual. (Orig.). 1982. 13.50 (0-686-82337-0) Natl Assn Women.

M

An Asterisk (*) at the beginning of an entry indicates that the title is appearing in BIP for the first time.

Moore, Kathryn M. & Twombly, Susan B., eds. Administrative Careers & the Marketplace. LC 85-644752. (New Directions for Higher Education Ser.: No. HE 72). 1990. 16.95 (1-55542-808-8) Jossey-Bass.

Moore, Kay. Gathering the Missing Pieces. LC 94-9667. 1995. 11.99 (0-8054-5355-5) Broadman.

— If You Lived at the Time of the Civil War. (J). (gr. 4-7). 1993. pap. 4.95 (0-590-45422-6) Scholastic Inc.

Moore, Keith D., jt. auth. see Coddington, Dean C.

Moore, Keith L. Clinically Oriented Anatomy. 3rd ed. (Illus.). 930p. 1992. 53.00 (0-683-06133-X) Williams & Wilkins.

Moore, Keith L. & Agur, Anne. Essential Clinical Anatomy. 3rd ed. 930p. 1992. 78.00 (0-683-06136-4) Williams & Wilkins.

Moore, Keith L. & Persaud, T. V. Before We Are Born: Basic Embryology & Birth Defects. 4th ed. LC 92-48476. (Illus.). 336p. 1993. pap. text ed. 28.50 (0-7216-4665-4) Saunders.

— The Developing Human: Clinically Oriented Embryology. 4th ed. LC 92-49327. (Illus.). 496p. 1993. pap. text ed. 18.95 (0-7216-4620-4) Saunders.

Moore, Keith L., et al. Color Atlas of Clinical Embryology. LC 93-26435. 1994. text ed. 93.50 (0-7216-4663-8) Saunders.

— Qur'an & Modern Science: Correlation Studies. (Illus.). 62p. (Orig.). (C). 1991. pap. text ed. 5.95 (0-9627236-0-6) Islamic Academy Sci Res.

Moore, Kelly. Deadly Medicine. 1989. mass mkt. 4.99 (0-312-91579-9) St Martin.

Moore, Ken. Bread Baking: Problems & Their Solutions. 2nd rev. ed. 32p. 1992. 2.25 (0-9632986-0-7) Moores Pub.

Moore, Kendall & Thompson, Sally. The Surgical Beauty Racket. LC 78-51044. 1979. 22.95 (0-87949-126-4) Ashley Bks.

Moore, Kenneth. Colt Single Action Army Revolvers & the London Agency. LC 90-60405. (Illus.). 144p. 1990. 35.00 (0-917218-43-4) A Mowbray.

Moore, Kenneth, ed. Waymarks: The Notre Dame Inaugural Lectures in Anthropology. LC 86-40339. 160p. 1988. text ed. 18.95 (0-268-01939-8); pap. text ed. 9.95 (0-268-01941-X) U of Notre Dame Pr.

Moore, Kenneth, ed. see Ortega y Gasset, Jose.

Moore, Kenneth C. Airport, Aircraft & Airline Security. 2nd ed. 424p. 1991. 49.95 (0-7506-9019-4) Buttrwrth-Heinemann.

Moore, Kenneth D. Classroom Teaching Skills. 3rd ed. LC 94-11081. 1994. pap. text ed. write for info. (0-07-042922-7) McGraw.

Moore, Kenneth D. & Quinn, Cheri L. Secondary Instructional Methods. 512p. 1994. pap. write for info. (0-697-11792-8) Brown & Benchmark.

Moore, Kenneth D., jt. auth. see Hopkins, W. Scott.

***Moore, Kenneth J., et al, eds.** Post-Harvest Physiology & Preservation of Forages: Proceedings of a Symposium Sponsored by C-6 of the Crop Science Society of America. LC 95-6087. (CSSA Special Publication: No. 22). 1995. write for info. (0-89118-539-9) Am Soc Agron.

Moore, Kenny. Best Efforts. LC 80-2057. 199p. 1992. reprint ed. pap. 12.95 (0-915297-10-8, BES) Cedarwinds.

Moore, Kevin, ed. Museum Management. LC 94-9057. (Leicester Readers in Museum Studies). 285p. 1995. 79.95 (0-415-11278-8, B4630, Routledge NY); pap. 29.95 (0-415-11279-6, B4634, Routledge NY) Routledge.

Moore, Kevin L. Iterative Learning Control for Deterministic Systems. Grimble, M. J. & Johnson, M., eds. LC 92-15936. (Advances in Industrial Control Ser.). (Illus.). 200p. 1992. 59.00 (0-387-19707-9) Spr-Verlag.

Moore, Kevin Z. The Descent of the Imagination: Postromantic Culture in the Later Novels of Thomas Hardy. 319p. 1993. pap. text ed. 22.50 (0-8147-5499-6) NYU Pr.

Moore, Kristin A. & Burt, Martha R. Private Crisis, Public Cost: Policy Perspectives on Teenage Childbearing. LC 82-60293. 166p. (Orig.). 1982. pap. text ed. 19.50 (0-87766-314-9) Urban Inst.

Moore, Kristin A., et al. Choice & Circumstance: Race Differences in Adolescent Sexuality & Fertility. 179p. 1986. pap. 19.95 (0-88738-773-X) Transaction Pubs.

***Moore, Kristina M., et al, eds.** Making Sense of Federal Employment & Training Policy for Youth & Adults Vol. II: Expert Recommendations to Create a Comprehensive & Unified System. 54p. 1995. pap. text ed. write for info. (1-887031-51-0) Am Youth Policy.

Moore, L. Baptism As Thirty Celebrations. 1990. pap. 3.95 (0-937032-74-3) Light&Life Pub Co MN.

Moore, L. David. The Christian Conspiracy: How the Teachings of Christ Have Been Altered by Christians. LC 94-66236. 360p. (Orig.). 1994. pap. 14.95 (0-9635665-2-0) Pendulum Plus.

— Christianity & the New Age Religion: A Bridge Toward Mutual Understanding. LC 92-82117. 248p. 1993. pap. 12.95 (0-9635665-0-4) Pendulum Plus.

— A Personal Pathway to God: Our Song of Freedom. (Illus.). 288p. (Orig.). 1995. pap. 13.95 (0-9635665-3-9) Pendulum Plus.

Moore, L. K. & Plung, D. L., eds. Marketing Technical Ideas & Products Successfully. LC 84-22414. (Reprint Ser.). 440p. 1985. 29.95 (0-87942-185-1, PC01792) Inst Electrical.

Moore, L. Tilden. Abstracts of Marriages & Deaths & Other Articles of Interest in the Newspapers of Frederick & Montgomery Counties, Maryland, 1831-1840. vi, 431p. 1991. pap. 26.50 (1-55613-478-9) Heritage Bk.

Moore-Landecker, Elizabeth. Fundamentals of the Fungi. 3rd ed. 544p. (C). 1990. Casebound. text ed. write for info. (0-13-332941-0) P-H.

Moore, Lane. The Talisman Technique: A Formula for Making Two Hundred Dollars a Hour. (Illus.). (Orig.). 1988. pap. text ed. 9.95 (0-945556-00-4) How-To Pubns.

Moore, Langdon W. His Own Story of His Eventful Life. LC 70-164617. (Select Bibliographies Reprint Ser.). 1977. reprint ed. 44.95 (0-8369-5901-9) Ayer.

Moore-Lanning, Linda. Breaking the Myth: The Truth about Texas Women. 240p. 1987. 14.95 (0-89015-565-8) Sunbelt Media.

Moore, Larry. Improving Workforce Basic Skills: The Foundation for Quality. 176p. 1992. text ed. 29.95 (0-527-91662-5, 916625) Qual Resc.

***Moore, Larry F. & Jennings, P. Devereaux, eds.** Human Resource Management on the Pacific Rim: Institutions, Practices, & Attitudes. LC 94-36058. (Studies in Organization: No. 60). 400p. (C). 1995. lib. bdg. 89.95 (3-11-014053-5) De Gruyter.

— Human Resource Management on the Pacific Rim: Institutions, Practices, & Attitudes. (Studies in Organization: No. 60). 400p. (C). 1995. pap. text ed. 32.95 (3-11-014747-5) De Gruyter.

Moore, Larry F., jt. ed. see Pinder, Craig C.

Moore, Laura & Skinner, Deborah. Simply Whidbey: A Collection of Regional Recipes from Whidbey Island, Washington. LC 90-81675. (Illus.). 224p. (Orig.). 1991. pap. 16.95 (0-9628766-0-7) Saratoga Pubs.

Moore, Laurence. Lightning Never Strikes Twice & Other False Facts. 256p. (Orig.). 1994. pap. 10.00 (0-380-77477-1) Avon.

Moore, Laurence J. & Taylor, Bernard W., III. Management Science. 4th ed. LC 92-20371. 1993. write for info. (0-205-14637-6) Allyn.

Moore, LaVoone B. Missouri Town Eighteen Fifty-Five: A Program in Architectural Preservation. (Illus.). 109p. 1987. pap. 14.95 (0-932845-26-6) Lowell Pr.

Moore, Lawrence C., jt. auth. see Smith, David A.

Moore, Lazarus. Sacred Tradition in the Orthodox Church. 1984. pap. 2.95 (0-937032-34-4) Light&Life Pub Co MN.

Moore, Leila V. & Young, Robert B., eds. Expanding Opportunities for Professional Education. LC 85-644751. (New Directions for Student Services Ser.: No. SS 37). 1987. 16.95 (1-55542-970-X) Jossey-Bass.

Moore, Lelia V., ed. Evolving Theoretical Perspectives on Students. LC 85-644751. (New Directions for Student Services Ser.: No. 51). 1991. 16.95 (1-55542-815-0) Jossey-Bass.

Moore, Leon R. & Moore, Orene, eds. Ancestors Charts of the Saline County History & Heritage Society Members. 120p. 1993. 17.50 (0-945183-17-8) Saline Cnty Hist Heritage Soc.

Moore, Leonard. Enciclopedia Juvenil De la Naturaleza. 2nd ed. 256p. (SPA.). (J). 1982. write for info. (0-7859-5097-4) Fr & Eur.

Moore, Leonard J. Citizen Klansmen: The Ku Klux Klan in Indiana, 1921-1928. LC 91-2602. xvi, 260p. (C). 1991. 37.50 (0-8078-1981-6) U of NC Pr.

***Moore, Les.** Letters to Henry. (Illus.). 360p. (Orig.). (C). 1995. pap. 15.95 (0-9647111-0-9) Little Lion.

Moore, Leslie E. Beautiful Sublime: The Making of "Paradise Lost," 1701-1734. 256p. 1990. 29.50 (0-8047-1632-3) Stanford U Pr.

***Moore, Lewis D.** Meditations on America: John D. MacDonald's Travis McGee Series & Other Fiction. 200p. (C). 1994. 39.95 (0-87972-663-6); pap. text ed. 17.95 (0-87972-664-4) Bowling Green Univ.

Moore, Lilian. Adam Mouse's Book of Poems. LC 91-42223. (Illus.). 64p. (J). (ps-5). 1992. text ed., lib. bdg. 12.95 (0-689-31765-4, Atheneum Bks Young) S&S Childrens.

— Don't Be Afraid, Amanda. LC 91-19661. (Illus.). 64p. (J). (gr. 2-5). 1992. text ed. 12.95 (0-689-31725-5, Atheneum Bks Young) S&S Childrens.

— I Never Did That Before: Poems. LC 95-2119. (Illus.). (J). 1995. write for info. (0-689-31889-8, Atheneum S&S) S&S Trade.

— I'll Meet You at the Cucumbers. (J). (gr. 1-4). 1989. pap. 2.99 (0-553-15705-1, Skylark) Bantam.

— I'll Meet You at the Cucumbers. LC 87-15195. (Illus.). 72p. (J). (gr. 2-6). 1988. text ed. 13.95 (0-689-31243-1, Atheneum Bks Young) S&S Childrens.

— Something New Begins: New & Selected Poems. LC 82-1723. (Illus.). 128p. (J). (gr. 3 up). 1982. text ed. 12.95 (0-689-30818-3, Atheneum Bks Young) S&S Childrens.

Moore, Lilian, jt. auth. see Charlip, Remy.

Moore, Lillian C. Images of the Dance: Historical Treasures of the Dance Collection, 1581-1861. LC 65-18552. (Illus.). 86p. 1965. 15.00 (0-87104-093-X) NY Pub Lib.

Moore, Lin. High Lakes Rider: Mountain Biking West of Bend. (Illus.). 96p. (Orig.). 1990. pap. 8.95 (0-9627569-0-3) Big Juniper Pr.

Moore, Lina E. Cuentos: An Anthology of Short Stories. iii, 131p. (Orig.). 1985. pap. text ed. 7.50 (971-10-0173-X, Pub. by New Day Pub PH) Cellar.

Moore, Linda. The Evil That Men Do. 1985. 12.00 (0-916620-59-X) Portals Pr.

— Yesterday's Children. 1986. 12.00 (0-916620-60-3) Portals Pr.

Moore, Lindy. Aberdeen University & the Education of Women, 1860-1920: Bajanellas & Semilinas. (Quincentennial Studies in the History of the University of Aberdeen). (Illus.). 192p. 1991. pap. text ed. 17.90 (0-08-040918-0, Pub. by Aberdeen U Pr) Macmillan.

— Bajanellas & Semilinas: Aberdeen University & the Education of Women 1860-1920. (SWSS Ser.). (Illus.). 192p. 1991. pap. text ed. 17.90 (0-08-041202-5, Pub. by Aberdeen U Pr) Macmillan.

Moore, Lloyd E. The Jury. Burden, William, ed. 1988. text ed. 19.50 (0-87084-577-2) Anderson Pub Co.

Moore, Lola & Quinn, Elizabeth. Osceola: Jewel of Tug Hill. (Illus.). 400p. 1985. pap. 14.95 (0-685-43033-2) Moore & Quinn.

Moore, Lorna G., et al. The Biocultural Basis of Health: Expanding Views of Medical Anthropology. (Illus.). 278p. (C). 1987. reprint ed. pap. text ed. 14.95 (0-88133-255-0) Waveland Pr.

Moore, Lorraine A. Back Roads & Buggy Trails: A Visitor's Guide to Ohio Amish Country. 2nd ed. LC 94-71491. (Illus.). 245p. (Orig.). 1994. pap. 9.95 (1-881122-01-8) Bluebrd Ohio.

Moore, Lorrie. Anagrams. 240p. 1987. pap. 10.95 (0-14-010328-7, Penguin Bks) Viking Penguin.

— Like Life. 178p. 1990. 18.95 (0-394-58101-6) Knopf.

— Like Life. 192p. 1991. reprint ed. pap. 9.95 (0-452-26637-8, Plume) NAL-Dutton.

— Who Will Run the Frog Hospital? LC 94-278. 1994. 20.00 (0-679-43484-4); 20.00 (0-679-43482-8) Knopf.

— Who Will Run the Frog Hospital? 160p. 1995. pap. 11.99 (0-446-67191-6) Warner Bks.

— Who Will Run the Frog Hospital? A Novel. large type ed. LC 95-719. 1995. pap. write for info. (0-7862-0416-8) Thorndike Pr.

Moore, Lorrie, ed. I Know Some Things: Contemporary Stories about Children Viewing the World. 270p. 1992. 19.95 (0-571-12945-5) Faber & Faber.

— I Know Some Things: Stories about Childhood by Contemporary Writers. 245p. 1993. pap. 12.95 (0-571-19802-3) Faber & Faber.

Moore, Louis & Land, Richard D. The Earth Is the Lord's: Christians & the Environment. (Orig.). 1992. pap. 10.99 (0-8054-1627-7) Broadman.

***Moore, Louis A. & Land, Richard D., eds.** Life at Risk: The Crisis in Medical Ethics. LC 94-42206. 1995. write for info. (0-8054-6265-1) Broadman.

Moore, Louis A., jt. ed. see Land, Richard D.

Moore, Louis C. The Impostors of Monterey: Bouchard & One-Eyed Charley. (Illus.). 232p. 1985. pap. text ed. 11.95 (0-9616361-0-6) L C Moore.

Moore, Lynda. Not As Far As You Think: The Realities of Working Women. LC 85-40109. 224p. (C). 1986. pap. text ed. 14.95 (0-685-11953-X) Free Pr.

Moore, Lynden. The Growth & Structure of International Trade since the Second World War. LC 84-11105. (Illus.). 414p. 1985. 58.50 (0-389-20498-6, BNB 08061) B&N Imports.

Moore, Lynn, jt. ed. see Taggart, Judith F.

Moore, M. Quarterly Review of Literature: The 1940s, Special Issue, Vol. IV, No. 2. 1940. pap. 50.00 (0-317-05284-5) Quarterly Rev.

— The Ultimate Sound Blaster Book. (Illus.). 512p. (Orig.). 1993. pap. 35.00 (1-56529-298-7) Que.

Moore, M., ed. Crystallography Reviews: A Special Issue of the Journal Crystallography Reviews, Issue 1. 84p. 1987. pap. text ed. 66.00 (2-88124-218-9) Gordon & Breach.

— Crystallography Reviews: A Special Issue of the Journal Crystallography Reviews, Vol. 2. 106p. 1987. Issue 2, 1987, 106p. pap. text ed. 66.00 (2-88124-217-0) Gordon & Breach.

Moore, M., ed. see Etter, M. C., et al.

Moore, M., jt. auth. see Vell.

Moore, M. H. Sketches of the Pioneers of Methodism in North Carolina & Virginia. 314p. 1977. reprint ed. 12.50 (0-87921-039-7) Attic Pr.

Moore, M. H., tr. see Cournot, Antoine A.

Moore, M. J. & Sieverding, C. H., eds. Aerothermodynamics of Low Pressure Steam Turbines & Condensers. (Von Karman Institute Bks.). 290p. 1986. 81.00 (0-89116-446-4) Hemisp Pub.

Moore, M. R., et al. Disorders of Porphyrin Metabolism. LC 87-14125. (Topics in Hematology Ser.). (Illus.). 396p. 1987. 89.50 (0-306-42625-0, Plenum Med Bk) Plenum.

Moore, MacDonald S. Yankee Blues: Musical Culture & American Identity. LC 83-49407. (Illus.). 223p. reprint ed. pap. 63.60 (0-7837-3720-3, 2057898) Bks Demand.

Moore, Madeleine H. & Moore, James R., Jr. Fats in Your Diet, Live a Longer Life: Guide to Lower Saturated Fat, Lower Cholesterol. LC 86-90364. (Orig.). 1986. pap. 8.95 (0-936833-00-9) MHM Pub.

Moore, Madeline. As You Desire. LC 93-84275. 180p. (Orig.). 1993. pap. 9.95 (0-933216-95-5) Spinsters Ink.

— The Short Season Between Two Silences. (Illus.). 240p. (C). 1984. text ed. 39.95 (0-04-800022-1) Routledge Chapman & Hall.

— The Short Season Between Two Silences: The Mystical & the Political in the Novels of Virginia Woolf. 216p. 1986. pap. text ed. 12.95 (0-04-800098-1) Routledge Chapman & Hall.

Moore, Maggie, jt. auth. see Wade, Barrie.

Moore, Malcolm, jt. auth. see Bassett, Patrick F.

Moore, Malcolm A., ed. Maturation Factors & Cancer. (Progress in Cancer Research & Therapy Ser.: Vol. 23). 406p. 1982. text ed. 126.00 (0-89004-596-8) Raven.

Moore, Malcolm T., jt. auth. see Fox, Edward J., Jr.

Moore, Mallie, et al. Talk Story. (Illus.). 115p. (Orig.). 1987. 7.95 (0-9618620-0-9) Bright Design.

Moore, Mamie. Make Way for August. Literacy Volunteers of New York City Staff, ed. (New Writers' Voices Ser.). (Illus.). 64p. (Orig.). 1991. pap. text ed. 3.50 (0-929631-36-6, Signal Hill) New Readers.

Moore, Mardell & Klein, Charna. Washington Foundation Directory, 1994: How to Get Your Slice of the Pie. 2nd ed. 456p. 1994. pap. 39.83 (0-9617216-2-6) Consult Serv NW.

Moore, Margaret. Dangerous Conceits. 204p. 1989. 17.95 (0-8027-5727-8) Walker & Co.

— Forests of the Night. LC 87-37265. 1988. 16.95 (0-8027-5707-3) Walker & Co.

— Forests of the Night. large type ed. 1990. 21.95 (0-7089-2175-2) Ulverscroft.

— Foundations of Liberalism. LC 92-22186. 240p. 1993. 48.00 (0-19-827385-1, Clarendon Pr) OUP.

— The Saxon. (Historical Ser.). 1995. pap. 4.50 (0-373-28868-9, 1-28868-7) Harlequin Bks.

— A Study of Young High School Graduates. LC 74-177081. (Columbia University. Teachers College. Contributions to Education Ser.: No. 583). reprint ed. 37.50 (0-404-55583-7) AMS Pr.

— The Viking. (Historical Ser.). 1993. mass mkt. 3.99 (0-373-28800-X, 1-28800-0) Harlequin Bks.

— Vows: (Weddings, Inc.) (Historical Ser.). 1994. mass mkt. 3.99 (0-373-28848-4, 1-28848-9) Harlequin Bks.

— A Warrior's Quest. (Historical Ser.). 1993. mass mkt. 3.99 (0-373-28775-5, 1-28775-4) Harlequin Bks.

— A Warrior's Way. 1994. mass mkt. 3.99 (0-373-28824-7, 1-28824-0) Harlequin Bks.

— The Welshman's Way. 1995. pap. 4.50 (0-373-28895-6, 1-28895-0) Harlequin Bks.

Moore, Margaret A., jt. auth. see Diamond, Barbara J.

Moore, Margaret E. Understanding British English. 1989. pap. 9.95 (0-8065-1149-4, Citadel Pr) Carol Pub Group.

Moore, Margaret F. & Brown, P. Hume. Lands of the Scottish Kings in England: The Honour of Huntington, the Liberty of Tyndale, & the Honour of Penrith. LC 70-91997. xii, 141p. 1973. reprint ed. lib. bdg. 29.50 (0-678-00728-4) Kelley.

Moore, Margaret S. Neath the Shadow of the Hills: Townscapes & Landscapes of Williamstown. LC 89-60885. (Illus.). 24p. 1989. pap. 4.00 (0-931102-25-1) S & F Clark Art.

Moore, Maria & Wright, Brianne, eds. The Handbook of Historically Black Colleges & Universities, Premier Edition 1992-94: Comprehensive Profiles & Photos of Black Colleges & Universities. LC 92-71364. (Illus.). 248p. (YA). (gr. 10 up). 1992. 19.95 (0-9632669-0-X) Jireh & Assocs.

Moore, Marianne. Complete Poems. 320p. 1994. 12.95 (0-14-018851-7, Penguin Classics) Viking Penguin.

— The Complete Poems of Marianne Moore. 1987. pap. 9.95 (0-14-058601-6, Penguin Bks) Viking Penguin.

Moore, Marianne & Wilson, Edmund. Homage to Henry James. 1971. 9.00 (0-911858-17-2) Appel.

Moore, Marie A. The Mastiff. LC 77-87765. (Breed Bks.). (Illus.). 112p. 1978. 29.95 (0-87714-059-6) Denlingers.

— Mastiffs. (Illus.). 160p. 1989. 11.95 (0-86622-335-5, KW180) TFH Pubns.

***Moore, MariJo.** Returning to the Homeland: Cherokee Poetry & Short Stories. LC 94-61389. (Illus.). 112p. (Orig.). 1995. pap. 9.95 (1-56664-073-3) WorldComm.

Moore, Marilyn. Gone to Missouri: From Whence They Came - to Where & When. 296p. (Orig.). 1991. pap. 19.95 (1-56524-050-2) InfoTech Pubns.

Moore, Marilyn A., ed. see Knight-Ridder Corporation Staff.

***Moore, Marilyn M.** The Self-Published Cook: How to Write, Publish & Sell Your Own Cookbook. (Illus.). 144p. (Orig.). 1995. pap. 14.95 (0-9603788-1-2) Wooden Spoon.

— Wooden Spoon Book of Home-Style Soups, Stews, Chowders, Chilis & Gumbos. LC 92-4961. 223p. 1993. pap. 13.00 (0-87113-555-8) Grove-Atltic.

— Wooden Spoon Bread Book: The Secrets of Successful Baking. 1992. pap. 15.00 (0-87113-505-1) Grove-Atltic.

— The Wooden Spoon Cookie Book: Favorite Home-Style Recipes from the Wooden Spoon Kitchen. LC 94-1256. 160p. 1994. 15.00 (0-87113-601-5) Grove-Atltic.

— The Wooden Spoon Dessert Book: The Best You Ever Ate. LC 95-993. 1995. pap. write for info. (0-87113-607-4, Atlntc Mnthly) Grove-Atltic.

— The Wooden Spoon Meat & Potatoes Cookbook: Traditional, Hearty Food from the Wooden Spoon Kitchen. LC 95-992. 1995. write for info. (0-87113-606-6, Atlntc Mnthly) Grove-Atltic.

Moore, Mark E. Come, Ye Faithful Wise Men. 1962. 4.25 (0-685-68592-6, MC-206) Lillenas.

***Moore, Mark H.** Creating Public Value: Strategic Management in Government. LC 95-18074. (Illus.). 416p. (C). 1995. text ed. 45.00 (0-674-17557-3) HUP.

— From Children to Citizens. LC 87-9976. 1987. 65.00 (0-387-96474-6) Spr-Verlag.

Moore, Mark H. & Gates, Margaret J. Inspectors General. LC 86-6728. (Social Science Perspectives Ser.). 112p. 1986. pap. text ed. 9.95 (0-87154-605-1) Russell Sage.

Moore, Mark H., ed. see National Research Council (U. S.), Panel on Alternative Policies Affecting the Prevention of Alcohol Abuse & Alcoholism Staff.

Moore, Mark H., et al. Dangerous Offenders: The Elusive Target of Justice. (Illus.). 264p. 1985. 28.50 (0-674-19065-3) HUP.

Moore, Maror, tr. see Galinas, Gratien.

Moore, Marsha L., jt. comp. see Davis, Lenwood G.

***Moore, Martha.** Under the Mermaid Angel. LC 95-1991. (J). 1995. write for info. (0-385-32160-0) Delacorte.

Moore, Martha M., et al, eds. Mammalian Cell Mutagenesis. LC 87-21784. (Banbury Report Ser.: No. 28). (Illus.). 280p. 1988. text ed. 77.00 (0-87969-228-6) Cold Spring Harbor.

Moore, Marti & Bostaph, Charles. Crossroads: A Back to School Career Guide for Adults. LC 79-2112. 128p. 1979. pap. 6.95 (0-910328-29-3) Sulzburger & Graham Pub.

Moore, Martin. Boston Revival Eighteen Forty-Two. 148p. 1980. 11.50 (0-939464-36-5) Labyrinth Pr.

— Boston Revival, Eighteen Forty-Two: A Brief History of the Evangelical Churches of Boston, Together with a More Particular Account of the Revival of 1842. (Revival Library). (Illus.). 148p. (C). 1980. reprint ed. lib. bdg. 11.50 (0-940033-16-X) R O Roberts.

Moore, Marvin. The Antichrist & the New World Order. LC 92-42089. 1993. 2.95 (0-8163-1150-1) Pacific Pr Pub Assn.

— Conquering the Dragon Within: God's Provision for Assurance & Victory in the End Time. LC 94-39860. 1995. 13.95 (0-8163-1252-4) Pacific Pr Pub Assn.

An Asterisk (*) at the beginning of an entry indicates that the title is appearing in BIP for the first time.

— The Crisis of the End Time. (Anchor Ser.). 253p. 1992. pap. 10.95 (0-8163-1085-8) Pacific Pr Pub Assn.
— The Gospel vs. Legalism: How to Deal with Legalism's Insidious Influence. LC 93-45399. 1994. write for info. (0-8280-0734-9) Review & Herald.
— How to Make a Decision. (Lifestyle Ser.). 30p. 1987. pap. 0.79 (0-8163-0714-8) Pacific Pr Pub Assn.
— When Religion Doesn't Work. Coffen, Richard W., ed. (Better Living Ser.). 32p. (Orig.). 1986. pap. 1.25 (0-8280-0314-9) Review & Herald.
Moore, Mary. Forever Black but Always Proud. 195p. 1988. pap. text ed. 19.95 (0-9638983-0-2) Moore-Ferguson.
— I'll Meet You in the Lobby. (American Autobiography Ser.). 250p. 1995. reprint ed. lib. bdg. 79.00 (0-7812-8596-8) Rprt Serv.
***Moore, Mary A.** Big Mary's Year O Fun '96. 370p. (Orig.). 1995. pap. text ed. 9.95 (1-56383-042-6, 9230) G & R Pub.
— Hide-&-Seek with God: A Collection of Stories for Children. LC 94-7551. 112p. (J). 1994. 14.00 (1-55896-277-8, Skinner Hse Bks) Unitarian Univ.
Moore, Mary A., jt. auth. see Duckett, Kermit E.
Moore, Mary B. & Philippides, Mary Z. Attic Black-Figured Pottery. LC 86-20615. (Athenian Agora Ser.: Vol. 23). (Illus.). xvi, 382p. 1986. 60.00 (0-87661-223-0) Am Sch Athens.
Moore, Mary B. & Von Bothmer, Dietrich. Attic Black-Figured Neck-Amphorae. LC 75-25613. (Illus.). 86p. 1976. 9.95 (0-87099-134-5) Metro Mus Art.
Moore, Mary B., ed. see Beazley, John D.
Moore, Mary C. David Rizzio. LC 81-1175. (Women Composers Ser.: No. 12). 1981. reprint ed. lib. bdg. 29.50 (0-306-76101-7) Da Capo.
— Pocket Guide to Nutrition & Diet Therapy. 2nd ed. LC 92-8484. 438p. 1992. spiral bd. 19.95 (0-8016-6690-2) Mosby Yr Bk.
— Twenty-Eight Songs. (Women Composers Ser.). 1988. 27.50 (0-306-79716-X) Da Capo.
Moore, Mary E. Teaching from the Heart: Theology & Educational Method. LC 91-17972. 246p. 1991. pap. 18.00 (0-8006-2497-1, 1-2497, Fortress Pr) Augsburg Fortress.
***Moore, Mary L. & Givens, Susan R.** Window of Opportunity: Interviewing by the Perinatal Nurse. Damus, Karla & Freda, Margaret C., eds. LC 94-39542. 1994. write for info. (0-86525-063-4) March of Dimes.
Moore, Mary Lou. Realities in Childbearing. 2nd ed. 1160p. 1983. text ed. 66.95 (0-7216-6498-9) Saunders.
Moore, Mary M., ed. see Bartholomew.
Moore, Mary-Margaret, ed. see Bartholomew.
Moore, Mary R. Zodiac: Exploring Human Qualities & Characteristics. rev. ed. LC 84-17977. (Vocabureader Workbook Ser.: No. 1). (Illus.). 112p. (J). (gr. 5 up). 1994. pap. 10.50 (0-86647-080-8) Pro Lingua.
Moore, Mary S. Fireside Tales. (Illus.). 21p. (Orig.). (J). (gr. 5-12). 1990. pap. 7.95 (0-913678-18-X); audio, pap. 10.00 (0-913678-19-8) New Day Pr.
— The Relationship Renewal Kit: Getting to the Heart of What Matters Most, 2 wkbks. LC 94-92391. 1995. pap. text ed. 11.95 (1-885574-00-2) Courage Press.
— Teen Self-Steam Pocket Coach: Exploring Life's Puzzles & Developing Personal Strength, 2 wkbks., Set. LC 94-92393. (YA). (gr. 6-12). 1994. pap. text ed. 11.95 (1-885574-01-0) Courage Press.
— Young Entrepreneur's Guide to Creating What Matters Most: Building Attitudes, Behaviors & an Action Plan for Success in Your Own Business. LC 94-92392. 64p. (YA). (gr. 6-12). 1994. pap. text ed. 9.95 (1-885574-03-7) Courage Press.
Moore, Mary V. Limited Liability Companies: Legal Research Guide - Pathfinder. LC 94-16191. (Legal Research Guides Ser.). iii, 100p. 1994. 40.00 (0-89941-872-4, 308250) W S Hein.
Moore, MaryAnn, jt. auth. see Kitchen, V. Rose.
Moore, Matthew S. & Levitan, Linda. For Hearing People Only: Answers to Some of the Most Commonly Asked Questions about the Deaf Community, Its Culture & the "Deaf Reality" (Illus.). 300p. (Orig.). 1992. pap. 14.95 (0-9634016-0-2) MSM Prods.
— For Hearing People Only: Answers to Some of the Most Commonly Asked Questions about the Deaf Community, Its Culture & the "Deaf Reality" 2nd ed. 336p. (Orig.). 1993. lib. bdg. 35.00 (0-9634016-2-9); pap. 19.95 (0-9634016-1-0) MSM Prods.
Moore, Maureen, ed. see Bessell, Harold.
***Moore, Maureen F.** Personnel Forms & Employment Checklists. 440p. 1994. disk, ring bd. 79.50 (0-614-05944-5) Michie Butterworth.
— Personnel Forms & Employment Checklists, 1990-1992. 280p. 1992. ring bd. 79.50 (0-88063-375-1) Butterworth Legal Pubs.
— Personnel Forms & Employment Checklists, 1990-1992. suppl. ed. 280p. 1993. 27.50 (0-250-48606-7) Butterworth Legal Pubs.
Moore, Maureen F. & Alder, Jonathan L. Family & Medical Leave: Federal & State Requirements. LC 93-35004. 540p. 1993. ring bd. 75.00 (0-250-48602-4) Michie Butterworth.
— Labor & Employment in Louisiana. LC 93-19122. 370p. 1994. ring bd. 89.50 (0-409-25716-8) Michie Butterworth.
Moore, Maureen F., jt. auth. see Alder, Jonathan L.
Moore, Maurice E., jt. auth. see Shaw, Clifford R.
Moore, Maurice G. Worlds in Motion. 46p. (Orig.). 1964. pap. text ed. 7.00 (0-943956-05-6) Trippensee Pub.
Moore, Maxine, jt. auth. see Moore, Bob.
Moore, Maxori, et al. Transformation: A Rites of Passage Manual for African American Girls. 2nd ed. (Illus.). 83p. 1987. reprint ed. pap. 15.00 (0-9621527-0-6) Stars Pr.
***Moore, Megan.** Thrift Store Prospecting. (Illus.). 95p. 1994. reprint ed. pap. 29.95 (1-879878-13-5) Penultimate Pr.
Moore, Melissa, ed. see Lafferty, Jerry.
Moore, Melita H., jt. auth. see Moore, Geoffrey H.
Moore, Meredith A., jt. ed. see Carlin, Diana P.
Moore, Michael. Battalion at War: Singapore 1942. (C). 1989. 59.00 (0-947893-11-3) St Mut.
— California Fishing & Hunting Guide: Outdoor Recreation by California Guides. 160p. 1988. reprint ed. pap. 12.95 (0-929237-00-5) Curtis CA.
— California Fishing & Hunting Guide: Outdoor Recreation by Western Guides. 2nd ed. (Illus.). 1990. pap. 12.95 (0-929237-01-3) Curtis CA.
— Knowing When...Being There. Perez, Barbara, ed. 73p. (Orig.). 1989. pap. 5.00 (0-9610702-2-6) Stugallz.
— Medicinal Plants of the Desert & Canyon West. (Illus.). 216p. 1989. text ed. 12.95 (0-89013-181-3); pap. text ed. 11.95 (0-89013-182-1) Museum NM Pr.
— Medicinal Plants of the Mountain West. 1979. pap. 12.95 (0-89013-104-X) Museum NM Pr.
— Medicinal Plants of the Pacific West. (Illus.). 360p. 1993. pap. 19.95 (1-878610-31-7) Red Crane Bks.
— Los Remedios: Traditional Herbal Remedies of the Southwest. LC 90-61682. (Illus.). 120p. (Orig.). 1990. pap. 9.95 (1-878610-06-6) Red Crane Bks.
— Staying Married Is the Best Revenge. 96p. 1987. 3.95 (1-55601-006-0) Great Sky.
Moore, Michael & Sawey, Ronald. BITNET for VMS Users. (Networking & Data Communications Ser.). (Illus.). 161p. 1992. pap. 25.95 (1-55558-094-7, EY-L464E-DP, Digital DEC) Buttrwrth-Heinemann.
Moore, Michael, tr. see Ceronetti, Guido.
Moore, Michael, jt. auth. see Geyerman, Chris.
Moore, Michael, jt. ed. see Kiernan, Kathy.
Moore, Michael C. Archeology of the Mixed Grass Prairie, Phases II & III: Hay & Cyclone Creeks Surveys & Predictive Modeling in the Quartermaster Watershed. (Archeological Resource Survey Report Ser.: No. 33). (Illus.). 244p. (C). 1988. pap. text ed. 10.00 (1-881346-22-6) Univ OK Archeol.
Moore, Michael C., et al. Archeological Investigations Within the Central Little River Draining Basin, Cleveland & Pottawatomie Counties, Oklahoma. (Archeological Resource Survey Report Ser.: No. 31). (Illus.). 186p. (C). 1988. pap. text ed. 6.00 (1-881346-20-X) Univ OK Archeol.
Moore, Michael G. The Unicorn Riders of the Orb. (Illus.). 227p. 1986. pap. 2.95 (0-9613282-1-5) MGM Bks.
Moore, Michael G., pref. Distance Education for Corporate & Military Training. 145p. (C). 1992. pap. text ed. 20.00 (1-877780-08-1) ACSDE.
***Moore, Michael G. & Koble, Margaret A., eds.** Video-Based Telecommunications in Distance Education. (Readings in Distance Education Ser.: No. 4). 144p. (Orig.). (C). 1995. pap. text ed. 20.00 (1-877780-12-X) ACSDE.
Moore, Michael G., et al, eds. Contemporary Issues in American Distance Education. 1990. 81.00 (0-08-040233-X, Pergamon Pr) Elsevier.
Moore, Michael J. & Viscusi, W. Kip. Compensation Mechanisms for Job Risks: Wages, Workers' Compensation & Product Liability. 224p. 1990. text ed. 37.50 (0-691-04247-0) Princeton U Pr.
Moore, Michael L. A Review of Search & Reconnaisance Theory Literature. LC 75-131015. 104p. 1970. 22.00 (0-403-04520-7) Scholarly.
***Moore, Michael L. & Outslay, Edmund.** U. S. Tax Aspects of Doing Business Abroad. 4th rev. ed. LC 95-5646. 1995. write for info. (0-87051-164-5) Am Inst CPA.
Moore, Michael P., ed. see Franz, Marion J.
Moore, Michael S. Act & Crime: The Theory of Action and Its Implications for Criminal Law. LC 92-41296. (Law Ser.). 1993. 69.00 (0-19-825791-0, Clarendon Pr) OUP.
Moore, Michael S. The Balaam Traditions: Their Character & Development. (Society of Biblical Literature Dissertation Ser.). 280p. 1990. 23.95 (1-55540-327-1, 06 21 13); pap. 15.95 (1-55540-328-X) Scholars Pr GA.
Moore, Michael T. & Geyerman, Chris. The Freshman Seminar: Surviving the First Year at Georgia Southern University. 208p. (C). 1993. per. 14.95 (0-8403-8615-X) Kendall-Hunt.
***Moore, Michalea.** Next Services. LC 80-5677. (Lucky Heart Book Ser.). (Illus.). reprint ed. pap. 25.00 (0-7837-9152-6, 2049852) Bks Demand.
Moore, Mickela, jt. ed. see Campbell, Dennis.
Moore, Mike. Marmosets in Captivity. (C). 1989. 35.00 (0-946873-95-X, Pub. by Basset Pubns UK) St Mut.
Moore, Mike, ed. Health Risks & the Press: Perspectives on Media Coverage of Risk Assessment & Health. LC 88-63767. 120p. (Orig.). (C). 1989. pap. 12.95 (0-937790-39-7, 4340) Media Institute.
Moore, Mike, jt. auth. see Burgard, Mike.
***Moore, Miles D.** The Bears of Paris. LC 95-61228. 80p. (Orig.). 1996. pap. 10.00 (0-915380-32-3) Word Works.
Moore, Milton T., Jr. Steve Reeves: One of Kind. LC 82-90099. 192p. (Orig.). 1983. pap. 14.95 (0-9608138-0-2) M T Moore.
Moore, Molly. Boomer's War. LC 92-31278. 352p. 1993. text ed. 22.50 (0-684-19418-X, Scribners) S&S Trade.
Moore, N., tr. see Windisch, Ernst W.
Moore, N. Hudson. The Collector's Manual. LC 76-30474. (Paperback Ser.). (Illus.). 1977. reprint ed. pap. 6.95 (0-306-80061-6) Da Capo.
Moore, N. M., Jr. & Darring, Walt. The Crossroader: Memoirs of a Professional Gambler. (Illus.). 177p. (Orig.). 1992. pap. 12.50 (0-9633399-6-6) Regency Pr AL.
Moore, Nancy. Machine-Quilted Jackets, Vests, & Coats. LC 90-55880. (Illus.). 184p. 1991. pap. 17.95 (0-8019-8117-4) Chilton.
Moore, Nancy & Komras, Henrietta. Patient-Focused Healing: Integrating Caring & Curing in Health Care. LC 93-4218. (Health-Management Ser.). 290p. 1993. 34.95 (1-55542-584-4) Jossey-Bass.
Moore, Nancy J. Maryland Employer's Guide, 1993-1994: A Handbook of Employment Laws & Regulations. LC 92-44472. 350p. 1994. ring bd. 89.50 (1-56759-004-7) Summers Pr.
***Moore, Nancy J., ed.** Virginia Employer's Guide: A Handbook of Employment Laws & Regulations. 500p. 1995. ring bd. 89.50 (1-56759-016-0) Summers Pr.
Moore, Nancy Y., et al. Assessment of the Economic Impacts of California's Drought on Urban Areas: A Research Agenda. LC 93-42318. 1993. write for info. (0-8330-1489-7, MR-251-CUWA) Rand Corp.
Moore, Nathaniel F. Ancient Mineralogy: An Inquiry Respecting Mineral Substances Mentioned by the Ancients. Albritton, Claude C., Jr., ed. LC 77-6532. (History of Geology Ser.). 1978. reprint ed. lib. bdg. 23.95 (0-405-10452-9) Ayer.
Moore, Nelwyn B., jt. auth. see Davidson, J. Kenneth.
Moore, Nick, jt. ed. see Hughes, Kirsty.
Moore, Noellene. Beyond Mayday. Caroland, Mary, ed. LC 90-71005. 291p. 1991. 8.95 (1-55523-366-X) Winston-Derek.
— Sim's Gold. LC 95-60769. 307p. 1996. 10.95 (1-55523-746-0) Winston-Derek.
Moore, Norman. The History of the Study of Medicine in the British Isles. LC 75-23746. reprint ed. 32.50 (0-404-13352-5) AMS Pr.
Moore, Olive. Collected Writings. LC 91-29755. 424p. 1992. 22.95 (1-56478-000-7) Dalkey Arch.
Moore, Opha. History of Franklin County, Ohio, 3 vols., Set. (Illus.). 1424p. 1993. reprint ed. lib. bdg. 139.00 (0-685-66022-2) Higginson Bk Co.
Moore, Orene, jt. ed. see Moore, Leon R.
Moore, Oscar. A Matter of Life & Sex. 336p. 1993. pap. 11.00 (0-452-27006-5, Plume) NAL-Dutton.
— Preachers: You Asked for It. 1975. pap. 2.00 (0-911866-79-5) LifeSprings Res.
Moore, P. B., jt. ed. see Nriagu, Jerome O.
Moore, P. D., jt. auth. see Cox, C. B.
Moore, P. D., et al. Pollen Analysis. 2nd ed. (Illus.). 224p. 1992. 85.00 (0-632-02176-4) Blackwell Sci.
Moore, P. G. & Seed, Raymond. The Ecology of Rock Coasts. 455p. 1986. text ed. 67.00 (0-231-06274-5) Col U Pr.
Moore, P. J., ed. Analysis & Design of Foundations for Vibration. 520p. (C). 1984. text ed. 165.00 (90-6191-525-2, Pub. by A A Balkema NE) Ashgate Pub Co.
Moore, P. W., jt. ed. see Nachfigall, P. E.
Moore, Pamela R. Safer Than a Known Way. LC 88-26514. 224p. 1988. 9.99 (0-8007-9175-4) Chosen Bks.
Moore, Pamela R., jt. auth. see Moore, Carey.
Moore, Patricia, ed. see Berlit, Peter.
Moore, Patricia, jt. auth. see Moore, John.
Moore, Patrick. A-Z of Astronomy. (Illus.). (Orig.). 1987. pap. 13.50 (0-393-30505-8) Norton.
— Amateur Astronomer. 1990. 35.00 (0-393-02864-X) Norton.
— Astronomy for the Beginner. (Illus.). 48p. (C). 1992. 12.95 (0-521-41833-X) Cambridge U Pr.
— Atlas of Solar System. rev. ed. 464p. 1990. 17.99 (0-517-00192-6) Random Hse Value.
— Atlas of the Universe. LC 94-22177. 1994. 29.95 (0-528-83704-4) Rand McNally.
— Exploring the Night Sky with Binoculars. (Illus.). 192p. 1989. pap. 17.95 (0-521-36866-9) Cambridge U Pr.
— Fireside Astronomy: An Anecdotal Tour Through the History & Lore of Astronomy. 212p. 1992. text ed. 24.95 (0-471-93164-0) Wiley.
— Fireside Astronomy: An Anecdotal Tour Through the History & Lore of Astronomy. 1993. pap. text ed. 14.95 (0-471-94202-2) Wiley.
— The Great Astronomical Revolution: 1534-1687 & the Space Age Epilogue. 256p. 1995. 34.95 (1-898563-18-7, Pub. by Albion Pubng UK); pap. 18.95 (1-898563-19-5, Pub. by Albion Pubng UK) Paul & Co Pubs.
— Mission to the Planets: The Illustrated Story of Man's Exploration of the Solar System. 1990. 24.95 (0-393-02872-0) Norton.
— Mission to the Planets: The Illustrated Story of the Exploration of Our Solar System. rev. ed. (Illus.). 128p. 1995. pap. 17.95 (0-304-34603-9, Pub. by Cassell UK) Sterling.
— The New Atlas of the Universe. 2nd rev. ed. (Illus.). 1988. 29.99 (0-517-55500-X) Random Hse Value.
— New Guide to the Planets. (Illus.). 228p. 1993. 37.50 (0-283-06145-6, Pub. by Sidgwick & Jackson UK) Trans-Atl Phila.
— Pocket Guide to Astronomy. 1980. pap. 7.95 (0-671-25309-3, 25309) S&S Trade.
— The Sky at Night Ten. 182p. (Orig.). 1993. pap. text ed. 19.95 (0-471-93763-0) Wiley.
— Space Travel for the Beginner. (Illus.). 48p. (C). 1992. 12.95 (0-521-41835-6) Cambridge U Pr.
— Stargazing: Astronomy Without a Telescope. (Illus.). 176p. 1985. 21.95 (0-8120-5644-2) Barron.
— Sun. (Illus.). 1968. 4.95 (0-393-06276-7) Norton.
— The Sun & Moon. (Starry Sky Ser.). (Illus.). 24p. (J). (gr. 5-7). 1995. 13.90 (1-56294-622-6) Millbrook Pr.
— Suns, Myths & Men. rev. ed. LC 68-27145. (Illus.). 1969. 7.95 (0-393-06364-X) Norton.
— The Universe for the Beginner. (Illus.). 48p. (C). 1992. 12.95 (0-521-41834-8) Cambridge U Pr.
Moore, Patrick & Jackson, Francis. Life on Mars. (Illus.). 1966. 4.50 (0-393-05225-7) Norton.
Moore, Patrick & Leventhal, Stan. This Every Night. 119p. (Orig.). 1990. pap. 8.95 (0-927200-06-6) Amethyst NY.
Moore, Patrick & Nicolson, Laian, eds. The Universe. (Illus.). 256p. 1985. text ed. 60.00 (0-02-922110-2) Macmillan.
Moore, Patrick, jt. auth. see Abrams, Bernard.
Moore, Patrick, jt. auth. see Cattermole, Peter.
Moore, Patrick, jt. auth. see Hunt, Garry E.
Moore, Patrick J. & Wheelock, Angela, eds. Wolverine Myths & Visions: Dene Traditions from Northern Alberta. LC 89-29379. (Studies in the Anthropology of North American Indians). (Illus.). xvi, 259p. 1990. 25.00 (0-8032-8161-7) U of Nebr Pr.
Moore, Paul, et al. All about Citrus & Subtropical Fruits. Bond, Richard H., ed. LC 85-70878. (Illus.). 96p. (Orig.). 1985. pap. 9.95 (0-89721-065-4) Ortho Info.
Moore, Paul L., ed. Managing the Political Dimension of Student Affairs. LC 85-644751. (New Directions for Student Services Ser.: No. SS 55). 1991. 16.95 (1-55542-779-0) Jossey-Bass.
Moore, Pauline. Milk-Free, Egg-Free Recipes for Children. 1994. pap. 7.95 (0-572-01401-5, Pub. by W Foulsham UK) Trans-Atl Phila.
Moore, Peggy. Before I Wake. 160p. 1991. per. 7.95 (0-8187-0136-6) Harlo Press.
Moore, Peggy, jt. auth. see Brigman, Greg.
Moore, Peggy A. How Not to Abuse Your Child. (Illus.). 60p. 1984. pap. text ed. 5.00 (0-9613078-3-8) Detroit Black.
— Neighbors & Family Coloring Book. (Illus.). 20p. (Orig.). (J). (gr. k up). 1989. pap. 2.50 (0-9613078-4-6) Detroit Black.
Moore, Peggy S. The Case of the Missing Bike & Other Things. 2nd rev. ed. (Illus.). 40p. (Orig.). (J). (gr. 4-6). 1992. pap. 5.95 (0-9613078-1-1) Detroit Black.
— My Very First book of Poetry & Other Things. (Poetry & Essays Ser.: No. I). (Illus.). 16p. (J). (gr. 3-5). 1982. pap. 1.98 (0-9613078-0-3) Detroit Black.
Moore, Perry. Evaluating Health Maintenance Organizations: A Guide for Employee Benefits Managers. LC 91-4719. 208p. 1991. text ed. 55.00 (0-89930-557-1, MHG/, Quorum Bks) Greenwood.
Moore, Peter. A Church to Believe In. 197p. (Orig.). 1994. pap. 9.95 (0-917851-76-5) Bristol Hse.
— European Mires. 1984. text ed. 161.00 (0-12-505580-3) Acad Pr.
— Litigation Management. 125p. (C). 1990. pap. 45.00 (1-875114-02-5, Blckstone AT) W W Gaunt.
— Managing Lawyers Information. 134p. (C). 1989. pap. 45.00 (1-875114-04-1, Blckstone AT) W W Gaunt.
— Precedents & Opinions. 92p. (C). 1989. pap. 45.00 (1-875114-03-3, Blckstone AT) W W Gaunt.
Moore, Peter, ed. Handbook of Botulinum Toxin Treatment. LC 95-184. 1995. write for info. (0-632-03616-8) Blackwell Sci.
— PASS: The Package & Sack Sequence System for Publications & Catalogs Mailings. 112p. 1989. 28.00 (0-89740-245-6) Graph Comm Assn.
Moore, Peter C. Disarming the Secular Gods: How to Talk So Skeptics Will Listen. LC 89-36756. 226p. (Orig.). 1989. pap. 9.99 (0-8308-1270-9, 1270) InterVarsity.
Moore, Peter D. Encyclopedia of Animal Ecology. (Encyclopedia of Animals Ser.). (Illus.). 150p. 1987. 29.95 (0-8160-1818-9) Facts on File.
Moore, Peter G. The Business of Risk. LC 82-23594. 200p. 1984. pap. 19.95 (0-521-28497-X) Cambridge U Pr.
Moore, Phil. Using Computers in English: A Practical Guide. (Teaching Secondary English Ser.). 200p. 1986. pap. 14.95 (0-416-36190-0, 9929) Routledge Chapman & Hall.
Moore, Philip. Total Bar & Beverage Management. 1981. pap. 23.95 (0-86730-238-0) Lebhar Friedman.
Moore, Philip S., jt. ed. see Corbett, James A.
Moore, Phillip, jt. auth. see Fairley, Alan.
Moore, Phyllis B. No Other Gods: An Interpretation of the Biblical Myth for a Transbiblical Age. (Chiron Monograph Ser.: Vol. VI). 208p. (Orig.). 1992. pap. 14.95 (0-933029-46-2) Chiron Pubns.
Moore, Phyllis B., ed. see Clarson, Laura E.
Moore Picture Trust Staff. Nelson Augustus Moore: Connecticut Landscape Painter. (Illus.). 144p. 1994. text ed. 40.00 (0-9637491-0-2) Moore Picture.
***Moore, Powell A.** Calumet Region, Indiana's Last Frontier. 685p. 1991. pap. 21.00 (1-885323-16-6) IN Hist Bureau.
Moore, Prentiss. The Garden in Winter & Other Poems. (University of Texas Press Poetry Ser.: No. 7). 116p. 1981. 14.95 (0-292-72721-6); pap. 7.95 (0-292-72722-4) U of Tex Pr.
— The Garden in Winter & Other Poems. LC 81-13117. (University of Texas Press Poetry Ser.: Vol. 7). 116p. 1981. reprint ed. pap. 33.10 (0-7837-8939-4, 2049649) Bks Demand.
— Mediterraneans: A Serenade. (Orig.). 1986. pap. text ed. 2.95 (0-941169-03-0) Black Chin Pr.
Moore, Preston. Drilling Practices Manual. 2nd ed. 606p. 1986. 89.95 (0-87814-292-4, P4344) PennWell Bks.
Moore, R. Pit-Men, Preachers & Politics. LC 73-88307. 1979. 42.50 (0-521-20356-2) Cambridge U Pr.
Moore, R. & Reppert, S. Suprachiasmatic Nucleus: The Mind's Clock. Klein, Donald F. et al, eds. (Illus.). 488p. 1991. 85.00 (0-19-506250-7) OUP.
Moore, R. E. Methods & Applications of Interval Analysis. LC 79-67191. (Studies in Applied Mathematics: No. 2). xi, 190p. 1979. text ed. 29.25 (0-89871-161-4) Soc Indus-Appl Math.
Moore, R. F., jt. ed. see Singh, P.
***Moore, R. I.** The Birth of Popular Heresy. (Medieval Academy Reprints for Teaching Ser.: MART 33). 176p. (C). 1995. pap. 14.95 (0-8020-7659-9) U of Toronto Pr.
— The Formation of a Persecuting Society: Power & Deviance in Western Europe. 192p. 1987. pap. 21.95 (0-631-17145-2) Blackwell Pubs.

An Asterisk (*) at the beginning of an entry indicates that the title is appearing in BIP for the first time.

— The Origins of European Dissent. (MART Thirty Medieval Academy Reprints for Teaching Ser.: No. 30). 322p. 1994. pap. 17.95 (*0-8020-7566-5*) U of Toronto Pr.

Moore, R. I., jt. ed. see Mayr-Harting, Henry.

Moore, R. J. Endgames of Empire: Studies of Britain's Indian Problem. 240p. 1989. 22.50 (*0-19-562143-3*) OUP.

Moore, R. J., jt. auth. see Wilkinson, J. B.

Moore, R. L. Control of Centrifugal Compressors. (Independent Learning Module Ser.). 305p. 1989. text ed. 60.00 (*1-55617-171-4*, A171-4) Instru Soc.

Moore, R. Laurence. Religious Outsiders & the Making of Americans. 272p. 1987. pap. 16.95 (*0-19-505188-2*) OUP.

— Selling God: American Religion in the Marketplace of American Culture. 288p. 1994. 25.00 (*0-19-508228-1*) OUP.

— Selling God: American Religion in the Marketplace of Culture. 334p. 1995. pap. 12.95 (*0-19-509838-2*) OUP.

Moore, R. T. Deuteromycete Studies: Collected Mycological Papers. (Bibliotheca Mycologica Ser.: Vol. 108). (Illus.). 180p. 1987. pap. text ed. 58.50 (*3-443-59009-8*) Lubrecht & Cramer.

— Measurable, Continuous & Smooth Vectors for Semigroups & Group Representations. LC 52-42839. (Memoirs Ser.: No. 1/78). 80p. 1968. pap. 16.00 (*0-8218-1278-5*, MEMO 1/78) Am Math.

Moore, Ralph. Financial Freedom. 177p. (Orig.). 1990. pap. 8.00 (*0-9628127-0-6*) Stright St Pubns.

— Let Go of the Ring: The Hope Chapel Story. 224p. (Orig.). 1993. pap. 10.00 (*0-9628127-1-4*) Stright St Pubns.

***Moore, Ralph & Tanner, Dinah.** Porcelain & Pottery Tea Tiles. (Illus.). 47p. 1994. pap. 12.95 (*1-57080-004-9*) Antique Pubns.

Moore, Ralph J. & Moore, Brooke N. The Cosmos, God & Philosophy. (American University Studies: Philosophy: Ser. V, Vol. 49). 312p. (C). 1989. text ed. 41.50 (*0-8204-0610-4*) P Lang Pubs.

Moore, Ralph L. Basic Instrumentation Lecture Notes & Study Guide, 2 vols., Vol. 1. 3rd ed. LC 82-81083. (Illus.). 187p. (Orig.). reprint ed. pap. 53.30 (*0-7837-4884-1*, 2044877) Bks Demand.

— Basic Instrumentation Lecture Notes & Study Guide, 2 vols., Vol. 2. LC 82-81083. (Illus.). 125p. (Orig.). reprint ed. pap. 35.70 (*0-7837-4885-X*, 2044877) Bks Demand.

— Environmental Protection by the Neutralization of Wastewater Using pH Control. LC 95-10626. 1995. write for info. (*1-55617-526-4*) Instru Soc.

— Neutralization of Waste Water by pH Control. LC 77-94491. (Instrument Society of America: Monograph: No. 1). (Illus.). 177p. reprint ed. pap. 50.50 (*0-7837-6058-2*, 2052504) Bks Demand.

Moore, Ralph L., ed. see Instrument Society of America Staff.

Moore, Ramon E., ed. Reliability in Computing: The Role of Interval Methods in Scientific Computing. (Perspectives in Computing Ser.: Vol. 19). 428p. 1988. text ed. 85.00 (*0-12-505630-3*) Acad Pr.

Moore, Randall C. Writing to Learn Botany. 112p. (C). 1995. spiral bd. write for info. (*0-697-17455-7*) Wm C Brown Pubs.

Moore, Randall c. & Lewis, Ricki. Life, 6 pts. 2nd ed. 936p. 1994. boxed write for info. (*0-697-15925-6*) Wm C Brown Pubs.

Moore, Randall c. & Vodopich, Darrell. Labman Biology. 368p. (C). 1995. spiral bd. write for info. (*0-697-03777-0*) Wm C Brown Pubs.

Moore, Randall c., jt. auth. see Lewis, Ricki.

Moore, Randall c., et al. Botany. 104p. (C). 1994. student ed write for info. (*0-697-24309-5*); boxed write for info. (*0-697-16957-X*) Wm C Brown Pubs.

— Botany. 208p. (C). 1995. student ed, spiral bd. write for info. (*0-697-03776-2*) Wm C Brown Pubs.

— Botany: Plant Diversity-Botany, Vol. 2. 384p. (C). 1994. pap. text ed. write for info. (*0-697-16657-0*) Wm C Brown Pubs.

— Botany: Plant Form & Function, Vol. 1. 592p. (C). 1994. pap. text ed. write for info. (*0-697-16656-2*) Wm C Brown Pubs.

Moore, Randall S., jt. auth. see Madsen, Clifford K.

Moore, Randy. Writing to Learn Biology. 352p. (C). 1992. pap. text ed. 17.00 (*0-03-074189-0*) SCP.

Moore, Randy, ed. Vegetative Compatibility Responses in Plants. LC 83-72004. (Illus.). 163p. 1983. pap. 19.50 (*0-918954-40-1*) Baylor Univ Pr.

Moore, Randy & Vodopich, Darrell S. The Living Desert. LC 90-42243. (Living World Ser.). (Illus.). 64p. (J). (gr. 6 up). 1991. lib. bdg. 15.95 (*0-89490-182-6*) Enslow Pubs.

***Moore, Ray A., ed.** Culture & Religion in Japanese-American Relations: Essays on Uchimura Kanzo, No. 5. x, 142p. 1981. pap. 8.95 (*0-939512-10-6*) U MI Japan.

Moore, Rayanne, jt. auth. see Stevens, Serita.

Moore, Rayburn S. Constance F. Woolson. (Twayne's United States Authors Ser.). 1963. pap. 13.95x (*0-8084-0092-4*, T34) NCUP.

— Constance Fenimore Woolson. LC 62-19478. (Twayne's United States Authors Ser.). 1963. lib. bdg. 8.95 (*0-89197-710-4*); pap. text ed. 4.95 (*0-8290-0008-9*) Irvington.

— Paul Hamilton Hayne. Bowman, Sylvia E., ed. LC 73-125818. (Twayne's United States Authors Ser.). 184p. (C). 1972. lib. bdg. 17.95 (*0-8290-1711-9*) Irvington.

Moore, Rayburn S., ed. Correspondence of Henry James & the House of Macmillan, 1877-1914: "All the Links in the Chain" LC 92-28962. xxvi, 275p. 1993. text ed. 40.00x (*0-8071-1834-6*) La State U Pr.

Moore, Rayburn S., ed. see James, Henry.

Moore, Rayburn S., ed. see Woolson, Constance F.

Moore, Raymond. Murmurs at Every Turn: The Photographs of Raymond Moore. 96p. 1981. 25.00 (*0-906333-12-1*); pap. 15.00 (*0-906333-15-6*) Jargon Soc.

Moore, Raymond & Moore, Dorothy. Home-Grown Kids. 253p. 1984. pap. text ed. 8.99 (*0-8499-3007-3*) Word Inc.

Moore, Raymond A., jt. auth. see Whicker, Marcia L.

Moore, Raymond C. Treatise on Invertebrate Paleontology, Pt. U: Echinodermata 3: Asterozoa-Echinozoa, 2 vols. LC 53-12913. (Illus.). 725p. 1966. reprint ed. 62.00 (*0-8137-3022-8*) Geol Soc.

Moore, Raymond C., ed. Treatise on Invertebrate Paleontology. LC 53-12913. 267p. reprint ed. pap. 76.10 (*0-7837-1257-X*, 2041394) Bks Demand.

— Treatise on Invertebrate Paleontology, Pt. D: Protista 3 (Chiefly Radiolaria, Tintinnina) LC 53-12913. (Illus.). 207p. 1954. reprint ed. 25.00 (*0-8137-3004-X*) Geol Soc.

— Treatise on Invertebrate Paleontology, Pt. F: Coelenterata. LC 53-12913. (Illus.). 508p. 1956. 27.50 (*0-8137-3006-6*) Geol Soc.

— Treatise on Invertebrate Paleontology, Pt. H: Brachiopoda, 2 vols. LC 53-12913. (Illus.). 959p. 1965. reprint ed. 65.00 (*0-8137-3008-2*) Geol Soc.

— Treatise on Invertebrate Paleontology, Pt. I: Mollusca 1. LC 53-12913. (Illus.). 374p. 1960. 43.75 (*0-8137-3009-0*) Geol Soc.

— Treatise on Invertebrate Paleontology, Pt. K: Mollusca 3. LC 53-12913. (Illus.). 547p. 1964. 44.00 (*0-8137-3011-2*) Geol Soc.

— Treatise on Invertebrate Paleontology, Pt. L: Mollusca 4. (Illus.). 511p. 1957. 55.00 (*0-8137-3012-0*) Geol Soc.

— Treatise on Invertebrate Paleontology, Pt. N: Mollusca 6, Bivalvia, Vols. 1-2. LC 53-12913. (Illus.). 989p. 1969. 44.25 (*0-8137-3014-7*) Geol Soc.

— Treatise on Invertebrate Paleontology, Pt. O: Arthropoda 1. LC 53-12913. (Illus.). 579p. 1959. 27.50 (*0-8137-3015-5*) Geol Soc.

— Treatise on Invertebrate Paleontology, Pt. P: Arthropoda 2. LC 53-12913. (Illus.). 198p. 1955. 24.50 (*0-8137-3016-3*) Geol Soc.

— Treatise on Invertebrate Paleontology, Pt. Q: Arthropoda 3: Crustacea: Ostracoda. LC 53-12913. (Illus.). 465p. 1961. 26.75 (*0-8137-3017-1*) Geol Soc.

— Treatise on Invertebrate Paleontology, Pt. S: Echinodermata 1: General Characters Homalozoa-Crinozoa (Except Crinoidea), 2 vols. LC 53-12913. (Illus.). 679p. 1967. 32.00 (*0-8137-3020-1*) Geol Soc.

— Treatise on Invertebrate Paleontology, Pt. W: Miscellanea. LC 53-12913. (Illus.). 284p. 1962. 18.00 (*0-8137-3024-4*) Geol Soc.

Moore, Raymond C. & Teichert, Curt, eds. Treatise on Invertebrate Paleontology, Pt. R: Arthropoda 4: Crustacea (Except Ostracoda): Myriapoda, Vols. 1-2. LC 53-12913. (Illus.). 687p. 1969. 32.00 (*0-8137-3018-X*) Geol Soc.

— Treatise on Invertebrate Paleontology, Pt. T: Echinodermata 2: Crinoidea, 3 vols., Set. LC 53-12913. (Illus.). 1978. 61.00 (*0-8137-3021-X*) Geol Soc.

— Treatise on Invertebrate Paleontology, Pt. T: Echinodermata 2: Crinoidea, Vol. 1. LC 53-12913. (Illus.). 439p. 1978. 31.00 (*0-686-82905-0*) Geol Soc.

— Treatise on Invertebrate Paleontology, Pt. T: Echinodermata 2: Crinoidea, Vol. 2. LC 53-12913. (Illus.). 411p. 1978. 30.00 (*0-686-82906-9*) Geol Soc.

— Treatise on Invertebrate Paleontology, Pt. T: Echinodermata 2: Crinoidea, Vol. 3. LC 53-12913. (Illus.). 215p. 1978. 17.00 (*0-686-82907-7*) Geol Soc.

Moore, Raymond C., ed. see Bulman, O. M.

Moore, Raymond C., ed. see Loeblich, Alfred R., Jr. & Tappan, Helen.

Moore, Raymond C., ed. see Stenzel, H. B.

Moore, Raymond C., et al. Invertebrate Fossils. 1952. text ed. write for info. (*0-07-043020-9*) McGraw.

Moore, Reavis. Native Artists of Africa. (Rainbow Warrior Artists Ser.). 48p. (J). (gr. 4-7). 1994. 14.95 (*1-56261-147-X*) John Muir.

— Native Artists of Europe. (Rainbow Warrior Artists Ser.). (Illus.). 48p. (J). (gr. 4-7). 1994. 14.95 (*1-56261-158-5*) John Muir.

— Native Artists of North America. (Rainbow Warrior Artists Ser.). (Illus.). 48p. (J). (gr. 4-7). 1993. 14.95 (*1-56261-105-4*) John Muir.

Moore, Rebecca. In Defense of People's Temple. LC 88-8933. (Studies in American Religion: Vol. 32). 150p. 1988. lib. bdg. 69.95 (*0-88946-676-9*) E Mellen.

— The Jonestown Letters: Correspondence of the Moore Family, 1970-1985. LC 86-18192. (Studies in American Religion: Vol. 23). (Illus.). 398p. 1986. lib. bdg. 109.95 (*0-88946-667-X*) E Mellen.

Moore, Rebecca & McGehee, Fielding M., III, eds. New Religious Movements, Mass Suicide & Peoples Temple: Scholarly Perspectives on a Tragedy. LC 88-34382. (Studies in American Religion). 256p. 1989. lib. bdg. 89.95 (*0-88946-680-7*) E Mellen.

Moore, Rebecca, ed. see Thomson, Andy.

Moore, Rebecca S., ed. see Fremont, Walter, et al.

Moore, Renee, tr. see Flynn, Ted & Flynn, Maureen.

***Moore, Rich & Rogalski, Ron.** Bow Down. 1991. 25.00 (*0-614-03115-X*) Lillenas.

Moore, Rich, jt. auth. see Rogalski, Ron.

Moore, Richard. Bottom Is Back. LC 94-6557. 96p. (Orig.). 1994. pap. 11.95 (*0-914061-43-7*) Orchises Pr.

— The High Blood Pressure Solution: Natural Prevention & Cure with the K Factor. 256p. (Orig.). 1993. pap. 12.95 (*0-89281-446-2*, Heal Arts VT) Inner Tradit.

— The Investigator. 220p. 1991. 18.95 (*0-934257-77-9*) Story Line.

— No More Bottom. LC 90-28176. 80p. (Orig.). 1991. pap. 10.00 (*0-914061-22-4*) Orchises Pr.

— Portugal. LC 91-26998. (World in View Ser.). (Illus.). 96p. (YA). (gr. 6-12). 1992. lib. bdg. 24.26 (*0-8114-2451-0*) Raintree Steck-V.

— The Rule That Liberates: New & Previously Published Essays. LC 93-41030. 1993. 10.95 (*0-929925-26-2*) Univ SD Pr.

Moore, Richard, photos. Gardens of Georgia. 1989. 50.00 (*0-934601-76-3*) Peachtree Pubs.

— Gardens of Georgia. limited ed. 1989. 75.00 (*1-56145-009-X*) Peachtree Pubs.

Moore, Richard, tr. see Fedorov, V. B., ed.

Moore, Richard, jt. auth. see Pagano, Michael A.

Moore, Richard B. The Name Negro. (African Studies). reprint ed. 18.00 (*0-938818-97-X*) ECA Assoc.

— The Name "Negro" - Its Origin & Evil Use. rev. ed. Turner, W. Burghardt & Turner, Joyce M., eds. LC 91-77147. 110p. 1992. reprint ed. 19.95 (*0-933121-36-9*); reprint ed. pap. 8.95 (*0-933121-35-0*) Black Classic.

Moore, Richard C., ed. Carlisle's Guide to Government. LC 93-85942. (Orig.). 1993. pap. 12.95 (*0-9639034-0-3*) Univ Wholesale.

— Carlisle's Guide to Government. 256p. (Orig.). 1994. pap. 12.95 (*0-9639034-4-6*) Univ Wholesale.

Moore, Richard C. & Ettore, Eugene. Anthology of French Horn Music. 1993. 15.00 (*1-56222-191-4*, 93801) Mel Bay.

Moore, Richard E. & Purcell, Nadine H., eds. Pacific Northwest Americana Supplement, 1949-1974. LC 81-65510. 372p. 1981. pap. 20.00 (*0-8323-0389-5*) Binford Mort.

Moore, Richard J., jt. auth. see Dietz, Henry A.

Moore, Richard V., ed. Nuclear Power. LC 77-142962. (Institution of Electrical Engineers Monograph Ser.: Vol. 6). (Illus.). 208p. reprint ed. pap. 59.30 (*0-8357-8975-6*, 2033453) Bks Demand.

Moore, Richard W., jt. ed. see Wilms, Wellford W.

Moore, Richter H., Jr., et al. Readings in Criminal Justice. LC 75-38727. 1976. pap. 10.95 (*0-672-61371-9*, Bobbs) Macmillan.

Moore, Rickie. A Goddess in My Shoes: Seven Steps to Peace. LC 88-9243. 160p. 1988. pap. 16.95 (*0-89334-109-6*) Humanics Ltd.

— Make the Circle Bigger: We Need Each Other. LC 90-4065. (Illus.). 128p. (Orig.). 1990. pap. 14.95 (*0-89334-133-9*) Humanics Ltd.

— Make the Circle Bigger: We Need Each Other. LC 90-4065. (Illus.). 128p. (Orig.). 1990. lib. bdg. 24.95 (*0-89334-193-2*, 193-2) Humanics Ltd.

Moore, Ricky D. The Lord's Rest. LC 91-90425. 80p. (Orig.). (C). 1991. pap. 5.95 (*0-9630110-0-6*) Am Network.

Moore-Rinvolucri, Mina, tr. see Veyne, Paul.

Moore, Rob & Ozga, Jenny, eds. Curriculum Policy. 160p. 1990. text ed. 33.00 (*0-08-041022-7*, Pergamon Pr); pap. text ed. 16.25 (*0-08-040818-4*, Pergamon Pr) Elsevier.

Moore, Robert. Logic & Representation. (CSLI Lecture Notes Ser.: No. 39). 210p. 1994. 39.95 (*1-881526-16-X*); pap. 16.95 (*1-881526-15-1*) Ctr Study Language.

— The Warrior Within: Accessing the Warrior in the Male Psyche. LC 92-9494. 1992. 22.00 (*0-688-09592-5*) Morrow.

Moore, Robert & Gillette, Doug. The Lover Within: Accessing the Romantic in the Male Psyche. LC 92-46193. 1993. 25.00 (*0-688-09593-3*) Morrow.

Moore, Robert & Gillette, Douglas. King, Warrior, Magician, Lover: Rediscovering the Archetypes of the Mature Masculine. LC 89-45991. (Illus.). 192p. 1991. reprint ed. pap. 10.00 (*0-06-250606-4*) Harper SF.

— The King Within: Accessing the King in the Male Psyche. 344p. 1993. pap. 11.00 (*0-380-72068-X*) Avon.

— The King Within: Accessing the King in the Male Psyche. (Illus.). 320p. 1992. 22.00 (*0-688-09591-7*) Morrow.

— The Lover Within: Accessing the Lover in the Male Psyche. 288p. 1995. pap. 12.50 (*0-380-72071-X*) Avon.

— The Magician Within: Accessing the Magician in the Male Psyche. LC 92-23557. 1993. 23.00 (*0-688-09594-1*) Morrow.

— The Magician Within: Accessing the Shaman in the Male Psyche. 304p. 1994. reprint ed. pap. 12.50 (*0-380-72070-1*) Avon.

— The Warrior Within: Accessing the Knight in the Male Psyche. 328p. 1993. pap. 11.00 (*0-380-72069-8*) Avon.

Moore, Robert, jt. auth. see Brown, Eleanor.

Moore, Robert A. A Life for the Confederacy: As Recorded in the Pocket Diaries of Pvt. Robert A. Moore, Co. G 17th Mississippi Regiment, Confederate Guards, Holly Springs, Mississippi. Silver, James W., ed. (Illus.). 182p. 1992. reprint ed. 25.00 (*0-916107-38-8*) Broadfoot.

Moore, Robert A., ed. Carl Jung & Christian Spirituality: A Reader. (Jung & Spirituality Ser.). 272p. 1988. pap. 12.95 (*0-8091-2950-7*) Paulist Pr.

Moore, Robert C. The Political Reality of Freedom of the Press in Zambia. 158p. (C). 1992. lib. bdg. 37.50 (*0-8191-8649-X*) U Pr of Amer.

Moore, Robert C., jt. ed. see Hobbs, Jerry.

Moore, Robert C., jt. ed. see Pisacane, Vincent L.

Moore, Robert E. Henry Purcell & the Restoration Theatre. LC 73-15057. (Illus.). 223p. (C). 1974. reprint ed. text ed. 55.00 (*0-8371-7155-5*, MOHQ, Greenwood Pr) Greenwood.

Moore, Robert H., II. The Charlottesville, Lee, Lynchburg & Johnson's Bedford Artillery. (Virginia Regimental Histories Ser.). (Illus.). 142p. 1990. 19.95 (*1-56190-008-7*) H E Howard.

— The Danville, Eighth Star New Market & Dixie Artillery. (Virginia Regimental Histories Ser.). (Illus.). 110p. 1989. 19.95 (*0-930919-72-6*) H E Howard.

Moore, Robert H. The Richmond, Fayette, Hampden, Thomas & Blount's Lynchburg Artillery. (Virginia Regimental Histories Ser.). (Illus.). 178p. 1991. 19.95 (*1-56190-018-4*) H E Howard.

Moore, Robert J. & Schwenz, Richard W., eds. Physical Chemistry: Developing a Dynamic Curriculum. LC 92-35619. (Illus.). 488p. 1992. 49.95 (*0-8412-2503-6*) Am Chemical.

Moore, Robert J., jt. auth. see Morton, Leslie T.

Moore, Robert L. Foundations of Point Set Theory. LC 62-8325. (Colloquium Publications: Vol. 13). 419p. 1987. reprint ed. pap. 83.00 (*0-8218-1013-8*, COLL-13) Am Math.

— John Wesley & Authority: A Psychological Perspective. LC 79-13709. (American Academy of Religion. Dissertation Ser.: No. 29). 255p. reprint ed. pap. 72.70 (*0-7837-5417-5*, 2045181) Bks Demand.

— Jung & Christianity in Dialogue: Faith, Feminism & Hermeneutics. Meckel, Daniel J., ed. 1990. pap. 12.95 (*0-8091-3187-0*) Paulist Pr.

— Self & Liberation: The Jung - Buddhism Dialogue. Meckel, Daniel J., ed. LC 91-40818. (Jung & Spirituality Ser.). 352p. 1992. pap. 19.95 (*0-8091-3301-6*) Paulist Pr.

Moore, Robert L., ed. Sources of Vitality in American Church Life. LC 78-71065. (Studies in Ministry & Parish Life). 1978. text ed. 14.95 (*0-913552-14-3*) Exploration Pr.

Moore, Robert L. & Studenmund, A. H. Instructor's Manual to Accompany Introduction to Economics: The Wealth & Poverty of Nations, by Gwartney & Stroup. 180p. (C). 1994. pap. text ed. 28.00 (*0-03-001836-6*) Dryden Pr.

Moore, Robert S., jt. ed. see Lupinski, John H.

Moore, Robert T., jt. auth. see Jorgensen, Palle E.

Moore, Roberta, jt. auth. see Herr, Edwin L.

Moore, Robin. Awakening the Hidden Storyteller: How to Build a Storytelling Tradition in Your Family. 1991. pap. 18.00 (*0-87773-599-9*) Shambhala Pubns.

— The Bread Sister of Sinking Creek. LC 89-36400. (Trophy Bk.). 160p. (J). (gr. 4-7). 1992. pap. 3.95 (*0-06-440357-2*, Trophy) HarpC Child Bks.

— The Devil to Pay. 415p. 1991. 19.95 (*1-879915-02-2*) Affil Writers America.

— Fiedler: The Colorful Mr. Pops. LC 79-24416. (Music Reprint Ser.). (Illus.). 1980. reprint ed. lib. bdg. 45.00 (*0-306-76008-8*) Da Capo.

— Grandpa's True Tales from the Woods. LC 94-19479. (J). 1995. 15.00 (*0-679-85641-2*) Knopf.

— Maggie among the Seneca. rev. ed. LC 89-77110. 112p. (J). (gr. 4-7). 1990. lib. bdg. 14.89 (*0-397-32456-1*, Lipp Jr Bks) HarpC Child Bks.

— The Moscow Connection. 500p. 1994. 20.00 (*1-879915-11-1*) Affil Writers America.

— When the Moon Is Full. 128p. (J). (gr. 5-9). 1994. 15.00 (*0-679-85642-0*) Knopf Bks Yng Read.

— The White Tribe. 550p. 1991. 24.95 (*1-879915-03-0*) Affil Writers America.

Moore, Robin & Dempsey, Al. Phase of Darkness. LC 73-92799. 1974. 30.00 (*0-89388-136-8*) Okpaku Communications.

Moore, Robin C. Plants for Play: A Plant Selection Guide for Children's Outdoor Environments. LC 92-62234. 1993. 16.95 (*0-944661-18-1*) MIG Comns.

Moore, Robin C., et al, eds. Play for All Guidelines: Planning, Design & Management of Outdoor Play Settings for All Children. 2nd ed. (Illus.). 300p. (Orig.). 1992. pap. 39.95 (*0-944661-17-3*) MIG Comns.

Moore, Rod. Monkey. 78p. (Orig.). 1985. pap. 4.95 (*0-933515-04-9*) Exile Pr.

Moore, Rod V. Igloo among Palms. LC 94-22499. (Iowa Short Fiction Award 1994 Ser.). 145p. 1994. 22.95 (*0-87745-475-2*) U of Iowa Pr.

Moore, Roger, ed. AGI Yearbook 1989. 250p. 1989. 105.00 (*0-85066-793-3*); pap. 53.00 (*0-85066-794-1*) Taylor & Francis.

Moore, Roger A., jt. auth. see Lake, Carol L.

Moore, Roger L., et al. Organizing Outdoor Volunteers: Building Grassroots Conservation Organizations. 2nd ed. LC 92-22621. (Illus.). 112p. 1992. pap. 4.95 (*1-878239-16-3*) AMC Books.

Moore, Ronald & Moore, Gloria. Margaret Sanger & the Birth Control Movement: A Bibliography, 1911-1984. LC 86-10119. 230p. 1986. 25.00 (*0-8108-1903-1*) Scarecrow.

Moore, Rosalie. Of Singles & Doubles. LC 78-68474. 1979. 7.95 (*0-913506-06-0*) Woolmer-Brotherson.

Moore, Rosalind, ed. The Dell Big Book of Crosswords & Pencil Puzzles, No. 6. (Orig.). 1987. mass mkt. 9.99 (*0-440-51899-7*) Dell.

— The Dell Big Book of Crosswords & Pencil Puzzles, No. 7. (Orig.). (J). 1989. mass mkt. 9.99 (*0-440-50161-X*) Dell.

— The Dell Big Book of Crosswords & Pencil Puzzles No. 5. (Orig.). 1985. mass mkt. 8.95 (*0-440-51877-6*, Dell Trade Pbks) Dell.

— The Dell Book of Logic Problems, No. 1. (Orig.). 1984. pap. 10.99 (*0-440-51891-1*, Dell Trade Pbks) Dell.

— The Dell Book of Logic Problems, No. 2. (Orig.). 1986. pap. 10.99 (*0-440-51875-X*, Dell Trade Pbks) Dell.

Moore, Rosalind, jt. ed. see Rafferty, Kathleen.

Moore, Rowan, ed. Structure, Space, & Skin: The Work of Nicholas Grimshaw & Partners. (Illus.). 256p. 1993. 60.00 (*0-7148-2850-5*, Pub. by Phaidon Press UK) Chronicle Bks.

Moore, Roy & Smith, F. T. Carpet Cleaners Guide to Increased Sales & Profit. Griffin, William R., ed. (Illus.). 38p. 1987. pap. text ed. 25.00 (*0-944352-01-4*) Cleaning Cons.

— Drapery Cleaning: On Location. Griffin, William R., ed. (Illus.). 36p. (C). 1987. pap. text ed. 25.00 (*0-944352-02-2*) Cleaning Cons.

— Professional Upholster Cleaning Techniques: The Basics. rev. ed. Griffin, W. R., ed. 35p. (C). 1987. pap. text ed. 25.00 (*0-944352-00-6*) Cleaning Cons.

An Asterisk (*) at the beginning of an entry indicates that the title is appearing in BIP for the first time.

Moore, Roy & Smith, F. W. Fire Restoration & Insurance Work. Griffin, William R., ed. 60p. 1987. pap. 25.00 (*0-9601054-6-8*) Cleaning Cons.

Moore, Roy L. Mass Communication Law & Ethics. (Communication Ser.). 616p. (C). 1993. text ed. 45.00 (*0-8058-0240-1*) L Erlbaum Assocs.

— Mass Communication Law & Ethics: 1995 Update. (LEA's Communication Ser.). 75p. 1994. pap. 10.00 (*0-8058-1927-4*) L Erlbaum Assocs.

— Mass Communication Law & Ethics: 1995 Update, Text & Supplement Set. suppl. ed. (LEA's Communication Ser.). 1994. pap. 45.00 (*0-8058-1928-2*) L Erlbaum Assocs.

Moore, Rudy. Arithmetic Series Two, Quarter Three. (J). (gr. 2). 1988. pap. 8.95 (*0-88062-238-5*) Mott Media.

— Arithmetic Series Two, Quarter Two. (J). (gr. 2). 1988. pap. 8.95 (*0-88062-237-7*) Mott Media.

Moore, Rudy & Moore, Betty. Arithmetic Series Four, Quarter Four. (J). (gr. 4). 1994. 8.95 (*0-88062-247-4*) Mott Media.

— Arithmetic Series Four, Quarter One. (J). (gr. 4). 1991. 8.95 (*0-88062-244-X*) Mott Media.

— Arithmetic Series Four, Quarter Three. (J). (gr. 4). 1994. 8.95 (*0-88062-246-6*) Mott Media.

— Arithmetic Series Four, Quarter Two. (J). (gr. 4). 1994. 8.95 (*0-88062-245-8*) Mott Media.

— Arithmetic Series One, Quarter Four. (J). (gr. 1). 1991. 8.95 (*0-88062-235-0*) Mott Media.

— Arithmetic Series One, Quarter One. (J). (gr. 1). 1988. pap. 8.95 (*0-88062-232-6*) Mott Media.

— Arithmetic Series One, Quarter Three. (J). (gr. 1). 1988. pap. 8.95 (*0-88062-234-2*) Mott Media.

— Arithmetic Series One, Quarter Two. (J). (gr. 1). 1988. pap. 8.95 (*0-88062-233-4*) Mott Media.

— Arithmetic Series Three, Quarter Four. (J). (gr. 3). 1991. 8.95 (*0-88062-243-1*) Mott Media.

— Arithmetic Series Three, Quarter One. (J). (gr. 3). 1988. pap. 8.95 (*0-88062-240-7*) Mott Media.

— Arithmetic Series Three, Quarter Three. (J). (gr. 3). 1991. 8.95 (*0-88062-242-3*) Mott Media.

— Arithmetic Series Three, Quarter Two. (J). (gr. 3). 1988. pap. 8.95 (*0-88062-241-5*) Mott Media.

— Arithmetic Series Two, Quarter Four. (J). (gr. 2). 1991. 8.95 (*0-88062-239-3*) Mott Media.

— Arithmetic Series Two, Quarter One. (J). (gr. 2). 1988. pap. 8.95 (*0-88062-236-9*) Mott Media.

— Reading Series Four, Quarter Four. (J). (gr. 4). 1994. 8.95 (*0-88062-215-6*) Mott Media.

— Reading Series Four, Quarter One. (J). (gr. 4). 1988. pap. 8.95 (*0-88062-212-1*) Mott Media.

— Reading Series Four, Quarter Three. (J). (gr. 4). 1988. pap. 8.95 (*0-88062-214-8*) Mott Media.

— Reading Series Four, Quarter Two. (J). (gr. 4). 1988. pap. 8.95 (*0-88062-213-X*) Mott Media.

— Reading Series One, Quarter Four. (J). (gr. 1). 1991. 8.95 (*0-88062-203-2*) Mott Media.

— Reading Series One, Quarter One. (J). (gr. 1). 1988. pap. 8.95 (*0-88062-200-8*) Mott Media.

— Reading Series One, Quarter Three. (J). (gr. 1). 1988. pap. 8.95 (*0-88062-202-4*) Mott Media.

— Reading Series One, Quarter Two. (J). (gr. 1). 1988. pap. 8.95 (*0-88062-201-6*) Mott Media.

— Reading Series Three, Quarter Four. (J). (gr. 3). 1994. 8.95 (*0-88062-211-3*) Mott Media.

— Reading Series Three, Quarter One. (J). (gr. 3). 1988. pap. 8.95 (*0-88062-208-3*) Mott Media.

— Reading Series Three, Quarter Three. (J). (gr. 3). 1988. pap. 8.95 (*0-88062-210-5*) Mott Media.

— Reading Series Three, Quarter Two. (J). (gr. 3). 1988. pap. 8.95 (*0-88062-209-1*) Mott Media.

— Reading Series Two, Quarter Four. (J). (gr. 2). 1991. 8.95 (*0-88062-207-5*) Mott Media.

— Reading Series Two, Quarter One. (J). (gr. 2). 1988. pap. 8.95 (*0-88062-204-0*) Mott Media.

— Reading Series Two, Quarter Three. (J). (gr. 2). 1988. pap. 8.95 (*0-88062-206-7*) Mott Media.

— Reading Series Two, Quarter Two. (J). (gr. 2). 1988. pap. 8.95 (*0-88062-205-9*) Mott Media.

— Writing Series Four, Quarter Four. (J). (gr. 4). 1994. 8.95 (*0-88062-231-8*) Mott Media.

— Writing Series Four, Quarter One. (J). (gr. 4). 1988. pap. 8.95 (*0-88062-228-8*) Mott Media.

— Writing Series Four, Quarter Three. (J). (gr. 4). 1988. pap. 8.95 (*0-88062-230-X*) Mott Media.

— Writing Series Four, Quarter Two. (J). (gr. 4). 1988. pap. 8.95 (*0-88062-229-6*) Mott Media.

— Writing Series One, Quarter Four. (J). (gr. 1). 1991. 8.95 (*0-88062-219-9*) Mott Media.

— Writing Series One, Quarter One. (J). (gr. 1). 1988. pap. 8.95 (*0-88062-216-4*) Mott Media.

— Writing Series One, Quarter Three. (J). (gr. 1). 1988. pap. 8.95 (*0-88062-218-0*) Mott Media.

— Writing Series One, Quarter Two. (J). (gr. 1). 1988. pap. 8.95 (*0-88062-217-2*) Mott Media.

— Writing Series Three, Quarter Four. (J). (gr. 3). 1991. 8.95 (*0-88062-227-X*) Mott Media.

— Writing Series Three, Quarter One. (J). (gr. 3). 1988. pap. 8.95 (*0-88062-224-5*) Mott Media.

— Writing Series Three, Quarter Three. (J). (gr. 3). 1991. 8.95 (*0-88062-226-1*) Mott Media.

— Writing Series Three, Quarter Two. (J). (gr. 3). 1988. pap. 8.95 (*0-88062-225-3*) Mott Media.

— Writing Series Two, Quarter Four. (J). (gr. 2). 1991. 8.95 (*0-88062-223-7*) Mott Media.

— Writing Series Two, Quarter One. (J). (gr. 2). 1988. pap. 8.95 (*0-88062-220-2*) Mott Media.

— Writing Series Two, Quarter Three. (J). (gr. 2). 1988. pap. 8.95 (*0-88062-222-9*) Mott Media.

— Writing Series Two, Quarter Two. (J). (gr. 2). 1988. pap. 8.95 (*0-88062-221-0*) Mott Media.

Moore, Russell, tr. see Amin, Samir.

Moore, Russell, jt. auth. see Richards, Sara.

Moore, Russell G. The Little Striker. LC 81-80507. (Illus.). 128p. (Orig.). 1981. pap. 5.00 (*0-936972-03-3*) Lower Cape.

Moore, Russell M. Multinational Corporations & the Regionalization of the Latin American Automotive Industry. Bruchey, Stuart, ed. LC 80-584. (Multinational Corporations Ser.). 1981. lib. bdg. 36.95 (*0-405-13376-6*) Ayer.

Moore, Russell M., jt. ed. see Lehman, Cheryl R.

Moore, Ruth. Candlemas Bay. 1994. pap. 10.95 (*0-942396-70-7*) Blackberry ME.

— Speak to the Winds. 1987. pap. 9.95 (*0-942396-54-5*) Blackberry ME.

— Spoonhandle. 1986. pap. 10.95 (*0-942396-49-9*) Blackberry ME.

— The Tired Apple Tree. 160p. (Orig.). 1990. pap. 8.50 (*0-942396-59-6*) Blackberry ME.

— The Walk Down Main Street. 386p. 1988. reprint ed. pap. 10.95 (*0-942396-56-1*) Blackberry ME.

— The Weir. 1986. pap. 10.95 (*0-942396-48-0*) Blackberry ME.

Moore, Ruth N. The Christmas Surprise. (Illus.). 160p. (Orig.). (J). (gr. 4-8). 1989. pap. 5.95 (*0-8361-3499-0*) Herald Pr.

— Distant Thunder: A Sequel to the Christmas Surprise. LC 91-10845. 160p. (Orig.). (J). (gr. 4-8). 1991. pap. 5.95 (*0-8361-3557-1*) Herald Pr.

— Ghost Town Mystery. LC 87-2874. (Sara & Sam Mysteries Ser.: No. 5). (Illus.). 144p. (J). (gr. 4 up). 1987. pap. 5.95 (*0-8361-3445-1*) Herald Pr.

— Mystery at Camp Ichthus. LC 86-25637. (Sara & Sam Mysteries Ser.: No. 4). (Illus.). 128p. (Orig.). (J). (gr. 3-9). 1986. pap. 5.95 (*0-8361-3421-4*) Herald Pr.

— Mystery at Captain's Cove. (Sara & Sam Mysteries Ser.: No. 7). 160p. (Orig.). (J). (gr. 4-7). 1992. pap. 5.95 (*0-8361-3581-4*) Herald Pr.

— Mystery at the Spanish Castle. 112p. (Orig.). (J). (gr. 4-8). 1990. pap. 5.95 (*0-8361-3515-6*) Herald Pr.

— Mystery of the Lost Heirloom. LC 85-27334. (Sara & Sam Mysteries Ser.: No. 3). (Illus.). 152p. (Orig.). (J). (gr. 6-9). 1985. pap. 5.95 (*0-8361-3408-7*) Herald Pr.

— Mystery of the Missing Stallions. LC 84-19. (Illus.). 136p. (Orig.). (J). (gr. 3-8). 1984. pap. 5.95 (*0-8361-3376-5*) Herald Pr.

— Mystery of the Secret Code. LC 85-5441. (Sara & Sam Mysteries Ser.: No. 2). (Illus.). 128p. (Orig.). (YA). (gr. 7-9). 1985. pap. 5.95 (*0-8361-3394-3*) Herald Pr.

— Where the Eagles Fly. 104p. (Orig.). (J). (gr. 4-7). 1994. pap. 5.95 (*0-8361-3664-0*) Herald Pr.

Moore, S. A. & Kimber, G. M. Secondary Co-Refining of Petroleum & Coal Distillates & the Evaluation of Coal Cleaning & Coal Liquisication, EUR 13973. 84p. 1992. pap. 13.00 (*92-826-3797-2*, CD-NA-13973-EN-C, Pub. by Europ Com) UNIPUB.

***Moore, S. Craig.** Framework for Characterization of Military Unit Training Status. LC 94-49663. 1995. write for info. (*0-8330-1625-3*) Rand Corp.

Moore, S. Craig, jt. auth. see Holroyd, Suzanne M.

Moore, S. Philip. Yachts in a Hurry. 160p. 1994. 40.00 (*0-393-03576-X*) Norton.

Moore, Sally. Country Roads of Pennsylvania. LC 93-11611. (Country Roads Ser.). (Illus.). 140p. (Orig.). 1993. pap. 9.95 (*1-56626-032-9*) Country Rds.

— Pennsylvania Outdoor Activity Guide. (Outdoor Activity Guide Ser.). 140p. 1995. pap. 9.95 (*1-56626-111-2*) Country Rds.

Moore, Sally F. Power & Property in Inca Peru. LC 72-5456. 190p. 1973. text ed. 35.00 (*0-8371-6441-9*, MOPO, Greenwood Pr) Greenwood.

— Social Facts & Fabrications: Customary Law on Kilimanjaro, Eighteen Eighty to Nineteen Eighty. LC 85-7897. 1986. pap. 32.95 (*0-521-31201-9*) Cambridge U Pr.

Moore, Sally F., ed. Moralizing States & the Ethnography of the Present. LC 93-33898. (American Ethnological Society Monograph Ser.: Vol. 5). 1993. write for info. (*0-913167-60-6*) Am Anthro Assn.

Moore, Sally F. & Puritt, Paul. The Chagga & Meru of Tanzania. LC 78-309993. (Ethnographic Survey of Africa: East Central Africa Ser.: No. 18). 156p. reprint ed. pap. 44.50 (*0-8357-6963-1*, 2039023) Bks Demand.

Moore, Sally Falk. Anthropology & Africa: Changing Perspectives on a Changing Scene. LC 93-40047. 205p. (C). 1994. 29.50 (*0-8139-1504-X*); pap. text ed. 9.95 (*0-8139-1505-8*) U Pr of Va.

Moore, Samuel & Knott, Thomas A. Elements of Old English. 1955. 15.00 (*0-911586-23-7*) Wahr.

Moore, Samuel, jt. auth. see Marckwardt, Albert H.

Moore, Samuel, tr. see Marx, Karl & Engels, Friedrich.

Moore, Samuel P. Confederate States Medical & Surgical Journal. (American Civil War Medical Ser.: No. 12). 272p. 1992. reprint ed. 95.00 (*0-930405-40-4*) Norman SF.

— Regulations of the C. S. A. Medical Department IN: Regulations for the Army of the Confederate States. (American Civil War Medical Ser.: No. 8). 420p. 1991. 50.00 (*0-930405-36-6*) Norman SF.

Moore, Samuel P. & Rutkow, Ira M., intros. A Manual of Military Surgery: Prepared for the Use of the Confederate States Army. LC 88-60874. (American Civil War Surgery Ser.: No. 2). (Illus.). 297p. 1989. reprint ed. 75.00 (*0-930405-14-5*) Norman SF.

Moore, Samuel T., ed. see Barron, Clarence W.

Moore, Sandra. High Country Cowboy. 1994. mass mkt. 3.50 (*0-373-09918-5*, 1-09918-3) Harlequin Bks.

Moore, Sandra C. Private Woods. 288p. 1988. 18.95 (*0-685-22051-6*) HarBrace.

— Private Woodsrors. 288p. 1988. 18.95 (*0-15-174710-5*) HarBrace.

Moore, Sara. Peace Without Victory for the Allies 1918-1932. 352p. Date not set. 59.95 (*1-85973-026-4*) Berg Pubs.

Moore, Sarah. Joyce Neimanas. (Illus.). 24p. 1984. pap. 7.95 (*0-938262-11-4*) Ctr Creat Photog.

***Moore, Sarah J. & Morfit, Christine A., eds.** Language & International Studies: A Richard Lambert Perspective. 386p. (C). 1993. pap. text ed. 12.00 (*1-880671-02-6*) NFLC Pubns.

Moore, Sarah J., jt. auth. see Tucson Museum of Art Staff.

Moore, Sarah J., et al. Introducing Chinese into High Schools: The Dodge Initiative. Yates, Mary V., ed. (National Foreign Language Center Monograph Ser.). 135p. (Orig.). (C). 1992. pap. text ed. 7.50 (*1-880671-01-8*) NFLC Pubns.

Moore, Sean, ed. Vascular Injury & Atherosclerosis. LC 81-15228. (Biochemistry of Disease Ser.: No. 9). (Illus.). 253p. reprint ed. pap. 72.20 (*0-7837-3344-5*, 2043302) Bks Demand.

Moore, Sean, ed. see Steiner, Josef & Steiner, Gerhard.

Moore, Sean A. Conan the Hunter. 256p. 1994. mass mkt. 4.99 (*0-8125-3531-6*) Tor Bks.

Moore, Sebastian. The Crucified Jesus Is No Stranger. 132p. 1993. pap. 6.95 (*0-8091-3401-2*) Paulist Pr.

Moore, Sharon. Meatloaf: From Downhome Classics to New Variations. 1991. 10.95 (*0-517-57494-2*, C P Pubs) Crown Pub Group.

Moore, Sharon, ed. see Moore, Herb.

Moore, Sheila & Frost, Roon. The Little Boy Book: A Guide to the First Eight Years. 320p. 1987. mass mkt. 4.95 (*0-345-34466-9*) Ballantine.

Moore, Shirley, ed. A French-English Music Dictionary. Austin, John & Chalifour, Martin, trs. LC 85-80710. 99p. (Orig.). (ENG & FRE.). (C). 1985. pap. text ed. 9.95 (*0-9615337-0-6*) Leihall Pubns.

Moore, Shirley, ed. see Corbett, Julia.

Moore, Shirley, ed. see Farley, Dale.

Moore, Shirley, ed. see Hartig, Louis F.

Moore, Shirley, ed. see Laven, Edward E.

Moore, Shirley T., ed. see Darvill, Fred T., Jr.

Moore, Shirley T., ed. see Driedger, Carolyn L.

Moore, Silas. Scarlet Arena 30303. Oddo, Genevieve, ed. LC 74-190272. (Illus.). 196p. (J). (gr. 8-12). 1972. lib. bdg. 3.95 (*0-87783-063-0*) Oddo.

Moore, Simon. Penknives & Other Folding Knives. 1989. pap. 25.00 (*0-85263-966-X*, Pub. by Shire UK) St Mut.

— Spoons 1650-1930. 1989. pap. 25.00 (*0-85263-910-4*, Pub. by Shire UK) St Mut.

Moore-Sines, Fay, jt. auth. see Johnson, Meldra.

Moore-Slater, Carole. Dana Doesn't Like Guns Anymore. (Illus.). (Orig.). (J). 1991. 10.95 (*0-377-00246-1*) Friendship Pr.

Moore, Sonia. The Stanislavski System: The Professional Training of an Actor. 2nd rev. ed. 144p. 1984. pap. 10.95 (*0-14-046660-6*, Penguin Bks) Viking Penguin.

— Stanislavsky Revealed: The Actor's Guide to Spontaneity on Stage. (Acting Ser.). 256p. 1991. pap. 9.95 (*1-55783-103-3*) Applause Theatre Bk Pubs.

Moore, Stanley. Marx vs. Markets. 136p. 1993. 22.50 (*0-271-00865-2*) Pa St U Pr.

Moore, Stanley B. Ornamental Horticulture As a Vocation. 2nd ed. (Illus.). (J). 1988. text ed. 11.95 (*0-912178-01-9*) Mor-Mac.

Moore, Stanley W., et al. The Child's Political World: A Longitudinal Perspective. LC 84-15975. 304p. 1985. text ed. 59.95 (*0-275-90167-X*, C0167, Praeger Pubs) Greenwood.

Moore, Stephen. Do We Need New Taxes? 1990. pap. 5.00 (*0-943802-84-9*, BG105) Natl Ctr Pol.

— Federal Budget Issue: Do We Need an Energy Tax? (BG127 Ser.). 18p. (Orig.). 1993. pap. text ed. 5.00 (*1-56808-010-7*) Natl Ctr Pol.

— Government: America's No. 1 Growth Industry: How the Relentless Growth of Government Is Impoverishing America. (Illus.). 98p. Date not set. pap. 9.95 (*0-9646127-0-4*) Instit Policy Innov. "Thorough but concise, easy-to-read overview of just how big & burdensome American government has become. Rich with enlightening graphs & tables, this volume documents the growing destructiveness of our fiscal & regulatory policies."--FORBES. "Timely & hard- hitting work. Should be read by every fed-up citizen & every responsive public official."--COMPETITIVE ENTERPRISE INSTITUTE. "America is suffering from a disturbing "economic growth deficit" that commands little public attention, but that has more impact of the nation's long-term economic well-being than any other socioeconomic trend in America today. The reason that America finds itself on an economic downward spiral is that today, Washington, D.C. is taxing, spending, borrowing, mandating, decreeing & regulating America to death. The private sector--businesses, entrepreneurs, investors, workers & families--is slowly suffocating under the weight of a relentlessly expanding government. Author Moore is director of fiscal policy studies for the Cato Institute. For orders & other additional information, contact the Institute for Policy Innovation, 250 S. Stemmons Frwy, Suite 306, Lewisville, TX, 75067. (214)-219-0811 ***Publisher Provided Annotation.***

— Social Welfare Alive! 256p. (C). 1993. 65.00x (*0-7487-1402-2*, Pub. by S Thornes Pubs UK) St Mut.

— Sociology Alive! 288p. (C). 1987. pap. 40.00x (*0-85950-661-4*, Pub. by S Thornes Pubs UK) St Mut.

— State Governments Turn to New Taxes. 1990. pap. 5.00 (*0-943802-85-7*, BG106) Natl Ctr Pol.

Moore, Stephen, jt. auth. see Briggs, Vernon M., Jr.

Moore, Stephen, jt. auth. see Murphy, Donn B.

Moore, Stephen C., jt. auth. see Agran, Martin.

Moore, Stephen D. Literary Criticism & the Gospels. LC 89-30951. 256p. (C). 1989. 35.00 (*0-300-04525-5*) Yale U Pr.

— Literary Criticism & the Gospels: The Theoretical Challenge. 248p. (C). 1992. reprint ed. pap. text ed. 13.00 (*0-300-05224-3*) Yale U Pr.

— Mark & Luke in Poststructuralist Perspectives: Jesus Begins to Write. 192p. (C). 1992. text ed. 25.00 (*0-300-05197-2*) Yale U Pr.

— Postructuralism & the New Testament: Derrida & Foucault at the Foot of the Cross. LC 94-2954. 1994. pap. 12.00 (*0-8006-2599-4*, Fortress Pr) Augsburg Fortress.

Moore, Stephen D., jt. ed. see Anderson, Janice C.

Moore, Steve. Designing with Analog Switches. (Electrical Engineering & Electronics Ser.: Vol. 68). 296p. 1991. 115.00 (*0-8247-8421-9*) Dekker.

— Where Golfers Go to Buy Their Pants & Other Collected Cartoons. LC 94-593. 1994. pap. 7.00 (*0-02-035127-5*) Macmillan.

Moore, Steve, et al. Absolom Daak: Dalek Killer. 96p. 1990. 8.95 (*1-85400-113-2*) Marvel Entmnt.

Moore, Steven. Born in the Bleachers. 96p. 1989. pap. 5.95 (*0-02-040631-2*, Collier S&S) S&S Trade.

— Revolution in the Bleachers: More Sports Cartoons by Steve Moore. (Illus.). 96p. (Orig.). 1991. pap. 5.95 (*0-02-070191-8*, Pub. by Gebrueder Borntraeger GW) Macmillan.

— William Gaddis. (United States Authors Ser.: No. 546). 176p. 1989. text ed. 20.95 (*0-8057-7534-X*, TUSAS 546, Pub. by Royal Botanic Garden UK) Macmillan.

Moore, Steven, ed. The Vampire in Verse: An Anthology. 196p. (Orig.). 1985. pap. 7.95 (*0-9611944-2-1*) Dracula Pr.

Moore, Steven, ed. see Dahlberg, Edward.

Moore, Steven, ed. see Firbank, Ronald.

Moore, Steven, jt. ed. see Kuehl, John.

Moore, Steven R., intro. Geriopharmacotherapy in Home Health Care: New Frontiers in Pharmaceutical Care. LC 93-6677. (Journal of Geriatric Drug Therapy: Vol. 7, No. 3). (Illus.). 71p. 1993. lib. bdg. 19.95 (*1-56024-415-1*) Haworth Pr.

Moore, Sue. Nursing Math Simplified: Math Magic. 2nd ed. Howland, Tom, ed. & illus. by. 70p. (Orig.). (C). 1992. pap. text ed. 8.95 (*0-943202-42-6*) H & H Pub.

Moore, Sue & Stephan, Naomi. The Finding Your Life Mission Workbook: A Guide for Self Study. (Illus.). 104p. (Orig.). (C). 1991. 14.95 (*0-9631262-0-2*) Life Mission.

Moore, Susan. Chiropractic. (Alternative Health Ser.). 1993. pap. 12.95 (*0-8048-1831-2*) C E Tuttle.

Moore, Susan, jt. auth. see Moore, Andy.

Moore, Susan, ed. see Roach, Margaret J.

***Moore, Susan, et al.** Orientation to Higher Education in California. 176p. (C). 1994. per., pap. text ed. 10.56 (*0-8403-9689-9*) Kendall-Hunt.

Moore, Susan G. Nursing Math Simplified: Math Magic. Howland, Joseph W. & Savige, Katherine, eds. (Illus.). 60p. (Orig.). (C). 1986. pap. text ed. 7.50 (*0-943202-22-1*) H & H Pubs.

Moore, Susan M. & Rosenthal, Doreen A. Adolescent Sexuality in Social Context. LC 93-9869. (Adolescence & Society Ser.). 272p. 1993. 59.95 (*0-415-07527-0*, B0890); pap. 17.95 (*0-415-07528-9*, B0894) Routledge.

Moore, Susanna. My Old Sweetheart. (Contemporary American Fiction Ser.). 224p. 1990. pap. 9.95 (*0-14-006783-3*, Penguin Bks) Viking Penguin.

— Sleeping Beauties. LC 93-12335. 1993. 22.00 (*0-394-58280-2*) Knopf.

— Sleeping Beauties. 1994. pap. 11.00 (*0-679-75539-X*, Vin) Random.

— Sleeping Beauties. large type ed. LC 94-2973. 1994. pap. 18.95 (*0-7862-0198-3*) Thorndike Pr.

— The Whiteness of Bones. 288p. 1990. pap. 10.95 (*0-14-013020-9*, Penguin Bks) Viking Penguin.

Moore, Suzanne. Looking for Trouble: Writings on Film, Shopping & Gender. 308p. (Orig.). (C). 1992. pap. 15.99 (*1-85242-242-4*) Serpents Tail.

Moore, Suzanne T. Coffee. (Illus.). 144p. 1974. pap. 4.95 (*0-938758-00-4*) MTM Pub Co.

— Coffee Too. 64p. (Orig.). 1975. pap. 3.95 (*0-938758-03-9*) MTM Pub Co.

— Palestina. 1983. 8.95 (*0-938758-13-6*) MTM Pub Co.

Moore, Sylvia, ed. No Bluebonnets, No Yellow Roses: Texas Women in the Arts. LC 87-63478. (Regional Women Artists Ser.). (Illus.). 144p. (Orig.). 1988. pap. 10.95 (*0-9602476-8-8*) Midmarch Arts Pr.

— Yesterday & Tomorrow: California Women Artists. LC 88-63871. (Regional Women Artists Ser.). (Illus.). 378p. (Orig.). 1989. 15.95 (*0-9602476-9-6*) Midmarch Arts-WAN.

Moore, Sylvia, jt. ed. see Faxon, Alicia.

Moore, T. Lalla Rookh. 304p. 1987. 80.00 (*1-85077-148-0*, Darf Pubs Ltd) St Mut.

— Soul Mates. 1994. pap. 13.00 (*0-06-092496-9*) HarpC.

Moore, T., jt. auth. see Woolley, P.
Moore, T. C. Biochemistry & Physiology of Plant Hormones. 2nd ed. (Illus.). xv, 330p. 1989. 69.00 (*0-387-96984-5*, 2731) Spr-Verlag.
— A Man May Fish. (Illus.). 226p. 1985. reprint ed. 27.00 (*0-86140-024-0*, Pub. by Colin Smythe Ltd UK) Dufour.
— Research Experiences in Plant Physiology: A Laboratory Manual. 2nd ed. (Illus.). 348p. 1981. pap. 48.00 (*0-387-90606-1*) Spr-Verlag.
Moore, T. E. & Waite, J. H., eds. Modeling Magnetospheric Plasma. (Geophysical Monograph Ser.: Vol. 44). 344p. 1989. 38.00 (*0-87590-070-4*) Am Geophysical.
***Moore, T. G., ed.** Anthony & Berryman's Magistrates' Court Guide. 510p. 1994. pap. 59.00 (*0-406-02873-7*) Butterworth Legal Pubs.
Moore, T. M. Making God's Good News Known. (Orig.). 1985. pap. text ed. 4.95 (*0-934688-18-4*); teacher ed, pap. text ed. 3.95 (*0-934688-19-2*) Great Comm Pubns.
Moore, T. O. & Hadlock, E. H. Complex Analysis. 404p. (C). 1991. text ed. 67.00 (*981-02-0246-6*); pap. text ed. 32.00 (*981-02-0247-4*) World Scientific Pub.
***Moore, T. Owens.** The Science of Melanin: Dispelling the Myths. 140p. 1995. pap. 12.95 (*0-931761-38-7*) Beckham House.
Moore, T. Sturge. Poems of T. Sturge Moore, 4 vols., Set. 1982. reprint ed. lib. bdg. 125.00 (*0-403-01114-0*) Scholarly.
***Moore, T. V.** Haggai, Zechariah & Malachi. (Geneva Series of Commentaries). 408p. 1993. reprint ed. 22.95 (*0-85151-666-1*) Banner of Truth.
— The Last Days of Jesus. 212p. (Orig.). 1981. pap. 8.95 (*0-85151-321-2*) Banner of Truth.
Moore, T. W. Philosophy of Education: An Introduction. (International Library of the Philosophy of Education). 100p. (Orig.). 1982. pap. 13.95 (*0-7100-9192-3*, RKP) Routledge.
***Moore, Terence.** The Captured Harvest: Creating Exquisite Objects from Nature. (Illus.). 160p. 1995. pap. 19.95 (*1-57076-012-8*, Trafalgar Sq Pub) Trafalgar.
— The New Captured Harvest: Creative Crafts from Nature. (Illus.). 160p. 1995. 29.95 (*1-57076-022-5*, Trafalgar Sq Pub) Trafalgar.
Moore, Terence & Carling, Chris. The Limitations of Language. LC 88-4372. 176p. 1988. text ed. 39.95 (*0-312-02039-2*) St Martin.
Moore, Terence F. Administrative Warfare. 114p. 1992. pap. 9.95 (*0-9633518-5-0*) Ivory Grp.
Moore, Terence F. & Simendinger, Earl A. The Effective Health Care Executive: A Guide to a Winning Management. 240p. 1986. 59.00 (*0-87189-386-X*) Aspen Pub.
Moore, Terence F. & Simendinger, Earl A., eds. Hospital Turnarounds: Lessons in Leadership. LC 92-49294. 236p. 1993. text ed. 42.00 (*0-910701-90-3*, 0925) Health Admin Pr.
— Managing the Nursing Shortage: A Guide to Recruitment & Retention. (Health Care Administration Ser.). 284p. 1989. 69.00 (*0-8342-0046-5*) Aspen Pub.
Moore, Teresa. Swords & Camellias. 400p. (Orig.). 1987. pap. 3.95 (*0-8439-2479-9*) Dorchester Pub Co.
***Moore, Terrence, photos.** Under the Sun: Desert Architecture & Style. LC 95-11432. (Illus.). 248p. 1995. 45.00 (*0-8212-2226-0*) Bulfinch Pr.
Moore, Terrence F., jt. ed. see Simendinger, Earl A.
Moore, Terris. Mt. McKinley: The Pioneer Climbs. LC 81-1002. (Illus.). 224p. 1981. reprint ed. pap. 9.95 (*0-89886-021-0*) Mountaineers.
Moore, Terry. Toothpaste & Peanut Butter. Bryce, Herb, ed. (Illus.). 140p. (Orig.). 1987. pap. 9.95 (*0-88839-207-9*) Hancock House.
Moore, Terry D., jt. auth. see Lloyd, Alwyn T.
Moore, Terry J. & Hampton, Anita B. Book Bridges: Story-Inspired Activities for Children Three Through Eight. (Illus.). 218p. (Orig.). 1991. pap. 19.50 (*0-87287-919-4*) Teacher Ideas Pr.
Moore, Thomas. Care of the Soul: A Guide for Cultivating Depth & Sacredness in Everyday Life. 1992. 25.00 (*0-06-016597-9*, HarpT) HarpC.
— Care of the Soul: A Guide for Cultivating Depth & Sacredness in Everyday Life. 336p. 1994. pap. 13.00 (*0-06-092224-9*, PL) HarpC.
— Care of the Soul: A Guide for Cultivating Depth & Sacredness in Everyday Life. large type ed. LC 93-13239. 496p. 1993. pap. 16.95 (*0-8027-2674-7*) Walker & Co.
— Care of the Soul & Soul Mates, 2 vols. 656p. 1994. 39.95 (*0-06-017173-1*, HarpT) HarpC.
— Dark Eros: The Imagination of Sadism. LC 90-43104. 190p. (Orig.). 1990. pap. 15.00 (*0-88214-343-3*) Spring Pubns.
— Dark Eros: The Imagination of Sadism. rev. ed. LC 94-35587. 200p. (Orig.). 1994. pap. 15.00 (*0-88214-365-4*) Spring Pubns.
— The Journal of Thomas Moore, Vol. 6: 1843-1847. Dowden, Wilfred S., ed. LC 79-13541. (Illus.). 408p. 1992. 70.00 (*0-87413-258-4*) U Delaware Pr.
— Lalla Rookh, an Oriental Romance. (BCL1-PR English Literature Ser.). 179p. 1992. reprint ed. lib. bdg. 69.00 (*0-7812-7605-5*) Rprt Serv.
— Life, Letters & Journals of Lord Byron. 735p. reprint ed. lib. bdg. 99.00 (*0-7812-0248-5*) Rprt Serv.
— Life of the Right Honorable Richard Brinsley Sheridan, 2 vols., Set. 1826. 59.00 (*0-403-00072-6*) Scholarly.
— Meditations: On the Monk Who Dwells in Daily Life. 96p. 1994. 15.00 (*0-06-017223-1*, HarpT) HarpC.
— Memoirs, Journal, & Correspondence of Thomas Moore, 8 vols., Set. (BCL1-PR English Literature Ser.). 1992. reprint ed. lib. bdg. 600.00 (*0-7812-7606-3*) Rprt Serv.
— Memoirs of Captain Rock (pseud.) the Celebrated Irish Chieftain: With Some Account of His Ancestors. LC 75-28831. reprint ed. 67.50 (*0-404-13821-7*) AMS Pr.
— Memoirs of the Life of the Right Honorable Richard Brinsley Sheridan, 2 vols. LC 79-152997. (Select Bibliographies Reprint Ser.). 1977. reprint ed. 44.95 (*0-8369-5749-0*) Ayer.
— Memoirs of the Life of the Right Honorable Richard Brinsley Sheridan, 2 vols. LC 69-14001. 1969. reprint ed. text ed. 19.75 (*0-8371-0573-0*, MORA, Greenwood Pr); reprint ed. Set. text ed. 37.50 (*0-8371-9944-1*, Greenwood Pr) Greenwood.
— Memoirs of the Life of the Right Honorable Richard Brinsley Sheridan, 2 vols., Vol. 2. LC 69-14001. 1969. reprint ed. text ed. 19.75 (*0-8371-0826-8*, MORB, Greenwood Pr) Greenwood.
— Memoirs of the Life of the Rt. Hon. Richard Brinlsey Sheridan, 2 vols., Set. (BCL1-PR English Literature Ser.). 1992. reprint ed. lib. bdg. 150.00 (*0-7812-7401-X*) Rprt Serv.
— Moore's Irish Melodies with Symphonies & Accompaniments. LC 81-81465. 261p. 1981. 40.00 (*0-89453-259-6*) Scholarly Res Inc.
— The Planets Within. 240p. 1993. reprint ed. pap. 14.95 (*0-940262-28-2*) Lindisfarne Pr.
— The Planets Within: Ficino's Astrological Psychology. LC 81-65457. (Illus.). 224p. 1982. 32.50 (*0-8387-5022-2*) Bucknell U Pr.
— Poetical Works of Thomas Little. LC 90-31439. 204p. 1990. reprint ed. 48.00 (*1-85477-050-0*, Pub. by Woodstock Bks UK) Cassell.
— The Poetical Works of Thomas Moore. Godley, A. D., ed. LC 75-41197. reprint ed. 42.50 (*0-404-14688-0*) AMS Pr.
— The Poetical Works of Thomas Moore. (BCL1-PR English Literature Ser.). 751p. 1992. reprint ed. lib. bdg. 109.00 (*0-7812-7604-7*) Rprt Serv.
— Soul Mates. large type ed. LC 94-19123. 1994. write for info. (*1-56895-110-8*) Wheeler Pub.
— Soul Mates: Honoring the Mysteries of Love & Relationship. 320p. 1994. 25.00 (*0-06-016928-1*, HarpT) HarpC.
— Soul Mates: Honoring the Mysteries of Love & Relationship. 1994. pap. 13.00 (*0-06-092575-2*, HarpT) HarpC.
— Soul Mates: Honoring the Mysteries of Love & Relationship. large type ed. 1994. write for info. (*0-318-72542-8*) Wheeler Pub.
— The Style of Connectedness: "Gravity's Rainbow" & Thomas Pynchon. LC 86-16093. 320p. 1987. text ed. 35.00 (*0-8262-0625-5*, 83-36331) U of Mo Pr.
— Tom Moore's Diary. Priestley, J. B., ed. LC 76-131783. 1971. reprint ed. 49.00 (*0-403-00670-8*) Scholarly.
— Tom Moore's Diary; a Selection. (BCL1-PR English Literature Ser.). 218p. 1992. reprint ed. lib. bdg. 79.00 (*0-7812-7607-1*) Rprt Serv.
Moore, Thomas, jt. auth. see Schiller, Pam.
Moore, Thomas A. Evidence in Negligence Cases. 463p. 1991. text ed. 50.00 (*0-87224-027-4*, H1-3002) PLI.
— A Traveler's Guide to Spacetime: An Introduction to the Special Theory of Relativity. LC 94-39850. 1995. pap. text ed. write for info. (*0-07-043027-6*) McGraw.
Moore, Thomas A. & Kramer, Daniel. Medical Malpractice. 6th ed. 583p. 1990. pap. text ed. 25.00 (*0-685-45801-6*, Q1-3006) PLI.
Moore, Thomas C. Challenges in Pediatric Surgery. (Medical Intelligence Unit Ser.). 130p. 1994. 89.95 (*1-57059-048-6*, LN9048) R G Landes.
Moore, Thomas F., jt. auth. see Watkins, Gary L.
Moore, Thomas G. The Economics of the American Theater. LC 68-28521. xv, 192p. 1968. 22.00 (*0-8223-0118-0*) Duke.
— Global Warming: A Boon to Humans & Other Animals. LC 95-12011. (Essays in Public Policy Ser.: No. 61). 1995. write for info. (*0-8179-5662-X*) Hoover Inst Pr.
Moore, Thomas G., jt. ed. see Leube, Kurt R.
Moore, Thomas H., ed. see Miller, Henry.
Moore, Thomas J. Amputation Surgery of the Lower Extremity. 400p. 1994. 115.00 (*0-8016-6926-X*) Mosby Yr Bk.
— Deadly Medicine: Why Tens of Thousands of Hearts Died in America's Worst Drug Disaster. 1995. 23.00 (*0-684-80417-4*) S&S Trade.
— Heart Failure. 1989. 19.95 (*0-394-56958-X*) Random.
— Lifespan: New Perspectives on Extending Human Longevity. 1994. pap. 12.00 (*0-671-88622-3*, Touchstone Bks) S&S Trade.
— Lifespan: What Really Affects Human Longevity. (Illus.). 352p. 1993. 23.00 (*0-671-72966-7*) S&S Trade.
Moore, Thomas M. & McKenna, Robert G., eds. Characterization of Integrated Circuit Packaging Materials. LC 93-7685. (Materials Characterization Ser.). 274p. 1993. 59.95 (*0-7506-9267-7*) Buttrwrth-Heinemann.
***Moore, Thomas R.** Plantagenet Descent: 31 Generations from William the Conqueror to Today. (Illus.). xviii, 242p. 1995. 49.50 (*0-9644929-0-3*) T R Moore.
— A Thick & Darksome Veil: The Rhetoric of Hawthorne's Sketches, Prefaces, & Essays. 192p. 1994. text ed. 37.50 (*1-55553-184-9*) NE U Pr.
Moore, Thomas R., et al, eds. Gynecology & Obstetrics: A Longitudinal Approach. (Illus.). 984p. 1993. text ed. 94.95 (*0-443-08811-X*) Churchill.
Moore, Thomas S., Jr. Lipid Metabolism in Plants. 1993. 189.95 (*0-8493-4907-9*, QK898) CRC Pr.
Moore, Thomas S. Some Soldier Poets. LC 68-16958. (Essay Index Reprint Ser.). 1977. 18.95 (*0-8369-0715-9*) Ayer.
Moore, Thomas V., jt. auth. see Bergman, Robert E.
Moore, Timothy E., ed. Cognitive Development & the Acquisition of Language. 1973. text ed. 55.00 (*0-12-505850-0*) Acad Pr.
Moore, Todd. The Dillinger Poems, Bk. One. 1978. pap. 2.00 (*0-930600-01-0*) Uzzano Pr.
— The Man in the Black Chevrolet. LC 76-29870. 1976. pap. 1.50 (*0-916918-04-1*) Duck Down.
— Watching. 36p. (Orig.). 1985. pap. 4.00 (*0-935390-10-3*) Wormwood Bks & Mag.
Moore, Tom. Rituals of the Imagination. 64p. 1984. pap. 8.00 (*0-911005-03-X*) Dallas Inst Pubns.
Moore, Tom I. Social Patterns in Australian Literature. LC 71-133027. 360p. reprint ed. pap. 102.60 (*0-318-34920-5*, 2031441) Bks Demand.
Moore, Tom I., jt. ed. see Wilde, William H.
***Moore, Tracy, ed.** Lesbiot. 1995. pap. 14.95 (*0-304-33158-9*) InBook.
***Moore, Tracy L.** Songs in the Night. 45p. 1995. 8.00 (*0-9646927-0-8*) T L Moore.
***Moore, Trevor.** Scraps. 160p. 1994. pap. 8.95 (*0-9643369-0-1*) Pointdexter Pr.
Moore, V. Farm Workshop & Maintenance. 3rd ed. (Book of the Farmers Weekly Ser.). (Illus.). 256p. 1992. pap. 34.95 (*0-632-02538-7*) Blackwell Sci.
— A Practical Approach to Planning Law. (C). 1991. text ed. 140.00 (*1-85431-185-9*, Pub. by Blackstone Pr UK) W W Gaunt.
Moore, Vic. Farm Workshop & Maintenance: The Book of the Farmers Weekly Series. 3rd ed. (Illus.). 248p. 1988. pap. 34.95 (*0-8464-1299-3*) Beekman Pubs.
Moore, Victor. A Practical Approach to Planning Law. 368p. (C). 1987. 180.00 (*1-85185-070-8*, Pub. by Blackstone Pr UK) St Mut.
— A Practical Approach to Planning Law. 3rd ed. xxvii, 381p. (C). 1992. pap. 40.00 (*1-85431-239-1*, Pub. by Blackstone Pr UK) W W Gaunt.
— A Practical Approach to Planning Law. 4th ed. 415p. 1994. pap. 42.00 (*1-85431-355-X*, Pub. by Blackstone Pr UK) W W Gaunt.
Moore, Victor & Hughes, David. Blackstone's Statutes on Planning Law. 444p. (C). 1995. pap. 30.00 (*1-85431-125-5*, Pub. by Blackstone Pr UK) W W Gaunt.
Moore, Virgilene. World Without End. 1995. 11.95 (*0-8062-5104-2*) Carlton.
Moore, Virginia. The Liberty Bell Papers: An Inquiry into American Values. 2nd ed. LC 80-66597. (Freedeeds Library). 96p. 1984. reprint ed. 7.00 (*0-8334-1010-5*, Freedeeds Libr); reprint ed. pap. 5.00 (*0-8334-1011-3*, Freedeeds Libr) Garber Comm.
— Life & Eager Death of Emily Bronte. LC 78-173844. (English Biography Ser.: No. 31). 1971. reprint ed. lib. bdg. 75.00 (*0-8383-1345-0*) M S G Haskell Hse.
Moore, Virginia, tr. see Castellon, Rolando, ed.
Moore, W. American Negro Slavery & Abolition. LC 73-148362. 1971. 29.95 (*0-89388-000-0*); pap. 14.95 (*0-89388-001-9*) Okpaku Communications.
Moore, W. C. Diccionario de Geografia: Dictionary of Geography. 158p. (SPA.). 1972. 19.95 (*0-8288-6354-7*, S-50246) Fr & Eur.
Moore, W. G. Clothing. (Man & His World Ser.). (Illus.). 112p. 1977. 15.95 (*0-7175-0772-6*) Dufour.
— Dictionary of Geography. rev. ed. (Reference Ser.). (Orig.). 1950. pap. 7.95 (*0-14-051002-8*, Penguin Bks) Viking Penguin.
— Fundamental Geography of the British Isles. 208p. (C). 1983. 49.00 (*0-7175-0884-6*, Pub. by S Thornes Pubs UK) St Mut.
— Homes. (Man & His World Ser.). (Illus.). 144p. 1976. 14.95 (*0-7175-0691-6*) Dufour.
— The Penguin Dictionary of Geography. rev. ed. (Illus.). 264p. 1989. pap. 8.95 (*0-14-051219-5*, Penguin Bks) Viking Penguin.
— The Tutorial System & Its Future. LC 67-30293. (C). 1968. 40.00 (*0-08-012659-6*, Pub. by Pergamon Repr UK) Franklin.
***Moore, W. G., ed.** Advances in Steam Turbine Technology for the Power Generation Industry: Proceedings of the International Joint Power Generation Conference, Phoenix, AZ, 1994. 330p. 1994. pap. 65.00 (*0-7918-1382-7*) ASME.
Moore, W. G., jt. auth. see Dittenhofer, M. A.
Moore, W. Harrison. Act of State in English Law. x, 178p. 1987. reprint ed. 25.00 (*0-8377-2433-3*) Rothman.
Moore, W. J. Diaries & Memoirs of a Sailor. 80p. (C). 1989. pap. 30.00 (*0-7223-1728-X*, Pub. by A H S Ltd UK) St Mut.
Moore, W. J. & Miljanic, P. N. The Current Comparator. 120p. 1987. boxed 64.00 (*0-86341-112-6*, EL004) Inst Elect Eng.
Moore, W. J., jt. auth. see Johnson, D. R.
Moore, W. Joan, et al. Homeboys: Gangs, Drugs & Prison in the Barrios of Los Angeles. LC 78-11808. (Illus.). 1978. pap. 16.95 (*0-87722-114-6*) Temple U Pr.
Moore, W. Kent, jt. auth. see Scott, David L.
Moore, W. R., jt. ed. see Delgado-Frias, J. G.
Moore, W. R., jt. ed. see Delgado-Frias, Jose G.
Moore, Waddy W. Arkansas in the Guilded Age, Eighteen Seventy-four to Nineteen Hundred. (Illus.). 229p. 1976. pap. 14.95 (*0-914546-08-2*) J W Bell.
Moore, Wallace. Wally Moore's Wedding & Banquet Reference. 154p. 1991. spiral bd. write for info. (*0-9631447-0-7*) T C & I.
Moore, Walter. A Life of Erwin Schrodinger. (Canto Bk.). (Illus.). 360p. (C). 1994. pap. 11.95 (*0-521-46934-1*) Cambridge U Pr.
— Schrodinger: Life & Thought. (Illus.). (C). 1989. 54.95 (*0-521-35434-X*) Cambridge U Pr.
— Schrodinger: Life & Thought. (Illus.). 513p. (C). 1992. pap. 22.95 (*0-521-43767-9*) Cambridge U Pr.
Moore, Walter J. Grundlagen der Physikalischen Chemie. xxiv, 819p. (C). 1990. lib. bdg. 67.70 (*3-11-009941-1*) De Gruyter.
— Physikalische Chemie. 3rd ed. 1236p. (GER.). 1983. 75.40 (*3-11-008554-2*) De Gruyter.
Moore, Ward. Greener Than You Think. 1993. reprint ed. lib. bdg. 18.95 (*0-89968-355-X*, Lghtyr Pr) Buccaneer Bks.
Moore, Warren. Mountain Voices: A Legacy of the Blue Ridge & Great Smokies. LC 88-11261. (Illus.). 288p. 1990. 34.95 (*0-87106-671-8*) Globe Pequot.
Moore, Wayne C. Small Computers in Construction: Proceedings of a Symposium Sponsored by the Construction Division. 89p. 1984. 16.00 (*0-87262-400-5*) Am Soc Civil Eng.
Moore, Wayne C., ed. Applications of Small Computers in Construction: Proceedings of a Session Sponsored by the Construction Division (A Follow-Up of a Symposium on Small Computers in Construction) 62p. 1984. 16.00 (*0-87262-416-1*) Am Soc Civil Eng.
Moore, Wendell, ed. see National Phonograph Company Staff.
Moore, Wendy. Malaysia: Land of Spice & Tropical Splendor. 2nd ed. 1993. pap. 14.95 (*0-8442-9682-1*, Passport Bks) NTC Pub Grp.
— West Malaysia & Singapore. (Passport's Regional Guides of Malaysia Ser.). (Illus.). 288p. 1993. pap. 17.95 (*0-8442-9891-3*, Passport Bks) NTC Pub Grp.
— West Malaysia & Singapore. 288p. 1993. pap. 19.95 (*0-945971-64-8*) Periplus.
Moore, Wesley & Gelabert, H. A. Antibiotic-Impregnated Vascular Grafts. (Medical Intelligence Unit Ser.). 125p. 1992. 89.95 (*1-879702-25-8*) R G Landes.
Moore, Wesley S., ed. Vascular Surgery: A Comprehensive Review. 4th ed. LC 92-49116. (Illus.). 816p. 1993. text ed. 164.00 (*0-7216-4841-X*) Saunders.
Moore, Wesley S. & Malone. Lower Extremity Amputation. 352p. 1989. text ed. 89.50 (*0-7216-6485-7*) Saunders.
Moore, Wesley S., jt. auth. see Ahn, Samuel S.
Moore, Wilbert E. American Negro Slavery & Abolition: A Sociological Study. Zuckerman, Harriet & Merton, Robert K., eds. LC 79-9015. (Dissertations on Sociology Ser.). 1980. lib. bdg. 19.95 (*0-405-12982-3*) Ayer.
— Economic Demography of Eastern & Southern Europe. LC 72-4283. (World Affairs Ser.: National & International Viewpoints). 304p. 1972. reprint ed. 23.95 (*0-405-04576-X*) Ayer.
— Industrial Relations & the Social Order. rev. ed. Stein, Leon, ed. LC 77-70517. (Work Ser.). (Illus.). 1977. reprint ed. lib. bdg. 59.95 (*0-405-10186-4*) Ayer.
— The Professions: Roles & Rules. LC 78-104184. 316p. 1970. 39.95 (*0-87154-604-3*) Russell Sage.
Moore, Wilbert E. & Feldman, Arnold S. Labor Commitment & Social Change in Developing Areas. LC 82-6144. xvi, 378p. 1982. reprint ed. text ed. 65.00 (*0-313-23572-4*, MOLC, Greenwood Pr) Greenwood.
Moore, Wilbert E., jt. auth. see Davis, Kingsley.
Moore, Wilbert E., jt. ed. see Gurvich, Georgy D.
Moore, Wilbert E., jt. ed. see Sheldon, Eleanor B.
Moore, Wilbert E., jt. auth. see Young, Donald R.
Moore, Wilbur E., jt. auth. see Black, John W.
Moore, Will G., et al, eds. French Mind: Studies in Honour of Gustave Rudler. LC 75-167386. (Essay Index Reprint Ser.). 1977. reprint ed. 22.95 (*0-8369-2464-9*) Ayer.
Moore, Will R., jt. ed. see Delgado-Frias, Jose G.
Moore, Willard. Molokan Oral Tradition: Legends & Memorates of an Ethnic Sect. LC 72-619685. (University of California Publications, Folklore Studies: No. 28). 93p. reprint ed. pap. 26.60 (*0-317-29038-X*, 2021207) Bks Demand.
Moore, Willard B., et al. Circles of Tradition: Folk Arts in Minnesota. LC 88-37753. (Illus.). 162p. 1989. pap. 18.95 (*0-87351-239-1*) Minn Hist.
Moore, William. Blind Man on a Freeway: The Community College Administrator. LC 72-168858. (Jossey-Bass Higher Education Ser.). 201p. reprint ed. pap. 57.30 (*0-8357-7320-5*, 2025664) Bks Demand.
— Home Beermaking. 3rd ed. (Illus.). 68p. 1991. pap. 5.95 (*0-9605318-1-5*) Ferment Pr.
— Microsoft Word 5 Mac: Quick Reference Guide. 1993. pap. 8.95 (*1-56243-088-2*) DDC Pub.
— Philadelphia Experiment. 1987. mass mkt. 5.99 (*0-449-21471-0*) Fawcett.
— The Sicarii. LC 89-63164. 192p. (Orig.). 1990. pap. 8.95 (*0-945563-01-9*) Penumbra Pub.
Moore, William & Wagstaff, Lonnie H. Black Educators in White Colleges. LC 73-12066. (Jossey-Bass Series in Higher Education). 240p. reprint ed. pap. 68.40 (*0-8357-4953-3*, 2037885) Bks Demand.
Moore, William A. History of Itsekiri. 2nd rev. ed. 224p. 1970. 35.00 (*0-7146-1701-6*, Pub. by F Cass Pubs UK) Intl Spec Bk.
Moore, William B., jt. auth. see Licht, Lilla M.
Moore, William C. Wall Street. LC 66-19018. 1969. reprint ed. 11.00 (*0-87034-041-7*) Fraser Pub Co.
Moore, William H. Chiefs, Agents & Soldiers: Conflict on the Navajo Frontier, 1868-1882. LC 93-35896. 380p. 1994. 45.00x (*0-8263-1475-9*) U of NM Pr.
— The Kefauver Committee & the Politics of Crime 1950-1952. LC 72-93923. 288p. 1974. 29.00 (*0-8262-0145-8*) U of Mo Pr.
Moore, William L. & Pessemier, Edgar A. Product Management: Planning & Analysis. LC 92-13522. (Marketing Ser.). 1992. text ed. write for info. (*0-07-043046-2*) McGraw.
Moore, William L., jt. ed. see Tushman, Michael L.
Moore, William V., jt. auth. see Graham, Cole B., Jr.
Moore, William W. Discover Creative Living. 64p. (Orig.). 1988. pap. 2.95 (*0-945563-00-0*) Penumbra Pub.
— The Little Church that Refused to Die. LC 93-30950. (Princeton Theological Monograph Ser.: No. 35). 1993. 16.00 (*1-55635-023-6*) Pickwick.

An Asterisk (*) at the beginning of an entry indicates that the title is appearing in BIP for the first time.

Moore, Winfred B., Jr. & Tripp, Joseph F., eds. Looking South: Chapters in the Story of an American Region. LC 89-1888. (Contributions in American History Ser.: No. 136). 301p. 1989. text ed. 59.95 (*0-313-26694-8*, MLU, Greenwood Pr) Greenwood.

Moore, Winfred B., Jr., jt. ed. see Fraser, Walter J., Jr.

Moore, Winfred B., Jr., et al, eds. Developing Dixie: Modernization in a Traditional Society. LC 87-24954. (Contributions in American History Ser.: No. 127). 380p. 1988. text ed. 59.95 (*0-313-26061-3*, MDX/, Greenwood Pr) Greenwood.

Moore, Wynn. Keeping It on the Road: How to Buy a Car You'll Love, Help It Live over 100,000 Miles, & Smile When You Kiss It Goodbye. LC 81-22754. 192p. (Orig.). 1982. pap. 5.25 (*0-688-01013-X*, Quill) Morrow.

Moore, Yvette. The Birth of Christ. (Jubilee Year Bible Stories Ser.). 16p. (J). 1993. pap. 6.00 (*0-9637273-0-3*) Jubilee Yr Bks.

— Freedom Songs. LC 88-43073. 176p. (YA). (gr. 7 up). 1991. 15.95 (*0-531-05812-3*); lib. bdg. 15.99 (*0-531-08412-4*) Orchard Bks Watts.

— Freedom Songs. LC 92-20289. 176p. (YA). (gr. 7 up). 1992. pap. 3.99 (*0-14-036017-4*) Puffin Bks.

Moorefield, A., ed. Galliculus: Gesamtausgabe, Isagoge de Composicione Cantus. (Gesamtausgaben - Collected Works Ser.: Vol. VIII, Pt. 4). 37p. (LAT.). 1992. 52.00 (*0-931902-74-6*) Inst Mediaeval Mus.

— Galliculus, Gesamtausgabe. (Gesamtausgaben - Collected Works Ser.: Vol. Viii, Pt. 1). 120p. (ENG & GER.). 1976. lib. bdg. 4.00 (*0-912024-69-0*) Inst Mediaeval Mus.

— Galliculus, Gesamtausgabe: The Magnificats. (Gesamtausgaben - Collected Works Ser.: Vol. VIII, Pt. 2). 120p. (ENG.). 1988. 80.00 (*0-931902-59-2*) Inst Mediaeval Mus.

— Galliculus, Gesamtausgabe: The Motets. (Gesamtausgaben - Collected Works Ser.: Vol. VIII, Pt. 3). 214p. (ENG.). 1988. 86.00 (*0-931902-66-5*) Inst Mediaeval Mus.

Moorefield, Arthur. An Introduction to Galliculus. (Wissenschaftliche Abhandlungen-Musicological Studies: Vol. 18). 100p. 1970. lib. bdg. 32.00 (*0-912024-79-8*) Inst Mediaeval Mus.

Moorefield, Arthur A., ed. see Galliculus, Johannes.

Moorefield, Emily, ed. see Feldstein, Sandy.

Moorehead, Alan. Blue Nile. 1976. 18.95 (*0-8488-0766-9*) Amereon Ltd.

— Cooper's Creek. 1976. 19.95 (*0-8488-0593-3*) Amereon Ltd.

— Fatal Impact. 256p. 1989. pap. 4.95 (*0-935180-77-X*) Mutual Pub HI.

— Gallipoli. (War Library). 352p. 1985. mass mkt. 5.99 (*0-345-33088-9*) Ballantine.

— Gallipoli. (War & Warriors Ser.). (Illus.). 384p. 1991. 18.95 (*0-939482-35-5*) Noontide.

— Gallipoli. LC 82-2242. (Great War Stories Ser.). (Illus.). 384p. 1982. reprint ed. 24.95 (*0-933852-28-2*) Nautical & Aviation.

— The Russian Revolution. (Illus.). 301p. 1987. pap. 10.95 (*0-88184-331-8*) Carroll & Graf.

— The White Nile. rev. ed. (Adventure Library). (Illus.). 384p. 1995. reprint ed. lib. bdg. 25.00 (*1-885283-03-2*) Advent Library.

Moorehead, Bob. Before You Throw in the Towel: Twelve Things You Should Consider Before Filing for Divorce. 1992. pap. 7.99 (*0-8499-3457-5*) Word Inc.

— How to Counsel Yourself & Others from the Bible. 284p. 1994. 16.99 (*0-88070-636-8*, Multnomah Bks) Questar Pubs.

Moorehead, Caroline. Namibia: Apartheid's Forgotten Children. (C). 1986. pap. text ed. 35.00 (*0-85598-111-3*, Pub. by Oxfam Pubns UK) St Mut.

Moorehead, Harold, ed. see Bodo, Martin.

***Moorehead, Monica.** South Africa: Which Road to Liberation? A Marxist View. 26p. 1993. pap. 2.50 (*0-89567-122-0*) World View Forum.

Moorehead, Warren K. American Indian in the United States, Period 1850-1914. LC 71-75512. (Select Bibliographies Reprint Ser.). 1977. 38.95 (*0-8369-5014-3*) Ayer.

— Archaeology of the Arkansas River Valley. LC 76-43780. reprint ed. write for info. (*0-404-15634-7*) AMS Pr.

— Fort Ancient, the Great Prehistoric Earthwork of Warren County, Ohio. LC 76-43781. (Illus.). reprint ed. 55.00 (*0-404-15637-1*) AMS Pr.

— The Hopewell Mound Group of Ohio. LC 76-43782. (Field Museum of Natural History. Publication Ser.: 211). (Illus.). reprint ed. 74.50 (*0-404-15638-X*) AMS Pr.

— The Indian Tribes of Ohio: Historically Considered, a Preliminary Paper. LC 76-43783. reprint ed. 31.50 (*0-404-15639-8*) AMS Pr.

— The Indian Tribes of Ohio: Historically Considered 1600-1840. (Historic Indians, Ohio History Ser.). (Illus.). 109p. (C). 1992. reprint ed. lib. bdg. 29.80 (*1-56651-059-7*); reprint ed. pap. 8.30 (*1-56651-080-5*) A W McGraw.

— Prehistoric Relics. (Shorey Historical Ser.). (Illus.). 165p. reprint ed. pap. 10.95 (*0-8466-0157-5*, S157) Shorey.

— Primitive Man in Ohio. LC 76-43787. reprint ed. 27.50 (*0-404-15642-8*) AMS Pr.

— Primitive Man in Ohio. (Ohio History, Prehistoric Indians, Archaeology Ser.). (Illus.). 276p. (C). 1991. reprint ed. lib. bdg. 48.90 (*1-56651-018-X*); reprint ed. pap. 31.80 (*1-56651-017-1*) A W McGraw.

— A Report on the Archaeology of Maine: Being a Narrative of Explorations in That State, 1912-1920, Together with Work at Lake Champlain, 1917. LC 76-43788. (Phillips Academy). reprint ed. 74.50 (*0-404-15643-6*) AMS Pr.

Moorehead, Warren K., et al. Prehistoric Implements. LC 76-43785. (Illus.). reprint ed. 115.00 (*0-404-15641-X*) AMS Pr.

— Stone Ornaments Used by Indians in the U. S. & Canada. LC 76-43790. reprint ed. 55.00 (*0-404-15645-2*) AMS Pr.

Moorehouse, Frank. Futility & Other Animals. 173p. 1991. pap. 9.95 (*0-207-15971-8*, Pub. by Angus & Robertson AT) HarpC.

Moores, Amanda. Dream Palace. 288p. 1994. 20.00 (*0-7867-0125-0*) Carroll & Graf.

— Dream Palace. 288p. 1993. 21.00 (*0-671-75919-1*) S&S Trade.

Moores, B. M., et al. Practical Guide to Quality Assurance in Medical Imaging. LC 86-24529. 139p. reprint ed. pap. 39.70 (*0-7837-6390-5*, 2046103) Bks Demand.

Moores, B. M., et al, eds. Physical Aspects of Medical Imaging: Proceedings of a Meeting Held at the University of Manchester, June 25-27, 1980. LC 82-116267. (Illus.). 354p. reprint ed. pap. 100.90 (*0-8357-8622-6*, 2035045) Bks Demand.

Moores, Dick. Jim Hardy: An Original Compilation of 1st Year 1936-1937. Blackbeard, Bill, ed. LC 76-53031. (Classic American Comic Strips Ser.). 1977. 16.50 (*0-88355-657-X*); pap. 10.00 (*0-88355-656-1*) Hyperion Conn.

Moores, Donald & Meadow-Orlans, Kathryn, eds. Educational & Developmental Aspects of Deafness. LC 90-14014. (Illus.). 451p. (C). 1990. text ed. 39.95 (*0-930323-52-1*) Gallaudet Univ Pr.

Moores, Donald F. Educating the Deaf: Psychology, Principles & Practices, 3 Vols. 3rd ed. LC 86-81340. 416p. (C). 1987. text ed. 61.16 (*0-395-35781-0*) HM.

Moores, Eldridge M. Shaping the Earth: Tectonics of Continents & Oceans. (C). 1995. text ed. write for info. (*0-7167-2141-4*) W H Freeman.

***Moores, Eldridge M., ed.** Volcanoes & Earthquakes. LC 95-12939. (Discoveries Ser.). (Illus.). 64p. (J). (gr. 4-7). 1995. write for info. (*0-7835-4764-1*) Time-Life.

Moores, Eldridge M., jt. auth. see Twiss, Robert J.

***Moores, John D.** Wrestling with Rationality in Paul: Romans 1-8 in a New Perspective. (Society for New Testament Studies Monograph: No. 82). 235p. (C). 1995. 54.95 (*0-521-47223-7*) Cambridge U Pr.

Moores, Lawrence. Thieves in the Schoolhouse. LC 78-50636. 1979. 22.95 (*0-87949-119-1*) Ashley Bks.

***Moores Rowland Staff.** Moores Rowland'S Yellow & Orange Tax Guides 1994-95: Orange, 2 pts. Incl. Moores Rowland's Yellow & Orange Tax Guides 1994-95: Yellow. 1995. pap. 31.95 (*0-406-03648-9*); 31.95 (*0-406-03647-0*) Butterworth Legal Pubs.

Moores, Shaun. Interpreting Audiences: The Ethnography of Media Consumption. (Media, Culture & Society Ser.). (C). Date not set. text ed. 59.95 (*0-8039-8446-4*); pap. text ed. 21.95 (*0-8039-8447-2*) Sage.

Moores, Shaun, jt. ed. see Jackson, Stevi.

Moores, T. & Mohr, M. Canoecraft, Woodstrip Construction. (Illus.). 148p. 1988. pap. 16.95 (*0-920656-24-2*, Pub. by Camden Hse CN) Firefly Bks Ltd.

***Moorey, James.** Living with Grief & Mourning. LC 94-40872. (Living With Ser.). 1995. text ed. write for info. (*0-7190-3944-4*); text ed. write for info. (*0-7190-3945-2*, Pub. by Manchester Univ Pr UK) St Martin.

Moorey, P. R. Ancient Egypt. (Illus.). 64p. 1995. pap. 12.95 (*0-907849-76-8*, 768, Pub. by Ashmolean Mus UK) A Schwartz & Co.

— Ancient Mesopotamian Materials & Industries: The Archaeological Evidence. (Illus.). 448p. 1994. 105.00 (*0-19-814921-2*) OUP.

— Ancient Near East. (Illus.). 58p. 1995. pap. 12.95 (*0-907849-58-X*, 58-X, Pub. by Ashmolean Mus UK) A Schwartz & Co.

— The Biblical Lands: The Making of the Past. (Illus.). 160p. (gr. 8 up). 1991. pap. 16.95 (*0-87226-247-2*) P Bedrick Bks.

— A Century of Biblical Archaeology. LC 92-19808. 208p. (Orig.). 1992. pap. 14.99 (*0-664-25392-X*) Westminster John Knox.

Moorhead, et al. The American Wine Society Presents the Complete Handbook of Winemaking. Reichwaye, Randall J., ed. (Illus.). 225p. (Orig.). 1993. pap. 15.95 (*0-9619072-2-3*) G W Kent.

Moorhead, A. J., et al, eds. Structural Ceramics Joining II. (Ceramic Transactions Ser.: Vol. 35). 334p. 1993. 69.00 (*0-944904-65-3*, TRANS035) Am Ceramic.

***Moorhead, Bruce B.** The Forest Elk: Roosevelt Elk in Olympic National Park. (Illus.). 62p. (Orig.). 1994. pap. text ed. 11.95 (*0-914019-34-1*, 5379) NW Interpretive.

Moorhead, Carol A. Colorado's Backyard Wildlife. (Illus.). 96p. (Orig.). (J). (gr. 6-8). 1992. pap. 10.95 (*1-879373-08-4*) R Rinehart.

— Wild Horses. (Wonder Ser.). (Illus.). 64p. (Orig.). (J). (gr. 1-6). 1994. pap. 7.95 (*1-879373-51-3*) R Rinehart.

Moorhead, Desiree, jt. auth. see Black, Peter.

Moorhead, E. J. Our Yesterdays: The History of the Actuarial Profession in North America, 1809-1979. LC 89-26100. 1989. text ed. 60.00 (*0-938959-08-5*) Soc Actuaries.

Moorhead, Elizabeth. Pittsburgh Portraits. (Orig.). 1955. pap. 1.95 (*0-910286-25-6*) Boxwood.

Moorhead, Gregory & Griffin, Ricky W. Organizational Behavior. 2nd ed. LC 88-81348. 1989. teacher ed 3.16 (*0-318-36899-4*); student ed write for info. (*0-318-63322-1*); trans. write for info. (*0-318-63323-X*) HM.

— Organizational Behavior: Managing People & Organizations, 3 Vols. 3rd ed. (C). 1992. text ed. 59.56 (*0-395-47282-2*) HM.

Moorhead, J. F., ed. see European Dialysis & Transplant Association Staff.

Moorhead, James H. American Apocalypse: Yankee Protestants & the Civil War, 1860-1869. LC 77-14360. 293p. reprint ed. pap. 83.60 (*0-8357-8016-3*, 2033832) Bks Demand.

Moorhead, John. Justinian. LC 93-33762. (Medieval World Ser.). (C). 1994. text ed. 38.95 (*0-582-06304-3*, 76703) Longman.

— Justinian. LC 93-33762. (Medieval World Ser.). (C). 1995. pap. text ed. 17.95 (*0-582-06303-5*, 76715) Longman.

Moorhead, John, tr. & intro. Victor of Vita: A History of the Vandal Persecution. (Translated Texts for Historians Ser.). 136p. (Orig.). (C). 1992. pap. text ed. 15.95 (*0-85323-127-3*, Pub. by Liverpool Univ Pr UK) U of Pa Pr.

Moorhead, John, ed. see European Dialysis & Transplant Association Staff.

Moorhead, John, tr. see Suger, Abbot of St. Denis.

Moorhead, John D., jt. auth. see Combs, Richard E.

Moorhead, Kelly J., jt. auth. see Morgan, Helen C.

***Moorhead, Max L.** New Mexico's Royal Road: Trade & Travel on the Chihuahua Trail. LC 94-35293. (Illus.). 256p. 1995. pap. 14.95 (*0-8061-2651-5*) U of Okla Pr.

— The Presidio: Bastion of the Spanish Borderlands. LC 74-15908. (Illus.). 304p. 1991. pap. 14.95 (*0-8061-2317-6*) U of Okla Pr.

Moorhead, Max L., ed. see Gregg, Josiah.

Moorhill, Mollie. A Few Late Leaves. 30p. 1978. 40.00 (*0-9506373-0-0*, Pub. by Yew Tree Bks UK) St Mut.

Moorhouse, A. C. Studies in the Greek Negatives. xi, 163p. 1959. 9.95 (*0-317-06158-5*, Pub. by U of Wales UK) Bks Intl VA.

Moorhouse, Asheleigh. Art, Sight, & Language. (Illus.). 164p. 1989. 21.95 (*0-921254-05-9*, Pub. by Penumbra Pr CN) U of Toronto Pr.

Moorhouse, Ashleigh, tr. see Schmemann, Alexander.

Moorhouse Crosswait, Helen G. Reflections of a Paleface from the Rosebud: Stories & Tales That Need to Be Told. (Illus.). 64p. (Orig.). 1992. pap. 9.00 (*0-9631143-1-X*) Paleface Pr.

Moorhouse, David M., tr. see Rozo, Teresa & Debicki, Andrew.

Moorhouse, E. Hallam. Samuel Pepys. LC 74-30375. (English Biography Ser.: No. 31). 1974. lib. bdg. 75.00 (*0-8383-1908-4*) M S G Haskell Hse.

Moorhouse, Frank. Forty-Seventeen. 175p. 1989. 16.95 (*0-15-132695-9*) HarBrace.

— Grand Days: A Novel. LC 93-39314. 592p. 1994. 25.00 (*0-679-43362-7*) Pantheon.

Moorhouse, Frank, ed. see Rudd, Steele.

Moorhouse, Geoffrey. The Boat & the Town. large type ed. 448p. 1983. 15.95 (*0-7089-0949-3*) Ulverscroft.

— Hell's Foundations: A Social History of the Town of Bury in the Aftermath of the Gallipoli Campaign. 272p. 1993. pap. 14.95 (*0-8050-2652-5*) H Holt & Co.

— Imperial City. large type ed. 1989. 17.95 (*0-7089-2093-4*) Ulverscroft.

Moorhouse, J. S., jt. ed. see Prout, N. M.

Moorhouse, John. A Historical Glossary of British Marxism. LC 87-29807. 48p. (C). 1987. reprint ed. lib. bdg. 23.00x (*0-8095-6750-4*) Borgo Pr.

— A Historical Glossary of British Marxism. 48p. (C). 1987. reprint ed. pap. 13.00x (*0-946650-06-3*) Borgo Pr.

Moorhouse, John & Newman, Paul. Colin Wilson, Two Essays: 'The English Existentialist' & 'Spiders & Outsiders' (Colin Wilson Studies: No. 1). 49p. (C). 1990. reprint ed. lib. bdg. 23.00x (*0-8095-6756-3*) Borgo Pr.

— Colin Wilson, Two Essays: 'The English Existentialist' & 'Spiders & Outsiders' (Colin Wilson Studies: No. 1). 49p. (C). 1990. reprint ed. pap. 13.00x (*0-946650-11-X*) Borgo Pr.

Moorhouse, Karin. A Child's Story of Canada. 72p. (J). (ps-8). 1987. 6.95 (*0-920806-50-3*, Pub. by Penumbra Pr CN) U of Toronto Pr.

Moorhouse, Mary F. & Doenges, Marilynn E. Nurse's Clinical Pocket Manual: Nursing Diagnoses, Care Planning & Documentation. 477p. (C). 1990. pap. text ed. 18.95 (*0-8036-6314-5*) Davis Co.

Moorhouse, Mary F., jt. auth. see Doenges, Marilynn E.

Moorhouse, Mary F., jt. auth. see Doenges, Maryilynn E.

Moorhouse, Mary F., et al. Critical Care Plans: Guidelines for Advanced Medical-Surgical Care. LC 87-6740. 472p. 1987. 29.95 (*0-8036-6311-0*) Davis Co.

Moorhouse, R. G., jt. auth. see Bransden, B. H.

Moorhouse, R. Gordon, jt. auth. see Bransden, B. H.

Moorhus, Donita M., jt. auth. see Grathwol, Robert P.

Mooring, Benjamin, et al. Fundamentals of Manipulator Calibration. 329p. 1991. text ed. 99.95 (*0-471-50864-0*) Wiley.

***Mooring, Linwood E., Jr.** Releasing Power from Within & the Real You. (Illus.). 230p. (Orig.). Date not set. pap. write for info. (*0-9646104-0-X*) Mooring Hse Pr.

Moorings Staff. Cruising Guide to the Vavu'u Island Group in the Kingdom of Tonga. 20p. 12.00 (*0-944428-17-7*) F Papy Cruising Guide.

Moorjani, Angela. Aesthetics of Loss & Lessness. LC 91-22390. 260p. 1991. text ed. 49.95 (*0-312-06827-1*) St Martin.

Moorjani, K. & Coey, J. M. Disordered Solids. write for info. (*0-318-56698-2*) Elsevier.

— Magnetic Glasses: Methods & Phenomena, Vol. 6. 1984. 187.25 (*0-444-42263-3*, I-452-84) Elsevier.

Moorman, Charles. The Pearl-Poet. Bowman, Sylvia E., ed. LC 68-17243. (Twayne's English Authors Ser.). 148p. (C). 1968. lib. bdg. 17.95 (*0-8290-1722-4*) Irvington.

— The Statistical Determination of Affiliation in the Landmark Manuscripts of the 'Canterbury Tales' LC 93-413. 224p. 1993. text ed. 89.95 (*0-7734-9276-3*) E Mellen.

Moorman, Charles, ed. The Works of the Gawain-Poet. LC 76-40190. (Illus.). 464p. reprint ed. pap. 132.30 (*0-8357-4347-0*, 2037150) Bks Demand.

Moorman, Charles & Minary, Ruth. Arthurian Dictionary. 1990. pap. 8.95 (*0-89733-348-9*) Academy Chi Pubs.

Moorman, Charles W. The Celtic Literature of Defeat: An Extraordinary Assortment of Irregularities. LC 93-24624. 176p. 1993. text ed. 79.95 (*0-7734-9332-8*) E Mellen.

Moorman, Chick. Talk Sense to Yourself: Language & Personal Power. 200p. 1985. 12.00 (*0-9616046-0-3*) Prsnl Power Pr.

— Your Family Matters. (Orig.). 1996. pap. write for info. (*0-9616046-4-6*) Prsnl Power Pr.

Moorman, Chick & Dishon, Dee. Our Classroom: We Can Learn Together. rev. ed. (Illus.). 218p. 1986. reprint ed. 18.00 (*0-9616046-1-1*) Prsnl Power Pr.

Moorman, Chick & Moorman, Nancy. Teacher Talk: What It Really Means. (Illus.). 160p. 1989. pap. 12.00 (*0-9616046-2-X*) Prsnl Power Pr.

Moorman, Donald. Harvest Waiting. LC 93-21088. 1993. 9.95 (*0-570-09936-6*) Concordia.

Moorman, Donald R. & Sessions, Gene A. Camp Floyd & the Mormons: The Utah War. LC 91-51098. (Utah Centennial Ser.: Vol. 7). (Illus.). 250p. (C). 1992. 29.95 (*0-87480-394-2*) U of Utah Pr.

Moorman, E. M. La Pitturs Parietale Romana Come Fonte Di Conoscenza per la Scultura Antica. (Scrinium (Monographs on History, Archaeology & Art History. Published under the Auspices of the Netherlands Institute & the Foundation of Friends of the Dutch Institute in Rome) Ser.: Vol. II). (Illus.). 288p. (ITA.). 1988. 88.00 (*90-232-2315-2*) IBD Ltd.

Moorman, Frederick W. Interpretation of Nature in English Poetry from Beowulf to Shakespeare. LC 78-172741. reprint ed. 36.00 (*0-404-04398-4*) AMS Pr.

Moorman, John. History of the Franciscan Order. 1988. 25.00 (*0-8199-0921-1*, Frncscn Herld) Franciscan Pr.

Moorman, John R. Anglican Spiritual Tradition. LC 82-229111. 240p. 1985. pap. text ed. 14.95 (*0-87243-139-8*) Templegate.

— Church Life in England in the Thirteenth Century. LC 76-29401. reprint ed. 49.50 (*0-404-15352-6*) AMS Pr.

— A History of the Church in England. 3rd rev. ed. 485p. 1980. pap. 22.50 (*0-8192-1282-2*) Morehouse Pub.

— Medieval Franciscan Houses. Marcel, George, ed. (History Ser.: No. 4). 1983. 40.00 (*0-318-00515-8*) Franciscan Inst.

— St. Francis of Assisi. 1986. 4.95 (*0-8199-0904-1*, Frncscn Herld) Franciscan Pr.

***Moorman, Madison.** Journal of Madison Berryman Moorman. (American Autobiography Ser.). 150p. 1995. reprint ed. lib. bdg. 69.00 (*0-7812-8597-6*) Rprt Serv.

Moorman, Margaret. Light the Lights! A Story about Celebrating Hanukkah & Christmas. (Illus.). 32p. (J). (ps-2). 1994. bds. 12.95 (*0-590-47003-5*, Cartwheel) Scholastic Inc.

— My Sister's Keeper: Learning to Cope with a Sibling's Mental Illness. 320p. 1993. pap. 11.00 (*0-14-023121-8*, Penguin Bks) Viking Penguin.

— My Sister's Keeper: Learning to Cope with a Sibling's Mental Illness. 320p. 1992. 21.95 (*0-393-02987-5*) Norton.

Moorman, Nancy, jt. auth. see Moorman, Chick.

Moorman, Robert. Cultural Anthropology: A Supplement. 100p. (C). 1992. per., pap. text ed. 14.95 (*0-8403-7902-1*) Kendall-Hunt.

Moorman, Robert B., jt. auth. see Parcel, John.

Moorman, Ruth & Williams, Lalla. A Salad a Day: Scrumptious Salads for Every Day of the Week. (Cookbook Ser.: No. 3). (Illus.). 80p. 1980. pap. 5.95 (*0-937552-02-X*) Quail Ridge.

— Seven Chocolate Sins: A Devilishly Delicious Collection of Chocolate Recipes. (Cookbook Ser.: No. 2). (Illus.). 80p. 1979. pap. 5.95 (*0-937552-01-1*) Quail Ridge.

— Twelve Days of Christmas Cookbook. (Cookbook Ser.: No. 1). (Illus.). 80p. 1978. pap. 5.95 (*0-937552-00-3*) Quail Ridge.

Moorman, Shar. Warm Glass. (Illus.). 127p. (C). 1988. pap. text ed. 18.95 (*0-935133-19-4*) CKE Pubns.

Moorman, Theo. Weaving As an Art Form. LC 86-61202. (Illus.). 104p. 1986. pap. 12.95 (*0-88740-068-X*) Schiffer.

***Moors, Annelies.** Women, Property & Islam: Palestinian Experiences, 1920-1990. (Middle East Studies: No. 3). 296p. (C). Date not set. write for info. (*0-521-47497-3*) Cambridge U Pr.

— Women, Property & Islam: Palestinian Experiences, 1920-1990. (Middle East Studies: No. 3). 296p. (C). 1995. write for info. (*0-521-48355-7*) Cambridge U Pr.

Moors, Hein G. Child Spacing & Family Size in the Netherlands. 1974. pap. 18.00 (*90-207-0491-5*) Kluwer Ac.

Moors, Hein G., et al, eds. Population & Family in the Low Countries, No. 1. (Publications of the Netherlands Inter-University Demographic Institute & the Population & Family Study Centre Ser.). 1976. pap. text ed. 33.50 (*90-247-1859-7*) Kluwer Ac.

— Population & Family in the Low Countries, No. 2. (Publications of the Netherlands Inter-University Demographic Institute & the Population & Family Study Centre Ser.: Vol. 6). 1978. pap. text ed. 31.00 (*90-207-0687-X*) Kluwer Ac.

***Moors, J. F.** Civil War Infantry, History of the 52nd Regiment, Mass. Volunteers. (Illus.). 283p. 1995. reprint ed. lib. bdg. 38.00 (*0-8328-4628-7*) Higginson Bk Co.

Moors, Joseph. French & Dutch Legal Dictionary: Dictionnaire Juridique. (DUT & FRE.). 1984. 125.00 (*0-8288-0975-5*, M521) Fr & Eur.

Moors, Kent. An Introduction to the Study of Politics. 180p. (Orig.). (C). 1988. pap. text ed. 19.50 (*0-8191-7185-9*) U Pr of Amer.

M

An Asterisk (*) at the beginning of an entry indicates that the title is appearing in BIP for the first time.

Moors, Kent, ed. Politokos I: Selected Papers of the North American Chapter of the Society for Greek Political Thought. LC 89-1075. 220p. 1989. text ed. 48.00x (*0-8207-0204-8*); pap. text ed. 21.95 (*0-8207-0212-9*) Duquesne.

Moorsom, Richard, jt. auth. see Eriksen, Tore L.

Moorsteen, Richard & Abramowitz, Morton. Remaking China Policy: U. S.-China Relations & Governmental Decisionmaking. LC 74-164428. (Rand Corporation Research Studies). 174p. 1971. 18.95 (*0-674-75981-8*) HUP.

Moorsteen, Richard H. & Powell, Raymond P. The Soviet Capital Stock, Nineteen Twenty-Eight to Nineteen Sixty-Two. LC 65-27841. (Economic Growth Center, Yale University Publication Ser.). 695p. reprint ed. pap. 180.00 (*0-8357-8328-6*, 2033833) Bks Demand.

***Moortgat, G. K., et al, eds.** Low-Temperature Chemistry of the Atmosphere. (Global Environmental Change Ser.). 544p. 1994. 222.00 (*0-387-58111-1*) Spr-Verlag.

Moortgat, M. Perspectives on Functional Grammar. 2nd ed. Hoekstra, T. et al, eds. x, 352p. 1983. reprint ed. pap. 41.45 (*90-70176-27-0*) Mouton.

Moortgat, Michael. Categorial Investigations: Logical & Linguistic Aspects of the Lambek Calculus. (Groningen-Amsterdam Studies in Semantics: No. 9). xiv, 278p. 1988. pap. 34.95 (*90-6765-387-X*) Mouton.

Moorthy, Vasantha. The Menu Book: A Comprehensive Guide to Authentic Indian Vegetarian Cuisine. 287p. 1992. 23.95 (*0-9634681-0-3*) G Moorthy.

— Vegetarian Menu Book: A Comprehensive Guide to Authentic Indian Vegetarian Cuisine. (C). 1993. pap. 14.00 (*81-85944-18-0*, Pub. by UBS Pubs Dist II) S Asia.

Moorton, Richard F., Jr., ed. Eugene O'Neill's Century: Centennial Views on America's Foremost Tragic Dramatist. LC 90-47536. (Contributions in Drama & Theatre Studies: No. 36). 264p. 1991. text ed. 49.95 (*0-313-26826-6*, MEF/, Greenwood Pr) Greenwood.

Moorty, D. N. The Feel of Feel. (Redbird Ser.). 1976. lib. bdg. 8.00 (*0-89253-097-9*); 4.80 (*0-89253-133-9*) Ind-US Inc.

Moos, David, jt. auth. see Crone, Rainer.

Moos, Elayne. The Herb Gardener's Mail Order Source Book. (Illus.). 176p. 1987. pap. 6.95 (*0-912661-08-9*) Woodsong Graph.

***Moos, Merry K. & Freda, Margaret C.** Preconceptional Health Promotion. Damus, Karla, ed. LC 94-37837. 1994. write for info. (*0-86525-061-8*) March of Dimes.

Moos, Merry-K., jt. auth. see Cefalo, Robert C.

Moos, Merry-K., jt. ed. see Miller, C. Arden.

Moos, Michael. Morning Windows. 80p. 1983. pap. 3.50 (*0-89823-051-9*) New Rivers Pr.

Moos, Michael & Francisco, Patricia W., eds. The Language of Light. (Illus.). 180p. (Orig.). 1983. pap. 5.00 (*0-927663-08-2*) COMPAS.

Moos, Michael, jt. ed. see Bradford, Gigi.

Moos, N. H. How to Acquire a Million. 1985. pap. 3.25 (*0-912576-08-1*) R Collier.

Moos, Rudolf H. Evaluating Correctional & Community Settings. LC 74-30267. 399p. reprint ed. pap. 113.80 (*0-317-07762-7*, 2015626) Bks Demand.

— Evaluating Educational Environments. LC 79-83568. (Jossey-Bass Higher Education & Social & Behavioral Science Ser.). 352p. reprint ed. pap. 100.40 (*0-7837-0185-3*, 2040481) Bks Demand.

— Evaluating Treatment Environments: A Social Ecological Approach. LC 73-17450. (Health, Medicine, & Society: A Wiley-Interscience Ser.). 409p. reprint ed. pap. 116.60 (*0-685-10850-3*, 2055756) Bks Demand.

Moos, Rudolf H., ed. Coping with Life Crises: An Integrated Approach. LC 85-28149. (Stress & Coping Ser.). 444p. 1986. 60.00 (*0-306-42133-X*, Plenum Pr); pap. 32.50 (*0-306-42144-5*, Plenum Pr) Plenum.

— Coping with Physical Illness, Vol. 2: New Perspectives. (Illus.). 452p. 1984. 49.50 (*0-306-41681-6*, Plenum Med Bk) Plenum.

— Coping with Physical Illness, Vol. 2: New Perspectives. (Illus.). 452p. 1989. pap. 29.50 (*0-306-43350-8*, Plenum Med Bk) Plenum.

Moos, Rudolf H. & Lemke, Sonne. Group Residences for Older Adults: Physical Features, Policies, & Social Climate. LC 93-32701. (Illus.). 304p. 1994. 55.00 (*0-19-506257-4*) OUP.

Moos, Rudolf H., et al. Alcoholism Treatment: Context, Process, & Outcome. (Illus.). 304p. 1990. 45.00 (*0-19-504362-6*) OUP.

Moos, Rudolph H. The Human Context. LC 83-17562. 460p. (C). 1986. reprint ed. lib. bdg. 38.50 (*0-89874-679-5*) Krieger.

Moosa, A. R., jt. auth. see Block, George E.

Moosa, Matti. The Early Novels of Naguib Mahfouz: Images of Modern Egypt. (Illus.). 304p. 1994. lib. bdg. 39.95 (*0-8130-1309-7*) U Press Fla.

— Extremist Shiites: The Ghulat Sects. (Contemporary Issues in the Middle East Ser.). 400p. 1987. text ed. 39.95x (*0-8156-2411-5*) Syracuse U Pr.

— The Maronites in History. 350p. 1986. text ed. 39.95x (*0-8156-2365-8*) Syracuse U Pr.

— Origins of Modern Arabic Fiction. rev. ed. 304p. 1995. pap. 16.00 (*0-89410-684-8*) Three Continents.

— Origins of Modern Arabic Fiction. 2nd rev. ed. 304p. 1995. 32.00 (*0-89410-683-X*) Three Continents.

Moosang, Faith, jt. auth. see Meyer, Christine.

Moose, Allan & Lorenz, Marian. Atari Assembly Language Programmer's Guide. 288p. 1986. pap. 26.95 (*0-938862-54-5*) Weber Systems.

***Moose, R.** Dreaming in Color. Date not set. pap. 3.99 (*0-517-13372-5*) Random.

— Wreath Ribbon Quilt. Date not set. pap. 2.99 (*0-517-13371-7*) Random.

***Moose, Ruth.** Making the Bed. 72p. (Orig.). 1994. pap. 8.95 (*1-885926-02-2*) Sandstone NC.

— The Wreath Ribbon Quilt. 126p. 1988. 14.00 (*0-932662-66-8*); pap. 10.00 (*0-932662-67-6*) St Andrews NC.

Mooser, Stephen. The Case of the Slippery Sharks. LC 87-3490. (Treasure Hounds Ser.). (Illus.). 96p. (J). (gr. 3-6). 1988. lib. bdg. 9.89 (*0-8167-1177-1*); pap. text ed. 2.95 (*0-8167-1178-X*) Troll Assocs.

— Disaster in Room 101. LC 93-24055. (Illus.). 80p. (J). (gr. 2-4). 1993. lib. bdg. 2.95 (*0-8167-3278-7*); pap. text ed. 2.95 (*0-8167-3279-5*) Troll Assocs.

— Elvis Is Back & He's in the Sixth Grade! (J). (gr. 4-7). 1994. pap. 3.50 (*0-553-48177-0*) Bantam.

— The Ghost with the Halloween Hiccups. (Illus.). 32p. (J). (gr. k-3). 1978. pap. 2.95 (*0-380-40287-4*, Camelot) Avon.

— The Mummy's Secret. LC 87-16152. (Treasure Hounds Ser.). (Illus.). 96p. (J). (gr. 3-6). 1988. lib. bdg. 9.89 (*0-8167-1181-X*); pap. text ed. 2.95 (*0-8167-1182-8*) Troll Assocs.

— The Secret Gold Mine. LC 87-16151. (Treasure Hounds Ser.). (Illus.). 96p. (J). (gr. 3-6). 1988. lib. bdg. 9.89 (*0-8167-1179-8*); pap. text ed. 2.95 (*0-8167-1180-1*) Troll Assocs.

— Secret in the Old Mansion. LC 87-15456. (Treasure Hounds Ser.). (Illus.). 96p. (J). (gr. 3-6). 1988. lib. bdg. 9.89 (*0-8167-1175-5*); pap. text ed. 2.95 (*0-8167-1176-3*) Troll Assocs.

— The Things Upstairs. LC 93-50676. (Illus.). 144p. (J). (gr. 3-6). 1994. pap. 2.95 (*0-8167-3421-6*) Troll Assocs.

Mooser, Stephen & Oliver, Lin. Tad & Dad. LC 87-40340. (Catch the Reading Bug Ser.). (Illus.). (J). (ps-2). 1990. 4.95 (*1-55782-023-6*, Warner Juvenile Bks) Little.

Moosewood Collective Staff. Moosewood Restaurant Cooks at Home: Fast & Easy Recipes for Any Day. 1994. 30.00 (*0-671-87954-5*, Fireside); pap. 16.00 (*0-671-67992-9*, Fireside) S&S Trade.

— New Recipes from Moosewood Restaurant. (Illus.). 320p. 1987. 19.95 (*0-89815-209-7*); pap. 15.95 (*0-89815-208-9*) Ten Speed Pr.

Moossa, A. R., et al. Comprehensive Textbook of Oncology, 2 vols. 2nd ed. 1918p. 1991. 199.00 (*0-683-06147-X*) Williams & Wilkins.

Moote, A. Lloyd. Louis XIII, The Just. 400p. (C). 1989. 50.00 (*0-520-06485-2*) U CA Pr.

— Louis XIII, The Just. (Illus.). 417p. 1991. reprint ed. pap. 15.00 (*0-520-07546-3*) U CA Pr.

Moote, Alanson L. The Revolt of the Judges: The Parlement of Paris & the Fronde, 1643-1652. LC 78-155003. 423p. reprint ed. pap. 120.60 (*0-8357-3851-5*, 2036584) Bks Demand.

***Moothart, Lorene.** Outstandingly His: The Life Story of Paul & Mary Williams (Uncle Paul & Aunt Mary) (Orig.). 1993. pap. 5.95 (*1-885729-02-2*) Toccoa Falls.

— Sunbursts: True Adventures of Toccoa Falls College Missionaries. (Illus.). 232p. (Orig.). 1992. pap. 5.95 (*1-885729-03-0*) Toccoa Falls.

Mootoo. Out on Main Street: And Other Stories. (NFS Canada Ser.). 1993. pap. 12.95 (*0-88974-052-6*, Pub. by Press Gang CN) InBook.

Mooy, John. The Tale of Boris: (A Fable of the Red-Tailed Hawk) (Illus.). 32p. (J). (gr. k-6). 1991. lib. bdg. 15.00 (*1-883960-06-1*); pap. 7.00 (*1-883960-07-X*) Henry Quill.

Mooy, John & Stroschin, Jane. Sidney: The Story of a Kingfisher. (Illus.). 32p. (J). (gr. k-6). 1991. text ed. 15.00 (*1-883960-08-8*) Henry Quill.

— Sidney: The Story of a Kingfisher. (Illus.). 32p. (J). (gr. k-6). 1991. pap. 7.00 (*1-883960-09-6*) Henry Quill.

Mooz, William E., Jr. Introduction to Doing Business in Mexico. LC 94-7487. 1994. 95.00 (*1-56425-037-7*) Transnatl Juris Pubns.

Mopris, James. You Can Win Big - Small Claims Court. 1995. write for info. (*1-56171-214-0*) Sure Sellers.

Mopsik, Wendy, jt. auth. see Robinson, Doris.

Moqbel, Redwan, ed. Allergy & Immunity to Helminths: Common Mechanisms or Divergent Pathways? LC 92-26365. 1992. 99.00 (*0-7484-0022-2*) Taylor & Francis.

Moquet, ed. see Rimbaud, Arthur.

Moquette-Magee, Elaine. Fight Fat & Win! How to Eat a Low-Fat Diet Without Changing Your Life. rev. ed. 277p. 1994. pap. 9.95 (*1-56561-047-4*) Chronimed.

— The Fight Fat & Win Cookbook: Timesaving Recipes for a Low-Effort, Low-Fat Lifestyle. 230p. 1994. 12.95 (*1-56561-055-5*) Chronimed.

— Two Hundred Kid-Tested Ways to Lower the Fat in Your Child's Favorite Foods: How to Make the Brand-Name & Homemade Foods Your Kids Love More Healthful - & Delicious. 297p. 1994. pap. 12.95 (*1-56561-034-2*, 004231) Chronimed.

***Moquin, Wayne & Van Doren, Charles.** Great Documents in American Indian History. (Illus.). 458p. 1995. reprint ed. pap. 16.95 (*0-306-80659-2*) Da Capo.

Moquist, Christopher. Words That Make Signs Sell. (Illus.). 88p. (Orig.). 1992. pap. 14.95 (*0-9629666-2-2*) Insignia Systs.

Moquist, Richard W. The Franklin Mysteries. (Illus.). 197p. 1994. pap. 8.95 (*1-56901-145-1*) NW Pub.

Mor-Barak, Michal E. Social Networks & Health of the Frail Elderly. LC 91-28275. (Studies on Elderly in America). 192p. 1991. 54.00 (*0-8153-0515-X*) Garland.

Mor, Barbara, jt. auth. see Sjoo, Monica.

Mor, Ben D. Decision & Interaction in Crisis: A Model of International Crisis Behavior. LC 92-31843. 192p. 1993. text ed. 52.95 (*0-275-94371-2*, C4371, Praeger Pubs) Greenwood.

***Mo'r, MacCarthy.** Historical Essays on the Kingdom of Munster. 315p. 1994. 30.00 (*0-940134-29-2*) Irish Genealog.

Mor, Menachem. Jewish Sects, Religious Movements, & Political Parties: Proceedings of the Third Annual Symposium of the Philip M. & Ethel Klutznick Chair in Jewish Civilization. LC 92-73317. 450p. (C). 1993. 30.00 (*1-881871-04-5*) Creighton U Pr.

Mor, Menachem, ed. Eretz Israel, Israel & the Jewish Diaspora Mutual Relations: Proceedings of the First Annual Symposium of the Philip M. & Ethel Klutznick Chair in Jewish Civilization Held on Sunday-Monday, October 9-10, 1988. (Studies in Jewish Civilizations: No. 1). 256p. (Orig.). (C). 1991. lib. bdg. 49.00 (*0-8191-8280-X*); pap. text ed. 24.00 (*0-8191-8281-8*) U Pr of Amer.

— International Perspectives on Church & State. LC 93-72313. (Klutznick Series in Jewish Civilization). xix, 330p. (C). 1994. lib. bdg. 30.00 (*1-881871-05-3*) Fordham.

— Jewish Assimilation, Acculturation, & Accommodation: Past Traditions, Current Issues, & Future Prospects. 340p. (C). 1991. lib. bdg. 54.00 (*0-8191-8456-X*) U Pr of Amer.

***Mor, Menachem, ed.** Crisis & Reaction: The Hero in Jewish History. (Studies in Jewish Civilization: No. 6). 420p. 1995. 30.00 (*1-881871-14-2*) Fordham.

Mor, Vincent. Hospice Care Systems: Structure, Process, Costs & Outcome. (Death & Suicide Ser.). 288p. 1987. 32.95 (*0-8261-5760-2*) Springer Pub.

Mor, Vincent, et al. The Hospice Experiment. LC 87-22580. (Contemporary Medicine & Public Health Ser.). 288p. 1988. text ed. 45.00x (*0-8018-3542-9*) Johns Hopkins.

— Networking AIDS Services. LC 93-37871. 238p. (Orig.). 1993. pap. text ed. 32.00 (*1-56793-006-9*, 0939) Health Admin Pr.

***Mora.** Tomas & the Library Lady. 15.00 (*0-679-80401-3*) Random.

Mora, Abdias A., tr. see Copeland, E. L.

Mora, Carl J. Mexican Cinema: Reflections of a Society. LC 81-7507. (Illus.). 392p. 1982. pap. 14.00 (*0-520-04304-9*) U CA Pr.

***Mora, Christina T., et al, eds.** Cardiopulmonary Bypass: Principles & Techniques of Extracorporeal Circulation. LC 94-29083. 535p. 1995. text ed. 139.00 (*0-387-94242-4*) Spr-Verlag.

Mora, E., jt. auth. see Pezzoli, F.

Mora, Elena S., tr. see Tarango, Yolanda, et al.

Mora, Emma. Animals of the Forest. (Illus.). 30p. (J). (ps-1). 1986. 3.95 (*0-8120-5722-8*) Barron.

— Cyril the Lion. (Once upon a Time Ser.). 30p. (J). (ps-1). 1987. 3.95 (*0-8120-5811-9*) Barron.

— Gideon the Little Bear Cub. (Illus.). 30p. (J). (ps-1). 1986. 3.95 (*0-8120-5728-7*) Barron.

— Mortimer Visits Santa Claus. (Illus.). (J). (ps-1). 1987. 3.95 (*0-8120-5808-9*) Barron.

— Snow White & the Seven Dwarfs. (Illus.). 30p. (J). (ps-1). 1986. 3.95 (*0-8120-5726-0*) Barron.

Mora, Fabio. Prosopografia Isiaca, 2 vols., Set. (Etudes Preliminaires aux Religions Orientales dans l'Empire Romain Ser.: Vol. 113). (Illus.). (ITA.). 1990. 188.75 (*90-04-09234-5*) E J Brill.

— Prosopografia Isiaca, 2 vols., Vol. I. (Etudes Preliminaires aux Religions Orientales dans l'Empire Romain Ser.: Vol. 113). (Illus.). xxii, 526p. (ITA.). 1990. 137.14 (*90-04-09233-1*) E J Brill.

— Prosopografia Isiaca, 2 vols., Vol. II. (Etudes Preliminaires aux Religions Orientales dans l'Empire Romain Ser.: Vol. 113). (Illus.). (ITA.). 1990. 51.43 (*90-04-09235-8*) E J Brill.

Mora, Francisco X. The Coyote Rings the Wrong Bell. LC 91-13163. (Adventures in Storytelling Ser.). (Illus.). 24p. (J). (ps-3). 1991. lib. bdg. 12.90 (*0-516-05136-9*); pap. 4.95 (*0-516-45136-7*) Childrens.

— La Gran Fiesta. LC 92-44365. (Illus.). 32p. (J). (ps-00). 1993. lib. bdg. 15.00 (*0-917846-19-2*, 95518) Highsmith Pr.

— Juan Tuza & the Magic Pouch. (Illus.). 32p. (J). (ps-1). 1993. lib. bdg. 15.00 (*0-917846-24-9*, 95563) Highsmith Pr.

— The Legend of the Two Moons. LC 92-31552. (Illus.). 32p. (J). (ps-00). 1993. lib. bdg. 15.00 (*0-917846-15-X*, 95517) Highsmith Pr.

— The Tiger & the Rabbit: A Puerto Rican Folk Tale. LC 91-3500. (Adventures in Storytelling Ser.). (Illus.). 32p. (J). (ps-3). 1991. lib. bdg. 13.95 (*0-516-05137-7*); pap. 5.95 (*0-516-45137-5*) Childrens.

Mora, Gabriela & Van Hooft, Karen S., eds. Theory & Practice of Feminist Literary Criticism. LC 81-67051. (Studies in Literary Analysis). 291p. (C). 1982. lib. bdg. 28.00 (*0-916950-23-9*); pap. 19.00 (*0-916950-22-0*) Biling Rev-Pr.

Mora, George, ed. On the Relations Between the Physical & Moral Aspects of Man, Vol. 2. Saidi, Margaret D., tr. LC 80-21694. 438p. reprint ed. pap. 124.90 (*0-317-08233-7*, 2019949) Bks Demand.

Mora, George, et al, eds. Witches, Devils, & Doctors in the Renaissance: Johann Weyer, "De Praestigiis Daemonum" Shea, John, tr. (Medieval & Renaissance Texts & Studies: Vol. 73). 896p. 1991. 45.00 (*0-86698-083-0*, MR73) MRTS.

Mora, George, ed. see Chiarugi, Vincenzo.

Mora, Gilles. Walker Evans: The Hungry Eye. LC 93-16399. 1993. 60.00 (*0-8109-3259-8*) Abrams.

***Mora, Gilles, ed.** Edward Weston: Forms of Passion. LC 95-10640. 1995. write for info. (*0-8109-3979-7*) Abrams.

Mora, I. English-Hungarian Law Dictionary. 208p. (ENG & HUN.). 1990. 40.00 (*963-622-117-0*, Pub. by Muszaki Fordito HU) IBD Ltd.

— Hungarian-English Law Dictionary. 261p. 1992. 43.00 (*963-622-136-7*, Pub. by Muszaki Fordito HU) IBD Ltd.

— Hungarian-English Law Dictionary. (ENG & HUN.). 1992. 43.00 (*0-7859-8903-X*) Fr & Eur.

***Mora, Imre.** Dictionnaire Pratique de l'Edition en 20 Langues. 3rd ed. 1984. write for info. (*0-7859-8669-3*, 3598104499) Fr & Eur.

— English-Hungarian Law Dictionary. 208p. (ENG & HUN.). 1992. 39.95 (*0-7859-7517-9*, 9636221170) Fr & Eur.

— Hungarian-English Legal Dictionary. 261p. (ENG & HUN.). 1992. 41.95 (*0-7859-7518-7*, 9636221367) Fr & Eur.

— Publisher's Practical Dictionary in 20 Languages. 3rd rev. ed. 418p. 1984. 250.00 (*0-8288-3399-0*, M6933) Fr & Eur.

***Mora, Jo.** Budgee Budgee Cottontail. Mitchell, Steve, ed. (Illus.). (J). (gr. 3). 1994. 24.95 (*0-922029-23-7*) D Stoecklein Photo.

— Californios. (Illus.). 1994. 24.95 (*0-922029-19-9*) D Stoecklein Photo.

— Trail Dust & Saddle Leather. 1994. 24.95 (*0-922029-18-0*) D Stoecklein Photo.

— Trail Dust & Saddle Leather. LC 86-19303. (Illus.). x, 246p. 1987. pap. 10.95 (*0-8032-8145-5*) U of Nebr Pr.

Mora, John, jt. auth. see Newby-Fraser, Paula.

Mora, Jose F. Diccionario De Filosofia, Vol. 2. 960p. 1991. 105.00 (*0-7859-6448-7*) Fr & Eur.

Mora, L., et al. Conservation of Wall Paintings. Plenderleith, H. J. & Schwartzbaum, E., trs. (Conservation in the Arts, Archaeology, & Architecture Ser.). 656p. 1984. text ed. 155.00 (*0-408-10812-6*) Buttrwrth-Heinemann.

Mora, Pat. Agua, Agua, Agua. 2nd ed. (Let Me Read Ser.). 16p. (J). (ps-1). 1994. text ed. 2.95 (*0-673-36195-0*) GdYrBks.

— Agua Agua Agua. 3rd ed. Ada, Alma F., tr. (Let Me Read, Level 2, Ser.). (Illus.). (SPA.). (J). 1995. bds. 2.95 (*0-673-36292-2*) GdYrBks.

— Agua Santa: Holy Water. LC 95-6024. 160p. (C). 1995. 17.95 (*0-8070-6828-4*) Beacon Pr.

— A Birthday Basket for Tia. LC 91-15753. (Illus.). 32p. (J). (ps-1). 1992. text ed. 13.95 (*0-02-767400-2*, Mac Bks Young Read) S&S Childrens.

— A Birthday Basket for Tia. (One World Friends & Neighbors Ser.). (Illus.). (J). (gr. k-4). 1993. 13.95 (*0-685-64816-8*); audio 11.00 (*1-882869-78-8*) Varsity Read Servs.

— Borders. 2nd ed. LC 85-73352. 88p. (Orig.). 1993. pap. 7.00 (*0-685-64977-6*) Arte Publico.

— Chants. 2nd ed. LC 83-70677. 52p. 1994. 7.00 (*0-934770-24-7*) Arte Publico.

— Communion. LC 91-305. 92p. 1991. pap. 7.00 (*1-55885-035-X*) Arte Publico.

— Confetti. LC 95-2038. 1995. 14.95 (*1-880000-25-3*) Lee & Low Bks.

— The Desert Is My Mother - el Desierto Es Mi Madre. LC 94-20047. (Illus.). (ENG & SPA.). (J). 1994. 14.95 (*1-55885-121-6*) Arte Publico.

— Listen to the Desert - Que Dice el Desierto? LC 93-31463. (Illus.). (ENG & SPA.). (J). (ps-2). 1994. 14.95 (*0-395-67292-9*, Clarion Bks) HM.

— Nepantla: Essays from the Land in the Middle. LC 92-39874. 190p. 1993. 19.95 (*0-8263-1454-6*) U of NM Pr.

— Pablo's Tree. LC 92-27145. (Illus.). 32p. (J). (ps-1). 1994. text ed. 14.95 (*0-02-767401-0*, Mac Bks Young Read) S&S Childrens.

— Uno, Dos, Tres: One, Two, Three. LC 94-15337. (Illus.). (J). (ps-3). Date not set. write for info. (*0-395-67294-5*, Clarion Bks) HM.

***Mora, Pat & Berg, Charles R.** The Gift of the Poinsettia. LC 94-37233. (ENG & SPA.). 1995. 14.95 (*1-55885-137-2*, Pinata Bks) Arte Publico.

Mora, Richard G. Shedding a Little Light on Your Skin. LC 91-67754. 126p. (Orig.). 1992. pap. 17.95 (*1-56002-162-4*) Aegina Pr.

Mora, Santiago, et al. Cultivars, Anthropic Soils & Stability: A Preliminary Report of Archaeological Research in Araracuara, Colombian Amazonia. (University of Pittsburgh Latin American Archaeology Reports: No. 2). (Illus.). 1991. pap. 13.00 (*1-877812-05-6*) UPLAAP.

Mora, Teo, ed. AAECC-6. (Lecture Notes in Computer Science Ser.: Vol. 357). ix, 481p. 1989. pap. 51.00 (*0-387-51083-4*, 3092) Spr-Verlag.

Mora, Teo & Traverso, C., eds. Effective Methods in Algebraic Geometry. (Progress in Mathematics Ser.: Vol. 94). 514p. 1991. 93.50 (*0-8176-3546-7*) Spr-Verlag.

Moracco, John C. & Higgins, Earl B. Comprehensive Approach to Human Relations Development. (Illus.). 388p. (C). reprint ed. 40.00 (*1-878907-38-7*) TechBooks.

Morace, G., jt. ed. see Sanna, A.

Morace, Robert A. The Dialogic Novels of Malcolm Bradbury & David Lodge. LC 88-29339. (Crosscurrents-Modern Critiques, Third Ser.). 256p. (C). 1989. 29.95 (*0-8093-1519-X*) S Ill U Pr.

Morace, Robert A. & VanSpanckeren, Kathryn, eds. John Gardner: Critical Perspectives. LC 81-16691. (Crosscurrents Modern Critiques, New Ser.). 199p. 1982. 19.95 (*0-8093-1031-7*) S Ill U Pr.

Morachevskii, V. G, jt. ed. see Kachurin, N. I.

Morack, K. Fiedler, ed. see Brown, Emily I.

Moraczewski, Albert S., jt. auth. see Atkinson, Gary M.

Moraczewski, Albert S., jt. ed. see Cataldo, Peter J.

Morad, M. & Agus, Z., eds. Intracellular Regulation of Ion Channels. (NATO ASI Series H: Cell Biology: Vol. 60). x, 251p. 1992. 139.00 (*0-387-54611-1*) Spr-Verlag.

Moraes, D. The Tempest Within: Account of East Pakistan. 102p. 1971. 8.95 (*0-318-37274-6*) Asia Bk Corp.

Moraes, Dom. Rajasthan: Splendour in the Wilderness. (Illus.). 144p. (C). 1988. 595.00 (*81-7002-027-1*, Pub. by Himalayan Bks II) St Mut.

Moraes, Frank & Howe, Ed, eds. John Kenneth Galbraith Introduces India. 232p. 1976. 17.95 (*0-318-36996-6*) Asia Bk Corp.

An Asterisk (*) at the beginning of an entry indicates that the title is appearing in BIP for the first time.

Moraes, George. The Kadamba Kula: A History of Ancient & Medieval Karnataka. 1990. reprint ed. 48.00 (*81-206-0595-0*, Pub. by Asian Educ Servs II) S Asia.

Moraff, Barbara. Deadly Nightshade. (Morning Chapbook Ser.). (Illus.). 17p. (Orig.). 1989. pap. 10.00 (*0-918273-61-7*) Coffee Hse.

— Learning to Move. 32p. (Orig.). 1982. pap. 5.50 (*0-937013-11-0*) Potes Poets.

— Telephone Company Repairman Poems. LC 82-19275. (Illus.). 17p. (Orig.). 1983. pap. 15.00 (*0-915124-75-0*, Toothpaste) Coffee Hse.

Morafka, David J. A Biogeographical Analysis of the Chihuahuan Desert Through Its Herpetofauna. (Biogeographica Ser.: No. 9). (Illus.). 1977. lib. bdg. 103.00 (*90-6193-210-6*) Kluwer Ac.

Morag, Shelomo. Vocalised Talmudic Manuscripts in the Cambridge Genizah Collections: Taylor-Schnechter Old Series, Vol. I: Taylor-Schechter Old Series. (Cambridge University Library Genizah Ser.: No. 4). 60p. 1988. 84.95 (*0-521-26863-X*) Cambridge U Pr.

— The Vocalization Systems of Arabic, Hebrew & Aramaic: Their Phonetic & Phonemic Principles. (Janua Linguarum, Ser. Minor: No. 13). 1972. pap. text ed. 16.95 (*90-279-1965-8*) Mouton.

Moraga, Cherrie. Heroes & Saints & Other Plays. 149p. (Orig.). 1994. pap. 14.95 (*0-931122-74-0*) West End.

— The Last Generation: Poetry & Prose. LC 93-703. 250p. (Orig.). 1993. 30.00 (*0-89608-467-1*); pap. 14.00 (*0-89608-466-3*) South End Pr.

— Loving in the War Years: Lo Que Nunca Paso Por Sus Labios. LC 86-61474. 153p. 1983. 30.00 (*0-89608-196-6*); pap. 12.00 (*0-89608-195-8*) South End Pr.

Moraga, Cherrie & Anzaldua, Gloria, eds. This Bridge Called My Back: Writings by Radical Women of Color. (Illus.). 261p. (Orig.). (C). 1984. reprint ed. lib. bdg. 21.95 (*0-913175-18-8*); reprint ed. pap. 9.95 (*0-913175-03-X*) Kitchen Table.

Moraga, Cherrie & Castillo, Ana, eds. The Sexuality of Latinas. (Illus.). 192p. 1991. pap. 10.95 (*0-943219-07-8*) Third Woman.

Moraglio, Joseph F. & Kerrigan, Harry D. The Federal Budget & Financial System: A Management Perspective. LC 85-12303. 276p. 1986. text ed. 55.00 (*0-89930-127-4*, MFB/, Quorum Bks) Greenwood.

Moragne, Lenora & Moragne, Rudolph. Baby's Early Years: A Record Book. (Illus.). 1975. spiral bd. 5.00 (*0-917230-02-7*) LenChamps Pubs.

— Our Baby's Early Years. (Illus.). 1988. spiral bd. 12.95 (*0-917230-01-9*) LenChamps Pubs.

Moragne, Rudolph, jt. auth. see Moragne, Lenora.

Morahg, Mordecai, jt. auth. see Morahg, Ruhama.

Morahg, Ruhama & Morahg, Mordecai. Towards Joy Profound. Freifield, Larry, ed. 282p. (Orig.). 1990. pap. 12.95 (*0-9625998-0-8*) M & R Project.

***Moraillon, Robert, et al.** Dictionnaire Pratique de Therapeutique Canine et Feline. 3rd rev. ed. 1992. 195.00 (*0-7859-7831-3*, 2-225-82579-3) Fr & Eur.

***Morain.** Human Cougar. 1981. 8.95 (*0-87975-062-6*) Prometheus Bks.

Morain, Mary, ed. Bridging Worlds Through General Semantics. LC 84-82325. 347p. 1984. 15.00 (*0-918970-34-2*) Intl Gen Semantics.

— Classroom Exercises in General Semantics. LC 80-80100. 162p. 1980. pap. 10.00 (*0-918970-26-1*) Intl Gen Semantics.

— Enriching Professional Skills Through General Semantics. LC 86-81557. xix, 326p. 1986. 15.00 (*0-918970-35-0*); pap. 10.00 (*0-685-14231-0*) Intl Gen Semantics.

— Teaching General Semantics. 2nd ed. LC 75-108193. 142p. 1977. reprint ed. pap. text ed. 10.00 (*0-918970-04-0*) Intl Gen Semantics.

Morain, Thomas J. Prairie Grass Roots: An Iowa Small Town in the Early Twentieth Century. LC 88-652. (Henry A. Wallace Series on Agricultural History & Rural Studies). (Illus.). 306p. 1988. 26.95 (*0-8138-0068-4*) Iowa St U Pr.

Morain, William D., ed. see Advances in Plastic & Reconstructive Surgery Staff.

Morais, Herbert, jt. auth. see Boyer, Richard.

Morais, Robert J. Social Relations in a Philippine Town. (Special Report Ser.: No. 19). (Illus.). 151p. (C). 1981. pap. 11.00 (*0-685-05867-0*) North Ill U Ctr SE Asian.

Moraitis, George & Pollock, George H., eds. Psychoanalytic Studies of Biography. LC 86-27750. (Emotions & Behavior Monographs: No. 4). 1987. 65.00 (*0-8236-4515-0*, BN#04515) Intl Univs Pr.

Morales, A., ed. Weak Interactions & Neutrinos: Proceedings of the 8th International Workshop, Javea, Spain, Sept. 5-11. 1982. 820p. 1983. 125.00 (*9971-950-89-8*) World Scientific Pub.

Morales, A., et al, eds. TAUP 91: Proceedings of the Second International Workshop on Theoretical & Phenomenological Aspects of Underground Physics, Toledo, Spain, 9-13 September 1991. LC 92-25597. 1992. write for info. (*0-444-89769-0*, North Holland) Elsevier.

Morales, Alejandro. The Brick People. 2nd ed. LC 88-10409. 320p. 1992. pap. 9.50 (*0-934770-91-3*) Arte Publico.

— Death of an Anglo. Ginsberg, Judith, tr. LC 88-70371. 241p. 1988. 22.00 (*0-916950-82-4*); pap. 14.00 (*0-916950-83-2*) Biling Rev-Pr.

— The Rag Doll Plagues. LC 91-2381. 200p. (Orig.). 1992. 17.95 (*1-55885-036-8*) Arte Publico.

— Rag Doll Plagues. LC 91-2381. 200p. (Orig.). 1992. pap. 9.95 (*1-55885-104-6*) Arte Publico.

— Reto en el Paraiso. LC 82-73753. 381p. (ENG & SPA.). 1983. pap. 17.00 (*0-916950-34-4*) Biling Rev-Pr.

Morales, Alejandro, ed. see Coleman, George.

Morales, Amparo & Vaquero, Maria. El Habla culta de San Juan: Materiales para su Estudio. LC 89-32488. 456p. (Orig.). 1990. pap. 12.50 (*0-8477-3641-5*) U of PR Pr.

Morales, Armando T. & Sheafor, Bradford W. Social Work: A Profession of Many Faces. 5th ed. 740p. 1989. teacher ed write for info. (*0-318-63867-3*, H18898); boxed 44.00 (*0-205-11888-7*, H18880) Allyn.

— Social Work: A Profession of Many Faces. 7th ed. LC 94-21177. 1994. text ed. write for info. (*0-205-16201-0*) Allyn.

Morales, Aurora L. & Morales, Rosario. Getting Home Alive. LC 86-22769. 216p. (Orig.). 1986. lib. bdg. 20.95 (*0-932379-20-6*); pap. 9.95 (*0-932379-19-2*) Firebrand Bks.

Morales, Carmen A., jt. auth. see Needham, Christina W.

Morales-Carrion, Arturo. Albores Historicos del Capitalismo en Puerto Rico. 2nd ed. (UPREX, Humanidades Ser.: No. 9). 140p. (C). 1980. pap. 1.50 (*0-8477-0009-7*) U of PR Pr.

— The Loneliness of Luis Munoz Rivera. 1976. lib. bdg. 59.95 (*0-8490-0554-X*) Gordon Pr.

— Puerto Rico & the United States: The Quest for a New Encounter. (Illus.). 120p. (C). 1990. text ed. 10.00 (*0-9622522-2-0*); pap. text ed. 8.00 (*0-9622522-3-9*) Editorial Academica.

— Testimonios de una Gestion Universitaria. LC 77-11056. (Illus.). 329p. 1978. pap. 3.00 (*0-8477-2740-8*) U of PR Pr.

Morales, Cecilio J., Jr., et al, eds. A Survey of Press Freedom in Latin America 1985-1986. 64p. (Orig.). 1986. pap. 8.95 (*0-937551-00-7*) Coun Hemispheric Aff.

***Morales, Dan.** The Evolving Protection of State Laws & the Environment: NAFTA from a Texas Perspective. (Occasional Paper Ser.: No. 5). 32p. 1994. 10.00 (*0-614-01227-9*) LBJ Sch Pub Aff.

Morales, Demetrio S. The Maya World. (Illus.). 144p. 1976. pap. 6.00 (*0-912434-21-X*) Ocelot Pr.

Morales, Ed & Morales, Mitzi. Defying the Odds. LC 91-68356. 224p. (Orig.). 1992. pap. 8.95 (*0-89221-219-5*) New Leaf.

Morales, Edgar, tr. see Hightower, J. A., Jr.

Morales, Edgar, tr. see White, Jerry.

Morales, Edgar O., tr. see Houk, Margaret.

Morales, Edgar O., tr. see Lester, Andrew D., ed.

Morales, Edgar O., tr. see Lowrie, D. L.

Morales, Edgar O., tr. see Shelley, Marshall.

Morales, Edmundo. Cocaine: White Gold Rush in Peru. LC 88-30303. 228p. 1990. pap. 14.95 (*0-8165-1159-4*) U of Ariz Pr.

— The Guinea Pig in the Andean Culture. LC 95-4343. 1995. write for info. (*0-8165-1479-8*); pap. write for info. (*0-8165-1558-1*) U of Ariz Pr.

Morales, Edna M., ed. see Moody, Ralph.

Morales, Francisco. Ethnic & Social Background of the Franciscan Friars in Seventeenth Century Mexico. (Monograph Ser.). 1973. 30.00 (*0-88382-060-9*) AAFH.

— Franciscan Presence in the Americas. 1983. 35.00 (*0-614-05572-5*) AAFH.

Morales, Goldie L. Eternal Etching. 24p. 1977. pap. 2.50 (*0-910083-00-2*) Heritage Trails.

— Floating Petals. (Illus.). 46p. (C). 1982. pap. 2.50 (*0-910083-09-6*) Heritage Trails.

— Moving Image. 24p. 1978. pap. 2.50 (*0-910083-02-9*) Heritage Trails.

— Poet Philosophers. (Illus.). 48p. (Orig.). 1983. pap. 3.00 (*0-910083-16-9*) Heritage Trails.

***Morales-Gomex, D. & Torres, A. Mario.** Social Policy in a Global Society: Parallels & Lessons from Canada-Latin America Experience. 220p. 1995. pap. 35.00 (*0-88936-761-2*, IDRC7612, Pub. by IDRC CN) UNIPUB.

Morales-Gomez, Daniel A. & Torres, Carlos A. The State, Corporatist Politics & Educational Policy Making in Mexico. LC 89-29986. 224p. 1990. text ed. 49.95 (*0-275-93484-5*, C3484, Praeger Pubs) Greenwood.

Morales-Gomez, Daniel A. & Torres, Carlos A., eds. Education, Policy & Social Change: Experiences from Latin America. LC 92-9544. 232p. 1992. text ed. 55.00 (*0-275-94080-2*, C4080, Praeger Pubs) Greenwood.

Morales-Gomez, Hildegard, jt. auth. see Gebel, Terri A.

Morales, Harry, tr. see Addison, Rita, et al.

Morales, Hector L., intro. Biotechnology & Food Systems in Latin America: A Planning Workshop. (Biotechnology & Food Systems in Latin America: No. 1). 468p. (Orig.). (ENG & SPA.). (C). 1986. ring bd. 20.00 (*0-935391-74-6*) UCSD Ctr US-Mex.

Morales, Hildegard, jt. auth. see Gebel, Terri A.

Morales, Humberto L. La Ensenanza Del Espanol Como Lengua Materna. 274p. 1990. pap. 15.50 (*0-8477-3615-6*) U of PR Pr.

— Espanol Basico One. 12th ed. 160p. (SPA.). (C). 1991. reprint ed. pap. text ed. 7.95 (*1-56328-018-3*) Edit Plaza Mayor.

— Redaccion One. 3rd ed. 144p. (SPA.). 1990. reprint ed. pap. 7.75 (*0-8477-3617-2*) U of PR Pr.

Morales, Humerto L. Redaccion II. 229p. 1990. pap. 9.25 (*0-8477-3624-5*) U of PR Pr.

Morales, Jorge & Villa, Eugenia, eds. El Folclor en la Construccion de las Americas: Memorias del VI Congreso de Antropologia en Colombia. (Memorias del VI Congreso de Antropologia en Colombia Ser.). 260p. (SPA.). 1993. pap. 12.00 (*958-95572-0-1*) UPLAAP.

Morales, Jorge L. Alfonso Reyes y la Literatural Espanola. LC 79-19455. (Mante y Palabra Ser.). 193p. (SPA.). (C). 1980. 5.00 (*0-8477-0558-7*); pap. 4.00 (*0-8477-0559-5*) U of PR Pr.

— Espana en Alfonso Reyes. LC 76-1892. (Coleccion Mente y Palabra). xiii, 181p. (Orig.). (SPA.). 1976. 5.00 (*0-8477-0522-6*); pap. 4.00 (*0-8477-0523-4*) U of PR Pr.

— Nueva Antologia Poetica. 368p. 1975. pap. 5.00 (*0-8477-3217-7*) U of PR Pr.

— Obelisco (Diosa-Madre-Poesia) (Poetry Ser.). 128p. 1990. 35.00 (*0-317-05414-7*); pap. 25.00 (*0-317-05415-5*) Instit Nacional.

— ORBE. (Poetry Ser.). 160p. 1992. 40.00 (*0-317-05418-X*); pap. 20.00 (*0-317-05419-8*) Instit Nacional.

— Ouranos (Cinabrio-Verb-Maria) (Poetry Ser.). 133p. 1991. 35.00 (*0-317-05416-3*); pap. 30.00 (*0-317-05417-1*) Instit Nacional.

— Poesia Afroantillana y Negrista: Puerto Rico, Republica Dominica, Cuba. LC 80-25893. 456p. 1981. pap. 10.00 (*0-8477-3230-4*) U of PR Pr.

— Los Rios Redimidos. (Illus.). 55p. (C). 1969. 1.75 (*0-8477-3209-6*) U of PR Pr.

Morales, Jose. El Cacao: A Novel on Migrants & Their Problem of Adaptation. 2nd ed. Uceda, Mario, ed. 114p. (SPA.). reprint ed. pap. 4.95 (*0-938693-01-8*) Maya Pubns.

Morales, Jose L., tr. see Arintero, Juan G.

***Morales, Juan A. & McMahon, Gary, eds.** Economic Policy & the Transition to Democracy: The Latin American Experience. LC 95-2567. (International Political Economy Ser.). 1995. write for info. (*0-312-12645-X*) St Martin.

Morales, Juan A., jt. ed. see Ladman, Jerry R.

Morales, Juan A., jt. auth. see Sachs, Jeffrey.

Morales, Julio, Jr. Puerto Rican Poverty & Migration: We Just Had to Try Elsewhere. LC 85-19439. 271p. 1986. text ed. 55.00 (*0-275-92020-8*, C2020, Praeger Pubs) Greenwood.

Morales, Karen. Take This Book to the Gynecologist with You. 1991. pap. 9.57 (*0-201-52380-9*) Addison-Wesley.

Morales, Laura, tr. see Smith, M. Sherry & Hanson, Karen.

Morales-Lebron, Mariano. Diccionario-Juridico Segun la Jurisprudencia Del Tribunal Supremo De Puerto Rico: Palabras, Frases y Doctrinas, 2 vols., Set. 925p. (SPA.). Date not set. 195.00 (*0-685-73078-6*) U Cinn Law.

— Diccionario-Juridico Segun la Jurisprudencia del Tribunal Supremo de Puerto Rico: Palabras, Frases y Doctrinas, 2 vols., Set. 925p. (SPA.). Date not set. 195.00 (*0-9626291-1-1*) U Cinn Law.

Morales, M. F., et al, eds. Annual Review of Biophysics & Bioengineering, Vol. 1. LC 79-188446. (Illus.). 1972. 55.00 (*0-8243-1801-3*) Annual Reviews.

Morales, Manual S. El Homero de Aristoteles. 200p. (SPA.). 1994. pap. 34.00 (*90-256-1064-1*, Pub. by A M Hakkert NE) Benjamins North Am.

Morales, Max, Jr. The Plano Diet. (Illus.). 87p. (Orig.). 1984. pap. 6.95 (*0-934157-00-6*) Morales Pubns.

Morales, Michael, ed. Aspects of Mesozoic Geology & Paleontology on the Colorado Plateau. (Bulletin Ser.). 192p. 1993. pap. 19.95 (*0-89734-114-7*, BS-59) Mus Northern Ariz.

Morales, Michael, jt. ed. see Beus, Stanley S.

Morales, Michael, jt. auth. see Colbert, Edwin H.

Morales, Mitzi, jt. auth. see Morales, Ed.

Morales, P. Gott'cha! Rubik's Cube. 1982. pap. 2.95 (*0-937816-17-5*) Tech Data.

Morales, Pablo. Victim for Hire. 1979. pap. 1.50 (*0-8439-0625-1*) Dorchester Pub Co.

***Morales Padron, F.** Canarias y America. (Gran Enciclopedia de Espana y America Ser.). (Illus.). (SPA.). 1989. 200.00x (*84-87053-12-2*) Elliots Bks.

— Historia Del Descubrimiento y Conquista de America. 720p. (SPA.). 1993. 150.00 (*84-249-1417-1*) Elliots Bks.

***Morales, Radames.** The Story Teller: A Collection of Short Stories, Bk. 1. LC 94-94610. 148p. (YA). (gr. 6 up). 1994. pap. 6.95 (*0-9642626-0-6*) R Morales.

Morales, Rafael C., tr. see Garmirian, Paul B.

Morales, Rebecca. Flexible Production: Restructuring of the International Automobile Industry. LC 94-6157. 220p. (C). 1994. write for info. (*0-7456-0752-7*) Blackwell Pubs.

Morales, Rebecca & Bonilla, Frank. Latinos in a Changing U. S. Economy: Comparative Perspectives on Growing Inequality. (Series on Race & Ethnic Relations: Vol. 7). (Illus.). 316p. (C). 1993. text ed. 49.95 (*0-8039-4923-5*); pap. text ed. 24.00 (*0-8039-4924-3*) Sage.

Morales, Rodney. Speed of Darkness. Chock, Eric & Lum, Darrell, eds. LC 88-24246. 200p. (Orig.). 1988. pap. 8.00 (*0-910043-16-7*) Bamboo Ridge Pr.

Morales, Rodney, ed. Ho'i Ho'i Hou, A Tribute to George Helm & Kimo Mitchell. LC 84-70273. (Illus.). 114p. (Orig.). 1984. pap. 6.00 (*0-910043-08-6*) Bamboo Ridge Pr.

Morales, Ronald J. Amateur Astronomer's Catalog of Five Hundred Deep-Sky Objects: Astronomy for the Serious Amateur. (Illus.). 128p. 1986. pap. 12.50 (*0-89404-076-6*) Aztex.

Morales, Rosario, jt. auth. see Morales, Aurora L.

Morales Santos, Francisco. Diccionario Escolar Centroamericano. 600p. 1988. pap. write for info. (*0-7859-6335-9*, 8483772310) Fr & Eur.

Morales, Vivian B. & Braidwood, Robert J. Figurines & Other Clay Objects from Sarab & Cayonu. (Oriental Institute Communications Ser.: No. 25). (Illus.). 85p. 1990. pap. 20.00 (*0-918986-59-1*) Orientl Inst Pr IT.

Morales, Waltraud Q. Bolivia: Land of Struggle. 202p. 1992. text ed. 46.00 (*0-8133-0197-1*) Westview.

Morales y Marin, Jose L. Los Toros en el Arte. 2nd ed. 310p. 1989. 295.00x (*84-239-5262-2*) Elliots Bks.

Moramarco, Fred & Zolynas, Al, eds. Men of Our Time: An Anthology of Male Poetry in Contemporary America. LC 91-31462. 472p. 1992. 45.00 (*0-8203-1404-8*); pap. 19.95 (*0-8203-1430-7*) U of Ga Pr.

Moramarco, Fred, et al. Modern American Poetry, 1865-1950. (Critical History of Poetry Ser.). 304p. 1989. text ed. 23.95 (*0-8057-8451-9*, Twayne) Macmillan.

***Moran.** Building Your Kevlar Canoe: A Foolproof Method & Three Foolproof Designs. 1995. pap. text ed. 19.95 (*0-07-043036-5*, Ragged Mntn) Intl Marine.

— A Little Rebellion. 1994. per. 12.95 (*0-88978-252-0*, Pub. by Arsenal Pulp CN) InBook.

Moran, Albert. Making a TV Series: The Bellamy Project. (C). 1990. 45.00 (*0-86819-061-6*, Pub. by Currency Pr AT) St Mut.

Moran, Albert, ed. Images & Industry: Television Drama Production in Australia. (C). 1990. 49.00 (*0-86819-073-X*, Pub. by Currency Pr AT) St Mut.

Moran, Albert & O'Regan, Tom. An Australian Film Reader. (C). 1990. 75.00 (*0-86819-123-X*, Pub. by Currency Pr AT) St Mut.

Moran, Albert & Tulloch, John. A Country Practice: Quality Soap. (C). 1990. 50.00 (*0-86819-142-6*, Pub. by Currency Pr AT) St Mut.

Moran, B., jt. ed. see Brinson, L. C.

Moran, Barbara, intro. Special Species by California Kids. 4th ed. (Anthology Ser.: No. 4). (Illus.). 90p. (J). (gr. k-12). 1994. pap. 14.95 (*0-9634474-2-4*) Ms B Bks.

Moran, Barbara, ed. see San Diego County School Children.

Moran, Barbara B. Academic Libraries: The Changing Knowledge Centers of Colleges & Universities. Fife, Jonathan D., ed. LC 85-61910. (ASHE-ERIC Higher Education Report Ser.: No. 8, 1984). 97p. (Orig.). 1985. pap. 7.50 (*0-913317-17-9*) GWU Schl E&HD.

Moran, Barbara B., jt. auth. see Stueart, Robert D.

Moran, Bill. The Mary Wanna Student Activity Book. (Illus.). 23p. (J). (gr. 4-6). 1989. pap. 2.50 (*0-942493-10-9*) Woodmere Press.

Moran, Bill & Mann, Peggy. The Mary Wanna Student Activity Book: Based Upon: The Sad Story of Mary Wanna Or How Marijuana Harms You. rev. ed. (Illus.). 26p. (J). (gr. 4-6). 1990. pap. text ed. 2.95 (*0-942493-11-7*) Woodmere Press.

Moran, Bob. A Closer Look at Catholicism: A Guide for Protestants. 192p. 1986. write for info. (*0-8499-0514-1*) Word Inc.

Moran, Brenda & Smith, Bob. Kingdom of Light. 48p. (J). (ps up). 1993. 12.95 (*0-9638144-3-5*) BrightWay Bks.

Moran, Brian. Battery Toys. LC 83-51743. (Illus.). 192p. 1984. 29.50 (*0-88740-003-5*) Schiffer.

Moran, Bruce T. Chemical Pharmacy Enters the University: Johannes Hartman & the Didactic Care of Chymiatria. 90p. (Orig.). 1991. 16.00 (*0-931292-24-7*) Am Inst Hist Pharm.

— Chemical Pharmacy Enters the University: Johannes Hartmann & the Didactic Care of Chymiatria. 90p. (Orig.). (C). 1991. pap. 8.50 (*0-931292-23-9*) Am Inst Hist Pharm.

Moran, Bruce T., ed. Patronage & Institutions: Science, Technology, & Medicine at the European Court, 1500-1750. 272p. (C). 1991. text ed. 79.00 (*0-85115-285-6*) Boydell & Brewer.

Moran, Carol, et al. Keys to the Classroom: A Teacher's Guide to the First Month of School. 192p. 1992. pap. text ed. 26.95 (*0-8039-6014-X*) Corwin Pr.

Moran, Cathleen, jt. auth. see Balkam, Jean.

Moran, Cathleen, et al. The Pediatric Nurse Practitioner Certification Review Guide. rev. ed. Millonig, Virginia L., ed. 582p. (Orig.). (C). 1991. pap. text ed. 43.95 (*1-878028-04-9*) Hlth Lead Assoc.

Moran, Charles & Penfield, Elizabeth, eds. Conversations: Contemporary Critical Theory & the Teaching of Literature. 237p. 1990. pap. 18.95 (*0-8141-0860-1*) NCTE.

Moran, Charles, jt. ed. see Herrington, Anne.

Moran, Chris, ed. see Langner, Lawrence & Robinson, Julian.

Moran, Christine A., ed. Hand Rehabilitation. (Clinics in Physical Therapy Ser.: Vol. 9). (Illus.). 232p. 1986. text ed. 42.00 (*0-443-08353-3*) Churchill.

Moran, Cynthia K., jt. auth. see Inlander, Charles B.

Moran, D. F., et al. Earthquake & Fire. 15p. 1958. 2.00 (*0-685-14382-1*) Earthquake Eng.

— Peru Earthquake of October, 1974. 85p. 1975. 12.00 (*0-318-16327-6*) Earthquake Eng.

Moran, D. P. & Rajah, K. K., eds. Fats in Food Products. LC 93-18951. 415p. 1994. 153.50 (*0-7514-0177-3*, Pub. by Blackie Acad & Prof UK) Routledge Chapman & Hall.

Moran, Daniel. The Flame Key. 224p. (Orig.). 1987. pap. 2.95 (*0-8125-4600-8*) Tor Bks.

— Toward the Century of Words: Johann Cotta & the Politics of the Public Realm in Germany, 1795-1832. 312p. 1990. 45.00 (*0-520-06640-5*) U CA Pr.

Moran, Daniel, jt. ed. see Paret, Peter.

Moran, Daniel, tr. see Paret, Peter & Moran, Daniel, eds.

Moran, Daniel K. Last Dancer. 1993. mass mkt. 5.99 (*0-553-56249-5*, Spectra) Bantam.

Moran, Daniel T. Dancing for Victoria: The Poems of Daniel Thomas Moran. LC 91-90156. 80p. 1992. 12.95 (*0-9629221-0-2*) D T Moran.

— Gone to Innisfree: Poems. Planz, Allen, ed. LC 93-91379. (Orig.). 1993. pap. 12.00 (*0-9629221-1-0*) D T Moran.

Moran, David T. & Rowley, J. Carter. Visual Histology. LC 87-3835. 299p. reprint ed. pap. 85.30 (*0-7837-2730-5*, 2043110) Bks Demand.

Moran, Denis M. The Allotment Movement in Britain. (American University Studies: Geography: Ser. XXV, Vol. 1). 200p. (C). 1989. text ed. 44.50 (*0-8204-0812-3*) P Lang Pubs.

Moran, Dennis P. Gabriel Marcel: Existentialist Philosopher, Dramatist, Educator. 140p. (Orig.). (C). 1992. lib. bdg. 39.50 (*0-8191-8821-2*); pap. text ed. 17.50 (*0-8191-8822-0*) U Pr of Amer.

Moran, Dennis W., jt. ed. see Hudson, Deal W.

Moran, Dermot. The Philosophy of John Scottus Eriugena. (Illus.). 450p. 1989. 79.95 (*0-521-34549-9*) Cambridge U Pr.

M

Moran, E. C., Jr. Bunker Genealogy, Ancestry & Descendants of Benjamin 3 (James 2, James 1) 232p. 1993. reprint ed. lib. bdg. 47.50 (*0-8328-3560-9*); reprint ed. pap. 37.50 (*0-8328-3561-7*) Higginson Bk Co.
— Bunker Genealogy, The Charlestown & Nantucket, Mass., Branches, & Some Unconnected Groups. 302p. 1993. reprint ed. lib. bdg. 56.50 (*0-8328-3558-7*); reprint ed. pap. 46.50 (*0-8328-3559-5*) Higginson Bk Co.
Moran, Ed, ed. see Lewis, Brad A.
Moran, Ed, ed. see Lowell, Ross.
Moran, Edward C., Jr. Bunker Genealogy, Dover Branch, Vol. III. 389p. 1993. reprint ed. lib. bdg. 69.50 (*0-8328-3554-4*); reprint ed. pap. 59.50 (*0-8328-3555-2*) Higginson Bk Co.
Moran, Edward G., ed. see Avery, Ron.
Moran, Eileen G., jt. ed. see Bart, Pauline B.
***Moran, Elizabeth.** Bradymania! Everything You Always Wanted To Know--and a Few Things You Probably Didn't. LC 94-35376. 1995. pap. 7.95 (*1-55850-418-4*) Adams Pubng.
Moran, Emilio F. Deforestation in the Brazilian Amazon. Conway, Dennis, ed. (Series on Environment & Development). 36p. (Orig.). 1992. pap. 2.00 (*1-881157-10-5*) In Ctr Global.
— Developing the Amazon. LC 80-8382. (Illus.). 320p. 1981. 35.00 (*0-253-14564-3*) Ind U Pr.
— Human Adaptability: An Introduction to Ecological Anthropology. (Illus.). 404p. (C). 1982. pap. text ed. 24. 95 (*0-86531-431-4*) Westview.
— Human Adaptability: An Introduction to Ecological Anthropology. 2nd ed. (C). 1929. text ed. 55.00 (*0-8133-1253-1*); pap. text ed. 21.95 (*0-8133-1254-X*) Westview.
— Through Amazonian Eyes: The Human Ecology of Amazonian Populations. LC 93-1148. (Illus.). 252p. 1993. text ed. 34.95 (*0-87745-417-5*); pap. 12.95 (*0-87745-418-3*) U of Iowa Pr.
Moran, Emilio F., ed. The Comparative Analysis of Human Societies: Toward Common Standards for Data Collection & Reporting. LC 94-3601. 202p. 1994. lib. bdg. 40.00 (*1-55587-514-9*) Lynne Rienner.
— The Ecosystem: Approach in Anthropology. rev. ed. 320p. 1990. pap. 18.95 (*0-472-08102-0*) U of Mich Pr.
Moran, Frances M. Subject & Agency in Psychoanalysis: Which Is to Be Master? LC 92-48288. (Psychoanalytic Crosscurrents Ser.). 208p. (C). 1993. text ed. 40.00 (*0-8147-5482-1*) NYU Pr.
Moran, Gabrial & Devitt, Patrick M. How Adult Is Are? 336p. 1989. pap. 45.00 (*1-85390-123-7*, Pub. by Veritas IE) St Mut.
Moran, Gabriel. Religious Education As a Second Language. LC 89-33871. 254p. (Orig.). 1989. pap. 17.95 (*0-89135-072-1*) Religious Educ.
— Uniqueness: Problem or Paradox in Jewish & Christian Traditions. LC 92-13009. (Faith Meets Faith Ser.). 215p. 1992. 39.95 (*0-88344-830-0*); pap. 16.95 (*0-88344-829-7*) Orbis Bks.
Moran, Gary T. & McGlynn, George. Dynamics of Strength Training. 176p. (C). 1990. pap. write for info. (*0-697-07638-5*) Brown & Benchmark.
Moran, Gary T., jt. auth. see Pearl, Bill.
Moran, Gary T., et al. Fit & Able. 224p. (C). 1995. pap. text ed. write for info. (*0-697-11286-1*) Brown & Benchmark.
Moran, George. Imagine Me on a Sit-Ski! A Concept Book. Grant, Christy, ed. (Illus.). 32p. (J). (gr. 2-5). 1994. lib. bdg. 13.95 (*0-8075-3618-0*) A Whitman.
Moran, George C. & Labine, Paul, eds. Corrosion Monitoring in Industrial Plants Using Nondestructive Testing & Electrochemical Methods: STP 908. LC 86-13994. (Special Technical Publication (STP) Ser.). (Illus.). 514p. 1986. text ed. 64.00 (*0-8031-0471-5*, 04-908000-27) ASTM.
Moran, Gerald F. & Vinovskis, Maris A. Religion, Family, & the Life Course: Explorations in the Social History of Early America. 326p. (C). 1992. text ed. 44.50 (*0-472-10312-1*) U of Mich Pr.
Moran, Gerard. Father Patrick Lavelle: The Rise & Fall of an Irish Nationalist 1825-86. (Illus.). 240p. 1994. 39.50 (*1-85182-163-5*, Pub. by Four Cts Pr IE) Intl Spec Bk.
Moran, J. Anthony. Pilgrims' Guide to America: U. S. Catholic Shrines & Centers of Devotion. LC 91-66664. (Illus.). 272p. (Orig.). 1992. pap. 7.95 (*0-87973-469-8*, 469) Our Sunday Visitor.
Moran, J. B. Moran Family: Two Hundred Years in Detroit. (Illus.). 152p. 1991. reprint ed. lib. bdg. 38.00 (*0-8328-2035-0*); reprint ed. pap. 28.00 (*0-8328-2036-9*) Higginson Bk Co.
Moran, J. F. The Japanese & the Jesuits: Alessandro Valignano in Sixteenth Century Japan. 208p. 1993. 67.50 (*0-415-08813-5*, A9698) Routledge.
Moran, J. M. & Hewitt, J. N., eds. Gravitational Lenses. (Lecture Notes in Physics Ser.: Vol. 330). xiv, 238p. 1989. 41.00 (*0-387-51061-3*) Spr-Verlag.
Moran, J. M., jt. auth. see Ho, P. T.
Moran, J. M., jt. ed. see Reid, M. J.
Moran, Jack. An Introduction to Theorectical & Computational Aerodynamics. LC 84-7243. 464p. (C). 1984. Net. text ed. write for info. (*0-471-87491-4*) Wiley.
Moran, James. The Double Crown Club: A History of Fifty Years. (Illus.). 128p. (C). 1989. 400.00 (*0-903696-03-7*, Pub. by Hurtwood Pr Ltd) St Mut.
— Fit to Be Styled a Typographer: History of the Society of Typographic Designers, 1928-78. 80p. (C). 1989. 95.00 (*0-903696-11-8*, Pub. by Hurtwood Pr Ltd) St Mut.
— U. S. Marine Corps Uniforms & Equipment in World War 2. (Illus.). 132p. 1992. 39.95 (*1-872004-57-1*, Pub. by Windrow & Green UK) Motorbooks Intl.
Moran, James P. Public Garden. LC 93-6221. 1994. 21.00 (*0-517-59606-7*, Crown) Crown Pub Group.
Moran, James P., jt. ed. see Simpson, Theresa C.
Moran, Jan. Fabulous Fragrances: How to Select Your Perfume Wardrobe-The Woman's Guide to Prestige Perfumes. Heyes, Eileen & Halper, Jan, eds. 240p. 1994. 29.00 (*0-9639065-5-0*) Crescent Hse.
***Moran, Jim.** Some Things Never Change: Classic Thoughts That Stand the Test of Time. 168p. 1995. pap. 5.95 (*1-56245-223-1*) Great Quotations.
— Why Men Shouldn't Marry. LC 69-10633. 1969. 3.00 (*0-8184-0094-3*) Carol Pub Group.
Moran, Jo Ann H. The Growth of English Schooling, 1340-1548. LC 84-42570. (Illus.). 352p. 1984. text ed. 55.00x (*0-691-05430-4*) Princeton U Pr.
Moran, Joan V., jt. ed. see Warner, Lou.
Moran, Joe, et al, contribs. Aqui Estamos...Y No Nos Vamos: Here We Are...& We're Not Leaving. LC 90-32219. (Illus.). 40p. (Orig.). 1990. pap. 10.00 (*0-945486-07-3*) CSU SBUAG.
Moran, John. Toward the World & Wisdom of Wittgenstein's "Tractatus" 1973. pap. text ed. 49.25 (*90-279-2394-9*) Mouton.
Moran, John, jt. auth. see Hoffherr, Glen.
Moran, John, et al. Daily Management: A System for Individual & Organizational Optimization. (Illus.). 100p. (Orig.). 1990. pap. 24.95 (*1-879364-07-7*) GOAL-QPC.
— Facilitating & Training in Quality Function Deployment. (Illus.). 152p. (Orig.). 1991. pap. 29.95 (*1-879364-18-2*) GOAL-QPC.
— Term Paper Study Aids. (J). 1986. pap. 2.25 (*0-87738-025-2*) Youth Ed.
Moran, John B. Creating a Legend: The Complete Record of Writing About the United States Marine Corps. LC 79-139570. (Illus.). 688p. 1973. lib. bdg. 24.95 (*0-912286-00-8*) Moran Andrews.
Moran, John C. An F. Marion Crawford Companion. LC 80-1707. (Illus.). 608p. 1981. text ed. 105.00 (*0-313-20926-X*, MCC/, Greenwood Pr) Greenwood.
— Last Days & Death of Dr. & Gen. William Walker. (Worthies Library: No. 3). (Illus.). 100p. 1988. 10.00 (*0-318-20644-7*) F M Crawford.
Moran, John C. & Herron, Don, eds. The Romantist: 1977, No. 1. 1977. 10.00 (*0-317-01472-2*) F M Crawford.
Moran, John C., ed. see Crawford, Anne & Von Rable, Baroness.
Moran, John C., ed. see Crawford, Marion F.
Moran, John C., ed. see Fraser, Hugh & Stahlmann, J. I.
Moran, John C., et al, eds. The Romantist: 1980-81, No. 4-5. 1982. 10.00 (*0-318-20641-2*) F M Crawford.
— The Romantist: 1982-84, No. 6-8. 1986. 10.00 (*0-318-20642-0*) F M Crawford.
— The Romantist: 1985-86, No. 9-10. 1988. 10.00 (*0-317-01473-0*) F M Crawford.
Moran, John H., tr. see Rousseau, Jean-Jacques & Herder, Johann G.
Moran, John J. A Defense of Edgar Allan Poe. LC 79-171361. reprint ed. 27.50 (*0-404-04399-2*) AMS Pr.
— Practical Business Law. 3rd ed. LC 94-25594. 1994. text ed. write for info. (*0-13-138660-3*) P-H.
Moran, John J., jt. auth. see Rosenau, Milton D., Jr.
Moran, John P. Living Our Life Story: Spiritual Transformation in a Turbulent World. Neary, R. Patrick & St. George, Michele, eds. (Illus.). 208p. 1994. pap. 12. 95 (*0-9640806-9-9*) Lightsmith Multimed.
Moran, John W. & Moreau, Nancy A. Experimental Physics. (Illus.). 1989. student ed 6.95 (*0-913811-06-8*) Northeast A S.
***Moran, John W. & ReVelle, Jack B.** The Executive's Handbook on Quality Function Deployment: Defining Managements' Roles & Responsibilities. 148p. (Orig.). 1994. pap. text ed. 29.95 (*0-9638223-3-0*) Markon.
Moran, John W., jt. auth. see Burton, Terrence T.
Moran, John W., et al. A Guide to Graphical Problem-Solving Processes. (Illus.). 73p. 1990. pap. 21.95 (*0-87389-079-5*) ASQC Qual Pr.
***Moran, Joseph J.** Assessing Adult Learning: A Guide for Practitioners. 1996. write for info. (*0-89464-938-8*) Krieger.
***Moran, Joseph M. & Morgan, Michael D.** Essentials of Atmosphere & Weather. (Illus.). 350p. (C). 1994. pap. text ed. write for info. (*0-02-383831-0*, Merrill Pub Co) Macmillan.
— Meteorology: The Atmosphere & the Science of Weather. 4th ed. LC 93-1035. (Illus.). 517p. (C). 1994. pap. write for info. (*0-02-383341-6*) Macmillan.
— Meteorology: The Atmosphere & the Science of Weather. 4th ed. LC 93-1035. (Illus.). 550p. (C). 1994. student ed, pap. write for info. (*0-02-383345-9*) Macmillan.
Moran, Joseph M., jt. auth. see Morgan, Michael D.
Moran, Judy, ed. New Langston Arts: The First Fifteen Years. (Illus.). 96p. (Orig.). 1990. pap. 30.00 (*0-9627010-0-9*) New Langston Arts.
Moran, K. D. & McGehee, M. A. Legal Aspects of School Communications. 1980. 4.95 (*1-56534-001-9*) NOLPE.
***Moran, Kate.** Investment Appraisal for Non-Financial Managers: A Step-by-Step Guide to Profitable Decisions. (Institute of Management Ser.). 250p. 1995. pap. 43.50 (*0-273-61245-X*, Pub. by Pitman Pub Ltd UK) Trans-Atl Phila.
***Moran, Kerry.** Hong Kong Handbook: Including Macau & Guangzhou. (Illus.). 300p. (Orig.). 1995. pap. 15.95 (*1-56691-056-0*) Moon Pubns CA.
— Nepal Handbook. 450p. (Orig.). 1991. pap. 12.95 (*0-918373-64-6*) Moon Pubns CA.
Moran, Kerry, jt. auth. see Johnson, Russell.
Moran, Leila, jt. ed. see Fusonie, Alan.
Moran-Lever, Tery, ed. Official Export Guide. rev. ed. (Illus.). 1500p. 1990. 349.00 (*0-912920-57-2*) North Am Pub Co.
— Official Export Guide. rev. ed. (Illus.). 1500p. 1991. 369. 00 (*0-912920-59-9*) North Am Pub Co.
— U. S. Custom House Guide. rev. ed. 1600p. 1990. 349.00 (*0-912920-56-4*) North Am Pub Co.
— U. S. Custom House Guide. rev. ed. 1800p. 1991. 369.00 (*0-912920-58-0*) North Am Pub Co.
Moran, Lois, ed. The Craftsman's Cookbook. LC 72-91347. (Illus.). 192p. 1972. 12.00 (*0-88321-000-2*) Am Craft.
***Moran-Lopez, J. L. & Sanchez, J. M., eds.** New Trends in Magnetism, Magnetic Materials, & Their Applications: Proceedings of II Latinamerica Workshop Held in Guanajua, Mexico, August 24-27, 1993. LC 94-39745. 475p. 1995. 125.00 (*0-306-44829-7*, Plenum Pr) Plenum.
Moran-Lopez, J. L. & Sanchez, Juan M., eds. Advanced Topics in Materials Science & Engineering. LC 93-12843. 1993. 95.00 (*0-306-44487-9*, Plenum Pr) Plenum.
Moran-Lopez, J. L. & Schuller, I. K., eds. Oxygen Disorder Effects in High Tc Superconductors. (Illus.). 228p. 1990. 65.00 (*0-306-43409-1*, Plenum Pr) Plenum.
Moran-Lopez, J. L., et al, eds. Structural & Phase Stability of Alloys. LC 92-8513. (Illus.). 278p. (C). 1992. 69.50 (*0-306-44211-6*, Plenum Pr) Plenum.
Moran, Louise. A Social History Approach to Research in Distance Education. (C). 1991. pap. 24.00x (*0-7300-1350-2*, IDE806, Pub. by Deakin Univ AT) St Mut.
Moran, Louise & Mugridge, Ian, eds. Collaboration in Distance Education: International Case Studies. LC 93-14950. (Studies in Distance Education). 192p. 1994. 59. 95 (*0-415-10098-4*, B2444) Routledge.
Moran, M. J., jt. ed. see Stecco, S. S.
Moran, Margaret, jt. ed. see Rempel, Richard A.
Moran, Marilyn A. Birth & the Dialogue of Love. LC 81-81200. (Illus.). 233p. (Orig.). (C). 1981. pap. 24.95 (*0-940128-01-2*) New Nativity.
Moran, Marilyn A., ed. Happy Birth Days: Personal Accounts of Birth at Home the Intimate, Husband-Wife Way. (Illus.). 134p. (Orig.). 1986. pap. 12.95 (*0-940128-02-0*) New Nativity.
Moran, Mark M., jt. auth. see Moran, Robert D.
***Moran, Martha.** Street Sharks: The Birth of Dr. Piranhoid. LC 95-4056. (Glowbacks Ser.). (J). 1995. 5.99 (*0-679-87714-2*) Random.
***Moran, Martin.** Alps 4000: 75 Peaks in 52 Days. (Pevensey Island Guides Ser.). (Illus.). 288p. 1995. 24.95 (*0-7153-0268-X*, Pub. by D & C Pub UK) Sterling.
— Tincture of Time: The Story of 150 Years of Medicine in Atlanta. 140p. 1995. 45.00 (*0-9647461-0-7*) Med Assn Atlanta.
Moran, Mary. Student Financial Aid & Women: Equity Dilemma? LC 86-72856. (ASHE-ERIC Higher Education Report Ser.: No. 5, 1986). 153p. (Orig.). 1987. pap. 10.00 (*0-913317-32-2*) GWU Schl E&HD.
Moran, Mary H. Civilized Women: Gender & Prestige in Southeastern Liberia. LC 89-22398. (Anthropology of Contemporary Issues Ser.). (Illus.). 208p. (Orig.). 1990. 36.95 (*0-8014-2293-0*); pap. 13.95 (*0-8014-9554-7*) Cornell U Pr.
— Margaret Drabble: Existing Within Structures. LC 83-332. 144p. 1983. 18.95 (*0-8093-1080-5*) S Ill U Pr.
— Penelope Lively. LC 93-7655. (Twayne's English Authors Ser.: Vol. 503). 192p. 1993. text ed. 22.95 (*0-8057-7028-3*, Twayne) Macmillan.
Moran, Michael. Nothing but Net! An Essay on the Culture of Pickup Basketball. 118p. (Orig.). 1991. pap. 7.95 (*0-9631597-0-4*) Full Ct TX.
— Politics & Society in Britain: An Introduction. LC 85-11718. 272p. 1985. text ed. 32.50 (*0-312-62629-0*) St Martin.
— The Politics of the Financial Services Revolution: The U. S. A., U. K. & Japan. LC 90-26391. 180p. 1991. text ed. 65.00 (*0-312-06112-9*) St Martin.
— Younger Than That Now: A Peace Corps Volunteer Remembers Morocco. LC 94-96345. 143p. (Orig.). 1994. pap. 12.95 (*0-9631597-8-X*) Full Ct TX.
***Moran, Michael & Brimer, Mark A.** Computer Principles for Physical & Occupational Therapists. 167p. 1994. pap. text ed. 45.00 (*0-88450-033-0*, 4298) Commun Skill.
Moran, Michael & Prosser, Tony, eds. Privatization & Regulatory Change in Europe. LC 93-30284. (Law & Political Change Ser.). 1994. 85.00 (*0-335-19073-1*, Open Univ Pr); pap. 34.00 (*0-335-19072-3*, Open Univ Pr) Taylor & Francis.
Moran, Michael & Wood, Bruce. States, Regulation & the Medical Profession. LC 92-23833. 1993. 90.00 (*0-335-15749-1*, Open Univ Pr); pap. 32.50 (*0-335-15748-3*, Open Univ Pr) Taylor & Francis.
Moran, Michael & Wright, Maurice, eds. The Market & the State: Studies in Interdependence. LC 91-24192. 280p. 1991. text ed. 69.95 (*0-312-06802-6*) St Martin.
Moran, Michael, jt. ed. see Parry, Geraint.
Moran, Michael, jt. ed. see Vogel, Ursula.
Moran, Michael C., ed. see Journal of Urban Law Editors.
Moran, Michael G., ed. Eighteenth Century British & American Rhetorics & Rhetoricians: Critical Studies & Sources. LC 93-35838. 328p. 1994. text ed. 85.00 (*0-313-27909-8*, Greenwood Pr) Greenwood.
Moran, Michael G. & Jacobi, Martin J., eds. Research in Basic Writing: A Bibliographic Sourcebook. LC 89-38229. 268p. 1990. text ed. 65.00 (*0-313-25564-4*, MRB/, Greenwood Pr) Greenwood.
Moran, Michael G. & Journet, Debra, eds. Research in Technical Communication: A Bibliographic Sourcebook. LC 84-8977. xxviii, 512p. 1985. text ed. 85.00 (*0-313-23431-0*, MRT/, Greenwood Pr) Greenwood.
Moran, Michael G. & Lunsford, Ronald F., eds. Research in Composition & Rhetoric: A Bibliographic Sourcebook. LC 83-22568. (Illus.). xviii, 506p. 1984. text ed. 89.50 (*0-313-23308-X*, MOR/, Greenwood Pr) Greenwood.
Moran, Michael J. Give Them Shelter: Responding to Hunger & Homelessness. Teutschman, Emilie L., ed. LC 90-60442. 128p. (Orig.). 1990. pap. 6.95 (*0-9623410-6-1*) Resurrection.
Moran, Michael J., ed. Availability Analysis: A Guide to Efficient Energy Use. rev. ed. 260p. 1989. 40.00 (*0-7918-0009-1*, 800091) ASME Pr.
Moran, Michael J. & Shapiro, Howard N. Fundamentals of Engineering Thermodynamics. 2nd ed. LC 87-23115. 816p. 1991. Net. text ed. write for info. (*0-471-53984-8*) Wiley.
— Fundamentals of Engineering Thermodynamics. 3rd ed. LC 95-16405. 1995. text ed. write for info. (*0-471-07681-3*) Wiley.
— Fundamentals of Engineering Thermodynamics: With Appendices. 2nd ed. 1993. text ed. write for info. (*0-471-03888-1*) Wiley.
Moran, Michael L., jt. auth. see Brimer, Mark A.
Moran, N. K. Singers in Late Byzantine & Slavonic Painting. (Byzantina Neerlandica Ser.: No. 9). (Illus.). xiv, 173p. 1986. 49.25 (*90-04-07809-6*) E J Brill.
Moran, P. A. An Introduction to Probability Theory. 1984. reprint ed. 35.00 (*0-19-853242-3*) OUP.
Moran, Pablo. A. Alekhine: Agony of a Chess Genius. Mur, Frank X. & Brandreth, Dale A., eds. LC 89-42737. 328p. 1989. lib. bdg. 38.50x (*0-89950-440-X*) McFarland & Co.
Moran, Pamela, ed. Marian Prayer Book. 265p. (Orig.). (C). 1991. pap. 7.99 (*0-89283-725-X*) Servant.
Moran, Pat. Painting the Beauty of Flowers with Oils. (Illus.). 134p. 1991. 27.95 (*0-89134-382-2*, 30325) North Light Bks.
***Moran, Patricia.** Painting the Beauty of Flowers in Oils. (Illus.). 144p. (Orig.). 1995. pap. 22.99 (*0-89134-649-X*) North Light Bks.
Moran, Patrick E., tr. Three Smaller Wisdom Books: Lao Zi's Dao De Jing, the Great Learning (Da Zue), & the Doctrine of the Mean (Zhong Yong) 310p. (Orig.). (C). 1993. lib. bdg. 48.50 (*0-8191-9214-7*); pap. text ed. 27. 50 (*0-8191-9215-5*) U Pr of Amer.
Moran, Patrick R. Lexicarry: An Illustrated Vocabulary-Builder for Second Languages. 2nd rev. ed. LC 84-1007. (Supplementary Materials Handbook Ser.: No. 2). (Illus.). 128p. (YA). (gr. 6 up). 1989. reprint ed. pap. text ed. 11.00 (*0-86647-032-8*) Pro Lingua.
— Lexicarry: Fifty-Four Function Flashcards. (Illus.). 56p. 1990. 25.00 (*0-86647-035-2*) Pro Lingua.
— Lexicarry: French Word List. rev. ed. Suquet, Annie, tr. LC 84-18026. 25p. 1991. pap. 4.00 (*0-86647-045-X*) Pro Lingua.
— Lexicarry: German Word List. Cammin, Renate, tr. 24p. (GER.). 1985. pap. 2.55 (*0-86647-013-1*) Pro Lingua.
— Lexicarry: Spanish Word List. rev. ed. DeFantini, Beatriz C., tr. LC 84-17939. 26p. 1991. pap. 4.00 (*0-86647-046-8*) Pro Lingua.
— Lexicarry Posters: Twenty-Five Wall Charts. (Illus.). 26p. 1990. 25.00 (*0-86647-034-4*) Pro Lingua.
Moran, Patrick R., ed. Lexicarry: Japanese Word List. rev. ed. Nishizawa, Tetsuo & Kubota, Ryuko, trs. 106p. (JPN.). 1991. pap. text ed. 15.00 (*0-86647-054-9*) Pro Lingua.
Moran, Patti J. Pet Sitting for Profit: A Complete Manual for Success. (Illus.). 192p. 1992. pap. 15.95 (*0-87605-770-9*) Howell Bk.
Moran, Peter. Hybrid Microelectric Technology. (Electrocomponent Science Monographs: Vol. 4). 225p. 1984. text ed. 149.00 (*0-677-06560-4*) Gordon & Breach.
Moran, Phillip, tr. see Bykhovsky, Bernard.
Moran, R. & Braaten, W. MCD Directory. 160p. 1995. write for info. (*0-88415-493-9*) Gulf Pub.
Moran, R., jt. auth. see Cullen, K.
Moran, Ran, ed. see Lira-Powell, Julianne H.
Moran, Richad D. & Hornung, Mark. Opportunities In Microelectronic Careers. (Illus.). 160p. 1987. 13.95 (*0-8442-6197-1*, VGM Career Bks); pap. 10.95 (*0-8442-6199-8*, VGM Career Bks) NTC Pub Grp.
Moran, Richard. Earth Winter. 320p. 1995. 22.95 (*0-312-85528-1*) Forge NYC.
— Earth Winter. 320p. 1996. mass mkt. write for info. (*0-614-05519-9*) Tor Bks.
— The Empire of Ice. 352p. 1994. 22.95 (*0-312-85527-3*) Forge NYC.
— The Empire of Ice. 1995. mass mkt. 5.99 (*0-8125-3009-8*) Tor Bks.
— Knowing Right from Wrong: The Insanity Defense of Daniel McNaughton. LC 81-65034. (Illus.). 1981. 27.95 (*0-02-921890-X*) Free Pr.
Moran, Richard A. Beware of Those Who Ask for Feedback. 1994. pap. 6.00 (*0-88730-710-8*) Harper Busn.
— Cancel the Meetings, Keep the Doughnuts. 176p. (Orig.). 1995. pap. 6.00 (*0-88730-730-2*) Harper Busn.
— Never Confuse a Memo with Reality: And Other Business Lessons Too Simple Not to Know. LC 93-14376. 160p. 1993. pap. 6.00 (*0-88730-669-1*) Harper Busn.
Moran, Robert. A Hiking Guide to Acadia National Park & Mount Desert Island. (Illus.). 24p. 1988. reprint ed. pap. 2.50 (*0-934745-07-2*) Acadia Pub Co.
***Moran, Robert & Grub, Phillip D., eds.** Global Business Strategies for the Year 2000, 2 vols., Set. 1200p. 1995. lib. bdg. 95.00 (*0-933833-36-9*) Beacham Pub.
Moran, Robert, jt. auth. see Hogan, Ben.
Moran, Robert D. How to Avoid OSHA. LC 80-39727. 264p. 1981. 69.00 (*0-87201-652-8*) Gulf Pub.
Moran, Robert D. & Moran, Mark M. The OSHA Five Hundred. 290p. 1991. 85.00 (*0-9632296-9-9*) Moran Assocs.
— OSHA Made Easy: A Guide to Recordkeeping, Reporting, & Compliance. LC 94-12508. 544p. 1994. pap. 99.95 (*0-442-01908-4*) Van Nos Reinhold.
Moran, Robert O. & Katzeff, Kathleen. The Healthcare Industry Guide to the Bloodborne Pathogens Standard. 290p. 1992. pap. 85.00 (*0-9632296-8-0*) Moran Assocs.

An Asterisk (*) at the beginning of an entry indicates that the title is appearing in BIP for the first time.

*Moran, Robert T. Getting Your Yen's Worth: How to Negotiate with Japan, Inc. fac. ed. LC 84-10882. 200p. Date not set. pap. 57.00 (0-7837-7428-1, 2047223) Bks Demand.

Moran, Robert T. & Abbott, Jeffrey D. NAFTA: Managing the Cultural Differences. LC 94-12482. 160p. 1994. 12.95 (0-88415-500-5) Gulf Pub.

Moran, Robert T. & Johnson, Michael. Cultural Guide to Doing Business in Europe. 2nd ed. 156p. 1992. pap. 24.95 (0-7506-0831-5) Buttrwrth-Heinemann.

Moran, Robert T. & Reisenberger, John R. The Global Challenge: Building the New Worldwide Enterprise. LC 94-10893. 1994. pap. text ed. 24.95 (0-07-709022-5) McGraw.

Moran, Robert T. & Stripp, William G. Dynamics of Successful International Business Negotiations. 256p. 1991. 27.50 (0-87201-196-8) Gulf Pub.

Moran, Robert T., jt. auth. see Harris, Philip R.

Moran, Robert T., et al. Developing Global Organizations: Strategies for Human Resource Professionals. LC 92-21197. 253p. 1993. 32.50 (0-88415-071-2) Gulf Pub.

— International Business Case Studies for the Multicultural Marketplace. LC 93-45859. 1994. 29.95 (0-88415-193-X) Gulf Pub.

Moran, Robert T., et al, eds. Global Business Management in the 1990s. 495p. (C). 1990. lib. bdg. 65.00 (0-933833-07-5) Beacham Pub.

Moran, Roberto E. Ninos con Problemas de Conducta y Aprendizaje: Temas Contemporaneos y Estrategias. 381p. 1984. pap. 12.50 (0-8477-2906-0) U of PR Pr.

Moran, Roberto F. Manual of Mental Subnormality. 482p. (SPA.). 1968. 7.00 (0-8477-2900-1) U of PR Pr.

*Moran, Ron. Getting the Body to Dance Again. 1995. pap. text ed. 6.95 (0-614-01214-7) Pudding Hse Pubns.

Moran, Ronald. Life on the Rim. (W.N.J. Ser.: No. 25). (Orig.). 1988. 18.00 (1-55780-103-7); pap. 9.00 (0-318-32676-0) Juniper Pr WI.

— So Simply Means the Rain. 1965. text ed. 4.95 (0-87511-087-8); pap. 2.95 (0-87511-086-X) Claitors.

— Sudden Fictions. 59p. pap. 6.00 (1-55780-130-4) Juniper Pr WI.

Moran, Ronald, jt. auth. see Lensing, George S.

Moran, S., ed. The Mathematical Theory of Knots & Braids: An Introduction. (Mathematical Studies: Vol. 82). 296p. 1983. pap. 56.50 (0-444-86714-7, I-274-83, North Holland) Elsevier.

Moran, Sally. A Woman for All Seasons: Reflections on Mary. LC 92-60892. 128p. (Orig.). 1993. pap. 7.95 (0-89622-531-3) Twenty-Third.

Moran, Sean F. Patrick Pearse & the Politics of Redemption: The Mind of the Easter Rising, 1916. LC 92-26449. 220p. 1994. 42.95 (0-8132-0775-4) Cath U Pr.

*Moran, Susan D. Gathered in the Spirit: Beginnings of the First Church in Cambridge. 192p. 1995. 18.95 (0-8298-1069-2) Pilgrim OH.

Moran, Theodore H. American Economic Policy & National Security. (Pew Project Ser.). 96p. 1992. pap. 10.95 (0-87609-137-0) Coun Foreign.

— Multinational Corporations: The Political Economy of Foreign Direct Investment. LC 85-45293. (Illus.). 304p. (C). 1985. pap. text ed. 24.95 (0-669-11242-9) Free Pr.

— Multinational Corporations & the Politics of Dependence: Copper in Chile. LC 74-2973. 303p. reprint ed. pap. 86.40 (0-8357-4289-X, 2037088) Bks Demand.

— Oil Prices & the Future of OPEC: The Political Economy of Tension & Stability in the Organization of Petroleum Exporting Countries. LC 78-2983. (Resources for the Future. Research Paper Ser.: No. R-8). 108p. reprint ed. pap. 30.80 (0-685-23704-4, 2032160) Bks Demand.

Moran, Theodore H., et al. Investing in Development: New Roles for Private Capital. 224p. (Orig.). 1986. 19.95 (0-88738-074-3); pap. 12.95 (0-88738-644-X) Transaction Pubs.

Moran, Thomas, illus. Watercolor Sketches of Thomas Moran: Yellowstone & Grand Teton National Park. 8p. 1991. pap. 9.95 (0-931895-21-9) Grand Teton NHA.

*Moran, Thomas & Morand, Anne. Thomas Moran, the Field Sketches, 1856-1923. LC 94-49719. 1995. write for info. (0-8061-2704-X) U of Okla Pr.

Moran, Thomas F. American Presidents: Their Individualities & Their Contributions to American Progress. (Essay Index Reprint Ser.). 1977. reprint ed. 21.95 (0-518-10157-6) Ayer.

Moran, Thomas P. & Carroll, John M., eds. Design Rationale: Concepts, Techniques, & Use. (Computers, Cognition, & Work Ser.). 600p. 1994. text ed. 100.00 (0-8058-1566-X); pap. 50.00 (0-8058-1567-8) L Erlbaum Assocs.

Moran, Tom. A Family in Ireland. (Families the World Over Ser.). (Illus.). 32p. (J). (gr. 2-5). 1986. lib. bdg. 14.95 (0-8225-1668-3, Lerner Publctns) Lerner Group.

— A Family in Mexico. (Families the World Over Ser.). (Illus.). 32p. (J). (gr. 2-5). 1987. 14.95 (0-8225-1677-2, Lerner Publctns) Lerner Group.

— Los Angeles International Airport: From Lindbergh's Landing Strip for World Air Center. LC 93-36904. 1993. 29.95 (1-884166-01-6) Preferred Mktg.

— The U. S. Army. (Armed Services Ser.). (Illus.). 88p. (YA). (gr. 5 up). 1990. lib. bdg. 22.95 (0-8225-1434-6, Lerner Publctns) Lerner Group.

Moran, Victoria. Compassion the Ultimate Ethic: An Exploration of Veganism. 3rd ed. 112p. 1991. reprint ed. pap. 6.95 (0-942401-12-3) Am Vegan Soc.

— Get the Fat Out: 501 Simple Ways to Cut the Fat in Any Diet. LC 93-39792. 1994. 9.00 (0-517-88184-5) Crown Pub Group.

— The Love-Powered Diet: A Revolutionary Approach to Healthy Eating & Recovery from Food Addiction. LC 91-30718. 336p. 1992. 12.95 (0-931432-75-8) New Wrld Lib.

Moran, W. Dean. It's about Time: Teacher's Time Teaching Resource Book & Student Work Sheets. 1988. 127.00 (0-317-93590-9) Time Teaching.

Moran, W. E. Settlements on the Eastern End of Long Island, Vol. 5, No. 2. 1993. reprint ed. lib. bdg. 89.00 (0-7812-5325-X) Rprt Serv.

Moran, William, jt. ed. see Pollington, Andrew.

Moran, William B., ed. Covert Surveillance & Electronic Penetration. (Illus.). 124p. 1983. pap. 12.95 (0-915179-20-2) Loompanics.

Moran, William C., ed. Workers' Compensation Law Review, 1974-93, 15 vols., Set. LC 73-93978. Vols. 1-15. lib. bdg. 695.00 (0-930342-54-2, 108550) W S Hein.

Moran, William F., Jr. & Phillips, Jim. The Blademaster. (Illus.). 200p. 1990. 19.95 (0-932572-11-1) Phillips Pubns.

Moran, William J., jt. auth. see Panje, William R.

Moran, William L. The Amarna Letters. 464p. 1992. text ed. 68.00 (0-8018-4251-4) Johns Hopkins.

Moran, William R., comp. Nellie Melba: A Contemporary Review. LC 83-26444. (Contributions to the Study of Music & Dance Ser.: No. 5). (Illus.). xxii, 491p. 1985. text ed. 65.00 (0-313-23893-6, MOM/, Greenwood Pr) Greenwood.

Moran, William R., ed. Herman Klein & the Gramophone. LC 89-36903. (Illus.). 620p. 1990. 54.95 (0-931340-18-7, Amadeus Pr) Timber.

Moran, William R., jt. comp. see Fagan, Ted.

*Moran-Zenteno, Dante. The Geology of the Mexican Republic. Wilson, James L. & Sanchez-Barreda, Luis, trs. (Studies in Geology: No. 39). (Illus.). vii, 160p. 1994. 67.00 (0-89181-047-1) AAPG.

Morand. Les Idees Politiques de Louis-Ferdinand Celene. 39.95 (0-685-37274-X) Fr & Eur.

*Morand & Ohayon. Interaction Fluids-Structures. Date not set. text ed. 65.95 (0-471-94459-9) Wiley.

Morand, Anne, jt. auth. see Moran, Thomas.

Morand, Anne R., et al. Splendors of the American West: Thomas Moran's Art of the Grand Canyon & Yellowstone. LC 90-1049. (Illus.). 96p. (Orig.). 1991. pap. 19.95 (0-295-97085-5) U of Wash Pr.

Morand, James M., jt. ed. see Cawley, William A.

Morand, Kathleen & Finn, David. Claus Sluter: Artist at the Court of Burgundy. (Illus.). 400p. 1991. 75.00 (0-292-71117-4) U of Tex Pr.

Morand, Martin J., jt. ed. see McCoy, Ramelle.

Morand, Paul. Closed All Night. LC 78-130067. (Short Story Index Reprint Ser.). 1977. 16.95 (0-8369-3648-5) Ayer.

— Fancy Goods - Open All Night. Pound, Ezra, tr. LC 83-23705. 160p. 1984. 16.00 (0-8112-0888-5); pap. 7.50 (0-8112-0889-3, NDP567) New Directions.

— Le Flagellant de Seville. (FRE.). 1982. pap. 13.95 (0-7859-4167-3) Fr & Eur.

— Green Shoots. LC 70-150553. (Short Story Index Reprint Ser.). 1977. reprint ed. 16.95 (0-8369-3850-X) Ayer.

— Nouvelles Completes, Vol. 1. Collomb, Michel, ed. (FRE.). 1992. lib. bdg. 160.00 (0-7859-3900-8) Fr & Eur.

— Tendres Stocks. (FRE.). 1981. pap. 8.95 (0-7859-4159-2) Fr & Eur.

Morand, Sheila. Santa Fe Then & Now. LC 84-2503. (Illus.). 96p. (Orig.). 1984. pap. 14.95 (0-86534-046-3) Sunstone Pr.

Moranda, Harold. The Hands of Time. 76p. 1976. 5.00 (0-87881-039-0) Mojave Bks.

Morandeira, J. R., et al, eds. European Society for Surgical Research (ESSR) Abstracts, 27th Congress, May 1992, Zaragoza, Spain: Journal: European Surgical Research, Vol. 24, Suppl. 2, 1992. (Illus.). xii, 124p. 1992. pap. 38.50 (3-8055-5615-2) S Karger.

Morandi, G. The Role of Topology in Classical & Quantum Physics. Beiglbock, W. et al, eds. (Lecture Notes in Physics, New Series, Monographs: Vol. M7). xiv, 239p. (C). 1992. text ed. 46.00 (0-387-55088-7) Spr-Verlag.

Morandi, Larry. Assessing the State Legislative Response to Global Warming. (State Legislative Reports: Vol. 17, No. 6). 4p. 1992. pap. 5.00 (1-55516-278-9, 7302-1706) Natl Conf State Legis.

— Financing Clean Water: Drinking Water. 13p. 1991. pap. text ed. 5.00 (1-55516-502-8, 4336) Natl Conf State Legis.

— Financing Clean Water: Wetlands. 14p. 1991. pap. text ed. 5.00 (1-55516-503-6, 4335) Natl Conf State Legis.

— Groundwater Protection Legislation: Survey of State Action 1988-1992. 65p. 1994. 15.00 (1-55516-504-4, 4340) Natl Conf State Legis.

— Legislative Guidance for Comprehensive State Groundwater Protection Programs. (State Legislative Report Ser.: Vol. 19, No. 3). 10p. 1994. 5.00 (1-55516-405-6, 7302-1903) Natl Conf State Legis.

— Rethinking Western Water Policy: Assessing the Limits of Legislation. 64p. 1994. pap. text ed. 10.00 (1-55516-404-8, 4339) Natl Conf State Legis.

— Superfund & Economic Development. (State Legislative Report Ser.: Vol. 19, No. 9). 7p. 1994. 5.00 (1-55516-227-4, 7302-1909) Natl Conf State Legis.

— Wastewater Permitting & Finance: New Issues in Water Quality Protection. (State Legislative Reports: Vol. 17, No. 8). 8p. 1992. pap. text ed. 5.00 (1-55516-280-0, 7302-1708) Natl Conf State Legis.

*Morandi, Larry & Azodmanesh, Sam. Financing Water Quality Infrastructure: An Update on State Revolving Funds. (State Legislative Report Ser.: Vol. 17, No. 20). 8p. 1992. 5.00 (1-55516-292-4, 7302-1720) Natl Conf State Legis.

*Morandi, Larry & Runyon, Cheryl. Protecting Estuaries: The Mix of Land & Sea. 30p. 1993. 10.00 (1-55516-376-9, 4338) Natl Conf State Legis.

*Morandi, Larry & Worthley, Justin. Rural Growth in Western States: Economic & Environmental Issues. 40p. 1995. 10.00 (1-55516-402-1, 4341) Natl Conf State Legis.

Morandi, Larry, jt. auth. see Doyle, Paul.

Morandini, Giuliana. Bloodstains. Kirschenbaum, Blossom S., tr. 1987. pap. 8.95 (0-89823-094-2) New Rivers Pr.

Morando, Bruno. Mouvement d'un Satellite Artificiel de la Terre. 270p. 1974. text ed. 207.00 (0-677-50750-X); pap. text ed. 48.00 (0-677-50755-0) Gordon & Breach.

Morano, Donald V., jt. ed. see Casey, Edward S.

Morano, John. A Wing & a Prayer. Van Treese, James B., ed. 148p. 1993. pap. 8.95 (1-56901-019-6) NW Pub.

Morano, Roy W. The Protestant Challenge to Corporate America: Issues of Social Responsibility. LC 84-8514. (Research for Business Decisions Ser.: No. 69). 256p. reprint ed. pap. 73.00 (0-8357-1592-2, 2070408) Bks Demand.

Morant, Geoffrey M. The Races of Central Europe: A Footnote to History. LC 77-87532. reprint ed. 16.50 (0-404-16598-2) AMS Pr.

Morant, Mack B. The Insane Nigger. 2nd ed. White, Mosezelle, ed. LC 82-62454. (Illus.). 75p. (Orig.). 1983. reprint ed. pap. 6.95 (0-936026-00-6) R&M Pub Co.

Morante, Elsa. L' Lle d'Arturo. 606p. (FRE.). 1979. pap. 15.95 (0-7859-4110-X, 2070370763) Fr & Eur.

— La Storia, Tome I. 1987. pap. 15.95 (0-7859-4132-0) Fr & Eur.

— La Storie, Tome II. 1987. pap. 13.95 (0-7859-4133-9) Fr & Eur.

Morante, Paolo, tr. see Igliori, Paola, ed.

Morantte, P. C. Remembering Carlos Bulosan. 164p. (Orig.). (C). 1984. pap. 8.75 (971-10-0184-5, Pub. by New Day Pub PH) Cellar.

Morantz & Walsh, eds. Brain Tumors: A Comprehensive Text. 864p. 1993. 215.00 (0-8247-8826-5) Dekker.

Morantz, Regina M., et al, eds. In Her Own Words: Oral Histories of Women Physicians. LC 81-13349. (Contributions in Medical History Ser.: No. 8.). (Illus.). xiv, 284p. 1982. text ed. 55.00 (0-313-22686-5, MHO/, Greenwood Pr) Greenwood.

— In Her Own Words: Oral Histories of Women Physicians. LC 81-13349. 290p. 1985. pap. 15.00 (0-300-03352-4, Y-534) Yale U Pr.

Morantz-Sanchez, Regina M. Sympathy & Science: Women Physicians in American Medicine. 480p. 1987. pap. 12.95 (0-19-504985-3) OUP.

Morantz, Toby, jt. auth. see Francis, Daniel.

Morari, M. & McAvoy, T. J., eds. Chemical Process Control - CPCIII: Proceedings of the Third International Conference, Asilomar, January 12-17, 1986. 932p. 1986. 184.75 (0-444-99532-3) Elsevier.

Morari, Manfred & Zafiriou, Evanghelos. Robust Process Control. 512p. 1988. text ed. 76.00 (0-13-782153-0) P-H.

Morari, Manfred, jt. auth. see Prett, David M.

Moras, D., et al, eds. Crystallographic Computing 5: From Chemistry to Biology. (IUCr Crystallographic Symposia Ser.: No. 5). (Illus.). 500p. 1992. 75.00 (0-19-855384-6) OUP.

Moras, Dino, et al, eds. Crystallography in Molecular Biology. LC 87-2509. (NATO ASI Series A, Life Sciences: Vol. 126). 454p. 1987. 125.00 (0-306-42497-5, Plenum Pr) Plenum.

Morash, Chris, ed. The Hungry Voice: Poetry of the Irish Famine. (Illus.). (C). 1989. text ed. 39.50 (0-7165-2437-6, Pub. by Irish Acad Pr IE) Intl Spec Bk.

*Morash, Christopher. Writing the Irish Famine. 256p. 1995. 40.00 (0-19-818279-1) OUP.

Morash, Marian. The Victory Garden Cookbook. LC 81-48132. (Illus.). 352p. 1982. 35.00 (0-394-50897-1); pap. 29.95 (0-394-70780-X) Knopf.

— Victory Garden Recipes for Vegetable & Fish Dishes. LC 92-44397. 1993. 35.00 (0-679-42362-1) Knopf.

Morash, Merry, jt. auth. see Trojanowicz, Robert C.

Morash, Ronald P. Bridge to Abstract Mathematics: Mathematical Proof & Structures. 2nd ed. 389p. 1991. text ed. write for info. (0-07-043043-8) McGraw.

Morasky, Robert L. Behavioral Systems. LC 82-12334. 192p. 1982. text ed. 45.00 (0-275-90863-1, C0863, Praeger Pubs) Greenwood.

Morassi, Antonio, jt. tr. see Ratti, Carlo G.

Morasso, P. & Tagliasco, V., eds. Human Movement Understanding: From Computational Geometry to Artificial Intelligence. 400p. 1986. 107.75 (0-444-70032-3, North Holland) Elsevier.

Morasso, P. G., jt. ed. see Marinaro, M.

Morasso, P. G., jt. auth. see Masulli, F.

Morath, Inge. Russian Journal. (Illus.). 128p. 1991. 40.00 (0-89381-473-3) Aperture.

Morath, Max. Best of Ragtime Piano. pap. 8.95 (0-89524-749-6) Cherry Lane.

— Max Morath - Cripple Creek. pap. 8.95 (0-89524-748-8) Cherry Lane.

Moratin. La Comedia Nueva O El Cafe - El Si De Las Ninas. 143p. (SPA.). 1979. 9.95 (0-8288-7061-6, S9170) Fr & Eur.

— Comedia Nueva O El Cafe - La Derrota de Los Pedantes. 126p. (SPA.). 1973. 7.95 (0-8288-7107-8) Fr & Eur.

— El Si de Las Ninas. 130p. (SPA.). 1980. 4.95 (0-8288-7104-3) Fr & Eur.

Moratto, Michael J. California Archaeology. LC 83-7141. (New World Archaeological Record Ser.). 1984. text ed. 114.00 (0-12-506180-3) Acad Pr.

— California Archaeology. LC 83-7141. (New World Archaeological Record Ser.). 1984. pap. text ed. 59.00 (0-12-506182-X) Acad Pr.

Moraux, Paul. Aristotelismus bei den Griechen von Andronikos bis Alexander von Aphrodisias, Vol. 1: Die Renaissance des Aristotelismus im 1.Jh.v.Chr. (Peripatoi: Vol. 5). 520p. (C). 1973. 161.55 (3-11-004361-0) De Gruyter.

— Le Commentaire D'Alexandre D'Aphrodise aux "Seconds Analytiques" D'Aristote. (Peripatoi Ser.). (C). 1979. text ed. 78.50 (3-11-007805-8) De Gruyter.

Moraux, Paul, et al, eds. Aristoteles Graecus. Die Griechischen Manuskripte des Aristoteles untersucht und beschrieben, Vol. 1, Vol. 1. (C). 1976. 315.40 (3-11-006732-3) De Gruyter.

— Zweifelhaftes im Corpus Aristotelicum - Studien zu einigen Dubia. 401p. (GER.). 1983. 176.95 (3-11-008980-7) De Gruyter.

Morava, Lillian, jt. auth. see Little, Mickey.

Morava, Lillian B. Camper's Guide to British Columbia Parks, Lakes, & Forests, Vol. 1: Vancouver, Lower Mainland, Cariboo-Shuswap-Okanagan. 152p. 1992. pap. 16.95 (0-87201-208-5) Gulf Pub.

— Camper's Guide to British Columbia Parks, Lakes, & Forests, Vol. 2: Kootenay & Northern British Columbia. 152p. 1992. pap. 16.95 (0-87201-215-8) Gulf Pub.

— Camper's Guide to Washington: Parks, Lakes, Forests, & Beaches. 176p. 1995. 16.95 (0-87201-212-3) Gulf Pub.

Morava, Lillian B. & Little, Mickey. Camper's Guide to U. S. National Parks: Where to Go & How to Get There. LC 92-43236. 192p. 1993. pap. 18.95 (0-88415-061-5) Gulf Pub.

Moravcik, Ivo, ed. see Englis, Karel.

*Moravcsik, G. Studia Byzantina: Studies in English, French, German, Italian, Russian & Neo-Greek. 438p. (C). 1967. 60.00x (963-05-2222-5, Pub. by Akad Kiado HU) St Mut.

Moravcsik, Gyula, ed. Constantine Porphyrogenitus, De Administrando Imperio. Jenkins, R. J., tr. LC 85-6950. (Dumbarton Oaks Texts: Vol. 1). 356p. (ENG & GRE.). 1985. reprint ed. 15.00 (0-88402-021-5) Dumbarton Oaks.

Moravcsik, J. M. Understanding Language: A Study of Theories of Language in Linguistics & in Philosophy. (Janua Linguarum, Ser. Minor: No. 169). 95p. 1977. pap. text ed. 29.25 (90-279-3111-9) Mouton.

Moravcsik, Julius. Plato & Platonism: Plato's Conception of Appearance & Reality in Ontology, Epistemology, & Ethics, & Its Modern Echoes. (Issues in Ancient Philosophy Ser.). (C). 1992. 54.95 (1-55786-202-8) Blackwell Pubs.

Moravcsik, Julius M. Thought & Language. 304p. 1990. 35.00 (0-415-04322-0, A4024) Routledge.

— Thought & Language. (Problems of Philosophy Series; Their Past & Present). 304p. 1992. pap. 16.95 (0-415-07105-4, A7121) Routledge.

Moravcsik, Julius M., ed. Patterns in Plato's Thought. LC 73-83566. (Synthese Historical Library: No. 6). 1973. lib. bdg. 84.00 (90-277-0286-1) Kluwer Ac.

Moravcsik, M. J., ed. Recent Developments in Particle Physics. (Nuclear Physics Ser.). 272p. (Orig.). 1966. text ed. 237.00 (0-677-11010-3) Gordon & Breach.

Moravec, Frantisek. Parasitic Nematodes of Freshwater Fishes of Europe. LC 93-215. 477p. (C). 1995. lib. bdg. 186.00 (0-7923-2172-3) Kluwer Ac.

Moravec, Hans. Mind Children: The Future of Robot & Human Intelligence. 224p. 1990. pap. text ed. 12.00 (0-674-57618-7) HUP.

Moravec, Hans P. Robot Rover Visual Navigation. LC 81-7512. (Computer Science: Artificial Intelligence Ser.: No. 3). (Illus.). 169p. reprint ed. pap. 48.20 (0-685-20337-9, 2070023) Bks Demand.

*Moravec, Marilyn. Facing down Our Fears: Finding Courage When Anxiety Grips the Heart Small Group Leader's Guide. (1995 50-Day Spiritual Adventure Ser.). (Illus.). 56p. (Orig.). 1994. student ed. pap. text ed. 6.99 (1-879050-51-X) Chapel of Air.

*Moravec, Randy. Claude. 1994. pap. 9.95 (0-425-14139-X) Berkley Pub.

— Claude. LC 92-15596. (Illus.). 64p. 1992. 14.95 (0-399-13792-0, Putnam) Putnam Pub Group.

Moravek, Otto. The Blue Warrior (above the Line of Duty) 1994. 17.50 (0-8062-4995-1) Carlton.

Moravek, T. M., jt. auth. see Jenson, Jack E.

Moravia, Alberto. L' Amour Conjugal. (FRE.). 1972. pap. 10.95 (0-7859-3988-1) Fr & Eur.

— Le Desobeissance. (FRE.). 1973. pap. 10.95 (0-7859-4022-7) Fr & Eur.

— Racconti di Alberto Moravia. Traversa, Vincenzo, ed. LC 68-11595. (Illus.). (Orig.). (ITA.). (C). 1979. reprint ed. pap. text ed. 12.95 (0-89197-368-0) Irvington.

— The Voyeur. Parks, Tim, tr. 280p. 1987. 18.95 (0-374-28544-6) FS&G.

*Moravia, Sergio. The Enigma of the Mind: The Mind-Body Problem in Contemporary Thought. 336p. (C). 1995. pap. 18.95 (0-521-40557-2) Cambridge U Pr.

— The Enigma of the Mind: The Mind-Body Problem in Contemporary Thought. 336p. (C). 1995. 54.95 (0-521-40550-5) Cambridge U Pr.

Moravscik, M., ed. On the Road to Worldwide Science. 576p. (C). 1989. pap. text ed. 44.00 (9971-5-0620-3) World Scientific Pub.

Morawetz, Anita & Walker, Gillian. Brief Therapy with Single-Parent Families. LC 83-21367. 294p. 1984. 36.95 (0-87630-350-5) Brunner-Mazel.

Morawetz, C. S. Lectures on Nonlinear Waves & Shocks. (Tata Institute Lectures on Mathematics Ser.). 137p. 1982. pap. 28.00 (0-387-10830-0) Spr-Verlag.

Morawetz, Cathleen S. Notes on Time Decay & Scattering for Some Hyperbolic Problems. (CBMS-NSF Regional Conference Ser.: No. 19). v, 81p. (Orig.). 1975. pap. text ed. 18.25 (0-89871-016-2) Soc Indus-Appl Math.

Morawetz, David. Go Gently. Johnson, Joy, ed. (Illus.). 24p. 1991. pap. 3.25 (1-56123-022-7) Centering Corp.

M

An Asterisk (*) at the beginning of an entry indicates that the title is appearing in BIP for the first time.

— Twenty-Five Years of Economic Development, 1950 to 1975. LC 77-17243. 139p. reprint ed. pap. 39.70 (*0-7837-4257-6*, 2043947) Bks Demand.

Morawetz, Herbert. Macromolecules in Solution. 2nd ed. LC 83-11991. (High Polymer Ser.: Vol. 21). 572p. (C). 1983. reprint ed. text ed. 57.50 (*0-89874-659-0*) Krieger.

— Polymers: The Origins & Growth of a Science. LC 95-6700. 1995. pap. write for info. (*0-486-68732-5*) Dover.

Morawetz, Herbert & Steinberg, I. Z., eds. Luminescence from Biological & Synthetic Macromolecules, Vol. 366. 414p. 1981. 82.00 (*0-89766-123-0*); pap. 82.00 (*0-89766-124-9*) NY Acad Sci.

Morawetz, Thomas, ed. Criminal Law. (International Library of Essays in Law & Legal Theory). 520p. 1991. text ed. 150.00 (*0-8147-5464-3*) NYU Pr.

— Justice. (International Library of Essays in Law & Legal Theory). 488p. 1991. text ed. 150.00 (*0-8147-5465-1*) NYU Pr.

Morawinska, Agnieszka. Nineteenth Century Polish Painting. 1989. pap. 30.00 (*0-87052-800-9*) Hippocrene Bks.

— Voices of Freedom: Polish Women Artists & the Avant-Garde. LC 91-34492. (Illus.). 56p. 1991. pap. 18.95 (*0-940979-19-5*) Natl Museum Women.

Morawska, L., ed. see International Workshop Indoor Air-an Integrated Approach Staff.

Morawski, Jill G. Practicing Feminisms, Reconstructing Psychology: Notes on a Liminal Science. LC 94-10786. (Critical Perspectives on Women & Gender Ser.). 260p. (C). 1994. text ed. 39.50x (*0-472-09481-5*); pap. text ed. 15.95 (*0-472-06481-9*) U of Mich Pr.

— The Rise of Experimentation in American Psychology. LC 87-18154. 256p. (C). 1988. text ed. 30.00 (*0-300-04153-5*) Yale U Pr.

Morawski, Stefan. Inquiries into the Fundamentals of Aesthetics. 1974. pap. 13.50x (*0-262-63066-4*) MIT Pr.

— The Trouble with Postmodernism. LC 95-16085. 1995. write for info. (*0-415-09386-4*) Routledge.

Morawski, Stefan, ed. see Marx, Karl & Engels, Friedrich.

Moray, Helga. Across the Years. large type ed. 320p. 1988. 15.95 (*0-7089-1917-0*) Ulverscroft.

— Beacon of Gold. large type ed. 483p. 1989. 17.95 (*0-7089-1979-0*) Ulverscroft.

— Blood on the Wind. large type ed. 400p. 1985. 15.95 (*0-7089-1270-2*) Ulverscroft.

— Footsteps in the Night. large type ed. 512p. 1988. 15.95 (*0-7089-1884-0*) Ulverscroft.

— The Harvest Burns. large type ed. 448p. 1984. 15.95 (*0-7089-1173-0*) Ulverscroft.

— Quest in the Sun. large type ed. 1991. 21.95 (*0-7089-2396-8*) Ulverscroft.

— The Savage Earth. large type ed. 400p. 1984. 15.95 (*0-7089-1116-1*) Ulverscroft.

— Tender Is the Search. large type ed. 288p. 1989. 17.95 (*0-7089-2030-6*) Ulverscroft.

— That Woman. large type ed. 384p. 1986. 15.95 (*0-7089-1449-7*) Ulverscroft.

— Tisa. large type ed. 496p. 1985. 15.95 (*0-7089-1314-8*) Ulverscroft.

— To Make a Light. large type ed. 393p. 1989. 17.95 (*0-7089-1947-2*) Ulverscroft.

— Trenfell Castle. large type ed. 416p. 1989. 17.95 (*0-7089-2016-0*) Ulverscroft.

— Untamed. large type ed. 512p. 1983. 15.95 (*0-7089-1046-7*) Ulverscroft.

Moray, N., jt. ed. see Senders, J.

Moraze, Charles. The Logic of History. Clough, Wilson, tr. (New Babylon Ser.: No. 11). 260p. 1976. text ed. 64.65 (*90-279-7781-X*) Mouton.

Morazzoni, Marta. The Girl in a Turban. Creagh, Patrick, tr. 157p. 1993. pap. 12.00 (*0-00-271270-9*, Pub. by HarpC UK) HarpC.

— His Mother's House. Rose, Emma, tr. 112p. 1995. 22.00 (*0-00-271254-7*, HarpT) HarpC.

— Invention of Truth: A Novel. LC 94-32219. 1995. pap. 10.00 (*0-88001-376-1*) Ecco Pr.

Morbeek, Kees & Moorbeek, Kees. Museum of Unnatural History. (Pop-up Ser.). (Illus.). 12p. (J). (ps up). 1993. 14.99 (*0-8431-3541-7*) Price Stern.

Morca, Teodoro. Becoming the Dance: Flamenco Spirit. 128p. (C). 1990. pap. 19.95 (*0-8403-5844-X*) Kendall-Hunt.

Morcay, Raoul & Muller, A. Histoire de la Litterature Francais - Renaissance. 487p. (FRE.). 1960. 24.95 (*0-8288-7421-2*) Fr & Eur.

Morch, Dea T. Evening Star. Tate, Joan, tr. LC 87-30083. (Modern Scandinavian Literature in Translation Ser.). (Illus.). 269p. reprint ed. pap. 76.70 (*0-7837-6173-2*, 2045895) Bks Demand.

— Winter's Child. Tate, Joan, tr. LC 85-24512. (Modern Scandinavian Literature in Translation Ser.). (Illus.). vi, 271p. 1986. reprint ed. 25.00 (*0-8032-3101-6*); reprint ed. pap. 7.95 (*0-8032-8133-1*) U of Nebr Pr.

Morch, Dea T., ed. see Nielson, Palle.

Morch, J., ed. Calcium Ion Antagonists in Cardiovascular Disease: Proceedings of an International Conference, 12-13 October 1979, Toronto, Canada. 200p. 1981. pap. 48.00 (*0-08-027376-9*, Pergamon Pr) Elsevier.

Morchin, William. Radar Engineer's Sourcebook. LC 92-18686. 1992. 88.00 (*0-89006-559-4*) Artech Hse.

Morchin, William C., Jr. Golden Age of Homespun. (Radar Ser.). 472p. 1993. reprint ed. per. 88.00 (*0-7812-5239-3*) Rprt Serv.

Morcira, Marcillo M. The Brazilian Quandary: A Twentieth Century Fund Paper. 87p. (Orig.). (C). 1986. pap. 7.00 (*0-87078-171-5*) TCFP-PPP.

Morcom & Parry. Capital Transfer Tax. 2nd ed. 336p. 1981. 65.00 (*0-85941-055-2*) St Mut.

***Morcom, John.** The John Morcom Collection of Western Greek Bronze Coins. Price, Martin, ed. (Sylloge of Coins of the British Isles). (Illus.). 96p. 1995. 49.95 (*0-19-726152-3*) OUP.

Morcos, Nabil, jt. ed. see Lambrecht, Richard M.

Mord, Jeanne & Millis, Bette R. Sentinels of Love: Rural Churches of California. LC 89-38422. (Illus.). 224p. (Orig.). 1990. pap. 9.95 (*0-931832-39-X*) Fithian Pr.

Mordan, C. B. American West Designs. (International Design Library). (Illus.). 48p. (Orig.). 1994. pap. 5.95 (*0-88045-127-0*) Stemmer Hse.

Mordarski, Sheila W., jt. auth. see Bond, Anita W.

Mordaunt, John. Facing up to AIDS. LC 89-85265. 141p. (Orig.). 1990. 16.95 (*0-86278-182-5*, Pub. by OBrien Pr IE); pap. 9.95 (*0-86278-191-4*, Pub. by OBrien Pr IE) Dufour.

Mordden, Ethan. Broadway Babies: The People Who Made the American Musical. 256p. 1988. pap. 10.95 (*0-19-505425-3*) OUP.

— Buddies. (Stonewall Inn Editions Ser.). 256p. 1987. pap. 8.95 (*0-312-01005-2*) St Martin.

— Everybody Loves You. (Stonewall Inn Editions Ser.). 1989. pap. 8.95 (*0-312-03334-6*) St Martin.

— A Guide to Opera Recordings. 352p. 1987. 30.00 (*0-19-504425-8*) OUP.

— A Guide to Orchestral Music: The Handbook for Non-Musicians. (Illus.). 592p. 1986. pap. 15.95 (*0-19-504041-4*) OUP.

— The Hollywood Studios: House Style in the Golden Age of Movies. LC 87-40488. 1988. 24.95 (*0-394-55404-3*) Knopf.

— How Long Has This Been Going On? 1995. 25.00 (*0-679-41529-7*) Random.

— I've a Feeling We're Not in Kansas Anymore. 204p. 1987. pap. 10.95 (*0-452-25929-0*, Plume) NAL-Dutton.

— One Last Waltz. 208p. 1986. 13.95 (*0-685-13215-3*) St Martin.

— One Last Waltz. (Stonewall Inn Editions Ser.). 1988. pap. 7.95 (*0-312-01801-0*) St Martin.

— Opera Anecdotes. 288p. 1988. pap. 9.95 (*0-19-505661-2*) OUP.

— Opera in the Twentieth Century: Sacred, Profane, Godot. 1978. 24.95 (*0-19-502288-2*) OUP.

— Rodgers & Hammerstein. (Illus.). 224p. 1992. 45.00 (*0-8109-1567-7*) Abrams.

— Rodgers & Hammerstein. LC 95-4039. 1995. write for info. (*0-8109-8144-0*) Abrams.

— Rodgers & Hammerstein: A Celebration. (Illus.). 224p. 1993. pap. 19.95 (*0-8065-1469-8*, Citadel Pr) Carol Pub Group.

— Waves: An Anthology of Gay Literature. LC 93-40349. 1994. pap. 12.00 (*0-679-74477-0*, Vin) Random.

Mordecai, Carolyn. Finding Love in the Eighties. LC 84-90643. 135p. (Orig.). 1984. pap. 4.95 (*0-9613823-0-9*) Nittany Pubs.

Mordecai, Pamela & Wilson, Betty, eds. Her True-True Name: An Anthology of Women's Writing from the Caribbean. (Caribbean Writers Ser.). 202p. (Orig.). 1990. pap. 9.95 (*0-435-98906-5*) Heinemann.

Mordecai, Samuel. Richmond in Be-Gone Days: Being Reminiscences of an Old Citizen. LC 75-1861. (Leisure Class in America Ser.). 1975. reprint ed. 23.95 (*0-405-06927-8*) Ayer.

Mordecai, Siegal, ed. Cornell Book of Cats. LC 89-40195. 1989. 30.00 (*0-394-56787-0*) Random.

Mordecai, Trevor T. Cut the Mustard: Create Your Own Destiny. LC 88-30239. (Illus.). 134p. (Orig.). (C). 1988. 19.95 (*0-9621302-0-6*) Chemam Pub Co.

Mordechai, Tova. Good Night My Friend Aleph. (Illus.). 32p. (J). (ps-1). 1989. 9.95 (*0-922613-12-5*); pap. 7.95 (*0-922613-13-3*) Hachai Pubns.

Mordell, Albert, ed. Notorious Literary Attacks. LC 69-18932. (Essay Index Reprint Ser.). 1977. 18.95 (*0-8369-0047-2*) Ayer.

Mordell, Albert, ed. see Hearn, Lafcadio.

Mordell, Albert, ed. see James, Henry.

Mordell, Klein, ed. Passover. 128p. pap. 4.50 (*0-686-95142-5*) ADL.

Morden, A. R. Business Strategy & Planning: A Strategic Management Approach. LC 92-40088. 1993. write for info. (*0-07-707718-0*) McGraw.

Morden, W. Across Asia's Snows & Deserts. deluxe limited ed. (Illus.). 413p. 1993. boxed 100.00 (*1-57157-006-3*) Safari Pr.

Mordfin, Leonard, ed. Mechanical Relaxation of Residual Stresses, STP 993. LC 88-15450. (Special Technical Publication (STP) Ser.). (Illus.). 128p. 1988. pap. text ed. 38.00 (*0-8031-1166-5*, 04-993000-23) ASTM.

Mordfin, Leonard, jt. ed. see Berger, Harold.

Mordi, A. Richard. Attitudes Toward Wildlife in Botswana. LC 91-20257. (Environment: Problems & Solutions Ser.). 240p. 1991. 58.00 (*0-8240-0471-X*) Garland.

Mordike, Barry L., ed. Laser Treatment of Materials: Proceedings of a Symposium, 1986. (Illus.). 480p. 1987. lib. bdg. 85.00 (*3-88355-117-1*, Pub. by DGM Metallurgy Info GW) IR Pubns.

Mordock, John, jt. auth. see Van Ornum, William E.

Mordock, John B. Counseling the Defiant Child: A Basic Guide to Helping Troubled & Aggressive Youth. LC 93-47043. (Formerly Counseling Children Ser.). 240p. 1994. reprint ed. pap. 12.95 (*0-8245-1407-6*) Crossroad NY.

Mordsley, Barry. Discrimination in Employment. 1993. U.K. pap. 51.00 (*0-406-16480-0*) Butterworth Legal Pubs.

Mordue, J. E. & Ainsworth, G. C., eds. Mycological Papers, No. 154: Ustilaginales of the British Isles. 96p. (C). 1984. pap. text ed. 25.00 (*0-00-000081-7*) CAB Intl.

Mordukhai-Boltovskoi, D., ed. The River Volga & Its Life. (Monographiae Biologicae: No. 33). 1979. lib. bdg. 140.00 (*90-6193-084-7*) Kluwer Ac.

More, Alan S., jt. ed. see Rice, Stan.

More, Carey & More, Julian. A Taste of Provence. (Illus.). 160p. 1991. pap. 24.95 (*1-85145-528-0*, Pub. by Pavilion UK) Trafalgar.

More, Charles. The Industrial Age. 449p. (C). 1989. pap. text ed. 25.95 (*0-582-49427-3*, 78243) Longman.

More, Charles, ed. Skill & the English Working Class 1870-1914. LC 80-51895. 1980. text ed. 29.95 (*0-312-72772-0*) St Martin.

More, David F. More: History of the More Family, & an Account of Their Reunion in 1890, with a Genealogical Record. (Illus.). 409p. 1992. reprint ed. lib. bdg. 73.00 (*0-8328-2428-3*); reprint ed. pap. 63.00 (*0-8328-2429-1*) Higginson Bk Co.

More, Elizabeth, jt. auth. see Irwin, Harry.

More, Ellen S. & Milligan, Maureen A., eds. The Empathic Practitioner: Empathy, Gender, & Medicine. LC 94-10061. 265p. (C). 1994. text ed. 45.00 (*0-8135-2118-1*); pap. text ed. 18.00 (*0-8135-2119-X*) Rutgers U Pr.

More, Grace V., ed. More: Chronicles of the More Family. (Illus.). 424p. 1993. reprint ed. lib. bdg. 73.50 (*0-8328-3375-4*); reprint ed. pap. 63.50 (*0-8328-3376-2*) Higginson Bk Co.

More, Hannah. Coelebs in Search of a Wife: Comprehending Observations on Domestic Habits & Manners, Religion & Morals, 2 vols. in 1. LC 79-8178. reprint ed. 44.50 (*0-404-62052-3*) AMS Pr.

— The Cottage Cook: Or, Mrs. Jones' Cheap Dishes. (Illus.). 16p. 1989. reprint ed. pap. 2.75 (*1-877984-08-6*) Hendricksn Group.

— Religion of the Heart. Helms, Hal M., ed. LC 93-84600. (Living Library). 250p. 1993. 8.95 (*1-55725-063-4*) Paraclete MA.

— Strictures on Female Education. LC 94-35575. (Revolution & Romanticism, 1789-1834 Ser.). 1995. 95.00 (*1-85477-186-8*, Pub. by Woodstock Bks UK) Cassell.

More, Hannah & Burney, Frances. Considerations on Religion & Public Education, with Remarks on the Speech of M. Dupont, Delivered in the National Convention of France: And Brief Reflections Relative to the Emigrant French Clergy. LC 92-23650. (Augustan Reprints Ser.: No. 262 (1990)). reprint ed. 12.00 (*0-404-70262-7*, BX1492) AMS Pr.

More, Harry W., Jr. Critical Issues in Law Enforcement. 4th ed. 350p. (C). 1985. pap. 19.95 (*0-87084-583-7*) Anderson Pub Co.

More, Harry W. Police Organization & Management, Instructor's Guide To. 8th ed. (Police Science Ser.). 93p. 1993. pap. text ed. write for info. (*1-56662-086-4*) Foundation Pr.

— Special Topics in Policing. LC 91-70608. 268p. (C). 1991. pap. text ed. 22.95 (*0-87084-574-8*) Anderson Pub Co.

More, Harry W. & Unsinger, Peter C. The Police Assessment Center. (Illus.). 232p. 1987. 51.95x (*0-398-05331-6*) C C Thomas.

— The Police Assessment Center. (Illus.). 232p. 1987. pap. 30.95 (*0-398-06299-4*) C C Thomas.

More, Harry W. & Unsinger, Peter C., eds. Managerial Control of the Police: Internal Affairs & Audits. 208p. (C). 1992. text ed. 41.95x (*0-398-05751-6*) C C Thomas.

— Managerial Control of the Police: Internal Affairs & Audits. 208p. 1992. pap. 24.95 (*0-398-06298-6*) C C Thomas.

More, Harry W. & Wegener, W. Fred. Behavioral Police Management. (Illus.). 576p. (C). 1992. teacher ed write for info. (*0-318-69531-6*); text ed. write for info. (*0-02-383350-5*) Macmillan.

More, Harry W., Jr. & Wegener, W. Fred. Effective Police Supervision. LC 88-71497. (Illus.). 300p. (C). 1989. text ed. 27.95 (*0-87084-588-8*) Anderson Pub Co.

More, Harry W., jt. auth. see Kenney, John P.

More, Harry W., Jr.

More, Harry W., jt. auth. see Leonard, V. A.

More, Harry W., jt. ed. see Unsinger, Peter C.

More, Henry. Democritus Platonissans: or An Essay upon the Infinity of Worlds Out of Platonick Principles. LC 92-24821. reprint ed. 12.00 (*0-404-70130-2*, PR3605) AMS Pr.

— Enthusiasmus Triumphatus: or A Brief Discourse of the Nature, Causes, Kinds, & Cure of Enthusiasm. LC 92-23647. (Augustan Reprints Ser.: No. 118 (1966)). reprint ed. 12.00 (*0-404-70118-3*, BR112) AMS Pr.

— Philosophical Writings of Henry More. MacKinnon, Flora I., ed. LC 78-95151. reprint ed. 42.50 (*0-404-04409-3*) AMS Pr.

More, Hilary. Ribbons. (Keepsake Crafts Ser.). 1995. pap. 9.99 (*0-376-04259-1*) Sunset Menlo Pk.

— Soft Furnishings. (Pleasures of Home Ser.). (Illus.). 128p. 1995. 21.95 (*0-304-34629-2*, Pub. by Cassell UK) Sterling.

***More, Hilary & Westland, Pamela.** Decorative Wreaths & Garlands. (Illus.). 96p. 1995. 19.99 (*0-89134-662-7*) North Light Bks.

More, Ian A. & Brown, Ian L. General Pathology. (Colour Aids Ser.). (Illus.). 130p. (Orig.). 1991. pap. text ed. 19.95 (*0-443-04057-5*) Churchill.

— General Pathology. LC 93-29877. (Colour Guide Ser.). (Orig.). 1994. 19.95 (*0-443-04949-1*) Churchill.

***More, James F.** History of Queens County, Nova Scotia. 255p. 1995. reprint ed. lib. bdg. 32.00 (*0-8328-4726-7*) Higginson Bk Co.

More, Jorge J. & Wright, D. Optimization Software Guide. LC 93-33771. (Frontiers in Applied Mathematics Ser.: No. 14). xii, 154p. 1993. pap. 24.50 (*0-89871-322-6*) Soc Indus-Appl Math.

***More, Julian.** Pagnol's Provence. (Illus.). 160p. 1995. 29.95 (*1-85793-356-7*, Pub. by Pavilion UK) Trafalgar.

— Taste of Burgundy. (Illus.). 160p. 1993. 27.50 (*1-55859-464-7*) Abbeville Pr.

— Views from a French Farmhouse. (Illus.). 144p. 1992. pap. 13.95 (*0-943955-55-6*, Trafalgar Sq Pub) Trafalgar.

More, Julian, jt. auth. see More, Carey.

More, Louise B. Wage Earners' Budgets: A Study of Standards & Cost of Living in New York City. LC 73-137178. (Poverty U. S. A. Historical Record Ser.). 1977. reprint ed. 23.95 (*0-405-03116-5*) Ayer.

More, Mary. A Way to God: A Biography of George More. (C). 1990. text ed. 35.00 (*0-947988-45-9*, Pub. by Wild Goose Pubns UK) St Mut.

More, Meredith. October Obsession. 192p. 1988. pap. 8.95 (*0-941483-18-5*) Naiad Pr.

More, Paul E. On Being Human. LC 68-57334. (Essay Index Reprint Ser.). 1977. 19.95 (*0-8369-0717-5*) Ayer.

— Selected Shelburne Essays. reprint ed. 39.00 (*0-403-07240-9*) Somerset Pub.

More, Paul E., ed. Shelburne Essays, 11 vols., Set. Incl. Vol. 1. 1904. LC 67-17764. 253p. 1967. 25.00 (*0-685-22556-9*); Vol. 2. 1905. LC 67-17764. 253p. 1967. 25.00 (*0-685-22557-7*); Vol. 3. 1906. LC 67-17764. 265p. 1967. 25.00 (*0-685-22558-5*); Vol. 4. 1906. LC 67-17764. 286p. 1967. 25.00 (*0-685-22559-3*); Vol. 5. 1908. LC 67-17764. 216p. 1967. 25.00 (*0-685-22560-7*); Vol. 6. Studies in Religious Dualism, 1909. LC 67-17764. 355p. 1967. 25.00 (*0-685-22561-5*); Vol. 7. 1910. LC 67-17764. 272p. 1967. 25.00 (*0-685-22562-3*); Vol. 8. Drift of Romanticism, 1913. LC 67-17764. 316p. 1967. 25.00 (*0-685-22563-1*); Vol. 9. Aristocracy & Justice, 1915. LC 67-17764. 253p. 1967. 25.00 (*0-685-22564-X*); Vol. 10. With the Wits, 1919. LC 67-17764. 323p. 1967. 25.00 (*0-685-22565-8*); Vol. 11. New England Group & Others, 1921. LC 67-17764. 300p. 1967. 25.00 (*0-685-22566-6*); LC 67-17764. 1967. reprint ed. 250.00 (*0-87753-028-9*) Phaeton.

***More, R. M., ed.** Laser Interactions with Atoms, Solids & Plasmas. (NATO ASI Series B, Physics: Vol. 327). (Illus.). 486p. 1994. 135.00 (*0-306-44801-7*, Plenum Pr) Plenum.

More, Richard. The Carpenters Rule to Measure Ordinarie Timber. LC 74-26026. (English Experience Ser.: No. 252). 56p. 1970. reprint ed. 8.00 (*90-221-0252-1*) Walter J Johnson.

More, Robert P., jt. auth. see Palmer, Philip M.

More, St. Thomas. Complete Works of St. Thomas More: The Debellation of Salem & Bizance, Vol. 10. Guy, John et al, eds. LC 63-7949. 600p. (C). 1988. text ed. 75.00 (*0-300-03376-1*) Yale U Pr.

— In Defense of Humanism: Letter to Martin Dorp, Letter to the University of Oxford, Letter to Edward Lee, Letter to a Monk, with a New Latin Text & Translation of "The History of Richard III" Kinney, Daniel, ed. LC 63-7949. (Complete Works of St. Thomas More: Vol. 15). 662p. 1986. text ed. 75.00 (*0-300-03161-0*) Yale U Pr.

— Letter to Bugenhagen: Supplication of Souls' & Letter Against Frith. Manley, Frank, ed. (Yale Edition of the Complete Works of St. Thomas More Ser.: Vol. 7). xxx, 752p. (C). 1990. text ed. 85.00 (*0-300-03809-7*) Yale U Pr.

More, T., tr. see Mirandola, Pico D. & Francesco, Giovanni.

More, Thomas. Answer to a Poisoned Book. Foley, Stepehn & Miller, Clarence H., eds. LC 63-7949. (Complete Works of St. Thomas More Ser.: Vol. II). 434p. 1985. text ed. 75.00 (*0-300-03129-7*) Yale U Pr.

— The Apology. Trapp, J. B., ed. LC 63-7949. (Complete Works of St. Thomas More: Vol. 9). (Illus.). 1979. text ed. 75.00 (*0-300-02067-8*) Yale U Pr.

— The Apolyge of Syr Thomas More. LC 72-221. (English Experience Ser.: No. 228). 1970. reprint ed. 65.00 (*90-221-0228-9*) Walter J Johnson.

— A Book for All Seasons. 1990. pap. 9.95 (*0-87243-184-3*) Templegate.

— A Concordance to the Utopia of St. Thomas More & a Frequency Word List. Bolchazy, Ladislaus J. et al, eds. (Alpha-Omega, Reihe B Ser.: Bd. II). vii, 332p. (GER.). 1978. lib. bdg. 63.70 (*3-487-06514-2*, Pub. by Georg Olms GW) Lubrecht & Cramer.

— The Correspondence of Sir Thomas More. Rogers, Elizabeth F., ed. LC 74-119961. (Select Bibliographies Reprint Ser.). 1977. reprint ed. 33.95 (*0-8369-5404-1*) Ayer.

— De Tristitia Christi: Complete Works of St. Thomas More, Vol. 14, Pts. 1 & 2. Miller, Clarence H., ed. LC 63-7949. 1976. 100.00 (*0-300-01793-6*) Yale U Pr.

— A Dialogue of Comfort Against Tribulation. (Complete Works of St. Thomas More: No. 12). 1976. 90.00 (*0-300-01609-3*) Yale U Pr.

— A Dyaloge of Syr T. More...Wherein Be Treatyd Dyvers Maters, As of the Veneration & Worshyp of Ymagys. LC 74-28873. (English Experience Ser.: No. 752). 1975. reprint ed. 26.50 (*90-221-0752-3*) Walter J Johnson.

— His Witness Is True: John & His Interpreters. (American University Studies: Theology & Religion: Ser. VII, Vol. 42). 242p. (C). 1988. text ed. 43.00 (*0-8204-0626-0*) P Lang Pubs.

— The History of King Richard III. Sylvester, Richard S., ed. (Complete Works of St. Thomas More Ser.: No. 2). (Illus.). (ENG & LAT.). 1963. 65.00 (*0-300-00984-4*) Yale U Pr.

— The History of King Richard III & Selections from the English & Latin Poems. (Selected Works of St. Thomas More). 1976. 35.00 (*0-300-01840-1*); pap. 16.00 (*0-300-01925-4*) Yale U Pr.

— Life of the R. Hon. Richard B. Sheridan, 2 vols. 1981. reprint ed. lib. bdg. 59.00 (*0-403-01763-7*) Scholarly.

— Responsio Ad Lutherum, 2 Vols, Set. Headley, John M., ed. LC 63-7949. (Complete Works of St. Thomas More Ser.: No. 5). 1969. 100.00 (*0-300-01123-7*) Yale U Pr.

— The Sadness of Christ. (Yale University Press Translation Ser.). 184p. 1993. 7.95 (*0-933932-66-9*) Scepter Pubs.

— Sir Thomas More: Selected Letters. LC 61-14944. (Yale Edition of the Works of St. Thomas More: Modernized Ser.). reprint ed. pap. 74.00 (*0-317-28285-9*, 2022022) Bks Demand.

An Asterisk (*) at the beginning of an entry indicates that the title is appearing in BIP for the first time.

— St. Thomas More: Selected Letters. Rogers, Elizabeth F., ed. LC 61-14944. (Yale Edition of the Works of St. Thomas More: Modernized Ser.). 297p. reprint ed. pap. 84.70 (*0-8357-8331-6*, 2033876) Bks Demand.
— St. Thomas More: Vol. 3, Pt. 2 - Latin Poems. Miller, Clarence H. et al, eds. LC 63-7949. (Yale Edition of the Complete Works of St. Thomas More Ser.). 800p. 1984. text ed. 85.00 (*0-300-02591-2*) Yale U Pr.
— The Supplycacyon of Soulys: Agaynst the Supplycacyon of Beggars. LC 72-220. (English Experience Ser.: No. 353). 88p. 1971. reprint ed. 25.00 (*90-221-0353-6*) Walter J Johnson.
— Thomas More's Prayer Book: A Facsimile Reproduction of the Annotated Pages. Martz, Louis L. & Sylvester, Richard S., trs. LC 69-15454. (Elizabethan Club Ser.: No. 4). (Illus.). (ENG & LAT.). 1969. 45.00 (*0-300-00179-7*) Yale U Pr.
— Treatise on the Passion: Complete Works of St. Thomas More, Vol. 13. Haupt, Garry E., ed. Incl. Treatise on the Passion. LC 63-7949. 1976. (*0-318-56514-5*); Treatise on the Blessed Body. LC 63-7949. 1976. (*0-318-56515-3*); Instructions & Prayers. LC 63-7949. 1976. (*0-318-56516-1*); LC 63-7949. 1976. Set text ed. 75.00 (*0-300-01794-4*) Yale U Pr.
— Utopia. Sacks, David H., ed. 208p. 1995. pap. text ed. 8.65 (*0-312-10145-7*) St Martin.
— Utopia: And Other Essential Writings. Greene, James, ed. 304p. 1984. mass mkt. 5.95 (*0-452-00920-0*, Mer) NAL-Dutton.
— Utopia: And Other Writings. Greene, James & Dolan, John P., eds. 304p. 1984. mass mkt. 4.95 (*0-452-00687-2*, Mer) NAL-Dutton.
— Utopia: Latin Text & English Translation. Logan, George M. et al, eds. LC 93-42534. 272p. (C). 1995. 79.95 (*0-521-40318-9*) Cambridge U Pr.
More, Thomas, et al, eds. A Dialogue Concerning Heresies: Complete Works of St. Thomas More, Set, Vol. 6, Pts. 1 & 2. LC 63-7949. (Illus.). 910p. (C). 1981. Set. text ed. 95.00 (*0-300-02211-5*) Yale U Pr.
More, Thomas G. Environmental Fundamentalism. LC 92-25696. (Essays in Public Policy Ser.: No. 33). 1992. 5.00 (*0-8179-5382-5*) Hoover Inst Pr.
More, Tracy, ed. see Morin, Katherine A., et al.
Morea, Deborah. Through the Doors of Truth, Find Thyself. 1978. 5.50 (*0-9603022-0-4*) Davida Pubns.
— The Transmutation of Attitudes. 1979. pap. 6.50 (*0-9603022-1-2*) Davida Pubns.
Moreau, jt. auth. see Cotteret.
***Moreau, A. Scott.** Spiritual Warfare. 96p. 1995. pap. 4.99 (*0-87788-777-2*) Shaw Pubs.
Moreau, Claude. Moulds, Toxins & Food. Moss, Maurice, tr. LC 78-8715. (Illus.). 491p. reprint ed. pap. 140.00 (*0-685-20666-1*, 2030454) Bks Demand.
Moreau, Dan. Kiplinger's Survive & Profit from a Mid-Career Change. 1994. pap. 12.95 (*0-938721-32-1*) Kiplinger Bks.
Moreau, Daniel. Kiplinger's Facing Forty: How To Deal Successfully With the Changes In Your Life. LC 93-21878. 284p. 1993. 19.95 (*0-938721-24-0*) Kiplinger Bks.
— Kiplinger's Facing 40. Date not set. 20.00 (*0-8129-2655-2*, Times Bks) Random.
— Kiplinger's Survive & Profit From a Mid-Career Change. Date not set. pap. 14.00 (*0-8129-2661-7*, Times Bks) Random.
Moreau, Emile. The Golden Franc: Memoirs of a Governor of the Bank of France: The Stabilization of the Franc (1926-1928) 574p. (C). 1991. text ed. 77.50 (*0-8133-8141-X*) Westview.
Moreau, Fernand. Botanique. (Methodique Ser.). 1534p. (FRE.). 1965. pap. 125.00 (*0-7859-1589-3*, 207010396X) Fr & Eur.
Moreau, J. F. & Mueller, G. O., trs. French Penal Code. (American Series of Foreign Penal Codes: Vol. 1). xviii, 258p. 1960. 15.00 (*0-8377-0021-3*) Rothman.
Moreau, J. J. & Panagiotopoulos, P. D., eds. Nonsmooth Mechanics & Applications. (CISM Courses & Lectures Ser.: Vol. 302). (Illus.). v, 462p. 1988. pap. 79.00 (*0-387-82066-3*) Spr-Verlag.
Moreau, J. J., et al. Topics in Nonsmooth Mechanics. 320p. 1988. 226.00 (*0-8176-1907-0*) Birkhauser.
Moreau, Jacqueline, jt. ed. see Kent, Sarah.
Moreau, Jacques. Die Christenverfolgung im roemischen Reich. 2nd ed. 119p. (C). 1971. 22.30 (*3-11-002456-X*) De Gruyter.
— Inscriptiones Latinae Christianae Veteres: Supplementband. Marrou, Henri-Irenee, ed. viii, 165p. 1985. write for info. (*3-296-13504-9*, Pub. by Georg Olms GW) Lubrecht & Cramer.
Moreau, Jeffrey, jt. auth. see Brueckman, Henry.
Moreau, Jeffrey, jt. auth. see Cushing, Raymond.
Moreau, Jeffrey, jt. auth. see Pope, Dan.
Moreau, Joseph. L' Ame du Monde de Platon aux Stoiciens. 200p. 1981. reprint ed. write for info. (*3-487-04094-8*, Pub. by Georg Olms GW) Lubrecht & Cramer.
— La Construction de l'Idealisme Platonicien. 515p. 1986. reprint ed. write for info. (*3-487-01830-6*, Pub. by Georg Olms GW) Lubrecht & Cramer.
— Dictionnaire de Geographie Historique de la Gaule et de la France: Historical Dictionary of the Geography of Gaul & France. 426p. (FRE.). 1972. pap. 99.50 (*0-8288-6371-7*, M-6593) Fr & Eur.
— L' Univers Leibnizien. 256p. 1988. reprint ed. write for info. (*3-487-07903-8*, Pub. by Georg Olms GW) Lubrecht & Cramer.
Moreau, Louis & Franck, Adolphe. Reflexions Sur les Idees De Saint-Martin & La Philosophie Mystique en France A la Fin Du Eighteenth Siecle, Vol. VII. Amadou, Robert, ed. 228p. reprint ed. write for info. (*0-318-71418-3*, Pub. by Georg Olms GW) Lubrecht & Cramer.
Moreau, M. Underground Storage Systems. (General Engineering Ser.). 1992. text ed. write for info. (*0-442-00390-0*) Van Nos Reinhold.
Moreau, M. & Turq, P., eds. Chemical Reactivity in Liquids: Fundamental Aspects. LC 88-17980. (Illus.). 642p. 1988. 135.00 (*0-306-42922-5*, Plenum Pr) Plenum.
Moreau, Michael, ed. see Fante, John & Mencken, H. L.
Moreau, Nancy. Physics. 2nd ed. Garnsey, Wayne, ed. (Science Ser.). (Illus.). 352p. pap. text ed. 4.13 (*0-935487-55-7*) N & N Pub Co.
Moreau, Nancy & Romano, Nicholas. A General Chemistry Review. 3rd ed. (Illus.). 148p. (gr. 9-12). 1987. pap. text ed. 4.69 (*0-9606036-4-5*) N & N Pub Co.
Moreau, Nancy A. General Physics Review Text. 2nd ed. (Illus.). 191p. 1991. pap. text ed. 4.72 (*0-685-59637-0*) N & N Pub Co.
Moreau, Nancy A., jt. auth. see Moran, John W.
Moreau, P., jt. ed. see Poirier, G.
Moreau, Patricia. Suzanne Masterson: Dangerous Games. 412p. (YA). 1994. pap. 8.99 (*0-88070-648-1*, Multnomah Bks) Questar Pubs.
Moreau, Philippe, tr. see Lewis, Lon D., et al.
Moreau, Pierre-Francois, jt. ed. see Curley, Edwin.
Moreau, R. Magnetohydrodynamics. (C). 1990. lib. bdg. 120.00 (*0-7923-0937-5*) Kluwer Ac.
Moreau, R. & Aubert, G. Neural Networks-Les Reseaux de Neurones: Biological Computers or Electronic Brains-Ordinateurs Biologiques Ou Cerveaux Electroniques. (Entretiens de Lyon Ser.). (Illus.). viii, 195p. 1990. pap. 51.00 (*0-387-59540-6*) Spr-Verlag.
Moreau, R., jt. ed. see Lielpeteris, J.
Moreau, R. J., ed. Measurement & Control in Liquid Metal Processing. (C). 1987. lib. bdg. 114.00 (*90-247-3510-6*) Kluwer Ac.
Moreau, Rene. The Computer Comes of Age: The People, the Hardware, & the Software. 225p. 1984. reprint ed. pap. 9.95x (*0-262-63103-2*) MIT Pr.
Moreau, W. M. Semiconductor Lithography: Principles, Practices, & Materials. LC 87-29077. (Microdevices: Physics & Fabrication Technologies Ser.). (Illus.). 952p. 1988. 145.00 (*0-306-42185-2*, Plenum Pr) Plenum.
Moreaux, Michel, jt. ed. see Laffont, Jean-Jacques.
Morecki, A. Biomechanics of Engineering. (CISM International Centre for Mechanical Sciences Ser.: No. 291). (Illus.). vi, 186p. 1987. pap. 35.00 (*0-387-81974-6*) Spr-Verlag.
Morecki, A., ed. Biomechanics of Motion. (CISM Courses & Lectures Ser.: Vol. 263). (Illus.). 217p. 1981. pap. 43.00 (*0-387-81611-9*) Spr-Verlag.
— Robotics & Manipulators: Theory & Practice. 36p. 1983. pap. 10.00 (*0-08-030530-X*, 11, Pergamon Pr) Elsevier.
Morecki, A., et al, eds. RoManSy Nine: Proceedings of the Ninth CISM-IFToMM Symposium on Theory & Practice of Robots & Manipulators, Udine, Italy, Sept. 1-4, 1992. (Lecture Notes in Control & Information Sciences Ser.: Vol. 187). (Illus.). xxxi, 438p. 1993. pap. 79.00 (*0-387-19834-2*) Spr-Verlag.
Morecroft, John D. & Sterman, John D., eds. Modeling for Learning Organization. (Illus.). 500p. 1994. 45.00 (*1-56327-060-9*) Prod Press.
Moree, Lowell. The Black Bahamian: His Indomitable Quest for Metaphysical, Ontological, & Political Balance. 1990. 10.95 (*0-533-08544-6*) Vantage.
Moreell, Ben & Hoover, Herbert C. Our Nation's Water Resources: Policies & Politics. LC 72-2857. (Use & Abuse of America's Natural Resources Ser.). 290p. 1972. reprint ed. 23.95 (*0-405-04521-2*) Ayer.
Moreen, Vera B. Iranian Jewry's Hour of Peril & Heroism. (Study of the American Academy for Jewish Research). 247p. 1987. text ed. 37.00 (*0-231-06578-7*) Col U Pr.
— Miniatures in Judaeo-Persian Manuscripts. (Bibliographica Judaica Ser.: No. 9). 56p. 1985. pap. 35.00 (*0-87820-907-7*) Hebrew Union Coll Pr.
Moreen, Vera B., jt. ed. see Mazzaoui, Michel M.
Moreen, Vera B., jt. ed. see Nemoy, Leon.
Moreh, S., tr. see Al-Jabarti, Abdal R.
Moreh, Shmuel. Live Theatre & Dramatic Literature in the Medieval Arabic World. 200p. 1991. text ed. 59.00 (*0-7486-0292-5*, Pub. by Edinburgh U Pr UK) Col U Pr.
— Live Theatre & Dramatic Literature in the Medieval Arabic World. (Eastern Civilization Ser.). 240p. (C). 1992. text ed. 45.00 (*0-8147-5481-3*) NYU Pr.
Morehart, Grover C. The Legal Status of City School Boards. LC 78-177082. (Columbia University. Teachers College. Contributions to Education Ser.: No. 270). reprint ed. 22.50 (*0-404-55270-6*) AMS Pr.
Morehart, Thomas B. A Health Maintenance Organization for the State of Georgia: Results of a Simulation. LC 77-4879. (Research Monograph: No. 76). 317p. 1977. spiral bd. 30.00 (*0-88406-113-2*) GA St U Busn Pr.
Morehead, Albert H. According to Hoyle. 1976. 21.95 (*0-8488-0348-5*) Amereon Ltd.
— The Complete Book of Solitaire & Patience Games. (Illus.). 192p. 1983. mass mkt. 5.50 (*0-553-26240-8*) Bantam.
— Complete Guide to Winning Poker. 1973. pap. 8.95 (*0-671-21646-5*, Fireside) S&S Trade.
— Hoyle's Rules of Games. 1983. pap. 11.95 (*0-452-26416-2*, Plume) NAL-Dutton.
Morehead, Albert H., ed. Official Rules of Card Games. 1986. mass mkt. 5.99 (*0-449-21381-1*, Crest) Fawcett.
Morehead, Albert H. & Morehead, Loy. New American Crossword Puzzle Dictionary. 1986. pap. 5.99 (*0-451-14503-8*, Sig) NAL-Dutton.
Morehead, Albert H. & Mott-Smith, Geoffrey. Hoyle Up-to-Date. 1970. 10.95 (*0-399-12827-1*, Perigree Bks) Berkley Pub.
Morehead, Albert H. & Mott-Smith, Geoffrey, eds. Hoyle's Rules of Games. 1946. pap. 4.99 (*0-451-16309-5*, Sig) NAL-Dutton.
— Hoyle's Rules of Games. 2nd rev. ed. LC 83-13297. 272p. 1983. pap. 7.95 (*0-452-26049-3*, Plume) NAL-Dutton.
Morehead, Albert L. New Complete Hoyle: The Authoritative Guide to the Official Rules of All Popular Games of Skill. 1991. 25.95 (*0-385-24962-4*) Doubleday.
Morehead, George, tr. see Leblanc, Maurice.
Morehead, James C., Jr. A Walking Tour of Rice University. exp. rev. ed. (Illus.). 108p. 1990. reprint ed. pap. 12.95 (*0-89263-301-8*) Rice Univ.
— A Walking Tour of Rice University. 2nd exp. rev. ed. (Illus.). 108p. 1990. reprint ed. 22.50 (*0-89263-300-X*) Rice Univ.
Morehead, Joe. Essays on Public Documents & Government Policies. LC 86-9840. (Technical Services Quarterly Ser.: Vol. 3, Nos. 3/4). 364p. 1986. 49.95 (*0-86656-248-6*) Haworth Pr.
Morehead, Joe & Fetzer, Mary. Introduction to United States Government Information Sources. 4th ed. LC 92-13251. (Library Science Text Ser.). 420p. 1992. lib. bdg. 45.00 (*0-87287-909-7*); pap. text ed. 37.50 (*1-56308-066-4*) Libs Unl.
Morehead, John W. Finding & Licensing New Products & Technology from the U. S. A. LC 82-50568. 387p. 1994. ring bd. 125.00 (*0-943420-00-8*) Tech Search Intl.
Morehead, Judith & Morehead, Richard. The New Texas Wild Game Cookbook. rev. ed. (Illus.). 104p. 1985. 12.95 (*0-89015-526-7*) Sunbelt Media.
Morehead, Loy, jt. auth. see Morehead, Albert H.
Morehead, Maureen. In a Yellow Room. Moremen, John S., ed. 65p. 1990. 13.50 (*0-9624086-1-1*) Sulgrave Pr.
Morehead, Philip D. The New American Roget's College Thesaurus in Dictionary Form. rev. ed. 1985. pap. 7.95 (*0-452-00732-1*, Mer) NAL-Dutton.
— The New International Dictionary of Music. LC 92-80541. (Illus.). 640p. 1992. pap. 15.00 (*0-452-01100-0*, Mer) NAL-Dutton.
***Morehead, Philip D., ed.** The New American Webster Handy College Dictionary. 800p. 1995. mass mkt. 4.99 (*0-451-18166-2*, Sig) NAL-Dutton.
Morehead, R., jt. ed. see Pennington, K.
Morehead, Richard. Fifty Years of Texas Politics. 1982. 16.95 (*0-89015-342-6*) Sunbelt Media.
Morehead, Richard, jt. auth. see Morehead, Judith.
Morehead, Ruth J. The Christmas Story with Holly Babes. LC 85-32305. (Pictureback Ser.). (Illus.). 32p. (J). (ps-1). 1987. 2.25 (*0-394-88051-X*); audio 5.95 (*0-394-89058-2*) Random Bks Yng Read.
— Holly Babes. (Christmas Ornament Bks.). (Illus.). 5p. (J). (ps). 1994. 1.99 (*0-679-83976-3*) Random Bks Yng Read.
Morehead, Ruth J., illus. A Christmas Countdown with Ruth J. Morehead's Holly Babes. LC 90-61905. (Chunky Shape Bks.). 22p. (J). (ps). 1991. bds. 2.95 (*0-679-81417-5*) Random Bks Yng Read.
— Christmas Is Coming with Ruth J. Morehead's Holly Babes: A Book of Poems & Songs. LC 89-3717. (Pictureback Ser.). 32p. (Orig.). (J). (ps-1). 1990. pap. 2.25 (*0-679-80075-1*) Random Bks Yng Read.
***Morehen, John, ed.** English Choral Practice, 1400-1650. (Cambridge Studies in Performance Practice: No. 5). (Illus.). 275p. (C). 1993. write for info. (*0-521-44143-9*) Cambridge U Pr.
Morehouse, Cynthia T., jt. ed. see Culligan, Michael.
Morehouse, Debra, jt. auth. see Capezio, Peter.
Morehouse, Frank, jt. auth. see Goodman, Murray.
***Morehouse, G. L., ed.** Maltby-Morehouse Family: A List of Pedigrees with Genealogical Notes. 157p. 1994. reprint ed. lib. bdg. 35.00 (*0-8328-4343-1*); reprint ed. pap. 25.00 (*0-8328-4344-X*) Higginson Bk Co.
Morehouse Hegne, Barbara. Unforgettable Pioneers. (Illus.). 119p. 1987. spiral bd. 10.00 (*0-9623847-0-4*) B Hegne.
— Yonder Hills: Shady Cove, Elk Creek, Persist, Trail, Etna. 128p. (Orig.). 1989. spiral bd. 10.95 (*0-9623847-1-2*) B Hegne.
Morehouse, Jayne, ed. Milady's Professional Barber-Styling Workbook. rev. ed. 193p. 1993. 16.50 (*1-56253-146-8*) Milady Pub.
Morehouse, Jayne, ed. see Milady Publishing Company Staff.
Morehouse, Joyce M. In Search of Yesterday. LC 87-14741. (Illus.). 136p. (Orig.). (YA). (gr. 9 up). 1987. pap. 4.99 (*0-932581-17-X*) Word Aflame.
Morehouse, Kathleen M. Rain on the Just: A Novel. LC 79-18762. (Lost American Fiction Ser.). 333p. 1980. reprint ed. 19.95 (*0-8093-0945-9*) S Ill U Pr.
Morehouse, Laurence E. Total Fitness in 30 Minutes. 1990. pap. 5.99 (*0-671-72993-4*) S&S Trade.
Morehouse, Lawrence G., jt. ed. see Wyllie, Thomas D.
***Morehouse, Matt, ed.** 1996 Nautical Almanac: Commercial Edition. (Illus.). 416p. (Orig.). 1995. reprint ed. spiral bd. 16.95 (*0-939837-07-2*) Paradise Cay Pubns.
Morehouse, Richard, jt. auth. see Maykut, Pamela.
Morehouse, Thomas A. The Alaska Native Claims Settlement Act, 1991, & Tribal Government. (Occasional Paper Ser.: No. 19). (Illus.). 29p. 1988. 2.00 (*0-88353-040-6*) U Alaska Inst Res.
— Alaska's Elections, Nineteen Fifty-Eight to Nineteen Eighty-Four. (Occasional Paper Ser.: No. 17). (Illus.). 37p. 2.00 (*0-88353-036-8*) U Alaska Inst Res.
— Native Claims & Political Development. (Occasional Paper Ser.: No. 18). (Illus.). 28p. 1987. 2.00 (*0-88353-039-2*) U Alaska Inst Res.
Morehouse, Thomas A. & Harrison, Gordon S. An Electoral Profile of Alaska: Interparty Competition Between 1958 & 1972. LC 73-620227. (ISER Reports: No. 37). (Illus.). 100p. 1973. pap. 3.00 (*0-88353-010-4*) U Alaska Inst Res.
Morehouse, Thomas A., jt. auth. see McBeath, Gerald A.
Morehouse, Thomas A., jt. ed. see McBeath, Gerald A.
Morehouse, Thomas A., et al. Alaska's Urban & Rural Governments. LC 83-25887. (Illus.). 272p. (Orig.). (C). 1984. pap. 25.00 (*0-8191-3771-5*) U Pr of Amer.
***Morehouse, Tim.** Basic Gardening Skills. (Illus.). 224p. 1996. pap. 14.95 (*0-8117-2508-1*) Stackpole.
— Basic Projects & Plantings for the Garden. LC 92-30915. (Illus.). 192p. (Orig.). 1993. pap. 12.95 (*0-8117-3048-4*) Stackpole.
Morehouse, Ward. George M. Cohan, Prince of the American Theater. LC 79-165445. (Illus.). 240p. 1972. reprint ed. text ed. 35.00 (*0-8371-6225-4*, MOGC, Greenwood Pr) Greenwood.
— Separate, Unequal, but More Autonomous. 50p. 1981. pap. text ed. 10.95 (*0-685-54936-4*) Transaction Pubs.
Morehouse, Ward, III. Waldorf-Astoria: America's Gilded Dream. LC 91-12084. 1991. 22.95 (*0-87131-663-3*) M Evans.
Morehouse, Ward, ed. Science & the Human Condition in India & Pakistan. LC 68-56606. (Illus.). 252p. 1968. 7.50 (*0-87470-010-8*) Rockefeller.
Morehouse, Ward & Subramaniam, Arun. The Bhopal Tragedy: What Really Happened & What It Means for American Workers & Communities at Risk. (Illus.). 190p. 1986. pap. 13.50 (*0-936876-47-6*) LRIS.
Morehouse, Ward, ed. see Benello, C. George, et al.
Morehouse, Ward, ed. see Carnegie Endowment for International Peace Staff.
Morehouse, Ward, jt. auth. see Dembo, David.
Morehouse, Ward, jt. ed. see Guiterrez, Ginny.
Morehouse, Ward, ed. see Nicholas, Marta R., et al.
Morein, B., jt. ed. see Dinter, Z.
Moreines, Robert N. Light up Your Blues: Understanding & Overcoming Seasonal Affective Disorders. 160p. (Orig.). 1989. pap. 7.95 (*0-929162-09-9*) PIA Pr.
***Moreira, Mauricio M.** Industrialization, Trade & Market Failures: The Role of Government Intervention in Brazil & South Korea. LC 94-18288. 1994. write for info. (*0-312-12223-3*) St Martin.
***Moreira, Paula.** Novell's Guide to NetWare Management. 1995. pap. write for info. (*0-7821-1601-9*) Sybex.
Morel. Hybridization Techniques for Electron Microscopy. 1993. 89.95 (*0-8493-4414-X*, QH452) CRC Pr.
Morel, A. Y., jt. auth. see Gordon, H. R.
Morel, Benedict A. Traite Des Degenerescences Physiques, Intellectuelles et Morales De L'espece Humaine, 2 vols. in 1. LC 75-16721. (Classics in Psychiatry Ser.). (Illus.). (FRE.). 1976. reprint ed. 62.95 (*0-405-07446-8*) Ayer.
Morel, Benoit & Olson, Kyle, eds. Shadows & Substance: The Chemical Weapons Convention. LC 93-8682. (Ridgeway International Security Studies). 345p. (C). 1993. pap. text ed. 63.00 (*0-8133-8735-3*) Westview.
Morel, Benoit, jt. ed. see Goodby, James E.
Morel, E. D. Affairs of West Africa. (Illus.). 382p. 1968. reprint ed. 35.00 (*0-7146-1702-4*, Pub. by F Cass Pubs UK) Intl Spec Bk.
— Great Britain & the Congo: The Pillage of the Congo Basin. LC 68-9619. 1969. reprint ed. 45.00 (*0-86527-088-0*) Fertig.
— Nigeria: Its Peoples & Its Problems. 3rd ed. (Illus.). 264p. 1968. reprint ed. 35.00 (*0-7146-1703-2*, BHA-01703, Pub. by F Cass Pubs UK) Intl Spec Bk.
Morel, Edmund. Red Rubber. LC 79-95442. (Studies in Russian Literature & Life: No. 100). 1970. reprint ed. lib. bdg. 75.00 (*0-8383-0995-X*) M S G Haskell Hse.
Morel, Edmund D. Black Man's Burden: The White Man in Africa from the Fifteenth Century to World War One. LC 74-81792. 240p. 1969. pap. 4.50 (*0-85345-115-X*, PB115X) Monthly Rev.
— King Leopold's Rule in Africa. LC 70-132078. 466p. 1971. reprint ed. text ed. 35.00 (*0-8371-4647-X*, MKL&, Negro U Pr) Greenwood.
— Red Rubber: The Story of the Rubber Slave Trade Flourishing on the Congo in the Year of Grace 1906. 2nd ed. LC 71-76859. (Illus.). 213p. 1969. reprint ed. text ed. 45.00 (*0-8371-1161-7*, MOR&, Greenwood Pr) Greenwood.
Morel, F., ed. Biochemistry of Kidney Functions. (INSERM Symposia Ser.: Vol. 21). 462p. 1982. 134.00 (*0-444-80417-X*) Elsevier.
Morel, Francois M. & Hering, Janet G. Principles & Applications of Aquatic Chemistry. 608p. 1993. text ed. 64.95 (*0-471-54896-0*) Wiley.
Morel, Francois, jt. auth. see Carrez, Maurice.
Morel, Francois M. Principles of Aquatic Chemistry. LC 83-6840. (Wiley-Interscience Publication Ser.). 456p. reprint ed. pap. 130.00 (*0-7837-2404-7*, 2040089) Bks Demand.
Morel, Gaud. Nature's Timekeeper: The Tree. (Young Discovery Library). (Illus.). 40p. (J). (gr. k-5). 1993. lib. bdg. 9.95 (*1-56674-072-X*, HTS Bks) Forest Hse.
— Nature's Timekeeper - The Tree. Bogard, Vicki, tr. LC 92-2710. (Illus.). 38p. (J). (gr. k-5). 1992. 5.95 (*0-944589-43-X*) Young Discovery Lib.
***Morel, Gerard.** Visualization of Nucleic Acids. LC 94-22190. 1995. write for info. (*0-8493-4781-5*) CRC Pr.
Morel, Hector V., tr. see Clymer, R. Swinburne.
***Morel, Jean-Michel & Solimini, Sergio.** Variational Models for Image Segmentation. LC 94-36639. (Progress in Nonlinear Differential Equations & Their Applications Ser.: 14). xvi, 245p. 1994. 59.50 (*0-8176-3720-6*) Birkhauser.
Morel, Lin M. Heaven's Helpful Hints: (There's God in Your Soup) (Illus.). 117p. (Orig.). 1990. pap. 14.95 (*1-879672-50-2*) L Morel Assocs.
Morel, Linda, ed. see Goble, Phillip E.
***Morel, Mina D.** Equine Reproductive Physiology: Breeding & Stud Management. (Illus.). 450p. 1993. text ed. 49.95 (*0-85236-255-2*, Pub. by Farming Pr UK) Diamond Farm Bk.
Morel-Seytoux, H. J., ed. Unsaturated Flow in Hydrologic Modeling: Theory & Practice. (C). 1989. lib. bdg. 172.00 (*0-7923-0211-7*) Kluwer Ac.

M

Morel-Seytoux, Hubert J., et al, eds. Modeling Hydrologic Processes. LC 78-68497. 1979. 32.00 (*0-918334-27-6*) WRP.

— Surface & Subsurface Hydrology. LC 78-68496. 1979. 30.00 (*0-918334-28-4*) WRP.

Morel, T. & Miller, J., eds. Aerodynamics of Transportation II. 89p. 1983. pap. text ed. 24.00 (*0-317-03525-8*, H00282) ASME.

Morel, Thomas, ed. see Fluids Engineering Conference Staff.

Moreland, A. Dickens Landmarks in London. 1972. 59.95 (*0-8490-0028-9*) Gordon Pr.

— Dickens Landmarks in London. LC 72-6291. (Studies in Dickens: No. 52). (Illus.). 1972. reprint ed. lib. bdg. 75.00 (*0-8383-1625-5*) M S G Haskell Hse.

Moreland, Carl & Bannister, David. Antique Maps. 3rd ed. (Illus.). 314p. (C). 1993. reprint ed. pap. 24.95 (*0-7148-2954-4*, Pub. by Phaidon Press UK) Chronicle Bks.

Moreland, Catherine. The Hawksmoor Heritage. (Orig.). 1981. pap. 2.50 (*0-89083-898-4*) Zebra.

Moreland, Dan, ed. see Christensen, Chris.

Moreland, Donald E., et al, eds. Biochemical Responses Induced by Herbicides. LC 81-20645. (ACS Symposium Ser.: No. 181). 274p. 1982. 43.95 (*0-8412-0699-6*) Am Chemical.

Moreland, Floyd, ed. Strategies in Teaching Greek & Latin: Two Decades of Experimentation. LC 81-18428. (American Philological Association Pamphlet Ser.). 1981. pap. 11.50 (*0-89130-556-4*, 40 06 07) Scholars Pr GA.

Moreland, Floyd L & Fleischer, Rita M. Latin: An Intensive Course. LC 75-36500. 1975. pap. 20.00 (*0-520-03183-0*) U CA Pr.

Moreland, George L. Balldom. 304p. 1989. reprint ed. 35.00 (*0-944786-46-4*) Horton Pub.

Moreland, J. P. Christianity & the Nature of Science: A Philosophical Investigation. LC 89-6719. 263p. (Orig.). 1989. pap. text ed. 14.99 (*0-8010-6249-7*) Baker Bk.

— Scaling the Secular City: A Defense of Christianity. LC 87-70626. 256p. (Orig.). 1987. pap. 12.99 (*0-8010-6222-5*) Baker Bk.

Moreland, J. P., ed. The Creation Hypothesis: Scientific Evidence for an Intelligent Designer. LC 93-42724. 240p. (Orig.). 1994. pap. 12.99 (*0-8308-1698-4*, 1698) InterVarsity.

Moreland, J. P. & Ciocchi, David M., eds. Christian Perspectives in Being Human: A Multidisciplinary Approach to Integration. LC 92-29773. 192p. (Orig.). 1993. pap. 15.99 (*0-8010-6300-0*) Baker Bk.

Moreland, J. P. & Geisler, Norman L. The Life & Death Debate: Moral Issues of Our Time. LC 90-37862. 192p. 1990. pap. text ed. 15.95 (*0-275-93702-X*, B3702, Praeger Pubs) Greenwood.

— The Life & Death Debate: Moral Issues of Our Time. LC 90-37842. (Contributions in Philosophy Ser.: No. 43). 192p. 1990. text ed. 55.00 (*0-313-27556-4*, MOO/, Greenwood Pr) Greenwood.

Moreland, J. P. & Nielsen, Kai. Does God Exist? The Debate Between Theists & Atheists. LC 92-41375. 320p. (C). 1993. reprint ed. pap. 16.95 (*0-87975-823-6*) Prometheus Bks.

Moreland, J. P., jt. ed. see Wilkins, Michael J.

Moreland, Jennifer. Industrial Revolution of the 19th Century 1760-1900. rev. ed. 72p. (J). (gr. k-8). 1992. pap. text ed. 19.95 (*0-913705-48-9*) Zephyr Pr AZ.

— The Renaissance A. D. 1300-1600. (Learning Packets - Anthropology Ser.). (Illus.). 60p. (J). (gr. k-8). 1992. pap. text ed. 19.95 (*0-913705-28-4*) Zephyr Pr AZ.

Moreland, Laurence W., et al. The Nineteen Eighty-Eight Presidential Election in the South: Continuity Amidst Change in Southern Party Politics. LC 90-23761. 320p. 1991. text ed. 59.95 (*0-275-93145-5*, C3145, Praeger Pubs) Greenwood.

Moreland, Laurence W., et al, eds. Blacks in Southern Politics. LC 87-15844. 312p. 1987. text ed. 65.00 (*0-275-92655-9*, C2655, Praeger Pubs) Greenwood.

— Contemporary Southern Political Attitudes & Behavior: Studies & Essays. LC 81-15694. 314p. 1982. text ed. 55.00 (*0-275-90864-X*, C0864, Praeger Pubs) Greenwood.

Moreland, Lisa A., jt. auth. see Kaplan, Laura G.

Moreland, Marylee M., jt. auth. see Temple, Gary L.

Moreland, Miles. Miles to Go: A Walk Across France. LC 92-44025. 1993. 21.00 (*0-679-42527-6*) Random.

Moreland, Paul A., jt. auth. see Place, Irene.

Moreland, Peggy. The Baby Doctor. (Desire Ser.). 1994. mass mkt. 2.99 (*0-373-05867-5*, 1-05867-6) Silhouette.

— Miss Lizzy's Legacy. (Desire Ser.). 1995. mass mkt. 3.25 (*0-373-05921-3*, 1-05921-1) Silhouette.

— Miss Prim. large type ed. (Silhouette Desire Ser.). 1994. 17.95 (*0-373-58893-3*, Silhouette Lrg Print) Chivers N Amer.

— Seven Year Itch. (Silhouette Desire Ser.). 1994. mass mkt. 2.99 (*0-373-05837-3*, 5-05837-5) Silhouette.

Moreland, R. S., ed. Regulation of Smooth Muscle Contraction. (Advances in Experimental Medicine & Biology Ser.: Vol. 304). (Illus.). 542p. 1991. 130.00 (*0-306-44041-5*, Plenum Pr) Plenum.

Moreland, Richard C. Faulkner & Modernism: Revision & Rewriting. LC 90-12049. 270p. (Orig.). (C). 1990. pap. text ed. 14.75 (*0-299-12504-1*) U of Wis Pr.

Moreland, W. H. India at the Death of Akbar: An Economic Study. (C). 1990. reprint ed. 12.50 (*81-85395-82-9*, Pub. by BR Pub II) S Asia.

***Moreland, William.** Captured Spirits: John Geldersma Sculpture 1964-1994. (Illus.). 44p. 1994. 20.00 (*0-936819-08-1*) USL Art Museum.

Moreland, William H. The Agrarian System of Moslem India. 314p. reprint ed. text ed. 27.50 (*0-685-13416-4*) Coronet Bks.

— From Akbar to Aurangzeb: A Study in Indian Economic History. (C). 1990. 12.75 (*81-85395-83-7*, Pub. by BR Pub II) S Asia.

— From Akbar to Aurangzeb: A Study in Indian Economic History. LC 77-180363. reprint ed. 47.50 (*0-404-56298-1*) AMS Pr.

— From Akbar to Aurangzeb: A Study in Indian Economic History. 372p. reprint ed. text ed. 28.50 (*0-685-13417-2*) Coronet Bks.

— India at the Death of Akbar: An Economic Study. 339p. reprint ed. text ed. 34.00 (*0-685-13418-0*) Coronet Bks.

Moreland, William M., jt. auth. see Eyers, Patricia S.

Moreland, Willis D. & Goldenstein, Erwin H. Pioneers in Adult Education. (Illus.). 280p. 1985. 34.95 (*0-8304-1082-1*) Nelson-Hall.

Morell, A., jt. auth. see Nydegger, U. E.

Morell, A., et al. IgG-Subklassen der Menschlichen Immunglobuline: Immunochemische Genetische, Biologische und Klinische Aspekte. (Illus.). 88p. 1975. pap. 23.25 (*3-8055-2153-7*) S Karger.

***Morell, Abelardo, photos.** A Camera in a Room. (Photographers at Work Ser.). (Illus.). 60p. 1995. pap. 15.95 (*1-56098-548-8*) Smithsonian.

Morell, B. A. The Actor's Little Instruction-Destruction Book. 100p. (Orig.). 1992. pap. 6.95 (*1-56850-030-0*) Chicago Plays.

Morell, Bernard B., jt. auth. see Bittinger, Marvin L.

Morell, Carolyn M. Unwomanly Conduct: The Challenges of Intentional Childlessness. LC 93-45984. 1994. 55.00 (*0-415-90677-6*, Routledge NY); pap. 16.95 (*0-415-90678-4*, Routledge NY) Routledge.

Morell, David, jt. auth. see Mazmanian, Daniel.

Morell, Franz. The MORA Concept: Patients' Own & Coloured Light Oscillations. Theory & Practice. Guest, Marion, tr. (Illus.). 158p. (Orig.). 1990. pap. text ed. 22.00 (*3-7760-1163-7*, Pub. by K F Haug Pubs) Medicina Bio.

Morell, H. Victorian Wooden Molding & Frame Designs: The 1887 Morell Catalog. (Illus.). 208p. 1992. reprint ed. pap. 11.95 (*0-486-26932-9*) Dover.

Morell, Hortensia R. Composicion Expresionista en "El Lugar sin Limites" de Jose Donoso. LC 85-1144. (UPREX, Estudios Literarios Ser.: No. 76). 122p. 1986. pap. 4.00 (*0-8477-0076-3*) U of PR Pr.

Morell, J. R. Algeria. 512p. 1984. 220.00 (*1-85077-017-4*, Darf Pubs Ltd) St Mut.

Morell, James B. The Law of the Sea: An Historical Analysis of the 1982 Treaty & Its Rejection by the United States. LC 91-52749. 496p. 1992. lib. bdg. 55.00x (*0-89950-634-8*) McFarland & Co.

Morell, John D. Elements of Psychology. LC 78-72813. (Brainedness, Handedness, & Mental Abilities Ser.). reprint ed. 28.50 (*0-404-60883-3*) AMS Pr.

Morell, Jonathan A., jt. ed. see Hermalin, Jared.

Morell, Martin, tr. see Yakubaitis, Eduard A.

Morell, Mary. Final Rest. LC 93-84276. 250p. (Orig.). 1993. pap. 9.95 (*0-933216-94-7*) Spinsters Ink.

— Final Session. LC 91-2066. 224p. (Orig.). 1991. pap. 9.95 (*0-933216-78-5*) Spinsters Ink.

Morell, Paul L. Living in the Lions' Den: How to Cope with Life's Stress. 1992. pap. 10.95 (*0-687-22295-8*) Abingdon.

Morell, Pierre, ed. Myelin. 2nd ed. LC 84-9975. 566p. 1984. 95.00 (*0-306-41540-2*, Plenum Pr) Plenum.

Morell-Romero, Jose. Revolution in Cuba - Memoirs of a Combatant. 1993. text ed. 19.95 (*0-937569-13-5*) Suncoast Prof Pub.

***Morell, Virginia.** Ancestral Passions: The Leakey Family & the Quest for Humankind's Beginnings. 1995. 30.00 (*0-684-80192-2*) S&S Trade.

Morella, Joe. Forever Lucy: The Life of Lucille Ball. 1990. pap. 4.95 (*0-425-12219-0*) Berkley Pub.

Morella, Joe & Barey, Patricia. Simon & Garfunkel: Old Friends a Dual Biography. (Illus.). 256p. 1991. 19.95 (*1-55972-089-1*, Birch Ln Pr) Carol Pub Group.

Morella, Joe & Epstein, E. Paulette. 1992. pap. 3.99 (*0-517-07913-5*) Random Hse Value.

Morella, Joe & Epstein, Edward Z. The Complete Films of Judy Garland. (Illus.). 204p. 1986. reprint ed. pap. 14.95 (*0-8065-1017-X*, Citadel Pr) Carol Pub Group.

— Lana. (Illus.). 1971. 6.95 (*0-8065-0258-4*, Citadel Pr) Carol Pub Group.

— Rebels: The Rebel Hero in Films. (Illus.). 224p. 1973. reprint ed. 9.95 (*0-685-29241-X*, Citadel Pr); reprint ed. pap. 7.95 (*0-8065-0360-2*, Citadel Pr) Carol Pub Group.

Morella, Joe, et al. The Amazing Careers of Bob Hope. (Illus.). 1978. pap. 5.95 (*0-89508-000-1*) Rainbow Bks.

***Morella, Joseph & Mazzei, George.** Noel & Cole: Their Sexuality, Their Genius. 304p. 1995. 23.00 (*0-7867-0237-0*) Carroll & Graf.

Morellet, Andre. Prospectus d'un Nouveau Dictionnaire de Commerce. (Economistes Francais du XVIIIe Siecle Ser.). 1990. reprint ed. pap. 44.00 (*0-8115-3802-8*) Periodicals Srv.

Morelli, Elizabeth A., ed. see Lonergan, Bernard J. F.

***Morelli, Jim.** Working Out on the Road. 256p. (Orig.). 1995. pap. 11.95 (*1-55650-695-3*) Hunter NJ.

Morelli, M. Computers & Electronics Dictionary: Dizionario di Informatica e Degli Elaboratori Elettronici. 3rd ed. 231p. (ENG & ITA.). 1982. pap. 24.95 (*0-8288-0904-6*, M7821) Fr & Eur.

Morelli, Mark D., ed. see Lonergan, Bernard J. F.

Morelli, Patricia L., comp. United States Department of Agriculture Pomological Watercolor Collection Index. 211p. 1987. 105.00 (*0-85964-206-2*) Chadwyck-Healey.

Morelli, Ralph, et al, eds. Minds, Brains & Computers: Perspectives in Cognitive Science & Artificial Intelligence. (Theoretical Issues in Cognitive Science Ser.). 240p. (C). 1992. text ed. 54.50 (*0-89391-793-1*); pap. text ed. 24.95 (*0-89391-962-4*) Ablex Pub.

Morelli, Ruey B., tr. see Pancaldi, Giuliano.

Morelli, Susan. Mrs. Funnywinkle. Weinberger, Jane, ed. (Illus.). 54p. (J). (ps-4). 1994. pap. 9.95 (*0-932433-62-6*) Windswept Hse.

Morelli, Val M. The Gates. (Renee Romance Ser.). 209p. 1993. pap. 5.95 (*0-9637810-0-6*) Not Aver Mind.

— Racing to the Moon. Spoon, ed. (Renee Romance Ser.). 266p. (Orig.). Date not set. pap. 5.95 (*0-9637810-1-4*) Not Aver Mind.

Morello, G. & Pluchino, F. Surgery of Peripheral Nerves. (Surgical Technique Ser.: Vol. XIV). 392p. 1988. text ed. 250.00 (*1-57235-043-1*) Piccin NY.

Morello, Jo, Inc. Staff, ed. see Mitchell, Gerald E.

Morello, Josephine A., et al. Microbiology in Patient Care. 5th ed. 592p. (C). 1993. Lab manual & wkbk. student ed write for info. (*0-697-13784-8*) Wm C Brown Pubs.

— Microbiology in Patient Care. 5th ed. 592p. (C). 1993. text ed. write for info. (*0-697-13302-8*) Wm C Brown Pubs.

***Morello, Sam A.** Lectio Divina: And the Practice of Tersian Prayer. LC 94-28368. (Pamphlet on American Writers Ser.). 32p. 1995. 3.50 (*0-935216-24-3*) ICS Pubns.

Morelock, J. D. The Army Times Book of Great Land Battles: From the Civil War to the Gulf War. Boyne, Walter J., ed. LC 94-8373. 352p. 1994. 29.95 (*0-425-14371-6*) Berkley Pub.

Moremen, John S., ed. Jack Daniel's Old Time Barbecue Cookbook. (Illus.). 192p. 1992. 24.95 (*0-9624086-2-X*) Sulgrave Pr.

— Our Brothers' War. 152p. 1993. pap. 14.95 (*0-9624086-5-4*) Sulgrave Pr.

Moremen, John S., ed. see Akers, Charles W. & Carter, John W.

Moremen, John S., ed. see Morehead, Maureen.

Moremen, John S., ed. see Pearce, J. E.

Moren, F., et al, eds. Aerosols in Medicine: Principles, Diagnosis, & Therapy. 2nd ed. LC 93-36576. 1993. 218.75 (*0-444-81332-2*) Elsevier.

— Aerosols in Medicine Principles Diagnosis & Therapy. 336p. 1985. 128.75 (*0-444-80610-5*) Elsevier.

Morena, John J. Advanced Composite Mold Making. LC 92-42441. 446p. (C). 1994. reprint ed. lib. bdg. 67.50 (*0-89464-825-X*) Krieger.

Morena, Miguel A. The Artistic History of Carlos Gardel: A Chronological Study with Filmography & Discography. (Latin American Music Ser.). 1980. lib. bdg. 75.00 (*0-8490-3059-5*) Gordon Pr.

***Morena Torres, Felipa.** Lexikon der Spanischen Redewendungen: Expresiones Idiomaticas. 312p. (GER & SPA.). 1990. 29.95 (*0-7859-8564-6*, 3927117498) Fr & Eur.

Morenberg, Max. Doing Grammar. 192p. (C). 1991. pap. text ed. 14.95 (*0-19-506427-5*) OUP.

Morenberg, Max, jt. ed. see Daiker, Donald A.

Morency, Claire, et al. Ready, Set, Listen! A Beginning Listening Program for Non-Readers. (Illus.). 200p. 1991. spiral bd. 29.95 (*1-55999-182-8*) LinguiSystems.

Morency, George, jt. auth. see Schonberger, Jane.

Moreng, Robert & Avens, John. Poultry Science & Production. (C). 1985. teacher ed write for info. (*0-8359-5562-1*, Reston); text ed. 47.20 (*0-8359-5559-1*, Reston) P-H.

— Poultry Science & Production. (Illus.). 438p. (C). 1991. reprint ed. text ed. 40.95 (*0-88133-634-3*) Waveland Pr.

***Moreno.** Arguing Euthanasia: Controversy over Mercy Killing, Suicide & Right to Die. 1995. pap. 11.00 (*0-684-80760-2*, Touchstone Bks) S&S Trade.

Moreno, Angel G., jt. auth. see Faulhaber, Charles B.

Moreno, Antonio. Jung, Gods, & Modern Man. LC 73-122047. 288p. reprint ed. pap. 82.10 (*0-317-29683-3*, 2022073) Bks Demand.

Moreno Baez, Enrique, ed. see Montemayor, Jorge de.

***Moreno, Barry.** Who Was Who at Ellis Island: A Survey. (Illus.). 150p. (Orig.). 1995. pap. 17.95 (*0-9646079-0-5*) Bellona Pr.

Moreno-Cabral, Carlos, et al. Manual of Postoperative Management in Adult Cardiac Surgery. (Illus.). 112p. 1988. pap. 28.00 (*0-683-06146-1*) Williams & Wilkins.

Moreno, Carlos. Algebraic Curves over Finite Fields: Error-Correcting Codes & Exponential Sums. (Tracts in Mathematics Ser.: No. 97). 255p. (C). 1994. pap. 27.95 (*0-521-45901-X*) Cambridge U Pr.

— Letter to Christopher Columbus: And Other Poems. 64p. (Orig.). 1993. pap. 4.95 (*1-880365-55-3*) Prof Pr NC.

Moreno, Carlos, ed. Algebraic Curves over Finite Fields: Error-Correcting Codes & Exponential Sums. (Tracts in Mathematics Ser.: No. 97). 272p. (C). 1991. 59.95 (*0-521-34252-X*) Cambridge U Pr.

Moreno, Carlos J. Advanced Analytic Number Theory, Pt. One: Ramification Theoretic Methods. LC 82-22620. (Contemporary Mathematics Ser.: No. 5). 190p. 1983. pap. 27.00 (*0-8218-5015-6*, CONM-15) Am Math.

Moreno, Cesar F., et al, eds. Latin America in Its Literature. Berg, Mary G., tr. LC 79-26626. (Latin America & Its Culture Ser.: Vol. I). Orig. Title: America Latina En Su Cultura. 350p. 1980. 54.50 (*0-8419-0530-4*) Holmes & Meier.

Moreno, Dario. The Struggle for Peace in Central America. LC 93-36885. 264p. (C). 1994. lib. bdg. 39.95 (*0-8130-1274-0*); pap. text ed. 19.95 (*0-8130-1275-9*) U Press Fla.

— U. S. Policy in Central America: The Endless Debate. 208p. (C). 1990. lib. bdg. 29.95 (*0-8130-1005-5*); pap. text ed. 17.95 (*0-8130-1020-9*) U Press Fla.

Moreno, Eduardo. The Films of Susan Hayward. (Illus.). 1979. 14.95 (*0-685-01098-8*, Citadel Pr); pap. 9.95 (*0-8065-0757-8*, Citadel Pr) Carol Pub Group.

Moreno, Enrique. Expanded Tunings in Contemporary Music: Theoretical Innovations & Practical Applications. LC 90-6025. (Studies in History & Interpretation of Music: Vol. 30). 156p. 1992. lib. bdg. 69.95 (*0-88946-485-5*) E Mellen.

Moreno, Fernando J., tr. see Palmer, Janice B., ed.

Moreno Fraginals, Manuel, et al, eds. Between Slavery & Free Labor: The Spanish-Speaking Caribbean in the Nineteenth Century. LC 84-23379. (Studies in Atlantic History & Culture). 320p. 1985. 43.50 (*0-8018-3224-1*) Johns Hopkins.

Moreno, G., et al. La Guia de Incafo de los Hongos de la Peninsula Iberica, 2 vols. (Illus.). 1276p. (SPA.). 1986. lib. bdg. 92.50 (*84-85389-44-1*) Lubrecht & Cramer.

Moreno, G., et al, eds. Photosensitisation. (NATO ASI Series H: Vol. 15). 521p. 1988. 153.00 (*0-387-18554-2*) Spr-Verlag.

***Moreno, H. J.** The A-Z of Alzheimer's Disease: A Caregiver's Guide & Planner. 38p. 1995. spiral bd. 16.95 (*0-9644962-0-8*) Alzheimers.

Moreno, J. L. The Classics of Sociometry, Vols. XI-XVIII, Set. pap. 110.00 (*0-685-22537-2*) Beacon Hse.

— Group Psychotherapy: A Symposium. pap. 16.00 (*0-685-06813-7*) Beacon Hse.

— Preludes to My Autobiography. 8.00 (*0-685-52594-5*) Beacon Hse.

— Psychodrama, 3 vols. Incl. Vol. 1. Collected Papers. pap. 20.00 (*0-685-22530-5*); Vol. 2. Foundations of Psychotherapy. 20.00 (*0-685-22531-3*); Vol. 2. Foundations of Psychotherapy. pap. 19.00 (*0-685-00718-9*); Vol. 3. Action-Therapy & Principles of Practice. 20.00 (*0-685-22532-1*); Vol. 3. Action-Therapy & Principles of Practice. pap. 19.00 (*0-685-22533-X*); write for info. (*0-318-51037-5*) Beacon Hse.

— Psychodrama & Sociodrama in American Education. 14.00 (*0-685-22536-4*) Beacon Hse.

— Sociometry, Experimental Method & the Science of Society. 16.00 (*0-685-06814-5*) Beacon Hse.

— Words of the Father. pap. 6.00 (*0-685-06818-8*) Beacon Hse.

Moreno, J. L., ed. Theater of Spontaneity. 3rd ed. 1983. pap. 15.00 (*0-685-42742-0*) Beacon Hse.

Moreno, Jaime H. & Lang, Tomas. Matrix Computations on Systolic-Type Arrays. LC 92-9868. (Kluwer International Series in Engineering & Computer Science: No. SECS 174). 320p. (C). 1992. lib. bdg. 93.50 (*0-7923-9237-X*) Kluwer Ac.

***Moreno, Jonathan D.** Deciding Together: Bioethics & Moral Consensus. 192p. 1995. 29.95 (*0-19-509218-X*) OUP.

Moreno, Jonathan D., ed. Paying the Doctor: Health Policy & Physician Reimbursement. LC 90-37837. 208p. 1990. text ed. 47.95 (*0-86569-006-5*, T006, Auburn Hse) Greenwood.

Moreno, Jonathan D. & Glassner, Barry. Discourse in the Social Sciences: Strategies for Translating Models of Mental Illness. LC 81-7092. (Contributions in Sociology Ser.: No. 40). (Illus.). 224p. 1981. text ed. 59.95 (*0-313-23159-1*, GLM/) Greenwood.

Moreno, Jose. Vuelta Al Hogar: Return Home. (SPA.). 3.25 (*84-7228-294-5*, 220951, Pub. by Edit Clie SP) TSELF.

Moreno, Jose A. Barrios in Arms: Revolution in Santo Domingo. LC 68-12723. 240p. reprint ed. pap. 68.40 (*0-8357-5970-9*, 2031902) Bks Demand.

***Moreno, Jose M. & Oechel, Walter C., eds.** Anticipated Effects of a Changing Global Environment in Mediterranean-Type Ecosystems. LC 95-5548. (Ecological Studies: Vol. 117). 1995. write for info. (*0-387-94352-8*) Spr-Verlag.

— The Role of Fire in Mediterranean-Type Ecosystems. LC 93-42622. (Ecological Studies). 1994. 79.00 (*0-387-94215-7*) Spr-Verlag.

Moreno, Leonard. The Life of Jesus Christ, Vol. 1. 108p. (Orig.). 1992. pap. text ed. 7.77 (*0-9631137-7-1*) Morenos Pub.

***Moreno, Leonardo.** Arqueologia de San Agustin: Pautas de Asentamiento Agustinianas en el Noroccidente de Saladoblanco (Huila) (Illus.). 144p. (SPA.). 1991. pap. 8.50 (*1-877812-16-1*) UPLAAP.

Moreno, Leonides. Of Stone & Tears. 1975. 2.00 (*0-912678-19-4*, Greenfld Rev Pr) Greenfld Rev Lit.

Moreno, Leslie, jt. auth. see Fulton, Susan.

Moreno, Leslie B. Companeros: Activity Book in Spanish & English for Children. 144p. (YA). (gr. 7-11). 1983. pap. 5.95 (*0-917168-09-7*) Executive Comm.

Moreno, Pepe. Rebel. (Illus.). 72p. (Orig.). 1986. pap. 10.95 (*0-87416-020-0*) Catalan Communs.

Moreno, Ralph. Berkeley Love & War Songs. 75p. 1957. pap. 4.00 (*0-317-57830-8*) Hartmus Pr.

Moreno, Rene, Jr. & Bailey, D. G. Alternative Transport Fuels from Natural Gas. (Technical Paper Ser.: No. 98). 98p. 1989. 7.95 (*0-8213-1230-8*, 11230) World Bank.

Moreno, Richard. The Backyard Traveler: Fifty-Four Outings in Northern Nevada. (Illus.). 268p. 1991. pap. 10.95 (*0-9631205-0-6*) Child Mus N Nev.

— The Backyard Traveler Returns: Sixty-Two Outings in Southern, Eastern & Historical Nevada. Meehan, Suzi, ed. (Illus.). 280p. (Orig.). 1992. pap. 10.95 (*0-9631205-1-4*) Child Mus N Nev.

— The Nevada Trivia Book. Jackson, Nancy & Mayerski, Kathy, eds. LC 95-75459. (Illus.). 176p. (Orig.). 1995. pap. 9.95 (*0-935182-79-9*) Gem Guides Bk.

Moreno, Richard, jt. auth. see Prosor, Larry.

Moreno, Rose M. Mental Health Planning in Texas: The Impact on Mexican-American Service Needs. 79p. (Orig.). 1982. pap. text ed. 9.95 (*1-878550-41-1*) Inter Dev Res Assn.

Moreno, Theodore. Microwave Transmission Design Data. (Microwave Library). 256p. 1989. text ed. 50.00 (*0-89006-346-X*) Artech Hse.

An Asterisk (*) at the beginning of an entry indicates that the title is appearing in BIP for the first time.

***Moreno Torres, Felipa.** Sinonimos, Lexikon der Spanischen Synonyme. 504p. (GER & SPA.). 1992. 29.95 (0-7859-8512-3, 3860470191) Fr & Eur.

***Morentz, James W.** SARA Title III Software: A Review of What's Available & What It Can Do for You. (Environmental Management Guides Ser.). 12p. 1994. pap. text ed. 17.50 (0-86587-438-7) Gov Insts.

Morentz, James W., Jr., jt. ed. see Chartrand, Robert L.

Morenus, Richard. Crazy-White-Man. 1994. reprint ed. lib. bdg. 32.95 (1-56849-315-0) Buccaneer Bks.

Morenz, Siegfried. Egyptian Religion. Keep, Ann E., tr. LC 73-8401. 400p. 1973. 49.95 (0-8014-0782-6) Cornell U Pr.

— Egyptian Religion. Keep, Ann E., tr. LC 73-8401. 400p. 1992. pap. 16.95 (0-8014-8029-9) Cornell U Pr.

Morer, J., jt. auth. see Chaussier, J. B.

Morera, Esteve. Gramsci's Historicism: A Realist Interpretation. 192p. 1990. 45.00 (0-685-26317-7, A3710) Routledge Chapman & Hall.

***Morere, Jean-Louis.** Dictionnaire de Sciences Biologiques du College a L'Universite. 320p. (FRE.). 1991. pap. 69.95 (0-7859-7978-6, 2729841261) Fr & Eur.

Mores, Deb. Babies First Year. 1994. 20.00 (0-517-59593-1) Crown Pub Group.

Moresby, Lily & Beck, Adams. Then Ninth Vibration, & Other Stories. Reginald, R. & Menville, Douglas, eds. LC 75-46251. (Supernatural & Occult Fiction Ser.). 1976. reprint ed. lib. bdg. 26.95 (0-405-08111-1) Ayer.

Moreschi, Robert W. Tort Liability Standards & the Firm's Response to Regulation. LC 90-44983. (Environment: Problems & Solutions Ser.: Vol. 22). 207p. 1990. 53.00 (0-8240-9299-6) Garland.

Moret, Alexandre. The Nile & Egyptian Civilization. (African Studies). reprint ed. 50.00 (0-938818-99-6) ECA Assoc.

Moret, Bernard. Algorithms from P to NP: Design & Efficiency, Vol. I. 450p. (C). 1991. text ed. 52.75 (0-8053-8008-6) Benjamin-Cummings.

Moret, P. R., et al, eds. Lactate: Physiologic, Methodologic & Pathologic Approach. (Illus.). 270p. 1980. pap. 39.00 (0-387-09829-1) Spr-Verlag.

Moreta, Andes, jt. auth. see Murphy, Merilene M.

***Moreto, Augustin.** Spite for Spite: El Desden Con el Desden. Matthews, Dakin, tr. (Great Translations for Actors Ser.). 112p. 1995. 11.95 (0-614-06679-4) Smith & Kraus.

Moreton, ed. see Robertson, J. D.

Moreton, C. A. Death in Practice. 249p. (C). 1989. 100.00 (0-7223-2179-1, Pub. by A H S Ltd UK) St Mut.

Moreton, C. E. The Townshends & Their World: Gentry, Law, & the Land in Norfolk C. 1450-1551. (Oxford Historical Monographs). (Illus.). 320p. 1992. 72.00 (0-19-820299-7) OUP.

Moreton, Edwina. Germany Between East & West. 194p. (C). 1989. pap. 17.95 (0-521-37891-5) Cambridge U Pr.

Moreton, Edwina & Segal, Gerald, eds. Soviet Strategy Toward Western Europe. 304p. (C). 1984. pap. text ed. 19.95 (0-04-330346-3) Routledge Chapman & Hall.

Moreton, Gill, jt. auth. see McNamara, Sylvia.

Moreton, Gill, jt. auth. see McNamara, Sylvie.

Moreton-Macdonald, John R. History of France, 3 Vols, Set. LC 76-142245. reprint ed. 210.00 (0-404-04430-1) AMS Pr.

Moreton, Pierre. MVP-FORTH File Management System. Haydon, Glen B., ed. (MVP-Forth Bks.: Vol. 5). 278p. (Orig.). 1984. pap. 30.00 (0-317-56529-X) Mntn View Pr.

***Moreton, T. Hugh.** The Temple in History & Prophecy. 40p. (Orig.). 1992. pap. 2.50 (1-879366-37-1) Hearthstone OK.

Moreton, Valerie S. New Day in Healing! Principles & Practices for Creating Health. (Transformational Healing Ser.: Bk. 1). 181p. 1993. pap. 12.00 (1-882590-01-5) Kalos Pub.

Moretti, Franco. Signs Taken for Wonders: Essays in the Sociology of Literary Forms. Fischer, Susan et al, trs. 336p. 1988. text ed. 50.00 (0-86091-210-8, A2102, Pub. by Verso UK); pap. text ed. 16.95 (0-86091-906-4, A1926, Pub. by Verso UK) Routledge Chapman & Hall.

— The Way of the World: The Bildungsroman in European Culture. 288p. 1987. 60.00 (0-86091-159-4, A1199, Pub. by Verso UK); pap. text ed. 16.95 (0-86091-891-2, A1128, Pub. by Verso UK) Routledge Chapman & Hall.

Moretti, G. P., ed. Proceedings. (Series Entomologica: No. 20). 471p. 1981. lib. bdg. 183.00 (90-6193-130-4) Kluwer Ac.

Moretti, Mickey, ed. see Engelbrecht, Charles V.

Moretti, Stephanie. The An Book. (Window on Words Ser.). (Illus.). 16p. (J). (ps-1). 1993. 18.95 (1-879567-09-1) Wonder Well.

— The At Book. (Window on Words Ser.). (Illus.). 18p. (J). (ps-1). 1991. 18.95 (1-879567-08-3, Valeria Bks) Wonder Well.

Moretti, Valerio. When Nuvolari Raced. (Illus.). 272p. 1994. 125.00 (1-874105-37-5, Pub. by Veloce Pub UK) Motorbooks Intl.

Moretto, L. G. & Ricci, R. A., eds. Nuclear Structure & Heavy Ion Dynamics: Proceedings of the International School of Physics "Enrico Fermi" Course LXXXVII, Varenna, Italy, 27 July-6 Aug, 1982. (Enrico Fermi International Summer School of Physics Ser.: Vol. 87). 492p. 1984. 159.00 (0-444-86826-7, North Holland) Elsevier.

Moretto, Lisa A., jt. auth. see Blicq, Ron S.

Morevski, Abraham. Shylock & Shakespeare. LC 67-19382. 112p. 1967. 3.35 (0-87527-056-5) Green.

Morewedge, Parviz, ed. Islamic Philosophical Theology. LC 79-14405. 265p. 1979. 64.50 (0-87395-242-1) State U NY Pr.

— Islamic Philosophy & Mysticism. LC 80-14364. (Studies in Islamic Philosophy & Science). 1981. 50.00 (0-88206-302-2) Caravan Bks.

— Neoplatonism & Islamic Thought. LC 92-388. (Studies in Neoplatonism: Ancient & Modern: Vol. 5). 267p. 1992. 59.50 (0-7914-1335-7); pap. 19.95 (0-7914-1336-5) State U NY Pr.

— Philosophies of Existence, Ancient & Medieval. LC 81-66643. 352p. reprint ed. pap. 100.40 (0-7837-5613-5, 2045519) Bks Demand.

Morewedge, Parviz, tr. see Mulla Sadra.

Morewedge, Parviz, tr. see Tusi, N.

Morewedge, Rosemarie T., ed. The Role of Woman in the Middle Ages. LC 74-23227. (Illus.). 195p. 1975. 44.50 (0-87395-274-X) State U NY Pr.

Morewitz, S., ed. see Johnson, Joe B.

Morewitz, Stephen. Sexual Harassment & Social Change in American Society. LC 93-48393. 350p. 1995. 64.95 (1-880921-77-4); pap. 44.95 (1-880921-76-6) Austin & Winfield.

Morewitz, Stephen, jt. auth. see Livingstone, Bruce.

***Morey.** Newnes Radio Amateur & Listeners Data Handbook. 1995. pap. write for info. (0-7506-2060-9, Focal) Buttrwrth-Heinemann.

Morey, ed. Early Proterozoic Rocks of the Great Lakes Region. (IGC Field Trip Guidebooks Ser.). 72p. 1989. 21.00 (0-87590-625-7, T145) Am Geophysical.

Morey, Ann-Janine. Religion & Sexuality in American Fiction. (Cambridge Studies in American Literature & Culture: No. 57). 340p. (C). 1992. 49.95 (0-521-41676-0) Cambridge U Pr.

Morey, Barbara, ed. see Ambrose, Paul V. & Algozzini, Joseph P.

Morey, Barbara, ed. see Weaver, Carl.

Morey, Carol, jt. auth. see Daum, David.

Morey, Cathy, ed. see Newlin, Lana S.

Morey, Clinton R. The Denial: A Play for Lent. 1980. 4.15 (0-89536-412-3, 0420) CSS OH.

Morey, Craig. Studio Nudes: Selected Photographs 1989-1992. (Illus.). 80p. 1992. 25.00 (0-9632813-0-5) C Morey Photo.

Morey, Earl W. Our God Reigns: An Inductive Approach to the Book of Revelation. 401p. (Orig.). 1992. pap. 18.95 (0-9634717-0-8) A Minis VA.

— Search the Scriptures: How To Study the Bible for Yourself. (Illus.). 333p. 1993. pap. 18.95 (0-9634717-1-6) A Minis VA.

Morey, Eileen. Amelia Earhart. LC 94-556. (Importance of... Biographies Ser.). (Illus.). 112p. (J). (gr. 5-8). 1995. 16.95 (1-56006-065-4) Lucent Bks.

Morey, G. B. & Hanson, Gilbert N., eds. Selected Studies of Archean Gneisses & Lower Proterozoic Rocks, Southern Canadian Shield. LC 80-67113. (Geological Society of America, Special Paper Ser.: No. 182). (Illus.). 181p. (Orig.). reprint ed. pap. 51.60 (0-8357-3147-2, 2039410) Bks Demand.

Morey, G. B., et al. Bibliography of Minnesota Geology, 1951-1980. (Bulletin: No. 46). 1981. 10.00 (0-934938-01-6) Minn Geol Surv.

Morey-Gaines, Ann-Janine. Apples & Ashes: Culture, Metaphor & Morality in the American Dream. LC 81-14346. (American Academy of Religion Academy Ser.). 1982. 19.95 (0-89130-535-1, 01-01-38) Scholars Pr GA.

Morey, Grace K., jt. auth. see Clymer, R. Swinburne.

Morey, James I., jt. auth. see Kirshner, Edward M.

Morey, Janet N. & Dunn, Wendy. Famous Asian Americans. (Illus.). 192p. (J). (gr. 5 up). 1992. 15.99 (0-525-65080-6, Cobblehill Bks) Dutton Child Bks.

— Famous Hispanic Americans. LC 95-10670. (J). 1996. write for info. (0-525-65190-X, Cobblehill Bks) Dutton Child Bks.

— Famous Mexican Americans. LC 89-7218. (Illus.). (J). (gr. 5 up). 1989. 14.99 (0-525-65012-1, Cobblehill Bks) Dutton Child Bks.

Morey, Kathy. Hawaii Trails: Walks, Strolls & Treks on the Big Island. LC 91-15130. (Illus.). 288p. (Orig.). 1992. pap. 12.95 (0-89997-134-2) Wilderness Pr.

— Kauai Trails: Walk, Strolls & Treks on the Garden Island. LC 90-45550. (Illus.). 224p. (Orig.). 1991. pap. 12.95 (0-89997-117-2) Wilderness Pr.

— Maui Trails: Walks, Strolls & Treks on the Valley Isle. LC 91-22224. (Illus.). 224p. (Orig.). 1991. 12.95 (0-89997-125-3) Wilderness Pr.

— Oahu Trails: Walks, Strolls & Treks on the Capital Isle. LC 91-42204. (Illus.). 212p. (Orig.). 1993. pap. 12.95 (0-89997-156-3) Wilderness Pr.

Morey, Philip R., et al, eds. Biological Contaminants in Indoor Environments. LC 90-21115. (Special Technical Publication Ser.: STP 1071). (Illus.). 260p. 1990. text ed. 49.00 (0-8031-1290-4, 04-010710-17) ASTM.

Morey, Rita, ed. see Gill, George.

Morey, Rita, ed. see Simmes, William.

***Morey, Robert.** La Invasion Islamica. 208p. (SPA.). 1995. pap. 8.99 (0-8254-1479-2) Kregel.

— The Islamic Invasion. 230p. 1992. reprint ed. pap. 7.99 (0-89081-983-1) Harvest Hse.

— Satan's Devices: Recognizing the Enemy & Knowing How to Defeat Him. LC 93-1132. 1993. pap. 8.99 (1-56507-142-5) Harvest Hse.

— The Truth about Masons. 1993. pap. 6.99 (1-56507-077-1) Harvest Hse.

Morey, Robert A. Battle of the Gods: The Emerging God of the New Age. 324p. (Orig.). (C). 1989. pap. 9.95 (0-925703-00-1) Crown MA.

— Death & the Afterlife. LC 84-15682. 322p. 1984. pap. 16.99 (0-87123-433-5) Bethany Hse.

— Here Is Your God. (Orig.). (C). 1989. pap. write for info. (0-925703-02-8) Crown MA.

— Horoscopes & the Christian. LC 81-18092. 64p. (Orig.). 1981. pap. 3.99 (0-87123-202-2) Bethany Hse.

— How to Answer a Jehovah's Witness. LC 79-25502. 112p. (Orig.). 1980. pap. 5.99 (0-87123-206-5) Bethany Hse.

— How to Answer a Mormon. LC 82-24315. 119p. (Orig.). 1983. pap. 5.99 (0-87123-260-X) Bethany Hse.

— How to Keep Your Faith While in College. 144p. (Orig.). (C). 1989. pap. write for info. (0-925703-03-6) Crown MA.

— How to Keep Your Kids Drug Free. 128p. (Orig.). 1989. pap. write for info. (0-925703-01-X) Crown MA.

— Introduction to Defending the Faith. 2nd ed. 52p. (Orig.). 1989. reprint ed. pap. text ed. write for info. (0-925703-09-5) Crown MA.

— The New Atheism & the Erosion of Freedom. 176p. 1994. reprint ed. pap. 8.99 (0-87552-362-5) Presby & Reformed.

— The Origins & Teachings of Freemasonry. 144p. (Orig.). 1990. pap. write for info. (0-925703-28-1) Crown MA.

— Reincarnation & Christianity. LC 80-24497. 60p. 1980. pap. 3.99 (0-87123-493-9) Bethany Hse.

— Studies in the Atonement. rev. ed. 320p. reprint ed. pap. write for info. (0-925703-07-9) Crown MA.

— When Is It Right to Fight? 1994. reprint ed. pap. 8.99 (0-87552-361-7) Presby & Reformed.

Morey, Shaun. Incredible Fishing Stories. White, Connie S., ed. LC 91-66632. (Illus.). 145p. (Orig.). 1991. pap. 12.95 (0-9633691-0-5) Incrdble Fish.

— Incredible Fishing Stories for Kids. LC 93-77082. (Illus.). 96p. (Orig.). (J). 1993. pap. 11.95 (0-9633691-1-3) Incrdble Fish.

Morey, Shaun, comp. Incredible Fishing Stories: Actual Tales by Real Anglers. LC 94-1329. 1994. pap. 8.95 (1-56305-637-2) Workman Pub.

Morey, Sylvester M., ed. Can the Red Man Help the White Man. LC 80-83370. (Illus.). 130p. (gr. 7-12). 1970. pap. 3.50 (0-913098-35-3) Myrin Institute.

Morey, Sylvester M. & Gilliam, Olivia L., eds. Respect for Life: The Traditional Upbringing of American Indian Children. LC 80-83371. (Illus.). 202p. (gr. 7-12). 1980. reprint ed. pap. text ed. 4.95 (0-913098-34-5) Myrin Institute.

Morey, W. C. Outlines in Roman History. 1972. 59.95 (0-8490-0789-5) Gordon Pr.

Morey, Walt. Angry Waters. (Walt Morey Adventure Library). (YA). (gr. 5-9). 1990. reprint ed. 7.95 (0-936085-10-X) Blue Heron OR.

— Canyon Winter. 208p. (J). (gr. 5 up). 1994. pap. 3.99 (0-14-036856-6) Puffin Bks.

— Death Walk. (Walt Morey Adventure Library). (Illus.). (YA). (gr. 5-12). 1991. 13.95 (0-936085-18-5) Blue Heron OR.

— Death Walk. 176p. (YA). 1993. pap. 7.95 (0-936085-55-X) Blue Heron OR.

— Deep Trouble. (Walt Morey Adventure Library). (YA). (gr. 5-9). 1989. reprint ed. pap. 7.95 (0-936085-15-0) Blue Heron OR.

— Gentle Ben. 192p. (J). (gr. 4 up). 1976. pap. 2.95 (0-380-00743-6, Camelot) Avon.

— Gentle Ben. (Illus.). 192p. (J). (gr. 5 up). 1992. pap. 3.99 (0-14-036035-2, Puffin) Puffin Bks.

— Gloomy Gus. (Walt Morey Adventure Library). 192p. (YA). (gr. 4-8). 1989. reprint ed. pap. 7.95 (0-936085-17-7) Blue Heron OR.

— Hero. 176p. (J). (gr. 3-7). 1995. pap. 3.99 (0-14-037793-X) Puffin Bks.

— Home Is the North. (Walt Morey Adventure Library). (YA). (gr. 4-9). 1989. reprint ed. pap. 7.95 (0-936085-11-8) Blue Heron OR.

— Kavik, the Wolf Dog. LC 68-24727. (Illus.). (J). (gr. 5-9). 1968. 14.95 (0-525-33093-3, DCB) Dutton Child Bks.

— Run Far, Run Fast. (Walt Morey Adventure Library). (YA). (gr. 4-9). 1989. reprint ed. pap. 6.95 (0-936085-16-9) Blue Heron OR.

— Runaway Stallion. (Walt Morey Adventure Library). 176p. (YA). (gr. 4-8). 1989. reprint ed. pap. 6.95 (0-936085-12-6) Blue Heron OR.

— Sandy & the Rock Star. LC 78-12375. (J). (gr. 4-7). 1979. 13.95 (0-525-38785-4, DCB) Dutton Child Bks.

— Scrub Dog of Alaska. (Walt Morey Adventure Library). 160p. (YA). (gr. 4-9). 1989. reprint ed. pap. 6.95 (0-936085-13-4) Blue Heron OR.

— Year of the Black Pony. (Walt Morey Adventure Library). 160p. (YA). (gr. 4-8). 1989. reprint ed. pap. 6.95 (0-936085-14-2) Blue Heron OR.

Morey, William C. Outlines of Roman Law Comprising Its Historical Growth & General Principles. 4th ed. xiii, 433p. 1985. reprint ed. lib. bdg. 35.00 (0-8377-0851-6) Rothman.

Moreyra, A. Manual of Surgical Clearance. (Illus.). 133p. 1989. 20.50 (0-912791-47-0) Ishiyaku Euro.

Morf, Gustav. Polish Heritage of Joseph Conrad. LC 65-26452. (Studies in Conrad: No. 8). 1969. reprint ed. lib. bdg. 75.00 (0-8383-0597-0) M S G Haskell Hse.

Morf, Martin. Optimizing Work Performance: A Look Beyond the Bottom Line. LC 85-23232. 205p. 1986. text ed. 45.00 (0-89930-143-6, MWK/, Quorum Bks) Greenwood.

— The Work-Life Dichotomy: Prospects for Reintegrating People & Jobs. LC 88-35739. 211p. 1989. text ed. 55.00 (0-89930-421-4, MUP/, Quorum Bks) Greenwood.

Morf, W. E. Principles of Ion-Selective Electrodes & of Membrane Transport. (Studies in Analytical Chemistry: Vol. 2). 434p. 1981. 113.00 (0-444-99749-0) Elsevier.

Morfaux, L. M. Vocabulary of Philosophy & Humanist Sciences: Vocabulaire de la Philosophie et des Sciences Humanies. 392p. (FRE.). 1979. reprint ed. 34.95 (0-7859-4857-0) Fr & Eur.

Morfett, John C., jt. auth. see Chadwick, A. J.

Morfett, John C., jt. auth. see Chadwick, Andrew.

Morfi, Fray J. History of Texas, Sixteen Seventy-Three to Seventeen Seventy-Nine, 2 pts. Castaneda, Carlos E., ed. LC 67-24718. (Quivira Society Publications, Vol. 6). 1967. reprint ed. 34.00 (0-405-19053-0) Ayer.

Morfi, Juan A. Excerpts from the Memoirs for the History of the Province of Texas. Chabot, Frederick C., tr. LC 76-43791. (ENG.). reprint ed. write for info. (0-404-15646-0) AMS Pr.

— History of Texas, 1673-1779, 2 vols., Set. 1993. reprint ed. lib. bdg. 180.00 (0-685-62348-3) Rprt Serv.

Morfill, G. E., ed. Dust in Space & Comets: Proceedings of the Topical Meeting of the COSPAR Interdisciplinary Scientific Commission B (Meetings B1 & B2) of the COSPAR 25th Plenary Meeting, Graz, Austria, 25 June-7 July 1984. (Illus.). 324p. 1985. pap. 54.00 (0-08-032745-1, Pub. by PPL UK) Elsevier.

Morfill, G. E. & Buccheri, R., eds. Galactic Astrophysics & Gamma Ray Astronomy. 1983. lib. bdg. 140.00 (90-277-1645-5) Kluwer Ac.

Morfill, W. R. The Book of the Secrets of Enoch. 100p. 1964. reprint ed. spiral bd. 6.60 (0-7873-0622-3) Mokelumne.

Morfill, William R. Poland. LC 75-39494. (Select Bibliographies Reprint Ser.). 1977. reprint ed. 23.95 (0-8369-9919-3) Ayer.

Morfit, Christine A., jt. ed. see Moore, Sarah J.

Morford, Henry. The Days of Shoddy: A Novel of the Great Rebellion in 1861. LC 73-164571. (American Fiction Reprint Ser.). 1977. reprint ed. 35.95 (0-8369-7048-9) Ayer.

Morford, Mark. Stoics & Neostoics: Rubens & the Circle of Lipsius. (Illus.). 256p. 1991. text ed. 45.00 (0-691-04081-8) Princeton U Pr.

***Morford, Mark & Lenardon, Robert.** Classical Mythology. 5th ed. 608p. (C). 1994. text ed. 26.00 (0-8013-1488-7) Longman.

Morford, Mark P. & Lenardon, Robert J. Classical Mythology. 4th ed. 703p. (C). 1991. pap. text ed. 33.95 (0-8013-0465-2, 78280) Longman.

— Classical Mythology. 5th ed. (Illus.). 608p. (C). 1995. pap. text ed. 31.95 (0-8013-1138-1) Longman.

Morford, T. C. Fifty Years Ago: A Brief History of the 29th Regiment New Jersey Volunteers in the Civil War. 60p. (C). 1990. reprint ed. pap. 8.00 (0-944413-16-1) Longstreet Hse.

***Morford, Ted R. & Mauer, Shelley M.** The Job World Instructor's Manual. 86p. 1987. 18.75 (1-55549-012-3) Ed Assocs KY.

— Job World Workbook. 3rd ed. (Job World Ser.). 86p. (Orig.). 1987. 6.75 (1-55549-013-1) Ed Assocs KY.

Morford, V. J. Metals & Welding. rev. ed. (Illus.). 236p. 1987. pap. text ed. 21.30 (0-913163-19-8, 170) Hobar Pubns.

Morford, Wanda L. Switzerland County Indiana Cemetery Inscriptions 1817-1985. LC 86-60482. 520p. 1986. 42.50 (0-9616543-0-9) W L Morford.

Morga, Robert. Magic Cauldron. Templar, Thorguard, ed. (Illus.). 105p. (Orig.). 1994. 9.00 (1-883147-74-3) Intern Guild ASRS.

— Magick of the Demon Ewaz. Templar, Thorguard, ed. (Illus.). 110p. (Orig.). 1994. 16.00 (1-883147-87-5) Intern Guild ASRS.

Morgado, E. M., jt. ed. see Martins, J. P.

Morgado, Martin. Junipero Serra. 1991. pap. 19.95 (0-9627216-0-3) Siempre Adelante.

Morgagni, Giambattista. Clinical Consultations: The Edition of Enrico Benassi (1935) rev. ed. Jarcho, Saul, tr. 450p. 1984. 25.00 (0-317-04057-X) F A Countway.

Morgaite, John-Paul. The Next Step, Pt. II. (Basic Christian Training Ser.). 64p. 1993. pap. 2.50 (1-880322-03-X) Champions Christ.

— Victory Christian Church Membership Manual. 41p. 1991. pap. 5.00 (1-880322-01-3) Champions Christ.

Morgall, Janine M. Technology Assessment: A Feminist Perspective. LC 93-9447. (Labor & Social Change Ser.). 288p. 1993. 39.95 (1-56639-090-7); pap. 18.95 (1-56639-091-5) Temple U Pr.

***Morgan.** Certain Magic. 1995. mass mkt. 5.50 (0-312-95423-9) St Martin.

— Community Mental Health: Practical Approaches to Long-Term Problems. 268p. 1993. pap. 44.75 (1-56593-138-6, 0450) Singular Publishing.

— Foundations of Wave Theory. 140p. 1988. text ed. 55.00 (0-13-330275-X) P-H.

— Home on the Range Cookbook. 1995. 9.97 (1-55748-654-9) Barbour & Co.

— Information Industry Directory, 2 vols. 14th ed. 1993. 495.00 (0-8103-8096-X) Gale.

— Information Industry Directory, 2 vols. 15th ed. (Encyclopedia of Info Systems & Services Ser.). 1994. 495.00 (0-8103-8513-9) Gale.

— Information Industry Directory, Vol. 1. 14th ed. 1993. write for info. (0-8103-8097-8) Gale.

— Information Industry Directory, Vol. 1. 15th ed. (Encyclopedia of Info Systems & Services Ser.). 1994. write for info. (0-8103-8514-7) Gale.

— Information Industry Directory, Vol. 2. 14th ed. 1993. write for info. (0-8103-8098-6) Gale.

— Information Industry Directory: Supplement 14, Vol. 2. 15th ed. (Encyclopedia of Info Systems & Services Ser.). 1993. 335.00 (0-8103-8515-5) Gale.

— Medieval Persia, 1040-1797. (History of the Near East Ser.). (Illus.). 197p. (C). 1988. pap. text ed. 25.95 (0-582-49324-2, 73578) Longman.

— Point Set Theory. (Pure & Applied Mathematics Ser.: Vol. 131). 296p. 1990. 125.00 (0-8247-8178-3) Dekker.

— Scars of Evolution. 1995. 17.95 (0-285-62996-4, Pub. by Souvenir UK) Atrium Pubs.

— Soil Erosion & Conservation. 2nd ed. Date not set. pap. text ed. 39.95 (0-470-23514-4) Wiley.

— Sports Fan's Connection. 2nd ed. 1996. 59.95 (*0-8103-8512-0*) Gale.

— Sports Fan's Connection: 1991. 1991. 62.00 (*0-8103-7954-6*) Gale.

Morgan & Kerr. Louisiana Scenes: The Lower Mississippi Valley. 1962. 14.95 (*0-87511-088-6*) Claitors.

***Morgan & Martorano.** Unmasking PMS: The Complete PMS Medical Treatment Plan. 272p. 1994. pap. text ed. 5.50 (*0-425-14401-1*) Berkley Pub.

Morgan, jt. auth. see Campbell, G.

Morgan, jt. auth. see Rosenbloom, David.

Morgan, tr. see Rubinstein, Anton.

Morgan, jt. auth. see Weinsier, Roland L.

Morgan, et al. What Made Them Great Series, 8 bks., Set. (Illus.). 832p. (J). (gr. 5-8). 1990. lib. bdg. 90.65 (*0-382-09983-4*); pap. 29.75 (*0-382-09984-2*) Silver Burdett Pr.

Morgan, et al, eds. The Public & Private Faces of Welfare: Social Policy in Transition. 1986. text ed. 49.95 (*0-435-82334-5*, Pub. by Dartmth Pub UK) Ashgate Pub Co.

Morgan, A. Daddy-Care. (Illus.). 24p. (J). (ps-8). 1986. 12.95 (*0-920303-58-7*, Pub. by Annick CN); pap. 4.95 (*0-920303-59-5*, Pub. by Annick CN) Firefly Bks Ltd.

— Matthew & the Midnight Money Van. (Illus.). 24p. (J). (ps-8). 1987. lib. bdg. 14.95 (*0-920303-75-7*, Pub. by Annick CN); pap. 4.95 (*0-920303-72-2*, Pub. by Annick CN) Firefly Bks Ltd.

— Matthew & the Midnight Tow Truck. (Illus.). 24p. (J). (ps-8). 1984. lib. bdg. 14.95 (*0-920303-00-5*, Pub. by Annick CN); pap. 4.95 (*0-920303-01-3*, Pub. by Annick CN) Firefly Bks Ltd.

— Matthew & the Midnight Turkeys. (Illus.). 24p. (J). (ps-8). 1985. lib. bdg. 14.95 (*0-920303-36-6*, Pub. by Annick CN); pap. 4.95 (*0-920303-37-4*, Pub. by Annick CN) Firefly Bks Ltd.

— Nicole's Boat. (Illus.). 24p. (J). (ps-8). 1986. 12.95 (*0-920303-60-9*, Pub. by Annick CN); pap. 4.95 (*0-920303-61-7*, Pub. by Annick CN) Firefly Bks Ltd.

Morgan, A. John. X-Ray Microanalysis in Electron Microscopy for Biologists. (Royal Microscopical Society Microscopy Handbooks Ser.). (Illus.). 1986. pap. 11.95 (*0-19-856409-0*) OUP.

Morgan, A. John, jt. auth. see Roos, Norbert.

Morgan, A. M. Forty-One Years with General Motors (& a Little Before & After) 1992. 16.95 (*0-533-09732-0*) Vantage.

Morgan, Adrian, jt. auth. see Morgan, Sally.

Morgan, Adrian, et al. Sail of the Century: America's Cup '87. 128p. 1987. pap. 11.95 (*0-911378-72-3*) Sheridan.

***Morgan, Albert W.** Memories of Old Sunrise: Gold Mining on Alaska's Turnagain Arm 1897-1901. Buzzell, Rolfe G., ed. & intro. by. LC 94-68464. (Illus.). 125p. (Orig.). 1994. pap. 18.95 (*1-878462-01-6*) Cook Inlet Hist Soc.

Morgan, Aled, photos. John Morgan's Wales: A Personal Anthology. (Illus.). 320p. (C). 1992. 69.00 (*0-7154-0686-8*, Pub. by C Davies Pubs) St Mut.

Morgan, Alexander. Vanilla Custard. (Orig.). 1987. pap. 10.00 (*0-912449-23-3*) Floating Island.

Morgan, Alfred. The Boys' First Book of Radio & Electronics. 1993. reprint ed. lib. bdg. 21.95 (*1-56849-181-6*) Buccaneer Bks.

Morgan, Alison. Dante & the Medieval Other World. (Studies in Medieval Literature: No. 8). (Illus.). 288p. (C). 1990. 59.95 (*0-521-36069-2*) Cambridge U Pr.

Morgan, Alistair. Case Study Research in Distance Education. (C). 1991. pap. 24.00x (*0-7300-1349-9*, IDE806, Pub. by Deakin Univ AT) St Mut.

— Improving Your Students' Learning. (Issues in Open & Distance Learning Ser.). 160p. 1993. pap. 32.50 (*0-7494-0712-3*, Pub. by Kogan Page Educ UK) Taylor & Francis.

— Research into Student Learning in Distance Education. (C). 1991. pap. 24.00x (*0-7300-1352-9*, IDE806, Pub. by Deakin Univ AT) St Mut.

Morgan, Allan. Sadie & the Snowman. (Illus.). 32p. (J). (ps-2). 1987. pap. 2.50 (*0-590-41826-2*) Scholastic Inc.

Morgan, Allen. Andrew & the Wild Bikes. (Illus.). 32p. (J). (ps-2). 1990. 12.95 (*1-55037-083-9*, Pub. by Annick CN); pap. 4.95 (*1-55037-082-0*, Pub. by Annick CN) Firefly Bks Ltd.

— Magic Hockey Skates. (J). (ps-3). 1994. pap. 6.95 (*0-19-540851-9*) OUP.

— Mateo y los Pavos de Medianoche: (Matthew & the Midnight Turkeys) Langer, Shirley, tr. (Illus.). 32p. (SPA.). (J). 1991. pap. 5.95 (*1-55037-188-6*, Pub. by Annick CN) Firefly Bks Ltd.

— Matthew & the Midnight Money Van. (Annick Press Ser.: Series 11). (Illus.). 24p. (J). (ps-2). 1991. pap. 0.99 (*1-55037-194-0*, Pub. by Annick CN) Firefly Bks Ltd.

— Matthew & the Midnight Tow Truck. (Annick Press Ser.: Series 11). (Illus.). 24p. (J). (ps-2). 1991. pap. 0.99 (*1-55037-192-4*, Pub. by Annick CN) Firefly Bks Ltd.

— Matthew & the Midnight Turkeys. (Annick Press Ser.: Series 11). (Illus.). 24p. (J). (ps-2). 1991. pap. 0.99 (*1-55037-193-2*, Pub. by Annick CN) Firefly Bks Ltd.

Morgan, Alton C., Jr., jt. ed. see Foon, Kenneth F.

Morgan, Alun. Inn of Fear. 206p. (C). 1989. pap. 29.00 (*0-905928-01-6*, Pub. by D Brown & Sons Ltd UK) St Mut.

— Legends of Porthcawl & the Glamorgan Coast. 120p. (C). 1989. 45.00 (*0-9504475-0-1*, Pub. by D Brown & Sons Ltd UK) St Mut.

— Portcawl, Newton & Nottage: A Concise Illustrated History. 120p. (C). 1989. 59.00 (*0-905928-73-3*, Pub. by D Brown & Sons Ltd UK) St Mut.

— The She-Goblin. 249p. (C). 1989. pap. 35.00 (*1-872808-02-6*, Pub. by D Brown & Sons Ltd UK) St Mut.

Morgan, Alun, ed. The Breakwater. 190p. (C). 1989. pap. 35.00 (*0-9500789-8-0*, Pub. by D Brown & Sons Ltd UK) St Mut.

Morgan, Alun & Horricks, Raymond. Modern Jazz: A Survey of Developments Since 1939. LC 77-8002. 240p. 1977. reprint ed. text ed. 55.00 (*0-8371-9674-4*, MOMO, Greenwood Pr) Greenwood.

Morgan, Alun, jt. auth. see Game, Victor.

Morgan, Alun, ed. see Gammond, Peter & Fox, Charles.

Morgan, Andrew J., ed. The Development of Epstein-Barr Virus Vaccines. (Medical Intelligence Unit Ser.). 126p. 1995. 59.00 (*1-57059-112-1*) R G Landes.

Morgan, Andy, jt. auth. see Nilson, Sue.

Morgan, Ann L., ed. Contemporary Architects. 2nd ed. 1987. 145.00 (*0-912289-26-0*) St James Pr.

— Dear Stieglitz, Dear Love. LC 87-5030. (American Art Ser.). (Illus.). 536p. 1988. 85.00 (*0-87413-292-4*) U Delaware Pr.

— International Contemporary Arts Directory. LC 84-40122. 393p. 1986. 65.00 (*0-312-41995-3*) St Martin.

Morgan, Anne, jt. auth. see High, Steven.

Morgan, Anne H. Robert S. Kerr: The Senate Years. LC 76-62514. (Illus.). 1977. 28.95 (*0-8061-1402-9*); pap. 14.95 (*0-8061-1635-8*) U of Okla Pr.

Morgan, Anne H. & Morgan, H. Wayne. Oklahoma: New Views of the Forty-Sixth State. LC 82-40327. (Illus.). 400p. (C). 1982. 24.95 (*0-8061-1651-X*) U of Okla Pr.

Morgan, Anne H. & Strickland, Rennard. Oklahoma Memories. LC 81-2777. 316p. 1977. pap. 14.95 (*0-8061-1767-2*) U of Okla Pr.

Morgan, Anne H. & Strickland, Rennard, eds. Arizona Memories. LC 84-8853. 354p. 1984. 40.00 (*0-8165-0869-0*) U of Ariz Pr.

Morgan, Anne H., jt. auth. see Morgan, H. Wayne.

Morgan, Annie L. Sunward I've Climbed: A Novel...Based on the True Story of yvette Hamel 7 the 371st Fighter Group. LC 94-6583. (Illus.). 320p. 1994. 22.00 (*1-881320-17-0*) Black Belt Pr.

Morgan, Anthony, jt. auth. see Engelmore, Robert.

***Morgan, Armand.** Drawing Dinosaurs: Activities & Investigations in Paleontology. LC 94-28175. (Museum of Science Book Ser.). (Illus.). 96p. (J). (gr. 5-8). 1995. lib. bdg. 18.90 (*1-56294-517-3*) Millbrook Pr.

Morgan, Arthur. Industries for Small Communities. 1953. 3.00 (*0-910420-19-X*) Comm Serv OH.

— It Can Be Done in Home & Community. 1961. pap. 1.00 (*0-910420-13-0*) Comm Serv OH.

— The Long Road. 1962. 3.50 (*0-910420-08-4*); pap. 2.50 (*0-910420-09-2*) Comm Serv OH.

— Search for Purpose. LC 55-10426. 1957. 5.00 (*0-317-06070-8*) Comm Serv OH.

Morgan, Arthur, jt. auth. see Morgan, Griscom.

Morgan, Arthur, jt. ed. see Morgan, Griscom.

Morgan, Arthur E. Community of the Future & the Future of Community. 1957. pap. 2.00 (*0-910420-02-5*) Comm Serv OH.

— Dams & Other Disasters: A Century of the Army Corps of Engineers in Civil Works. LC 74-172688. (Extending Horizons Ser.). 448p. (C). 1971. 7.50 (*0-87558-066-1*); pap. 3.95 (*0-87558-094-7*) Porter Sargent.

— Great Community. 1946. pap. 1.00 (*0-910420-03-3*) Comm Serv OH.

— Plagiarism in Utopia. 1944. pap. 1.00 (*0-910420-16-5*) Comm Serv OH.

— Scott & His Poetry. LC 79-120980. (Poetry & Life Ser.). reprint ed. 16.00 (*0-404-52526-1*) AMS Pr.

— Tendencies of Modern English Drama. LC 68-29233. (Essay Index Reprint Ser.). 1977. 21.95 (*0-8369-1061-3*) Ayer.

Morgan, Arthur E. & Szantho, Donald Harrington. The Small Community: Foundation of Democratic Life. LC 83-73240. 336p. 1984. reprint ed. pap. 10.00 (*0-910420-28-9*) Comm Serv OH.

Morgan, Arthur N., jt. auth. see LaFarge, Oliver.

Morgan, Austen. Harold Wilson: A Life. 625p. (C). 1992. text ed. 53.50 (*0-7453-0635-7*) Westview.

— James Ramsay MacDonald. (Lives of the Left Ser.). 320p. 1988. text ed. 55.00 (*0-7190-2168-5*, Pub. by Manchester Univ Pr UK) St Martin.

— Labour & Partition: The Belfast Working Class 1905-23. 358p. (C). 1991. text ed. 63.00 (*0-7453-0326-9*) Westview.

Morgan, B. Keyguide to Information Sources in Agricultural Engineering. 216p. 1985. text ed. 90.00 (*0-7201-1720-8*, Mansell Pub) Cassell.

Morgan, B., ed. Photoelectronic Image Devices: Proceedings of the 10th Symposium on Photoelectronic Image Devices, "The McGee Symposium" Held 6 September 1991 at Imperial College. (Institute of Physics Conference Ser.: No. 121). (Illus.). 456p. 1992. 110.00 (*0-85498-411-9*) IOP Pub.

Morgan, B. A., tr. see Von Kleist, Heinrich.

Morgan, B. J. Analysis of Quatal Response Data. (Monographs on Statistics & Applied Probability: No. 44). 250p. 1991. 49.95 (*0-412-31750-8*, A4554) Chapman & Hall.

Morgan, B. J. & North, P. M., eds. Statistics in Ornithology. LC 85-10052. (Lecture Notes in Statistics Ser.: Vol. 29). xxv, 418p. 1985. pap. 59.00 (*0-387-96189-5*) Spr-Verlag.

Morgan, B. Q., tr. see Goethe, Johann Wolfgang Von.

Morgan, Barbara. Martha Graham: Sixteen Dances in Photographs. rev. ed. LC 80-81766. (Illus.). 168p. 1980. reprint ed. 125.00 (*0-87100-176-4*, 2176) Morgan.

— Prints, Drawings, Watercolors & Photographs. LC 88-62482. (Illus.). 128p. 1988. pap. 35.00 (*0-87100-261-2*) Morgan.

Morgan, Barbara, ed. Photomontage: Barbara Morgan. LC 80-81142. 64p. (Orig.). 1980. pap. 15.00 (*0-87100-171-3*) Morgan.

Morgan, Barbara, jt. auth. see Green Group Staff.

Morgan, Barbara K. Desserts. 36p. (Orig.). 1989. pap. 2.75 (*0-940844-33-8*) Wellspring.

— Potatoes. 36p. (Orig.). 1990. pap. 2.75 (*0-940844-37-0*) Wellspring.

Morgan, Bessie C. New Directions in Healthful Cooking: A Guide to Low Fat, Low Sodium Low Cholesterol Eating. Renkoski, Angela, ed. (Illus.). 80p. (Orig.). 1988. pap. write for info. (*0-9621450-0-9*) DSK International.

Morgan, Beth, ed. see Bordeaux, Darlene B.

Morgan, Beth, jt. ed. see Eidenbach, Peter L.

Morgan, Betsy & Jackson, Laura, eds. Going Home: Building Peace in El Salvador - The Story of Repatriation. LC 91-10917. (Illus.). 160p. (Orig.). 1991. pap. 17.50 (*0-945257-21-X*) Apex Pr.

Morgan, Betty. The Professional Manicure Bible. (Illus.). 300p. 1985. text ed. write for info. (*0-318-60426-4*); pap. text ed. 45.00 (*0-936789-01-8*) Ramif Hl.

Morgan, Bill. Incredible Captures. (J). (gr. 4-7). 1993. pap. 2.95 (*0-590-47142-2*) Scholastic Inc.

— The Magic: Earvin Johnson. (J). 1992. 2.95 (*0-590-46050-1*, 063) Scholastic Inc.

— The Works of Allen Ginsberg, 1941-1994: A Descriptive Bibliography. LC 94-41266. (Bibliographies & Indexes in American Literature Ser.: Vol. 19). 457p. 1995. text ed. 75.00 (*0-313-29389-9*, Greenwood Pr) Greenwood.

Morgan, Bradley. Education Career Directory: A Practical, One-Step Guide to Getting a Job in the Field of Education. 335p. 1994. pap. (*0-8103-9493-6*) Gale.

Morgan, Bradley, Jr. Film & Video Career Directory. 1994. pap. 17.95 (*0-8103-9492-8*) Gale.

Morgan, Bradley. Performing Arts Career Directory. 1994. pap. 17.95 (*0-8103-9491-X*) Gale.

— Physical Science Career Directory. 1994. pap. 17.95 (*0-8103-9494-4*) Gale.

— Public Administration Career Directory: A Practical, One-Step Guide to Getting a Job in Public Administration. (Career Advisory Ser.). 315p. 1994. pap. 17.95 (*0-8103-9495-2*) Gale.

Morgan, Bradley J. Healthcare Career Directory - Nurses & Physicians. Dupuis, Diane, ed. (Career Advisor Ser.). 1993. pap. 17.95 (*0-8103-9437-5*, 089146) Visible Ink Pr.

— Magazine Careers Directory. 5th ed. Dupuis, Diane, ed. (Career Advisor Ser.). 1993. pap. 17.95 (*0-8103-9440-5*, 089143) Visible Ink Pr.

— Newspapers Career Directory. 4th ed. Dupuis, Diane, ed. (Career Advisor Ser.). 1990. pap. 17.95 (*0-8103-9438-3*, 089142) Visible Ink Pr.

— Public Relations Career Directory: A Practical One-Stop Guide to Getting a Job in Public Relations. 5th ed. Dupuis, Diane, ed. (Career Advisor Ser.). 1993. pap. 17.95 (*0-8103-9439-1*, 089141) Visible Ink Pr.

— Radio Television Career Directory: A Practical One-Stop Guide to Getting a Job. Dupuis, Diane, ed. (Career Advisor Ser.). 1993. pap. 17.95 (*0-8103-9441-3*, 089144) Visible Ink Pr.

Morgan, Bradley J., ed. Advertising Career Directory. 5th ed. (Career Advisor Ser.). 300p. 1992. pap. 39.00 (*0-8103-5606-6*, 101578) Visible Ink Pr.

— Book Publishing Career Directory. 5th ed. (Career Advisor Ser.). 300p. 1992. pap. text ed. 39.00 (*0-8103-5611-2*, 101583) Visible Ink Pr.

— Business & Finance Career Directory. 2nd ed. (Career Advisor Ser.). 300p. 1992. 39.00 (*0-8103-5604-X*, 101576) Gale.

— Healthcare Career Directory - Nurses & Physicians: A Practical One-Stop Guide to Getting a Job in Public Relations. 2nd ed. (Career Advisor Ser.). 300p. 1993. 39.00 (*0-8103-5613-9*, 101585) Gale.

— Magazines Career Directory: A Practical One-Stop Guide to Getting a Job in Public Relations. 5th ed. (Career Advisor Ser.). 300p. 1993. text ed. 39.00 (*0-8103-5610-4*, 101582) Gale.

— Marketing & Sales Career Directory. 4th ed. (Career Advisor Ser.). 300p. 1992. pap. 39.00 (*0-8103-5609-0*, 101581) Visible Ink Pr.

— Newspapers Career Directory: A Practical One-Stop Guide to Getting a Job in Newspaper Publishing. 4th ed. (Career Advisor Ser.). 300p. 1993. 39.00 (*0-8103-5608-2*, 101580) Gale.

— Public Relations Career Directory: A Practical One-Stop Guide to Getting a Job in Public Relations. 5th ed. (Career Advisor Ser.). 300p. 1993. 39.00 (*0-8103-5607-4*, 101579) Gale.

— Radio & Television Career Directory: A Practical One-Stop Guide to Getting a Job in Public Relations. 2nd ed. (Career Advisor Ser.). 300p. 1993. 39.00 (*0-8103-5612-0*, 101584) Gale.

— Travel & Hospitality Career Directory. 2nd ed. (Career Advisor Ser.). 300p. 1992. pap. 39.00 (*0-8103-5605-8*, 101577) Visible Ink Pr.

Morgan, Bradley J. & Palmisano, Joseph M., eds. Computing & Software Career Directory. (Career Advisor Ser.). 300p. 1993. 39.00 (*0-8103-9152-X*, 101797) Gale.

— Computing & Software Career Directory. (Career Advisor Ser.). 300p. 1993. pap. 17.95 (*0-8103-9448-0*, 089162) Visible Ink Pr.

— Education Career Directory. (Career Advisor Ser.). 300p. 1994. 39.00 (*0-8103-9158-9*, M89334-101793) Gale.

— Environmental Career Directory. (Career Advisor Ser.). 300p. 1993. 39.00 (*0-8103-9153-8*, 101798) Gale.

— Environmental Career Directory. (Career Advisor Ser.). 300p. 1993. pap. 17.95 (*0-8103-9447-2*, 089163) Visible Ink Pr.

— Healthcare Career Directory - Allied Health. (Career Advisor Ser.). 300p. 1993. 39.00 (*0-8103-9155-4*, 101800) Gale.

— Healthcare Career Directory - Allied Health. (Career Advisor Ser.). 300p. 1993. pap. 17.95 (*0-8103-9449-9*, 089167) Visible Ink Pr.

— Healthcare Career Directory - Medical-Technical. (Career Advisor Ser.). 300p. 1993. 39.00 (*0-8103-9154-6*, 101799) Gale.

— Healthcare Career Directory - Medical-Technical. (Career Advisor Ser.). 300p. 1993. pap. 17.95 (*0-8103-9446-4*) Visible Ink Pr.

— Performing Arts Career Directory. (Career Advisor Ser.). 300p. 1994. 39.00 (*0-8103-9160-0*, M89334-101795) Gale.

— Physical Sciences Career Directory. (Career Advisor Ser.). 300p. 1994. 39.00 (*0-8103-9157-0*, M89334-101792) Gale.

— Psychology & Social Work Career Directory. (Career Advisor Ser.). 300p. 1993. 39.00 (*0-8103-9156-2*, 101801) Gale.

— Psychology & Social Work Career Directory. (Career Advisor Ser.). 300p. 1993. pap. 17.95 (*0-8103-9445-6*, 089164) Visible Ink Pr.

— Public Administration Career Directory. (Career Advisor Ser.). 300p. 1994. 39.00 (*0-8103-9161-9*, M89334-101796) Gale.

Morgan, Bradley J., et al, eds. Film & Video Career Directory: A Practical, One-Step Guide to Getting a Job in Film and Video. (Career Advisor Ser.). 300p. 1994. 39.00 (*0-8103-9159-7*, M89334-101794) Gale.

Morgan, Brandt. The Santa Fe & Taos Book: A Complete Guide. rev. ed. LC 94-1511. (Orig.). 1994. pap. 16.95 (*0-936399-59-7*) Berkshire Hse.

Morgan, Brandt, jt. auth. see Brown, Tom, Jr.

Morgan, Brian, jt. auth. see Campbell, Malcolm.

Morgan, Brian, jt. auth. see Levy, Lawrence.

Morgan, Brian, jt. auth. see Morgan, Roberta.

Morgan, Brian, jt. auth. see Wheatley, Richard C.

Morgan, Brian L. Advances in Electronics & Electron Physics: Ninth Symposium on Photo-Electronic Image Devices, Vol. 74. Hawkes, Peter W., ed. 508p. 1988. text ed. 176.00 (*0-12-014674-6*) Acad Pr.

— Nutrition Prescription. 1988. mass mkt. 4.95 (*0-449-21671-3*) Fawcett.

Morgan, Brian L., ed. Advances in Electronics & Electron Physics, Vol. 64A. (Serial Publication Ser.). 1985. text ed. 222.00 (*0-12-014664-9*) Acad Pr.

Morgan, Brian L. G. & Morgan, Roberta. Nutri-Tips. 204p. (Orig.). 1992. pap. 7.95 (*0-681-41184-8*) Longmeadow Pr.

Morgan, Buford. Quest for Quivera: Coronado's Exploration into Southern U. S. 189p. (YA). (gr. 10 up). 1990. 15.95 (*0-89992-425-5*); pap. 9.95 (*0-89992-125-6*) Coun India Ed.

Morgan, Burton D. Mackinac to Miami: Exploring the Mississippi River. (Illus.). 96p. 1983. 45.00 (*0-9609310-1-5*) Summit Pub OH.

— Start at the Top. (Illus.). 131p. (C). 1982. 14.95 (*0-9609310-0-7*) Summit Pub OH.

Morgan, C. Lloyd. Habit & Instinct. LC 73-2978. (Classics in Psychology Ser.). 1977. reprint ed. 25.95 (*0-405-05150-6*) Ayer.

— Introduction to Comparative Psychology, Vol. 2. LC 77-72191. (Contributions to the History of Psychology Ser.: Pt. D, Vol. II, Comparative Psychology). 240p. 1977. reprint ed. text ed. 65.00 (*0-313-26946-7*, U6946, Greenwood Pr) Greenwood.

Morgan, C. W. Morgan: A History of That Branch of the Morgan Family Beginning with James of New London & Continued Through Line of Col. Samuel & Sybil Huntington Morgan of Weathersfield, VT to 1911. 100p. 1991. reprint ed. pap. 15.00 (*0-8328-1756-2*) Higginson Bk Co.

Morgan, Campbell G. The Westminster Pulpits: The Preaching of G. Campbell Morgan, 10 vols., Set. 1992. 139.99 (*0-8010-6155-5*) Baker Bk.

Morgan-Capner, Peter, ed. Current Topics in Clinical Virology. (Public Health Laboratory Service Publication Ser.). 320p. (C). 1992. pap. 54.95 (*0-521-42710-X*) Cambridge U Pr.

Morgan, Carl H. The Layperson's Introduction to the New Testament. rev. ed. 1990. pap. 9.00 (*0-8170-1162-5*) Judson.

Morgan, Carol, jt. auth. see Byram, Michael.

Morgan, Carol E., ed. see Aptheker, Herbert.

Morgan, Carol J. Managing for Success. 54p. (C). 1994. pap. text ed. 16.50 (*0-03-007482-7*) Dryden Pr.

Morgan, Carol M. & Levy, Doran J. Segmenting the Mature Market: Identifying, Targeting & Reaching America's Diverse, Booming Senior Markets. 300p. 1993. 32.50 (*1-55738-448-7*) Probus Pub Co.

Morgan, Carroll. Programming from Specifications. 2nd ed. LC 94-6077. (International Series in Computer Science). 340p. 1994. pap. text ed. 40.00 (*0-13-123274-6*) P-H.

— Using Robots. 250p. 1985. 79.00 (*0-387-12584-1*) Spr-Verlag.

Morgan, Carroll & Vickers, Trevor, eds. On the Refinement Calculus. LC 92-40591. (Formal Applications of Computing & Information Technology Ser.). 1994. 49.00 (*0-387-19809-1*) Spr-Verlag.

Morgan, Carroll & Woodcock, J. C., eds. Refinement Workshop, Third: Organised by the Programming Research Group, Oxford & IBM UK Laboratories, Hursley Park, 9-11 January 1990. (Workshops in Computing Ser.). viii, 199p. 1991. pap. 39.00 (*0-387-19624-2*) Spr-Verlag.

Morgan, Catherine. Athletes & Oracles: The Transformation of Olympia & Delphi in the Eighth Century B. C. (Illus.). 270p. (C). 1990. 54.95 (*0-521-37451-0*) Cambridge U Pr.

Morgan, Catrin. Comfort Me with Apples. large type ed. (Magna General Fiction Ser.). 423p. 1992. 21.95 (*0-7505-0268-1*) Ulverscroft.

— Lily among Thorns. large type ed. 1993. 18.95 (*0-7505-0266-5*, Pub. by Magna Print Bks) Ulverscroft.

An Asterisk (*) at the beginning of an entry indicates that the title is appearing in BIP for the first time.

— Lily of the Valleys. large type ed. 1993. 18.95 (*0-7505-0264-9*, Pub. by Magna Print Bks) Ulverscroft.

***Morgan, Cecil.** The First Constitution of the State of Louisiana. fac. ed. LC 76-354043. (Historic New Orleans Collection Monograph Ser.). (Illus.). 147p. 1975. reprint ed. pap. 41.90 (*0-7837-7811-2*, 2047567) Bks Demand.

Morgan, Charles. Challenge to Venus. 240p. 1989. pap. 3.95 (*0-345-35882-1*) Ballantine.

— Experiments in Biology. 64p. (C). 1992. student ed 18.29 (*1-56870-025-3*) RonJon Pub.

— The Fountain. 408p. 1987. mass mkt. 4.95 (*0-345-34549-5*) Ballantine.

— My Name Is Legion. (Literature Ser.). 346p. 1972. reprint ed. 39.00 (*0-403-01115-9*) Scholarly.

Morgan, Charles, ed. see Bellows, George.

Morgan, Charles J., jt. auth. see Siegel, Andrew F.

***Morgan, Charles O., Jr.** Down-to-Earth Jesus. (Illus.). 192p. (Orig.). 1995. pap. 12.99 (*0-8007-5553-7*) Revell.

Morgan, Charles R. Gate of Hope. LC 88-63172. 230p. (Orig.). 1989. pap. 7.95 (*0-922753-01-6*) Pinnacle MO.

Morgan, Charlie. Earthworm Feeds & Feeding. 1978. pap. 6.00 (*0-914116-02-9*) Shields.

— Earthworm Selling & Shipping Guide. 1978. pap. 5.00 (*0-914116-01-0*) Shields.

— How to Raise, Store & Sell Nightcrawlers. 1984. pap. 4.00 (*0-914116-17-7*) Shields.

— Manual of Therapeutic Medications & Pesticides for Worm Growers. (Illus.). 1979. pap. 7.50 (*0-914116-16-9*) Shields.

— Profitable Earthworm Farming. 1975. pap. 6.00 (*0-914116-06-1*) Shields.

— Raising the African Nightcrawler. 1978. pap. 5.00 (*0-9600102-9-7*) Shields.

— The Worm Farm. 1962. pap. 5.00 (*0-914116-00-2*) Shields.

Morgan, Charlotte E. Origin & History of the New York Employing Printers' Association. LC 68-58608. (Columbia University. Studies in the Social Sciences: No. 319). reprint ed. 15.00 (*0-404-51319-0*) AMS Pr.

Morgan, Cheryl. Dangerous Innocence. 137p. (Orig.). 1988. pap. 7.50 (*0-943487-09-9*) Sevgo Pr.

Morgan, Cheryl K. The Everglades. LC 89-5175. (Let's Take a Trip Ser.). (Illus.). 32p. (J). (gr. 3-6). 1990. lib. bdg. 10.79 (*0-8167-1733-8*); pap. text ed. 2.95 (*0-8167-1734-6*) Troll Assocs.

***Morgan, Chester M.** Redneck Liberal: Theodore G. Bilbo & the New Deal. LC 85-11023. 288p. 1985. pap. 82.10 (*0-7837-8516-X*, 2049325) Bks Demand.

Morgan, Chris. Future Man. (Illus.). 208p. 1979. 19.00 (*0-8290-0144-1*) Irvington.

— Future Man. (Illus.). 208p. 1987. reprint ed. pap. 6.95 (*0-8290-2117-5*) Irvington.

— Handwriting Analysis. (Illus.). 80p. 1993. 9.98 (*0-8317-4205-4*) Smithmark.

Morgan, Chris & Patient, Matthew. Auditing Investment Businesses. 1989. U.K. pap. 101.00 (*0-406-53109-9*) Butterworth Legal Pubs.

Morgan, Christopher. The Fire Jump & Other Poems. 79p. (C). 1989. 40.00 (*0-9502723-6-1*, Pub. by Brynmill Pr Ltd UK) St Mut.

— Muscle Bound. (Orig.). 1992. pap. 4.95 (*1-56333-028-8*) Masquerade.

***Morgan, Christopher, ed.** Sportsmen. (Orig.). Date not set. mass mkt., pap. 5.95 (*1-56333-385-6*) Masquerade.

Morgan, Christopher, jt. auth. see Van Devanter, Lynda.

Morgan, Claire. The Price of Salt. LC 75-12340. (Homosexuality Ser.). 1979. reprint ed. 19.95 (*0-405-07384-4*) Ayer.

***Morgan, Clay.** Idaho Unbound: A Scrapbook & Guide. Mitchell, Steve, ed. (Illus.). 240p. (Orig.). 1995. pap. 19.95 (*1-887504-00-1*) West Bound.

— Santiago & the Drinking Party. (Contemporary American Fiction Ser.). 288p. 1993. reprint ed. pap. 10.00 (*0-14-016732-3*, Penguin Bks) Viking Penguin.

Morgan, Clay & Bly, Steve. Boise: The City & the People. (Illus.). 112p. (Orig.). 1993. 22.95 (*1-56037-053-X*) Am Wrld Geog.

Morgan, Cleona. Daniel Meets a Lion. 1993. pap. 2.95 (*0-88494-885-4*) Bookcraft Inc.

Morgan, Clifford T., et al. How to Study. 3rd ed. (Illus.). 1979. pap. text ed. 5.95 (*0-07-043115-9*) McGraw.

Morgan, Colin & Murgatroyd, Stephen. Total Quality Management in the Public Sector: An International Perspective. LC 93-24014. 208p. 1994. 85.00 (*0-335-19103-7*, Open Univ Pr); pap. 29.50 (*0-335-19102-9*, Open Univ Pr) Taylor & Francis.

Morgan, Colin, jt. auth. see Murgatroyd, Stephen.

Morgan, Colin, jt. auth. see Riches, Colin.

Morgan, Colin, et al. A Handbook on Selecting Senior Staff for Schools. 136p. 1984. pap. 41.00 (*0-335-10596-3*, Open Univ Pr) Taylor & Francis.

— The Selection of Secondary School Headteachers. 192p. 1983. pap. 32.00 (*0-335-10410-X*, Open Univ Pr) Taylor & Francis.

Morgan, Conwy L. Emergent Evolution. 2nd ed. LC 77-27209. (Gifford Lectures: 1922). reprint ed. 42.50 (*0-404-60468-4*) AMS Pr.

— Life, Mind & Spirit. LC 77-27207. (Gifford Lectures: 1923). reprint ed. 32.50 (*0-404-60473-0*) AMS Pr.

Morgan, Cynthia. If You Love Somebody Who Smokes: Confessions of a Nicotine Addict. LC 87-71061. 112p. (Orig.). 1987. pap. 5.95 (*0-933944-14-4*) City Miner Bks.

Morgan, D., jt. auth. see Pearce, David.

Morgan, D. J., jt. ed. see Wickramasinghe, Nalin C.

Morgan, D. Lloyd, tr. see Nordenskiold, Gustaf E.

Morgan, D. P. Surface-Wave Devices for Signal Processing. LC 85-10330. (Studies in Electrical & Electronic Engineering: No. 19). 432p. 1985. 133.50 (*0-444-42511-X*) Elsevier.

— Surface-Wave Devices for Signal Processing. (Studies in Electrical & Electronic Engineering: No. 19). 432p. 1990. reprint ed. pap. 59.50 (*0-444-88845-4*) Elsevier.

Morgan, D. V. & Board, K. An Introduction to Semiconductor Microtechnology. 2nd ed. 208p. 1990. pap. text ed. 54.95 (*0-471-92478-4*) Wiley.

Morgan, D. V., jt. ed. see Howes, M. J.

Morgan, Dale, ed. Overland in Eighteen Forty-Six: Diaries & Letters of the California-Oregon Trail, 2 vols. LC 93-8247. 475p. 1993. 90.00 (*0-8032-3178-4*); pap. 29.90 (*0-8032-8202-8*) U of Nebr Pr.

— Overland in Eighteen Forty-Six: Diaries & Letters of the California-Oregon Trail, 2 vols., 1. LC 93-8247. 475p. 1993. 45.00 (*0-8032-3176-8*) U of Nebr Pr.

— Overland in Eighteen Forty-Six: Diaries & Letters of the California-Oregon Trail, 2 vols., 2. LC 93-8247. vii, 368p. 1993. 45.00 (*0-8032-3177-6*) U of Nebr Pr.

— Overland in Eighteen Forty-Six: Diaries & Letters of the California-Oregon Trail, 2 vols., Vol. 1. LC 93-8247. 475p. 1993. pap. 14.95 (*0-8032-8200-1*) U of Nebr Pr.

— Overland in Eighteen Forty-Six: Diaries & Letters of the California-Oregon Trail, 2 vols., Vol. 2. LC 93-8247. vii, 368p. 1993. pap. 14.95 (*0-8032-8201-X*) U of Nebr Pr.

Morgan, Dale L. Dale Morgan on Early Mormonism: Correspondence & a New History. Walker, John P., ed. LC 86-60251. 413p. 1986. 25.95 (*0-941214-36-2*) Prometheus Bks.

— The Great Salt Lake. (Illus.). 440p. 1995. pap. 14.95 (*0-87480-478-7*) U of Utah Pr.

— The Humboldt: Highroad of the West. LC 85-8108. (Illus.). viii, 374p. 1985. reprint ed. pap. 8.95 (*0-8032-8128-5*, Bison Books) U of Nebr Pr.

— Humboldt, Highroad of the West. LC 70-146867. (Select Bibliographies Reprint Ser.). 1977. 26.95 (*0-8369-5634-6*) Ayer.

— Jedediah Smith & the Opening of the West. LC 53-10550. (Illus.). 468p. 1964. pap. 11.95 (*0-8032-5138-6*, Bison Books) U of Nebr Pr.

— The State of Deseret. LC 87-21632. 215p. reprint ed. pap. 61.30 (*0-7837-7063-4*, 2046875) Bks Demand.

Morgan, Dale L., ed. see Anderson, William M.

Morgan, Dan. Rising in the West: An "Okie" Family & the Origins of the New Populism. LC 89-445314. (Illus.). 512p. 1992. 24.50 (*0-394-57453-2*) Knopf.

— Rising in the West: The True Story of an "Okie" Family in Search of the American Dream. LC 93-13115. 1993. pap. 15.00 (*0-679-74593-9*, Vin) Random.

Morgan, Daniel C. Retail Sales Tax: An Appraisal of New Issues. (Illus.). 204p. 1964. 14.00 (*0-299-03100-4*) U of Wis Pr.

Morgan, Daniel P. & Jenson, William R. Teaching Behaviorally Disordered Students: Preferred Practices. 480p. (C). 1988. write for info. (*0-675-20543-3*, Merrill Pub Co) Macmillan.

Morgan, Dave. Door Slammers: The Chassis Book. (Illus.). 188p. (Orig.). reprint ed. pap. 30.00 (*0-9631217-0-7*) Lamplighter MI.

Morgan, David. The Capitol Press Corps: Newsmen & the Governing of New York State. LC 77-84771. (Contributions in Political Science Ser.: No. 2). 177p. 1978. text ed. 49.95 (*0-8371-9883-6*, MCP/, Greenwood Pr) Greenwood.

— Discovering Men. 240p. 1992. 39.95 (*0-04-445599-2*, A8163); pap. 15.95 (*0-04-445598-4*, A8164) Routledge Chapman & Hall.

— The Flacks of Washington: Government Information & the Public Agenda. LC 85-5577. (Contributions in Political Science Ser.: No.137). (Illus.). 176p. 1986. text ed. 49.95 (*0-313-24856-7*, MFW/, Greenwood Pr) Greenwood.

— A Handbook of EMC Testing & Measurement. (IEE Electrical Measurement Ser.: No. 8). 320p. 1994. 149.00 (*0-86341-262-9*, Pub. by Peregrinus UK) Inst Elect Eng.

— The Mongols. 256p. 1987. 24.95 (*0-631-13556-1*) Blackwell Pubs.

— Mongols. 1990. pap. 21.95 (*0-631-17563-6*) Blackwell Pubs.

— Whips & Whipmaking: With a Practical Introduction to Braiding. LC 72-78240. (Illus.). 144p. 1972. pap. 9.95 (*0-87033-270-8*) Cornell Maritime.

Morgan, David & Benton, J. Edwin, eds. Intergovernmental Relations & Public Policy. 208p. (Orig.). 1985. pap. 12.00 (*0-918592-82-8*) Pol Studies.

Morgan, David & Evans, Mary. The Battle for Britain: Citizenship & Ideology in the Second World War. LC 92-11717. 1993. 62.50 (*0-415-01722-X*, A5913) Routledge.

Morgan, David & Stanley, Liz, eds. Challenge & Change: Debates in Sociology, 1967 to 1992. LC 92-36829. 1993. text ed. 59.95 (*0-7190-3830-8*, Pub. by Manchester Univ Pr UK); text ed. 19.95 (*0-7190-3831-6*, Pub. by Manchester Univ Pr UK) St Martin.

Morgan, David, jt. ed. see Scott, Sue.

Morgan, David H., jt. auth. see Hearn, Jeff.

Morgan, David J. The Mississippi River Delta: Legal-Geomorphologic Evaluation of Historic Shoreline Changes. (Geoscience & Man Ser.: Vol. 16). 196p. 1977. pap. 15.00 (*0-938909-15-0*) Geosci Pubns LSU.

— Patterns of Population Distribution: A Residential Preference Model & Its Dynamic. LC 78-18794. (Research Papers Ser.: No. 176). (Illus.). 1978. pap. 12.00 (*0-89065-083-7*) U Chicago Comm Geo.

Morgan, David L. Focus Groups As Qualitative Research. (Qualitative Research Methods Ser.: Vol. 16). 96p. (C). 1988. text ed. 21.50 (*0-8039-3208-1*); pap. text ed. 9.50 (*0-8039-3209-X*) Sage.

Morgan, David L., ed. Successful Focus Groups: Advancing the State of the Art. LC 93-6872. (Focus Editions Ser.: Vol. 156). (Illus.). 320p. (C). 1993. text ed. 49.95 (*0-8039-4873-5*); pap. text ed. 24.95 (*0-8039-4874-3*) Sage.

Morgan, David P. & Scofield, Christopher L. Neural Networks & Speech Processing. (International Series in Engineering & Computer Science, VLSI, Computer Architecture, & Digital Screen Processing). 416p. (C). 1991. lib. bdg. 86.00 (*0-7923-9144-6*) Kluwer Ac.

Morgan, David R., ed. Urban Management. LC 72-8662. 183p. 1973. text ed. 34.50 (*0-8422-5065-4*); pap. text ed. 9.95 (*0-8422-0249-8*) Irvington.

Morgan, David R. & Caddy, David. Almost Alchemy. 52p. (C). 1988. 75.00 (*0-947612-31-9*, Pub. by Rivelin Grapheme Pr) St Mut.

***Morgan, David R. & England, Robert E.** Managing Urban America. 4th ed. (Illus.). 368p. (C). 1995. pap. text ed. 29.95x (*1-56643-019-4*) Chatham Hse Pubs.

Morgan, David R. & Kirkpatrick, Samuel A. Urban Political Analysis. LC 74-156838. 1972. 24.95 (*0-02-922060-2*) Free Pr.

Morgan, David R., jt. ed. see Benton, J. Edwin.

Morgan, David R., et al. Oklahoma Politics & Policies: Governing the Sooner State. LC 90-13044. (Politics & Governments of the American States Ser.). (Illus.). xxviii, 264p. 1991. 35.00 (*0-8032-3106-7*); pap. 15.95 (*0-8032-8136-6*) U of Nebr Pr.

***Morgan, David T.** The New Crusades, the New Holy Land: The Southern Baptist Convention, 1969-1991. LC 95-12245. 1996. write for info. (*0-8173-0804-0*) U of Ala Pr.

Morgan, David T., ed. The John Gray Blount Papers, Vol. 4, 1803-1833. (Illus.). xxxiv, 662p. 1982. 28.00 (*0-86526-189-X*) NC Archives.

Morgan, David T. & Stafford, C. Russell, eds. Early Late Woodland Occupations in the Fall Creek Locality of the Mississippi Valley. LC 87-6584. (Kampsville Archeological Center Technical Reports: No. 3). (Illus.). 145p. (Orig.). 1987. pap. 7.95 (*0-942118-26-X*) Ctr Amer Arche.

Morgan, David W. The Socialist Left & the German Revolution: A History of the German Independent Social Democratic Party, 1917-1922. LC 75-5393. 520p. 1975. 59.95 (*0-8014-0851-2*) Cornell U Pr.

Morgan, Deborah & Engler, Nick. How to Build Outdoor Structures. (Popular Science Ser.). 416p. (Orig.). 1988. pap. 21.95 (*0-8069-6742-0*) Sterling.

Morgan, Dennis. The Cardiff Story. 272p. (C). 1989. 90.00 (*0-685-61446-8*, Pub. by D Brown & Sons Ltd UK) St Mut.

— Life in Process. 1993. 9.99 (*1-56476-125-8*, Victor Books) SP Pubns.

Morgan, Dennis L. The Complete Guide to Marketing a Small Business or Product Successfully. 269p. (Orig.). 1993. 29.95 (*0-9640823-0-6*) Morgan Mktg.

Morgan, Derec L. Kate Roberts. v, 69p. 1991. pap. 9.95 (*0-7083-1115-6*, Pub. by U of Wales UK) Bks Intl VA.

Morgan, Derek, ed. Personal Injury. (C). 1991. text ed. 22.00 (*1-85431-133-6*, Pub. by Blackstone Pr UK) W W Gaunt.

Morgan, Derek & Lee, Robert G., eds. Blackstone's Guide to the Human Fertilisation & Embryology Act 1990: Abortion & Embryo Research, the New Law. 276p. (C). 1991. text ed. 33.00 (*1-85431-105-0*, Pub. by Blackstone Pr UK) W W Gaunt.

***Morgan, Derek & Stephenson, Geoffrey, eds.** Suspicion & Silence: The Right to Silence in Criminal Investigations. 1994. text ed. 38.00 (*1-85431-380-0*, Pub. by Blackstone Pr UK) W W Gaunt.

Morgan, Derek, jt. ed. see Lee, Robert.

Morgan, Diana. Chapel Hill. 256p. (Orig.). 1992. mass mkt. 4.99 (*0-446-35771-5*) Warner Bks.

— The Lost Years. large type ed. (General Ser.). 464p. 1993. 21.95 (*0-7089-2882-X*) Ulverscroft.

Morgan, Diane. Understanding Your Horse's Lameness. LC 92-13128. (Illus.). 152p. 1992. 19.95 (*0-939481-26-X*) Half Halt Pr.

Morgan, Diane, et al. The Basic Gourmet: One Hundred Foolproof Recipes & Essential Techniques for the Beginning Cook. LC 94-18470. (Illus.). 1994. 15.95 (*0-8118-0476-3*) Chronicle Bks.

— Very Entertaining: Menus for Special Occasions. Lustburg, Lynn, ed. LC 89-81843. (Illus.). 174p. (Orig.). 1990. pap. 19.95 (*0-9620937-1-8*) Entertaining People.

Morgan, Don. Practical DSP Modeling, Techniques & PRogramming in C. 1994. pap. text ed. 36.95 (*0-471-00606-8*) Wiley.

— Practical DSP Modeling, Techniques, & Programming in C. 1994. text ed. 49.95 (*0-471-00434-0*) Wiley.

— Practical DSP Modeling, Techniques, & Programming in C. 1994. text ed. 13.00 (*0-471-00613-0*) Wiley.

Morgan, Don, jt. auth. see Lacy, Madison S.

Morgan, Donald G. Congress & the Constitution: A Study of Responsibility. LC 66-18252. 506p. reprint ed. pap. 144.30 (*0-317-09466-1*, 2005245) Bks Demand.

Morgan, Donald P. Recognition & Management of Pesticide Poisonings. 4th ed. 218p. 1993. 49.95 (*0-912702-81-8*) Global Eng Doc.

— Recognition & Management of Pesticide Poisonings. 4th ed. (Illus.). 217p. 1990. per. 8.00 (*0-16-021031-3*, S/N 055-000-00359-9) USGPO.

Morgan, Donn F. Between Text & Community. LC 89-37528. 176p. 1990. pap. 13.00 (*0-8006-2406-8*, 1-2406) Augsburg Fortress.

Morgan, Dorothy H. When Servants Ride Horses: One Version of the David Dickson Story. rev. ed. (Illus.). 208p. (Orig.). 1992. Perfect bdg. per. 15.00 (*0-9632936-0-5*) D H Morgan.

Morgan, E. B., jt. auth. see Andrews, C. F.

Morgan, E. David, jt. ed. see Mandava, N. Bhushan.

Morgan, Ed. Chemometrics: Experimental Design. (Analytical Chemistry by Open Learning Ser.). 275p. 1991. text ed. 74.95 (*0-471-92903-4*) Wiley.

Morgan, Edith, jt. auth. see Jasper, James M.

Morgan, Edith, jt. auth. see Jasper, James.

Morgan, Edmund, ed. see Wigglesworth, Michael.

Morgan, Edmund M., ed. Some Problems of Proof Under the Anglo-American System of Litigation. LC 75-31438. (James S. Carpentier Lectures Ser.: 1955). 207p. 1976. reprint ed. text ed. 35.00 (*0-8371-8517-3*, MOSP, Greenwood Pr) Greenwood.

Morgan, Edmund M., jt. auth. see Joughin, Louis.

Morgan, Edmund S. American Slavery - American Freedom: The Ordeal of Colonial Virginia. 454p. (C). 1976. pap. text ed. 10.95 (*0-393-09156-2*) Norton.

— American Slavery - American Freedom: The Ordeal of Colonial Virginia. 464p. 1995. pap. 14.95 (*0-393-31288-7*, Norton Paperbks) Norton.

— The Birth of the Republic, 1763-89. LC 92-8871. (Chicago History of American Civilization Ser.). 224p. (C). 1992. pap. text ed. 9.95 (*0-226-53757-9*) U Ch Pr.

— The Birth of the Republic, 1763-89. 3rd ed. LC 92-8871. (Chicago History of American Civilization Ser.). 224p. (C). 1992. lib. bdg. 29.95 (*0-226-53756-0*) U Ch Pr.

— The Challenge of the American Revolution. 1976. 10.95 (*0-393-05603-1*) Norton.

— The Challenge of the American Revolution. (C). 1978. pap. text ed. 8.95 (*0-393-00876-2*) Norton.

— The Genius of George Washington. (Illus.). 104p. 1982. pap. 7.95 (*0-393-00060-5*) Norton.

— The Genius of George Washington. (George Rogers Clark Lecture November 11, 1977 Ser.: No. 3). (Illus.). 104p. 1985. reprint ed. lib. bdg. 22.50 (*0-8191-4871-7*) U Pr of Amer.

— The Gentle Puritan: A Life of Ezra Stiles, 1727-1795. LC 62-8257. (Illus.). 508p. 1974. reprint ed. pap. 144.80 (*0-8357-3923-6*, 2036658) Bks Demand.

— Inventing the People. 1989. pap. 10.95 (*0-393-30623-2*) Norton.

— The Meaning of Independence: John Adams, George Washington, Thomas Jefferson. LC 76-8438. (Richard Lectures for 1975, University of Virginia Ser.). 95p. reprint ed. pap. 27.10 (*0-7837-4227-4*, 2043914) Bks Demand.

— The Puritan Dilemma: The Story of John Winthrop. (Library of American Biography). (C). 1987. pap. text ed. 16.00 (*0-673-39347-X*) HarpCollege.

***Morgan, Edmund S.** The Puritan Dilemma: The Story of John Winthrop. (Library of American Biography). 224p. 1995. reprint ed. pap. 15.95 (*1-886746-23-0*) Talman Pub.

Morgan, Edmund S. The Puritan Family: Religion & Domestic Relations in Seventeenth-Century New England. LC 80-18819. x, 196p. 1980. reprint ed. text ed. 38.50 (*0-313-22703-9*, MOPFA, Greenwood Pr) Greenwood.

— Roger Williams: The Church & the State. 1988. 18.50 (*0-8446-6321-2*) Peter Smith.

— Roger Williams: The Church & the State. 176p. 1987. reprint ed. pap. 6.95 (*0-393-30403-5*) Norton.

Morgan, Edmund S. Virginians at Home: Family Life in the Eighteenth Century. LC 52-14250. (America Ser.: Vol. 2). (Illus.). 101p. (Orig.). 1952. 14.95 (*0-910412-52-9*) Colonial Williamsburg.

Morgan, Edmund S. Visible Saints: The History of a Puritan Idea. LC 63-9999. 168p. 1965. pap. 9.95 (*0-8014-9041-3*) Cornell U Pr.

Morgan, Edmund S., ed. Puritan Family: Religion & Domestic Relations in 17th-Century New England. rev. ed. 1942. pap. text ed. 12.00 (*0-06-131227-4*, TB1227, Torch) HarpC.

— Puritan Political Ideas 1558-1794. LC 65-22347. (Orig.). 1965. pap. 7.35 (*0-672-60042-0*, AHS33, Bobbs) Macmillan.

***Morgan, Edmund S & Morgan, Helen M.** The Stamp Act Crisis: Prologue to Revolution. LC 94-31357. (Institute of Early American History & Culture Ser.). 350p. 1995. pap. text ed. 14.95x (*0-8078-4513-2*) U of NC Pr.

Morgan, Edward, pref. The Apple Tree. 24p. 1982. 30.00 (*0-906474-25-6*, Pub. by Third Eye Centre UK) St Mut.

Morgan, Edward E., Jr. & Hiltner, John. Managing Aging & Human Service Agencies. LC 91-5227. 168p. 1992. 27.95 (*0-8261-7810-3*) Springer Pub.

Morgan, Edward H., jt. auth. see Warlick, Roger.

Morgan, Edward P. The Sixties Experience: Hard Lessons about Modern America. (Illus.). 330p. 1991. 39.95 (*0-87722-805-1*) Temple U Pr.

— Sixties Experience: Hard Lessons about Modern America. 1992. pap. 19.95 (*1-56639-014-1*) Temple U Pr.

Morgan, Edward V. Theory & Practice of Central Banking, 1797-1913. 252p. 1965. 35.00 (*0-7146-1237-5*, Pub. by F Cass Pubs UK) Intl Spec Bk.

Morgan, Edwin. Flower of Evil: Life of Charles Baudelaire. LC 75-114889. (Select Bibliographies Reprint Ser.). 1977. 21.95 (*0-8369-5293-6*) Ayer.

— Stargate. 1989. 45.00 (*0-906474-10-8*, Pub. by Third Eye Centre UK) St Mut.

Morgan, Edwin, tr. The Apple Tree. 1989. 50.00 (*0-906474-24-8*, Pub. by Third Eye Centre UK) St Mut.

— Beowulf: A Verse Translation into Modern English. (C). 1952. pap. 11.00 (*0-520-00881-2*) U CA Pr.

— Master Peter Pathelin: A Mid 15th Century French Farce. 64p. 1983. 24.00 (*0-906474-36-1*, Pub. by Third Eye Centre UK) St Mut.

Morgan, Eileen, jt. auth. see Tourevski, Mark.

***Morgan, Elaine.** The Descent of the Child. 208p. 1995. 19.95 (*0-19-509895-1*) OUP.

— The Scars of Evolution: What Our Bodies Tell Us about Human Origin. (Illus.). 208p. 1994. reprint ed. pap. 12.95 (*0-19-509431-X*) OUP.

Morgan, Elaine & Davies, Stephen. Red Sea Pilot: Aden to Cyprus. (Illus.). 260p. 1995. 69.95 (*0-85288-253-X*, Pub. by Imray Laurie Norie & Wilson UK) Bluewater Bks.

M

An Asterisk (*) at the beginning of an entry indicates that the title is appearing in BIP for the first time.

Morgan, Eleanor. Corporate Taxation & Investment: The Implications of the 1984 Tax Reform. 130p. 1986. text ed. 66.00 (0-566-05265-2, Pub. by Avebury Pub UK) Ashgate Pub Co.

***Morgan, Elemore.** The Face of Louisiana. LC 78-86493. 176p. 1969. pap. 50.20 (0-7837-8467-8, 2049272) Bks Demand.

— Five Days in Baton Rouge. 1951. pap. 2.50 (0-685-08170-2) Claitors.

Morgan, Elisa. Chronicles of Childhood: Recording Your Child's Spiritual Journey. LC 91-61427. 144p. 1991. 12.00 (0-89109-630-2) NavPress.

***Morgan, Elisa & Kuykendall, Carol.** What Every Mom Needs. 192p. 1995. 14.99 (0-310-20097-0); audio 12.99 (0-310-20417-8) Zondervan.

Morgan, Elise N. The Angel of the Presence. (Meditation Ser.). 1922. 6.95 (0-87516-327-0) DeVorss.

— Communion. (Meditation Ser.). 1928. 6.95 (0-87516-328-9) DeVorss.

— The Illimitable One. (Meditation Ser.). 1934. 6.95 (0-87516-329-7) DeVorss.

— Now This Day. 1948. 6.95 (0-87516-330-0) DeVorss.

— That We May Be Willing to Receive. (Meditation Ser.). 1938. 6.95 (0-87516-331-9) DeVorss.

— The Way. (Meditation Ser.). 1972. 6.95 (0-87516-332-7) DeVorss.

— Your Own Path. (Meditation Ser.). 1928. pap. 6.95 (0-87516-333-5) DeVorss.

Morgan, Elizabeth. Amandas Folly. 1991. pap. 3.50 (0-8217-3604-3) Zebra.

Morgan, Elizabeth, et al. Global Poverty & Personal Responsibility: Integrity Through Commitment. 1989. pap. 9.95 (0-8091-3097-1) Paulist Pr.

Morgan, Elizabeth D. Jane Long: A Child's Pictorial History. LC 92-17739. (Illus.). 96p. (J). (gr. 4-7). 1992. 12.95 (0-89015-861-4) Sunbelt Media.

— President Mirabeau B. Lamar: Father of Texas Education. LC 94-2641. (Illus.). (J). 1994. 12.95 (0-89015-963-7) Sunbelt Media.

Morgan, Elizabeth S. The Governor of Desire. Poems. LC 92-37785. ix, 64p. (C). 1993. text ed. 15.95 (0-8071-1811-7); pap. 8.95 (0-8071-1812-5) La State U Pr.

— Parties. Poems. LC 88-1390. 53p. 1988. pap. 6.95 (0-8071-1475-8) La State U Pr.

— Uncertain Seasons. LC 93-18428. 176p. (C). 1994. 24.95 (0-8173-0702-8) U of Ala Pr.

Morgan, Ella J., jt. auth. see O'Neill, Erin.

Morgan, Elmer. Making a Difference. 122p. 1992. pap. 5.95 (0-940999-95-1, C2265) Star Bible.

— Near to the Heart of God. 342p. (Orig.). 1990. pap. 9.95 (1-56794-012-9, C2273) Star Bible.

— The Quest for Something More. 1994. pap. 6.95 (1-56794-059-5) Star Bible.

— Sibling Rivalry in God's Family. 147p. (Orig.). 1993. pap. 5.95 (1-56794-033-1, C2292) Star Bible.

Morgan, Elmer & Tudor, Don, eds. Teenage Tenderness. 115p. (Orig.). 1991. pap. 6.95 (1-56794-013-7, C2274) Star Bible.

Morgan, Emma. Gooseflesh. 53p. (Orig.). 1993. pap. 7.95 (1-878533-06-1) Clothespin Fever Pr.

Morgan, Ernest. Arthur Morgan Remembered. 1991. 6.00 (0-910420-31-9) Comm Serv OH.

— Dealing Creatively with Death: A Manual of Death Education & Simple Burial. 11th rev. ed. Morgan, Jenifer, ed. LC 87-32573. (Illus.). 186p. 1988. pap. 9.00 (0-914064-26-6) Celo Pr.

— Dealing Creatively with Death: A Manual of Death Education & Simple Burial. 12th ed. Morgan, Jenifer, ed. 167p. 1990. pap. 11.95 (0-935016-79-1, Barclay House) Excelsior Music Pub Co.

— Dealing Creatively with Death: A Manual of Death Education & Simple Burial. 13th ed. 1994. pap. 12.95 (0-935016-89-9, Barclay House) Excelsior Music Pub Co.

Morgan, Evan, et al. The Dawn of Chinese Civilization. American Woman's Club, Literary Department, Shanghai Staff, ed. 1976. lib. bdg. 59.95 (0-87968-999-4) Gordon Pr.

Morgan, F., jt. ed. see Vinogradoff, P.

Morgan, Faye. Riding the Gold Curve. 384p. 1994. 25.00 (0-89672-326-7) Tex Tech Univ Pr.

***Morgan, Faye, pseud.** Trial by Fire. 192p. 1994. mass mkt. 3.99 (0-8439-3717-3) Dorchester Pub Co.

Morgan, Felix R. De Mujeres y Perros. LC 89-81221. (Coleccion Caniqui Ser.). (Illus.). 101p. (Orig.). (SPA.). 1990. pap. 9.95 (0-89729-555-2) Ediciones.

Morgan, Ffiona. Daughters of the Moon Tarot: Tarot of the Goddess. Pei, Cherie, ed. (Illus.). 96p. 1991. reprint ed. pap. 9.95 (1-880130-01-7); reprint ed. 21.95 (1-880130-00-9) Daughters Moon.

— Goddess Spirituality Book: Rituals, Holydays & Moon Magic. (Illus.). 194p. (Orig.). 1995. pap. 13.00 (1-880130-06-8) Daughters Moon.

— Mysteries of the Goddess: Astrology, Tarot & the Magical Arts. (Illus.). 194p. (Orig.). 1995. pap. 13.00 (1-880130-37-8) Daughters Moon.

— Wild Witches Don't Get the Blues: Astrology, Rituals & Healing. Rifkin, Ellen & Leavitt, Susan, eds. LC 84-90579. (Illus.). 284p. (Orig.). 1991. pap. 14.95 (1-880130-03-3) Daughters Moon.

Morgan, Fidelis. Bluff Your Way in British Theatre. (Bluffers Ser.). 74p. (Orig.). 1993. pap. 3.95 (1-57143-001-6) RDR Bks.

— The Female Wits: Women Playwrights of the Restoration. 468p. 1991. pap. 39.95 (0-86068-231-5, Pub. by Virago Pr UK) Trafalgar.

Morgan, Fidelis, ed. & intro. The Female Tatler. 242p. (Orig.). 1992. pap. 6.95 (0-460-87074-2, Everyman's Classic Lib) C E Tuttle.

Morgan, Forrest E. Living the Martial Way: A Manual for the Way a Modern Warrior Should Think. LC 92-16969. 1992. 25.00 (0-942637-61-5); pap. 16.95 (0-942637-76-3) Barricade Bks.

Morgan, Frank. Calculus Lite. 300p. 1995. text ed. 29.95 (1-56881-037-7) AK Peters.

— Riemannian Geometry: A Beginner's Guide. LC 92-13261. (Illus.). 128p. (C). 1992. text ed. 29.95 (0-86720-242-4) AK Peters.

***Morgan, Frank, ed.** Geometric Measure Theory: A Beginner's Guide. 2nd ed. (Illus.). 175p. 1995. boxed 34.95 (0-12-506857-3) Acad Pr.

Morgan, Fred. Here & Now III: An Approach to Writing Through Perception. 238p. (C). 1979. pap. text ed. 21.50 (0-15-535624-0) HB Coll Pubs.

— Here & Now III: An Approach to Writing Through Perception. 3rd ed. 238p. (C). 1979. pap. text ed. 1.50 (0-15-535625-9) HB Coll Pubs.

Morgan, Fred & Pohlman, Richard W. Education & Practice: The Critical Interface. (Illus.). 250p. 1993. pap. text ed. 50.00 (1-880250-02-0) Assoc Comp Aid Des.

Morgan, Fred T. Ghost Tales of the Uwharries. LC 68-58501. 152p. 1991. pap. 7.95 (0-89587-083-5) Blair.

— Haunted Uwharries: Ghost Stories, Witch Tales & Other Happenings from North America's Oldest Mountains. Bledsoe, Jerry, ed. LC 92-72657. (Illus.). 173p. (Orig.). 1992. pap. 10.95 (1-878086-13-8) Down Home NC.

Morgan, Frederick. A Book of Change (Poems) LC 72-2214. 160p. 1972. 16.00 (0-684-12950-7); pap. 8.00 (0-684-13962-6) Hudson Rev.

— The Fountain & Other Fables. 66p. 1985. 20.00 (0-931757-00-2); pap. 15.00 (0-931757-01-0) Pterodactyl Pr.

— Northbrook. Poems. LC 81-14664. 88p. 1982. 14.95 (0-252-00947-9); pap. 9.95 (0-252-00948-7) U of Ill Pr.

— Poems: New & Selected. LC 86-30844. 280p. 1987. 24.95 (0-252-01433-2); pap. 12.95 (0-252-01434-0) U of Ill Pr.

— Poems for Paula. 78p. (Orig.). 1995. 14.00 (1-885266-14-6); pap. 8.00 (1-885266-18-9) Story Line.

— Poems of the Two Worlds. LC 76-51907. 132p. 1977. 14.95 (0-252-00604-6) U of Ill Pr.

— Refractions: Poems. 1981. 25.00 (0-317-40789-9) Abattoir.

— The Tarot of Cornelius Agrippa. LC 77-94782. (Illus.). 50p. (Orig.). 1978. pap. 75.00 (0-915298-11-2) Hudson Rev.

Morgan, G., et al. Child Care Handbook. (Illus.). 32p. 1988. reprint ed. write for info. (0-9618201-1-X) Work Family Direct.

Morgan, G. Campbell. Acts of the Apostles. 560p. 1924. 21.99 (0-8007-0000-7) Revell.

— The Best of G. Campbell Morgan. Turnbull, Ralph G., ed. (Best Ser.). 232p. 1991. reprint ed. pap. 7.99 (0-8010-6282-9) Baker Bk.

— El Corazon de Dios. (SPA.). 1980. pap. 3.75 (0-8254-1494-6) Kregel.

— Corinthian Letters of Paul. 288p. 1946. 16.99 (0-8007-0051-1) Revell.

— The Crises of the Christ. LC 89-8429. 1989. pap. 9.99 (0-8007-5307-0) Revell.

— Crises of the Christ: The Seven Greatest Events of His Life. LC 89-2565. 344p. 1989. reprint ed. pap. 12.99 (0-8254-3258-8) Kregel.

— Las Crisis de Cristo, Vol. 2. Orig. Title: Crises of the Christ. 192p. (SPA.). 1993. pap. 4.75 (0-8254-1496-2) Kregel.

— Discipleship: Growing up As a Christian. LC 91-15196. 121p. 1991. reprint ed. pap. 7.99 (0-8254-3259-6) Kregel.

— El Discipulado Cristiano: The Christian Disciple. (SPA.). 3.25 (84-7228-826-9, 220312, Pub. by Edit Clie SP) TSELF.

— Las Ensenanzas De Cristo: The Teachings of Christ. (SPA.). 7.50 (84-7228-794-7, 220366, Pub. by Edit Clie SP) TSELF.

— El Espiritu De Dios: The Spirit of God. (SPA.). 5.50 (84-7228-829-3, 222328, Pub. by Edit Clie SP) TSELF.

— El Evangelismo: Evangelism. (SPA.). 3.25 (84-7228-933-8, 223002, Pub. by Edit Clie SP) TSELF.

— Exposition of the Whole Bible. LC 59-8719. 544p. 1959. 24.99 (0-8007-0088-0) Revell.

— The Gospel According to John. Fang, Carl, tr. (G. Campbell Morgan's Expository Ser.). 1985. write for info. (0-941598-94-2); pap. write for info. (0-941598-18-7) Living Spring Pubns.

— The Gospel According to Luke. Chao, Lorna, tr. (G. Campbell Morgan's Expository Ser.). 1985. write for info. (0-941598-95-0); pap. write for info. (0-941598-17-9) Living Spring Pubns.

— The Gospel According to Luke. reprint ed. 18.99 (0-8007-0120-8) Revell.

— The Gospel According to Mark. Chan, Silas, tr. (G. Campbell Morgan's Expository Ser.). (CHI.). 1984. write for info. (0-941598-96-9); pap. write for info. (0-941598-16-0) Living Spring Pubns.

— The Gospel According to Mark. reprint ed. 18.99 (0-8007-0121-6) Revell.

— The Gospel According to Matthew. Chang, David, tr. (G. Campbell Morgan's Expository Ser.). (CHI.). 1984. write for info. (0-941598-97-7); pap. write for info. (0-941598-15-2) Living Spring Pubns.

— The Gospel According to Matthew. reprint ed. 18.99 (0-8007-0122-4) Revell.

— The Gospels, 4 vols., Set. reprint ed. 69.95 (0-8007-1687-6) Revell.

— Los Grandes Capitulos De la Biblia: Great Chapters of the Bible, 2 bks., Bk. I. (SPA.). 5.00 (84-7228-881-1, 222330, Pub. by Edit Clie SP) TSELF.

— Los Grandes Capitulos De la Biblia: Great Chapters of the Bible, 2 bks., Bk. II. (SPA.). 5.25 (84-7228-882-X, 222331, Pub. by Edit Clie SP) TSELF.

— Great Chapters of the Bible. 16.99 (0-8007-1040-1) Revell.

— The Great Physician. 416p. 1982. reprint ed. 17.99 (0-8007-0485-1) Revell.

— Handbook for Bible Teachers & Preachers: Applications to Life from Every Book of the Bible. 312p. 1982. pap. 10.99 (0-8010-6190-3) Baker Bk.

— Isaiah. Chao, Lorna, tr. (G. Campbell Morgan's Expository Ser.). 1985. write for info. (0-941598-93-4); pap. write for info. (0-941598-20-9) Living Spring Pubns.

— Jeremiah. Chan, Silas, tr. (Morgan's Expository Ser.). 1987. write for info. (0-941598-90-X); pap. write for info. (0-941598-42-X) Living Spring Pubns.

— Jesus Responde a Job. Orig. Title: The Answer of Jesus to Job. (SPA.). pap. 2.75 (0-8254-1447-4) Kregel.

— Life Applications from Every Chapter of the Bible. 384p. 1994. reprint ed. pap. 11.99 (0-8007-5535-9) Revell.

— Me Han Defraudado! Orig. Title: Wherein!. 96p. (SPA.). 1984. pap. 2.75 (0-8254-1497-0) Kregel.

— Mensaje de Apocalipsis a las Iglesias: Message of Revelation to the... (SPA.). 3.95 (84-7228-822-6, 222348, Pub. by Edit Clie SP) TSELF.

— Ministerio de la Predicacion: Ministering Through Preaching. (SPA.). 3.95 (84-7228-848-X, 220596, Pub. by Edit Clie SP) TSELF.

— Notes on the Psalms. 288p. 1947. 16.99 (0-8007-0241-7) Revell.

— Pedro & la Iglesia: Peter & the Church. (SPA.). 2.95 (84-7228-838-2, 220675, Pub. by Edit Clie SP) TSELF.

— Perfecta Voluntad de Dios: God's Perfect Will. (SPA.). 3.25 (84-7228-861-7, 222361, Pub. by Edit Clie SP) TSELF.

— El Plan de Dios para las Edades: God's Plan for the Ages. (SPA.). 4.25 (84-7228-885-4, 220692, Pub. by Edit Clie SP) TSELF.

— Preaching. Low, John J., tr. 78p. (CHI.). 1993. pap. 4.00 (0-614-01910-9) Christ Renew Min.

— Preaching. Low, John J., tr. 78p. (CHI.). 1993. 6.00 (1-56582-031-2) Christ Renew Min.

— Principios Basicos de la Vida: Basics of Christian Living. (SPA.). 3.25 (84-7228-845-5, 220712, Pub. by Edit Clie SP) TSELF.

— Profetas Menores: Minor Prophets. (SPA.). 3.25 (84-7228-837-4, 220726, Pub. by Edit Clie SP) TSELF.

— Pulpit Legends. 1994. reprint ed. 19.99 (0-89957-200-6) AMG Pubs.

— The Simple Things of the Christian Life. 1984. pap. 2.50 (0-915374-40-4) Rapids Christian.

— Survey of the Bible. (World Classic Library). 639p. 1994. reprint ed. 19.99 (0-529-10061-4) World Bible.

— The Teaching of Christ. 352p. 1984. 16.99 (0-8007-0395-2) Revell.

— Triunfos de la Fe: Triumphs of Faith. (SPA.). 4.95 (84-7228-921-4, 220908, Pub. by Edit Clie SP) TSELF.

— Ultimo Mansaje de Dios al Hombre: God's Last Word to Man. (SPA.). 4.25 (84-7228-852-8, 220919, Pub. by Edit Clie SP) TSELF.

Morgan, G. Edward, Jr. & Mikhail, Maged S. Clinical Anesthesiology. (Illus.). 747p. (C). 1992. pap. text ed. 41.95 (0-8385-1324-7, A1324-1) Appleton & Lange.

Morgan, G. G., jt. ed. see Boim, L.

Morgan, G. G., ed. see Leith, Philip.

Morgan, G. R., jt. ed. see Pauly, D.

***Morgan, Gareth.** Athos Sixty. 144p. 1994. pap. 10.95 (1-57087-069-1) Prof Pr NC.

— Church Computing: A Strategy. (C). 1989. 49.00 (1-870404-02-5, Pub. by Jay Bks UK) St Mut.

— Creative Organization Theory: A Resource Book. 376p. (C). 1989. text ed. 55.00 (0-8039-3444-0); pap. text ed. 25.00 (0-8039-3438-6) Sage.

— Images of Organization. 432p. (C). 1986. text ed. 55.00 (0-8039-2830-0); pap. text ed. 25.00 (0-8039-2831-9) Sage.

— Imaginization: The Art of Creative Management. LC 93-12148. (Illus.). 320p. (C). 1993. text ed. 28.00 (0-8039-5299-6) Sage.

— Riding the Waves of Change: Developing Managerial Competencies for a Turbulent World. LC 87-46337. (Management Ser.). 230p. 1988. 28.95x (1-55542-093-1) Jossey-Bass.

Morgan, Gareth, ed. Beyond Method: Strategies for Social Research. 424p. 1983. 49.95 (0-8039-1973-5); pap. 22.50 (0-8039-2078-4) Sage.

Morgan, Gareth, jt. auth. see Harlow, Rosie.

Morgan, Gary. There Was So Much Laughter. 50p. 1984. pap. 2.95 (0-942424-03-4) W Anglia Pubns.

Morgan, Geoffrey. Tea with Mr. Timothy. 2nd large type ed. (Illus.). 111p. (J). 1993. 18.95 (1-85695-300-9, Pub. by ISIS UK) Transaction Pubs.

Morgan, George. Life of James Monroe. LC 76-106979. reprint ed. 74.50 (0-404-00594-2) AMS Pr.

Morgan, George, jt. auth. see Morgan, Peg.

Morgan, George, tr. see Tillman, Terry.

Morgan, George A. Speech & Society: The Christian Linguistic Social Philosophy of Eugen Rosenstock-Huessy. 192p. 1987. 29.95 (0-8130-0852-2) U Press Fla.

Morgan, George A., Jr. What Nietzsche Means. LC 74-2555. 408p. 1975. reprint ed. text ed. 35.00 (0-8371-7404-X, MOWN, Greenwood Pr) Greenwood.

Morgan, George A., ed. see Pdersen, Frank A., et al.

Morgan, George H. Annals, Comprising Memoirs, Incidents, & Statistics of Harrisburg, from the Period of Its First Settlement (Pennsylvania) 446p. (Orig.). reprint ed. pap. text ed. 29.00 (1-55613-931-4) Heritage Bk.

Morgan, George T., Jr. & King, John O. The Woodlands: New Community Development, 1964-1983. LC 86-23081. (Illus.). 176p. 1987. 27.50 (0-89096-306-1) Tex A&M Univ Pr.

Morgan, George W. The Human Predicament: Dissolution & Wholeness. LC 68-23791. 360p. reprint ed. pap. 102.60 (0-317-41777-0, 2025641) Bks Demand.

Morgan, Gerald. Anglo-Russian Rivalry in Central Asia 1810-1895. (Illus.). 284p. 1981. text ed. 38.00 (0-7146-3179-5, Pub. by F Cass Pubs UK) Intl Spec Bk.

— Sir Gawain & the Green Knight & the Idea of Righteousness. (Dublin Studies in Medieval Renaissance Literature). 192p. 1992. text ed. 39.50 (0-7165-2470-8, Pub. by Irish Acad Pr IE) Intl Spec Bk.

Morgan, Gerald, ed. see Chaucer, Geoffrey.

Morgan, Gillian. The Complete Galley Slave. 144p. 1987. 40.00 (0-85937-123-9, Pub. by K Mason Pubns Ltd UK) St Mut.

Morgan, Glenn. Organizations in Society. LC 89-70084. 296p. 1990. text ed. 45.00 (0-312-04253-1) St Martin.

Morgan, Glenn G. Soviet Administrative Legality: The Role of the Attorney General's Office. x, 281p. 1962. 39.50 (0-8047-0143-1) Stanford U Pr.

Morgan, Gordon D. Sociology by the Discovery Method: Cutting Costs & Teaching More. LC 83-62300. 125p. (Orig.). (C). 1985. pap. text ed. 5.95 (0-88247-726-9) R & E Pubs.

— Tilman C. Cothran: Second Generation Sociologist. 225p. (C). 1995. text ed. 39.95 (1-55605-252-9); pap. text ed. 29.95 (1-55605-251-0) Wyndhall Pr.

Morgan, Gordon D. & Preston, Izola. The Edge of Campus: A Journal of Black Experience at the University of Arkansas. LC 89-28619. 247p. 1990. 19.95 (1-55728-117-3); pap. 11.95 (1-55728-118-1) U of Ark Pr.

Morgan, Gordon N. Over My Shoulder. York, Sherri, ed. LC 87-50982. 70p. 1987. pap. 6.95 (1-55523-089-X) Winston-Derek.

Morgan, Griscom. The Community's Need for an Economy. 1969. pap. 1.00 (0-910420-17-3) Comm Serv OH.

— Future of the Community Heritage. 1971. pap. 1.00 (0-910420-04-1) Comm Serv OH.

— Small Community, Population & the Economic Order. rev. ed. 1975. pap. 2.00 (0-910420-22-X) Comm Serv OH.

— Vitality & Civilization. 1947. pap. 1.00 (0-910420-06-8) Comm Serv OH.

Morgan, Griscom & Morgan, Arthur. Future of Cities & Future of Man. 1993. pap. 5.00 (0-910420-05-X) Comm Serv OH.

Morgan, Griscom & Morgan, Arthur, eds. Heritage of Community. rev. ed. (Orig.). 1971. pap. 2.00 (0-910420-00-9) Comm Serv OH.

Morgan, Griscom, ed. see Community Service Editors.

Morgan, Griscom, et al. Human Scale in Schools. rev. ed. 1988. pap. 2.50 (0-910420-29-7) Comm Serv OH.

— Shaping Things to Come. 1980. pap. 1.00 (0-910420-27-0) Comm Serv OH.

Morgan, Gwen. The National State of Child Care Regulation, 1986. 250p. 1987. write for info. (0-9618201-0-1) Work Family Direct.

Morgan, Gwen & Veysey, Arthur. Poor Little Rich Boy: The Saga of America's Foremost Newspaper Dynasty - Col. Robert R. McCormick. LC 85-70124. (Illus.). 500p. (Orig.). 1985. pap. 10.95 (0-916445-11-9) Crossroads Comm.

Morgan, Gwen, et al. Quality in Early Childhood Programs: Four Perspectives. 70p. (Orig.). 1985. pap. 10.95 (0-931114-35-7) High-Scope.

Morgan, Gwen G. Managing the Day Care Dollars: A Financial Handbook. rev. ed. LC 82-50691. 112p. 1992. pap. 7.95 (0-942820-02-9) Steam Pr MA.

Morgan, Gwenda. The Hegemony of the Law: Richmond County, Virginia, 1642-1776. (Outstanding Studies in Early American History). 242p. 1989. reprint ed. 15.00 (0-8240-6192-6) Garland.

Morgan, Gwendolyn A. Medieval Balladry & the Courtly Tradition: Literature of Revolt & Assimilation. LC 92-28130. (American University Studies: English Language & Literature: Ser. IV, Vol. 160). 148p. 1992. 36.95 (0-8204-2042-5) P Lang Pubs.

Morgan, Gwyneth. Life in Medieval Village. 1975. pap. 8.25 (0-521-20404-6) Cambridge U Pr.

Morgan, H. E., ed. Cellular Biology of the Heart: Supplement to Journal of Molecular & Cellular Cardiology. 1982. text ed. 57.00 (0-12-506960-X) Acad Pr.

Morgan, H. G. Aids to Psychiatry. 3rd ed. (Illus.). 224p. 1989. pap. text ed. 24.00 (0-443-03928-3) Churchill.

Morgan, H. Wayne. America's Road to Empire: The War with Spain & Overseas Expansion. 124p. (C). 1965. pap. text ed. write for info. (0-07-554680-9) McGraw.

— Drugs in America: A Social History, 1800-1980. LC 81-14531. (Illus.). 248p. 1982. pap. 14.95 (0-8156-2282-1) Syracuse U Pr.

— Keepers of Culture: The Art-Thought of Kenyon Cox, Royal Cortissoz, & Frank Jewett Mather, Jr. LC 89-32669. (Illus.). 204p. 1989. 25.00 (0-87338-390-7) Kent St U Pr.

— Kenyon Cox, 1856-1919: A Life in American Art. LC 93-33967. (Illus.). 304p. (C). 1994. lib. bdg. 32.00 (0-87338-485-7) Kent St U Pr.

— Yesterday's Addicts: American Society & Drug Abuse, 1865-1920. LC 73-7421. 220p. 1974. pap. 12.95 (0-8061-1636-6) U of Okla Pr.

Morgan, H. Wayne, ed. An American Art Student in Paris: The Letters of Kenyon Cox, 1877-1882. LC 86-4702. (Illus.). 226p. 1986. 35.00 (0-87338-333-8) Kent St U Pr.

— An Artist of the American Renaissance: The Letters of Kenyon Cox, 1883-1919. LC 95-1587. (Illus.). 312p. 1995. text ed. 35.00x (0-87338-517-9) Kent St U Pr.

— Victorian Culture in America, 1865-1914. LC 72-89722. (Primary Sources in American History Ser.). 1973. pap. text ed. write for info. (0-88295-787-2) Harlan Davidson.

Morgan, H. Wayne & Morgan, Anne H. Oklahoma: A History. (States & the Nation Ser.). (Illus.). 1984. pap. 7.95 (0-393-30181-8) Norton.

An Asterisk (*) at the beginning of an entry indicates that the title is appearing in BIP for the first time.

Morgan, H. Wayne, jt. auth. see Morgan, Anne H.

Morgan, Hal. Symbols of America. (Illus.). 240p. 1986. pap. 40.00 (*0-670-80667-6*) Viking Penguin.

— Symbols of America. (Illus.). 240p. 1987. pap. 22.50 (*0-14-008077-5*, Penguin Bks) Viking Penguin.

***Morgan, Harry.** Historical Perspectives on the Education of Black Children. LC 94-42843. 248p. 1995. text ed. 49.95 (*0-275-95071-9*, Praeger Pubs) Greenwood.

Morgan, Hazel, ed. Through Peter's Eyes. (C). 1990. pap. 24.00 (*0-85305-305-7*, Pub. by J Arthur Ltd UK) St Mut.

Morgan, Helen. Who'd Stay a Missionary? 1979. pap. 1.95 (*0-87508-366-8*) Chr Lit.

— The Witch Doll. 144p. (J). (gr. 3-7). 1994. pap. 3.99 (*0-14-037146-X*) Puffin Bks.

Morgan, Helen, ed. see Davis, Alvis O.

Morgan, Helen C. & Moorhead, Kelly J. Spirulina - Nature's Superfood. 43p. 1993. pap. 2.95 (*0-9637511-3-1*) Nutrex.

Morgan, Helen M., jt. auth. see Morgan, Edmund S.

Morgan, Helene, jt. auth. see Morgan, Paul.

Morgan, Henry. Here's Morgan! LC 93-45406. 1994. 22.00 (*1-56980-001-4*) Barricade Bks.

Morgan, Henry, ed. Approaches to Prayer: A Resource Book for Groups & Individuals. LC 92-35257. (Illus.). 160p. (Orig.). 1993. pap. 11.95 (*0-8192-1599-6*) Morehouse Pub.

Morgan, Henry J. The Canadian Legal Directory. (Biographical Reference Work Ser.). xii, 279p. 1989. reprint ed. 59.00 (*0-7812-0696-0*, Am Repr Serv) Rprt Serv.

Morgan, Hilary. Burne-Jones, the Pre-Raphaelites & Their Century, 2 Vols., Set. (Illus.). (C). 1989. 195.00 (*0-685-75371-9*) St Mut.

— Burne-Jones, the Pre-Raphaelites & Their Century, 2 Vols., Vol. 1: The Text. (Illus.). (C). 1989. write for info. (*1-872508-01-4*) St Mut.

— Burne-Jones, the Pre-Raphaelites & Their Century, 2 Vols., Vol. 2: The Plates. (Illus.). (C). 1989. write for info. (*1-872508-02-2*) St Mut.

Morgan, Hiram. Tyrone's Rebellion: The Outbreak of the Nine Years War in Tudor Ireland. (Royal Historical Society: Studies in History: Vol. 67). (Illus.). (C). 1992. text ed. 63.00 (*0-86193-224-2*) Boydell & Brewer.

Morgan, Howard G. Death Wishes? The Understanding & Management of Deliberate Self-Harm. LC 79-1044. (Illus.). 182p. reprint ed. pap. 51.90 (*0-8357-3101-4*, 2039357) Bks Demand.

Morgan, Howard M. & Morgan, John C. The God-Man of Galilee: Studies in Christian Living (Sermons) 100p. 1983. 4.95 (*0-913029-14-9*) Stevens Bk Pr.

Morgan, Howard W. From Hayes to McKinley: National Party Politics, 1877-1896. LC 69-17074. 678p. reprint ed. pap. 180.00 (*0-317-51996-4*, 2027392) Bks Demand.

— William McKinley & His America. LC 63-19723. 623p. reprint ed. pap. 177.60 (*0-317-29726-0*, 2022207) Bks Demand.

Morgan, Howard W., ed. The Gilded Age. enl. rev. ed. LC 75-113203. 341p. reprint ed. pap. 97.20 (*0-317-51997-2*, 2027393) Bks Demand.

***Morgan, Hugh.** Me 262: Stormbird Rising. (Illus.). 224p. 1994. 29.95 (*0-87938-965-6*) Motorbooks Intl.

Morgan, Huw. Let Them Live. 1985. pap. 0.99 (*0-85234-199-7*, Pub. by Evangel Pr UK) Presby & Reformed.

Morgan, Iwan W. Beyond the Liberal Consensus: A Political History of the United States since 1965. LC 93-44098. 1994. write for info. (*0-312-10747-1*); pap. 18.95 (*0-312-12015-X*) St Martin.

— Deficit Government: Taxing & Spending in Modern America. LC 94-46129. (American Ways Ser.). 1995. write for info. (*1-56663-081-9*); pap. write for info. (*1-56663-082-7*) I R Dee.

— Ike Versus the Spenders: Eisenhower Economic Conservatism & the Liberal Response. 256p. 1990. text ed. 39.95 (*0-312-03176-9*) St Martin.

Morgan, Iwan W. & Wynn, Neil A., eds. America's Century: Perspectives on Twentieth-Century American History. LC 91-29508. 340p. (C). 1993. 45.00 (*0-8419-1303-X*); pap. 19.95 (*0-8419-1304-8*) Holmes & Meier.

Morgan, J. Canadian Cancer Conference: Proceedings of the 8th Canadian Cancer Res. Conference Saskatoon Saskatch 1969, No. 8. LC 55-8263. 1969. 189.00 (*0-08-006791-3*, Pub. by Pergamon Repr UK) Franklin.

Morgan, J., jt. auth. see Griffiths, P. A.

Morgan, J., jt. auth. see Turland, B. D.

Morgan, J., et al. The L Squared Moduli Space & a Vanishing Theorem for Donaldson Polynomial Invariants. (Monographs in Geometry & Topology). 232p. (C). 1994. text ed. 22.00 (*1-57146-006-3*) Intl Pr Boston.

Morgan, J. Brian. The Police Function & the Investigation of Crime. (Illus.). 201p. 1990. text ed. 60.00 (*0-566-07127-4*) Ashgate Pub Co.

Morgan, J. Derald & Abdullah, Mohammed. Dielectric Engineering Practice in Power Apparatus. 450p. 1984. pap. text ed. write for info. (*0-317-05122-9*) Macmillan.

Morgan, J. Derald, jt. auth. see Matsch, Leander W.

Morgan, J. Jeffrey, jt. auth. see Morgan, James C.

Morgan, J. L. The Elite of the Fleet, Vol. 1: Insignia of U. S. Naval Aviation. LC 90-81998. (Insignia Identification Ser.). (Illus.). 128p. 1990. write for info. (*0-9626310-0-0*) Intl Trade Assn.

Morgan, J. M. Beyond Eden. 1992. mass mkt. 4.99 (*1-55817-602-0*, Pinnacle NY) Windsor NY.

— Desert Eden. 1991. mass mkt. 4.95 (*1-55817-542-3*, Pinnacle NY) Windsor NY.

— Economics. 2nd ed. 1988. pap. text ed. write for info. (*0-07-017783-X*) McGraw.

— Future Eden. 320p. 1992. mass mkt. 4.99 (*1-55817-653-5*, Pinnacle NY) Windsor NY.

Morgan, J. R. & Stoneman, Richard, eds. Greek Fiction: The Greek Novel in Context. LC 93-28137. 1994. write for info. (*0-415-08506-3*); write for info. (*0-415-08507-1*) Routledge.

***Morgan, J. S. & Schonfelder, J. L.** Programming in Fortran 90. 350p. Date not set. pap. 26.00 (*1-872474-06-3*, Pub. by Alfred Waller UK) Paul & Co Pubs.

Morgan, J. T., ed. see Easter School in Agricultural Science (8th 1961, University of Nottingham) Staff.

Morgan, J. Tom, Jr. Kiss Impressions: My Love Affair with Lithography. LC 82-99983. 1983. 50.00 (*0-89938-014-X*) Tech & Ed Ctr Graph Arts RIT.

Morgan, J. W. California Impressions. Perkins, David, ed. (Illus.). 1886. 71.00 (*0-937048-46-1*) CSUN.

— A Product Formula for Surgery Obstructions. LC 78-4581. (Memoirs Ser.: No. 14/201). 90p. 1978. pap. 19.00 (*0-8218-2201-2*, MEMO 14/201) Am Math.

Morgan, Jacques J. Prehistoric Man. Paxton, J. H. & Collum, V. C., trs. LC 76-44763. reprint ed. 22.00 (*0-404-15954-0*) AMS Pr.

Morgan, Jacqui. Watercolor for Illustration. (Illus.). 144p. 1986. 29.95 (*0-8230-5658-9*, Watsn-Guptill) Watsn-Guptill.

Morgan, James. The Adorers of Dionysos, Bakchai. Pryse, tr. 164p. 1972. reprint ed. spiral bd. 9.35 (*0-7873-0318-6*) Mokelumne.

— Application Cases in MIS: Using Spreadsheet & Database Software. 130p. (C). 1993. pap. text ed. 22.95 (*0-256-13389-1*) Irwin.

Morgan, James, jt. auth. see Flanagan, John.

Morgan, James, jt. auth. see Kelley, Virginia C.

Morgan, James A., ed. Digest Shakespeareanae. LC 75-172743. (Shakespeare Society of New York. Publications: No. 4, Pts. 1 & 7). reprint ed. 37.50 (*0-404-04419-0*) AMS Pr.

— Mrs. Shakespeare's Second Marriage. LC 75-170138. (Shakespeare Society of New York. Publications: No. 14). reprint ed. 27.50 (*0-404-54214-X*) AMS Pr.

— Study in the Warwickshire Dialect. 3rd ed. LC 76-169927. (Shakespeare Society of New York. Publications: No. 10). reprint ed. 45.00 (*0-404-54210-7*) AMS Pr.

— Venus & Adonis: A Study in Warwickshire Dialect. LC 76-169261. (Shakespeare Society of New York. Publications: No. 2). reprint ed. 27.50 (*0-404-54202-6*) AMS Pr.

Morgan, James A., ed. see Shakespeare, William.

***Morgan, James C.** Jesus & Mastership: The Gospel According to Jesus of Nazareth, As Dictated Through James Coyle Morgan. 2nd ed. 389p. (C). 1992. pap. 14.95 (*1-878555-00-6*) Oakbridge Univ Pr.

— The New Book of Revelation: From John, the Disciple of Jesus the Christ, Through James Coyle Morgan. 100p. (Orig.). (C). 1991. pap. 9.95 (*1-878555-01-4*) Oakbridge Univ Pr.

— Slavery in the United States: Four Views. LC 84-43220. 214p. 1985. lib. bdg. 27.50x (*0-89950-162-1*) McFarland & Co.

Morgan, James C. & Morgan, J. Jeffrey. Cracking the Japanese Market: Strategies for Success in the New Global Economy. 288p. 1991. 32.95 (*0-02-921691-5*) Free Pr.

Morgan, James J., jt. auth. see Stumm, Werner.

Morgan, James L. Arkansas Marriage Records, 1808-1835. 90p. reprint ed. pap. 15.00 (*0-941765-91-1*) Arkansas Res.

— Arkansas Newspaper Abstracts, 1819-1845. 364p. 1992. reprint ed. text ed. 42.00 (*0-941765-74-1*); reprint ed. pap. 32.00 (*0-941765-73-3*) Arkansas Res.

— Arkansas Newspaper Index, 1819-1845. 100p. 1992. reprint ed. pap. 16.00 (*0-941765-75-X*) Arkansas Res.

— Arkansas Volunteers of 1836-1837. 81p. 1992. reprint ed. pap. 14.00 (*0-941765-79-2*) Arkansas Res.

— Census of the Territory of Arkansas, 1820 (Reconstructed) 108p. 1992. reprint ed. pap. 16.00 (*0-941765-77-6*) Arkansas Res.

— Early Arkansas Marriage Notices, 1819-1845. 86p. 1992. reprint ed. pap. 14.00 (*0-941765-78-4*) Arkansas Res.

— Families of Confederate Soldiers of Prairie County, Arkansas, 1861-1867. 53p. 1992. reprint ed. pap. 12.00 (*0-941765-82-2*) Arkansas Res.

— From Simple Input to Complex Grammar. (Learning, Development, & Conceptual Change). (Illus.). 232p. 1986. 30.00 (*0-262-13217-6*, Bradford Bks) MIT Pr.

***Morgan, James L. & Demuth, Katherine, eds.** Signal To Syntax: Bootstrapping from Speech to Grammar in Early Acquisition. 500p. 1995. text ed. 120.00 (*0-8058-1265-2*) L Erlbaum Assocs.

— Signal To Syntax: Bootstrapping from Speech to Grammar in Early Acquisition. 500p. 1995. pap. text ed. 60.00 (*0-8058-1266-0*) L Erlbaum Assocs.

Morgan, James N., ed. A Panel Study of Income Dynamics: Complete Documentation for Interviewing Years 1968-1981, 2 vols. & 9 suppls. suppl. ed. Incl. Vol. 1. Study Design, Procedures & Available Data for 1968-1972 Interviewing Years. 392p. (C). 1973. pap. 40.00 (*0-87944-141-0*); 1973 Supplement. 240p. (C). 1974. pap. 35.00 (*0-87944-155-0*); 1975 Supplement. 298p. (C). 1976. pap. 35.00 (*0-87944-200-X*); 1976 Supplement. 516p. (C). 1977. pap. 35.00 (*0-87944-215-8*); 1977 Supplement. 354p. (C). 1978. pap. 35.00 (*0-87944-225-5*); 1978 Supplement. 416p. (C). 1979. pap. 35.00 (*0-87944-243-3*); 1979 Supplement. 512p. (C). 1980. pap. 35.00 (*0-87944-258-1*); 1980 Supplement. 590p. (C). 1981. pap. 35.00 (*0-87944-271-9*); 500p. (C). 1981. reprint ed. Supplement 1981. Set pap. 35.00 (*0-87944-279-4*) Inst Soc Res.

Morgan, James N. & Duncan, Greg J. The Economics of Personal Choice. 272p. 1980. 27.95 (*0-472-08007-5*) U of Mich Pr.

— Making Your Choices Count: Economic Principles for Everyday Decisions. 1982. pap. 16.95 (*0-472-06305-7*) U of Mich Pr.

Morgan, James N. & Duncan, Greg J., eds. Five Thousand American Families: Patterns of Economic Progress, 10 vols., Set. Incl. Vol. 1. Analysis of the First Five Years of the Panel Study of Income Dynamics. 436p. 1973. (*0-318-53546-7*); Set, Vols. 1 & 2. Special Studies of the First Five Years of the Panel Study of Income Dynamics. 376p. 1974. Set Vols. 1 & 2. 30.00 (*0-87944-154-2*); Vol. 2. Special Studies of the First Five Years of the Panel Study of Income Dynamics. 376p. 1974. pap. 22.00 (*0-87944-153-4*); Vol. 3. Analyses of the First Six Years of the Panel Study of Income Dynamics. 496p. 1975. pap. 14.00 (*0-87944-175-5*); Vol. 4. Family Composition Change & Other Analyses of the First Seven Years of the Panel Study of Income Dynamics. 536p. 1976. pap. 14.00 (*0-87944-196-8*); Vol. 5. Components of Change in Family Well-Being & Other Analyses of the First Eight Years of the Panel Study of Income Dynamics. 534p. 1977. pap. 14.00 (*0-87944-211-5*); Vol. 6. Accounting for Race & Sex Differences in Earnings & Other Analyses of the First Nine Years of the Panel Study of Income Dynamics Vol. 7: Analyses of the First Ten Years of the Panel Study of Income Dynamics. 502p. 1978. 22.00 (*0-87944-223-9*); Vol. 6. Accounting for Race & Sex Differences in Earnings & Other Analyses of the First Nine Years of the Panel Study of Income Dynamics Vol. 7: Analyses of the First Ten Years of the Panel Study of Income Dynamics. 390p. 1979. Vol. 7. Analyses of the First Ten Years of The Panel Study Of Income Dynamics, 390p. 1979. 22.00 (*0-87944-234-4*); Vol. 8. Analyses of the First Eleven Years of the Panel Study of Income Dynamics. 458p. 1980. 22.00 (*0-87944-250-6*); Vol. 9. Analyses of the First Twelve Years of the Panel Study of Income Dynamics. 546p. 1981. 22.00 (*0-87944-267-0*); Vol. 10. Analysis of the First Thirteen Years of the Panel Study of Income Dynamics. (Illus.). 416p. 1983. pap. 20.00 (*0-87944-310-3*); 160.00 (*0-87944-268-9*) Inst Soc Res.

Morgan, James N. & Messenger, Robert C. THAID: A Sequential Analysis Program for the Analysis of Nominal Scale Dependent Variables. LC 72-619720. 98p. 1973. 12.00 (*0-87944-137-2*) Inst Soc Res.

Morgan, James N., jt. auth. see Barfield, Richard E.

Morgan, James N., jt. auth. see Burpee, C. Gaye.

Morgan, James N., jt. auth. see Economic Behavior Program Staff.

Morgan, James N., jt. auth. see Lansing, John B.

Morgan, James N., et al. Results from Two National Surveys of Philanthropic Activity. 204p. (Orig.). 1979. pap. 12.00 (*0-87944-246-8*) Inst Soc Res.

— Results from Two National Surveys of Philanthropic Activity. LC 79-53850. (Institute for Social Research, Research Report Ser.). 173p. (Orig.). reprint ed. pap. 49.40 (*0-7837-5254-7*, 2044991) Bks Demand.

Morgan, James P. & Shaver, Robert H., eds. Deltaic Sedimentation: Modern & Ancient. LC 72-191407. (Society of Economic Paleontologists & Mineralogists, Special Publication Ser.: No. 15). 332p. reprint ed. pap. 94.70 (*0-317-27153-9*, 2024740) Bks Demand.

***Morgan, James T.** Passport: Mark's Gospel. 32p. 1994. 2.95 (*0-89944-311-7*) Don Bosco Multimedia.

— Passport: Relationships. 32p. 1994. 2.95 (*0-89944-312-5*) Don Bosco Multimedia.

— Passport: the Good News. 32p. 1994. 2.95 (*0-89944-310-9*) Don Bosco Multimedia.

— Passport: the Image Industry. 32p. 1994. 2.95 (*0-89944-313-3*) Don Bosco Multimedia.

— Passport: the Sacraments. 32p. 1994. 2.95 (*0-89944-314-1*) Don Bosco Multimedia.

— Passport: Violence. 32p. 1994. 2.95 (*0-89944-315-X*) Don Bosco Multimedia.

Morgan, James W., ed. Naval Documents of the American Revolution, Vol. 9. LC 64-60087. (Illus.). 1171p. 1986. 44.00 (*0-16-002037-9*, S/N 008-046-00097-2) USGPO.

Morgan, Jane. Conflict & Order: The Police & Labour Disputes in England & Wales 1900-1939. (Illus.). 320p. 1988. 69.00 (*0-19-820128-1*) OUP.

Morgan, Jane, ed. see Miller, Bob.

Morgan, Janet, ed. The Backbench Diaries of Richard Crossman. 1136p. 1981. 55.00 (*0-8419-0686-6*) Holmes & Meier.

Morgan, Janet L., jt. auth. see Swan, William W.

Morgan, Janice & Hall, Colette, eds. Redefining Autobiography in Twentieth-Century Women's Fiction. LC 90-49120. (Gender & Genre in Literature Ser.: Vol. 3). 336p. 1991. 50.00 (*0-8240-7392-4*, H1386) Garland.

Morgan, Jason P., et al, eds. Mantle Flow & Melt Generation at Mid-Ocean Ridges. LC 93-812. (Geophysical Monograph Ser.: No. 71). 1993. 46.00 (*0-87590-035-6*) Am Geophysical.

Morgan, Jeff. The Rescue. (Survive! Ser.). (Illus.). 160p. (J). (gr. 3-7). 1994. pap. 3.50 (*0-448-40436-2*, G&D) Putnam Pub Group.

Morgan, Jenifer, ed. see Morgan, Ernest.

Morgan, Jenny. Herbs for Horses, No. 27: Threshold Picture Guide. (Illus.). 24p. (Orig.). (YA). 1993. pap. 12.00 (*1-872082-46-7*, Pub. by Kenilworth Pr UK) Half Halt Pr.

Morgan, Jenny, jt. auth. see Graycar, Regina.

***Morgan, Jill.** Victorian Shadows, No. 1. Date not set. write for info. (*0-679-87457-7*) Random.

— Victorian Shadows, No. 2. Date not set. write for info. (*0-679-87458-5*) Random.

— Victorian Shadows, No. 3. Date not set. write for info. (*0-679-87459-3*) Random.

— Victorian Shadows, No. 4. Date not set. write for info. (*0-679-87460-7*) Random.

Morgan, Jo A. Fair Play: One Hundred Ninety-Nine of the Single Hottest Jocks in the NBA. JBJ Enterprises, Inc. Staff, ed. (NFL, Major League Baseball Ser.). 200p. (Orig.). 1992. pap. text ed. 9.95 (*0-9631975-0-9*) J B J Ent.

Morgan, Jo-Anne. Fair Play: One Hundred Ninety-Seven of the Hottest Single Athletes in the NBA. (Illus.). 160p. (Orig.). Date not set. pap. write for info. (*0-318-69418-2*) J B J Ent.

Morgan, Joan & Richards, Alison. The Book of Apples. (Illus.). 288p. 1994. 29.95 (*0-09-177759-3*, Pub. by Ebury Pr UK) Trafalgar.

***Morgan, Joe.** Dreams. 190p. 1993. pap. 7.95 (*1-56901-404-3*) NW Pub.

— A Series to Remember: Toronto & Philadelphia, 1993: The Official Book of the 1993 World Series. Hyman, Laurence J. & Rochmis, Jon, eds. LC 93-61703. 144p. 1993. 29.95 (*0-942627-19-9*) Woodford Pub.

Morgan, Joe & Falkner, David. Joe Morgan: A Life in Baseball. LC 92-40151. 404p. 1993. 21.95 (*0-393-03469-0*) Norton.

Morgan, Joe P. Radiology in Veterinary Orthopedics. LC 71-175464. 415p. reprint ed. pap. 118.30 (*0-685-15883-7*, 2056191) Bks Demand.

Morgan, Joe P., ed. Techniques of Veterinary Radiography. 5th ed. LC 92-41342. (Illus.). 450p. (C). 1993. pap. text ed. 69.95 (*0-8138-1727-7*) Iowa St U Pr.

Morgan, Joe P. & Leighton, Robert L. Radiology of Small Animal Fracture Management. LC 94-13109. (Illus.). 400p. 1994. text ed. 70.00 (*0-7216-5455-X*) Saunders.

***Morgan, Joe P. & Wolvekamp, W. T.** An Atlas of Radiology of the Traumatized Dog & Cat. LC 94-22818. (Illus.). 1994. write for info. (*0-397-51483-2*) Lippincott.

Morgan, Joe P., et al. Equine Radiography. (Venture Series in Veterinary Medicine). (Illus.). 384p. (C). 1991. pap. text ed. 89.95 (*0-8138-0257-1*) Iowa St U Pr.

Morgan, Joe R. Potato Branch: Sketches of Mountain Memories. LC 92-24274. 176p. 1992. 14.95 (*0-914875-20-5*) Bright Mtn Bks.

Morgan, John. The Arctic Herd. LC 83-9130. (Alabama Poetry Ser.). x, 64p. 1984. 15.95x (*0-8173-0195-X*) U of Ala Pr.

— The Bone-Duster. (QRL Poetry Book Ser.: Vol. XXI). 20.00 (*0-614-06380-9*); pap. 15.00 (*0-614-06381-7*) Quarterly Rev.

— A Discourse Upon the Institution of Medical Schools in America. LC 74-26276. (History, Philosophy & Sociology of Science Ser.). 1975. reprint ed. 16.95 (*0-405-06604-X*) Ayer.

— Godly Learning: Puritan Attitudes Towards Reason, Learning, & Education, 1560-1640. 378p. 1988. pap. 24.95 (*0-521-35700-4*) Cambridge U Pr.

— Golf. (EP Sports Ser.). (Illus.). 112p. 1976. 6.95 (*0-7158-0596-7*) Charles River Bks.

— The Inside Passage. (Poetry Chapbook Ser.). 20p. (Orig.). 1985. pap. 4.00 (*0-937669-16-4*) Owl Creek Pr.

— The Log House in East Tennessee. LC 90-11912. 192p. 1990. lib. bdg. 30.00x (*0-87049-652-2*); pap. text ed. 15.00x (*0-87049-653-0*) U of Tenn Pr.

— Skilful Golf. (Skilful Ser.). (Illus.). 96p. 1991. pap. 14.95 (*0-7136-3394-8*, Pub. by A&C Black UK) Talman.

Morgan, John & Rinvolucri, Mario. Once upon a Time: Using Stories in the Language Classroom. (Cambridge Handbooks for Language Teachers Ser.). 120p. 1984. pap. 13.95 (*0-521-27262-9*) Cambridge U Pr.

Morgan, John & Welton, Peter. See What I Mean? An Introduction to Visual Communication. 2nd ed. 160p. 1992. pap. 16.95 (*0-340-55781-8*, A7066, Pub. by E Arnold UK) Routledge Chapman & Hall.

Morgan, John, jt. auth. see Friedman, John.

Morgan, John, jt. auth. see Hess, Robert E.

Morgan, John, ed. see Johnson County Historical Society Staff.

Morgan, John, jt. auth. see Sofie, Harold.

***Morgan, John C.** The Devotional Heart: Pietism & the Renewal of American Unitarian Universalism. 1995. pap. 14.00 (*1-55896-333-2*) Unitarian Univ.

Morgan, John C., jt. auth. see Morgan, Howard M.

Morgan, John D., ed. The Dying & the Bereaved Teenager. LC 90-35058. 168p. (Orig.). (C). 1990. pap. 16.95 (*0-914783-44-0*) Charles.

— Personal Care in an Impersonal World: A Multidimensional Look at Bereavement. LC 92-37430. (Death, Value, & Meaning Ser.). 267p. 1993. text ed. 31.95 (*0-89503-109-4*); pap. text ed. 23.95 (*0-89503-110-8*) Baywood Pub.

— Young People & Death. LC 90-28402. 224p. (Orig.). 1991. pap. 18.95 (*0-914783-49-1*) Charles.

Morgan, John D., jt. ed. see Doka, Kenneth J.

Morgan, John H. Catholic Spirituality: A Guide for Protestants. 126p. (Orig.). (C). Date not set. text ed. 24.95 (*1-55605-238-3*); pap. text ed. 14.95 (*1-55605-236-7*) Wyndhall Pr.

— From Freud to Frankl: Our Modern Search for Personal Meaning. LC 86-50580. 179p. (Orig.). (C). 1988. text ed. 24.95 (*1-55605-062-3*); pap. text ed. 14.95 (*0-932269-92-3*) Wyndhall Pr.

— Gilbert Stuart & His Pupils. LC 72-96440. (Library of American Art Ser.). 1969. reprint ed. lib. bdg. 25.00 (*0-306-71827-8*) Da Capo.

— Library Research in Psychology: A Student Manual of Information Retrieval & Utilization Skills. LC 86-50581. (Illus.). 56p. (Orig.). 1987. pap. text ed. 14.95 (*0-932269-91-5*) Wyndhall Pr.

— Women Priests: An Emerging Ministry in the Episcopal Church (1960 to 1980) 185p. (Orig.). (C). 1985. pap. 14.95 (*0-932269-48-6*) Wyndhall Pr.

An Asterisk (*) at the beginning of an entry indicates that the title is appearing in BIP for the first time.

Morgan, John H., ed. Celebration in Poetry: Wyndham Hall Press Inaugural Edition. 180p. (Orig.). 1988. pap. 14.95 (*0-932269-38-9*) Wyndhall Pr.

— Church Divinity, 1985. 109p. (Orig.). 1985. pap. 14.95 (*0-932269-61-3*) Wyndhall Pr.

— Church Divinity, 1986. 108p. 1986. pap. text ed. 14.95 (*0-932269-98-2*) Wyndhall Pr.

— Church Divinity, 1987. (Church Divinity Monograph Ser.). 154p. (C). 1987. pap. text ed. 14.95 (*1-55605-033-X*) Wyndhall Pr.

— Church Divinity, 1988. (Church Divinity Monograph Ser.). 125p. (C). 1988. pap. text ed. 14.95 (*1-55605-058-5*) Wyndhall Pr.

— The Cloverdale Review of Criticism & Poetry: James Joyce (1882-1941) in Memoriam. (Nineteen Ninety-One Ser.). 104p. (Orig.). (C). 1992. pap. text ed. 14.95 (*1-55605-199-9*) Wyndhall Pr.

— The Cloverdale Review of Poetry & Criticism, 1992-1993. (Illus.). 178p. (C). Date not set. pap. text ed. 14.95 (*1-55605-227-8*) Wyndhall Pr.

— Frost in Spring: An Anthology in Memoriam to Robert Frost. LC 89-40278. 245p. (C). 1989. pap. text ed. 14.95 (*1-55605-067-4*) Wyndhall Pr.

— Lutheran-Anglican-Roman Catholic Fellows: Yearbook 1988. 154p. (Orig.). (C). 1988. pap. 14.95 (*1-55605-047-X*) Wyndhall Pr.

— New Poets of Summer, Nineteen Eighty Five. LC 85-51482. 235p. 1985. pap. 14.95 (*0-932269-54-0*) Wyndhall Pr.

— Newman of Oxford: A Centennial Celebration in Poetry. LC 89-40612. 394p. 1990. text ed. 24.95 (*1-55605-117-4*); pap. text ed. 14.95 (*1-55605-116-6*) Wyndhall Pr.

— The Poetic Churchman: A Memorial Anthology to George Herbert (1593-1633) (Illus.). 110p. (Orig.). 1983. pap. text ed. 14.95 (*1-55605-140-9*) Wyndhall Pr.

— Riley in Memoriam (1849-1916) A Sesquicentennial Celebrative Anthology by the Poets of Indiana. LC 89-40432. (Illus.). 205p. 1989. text ed. 34.95 (*1-55605-099-2*); pap. text ed. 24.95 (*1-55605-100-X*) Wyndhall Pr.

— Seabury in Memoriam: A Bicentennial Anthology of Poetry to Samuel Seabury. (Illus.). 165p. (Orig.). 1984. pap. 14.95 (*1-55605-137-9*) Wyndhall Pr.

Morgan, John H., intro. The Anglican Mind: A Theological Compendium of the Classic Statements (from the 17th Century) LC 90-50109. 500p. (C). 1990. text ed. 37.95 (*1-55605-148-4*); pap. text ed. 27.95 (*1-55605-147-6*) Wyndhall Pr.

— Church Divinity, 1981. (Church Divinity Monograph Ser.). 160p. (Orig.). 1981. pap. text ed. 14.95 (*1-55605-141-7*) Wyndhall Pr.

— Church Divinity, 1982. (Church Divinity Monograph Ser.). 175p. (Orig.). 1982. pap. text ed. 14.95 (*1-55605-142-5*) Wyndhall Pr.

— Church Divinity, 1983. (Church Divinity Monograph Ser.). 150p. (Orig.). (C). 1983. pap. text ed. 14.95 (*1-55605-143-3*) Wyndhall Pr.

— Church Divinity, 1984. (Church Divinity Monograph Ser.). 240p. (Orig.). (C). 1984. pap. text ed. 14.95 (*1-55605-144-1*) Wyndhall Pr.

— Church Divinity, 1989-90. (Church Divinity Monograph Ser.). 250p. (Orig.). (C). 1990. pap. text ed. 14.95 (*1-55605-145-X*) Wyndhall Pr.

— Church Divinity, 1990-1991: Student Essays in Divinity. (Church Divinity Monograph Ser.). 96p. (Orig.). (C). 1991. pap. text ed. 14.95 (*1-55605-189-1*) Wyndhall Pr.

Morgan, John H. & Morgan, Linda B. Wives of Priests: A Study of Clergy Wives in the Episcopal Church. 185p. (Orig.). (C). 1988. pap. 14.95 (*1-55605-059-3*) Wyndhall Pr.

Morgan, John H., jt. auth. see Abraham, Francis.

Morgan, John H., jt. auth. see Barnes, William H.

Morgan, John J. & Webb, Ewing T. Making the Most of Your Life. LC 70-152199. (Essay Index Reprint Ser.). 1977. reprint ed. 23.95 (*0-8369-2248-4*) Ayer.

***Morgan, John M., 4th & Bennett, Genevieve R.** Directory of Colleges & Universities Offering GIS Courses. 70p. 1990. pap. 25.00 (*0-614-06095-8*, L333) Am Congrs Survey.

Morgan, John M., jt. auth. see Stevenson, Marshall L.

Morgan, John P. & Kagan, Doreen V., eds. Phenylpropanolamine: Risks, Benefits & Controversies. LC 85-6590. (Clinical Pharmacology & Therapeutics Ser.: Vol. 5). 440p. 1985. text ed. 79.50 (*0-275-91336-8*, C1336, Praeger Pubs) Greenwood.

Morgan, John S. Americans at War. 120p. (Orig.). 1991. pap. 13.76 (*0-685-48272-3*) Dayspring Pr.

— Business Faces the Urban Crisis. LC 74-86626. 264p. reprint ed. pap. 75.30 (*0-8357-7491-0*, 2051873) Bks Demand.

— Getting a Job after Fifty. (Illus.). 276p. 1990. text ed. 27.95 (*0-89433-311-9*, 8251); pap. text ed. 14.95 (*0-8306-8251-1*) Petrocelli.

— Getting a Job after Fifty. 1990. 27.95 (*0-685-32940-2*); pap. 14.60 (*0-685-32941-0*) TAB Bks.

— Getting a Job after 50. 1988. text ed. 27.95 (*0-07-156508-6*) McGraw.

— Unlimited Human Potential: A New Definition. LC 94-7645. 224p. (Orig.). 1994. pap. 14.95 (*1-56825-019-3*) Rainbow Books.

Morgan, John W. & Bass, Hyman. The Smith Conjecture. LC 83-15846. (Pure & Applied Mathematics Ser.). 1984. text ed. 91.00 (*0-12-506980-4*) Acad Pr.

Morgan, John W. & O'Grady, Kieran G. Differential Topology of Complex Surfaces. (Lecture Notes in Mathematics Ser.: Vol. 1545). (Illus.). viii, 224p. 1993. pap. write for info. (*3-540-56674-0*) Spr-Verlag.

— Differential Topology of Complex Surfaces: Elliptic Surfaces with Pg Equals 1: Smooth Classification. LC 93-16063. (Lecture Notes in Mathematics Ser.: Vol. 1545). 1993. 36.00 (*0-387-56674-0*) Spr-Verlag.

Morgan, Joseph. The Physical Basis of Musical Sound. LC 78-5508. (Illus.). 168p. (Orig.). 1980. lib. bdg. 16.50 (*0-88275-656-7*) Krieger.

***Morgan, Joseph R.** Porpoises among the Whales: Small Navies in Asia & the Pacific. (Illus.). 53p. (Orig.). (C). 1994. pap. text ed. 30.00x (*0-7881-0888-3*) Diane Pub.

Morgan, Joseph R. & Valencia, Mark J., eds. Atlas for Marine Policy in East Asian Seas. LC 91-29923. (C). 1992. 175.00 (*0-520-07798-9*) U CA Pr.

— Atlas for Marine Policy in Southeast Asian Seas. LC 83-47891. (Illus.). 1983. 160.00 (*0-520-05005-3*) U CA Pr.

Morgan, Joyce V. Stanislavski's Encounter with Shakespeare: The Evolution of a Method. LC 83-17979. (Theater & Dramatic Studies: No. 14). (Illus.). 186p. reprint ed. pap. 53.10 (*0-8357-1485-3*, 2070485) Bks Demand.

Morgan, Judith. An Art Text-Workbook: Calligraphy (Introduction) Wallace, Dorathye, ed. (Illus.). 134p. (Orig.). (YA). (gr. 8-10). 1990. student ed, pap. 14.35 (*0-914127-31-4*); teacher ed, pap. 16.95 (*0-914127-37-3*) Univ Class.

— An Art Text-Workbook: Ceramics (Introduction) Wallace, Dorathye, ed. (Illus.). 123p. (Orig.). (YA). (gr. 8-10). 1990. student ed, pap. 14.35 (*0-914127-24-1*); teacher ed, pap. 6.95 (*0-914127-26-8*) Univ Class.

— An Art Text-Workbook: Crafts (Introduction) Wallace, Dorathye, ed. (Illus.). 157p. (Orig.). (YA). (gr. 8-10). 1990. student ed, pap. 14.35 (*0-914127-32-2*); teacher ed, pap. 16.95 (*0-914127-38-1*) Univ Class.

— An Art Text-Workbook: Drawing (Introduction) Wallace, Dorathye, ed. (Illus.). 150p. (Orig.). (YA). (gr. 8-10). 1990. student ed, pap. 14.35 (*0-914127-51-9*); teacher ed, pap. 16.95 (*0-914127-52-7*) Univ Class.

— An Art Text-Workbook: Film Making (Introduction) Wallace, Dorathye, ed. (Illus.). 146p. (Orig.). (YA). (gr. 8-10). 1990. student ed, pap. 14.35 (*0-914127-36-5*); teacher ed, pap. 16.95 (*0-914127-40-3*) Univ Class.

— Art Text-Workbook: General Art (Introduction) Wallace, Dorathye, ed. (Illus.). 100p. (Orig.). (YA). (gr. 8-10). 1990. student ed, pap. 1,435.27 (*0-914127-54-3*); teacher ed, pap. 16.95 (*0-914127-53-5*) Univ Class.

— An Art Text-Workbook: Metalsmithing (Introduction) Wallace, Dorothy, ed. (Illus.). 142p. (Orig.). (YA). (gr. 8-10). 1990. student ed, pap. 13.27 (*0-914127-33-0*) Univ Class.

— An Art Text-Workbook: Metalsmithing (Introduction) Wallace, Dorothy, ed. (Illus.). 142p. (Orig.). (YA). (gr. 8-10). 1990. teacher ed 16.95 (*0-914127-41-1*) Univ Class.

— An Art Text-Workbook: Painting (Introduction) Wallace, Dorathye, ed. (Illus.). 127p. (Orig.). (YA). (gr. 8-10). 1990. teacher ed 16.95 (*0-914127-58-6*); student ed, pap. 14.35 (*0-914127-57-8*) Univ Class.

— An Art Text-Workbook: Photography (Introduction) Baird, Tate, ed. (Illus.). 178p. (Orig.). (YA). (gr. 8-10). 1990. teacher ed 16.95 (*0-914127-42-X*); student ed, pap. text ed. 14.35 (*0-914127-23-3*) Univ Class.

— An Art Text-Workbook: Printmaking (Introduction) Wallace, Dorathye, ed. (Illus.). 124p. (Orig.). (YA). (gr. 8-10). 1990. teacher ed 16.95 (*0-914127-28-4*); student ed, pap. 14.35 (*0-914127-27-6*) Univ Class.

— An Art Text-Workbook: Sculpture (Introduction) Wallace, Dorathye, ed. (Orig.). 1990. student ed 14.35 (*0-914127-43-8*) Univ Class.

— An Art Text-Workbook: Sculpture (Introduction) Wallace, Dorathye, ed. (Illus.). 113p. (Orig.). (YA). (gr. 8-10). 1990. teacher ed 16.95 (*0-914127-34-9*) Univ Class.

— An Art Text-Workbook: Weaving (Introduction) Wallace, Dorathye, ed. (Illus.). 144p. (Orig.). (YA). (gr. 8-10). 1990. teacher ed 16.95 (*0-914127-62-4*); student ed, pap. 14.35 (*0-914127-61-6*) Univ Class.

Morgan, Judith & Morgan, Neil. Dr. Seuss & Mr. Geisel: A Biography. 1995. 25.00 (*0-679-41686-2*) Random.

Morgan, Julia, jt. auth. see Bye, L. Dean.

Morgan, K., jt. auth. see Marley, W.

Morgan, K., ed. see Schrefler, B. A.

***Morgan, K., et al.** Interactive Technology in Health Care. LC 94-73352. 300p. 1995. 82.00 (*90-5199-201-7*) IOS Press.

Morgan, K. O., ed. see Ramm, Agatha.

Morgan, K. O., ed. see Wrigley, Chris.

Morgan, Kate. Days of Crime & Roses. 192p. (Orig.). 1992. pap. 3.99 (*0-425-13471-7*) Berkley Pub.

— The Story of Things. (Illus.). 32p. (J). (gr. 3-7). 1991. 14.95 (*0-8027-6918-7*); lib. bdg. 15.85 (*0-8027-6919-5*) Walker & Co.

— Wanted: Dude or Alive. 208p. (Orig.). 1994. pap. 4.50 (*0-425-14330-9*, Prime Crime) Berkley Pub.

Morgan, Kathleen. Child of the Mist. 400p. (Orig.). 1993. pap. 4.50 (*0-8439-3379-8*) Dorchester Pub Co.

— Crystal Fire. 448p. (Orig.). 1992. pap. 4.50 (*0-8439-3285-6*) Dorchester Pub Co.

— Crystal Fire. 448p. (Orig.). 1995. mass mkt., pap. 5.50 (*0-505-52065-6*) Dorchester Pub Co.

— Demon Prince. 448p. (Orig.). 1994. pap. 4.99 (*0-505-51941-0*, Love Spell) Dorchester Pub Co.

— Enchant the Heavens. 480p. 1995. mass mkt. 4.99 (*0-8217-4799-1*) Zebra.

— Fire Queen. 1994. mass mkt. 4.99 (*0-312-95268-6*) St Martin.

— Firestar. 448p. (Orig.). 1993. pap. 4.99 (*0-505-51908-9*, Love Spell) Dorchester Pub Co.

— Firestorm. 448p. 1995. pap. 4.99 (*0-7860-0175-5*) Windsor NY.

— Fun with the Alphabet. (Illus.). 64p. (J). (ps-1). 1987. teacher ed, pap. 6.95 (*1-55799-068-9*, EMC 214) Evan-Moor Corp.

— Heart's Lair. 368p. 1994. reprint ed. mass mkt., pap. text ed. 4.50 (*0-8439-3549-9*) Dorchester Pub Co.

— Heart's Surrender. 480p. 1994. mass mkt. 5.99 (*0-7860-0052-X*) Windsor NY.

— The Knowing Crystal. 368p. 1994. mass mkt., pap. text ed. 4.50 (*0-8439-3548-0*) Dorchester Pub Co.

— Math Readiness. (Illus.). 48p. (J). (ps-1). 1990. pap. text ed. 5.95 (*1-55799-157-X*) Evan-Moor Corp.

— Simple Games for Practicing Basic Skills. (Illus.). 48p. (J). (ps-1). 1989. pap. text ed. 5.95 (*1-55799-147-2*) Evan-Moor Corp.

— Tales Plainly Told: The Eyewitness Narratives of Hemingway & Homer. (Studies in English & American Literature, Linguistics & Culture: Vol. 7). 102p. 1991. 44.00 (*0-938100-81-5*) Camden Hse.

Morgan, Kathleen O., ed. District of Columbia Crime in Perspective 1994: Crime in the "Capital City" 23p. 1994. pap. text ed. 18.00 (*1-56692-300-X*) Morgan Quitno Corp.

Morgan, Kathleen O., et al, eds. California Health Care Perspective, 1994. 24p. 1994. 18.00 (*1-56692-154-6*) Morgan Quitno Corp.

***Morgan, Kathleen O., et al.** District of Columbia Crime in Perspective. 1995. pap. 18.00 (*1-56692-308-5*) Morgan Quitno Corp.

Morgan, Kathleen O., et al, eds. Alabama Crime Perspective, 1994. 24p. 1994. 18.00 (*1-56692-250-X*) Morgan Quitno Corp.

— Alabama Crime Perspective, 1995. 24p. 1995. 18.00 (*1-56692-350-6*) Morgan Quitno Corp.

— Alabama Health Care Perspective, 1994. 24p. 1994. 18.00 (*1-56692-150-3*) Morgan Quitno Corp.

— Alabama Health Care Perspective 1995. 24p. 1995. 18.00 (*1-56692-400-6*) Morgan Quitno Corp.

— Alabama in Perspective, 1994. 26p. 1994. pap. 18.00 (*1-56692-200-3*) Morgan Quitno Corp.

— Alabama in Perspective 1995. 26p. 1995. pap. 18.00 (*1-56692-450-2*) Morgan Quitno Corp.

— Alaska Crime Perspective, 1994. 24p. 1994. 18.00 (*1-56692-251-8*) Morgan Quitno Corp.

— Alaska Crime Perspective 1995. 24p. 1995. 18.00 (*1-56692-351-4*) Morgan Quitno Corp.

— Alaska Health Care Perspective, 1994. 24p. 1994. 18.00 (*1-56692-151-1*) Morgan Quitno Corp.

— Alaska Health Care Perspective 1995. 24p. 1995. 18.00 (*1-56692-401-4*) Morgan Quitno Corp.

— Alaska in Perspective, 1994. 26p. 1994. 18.00 (*1-56692-201-1*) Morgan Quitno Corp.

— Alaska in Perspective 1995. 26p. 1995. pap. 18.00 (*1-56692-451-0*) Morgan Quitno Corp.

— Arizona Crime Perspective, 1994. 24p. 1994. 18.00 (*1-56692-252-6*) Morgan Quitno Corp.

— Arizona Crime Perspective 1995. 24p. 1995. 18.00 (*1-56692-352-2*) Morgan Quitno Corp.

— Arizona Health Care Perspective, 1994. 24p. 1994. 18.00 (*1-56692-152-X*) Morgan Quitno Corp.

— Arizona Health Care Perspective 1995. 24p. 1995. 18.00 (*1-56692-402-2*) Morgan Quitno Corp.

— Arizona in Perspective, 1994. 26p. 1994. 18.00 (*1-56692-202-X*) Morgan Quitno Corp.

— Arizona in Perspective 1995. 26p. 1995. pap. 18.00 (*1-56692-452-9*) Morgan Quitno Corp.

— Arkansas Crime Perspective, 1994. 24p. 1994. 18.00 (*1-56692-253-4*) Morgan Quitno Corp.

— Arkansas Crime Perspective, 1995. 24p. 1995. 18.00 (*1-56692-353-0*) Morgan Quitno Corp.

— Arkansas Health Care Perspective, 1994. 24p. 1994. 18.00 (*1-56692-153-8*) Morgan Quitno Corp.

— Arkansas Health Care Perspective 1995. 24p. 1995. 18.00 (*1-56692-403-0*) Morgan Quitno Corp.

— Arkansas in Perspective 1994. 26p. 1994. 18.00 (*1-56692-203-8*) Morgan Quitno Corp.

— Arkansas in Perspective 1995. 26p. 1995. pap. 18.00 (*1-56692-453-7*) Morgan Quitno Corp.

— California Crime Perspective, 1994. 24p. 1994. 18.00 (*1-56692-254-2*) Morgan Quitno Corp.

— California Crime Perspective 1995. 24p. 1995. 18.00 (*1-56692-354-9*) Morgan Quitno Corp.

— California Health Care Perspective 1995. 24p. 1995. 18.00 (*1-56692-404-9*) Morgan Quitno Corp.

— California in Perspective 1994. 26p. 1994. 18.00 (*1-56692-204-6*) Morgan Quitno Corp.

— California in Perspective 1995. 26p. 1995. pap. 18.00 (*1-56692-454-5*) Morgan Quitno Corp.

— City Crime Rankings: Crime in Metropolitan America. 300p. (Orig.). 1995. pap. 19.95 (*1-56692-307-7*) Morgan Quitno Corp.

— Colorado Crime Perspective, 1994. 24p. 1994. 18.00 (*1-56692-255-0*) Morgan Quitno Corp.

— Colorado Crime Perspective 1995. 24p. 1995. 18.00 (*1-56692-355-7*) Morgan Quitno Corp.

— Colorado Health Care Perspective, 1994. 24p. 1994. 18.00 (*1-56692-155-4*) Morgan Quitno Corp.

— Colorado Health Care Perspective 1995. 24p. 1995. 18.00 (*1-56692-405-7*) Morgan Quitno Corp.

— Colorado in Perspective, 1994. 26p. 1994. 18.00 (*1-56692-205-4*) Morgan Quitno Corp.

— Colorado in Perspective 1995. 26p. 1995. pap. 18.00 (*1-56692-455-3*) Morgan Quitno Corp.

— Connecticut Crime Perspective, 1994. 24p. 1994. 18.00 (*1-56692-256-9*) Morgan Quitno Corp.

— Connecticut Crime Perspective 1995. 24p. 1995. 18.00 (*1-56692-356-5*) Morgan Quitno Corp.

— Connecticut Health Care Perspective, 1994. 24p. 1994. 18.00 (*1-56692-156-2*) Morgan Quitno Corp.

— Connecticut Health Care Perspective 1995. 24p. 1995. 18.00 (*1-56692-406-5*) Morgan Quitno Corp.

— Connecticut in Perspective, 1994. 26p. 1994. 18.00 (*1-56692-206-2*) Morgan Quitno Corp.

— Connecticut in Perspective 1995. 26p. 1995. pap. 18.00 (*1-56692-456-1*) Morgan Quitno Corp.

— Crime State Rankings 1995. 544p. 1995. pap. 43.95 (*1-56692-301-8*) Morgan Quitno Corp.

— Crime State Rankings 1995. 544p. 1995. 67.95 (*1-56692-305-0*) Morgan Quitno Corp.

— Delaware Crime Perspective, 1994. 24p. 1994. 18.00 (*1-56692-257-7*) Morgan Quitno Corp.

— Delaware Crime Perspective 1995. 24p. 1995. 18.00 (*1-56692-357-3*) Morgan Quitno Corp.

— Delaware Health Care Perspective, 1994. 24p. 1994. 18.00 (*1-56692-157-0*) Morgan Quitno Corp.

— Delaware Health Care Perspective 1995. 24p. 1995. 18.00 (*1-56692-407-3*) Morgan Quitno Corp.

— Delaware in Perspective, 1994. 26p. 1994. 18.00 (*1-56692-207-0*) Morgan Quitno Corp.

— Delaware in Perspective 1995. 26p. 1995. pap. 18.00 (*1-56692-457-X*) Morgan Quitno Corp.

— Florida Crime Perspective, 1994. 24p. 1994. 18.00 (*1-56692-258-5*) Morgan Quitno Corp.

— Florida Crime Perspective 1995. 24p. 1995. 18.00 (*1-56692-358-1*) Morgan Quitno Corp.

— Florida Health Care Perspective, 1994. 24p. 1994. 18.00 (*1-56692-158-9*) Morgan Quitno Corp.

— Florida Health Care Perspective 1995. 24p. 1995. 18.00 (*1-56692-408-1*) Morgan Quitno Corp.

— Florida in Perspective, 1994. 26p. 1994. 18.00 (*1-56692-208-9*) Morgan Quitno Corp.

— Florida in Perspective 1995. 26p. 1995. pap. 18.00 (*1-56692-458-8*) Morgan Quitno Corp.

— Georgia Crime Perspective, 1994. 24p. 1994. 18.00 (*1-56692-259-3*) Morgan Quitno Corp.

— Georgia Crime Perspective 1995. 24p. 1995. 18.00 (*1-56692-359-X*) Morgan Quitno Corp.

— Georgia Health Care Perspective, 1994. 24p. 1994. 18.00 (*1-56692-159-7*) Morgan Quitno Corp.

— Georgia Health Care Perspective 1995. 24p. 1995. 18.00 (*1-56692-409-X*) Morgan Quitno Corp.

— Georgia in Perspective, 1994. 26p. 1994. 18.00 (*1-56692-209-7*) Morgan Quitno Corp.

— Georgia in Perspective 1995. 26p. 1995. pap. 18.00 (*1-56692-459-6*) Morgan Quitno Corp.

— Hawaii Crime Perspective 1995. 24p. 1995. 18.00 (*1-56692-360-3*) Morgan Quitno Corp.

— Hawaii Crime Perspective, 1994. 24p. 1994. 18.00 (*1-56692-260-7*) Morgan Quitno Corp.

— Hawaii Health Care Perspective 1995. 24p. 1995. 18.00 (*1-56692-410-3*) Morgan Quitno Corp.

— Hawaii Health Care Perspective, 1994. 24p. 1994. 18.00 (*1-56692-160-0*) Morgan Quitno Corp.

— Hawaii in Perspective 1995. 26p. 1995. pap. 18.00 (*1-56692-460-X*) Morgan Quitno Corp.

— Hawaii in Perspective, 1994. 26p. 1994. 18.00 (*1-56692-210-0*) Morgan Quitno Corp.

— Health Care State Rankings, 1993: Health Care in the 50 United States. 512p. 1992. pap. text ed. 43.95 (*0-9625531-4-X*) Morgan Quitno Corp.

— Health Care State Rankings, 1994. 540p. 1994. pap. 43.95 (*0-9625531-8-2*) Morgan Quitno Corp.

— Health Care State Rankings 1995. 540p. 1995. pap. 43.95 (*1-56692-302-6*) Morgan Quitno Corp.

— Health Care State Rankings 1995. 540p. 1995. 67.95 (*1-56692-306-9*) Morgan Quitno Corp.

— Idaho Crime Perspective, 1994. 24p. 1994. 18.00 (*1-56692-261-5*) Morgan Quitno Corp.

— Idaho Crime Perspective 1995. 24p. 1995. 18.00 (*1-56692-361-1*) Morgan Quitno Corp.

— Idaho Health Care Perspective, 1994. 24p. 1994. 18.00 (*1-56692-161-9*) Morgan Quitno Corp.

— Idaho Health Care Perspective 1995. 24p. 1995. 18.00 (*1-56692-411-1*) Morgan Quitno Corp.

— Idaho in Perspective, 1994. 26p. 1994. 18.00 (*1-56692-211-9*) Morgan Quitno Corp.

— Idaho in Perspective 1995. 26p. 1995. pap. 18.00 (*1-56692-461-8*) Morgan Quitno Corp.

— Illinois Crime Perspective, 1994. 24p. 1994. 18.00 (*1-56692-262-3*) Morgan Quitno Corp.

— Illinois Crime Perspective 1995. 24p. 1995. 18.00 (*1-56692-362-X*) Morgan Quitno Corp.

— Illinois Health Care Perspective, 1994. 24p. 1994. 18.00 (*1-56692-162-7*) Morgan Quitno Corp.

— Illinois Health Care Perspective 1995. 24p. 1995. 18.00 (*1-56692-412-X*) Morgan Quitno Corp.

— Illinois in Perspective, 1994. 26p. 1994. 18.00 (*1-56692-212-7*) Morgan Quitno Corp.

— Illinois in Perspective 1995. 26p. 1995. pap. 18.00 (*1-56692-462-6*) Morgan Quitno Corp.

— Indiana Crime Perspective, 1994. 24p. 1994. 18.00 (*1-56692-263-1*) Morgan Quitno Corp.

— Indiana Crime Perspective 1995. 24p. 1995. 18.00 (*1-56692-363-8*) Morgan Quitno Corp.

— Indiana Health Care Perspective, 1994. 24p. 1994. 18.00 (*1-56692-163-5*) Morgan Quitno Corp.

— Indiana Health Care Perspective 1995. 24p. 1995. 18.00 (*1-56692-413-8*) Morgan Quitno Corp.

— Indiana in Perspective, 1994. 26p. 1994. 18.00 (*1-56692-213-5*) Morgan Quitno Corp.

— Indiana in Perspective 1995. 26p. 1995. pap. 18.00 (*1-56692-463-4*) Morgan Quitno Corp.

— Iowa Crime Perspective, 1994. 24p. 1994. 18.00 (*1-56692-264-X*) Morgan Quitno Corp.

— Iowa Crime Perspective, 1995. 24p. 1995. 18.00 (*1-56692-364-6*) Morgan Quitno Corp.

— Iowa Health Care Perspective, 1994. 24p. 1994. 18.00 (*1-56692-164-3*) Morgan Quitno Corp.

— Iowa Health Care Perspective 1995. 24p. 1995. 18.00 (*1-56692-414-6*) Morgan Quitno Corp.

— Iowa in Perspective 1994. 26p. 1994. 18.00 (*1-56692-214-3*) Morgan Quitno Corp.

— Iowa in Perspective 1995. 26p. 1995. pap. 18.00 (*1-56692-464-2*) Morgan Quitno Corp.
— Kansas Crime Perspective, 1994. 24p. 1994. 18.00 (*1-56692-265-8*) Morgan Quitno Corp.
— Kansas Crime Perspective 1995. 24p. 1995. 18.00 (*1-56692-365-4*) Morgan Quitno Corp.
— Kansas Health Care Perspective, 1994. 24p. 1994. 18.00 (*1-56692-165-1*) Morgan Quitno Corp.
— Kansas Health Care Perspective 1995. 24p. 1995. 18.00 (*1-56692-415-4*) Morgan Quitno Corp.
— Kansas in Perspective, 1994. 26p. 1994. 18.00 (*1-56692-215-1*) Morgan Quitno Corp.
— Kansas in Perspective 1995. 26p. 1995. pap. 18.00 (*1-56692-465-0*) Morgan Quitno Corp.
— Kentucky Crime Perspective, 1994. 24p. 1994. 18.00 (*1-56692-266-6*) Morgan Quitno Corp.
— Kentucky Crime Perspective 1995. 24p. 1995. 18.00 (*1-56692-366-2*) Morgan Quitno Corp.
— Kentucky Health Care Perspective, 1994. 24p. 1994. 18.00 (*1-56692-166-X*) Morgan Quitno Corp.
— Kentucky Health Care Perspective 1995. 24p. 1995. 18.00 (*1-56692-416-2*) Morgan Quitno Corp.
— Kentucky in Perspective, 1994. 26p. 1994. 18.00 (*1-56692-216-X*) Morgan Quitno Corp.
— Kentucky in Perspective 1995. 26p. 1995. pap. 18.00 (*1-56692-466-9*) Morgan Quitno Corp.
— Louisiana Crime Perspective, 1994. 24p. 1994. 18.00 (*1-56692-267-4*) Morgan Quitno Corp.
— Louisiana Crime Perspective 1995. 24p. 1995. 18.00 (*1-56692-367-0*) Morgan Quitno Corp.
— Louisiana Health Care Perspective, 1994. 24p. 1994. 18.00 (*1-56692-167-8*) Morgan Quitno Corp.
— Louisiana Health Care Perspective 1995. 24p. 1995. 18.00 (*1-56692-417-0*) Morgan Quitno Corp.
— Louisiana in Perspective, 1994. 26p. 1994. 18.00 (*1-56692-217-8*) Morgan Quitno Corp.
— Louisiana in Perspective 1995. 26p. 1995. pap. 18.00 (*1-56692-467-7*) Morgan Quitno Corp.
— Maine Crime Perspective, 1994. 24p. 1994. 18.00 (*1-56692-268-2*) Morgan Quitno Corp.
— Maine Crime Perspective 1995. 24p. 1995. 18.00 (*1-56692-368-9*) Morgan Quitno Corp.
— Maine Health Care Perspective, 1994. 24p. 1994. 18.00 (*1-56692-168-6*) Morgan Quitno Corp.
— Maine Health Care Perspective 1995. 24p. 1995. 18.00 (*1-56692-418-9*) Morgan Quitno Corp.
— Maine in Perspective, 1994. 26p. 1994. 18.00 (*1-56692-218-6*) Morgan Quitno Corp.
— Maine in Perspective 1995. 26p. 1995. pap. 18.00 (*1-56692-468-5*) Morgan Quitno Corp.
— Maryland Crime Perspective, 1994. 24p. 1994. 18.00 (*1-56692-269-0*) Morgan Quitno Corp.
— Maryland Crime Perspective 1995. 24p. 1995. 18.00 (*1-56692-369-7*) Morgan Quitno Corp.
— Maryland Health Care Perspective, 1994. 24p. 1994. 18.00 (*1-56692-169-4*) Morgan Quitno Corp.
— Maryland Health Care Perspective 1995. 24p. 1995. 18.00 (*1-56692-419-7*) Morgan Quitno Corp.
— Maryland in Perspective, 1994. 26p. 1994. 18.00 (*1-56692-219-4*) Morgan Quitno Corp.
— Maryland in Perspective 1995. 26p. 1995. pap. 18.00 (*1-56692-469-3*) Morgan Quitno Corp.
— Massachusetts Crime Perspective, 1994. 24p. 1994. 18.00 (*1-56692-270-4*) Morgan Quitno Corp.
— Massachusetts Crime Perspective 1995. 24p. 1995. 18.00 (*1-56692-370-0*) Morgan Quitno Corp.
— Massachusetts Health Care Perspective, 1994. 24p. 1994. 18.00 (*1-56692-170-8*) Morgan Quitno Corp.
— Massachusetts Health Care Perspective 1995. 24p. 1995. 18.00 (*1-56692-420-0*) Morgan Quitno Corp.
— Massachusetts in Perspective, 1994. 26p. 1994. 18.00 (*1-56692-220-8*) Morgan Quitno Corp.
— Massachusetts in Perspective 1995. 26p. 1995. pap. 18.00 (*1-56692-470-7*) Morgan Quitno Corp.
— Michigan Crime Perspective, 1994. 24p. 1994. 18.00 (*1-56692-271-2*) Morgan Quitno Corp.
— Michigan Crime Perspective 1995. 24p. 1995. 18.00 (*1-56692-371-9*) Morgan Quitno Corp.
— Michigan Health Care Perspective, 1994. 24p. 1994. 18.00 (*1-56692-171-6*) Morgan Quitno Corp.
— Michigan Health Care Perspective 1995. 24p. 1995. 18.00 (*1-56692-421-9*) Morgan Quitno Corp.
— Michigan in Perspective, 1994. 26p. 1994. 18.00 (*1-56692-221-6*) Morgan Quitno Corp.
— Michigan in Perspective 1995. 26p. 1995. pap. 18.00 (*1-56692-471-5*) Morgan Quitno Corp.
— Minnesota Crime Perspective, 1994. 24p. 1994. 18.00 (*1-56692-272-0*) Morgan Quitno Corp.
— Minnesota Crime Perspective 1995. 24p. 1995. 18.00 (*1-56692-372-7*) Morgan Quitno Corp.
— Minnesota Health Care Perspective, 1994. 24p. 1994. 18.00 (*1-56692-172-4*) Morgan Quitno Corp.
— Minnesota Health Care Perspective 1995. 24p. 1995. 18.00 (*1-56692-422-7*) Morgan Quitno Corp.
— Minnesota in Perspective, 1994. 26p. 1994. 18.00 (*1-56692-222-4*) Morgan Quitno Corp.
— Minnesota in Perspective 1995. 26p. 1995. pap. 18.00 (*1-56692-472-3*) Morgan Quitno Corp.
— Mississippi Crime Perspective, 1994. 24p. 1994. 18.00 (*1-56692-273-9*) Morgan Quitno Corp.
— Mississippi Crime Perspective 1995. 24p. 1995. 18.00 (*1-56692-373-5*) Morgan Quitno Corp.
— Mississippi Health Care Perspective, 1994. 24p. 1994. 18.00 (*1-56692-173-2*) Morgan Quitno Corp.
— Mississippi Health Care Perspective 1995. 24p. 1995. 18.00 (*1-56692-423-5*) Morgan Quitno Corp.
— Mississippi in Perspective, 1994. 26p. 1994. 18.00 (*1-56692-223-2*) Morgan Quitno Corp.
— Mississippi in Perspective 1995. 26p. 1995. pap. 18.00 (*1-56692-473-1*) Morgan Quitno Corp.
— Missouri Crime Perspective, 1994. 24p. 1994. 18.00 (*1-56692-274-7*) Morgan Quitno Corp.
— Missouri Crime Perspective 1995. 24p. 1995. 18.00 (*1-56692-374-3*) Morgan Quitno Corp.
— Missouri Health Care Perspective, 1994. 24p. 1994. 18.00 (*1-56692-174-0*) Morgan Quitno Corp.
— Missouri Health Care Perspective 1995. 24p. 1995. 18.00 (*1-56692-424-3*) Morgan Quitno Corp.
— Missouri in Perspective, 1994. 26p. 1994. 18.00 (*1-56692-224-0*) Morgan Quitno Corp.
— Missouri in Perspective 1995. 26p. 1995. pap. 18.00 (*1-56692-474-X*) Morgan Quitno Corp.
— Montana Crime Perspective, 1994. 24p. 1994. 18.00 (*1-56692-275-5*) Morgan Quitno Corp.
— Montana Crime Perspective 1995. 24p. 1995. 18.00 (*1-56692-375-1*) Morgan Quitno Corp.
— Montana Health Care Perspective, 1994. 24p. 1994. 18.00 (*1-56692-175-9*) Morgan Quitno Corp.
— Montana Health Care Perspective 1995. 24p. 1995. 18.00 (*1-56692-425-1*) Morgan Quitno Corp.
— Montana in Perspective, 1994. 26p. 1994. 18.00 (*1-56692-225-9*) Morgan Quitno Corp.
— Montana in Perspective 1995. 26p. 1995. pap. 18.00 (*1-56692-475-8*) Morgan Quitno Corp.
— Nebraska Crime Perspective, 1994. 24p. 1994. 18.00 (*1-56692-276-3*) Morgan Quitno Corp.
— Nebraska Crime Perspective 1995. 24p. 1995. 18.00 (*1-56692-376-X*) Morgan Quitno Corp.
— Nebraska Health Care Perspective, 1994. 24p. 1994. 18.00 (*1-56692-176-7*) Morgan Quitno Corp.
— Nebraska Health Care Perspective 1995. 24p. 1995. 18.00 (*1-56692-426-X*) Morgan Quitno Corp.
— Nebraska in Perspective, 1994. 26p. 1994. 18.00 (*1-56692-226-7*) Morgan Quitno Corp.
— Nebraska in Perspective 1995. 26p. 1995. pap. 18.00 (*1-56692-476-6*) Morgan Quitno Corp.
— Nevada Crime Perspective, 1994. 24p. 1994. 18.00 (*1-56692-277-1*) Morgan Quitno Corp.
— Nevada Crime Perspective 1995. 24p. 1995. 18.00 (*1-56692-377-8*) Morgan Quitno Corp.
— Nevada Health Care Perspective, 1994. 24p. 1994. 18.00 (*1-56692-177-5*) Morgan Quitno Corp.
— Nevada Health Care Perspective 1995. 24p. 1995. 18.00 (*1-56692-427-8*) Morgan Quitno Corp.
— Nevada in Perspective, 1994. 26p. 1994. 18.00 (*1-56692-227-5*) Morgan Quitno Corp.
— Nevada in Perspective 1995. 26p. 1995. pap. 18.00 (*1-56692-477-4*) Morgan Quitno Corp.
— New Hampshire Crime Perspective, 1994. 24p. 1994. 18.00 (*1-56692-278-X*) Morgan Quitno Corp.
— New Hampshire Crime Perspective 1995. 24p. 1995. 18.00 (*1-56692-378-6*) Morgan Quitno Corp.
— New Hampshire Health Care Perspective, 1994. 24p. 1994. 18.00 (*1-56692-178-3*) Morgan Quitno Corp.
— New Hampshire Health Care Perspective 1995. 24p. 1995. 18.00 (*1-56692-428-6*) Morgan Quitno Corp.
— New Hampshire in Perspective, 1994. 26p. 1994. 18.00 (*1-56692-228-3*) Morgan Quitno Corp.
— New Hampshire in Perspective 1995. 26p. 1995. pap. 18.00 (*1-56692-478-2*) Morgan Quitno Corp.
— New Jersey Crime Perspective, 1994. 24p. 1994. 18.00 (*1-56692-279-8*) Morgan Quitno Corp.
— New Jersey Crime Perspective 1995. 24p. 1995. 18.00 (*1-56692-379-4*) Morgan Quitno Corp.
— New Jersey Health Care Perspective, 1994. 24p. 1994. 18.00 (*1-56692-179-1*) Morgan Quitno Corp.
— New Jersey Health Care Perspective 1995. 24p. 1995. 18.00 (*1-56692-429-4*) Morgan Quitno Corp.
— New Jersey in Perspective, 1994. 26p. 1994. 18.00 (*1-56692-229-1*) Morgan Quitno Corp.
— New Jersey in Perspective 1995. 26p. 1995. pap. 18.00 (*1-56692-479-0*) Morgan Quitno Corp.
— New Mexico Crime Perspective, 1994. 24p. 1994. 18.00 (*1-56692-280-1*) Morgan Quitno Corp.
— New Mexico Crime Perspective 1995. 24p. 1995. 18.00 (*1-56692-380-8*) Morgan Quitno Corp.
— New Mexico Health Care Perspective, 1994. 24p. 1994. 18.00 (*1-56692-180-5*) Morgan Quitno Corp.
— New Mexico Health Care Perspective 1995. 24p. 1995. 18.00 (*1-56692-430-8*) Morgan Quitno Corp.
— New Mexico in Perspective, 1994. 26p. 1994. 18.00 (*1-56692-230-5*) Morgan Quitno Corp.
— New Mexico in Perspective 1995. 26p. 1995. pap. 18.00 (*1-56692-480-4*) Morgan Quitno Corp.
— New York Crime Perspective, 1994. 24p. 1994. 18.00 (*1-56692-281-X*) Morgan Quitno Corp.
— New York Crime Perspective 1995. 24p. 1995. 18.00 (*1-56692-381-6*) Morgan Quitno Corp.
— New York Health Care Perspective, 1994. 24p. 1994. 18.00 (*1-56692-181-3*) Morgan Quitno Corp.
— New York Health Care Perspective 1995. 24p. 1995. 18.00 (*1-56692-431-6*) Morgan Quitno Corp.
— New York in Perspective, 1994. 26p. 1994. 18.00 (*1-56692-231-3*) Morgan Quitno Corp.
— New York in Perspective 1995. 26p. 1995. pap. 18.00 (*1-56692-481-2*) Morgan Quitno Corp.
— North Carolina Crime Perspective, 1994. 24p. 1994. 18.00 (*1-56692-282-8*) Morgan Quitno Corp.
— North Carolina Crime Perspective 1995. 24p. 1995. 18.00 (*1-56692-382-4*) Morgan Quitno Corp.
— North Carolina Health Care Perspective, 1994. 24p. 1994. 18.00 (*1-56692-182-1*) Morgan Quitno Corp.
— North Carolina Health Care Perspective 1995. 24p. 1995. 18.00 (*1-56692-432-4*) Morgan Quitno Corp.
— North Carolina in Perspective, 1994. 26p. 1994. 18.00 (*1-56692-232-1*) Morgan Quitno Corp.
— North Carolina in Perspective 1995. 26p. 1995. pap. 18.00 (*1-56692-482-0*) Morgan Quitno Corp.
— North Dakota Crime Perspective, 1994. 24p. 1994. 18.00 (*1-56692-283-6*) Morgan Quitno Corp.
— North Dakota Crime Perspective 1995. 24p. 1995. 18.00 (*1-56692-383-2*) Morgan Quitno Corp.
— North Dakota Health Care Perspective, 1994. 24p. 1994. 18.00 (*1-56692-183-X*) Morgan Quitno Corp.
— North Dakota Health Care Perspective 1995. 24p. 1995. 18.00 (*1-56692-433-2*) Morgan Quitno Corp.
— North Dakota in Perspective, 1994. 26p. 1994. 18.00 (*1-56692-233-X*) Morgan Quitno Corp.
— North Dakota in Perspective 1995. 26p. 1995. pap. 18.00 (*1-56692-483-9*) Morgan Quitno Corp.
— Ohio Crime Perspective, 1994. 24p. 1994. 18.00 (*1-56692-284-4*) Morgan Quitno Corp.
— Ohio Crime Perspective 1995. 24p. 1995. 18.00 (*1-56692-384-0*) Morgan Quitno Corp.
— Ohio Health Care Perspective, 1994. 24p. 1994. 18.00 (*1-56692-184-8*) Morgan Quitno Corp.
— Ohio Health Care Perspective 1995. 24p. 1995. 18.00 (*1-56692-434-0*) Morgan Quitno Corp.
— Ohio in Perspective, 1994. 26p. 1994. 18.00 (*1-56692-234-8*) Morgan Quitno Corp.
— Ohio in Perspective 1995. 26p. 1995. pap. 18.00 (*1-56692-484-7*) Morgan Quitno Corp.
— Oklahoma Crime Perspective, 1994. 24p. 1994. 18.00 (*1-56692-285-2*) Morgan Quitno Corp.
— Oklahoma Crime Perspective 1995. 24p. 1995. 18.00 (*1-56692-385-9*) Morgan Quitno Corp.
— Oklahoma Health Care Perspective, 1994. 24p. 1994. 18.00 (*1-56692-185-6*) Morgan Quitno Corp.
— Oklahoma Health Care Perspective 1995. 24p. 1995. 18.00 (*1-56692-435-9*) Morgan Quitno Corp.
— Oklahoma in Perspective, 1994. 26p. 1994. 18.00 (*1-56692-235-6*) Morgan Quitno Corp.
— Oklahoma in Perspective 1995. 26p. 1995. pap. 18.00 (*1-56692-485-5*) Morgan Quitno Corp.
— Oregon Crime Perspective, 1994. 24p. 1994. 18.00 (*1-56692-286-0*) Morgan Quitno Corp.
— Oregon Crime Perspective 1995. 24p. 1995. 18.00 (*1-56692-386-7*) Morgan Quitno Corp.
— Oregon Health Care Perspective, 1994. 24p. 1994. 18.00 (*1-56692-186-4*) Morgan Quitno Corp.
— Oregon Health Care Perspective 1995. 24p. 1995. 18.00 (*1-56692-436-7*) Morgan Quitno Corp.
— Oregon in Perspective, 1994. 26p. 1994. 18.00 (*1-56692-236-4*) Morgan Quitno Corp.
— Oregon in Perspective 1995. 26p. 1995. pap. 18.00 (*1-56692-486-3*) Morgan Quitno Corp.
— Pennsylvania Crime Perspective, 1994. 24p. 1994. 18.00 (*1-56692-287-9*) Morgan Quitno Corp.
— Pennsylvania Crime Perspective 1995. 24p. 1995. 18.00 (*1-56692-387-5*) Morgan Quitno Corp.
— Pennsylvania Health Care Perspective, 1994. 24p. 1994. 18.00 (*1-56692-187-2*) Morgan Quitno Corp.
— Pennsylvania Health Care Perspective 1995. 24p. 1995. 18.00 (*1-56692-437-5*) Morgan Quitno Corp.
— Pennsylvania in Perspective, 1994. 26p. 1994. 18.00 (*1-56692-237-2*) Morgan Quitno Corp.
— Pennsylvania in Perspective 1995. 26p. 1995. pap. 18.00 (*1-56692-487-1*) Morgan Quitno Corp.
— Rhode Island Crime Perspective, 1994. 24p. 1994. 18.00 (*1-56692-288-7*) Morgan Quitno Corp.
— Rhode Island Crime Perspective 1995. 24p. 1995. 18.00 (*1-56692-388-3*) Morgan Quitno Corp.
— Rhode Island Health Care Perspective, 1994. 24p. 1994. 18.00 (*1-56692-188-0*) Morgan Quitno Corp.
— Rhode Island Health Care Perspective 1995. 24p. 1995. 18.00 (*1-56692-438-3*) Morgan Quitno Corp.
— Rhode Island in Perspective, 1994. 26p. 1994. 18.00 (*1-56692-238-0*) Morgan Quitno Corp.
— Rhode Island in Perspective 1995. 26p. 1995. pap. 18.00 (*1-56692-488-X*) Morgan Quitno Corp.
— South Carolina Crime Perspective, 1994. 24p. 1994. 18.00 (*1-56692-289-5*) Morgan Quitno Corp.
— South Carolina Crime Perspective 1995. 24p. 1995. 18.00 (*1-56692-389-1*) Morgan Quitno Corp.
— South Carolina Health Care Perspective, 1994. 24p. 1994. 18.00 (*1-56692-189-9*) Morgan Quitno Corp.
— South Carolina Health Care Perspective 1995. 24p. 1995. 18.00 (*1-56692-439-1*) Morgan Quitno Corp.
— South Carolina in Perspective, 1994. 26p. 1994. 18.00 (*1-56692-239-9*) Morgan Quitno Corp.
— South Carolina in Perspective 1995. 26p. 1995. pap. 18.00 (*1-56692-489-8*) Morgan Quitno Corp.
— South Dakota Crime Perspective, 1994. 24p. 1994. 18.00 (*1-56692-290-9*) Morgan Quitno Corp.
— South Dakota Crime Perspective 1995. 24p. 1995. 18.00 (*1-56692-390-5*) Morgan Quitno Corp.
— South Dakota Health Care Perspective, 1994. 24p. 1994. 18.00 (*1-56692-190-2*) Morgan Quitno Corp.
— South Dakota Health Care Perspective 1995. 24p. 1995. 18.00 (*1-56692-440-5*) Morgan Quitno Corp.
— South Dakota in Perspective, 1994. 26p. 1994. 18.00 (*1-56692-240-2*) Morgan Quitno Corp.
— South Dakota in Perspective 1995. 26p. 1995. pap. 18.00 (*1-56692-490-1*) Morgan Quitno Corp.
— State Rankings, 1990: A Statistical View of the 50 United States. 316p. (Orig.). 1990. pap. 39.95 (*0-9625531-0-7*) Morgan Quitno Corp.
— State Rankings, 1991: A Statistical View of the 50 United States. 400p. (Orig.). 1991. pap. 39.95 (*0-9625531-1-5*) Morgan Quitno Corp.
— State Rankings 1992: A Statistical View of the Fifty United States. 504p. (Orig.). 1992. pap. 39.95 (*0-9625531-2-3*) Morgan Quitno Corp.
— State Rankings, 1994. 560p. 1994. pap. 43.95 (*0-9625531-7-4*) Morgan Quitno Corp.
— State Rankings 1995. 612p. 1995. pap. 43.95 (*1-56692-303-4*) Morgan Quitno Corp.
— State Rankings 1995. 612p. 1995. 67.95 (*1-56692-304-2*) Morgan Quitno Corp.
— Tennessee Crime Perspective, 1994. 24p. 1994. 18.00 (*1-56692-291-7*) Morgan Quitno Corp.
— Tennessee Crime Perspective 1995. 24p. 1995. 18.00 (*1-56692-391-3*) Morgan Quitno Corp.
— Tennessee Health Care Perspective, 1994. 24p. 1994. 18.00 (*1-56692-191-0*) Morgan Quitno Corp.
— Tennessee Health Care Perspective 1995. 24p. 1995. 18.00 (*1-56692-441-3*) Morgan Quitno Corp.
— Tennessee in Perspective, 1994. 26p. 1994. 18.00 (*1-56692-241-0*) Morgan Quitno Corp.
— Tennessee in Perspective 1995. 26p. 1995. pap. 18.00 (*1-56692-491-X*) Morgan Quitno Corp.
— Texas Crime Perspective, 1994. 24p. 1994. 18.00 (*1-56692-292-5*) Morgan Quitno Corp.
— Texas Crime Perspective 1995. 24p. 1995. 18.00 (*1-56692-392-1*) Morgan Quitno Corp.
— Texas Health Care Perspective, 1994. 24p. 1994. 18.00 (*1-56692-192-9*) Morgan Quitno Corp.
— Texas Health Care Perspective 1995. 24p. 1995. 18.00 (*1-56692-442-1*) Morgan Quitno Corp.
— Texas in Perspective, 1994. 26p. 1994. 18.00 (*1-56692-242-9*) Morgan Quitno Corp.
— Texas in Perspective 1995. 26p. 1995. pap. 18.00 (*1-56692-492-8*) Morgan Quitno Corp.
— Utah Crime Perspective, 1994. 24p. 1994. 18.00 (*1-56692-293-3*) Morgan Quitno Corp.
— Utah Crime Perspective 1995. 24p. 1995. 18.00 (*1-56692-393-X*) Morgan Quitno Corp.
— Utah Health Care Perspective, 1994. 24p. 1994. 18.00 (*1-56692-193-7*) Morgan Quitno Corp.
— Utah Health Care Perspective 1995. 24p. 1995. 18.00 (*1-56692-443-X*) Morgan Quitno Corp.
— Utah in Perspective, 1994. 26p. 1994. 18.00 (*1-56692-243-7*) Morgan Quitno Corp.
— Utah in Perspective 1995. 26p. 1995. pap. 18.00 (*1-56692-493-6*) Morgan Quitno Corp.
— Vermont Crime Perspective, 1994. 24p. 1994. 18.00 (*1-56692-294-1*) Morgan Quitno Corp.
— Vermont Crime Perspective 1995. 24p. 1995. 18.00 (*1-56692-394-8*) Morgan Quitno Corp.
— Vermont Health Care Perspective, 1994. 24p. 1994. 18.00 (*1-56692-194-5*) Morgan Quitno Corp.
— Vermont Health Care Perspective 1995. 24p. 1995. 18.00 (*1-56692-444-8*) Morgan Quitno Corp.
— Vermont in Perspective, 1994. 26p. 1994. 18.00 (*1-56692-244-5*) Morgan Quitno Corp.
— Vermont in Perspective 1995. 26p. 1995. pap. 18.00 (*1-56692-494-4*) Morgan Quitno Corp.
— Virginia Crime Perspective, 1994. 24p. 1994. 18.00 (*1-56692-295-X*) Morgan Quitno Corp.
— Virginia Crime Perspective 1995. 24p. 1995. 18.00 (*1-56692-395-6*) Morgan Quitno Corp.
— Virginia Health Care Perspective, 1994. 24p. 1994. 18.00 (*1-56692-195-3*) Morgan Quitno Corp.
— Virginia Health Care Perspective 1995. 24p. 1995. 18.00 (*1-56692-445-6*) Morgan Quitno Corp.
— Virginia in Perspective, 1994. 26p. 1994. 18.00 (*1-56692-245-3*) Morgan Quitno Corp.
— Virginia in Perspective 1995. 26p. 1995. pap. 18.00 (*1-56692-495-2*) Morgan Quitno Corp.
— Washington Crime Perspective, 1994. 24p. 1994. 18.00 (*1-56692-296-8*) Morgan Quitno Corp.
— Washington Crime Perspective 1995. 24p. 1995. 18.00 (*1-56692-396-4*) Morgan Quitno Corp.
— Washington Health Care Perspective, 1994. 24p. 1994. 18.00 (*1-56692-196-1*) Morgan Quitno Corp.
— Washington Health Care Perspective 1995. 24p. 1995. 18.00 (*1-56692-446-4*) Morgan Quitno Corp.
— Washington in Perspective, 1994. 26p. 1994. 18.00 (*1-56692-246-1*) Morgan Quitno Corp.
— Washington in Perspective 1995. 26p. 1995. pap. 18.00 (*1-56692-496-0*) Morgan Quitno Corp.
— West Virginia Crime Perspective, 1994. 24p. 1994. 18.00 (*1-56692-297-6*) Morgan Quitno Corp.
— West Virginia Crime Perspective 1995. 24p. 1995. 18.00 (*1-56692-397-2*) Morgan Quitno Corp.
— West Virginia Health Care Perspective, 1994. 24p. 1994. 18.00 (*1-56692-197-X*) Morgan Quitno Corp.
— West Virginia Health Care Perspective 1995. 24p. 1995. 18.00 (*1-56692-447-2*) Morgan Quitno Corp.
— West Virginia in Perspective, 1994. 26p. 1994. 18.00 (*1-56692-247-X*) Morgan Quitno Corp.
— West Virginia in Perspective 1995. 26p. 1995. pap. 18.00 (*1-56692-497-9*) Morgan Quitno Corp.
— Wisconsin Crime Perspective, 1994. 24p. 1994. 18.00 (*1-56692-298-4*) Morgan Quitno Corp.
— Wisconsin Crime Perspective, 1995. 24p. 1995. 18.00 (*1-56692-398-0*) Morgan Quitno Corp.
— Wisconsin Health Care Perspective, 1994. 24p. 1994. 18.00 (*1-56692-198-8*) Morgan Quitno Corp.
— Wisconsin Health Care Perspective 1995. 24p. 1995. 18.00 (*1-56692-448-0*) Morgan Quitno Corp.
— Wisconsin in Perspective, 1994. 26p. 1994. 18.00 (*1-56692-248-8*) Morgan Quitno Corp.
— Wisconsin in Perspective, 1995. 26p. 1995. pap. 18.00 (*1-56692-498-7*) Morgan Quitno Corp.
— Wyoming Crime Perspective, 1994. 24p. 1994. 18.00 (*1-56692-299-2*) Morgan Quitno Corp.
— Wyoming Crime Perspective, 1995. 24p. 1995. 18.00 (*1-56692-399-9*) Morgan Quitno Corp.
— Wyoming Health Care Perspective 1995. 24p. 1995. 18.00 (*1-56692-449-9*) Morgan Quitno Corp.
— Wyoming in Perspective 1995. 26p. 1995. pap. 18.00 (*1-56692-499-5*) Morgan Quitno Corp.

Morgan, Kathryn L. Children of Strangers: The Stories of a Black Family. LC 80-21144. 122p. 1981. pap. 14.95 (*0-87722-240-1*) Temple U Pr.

***Morgan, Kathy J. & McClain, Sandra L.** Core Curriculum for Home Health Care Nursing, 1995. 1995. 79.00 (*0-8342-0725-7*) Aspen Pub.

Morgan, Keith. Boston Architecture Nineteen Seventy-Five to Nineteen Ninety. Miller, Naomi, ed. (Illus.). 272p. 1990. 65.00 (*3-7913-1097-6*, Pub. by Prestel) TeNeues.

— Charles Platt: The Artist As Architect. (American Monographs). (Illus.). 265p. 1985. 37.50 (0-262-13188-9) MIT Pr.

Morgan, Keith, jt. ed. see Lewis, Arnold.

*__Morgan, Keith N.__ Shaping an American Landscape: The Art & Architecture of Charles A. Platt. LC 94-31831. 216p. 1995. 50.00 (0-87451-704-4); pap. 29.95 (0-87451-705-2) U Pr of New Eng.

Morgan, Kenneth. Bristol & the Atlantic Trade in the Eighteenth Century. LC 92-27535. (Illus.). 272p. (C). 1994. 59.95 (0-521-33017-3) Cambridge U Pr.

— Introduction to Structured Programming Using Turbo Pascal on the IBM PC. 752p. (C). 1990. pap. write for info. (0-675-20770-3, Merrill Pub Co) Macmillan.

— The Religion of the Hindus. 1987. reprint ed. 26.00 (81-208-0387-6, Pub. by Motilal Banarsidass II) S Asia.

Morgan, Kenneth, ed. see Fisher, Jabez M.

Morgan, Kenneth O. David Lloyd George: Welsh Radical As World Statesman. LC 82-2988. 85p. 1982. reprint ed. text ed. 49.75 (0-313-23453-1, MODG, Greenwood Pr) Greenwood.

— Labour in Power: 1945-1951. (Illus.). (C). 1985. pap. 17.95 (0-19-285150-0) OUP.

— The People's Peace: British History 1945-1989. (Illus.). 600p. 1991. 35.00 (0-19-822764-7) OUP.

— The People's Peace: British History 1945-1990. (Illus.). 576p. 1992. reprint ed. pap. 14.95 (0-19-285252-3) OUP.

— Rebirth of a Nation: Wales, 1880-1890. (Oxford History of Wales Ser.: Vol. VI). (Illus.). 480p. 1987. pap. 15.95 (0-19-821760-9) OUP.

Morgan, Kenneth O., ed. The Oxford History of Britain. 760p. 1988. pap. 16.95 (0-19-285202-7) OUP.

— The Oxford Illustrated History of Britain. LC 83-21990. 1984. 49.95 (0-19-822684-5) OUP.

— The Oxford Illustrated History of Britain. LC 83-21990. 1986. pap. 22.95 (0-19-285174-8) OUP.

Morgan, Kenneth O., ed. see Guy, John S. & Morrill, John.

Morgan, Kenneth O., ed. see Langford, Paul & Harvie, Christopher T.

Morgan, Kenneth O., jt. auth. see Matthew, H. C.

Morgan, Kenneth O., ed. see Salway, Peter & Blair, John.

Morgan, Kenneth W. Islam: The Straight Path. (C). 1987. 26.00 (81-208-0403-1, Pub. by Motilal Banarsidass II) S Asia.

— The Path of the Buddha: Buddhism Interpreted by Buddhists. 1986. 24.00 (81-208-0030-3, Pub. by Motilal Banarsidass II) S Asia.

— Reaching for the Moon: On Asian Religious Paths. LC 90-751. 1990. 18.95 (0-89012-059-5) Anima Pubns.

Morgan, Kenneth W., ed. Islam the Straight Path: Islam Interpreted by Muslims. LC 58-9807. 463p. reprint ed. pap. 132.00 (0-317-08489-5, 2012383) Bks Demand.

— The Religion of the Hindus: Interpreted by Hindus. LC 53-10466. 448p. reprint ed. 127.70 (0-8357-9975-1, 2015620) Bks Demand.

Morgan, Kenneth W. & Smith, Daniel. Focus on Hinduism: Audio Visual Resources for Teaching Religion. enl. ed. McDermott, Robert A., ed. LC 81-8085. 160p. 1981. pap. text ed. 2.50 (0-89012-019-6) Anima Pubns.

— Focus on Hinduism: Audio Visual Resources for Teaching Religion. 2nd enl. ed. McDermott, Robert A., ed. LC 81-8085. 160p. 1981. text ed. 4.95 (0-89012-018-8) Anima Pubns.

Morgan, Kevin. Harry Pollitt. LC 92-35132. (Lives of the Left Ser.). 1993. text ed. 69.95 (0-7190-3243-1, Pub. by Manchester Univ Pr UK) St Martin.

— Harry Pollitt Vol. 1. 1994. text ed. 19.95 (0-7190-3247-4, Pub. by Manchester Univ Pr UK) St Martin.

— Sleep & Aging: A Research-Based Guide to Sleep in Later Life. LC 87-45486. 160p. 1987. text ed. 36.50 (0-8018-3564-X) Johns Hopkins.

Morgan, Kevin, ed. Gerontology: Responding to an Aging Society. 200p. 1992. 49.50 (1-85302-117-2, Pub. by J Kingsley Pubs UK) Taylor & Francis.

Morgan, Kitty, jt. auth. see Littlefield, Kinney.

Morgan, Kris, illus. Lentil & Split Pea Cookbook: The Pulse of Life. 193p. (Orig.). 1990. pap. text ed. 12.95 (0-89716-352-4) P B Pubng.

*__Morgan, Kristin.__ A Bride to Be. (Romance Ser.). 1995. pap. 2.75 (0-373-19055-7, 1-19055-2) Silhouette.

— Make Room for Baby. (Romance Ser.). 1995. mass mkt. 2.99 (0-373-19084-0, 1-19084-2) Silhouette.

— Rebel Dad: (Fabulous Fathers) (Silhouette Romance Ser.). 1994. pap. 2.75 (0-373-08982-1, 5-08985-6) Silhouette.

— Who's That Baby? (Silhouette Romance Ser.). 1993. pap. 2.69 (0-373-08929-5, 5-08929-7) Silhouette.

Morgan, L. A., jt. ed. see Ehrhardt, H.

Morgan, L. H. Ancient Society: or Researches in the Lines of Human Progress from Savagery Through Barbarism to Civilization. Leacock, E. G., ed. 19.50 (0-8446-2611-2) Peter Smith.

— League of the Iroquois. (Illus.). 15.50 (0-8446-2612-0) Peter Smith.

Morgan, Lael. Art & Eskimo Power: The Life & Times of Alaskan Howard Rock. Sims, Virginia, ed. LC 88-24408. (Illus.). 260p. (Orig.). (YA). (gr. 9-12). 1988. 24.95 (0-945397-02-X); pap. 16.95 (0-945397-03-8) Epicenter Pr.

— Earthquake Survival Manual. Graydon, Don, ed. (Illus.). 160p. (Orig.). 1993. pap. 14.95 (0-945397-20-8) Epicenter Pr.

Morgan, Lael, ed. Alaska's Native People. LC 78-10528. (Alaska Geographic Ser.: Vol. 6, No. 3). (Illus.). (Orig.). 1979. pap. 24.95 (0-88240-104-1) Alaska Geog Soc.

Morgan, Lael, ed. see Birdsall, Byron.

Morgan, Lane. Winter Harvest Cookbook: How to Select & Prepare Fresh Seasonal Produce All Winter Long. LC 90-47422. (Illus.). 280p. (Orig.). 1990. pap. 14.95 (0-912365-35-8) Sasquatch Bks.

Morgan, Lane, ed. Good Food Guide to Washington & Oregon: Discover the Finest, Freshest Foods Grown & Harvested in the Northwest. (Illus.). 260p. (Orig.). 1992. pap. 14.95 (0-912365-50-1) Sasquatch Bks.

— Northwest Experience One. (Northwest Experience Ser.). 192p. (gr. 12). 1980. lib. bdg. 10.95 (0-914842-47-1); pap. 5.95 (0-914842-46-3) Madrona Pubs.

— The Northwest Experience Two. 192p. 1981. lib. bdg. 10.95 (0-914842-61-7); pap. 5.95 (0-914842-60-9) Madrona Pubs.

Morgan, Lane, text. Greetings from Washington. LC 88-80539. (Illus.). 112p. 1988. 24.95 (0-932575-69-2) Gr Arts Ctr Pub.

Morgan, Lanier. Understanding & Modification of Delinquent Behavior. LC 84-90339. 1984. 15.00 (0-87212-181-X) Libra.

— Understanding & Modification of Delinquent Behavior. rev. ed. LC 91-61814. 1992. 20.00 (0-87212-251-4) Libra.

*__Morgan, Lee.__ McMasters. 320p. (Orig.). 1995. pap. text ed. 4.99 (0-515-11632-7) Jove Pubns.

— McMasters No. 2: Silver Creek Showdown. 192p. (Orig.). 1995. pap. text ed. 3.99 (0-515-11682-3) Jove Pubns.

— Plunder Valley. (McMasters Ser.: No. 3). 192p. (Orig.). 1995. pap. 3.99 (0-515-11731-5) Jove Pubns.

Morgan, Lee & Cattaneo, Pietro. Abraham Lincoln. (What Made Them Great Ser.). (Illus.). 104p. (J). (gr. 5-8). 1990. lib. bdg. 12.95 (0-382-09973-7) Silver Burdett Pr.

Morgan, Lee & Solarino, Claudio. Christopher Columbus. (What Made Them Great Ser.). (Illus.). 104p. (J). (gr. 5-8). 1990. 12.95 (0-382-09974-5); pap. 5.95 (0-382-24001-4) Silver Burdett Pr.

Morgan, Len. The P-51 Mustang. LC 63-14945. (Famous Aircraft Ser.). (Illus.). 1979. pap. 7.95 (0-8168-5647-8, 25647, TAB-Aero) TAB Bks.

— Reflections of a Pilot. (Illus.). 224p. (Orig.). 1987. 16.95 (0-8306-2098-2); pap. 12.95 (0-8306-2398-1) TAB Bks.

— Vectors: The Best of Len Morgan. 1991. text ed. 22.95 (0-07-157707-6); pap. text ed. 14.95 (0-07-157706-8) McGraw.

— Vectors: The Best of Len Morgan. 1991. 22.95 (0-8306-2087-7); pap. 14.95 (0-8306-2083-4) TAB Bks.

— View from the Cockpit. 112p. 1985. pap. 5.95 (0-89745-072-8) Sunflower U Pr.

Morgan, Len & Morgan, Terry. Boeing 727 Scrapbook. LC 78-72164. 1978. pap. 12.60 (0-8168-8349-1, TAB-Aero) TAB Bks.

Morgan, Lenore. Dragons & Stuff. LC 70-108725. (Illus.). 32p. (J). (gr. 2-4). 1970. lib. bdg. 9.95 (0-87783-012-6) Oddo.

— Dragons & Stuff. deluxe ed. LC 70-108725. (Illus.). 32p. (J). (gr. 2-4). 1970. pap. 3.94 (0-87783-091-6) Oddo.

— Peter's Pockets. LC 65-27622. (Illus.). 32p. (J). (gr. k-2). 1968. lib. bdg. 9.95 (0-87783-029-0) Oddo.

— Peter's Pockets. (Illus.). (J). (gr. k-2). 1978. pap. 1.25 (0-89508-063-X) Rainbow Bks.

Morgan, Les. Dancing Against the Devil. LC 92-5700. (Straight Talk Ser.). (Orig.). 1992. pap. 1.00 (1-56476-000-6, Victor Books) SP Pubns.

— Pulling Weeds. LC 88-93031. 124p. (Orig.). (YA). (gr. 9-12). 1989. pap. 5.99 (0-87509-414-7) Chr Pubns.

— Taming the Lions in Your Life. LC 91-58677. 160p. (Orig.). (YA). (gr. 8-12). 1992. pap. 6.99 (0-87509-479-1) Chr Pubns.

Morgan, Leslie. Desert Lights. (Rapture Romance Ser.: No. 65). 192p. 1984. pap. 1.95 (0-317-00765-3, Sig) NAL-Dutton.

Morgan, Leslie A. After Marriage Ends: Economic Consequences for Midlife Women. (New Perspectives on Family Ser.). (Illus.). 240p. 1991. 46.00 (0-8039-3548-X); pap. 21.95 (0-8039-3549-8) Sage.

*__Morgan, Leslie A., et al.__ Small Board-&-Care Homes: Residential Care in Transition. LC 94-38059. (Illus.). 264p. 1995. text ed. 47.50x (0-8018-4996-9) Johns Hopkins.

Morgan, Leslie Z., tr. see Ariosto, Lodovico.

Morgan, Lewis. Ancient Society. 1974. lib. bdg. 150.00 (0-87968-630-8) Gordon Pr.

Morgan, Lewis B., jt. auth. see Maslowski, Raymond M.

Morgan, Lewis H. The American Beaver: A Classic of Natural History & Ecology. 384p. 1986. reprint ed. pap. 10.95 (0-486-24995-6) Dover.

— Ancient Society. 1978. pap. 14.00 (0-935534-02-4) NY Labor News.

— Ancient Society. LC 85-1121. (Classics of Anthropology Ser.). 560p. 1985. reprint ed. pap. 19.95 (0-8165-0924-7) U of Ariz Pr.

— The Indian Journals, Eighteen Fifty-Nine to Sixty-Two. White, Leslie A. & Walton, Clyde, eds. LC 58-10122. 269p. reprint ed. pap. 76.70 (0-317-29147-5, 2055633) Bks Demand.

— The Indian Journals,1859-62. LC 92-42188. (Illus.). 272p. 1993. reprint ed. pap. 10.95 (0-486-27599-X) Dover.

— League of the Iroquois. (Illus.). 477p. 1984. reprint ed. pap. 8.95 (0-8065-0917-1, Citadel Pr) Carol Pub Group.

— League of the Iroquois, 2 vols., Set. 1993. reprint ed. lib. bdg. 150.00 (0-7812-5160-5) Rprt Serv.

— Montezuma's Dinner. 2nd ed. 1967. pap. text ed. 0.75 (0-935534-21-0) NY Labor News.

Morgan, Linda B., jt. auth. see Morgan, John H.

Morgan, Lorraine L., et al. Beyond the Open Classroom: Toward Informal Education. LC 80-69235. 1981. 10.50 (0-86548-050-8) R & E Pubs.

*__Morgan, Lorrie.__ Self-Help. 176p. 1995. pap. 10.99 (0-446-67192-4) Warner Bks.

Morgan, Louise. Westward H-O-O-O-o-o-o-o-o! The Olivers. LC 89-61486. (Illus.). 208p. 1989. 24.95 (0-8323-0472-7) Binford Mort.

Morgan, Lyle. Homeopathic Medicine: First Aid & Emergency Care. (Orig.). 1989. pap. 10.95 (0-89281-249-4, Heal Arts VT) Inner Tradit.

Morgan, Lyle W. Homeopathic Treatment of Sports Injuries. 144p. 1987. pap. 9.95 (0-89281-227-3, Heal Arts VT) Inner Tradit.

Morgan, Lyle W., II. Homeopathy & Your Child: A Parent's Guide to Homeopathic Treatment from Infancy Through Adolescence. 128p. (Orig.). 1992. pap. 9.95 (0-89281-330-X) Inner Tradit.

*__Morgan, Lyle W.__ La Homeopatia y Su Hijo-Homeopathy & Your Child. 1995. pap. 9.95 (0-89281-468-3) Inner Tradit.

Morgan, Lynda J. Emancipation in Virginia's Tobacco Belt, 1850-1870. LC 91-35702. (Illus.). 400p. 1992. 45.00 (0-8203-1415-3) U of Ga Pr.

Morgan, Lynn M. Community Participation in Health: The Politics of Primary Care in Costa Rica. LC 92-9575. (Studies in Medical Anthropology). (Illus.). 208p. (C). 1993. 54.95 (0-521-41898-4) Cambridge U Pr.

Morgan, Lyvia. The Miniature Wall Paintings of Thera: A Study in Aegean Culture & Iconography. (Cambridge Classical Studies). (Illus.). 320p. 1989. 105.00 (0-521-24727-6) Cambridge U Pr.

Morgan, M., jt. auth. see Hake, H.

Morgan, M. G., ed. Energy & Man: Technical & Social Aspects of Energy. LC 74-27680. 536p. 1975. pap. 39.95 (0-87942-042-1, PP00513) Inst Electrical.

Morgan, M. Granger & Henrion, Max. Uncertainty: A Guide to Dealing with Uncertainty in Quantitative Risk & Policy Analysis. (Illus.). 250p. (C). 1990. 59.95 (0-521-36542-2) Cambridge U Pr.

— Uncertainty: A Guide to Dealing with Uncertainty in Quantitative Risk & Policy Analysis. (C). 1992. pap. 17.95 (0-521-42744-4) Cambridge U Pr.

Morgan, Mal, ed. La Mama Poetica, the Anthology. 1990. pap. 19.95 (0-522-84396-4) Intl Spec Bk.

Morgan, Mar Lou, jt. auth. see MacDonald, Kathryn.

Morgan, Marabel. The Total Woman. LC 73-11474. 192p. 1973. 4.99 (0-8007-8218-6) Revell.

— Total Woman. 1990. pap. 5.50 (0-671-73211-0) S&S Trade.

Morgan, Marc S., jt. auth. see Johnson, Howard D.

*__Morgan, Marcia.__ How to Interview Sexual Abuse Victims: With a Special Segment on Appropriate Use of Anatomical Dolls. (Interpersonal Violence: The Practice Ser.: Vol. 7). 1994. 42.95 (0-8039-5288-0) Sage.

— How to Interview Sexual Abuse Victims: With a Special Segment on Appropriate Use of Anatomical Dolls. (Interpersonal Violence: the Practice Ser.: Vol. 7). 1994. pap. 18.95 (0-8039-5289-9) Sage.

Morgan, Marcia, jt. auth. see Friedemann, Virginia.

Morgan, Marcia K. My Feelings. 2nd ed. (Illus.). (J). (ps-5). 1984. reprint ed. pap. text ed. 3.95 (0-930413-00-8, TX-1-361-947) Equal Just Con.

Morgan, Margery. The Well-Woman. 128p. (Orig.). 1993. pap. 9.95 (0-563-36307-X, BBC-Parkwest) Parkwest Pubns.

Morgan, Margery, jt ed. see Page, Malcolm.

Morgan, Margery M., ed. see Shaw, George Bernard.

Morgan, Marian & Preston, Izola. The Arkansas African-American Quizbook. 40p. (Orig.). 1993. pap. 10.00 (0-938041-12-6) Arc Pr AR.

*__Morgan, Marilyn.__ Alaska Alphabet: Stories & Activities. (Illus.). 423p. (Orig.). (C). 1994. teacher ed. pap. text ed. 34.95 (1-878051-18-0) Circumpolar Pr.

— Diagnosis: Murder. 200p. (Orig.). Date not set. pap. 7.95 (0-7610-0250-2) NW Pub.

Morgan, Marilyn S., jt. auth. see Steele, John E.

Morgan, Marjorie. Manners, Morals, & Class in England, 1774-1858. LC 93-5864. 1994. text ed. 59.95 (0-312-10584-3) St Martin.

Morgan, Mark D. Ecology of Mysidacea. 1982. lib. bdg. 117.00 (90-6193-761-2) Kluwer Ac.

Morgan, Marlo. Mutant Message Down Under. LC 94-17930. 1994. 18.00 (0-06-017192-8) HarpC.

— Mutant Message Down Under. 1995. pap. 10.00 (0-06-092631-7, PL) HarpC.

— Mutant Message Down Under. large type ed. LC 94-33225. 289p. 1994. lib. bdg. 19.95 (0-7862-0330-7) Thorndike Pr.

Morgan, Martha, jt. auth. see Fibush, Esther.

Morgan, Martha M. A Trip Across the Plains in Eighteen Forty-Nine. 32p. 1983. pap. 4.95 (0-87770-295-0) Ye Galleon.

*__Morgan, Marv L.__ A Peek at the People: Australia. (Cultural Workbooks for Students Ser.). 35p. 1995. student ed 11.00 (1-885272-07-3) Eclectic Trvl.

Morgan, Mary. Benjamin's Bugs. LC 93-22911. (Illus.). 44p. (J). (ps-1). 1994. text ed. 12.95 (0-02-767450-9, Bradbury S&S) S&S Childrens.

— The History of Econometric Ideas. (Historical Perspectives on Modern Economics Ser.). (Illus.). 300p. (C). 1991. pap. 22.95 (0-521-42465-8) Cambridge U Pr.

— Patterns & Sources of Zuni Kachinas. 1989. 40.00 (0-9601322-4-4) Harmsen.

— Wee Seasons. (Wee Pudgy Board Bks.). (Illus.). 24p. (J). (ps). 1990. bds. 2.50 (0-448-02261-3, G&D) Putnam Pub Group.

Morgan, Mary, illus. Baby's First Mother Goose. (My First Golden Board Bks.). 24p. (J). (ps). 1993. bds. 3.50 (0-307-06143-4, 6143, Golden Pr) Western Pub.

— Guess Who I Love? (Pudgy Board Bks.). 18p. (J). (ps). 1992. bds. 2.95 (0-448-40313-7) Putnam Pub Group.

— My Little Prayer. (Jewelry Board Bks.). 8p. (J). (ps up). 1994. bds. 3.99 (0-679-85864-4) Random Bks Yng Read.

— The Pudgy Merry Christmas Book. (Pudgy Board Bks.). 16p. (J). 1989. bds. 2.95 (0-448-02262-1, G&D) Putnam Pub Group.

Morgan, Mary & Shermis, Michael. Critical Thinking, Reading & Writing. LC 89-49156. (Teaching Resources in the ERIC Database (TRIED) Ser.). 1989. pap. 14.95 (0-927516-08-X) ERIC-REC.

Morgan, Mary, ed. see Alano, Becky.

Morgan, Mary, ed. see Saint Louis Art Museum Staff.

Morgan, Mary E. Annette von Droste-Huelshoff: A Biography. LC 83-48746. (American University Studies: Germanic Languages & Literature: Ser. I, Vol. 23). 221p. (Orig.). (C). 1984. text ed. 26.10 (0-8204-0036-X) P Lang Pubs.

Morgan, Mary H. How to Dress an Old-Fashioned Doll. LC 72-93612. Orig. Title: How to Dress a Doll. (Illus.). 96p. (J). (gr. 5-8). 1973. reprint ed. pap. 2.95 (0-486-22912-2) Dover.

Morgan, Mary M., comp. The Indiana Eighteen Twenty Enumeration of Males. 173p. 1988. 12.00 (0-87195-010-3) Ind Hist Soc.

Morgan, Mary S., jt. ed. see De Marchi, Neil.

Morgan, Mary S., jt. ed. see Hendry, David F.

Morgan, Maryanne, jt. auth. see Thompson, Simon B.

Morgan, Marycyliena, ed. Language & the Social Construction of Identity in Creole Situations. (Special Publications: Vol. 8). 148p. (Orig.). (C). 1994. pap. text ed. 15.95 (0-934934-40-1) UCLA CAAS.

*__Morgan, Maud.__ Maud's Journey: A Life from Art. (Illus.). 272p. (Orig.). Date not set. pap. 14.95 (0-915117-16-9) New Earth Pubns.

Morgan, Maurice & Richardson, W. Essays on Shakespeare's Falstaff. 1972. 59.95 (0-8490-0130-7) Gordon Pr.

Morgan, McClymont. Taos Treasure. abr. ed. 140p. 1995. pap. 7.95 (1-56901-510-4) NW Pub.

Morgan, Meg P., et al. Strategies for Technical Communication: A Collection of Teaching Tips. 112p. Date not set. pap. text ed. 25.00 (0-914548-76-X) Soc Tech Comm.

Morgan, Melissa, jt. auth. see Chant, Ben.

*__Morgan, Melody.__ Abiding Love. 400p. (Orig.). 1995. mass mkt. 4.99 (0-8439-3825-0) Dorchester Pub Co.

— Jauncey. 400p. (Orig.). 1994. mass mkt. 4.99 (0-505-51992-5, Love Spell) Dorchester Pub Co.

Morgan, Melvin D., jt. auth. see Volk, Michael D.

Morgan, Meredith. Emerald Destiny. 352p. 1989. pap. 3.95 (0-8217-2556-4) Zebra.

Morgan, Meredith W., jt. auth. see Rosenbloom, Alfred J.

Morgan, Michael. Creating Workforce Innovation: Turning Individual Creativity into Organizational Innovation. 1993. 25.95 (1-875680-02-0, Pub. by Busn & Prof Pubng AT) Pubs Dist MI.

— Lenin. 1972. 20.00 (0-8214-0094-0) Lib Soc Sci.

— Magic. (Illus.). 76p. (Orig.). (YA). (gr. 7-12). 1986. pap. 3.95 (0-89872-202-0) Turman Pub.

— Prince. (Illus.). 75p. (Orig.). (YA). (gr. 7-12). 1987. pap. 3.95 (0-89872-203-9) Turman Pub.

*__Morgan, Michael & Shanahan, James.__ Democrary Tango: Television, Adolescents, & Authoritarian Tensions in Argentina. Good, Leslie, ed. (Communication Ser.: Critical Studies in Communication). 256p. 1995. text ed. 55.00 (1-881303-90-X) Hampton Pr NJ.

— Democrary Tango: Television, Adolescents, & Authoritarian Tensions in Argentina. Good, Leslie, ed. (Communication Ser.: Critical Studies in Communication). 256p. 1995. pap. text ed. 19.95 (1-881303-91-8) Hampton Pr NJ.

Morgan, Michael, ed. see Rutstein, Nathan.

Morgan, Michael, jt. ed. see Signorielli, Nancy.

Morgan, Michael A., ed. Finite Elements & Finite Difference Methods in Electromagnetic Scattering, Vol. 2. (Progress in Electromagnetics Research Ser.). 410p. 1989. 62.00 (0-444-01518-3) Elsevier.

Morgan, Michaei D. & Moran, Joseph M. Student Study Guide to Accompany Environmental Science: Managing Biological & Physical Resources. 136p. (C). 1992. spiral bd. write for info. (0-697-10834-1) Wm C Brown Pubs.

Morgan, Michael D., jt. auth. see Moran, Joseph M.

Morgan, Michael H. The Twilight War. 464p. 1992. pap. 5.99 (0-451-17228-0, Sig) NAL-Dutton.

Morgan, Michael J. Molyneux's Question: Vision, Touch & the Philosophy of Perception. LC 76-54066. 222p. reprint ed. pap. 63.30 (0-317-08116-0, 2022463) Bks Demand.

Morgan, Michael J., ed. Carbohydrate Metabolism in Cultured Cells. LC 86-12170. 536p. 1986. 125.00 (0-306-42240-9, Plenum Pr) Plenum.

Morgan, Michael L. Dilemmas in Modern Jewish Thought: The Dialectics of Revelation & History. LC 92-7724. 224p. 1992. 35.00 (0-253-33878-6) Ind U Pr.

— Platonic Piety: Philosophy & Ritual in Fourth-Century Athens. LC 89-38418. 288p. (C). 1990. text ed. 37.00 (0-300-04517-4) Yale U Pr.

Morgan, Michael L., ed. Classics of Moral & Political Theory. LC 91-38760. 1280p. (C). 1992. lib. bdg. 48.50 (0-87220-127-9); pap. text ed. 29.50 (0-87220-126-0) Hackett Pub.

Morgan, Michael L. & Fackenheim, Emil, eds. The Jewish Thought of Emil Fackenheim: A Reader. LC 87-2116. 400p. 1987. 44.95 (0-8143-1820-7); pap. 19.95 (0-8143-1821-5) Wayne St U Pr.

Morgan, Michael V., ed. Michigan Drunk Driving Law & Practice. 2nd ed. LC 91-78184. 624p. 1992. ring bd. 95.00 (0-685-65989-5, 92-007) U MI Law CLE.

Morgan, Michaela. Dinostory. LC 90-44935. (Illus.). 32p. (J). (ps-4). 1991. 13.95 (0-525-44726-1, DCB) Dutton Child Bks.

— Helpful Betty to the Rescue. LC 93-39885. (Illus.). (J). (gr. k-3). 1994. 15.95 (0-87614-831-3, Carolrhoda) Lerner Group.

Morgan, Michaela & Kemp, Moira. Helpful Betty Solves a Mystery. LC 93-39050. (J). (gr. k-3). 1994. 15.95 (0-87614-832-1, Carolrhoda) Lerner Group.

*__Morgan, Mike.__ Introduction to Electronic Assembly: TE-1000. Ager, Rick, ed. (Electronic Technology Ser.). (Illus.). (J). (gr. 6-8). Date not set. teacher ed 2.00 (1-884268-19-6); pap. text ed. 19.95 (1-884268-18-8) Marcraft Intl.

An Asterisk (*) at the beginning of an entry indicates that the title is appearing in BIP for the first time.

Morgan, Millard. American Guide to Hotels, Motels, Resorts & Inns. (Western Edition Ser.). 180p. (Orig.). 1989. pap. 6.95 (*0-685-29015-8*) Guide Pr CA.

— American Guide to Hotels, Motels, Resorts & Inns: Central Edition. 180p. 1989. pap. 6.95 (*0-685-29018-2*) Guide Pr CA.

— American Guide to Hotels, Motels, Resorts & Inns: Eastern Edition. 180p. (Orig.). 1989. pap. 6.95 (*0-685-29017-4*) Guide Pr CA.

— American Guide to Hotels, Motels, Resorts & Inns: Southern Edition. 180p. (Orig.). 1989. pap. 6.95 (*0-685-29016-6*) Guide Pr CA.

Morgan, Mona M., ed. Growing Up in Kilvert Country. 150p. (C). 1990. 30.00x (*0-86383-680-1*, Pub. by Gomer Pr UK) St Mut.

Morgan, Monroe T. Environmental Health. 320p. (C). 1993. pap. text ed. write for info. (*0-697-14955-2*) Brown & Benchmark.

Morgan, Morris H., tr. see Vitruvius.

***Morgan, Moshe.** A Guide to the Laws of Sukkos. LC 94-68426. (Illus.). 400p. (C). Date not set. write for info. (*1-56062-275-X*) CIS Comm.

***Morgan, Murray.** Confederate Raider in the North Pacific: The Saga of the C.S.S. "Shenandoah," 1864-65. (Illus.). 352p. Date not set. reprint ed. pap. 19.95 (*0-87422-123-4*) Wash St U Pr.

— The Last Wilderness. LC 76-41. 290p. 1976. pap. 10.95 (*0-295-95319-5*) U of Wash Pr.

— The Mill on the Boot: The Story of the St. Paul & Tacoma Lumber Company. LC 82-16107. (Illus.). 296p. 1985. pap. 17.50 (*0-295-96273-9*) U of Wash Pr.

— The Mill on the Boot: The Story of the St. Paul & Tacoma Lumber Company. LC 82-16107. (Illus.). 286p. 1982. 19.95 (*0-685-38498-5*) Wash St Hist Soc.

— One Man's Gold Rush: A Klondike Album. rev. ed. LC 67-13109. (Illus.). 224p. (C). 1995. reprint ed. pap. 24.95 (*0-295-95187-7*) U of Wash Pr.

— Over Washington. Barnes, Beverley & Dow, Lesley, eds. (Wings over America Ser.). (Illus.). 1995. pap. 35.00 (*1-887451-01-3*) Wldon Owen Ref.

— Over Washington. Barnes, Beverley & Dow, Lesley, eds. (Wings over America Ser.). (Illus.). 256p. 1995. reprint ed. 45.00 (*1-887451-07-2*) Wldon Owen Ref.

— Puget's Sound: A Narrative of Early Tacoma & the Southern Sound. LC 79-4844. (Illus.). 370p. 1981. pap. 17.50 (*0-295-95842-1*) U of Wash Pr.

— The Viewless Winds. LC 89-16355. (Northwest Reprints Ser.). 240p. 1990. reprint ed. text ed. 24.95 (*0-87071-504-6*); reprint ed. pap. 13.95 (*0-87071-505-4*) Oreg St U Pr.

Morgan, Murray & Morgan, Rose. Tacoma: South on the Sound: An Illustrated History of Tacoma & Pierce County. 199p. 1984. 22.95 (*0-89781-074-0*) Preferred Mktg.

Morgan, Murray, jt. auth. see Norden, Linda.

Morgan, Murry. Skid Road: An Informal Portrait of Seattle. rev. ed. LC 81-11701. (Illus.). 296p. 1982. reprint ed. pap. text ed. 14.95 (*0-295-95846-4*) U of Wash Pr.

Morgan, Myfanwy, et al. Sociological Approaches to Health & Medicine. LC 85-48015. (Social Analysis Ser.). 297p. (C). 1985. 24.50 (*0-7099-1705-8*, Pub. by Croom Helm UK); pap. 11.50 (*0-7099-3514-5*, Pub. by Croom Helm UK) Routledge Chapman & Hall.

Morgan, N. G. Hormones & Cell Signalling. 208p. 1989. write for info. (*0-318-65444-X*, Open Univ Pr); pap. write for info. (*0-335-15820-X*, Open Univ Pr) Taylor & Francis.

Morgan, N. J. The Medieval Glass of Lincoln Cathedral. (Corpus Vitrearum Medii Aevi Occasional Papers: No. 3). (Illus.). 1984. 45.00 (*0-19-726021-7*) OUP.

— Printed in Germany, Bk. 1. 1989. pap. text ed. 10.84 (*0-582-01450-6*, 78051) Longman.

— Printed in Germany, Bk. 2. 1989. pap. 10.84 (*0-685-32947-X*, 78050) Longman.

Morgan, Nancy, ed. see Dunn, Hampton.

Morgan, Nancy, ed. see Foss, William O.

Morgan, Nancy M., ed. see Kale, Wilford.

Morgan, Nathaniel H. A History of James Morgan of New London, Connecticut, & His Descendants from 1607 to 1869. (Illus.). 306p. 1992. reprint ed. pap. 22.00 (*1-55613-578-5*) Heritage Bk.

Morgan, Neal. Karankawa County: Short Stories from a Corner of Texas. LC 89-48086. 152p. 1990. 16.95 (*0-89096-423-8*) Tex A&M Univ Pr.

Morgan, Neil. Professional Services Marketing. 256p. 1991. pap. 37.95 (*0-7506-0090-X*) Buttrwrth-Heinemann.

Morgan, Neil, jt. auth. see Morgan, Judith.

Morgan, Nelson. Artificial Neural Networks - Electronic Implementation. (Neural Networks Technology Ser.). 120p. 1990. pap. 32.00 (*0-8186-2029-3*, 2029) IEEE Comp Soc.

— Talking Chips: IC Speech Synthesis. 1984. 40.00 (*0-07-043107-8*) McGraw.

Morgan, Nicholas. Secret Journeys: Theory & Practice in Reading Dickens. LC 91-55022. (Illus.). 152p. 1992. 29.50 (*0-8386-3447-8*) Fairleigh Dickinson.

Morgan, Nicholas, jt. ed. see Jones, Geoffrey.

Morgan, Nicola. Louis & the Night Sky. (Illus.). 32p. (J). 1991. bds. 13.95 (*0-19-540746-6*) OUP.

Morgan, Nigel. Deadly Dwellings. (C). 1993. 45.00 (*1-873424-01-9*, Pub. by Mullion Bks UK) St Mut.

Morgan, Nigel, jt. auth. see Marks, Richard.

***Morgan, Nina.** Chemistry in Action: The Molecules of Everyday Life. (The New Encyclopedia of Science Ser.). (Illus.). 160p. 1995. text ed. 35.00 (*0-19-521086-7*) OUP.

— The Human Cycle. LC 93-5265. (Natural Cycles Ser.). (Illus.). 32p. (J). (gr. 2-5). 1993. 12.95 (*1-56847-094-0*) Thomson Lrning.

— Marine Technology Reference Book. (Illus.). 500p. 1990. text ed. 225.00 (*0-408-02784-3*) Buttrwrth-Heinemann.

— The Mississippi. LC 92-39950. (Rivers of the World Ser.). (Illus.). 48p. (J). (gr. 5-6). 1993. lib. bdg. 22.80 (*0-8114-3103-7*) Raintree Steck-V.

— The Plant Cycle. LC 93-977. (Natural Cycles Ser.). (Illus.). 32p. (J). (gr. 2-5). 1993. 12.95 (*1-56847-091-6*) Thomson Lrning.

— The Sea. LC 94-9084. (First Facts Ser.). (Illus.). 128p. (J). (gr. k-4). 1994. pap. 5.95 (*1-85697-526-6*, Kingfisher LKC) LKC.

Morgan, Noel G. Cell Signalling. LC 89-11931. (Guilford Molecular Cell Biology Ser.). i, 203p. 1990. pap. text ed. 22.95 (*0-89862-518-1*) Guilford Pr.

Morgan, Noja. Expressions from My Heart. 60p. 1993. 5.95 (*0-9622849-9-8*) Papito.

Morgan, Norah & Saxton, Juliana. Teaching Drama. x, 230p. (Orig.). 1987. pap. text ed. 18.50 (*0-435-08458-5*) Heinemann.

— Teaching Drama. 230p. (Orig.). 1987. pap. 36.50 (*0-7487-0243-1*, Pub. by Stanley Thornes UK) Trans-Atl Phila.

Morgan, Norah H. & Saxton, Juliana. Teaching, Questioning & Learning. 192p. 1991. 74.50 (*0-415-06465-1*, A5611); pap. 16.95 (*0-415-06466-X*, A5615) Routledge.

Morgan, Ora S., ed. Agricultural Systems of Middle Europe: A Symposium. LC 72-94470. reprint ed. 31.50 (*0-404-04434-4*) AMS Pr.

Morgan, P. D., jt. ed. see Berlin, Ira.

Morgan, Pat. My Love, My Enemy: Meditations for the Separation. 1992. pap. 7.99 (*1-881273-03-2*) Northfield Pub.

Morgan, Patricia. Battle for the Seed. 112p. (Orig.). 1992. pap. 8.99 (*1-56043-099-0*) Destiny Image.

— Delinquent Fantasies. LC 78-309292. 1979. 21.00 (*0-85117-116-8*) Transatl Arts.

— How to Raise Children of Destiny. 210p. (Orig.). 1994. pap. 8.99 (*1-56043-134-2*) Destiny Image.

Morgan, Patricia, jt. auth. see Ruggiero, Vincent.

Morgan, Patricia G. A Mountain Adventure. LC 87-3486. (Let's Take a Trip Ser.). (Illus.). 32p. (J). (gr. 3-6). 1988. lib. bdg. 10.79 (*0-8167-1173-9*); pap. text ed. 2.95 (*0-8167-1174-7*) Troll Assocs.

— A River Adventure. LC 87-3485. (Let's Take a Trip Ser.). (Illus.). 32p. (J). (gr. 3-6). 1988. lib. bdg. 10.79 (*0-8167-1171-2*); pap. text ed. 2.95 (*0-8167-1172-0*) Troll Assocs.

Morgan, Patricia T. Tax Fraud & Procedure in a Nutshell. (Nutshell Ser.). 400p. 1991. reprint ed. pap. text ed. 18.00 (*0-314-73300-0*) West Pub.

Morgan, Patrick A., jt. ed. see Kolodziej, Edward A.

Morgan, Patrick M. Arms Control in International Politics: Some Theoretical Reflections. (CISA Working Paper Ser.: No. 48). 34p. (Orig.). Date not set. pap. 10.00 (*0-86682-061-2*) Ctr Intl Relations.

— Theories & Approaches to International Politics. 4th ed. 314p. 1986. 24.95 (*0-88738-093-X*); pap. text ed. 16.95 (*0-88738-630-X*) Transaction Pubs.

Morgan, Patrick M., jt. auth. see Knorr, Klaus.

Morgan, Patrick M., jt. ed. see Kolodziej, Edward A.

Morgan, Patti, ed. see De Sanchez, Victoria D.

Morgan, Paul. The Art of Richard Hughes: A Study of the Novels. viii, 177p. 1993. pap. 26.00 (*0-7083-1192-X*, Pub. by U of Wales UK) Bks Intl VA.

— Complement: Clinical Aspects & Relevance to Disease. 215p. 1991. text ed. 55.00 (*0-12-506955-3*) Acad Pr.

Morgan, Paul & Morgan, Helene. The Ultimate Kite Book: The Complete Guide to Choosing, Making, & Flying Kites of All Kinds - from Boxes & Sleds to Diamonds & Deltas, from Stunts & Fighters to Parachutes & More! (Illus.). 80p. 1992. 19.95 (*0-671-74443-7*) S&S Trade.

Morgan, Paul, jt. auth. see Barhydt, Frances B.

Morgan, Peg & Morgan, George. The Morgan-Collins-Teeples Book: Idaho Pioneers. 82p. 1992. pap. 20.00 (*0-9634328-0-X*) Knit-Toons.

Morgan, Peggy. Being a Buddhist. (Looking into World Religions Ser.). (Illus.). 72p. (YA). (gr. 7-10). 1989. 19.95 (*0-7134-6015-6*, Pub. by Batsford UK) Trafalgar.

— Buddhism in the Twentieth Century. (Illus.). 64p. 1985. pap. 8.95 (*0-7175-1394-7*, Pub. by S Thornes UK) Dufour.

Morgan, Peggy, jt. auth. see Cole, W. Owen.

Morgan, Peter. The Critical Idyll: Traditional Values & the French Revolution in Goethe's Hermann und Dorothea. (Studies in German Literature, Linguistics & Culture: Vol. 59). 186p. 1991. 43.00 (*0-938100-85-8*) Camden Hse.

— The Nations. 154p. (Orig.). 1992. pap. 7.99 (*1-56043-090-7*) Destiny Image.

— Nations, the Workbook. 48p. (Orig.). 1993. pap. 5.99 (*1-56043-096-6*) Destiny Image.

— Original Porsche 911: The Restorers Guide. (Illus.). 96p. 1995. pap. 34.95 (*1-870979-57-5*, Pub. by Bay View Bks UK) Motorbooks Intl.

— Story Weaving. LC 86-6079. 128p. (Orig.). 1986. pap. 8.99 (*0-8272-3423-6*) Chalice Pr.

Morgan, Peter & Nott, Susan. Development Control. 1988. 70.00 (*0-406-50250-1*); pap. 38.00 (*0-406-50251-X*, U.K.) Butterworth Legal Pubs.

Morgan, Peter, jt. auth. see Porter, Lindsay.

Morgan, Peter F. The Poetic & Pictorial Elements in Works by Five Writers in English - Milton, Pope, Wordsworth, Ruskin, Pound. LC 92-9968. (Illus.). 268p. 1992. lib. bdg. 89.95 (*0-7734-9503-7*) E Mellen.

Morgan, Peter M., ed. Disciples Family Album. 96p. (Orig.). 1990. pap. 7.99 (*0-8272-0617-8*) Chalice Pr.

***Morgan, Philip.** Italian Fascism, 1919-1945. LC 94-29898. 1995. write for info. (*0-312-12321-3*) St Martin.

Morgan, Philip D., ed. Diversity & Unity in Early North America. LC 93-16763. (Re-writing Histories Ser.). 296p. 1993. 59.95 (*0-415-08798-8*, B2408); pap. 16.95 (*0-415-08799-6*, B2412) Routledge.

Morgan, Philip D., jt. ed. see Ammerman, David L.

Morgan, Philip D., jt. ed. see Bailyn, Bernard.

Morgan, Philip D., jt. ed. see Berlin, Ira.

***Morgan, Philip I.** Privatization & the Welfare State: Implications for Consumerism & the Workforce. (Illus.). 320p. 1995. text ed. 59.95 (*1-85521-404-0*) Ashgate Pub Co.

Morgan, Pierr. Supper for Crow: A Northwest Coast Indian Tale. LC 93-41665. (J). 1994. 15.00 (*0-517-59378-5*); lib. bdg. 15.99 (*0-517-59379-3*) Crown Bks Yng Read.

Morgan, R. A. Plasma Etching in Semiconductor Fabrication: Plasma Technology, Vol. 1. 1985. 107.75 (*0-444-42419-9*) Elsevier.

Morgan, R. P. Soil Conservation Problems & Prospects. 576p. (C). 1981. text ed. 550.00 (*81-7089-121-3*, Pub. by Intl Bk Distr II) St Mut.

— Soil Conservation Problems & Prospects. 576p. (C). 1992. write for info. (*0-318-69592-8*, Pub. by Intl Bk Distr II) St Mut.

Morgan, R. P., jt. ed. see Chisci, G.

Morgan, R. P., ed. see International Conference on Soil Conservation Staff.

Morgan, R. W. St. Paul in Britain. LC 83-73168. 128p. 1984. reprint ed. pap. 4.50 (*0-934666-12-1*) Artisan Sales.

Morgan, Rachel & McGilton, Henry. Introducing the UNIX System V. 640p. 1987. pap. text ed. 29.95 (*0-07-043152-3*) McGraw.

Morgan, Rachel, jt. auth. see McGilton, Henry.

Morgan, Raleigh, Jr. The Regional French of County Beauce, Quebec. LC 74-78061. (Janua Linguarum, Series Practica: No. 177). 128p. 1975. pap. text ed. 64.65 (*90-279-3107-0*) Mouton.

Morgan, Randy. Truth Is Truth: What Americans Are Really Thinking about Black People & Feminist Women These Days. 168p. (Orig.). 1994. pap. write for info. (*0-9639888-0-8*) Mens Alliance.

Morgan, Raye. Babies on the Doorstep. 1994. mass mkt. 2.99 (*0-373-05886-1*, 1-05886-6) Harlequin Bks.

— Baby Aboard. large type ed. (Silhouette Desire Ser.). 1994. 17.95 (*0-373-58856-9*, Silhouette Lrg Print) Chivers N Amer.

— Caution: Charm at Work. (Silhouette Desire Ser.). 1993. mass mkt. 2.99 (*0-373-05807-1*, 5-05807-8) Silhouette.

— The Daddy Due Date. (Silhouette Desire Ser.). 1994. mass mkt. 2.99 (*0-373-05843-8*, 5-05843-3) Silhouette.

— Sorry, the Bride Has Escaped. 1994. mass mkt. 2.99 (*0-373-05892-6*, 1-05892-4) Harlequin Bks.

— Yesterday's Outlaw. (Silhouette Desire Ser.). 1994. mass mkt. 2.99 (*0-373-05836-5*, 5-05836-7) Silhouette.

Morgan, Raymond C. The Angels Do Not Forget. (Illus.). (Orig.). 1979. pap. text ed. 7.95 (*0-9602718-0-5*) Law & Justice.

Morgan, Raymond F., jt. auth. see Richardson, Judy S.

Morgan, Rebecca. Calming Upset Customers. Crisp, Michael G., ed. LC 88-72256. (Fifty-Minute Ser.). (Illus.). 96p. (Orig.). 1989. pap. 9.95 (*0-931961-65-3*) Crisp Pubns.

— Professional Selling. Crisp, Michael G., ed. LC 87-72479. (Fifty-Minute Ser.). (Illus.). 110p. (Orig.). 1988. pap. 9.95 (*0-931961-42-4*) Crisp Pubns.

Morgan, Rhea V. Handbook of Small Animal Practice. LC 87-16821. 1281p. reprint ed. pap. 180.00 (*0-7837-2592-2*, 2042755) Bks Demand.

Morgan, Richard. J. Walter Takeover: From Divine Right to Common Stock. 240p. 1990. text ed. 30.00 (*1-55623-403-1*) Irwin Prof Pubng.

— Kenneth Patchen: An Annotated Descriptive Bibliography. 1978. 25.00 (*0-911858-36-9*) Appel.

Morgan, Richard, ed. see Patchen, Kenneth.

Morgan, Richard E. Domestic Intelligence: Monitoring Dissent in America. LC 80-13254. 204p. 1980. text ed. 14.95 (*0-292-76463-4*); pap. 6.95 (*0-292-71529-3*) U of Tex Pr.

Morgan, Richard E., et al. American Politics: Directions of Change, Dynamics of Choice. 2nd ed. 672p. (C). 1982. student ed 5.75 (*0-394-34931-8*); text ed. 20.00 (*0-394-34930-X*) Random.

Morgan, Richard G., ed. Kenneth Patchen: A Collection of Essays. LC 77-78319. (Studies in Modern Literature: No. 2). (Illus.). 1977. lib. bdg. 29.50 (*0-404-16005-0*) AMS Pr.

Morgan, Richard L. From Grim to Green Pastures. 176p. 1994. pap. 8.95 (*0-8358-0708-8*) Upper Room Bks.

— I Never Found That Rocking Chair: God's Call at Retirement. LC 92-61442. 144p. 1993. pap. 8.95 (*0-8358-0663-4*) Upper Room Bks.

— No Wrinkles on the Soul. LC 89-51765. 144p. (Orig.). 1990. pap. 8.95 (*0-8358-0610-3*) Upper Room Bks.

— No Wrinkles on the Soul: A Book of Readings for Older Adults. 1990. pap. 8.95 (*0-687-60809-0*) Abingdon.

Morgan, Robert. All Things under the Moon. 224p. (Orig.). 1994. pap. text ed. 4.99 (*0-425-14302-3*, Prime Crime) Berkley Pub.

— At the Edge of the Orchard Country. LC 85-29506. (Wesleyan Poetry Ser.). 75p. 1987. 22.50 (*0-8195-5158-9*, Wesleyan Univ Pr); pap. 10.95 (*0-8195-6164-9*, Wesleyan Univ Pr) U Pr of New Eng.

— The Blue Valleys. 192p. 1989. 15.95 (*0-934601-71-2*) Peachtree Pubs.

— Good Measure: Essays, Interviews, & Notes on Poetry. LC 92-34860. 192p. 1993. text ed. 35.00 (*0-8071-1798-6*) La State U Pr.

— Green River: New & Selected Poems. LC 90-50912. (Wesleyan Poetry Ser.). 98p. 1991. 22.50 (*0-8195-2179-5*, Wesleyan Univ Pr); pap. 10.95 (*0-8195-1181-1*, Wesleyan Univ Pr) U Pr of New Eng.

— Groundwork. LC 79-55810. 1979. 15.00 (*0-917788-22-2*); pap. 10.50 (*0-917788-21-4*) Gnomon Pr.

— The Hinter Lands: A Novel. LC 93-33728. 1994. write for info. (*1-56512-021-3*) Algonquin Bks.

— Land Diving. Poems. LC 76-28168. viii, 70p. 1977. pap. 6.95 (*0-8071-0274-1*) La State U Pr.

— The Mountains Won't Remember Us: And Other Stories. 176p. 1992. 15.95 (*1-56145-049-9*) Peachtree Pubs.

— My Lamp Still Burns. 141p. (C). 1981. text ed. 39.00 (*0-85088-504-3*, Pub. by Gomer Pr UK) St Mut.

— The Only Thing to Fear. 256p. 1994. pap. 4.99 (*0-425-14468-2*, Prime Crime) Berkley Pub.

— Red Owl. 88p. (Orig.). (C). 1972. pap. text ed. 1.95 (*0-393-04136-0*) Norton.

— Sigodlin: Poems. LC 89-30431. (Wesleyan Poetry Ser.). 72p. 1990. 22.50 (*0-8195-2178-7*, Wesleyan Univ Pr); pap. 10.95 (*0-8195-1180-3*, Wesleyan Univ Pr) U Pr of New Eng.

— Some Things Come Back. 256p. (Orig.). 1995. pap. text ed. 4.99 (*0-425-14690-1*, Prime Crime) Berkley Pub.

— Some Things Never Die. 208p. (Orig.). 1993. pap. 3.99 (*1-55773-887-4*) Diamond.

— Thing That Darkness Hides. 1993. pap. 4.50 (*1-55773-960-9*) Diamond.

— Things That Are Not There. 208p. (Orig.). 1992. pap. 3.99 (*1-55773-827-0*) Diamond.

— The Truest Pleasure. 336p. 1995. write for info. (*1-56512-105-8*) Algonquin Bks.

Morgan, Robert & Barton, John. Biblical Interpretation. 352p. (C). 1988. 62.00 (*0-19-213256-3*); pap. text ed. 19.95 (*0-19-213257-1*) OUP.

Morgan, Robert, jt. ed. see Pye, Michael.

Morgan, Robert, tr. see Troeltsch, Ernst.

Morgan, Robert C. Commentaries on the New Media Arts: Fluxus & Conceptual, Artists' Books, MailArt, Correspondence Art, Audio & Video Art. 64p. (Orig.). 1992. pap. 9.95 (*0-9635042-0-7*) Umbrella Assocs.

— Concept Decoratif Anti-Formalist Art of the Seventies. (Illus.). 28p. (Orig.). 1990. pap. 10.00 (*0-9624615-5-5*) Nahan Contemporary.

— Conceptual Art: An American Perspective. 216p. 1994. lib. bdg. 35.00 (*0-89950-950-9*) McFarland & Co.

— Dorothea Tanning "Messages" (Illus.). 24p. 1989. pap. write for info. (*0-9624615-7-1*) Nahan Contemporary.

— Lift High the Cross. LC 94-40486. 144p. (Orig.). 1995. pap. 11.95 (*0-687-21851-9*) Abingdon.

— Nancy Grossman, Ariane Lopez-Huici, Aura Rosenberg, Carolee Schneemann, Joan Semmel. (Illus.). 7p. 1989. pap. 2.00 (*0-9624615-6-3*) Nahan Contemporary.

Morgan, Robert C., intro. Franz Erhard Walther. (Illus.). 32p. (Orig.). 1988. pap. 12.00 (*0-929687-00-0*) E & C Zilkha Gal.

Morgan, Robert C., jt. auth. see Carmean, E. A., Jr.

***Morgan, Robert F.** The Adult Growth Examination: Test Manual for Measuring Body Age. 78p. 1994. student ed 55.00 (*1-885679-00-9*) Morgan Fnd Pubs.

— Effective Verbal Adaptation (EVA) Test Manual for Personnel Selection & Screening: Executive & Professional Screening by Structured Scored Group Test Forms A&B. 70p. 1994. 85.00 (*1-885679-01-7*) Morgan Fnd Pubs.

— The Partners: A Three Act Play. 20p. (J). (gr. 6). 1994. pap. 20.00 (*1-885679-05-X*) Morgan Fnd Pubs.

— Training the Time Sense: Hypnotic & Conditioning Approaches. (Illus.). 220p. (Orig.). 1983. pap. 10.00 (*0-317-18296-X*) CSPP-Fresno Pubns.

— Uncas Slattery: A Two Act Play. 90p. 1994. pap. 34.00 (*1-885679-07-6*) Morgan Fnd Pubs.

***Morgan, Robert F., ed.** Iatrogenics in Professional Practice & Education: When Helping Hurts: A Handbook. 466p. (C). 1994. pap. text ed. 66.00 (*1-885679-04-1*) Morgan Fnd Pubs.

***Morgan, Robert F. & Wilson, Jane.** How to Measure & Change Your Body's Age. 263p. 1994. pap. 72.00 (*1-885679-03-3*) Morgan Fnd Pubs.

***Morgan, Robert F., et al.** Electroshock Treatment over Four Decades: The Case Against. 93p. (C). 1994. pap. text ed. 20.00 (*1-885679-02-5*) Morgan Fnd Pubs.

— Training the Time Sense: Hypnotic & Conditioning Approaches. 219p. (C). 1994. pap. text ed. 65.00 (*1-885679-06-8*) Morgan Fnd Pubs.

Morgan, Robert J. James Madison on the Constitution & the Bill of Rights. LC 88-10243. (Contributions in Legal Studies: No. 48). 235p. 1988. text ed. 49.95 (*0-313-26394-9*, MJM/, Greenwood Pr) Greenwood.

Morgan, Robert M. Water & the Land: A History of Irrigation in America. Shank, Bruce M., ed. (Illus.). 200p. 1993. 36.95 (*0-935030-02-6*); 12.00 (*0-317-36872-9*) Irrigation.

Morgan, Robert P. Anthology of Twentieth Century Music. (C). 1992. pap. text ed. 30.95 (*0-393-95284-3*) Norton.

— Modern Times. 416p. (C). 1993. pap. text ed. write for info. (*0-13-590159-6*) P-H.

Morgan, Robert P., ed. see Cone, Edward T.

Morgan, Robert P., jt. auth. see Norton Staff.

***Morgan, Robert W.** Genesis: Act II: The Ultimate Legend Quest. 300p. 1994. pap. text ed. 12.95 (*1-885969-02-3*) Talisman Media.

Morgan, Roberta. It's Better at Burdines. (Illus.). 152p. (Orig.). 1992. pap. 12.95 (*0-940495-25-2*) Pickering Pr.

Morgan, Roberta & Morgan, Brian. Hormones: How They Affect Behavior, Metabolism, Growth, Development & Relationships. (Illus.). 224p. 1989. 12.95 (*0-89586-662-5*, Body Pr-Perigree) Berkley Pub.

Morgan, Roberta, ed. see Despierres, G.

Morgan, Roberta, jt. auth. see Morgan, Brian L. G.

Morgan, Robin. Anatomy of Freedom: Feminism in Four Dimensions. 1994. pap. 10.95 (*0-393-31161-9*) Norton.

— The Anatomy of Freedom: Feminism in Four Dimensions. 2nd ed. 1995. 21.00 (*0-8446-6853-2*) Peter Smith.

— Demon Lover: On the Sexuality of Terrorism. 1990. pap. 9.95 (*0-393-30677-1*) Norton.

M

— The Mer-Child: A Legend for Children & Other Adults. (Illus.). 64p. (J). 1991. 17.95 (1-55861-053-7); 8.95 (1-55861-054-5) Feminist Pr.

— Upstairs in the Garden. 1991. pap. 9.95 (0-393-30760-3) Norton.

— The Word of a Woman: Feminist Dispatches 1968-1992. 304p. 1994. pap. 10.95 (0-393-31099-X) Norton.

— The Word of a Woman: Selected Prose, 1968-1991. 288p. 1992. 19.95 (0-393-03427-5) Norton.

Morgan, Robin, ed. Sisterhood Is Global: The First Anthology of Writings from The International Women's Movement. LC 82-45332. 840p. 1984. pap. 19.95 (0-385-17797-6, Anchor NY) Doubleday.

— Sisterhood Is Powerful: An Anthology of Writings from the Women's Liberation Movement. 1970. pap. 15.00 (0-394-70539-4, Vin) Random.

Morgan, Rod, jt. ed. see Clarkson, C. M.

Morgan, Roger. School Life: Pupils' View on Boarding. 105p. 1993. pap. 17.00 (0-11-321591-6, HM15916, Pub. by HMSO UK) UNIPUB.

Morgan, Roger & Silvestri, Stefano. Moderates & Conservatives in Western Europe. LC 83-5662. 288p. 1983. 37.50 (0-8386-3201-7) Fairleigh Dickinson.

Morgan, Roger, et al, eds. New Diplomacy in a Post-Cold-War World: Essays for Susan Strange. LC 93-7293. 300p. 1993. text ed. 69.95 (0-312-09683-6) St Martin.

***Morgan, Ronald B. & Smith, Jack E.** Staffing the New Workplace: Selecting & Promoting for Quality Improvement. 1995. 32.00 (0-87389-307-7) ASQC Qual Pr.

Morgan, Ronald R., jt. auth. see Miller, Steven I.

Morgan, Rose, jt. auth. see Morgan, Murray.

Morgan, Rosemarie. Cancelled Words: Rediscovering Thomas Hardy. LC 91-38326. (Illus.). 240p. 1992. 39.95 (0-415-06825-8, A6569) Routledge.

— Women & Sexuality in the Novels of Thomas Hardy. 224p. 1988. text ed. 45.00 (0-415-00268-0) Routledge.

— Women & Sexuality in the Novels of Thomas Hardy. 224p. 1991. pap. 14.95 (0-415-05850-3, A5669) Routledge.

Morgan, Rowland, et al. Planet Gauge 1994: The Trends That Are Shaping Our Future. 160p. 1993. 12.95 (1-85383-172-7, Pub. by Erthscan Pubns UK) Island Pr.

Morgan, Roy, jt. auth. see Peters, Ellis.

Morgan, Royston P. Soil Erosion & Conservation. 1986. pap. text ed. 59.95 (0-470-20671-3) Halsted Pr.

Morgan, S. J. & Darling, D. C. Animal Cell Structure. (Introduction to Biotechniques Ser.). 176p. (Orig.). 1993. pap. 47.50x (1-872748-16-3, Pub. by Bios Scientific UK) Coronet Bks.

Morgan, S. J., jt. auth. see Darling, D. C.

***Morgan, S. Keith & Seaton, Anthony.** Occupational Lung Diseases. 3rd ed. LC 94-19777. (Illus.). 624p. 1995. text ed. 85.00 (0-7216-4671-9) Saunders.

Morgan, S. L., jt. auth. see Deming, Stanley N.

Morgan, Sally. Circles & Spheres. (World of Shapes Ser.). (Illus.). 32p. (J). (gr. 1-3). 1994. 14.95 (1-56847-235-8) Thomson Lrning.

— Ecology & Environment: The Cycles of Life. (The New Encyclopedia of Science Ser.). (Illus.). 160p. 1995. 35.00 (0-19-521140-5) OUP.

— The Flying Emu & Other Australian Stories. LC 92-37880. (Illus.). 128p. (J). (gr. k-7). 1993. 18.00 (0-679-84705-7) Knopf Bks Yng Read.

— My Place, Vol. 1. 1993. pap. 12.95 (0-316-58289-1) Little.

— Spirals. (World of Shapes Ser.). (Illus.). 32p. (J). (gr. 1-3). 1995. 14.95 (1-56847-278-1) Thomson Lrning.

— Squares & Cubes. (World of Shapes Ser.). (Illus.). 32p. (J). (gr. 1-3). 1994. 14.95 (1-56847-234-X) Thomson Lrning.

— The Super Science Book of the Environment. LC 93-41696. (Super Science Ser.). (Illus.). 32p. (J). (gr. 4-8). 1994. 14.95 (1-56847-095-9) Thomson Lrning.

— Triangles & Pyramids. LC 94-31055. (World of Shapes Ser.). (Illus.). 32p. (J). (gr. 1-3). 1995. 14.95 (1-56847-277-3) Thomson Lrning.

Morgan, Sally & Morgan, Adrian. Colour in Art & Advertising. (Wonderful World of Colour Ser.). (Illus.). 48p. (YA). (gr. 7-10). 1994. 19.95 (0-237-51277-7, Pub. by Ebury Pr UK) Trafalgar.

— Materials. LC 93-31722. (Designs in Science Ser.). (Illus.). 48p. (YA). (gr. 5-9). 1994. 14.95 (0-8160-2985-7) Facts on File.

— Movement. LC 93-20162. (J). 1993. write for info. (0-8160-2979-2) Facts on File.

— Structures. LC 93-20164. (J). 1993. write for info. (0-8160-2983-0) Facts on File.

— Technology in Action. (Designs in Science Ser.). (Illus.). 48p. (YA). (gr. 5-9). 1994. 14.95 (0-8160-3126-6) Facts on File.

— Using Energy. LC 93-20407. (Designs in Science Ser.). (J). (gr. 4 up). 1993. write for info. (0-8160-2984-9) Facts on File.

— Using Light. LC 93-21535. (Designs in Science Ser.). (J). 1993. write for info. (0-8160-2980-6) Facts on File.

— Using Sound. LC 93-31720. (Designs in Science Ser.). (Illus.). 48p. (YA). (gr. 5-9). 1994. 14.95 (0-8160-2981-4) Facts on File.

— Water. LC 93-31721. (Designs in Science Ser.). (Illus.). 48p. (YA). (gr. 5-9). 1994. 14.95 (0-8160-2982-2) Facts on File.

Morgan, Sally, jt. auth. see Harlow, Rosie.

Morgan, Sam B. & Okwumabua, Theresa M., eds. Child & Adolescent Disorders: Developmental & Health Psychology Perspectives. 480p. 1990. 79.95 (0-8058-0514-1) L Erlbaum Assocs.

Morgan, Sampson. Clean Culture: The New Soil Science. Bernard, Raymond W., ed. 1985. spiral bd. 6.60 (0-7873-1005-0) Mokelumne.

— How to Make the Most of the Land. 100p. 1974. reprint ed. spiral bd. 6.60 (0-7873-0624-X) Mokelumne.

— How to Make the Most of the Land: A Textbook of the Fruit & Vegetable Growing Movement for Private Gardeners & Commercial Growers. 1991. lib. bdg. 250.00 (0-87700-996-1) Revisionist Pr.

Morgan, Sandra K., ed. The J. Paul Getty Museum Journal, Vol. 6-7. LC 76-642750. (Illus.). 216p. 1979. pap. 25.00 (0-89236-018-6) J P Getty Trust.

— J. Paul Getty Museum Journal, Vol. 8. (Illus.). 212p. 1980. pap. 25.00 (0-89236-030-5) J P Getty Trust.

— J. Paul Getty Museum Journal, Vol. 9. (Illus.). 178p. 1981. pap. 25.00 (0-89236-032-1) J P Getty Trust.

— J. Paul Getty Museum Journal, Vol. 10. (Illus.). 202p. 1982. pap. 25.00 (0-89236-048-8) J P Getty Trust.

— J. Paul Getty Museum Journal, Vol. 11. (Illus.). 224p. 1983. pap. 30.00 (0-89236-067-4) J P Getty Trust.

— J. Paul Getty Museum Journal: Includes Acquisitions 1984, Vol. 13. (Illus.). 260p. 1985. 62.00 (0-89236-090-9) J P Getty Trust.

— J. Paul Getty Museum Journal: Includes 1983 Acquisitions, Vol. 12. (Illus.). 318p. 1984. 62.00 (0-89236-079-8) J P Getty Trust.

Morgan, Sarah. Bread. (Illus.). 120p. 1975. 15.00 (0-88426-042-9) Encino Pr.

— The Civil War Diary of Sarah Morgan. East, Charles, ed. LC 91-2161. 688p. 1991. 34.95 (0-8203-1357-2) U of Ga Pr.

— Dining with the Cattle Barrons. 1981. 13.95 (0-87244-064-8) Texian.

— Sarah Morgan: The Civil War Diary of a Southern Woman. East, Charles, ed. LC 92-21798. (Illus.). 688p. 1992. pap. 15.00 (0-671-78503-6, Touchstone Bks) S&S Trade.

Morgan, Sarah, jt. auth. see Vivion, Michael J.

Morgan, Sarah J. & Okerstrom, Dennis. The Endangered Earth: Readings for Writers. 512p. (C). 1991. pap. text ed. 22.00 (0-205-13218-9) Allyn.

Morgan, Sarah J., jt. auth. see Okerstrom, Dennis.

Morgan, Scott & Colson, Elizabeth, eds. People in Upheaval. LC 86-33354. 228p. 1987. 19.50 (0-934733-17-1) Ctr Migration.

Morgan, Scott M. & Colson, Elizabeth, eds. People in Upheaval. LC 86-33354. 228p. 1987. pap. 14.50 (0-934733-16-3) Ctr Migration.

Morgan, Seth. Homeboy. 1990. 19.95 (0-394-57577-6) Random.

— Homeboy. LC 90-55669. 400p. 1991. pap. 12.00 (0-679-73395-7, Vin) Random.

Morgan, Seth A. Manual for the Laboratory Assistant. pap. 4.95 (0-89741-007-6) Roadrunner Tech.

Morgan, Sharon. Land Settlement in Early Tasmania: Creating an Antipodean England. (Studies in Australian History). 270p. (C). 1992. 59.95 (0-521-39031-1) Cambridge U Pr.

Morgan, Sharon & Reinhart, Jo An. Interventions for Students with Emotional Disorders. LC 89-29103. 212p. (C). 1991. text ed. 34.00 (0-89079-296-8, 1592) PRO-ED.

Morgan, Sharon R. At Risk Youth in Crises: A Team Approach in the Schools. LC 93-41948. (C). 1994. pap. 28.00 (0-89079-574-6, 6719) PRO-ED.

— Children in Crisis: A Team Approach in the Schools. LC 90-20860. 253p. (Orig.). (C). 1985. pap. text ed. 28.00 (0-89079-289-5, 1747) PRO-ED.

Morgan, Sherm. The Aviation Humor of 1987. LC 87-91286. 128p. (Orig.). (C). 1987. pap. 5.95 (0-944792-00-6) Pendragon TX.

— Classic Aviation Humor Bk. II. 1989. pap. 5.95 (0-944792-01-4) Pendragon TX.

— Sherm Morgan's Classic Aviation Humor Bk. III. 1992. pap. 6.95 (1-881001-06-7) Pendragon TX.

Morgan, Sherman. Old Planes, Young Men & Red Wooden Shoes. 227p. (Orig.). 1993. pap. 10.00 (0-944792-26-X) Pendragon TX.

Morgan, Sherman F. Good Sticks. LC 89-92016. 364p. 1991. 19.95 (0-944792-02-2) Pendragon TX.

Morgan, Speer. The Assemblers. 304p. 1989. reprint ed. pap. 3.95 (0-373-97098-6) Harlequin Bks.

— The Whipping Boy. LC 93-40836. 1994. 21.95 (0-395-67725-4) HM.

Morgan, Speer, et al. The Best of the Missouri Review: Fiction, 1978-1990. 320p. (Orig.). 1991. text ed. 32.50 (0-8262-0773-1); pap. 15.95 (0-8262-0784-7) U of Mo Pr.

Morgan, Stacy T. The Cuddlers. LC 92-75695. (Illus.). 1993. 12.95 (0-912500-41-7) La Leche.

Morgan, Stanley. Too Rich to Live. (Orig.). 1979. pap. 2.25 (0-449-14269-8, GM) Fawcett.

Morgan, Stephanie, tr. see Sellato, Bernard.

Morgan, Stephen L., jt. auth. see Deming, Stanley N.

***Morgan, Steve.** Performance Assessment in Academic Libraries. LC 94-45209. 160p. 1995. 52.50 (0-7201-2188-4, Mansell Pub) Cassell.

Morgan, Steven M. Conjugal Terrorism: A Psychological & Community Treatment Model of Wife Abuse. Reed, R., ed. LC 81-83615. (Illus.). 125p. (C). 1982. pap. 12.00 (0-88247-623-8) R & E Pubs.

Morgan, Sue. Plaster Casting: Patient Problems & Nursing Care. 204p. 1990. pap. text ed. 34.95 (0-433-00082-1) Buttrwrth-Heinemann.

***Morgan, Susan.** Place Matters: Victorian Women's Travel Books on Southeast Asia. 350p. (C). 1996. text ed. 50.00 (0-8135-2248-X); pap. text ed. 19.95 (0-8135-2249-8) Rutgers U Pr.

— Sisters in Time: Imagining Gender in Nineteenth-Century British Fiction. 272p. 1989. 42.00 (0-19-505822-4) OUP.

Morgan, Susan, ed. see North, Marianne.

Morgan, Susan B. Ladybug. 1989. 1.98 (0-945603-01-0) Dinnerman Bks.

— Smooth & Round in the Ground. 1989. 1.98 (0-945603-04-5) Dinnerman Bks.

Morgan, Sydney. Woman & Her Master, 2 vols. LC 75-21813. (Pioneers of the Woman's Movement: an International Perspective Ser.). viii, 429p. 1976. reprint ed. 30.25 (0-88355-267-1) Hyperion Conn.

Morgan, Sydney O. Lady Morgan's Memoirs, 2 vols., Set. LC 76-37705. (Women of Letters Ser.). reprint ed. 145.00 (0-404-56793-2) AMS Pr.

— Missionary: An Indian Tale, 3 vols. in 1. LC 80-20308. 1980. reprint ed. 50.00 (0-8201-1358-1) Schol Facsimiles.

— The O'Briens & the O'Flahertys: A National Tale, 4 vols. in 2, 1. LC 79-8175. reprint ed. write for info. (0-404-62056-6) AMS Pr.

— The O'Briens & the O'Flahertys: A National Tale, 4 vols. in 2, 2. LC 79-8175. reprint ed. write for info. (0-404-62057-4) AMS Pr.

— The O'Briens & the O'Flahertys: A National Tale, 4 vols. in 2, Set. LC 79-8175. reprint ed. 84.50 (0-404-62055-8) AMS Pr.

— O'Donnel: A National Tale, 3 vols. in 2, 1. LC 79-8176. reprint ed. write for info. (0-404-62061-2) AMS Pr.

— O'Donnel: A National Tale, 3 vols. in 2, 2. LC 79-8176. reprint ed. write for info. (0-404-62062-0) AMS Pr.

— O'Donnel: A National Tale, 3 vols. in 2, Set. LC 79-8176. reprint ed. 84.50 (0-404-62060-4) AMS Pr.

— The Wild Irish Girl: A National Tale. LC 79-8177. reprint ed. 44.50 (0-404-62064-7) AMS Pr.

Morgan, T., jt. ed. see Horster, M. F.

Morgan, T. Clifton. Untying the Knot of War: A Bargaining Theory of International Crises. 240p. (C). 1994. text ed. 44.50x (0-472-10277-X) U of Mich Pr.

Morgan, T. J., jt. ed. see Cisneros, C.

Morgan, T. R., jt. auth. see Slater, R. H.

Morgan, Ted. Literary Outlaw: The Life & Times of William S. Burroughs. (Illus.). 1990. pap. 12.95 (0-380-70882-5) Avon.

— Shovel of Stars. 1995. 30.00 (0-671-79439-6) S&S Trade.

— Wilderness At Dawn. 1994. pap. 15.00 (0-671-88237-6, Touchstone Bks) S&S Trade.

— Wilderness at Dawn: The Settling of the North American Continent. (Illus.). 560p. 1993. 27.50 (0-671-69088-4) S&S Trade.

Morgan, Teresa. Days on the Farm with Annette & Samuel. 1987. 7.15 (0-318-37713-6) Rod & Staff.

Morgan, Terrell A., jt. ed. see Laeufer, Christiane.

Morgan, Terrell A., et al, eds. Language & Language Use: Studies in Spanish. (Illus.). 346p. (Orig.). (C). 1988. lib. bdg. 52.50 (0-8191-6697-9); pap. text ed. 29.50 (0-8191-6698-7) U Pr of Amer.

Morgan, Terri. Photography: Terri Morgan. (YA). (gr. 5 up). 1991. pap. 8.95 (0-8225-9605-9, Lerner Publctns) Lerner Group.

Morgan, Terri & Thaler, Shmuel. Photography: Take Your Best Shot. (Media Workshop Ser.). 80p. (J). (gr. 5 up). 1991. lib. bdg. 19.95 (0-8225-2302-7, Lerner Publctns) Lerner Group.

Morgan, Terri & Thaler, Shuel. Chris Mullin: Sure Shot. LC 94-2704. (Achievers Ser.). (Illus.). 64p. (J). (gr. 4-9). 1994. lib. bdg. 13.50 (0-8225-2882-7, Lerner Publctns); pap. 5.95 (0-8225-9664-4, Lerner Publctns) Lerner Group.

Morgan, Terry, jt. auth. see Morgan, Len.

Morgan, Terry, jt. auth. see Shonkwiler, John W.

Morgan, Thais, jt. ed. see Henricksen, Bruce.

Morgan, Thais E., ed. Men Writing the Feminine: Literature, Theory, & the Question of Genders. LC 93-43224. 207p. (C). 1994. 49.50 (0-7914-1993-2); pap. 16.95 (0-7914-1994-0) State U NY Pr.

— Victorian Sages & Cultural Discourse: Renegotiating Gender & Power. LC 90-30977. (Illus.). 320p. (C). 1990. text ed. 38.00 (0-8135-1600-5); pap. text ed. 15.00 (0-8135-1601-3) Rutgers U Pr.

Morgan, Thais E., tr. see Genette, Gerard.

Morgan, Theodore & Spoelstra, Nyle, eds. Economic Interdependence in Southeast Asia: Proceedings of a Conference Held at Bangkok, 1967. LC 68-9021. 442p. reprint ed. pap. 126.00 (0-317-29005-3, 2023725) Bks Demand.

Morgan, Theron, ed. see Taylor, Lynn E.

Morgan, Thomas. The Moral Philosopher in a Dialogue Between Philalethes, a Christian Deist, & Theophanes, a Christian Jew. LC 75-11239. (British Philosophers & Theologians of the 17th & 18th Centuries Ser.: Vol. 39). 463p. 1977. reprint ed. lib. bdg. 15.00 (0-8240-1791-9) Garland.

Morgan, Thomas & Barlow, William. From Cakewalks to Concert Halls: An Illustrated History of African American Popular Music from 1895 to 1930. (Illus.). 132p. 1993. reprint ed. pap. 21.95 (1-880216-17-5) Elliott & Clark.

Morgan, Thomas B. Speaking of Cardinals. LC 70-134119. (Essay Index Reprint Ser.). 1977. 20.95 (0-8369-2002-3) Ayer.

Morgan, Thomas D. Antitrust Law, Teacher's Manual to Accompany Cases & Materials on. (American Casebook Ser.). 150p. 1994. pap. text ed. write for info. (0-314-04199-0) West Pub.

— Cases & Materials on Antitrust Law. LC 93-50856. (American Casebook Ser.). 908p. 1994. text ed. 46.00 (0-314-03343-2) West Pub.

***Morgan, Thomas D. & Rotunda, Ronald D.** Selected Standards on Professional Responsibility, Including California Rules: Including California Rules. 613p. (C). 1994. pap. text ed. 16.95 (1-56662-250-6) Foundation Pr.

— Professional Responsibility: Problems & Materials. 6th ed. (Illus.). 598p. 1995. text ed. 38.50 (1-56662-254-9) Foundation Pr.

— Professional Responsibility, Problems & Materials On. 5th ed. (University Casebook Ser.). 571p. 1990. text ed. 34.50 (0-88277-861-7) Foundation Pr.

— Professional Responsibility, Revised Teacher's Manual to Accompany. 5th ed. (University Casebook Ser.). 363p. 1993. pap. text ed. write for info. (1-56662-123-2) Foundation Pr.

— Selected Standards on Professional Responsibility, Including California Rules. 575p. 1992. pap. text ed. 14.95 (1-56662-052-X) Foundation Pr.

— Selected Standards on Professional Responsibility, Including California Rules, 1994. 5th ed. 607p. 1991. pap. text ed. 16.00 (1-56662-141-0) Foundation Pr.

Morgan, Thomas D., et al. The Economic Regulation of Business: Cases & Materials. 2nd ed. (American Casebook Ser.). 666p. (C). 1985. text ed. 45.50 (0-314-89739-9) West Pub.

Morgan, Thomas L. & Barlow, William. From Cakewalks to Concert Halls: An Illustrated History of African American Popular Music from 1895 to 1930. (Illus.). 132p. 1992. 32.50 (1-880216-06-X) Elliott & Clark.

Morgan, Thomas R. Foundations of Wave Theory for Seismic Exploration. LC 82-83805. (Illus.). 140p. 1983. text ed. 40.00 (0-934634-34-3) Intl Human Res.

Morgan, Thomas S. Juvenile Law & Practice. (Illus.). 678p. write for info. (0-318-59331-9) West Pub.

Morgan, Tom. Not of Our Time. Pickup, Ronald, ed. 124p. (Orig.). 1989. pap. text ed. 10.00 (0-9623094-0-0) GlenHill Prodns.

— Saints: A Visual Almanac of the Virtuous, Pure, Praiseworthy, & Good. LC 94-7244. 1994. 16.95 (0-8118-0549-2) Chronicle Bks.

Morgan, Tracy. Michael's Wife. (Temptation Ser.). 1993. mass mkt. 2.99 (0-373-25530-6, 1-25530-6) Harlequin Bks.

***Morgan, Trevor.** Physiology Through Questions. 200p. 1995. pap. text ed. write for info. (0-07-470196-7) Hlth Prof Div.

***Morgan, Trudy.** Alex Best & Friends. (J). 1994. write for info. (0-8280-0849-3) Review & Herald.

— Facing the Music. LC 95-7755. (J). 1995. write for info. (0-8280-0880-9) Review & Herald.

— Where's Alex Best? LC 93-35925. (J). 1994. write for info. (0-8280-0736-5) Review & Herald.

Morgan, Valerie, jt. auth. see Dunn, Seamus.

Morgan, Vance G. Foundations of Cartesian Ethics. LC 92-34250. 256p. (C). 1994. text ed. 49.95 (0-391-03804-4) Humanities.

Morgan, Vincent T. Thermal Behaviour of Electrical Conductors: Steady, Dynamic & Fault-Current Ratings. (Electronic & Electrical Engineering Research Ser.: No. 1744). 741p. 1991. text ed. 250.00 (0-471-93071-7) Wiley.

Morgan, W. B., jt. ed. see Billet, M. L.

Morgan, W. B., ed. see Fluids Engineering Conference Symposium on Cavity Flows Staff.

Morgan, W. B., jt. auth. see Moss, R. P.

Morgan, W. H. La Administracion En Extension. pap. 3.10 (0-8477-2209-0) U of PR Pr.

Morgan, W. J. Curricular Issues for the Nineteen Nineties. (C). 1989. 50.00 (1-85041-059-3, Pub. by Univ Nottingham UK) St Mut.

Morgan, W. J., jt. auth. see Coates, K.

Morgan, W. J., jt. ed. see Hake, B. J.

Morgan, W. John & Preston, Peter, eds. Raymond Williams: Politics, Education, Letters. LC 92-34122. 232p. 1993. text ed. 45.00 (0-312-08357-2) St Martin.

Morgan, W. John, jt. ed. see Hake, Barry.

Morgan, W. P. Piety: Partial History of James Duncan Piety, His Forebears & Descendants, 1796-1948. (Illus.). 150p. 1994. reprint ed. lib. bdg. 33.00 (0-8328-4231-1); reprint ed. pap. 23.00 (0-8328-4232-X) Higginson Bk Co.

— Piety - Partial History of James Duncan Piety, His Forebears & Descendants, 1796-1948. (Illus.). 150p. 1994. reprint ed. lib. bdg. 33.00 (0-8328-4519-1); reprint ed. pap. 23.00 (0-8328-4520-5) Higginson Bk Co.

Morgan, W. Roy. Fat Suction. 1985. 19.95 (0-918227-00-3) Body Sculpt.

Morgan, W. T., jt. auth. see Stamp, L. Dudley.

Morgan, Walter L. & Gordon, Gary D. Communications Satellite Handbook. LC 88-6077. 900p. 1989. text ed. 115.00 (0-471-31603-2) Wiley.

Morgan, Walter L. & Rouffet, Denis. Business Earth Stations for Telecommunications. (Telecommunications Ser.). 234p. 1988. text ed. 79.95 (0-471-63556-1) Wiley.

Morgan, Walter L., jt. auth. see Gordon, Gary D.

Morgan, Wendy. Ned Kelly Reconstructed. LC 93-48705. (J). 1995. pap. 17.95 (0-521-43783-0) Cambridge U Pr.

***Morgan, Willard.** From Critic to Convert: A Skeptic Questions His Way to Mormonism. 1995. 14.98 (0-88290-517-1, 1056) Horizon Utah.

Morgan, William. Collegiate Gothic: The Architecture of Rhodes College. LC 89-4861. (Illus.). 128p. 1989. text ed. 28.00 (0-8262-0699-9) U of Mo Pr.

— Freemasonry Exposed. 13.00 (0-685-19475-2) Powner.

— How to Help Your Child Learn to Read. 1978. 2.50 (0-685-66030-3) Delta Sales.

— Louisville: Architecture & the Urban Environment. LC 79-631. 1979. 8.95 (0-87233-050-8) Bauhan.

— Morgan's Freemasonry Exposed & Explained. 131p. 1993. reprint ed. spiral bd. 8.80 (0-7873-0623-1) Mokelumne.

— Navajo Coyote Tales. Thompson, Hildegard, ed. & tr. by. LC 88-72048. (Illus.). 50p. (J). (gr. 2 up). 1988. reprint ed. pap. 8.95 (0-941270-52-1) Ancient City Pr.

Morgan, William, photos. Portals. 1981. pap. 4.75 (0-87233-057-5) Bauhan.

Morgan, William, jt. ed. see Brask, Per.

Morgan, William, tr. see Crowder, Jack L., et al.

Morgan, William, jt. auth. see Young, Robert W.

Morgan, William, Sr.

Morgan, William, jt. auth. see Young, Robert.

Morgan, William A. The Joshua Line. Ingram, tr. 256p. 1995. pap. 8.95 (1-56901-304-7) NW Pub.

An Asterisk (*) at the beginning of an entry indicates that the title is appearing in BIP for the first time.

Morgan, William D. & Kennedy, Charles S. The U. S. Consul at Work. LC 90-19910. (Contributions in Political Science Ser.: No. 275). 272p. 1991. text ed. 59. 95 (*0-313-27796-6*, MUW/, Greenwood Pr) Greenwood.

Morgan, William H. Personal Reminiscences of the War of 1861-5. LC 74-146868. (Select Bibliographies Reprint Ser.). 1977. reprint ed. 19.95 (*0-8369-5635-4*) Ayer.

Morgan, William J. Leftist Theories of Sport: A Critique & Reconstruction. LC 93-24135. (Sport & Society Ser.). 288p. 1994. 49.50 (*0-252-02068-5*); pap. 17.95 (*0-252-06361-9*) U of Ill Pr.

Morgan, William J., Jr. Supervision & Management of Quantity Food Preparation. 3rd ed. LC 88-60453. (Illus.). (C). 1988. 36.00 (*0-8211-1260-0*); teacher ed write for info. (*0-685-45510-6*) McCutchan.

***Morgan, William J. & Deier, Klaus V., eds.** Philosophic Inquiry in Sport. 2nd ed. LC 95-10920. (Illus.). 458p. 1995. text ed. write for info. (*0-87322-716-6*, BMOR0716) Human Kinetics.

Morgan, William J. & Meier, Klaus V., eds. Philosophic Inquiry in Sport. LC 87-2767. 560p. 1988. text ed. 42.00 (*0-87322-119-2*, BMOR0119) Human Kinetics.

Morgan, William N. The Almighty Wall: The Architecture of Henry Vaughan. 1982. 40.00 (*0-262-13187-0*) MIT Pr.

— Ancient Architecture of the Southwest. LC 93-21256. (Illus.). 320p. (C). 1994. 55.00 (*0-292-75159-1*) U of Tex Pr.

— Prehistoric Architecture in Micronesia. (Illus.). 180p. 1988. 55.00 (*0-292-76506-1*) U of Tex Pr.

Morgan, William P. & Goldston, Stephen E. Exercise & Mental Health. (Series in Health Psychology & Behavioral Medicine). 196p. 1987. 48.00 (*0-89116-564-9*) Hemisp Pub.

Morgan, William T. East Africa. LC 74-161775. (Geographies for Advanced Study Ser.). (Illus.). 430p. reprint ed. pap. 122.60 (*0-685-20300-X*, 2030336) Bks Demand.

Morgan, William T., jt. auth. see Brinkman, Marilyn S.

Morgan, William W., ed. Retinal Transmitters & Modulators: Models for the Brain, Vol. I. 176p. 1985. 132.00 (*0-8493-5691-1*, QP479) CRC Pr.

— Retinal Transmitters & Modulators: Models for the Brain, Vol. II. 176p. 1985. 132.00 (*0-8493-5692-X*, QP479) CRC Pr.

Morgan, William W., ed. see Fisher, Donald W.

Morgan-Williams, Louise. I Can Sing en Espanol: Fun Songs for Learning Spanish. (J). (gr. 4-7). 1994. pap. 12.95 (*0-8442-7172-1*) NTC Pub Grp.

— I Can Sing En Francais! Fun Songs for Learning French. (J). (gr. 4-7). 1993. 8.95 (*0-8442-1457-4*, Natl Textbk) NTC Pub Grp.

— I Can Sing En Francais: Fun Songs for Learning French. (J). (gr. 4-7). 1994. pap. 12.95 (*0-8442-1459-0*) NTC Pub Grp.

— I Can Sing Ien Espanol! Fun Songs for Learning Spanish. (J). (gr. 4-7). 1994. 8.95 (*0-8442-7168-3*, Natl Textbk) NTC Pub Grp.

Morgan, Winifred. An American Icon: Brother Jonathan & American Identity. LC 86-40597. (Illus.). 224p. 1988. 32.50 (*0-87413-307-6*) U Delaware Pr.

Morgan, Winona L. The Family Meets the Depression: A Study of a Group of Highly Selected Families, Vol. 19. LC 79-141550. (Child Welfare Ser.). (Illus.). 126p. (C). 1972. reprint ed. text ed. 22.50 (*0-8371-5897-4*, CWMF, Greenwood Pr) Greenwood.

Morgan Witts, Max, jt. auth. see Thomas, Gordon.

Morgan-Witts, Max

Morgan, Wm. B., ed. see International Symposium on Cavitation Inception Staff.

Morgan, Wyn, jt. auth. see Sapsford, David.

Morgan, Yarrow, jt. ed. see McNaron, Toni A.

Morgane & Panksepp. Handbook of the Hypothalamus: Behavioral Studies of the Hypothalmus, Vol. 3, Pt. A. 512p. 1980. 170.00 (*0-8247-6904-X*) Dekker.

— Handbook of the Hypothalamus: Behavioral Studies of the Hypothalmus, Vol. 3, Pt. B. 480p. 1981. 170.00 (*0-8247-6905-8*) Dekker.

— Handbook of the Hypothalamus: Physiology of the Hypothalamus, Vol. 2. 688p. 1980. 250.00 (*0-8247-6881-7*) Dekker.

Morgane, P. & Panksepp, J., eds. Anatomy of the Hypothalmus. (Handbook of the Hypothalamus Ser.: Vol. 1). 756p. 250.00 (*0-8247-6834-5*) Dekker.

***Morganett, Rosemarie S.** Skills & Techniques for Group Work with Youth. 200p. (Orig.). 1995. pap. text ed. write for info. (*0-87822-352-5*) Res Press.

— Skills for Living: Group Counseling Activities for Elementary Students. LC 94-65700. 238p. (Orig.). 1994. pap. text ed. 24.95 (*0-87822-347-9*, 4761) Res Press.

— Skills for Living: Group Counseling Activities for Young Adolescents. LC 89-61588. 216p. (Orig.). 1989. pap. text ed. 24.95 (*0-87822-318-5*, 3184) Res Press.

Morgani, Giambattista. The Clinical Consultations of Giambattista Morgagni: The Edition of Enrico Benassi, 1935. Jarcho, Saul, tr. & intro. by. c, 450p. 1984. 25.00 (*0-88135-103-2*, Sci Hist) Watson Pub Intl.

Morgann, Maurice. Essay on the Dramatic Character of Sir John Falstaff. Gill, William A., ed. LC 72-109657. (Select Bibliographies Reprint Ser.). 1977. 20.95 (*0-8369-5266-9*) Ayer.

— Essay on the Dramatic Character of Sir John Falstaff. LC 79-115363. reprint ed. 20.00 (*0-404-04435-2*) AMS Pr.

Morgano, M., ed. The U. K. Finance Directory: A Directory of Sources of U. K. Corporate Finance. 600p. 1990. 695. 00 (*0-86010-342-0*, Pub. by Graham & Trotman UK); pap. 395.00 (*0-86010-341-2*, Pub. by Graham & Trotman UK) St Mut.

Morganroth, Joel, ed. Congestive Heart Failure: Proceedings of Symposium on New Drugs & Devices, October 30-31, 1986, Philadelphia, PA. (Developments in Cardiovascular Medicine Ser.). (C). 1987. lib. bdg. 92.00 (*0-89838-955-0*) Kluwer Ac.

— The Evaluation of New Antiarrhythmic Drugs. 340p. 1981. 39.95 (*0-686-34396-4*) Kluwer Ac.

Morganroth, Joel & Horowitz, Leonard, eds. Sudden Cardiac Death. LC 79-2965. 352p. 1985. text ed. 79.95 (*0-8089-1725-0*, 792965, Grune) Saunders.

Morganroth, Joel & Moore, E. Neil. The Evaluation of Beta Blocker & Calcium Antagonist Drugs. 1982. lib. bdg. 117.00 (*90-247-2642-5*) Kluwer Ac.

— Sudden Cardiac Death & Congestive Heart Failure. 1983. lib. bdg. 80.00 (*0-89838-580-6*) Kluwer Ac.

Morganroth, Joel & Moore, E. Neil, eds. Cardiac Arrhythmias: New Therapeutic Drugs & Devices. (Developments in Cardiovascular Medicine Ser.). 1985. lib. bdg. 88.00 (*0-89838-716-7*) Kluwer Ac.

— Interventions in the Acute Phase of Myocardial Infarction. 320p. 1984. lib. bdg. 72.00 (*0-89838-659-4*) Kluwer Ac.

— Risk-Benefit Analysis for the Use & Approval of Thrombolytic, Antiarrhythmic, & Hypolipidemic Agents. (C). 1989. lib. bdg. 97.00 (*0-7923-0294-X*) Kluwer Ac.

— Use & Approval of Antihypertensive Agents & Surrogate Endpoints for the Approval of Drugs Affecting Antiarrhythmic Heart Failure & Hypolipidemia: Proceedings of the Tenth Annual Symposium on New Drugs & Devices, Oct. 31-Nov. 1, 1989. (C). 1990. lib. bdg. 89.50 (*0-7923-0756-9*) Kluwer Ac.

Morganroth, Joel, et al, eds. Noninvasive Cardiac Imaging. LC 82-11095. (Illus.). 458p. reprint ed. pap. 130.60 (*0-8357-7624-7*, 2056947) Bks Demand.

Morgans, W. M. Outlines of Paint Technology. 3rd ed. 503p. 1990. text ed. 139.00 (*0-470-21654-9*) Wiley.

Morgans, William. Illustrations of Masonry by One of the Fraternity Who Has Devoted Thirty Years to the Subject. Obaba, Al Imam, ed. 1991. pap. text ed. write for info. (*0-916157-96-2*) African Islam Miss Pubns.

Morganstern, Michael. How to Make Love to a Woman. 144p. 1985. mass mkt. 5.99 (*0-345-33206-7*) Ballantine.

Morganstern, Stanley, jt. ed. see Sowald, Beatrice K.

Morganstern, Steven. Overcoming Impotence: Doctor's Guide to Regaining Sexual Vitality. 2nd ed. 1994. pap. 15.95 (*0-13-146978-9*) P-H.

— The Prostate Sourcebooks: Everything You Need to Know. 252p. 1994. reprint ed. pap. 12.95 (*1-56565-117-0*) Lowell Hse.

Morganstern, Steven & Abrahams, Allen. Love Again, Live Again. 176p. 1988. 16.95 (*0-13-540758-3*) P-H.

— The Prostate Sourcebook: Everything You Need to Know. LC 93-16403. 288p. 1993. 23.95 (*1-56565-007-7*) Lowell Hse.

Morgante, John-Paul. First Things First, Pt. 1. (Basic Christian Training Ser.). 64p. 1991. pap. 2.50 (*1-880322-02-1*) Champions Christ.

— Follow-Up Manual. 50p. 1991. pap. 5.00 (*1-880322-00-5*) Champions Christ.

Morganthal, Deborah, ed. see Sturges, Norma.

Morganti, P. & Montagna, W., eds. A New Look at Old Skin, a Challenge to Cosmetology: 1st International Meeting on Cosmetic Dermatology, Rome, Italy, March 7-9, 1985. 300p. 1986. text ed. 120.00 (*0-87936-017-8*) Scholium Intl.

***Morgart, Marie.** Abandoned Child. Hammond, Deanna, ed. 130p. (Orig.). Date not set. pap. text ed. 9.95 (*1-882185-26-9*) Crnrstone Pub.

— Sunrise at Ten: Johnstown - Another Age. LC 90-71995. 203p. (Orig.). 1991. pap. 10.00 (*1-56002-093-8*) Aegina Pr.

Morgen, Howard. 10 from Guitar Player. Stang, Aaron, ed. 72p. (Orig.). (YA). 1992. pap. text ed. 12.95 (*0-89898-575-7*) CPP Belwin.

***Morgen, Kenneth B.** Getting Simon: Two Gay Doctors' Journey to Fatherhood. LC 95-13177. 232p. (Orig.). 1995. pap. 14.95 (*1-883647-04-5*, Bramble Bks) Bramble Co.

Morgen, Sandra, ed. Gender & Anthropology. 1989. 20.00 (*0-913167-33-9*) Am Anthro Assn.

Morgen, Sandra, jt. ed. see Bookman, Ann.

Morgen, Sharon D. Sales on the Line: Meeting the Business Demands of the '90s Through Phone Partnering. 248p. (Orig.). 1993. pap. 14.95 (*1-55552-047-2*) Metamorphous Pr.

Morgenbesser, Mel & Nehls, Nadine. Joint Custody: An Alternative for Divorcing Families. LC 80-22182. (Illus.). 176p. 1981. 27.95 (*0-88229-620-5*) Nelson-Hall.

Morgenbesser, Sidney, ed. see Dewey, John.

Morgenfrug, Rudolph A., jt. auth. see Dominy, Arthur L.

Morgenroth, Barbara. Get Inside a Ranch. LC 93-41626. (Get Inside Ser.). (Illus.). 64p. (J). (gr. 4-6). 1994. lib. bdg. 12.95 (*1-881889-56-4*) Silver Moon.

Morgenroth, Barbara, jt. auth. see Layman, Teresa.

Morgenroth, Hermann & Najock, Dietmar, eds. Priapea - Concordantiae In Corpus Priapeorum et In Pervigilium Veneris. (Alpha-Omega, Reihe A Ser.: Bd. LIX). 181p. (LAT.). 1983. 52.50 (*3-487-07328-5*, Pub. by Georg Olms GW) Lubrecht & Cramer.

— Vergilius: Concordantia in Appendicem Vergilianam. Vol. LXVIII. 750p. Date not set. write for info. (*0-318-71981-9*, Pub. by Georg Olms GW) Lubrecht & Cramer.

— Vergilius - Concordantia in Appendicem Vergilianam. (Alpha-Omega, Reihe A Ser.: Bd. LXVIII). x, 542p. (GER.). 1992. write for info. (*3-487-09592-0*, Pub. by Georg Olms GW) Lubrecht & Cramer.

Morgenroth, Joyce. Dance Improvisations. LC 86-19318. (Illus.). 160p. (C). 1987. 29.95 (*0-8229-3550-3*); pap. 16. 95x (*0-8229-5386-2*) U of Pittsburgh Pr.

Morgenroth, Konrad & Newhouse, M. The Surfactant System of the Lungs. viii, 112p. (C). 1988. lib. bdg. 79. 25 (*0-89925-377-6*) De Gruyter.

— The Surfactant System of the Lungs. viii, 112p. (C). 1988. lib. bdg. 79.25 (*3-11-011387-2*) De Gruyter.

— Das Surfactantsystem der Lunge. viii, 110p. (C). 1986. lib. bdg. 79.25 (*3-11-011015-6*) De Gruyter.

Morgensen, Gunnar V. Danes & Their Politicians: A Summary of the Findings of a Research Project on Political Credibility in Denmark. (Voters in Scandinavia Ser.: No. 2). 85p. (Orig.). 1993. pap. 26.50 (*87-7288-451-7*, Pub. by Aarhus Univ Pr DK) Coronet Bks.

Morgensen, Gunnar V., jt. ed. see Atkinson, A. B.

***Morgensen, O.E.** Positron Annihilation in Chemistry. LC 94-27490. (Chemical Physics Ser.). 1994. 99.00 (*0-387-57853-6*) Spr-Verlag.

Morgenson, Dana C. Yosemite Wildflower Trails. (Illus.). 88p. (Orig.). 1975. pap. 6.95 (*0-939666-27-8*) Yosemite Assn.

Morgenstein, Melvin. Career Accounting Fundamentals. 559p. (C). 1988. text ed. 44.00 (*0-15-505778-2*); disk write for info. (*0-318-64533-5*); disk write for info. (*0-318-64534-3*); 5.50 (*0-15-505782-0*) Dryden Pr.

Morgenstein, Melvin & Strongin, Harriet. Modern Retailing: Management Principles & Practices. 3rd ed. 640p. (C). 1992. text ed. write for info. (*0-13-588120-X*) P-H.

Morgenstern, Barbara L., jt. auth. see Mirabito, Michael M.

***Morgenstern, Christian.** Christian Morgenstern: Lullabies, Lyrics & Gallows Songs. Bell, Anthea, tr. LC 94-40351. (Illus.). 48p. (J). (gr. 1-4). 1995. 16.95 (*1-55858-364-5*); lib. bdg. 16.88 (*1-55858-365-3*) North-South Bks NYC.

— Christian Morgenstern's Galgenlieder (Gallows Songs) Knight, Max, tr. & intro. by. (Illus.). (ENG & GER.). 1963. pap. 11.00 (*0-520-00884-7*) U CA Pr.

— Songs from the Gallows: Galgenlieder. Arndt, Walter, tr. LC 93-3459. 160p. (C). 1993. 20.00 (*0-300-05278-2*) Yale U Pr.

Morgenstern, Claudia, jt. ed. see Calleo, David P.

Morgenstern, Dan. Jazz People. (Illus.). 301p. 1993. reprint ed. pap. 24.50 (*0-306-80527-8*) Da Capo.

— Jazz People. (Illus.). 1978. reprint ed. pap. text ed. write for info. (*0-13-511352-0*) P-H.

Morgenstern, Felice. International Conflicts of Labour Law: A Survey of the Law Applicable to the International Employment Relation. 2nd ed. ix, 129p. 1986. text ed. 22.00 (*92-2-103593-X*) Intl Labour Office.

— Legal Problems of International Organizations. 163p. (C). 1986. 135.00 (*0-906496-24-1*, Pub. by Grotius Pubns UK) St Mut.

Morgenstern, George. Pearl Harbor: The Story of the Secret War. 425p. reprint ed. pap. 14.95 (*0-939484-38-2*) Inst Hist Rev.

Morgenstern, I., jt. ed. see Van Hemmen, J. L.

Morgenstern, Julian. Rites of Birth, Marriage, Death, & Kindred Occasions among the Semites. 1966. 25.00 (*0-87068-230-X*) Ktav.

Morgenstern, Michael. How to Make Love to a Woman. 1988. 6.99 (*0-517-60525-2*) Random Hse Value.

Morgenstern, Oskar. International Financial Transactions & Business Cycles. (Studies in Business Cycles: No. 8). 671p. 1959. reprint ed. 160.00 (*0-87014-091-4*) Natl Bur Econ Res.

— On the Accuracy of Economic Observations. LC 63-15358. 336p. reprint ed. pap. 95.80 (*0-8357-8977-2*, 2033408) Bks Demand.

Morgenstern, Oskar, jt. auth. see Kemmerer, Edwin W.

Morgenstern, Oskar, jt. auth. see Von Neumann, John.

Morgenstern, Sam, jt. auth. see Barlow, Harold.

Morgenstern, Sam, jt. comp. see Barlow, Harold.

Morgenstern, Steve. No-Sweat Desktop Publishing: A Guide from Home Office Computing Magazine. 224p. (Orig.). 1992. pap. 22.95 (*0-8144-7729-1*) AMACOM.

Morgenstern, Susie. Oukele la Tele. (Folio - Cadet Bleu Ser.: No. 190). (Illus.). 54p. (FRE.). (J). (gr. 1-5). 1991. pap. 9.95 (*2-07-031190-2*) Schoenhof.

Morgenstern, W., et al, eds. CINDI: Country Integrated Noncommunicable Diseases Intervention Programme, Baseline Evaluation. (Sitzungsberichte der Heidelberger Akademie der Wissenschaften Ser., Mathematisch-Naturwissenschaftliche Klasse, Jahrgang 1991: Suppl. 3). (Illus.). 70p. 1991. pap. 14.00 (*0-387-54646-4*) Spr-Verlag.

— Models of Noncommunicable Diseases: Health Status & Health Service Requirements. LC 92-2326. (Supplement zu den Sitzungsberichten der Mathematisch-Naturwissenschaftlichen Klasse Ser.: Vol. 1992). (Illus.). 196p. 1993. 22.00 (*3-540-55217-0*); pap. 15.00 (*0-387-55217-0*) Spr-Verlag.

Morgentaler, Abraham. The Male Body: A Physician's Guide to what Every Man Should Know. LC 93-18035. 1993. pap. 10.00 (*0-671-86426-2*) S&S Trade.

***Morgenthal, Deborah.** A Crafter's Book of Angels. LC 95-6210. (Illus.). 160p. 1995. 27.95 (*0-8069-3156-6*, Lark Bks) Sterling.

— Wreaths Around the House: More Than 80 Distinctive Wreaths to Make, Enjoy & Give as Gifts. LC 93-39715. (Illus.). 144p. 1994. 21.95 (*0-8069-0712-6*) Sterling.

— Wreaths Around the House: More Than 80 Distinctive Wreaths to Make, Enjoy & Give As Gifts. (Illus.). 144p. (Orig.). 1995. pap. 14.95 (*0-8069-0713-4*, Lark Bks) Sterling.

***Morgenthal, Deborah, ed.** Making Simple Musical Instruments: A Melodious Collection of Strings, Winds, Drums & More. LC 94-3543. (Illus.). 144p. (Orig.). (YA). 1995. 24.95 (*0-937274-80-1*) Lark Books.

Morgenthaler, Fritz. Homosexuality, Heterosexuality, Perversion. Moor, Paul, ed. Aebi, Andreas, tr. 160p. 1987. 24.95 (*0-88163-060-8*) Analytic Pr.

Morgenthaler, G. W., ed. Exploration of Mars. (Advances in the Astronautical Sciences Ser.: Vol. 15). 1963. 45.00 (*0-87703-016-2*, Pub. by Am Astro Soc) Univelt Inc.

Morgenthaler, G. W. & Hollstein, M., eds. Space Shuttle & Spacelab Utilization: Near-Term & Long-Term Benefits for Mankind, Pt. I, Vol. 37. (Advances in the Astronautical Sciences Ser.). 400p. 1978. Pt. I, 400p. lib. bdg. 40.00 (*0-87703-096-0*, Pub. by Am Astro Soc) Univelt Inc.

— Space Shuttle & Spacelab Utilization: Near-Term & Long-Term Benefits for Mankind, Pt. II, Vol. 37. (Advances in the Astronautical Sciences Ser.). 465p. 1978. Pt. II, 465p. lib. bdg. 45.00 (*0-87703-097-9*, Pub. by Am Astro Soc) Univelt Inc.

Morgenthaler, G. W. & Morra, R. G., eds. Unmanned Exploration of the Solar System. (Advances in the Astronautical Sciences Ser.: Vol. 19). 1965. 45.00 (*0-87703-021-9*, Pub. by Am Astro Soc) Univelt Inc.

Morgenthaler, G. W., ed. see Manned Lunar Flight Symposium Staff.

Morgenthaler, G. W., et al, eds. Space Shuttle Payloads. (Science & Technology Ser.: Vol. 30). 530p. 1973. lib. bdg. 40.00 (*0-87703-063-4*, Pub. by Am Astro Soc) Univelt Inc.

Morgenthaler, George W., ed. Future Space Program & Impact on Range & Network Development. (Science & Technology Ser.: Vol. 15). 1967. 40.00 (*0-87703-043-X*, Pub. by Am Astro Soc) Univelt Inc.

Morgenthaler, George W. & Greyber, Howard D., eds. Astronomy from a Space Platform. (Science & Technology Ser.: Vol. 28). 1972. lib. bdg. 35.00 (*0-87703-061-8*, Am Astronaut) Univelt Inc.

Morgenthaler, George W. & Morra, Robert, eds. Planning Challenges of the Seventies in Space. LC 57-43769. (Advances in the Astronautical Sciences Ser.: Vol. 26). (Illus.). 1970. lib. bdg. 35.00 (*0-87703-053-7*, Pub. by Am Astro Soc) Univelt Inc.

— Planning Challenges of the Seventies in Space. suppl. ed. LC 57-43769. (Advances in the Astronautical Sciences Ser.: Vol. 26). (Illus.). 1970. fiche 20.00 (*0-87703-130-4*, Pub. by Am Astro Soc) Univelt Inc.

Morgenthaler, George W. & Silver, Aaron N., eds. Energy Delta, Supply vs. Demand. (Science & Technology Ser.: Vol. 35). 604p. 1975. lib. bdg. 35.00 (*0-87703-070-7*, Pub. by Am Astro Soc); pap. 25.00 (*0-87703-082-0*, Pub. by Am Astro Soc) Univelt Inc.

Morgenthaler, George W., et al, eds. Aerospace Century XXI: Advances in Astronautical Sciences Ser. Pts I, II, III, Vol. 64. (Illus.). 1987. lib. bdg. 225.00 (*0-87703-276-9*, Amer Astro Soc); pap. 180.00 (*0-87703-277-7*, Amer Astro Soc); fiche 25.00 (*0-87703-278-5*, Amer Astro Soc) Univelt Inc.

— Aerospace Century XXI: Space Flight Technologies, Vol. 64. (Advances in the Astronautical Sciences Ser.: Pt. II). (Illus.). 608p. 1987. lib. bdg. 75.00 (*0-87703-280-7*, Amer Astro Soc); pap. 60.00 (*0-87703-283-1*, Amer Astro Soc) Univelt Inc.

— Aerospace Century XXI: Space Missions & Policy, Vol. 64. (Advances in the Astronautical Sciences Ser.: Pt. I). (Illus.). 686p. 1987. lib. bdg. 75.00 (*0-87703-279-3*, Amer Astro Soc); pap. 60.00 (*0-87703-282-3*, Amer Astro Soc) Univelt Inc.

— Aerospace Century XXI: Space Sciences,Applications, & Commercial Developments, Vol. 64. (Advances in the Astronautical Sciences Ser.: Pt. III). (Illus.). 724p. 1987. lib. bdg. 75.00 (*0-87703-281-5*, Amer Astro Soc); pap. 60.00 (*0-87703-284-X*, Amer Astro Soc) Univelt Inc.

Morgenthaler, Hans R. The Early Sketches of German Architect Erich Mendelsohn (1887-1953) No Compromise with Reality. LC 92-14574. 168p. 1992. 79. 95 (*0-7734-9535-5*) E Mellen.

Morgenthaler, J. J., ed. Virus Inactivation in Plasma Products. (Current Studies in Hematology & Blood Transfusion: No. 56). (Illus.). x, 158p. 1988. 113.75 (*3-8055-4836-2*) S Karger.

Morgenthaler, John & Fowkes, Steven W., eds. Stop the FDA: Save Your Health Freedom. 192p. 1993. pap. 9.95 (*0-9627418-8-4*) Hlth Freedom.

Morgenthaler, John, jt. auth. see Dean, Ward.

Morgenthaler, John, et al. Better Sex Through Chemistry: A Guide to the New Prosexual Drugs & Nutrients. 240p. 1995. 14.95 (*0-9627418-2-5*, Smart Pubns) Hlth Freedom.

Morgenthaler, S. & Tukey, John W., eds. Configural Polysampling: A Route to Practical Robustness. (Series in Probability & Mathematics). 228p. 1991. text ed. 69. 95 (*0-471-52372-0*) Wiley.

Morgenthaler, S., et al, eds. New Directions in Statistical Data Analysis & Robustness. LC 93-8952. (Monte Verita, Proceedings of the Centro Stefano Franscini Ascona Ser.). 284p. 1993. 69.00 (*0-8176-2923-8*) Birkhauser.

***Morgenthaler, Sally.** Worship Evangelism: Inviting Unbelievers into the Presence of God. 224p. 1995. pap. 19.99 (*0-310-48561-4*) Zondervan.

Morgenthaler, Walter. Madness & Art: The Life & Works of Adolf Wolfli. Esman, Aaron H., tr. LC 91-46761. (Texts & Contexts Ser.). (Illus.). xviii, 156p. 1992. 40.00 (*0-8032-3156-3*) U of Nebr Pr.

Morgenthau, Hans J. In Defense of the National Interest: A Critical Examination of American Foreign Policy. LC 82-18295. 306p. (C). 1983. reprint ed. pap. text ed. 22. 00 (*0-8191-2846-5*) U Pr of Amer.

— Politics among Nations. 6th rev. ed. Thompson, Kenneth W., ed. 688p. (C). 1985. text ed. write for info. (*0-07-554469-5*) McGraw.

— Politics among Nations: The Struggle for Power & Peace. rev. ed. 1978. text ed. 20.00 (*0-394-32193-6*) Knopf.

— The Purpose of American Politics. LC 82-20057. 382p. (C). 1983. reprint ed. pap. text ed. 27.00 (*0-8191-2847-3*) U Pr of Amer.

M

Morgenthau, Hans J., ed. Peace, Security & the United Nations. LC 72-10841. (Essay Index Reprint Ser.). 1977. reprint ed. 18.95 (*0-8369-7232-5*) Ayer.

Morgenthau, Hans J. & Thompson, Kenneth W. Politics among Nations: The Struggle for Power & Peace. 1992. pap. text ed. write for info. (*0-07-043306-2*) McGraw.

Morgenthau, Hans W. Scientific Man vs. Power Politics. (Midway Reprint Ser.). 1974. reprint ed. pap. text ed. 13.95 (*0-226-53826-5*) U Ch Pr.

Morgenthau, Nans J. The Twilight of International Morality. (Reprint Series in Social Sciences). (C). 1993. reprint ed. pap. text ed. 1.00 (*0-8290-2765-3*, PS-211) Irvington.

Morgenthau, Ruth S. Pride Without Prejudice: The Life of John O. Pastore. (Illus.). 201p. 1989. 30.00 (*0-685-32876-7*) RI Hist Soc.

Morgera, Salvatore D. & Krishna, Hari. Digital Signal Processing: Applications to Communications & Algebraic Coding Theories. 233p. 1989. text ed. 66.00 (*0-12-506995-2*) Acad Pr.

Morgereth, Timothy A., comp. Bing Crosby: A Discography, Radio Program List & Filmography. LC 85-43582. 572p. 1987. lib. bdg. 55.00x (*0-89950-210-5*) McFarland & Co.

Morgolis, Matthew, jt. auth. see Siegal, Mordecai.

Morgridge, Barbara G., ed. see Hamsun, Knut.

Morgridge, Tashia. Award-Winning Activities for All Curriculum Areas. 1990. pap. 12.99 (*0-8224-7336-4*) Fearon Teach Aids.

Morhange-Begue, Claude. Chamberet: Recollections from an Ordinary Childhood. Wainhouse, Austryn, tr. LC 87-81087. 130p. 1987. 14.95 (*0-910395-25-X*); pap. 9.00 (*0-910395-26-8*) Marlboro Pr.

Morhardt, David. Encyclopedia of Bird Reference Drawings. 2nd ed. (Illus.). 80p. 1985. pap. 14.95 (*1-56523-009-4*) Fox Chapel Pub.

Morholt, Evelyn & Brandwein, Paul F. A Sourcebook for the Biological Sciences. 3rd ed. 813p. (C). 1986. text ed. 41.25 (*0-15-582852-5*) HB Coll Pubs.

*__Morhous, Henry C.__ Reminiscences of the 123rd Regiment, N.Y.S.V., Giving a Complete History of Its Three Years Service in the War. (Illus.). 220p. 1995. 30.00 (*1-881868-01-X*) Wash Cnty Hist.

Mori, A., et al. Guanidines, Vol. 2: Further Explorations of the Biological & Clinical Significance. (Illus.). 380p. 1989. 95.00 (*0-306-43223-4*, Plenum Pr) Plenum.

Mori, Barbara L. Americans Studying the Traditional Japanese Art of the Tea Ceremony. LC 92-4379. 216p. 1992. lib. bdg. 89.95 (*0-7734-9853-2*) E Mellen.

Mori, Brian R. Dreams of Flight. 1984. pap. 2.75 (*0-8222-0333-2*) Dramatists Play.

Mori, H. & Miyake, A., eds. New Aspects of Physiology & Pathology of Luteal Phase: Journal: Hormone Research, Vol. 37, Suppl. 1, 1992. (Illus.). iv, 80p. 1992. pap. 33.75 (*3-8055-5625-X*) S Karger.

Mori, H. & Yoshimura, Y., eds. Local Regulators in the Ovary - Paracrine & Autocrine Control. (Journal: Hormone Research Ser.: Vol. 41, Suppl. 1, 1994). (Illus.). iv, 68p. 1994. pap. 29.00 (*3-8055-5994-1*) S Karger.

Mori, Hana. Jirohattan. Kurosaki, Tamiko & Crowe, Elizabeth, trs. LC 93-72833. (Illus.). 80p. (J). (gr. 4-8). 1993. pap. 6.95 (*1-880188-69-4*) Bess Pr.

Mori, Hisashi. Sculpture of the Kamakura Period. Eickmann, Katherine A., tr. LC 73-88470. (Heibonsha Survey of Japanese Art Ser.: Vol. 11). (Illus.). 176p. 1974. 20.00 (*0-8348-1017-4*) Weatherhill.

Mori, Joseph E., jt. auth. see Pahler, Arnold J.

Mori, Joyce. Applique Patterns from Native American Beadwork Designs. LC 93-44235. 1994. 14.95 (*0-89145-826-3*) Collector Bks.

— Quilting Patterns from Native American Designs. LC 92-46892. 1993. 12.95 (*0-89145-813-1*) Collector Bks.

Mori, K., ed. MRI of the Central Nervous System: A Pathology Atlas. (Illus.). ix, 241p. 1991. 149.00 (*0-387-70069-2*) Spr-Verlag.

Mori, Kyoko. The Dream of Water. 288p. 1995. 22.50 (*0-8050-3260-6*) H Holt & Co.

— Fallout. 96p. (Orig.). 1994. pap. 7.95 (*1-882688-04-X*) Tia Chucha Pr.

— One Bird. LC 95-2926. (Edge Bks.). (J). 1995. 15.95 (*0-8050-2983-4*) H Holt & Co.

— Shizuko's Daughter. LC 92-26956. 240p. (YA). (gr. 7 up). 1993. 15.95 (*0-8050-2557-X*, Bks Young Read) H Holt & Co.

Mori, M., jt. ed. see Piessens, R.

Mori, M., et al, eds. The LEC Rat: A New Model for Hepatitis & Liver Cancer. (Illus.). 360p. 1992. 179.00 (*0-387-70079-X*) Spr-Verlag.

Mori, Masahiko. Histochemistry of the Salivary Glands. (Illus.). 288p. 1991. 205.00 (*0-8493-6244-X*, QM576) CRC Pr.

Mori, Masahiro. The Buddha in the Robot: A Robot Engineer's Thoughts on Science & Religion. Terry, Charles S., tr. 192p. 1981. pap. 9.95 (*4-333-01002-0*, Pub. by Kosei Pub Co JA) C E Tuttle.

Mori, Masatoshi G. Buddhism & Faith. LC 78-70102. reprint ed. 21.50 (*0-404-17353-5*) AMS Pr.

*__Mori, Michael T. & Welder, W. Dean.__ The PCMCIA Developer's Guide. 2nd ed. LC 94-93969. (Illus.). 618p. (C). 1995. pap. 89.95 (*0-9640342-1-2*) Sycard Tech.

Mori, Ogai. The Incident at Sakai & Other Stories. Dilworth, David, ed. LC 76-58462. (Unesco Collection of Representative Works, Series of Translations from the Literature of the Union of Soviet Socialist Republics: No. 1). (Illus.). 240p. reprint ed. pap. 68.40 (*0-8357-6154-1*, 2034643) Bks Demand.

— Vita Sexualis. Ninomiya, Kazuji & Goldstein, Sanford, trs. LC 72-79020. 156p. 1972. pap. 8.95 (*0-8048-1048-6*) C E Tuttle.

— The Wild Geese. Goldstein, Sanford & Ochiai, Kingo, trs. LC 59-14087. 119p. 1974. pap. 8.95 (*0-8048-1070-2*) C E Tuttle.

Mori, S. & Yamamoto, G., eds. Productivity of Communities in Japanese Inland Waters, Vol. 10. (Japan International Biological Program Synthesis Ser.). 436p. 1975. pap. 72.50 (*0-86008-220-2*, Pub. by U of Tokyo JA) Col U Pr.

Mori, S., jt. auth. see Furtado, J. I.

Mori, S. A. The Lecythidaceae of a Lowland Neotropical Forest: La Fumee Mountain French Guiana. LC 87-11182. (Memoirs Ser.: Vol. 44). (Illus.). 190p. 1987. pap. 37.00 (*0-89327-315-5*) NY Botanical.

Mori, S. A. & Prance, G. T. Flora of the Guianas: Series A: Phanerogams: Lecythidaceae, Fascicle 12. Gorts Van Rijn, A. R., ed. (Illus.). 87p. 1992. pap. text ed. 119.00 (*1-878762-33-8*, 047883) Koeltz Sci Bks.

Mori, S. A., jt. auth. see Mitchell, J.

Mori, Scott A. & Prance, Ghillean. Lecythidaceae, Pt. Two: The Zygomorphic-Flowered New World Genera (Couroupita, Corythophora, Bertholletia, Couratari, Eschweilera & Lecythis) LC 85-647083. (Flora Neotropica Monograph Ser.: No. 21). (Illus.). 376p. 1990. pap. text ed. 69.00 (*0-89327-345-7*) NY Botanical.

Mori, Scott A., jt. auth. see Prance, Ghillean T.

Mori, Takahide, jt. ed. see Yoshinaga, Koji.

Mori, Takao & Nagasawa, Hiroshi, eds. Toxicity of Hormones in Perinatal Life. 208p. 1988. 114.00 (*0-8493-6862-6*, RG627, CRC Reprint) Franklin.

Mori, Takeo & Milenkovic, Dragen. Secrets of Japanese Astrology: The Science of Kigaku. Robinson, Patricia, tr. LC 92-46664. (Illus.). 144p. (ENG & JPN.). 1993. pap. 9.95 (*0-8348-0290-2*, Tengu Bks) Weatherhill.

Mori, Teruo. The New Experimental Design: Taguchi's Approach to Quality Engineering. 320p. 1993. 45.00 (*0-941243-13-3*) ASI Pr.

— Taguchi Techniques for Image & Pattern Developing Technology. LC 94-17392. 304p. 1994. text ed. 56.00 (*0-13-142747-4*) P-H Gen Ref & Trav.

Mori, Toshio. The Chauvinist & Other Stories. LC 79-52265. (C). 1979. pap. 10.00 (*0-934052-01-8*) UCLA Asian Am Studies Ctr.

Mori, Toshio & Inada, Lawson F. Yokohama, California. LC 84-21987. 176p. (Orig.). 1985. reprint ed. pap. 12.95 (*0-295-96167-8*) U of Wash Pr.

Mori, Y. & Yang, W., eds. Thermal Engineering Joint Conference: Proceedings of the ASME-JSME, 4 vols., 1. 2005p. 1983. pap. text ed. 10.00 (*0-317-02653-4*, I00158A) ASME.

— Thermal Engineering Joint Conference: Proceedings of the ASME-JSME, 4 vols., 2. 2005p. 1983. pap. text ed. 10.00 (*0-317-02654-2*, I00158B) ASME.

— Thermal Engineering Joint Conference: Proceedings of the ASME-JSME, 4 vols., 3. 2005p. 1983. pap. text ed. 10.00 (*0-317-02655-0*, I00158C) ASME.

— Thermal Engineering Joint Conference: Proceedings of the ASME-JSME, 4 vols., 4. 2005p. 1983. pap. text ed. 10.00 (*0-317-02656-9*, I00158D) ASME.

— Thermal Engineering Joint Conference: Proceedings of the ASME-JSME, 4 vols., Set. 2005p. 1983. pap. text ed. 30.00 (*0-317-02652-6*, I00158) ASME.

Mori, Y. & Yang, Wen-Jei, eds. Heat Transfer in High Technology & Power Engineering. (Illus.). 602p. 1986. 131.00 (*0-89116-645-9*) Hemisp Pub.

Mori, Y., et al, eds. High-Temperature Heat Exchangers. (Proceedings of the International Center for Heat & Mass Transfer Ser.). 606p. 1986. 131.00 (*0-89116-565-7*) Hemisp Pub.

Mori, Yasuo, jt. ed. see Hatta, Keizo.

Moriarity, Brian, jt. auth. see Roland, Harold E.

Moriarity, David M. Psychic Energy & Aggression. 188p. (C). 1991. 32.50 (*0-87527-486-2*) Green.

Moriarity, Gene M., jt. auth. see O'Flynn, Michael F.

Moriarity, Joe, jt. auth. see Lucas, John.

Moriarity, Shane, ed. Cases from Management Accounting Practice, 2 vols., Vol. 1. 35p. 4.95 (*0-86641-133-X*, 86198) Inst Mgmt Account.

— Cases from Management Accounting Practice, 2 vols., Vol. 2. 42p. 4.95 (*0-86641-143-7*) Inst Mgmt Account.

— Joint Cost Allocations. 1981. 14.95 (*0-317-02579-1*) U OK Ctr Econ.

— Laboratory Market Research. 222p. 1986. 15.00 (*0-931880-05-X*) U OK Ctr Econ.

Moriarity, Shane & Joyce, Edward, eds. Decision Making & Accounting: Current Research. 217p. 1984. 14.95 (*0-931880-04-1*) U OK Ctr Econ.

Moriarty, Alice, jt. auth. see Gardner, Riley W.

Moriarty, Alice E., jt. auth. see Murphy, Lois B.

Moriarty, Anthony. The Psychology of Adolescent Satanism: A Guide for Parents, Counselors, Clergy, & Teachers. LC 92-12731. 168p. 1992. text ed. 39.95 (*0-275-94307-0*, C4307, Praeger Pubs) Greenwood.

Moriarty, Anthony R. & Field, Mark W. Police Officer Selection: A Handbook for Law Enforcement Administrators. LC 94-17514. (Illus.). 372p. (C). 1994. 76.95 (*0-398-05922-5*) C C Thomas.

— Police Officer Selection: A Handbook for Law Enforcement Administrators. LC 94-17514. (Illus.). 372p. (C). 1994. pap. 39.95 (*0-398-05970-5*) C C Thomas.

Moriarty, Barry M. Industrial Location & Community Development. LC 79-16029. xvii, 381p. 1980. pap. 13.95 (*0-8078-4064-5*) U of NC Pr.

Moriarty, Brian, jt. auth. see Roland, Harold E.

Moriarty, Catherine, ed. The Voice of the Middle Ages: In Personal Letters 1100-1500. (Illus.). 352p. 1991. 29.95 (*0-87226-343-6*) P Bedrick Bks.

— The Voice of the Middle Ages: In Personal Letters, 1100-1500. (Illus.). 352p. 1991. pap. 12.95 (*0-87226-252-9*) P Bedrick Bks.

Moriarty, Christopher. By-Ways Rather Than Highways: Exploring Ireland's Hidden Places. (Illus.). 128p. 1994. pap. 19.95 (*0-86327-373-4*, Pub. by Wolfhound Pr IE) Dufour.

— On Foot in Dublin & Wicklow. 1989. pap. 8.95 (*0-86327-226-6*) Dufour.

— On Foot in Dublin & Wicklow: Exploring the Wilderness. 144p. 1989. pap. 7.95 (*0-685-33534-8*, Pub. by Wolfhound Pr IE) Dufour.

Moriarty, D. J. & Pullin, R. S., eds. Detritus & Microbial Ecology in Aquaculture. (Conference Proceedings Ser.: No. 14). 1987. pap. 28.50 (*971-10-2229-X*, Pub. by ICLARM PH) Intl Spec Bk.

Moriarty, Daniel P. How to Help Your Kids Through College. 1978. pap. 2.00 (*0-933968-01-9*) D Moriarty.

— How to Publish a Worldwide Family-Name Newsletter. 1979. pap. 10.00 (*0-933968-02-7*) D Moriarty.

— How to Raise Money at Church Without Sales or Bingo. 1977. pap. 4.00 (*0-933968-00-0*) D Moriarty.

— Ten Ways to Lobby Your Representatives from Home. 1979. pap. 2.00 (*0-933968-03-5*) D Moriarty.

Moriarty, David. King Phillip's War. 425p. (Orig.). (C). 1995. pap. 32.50 (*0-87527-493-5*) Green.

Moriarty, David M. The Loss of Loved Ones. 2nd ed. LC 79-50189. 312p. 1983. 27.50 (*0-87527-161-8*) Green.

— A Psychological Study of Adolf Hitler. (Illus.). 302p. (Orig.). 1993. pap. text ed. 27.50 (*0-87527-491-9*) Green.

— Rudolf Hess, Deputy Fuhrer: A Psychological Study. (Illus.). 325p. (Orig.). (C). 1996. pap. 35.00 (*0-87527-489-7*) Green.

Moriarty, Dorothy. Dorothy. large type ed. (Illus.). 368p. 1992. 21.95 (*0-7089-2591-X*) Ulverscroft.

Moriarty, Ernest T. One Day into Twenty Three. 164p. (Orig.). 1987. pap. text ed. 13.95 (*0-9620139-0-0*) E T Moriarty.

Moriarty, F. Ecotoxicology: The Study of Pollutants in Ecosystems. 2nd ed. 289p. 1988. text ed. 68.00 (*0-12-506761-5*); pap. text ed. 34.95 (*0-12-506762-3*) Acad Pr.

*__Moriarty, Frank.__ Supercars: The Story of the Dodge Charger Daytona & Plymouth Superbird. (Illus.). 160p. 1995. 34.95 (*1-57427-043-5*) Howell Pr VA.

Moriarty, G. P. Dean Swift & His Writings. LC 70-130247. (English Literature Ser.: No. 33). 1970. reprint ed. lib. bdg. 53.95 (*0-8383-1137-7*) M S G Haskell Hse.

Moriarty, Gerald P. The Paris Law Courts: Sketches of Men & Manners. (Illus.). viii, 293p. 1987. reprint ed. lib. bdg. 37.50 (*0-8377-2434-1*) Rothman.

Moriarty, J. M. Ground Attack - Vietnam: The Marines Who Controlled the Skies. (Orig.). 1993. mass mkt. 5.99 (*0-8041-1065-4*) Ivy Books.

*__Moriarty, Jane.__ Technical Evidence in Criminal Trials, 3 vols., Set. (Criminal Ser.). 1995. ring bd. write for info. (*0-614-06275-6*) Clark Boardman Callaghan.

Moriarty, Jim. Tee Off: America's Most Public Golf Courses. (Illus.). 144p. 1991. 15.99 (*0-517-06574-6*, Crescent) Random Hse Value.

Moriarty, John. Diction: Italian, Latin, French, German . . . the Sounds & 81 Exercises for Singing Them. LC 74-17158. 1975. pap. 15.00 (*0-911318-09-7*) E C Schirmer.

Moriarty, John D. Psychiatric Treatment Is Much More Than Psychotherapy. 300p. 1993. 24.00 (*0-9633747-0-2*); pap. 16.95 (*0-9633747-1-0*) SoCal Med Pr.

Moriarty, John J., jt. auth. see Oldfield, Barney.

Moriarty, John P. & McNeily, Curtlan R. Regulation of Financial Planners. LC 91-26315. (Securities Law Ser.). 1991. ring bd. 145.00 (*0-87632-816-8*) Clark Boardman Callaghan.

Moriarty, Kathleen. A Shaker Sampler Coloring Book. 2.25 (*0-937942-11-1*) Shaker Mus.

Moriarty, Kathleen M. A Shaker Sampler: Coloring Book. 2nd ed. (Illus.). 30p. (J). (gr. k-6). 1991. pap. 4.95 (*0-915836-15-7*) United Soc Shakers.

Moriarty, Laura. L' Archiviste. 32p. 1991. pap. 8.00 (*84-87467-10-5*) SPD-Small Pr Dist.

— Like Roads. Dienstfrey, Pat, ed. LC 89-49484. 74p. (Orig.). (C). 1990. pap. text ed. 8.00 (*0-932716-24-5*) Kelsey St Pr.

— Rondeaux. LC 90-61555. (Roof Bks.). 88p. (Orig.). 1990. pap. text ed. 8.00 (*0-937804-39-8*) Segue NYC.

— Symmetry. Chadwick, Cydney, ed. 120p. (Orig.). 1995. pap. text ed. 9.95 (*1-880713-04-7*) AVEC Bks.

Moriarty, Laura, ed. The American Poetry Archives Videotape Catalogue: 1974-1990. 120p. 1991. per., pap. 3.00 (*0-685-56990-X*) Poetry Ctr Pr.

Moriarty, Linda P. Ni'ihau Shell Leis. LC 86-50306. (Illus.). 104p. 1986. 39.95 (*0-8248-0998-X*) UH Pr.

Moriarty, Margaret, tr. see Jacquard, Albert.

Moriarty, Mary & Sweeney, Catherine. Bob Geldof. LC 89-50965. (O'Brien Press Junior Biography Ser.). (Illus.). 80p. (Orig.). (YA). (gr. 9-12). 1990. pap. 8.95 (*0-86278-163-9*, Pub. by OBrien Pr IE) Dufour.

— Granuaile: Chieftain Pirate Trader. 76p. 1989. pap. 8.95 (*0-86278-162-0*, Pub. by OBrien Pr IE) Dufour.

— Jonathan Swift: The Man Who Wrote Gulliver. 64p. 1990. pap. 8.95 (*0-86278-210-4*, Pub. by OBrien Pr IE) Dufour.

— The Rebel Countess. (Junior Biography Library). (Illus.). 80p. (Orig.). (J). (gr. 1-7). 1992. pap. 8.95 (*0-86278-211-2*, Pub. by OBrien Pr IE) Dufour.

— Theobald Wolfe Tone. (Illus.). 64p. (J). 1989. pap. 8.95 (*0-86278-160-4*, Pub. by OBrien Pr IE) Dufour.

— W. B. Yeats. 58p. 1989. pap. 8.95 (*0-86278-161-2*, Pub. by OBrien Pr IE) Dufour.

Moriarty, Mary, tr. see Jacquard, Albert.

Moriarty, Michael. Roland Barthes. LC 90-72070. (Key Contemporary Thinkers Ser.). 280p. 1992. 39.50 (*0-8047-1932-2*); pap. 12.95 (*0-8047-1933-0*) Stanford U Pr.

— Taste & Ideology in Seventeenth-Century France. (Cambridge Studies in French: No. 25). 244p. (C). 1989. 64.95 (*0-521-30686-8*) Cambridge U Pr.

Moriarty, Michael G. The New Charismatics: A Concerned Voice Responds to Dangerous New Trends. LC 92-12287. 1992. write for info. (*0-310-50375-2*) Zondervan.

— The New Charismatics: A Concerned Voice Responds to Dangerous New Trends. 336p. 1992. pap. 17.99 (*0-310-53431-3*) Zondervan.

Moriarty, Mike, jt. auth. see Goya, Fred.

Moriarty, Patrick J., ed. Evening Prayers Morning Promises: Understanding 12 Step Spirituality. LC 89-37966. 168p. (Orig.). 1989. pap. 7.95 (*0-934125-14-7*) Hazelden.

Moriarty, Richard C. New York Understanding the Penal Law. 1994. 23.95 (*0-87526-416-6*) Gould.

*__Moriarty, Sandra & Duncan, Tom.__ How to Create & Deliver Winning Advertising & Marketing Presentations. 2nd ed. Knudsen, Anne, ed. LC 94-30848. 1995. 49.95 (*0-8442-3529-6*, NTC Busn Bks) NTC Pub Grp.

— How to Create & Deliver Winning Advertising Presentations. 192p. 1989. pap. 19.95 (*0-8442-3196-7*, NTC Busn Bks) NTC Pub Grp.

Moriarty, Sandra E. Creative Advertising: Theory & Practice. 2nd ed. 448p. (C). 1990. text ed. 56.00 (*0-13-189911-2*) P-H.

Moriarty-Schieven, Cindy. In Celebration of Life. (Illus.). 154p. 1991. 19.95 (*0-87527-474-9*) Green.

Moriarty, Tim. Vampire Nights. 1989. pap. 3.95 (*1-55817-180-0*, Pinnacle NY) Windsor NY.

Moriber, Harry. Structured BASIC Programming. 2nd ed. 480p. (C). 1989. pap. write for info. (*0-675-20715-0*, Merrill Pub Co) Macmillan.

Morice, Anne. Fatal Charm. large type ed. (Nightingale Ser.). 276p. 1990. pap. 13.95 (*0-8161-4925-9*) G K Hall.

— Planning for Murder. large type ed. (Nightingale Ser.). 267p. 1991. pap. 14.95 (*0-8161-5246-2*) G K Hall.

*__Morice, Dave.__ The Adventures of Dr. Alphabet: 104 Unusual Ways to Write Poetry in the Classroom & the Community. (Illus.). 276p. (Orig.). 1995. pap. 15.95 (*0-915924-44-7*) Tchrs & Writers Coll.

— How to Make Poetry Comics. 64p. 1983. pap. 5.95 (*0-915924-31-5*) Tchrs & Writers Coll.

— Quicksand Through the Hourglass. LC 79-25714. (Illus.). 57p. (Orig.). 1979. pap. 4.50 (*0-915124-27-0*, Toothpaste) Coffee Hse.

— A Visit from St. Alphabet. LC 80-24865. (Illus.). 24p. (Orig.). 1994. reprint ed. pap. 5.95 (*1-55652-201-0*) A cappella Bks.

Morice, David. More Poetry Comics. LC 94-16563. (Illus.). 176p. 1994. 14.95 (*1-55652-220-7*) A cappella Bks.

Morice, E. Diccionario de Estadistica. 220p. (SPA.). 1975. pap. 18.50 (*0-8288-5808-X*, S50210) Fr & Eur.

Morice, Sidney B. Geriatric Nursing. (Outline Ser.). (Illus.). 300p. (Orig.). (C). 1994. pap. text ed. 16.95 (*0-944132-90-1*) Skidmore Roth Pub.

Morici, Peter. Free Trade in the Americas. LC 94-7627. 1994. 8.95 (*0-87078-187-1*) TCFP-PPP.

— A New Special Relationship: Free Trade & U. S.-Canada Economic Relations in the... 153p. 1991. pap. 23.95 (*0-88645-132-9*, Pub. by Inst Res Pub CN) Ashgate Pub Co.

— Trade Talks with Mexico: A Time for Realism. 124p. (Orig.). 1991. pap. text ed. 15.00 (*0-89068-110-4*, CIR 22 (NPA253)) Natl Planning.

Morici, Peter, ed. Making Free Trade Work: The Canada-U. S. Agreement. LC 89-71317. 200p. 1990. pap. 17.95 (*0-87609-078-1*) Coun Foreign.

Morici, Peter & Megna, Laura L. Canada: United States Trade & Economic Interdependence. (Canadian-U. S. Prospect Ser.). 64p. (Orig.). 1980. pap. 5.00 (*0-88806-072-6*) Natl Planning.

— U. S. Economic Policies Affecting Industrial Trade: A Quantitative Assessment. LC 83-60013. (Committee on Changing International Realities Ser.). 140p. (Orig.). 1983. pap. 12.00 (*0-89068-068-X*, CIR-13) Natl Planning.

Morici, Peter, jt. auth. see Mutti, John.

Morick, Harold. Challenges to Empiricism. LC 72-10731. 339p. (C). 1980. reprint ed. 34.95 (*0-915144-89-1*); reprint ed. pap. text ed. 12.95 (*0-915144-90-5*) Hackett Pub.

Morieda, Takashi. Children of the World: Burma. LC 86-42799. (Illus.). 64p. (J). (gr. 5-6). 1987. lib. bdg. 21.26 (*1-55532-159-3*) Gareth Stevens Inc.

Moriei, Peter, et al. Canadian Industrial Policy. LC 82-81566. 116p. (Orig.). 1982. pap. 10.00 (*0-89068-063-9*) Natl Planning.

Moriello, K. A. & Mason, I. S. Handbook of Small Animal Dermatology. LC 94-18014. (Pergamon Veterinary Handbook Ser.: No. 11). 1995. 77.00 (*0-08-042281-0*, Pergamon Pr); pap. 53.00 (*0-08-042280-2*, Pergamon Pr) Elsevier.

Morier, Henri. Dictionnaire De Poetique et De Rhetorique. 4th ed. 1320p. (FRE.). 1989. 350.00 (*0-7859-0469-7*, 2130400973) Fr & Eur.

Morier, J. The Adventure of Hajji Baba of Ispahan. 464p. 1987. 100.00 (*1-85077-145-6*, Darf Pubs Ltd) St Mut.

*__Mories, John, contrib.__ One Hundred Plus Essential Guitar Chords. 1994. 7.95 (*0-7119-3935-7*, AM91816) Omnibus NY.

Moriet, Marie-Therese. Dictionnaire Etymologique des Noms de Famille. 1120p. (FRE.). 1991. 150.00 (*0-8288-9497-3*) Fr & Eur.

Morieux, Yves, jt. ed. see Sutherland, Ewan.

Morigaki, K. Physics of Amorphous Semiconductors. 300p. 1996. text ed. 55.00 (*981-02-1381-6*) World Scientific Pub.

Morigi, Paolo. Raccolta di un Amatore: D'arte Primtiva. (Illus.). 475p. (ENG, FRE, GER & ITA.). 1980. lib. bdg. 195.00 (*0-87817-286-6*) Hacker.

An Asterisk (*) at the beginning of an entry indicates that the title is appearing in BIP for the first time.

Moriguchi, Yasuhiko & Jenkins, David, trs. The Song in the Dream of the Hermit: Selections from the Kanginshu. LC 93-71568. (International Ser.). 128p. (Orig.). 1994. pap. 12.95 (*0-913089-35-4*) Broken Moon.
Moriguchi, Yasuhiko, jt. tr. see Jenkins, David.
Moriguti, S., et al, eds. Microcomputers in Secondary Education: Proceedings of the IFIP TC 3 Regional Conference, MCSE'86 Tokyo, Japan, 18-22 August, 1986. 546p. 1987. 107.75 (*0-444-70220-2*, North Holland) Elsevier.
Morihara, Bonnie V., jt. auth. see McSwain, Mary E.
Morihisa, John M., ed. Brain Imaging in Psychiatry. LC 84-6303. (Clinical Insights Ser.). 103p. reprint ed. pap. 29.40 (*0-8357-7812-6*, 2036184) Bks Demand.
Morii, H., ed. Calcium-Regulating Hormones, Vol. I: Role in Disease & Aging. (Contributions to Nephrology Ser.: Vol. 90). (Illus.). xiv, 230p. 1991. 167.25 (*3-8055-5371-4*) S Karger.
— Calcium-Regulating Hormones, Vol. II: Calcium Transport, Bone Metabolism & New Drugs. (Contributions to Nephrology Ser.: Vol. 91). (Illus.). viii, 152p. 1991. 109.00 (*3-8055-5372-2*) S Karger.
***Morii, H., et al, eds.** New Actions of Parathyroid Hormone. (Journal: Mineral & Electrolyte Metabolism Ser.: Vol. 21, Nos. 1-3, 1995). (Illus.). 244p. 1995. pap. 129.75 (*3-8055-6195-4*) S Karger.
Morik, K., ed. Knowledge Representation & Organization in Machine Learning. (Lecture Notes in Artificial Intelligence Ser.: Vol. 347). 319p. 1989. pap. 40.00 (*0-387-50768-X*) Spr-Verlag.
Morik, Katharina, ed. EWSL-89: Proceedings of the Fourth European Working Session on Learning, Montpellier. 272p. (C). 1989. text ed. 350.00 (*0-273-08811-4*, Pub. by Pitman Pubng UK) St Mut.
Morik, Katherina, et al. Knowledge Acquisition & Machine Learning. (Knowledge Based Systems Ser.). (Illus.). 320p. 1993. text ed. 55.00 (*0-12-506230-3*) Acad Pr.
Morikawa, Hidemasa, jt. ed. see Kobayashi, Kesaji.
Morike, Eduard. Morike: Poems. Thomas, Lionel, ed. (Bristol German Texts Ser.). 152p. (GER.). 1960. 11.95 (*0-631-01660-0*, Pub. by Brstl Class Pr UK) Focus Info Gr.
***Morillo, Carolyn R.** Contingent Creatures: A Reward Event Theory of Motivation. 206p. (C). 1995. text ed. 59.50 (*0-8226-3040-0*); pap. text ed. 22.95 (*0-8226-3041-9*) Littlefield.
Morillo, Stephen. Warfare under the Anglo-Norman Kings, 1066-1135. LC 94-18931. (Illus.). 192p. (C). 1994. text ed. 53.00 (*0-85115-555-3*, Boydell Pr) Boydell & Brewer.
***Morillo, Stephen, ed.** Battle of Hastings: Sources & Interpretations. (Warfare in History: Sources & Interpretations Ser.: vol. 1). (Illus.). 272p. (Orig.). 1995. text ed. 45.00 (*0-85115-593-6*) Boydell & Brewer.
— Battle of Hastings: Sources & Interpretations. (Warfare in History: Sources & Interpretations Ser.: vol. 1). (Illus.). 272p. (Orig.). 1995. pap. text ed. 27.00 (*0-85115-619-3*) Boydell & Brewer.
Morimitsu, Phil. In the Company of ECK Masters. 288p. 1988. pap. 11.00 (*1-57043-058-6*) ECKANKAR.
— In the Company of ECK Masters. LC 87-80798. 288p. 1987. pap. 11.00 (*0-88155-048-5*) Illum Way Pub.
— The Seeker. 174p. 1992. pap. 11.00 (*1-57043-061-6*) ECKANKAR.
— The Seeker. LC 92-71541. 177p. 1992. pap. 11.00 (*0-88155-098-1*) Illum Way Pub.
Morimore, Peter & Mortimore, Jo. The Primary Head: Roles, Responsibilities & Reflections. 144p. 1991. pap. 27.00 (*1-85396-140-X*, Pub. by P Chapman Pub UK) Taylor & Francis.
— The Secondary Head: Roles, Responsibilities & Reflections. 176p. 1991. pap. 27.00 (*1-85396-141-8*, Pub. by P Chapman Pub UK) Taylor & Francis.
***Morimoto, Anri.** Jonathan Edwards & the Catholic Vision of Salvation. LC 94-40824. 200p. 1995. pap. 33.50 (*0-271-01453-9*) Pa St U Pr.
Morimoto, Junko. The Inch Boy. (J). (ps-3). 1988. pap. 4.99 (*0-14-050677-2*, Puffin) Puffin Bks.
— Mouse's Marriage. (Illus.). 32p. (Orig.). (J). (ps-1). 1988. pap. 4.99 (*0-14-050678-0*, Puffin) Puffin Bks.
— My Hiroshima. (Illus.). 32p. (J). (ps up). 1990. pap. 13.95 (*0-670-83181-6*) Viking Child Bks.
Morimoto, Junko, jt. auth. see Martin, Rafe.
Morimoto, Kiyo, ed. see Burkle, Candace R. & Marshak, David.
Morimoto, Kiyo, ed. see Tobin, Catherine.
Morimoto, Kokichi. The Standard of Living in Japan. LC 78-63963. (Johns Hopkins University. Studies in the Social Sciences. Thirtieth Ser. 1912: No. 2). reprint ed. 17.50 (*0-404-61210-5*) AMS Pr.
Morimoto, Mitsuo. An Introduction to Sato's Hyperfunctions. LC 93-21490. (Translations of Mathematical Monographs: Vol. 128). 296p. 1993. 87.00 (*0-8218-4571-3*) Am Math.
Morimoto, Richard I., et al, eds. The Biology of Heat Shock Proteins & Molecular Chaperones. LC 93-46368. (Monograph Ser.: Vol. 26). (Illus.). 593p. (C). 1994. text ed. 97.00 (*0-87969-427-0*) Cold Spring Harbor.
Morimoto, Richard J., et al, eds. Stress Proteins in Biology & Medicine. 1990. pap. text ed. 97.00 (*0-87969-337-1*) Cold Spring Harbor.
***Morimoto, Toshifumi, et al, eds.** Brain & Oral Functions: Oral Motor Function & Dysfunction: Selected Papers from the Osaka International Oral Physiology Symposium on Brain & Oral Function, Osaka, 3-5 September 1994. LC 95-8197. (International Congress Ser.: No. 1079). 1995. write for info. (*0-444-81963-0*) Elsevier.
Morin. The Eye in Pediatric Disease. (Illus.). 400p. 1991. 60.00 (*0-8016-3553-5*) Mosby Yr Bk.
— The Eye in Pediatric Disease. 400p. 1993. 60.00 (*0-8016-7481-6*) Mosby Yr Bk.
— Silent Sabotage: The Value of Values. 1994. pap. text ed. 10.95 (*1-880030-29-2*) DBM Pub.
— Successful Termination: A DBM Training Program. 1994. pap. text ed. 10.95 (*1-880030-06-3*) DBM Pub.
— Testbank to Accompany Nursing Care of the Childbearing Family. 2nd ed. (C). 1995. teacher ed write for info. (*0-8385-7089-5*) Appleton & Lange.
Morin, Alexander J. Science Policy & Politics. 208p. 1992. pap. text ed. write for info. (*0-13-795246-5*) P-H.
Morin, Alice. Newspaper Theatre. (J). (gr. 1-8). 1989. pap. 9.99 (*0-8224-6349-0*) Fearon Teach Aids.
***Morin, Ann M.** Her Excellency. (Twayne's Oral History Ser.: No. 14). (Illus.). 336p. 1994. text ed. 27.95x (*0-8057-9118-3*, Twayne) Macmillan.
— Her Excellency. (Twayne's Oral History Ser.: No. 14). (Illus.). 336p. 1994. pap. 16.95 (*0-8057-9142-6*, Twayne) Macmillan.
Morin, Beatrice, jt. auth. see Colin, Eric.
Morin, Carol, jt. auth. see Meisels, Alexander.
Morin Center for Banking Law Studies. Annual Review of Banking Law, Vol. 10. 270p. 1991. boxed 80.00 (*0-88063-782-X*) Butterworth Legal Pubs.
***Morin Center for Banking Law Studies Staff.** Annual Review of Banking Law. 1987. boxed 400.00 (*0-614-05779-5*) Michie Butterworth.
— Annual Review of Banking Law, Vols. 6-13, Set. 1992. text ed. 400.00 (*0-88063-162-7*) Butterworth Legal Pubs.
— Annual Review of Banking Law, Vol. 6. 500p. 1987. 50.00 (*0-88063-168-6*) Butterworth Legal Pubs.
— Annual Review of Banking Law, Vol. 7. 600p. 1988. 50.00 (*0-88063-224-0*) Butterworth Legal Pubs.
— Annual Review of Banking Law, Vol. 8. 700p. 1989. 50.00 (*0-88063-273-9*) Butterworth Legal Pubs.
— Annual Review of Banking Law, Vol. 9. 700p. 1990. 50.00 (*0-88063-394-8*) Butterworth Legal Pubs.
Morin, Charles M. Insomnia: Psychological Assessment & Management. LC 93-6564. (Treatment Manuals for Practitioners Ser.). 231p. 1993. lib. bdg. 27.95 (*0-89862-210-7*) Guilford Pr.
Morin, Dominique. How to Understand God. (How to Understand Ser.). (Illus.). 144p. (Orig.). 1990. pap. 12.95 (*0-8245-1047-X*) Crossroad NY.
Morin, Douglas J. No Less Zeal: A Spiritual Guide for Catholic Lay People. LC 92-34242. 145p. (Orig.). 1993. pap. 7.95 (*0-8189-0631-6*) Alba.
Morin, Ed, jt. auth. see Morin, Selma.
Morin, Edgar. Method: Towards a Study of Humankind, Vol. 1: The Nature of Nature. Belanger, J. L., tr. LC 91-45484. (American University Studies: Philosophy: Ser. V, Vol. 111). 435p. (C). 1992. text ed. 63.95 (*0-8204-1878-1*) P Lang Pubs.
Morin, Edward, ed. & tr. The Red Azalea: Chinese Poetry Since the Cultural Revolution. Fang Dai et al, trs. LC 90-41829. 256p. 1990. text ed. 35.00 (*0-8248-1256-5*); pap. 14.95 (*0-8248-1320-0*) UH Pr.
Morin, Edward, jt. auth. see Morin, Selma.
Morin, France, et al. The Interrupted Life. Levi, Jan H., ed. (Illus.). 239p. 1991. 35.00 (*0-915557-74-6*) New Mus Contemp Art.
Morin, Gavino, jt. auth. see Cavazos, Edward A.
Morin, Gustave. Rusted Childhood Memoirs. 17p. (Orig.). 1994. pap. 7.00 (*0-926935-96-8*) Runaway Spoon.
Morin, Isobel V. Days of Judgment: The World War II War Crimes Trials. LC 94-11295. (Illus.). 144p. (YA). (gr. 7 up). 1995. 15.90 (*1-56294-442-8*) Millbrook Pr.
— Women Chosen for Public Office. LC 94-22097. (Profiles Ser.). (Illus.). 160p. (YA). 1995. 14.95 (*1-881508-20-X*) Oliver Pr MN.
— Women of the U. S. Congress. LC 93-26068. (Profiles Ser.). (Illus.). 160p. (YA). (gr. 5-12). 1994. lib. bdg. 14.95 (*1-881508-12-9*) Oliver Pr MN.
— Women Who Reformed Politics. LC 93-46336. (Profiles Ser.). (Illus.). 160p. (YA). (gr. 5-12). 1994. lib. bdg. 14.95 (*1-881508-16-1*) Oliver Pr MN.
Morin, J. Erotic Mind. Date not set. 20.00 (*0-06-016975-3*, HarpT) HarpC.
Morin, J. B. Morinus System of Interpretation. 116p. 1974. 7.00 (*0-86690-132-9*, M1348-014) Am Fed Astrologers.
Morin, Jack. Anal Pleasure & Health: A Guide for Men & Women. 2nd rev. ed. LC 81-9789. (Illus.). 278p. (Orig.). 1986. reprint ed. pap. 12.50 (*0-940208-08-3*, Yes Pr) Down There Pr.
— Men Loving Themselves. LC 80-52942. (Illus.). 104p. 1988. pap. 15.00 (*0-9602324-5-1*) Down There Pr.
Morin, Jacques, jt. ed. see Fossey, John M.
***Morin, Jean-Baptiste.** Astrologia Gallica Book Twenty-Two Directions. Holden, James H., tr. 294p. 1994. 16.00 (*0-86690-425-5*, M3463-014) Am Fed Astrologers.
Morin, Jim. Line of Fire: Political Cartoons by Jim Morin. (Illus.). 264p. 1991. lib. bdg. 29.95 (*0-8130-1081-0*); pap. 15.95 (*0-8130-1101-9*) U Press Fla.
Morin, John B. Sea-Lords of Gondor. Fenlon, Peter C., Jr., ed. (Middle-Earth Campaign Module Ser.). 64p. (Orig.). (YA). (gr. 10-12). 1987. pap. 12.00 (*0-915795-88-4*, 3400) Iron Crown Ent Inc.
Morin, Joseph F., jt. auth. see Morris, Paul C.
***Morin, Katherine A., et al.** Distinguished African American Scientists of the Twentieth Century. More, Tracy, ed. (Illus.). 384p. 1995. 49.95 (*0-89774-955-3*, 2309) Oryx Pr.
***Morin, Kimberly A.** 1994 State Legislation on Native American Issues. 35p. 1994. 10.00 (*1-55516-924-4*, 9369) Natl Conf State Legis.
Morin, Laura. Every Woman's Essential Job Hunting & Resume Book. 1994. pap. 10.95 (*1-55850-382-X*) Adams Pubng.
Morin, Laura, jt. auth. see Adams, Bob.
Morin, Nancy R. Flora of North America, Vol. 2: Ferns & Gymnosperms. (Illus.). 496p. 1993. 75.00 (*0-19-508242-7*) OUP.
Morin, Nancy R., jt. ed. see Flora of North America Editorial Committee.
Morin, Patrice T. CP "Teach" Workbook with Answers. (Illus.). 96p. 1995. pap. 29.95 (*0-923369-30-9*) MedBooks.
— CP"Teach" Instructor's Manual. (Illus.). 350p. 1993. reprint ed. teacher ed 149.95 (*0-685-65111-8*) MedBooks.
Morin, Rich, ed. Prime Time Freeware for UNIX, Issue 2-2. (Orig.). (C). 1993. pap. 60.00 (*1-881957-03-9*) PT Freeware.
Morin, Richard L., ed. Monte Carlo Simulation in the Radiological Sciences. 240p. 1988. 180.00 (*0-8493-5559-1*, R905) CRC Pr.
Morin, Robert B. & Gorman, Marvin, eds. Chemistry & Biology of B-Lactam Antibiotics, 1. 402p. 1982. text ed. 156.00 (*0-12-506301-6*) Acad Pr.
— Chemistry & Biology of B-Lactam Antibiotics, 2. 402p. 1982. text ed. 146.00 (*0-12-506302-4*) Acad Pr.
— Chemistry & Biology of B-Lactam Antibiotics, 3. 402p. 1982. text ed. 146.00 (*0-12-506303-2*) Acad Pr.
Morin, Robert J. & Bing, Richard J., eds. Frontiers in Medicine: Implications for the Future. 272p. 1984. 45.95 (*0-89885-209-9*) Human Sci Pr.
Morin, Robert J., jt. auth. see Peng Shi-Kaung.
Morin, Roger. Regulatory Finance. 560p. 1994. pap. 89.00 (*0-910325-46-4*) Public Util.
Morin, Selma & Morin, Ed. Complete Book of Jiffy Needle Tatting. Workbasket Magazine Staff, ed. (Illus.). 156p. (Orig.). 1992. pap. 18.95 (*0-86675-338-9*) KC Pub.
Morin, Selma & Morin, Edward. Jiffy Needle Tatting: A to Z. Workbasket Magazine Staff, ed. (Illus.). 112p. (Orig.). 1992. pap. 8.95 (*0-86675-340-0*) KC Pub.
— Jiffy Needle Tatting: Fashion Accessories. Workbasket Magazine Staff, ed. (Illus.). 96p. (Orig.). 1992. pap. 8.95 (*0-86675-341-9*) KC Pub.
— Jiffy Needle Tatting: Holiday Collection. Workbasket Magazine Staff, ed. (Illus.). 96p. (Orig.). 1992. pap. 8.95 (*0-86675-342-7*) KC Pub.
— Jiffy Needle Tatting: Quick & Easy. Workbasket Magazine Staff, ed. (Illus.). 112p. (Orig.). 1992. pap. 8.95 (*0-86675-339-7*) KC Pub.
***Morin-Spatz, Patrice.** CP "Teach" Expert Coding Made Easy: 1995 Version. rev. ed. (Illus.). 357p. (C). 1994. pap. text ed. 44.95 (*0-923369-27-9*) MedBooks.
— CP "Teach" Instructor's Manual. (Illus.). 447p. (C). 1995. ring bd. 199.95 (*0-614-06571-2*) MedBooks.
— CP "Teach" Student Workbook. rev. ed. (Illus.). 96p. (C). 1995. pap. text ed. 19.95 (*0-923369-28-7*) MedBooks.
Morin, Suzann. Dicey's Song: A Study Guide. (Novel-Ties Ser.). (gr. 6-10). 1987. student ed, teacher ed 15.95 (*0-88122-112-0*) Lrn Links.
***Morin, Suzanne.** How to Survive Airline Travel. 1995. 12.95 (*0-8062-5154-9*) Carlton.
Morin, Thomas, II. Art Glass Images. Churilla, Kenneth R., ed. (Illus.). 80p. 1986. pap. 9.95 (*0-913417-03-3*) Aurora Pubns.
Morin, Thomas E., ed. Information Management: Strategy, Systems & Technologies, 2 vols. write for info. (*0-318-72268-2*, ADPM) Warren Gorham & Lamont.
Morin, Virginia K. Messy Activities & More. LC 92-41453. (Illus.). 144p. (Orig.). (J). (ps-5). 1993. pap. 9.95 (*1-55652-173-1*) Chicago Review.
Morin, William J. Dismissal: There Is No Easy Way but There Is a Better Way. 1990. 19.95 (*0-15-125740-X*) HarBrace.
— Silent Sabotage: Rescuing Our Companies & Our Lives from the Creeping Paralysis of Anger & Bitterness. 192p. 1995. 19.95 (*0-8144-0300-X*) AMACOM.
— Successful Termination. rev. ed. (Illus.). 44p. (C). 1993. pap. text ed. 10.95 (*1-880030-60-8*) DBM Pub.
— Trust Me. Lynch, Tim, ed. LC 89-92534. 117p. 1990. 17.95 (*0-9622292-1-0*) DBM Pub.
— Trust Me. 117p. 1990. 17.95 (*0-15-191314-5*) HarBrace.
Morin, William J. & Cabrera, James C. Parting Company: How to Survive the Loss of a Job & Find Another Successfully. 2nd ed. 1991. pap. 10.00 (*0-15-671047-1*, Harvest Bks) HarBrace.
— Trust Me. 1992. pap. 9.95 (*0-15-691350-X*, Harvest Bks) HarBrace.
Morin, William J. & Yorks. Dismissal: There is No Easy Way, but There is a Better Way. 1992. pap. 9.95 (*0-15-626103-0*, Harvest Bks) HarBrace.
Morin, William J. & Yorks, Lyle. Dismissal: There Is No Easy Way, but There Is a Better Way. 290p. 1990. text ed. 19.95 (*0-9622292-0-2*) DBM Pub.
Morinaga, H. & Yamazaki, T. In-Beam Gamma-Ray Spectroscopy. 528p. 1977. 146.25 (*0-444-10569-7*, North Holland) Elsevier.
Morine, Dave. The Class Choregus. 244p. 1993. 20.00 (*1-55643-122-8*) North Atlantic.
Morine, David E. Good Dirt: Confessions of a Conservationist. 208p. 1993. pap. 9.00 (*0-345-38147-5*, Ballantine Trade) Ballantine.
Morine, L. A., ed. Guidance & Control, 1980. (Advances in the Astronautical Sciences Ser.: Vol. 42). (Illus.). 738p. 1980. lib. bdg. 60.00 (*0-87703-137-1*, Pub. by Am Astro Soc); pap. text ed. 45.00 (*0-87703-138-X*, Pub. by Am Astro Soc) Univelt Inc.
Moring, jt. auth. see Crowell.
Moring, John. Arthur Hill: Western Actor, Miner, & Law Officer. (Illus.). 115p. 1994. pap. text ed. 16.95 (*0-89745-175-9*) Sunflower U Pr.
***Moring, Marcel.** The Great Longing. 1995. 20.00 (*0-06-017243-6*) HarpC.
Morini, Simona. Enciclopedia de la Salud y la Belleza: Encyclopedia of Health & Beauty. 448p. (SPA.). 1977. pap. 19.95 (*0-8288-5409-2*, S50037) Fr & Eur.
— Simona Morini's Encyclopedia of Beauty & Health for Women. LC 75-6403. (Illus.). 512p. 1976. 17.50 (*0-672-51913-5*, Bobbs) Macmillan.
Morinigo, Fernando B., comp. The Acronym Book: Acronyms in Aerospace & Defense. 2nd ed. 210p. 1992. 39.95 (*0-930403-63-0*) AIAA.
Morinigo, Marcos A. Dictionary of Americanisms: Diccionario de Americanismos. 400p. (SPA.). 1985. 75.00 (*0-8288-1205-5*, S12121) Fr & Eur.
Morinis, Alan. Sacred Journeys: The Anthropology of Pilgrimage. LC 91-36833. (Contributions to the Study of Anthropology Ser.: No. 7). 336p. 1992. text ed. 55.00 (*0-313-27879-2*, MJU/, Greenwood Pr) Greenwood.
Morino, L., ed. Computational Methods in Potential Aerodynamics. (Computational Methods in Aerodynamics Ser.). 1986. 120.00 (*0-931215-06-4*) Computational Mech MA.
Morino, L. & Piva, R., eds. Boundary Integral Methods: Theory & Applications: Proceedings of the IABEM Symposium Rome, Italy, October 15-19, 1990. (Illus.). 544p. 1991. 105.00 (*0-387-53773-2*) Spr-Verlag.
Morino, L., jt. ed. see Banerjee, P. K.
Morino, Marianne & Salvatore, Robert. Max Factor: The Man Who Changed the Face of the World. 300p. 1989. 19.95 (*0-942139-08-9*) Tale Weaver.
***Morino, Mitchell Lawrence.** The American Response: The Last Laugh Must be Ours. LC 93-85076. 224p. (Orig.). 1993. pap. 14.99 (*1-884176-01-1*) Thee Am Response.
Morio, Simone & Zoctizum, Yarrise. Two Studies on Unemployment Among Educated Young People Pt. 1: Unemployment in the Developed Market Economy Countries, Set: 2 Pts. (Illus.). 1980. pap. 5.00 (*92-3-101618-0*, U996) UNIPUB.
— Two Studies on Unemployment Among Educated Young People Pt. 2: Unemployment in the French-Speaking Developing Countries, Set: 2 Pts. (Illus.). 1980. pap. write for info. (*0-318-60625-9*) UNIPUB.
Morioka, Heinz & Sasaki, Miyoko. Rakugo: The Popular Narrative Art of Japan. (East Asian Monographs: No. 138). 470p. 1990. 38.00 (*0-674-74725-9*) HUP.
Morioka, Kiyomi, jt. ed. see Fukutake, Tadashi.
Morioka, Shigeki, ed. see IUTAM Symposium on Waves in Liquid/Gas & Liquid/Vapor Two-Phase Systems Staff.
Moris, Jan, ed. see Ruskin, John.
Moris, Jon & Copestake, James. Qualitative Enquiry for Rural Development: A Review. 128p. (Orig.). 1994. pap. 17.50 (*1-85339-215-4*, Pub. by Intermed Tech UK) Women Ink.
Moris, Max & Griggs, Clive, eds. Education: The Wasted Years? 1973-1986. 270p. 1988. pap. 38.00 (*1-85000-341-6*, Falmer Pr) Taylor & Francis.
Moris, Zailan, ed. see Mushtaq, Q. & Tan, A. L.
Morisawa, M., ed. see Binghamton Symposium in Geomorphology Staff.
Morisawa, Marie, ed. Fluvial Gemorphology: Binghamton Symposia in Geomorphology. (International Ser.: No. 4). 304p. (C). 1981. reprint ed. text ed. 65.00 (*0-04-551046-6*) Routledge Chapman & Hall.
Morishige, Reiko & Mende, Kazuko. Sashiko: Blue-&-White Quilt Art of Japan. (Illus.). 128p. 1991. 45.50 (*0-87040-828-3*) Japan Pubns USA.
Morishima, James K., jt. auth. see Sue, Stanley.
Morishima, Michio. Capital & Credit: A New Formulation of General Equilibrium Theory. 270p. (C). 1992. 54.95 (*0-521-41840-2*) Cambridge U Pr.
— Capital & Credit: A New Formulation of General Equilibrium Theory. 224p. (C). 1994. pap. 19.95 (*0-521-46638-5*) Cambridge U Pr.
— The Economics of Industrial Society. (Illus.). 320p. 1985. 64.95 (*0-521-26700-5*); pap. 22.95 (*0-521-31823-8*) Cambridge U Pr.
— Ricardo's Economics: A General Equilibrium Theory of Distribution & Growth. (Illus.). (C). 1989. 59.95 (*0-521-36630-5*) Cambridge U Pr.
— Ricardo's Economics: A General Equilibrium Theory of Distribution & Growth. (Illus.). 256p. (C). 1990. pap. 22.95 (*0-521-39688-3*) Cambridge U Pr.
— Why Has Japan Succeeded? Western Technology & the Japanese Ethos. LC 81-15544. (Illus.). 219p. 1984. pap. 15.95 (*0-521-26903-2*) Cambridge U Pr.
Morishita. Hidden Truth of Cancer. 1984. pap. 4.50 (*0-916508-28-5*) Happiness Pr.
Morisita, T., ed. Studies on Methods of Estimating Population Density, Biomass & Productivity in Terrestrial Animals, Vol. 17. (Japan International Biological Program Synthesis Ser.). 237p. 1977. pap. 42.50 (*0-86008-227-X*, Pub. by U of Tokyo JA) Col U Pr.
Morison, A. Blackhall, the Blackhalls of That Ilk & Barra: Hereditary Coroners & Foresters of the Barioch. (Illus.). 180p. 1992. reprint ed. lib. bdg. 38.00 (*0-8328-2639-1*); reprint ed. pap. 28.00 (*0-8328-2640-5*) Higginson Bk Co.
Morison, Alexander. The Physiognomy of Mental Diseases. 2nd ed. LC 75-16723. (Classics in Psychiatry Ser.). (Illus.). 1976. reprint ed. 23.95 (*0-405-07447-6*) Ayer.
Morison, B. J. The Martini Effect. LC 92-31610. (Little Maine Murder Ser.). 1992. 17.95 (*0-945980-38-8*) Nrth Country Pr.
— Port & a Star Boarder. LC 84-24. 244p. 1984. 12.95 (*0-89621-081-2*) Nrth Country Pr.
— Reality & Dream: A Christmas Story. LC 85-20870. (Illus.). 63p. (Orig.). 1985. pap. 3.95 (*0-89621-096-0*) Nrth Country Pr.
— The Voyage of the Chianti. LC 87-24888. 300p. 1987. 15.95 (*0-89621-110-X*); pap. 8.95 (*0-89621-112-6*) Nrth Country Pr.
Morison, Bradley G. & Dalgleish, Julie G. Waiting in the Wings: A Larger Audience for the Arts & How to Develop It. LC 87-940. (Illus.). 176p. (Orig.). 1987. pap. 14.95 (*0-915400-54-5*, 9453, ACA Bks) Am Council Arts.
Morison, Bradley L. Sunlight on Your Doorstep. 1966. 6.95 (*0-87018-044-4*); pap. 2.95 (*0-87018-073-8*) Ross.
Morison, Elting E. Men, Machines, & Modern Times. 1966. pap. 12.50 (*0-262-63018-4*) MIT Pr.

M

An Asterisk (*) at the beginning of an entry indicates that the title is appearing in BIP for the first time.

Morison, Elting E., jt. auth. see Wright, James.

Morison, Frank. Quien Movio la Piedra? Ward, Rhode, tr. LC 77-11752. 206p. (SPA.). 1977. pap. 6.25 (*0-89922-100-9*) Edit Caribe.

— Who Moved the Stone? 193p. 1987. pap. 9.99 (*0-310-29561-0*, 10373P) Zondervan.

Morison, George S. The New Epoch: As Developed by the Manufacture of Power. LC 72-5064. (Technology & Society Ser.). (Illus.). 148p. 1972. reprint ed. 15.95 (*0-405-04715-0*) Ayer.

Morison, J. D. & Clarke, A. S. ELLA 2000: A Language for Electronic System Design. LC 93-1998. 1993. write for info. (*0-07-707821-7*) McGraw.

Morison, Jacquelyne A., ed. Pocket Guide: IBM Displaywriter. (C). 1983. pap. text ed. 40.00 (*0-273-01994-5*, Pub. by Pitman Pubng UK) St Mut.

Morison, James C. The Life & Times of St. Bernard of Clairvaux. 1977. lib. bdg. 59.95 (*0-8490-2162-6*) Gordon Pr.

Morison, John, ed. The Czech & Slovak Experience. LC 92-4308. 256p. 1992. text ed. 65.00 (*0-312-07992-3*) St Martin.

— Eastern Europe & the West. LC 92-2776. (Selected Papers from the Fourth World Congress for Soviet & East European Studies, Harrogate, 1990). 296p. 1992. text ed. 69.95 (*0-312-08040-9*) St Martin.

Morison, John & Leith, Philip. The Barrister's World: And the Nature of Law. 256p. 1991. 95.00 (*0-335-09396-5*, Open Univ Pr); pap. 39.00 (*0-335-09395-7*, Open Univ Pr) Taylor & Francis.

Morison, John, jt. auth. see Livingstone, Stephen.

Morison, John E. Foetal & Neonatal Pathology. 3rd ed. LC 72-500929. (Illus.). 655p. reprint ed. pap. 180.00 (*0-317-41716-9*, 2025726) Bks Demand.

Morison, John H. The Great Poets As Religious Teachers. LC 72-286. (Essay Index Reprint Ser.). 1977. reprint ed. 19.95 (*0-8369-2809-1*) Ayer.

***Morison, Kay.** Homework: Bridging the Gap; a Guide for Building Homework Partnerships. 1994. student ed. pap. 12.99 (*0-9639882-5-5*) Goodfellow Pr.

Morison, Patrick H. Forgive! As the Lord Forgave You. LC 87-6961. 32p. 1987. pap. 1.99 (*0-87552-293-9*) Presby & Reformed.

Morison, Richard. An Exhortation to Styre All Englyshe Men to the Defense of Theyr Countreye. LC 79-38211. (English Experience Ser.: No. 476). 64p. 1972. reprint ed. 9.50 (*90-221-0476-1*) Walter J Johnson.

— Humanist Scholarship & Public Order: Two Tracts Against the Pilgrimage of Grace, & a Collection of Related Contemporary Documents. Berkowitz, David S., ed. LC 79-89983. 280p. 1984. text ed. 39.50 (*0-918016-01-0*) Folger Bks.

— An Invective Agenste Treason. LC 72-38212. (English Experience Ser.: No. 477). 104p. 1972. reprint ed. 9.50 (*90-221-0477-X*) Walter J Johnson.

Morison, Robert S., jt. ed. see Lappe, Marc.

Morison, S. & Jackson, H. A. Brief Survey of Printing. 1972. 59.95 (*0-87968-788-6*) Gordon Pr.

Morison, Samuel E. Admiral of the Ocean Sea: A Life of Christopher Columbus. abr. ed. (Illus.). 704p. 1991. pap. 24.95 (*0-316-58478-9*) Little.

— Builders of the Bay Colony. LC 75-41198. reprint ed. 26.45 (*0-404-14741-0*) AMS Pr.

— Builders of the Bay Colony. LC 81-9649. (Illus.). 418p. 1982. reprint ed. pap. 15.95 (*0-930350-22-7*) NE U Pr.

— Christopher Columbus, Mariner. (Illus.). 192p. (YA). (gr. 9-12). 1983. pap. 9.00 (*0-452-00992-8*, Mer) NAL-Dutton.

— The Conservative American Revolution. (George Rogers Clark Lecture April 22, 1975 Ser.: Inaugural). (Illus.). 48p. 1985. reprint ed. lib. bdg. 22.50 (*0-8191-4875-X*) U Pr of Amer.

— The European Discovery of America, 2 vols., Vol. 1, The Northern Voyages A. D. 500-1600. LC 93-20183. 736p. (C). 1993. Vol. 1, The Northern Voyages A.D. 500-1600. pap. 19.95 (*0-19-508271-0*) OUP.

— The European Discovery of America, 2 vols., Vol. 2, The Southern Voyages 1492-1616. LC 93-20183. 736p. (C). 1993. pap. 19.95 (*0-19-508272-9*) OUP.

— European Discovery of America: The Northern Voyages. 1971. 39.95 (*0-19-501377-8*) OUP.

— The European Discovery of America: The Southern Voyages. (Illus.). 1974. 39.95 (*0-19-501823-0*) OUP.

— Founding of Harvard College. LC 35-4941. (Illus.). 453p. 1990. text ed. 37.00 (*0-674-31450-6*) HUP.

— The Founding of Harvard College. LC 95-16667. (Illus.). 592p. (Orig.). (C). 1995. reprint ed. pap. text ed. 19.95 (*0-674-31451-4*) HUP.

— Freedom in Contemporary Society. LC 69-17586. (Essay Index Reprint Ser.). 1977. 17.95 (*0-8369-0049-9*) Ayer.

— The Great Explorers: The European Discovery of America. (Illus.). 784p. 1986. pap. 18.95 (*0-19-504222-0*) OUP.

— History of the United States Naval Operations in World War Two, 15 vols, Set. Incl. Vol. 1. Battle of the Atlantic, 1939-1943. 1947. 45.00 (*0-316-58301-4*); Vol. 2. Operations in North African Waters, October 1942-June 1943. 1947. 45.00 (*0-316-58302-2*); Vol. 3. Rising Sun in the Pacific, 1931-April 1942. 1948. 45.00 (*0-316-58303-0*); Vol. 4. Coral Sea, Midway & Submarine Actions, May 1942-August 1942. 1949. 45.00 (*0-316-58304-9*); Vol. 5. Struggle for Guadalcanal, August 1942-February 1943. 1949. 45.00 (*0-316-58305-7*); Vol. 6. Breaking the Bismarck's Barrier, 22 July 1942-May 1944. 1950. 45.00 (*0-316-58306-5*); Vol. 7. Aleutians, Gilberts & Marshalls, June 1942-April 1944. 1951. 45.00 (*0-316-58307-3*); Vol. 8. New Guinea & the Marianas, March 1944-August 1944. 1953. 45.00 (*0-316-58308-1*); Vol. 9. Sicily-Salerno-Anzio, January 1943-June 1944. 1954. 45.00 (*0-316-58316-2*); Vol. 10. Atlantic Battle Won, May 1943-May 1945. 1956. 45.00 (*0-316-58310-3*); Vol. 11. Invasion of France & Germany, 1944-1945. 1957. 45.00 (*0-316-58311-1*); Vol. 12. Leyte, June 1944-January 1945. 1958. 45.00 (*0-316-58317-0*); Vol. 13. Liberation of the Philippines: Luzon, Mindanao, the Visayas, 1944-1945. 1959. 45.00 (*0-316-58313-8*); Vol. 14. Victory in the Pacific, 1945. 1960. 45.00 (*0-316-58314-6*); Vol. 15. Supplement & General Index. 1962. 45.00 (*0-316-58315-4*); (Illus.). 375.00 (*0-316-58300-6*) Little.

— Intellectual Life of Colonial New England. 288p. 1960. pap. 14.95 (*0-8014-9011-1*) Cornell U Pr.

— The Intellectual Life of Colonial New England. LC 79-20246. 288p. 1980. reprint ed. text ed. 35.00 (*0-313-22032-8*, MOIL, Greenwood Pr) Greenwood.

— John Paul Jones: A Sailor's Biography. LC 89-13423. (Classics of Naval Literature Ser.). 300p. 1990. 32.95 (*0-87021-323-7*) Naval Inst Pr.

— John Paul Jones: A Sailor's Biography. 474p. 1985. reprint ed. pap. 15.95 (*0-930350-70-7*) NE U Pr.

— The Maritime History of Massachusetts: 1783-1860. LC 79-5422. 433p. 1979. reprint ed. 37.50 (*0-930350-06-5*); reprint ed. pap. 16.95 (*0-930350-04-9*) NE U Pr.

— Oxford History of the American People, 3 vols., 2. 1972. pap. 4.95 (*0-451-62408-4*, ME2254, Ment) NAL-Dutton.

— Oxford History of the American People, 3 vols., 3. 1972. pap. 4.95 (*0-451-62446-7*, ME2255, Ment) NAL-Dutton.

— The Oxford History of the American People: Prehistory to 1789, Vol. 1. (Illus.). 432p. 1994. pap. 13.95 (*0-452-01130-2*, Mer) NAL-Dutton.

— The Oxford History of the American People: 1789 Through the Reconstruction, Vol. II. (Illus.). 540p. 1994. pap. 13.95 (*0-452-01131-0*, Mer) NAL-Dutton.

— The Oxford History of the American People: 1869 Through the Death of John F. Kennedy, Vol. III. (Illus.). 520p. 1994. pap. 13.95 (*0-452-01132-9*, Mer) NAL-Dutton.

— Plymouth Colony Beachhead. (Pilgrim Society Notes Ser.: No. 25). 1986. 2.00 (*0-940628-33-3*) Pilgrim Soc.

— The Ropemakers of Plymouth: A History of the Plymouth Cordage Company, 1824-1949. LC 75-41772. (Companies & Men: Business Enterprises in America Ser.). (Illus.). 1976. reprint ed. 23.95 (*0-405-08086-7*) Ayer.

— Three Centuries of Harvard. 520p. 1986. pap. 19.95 (*0-674-88891-X*) Belknap Pr.

— Two Ocean War, Vol. 1. 1989. pap. 21.95 (*0-316-58352-9*) Little.

Morison, Samuel E., ed. Sources & Documents Illustrating the American Revolution, 1764-1788, & the Formation of the Federal Constitution. 2nd ed. (YA). (gr. 9 up). 1965. pap. 17.95 (*0-19-500262-8*) OUP.

Morison, Samuel E., ed. see Bradford, William.

Morison, Samuel E., tr. see Columbus, Christopher.

Morison, Samuel E., et al. A Concise History of the American Republic, 2 vols. in 1. LC 82-3621. (Illus.). 1983. pap. 31.00 (*0-19-503180-6*) OUP.

— A Concise History of the American Republic, 2 vols. in 1, 1. LC 82-3621. (Illus.). 1983. pap. 23.00 (*0-19-503181-4*) OUP.

— A Concise History of the American Republic, 2 vols. in 1, 2. LC 82-3621. (Illus.). 1983. pap. 23.00 (*0-19-503182-2*) OUP.

— The Growth of the American Republic, 2 vols., 1. 7th ed. (Illus.). 1980. 32.50 (*0-19-502593-8*) OUP.

— The Growth of the American Republic, 2 vols., 2. (Illus.). 1980. 32.50 (*0-19-502594-6*) OUP.

Morison, Stanley. Early Italian Writing Books. 220p. 1991. 65.00 (*0-87923-880-1*) Godine.

— German Incunabula in the British Museum. LC 73-143358. (Illus.). 1975. reprint ed. 150.00 (*0-87817-077-4*) Hacker.

— The Likeness of Thomas More: An Iconographical Survey of Three Centuries. Barker, Nicolas, ed. LC 64-4266. 134p. reprint ed. pap. 38.20 (*0-7837-5614-3*, 2045521) Bks Demand.

— Pacioli's Classic Roman Alphabet. (Illus.). 128p. 1994. reprint ed. pap. 7.95 (*0-685-75327-1*) Dover.

— Selected Essays on the History of Letter-Forms in Manuscript & Print, 2 vols., Set. McKitterick, David, ed. LC 78-54718. (Illus.). 543p. 1981. 350.00 (*0-521-22338-5*) Cambridge U Pr.

— A Tally of Types. Crutchley, Brooke, ed. 144p. 1995. pap. 15.95 (*1-56792-004-7*) Godine.

— A Tally of Types, with Additions by Several Hands. rev. ed. Crutchley, Brooke, ed. LC 72-90486. (Illus.). 138p. 1973. 55.00 (*0-521-20043-1*) Oak Knoll.

Morison, W. & Sappideen, C. Torts: Commentary & Materials. 8th ed. 1993. 130.00 (*0-455-21172-8*, Pub. by Law Bk Co); pap. 94.00 (*0-455-21173-6*, Pub. by Law Bk Co) W W Gaunt.

Morison, W. L. & Sappideen, C. Torts: Commentary & Materials. 7th ed. li, 936p. 1989. 120.00 (*0-455-20826-3*, Pub. by Law Bk Co); pap. 84.00 (*0-455-20827-1*, Pub. by Law Bk Co) W W Gaunt.

Morison, Walter, ed. see Babel, Isaac.

Morison, Warwick L. Phototherapy & Photochemotherapy of Skin Disease. 2nd ed. 304p. 1991. 82.00 (*0-88167-723-X*) Raven.

Morison, William L. John Austin. LC 82-80924. (Jurists: Profiles in Legal Theory Ser.). x, 239p. 1982. 32.50 (*0-8047-1141-0*) Stanford U Pr.

Morisseau-Leroy, Felix. Dyakout 1, 2, 3, 4. 177p. (CRP.). 1992. pap. text ed. 11.95 (*0-944987-69-9*) Haitiana Pubns.

— Works by Felix Morisseau-Leroy: Recolte, Natif-Natal, Antigone en Creole, Diacoute, 4 vols. in 1. (B. E. Ser.: No. 12). 1954. Four works in one unit. 24.00 (*0-8115-2963-0*) Periodicals Srv.

Morisseau-Leroy, Felix, et al. First Works of Caribbean Writers. (B. E. Ser.: No. 111). 1970. 18.00 (*0-8115-3042-6*) Periodicals Srv.

Morisset, ed. Growth of the Gastrointestinal Test. 1990. 133.00 (*0-8493-4617-7*, R) CRC Pr.

Morisset, R. & Kurstak, E., eds. Advances in Sexually Transmitted Diseases: Diagnosis & Treatment. 237p. 1986. lib. bdg. 110.00 (*90-6764-059-X*, Pub. by VSP NE) Coronet Bks.

Morita, Akio, et al. Made in Japan: Akio Morita & Sony. 1989. pap. 9.95 (*0-317-02806-5*) NAL-Dutton.

Morita, James, tr. see Hara, Shiro.

Morita, James R. Kaneko Mitsuharu. (World Authors Ser.). 1980. text ed. 21.95 (*0-8057-6397-X*, Pub. by Royal Botanic Garden UK) Macmillan.

Morita, K., ed. Applied Fourier Transforms. LC 94-76401. 433p. 1995. 93.00 (*90-5199-166-5*) IOS Press.

Morita, K. & Nagata, J., eds. Topics in General Topology. (Mathematical Library: No. 41). 760p. 1989. 183.00 (*0-685-28251-1*, North Holland) Elsevier.

Morita, Kiyoko. The Book of Incense: Enjoying the Traditional Art of Japanese Scents. Calogeras, Meagan, ed. LC 92-11064. (Illus.). 144p. 1992. 15.00 (*4-7700-1557-7*) Kodansha.

Morita, Nagayoshi, et al. Integral Equation Methods for Electromagnetics. (Microwave Library). 300p. 1991. text ed. 75.00 (*0-89006-482-2*) Artech Hse.

Morita, S., jt. ed. see Matsumoto, Y.

Moritani, Mineo. A Theoretical Study of Milton's Art, Vol. 1. 1987. 22.50 (*4-7952-6810-X*) World Univ AZ.

Moritsch, Andreas, jt. auth. see Barker, Thomas M.

Moritz, jt. auth. see Zeller.

Moritz, A. F. The Tradition. LC 85-43203. (Contemporary Poets Ser.). 128p. 1986. text ed. 26.95 (*0-691-06667-1*); pap. 10.95 (*0-691-01427-2*) Princeton U Pr.

Moritz, Carl P. Journeys of a German in England: A Walking Tour of England in 1782. (Eland Travel Classics Ser.). 198p. 1984. pap. 14.95 (*0-907871-50-X*) Hippocrene Bks.

Moritz, Craig, jt. auth. see Hillis, David M.

Moritz, Craig, et al, eds. Conservation Biology in Australia & Oceania. 500p. (C). 1993. text ed. 200.00 (*0-949324-48-5*, Pub. by Surrey Beatty & Sons AT) St Mut.

Moritz, Cynthia. About Cancer. LC 93-37166. (For Your Information Ser.). 1993. 5.95 (*1-56420-031-0*); audio 16.00 (*1-56420-032-9*) New Readers.

Moritz, Derry A., jt. ed. see Kim, Mi J.

Moritz, Fred. Be Ye Holy: The Call to Christian Separation. LC 93-50169. 1994. pap. 8.95 (*0-89084-737-1*) Bob Jones Univ Pr.

— Tragedy of Compromise. Sidwell, Mark, ed. (Orig.). 1994. pap. 9.95 (*0-89084-757-6*) Bob Jones Univ Pr.

Moritz, H. & Torok, T. Technical Dictionary of Spectroscopy & Spectral Analysis: English, German, French, Russian. 1971. 88.00 (*0-08-015864-1*, Pub. by Pergamon Repr UK) Franklin.

Moritz, Helmut & Mueller, Ivan I. Earth Rotation. (Illus.). 600p. (C). 1987. 85.00 (*0-8044-4671-7*, F Ungar Bks) Continuum.

Moritz, Helmut, jt. auth. see Heiskanen, Weikko A.

Moritz, John, ed. see McCrary, Jim.

Moritz, Karl P. Anton Reiser: A Psychological Novel. Matheson, P. E., tr. LC 76-48443. (Library of World Literature Ser.). 1986. reprint ed. 37.00 (*0-88355-582-4*) Hyperion Conn.

Moritz, L. A. Grain-Mills & Flour in Classical Antiquity. Finley, Moses, ed. LC 79-4994. (Ancient Economic History Ser.). (Illus.). 1979. reprint ed. lib. bdg. 35.95 (*0-405-12381-7*) Ayer.

Moritz, Robert, et al. SPONGING: A Guide to Living Off Those You Love. (Illus.). 112p. 1995. pap. 9.95 (*1-886186-00-6*) Dune Rd Bks. SOON TO BE A MAJOR MOTION PICTURE! In a deal worth $350,000, Carousel Entertainment ("Jade") has purchased the movie rights to SPONGING & is negotiating with Keanu Reeves to star in this "Day In The Life Of..." movie (think "Ferris Bueller's Day Off"). LOCK YOUR REFRIGERATORS & HOLD ONTO YOUR REMOTE CONTROLS, here comes SPONGING: A GUIDE TO LIVING OFF THOSE YOU LOVE. The motto is "maximize output/ minimize input" in this catchy, hilarious, tongue-in-cheek look at the day in the life of a Sponger (defined as one who lives off the hospitalities of others--especially parents & friends). "If you've ever raided a refrigerator or had yours raided this book will make you laugh."--ROLLING STONE. Awarded the "Most Ungrateful Dedication of the Week" by ENTERTAINMENT WEEKLY, SPONGING is quickly becoming notorious within the very broad Sponger demographic (male & female, all ages). Spongers are redefining the American Dream--they want to have their cake & eat it too...& then find someone else to do the dishes. But it's hard to hate a Sponger -- just ask all the parents, siblings, friends, husbands & wives who put up with the Spongers in their lives. They're lovable & harmless. And this book is very funny. Dune Road Books, 40 Park Ave., Venice, CA 90291. 800-804-DUNE. Wholesalers: Ingram, Koen, Pacific Pipeline & Baker & Taylor.** ***Publisher Provided Annotation.

Moritz, Robert E., ed. Memorabilia Mathematics: The Philomath's Quotation Book. (Spectrum Ser.). 440p. 1993. reprint ed. pap. 26.00 (*0-88385-321-3*) Math Assn.

Moritz, Robin F. & Southwick, Edward E. Bees as Superorganisms: An Evolutionary Reality. LC 92-14560. (Illus.). 304p. 1992. 129.00 (*3-540-54821-1*); 129.00 (*0-387-54821-1*) Spr-Verlag.

Moritz, S. Mrs. Molnar's Daughter Julie. 1993. 18.95 (*0-533-10700-8*) Vantage.

Moritz, Theresa A., jt. auth. see Allen, Judson B.

Moritz, Tom, jt. ed. see Wilson, Sam.

Moriwaki, A. Banking Dictionary. (ENG & JPN.). 1990. lib. bdg. 85.00 (*0-8288-3900-X*, F117170) Fr & Eur.

Moriwaki, Glenda. Love for Priscilla. (Illus.). 28p. (Orig.). (J). (ps-3). 1991. pap. 4.95 (*0-9627956-7-4*) Meadora Pub.

Moriya, T. Spin Fluctuations in Itinerant Electron Magnetism. (Solid-State Sciences Ser.: Vol. 56). (Illus.). 260p. 1985. 78.00 (*0-387-15422-1*) Spr-Verlag.

Moriya, T., ed. Electron Correlation & Magnetism in Narrow Band Systems. (Solid-State Sciences Ser.: Vol. 29). (Illus.). 257p. 1981. 62.00 (*0-387-10767-3*) Spr-Verlag.

Moriyama, Alan T. Imingaisha: Japanese Emigration Companies & Hawaii, 1894-1908. LC 85-8694. (Illus.). 290p. 1985. text ed. 19.95 (*0-8248-1004-X*) UH Pr.

Moriyama, Iwao, et al. Cardiovascular Diseases in the United States. LC 73-154498. (Vital & Health Statistics Monographs, American Public Health Association). (Illus.). 524p. 1971. 45.00 (*0-674-09640-1*) HUP.

Moriyama, J. Process Architecture: Moriyama & Teshima, No. 107. (Illus.). 155p. 1993. pap. 46.95 (*4-89331-107-7*, Pub. by Process Archit JA) Bks Nippan.

Moriyama, Sachiko. Cakes You Can Make: A Step-by-Step Illustrated Cookbook. (Illus.). 48p. (Orig.). 1989. pap. 10.95 (*0-87040-800-3*) Japan Pubns USA.

— Cookies You Can Make: A Step-by-Step Illustrated Cookbook. (Illus.). 48p. (Orig.). 1989. pap. 10.95 (*0-87040-801-1*) Japan Pubns USA.

Moriyama, Tae. The Practical Guide to Japanese Signs: Especially for Newcomers. LC 86-45788. 200p. (Orig.). 1987. pap. 10.00 (*0-87011-790-4*) Kodansha.

— The Practical Guide to Japanese Signs: Making Life Easier, Pt. 2. LC 86-45788. 200p. (Orig.). 1987. pap. 9.95 (*0-87011-791-2*) Kodansha.

— Tokyo Adventures: Glimpses of the City in Bygone Eras. Garvey, Bob & Garvey, Reiko, trs. (Illus.). 376p. 1993. 19.95 (*4-07-975842-1*, Pub. by Shufunomoto Co Ltd JA) C E Tuttle.

— Weekend Adventures Outside Tokyo: Travel with a Historical Twist. (Illus.). 358p. (Orig.). 1990. pap. 19.95 (*4-07-975049-8*, Pub. by Shufunomoto Co Ltd JA) C E Tuttle.

Moriyasu, ed. see Yoshikawa, Eiji.

Moriyasu, K. An Elementary Primer for Gauge Theory. 192p. 1983. text ed. 41.00 (*9971-950-83-9*); pap. text ed. 21.00 (*9971-950-94-4*) World Scientific Pub.

Moriyasu, Ushio. The Ume Plum's Secrets. 1992. per. 4.75 (*0-916508-40-4*) Happiness Pr.

Moriyoshi, jt. ed. see Somiya, S.

Morize, Andre. Problems & Methods of Literary History. LC 66-13475. 1922. 24.00 (*0-8196-0168-3*) Biblo.

Morizet, Jacques, jt. ed. see Dreyfus, Francois-Georges.

Morizio, Diane. So, You Want to Do Bread Dough Art. 1992. student ed 8.95 (*0-9632807-6-7*) J&D Ent.

Morizot, Pierre. School of Chartres. 1987. pap. 6.95 (*0-916786-97-8*, Saint George Pubns) R Steiner Col Pubns.

Mork, Ebbe. Tivoli: The Magic Garden. (Illus.). 60p. 1988. pap. 24.00 (*87-14-28861-3*) IBD Ltd.

Mork, Knut A. Macroeconomics for Managers. 500p. (C). 1992. text ed. 53.95 (*0-534-13794-6*) Intl Thomson.

Mork, Wulstan. The Benedictine Way. 15.75 (*0-8446-6394-8*) Peter Smith.

Morkel, D. W., jt. auth. see Snyman, J.

Morken, Ken E., ed. The Bazaar Book for Festivals & Craft Fairs in Greater Washington State for 1991. (Illus.). 192p. 1990. 19.00 (*0-685-39514-6*) Capital WA.

An Asterisk (*) at the beginning of an entry indicates that the title is appearing in BIP for the first time.

Morkert, A. S., illus. Once Upon a (Life) Time: Stories from Western Montana 1908-1960. 96p. (Orig.). 1990. pap. text ed. write for info. (0-9620902-6-3) Vernon Print & Pub.

Morkholm, Otto. Early Hellenistic Coinage from the Accession of Alexander to the Peace of Apamaea (336-188 BC) Grierson, Philip & Westermark, Ulla, eds. (Illus.). 336p. (C). 1991. 105.00 (0-521-39504-6) Cambridge U Pr.

Morkholm, Otto & Waggoner, Nancy M., eds. Greek Numismatics & Archaeology: Essays in Honor of Margaret Thompson. (Editions NR, 1979 Ser.). 326p. 1994. 75.00 (0-685-72018-7) Am Numismatic.

Morkoc, jt. ed. see Gunshor.

Morkoc, H., et al. Principles & Technology of MODFETS, Vols. 1 & 2. (Design & Measurement in Electronic Engineering Ser.: No. 1795). 526p. 1991. text ed. 275.00 (0-471-92995-6) Wiley.

Morkot, Robert. Egypt: Gift of the Nile. 2nd ed. 1993. pap. 16.95 (0-8442-9665-1, Passport Bks) NTC Pub Grp.

***Morkovine, Sergey, ed.** Russian Cookbook. (Illus.). 32p. (Orig.). 1994. pap. 4.99 (0-9643971-2-9) Isometry.

Morkovkin, V. Lexical Basis of the Russian Language: Learner's Dictionary. 1168p. (RUS.). (C). 1984. 95.00 (0-685-54115-0, Pub. by Collets) St Mut.

Morkovsky, Christine, tr. see Dussel, Enrique.

***Morkre, Morris E. & Kelly, Kenneth H.** Effects of Unfair Imports on Domestic Industries: U. S. Antidumping & Countervailing Duty Cases, 1980 to 1988. (Illus.). 120p. (Orig.). (C). 1994. pap. text ed. 47.95x (0-7881-1174-4) Diane Pub.

Morlacchi, Francesco. Tebaldo ed Isolina. Gossett, Philip, ed. (Italian Opera Ser., 1810-1840). 260p. 1990. 97.00 (0-8240-6573-5) Garland.

Morlan, Don M. & Tuttle, George E., Jr. Specific Situations in Effective Oral Communication. (gr. 12). 1977. teacher ed 3.33 (0-672-61411-1, Bobbs); pap. 9.50 (0-672-61410-3, Bobbs) Macmillan.

Morlan, George K. America's Heritage from John Stuart Mill. LC 72-987. reprint ed. 20.00 (0-404-04436-0) AMS Pr.

Morlan, John E., jt. auth. see Espinosa, Leonard J.

Morlan, Michael. American Automobile Collections & Museums: A Guide to U. S. Exhibits. (American Travel Themes Ser.). (Illus.). 256p. (Orig.). 1992. pap. 15.95 (1-878446-10-X) Bon A Tirer Pub.

— Kitty Hawk to NASA: A Guide to U. S. Air & Space Museums & Exhibits. (American Travel Themes Ser.). (Illus.). 320p. (Orig.). 1991. pap. 15.95 (1-878446-04-5, A&S-1) Bon A Tirer Pub.

Morlan, Robert L. Political Prairie Fire: The Nonpartisan League, 1915-1922. LC 74-9275. (Illus.). 408p. 1974. reprint ed. text ed. 35.00 (0-8371-7639-5, MOPF, Greenwood Pr) Greenwood.

— Political Prairie Fire: The Nonpartisan League, 1915-1922. LC 85-18792. 414p. 1985. reprint ed. pap. 10.95 (0-87351-186-7, Borealis Book) Minn Hist.

Morlan, Terry H., ed. Energy Forecasting. 57p. 1985. 13.00 (0-87262-498-6) Am Soc Civil Eng.

Morland, Andrew. Farm Tractors. LC 93-17026. (Enthusiast Color Ser.). (Illus.). 1993. 12.95 (0-87938-824-2) Motorbooks Intl.

— Ford & Fordson Tractors. (Enthusiast Color Ser.). (Illus.). 96p. 1995. pap. 12.95 (0-7603-0044-5) Motorbooks Intl.

— Harley Davidson. 1991. 9.99 (0-517-06683-1) Random Hse Value.

— Lotus Seven. (Color Library). (Illus.). 128p. 1994. pap. 15.95 (1-85532-490-3, Pub. by Osprey Pubng Ltd UK) Motorbooks Intl.

— Modern American Farm Tractors. (Enthusiast Color Ser.). (Illus.). 96p. 1994. pap. 12.95 (0-87938-926-5) Motorbooks Intl.

— Triumph Triples. (Osprey Color Ser.). (Illus.). 128p. 1995. pap. 15.95 (1-85532-428-8) Motorbooks Intl.

Morland, Andrew & Pripps, Robert. Threshers. (Illus.). 128p. 1992. pap. 19.95 (0-87938-617-7) Motorbooks Intl.

Morland, Andrew & Wendel, C. H. Allis Chalmers Tractors. (Illus.). 128p. 1992. pap. 19.95 (0-87938-628-2) Motorbooks Intl.

Morland, Andrew, jt. auth. see Pripps, Robert N.

Morland, Andrew, jt. auth. see Propps, Robert.

Morland, Andrew, jt. auth. see Wendel, C. H.

Morland, Cary. Because Their Hearts Were Pure: or The Secret of the Mine. 1952. pap. 4.75 (0-8222-0102-X) Dramatists Play.

Morland, Harold, tr. see Borges, Jorge L.

Morland, J. K., jt. auth. see Williams, John E.

Morland, J. Kenneth. Social Problems in the United States. LC 74-22542. (Illus.). 694p. reprint ed. pap. 180.00 (0-317-09589-7, 2012515) Bks Demand.

Morland, J. Kenneth, jt. auth. see Balswick, Jack O.

Morland, John, et al. Classroom Learning Centers. LC 73-77592. (J). (gr. 1-6). 1973. pap. 10.99 (0-8224-1410-4) Fearon Teach Aids.

Morland, John K. Millways of Kent. 1958. pap. 14.95x (0-8084-0219-6) NCUP.

Morland, Kjell A. The Rhetoric of Curse in Galatian: Paul Confronts Another Gospel. LC 93-39947. 1993. write for info. (1-55540-923-7) Scholars Pr GA.

Morland, Miles. A Walk Across France. Orig. Title: Miles Away. 256p. 1994. reprint ed. pap. 10.00 (0-449-90945-X) Fawcett.

Morland, Nigel. Sing a Song of Cyanide. (Black Dagger Crime Ser.). 240p. 1989. reprint ed. text ed. 16.50 (0-86220-757-6, Black Dagger) Chivers N Amer.

— That Nice Miss Smith. large type ed. 1990. 21.95 (0-7089-2337-2) Ulverscroft.

Morland, Samuel. History of the Evangelical Churches of the Valleys of Piemont. 1983. reprint ed. 32.00 (0-686-42929-X) Church History.

Morlands, Andrew, jt. auth. see Pripps, Robert.

***Morlay, Jacqueline.** Clothes for Work, Play & Display: For Work, Play & Display. (Timelines Ser.). (Illus.). 48p. (J). (gr. 4-7). 1995. pap. 7.95 (0-531-15740-7) Orchard Bks Watts.

***Morledge, G. Alan.** Home Design Guide: Planning, Building or Buying Your Dream Home. 1995. pap. 15.95 (0-7931-1283-4, Real Estate Ed) Dearborn Finan.

Morler, Patty, jt. auth. see Mattia, Jan B.

***Morley.** Farmyard Song. (J). 1995. 14.00 (0-671-89551-6, S&S Bks Young Read) S&S Childrens.

— Geriatric Medicine. 816p. Date not set. 79.95 (0-8016-3526-8) Mosby Yr Bk.

Morley, jt. auth. see Turnbull.

Morley, Andrew, jt. auth. see Brown, Stephen W.

Morley, Andrew P., Jr., jt. auth. see Brown, Stephen W.

Morley, Barry. Beyond Consensus: Salvaging Sense of the Meeting. LC 73-84214. 32p. (Orig.). 1993. pap. 3.00 (0-87574-307-2) Pendle Hill.

Morley, Becky, jt. ed. see Mullender, Audrey.

Morley, C. B. Hymenoptera: Ichueumonidae: 1 Ichneumones Deltoidei, Vol. 3. (Illus.). xxxvi, 536p. 1973. reprint ed. 25.00 (0-88065-162-8, Messers Today & Tomorrow) Scholarly Pubns.

Morley, Carol. A Spider & a Pig. LC 92-53215. (J). 1993. 14.95 (0-316-58405-3) Little.

Morley, Carolyn A. Transformation, Miracles, & Mischief: The Mountain Priest Plays of Kyogen. (Cornell East Asia Ser.: No. 62). (Illus.). 248p. (Orig.). (C). 1993. pap. 12.00 (0-939657-62-7) Cornell East Asia Pgm.

Morley, Christopher. Christopher Morley's New York. LC 88-81015. (Illus.). xx, 379p. 1988. 19.95 (0-8232-1214-9) Fordham.

— Christopher Morley's Philadelphia. Kalfus, Ken, ed. LC 90-80081. (Illus.). xx, 329p. (C). 1993. pap. 15.00 (0-8232-1270-X) Fordham.

— The Haunted Bookshop. 20.95 (0-88411-887-8, Aeonian Pr) Amereon Ltd.

— The Haunted Bookshop. (Illus.). 240p. reprint ed. pap. 13.95 (1-879923-02-5) Booksellers Pub.

— Kitty Foyle. 23.95 (0-88411-888-6, Aeonian Pr) Amereon Ltd.

— Kitty Foyle. 1993. reprint ed. lib. bdg. 89.00 (0-7812-5493-0) Rprt Serv.

— Parnassus on Wheels. 1976. 16.95 (0-8488-0594-1) Amereon Ltd.

— Parnassus on Wheels. (Illus.). 150p. 1992. reprint ed. pap. 12.95 (1-879923-01-7) Booksellers Pub.

— Prefaces Without Books: Prefaces & Introductions to Thirty Books. Abromson, Herman, ed. LC 76-14891. (Illus.). 1970. 15.00 (0-87959-062-9) U of Tex H Ransom Ctr.

— Thunder on the Left. (Sun & Moon Classics Ser.: No. 68). 276p. (Orig.). 1995. pap. 12.95 (1-55713-190-2) Sun & Moon CA.

— Thunder on the Left. (Sun & Moon Classics Ser.: No. 68). 276p. 1995. 21.95 (1-55713-088-4) Sun & Moon CA.

— Travels in Philadelphia. 1993. reprint ed. lib. bdg. 89.00 (0-7812-5492-2) Rprt Serv.

Morley, Christopher D. Ironing Board. LC 68-8483. (Essay Index Reprint Ser.). 1977. 20.95 (0-8369-0718-3) Ayer.

— Thunder on the Left. LC 83-45821. reprint ed. 27.00 (0-404-20185-7) AMS Pr.

***Morley, Cindy L.** How to Get the Most Out of Meetings. LC 94-28351. 1994. pap. text ed. 6.95 (0-87120-231-X) Assn Supervision.

Morley, Cindy L., jt. auth. see Ohle, Nancy.

Morley College for Working Men & Women, London Staff. Science To-Day & To-Morrow, Compiled from a Series of Lectures Delivered at Morley College. LC 67-30231. (Essay Index Reprint Ser.). 1977. 19.95 (0-8369-0857-0) Ayer.

Morley, D. A. Mathematical Modelling in Water & Wastewater Treatment. (Illus.). 366p. 1979. 97.25 (0-85334-842-1, Pub. by Elsevier Applied Sci UK) Elsevier.

Morley, David. Family Television: Cultural Power & Domestic Leisure. 192p. 1988. pap. 14.95 (0-906890-73-X) Routledge.

— Television, Audiences, & Cultural Studies. LC 92-10404. 304p. 1993. 69.95 (0-415-05444-3, A7917); pap. 16.95 (0-415-05445-1, A7921) Routledge.

***Morley, David & Chen, Kuan-Hsing, eds.** Stuart Hall: Critical Dialogues. LC 95-16455. (Comedia Ser.). 1995. write for info. (0-415-08803-8); pap. write for info. (0-415-08804-6) Routledge.

***Morley, David & Robins, Kevin.** Spaces of Identity: Global Media, Electronic Landscapes & Cultural Boundaries. LC 94-42068. (International Library of Sociology). 1995. 59.00 (0-415-09596-4); pap. text ed. 17.95 (0-415-09597-2) Routledge.

Morley, Don. BMW Motorcycles-OCL. (Osprey Colour Library). (Illus.). 128p. 1993. pap. 15.95 (1-85532-275-7, Pub. by Osprey Pubng Ltd UK) Motorbooks Intl.

— BSA. (Osprey Colour Library). (Illus.). 1991. pap. 15.95 (1-85532-118-1, Pub. by Osprey Pubng Ltd UK) Motorbooks Intl.

— Honda Motorcycles - OCL. (Osprey Colour Library). (Illus.). 128p. 1993. pap. 15.95 (1-85532-276-5, Pub. by Osprey Pubng Ltd UK) Motorbooks Intl.

Morley, Edith J. Life & Times of Henry Crabb Robinson. LC 71-115396. 1970. reprint ed. 32.50 (0-404-05368-8) AMS Pr.

Morley, Edith J., ed. see Robinson, Henry C.

Morley, Elaine J. A Practitioner's Guide to Public Sector Productivity Improvement. LC 87-19388. 272p. (C). 1987. reprint ed. lib. bdg. 30.50 (0-89464-252-9) Krieger.

Morley, F. H. W., ed. Grazing Animals. (World Animal Science Ser.: Vol. 1B). 412p. 1981. 133.50 (0-444-41835-0) Elsevier.

Morley, Felix. For the Record. LC 78-74437. 476p. 1979. 15.00 (0-89526-687-3) Regnery Pub.

— Freedom & Federalism. LC 80-82575. 352p. 1981. 12.00 (0-913966-86-X); pap. 5.50 (0-913966-87-8) Liberty Fund.

Morley, Felix, ed. Aspects of the Depression. LC 68-22932. (Essay Index Reprint Ser.). 1977. 17.95 (0-8369-0719-1) Ayer.

— Essays on Individuality. LC 76-58027. 1977. 12.00 (0-913966-27-4); pap. 5.00 (0-913966-28-2) Liberty Fund.

Morley, Fran & Skarmeas, Nancy, eds. Hymns of Faith & Inspiration. (Illus.). 180p. 1991. 22.95 (0-8249-4041-5) Ideals.

Morley, Fran, jt. ed. see Skarmeas, Nancy.

Morley, Frank, ed. see Boswell, James.

Morley, Geoffrey. Smuggling in Hampshire & Dorset: 1700-1850. 224p. 1987. pap. 30.00 (0-905392-24-8) St Mut.

Morley, George. Shakespeare's Greenwood: The Customs in the Country, the Language, the Superstitions. LC 70-185021. (Studies in Shakespeare: No. 24). 289p. 1972. reprint ed. lib. bdg. 75.00 (0-8383-1381-7) M S G Haskell Hse.

***Morley, Helena.** The Diary of "Helena Morley" Bishop, Elizabeth, tr. 281p. 1995. pap. text ed. 11.00 (0-374-52435-1, Noonday) FS&G.

Morley, Henry. The Life of Henry Cornelius Agrippa: Doctor & Knight, Commonly Known As a Magician. 342p. 1993. reprint ed. pap. 24.95 (1-56459-388-6) Kessinger Pub.

Morley, Hilda. Cloudless at First. 302p. 1989. 22.50 (0-918825-71-7); pap. 12.95 (0-918825-72-5) Moyer Bell.

— To Hold in My Hand: Selected Poems, 1955-1983. LC 83-40199. 213p. 1983. 14.95 (0-935296-46-8) Sheep Meadow.

— What Are Winds & What Are Waters. 72p. (Orig.). 1993. pap. 9.95 (1-55921-089-3, Asphodel Pr) Moyer Bell.

Morley, Iris. Proud Paladin. LC 70-144164. (Short Story Index Reprint Ser.). 1977. reprint ed. 20.95 (0-8369-3779-1) Ayer.

Morley, J., jt. ed. see Bray, M. A.

Morley, J. E. & Korenman, S. G., eds. Endocrinology & Metabolism in the Elderly. (Current Issues in Endocrinology & Metabolism Ser.). (Illus.). 592p. 1992. 135.00 (0-86542-148-X) Blackwell Sci.

Morley, J. S., jt. ed. see Andrews, P. R.

Morley, J. T. Secular Socialists: The CCF-NDP in Ontario, a Biography. 283p. 1984. 29.95 (0-7735-0389-7, Pub. by McGill CN); pap. 24.95 (0-7735-0390-0, Pub. by McGill CN) U of Toronto Pr.

Morley, Jacqueline. An Egyptian Pyramid. (Inside Story Ser.). (Illus.). 48p. (J). (gr. 5 up). 1993. pap. 8.95 (0-87226-255-3) P Bedrick Bks.

— An Egyptian Pyramid: Inside Story. (Inside Story Ser.). (Illus.). 48p. (J). (gr. 5 up). 1991. 17.95 (0-87226-346-0) P Bedrick Bks.

— Entertainment: Screen, Stage & Stars. (Timelines Ser.). (Illus.). 48p. (J). (gr. 5-8). 1994. lib. bdg. 14.98 (0-531-14311-2); pap. 7.95 (0-531-15710-5) Watts.

— How Would You Survive As a Viking? LC 94-26161. (How Would You Survive? Ser.). (Illus.). 48p. (J). (gr. 5-8). 1995. lib. bdg. 14.98 (0-531-14344-9) Watts.

— How Would You Survive As an Ancient Egyptian? LC 94-26157. (How Would You Survive Ser.). (Illus.). 48p. (J). (gr. 5-8). 1995. lib. bdg. 14.98 (0-531-14345-7) Watts.

— Shakespeare's Theater. LC 94-16386. (Inside Story Ser.). (Illus.). 48p. (J). (gr. 5 up). 1994. lib. bdg. 17.95 (0-87226-309-6) P Bedrick Bks.

Morley, Jacqueline & James, John. A Roman Villa: Inside Story. LC 92-15279. (Illus.). 48p. (J). (gr. 5 up). 1992. 17.95 (0-87226-360-6) P Bedrick Bks.

Morley, James, ed. Deterrent Diplomacy: Japan, Germany & the U. S. S. R., 1935-1940. LC 75-25524. (Japan's Road to the Pacific War Ser.). 380p. reprint ed. pap. 108.30 (0-317-26658-6, 2025109) Bks Demand.

Morley, James M. Muir Woods: The Ancient Redwood Forest near San Francisco. 2nd ed. 1992. pap. 10.95 (0-938765-53-1) Smith Novelty.

Morley, James W. Forecast for Japan: Security in the 1970's. LC 79-155964. 256p. 1972. 39.50 (0-691-03091-X) Princeton U Pr.

— Japan & Korea: America's Allies in the Pacific. LC 81-4196. (Illus.). 152p. 1981. reprint ed. text ed. 49.75 (0-313-23033-1, MOJK, Greenwood Pr) Greenwood.

— The Japanese Thrust into Siberia, 1918. LC 75-38115. (Select Bibliographies Reprint Ser.). 1980. reprint ed. 28.95 (0-8369-9966-5) Ayer.

— Security Interdependence in the Asia Pacific Region. LC 86-45053. 208p. 1986. text ed. 29.95 (0-669-13090-7) Free Pr.

Morley, James W., ed. Driven by Growth: Political Change in the Asia-Pacific Region. LC 91-28995. 382p. 1992. 62.95 (1-56324-013-0); pap. text ed. 23.95 (1-56324-014-9) M E Sharpe.

— The Fateful Choice: Japan's Advance into Southeast Asia, Nineteen Thirty-Nine to Nineteen Forty-One. Burton, Peter A. & Scalapino, Robert A., trs. LC 79-23486. (Studies of the East Asian Institute: Vol. 2). 1980. text ed. 55.00 (0-231-04804-1) Col U Pr.

— The Final Confrontation: Japan's Negotiations with the United States, 1941. LC 94-1392. (Japan's Road to the Pacific War Ser.). 1994. write for info. (0-231-08024-7) Col U Pr.

— Forecast for Japan: Security in the 1970's. LC 71-37578. 255p. 1972. reprint ed. pap. 72.70 (0-7837-8594-1, 2049409) Bks Demand.

— Japan's Road to the Pacific War: Japan Erupts (Selected Translations from Taiheiyo senso e no michi: Kaisen Gaiko shi), Vol. 4. LC 83-27320. (Studies of the East Asian Institute). 384p. 1984. text ed. 52.50 (0-231-05782-2) Col U Pr.

Morley, Jane, et al, eds. Isis Cumulative Index: 1953-1982. 168p. 1985. lib. bdg. 36.00 (0-934235-00-7); pap. text ed. 15.00 (0-934235-01-5) Hist Sci Soc.

Morley, Janet. All Desires Known. enl. ed. LC 93-45039. 128p. 1994. pap. 10.95 (0-8192-1610-0) Morehouse Pub.

Morley, Janet, ed. Bread of Tomorrow: Prayers for the Church Year. LC 92-5619. 192p. 1992. pap. 8.95 (0-88344-831-9) Orbis Bks.

Morley, Jim, ed. PFD Wedding Design Manual. (Illus.). 104p. (C). 1993. text ed. 30.95 (0-944074-02-2) AFS Education.

— Professional Floral Design Manual. (Illus.). 72p. (C). 1989. text ed. 24.95 (0-944074-01-4) AFS Education.

Morley, Jim, ed. see American Floral Services, Inc. Staff.

Morley, Jim, ed. see American Floral Services Staff.

Morley, Joan. Consonants in Context, Bk. 1: Rapid Review of Vowel & Prosodic Contexts. 76p. (C). 1992. pap. text ed. 9.95 (0-472-08127-6) U of Mich Pr.

— Consonants in Context, Bk. 2: Intensive Consonant Pronunciation Practice. 350p. (C). 1992. pap. text ed. 17.95 (0-472-08128-4) U of Mich Pr.

— Consonants in Context, Bk. 3: Extempore Speaking Practice. 200p. 1992. pap. text ed. 13.95 (0-472-08129-2) U of Mich Pr.

— Improving Aural Comprehension's Student's Workbook: Teacher's Book of Readings. LC 70-185904. 1972. teacher ed 11.95 (0-472-08666-9); student ed 14.95 (0-472-08665-0) U of Mich Pr.

— Improving Spoken English. LC 76-49151. 1979. pap. text ed. 15.95 (0-472-08660-X) U of Mich Pr.

— Listening & Language Learning in ESL. (Language in Education Ser.: No. 59). 163p. 1986. pap. text ed. 12.00 (0-13-537531-2) P-H.

— Listening Dictation: Understanding English Sentence Structure. 1976. pap. 11.95x (0-472-08667-7) U of Mich Pr.

Morley, Joan, ed. Current Perspectives on Pronunciation: Practices Anchored in Theory. 121p. 1987. pap. 14.00 (0-939791-28-5) Tchrs Eng Spkrs.

— Pronunciation Pedagogy & Theory: New Views, New Directions. 511p. 1994. pap. 15.95 (0-939791-55-2) Tchrs Eng Spkrs.

Morley, John. Asthma Reviews, Vol. 1. 181p. 1988. text ed. 60.00 (0-12-040921-6) Acad Pr.

— Burke. LC 68-58388. (English Men of Letters Ser.). reprint ed. 27.50 (0-404-51720-X) AMS Pr.

— The Diary of a District Officer. (Illus.). 200p. 1992. text ed. 39.50 (1-85043-526-X, Pub. by I B Tauris UK) St Martin.

— The Life of William Ewart Gladstone, 3 vols., Set. LC 70-145193. 1966p. 1972. reprint ed. 125.00 (0-403-01117-5) Scholarly.

— Recollections, 2 vols. LC 75-30034. reprint ed. 95.00 (0-404-14080-7) AMS Pr.

— Regency Design, 1790-1840: Gardens, Buildings, Interiors, Furniture. LC 92-28364. (Illus.). 448p. 1993. 150.00 (0-8109-3768-9) Abrams.

— Scriptwriting for High-Impact Videos: Imaginative Approaches to Delivering Factual Information. 272p. (C). 1992. pap. 28.95 (0-534-15066-7) Intl Thomson.

Morley, John, ed. Asthma Reviews, Vol. 2. 209p. 1989. text ed. 92.00 (0-12-040922-4) Acad Pr.

— Beta Adrenoceptors in Asthma. (Perspectives in Asthma Ser.). 1984. text ed. 69.00 (0-12-506440-3) Acad Pr.

— High-Performance Fibre Composites. 1987. text ed. 94.00 (0-12-506445-4) Acad Pr.

— Preventive Therapy in Asthma. (Perspectives in Asthma Ser.: Vol. 5). (Illus.). 300p. 1991. text ed. 72.00 (0-12-506448-9) Acad Pr.

Morley, John & Colditz, I., eds. Eosinophils in Asthma. (Perspectives in Asthma Ser.: No. 4). 300p. 1989. text ed. 73.00 (0-12-506452-7) Acad Pr.

Morley, John & Rainsford, Kim, eds. Pharmacology of Asthma. (Agents & Actions Supplements Ser.: Vol. 13). 228p. 1983. 74.00 (0-8176-1503-2) Birkhauser.

Morley, John, ed. see Ainger, Alfred.

Morley, John, ed. see Black, William.

Morley, John, ed. see Church, Richard W.

Morley, John, ed. see Colvin, Sidney.

Morley, John, ed. see Courthope, William J.

Morley, John, ed. see Dobson, Austin.

Morley, John, ed. see Dowden, Edward.

Morley, John, ed. see Fowler, Thomas.

Morley, John, ed. see Froude, James A.

Morley, John, jt. ed. see Hansel, Trevor T.

Morley, John, jt. ed. see Holme, G.

Morley, John, ed. see Hutton, Richard H.

Morley, John, ed. see Huxley, Thomas H.

Morley, John, ed. see Masson, David.

Morley, John, ed. see Minto, William.

Morley, John, ed. see Nichol, John.

Morley, John, ed. see Pattison, Mark.

Morley, John, ed. see Saintsbury, George E.

Morley, John, ed. see Shairp, John C.

Morley, John, ed. see Smith, Goldwin.

Morley, John, ed. see Stephen, Leslie.

Morley, John, ed. see Traill, H. D.

Morley, John, ed. see Trollope, Anthony.

Morley, John, ed. see Ward, Adolphus W.

***Morley, John D.** Feast of Fools. 1994. 23.95 (0-312-11786-8) St Martin.

***Morley, John E., ed.** Geriatric Nutrition. 2nd ed. LC 95-3911. 1995. write for info. (0-7817-0169-4) Raven.

Morley, John E., et al, eds. Memory Function & Aging-Related Disorders. LC 91-5089. 352p. 1992. 48.95 (0-8261-7710-7) Springer Pub.

M

— Nutritional Modulation of Neural Function. (UCLA Forum in Medical Sciences Ser.: Vol. 28). 325p. 1988. text ed. 79.00 (0-12-506455-1) Acad Pr.

Morley, John F. Vatican Diplomacy & the Jews During the Holocaust, 1939-1943. 1980. 35.00 (0-87068-701-8) Ktav.

— Vatican Diplomacy & the Jews During the Holocaust 1939-1943. 320p. 25.00 (0-685-05993-6) ADL.

Morley, John M. Critical Miscellanies. LC 68-29234. (Essay Index Reprint Ser.). 1977. reprint ed. 25.95 (0-8369-2417-7) Ayer.

— Edmund Burke: A Historical Study. Mayer, J. P., ed. LC 78-67372. (European Political Thought Ser.). 1980. reprint ed. lib. bdg. 25.95 (0-405-11722-1) Ayer.

— Life of William Ewart Gladstone, 3 Vols, 1. LC 68-57630. (Illus.). 1971. reprint ed. lib. bdg. 24.00 (0-313-21287-2, MOWA) Greenwood.

— Life of William Ewart Gladstone, 3 Vols, Set. LC 68-57630. (Illus.). 1971. reprint ed. text ed. 125.00 (0-8371-0576-5, MOWG) Greenwood.

— Life of William Ewart Gladstone, 3 Vols, Vol. 2. LC 68-57630. (Illus.). 1971. reprint ed. text ed. 45.00 (0-8371-0827-6, MOWB) Greenwood.

— Life of William Ewart Gladstone, 3 Vols, Vol. 3. LC 68-57630. (Illus.). 1971. reprint ed. text ed. 45.00 (0-8371-0828-4, MOWC) Greenwood.

— Oracles on Man & Government. LC 68-22933. (Essay Index Reprint Ser.). 1977. reprint ed. 19.95 (0-8369-0720-5) Ayer.

— Walpole. LC 76-110858. 251p. 1971. reprint ed. text ed. 59.75 (0-8371-4527-9, MOHW, Greenwood Pr) Greenwood.

Morley, John M., ed. English Men of Letters, 41 vols, Set. LC 77-166037. reprint ed. lib. bdg. write for info. (0-404-51700-5) AMS Pr.

Morley, John T. Secular Socialists: The CCF-NDP in Ontario: a Biography. LC 85-160769. (Illus.). 283p. reprint ed. pap. 80.70 (0-7837-6906-7, 2046736) Bks Demand.

Morley, Kevin, jt. auth. see Linton, Ian.

***Morley, Larry.** Programmer's Guide to C++ & Object-Oriented Programming. 1995. pap. 39.95 (0-442-02003-1) Van Nos Reinhold.

Morley, Laurene S. Hors d'Oeuvres: Easy Elegance. Petruzzini, Diane M., ed. (Orig.). 1986. pap. 6.95 (0-9617473-0-7) Creative Cookery.

Morley, Lewis. Out of Weakness...Strength. LC 86-32417. (Illus.). 160p. (Orig.). 1987. pap. 5.99 (0-932581-02-1) Word Aflame.

***Morley, Louise & Walsh, Val, eds.** Feminist Academics: Creative Agents for Change. LC 95-1200. (Gender & Society Ser.). 240p. 1995. 75.00 (0-7484-0299-3); pap. 24.95 (0-7484-0300-0) Taylor & Francis.

Morley, Mary, jt. auth. see Jenkins, Clare.

Morley, Michael D., ed. Studies in Model Theory. LC 73-86564. (MAA Studies: No. 8). 197p. 1974. 12.00 (0-88385-108-3) Math Assn.

Morley, Michael S. The Linear IC Handbook. (Illus.). 624p. 1986. 49.50 (0-8306-0472-3, NO. 2672, TAB/TPR) TAB Bks.

Morley, Morris, jt. auth. see Petras, James.

Morley, Morris H. Imperial State & Revolution: The United States & Cuba, 1952-1986. 575p. 1988. pap. 24.95 (0-521-35762-4) Cambridge U Pr.

— Washington, Somoza, & the Sandinistas: State & Regime in U. S. Policy Toward Nicaragua, 1969-1981. LC 93-34540. 352p. (C). 1994. 69.95 (0-521-45081-0) Cambridge U Pr.

Morley, Morris H., ed. Crisis & Confrontation: Ronald Reagan's Foreign Policy. 264p. 1988. 51.25 (0-8476-7432-0, CR7432) Rowman.

Morley-Mower, Geoffrey. Cabell under Fire. 1974. lib. bdg. 250.00 (0-87700-214-2) Revisionist Pr.

— Messerschmitt Routlette: The Western Desert 1941-42. LC 93-85728. (Illus.). 1993. 24.95 (1-883809-01-0) Phalanx Pub.

***Morley, N. T.** Noirotica. (Orig.). Date not set. pap. write for info. (1-56333-390-2) Masquerade.

***Morley, Nicholas.** The Parlour. (Orig.). 1995. pap. text ed. 4.95 (1-56333-291-4) Masquerade.

Morley, Patricia. As Though Life Mattered: Leo Kennedy's Story. LC 93-90597. (Illus.). 264p. 1994. 29.95 (0-7735-1147-4, Pub. by McGill CN) U of Toronto Pr.

— Margaret Laurence: The Long Journey Home. rev. ed. 192p. (C). 1991. reprint ed. pap. text ed. 6.95 (0-7735-0856-2, Pub. by McGill CN) U of Toronto Pr.

— My Other Family: An Artist-Wife in Singapore, 1946-48. (Illus.). 160p. 1994. text ed. 39.50 (1-85043-823-4, Pub. by I B Tauris UK) St Martin.

— The Mystery of Unity: Theme & Technique in the Novels of Patrick White. 1972. 24.95 (0-7735-0112-6, Pub. by McGill CN) U of Toronto Pr.

Morley, Patricia A. The Mystery of Unity: Theme & Technique in the Novels of Patrick White. LC 77-188136. 261p. reprint ed. pap. 74.40 (0-7837-6932-6, 2046761) Bks Demand.

Morley, Robert. Aerobics for the Spirit. 1990. pap. write for info. (0-8499-3224-6) Word Inc.

— The Pleasures of Age. large type ed. 1990. 21.95 (0-7089-2338-0) Ulverscroft.

Morley, S., et al. Industrial & Business Space Development: A Practical Guide to Implementation. 350p. 1989. 67.50 (0-685-24722-8, E & FN Spon) Routledge Chapman & Hall.

Morley, S. G., ed. Spanish Ballads. 1977. lib. bdg. 59.95 (0-8490-2647-4) Gordon Pr.

Morley, S. G. & Bruerton, C. Chronology of Lope De Vega's Comedies. (MLA Ser.). 1940. 37.00 (0-527-65200-8) Periodicals Srv.

Morley, S. Griswold. The Covered Bridges of California. 1992. reprint ed. lib. bdg. 75.00 (0-7812-5066-8) Rprt Serv.

Morley, S. Griswold & Hills, E. C. Modern Spanish Lyric. 1972. 59.95 (0-8490-0652-X) Gordon Pr.

***Morley, Sam.** Ninety-Nine Years of Navy: From Victoria to VJ Day Through Three Pairs of Eyes. 1995. 19.95 (1-899163-07-7) Cimino Pub Grp.

***Morley, Samuel A.** Poverty & Inequality in Latin America: Past Evidence, Future Prospects, Vol. 13. LC 94-35166. (Policy Essay Ser.). (Orig.). 1994. pap. 9.95 (1-56517-020-2) Overseas Dev Council.

— Poverty & Inequality in Latin America: The Impact of Adjustment & Recovery. 288p. 1995. text ed. 42.50x (0-8018-5064-9) Johns Hopkins.

Morley, Sheridan. Audrey Hepburn: A Celebration. (Illus.). 160p. 1994. 24.95 (1-85793-136-X, Pub. by Pavilion UK) Trafalgar.

— Audrey Hepburn: A Celebration. (Illus.). 192p. 1995. pap. 15.95 (1-85793-267-6, Pub. by Pavilion UK) Trafalgar.

— Elizabeth Taylor: A Celebration. 19.95 (0-685-39949-4, M Joseph) Viking Penguin.

— The Great Stage Stars. (Illus.). 484p. 1986. 29.95 (0-8160-1401-9) Facts on File.

— Odd Man Out: James Mason. large type ed. 288p. 1990. 19.95 (1-85089-376-4, Pub. by ISIS UK) Transaction Pubs.

— Robert, My Father. (Illus.). 240p. 1994. 34.95 (0-297-81329-3) Trafalgar.

Morley, Stephen, jt. ed. see Miller, Edgar.

Morley, Sylvanus G. The Inscriptions at Copan. LC 77-11506. (Carnegie Institution of Washington. Publications: No. 219). reprint ed. 57.00 (0-404-16271-1) AMS Pr.

— The Inscriptions of Peten, 5 vols. in 6, Set. LC 77-11510. (Carnegie Institution of Washington. Publications: No. 437). reprint ed. 253.00 (0-404-16290-8) AMS Pr.

— Introduction to the Study of Maya Hieroglyphs. (Bureau of American Ethnology Bulletins Ser.: No. 57). 284p. 1995. lib. bdg. 89.00 (0-7812-4057-3) Rprt Serv.

— An Introduction to the Study of the Maya Hieroglyphs. LC 74-82503. (Illus.). 384p. 1975. reprint ed. pap. 8.95 (0-486-23108-9) Dover.

— Introduction to the Study of the Maya Hieroglyphs. 1988. reprint ed. lib. bdg. 75.00 (0-685-21387-0) Rprt Serv.

Morley, Sylvanus G., ed. Spanish Ballads. LC 78-137068. 226p. 1977. reprint ed. text ed. 55.00 (0-8371-5531-2, MOSB, Greenwood Pr) Greenwood.

Morley, Sylvanus G. & Brainerd, George W. The Ancient Maya. 4th rev. ed. LC 81-85451. (Illus.). xx, 708p. 1983. 45.00 (0-8047-1137-2); pap. 19.95 (0-8047-1288-3) Stanford U Pr.

Morley, Sylvanus G., tr. see Cervantes Saavedra, Miguel de.

Morley, Thomas. Memecyleae. LC 76-13371. (Flora Neotropica Monograph Ser.: No. 15). (Illus.). 295p. 1976. pap. 22.00 (0-89327-000-8) NY Botanical.

Morley, Thomas, jt. auth. see Ownbey, Gerald B.

Morley, W. F., ed. see Waldon, Freda F.

Morley, William F. The Atlantic Provinces: Newfoundland, Nova Scotia, New Brunswick, Prince Edward Island. LC 68-90634. (Canadian Local Histories to 1950: A Bibliography Ser.: No. 1). 183p. reprint ed. pap. 52.20 (0-8357-8031-7, 2034020) Bks Demand.

Morley, William F., jt. auth. see Beaulieu, Andre.

Morlock, Henry, jt. auth. see Harless, Marion.

Morlok, E. K. Introduction to Transportation System Engineering & Planning. (Illus.). 1978. text ed. write for info. (0-07-043132-9) McGraw.

Morlok, Edward K. Introduction to Transportation System Engineering & Planning. 2nd ed. 1991. text ed. write for info. (0-07-043143-4) McGraw.

Morman, Edward T., ed. Efficiency, Science Management, & Hospital Standardization. (Medical Care in the United States Ser.). 288p. 1989. reprint ed. lib. bdg. 25.00 (0-8240-8338-5) Garland.

Morman, Jean M. Art: Tempo of Today. rev. ed. (Illus.). 1978. teacher ed 4.70 (0-685-62931-7); text ed. 17.20 (0-912242-14-0) Art Educ.

Morman, Paul, tr. see De La Barre, Poullain.

Morman, Robert, ed. see Pyrczak, Fred.

Mormile, M. Italian-French - French-Italian Commercial Dictionary. 650p. 1978. 42.50 (2-85608-008-1) IBD Ltd.

Mormile, Mario. Dictionnaire Commercial: Francais-Italien, Italien-Francais. (FRE & ITA.). 1978. lib. bdg. 125.00 (0-7859-3907-5) Fr & Eur.

Mormillo, F. B. F-4 Phantom. (Illus.). 64p. 1990. pap. 9.95 (0-7110-1928-2) Motorbooks Intl.

Mormillo, Frank B., jt. auth. see Thornborough, Tony.

Mormino, Gary R. Immigrants on the Hill: Italian-Americans in St. Louis, 1882-1982. (Illus.). 304p. 1986. 24.95 (0-252-01261-5) U of Ill Pr.

Mormino, Gary R. & Pozzetta, George E. The Immigrant World of Ybor City: Italians & Their Latin Neighbors in Tampa, 1885-1985. LC 86-7115. (Statue of Liberty-Ellis Island Centennial Ser.). (Illus.). 388p. 1987. 34.95 (0-252-01351-4); pap. 14.95 (0-252-06123-3) U of Ill Pr.

Mormino, Gary R., jt. ed. see Henderson, Ann L.

Mormon Handicraft Staff & Danzig, Ann, eds. The Utah Sampler Quilt. (Illus.). 56p. 1990. pap. 11.95 (0-87579-349-5) Deseret Bk.

Mormon, Paul J. Noel Aubert de Verse: A Study in the Concept of Toleration. LC 87-21643. (Texts & Studies in Religion: Vol. 32). 290p. 1986. lib. bdg. 89.95 (0-88946-822-2) E Mellen.

Morn, Frank. Academic Politics & History of Criminal Justice Education. LC 94-18557. (Contributions in Criminology & Penalogy: No. 46). 256p. 1995. text ed. 55.00 (0-313-29316-3, Greenwood Pr) Greenwood.

— The Eye That Never Sleeps: A History of the Pinkerton National Detective Agency. LC 81-47776. 255p. reprint ed. pap. 72.70 (0-8357-3959-7, 2057055) Bks Demand.

***Morn, September B.** Dogs Love to Please...We Teach Them How! The Safe & Gentle Guide to Dog Obedience Through Interspecies Communication. 4th rev. ed. (Illus.). 248p. 1994. per., pap. 15.95 (0-9633884-1-X) Pawprince Pr.

— Dogs Love to Please...We Teach Them How! The Safe & Gentle Guide to Dog Obedience Training Through Interspecies Communication. 3rd rev. ed. (Illus.). 144p. 1992. pap. text ed. 15.00 (0-9633884-0-1) Pawprince Pr.

Mornand, Pierre. In the Forest of the Golden Dragon. LC 73-76776. (Illus.). (ENG & FRE.). 1973. 35.00 (0-933652-04-6) Domjan Studio.

Morneau, Claude. Martinique Travel Guide. (Illus.). 176p. (Orig.). 1994. pap. 14.95 (2-921444-87-9, Pub. by Editions Ulysse CN) Ulysses Travel.

Morneau, Paul. PC Assembly Language: An Introduction to Computer Systems. Gordon, Robert J., ed. LC 92-13906. 750p. (C). 1993. text ed. 53.75 (0-314-01003-3) West Pub.

***Morneau, Robert.** Gift, Mystery, & Calling: Prayers & Reflections. Koch, Carl, ed. (Illus.). 111p. (Orig.). 1994. pap. 6.95 (0-88489-346-4) St Marys.

— Gift, Mystery, & Calling: Prayers & Reflections. Koch, Carl, ed. (Illus.). 111p. (Orig.). 1994. spiral bd. 8.95 (0-88489-355-3) St Marys.

— Mantras from a Poet: Jessica Powers. LC 90-64032. 128p. (Orig.). 1991. pap. 8.95 (1-55612-420-1, LL1420) Sheed & Ward MO.

Morneau, Robert, jt. ed. see Siegfried, Regina.

***Morneau, Robert F.** The Gift. LC 94-78138. 32p. (J). (gr. k-4). 1995. text ed. 16.00 (0-9642140-6-7) Kodomo Pr.

— Mantras for the Midnight. 112p. 1985. pap. 4.95 (0-8146-1404-3) Liturgical Pr.

— Mantras for the Morning: An Introduction to Holistic Prayer. LC 81-1085. (Illus.). 116p. 1981. pap. 4.95 (0-8146-1210-5) Liturgical Pr.

— Spiritual Aids for Those in Renew: Ponderings, Poems & Promises. LC 84-12299. 111p. (Orig.). 1984. pap. 4.50 (0-8189-0473-9) Alba.

— Spiritual Direction: Principles & Practices. 144p. (Orig.). 1992. pap. 10.95 (0-8245-1202-2) Crossroad NY.

— Themes & Theses of Six Recent Papal Documents: A Commentary. LC 84-29034. 160p. (Orig.). 1985. pap. 5.95 (0-8189-0482-8) Alba.

— There Is a Season: An Inspirational Journal. LC 84-11622. (Illus.). 175p. 1986. 18.95 (0-13-914755-1, Busn); 9.95 (0-13-914706-3, Busn) P-H.

Morneau, Roger J. More Incredible Answers to Prayer. LC 93-18276. 1993. pap. 7.95 (0-8280-0719-5) Review & Herald.

Mornell, Pierre. Passive Men, Wild Women. 160p. 1987. mass mkt. 4.99 (0-345-34523-1) Ballantine.

Morner, Kathleen & Rausch, Ralph. NTC's Dictionary of Literary Terms. 304p. 1991. 16.95 (0-8442-5465-7, Natl Textbk); pap. 12.95 (0-8442-5464-9, Natl Textbk) NTC Pub Grp.

Morner, M., jt. ed. see Emmer, P. C.

Morner, Magnus. Adventurers & Proletarians: The Story of Migrants in Latin America. Sims, Harold, tr. LC 84-19597. (Latin American Ser.). (Illus.). 195p. 1985. 49.95 (0-8229-3505-8) U of Pittsburgh Pr.

— The Andean Past: Land, Societies & Conflicts. LC 83-23136. 316p. reprint ed. pap. 90.10 (0-7837-0421-6, 2040744) Bks Demand.

— The Political & Economic Activities of the Jesuits in the Plata Region. 1976. lib. bdg. 59.95 (0-8490-2451-X) Gordon Pr.

— Region & State in Latin America's Past. LC 92-28774. (Symposia in Comparative History Ser.). 168p. 1993. text ed. 32.50 (0-8018-4478-9) Johns Hopkins.

Morner, Magnus & Svensson, Thommy. The Transformation of Rural Society in the Third World. 352p. (C). 1991. text ed. 65.00 (0-415-03632-1, A5218) Routledge.

Morner, Magnus & Svensson, Thommy, eds. The History of the Third World in Nordic Research. (Acta Regiae Societatis Scientiarum Humaniora Ser.: No. 25). 202p. (Orig.). 1986. pap. text ed. 83.50x (91-85252-36-0, Pub. by Vetenskaps SW) Coronet Bks.

Morner, Nils-Axel, ed. Earth Rheology, Isostasy & Eustasy: Proceedings of Earth Rheology & Late Cenozoic Isostatic Movements an Interdisciplinary Symposium Held in Stockholm, Sweden, July 31-August 8, 1977. LC 79-1473. (Geodynamics Project: Scientific Report Ser.: No. 49). (Illus.). 621p. reprint ed. pap. 177.00 (0-685-44065-6, 2030415) Bks Demand.

Mornex, R., jt. auth. see Hermann, H.

Mornex, Rene, et al, eds. Progress in Endocrinology: The Proceedings of the Ninth International Congress of Endocrinology Held in Nice, France, September, 1992. LC 93-22896. (International Congress, Symposium & Seminar Ser.). (Illus.). 800p. (C). 1993. 125.00 (1-85070-469-4) Prthnon Pub.

Mornin, Daniel. All Our Fault. 218p. 1992. 22.95 (0-09-174678-7, Pub. by Hutchinson & Co UK) Heinemann.

***Morning, Barbara.** Grandfather's Shirt. Johnson, Joy, ed. (Illus.). 16p. (J). (gr. k-3). Date not set. pap. 4.95 (1-56123-074-X) Centering Corp.

Morning Star, Inc., Staff, jt. auth. see Remaley, William A.

Morninghouse, Sundaira. Habari Gani? What's the News? (Illus.). 32p. (J). (gr. k-4). 1992. 14.95 (0-940880-39-3) Open Hand.

— Nightfeathers: Black Goose Rhymes. LC 89-63264. (Illus.). 32p. (J). (gr. 1-4). 1989. 9.95 (0-940880-27-X); pap. text ed. 4.95 (0-940880-28-8) Open Hand.

***Morninghouse, Sunsaira.** Nightfeathers. (Illus.). 32p. (J). (gr. k-3). 1995. 9.95 (0-940880-60-1) Open Hand.

Morningland Publications, Inc. Staff. Healing: As It Is, 2 vols., Set. (Illus.). 320p. (Orig.). 1981. pap. 10.00 (0-935146-59-8) Morningland.

— Morningland Astrology Chart Construction. (Illus.). 100p. (Orig.). 1980. spiral bd., pap. 3.50 (0-935146-10-5) Morningland.

Morningland Publications, Inc. Staff & Donato, Gopi G. Lord Jupiter. (Astrology Ser.). (Illus.). 283p. (Orig.). 1980. pap. 6.95 (0-935146-50-4) Morningland.

Morningland Publications, Inc. Staff, ed. see Donato, Gopi G.

Morningland Publications, Inc. Staff, ed. see Donato, Sri.

Morningland Publications, Inc. Staff, ed. see Donato, Sri & Donato, Gopi G.

Morningland Publications, Inc. Staff, ed. see Donato, Sri.

Morningland Publications, Inc. Staff, ed. see Donato, Sri.

Morningland Publications, Inc. Staff, ed. see Gyan, Gopi.

Morningland Publications, Inc. Staff, ed. see Kamazi, I.

Morningland Publications, Inc. Staff, ed. see Patricia.

Morningland Publications, Inc. Staff, ed. see Sri, Patricia.

***Morningstar, Amadea.** Ayurvedic Cooking for Westerners: Familiar Western Food Prepared with Ayurvedic Principles. 400p. (Orig.). 1995. pap. 19.95 (0-914955-14-4) Lotus Pr WI.

Morningstar, Amadea & Desai, Urmila. Ayurvedic Cookbook. LC 90-35806. 351p. (Orig.). (C). 1990. pap. 16.95 (0-914955-06-3) Lotus Light.

Morningstar, Amadea, jt. auth. see Gagnon, Daniel.

Morningstar, Gersh, jt. auth. see Tropman, John E.

Morningstar, Heather. How to Enroll in an Indian Tribe. Frazier, Gregory W., ed. 95p. (Orig.). 1993. pap. 19.95 (0-935151-20-6) Arrowstar Pub.

Morningstar, Inc. Staff. Morningstar Mutal Fund 500: An in-Depth Loodk at 500 Select Mutual Funds from the Leading Authority in Mutual-Fund Analysis 1994 Edition. 2nd ed. 1994. 35.00 (0-7863-0136-8) Irwin Prof Pubng.

***Morningstar Inc. Staff, ed.** Morningstar Closed-End Fund 250: 1995 Edition. 500p. 1995. pap. 35.00 (0-7863-0451-0) Irwin Prof Pubng.

— Morningstar Mutual Fund 500: 1995 Edition. 3rd ed. 525p. 1995. pap. 35.00 (0-7863-0431-6) Irwin Prof Pubng.

Morningstar, Inc., Staff, jt. ed. see Dow Jones.

Morningstar, Jean. Clip Art for Communicating the Good News. LC 89-10624. (Illus.). 128p. (Orig.). (C). 1989. pap. 14.95 (0-89390-160-1) Resource Pubns.

***Morningstar, Jim.** Breathing in Light & Love: Your Call to Breath & Body Mastery. 224p. (Orig.). 1994. pap. text ed. 10.00 (0-9604856-2-7) Transform Inc.

— Family Awakening in Body, Mind, & Spirit. 60p. 1984. pap. 6.00 (0-9604856-1-9) Transform Inc.

— Spiritual Psychology: A New Age Course for Body, Mind & Spirit. 2nd ed. (Illus.). 119p. (C). 1981. pap. 10.00 (0-9604856-0-0) Transform Inc.

Morningstar, Ramon S. Zero Weather. King, Una & Moon, Delia, eds. LC 80-20072. 367p. (Orig.). 1980. pap. 3.95 (0-937770-00-0) Family Pub CA.

Morningstar Staff. Morningstar Mutal Fund 500. 1993. pap. 35.00 (1-55623-072-9) Irwin Prof Pubng.

Morns, Jan. Dakota & the Wolf Pack. (Friends of the Forest Adventure Bks.). (Illus.). (J). (ps-8). 1994. 16.95 (0-9641742-0-0) Pequot Pubng.

Moro, Cesar. Love till Death. Lefevre, Frances, tr. 140p. 1971. 25.00 (0-931106-05-2) TVRT.

— The Scandalous Life of Cesar Moro in His Own Words: Peruvian Surrealist Poetry. Ward, Philip, tr. (Modern Poets Ser.: Vol. 6). 1976. pap. 4.95 (0-902675-73-7) Oleander Pr.

Moro, F. T. Diccionario Juridico Espasa. 1010p. (SPA.). 1991. 119.50x (84-239-5988-0) IBD Ltd.

***Moro, Ginger H.** European Designer Jewelry of the 20th Century. LC 95-2180. (Illus.). 304p. 1995. 79.95 (0-88740-823-0) Schiffer.

Moro-oka, Y., jt. ed. see Ando, W.

Moro-Oka, Y., et al, eds. Hydrogen Absorbing Materials-Catalytic Materials: Materials Research Society International Symposium Proceedings - IMAM, No. 2. 396p. 1989. text ed. 60.00 (1-55899-031-3) Materials Res.

Moro, Oscar P. Rios y Palmas: Poesias. LC 85-80622. (Coleccion Espejo de Paciencia Ser.). 127p. (Orig.). (SPA.). 1985. pap. 8.95 (0-89729-377-0) Ediciones.

Moro, Oscar P. & Perez, Dario E. Lira Criolla (Decimas Cubanas) LC 86-83149. (Coleccion Espejo de Paciencia Ser.). 85p. (Orig.). 1987. pap. 9.95 (0-89729-430-0) Ediciones.

Moro, Ruben O. The History of the South Atlantic Conflict: The War for the Malvinas. LC 88-38300. 376p. 1989. text ed. 69.50 (0-275-93081-5, C3081, Praeger Pubs) Greenwood.

Morocutti, C. & Rizzo, P. A., eds. Evoked Potentials: Neurphysiological & Clinic Aspects. 436p. 1985. 184.00 (0-444-80658-X) Elsevier.

Moroi, Y. Micelles: Theoretical & Applied Aspects. (Illus.). 248p. (C). 1992. 59.50 (0-306-43996-4, Plenum Pr) Plenum.

***Moroji, T., ed.** The Biology of Schizophrenia: Proceedings of the 7th International Symposium of the Tokyo Institute of Psychiatry, Tokyo, Japan, October 19-20, 1992. LC 94-3420. (Developments in Psychiatry Ser.). 1994. write for info. (0-444-81772-7) Elsevier.

Morokoff, William J., jt. auth. see Kersch, Alfred.

Morokuma, K., jt. auth. see Ohno, K.

Morokuma, Keiji, jt. ed. see Van Leeuwen, Piet W.N.M.

Moron Arroyo, Ciriaco, ed. see De Unamuno, Miguel.

***Moron, Guillermo.** History of Venezuela. Street, John, tr. 268p. 1964. 69.50 (0-614-00156-0) Elliots Bks.

Morone, James A. The Democratic Wish: Popular Participation & the Limits of American Government. LC 90-80250. 402p. 1992. reprint ed. pap. text ed. 16.00 (0-465-01602-2) Basic.

An Asterisk (*) at the beginning of an entry indicates that the title is appearing in BIP for the first time.

Morone, James A. & Belkin, Gary S., eds. The Politics of Health Care Reform: Lessons from the Past, Prospects for the Future. LC 94-10005. 552p. 1994. lib. bdg. 49.95 (*0-8223-1461-4*); pap. text ed. 19.95 (*0-8223-1489-4*) Duke.

Morone, John J. & Hilbush, Mark R. Experiencing Artificial Intelligence: An Interactive Approach for the Apple. (Illus.). 190p. (Orig.). 1987. pap. 36.95 (*0-8306-2860-6*, 2860C) TAB Bks.

— Experiencing Artificial Intelligence: An Interactive Approach for the IBM PC. (Illus.). 190p. (Orig.). 1987. disk 29.95 (*0-8306-2830-4*, 2830C) TAB Bks.

Morone, Joseph & Woodhouse, Edward. The Demise of American Nuclear Power: Learning from the Failure of a Politically Unsafe Technology. LC 88-39306. 168p. (C). 1989. text ed. 8.00 (*0-300-04448-8*); pap. 8.00 (*0-300-04449-6*) Yale U Pr.

Morone, Joseph G. Winning in High-Tech Markets: The Role of General Management. LC 92-15842. 304p. (C). 1993. 29.95 (*0-87584-325-5*) Harvard Busn.

Moroney, John R., ed. Advances in the Economics of Energy & Resources, Vol. 6. 1987. 73.25 (*0-89232-584-4*) Jai Pr.

— Econometric Models of the Demand for Energy. (Advances in the Economics of Energy & Resources Ser.: Vol. 5). 210p. 1983. 73.25 (*0-89232-327-2*) Jai Pr.

— Economic Aspects of New Technology. (Advances in the Economics of Energy & Resources Ser.: Vol. 3). 274p. 1980. 73.25 (*0-89232-175-X*) Jai Pr.

— Formal Energy & Resource Models. (Advances in the Economics of Energy & Resources Ser.: Vol. 4). 275p. 1982. 73.25 (*0-89232-215-2*) Jai Pr.

Moroney, John R., jt. ed. see Khazzoom, J. Daniel.

***Moroney, Lynn.** Moontellers: Myths of the Moon from Around the World. Murphy, Erin, ed. LC 95-2418. (Illus.). 32p. (J). (ps up). 1995. 14.95 (*0-87358-601-8*) Northland AZ.

Moroney, Paul. Issues in the Implementation of Digital Feedback Compensators. (Signal Processing, Optimization, & Control Ser.). (Illus.). 224p. 1983. 37.50 (*0-262-13185-4*) MIT Pr.

Moroney, Robert. The Family & the State: Considerations for Social Policy. LC 75-45230. 154p. reprint ed. pap. 43.90 (*0-317-27861-4*, 2025262) Bks Demand.

Moroney, Robert M. Shared Responsibility: Families & Social Policy. Whittaker, James K., ed. LC 85-20950. (Modern Applications of Social Work Ser.). (Illus.). 229p. (Orig.). 1986. lib. bdg. 44.95 (*0-202-36041-5*); pap. text ed. 22.95 (*0-202-36042-3*) Aldine de Gruyter.

— Social Policy & Social Work: Critical Essays on the Welfare State. (Modern Applications of Social Work Ser.). 270p. 1991. lib. bdg. 47.95 (*0-202-36061-X*); pap. text ed. 25.95 (*0-202-36062-8*) Aldine de Gruyter.

Moroney, Sean, ed. Africa, 2 vols. (Handbooks to the Modern World Ser.). (Illus.). 1248p. 1989. 110.00 (*0-8160-1623-2*) Facts on File.

Morong, Bill. Yo - Pho's: Young Photographers. Berk, Judy, ed. (Illus.). 145p. 1989. 29.95 (*0-923486-00-3*) F-Stop Pubns.

Morony, Michael G. Iraq after the Muslim Conquest. LC 83-42569. (Illus.). 702p. reprint ed. pap. 180.00 (*0-8357-3848-5*, 2036581) Bks Demand.

Morony, Michael G., tr. The History of al-Tabari, Vol. 18: Between Civil Wars: The Caliphate of Mu'awiyah 40 A.H., 66 A.D.-60 A.H., 680 A.D. LC 85-2823. (SUNY Series in Near Eastern Studies). 261p. (C). 1986. 49.50 (*0-87395-933-7*); pap. 16.95 (*0-88706-314-4*) State U NY Pr.

***Morosan, Vladimir.** Choral Performance in Pre-Revolutionary Russia. LC 86-1266. (Illus.). xxi, 376p. 1994. pap. 39.00 (*0-9629460-2-8*) Musica Russica.

Morosan, Vladimir, ed. One Thousand Years of Russian Church Music, 988-1988. LC 89-63652. (Monuments of Russian Sacred Music Ser.). (Illus.). xlviii, 774p. (ENG & RUS.). 1991. lib. bdg. 129.00 (*0-9629460-0-1*) Musica Russica.

Morosani, Roopa, ed. see Ananda Yogi, Gururaj.

Morosanu, C. E. Thin Films by Chemical Vapour Deposition. (Thin Films Science & Technology Ser.: Vol. 7). 718p. 1990. 192.50 (*0-444-98801-7*, TFS 7) Elsevier.

Morosanu, Gheorghe. Nonlinear Evolution Equations & Applications. (C). 1988. lib. bdg. 140.00 (*90-277-2486-5*) Kluwer Ac.

Morosco, Anthony B. Prosecution & Defense of Sex Crimes. 1976. Looseleaf updates avail. write for info. (*0-8205-1562-0*) Bender.

Morot-Sir, Edouard. The Imagination of Reference: Meditating the Linguistic Condition. LC 92-22881. (University of Florida Humanities Monographs: No. 67). 184p. 1993. 24.95 (*0-8130-1171-X*) U Press Fla.

— The Imagination of Reference II: Perceiving, Indicating, Naming. 240p. 1995. lib. bdg. 49.95 (*0-8130-1406-9*) U Press Fla.

Morowitz, David A. Clinical Implications of Abnormal Digestive Tract Radiographs. LC 89-12982. (Illus.). 235p. 1990. text ed. 45.00 (*0-8121-1268-7*) Williams & Wilkins.

***Morowitz, Harold & Singer, Jerome L.** The Mind, the Brain, & Complex Adaptive Systems. 256p. (C). 1995. 55.95 (*0-201-40988-7*); pap. 31.95x (*0-201-40986-0*) Addison-Wesley.

Morowitz, Harold J. Beginnings of Cellular Life: Metabolism Recapitulates Biogenesis. (Illus.). 208p. (C). 1993. text ed. 30.00 (*0-300-05483-1*) Yale U Pr.

— Cosmic Joy & Local Pain: Musings of a Mystic Scientist. LC 86-26020. 1987. 18.95 (*0-684-18443-5*) Ox Bow.

— Ego Niches: An Ecological View of Organizational Behavior. LC 76-48588. (Illus.). 96p. 1977. pap. 8.95 (*0-918024-01-3*) Ox Bow.

— Energy Flow in Biology. LC 79-89841. 1979. 24.00 (*0-918024-12-9*); pap. 12.00 (*0-918024-13-7*) Ox Bow.

— Entropy & the Magic Flute. LC 92-27935. 240p. 1993. 22.00 (*0-19-508199-4*) OUP.

— Foundations of Bioenergetics. 1978. 55.00 (*0-12-507250-3*) Ox Bow.

— Mayonnaise & the Origin of Life: Thoughts of Minds & Molecules. LC 90-25713. vii, 244p. 1991. reprint ed. pap. 14.95 (*0-918024-82-X*) Ox Bow.

— The Thermodynamics of Pizza. 258p. (Orig.). 1992. reprint ed. pap. 11.95 (*0-8135-1774-5*) Rutgers U Pr.

— The Wine of Life: And Other Essays on Societies, Energy & Living Things. LC 79-16404. 1979. 18.95 (*0-312-88227-0*) Ox Bow.

Morowitz, Harold J. & Trefil, James. The Facts of Life: Science & the Abortion Controversy. (Illus.). 192p. 1992. 25.00 (*0-19-507927-2*) OUP.

— The Facts of Life: Science & the Abortion Controversy. (Illus.). 192p. 1994. reprint ed. pap. 9.95 (*0-19-509046-2*) OUP.

Moroy, T., jt. auth. see Sedlacek, H. H.

Moroz, Andrew R., jt. auth. see Salembier, G. E.

Moroz, B. Z. Analytic Arithmetic in Algebraic Number Fields. (Lecture Notes in Mathematics Ser.: Vol. 1205). vii, 177p. 1986. pap. 31.30 (*0-387-16784-6*) Spr-Verlag.

Morozov. Regularization Methods for Ill-Proposed Problems. 1993. 69.95 (*0-8493-9311-6*) CRC Pr.

Morozov, jt. auth. see Elion.

Morozov, E. M., jt. auth. see Parton, V. Z.

***Morozov, Kostiantyn, et al.** The Military Tradition in Ukraine: Its Role in the Construction of Ukraine's Armed Forces (Conference Proceedings, Harvard University, 12-13 May 1994) (Harvard Papers in Ukrainian Studies). (Illus.). 110p. 1995. pap. 5.00 (*0-916458-73-3*) Harvard Ukrainian.

Morozov, P. V., ed. Research on the Viral Hypothesis of Mental Disorders. (Advances in Biological Psychiatry Ser.: Vol. 12). (Illus.). x, 178p. 1983. pap. 73.00 (*3-8055-3706-9*) S Karger.

Morozov, V. A. Methods for Solving Incorrectly Posed Problems. Nashed, Z., ed. Aries, A. B., tr. (Illus.). 270p. 1984. pap. 76.00 (*0-387-96059-7*) Spr-Verlag.

Morozowich, Walter, jt. ed. see Tsuji, Kiyoski.

Morozumi, Atsuko. One Gorilla. (J). (ps). 1993. pap. 4.95 (*0-374-45646-1*, Sunburst Bks) FS&G.

— One Gorilla: A Counting Book. (Illus.). 26p. (J). (ps-1). 1990. 15.00 (*0-374-35644-0*) FS&G.

Morpeau, Louis. Anthologie d'un Siecle de Poesie Haitienne, 1817-1925, avec une Etude sur la Muse Haitienne d'Expression Franciase et une Etude sur la Muse Haitienne d'Expression Creole. (B. E. Ser.: No. 10). (FRE.). 1925. 30.00 (*0-8115-2961-4*) Periodicals Srv.

***Morphet.** Windows on the Internet. 1995. cd-rom, pap. text ed. 34.95 (*0-07-912173-X*) McGraw.

Morphet, Edgar L. The Measurement & Interpretation of School Building Utilization. LC 75-177084. (Columbia University. Teachers College. Contributions to Education Ser.: No. 264). reprint ed. 37.50 (*0-404-55264-1*) AMS Pr.

***Morphet, John P.** The Complete Internet Kit for Windows. 352p. 1994. pap. 34.95 (*0-9642539-0-9*) Advnced Systs.

***Morphet, Richard, ed.** R. B. Kitaj. (Illus.). 240p. 1995. 60.00 (*0-8478-1846-2*) Rizzoli Intl.

Morpheus. No Lover Ever Dies. (Illus.). 80p. 1985. 11.99 (*0-9604512-1-8*) Mortal Pr.

Morphew, Carol, jt. auth. see Jacob, Bernard.

Morphonios, Ellen & Wilson, Mike. Maximum Morphonios: The Life & Times of America's Toughest Judge. (Illus.). 320p. 1991. 19.95 (*0-688-09155-5*) Morrow.

Morphy, Guillermo. Les Luthistes espagnols du XVIe siecle, 2 vols in 1. (Illus.). 306p. (FRE & GER.). 1967. reprint ed. lib. bdg. 95.00 (*0-8450-1008-5*) Broude.

Morphy, H. Animals into Art. 350p. 1988. text ed. 90.00 (*0-04-445030-3*) Routledge Chapman & Hall.

Morphy, Howard. Ancestral Connections: Art & an Aboriginal System of Knowledge. (Illus.). 336p. 1991. pap. text ed. 19.95 (*0-226-53866-4*) U Ch Pr.

— Ancestral Connections: Art & an Aboriginal System of Knowledge. (Illus.). 336p. 1992. lib. bdg. 47.50 (*0-226-53865-6*) U Ch Pr.

Morpugo, Michael. The War of Jenkins' Ear. LC 94-7602. (J). 1995. 15.95 (*0-399-22735-0*, Philomel Bks) Putnam Pub Group.

Morpurgo, Annselm L., see Artemis Smith, pseud..

Morpurgo, M., et al, eds. Pulmonary Circulation. (Current Topics in Rehabilitation Ser.). 192p. 1990. 56.00 (*0-387-19542-4*) Spr-Verlag.

Morpurgo, Mario. Pulmonary Embolism. LC 93-46951. (Lung Biology in Health & Disease Ser.: Vol. 75). 376p. 1994. 150.00 (*0-8247-9178-9*) Dekker.

Morpurgo, Michael. Arthur, High King of Britain. LC 93-33620. (Illus.). 144p. (J). (gr. 4-9). 1995. 19.95 (*0-15-200080-1*) HarBrace.

— Blodin the Beast. (Illus.). 32p. 1995. 15.95 (*1-55591-211-7*) Fulcrum Pub.

— King of the Cloud Forests. (J). (gr. 10 up). 1988. pap. 12.95 (*0-670-82069-5*) Viking Child Bks.

— My Friend Walter. large type ed. 216p. (J). 1991. 16.95 (*0-7451-1408-3*, Galaxy Child Lrg Print) Chivers N Amer.

— The Sandman & the Turtles. LC 93-21531. 80p. (J). (gr. 3-7). 1994. 14.95 (*0-399-22672-9*, Philomel Bks) Putnam Pub Group.

— Waiting for Anya. (J). 1991. 13.99 (*0-670-83735-0*) Viking Child Bks.

— The Wreck of the Zanzibar. (Illus.). 80p. (J). (gr. 5-9). 1995. 14.99 (*0-670-86360-2*) Viking Child Bks.

***Morpurgo, Michael, ed.** Ghostly Haunts. (Illus.). 160p. (J). 1995. 22.95 (*1-85793-158-0*, Pub. by Pavilion UK) Trafalgar.

***Morr, Mary L. & Irmiter, Theodore.** Introductory Foods. 6th ed. (Illus.). 320p. (C). 1994. student ed, pap. text ed. write for info. (*0-02-384142-7*, Merrill Pub Co) Macmillan.

Morr, Mary L. & Irmiter, Theodore F. Introductory Foods: A Laboratory Manual of Food Preparation & Evaluation. 5th ed. 352p. (C). 1990. pap. write for info. (*0-02-384131-1*) Macmillan.

Morra, Marion & Potts, Eve. Choices. rev. ed. 976p. (Orig.). 1994. pap. 15.00 (*0-380-77620-0*) Avon.

— Choices: Realistic Alternatives in Cancer Treatment. rev. ed. 976p. 1980. pap. 12.95 (*0-380-75308-1*) Avon.

— Triumph: Getting Back to Normal When You Have Cancer. 304p. 1990. pap. 9.95 (*0-380-75503-3*) Avon.

Morra, Marion, jt. auth. see Potts, Eve.

Morra, R. G., jt. ed. see Morgenthaler, G. W.

Morra, Robert, jt. ed. see Morgenthaler, George W.

Morra-Yoe, Janet, jt. auth. see Yoe, Craig.

Morra-Yoe, Janet, jt. ed. see Yoe, Craig.

Morrah, Patrick. Restoration England. LC 79-317995. 252p. reprint ed. pap. 71.90 (*0-318-34738-5*, 2031995) Bks Demand.

***Morral, J. E., ed.** Experimental Methods of Phase Determination: Proceedings of a Symposium Sponsored by a Committee of the Material Science Division of ASM International. 210p. 1994. 44.00 (*0-87339-226-4*) Minerals Metals.

Morral, J. E., ed. see International Symposium on Boron Steels (September 18, 1979: Milwaukee, WI Staff.

Morrall, John B. Political Thought in Medieval Times. (Medieval Academy Reprints for Teaching Ser.). 1980. pap. 8.95 (*0-8020-6413-2*) U of Toronto Pr.

Morrall, John B., jt. auth. see Ehler, Sidney Z.

Morrall, June. The Coburn Mystery: Northern California's Unsolved Murder. LC 92-81071. (Illus.). 228p. (Orig.). 1992. pap. write for info. (*0-9602088-1-X*) Moonbeam CA.

— Costside Memories: Motoring South of San Francisco, 1850-1950. Mannett, Luana, ed. (Illus.). 176p. (Orig.). 1994. write for info. (*0-9602088-2-8*) Moonbeam CA.

— Half Moon Bay Memories: The Coastside's Colorful Past. (Illus.). 176p. 1987. reprint ed. pap. 12.95 (*0-9602088-0-1*) Moonbeam CA.

Morray, David. An Ayyubid Notable & His World: Ibn Al-Adim & Aleppo as Portrayed in His Biological Dictionary of People Associated with the City. LC 93-47288. (Islamic History & Civilization, Studies & Texts Ser.: Vol. 5). 1994. 83.00 (*90-04-09956-5*) E J Brill.

Morray, J. P. Project Kuzbas: American Workers in Siberia, 1921-1926. LC 83-12607. (Illus.). 204p. 1983. pap. 4.75 (*0-7178-0606-5*) Intl Pubs Co.

Morray, Jeffrey P. Pediatric Intensive Care. (Illus.). 581p. 1987. boxed 90.00 (*0-8385-7800-4*, A7800-4) Appleton & Lange.

Morray, Joseph P. From Yalta to Disarmament: Cold War Debate. LC 73-19225. 368p. 1974. reprint ed. text ed. 39.75 (*0-8371-7306-X*, MOYD, Greenwood Pr) Greenwood.

Morre, Alvin, tr. see Guenon, Rene & Lings, Martin, eds.

Morre, D. J., et al, eds. Molecular Mechanisms of Membrane Traffic. LC 93-1200. 1993. 171.00 (*0-387-53096-7*) Spr-Verlag.

Morre, Roger, jt. auth. see Day, Chris.

Morreale, Ben, jt. auth. see Mangione, Jerre.

Morreale, Cyndy & Morreale, Sam. Twenty-Two Days in the West Indies: The Itinerary Planner. (Illus.). 136p. (Orig.). 1987. pap. 7.95 (*0-912528-74-5*) John Muir.

Morreale, Joanne. A New Beginning: A Textual Frame Analysis of the Political Campaign Film. LC 90-9904. (SUNY Series in Speech Communication). 154p. 1991. 57.50 (*0-7914-0608-3*); pap. 18.95 (*0-7914-0609-1*) State U NY Pr.

— The Presidential Campaign Film: A Critical History. LC 93-20129. (Praeger Series in Political Communication). 224p. 1993. text ed. 49.95 (*0-275-93882-4*, C3882, Praeger Pubs) Greenwood.

Morreale, Sam, jt. auth. see Morreale, Cyndy.

Morreale, Sherwyn P., et al, eds. The Competent Speaker Speech Evaluation Form. 65p. (Orig.). (C). 1993. pap. text ed. 20.00 (*0-944811-13-2*) Speech Commun Assn.

Morreale, Vin, Jr. Breaking & Entering. 1994. 4.95 (*0-87129-284-X*, B75) Dramatic Pub.

— The Day the Woods Were One. (Orig.). (J). (gr. 3 up). 1985. pap. 6.00 (*0-88734-507-7*) Players Pr.

— It'll All Come Out in the Wash. (Orig.). 1985. pap. 6.00 (*0-88734-207-8*) Players Pr.

Morreall, John. Taking Laughter Seriously. LC 82-5858. 144p. (C). 1983. 64.50 (*0-87395-642-7*); pap. 21.95 (*0-87395-643-5*) State U NY Pr.

Morreall, John, ed. The Philosophy of Laughter & Humor. LC 86-14498. (SUNY Series in Philosophy). 270p. (C). 1986. 64.50 (*0-88706-326-8*); pap. 21.95 (*0-88706-327-6*) State U NY Pr.

Morreau, Jacqueline. Jacqueline Morreau. LC 86-4000. (Drawings & Graphics Ser.). (Illus.). 192p. 1986. 32.50 (*0-8108-1888-4*) Scarecrow.

Morreau, Jacqueline, jt. auth. see Kent, Sarah.

Morreau, M., jt. ed. see Fuhrmann, A.

Morreau, Michael, tr. see Gamut, L. T.

Morreim, Dennis. The Road to Recovery: Bridges Between the Bible & the Twelve Steps. LC 89-49091. 144p. (Orig.). 1990. pap. 5.99 (*0-8066-2456-6*, 9-2456) Augsburg Fortress.

Morreim, Dennis C. Changed Lives: The Story of Alcoholics Anonymous. (J). (ps-3). 1991. pap. 8.99 (*0-8066-2548-1*, 9-2548) Augsburg Fortress.

Morreim, E. Haavi. Balancing Act: The New Medical Ethics of Medicine's New Economics. (C). 1991. lib. bdg. 67.50 (*0-7923-1170-1*) Kluwer Ac.

— Balancing Act: The New Medical Ethics of Medicine's New Economics. 1995. 17.95 (*0-87840-584-4*) Georgetown U Pr.

Morrell, Anne. Contemporary Embroidery: Exciting & Innovative Textile Art. (Illus.). 160p. 1994. 29.95 (*0-289-80105-2*, Pub. by Studio Vista Bks UK) Sterling.

— Techniques of Indian Embroidery. (Illus.). 128p. 1994. 34.95 (*0-7134-6410-0*, Pub. by Batsford UK) Trafalgar.

— Techniques of Indian Embroidery. 144p. 1995. pap. 18.95 (*1-883010-08-X*) Interweave.

Morrell, Bernard B., jt. auth. see Bittinger, Marvin L.

***Morrell, Brad.** Pearl Jam Illustrated Biography. Date not set. pap. 9.95 (*0-7119-3457-6*) Omnibus NY.

***Morrell, Carol, ed.** Grammar of Dissent. 1995. pap. 14.95 (*0-86492-141-1*) InBook.

Morrell, David. The Art of General Practice. (Illus.). 168p. 1991. 45.00 (*0-19-261988-8*); pap. 19.95 (*0-19-261990-X*) OUP.

— Assumed Identity. 512p. 1994. mass mkt. 6.50 (*0-446-60070-9*, Warner Vision) Warner Bks.

— Assumed Identity. large type ed. 1994. 23.95 (*0-7927-1959-X*, Paragon Lrg Print) Chivers N Amer.

— Blood Oath. 240p. 1983. mass mkt. 4.95 (*0-449-20391-3*) Fawcett.

— Blood Oath Vol. 1. 1994. pap. 5.99 (*0-312-95345-3*) St Martin.

— The Brotherhood of the Rose. 352p. 1984. mass mkt. 5.95 (*0-449-20661-0*, Crest) Fawcett.

— The Brotherhood of the Rose. large type ed. 496p. 1987. 23.95 (*0-7089-8381-2*, Charnwood) Ulverscroft.

— The Covenant of the Flame. 1991. 19.95 (*0-446-51563-9*) Warner Bks.

— The Covenant of the Flame. 480p. 1992. mass mkt. 6.50 (*0-446-36292-1*) Warner Bks.

— Desperate Measures. 416p. 1994. 22.95 (*0-446-51791-7*) Warner Bks.

— Desperate Measures. 1995. mass mkt. 6.99 (*0-446-60239-6*, Warner Vision) Warner Bks.

— The Fifth Profession. 1990. 19.95 (*0-446-51562-0*) Warner Bks.

— The Fifth Profession. 512p. 1991. mass mkt. 6.50 (*0-446-36087-2*) Warner Bks.

— First Blood. deluxe ed. LC 90-45660. 256p. 1990. 25.00 (*0-922890-64-1*) Armchair Detective.

— First Blood. limited ed. LC 90-45660. 256p. 1990. 75.00 (*0-922890-65-X*) Armchair Detective.

— First Blood. LC 90-45660. 256p. 1990. reprint ed. 18.95 (*0-922890-63-3*) Armchair Detective.

— Fraternity of the Stone. 1986. mass mkt. 4.50 (*0-449-44505-4*, Crest); mass mkt. 5.99 (*0-449-20973-3*) Fawcett.

— The Fraternity of the Stone. large type ed. 560p. 1987. 23.95 (*0-7089-8397-9*, Charnwood) Ulverscroft.

— Last Reveille. 272p. 1994. mass mkt. 5.99 (*0-446-36442-8*) Warner Bks.

— The League of Night & Fog. large type ed. 532p. 1989. 17.95 (*0-7089-1936-7*) Ulverscroft.

— Testament. 352p. 1993. mass mkt. 5.99 (*0-446-36448-7*) Warner Bks.

— The Totem. 352p. 1995. mass mkt. 6.50 (*0-446-36446-0*) Warner Bks.

— The Totem (Complete & Unaltered) (Illus.). 1994. boxed 100.00 (*1-880418-25-8*) D M Grant.

— The Totem (Complete & Unaltered) deluxe ed. (Illus.). 1994. 24.95 (*1-880418-26-6*) D M Grant.

Morrell, David, ed. Epidemiology in General Practice. (Oxford General Practice Ser.: No. 14). (Illus.). 176p. 1988. pap. 33.50 (*0-19-261603-X*) OUP.

Morrell, F., ed. Kindling & Synaptic Plasticity: The Legacy of Graham Goddard. xvi, 304p. 1991. 105.00 (*0-8176-3466-5*) Spr-Verlag.

***Morrell, Gordon W.** Britain Confronts the Stalin Revolution: Anglo-Soviet Relations & the Metro-Vickers' Crisis. 232p. (C). 1995. text ed. 35.00 (*0-88920-250-8*, Pub. by Wilfrid Laurier CN) Humanities.

Morrell, Jack & Thackray, Arnold, eds. Gentlemen of Science: Early Correspondence of the British Association for the Advancement of Science. (Royal Historical Society: Camden Fourth Ser.: No. 30). 382p. 1985. 30.00 (*0-86193-103-3*) Boydell & Brewer.

Morrell, Jack, jt. auth. see Inkster, Ian.

Morrell, James R. Spiritism & the Beginnings of Christianity. 87p. 1963. reprint ed. spiral bd. 3.30 (*0-7873-0625-8*) Mokelumne.

Morrell, Janet M. Four English Comedies. 1982. pap. 9.05 (*0-14-043158-6*, Penguin Classics) Viking Penguin.

Morrell, Jeffrey J., jt. auth. see Zabel, Robert A.

Morrell, Karen. Bachelor for Rent. 1993. 13.95 (*0-8034-9011-9*) Bouregy.

— Twice in a Blue Moon. 1993. 13.95 (*0-8034-9021-6*) Bouregy.

Morrell, L. C., ed. Holloway - Amiss - Leavell Family. 62p. 1994. reprint ed. pap. 13.00 (*0-8328-4135-8*) Higginson Bk Co.

Morrell, Louis, ed. It's Your Future: Financial Planning for Retirement. 2nd ed. 16p. 1992. 4.00 (*1-878240-14-5*) Coll & U Personnel.

Morrell, Louis R. Retirement Plan Alternatives: The Role of the Business Officer. LC 94-20948. 1994. write for info. (*0-915164-95-7*) NACUBO.

Morrell, Martha J., jt. auth. see Sperling, Michael R.

Morrell, Patrick. Design of Reinforced Concrete Elements. (Illus.). 1977. pap. 26.95 (*0-8464-0320-X*) Beekman Pubs.

Morrell, Robert E. Sand & Pebbles: The Tales of Muju Ichien, a Voice for Pluralism in Kamakura Buddhism. LC 84-16348. (SUNY Series in Buddhist Studies). 383p. 1985. 64.50 (*0-88706-059-5*); pap. 21.95 (*0-88706-060-9*) State U NY Pr.

M

Morrell, Samuel. Precedent & Judicial Discretion: The Case of Joseph ibn Lev. (USF Studies in the History of Judaism). 213p. 1991. 59.95 (*1-55540-616-5*, 240026) Scholars Pr GA.

Morrell, Sydney. Spheres of Influence. LC 70-142672. (Essay Index Reprint Ser.). 1977. 23.95 (*0-8369-2197-6*) Ayer.

Morrell, W. P. Gold Rushes. 2nd ed. LC 67-23287. (Illus.). 1968. 18.95 (*0-8023-1140-7*) Dufour.

Morrell, Z. N. Flowers & Fruits from the Wilderness; or Thirty-six Years in Texas & Two Winters in Honduras. LC 76-12002. (Illus.). 428p. 1976. reprint ed. pap. 5.95 (*0-918954-17-7*) Baylor Univ Pr.

Morren, George E., Jr. The Miyanmin: Human Ecology of a Papua New Guinea Society. Kottak, Conrad P., ed. LC 85-20817. (Studies in Cultural Anthropology Ser.). (Illus.). 374p. (C). 1986. reprint ed. text ed. 32.95 (*0-8138-0579-1*) Iowa St U Pr.

Morren, George E., Jr., jt. auth. see Wilson, Kathleen.

Morresi, Angelo, jt. auth. see Cheremisinoff, Paul N.

Morresi, W., jt. auth. see Salmons, J.

Morrett, John J. Soldier Priest. Jones, M. L., ed. 304p. (Orig.). 1992. pap. 12.95 (*1-882270-01-0*) Old Rugged Cross.

Morrey-Bailey, Alice. Stellarian. LC 86-81777. 158p. 1986. 9.98 (*0-88290-279-2*) Horizon Utah.

Morrey, Bernard F. The Elbow & Its Disorders. 2nd ed. (Illus.). 944p. 1993. text ed. 175.00 (*0-7216-6794-5*) Saunders.

Morrey, Bernard F., ed. Biological, Material, & Mechanical Considerations of Joint Replacement. LC 93-20466. (Bristol-Myers - Squibb-Zimmer Orthopaedic Research Symposia Ser.). 480p. 1993. 103.00 (*0-7817-0008-6*) Raven.

— The Elbow. LC 93-4630. (Master Techniques in Orthopaedic Surgery Ser.). (Illus.). 368p. 1994. 189.00 (*0-7817-0036-1*) Raven.

— Joint Replacement Arthroplasty. (Illus.). 1252p. 1991. text ed. 220.00 (*0-443-08725-3*) Churchill.

Morrey, C. B., Jr., ed. see Pure Mathematics Symposium Staff.

Morrey, Charles B., Jr. Multiple Integrals in the Calculus of Variations. (Grundlehren der Mathematischen Wissenschaften Ser.: Vol. 130). 1966. 98.00 (*0-387-03524-9*) Spr-Verlag.

Morrey, Charles B., Jr., jt. auth. see Protter, Murray H.

***Morrical, Guy.** Geometry Flipper No. 2. 49p. (YA). (gr. 9 up). 1994. 6.25 (*1-878383-28-0*) C Lee Pubns.

Morrical, Guy & Churchill, Eric R. Geometry Flipper, Vol. 1. 49p. (YA). (gr. 7 up). 1989. reprint ed. 6.25 (*1-878383-04-3*) C Lee Pubns.

Morrice. Tale of Two Cities (Dickens) (Book Notes Ser.). (C). 1984. pap. 2.50 (*0-8120-3444-9*) Barron.

Morrice, J. K. Crisis Intervention: Case Histories. Kahn, J. H., ed. 117p. 1976. 51.00 (*0-08-019742-6*, Pub. by Pergamon Repr UK) Franklin.

Morrice, Ken. The Scampering Marmoset. 60p. 1990. pap. text ed. 12.00 (*0-08-040927-X*, Pub. by Aberdeen U Pr) Macmillan.

Morrice, Ken, ed. When Truth Is Known. 72p. 1986. pap. text ed. 5.75 (*0-08-032451-7*, R140, K150, Pergamon Pr) Elsevier.

Morrice, Nancy, ed. see Chirlian, Paul.

Morrice, Polly & Moynihan, Daniel P. The French Americans. (Peoples of North America Ser.). (Illus.). 112p. (J). (gr. 5 up). 1988. lib. bdg. 17.95 (*0-87754-878-1*) Chelsea Hse.

Morrice, Thomas. An Apology for Schoole-Masters. LC 76-57401. (English Experience Ser.: No. 817). 1977. reprint ed. lib. bdg. 20.00 (*90-221-0817-1*) Walter J Johnson.

***Morrice, William G.** The Durham New Testament Greek Course: A Three Month Introduction. 127p. 1993. pap. 12.95 (*0-85364-556-6*, Pub. by Paternoster UK) Attic Pr.

— Joy in the New Testament. 144p. (Orig.). 1982. pap. 13.50 (*0-85364-340-7*) Attic Pr.

Morrien, Adrian. Use of a Wall Mirror. Leigh-Loohuizen, Ria, tr. 1970. pap. 6.00 (*0-912136-17-0*) Twowindows Pr.

Morrill, B. & Irvine, T. N. Introduction to Equilibrium Thermodynamics. LC 73-173824. (Pergamon Unified Engineering Ser.). 1972. 154.00 (*0-08-016891-4*, Pub. by Pergamon Repr UK) Franklin.

***Morrill, Calvin.** The Executive Way: Conflict Management in Corporations. LC 94-33344. 1995. pap. text ed. 29.95 (*0-226-53873-7*) U Ch Pr.

Morrill, Dan. Southern Campaigns of the American Revolution. 300p. 1993. 26.95 (*1-877853-21-6*) Nautical & Aviation.

Morrill, Dexter, comp. Woody Herman: A Guide to the Big Band Recordings, 1936-1987. LC 90-13989. (Discographies Ser.: No. 40). 144p. 1990. text ed. 39.95 (*0-313-27756-7*, MGJ/, Greenwood Pr) Greenwood.

Morrill, Georgiana L., ed. Speculum Guidonis de Warewyke. (EETS, ES Ser.: No. 75). 1974. reprint ed. 42.00 (*0-527-00277-1*) Periodicals Srv.

***Morrill, Glyn V.** Type Logical Grammar: Categorical Logic of Signs. LC 94-33169. 1994. lib. bdg. 99.00 (*0-7923-3095-1*) Kluwer Ac.

Morrill, Harriet. Structured Programming with True BASIC. (C). 1987. pap. text ed. 24.25 (*0-673-39061-6*) HarpCollege.

Morrill, James L. The Ongoing State University. LC 60-9636. 153p. reprint ed. pap. 43.70 (*0-317-29450-4*, 2055892) Bks Demand.

Morrill, John. The Nature of the English Revolution: Essays. LC 92-25941. 480p. (C). 1992. text ed. 62.95 (*0-582-08941-7*, 79647) Longman.

— The Nature of the English Revolution: Essays. LC 92-25941. 480p. (C). 1994. pap. text ed. 31.50 (*0-582-08942-5*, 79646) Longman.

— Oliver Cromwell & the English Revolution. 352p. (C). 1990. pap. text ed. 25.95 (*0-582-01675-4*, 78528) Longman.

Morrill, John, ed. The National Convenant in Its British Context, Sixteen Thirty-Eight to Fifty-One. 1990. text ed. 45.00 (*0-685-54170-3*, Pub. by Edinburgh U Pr UK) Col U Pr.

— The National Convenant in Its British Context 1638-51. 240p. 1990. 45.00 (*0-7486-0203-8*, Pub. by Edinburgh U Pr UK) Col U Pr.

— Revolution & Restoration. (History Today Book Ser.). (Illus.). 160p. 1993. pap. 22.95 (*1-85585-137-7*) Trafalgar.

Morrill, John, jt. auth. see Du Pont, Peter.

Morrill, John, jt. auth. see Guy, John S.

Morrill, John, ed. see Jones, Norman.

Morrill, John, jt. auth. see Wilson, Alex.

Morrill, John, et al, eds. Public Duty & Private Conscience in Seventeenth-Century England: Essays Presented to G. E. Aylmer. LC 92-32519. (Illus.). 352p. 1993. 55.00 (*0-19-820229-6*, Clarendon Pr) OUP.

Morrill, Judi S., jt. auth. see Deutsch, Ronald M.

Morrill, Paul H. & Spees, Emil R. The Academic Profession: Teaching in Higher Education. LC 81-4136. 363p. 1982. 35.95 (*0-89885-008-8*) Human Sci Pr.

Morrill, Penny C. Mexican Silver: Twentieth Century Handwrought Jewelry & Metalwork. LC 94-65616. (Illus.). 224p. 1994. 59.95 (*0-88740-610-6*) Schiffer.

Morrill, Peter & Thio, Alex. Sociology: Student Review Manual. 2nd ed. (C). 1990. student ed, text ed. 11.25 (*0-06-044662-5*) HarpCollege.

Morrill, Richard L. Political Redistricting & Geographic Theory. Knight, C. Gregory, ed. LC 81-69235. (Resource Publications in Geography). (Orig.). 1981. pap. 10.00 (*0-89291-159-X*) Assn Am Geographers.

— Teaching Values in College. LC 80-8003. (Jossey-Bass Series in Higher Education). 191p. reprint ed. pap. 54.50 (*0-8357-4692-5*, 2052347) Bks Demand.

Morrill, Sibley S. The Texas Cannibals, or, Why Father Serra Came to California. 28p. 1964. 5.00 (*0-910740-04-6*) Holmes.

Morrill, Terence C. Lanthanide Shift Reagents in Stereochemical Analysis, Vol. 5. (Illus.). 193p. 1987. lib. bdg. 65.00 (*0-89573-119-3*) VCH Pubs.

***Morrill, Wendell J., ed.** Insect Pests of Small Grains. 145p. Date not set. 57.00 (*0-89054-200-7*) Am Phytopathol Soc.

Morrione, Thomas J., ed. see Blumer, Herbert.

Morris. Adult Education Procedures. 1985. pap. 5.95 (*0-8164-2000-9*) Harper SF.

— Art of Conversation. 1986. pap. 7.95 (*0-671-63275-2*) S&S Trade.

— Artificial Flower Arranger's Companion. 1995. (*0-7858-0312-2*) Bk Sales Inc.

— At the Head of the Class. 1995. 22.95 (*0-8057-9129-9*, Twayne); pap. 15.95 (*0-8057-9130-2*, Twayne) Macmillan.

— Canadian Nurses & the Law. 256p. 1991. 49.00 (*0-409-80190-9*) Butterworth Legal Pubs.

— Cancer Risk Assessment: A Quantitative Approach. (Occupational Safety & Health Ser.: Vol. 20). 416p. 1990. 125.00 (*0-8247-8239-9*) Dekker.

— Candlestick Charting Explained: Timeless Techniques for Trading Stocks & Futures. 1995. pap. text ed. 35.00 (*1-55738-891-1*) Probus Pub Co.

— The Candywine Development. 5.95 (*0-8065-0149-9*, Citadel Pr) Carol Pub Group.

— Color Atlas of Baby Delivery. (Illus.). 1991. write for info. (*0-8151-5953-6*, Yr Bk Med Pubs) Mosby Yr Bk.

— Crime & Punishment (Dostoevski) (Book Notes Ser.). (C). 1984. pap. 2.50 (*0-8120-3409-0*) Barron.

— Dictionary of Communication Disorders. 2nd ed. 244p. 1992. pap. 37.75 (*1-56593-371-0*, 0319) Singular Publishing.

— Drummer Boy at Bull Run. (Bonnets & Bugles Ser.: No. 1). 1995. pap. 5.99 (*0-8024-0911-3*) Moody.

— ICH in Gastroenterology. 1993. 24.95 (*0-8151-6222-7*, Yr Bk Med Pubs) Mosby Yr Bk.

— Introductory Astronomy for Nonscience Majors. 640p. 1995. 45.95 (*0-8016-2689-7*) Mosby Yr Bk.

— Karate Kata. 1995. pap. 12.99 (*0-517-12350-9*) Random.

— Lettering Book of Alphabets. 1995. pap. (*0-590-20514-5*) Scholastic Inc.

— Lotus Symphony Two Handbook. 1990. pap. 47.95 (*0-434-91302-2*) Buttrwrth-Heinemann.

— Measurement & Calibration for Quality Assurance. 300p. 1991. pap. text ed. 57.00 (*0-13-567652-5*) P-H.

— Microscopic & Spectroscopic Imaging of the Chemical State. (Practical Spectroscopy Ser.: Vol. 16). 512p. 1993. 190.00 (*0-8247-9104-5*) Dekker.

— Monkeys & Apes. 1984. pap. text ed. (*0-8393-0286-X*) Raintree Steck-V.

— Newnes PC User's Pocket Book. 1991. 29.95 (*0-7506-0085-3*) Buttrwrth-Heinemann.

— Nixon Bio, Vol. 2. 1992. 26.95 (*0-8050-1365-2*) H Holt & Co.

— No Acting Please. 1995. pap. text ed. 11.95 (*0-9629709-3-X*) Ermor Enter.

— One Hundred Ninety-Eight Easy Wood Projects. 1989. pap. 11.00 (*0-87006-629-3*) Goodheart.

— Runaway Balloon, Rescue in the Trinity River, Apartment Inferno. (Real Kids, Real Adventures Ser.: No. 3). (J). 1995. pap. text ed. (*0-8054-4053-4*) Broadman.

— Scientific Creationism. 1986. 8.95 (*0-89051-003-2*) Master Bks.

— Seven Sleepers the Sword of Camelot. 1995. pap. 5.99 (*0-8024-3683-8*) Moody.

— Shark Attack, Rescue at Nordic Valley, Emergency at Chitek Lake. (Real Kids, Real Adventures Ser.: No. 4). (J). 1995. pap. text ed. (*0-8054-4054-2*) Broadman.

— Skybusters. 1995. pap. (*0-590-22285-6*) Scholastic Inc.

— Spacebusters. 1995. pap. (*0-590-22284-8*) Scholastic Inc.

— Special Education. (C). 1986. 65.95 (*0-205-14423-3*, H4423) Allyn.

— Supplement Real Estate Tax '81. 1981. 15.00 (*0-316-58393-6*) Little.

— Sydney. 1994. pap. 4.99 (*0-517-13037-8*) Random.

— Taste the Good Life: New Checking. 1992. ring bd., pap. 10.95 (*0-9631249-0-0*) Morris Pubng.

— Three Works. (C). 1968. pap. 15.00 (*0-85315-170-9*, Pub. by Lawrence & Wishart UK) Humanities.

— Using Gem Paint on the Amstrad 1512. 2nd ed. 1987. 24.95 (*0-685-63315-2*) Buttrwrth-Heinemann.

— Watt Pottery Identification & Value Guide. 160p. 1992. 19.95 (*0-89145-527-2*) Collector Bks.

— Women in Computing. 124p. 1989. pap. 24.95 (*1-85384-004-1*) Buttrwrth-Heinemann.

***Morris & Kinder.** Accident & Emergency Data & Drug Guide. 1995. pap. write for info. (*0-7506-2035-8*, Focal) Buttrwrth-Heinemann.

Morris & Sawyer. A Walk in the Garden: Biblical Iconographical & Literary Images of Eden. (JSOT Supplement Ser.: No. 136). 370p. (C). 1992. 35.00 (*1-85075-338-5*, Pub. by Sheffield Acad UK) CUP Services.

Morris & Tilney. Transplantation Reviews. 2nd ed. 240p. 1988. text ed. 71.50 (*0-7216-2869-9*) Saunders.

— Transplantation Reviews, Vol. 1. 1987. text ed. 75.00 (*0-8089-1884-2*, Grune) Saunders.

— Transplantation Reviews, Vol. 3. (Illus.). 240p. 1989. text ed. 77.95 (*0-7216-3288-2*) Saunders.

Morris, jt. auth. see Bardach.

Morris, jt. auth. see Berry.

Morris, jt. auth. see Lawrie.

Morris, jt. auth. see Mishkin.

Morris, et al. Complications of Plastic Surgery. 504p. 1989. text ed. 121.00 (*0-7020-1360-9*) Saunders.

Morris, A., jt. auth. see Gardiner, G.

Morris, A. E. A History of Urban Form: Before the Industrial Revolution. 3rd ed. LC 92-30438. 444p. 1994. pap. text ed. 41.95 (*0-470-21962-9*) Halsted Pr.

Morris, A. Earl. The Long Road. Jones, M. L., ed. 336p. (Orig.). 1993. pap. text ed. 12.95 (*1-882270-10-X*) Old Rugged Cross.

***Morris, A. I. & Quest, Barry.** Design: The Modern Law & Practice. 2nd ed. 1995. ring bd. write for info. (*0-406-01359-4*, UK) Butterworth Legal Pubs.

— Design - the Modern Law & Practice. 1987. 132.00 (*0-406-10320-8*, U.K.) Butterworth Legal Pubs.

Morris, A. J. C. P. Trevelyan, Eighteen Seventy to Nineteen Fifty-Eight: Portrait of a Radical. 1979. text ed. 29.95 (*0-312-11242-4*) St Martin.

Morris, A. L. & Barras, R. C., eds. Air Quality Meteorology & Atmospheric Ozone - STP 653. 639p. 1978. 55.00 (*0-8031-0275-5*, 04-653000-17) ASTM.

Morris, A. S., jt. ed. see Zalala, A. M.

Morris, A. V., jt. auth. see Collinson, William E.

Morris, Adalaide K. Wallace Stevens: Imagination & Faith. LC 73-2495. (Essays in Literature Ser.). 192p. 1974. 35.00x (*0-691-06265-X*) Princeton U Pr.

— Wallace Stevens: Imagination & Faith. LC 73-2495. (Princeton Essays in Literature Ser.). reprint ed. pap. 62.20 (*0-7837-9288-3*, 2060027) Bks Demand.

Morris, Adrian, tr. see Mesina, M., et al, eds.

Morris, Adriana, tr. see Anink, David, et al.

Morris, Alan. Collaboration & Resistance Reviewed: Writers & 'la Mode Retro' in Post-Gaullist France. 210p. 1992. 35.95 (*0-85496-634-X*) Berg Pubs.

Morris, Alan S. Principles of Measurement & Instrumentation. 2nd ed. LC 93-3286. 1993. pap. text ed. 72.00 (*0-13-489709-9*) P-H.

Morris, Aldon & Mueller, Carol M., eds. Frontiers in Social Movement Theory. 400p. (C). 1992. pap. text ed. 22.00 (*0-300-05486-6*) Yale U Pr.

Morris, Aldon D. The Origins of the Civil Rights Movement: Black Communities Organizing for Change. LC 84-10272. (Illus.). 368p. 1984. 24.95 (*0-02-922120-X*) Free Pr.

— The Origins of the Civil Rights Movement: Black Communities Organizing for Change. 1986. pap. 14.95 (*0-02-922130-7*) Free Pr.

***Morris, Aldyth.** Captain James Cook. LC 94-48698. (Illus.). 1995. pap. 8.95 (*0-8248-1670-6*) UH Pr.

— Damien. LC 79-22915. 44p. 1980. pap. text ed. 7.00 (*0-8248-1323-5*) UH Pr.

— Lili'uokalani. LC 93-3717. (Illus.). 88p. (C). 1993. pap. 9.95 (*0-8248-1543-2*) UH Pr.

— Robert Louis Stevenson - Appointment on Moloka'I. LC 94-48702. (Illus.). 60p. 1995. pap. 8.95 (*0-8248-1671-4*) UH Pr.

Morris, Alexander. The Treaties of Canada with the Indians of Manitoba & North-West Territories. LC 76-43792. reprint ed. write for info. (*0-404-15647-9*) AMS Pr.

Morris, Alfred & Sizer, John. Resources & Higher Education. 226p. 1983. 29.00 (*0-900868-90-2*, Open Univ Pr) Taylor & Francis.

Morris, Alfred F. Sports Medicine & Athletic Injuries. 396p. (C). 1984. pap. write for info. (*0-697-00087-7*) Brown & Benchmark.

Morris, Alison, jt. auth. see Giller, Henri.

Morris, Alistair & Gardiner, Gordon. Automobilia of Europe: Reference & Price Guide. (Illus.). 256p. 1992. reprint ed. 49.50 (*1-85149-163-5*) Antique Collect.

***Morris, Allen.** The Florida Handbook 1991-1992. (Illus.). 720p. 1991. text ed. 37.95 (*0-9616000-3-9*) Peninsular Pub Co.

— The Florida Handbook, 1993-1994. (Illus.). 725p. reprint ed. text ed. 37.95 (*0-9616000-4-7*) Peninsular Pub Co.

— The Florida Handbook 1995-96. 25th ed. (Illus.). 700p. 1995. text ed. 38.95 (*0-9616000-5-5*) Peninsular Pub Co.

— Florida Place Names: Alachua to Zolfo Springs. Morris, Joan P., ed. (Illus.). 250p. 1995. 21.95 (*1-56164-084-0*) Pineapple Pr.

Morris, Allison. Women Crime & Criminal Justice. 256p. (Orig.). (C). 1987. pap. text ed. 24.95 (*0-631-15445-0*) Blackwell Pubs.

Morris, Allison, jt. ed. see Gelsthorpe, Loraine.

Morris, Alton C., ed. Folksongs of Florida: A Florida Sand Dollar Book. 488p. 1990. pap. 19.95 (*0-8130-0983-9*) U Press Fla.

Morris, Alton C., jt. auth. see Bloodworth, Bertha E.

Morris, Alton C., et al. College English. 8th ed. 839p. (C). 1983. text ed. 33.25 (*0-15-508209-4*) HB Coll Pubs.

— Imaginative Literature: Fiction, Drama, Poetry. 4th ed. 829p. (C). 1983. pap. text ed. 21.50 (*0-15-540732-5*) HB Coll Pubs.

Morris, Andrew. ULTIMA VII Clue Book: Key to the Black Gate. (Illus.). 64p. (Orig.). 1992. pap. 14.95 (*0-929373-09-X*) Origin Syst.

Morris, Andrew, jt. auth. see Hobbs, Sheri.

Morris, Andrew J., jt. auth. see Larimer County Heritage Association Staff.

***Morris, Ann.** The Animal Book. LC 95-13804. (World's Family Ser.). (J). 1995. write for info. (*0-382-24701-9*); lib. bdg. write for info. (*0-382-24702-7*); pap. write for info. (*0-382-24703-5*) Silver Burdett Pr.

— Bread, Bread, Bread. LC 82-26677. (Illus.). 32p. (J). (ps-2). 1989. 16.00 (*0-688-06334-9*); lib. bdg. 15.93 (*0-688-06335-7*) Lothrop.

— Bread, Bread, Bread. LC 92-25547. (Illus.). 32p. (J). (gr. k up). 1993. reprint ed. pap. 4.95 (*0-688-12275-2*, Mulberry) Morrow.

— Bread, Bread, Bread: Big Book Edition. 32p. (J). (gr. k up). 1993. pap. 18.95 (*0-688-12939-0*, Mulberry) Morrow.

— Dancing to America. (Illus.). 40p. (J). (gr. 2-7). 1994. 15.99 (*0-525-45128-5*) Dutton Child Bks.

— Hats, Hats, Hats. LC 88-26676. (Illus.). 32p. (J). (ps-2). 1989. 16.00 (*0-688-06338-1*); lib. bdg. 15.93 (*0-688-06339-X*) Lothrop.

— Hats, Hats, Hats. LC 92-25548. (Illus.). 32p. (J). (ps up). 1993. reprint ed. pap. 4.95 (*0-688-12274-4*, Mulberry) Morrow.

— Hats, Hats, Hats: Big Book Edition. 32p. (J). (ps up). 1993. pap. 18.95 (*0-688-12938-2*, Mulberry) Morrow.

— Houses & Homes. Pearson, Susan, ed. LC 92-1365. (Illus.). 32p. (J). (ps-2). 1992. 14.00 (*0-688-10168-2*); lib. bdg. 13.93 (*0-688-10169-0*) Lothrop.

— Houses & Homes. Cohn, Amy, ed. LC 92-1365. (Illus.). 32p. (J). (gr. k up). 1995. reprint ed. pap. 4.95 (*0-688-13578-1*, Mulberry) Morrow.

— How Teddy Bears Are Made. LC 93-44617. (Illus.). (J). 1994. 10.95 (*0-590-47152-X*, Cartwheel) Scholastic Inc.

— I Am Six. LC 94-30495. (J). 1995. 16.95 (*0-382-24686-1*); lib. bdg. 14.95 (*0-382-24759-0*); pap. 3.95 (*0-382-24688-8*) Silver Burdett Pr.

— Just One Seed. (ESL Theme Links Ser.). (Illus.). (J). (gr. k-3). 1993. 99.50 (*1-56334-308-8*); audio 10.50 (*1-56334-306-1*); 35.00 (*1-56334-307-X*) Hampton-Brown.

— Loving. (Illus.). 32p. (J). 1990. 13.95 (*0-688-06340-3*); lib. bdg. 13.88 (*0-688-06341-1*) Lothrop.

— Loving. Cohn, Amy, ed. LC 90-33844. (Illus.). 32p. (J). (gr. k up). 1994. reprint ed. pap. 4.95 (*0-688-13613-3*, Mulberry) Morrow.

— Machines. 2nd ed. (Let Me Read, Level 1, Ser.). (Illus.). (J). 1995. bds. 2.95 (*0-673-36268-X*) GdYrBks.

— The Mommy Book. LC 95-12237. (World's Family Ser.). (Illus.). (J). 1996. write for info. (*0-382-24692-6*); lib. bdg. write for info. (*0-382-24693-4*); pap. write for info. (*0-382-24694-2*) Silver Burdett Pr.

— On the Go. Cohn, Amy, ed. LC 90-33842. (Illus.). 32p. (J). (gr. k up). 1994. reprint ed. pap. 4.95 (*0-688-13637-0*, Mulberry) Morrow.

— On Their Toes: A Russian Ballet School. LC 91-11903. (Illus.). 56p. (J). (gr. 3-7). 1991. text ed. 14.95 (*0-689-31660-7*, Atheneum Bks Young) S&S Childrens.

— Puddle Jumper. LC 92-14763. (Illus.). 1993. write for info. (*0-688-10204-2*); lib. bdg. write for info. (*0-688-10205-0*) Lothrop.

— Seven Hundred Kids on Grandpa's Farm. (Illus.). 32p. (J). (ps-3). 1994. 14.99 (*0-525-45162-5*, DCB) Dutton Child Bks.

— Shoes, Shoes, Shoes. LC 94-46649. (Illus.). 1885. lib. bdg. write for info. (*0-688-13667-2*) Lothrop.

— Shoes, Shoes, Shoes. LC 94-46649. (Illus.). (J). 1995. write for info. (*0-688-13666-4*) Lothrop.

— Tools. (ESL Theme Links Ser.). (Illus.). 24p. (J). (gr. k-3). 1993. teacher ed 15.00 (*1-56334-302-9*); Big Book. pap. text ed. 29.95 (*1-56334-300-2*); Small Book. pap. text ed. 6.00 (*1-56334-301-0*); student ed, teacher ed 10.50 (*1-56334-303-7*); student ed, teacher ed 35.00 (*1-56334-304-5*); student ed, teacher ed 99.50 (*1-56334-305-3*) Hampton-Brown.

— Tools. LC 92-3871. (Illus.). 32p. (J). (ps-2). 1992. 14.00 (*0-688-10170-4*); lib. bdg. 13.93 (*0-688-10171-2*) Lothrop.

— Weddings. LC 94-48040. (J). 1995. write for info. (*0-688-13272-3*); lib. bdg. write for info. (*0-688-13273-1*) Lothrop.

Morris, Ann & Ambrose, Henrietta. North Webster: A Photographic History of a Black Community. LC 93-9619. 1993. 35.00 (*0-253-33895-6*); pap. 19.95 (*0-253-28601-8*) Ind U Pr.

Morris, Ann R. Winesburg, Ohio Notes. 61p. (Orig.). (C). 1974. pap. text ed. 3.75 (*0-8220-1382-7*) Cliffs.

Morris, Ann R., jt. auth. see Dunn, Margaret M.

Morris, Anne, ed. Application of Expert Systems in Library & Information Centres. 247p. 1992. 65.00 (*0-86291-276-8*) Bowker-Saur.

Morris, Anne, jt. auth. see Dyer, Hilary.

Morris, Anne, jt. ed. see Jones, Michael.
Morris, Anne C., ed. see Morris, Gouverneur.
Morris, Anne E. & Nott, Susan M. Working Women & the Law: Equality & Discrimination in Theory & Practice. 272p. (C). 1991. text ed. 55.00 (*0-415-05739-6*, A4904) Routledge.
— Working Women & the Law: Equality & Discrimination in Theory & Practice. 272p. 1992. pap. 17.95 (*0-415-00937-5*, A9855) Routledge.
Morris, Arthur. Latin America: Economic Development & Regional Differentiation. 256p. (C). 1981. text ed. 56.00 (*0-389-20194-4*, N6976) B&N Imports.
— South America. 3rd ed. (Illus.). 285p. 1991. pap. text ed. 36.00 (*0-340-40607-0*, Pub. by Hodder & Stoughton Ltd UK) Lubrecht & Cramer.
Morris, Arthur & Lowder, Stella, eds. Decentralization in Latin America: An Evaluation. LC 91-17806. 240p. 1992. text ed. 55.00 (*0-275-94021-7*, C4021, Praeger Pubs) Greenwood.
Morris, Arval A. The Constitution & American Public Education. LC 89-62026. 652p. 1989. lib. bdg. 37.50 (*0-89089-348-9*) Carolina Acad Pr.
— Dismissal of Tenured Higher Education Faculty: Legal Implications of the Elimination of Mandatory Retirement. 97p. (Orig.). 1992. pap. 25.95 (*1-56534-052-3*) NOLPE.
Morris, B. A. & Clifford, M. N., eds. Immunoassays in Food Analysis. 240p. 1985. 61.25 (*0-85334-321-7*, Pub. by Elsevier Applied Sci UK) Elsevier.
Morris, B. A., et al, eds. Immunoassays for Veterinary & Food Analysis - 1: Based on the Proceedings of the 2nd International Symposium held at the University of Surrey, Guilford, UK 15-17 July 1986. 384p. 1988. 106. 25 (*1-85166-138-7*) Elsevier.
Morris, B. J., jt. ed. see Wisden, W.
Morris, Barbara. Trim a Tree. LC 89-81054. (Illus.). 106p. (Orig.). 1989. pap. 9.95 (*0-944419-22-4*) Everett Cos Pub.
Morris, Barbara, jt. auth. see Vernon, Kathleen.
Morris, Barbara A., jt. auth. see Morris, Wesley.
Morris, Barbara B. The Kennedy Center: An Insider's Guide to Washington's Liveliest Memorial. LC 94-1836. (Illus.). 120p. 1994. pap. 10.95 (*0-939009-79-X*) EPM Pubns.
Morris, Barry. The Domestication of Resistance: The Dhan-Gadi & the Australian State. LC 88-39473. (Explorations in Anthropology Ser.). (Illus.). 262p. 1989. 65.00 (*0-85496-271-9*) Berg Pubs.
Morris, Benny. The Birth of the Palestinian Refugee Problem, 1947-1949. (Cambridge Middle East Library: No. 15). 416p. 1989. pap. 21.95 (*0-521-33889-1*) Cambridge U Pr.
— Israel's Border Wars, 1949-1956: Arab Infiltration, Israeli Retaliation, & the Countdown to the Suez War. (Illus.). 472p. 1994. 39.95 (*0-19-827850-0*) OUP.
— Nineteen Forty-Eight & After: Israel & the Palestinians. (Illus.). 192p. 1991. 69.00 (*0-19-828784-4*) OUP.
— Nineteen Forty-Eight & After: Israel & the Palestinians. (Illus.). 312p. 1994. reprint ed. pap. 24.00 (*0-19-827929-9*) OUP.
— The Roots of Appeasement: The British Weekly Press & Nazi Germany During the 1930s. 1991. text ed. 40.00 (*0-7146-3417-4*, Pub. by F Cass Pubs UK) Intl Spec Bk.
Morris, Bernard E. A Guide to Writing. 209p. (C). 1991. pap. text ed. 27.95x (*1-880157-00-4*) Ardsley.
Morris, Bernard S. Communism, Revolution, & American Policy. LC 86-29214. xiv, 200p. 1987. lib. bdg. 37.00 (*0-8223-0706-5*); pap. 16.95 (*0-8223-0760-X*) Duke.
— Imperialism & Revolution: An Essay for Radicals. LC 73-81164. (Midland Bks.: No. 170). 93p. reprint ed. pap. 26.60 (*0-8357-9217-X*, 2017632) Bks Demand.
Morris, Bertram. Aesthetic Process. LC 75-12900. (Northwestern University. Humanities Ser.: No. 8). reprint ed. 25.00 (*0-404-50708-5*) AMS Pr.
Morris, Beryl. Biotechnology. LC 93-41597. (Science & Our Future Ser.). (J). 1995. pap. 16.95 (*0-521-43785-7*) Cambridge U Pr.
— Training & Development for Women. 64p. 1993. pap. 35. 00 (*1-85604-080-1*, LAP0801, Pub. by Lib Assn Pub UK) UNIPUB.
Morris, Beryl, et al. The Greenhouse Effect: Exploring the Theory. (Illus.). 48p. 1990. pap. 14.95 (*0-643-05056-6*, Pub. by CSIRO AT) Intl Spec Bk.
Morris, Betty J., et al. Administering the School Library Media Center. 3rd ed. 567p. 1992. 45.00 (*0-8352-3092-9*) Bowker.
***Morris, Bill.** The Astral Zoo. 190p. (Orig.). 1995. pap. 11. 95 (*0-9639775-1-2*) New Sun Pubns.
— Motor City. Rubenstein, Julie, ed. LC 93-7428. 352p. 1993. reprint ed. pap. 10.00 (*0-671-86813-6*, WSP) PB.
— Notes to a Five-Year-Old. LC 94-69059. 90p. 1995. pap. 11.95 (*1-885340-09-5*) Coming Age Pr.
Morris, Bonnie. Bulletin Board Ideas. 48p. (Orig.). 1991. pap. 6.95 (*0-687-04553-3*) Abingdon.
***Morris, Brenda G.** The Gift Bearers: A Sculptural Interpretation of Christmas Traditions Through the Centuries. LC 94-96636. (Illus.). 100p. 1995. 39.95 (*0-9643930-0-X*) Brenmor Bks.
Morris, Brian. Anthropological Studies of Religion: An Introductory Text. (Illus.). 384p. 1987. pap. 15.95 (*0-521-33991-X*) Cambridge U Pr.
— Anthropological Studies of Religion: An Introductory Text. (Illus.). 384p. 1987. 69.95 (*0-521-32794-6*) Cambridge U Pr.
— Anthropology of the Self. (Anthropology, Culture & Society Ser.). (C). 1994. pap. text ed. 19.95 (*0-7453-0858-9*) Westview.
— Anthropology of the Self: The Individual in Cultural Perspective. LC 94-9670. (Anthropology, Culture, & Society Ser.). (C). 1994. text ed. 69.95 (*0-7453-0857-0*, Pub. by Pluto Pr UK) Westview.
— Australia: Take a Bow. 1990. pap. 5.00 (*0-517-03702-5*) Random Hse Value.
— Common Mushrooms of Malawi. 108p. (C). 1987. pap. text ed. 31.80 (*82-90724-00-4*) Lubrecht & Cramer.
— Harri Webb. 113p. 1993. pap. 9.95 (*0-7083-1225-X*, Pub. by U of Wales UK) Bks Intl VA.
— Tide Race. (C). 1976. pap. 20.00x (*0-85088-420-9*, Pub. by Gomer Pr UK) St Mut.
— Western Conceptions of the Individual. 500p. 1992. 75.00 (*0-85496-698-6*) Berg Pubs.
— Western Conceptions of the Individual. 528p. (C). 1992. pap. text ed. 19.95 (*0-85496-801-6*) Berg Pubs.
Morris, Brian, ed. see Ford, John.
Morris, Brian, ed. see Shakespeare, William.
Morris, Brian, ed. see Tourneur, Cyril.
Morris, Bruce R. The Economics of the Special Taxation of Chain Stores. Bruchey, Stuart & Carosso, Vincent P., eds. LC 78-18971. (Small Business Enterprise in America Ser.). (Illus.). 1979. lib. bdg. 25.95 (*0-405-11474-5*) Ayer.
Morris, Burnis R. Nonprofit News Coverage: A Guide for Journalists. (Illus.). 64p. (Orig.). 1993. pap. 12.00 (*0-929556-13-5*, P91) Ind Sector.
Morris, C. Aryan Sun Myths: The Origins of Religion. 1991. lib. bdg. 79.95 (*0-8490-4286-0*) Gordon Pr.
— Com. Bib. Continente Nuevo (New Continent Com) Marcos (Mark) (SPA.). Date not set. 12.99 (*1-56063-269-0*, 498637); pap. 8.99 (*0-685-74917-7*, 498638) Editorial Unilit.
— The True History of Mexico. 1976. lib. bdg. 59.95 (*0-8490-2772-1*) Gordon Pr.
Morris, C., ed. Academic Press Dictionary of Science & Technology. (Illus.). 2432p. 1992. text ed. 115.00 (*0-12-200400-0*) Acad Pr.
Morris, C. G., jt. ed. see Halsey, W. D.
Morris, C. J. Gurkhas: An Ethnology. (C). 1993. text ed. 11. 00 (*81-85418-98-5*, Pub. by Low Price II) S Asia.
Morris, C. J., jt. ed. see Catterall, Peter.
Morris, C. Robert, jt. auth. see Morris, Clarence R.
Morris, C. Spencer & Beers, V. Gilbert. Beginners ABC Bible Memory Book. 287p. (Orig.). (J). (ps-3). 12.99 (*0-945564-41-4*, Gold & Honey) Questar Pubs.
Morris, Calvin S. Reverdy C. Ransom: Black Advocate of the Social Gospel. 212p. (Orig.). (C). 1990. lib. bdg. 44. 50 (*0-8191-7766-0*) U Pr of Amer.
Morris, Campbell. Best Jumbo Paper Aircraft. LC 92-40581. (Illus.). 32p. (Orig.). 1993. pap. 6.95 (*0-399-51801-0*, Perigee Bks) Berkley Pub.
— The Best Paper Aircraft. (Illus.). 64p. (Orig.). 1986. pap. 7.95 (*0-399-51301-9*, Perigee Bks) Berkley Pub.
— Fold Your Own Dinosaurs. LC 92-32894. (Illus.). 48p. (Orig.). (J). 1993. pap. 7.95 (*0-399-51794-4*, Perigee Bks) Berkley Pub.
— More Best Paper Aircraft. (Illus.). 32p. 1988. pap. 5.95 (*0-399-51446-5*, Perigee Bks) Berkley Pub.
— Three D Magic Portfolio. 1994. pap. 15.95 (*0-8050-3755-1*) H Holt & Co.
***Morris, Carla D. & Morris, Stephen R.** How to Index Newspapers Using Wordperfect Microsoft Word. 100p. 1995. disk, pap. text ed. 40.00 (*1-56308-305-1*) Libs Unl.
Morris, Carlos A. Mensajes Mayores de los Profetas: Major Messages from the Minor. (SPA.). 5.50 (*84-7645-086-9*, 223135, Pub. by Edit Clie SP) TSELF.
Morris, Carol. Sweet Uprisings. (Illus.). 18p. (Orig.). 1990. pap. 5.00 (*0-9608802-7-5*) Years Pr.
Morris, Carol, ed. see Hurst, John A.
Morris, Carroll. A Suzuki Parent's Diary. 88p. 1984. pap. text ed. 8.95 (*0-87487-590-0*) Summy-Birchard.
Morris, Carroll H. If the Gospel Is True, Why Do I Hurt So Much? Help for Dysfunctional LDS Families. LC 91-28889. 172p. 1991. 10.95 (*0-87579-539-0*) Deseret Bk.
— The Merry-Go-Round. LC 88-14885. 244p. 1988. 10.95 (*0-87579-152-2*) Deseret Bk.
Morris, Cedric, tr. see Henning, Harald, Jr., et al.
***Morris, Celia.** Bearing Witness: Sexual Harassment & Beyond. 1995. pap. 12.95 (*0-316-58423-1*) Little.
— Bearing Witness: Sexual Harassment & Beyond - Everywoman's Story. 1994. 21.95 (*0-316-58422-3*) Little.
— Fanny Wright: Rebel in America. (Illus.). 352p. 1992. pap. 16.95 (*0-252-06249-3*) U of Ill Pr.
— Storming the Statehouse: Running for Governor with Ann Richards & Dianne Feinstein. (Illus.). 352p. 1992. text ed. 25.00 (*0-684-19328-0*, Scribners) S&S Trade.
Morris, Charles. Aryan Sun-Myths: The Origins of Religions. 177p. 1977. reprint ed. spiral bd. 8.25 (*0-7873-1267-3*) Mokelumne.
— The San Francisco Calamity by Earthquake & Fire. (Illus.). 224p. 1986. pap. 9.95 (*0-8065-0984-8*, Citadel Pr) Carol Pub Group.
Morris, Charles & Coleman, James C. Contemporary Psychology Plus Discovery Journal. 7th ed. (C). 1990. text ed. 53.00 (*0-673-46051-7*) HarpCollege.
Morris, Charles E., jt. ed. see Haberstroh, Chuck.
Morris, Charles G. Psychology: An Introduction. 8th ed. LC 92-15579. 768p. (C). 1992. text ed. write for info. (*0-13-735465-7*) P-H.
— Signification & Significance: A Study of the Relations of Signs & Values. 1964. pap. 9.95 (*0-262-63014-1*) MIT Pr.
— Understanding Psychology. 2nd ed. LC 92-15582. 736p. (C). 1992. pap. text ed. write for info. (*0-13-951484-8*) P-H.
Morris, Charles G., jt. auth. see Sashkin, Marshal.
Morris, Charles J., ed. American Labor Policy: A Critical Appraisal of the NLRA. 484p. 1987. text ed. 62.00 (*0-87179-532-9*, 0532) BNA.
Morris, Charles R. Locke, Berkeley, Hume. LC 79-17847. 174p. 1979. reprint ed. text ed. 38.50 (*0-313-22091-3*, MOLO, Greenwood Pr) Greenwood.
Morris, Charles W. Logical Positivism, Pragmatism & Scientific Empiricism. LC 75-3285. reprint ed. 29.50 (*0-404-59273-2*) AMS Pr.
— Symbolism & Reality: A Study in the Nature of Mind. LC 86-17602. (Foundations of Semiotics Ser.: No. 15). v, 105p. (C). 1993. 153.00 (*90-272-3287-3*) Benjamins North Am.
— Varieties of Human Value. LC 56-6641. (Midway Reprint Ser.: 1973). 225p. reprint ed. 64.20 (*0-8357-9660-4*, 2016989) Bks Demand.
Morris, Charles W., ed. see Mead, George H.
Morris, Charles W. E. The Gurnet. (Pilgrim Society Notes Ser.: No. 30). 1982. 2.00 (*0-940628-47-3*) Pilgrim Soc.
***Morris, Chris.** So You Have to Write an Essay. 144p. (C). 1995. pap. text ed. 15.95 (*0-7872-0821-3*) Kendall-Hunt.
Morris, Chris, jt. auth. see Morris, Janet.
***Morris, Chris, et al.** Weapons of Mass Destruction: Nonlethality, Information Warfare, & Airpower in the Age of Chaos. (Illus.). 47p. (Orig.). (C). 1995. pap. text ed. 30.00x (*0-7881-1670-3*) Diane Pub.
Morris, Christopher. Becoming Southern: Warren County & Vicksburg, Mississippi, 1760-1860. LC 93-37916. (Illus.). 336p. 1995. 35.00 (*0-19-508366-0*) OUP.
— Models of Misrepresentation: On the Fiction of E. L. Doctorow. LC 91-3730. 1991. 35.00 (*0-87805-524-X*) U Pr of Miss.
— The Oxford Book of Tudor Anthems. 1978. pap. 14.95 (*0-19-353325-1*) OUP.
***Morris, Christopher, ed.** Academic Press Dictionary of Science & Technology CD-ROM Version. (Illus.). 1995. cd-rom 79.95 (*0-12-200401-9*) Acad Pr.
— Anthems for Choirs Four. 1976. pap. 16.95 (*0-19-353018-X*) OUP.
Morris, Christopher, jt. ed. see Jovanovich, Peter.
Morris, Christopher D. The Birsay Bay Project, Vol. 1: Excavations 1976-1982. (Illus.). 334p. 1993. text ed. 66. 00 (*0-905096-08-8*) A Sutton Pub.
Morris, Christopher D., et al, eds. The Viking Age in Caithness, Orkney, & the North Atlantic. (Illus.). 528p. 1993. 45.00 (*0-7486-0430-8*, Pub. by Edinburgh U Pr UK) Col U Pr.
Morris, Christopher W., jt. ed. see Frey, R. G.
Morris, Clare. Quantitative Approaches in Business Studies. 3rd ed. 384p. 1993. pap. 43.50 (*0-273-60116-4*, Pub. by Pitman Pub Ltd UK) Trans-Atl Phila.
***Morris, Clarence.** How Lawyers Think. xiv, 144p. 1995. reprint ed. lib. bdg. 32.50 (*0-8377-2475-9*) Rothman.
— Modern Defamation Law: Torts Practice Handbook, 1978. LC 78-55262. 76p. 1978. pap. 2.00 (*0-685-09811-7*, B247) Am Law Inst.
Morris, Clarence, ed. Great Legal Philosophers: Selected Readings in Jurisprudence. LC 57-11955. 582p. 1971. reprint ed. pap. 21.95 (*0-8122-1008-5*) U of Pa Pr.
Morris, Clarence R., intro. Trends in Modern American Society. LC 86-22762. (Benjamin Franklin Lectures of the University of Pennsylvania, 7th Series). 191p. 1986. reprint ed. text ed. 49.75 (*0-313-22106-5*, MOTM, Greenwood Pr) Greenwood.
Morris, Clarence R. & Morris, C. Robert. Morris on Torts. 2nd ed. LC 80-170. (University Textbook Ser.). 443p. 1980. text ed. 24.95 (*0-88277-002-0*) Foundation Pr.
Morris, Clarice. Classroom Experiments in Hair Structure & Chemistry. (Illus.). 1976. 37.50 (*0-87350-068-7*) Milady Pub.
Morris, Colin. The Discovery of the Individual 1051-1200. (Medieval Academy Reprints for Teaching Ser.). 188p. 1987. reprint ed. pap. text ed. 10.95 (*0-8020-6665-8*) U of Toronto Pr.
— The Papal Monarchy: The Western Church from 1050 to 1250. (Oxford History of the Christian Church Ser.). 696p. 1989. 105.00 (*0-19-826907-2*) OUP.
— The Papal Monarchy: The Western Church from 1050 to 1250. (Oxford History of the Christian Church Ser.). 696p. 1991. reprint ed. pap. 35.00 (*0-19-826925-0*, 12306) OUP.
— Starting from Scratch. 96p. (Orig.). (C). 1991. pap. 9.95 (*0-7162-0473-8*, Epworth Pr) TPI PA.
Morris, Colton G. & Cave, Hugh B. Fightin'est Ship: The Story of the Cruiser Helena in World War II. LC 79-20662. reprint ed. 15.95 (*0-89201-083-5*) Zenger Pub.
Morris, Constance L., tr. see Celarie, Henriette.
Morris, Corbyn. Essay Towards Fixing the True Standards of Wit & Humor. LC 70-172747. reprint ed. 29.50 (*0-404-04501-4*) AMS Pr.
Morris, Corliss. Behind the Badge: A Policewoman's Ordeal. 254p. (Orig.). 1990. pap. 4.95 (*1-879331-09-8*) Marciel Pub & Print.
— With Love to the Monsters under My Bed. 2nd ed. (Illus.). 60p. (Orig.). reprint ed. pap. 7.95 (*1-879331-08-X*) Marciel Pub & Print.
Morris, Craig. Inka Empire & Its Andean Origins. 1993. 50. 00 (*1-55859-556-2*) Abbeville Pr.
Morris, Craig & Thompson, Donald E. Huanuco Pampa: An Inca City & Its Hinterland. LC 84-52180. (Ancient Peoples & Places Ser.). (Illus.). 181p. 1985. 29.95 (*0-500-39020-7*) Thames Hudson.
Morris, Curtis. Skillet & Trophy Fishing Texas. (Illus.). 256p. (Orig.). 1989. pap. text ed. 10.95 (*1-877740-00-4*) Nel-Mar Pub.
Morris, Cynthia T. & Adelman, Irma. Comparative Patterns of Economic Development, 1850-1914. LC 87-45480. (Johns Hopkins Studies in Development). 528p. 1988. text ed. 55.00 (*0-8018-3507-0*) Johns Hopkins.
Morris, Cynthia T., jt. auth. see Adelman, Irma.
Morris, D. Communicate in French: Writing. (C). 1989. 40. 00 (*0-09-173081-3*, Pub. by S Thornes Pubs UK) St Mut.
Morris, D. & Tamm, B., eds. Concise Encyclopedia of Software Engineering. LC 92-27942. (Advances in Systems Control, & Information Engineering Ser.). 1992. 345.00 (*0-08-036214-1*, Pergamon Pr) Elsevier.
Morris, D. Hampton. Stephane Mallarme, Twentieth-Century Criticism, 1972-1979. LC 89-34656. (Romance Monographs: No. 48). 1989. pap. 22.00 (*84-599-2717-2*) Romance.
Morris, D. L. & Richards, K. S. Hydatid Disease: Current Medical & Surgical Management. (Illus.). 104p. 1992. 95.00 (*0-7506-1379-3*) Buttrwrth-Heinemann.
***Morris, D. L., et al, eds.** Hepatic Metastases: Diagnosis & Management. LC 95-7176. 1995. write for info. (*0-7506-0879-X*) Buttrwrth-Heinemann.
Morris, D. S. & Haigh, R. H. Britain, Spain & Gibraltar 1945-1990: The Eternal Triangle. LC 91-20990. (Illus.). 224p. 1992. 69.95 (*0-415-07145-3*, A6671) Routledge.
Morris, D. W., jt. auth. see Cooper, M. McG.
Morris, D. W., et al, eds. Patterns in the Structure of Mammalian Communities. LC 89-32598. (Special Publications: No. 28). iv, 266p. (C). 1989. 30.00 (*0-89672-173-6*); pap. 20.00 (*0-89672-174-4*) Tex Tech Univ Pr.
Morris, Dan & Morris, Inez. Complete Fish Cookbook. LC 73-161249. 1972. 10.00 (*0-672-51421-4*, Bobbs) Macmillan.
— Complete Fish Cookbook. rev. ed. 436p. 1989. reprint ed. pap. 16.95 (*0-88317-155-4*) Stoeger Pub Co.
Morris, Daniel. Painless Publishing. (Illus.). 60p. (C). 1988. write for info. (*0-318-62977-1*) Osage Pr.
— Presque Isle. (Illus.). 102p. (Orig.). 1988. pap. write for info. (*0-318-62978-X*) Osage Pr.
— The Writings of William Carlos Williams: Publicity for the Self. 224p. 1995. 34.95 (*0-8262-1002-3*) U of Mo Pr.
Morris, Daniel A. Federal Tort Claims, 1 vol. 1993. ring bd. 135.00 (*0-685-68851-8*) Clark Boardman Callaghan.
***Morris, Daniel C.** Re-Engineering Your Business. 1994. pap. 14.95 (*0-07-043179-5*) McGraw.
Morris, Daniel C. & Brandon, Joel S. Reengineering Your Business. 256p. 1993. text ed. 24.95 (*0-07-043178-7*) McGraw.
— Relational Diagramming: Enchancing the Software Development Process. 320p. 1989. text ed. 45.00 (*0-07-043198-1*) McGraw.
Morris, Daniel R. From Heaven to Hell: Imagery of Earth, Air, Water & Fire in the Novels of Georges Bernanos. (American University Studies: Romance Languages & Literature: Ser. II, Vol. 86). 332p. (C). 1989. text ed. 41. 95 (*0-8204-0691-0*) P Lang Pubs.
Morris, Danny. Aces & Wingmen II, Vol. I. Frisque, Thomas A., ed. (Illus.). 256p. (C). 1989. lib. bdg. 39.95 (*0-9623080-1-3*) Aviation Usk.
— Yearning to Know God's Will: A Workbook for Discerning God's Guidance for Your Life. 144p. 1991. pap. 7.99 (*0-310-75491-7*) Zondervan.
Morris, Daphne K., jt. auth. see Averill, Lloyd J.
Morris, Darlene. House of Seven Gables Notes. 1984. pap. 3.75 (*0-8220-0595-6*) Cliffs.
Morris, Darrell. Case Studies in Teaching Beginning Readers: The Howard Street Tutoring Manual. LC 92-71181. (Illus.). 258p. (Orig.). (C). 1992. pap. text ed. 23. 00 (*0-9632376-0-8*) Fieldstream.
Morris, David. Dalesmen of the Mississippi. (C). 1990. 90. 00 (*1-85072-062-2*, Pub. by W Sessions UK) St Mut.
— The End of Marriage: The Development of European Divorce Law 1550-1970. 1971. 22.95 (*0-8464-0375-7*) Beekman Pubs.
— Getting from Here to There: Building a Rational Transportation System. 9p. (Orig.). 1992. pap. 4.50 (*0-917582-28-4*) Inst Local Self Re.
— Guidelines for Writing a Qualitative Research Report. LC 94-26179. 1994. 7.00 (*0-87757-243-7*) Am Mktg.
— Hunting Trophy Whitetails. LC 92-60822. (Illus.). 528p. 1993. reprint ed. 29.95 (*0-9633315-0-7*) Venture Pr MT.
— Self-Reliant Cities: Energy & the Transformation of Urban America. LC 81-18301. (Illus.). 256p. 1982. 19.95 (*0-87156-296-0*); pap. 8.95 (*0-87156-309-6*) Sierra.
— Thomas Hearne & His Landscape. (Illus.). 160p. 1990. text ed. 50.00 (*0-295-97040-5*) U of Wash Pr.
Morris, David & Abeles, Tom. Substituting Agricultural Materials for Petroleum-Based Industrial Products. LC 86-21350. 33p. 1986. 20.00 (*0-917582-46-2*) Inst Local Self Re.
Morris, David & Ahmed, Irshad. The Carbohydrate Economy: Making Chemicals & Industrial Materials from Plant Matter. LC 92-18177. (Illus.). 70p. 1992. pap. text ed. 25.00 (*0-917582-25-X*) Inst Local Self Re.
***Morris, David & Chandra, Satish.** Guidelines for Case Analysis. LC 94-25037. 1994. 7.00 (*0-87757-241-0*) Am Mktg.
— Guidelines for Writing a Research Report. LC 92-45550. 1992. 5.00 (*0-87757-232-1*) Am Mktg.
Morris, David & Platt, Brenda. Garbage Disposal Economics: A Statistical Snapshot. LC 87-4182. (Illus.). 110p. 1987. pap. 20.00 (*0-917582-44-6*) Inst Local Self Re.
Morris, David, jt. auth. see Ahmed, Irshad.
Morris, David, et al. Getting the Most from Our Materials: Making New Jersey the State of the Art. LC 91-22240. (Illus.). 85p. (Orig.). 1991. pap. text ed. 25.00 (*0-917582-33-0*) Inst Local Self Re.
Morris, David B. Alexander Pope: The Genius of Sense. LC 83-18577. 384p. reprint ed. pap. 109.50 (*0-7837-4474-9*, 2044182) Bks Demand.
— The Culture of Pain. LC 90-11305. (Illus.). 354p. 1991. 30.00 (*0-520-07266-9*) U CA Pr.
— The Culture of Pain. 1993. pap. 14.00 (*0-520-08276-1*) U CA Pr.
— Earth Warrior: Overboard with Paul Watson & the Sea Shepherd Conservation Society. LC 94-37952. (Illus.). 224p. 1995. pap. 14.95 (*1-55591-203-6*) Fulcrum Pub.
Morris, David G., jt. auth. see Webb, G. L.
***Morris, David J., Jr.** Getting the Most from Your Textbooks. LC 94-25041. 1994. 7.00 (*0-87757-247-X*) Am Mktg.

— Marketing As a Means to Achieve Organizational Ends. 3rd ed. (Illus.). 232p. 1992. pap. text ed. 22.00 (*0-936285-17-6*) U New Haven Pr.

Morris, David J. Pulse Code Formats for Fiber Optical Data Communication. (Optical Engineering Ser.: Vol. 5). 224p. 1983. 110.00 (*0-8247-7067-6*) Dekker.

Morris, David J., ed. see Masie, Elliott & Wolman, Rebekah.

Morris, David J., Jr., jt. auth. see Rigall, Mary O.

Morris, David M., ed. Asset Securitization: Principles & Practice. 1990. pap. 75.00 (*1-55840-441-4*) Exec Ent Pubns.

— Asset Securitization: Principles & Practice. 1994. pap. text ed. 75.00 (*0-471-11236-4*) Wiley.

Morris, David R. & Marton, Laurence J., eds. Polyamines in Biology & Medicine. LC 81-9757. (Biochemistry of Disease Ser.: No. 8). 477p. reprint ed. pap. 136.00 (*0-7837-3362-3*, 2043320) Bks Demand.

Morris, David W. Dictionary of Speech Therapy. 200p. 1988. pap. 27.00 (*0-85066-444-6*) Singular Publishing.

Morris, Dean. Animals That Burrow. rev. ed. LC 87-16694. (Read about Animals Ser.). (Illus.). 48p. (J). (gr. 2-6). 1987. lib. bdg. 10.95 (*0-8172-3201-X*) Raintree Steck-V.

— Animals That Live in Shells. rev. ed. LC 87-20556. (Read about Animals Ser.). (Illus.). 48p. (J). (gr. 2-6). 1987. lib. bdg. 10.95 (*0-8172-3202-8*) Raintree Steck-V.

— Birds. rev. ed. LC 87-16672. (Read about Animals Ser.). (Illus.). 48p. (J). (gr. 2-6). 1987. lib. bdg. 10.95 (*0-8172-3203-6*) Raintree Steck-V.

— Butterflies & Moths. rev. ed. LC 87-16666. (Read about Animals Ser.). (Illus.). 48p. (J). (gr. 2-6). 1987. lib. bdg. 10.95 (*0-8172-3204-4*) Raintree Steck-V.

— Cats. rev. ed. LC 87-16699. (Read about Animals Ser.). (Illus.). 48p. (J). (gr. 2-6). 1987. lib. bdg. 10.95 (*0-8172-3205-2*) Raintree Steck-V.

— Dinosaurs & Other First Animals. LC 87-16670. (Read about Animals Ser.). (Illus.). 48p. (J). (gr. 2-6). 1987. lib. bdg. 10.95 (*0-8172-3206-0*) Raintree Steck-V.

— Endangered Animals. (J). (ps-3). 1990. pap. 4.95 (*0-8114-8220-0*) Raintree Steck-V.

— Endangered Animals. 1983. 14.25 (*0-8393-0011-5*) Raintree Steck-V.

— Endangered Animals. rev. ed. LC 87-20459. (Read about Animals Ser.). (Illus.). 48p. (J). (gr. 2-6). 1987. lib. bdg. 10.95 (*0-8172-3207-9*) Raintree Steck-V.

— Frogs & Toads. rev. ed. LC 87-16698. (Read about Animals Ser.). (Illus.). 48p. (J). (gr. 2-6). 1987. lib. bdg. 10.95 (*0-8172-3208-7*) Raintree Steck-V.

— Horses. rev. ed. LC 87-16690. (Read about Animals Ser.). (Illus.). 48p. (Orig.). (J). (gr. 2-6). 1987. lib. bdg. 10.95 (*0-8172-3209-5*) Raintree Steck-V.

— Insects That Live in Families. rev. ed. LC 87-16696. (Read about Animals Ser.). (Illus.). 48p. (J). (gr. 2-6). 1987. lib. bdg. 10.95 (*0-8172-3210-9*) Raintree Steck-V.

— Monkeys & Apes. rev. ed. LC 87-16688. (Read about Animals Ser.). (Illus.). 48p. (J). (gr. 3). 1987. lib. bdg. 10.95 (*0-8172-3211-7*) Raintree Steck-V.

— Snakes & Lizards. rev. ed. LC 87-16697. (Read about Animals Ser.). (Illus.). 48p. (J). (gr. 2-6). 1987. lib. bdg. 10.95 (*0-8172-3212-5*) Raintree Steck-V.

— Spiders. rev. ed. LC 87-16695. (Read about Animals Ser.). (Illus.). 48p. (J). (gr. 2-6). 1987. lib. bdg. 10.95 (*0-8172-3213-3*) Raintree Steck-V.

— Underwater Life. (J). (ps-3). 1990. pap. 4.95 (*0-8114-8219-7*) Raintree Steck-V.

— Underwater Life. rev. ed. LC 87-16693. (Read about Animals Ser.). (Illus.). 48p. (J). (gr. 2-6). 1987. lib. bdg. 10.95 (*0-8172-3214-1*) Raintree Steck-V.

Morris, Deborah. Real Kids, Real Adventures. LC 94-11741. 112p. (J). (gr. 3-10). 1994. 5.99 (*0-8054-4051-8*, 4240-51) Broadman.

— Real Kids, Real Adventures, No. 2. 112p. (J). (gr. 3-10). 1994. 5.99 (*0-8054-4052-6*, 4240-52) Broadman.

— Trapped In A Cave! A True Story. LC 92-40731. (J). 1993. 7.99 (*0-8054-4003-8*) Broadman.

Morris, Deidre, comp. Contemporary Australian Issues. 140p. 1993. pap. 25.00 (*1-875589-29-5*) D W Thorpe.

Morris, Dennis. The Sex Pistols Never Mind the B ll cks: A Photographic Record Of. (Illus.). 96p. 1991. pap. 19.95 (*0-7119-2555-0*, OP46416) Omnibus NY.

Morris, Derek J., jt. auth. see Hay, Donald A.

***Morris, Desmond.** Animal Watching. 1992. pap. 17.99 (*0-517-08338-8*) Random.

— The Animals Roadshow. large type ed. (Illus.). 213p. 1990. 15.95 (*1-85089-355-1*, Pub. by ISIS UK) Transaction Pubs.

— Animalwatching: A Field Guide to Animal Behavior. (Illus.). 1990. 35.00 (*0-517-57859-X*, Crown) Crown Pub Group.

— Babywatching. (Illus.). 1992. 15.00 (*0-517-58845-5*, Crown) Crown Pub Group.

— Bodytalk: The Meaning of Human Gestures. LC 94-30719. 1995. pap. 14.00 (*0-517-88355-4*, Crown) Crown Pub Group.

— Catlore. (Illus.). 192p. 1988. 12.95 (*0-517-56903-5*, Crown) Crown Pub Group.

— Catlore. 1993. pap. 8.00 (*0-517-88057-1*, Crown) Crown Pub Group.

— Catwatching. 1987. 13.00 (*0-517-56518-8*, Crown) Crown Pub Group.

— Catwatching. 1993. pap. 8.00 (*0-517-88053-9*, Crown) Crown Pub Group.

— Catwatching. 1994. 17.99 (*0-517-12065-8*) Random Hse Value.

— Dogwatching. 1987. 13.00 (*0-517-56519-6*, Crown) Crown Pub Group.

— Dogwatching. 1993. pap. 8.00 (*0-517-88055-5*, Crown) Crown Pub Group.

— Horsewatching. (Illus.). 1989. 14.00 (*0-517-57267-2*, Crown) Crown Pub Group.

— The Human Animal: A Personal View of the Human Species. LC 94-33602. 1995. 25.00 (*0-517-70090-5*) Crown Pub Group.

— The Human Zoo: A Zoologist's Study of the Urban Animal. Turner, Philip, ed. (Kodansha Globe Ser.). 272p. 1996. pap. 13.00 (*1-56836-104-1*, Kodansha Globe) Kodansha.

— The Naked Ape. 1980. mass mkt. 5.99 (*0-440-36266-0*, LE) Dell.

— The World of Animals. (Illus.). 128p. (J). 1993. 22.50 (*0-670-85184-1*) Viking Child Bks.

***Morris, Desmond & Reid, Beryl.** A Passion for Cats Forewords. 1994. pap. 17.95 (*0-7153-9980-2*, Pub. by D & C Pub UK) Sterling.

Morris, Desmond, jt. auth. see Boyle, Katie.

Morris, Diana, intro. Miriam Laufer: A Retrospective. LC 81-66864. (Illus.). 80p. 1981. pap. text ed. 12.95 (*0-940220-04-0*) Asylums Pr-Language.

Morris, Diane H., jt. auth. see Boyle, Marie A.

Morris, Dirk. Government Debt in International Financial Markets. 220p. 1992. 54.00 (*0-86187-994-5*, Pub. by Pinter Pubs UK) St Martin.

Morris, Dixie G. Who is Santa? (Illus.). 25p. (Orig.). (J). (ps-3). 1988. spiral bd. 7.50 (*0-929946-04-9*) L P T C.

Morris, Dixie G., jt. auth. see Morris, Frank R.

Morris, Donald, jt. auth. see Jamieson, Paul.

Morris, Donald F. Small Local Governments & Information Management. 17p. (Orig.). 1984. pap. 2.00 (*1-55719-078-X*) U NE CPAR.

Morris, Donald R. The Washing of the Spears: The Rise & Fall of the Zulu Nation. 688p. 1986. pap. 16.95 (*0-671-62822-4*, Touchstone Bks) S&S Trade.

Morris, Doris, ed. see Sweet, Orville K.

Morris, Dorothy. A Garland of Green Gold. large type ed. 224p. 1992. pap. 14.95 (*0-7089-7189-X*, Trailtree Bookshop) Ulverscroft.

— None of Your Black Business. LC 90-82800. 105p. (Orig.). (C). 1991. pap. 12.95 (*0-9627732-0-4*) Dell-Morse.

Morris, Dwight & Gamache, Murielle E. Handbook of Campaign Spending: Money in the 1992 Congressional Races. LC 93-50217. 570p. 1994. 139.95 (*0-87187-997-2*) Congr Quarterly.

Morris, Dwight, jt. auth. see Fritz, Sara.

Morris, E. & Sadler, T. Our Rainforests & the Issues. (Illus.). 54p. (J). (gr. 6-11). 1992. pap. 14.95 (*0-643-05141-4*, Pub. by CSIRO AT) Intl Spec Bk.

Morris, E. E. Australasian England. 1970. 59.95 (*0-87968-678-2*) Gordon Pr.

Morris, E. K. & Braukmann, C. J., eds. Behavioral Approaches to Crime & Delinquency: A Handbook of Application, Research, & Concepts. LC 87-29081. 652p. 1988. 90.00 (*0-306-42632-3*, Plenum Pr) Plenum.

Morris, Earl H. The Temple of the Warriors: The Adventure of Exploring & Restoring a Masterpiece of Native American Architecture in the Ruined City of Chichen Itza, Yucatan. LC 76-44764. (Illus.). reprint ed. 55.00 (*0-404-15871-4*) AMS Pr.

Morris, Earl H., et al. The Temple of the Warriors at Chichen Itza, Yucatan, 2 vols., Set. LC 77-11511. (Carnegie Institution of Washington. Publications: No. 406). reprint ed. 104.50 (*0-404-16280-0*) AMS Pr.

Morris, Ed. Garth Brooks, Platinum Cowboy. LC 92-43645. 1992. pap. 10.95 (*0-312-08788-8*) St Martin.

Morris, Edmund. The Rise of Theodore Roosevelt. 1986. pap. 16.00 (*0-345-33902-9*, Ballantine Trade) Ballantine.

— The Wooden Dish. 1956. pap. 4.75 (*0-8222-1276-5*) Dramatists Play.

***Morris, Edward.** The Walker Art Gallery. (Illus.). 96p. 1994. 25.00 (*1-85759-036-8*, Pub. by P Wilson Pubs) Sothebys Pubns.

Morris, Edward A. The Demagogue's Disease. LC 79-64157. (Illus.). 1979. 7.95 (*0-934062-00-5*); pap. 4.50 (*0-934062-01-3*) World Wide Prods.

Morris, Edward K., jt. ed. see Todd, James T.

Morris, Edwin L. Fish, Fiber, & Fitness: Magic Keys to a Healthy, Vigorous, Happy Life. McKinney, Aubrey R., ed. (Adventures in Science Ser.). (Illus.). 160p. 1989. 24.95 (*0-914587-05-6*) Helix Pr.

Morris, Eileen. Crafts Kids Can Eat, Play with, or Wear. (J). (gr. k-3). 1991. pap. 11.99 (*0-86653-979-4*) Fearon Teach Aids.

Morris, Eleanor. Country Roads of Texas. LC 94-4403. (Country Roads Ser.). 140p. 1994. pap. 9.95 (*1-56626-100-7*) Country Rds.

— Country Towns of Northern California. LC 94-11543. (Country Towns Ser.). (Illus.). (Orig.). 1995. pap. 9.95 (*1-56626-101-5*) Country Rds.

— Country Towns of Texas. (Illus.). (Orig.). 1995. pap. 9.95 (*0-614-00764-X*) Country Rds.

***Morris, Eleanor S.** Recommended Country Inns: The Southwest-AZ, NM, TX. 5th ed. LC 92-25077. (Recommended Country Inns Ser.). (Illus.). 416p. 1994. pap. 14.95 (*1-56440-513-3*) Globe Pequot.

Morris, Elias C. Sermons, Addresses & Reminiscences & Important Correspondence, with a Picture Gallery of Eminent Ministers & Scholars. Gaustad, Edwin S., ed. LC 79-52598. (Baptist Tradition Ser.). (Illus.). 1980. reprint ed. lib. bdg. 30.95 (*0-405-12465-1*) Ayer.

Morris, Elizabeth. Days Out & Other Papers. LC 67-26767. (Essay Index Reprint Ser.). 1977. 18.95 (*0-8369-0721-3*) Ayer.

— Jonathan Papers. LC 70-152200. (Essay Index Reprint Ser.). 1977. reprint ed. 20.95 (*0-8369-2249-2*) Ayer.

— More Jonathan Papers. LC 68-8484. (Essay Index Reprint Ser.). 1977. 19.95 (*0-8369-0722-1*) Ayer.

Morris, Elizabeth A. Basketmaker Caves in the Prayer Rock District, Northeastern Arizona. LC 79-20149. (Anthropological Papers: No. 35). 158p. 1980. pap. 14.95 (*0-8165-0499-7*) U of Ariz Pr.

Morris, Elizabeth H. Personal Traits & Success in Teaching. LC 76-177087. (Columbia University. Teachers College. Contributions to Education Ser.: No. 342). reprint ed. 37.50 (*0-404-55342-7*) AMS Pr.

Morris, Ellen, comp. Monmouth County, New Jersey: Families of Color in 1880. (New Jersey, 1880: Afro-Americans & Native Americans Ser.). (Illus.). 134p. 1992. pap. 20.00 (*0-317-04688-8*) Morris Genealog Lib.

Morris, Ellen M. & Pasteris, Jill D., eds. Mantle Metasomatism & Alkaline Magmatism. (Special Paper Ser.: No. 215). (Illus.). 392p. 1987. pap. 18.00 (*0-8137-2215-2*) Geol Soc.

Morris, Emily. Cuba. LC 90-10354. (World in View Ser.). (Illus.). 96p. (YA). (gr. 6-12). 1991. lib. bdg. 24.26 (*0-8114-2439-1*) Raintree Steck-V.

Morris, Erdie & Weldon, Kimberly J. Biology Concepts: The Laboratory Manual. (Illus.). 80p. (C). 1992. 16.00 (*1-880948-01-X*) Bold Ent.

Morris, Eric. Acting from the Ultimate Consciousness. 1992. pap. 11.95 (*0-9629709-1-3*) Ermor Enter.

— Being & Doing: A Workbook for Actors. 190p. 1990. pap. text ed. 12.95 (*0-9629709-0-5*) Ermor Enter.

— Irreverent Acting. (Orig.). 1992. pap. 11.95 (*0-9629709-2-1*) Ermor Enter.

Morris, Eric & Hoe, Alan. Terrorism: Threat & Response. LC 87-30696. 180p. 1988. text ed. 55.00 (*0-312-01594-1*) St Martin.

Morris, Eugene J., et al. New York Practice Guide: Real Estate, 4 vols. 1986. Updates. ring bd. write for info. (*0-8205-1523-X*) Bender.

— Real Estate Development: Business, Commercial, Industrial & Major Residential Properties, 4 vols. 1987. Updates. ring bd. write for info. (*0-8205-1570-1*) Bender.

Morris, Felipe. Latin America's Banking Systems in the 1980s: A Cross-Country Comparison. (Discussion Paper Ser.: No. 81). 122p. 1990. 7.95 (*0-8213-1560-9*, 11560) World Bank.

Morris, Florence T. A Walk in the Woods. 1993. 10.00 (*0-533-10139-5*) Vantage.

Morris, Floyd. 272 Artistic Silhouettes. (Illus.). 1972. 11.00 (*0-87006-158-5*) Goodheart.

Morris, Frances, jt. auth. see Clouzot, Henri.

Morris, Francis & Moore, Fionna. Case Presentations in Accident & Emergency Medicine. LC 92-49711. 1992. 30.00 (*0-7506-1378-5*) Buttrwrth-Heinemann.

Morris, Frank. The Divine Epic. LC 72-96118. 539p. 1973. pap. 8.95 (*0-913382-18-3*, 101-18) Prow Bks-Franciscan.

Morris, Frank R. & Morris, Dixie G. Grandparent Wisdom. 39p. 1988. pap. text ed. 5.95 (*0-929946-03-0*) L P T C.

— Liberation Psychology. 147p. 1988. spiral bd. 20.00 (*0-929946-02-2*) L P T C.

— The Logic of Feelings: A Companion for therapeutic Adventurers. rev. ed. Orig. Title: Therapeutic Feelings. (Illus.). 110p. (C). 1993. spiral bd. 20.00 (*0-929946-00-6*) L P T C.

— Who Am I, Anyway? 115p. 1989. spiral bd. 20.00 (*0-929946-01-4*) L P T C.

Morris, Frank T. Finches of Australia: A Folio. (Illus.). 124p. 65.00 (*0-7018-1000-9*) Eastview.

Morris, Freda. Self-Hypnosis in Two Days. 1975. pap. 7.95 (*0-525-48364-0*, Dutton) NAL-Dutton.

Morris, Frederick M. Bishop Pike: Ham, Heretic, or Hero. LC 67-28381. 32p. reprint ed. pap. 25.00 (*0-8357-7278-0*, 2012934) Bks Demand.

***Morris, G.** Laying down the Law. 3rd ed. 352p. 1992. pap. 51.00 (*0-409-30541-3*, Austral) Butterworth Legal Pubs.

Morris, G. H. & Chenail, Ronald U., eds. The Talk of the Clinic: Exploration in the Analysis of Medical & Therapeutic Discourse. (Communication Ser.). 352p. 1995. text ed. 79.95 (*0-8058-1372-1*); pap. 29.95 (*0-8058-1373-X*) L Erlbaum Assocs.

Morris, G. J. & Clarke, A., eds. Effects of Low Temperature on Biological Membranes. LC 81-67921. 1982. text ed. 134.00 (*0-12-507650-9*) Acad Pr.

Morris, G. J., jt. ed. see Grout, B. W.

Morris, G. M. Holographic Optics Three, Vol. 1507: Principles & Applications. 1991. 95.00 (*0-8194-0616-3*) SPIE.

Morris, G. M., ed. Statistical Optics, Vol. 976. 1988. 51.00 (*0-8194-0011-4*) SPIE.

Morris, G. Michael, ed. Holographic Optics II: Principles & Applications. 380p. 1989. 77.00 (*0-8194-0172-2*, VOL. 1136) SPIE.

Morris, G. S. Strikes in Essential Services. Hepple, Bob & O'Higgins, Paul, eds. (Studies in Labour & Social Law). 232p. 1986. pap. text ed. 50.00 (*0-7201-1869-7*, Mansell Pub) Cassell.

Morris, G. S. & Stiehl, Jim. Changing Kids' Games. LC 88-22097. (Illus.). 160p. 1989. pap. text ed. 15.00x (*0-87322-187-7*, BMOR0187) Human Kinetics.

— Physical Education: From Intent to Action. 464p. (C). 1985. write for info. (*0-675-20115-2*, Merrill Pub Co) Macmillan.

Morris, Gabrielle, jt. auth. see Margolis, Jonathan.

Morris, Gareth. Flute Technique: New Edition. (Illus.). 80p. 1992. pap. 26.95 (*0-19-318432-X*) OUP.

Morris, Gareth, jt. ed. see Rose, A. H.

Morris, Gene, jt. auth. see Morris, Michael H.

Morris, Geoffrey. The Rise of the Labour Movement. 128p. (C). 1986. 45.00 (*0-317-89992-9*) St Mut.

Morris, Geoffrey, jt. auth. see King, Howard.

Morris, George. Rebellion in the Unions: A Handbook for Rank & File Action. LC 74-173354. 160p. 1971. pap. 2.75 (*0-685-23466-5*) New Outlook.

— Social Democrats -U. S. A. in the Service of Reaction: A Record of Racism, Low Wages, Bureaucracy & Betrayal of Socialism. 1976. pap. 0.50 (*0-87898-119-5*) New Outlook.

Morris, George E. & Fox, H. Eddie. Faith-Sharing: Dynamic Christian Witnessing By Invitation. LC 86-71913. 144p. (Orig.). 1986. pap. 6.95 (*0-88177-039-6*, DR039B) Discipleship Res.

Morris, George G. & Foutz, Susan L. Lynchburg in the Civil War. (Virginia Civil War Battles & Leaders Ser.). (Illus.). 146p. 1984. 19.95 (*0-930919-11-4*) H E Howard.

Morris, George H. The American Show Jumping Style: Modern Techniques of Successful Horsemanship. LC 92-42850. 1993. 27.50 (*0-385-41082-4*) Doubleday.

— Hunter Seat Equitation. 3rd ed. 1990. 27.50 (*0-385-41368-8*) Doubleday.

Morris, George S. British Thought & Thinkers: From John of Salisbury & Roger Bacon to John Stuart Mill & Herbert Spencer. 1977. lib. bdg. 59.95 (*0-8490-1557-X*) Gordon Pr.

— British Thought & Thinkers: Introductory Studies, Critical, Biographical & Philosophical. LC 75-3286. reprint ed. 26.00 (*0-404-59274-0*) AMS Pr.

— Hegel's Philosophy of the State & of History: An Exposition. 2nd ed. LC 75-3287. reprint ed. 32.50 (*0-404-59275-9*) AMS Pr.

Morris, George S., tr. see Ueberweg, Friedrich.

Morris, George W., et al. Russian: Face to Face: Beginning. (RUS.). (YA). 1993. student ed 9.25 (*0-8442-4301-9*, Natl Textbk); teacher ed 13.25 (*0-8442-4307-8*, Natl Textbk); text ed. 33.25 (*0-8442-4300-0*, Natl Textbk); audio 106.60 (*0-8442-4303-5*, Natl Textbk) NTC Pub Grp.

— Russian: Face to Face: Beginning. annot. ed. (RUS.). (YA). 1993. teacher ed 41.25 (*0-8442-4302-7*, Natl Textbk) NTC Pub Grp.

Morris, Georgia & Pollard, Mark. Roy Rogers: King of the Cowboys. LC 93-35483. 1994. 24.95 (*0-00-255334-1*) Collins SF.

Morris, Gerald E. & Howland, Llewellyn, III. Yachting in America: A Bibliography. x, 398p. 1991. 49.95 (*0-913372-49-8*) Mystic Seaport.

Morris, Gerald E., ed. see Ray, Roger B.

Morris, Gilbert. Boomtown, No. 4. 1992. pap. 9.99 (*0-8423-7789-1*) Tyndale.

— The Bucks of Goober Hollow. LC 94-7012. (Ozark Adventures Ser.: Vol. 1). (J). (gr. 3-7). 1994. pap. 4.99 (*0-8423-4392-X*) Tyndale.

— Captain Chip & the March to Victory. (Captain Chip & His Rag Tag Band Ser.). (J). (gr. 4-7). 1994. pap. 5.99 (*0-8024-1584-9*) Moody.

— The Captive Bride. LC 87-15782. (House of Winslow Ser.: Bk. 2). 228p. (Orig.). 1987. pap. 8.99 (*0-87123-978-7*) Bethany Hse.

— Corporal Chip & the Call to Battle. (Captain Chip & His Rag Tag Band Ser.). (J). (gr. 4-7). 1994. pap. 5.99 (*0-8024-1585-7*) Moody.

— A Covenant of Love. LC 92-5584. (Appomattox Saga Ser.: Vol. 1). 352p. 1992. pap. 10.99 (*0-8423-5497-2*) Tyndale.

— The Crossed Sabres. (House of Winslow Ser.). 304p. (Orig.). (YA). 1993. pap. 8.99 (*1-55661-309-1*) Bethany Hse.

— Danielle Ross Mystery Series, 3 vols., Set. 1992. pap. 24.00 (*0-8007-5454-9*) Revell.

— Deadly Deception. LC 91-36737. (Danielle Ross Mystery Ser.: No. 3). 1992. pap. 8.99 (*0-8007-5419-0*) Revell.

— The Dixie Widow. (House of Winslow Ser.: Bk. 9). 302p. (Orig.). (YA). (gr. 9-12). 1991. text ed. 8.99 (*1-55661-115-3*) Bethany Hse.

— The Final Adversary. LC 92-16172. (House of Winslow Ser.: Bk. 12). 302p. (Orig.). 1992. pap. 8.99 (*1-55661-261-3*) Bethany Hse.

— The Final Curtain. LC 91-18713. 256p. 1991. pap. 8.99 (*0-8007-5411-5*) Revell.

— Flight of the Eagles. (YA). 1994. pap. 5.99 (*0-8024-3681-1*) Moody.

— The Gallant Outlaw. LC 93-45364. (House of Winslow Ser.: No. 15). 1994. pap. 8.99 (*1-55661-311-3*) Bethany Hse.

— The Gates of His Enemies. LC 92-17784. (Appomattox Sage Ser.). 1992. 10.99 (*0-8423-1069-X*) Tyndale.

— The Gates of Neptune. (Seven Sleepers Ser.). 180p. 1994. pap. 5.99 (*0-8024-3682-X*) Moody.

— The Gentle Rebel. LC 88-18712. (House of Winslow Ser.). 240p. (Orig.). 1988. pap. 8.99 (*1-55661-006-8*) Bethany Hse.

— Guilt by Association. LC 90-26028. 1991. pap. 8.99 (*0-8007-5395-X*) Revell.

— The Holy Warrior. (House of Winslow Ser.). 288p. (Orig.). 1989. pap. 8.99 (*1-55661-054-8*) Bethany Hse.

— The Honorable Imposter. 331p. 1986. pap. 8.99 (*0-87123-933-7*) Bethany Fellow.

— The Honorable Imposter. large type ed. LC 92-36473. (General Ser.). 464p. 1993. 20.95 (*0-8161-5672-7*) G K Hall.

— House of Winslow, 5 vols., Set, Vols. 1-5. 1992. Gift set. 44.99 (*1-55661-767-4*) Bethany Hse.

— House of Winslow, Vols. 6-10. (House of Winslow Ser.). (Orig.). (YA). 1993. 44.99 (*1-55661-768-2*) Bethany Hse.

— How to Write - & Sell - a Christian Novel: Proven & Practical Advice from a Bestselling Author. 180p. 1994. pap. 8.99 (*0-89283-878-7*, Vine Bks) Servant.

— The Indentured Heart. LC 87-34128. (House of Winslow Ser.). 272p. 1988. pap. 8.99 (*1-55661-003-3*) Bethany Hse.

— Jeweled Spur. 1994. pap. 8.99 (*1-55661-392-X*) Bethany Hse.

— Land of the Shadow. LC 93-13781. (Appomattox Saga Ser.: Vol. 4). 1993. 10.99 (*0-8423-5742-4*) Tyndale.

— The Last Confederate. (House of Winslow Ser.). 302p. (Orig.). 1990. pap. 8.99 (*1-55661-109-9*) Bethany Hse.

— Lone Wolf. LC 95-7541. (Reno Western Saga Ser.: Vol. 6). 1995. write for info. (*0-8423-1997-2*) Tyndale.

An Asterisk (*) at the beginning of an entry indicates that the title is appearing in BIP for the first time.

— Out of the Whirlwind. LC 93-35507. (Appomattox Saga Ser.: No. 5). (Illus.). 1994. pap. 9.99 (*0-8423-1658-2*) Tyndale.
— The Phantom of the Circus. LC 94-9212. (Ozark Adventures Ser.: Vol. 3). (J). (gr. 3-7). 1994. pap. 4.99 (*0-8423-5097-7*) Tyndale.
— The Quality of Mercy. LC 93-32432. (Danielle Ross Mystery Ser.). 288p. 1993. pap. 8.99 (*0-8007-5474-3*) Revell.
— Race with Death. LC 94-14532. (Danielle Ross Ser.: No. 6). 288p. (Orig.). 1994. pap. 8.99 (*0-8007-5498-0*) Revell.
— The Reluctant Bridegroom. (House of Winslow Ser.). 302p. (Orig.). 1990. pap. 8.99 (*1-55661-069-6*) Bethany Hse.
— Reno. LC 92-9438. (Jim Reno Westerns Ser.: Vol. 1). 1992. 9.99 (*0-8423-1058-4*) Tyndale.
— Revenge at the Rodeo. LC 92-591. (Danielle Ross Mystery Ser.). 320p. (Orig.). 1993. pap. 8.99 (*0-8007-5457-3*) Revell.
— Ride the Wild River. LC 92-9437. (Jim Reno Westerns Ser.: No. 3). Orig. Title: The Runaway. 1992. 9.99 (*0-8423-5795-5*) Tyndale.
— Rimrock. LC 92-9439. (Jim Reno Westerns Ser.: Vol. 2). 1992. 9.99 (*0-8423-1059-2*) Tyndale.
— The Rustlers of Panther Gap. LC 94-7128. No. 2. (J). (gr. 3-7). 1994. pap. 4.99 (*0-8423-4393-8*) Tyndale.
— The Saintly Buccaneer. LC 88-33337. (House of Winslow Ser.). 288p. (Orig.). (YA). (gr. 11 up). 1989. pap. 8.99 (*1-55661-048-3*) Bethany Hse.
— The Shadow of His Wings. LC 94-28708. (Appomattox Saga Ser.: No. 6). 352p. 1994. pap. 10.99 (*0-8423-5987-7*) Tyndale.
— The Shield of Honor. LC 94-45604. (Wakefield Dynasty Ser.: Vol. 3). 1995. pap. 10.99 (*0-8423-5930-3*) Tyndale.
— Silence in Heaven. 1994. pap. 9.99 (*0-8499-3511-3*) Word Inc.
— Sound the Trumpet. (Liberty Bell Ser.: Bk. 1). 320p. 1995. pap. 8.99 (*1-55661-565-5*) Bethany Hse.
— A Time to Be Born. LC 93-26089. (American Odyssey Ser.). 336p. (Orig.). (YA). 1994. pap. 9.99 (*0-8007-5497-2*) Revell.
— A Time to Die. LC 93-36519. (American Odyssey Ser.: No. 2). 288p. (Orig.). (YA). 1994. pap. 9.99 (*0-8007-5521-9*) Revell.
— A Time to Laugh. (American Odyssey Ser.: Bk. 3). 304p. (Orig.). 1995. pap. 9.99 (*0-8007-5566-9*) Revell.
— The Union Belle. (House of Winslow Ser.: No. 11). 302p. (Orig.). (YA). 1992. pap. 8.99 (*1-55661-186-2*) Bethany Hse.
— The Valiant Gunman. LC 93-2416. (House of Winslow Ser.: Bk. 14). 1993. pap. 8.99 (*1-55661-310-5*) Bethany Hse.
— Valley Justice. LC 94-26129. (Reno Western Saga Ser.: Vol. 5). 1995. 9.99 (*0-8423-7756-5*) Tyndale.
— Wall of Fire. LC 94-43872. (Appomattox Saga Ser.: Vol. 7). 1995. 10.99 (*0-8423-8126-0*) Tyndale.
— Where Honor Dwells. LC 92-36469. 1993. 9.99 (*0-8423-6799-3*) Tyndale.
— The Winds of God. LC 94-28712. (Wakefield Dynasty Ser.: No. 2). 422p. 1994. pap. 10.99 (*0-8423-7953-3*) Tyndale.
— Wounded Yankee. (House of Winslow Ser.: Bk. 11). 320p. (Orig.). 1991. pap. 8.99 (*1-55661-116-1*) Bethany Hse.
— The Yukon Queen. (House of Winslow Ser.: Bk. 17). 320p. 1995. pap. 8.99 (*1-55661-393-8*) Bethany Hse.
Morris, Gilbert, ed. The Sword of Truth. LC 94-7013. (Wakefield Dynasty Ser.). 422p. 1994. pap. 10.99 (*0-8423-6228-2*) Tyndale.
Morris, Gilbert & Funderburk, Bobby. All the Shining Young Men. LC 93-24235. (Price of Liberty Ser.: No. 3). 1993. 8.99 (*0-8499-3496-6*) Word Pub.
— A Call to Honor. LC 92-44517. (Price of Liberty Ser.: No. 1). 224p. (Orig.). 1993. pap. 8.99 (*0-8499-3494-X*) Word Inc.
— The Color of the Star. LC 92-44518. (Price of Liberty Ser.: No. 2). 1993. pap. 8.99 (*0-8499-3495-8*) Word Pub.
— The Color of the Star. No. 2. 220p. 1993. pap. write for info. (*0-318-70296-7*) Word Inc.
— An End to Glory. LC 93-24236. (Price of Liberty Ser.: No. 4). 1993. 8.99 (*0-8499-3825-2*) Word Pub.
— A Time To Heal. LC 94-27309. 1994. write for info. (*0-8499-3512-1*) World Pub FL.
Morris, Gilbert & Funderburtk, Bobby. Beyond the River. 288p. 1994. pap. 8.95 (*0-914984-51-9*) Starburst.
Morris, Gilbert & Morris, Lynn. Shadow of the Mountain. (Cheny Duvall, M. D. Ser.: No. 2). 1994. pap. 8.99 (*1-55661-423-3*) Bethany Hse.
Morris, Gilbert, jt. auth. see Morris, Lynn.
***Morris, Gilbert, et al.** A City Not Forsaken. (M. D. Ser.: Bk. 2). 320p. 1995. pap. 8.99 (*1-55661-424-1*) Bethany Hse.
Morris, Gillian S. & Archer, Timothy J. Trade Unions, Employers & the Law. 384p. 1991. 139.95 (*0-632-02966-8*) Blackwell Sci.
— Trade Unions, Employers & the Law. 2nd ed. 1993. boxed 135.00 (*0-406-02448-0*, UK) Butterworth Legal Pubs.
***Morris, Gillian S. & Deakin, Simon.** Labour Law. 1995. pap. text ed. write for info. (*0-406-01025-0*, UK) Butterworth Legal Pubs.
Morris, Gillian S., jt. auth. see Fredman, Sandra.
Morris, Glen. Country Roads of North Carolina. LC 94-14329. (Illus.). 144p. (Orig.). 1994. pap. 9.95 (*1-56626-067-1*) Country Rds.
Morris, Glenda, jt. auth. see Early, Howard.
Morris, Glenn. North Carolina Beaches: A Guide to Coastal Access. LC 92-50813. (Illus.). xviii, 294p. (Orig.). 1993. pap. 16.95 (*0-8078-4413-6*) U of NC Pr.
— Path Notes of an American Ninja Master. LC 93-8031. 264p. (Orig.). 1993. pap. 12.95 (*1-55643-157-0*) North Atlantic.
— Shadow Strategies of an American Ninja Master. 250p. (Orig.). (C). 1995. pap. 12.95 (*1-883319-29-3*) Frog CA.
Morris, Gordon, ed. Shaw's Directory of Courts. (C). 1988. pap. 110.00 (*0-7219-0983-3*, Scientific) St Mut.
— Shaw's Directory of Courts in the United Kingdom. (C). 1987. pap. 75.00 (*0-7219-0980-9*, Scientific) St Mut.
Morris, Gouverneur. Diary & Letters of Gouverneur Morris, 2 Vols. Morris, Anne C., ed. LC 70-98691. (American Public Figures Ser.). 1970. reprint ed. lib. bdg. 130.00 (*0-306-71835-9*) Da Capo.
— Diary of the French Revolution, 2 vols. Davenport, Beatrix C., ed. LC 70-110859. (Illus.). 1972. reprint ed. text ed. 75.00 (*0-8371-4528-7*, MOFR) Greenwood.
— Diary of the French Revolution, 2 vols, 1. Davenport, Beatrix C., ed. LC 70-110859. (Illus.). 1972. reprint ed. text ed. 45.00 (*0-8371-4529-5*, MOFS) Greenwood.
— A Diary of the French Revolution, 2 vols., Set. Davenport, Beatrix C., ed. LC 71-157348. (Select Bibliographies Reprint Ser.). 1977. reprint ed. 72.95 (*0-8369-5809-8*) Ayer.
— Diary of the French Revolution, 2 vols, Vol. 2. Davenport, Beatrix C., ed. LC 70-110859. (Illus.). 1972. reprint ed. text ed. 45.00 (*0-8371-4530-9*, MOFT) Greenwood.
— Footprint, & Other Stories. LC 70-142270. (Short Story Index Reprint Ser.). 1977. 23.95 (*0-8369-3754-6*) Ayer.
— Incandescent Lily, & Other Stories. LC 73-142271. (Short Story Index Reprint Ser.). 1977. 20.95 (*0-8369-3755-4*) Ayer.
Morris, Grant H. & Snyder, Allen C. Mental Disorder in the Criminal Process: Stan Stress & the Vietnam-Sports Conspiracy. LC 92-21355. (Contributions in Legal Studies: No. 72). 324p. 1993. text ed. 55.00 (*0-313-28761-9*, GM8761, Greenwood Pr) Greenwood.
Morris, Greggory. Basketball Basics. LC 75-34142. (Illus.). (J). (gr. 2-6). 1979. 6.95 (*0-13-072256-1*, Pub. by Treehouse Paperback) P-H.
Morris, Greggory W. & Waters, Thomas J. Unspeakable Acts: The Ordeal of Thomas Waters-Rimmer. 1993. 23.00 (*0-688-09483-X*) Morrow.
Morris, Gregory ., jt. auth. see Baldwin, Dean.
***Morris, Gregory A.** Too Fresh the Grudge. 290p. 1995. pap. 8.95 (*1-56901-672-0*) NW Pub.
Morris, Gregory L. Candlepower: Advanced Candlestick Pattern Recognition & Filtering Techniques for Trading Stocks & Futures. 275p. 1992. 50.00 (*1-55738-458-4*, 458) Probus Pub Co.
— Talking Up a Storm: Voices of the New West. LC 93-46326. (Illus.). 288p. 1994. text ed. 25.00 (*0-8032-3169-5*) U of Nebr Pr.
Morris, Guy V. Airborne Pulsed Doppler Radar. (Radar Library). 416p. 1988. text ed. 79.00 (*0-89006-272-2*) Artech Hse.
Morris, H. C., jt. ed. see Lam, Lui.
Morris, H. H. Demystifying the Congregational Budget. LC 88-70759. 62p. (Orig.). 1988. pap. 6.95 (*1-56699-066-1*, OD75) Alban Inst.
Morris, H. R., ed. see Symposium on Advances in Mass Spectrometry Soft Ionization Methods Staff.
Morris, Harold. Duplamente Perdoado. 240p. (POR.). 1990. pap. 9.95 (*0-8297-1629-7*) Life Pubs Intl.
***Morris, Harold & Barker, Dianne.** Twice Pardoned. 258p. Date not set. pap. 4.99 (*0-8423-7396-9*) Tyndale.
Morris, Harry. Birth, & Copulation, & Death. LC 79-94804. 68p. reprint ed. pap. 25.00 (*0-7837-5079-X*, 2044777) Bks Demand.
— Last Things in Shakespeare. 1985. 39.95 (*0-685-58690-1*) U Press Fla.
— Richard Barnfield: Colin's Child. LC 63-63443. (Florida State University Studies: No. 38). 217p. reprint ed. pap. 61.90 (*0-7837-4928-7*, 2044594) Bks Demand.
Morris, Harvey, jt. auth. see Bulloch, John.
Morris, Henry. Amostra de Salmos. Orig. Title: Sampling the Psalms. 180p. (POR.). 1986. 7.95 (*0-8297-0698-4*) Life Pubs Intl.
— The Bible, Science & Creation. 1991. pap. 1.99 (*0-8474-0868-X*) Back to Bible.
— Geologia: Actualismo O Diluvianismo? Geology: Actualism. (SPA.). 3.95 (*84-7228-515-4*, 220425, Pub. by Edit Clie SP) TSELF.
— El Mundo en Sus Comienzos: Beginning of the World. (SPA.). 5.25 (*84-7228-631-2*, 220614, Pub. by Edit Clie SP) TSELF.
— Psaumes Choisis. 192p. (FRE.). 1986. 6.95 (*0-8297-0697-6*) Life Pubs Intl.
Morris, Henry, ed. Proceedings of the Tenth Annual Control Engineering Conference: Held As Part of the Control Engineering Conference & Exposition, O'Hare Exposition Center, Rosemont, IL May 21-23, 1991. (Illus.). 500p. (Orig.). (C). 1991. pap. write for info. (*0-914331-60-4*, Control Engrng) Cahners Des Plaines.
Morris, Henry I., jt. auth. see Phillips, Arthur.
Morris, Henry M. The Beginning of the World. 184p. 1991. reprint ed. pap. 8.95 (*0-89051-162-4*) Master Bks.
Morris, Henry M. Bible Has the Answer. 1971. pap. 11.99 (*0-8010-5905-4*) Baker Bk.
Morris, Henry M. The Biblical Basis of Modern Science. LC 84-72122. (C). 1984. 24.99 (*0-8010-6178-4*) Baker Bk.
— Biblical Creationism: What Each Book of the Bible Teaches about Creation & the Flood. LC 93-13462. 320p. 1993. text ed. 21.99 (*0-8010-6298-5*) Baker Bk.
— Christian Education for the Real World. LC 77-78017. 295p. 1991. reprint ed. pap. 10.95 (*0-89051-160-8*) Master Bks.
— Creation & the Modern Christian. 298p. 1985. pap. 8.95 (*0-89051-111-X*) Master Bks.
— Creation & the Second Coming. 194p. 1991. 12.95 (*0-89051-163-2*) Master Bks.
***Morris, Henry M.** The Defender's Study Bible. 1700p. 1995. 34.99 (*0-529-10444-X*) World Bible.
Morris, Henry M. Evolution & the Modern Christian. 1967. pap. 3.99 (*0-87552-337-4*) Presby & Reformed.
— Genesis Record. LC 76-2265. 1976. 24.99 (*0-8010-6004-4*) Baker Bk.
— The God Who Is Real: A Creationist Approach to Evangelism & Missions. 104p. (Orig.). 1988. pap. 5.99 (*0-8010-6233-0*) Baker Bk.
— The Long War Against God: The History & Impact of the Creation - Evolution Conflict. LC 89-39261. 368p. 1989. 21.99 (*0-8010-6257-8*) Baker Bk.
— Many Infallible Proofs. LC 74-81484. 381p. 1974. pap. 8.95 (*0-89051-005-9*) Master Bks.
— Men of Science, Men of God. rev. ed. LC 82-70271. (Illus.). 126p. 1988. pap. 6.95 (*0-89051-080-6*) Master Bks.
— The Remarkable Record of Job: The Ancient Wisdom, Scientific Accuracy, & Life-Changing Message of an Amazing Book. 1988. 12.99 (*0-8010-6238-1*) Baker Bk.
— The Revelation Record. 1983. 24.99 (*0-8423-5511-1*) Tyndale.
— Sampling the Psalms. LC 78-55613. 269p. 1991. reprint ed. pap. 8.95 (*0-89051-049-0*) Master Bks.
— Science & the Bible. rev. ed. 1986. pap. 8.99 (*0-8024-0656-4*) Moody.
— Scientific Creationism. Han, Paul, tr. 223p. (CHI.). 1993. pap. 6.50 (*1-56582-039-8*) Christ Renew Min.
— Twilight of Evolution. LC 63-21471. (C). 1963. pap. 6.99 (*0-8010-5862-7*) Baker Bk.
— What Is Creation Science. rev. ed. LC 82-70114. (Illus.). 1987. pap. 10.95 (*0-89051-081-4*) Master Bks.
Morris, Henry M., ed. Proceedings of the Ninth Annual Control Engineering Conference: Held as Part of the Control Engineering Conference & Exposition, O'Hare Exposition Center, Rosemont, Illinois, May 22-24, 1990. (Illus.). 500p. (Orig.). (C). 1990. pap. text ed. 120.00 (*0-914331-59-0*, Control Engrng) Cahners Des Plaines.
Morris, Henry M. & Clark, Martin. The Bible Has the Answer. rev. ed. LC 76-20206. 408p. 1987. pap. 10.95 (*0-89051-018-0*) Master Bks.
Morris, Henry M. & Wiggert, James M. Applied Hydraulics in Engineering. 2nd ed. 629p. 1972. Net. text ed. write for info. (*0-471-06669-9*); 3.00 (*0-471-07503-5*) Wiley.
Morris, Henry M., jt. auth. see Whitcomb, John C.
Morris, Henry M., jt. auth. see Whitcomb, John C., Jr.
Morris, Henry M., et al, eds. Advanced Control in Computer Integrated Manufacturing. (Proceedings of the 13th. Annual Advanced Control Conference). 200p. 1987. 30.00 (*0-931682-23-1*) Purdue U Pubns.
Morris, Herbert. Afghanistan. 1984. pap. 10.00 (*0-89807-016-3*) Illuminati.
— Afghanistan. limited ed. 1984. 20.00 (*0-89807-017-1*) Illuminati.
— Intimate Letters. LC 79-14341. 1991. 20.00 (*0-89807-021-X*); pap. 8.95 (*0-89807-020-1*) Illuminati.
— The Masked Citadel: The Significance of the Title of Stendhal's La Chartreuse de Parme. LC 68-65298. 38p. 1983. reprint ed. lib. bdg. 23.00x (*0-89370-762-7*) Borgo Pr.
— On Guilt & Innocence: Essays in Legal Philosophy & Moral Psychology. 1976. pap. 11.00 (*0-520-03944-0*) U CA Pr.
Morris, Herbert, ed. Freedom & Responsibility: Readings in Philosophy & Law. LC 61-8469. 111p. reprint ed. pap. 30.00 (*0-7837-2163-3*, 2042469) Bks Demand.
***Morris, Holly, ed.** A Different Angle: Fly Fishing Stories by Women. LC 94-39386. 288p. (Orig.). 1995. 22.95 (*1-878067-63-X*) Seal Pr Feminist.
— Uncommon Waters: Women Write about Fishing. LC 91-21455. (Women in Sports Ser.). (Illus.). 320p. (Orig.). 1991. pap. 14.95 (*1-878067-10-9*) Seal Pr Feminist.
Morris, Holly, jt. auth. see Reiser, David.
Morris, Humphrey, jt. ed. see Smith, Joseph H.
Morris, I., ed. The Physiological Ecology of Phytoplankton. (Studies in Ecology: Vol. 7). 1981. 95.00 (*0-520-04308-1*) U CA Pr.
Morris, Ian. Burial & Ancient Society: The Rise of the Greek City State. (New Studies in Archaeology). (Illus.). 288p. (C). 1990. pap. 21.95 (*0-521-38738-8*) Cambridge U Pr.
— Death-Ritual & Social Structure in Classical Antiquity. (Key Themes in Ancient History Ser.). (Illus.). 288p. (C). 1992. pap. 21.95 (*0-521-37611-4*) Cambridge U Pr.
Morris, Ian, ed. Classical Greece: Ancient Histories & Modern Archaeologies. LC 93-6625. (New Directions in Archaeology Ser.). (Illus.). 250p. (C). 1994. 64.95 (*0-521-39279-9*); pap. 19.95 (*0-521-45678-9*) Cambridge U Pr.
Morris, Ian, jt. auth. see Ross, Sydney.
Morris, Inez, jt. auth. see Morris, Dan.
Morris, Irvin, jt. ed. see Eteitly, Henry.
Morris, Ivan. Pillow Book of Sei Shonagon. 1991. text ed. 50.00 (*0-231-07336-4*) Col U Pr.
— World of the Shining Prince: Court Life in Ancient Japan. De Angelis, Paul, ed. 352p. 1994. pap. 15.00 (*1-56836-029-0*) Kodansha.
Morris, Ivan, ed. Madly Singing in the Mountains: An Appreciation & Anthology of Arthur Waley. 404p. 1981. reprint ed. pap. 9.95 (*0-916870-35-9*) Creat Arts Bk.
— Modern Japanese Stories: An Anthology. LC 61-11971. (Illus.). 512p. 1977. pap. 16.95 (*0-8048-1226-8*) C E Tuttle.
Morris, Ivan, tr. & intro. As I Crossed a Bridge of Dreams: Recollections of a Woman in Eleventh-Century Japan. 176p. 1989. pap. 7.95 (*0-14-044282-0*, Penguin Classics) Viking Penguin.
Morris, Ivan, tr. The Pillow Book of Sei Shonagon. 411p. 1991. pap. text ed. 12.00 (*0-231-07337-2*) Col U Pr.
Morris, Ivan, tr. see Kenzaburo Oe, ed.
Morris, Ivan, tr. see Mishima, Yukio.
Morris, Ivan, tr. see Ooka, Shohei.
Morris, Ivan, tr. see Osaragi, Jiro.
Morris, Ivan, ed. see Saikaku, Ihara.
Morris, J. Managing the Library Fire Risk. 2nd rev. ed. LC 78-22603. (Illus.). 1979. 15.50 (*0-9602278-1-4*) J Morris.
Morris, J. Bayard, tr. Hernando Cortes: Five Letters. Orig. Title: Hernando Cortes Five Letters, 1519-1526. (C). 1991. pap. 10.95 (*0-393-09877-X*) Norton.
Morris, J. Bayard, tr. see Cortes, Hernan.
Morris, J. C., tr. see Lilie, Ralph-J.
Morris, J. E. The Felt Genealogy: A Record of the Descendants of George Felt of Casco Bay. 568p. 1989. reprint ed. lib. bdg. 97.00 (*0-8328-0542-4*); reprint ed. pap. 87.00 (*0-8328-0543-2*) Higginson Bk Co.
Morris, J. F. A Genealogical & Historical Register of the Descendants of Edward Morris of Roxbury, Massachusetts, & Woodstock, Connecticut. (Illus.). 423p. 1989. reprint ed. lib. bdg. 76.50 (*0-8328-0882-2*); reprint ed. pap. 66.50 (*0-8328-0883-0*) Higginson Bk Co.
Morris, J. G., ed. see Metallurgical Society of AIME Staff.
Morris, J. G., jt. ed. see Rose, A. H.
Morris, J. Gareth, jt. ed. see Rose, A. H.
Morris, J. H. & North, P. M. Cases & Materials on Private International Law. 786p. 1984. U.K. pap. text ed. 68.00 (*0-406-25265-3*, UK) Butterworth Legal Pubs.
Morris, J. L. Computational Methods in Elementary Numerical Analysis. LC 82-2778. 410p. 1983. pap. text ed. 53.95 (*0-471-10420-5*, Wiley-Interscience) Wiley.
Morris, J. L., jt. auth. see Rushforth, J. M.
Morris, J. M., et al, eds. Fourth Refinement Workshop: Proceedings of the 4th Refinement Workshop Organised by BCS-FACS 9-11 January 1991, Cambridge, UK. (Workshops in Computing Ser.). (Illus.). viii, 479p. 1991. pap. 59.00 (*0-387-19657-9*) Spr-Verlag.
Morris, J. N. Religion & Urban Change: Croydon, 1840-1914. LC 92-27759. (Royal Historical Society: Studies in History: No. 65). (Illus.). 224p. (C). 1992. text ed. 63.00 (*0-86193-222-6*, Royal Historical Soc) Boydell & Brewer.
Morris, J. R., jt. ed. see Johnston, C. S.
Morris, J. Scott. Real Estate Tax Forms. LC 80-84025. 1981. 65.00 (*0-316-58382-0*) Little.
Morris, J. W., jt. ed. see Chipman, R. A.
Morris, Jack. The Bushido Thing. (Illus.). 350p. 1994. 25.00 (*0-912479-08-6*) Palmer Pr.
— The Crime Analysis Charting. (Illus.). 116p. 1994. pap. 16.00 (*0-912479-01-9*) Palmer Pr.
— The Criminal Intelligence File. (Illus.). 100p. 1992. 20.00 (*0-912479-00-0*) Palmer Pr.
— The Deadly Routine. LC 80-82429. (Illus.). 154p. 1980. pap. 17.00 (*0-912479-04-3*) Palmer Pr.
— Master Criminals among the Gypsies. (Illus.). 200p. 1994. text ed. 20.00 (*0-912479-11-6*) Palmer Pr.
— Police Informant Management. LC 83-63214. (Illus.). 95p. 1983. pap. 15.00 (*0-912479-02-7*) Palmer Pr.
Morris, Jack, jt. auth. see Frost, Charles C.
Morris, Jack J. Disaster Zone - U.S.A. LC 90-85799. 192p. (Orig.). 1991. pap. text ed. write for info. (*0-9628670-0-4*) Avanti Pub Hse.
***Morris, Jackie.** Bears, Bears & More Bears. LC 94-42980. (J). 1995. write for info. (*0-8120-6516-6*); pap. write for info. (*0-8120-9349-6*) Barron.
Morris, Jacqueline, jt. ed. see Callison, Daniel.
Morris, James. America's Armed Forces: A History. 1991. pap. text ed. 20.00 (*0-13-029265-6*, 680105) P-H.
— Farewell the Trumpets: The Decline of an Empire. LC 79-24253. (Illus.). 576p. 1980. pap. 16.00 (*0-15-630286-1*, Harvest Bks) HarBrace.
— Heaven's Command: An Imperial Progress. LC 79-24327. (Illus.). 554p. 1980. pap. 14.95 (*0-15-640006-5*, Harvest Bks) HarBrace.
— History of the U.S. Army. 1992. 19.99 (*0-517-06723-4*) Random Hse Value.
— Pax Britannica: The Climax of an Empire. LC 79-24725. (Illus.). 544p. 1980. pap. 14.95 (*0-15-671466-3*, Harvest Bks) HarBrace.
— The World of Venice. rev. ed. LC 73-18461. (Illus.). 328p. 1995. reprint ed. pap. 13.00 (*0-15-698356-7*, Harvest Bks) HarBrace.
Morris, James & Cave-Penny, Toney, eds. Goats for Fibre. (Illus.). 115p. (Orig.). 1987. pap. text ed. 14.50 (*0-9512543-0-8*) Scholium Intl.
Morris, James, jt. auth. see Kish, Joseph L.
Morris, James, jt. auth. see Schuette, Donald.
Morris, James A., Jr. Art of Conversation: The Magic Key to Personal & Social Popularity. 1976. 19.95 (*0-13-046698-0*) P-H.
Morris, James A. History of U. S. Navy: An Illustrated History. 1984. 14.98 (*0-671-06980-2*) S&S Trade.
Morris, James A., jt. ed. see Baloyra, Enrique A.
Morris, James C. Dusty Shells from the Peanut Gallery. LC 92-30750. 114p. 1993. 7.95 (*0-944957-15-3*) Rivercross Pub.
— Potpourri from a Black Pen: Many Musings That Have Passed Through the Years. LC 95-16113. 1995. write for info. (*0-944957-53-6*) Rivercross Pub.
Morris, James E., ed. Electronics Packaging Forum: Multichip Module Technology Issues. LC 93-23146. (Illus.). 400p. 1994. text ed. 69.95 (*0-7803-0439-X*, PC03368) Inst Electrical.
Morris, James G., ed. see AIME, Metallurgical Society Staff.
***Morris, James H.** A Life after Death & the Image of My Soul. 1995. 8.50 (*0-533-11246-X*) Vantage.
***Morris, James M., ed.** Legacies of Woodrow Wilson. LC 94-47449. 1995. pap. write for info. (*0-943875-70-6*) W Wilson Ctr Pr.
— On Mozart. (Woodrow Wilson Center Press Ser.). (Illus.). 250p. (C). 1994. 54.95 (*0-521-47065-X*); pap. 15.95 (*0-521-47661-5*) Cambridge U Pr.

M

***Morris, James M. & Adler, Laura.** Grant Seekers Guide. 4th ed. 1200p. 1995. 49.95 (1-55921-138-5) Moyer Bell.

— Grant Seekers Guide. 4th ed. 1200p. 1995. pap. 39.95 (1-55921-139-3) Moyer Bell.

Morris, James M., ed. see Jefferson, Thomas.

Morris, James O. A Bibliography of Industrial Relations in the Railroad Industry. LC 75-8878. (ILR Bibliography Ser.: No. 12). 172p. 1975. 1.00 (0-87546-058-5) ILR Pr.

— Conflict Within the AFL. LC 73-22506. (Cornell Studies in Industrial & Labor Relations: Vol. 10). 319p. 1974. reprint ed. text ed. 75.00 (0-8371-6371-4, MOCA, Greenwood Pr) Greenwood.

Morris, James P. History of the U. S. Army. 1987. 14.98 (0-671-08191-8) S&S Trade.

Morris, James W. K. N. Pepper. LC 73-166813. 1971. reprint ed. 29.00 (0-403-01458-1) Scholarly.

Morris, James W., tr. see Mulla Sadra.

Morris, Jan. Among the Cities. LC 85-13739. 1985. 25.00 (0-19-520489-1) OUP.

— Conundrum. LC 87-8668. 192p. 1987. pap. 9.95 (0-8050-0361-4, Owl) H Holt & Co.

— Destinations. 1982. pap. 9.95 (0-19-503069-9) OUP.

— Destinations: Essays from Rolling Stone. (Illus.). 1980. 21.95 (0-19-502708-6) OUP.

— Fisher's Face. LC 94-34174. 1995. 23.00 (0-679-41609-9) Random.

— The Great Port: A Passage Through New York. (Illus.). 1985. pap. 8.95 (0-19-503576-3) OUP.

— Hong Kong. LC 88-42677. (Illus.). 352p. 1988. 22.50 (0-394-55097-8) Random.

— Hong Kong. 1989. pap. 13.00 (0-679-72486-9, Vin) Random.

— Journeys. 192p. 1984. 25.00 (0-19-503452-X) OUP.

— Journeys. 192p. 1985. pap. 8.95 (0-19-503606-9) OUP.

— Last Letters from Hav. 1989. pap. 6.95 (0-394-75564-2, Vin) Random.

— Locations. 160p. 1992. 25.00 (0-19-212996-1) OUP.

— Locations. LC 92-45098. 160p. (C). 1993. pap. 9.95 (0-19-283136-4) OUP.

— Manhattan, 'Forty-Five. (Illus.). 288p. 1987. 25.00 (0-19-503870-3) OUP.

— Manhattan 'Forty-Five. 288p. 1990. reprint ed. pap. 9.95 (0-19-506664-2) OUP.

— Over Europe. Earley, Mary-Dawn & Frasier, Jane, eds. (Illus.). 288p. 1995. reprint ed. 45.00 (1-887451-00-5), Wldon Owen Ref.

— Oxford. 3rd ed. (Illus.). 304p. 1988. pap. 12.95 (0-19-282065-6) OUP.

— Pleasures of a Tangled Life. 1989. 18.95 (0-394-57649-7) Random.

— Pleasures of a Tangled Life. LC 90-50172. 224p. 1990. pap. 12.95 (0-679-73131-8, Vin) Random.

— The Venetian Empire: A Sea Voyage. (Illus.). 208p. 1990. pap. 12.00 (0-14-011994-9, Penguin Bks) Viking Penguin.

Morris, Jane A. Not in My Backyard: The Handbook. 308p. (Orig.). 1994. pap. 14.95 (0-9624945-7-7) Silvercat Pubns.

Morris, Janet. How to Develop Problem Solving Using a Calculator. LC 81-9569. (Illus.). 40p. 1981. pap. 6.00 (0-87353-175-2) NCTM.

Morris, Janet & Drake, David. Active Measures. 1985. pap. 3.95 (0-317-18176-9) S&S Trade.

Morris, Janet & Morris, Chris. The American Warrior. 288p. 1992. 18.95 (0-681-41401-4) Longmeadow Pr.

— The Stalk. 256p. 1994. 4.99 (0-451-45307-7, ROC) NAL-Dutton.

— Threshold. 256p. 1991. pap. 5.50 (0-451-45084-1, ROC) NAL-Dutton.

— Trust Territory. (Threshold Ser.: No. 2). 336p. 1992. pap. 20.00 (0-451-45126-0, ROC) NAL-Dutton.

— Trust Territory. 272p. 1993. pap. 4.99 (0-451-45236-4, ROC) NAL-Dutton.

Morris, Janet, jt. auth. see Drake, David.

***Morris, Jeannie.** Brian Piccolo: A Short Season. 25th ed. (Illus.). 200p. 1995. pap. text ed. 12.95 (1-56625-024-2) Bonus Books.

Morris, Jeff. Petroleum Geology & Reservoirs: Oil Well Servicing & Workover, Lesson 2. 2nd ed. (Illus.). 116p. (Orig.). 1992. pap. text ed. 25.00 (0-88698-156-5, 3.70220) PETEX.

Morris, Jeff, et al. Practical Petroleum Geology. Leecraft, Jodie, ed. (Illus.). 234p. (Orig.). 1985. pap. text ed. 35.00 (0-88698-097-6, 1.00210) PETEX.

Morris, Jeffrey. The Jefferson Way. LC 94-923. (Great Presidential Decisions Ser.). (Illus.). 112p. (YA). (gr. 5 up). 1994. 22.95 (0-8225-2926-2, Lerner Publctns) Lerner Group.

— The Lincoln Way. LC 94-23754. (Great Presidential Decisions Ser.). (J). 1995. write for info. (0-8225-2930-0) Lerner Group.

— The Truman Way. (Great Presidential Decisions Ser.). (Illus.). 128p. (YA). (gr. 5 up). 1994. 22.95 (0-8225-2927-0, Lerner Publctns) Lerner Group.

— The Washington Way. (Great Presidential Decisions Ser.). (Illus.). 128p. (J). (gr. 5 up). 1994. 22.95 (0-8225-2928-9, Lerner Publctns) Lerner Group.

***Morris, Jeffrey B.** The FDR Way. LC 95-12575. (Great Presidential Decisions Ser.). (J). 1995. write for info. (0-8225-2929-7, Lerner Publctns) Lerner Group.

— The Reagan Way. LC 94-24644. (Great Presidential Decisions Ser.). (J). 1995. write for info. (0-8225-2931-9, Lerner Publctns) Lerner Group.

Morris, Jeffrey W., jt. auth. see Anderson, John C.

Morris, Jeffrey W., jt. auth. see Drake, William.

Morris, Jenny. Pride against Prejudice: Transforming Attitudes toward Disability. 208p. 1993. 39.95 (0-86571-278-6); pap. 12.95 (0-86571-279-4) New Soc Pubs.

— The Shape of Things to Come? User-Led Social Services. 1994. pap. 24.00 (0-902789-94-5, Pub. by Natl Inst Soc Work) St Mut.

Morris, Jerry. The Boston Globe Guide to Boston. 2nd ed. LC 92-31222. (Illus.). 256p. 1993. pap. 11.95 (1-56440-148-0) Globe Pequot.

— New England under Sail. LC 92-72758. (Under Sail Ser.). (Illus.). 120p. (Orig.). 1993. pap. 12.95 (1-56626-013-2) Country Rds.

Morris, Jerry, ed. see Pratson, Frederick.

Morris, Jill. Creative Breakthroughs: Tap the Power of Your Unconscious Mind. 272p. (Orig.). 1992. pap. 12.99 (0-446-39217-0) Warner Bks.

— The Dream Workbook. 1986. mass mkt. 4.95 (0-449-21041-3, Crest) Fawcett.

Morris, Jim. Fighting Men. 1993. mass mkt. 4.99 (0-440-21150-6) Dell.

— War Story. 308p. 1994. text ed. 29.95 (0-87364-147-7) Paladin Pr.

Morris, Jo. No More Peanuts. (C). 1988. 21.00 (0-946088-08-X, Pub. by NCCL UK) St Mut.

Morris, Joan P. & Warner, Lee H., eds. The Photographs of Alvan S. Harper: Tallahassee, 1885-1910. LC 82-24765. (Illus.). 152p. 1983. 37.95 (0-8130-0737-2) U Press Fla.

Morris, Joan P., ed. see Morris, Allen.

Morris, Joe A. Deadline Every Minute: The Story of the United Press. LC 69-10137. 356p. 1968. reprint ed. text ed. 65.00 (0-8371-0175-1, MOUP, Greenwood Pr) Greenwood.

Morris, Joe L., jt. auth. see Collins, James C.

***Morris, John.** Earth Roads. 242p. 1995. pap. 34.95 (1-85628-989-3, Pub. by Avebury Pub UK) Ashgate Pub Co.

— From Coronado to Escalante: The Explorers of the Spanish Southwest. (World Explorers Ser.). (Illus.). 112p. (YA). (gr. 5 up). 1992. lib. bdg. 18.95 (0-7910-1300-6) Chelsea Hse.

— The Library Disaster Preparedness Handbook. LC 86-1155. 176p. 1986. pap. text ed. 25.00 (0-8389-0438-6) ALA.

— Noah's Ark & the Ararat Adventure. rev. ed. (Illus.). 64p. (J). (gr. 3-5). 1994. 10.95 (0-89051-166-7) Master Bks.

— Welsh Wars of Edward First: Medieval Military History. LC 68-25253. (British History Ser.: No. 30). 1969. reprint ed. lib. bdg. 75.00 (0-8383-0221-1) M S G Haskell Hse.

Morris, John, ed. Exploring Stereotyped Images in Victorian & Twentieth-Century Literature & Society. LC 93-29916. 304p. 1993. pap. 79.95 (0-7734-9325-5) E Mellen.

Morris, John, jt. auth. see Dunn, Ruben J.

Morris, John, et al. What Really Happened to the Dinosaurs? (Illus.). 24p. (J). (ps-2). 1990. pap. 9.95 (0-89051-159-4) Master Bks.

Morris, John B., jt. auth. see MacKinnon, Pamela C.

Morris, John C. Analogue Electronics. 256p. 1991. pap. 25.00 (0-340-54461-9, A6450, Pub. by E Arnold UK) Routledge Chapman & Hall.

— Digital Electronics. (Illus.). 244p. 1992. pap. 25.00 (0-340-55638-2, A9676, Pub. by E Arnold UK) Routledge Chapman & Hall.

Morris, John C., ed. Handbook of Dementing Illnesses. LC 93-38090. (Neurological Disease & Therapy Ser.: Vol. 22). 688p. 1994. 175.00 (0-8247-8837-0) Dekker.

Morris, John E. Bontecou Genealogy: A Records of the Descendants of Pierre Bontecou, Huguenot Refugee from France, in the Lines of His Sons. (Illus.). 271p. 1994. reprint ed. lib. bdg. 53.00 (0-8328-4256-7); reprint ed. pap. 43.00 (0-8328-4255-9) Higginson Bk Co.

Morris, John E., jt. auth. see Ellis, George W.

Morris, John F., jt. auth. see Mackinnon, Pamela C.

Morris, John S. Bean Street. LC 77-79214. (Lost Roads Poetry Ser.: No. 4). 1978. 6.00 (0-918786-06-1); pap. 3.00 (0-918786-07-X) Lost Roads.

Morris, John W. The Charismatic Movement. 43p. 1984. pap. 2.00 (0-916586-72-3) Holy Cross Orthodox.

— Ghost Towns of Oklahoma. LC 77-22439. (Illus.). 1978. pap. 18.95 (0-8061-1420-7) U of Okla Pr.

Morris, John W., jt. auth. see Goins, Charles R.

Morris, John W., et al. Historical Atlas of Oklahoma. 3rd ed. LC 86-40077. (Illus.). 208p. 1986. 32.95 (0-8061-1991-8); pap. 18.95 (0-8061-2001-0) U of Okla Pr.

Morris, Johnathan, et al. Working for the Japanese: The Economic & Social Consequences of Japanese Investment in Wales. LC 93-14561. (Illus.). 180p. (C). 1993. text ed. 65.00 (0-485-11438-0, Pub. by Athlone Pr UK) Humanities.

Morris, Johnny. Animal-Go-Round. LC 93-12376. (Illus.). 18p. (J). (gr. k-3). 1993. 12.95 (1-56458-329-5) Dorling Kindersley.

— Animal-Go-Round. (Illus.). 16p. (J). (ps). 1993. 12.98 (1-881445-14-3) Sandvik Pub.

— Just Like You & Me. 1985. 30.00 (0-900873-66-3, Pub. by Bishopsgate Pr Ltd UK) St Mut.

Morris, Jonathan. The Political Economy of Shopkeeping in Milan, 1886-1922. (Past & Present Publications). (Illus.). 320p. (C). 1993. 64.95 (0-521-39119-9) Cambridge U Pr.

Morris, Jonathan, ed. Japan & the Global Economy: Issues & Trends in the 1990s. 240p. 1991. 59.95 (0-415-06456-2, A5778) Routledge.

Morris, Jonathan, jt. ed. see Blyton, Paul.

Morris, Jonathan, ed. see Shakespeare, William.

Morris Jones, John, jt. ed. see Rhys, John.

Morris-Jones, W. H. Politics Mainly Indian. 392p. 1978. 19.95 (0-318-36605-3) Asia Bk Corp.

Morris-Jones, W. H., ed. From Rhodesia to Zimbabwe: Behind & Beyond Lancaster House. (Studies in Commonwealth Politics & History: No. 9). (Illus.). 123p. 1980. 35.00 (0-7146-3167-1, Pub. by F Cass Pubs UK) Intl Spec Bk.

Morris-Jones, W. H. & Fischer, Georges, eds. Decolonization & After: The British & French Experience. (Studies in Commonwealth Politics & History: No. 7). 369p. 1980. 40.00 (0-7146-3095-0, Pub. by F Cass Pubs UK) Intl Spec Bk.

Morris-Jones, W. H., jt. auth. see Dasgupta, Biplab.

Morris-Jones, W. H., jt. ed. see Madden, A. F.

Morris, Joodi, intro. From Wimberley's Kitchens: A Small Town in Texas. 1993. spiral bd. 4.95 (0-9636364-0-5) Wimb Chamb Com.

***Morris, Joseph M. & Blackton, Mark A.** Accountant's Merger & Acquisition Handbook. LC 94-29853. 1994. text ed. 95.00 (0-471-57017-6) Wiley.

Morris, Joseph M., et al. Software Industry Accounting. 320p. 1992. text ed. 110.00 (0-471-55931-8) Wiley.

Morris, Juddi. The Harvey Girls: The Women Who Civilized the West. 144p. (J). (gr. 4-6). 1994. 15.95 (0-8027-8302-3); lib. bdg. 16.85 (0-8027-8303-1) Walker & Co.

Morris, Judith, jt. auth. see Gasson, Andrew.

Morris, Judy K. The Kid Who Ran for Principal. LC 89-2729. 224p. (J). (gr. 3-7). 1989. lib. bdg. 12.89 (0-397-32360-3, Lipp Jr Bks) HarpC Child Bks.

***Morris, Julianna.** Baby Talk. (Romance Ser.). 1995. mass mkt. 2.99 (0-373-19097-2, 1-19097-4) Silhouette.

Morris, Julius A. & Ward, Emit K. A History One Hundred Ninety-Third General Hospital 1944-1946. (Illus.). 130p. 1989. write for info. (0-318-65421-0) E K Ward.

***Morris, June.** Sexfacts: The Handbook for Healthy Sexuality. (Illus.). 44p. (Orig.). 1995. pap. 10.95 (0-85572-244-4) Seven Hills Bk.

Morris, June, jt. auth. see Schmidt, Mary M.

***Morris, Karen.** Smith & Kraus Monologue Index. 1995. pap. 9.95 (1-880399-75-X) Smith & Kraus.

Morris, Karen S. & Craker, Lyle E. Herb Gardens in America: A Visitor's Guide. 191p. (Orig.). 1991. pap. 9.95 (0-9629868-0-1) HSMP Pr.

Morris, Katherine. Sorceress or Witch: The Image of Gender in Medieval Iceland & Northern Europe. 262p. (C). 1991. lib. bdg. 53.00 (0-8191-8256-7); pap. text ed. 32.50 (0-8191-8257-5) U Pr of Amer.

***Morris, Katherine, ed.** Odyssey of Exile: Jewish Women Flee the Nazis for Brazil. (Illus.). 288p. 1995. 38.95 (0-8143-2562-9); pap. 18.95 (0-8143-2563-7) Wayne St U Pr.

Morris, Katherine, et al. Database Management Systems in Engineering. (Illus.). 175p. (Orig.). (C). 1994. pap. text ed. 60.00 (1-56806-363-6) Diane Pub.

***Morris-Keitel, Helen G.** Identity in Transition: The Images of Working-Class Women in Social Prose of the Vormarz (1840-1848) (North American Studies in Nineteenth-Century German Literature: Vol. 15). 216p. (C). 1995. text ed. 60.95 (0-8204-2256-8) P Lang Pubs.

Morris-Keitel, Peter. Die Verbrechensthematik im Modernen Roman. Hermand, Jost, ed. LC 89-12146. (German Life & Civilization Ser.: Vol. 4). 210p. 1990. text ed. 42.95 (0-8204-1106-X) P Lang Pubs.

Morris, Keith. The Story of the Canadian Pacific Railway. Bruchey, Stuart, ed. LC 80-1332. (Railroads Ser.). (Illus.). 1981. reprint ed. lib. bdg. 20.95 (0-405-13806-7) Ayer.

Morris, Kelly, ed. see Finkelstein, Irving L.

Morris, Kelly, ed. see Kreamer, Christine M.

Morris, Kelly, ed. see Peet, Phyllis.

Morris, Kelly, ed. see Rosenthal, Donald.

Morris, Kelly, ed. see Zafran, Eric & Ackerman, Gerald M.

Morris, Kelso B. Fundamental Chemical Equilibria: Nonionic-Ionic. (Illus.). 120p. 1971. text ed. 105.00 (0-677-03090-8); pap. text ed. 59.00 (0-677-03095-9) Gordon & Breach.

Morris, Kenneth. Book of the Three Dragons. Reginald, R. & Melville, Douglas, eds. LC 77-84257. (Lost Race & Adult Fantasy Ser.). 1978. reprint ed. lib. bdg. 23.95 (0-405-11001-4) Ayer.

— The Chalchiuhite Dragon. 304p. 1993. pap. 12.95 (0-312-89001-X) Orb NYC.

— Collected Stories. 1995. pap. 13.95 (0-312-89029-X) Orb NYC.

— The Dragon Path: The Collected Tales of Kenneth Morris. 384p. 1995. 23.95 (0-312-85309-2) Tor Bks.

— The Wall Street Journal Guide to Money & Investment. 1994. pap. 13.95 (0-671-89451-X, Fireside) S&S Trade.

— Wall Street Journal Guide to Understanding Personal Finance. 1993. pap. 14.95 (0-671-87964-2, Fireside) S&S Trade.

— Wall Street Journal Guide to Understanding Taxes. 1995. pap. 14.95 (0-671-50235-2, Fireside) S&S Trade.

Morris, Kenneth & Inverson, Harris L. Golden Threads in the Tapestry of History. (Illus.). 246p. 1975. reprint ed. pap. 5.25 (0-913004-27-8) Point Loma Pub.

Morris, Kenneth, et al. American Dreams: One Hundred Years of Business Ideas & Innovation from The Wall Street Journal. (Illus.). 224p. 1991. 35.00 (0-8109-3656-9) Abrams.

Morris, Kenneth E. Bonhoeffer's Ethic of Discipleship: A Study in Social Psychology, Political Thought, & Religion. LC 85-31949. 160p. 1986. 25.00 (0-271-00428-2) Pa St U Pr.

***Morris, Kenneth M. & Siegel, Alan M.** The Wall Street Journal Guide to Planning Your Financial Future: The Easy-to-Read Guide to Lifetime Planning for Retirement. 1995. pap. 14.95 (0-684-80202-3, Fireside) S&S Trade.

Morris, Kevin L. The Image of the Middle Ages in Romantic & Victorian Literature. 272p. 1984. 45.00 (0-7099-3511-0, Pub. by Croom Helm UK) Routledge Chapman & Hall.

Morris, Kimberly. Wild Hearts. (Changes Romance Ser.: No. 6). (YA). 1992. mass mkt. 3.50 (0-06-106781-4, Harp PBks) HarpC.

Morris, Kirsten A., ed. Control of Flexible Structures. LC 93-11354. (Fields Institute Communications Ser.: Vol. 2). 243p. 1993. 82.00 (0-8218-9201-0, FIC/2) Am Math.

Morris, L. Poetry of Edwin Arlington Robinson. LC 73-92976. (Studies in Poetry: No. 38). (C). 1969. reprint ed. lib. bdg. 75.00 (0-8383-0996-8) M S G Haskell Hse.

Morris, L. A. Communicating Therapeutic Risks. (Recent Research in Psychology Ser.). xii, 186p. 1989. pap. 54.00 (0-387-97192-0, 3675) Spr-Verlag.

Morris, L. Delyte, jt. auth. see Diehl, Pamela.

Morris, L. Delyte, jt. auth. see Johnson, Pamela.

Morris, L. J., jt. auth. see Horne, M. R.

Morris, L. J., jt. auth. see Plum, D. R.

Morris, L. Robert. Lawrence of Arabia: The Official Thirtieth Anniversary Pictorial History. (Illus.). 1992. pap. 19.50 (0-385-42479-5) Doubleday.

Morris, L. W. Critical Path: Construction & Analysis. 1967. 54.00 (0-08-012472-0, Pub. by Pergamon Repr UK) Franklin.

Morris, Lacey M., jt. ed. see Verlenden, Jeanne S.

***Morris, Langdon.** Managing the Evolving Corporation. (Industrial Engineering Ser.). 256p. 1994. text ed. 24.95 (0-442-01906-8) Van Nos Reinhold.

Morris, Larry. New Riders Guide to E-Mail & Messaging. 900p. 1994. pap. 35.00 (1-56205-369-8) New Riders Pub.

Morris, Larry E. Industrial Stress Injuries: Dynamic Understanding, Clinical Illustrations & Logical Management. 185p. (C). 1989. 35.00 (0-685-26951-5) Bourne & Atherton Pubns.

Morris, Laurel, jt. auth. see Montgomery, Bob.

Morris, Laurence. Pilgrim's Progress (Retold for Children) (J). (gr. 1-5). 1993. pap. 3.95 (0-87508-747-7) Chr Lit.

Morris, Lawrence, tr. see Ansarti, Khwajih A.

Morris, Leon. Apostolic Preaching of the Cross. 1955. pap. 12.99 (0-8028-1512-X) Eerdmans.

— The Atonement. LC 83-20649. 219p. 1984. pap. 14.99 (0-87784-826-2, 826) InterVarsity.

— Creo en la Revelacion. Blanch, Miguel, tr. (Serie Creo). 223p. (SPA.). 1979. pap. 6.25 (0-89922-140-8) Edit Caribe.

— The Cross of Jesus. LC 88-371. 126p. reprint ed. pap. 36.00 (0-7837-6565-7, 2046130) Bks Demand.

— The Epistle to the Romans. 640p. 1988. 29.99 (0-8028-3636-4) Eerdmans.

— Expository Reflections on the Gospel of John, 4 vols. in 1. LC 90-964. 760p. 1990. text ed. 32.99 (0-8010-6255-1) Baker Bk.

— Expository Reflections on the Letter to the Ephesians. LC 93-28253. 240p. (Orig.). 1994. pap. 17.99 (0-8010-6312-4) Baker Bk.

— The First & Second Epistles to the Thessalonians. 2nd rev. ed. Bruce, F. F., ed. (New International Commentary on the New Testament Ser.). xvi, 280p. 1991. 27.99 (0-8028-2168-5) Eerdmans.

— First & Second Thessalonians. rev. ed. Tasker, R. V., ed. (Tyndale New Testament Commentaries Ser.). 160p. 1984. pap. 9.99 (0-8028-0034-3) Eerdmans.

— First Corinthians. rev. ed. Tasker, R. V., ed. (Tyndale New Testament Commentaries Ser.). 224p. 1986. pap. 9.99 (0-8028-0064-5) Eerdmans.

— Gospel According to John. 1994. student ed 39.99 (0-8028-2504-4) Eerdmans.

— The Gospel According to Matthew. LC 92-15806. (Pillar New Testament Commentary Ser.). xvi, 782p. 1992. text ed. 39.99 (0-8028-3696-8) Eerdmans.

— The Gospel According to St. Luke. rev. ed. (Tyndale New Testament Commentaries Ser.). 1988. pap. 9.99 (0-8028-0419-5) Eerdmans.

— Gospel of John. (New International Commentary on the New Testament Ser.). 1971. 34.99 (0-8028-2296-7) Eerdmans.

— New Testament Theology. 1990. 18.99 (0-310-45571-5) Zondervan.

— Reflections on the Gospel of John, Vol. 4: Crucified & Risen, John 17-21. LC 85-73360. 1989. 8.99 (0-8010-6245-4) Baker Bk.

— Revelation. rev. ed. (Tyndale New Testament Commentaries Ser.). 1987. pap. text ed. 9.99 (0-8028-0273-7) Eerdmans.

— WBT: First & Second Thessalonians. 105p. 1989. 9.99 (0-8499-0797-7) Word Inc.

Morris, Leon, ed. see Cole, R. Alan.

Morris, Leon, jt. auth. see Cundall, Arthur E.

Morris, Leon, ed. see France, Richard.

Morris, Leon, ed. see Guthrie, Donald.

Morris, Leon, et al. The Expositor's Bible Commentary, Vol. 12. 1986. 31.99 (0-88469-198-5) BMH Bks.

***Morris, Leonard.** The Life of Marcus Garvey. (Illus.). 1995. 9.95 (0-8062-5256-1) Carlton.

Morris, Leslie A. Rosenbach Abroad: In Pursuit of Books in Private Collections. (Illus.). 64p. 1988. pap. 12.50 (0-939084-22-8) R Mus & Lib.

— Rosenbach Redux: Further Book Adventures in England & Ireland. (Illus.). 111p. 1989. pap. 14.95 (0-939084-25-2) R Mus & Lib.

Morris, Leslie R., ed. Choosing a Bibliographic Utility: User Views of Current Choices. 200p. (Orig.). 1990. pap. text ed. 37.50 (1-55570-044-6) Neal-Schuman.

— Interlibrary Loan Policies Directory. 5th rev. ed. LC 94-45805. 1995. write for info. (1-55570-198-1) Neal-Schuman.

Morris, Leslie R. & Morris, Sandra C. Interlibrary Loan Policies Directory. 4th ed. 785p. 1991. 99.95 (1-55570-090-X) Neal-Schuman.

Morris, Lewis. The Papers of Lewis Morris. LC 73-117885. (Select Bibliographies Reprint Ser.). 1977. reprint ed. 25.95 (0-8369-5338-X) Ayer.

Morris, Linda, tr. see Kruglikov, Alexander.

An Asterisk (*) at the beginning of an entry indicates that the title is appearing in BIP for the first time.

Morris, Linda A. Women's Humor in the Age of Gentility: The Life & Works of Frances Miriam Whitcher. (Illus.). 256p. 1992. text ed. 32.50 (*0-8156-2562-6*) Syracuse U Pr.

Morris, Linda A., ed. American Women Humorists: Critical Essays. LC 93-21788. (Studies in Humor: Vol. 4). 480p. 1993. 72.00 (*0-8153-0622-9*, H1500) Garland.

Morris, Linda A., jt. auth. see Zender, Karl.

Morris, Linda L. Morning Milking. LC 91-13103. (Illus.). 32p. (J). (gr. k up). 1991. pap. 16.95 (*0-88708-173-8*, Picture Book Studio) S&S Childrens.

Morris-Lipsman, Arlene J. Notable Women, Grades Four-Six. 112p. 1989. pap. 9.95 (*0-673-38743-7*) GdYrBks.

Morris, Lisa R., jt. auth. see Schulz, Linda.

Morris, Lloyd. Incredible New York: High Life & Low Life of the Last Hundred Years. LC 75-1862. (Leisure Class in America Ser.). (Illus.). 1975. reprint ed. 26.95 (*0-405-06928-6*) Ayer.

— Poetry of Edwin Arlington Robinson. LC 70-99664. (Select Bibliographies Reprint Ser.). 1977. 20.95 (*0-8369-5093-3*) Ayer.

Morris, Lloyd & Whitall, W. Van. The Poetry of Edwin Arlington Robinson: An Essay in Appreciation. LC 70-99664. (Select Bibliographies Reprint Ser.). 116p. reprint ed. 13.50 (*0-8290-0486-6*) Irvington.

Morris, Lloyd R. Not So Long Ago. (History - United States Ser.). 504p. 1993. reprint ed. lib. bdg. 99.00 (*0-7812-4845-0*) Rprt Serv.

— The Rebellious Puritan: Portrait of Mr. Hawthorne. (BCL1-PS American Literature Ser.). 369p. 1992. reprint ed. lib. bdg. 89.00 (*0-7812-6730-7*) Rprt Serv.

Morris, Lois B., jt. auth. see Gold, Mark S.

Morris, Lois B., jt. auth. see Oldham, John M.

Morris, Lois B., jt. auth. see Oldham, John.

Morris, Lorenzo, ed. The Social & Political Implications of the 1984 Jesse Jackson Presidential Campaign. LC 89-27476. (Praeger Series in Political Economy). 288p. 1990. text ed. 57.60 (*0-275-92785-7*, C2785, Praeger Pubs) Greenwood.

Morris, Louis, et al, eds. Product Labeling & Health Risks. LC 80-22728. (Banbury Report Ser.: Report 6). 328p. 1980. 52.00 (*0-87969-205-7*) Cold Spring Harbor.

Morris, Louis A. The Morris, Arnold & Related Families. (Illus.). 288p. 1985. 25.00 (*0-89308-550-2*) Southern Hist Pr.

Morris, Louise. The Crucifixion & the Resurrection of Jesus. 94p. 1993. spiral bd. 5.50 (*0-7873-0626-6*) Mokelumne.

Morris, Lucy W., ed. Old Rail Fence Corners: Frontier Tales Told by Minnesota Pioneers. xxv, 344p. 1976. reprint ed. pap. 9.50 (*0-87351-109-3*, Borealis Book) Minn Hist.

Morris, Lydia. Dangerous Classes: The Underclass & Social Citizenship. LC 93-24569. 1993. 45.00 (*0-415-05013-8*, Routledge NY); pap. 14.95 (*0-415-05014-6*, Routledge NY) Routledge.

— Social Divisions: Economic Decline & Social Structural Change. 224p. 1995. 65.00x (*1-85728-201-9*, Pub. by UCL Pr UK) Taylor & Francis.

— Social Divisions: Economic Decline & Social Structural Change. 224p. 1995. pap. 24.95x (*1-85728-202-7*, Pub. by UCL Pr UK) Taylor & Francis.

— The Workings of the Household: A U. S.-U. K. Comparison. (Family Life Ser.). (Illus.). 260p. 1990. text ed. 54.95 (*0-7456-0441-2*); pap. text ed. 21.95 (*0-7456-0442-0*) Blackwell Pubs.

Morris, Lyle L. The Single Salary Schedule: An Analysis & Evaluation. LC 72-177086. (Columbia University. Teachers College. Contributions to Education Ser.: No. 413). reprint ed. 37.50 (*0-404-55413-X*) AMS Pr.

***Morris, Lynda & Radford, Robert.** AIA: The Story of the Artists International Association 1933-1953. 96p. 1983. 32.00 (*0-905836-35-9*, Pub. by Museum Modern Art UK) St Mut.

Morris, Lynn. Stars for a Light. 1994. pap. 8.99 (*1-55661-422-5*) Bethany Hse.

***Morris, Lynn & Morris, Gilbert.** The Stars for a Light. large type ed. LC 95-8901. 1995. write for info. (*0-7838-1376-7*) Hall.

Morris, Lynn, jt. auth. see Morris, Gilbert.

Morris, Lynn A., ed. Research about Leisure: Past, Present & Future. 2nd ed. 1994. pap. 24.95 (*0-915611-96-1*) Sagamore Pub.

Morris, Lynn L. & Fitz-Gibbon, Carol T. Evaluator's Handbook. LC 78-58658. (Program Evaluation Kit Ser.: No. 1). (Illus.). 133p. reprint ed. pap. 38.00 (*0-8357-4832-4*, 2037769) Bks Demand.

— How to Deal with Goals & Objectives. LC 78-57012. (Program Evaluation Kit Ser.: No. 2). (Illus.). 78p. reprint ed. pap. 25.00 (*0-8357-4833-2*, 2037770) Bks Demand.

— How to Measure Achievement. LC 78-58656. (Program Evaluation Kit Ser.). (Illus.). 159p. reprint ed. pap. 45.40 (*0-8357-4835-9*, 2037772) Bks Demand.

— How to Measure Program Implementation. LC 78-58656. (Program Evaluation Kit Ser.). (Illus.). 140p. reprint ed. pap. 39.90 (*0-8357-4834-0*, 2037771) Bks Demand.

Morris, Lynn L., jt. auth. see Fitz-Gibbon, Carol T.

Morris, Lynn L., et al. How to Communicate Evaluation Findings. 2nd ed. (Program Evaluation Kit Ser.: Vol. 9). 64p. (C). 1987. pap. text ed. 12.95 (*0-8039-3134-4*) Sage.

— How to Measure Performance & Use Tests. 2nd ed. (Program Evaluation Kit Ser.: Vol. 7). 176p. (C). 1987. text ed. 12.95 (*0-8039-3132-8*) Sage.

Morris, M. Amateur Stage: A Practical Handbook for Directors & Producers. 1990. 30.00 (*0-7463-0646-6*, Pub. by Northcote UK) St Mut.

Morris, M., jt. auth. see Crawford, D. A.

Morris, M. C., jt. auth. see Bosschere, Jean de.

Morris, M. E. The Last Kamikaze. 368p. 1990. 19.95 (*0-394-57634-9*) Random.

Morris, M. F. An Introduction to the History of the Development of Law. 315p. 1982. reprint ed. lib. bdg. 30.00 (*0-8377-0844-3*) Rothman.

Morris, M. J. & Carrol, B. F., eds. Turbulent Flows, 1993. LC 87-71097. (FED Ser.: Vol. 155). 189p. 1993. pap. 40.00 (*0-7918-0963-3*, H00795) ASME.

***Morris, M. J. & Carroll, B. F., eds.** Turbulent Flows 1994. LC 87-71097. (Fluid Engineering Division Conference Ser.: Vol. 188). 83p. 1994. pap. 30.00 (*0-7918-1371-1*) ASME.

Morris, M. J., jt. ed. see Parekh, D. E.

Morris, M. M. Fellows: Joseph & Philena (Elton) Fellows: Their Ancestors & Descendants. (Illus.). 404p. 1993. reprint ed. lib. bdg. 71.00 (*0-8328-3310-X*); reprint ed. pap. 61.00 (*0-8328-3311-8*) Higginson Bk Co.

Morris, M. Wayne. Stalin's Famine & Roosevelt's Recognition of Russia. LC 93-45822. 234p. (C). 1994. lib. bdg. 34.50 (*0-8191-9379-8*) U Pr of Amer.

Morris, Manuel, comp. The Recorded Performances of Gerard Souzay: A Discography. LC 90-13978. (Discographies Ser.: No. 41). 260p. 1990. text ed. 49.95 (*0-313-27392-8*, MGG/, Greenwood Pr) Greenwood.

Morris, Marcia A. Saints & Revolutionaries: The Ascetic Hero in Russian Fiction. LC 92-279. 256p. (C). 1993. 59.50 (*0-7914-1299-7*); pap. 19.95 (*0-7914-1300-4*) State U NY Pr.

Morris, Margaret. Georgia O'Keeffe: Selected Paintings & Works on Paper. (Illus.). 96p. (Orig.). 1986. pap. 18.00 (*0-935037-14-4*) G Peters Gallery.

— Leon Gaspard. 16p. 1984. pap. 10.00 (*0-935037-08-X*) G Peters Gallery.

— Private Journal of Margaret Morris, Kept During a Portion of the Revolutionary War. Decker, Peter, ed. LC 71-77107. (Eyewitness Accounts of the American Revolution Ser., No. 1). 1977. reprint ed. 16.95 (*0-405-01168-7*) Ayer.

Morris, Margaret F., ed. Essays on the Gilded Age. LC 72-8266. (Walter Prescott Webb Memorial Lectures: No. 7). 108p. 1973. 10.95 (*0-292-72004-1*) Tex A&M Univ Pr.

Morris, Margaret F. & Myres, Sandra L., eds. Essays on American Foreign Policy. LC 73-19500. (Walter Prescott Webb Memorial Lectures: No. 8). 146p. 1974. 10.95 (*0-292-72009-2*) Tex A&M Univ Pr.

Morris, Margaret F. & West, Elliott, eds. Essays on Urban America. LC 74-31058. (Walter Prescott Webb Memorial Lectures: No. 9). 147p. 1975. 10.95 (*0-292-72011-4*) Tex A&M Univ Pr.

Morris, Margie. Helping Children Feel at Home in Church. LC 87-73377. 72p. (Orig.). 1988. pap. 5.95 (*0-88177-054-X*, DR054) Discipleship Res.

— Tools for Building Your Volunteer Ministries. 148p. (Orig.). 1991. pap. 17.95 (*0-9620898-6-9*) Newton-Cline.

— Volunteer Ministries: New Strategies for Today's Church. 156p. (Orig.). 1990. pap. 15.95 (*0-9620898-1-8*) Newton-Cline.

— Volunteer Ministries: New Strategies for Today's Church. Brewer, Karen, ed. (Illus.). 160p. (Orig.). 1994. pap. text ed. 12.99 (*0-7847-0068-0*, 18-03206) Standard Pub.

— Volunteer Ministries: New Strategies for Today's Church. 152p. (Orig.). 1991. reprint ed. pap. 12.95 (*0-9620898-7-7*) Newton-Cline.

— Volunteer Programs That Work. (Orig.). 1992. pap. write for info. (*0-9620898-3-4*) Newton-Cline.

Morris, Margie & Stephens, Jessie G. Volunteer Management: Workshop Leader's Guide. 65p. (Orig.). 1991. ring bd. 14.95 (*0-9620898-5-0*) Newton-Cline.

Morris, Marianne. Sins of the Father. LC 92-42184. 1993. pap. 9.95 (*0-8163-1146-3*) Pacific Pr Pub Assn.

Morris, Marie & Mark, Norm. The Conzack Mine Incident: A Fictional Alaskan Adventure Inspired by the History of the Famous Kennicott Mine. (Illus.). 116p. (Orig.). 1993. pap. 7.95 (*1-883630-03-7*) Polo Prods.

Morris, Mark. Ireland: Emerald Isle. 1994. pap. 16.95 (*0-8442-9669-4*, Passport Bks) NTC Pub Grp.

Morris, Mark, ed. The Center of the Galaxy. (C). 1989. lib. bdg. 186.50 (*0-7923-0221-4*); pap. text ed. 80.50 (*0-7923-0222-2*) Kluwer Ac.

***Morris, Mark & Drosdick, Nan.** Atlantic Canada Handbook: New Brunswick, Nova Scotia, Newfoundland, Prince Edward Island & Labrador. (Moon Travel Handbooks Ser.). (Illus.). 450p. (Orig.). 1995. pap. 17.95 (*1-56691-007-2*) Moon Pubns CA.

Morris, Mark & Zuckerson, Ben, eds. Mass Loss from Red Giants. 1985. lib. bdg. 110.00 (*90-277-2075-4*) Kluwer Ac.

Morris, Mark S. How to Become a Professional Bartender: Plus: the New up-to-Date List of Todays Most Popular Drink Recipes. (Illus.). 96p. (Orig.). 1992. pap. 9.95 (*0-9632492-0-7*) Morris Ent.

Morris, Mark W., jt. auth. see Daye, Charles E.

Morris, Marlene B. The Flying Gourmet: Just Plane Good. LC 88-90622. (Illus.). 300p. (Orig.). 1988. pap. 14.95 (*0-9620398-0-2*) M & M Pubns.

Morris, Marshall. Saying & Meaning in Puerto Rico: Some Problems in the Ethnography of Discourse. (Language & Communication Library: Vol. 1). 186p. 1981. text ed. 79.00 (*0-08-025822-0*, CRC Reprint) Franklin.

Morris, Martha. Katherine & the Garbage Dump. (Illus.). 24p. (J). (gr. 1-4). Date not set. 12.95 (*0-929005-39-2*, Pub. by Second Story Pr CN); pap. 5.95 (*0-929005-38-4*, Pub. by Second Story Pr CN) InBook.

***Morris, Mary.** HTML Authoring for Fun & Profit. 1995. pap. 35.95 (*0-13-359290-1*) P-H.

— Maiden Voyages. 1993. pap. 14.00 (*0-679-74030-9*) McKay.

— A Mother's Love. LC 92-25031. 1993. 17.50 (*0-385-42409-4*, N A Talese) Doubleday.

— Mother's Love. 1994. pap. 9.95 (*0-385-31219-9*, Delta) Dell.

— Nothing to Declare. 1989. pap. 10.95 (*0-14-009587-X*, Penguin Bks) Viking Penguin.

— Nothing to Declare: Memoirs of a Woman Traveling Alone. large type ed. (General Ser.). 355p. 1989. 19.95 (*0-8161-4730-2*, Large Print Bks) Hall.

— Real Life System Administration with Solaris. 1994. pap. text ed. 27.75 (*0-13-125543-6*) P-H.

— Wall to Wall: From Beijing to Berlin by Rail. 272p. 1992. pap. 10.00 (*0-14-019939-X*, Penguin Bks) Viking Penguin.

Morris, Mary, jt. auth. see Morris, William.

Morris, Mary A., ed. Glorious Liqueurs: One Hundred Fifty Recipes for Spirited Desserts, Drinks, & Gifts of Food. LC 91-60332. (New Country Fare Ser.). (Illus.). 200p. 1991. 22.95 (*0-9627403-1-4*) Lake Isle Pr.

Morris, Mary E. New Political Realities & the Gulf: Egypt, Syria, & Jordan. LC 92-46989. 1993. write for info. (*0-8330-1315-7*, MR-127-AF) Rand Corp.

— The Persistence of External Interest in the Middle East. LC 93-31042. 1993. 15.00 (*0-8330-1486-2*, MR-318) Rand Corp.

Morris, Mary M. A Dangerous Woman. LC 90-50405. 384p. 1991. 19.95 (*0-670-83699-0*) Viking Penguin.

— A Dangerous Woman. 368p. 1992. pap. 10.00 (*0-14-016764-1*, Penguin Bks) Viking Penguin.

— A Dangerous Woman. 370p. 1994. pap. 10.95 (*0-14-023669-4*, Penguin Bks) Viking Penguin.

— Dangerous Woman. 1993. pap. 5.99 (*0-451-18236-7*, Sig) NAL-Dutton.

— Songs in Ordinary Time. LC 94-44071. 1995. 24.95 (*0-670-86014-X*, Viking) Viking Penguin.

— Vanished. 1989. pap. 8.95 (*0-671-67943-0*, WSP) PB.

— Vanished. 1988. 16.95 (*0-670-82216-7*) Viking Penguin.

***Morris, Mary T.** Connections & Partings: Abstracts of Marriage, Divorce, Death, & Legal Notices Regarding Clarke County, Virginia, 1857-1884 (Derived from Local & Regional Newspapers) 210p. 1990. lib. bdg. 37.00 (*0-8095-8186-8*); pap. 15.00 (*0-8095-8549-9*) Borgo Pr.

Morris, Maryke, jt. ed. see Crawford, Doreen.

Morris, May, ed. Collected Works of William Morris: Introductions by His Daughter, May Morris, 24 vols., Set. 8000p. 1992. Boxed set. boxed 2,650.00 (*0-415-07972-1*, B0563, Pub. by Thoemmes Pr UK) Routledge.

Morris-McKinsey, Jill, ed. Religiously Speaking: Plays & Poems for Children's Church. 48p. (Orig.). (J). 1992. pap. 7.98 (*1-877588-03-2*) Creatively Yours.

Morris, Meaghan. The Pirate's Fiancee: Feminism, Reading, Postmodernism. (Questions for Feminism Ser.). 352p. 1988. text ed. 50.00 (*0-86091-212-4*, Pub. by Verso UK); pap. text ed. 16.95 (*0-86091-926-9*, Pub. by Verso UK) Routledge Chapman & Hall.

Morris, Meaghan, jt. ed. see Frow, John.

Morris, Melinda, ed. see Swinney, Bridget & Anderson, Tracey.

Morris, Mervyn, ed. The Faber Book of Contemporary Caribbean Short Stories. 250p. 1991. pap. 10.95 (*0-571-15299-6*) Faber & Faber.

Morris, Michael. The Good & the True. LC 92-462. (Oxford Philosophical Monographs). 304p. 1992. 69.00 (*0-19-823944-0*, Clarendon Pr) OUP.

— Madam Valentino: The Many Lives of Natacha Rambova. (Illus.). 272p. 1991. 15.98 (*1-55859-136-2*) Abbeville Pr.

Morris, Michael, tr. Contemporary Basque Fiction: An Anthology. LC 90-11921. (Basque Ser.). 112p. (C). 1990. 17.95 (*0-87417-158-X*) U of Nev Pr.

Morris, Michael & Williamson, John B. Poverty & Public Policy: An Analysis of Federal Intervention Efforts. LC 86-398. (Studies in Social Welfare Policies & Programs: No. 3). 248p. 1986. text ed. 55.00 (*0-313-24942-3*, MPV/, Greenwood Pr) Greenwood.

Morris, Michael A. Caribbean Maritime Security. LC 93-3841. 270p. 1994. text ed. 65.00 (*0-312-12057-5*) St Martin.

— Expansion of Third World Navies. 230p. 1988. text ed. 39.95 (*0-312-00074-X*) St Martin.

— The Strait of Magellan. (C). 1989. lib. bdg. 102.00 (*0-7923-0181-1*) Kluwer Ac.

Morris, Michael A., ed. Great Power Relations in Argentina, Chile & Antarctica. LC 89-34721. 280p. 1990. text ed. 55.00 (*0-312-03610-8*) St Martin.

Morris, Michael G., jt. auth. see Collins, N. Mark.

Morris, Michael H. Industrial & Organizational Marketing. 2nd ed. (Illus.). 800p. (C). 1992. text ed. write for info. (*0-02-384135-4*) Macmillan.

— Market Oriented Pricing: Strategies for Management. 1992. pap. 27.95 (*0-8442-3460-5*, NTC Busn Bks) NTC Pub Grp.

Morris, Michael H. & Morris, Gene. Market-Oriented Pricing: Strategies for Management. LC 89-10712. 218p. 1990. text ed. 55.00 (*0-89930-402-8*, MBY/, Greenwood Pr) Greenwood.

Morris, Michele. Cowboy Life. 1993. pap. 12.00 (*0-671-86682-6*, Fireside) S&S Trade.

Morris, Michele, jt. auth. see Cheng, Rose.

Morris, Michele R. Mieux Ecrire en Francais: Manuel de Composition et Guide Pratique a l'Usage des Etudiants Anglophones. 2nd ed. LC 88-21287. 323p. (Orig.). (C). 1988. teacher ed, pap. 4.50 (*0-87840-226-8*); pap. text ed. 9.95 (*0-87840-225-X*) Georgetown U Pr.

Morris, Michele R., ed. Images of America in Revolutionary France. LC 90-3689. (Illus.). 225p. (Orig.). (ENG & FRE.). 1990. 19.95 (*0-87840-497-X*) Georgetown U Pr.

Morris, Michelle, jt. auth. see O'Donnell, Michael.

Morris, Mike. Confirmed Kill, No. 4: Point Blank. 208p. (Orig.). 1993. pap. 4.50 (*1-55773-898-X*) Diamond.

Morris, Milford J. The History of St. Mark's Church. (Illus.). 85p. (Orig.). 1990. pap. text ed. 10.00 (*0-685-58725-8*) SCP Third.

Morris, Milton, jt. auth. see Bostis, David.

Morris, Milton D. Blacks & the Nineteen Eighty-Eight Republican National Convention. 50p. 1988. pap. 10.50 (*0-941410-70-6*) Jt Ctr Pol Studies.

— Immigration-The Beleaguered Bureauracy. LC 84-22962. 150p. 1985. 26.95 (*0-8157-5838-3*); pap. 9.95 (*0-8157-5837-5*) Brookings.

Morris, Milton D. & Rubin, Gary E. Blacks & Jews: A Dialogue. 90p. (C). 1991. lib. bdg. 38.00 (*0-941410-64-1*); pap. text ed. 12.50 (*0-941410-99-4*) Jt Ctr Pol Studies.

Morris, Milton D., et al. Curbing Illegal Immigration. LC 82-70892. 38p. 1982. pap. 6.95 (*0-8157-5839-1*) Brookings.

Morris, Monica. Last-Chance Children: Growing Up with Older Parents. 176p. 1988. 14.95 (*0-231-06694-5*) Col U Pr.

Morris, Morris D. Measuring the Condition of the World's Poor: The Physical Quality of Life Index. LC 79-16613. 190p. 1979. pap. 5.95 (*0-08-023889-0*) Overseas Dev Council.

Morris, N. Hawaii. (World Bibliographical Ser.). 1993. lib. bdg. 91.50 (*1-85109-175-0*); lib. bdg. 91.50 (*0-685-75411-1*) ABC-CLIO.

— Hawaii: World Bibliographical Series. 1993. lib. bdg. 91.50 (*0-685-70606-0*) ABC-CLIO.

Morris, N. & Perlman, M. Law & Crime: Essays in Honor of Sir John Barry. 270p. 1972. text ed. 77.00 (*0-677-15270-1*) Gordon & Breach.

Morris, N. Ronald, jt. ed. see Cappuccinelli, Piero.

***Morris, Nancy.** Puerto Rico: Culture, Politics, & Identity. LC 95-14416. 1995. text ed. write for info. (*0-275-95228-2*, Praeger Pubs) Greenwood.

— Through the Valley. LC 91-66013. 85p. 1992. pap. 6.95 (*1-55523-453-4*) Winston-Derek.

***Morris, Neil.** Caves. (Wonders of Our World Ser.). (Illus.). 50p. (J). (gr. 1-4). 1995. lib. bdg. 17.95 (*0-86505-830-X*) Crabtree Pub Co.

— Caves. (Wonders of Our World Ser.). (Illus.). 50p. (J). (gr. 1-4). 1995. pap. 6.95 (*0-86505-842-3*) Crabtree Pub Co.

— Deserts. (Wonders of Our World Ser.). (Illus.). 50p. (J). (gr. 1-4). 1995. lib. bdg. 17.95 (*0-86505-827-X*) Crabtree Pub Co.

— Deserts. (Wonders of Our World Ser.). (Illus.). 50p. (J). (gr. 1-4). 1995. pap. 6.95 (*0-86505-839-3*) Crabtree Pub Co.

— Do Animals Take Baths? Questions Kids Ask about Animals. LC 94-14119. (Tell Me Why Ser.). (Illus.). 32p. (J). (ps-2). 1994. 7.99 (*0-89577-610-3*, Readers Digest Kids) RD Assn.

— Feel! A Fun Book of Touch. (Fun Books of Learning). (Illus.). 32p. (J). (ps-2). 1991. lib. bdg. 13.50 (*0-87614-672-8*, Carolrhoda) Lerner Group.

— Feel! A Fun Book of Touch. (J). (ps). 1992. pap. 6.95 (*0-87614-569-1*, Carolrhoda) Lerner Group.

— The Golden Atlas for Children. (Reference Bks.). (Illus.). 48p. (J). (gr. 1-6). 1992. 8.95 (*0-307-17876-5*, 17876, Golden Pr) Western Pub.

— Holly & Harry: A Fun Book of Sizes. (Fun Books of Learning). (Illus.). 32p. (J). (ps-2). 1991. lib. bdg. 13.50 (*0-87614-673-6*, Carolrhoda) Lerner Group.

— Holly & Harry: A Fun Book of Sizes. (J). (ps). 1992. pap. 6.95 (*0-87614-570-5*, Carolrhoda) Lerner Group.

— Home on the Prairie. LC 89-987. (Tales of the Old West Ser.). (Illus.). 32p. (J). (gr. 4-8). 1989. lib. bdg. 9.95 (*1-85435-165-6*) Marshall Cavendish.

— I'm Big: A Fun Book of Opposites. (Fun Books of Learning). (Illus.). 32p. (J). (ps-2). 1991. lib. bdg. 13.50 (*0-87614-674-4*, Carolrhoda) Lerner Group.

— I'm Big: A Fun Book of Opposites. (J). (ps). 1992. pap. 6.95 (*0-87614-571-3*, Carolrhoda) Lerner Group.

— Jump Along: A Fun Book of Movement. (Fun Books of Learning). (Illus.). 32p. (J). (ps-2). 1991. lib. bdg. 13.50 (*0-87614-671-X*, Carolrhoda) Lerner Group.

— Linda's Late: A Fun Book of Time. (Fun Books of Learning). (Illus.). 32p. (J). (ps-2). 1991. lib. bdg. 13.50 (*0-87614-675-2*, Carolrhoda) Lerner Group.

— Linda's Late: A Fun Book of Time. (J). (ps). 1992. pap. 6.95 (*0-87614-573-X*, Carolrhoda) Lerner Group.

— Longhorn on the Move. LC 89-7153. (Tales of the Old West Ser.). (Illus.). 32p. (J). (gr. 3-8). 1989. lib. bdg. 9.95 (*1-85435-166-4*) Marshall Cavendish.

— Magic Monkey: A Fun Book of Numbers. (Fun Books of Learning). (Illus.). 32p. (J). (ps-2). 1991. lib. bdg. 13.50 (*0-87614-677-9*, Carolrhoda) Lerner Group.

— Magic Monkey: A Fun Book of Shapes & Colors. (J). (ps). 1992. pap. 6.95 (*0-87614-574-8*, Carolrhoda) Lerner Group.

— Mountains. (Wonders of Our World Ser.). (Illus.). 50p. (J). (gr. 1-4). 1995. lib. bdg. 17.95 (*0-86505-829-6*) Crabtree Pub Co.

— Mountains. (Wonders of Our World Ser.). (Illus.). 50p. (J). (gr. 1-4). 1995. pap. 6.95 (*0-86505-841-5*) Crabtree Pub Co.

— Oceans. (Wonders of Our World Ser.). (Illus.). 50p. (J). (gr. 1-4). 1995. lib. bdg. 17.95 (*0-86505-828-8*) Crabtree Pub Co.

— Oceans. (Wonders of Our World Ser.). (Illus.). 50p. (J). (gr. 1-4). 1995. pap. 6.95 (*0-86505-840-7*) Crabtree Pub Co.

— On the Trapping Trail. LC 89-989. (Tales of the Old West Ser.). (Illus.). 32p. (J). (gr. 3-8). 1989. lib. bdg. 9.95 (*1-85435-164-8*) Marshall Cavendish.

— Rummage Sale: A Fun Book of Shapes & Colors. (Fun Books of Learning). (Illus.). 32p. (J). (ps-2). 1991. lib. bdg. 13.50 (*0-87614-676-0*, Carolrhoda) Lerner Group.

— Rummage Sale: A Fun Book of Shapes & Colors. (J). (ps). 1992. pap. 6.95 (*0-87614-575-6*, Carolrhoda) Lerner Group.

— The Student's Activity Atlas. (Illus.). 48p. (J). (gr. 3 up). 1993. lib. bdg. 21.26 (*0-8368-1041-4*) Gareth Stevens Inc.

— Tales of the American West. 1989. 5.99 (*0-517-68024-6*) Random Hse Value.

— Volcanoes. (Wonders of Our World Ser.). (Illus.). 50p. (J). (gr. 1-4). 1995. lib. bdg. 17.95 (*0-86505-826-1*) Crabtree Pub Co.

— Volcanoes. (Wonders of Our World Ser.). (Illus.). 50p. (J). (gr. 1-4). 1995. pap. 6.95 (*0-86505-838-5*) Crabtree Pub Co.

— Wagon Wheels Roll West. LC 89-988. (Tales of the Old West Ser.). (Illus.). 32p. (J). (gr. 3-8). 1989. lib. bdg. 9.95 (*1-85435-167-2*) Marshall Cavendish.

— What a Noise: A Fun Book of Sounds. (Fun Books of Learning). (Illus.). 32p. (J). (ps-2). 1991. lib. bdg. 13.50 (*0-87614-670-1*, Carolrhoda) Lerner Group.

— What a Noise: A Fun Book of Sounds. (J). (ps). 1992. pap. 6.95 (*0-87614-576-4*, Carolrhoda) Lerner Group.

— What Is My Shadow Made Of? Questions Kids Ask about Everyday Science. LC 94-14120. (Tell Me Why Ser.). (Illus.). 32p. (J). (ps-2). 1994. 7.99 (*0-89577-609-X*, Readers Digest Kids) RD Assn.

— Where Do Ants Live? Questions Kids Ask about Backyard Nature. LC 94-14122. (Tell Me Why Ser.). (Illus.). 32p. (J). (ps-2). 1994. 7.99 (*0-89577-607-3*, Readers Digest Kids) RD Assn.

— Where Does My Spaghetti Go When I Eat? Questions Kids Ask about the Human Body. LC 94-14121. (Illus.). 32p. (J). (ps-2). 1994. 7.99 (*0-89577-608-1*, Readers Digest Kids) RD Assn.

— Wildlife Homes. LC 94-66822. (Nature Search Ser.). (Illus.). 32p. (J). 1994. 14.00 (*0-89577-645-6*) RD Assn.

Morris, Neil, jt. auth. see Morris, Ting.

Morris, Noel. Computer Graphics & CAD Fundamentals. 224p. (Orig.). 1986. pap. text ed. 39.50 (*0-273-02517-1*) Trans-Atl Phila.

— Pocket Guide: Assembly Language for the 8085. (C). 1984. pap. text ed. 45.00 (*0-273-02123-0*, Pub. by Pitman Pubng UK) St Mut.

Morris, Noel M. Mastering Electrical Engineering. 2nd ed. 1991. pap. text ed. 22.95 (*0-07-043296-1*) McGraw.

Morris, Noel M., ed. Computer Graphics & CAD Fundamentals. 240p. (Orig.). (C). 1986. pap. text ed. 110.00 (*0-685-47903-X*, Pub. by Pitman Pubng UK) St Mut.

Morris, Noelene, jt. auth. see Morris, William.

Morris, Norman, ed. see International Congress of Psychosomatic Medicine in Obstetrics & Gynecology Staff.

Morris, Norval. The Brothel Boy & Other Parables of the Law. 336p. 1992. 30.00 (*0-19-507443-2*) OUP.

— The Brothel Boy & Other Parables of the Law. 352p. 1994. reprint ed. pap. 14.95 (*0-19-509386-0*) OUP.

— The Habitual Criminal. LC 72-9831. 395p. 1973. reprint ed. text ed. 83.50 (*0-8371-6601-2*, MOHC, Greenwood Pr) Greenwood.

— Madness & the Criminal Law. LC 82-13435. (Studies in Crime & Justice). 168p. (C). 1982. lib. bdg. 20.00 (*0-226-53907-5*) U Ch Pr.

Morris, Norval & Hawkins, Gordon J. The Honest Politican's Guide to Crime Control. LC 76-101467. 272p. 1972. pap. 4.50 (*0-226-53902-4*, P460) U Ch Pr.

***Morris, Norval & Rothman, David J., eds.** The Oxford History of the Prison. (Illus.). 528p. 1995. 39.95 (*0-19-506153-5*) OUP.

Morris, Norval & Tonry, Michael H. Between Prison & Probation: Intermediate Punishments in a Rational Sentencing System. (Illus.). 296p. 1991. reprint ed. pap. 9.95 (*0-19-507138-7*) OUP.

— Crime & Justice: An Annual Review of Research, Vol. 11. 480p. (C). 1981. reprint ed. lib. bdg. 19.50 (*0-226-53957-1*) U Ch Pr.

— Crime & Justice: An Annual Review of Research, Vol. 11. 480p. (C). 1981. reprint ed. pap. text ed. 7.95 (*0-226-53959-8*) U Ch Pr.

Morris, Norval & Tonry, Michael H., eds. Crime & Justice: An Annual Review of Research, Vol. 1. 1979. lib. bdg. 14.00 (*0-226-53955-5*, P903) U Ch Pr.

— Crime & Justice: An Annual Review of Research, Vol. 1. 1980. pap. text ed. 6.95 (*0-226-53956-3*, P903) U Ch Pr.

Morris, Norval, jt. auth. see Tonry, Michael H.

Morris, Norval, jt. ed. see Tonry, Michael H.

Morris, Oradel N. I Hear the Song of the Houmas: J'Entends la Chanson des Houmas. LC 88-92449. (Gens de la Louisiane - Peoples of Louisiana Ser.: Bk. 2). (Illus.). 160p. (ENG & FRE.). 1992. 29.95 (*0-944064-04-3*) Paupieres Pub.

— Little Angel Dancer. (Illus.). (Orig.). (J). (gr. 1-8). Date not set. pap. write for info. (*0-944064-06-X*) Paupieres Pub.

— Le Monde Acadien de Ti-Jean. LC 81-107884. (Gens de la Louisiane - Peoples of Louisiana Ser.: Bk. 1). (Illus.). 81p. (ENG & FRE.). (J). (gr. k-8). 1980. reprint ed. 8.95 (*0-944064-01-9*) Paupieres Pub.

— Le Reve de Ti-Jean: (Ti-Jean's Dream) (Orig.). (ENG & FRE.). 1983. pap. 4.50 (*0-944064-02-7*) Paupieres Pub.

Morris, P. A. The Hedgehog. 1989. pap. 25.00 (*0-85263-958-9*, Pub. by Shire UK) St Mut.

Morris, P. J., jt. auth. see Hill, C. M.

Morris, P. J., jt. ed. see Mossman, S. T.

***Morris, Pam.** The Bakhtin Reader. 256p. 1994. pap. 16.95 (*0-340-59267-2*, B3437, Pub. by E Arnold UK) Routledge Chapman & Hall.

— Dickens's Class Consciousness: A Marginal View. LC 90-8900. 180p. 1991. text ed. 45.00 (*0-312-05353-3*) St Martin.

— Literature & Feminism: An Introduction. LC 92-41839. 220p. 1993. pap. 16.95 (*0-631-18421-X*) Blackwell Pubs.

Morris, Pat, jt. auth. see Burgis, Mary J.

Morris, Patricia, jt. auth. see Brody, Helen.

Morris, Patricia J. Ins & Outs of Perfecting Quilting Stitch. 1990. pap. 9.95 (*0-89145-962-6*) Collector Bks.

Morris, Patricia M., et al. Trying to Take Root: Sustainable Agriculture in the U. S. Heartland. (Illus.). 94p. (Orig.). 1992. pap. 15.00 (*1-881360-00-8*) Public Voice.

***Morris, Paul.** Curriculum in Hong Kong: Development, Issues & Policies. 160p. 1995. pap. 26.50 (*962-209-370-1*, Pub. by Hong Kong Univ Pr HK) Coronet Bks.

— Kingdom of God. 1994. pap. 7.99 (*0-85234-232-2*, Pub. by Evangel Pr UK) Presby & Reformed.

— Telling Jews about Jesus. 1994. pap. 8.99 (*0-85234-532-1*, Pub. by Evangel Pr UK) Presby & Reformed.

***Morris, Paul & Sweeting, Anthony, eds.** Education & Development in East Asia. LC 95-1545. (Reference Books in International Education: Vol. 31). (Illus.). 312p. 1995. 47.00 (*0-8153-1598-8*, SS942) Garland.

Morris, Paul, jt. ed. see Marsh, Colin J.

Morris, Paul, jt. auth. see Rosenstein, Milton.

Morris, Paul C. Maritime Sketches. LC 85-50662. (Illus.). 88p. 1985. pap. 8.50 (*0-936972-07-6*) Lower Cape.

— A Portrait of a Ship, the Benj. F. Packard. LC 87-80164. (Illus.). 200p. 1987. 30.00 (*0-936972-09-2*) Lower Cape.

— Schooners & Schooner Barges. LC 84-81110. (Illus.). 160p. 1984. 25.00 (*0-936972-06-8*) Lower Cape.

Morris, Paul C. & Morin, Joseph F. The Island Steamers: A Chronology of Steam Transportation to & from the Offshore Islands of Martha's Vineyard & Nantucket. 2nd ed. Towne, Sumner A., Jr., ed. LC 77-79090. (Illus.). 196p. 1977. pap. 11.95 (*0-686-28900-5*) Nantucket Nautical.

Morris, Paul C. & Quinn, William P. Shipwrecks in New York Waters. (Illus.). 240p. 1989. 34.95 (*0-940160-44-7*) Parnassus Imprints.

Morris, Paulette, jt. auth. see Skellington, Richard.

Morris, Percy A. Field Guide to Atlantic Coast Shells. 3rd ed. LC 72-75612. (Illus.). 1973. 15.95 (*0-685-02290-0*) HM.

— A Field Guide to Pacific Coast Shells. LC 72-75612. (Peterson Field Guide Ser.). (Illus.). 442p. 1974. 21.95 (*0-395-08029-0*) HM.

— A Field Guide to Pacific Coast Shells. LC 72-75612. (Peterson Field Guide Ser.). (Illus.). 442p. 1974. pap. 15.95 (*0-395-18322-7*) HM.

Morris, Percy A., jt. auth. see Abbott, R. Tucker.

Morris, Peter. David Cronenberg: A Delicate Balance. (Illus.). 160p. 1994. pap. 9.95 (*1-55022-191-4*, Pub. by Jon Pubng UK) InBook.

— Embattled Shadows: A History of Canadian Cinema, 1895-1939. (Illus.). 1993. reprint ed. pap. 18.95 (*0-7735-0323-4*, Pub. by McGill CN) U of Toronto Pr.

— Fountains Dyed Blue for a Day. Hathaway, Michael, ed. 56p. (Orig.). 1992. pap. 6.00 (*0-943795-21-4*) Chiron Rev.

— French Politics Today. LC 93-40663. 1994. text ed. 16.95 (*0-7190-3764-6*, Pub. by Manchester Univ Pr UK) St Martin.

— Introduction to Game Theory. LC 94-6515. (Universitext Ser.). 1994. text ed. 29.00 (*0-387-94284-X*) Spr-Verlag.

— Windows: Advanced Programming & Design. (Illus.). 900p. 1993. pap. 39.95 (*0-7506-0636-3*) Buttrwrth-Heinemann.

Morris, Peter, ed. Cantonese Love Songs: An English Translation of Jiu Ji-yung's Cantonese Songs of the Early 19th Century. 216p. (C). 1992. pap. text ed. 72.00 (*962-209-284-5*, Pub. by Hong Kong U Pr HK) St Mut.

***Morris, Peter & Gruneberg, Michael, eds.** Theoretical Aspects of Memory Vol. 2. 1994. pap. 18.95 (*0-415-06958-0*, B3706) Routledge.

— Theoretical Aspects of Memory Vol. 2. 2nd ed. 336p. 1994. 59.95x (*0-415-06957-2*, B7302) Routledge.

***Morris, Peter & Jacobs, Daniel.** The Rough Guide to Tunisia. (Illus.). 448p. 1995. pap. 16.95 (*1-85828-139-3*, Penguin Bks) Viking Penguin.

***Morris, Peter & Therivel, Riki, eds.** Methods of Environment Impact Assessment. 256p. 1994. 75.00x (*1-85728-214-0*, Pub. by UCL Pr UK) Taylor & Francis.

— Methods of Environment Impact Assessment. 256p. 1994. pap. 27.50x (*1-85728-215-9*, Pub. by UCL Pr UK) Taylor & Francis.

Morris, Peter, tr. see Berstein, Serge.

Morris, Peter, jt. auth. see Cornick, Martyn.

Morris, Peter, jt. ed. see Gruneberg, Michael M.

Morris, Peter, jt. ed. see Gruneberg, Michael.

Morris, Peter, jt. auth. see Kavanagh, Dennis A.

Morris, Peter, jt. auth. see Kavanagh, Dennis.

Morris, Peter, jt. auth. see McDonald, Malcolm.

Morris, Peter, tr. see Sadoul, Georges.

Morris, Peter A., ed. Netherlands International Law Review: Index to Volume I - XXX. (C). 1991. lib. bdg. 125.50 (*0-7923-0906-5*) Kluwer Ac.

Morris, Peter E. Modelling Cognition. LC 86-28229. 309p. 1987. text ed. 165.00 (*0-471-91432-0*) Wiley.

Morris, Peter E. & Conway, Martin E., eds. The Psychology of Memory, 3 vols. LC 92-45221. (International Library of Critical Writings in Business History). 1993. 375.00 (*0-8147-5496-1*) NYU Pr.

Morris, Peter E. & Hampson, Peter J. Imagery & Consciousness. LC 82-74571. 1984. text ed. 94.00 (*0-12-507680-0*) Acad Pr.

Morris, Peter E., jt. auth. see Hampson, Peter J.

Morris, Peter E., jt. auth. see Harris, John E.

Morris, Peter J. Kidney Transplantation. 4th ed. (Illus.). 576p. 1994. text ed. 150.00 (*0-7216-4557-7*) Saunders.

— Polymer Pioneers: A Popular History of the Science & Technology of Large Molecules. (BCHOC Publication Ser.: No. 5). (Illus.). 88p. (Orig.). 1986. pap. 10.00 (*0-941901-03-3*, TP1116.M67 1986) Chem Heritage Fnd.

Morris, Peter J. & Malt, Ronald A., eds. Oxford Textbook of Surgery. (Illus.). 3104p. 1994. 199.00 (*0-19-261800-8*) OUP.

Morris, Peter J., jt. ed. see Warlow, Charles.

Morris, Peter M. The Days of Visitation: A Practical & Statistical Study of the Parishes of the Diocese of Swansea & Brecon Based on the Returns to the Visitation Questionnaire of Bishop Vaughan from 1977 to 1987. LC 89-48075. (Welsh Studies: Vol. 2). 272p. 1990. lib. bdg. 89.95 (*0-88946-065-5*) E Mellen.

Morris, Peter M. & James, Edward. A Critical Word Book of Leviticus, Numbers, Deuteronomy. (Computer Bible Ser.: Vol. VIII). 1975. pap. 20.00 (*0-935106-13-8*) Biblical Res Assocs.

— A Critical Word Book of the Pentateuch. (Computer Bible Ser.: Vol. XVII). 1980. pap. 25.00 (*0-935106-03-0*) Biblical Res Assocs.

Morris, Phil & Phillips, Dennis. How to Operate a Financially Successful Haunted House. LC 87-80906. 136p. 1987. pap. 9.95 (*0-911137-11-4*) Imagine.

Morris, Philip & Weston, Geoff, eds. Directory of Translators & Translating Agencies in the United Kingdom. 2nd ed. 352p. 1990. lib. bdg. 65.00 (*0-86291-277-6*) Bowker-Saur.

Morris, Philip A. & White, Marjorie L., eds. Designs on Birmingham: A Landscape History of a Southern City & Its Suburbs. (Illus.). (Orig.). 1989. 28.00 (*0-943994-14-4*); pap. 14.95 (*0-943994-15-2*) Birmingham Hist Soc.

Morris, Philip A., jt. auth. see White, Marjorie L.

Morris, Phyllis S. Sartre's Concept of a Person: An Analytic Approach. LC 75-8451. 184p. 1976. 25.00 (*0-87023-185-5*) U of Mass Pr.

Morris, R. Bare Ruined Choirs. (World of Change Ser.). (C). 1987. 40.00 (*0-685-47491-7*, Pub. by S Thornes Pubs UK) St Mut.

— Ocean Life. (Mysteries & Marvels Ser.). (Illus.). 32p. (J). (gr. 3-6). 1983. lib. bdg. 13.96 (*0-88110-149-4*, Usborne); pap. 5.95 (*0-86020-753-6*, Usborne) EDC.

— Perspectives in Abnormal Behavior. LC 73-7975. (Pergamon General Psychology Ser.: Vol. 37). 1974. 234.00 (*0-08-017738-7*, Pub. by Pergamon Repr UK) Franklin.

***Morris, R., Jr.** Sheridan: Life & Wars. Date not set. pap. 9.99 (*0-517-13175-7*) Random.

Morris, R. The Works of Edmund Spencer. 1988. reprint ed. lib. bdg. 99.00 (*0-7812-0237-X*) Rprt Serv.

Morris, R., ed. The Blickling Homilies, Pts. I-III. (EETS, OS Ser.: Vols. 58 & 63, 73). 1874. 45.00 (*0-8115-3354-9*) Periodicals Srv.

— Early English Alliterative Poems. (EETS, OS Ser.: Vol. 1). 1972. reprint ed. 22.00 (*0-8115-3340-9*) Periodicals Srv.

— Encyclopedia of American History. 7th ed. Date not set. 40.00 (*0-06-270055-3*, Harper Ref) HarpC.

— The Story of Genesis & Exodus an Early English Song. (EETS, OS Ser.: No. 7). 1974. reprint ed. 42.00 (*0-527-00006-X*) Periodicals Srv.

***Morris, R. & Payne, R.** An Anthology of Machine Postal Markings, 5. Billings, Bart, ed. (Illus.). 83p. 1994. pap. 12.50 (*1-880065-08-8*) Machine Cancel Soc.

— The Columbia Story: Early History, Etc. of the Columbia Postal Supply Co. (Illus.). 244p. 1994. pap. 21.00 (*1-880065-09-6*) Machine Cancel Soc.

Morris, R., jt. auth. see Cork, Barbara.

Morris, R., et al, eds. Acid Toxicity & Aquatic Animals. (Society for Experimental Biology Seminar Ser.: No. 34). 300p. 1989. 79.95 (*0-521-33435-7*) Cambridge U Pr.

Morris, R. A. & Andre, J., eds. Raster Imaging & Digital Typography II. (Cambridge Series on Electronic Publishing). (Illus.). 250p. (C). 1991. 59.95 (*0-521-41764-3*) Cambridge U Pr.

Morris, R. C., jt. ed. see Trendall, A. F.

Morris, R. G., ed. Parallel Distributed Processing: Implications for Psychology & Neurobiology. (Illus.). 352p. 1990. 69.50 (*0-19-852178-2*) OUP.

Morris, R. J. Cholera, Eighteen Thirty-Two: Social Response to an Epidemic. LC 76-25452. (Illus.). 230p. 1976. 39.50 (*0-8419-0288-7*) Holmes & Meier.

Morris, R. J. & MacSweeney, J. E. Medical Ophthalmology for Postgraduate Examinations. (Illus.). 206p. 1991. pap. text ed. 36.00 (*0-443-04049-4*) Churchill.

Morris, R. J. & Rodger, Richard, eds. The Victorian City: A Reader in British Urban History, 1820-1914. LC 92-28232. (Readers in Urban History Ser.). (C). 1993. text ed. 51.50 (*0-582-05133-9*, 79760); pap. text ed. 27.50 (*0-582-05132-0*, 79759) Longman.

Morris, R. J., jt. auth. see Langton, John.

Morris, R. J., jt. ed. see McKinlay, Alan.

Morris, R. M., jt. auth. see Chisholm, J. S.

Morris, R. W., et al, eds. Health-Related Water Microbiology 1992. (Water Science & Technology Ser.: Vol. 27). 500p. 1993. pap. 220.00 (*0-08-042207-1*, Pergamon Pr) Elsevier.

***Morris, R. Winston & Goldstein, Edward R., eds.** The Tuba Source Book. LC 94-48097. 1995. write for info. (*0-253-32889-6*) Ind U Pr.

Morris, Raimundo. Ensenanzas Falsas (Modulo) Los Adventistas Del Septimo Dia. rev. ed. (SPA.). 1990. 0.50 (*1-55955-077-5*) CITE MI.

— Ensenanzas Falsas (Modulo) Los Catolicoromanos. rev. ed. (SPA.). 1990. 0.40 (*1-55955-078-3*) CITE MI.

— Ensenanzas Falsas (Modulo) Los Mormones. rev. ed. (SPA.). 1990. 0.35 (*1-55955-080-5*) CITE MI.

— Ensenanzas Falsas (Modulo) Los Testigos De Jehova. rev. ed. (SPA.). 1990. 0.35 (*1-55955-081-3*) CITE MI.

— Evangelismo Personal, Tomo I. rev. ed. (SPA.). 1988. 4.85 (*1-55955-075-9*) CITE MI.

— Evangelismo Personal, Tomo II. rev. ed. (SPA.). 1989. 4.80 (*1-55955-076-7*) CITE MI.

Morris, Ralph. The Life & Astonishing Adventures of John Daniel. LC 74-16398. (Science Fiction Ser.). (Illus.). 276p. 1975. reprint ed. 26.95 (*0-405-06307-5*) Ayer.

Morris, Ralph C. Air Conditioning Cutter's Ready Reference. rev. ed. LC 73-148571. (Illus.). 363p. 1971. 27.95 (*0-912524-02-2*) Busn News.

Morris, Randall C. Process Philosophy & Political Ideology: The Social & Political Thought of Alfred North Whitehead & Charles Hartshorne. LC 89-49229. 289p. (C). 1991. 59.50 (*0-7914-0415-3*); pap. 19.95 (*0-7914-0416-1*) State U NY Pr.

Morris, Raymond N. Behind the Jester's Mask: Canadian Editorial Cartoons about Dominant & Minority Groups 1960-1979. 230p. 1989. text ed. 40.00 (*0-8020-5806-X*) U of Toronto Pr.

Morris, Reg & Payne, Bob. American Service Markings. 2nd ed. 102p. 1992. pap. 10.00 (*1-880065-02-9*) Machine Cancel Soc.

Morris, Reg & Payne, Robert. Barr-Fyke Machines & Postal Markings, 3 vols., Set. (Illus.). 116p. 1990. pap. 26.00 (*0-9621481-4-8*); pap. 26.00 (*0-9621481-5-6*); pap. 26.00 (*0-9621481-6-4*) Machine Cancel Soc.

— Hampden: Machines & Postal Markings. 206p. (C). 1991. pap. 17.50 (*1-880065-01-0*) Machine Cancel Soc.

— Perfection Mechanical Hand Stamp Machine. (Illus.). 63p. 1991. pap. 8.00 (*0-9621481-9-9*) Machine Cancel Soc.

— Pneumatic: Machines & Postal Markings. 176p. (C). 1992. pap. 15.00 (*1-880065-00-2*) Machine Cancel Soc.

Morris, Reg & Payne, Robert J. Groth-Constantine Machines & Postal Markings. (Illus.). 95p. (Orig.). 1990. pap. text ed. 7.00 (*0-9621481-1-3*) Machine Cancel Soc.

Morris, Reg, ed. see Billings, Bart.

Morris, Reginald O. Figured Harmony at the Keyboard, 2 Vols, Pt. 1. 1968. 14.95 (*0-19-321471-7*) OUP.

— Figured Harmony at the Keyboard, 2 Vols, Pt. 2. 1968. 12.95 (*0-19-321472-5*) OUP.

— Introduction to Counterpoint: Music Book Index. 55p. 1993. reprint ed. lib. bdg. 69.00 (*0-7812-9677-3*) Rprt Serv.

Morris, Reginald O. & Ferguson, Howard. Preparatory Exercises in Score Reading. 1968. 14.95 (*0-19-321475-X*) OUP.

Morris, Richard. The Adventures of God. 1993. 2.00 (*0-939520-04-4*) Ghost Dance.

— Assyrians. 112p. (Orig.). pap. 10.95 (*0-912292-92-X*) The Smith.

— The Autobiography. 1994. 15.00 (*0-939520-01-X*) Ghost Dance.

— Board of Directors. 1977. pap. 1.50 (*0-686-22678-X*) Ghost Dance.

— Cosmic Questions: Galactic Halos, Cold Dark Matter, & the End of Time. LC 93-13373. 208p. 1993. text ed. 24.95 (*0-471-59521-7*) Wiley.

— Light: From Genesis to Modern Physics. LC 78-11206. (Illus.). 1979. 10.95 (*0-672-52557-7*, Bobbs) Macmillan.

Morris, Richard, ed. Labor & Management. LC 76-183137. (Great Contemporary Issues Ser.). (Illus.). 500p. (C). 1973. 30.00 (*0-685-41643-7*, New York Times Co Bk) Ayer.

— Labor & Management. LC 76-183137. (Great Contemporary Issues Ser.). (Illus.). 500p. (C). 1973. 27.95 (*0-405-04163-2*, New York Times Co Bk) Ayer.

— Legends of the Holy Rood: Symbols of the Passion & Cross-Poems. (EETS, OS Ser.: No. 46). 1969. reprint ed. 40.00 (*0-527-00043-4*) Periodicals Srv.

— Old English Homilies & Homiletic Treatises, Pts. I & II. (EETS, OS Ser.: No. 29, 31, 34). 1974. reprint ed. 45.00 (*0-527-00029-9*) Periodicals Srv.

— Old English Homilies of the 13th Century. (EETS, OS Series II: No. 53). 1974. reprint ed. 42.00 (*0-527-00048-5*) Periodicals Srv.

— Old English Miscellany Containing a Bestiary, Etc. (EETS, OS Ser.: No. 49). 1974. reprint ed. 44.00 (*0-527-00045-0*) Periodicals Srv.

— The Puggala-Pannatti. LC 78-70109. reprint ed. 20.00 (*0-404-17359-4*) AMS Pr.

Morris, Richard, et al, eds. Cultural Legacies of Vietnam: Uses of the Past in the Present. LC 90-971. (Communication & Information Science Ser.). 256p. (C). 1990. text ed. 42.50 (*0-89391-635-8*); pap. text ed. 24.95 (*0-89391-713-3*) Ablex Pub.

Morris, Richard & Colman, Hila. Thoroughly Modern Millie. 15.95 (*0-88411-449-X*, Aeonian Pr) Amereon Ltd.

Morris, Richard & Zerchykov, Ross, comps. Community Councils. (Working Papers). 21p. 1980. pap. 2.50 (*0-317-00494-8*) Inst Responsive.

Morris, Richard, jt. ed. see Addyman, Peter.

Morris, Richard, ed. see Buddhavamsa.

Morris, Richard, ed. see Granger, James R., Jr.

Morris, Richard A. Old Russian Ways: Cultural Variations among Three Russian Groups in Oregon. LC 91-8067. (Immigrant Communities & Ethnic Minorities in the U. S. & Canada Ser.: No. 74). 1991. 64.50 (*0-404-19484-2*) AMS Pr.

Morris, Richard B. The American Revolution. rev. ed. LC 85-12878. (American History Topic Bks.). (Illus.). 72p. (J). (gr. 5-10). 1985. lib. bdg. 13.50 (*0-8225-1701-9*, Lerner Publctns) Lerner Group.

— The American Revolution: A Short History. LC 78-24604. (Anvil Ser.). 192p. 1979. reprint ed. pap. text ed. 10.50 (*0-88275-812-8*) Krieger.

— The American Revolution Reconsidered. LC 78-27608. 178p. 1979. reprint ed. text ed. 41.50 (*0-313-20909-X*, MOAM, Greenwood Pr) Greenwood.

— Basic Documents in American History. LC 80-12822. (Anvil Ser.). 194p. 1980. reprint ed. pap. text ed. 10.50 (*0-89874-202-1*) Krieger.

— Basic Documents on the Confederation & Constitution. LC 84-28908. 254p. (C). 1985. reprint ed. pap. 12.50 (*0-89874-839-9*) Krieger.

An Asterisk (*) at the beginning of an entry indicates that the title is appearing in BIP for the first time.

— The Constitution. rev. ed. (American History Topic Bks.). (Illus.). 72p. (YA). (gr. 5 up). 1985. lib. bdg. 13.50 (*0-8225-1702-7*, Lerner Publctns) Lerner Group.

— Independence: A Guide to Independence National Historic Park, Philadelphia, Pennsylvania. (National Park Service Handbook Ser.: No. 115). (Illus.). 65p. 1982. pap. 3.25 (*0-16-003497-3*, S/N 024-005-00913-2) USGPO.

— The War of Eighteen Twelve. rev. ed. (American History Topic Bks.). (Illus.). 72p. (YA). (gr. 5 up). 1985. lib. bdg. 13.50 (*0-8225-1705-1*, Lerner Publctns) Lerner Group.

Morris, Richard B., ed. Era of the American Revolution. 11. 25 (*0-8446-0212-4*) Peter Smith.

— A History of the American Worker. LC 82-48564. 328p. 1983. reprint ed. pap. 14.95 (*0-691-00593-1*) Princeton U Pr.

Morris, Richard B. & Baskin, Leonard. Framing of the Federal Constitution. LC 76-608411. (National Park Service Handbook Ser.: No. 103). (Illus.). 112p. 1986. pap. 4.75 (*0-16-003528-7*, S/N 024-005-01000-9) USGPO.

Morris, Richard B., jt. ed. see Commager, Henry S.

Morris, Richard B., jt. ed. see Leab, Daniel J.

Morris, Richard B., ed. see Thomas, Emory M.

Morris, Richard B., et al, eds. Dissertations in American Biography Series, 38 bks. 1982. write for info. (*0-318-50808-7*) Ayer.

Morris, Richard E., jt. auth. see Ferris, Robert G.

Morris, Richard J. & Kratochwill, Thomas R., eds. The Practice of Child Therapy. (General Psychology Ser.: No. 124). (Illus.). 360p. 1983. text ed. 100.00 (*0-08-028033-1*, Pergamon Pr); pap. text ed. 40.00 (*0-08-028032-3*, Pergamon Pr) Elsevier.

***Morris, Richard J. & McReynolds, Rebecca A.** Managing Aggressive & Disruptive Behavior in the Classroom. 150p. Date not set. pap. text ed. write for info. (*0-87822-353-3*) Res Press.

Morris, Richard J., jt. ed. see Kratochwill, Thomas R.

Morris, Richard K. John P. Holland, Eighteen Forty-One to Nineteen Fourteen. LC 79-6120. (Navies & Men Ser.). (Illus.). 1980. reprint ed. lib. bdg. 23.95 (*0-405-13048-1*) Ayer.

Morris, Richard L. Runic & Mediterranean Epigraphy. (NOWELE Ser.: Suppl. Vol. 4). 178p. (Orig.). 1988. pap. 42.50 (*87-7492-683-7*, Pub. by Odense Universitets Forlag DK) Coronet Bks.

Morris, Richard M. Developing a Charter for an Internal Adiut Function. Holman, Richard, ed. (IIA Monograph: No. 1). (Illus.). 29p. (Orig.). 1983. pap. text ed. 15.00 (*0-89413-101-X*) Inst Inter Aud.

Morris, Richard S. Bum Rap on America's Cities: The Real Cause of Urban Decay. 204p. 1980. pap. text ed. write for info. (*0-13-089219-X*) P-H.

Morris, Robert. Bare Ruined Choirs: The Fate of a Welsh Abbey. 52p. (YA). (gr. 11 up). 1987. pap. 7.95 (*0-85950-544-8*, Pub. by S Thornes UK) Dufour.

— Continuous Project Altered Daily: The Writings of Robert Morris. (October Ser.). (Illus.). 400p. 1993. 45. 00x (*0-262-13294-X*) MIT Pr.

— Continuous Project Altered Daily: The Writings of Robert Morris. (Illus.). 338p. 1995. pap. 25.00 (*0-262-63163-6*) MIT Pr.

— The Faithful Slave. LC 72-1562. (Black Heritage Library Collection). (Illus.). 1977. reprint ed. 17.95 (*0-8369-9039-0*) Ayer.

— Freemasonry in the Holy Land: Handmarks of Hiram's Builders. Davis, Moshe, ed. LC 77-70731. (America & the Holy Land Ser.). (Illus.). 1977. reprint ed. lib. bdg. 51.95 (*0-405-10270-4*) Ayer.

— Our Globe under Siege III. 200p. 1988. pap. 9.95 (*0-936676-75-2*) Better Baby.

— Select Architecture. LC 72-87427. (Architecture & Decorative Art Ser.). 102p. 1973. reprint ed. lib. bdg. 35. 00 (*0-306-71573-2*) Da Capo.

— Toward a Caring Society. 1974. 2.50 (*0-686-09284-8*) Univ Bk Serv.

— The Truth about the American Flag. LC 76-12730. (Illus.). 1976. 10.80 (*0-9601476-1-6*); pap. 7.65 (*0-9601476-2-4*) Wynnehaven.

— The Truth about the Betsy Ross Story. LC 82-70798. (Illus.). 1982. 15.95 (*0-9601476-3-2*); pap. 12.95 (*0-9601476-4-0*) Wynnehaven.

Morris, Robert, ed. Testing the Limits of Social Welfare: International Perspectives on Policy Changes in Nine Countries. LC 88-5559. (Illus.). 327p. 1988. text ed. 45. 00 (*0-87451-455-X*) U Pr of New Eng.

— Umbral Calculus & Hopf Algebras. LC 81-22756. (Contemporary Mathematics Ser.: Vol. 6). 84p. 1982. pap. 17.00 (*0-8218-5003-2*, CONM-6) Am Math.

Morris, Robert & Bass, Scott, eds. Retirement Reconsidered: Economic & Social Roles for Older People. 272p. 1988. 33.95 (*0-8261-5870-6*) Springer Pub.

Morris, Robert A. Dolphin. LC 75-6292. (Trophy I Can Read Bk.). (Illus.). 64p. (J). (gr. k-3). 1983. pap. 3.50 (*0-06-444043-5*, Trophy) Irwin Prof Pubng.

Morris, Robert A., ed. see Ring Theory Conference Staff.

Morris, Robert, Associates Staff. Computerized Credit Analysis. LC 83-9370. (High Technology in Banking Ser.). (Illus.). 44p. (Orig.). 1983. pap. text ed. 13.00 (*0-936742-08-9*) Robt Morris Assocs.

— Controlling Credit Department Functions. LC 86-5115. (Illus.). 52p. (Orig.). 1986. pap. text ed. 32.00 (*0-936742-29-1*) Robt Morris Assocs.

— Information on Deteriorating Accounts. LC 82-81367. 128p. 1982. 54.00 (*0-936742-05-4*) Robt Morris Assocs.

Morris, Robert B. Principles of Dental Treatment Planning. LC 82-15370. 252p. reprint ed. pap. 71.90 (*0-7837-2731-3*, 2043111) Bks Demand.

Morris, Robert C. Reading, Riting & Reconstruction: The Education of Freedmen in the South, 1861-1870. LC 80-25370. (Illus.). (C). 1981. 28.00 (*0-226-53928-8*) U Ch Pr.

— Solving the Problems of Youth At-Risk: Involving Parents & Community Resources. LC 91-67282. 232p. 1991. pap. text ed. 35.00 (*0-87762-915-3*) Technomic.

Morris, Robert C., ed. Freedmen's Schools & Textbooks: Black Education in the South, 1861-1870, 6 vols., Set. Incl. Vol. 1. 62.50 (*0-404-60761-6*); Vol. 2. 62.50 (*0-404-60762-4*); Vol. 3. 62.50 (*0-404-60763-2*); Vol. 4. 37.50 (*0-404-60764-0*); Vol. 5. 42.50 (*0-404-60765-9*); Vol. 6. 37.50 (*0-404-60766-7*); reprint ed. 305.00 (*0-404-19519-9*) AMS Pr.

— Using What We Know about At-Risk Youth: Lessons from the Field. 272p. 1994. pap. 29.00 (*1-56676-147-6*) Technomic.

Morris, Robert C. & Schultz, Nelda, eds. A Resource Guide for Working with Youth at Risk. 263p. 1993. pap. 24.50 (*1-56676-098-4*) Technomic.

Morris, Robert D. Composition with Pitch-Classes: A Theory of Compositional Design. 416p. 1987. text ed. 47.50 (*0-300-03684-1*) Yale U Pr.

Morris, Robert H., et al. Intertidal Invertebrates of California. LC 77-92946. (Illus.). 904p. 1980. 69.50 (*0-8047-1045-7*) Stanford U Pr.

Morris, Robert J. The Contemporary Peruvian Theatre. (Graduate Studies: No. 15). 98p. (Orig.). 1977. pap. 9.00 (*0-89672-025-X*) Tex Tech Univ Pr.

Morris, Robert K. Paradoxes of Order: Some Perspectives on the Fiction of V. S. Naipaul. LC 74-23752. (Literary Frontiers Ser.). 112p. 1975. pap. 9.95 (*0-8262-0172-5*) U of Mo Pr.

Morris, Robert K., ed. Old Lines, New Forces: Essays on the Contemporary British Novel, 1960-1970. LC 75-18243. 211p. 1976. 32.50 (*0-8386-1771-9*) Fairleigh Dickinson.

Morris, Robert L., ed. Perspectives in Psychical Research Series, 34 vols., Set. 1975. 1,049.00 (*0-405-07020-9*) Ayer.

Morris, Robin. The Marketing Principle. 168p. 1989. pap. text ed. 32.95 (*0-409-10735-2*) Buttrwrth-Heinemann.

Morris, Robin, jt. auth. see Miller, Edgar.

Morris, Robin D., jt. auth. see Horchler, Joani N.

Morris, Rod, ed. see Alcorn, Randy.

Morris, Rod, ed. see Bergstrom, Richard L., et al.

Morris, Rod, ed. see Dunnam, Maxie A., et al.

Morris, Rodler F. From Weimar Philosemite to Nazi Apologist: The Case of Walter Bloem. LC 88-14751. (Studies in German Thought & History: Vol. 7). 264p. 1988. lib. bdg. 89.95 (*0-88946-349-2*) E Mellen.

Morris, Rodney, ed. see Dobson, Edward G., et al.

Morris, Rodney L., ed. see Anderson, Leith, et al.

Morris, Rodney L., ed. see Briscsoe, Stuart, et al.

Morris, Rodney L., ed. see Hayford, Jack, et al.

Morris, Roger. Atlantic Seafaring: Ten Centuries of Exploration & Trade in the North Atlantic. (Illus.). 1992. 29.95 (*0-87742-337-7*, 60334) Intl Marine.

— Atlantic Seafaring: Ten Centuries of Exploration & Trade in the North Atlantic. 1992. 34.95 (*0-07-043298-8*) McGraw.

— The Devil's Butcher Shop: The New Mexico Prison Uprising. LC 88-4005. 277p. 1988. reprint ed. pap. 16.95 (*0-8263-1062-1*) U of NM Pr.

— Promises of Change: Clinton Admin., Politics of Renewal. 314p. 1996. 27.50 (*0-8050-2804-8*) H Holt & Co.

— Richard Milhous Nixon: The Rise of an American Politician. LC 89-7451. (Illus.). 944p. 1989. 29.95 (*0-8050-1121-8*) H Holt & Co.

— Richard Milhous Nixon: The Rise of an American Politician. (Illus.). 1024p. 1991. pap. 15.95 (*0-8050-1834-4*, Owl) H Holt & Co.

Morris, Roger, jt. auth. see Sheets, Hal.

Morris, Roland, jt. auth. see U. S. Department of State Staff.

Morris, Ron, et al. ACC Basketball: An Illustrated History. 304p. 1988. 39.95 (*0-9609548-9-9*) Village Sports.

Morris, Ronald A., et al. Federal Taxation of Real Estate. LC 89-50355. 468p. 1989. text ed. 10.00 (*0-318-42523-8*, J1-1467) PLI.

Morris, Ronald W. Values in Sexuality Education: A Philosophical Study. 132p. (Orig.). 1994. lib. bdg. 37.50 (*0-8191-9556-1*); pap. text ed. 18.50 (*0-8191-9557-X*) U Pr of Amer.

Morris, Rosalind C. New Worlds from Fragments: Film, Ethnography, & the Representation of Northwest Coast Cultures. LC 93-47668. (Studies in the Ethnographic Imagination). 194p. (C). 1994. text ed. 52.00 (*0-8133-8574-1*) Westview.

— New Worlds from Fragments: Film, Ethnography, & the Representation of Northwest Coast Cultures. LC 93-47668. (Studies in the Ethnographic Imagination). 194p. (C). 1994. pap. text ed. 22.95 (*0-8133-8783-3*) Westview.

Morris, Rosemary. The Character of King Arthur in Medieval Literature. (Arthurian Studies: No. IV). 175p. 1985. 70.00 (*0-85991-088-1*) Boydell & Brewer.

— Monks & Laymen in Byzantium, 843-1118. (Illus.). 365p. (C). 1995. write for info. (*0-521-26558-4*) Cambridge U Pr.

Morris, Rosemary, tr. see Farge, Arlette.

Morris, Rosemary, tr. see Gelis, Jacques.

Morris, Rosemary, tr. see Pinguet, Maurice.

Morris, Rosemary, tr. see Pouchelle, Marie-Christien.

Morris, Roy. Sheridan. 1994. 23.00 (*0-8446-6753-6*) Peter Smith.

— Sheridan: The Life & Wars of General Phil Sheridan. 1992. 25.00 (*0-517-58070-5*, Crown) Crown Pub Group.

Morris, Roy, Jr. Sheridan: The Life & Wars of General Phil Sheridan. LC 92-50621. (Civil War Library). 1993. 14.00 (*0-679-74398-7*, Vin) Random.

***Morris, Ruth.** Crumbling Walls: Why Prisons Fail. 166p. 1995. lib. bdg. 27.00 (*0-8095-4928-X*) Borgo Pr.

***Morris, Ruth & Heffren, Colleen.** Street People Speak. (Illus.). 96p. 1995. 27.00 (*0-8095-4931-X*) Borgo Pr.

Morris, Sally M. Favorite Seafood Recipes: Enjoy Your Restaurant Favorites at Home. rev. ed. (Illus.). 176p. 1989. pap. 8.95 (*1-55867-000-9*) Bristol Pub Ent CA.

Morris, Samuel M. Cardiopulmonary Bypass: Index of Modern Information. LC 88-47962. 150p. 1988. 44.50 (*0-88164-970-8*); pap. 39.50 (*0-88164-971-6*) ABBE Pubs Assn.

— Coronary Disease: Medical Subject Analysis with Reference Bibliography. rev. ed. LC 85-48190. 159p. 1991. 39.50 (*1-55914-474-2*); pap. 34.50 (*1-55914-475-0*) ABBE Pubs Assn.

— Health Care Financing in the U. S. Index of New Information with Authors & Subjects. LC 92-54239. 180p. 1992. 44.50 (*1-55914-626-5*); pap. 39.50 (*1-55914-627-3*) ABBE Pubs Assn.

— Medical Treatment of Self & Hypochondria: Index of Modern Authors & Subjects with Guide for Rapid Research. LC 90-56315. 160p. 1991. 44.50 (*1-55914-414-9*); pap. 39.50 (*1-55914-415-7*) ABBE Pubs Assn.

— Phobias & Disorders: Index of Modern Information. LC 88-47614. 150p. 1988. 37.50 (*0-88164-834-5*); pap. 34.50 (*0-88164-835-3*) ABBE Pubs Assn.

Morris, Sandra C., jt. auth. see Morris, Leslie R.

Morris, Sandra K., jt. auth. see Bunzel, Mark J.

Morris, Sandra M. A Message for All. LC 91-76391. 96p. (Orig.). 1993. pap. 7.95 (*1-55618-103-5*) Brunswick Pub.

Morris, Sarah P. Daidalos & the Origins of Greek Art. (Illus.). 498p. 1992. text ed. 75.00 (*0-691-03599-7*) Princeton U Pr.

— Daidalos & the Origins of Greek Art. (Illus.). 498p. 1995. pap. 35.00 (*0-691-00160-X*) Princeton U Pr.

Morris, Scott. Go Big Red: Recipes & Traditions from the Hearts of Huskers. LC 92-64319. 248p. 1992. 16.95 (*0-9631249-2-7*) Morris Pubng.

— How to Read a Map. LC 92-22824. (Using & Understanding Maps Ser.). (Illus.). 48p. (YA). (gr. 5 up). 1993. lib. bdg. 15.95 (*0-7910-1812-1*, Am Art Analog); pap. write for info. (*0-7910-1825-3*, Am Art Analog) Chelsea Hse.

— The Oregon Trail Cookbook: A Historical View of Cooking, Traveling & Surviving on the Trail. LC 93-78500. 200p. 1993. 10.95 (*0-9631249-3-5*) Morris Pubng.

Morris, Scott, ed. Agriculture & Vegetation of the World. LC 92-22290. (Using & Understanding Maps Ser.). (Illus.). (J). 1993. pap. write for info. (*0-7910-1817-2*, Am Art Analog) Chelsea Hse.

— Agriculture & Vegetation of the World. LC 92-22290. (Using & Understanding Maps Ser.). (Illus.). 48p. (YA). (gr. 5 up). 1993. lib. bdg. 15.95 (*0-7910-1804-0*, Am Art Analog) Chelsea Hse.

— The Economy of the World. LC 92-22291. (Using & Understanding Maps Ser.). (Illus.). 48p. (YA). (gr. 5 up). 1993. lib. bdg. 15.95 (*0-7910-1809-1*, Am Art Analog); pap. write for info. (*0-7910-1822-9*, Am Art Analog) Chelsea Hse.

— The Endangered World. LC 92-22289. (Using & Understanding Maps Ser.). (Illus.). 48p. (YA). (gr. 5 up). 1993. lib. bdg. 15.95 (*0-7910-1806-7*, Am Art Analog); pap. write for info. (*0-7910-1819-9*, Am Art Analog) Chelsea Hse.

— Industry of the World. LC 92-22288. (Using & Understanding Maps Ser.). (Illus.). 48p. (YA). (gr. 5 up). 1993. lib. bdg. 15.95 (*0-7910-1807-5*, Am Art Analog); pap. write for info. (*0-7910-1820-2*, Am Art Analog) Chelsea Hse.

— Languages of the World. LC 92-22287. (Using & Understanding Maps Ser.). (Illus.). 48p. (YA). (gr. 5 up). 1993. lib. bdg. 15.95 (*0-7910-1811-3*, Am Art Analog); pap. write for info. (*0-7910-1824-5*, Am Art Analog) Chelsea Hse.

— The Military World. LC 92-22286. (Using & Understanding Maps Ser.). (Illus.). 48p. (YA). (gr. 5 up). 1993. lib. bdg. 15.95 (*0-7910-1808-3*, Am Art Analog); pap. write for info. (*0-7910-1821-0*, Am Art Analog) Chelsea Hse.

— The Physical World. LC 92-22285. (Using & Understanding Maps Ser.). (Illus.). 48p. (YA). (gr. 5 up). 1993. lib. bdg. 15.95 (*0-7910-1801-6*, Am Art Analog); pap. write for info. (*0-7910-1814-8*, Am Art Analog) Chelsea Hse.

— The Political World. LC 92-22284. (Using & Understanding Maps Ser.). (Illus.). 48p. (YA). (gr. 5 up). 1993. lib. bdg. 15.95 (*0-7910-1802-4*, Am Art Analog); pap. write for info. (*0-7910-1815-6*, Am Art Analog) Chelsea Hse.

— Populations of the World. LC 92-22283. (Using & Understanding Maps Ser.). (Illus.). 48p. (YA). (gr. 5 up). 1993. lib. bdg. 15.95 (*0-7910-1805-9*, Am Art Analog) Chelsea Hse.

— Religions of the World. LC 92-22282. (Using & Understanding Maps Ser.). (Illus.). 48p. (YA). (gr. 5 up). 1993. lib. bdg. 15.95 (*0-7910-1810-5*, Am Art Analog); pap. write for info. (*0-7910-1823-7*, Am Art Analog) Chelsea Hse.

— Rocks & Minerals of the World. LC 92-22910. (Using & Understanding Maps Ser.). (Illus.). 48p. (YA). (gr. 5 up). 1993. lib. bdg. 15.95 (*0-7910-1803-2*, Am Art Analog); pap. write for info. (*0-7910-1816-4*, Am Art Analog) Chelsea Hse.

— Using & Understanding Maps, 12 vols., Set. (Using & Understanding Maps Ser.). (Illus.). 48p. (YA). (gr. 5 up). 1994. lib. bdg. write for info. (*0-7910-1800-8*, Am Art Analog) Chelsea Hse.

Morris, Shirley, ed. Thoughts. (C). 1989. 30.00 (*0-7223-2352-2*, Pub. by A H S Ltd UK) St Mut.

***Morris, Sidney.** If This Isn't Love. LC 94-62042. (Gay Play Script Ser.). (Illus.). 101p. 1985. pap. 8.95 (*1-886586-01-2*) T n T Class.

Morris, Simon C., jt. ed. see Simonetta, Alberto.

Morris, Skip. The Art of Tying the Dry Fly. (Illus.). 112p. (Orig.). 1993. 39.95 (*1-878175-37-8*); pap. 29.95 (*1-878175-36-X*) F Amato Pubns.

— The Art of Tying the Nymph. 112p. 1994. pap. 29.95 (*1-878175-51-3*) F Amato Pubns.

— The Custom Graphite Fly Rod: Design & Construction. (Illus.). 112p. 1989. 24.95 (*1-55821-011-3*) Lyons & Burford.

— Fly Proportion Chart. (Illus.). 1994. 3.95 (*1-878175-69-6*) F Amato Pubns.

— Fly Tying Made Clear & Simple. (Illus.). 80p. (Orig.). 1992. 29.95 (*1-878175-14-9*); pap. 19.95 (*1-878175-13-0*) F Amato Pubns.

— Tying Foam Flies. (Illus.). 48p. 1994. 29.95 (*1-878175-90-4*); pap. 16.95 (*1-878175-89-0*) F Amato Pubns.

***Morris, Sonia, et al, eds.** Aboriginal Languages & Education: The Canadian Experience. 150p. 1995. lib. bdg. 45.00 (*0-8095-4815-1*) Borgo Pr.

***Morris, Sonia V., ed. & pref.** Multicultural & Intercultural Education: Building Canada. 255p. (Orig.). (C). 1989. pap. text ed. 10.95x (*1-55059-006-5*) Temeron Bks.

***Morris Staff.** The Constitution of the United States of America. 32p. 1995. pap. text ed. 8.95 (*1-55709-105-6*) Applewood.

Morris, Stephanie, jt. auth. see Crilly, Eileen.

Morris, Stephanie A., jt. auth. see McMahon, A. Michael.

Morris, Stephen. Newnes PC Printers Pocketbook. 352p. 1992. 27.95 (*0-7506-0197-3*) Buttrwrth-Heinemann.

— Newness PC Programmer's Pocket Book. 399p. 19.95 (*0-7506-1386-6*) Buttrwrth-Heinemann.

— Object Oriented Programming under Windows: A Practical Handbook. (Illus.). 350p. 1994. pap. 29.95 (*0-7506-1792-6*) Buttrwrth-Heinemann.

— Using Quick BASIC 4.5: Step-by-Step. 256p. 1991. pap. 32.95 (*0-7506-0220-1*) Buttrwrth-Heinemann.

Morris, Stephen D. Corruption & Politics in Contemporary Mexico. 224p. 1991. pap. 19.95 (*0-8173-0525-4*) U of Ala Pr.

— Political Reformism in Mexico: An Overview of Contemporary Mexican Politics. LC 95-3472. 320p. 1995. lib. bdg. 48.00 (*1-55587-572-6*); pap. text ed. 19. 95 (*1-55587-594-7*) Lynne Rienner.

Morris, Stephen R., jt. auth. see Morris, Carla D.

***Morris, Steve.** Leadership Skills for Team Management: An Action Guide. Knasel, Eddy & Wilcox, Graham, eds. 192p. (C). 1995. 48.00x (*0-273-61093-7*, Pub. by Pitman Pubng UK) St Mut.

***Morris, Steve & Willcocks, Graham.** Creating a Safe & Healthy Culture. 300p. 1995. pap. 36.50 (*0-273-61687-0*, Pub. by Pitman Pub Ltd UK) Trans-Atl Phila.

Morris, Sue, ed. see Rowe, William.

Morris, Susan. Purinton Pottery. 1994. 24.95 (*0-89145-594-9*) Collector Bks.

— Thomas Girtin (1775-1802) LC 85-51651. (Illus.). 79p. (Orig.). 1986. pap. 12.00 (*0-930606-50-7*) Yale Ctr Brit Art.

Morris, Susan, jt. auth. see Cooper, John.

Morris, Susan, jt. auth. see McCarthy, Bernice.

Morris, Suzanne. Keeping Secrets. 1983. pap. 3.75 (*0-8217-1291-8*) Zebra.

— Wives & Mistresses. 1988. mass mkt. 4.95 (*1-55817-120-7*, Pinnacle NY) Windsor NY.

Morris-Suzuki, Tessa. Beyond Computopia: Information, Automation & Democracy in Japan. (Japanese Studies). 280p. 1988. lib. bdg. 59.95 (*0-7103-0293-2*, A2124) Routledge Chapman & Hall.

— A History of Japanese Economic Thought. (Nissan Institute Japanese Studies). 256p. 1988. text ed. 35.00 (*0-415-01264-3*) Routledge.

— A History of Japanese Economic Thought. 240p. 1992. pap. 16.95 (*0-415-07168-2*, A6625) Routledge.

— The Technological Transformation of Japan from the Seventeenth to the Twenty-First Century. LC 94-10310. (Illus.). 328p. (C). 1994. pap. 18.95 (*0-521-42492-5*) Cambridge U Pr.

— The Technological Transformation of Japan from the Seventeenth to the Twenty-First Century. LC 94-10310. (Illus.). 328p. (C). 1995. 59.95 (*0-521-41463-6*) Cambridge U Pr.

Morris-Suzuki, Tessa & Takuro, Seiyama, eds. Japanese Capitalism since 1945: Critical Perspectives. LC 89-4297. 252p. 1990. 57.50 (*0-87332-551-6*); pap. text ed. 25.95 (*0-87332-834-5*) M E Sharpe.

Morris, Sylvia, ed. Use of Group Services in Permanency Planning for Children. LC 82-23389. (Social Work with Groups Ser.: Vol. 5, No. 4). 109p. 1983. text ed. 32.95 (*0-86656-199-4*) Haworth Pr.

Morris, Sylvia J. Edith Kermit Roosevelt. LC 89-40498. 592p. 1990. pap. 15.95 (*0-679-72863-5*, Vin) Random.

Morris, Sylvia S., ed. William Marsh Rice & His Institute: A Biographical Study. LC 72-87103. (Rice University Studies: Vol. 58, No. 2). 171p. 1972. pap. 12.95 (*0-89263-212-7*) Rice Univ.

Morris, T., jt. ed. see Watson, M.

Morris, T. S. The Tucker Genealogy: A Record of Gilbert Ruggles & Evelina Christina (Snyder) Tucker, Their Ancestors & Descendants. (Illus.). 305p. 1989. reprint ed. lib. bdg. 53.50 (*0-8328-1186-6*); reprint ed. pap. 45. 50 (*0-8328-1187-4*) Higginson Bk Co.

Morris, T. V. The Bluffer's Guide to Philosophy. LC 89-1414. 129p. 1989. pap. 6.95 (*0-912083-35-2*) Diamond Communications.

Morris, Ted. Snapshot. 345p. (C). 1990. pap. 35.00 (*0-318-71718-2*, Pub. by IMMEL Pubng UK) St Mut.

An Asterisk (*) at the beginning of an entry indicates that the title is appearing in BIP for the first time.

Morris, Terence. Crime & Criminal Justice Since 1945. (Making Contemporary Britain Ser.). (Illus.). 160p. 1989. pap. 16.95 (*0-631-16109-0*) Blackwell Pubs.
— The Criminal Area: A Study in Social Ecology. LC 85-8015. (International Library of Sociology & Social Reconstruction). xiv, 202p. 1985. reprint ed. text ed. 75.00 (*0-313-24427-8*, MCRA, Greenwood Pr) Greenwood.
Morris, Terry. No Justice No Peace: From Emmett Till - Rodney King. 128p. (Orig.). 1993. pap. 10.95 (*0-9635878-0-3*) Africentric.
***Morris, Thomas D.** The Institution of African Service: Southern Slavery & the Law, 1619-1860. LC 95-6565. (Studies in Legal History). 1995. write for info. (*0-8078-2238-8*) U of NC Pr.
Morris, Thomas H. The RCIA: Transforming the Church: A Resource for Pastoral Implementation. 1989. pap. 10.95 (*0-8091-3047-5*) Paulist Pr.
— Walking Together in Faith: A Workbook for Sponsors of Christian Initiation. 224p. 1992. pap. 12.95 (*0-8091-3289-3*) Paulist Pr.
Morris, Thomas R. The Virginia Supreme Court: An Institutional & Political Analysis. LC 75-1158. 207p. reprint ed. pap. 59.00 (*0-8357-2714-9*, 2039828) Bks Demand.
Morris, Thomas R. & Sabato, Larry, eds. Virginia Government & Politics: Readings & Comments. 3rd rev. ed. 231p. 1990. pap. 25.00 (*0-318-04190-1*) U VA Ctr Pub Serv.
Morris, Thomas R., jt. ed. see Cooper, Weldon.
Morris, Thomas V. Anselmian Explorations: Essays in Philosophical Theology. LC 86-40239. 264p. (C). 1989. text ed. 29.95 (*0-268-00616-4*); pap. text ed. 12.95 (*0-268-00621-0*) U of Notre Dame Pr.
— God & the Philosophers: The Reconciliation of Faith & Reason. 304p. 1994. 25.00 (*0-19-508822-0*) OUP.
— The Logic of God Incarnate. LC 85-21252. 224p. 1986. 33.50 (*0-8014-1846-1*); pap. 11.95 (*0-8014-9474-5*) Cornell U Pr.
— Making Sense of It All: Pascal & the Meaning of Life. 208p. (Orig.). 1992. pap. 12.99 (*0-8028-0652-X*) Eerdmans.
— Our Idea of God. LC 90-19145. 216p. (C). 1991. text ed. 12.95 (*0-268-01504-X*) U of Notre Dame Pr.
— Our Idea of God: An Introduction to Philosophical Theology. Evans, C. Stephen, ed. LC 90-19145. (Contours of Christian Philosophy Ser.). 180p. (Orig.). (C). 1991. pap. 11.99 (*0-87784-346-5*, 346) InterVarsity.
— True Success: A New Philosophy of Excellence. LC 93-38664. 256p. 1994. 22.95 (*0-399-13943-5*, Grosset-Putnam) Putnam Pub Group.
Morris, Thomas V., ed. Divine & Human Action: Essays in the Metaphysics of Theism. LC 88-47738. 368p. 1988. 46.50 (*0-8014-2197-7*); pap. 17.95 (*0-8014-9517-2*) Cornell U Pr.
— God & the Philosophers: The Reconciliation of Faith & Reason. 304p. 1996. reprint ed. pap. 12.95 (*0-19-510119-7*) OUP.
— Philosophy & the Christian Faith. LC 87-40618. (Studies in Philosophy of Religion: No. 5). 336p. (C). 1990. text ed. 31.95 (*0-268-01570-8*); pap. text ed. 14.95 (*0-268-01571-6*) U of Notre Dame Pr.
Morris-Tigerman, Ellen, jt. auth. see Lynch-Fraser, Diane.
Morris, Timothy. Becoming Canonical in American Poetry. LC 94-12411. 1995. write for info. (*0-252-02136-3*); pap. write for info. (*0-252-06428-3*) U of Ill Pr.
— The Despairing Developer: Diary of an Aid Worker in the Middle East. 224p. 1991. 49.95 (*1-85043-486-7*, Pub. by I B Tauris UK); text ed. 16.95 (*1-85043-350-X*, Pub. by I B Tauris UK) St Martin.
***Morris, Ting.** Communication. LC 95-11620. (Craft Topics Ser.). (J). 1995. write for info. (*0-531-14385-6*) Watts.
Morris, Ting & Morris, Neil. Animals. LC 93-20415. (Sticky Fingers Ser.). (Illus.). 32p. (J). (gr. 2-4). 1993. lib. bdg. 13.23 (*0-531-14268-X*) Watts.
— Dinosaurs. LC 92-32915. (Sticky Fingers Ser.). (J). 1993. lib. bdg. 12.95 (*0-531-14258-2*) Watts.
— Growing Things. (Sticky Fingers Ser.). (Illus.). 32p. (J). (gr. 2-4). 1994. lib. bdg. 13.23 (*0-531-14284-1*) Watts.
— Masks. LC 92-32916. (Sticky Fingers Ser.). (J). 1993. lib. bdg. 13.23 (*0-531-14259-0*) Watts.
— Music. LC 93-20424. (Sticky Fingers Ser.). (Illus.). 32p. (J). (gr. 2-4). 1993. lib. bdg. 13.23 (*0-531-14269-8*) Watts.
— No-Cook Cooking. LC 93-31801. (Sticky Fingers Ser.). (Illus.). 32p. (J). (gr. 2-4). 1994. lib. bdg. 13.23 (*0-685-70145-X*) Watts.
— Rain Forest. LC 93-26686. (Sticky Fingers Ser.). (Illus.). 32p. (J). (gr. 2-4). 1994. lib. bdg. 13.23 (*0-531-14281-7*) Watts.
— Space. LC 93-24435. (Sticky Fingers Ser.). (Illus.). 32p. (J). (gr. 2-4). 1994. lib. bdg. 13.23 (*0-531-14282-5*) Watts.
Morris, Tom. Bursting the Foundations: A Bibliographical Primer on the Criticism of Culture. LC 81-82009. (Paunch Ser.: No. 55-56). (Illus.). 164p. 1981. pap. 7.00 (*0-9602478-5-8*) Paunch.
— True Success: A New Philosophy of Excellence. 288p. (Orig.). 1995. pap. 14.00 (*0-425-14615-4*, Berkley Trade) Berkley Pub.
Morris, Tom, jt. auth. see Miles, John.
Morris, Tracie. Chap-T-Her Won: Some Poems by Tracie Morris. 46p. 1993. pap. text ed. 7.00 (*1-883676-00-2*) TM Ink.
Morris, V. J., jt. auth. see Jennings, B. R.
Morris, Valerie B., jt. ed. see Pankratz, David B.
Morris, Van C. Deaning: Middle Management in Academe. LC 80-26119. 192p. 1981. 24.95 (*0-252-00871-5*) U of Ill Pr.
— Existentialism in Education: What It Means. (Illus.). 163p. (C). 1990. reprint ed. pap. text ed. 12.95 (*0-88133-497-9*) Waveland Pr.
Morris, Van Cleave & Pai, Young. Philosophy & the American School: An Introduction to the Philosophy of Education. 2nd ed. LC 93-4902. 1993. 36.00 (*0-8191-9005-5*) U Pr of Amer.
Morris-Vann, Artie M. My Dad Is Unemployed... But. (It's Not the End of the World Ser.). (Illus.). 40p. (Orig.). (J). (ps-5). 1981. pap. 6.50 (*0-940370-01-8*); 6.50 (*0-685-00149-0*) Aid-U Pub.
— My Mom Keeps Hitting Me...But. (It's Not the End of the World Ser.). (Illus.). 32p. (Orig.). (J). (ps-5). 1981. pap. 6.50 (*0-940370-02-6*); 6.50 (*0-940370-06-9*) Aid-U Pub.
— My Parents Are Drug Abusers. (It's Not the End of the World Ser.). 40p. (Orig.). (J). (ps-5). pap. 6.50 (*0-317-02490-6*) Aid-U Pub.
— Once upon a Time... A Guide to the Use of Bibliotherapy. (Illus.). 100p. (Orig.). 1979. pap. text ed. 15.00 (*0-940370-00-X*) Aid-U Pub.
Morris, Victor P. Oregon's Experience with Minimum Wage Legislation. LC 68-58609. (Columbia University. Studies in the Social Sciences: No. 320). reprint ed. 20.00 (*0-404-51320-4*) AMS Pr.
Morris, Vince. Zanshin: Meditation & the Mind in Modern Martial Arts. (Illus.). 108p. (Orig.). 1992. pap. 7.95 (*0-87728-756-2*) Weiser.
Morris, Virginia. The Complete Primer: Caring for Aging Parents. (Illus.). 480p. (Orig.). 1994. pap. 12.95 (*1-56305-435-3*) Workman Pub.
— Double Jeopardy: Women Who Kill in Victorian Fiction. LC 90-32879. 192p. 1990. text ed. 21.00 (*0-8131-1751-8*) U Pr of Ky.
Morris, Virginia & Schaef, Michael. The Yugoslavia War Crimes Tribunal: A Documentary History & Analysis. 1994. lib. bdg. 165.00 (*0-941320-92-8*) Transnatl Pubs.
Morris, Vivian G., jt. auth. see Jaisinghani, Vijay T.
Morris, W. A., et al, eds. English Government at Work, 1327-1336, Vol. 2 Fiscal Administration. (Medieval Academy Bks.: No. 48). 1968. reprint ed. 25.00 (*0-910956-22-7*) Medieval Acad.
Morris, W. A., jt. ed. see Willard, J. F.
Morris, W. G. & Hough, George H. The Anatomy of Major Projects: A Study of the Reality of Project Management. LC 87-8176. 336p. 1988. text ed. 76.95 (*0-471-91551-3*) Wiley.
Morris, W. H. Old Time Violin Melodies, Bk. 1. 25p. 1992. pap. 10.00 (*0-9637812-1-9*) MO St Old Time.
Morris, W. N. Mood. (Social Psychology Ser.). (Illus.). 248p. 1989. 65.00 (*0-387-96978-0*) Spr-Verlag.
Morris, W. R. Beyond the Storm: True Story of Jack McWilliams. 200p. Date not set. 14.95 (*0-9634779-7-8*) Cherokee Pr.
— Buford: True Story of "Walking Tall" Sheriff Buford Pusser. LC 83-62125. 215p. 1984. 14.95 (*0-915045-00-1*) Poplar Bks.
— The Twelfth of August. 1994. 14.95 (*0-9634779-9-4*) Cherokee Pr.
Morris, W. S., et al. History Thirty-First Regiment Illinois Volunteers Organized by John A. Logan. 302p. 1991. reprint ed. 24.95 (*0-9623990-5-1*); reprint ed. pap. 12.95 (*0-9623990-4-3*) Crossfire Pr.
Morris, W. Sidney. Carmina Latina. (C). 1982. pap. text ed. 39.00 (*0-900269-13-8*, Pub. by Old Vicarage UK) St Mut.
Morris, Walter D., tr. see Mann, Thomas.
Morris, Warren B. The Revisionist Historians & German War Guilt. 1976. lib. bdg. 250.00 (*0-87700-257-6*) Revisionist Pr.
— The Road to Olmutz: The Political Career of Joseph Maria Von Radowitz. 1975. lib. bdg. 250.00 (*0-87700-230-4*) Revisionist Pr.
— The Weimar Republic & Nazi Germany. LC 81-14179. 400p. 1982. 30.95 (*0-88229-336-2*); pap. 19.95 (*0-88229-797-X*) Nelson-Hall.
Morris, Wesley. Toward a New Historicism. LC 77-166384. 228p. 1972. 42.50x (*0-691-06223-4*) Princeton U Pr.
— Toward a New Historicism. LC 77-166384. Date not set. reprint ed. pap. 79.00 (*0-7837-9394-4*, 2060139) Bks Demand.
Morris, Wesley & Morris, Barbara A. Reading Faulkner. LC 89-4806. (Wisconsin Project on American Writers Ser.). 304p. (C). 1989. text ed. 24.95 (*0-299-12220-4*) U of Wis Pr.
Morris, William. Art & Society: Lectures & Essays by William Morris. 176p. (C). 1993. pap. 16.00 (*0-9635308-0-1*) Georges Hill.
— A Book of Verse. 1980. 424.95 (*0-85967-606-4*, Pub. by Scolar Pr UK) Ashgate Pub Co.
— The Collected Letters of William Morris, Vol. 1. Kelvin, Norman, ed. LC 82-47604. (Collected Letters of William Morris Ser.). (Illus.). 626p. 1984. 87.50 (*0-691-06501-2*) Princeton U Pr.
— Collected Works. 1973. 600.00 (*0-87968-895-5*) Gordon Pr.
— The Collected Works of William Morris, 24 vols., Set. (BCL1-PR English Literature Ser.). 1992. reprint ed. lib. bdg. 1,800.00 (*0-7812-7608-X*) Rprt Serv.
— Golden Wings & Other Stories. (Forgotten Fantasy Library: Vol. 8). 168p. 1976. pap. 5.95 (*0-87877-107-7*, F-107) Newcastle Pub.
— The Ideal Book: Essays & Lectures on the Arts of the Book. Peterson, William S., ed. LC 81-51339. (Illus.). 176p. 1982. 48.00 (*0-520-04563-7*); pap. 17.00 (*0-520-05625-6*) U CA Pr.
— The Letters of William Morris to His Family & Friends. Henderson, Philip, ed. LC 75-41199. reprint ed. 69.50 (*0-404-14711-9*) AMS Pr.
— News from Nowhere. Kumar, Krishan, ed. (Texts in the History of Political Thought Ser.). 230p. (C). 1995. 54.95 (*0-521-42007-5*); pap. 16.95 (*0-521-42233-7*) Cambridge U Pr.
— News from Nowhere. Redmond, James, ed. (English Texts Ser.). 1972. pap. 10.95 (*0-7100-6756-9*, RKP) Routledge.
— News from Nowhere & Other Writings. 480p. 1994. pap. 9.95 (*0-14-043330-9*, Penguin Classics) Viking Penguin.
— News from Nowhere & Selected Writings & Design. Briggs, Asa, ed. (English Library). 352p. 1984. mass mkt. 6.95 (*0-14-043115-2*, Penguin Classics) Viking Penguin.
— Old French Romances, Done into English. LC 75-113680. (Short Story Index Reprint Ser.). 1977. 19.95 (*0-8369-3409-1*) Ayer.
— Ornamentation & Illustrations from the Kelmscott Chaucer. 1973. pap. 7.95 (*0-486-22970-X*) Dover.
— Stoked. 350p. 1994. pap. 19.95 (*0-9639775-0-4*) New Sun Pubns.
— Stories in Prose, Stories in Verse, Shorter Poems, Lectures & Essays. Cole, G. D., ed. LC 75-41200. reprint ed. 94.50 (*0-404-14690-2*) AMS Pr.
— Story of the Glittering Plain: Which Has Also Been Called the Land of the Living or the Acre of the Dying. Reginald, R. & Menville, Douglas, eds. LC 80-19460. (Forgotten Fantasy Library: Vol. 1). xvi, 174p. 1980. reprint ed. 31.00x (*0-89370-500-4*) Borgo Pr.
— The Story of the Glittering Plain or the Land of Living Men: The 1894 Kelmscott Edition-with 23 Woodcuts by Walter Crane. (Illus.). 192p. 1987. reprint ed. pap. 7.95 (*0-486-25467-4*) Dover.
— Three Works. Morton, A. L., ed. 404p. 1987. reprint ed. pap. 4.95 (*0-7178-0202-7*) Intl Pubs Co.
— The Unpublished Lectures of William Morris. LC 69-19307. 332p. reprint ed. pap. 94.70 (*0-7837-3609-6*, 2043475) Bks Demand.
— The Widow's House by the Great Water. Timo, Helen, ed. 64p. (Orig.). (C). 1991. pap. 8.50 (*0-931332-07-9*) Wm Morris Soc.
— William Morris Full-Color Patterns & Design. (Illus.). 48p. 1988. reprint ed. pap. 7.95 (*0-486-25645-6*) Dover.
— The Wood Beyond the World. 261p. 1972. reprint ed. pap. 8.95 (*0-486-22791-X*) Dover.
Morris, William & Morris, Mary. Morris Dictionary of Word & Phrase Origins. 2nd ed. LC 87-45651. 736p. 1988. 35.00 (*0-06-015862-X*, HarpT) HarpC.
***Morris, William & Morris, Noelene.** A Pocketful of Stars. 252p. (Orig.). 1995. pap. 5.95 (*1-86429-010-2*, Pub. by Millennium Bks AT) Seven Hills Bk.
Morris, William, jt. auth. see Barr, Ben.
Morris, William, jt. ed. see Fulford, William.
Morris, William, jt. tr. see Magnusson, Eirikr.
Morris, William C. & Sashkin, Marshal. Organization Behavior in Action: Skill Building Experiences. LC 76-490. (Illus.). 292p. 1976. pap. text ed. 38.25 (*0-8299-0080-2*) West Pub.
Morris, William C., jt. auth. see Sashkin, Marshal.
Morris, William D. Heat Transfer & Fluid Flow in Rotating Coolant Channels. LC 82-139168. (Mechanical Engineering Research Studies Ser.: No. 2). (Illus.). 244p. reprint ed. pap. 69.60 (*0-8357-6139-8*, 2034231) Bks Demand.
Morris, William O. Hannibal. LC 73-14457. (Heroes of the Nations Ser.). reprint ed. 30.00 (*0-404-58275-3*) AMS Pr.
— Moltke: A Biographical & Critical Study. LC 68-25254. (World History Ser.: No. 48). 1969. reprint ed. lib. bdg. 75.00 (*0-8383-0222-X*) M S G Haskell Hse.
— Napoleon. LC 73-14458. (Heroes of the Nations Ser.). reprint ed. 30.00 (*0-404-58276-1*) AMS Pr.
— Wellington. LC 73-14459. (Heroes of the Nations Ser.). reprint ed. 30.00 (*0-404-58277-X*) AMS Pr.
Morris, William S. The Young Jonathan Edwards: A Reconstruction. LC 91-28030. (Chicago Studies in the History of American Religion Ser.: Vol. 14). 700p. 1991. 125.00 (*0-926019-50-3*) Carlson Pub.
Morris, William T., jt. auth. see Sink, D. Scott.
Morris, Willie. After All, It's Only a Game. LC 92-19542. (Author & Artist Ser.). (Illus.). 100p. 1992. 25.00 (*0-87805-600-9*) U Pr of Miss.
— Always Stand in Against the Curve & Other Sports Stories. (Illus.). 144p. 1983. 15.95 (*0-916242-25-0*) Yoknapatawpha.
— The Courting of Marcus Dupree. LC 92-27510. 464p. 1992. reprint ed. 37.50 (*0-87805-610-6*); reprint ed. pap. 17.95 (*0-87805-585-1*) U Pr of Miss.
— Good Old Boy: A Delta Boyhood. LC 80-52627. 143p. 1980. 14.95 (*0-916242-09-9*); pap. 8.95 (*0-916242-10-2*) Yoknapatawpha.
— Good Old Boy & the Witch of Yazoo. 1989. 15.95 (*0-916242-60-9*) Yoknapatawpha.
— Homecomings. LC 89-16683. (Author & Artist Ser.). (Illus.). 90p. 1990. 25.00 (*0-87805-416-2*) U Pr of Miss.
— Homecomings. limited ed. LC 89-16683. (Author & Artist Ser.). (Illus.). 90p. 1990. boxed 65.00 (*0-87805-417-0*) U Pr of Miss.
— Last of the Southern Girls. LC 72-11040. (Voices of the South Ser.). 304p. 1994. pap. 11.95 (*0-8071-1956-3*) La State U Pr.
— My Dog Skip. 1995. 15.00 (*0-679-44144-1*) Random.
— New York Days, Vol. 1. 1993. 24.95 (*0-316-58421-5*) Little.
— New York Days Vol. 1. 1994. pap. 12.95 (*0-316-58398-7*) Little.
— North Toward Home. 2nd ed. LC 67-25803. 438p. (C). 1983. reprint ed. pap. 14.95 (*0-916242-16-1*) Yoknapatawpha.
— Prayer for the Opening of Little League Season. LC 94-14471. (Illus.). (J). 1995. 15.00 (*0-15-200892-6*) HarBrace.
— Prayer for the Opening of Little League Season. limited ed. (Illus.). 1995. 60.00 (*0-15-200781-4*) HarBrace.
— Terrains of the Heart & Other Essays on Home. LC 81-50423. 288p. 1981. pap. 8.95 (*0-916242-23-4*) Yoknapatawpha.
Morris, Willie, ed. American Classrooms: Photographs by Catherine Wagner. (Illus.). 96p. (Orig.). 1988. pap. 25.00 (*0-89381-338-9*) Aperture.
Morris, Winifred. The Future of Yen-tzu. LC 90-26989. (Illus.). 32p. (J). (ps-3). 1992. text ed. 13.95 (*0-689-31501-5*, Atheneum Bks Young) S&S Childrens.
— What If the Shark Wears Tennis Shoes? LC 89-38150. (Illus.). 32p. (J). (gr. k-3). 1990. text ed. 13.95 (*0-689-31587-2*, Atheneum Bks Young) S&S Childrens.
— What If the Shark Wears Tennis Shoes? (Illus.). (J). (ps-3). 1995. pap. 4.95 (*0-689-71894-2*, Aladdin Paperbacks) S&S Childrens.
Morris, Woodrow W. The Greatest of These: Quotations on Fundamental Truths of Charity - The Teaching of Freemasonry. (Illus.). xiv, 111p. 1985. 11.50 (*0-88053-080-4*, M 328) Macoy Pub.
Morris, Wright. A Bill of Rites, a Bill of Wrongs, a Bill of Goods. LC 80-389. x, 177p. 1980. reprint ed. 17.95 (*0-8032-3065-6*); reprint ed. pap. 5.95 (*0-8032-8107-2*) U of Nebr Pr.
— Cause for Wonder. LC 77-14594. vi, 272p. 1978. 22.50 (*0-8032-0966-5*); pap. 5.95 (*0-8032-5885-2*) U of Nebr Pr.
— Ceremony in Lone Tree. LC 60-7775. viii, 304p. 1973. reprint ed. pap. 9.95 (*0-8032-5782-1*, Bison Books) U of Nebr Pr.
— Collected Stories, 1948-1986. LC 88-45282. 274p. 1989. pap. 10.95 (*0-87923-752-X*) Godine.
— Conversations with Wright Morris: Critical Views & Responses. Knoll, Robert E., ed. LC 76-25497. 329p. reprint ed. pap. 93.80 (*0-7837-6028-0*, 2045840) Bks Demand.
— The Deep Sleep. LC 75-5746. viii, 312p. 1975. reprint ed. pap. 7.95 (*0-8032-5823-2*, Bison Books) U of Nebr Pr.
— The Field of Vision. LC 56-8525. 251p. 1974. reprint ed. 25.00 (*0-8032-3060-5*); reprint ed. pap. 9.95 (*0-8032-5789-9*) U of Nebr Pr.
— Fire Sermon. LC 79-14763. iv, 155p. 1979. reprint ed. pap. 3.50 (*0-8032-8104-8*) U of Nebr Pr.
— The Fork River Space Project. LC 81-7540. vi, 185p. 1981. reprint ed. pap. 7.95 (*0-8032-8112-9*, Bison Books) U of Nebr Pr.
— The Huge Season. LC 54-10858. viii, 306p. 1975. reprint ed. pap. 7.95 (*0-8032-5805-4*, Bison Books) U of Nebr Pr.
— The Inhabitants. LC 70-115681. (Photography Ser.). (Illus.). 114p. 1972. reprint ed. lib. bdg. 25.00 (*0-306-71931-2*) Da Capo.
— A Life. LC 79-18304. vi, 152p. 1980. pap. 5.95 (*0-8032-8106-4*) U of Nebr Pr.
— The Loneliness of the Long Distance Writer: The Works of Love & the Huge Season. 575p. (C). 1995. 30.00 (*0-87685-991-0*); 40.00 (*0-87685-992-9*); pap. 17.50 (*0-87685-990-2*) Black Sparrow.
— Man & Boy. LC 51-2263. viii, 212p. 1974. reprint ed. pap. 6.95 (*0-8032-5787-2*, Bison Books) U of Nebr Pr.
— The Man Who Was There. LC 76-16590. viii, 237p. 1977. reprint ed. pap. 4.95 (*0-8032-5813-5*) U of Nebr Pr.
— My Uncle Dudley. LC 75-5696. viii, 210p. 1975. reprint ed. pap. 7.50 (*0-8032-5804-6*, Bison Books) U of Nebr Pr.
— One Day. LC 76-3766. viii, 435p. 1976. 33.50 (*0-8032-0879-0*); pap. 7.95 (*0-8032-5841-0*) U of Nebr Pr.
— Photographs & Words. Alinder, James, ed. LC 82-82471. (Illus.). 120p. 1982. 40.00 (*0-933286-28-7*) Frnds Photography.
— Plains Song. LC 89-46184. 232p. 1991. reprint ed. pap. 10.95 (*0-87923-835-6*) Godine.
— The Territory Ahead. LC 77-27989. xvi, 245p. 1978. 21.00 (*0-8032-3050-8*); pap. 5.50 (*0-8032-8100-5*) U of Nebr Pr.
— Three Easy Pieces. LC 93-35699. 328p. (Orig.). (C). 1993. 25.00 (*0-87685-924-4*); pap. 15.00 (*0-87685-923-6*) Black Sparrow.
— Three Easy Pieces, signed ed. deluxe ed. LC 93-35699. 328p. (Orig.). (C). 1993. 35.00 (*0-87685-925-2*) Black Sparrow.
— Time Pieces: Word & Image. (Writers & Artists on Photography Ser.). (Illus.). 126p. 1989. 35.00 (*0-89381-381-8*); pap. 14.95 (*0-89381-382-6*) Aperture.
— Two for the Road. LC 94-38984. 304p. (Orig.). (C). 1994. 25.00 (*0-87685-945-7*); pap. 15.00 (*0-87685-944-9*) Black Sparrow.
— Two for the Road, signed ed. deluxe ed. LC 94-38984. 304p. (Orig.). (C). 1994. 40.00 (*0-87685-946-5*) Black Sparrow.
— War Games. LC 78-5603. x, 164p. 1978. reprint ed. 16.50 (*0-8032-0950-9*); reprint ed. pap. 3.95 (*0-8032-5878-X*) U of Nebr Pr.
— What a Way to Go. LC 78-26760. viii, 311p. 1979. reprint ed. 25.95 (*0-8032-0915-0*); reprint ed. pap. 7.95 (*0-8032-5862-3*) U of Nebr Pr.
— The World in the Attic. LC 49-5058. x, 189p. 1971. 20.00 (*0-8032-3053-2*) U of Nebr Pr.
— Writing My Life: An Autobiography. LC 93-13802. 484p. (Orig.). (C). 1993. 25.00 (*0-87685-909-0*); pap. 15.00 (*0-87685-908-2*) Black Sparrow.
— Writing My Life: An Autobiography, signed ed. deluxe ed. LC 93-13802. 484p. (Orig.). (C). 1993. 35.00 (*0-87685-910-4*) Black Sparrow.
Morris, Wright, et al. Wright Morris: Origin of a Species. LC 92-16260. (Illus.). 96p. 1992. pap. 19.95 (*0-918471-24-9*) San Fran MOMA.
Morris-Wu, Eleanor B. Human Efflorescence: A Study in Man's Evolutionary & Historical Development. 352p. (C). 1983. 27.50 (*0-87527-323-8*) Green.

An Asterisk (*) at the beginning of an entry indicates that the title is appearing in BIP for the first time.

Morrisby, Edwin. Unpackaged Tours: World Travels off the Beaten Track. (Illus.). 400p. 1988. 17.95 (*0-8008-7939-2*) Taplinger.

*__Morrisey, George.__ Morrisey on Planning. (Management Ser.). 1995. 22.50 (*0-7879-0169-5*); 22.50 (*0-7879-0170-9*); 54.00 (*0-7879-0115-6*) Jossey-Bass.

— Morrisey on Planning Vol. I: A Manager's. 1995. 22.50 (*0-614-07238-7*) Jossey-Bass.

Morrisey, George L. Creating Your Future: Personal Strategic Planning for Professionals. LC 92-19057. 216p. (Orig.). 1992. pap. 15.95 (*1-881052-06-0*) Berrett-Koehler.

— Effective Business & Technical Presentations. 2nd ed. LC 74-24920. 224p. 1975. pap. text ed. write for info. (*0-201-04828-0*) Addison-Wesley.

— Management by Objectives & Results for Business & Industry. 2nd ed. (Illus.). 260p. 1977. pap. 20.95 (*0-201-04906-6*) Addison-Wesley.

— Management by Objectives & Results in the Public Sector. LC 76-1746. (Illus.). 204p. 1976. pap. 20.95 (*0-201-04825-6*) Addison-Wesley.

— Performance Appraisals in Business Industry: Keys to Effective Supervision. 1983. teacher ed write for info. (*0-201-13982-0*); pap. write for info. (*0-201-04831-0*) Addison-Wesley.

— Performance Appraisals in the Public Sector: Key to Effective Supervision. (Illus.). 160p. 1983. pap. write for info. (*0-201-04847-7*) Addison-Wesley.

Morrisey, George L. & Sechrest, Thomas L. Effective Business & Technical Presentations. 3rd ed. LC 87-1814. (Illus.). 163p. 1987. pap. 20.95 (*0-201-15852-3*) Addison-Wesley.

Morrisey, Michael A. Cost Shifting in Health Care: Separating Evidence from Rhetoric. LC 94-14605. Date not set. pap. write for info. (*0-8447-3861-1*) Am Enterprise.

— Cost Shifting in Health Care: Separating Evidence from Rhetoric. LC 94-14605. 1994. 19.95 (*0-8447-3860-3*, AEI Pr) Am Enterprise.

Morrisey, Patricia A. Disability Etiquette in the Workplace: Special Legi-Slate Edition. 64p. 1993. pap. text ed. write for info. (*1-880955-02-4*) Legi-Slate.

Morrisey, Thomas J., jt. auth. see Miller, Rex.

*__Morrisey, Will.__ A Political Approach to Pacifism, Bk. 1. LC 95-12482. (Studies in World Peace: Vol. 6a). 472p. 1996. text ed. 109.95 (*0-7734-8910-X*) E Mellen.

— A Political Approach to Pacifism, Bk. 2. LC 95-12482. (Studies in World Peace: Vol. 6b). 460p. 1996. text ed. 109.95 (*0-7734-8912-6*) E Mellen.

Morrisey, Will, jt. auth. see Eidelberg, Paul.

*__Morrish, Allan H.__ Canted Antiferromagnetism: Hematite. LC 94-35067. 200p. 1995. text ed. 46.00 (*981-02-2007-3*) World Scientific Pub.

Morrish, George. A Concordance of the Septuagint. 1976. 29.99 (*0-310-20300-7*, 6512) Zondervan.

*__Morrish, John.__ Fender Amp Book: A Complete History of Fender Amplifiers. (Illus.). 96p. 1995. 17.95 (*0-87930-345-X*) Miller Freeman.

Morrish, Robert & Enfantino, Peter, eds. Quick Chills II: The Best Horror Fiction from the Specialty Press. (Quick Chills Ser.: Vol. II). (Illus.). 356p. 1992. 45.00 (*0-9631367-3-9*) Deadline Pr.

*__Morrish, William R.__ Civilizing Terrains: Mountains, Mounds & Mesas. (Illus.). 102p. (C). 1990. pap. text ed. 25.00 (*0-9625974-0-6*) Design Ctr Amer Urban Land.

*__Morrish, William R. & Brown, Catherine R.__ Planning to Stay: Learning to See the Physical Features of Your Neighborhood. LC 94-25402. 1994. pap. 16.95 (*1-57131-203-X*) Milkweed Ed.

Morrison. Bacterial Endotoxic Lipopolysaccarides, 2 vols., 1. 1992. 207.00 (*0-8493-6787-5*, QP632) CRC Pr.

— Bacterial Endotoxic Lipopolysaccarides, 2 vols., 2. 1992. 207.00 (*0-8493-6788-3*) CRC Pr.

— Leadership & Management Skills for Practical - Vocational. 320p. 1994. pap. 17.95 (*0-8016-7235-X*) Mosby Yr Bk.

— Morrison on James to Revelation. 1984. pap. 4.99 (*0-89957-563-3*) AMG Pubs.

— Negotiations Set. 508p. 1994. 50.00 (*0-89464-925-6*) Krieger.

— New Improved Data Factory. 1994. pap. 39.95 (*0-442-01771-5*) Van Nos Reinhold.

— Powers of Ten. 1995. pap. text ed. write for info. (*0-7167-1500-7*) W H Freeman.

Morrison & Boyd, A. W. Organic Chemistry. 5th ed. 1987. student ed, pap. 35.00 (*0-685-18128-6*, H8454-4); trans. 70.00 (*0-685-18129-4*, H0525-9); write for info. (*0-318-61878-8*, H0524-2) P-H.

*__Morrison & Ryan.__ Novel Therapeutic Strategies in the Treatment of Sepsis. (Infectious Disease & Therapy Ser.). 511p. 1995. write for info. (*0-8247-9661-6*) Dekker.

Morrison & Serruys, eds. Medically Refractory Rest Angina. 480p. 1992. 175.00 (*0-8247-8630-0*) Dekker.

Morrison, jt. auth. see Carlson.

Morrison, ed. see Klusacek.

Morrison, et al. Powers of Ten: About the Relative Size of Things in the Universe. LC 82-5504. (Scientific American Library). (Illus.). 164p. (C). 1995. pap. text ed. write for info. (*0-7167-6003-7*); vhs 35.00 (*0-7167-5029-5*) W H Freeman.

— Powers of Ten: About the Relative Size of Things in the Universe. LC 82-5504. (Scientific American Library). (Illus.). 164p. (C). 1995. text ed. write for info. (*0-7167-1409-4*) W H Freeman.

— Remember to Read the Question: A Thinking Student's Guide to the S.A.T. & Beyond. 192p. (C). 1992. pap. text ed. 14.95 (*0-8403-7098-9*) Kendall-Hunt.

Morrison & Foerster Staff. CA Employer's Guide to Employee Handbook & Personnel Policy Manual. 1989. write for info. (*0-8205-1072-6*) Bender.

Morrison, A. J., tr. see Von Schlegel, Friedrich.

Morrison, A. W., jt. ed. see Ballantyne, John.

Morrison, Adrian, jt. ed. see Epstein, Alan N.

Morrison, Al H., ed. see Gregory, Eve S., et al.

Morrison, Al H., ed. see O'Clery, Helen.

Morrison, Al H., ed. see Tilton, Matt.

Morrison, Alan S. Screening in Chronic Disease. 2nd ed. (Monographs in Epidemiology & Biostatistics: No. 19). (Illus.). 256p. 1992. 45.00 (*0-19-506390-2*) OUP.

Morrison, Alastair. Fair Land Sarawak. (Studies on Southeast Asia: No. 13). (Illus.). 196p. (Orig.). 1993. pap. text ed. 16.00 (*0-87727-712-5*) Cornell SE Asia.

Morrison, Alastair M., jt. auth. see Mill, Robert C.

Morrison, Alec, ed. The Impossible Art of Golf: An Anthology of Golf Writing. 352p. 1994. 25.00 (*0-19-211698-3*) OUP.

*__Morrison, Alec, sel.__ The Impossible Art of Golf: An Anthology of Golf Writing. 328p. 1995. reprint ed. pap. 12.95 (*0-19-282503-8*) OUP.

*__Morrison, Alex, ed.__ The Changing Face of Peacekeeping: Proceedings of Peacekeeping '93. 243p. (Orig.). (C). 1994. pap. 45.00x (*0-7881-1286-4*) Diane Pub.

— Peacekeeping, Peacemaking or War: International Security Enforcement. 159p. 1994. reprint ed. pap. 40.00x (*0-7881-1287-2*) Diane Pub.

Morrison, Alex, jt. auth. see Jessop, David.

Morrison, Alexander B. The Dawning of a Brighter Day. LC 90-35883. (Illus.). 149p. 1990. 9.95 (*0-87579-338-X*) Deseret Bk.

— Feed My Sheep. LC 92-25690. 182p. 1992. 11.95 (*0-87579-605-2*) Deseret Bk.

— Visions of Zion. LC 93-36628. vii, 139p. 1993. 12.95 (*0-87579-788-1*) Deseret Bk.

Morrison, Alick. The Clan Morrison. (Johnston & Bacon Clan Histories Ser.). (Illus.). 32p. 1993. reprint ed. pap. 8.95 (*0-685-69989-7*, 9619) Clearfield Co.

Morrison, Allen. The Tramways of Chile, 1858-1978. LC 92-73238. (Illus.). 144p. (Orig.). 1992. pap. 20.00 (*0-9622348-2-6*) Bonde Pr.

Morrison, Allen J. Strategies in Global Industries: How U. S. Businesses Compete. LC 89-24370. 216p. 1990. text ed. 55.00 (*0-89930-528-8*, MBG/, Greenwood Pr) Greenwood.

***Morrison, Alwyn R. Thoughts to Dwell On. LC 94-69160. 125p. 1995. pap. 9.95 (*0-9643939-0-5*) Shepard Edge. THOUGHTS TO DWELL ON is a book of thoughts designed to motivate its readers to success. The thoughts were created by the author who has used & continues to use them as basic guidelines for success. The thoughts are expressed from different standpoints, from simple common sense to ideas that force us to think. It motivates, teaches, inspires, & sometimes attacks the way we normally look at life. It looks at our existence from the point of view that life is either everything or life is nothing. The primary view of the author is "life is what you make it." This is expressed to the readers from a number of angles. Every problem, no matter how large or how small, has a solution. Once this concept is accepted it eliminates the view "there's nothing I can do." An area of great importance in the book is our value to ourselves. Once we realize our own personal value, we begin to utilize our unlimited minds. Many of the thoughts deal with constant never-ending growth. The more we grow, the better people we become. Another important point of view in the book is "the more you save, the more independent you become." Society as a whole teaches that spending is a normal part of life. This allows growth for those at the top, but at the cost of millions of people without any level of financial independence. Once these thoughts are understood & acted upon, steps can then be taken toward success & happiness.**
Publisher Provided Annotation.

Morrison, Andrew, jt. ed. see Lansky, Melvin.

Morrison, Andrew, jt. ed. see Lutwack, Ralph.

*__Morrison, Andrew P.__ Lifting Burden Shame. Date not set. write for info. (*0-345-37484-3*) Ballantine.

— Shame: The Underside of Narcissism. 238p. 1989. text ed. 32.50 (*0-88163-082-9*) Analytic Pr.

Morrison, Andrew P., ed. Essential Papers on Narcissism. (Essential Papers in Psychoanalysis). 496p. 1986. 75.00x (*0-8147-5394-9*); pap. 25.00 (*0-8147-5395-7*) NYU Pr.

Morrison, Ann, jt. ed. see Black, Patti.

Morrison, Ann, et al. Performance Appraisal on the Line. 160p. 1981. pap. 15.00 (*0-912879-93-9*) Ctr Creat Leader.

Morrison, Ann M. Developing Leadership Diversity in Organizations. (Philip Morris Lectures on Business & Society Ser.). 25p. 1993. pap. write for info. (*1-884663-02-8*) Baruch Coll Cty U.

— The New Leaders: Guidelines on Leadership Diversity in America. LC 92-20107. (Management Ser.). 343p. 1992. 29.00 (*1-55542-459-7*) Jossey-Bass.

Morrison, Ann M. & Crabtree, Kristen M. Developing Diversity in Organizations: A Digest of Selected Literature. LC 93-144970. (Special Report Ser.: No. 317G). 138p. 1992. pap. text ed. 20.00 (*0-912879-70-X*) Ctr Creat Leader.

Morrison, Ann M., et al. Breaking the Glass Ceiling: Can Women Reach the Top of America's Largest Corporations? 2nd rev. ed. (Illus.). 1992. 19.18 (*0-201-63214-4*) Addison-Wesley.

Morrison, Ann M., et al, eds. Making Diversity Happen: A Forum on Controversies, Dilemmas, & Solutions. LC 93-40166. (Special Report Ser.: No. 320G). 127p. 1993. pap. text ed. 20.00 (*0-912879-72-6*) Ctr Creat Leader.

Morrison, Arthur. A Child of the Jago. (Victorian Classics Ser.). 208p. 1994. pap. 10.00 (*0-89733-392-6*) Academy Chi Pubs.

— Chronicles of Martin Hewitt. LC 74-144165. (Short Story Index Reprint Ser.). 1977. reprint ed. 18.95 (*0-8369-3780-5*) Ayer.

— The Hole in the Wall. 179p. 1994. reprint ed. pap. 10.00 (*0-89733-393-4*) Academy Chi Pubs.

— Martin Hewitt, Investigator. LC 75-32769. (Literature of Mystery & Detection Ser.). (Illus.). 1976. reprint ed. 19.95 (*0-405-07888-9*) Ayer.

— Martin Hewitt, Investigator. LC 74-10488. (Milestones of Mystery Ser.). (Illus.). v, 216p. 1975. reprint ed. 15.00 (*0-88355-203-5*) Hyperion Conn.

— Red Triangle. LC 75-116962. (Short Story Index Reprint Ser.). 1977. 21.95 (*0-8369-3466-0*) Ayer.

— Tales of Mean Streets. LC 78-128742. (Short Story Index Reprint Ser.). 1977. 19.95 (*0-8369-3633-7*) Ayer.

Morrison, Barrie M. Lalmai, a Cultural Center of Early Bengal: An Archaeological Report & Historical Analysis. LC 74-9892. (Publications on Asia of the School of International Studies: No. 24). (Illus.). 160p. 1974. 25.00 (*0-295-95342-X*) U of Wash Pr.

Morrison, Beverly H., jt. ed. see Bakker, Martinus A.

Morrison, Bill, jt. auth. see Coates, Ken.

*__Morrison, Blake.__ And When Did You Last See Your Father? A Son's Memoir of Love & Loss. 224p. 1995. 21.00 (*0-312-13023-6*) St Martin.

— The Yellow House. LC 93-36274. (Illus.). 32p. (J). (ps up). 1994. 4.99 (*1-56402-385-0*) Candlewick Pr.

Morrison, Bob, jt. auth. see Taylor, James.

Morrison, Bradley G. & Dalgleish, Julie G. Waiting in the Wings: A Larger Audience for the Arts & How to Develop It. rev. ed. LC 92-33800. 178p. (Orig.). 1992. pap. 14.95 (*1-879903-03-2*) Am Council Arts.

Morrison, Brenda, intro. S. C. Yuan. LC 94-72075. 200p. (Orig.). 1994. write for info. (*1-885666-06-3*); pap. write for info. (*1-885666-07-1*) Carmel Art.

Morrison, Brian. Cause for Dying. 1992. mass mkt. 5.50 (*0-06-104124-6*, Harp PBks) HarpC.

Morrison, Brian, jt. auth. see Fink, Howard.

Morrison, Bruce. 26.2: Trail of Truth. 96p. (Orig.). 1991. pap. 9.95 (*1-878901-20-6*) Hampton Roads Pub Co.

Morrison, Bryce. Liszt. (Illustrated Lives of the Great Composers Ser.). (Illus.). 112p. 1989. pap. 14.95 (*0-7119-1682-9*, OP44999) Omnibus NY.

Morrison, C. L. Defilement. LC 78-64744. (Illus.). 1979. 18.95 (*0-932508-02-2*) Seven Oaks.

Morrison, C. L., ed. Pithy Sayings from FORMAT Interviews, Vol. I. 1979. pap. 3.95 (*0-932508-06-5*) Seven Oaks.

— Pithy Sayings from FORMAT Interviews, Vol. II. 1980. pap. 3.95 (*0-932508-07-3*) Seven Oaks.

Morrison, Carlton A., jt. auth. see Mills, Margie B.

Morrison, Catherine. Managing Corporate Political Action Committees. (Report Ser.: No. 880). (Illus.). vii, 27p. (Orig.). 1986. pap. text ed. 60.00 (*0-8237-0322-3*) Conference Bd.

Morrison, Catherine, jt. auth. see Murray, John.

Morrison, Charles. The Fairfax Line: A Profile in History & Geography. (Illus.). 1974. pap. 2.00 (*0-87012-085-9*) McClain.

Morrison, Charles C. An Essay on the Relations Between Labor & Capital. LC 70-38273. (Evolution of Capitalism Ser.). 348p. 1979. reprint ed. 26.95 (*0-405-04128-4*) Ayer.

— Outlawry of War: A Constructive Policy for World Peace. Bd. with Outlawry of War. LC 71-147607. LC 71-147607. (Library of War & Peace; Kellogg Pact & the Outlawry of War). 1972. Set lib. bdg. 46.00 (*0-8240-0367-5*) Garland.

— Unfinished Reformation. LC 68-20322. (Essay Index Reprint Ser.). 1977. 20.95 (*0-8369-0723-X*) Ayer.

Morrison, Charles E. Japan, the United States & a Changing Southeast Asia. (Illus.). 82p. (Orig.). 1985. pap. text ed. 8.50 (*0-8191-4595-5*) U Pr of Amer.

Morrison, Charles E., ed. Asia-Pacific Report Nineteen Eighty-Seven thru Nineteen Eighty-Eight: Trends, Issues, Challenges. LC 87-20074. vi, 84p. 1987. pap. 10.00 (*0-86638-098-1*) EW Ctr HI.

— Asia-Pacific Report, 1986: Trends, Issues, Challenges. LC 85-27538. viii, 104p. 1986. pap. 10.00 (*0-86638-071-X*) EW Ctr HI.

— Japan, China & the Newly Industrialized Economies of East Asia, 1989. 1990. 5.00 (*0-685-34498-3*) Southern Ctr Intl Stud.

Morrison, Charles E., ed. & intro. Threats to Security in East Asia-Pacific. 221p. (C). 1983. text ed. 27.95 (*0-317-91349-2*) Pac Forum.

Morrison, Charles E. & Dernberger, Robert F., eds. Asia-Pacific Report, 1989: Focus: China in the Reform Era. LC 89-1103. vi, 126p. 1989. pap. 15.00 (*0-86638-111-2*) EW Ctr HI.

Morrison, Chris. PC Care Manual. 1991. 24.95 (*0-8306-6650-8*) TAB Bks.

Morrison, Chris & Stover, T. Commodore Care Manual: 64 System. 1991. 24.95 (*0-8306-6432-7*) TAB Bks.

Morrison, Chris & Stover, T. S. Commodore Care Manual: Diagnosing & Maintaining Your 64 or 128 System. 1988. pap. 16.95 (*0-07-155997-3*) McGraw.

Morrison, Chris & Stover, Teresa S. Apple Care Manual. 1991. 5.25 hd 24.95 (*0-8306-4252-8*) TAB Bks.

— Commodore Care Manual: Diagnosing & Maintaining Your 64 or 128 System. (Illus.). 224p. 1988. pap. 16.95 (*0-8306-3141-0*, 3141) TAB Bks.

— Commodore Care Manual: 128 System. 1991. 24.95 (*0-8306-6433-5*) TAB Bks.

— PC Care Manual: Diagnosing & Maintaining Your MS-DOS, CAM or Macintosh System. 1988. pap. 24.95 (*0-07-155792-X*) McGraw.

— PC Care Manual: Diagnosing & Maintaining Your MS-DOS CP-M or Macintosh System. LC 87-26235. (Illus.). 224p. 1987. 24.95 (*0-8306-0991-1*, 2991) TAB Bks.

Morrison, Christian. Adjustment & Equity in Morocco. (Adjustment & Equity in Developing Countries Ser.). 150p. (Orig.). 1991. pap. text ed. 31.00 (*92-64-13589-8*, 41-91-21-1) OECD.

Morrison, Clinton. An Analytical Concordance to the Revised Standard Version of the New Testament. LC 77-26210. 800p. 1979. 20.00 (*0-664-20773-1*, Westminster) Westminster John Knox.

Morrison, Clinton D., jt. tr. see Lammers, Wayne.

Morrison, Clyde A. Crystal Fields for Transition-Metal Ions in Laser Host Materials. LC 92-15276. viii, 190p. 1992. 69.00 (*0-387-55465-3*) Spr-Verlag.

Morrison, Colin, intro. Christmas in Ireland. (Illus.). 94p. 1990. 26.00 (*0-85342-908-1*, Pub. by Mercier Pr IE); pap. 13.95 (*0-85342-950-2*, Pub. by Mercier Pr IE) Dufour.

Morrison, Connie. Microsoft Word: Easy Reference Guides for IBM & Macintosh. 1992. text ed., mac hd 5.95 (*0-538-61758-6*); text ed., disk 5.95 (*0-538-61757-8*) S-W Pub.

— Microsoft Word for Windows 2.0: Easy Reference Guide. LC 93-33039. 1995. text ed. 5.95 (*0-538-63383-2*) S-W Pub.

— Microsoft Word 5.1 - Macintosh: Easy Reference Guide. LC 93-19714. 1994. text ed. 5.95 (*0-538-62676-3*) S-W Pub.

Morrison, Constance. Claudette of the Vieux Carre. Ingram, tr. 110p. (YA). 1995. pap. 7.95 (*1-56901-405-1*) NW Pub.

Morrison, Crystal D. Trial of Cristobal Colon: An Historical Play. LC 93-84327. 160p. (Orig.). 1994. pap. 15.98 (*1-879289-04-0*) Native Sun Pubs.

Morrison, D., jt. ed. see Chapman, C. P.

Morrison, D. C., ed. Organizing Early Experience: Imagination & Cognition in Childhood. 247p. 1988. pap. 24.95 (*0-89503-051-9*) Baywood Pub.

*__Morrison, Dane A.__ A Praying People: Massachusett Acculturation & the Failure of the Puritan Mission, 1600-1690. (American Indian Studies: Vol. 2). 304p. (C). 1995. text ed. 61.95 (*0-8204-1808-0*) P Lang Pubs.

Morrison, Daniel. Trading Peasants & Urbanization in Eighteenth-Century Russia: The Central Industrial Region. McNeill, William H. & Jelavich, Barbara, eds. (Modern European History Ser.). 440p. 1987. lib. bdg. 15.00 (*0-8240-8059-9*) Garland.

Morrison, Danny. West Belfast. LC 89-82069. 200p. 1990. pap. 12.95 (*0-85342-910-3*, Pub. by Mercier Pr IE) Dufour.

Morrison, Daphne. Being Pregnant: Conversations with Women. (Illus.). 201p. 1987. 19.95 (*0-919573-72-X*); pap. 5.00 (*0-919573-71-1*) Left Bank.

Morrison, David. Exploring Planetary Worlds. LC 92-46641. (Scientific American Library). 1995. text ed. write for info. (*0-7167-5043-0*) W H Freeman.

— Frontiers of Astronomy. 2nd ed. (C). 1993. pap. 29.00 (*0-03-093933-X*) HB Coll Pubs.

— Heroes, Antiheroes & the Holocaust: American Jewry & Historical Choice. LC 95-76846. 344p. (Orig.). 1995. 24.95 (*0-9646886-0-3*) Milah.

— The Planetary System. 2nd ed. (Illus.). 576p. (C). 1996. text ed. write for info. (*0-201-55450-X*) Addison-Wesley.

Morrison, David, ed. Satellites of Jupiter. LC 81-13050. (Space Science Ser.). (Illus.). 982p. reprint ed. pap. 180.00 (*0-7837-1909-4*, 2042113) Bks Demand.

Morrison, David & Samz, Jane. Voyage to Jupiter. (NASA SP Ser.: No. 439). 211p. 1980. pap. 9.00 (*0-16-004136-8*, S/N 033-000-00797-3) USGPO.

Morrison, David & Wolff, Sidney C. Frontiers of Astronomy. 475p. (C). 1990. pap. text ed. 36.00 (*0-03-030348-6*) SCP.

Morrison, David, jt. ed. see Friedman, Robert.

Morrison, David, jt. auth. see Owen, Tobias.

Morrison, David, jt. auth. see Pilon, Jean-Luc.

Morrison, David A. The Diamond Jenness Collections from Bering Strait. (Canadian Museum of Civilization Mercury Ser.). (Illus.). 171p. 1992. pap. 19.95 (*0-660-12922-1*) U Ch Pr.

— Iglulualumiut Prehistory: The Lost Inuit of Franklin Bay. (Canadian Museum of Civilization Mercury Ser.). (Illus.). 212p. 1991. pap. 17.95 (*0-660-10794-5*) U Ch Pr.

— The Kugaluk Site & the Nuvorugmiut. (Canadian Museum of Civlization Mercury Series-Canadian Ethnology Service). (Illus.). 116p. 1988. pap. text ed. 12.95 (*0-660-10778-3*, Pub. by CN Mus Civilization CN) U Ch Pr.

Morrison, David D. Long Island Rail Road Steam Locomotive Pictorial. Valenti, Linda A., ed. LC 87-36821. (Illus.). 60p. (Orig.). 1987. pap. 9.95 (*0-945089-00-7*) Cannon Ball.

Morrison, David E. & Tumbler, Howard. Journalists at War: The Dynamic of News Reporting During the Falklands Conflict. 384p. 1988. text ed. 49.95 (*0-8039-8057-4*); pap. text ed. 18.95 (*0-8039-8058-2*) Sage.
Morrison, David J., jt. auth. see Martin, Edmund F.
***Morrison, Deborah.** OS-2 Warp Internet Connection. 1995. pap. 24.99 (*1-56884-465-4*) IDG Bks.
Morrison, Delmont C. Neurobehavioral & Perceptual Dysfunction in Learning Disabled Children. LC 85-8656. 180p. (C). 1985. text ed. 23.00 (*0-88937-014-1*) Hogrefe & Huber Pubs.
Morrison, Dennis. Secret Society of the Shamans - Mystery Religions of the North American Indians Revealed. (Illus.). 112p. 1992. 10.95 (*0-938294-44-X*) Glob Comm-Inner Lght.
— Woman of Conscience: Margaret Chase Smith of Maine. (Illus.). 140p. (C). Date not set. pap. 17.95 (*1-881089-33-9*) Brandywine Press.
— Woman of Conscience: Margaret Chase Smith of Maine. (Illus.). (C). 1994. pap. text ed. 11.96 (*0-614-03061-7*) Brandywine Press.
Morrison, Denton E., jt. ed. see Ghosh, Pradip K.
Morrison, Diana. A Glossary of Sanskrit from the Spiritual Tradition of India. LC 77-27959. 40p. (ENG & SAN.). 1977. pap. 4.00 (*0-915132-12-5*) Nilgiri Pr.
Morrison, Donald. Mikhail S. Gorbachev: An Intimate Biography. pap. 4.50 (*0-318-50012-4*, Sig) NAL-Dutton.
Morrison, Donald, ed. Mikhail S. Gorbachev: An Intimate Biography. 288p. 1988. 14.95 (*0-317-70076-6*, Sig) NAL-Dutton.
Morrison, Donald F. Multivariate Statistical Methods. 3rd ed. 560p. (C). 1990. text ed. write for info. (*0-07-043187-6*) McGraw.
Morrison, Donald G., et al. Black Africa: A Comparative Handbook. 2nd ed. LC 89-2879. (Illus.). 768p. 1989. disk 249.50 (*0-8290-2477-8*); text ed. 169.50 (*0-8290-2466-2*) Irvington.
— Black Africa: A Comparative Handbook. 2nd ed. LC 89-2879. 716p. 1989. 169.50 (*0-88702-042-9*) Washington Inst Pr.
— Understanding Black Africa: Data & Analysis of Social Change & Nation Building. LC 88-33052. (Illus.). 253p. (C). 1989. text ed. 39.50 (*0-8290-2228-7*); pap. text ed. 19.95 (*0-8290-1371-7*) Irvington.
— Understanding Black Africa: Data & Analysis of Social Change & Nation Building. LC 88-33052. 255p. 1988. 39.50 (*0-88702-052-6*) Washington Inst Pr.
Morrison, Donald R., comp. Bibliography of Editions, Translations, & Commentary on Xenophon's Socratic Writings 1600-Present. 120p. 1988. 15.00 (*0-935225-02-1*) Mathesis Pubns.
Morrison, Donald W. Personal Problem Solving in the Classroom: The Reality Technique. LC 76-28419. 200p. reprint ed. pap. 57.00 (*0-317-09868-3*, 2015848) Bks Demand.
Morrison, Donita. Picking up the Pieces: How Survivors Survive. 1994. 14.95 (*0-533-10934-5*) Vantage.
Morrison, Dorothy. The Rise of Modern China. 1988. pap. text ed. 13.98 (*0-05-004183-5*, 78260) Longman.
Morrison, Dorothy N. Chief Sarah: Sarah Winnemucca's Fight for Indian Rights. (Eager Beaver Bks.). (Illus.). 192p. (J). (gr. 4 up). 1990. reprint ed. pap. 7.95 (*0-87595-204-6*) Oregon Hist.
— The Eagle & the Fort: The Story of John McLoughlin. (Illus.). 192p. 1984. reprint ed. pap. 5.95 (*0-87595-167-8*) Oregon Hist.
— Somebody's Horse. 224p. (J). (gr. 4-8). 1987. reprint ed. pap. 2.95 (*0-8167-1046-5*) Troll Assocs.
— Under a Strong Wind: The Adventures of Jessie Benton Fremont. LC 83-6356. (Illus.). 192p. (J). (gr. 5-9). 1983. lib. bdg. 14.95 (*0-689-31004-8*, Atheneum Bks Young) S&S Childrens.
— Whisper Again. 208p. (J). (gr. 2-9). 1989. reprint ed. pap. 2.95 (*0-8167-1307-3*) Troll Assocs.
— Whisper Goodbye. 192p. (J). (gr. 2-9). 1988. reprint ed. pap. 2.95 (*0-8167-1045-7*) Troll Assocs.
Morrison, Elizabeth, ed. see Cambridge, Ada.
Morrison, Elizabeth, ed. see Garzarelli, Bernadette.
Morrison, Elizabeth, jt. ed. see Purcell, Randall B.
Morrison, Ellen E. The Church That Keeps Memories Alive: The Story of Christ Church, Alexandria, Virginia. 2nd rev. ed. LC 79-114253. (Illus.). 12p. (J). (gr. 6). 1979. 1.75 (*0-9622537-0-7*) Morielle Pr.
— Gentle Man of Destiny: A Portrait of Robert E. Lee. 2nd rev. ed. LC 80-201289. (Illus.). 16p. (J). (gr. 6). 1984. 1.75 (*0-9622537-1-5*) Morielle Pr.

—Guardian of the Forest: A History of Smokey Bear & the Cooperative Forest Fire Prevention Program. 3rd rev. ed. (Illus.). 200p. 1995. lib. bdg. 18.95 (*0-9622537-5-8*) Morielle Pr. GUARDIAN OF THE FOREST is the only officially accepted, definitive history of the U.S. Forest Service's Cooperative Forest Fire Prevention Program. First published in 1976, it was updated & republished in the 1989 Second Edition, at the request of the U.S. Forest Service, & is widely recognized as a valuable reference book about the CFFP Program & its advertising symbol, Smokey Bear. The new revised, updated & enlarged Third Edition carries the history beyond the 1994 celebration of Smokey Bear's 50th birthday. Profusely illustrated, the book tells of people who have worked with the Program, adoption of the Smokey Bear symbol, introduction of the live bear, laws & regulations governing the Program, the 50th Birthday celebration, & the reasons for Smokey Bear's continued popularity for over half a century. The new edition contains many pages of additional text & illustrations. An Index has been included, by popular request. Order from Morielle Press, P.O. Box 10612, Alexandria, VA 22310-0612. (Tel. 703-960-2638). ***Publisher Provided Annotation.***

— Guardian of the Forest: A History of the Smokey Bear Program. 2nd rev. ed. LC 89-60719. (Illus.). 144p. (J). (gr. 6). 1989. 12.95 (*0-9622537-3-1*) Morielle Pr.
— Lady of Legend: The Mystery of the Female Stranger of Gadsby's Tavern. 2nd rev. ed. LC 87-460803. (Illus.). 16p. (J). (gr. 6). 1986. 1.75 (*0-9622537-2-3*) Morielle Pr.

—The Smokey Bear Story. (Illus.). 64p. (J). (gr. 1 up). 1995. lib. bdg. 15.95 (*0-9622537-4-X*) Morielle Pr. THE SMOKEY BEAR STORY tells young readers how Smokey Bear originated in 1944 as the advertising symbol of the U.S. Forest Service's Cooperative Forest Fire Prevention Program. It also gives a true account of the bear cub who was rescued after being burned in a 1950 forest fire, & later was sent to the National Zoo in Washington, D.C., as the living Smokey Bear, staying there until his death in 1976. Meanwhile, the original advertising symbol continued to campaign actively for forest fire prevention through the years, even when there was a live bear at the Zoo. Smokey Bear celebrated his 50th birthday in 1994, & is one of the most widely-recognized advertising symbols in the world. He receives so much mail that he has his own zip code. His most famous message, "Remember - only YOU can prevent forest fires!" is well-known to both children & adults. THE SMOKEY BEAR STORY is by the author of the popular adult reference book, GUARDIAN OF THE FOREST: A HISTORY OF THE SMOKEY BEAR PROGRAM. Order from Morielle Press, P.O. Box 10612, Alexandria, VA 22310-0612; tel. 703-960-2638. ***Publisher Provided Annotation.***

Morrison, Ellen M., jt. auth. see Shortell, Stephen M.
Morrison, Emily K. Leadership Skills: Developing Volunteers for Organizational Success. LC 94-9333. 236p. 1994. pap. 16.95 (*1-55561-066-8*) Fisher Bks.
Morrison, Emmeline. No More Such Days. large type ed. 368p. 1985. 15.95 (*0-7089-1352-0*) Ulverscroft.
***Morrison, Ernest.** The City on the Hill: History of the Harrisburg State Hospital. 262p. 1995. 25.00 (*0-9644246-0-6*); pap. 10.00 (*0-9644246-1-4*) Hist Committ HSH.
Morrison, F. J., jt. ed. see Siegel, L. S.
Morrison, Florence. The Cockeyed Boom Shack Cat & Other Stories. (Illus.). 48p. 1974. 5.00 (*0-87881-009-9*) Mojave Bks.
— The Devil's Bouquet. 70p. 1974. 5.75 (*0-87881-018-8*) Mojave Bks.
Morrison, Foster. The Art of Modeling Dynamic Systems: Forecasting for Chaos, Randomness, & Determinism. (Scientific & Technical Computation Ser.). 387p. 1991. text ed. 69.95 (*0-471-52004-7*) Wiley.
Morrison, Fred W. Equalization of the Financial Burden of Education among Counties in North Carolina: A Study of the Equalizing Fund. LC 73-177089. (Columbia University. Teachers College. Contributions to Education Ser.: No. 184). reprint ed. 37.50 (*0-404-55184-X*) AMS Pr.
Morrison, Frederick, tr. see Orlova, Alexandra, ed.
Morrison, Frederick J. Applied Developmental Psychology, Vol. 1. (Serial Publication Ser.). 1984. text ed. 91.00 (*0-12-041201-2*) Acad Pr.
Morrison, Frederick J. & Keating, Daniel P., eds. Applied Developmental Psychology, Vol. 2. (Serial Publication Ser.). 1985. text ed. 91.00 (*0-12-041202-0*) Acad Pr.
Morrison, Frederick J., et al, eds. Applied Developmental Psychology: Psychological Development in Infancy, Vol. 3. 267p. 1989. text ed. 92.00 (*0-12-041203-9*) Acad Pr.
***Morrison, G.** The Mystery Play. Kahan, B., ed. (Illus.). 80p. 1995. pap. 9.95 (*1-56389-189-1*, Vertigo) DC Comics.
***Morrison, G. A., Jr.** King: Clement King of Marshfield, MA, 1668, & His Descendants. (Illus.). 65p. 1994. reprint ed. lib. bdg. 23.00 (*0-8328-4337-7*); reprint ed. pap. 13.00 (*0-8328-4338-5*) Higginson Bk Co.
Morrison, G. E. The Correspondence of G. E. Morrison, 2 Vols., Set. Lo Hui-Min, ed. LC 74-31805. 825p. 1978. 265.00 (*0-521-08779-1*) Cambridge U Pr.
Morrison, G. H. Morrison: Genealogy of the Descendants of John Morrison & Prudence Gwyn. 31p. 1994. reprint ed. pap. 6.00 (*0-8328-4163-3*) Higginson Bk Co.
— Morrison on Galations Through Hebrews. LC 82-71841. (Glasgow Pulpit Ser.). 1982. pap. 4.99 (*0-89957-582-X*) AMG Pubs.
— Morrison on John, Vol. I. (Glasgow Pulpit Ser.). 1979. pap. 4.99 (*0-89957-534-X*) AMG Pubs.
— Morrison on John, Vol. II. (Glasgow Pulpit Ser.). 1979. pap. 4.99 (*0-89957-535-8*) AMG Pubs.
— Morrison on Luke, Vol. I. (Glasgow Pulpit Ser.). 1979. pap. 4.99 (*0-89957-532-3*) AMG Pubs.
— Morrison on Luke, Vol. II. (Glasgow Pulpit Ser.). 1979. pap. 4.99 (*0-89957-533-1*) AMG Pubs.
— Morrison on Mark. (Glasgow Pulpit Ser.). 1979. pap. 4.99 (*0-89957-531-5*) AMG Pubs.
— Morrison on Matthew, Vol. I. (Glasgow Pulpit Ser.). 1979. pap. 4.99 (*0-89957-528-5*) AMG Pubs.
— Morrison on Matthew, Vol. II. (Glasgow Pulpit Ser.). 1979. pap. 4.99 (*0-89957-529-3*) AMG Pubs.
— Morrison on Matthew, Vol. III. (Glasgow Pulpit Ser.). 1979. pap. 4.99 (*0-89957-530-7*) AMG Pubs.
— Morrison on Romans & Corinthians. (Glasgow Pulpit Ser.). 96p. 1982. pap. 4.99 (*0-89957-547-1*) AMG Pubs.
Morrison, G. H., ed. Morrison on Genesis. (Glasgow Pulpit Ser.). 72p. 1976. pap. 4.99 (*0-89957-520-X*) AMG Pubs.
Morrison, Gail M. The Sound & the Fury. 300p. Date not set. 54.00 (*0-8240-4236-0*) Garland.
Morrison, Gayle. To Move the World: Louis G. Gregory & the Advancement of Racial Unity in America. LC 81-22763. 367p. 1983. pap. 14.50 (*0-87743-188-4*, 332-073) Bahai.
Morrison, George H. Highways of the Heart. LC 93-37827. 208p. 1993. pap. 9.99 (*0-8254-3290-1*) Kregel.
— Morrison on Acts. rev. ed. Zodhiates, Joan, ed. LC 80-69541. (Glasgow Pulpit Ser.). 1981. pap. 4.99 (*0-89957-050-X*) AMG Pubs.
— The Weaving of Glory. 192p. 1994. pap. 9.99 (*0-8254-3291-X*) Kregel.
— The Wind on the Heath. LC 93-37826. 176p. 1993. pap. 9.99 (*0-8254-3289-8*) Kregel.
— Wings of the Morning. 192p. 1994. pap. 9.99 (*0-8254-3288-X*) Kregel.
Morrison, George R. Liquidity Preferences of Commercial Banks. LC 66-13882. (Chicago University Economics Research Center Studies). 175p. reprint ed. pap. 49.90 (*0-317-09091-7*, 2020130) Bks Demand.
Morrison, George S. Contemporary Curriculum K-Eight. LC 92-35298. 1993. text ed. write for info. (*0-205-14523-X*) Allyn.
— Early Childhood Education Today. 5th ed. 576p. (C). 1990. write for info. (*0-675-21342-8*, Merrill Pub Co) Macmillan.
— Early Childhood Education Today. 6th ed. LC 94-8332. 640p. (C). 1994. write for info. (*0-02-384151-6*) Merrill.
— Education & Development of Infants, Toddlers, & Preschoolers. (C). 1988. text ed. 51.00 (*0-673-39741-6*) HarpCollege.
Morrison, Glenn H. The Morrisons: They Came to the Land That Hudgin Drains. (Orig.). 1994. pap. 15.95 (*0-9640081-0-6*) G H Morrison.
Morrison, Gordon, jt. auth. see Kricher, John C.
Morrison, Gordon, jt. auth. see Walton, Richard K.
Morrison, Grant. Animal Man. Hill, Michael, ed. (Illus.). 240p. 1991. pap. 19.95 (*1-56389-005-4*, Vertigo) DC Comics.
— Batman: Arkham Asylum. Berger, Karen, ed. 128p. 1990. pap. 14.95 (*0-930289-56-0*) DC Comics.
— Doom Patrol: Crawling from the Wreckage. Kahan, Bob, ed. 192p. 1992. pap. 19.95 (*1-56389-034-8*, Vertigo) DC Comics.
— Isaac Bronson & the Search for System in American Capitalism, 1789-1838. (Dissertations in American Economic History Ser.). 1978. 39.95 (*0-405-11050-2*) Ayer.
Morrison, Grant & Janson, Klaus. Batman Gothic. (Illus.). (Orig.). 1992. pap. 12.99 (*0-446-39428-9*) Warner Bks.
Morrison, Grant & McKeon, David. Batman: Arkham Asylum. 1990. pap. 14.95 (*0-446-39189-1*) Warner Bks.
Morrison, Greg, jt. auth. see Fortschen, William R.
Morrison, Greg, jt. auth. see Fortschen, William R.
Morrison, Gregory B. The Modern Technique of the Pistol. LC 91-72644. 175p. 1991. write for info. (*0-9621342-3-6*) Gunsite Pr.
Morrison, H. C. Remarkable Conversions & Striking Illustrations. pap. 3.99 (*0-88019-102-3*) Schmul Pub Co.
***Morrison, Harriet B.** Seven Gifts: A New View of Teaching Inspired by the Philosophy of Maurice Merleau-Ponty. LC 88-13089. 201p. 1988. lib. bdg. 15.95 (*0-934328-09-9*) LEPS Pr.
Morrison, Harry. Biorganic Photochemistry, Vol. 1: Photochemistry & the Nucleic Acids. 437p. 1990. text ed. 94.95 (*0-471-62987-1*) Wiley.
Morrison, Harry, ed. Biological Applications of Photochemical Switches. 316p. 1993. text ed. 84.95 (*0-471-57293-4*) Wiley.
— Quantum Theory of Many-Particle Systems. (International Science Review Ser.). (Illus.). 360p. 1968. text ed. 145.00 (*0-677-00550-4*) Gordon & Breach.
Morrison, Hedda. Travels of a Photographer in China, 1933-1946. (Illus.). 276p. 1987. 29.95 (*0-19-584098-4*) OUP.
Morrison, Henry C. The Practice of Teaching in the Secondary School. rev. ed. LC 31-9855. 698p. reprint ed. pap. 180.00 (*0-317-28133-X*, 2024101) Bks Demand.
— School & Commonwealth. LC 73-142673. (Essay Index Reprint Ser.). 1977. 20.95 (*0-8369-2063-5*) Ayer.
Morrison, Howard. American Encounters. (Illus.). 80p. (Orig.). 1992. pap. write for info. (*0-929847-05-9*) Natl Mus Am.
Morrison, Hugh. Acting Skills. (Illus.). 150p. 1992. pap. text ed. 13.95 (*0-87830-034-1*, A9672, Theatre Arts Bks) Routledge Chapman & Hall.
— Directing in the Theatre. LC 73-83996. 1974. pap. 10.95 (*0-87830-587-4*, Theatre Arts Bks) Routledge Chapman & Hall.
— Early American Architecture: From the First Colonial Settlements to the National Period. (Illus.). 640p. 1987. reprint ed. pap. 14.95 (*0-486-25492-5*) Dover.
Morrison, Hugh A. List of Books & of Articles in Periodicals Relating to Interoceanic Canal & Railway Routes. 174p. 1988. reprint ed. 17.50 (*0-913129-21-6*) La Tienda.
Morrison, Ian. The Crannogs of Scotland: Lake Dwellings in a Landscape. 80p. (Orig.). 1983. pap. 16.50 (*0-85224-472-X*, Pub. by Edinburgh U Pr UK) Col U Pr.
— Golf. rev. ed. (Play the Game Ser.). (Illus.). 80p. 1994. pap. 7.95 (*0-7137-2442-0*, Pub. by Blandford Pr UK) Sterling.
— One Hundred Greatest Golfers. 1988. 9.99 (*0-517-65839-9*) Random Hse Value.
— Radio Times Book of Sporting Dates: Sporting Facts & Figures for 366 Days a Year. 256p. (Orig.). 1995. pap. 9.95 (*0-563-36959-0*, Pub. by BBC UK) Parkwest Pubns.
Morrison, Ian & Schmid, Gregory. Future Tense: Preparing for the Business Realities in the Next Ten Years. 1994. 25.00 (*0-688-12351-1*) Morrow.
Morrison, Ian A. Egypt. LC 91-7791. (World in View Ser.). (Illus.). 96p. (YA). (gr. 6-12). 1991. lib. bdg. 24.26 (*0-8114-2445-6*) Raintree Steck-V.
— Middle East. LC 90-24433. (World in View Ser.). (Illus.). 96p. (YA). (gr. 6-12). 1991. lib. bdg. 24.26 (*0-8114-2440-5*) Raintree Steck-V.
Morrison, Ian A., et al. Continuing Care Retirement Communities: Political, Social & Financial Issues. LC 85-8669. (Journal of Housing for the Elderly: Vol. 3, No. 1-2). 188p. 1986. text ed. 39.95 (*0-86656-384-9*) Haworth Pr.
Morrison, Ian M., ed. Advances in Plant Cell Biochemistry & Biotechnology, Vol. 1. 1991. 90.25 (*1-55938-357-7*) Jai Pr.
Morrison, Irma L., jt. auth. see Freedman, Alan.
Morrison, J., jt. auth. see Lindgren, I.
Morrison, J. Cayce. The Puerto Rican Study, 1953-1957. Cortes, Carlos E., ed. LC 79-6217. (Hispanics in the United States Ser.). (Illus.). 1981. reprint ed. lib. bdg. 31.95 (*0-405-13165-8*) Ayer.
Morrison, J. F., jt. ed. see Cervero, F.
Morrison, J. F., jt. ed. see Torrens, M. J.
Morrison, J. M. Virus Induced Enzymes. 655p. 1991. text ed. 259.95 (*0-471-92339-7*, Wiley-Liss) Wiley.
***Morrison, James.** DSM-IV Made Easy. 1995. lib. bdg. 38.95 (*0-89862-568-8*) Guilford Pr.
Morrison, James & Munoz, Rodrigo. Boarding Time: A Psychiatry Candidate's Guide to Part II of the ABPN Examination. LC 90-564. 175p. 1990. pap. text ed. 24.50 (*0-88048-366-0*) Am Psychiatric.
Morrison, James, jt. auth. see Morrison, Rob.
Morrison, James C. Meaning & Truth in Wittgenstein's Tractatus. LC 68-15536. (Janua Linguarum, Series Minor: No. 64). 1968. pap. text ed. 35.40 (*90-279-0592-4*) Mouton.
Morrison, James D., ed. Asymmetric Synthesis, Vol. 1: Analytical Methods. LC 83-4620. 1983. text ed. 79.00 (*0-12-507701-7*) Acad Pr.
— Asymmetric Synthesis, Vol. 5: Chiral Catalysis. 1985. text ed. 158.00 (*0-12-507705-X*) Acad Pr.
Morrison, James D. & Mosher, Harry S. Asymmetric Organic Reactions. LC 75-21608. 465p. 1976. reprint ed. pap. 16.95 (*0-8412-0296-6*) Am Chemical.
Morrison, James D. & Scott, John W. Asymetric Synthesis, Vol. 4: The Chiral Carbon Pool & Chiral Sulfur, Nitrogen, Phosphorus & Silicon Centers. 1984. text ed. 158.00 (*0-12-507704-1*) Acad Pr.
Morrison, James E. Blood Rain. 350p. 1994. pap. 9.95 (*1-56901-309-8*) NW Pub.
— Twenty-Four Early American Country Dances: Cotillions & Reels for the Year 1976. LC 76-3969. (Illus.). 72p. Date not set. spiral bd. 6.00 (*0-917024-04-4*) Country Dance & Song.
Morrison, James F. The Polish People's Republic. LC 68-10209. (Integration & Community Building in Eastern Europe Ser.: No. 2). 184p. reprint ed. pap. 52.50 (*0-317-09029-1*, 2002280) Bks Demand.
Morrison, James H. Missionary Heroes of Africa. LC 79-89010. 267p. 1969. reprint ed. text ed. 52.50 (*0-8371-1738-0*, MOM&, Negro U Pr) Greenwood.
Morrison, James L. The Best School in the World: West Point, the Pre-Civil War Years, 1833-1866. LC 85-12625. 267p. reprint ed. pap. 76.10 (*0-7837-1982-5*, 2042256) Bks Demand.
Morrison, James L., Jr. Memoirs of Henry Heth. LC 72-820. (Contributions in Military History Ser.: No. 6). 303p. 1974. text ed. 42.95 (*0-8371-6389-7*, MHH/, Greenwood Pr) Greenwood.
Morrison, James L., et al. Futures Research & the Strategic Planning Process: Implications for Higher Education. LC 85-61908. (ASHE-ERIC Higher Education Report Ser.: No. 9, 1984). (Illus.). 141p. (Orig.). 1985. pap. 7.50 (*0-913317-18-7*) GWU Schl E&HD.
Morrison, James L., et al, eds. Applying Methods & Techniques of Futures Research. LC 82-84194. (New Directions for Institutional Research Ser.: No. IR 39). 1983. pap. 16.95x (*0-87589-957-9*) Jossey-Bass.
Morrison, James O. Math, the Exciting Language. 120p. 1986. pap. text ed. 6.50 (*0-935920-42-0*, Ntl Pubs Blck) P-H.
Morrison, James R. Your Brother's Keeper: A Guide for Families Confronting Psychiatric Illness. LC 79-27810. 352p. 1981. 27.95 (*0-88229-563-2*) Nelson-Hall.

An Asterisk (*) at the beginning of an entry indicates that the title is appearing in BIP for the first time.

Morrison, James V. Homeric Misdirection: False Predictions in the Iliad. LC 92-27449. (Monographs in Classical Antiquity). 130p. (C). 1992. text ed. 32.50 (*0-472-10352-0*) U of Mich Pr.

Morrison, Jan. A Safe Place: Beyond Sexual Abuse. 180p. (Orig.). (YA). 1990. pap. 7.99 (*0-87788-747-0*) Shaw Pubs.

Morrison, Jaydene, jt. auth. see Clayton, Lawrence.

Morrison, Jim. The American Night. 1993. pap. 3.99 (*0-517-08683-2*) Random Hse Value.

— The American Night: The Writings of Jim Morrison. LC 90-50901. 224p. 1991. pap. 9.00 (*0-679-73462-7*, Vin) Random.

— The Lords & the New Creatures. 1971. pap. 9.00 (*0-671-21044-0*, Touchstone Bks) S&S Trade.

— Wilderness: The Lost Writings of Jim Morrison, Vol. 1. 1989. pap. 9.00 (*0-679-72622-5*, Vin) Random.

Morrison, Joan. ShareHouse Blues. 160p. (C). 1990. pap. 30.00 (*0-86439-002-5*, Pub. by Boolarong Pubns AT) St Mut.

Morrison, Joan & Morrison, Robert K. From Camelot to Kent State: The Sixties Experience in the Words of Those Who Lived It. LC 87-9978. 384p. 1987. pap. 15.00 (*0-8129-1715-4*, Times Bks) Random.

Morrison, Joan & Zabusky, Charlotte F. American Mosaic: The Immigrant Experience in the Worlds of Those Who Lived It. 2nd ed. LC 92-50274. (Social & Labor History Ser.). 480p. 1993. reprint ed. 49.95 (*0-8229-3753-0*); reprint ed. pap. 10.95 (*0-8229-5488-5*) U of Pittsburgh Pr.

Morrison, Joel L. Rand McNally Goode's World Atlas. 18th ed. Epenshade, Edward, Jr., ed. (Illus.). 384p. 1989. text ed. 28.95 (*0-528-83128-3*) Rand McNally.

***Morrison, Joel L. & Wortman, Kathryn, eds.** Implementing the Spatial Data Transfer Standard. (Cartography & Geographic Information Systems Journal Ser.: Vol. 19, No. 5). 64p. 1992. 20.00 (*0-614-06099-0*, AC195) Am Congrs Survey.

Morrison, John. The Happy Warrior. 160p. (C). 1990. 27.00 (*0-947087-08-7*, Pub. by Pascoe Pub AT) St Mut.

— Learning AutoCAD. (C). pap. text ed. 27.00 (*0-13-031253-3*) P-H.

Morrison, John, ed. The Age of the Galley: Mediterranean Vessels since Pre-Classical Times. (Conway's History of the Ship Ser.). (Illus.). 208p. 1994. 44.95 (*1-55750-024-X*) Naval Inst Pr.

Morrison, John & Coates, John. The Athenian Trireme: The History & Reconstruction of an Ancient Greek Warship. (Illus.). 288p. 1986. pap. 21.95 (*0-521-31100-4*) Cambridge U Pr.

Morrison, John, jt. auth. see Albrecht, Steven.

Morrison, John, jt. ed. see Mizrahi, Terry.

Morrison, John A. The Deacon of Dobbinsville. 64p. pap. 1.00 (*0-686-29146-8*) Faith Pub Hse.

— The Educational Philosophy of Saint John Bosco. LC 79-54817. 258p. (Orig.). 1979. pap. 6.95 (*0-89944-050-9*) Don Bosco Multimedia.

Morrison, John C., jt. auth. see Smith, Philip H.

Morrison, John E., ed. Training for Performance: Principles of Applied Human Learning. (Series on Studies in Human Performance & Cognition: No. 1507). 311p. 1991. text ed. 104.95 (*0-471-92248-X*) Wiley.

Morrison, John H. History of American Steam Navigation, 2 vols. 1977. lib. bdg. 200.00 (*0-8490-1965-6*) Gordon Pr.

— History of Steam Navigation. (Illus.). 1967. reprint ed. 25.00 (*0-87266-023-0*) Argosy.

Morrison, John S. & Williams, R. T. Greek Oared Ships, Nineteen Hundred to Three Twenty-Two B. C. LC 67-19504. 397p. reprint ed. pap. 113.20 (*0-317-27550-X*, 2024499) Bks Demand.

Morrison, Joseph L. Governor O. Max Gardner: A Power in North Carolina & New Deal Washington. LC 74-132253. (Illus.). 340p. reprint ed. pap. 96.90 (*0-8357-3865-5*, 2036597) Bks Demand.

***Morrison, Judith.** The Book of Ayurveda: A Holistic Approach to Health & Longevity. 1995. pap. 15.00 (*0-684-80017-9*) S&S Trade.

Morrison, Karin. Compassion Seeds. 101p. (Orig.). 1994. pap. 6.95 (*0-9645283-0-4*) K Morrison. COMPASSION SEEDS takes a new approach to reach the toughest man, to melt the hardest heart, to plant seeds that will awaken feelings you never thought you had. COMPASSION SEEDS makes grown men cry. The books reminds mankind that there are more important things than man-made treasures. COMPASSION SEEDS is possibly one of the first books to bring peace to all living creatures. COMPASSION SEEDS message is powerful! It glorifies God, embraces all life & gives strength to all those doubting in God's love & His concern for all creatures. Simple, yet rich in wisdom! To order: Karin Morrison Publishing, 405-229-0400.** ***Publisher Provided Annotation.

Morrison, Karl F. Conversion & Text: The Cases of Augustine of Hippo, Herman-Judah, & Constantine Tsatsos. 208p. 1992. text ed. 35.00 (*0-8139-1359-4*); pap. 16.95 (*0-8139-1393-4*) U Pr of Va.

— History of a Visual Art in the Twelfth-Century Renaissance. (Illus.). 258p. (C). 1990. text ed. 39.50 (*0-691-05582-3*) Princeton U Pr.

— Holiness & Politics in Early Medieval Thought. (Collected Studies: No. CS219). 302p. (C). 1985. reprint ed. lib. bdg. 87.50 (*0-86078-167-4*, Pub. by Variorum UK) Ashgate Pub Co.

— I Am You: The Hermeneutics of Empathy in Western Literature, Theology, & Art. (Illus.). 430p. 1988. text ed. 52.50 (*0-691-05510-6*) Princeton U Pr.

— The Mimetic Tradition of Reform in the West. LC 81-47935. 426p. 1982. 57.50 (*0-691-05350-2*) Princeton U Pr.

— Understanding Conversion. 272p. 1992. text ed. 40.00 (*0-8139-1360-8*) U Pr of Va.

Morrison, Kathy & Reader, Alice. Beginning Science. (Early Childhood Science Ser.). 80p. 1987. 9.95 (*0-317-58254-2*) Denison.

***Morrison, Keith.** Implementing Cross-Curricular Themes. 160p. 1994. pap. 29.00x (*1-85346-313-2*, Pub. by D Fulton UK) Taylor & Francis.

Morrison, Keith & Ridley, Ken. Curriculum Planning & the Primary School. 208p. (C). 1988. 45.00 (*1-85396-009-8*, Pub. by P Chapman Pub UK) St Mut.

Morrison, Kenneth & Thompson, Marcia. Feeling Good about Me. Sorenson, Don L., ed. LC 79-55664. (Illus.). 224p. (Orig.). 1980. pap. text ed. 8.95 (*0-932796-05-2*) Ed Media Corp.

Morrison, Kenneth M. The Embattled Northeast: The Elusive Ideal of Alliance in Abenaki-Euramerican Relations. LC 83-18002. 1984. 45.00 (*0-520-05126-2*) U CA Pr.

***Morrison, Kevin M.** Speed Measurement in Traffic Law Enforcement from Radar to Laser. (Illus.). 107p. (C). 1994. pap. text ed. 24.95 (*1-884566-17-0*) Inst Police Tech.

Morrison, Kristin. Canters & Chronicles: The Use of Narrative in the Plays of Samuel Beckett & Harold Pinter. LC 82-16086. viii, 228p. (C). 1986. pap. text ed. 9.95 (*0-226-54131-2*) U Ch Pr.

— William Trevor. (Twayne's English Authors Ser.). 208p. 1993. text ed. 22.95 (*0-8057-7032-1*, Pub. by Royal Botanic Garden UK) Macmillan.

Morrison, L. A. The History of the Sinclair Family in Europe & America for 1100 Years. (Illus.). 453p. 1989. reprint ed. lib. bdg. 76.00 (*0-8328-1074-6*); reprint ed. pap. 68.00 (*0-8328-1075-4*) Higginson Bk Co.

Morrison, L. V. & Gilmore, G. F., eds. Galactic & Solar System Optical Astrometry: Proceedings of the Royal Greenwich Observatory & the Institute of Astronomy Workshop Held in Cambridge, June 21-24, 1993. LC 94-9034. (Illus.). 336p. (C). 1994. 59.95 (*0-521-46240-1*) Cambridge U Pr.

***Morrison, Laura L. & DeCiani, Gina.** Legal Ethics for Paralegals & the Law Office. LC 94-27670. 350p. (Orig.). 1994. pap. text ed. 29.50 (*0-314-04173-7*) West Pub.

Morrison, Laura M. Integration in Thought & Behavior: A Neuropsychological Theory. LC 81-83785. (Illus.). 357p. 1984. 29.95 (*0-937638-01-3*); pap. 24.95 (*0-937638-00-5*) Harbor Pub.

Morrison, Leger. TFB: Typewriting for Business. 208p. 1985. reprint ed. student ed. 5.00 (*0-935920-35-8*, Ntl Pubs Blck); reprint ed. pap. text ed. 11.50 (*0-935920-34-X*, Ntl Pubs Blck) P-H.

Morrison, Leger & Birt, Robert F. Illustrated Guide for Term Papers, Reports, Theses, & Dissertations, with Index & Rules for Punctuation & for Expression of Numbers. enl. ed. (Illus.). ix, 102p. (C). 1971. pap. text ed. 4.95 (*0-911593-02-0*) Morrison Pub Co.

Morrison, Leger R. & Birt, Robert F. End-of-Line Division Manual. xx, 342p. (Orig.). (C). pap. text ed. 9.50 (*0-911593-03-9*) Morrison Pub Co.

— Guide to Confused Words. xxvi, 272p. (Orig.). (C). 1972. pap. 7.85 (*0-911593-04-7*) Morrison Pub Co.

Morrison, Leonard A. History of the Alison or Allison Family in Europe & America, A. D. 1135 to 1893. (Illus.). 328p. 1988. reprint ed. lib. bdg. 57.00 (*0-8328-0114-3*); reprint ed. pap. 49.00 (*0-8328-0115-1*) Higginson Bk Co.

— The History of Windham, New Hampshire, 1719-1883, with the History & Genealogy of Its First Settlers. (Illus.). 862p. 1988. reprint ed. lib. bdg. 88.00 (*0-8328-0056-2*, NH0028) Higginson Bk Co.

Morrison, Lillian. At the Crack of the Bat. LC 91-28946. (Illus.). 64p. (J). (gr. 3-7). 1994. pap. 5.95 (*1-56282-670-0*) Hyprn Ppbks.

— Rhythm Road: Poems to Move To. LC 87-4071. (J). (gr. 4 up). 1988. lib. bdg. 13.95 (*0-688-07098-1*) Lothrop.

— Whistling the Morning in New Poems by Lillian Morrison: New Poems. (Illus.). 40p. (J). 1992. lib. bdg. 16.95 (*1-56397-035-X*, Wordsong) Boyds Mills Pr.

Morrison, Liz, jt. auth. see Devereux, Sue.

Morrison, Louis. Monarch Notes on Tolkien's Fellowship of the Ring. 1975. pap. 3.25 (*0-671-00971-0*, Arco Test) P-H Gen Ref & Trav.

Morrison, M., jt. ed. see Jessop, J.

Morrison, M. A. & Owen, D. I., eds. Studies on the Civilization & Culture of Nuzi & the Hurrians, Vol. 1: In Honor of Ernest R. Lacheman on His Seventy-Fifth Birthday, April 29, 1981. LC 81-15123. xxi, 496p. 1981. text ed. 52.50 (*0-931464-08-0*) Eisenbrauns.

Morrison, M. A., jt. ed. see Owen, D. I.

***Morrison, M. E., ed.** Directory of Traditional Latin Masses, 1994-1995. 80p. (Orig.). 1994. pap. 10.00 (*1-883511-05-4*) Veritas Pr CA.

Morrison, M. E. S., jt. auth. see Lind, Edna M.

Morrison, Madison. Soluna: Collected Earlier Poems. 287p. 1989. text ed. 30.00 (*81-207-1035-5*, Pub. by Sterling Pubs II) Apt Bks.

Morrison, Maighan. Long Live Earth. (J). (ps-3). 1994. pap. 4.95 (*0-590-48012-X*) Scholastic Inc.

***Morrison, Margaret.** Hello Out There. 128p. 1992. pap. 5.95 (*1-57087-104-3*) Prof Pr NC.

Morrison, Margaret N. A Simplified Guide to Using Statistical Techniques with Computer Applications. LC 86-3242. 206p. 1986. text ed. 29.95 (*0-13-810185-X*, Busn) P-H.

Morrison, Marion. The Amazon Rain Forest & Its People. LC 93-20410. (People & Places Ser.). 48p. (J). (gr. 5-8). 1993. 15.95 (*1-56847-087-8*) Thomson Lrning.

— The Amazon Rain Forest & Its People. (People & Places Ser.). (Illus.). 48p. (J). (gr. 5-8). 1995. reprint ed. pap. 6.95 (*1-56847-307-9*) Thomson Lrning.

— Argentina. (People & Places Ser.). (Illus.). 48p. (J). (gr. 4-8). 1989. lib. bdg. 12.95 (*0-382-09793-9*) Silver Burdett Pr.

— Bolivia. LC 88-10877. (Enchantment of the World Ser.). (Illus.). 128p. (J). (gr. 5-9). 1988. lib. bdg. 20.55 (*0-516-02705-0*) Childrens.

— Brazil. LC 93-26100. (Country Fact Files Ser.). (J). 1993. lib. bdg. 22.80 (*0-8114-1842-1*) Raintree Steck-V.

— Brazil. LC 88-18294. (People & Places Ser.). (Illus.). 48p. (J). (gr. 4-8). 1988. lib. bdg. 12.95 (*0-382-09516-2*) Silver Burdett Pr.

— Central America. LC 92-14537. (World in View Ser.). 96p. (J). 1992. lib. bdg. 24.26 (*0-8114-2458-8*) Raintree Steck-V.

— Central America. (People & Places Ser.). (Illus.). 48p. (J). (gr. 4-8). 1989. lib. bdg. 12.95 (*0-382-09824-2*) Silver Burdett Pr.

— Colombia. LC 90-36528. (Enchantment of the World Ser.). (Illus.). 128p. (J). (gr. 5-9). 1990. lib. bdg. 20.55 (*0-516-02722-0*) Childrens.

— Ecuador, Peru, Bolivia. (World in View Ser.). (Illus.). 96p. (YA). (gr. 6-12). 1992. lib. bdg. 24.26 (*0-8114-2453-7*) Raintree Steck-V.

— French Guiana. LC 94-37950. (Enchantment of the World Ser.). 172p. (J). (gr. 5-9). 1995. lib. bdg. 20.55 (*0-516-02633-X*) Childrens.

— Indians of the Andes. (Original People Ser.). (Illus.). 48p. (J). (gr. 4-8). 1987. 12.50 (*0-685-67605-6*); lib. bdg. 16.67 (*0-86625-260-6*) Rourke Corp.

— Italy. LC 88-18317. (People & Places Ser.). (Illus.). 48p. (J). (gr. 4-8). 1988. lib. bdg. 12.95 (*0-382-09517-0*) Silver Burdett Pr.

— Mexico & Central America. LC 94-37192. (Places & People Ser.). (J). 1995. lib. bdg. 13.16 (*0-531-14366-X*) Watts.

— Paraguay. LC 93-754. (Enchantment of the World Ser.). (Illus.). 128p. (J). (gr. 5-9). 1993. lib. bdg. 20.55 (*0-516-02619-4*) Childrens.

— Uruguay. LC 91-35144. (Enchantment of the World Ser.). 128p. (J). (gr. 5-9). 1992. lib. bdg. 20.55 (*0-516-02607-0*) Childrens.

— Venezuela. LC 88-30493. (Enchantment of the World Ser.). (Illus.). 128p. (J). (gr. 5-9). 1989. lib. bdg. 20.55 (*0-516-02711-5*) Childrens.

Morrison, Mark. Waterfall Walks & Drives in Northeast Georgia & the Western Carolinas. 76p. 1992. pap. 7.95 (*0-9636070-0-6*) H F Pub GA.

— Waterfall Walks & Drives in the Western Carolinas. (Illus.). 128p. (Orig.). 1994. pap. write for info. (*0-9636070-1-4*) H F Pub GA.

Morrison, Mark, et al. Sorcerers of Pan Tang. (Stormbringer Roleplaying Game System Ser.). (Illus.). 128p. (Orig.). 1991. pap. 18.95 (*0-933635-79-6*, 2112) Chaosium.

Morrison, Marlene, jt. ed. see Galloway, Shiela.

Morrison, Marsh. Doctor Morrison's Amazing Healing Foods: With Miracle Health Promoter M. 1982. 19.95 (*0-13-217125-2*, Parker Publishing Co) P-H.

— Doctor Morrison's Miracle Body Tune-up for Rejuvenated Health. 224p. 1973. text ed. 27.95 (*0-13-216366-7*, Reward) P-H.

Morrison, Martha. White Rabbit. 1991. pap. 4.95 (*0-425-12847-4*) Berkley Pub.

Morrison, Martin E., ed. Official Rules of Chess. (Tartan Paperback Ser.). (Illus.). 1978. 3.95 (*0-679-14043-3*) McKay.

Morrison, Marvin L. Word Finder: The Phonic Key to the Dictionary. rev. ed. LC 86-61846. 408p. 1987. pap. 14.95 (*0-9608376-1-2*) Pilot Light.

Morrison, Mary. The Journal & the Journey. LC 81-85559. 32p. (Orig.). 1982. pap. 3.00 (*0-87574-242-4*) Pendle Hill.

— Re-Conciliation: The Hidden Hyphen. LC 74-24007. 24p. (Orig.). 1974. pap. 3.00 (*0-87574-198-3*) Pendle Hill.

— Snow Babies, Santas & Elves: Collecting Christmas Bisque Figures. (Illus.). 160p. 1993. pap. 29.95 (*0-88740-493-6*) Schiffer.

— Without Nightfall upon the Spirit: Reflections on Aging. LC 93-85962. 32p. 1993. pap. 3.00 (*0-87574-311-0*) Pendle Hill.

Morrison, Mary, ed. see Ibsen, Henrik.

Morrison, Mary, ed. see Law, William.

Morrison, Mary C. Approaching the Gospels Together: A Leaders' Guide to Group Gospels Study. LC 86-62204. (Orig.). 1987. pap. 10.95 (*0-87574-910-0*) Pendle Hill.

— A Fresh Look at the Gospels. LC 78-51385. 32p. (Orig.). 1978. pap. 3.00 (*0-87574-219-X*) Pendle Hill.

— The Way of the Cross. LC 85-60516. 32p. (Orig.). 1985. pap. 3.00 (*0-87574-260-2*) Pendle Hill.

Morrison, Mary C., jt. auth. see Bonfield, Lynn A.

Morrison, Mary E., ed. Adaptations & Acting Versions. (Shakespeariana Ser.). xiii, 64p. (Orig.). 1990. 15.00 (*0-8357-0931-0*) Univ Microfilms.

— Alan Barbour's Screen Facts & Screen Nostalgia Illustrated Collection. (Guide to the Microfiche Collection Ser.). 11p. (Orig.). 1987. 10.00 (*0-685-46000-2*) Univ Microfilms.

— Albany Medical Center Inaugural Theses, 1839-1891. (Guide to the Microfiche Collection Ser.). 218p. 1989. 15.00 (*0-8357-0870-5*) Univ Microfilms.

— Crime & Juvenile Delinquency, 1984-1985: A Bibliographic Guide. iv, 42p. 1986. 30.00 (*0-8357-0704-0*) Univ Microfilms.

— Crime & Juvenile Delinquency, 1986: A Bibliographic Guide. iv, 42p. 1986. 30.00 (*0-8357-0720-2*) Univ Microfilms.

— Crime & Juvenile Delinquency, 1987: A Bibliographic Guide. iv, 40p. 1987. 30.00 (*0-8357-0755-5*) Univ Microfilms.

— Crime & Juvenile Delinquency, 1988: A Bibliographic Guide. iv, 42p. (Orig.). 1989. 30.00 (*0-8357-0802-0*) Univ Microfilms.

— Folklore, Superstition & Witchcraft in Shakespeare's Time. (Shakespeariana Ser.). x, 41p. (Orig.). 1989. 15.00 (*0-8357-0875-6*) Univ Microfilms.

— An Index to the Abstracts on Crime & Juvenile Delinquency, 1986. viii, 324p. 1987. 120.00 (*0-8357-0716-4*) Univ Microfilms.

— An Index to the Abstracts on Crime & Juvenile Delinquency, 1987. ix, 298p. 1988. 120.00 (*0-8357-0829-2*) Univ Microfilms.

— An Index to the Abstracts on Crime & Juvenile Delinquency 1988. v, 350p. (Orig.). 1990. pap. 250.00 (*0-8357-2121-3*) Univ Microfilms.

— An Index to the Abstracts on Crime & Juvenile Deliquency 1983-1984. 435p. 1986. 120.00 (*0-8357-0701-6*) Univ Microfilms.

— The John M. Echols Collection, Cornell University: Selections on the Vietnam War. (Guide to the Microfiche Collection Ser.: Unit 1). v, 59p. (Orig.). 1989. 20.00 (*0-8357-0881-0*) Univ Microfilms.

— The John M. Echols Collection, Cornell University: Selections on the Vietnam War. (Guide to the Microfiche Collection Ser.: Unit 2). v, 64p. (Orig.). 1989. 20.00 (*0-8357-0891-8*) Univ Microfilms.

— MusiCache: An Index to the Microfiche Collection. iv, 216p. reprint ed. 40.00 (*0-8357-0927-2*) Univ Microfilms.

— Prose Fiction of Shakespeare's Time. (Shakespeariana Ser.). xiii, 35p. (Orig.). 1989. 15.00 (*0-8357-0888-8*) Univ Microfilms.

— The Pulitzer Prizes in Journalism-1917-1985: A Guide to the Microfilm Edition. 187p. 1986. 70.00 (*0-8357-0709-1*) Univ Microfilms.

— Rehabilitation & Handicapped Literature, 1982-1985 Update: A Bibliographic Guide to the Microfiche Collection. (Orig.). 1987. 20.00 (*0-8357-0732-6*) Univ Microfilms.

— Working Papers in Economics. (Guide to the Microfiche Collection Ser.: Ser. 1). v, 110p. 1989. 20.00 (*0-8357-0882-9*) Univ Microfilms.

— Working Papers in Economics. (Guide to the Microfiche Collection Ser.: Ser. 2). v, 95p. 1989. 20.00 (*0-8357-0890-X*) Univ Microfilms.

Morrison, Mary G., ed. see Garnier, Robert.

Morrison, Matthew C., ed. Sparks That Leap. LC 91-73112. 1991. pap. 10.95 (*0-89112-225-7*) Abilene Christ U.

***Morrison, Melanie.** The Grace of Coming Home: Spirituality, Sexuality, & the Struggle for Justice. 112p. (Orig.). 1995. pap. 10.95 (*0-8298-1071-4*) Pilgrim OH.

Morrison, Micah. Fire in Paradise: The Yellowstone Fires & the Politics of Environmentalism. LC 92-53358. 288p. 1993. 22.00 (*0-06-016303-8*, HarpT) HarpC.

Morrison, Michael A. Understanding Quantum Physics: A User's Manual, Vol. I. 500p. (C). 1990. text ed. 73.00 (*0-13-747908-5*) P-H.

Morrison, Michael A., ed. see Gray, Ralph D.

Morrison, Michael A., et al. Understanding More Quantum Physics, Vol. 1. 1991. pap. text ed. 27.20 (*0-13-928300-5*, 530502) P-H.

Morrison, Michael L., et al. Wildlife-Habitat Relationships: Concepts & Applications. LC 91-37591. (Illus.). 364p. (C). 1992. text ed. 26.95 (*0-299-13200-5*) U of Wis Pr.

Morrison, Mike. Becoming a Computer Animator with CD-ROM. 1994. pap. 39.99 (*0-672-30463-5*) Sams.

— The Magic of Computer Graphics. (Illus.). 400p. (Orig.). 1995. pap. text ed. 45.00 (*0-672-30612-3*) Sams.

— Magic of Image Processing. 1993. pap. 39.95 (*0-672-30315-9*) Sams.

— Magic of Interactive Entertainment. 1994. cd-rom, pap. 39.95 (*0-672-30456-2*) Sams.

— Magic of Interactive Entertainment. 2nd ed. (Illus.). 1994. pap. 39.99 (*0-672-30590-9*) Sams.

Morrison, Minion K. Black Political Mobilization, Leadership, Power, & Mass Behavior. LC 86-30051. (Afro-American Studies). 303p. 1987. 64.50 (*0-88706-515-5*); pap. 21.95 (*0-88706-516-3*) State U NY Pr.

— Ethnicity & Political Integration: The Case of Ashanti, Ghana. LC 82-23239. (Foreign & Comparative Studies Program, African Ser.: No. 38). (Orig.). (C). 1982. pap. text ed. 8.00 (*0-915984-59-8*) Syracuse U Foreign Comp.

Morrison, Minion K., et al, eds. Housing the Urban Poor in Africa. LC 82-21636. (Foreign & Comparative Studies Program, African Ser.: No. 37). (Orig.). (C). 1982. pap. text ed. 8.00 (*0-915984-61-X*) Syracuse U Foreign Comp.

Morrison, Morag. The Lockerbie Legend. 100p. 1993. 14.95 (*0-8059-3395-6*) Dorrance.

Morrison, Morris R. Poetry As Therapy. LC 86-15281. 229p. 1987. 35.95 (*0-89885-312-5*) Human Sci Pr.

Morrison, Murray, et al. Management of Voice Disorders. LC 93-32952. 1993. write for info. (*0-412-35090-4*, Chap & Hall NY) Chapman & Hall.

Morrison, Neil, jt. auth. see Moore, John.

Morrison, Norman. Introduction to Fourier Analysis: With Full-System FFT Disk. LC 93-44637. 1994. 69.95 (*0-471-01737-X*) Wiley.

Morrison, Nyla. Minna's Kitchen. rev. ed. 1994. 9.95 (*0-8062-4940-4*) Carlton.
Morrison, Pam, jt. auth. see Light, H. Wayne.
***Morrison, Paul.** The Poetics of Fascism: Ezra Pound, T. S. Eliot, Paul de Man. 192p. 1995. 35.00 (*0-19-508085-8*) OUP.
— Professional Caring in Practice: A Psychological Analysis. 307p. 1992. 63.95 (*1-85628-355-0*, Pub. by Avebury Pub UK) Ashgate Pub Co.
Morrison, Paul & Burnard, Philip, eds. Aspects of Forensic Psychiatric Nursing. 192p. 1992. 55.95 (*1-85628-371-2*, Pub. by Avebury Pub UK) Ashgate Pub Co.
Morrison, Paul, jt. auth. see Burnard, Philip.
Morrison, Penelope, jt. auth. see Morrison, Rob.
Morrison, Perry, jt. auth. see Forester, Tom.
Morrison, Peter. Basic Math Skills. 1972. text ed. 17.75 (*0-07-043197-3*) McGraw.
Morrison, Peter A., ed. see Beale, Calvin.
Morrison, Philip. Nothing Is Too Wonderful To Be True. LC 94-17906. (Masters of Modern Physics Ser.). 1994. 29.95 (*1-56396-363-9*) Am Inst Physics.
Morrison, Philip & Morrison, Phylis. Primary Science: Symbol Or Substance? 20p. (Orig.). (C). 1984. pap. 3.00 (*0-317-45086-7*) City Coll Wk.
— Ring of Truth. LC 88-40257. 320p. 1989. pap. 15.95 (*0-679-72130-4*, Vin) Random.
***Morrison, Philip, et al.** Powers of Ten: About the Relative Size of Things in the Universe. LC 82-5504. (Illus.). 159p. (C). 1995. pap. text ed. 19.95 (*0-7167-6008-8*) W H Freeman.
Morrison, Phylis, jt. auth. see Morrison, Philip.
Morrison, Phylis S., jt. auth. see Holden, Alan.
Morrison, R., jt. auth. see Sommerville, Ian.
Morrison, R. B., ed. Quaternary Nonglacial Geology: Conterminous U. S. (DNAG, Geology of North America Ser.: Vol. K2). 670p. 1991. 85.00 (*0-8137-5215-9*) Geol Soc.
Morrison, R. H., tr. Poems from Mandelstam. LC 88-46184. 120p. 1990. 26.50 (*0-8386-3382-X*) Fairleigh Dickinson.
Morrison, Ralph. Grounding & Shielding Techniques in Instrumentation. 3rd ed. LC 85-22456. 172p. 1986. text ed. 64.95 (*0-471-83805-5*) Wiley.
— Instrumentation Fundamentals & Applications. LC 83-21696. 157p. reprint ed. pap. 44.80 (*0-7837-2810-7*, 2057662) Bks Demand.
— Noise & Other Interfering Signals. 160p. 1991. text ed. 59.95 (*0-471-54288-1*) Wiley.
— Solving Interference Problems in Electronics. LC 95-12074. 1996. 64.95 (*0-471-12796-5*) Wiley-Interscience.
Morrison, Randall L. & Bellack, Alan S., eds. Medical Factors & Psychological Disorders: A Handbook for Psychologists. LC 87-7903. 392p. 1987. 75.00 (*0-306-42425-8*, Plenum Pr) Plenum.
Morrison-Reed, Mark & James, Jacqui, eds. Been in the Storm So Long: A Meditation Manual. 53p. 1991. 6.00 (*1-55896-202-6*, Skinner Hse Bks) Unitarian Univ.
***Morrison-Reed, Mark D. & Young, Andrew J.** Black Pioneers in a White Denomination. 3rd ed. LC 94-32438. 1994. 17.00 (*1-55896-250-6*) Unitarian Univ.
Morrison, Richard. Best Books on the West: A Guide to a Core Collection of 1700 Works. 100p. 1989. 42.50 (*0-926158-02-3*); pap. 22.50 (*0-926158-03-1*) W M Morrison.
— Eyewitness Texana: A Bibliography of Nine Hundred First Hand Accounts of Texas Before 1860. 2nd enl. rev. ed. 68p. 1992. pap. 22.50 (*0-926158-17-1*) W M Morrison.
— Eyewitness Texana: Checklist of Firsthand Accounts of Texas Before 1860. 75p. (Orig.). 1988. pap. 12.50 (*0-317-93434-1*) W M Morrison.
— Howes U. S. - Iana Catalogue Prices, 1987-89: Price Entries on over 3,000 Different Western Americana Homes Entries. 90p. (Orig.). 1990. pap. 22.50 (*0-926158-09-0*) W M Morrison.
Morrison, Richard, ed. Best Books on Texas & the West: A Guide to 1,100 Most Recommended Works on Texas & the West. 60p. (Orig.). 1987. pap. 12.50 (*0-317-93432-5*) W M Morrison.
Morrison, Richard & Morrison, Shelly. Nineteenth Century Texana: A Checklist of Books & Pamphlets Relating to Texas Published Before 1900. 200p. 1991. 75.00 (*0-926158-13-9*); pap. 40.00 (*0-926158-14-7*) W M Morrison.
— Texana Catalogue Prices 1990, Vol. 8: Ten Thousand Price Entries on Texana Offered for Sale in 1990. 150p. (Orig.). 1991. pap. 38.50 (*0-926158-08-2*) W M Morrison.
— Texana Catalogue Prices, 1991, Vol. 9. 136p. (Orig.). 1991. pap. 38.50 (*0-926158-40-6*) W M Morrison.
— Texas & Western American Maps, Catalogue Prices, 1987-1990: Chronological Listing of over 3,000 Price Entries on Maps Featuring the U. S. West of the Mississippi. 75p. (Orig.). 1991. pap. 22.50 (*0-926158-12-0*) W M Morrison.
— Western Americana Catalogue Prices, 1990, Vol. 4: Fifteen Thousand Price Entries for Works Offered for Sale in 1990. 250p. (Orig.). 1991. pap. 38.50 (*0-926158-07-4*) W M Morrison.
— Western Americana Catalogue Prices, 1991, Vol. 5. 240p. (Orig.). 1991. pap. 38.50 (*0-926158-41-4*) W M Morrison.
Morrison, Richard, jt. auth. see Morrison, Shelly.
***Morrison, Richard D.** History of Alabama Agricultural & Mechanical University 1875-1992. 500p. (C). 1995. 25.00 (*0-9623627-1-9*) Liberal Arts Pr.
Morrison, Richard J., jt. auth. see Lewis, Gordon H.
Morrison, Richard K. & Morrison, Shelly. Texana & Western Americana Catalogue Prices, Vol. 4. 250p. (Orig.). 1987. pap. 60.00 (*0-317-93435-X*) W M Morrison.
Morrison, Rob. X-Rays. LC 93-28983. (Voyages Ser.). (Illus.). (J). 1994. 4.25 (*0-383-03789-1*) SRA Schl Grp.
Morrison, Rob & Morrison, James. Monsters! Just Imagine. LC 93-26927. (Voyages Ser.). (Illus.). (J). 1994. 4.25 (*0-383-03763-8*) SRA Schl Grp.
Morrison, Rob & Morrison, Penelope. Snorkels for Tadpoles. LC 93-28967. (Voyages Ser.). (Illus.). (J). 1994. 4.25 (*0-383-03775-1*) SRA Schl Grp.
***Morrison, Robert & Baldick, Chris, eds.** Tales of Terror from Blackwood's Magazine. (The World's Classics Ser.). 384p. 1995. pap. 10.95 (*0-19-282366-3*) OUP.
Morrison, Robert & Vosburgh, Richard. Career Development of Engineers & Scientists: Organizational Programs & Individual Choices. (Professional Bks.). (Illus.). 288p. (C). 1987. text ed. 59.95 (*0-442-26351-1*) Van Nos Reinhold.
Morrison, Robert, et al. High Stakes to High Risk: The Strange Story of Resorts International & the Taj Mahal. 1994. 21.95 (*0-317-05740-5*) Lake Erie Pr.
Morrison, Robert D. Ground Water Monitoring: Procedures, Equipment & Applications. (Illus.). 132p. (C). 1983. text ed. 33.00 (*0-9611060-0-X*, 83-070805) Timco Mfg.
Morrison, Robert D., jt. auth. see Erickson, Randall L.
Morrison, Robert F. & Adams, Jerome, eds. Contemporary Career Development Issues. 192p. 1991. text ed. 29.95 (*0-8058-0945-7*) L Erlbaum Assocs.
Morrison, Robert H. Internal Administrative Organization in Teachers Colleges. LC 78-177090. (Columbia University. Teachers College. Contributions to Education Ser.: No. 592). reprint ed. 37.50 (*0-404-55592-6*) AMS Pr.
Morrison, Robert K., jt. auth. see Morrison, Joan.
Morrison, Robert S. Handbook for Manufacturing Entrepreneurs. LC 73-91212. (Illus.). 1973. pap. 12.50 (*0-912400-09-9*) Western Res Pr.
— Inflation Can Be Stopped. LC 73-91213. (Illus.). 1973. 4.95 (*0-912400-05-6*); pap. 2.00 (*0-912400-04-8*) Western Res Pr.
— The Real War on Inflation Has Not Begun. LC 82-5057. (Illus.). 1982. 15.00 (*0-912400-25-0*); pap. 9.50 (*0-912400-26-9*) Western Res Pr.
Morrison, Robert T. & Boyd, Robert K. Organic Chemistry. 6th ed. 1300p. 1992. text ed. 64.67 (*0-13-643669-2*) P-H.
Morrison, Rodney J. Portugal: Revolutionary Change in an Open Economy. LC 81-2099. 184p. (C). 1981. text ed. 39.95 (*0-86569-077-4*, Auburn Hse) Greenwood.
Morrison, Roger. Desktop Guide: To Keynotes & Confirmatory Symptoms. 448p. 1993. 65.00 (*0-9635368-0-X*) Hahnemann Clinic.
Morrison, Roger B. & Davis, Jonathan O. Supplementary Guidebook for Field Trip 13: Quaternary Stratigraphy & Archaeology of the Lake Lahontan Area. 2nd ed. (Social Sciences Center Technical Report Ser.: No. 41). (Illus.). 54p. (Orig.). (C). 1984. pap. 5.00 (*0-945920-41-5*) Desert Rsch Inst.
Morrison, Ron, jt. ed. see Albano, Antonio.
***Morrison, Roy.** Ecological Democracy. 250p. (Orig.). (C). Date not set. text ed. 40.00 (*0-89608-514-7*); pap. text ed. 15.00 (*0-89608-513-9*) South End Pr.
— We Build the Road As We Travel: Mondragon's Cooperative Society. 288p. (Orig.). 1990. lib. bdg. 39.95 (*0-86571-172-0*); pap. 16.95 (*0-86571-173-9*) New Soc Pubs.
Morrison, Rusane. Summer Patchwork. 1976. 1.50 (*0-685-79010-X*) Oyez.
Morrison, Ruth & Radtke, Dawn. Aging with Joy. LC 87-51567. 112p. (Orig.). 1988. pap. 5.95 (*0-89622-360-4*) Twenty-Third.
Morrison, Ruth & Radtke, Dawn D. From Worry to Wellness: Twenty-One People Who Changed Their Lives. LC 90-70559. 192p. (Orig.). 1990. pap. 7.95 (*0-89622-443-0*) Twenty-Third.
Morrison, S. Roy. The Chemical Physics of Surfaces. 2nd ed. LC 90-42068. (Illus.). 400p. 1990. 79.50 (*0-306-43549-7*, Plenum Pr) Plenum.
— Electrochemistry at Semiconductor & Oxidized Metal Electrodes. LC 80-20416. 416p. 1980. 95.00 (*0-306-40524-5*, Plenum Pr) Plenum.
Morrison, S. Roy, jt. auth. see Madou, Marc J.
Morrison, Sally. Cross Creek Kitchens: Seasonal Recipes & Reflections. (Illus.). 224p. 1983. 24.95 (*0-937404-50-0*) Triad Pub FL.
Morrison, Sarah L. The Modern Witch's Book of Home Remedies. 224p. 1991. pap. 8.95 (*0-8065-1265-2*, Citadel Pr) Carol Pub Group.
— The Modern Witch's Dreambook. 1990. pap. 7.95 (*0-8065-1203-2*, Citadel Pr) Carol Pub Group.
— The Modern Witch's Spellbook. LC 71-135588. 256p. 1973. reprint ed. pap. 6.95 (*0-8065-0372-6*, Citadel Pr) Carol Pub Group.
— The Modern Witch's Spellbook, Vol. 2. 224p. 1986. pap. 6.95 (*0-8065-1015-3*, Citadel Pr) Carol Pub Group.
— The New Modern Witch's Dreambook. rev. ed. LC 93-43437. Orig. Title: The Modern Witch's Dreambook. 1994. reprint ed. 8.95 (*0-8065-1471-X*, Citadel Pr) Carol Pub Group.
Morrison, Scott. Open & Innocent: The Gentle, Passionate Art of Not-Knowing. 2nd ed. LC 92-85577. 80p. 1992. pap. 7.50 (*1-882496-00-0*) Am Zen Soc.
***Morrison, Scott, ed. & intro.** The Code Book of America. 2nd ed. (Illus.). (Orig.). 1995. pap. 6.95 (*0-929150-50-3*) Castalia CA.
— The Code Book of America: Pocket Size. 2nd ed. (Illus.). 96p. (Orig.). 1995. pap. 5.95 (*0-929150-51-1*) Castalia CA.
Morrison, Shelly & Morrison, Richard. Texana Catalogue Prices, Vol. 7 - 1989: Price Entries for 12,000 Works. 210p. 1990. pap. 38.50 (*0-926158-06-6*) W M Morrison.
— Texana Catalogue Prices, 1992, Vol. 10. 144p. 1993. pap. 38.50 (*0-926158-18-X*) W M Morrison.
— Texana Catalogue Prices 1993, Vol. 11. 150p. (Orig.). 1994. pap. 38.50 (*0-926158-20-1*) W M Morrison.
— Western Americana Catalogue Prices, Vol. 3 - 1989: 15,000 Price Entries for Books, Pamphlets, Etc. 270p. (Orig.). 1990. pap. 38.50 (*0-926158-05-8*) W M Morrison.
— Western Americana Catalogue Prices, 1992, Vol. 6. 250p. 1993. pap. 38.50 (*0-926158-19-8*) W M Morrison.
— Western Americana Catalogue Prices 1993, Vol. 7. 250p. (Orig.). Date not set. pap. 38.50 (*0-926158-21-X*) W M Morrison.
Morrison, Shelly, jt. auth. see Morrison, Richard K.
Morrison, Shelly, jt. auth. see Morrison, Richard.
Morrison, Shelly, ed. see Ross, Lawrence S.
Morrison, Shelly O., ed. Texana Catalogue Prices 1987, Vol. 5. 230p. (Orig.). 1989. pap. 42.50 (*0-926158-01-5*) W M Morrison.
— Western Americana Catalogue Prices, 1987. 200p. (Orig.). 1988. pap. 25.00 (*0-926158-00-7*) W M Morrison.
Morrison, Shirley L. The Pearl & the Princes. LC 84-23349. vi, 170p. 1985. 14.95 (*0-9613978-0-2*); pap. 7.95 (*0-9613978-1-0*) Laurel Pr.
***Morrison, Sol.** The World's Greatest Book of Chicken Jokes & Other Fowl Humor. (Illus.). 124p. (Orig.). 1995. pap. 9.95 (*0-940861-57-7*) Poetry Ctr Pr.
Morrison, Stanley, jt. auth. see Fairman, Charles.
Morrison, Steven & Winston, Clifford. The Economic Effects of Airline Deregulation. LC 85-48202. (Studies in the Regulation of Economic Activity). 84p. 1986. pap. 8.95 (*0-8157-5845-6*) Brookings.
***Morrison, Steven A. & Winston, Clifford.** The Evolution of the Airline Industry. 130p. (C). Date not set. 28.95x (*0-8157-5844-8*); pap. 10.95x (*0-8157-5843-X*) Brookings.
Morrison, Susan. Arkansas Wildlife. LC 80-52076. 64p. 1980. 14.95 (*0-914546-32-5*) Rose Pub.
Morrison, Susan D. The Passenger Pigeon. LC 89-31839. (Gone Forever Ser.). (Illus.). 48p. (J). (gr. 5-6). 1989. text ed. 12.95 (*0-89686-457-X*, Crstwood Hse) Silver Burdett Pr.
***Morrison, Terri, et al.** Kiss Bow or Shake Hands: How to Do Business in Sixty Countries. 1994. pap. 17.95 (*1-55850-444-3*) Adams Pubng.
Morrison, Theodore, ed. see Chaucer, Geoffrey.
Morrison, Tom. Hardrock Gold: A Miner's Tale. LC 92-54130. (Illus.). 304p. (C). 1992. 24.95 (*0-8061-2442-3*) U of Okla Pr.
— Root Beer Advertising & Collectibles. LC 92-60625. (Illus.). 128p. 1992. pap. 24.95 (*0-88740-421-9*) Schiffer.
— To Fly Through the Air: The Experience of Learning to Fly. LC 91-8191. 200p. 1991. 23.95 (*0-8138-0348-9*) Iowa St U Pr.
— Weather for the New Pilot. LC 91-19260. (Illus.). 186p. 1991. 22.95 (*0-8138-1773-0*); pap. 13.95 (*0-8138-1772-2*) Iowa St U Pr.
Morrison, Toni. Beloved. LC 87-46157. 288p. 1987. 27.50 (*0-394-53597-9*) Knopf.
— Beloved. 1988. pap. 10.95 (*0-452-26446-4*, Plume) NAL-Dutton.
— Beloved. 1991. pap. 5.99 (*0-451-15659-5*) NAL-Dutton.
— The Bluest Eye: A Novel. LC 93-43124. 1993. 22.00 (*0-679-43373-2*) Knopf.
— Jazz. 229p. 1992. 21.00 (*0-685-53430-8*) Knopf.
— Jazz. 1992. pap. 21.00 (*0-679-41167-4*) McKay.
— Jazz. 240p. 1993. pap. 10.95 (*0-452-26965-2*, Plume) NAL-Dutton.
— Jazz. Date not set. pap. 5.99 (*0-517-11255-8*) Random Hse Value.
— Jazz. braille ed. 326p. 1994. text ed., vinyl bd. 26.08 (*1-56956-549-X*, BR9346) W A T Braille.
— Jazz. large type ed. LC 92-35901. (General Ser.). 1993. 21.95 (*0-8161-5624-7*, Large Print Bks) Hall.
— Nobel Prize Speech. 1994. 12.00 (*0-679-43437-2*) Knopf.
— Noble Prize Boxed Set. 1994. 125.00 (*0-679-43436-4*) Knopf.
— Playing in the Dark: Whiteness & the Literary Imagination. (Massey Lectures). 91p. 1992. text ed. 14.95 (*0-674-67377-8*) HUP.
— Playing in the Dark: Whiteness & the Literary Imagination. LC 92-50581. 1993. pap. 9.00 (*0-679-74542-4*, Vin) Random.
— Song of Solomon. 1977. 24.00 (*0-394-49784-8*) Knopf.
— Song of Solomon. 352p. 1978. pap. 4.50 (*0-451-12933-4*, AE2933, Sig) NAL-Dutton.
— Song of Solomon. LC 87-5809. 320p. 1987. pap. 10.95 (*0-452-26011-6*, Plume) NAL-Dutton.
— Song of Solomon. 1989. pap. 4.50 (*0-451-15261-1*) NAL-Dutton.
— Song of Solomon. large type ed. LC 93-43970. 1994. 24.95 (*0-7927-1936-0*, Contemp Lrg Print); pap. 22.95 (*0-7927-1935-2*, Contemp Lrg Print) Chivers N Amer.
— Sula. 1973. 24.00 (*0-394-48044-9*) Knopf.
— Sula. 1987. pap. 10.00 (*0-452-26349-2*); mass mkt. 6.95 (*0-452-26010-8*, Z5476, Plume) NAL-Dutton.
— Sula. braille ed. 240p. 1994. text ed., vinyl bd. 19.20 (*1-56956-566-X*, BR9661) W A T Braille.
— Tar Baby. LC 80-22821. 320p. 1981. 25.00 (*0-394-42329-1*) Knopf.
— Tar Baby. LC 87-15238. 352p. 1987. pap. 7.95 (*0-452-26012-4*, Z5326, Plume); pap. 10.95 (*0-452-26479-0*, Plume) NAL-Dutton.
— Toni Morrison Boxed Set: Song of Solomon; Beloved; Jazz, 3 vols., Set. 1994. pap. 32.85 (*0-452-15455-3*, Plume) NAL-Dutton.
Morrison, Toni, aft. The Bluest Eye. LC 94-14448. 1994. pap. 9.95 (*0-452-27305-6*, Plume) NAL-Dutton.
Morrison, Toni, intro. Race-ing Justice, En-Gendering Power: Essays on Anita Hill, Clarence Thomas, & the Construction of Social Reality. LC 92-54119. 512p. (Orig.). 1992. pap. 15.00 (*0-679-74145-3*) Pantheon.
Morrison, Toni, ed. see Newton, Huey P.
Morrison, Tony. Pathways to the Gods: The Mystery of the Andes Lines. (Illus.). 256p. 1988. reprint ed. pap. 9.95 (*0-685-07947-3*) Academy Chi Pubs.
Morrison, Tony, et al, eds. Sexual Offending Against Children: Assessment & Treatment of Male Abusers. LC 94-1687. 240p. 1994. 59.95x (*0-415-05504-0*, B4369); pap. 19.95 (*0-415-05505-9*, B4373) Routledge.
Morrison, Veronique, jt. auth. see Marlow, Elisabeth.
Morrison, Veronique, et al, eds. Tout a Fait Francais. (Illus.). (C). 1979. pap. text ed. 16.95 (*0-393-09005-1*) Norton.
***Morrison, Vicki F.** For the Birds. 52p. 1994. 10.95 (*0-936459-27-1*) Stained Glass.
— The Stained Glass Village. (Illus.). 52p. 1993. 10.95 (*0-936459-21-2*) Stained Glass.
Morrison, W. D., ed. see Pfleiderer, Otto.
Morrison, W. L. The System of Law & Courts Governing New South Wales. 2nd ed. 1985. Australia. pap. 71.00 (*0-409-49263-9*) Butterworth Legal Pubs.
Morrison, W. R., jt. auth. see Coates, K. S.
Morrison, Wayne A., jt. auth. see O'Brien, Bernard M.
***Morrison, Wendy.** Treats Nutritional Treats: A Dynamite Cookbook for Nutritional Sweet Treats, Drinks, Breads & Muffins. 72p. 1980. spiral bd. 7.95 (*0-920490-05-0*, Pub. by Detselig CN) Temeron Bks.
Morrison, Wilbur H. Adventure Guide to Baja California. 2nd ed. (Adventure Guides Ser.). (Illus.). 320p. (Orig.). 1993. pap. 11.95 (*1-55650-590-6*) Hunter NJ.
— Catskills & Adirondacks Adventure Guide. (Adventure Guide Ser.). (Illus.). 224p. (Orig.). 1995. pap. 9.95 (*1-55650-681-3*) Hunter NJ.
— Donald W. Douglas: A Heart with Wings. LC 90-48685. (Illus.). 280p. 1991. 29.95 (*0-8138-1834-6*) Iowa St U Pr.
— Fortress Without a Roof: The Allied Bombing of the Third Reich. 1986. mass mkt. 4.95 (*0-312-90179-8*) St Martin.
— Hellbirds: The Story of the B-29's in Combat. LC 79-20016. reprint ed. 16.95 (*0-89201-062-2*) Zenger Pub.
— Twentieth Century Wars: Their Causes & Their Effects on American Life. LC 93-5305. 436p. 1993. 29.50 (*0-7818-0120-6*) Hippocrene Bks.
Morrison, William D. Juvenile Offenders. LC 75-156029. reprint ed. 27.50 (*0-404-09130-X*) AMS Pr.
— Juvenile Offenders: With Intro. & Index Added. LC 70-172589. (Criminology, Law Enforcement, & Social Problems Ser.: No. 179). 1975. 10.00 (*0-87585-179-7*) Patterson Smith.
Morrison, William F. The Prenegotiation Planning Book. LC 91-32393. 272p. (C). 1992. reprint ed. lib. bdg. 31.50 (*0-89464-671-0*) Krieger.
Morrison, William F. & Calero, Henry H. The Human Side of Negotiations. LC 92-47483. 236p. (C). 1994. 32.50 (*0-89464-836-5*) Krieger.
Morrison, William J., ed. see Wourms, John P., et al.
Morrison, William J., ed. see Wright, James E., et al.
Morrison, William R. & Coates, Kenneth A. Working the North: Labor & the Northwest Defense Projects, 1942-1946. LC 93-41687. (Illus.). xiv, 270p. 1994. 30.00 (*0-912006-72-2*); pap. 20.00 (*0-912006-73-0*) U of Alaska Pr.
Morrisroe, Patricia. Mapplethorpe: A Biography. 1995. 27.50 (*0-394-57650-0*) Random.
Morriss, Frank. The Catholic As Citizen. 141p. 1980. 6.95 (*0-8199-0775-8*, Frncscn Herld) Franciscan Pr.
Morriss, Frank, ed. A Christmas Celebration: The Wanderer's Christmas Anthology. LC 83-51146. 334p. 1983. 14.95 (*0-915245-00-0*) Wanderer Pr.
Morriss, James E., jt. auth. see Boyle, Joan M.
Morriss-Kay, Gillian, ed. Retinoids in Normal Development & Teratogenesis. (Illus.). 320p. 1992. 89.00 (*0-19-854770-6*) OUP.
Morriss, Margaret S. Colonial Trade of Maryland, 1689-1715. LC 76-49477. (Perspectives in American History Ser.: No. 46). viii, 157p. 1977. reprint ed. lib. bdg. 27.50 (*0-87991-370-3*) Porcupine Pr.
Morriss, Peter. Power: A Philosophical Analysis. LC 87-9837. 350p. 1988. text ed. 39.95 (*0-312-00943-7*) St Martin.
— Power: A Philosophical Analysis. LC 87-9837. 276p. 1989. text ed. 17.95 (*0-7190-2359-9*, Pub. by Manchester Univ Pr UK) St Martin.
***Morriss, Richard.** Attention Disorders in Children: School-Based Assessment, Diagnosis, & Treatment. 1995. 49.50 (*0-614-06076-1*, W-314A) Western Psych.
Morriss, Richard K. The Buildings of Bath. (Buildings of... Ser.). (Illus.). 128p. 1993. pap. 15.99 (*0-7509-0256-6*) A Sutton Pub.
— The Buildings of Chester. (Buildings of...Ser.). (Illus.). 128p. 1993. pap. 15.99 (*0-7509-0255-8*) A Sutton Pub.
— The Buildings of Ludlow. (Buildings of...Ser.). (Illus.). 128p. 1993. pap. 15.99 (*0-7509-0254-X*) A Sutton Pub.
— The Buildings of Shrewsbury. (Buildings of...Ser.). (Illus.). 128p. 1993. pap. 15.99 (*0-7509-0253-1*) A Sutton Pub.
— The Buildings of Stratford-upon-Avon. (Buildings of... Ser.). (Illus.). 128p. (Orig.). 1994. pap. 16.00 (*0-7509-0559-X*) A Sutton Pub.
— The Buildings of Warwick. (Buildings of...Ser.). (Illus.). 128p. (Orig.). 1994. pap. 16.00 (*0-7509-0558-1*) A Sutton Pub.
— The Buildings of Worcester. (Buildings of...Ser.). (Illus.). 128p. (Orig.). 1994. pap. 16.00 (*0-7509-0557-3*) A Sutton Pub.
Morriss, Roger & Bursey, Peter, comps. Guide to British Naval Papers in North America. LC 94-2456. 416p. 1995. 120.00 (*0-7201-2162-0*, Mansell Pub) Cassell.
Morriss, S. Brian. Industrial Automation: Components & Control. LC 93-49739. 1994. write for info. (*0-02-802331-5*) Glencoe.

An Asterisk (*) at the beginning of an entry indicates that the title is appearing in BIP for the first time.

Morrissett, Irving, ed. Social Studies in the 1980s: A Report of Project SPAN. LC 82-72766. 147p. (Orig.). 1982. pap. text ed. 8.75 (0-87120-114-3, 611-82270) Assn Supervision.

Morrissette, Bruce. Novel & Film: Essays in Two Genres. LC 85-995. (Illus.). xii, 182p. 1985. lib. bdg. 26.00 (0-226-54023-5) U Ch Pr.

Morrissette, Mikki. Nancy Kerrigan: Heart of a Champion. (J). (gr. 4-7). 1994. mass mkt. 3.99 (0-553-48254-8) Bantam.

Morrissette, Nan H. Setting up a Bank Records Management Program. LC 92-37466. 192p. 1993. text ed. 55.00 (0-89930-748-5, MTX/, Quorum Bks) Greenwood.

Morrissey, Brendan. Boston 1775. (Campaign Ser.). (Illus.). 96p. 1994. pap. 14.95 (1-85532-362-1, 9531, Pub. by Osprey UK) Stackpole.

***Morrissey, Dean.** Ship of Dreams. (Illus.). 37p. (J). 1994. 17.95 (0-8109-3848-0) Abrams.

Morrissey, Dianne J. Reflections of a Young Woman. 1978. pap. 4.95 (0-686-24550-4) Aaron-Jenkins.

Morrissey, Gerard. The Crisis of Dissent. 128p. (Orig.). 1985. pap. 5.95 (0-931888-19-0) Christendom Pr.

— Defending the Papacy. 96p. (Orig.). 1984. pap. 5.95 (0-931888-15-8) Christendom Pr.

— What the Catholic Faithful Can Do. 128p. (Orig.). 1987. pap. 5.95 (0-931888-23-9) Christendom Pr.

Morrissey, James M., et al. Consent & Confidentiality in the Health Care of Children & Adolescents: A Legal Guide. 304p. 1986. text ed. 49.95 (0-02-921800-4) Free Pr.

Morrissey, Kevin, jt. auth. see Bluestein, Barry.

Morrissey, Kevin, ed. see Chicago Architecture Foundation Staff.

Morrissey, Kevin, jt. auth. see Levin, Keren.

Morrissey, Kirkie. Designed by God: A Woman's Workshop on Wholeness. (Woman's Workshop Ser.). 160p. (Orig.). 1985. pap. 7.99 (0-310-45011-X, 16246P) Zondervan.

Morrissey, Lee, ed. The Kitchen Turns Twenty: A Retrospective Anthology. (Illus.). 120p. (Orig.). 1992. pap. 10.00 (0-9634456-1-8) Kitchen Ctr.

Morrissey, Maria & Mitchell, Jack. VersaCAD Corporation's Training Guide: 2D & 3D Tutorials. (Orig.). (C). 1989. teacher ed 15.00 (0-8273-3563-6) Delmar.

Morrissey, Martin. The Changing Years. 158p. 1993. pap. 13.95 (0-86278-279-1, Pub. by OBrien Pr IE) Dufour.

— Land of My Cradle Days: Recollections from a Country Childhood. 160p. 1990. pap. 12.95 (0-86278-229-5, Pub. by OBrien Pr IE) Dufour.

***Morrissey, Mary M.** Alchemy of the Heart: The Transformative Power of Love in Everyday Life. LC 95-67928. 208p. 1995. pap. 12.00 (0-89716-562-4) P B Pubng.

Morrissey, Michael P. Consciousness & Transcendence: The Theology of Eric Voegelin. LC 92-50159. (C). 1994. text ed. 41.95 (0-268-00793-4) U of Notre Dame Pr.

Morrissey, Michael T. & Pollnac, Richard B., eds. Aspects of Small-Scale Fisheries Development. 154p. (C). 1989. pap. 7.00 (1-882027-00-0) URI ICMRD.

Morrissey, Michael T., jt. ed. see Sylvia, Gilbert.

Morrissey, Mike & Gaffikin, Frank. Northern Ireland: The Thatcher Years. LC 89-25027. (Illus.). 160p. (C). 1990. text ed. 45.00 (0-86232-906-X, Pub. by Zed Books UK); pap. 15.00 (0-86232-907-8, Pub. by Zed Books UK) Humanities.

Morrissey, Mike, jt. ed. see Gaffikin, Frank.

Morrissey, Muriel E. Amelia Earhart. (Illus.). 1977. pap. 3.95 (0-88388-044-X) Bellerophon Bks.

Morrissey, Muriel E. & Osborne, Carol L. Amelia, My Courageous Sister: Biography of Amelia Earhart. (Biography Ser.). (Illus.). 320p. 1987. pap. 19.95 (0-940997-02-9) Aviation.

— Amelia, My Courageous Sister: Biography of Amelia Earhart, Set. (Biography Ser.). (Illus.). 320p. 1987. pap. 29.95 (0-685-17989-3) Aviation.

***Morrissey, Oliver & Stewart, Frances, eds.** Economic & Political Reform in Developing Countries. LC 95-2568. 1995. write for info. (0-312-12606-9) St Martin.

Morrissey, Oliver, jt. ed. see Lloyd, Tim.

Morrissey, Oliver, et al. British Aid & International Trade: Aid Policy Making, 1979-89. LC 92-11902. (Public Policy & Management Ser.). 1992. 95.00 (0-335-15652-5, Open Univ Pr) Taylor & Francis.

***Morrissey, Patricia.** Disability Etiquette in the Workplace. 38p. 1991. 20.00 (0-916559-35-1, 2032-TM-4045) EPF.

Morrissey, Patricia A. ADA News & Regulations: For the Private Sector. 350p. 1993. 350.00 (1-880955-01-6) Legi-Slate.

— Human Resource Executive's Survival Guide to the Americans with Disabilities Act. LC 91-38253. 500p. 1992. ring bd. 135.00 (0-934753-63-6) LRP Pubns.

— A Primer for Corporate America on Civil Rights for the Disabled. LC 91-25397. 139p. (Orig.). 1991. pap. 12.95 (0-934753-49-0) LRP Pubns.

Morrissey, Paul F. Let Someone Hold You: The Journey of a Hospice Priest. LC 93-45874. 240p. (Orig.). 1994. pap. 16.95 (0-8245-1408-4) Crossroad NY.

Morrissey, R. Sterilization Technology: A Practical Guide for Manufacturers & Users of Health Care Products. Phillips, G. Briggs, ed. LC 92-17950. 1992. text ed. 95.00 (0-442-23832-0) Chapman & Hall.

Morrissey, Robert J. La Reverie Jusqu'a Rousseau: Recherches sur un topos Litteraire. LC 84-81406. (French Forum Monographs: No. 55). 184p. (Orig.). 1984. pap. 13.45 (0-917058-55-0) French Forum.

***Morrissey, Sally.** Mud Stoves & Strawberry Jam. 240p. Date not set. pap. 14.95 (0-9643963-0-0) R Paul Pr.

Morrissey, Thomas. A Man Called Hughes. 512p. 1989. 75.00 (1-85390-138-5, Pub. by Veritas IE) St Mut.

Morrissey, W. D. Heavy Dues. LC 91-67757. 144p. 1993. pap. 9.00 (1-56002-129-2, Univ Edtns) Aegina Pr.

Morrisson, Cecile. La Monnaie a Byzance: Finances, Analyses, Techniques. (Collected Studies: CS 461). 336p. 1994. 95.00 (0-86078-401-0, Pub. by Variorum UK) Ashgate Pub Co.

Morrisson, Christian, jt. auth. see Bourguignon, Francois.

Morrisson, Christian, ed. see Lafary, J. D. & Lecaillon, J.

Morrisson, Christian, ed. see OECD Staff, et al.

Morrisson, Clovis C. The Dynamics of Development in the European Human Rights Convention System. 192p. 1981. lib. bdg. 94.00 (90-247-2546-1) Kluwer Ac.

Morrissy. Atlas of Pediatric Orthopaedic Surgery. (Illus.). 800p. 1992. text ed. 150.00 (0-397-50969-3) Lippincott.

— Lovell & Winter's Pediatric Orthopaedics, 2 vols., Set. 3rd ed. (Illus.). 1400p. 1989. text ed. 260.00 (0-397-50914-6) Lippincott.

***Morrissy, Mary.** Mother of Pearl: A Novel. LC 94-42084. 1995. 20.00 (0-684-19667-0, Scribners) S&S Trade.

Morrissy, Una. Great Irish Love Stories. 1990. pap. 9.95 (0-85342-890-5, Pub. by Mercier Pr IE) Dufour.

Morro, A., jt. auth. see Caviglia, G.

Morro, Angelo, jt. auth. see Fabrizio, Mauro.

Morrocco, John. Air Power Unleashed: The Air War, 1968-1975. Boston Publishing Company Editors, ed. (Illus.). 192p. 1985. 16.30 (0-201-11268-X) Addison-Wesley.

— Rain of Fire, Air War. Manning, Robert, ed. LC 84-73511. (Vietnam Experience Ser.: Vol. XIV). (Illus.). 192p. 1984. 16.95 (0-939526-14-X) Boston Pub Co.

— Thunder from Above, Vol. 9. Dreyfus, Paul, ed. LC 84-70448. (Vietnam Experience Ser.). (Illus.). 192p. 1984. 16.95 (0-939526-09-3) Boston Pub Co.

Morron, Bradford, ed. Conjunctions Fifteen: Biannual Volumes of New Writing. (Illus.). 415p. (Orig.). (C). 1991. pap. 9.95 (0-685-49112-9) Random.

Morrone, Francis. The Architectural Guidebook to New York City. LC 93-42964. (Illus.). 400p. 1994. pap. 21.95 (0-87905-629-0) Gibbs Smith Pub.

— Night Before Christmas in New York City. (Illus.). 1994. pap. 5.95 (0-87905-615-0, Peregrine Smith) Gibbs Smith Pub.

Morrone, Joan. Addicted. LC 85-82145. 125p. (Orig.). 1986. pap. 6.00 (0-9616771-0-4) J & R Pub.

— The Age of Reason: A Scientific Study of the Evolutionary Potential of Man - The Revelation of Cosmic Consciousness. (Illus.). 72p. (Orig.). 1988. pap. 8.50 (0-9616771-1-2) J & R Pub.

Morrone, John, ed. see PEN American Center Staff.

Morroni, Mario. Production Process & Technical Change. (Illus.). 232p. (C). 1992. 49.95 (0-521-41001-0) Cambridge U Pr.

Morrow. Interfacial Phenomena in Petroleum Recovery. (Surfactant Science Ser.: Vol. 36). 464p. 1990. 160.00 (0-8247-8385-9) Dekker.

Morrow, ed. Dental Laboratory Procedures: Complete Dentures, Vol. 1. 600p. 1985. 89.00 (0-8016-3519-5) Mosby Yr Bk.

— Nebula Awards Twenty-Six: SFWA's Choices for the Best Science Fiction & Fantasy of the Year. 1992. 24.95 (0-15-164934-0, Harvest Bks); pap. 12.95 (0-15-665472-5, Harvest Bks) HarBrace.

Morrow, Alexander. Inside the Sanctuary. LC 86-42954. 260p. 1987. 15.95 (0-88400-124-5) Shengold.

Morrow, Ann. Highness: The Maharajahs of India. large type ed. (Illus.). 448p. 1987. 23.95 (0-7089-8441-X, Trail West Pubs) Ulverscroft.

— Princess. large type ed. 541p. 1992. 21.95 (0-7505-0398-X, Pub. by Magna Print Bks) Ulverscroft.

— The Queen Mother. large type ed. (Illus.). 416p. 1985. 23.95 (0-7089-8257-3, Trail West Pubs) Ulverscroft.

Morrow, Ann, jt. auth. see Cerulean, Susan.

Morrow, Anne. A Case of Injustice: A True Story of a Woman Scorned. Amsbary, George, ed. 502p. 1991. 19.95 (0-9628704-0-4) Palatine Pr.

Morrow, Arthur E. & Morrow, Edith M. Two Morrow's Legacy. (Illus.). 1988. 10.95 (0-9620550-0-X) Dodson Assocs.

***Morrow, B.** Edwards Portrait. Date not set. pap. 3.99 (0-517-13321-0) Random.

— Help for Mr. Peale. Date not set. pap. 3.99 (0-517-13326-1) Random.

***Morrow, Baker H.** Best Plants for New Mexico Gardens & Landscapes: Keyed to Cities & Regions in New Mexico & Adjacent Areas. (Illus.). 300p. 1995. pap. 24.95 (0-8263-1595-X) U of NM Pr.

***Morrow, Barbara.** Indiana's Authors. (Illus.). 150p. 1995. 21.95 (1-878208-60-8) Guild Pr IN.

Morrow, Bardford. Trinity Fields. LC 94-20125. 448p. 1995. 22.95 (0-670-85728-9, Viking) Viking Penguin.

Morrow, Blaine V. CD-ROM for Information Distribution. Wicks, Wendy & Cunningham, Ann M., eds. (Report Series, 1992: No. 2). 160p. (Orig.). 1992. pap. text ed. 100.00 (0-942308-35-2) NFAIS.

Morrow, Bradford. The Almanac Branch. 288p. 1992. pap. 8.95 (0-393-30921-5) Norton.

— Conjunctions, No. 22. 1994. pap. 10.00 (0-679-75581-0) Random.

— Conjunctions 23: New World Writing. 1994. 10.00 (0-679-75820-8) Random.

— Posthumes. 52p. 1982. pap. 5.00 (0-932274-25-0) Cadmus Eds.

Morrow, Bradford, ed. Conjunction: Bi-Annual Volumes of New Writing, Vol. 16. 350p. 1991. pap. 10.00 (0-679-73541-0) Conjunctions.

— Conjunctions: Bi-Annual Volumes of New Writing, Vol. 8. (Illus.). 262p. 1985. 25.00 (0-941964-18-3); pap. 10.00 (0-941964-17-5) Conjunctions.

— Conjunctions: Bi-Annual Volumes of New Writing, Vol. 9. (Illus.). 289p. 1986. 25.00 (0-941964-16-7); pap. 10.00 (0-941964-15-9) Conjunctions.

— Conjunctions: Bi-Annual Volumes of New Writing, Vol. 11. (Illus.). 288p. 1988. 25.00 (0-941964-24-8); pap. 10.00 (0-941964-23-X) Conjunctions.

— Conjunctions: Bi-Annual Volumes of New Writing, Vol. 12. 312p. 1988. 25.00 (0-684-58712-2); pap. 10.00 (0-02-035281-6) Conjunctions.

— Conjunctions: Bi-Annual Volumes of New Writing, Vol. 13. 275p. 1989. pap. 10.00 (0-02-035282-4) Conjunctions.

— Conjunctions: Bi-Annual Volumes of New Writing, Vol. 14. 287p. 1989. 25.00 (0-684-19149-0); pap. 10.00 (0-02-035290-5) Conjunctions.

— Conjunctions: Bi-Annual Volumes of New Writing, Vol. 15. 415p. 1990. pap. 10.00 (0-679-73515-1) Conjunctions.

— Conjunctions: Bi-Annual Volumes of New Writing, Vol. 17. 414p. 1991. pap. 10.00 (0-679-73774-X) Conjunctions.

— Conjunctions: Bi-Annual Volumes of New Writing, Vol. 18. 370p. 1992. pap. 10.00 (0-679-74051-1) Conjunctions.

— Conjunctions: Bi-Annual Volumes of New Writing, Vol. 19. 324p. 1992. pap. 10.00 (0-679-74399-5) Conjunctions.

— Conjunctions: Bi-Annual Volumes of New Writing, Vol. 20. 341p. 1993. pap. 10.00 (0-679-74710-9) Conjunctions.

— Conjunctions: Bi-Annual Volumes of New Writing, Vol. 21. 360p. 1994. pap. text ed. 10.00 (0-679-75112-2) Conjunctions.

— Conjunctions: 1. (Bi-Annual Volumes of New Writing Ser.). (Illus.). 312p. 1981. pap. 9.00 (0-941964-01-9) Conjunctions.

— Conjunctions: 2. (Bi-Annual Volumes of New Writing Ser.). (Illus.). 240p. 1982. 22.50 (0-941964-04-3); pap. 7.50 (0-941964-03-5) Conjunctions.

— Conjunctions: 3. (Bi-Annual Volumes of New Writing Ser.). (Illus.). 240p. 1982. 22.50 (0-941964-06-X); pap. 7.50 (0-941964-05-1) Conjunctions.

— Conjunctions: 4. (Bi-Annual Volumes of New Writing Ser.). (Illus.). 240p. 1983. 22.50 (0-941964-08-6); pap. 7.50 (0-941964-07-8) Conjunctions.

— Conjunctions: 5. (Bi-Annual Volumes of New Writing Ser.). (Illus.). 248p. (C). 1983. 22.50 (0-941964-10-8); pap. 7.50 (0-941964-09-4) Conjunctions.

— Conjunctions: 6. (Bi-Annual Volumes of New Writing Ser.). (Illus.). 316p. 1984. 22.50 (0-941964-12-4); pap. 7.50 (0-941964-11-6) Conjunctions.

— Conjunctions: 7. (Bi-Annual Volumes of New Writing Ser.). (Illus.). 282p. 1985. 20.00 (0-941964-14-0); pap. 8.95 (0-941964-13-2) Conjunctions.

— Conjunctions 12. Date not set. pap. 12.00 (0-941964-26-4) Conjunctions.

— Conjunctions 13. Date not set. pap. 12.00 (0-941964-30-2) Conjunctions.

— Conjunctions 14: The New Gothic. Date not set. pap. 12.00 (0-941964-31-0) Conjunctions.

— Conjunctions 15: The Poetry Issue. Date not set. pap. 12.00 (0-941964-32-9) Conjunctions.

— Conjunctions 16: The Music Issue. Date not set. pap. 12.00 (0-941964-33-7) Conjunctions.

— Conjunctions 17: Tenth Anniversary Issue. Date not set. pap. 12.00 (0-941964-34-5) Conjunctions.

— Conjunctions 18: Fables, Yarns, Fairy Tales. Date not set. pap. 12.00 (0-941964-35-3) Conjunctions.

— Conjunctions 19: Other Worlds. Date not set. pap. 12.00 (0-941964-36-1) Conjunctions.

— Conjunctions 20: Unfinished Business: Novels-in-Progress. Date not set. pap. 12.00 (0-941964-37-X) Conjunctions.

— Conjunctions 21: The Credos Issue. Date not set. pap. 12.00 (0-941964-38-8) Conjunctions.

— Conjunctions 22: The Novellas Issue. Date not set. pap. 12.00 (0-941964-39-6) Conjunctions.

— Conjunctions 23: New World Writing. Date not set. pap. 12.00 (0-941964-40-X) Conjunctions.

— Conjunctions 24: Critical Mass. 1995. pap. 12.00 (0-941964-29-9) Conjunctions.

Morrow, Bradford & Cooney, Seamus. A Bibliography of the Black Sparrow Press 1966-1978. LC 80-24229. (Illus.). 302p. 1981. 40.00 (0-87685-465-X) Black Sparrow.

Morrow, Bradford & Lafourcade, Bernard. A Bibliography of the Writings of Wyndham Lewis. LC 78-12751. (Illus.). 350p. 1978. 40.00 (0-87685-419-6) Black Sparrow.

Morrow, Bradford & McGrath, Patrick, eds. A Collection of Contemporary Gothic Fiction. LC 91-52673. 337p. 1991. 21.50 (0-394-58767-7) Random.

— The New Gothic: A Collection of Contemporary Gothic Fiction. LC 92-50089. 1992. 13.00 (0-679-73075-3, Vin) Random.

Morrow, Bradford, ed. see Rexroth, Kenneth.

Morrow, Bradford, et al, eds. Conjunctions: Bi-Annual Volumes of New Writing, Vol. 10. (Conjunctions--Bi-Annual Volumes of New Writing Ser.). (Illus.). 304p. 1987. 25.00 (0-941964-22-1); pap. 10.00 (0-941964-21-3) Conjunctions.

Morrow, C. Paul & Townsend, Duane E. Synopsis of Gynecologic Oncology. 3rd ed. LC 87-2112. (Illus.). 602p. reprint ed. pap. 171.60 (0-7837-6248-8, 2045960) Bks Demand.

Morrow, C. Paul, et al. Synopsis of Gynecologic Oncology. 4th ed. LC 93-50. 576p. 1993. text ed. 92.00 (0-443-08861-6) Churchill.

Morrow, C. Paul, et al, eds. Recent Clinical Developments in Gynecologic Oncology. (Progress in Cancer Research & Therapy Ser.: Vol. 24). 224p. 1983. text ed. 98.00 (0-89004-810-X) Raven.

— Recent Clinical Developments in Gynecologic Oncology. LC 83-3312. (Progress in Cancer Research & Therapy Ser.: No. 24). (Illus.). Date not set. reprint ed. pap. 66.50 (0-7837-9517-3, 2060266) Bks Demand.

***Morrow, Carolyn C.** National Conference on the Development of Statewide Preservation Programs. 108p. 1991. pap. 10.00 (1-887334-05-X) Comm Preserv & Access.

Morrow, Carolyn C. & Dyal, Carole. Conservation Treatment Procedures: A Manual of Step-by-Step Procedures for the Maintenance & Repair of Library Materials. 2nd ed. LC 86-20948. 225p. 1986. lib. bdg. 32.00 (0-87287-437-0) Libs Unl.

Morrow, Carolyn C. & Walker, Gay. The Preservation Challenge: A Guide to Conserving Library Materials. LC 82-18726. (Professional Librarian Ser.). (Illus.). 231p. 1982. Professional. lib. bdg. 37.50 (0-86729-003-X); pap. 30.50 (0-86729-002-1) G K Hall.

Morrow, Catherine. The Jellybean Principal. LC 93-26537. (Step into Reading Bks.). (Illus.). 48p. (J). (gr. 1-3). 1994. 7.99 (0-679-94743-4); pap. 3.50 (0-679-84743-X) Random Bks Yng Read.

Morrow, Charles T. Shock & Vibration Engineering. LC 63-7556. 404p. reprint ed. pap. 115.20 (0-317-08532-8, 2011956) Bks Demand.

Morrow, Christine, jt. auth. see Picton, Bernard.

***Morrow, Cliff.** Cold Boiled Potatoes & Buttermilk. 1994. 12.95 (0-533-11142-0) Vantage.

Morrow, Cucuel. Bohemian Paris of Today. 1977. lib. bdg. 59.95 (0-8490-1520-0) Gordon Pr.

Morrow, Danny R. Silhouette of a Saint: Albert Pepper. 1985. 5.95 (0-86544-027-1) Salv Army Suppl South.

Morrow, David A. Current Therapy in Theriogenology Two: Diagnosis, Treatment, & Prevention of Reproductive Diseases in Small & Large Animals. 2nd ed. (Illus.). 1143p. 1986. text ed. 140.00 (0-7216-6580-2) Saunders.

Morrow, David C. The Once & Future Nerd. 20p. (Orig.). 1994. pap. 5.00 (0-9641836-0-9) Textar Media.

— Shondan Language. 20p. (Orig.). 1995. pap. 5.00 (0-9641836-2-5) Textar Media.

— Thomas Morrow: Pioneer of Alabama & Texas. 18p. (Orig.). 1994. pap. 18.00 (0-9641836-1-7) Textar Media.

Morrow, Don, et al. A Concise History of Sport in Canada. (Illus.). 400p. 1990. pap. 19.95 (0-19-540693-1) OUP.

***Morrow, Ed.** Born This Day: A Daily Celebration of Famous Beginnings. (Illus.). 324p. 1995. pap. 10.95 (0-8065-1648-8, Citadel Pr) Carol Pub Group.

— The Grim Reaper's Book of Days: A Cautionary Record of Famous, Infamous & Unconventional Exits. (Illus.). 256p. 1992. pap. 9.95 (0-8065-1364-0, Citadel Pr) Carol Pub Group.

Morrow, Edith M., jt. auth. see Morrow, Arthur E.

Morrow, Felix. Revolution & Counter-Revolution in Spain. 2nd ed. LC 74-80372. 272p. 1976. reprint ed. lib. bdg. 50.00 (0-87348-401-0); reprint ed. pap. 17.95 (0-87348-402-9) Pathfinder NY.

Morrow, France. Unleashing Our Unknown Selves: An Inquiry into the Future of Feminity & Masculinity. LC 90-39262. 288p. 1990. text ed. 59.95 (0-275-93587-6, C3587, Praeger Pubs); pap. text ed. 17.95 (0-275-93837-9, B3837, Praeger Pubs) Greenwood.

Morrow, G. J. & Yang, W. S., eds. Probability Models in Mathematical Physics: Proceedings of the Conference on Probability Models in Mathematical Physics, Colorado Springs, May 16-24, 1990. 252p. 1991. text ed. 104.00 (981-02-0394-2) World Scientific Pub.

Morrow, Gerald S., jt. auth. see Edwards, John C.

Morrow, Gertrude. The Compassionate School: A Practical Guide to Educating Abused & Traumatized Children. 250p. 1987. text ed. 27.95 (0-13-154742-9) P-H.

— Helping the Chronically Ill Child in School: A Handbook for Teachers, Counselors & Administrators. 1985. pap. text ed. 21.95 (0-13-386053-1, Parker Publishing Co) P-H.

Morrow, Glenn R. Plato's Cretan City: A Historical Interpretation of the Laws. 646p. 1993. pap. text ed. 24.95 (0-691-02484-7) Princeton U Pr.

— Plato's Law of Slavery in Its Relation to Greek Law. LC 75-13283. (History of Ideas in Ancient Greece Ser.). 1976. reprint ed. 15.95 (0-405-07325-9) Ayer.

Morrow, Glenn R., tr. see Proclus.

Morrow, Harold W. Statics & Strength of Materials. 2nd ed. 640p. 1992. text ed. 73.00 (0-13-845835-9) P-H.

Morrow, Honore. On to Oregon. (Illus.). (J). (gr. 5-9). 1946. reprint ed. 16.00 (0-688-21639-0); reprint ed. pap. 4.95 (0-688-10494-0, Pub. by Beech Tree Bks) Morrow Jr Bks.

Morrow, Honore W. Splendor of God. 24.95 (0-89190-310-0, Am Repr) Amereon Ltd.

Morrow, I. F., tr. see Von Salomon, Ernst.

Morrow, Ian F., tr. see Paleologue, Maurice.

Morrow, James. City of Truth. LC 92-43161. 1993. pap. 7.95 (0-15-618042-1) HarBrace.

— Nebula Awards Twenty-Eight: SFWA's Choice for the Best Science Fiction & Fantasy of the Year. 1994. 24.95 (0-15-100082-4); pap. 12.95 (0-15-600039-3) HarBrace.

— This Is the Way the World Ends. LC 85-24773. 1995. pap. 11.00 (0-15-600208-6) HarBrace.

— Towing Jehovah. LC 93-35022. 1994. 23.95 (0-15-190919-9) HarBrace.

— Towing Jehovah. LC 93-35022. 1995. pap. 12.00 (0-15-600210-8) HarBrace.

Morrow, James D. Game Theory for Political Scientists. LC 94-9256. 1994. 35.00 (0-691-03430-3) Princeton U Pr.

Morrow, James R., Jr. & Pivarnik, James M. Simulated Exercise Physiology Laboratories. LC 89-1913. (C). 1989. student ed, disk 36.00x (0-87322-232-6, BMOR0232); student ed, disk 36.00x (0-87322-234-2, BMOR0234) Human Kinetics.

M

An Asterisk (*) at the beginning of an entry indicates that the title is appearing in BIP for the first time.

*Morrow, James R., Jr., et al. Measurement & Evaluation in Human Performance. (Illus.). 488p. (C). 1995. disk 49.00 (0-87322-731-X, BMOR0731); disk 49.00 (0-87322-961-4) Human Kinetics.

Morrow, James S., jt. auth. see Stern, Uri.

Morrow, Jodie B. & Lebov, Myrna. Not Just a Secretary: Using the Job to Get Ahead. LC 82-24744. (General Trade Bks.). 182p. 1984. pap. text ed. 12.95 (0-471-87060-9, 1-999) Wiley.

Morrow, John, ed. Coleridge's Writings Vol. I: On Politics & Society. 352p. 1991. text ed. 39.95 (0-691-06887-9); pap. text ed. 13.95 (0-691-01503-1) Princeton U Pr.

Morrow, John, jt. auth. see Francis, Mark.

Morrow, John, ed. see Green, T. H.

Morrow, John H. Building German Airpower, 1909-1914. LC 76-15287. 164p. reprint ed. pap. 46.80 (0-8357-7466-X, 2023171) Bks Demand.

— German Air Power in World War I. LC 81-11588. 289p. reprint ed. pap. 82.40 (0-7837-6466-9, 2046470) Bks Demand.

Morrow, John H., Jr. The Great War in the Air: Military Aviation from 1909 to 1921. LC 92-17437. (History of Aviation Ser.). (Illus.). 464p. 1993. 29.95 (1-56098-238-1) Smithsonian.

Morrow, John H., jt. ed. see Rivkin, Arnold.

Morrow, Katherine D. Greek Footwear & the Dating of Sculpture. LC 84-40500. (Illus.). 272p. 1986. text ed. 35.00 (0-299-10190-8) U of Wis Pr.

*Morrow, Lance. Heart: A Memoir. 336p. 1995. 22.95 (0-446-51870-0) Warner Bks.

Morrow, Lance, jt. auth. see Leifer, Neil.

Morrow, Laura, jt. ed. see Atkins, G. Douglas.

Morrow, Laurie, ed. see Ford, Corey.

Morrow, Laurie, jt. auth. see Smith, Steve.

Morrow, Lee A. & Pike, Frank. Creating Theatre: The Professionals' Approach to New Plays. LC 86-40149. 320p. 1986. pap. 9.95 (0-394-74279-6, Vin) Random.

Morrow, Lesley M. Literacy Development in the Early Years: Helping Children Read & Write. 2nd ed. 448p. (C). 1992. pap. text ed. 34.95 (0-205-14043-2, H40439) Allyn.

— Promoting Voluntary Readers in School & Home. LC 85-61796. (Fastback Ser.: No. 225). 50p. (Orig.). 1985. pap. 1.25 (0-87367-225-9) Phi Delta Kappa.

*Morrow, Lesley M., ed. Family Literacy. 280p. 1995. pap. 18.00 (0-87207-127-8) Intl Reading.

— A Survey of Family Literacy in the United States. 140p. 1995. pap. 12.00 (0-87207-131-6) Intl Reading.

Morrow, Lesley M., jt. ed. see Strickland, Dorothy S.

Morrow, Leslie & Smith, Jeffrey. Assessment for Instruction in Early Literacy. 256p. (C). 1989. Casebound. text ed. 54.00 (0-13-050428-9) P-H.

Morrow, Leslie M., et al, eds. Integrated Language Arts: Controversy to Consensus. LC 93-22944. 348p. 1993. 38.95 (0-205-14736-4); pap. write for info. (0-205-14735-6) Allyn.

Morrow, Linda, ed. see Adams, Faye.

Morrow, Linda, ed. see Deveraux, Jude.

*Morrow, Liza K. Allergic to My Family. (J). (gr. 3-6). 1995. reprint ed. pap. 3.50 (0-671-86505-6, Minstrel Bks) PB.

Morrow, Lorna J., jt. ed. see Rowan, Thomas E.

Morrow, Lynn, ed. The White River Chronicles of S. C. Turnbo: Man & Wildlife on the Ozarks Frontier. LC 93-49518. 356p. 1994. 44.00 (1-55728-307-9) U of Ark Pr.

Morrow, Lynn, jt. ed. see Keefe, James F.

Morrow, M. E., ed. & intro. St. Augustine Today. (Illus.). 1985. write for info. (0-933959-01-X) Merton Pr.

Morrow, Mable. Indian Rawhide: An American Folk Art. LC 73-7427. (Civilization of the American Indian Ser.: Vol. 132). (Illus.). 200p. 1975. pap. 24.95 (0-8061-1637-4) U of Okla Pr.

Morrow, Mark. Images of the Southern Writer: Photographs by Mark Morrow. LC 85-8629. (Illus.). 112p. 1985. 27.95 (0-8203-0810-2) U of Ga Pr.

Morrow, Mary F. Sarah Winnemucca. (Raintree-Rivilo American Indian Stories Ser.). (Illus.). 32p. (J). (gr. 3-6). 1990. lib. bdg. 19.97 (0-8172-3402-0); pap. 4.95 (0-8114-4095-8) Raintree Steck-V.

Morrow, Matthew E. Ghosts on the Run II. limited ed. 120p. 1985. 12.00 (0-933959-00-1) Merton Pr.

Morrow, Muriel M., tr. see Paleoloque, Maurice.

Morrow, Nancy. Dreadful Games: The Play of Desire in the Nineteenth-Century Novel. LC 87-35902. 209p. 1988. 24.00 (0-87338-358-3) Kent St U Pr.

Morrow, Nancy, ed. see Overlook Hospital Auxilary Staff.

Morrow, Norma L. Being a Medical Transcriptionist. 208p. 1991. pap. 19.80 (0-89303-082-1) P-H.

*Morrow, Ord L. Gigantes Al Acecho. 128p. (SPA.). 1995. mass mkt., pap. 4.50 (0-8254-1481-4) Kregel.

Morrow, Patrick. Beyond Everest. (Illus.). 176p. 1986. pap. 19.95 (0-920656-46-3) Firefly Bks Ltd.

— Bret Harte. LC 72-619588. (Western Writers Ser.: No. 5). (Illus.). 51p. (Orig.). (C). 1972. pap. 3.95 (0-88430-004-8) Boise St U W Writ Ser.

— Katherine Mansfield's Fiction. LC 92-74783. 1993. 29.95 (0-87972-563-X); pap. 10.95 (0-87972-564-8) Bowling Green Univ.

Morrow, Patrick, tr. Porcelain Butterfly. 1972. pap. 2.00 (0-88031-005-7) Invisible-Red Hill.

Morrow, Patrick D. The Popular & the Serious in Select Twentieth-Century American Novels. LC 92-4342. 162p. 1992. lib. bdg. 79.95 (0-7734-9496-0) E Mellen.

Morrow, Paula C. The Theory & Measurement of Work Commitment. LC 93-920. (Monographs in Organizational Behavior & Industrial Relations: Vol. 15). 1993. write for info. (1-55938-572-3) Jai Pr.

*Morrow, Phyllis & Sshneider, William. When Our Words Return. 1995. write for info. (0-614-07176-3) Utah St U Pr.

Morrow, R. H., jt. auth. see Smith, P. G.

Morrow, Raymond A. & Brown, David A. Critical Theory & Methodology: Interpretive Structuralism As a Research Program. LC 94-10888. (Contemporary Social Theory Ser.: Vol. 3). 320p. 1994. 55.00 (0-8039-4682-1); pap. 26.95 (0-8039-4683-X) Sage.

Morrow, Raymond A. & Torres, Carlos A., eds. Social Theory & Education: A Critique of Theories of Social & Cultural Reproduction. LC 94-3956. (Teacher Empowerment & School Reform Ser.). 448p. (C). 1995. text ed. 74.50x (0-7914-2251-8); pap. 24.95 (0-7914-2252-6) State U NY Pr.

Morrow, Rob, photos. Northern Exposures. (Illus.). 96p. 1994. pap. 9.95 (0-7868-6064-2) Hyperion.

Morrow, Robert. First Hand Knowledge: How I Participated in the CIA-Mafia Murder of President Kennedy. 1992. 22.95 (1-56171-179-9) Sure Sellers.

Morrow, Robert, ed. The Indoor Air Quality Directory, 1992-1993. 375p. (Orig.). 1992. pap. 75.00 (0-9633003-1-8) IAQ Pubns.

— Lead Tech '92 Proceedings: Solutions for a Nation at Risk, 1992-1993. (Illus.). 650p. 1992. pap. 50.00 (0-9633003-3-4) IAQ Pubns.

Morrow, Robert D. First-Hand Knowledge: How I Participated in the CIA-Mafia Murder of President Kennedy. 1993. pap. 5.99 (1-56171-274-4) Sure Sellers.

— The Senator Must Die. LC 88-61816. (Illus.). 368p. 1988. 22.95 (0-915677-39-3) Roundtable Pub.

Morrow, Rodger, ed. see Ryder, Thomas.

Morrow, Roger & Glenn, Monica. Let's Talk. 160p. (Orig.). (YA). (gr. 7-12). 1991. pap. 4.95 (0-8474-6625-6) Back to Bible.

Morrow, Rosemary. Earth User's Guide to Permaculture. (Illus.). 144p. (Orig.). 1994. pap. 15.95 (0-86417-514-0, Pub. by Kangaroo Pr AT) Seven Hills Bk.

Morrow, Steve, tr. see Shiv Brat Lal.

Morrow, Sue A. The Beginning of Wisdom: Sermons for Pentecost Middle Third. LC 92-45764. (Cycle B First Lesson Texts Ser.). 1993. pap. 6.25 (1-55673-614-2, 9339) CSS OH.

Morrow, T. B., jt. ed. see Bajura, R. A.

*Morrow, T. B., et al, eds. Fluid Measurement & Instrumentation 1994. LC 86-70582. (Fluid Engineering Division Conference Ser.: Vol. 183). 109p. 1994. pap. 35.00 (0-7918-1366-5) ASME.

— Industrial & Environmental Application of Fluid Mechanics 1994. LC 92-54703. (Fluid Engineering Division Conference Ser.: Vol. 186). 197p. 1994. pap. 37.50 (0-7918-1369-X) ASME.

Morrow, Theodore, tr. see Boff, Leonardo.

Morrow, Theodore, tr. see Libanio, J. B.

Morrow, Theresa. Seattle Survival Guide II: The Essential Handbook for City Living. 2nd rev. ed. (Illus.). 380p. 1993. pap. 17.95 (0-912365-84-6) Sasquatch Bks.

Morrow, Thomas J., jt. auth. see Kennedy, Joyce L.

Morrow, Toby. Iowa Projectile Points. 1986. pap. 10.00 (0-87414-034-X) U IA Pubns Dept.

Morrow, Vincent. Handbook of Financial Analysis for Corporate Managers. 1991. 89.95 (0-13-318346-7, Busn) P-H.

Morrow, W. John & Haigwood, Nancy L., eds. HIV Molecular Organization, Pathogenesis & Treatment. 284p. 1993. 162.75 (0-444-89521-3) Elsevier.

*Morrow, Will, ed. Northern Justice: The Memoirs of Justice William G. Morrow. 184p. (C). 1995. 35.00 (0-8020-0788-0) U of Toronto Pr.

*Morrow, William S. Scribing the Center: Organization & Redaction in Deuteronomy 14:1-17:13. (Society of Biblical Literature Ser.: No. 49). 1995. write for info. (0-7885-0064-3) Scholars Pr GA.

Morrs, Hein & Palomba, Rossella, eds. Population, Family, & Welfare, Vol. 1. 250p. 1995. 45.00 (0-19-828846-8) OUP.

Mors, A. & Williams, J. Americans at School. (American Background Readers Ser.). (YA). 1991. pap. text ed. 5.25 (0-582-01714-9) Longman.

Mors, Walter B. & Rizzini, Carlos T. Useful Plants of Brazil. LC 66-17891. 181p. reprint ed. pap. 51.60 (0-317-28317-0, 2016293) Bks Demand.

Mors, Walter B., et al. Medicinal Plants of Brazil. DeFilipps, Robert A., ed. (Medicinal Plants of the World Ser.: No. 6). (Illus.). 1996. 39.95 (0-917256-42-5) Ref Pubns.

Mors, Walter P. Consumer Credit Finance Charges: Rate Information & Quotation. (Financial Research Program II: Studies in Consumer Installment Financing: No. 12). 150p. 1965. 39.30 (0-87014-128-7) Natl Bur Econ Res.

Morsbach, Helmut. Simple Etiquette in Japan. 1988. pap. 20.00 (0-904404-46-3, Pub. by P Norbury Pubns Ltd UK) St Mut.

Morsbach, Helmut & Kurebayashe, Kazue, eds. Essential Japanese. 256p. 1990. pap. 8.95 (0-14-010188-8, Penguin Bks) Viking Penguin.

Morsbach, Helmut & Stach, Babett, eds. Posters of GDR Films, 1945-1990. (Film-Television-Sound Archive Ser.: Vol. 2). 149p. 1991. lib. bdg. 60.00 (3-598-22591-1) K G Saur.

Morsbach, Helmut, jt. ed. see Stack, Babett.

Morsbach, Helmut, et al. Remembering the Katakana. 96p. 1990. Incl. suppl. "Learning How to Remember". pap. 7.00 (0-87040-860-7) Japan Pubns USA.

Morsberger, Robert & Lesser, Stephen, eds. American Screenwriters, Vol. 26. (Dictionary of Literary Biography Ser.: Vol. 26). (Illus.). 400p. 1984. 128.00 (0-8103-0917-3) Gale.

Morsberger, Robert E. James Thurber. (United States Authors Ser.). 232p. 1964. text ed. 21.95 (0-8057-0728-X, 62, Pub. by Royal Botanic Garden UK) Macmillan.

Morsch, Gary & Hall, Eddy. Ministry: It's Not Just for Ministers. 127p. (Orig.). 1993. pap. 6.95 (0-8341-1510-7) Beacon Hill.

Morsch, Gary, jt. auth. see Hall, Eddy.

Morsch, Lucille M. Historical Records Survey: Check List of New Jersey Imprints, 1784-1800. 1939. 16.00 (0-527-01906-2) Periodicals Srv.

Morschauser, Joseph, III, jt. auth. see Becton, F. Julian.

Morschauser, Scott. Threat-Formulae in Ancient Egypt. xvi, 268p. (Orig.). 1991. pap. 72.00 (0-9613805-5-1) Halgo Inc.

Morschauser, Scott, jt. ed. see Kort, Ann.

*Morse. Into the Storm. (Loveswept Ser.: No. 745). 1995. mass mkt. (0-553-44509-X, Loveswept) Bantam.

— Nursing Research. 208p. 1995. pap. 37.95 (1-56593-586-1, 1194) Singular Publishing.

— Parting Visions. 1995. mass mkt. 5.99 (0-8041-1366-1) Ivy Books.

Morse, jt. auth. see Dyckman, Thomas R.

Morse, jt. auth. see Tse.

Morse, A. Genealogical Register of Several Ancient Puritans, Vol. 2. 228p. 1988. reprint ed. lib. bdg. 46.00 (0-8328-0318-9); reprint ed. pap. 38.00 (0-8328-0319-7) Higginson Bk Co.

Morse, A. P. A Theory of Sets: Monographs. 2nd ed. (Pure & Applied Mathematics Ser.). 1986. text ed. 91.00 (0-12-507952-4) Acad Pr.

Morse, A. Reynolds. Lewd Limericks & Worse Verse. Aman, Reinhold A., ed. Date not set. pap. 15.00 (0-916500-10-1) Maledicta.

— The Quest for Redonda. (Illus.). 160p. 1986. pap. 10.00 (0-317-39306-5) Reynolds Morse.

— The Works of M. P. Shiel, 2 vols., Vol. 2, Pts. 1 & 2. rev. ed. Orig. Title: Works of M. P. Shiel, a Study in Bibliography 1948. (Illus.). 864p. 1980. 90.00 (0-686-62335-5); pap. 65.00 (0-686-62336-3); 75.00 (0-685-04347-9) Reynolds Morse.

Morse, Abner. Genealogical Register of the Inhabitants & History of the Town of Sherborn & Hollister, Ma. (Illus.). 340p. 1993. reprint ed. lib. bdg. 39.00 (0-8328-2889-0) Higginson Bk Co.

Morse, Albert L. The Tattooists. Walsh, John A., ed. (Illus.). 1977. 79.95 (0-918320-01-1) A L Morse.

*Morse, Ann. America's Newcomers: Employment & Training Programs for Refugees & Immigrants. 18p. 1993. 10.00 (1-55516-927-9, 9360) Natl Conf State Legis.

*Morse, Ann, ed. America's Newcomers: An Immigrant Policy Handbook. 108p. 1994. 35.00 (1-55516-996-1, 9366) Natl Conf State Legis.

*Morse, Ann & Dunlap, Jonathan C. America's Newcomers: Community Relations & Ethnic Diversity. 20p. 1994. 10.00 (1-55516-995-3, 9365) Natl Conf State Legis.

Morse, Anthony P., jt. auth. see Kenyon, Hewitt.

Morse, Arthur D. While Six Millon Died: A Chronicle of American Apathy. LC 82-22291. 432p. 1985. 22.95 (0-87951-174-5); pap. 9.95 (0-87951-973-8) Overlook Pr.

Morse, B. William, jt. auth. see Drew, Shirley.

Morse, Barbara, jt. auth. see Goodman, Harriet W.

Morse-Boycott, Desmond L. Lead, Kindly Light. LC 70-107728. (Essay Index Reprint Ser.). 1977. 18.95 (0-8369-1529-1) Ayer.

Morse, C. G. Torts in Private International Law. LC 78-5881. (Problems in Private International Law Ser.: Vol. 2). 412p. 1979. 100.00 (0-444-85168-2, North Holland) Elsevier.

Morse, C. G., jt. auth. see Rubino-Sammartano, M.

Morse, C. Wesley. Environmental Consultation. LC 83-24802. 208p. 1984. text ed. 55.00 (0-275-91233-7, C1233, Praeger Pubs) Greenwood.

Morse, Carl & Larkin, Joan, eds. Gay & Lesbian Poetry in Our Time. (Stonewall Inn Editions Ser.). 432p. 1989. pap. 14.95 (0-312-03836-4) St Martin.

— Gay & Lesbian Poetry in Our Time: An Anthology. 448p. 1988. 29.95 (0-312-02213-1) St Martin.

Morse, Carlton E. Killer at the Wheel. 400p. 1987. 16.95 (0-940249-01-4) Seven Stones Pr.

— A Lavish of Sin. 224p. 1987. 14.95 (0-940249-02-2) Seven Stones Pr.

— One Man's Family Album. (Illus.). 160p. (Orig.). 1988. pap. 8.95 (0-940249-05-7) Seven Stones Pr.

— Stuff the Lady's Hatbox. (I Love a Mystery Novel Ser.). 342p. (Orig.). 1988. 16.95 (0-940249-03-0); pap. 9.95 (0-940249-04-9) Seven Stones Pr.

Morse, Carmel L. Audio-Visual Primer. LC 82-84727. (Illus.). 75p. (Orig.). 1983. pap. 5.95 (0-911997-00-8) Backwoods Pubns.

Morse, Chandler, jt. auth. see Barnett, Harold J.

Morse, Chandler, ed. see Copeland, Morris A.

Morse, Charlotte C., et al, eds. Uses of Manuscripts in Literary Studies: Essays in Memory of Judson Boyce Allen. (Studies in Medieval Culture: No. 31). 1992. pap. 15.00 (1-879288-14-1); boxed 35.00 (1-879288-13-3) Medieval Inst.

Morse, Christopher. Not Every Spirit: A Dogmatics of Christian Disbelief. LC 93-45865. 432p. (C). 1994. 40.00 (1-56338-086-2); pap. 22.00 (1-56338-087-0) TPI PA.

Morse-Cluley, Elizabeth & Read, Richard. Webster's New World Power Vocabulary. 2nd ed. LC 93-47434. (Orig.). 1994. pap. 10.00 (0-671-88821-8) P-H Gen Ref & Trav.

Morse, Constance. Music & Music-Makers. LC 68-54363. (Essay Index Reprint Ser.). 1977. 22.95 (0-8369-0724-8) Ayer.

Morse, D., et al, eds. Guide to Prosthetic Cardiac Valves. (Illus.). xvi, 362p. 1985. 164.00 (0-387-96123-2) Spr-Verlag.

Morse, D. R. & Pollack, R. L. The Stress-Free, Anti-Aging Diet. (Stress in Modern Society Ser.: No. 19). 1989. 32.50 (0-404-63270-X) AMS Pr.

Morse, Dan F. The Steuben Village & Mounds: A Multicomponent Late Hopewell Site in Illinois. LC 64-7124. (Anthropological Papers: No. 21). (Illus.). 176p. reprint ed. 50.20 (0-8357-9613-2, 2011182) Bks Demand.

Morse, Daniel P., Jr. The History of the Fiftieth Aero Squadron. (Great War Ser.: No. 6). (Illus.). 110p. 1990. reprint ed. 27.95 (0-89839-151-2) Battery Pr.

Morse, David. American Romanticism, Vol. 2. LC 85-13424. 144p. 1986. 52.00 (0-389-20587-7, N8145 3) B&N Imports.

— England's Time of Crisis: From Shakespeare to Milton: a Cultural History. LC 88-18292. 320p. 1989. text ed. 45.00 (0-312-02413-4) St Martin.

— High Victorian Culture. LC 92-18942. 568p. (C). 1992. text ed. 60.00 (0-8147-5487-2) NYU Pr.

— High Victorian Culture. LC 92-18942. 1994. pap. 20.00 (0-8147-5504-6) NYU Pr.

— Perspectives on Romanticism: A Transformational Analysis. 324p. 1981. 45.00 (0-389-20164-2, N6934) B&N Imports.

Morse, Dean. The Peripheral Worker. LC 73-76251. 222p. reprint ed. pap. 63.30 (0-318-34935-3, 2030717) Bks Demand.

Morse, Dean & Gray, Susan. Early Retirement: Boon or Bane?, a Study of Three Large Corporations. LC 79-54970. (Conservation of Human Resources Ser.: No. 14). (Illus.). 154p. 1981. text ed. 38.50 (0-916672-44-1) Rowman.

Morse, Dean W. Pride Against Prejudice: Work in the Lives of Older Blacks & Young Puerto Ricans. LC 78-65534. (Conservation of Human Resources Ser.: No. 9). 254p. 1981. text ed. 38.50 (0-916672-67-0) Rowman.

Morse, Dean W., et al. Life after Early Retirement: The Experiences of Lower Level Workers. LC 81-70970. (Conservation of Human Resources Ser.: Vol. 17). 206p. 1983. text ed. 53.50 (0-916672-62-X) Rowman.

Morse, Deborah D. Women in Trollope's Palliser Novels. McMaster, Juliet, ed. LC 87-21497. (Nineteenth-Century Studies). 174p. 1991. 39.00 (0-8357-1847-6) Univ Rochester Pr.

Morse, Don. Deadly Reaction. Bettendorf, Joan, ed. 306p. 1990. 17.95 (1-878869-00-0) Cryptic Pr.

— Eye to Eye. Bettendorf, Joan, ed. 1991. 19.95 (1-878869-01-9) Cryptic Pr.

Morse, Donald E. Kurt Vonnegut. LC 93-201941. (Starmont Reader's Guide Ser.: Vol. 61). iv, 128p. (Orig.). 1992. lib. bdg. 27.00x (1-55742-219-2); pap. 17.00x (1-55742-220-6) Borgo Pr.

Morse, Donald E., ed. The Fantastic in World Literature & the Arts: Selected Essays from the Fifth International Conference on the Fantastic in the Arts. LC 87-7424. (Contributions to the Study of Science Fiction & Fantasy Ser.: No. 28). 272p. 1987. text ed. 65.00 (0-313-25526-1, MFA/) Greenwood.

Morse, Donald E. & Csilla, Bertha, eds. More Real Than Reality: The Fantastic in Irish Literature & the Arts. LC 90-47537. (Contributions to the Study of Science Fiction & Fantasy Ser.: No. 45). 288p. 1991. text ed. 55.00 (0-313-26612-3, MFM/, Greenwood Pr) Greenwood.

Morse, Donald E., et al, eds. The Celebration of the Fantastic: Selected Papers from the Tenth Anniversary International Conference on the Fantastic in the Arts. LC 91-37133. (Contributions to the Study of Science Fiction & Fantasy Ser.: No. 49). 328p. 1992. text ed. 59.95 (0-313-27814-8, MFO/, Greenwood Pr) Greenwood.

— A Small Nation's Contribution to the World: Essays on Anglo-Irish Literature & Language. (Irish Literary Studies Ser.). 250p. (C). 1994. lib. bdg. 55.00 (0-86140-375-4, Pub. by C Smythe Ltd UK) B&N Imports.

Morse, Donald R. & Pollack, Robert L. Nutrition, Stress & Aging: An Holistic Approach. LC 87-45805. (Stress in Modern Society Ser.: No. 17). 1988. 32.50 (0-404-63268-8) AMS Pr.

Morse, Douglass H. American Warblers: An Ecological & Behavioral Perspective. LC 89-31622. (Illus.). 424p. 1989. 42.50 (0-674-03035-4) HUP.

— Behavioral Mechanisms in Ecology. LC 80-12130. 391p. 1980. 40.00 (0-674-06460-7) HUP.

— Behavioral Mechanisms in Ecology. LC 80-12130. 391p. 1982. pap. 16.95 (0-674-06461-5) HUP.

Morse, Dryden, et al. A Guide to Cardiac Pacemakers. LC 82-7302. (Illus.). 544p. (C). 1983. text ed. 90.00 (0-8036-6323-4) Davis Co.

— A Guide to Cardiac Pacemakers. 3rd ed. (Illus.). 1000p. 1991. pap. write for info. (1-879976-01-3); ring bd. 179.00 (1-879976-00-5); disk 229.00 (1-879976-02-1) Droege Computing.

— A Guide to Cardiac Pacemakers: Supplement, 1986-1987. LC 85-31126. (Illus.). 207p. 1986. text ed. 50.00 (0-8036-6326-9) Davis Co.

Morse, Edgar & Curran, Thomas, eds. Silver in the Golden State: Images & Essays Celebrating the History & Art of Silver in California. (Artisans & the Arts Ser.). (Illus.). 130p. 1986. lib. bdg. 43.00 (0-8026-0021-2) Univ Pub Assocs.

Morse, Edward L. Foreign Policy & Interdependence in Gaullist France. LC 72-5391. (Center of International Studies). 388p. 1973. 52.50 (0-691-05209-3) Princeton U Pr.

— Foreign Policy & Interdependence in Gaullist France. LC 72-5391. Date not set. reprint ed. pap. 100.10 (0-7837-9395-2, 2060140) Bks Demand.

Morse, Edward L., ed. see Morse, Samuel F.

Morse, Edward S. Catalogue of the Morse Collection of Japanese Pottery. LC 77-83037. (Illus.). 544p. 1979. reprint ed. boxed 60.00 (0-8048-1299-3) C E Tuttle.

— Glimpses of China & Chinese Homes. (Illus.). 216p. 1993. reprint ed. lib. bdg. 35.00 (0-8328-3102-6) Higginson Bk Co.

— Japan, Day by Day. LC 90-47731. (Illus.). 908p. 1990. reprint ed. 39.95 (0-87797-190-0) Cherokee.

— Japanese Homes & Their Surroundings. LC 76-157262. (Illus.). 408p. 1971. reprint ed. pap. 16.95 (0-8048-0998-4) C E Tuttle.

An Asterisk (*) at the beginning of an entry indicates that the title is appearing in BIP for the first time.

— Japanese Homes & Their Surroundings. (Illus.). 1961. reprint ed. pap. 8.95 (*0-486-20746-3*) Dover.

Morse, Elenir. A Quest of Existence. LC 89-81908. 1991. 7.95 (*0-8158-0458-X*) Chris Mass.

Morse, Elisabeth, jt. ed. see Hollingsworth, Dorothy.

Morse, Eric. Freshwater Saga. 180p. 1987. pap. 9.95 (*0-942802-55-1*) NorthWord.

— Friday the Thirteenth: Jason's Curse. (Tales from Camp Crystal Lake Ser.: Bk. 2). 192p. (Orig.). (YA). 1994. pap. text ed. 3.99 (*0-425-14339-2*) Berkley Pub.

— Friday the Thirteenth: Mother's Day. (Tales from Camp Crystal Lake Ser.: Bk. 1). 192p. (Orig.). (YA). 1994. pap. text ed. 3.50 (*0-425-14292-2*) Berkley Pub.

— Friday the Thirteenth: The Carnival. (Tales from Camp Crystal Lake Ser.: Bk. 3). 192p. (Orig.). (J). 1994. pap. text ed. 3.99 (*0-425-15825-X*) Berkley Pub.

— Friday the 13th: Tales from Camp Crystal Lake Bk. 4: Road Trip. 192p. (Orig.). (YA). (gr. 7 up). 1994. pap. text ed. 3.50 (*0-425-14383-X*) Berkley Pub.

Morse, Eric W. Fur Trade Canoe Routes of Canada: Then & Now. rev. ed. (Illus.). 1979. pap. 12.95 (*0-8020-6384-5*) U of Toronto Pr.

— Fur Trade Canoe Routes of Canada: Then & Now. 2nd ed. LC 80-478235. (Canadian University Paperbooks Ser.: 239). 136p. reprint ed. pap. 38.80 (*0-317-28761-3*, 2055477) Bks Demand.

Morse, Flo. The Shakers & the World's People. LC 87-8223. (Illus.). 399p. 1987. pap. 18.95 (*0-87451-426-6*) U Pr of New Eng.

— The Story of the Shakers. LC 85-31430. (Illus.). 128p. 1986. pap. 8.00 (*0-88150-062-3*) Countryman.

Morse, G. Company Law, Charlesworth. (C). 1987. 100.00 (*0-685-33727-8*, Pub. by Witherby & Co UK) St Mut.

Morse, Geoffrey. Partnership Law. 200p. (C). 1991. 32.00 (*1-85431-115-8*, Pub. by Blackstone Pr UK) W W Gaunt.

Morse, Geoffrey, jt. auth. see Whittaker, Andrew M.

***Morse, George P.** America Twice Betrayed: Reversing Fifty Years of Government Security Failure. LC 95-14067. 400p. 1995. 23.50 (*0-910155-32-1*) Bartleby Pr.

Morse, Gladys K. A Potpourri of Pleasantries. (Illus.). 64p. (Orig.). 1993. pap. 6.00 (*0-945069-01-4*) Freedom Pr Assocs.

Morse, H. K. Elizabethan Pageantry. LC 68-56511. (Illus.). 1972. reprint ed. 27.95 (*0-405-08798-5*, Pub. by Blom Pubns UK) Ayer.

***Morse, H. Newcomb.** The Thinkers. 270p. (C). 1994. lib. bdg. 48.00 (*0-8191-9666-5*) U Pr of Amer.

Morse, Harriet. Gardening in the Shade. LC 81-23231. (Illus.). 242p. 1962. pap. 13.95 (*0-917304-16-0*) Timber.

Morse, Harry N. Graphic Description of Pacific Coast Outlaws. (Great West & Indian Ser.: Vol. 11). (Illus.). 1990. 23.95 (*0-87026-074-X*) Westernlore.

Morse, Howard H. & Kelly, Arthur C. Historic Old Rhinebeck, Echoes of Two Centuries: A Hudson River & Post Road Colonial Town. (Illus.). 509p. 1977. reprint ed. lib. bdg. 21.00 (*1-56012-035-5*) Kinship Rhinebeck.

Morse, J. G., ed. Industry-University Advanced Materials Conference: Proceedings of a Conference. LC 87-1716. (Illus.). 410p. reprint ed. pap. 116.90 (*0-685-23388-X*, 2032590) Bks Demand.

Morse, J. H. & Leavitt, Emily W. Morse Genealogy, Being a Revision of the Memorial of the Morse Publication by Abner Morse in 1850, 2 vols. in 1. 596p. 1989. reprint ed. lib. bdg. 98.00 (*0-8328-0884-9*); reprint ed. pap. 90.00 (*0-8328-0885-7*) Higginson Bk Co.

Morse, J. M., ed. Cross-Cultural Nursing: Anthropological Approaches to Nursing. vi, 144p. 1989. pap. text ed. 21.00 (*2-88124-383-5*) Gordon & Breach.

Morse, J. N., ed. Organizations: Multiple Agents with Multiple Criteria, Newark, 1980. Proceedings. (Lecture Notes in Economics & Mathematical Systems Ser.: Vol. 190). (Illus.). 509p. 1981. pap. 55.50 (*0-387-10821-1*) Spr-Verlag.

***Morse, J. Stephen.** Practical Parallel Computing. LC 94-32053. (Illus.). 401p. 1994. pap. 39.95 (*0-12-508160-X*, AP Prof) Acad Pr.

Morse, J. Thomas, ed. see Gouge, Betty, et al.

Morse, J. Thomas, et al. KidSkills Interpersonal Skill Series, A Lasting Friend: Friendship: Making Friends. Gouge, Betty et al, eds. LC 85-45422. (Illus.). 45p. (J). (gr. 2-3). 1985. lib. bdg. 9.95 (*0-934275-06-8*); audio 13.95 (*0-934275-20-3*) Fam Skills.

— KidSkills Interpersonal Skill Series, An Island Adventure: Self-Esteem: Being a Friend to Myself. Gouge, Betty et al, eds. LC 85-47429. (Illus.). 47p. (J). (gr. 2-3). 1985. lib. bdg. 9.95 (*0-934275-01-7*); audio 13.95 (*0-934275-14-9*) Fam Skills.

— KidSkills Interpersonal Skill Series, Lair of the Jade Tiger: Friendship: Keeping Friends. Gouge, Betty et al, eds. LC 85-81270. (Illus.). 48p. (J). (gr. 2-3). 1986. lib. bdg. 9.95 (*0-934275-07-6*); audio 13.95 (*0-934275-21-1*) Fam Skills.

— KidSkills Interpersonal Skill Series, The Feeling Fun House: Feelings: Dealing with Feelings. Gouge, Betty et al, eds. LC 85-45423. (Illus.). 45p. (J). (gr. 2-3). 1985. lib. bdg. 9.95 (*0-934275-03-3*); audio 13.95 (*0-934275-17-3*) Fam Skills.

— KidSkills Interpersonal Skill Series, The Land of Listening: Listening: Getting & Giving Attention. Gouge, Betty et al, eds. LC 85-45429. (Illus.). 45p. (J). (gr. 2-3). 1985. lib. bdg. 9.95 (*0-934275-00-9*); audio 13.95 (*0-934275-15-7*) Fam Skills.

Morse, J. W. & Mackenzie, Fred T., eds. Geochemistry & Sedimentary Carbonates: Developments in Sedimentology, No. 48. 696p. 1990. 113.00 (*0-444-87391-0*); pap. 56.50 (*0-444-88781-4*) Elsevier.

Morse, James K. Jedidiah Morse: A Champion of New England Orthodoxy. LC 39-11247. reprint ed. 20.00 (*0-404-04504-9*) AMS Pr.

Morse, James S., ed. see Germroth, David S. & Hudson, Rebecca J.

Morse, Jane C., ed. Beatrix Potter's Americans: Selected Letters. LC 81-7258. (Illus.). 232p. 1982. 35.95 (*0-87675-282-2*) Horn Bk.

Morse, Janice M., ed. Critical Issues in Qualitative Research Methods. (C). 1993. text ed. 55.00 (*0-8039-5042-X*); pap. text ed. 26.00 (*0-8039-5043-8*) Sage.

— Qualitative Health Research. (Illus.). 272p. (C). 1992. 55.00 (*0-8039-4774-7*); pap. 26.00 (*0-8039-4775-5*) Sage.

— Qualitative Nursing Research: A Contemporary Dialogue. rev. ed. (Illus.). 360p. (C). 1990. text ed. 49.95 (*0-8039-4078-5*); pap. text ed. 24.00 (*0-8039-4079-3*) Sage.

***Morse, Janice M. & Field, Peggy A.** Qualitative Research Methods. 2nd ed. (Illus.). 304p. 1995. 46.00 (*0-8039-7326-8*) Sage.

— Qualitative Research Methods. 2nd ed. (Illus.). 304p. 1995. pap. 22.95 (*0-8039-7327-6*) Sage.

Morse, Janice M. & Johnson, Joy L., eds. The Illness Experience: Expressions of Suffering. (Illus.). 320p. 1991. 44.00 (*0-8039-4053-X*); pap. 21.50 (*0-8039-4054-8*) Sage.

Morse, Jedidiah. American Gazetteer. LC 71-146409. (First American Frontier Ser.). (Illus.). 1971. reprint ed. 52.95 (*0-405-02871-7*) Ayer.

— American Gazetteer, 1797. 629p. 1979. 23.20 (*0-686-27821-6*) Bookmark.

— American Geography: Or, a View of the Present Situation of the United States of America. LC 70-125754. (American Environmental Studies). 1976. reprint ed. 33.95 (*0-405-02680-3*) Ayer.

— Annals of the American Revolution. 1971. 59.95 (*0-87968-640-5*) Gordon Pr.

— Annals of the American Revolution. LC 87-50059. 1987. reprint ed. pap. 19.95 (*0-940561-05-0*) White Rose Pr.

— A Report to the Secretary of War of the U. S. on Indian Affairs. LC 70-108516. (Illus.). 400p. 1972. reprint ed. 69.00 (*0-403-00345-8*) Scholarly.

— Report to the Secretary of War of the United States on Indian Affairs: Comprising a Narrative of a Tour Performed in the Summer of 1820. LC 68-27675. (Illus.). 400p. 1970. reprint ed. 49.50 (*0-678-00548-6*) Kelley.

***Morse, Jeremy.** Chess Problems. (Orig.). 1995. pap. 29.95 (*0-571-15363-1*) Faber & Faber.

Morse, Jerome G. Nuclear Methods in Mineral Exploration & Production. (Developments in Economic Geology Ser.: Vol. 7). 280p. 1977. 92.50 (*0-444-41567-X*) Elsevier.

Morse, Jerome G. & Olerud, Lesley A. Industry-University Advanced Materials Conference Two, 1989: Proceedings. (Illus.). 888p. 1989. pap. text ed. 25.00 (*0-9624027-0-2*) Advan Mat Inst.

Morse, Jim. Big Band Era. Skogen, Kirsten, ed. (Illus.). 120p. (Orig.). 1992. 5.95 (*1-881550-00-1*) Hiawatha Pubs.

Morse, John C., ed. Trichoptera, Fourth International Symposium: Proceedings: Clemson, South Carolina, 11-16 July 1983. (Entomologica Ser.: No. 30). 512p. 1984. lib. bdg. 170.00 (*90-6193-003-0*) Kluwer Ac.

Morse, John T., Jr. Abraham Lincoln, 2 Vols, Set. LC 73-128958. (American Statesmen Ser.: Nos. 25, 26). reprint ed. 95.00 (*0-404-50892-8*) AMS Pr.

— American Statesmen, 40 vols. Incl. First Series, 31 vols. (*0-318-50521-5*); Second Series, 9 vols. (*0-318-50522-3*); reprint ed. 1,873.00 (*0-404-50850-2*) AMS Pr.

— Benjamin Franklin. LC 74-128926. (American Statesmen Ser.: No. 1). reprint ed. 49.50 (*0-404-50851-0*) AMS Pr.

— Famous Trials: The Tichborne Claimant, Troppmann, Prince Pierre Bonaparte, Mrs. Wharton, the Meteor, Mrs. Fair. v, 342p. 1992. reprint ed. 37.50 (*0-8377-2444-9*) Rothman.

— John Adams. LC 79-128970. (American Statesmen Ser.: No. 6). reprint ed. 45.00 (*0-404-50856-1*) AMS Pr.

— John Quincy Adams. LC 77-128967. (American Statesmen Ser.: No. 15). reprint ed. 45.00 (*0-404-50866-9*) AMS Pr.

— Thomas Jefferson. LC 77-128975. (American Statesmen Ser.: No. 11). reprint ed. 45.00 (*0-404-50861-8*) AMS Pr.

***Morse, John T., Jr., intro.** Diary of Gideon Welles, Secretary of the Navy under Lincoln & Johnson Vol. I: 1861 to 1864. (Illus.). 549p. 1995. reprint ed. lib. bdg. 62.50 (*0-8328-4501-9*) Higginson Bk Co.

— Diary of Gideon Welles, Secretary of the Navy under Lincoln & Johnson Vol. II: 1864 to 1866. (Illus.). 653p. 1995. reprint ed. lib. bdg. 72.50 (*0-8328-4500-0*) Higginson Bk Co.

— Diary of Gideon Welles, Secretary of the Navy under Lincoln & Johnson Vol. III: 1867 to 1869. (Illus.). 671p. 1995. reprint ed. lib. bdg. 75.00 (*0-8328-4499-3*) Higginson Bk Co.

Morse, John T., Jr., ed. see Adams, Charles F.

Morse, John T., Jr., ed. see Adams, Henry.

Morse, John T., Jr., ed. see Burton, Theodore E.

Morse, John T., Jr., ed. see Coolidge, Louis A.

Morse, John T., ed. see Gay, Sydney H.

Morse, John T., Jr., ed. see Gilman, Daniel C.

Morse, John T., Jr., ed. see Hart, Albert B.

Morse, John T., Jr., ed. see Hosmer, James K.

Morse, John T., Jr., ed. see Lodge, Henry C.

Morse, John T., Jr., ed. see Lothrop, Thorton K.

Morse, John T., Jr., ed. see Magruder, Allan B.

Morse, John T., Jr., ed. see McCall, Samuel W.

Morse, John T., Jr., ed. see McLaughlin, Andrew C.

Morse, John T., Jr., ed. see Pellew, George.

Morse, John T., Jr., ed. see Roosevelt, Theodore.

Morse, John T., Jr., ed. see Schurz, Carl.

Morse, John T., Jr., ed. see Shepard, Edward M.

Morse, John T., Jr., ed. see Smith, Theodore C.

Morse, John T., Jr., ed. see Stanwood, Edward.

Morse, John T., Jr., ed. see Stevens, John A.

Morse, John T., Jr., ed. see Storey, Moorfield.

Morse, John T., Jr., ed. see Sumner, William G.

Morse, John T., Jr., ed. see Thayer, William R.

Morse, John T., Jr., ed. see Tyler, Moses C.

Morse, John T., Jr., ed. see Von Holst, Hermann E.

Morse, Johnathan. Word by Word: The Language of Memory. LC 89-23931. (Illus.). 272p. 1990. 29.95 (*0-8014-2383-X*) Cornell U Pr.

Morse, Joyce S., jt. ed. see Roth, Shirley P.

Morse, Kendall. Stories Told in the Kitchen. LC 81-8775. (Illus.). 95p. (Orig.). 1981. pap. 4.95 (*0-945980-19-1*) Nrth Country Pr.

Morse, Kenneth I. Listen to the Sunrise: Hymns & Prayers. 96p. (Orig.). 1991. pap. 9.95 (*0-87178-527-7*) Brethren.

Morse, Kitty. The California Farm Cookbook. LC 93-14992. (Illus.). 208p. 1993. 26.95 (*0-88289-911-2*) Pelican.

— Edible Flowers: A Kitchen Companion. 64p. 1995. 9.95 (*0-89815-754-4*) Ten Speed Pr.

— Three Hundred Sixty-Five Ways to Cook Vegetarian. 288p. 1994. 17.95 (*0-06-016958-3*, HarpT) HarpC.

Morse, L. A. Video Trash & Treasures, 2 vols., Vol. I. 370p. (Orig.). 1992. mass mkt. 5.95 (*0-00-215439-0*, Pub. by HarpC CN) HarpC.

— Video Trash & Treasures, 2 vols., Vol. II. 402p. (Orig.). 1992. mass mkt. 5.95 (*0-00-637635-5*, Pub. by HarpC CN) HarpC.

Morse, L. A., jt. auth. see Yorio, Carlos A.

Morse, L. E. & Henifin, M. S., eds. Rare Plant Conservation: Geographic Data Organization. LC 80-19361. 377p. 1981. pap. 25.00 (*0-89327-223-X*) NY Botanical.

Morse, Laurie, jt. auth. see Greising, David.

Morse, Lawrence. Writing the Economics Paper. 1981. pap. text ed. 6.95 (*0-8120-2113-4*) Barron.

Morse, Lawrence B. Statistics for Business & Economics. (C). 1992. 68.50 (*0-06-044617-X*) HarpCollege.

— Statistics for Business & Economics: Back to Basics, 3.5 IBM. (C). 1993. 5.50 (*0-06-501661-0*) HarpCollege.

— Statistics for Business & Economics: Stat Workbook. (C). 1994. 15.50 (*0-06-501762-5*) HarpCollege.

Morse, Leon W. Practical Handbook of Industrial Traffic Management. 6th ed. LC 77-9240. 532p. 1980. text ed. 32.50 (*0-87408-020-7*) Intl Thom Trans Pr.

Morse, Linda, jt. auth. see LaForge, Carol.

Morse, Linda A., jt. auth. see Graver, Carl M.

Morse, M., et al, eds. The Banks & the Public. (C). 1989. 40.00 (*0-85297-060-9*, Pub. by Inst Bankers UK) St Mut.

Morse, Marcia, illus. The Eight Rainbows of 'Umi, Ku'ulei Ihara & 'Iliahi Johnson. 1976. pap. 2.95 (*0-914916-14-9*) Ku Paa.

Morse, Margaret, ed. see Junior League of Elmira, Inc. Staff.

Morse, Marjorie J. Selected Papers. (Illus.). 882p. 1981. 94.00 (*0-387-90532-4*) Spr-Verlag.

Morse, Marston. The Calculus of Variations in the Large. 8th ed. LC 34-40909. (Colloquium Publications: Vol. 18). 368p. 1990. reprint ed. pap. 55.00 (*0-8218-1018-9*, COLL-18) Am Math.

— Global Variational Analysis: Weierstrass Integrals on a Riemannian Manifold. LC 76-836. (Mathematical Notes Ser.: No. 16). 264p. 1976. pap. 39.50 (*0-691-08181-6*) Princeton U Pr.

— Topological Methods in the Theory of Functions of a Complex Variable. (Annals of Mathematics Studies). 1947. 15.00 (*0-527-02731-6*) Periodicals Srv.

— Variational Analysis: Critical Extremals & Sturmian Extensions. LC 72-8368. (Pure & Applied Mathematics Ser.). 272p. reprint ed. 77.60 (*0-8357-9998-0*, 2019523) Bks Demand.

***Morse, Mary.** Women Changing Science: Voices from a Field in Transition. 305p. 1995. 27.95 (*0-306-45081-X*, Plenum Pr) Plenum.

Morse, Mary, ed. see Kincher, Jonni.

Morse, Melvin. Closer to the Light: Learning from Near Death Experiences of Children. 1991. mass mkt. 5.99 (*0-8041-0832-3*) Ivy Books.

— Parting Visions: Pre-Death Visions & Spiritual Experiences. 1994. 20.00 (*0-679-42754-6*, Villard Bks) Random.

Morse, Melvin & Perry, Paul. Transformed by the Light: The Powerful Effect of Near-Death Experiences on People's Lives. 1994. reprint ed. mass mkt. 5.99 (*0-8041-1183-9*) Ivy Books.

Morse, Melvin L. Transformed by the Light: A Study of the Powerful Effect of Near Death Experiences on Peoples. 1992. 19.50 (*0-679-40443-0*, Villard Bks) Random.

Morse, Melvin L. & Perry, Paul J. Closer to the Light: Learning from the Near-Death Experiences of Children. large type ed. (General Ser.). 293p. 1991. text ed. 20.95 (*0-8161-5183-0*, Large Print Bks) Hall.

Morse, Merrill. The Ministry to the Single Person. 56p. 1988. pap. text ed. 1.95 (*0-8146-1586-4*) Liturgical Pr.

— Psalms for Troubled Times. 192p. (Orig.). 1991. pap. 6.95 (*0-8146-1968-1*) Liturgical Pr.

Morse, Michael. Build a Doll's House. LC 93-25460. 1993. reprint ed. 19.95 (*0-89024-188-0*) Kalmbach.

Morse, Michael J., jt. auth. see Rynecki, Steven B.

Morse, Michael L., jt. auth. see Montell, William L.

***Morse, Michael.** Furnish a Doll's House. (Illus.). 112p. 1995. pap. 19.95 (*0-89024-259-3*, 12155) Kalmbach.

Morse, Miranda. Mailmerge Without Hassles. 42p. (Orig.). 1986. pap. 6.95 (*0-930545-04-4*) Maple Hill Pr.

— WordStar in Three Days & What to Do When Things Go Wrong. 218p. 1984. pap. 14.95 (*0-930545-02-8*) Maple Hill Pr.

Morse, Miranda & Fleck, Christopher. PageMaker 4 with Ease: Step-by-Step Learning, Problem-Solving & Upgraders' Reference (PC & MacIntosh) 302p. (Orig.). 1991. pap. 19.95 (*0-930545-12-5*) Maple Hill Pr.

Morse, Nancy. Echoes. 224p. (Orig.). 1992. pap. 2.95 (*1-878702-83-1*, Kismet) Meteor Pub.

— The Mom Who Came to Stay. 1995. pap. 3.75 (*0-373-07683-5*, 1-07683-5) Silhouette.

Morse, Nancy C. Satisfactions in White-Collar Job. Stein, Leon, ed. LC 77-70518. (Work Ser.). (Illus.). 1977. reprint ed. lib. bdg. 23.95 (*0-405-10187-2*) Ayer.

Morse, Peggy. The Stillman Curse. 224p. (Orig.). 1992. pap. 2.95 (*1-56597-012-8*, Kismet) Meteor Pub.

Morse, Peter. Hokusai: One Hundred Poets. LC 88-25175. (Illus.). 222p. 1989. 80.00 (*0-8076-1213-8*) Braziller.

— Illustrated Bartsch, Vol. 2, Part 1 Commentary: Netherlandish Artists - Anthonie Waterloo. (C). 1992. 140.00 (*0-89835-101-4*) Abaris Bks.

— Jean Charlot's Prints: A Catalogue Raisonne. limited ed. (Illus.). 472p. 1976. boxed 175.00 (*0-8248-0474-0*) UH Pr.

— Jean Charlot's Prints: Supplement. (Illus.). 32p. 1983. pap. 5.00 (*0-8248-0874-6*) UH Pr.

Morse, Peter, jt. ed. see Leach, Mark C.

Morse, Peter H. Vitreo-Retinal Disease: A Manual for Diagnosis & Treatment. 2nd ed. 624p. 1989. 99.95 (*0-8151-5963-3*, Yr Bk Med Pubs) Mosby Yr Bk.

Morse, Peter H., jt. ed. see Kanski, Jack J.

Morse, Philip A., ed. see Kenig, J., et al.

Morse, Philip M. In at the Beginnings: A Physicist's Life. LC 76-40010. 1977. 32.50 (*0-262-13124-2*) MIT Pr.

— Thermal Physics. 2nd ed. 432p. (C). 1969. 52.95 (*0-8053-7202-4*, Adv Bk Prog) Addison-Wesley.

— Vibration & Sound. LC 81-68618. 468p. 1981. Prepaid. 25.00 (*0-88318-287-4*); 20.00 (*0-317-03277-1*) Acoustical Soc Am.

Morse, Philip M. & Feshbach, Herman. Methods of Theoretical Physics, 2 Pts, Pt. 1. (International Series in Pure & Applied Physics). (Illus.). 1953. text ed. write for info. (*0-07-043316-X*) McGraw.

— Methods of Theoretical Physics, 2 Pts, Pt. 2. (International Series in Pure & Applied Physics). (Illus.). 1953. pap. text ed. write for info. (*0-07-043317-8*) McGraw.

Morse, Philip M. & Ingard, K. Uno. Theoretical Acoustics. 960p. 1987. pap. text ed. 45.00 (*0-691-02401-4*) Princeton U Pr.

Morse, Philip M. & Kimball, George E. Methods of Operations Research. LC 80-83558. (Illus.). 179p. 1980. reprint ed. 23.95 (*0-932146-03-1*) Peninsula CA.

***Morse, Philip S. & Brand, Lillian B.** Young Children at Home & in School: 212 Educational Activities for Their Parents, Teachers, & Caregivers. 1995. pap. 14.95 (*0-205-15419-0*); pap. 15.95 (*0-205-15420-4*) Allyn.

Morse, Richard L. D. Truth in Savings with Centsible Interest & Morse Rate Tables. iv, 104p. (Orig.). 1992. pap. 11.95 (*1-881331-00-8*) Family Econ Trust.

Morse, Richard M. New World Soundings: Culture & Ideology in the Americas. LC 89-1730. (Studies in Atlantic History & Culture). 320p. 1989. text ed. 46.50x (*0-8018-3376-0*) Johns Hopkins.

Morse, Richard M., ed. Haiti's Future: Views of Twelve Haitian Leaders. LC 87-30533. (Woodrow Wilson Center Perspectives Ser.). (Illus.). 144p. (Orig.). (C). 1988. lib. bdg. 29.25 (*0-943875-06-4*, Johns Hopkins); pap. text ed. 12.00 (*0-943875-03-X*, Johns Hopkins) W Wilson Ctr Pr.

Morse, Richard M. & Hardoy, Jorge E., eds. Rethinking the Latin American City. (Woodrow Wilson Center Press Ser.). 190p. 1992. text ed. 27.50 (*0-943875-43-9*) Johns Hopkins.

Morse, Robert E. Evocation of Virgil in Tolkien's Art. LC 86-71230. 80p. (Orig.). 1986. 19.00 (*0-86516-175-5*); pap. 9.00 (*0-86516-176-3*) Bolchazy-Carducci.

— Fabulae Latinae. 36p. (Orig.). (LAT.). (YA). (gr. 9-12). 1992. spiral bd., pap. 2.50 (*0-939507-42-0*, B729) Amer Classical.

Morse, Robert S. Twenty-Five Mountain Bike Tours in Massachusetts. LC 91-15374. 176p. 1991. pap. 11.00 (*0-88150-191-3*, Backcountry) Countryman.

Morse, Roger & Flottum, Kim, eds. The ABC & XYZ of Bee Culture: An Encyclopedia of Beekeeping. 40th rev. ed. (Illus.). 528p. 1990. 25.00 (*0-936028-01-7*) A I Root.

Morse, Roger A. Making Mead (Honey Wine) History, Recipes, Methods & Equipment. (Illus.). 128p. 1992. reprint ed. pap. text ed. 10.95 (*1-878075-04-7*) Wicwas Pr.

— The New Complete Guide to Beekeeping. (Illus.). 208p. 1994. pap. 15.00 (*0-88150-315-0*) Countryman.

— Raising Queen Honey Bees. 2nd rev. ed. (Illus.). 128p. 1994. pap. text ed. 12.95 (*1-878075-05-5*) Wicwas Pr.

Morse, Ronald A., ed. Japan & the Middle East in Alliance Politics. LC 86-1512. (Illus.). 124p. (Orig.). 1986. pap. text ed. 22.00 (*0-8191-5266-8*) U Pr of Amer.

— Korean Studies in America: Options for the Future. LC 83-13996. 164p. (Orig.). 1983. pap. text ed. 25.00 (*0-8191-3409-0*) U Pr of Amer.

— The Politics of Japan's Energy Strategy. (Research Papers & Policy Studies: No. 3). (Orig.). 1981. pap. 3.50 (*0-912966-45-9*) IEAS.

— Southeast Asian Studies: Options for the Future. Report of a Conference at the Wilson Center March 1984. 192p. (Orig.). 1985. lib. bdg. 55.00 (*0-8191-4317-0*, Woodrow Wilson Schl); pap. text ed. 23.00 (*0-8191-4318-9*, Woodrow Wilson Schl) U Pr of Amer.

— U. S.-Japan Relations: An Agenda for the Future. LC 88-36667. 80p. (Orig.). (C). 1989. lib. bdg. 29.00 (*0-8191-7348-7*); pap. text ed. 15.00 (*0-8191-7349-5*) U Pr of Amer.

Morse, Ronald A., jt. auth. see Coleman, Edwin J.

Morse, Ronald A., et al, eds. Burma: A Study Guide. LC 88-5441. 332p. (C). 1988. text ed. 43.50 (*0-943875-04-8*, Johns Hopkins) W Wilson Ctr Pr.

Morse, Russell A., Jr. Tax Sales Manual 1983-84. (Mining District Record Ser.). 8p. 1983. pap. 25.00 (*0-943714-00-1*) Cmdrs-Rusty's.
— Tax Sales Manual, 1984-85. 32p. 1984. pap. 17.50 (*0-943714-01-X*) Cmdrs-Rusty's.

Morse, Rusty. The Armchair Quarterback's Guide to the Football Cards of the Denver Broncos. (Illus.). 24p. (Orig.). 1986. pap. 3.00 (*0-943714-02-8*) Cmdrs-Rusty's.

Morse, Ruth. Truth & Convention in the Middle Ages: Medieval Rhetoric & Representation. (Illus.). 304p. (C). 1990. 69.95 (*0-521-30211-0*) Cambridge U Pr.

Morse, Ruth & Windeatt, Barry, eds. Chaucer Traditions: Studies in Honour of Derek Brewer. (Illus.). 292p. (C). 1990. 69.95 (*0-521-35247-9*) Cambridge U Pr.

Morse, S. A. Basalts & Phase Diagrams: An Introduction to the Quantitative Use of Phase Diagrams in Igneous Petrology. LC 93-33966. 493p. (C). 1994. text ed. 61.50 (*0-89464-857-8*) Krieger.

Morse, Samuel F. Foreign Conspiracy Against the Liberties of the United States. 1980. lib. bdg. 59.95 (*0-87700-270-3*) Revisionist Pr.
— Foreign Conspiracy Against the Liberties of the United States: The Numbers of Brutus. LC 76-46090. (Anti-Movements in America Ser.). 1977. lib. bdg. 20.95 (*0-405-09963-0*) Ayer.
— Imminent Dangers to the Free Institutions of the United States Through Foreign Immigration & the Present State of the Naturalization Laws. LC 69-18785. (American Immigration Collection Ser., No. 1). 1969. reprint ed. 13.95 (*0-405-00533-4*) Ayer.
— Samuel F. B. Morse: His Letters & Journals, 2 vols, Set. Morse, Edward L., ed. LC 76-75279. (Library of American Art Ser.). (Illus.). 1080p. 1973. reprint ed. lib. bdg. 110.00 (*0-306-71304-7*) Da Capo.

Morse, Sarah, jt. auth. see Cross, David.

Morse, Sidney. Freemasonry in the American Revolution. 134p. 1992. pap. 12.95 (*1-56459-047-X*) Kessinger Pub.

Morse, Sidney H. Selected Writings of Sidney H. Morse. 1977. lib. bdg. 59.95 (*0-8490-2590-7*) Gordon Pr.

Morse, Stearns, ed. Lucy Crawford's History of the White Mountains. LC 66-17763. (Illus.). 260p. 1979. 10.95 (*0-910146-16-0*) AMC Books.

Morse, Stearns A., jt. auth. see Stoiber, Richard E.

Morse, Stephen. Management Skills in Marketing. 224p. 1993. pap. 14.95 (*0-89384-252-4*) Pfeiffer & Co.

Morse, Stephen, jt. auth. see Shapiro, Michael H.

Morse, Stephen A., jt. auth. see Rest, Richard F.

Morse, Stephen S., ed. Emerging Viruses. (Illus.). 352p. 1993. 39.95 (*0-19-507444-0*) OUP.
— Evolutionary Biology of Viruses. LC 93-29820. 368p. 1994. 69.00 (*0-7817-0119-8*) Raven.

Morse, Suzanne W. Renewing Civic Capacity: Preparing Students for Service & Citizenship. Fife, Jonathan D., ed. & frwd. by. LC 89-63528. (ASHE-ERIC Higher Education Report Ser.: No. 8, 1989). 133p. (Orig.). (C). 1990. pap. 15.00 (*0-9623882-7-0*) GWU Schl E&HD.

Morse, Theoda M. & White, Charles. A Genealogical History of the Families of Morrill, Maine. (Illus.). 461p. 1992. reprint ed. lib. bdg. 48.00 (*0-8328-2335-X*) Higginson Bk Co.

Morse, Theodore F. Excellence in United States History. 1986. pap. text ed. 12.81 (*0-88334-193-X*, 76158) Longman.

Morse, Wayne J. & Roth, Harold P. Cost Accounting: Processing, Evaluating, & Using Cost Data. 3rd ed. LC 85-6153. 1040p. (C). 1986. teacher ed write for info. (*0-201-13997-9*); text ed. 51.95 (*0-201-13995-2*); Study guide. student ed 24.75 (*0-201-13996-0*); write for info. (*0-201-13979-0*); write for info. (*0-201-13998-7*); Check list key figure. 27.95 (*0-201-13745-3*) Addison-Wesley.

Morse, Wayne J., et al. Management Accounting. (C). 1986. pap. text ed. write for info. (*0-201-15870-1*) Addison-Wesley.
— Management Accounting. 2nd ed. (Illus.). 736p. (C). 1988. text ed. 39.96 (*0-201-15760-8*) Addison-Wesley.
— Management Accounting. 3rd ed. (Illus.). 896p. (C). 1991. text ed. 61.25 (*0-201-52827-4*) Addison-Wesley.

Morse, Wayne L. & Beattie, Ronald H. Survey of the Administration of Criminal Justice in Oregon: Final Report on 1771 Felony Cases in Multnomah County Report Number One. LC 74-3838. (Criminal Justice in America Ser.). 1974. reprint ed. 24.95 (*0-405-06155-2*) Ayer.

Morse, Whit, jt. auth. see Firestone, Linda.

Morse, Willard S. & Brinckle, Gertrude. Howard Pyle. 1995. reprint ed. 35.00 (*1-55888-995-7*) Omnigraphics Inc.

Morse, William C. Crisis Intervention in Residential Treatment: The Clinical Innovations of Fritz Redl. LC 91-25834. (Residential Treatment for Children & Youth Ser.). (Illus.). 107p. 1991. lib. bdg. 29.95 (*1-56024-215-9*) Haworth Pr.
— The Education & Treatment of Socioemotionally Impaired Children & Youth. LC 85-2842. (Illus.). 384p. 1985. text ed. 39.95x (*0-8156-2268-6*); pap. text ed. 16.95 (*0-8156-2269-4*) Syracuse U Pr.

Morse, William C., ed. Humanistic Teaching for Exceptional Children: An Introduction to Special Education. (Illus.). 344p. (C). 1979. pap. 14.95x (*0-8156-2215-5*) Syracuse U Pr.

Morse, William C. & Smith, Judith M. Understanding Child Variance. LC 79-57303. 117p. (Orig.). 1980. pap. 11.90 (*0-86586-099-8*, P200) Coun Exc Child.

Morse, William C., et al. Studies in Psychology of Reading. LC 68-54427. (Michigan University Monographs in Education: No. 4). 188p. 1968. reprint ed. text ed. 38.50 (*0-8371-0176-X*, MOPR, Greenwood Pr) Greenwood.

Morse, William E., jt. auth. see Russel, J. C.

Morse, William R. Chinese Medicine. LC 75-23661. (Clio Medica Ser.: 11). (Illus.). reprint ed. 36.00 (*0-404-58911-1*) AMS Pr.

***Morse, William S.** A Country Life. LC 94-43017. (Illus.). 136p. (Orig.). 1995. pap. 9.95 (*0-9642213-1-4*) Moose Cntry.

Morselli, Guido. Past Conditional. 224p. 1991. 23.95 (*0-7011-2917-4*, Pub. by Chatto & Windus UK) Trafalgar.

Morselli, Henry. Suicide: An Essay on Comparative Moral Statistics. LC 74-25770. (European Sociology Ser.). 402p. 1975. reprint ed. 29.95 (*0-405-06524-8*) Ayer.

Morselli, Mario. Amadeo Avogadro. 1984. lib. bdg. 136.50 (*90-277-1624-2*) Kluwer Ac.

Morselli, Paolo L., jt. auth. see Porter, Roger J.

Morselli, Paolo L., jt. ed. see Schmidt, Dieter.

Morshead, Ian. The Life & Murder of Henry Morshead: A True Story of the Raj. (Illus.). 220p. 1982. 27.00 (*0-900891-76-9*) Oleander Pr.

Morshead, O. F., ed. see Pepys, Samuel.

Morsi, Pamela. Courting Miss Hattie. 1991. mass mkt. 5.50 (*0-553-29000-2*) Bantam.
— Garters. 336p. (Orig.). 1992. mass mkt. 5.50 (*0-515-10895-2*) Jove Pubns.
— Garters. large type ed. LC 93-18606. (Orig.). 1993. 19.95 (*1-56054-725-1*) Thorndike Pr.
— Heaven Sent. 1991. mass mkt. 4.50 (*0-553-28944-6*) Bantam.
— Marrying Stone. 336p. (Orig.). 1994. pap. text ed. 5.50 (*0-515-11431-6*) Jove Pubns.
— Runabout. 304p. (Orig.). 1994. mass mkt. 4.99 (*0-515-11305-0*) Jove Pubns.
— Runabout. large type ed. LC 94-32215. 400p. 1994. pap. 17.95 (*0-7838-1126-8*) Hall.
— Something Shady. 336p. (Orig.). Date not set. pap. text ed. 7.99 (*0-515-11628-9*) Jove Pubns.
— Wild Oats. 336p. (Orig.). 1993. mass mkt. 4.99 (*0-515-11185-6*) Jove Pubns.
— Wild Oats. large type ed. LC 93-37210. (Orig.). 1994. pap. 17.95 (*0-7862-0099-5*) Thorndike Pr.

Morsi, Pamela, et al. Summer Magic. 304p. (Orig.). 1993. mass mkt. 4.99 (*0-515-11116-3*) Jove Pubns.

Morsiani, Mario. Epidemiology & Screening of Diabetes. 320p. 1988. 144.00 (*0-8493-4971-0*, RC660) CRC Pr.

Morsink, Catherine. Interactive Teaming: Consultant & Collaborator in Special Programs. 400p. (C). 1990. write for info. (*0-675-21218-9*, Merrill Pub Co) Macmillan.

Morsink, Catherine V. Teaching Special Needs Students in Regular Classrooms. (C). 1987. text ed. 27.75 (*0-673-39173-6*) HarpCollege.

Morsink, Deborah H. Tournants: Conversation en Culture. LC 92-24486. 1992. pap. text ed. write for info. (*0-13-927682-3*) P-H.

Morsink, Hubert, jt. ed. see Allen, Tim.

Morskaya, Larisa. Za Grekhi Roditelei (For the Parents Sins) Povesti I Rasskazy (Novels & Stories) (Illus.). 224p. (C). 1991. pap. 14.00 (*0-911971-55-6*) Effect Pub.

Morsman, Edgar M., Jr. Commercial Loan Portfolio Management. Behr, Joan, ed. LC 93-16711. (Illus.). 136p. 1993. pap. text ed. 58.00 (*0-936742-95-X*, 31181) Robt Morris Assocs.
— Effective Loan Management. LC 81-84671. (Illus.). 224p. 1982. text ed. 59.00 (*0-936742-06-2*) Robt Morris Assocs.

Morson. Color Atlas of Gastrointestinal Pathology. 300p. 1988. text ed. 205.00 (*0-7216-2607-6*) Saunders.

Morson & Jass, J. R. Precancerous Lesions of the Gastrointestinal Tract. 1985. text ed. 79.50 (*0-7020-1053-7*, Bailliere-Tindall) Saunders.

Morson, B., et al. Morson & Dawson's Gastrointestinal Pathology. 3rd ed. 1990. 245.00 (*0-632-01693-0*) Blackwell Sci.

Morson, Basil C., ed. Alimentary Tract. (Symmers Systemic Pathology Ser.: Vol. 3). (Illus.). 472p. 1987. text ed. 185.00 (*0-443-03095-2*) Churchill.

Morson, Gary S. The Boundaries of Genre. 219p. 1988. pap. 12.95 (*0-8101-0811-9*) Northwestern U Pr.
— The Boundaries of Genre: Dostoevsky's "Diary of a Writer" & the Traditions of Literary Utopia. (Slavic Ser.: No. 4). 230p. 1981. 25.00 (*0-292-70732-0*) U of Tex Pr.
— Hidden in Plain View: Narrative & Creative Potentials in 'War & Peace' LC 87-6471. 336p. 1987. 42.50 (*0-8047-1387-1*); pap. 13.95 (*0-8047-1718-4*) Stanford U Pr.
— Narrative & Freedom: The Shadows of Time. LC 94-7065. 336p. 1994. 30.00 (*0-300-05882-9*) Yale U Pr.

Morson, Gary S., ed. Bakhtin: Essays & Dialogues on His Work. LC 85-24624. xiv, 192p. 1986. lib. bdg. 22.95 (*0-226-54132-0*); pap. text ed. 11.50 (*0-226-54133-9*) U Ch Pr.
— Literature & History: Theoretical Problems & Russian Case Studies. LC 85-27843. 352p. 1986. 42.50 (*0-8047-1302-2*); pap. 14.95 (*0-8047-1470-3*) Stanford U Pr.

Morson, Gary S. & Emerson, Caryl. Mikhail Bakhtin: Creation of a Prosaics. LC 90-39855. 560p. 1990. 52.50 (*0-8047-1821-0*); pap. 16.95 (*0-8047-1822-9*) Stanford U Pr.

Morson, Gary S. & Emerson, Caryl, eds. Rethinking Bakhtin: Extensions & Challenges. (Studies in Russian Literature & Theory). 330p. 1989. pap. 16.95 (*0-8101-0810-0*) Northwestern U Pr.

Morson, Gary S., jt. ed. see Allen, Elizabeth C.

***Morson, Ian.** Falconer's Crusade. 1995. 18.95 (*0-312-11784-1*) St Martin.

Morson, Jamie, jt. ed. see Kalb, Marion.

Morson, John. Christ the Way: The Christology of Guerric of Igny. (Cistercian Studies: N0.25). 1978. 11.95 (*0-87907-825-1*) Cistercian Pubns.

Morss, John R. The Biologising of Childhood: Developmental Psychology & the Darwinian Myth. 320p. 1990. 59.95 (*0-86377-129-7*) L Erlbaum Assocs.
— Growing Critical: Alternatives to Developmental Psychology. LC 95-8132. (Critical Psychology Ser.). 1995. write for info. (*0-415-06108-3*); pap. write for info. (*0-415-06109-1*) Routledge.

Morss, L. R., jt. ed. see Meyer, G.

Morss, Lester R. & Fuger, Jean, eds. Transuranium Elements: A Half Century. LC 92-7475. (Illus.). 590p. 1992. 99.95 (*0-8412-2219-3*) Am Chemical.

Morss, Martha. When Dinosaurs Ruled the Earth. (Really Reading Ser.: Level 1). (Illus.). 32p. (J). (gr. 1-2). 1991. pap. 2.99 (*0-87406-560-7*) Willowisp Pr.

Morss, Noel. Ancient Culture of the Fremont River in Utah. (HUPMP Ser.: Vol. 12, No. 3). 1931. 26.00 (*0-527-01226-2*) Periodicals Srv.
— Archaeological Explorations on the Middle Chinlee. LC 28-11557. (American Anthropological Association Memoirs Ser.). 1927. pap. 16.00 (*0-527-00533-9*) Periodicals Srv.
— Notes on the Archaeology of the Kaibito & Rainbow Plateaus in Arizona. (Harvard University Peabody Museum of Archaeology & Ethnology Papers: Vol. 12, No. 3). 1974. reprint ed. pap. 26.00 (*0-527-01225-4*) Periodicals Srv.

Morss, Willard N. & Herren, Janet M. Stolen Princess: A Northwest Indian Legend. LC 83-82920. (Illus.). 79p. (Orig.). (J). (gr. 4-8). 1983. pap. 8.95 (*0-9613025-0-X*) J M Herren.

Morstyn & Dexter, eds. Filgrastim in Clinical Practice. LC 93-5548. (Basic & Clinical Oncology: Vol. 5). 368p. 1994. 140.00 (*0-8247-8832-X*) Dekker.

Morstyn, G. & Kaye, A. H., eds. Phototherapy of Cancer. 240p. 1990. text ed. 123.00 (*3-7186-0510-4*) Gordon & Breach.

Morsy, E. M. Aloe Vera: Literature Index & Abstract 1980-1992. 450p. 1992. 285.00 (*0-937425-06-0*) CITA Intl.
— Aloe Vera, Farming, Processing & Applications, A Technical Guide. 400p. 1992. write for info. (*0-937425-07-9*) CITA Intl.
— Aloe Vera, Science & Technology, 1980-1993. 7th ed. (Illus.). 579p. 1993. pap. text ed. 285.00 (*0-937425-26-5*) CITA Intl.
— Aloe Vera, Stabilization & Processing for the Cosmetic & Beverage. 1,992th rev. ed. 200p. 1992. 135.00 (*0-937425-05-2*) CITA Intl.

Morsy, E. M., ed. For Formulation Chemists Only, 3 vols., Set. (F2CO Ser.). (Illus.). 144p. 1991. pap. 285.00 (*0-685-52445-0*) CITA Intl.
— For Formulation Chemists Only, Vol. 1. (F2CO Ser.). 150p. 1991. pap. text ed. 95.00 (*0-937425-02-8*) CITA Intl.
— For Formulation Chemists Only, 3 vols., Vol. 2. (F2CO Ser.). (Illus.). 144p. 1991. pap. 95.00 (*0-937425-14-1*) CITA Intl.
— For Formulation Chemists Only, Vol. 2. (F2CO Ser.). 148p. 1992. pap. text ed. 95.00 (*0-937425-03-6*) CITA Intl.

Morsy, Esam M. Aloe Vera: Stabilization & Processing for the Cosmetic, Food & Beverage Industries. 3rd ed. LC 82-84430. (Illus.). 1985. lib. bdg. 85.00 (*0-317-14729-3*) CITA Intl.

Morsy, Soheir A. Gender, Sickness, & Healing in Rural Egypt: Ethnography in Historical Context. (Conflict & Social Change Ser.). 237p. (C). 1993. text ed. 52.00 (*0-8133-8166-5*) Westview.

***Morsy, Zaghloul, ed.** The Challenge of Illiteracy: From Reflection to Action. LC 94-32885. (IBE Studies on Education: Vol. 1). 352p. 1994. 40.00 (*0-8153-1854-5*, SS995) Garland.

Morsy, Zhagloul & Altbach, Philip G., eds. Higher Education in International Perspective: Toward the 21st Century. 250p. 1993. text ed. 37.50 (*0-89891-066-8*) Advent Bks Div.

Mort, D., jt. auth. see Aldcroft, D. H.

Mort, D. M. Developmental Concordance & Discordance During Puberty & Early Adolesence. (SRCD Ser.: Vol. 18, No. 1). 1953. 12.00 (*0-527-01557-1*) Periodicals Srv.

Mort, David. European Market Information: A Handbook for Managers. 288p. 1992. 111.00x (*0-273-03736-6*, Pub. by Pitman Pubng UK) St Mut.
— U.K. Statistics: A Guide for Business Users. 300p. 1992. 72.95 (*0-566-02971-5*, Pub. by Gower UK) Ashgate Pub Co.

Mort, David, ed. European Directory of Non-Official Statistical Sources Nineteen Ninety. 281p. 1990. pap. 230.00 (*0-685-50202-3*, 073127-M99348, Pub. by Euromonitor Pubns UK) Gale.

Mort, David & Woolley, Marcus. Counties & Regions of the U. K. 3rd ed. 250p. 1994. 76.95 (*0-566-02972-3*, Pub. by Avebury Pub UK) Ashgate Pub Co.

Mort, J. The Anatomy of Xerography: Its Invention & Evolution. LC 89-42739. 240p. 1989. lib. bdg. 32.50x (*0-89950-442-6*) McFarland & Co.

Mort, J. & Jansen, F. Plasma Deposited Thin Films. LC 86-23264. 1986. reprint ed. 138.00 (*0-8493-5119-7*, CRC Reprint) Franklin.

Mort, John. Tanks: Vietnam Stories. LC 85-73391. 88p. 1986. pap. 9.50 (*0-933532-55-5*) BkMk.
— The Walnut King: And Other Stories. 184p. (Orig.). 1990. pap. 8.00 (*0-9617499-2-X*) Woods Colt Pr.

Mort, S. R. Coins of the Hapsburg Emperors & Related Issues 1619-1919. (Illus.). 1990. reprint ed. lib. bdg. 30.00 (*0-942666-15-1*) S J Durst.

Mort, S. W. Bluewater Seamanship. (C). 1987. 42.00 (*0-85174-403-6*, Pub. by Brwn Son Ferg) St Mut.

Mort, Simon. The Minutes. 128p. 1991. text ed. 54.95 (*0-566-02708-9*, Pub. by Gower UK) Ashgate Pub Co.
— Professional Report Writing. 300p. 1992. 56.95 (*0-566-02712-7*, Pub. by Gower UK) Ashgate Pub Co.

Mort, Terry A. Systematic Selling: How to Influence the Buying Decision Process. LC 77-5937. 198p. reprint ed. pap. 56.50 (*0-317-26910-0*, 2023552) Bks Demand.

***Mortalsin, Mary.** Celibacy Is Hard, Right? 1994. pap. 4.99 (*0-671-52422-4*) PB.

***Mortazavi, Ali.** The Fine Art of Swindling. 144p. 1994. pap. 17.95 (*1-85744-105-2*, Pub. by Cadogan Books UK) Macmillan.

***Morteani, Giulio, ed.** Prehistoric Gold in Europe: Mines, Metallurgy & Manufacture: Proceedings of the NATO Advanced Research Workshop, Seeon, Germany, September 27-October 1, 1993. LC 94-23902. (NATO Advanced Science Instututes Series E: Vol. 280). 632p. (C). 1994. lib. bdg. 285.00 (*0-7923-3255-5*) Kluwer Ac.

Mortell, Art. Courage to Fail: Art Mortell's Secrets for Business Success. 1993. text ed. 18.95 (*0-07-043392-5*) McGraw.
— World Class Selling. 224p. 1991. 19.95 (*0-7931-0275-8*, 2401-28) Dearborn Finan.

Morten, Baker E. The First Step to Recovery. 200p. 1992. pap. text ed. 19.95 (*0-9633004-3-1*) Integ Pub DC.
— Unlock Your Happiness. 104p. 1994. pap. 10.95 (*0-9633004-8-2*) Integ Pub DC.

Mortensen, Brita M. & Downs, Brian W. Strindberg: An Introduction to His Life & Work. 246p. reprint ed. pap. 70.20 (*0-317-09198-0*, 2051420) Bks Demand.

Mortensen, C. D. Violence & Communication: Public Reactions to an Attempted Presidential Assassination. (Illus.). 232p. (Orig.). (C). 1988. pap. text ed. 22.00 (*0-8191-6688-X*) U Pr of Amer.

Mortensen, C. David. Problematic Communication: The Construction of Invisible Walls. LC 93-23671. 256p. 1994. text ed. 55.00 (*0-275-94632-0*, Praeger Pubs) Greenwood.

Mortensen, Carl E. The Healing of America, Vol. 1. 55p. 1993. pap. 7.95 (*0-9636251-0-1*) C E Mortensen.

***Mortensen, Chris.** Inconsistent Mathematics. LC 94-37996. (Mathematics & Its Applications Ser.: Vol.312). 1994. lib. bdg. 77.00 (*0-7923-3186-9*) Kluwer Ac.

Mortensen, Daniel B. Pattern for Joint Operations: World War 2 Close Air Support, North Africa. LC 87-19335. (Illus.). 104p. (Orig.). 1987. pap. 5.50 (*0-16-001963-X*, 008-029-00161-6) USGPO.

Mortensen, Donald G. & Schmuller, Alan M. Guidance in Today's Schools. 3rd ed. LC 75-35989. 564p. reprint ed. pap. 160.80 (*0-317-09829-2*, 2055397) Bks Demand.

Mortensen, Douglas L., jt. auth. see Root, Jack B., Sr.

Mortensen, E., ed. Nutrient Dynamics & Biological Structure in Shallow Freshwater & Brackish Lakes. LC 93-47528. (Developments in Hydrobiology Ser.: No. 94). 528p. (C). 1994. lib. bdg. 280.00 (*0-7923-2677-6*) Kluwer Ac.

Mortensen, Enok. Danish-American Life & Letters: A Bibliography. Scott, Franklyn D., ed. LC 78-15200. (Scandinavians in America Ser.). 1979. reprint ed. lib. bdg. 15.95 (*0-405-11652-7*) Ayer.

Mortensen, Inge Demant. Nomads of Luristan & Their Material Culture. LC 93-60435. (Carlsberg Nomad Ser.). (Illus.). 496p. 1993. 50.00 (*0-500-01572-4*) Thames Hudson.

Mortensen, Jorgan, ed. The Future of Pensions in the European Community. 231p. 1992. 37.00 (*1-85753-057-8*, Pub. by Brasseys UK) Brasseys Inc.

Mortensen, Jorgen, ed. Improving Economic & Social Cohesion in the European Community. LC 94-1155. 1994. text ed. 75.00 (*0-312-12174-1*) St Martin.

Mortensen, K. & Skamris, C. Masnedoe Wind Farm, No. EUR 13228. 59p. 1991. pap. 9.00 (*92-826-2162-6*, CD-NA-13228-EN-C, Pub. by Europ Com) UNIPUB.

Mortensen, Karen. Form & Content in Children's Human Figure Drawings. 256p. 1991. 45.00 (*0-8147-5456-2*); pap. text ed. 16.50 (*0-8147-5500-3*) NYU Pr.

Mortensen, Kay S., jt. auth. see Allen, Dell K.

Mortensen, Lynn O. Whitecaps in the Icebox. (Illus.). 108p. 1990. spiral bd. 9.95 (*0-945265-11-5*) Accord Comm.

Mortensen, Pauline. Back Before the World Turned Nasty. LC 89-4739. 115p. 1989. 17.95 (*1-55728-104-1*); pap. 8.95 (*1-55728-105-X*) U of Ark Pr.

Mortensen, Richard E. Random Signals & Systems. LC 86-19007. (Illus.). 246p. reprint ed. pap. 70.40 (*0-7837-3528-6*, 2057864) Bks Demand.

Mortensen, Richard F., jt. auth. see Krier, Julius P.

Mortensen, Robert K. In the Cause of Progress: A History of the New Mexico Cattle Growers Association. (Illus.). 128p. 1983. 17.95 (*0-9627417-2-8*) Athena NM.

Mortensen, Susan. Burgess Families in the Nineteen Hundred Soundex. (Borgo Family Histories Ser.: No. 5). 160p. Date not set. lib. bdg. write for info. (*0-89370-823-2*); pap. write for info. (*0-89370-923-9*) Borgo Pr.

Mortensen, Viggo & Sorensen, Robert C., eds. Free Will & Determinism: Papers from an Interdisciplinary Research Conference. 214p. (Orig.). 1987. pap. 28.50 (*87-7288-095-3*) Coronet Bks.

Mortensen, William. Monsters & Madonnas. LC 72-9220. (Literature of Photography Ser.). 1977. reprint ed. 18.95 (*0-405-04927-7*) Ayer.

Mortenson, Kenneth E. Variable Capacitance Diodes: The Operation & Characterization of Varactor, Charge Storage & PIN Diodes for RF & Microwave Applications. LC 74-189395. (Modern Frontiers in Applied Science Ser.). 142p. reprint ed. pap. 40.50 (*0-317-39628-5*, 2025053) Bks Demand.

Mortenson, Kenneth E. & Borrego, Jose M. Design, Performance, & Applications of Microwave Semiconductor Control Components. LC 70-189394. (Modern Frontiers in Applied Science Ser.). (Illus.). 294p. reprint ed. pap. 83.80 (*0-8357-4176-1*, 2036954) Bks Demand.

Mortenson, Michael. Geometric Modeling. LC 84-29940. 763p. 1985. Net. text ed. write for info. (*0-471-88279-8*); 50.00 (*0-471-81872-0*) Wiley.

Mortenson, Michael E. Computer Graphics: An Introduction to the Mathematics & Geometry. 396p. (C). 1989. 32.95 (*0-8311-1182-8*) Indus Pr.
— Computer Graphics Handbook. (Illus.). 288p. 1990. 26.95 (*0-8311-1002-3*) Indus Pr.
— Geometric Transformations. (Illus.). 312p. (C). 1995. text ed. 49.95 (*0-8311-3057-1*) Indus Pr.
Mortenson, Ray. Meadowland. LC 83-80569. (Illus.). 80p. 1983. 25.00 (*0-912810-40-8*) Lustrum Pr.
***Mortenson, Vernon.** God Made It Grow: The History of T. E. A. M. (Illus.). 1024p. (Orig.). 1994. pap. text ed. 17.95 (*0-87808-257-3*, WCL257-3) William Carey Lib.
Mortenson, W. P., jt. auth. see Brickbaurer, E. A.
Mortenson, W. P., jt. auth. see Juergenson, E. M.
Morter, M. T., Jr. Chiropractic Physiology: A Review of Scientific Principles As Related to the Chiropractic Adjustment with Emphasis on the Bio Energetic Synchronization Technique. LC 88-70369. 120p. 1988. 32.00 (*0-944994-01-6*) BEST Research.
— Correlative Urinalysis: The Body Knows Best. LC 87-51116. 150p. 1988. 32.00 (*0-944994-00-8*) BEST Research.
— Correlative Urinalysis: The Body Knows Best. LC 87-51116. 200p. 1988. pap. 32.00 (*0-944994-02-4*) BEST Research.
— The Healing Field. 146p. (Orig.). 1991. pap. 24.95 (*0-944994-03-2*) BEST Research.
— Your Health, Your Choice: A New Holistic Approach to Disease Prevention & a Healthier You. 224p. 1990. 17.95 (*0-8119-0655-8*); pap. 12.95 (*0-8119-0667-1*) LIFETIME.
Morterra, C., et al, eds. Structures & Reactivity of Surfaces: Proceedings of a European Conference, Trieste, Italy, September 13-16. (Studies in Surface Science & Catalysis: Vol. 48). 970p. 1989. 179.50 (*0-444-87465-8*) Elsevier.
Mortgage Bankers Assoc. Staff. Residential Mortgage Loan Underwriting Casebook. (Illus.). 200p. (Orig.). (C). 1989. student ed, pap. 100.00 (*0-945359-02-0*) Mortgage Bankers.
Mortgage Bankers Association Staff. HUD Compendium, 1993: A Compilation of Processing Directives DE Updates Policy Memoranda & CHUMS Updates. rev. ed. 110p. (C). 1993. pap. text ed. 60.00 (*0-945359-17-9*) Mortgage Bankers.
Mortier, K. M. & Orszulik, S. T., eds. Chemistry & Technology of Lubricants. LC 91-44485. 302p. 1993. 110.00 (*1-56081-594-9*) VCH Pubs.
Mortier, R. Shamms. Amiga Desktop Videography. (Illus.). (Orig.). 1991. pap. 39.95 (*0-944500-62-5*) MichTron.
Mortifee, Ann, jt. auth. see Robbins, John.
Mortillaro, Nicholas A. The Pathophysiology of the Microcirculation. 1994. 189.95 (*0-8493-4547-2*, RC700) CRC Pr.
***Mortimer.** Titmuss Regained. 3.99 (*0-517-13581-7*) Random Hse Value.
Mortimer, A. M. & Rix, K. J., eds. The Psychopathology of Perception: Proceedings of the Third Leeds Psychopathology Symposium, September 1988 - Psychopathology Journal, Vol. 24, No. 6. (Illus.). 36p. 1991. pap. 50.50 (*3-8055-5536-9*) S Karger.
Mortimer, Andrew. Information Structure Design for Databases: A Practical Approach. (Computer Weekly Professional Ser.). (Illus.). 300p. 1993. pap. 45.00 (*0-7506-0683-5*) Buttrwrth-Heinemann.
Mortimer, Armine K. The Gentlest Law: Roland Barthes's The Pleasure of the Text. (American University Studies: General Literature: Ser. XIX, Vol. 22). 254p. (C). 1989. text ed. 38.95 (*0-8204-0944-8*) P Lang Pubs.
— Plotting to Kill. LC 90-19208. (Writing about Women Ser.: Vol. 1). 220p. (C). 1991. text ed. 41.95 (*0-8204-1435-2*) P Lang Pubs.
Mortimer, Bunny, jt. auth. see Mortimer, John.
Mortimer, C. Reaction Heats & Bond Strengths. LC 61-17034. 1962. 100.00 (*0-08-013769-5*, Pub. by Pergamon Repr UK) Franklin.
Mortimer, C. H., jt. ed. see Graf, W. H.
Mortimer, Carole. A Christmas Affair. 1990. pap. 2.50 (*0-373-11325-0*) Harlequin Bks.
— Darkness into Light. large type ed. (Nightingale Series Large Print Bks.). 233p. 1991. pap. 14.95 (*0-8161-5179-2*, Nightingale) Hall.
— Elusive Obsession. (Presents Ser.). 1994. mass mkt. 2.99 (*0-373-11631-4*, 1-11631-8) Harlequin Bks.
— Elusive Obsession. large type ed. (Harlequin Ser.). 1993. 18.95 (*0-263-13413-X*) Thorndike Pr.
— Fated Attraction. 1994. mass mkt. 2.99 (*0-373-11689-6*, 1-11689-6) Harlequin Bks.
— Fated Attraction. large type ed. 1992. reprint ed. lib. bdg. 18.95 (*0-263-13031-2*, Pub. by Mills & Boon UK) Thorndike Pr.
— Glass Slippers & Unicorns. large type ed. (Nightingale Series Large Print Bks.). 226p. 1991. pap. 14.95 (*0-8161-5187-3*, Nightingale) Hall.
— Gracious Lady. 1994. mass mkt. 2.99 (*0-373-11657-8*, 1-11657-3) Harlequin Bks.
— Hunter's Moon. large type ed. 1994. 17.95 (*0-263-13652-3*, Pub. by Mills & Boon Ltd UK) Chivers N Amer.
— Hunter's Moon: (Presents Plus) (Presents Ser.). 1994. mass mkt. 2.99 (*0-373-11703-5*, 1-11703-5) Harlequin Bks.
— The Jilted Bridegroom. (Presents Ser.). 1993. mass mkt. 2.99 (*0-373-11559-8*, 1-11559-1) Harlequin Bks.
— Memories of the Past. large type ed. 1991. reprint ed. lib. bdg. 18.95 (*0-263-12686-2*, Pub. by Mills & Boon UK) Thorndike Pr.
— Mother of the Bride. (Presents Plus Ser.). 1993. mass mkt. 2.99 (*0-373-11607-1*, 1-11607-8) Harlequin Bks.
— Mother of the Bride. large type ed. (Harlequin Ser.). 1993. reprint ed. lib. bdg. 18.95 (*0-263-13266-8*, Pub. by Mills & Boon UK) Thorndike Pr.
— Private Lives. large type ed. 1993. 17.95 (*0-263-13318-4*, Pub. by Mills & Boon Ltd UK) Chivers N Amer.
— Private Lives: Presents Plus. (Presents Ser.). 1993. mass mkt. 2.99 (*0-373-11583-0*, 1-11583-1) Harlequin Bks.
— Return Engagement. large type ed. (Harlequin Ser.). 1994. 18.95 (*0-263-13717-1*) Thorndike Pr.
— Return Engagement: (Presents Plus) (Presents Ser.). 1994. mass mkt. 2.99 (*0-373-11671-3*, 1-11671-4) Harlequin Bks.
— A Rogue & a Pirate. large type ed. (Magna Large Print Ser.). 1994. 18.95 (*0-7505-0741-1*, Pub. by Magna Print Bks) Ulverscroft.
— Romance of a Lifetime. large type ed. 285p. 1992. reprint ed. lib. bdg. 18.95 (*0-263-12812-1*) Thorndike Pr.
— Saving Grace. (Presents Ser.). 1993. pap. 2.89 (*0-373-11543-1*, 1-11543-5) Harlequin Bks.
— Saving Grace. large type ed. 1992. reprint ed. lib. bdg. 18.95 (*0-263-13090-8*, Pub. by Mills & Boon UK) Thorndike Pr.
— Le Visage du Passe. (Azur Ser.). (FRE.). 1994. pap. 3.50 (*0-373-34433-3*, 1-34433-2) Harlequin Bks.
— War of Love: (Presents Plus) (Presents Ser.). 1995. pap. 3.25 (*0-373-11727-2*, 1-11727-4) Harlequin Bks.
Mortimer, Charlotte. Marrying by Lot. 1993. reprint ed. lib. bdg. 89.00 (*0-7812-5494-9*) Rprt Serv.
Mortimer, Colin. Elements of Pronounciation. 100p. 1985. pap. 11.95 (*0-521-26938-5*) Cambridge U Pr.
— Elements of Pronounciation, Set. 100p. 1985. pap. 54.95 (*0-521-26334-4*) Cambridge U Pr.
Mortimer, Curtis. Dinosaur Journal: Making Sense of a Young Son's Death. (Illus.). 150p. 1995. pap. 12.95 (*0-940895-19-6*) Cornerstone IL.
Mortimer, David. Practical Laboratory Andrology. LC 92-48921. (Illus.). 416p. 1994. 65.00 (*0-19-506595-6*) OUP.
Mortimer, Dolores A. Together As Parish: An Innovative Strategy to Nourish Family & Parish. LC 91-76777. (Illus.). 136p. (Orig.). 1992. 2.95 (*0-87793-476-2*); spiral bd. 12.95 (*0-87793-475-4*) Ave Maria.
Mortimer, Edward. Faith & Power: The Politics of Islam. (Illus.). 425p. 1982. pap. 11.96 (*0-394-71173-4*) Random.
Mortimer, Edward A., Jr., jt. auth. see Plotkin, Stanley A.
Mortimer, Eunice. Working with the Elderly. Davies, Martin, ed. (Community Care Practice Handbook Ser.: No. 9). vi, 91p. (Orig.). (C). 1982. pap. text ed. 16.50 (*0-566-05171-0*) Ashgate Pub Co.
Mortimer, Gail L. Daughter of the Swan: Legacies of Love & Knowledge in Eudora Welty's Fiction. LC 93-41117. 264p. 1994. 40.00 (*0-8203-1633-4*) U of Ga Pr.
Mortimer, Gail L., ed. see Gallagher, Philip J.
Mortimer, Geoffrey. Chapters on Human Love. 1972. 59.95 (*0-87968-836-X*) Gordon Pr.
Mortimer, George. Observations & Remarks Made During a Voyage to the Islands of Teneriffe, Amsterdam, Maria's Islands Near Van Dieman's Land, Otaheita, Sandwich Islands, Owyhee, the Fox Islands on the Northwest Coast of America, Tinian, & from Thence to Canton, in the Brig Mercury, Commanded by John Henry Cox, Esq. 80p. 1989. 22.50 (*0-87770-456-2*) Ye Galleon.
Mortimer, J. & Rooks, B., eds. The International Robot Industry Report. (Illus.). 260p. 1987. pap. 166.00 (*0-387-16353-0*) Spr-Verlag.
Mortimer, J., ed. see Ingersoll Engineers Staff.
Mortimer, J. E., jt. auth. see Jenkins, C.
Mortimer, J. Peter, ed. see Hirsch, Bob.
Mortimer, J. W., jt. auth. see Hurst, W. J.
Mortimer, James, tr. see Dreyfus, Alfred.
Mortimer, James, et al, eds. The Aging Motor System, Vol. 3. LC 82-598. 270p. 1982. text ed. 55.00 (*0-275-90865-8*, C08653, Praeger Pubs) Greenwood.
Mortimer, James A. & Schuman, Leonard M., eds. The Epidemiology of Dementia. (Illus.). (C). 1981. text ed. 29.95 (*0-19-502906-2*) OUP.
Mortimer, Jeylan, et al. Work, Family & Personality. Platt, Gerald, ed. LC 85-20951. (Modern Sociology Ser.). 272p. 1986. text ed. 39.50 (*0-89391-293-X*) Ablex Pub.
Mortimer, Jeylan T. Changing Attitudes Toward Work. (Studies in Productivity: Highlights of the Literature Ser.: Vol. 11). 55p. 1979. pap. 55.00 (*0-08-029492-8*) Work in Amer.
Mortimer, Jeylan T., jt. ed. see Petersen, Anne C.
Mortimer, John. The Best of Rumpole. 288p. 1994. reprint ed. pap. 10.95 (*0-14-017684-5*, Penguin Bks) Viking Penguin.
— Character Parts. write for info. (*0-670-81124-6*) Viking Penguin.
— Charade. 1976. 18.95 (*0-8488-0595-X*) Amereon Ltd.
— Charade. 192p. 1988. mass mkt. 5.95 (*0-14-009267-6*, Penguin Bks) Viking Penguin.
— Clinging to the Wreckage. 1987. pap. 8.00 (*0-14-006383-8*, Penguin Bks) Viking Penguin.
— Clinging to the Wreckage: A Part of Life. LC 83-13078. 224p. 1984. mass mkt. 11.95 (*0-14-006860-0*, Penguin Bks) Viking Penguin.
— Dunster. 304p. 1994. pap. 10.95 (*0-14-023270-2*, Penguin Bks) Viking Penguin.
— A First Rumpole Omnibus. (Crime Monthly Ser.). 560p. 1984. pap. 13.95 (*0-14-006768-X*, Penguin Bks) Viking Penguin.
— Like Men Betrayed. large type ed. LC 93-45297. 1994. 21.95 (*0-7927-1930-1*, Curley Lrg Print); pap. 19.95 (*0-7927-1929-8*, Curley Lrg Print) Chivers N Amer.
— Murderers & Other Friends: Another Part of Life. (Illus.). 320p. 1995. 23.95 (*0-670-84902-2*, Viking) Viking Penguin.
— The Narrowing Stream. large type ed. LC 93-11689. 1993. pap. 17.95 (*0-7927-1798-8*, Curley Lrg Print) Chivers N Amer.
— The Rapstone Chronicles: Paradise Postponed & Titmuss Regained. LC 92-39686. 704p. 1993. pap. 14.00 (*0-14-017595-4*, Penguin Bks) Viking Penguin.
— Rumpole a la Carte. braille ed. 501p. 1992. vinyl bd. 40.08 (*1-56956-085-4*, BR8651) W A T Braille.
— Rumpole a la Carte. large type ed. 1992. 18.95 (*0-7927-1001-0*, E0023, Eagle Lrg Print) Chivers N Amer.
— Rumpole a la Carte. large type ed. 1992. pap. 14.95 (*0-7927-1002-9*, Paragon Lrg Print) Chivers N Amer.
— Rumpole a la Carte. 256p. 1991. reprint ed. pap. 10.00 (*0-14-015609-7*, Penguin Bks) Viking Penguin.
— Rumpole & the Age of Miracles. (Orig.). 1989. pap. 6.00 (*0-14-013116-7*, Penguin Bks) Viking Penguin.
— Rumpole & the Age of Miracles. large type ed. 1995. pap. 18.95 (*0-7838-1188-8*, Large Print Bks) Hall.
— Rumpole & the Golden Thread. (Crime Ser.). 256p. 1984. mass mkt. 5.95 (*0-14-006331-5*, Penguin Bks) Viking Penguin.
— Rumpole & the Golden Thread. large type ed. LC 92-18447. 1992. 18.95 (*0-7927-1371-0*, Eagle Lrg Print) Chivers N Amer.
— Rumpole & the Golden Thread. large type ed. 1993. pap. 16.95 (*0-7927-1370-2*, Paragon Lrg Print) Chivers N Amer.
— Rumpole for the Defence. (Crime Monthly Ser.). 192p. 1984. mass mkt. 5.95 (*0-14-006060-X*, Penguin Bks) Viking Penguin.
— Rumpole for the Defence. large type ed. LC 93-12730. 1993. 18.95 (*0-7927-1605-1*, Eagle Lrg Print) Chivers N Amer.
— Rumpole for the Defence. large type ed. 1994. pap. 16.95 (*0-7927-1604-3*, Paragon Lrg Print) Chivers N Amer.
— Rumpole of the Bailey. 15.95 (*0-89190-275-9*, Am Repr) Amereon Ltd.
— Rumpole of the Bailey. LC 90-28741. 216p. 1991. 18.95 (*0-922890-81-1*); 25.00 (*0-922890-82-X*) Armchair Detective.
— Rumpole of the Bailey. 1980. mass mkt. 5.95 (*0-14-004670-4*, Penguin Bks) Viking Penguin.
— Rumpole of the Bailey. large type ed. LC 92-43129. (Eagle Large Print Ser.). 1993. 19.95 (*0-7927-1532-2*, Eagle Lrg Print); pap. write for info. (*0-7927-1531-4*, Eagle Lrg Print) Chivers N Amer.
— Rumpole of the Bailey. limited ed. LC 90-28741. 216p. 1991. 75.00 (*0-922890-83-8*) Armchair Detective.
— Rumpole on Trial. large type ed. LC 93-7198. 1993. 20.95 (*1-56054-727-8*) Thorndike Pr.
— Rumpole on Trial. 256p. 1993. reprint ed. pap. 10.00 (*0-14-017510-5*, Penguin Bks) Viking Penguin.
— Rumpole's Last Case. 288p. 1988. pap. 3.95 (*0-14-010447-X*, Penguin Bks) Viking Penguin.
— Rumpoles Last Case. 1990. pap. 9.95 (*0-14-012695-3*, Penguin Bks) Viking Penguin.
— Rumpole's Return. 16.95 (*0-89190-277-5*, Am Repr) Amereon Ltd.
— Rumpole's Return. 160p. 1982. mass mkt. 6.00 (*0-14-005571-1*, Penguin Bks) Viking Penguin.
— Rumpole's Return. limited ed. 176p. 1993. 75.00 (*1-56287-039-4*) Armchair Detective.
— Rumpole's Return. 176p. 1993. reprint ed. 19.95 (*1-56287-037-8*); reprint ed. 25.00 (*1-56287-038-6*) Armchair Detective.
— The Second Rumpole Omnibus. 672p. 1988. pap. 13.00 (*0-14-008958-6*, Penguin Bks) Viking Penguin.
— Summer's Lease. 288p. 1991. pap. 10.95 (*0-14-015827-8*, Penguin Bks) Viking Penguin.
— Titmuss Regained. large type ed. 1992. pap. 15.95 (*0-7927-0666-8*, Paragon Lrg Print) Chivers N Amer.
— Titmuss Regained: Movie-TV Tie-in. 1992. pap. 10.00 (*0-14-017185-1*, Penguin Bks) Viking Penguin.
— The Trials of Rumpole. 18.95 (*0-89190-276-7*, Am Repr) Amereon Ltd.
— The Trials of Rumpole. 206p. 1981. mass mkt. 6.00 (*0-14-005162-7*, Penguin Bks) Viking Penguin.
— The Trials of Rumpole. limited ed. 224p. 1991. 75.00 (*1-56287-007-6*) Armchair Detective.
— The Trials of Rumpole. 224p. 1991. reprint ed. 19.95 (*1-56287-006-8*); reprint ed. 25.00 (*1-56287-015-7*) Armchair Detective.
Mortimer, John, ed. Famous Trials. 376p. 1986. 16.95 (*0-88029-080-3*) Dorset Pr.
— Famous Trials. (Nonfiction Ser.). 384p. 1984. pap. 11.95 (*0-14-006924-0*, Penguin Bks) Viking Penguin.
— The Oxford Book of Villains. 448p. 1992. 24.00 (*0-19-214195-3*) OUP.
— The Oxford Book of Villains. 448p. 1993. reprint ed. pap. 11.95 (*0-19-282277-2*) OUP.
Mortimer, John, intro. & sel. Great Law & Order Stories. 352p. 1992. 25.00 (*0-393-03079-2*) Norton.
Mortimer, John & Mortimer, Bunny. Trees for the New Zealand Countryside: A Planter's Guide. (Illus.). 272p. 1987. text ed. 69.95 (*0-409-60478-X*) Buttrwrth-Heinemann.
***Mortimer, John C.** Dunster. large type ed. LC 94-26347. 407p. 1994. pap. 18.95 (*0-8161-7476-8*) Hall.
Mortimer, Katharine. Sting of the Wasp. 224p. 1987. 17.95 (*0-88191-047-3*) Freundlich.
Mortimer, Kenneth P. & McConnell, T. R. Sharing Authority Effectively. LC 76-50721. (Jossey-Bass Series in Higher Education). 344p. reprint ed. pap. 98.10 (*0-8357-4913-4*, 2037843) Bks Demand.
Mortimer, Kenneth P., et al. Flexibility in Academic Staffing: Effective Policies & Practices. Fife, Jonathan D., ed. & frwd. by. LC 85-72832. (ASHE-ERIC Higher Education Report Ser.: No. 1, 1985). 121p. (Orig.). 1985. pap. 10.00 (*0-913317-20-9*) GWU Schl E&HD.
Mortimer, Kristin A. Harvard University Art Museums: A Guide to the Collections. LC 85-22910. (Illus.). 344p. 1995. 29.95 (*0-89659-600-1*, 601) A Schwartz & Co.
— Harvard University Art Museums: A Guide to the Collections. (Illus.). 344p. 1995. pap. 14.95 (*0-89659-601-X*) A Schwartz & Co.
Mortimer, M., jt. ed. see Begon, M.
Mortimer, Martin, jt. auth. see Cousens, Roger.
Mortimer, Mildred. Journeys Through the French African Novel. LC 90-4416. (Studies in African Literature). 230p. (Orig.). (C). 1990. pap. text ed. 18.50 (*0-435-08042-3*, 08042) Heinemann.
***Mortimer, Mildred, ed.** Critical Perspectives on Algerian Literature. 320p. 1996. 36.00 (*0-89410-797-6*); pap. 18.00 (*0-89410-798-4*) Three Continents.
Mortimer, Mildred, et al, eds. The Literature of Africa & the African Continuum. LC 84-51450. (African Literature Association Annuals Ser.). 140p. (Orig.). 1988. 22.00 (*0-89410-460-8*); pap. 14.00 (*0-89410-461-6*) Three Continents.
Mortimer, Monty. Competition Training: For Horse & Rider. (Illus.). 192p. 1993. 29.95 (*0-7153-9961-6*, Pub. by David & Charles UK) Trafalgar.
Mortimer, Pamela, ed. see Long, David M.
Mortimer, Raymond, jt. auth. see Todd, Dorothy.
Mortimer, Rex. Indonesian Communism Under Sukarno: Ideology & Politics, 1959-1965. LC 73-19372. 448p. 1974. 52.50 (*0-8014-0825-3*) Cornell U Pr.
Mortimer, Richard. Angevin England, 1154-1258. (History of Medieval Britain Ser.). (Illus.). 256p. 1994. 39.95 (*0-631-16388-3*) Blackwell Pubs.
Mortimer, Richard, ed. Leiston Abbey Cartulary & Butley Priory Charters. (Suffolk Charters Ser.: No. I). 176p. 1979. 39.00 (*0-85115-106-X*) Boydell & Brewer.
Mortimer, Richard, jt. auth. see Harper-Bill, Christopher.
Mortimer, Richard, jt. ed. see Harper-Bill, Christopher.
Mortimer, Richard, jt. ed. see Harvey, Anthony.
Mortimer, Richard, tr. see Haverkamp, Alfred.
Mortimer, Robert G. Physical Chemistry. LC 92-40711. 1993. 13.75 (*0-8053-4650-3*) Benjamin-Cummings.
Mortimer, Ruth, intro. The Selma Erving Collection: Modern Illustrated Books. 60p. 1977. pap. 7.00 (*0-87391-037-0*) Smith Coll Mus Art.
***Mortimer, Sheila.** Fred the Frog. (Illus.). 32p. (J). (ps-2). 1995. 8.95 (*0-7078-0235-0*, Pub. by Natl Trust UK) Trafalgar.
***Mortimer, Stuart.** Techniques of Spiral Work: A Practical Guide to the Craft of Making Twists by Hand. (Illus.). 175p. 1995. pap. write for info. (*0-941936-34-1*) Linden Pub Fresno.
Mortimer, W. Golden. Peru & the History of Coca: Divine Plant of the Incas. 1976. lib. bdg. 75.00 (*0-8490-0821-2*) Gordon Pr.
Mortimer, William G. Peru: History of Coca, "the Divine Plant" of the Incas. LC 74-15120. reprint ed. 69.50 (*0-404-11980-8*) AMS Pr.
Mortimore, Jo & Blackstone, Tessa. Disadvantage & Education. (SSRC-DHSS Studies in Deprivation & Disadvantage: No. 4). 216p. 1982. text ed. 28.95 (*0-435-82608-5*) Ashgate Pub Co.
Mortimore, Jo, jt. auth. see Morimore, Peter.
Mortimore, Michael, jt. auth. see Tiffen, Mary.
Mortimore, Peter, et al. Managing Associate Staff: Innovation in Primary & Secondary Schools. 192p. 1993. pap. 37.50 (*1-85396-231-7*, Pub. by Paul Chapman UK) Taylor & Francis.
— School Matters. 1988. 45.00 (*0-520-06502-6*); pap. 17.00 (*0-520-06503-4*) U CA Pr.
— School Matters: The Junior Years. 314p. 1988. pap. 22.00 (*0-7291-0194-0*, Pub. by Paul Chapman UK) Taylor & Francis.
Mortis, Joseph, ed. see Society of Biological Psychiatry Staff.
Mortland, Donald, ed. see Colcord, Lincoln.
Mortley. Womanhood the Feminine in Ancient Hellenism Gnosticism Christianity & Islam. 1981. 18.50 (*0-85668-912-2*, Pub. by Aris & Phillips UK); pap. write for info. (*0-85668-913-0*, Pub. by Aris & Phillips UK) David Brown.
Mortley, Raoul. French Philosophers in Conversation. 108p. 1991. 42.50 (*0-415-05254-8*, A5106); pap. 11.95 (*0-415-05255-6*, A5110) Routledge.
Mortlock. Evolution of Metabolic Function. 1992. 156.95 (*0-8493-8863-5*) CRC Pr.
Mortlock, Robert P., ed. Microorganisms As Model Systems for Studying Evolution. LC 84-17938. (Monographs in Evolutionary Biology). 344p. 1984. 85.00 (*0-306-41788-X*, Plenum Pr) Plenum.
Mortman, Doris. Circles. (Orig.). 1988. mass mkt. 6.50 (*0-553-27197-0*) Bantam.
— First Born. 1988. mass mkt. 5.99 (*0-553-27032-X*) Bantam.
— Rightfully Mine. 1990. mass mkt. 6.50 (*0-553-28416-9*) Bantam.
— True Colors: A Novel. LC 94-13068. 1994. 24.00 (*0-517-59262-2*) Crown Pub Group.
— Wild Rose. 1992. mass mkt. 6.99 (*0-553-29761-9*) Bantam.
Morton. British Labour Movement. (C). 1979. pap. 19.95 (*0-85315-286-1*, Pub. by Lawrence & Wishart UK) Humanities.
— Health Assessment in Nursing. 2nd ed. 1992. 44.95 (*0-87434-425-5*) Springhouse Pub.
— A History of Monroe County, West Virginia. (Illus.). 510p. 1988. 25.00 (*0-614-03820-0*, 3900) Genealog Pub.
— Nurses Clinical Guide to Health Assessment. 306p. 1990. 24.95 (*0-87434-233-3*) Springhouse Pub.
— Self Assessment Picture Tests in Dentistry. 144p. 1994. pap. 19.95 (*0-8151-6223-5*, Yr Bk Med Pubs) Mosby Yr Bk.
Morton, jt. auth. see Dillon.
Morton, jt. auth. see Enright.
Morton, jt. auth. see Trowbridge.

M

Morton, A. Mechanical Composition, 3 pts. Incl. Pt. 2. Monotype Keyboard. 52p. 1969. pap. 30.00 (0-08-013965-5); 1969. Set pap. write for info. (0-318-55181-0, Pub. by Pergamon Repr UK) Franklin.

Morton, A. A., jt. auth. see Broderick, M.

Morton, A. C., et al, eds. Developments in Sedimentary Provenance Studies. (Geological Society Special Publications: No. 57). (Illus.). 376p. 1991. 130.00 (0-903317-56-7, Pub. by Geol Soc Pub Hse UK) AAPG.

— Geology of the Brent Group. (Geological Society Special Publications: No. 61). (Illus.). vi, 506p. (C). 1992. 125.00 (0-903317-68-0, Pub. by Geol Soc Pub Hse UK) AAPG.

Morton, A. G. History of Botanical Science: An Account of the Development of Botany from the Ancient Time to the Present. LC 81-67891. 1981. pap. text ed. 53.00 (0-12-508382-3) Acad Pr.

Morton, A. L. Everlasting Gospel. (Studies in Blake: No. 3). 1958. pap. 39.95 (0-8383-0098-7) M S G Haskell Hse.

— History & the Imagination: The Selected Writings of A. L. Morton. (C). 1990. text ed. 39.95 (0-85315-719-7, Pub. by Lawrence & Wishart UK) Humanities.

— Life & Ideas of Robert Owen. 239p. 1969. 12.95 (0-8464-1111-3) Beekman Pubs.

— The Matter of Britain. 166p. 1966. 24.95 (0-8464-1427-9) Beekman Pubs.

— A People's History of England. 2nd ed. 588p. 1938. pap. 19.95 (0-85315-723-5, Pub. by Lawrence & Wishart UK) Humanities.

***Morton, A. L., ed. & intro.** The Political Writings of William Morris. 246p. Date not set. pap. write for info. (0-85315-257-8, Pub. by Lawrence & Wishart UK) Humanities.

Morton, A. L., ed. see Morris, William.

Morton, A. L., tr. see Sperber, Dan.

Morton, A. Q., et al. Critical Concordance to the Letter of Paul to the Romans. Baird, J. Arthur & Freedman, David Noel, eds. (Computer Bible Ser.: Vol. XIII). 1977. pap. 27.50 (0-935106-08-1) Biblical Res Assocs.

Morton, A. Q. & Michaelson, Sidney. A Critical Concordance to the Acts of the Apostles. (Computer Bible Ser.: Vol. VII). 1976. pap. 15.00 (0-935106-14-6) Biblical Res Assocs.

Morton, A. Q., et al. A Critical Concordance to I & II Corinthians. (Computer Bible Ser.: Vol. XIX). 1979. pap. 30.00 (0-935106-01-4) Biblical Res Assocs.

— A Critical Concordance to I, II Thessalonians. Baird, J. Arthur & Freedman, David N., eds. (Computer Bible Ser.: Vol XXVI). 136p. (Orig.). 1983. pap. 25.00 (0-935106-21-9) Biblical Res Assocs.

— A Critical Concordance to the Epistle of Paul to the Galatians. Baird, J. Arthur & Freedman, David, eds. (Computer Bible Ser.: Vol. XXI). (Orig.). 1980. pap. text ed. 20.00 (0-935106-16-2) Biblical Res Assocs.

— Critical Concordance to the Letter of Paul to the Colossians. Baird, J. Arthur & Freedman, David, eds. (Computer Bible Ser.: Vol. XXIV). (Orig.). 1981. pap. text ed. 20.00 (0-935106-19-7) Biblical Res Assocs.

— A Critical Concordance to the Letter of Paul to the Ephesians. Baird, J. Arthur & Freedman, David, eds. (Computer Bible Ser.: Vol. XXII). (Orig.). 1980. pap. text ed. 20.00 (0-935106-17-0) Biblical Res Assocs.

— Critical Concordance to the Letter of Paul to the Philippians. Baird, J. Arthur & Freedman, David, eds. (Computer Bible Ser.: Vol. XXIII). (Orig.). 1980. pap. text ed. 20.00 (0-935106-18-9) Biblical Res Assocs.

— Critical Concordance to the Pastoral Epistles, I, II Timothy, Titus, Philemon. Baird, J. Arthur & Freedman, David N., eds. (Computer Bible Ser.: Vol. XXV). 1982. pap. 35.00 (0-935106-20-0) Biblical Res Assocs.

***Morton, Adam.** Philosophy in Practice: An Introduction to the Main Question. (Illus.). 500p. (C). 1996. write for info. (0-631-18864-9); pap. write for info. (0-631-18865-7) Blackwell Pubs.

Morton, Alan Q. & Wess, Jane A. Public & Private Science: The King George III Collection. (Illus.). 704p. 1993. boxed 85.00 (0-19-856392-2) OUP.

***Morton, Alexander.** In the Company of Whales: From the Diary of a Whalewatcher. (Illus.). 64p. (YA). 1995. pap. write for info. (1-55143-058-4) Orca Bk Pubs.

Morton, Alexander C. The Official Guide to Airline Careers. write for info. (0-318-59582-6) S&S Trade.

Morton, Alexander L., jt. auth. see Meyer, John R.

***Morton, Alexandra.** In the Company of Whales: From the Diary of a Whale Watcher. 64p. (YA). (gr. 8-12). 1993. lib. bdg. 15.95 (1-55143-000-2) Orca Bk Pubs.

— Siwiti: A Whale's Story. (Illus.). 48p. (Orig.). (YA). (gr. 8-12). 1991. pap. 9.95 (0-920501-97-4) Orca Bk Pubs.

Morton, Alice, tr. see De Heusch, Luc.

***Morton, Andrew.** Diana: Her New Life. 1994. 23.00 (0-684-80009-8) S&S Trade.

— Diana: Her New Life. large type ed. LC 95-2572. 1995. write for info. (0-7862-0425-7) Thorndike Pr.

— Diana: Her True Story. Rubenstein, Julie & Peters, Sally, eds. 288p. 1992. mass mkt. 5.99 (0-671-79878-2) PB.

— Diana: Her True Story. large type ed. 304p. 1993. reprint ed. lib. bdg. 21.95 (1-56054-608-5); reprint ed. pap. 13.95 (1-56054-889-4) Thorndike Pr.

— Duchess. large type ed. (Large Print Contemporary Ser.). (Illus.). 193p. 1989. 23.95 (0-7089-8514-9, Charnwood) Ulverscroft.

— Inside Buckingham Palace: The Private World of the Royal Family. (Illus.). 96p. (Orig.). 1993. pap. 28.50 (1-85479-921-5, Pub. by M OMara Books UK) Trans-Atl Phila.

— The Wealth of the Windsors. (Illus.). 192p. 1994. reprint ed. pap. 10.95 (1-55970-261-3) Arcade Pub Inc.

Morton, Andrew B. Food Contamination: Medical Subject Analysis with Bibliography. LC 87-47612. 160p. 1987. 39.50 (0-88164-536-2); pap. 34.50 (0-88164-537-0) ABBE Pubs Assn.

***Morton, Andrew R.** Food-Calorie Intake & Effects on Diet, Energy & Metabolism: Index of New Information with Authors & Subjects. rev. ed. LC 94-34922. 163p. 1994. 49.50 (0-7883-0444-5); pap. 39.50 (0-7883-0445-3) ABBE Pubs Assn.

Morton, Anne. Canadian Office Management Manual: An on-the-Job Guide for Office Professionals. 2nd ed. (Reference Ser.). 288p. 1993. Canadian ed. pap. 9.95 (0-88908-537-4) Self-Counsel Pr.

— The Office Management Manual: A Guide for Secretaries, Administrative Assistants, & Other Office Professionals. (Reference Ser.). 336p. (Orig.). 1990. pap. text ed. 9.95 (0-88908-927-2) Self-Counsel Pr.

— The Secretary's Friend: The Office Management Manual. LC 86-45541. 256p. 1986. 14.95 (0-933051-16-6) Lowen Pub.

— Secretary's Friend: The Office Management Manual. 2nd rev. ed. 256p. 1987. pap. 9.95 (0-933051-33-6) Lowen Pub.

Morton, Annie, et al. Great Special Events. LC 91-65991. 112p. 1991. pap. 16.95 (0-910251-45-2) Venture Pub PA.

Morton, Arthur L. & Tate, George. British Labour Movement, 1770-1920. 313p. 1974. pap. 22.00 (0-8464-0215-7) Beekman Pubs.

— The British Labour Movement, 1770-1920: A Political History. LC 74-25892. 313p. 1975. reprint ed. text ed. 35.00 (0-8371-7865-7, MOBL, Greenwood Pr) Greenwood.

Morton, Avery A. Solid Organoalkali Metal Reagents. 256p. 1967. text ed. 207.00 (0-677-00560-1) Gordon & Breach.

Morton, Barbara M. Down East Netting: A History & How-To of Netmaking. (Illus.). 1988. pap. 9.95 (0-89272-246-0) Down East.

— Down East Netting: A History & How-to of Netmaking. LC 88-51283. (Illus.). 1988. pap. 9.95 (0-89272-231-2) Down East.

Morton, Brian. Asian Marine Biology, 8 Vols., Vol. 1: 1984. 192p. (C). 1992. Vol. 1, 1984, 192p. pap. 80.00 (962-209-113-X, Pub. by Hong Kong U Pr HK) St Mut.

— Asian Marine Biology, 8 Vols., Vol. 2: 1985. 152p. (C). 1992. Vol. 2, 1985, 152p. pap. 80.00 (962-209-126-1, Pub. by Hong Kong U Pr HK) St Mut.

— Asian Marine Biology, 8 Vols., Vol. 3: 1986. 192p. (C). 1992. Vol. 3, 1986, 192p. pap. 80.00 (962-209-187-3, Pub. by Hong Kong U Pr HK) St Mut.

— Asian Marine Biology, 8 Vols., Vol. 4: 1987. 170p. (C). 1992. Vol. 4, 1987, 170p. pap. 80.00 (962-209-198-9, Pub. by Hong Kong U Pr HK) St Mut.

— Asian Marine Biology, 8 Vols., Vol. 5: 1988. 146p. (C). 1992. Vol. 5, 1988, 146p. pap. 80.00 (962-209-218-7, Pub. by Hong Kong U Pr HK) St Mut.

— Asian Marine Biology, 8 Vols., Vol. 6: 1989. 256p. (C). 1992. Vol. 6, 1989, 256p. pap. 80.00 (962-209-240-3, Pub. by Hong Kong U Pr HK) St Mut.

— Asian Marine Biology, 8 Vols., Vol. 7: 1990. 214p. (C). 1992. Vol. 7, 1990, 214p. pap. 80.00 (962-209-273-X, Pub. by Hong Kong U Pr HK) St Mut.

— Asian Marine Biology, 8 Vols., Vol. 8: 1991. 232p. (C). 1992. Vol. 8, 1991, 232p. pap. 80.00 (962-209-297-7, Pub. by Hong Kong U Pr HK) St Mut.

— The Bivalve: Proceedings of a Memorial Symposium in Honour of Sir Charles Maurice Yonge. 364p. (C). 1990. pap. text ed. 144.00 (962-209-254-3, Pub. by Hong Kong U Pr HK) St Mut.

— The Blackwell Guide to Contemporary Composers on Disc. (Blackwell Guides Ser.). 352p. 1995. 24.95 (0-631-18881-9) Blackwell Pubs.

— The Malacofauna of Hong Kong & Southern China: Proceedings of International Workshops, 1st, Hong Kong, March 23-April 8, 1977, 2 vols., Set. 2nd ed. (Illus.). vi, 345p. 1986. pap. 62.75 (962-209-021-4) E J Brill.

Morton, Brian, comp. A Bibliography of Hong Kong Marine Science: 1842-1990. 148p. (C). 1990. pap. text ed. 69.00 (962-209-275-6, Pub. by Hong Kong U Pr HK) St Mut.

Morton, Brian, ed. The Malacofauna of Hong Kong & Southern China 11. 700p. (C). 1985. pap. text ed. 240.00 (962-209-120-2, Pub. by Hong Kong U Pr HK) St Mut.

— Marine Biology of the South China Sea, 2 vols., Set. (Illus.). 656p. (Orig.). 1993. pap. 125.00x (962-209-339-6, Pub. by Hong Kong Univ Pr HK) Coronet Bks.

— The Marine Flora & Fauna of Hong Kong & Southern China, 2 vols., Set. (Illus.). 928p. (Orig.). 1993. pap. 275.00x (962-209-293-4, Pub. by Hong Kong Univ Pr HK) Coronet Bks.

— The Marine Flora & Fauna of Hong Kong & Southern China 11, 3 vols., Set. 1322p. (C). 1990. pap. text ed. 600.00 (962-209-241-1, Pub. by Hong Kong U Pr HK) St Mut.

Morton, Brian & Collins, Pamela, eds. Contemporary Composers. 1000p. 1992. 125.00 (1-55862-085-0, 200105) St James Pr.

Morton, Brian & Morton, John. The Sea Shore Ecology of Hong Kong. (Illus.). 366p. 1983. 62.50 (962-209-028-1, Pub. by Hong Kong Univ Pr HK) Coronet Bks.

— The Sea Shore Ecology of Hong Kong. 366p. (C). 1983. text ed. 75.00 (0-685-65778-7, Pub. by Hong Kong U Pr HK); pap. text ed. 60.00 (962-209-027-3, Pub. by Hong Kong U Pr HK) St Mut.

Morton, Brian, jt. auth. see Britton, Joseph C.

Morton, Brian, jt. auth. see Cook, Richard.

Morton, Brian, ed. see International Marine Biological Workshop Staff.

Morton, Brian, tr. see Lie, Jonas L.

Morton, Brian N. Americans in London: A Street-By-Street Guide. LC 86-6621. (Illus.). 296p. 1986. pap. 12.95 (0-688-06555-4) Olivia & Hill.

— Americans in Paris: An Anecdotal Street Guide. (Illus.). 313p. 1986. 20.00 (0-934034-06-0); pap. 12.95 (0-934034-05-2) Olivia & Hill.

Morton, Brian N. & Morton, Jacqueline. La Presse Deux: Contemporary Issues in French Newspapers. 2nd ed. 237p. (ENG & FRE.). (C). 1977. pap. text ed. 16.50 (0-669-01636-5) Heath.

Morton, Brian N. & Spinelli, Donald C. Beaumarchais: A Bibliography. xxiv, 374p. 1988. 50.00 (0-934034-08-7) Olivia & Hill.

Morton, Brian N., ed. see De Beaumarchais, Pierre-Augustin C.

Morton, Brian N., ed. see De Beaumarchais, Pierre.

Morton, Bruce. John Gould Fletcher: A Bibliography. LC 79-10877. (Serif Series, Bibliographies & Checklists: No. 37). 219p. reprint ed. pap. 62.50 (0-7837-0295-7, 2040616) Bks Demand.

Morton, Bruce, comp. Halley's Comet, Seventeen Fifty-Five to Nineteen Eighty-Four: A Bibliography. LC 84-19716. (Illus.). xvi, 280p. 1985. text ed. 36.95 (0-313-24022-1, MOH/, Greenwood Pr) Greenwood.

Morton, C., jt. auth. see Morton, I. D.

Morton, C., jt. auth. see Morton, Ian D.

Morton, Carlos. Los Dorados. Landes, William A., ed. LC 90-53688. 30p. (Orig.). 1991. pap. 5.00 (0-88734-321-X) Players Pr.

— El Jardin. LC 90-53686. 34p. (Orig.). 1991. pap. 5.00 (0-88734-320-1) Players Pr.

— Johnny Tenorio. LC 93-19387. 1993. pap. 5.00 (0-88734-339-2) Players Pr.

— Johnny Tenorio & Other Plays. LC 91-40493. (Orig.). 1992. 11.00 (1-55885-047-3) Arte Publico.

— The Many Deaths of Danny Rosales. LC 90-53684. 50p. (Orig.). 1991. pap. 6.00 (0-88734-232-9) Players Pr.

— The Many Deaths of Danny Rosales, & Other Plays. LC 82-72277. 160p. (Orig.). (C). 1983. 11.00 (0-934770-16-6) Arte Publico.

— The Miser of Mexico. LC 93-19388. (Orig.). 1993. pap. 6.00 (0-88734-270-1) Players Pr.

— Pancho Diablo. LC 93-15620. 1993. pap. 5.00 (0-88734-340-6) Players Pr.

— Rancho Hollywood. LC 90-53687. 50p. (Orig.). 1991. pap. 6.00 (0-88734-233-7) Players Pr.

— The Savior. LC 93-15619. 1993. pap. 6.00 (0-88734-271-X) Players Pr.

Morton, Charles. Charles Morton's Compendium Physicae. Hornberger, Theodore, ed. (Publications - Colonial Society of Massachusetts: Vol. 33). 277p. reprint ed. pap. 79.00 (0-7837-0267-1, 2040576) Bks Demand.

Morton, Chris & Beverly, Don. School District Instructional Computer-Use Evaluation Manual. LC 88-24682. (Illus.). 61p. 1989. pap. 19.95 (0-87778-214-8) Educ Tech Pubns.

Morton, Christine. The Pig That Barked. (Illus.). 32p. (J). (gr. 2-4). 1994. 11.95 (0-340-56814-3, Pub. by H & S UK); pap. 6.95 (0-340-58659-1, Pub. by H & S UK) Trafalgar.

Morton, Chuck. Ferrets. (Pet Care Ser.). 80p. 1985. pap. 5.95 (0-8120-2976-3) Barron.

***Morton, Chuck & Morton, E. Lynn.** Ferrets: Everything about Purchase, Care, Nutrition, Diseases, Behavior, & Breeding. 2nd rev. ed. Vriends, Mattew M., ed. LC 94-37728. 1995. pap. 5.95 (0-8120-9021-7) Barron.

Morton-Cooper, Alison & Palmer, Anne. Mentoring & Preceptorship: A Guide to Support Roles in Clinical Practice. LC 93-19829. 1993. write for info. (0-632-03596-X) Blackwell Sci.

Morton, D. Morton: The Mortons & Their Kin: A Genealogy & a Source Book. 899p. 1992. reprint ed. lib. bdg. 129.00 (0-8328-2297-3); reprint ed. pap. 119.00 (0-8328-2298-1) Higginson Bk Co.

Morton, Daniel. Marti & the Mango. LC 92-25149. (Illus.). 32p. 1993. 8.95 (1-55670-264-7) Stewart Tabori & Chang.

Morton, Daniel O. Memoir of Rev. Levi Parsons: Late Missionary to Palestine. Davis, Moshe, ed. (America & the Holy Land Ser.). 1977. reprint ed. lib. bdg. 36.95 (0-405-10271-2) Ayer.

Morton, David, ed. Selected Reports in Ethnomusicology, Vol. II, No. 2. LC 75-24270. (Illus.). xii, 259p. (Orig.). 1975. pap. text ed. 9.50 (0-88287-005-X) UCLA Dept Ethnom.

— Shorter Modern Poems: 1900-1931. LC 74-116411. (Granger Index Reprint Ser.). 1977. 15.95 (0-8369-6152-8) Ayer.

Morton, David A. How to Qualify for Social Security Disability: And Protect Your Rights. LC 92-93518. 224p. (Orig.). 1992. pap. 15.00 (0-9634464-0-1) Fine Bks.

Morton, David A., III. Medical Proof of Social Securities Disability. LC 83-16800. 585p. 1992. reprint ed. text ed. write for info. (0-314-72082-0) West Pub.

Morton, David C. & Wolfe, Charles K. DeFord Bailey: A Black Star in Early Country Music. LC 90-22519. (Illus.). 224p. (C). 1993. pap. 14.95 (0-87049-792-8) U of Tenn Pr.

Morton, Davis L. Traveler's Guide to the Great Art Treasures of Europe. 575p. 1987. lib. bdg. 45.00 (0-8161-8733-9, Hall Reference); pap. 12.95 (0-8161-8931-5, Hall Reference) Macmillan.

Morton, Desmond. Ministers & Generals: Politics & the Canadian Militia 1868-1904. LC 79-135208. 272p. reprint ed. pap. 77.60 (0-317-08273-6, 2014374) Bks Demand.

— A Peculiar Kind of Politics: Canada's Overseas Ministry in the First World War. 280p. 1982. 30.00 (0-8020-5586-9) U of Toronto Pr.

— A Short History of Canada. 300p. 1992. pap. 12.95 (0-88830-252-5, Pub. by McClelland & Stewart CN) Firefly Bks Ltd.

— A Short History of Canada. 351p. (Orig.). 1995. pap. 14.95 (0-7710-6516-7, Pub. by McClelland & Stewart CN) Firefly Bks Ltd.

Morton, Desmond & Wright, Glenn. Winning the Second Battle: Canadian Veterans & the Return to Civilian Life, 1915-1930. 328p. 1987. 45.00 (0-8020-5705-5); pap. 18.95 (0-8020-6634-8) U of Toronto Pr.

Morton, Don & Tsunoi, Naoko. The Best of Tokyo. rev. ed. (Illus.). 208p. 1993. pap. 12.95 (0-8048-1919-X) C E Tuttle.

Morton, Donald & Zavarzadeh, Mas'ud, eds. Theory - Pedagogy - Politics: Texts for Change. 264p. 1991. 29.95 (0-252-01761-7); pap. 12.50 (0-252-06157-8) U of Ill Pr.

Morton, Donald, jt. auth. see Zavarzadeh, Mas'ud.

Morton, Douglas R., Jr., jt. ed. see Pike, John E.

Morton, E. D., jt. auth. see Simmonds, A. T.

Morton, E. Lynn, jt. auth. see Morton, Chuck.

Morton, E. Reginald. Essentials of Medical Electricity. 1991. lib. bdg. 88.95 (0-8490-5014-6) Gordon Pr.

Morton, E. Susan & Grigsby, R. Kevin. Advancing Family Preservation Practice. (Focus Editions Ser.: Vol. 150). (Illus.). 196p. (C). 1992. 49.95 (0-8039-4570-1); pap. 24.95 (0-8039-4571-X) Sage.

Morton, Eugene S. Animal Talk. 1992. 19.50 (0-394-58337-X) Random.

Morton, Eugene S., jt. ed. see Keast, Allen.

Morton, Eugene S., jt. auth. see Page, Jake.

Morton, F. L. Pro-Choice vs. Pro-Life: The Abortion Debate in Canada. LC 92-34959. 1993. pap. 19.95 (0-8061-2522-5) U of Okla Pr.

Morton, F. L., ed. Law, Politics & the Judicial Process in Canada. 2nd ed. 502p. 1993. pap. 29.95 (0-919813-83-6, Pub. by Univ Calgary CN) Paul & Co Pubs.

Morton, Fred, jt. ed. see Eldredge, Elizabeth A.

Morton, Fred, et al. Historical Dictionary of Botswana. LC 89-36098. (African Historical Dictionaries Ser.: No. 44). (Illus.). 244p. 1989. 29.50 (0-8108-2224-5) Scarecrow.

Morton, Frederic. A Nervous Splendor: Vienna 1888-1889. 1980. pap. 11.95 (0-14-005667-X, Penguin Bks) Viking Penguin.

— The Rothschilds: A Family Portrait. LC 83-6328. (Illus.). 352p. 1983. pap. 9.95 (0-689-70657-X, 301, Atheneum S&S) S&S Trade.

— The Rothschilds: A Family Portrait. 304p. 1991. reprint ed. pap. 12.95 (0-02-023002-8, Pub. by Gebrueder Borntraeger GW) Macmillan.

— Thunder at Twilight: Vienna, Nineteen Thirteen to Nineteen Fourteen. 384p. 1991. reprint ed. pap. 9.95 (0-02-035300-6, Pub. by Gebrueder Borntraeger GW) Macmillan.

Morton, Friedrich. In the Land of the Quetzal Feather. (Illus.). 1960. 10.00 (0-8159-5807-2) Devin.

Morton, Gene A., jt. auth. see Long, Dani L.

Morton, George, ed. see Riegel, E. C.

Morton, George A. & Malloch, D. Macleod. Law & Laughter. (Illus.). x, 259p. 1989. reprint ed. lib. bdg. 27.50 (0-8377-2439-2) Rothman.

Morton, Gerald & O'Brien, George. Wrestling to Rasslin. LC 85-70425. 169p. 1985. 19.95 (0-87972-323-8) Bowling Green Univ.

Morton, Gerald W. A Biography of Mildmay Fane, Second Earl of Westmorland (1601-1666) The Unknown Cavalier. LC 90-24436. (Studies in British History: Vol. 22). (Illus.). 168p. 1991. lib. bdg. 79.95 (0-88946-261-5) E Mellen.

— Critical Edition of Midmay Fane's Vertues Triumph (1644) (American University Studies: English Language & Literature: Ser. IV, Vol. 75). 222p. (C). 1989. text ed. 32.50 (0-8204-0809-3) P Lang Pubs.

Morton, Gerald W., jt. ed. see Helgeson, Karin P.

Morton, Grace, jt. auth. see Morton, Lucy.

Morton, Gregory. Family. (Illus.). 1980. 8.95 (0-8065-0691-1, Citadel Pr) Carol Pub Group.

Morton, Harold. Flying for God: ...into the Son. 208p. (C). 1990. pap. text ed. 35.00 (0-685-40843-4) St Mut.

Morton, Harry. The Whale's Wake. (Illus.). 396p. 1982. text ed. 32.50 (0-8248-0830-4) UH Pr.

Morton, Helen. Highlights: Eighty Years Worth Living. (Illus.). 272p. 1989. pap. 17.95 (0-933858-05-1) Kennebec River.

Morton, Henry W. & Stuart, Robert C., eds. The Contemporary Soviet City. LC 83-8543. 288p. 1984. pap. 44.95 (0-87332-254-1) M E Sharpe.

Morton, Henry W. & Tokes, Rudolf L. Soviet Politics & Society in the 1970's. LC 73-10575. (Illus.). 1974. 24.95 (0-02-922090-4) Free Pr.

Morton, Herbert C. The Story of Webster's Third: Philip Gove's Controversial Dictionary & Its Critics. (Illus.). 368p. (C). 1994. 29.95 (0-521-46146-4) Cambridge U Pr.

— The Story of Webster's Third: Philip Gove's Controversial Dictionary & Its Critics. (Illus.). 360p. (C). 1995. pap. 18.95 (0-521-55869-7) Cambridge U Pr.

Morton, Herbert C. & Price, Anne J. The ACLS Survey of Scholars: Final Report of Views on Publications, Computers, & Libraries. (Illus.). 148p. (Orig.). (C). 1989. pap. text ed. 23.00 (0-8191-7261-8) Am Coun Lrnd Soc.

Morton, Hugh, jt. photos see Donnan, Bob.

Morton, I. & Rhodes, D. N., eds. Contribution of Chemistry to Food Supplies: Proceedings of a Symposium, Hamburg, 1973. 448p. 1974. 188.00 (0-08-020748-0, Pub. by Pergamon Repr UK) Franklin.

Morton, I. D. Cereals in a European Context: First European Conference on Food Science & Technology. (Ellis Horwood Series in Food Science & Technology). 523p. 1987. lib. bdg. 220.00 (0-89573-523-7) VCH Pubs.

Morton, I. D. & Lenges, J. J., eds. Education & Training in Food Science: A Changing Scene. LC 92-20703. (Ellis Horwood Series in Food Science & Technology). 300p. 1992. 75.00 (0-13-802273-9, Tavistock-E Horwood) Routledge Chapman & Hall.

An Asterisk (*) at the beginning of an entry indicates that the title is appearing in BIP for the first time.

Morton, I. D. & MacLeod, A. J., eds. Food Flavours, Part B: The Flavour of Beverages. (Developments in Food Science Ser.: No. 3B). 384p. 1986. 133.50 (*0-444-42599-3*) Elsevier.

— Food Flavours, Pt. C: The Flavour of Fruits. (Developments in Food Science Ser.: 3C). 372p. 1990. 141.00 (*0-444-87362-7*) Elsevier.

Morton, I. D. & Morton, C. Elsevier's Dictionary of Food Science & Technology. 208p. (ENG, FRE, GER & SPA.). 1990. 195.00 (*0-8288-9213-X*, M7929) Fr & Eur.

Morton, Ian D. & Morton, C. Elsevier's Dictionary of Food Science & Technology. 208p. (ENG, FRE, GER, ITA & SPA.). 1977. 84.75 (*0-444-41559-9*) Elsevier.

Morton, Ira. The Galloping Ghost: Biography of Harold "Red" Grange, First Football Superstar. (Illus.). 1984. 10. 50 (*0-916445-04-6*) Crossroads Comm.

Morton, Ira, aft. & told to. The Red Grange Story: An Autobiography. LC 93-11212. (Illus.). 232p. 1993. reprint ed. pap. 9.95 (*0-252-06329-5*) U of Ill Pr.

Morton, J. Criminal Justice Act, 1987: A Commentary. (Criminal Law Guides Ser.). 128p. 1988. pap. 34.00 (*0-08-033088-6*, Pergamon Pr) Elsevier.

— A Guide to Sentencing. (Waterlow Criminal Law Guide Ser.). 160p. 1990. pap. 29.95 (*0-08-040117-1*, Pergamon Pr) Elsevier.

Morton, J., ed. Structural Impact & Crashworthiness, Vol. 2. 556p. 1984. 97.25 (*0-85334-293-8*, I-259-84, Pub. by Elsevier Applied Sci UK) Elsevier.

Morton, J., jt. auth. see Duckers, L. J.

Morton, J., jt. ed. see Duckers, L. J.

Morton, J., jt. auth. see Gillett, W. B.

Morton, J., jt. auth. see Hall, D. O.

Morton, J., jt. auth. see McNelis, B.

Morton, J., jt. ed. see McNelis, B.

Morton, J., jt. auth. see Rosenfeld, J. L.

Morton, J. B. Brumaire: The Rise of Bonaparte. (Select Bibliographies Reprint Ser.). 1977. reprint ed. 25.95 (*0-518-19075-7*) Ayer.

— Hilaire Belloc: A Memoir. 1984. lib. bdg. 90.00 (*0-8490-3236-9*) Gordon Pr.

Morton, J. D. & MacLeod, A. J., eds. Food Flavors: Pt. A: Introduction. (Developments in Food Science Ser.: Vol. 3A). 474p. 1982. 159.00 (*0-444-41857-1*) Elsevier.

Morton, J. E. Urban Mortgage Lending: Comparative Markets & Experience. (Financial Research Program IV: Studies in Urban Mortgage Financing: No. 6). 212p. 1956. reprint ed. 55.20 (*0-87014-144-9*) Natl Bur Econ Res.

Morton, Jacqueline. English Grammar for Students of French: The Study Guide for Those Learning French. 3rd ed. 182p. 1993. pap. 9.95 (*0-934034-18-4*) Olivia & Hill.

Morton, Jacqueline, ed. see Cruise, Edwina.

Morton, Jacqueline, ed. see Levenson, Ana & Eggly, Susan.

Morton, Jacqueline, jt. auth. see Morton, Brian N.

Morton, Jacqueline, ed. see Primorac, Karen & Adorni, Sergio.

Morton, Jacqueline, ed. see Simon, Mutsuko E.

Morton, Jacqueline, ed. see Spinelli, Emily.

Morton, Jacqueline, ed. see Zorach, Cecile & Melin, Charlotte.

Morton, James. Anthology of Rock Drumming. 1993. 9.95 (*0-87166-861-0*, 93802) Mel Bay.

— Easiest Drum Set Book. 1993. 2.95 (*1-56222-027-6*, 94494) Mel Bay.

— Fusion Drum Styles. 1993. 6.95 (*0-87166-508-5*, 93866); audio 9.98 (*0-87166-509-3*, 93866); audio 15.95 (*0-87166-510-7*, 93866) Mel Bay.

— Jazz & Rock Beats for the New Drummer. 1993. 3.95 (*0-87166-287-6*, 93741); audio 9.98 (*0-87166-288-4*, 93741); audio 12.95 (*0-87166-289-2*, 93741) Mel Bay.

— Jazz & Swing Drum Patterns Flip Book. 1993. 3.95 (*0-685-64645-9*, 94376) Mel Bay.

— Killer-Fillers. 1993. 4.95 (*0-87166-379-1*, 93687); audio 9.98 (*0-87166-380-5*, 93687); audio 13.95 (*0-87166-381-3*, 93687) Mel Bay.

— Linear Fusion Drum Patterns Flip Book. 1993. 3.95 (*0-685-64646-7*, 94377) Mel Bay.

— Rhythm Sight Reading Flip Book. 1993. 3.95 (*0-685-64616-5*, 94378) Mel Bay.

— Rock & Funk Drum Patterns Flip Book. 1993. 3.95 (*0-685-64647-5*, 94375) Mel Bay.

— Rock Studies for Drum Set. 1993. 3.95 (*0-87166-813-0*, 94379); audio 9.98 (*1-56222-116-7*, 94379) Mel Bay.

Morton, James, ed. Ancren Riwle, a Treatise on the Rules & Duties of Monastic Life from a Semi-Saxon MS. of the Thirteenth Century. LC 72-158250. (Camden Society, London. Publications, First Ser.: No. 1). reprint ed. 115. 00 (*0-404-50157-5*) AMS Pr.

— Financial Times Global Guide to Investing. 628p. 1995. 75.00 (*0-273-61414-2*, Pub. by Pitman Pub UK) Natl Bk Netwk.

Morton, James P., jt. auth. see Sandys, Edwina.

Morton, Jane. No Place for Cal. 112p. (Orig.). (J). 1989. pap. 2.75 (*0-380-75548-3*, Camelot) Avon.

— Noah's Amazing Ark. (Illus.). 6p. (J). 1994. 4.99 (*1-56476-170-3*, Victor Books) SP Pubns.

— What Babies Can Do. (Illus.). 12p. (J). (ps). 1993. bds. 0.60 (*1-56476-081-2*, Victor Books) SP Pubns.

— What Ones Can Do. (Illus.). 12p. (J). (ps). 1993. bds. 0.60 (*1-56476-082-0*, Victor Books) SP Pubns.

— What Threes Can Do. (Illus.). 12p. (J). (ps). 1993. bds. 0.60 (*1-56476-084-7*, Victor Books) SP Pubns.

— What Twos Can Do. (Illus.). 12p. (J). (ps). 1993. bds. 0.60 (*1-56476-083-9*, Victor Books) SP Pubns.

Morton, Jane, jt. auth. see Preston, Marianne.

Morton, Janet L., et al, eds. Geologic, Hydrothermal, & Biologic Studies at Escanaba Trough, Gorda Ridge, Offshore Northern California. (U. S. Geological Survey Bulletin Ser.: Vol. 2022). 1994. write for info. (*0-318-72781-1*) US Geol Survey.

Morton, Janice. Complete Preparation for Childbirth: A Self Help Manual for Expectant Parents. 240p. (C). 1990. pap. text ed. 80.00 (*962-209-220-9*, Pub. by Hong Kong U Pr HK) St Mut.

Morton, Jeffrey B. BASIC: Step-by-Step Programming. (Illus.). 206p. 1977. pap. 21.95 (*0-916460-22-3*, Matrix Pubs Inc) Weber Systems.

Morton, Joann B., ed. Change, Challenge, & Choices: Women's Role in Modern Corrections. (Illus.). 117p. 1991. 16.80 (*0-929310-54-3*, 322) Am Correctional.

— Public Policy for Corrections: Ratified Public Correctional Policies of the American Correctional Association. 2nd ed. 93p. 1991. pap. 14.75 (*0-929310-46-2*, 311) Am Correctional.

Morton, John. Don't Look Back: Olympic Skiing Competitor & Coach Shares His Story & Training Program. LC 91-34326. (Illus.). 272p. 1992. pap. 14.95 (*0-8117-2434-4*) Stackpole.

Morton, John, ed. Biological & Social Factors in Psycholinguistics. LC 70-137819. (Illus.). 215p. reprint ed. 61.30 (*0-8357-9666-3*, 2014924) Bks Demand.

Morton, John & Marshall, John C., eds. Psycholinguistics: Developmental & Pathological. LC 76-280199. 152p. 1977. 31.95 (*0-8014-1075-4*) Cornell U Pr.

Morton, John, jt. auth. see Johnson, Mark H.

Morton, John, jt. auth. see Morton, Brian.

Morton, John K. Faded Glory: Airline Colour Schemes: View of the Past. (Illus.). 136p. 1991. 19.95 (*0-87938-563-4*, Pub. by Airlife UK) Motorbooks Intl.

— Flying Colors. LC 93-46379. 1994. pap. 19.95 (*0-87938-903-6*) Motorbooks Intl.

Morton, John W. Artillery of Nathan Bedford Forrest. 374p. 1993. pap. 10.95 (*0-89176-042-3*, Bellum Edits) R Bemis Pub.

— The Artillery of Nathan Bedford Forrest's Cavalry. 376p. 1994. 31.95 (*1-55793-019-8*) Guild Bindery Pr.

— The Artillery of Nathan Bedford Forrest's Cavalry. 374p. 1909. 35.00 (*1-56013-008-3*) Olde Soldier Bks.

Morton, Joyce. Legal Secretarial Procedures. 3rd ed. 400p. 1992. pap. text ed. 47.00 (*0-13-529736-2*) P-H.

Morton, Jude, jt. ed. see Jones, Lisa.

Morton, Julia F. Atlas of Medicinal Plants of Middle America: Bahamas to Yucatan. fac. ed. (Illus.). 1448p. 1981. 218.95 (*0-398-04036-2*) C C Thomas.

— Fruits of Warm Climates. Dowling, Curtis F., ed. (Illus.). 500p. 1987. 75.00 (*0-9610184-1-0*) J F Morton.

— Major Medicinal Plants: Botany, Culture & Uses. fac. ed. (Illus.). 448p. 1978. 94.95 (*0-398-03673-X*) C C Thomas.

— Plants Poisonous to People in Florida & Other Warm Areas. 2nd rev. ed. LC 81-71614. (Illus.). 170p. 1982. pap. 19.75 (*0-9610184-0-2*) J F Morton.

Morton, K. W., ed. International Conference on Numerical Methods in Fluid Dynamics, Twelfth: Proceedings of the Conference Held at the University of Oxford, England, on 9-13 July 1990. (Lecture Notes in Physics Ser.: Vol. 371). xiv, 562p. 1991. 75.00 (*0-387-53619-1*) Spr-Verlag.

Morton, K. W. & Baines, M. J. Numerical Methods for Fluid Dynamics II. 2nd ed. (Institute of Mathematics & Its Applications Conference Series, New Ser.: New Series 7). (Illus.). 679p. 1986. 95.00 (*0-19-853610-0*) OUP.

Morton, K. W. & Baines, M. J., eds. Numerical Methods for Fluid Dynamics. LC 82-11627. 1983. text ed. 126.00 (*0-12-508360-2*) Acad Pr.

— Numerical Methods for Fluid Dynamics III. (Institute of Mathematics & Its Applications Conference Series, New Ser.: New Series 17). (Illus.). 552p. 1989. 95.00 (*0-19-853632-1*) OUP.

Morton, K. W. & Mayers, D. F. Numerical Solution of Partial Differential Equations. (Illus.). 240p. (C). 1995. 54.95 (*0-521-41855-0*); pap. 22.95 (*0-521-42922-6*) Cambridge U Pr.

Morton, K. W., jt. ed. see Baines, M. J.

Morton, K. W., jt. auth. see Richtmyer, Robert D.

Morton, Kati & Bierman, John. Missing Hero: The Story of Raoul Wallenberg. (Illus.). 224p. 1995. reprint ed. pap. 11.95 (*1-55970-276-1*) Arcade Pub Inc.

Morton, Kelsey. The Redwood Seed. (Wellspring Bks.). (Illus.). 128p. 1988. pap. 8.95 (*0-916349-45-4*) Amity Hse Inc.

Morton, L., tr. see Dumont, Louis.

Morton, L. L. A Make-Believe Face. 241p. (Orig.). 1993. pap. 4.95 (*0-9634673-0-1*) Indep-Hse Pr.

Morton, Larry, jt. auth. see Appleby, Martha.

Morton, Leah, pseud. I Am a Woman - & a Jew. (American Biography Ser.). 362p. 1991. reprint ed. lib. bdg. 79.00 (*0-7812-8364-7*) Rprt Serv.

— I Am a Woman & a Jew. LC 86-50263. (Masterworks of Modern Jewish Writing Ser.). (Illus.). 372p. (C). 1986. reprint ed. pap. 9.95 (*0-910129-56-8*) Wiener Pubs Inc.

Morton, Leith. Divided Self: A Biography of Arishma Takeo. 288p. (Orig.). 1989. pap. text ed. 24.95 (*0-04-378006-7*, Pub. by Allen Unwin AT) Paul & Co Pubs.

Morton, Leith, ed. & tr. An Anthology of Contemporary Japanese Poetry. LC 93-19734. (World Literature in Translation Ser.: Vol. 25). (Illus.). 486p. 1993. 75.00 (*0-8240-0037-4*) Garland.

— Seven Stories of Modern Japan. Clarke, H. D. et al, trs. 96p. 1991. pap. text ed. 15.95 (*0-9590735-9-0*, Pub. by Wild Peony Pty AT) UH Pr.

Morton, Leith, tr. see Kusano, Shimpei.

Morton, Lena Beatrice. The Influence of the Sea Upon English Literature from the Anglo-Saxon to the Victorian Period. 1974. lib. bdg. 250.00 (*0-87700-223-1*) Revisionist Pr.

Morton, Leslie & Godbolt, Shane, eds. Information Sources in the Medical Sciences. 4th ed. (Guides to Information Sources Ser.). 624p. 1992. lib. bdg. 100.00 (*0-86291-596-1*) Bowker-Saur.

Morton, Leslie T. & Moore, Robert J. A Bibliography of Medical & Biomedical Biography. 2nd ed. LC 94-8284. 1994. 99.95 (*0-85967-981-0*, Pub. by Scolar Pr UK) Ashgate Pub Co.

Morton, Lois W., jt. auth. see Baskin, Maria M.

Morton, Lone. Goodnight Everyone (Bonne Nuit a Tous) Bougard, Marie-Therese, tr. LC 94-2434. (Language Learning Story Books: I Can Read Spanish - I Can Read French). (Illus.). 28p. (ENG & FRE.). (J). (ps up). 1994. 6.95 (*0-8120-6453-4*) Barron.

— Goodnight Everyone (Buenos Noches a Todos) LC 94-2433. (Language Learning Story Books: I Can Read Spanish - I Can Read French). (Illus.). 28p. (ENG & SPA.). (J). (ps up). 1994. 6.95 (*0-8120-6452-6*) Barron.

— I'm Too Big (Je Suis Trop Gros) Helie, Ide M., tr. LC 94-561. (Language Learning Story Books: I Can Read Spanish - I Can Read French). (Illus.). 28p. (ENG & FRE.). (J). (ps up). 1994. 6.95 (*0-8120-6454-2*) Barron.

— I'm Too Big (Soy Demasiado Grande) LC 94-563. (Language Learning Story Books: I Can Read Spanish - I Can Read French). (Illus.). 28p. (ENG & SPA.). (J). (ps up). 1994. 6.95 (*0-8120-6451-8*) Barron.

— My First Design Book: Projects to Make with Stencil Shapes. (Illus.). 24p. (J). (gr. 1-4). pap. 4.95 (*0-8120-1744-7*) Barron.

— My Second Design Book. 24p. (J). (gr. 1-4). 1994. pap. 4.95 (*0-8120-1262-3*) Barron.

Morton, Lone, jt. auth. see Bruzzone, Catherine.

Morton, Louis. Robert Carter of Nomini Hall: A Virginia Tobacco Planter of the 18th Century. LC 83-45824. 1983. reprint ed. 31.00 (*0-404-20187-3*) AMS Pr.

Morton, Louis, ed. see Trask, David F.

Morton, Lucie T. Winegrowing in Eastern America: An Illustrated Guide to Viniculture East of the Rockies. LC 85-47696. (Illus.). 208p. (C). 1985. 32.50 (*0-8014-1290-0*) Cornell U Pr.

Morton, Lucy & Morton, Grace. Cloth Marionettes: Sewing, Stringing, Staging. (Illus.). 96p. (Orig.). 1984. pap. 10.95 (*0-938432-20-6*) Mother Earth.

Morton, Lyman. Yucatan Cookbook. (Illus.). 1996. pap. 22. 50 (*1-878610-51-1*) Red Crane Bks.

Morton, Lynne, jt. auth. see Schneider, Stephen H.

Morton, Malvin, ed. Can Public Welfare Keep Pace? LC 76-89859. 189p. reprint ed. pap. 53.90 (*0-8357-7985-8*, 2030713) Bks Demand.

Morton, Margaret, jt. auth. see Balmori, Diana.

Morton, Margaret A., jt. auth. see Green, Helen H.

Morton, Margaret A., jt. auth. see Hopkins, Charles R.

Morton, Marian. Emma Goldman. (Twayne's Twentieth Century American Biography Ser.). 200p. 1992. text ed. 26.95 (*0-8057-7794-6*, Pub. by Royal Botanic Garden UK); pap. 14.95 (*0-8057-7795-4*, Twayne) Macmillan.

Morton, Marian J. And Sin No More: Social Policy & Unwed Mothers in Cleveland, 1855-1990. LC 92-39087. (Women & Health Ser.). (Illus.). 216p. 1993. 39.50 (*0-8142-0602-6*) Ohio St U Pr.

— Women in Cleveland: An Illustrated History. LC 94-48852. (Encyclopedia of Cleveland History Ser.). (Illus.). 1995. write for info. (*0-253-32896-9*); pap. write for info. (*0-253-20972-2*) Ind U Pr.

Morton, Marian J. & Duncan, Russell, eds. First Person Past, Vol. Two: American Autobiographies. (Illus.). 300p. (Orig.). (C). 1994. pap. text ed. 13.50 (*1-881089-29-0*) Brandywine Press.

Morton, Marian J., jt. auth. see Frey, Sylvia R.

Morton, Mark J., jt. ed. see Kron, Jack.

Morton, Maurice. Rubber Technology. 3rd ed. (Illus.). 1987. text ed. 62.95 (*0-442-26422-4*) Chapman & Hall.

Morton, Maurice, ed. Anionic Polymerization. LC 82-11627. 268p. 1983. text ed. 95.00 (*0-12-508080-8*) Acad Pr.

Morton, Michael. The Critical Turn: Studies in Kant, Herder, Wittgenstein, & Contemporary Theory. LC 92-13153. (Kritik: German Literary Theory & Cultural Studies). 346p. (C). 1992. 39.95 (*0-8143-2376-6*) Wayne St U Pr.

Morton, Michael M. Herder & the Poetics of Thought: Unity & Diversity in "On Diligence in Several Learned Languages" LC 88-7697. 208p. 1989. lib. bdg. 27.50 (*0-271-00663-3*) Pa St U Pr.

Morton, Michael S., ed. The Corporation of the 1990s: Information Technology & Organizational Transformation. (Illus.). 352p. 1991. 27.50 (*0-19-506358-9*) OUP.

Morton, Michael S., jt. ed. see Allen, Thomas J.

Morton, Miriam, ed. Russian Plays for Young Audiences. 401p. 1977. 13.95 (*0-932720-62-5*); pap. 9.95 (*0-932720-61-7*) New Plays Inc.

Morton, Miriam, ed. see Chukovsky, Kornei.

Morton, Moira. Blossoming Romance. large type ed. (Linford Romance Library). 256p. 1989. pap. 11.95 (*0-7089-6693-4*, Linford) Ulverscroft.

Morton, N. E., et al. Methods in Genetic Epidemiology. (Contributions to Epidemiology & Biostatistics Ser.: Vol. 4). (Illus.). x, 262p. 1983. pap. 131.25 (*3-8055-3668-2*) S Karger.

***Morton, N. S. & Doyle, E.** Case Presentations in Paediatric Anaesthesia & Intensive Care. LC 94-28685. (Case Presentations Ser.). 1994. write for info. (*0-7506-1651-2*) Buttrwrth-Heinemann.

Morton, N. S. & Raine, P. A., eds. Paediatric Day Case Surgery. LC 93-23712. (Oxford Medical Publications). 1994. write for info. (*0-19-262255-2*) OUP.

— Pediatric Day Case Surgery. (Illus.). 136p. 1994. bds. 65. 00 (*0-19-262256-0*) OUP.

Morton, Nathaniel. New-Englands Memorial. LC 75-31124. reprint ed. 16.50 (*0-404-13605-2*) AMS Pr.

— New England's Memorial. LC 38-10717. 1979. reprint ed. 50.00 (*0-8201-1184-8*) Schol Facsimiles.

Morton, Nelle. The Journey Is Home: The Distinguished Feminist Theologian Traces the Development of Her Personal & Theoretical Vision. LC 85-42342. 285p. 1986. reprint ed. pap. 14.00 (*0-8070-1133-9*, BP 718) Beacon Pr.

Morton, Oren F. Annals of Bath County, Virginia. 208p. 1990. reprint ed. 21.00 (*0-685-60473-X*, 9260) Clearfield Co.

— A History of Highland County, Virginia: With a New 112-Page Index to Names. (Illus.). 532p. 1994. reprint ed. pap. 39.95 (*0-685-75096-5*, 3895) Clearfield Co.

— A History of Monroe County, West Virginia. LC 73-16338. (Illus.). 510p. 1980. reprint ed. 25.00 (*0-8063-0592-4*) Regional.

— History of Monroe County, West Virginia. (Illus.). 510p. 1993. reprint ed. lib. bdg. 52.50 (*0-8328-2940-4*) Higginson Bk Co.

— A History of Rockbridge County, Virginia. (Illus.). 574p. 1994. reprint ed. pap. 45.00 (*0-685-75097-3*, 3910) Clearfield Co.

— A History of Rockbridge County, Virginia. 574p. 1994. reprint ed. lib. bdg. 59.50 (*0-8328-4258-3*) Higginson Bk Co.

Morton, P., jt. auth. see Brittain, A.

Morton, Pamela. Basics of Disco Dancing. (Illus.). 56p. 1982. pap. text ed. 5.95x (*0-89641-092-7*) American Pr.

— The Basics of Square Dancing. (Illus.). 67p. (Orig.). 1981. pap. text ed. 5.95x (*0-89641-084-6*) American Pr.

***Morton, Pat & Fox, Marcia R.** The First-Job Survival Guide: Winning Advice on Choosing & Getting the Job You Want. (Career Works Ser.). 176p. 1995. pap. 11.00 (*1-880030-44-6*) DBM Pub.

Morton, Pat, jt. auth. see Stirling, Bob.

Morton, Patricia. Disfigured Images: The Historical Assault on Afro-American Women. LC 90-20701. (Contributions in Afro-American & African Studies: No. 144). 192p. 1991. text ed. 49.95 (*0-313-27296-4*, MBW/, Greenwood Pr); pap. text ed. 15.95 (*0-275-93885-9*, B3885, Praeger Pubs) Greenwood.

***Morton, Patricia, ed.** Discovering the Women in Slavery: Emancipating Perspectives on the American Past. LC 95-14154. 1996. write for info. (*0-8203-1756-X*); pap. write for info. (*0-8203-1757-8*) U of Ga Pr.

Morton, Patricia G. Health Assessment & Nursing. 2nd ed. (Illus.). 681p. 1993. text ed. 46.95 (*0-685-72893-5*) Davis Co.

***Morton, Patricia G., ed.** Nurse's Clinical Guide to Health Assessment. 2nd ed. LC 94-28318. (C). 1994. write for info. (*0-87434-704-1*) Springhouse Pub.

***Morton, Patricia G., et al, eds.** Davis's Clinical Guide to Health Assessment. 2nd ed. (Illus.). 340p. (C). 1995. pap. text ed., spiral bd. 26.95 (*0-8036-0119-0*) Davis Co.

***Morton, Paul.** It's Time for the Outpouring. 1994. pap. 8.00 (*0-927936-59-3*) Vincom Inc.

Morton, Peter, ed. see Baker, Chuck.

Morton, Phyllis D., jt. ed. see Ballam, Harry.

Morton Press Staff. Chicago Works: A Collection of Chicago Author's Best Stories. Levy, Laurie, ed. 270p. (Orig.). 1990. 18.95 (*0-9625446-0-4*); pap. 10.00 (*0-9625446-1-2*) Morton Pr.

Morton, R. & Sinclair, H. Fat Soluble Vitamins. LC 72-89945. (International Encyclopedia of Food & Nutrition Ser.: Vol. 9). 1970. 219.00 (*0-08-012708-8*, Pub. by Pergamon Repr UK) Franklin.

Morton, R. A. & Ayers, W. B., Jr. Plio-Pleistocene Genetic Sequences of the South-Western Louisiana Continental Shelf & Slope: Geologic Framework, Sedimentary Facies, & Hydrocarbon Distribution. (Illus.). 74p. 1992. pap. 7.00 (*0-317-05177-6*, RI 210) Bur Econ Geology.

— Plio-Pleistocene Genetic Sequences of the Southwestern Louisiana Continental Shelf & Slope: Geologic Framework, Sedimentary Facies, & Hydrocarbon Distribution. (Report of Investigations Ser.: RI 210). (Illus.). 74p. 1992. 7.00 (*0-317-05187-3*) Bur Econ Geology.

Morton, R. A. & McGowen, J. H. Modern Depositional Environments of the Texas Coast. (Guidebook Ser.: GB 20). (Illus.). 167p. 1983. reprint ed. 4.50 (*0-318-03129-9*) Bur Econ Geology.

Morton, R. A., jt. auth. see Paine, J. G.

Morton, R. A., et al. Continuity & Internal Properties of Gulf Coast Sandstones & Their Implications for Geopressured Fluid Production. (Report of Investigations Ser.: RI 132). (Illus.). 70p. 1983. 3.00 (*0-318-03287-2*) Bur Econ Geology.

Morton, R. J. Accidents & Emergencies in Children. (Oxford Handbooks in Emergency Medicine Ser.). 1992. pap. 32.50 (*0-19-261929-2*) OUP.

Morton, R. J. & Phillips, B. M. Accidents & Emergencies in Children. (Oxford Handbooks in Emergency Medicine Ser.: No. 2). (Illus.). 208p. 1992. 55.00 (*0-19-262222-6*) OUP.

Morton, Ralph, tr. see Satoh, Akira.

Morton, Richard. Anne Sexton's Poetry. LC 88-39019. (Studies in Art & Religious Interpretation: Vol. 11). 150p. 1988. lib. bdg. 69.95 (*0-88946-563-0*) E Mellen.

Morton, Richard F., et al. A Study Guide to Epidemiology & Biostatistics. 3rd ed. 196p. (C). 1990. 32.00 (*0-8342-0157-7*) Aspen Pub.

Morton, Richard L. Struggle Against Tyranny, & the Beginning of a New Era: Virginia, 1677-1699. (Jamestown 350th Anniversary Historical Booklet Ser.: No. 9). 90p. reprint ed. pap. 25.70 (*0-7837-2023-8*, 2042298) Bks Demand.

Morton, Robert. Robert Morton: The Collected Works. Atlas, Allan, ed. (Masters & Monuments of the Renaissance Ser.: Vol. 2). xxxvi, 105p. 1982. pap. 47.50 (*0-8450-7302-8*) Broude.

Morton, Robert, et al. Living with the Texas Shore. LC 83-1753. (Living with the Shore Ser.). (Illus.). xii, 180p. (C). 1983. 31.95 (*0-8223-0499-6*); pap. 16.95 (*0-8223-0500-3*) Duke.

Morton, Robert J., jt. ed. see Karzmark, C. J.

Morton, Roger R. & Hsieh, Robert C., eds. Imaging Workstations & Document Input Systems. 208p. 1989. 53.00 (*0-8194-0109-9*, VOL. 1074) SPIE.

***Morton, Ron & Lloyd, John, eds.** The Health-Promoting Primary School. 160p. 1994. pap. 24.95x (*1-85346-325-6*, Pub. by D Fulton UK) Taylor & Francis.

Morton, Ruth. Interior Design: The Home-Its Furnishing & Equipment. Zinkus, Dan & Newman, Carol, eds. (Illus.). 184p. (Orig.). (gr. 9-12). 1979. pap. text ed. 18.60 (*0-07-043426-3*) McGraw.

Morton, Ruth, et al. The Home, It's Furnishings & Equipment. 1979. text ed. 33.96 (*0-07-043417-4*) McGraw.

Morton, Sarah W. My Mind & Its Thoughts, in Sketches, Fragments, & Essays. LC 74-28388. 336p. 1975. reprint ed. lib. bdg. 50.00 (*0-8201-1150-3*) Schol Facsimiles.

Morton-Schwalb, Sandy, jt. auth. see Emmolo, Lauren M.

Morton, Sharon E., ed. Heaven - Fact Or Fiction. 2nd rev. ed. 49p. 1990. reprint ed. pap. 6.95 (*0-9628047-0-3*) T J Simmons.

***Morton, Suzanne.** Ideal Surroundings: Domestic Life in a Working-Class Suburb in the 1920s. (Studies in Gender & History). (Illus.). 200p. 1995. 40.00 (*0-8020-0474-1*); pap. 17.95 (*0-8020-7575-4*) U of Toronto Pr.

Morton, Thomas. Cash Flow Letter Book for the Small Business. 194p. 1993. disk 75.00 (*0-471-58079-1*) Wiley.

— Financial Letters for the Small Business. 208p. 1992. text ed. 80.00 (*0-471-57115-6*) Wiley.

Morton, Thomas, jt. auth. see Colman, George.

Morton, Thomas D. & Green, Ronald K., eds. Training in Human Services, Vol. I. 223p. (Orig.). 1978. pap. text ed. 5.00 (*0-89695-002-6*) U Tenn CSW.

Morton, Thomas E. & Pentico, David W. Heuristic Scheduling Systems: With Applications to Production Systems & Project Management. (Series in Engineering & Technology Management). 722p. 1993. text ed. 89.95 (*0-471-57819-3*) Wiley.

Morton, Thomas G. The History of the Pennsylvania Hospital, 1751-1895. LC 73-2408. (Mental Illness & Social Policy; the American Experience Ser.). 1973. reprint ed. 48.95 (*0-405-05218-9*) Ayer.

— New English Canaan or New Canaan. LC 73-141136. (Research Library of Colonial Americana: Personal Narratives & Promotional Literature). 196p. 1972. reprint ed. 23.95 (*0-405-03309-5*) Ayer.

Morton, Thomas H., Jr., et al. Principles of Biopsy: A Self-Instructional Guide, Bk. 8. 3rd rev. ed. (Illus.). 94p. 1983. pap. 14.95 (*0-89939-081-1*) Stoma Pr.

Morton-Thompson, Diana & Woods, Arnold M., eds. Development Geology Reference Manual. (Methods in Exploration Ser.: No. 10). (Illus.). xv, 550p. 1993. ring bd. 96.00 (*0-89181-660-7*) AAPG.

***Morton, Timothy.** Shelley & the Revolution in Taste: The Body & the Natural World. (Studies in Romanticism: No. 10). (Illus.). 320p. (C). 1995. 54.95 (*0-521-47135-4*) Cambridge U Pr.

Morton, Tom. Spirit of Adventure: A Journey Beyond the Whiskey Trails. (Illus.). 224p. 1993. 29.95 (*1-85158-496-6*, Pub. by Mnstream UK) Trafalgar.

— Spirit of Adventure: A Journey Beyond the Whisky Trails. (Illus.). 203p. 1994. pap. 13.95 (*1-85158-549-4*, Pub. by Mnstream UK) Trafalgar.

— The Survivor's Guide to Unemployment. LC 92-64091. 224p. (Orig.). 1992. pap. 10.00 (*0-89109-701-5*) Pinon Press.

Morton, Tom J. Texas Real Estate Finance. 4th rev. ed. 384p. 1992. pap. 38.95 (*0-7931-0421-1*, 1557-17, Real Estate Ed) Dearborn Finan.

— Texas Real Estate Finance. 5th ed. LC 94-6528. 1994. 38.95 (*0-7931-1020-3*, 1557-1705) Dearborn Finan.

Morton, Tom J. & Stout, Dean. Real Estate Marketing. (C). 1985. teacher ed write for info. (*0-8359-6491-4*, Reston) P-H.

***Morton, W.** Morton, the Stem of Morton: Collection of Genealogical Notes Respecting the Family of Morton, Chiefly Seated in the Wapentake of Strafford-cum-Tickhill, S. Yorkshire. 311p. 1995. lib. bdg. 57.50 (*0-8328-4450-0*) Higginson Bk Co.

— Morton, the Stem of Morton: Collection of Genealogical Notes Respecting the Family of Morton, Chiefly Seated in the Wapentake of Strafford-cum-Tickhill, S. Yorkshire. 311p. 1995. reprint ed. pap. 47.50 (*0-8328-4451-9*) Higginson Bk Co.

Morton, W. E. Physical Properties of Textile Fibres. 660p. 1975. 125.00 (*0-686-63781-X*) St Mut.

Morton, W. E. & Hearle, J. W. Physical Properties of Textile Fibres. 660p. (C). 1975. 160.00 (*0-900739-87-8*, Pub. by Textile Institue UK) St Mut.

Morton, W. L., ed. see Begg, Alexander.

Morton, W. Scott. China: Its History & Culture. (Illus.). 1982. pap. text ed. 9.95 (*0-07-043421-2*) McGraw.

— China: Its History & Culture. 3rd ed. 1995. pap. text ed. 12.95 (*0-07-043424-7*) McGraw.

— Japan: Its History & Culture. 3rd ed. 1994. pap. text ed. 11.95 (*0-07-043423-9*) McGraw.

Morton, Walter A. British Finance, 1930-1940. Wilkins, Mira, ed. LC 78-3942. (International Finance Ser.). (Illus.). 1979. reprint ed. lib. bdg. 35.95 (*0-405-11242-4*) Ayer.

Morton, Ward M. Woman Suffrage in Mexico. LC 62-20735. (Illus.). 174p. reprint ed. pap. 49.60 (*0-8357-6721-3*, 2035356) Bks Demand.

Morton, William C. The Harmony of Verse. LC 68-85787. 245p. reprint ed. pap. 69.90 (*0-317-09482-3*, 2014375) Bks Demand.

Morton, William F. Tanaka Giichi & Japan's China Policy. LC 79-27570. 330p. 1980. text ed. 35.00 (*0-312-78500-3*) St Martin.

Morton, William J. & Hammer, Edwin W. The X-Ray or Photography of the Invisible & Its Value in Surgery. (Illus.). 196p. 1995. 125.00 (*0-930405-51-X*) Norman SF.

Morton, William L. The Canadian Identity. 2nd ed. 1972. 13.95 (*0-8020-6139-7*) U of Toronto Pr.

— Henry Youle Hind, Eighteen Twenty-Three to Nineteen Eight. LC 81-113864. (Canadian Biographical Studies: No. 7). 171p. reprint ed. pap. 48.80 (*0-317-27009-5*, 2023653) Bks Demand.

— Manitoba: A History. LC 67-4598. 561p. reprint ed. pap. 159.90 (*0-317-27008-7*, 2023654) Bks Demand.

Morton-Williams, Jean. Interviewer Approaches. LC 93-20002. 250p. 1993. 57.95 (*1-85521-339-7*, Pub. by Dartmth Pub UK) Ashgate Pub Co.

Morton-Williams, Peter, ed. see Bradbury, R. E.

***Morton-Young, Tommie.** After-School & Parent Education Programs for At-Risk Youths & Their Families: A Guide to Organizing & Operating Community-Based Center for Basic Educational Skills Reinforcement, Homework Assistance, Cultural Enrichment & A Parent Involvement Focus. LC 94-38716. (Illus.). 144p. (C). 1995. text ed. 37.95x (*0-398-05961-6*); pap. text ed. 22.95x (*0-398-05962-4*) C C Thomas.

***Mortonson, Kenneth.** The Advent Instructor. 1995. pap. write for info. (*0-7880-0562-6*) CSS OH.

Mortonson, Kenneth A. That Seeing, They May Believe: Children's Object Lessons. LC 93-18007. 1993. pap. 8.95 (*1-55673-652-5*, 9352) CSS OH.

Mortreux, Andre & Petit, Francis, eds. Industrial Applications of Homogeneous Catalysis. (C). 1987. lib. bdg. 133.00 (*90-277-2520-9*) Kluwer Ac.

Mortz, John R. How to Moonlight with Your Computer. rev. ed. 356p. 1990. pap. 39.95 (*0-9623722-3-4*) Amer Inst Comput Tech.

— Insider Secrets for the Desktop Publisher: How to Turn Your PC into an 89,378 Dollars per Year Profit Center. 1990. pap. write for info. (*0-9623722-4-2*) Amer Inst Comput Tech.

— Make Money Moonlighting! The Four Best Ways to Earn Money with Your Computer & the Four Traps to Avoid. 121p. 1989. pap. 9.95 (*0-9623722-2-6*) Amer Inst Comput Tech.

Mortz, Mary. Overcoming Our Compulsions: Using the Twelve Steps & the Enneagram As Spiritual Tools for Life. LC 94-7494. 288p. (Orig.). 1994. pap. 12.95 (*0-89243-688-3*, Triumph Bks) Liguori Pubns.

Mortzfeld, Peter. Katalog der Graphischen Portrats in der Herzog August Bibliothek Wolfenbuttel, 40 vols., Set. Bibliothek, Herzog A., ed. (Portraitsammlung Series A). 1986. lib. bdg. 6,500.00 (*3-598-31480-9*) K G Saur.

Moruzzi, Giuseppe, jt. auth. see Dow, Robert.

***Moruzzi, James M.** Nazi Trials: A Soldier's Story of Terror. Brown, Victoria M. et al, eds. (Criminal Justice & Law Ser.). 224p. (Orig.). (C). 1995. text ed. write for info. (*0-938993-23-2*) Coral Gables Pub.

***Moruzzi, V. L. & Sommers, C. B.** Calculated Electronic Properties of Ordered Alloys. 420p. (C). 1995. text ed. 86.00 (*981-02-1918-0*) World Scientific Pub.

***Morvan, Christiane.** Dictionnaire Cegos. 1986. write for info. (*0-7859-8642-1*, 271240307X) Fr & Eur.

Morvan, Michael, jt. ed. see Bouchitte, Vincent.

Morvan, P. Cegos Dictionary: Definition of Micro - Computer & Electronic Vocabulary: Dictionnaire Cegos: Definition Du Vocabulaire Micro-Informatique - Electronique. 322p. (ENG & FRE.). 1986. 65.00 (*0-8288-1375-2*, M8340) Fr & Eur.

Morvillo, Robert G., jt. ed. see Obermaier, Otto G.

Morway, Richard J., ed. Classic Brain Teasers of the Twentieth Century, Vols. 1 & 2: A Selection of the Best Puzzles in Logic, Math, & Deductive Reasoning, Vol. 1. 48p. 1992. pap. 2.95 (*0-9632528-0-1*) Madisn Hse NH.

— Classic Brain Teasers of the Twentieth Century, Vols. 1 & 2: A Selection of the Best Puzzles in Logic, Math, & Deductive Reasoning, Vol. 2. 48p. 1992. pap. 2.95 (*0-9632528-1-X*) Madisn Hse NH.

Morwin, S., et al, eds. The Chernobyl Papers: Doses to the Soviet Population & Early Health Effects Studies. 500p. 1993. 75.00 (*1-883021-02-2*) Research Ent.

Morwitz, Ernst, tr. see George, Stefan.

Morwood, J. H., ed. see Apuleius, Lucius.

***Morwood, James.** The Oxford Latin Minidictionary. 1995. 5.95 (*0-19-864225-3*) OUP.

***Morwood, James, ed.** The Pocket Oxford Latin Dictionary. (Illus.). 368p. 1995. reprint ed. pap. text ed. 11.95 (*0-19-864228-8*) OUP.

***Morwood, James & Crane, David, eds.** Sheridan Studies. (Illus.). 275p. (C). 1996. write for info. (*0-521-46466-8*) Cambridge U Pr.

Morwood, James & Warman, Mark. Our Greek & Latin Roots. Phinney, Ed, ed. (Awareness of Language Ser.). (Illus.). 64p. (C). 1990. pap. 8.50 (*0-521-37841-9*) Cambridge U Pr.

Morwood, James, jt. auth. see Balme, Maurice G.

Morwood, James, jt. ed. see Woodhouse, S. E.

Morwood, Peter. Rules of Engagement. (Star Trek Ser.: No. 48). 288p. 1990. pap. 4.50 (*0-685-28839-0*) PB.

Morwood, Peter, jt. auth. see Duane, Diane.

Morwyn. Secrets of a Witch's Coven. Alexander, Skye, ed. LC 88-50422. (Illus.). 400p. (Orig.). 1988. pap. 19.95 (*0-914918-80-X*, Whitford Pr) Schiffer.

Morwyng, P., tr. see Gesner, Conrad.

Morya, El. Ashram Notes. Prophet, Elizabeth C., ed. 224p. 1990. 19.95 (*0-922729-02-6*) Summit Univ.

Morykan, Dana G. & Rinker, Harry L. Warman's Country Antiques & Collectibles. 2nd ed. LC 93-45256. (Encyclopedia of Antiques & Collectibles Ser.). 384p. 1994. 14.95 (*0-87069-699-8*, Wallace-Hmestead) Chilton.

Moryson, Fynes. An Itinerary. LC 70-38150. (English Experience Ser.: No. 387). 1971. reprint ed. 175.00 (*90-221-0387-0*) Walter J Johnson.

— Shakespeare's Europe. rev. ed. LC 66-12287. (Illus.). 1972. 38.95 (*0-405-08799-3*, Pub. by Blom Pubns UK) Ayer.

Morzik, Fritz. German Air Force Airlift Operations. LC 68-22555. (German Air Force in World War 2 Ser.). (Illus.). 1968. reprint ed. 24.95 (*0-405-00042-1*) Ayer.

***Morzoeff, Nicholas.** Silent Poetry: Deafness, Sign, & Visual Culture in Modern France. LC 94-42545. 1995. text ed. write for info. (*0-691-03789-2*) Princeton U Pr.

Mos, Leendert P. & Royce, Joseph R., eds. Annals of Theoretical Psychology, Vol. 1. LC 84-644088. 346p. 1984. 85.00 (*0-306-41327-2*, Plenum Pr) Plenum.

Mos, Leendert P., jt. ed. see Madsen, K. B.

Mos, Leendert P., jt. ed. see Robinson, Daniel N.

Mos, Leendert P., jt. ed. see Royce, Joseph R.

Mos, Leendert P., jt. ed. see Staats, Arthur W.

Mos, Leendert P., jt. ed. see Van Geert, Paul.

Mos, Leendert P., et al, eds. Annals of Theoretical Psychology, Vol. 2. LC 84-644088. 390p. 1984. 85.00 (*0-306-41692-1*, Plenum Pr) Plenum.

— Annals of Theoretical Psychology, Vol. 4. LC 84-644088. 420p. 1986. 85.00 (*0-306-42327-8*, Plenum Pr) Plenum.

Mosaic Software, Inc. Staff. The Twin Educational Version. (Illus.). 208p. (C). 1987. pap. text ed. 22.60 (*0-13-935370-4*) P-H.

Mosak, Harold. Ha Ha & Aha: The Role of Humor in Psychotherapy. LC 87-70349. viii, 152p. 1987. text ed. 21.95 (*0-915202-65-4*) Accel Devel.

Mosak, Harold H. A Child's Guide to Parent Rearing. LC 80-66084. (Illus.). 79p. (Orig.). (C). 1980. pap. text ed. 3.50 (*0-918560-27-6*) Adler Sch Prof Psy.

— On Purpose: Collected Papers. LC 76-42942. 1977. pap. 14.95 (*0-918560-19-5*) Adler Sch Prof Psy.

Mosak, Harold H., jt. auth. see Shulman, Bernard H.

Mosala, Itumeleng, jt. ed. see Tlhagale, Buti.

Mosala, Itumeleng J. Biblical Hermeneutics & Black Theology in South Africa. 1989. pap. 14.99 (*0-8028-0372-5*) Eerdmans.

Mosala, Itumeleng J., jt. ed. see Tlhagale, Buti.

Mosalakae, Kenosi. Introspection of an African. 1993. 15.95 (*0-533-10611-7*) Vantage.

Mosallan, K. H., jt. auth. see Chen, W. F.

Mosatche, Harriet S. Searching: Practices & Beliefs of the Religious Cults & Human Potential Movements. LC 83-4829. (Illus.). 437p. 1984. 14.95 (*0-87396-092-0*) Stravon.

Mosbach, Klaus, ed. Methods in Enzymology, Vol. 135. 675p. 1987. text ed. 106.00 (*0-12-182035-1*) Acad Pr.

Mosbach, Klaus, et al, eds. Methods in Enzymology: Immobilized Enzymes & Cells, Vol. 137, Pt. D. 767p. 1988. text ed. 136.00 (*0-12-182037-8*) Acad Pr.

Mosbacher, E., tr. see Giglio, Giovanni.

Mosbacher, Eric, tr. see Aichinger, Ilse.

Mosbacher, Eric, tr. see Perutz, Leo.

Mosbacher, Eric, tr. see Strasser, Otto.

Mosbacher, Georgette. Feminine Force. 1994. pap. 12.00 (*0-671-89934-1*, Fireside) S&S Trade.

— Feminine Force: Release the Power Within To Create the Life You Deserve. (Illus.). 352p. 1993. 22.00 (*0-671-79896-0*) S&S Trade.

Mosbacher, Rob. Deep in the Heart: A Remedy for an Ailing Texas. LC 93-42367. 1993. pap. 9.95 (*1-56530-122-6*) Summit TX.

Mosbrooker, Michael. Implementation of Project Management. 2nd ed. 1995. write for info. (*0-201-52388-4*) Addison-Wesley.

Mosbrugger, V. The Tree Habit in Land Plants: A Functional Comparison of Trunk Construction with a Brief Introduction into the Biomechanics of Trees. Bhattacharji, S. et al, eds. (Lecture Notes in Earth Sciences Ser.: Vol. 28). v, 161p. 1990. pap. 26.00 (*0-387-52374-X*) Spr-Verlag.

Mosburg, Earl R. Dictionary of Spoken Nepali: Nepali-English, English-Nepali, with Phrases & Grammar Reference Notes. viii, 111p. (Orig.). (ENG & NEP.). 1991. pap. 14.95 (*0-9629545-2-7*) E R Mosburg.

Mosby. Enciclopedia Mosby de Medicina y Enfermeria, 3 vols., Set. (SPA.). 1990. 495.00 (*0-8288-8235-5*, 8477642184) Fr & Eur.

— Mosby's Nursing Almanac. 700p. Date not set. pap. 19.95 (*0-8016-3503-9*) Mosby Yr Bk.

— Nursing: Illustrated Desk Diary 1993. (Illus.). 144p. 1992. spiral bd. 19.95 (*0-8016-7290-2*) Mosby Yr Bk.

— Nursing Illustrated Desk Diary 1994. (Illus.). 144p. 1993. 19.95 (*0-8016-8015-8*) Mosby Yr Bk.

— Oropharyngeal, Nasopharyngeal, & Nasotracheal Su. 1993. 100.00 (*0-8016-7118-3*) Mosby Yr Bk.

— Pharmacology Newsletter Packet Spring 1993. 1993. write for info. (*0-8016-7929-X*) Mosby Yr Bk.

— Putting It All Together - Phy. Assess. of the Adult. 1994. 100.00 (*0-8016-7091-8*) Mosby Yr Bk.

Mosby & Anderson. Mosby's Medical, Nursing, & Allied Health Dictionary. 4th ed. 2208p. 1993. 28.95 (*0-8016-7225-2*) Mosby Yr Bk.

— Mosby's Pocket Dictionary of Medicine, Nursing. 2nd ed. 1040p. 1994. pap. 19.95 (*0-8016-7226-0*) Mosby Yr Bk.

***Mosby, C. V.** Mosby's Home Health Nursing Pocket Consultant. 1994. pap. 23.95 (*0-8151-6125-5*) Mosby Yr Bk.

***Mosby, Dewey F.** Across Continents & Cultures: The Art & Life of Henry Ossawa Tanner. LC 95-4078. (Illus.). 128p. 1995. pap. 25.00 (*0-942614-24-0*) Nelson-Atkins.

Mosby, Dewey F. & Rossen, Susan F., comments. The Figure in 19th-Century French Painting. (Illus.). 60p. 1979. pap. 7.50 (*0-89558-074-8*) Det Inst Arts.

Mosby, George, Jr. Population. 1983. pap. 7.00 (*0-914610-35-X*) Hanging Loose.

Mosby, Jack & Dapkus, Dave. Alaska Paddling Guide. 3rd rev. ed. LC 86-11669. (Illus.). 113p. 1992. pap. 7.95 (*0-9608550-2-5*) J & R Enter.

Mosby, John S. Memoirs. Russell, Charles W., ed. LC 59-5903. (Indiana University Civil War Centennial Ser.). (Illus.). 1968. reprint ed. 37.00 (*0-527-65350-0*) Periodicals Srv.

— Mosby's Memoirs. 1995. pap. 11.95 (*1-879941-27-9*) J S Sanders.

— Mosby's War Reminiscences. (Illus.). 256p. 1992. reprint ed. pap. 20.00 (*1-55613-643-9*) Heritage Bk.

— Stuart's Cavalry in the Gettysburg Campaign. 228p. 1987. reprint ed. 25.00 (*0-942211-28-6*) Olde Soldier Bks.

Mosby, Katherine. Private Altars. LC 94-17412. 1994. 21.00 (*0-679-42896-8*) Random.

Mosby Staff. Mosby's Medical Dictionary. 3rd ed. 1989. 21.95 (*0-8016-3489-X*) Mosby Yr Bk.

Mosby-Year Book Staff. Illustrated Desk Diary, 1993. 144p. 1992. spiral bd. 19.95 (*0-8016-7163-9*) Mosby Yr Bk.

— Illustrated Desk Diary, 1993. 144p. 1992. 39.95 (*0-8016-7162-0*) Mosby Yr Bk.

Mosca, Edoardo. Optimal, Predictive, & Adaptive Control. LC 94-6082. 1994. text ed. 74.00 (*0-13-847609-8*) P-H.

Mosca, Frank. All American Boys. 116p. (Orig.). (J). (gr. 7-12). 1983. pap. 5.95 (*0-932870-44-9*) Alyson Pubns.

Mosca, Gaetano. Partiti & Sindacati Nella Crisi del Regime Parlamentare: Parties & Labor Unions in the Crisis of the Parliamentary Regime. LC 74-25771. (European Sociology Ser.). 348p. 1975. reprint ed. 28.95 (*0-405-06525-6*) Ayer.

— The Ruling Class. Livingston, Arthur, ed. Kahn, Hannah D., tr. LC 80-17230. xli, 514p. 1980. reprint ed. text ed. 45.50 (*0-313-22617-2*, MORU, Greenwood Pr) Greenwood.

Mosca, Mark. Hole in the Heart. (Mystery on the Monterey Peninsula Ser.). 240p. (Orig.). 1994. pap. 9.95 (*0-9617681-7-7*) Otter B Bks.

Moscardini, A. O., jt. ed. see Esroy, Yasar.

***Moscatelli, Robert G.** Too Soon Old, Too Late Smart: How to Get Control of Your Money (Before Your Money Gets Control of You) (Illus.). 280p. (Orig.). 1995. pap. 14.95 (*0-9643601-0-1*) Blck Knight.

Moscatelli, V. B., jt. auth. see Hogbe-Nlend, H.

Moscati, Sabatino. Semites in Ancient History. 142p. 1959. 10.50 (*0-7083-0074-X*, Pub. by U of Wales UK) Bks Intl VA.

Moscato, Donald R. Building Financial Decision-Making Models: An Introduction to Principles & Procedures. LC 80-65704. 160p. reprint ed. pap. 45.60 (*0-8357-7465-1*, 2023581) Bks Demand.

Moscato, Michael & LeBlanc, Leslie. The United States of America vs. One Book Entitled Ulysses by James Joyce: Documents & Commentary : 50-Year Retrospective. LC 83-25929. 482p. 1984. text ed. 75.00 (*0-313-27065-1*, U7065) Greenwood.

Moschandreas, Maria. Business Economics. LC 93-38120. 1994. write for info. (*0-415-10909-4*); pap. write for info. (*0-415-10910-8*) Routledge.

Moscheles, Felix, ed. see Mendelssohn, Felix.

Moscheles, Ignatz. Recent Music & Musicians As Described in the Diaries & Correspondence of Ignatz Moscheles. LC 73-125057. (Music Ser.). 1970. reprint ed. lib. bdg. 45.00 (*0-306-70022-0*) Da Capo.

Moscheles, Ignaz & Kann, Hans. Piano Concerto No. 3 in G Minor, Op. 58 Two-Piano Score. LC 79-155179. (Illus.). (Orig.). 1971. pap. 6.50 (*0-912028-03-3*) Music Treasure.

Moschella, Samuel L. & Hurley, Harry J. Dermatology, 2 vols., Set. 3rd ed. (Illus.). 2767p. 1992. text ed. 315.00 (*0-7216-3263-7*) Saunders.

Moscherosch, Johann M., pseud. Visiones De Don Quevedo, 2 vols. in 1. xliv, 976p. 1974. reprint ed. write for info. (*3-487-05288-1*, Pub. by Georg Olms GW) Lubrecht & Cramer.

Moschetta, Evelyn F. & Moschetta, Paul. Caring Couples. 190p. (Orig.). 1984. pap. 9.95 (*0-942494-98-9*) P & E Moschetta.

Moschetta, Paul, jt. auth. see Moschetta, Evelyn F.

Moschis, George P. Acquisition of the Consumer Role by Adolescents. LC 78-10344. (Research Monograph: No. 82). 139p. 1978. pap. 20.00 (*0-88406-124-8*) GA St U Busn Pr.

— Consumer Socialization: A Life Cycle Perspective. LC 85-45165. 368p. 1987. text ed. 45.00 (*0-669-11244-5*) Free Pr.

— Marketing Strategies for the Mature Market. LC 94-8542. 216p. 1994. text ed. 55.00 (*0-89930-887-2*, Quorum Bks) Greenwood.

— Marketing to Older Consumers: A Handbook of Information for Strategy Development. LC 91-47642. 352p. 1992. text ed. 59.95 (*0-89930-764-7*, MOV, Quorum Bks) Greenwood.

Moschos, John. The Spiritual Meadow (Pratum Spirituale) Wortley, John, tr. & intro. by. (Cistercian Studies). 261p. 1992. write for info. (*0-87907-439-6*); pap. write for info. (*0-87907-539-2*) Cistercian Pubns.

Moschovakis, Y. N. Descriptive Set Theory. (Studies in Logic & the Foundations of Mathematics: Vol. 100). 638p. 1980. 128.25 (*0-444-85305-7*, North Holland) Elsevier.

— Descriptive Set Theory. (Studies in Logic & the Foundations of Mathematics: No. 100). 638p. 1987. reprint ed. pap. 49.50 (*0-444-70199-0*, North Holland) Elsevier.

Moschovakis, Y. N., jt. ed. see Kechris, A. S.

An Asterisk (*) at the beginning of an entry indicates that the title is appearing in BIP for the first time.

Moschovakis, Y. N., et al, eds. Logic from Computer Science: Proceedings of a Workshop Held November 13-17, 1989. (Mathematical Sciences Research Institute Publications: Vol. 21). (Illus.). 624p. 1991. 69.00 (*0-387-97667-1*) Spr-Verlag.

Moschovakis, Yiannis. Notes on Set Theory. LC 93-35825. (University Texts in Mathematics Ser.). 1994. 39.00 (*0-387-94180-0*) Spr-Verlag.

Moschus. Europa. Bd. 19. xii, 144p. (GER.). 1991. write for info. (*0-318-70420-X*, Pub. by Georg Olms GW) Lubrecht & Cramer.

— Moschus Europa. (Altertumswissenschaftliche Texte und Studien Ser.: Vol. 19). xii, 144p. (GER.). 1991. pap. text ed. 20.00 (*3-487-09432-0*, Pub. by Georg Olms GW) Lubrecht & Cramer.

Moschus, John. Spiritual Meadow: The Pratum Spirituale. pap. 1.25 (*0-89981-100-0*) Eastern Orthodox.

***Moschwitzer, Albrecht.** Parat Lexikon Elektronik. 1000p. (GER.). 1993. 225.00 (*0-7859-8415-1*, 3527281533) Fr & Eur.

— Semiconductor Devices, Circuits & Systems. (Monographs in Electrical & Electronic Engineering). (Illus.). 368p. 1991. 79.00 (*0-19-859374-0*) OUP.

Moschytz, G. M., ed. MOS Switched-Capacitor Filters: Analysis & Design. LC 84-9055. 512p. 1984. 69.95 (*0-87942-177-0*, PC01701) Inst Electrical.

Moschytz, George S. & Horn, P. Active Filter Design Handbook: For Use with Programmable Pocket Calculators & Minicomputers. LC 80-40845. (Illus.). 324p. reprint ed. pap. 92.40 (*0-7837-6732-3*, 2046360) Bks Demand.

***Moscinski, Sharon.** 101 Crafty Creatures in Your Neighborhood. LC 95-4030. (Illus.). (J). 1995. write for info. (*1-56261-227-1*) John Muir.

— Tracing Our Irish Roots. LC 93-2070. (American Origins Ser.). (Illus.). 48p. (J). 1993. text ed. 12.95 (*1-56261-148-8*) John Muir.

— Tracing Our Polish Roots. (American Origins Ser.). (Illus.). 48p. (J). (gr. 4-7). 1994. 12.95 (*1-56261-161-5*) John Muir.

***Mosciuski, Sharon.** Tracing Our English Roots. LC 94-26925. (American Origins Ser.). (Illus.). (J). 1995. (*1-56261-188-7*) John Muir.

Mosco, M. Price of Fame. 1994. mass mkt. 5.50 (*0-06-100625-4*, Harp PBks) HarpC.

Mosco, Maisie. Almonds & Raisins. 1991. mass mkt. 5.50 (*0-06-100142-2*, PL) HarpC.

— Children's Children. 1991. mass mkt. 5.50 (*0-06-100209-7*, Harp PBks) HarpC.

— For Love & Duty. 1992. mass mkt. 5.50 (*0-06-100395-6*, Harp PBks) HarpC.

— For Love & Duty. large type ed. 1992. pap. 15.95 (*0-7927-0820-2*, Paragon Lrg Print) Chivers N Amer.

— New Beginnings. 1993. mass mkt. 5.50 (*0-06-100525-8*, Harp PBks) HarpC.

— New Beginnings. large type ed. (General Fiction Ser.). 400p. 1992. 23.95 (*0-7089-8657-9*) Ulverscroft.

— Out of the Ashes. 1990. mass mkt. 5.50 (*0-06-100021-3*, Harp PBks) HarpC.

— Out of the Ashes. large type ed. (Charnwood Library). 1991. 23.95 (*0-7089-8559-9*, Charnwood) Ulverscroft.

— Scattered Seed. 1991. mass mkt. 4.95 (*0-06-100185-6*, Harp PBks) HarpC.

— Sense of Place. 1994. mass mkt. 5.50 (*0-06-100624-6*, Harp PBks) HarpC.

Mosco, U., ed. see Fabes, E., et al.

Mosco, Vincent. The Pay-Per Society: Computers & Communication in the Information Age. Dervin, Brenda, ed. LC 89-6665. (Communication & Information Science Ser.). 224p. (C). 1989. pap. text ed. 19.95 (*0-89391-604-8*) Ablex Pub.

— Policy Research in Telecommunications: Proceedings, Telecommunications Policy Research Conference Annual 11th. Voigt, Melvin J., ed. LC 83-12340. (Communication & Information Science Ser.). 472p. 1984. text ed. 75.00 (*0-89391-260-3*) Ablex Pub.

— Pushbutton Fantasies. Voigt, Melvin J., ed. LC 82-11601. (Communication & Information Science Ser.). 240p. (C). 1982. text ed. 55.00 (*0-89391-125-9*); pap. text ed. 22.50 (*0-89391-132-1*) Ablex Pub.

Mosco, Vincent & Wasko, Janet, eds. The Changing Patterns of Communication Control. LC 82-11592. (Critical Communication Review Ser.: Vol. 2). 320p. 1984. text ed. write for info. (*0-89391-153-4*) Ablex Pub.

— Critical Communication Review. write for info. (*0-318-50148-1*) Ablex Pub.

— Labor, the Working Class & Media. LC 82-11592. (Critical Communication Review Ser.: Vol. 1). 340p. 1983. text ed. 75.00 (*0-89391-122-4*); pap. 39.50 (*0-89391-212-3*) Ablex Pub.

— The Political Economy of Information. LC 87-40369. (Studies in Communication & Society). 368p. (C). 1988. pap. text ed. 17.50 (*0-299-11574-7*) U of Wis Pr.

— Popular Culture & Media Events. LC 82-11592. (Critical Communication Review Ser.: Vol. 3). 344p. 1985. text ed. 75.00 (*0-89391-279-4*) Ablex Pub.

Moscona, Aron, ed. The Cell Surface in Development. LC 74-7308. 348p. reprint ed. 99.20 (*0-685-07768-3*, 2015197) Bks Demand.

Moscona, Aron A., ed. Current Topics in Developmental Biology: Recent Advances in Mammalian Development, Vol. 23. Monroy, Alberto, tr. (Illus.). 268p. 1987. text ed. 96.00 (*0-12-153123-6*) Acad Pr.

Moscona, Aron A., jt. ed. see Monroy, Alberto.

Moscona, Aron A., et al, eds. Current Topics in Developmental Biology, Vol. 21. (Serial Publication Ser.). 426p. 1987. text ed. 138.00 (*0-12-153121-X*) Acad Pr.

— Current Topics in Developmental Biology, Vol. 22. (Serial Publication Ser.). 254p. 1987. text ed. 96.00 (*0-12-153122-8*) Acad Pr.

Mosconi, William, jt. auth. see McNair, Carol J.

Mosconi, Willie. Willie Mosconi on Pocket Billiards. (Illus.). 1948. 7.00 (*0-517-50779-X*, Crown) Crown Pub Group.

— Willie Mosconi on Pocket Billiards. Date not set. 9.00 (*0-517-88428-3*) Random.

— Winning Pocket Billiards. (Illus.). 1965. 7.95 (*0-517-50454-5*, Crown) Crown Pub Group.

— Winning Pocket Billiards. Date not set. 9.00 (*0-517-88427-5*) Random.

Mosconi, Willie & Cohen, Stanley. Willie's Game: An Autobiography of Willie Mosconi. 256p. 1993. text ed. 20.00 (*0-02-587495-0*) Macmillan.

Moscotti, Albert D. British Policy & the Nationalist Movement in Burma, 1917-1937. LC 73-86163. (Asian Studies at Hawaii: No. 11). 281p. reprint ed. pap. 80.10 (*0-8357-7426-0*, 2027030) Bks Demand.

Moscove, Stephen A. Accounting Fundamentals: A Self-Instructional Approach. 2nd ed. 1981. teacher ed write for info. (*0-8359-0062-2*, Reston) P-H.

— Accounting Fundamentals for Non-Accountants. 2nd ed. (Illus.). 320p. 1984. 25.95 (*0-8359-0036-3*, Reston) P-H.

Moscove, Stephen A. & Wright, Arnold. Cost Accounting with Managerial Applications. 6th ed. LC 88-81349. 1989. text ed. 49.16 (*0-318-36900-1*) HM.

Moscove, Stephen A., et al. Accounting Information Systems: Concepts & Practice for Effective Decisions. 4th ed. 774p. 1990. Net. teacher ed write for info. (*0-471-51626-0*); Net. text ed. write for info. (*0-471-50449-1*) Wiley.

— Cost Accounting: With Managerial Applications. 5th ed. LC 84-80701. 928p. (C). 1985. 6.36 (*0-685-09608-4*) HM.

***Moscovice, Ira, et al.** Building Rural Hospital Networks: Lessons in Providing Care to Underserved Populations. LC 95-174. 1995. pap. write for info. (*1-56793-028-X*) Health Admin Pr.

Moscovich, Ivan. Fiendishly Difficult Math Puzzles. LC 90-24767. (Illus.). 64p. 1991. pap. 6.95 (*0-8069-8270-5*) Sterling.

— Fiendishly Difficult Visual Perception Puzzles. LC 90-24662. (Illus.). 64p. 1991. pap. 6.95 (*0-8069-8268-3*) Sterling.

— The Magic Cylinder Book: Hidden Pictures to Color & Discover. (J). 1991. pap. 6.95 (*0-906212-67-7*, Pub. by Tarquin UK) Parkwest Pubns.

— Puzzling Reflections: Test Your Thinking Powers with Mirror-Cubes. (J). 1991. pap. 6.95 (*0-906212-72-3*, Pub. by Tarquin UK) Parkwest Pubns.

Moscovici, S., jt. auth. see Graumann, Carl F.

Moscovici, S., jt. ed. see Graumann, Carl F.

Moscovici, Serge. The Invention of Society: Psychological Explanations for Social Phenomena. Leigh, Sue, ed. Halls, W. D., tr. 360p. 1993. 44.95 (*0-7456-0814-0*) Blackwell Pubs.

Moscovici, Serge, et al, eds. Perspectives on Minority Influence. (European Studies in Social Psychology). 450p. 1985. 64.95 (*0-521-24695-4*) Cambridge U Pr.

Moscovici, Serge & Doise, Willem. Conflict & Consensus: A General Theory of Collective Decisions. 240p. 1994. 69.95 (*0-8039-8456-1*); pap. 21.95 (*0-8039-8457-X*) Sage.

Moscovici, Serge, et al, eds. Minority Influence. LC 94-15802. 1994. write for info. (*0-8304-1281-6*) Nelson-Hall.

Moscovit, Andrei, pseud. The Seventh Wife. Olcott, Anthony, tr. 466p. 1994. 23.00 (*1-880909-16-2*) Baskerville.

Moscovitch, Allan, et al. The Welfare State in Canada: A Selected Bibliography, 1840-1978. 3rd ed. 288p. (C). 1983. text ed. 28.50 (*0-88920-114-5*, Pub. by Wilfrid Laurier CN) Humanities.

Moscovitch, Allan & Drover, Glenn, eds. Inequality: Essays on the Political Economy of Social Welfare. (Studies in the Political Economy of Canada). 408p. 1981. pap. 15.95 (*0-8020-6426-4*) U of Toronto Pr.

Moscovitch, Edward. Mental Retardation Programs: How Does Massachusetts Compare? (Pioneer Paper Ser.: No. 4). 100p. (Orig.). 1991. pap. 10.00 (*0-929930-06-1*) Pioneer Inst.

— Special Education: Good Intentions Gone Awry. (Pioneer Paper Ser.: No. 8). 165p. 1993. pap. 10.00 (*0-929930-10-X*) Pioneer Inst.

***Moscovitch, Henry.** Newpoems. 128p. 1995. lib. bdg. 25.00 (*0-8095-4569-1*) Borgo Pr.

Moscovitch, Morris, ed. Infant Memory: Its Relation to Normal & Pathological Memory in Humans & Other Animals. LC 84-9844. (Advances in the Study of Communication & Affect Ser.: Vol. 9). 236p. 1984. 59.50 (*0-306-41588-7*, Plenum Pr) Plenum.

Moscovitz, H. S., jt. ed. see Brodersen, R. W.

Moscovitz, H. S., et al, eds. VLSI Signal Processing, Four. LC 90-5252. 480p. 1991. 49.95 (*0-87942-271-8*, PC02659) Inst Electrical.

Moscovitz, Judy. The Dieter's Companion: How to Make Any Diet Work. 192p. (Orig.). 1989. mass mkt. 6.95 (*0-380-75460-6*) Avon.

— Rice Diet Report. 224p. 1987. mass mkt. 5.50 (*0-380-70286-X*) Avon.

Moscow. Rare Earth Elements. 368p. reprint ed. text ed. 88.50 (*0-7065-0095-4*, Pub. by Keter Pub IS) Coronet Bks.

Moscow, Alvin, jt. auth. see Geneen, Harold.

Moscow, Alvin, jt. auth. see Hearst, Patricia C.

Moscow, Bradford. Book of New York Firsts. 1989. 9.95 (*0-685-46247-1*, Collier S&S) S&S Trade.

***Moscow, Henry.** The Book of New York Firsts: Unusual, Arcane, & Fascinating Facts in the Life of New York City. LC 94-39250. (Illus.). 133p. 1995. pap. 14.95 (*0-8156-0308-8*) Syracuse U Pr.

— The Street Book: An Encyclopedia of Manhattan's Street Names & Their Origins. LC 78-66990. (Illus.). 119p. 1990. pap. 14.95 (*0-8232-1275-0*) Fordham.

***Moscow Museum of Art & Industry Staff.** Medieval Russian Ornament in Full Color: From Illuminated Manuscripts. LC 94-32632. (Pictorial Archive Ser.). (Illus.). 1994. pap. 21.95 (*0-486-28258-9*) Dover.

Moscow Synod Staff, ed. Bogojavlenije Gospodnje. 194p. reprint ed. pap. 8.00 (*0-317-29167-X*) Holy Trinity.

— Preobrazhenije Gospodnje. 128p. pap. 6.00 (*0-317-29169-6*) Holy Trinity.

Moscow, Vsesoiuznyi Nauchno-issledovatel'skii Institut Mineral'nogo Syr'ia. New Data on Rare Element Mineralogy (Authorized Translation from the Russian) Ginzburg, A. I., ed. LC 61-18756. 144p. reprint ed. pap. 41.10 (*0-317-10653-8*, 2003368) Bks Demand.

Moscowitz, David S. Amulet of the Salkti. (Illus.). 1984. 6.95 (*0-940244-20-9*) Flying Buffalo.

Moscowitz, Ellyn. Legal Research & Writing for Paralegals. LC 93-72659. 315p. (C). 1993. pap. text ed. write for info. (*0-87084-132-7*) Anderson Pub Co.

Moscowitz, Harold, ed. see Bdolak, Levanah S.

Moscowitz, Raymond. Small School, Giant Dream: A Year of Hoosier High School Hoopla. (Illus.). (Orig.). 1990. pap. 7.95 (*0-9627117-0-5*) Littleguy Enter.

Moscrip, F. A., jt. auth. see Battin, George W.

Moscrop. Sinhalese-English, English-Sinhalese Dictionary. rev. ed. 336p. (ENG & SNH.). 1992. 49.95 (*0-8288-6986-3*) Fr & Eur.

Moscrop, J. E., jt. auth. see Robbins, J.

***Moscrop, T.** Sinhalese-English--English Sinhalese Dictionary. (ENG & SNH.). 1992. 31.00 (*0-7859-8920-X*) Fr & Eur.

Moscrop, T. & Vijairantne. Sinhalese-English - English-Sinhalese Dictionary. 335p. (ENG & SNH.). 1992. 31.00 (*81-85243-66-2*) IBD Ltd.

Moscucci, Ornella. The Science of Woman: Gynaecology & Gender in England, 1800-1929. (History of Medicine Ser.). (Illus.). 296p. (C). 1993. pap. 17.95 (*0-521-44795-X*) Cambridge U Pr.

Mose, D. G., jt. auth. see Bickford, Marion E.

Mose, Kenrick. Defamiliarization in the Work of Gabriel Garcia Marquez from 1947-1967. LC 89-9406. (Hispanic Literature Ser.). 350p. 1989. lib. bdg. 99.95 (*0-88946-387-5*) E Mellen.

Mose, Kenrick E. Shades of Darkness: Poems. LC 92-40838. 1993. pap. 12.95 (*0-7734-0029-X*, Mellen Poetry Pr) E Mellen.

Mosedale, F. Philosophy & Science: The Wide Range of Interaction. 1979. pap. text ed. write for info. (*0-13-662577-0*) P-H.

Mosekilde. European Simulation Multiconference, 1991 Proceedings. 968p. 1991. pap. 150.00 (*0-911801-92-8*, ESM91-1) Soc Computer Sim.

Mosekilde, E. & Mosekilde, L., eds. Complexity, Chaos & Biological Evolution. (NATO ASI Series B, Physics: Vol. 270). (Illus.). 424p. 1991. 110.00 (*0-306-44026-1*, Plenum Pr) Plenum.

***Mosekilde, Erik & Mouritsen, Ole G.** Modeling the Dynamics of Living Systems: Nonlinear Phenomena & Pattern Formation. (Series in Synergetics: Vol. 65). 1994. write for info. (*0-387-58480-3*); 69.00 (*3-540-58480-3*) Spr-Verlag.

Mosekilde, L., jt. ed. see Mosekilde, E.

Mosel, Arlene. The Funny Little Woman. LC 75-179046. (Illus.). 40p. (J). (ps-4). 1972. 16.00 (*0-525-30265-4*, 01258-370, DCB); pap. 4.95 (*0-525-45036-X*, DCB) Dutton Child Bks.

— Funny Little Woman. (J). (ps-3). 1993. pap. 4.99 (*0-14-054753-3*, Puffin) Puffin Bks.

— Tikki Tikki Tembo. LC 68-11839. (Illus.). 48p. (J). (ps-2). 1968. 14.95 (*0-8050-0662-1*, Bks Young Read) H Holt & Co.

— Tikki Tikki Tembo. Alonso, Liwayway, tr. LC 68-11839. (Illus.). 48p. (J). Date not set. 14.95 (*1-880507-13-7*) Lectorum Pubns.

— Tikki Tikki Tembo: Big Book. LC 68-11839. (Illus.). 32p. (J). (ps-2). 1992. pap. 18.95 (*0-8050-2345-3*, Bks Young Read) H Holt & Co.

Mosel, Doug, jt. auth. see Gift, Robert G.

Mosel, Tad. All the Way Home. 1961. 15.00 (*0-8392-1003-5*) Astor-Honor.

— Impromptu. 1961. pap. 2.75 (*0-8222-0557-2*) Dramatists Play.

— That's Where the Town's Going. 1963. pap. 4.75 (*0-8222-1130-0*) Dramatists Play.

Mosel, Ulrich. Fields Symmetries & Quarks. 450p. 1989. text ed. write for info. (*0-07-092200-4*) McGraw.

Moselage, John. The Lawhorn Site, Vol. 24. Bray, Robert T., ed. (Missouri Archaeologist Ser.). (Illus.). 110p. (Orig.). 1962. pap. 3.50 (*0-943414-40-7*) MO Arch Soc.

Moselev, George. The Consolidation of the South China Frontier. LC 73-170719. (Center for Chinese Studies Publications). 206p. reprint ed. pap. 58.80 (*0-318-34921-3*, 2031442) Bks Demand.

Moseley, Ann. Ole Edvart Rolvaag. LC 87-70033. (Western Writers Ser.: No. 80). (Illus.). 52p. (Orig.). 1987. pap. 3.95 (*0-88430-079-X*) Boise St U W Writ Ser.

Moseley, Ann & Harris, Jeanette. Interactions. (C). 1991. write for info. (*0-395-55425-X*) HM Soft Schl Col Div.

Moseley, Ann, jt. auth. see Harris, Jeanette.

***Moseley, Antony.** Learn dBASE 5.5 for Windows in a Day. 1995. disk, pap. 15.95 (*1-55622-469-9*) Wordware Pub.

Moseley, Barbara, ed. Best of the Best from Mississippi: Selected Recipes from Mississippi's Favorite Cookbooks. rev. ed. (Best of the Best Ser.). (Illus.). 288p. 1987. pap. 14.95 (*0-937552-19-4*) Quail Ridge.

— Best of the Best from Tennessee: Selected Recipes from Tennessee's Favorite Cookbooks. (Best of the Best Ser.). (Illus.). 288p. (Orig.). 1987. pap. 14.95 (*0-937552-20-8*) Quail Ridge.

Moseley, Barbara, jt. ed. see McKee, Gwen.

Moseley, C. W. The Poetic Birth: Milton's Poems of 1645. 256p. 1991. text ed. 59.95 (*0-85967-868-7*, Pub. by Scolar Pr UK) Ashgate Pub Co.

Moseley, Charles. A Century of Emblems: Curiously Culled & Delightfully Displayed. An Introductory Anthology. (Illus.). 250p. 1989. text ed. 54.95 (*0-85967-750-8*, Pub. by Scolar Pr UK) Ashgate Pub Co.

Moseley, Charles J., ed. Official World Wildlife Fund Guide to Endangered Species of North America, Vol. 3. LC 89-29757. (Illus.). 546p. 1992. lib. bdg. 85.00 (*0-933833-29-6*) Beacham Pub.

Moseley, Charles J., et al, eds. Beacham's Guide to Environmental Issues & Sources, 5 vols., Set. LC 92-42027. 1993. 240.00 (*0-933833-31-8*) Beacham Pub.

Moseley, Charles W., tr. see Mandeville, John.

Moseley, Chris. Colloquial Estonian. LC 93-11594. (Colloquial Ser.). 1994. write for info. (*0-415-08743-0*, Routledge NY); audio write for info. (*0-415-08744-9*, Routledge NY); audio write for info. (*0-415-08745-7*, Routledge NY) Routledge.

Moseley, Chris & Asher, R. E., eds. Atlas of the World's Languages. (Illus.). 182p. 1993. 599.95 (*0-415-01925-7*, A7190) Routledge.

***Moseley, Christopher, ed. & tr.** From Baltic Shores: Short Stories from Denmark, Estonia, Finland, Latvia, Lithuania, Sweden. 264p. 1995. pap. 24.00 (*1-870041-25-9*, Pub. by Norvik Pr UK) Dufour.

Moseley, Dana. A Fiesta at Twilight. LC 92-81048. 1993. 18.95 (*0-87212-258-1*) Libra.

Moseley, Douglas, jt. auth. see Moseley, Naomi.

Moseley, Edward H. & Huck, Eugene R., eds. Militarists, Merchants & Missionaries: United States Expansion in Middle America. LC 68-14556. 184p. reprint ed. 52.50 (*0-8357-9620-5*, 2050450) Bks Demand.

Moseley, Edward H. & Terry, Edward D., eds. Yucatan: A World Apart. LC 79-26492. (Illus.). 352p. 1980. 29.95 (*0-8173-0025-2*) U of Ala Pr.

Moseley, Elizabeth R. Davy Crockett: Hero of the Wild Frontier. (Discovery Biographies Ser.). (Illus.). 80p. (J). (gr. 2-6). 1991. reprint ed. lib. bdg. 12.95 (*0-7910-1409-6*) Chelsea Hse.

***Moseley, Eva S., ed.** Women, Information & the Future: Collecting & Sharing Resources Worldwide. LC 95-8890. 1995. write for info. (*0-917846-67-2*) Highsmith Pr.

Moseley, Fred. The Falling Rate of Profit in the Postwar United States Economy. LC 91-25750. 180p. 1992. text ed. 65.00 (*0-312-06888-3*) St Martin.

***Moseley, Fred, ed.** Heterodox Economic Theories: True or False? LC 94-49056. 1995. 61.95 (*1-85278-841-0*, Pub. by E Elgar Pub UK) Ashgate Pub Co.

— Marx's Method in Capital: A Reexamination. LC 92-22220. 240p. (C). 1993. text ed. 45.00 (*0-391-03785-4*) Humanities.

Moseley, Fred B. & Wolfe, Edward N. International Perspectives on Profitability & Accumulation. 289p. 1992. text ed. 69.95 (*1-85278-557-8*, Pub. by E Elgar Pub UK) Ashgate Pub Co.

Moseley, G. C. Leather Goods Manufacture: Methods & Processes. 340p. 1986. reprint ed. pap. text ed. 25.00 (*0-87556-389-9*) Saifer.

Moseley, George. Sino-Soviet Cultural Frontier: The Ili Kazakh Autonomous Chou. LC 67-827. (East Asian Monographs: No. 22). 171p. 1966. pap. 11.00 (*0-674-80925-4*) HUP.

— Sometimes a Little Justice. Van Treese, James B., ed. 240p. 1993. pap. 8.95 (*1-56901-030-7*) NW Pub.

Moseley, H. Non-ionising Radiation: Microwaves, Ultraviolet & Laser Radiation. (Medical Physics Handbook Ser.: No. 18). (Illus.). 308p. 1988. 105.00 (*0-85274-166-9*) IOP Pub.

Moseley, H. F., ed. see Hermodsson, Ivan.

Moseley, Henry. The Mechanical Principles of Engineering & Architecture. (Industrial Antiquities Ser.). (Illus.). 656p. (C). 1989. reprint ed. 135.00 (*1-85297-017-0*, Pub. by Archival Facs UK) St Mut.

Moseley, Henry N. Notes by a Naturalist. rev. ed. LC 72-1710. Orig. Title: Notes by a Naturalist on the Challenger. (Illus.). reprint ed. 65.00 (*0-404-08159-2*) AMS Pr.

Moseley, Herbert F. Recurrent Dislocation of the Shoulder. 175p. reprint ed. pap. 49.90 (*0-317-20727-X*, 2023824) Bks Demand.

Moseley, James G. A Complex Inheritance: The Idea of Self-Transcendence in the Theology of Henry James, Sr., & the Novels of Henry James. LC 75-8955. (American Academy of Religion. Dissertation Ser.: No. 4). 179p. reprint ed. pap. 51.10 (*0-7837-5469-8*, 2045234) Bks Demand.

— A Cultural History of Religion in America. LC 80-23609. (Contributions to the Study of Religion Ser.: No. 2). 216p. 1981. text ed. 49.95 (*0-313-22479-X*, MRA/, Greenwood Pr) Greenwood.

— John Winthrop's World: History As a Story; the Story As History. LC 92-20629. (History of American Thought & Culture Ser.). 202p. (Orig.). (C). 1992. lib. bdg. 42.50 (*0-299-13530-6*); pap. 14.95 (*0-299-13534-9*) U of Wis Pr.

Moseley, James W. UFO Crash Secrets at Wright-Patterson Air Force Base. 9.95 (*0-938294-71-7*) Glob Comm-Inner Lght.

— UFO Crash Secrets at Wright Patterson Air Force Base. 100p. 1992. 9.95 (*0-685-64743-9*) Glob Comm-Inner Lght.

Moseley, Keith. The Door under the Stairs. (Spooky Pop-Ups Ser.). (Illus.). 12p. (J). (gr. 1-4). 1994. 4.95 (*0-448-40834-1*, G&D) Putnam Pub Group.

— The Ghosts of Creepy Castle. (Spooky Pop-Ups Ser.). (Illus.). 12p. (J). (gr. 1-4). 1994. 4.95 (*0-448-40833-3*, G&D) Putnam Pub Group.

M

An Asterisk (*) at the beginning of an entry indicates that the title is appearing in BIP for the first time.

— It Was a Dark & Stormy Night: A Pop-up Mystery Whodunit. (Illus.). 14p. (J). (gr. 1-4). 1991. 12.95 (0-8037-1021-6) Dial Bks Young.
— Some Bodies in the Attic. (Spooky Pop-Ups Ser.). (Illus.). 12p. (J). (gr. 1-4). 1994. 4.95 (0-448-40836-8, G&D) Putnam Pub Group.
— The Things in Mouldy Manor. (Spooky Pop-Ups Ser.). (Illus.). 12p. (J). (gr. 1-5). 1994. 4.95 (0-448-40835-X, G&D) Putnam Pub Group.
Moseley, Keith & Everitt-Stewart, Andy. The Door under the Stairs. (Illus.). 12p. (J). 1990. 8.95 (0-448-40044-8, G&D) Putnam Pub Group.
Moseley, Lloyd W. Customer Relations: The Road to Greater Profits. rev. ed. LC 72-85929. (Illus.). 1990. pap. 36.95 (0-912016-79-5) Lebhar Friedman.
Moseley, Malcolm. Growth Centres in Spatial Planning. LC 74-9962. 1974. 84.00 (0-08-018055-8, Pub. by Pergamon Repr UK) Franklin.
Moseley, Marshall L. Windows 3.1 Instant Reference. 2nd ed. LC 91-67705. 262p. 1992. pap. 9.95 (0-89588-844-0) Sybex.
Moseley, Marshall L. & Rathbone, Andrew. Working with Windows(TM) 3.1. 352p. 1992. pap. 19.95 (0-8306-7722-4, 3722, Windcrest) TAB Bks.
Moseley, Marshall L. & Rathbone, R. Andrew. Working with Windows 3.1. 1992. pap. text ed. 19.95 (0-07-157694-0) McGraw.
Moseley, Mary. The Bahamas Handbook. 1976. lib. bdg. 69. 95 (0-8490-1472-7) Gordon Pr.
Moseley, Mary, jt. auth. see Sutton, Edna.
Moseley, Merritt. David Lodge: How Far Can You Go? LC 89-29632. (Milford Ser.: Popular Writers of Today: Vol. 16). viii, 112p. 1991. lib. bdg. 25.00x (0-8095-5204-3); pap. 15.00x (0-8095-5229-9) Borgo Pr.
— Understanding Kingsley Amis. LC 92-37274. (Understanding Contemporary British Literature Ser.). 192p. (C). 1993. text ed. 34.95 (0-87249-861-1) U of SC Pr.
Moseley, Merritt, ed. Proceedings of the 1991 Asheville Institute on General Education. 87p. (Orig.). 1992. pap. 15.00 (0-911696-54-7) Assn Am Coll.
Moseley, Michael E. The Incas & Their Ancestors: The Archaeology of Peru. LC 91-65309. (Illus.). 272p. 1993. pap. 19.95 (0-500-27723-0) Thames Hudson.
Moseley, Michael E. & Cordy-Collins, Alana, eds. Northern Dynasties: Kingship & Statecraft in Chimor: Symposium at Dumbarton Oaks, October 12 & 13, 1985. LC 89-23336. (Illus.). 560p. 1990. 40.00 (0-88402-180-7, MCND) Dumbarton Oaks.
Moseley, Naomi & Moseley, Douglas. Dancing in the Dark: The Shadow Side of Intimate Relationship. Niendorff, John S., ed. LC 93-85994. 252p. 1993. pap. 14.95 (1-880823-08-X) N Star Pubns.
Moseley, Nicholas, ed. see Plautus, T. Maccius.
Moseley, P. T. & Tofield, B. C., eds. Solid State Gas Sensors. (Sensors Ser.). (Illus.). 264p. 1987. 101.00 (0-85274-514-1) IOP Pub.
Moseley, P. T., et al, eds. Techniques & Mechanisms in Gas Sensing. (Sensors Ser.). (Illus.). 408p. 1991. 137.00 (0-7503-0074-4) IOP Pub.
Moseley, Robert K., jt. auth. see Duft, Joseph F.
Moseley, Romney M. Becoming a Self Before God: Critical Transformations. 1991. pap. 13.95 (0-687-02504-4) Abingdon.
Moseley, Roy. Bette Davis: An Intimate Memoir. 1990. 18. 95 (1-55611-218-1) D I Fine.
Moseley, Roy, jt. auth. see Higham, Charles.
Moseley, Rufas. Manifest Victory. 1985. pap. 9.95 (0-910924-92-9) Macalester.
Moseley, Rufus. Perfect Everything. 230p. pap. 7.95 (0-910924-29-5) Macalester.
Moseley, S. Kelley. Managing Seniors Housing. LC 88-61093. (Illus.). 214p. 1988. pap. 40.00 (0-86718-323-3) Home Builder.
Moseley, Spencer & Reed, Gervais. Walter F. Isaacs: An Artist in America, 1886-1964. LC 74-28489. (Index of Art in the Pacific Northwest Ser.: No. 8). (Illus.). 124p. 1982. 20.00 (0-295-95950-9) U of Wash Pr.
Moseley, Spencer & Rogers, Millard B. Wendell Brazeau: A Search for Form. LC 76-49167. (Index of Art in the Pacific Northwest Ser.: No. 12). (Illus.). 96p. 1977. 16. 50 (0-295-95555-4); pap. 8.95 (0-295-95546-5) U of Wash Pr.
***Moseley, Tom.** Clarion Program for Dummies, Windows Edition. 1995. pap. 22.99 (1-56884-334-8) IDG Bks.
Moseley, William W., et al, comps. Spanish Literature, 1500-1700: A Bibliography of Golden Age Studies in Spanish & English, 1925-1980. LC 84-8965. (Bibliographies & Indexes in World Literature Ser.: No. 3). lxiii, 765p. 1984. text ed. 115.00 (0-313-21491-3, MSL/) Greenwood.
Moseley, Willie G. Classic Guitars, U. S. A. A Primer for the Vintage Guitar Collector. LC 91-70519. (Illus.). 160p. (C). 1992. pap. text ed. 19.95 (0-931759-52-8, 00000139, Ctrstream) H Leonard.
— Stellas & Stratocasters. (Illus.). 292p. 1994. pap. 19.95 (0-7935-3492-5, HL00330115) H Leonard.
— Stellas & Stratocasters. 292p. Date not set. pap. 19.95 (1-884883-00-1) Vintage Guitar.
Mosely, Donald C., et al. Supervisory Management: The Art of Empowering & Developing People. 3rd ed. LC 92-24127. 1993. text ed. 44.95 (0-538-82246-5) S-W Pub.
Mosely Education Commission. Reports of the Mosely Education Commission to the United States of America, October-December, 1903. LC 73-89223. (American Education: Its Men, Institutions & Ideas, Ser. 1). 1978. reprint ed. 20.95 (0-405-01445-7) Ayer.
Mosely, F., jt. auth. see Meredith, S.
Mosely Industrial Commission. Reports of the Delegates of the Mosely Industrial Commission to the United States of America, Oct.-Dec., 1902. LC 73-2526. (Big Business; Economic Power in a Free Society Ser.). 1973. reprint ed. 19.95 (0-405-05105-0) Ayer.
Mosely, Jane, ed. see Lynch, Daniel.
Mosely, Ralph, ed. Readings in Noise Control & Hearing Conservation. 56p. 1985. 10.00 (0-939874-65-2) ASSE.
Mosely, Walter M. An Essay on Archery. 1976. reprint ed. 17.50 (0-85409-968-9) Charles River Bks.
Moseman, C. M. Moseman's Illustrated Guide for Purchasers of Horse Furnishing Goods. (Illus.). 304p. 1990. 15.99 (0-517-67575-7) Random Hse Value.
Moseman, C. M. & Brother Staff. Mosemans' Illustrated Catalog of Horse Furnishing Goods: An Unabridged Republication of the Fifth Edition. 320p. 1987. reprint ed. pap. 14.95 (0-486-25381-3) Dover.
Mosemann, John H. Russell's Hell vs. the Bible Hell. 15p. 1988. reprint ed. pap. 0.95 (1-883858-54-2) Witness CA.
Mosenson, Cecil. From the "Pit" to the Rose Garden. (Orig.). 1991. pap. 11.95 (0-9629935-1-4) Woodruff PA.
— Mr. Principal, Your Activity Period Sucks. (Illus.). (Orig.). 1991. pap. 11.95 (0-9629935-0-6) Woodruff PA.
Mosenthal, Basil. Young Sailor: An Introduction to Sailing & the Sea. (Illus.). 48p. (YA). (gr. 8 up). 1993. 13.95 (0-924486-61-9) Sheridan.
***Mosenthal, W. T.** Textbook of Neuroanatomy: With an Atlas & Dissection Guide. (Illus.). 525p. (C). 1994. pap. text ed. 32.95 (1-85070-587-9) Prthnon Pub.
Moser, jt. auth. see Carroll, Lewis.
Moser, A. Bioprocess Technology - Kinetics & Reactors. (Illus.). 455p. 1988. 189.00 (0-387-96603-X) Spr-Verlag.
Moser, A. P. Buried Pipe Design. 240p. 1990. text ed. 48.00 (0-07-043490-5) McGraw.
***Moser, Adolph.** Don't Despair on Thursdays! The Children's Grief-Management Book. Thatch, Nancy R., ed. LC 95-8653. (Emotional Impact Ser.). (Illus.). 60p. (J). (gr. k-8). 1995. lib. bdg. 14.95 (0-933849-60-5) Vanderbilt U Pr.
— Don't Feed the Monster on Tuesdays! The Children's Self-Esteem Book. Thatch, Nancy R., ed. LC 91-12941. (Emotional Impact Ser.). (Illus.). 55p. (J). (gr. k-12). 1991. lib. bdg. 14.95 (0-933849-38-9) Landmark Edns.
— Don't Rant & Rave on Wednesdays! The Children's Anger-Control Book. Thatch, Nancy R., ed. LC 94-22775. (Illus.). 61p. (J). 1994. lib. bdg. 14.95 (0-933849-54-0) Landmark Edns.
Moser, Adolph J. Don't Pop Your Cork on Mondays! The Children's Anti-Stress Book. LC 88-13912. (Emotional Impact Ser.). (Illus.). 48p. (J). (gr. k up). 1988. lib. bdg. 14.95 (0-933849-18-4) Landmark Edns.
Moser, Allison. Designing Woman. 1990. mass mkt. 4.50 (1-55817-337-4, Pinnacle NY) Windsor NY.
Moser, Antonio & Leers, Bernadino. Moral Theology: Dead Ends & Alternatives. (Theology & Liberation Ser.). 1990. 39.95 (0-88344-680-4); pap. 16.95 (0-88344-665-0) Orbis Bks.
Moser, Barry. The Barry Moser Engagement Calendar for 1992. 1991. pap. 12.95 (0-15-610694-9) HarBrace.
— Fly! A Brief History of Flight Illustrated. LC 92-30960. (Willa Perlman Bks.). (Illus.). 56p. (J). (gr. 1 up). 1993. lib. bdg. 15.89 (0-06-022894-6) HarpC Child Bks.
— Gold Rush: Twenty-Five Wood Engravings on a Theme of the Discovery & Mining of Gold in America, Africa & Australia. limited ed. (Illus.). 32p. (C). 1985. 600.00 (0-923980-02-4) Arundel Pr.
— Good & Perfect Gifts: A Retelling of O. Henry's the Gift of the Magi. LC 94-39168. (J). 1996. 15.95 (0-316-58543-2) Little.
— Tales of Edgar Allan Poe. LC 91-3277. (Books of Wonder). (Illus.). 312p. (J). 1991. 20.00 (0-688-07509-6) Morrow Jr Bks.
— Tucker Pfeffercorn. LC 92-34340. (J). 1994. 15.95 (0-316-58542-4) Little.
Moser, Barry, illus. Fifty Years of American Poetry: Anniversary Volume for the Academy of American Poets. 260p. 1984. 35.00 (0-8109-0934-0) Abrams.
— The Other Wise Man. LC 93-16259. (J). (ps-8). 1993. 16. 95 (0-88708-329-3, Picture Book Studio) S&S Childrens.
Moser, Barry, illus. & ret. Polly Vaughn: A Traditional British Ballad. 32p. (J). (gr. 2 up). 1992. 15.95 (0-316-58541-6) Little.
Moser, Barry, illus. St. Jerome & the Lion. LC 90-22142. 32p. (J). (ps-2). 1991. 16.95 (0-531-05938-3); 16.99 (0-531-08538-4) Orchard Bks Watts.
Moser, Barry, jt. auth. see Harper, Isabelle.
Moser, Caroline & Peake, Linda, eds. Women, Human Settlements, & Housing. 256p. (C). 1988. text ed. 55.00 (0-422-61860-8, Pub. by Tavistock UK); pap. text ed. 14. 95 (0-422-61980-9, Pub. by Tavistock UK) Routledge Chapman & Hall.
Moser, Caroline O. Gender Planning & Development: Theory, Practice & Training. LC 92-37648. 272p. 1993. 49.95 (0-415-05620-9, A5974, Routledge NY); pap. 17. 95 (0-415-05621-7, A5978, Routledge NY) Routledge.
Moser, Caroline O., ed. Community Participation in Urban Projects in the Third World. (Progress in Planning Ser.: No. 32). (Illus.). 68p. 1990. pap. 30.00 (0-08-040159-7, Pergamon Pr) Elsevier.
Moser, Charles. Dimitrov of Bulgaria. LC 79-90385. 360p. 1979. 14.95 (0-89803-011-0) Green Hill.
Moser, Charles A. Esthetics As Nightmare: Russian Literary Theory, 1855-1870. 248p. 1989. text ed. 42.50 (0-691-06763-5) Princeton U Pr.
— A History of Bulgarian Literature 1865-1944. LC 76-170000. (Slavistic Printings & Reprintings Ser.: No. 112). 282p. 1972. text ed. 67.70 (90-279-2008-7) Mouton.
— Pisemsky: A Provincial Realist. LC 78-78521. 283p. reprint ed. pap. 80.70 (0-7837-5938-X, 2045737) Bks Demand.
Moser, Charles A., ed. The Cambridge History of Russian Literature. 628p. (C). 1992. pap. 29.95 (0-521-42567-0) Cambridge U Pr.
— The Cambridge History of Russian Literature. 628p. (C). 1992. 94.95 (0-521-41554-3) Cambridge U Pr.
— The Russian Short Story: A Critical History. (Twayne's Critical History of the Short Story Ser.). 289p. 1986. lib. bdg. 22.95 (0-8057-9360-7, Twayne) Macmillan.
Moser, Charlotte. Clyde Connell: The Art & Life of a Louisiana Woman. (Illus.). 94p. 1991. pap. 19.95 (0-292-71141-7) U of Tex Pr.
***Moser, Cheri.** The Adventures of Fred & Ned. 1995. 9.95 (0-8062-5300-2) Carlton.
Moser, Christopher. Nuine Writing & Iconography of the Mixteca Baja. (Publications in Anthropology: No. 19). (Illus.). 246p. 1977. pap. 14.75 (0-935462-08-2) Vanderbilt Pubns.
Moser, Christopher L. Basketry of the Indians of California, 3 vols. (Illus.). 363p. (Orig.). 1993. Boxed Set. boxed 130.00 (0-935661-22-0) Riverside Mus Pr.
— Baskerty of the Indians of California, 3 vols., Vol. 1: Native American Basketry of Central Califo. (Illus.). 363p. (Orig.). 1993. pap. 30.00 (0-935661-12-3) Riverside Mus Pr.
— Basketry of the Indians of California, 3 vols., Vol. 2: Northern California Indian Basketry. (Illus.). 363p. (Orig.). 1993. Vol. 2, Northern California Indian Basketry. pap. 30.00 (0-935661-18-2) Riverside Mus Pr.
— Basketry of the Indians of California, 3 vols., Vol. 3: Native American Basketry of Southern Calif. (Illus.). 363p. (Orig.). 1993. Vol. 3, Native American Basketry of Southern California. pap. 45.00 (0-935661-20-4) Riverside Mus Pr.
Moser, Curtis C. How to Save Thousands When You Buy a Mobile Home. rev. ed. 96p. pap. 14.95 (0-9628152-0-9) CCM Advrtsng.
Moser, Diane, jt. auth. see Spangenberg, Ray.
Moser, Diane, jt. auth. see Spangenburg, Ray.
Moser, Diane K., jt. auth. see Spangenburg, Ray.
Moser, Diane R., jt. auth. see Spangenburg, Ray.
Moser, Dietz-Ruediger. Die Tannhaeuser Legende. (Fabula Supplement Ser.: Vol. 4). (C). 1977. 80.00 (3-11-005957-6) De Gruyter.
Moser, Edward P. Willy Nilly: Bill Clinton Speaks Out. 1994. pap. 8.95 (1-879941-25-2, Caliban Bks) J S Sanders.
Moser, Erwin. The Crow in the Snow & Other Bedtime Stories. Agee, Joel, tr. LC 86-10740. (Illus.). 48p. (J). (ps up). 1986. 10.95 (0-915361-49-3) Modan-Adama Bks.
— Wilma the Elephant. Agee, Joel, tr. LC 86-1145. (J). (gr. 3-8). 1986. 9.95 (0-915361-45-0) Modan-Adama Bks.
Moser, F. E. & Schnitzer, H. Heat Pumps in Industry. (Chemical Engineering Monographs: Vol. 20). 1985. 92. 50 (0-444-42452-0) Elsevier.
Moser, Frank H. & Thomas, Arthur L. The Phthalocyanines, Vol. I. 248p. 1983. 156.00 (0-8493-5677-6, QD441, CRC Reprint) Franklin.
— The Phthalocyanines, Vol. II. 184p. 1983. 115.00 (0-8493-5678-4, CRC Reprint) Franklin.
Moser, G. & Woodbridge, H. C. Ruben Dario y "El Cojo Ilustrado" 69p. 1.00 (0-318-22350-3) Hispanic Inst.
Moser, G. Paul, ed. Journal of the Johannes Schwalm Historical Association, Inc., Vol. 1, Nos. 1-3. Freund, H. H., tr. (Illus.). 106p. (Orig.). 1988. reprint ed. pap. 12.00 (0-939016-14-1) Johannes Schwalm Hist.
Moser, Gerald. A New Bibliography of the Lusophone Literatures of Africa. 2nd rev. ed. LC 93-19931. (Bibliographical Research in African Literatures Ser.: No. 2). 432p. 1993. 90.00 (1-873836-85-6, Pub. by H Zell Pubs UK) Bowker-Saur.
Moser, Gerald M. Changing Africa: The First Literary Generation of Independent Cape Verde. LC 92-72961. (Transactions Ser.: Vol. 82, Pt. 4). (Illus.). 102p. (C). 1992. pap. 15.00 (0-87169-824-2, T824-MOG) Am Philos.
Moser, Gerd, jt. auth. see Lange-Bertalot, H.
Moser, H. Geoffrey. Dawn Fish. LC 78-56849. 1979. 6.95 (0-87212-109-7) Libra.
Moser, H. O. A History of Delano, Pennsylvania. (Illus.). 227p. 1993. reprint ed. lib. bdg. 33.00 (0-8328-3549-8) Higginson Bk Co.
Moser, Hans J. Paul Hofhaimer: Ein Lied- und Orgelmeister des Deutschen Humanismus. ix, 231p. 1966. write for info. (0-318-71931-2, Pub. by Georg Olms GW) Lubrecht & Cramer.
Moser, Harold D., ed. see Webster, Daniel.
Moser, Harold D., et al. The Papers of Andrew Jackson: 1804-1813. LC 79-15078. (Andrew Jackson Ser.). 664p. (C). 1985. 49.50 (0-87049-441-4) U of Tenn Pr.
Moser, Harold D., et al, eds. The Papers of Andrew Jackson: Guide & Index to the Microfilm Editions. LC 86-33831. 343p. 1987. 50.00 (0-8420-4007-2) Scholarly Res Inc.
— The Papers of Andrew Jackson: 1816-1820, Vol. 4. LC 79-15078. (Illus.). 592p. (C). 1993. text ed. 49.50 (0-87049-778-2) U of Tenn Pr.
— The Papers of Andrew Jackson, 1814-1815, Vol. 3. LC 79-15078. (Illus.). 648p. 1991. text ed. 49.50x (0-87049-650-6) U of Tenn Pr.
Moser, Ingunn, jt. ed. see Shiva, Vandana.
Moser, J. Problems & Programmes Related to Alcohol & Drug Dependence in 33 Countries. (Offset Publication Ser.: No. 6). 1974. pap. 8.00 (92-4-170006-8) World Health.
Moser, J. K., jt. auth. see Siegel, C. L.
Moser, Joann. Visual Poetry: The Drawings of Joseph Stella. LC 89-11520. (Illus.). 208p. 1990. 45.00 (0-87474-738-4) Smithsonian.
Moser, Johann, ed. see St. Thomas Aquinas.
Moser, Johann, tr. see St. Thomas Aquinas.
Moser, Johann M. Most Ancient of All Splendors. LC 88-34644. 120p. 1989. 14.95 (0-918477-07-7) Sophia Inst Pr.
***Moser, Johann M., ed.** O Holy Night: Masterworks of Christmas Poetry. LC 94-34707. 115p. 1995. write for info. (0-918477-24-7) Sophia Inst Pr.
***Moser, Joyce & Watters, Ann, eds.** Creating America: Reading & Writing Arguments. LC 94-23916. 768p. 1995. pap. text ed. write for info. (0-13-061557-9) P-H.
Moser, Juelich W., jt. auth. see Moser, M.
Moser, Juergen K., jt. auth. see Siegel, Carl L.
Moser, Jurgen, ed. Fritz John: Collected Papers, 2 vols., Vol. I. (Contemporary Mathematicians Ser.). 648p. 1980. lib. bdg. 115.00 (0-8176-3266-2) Birkhauser.
— Fritz John: Collected Papers, 2 vols., Vol. II. (Contemporary Mathematicians Ser.). 760p. 1980. lib. bdg. 115.00 (0-8176-3267-0) Birkhauser.
Moser, Jurgen & Kyner, Walter T. Lectures on Hamiltonian Systems, & Rigorous & Formal Stability of Orbits about an Oblate Planet. LC 52-42839. (Memoirs Ser.: No. 1/ 81). 87p. 1989. reprint ed. pap. 19.00 (0-8218-1281-5, MEMO 1/81) Am Math.
Moser, K. Pulmonary Vascular Diseases. (Lung Biology in Health & Disease Ser.: Vol. 14). 728p. 1979. 215.00 (0-8247-6609-1) Dekker.
Moser, Kay. Celebration. LC 93-1662. 1993. 9.95 (1-56233-044-6) Star Song TN.
— Celebration. 1994. pap. 7.99 (1-56233-300-3, Star Song Contemp) Star Song TN.
Moser, Kenneth E. Shortness of Breath: A Guide to Better Living & Breathing. 144p. 1991. pap. 14.95 (0-8016-9055-2) Mosby Yr Bk.
Moser, Leo, jt. ed. see Bendahmane, Diane B.
Moser, Leslie E. Crack, Cocaine, Methamphetamine & Ice: What Every One of Us Must Know about These Public Enemies. 336p. 1990. 19.95 (1-878938-00-2) Mlti-Media Prodns.
— Older & Growing: Your Eternal Life Beginning Now. 1990. 14.95 (1-878938-01-0) Mlti-Media Prodns.
Moser, Louise E. & Turnbull, Andrew A. Proverbs for Programming in Pascal. LC 85-16870. 320p. 1990. pap. 24.50 (0-471-82309-0) Krieger.
Moser, M. Fungorum Rariorum Icones Coloratae, Part 7. (Illus.). 1979. pap. text ed. 24.00 (3-7682-0413-8) Lubrecht & Cramer.
***Moser, M., ed.** Microstructures of Ceramics: Structures & Properties of Grinding Tools. 364p. (C). 1980. 105.00x (963-05-1576-8, Pub. by Akad Kiado HU) St Mut.
Moser, M. & Horak, E. Cortinarius Fr. und Nahe Verwandte Gottungen in Suedamerika. 1975. 162.50 (3-7682-5452-6) Lubrecht & Cramer.
Moser, M. & Juelich, W. Farbatlas der Basidiomyceten (Color Atlas of Basidiomycetes), Fasc. 3. (Illus.). 30p. (ENG, FRE, GER & ITA.). 1986. ring bd. 64.00 (3-437-30513-1) Lubrecht & Cramer.
Moser, M. & Moser, Juelich W. Farbatlas der Basidiomyceten: Fasc. 1 & 2. (Illus.). 93p. (FRE, GER & ITA.). 1985. 130.00 (3-437-30438-0) Lubrecht & Cramer.
Moser, M. E. & Finlayson, C. A., eds. Wetlands: A Global Perspective. (Illus.). 224p. 1991. 45.00 (0-8160-2556-8) Facts on File.
Moser, Marvin. Lower Your Blood Pressure & Live Longer. 1991. pap. 4.50 (0-425-12675-7) Berkley Pub.
— Lower Your Blood Pressure & Live Longer: A Simple & Effective Program Developed by a Leading Specialist in Hypertension. 288p. 1989. 18.95 (0-394-56876-1, Villard Bks) Random.
Moser, Marvin & Becker, Brenda L. Week by Week to a Strong Heart. 336p. 1994. mass mkt. 5.50 (0-380-72089-2) Avon.
— Week-by-Week to a Strong Heart: An Action Plan for Preventing & Treating Heart Disease & Other Circulatory Diseases. (Illus.). 288p. 1992. 22.95 (0-87596-133-9, 05-363-0) Rodale Pr Inc.
***Moser, Mary A. & MacLeod, Douglas, eds.** Immersed in Technology: Art & Virtual Environments. (Illus.). 336p. 1995. 40.00 (0-262-13314-8) MIT Pr.
Moser, Mary B., jt. auth. see Felger, Richard S.
Moser, Maynard. Jacob Gould Schurman: Scholar, Political Activist & Ambassador of Good Will, 1892-1942. 1981. 30.95 (0-405-14100-9) Ayer.
Moser, Meinhard. Die Pilze Mitteleuropas: Vol. 4, Die Gattung Phlegmacium (Schleimkoepfe) (Illus.). 1960. 143.00 (3-7682-0523-1) Lubrecht & Cramer.
— The Polypores, Boletes & Agarica. Kibby, G. & Rayner, R., trs. (Illus.). 355p. (C). 1983. text ed. 51.95x (0-916422-43-7) Mad River.
Moser-Mercer, Barbara, jt. ed. see Lambert, Sylvie.
***Moser, Michael.** Arbitration in the People's Republic of China. 1995. write for info. (0-409-99698-X, SI) Butterworth Legal Pubs.
Moser, Michael J. & Change, Jessie T., eds. Foreign Trade Investment & the Law in the People's Republic of China. 2nd ed. LC 87-11272. 1987. 45.00 (0-19-584058-5) OUP.
Moser, Michael J. & Moser, Yeone W. Foreigners Within the Gates: The Legations at Peking. LC 92-39882. (Illus.). 176p. 1993. 32.00 (0-19-585702-X) OUP.
Moser, Michael J. & Zee, Winston K. China Tax Guide. 2nd ed. LC 92-29434. 328p. (C). 1993. 79.00 (0-19-585724-0) OUP.
Moser, Norm, ed. The Shorter Plays & Scenarios of Norm Moser. 48p. (Orig.). 1981. pap. 3.00 (0-941442-00-4) Illuminations Pr.
Moser, Norman. El Grito del Norte & Other Stories: Stories, Tales & Fables. (New 80's Bk.). (Illus.). 172p. (Orig.). 1983. pap. 6.00 (0-941442-02-0) Illuminations Pr.

An Asterisk (*) at the beginning of an entry indicates that the title is appearing in BIP for the first time.

— Open Season: Selected Poems. (New 80's Bk.). (Illus.). 60p. (Orig.). 1980. 3.00 (*0-686-29369-X*) Illuminations Pr.

Moser, Paul & Mulder, Dwayne. Contemporary Approaches to Philosophy. (Illus.). 450p. (Orig.). (C). 1994. pap. write for info. (*0-02-384171-0*) Macmillan.

Moser, Paul K. Empirical Justification. 1985. lib. bdg. 91.50 (*90-277-2041-X*); pap. text ed. 47.00 (*90-277-2042-8*) Kluwer Ac.

— Empirical Knowledge: Readings in Contemporary Epistemology. LC 86-3197. 296p. (C). 1986. 49.00 (*0-8476-7492-4*); pap. 24.95 (*0-8476-7493-2*) Rowman.

— Knowledge & Evidence. (Studies in Philosophy). (C). 1989. 64.95 (*0-521-37028-0*) Cambridge U Pr.

— Knowledge & Evidence. (Studies in Philosophy). 285p. (C). 1991. pap. 22.95 (*0-521-42363-5*) Cambridge U Pr.

— Philosophy after Objectivity: Making Sense in Perspective. LC 92-38864. 280p. 1993. 42.00 (*0-19-508109-9*) OUP.

Moser, Paul K., ed. Rationality in Action: Contemporary Approaches. 450p. (C). 1990. 79.95 (*0-521-38572-5*); pap. 29.95 (*0-521-38598-9*) Cambridge U Pr.

***Moser, Paul K. & Trout, J. D., eds.** Contemporary Materialism: A Reader. LC 94-32686. 400p. 1995. 65.00x (*0-415-10863-2*, B7037); pap. 22.95 (*0-415-10864-0*, B7041, Routledge NY) Routledge.

Moser, Paul K. & Vander Nat, Arnold. Human Knowledge: Classical & Contemporary Approaches. 480p. (C). 1995. pap. text ed. 24.95 (*0-19-508625-2*) OUP.

— Human Knowledge: Classical & Contemporary Approaches. 2nd ed. 480p. (C). 1995. 45.00 (*0-19-508626-0*) OUP.

***Moser, Richard.** The New Winter Soldiers: GI & Veteran Dissent During the Vietnam Era. (Sights on the Sixties Ser.). (Illus.). 300p. (C). 1996. text ed. 50.00 (*0-8135-2241-2*); pap. text ed. 18.95 (*0-8135-2242-0*) Rutgers U Pr.

Moser, Robert H. A Decade of Decision: A Physician Remembers the American College of Physicians 1977-1986. 336p. 1991. 38.00 (*0-943126-17-7*, DDS91) Amer Coll Phys.

— A Decade of Decision: A Physician Remembers the American College of Physicians 1977-1986. limited ed. 336p. 1991. 49.00 (*0-685-49577-9*, DDH91) Amer Coll Phys.

Moser, Robert V. Different Views for Christian Thinking. 72p. 1988. 6.95 (*0-9621065-0-X*) R V Moser.

Moser, Sally, ed. see Bridwell, Jim & Peall, Keith.

Moser, Thomas. How to Build Shaker Furniture. LC 76-46809. (Illus.). 224p. 1980. pap. 14.95 (*0-8069-8392-2*) Sterling.

— Measured Shop Drawings for American Furniture. LC 84-26872. (Illus.). 328p. 1988. pap. 19.95 (*0-8069-6792-7*) Sterling.

Moser, Thomas C. The Life in the Fiction of Ford Madox Ford. LC 80-7548. 370p. reprint ed. pap. 105.50 (*0-8357-4645-3*, 2037576) Bks Demand.

Moser, Thomas C., ed. see Conrad, Joseph.

Moser, Thomas C., ed. see Ford, Ford M.

Moser, U. & Von Zeppelin, I., eds. Cognitive-Affective Processes: New Ways of Psychoanalytic Modeling. (Monographien der Breuninger-Stiffung Stuttgart Ser.). (Illus.). vii, 183p. 1991. pap. 51.00 (*0-387-53993-X*) Spr-Verlag.

Moser, W. O., jt. auth. see Coxeter, H. S.

Moser, W. R. & Pfeffer, R., eds. Honoring the Eightieth Birthday of John Happel: Special Issues of the Journal Chemical Engineering Communications, 2 vols., Set. ii, 566p. 1989. pap. text ed. 622.00 (*2-88124-380-0*) Gordon & Breach.

Moser, William D. Elsinore Revisited. 28p. (Orig.). 1992. pap. text ed. 5.00 (*0-9633307-0-5*, P921) Poets Farm Pr.

Moser, William D., ed. see Giusto, Joan M.

Moser, William R., ed. Catalysis of Organic Reactions. LC 81-15172. (Chemical Industries Ser.: Vol. 5). (Illus.). 496p. 1981. 175.00 (*0-8247-1341-9*) Dekker.

Moser, William R. & Happel, John R., eds. Catalytic Chemistry of Solid-State Inorganics, Vol. 272. (Annals Ser.). 1976. 10.00 (*0-89072-051-7*) NY Acad Sci.

Moser, William R. & Slocum, Donald W., eds. Homogeneous Transition Metal Catalyzed Reactions: Developed from a Symposium Sponsored by the Catalysis Secretariat at the 199th National Meeting of the American Chemical Society, Boston, Massachusetts, April 22-27, 1990. LC 92-356. (Advances in Chemistry Ser.: Vol. 230). (Illus.). 602p. 1992. 139.95 (*0-8412-2007-7*) Am Chemical.

Moser, William R., jt. ed. see Slocum, D. W.

Moser, Yeone W., jt. auth. see Moser, Michael J.

Moserova, J. & Houskova, E. The Healing & Treatment of Skin Defects. (Illus.). viii, 163p. 1989. 60.00 (*3-8055-4704-8*) S Karger.

Moses. The South Carolina Probate Practice Manual. 1990. 125.00 (*0-685-46188-2*, NO. 421) SC Bar CLE.

Moses, jt. auth. see Patterson.

Moses, A. Elfin & Hawkins, Robert O., Jr. Counseling Lesbian Women & Gay Men: A Life-Issues Approach. 263p. (C). 1982. pap. write for info. (*0-675-20599-9*, Merrill Pub Co) Macmillan.

Moses, A. J. Nuclear Techniques in Analytical Chemistry. LC 64-15736. (International Series of Monographs on Analytical Chemistry: Vol. 20). 1964. 69.00 (*0-08-010695-1*, Pub. by Pergamon Repr UK) Franklin.

Moses, A. J. & Belcher, R. Analytical Chemistry of the Actinide Elements. LC 63-12697. (International Series of Monographs on Analytical Chemistry: Vol. 9). 1963. 71.00 (*0-08-009915-7*, Pub. by Pergamon Repr UK) Franklin.

Moses, A. M., ed. see International Conference on the Neurohypophysis Staff.

Moses, Abayomi. U. S. Law Schools: A Directory of Courses & Other Special Programs Available at the American Law Schools. LC 81-52882. 180p. 1981. 14.00 (*0-9606958-0-X*); pap. 11.00 (*0-9606958-1-8*) Sekoni Pubs.

Moses, Albert L. South Carolina Probate Practice Manual. 1990. ring bd. 125.00 (*0-943856-33-7*, 421) SC Bar CLE.

Moses, Amy. I Am an Explorer. LC 90-38374. (Rookie Reader Ser.). (Illus.). 32p. (J). (ps-2). 1990. lib. bdg. 10.35 (*0-516-02059-5*); pap. 2.95 (*0-516-42059-3*) Childrens.

— I Am an Explorer Big Book. (Rookie Readers Big Bks.). (Illus.). 32p. (J). (ps-2). 1991. lib. bdg. 22.95 (*0-516-49517-8*) Childrens.

— If I Were an Ant. LC 92-12947. (Rookie Reader Ser.). (Illus.). 32p. (J). (ps-2). 1992. lib. bdg. 10.35 (*0-516-02011-0*) Childrens.

— If I Were an Ant. LC 92-12947. (Rookie Reader Ser.). (Illus.). 32p. (J). (ps-2). 1993. pap. 2.95 (*0-516-42011-9*) Childrens.

***Moses, Barbara.** Discover Seashores: A Discovery Book. (Illus.). 32p. (J). (gr. 5-7). 1995. pap. 3.75 (*0-915992-72-8*) Eastern Acorn.

Moses, Bernard. Democracy & Social Growth in America. 1977. 59.95 (*0-8490-1706-8*) Gordon Pr.

— The Railway Revolution in Mexico. 1976. lib. bdg. 59.95 (*0-8490-2499-4*) Gordon Pr.

— Spain's Declining Power in South America 1730-1806. LC 65-21911. reprint ed. 52.25 (*0-8154-0158-2*) Cooper Sq.

Moses, Brian. Hippopotamus Dancing & Other Poems. LC 93-43968. (J). 1994. 14.95 (*0-521-44141-2*); 7.95 (*0-521-44684-8*) Cambridge U Pr.

— Knock Down Ginger & Other Poems. LC 93-43969. (J). 1994. 14.95 (*0-521-44140-4*); pap. 7.95 (*0-521-44683-X*) Cambridge U Pr.

Moses, Bruce E. How to Market Yourself, Yourself! The Executive Job Changing Guide Book. LC 79-63505. (Illus.). 1979. 14.95 (*0-9602540-0-5*) Pro-Search.

Moses, Carole. Melville's Use of Spenser. (American University Studies: American Literature: Ser. XXIV, Vol. 6). 235p. (C). 1989. text ed. 39.95 (*0-8204-0832-8*) P Lang Pubs.

— Process, Purpose, Practice: A Basic Writer's Guide. 411p. (C). 1991. Instr.'s guide/wkbk. teacher ed write for info. (*0-669-19819-6*); pap. text ed. write for info. (*0-669-19818-8*); Instr.'s ed. teacher ed write for info. (*0-669-24709-X*) Heath.

Moses, Claire G. French Feminism in the 19th Century. LC 83-18040. (SUNY Series in European Social History). 311p. 1985. 64.50 (*0-87395-859-4*); pap. 21.95 (*0-87395-860-8*) State U NY Pr.

***Moses, Claire G. & Hartman, Heidi, eds.** U. S. Women in Struggle: A Feminist Studies Anthology. (Women in American History Ser.). 1995. write for info. (*0-252-02166-5*) U of Ill Pr.

***Moses, Claire G. & Hartmann, Heidi, eds.** U. S. Women in Struggle: A Feminist Studies Anthology. (Women in American History Ser.). 1995. pap. write for info. (*0-252-06462-3*) U of Ill Pr.

Moses, Claire G. & Rabine, Leslie W. Feminism, Socialism, & French Romanticism. 384p. (C). 1993. 39.95 (*0-253-33889-1*, MB-818) Ind U Pr.

Moses, Don V., jt. auth. see Demaree, Robert W., Jr.

Moses, Earl C., Jr. An Introduction to the Christian Faith: A Biblical Perspective. 1993. 16.95 (*0-533-10329-0*) Vantage.

Moses, Edward, jt. auth. see Getz, Robert.

Moses, Edward A., jt. auth. see Cheney, John M.

Moses, Edward A., et al. Cases in Investments. 2nd ed. Fenton, ed. 247p. (C). 1989. pap. text ed. 33.00 (*0-314-48128-1*) West Pub.

Moses, Edward P. & Warda, Mark. How to Make a Georgia Will. LC 93-86527. 94p. (Orig.). 1993. pap. 9.95 (*0-913825-77-8*) Sphinx Pub FL.

Moses, Elbert R., Jr. Adventure in Reasoning. 80p. 1988. 15.00 (*0-9621305-0-8*) Moses Pubns.

Moses, Elbert R. Beating the Odds: A Mini Autobiography. (Illus.). 50p. (Orig.). (YA). 1992. pap. text ed. 3.95 (*0-922484-03-1*) Poligion Pub.

Moses, Elbert R., Jr. Three Attributes of God. LC 83-90115. 61p. 1983. 9.95 (*0-9621305-1-6*) Moses Pubns.

Moses, Gavriel. The Nickel Was for the Movies - Film in the Novel: Pirandello to Pulg. LC 93-16283. 1994. 40.00 (*0-520-07943-4*) U CA Pr.

Moses, George. Those Good Old Days in the Black Hills. 120p. (Orig.). 1991. pap. text ed. write for info. (*0-913062-01-4*) Fenwyn Pr.

Moses, George D. Vietnam, an American Ordeal. 2nd ed. LC 92-46988. 1993. pap. text ed. write for info. (*0-13-221151-3*) P-H Gen Ref & Trav.

Moses, Grace E. Rooster Strut on the Suwannee & Two Short Stories. LC 88-3458. 149p. 1988. 13.75 (*0-930950-15-1*); pap. 8.75 (*0-930950-16-X*) Nopoly Pr.

Moses, Grace M. The Welsh Lineage of John Lewis (1592-1657), Emigrant to Gloucester, Virginia. rev. ed. 68p. 1992. reprint ed. pap. 10.00 (*0-685-62585-0*, 9263) Clearfield Co.

Moses, Gregory A. Engineering Applications Software Development Using FORTRAN 77. LC 88-20887. 320p. 1988. text ed. 69.95 (*0-471-63851-X*) Wiley.

Moses, H. & Patterson, C. H. Research Readings in Rehabilitation Counseling. 1973. pap. 9.80 (*0-87563-054-5*) Stipes.

Moses, H., jt. auth. see Kay, I.

***Moses, H. Weston, et al.** A Practical Guide to Cardiac Pacing. 4th ed. LC 94-3383. 1994. 32.95 (*0-316-58552-1*) Little.

Moses, Halsey H. The Law of Mandamus & the Practice Connected with It, with an Appendix of Forms. iv, 268p. 1981. reprint ed. lib. bdg. 27.50 (*0-8377-0838-9*) Rothman.

***Moses, Harry M.** It's So Easy When You Know How. 159p. (Orig.). 1994. pap. 12.00 (*1-886578-00-1*) New Thought.

Moses, Henry C. Inside College: New Freedom, New Responsibility. 240p. (C). 1990. pap. 10.95 (*0-87447-383-7*) College Bd.

Moses-Hrushovski, Rena. Deployment: Hiding Behind Power Struggles As a Character Defense. LC 94-98. 344p. 1994. 40.00 (*1-56821-042-6*) Aronson.

Moses, Ingrid. Academic Staff Evaluation & Development: A University Case Study. LC 87-30074. (Illus.). 318p. (Orig.). (C). 1988. pap. text ed. 32.95 (*0-7022-2117-1*, Pub. by Univ Queensland Pr AT) Intl Spec Bk.

Moses, Ingrid & Roe, Ernest. Heads & Chairs: Managing Academic Departments. 1990. pap. 29.95 (*0-7022-2263-1*, Pub. by Univ Queensland Pr AT) Intl Spec Bk.

***Moses, James.** Children's Publishing, Media & Entertainment. 252p. Date not set. 265.00 (*0-9626749-7-4*) Primary Research.

— Reference & Professional Information Business: A Study of Reference, Professional, Scientific, Technical, Directory & Database Publishing, 1990 Edition. 218p. 1991. ring bd. 125.00 (*0-9626749-1-5*) Primary Research.

— The Reference Book & Technology Report. 218p. 1990. per. write for info. (*0-9626749-0-7*) Primary Research.

***Moses, James & Flicek, Joseph.** Free Markets Emerge in the Electric Power Industry: Bottom Line Consequences for American Corporations, Utilities & Their Investors, Government Agencies & Other Producers & Consumers of Electricity. 178p. (Orig.). 1995. pap. 68.50 (*0-926674-99-4*) Primary Research.

Moses, James & Katos, Demetrios. The Corporate - Business Library Budget & Materials Expenditure Report. 100p. 1991. ring bd. 145.00 (*0-9626749-2-3*) Primary Research.

Moses, James & Park, Peter. The Public Library Budget & Materials Expenditure Report. 150p. 1991. ring bd. 95.00 (*0-9626749-3-1*) Primary Research.

Moses, James, jt. auth. see Flicek, Joseph.

Moses, James A., jt. auth. see Strickland, Winifred G.

Moses, Jeff, jt. auth. see Welch, Bill.

Moses, Jeffrey. Oneness: Great Principles Shared by All Religions. 128p. 1992. mass mkt. 6.00 (*0-449-90760-0*, Columbine) Fawcett.

Moses, Jeffrey S., jt. auth. see Harris, George A.

Moses, Joel, jt. ed. see Dertouzos, Michael L.

Moses, Joel C. The Politics of Female Labor in the Soviet Union. (Western Societies Papers). 76p. 1978. pap. 11.95 (*0-8014-9632-2*) Cornell U Pr.

— The Politics of Women & Work in the Soviet Union & the United States: Alternative Work Schedules & Sex Discrimination. LC 82-23307. (Research Ser.: No. 50). xii, 184p. 1983. pap. 9.50 (*0-87725-150-9*) U of Cal IAS.

Moses, Joel C., jt. ed. see Bahry, Donna L.

Moses, Joel C., jt. auth. see Rasmussen, Jorgen S.

Moses, John. Trade Unionism in Germany from Bismarck to Hitler: 1869-1933, 2 vols. Incl. Vol. 1. Eighteen Sixty-Nine to Nineteen Eighteen. 314p. 1982. 53.00 (*0-389-20072-7*, 06843); Vol. 2. Nineteen Nineteen to Nineteen Thirty-Three. 295p. 1982. 50.00 (*0-389-20073-5*, 06844); 1982. 25.00 (*0-685-00695-6*) B&N Imports.

Moses, John A. Trade Union Theory from Marx to Walesa. LC 89-39266. 264p. 1990. 59.95 (*0-85496-186-0*) Berg Pubs.

Moses, John G. & Nassar, Eugene P. Annotated Index to the "Syrian World," 1926-1932. Rosenblatt, Judith, ed. LC 93-80115. (Illus.). xiii, 129p. 1994. spiral bd. 18.00 (*0-932833-13-6*) Immig His Res.

Moses, Julian M. Price Guide to Collectors' Records with New Revised Value Chart. 3rd ed. 32p. 1976. pap. 9.95 (*0-914652-03-6*) Am Record.

Moses, Julian M. & De Luca, Giuseppe. American Celebrity Recordings 1900-1925. 3rd ed. LC 93-78789. 208p. 1993. pap. 12.95 (*0-9632903-1-2*) Monarch Rec Ent.

Moses, Kathy. It's a Child's World: The Complete Guide to Day-Care; an Operational Manual for Providers, an Informational Guide for Parents. (Illus.). 184p. (Orig.). 1989. pap. 11.95 (*0-942323-06-8*) N Amer Heritage Pr.

Moses, L. & Tomikel, John. Basic Meteorology, an Introduction to the Science. (Illus.). 130p. (C). 1981. pap. text ed. 14.95 (*0-910042-39-X*) Allegheny.

Moses, L. G. The Indian Man: A Biography of James Mooney. LC 83-6481. (Illus.). 320p. 1984. 29.95 (*0-252-01040-X*) U of Ill Pr.

Moses, L. G. & Wilson, Raymond, eds. Indian Lives: Essays on Nineteenth & Twentieth Century Native American Leaders. LC 85-1188. (Illus.). 239p. 1985. pap. 14.95 (*0-8263-0815-5*) U of NM Pr.

Moses, Larry & Halkovic, Stephen A., Jr. Introduction to Mongolian History & Culture. LC 86-620695. (Uralic & Altaic Ser.: Vol. 149). 305p. (Orig.). (C). 1985. pap. 10.00 (*0-933070-18-7*) Res Inst Inner Asian Studies.

Moses, Larry, ed. see Halkovic, Stephen A., Jr.

Moses, Larry W. The Political Role of Mongol Buddhism. LC 81-622859. (Uralic & Altaic Ser.: Vol. 133). x, 299p. 1977. 15.00 (*0-933070-01-2*) Res Inst Inner Asian Studies.

Moses, Leon N. & Lindstrom, Dan, eds. Transportation of Hazardous Materials: Issues in Law, Social Science, & Engineering Ser. LC 93-20447. 365p. (C). 1993. lib. bdg. 89.95 (*0-7923-9340-6*) Kluwer Ac.

Moses, Leon N. & Savage, Ian, eds. Transportation Safety in an Age of Deregulation. (Illus.). 368p. 1989. 55.00 (*0-19-505797-X*) OUP.

Moses, Libby, jt. auth. see Scalisi, Danny.

Moses, Lincoln E. & Oakford, Robert V. Tables of Random Permutations. LC 63-12041. 233p. 1963. 32.50 (*0-8047-0148-2*) Stanford U Pr.

Moses, Lincoln E., jt. auth. see Chernoff, Herman.

Moses, Lloyd R. Whatever It Takes: The Autobiography of Lloyd R. Moses. 1991. 35.95 (*0-929925-06-8*) Univ SD Pr.

Moses, Lucille, jt. auth. see Osborn, Susan Titus.

Moses, M. Famous Actor Families in America. 1972. 59.95 (*0-8490-0153-6*) Gordon Pr.

Moses, Marion. Cosecha Dolorosa: Campesinos y Pesticidas, Parte I Trabajadores en el Fil. Abello, Elizabeth, tr. (Illus.). 120p. (SPA.). 1992. 10.00 (*1-881510-02-6*) Pesticide Educ Ctr.

— Cosecha Dolorosa: Campesinos y Pesticidas, Parte II Mezcladores, Cargadores, Aplicadores. Abello, Elizabeth, tr. (Illus.). 120p. (SPA.). 1992. 10.00 (*1-881510-04-2*) Pesticide Educ Ctr.

— Harvest of Sorrow: Farm Workers & Pesticides, Part I Field Workers. (Illus.). 72p. 1992. student ed 10.00 (*1-881510-01-8*) Pesticide Educ Ctr.

— Harvest of Sorrow: Farm Workers & Pesticides, Part II Mixers, Loaders, Applicators. (Illus.). 72p. 1992. student ed 10.00 (*1-881510-03-4*) Pesticide Educ Ctr.

Moses, Mary J. & Martindale, Judith A. Fifty-Two Simple Ways to Manage Your Money. LC 93-31430. 224p. 1994. 19.95 (*0-942061-63-2*); pap. 9.95 (*0-942061-62-4*) Sourcebks.

Moses, Mary J., jt. auth. see Martindale, Judith A.

***Moses, Michael V.** The Novel & the Globalization of Culture. 224p. 1995. text ed. 35.00 (*0-19-508951-0*); pap. 17.95 (*0-19-508952-9*) OUP.

Moses Monk of the Holy Mountain. Married Saints of the Church. Reed, Melania & Simonsson, Maria, eds. LC 91-68400. (Illus.). 182p. (Orig.). 1992. pap. 6.95 (*0-938635-46-8*) St Herman AK.

Moses, Monte C., jt. auth. see Whitaker, Kathryn S.

Moses, Montrose. American Theater As Seen by Its Critics, 1752-1934. 391p. 1993. reprint ed. lib. bdg. 89.00 (*0-7812-5279-2*) Rprt Serv.

— Fabulous Forrest. 1993. reprint ed. lib. bdg. 89.00 (*0-7812-5495-7*) Rprt Serv.

Moses, Montrose J. American Dramatist. rev. ed. LC 64-14706. (Illus.). 1972. reprint ed. 24.95 (*0-405-08800-0*, Pub. by Blom Pubns UK) Ayer.

— Fabulous Forrest. LC 72-91909. (Illus.). 1972. reprint ed. 24.95 (*0-405-08801-9*, Pub. by Blom Pubns UK) Ayer.

— Famous Actor-Families in America. LC 68-58994. (Illus.). 1972. reprint ed. 23.95 (*0-405-08802-7*, Pub. by Blom Pubns UK) Ayer.

— The Life of Heinrich Conried. Farkas, Andrew, ed. LC 76-29959. (Opera Biographies Ser.). (Illus.). 1977. reprint ed. lib. bdg. 35.95 (*0-405-09699-2*) Ayer.

— Representative Plays by American Dramatists. 1972. 132.00 (*0-685-43147-9*, 1026) Ayer.

— Representative Plays by American Dramatists, 3 vols. (BCL1-PS American Literature Ser.). 1992. reprint ed. lib. bdg. 225.00 (*0-7812-6654-8*) Rprt Serv.

Moses, Montrose J., tr. see Maeterlinck, Maurice.

Moses, Nelson, jt. auth. see Klein, Harriet B.

Moses of Khoren. Patmowt'iwn Hayots: History of the Armenians. Thomson, Robert W., ed. LC 81-3869. (Classical Armenian Texts Ser.). 1981. reprint ed. 50.00 (*0-88206-032-5*) Caravan Bks.

Moses, Phillip J. How to Build a Dynamic Real Estate Listing Machine. 1980. 49.50 (*0-13-402446-X*) Exec Reports.

— How to Use the Inside Secrets of a Super Land Salesman to Make Big Money in Any Kind of Real Estate. 1976. 79.50 (*0-13-436188-1*) Exec Reports.

Moses, Rafael, ed. Persistent Shadows of the Holocaust: The Meaning to Those Not Directly Affected. 288p. 1993. text ed. 37.50 (*0-8236-4062-0*) Intl Univs Pr.

Moses, Robb E. & Summers, William C., eds. DNA Replication & Mutagenesis. (Illus.). 515p. 1988. text ed. 49.00 (*1-55581-003-9*) Am Soc Microbio.

Moses, Robert. Civil Service of Great Britain. LC 14-2375. (Columbia University. Studies in the Social Sciences: No. 139). reprint ed. 34.50 (*0-404-51139-2*) AMS Pr.

Moses, Robert, ed. see Ken, Light.

Moses, Russell L. Mediation & Private Contacts in the Iran Hostage Crisis, April 1980-January 1981. (Pew Case Studies in International Affairs). 94p. (C). 1989. pap. text ed. 2.50 (*1-56927-316-2*) Geo U Inst Dplmcy.

Moses, Ryan O. Evilway. 1990. pap. 3.95 (*0-8217-3042-8*) Zebra.

Moses, Sam. Fast Guys, Rich Guys & Idiots: A Racing Odyssey on the Border of Obsession. LC 86-60155. (Illus.). 352p. 1986. 17.95 (*0-937159-09-3*) September Pr.

***Moses, Shelia P.** One More River to Cross. Justice, Felix, ed. 80p. (YA). 1994. pap. 12.00 (*0-9644197-0-X*) M-Promotions.

Moses, Stanley, jt. auth. see Margolis, Edwin.

Moses, Stephane. System & Revelation: The Philosophy of Franz Rosenzweig. Tihanyi, Catherine, tr. LC 91-29532. 318p. 1992. 39.95 (*0-8143-2128-3*) Wayne St U Pr.

Moses, V. & Springham, D. G. Bacteria & the Enhancement of Oil Recovery. 178p. 1982. 54.00 (*0-85334-995-9*, Pub. by Elsevier Applied Sci UK) Elsevier.

Moses, W. R. Double View. (Inland Seas Ser.: No. 3). 1984. pap. 10.00 (*1-55780-083-9*) Juniper Pr WI.

— Edges. (Juniper Book Ser.: No. 60). 1994. pap. 9.00 (*1-55780-143-6*) Juniper Pr WI.

Moses, W. Stainton. Direct Spirit Writing (Psychography) A Treatise on One of the Objective Forms: Psychic or Spiritual Phenomena. 152p. 1972. reprint ed. spiral bd. 6.60 (*0-7873-0627-4*) Mokelumne.

Moses, Walter F., ed. Artistic Anatomy. 1939. pap. 8.95 (*0-685-00796-0*) Borden.

Moses, William F. A Guide to American State & Local Laws on South Africa: 1992 Edition. 156p. (Orig.). 1992. pap. 95.00 (*0-931035-99-6*) IRRC Inc DC.

— A Guide to American State & Local Laws on South Africa - 1993 Edition. 160p. (Orig.). 1993. pap. 125.00 (*1-879775-06-9*) IRRC Inc DC.

— A Guide to American State & Local Laws on South Africa 1991. Voorhes, Meg, ed. 104p. 1991. reprint ed. pap. 95.00 (*0-931035-89-9*) IRRC Inc DC.

Moses, William F. & Voorhes, Meg. The Statement of Principles & Corporate Social Responsibility in a Changing South Africa. 64p. 1991. pap. 35.00 (*0-931035-91-0*) IRRC Inc DC.

Moses, William S. Spirit Teachings Through the Mediumship of William Stainton Moses. LC 75-36910. (Occult Ser.). 1976. reprint ed. 26.95 (*0-405-07968-0*) Ayer.

Moses, Wilson J. Black Messiahs & Uncle Toms: Social & Literary Manipulations of a Religious Myth. (C). 1993. pap. 14.95 (*0-271-00933-0*) Pa St U Pr.

— The Golden Age of Black Nationalism, 1850-1925. (Illus.). 348p. 1988. pap. 11.95 (*0-19-520639-8*) OUP.

— Selections from Philosophy & Opinions of Marcus Garvey. 160p. 1995. pap. text ed. 8.65 (*0-312-10665-3*) St Martin.

***Moses, Wilson J., ed.** Classical Black Nationalism: From the American Revolution to Marcus Garvey. 200p. 1996. 50.00 (*0-8147-5524-0*); pap. 15.95 (*0-8147-5533-X*) NYU Pr.

Moses, Wilson J., ed. see Crummell, Alexander.

Moses, Yoram, ed. Theoretical Aspects of Reasoning about Knowledge: Proceedings of the Fourth Conference (TARK 1992), Monterey, California, March 22-25, 1992. LC 92-12306. 1992. 39.95 (*1-55860-243-7*) Morgan Kaufmann.

Mosesson, M. W., et al, eds. Fibrinogen 3 - Biochemistry, Biological, Functions, Gene Regulation & Expression: Proceedings of the International Fibrinogen Workshop, Milwaukee, WI, 13-15 June, 1988. (International Congress Ser.: No. 801). 364p. 1989. 120.00 (*0-444-81055-2*, Excerpta Medica) Elsevier.

Mosesson, Michael W. & Doolittle, Russell F., eds. Molecular Biology of Fibrinogen & Fibrin. 1983. 135.00 (*0-89766-208-3*); pap. 135.00 (*0-89766-209-1*, VOL. 408) NY Acad Sci.

Mosey. Reactor Accidents. 1990. 62.95 (*0-408-06198-7*) Buttrwrth-Heinemann.

Mosey, Anne C. Activities Therapy. LC 73-79286. 205p. 1973. 28.00 (*0-911216-41-3*) Raven.

— Applied Scientific Inquiry in the Health Professions: An Epistemological Orientation. 280p. (C). 1992. pap. text ed. 38.00 (*0-910317-74-7*) Am Occup Therapy.

— Occupational Therapy: Configuration of a Profession. 186p. 1981. text ed. 30.00 (*0-89004-655-7*) Raven.

— Psychosocial Components of Occupational Therapy. 624p. 1986. text ed. 50.00 (*0-89004-334-5*) Raven.

Mosey, Caron. American Pictorial Quilts. (Illus.). 112p. 1986. 19.95 (*0-89145-910-3*, 1662) Collector Bks.

Mosey, Chris. Cruel Awakening: Sweden & the Killing of Olof Palme. LC 91-15981. 208p. 1991. text ed. 49.95 (*0-312-06711-9*) St Martin.

Mosey, Don, jt. auth. see Oslear, Don.

***Mosgofian.** Sexual Misconduct in Counseling & Ministry. 1995. pap. text ed. (*0-8499-3676-4*) Word Inc.

***Mosgofian, Peter T. & Ohlschlager, George W.** Sexual Misconduct in Counseling. LC 94-41599. (Contemporary Christian Counseling Ser.). 1994. 15.99 (*0-8499-1073-0*) Word Inc.

Mosgofian, Peter T., jt. auth. see Ohlschlager, George W.

Mosgrove, George D. Kentucky Cavaliers in Dixie: Reminiscences of a Confederate Cavalryman. (Illus.). 281p. 1991. reprint ed. 30.00 (*0-916107-39-6*) Broadfoot.

Moshansky, Mozelle. Mendelssohn. (Illustrated Lives of the Great Composers Ser.). (Illus.). 144p. 1984. pap. 14.95 (*0-7119-0252-6*, OP42381) Omnibus NY.

Moshaver, Ziba. Nuclear-Weapons Proliferation in the Indian Sub-Continent. 290p. 1991. text ed. 65.00 (*0-312-05781-4*) St Martin.

Moshe, Beth. Judaism's Truth Answers the Missionaries. 276p. 1987. 24.95 (*0-8197-0520-9*); pap. 16.95 (*0-8197-0515-2*) Bloch.

Moshe, Carmilly-Weinberger. Fear of Art. 249p. 1986. lib. bdg. 39.95 (*0-8352-2241-1*) Bowker.

Moshe, Davis, jt. ed. see Fink, Reuben.

Moshe, Karp, ed. see International Beilinson Symposium Staff.

***Moshe, Max & Jacoby, Hill, photos.** Next Year in Jerusalem. (Illus.). 1995. 49.99 (*1-56507-342-8*) Harvest Hse.

Moshe, Solomon, et al, eds. The Parke-Davis Manual on Epilepsy: Useful Tips That Help You Get the Best Out of Life. LC 92-74838. (Illus.). 80p. (Orig.). 1992. pap. 9.95 (*0-9634953-1-3*) KSF Grp.

Moshe, Zeyda. The Encyclopedia of Biblical Humor. 376p. 1990. pap. 10.95 (*0-944007-91-0*) Sure Sellers.

Moshell, Michael. Computer Power. 224p. 1982. text ed. 18. 80 (*0-07-065773-4*) McGraw.

Mosher, Arthur T. Technical Co-Operation in Latin-American Agriculture. LC 75-26310. (World Food Supply Ser.). (Illus.). 1976. reprint ed. 40.95 (*0-405-07788-2*) Ayer.

***Mosher, Bill.** Visionaries. 200p. 1995. 17.95 (*1-57075-024-6*) Orbis Bks.

Mosher, Clelia D. The Mosher Survey. MaHood, James & Wanburg, Kristine, eds. LC 79-48014. 490p. 1980. lib. bdg. 30.95 (*0-405-13090-2*) Ayer.

Mosher, Deane R., ed. Fibronectin. (Biology of Extracellular Matrix Ser.). 500p. 1988. text ed. 140.00 (*0-12-508470-6*) Acad Pr.

Mosher, Edith A. & Williams, Nella D. From Indian Legends to the Modern Bookshelf. 1931. 12.50 (*0-911586-24-5*) Wahr.

Mosher, Edith K., jt. auth. see Bailey, Stephen K.

Mosher, Elizabeth & Watts, Jacqueline, eds. Vital Records of Lincolnville, Maine. (Illus.). 394p. 1993. lib. bdg. 75. 00 (*0-89725-098-2*) Picton Pr.

Mosher, Elizabeth M. Vital Records of Swanville Maine Prior to 1892. 209p. 1990. lib. bdg. 55.00 (*0-929539-27-3*) Picton Pr.

Mosher, Elizabeth M., comp. Vital Records of Thorndike, Maine Prior to 1892. 229p. 1993. lib. bdg. 55.00 (*0-89725-097-4*) Picton Pr.

***Mosher, Elizabeth M., contrib.** Vital Records of Searsport, Waldo County, ME, Prior to 1892. 352p. 1993. 65.00 (*0-89725-135-0*) Picton Pr.

Mosher, Elizabeth M., ed. Records of Rev. Edward F. Cutter of Maine, 1833-1856. LC 88-63777. 96p. 1989. 20.00 (*0-929539-19-2*) Picton Pr.

Mosher, Elizabeth M., tr. Vital Records of Freedom, Waldo County, Maine Prior to 1892. (Illus.). 194p. 1991. 65.00 (*0-929539-81-8*) Picton Pr.

Mosher, Fred & Schneider, David I. Handbook of BASIC for the Commodore 64. (Illus.). 350p. 14.95 (*0-317-12840-X*) P-H.

Mosher, Frederick C. Democracy & the Public Service. (Public Administration & Democracy Ser.). 1968. 12.95 (*0-19-500031-5*) OUP.

— Democracy & the Public Service. 2nd ed. (Public Administration & Democracy Ser.). (Illus.). (C). 1982. pap. text ed. 14.95 (*0-19-503018-4*) OUP.

— Tale of Two Agencies: A Comparative Analysis of the General Accounting Office & the Office of Management & Budget. LC 83-10634. (Miller Center Series on the American Presidency). xxvi, 219p. 1986. pap. text ed. 11.95 (*0-8071-1305-0*) La State U Pr.

Mosher, Frederick C., ed. American Public Administration: Past, Present, Future. LC 74-17916. 312p. 1975. pap. 14. 95 (*0-8173-4829-8*) U of Ala Pr.

— Basic Documents of American Public Administration, 1776-1950. LC 76-13866. 225p. (C). 1976. text ed. 27.95 (*0-8419-0275-5*); pap. 15.95 (*0-8419-0276-3*) Holmes & Meier.

— Basic Literature of American Public Administration, 1787-1950. LC 79-28553. 314p. (C). 1981. 34.50 (*0-8419-0574-6*); pap. 15.95 (*0-8419-0575-4*) Holmes & Meier.

— The President Needs Help: Proceedings of a Conference Held on January 15, 1987. (Miller Center Tenth Anniversary Commemorative Publication, 1975-1985). 98p. (Orig.). (C). 1988. lib. bdg. 29.50 (*0-8191-6780-0*, Pub. by White Miller Center) U Pr of Amer.

Mosher, Frederick C., ed. see Price, Don K. & Evans, Robert H.

Mosher, Frederick C., jt. ed. see Stillman, Richard.

Mosher, Fredrick C. & Thompson, Kenneth W., eds. Some Views from the Campus. LC 87-8193. (Papers on Presidential Transitions & Foreign Policy: Vol. IV). 128p. (Orig.). (C). 1987. lib. bdg. 35.50 (*0-8191-6331-7*, Pub. by White Miller Center) U Pr of Amer.

Mosher, Gouverneur. Kyoto: A Contemplative Guide. rev. ed. LC 64-24951. (Illus.). 372p. 1978. pap. 14.95 (*0-8048-1294-2*) C E Tuttle.

Mosher, Harry S., jt. auth. see Morrison, James D.

Mosher, Howard. Disappearances. LC 77-22083. 272p. 1984. pap. 12.95 (*0-87923-524-1*) Godine.

Mosher, Howard F. Marie Blythe. (Contemporary American Fiction Ser.). 112p. 1989. pap. 10.95 (*0-14-007659-X*, Penguin Bks) Viking Penguin.

— Northern Borders. LC 94-6443. 1994. 22.95 (*0-385-47337-0*) Doubleday.

— Northern Borders. large type ed. LC 95-1978. 1995. write for info. (*0-7862-0421-4*) Thorndike Pr.

— Where the Rivers Flow North. (Contemporary American Fiction Ser.). 224p. 1989. pap. 10.95 (*0-14-007748-0*, Penguin Bks) Viking Penguin.

Mosher, James F. Liquor Liability Law, 2 vols. 1987. Updates. ring bd. write for info. (*0-8205-1498-5*) Bender.

— Responsible Beverage Service: An Implementation Handbook for Communities. (Illus.). 108p. (Orig.). 1991. pap. 12.50 (*1-879552-37-X*) Stanford CRDP.

Mosher, Jerry, ed. see Ashmore, Nancy V.

Mosher, Jerry, ed. see Reinstedt, Randall A.

Mosher, Joseph A. Exemplum in the Early Religious & Didactic Literature of England. LC 11-32391. reprint ed. 32.50 (*0-404-04505-7*) AMS Pr.

Mosher, Linda L. Going Home: Memories of West Virginia. 1992. pap. 7.50 (*1-880631-01-6*) Shuffaloff Bks.

Mosher, Loren & Burti, Lorenzo. Community Mental Health: A Practical Guide. 224p. (C). 1994. pap. 15.00 (*0-393-70165-4*) Norton.

Mosher, Loren R., jt. auth. see Gunderson, John G.

Mosher, Lynn. Automotive Fundamentals: Text-Laboratory Activities Manual. 160p. (C). 1991. pap. text ed. 14.95 (*0-8403-6780-5*) Kendall-Hunt.

— Industrial Processes. 52p. 1993. per. 8.76 (*0-8403-8865-9*) Kendall-Hunt.

Mosher, M., jt. auth. see Smith, S.

***Mosher, Merrill H.** John Freeman of Norfolk County, VA: His Descendants in North Carolina & Virginia & Other Colonial N.C. Freeman Families. (Illus.). 236p. (Orig.). 1994. pap. text ed. 18.50 (*0-7884-0109-2*) Heritage Bk.

Mosher, Michael, jt. auth. see Smith, David.

Mosher, Nicole M. Le Texte Visualise: Le Calligramme de l'Epoque Alexandrine a l'Epoque Cubiste. (American University Studies: Romance Languages & Literature: Ser. II, Vol. 119). 188p. (C). 1989. text ed. 42.95 (*0-8204-0924-3*) P Lang Pubs.

Mosher, Paul W., ed. Title Key Word & Author Index to Psychoanalytic Journals. 1988. 38.00 (*0-318-32967-0*) Am Psychoanalytic.

***Mosher, Ralph.** Preparing for Citizenship: Teaching Youth to Live Democratically. LC 94-6379. 216p. 1994. pap. text ed. 17.95 (*0-275-95096-4*, Praeger Pubs) Greenwood.

Mosher, Ralph, ed. Moral Education: A First Generation of Research & Development. LC 80-18607. 426p. 1980. text ed. 42.95 (*0-275-90528-4*, C0528, Praeger Pubs) Greenwood.

Mosher, Ralph, et al. Preparing for Citizenship: Schools for Democracy. LC 94-6379. 216p. 1994. text ed. 55.00 (*0-275-94606-1*, Praeger Pubs) Greenwood.

***Mosher, Randy.** The Brewer's Companion. rev. ed. (Illus.). 1995. pap. 19.95 (*0-9640410-1-4*) Alephenalia.

Mosher, Steven W. Broken Earth: The Rural Chinese. LC 83-47982. 336p. (C). 1983. 27.95 (*0-02-921700-8*) Free Pr.

— Broken Earth: The Rural Chinese. LC 84-47982. (Illus.). 317p. 1984. pap. 14.95 (*0-02-921720-2*) Free Pr.

— Journey to the Forbidden China. (Illus.). 208p. 1985. 27. 95 (*0-02-921710-5*) Free Pr.

— A Mother's Ordeal. LC 93-16394. 1993. 21.95 (*0-15-162662-6*) HarBrace.

— A Mother's Ordeal: One Woman's Fight Against China's One-Child Policy. LC 94-903. 352p. 1994. pap. 12.00 (*0-06-097614-4*, PL) HarpC.

Mosher, Steven W., ed. Korea in the 1990s: Prospects for Unification. 172p. (C). 1992. text ed. 32.95 (*1-56000-010-4*) Transaction Pubs.

— The United States & the Republic of China: Democratic Friends, Strategic Allies & Economic Partners. 176p. (C). 1991. text ed. 32.95 (*0-88738-410-2*); pap. 21.95 (*0-88738-893-0*) Transaction Pubs.

Mosher, Terry W. Harsh: The Life, Times & Philosophy of Hall of Fame Coach Marv Harshman. 166p. 1994. 21.50 (*0-9639827-0-2*) Mo Bks.

Moshi, Lioba, jt. ed. see Mufwene, Salikoko.

Moshi, Lioba J. Mazoezi Ya Kiswahili: Kitabu Cha Wanafunzi Wa Mwaka Wa Kwanza: Swahili Exercises: A Workbook for First Year Students. LC 88-27671. 244p. (Orig.). (C). 1989. pap. text ed. 26.50 (*0-8191-7215-4*) U Pr of Amer.

Moshier. Methods & Programs for Mathematical Functions. 1990. pap. write for info. (*0-318-68280-X*) P-H.

Moshier, R. & Belcher, R. Analytical Chemistry of Niobium & Tantalum. LC 63-20874. (International Series of Monographs on Analytical Chemistry: Vol. 16). 1964. 118.00 (*0-08-010418-5*, Pub. by Pergamon Repr UK) Franklin.

Moshimer, Joan. The Complete Book of Rug Hooking. (Illus.). 176p. 1989. pap. 9.95 (*0-486-25945-5*) Dover.

Moshinsky, George. Behind the Masonic Curtain: The Soviet Attack on Masonry. (Illus.). 61p. (Orig.). 1986. pap. 6.95 (*0-938103-00-8*) ZZYZX Pub.

— General Erich Ludendorff: The Nazi Persecution of Masonry, Vol. I. (Illus.). 300p. 1988. write for info. (*0-938103-02-4*) ZZYZX Pub.

— Without Christ in Their Hearts: Religion in the Soviet Union. 250p. 1988. write for info. (*0-938103-01-6*) ZZYZX Pub.

Moshinsky, Julius. A Grammar of Southeastern Pomo. (Publications in Linguistics: Vol. 72). 1974. pap. 30.00 (*0-520-09450-6*) U CA Pr.

Moshinsky, M. Group Theory & the Many-Body Problem. 188p. 1968. text ed. 121.00 (*0-677-01740-5*) Gordon & Breach.

Moshinsky, M. Harmonic Oscillator in Modern Physics: From Atoms to Quarks. (Documents on Modern Physics Ser.). 100p. 1969. text ed. 87.00 (*0-677-02450-9*) Gordon & Breach.

Moshinsky, M., jt. auth. see Brody, T. A.

Moshinsky, M., ed. see Latin American School of Physics-University of Mexico, 1965 Staff.

Moshiri, Gerald A. Constructed Wetlands for Water Quality Improvement. 1993. 79.95 (*0-87371-550-0*, TD756) Lewis Pubs.

Moshiri, Leila. Colloquial Persian. 2nd ed. 200p. 1988. pap. 17.95 (*0-415-00886-7*, A1402); audio 17.95 (*0-415-00887-5*, A1406) Routledge.

— Colloquial Persian, Set. 2nd ed. 200p. 1988. audio 29.95 (*0-415-02618-0*, A2659) Routledge.

Moshkin, V. A., ed. Castor. (C). 1986. 31.00 (*0-685-22789-8*, Pub. by Oxford IBH II) S Asia.

Moshman, David. Children, Education, & the First Amendment: A Psycholegal Analysis. LC 88-29094. (Children & the Law Ser.). xviii, 218p. 1989. 30.00 (*0-8032-3110-5*) U of Nebr Pr.

Moshman, David S., et al. Developmental Psychology: A Topical Approach. (C). 1987. text ed. 52.00 (*0-673-39087-X*) HarpCollege.

Moshy, Roger E., jt. auth. see Friedman, Ellis H.

Mosich, A. N. & Davis, Charles. Intermediate Accounting. rev. ed. 1989. Working papers, Chapters 1-15. write for info. (*0-07-041857-8*); Working papers, Chapters 16-25. write for info. (*0-07-041858-6*); Accounting worksheets, Chapters 1-14. write for info. (*0-07-041862-4*) McGraw.

— Intermediate Accounting. 6th ed. 1989. Study guide. student ed, pap. text ed. write for info. (*0-07-041856-X*) McGraw.

— Intermediate Accounting. 6th rev. ed. 1989. Accounting worksheets, Chapters 15-23. pap. text ed. write for info. (*0-07-041863-2*) McGraw.

— Intermediate Accounting. 6th rev. ed. 1989. text ed. write for info. (*0-07-041855-1*) McGraw.

Mosich, A. N. & Larsen, E. A. Intermediate Accounting. 1982. Accounting worksheets, Chapters 14-25. write for info. (*0-07-041583-8*) McGraw.

Mosich, A. N. & Larsen, E. John. Intermediate Accounting. 6th rev. ed. 1248p. 1986. Instr's. guide. teacher ed write for info. (*0-07-041621-4*); Overhead transparencies. trans. write for info. (*0-07-041612-5*); Exam questions. write for info. (*0-07-041611-7*) McGraw.

Mosich, Donna & Adams-Regan, Pamela. WordPerfect 5.0 Macros. 1989. pap. text ed. 22.95 (*0-07-157273-2*) McGraw.

Mosich, Donna, et al. WordPerfect Macros: The Windows Version. 1992. pap. 29.95 (*0-07-157888-9*) McGraw.

Mosich, Donna M. WordPerfect 4.2 Macros. 1991. 24.95 (*0-8306-6651-6*) TAB Bks.

— WordPerfect 5.0: New Features & Advanced Techniques. (Illus.). 300p. 1988. 29.95 (*0-8306-3084-8*, 3084) TAB Bks.

Mosich, Donna M. & Adams-Regan, Pamela. WordPerfect Macros 5.0. (Illus.). 304p. (Orig.). 1989. pap. 22.95 (*0-8306-3254-9*, Windcrest) TAB Bks.

Mosich, Donna M., et al. Advanced Turbo C Programmers Guide. 339p. 1988. pap. text ed. 21.95 (*0-471-63742-4*) Wiley.

— WordPerfect Macros: The Windows Version. 576p. 1992. pap. 29.95 (*0-8306-2501-1*, 3945, Windcrest) TAB Bks.

Mosich, S. Kathena. Through the Eyes of the Goddess: How to Give Life to the Spirit of Aphrodite in You. (Illus.). 167p. (Orig.). 1990. pap. 12.99 (*0-9634361-0-4*) Shapes of Spirit.

Mosier, Alice & Pace, Frank J. Medical Records Technology. LC 74-18676. (Allied Health Ser.). 1975. pap. 9.95 (*0-672-61396-4*, Bobbs) Macmillan.

Mosier, C. H. Practice & Procedure in Magistrates Courts. 216p. 1986. 104.00 (*1-85190-013-6*, Pub. by Fourmat Pub UK) St Mut.

Mosillo & Pancner. Engineering Graphics: Multiview Visualization with Computer Drawing Logic. 176p. 1989. 22.95 (*0-8403-5391-X*) Kendall-Hunt.

Mosiman, Billie S. Night Cruise. 288p. (Orig.). 1992. mass mkt. 4.99 (*0-515-10977-0*) Jove Pubns.

— Widow. 384p. (Orig.). 1995. pap. text ed. 5.99 (*0-425-14683-9*) Berkley Pub.

Mosimann, Anton. Anton Mosimann's Fish Cuisine. (Illus.). 256p. 1993. 24.95 (*0-89815-543-6*) Ten Speed Pr.

— The Essential Mosimann. (Illus.). 160p. 1994. 45.00 (*0-09-175379-1*, Pub. by Ebury Pr UK) Trafalgar.

— The Essential Mosimann. (Illus.). 192p. 1995. pap. 17.95 (*0-09-180663-1*, Vermillion) Trafalgar.

Mosimann, E. A., jt. comp. see Callery, B. G.

Mosin, V. A., intro. Greek Charters of Serbian Rulers. 696p. (C). 1974. reprint ed. lib. bdg. 130.00 (*0-902089-65-X*, Pub. by Variorum UK) Ashgate Pub Co.

Mosing, Lisa. Sharpening Your Image: How to Get, Keep & Expand a Healthcare Business. 238p. 1992. pap. 29.95 (*0-9633990-0-4*) Nutrition Wks.

***Mosk, Carl.** Competition & Cooperation in Japanese Labour Markets. LC 95-4170. (Studies in the Modern Japanese Economy). 1995. write for info. (*0-312-12683-2*) St Martin.

Mosk, Sanford A. Land Tenure Problems in the Santa Fe Railroad Grant Area. Bruchey, Stuart, ed. LC 80-1333. (Railroads Ser.). (Illus.). 1981. reprint ed. lib. bdg. 15.95 (*0-405-13807-5*) Ayer.

***Mosk, Stanley.** Democracy in America-Day by Day. 1995. 19.95 (*0-533-11204-4*) Vantage.

Moskal, Jeanne. Blake, Ethics, & Forgiveness. 240p. (C). 1994. 32.95 (*0-8173-0678-1*) U of Ala Pr.

Moskalenko, Yu E., ed. Biophysical Aspects of Cerebral Circulation. LC 78-41243. (Illus.). 174p. 1980. 74.00 (*0-08-022672-8*, Pub. by Pergamon Repr UK) Franklin.

Moskaliuk, Stepan S. Group Theoretical Methods in Physics: Proceedings of the Eleventh International Hutsulian Workshop Held in Rakhiv, Ukraine, Oct. 1992. (Monographs in Physics). 280p. (C). Date not set. lib. bdg. 80.00 (*0-911767-74-6*) Hadronic Pr Inc.

Moskin, J. Robert. The Meaning of CAPHE: A Report on the First Five Years of the Consortium for the Advancement of Private Higher Education. ix, 147p. (Orig.). 1990. 3.00 (*1-879994-01-1*) Consortium Advan.

— Report from Jerusalem: City at the Crossroads. LC 77-79877. (Illus.). 64p. 1977. pap. 1.50 (*0-87495-013-9*) Am Jewish Comm.

— U. S. Marine Corps Story. 1992. pap. 24.95 (*0-316-58558-0*) Little.

Moskin, J. Robert, jt. auth. see Vitullo-Martin, Julia.

Moskin, Marietta D. Margaret Thatcher. (In Focus Biographies Ser.). (Illus.). 128p. (J). 1990. lib. bdg. 13.98 (*0-671-69632-7*, Julian Messner); pap. 7.95 (*0-671-69633-5*, Julian Messner) Silver Burdett Pr.

Moskin, Marietta D., jt. auth. see Worth, Richard.

Moskin, V. A., ed. Castor. Dhote, R. K., tr. 329p. (C). 1986. text ed. 95.00 (*90-6191-466-3*, Pub. by A A Balkema NE) Ashgate Pub Co.

Mosko, Joseph A., jt. auth. see Corzine, Robert G.

Moskoff, William. The Bread of Affliction: The Food Supply in the U. S. S. R. During World War II. (Cambridge Russian, Soviet & Post-Soviet Studies: No. 76). (Illus.). 576p. (C). 1990. 69.95 (*0-521-37499-5*) Cambridge U Pr.

— Hard Times: Impoverishment & Protest in the Perestroika Years: The Soviet Union 1985-1991. LC 93-20098. 260p. 1993. 62.95 (*1-56324-213-3*); pap. text ed. 20.95 (*1-56324-214-1*) M E Sharpe.

Moskoff, William, ed. Perestroika in the Countryside: Agricultural Reform in the Gorbachev Era. LC 90-8603. 144p. 1990. 62.95 (*0-87332-767-5*) M E Sharpe.

Moskoff, William, jt. auth. see Jones, Anthony.

Moskoff, William, jt. ed. see Jones, Anthony.

Moskoff, William, jt. ed. see Linz, Susan.

Moskop, John C. Divine Omniscience & Human Freedom: Thomas Aquinas & Charles Hartshorne. LC 84-1172. xviii, 105p. 1984. 14.95 (*0-86554-123-X*, MUP/H102) Mercer Univ Pr.

Moskop, John C., jt. ed. see Kopelman, Loretta M.

Moskop, Ruth W., tr. see Delkeskamp-Hayes, Corinna & Cutter, Mary A., eds.

Moskos, C. C. & Wood, Frank R. The Military: More Than Just a Job? (Illus.). 322p. 1988. 33.00 (*0-08-034321-X*) Brasseys Inc.

An Asterisk (*) at the beginning of an entry indicates that the title is appearing in BIP for the first time.

Moskos, C. C., Jr., et al. Greek Orthodox Youth Today. (Saints Peter & Paul Youth Ministry Lectures). 56p. (Orig.). 1983. pap. 2.50 (*0-916586-56-1*) Holy Cross Orthodox.

Moskos, Charles C. A Call to Civic Service: National Service for Country & Community. 224p. 1988. text ed. 29.95 (*0-02-921991-4*) Free Pr.

— Greek Americans: Struggle & Success. enl. rev. ed. 176p. 1989. pap. 21.95 (*0-88738-778-0*) Transaction Pubs.

Moskos, Charles C., II & Chambers, John W., eds. The New Conscientious Objection: From Sacred to Secular Resistance. LC 92-20615. (Illus.). 296p. 1993. 45.00 (*0-19-507954-X*); pap. 18.95 (*0-19-507955-8*) OUP.

Moskos, Charles C., jt. ed. see Georgakas, Dan.

Moskosky, Susan, ed. see Cassidy, Jean, et al.

Moskovitch, Morris, jt. ed. see Umlita, Carlo.

Moskovits, M., jt. ed. see Andrews, L.

Moskovits, Malka. The World That Crumbled. LC 93-6758. 1993. pap. 13.95 (*0-89604-155-7*) Holocaust Pubns.

Moskovitz, Denise P., ed. Chicago Ancestor File 1974-1984. 381p. 1985. pap. 12.00 (*1-881125-08-4*) Chi Geneal Soc.

Moskovitz, Jack. Artist As Autist. (Illus.). 59p. (Orig.). 1989. pap. 3.00 (*0-926935-14-3*) Runaway Spoon.

— Isis Slices. (Illus.). 31p. (Orig.). 1992. pap. 3.00 (*0-926935-66-6*) Runaway Spoon.

Moskovitz, Myron. Cases & Problems in Criminal Law. 397p. 1989. 45.00 (*0-87084-592-6*) Anderson Pub Co.

— Cases & Problems in Criminal Procedure: The Police. LC 95-5354. (Analysis & Skills Ser.). 1995. write for info. (*0-256-18479-8*) Bender.

— Winning an Appeal: A Step-by-Step Explanation of How to Prepare & Present your Case Efficiently & with Maximum Effectiveness, with a Sample Brief. rev. ed. 172p. 1985. 15.00 (*0-87215-878-0*) Michie Butterworth.

***Moskovitz, Myron & Warner, Ralph.** Tenants' Rights: California Edition. 12th ed. Elias, Stephen, ed. LC 94-27465. 1994. 18.95 (*0-87337-270-0*) Nolo Pr.

***Moskow, Eric & Biracree, Tom.** Heart Smart: The Family Doctor's Guide to Cholesterol & Your Heart. 144p. 1995. 18.95 (*0-312-13085-6*, Pub. by Thomas Dunne Bks) St Martin.

Moskow, Michael H. & Holland, Robert C. Strategic Planning in Business & Government. LC 78-23401. (CED Supplementary Paper). 86p. 1978. pap. 3.50 (*0-87186-241-7*) Comm Econ Dev.

Moskow, Shirley B. Emma's World: An Intimate Look at Lives Touched by the Civil War Era. LC 90-60916. 294p. 1990. 20.95 (*0-88282-059-1*) New Horizon NJ.

Moskow, Shirley B., ed. Hunan Hand & Other Ailments: Letters to the New England Journal of Medicine. 1987. 15.95 (*0-316-58533-5*) Little.

Moskow, Shirley B., ed. see Booth, Robert.

Moskowitz. Food Texture. (Food Science & Technology Ser.: Vol. 22). 352p. 1987. 150.00 (*0-8247-7585-6*) Dekker.

Moskowitz, et al. Shiel in Diverse Hands: A Collection of Essays. LC 82-61695. 501p. 1983. pap. 32.50 (*0-685-04346-0*) Reynolds Morse.

Moskowitz, Addie A., jt. auth. see Laskin, Pamela L.

Moskowitz, Anita F. Nicola Pisano's Arca di San Domenico & Its Legacy. LC 92-35734. (College Art Association Monographs on the Fine Arts: Vol. L). (Illus.). 160p. (C). 1994. 55.00 (*0-271-00946-2*) Pa St U Pr.

— The Sculpture of Andrea & Nino Pisano. (Illus.). 504p. 1987. 205.00 (*0-521-30754-6*) Cambridge U Pr.

***Moskowitz, David.** EarthSiege: Official Players Guide. (Illus.). 256p. (Orig.). 1995. pap. 18.95 (*1-57280-009-7*) IFTW Bks.

Moskowitz, David & Ivens, Kathy. OS-2 Power Tools. 400p. 1989. disk 44.95 (*0-13-643065-1*) P-H.

***Moskowitz, Dvid & Kerr, David.** OS-2 Unleashed. deluxe ed. (Illus.). 1400p. (Orig.). 1995. pap. text ed. 45.00 (*0-672-30545-3*) Sams.

Moskowitz, Faye. And the Bridge Is Love: Life Stories. LC 91-14217. 160p. 1993. pap. 12.00 (*0-8070-6327-4*) Beacon Pr.

— A Leak in the Heart: Tales from a Woman's Life. LC 84-48298. 176p. 1987. pap. 10.95 (*0-87923-659-6*) Godine.

— Whoever Finds This: I Love You. 1992. pap. 11.95 (*0-87923-936-0*) Godine.

Moskowitz, Faye, ed. Her Face in the Mirror: Jewish Women on Mothers & Daughters. LC 94-8426. 336p. 1994. 24.00 (*0-8070-3614-5*) Beacon Pr.

— Her Face in the Mirror: Jewish Women on Mothers & Daughters. 336p. (C). 1995. pap. 14.00 (*0-8070-3615-3*) Beacon Pr.

Moskowitz, Francine & Moskowitz, Robert. Parenting Your Aging Parents. LC 90-92272. 296p. 1995. 21.95 (*0-9624415-0-3*) Key Pubns Woodland Hills.

Moskowitz, Gertrude. Caring & Sharing in the Foreign Language Class: A Sourcebook on Humanistic Techniques. 360p. (C). 1978. pap. 22.95 (*0-8384-2771-5*, Newbury) Heinle & Heinle.

Moskowitz, H. R. New Directions for Product Testing & Sensory Analysis of Foods. 370p. 1985. 73.00 (*0-917678-18-4*) Food & Nut Pr.

— Product Testing & Sensory Evaluation of Foods: Marketing & R&D Approaches. 605p. 1983. 87.00 (*0-917678-16-8*) Food & Nut Pr.

Moskowitz, H. R., et al, eds. Sensation & Measurement: Papers in Honor of S. S. Stevens. LC 74-77966. 550p. 1974. lib. bdg. 149.50 (*90-277-0474-0*) Kluwer Ac.

Moskowitz, H. R. & Warren, Craig, eds. Odor Quality & Chemical Structure. LC 80-28633. (ACS Symposium Ser.: No. 148). 1981. 38.95 (*0-8412-0607-4*) Am Chemical.

Moskowitz, Harvey S. & Lindbloom, Carl G. The Illustrated Book of Development Definitions. (Illus.). 263p. 1981. pap. text ed. 18.95 (*0-88285-070-9*) Transaction Pubs.

— The New Illustrated Book of Development Definitions. LC 92-19394. 328p. (C). 1993. pap. text ed. 29.95 (*0-88285-144-6*) Ctr Urban Pol Res.

Moskowitz, Herbert & Wright, Gordon. Statistics for Management & Economics. 768p. (C). 1985. write for info. (*0-675-20211-6*, Merrill Pub Co) Macmillan.

Moskowitz, Howard, ed. Applied Sensory Analysis of Foods, Vol. I. 272p. 1988. 174.00 (*0-8493-6705-0*, TX546) CRC Pr.

— Applied Sensory Analysis of Foods, Vol. II. 192p. 1988. 174.00 (*0-8493-6706-9*, TX546) CRC Pr.

Moskowitz, Howard R. Cosmetic Product Testing: A Modern Psychophysical Approach. LC 84-17660. (Cosmetic Science & Technology Ser.: No. 3). 477p. reprint ed. pap. 136.00 (*0-7837-2025-4*, 2052451) Bks Demand.

— Food Concepts & Products: Just in Time Development. LC 93-71709. (Publications in Food Science & Nutrition Ser.). 502p. 1993. 110.00 (*0-917678-32-X*) Food & Nut Pr.

***Moskowitz, Ira, illus.** Patterns & Ceremonials of the Indians of the Southwest. LC 95-6513. 1995. pap. write for info. (*0-486-28692-4*) Dover.

Moskowitz, Jane M., jt. auth. see Bloomfield, Brynna C.

Moskowitz, Joel. The Paper Machine Series, Vol 2: The Working Piston Engine. 96p. 1986. pap. 79.50 (*0-671-93855-X*) S&S Trade.

Moskowitz, Joel S. Environmental Liability & Real Property Transactions: Law & Practice. 384p. 1989. text ed. 125.00 (*0-471-61390-8*) Wiley.

— Environmental Liability & Real Property Transactions: Law & Practice. 2nd ed. LC 95-16512. (Environmental Law Library). 1995. text ed. 125.00 (*0-471-10628-3*) Wiley.

Moskowitz, Karl, ed. From Patron to Partner: The Development of U. S.-Korean Business & Trade Relations. LC 83-48028. 256p. 1984. text ed. 45.00 (*0-669-06837-3*) Free Pr.

Moskowitz, Ken. Greater Washington Area Bicycle Atlas. 3rd rev. ed. (Illus.). 254p. 1985. pap. 9.95 (*0-9614892-0-0*) Potomac Area.

Moskowitz, Kerr. OS - 2 Unleashed. 1992. disk 34.95 (*0-672-30240-3*) Sams.

— Os 2 2.1 Unleashed. deluxe ed. 1994. cd-rom 39.95 (*0-672-30445-7*) Sams.

Moskowitz, Lawrence A. Unfair Tactics in Matrimonial Cases. (Trial Practice Library). 298p. 1990. text ed. 128.00 (*0-471-50117-4*) Wiley.

***Moskowitz, Lester R.** Permanent Magnet & Application Handbook. 2nd ed. LC 85-5629. (Illus.). (C). 1995. lib. bdg. write for info. (*0-89464-768-7*) Krieger.

— Permanent Magnet & Application Handbook. LC 85-5629. 454p. (C). 1986. reprint ed. 57.50 (*0-89874-863-1*) Krieger.

Moskowitz, Lisa, jt. auth. see Timerbaev, Roland.

Moskowitz, Michael A., jt. ed. see Olesen, Jes.

Moskowitz, Milton. The Global Marketplace: One Hundred & Two of the Most Influential Companies Outside of America. 1988. 22.50 (*0-317-66939-7*, Scribners) S&S Trade.

Moskowitz, Milton, jt. auth. see Levering, Robert.

Moskowitz, Milton, et al, eds. Everybody's Business: An Almanac the Irreverent Guide to Corporate America. LC 80-7736. (Illus.). 916p. 1980. 23.00 (*0-06-250620-X*); pap. 9.95i (*0-06-250621-8*, CN 4002) Harper SF.

Moskowitz, Moses. The Roots & Reaches of United Nations Actions & Decisions. LC 80-51741. 220p. 1980. lib. bdg. 63.00 (*90-286-0140-6*) Kluwer Ac.

Moskowitz, Nachama S. Bridge to Prayer: The Jewish Worship Workbook, Vol. II. (Amidah, Torah Service, & Concluding Prayers Ser.). (Illus.). 144p. (J). (gr. 6-7). 1989. pap. text ed. 6.00 (*0-8074-0432-2*, 123596) UAHC.

— A Bridge to Prayer: The Jewish Worship Workbook: God, Prayer, & the Shema, Vol. 1. (J). (gr. 4-6). 1988. pap. text ed. 6.00 (*0-8074-0417-9*, 123594) UAHC.

— Games, Games, & More Games for the Jewish Classroom. 306p. (Orig.). (J). (gr. 4-6). 1994. pap. 8.00 (*0-8074-0504-3*, 201000) UAHC.

— Original Bulletin Boards on Jewish Themes. 128p. (Orig.). 1986. pap. text ed. 12.50 (*0-86705-019-5*) A R E Pub.

Moskowitz, Nathan. Molecular Modulation of Chemical Presynaptic Neurotransmission. 258p. 1985. text ed. 59.95 (*0-275-91320-1*, C1320, Praeger Pubs) Greenwood.

Moskowitz, Reed C. Your Healing Mind. 288p. 1992. 22.00 (*0-688-10461-4*) Morrow.

— Your Healing Mind. 304p. 1993. reprint ed. pap. 10.00 (*0-380-71470-1*) Avon.

Moskowitz, Richard & Boston Women's Health Book Collective Staff. Homeopathic Medicines for Pregnancy & Childbirth. 300p. (Orig.). 1992. pap. 14.95 (*1-55643-137-6*) North Atlantic.

Moskowitz, Robert. How to Organize Your Work & Your Life. 2nd rev. ed. LC 92-27756. 1981. 14.95 (*0-385-42480-9*) Doubleday.

Moskowitz, Robert, jt. auth. see Moskowitz, Francine.

Moskowitz, Robert K. The Small Business Computer Book: A Guide in Plain English. 192p. (Orig.). 1993. pap. 19.95 (*0-936894-44-X*) Upstart Pub.

Moskowitz, Roland W. & Haug, Marie R. Arthritis & the Elderly. LC 85-22092. 208p. 1985. 24.95 (*0-8261-4710-0*) Springer Pub.

Moskowitz, Sam. After All These Years. 96p. 1991. reprint ed. lib. bdg. 23.00x (*0-8095-6857-8*) Borgo Pr.

— Explorers of the Infinite. LC 73-15068. (Classics of Science Fiction Ser.). 353p. 1986. reprint ed. 24.00 (*0-88355-130-6*); reprint ed. pap. 10.00 (*0-88355-159-4*) Hyperion Conn.

— History of the Movement 1854-1890. (Illus.). 1980. 15.00 (*0-937986-40-2*) D M Grant.

— The Immortal Storm: A Lively History of the Science Fiction Movement. LC 73-15069. (Classics of Science Fiction Ser.). 1989. reprint ed. 34.00 (*0-88355-131-4*) Hyperion Conn.

— Seekers of Tomorrow. LC 73-15073. (Classics of Science Fiction Ser.). 441p. 1986. reprint ed. 26.00 (*0-88355-129-2*); reprint ed. pap. 10.00 (*0-88355-158-6*) Hyperion Conn.

Moskowitz, Sam, ed. A. Merritt: Reflections in the Moon Pool. 20.00 (*1-880418-13-4*) D M Grant.

— Masterpieces of Science Fiction. LC 73-15070. (Classics of Science Fiction Ser.). 522p. 1985. reprint ed. 38.00 (*0-88355-127-6*) Hyperion Conn.

— Modern Masterpieces of Science Fiction. LC 73-15071. (Classics of Science Fiction Ser.). 518p. 1985. reprint ed. 37.25 (*0-88355-126-8*) Hyperion Conn.

— Science Fiction by Gaslight. LC 73-15074. 364p. 1986. 25.25 (*0-88355-128-4*) Hyperion Conn.

Moskowitz, Sam, ed. see Keller, David H.

Moskowitz, Seymour. Thermodynamics of the Future, 2 vols., 1. (Illus.). 257p. (C). 1989. reprint ed. text ed. 160.00 (*0-9630456-0-1*); reprint ed. pap. text ed. 150.00 (*0-9630456-3-6*) S Moskowitz.

— Thermodynamics of the Future, 2 vols., 2. (Illus.). 257p. (C). 1989. reprint ed. text ed. 160.00 (*0-9630456-1-X*); reprint ed. pap. text ed. 150.00 (*0-9630456-4-4*) S Moskowitz.

— Thermodynamics of the Future, 2 vols., Set. (Illus.). 257p. (C). 1989. reprint ed. text ed. 300.00 (*0-9630456-2-8*); reprint ed. pap. text ed. 275.00 (*0-9630456-5-2*) S Moskowitz.

Moskowitz, Seymour H., et al, eds. New York Trial Guide, 5 vols., Set. 1990. write for info. (*0-8205-1599-X*, 599) Bender.

Moskuina, Tamara. Secrets of the Soviet Skaters: Off-Ice Training Methods. Copley-Graves, L., ed. (Illus.). 1995. pap. 40.00 (*1-882849-03-5*) Platoro Pr.

Moskvin, L., ed. Working Class & Its Allies. 284p. (C). 1980. 50.00 (*0-685-31640-8*, Pub. by Collets UK) Pro-Am Music.

Moskvitin, N. I. Physicochemical Principles of Gluing & Adhesion Processes. 193p. 1968. text ed. 49.00 (*0-7065-0669-3*, Pub. by Keter Pub IS) Coronet Bks.

***Moslander, Marie.** Life's Path Unfolding. 200p. 1994. pap. 12.95 (*1-884954-00-6*) Evergreen WA.

Mosle, Mira & Crisler, Shirley. In the Midst of His People: The Authorized Biography of Bishop Maurice J. Dingman. LC 94-26663. (Illus.). 300p. (Orig.). 1994. pap. 14.95 (*0-945213-13-1*) Rudi Pub.

Mosle, Mira, jt. auth. see Crisle, Shirley.

Moslehi, M. M. & Singh, R. Rapid Thermal & Related Processing Techniques, Vol. 1393. 1991. 62.00 (*0-8194-0462-4*) SPIE.

Moslehi, Shahnaz. Ask Me, about Me: A Look at the Psychology of Iranians & Iranian Immigrants. LC 87-91341. (Illus.). 100p. (Orig.). (C). 1988. pap. 10.00 (*0-9619523-2-6*) Shahnaz Inc.

Moslem. Free Radical Mechanisms of Tissue Injury. 1992. 104.95 (*0-8493-5161-8*, RB170) CRC Pr.

Moslemi, A. A. Particleboard, Vol. 1: Materials. LC 74-2071. (Illus.). 256p. 1974. 19.95 (*0-8093-0655-7*) S Ill U Pr.

— Particleboard, Vol. 2: Technology. LC 74-2071. (Illus.). 252p. 1974. 19.95 (*0-8093-0656-5*) S Ill U Pr.

Mosler, H., ed. see International Symposium on the Judicial Settlement of International Disputes Staff.

Mosler, Hermann. The International Society As a Legal Community. LC 80-50454. (Collected Courses, the Hague Academy of International Law: Vol. 140, 1974-IV). 327p. 1980. pap. text ed. 58.00 (*90-286-0080-9*) Kluwer Ac.

Mosler, K. & Scarsini, M., eds. Stochastic Orders & Decision under Risk. LC 91-77909. (IMS Lecture Notes - Monograph Ser.: Vol. 19). xiv, 392p. 1991. pap. 30.00 (*0-940600-26-9*) Inst Math.

Mosler, K. C. Cinitnous Location of Transportation Networks. (Texts & Monographs in Economics & Mathematical Systems). (Illus.). x, 158p. 1987. 49.00 (*0-387-17297-1*) Spr-Verlag.

Mosler, Karl & Scarsini, Marco. Stochastic Orders & Applications: A Classified Bibliography. (Lecture Notes in Economics & Mathematical Systems Ser.: Vol. 401). vi, 379p. 1993. pap. write for info. (*3-540-56956-1*) Spr-Verlag.

— Stochastic Orders & Applications: A Classified Biography. LC 93-8817. (Lecture Notes in Economics & Mathematical Systems Ser.: Vol. 401). 1993. pap. 65.00 (*0-387-56956-1*) Spr-Verlag.

Mosley, Albert. Introduction to Logic. 1989. 18.00 (*0-536-57394-8*) Ginn Pr.

***Mosley, Albert G.** African Philosophy: Selected Readings. LC 95-2731. 1995. pap. text ed. 33.33 (*0-02-384181-8*) P-H.

Mosley, Charlotte. Love from Nancy: The Letters of Nancy Mitford. 1993. 35.00 (*0-395-57041-7*) HM.

Mosley, Daniel J. Handbook of MIS Application Software Testing: Methods, Techniques, & Tools for Assuring Quality Through Testing. 352p. 1992. text ed. 54.00 (*0-13-907007-9*) P-H.

Mosley, David L. Gesture, Sign, & Song: An Interdisciplinary Approach to Schumann's Liederkreis Opus 39. LC 89-32372. (New Connections: Studies in Interdisciplinarity: Vol. 3). 214p. (C). 1990. text ed. 46.95 (*0-8204-1102-7*) P Lang Pubs.

Mosley, Derek J. Envoys & Diplomacy in Ancient Greece. 107p. (Orig.). 1973. pap. text ed. 37.50 (*3-515-01194-3*) Coronet Bks.

Mosley, Diana. The Writing of Rebecca West. 48p. 1986. 30.00 (*0-930126-18-1*) Typographeum.

***Mosley, Donald C., et al.** Management, Leadership in Action. 5th rev. ed. LC 95-8641. Orig. Title: Management, Concepts & Applications. 1995. write for info. (*0-673-99264-0*, HarpT) HarpC.

Mosley, Donald C., jt. auth. see Megginson, Leon C.

Mosley, Donald C., et al. Supervisory Management: The Art of Work with & Through People. (C). 1985. write for info. (*0-538-07660-7*, G66) S-W Pub.

Mosley, Francis. The Dinosaur Eggs. (Illus.). 32p. (J). (ps-2). 1992. pap. 5.95 (*0-8120-4959-4*) Barron.

Mosley, Francis, illus. Myths & Legends. LC 93-11878. (Story Library). 256p. (Orig.). (J). (gr. 4-9). 1994. pap. 6.95 (*1-85697-975-X*, Kingfisher LKC) LKC.

***Mosley-Howard, Susan.** Human Development in Education. 112p. (C). 1995. pap. text ed., spiral bd. 18.00 (*0-7872-1035-8*) Kendall-Hunt.

Mosley, J. G. Palliation in Malignant Disease. (Illus.). 170p. 1988. text ed. write for info. (*0-443-03690-X*) Churchill.

Mosley, J. R., Sr. Biblical Explanation of the Church's Covenant: Preaching from the Covenant. 1990. pap. text ed. write for info. (*0-9627958-2-8*) J R Mosleys Pr.

— Christian Men's Union Brotherhood Guide. 51p. 1990. pap. text ed. 3.50 (*0-9627958-0-1*, TXU 371-442) J R Mosleys Pr.

— Resolutions for Funeral, Welcome Addresses, & Responses for Special Occasions & Annual Days. 1990. pap. text ed. 2.50 (*0-9627958-1-X*) J R Mosleys Pr.

Mosley, James & Chambers, David. Charles Holtzappfel's Printing Apparatus for the Use of Amateurs. 126p. 1971. 20.00 (*0-900002-60-3*, Pub. by Priv Lib Assn UK) Oak Knoll.

Mosley, James L. Snore No More. (Modern Technology & Information Ser.). (Illus.). 80p. 4.95 (*0-685-51586-9*) Son Rise Pubns.

Mosley, Janice, jt. auth. see Breeden, Terri.

Mosley, Jean B. Seeds on the Wind. 220p. 1994. text ed. 25.00 (*0-9642039-0-1*) Concord Prnting.

***Mosley, Joe.** Understanding Sentence Structure: A Simplified Approach. 68p. (C). 1994. 7.96 (*0-8403-9656-2*) Kendall-Hunt.

Mosley, John, et al. Aid & Power, Vol. 1: The World Bank & Policy-Based Lending. 304p. 1991. 89.95 (*0-415-01095-0*, A5484); pap. 22.50 (*0-415-01548-0*, A5488) Routledge.

Mosley, John. The Christmas Star. (Illus.). 76p. (Orig.). 1988. pap. 3.95 (*0-9619874-0-5*) Griffith Observ.

Mosley, K. F. The Human Dilemma. 128p. 1984. 35.00 (*0-7212-0658-1*, Pub. by Regency Press) St Mut.

Mosley, Leonard. Duel for Kilemanjaro. 19.95 (*0-89190-158-2*, Am Repr) Amereon Ltd.

Mosley, Marilyn C. Dachshund Tails Down the Yukon. (Dachshund Tails Ser.: No. 3). (Illus.). 112p. (Orig.). (J). (gr. 5). 1988. pap. 5.95 (*0-9614850-2-7*) M C Mosley.

— Dachshund Tails North. LC 82-90167. (Dachshund Tails Ser.: No. 1). (Illus.). 50p. (Orig.). (J). (gr. 5). 1982. pap. 4.95 (*0-9614850-0-0*) M C Mosley.

— Dashchund Tails up the Inside Passage. LC 84-90672. (Dachshund Tails Ser.: No. 2). (Illus.). 95p. (Orig.). (J). (gr. 5). 1984. pap. 4.95 (*0-9614850-1-9*) M C Mosley.

Mosley, Marilyn C., et al, eds. Alaskan Ferry Tales for Children. LC 89-80605. (Illus.). 112p. (Orig.). 1989. pap. 6.95 (*0-9614850-3-5*) M C Mosley.

Mosley, Nicholas. Accident. LC 85-72479. 195p. 1985. reprint ed. 20.00 (*0-916583-10-4*); reprint ed. pap. 9.95 (*0-916583-11-2*) Dalkey Arch.

— Catastrophe Practice. rev. ed. LC 88-30391. 342p. 1989. 19.95 (*0-916583-35-X*) Dalkey Arch.

— Efforts at Truth. 345p. 1995. 22.95 (*1-56478-075-9*) Dalkey Arch.

— Hopeful Monsters. LC 91-13076. 551p. 1991. 21.95 (*0-916583-85-6*) Dalkey Arch.

— Hopeful Monsters: A Novel. LC 92-50063. 1993. pap. 13.00 (*0-679-73929-7*) Vintage NY.

— Imago Bird. rev. ed. LC 88-30392. 180p. 1989. 19.95 (*0-916583-36-8*) Dalkey Arch.

— Impossible Object. LC 85-72480. 219p. 1985. reprint ed. 20.00 (*0-916583-08-2*); reprint ed. pap. 9.95 (*0-916583-09-0*) Dalkey Arch.

— Judith. rev. ed. LC 90-3636. 298p. 1991. 19.95 (*0-916583-69-4*) Dalkey Arch.

— Judith. 298p. 1992. reprint ed. pap. 10.95 (*0-916583-77-5*) Dalkey Arch.

— Rules of the Game - Beyond the Pale: Memoirs of Sir Oswald Mosley & Family. LC 90-14042. (Illus.). 600p. 1991. 27.50 (*0-916583-75-9*) Dalkey Arch.

— Serpent. rev. ed. LC 89-35214. 190p. 1990. 19.95 (*0-916583-49-X*) Dalkey Arch.

Mosley, O. The Greater Britain. 1972. 59.95 (*0-8490-0263-X*) Gordon Pr.

— Policy & Debate. 1972. 59.95 (*0-8490-0869-7*) Gordon Pr.

— Tomorrow We Live. 1973. 59.95 (*0-8490-1221-X*) Gordon Pr.

Mosley, Oswald. Britain First. 1984. lib. bdg. 79.95 (*0-87700-612-1*) Revisionist Pr.

— Two Germans of Genius. 44p. 1987. 30.00 (*0-930126-22-X*) Typographeum.

Mosley, Oswald E. The Alternative. 1972. 59.95 (*0-87968-592-1*) Gordon Pr.

Mosley, Patrick A. The Lighter Side of Stained Glass. (Illus.). 90p. 1984. pap. 6.95 (*0-917661-00-1*) P Mosley.

Mosley, Paul. Conditionality As Bargaining Process: Structural-Adjustment Lending. LC 87-25806. (Essays in International Finance Ser.: No. 168). 1987. pap. text ed. 8.00 (*0-88165-075-7*) Princeton U Int Finan Econ.

— Foreign Aid: Its Defense & Reform. LC 86-23400. 280p. 1987. 31.00 (*0-8131-1608-2*) U Pr of Ky.

— The Making of Economic Policy: Theory & Evidence from Britain & the United States since 1945. LC 83-40518. 240p. 1984. text ed. 29.95 (*0-312-50688-0*) St Martin.

M

— The Settler Economies: Studies in the Economic History of Kenya & Southern Rhodesia, 1900-1963. LC 82-12896. (African Studies: No. 35). (Illus.). 336p. 1983. 74.95 (*0-521-24339-4*) Cambridge U Pr.

Mosley, Paul, et al. Aid & Power, Vol. 2: The World Bank & Policy-Based Lending. 416p. 1991. 89.95 (*0-415-06077-X*, A5485); pap. 27.50 (*0-415-06246-2*, A5724) Routledge.

Mosley, Philip, tr. see Rodenbach, Georges.

Mosley, R. J., tr. see Moiseev, Yu V. & Zaikov, G. E.

Mosley, R. K. Westminster Workshop: A Student's Guide to British Government. 205p. 1985. text ed. 50.00 (*0-08-031834-7*, Pergamon Pr) Elsevier.

Mosley, Steve. If Only God Would Answer: What to do When You Ask, Speak & Knock--And Nothing Happens. LC 92-62811. 193p. (Orig.). 1993. pap. 9.00 (*0-89109-712-0*) NavPress.

Mosley, Steve, jt. auth. see Finley, Mark.

***Mosley, Steven.** Deepen My Heart: Discovering a Sense of Intimacy with God. 1995. pap. 10.99 (*0-88070-734-8*) Questar Pubs.

Mosley, Steven, jt. auth. see Finley, Mark.

Mosley, Steven R. There I Go Again. 1991. pap. write for info. (*0-8499-3270-X*) Word Inc.

Mosley, Steven R., jt. auth. see Finley, Mark.

Mosley, Thomas E., Jr. Marketing Your Invention. 232p. 1992. pap. 19.95 (*0-936894-33-4*) Upstart Pub.

Mosley, W. H. & Bungey, J. H. Reinforced Concrete Design. 3rd ed. (Illus.). 399p. (C). 1987. pap. text ed. 31.50 (*0-333-45183-X*, Pub. by Macmill Press UK) Scholium Intl.

— Reinforced Concrete Design. 4th ed. (Civil Engineering Ser.). (Illus.). 401p. (C). 1991. pap. text ed. 32.50 (*0-333-53718-1*, Pub. by Macmill Press UK) Scholium Intl.

Mosley, W. H. & Spencer, W. J. Microcomputer Applications in Structural Engineering. 250p. 1985. 49.50 (*0-444-00919-1*); disk 30.25 (*0-444-00948-5*) Elsevier.

Mosley, W. H., jt. auth. see Hulse, R.

Mosley, W. Henry & Chen, Lincoln C., eds. Child Survival: Strategies for Research - Supplement to Population & Development Review, Vol. 10. LC 84-15985. 401p. 1992. reprint ed. pap. text ed. 12.00 (*0-685-66120-2*) Population Coun.

Mosley, Walter. Black Betty. LC 94-6839. 1994. 19.95 (*0-393-03644-8*) Norton.

— Black Betty. large type ed. LC 94-5385. 520p. 1994. 21.95 (*0-7862-0323-4*) Thorndike Pr.

— Devil in a Blue Dress. 1990. 19.95 (*0-393-02854-2*) Norton.

— Devil in a Blue Dress. large type ed. LC 93-16667. 1993. lib. bdg. 19.95 (*1-56054-722-7*) Thorndike Pr.

— Devil in a Blue Dress. Chelius, Jane, ed. 224p. 1991. reprint ed. mass mkt. 5.99 (*0-671-74050-4*) PB.

— Devil in a Blue Dress. Ryan, Kevin, ed. 1995. reprint ed. mass mkt. 5.99 (*0-671-51142-4*) PB.

— Red Death. 1991. 19.95 (*0-393-02998-0*) Norton.

— A Red Death. large type ed. LC 93-18588. 1993. bds. 20.95 (*1-56054-723-5*) Thorndike Pr.

— A Red Death. Chelius, Jane, ed. 256p. 1992. reprint ed. mass mkt. 5.99 (*0-671-74989-7*) PB.

— RL's Dream: A Novel. 288p. 1995. 22.00 (*0-393-03802-5*) Norton.

— White Butterfly. large type ed. LC 93-16668. 1993. 19.95 (*1-56054-724-3*) Thorndike Pr.

— White Butterfly. Chelius, Jane, ed. 394p. 1993. reprint ed. mass mkt. 5.99 (*0-671-86787-3*) PB.

— White Butterfly: An Easy Rawlins Mystery. 256p. 1992. 19.95 (*0-393-03366-X*) Norton.

Mosley, William. What Color Was Jesus. 67p. 1987. pap. 6.95 (*0-913543-09-8*) African Am Imag.

Moslow, T. F., jt. auth. see Rhodes, E. G.

Moslow, Thomas F. & Rhodes, Eugene G. Modern & Ancient Shelf Clastics. (Core Workshop Notes Ser.: No. 9). 459p. 1986. pap. 42.00 (*0-918985-61-7*) SEPM.

Mosman, Chesley A. The Rough Side of War: The Civil War Journal of Chesley A. Mosman, 1st Lieutenant, Company D, 59th Illinois Volunteer Infantry Regiment, 1862-1866. (Illus.). 448p. 1987. 25.00 (*0-940591-06-5*) Basin Pub.

Mosman, Richard A. This Irritating World We Live In. (Illus.). 1989. pap. write for info. (*0-318-65828-3*) R A Mosman.

Mosmann, Charles. Evaluating Instructional Computing: Measuring Needs & Resources for Computing in Higher Education. 88p. 1977. 12.00 (*0-318-14018-7*); 6.00 (*0-318-14019-5*) EDUCOM.

Mosmann, Charles, jt. ed. see Feldman, Julian.

Mosmann, Charles J. Academic Computers in Service. LC 72-13602. (Jossey-Bass Higher Education Ser.). 202p. reprint ed. pap. 57.60 (*0-8357-5027-2*, 2025665) Bks Demand.

Mosmann, Charles J., ed. Statewide Computing Systems: Coordinating Academic Computer Planning. LC 74-24337. (Books in Library & Information Science: Vol. 10). 215p. reprint ed. pap. 61.30 (*0-685-16299-0*, 2027119) Bks Demand.

Mosmiller, Thomas E., jt. ed. see Kimmel, Michael S.

Mosnaim & Wolf. Noncatecholic Phenylethylamines. (Modern Pharmacology-Toxicology Ser.: Vol. 12). 552p. 1978. 190.00 (*0-8247-6616-4*) Dekker.

— Noncatecholic Phenylethylamines, Pt. 2. (Modern Pharmacology-Toxicology Ser.: Vol. 12). 400p. 1980. 140.00 (*0-8247-6721-7*) Dekker.

Mosnaim, Aron, jt. ed. see Wolf, Marion.

Mosnaim, Aron D., jt. ed. see Wolf, Marion.

Mosocco, Ronald A. The Chronological Tracking of the American Civil War Per the Official Records of the War of the Rebellion. LC 94-76315. 400p. (C). Date not set. student ed, spiral bd. 34.95 (*0-9641675-6-5*) James River.

— The Chronological Tracking of the American Civil War Per the Official Records of the War of the Rebellion. LC 94-76315. (Illus.). 400p. (C). 1994. 39.95 (*0-9641675-9-X*) James River.

Mosokovitz, Faye. Whoever Finds This: I Love You. LC 87-46372. 224p. 1988. 15.95 (*0-87923-746-5*) Godine.

Mosonyi, E. Water Power Development, Vol. 1. 1074p. (C). 1987. 350.00 (*0-569-09084-9*, Pub. by Collets) St Mut.

— Water Power Development, Vol. 2. 748p. (C). 1965. 350.00 (*0-685-36847-5*, Pub. by Collets) St Mut.

— Water Power Development: Low-Head Power Plants, Vol. 1. 1074p. (C). 1987. 300.00x (*963-05-4271-4*) St Mut.

Mosonyi, Emil. Water Power Development Vol. 11: High Head Power Plants. 1091p. (C). 1991. 500.00 (*963-05-5885-8*, Pub. by Akad Kiado HU) St Mut.

***Mosquera, Cristobal.** Poesias Ineditas de Cristobal Mosquera. Diaz Plaja, Guillermo, ed. 239p. (SPA.). 1968. pap. 100.00 (*0-614-00213-3*) Elliots Bks.

***Moss.** Forts & Castles. (Illus.). (J). 1995. pap. text ed. (*0-8114-6339-7*) Raintree Steck-V.

— Jean Moss Designer Knits. 2nd ed. 1995. pap. text ed. 17.95 (*0-02-860425-3*) Macmillan.

— Town House. 1997. 39.95 (*0-8050-1398-9*) H Holt & Co.

Moss & Cox. Radiation Oncology: Rationale Technique Results. (Illus.). 816p. 1988. 99.00 (*0-8016-3570-5*) Mosby Yr Bk.

Moss & Winkler. Presidential Houses. 1995. 29.95 (*0-8050-0734-2*) H Holt & Co.

Moss, jt. auth. see Fanshal, David.

Moss, jt. auth. see Pierce.

***Moss, Adam.** The Sport Summit Sports Business Directory. 700p. 1995. pap. text ed. 129.00 (*0-9644259-0-4*) E J Krause.

Moss, Adrian. HIV & AIDS: Management by the Primary Care Team. (Practical Guides for General Practice Ser.: No. 16). 112p. 1992. pap. 19.95 (*0-19-262216-1*) OUP.

Moss, Alan. Beginner's Guide to Still Life Drawing. 1993. 12.98 (*1-55521-852-0*) Bk Sales Inc.

***Moss, Alfred A.** The American Negro Academy: Voice of the Talented Tenth. fac. ed. LC 80-18026. 349p. 1981. reprint ed. pap. 99.50 (*0-7837-7806-6*, 2047562) Bks Demand.

Moss, Alfred A., Jr., jt. ed. see Anderson, Eric.

Moss, Alfred A., Jr., jt. auth. see Franklin, John H.

Moss, Alison, ed. Catalogue of British Official Publications Not Published by HMSO, 1983. 500p. 1984. lib. bdg. 290.00 (*0-85964-132-5*) Chadwyck-Healey.

Moss, Alwyn, ed. see Moss, Ann E.

Moss, Ambler H., Jr., ed. NAFTA: Assessments of the North American Free Trade Agreement. LC 93-39473. 120p. (C). 1994. pap. 16.95 (*1-56000-730-3*, U Miami North-South Ctr) Transaction Pubs.

Moss, Anita & Stott, Don. The Family of Stories: An Anthology of Children's Literature. 672p. (C). 1986. pap. text ed. 32.75 (*0-03-921832-5*) HB Coll Pubs.

Moss, Ann E. Friends of Tinkle Rescue Club. Moss, Alwyn, ed. LC 90-24192. (Illus.). 88p. 1991. pap. 8.95 (*0-936015-27-6*) Pocahontas Pr.

Moss, Anne, jt. auth. see Church, Nancy.

Moss, Anne, jt. auth. see Zimmer-Loew, Helene.

Moss, Austin P., ed. The Wines & Wines of Sonoma County. LC 90-1763. (Insiders Guide Ser.). 288p. (Orig.). 1990. pap. 9.95 (*0-929635-01-9*) Cole Pub Co Inc.

Moss, B. Ecology of Fresh Waters: Man & Medium. 2nd ed. (Illus.). 432p. 1989. pap. text ed. 49.95 (*0-632-01642-6*) Blackwell Sci.

Moss, B., jt. auth. see Eliot, J.

Moss, Beverly J. Literacy Across Communities. Farr, Marcia, ed. LC 94-7395. (Written Language Ser.). 240p. (C). 1994. text ed. 45.00 (*1-881303-61-6*); pap. text ed. 18.95 (*1-881303-62-4*) Hampton Pr NJ.

Moss, Bill, jt. auth. see Applewhaite, Charles.

Moss, Bobby G. Roster of South Carolina Patriots in the American Revolution. LC 82-83584. (Illus.). 1023p. 1994. reprint ed. 50.00 (*0-8063-1005-7*, 3915) Genealog Pub.

Moss, C., jt. auth. see Savin, J. A.

Moss, Carol. Science in Ancient Mesopotamia. LC 88-2649. (First Bks.). (Illus.). 72p. (J). (gr. 5-8). 1988. lib. bdg. 11.62 (*0-531-10594-6*) Watts.

Moss, Carolyn J. Bibliographical Guide to Self-Disclosure Literature Nineteen Fifty-Six to Nineteen Seventy-Six. LC 77-89643. 219p. 1978. 15.00 (*0-87875-132-7*) Whitston Pub.

Moss, Carolyn J., jt. auth. see Moss, Sidney P.

Moss, Charlotte. Passion for Detail. 1991. 40.00 (*0-385-26760-6*) Doubleday.

— Room Service: A Step-by-Step Guide to Accessorizing Your Home. LC 94-16052. (Illus.). 1995. write for info. (*0-670-84799-2*, Viking Studio) Studio Bks.

Moss, Chris. Prolog Plus Plus: The Power of Object Oriented & Logic Programming. (C). 1993. text ed. 36.75 (*0-201-56507-2*) Addison-Wesley.

Moss, Claude S. Dreams, Images, & Fantasy: A Semantic Differential Casebook. LC 79-105543. 317p. reprint ed. pap. 90.40 (*0-317-07824-0*, 2022781) Bks Demand.

Moss, Cynthia. Echo of the Elephants: The Story of an Elephant Family. 1994. pap. 15.00 (*0-688-13513-7*, Quill) Morrow.

— Portraits in the Wild: Animal Behavior in East Africa. LC 81-23092. (Illus.). 1982. pap. 14.95 (*0-226-54233-5*) U Ch Pr.

Moss, Cynthia & Colbeck, M. Echo of the Elephants: The Story of an Elephant Family. LC 92-33463. (Illus.). 192p. 1993. 30.00 (*0-688-12103-9*) Morrow.

Moss, Cynthia A. Elephant Memories. large type ed. (Charnwood Library). 448p. 1992. 23.95 (*0-7089-8638-2*, Trail West Pubs) Ulverscroft.

Moss, D. S., jt. auth. see Goodfellow, J. M.

Moss, D. W. & Butterworth, P. J. Enzymology & Medicine. (Illus.). 1974. pap. text ed. 60.00 (*0-272-00094-9*) St Mut.

Moss, Danny, ed. Public Relations in Practice: A Casebook. 240p. (C). 1991. text ed. 74.00 (*0-415-05528-8*, A4893) Routledge.

Moss, David. Colors. (Pull the Tab Bks.). 10p. (J). 1989. 4.99 (*0-517-69421-2*) Random Hse Value.

— Numbers. (Pull the Tab Bks.). 10p. (J). (ps). 1989. 4.99 (*0-517-69423-9*) Random Hse Value.

— The Politics of Left-Wing Violence in Italy, 1969-85. LC 89-30611. (Illus.). 224p. 1989. text ed. 45.00 (*0-312-02814-8*) St Martin.

— Shapes. (Pull the Tab Bks.). (Illus.). 10p. (J). (ps). 1989. 4.99 (*0-517-69422-0*) Random Hse Value.

— The Song of David: The Moss Haggadah, 2. (Illus.). 340p. (ENG & HEB.). 1987. pap. write for info. (*0-318-65919-0*) Bet Alpha Editions.

— The Song of David: The Moss Haggadah, I. (Illus.). 340p. (ENG & HEB.). 1987. write for info. (*0-318-65918-2*) Bet Alpha Editions.

— The Song of David: The Moss Haggadah, Set, Vols. 1 & 2. deluxe limited ed. LC 87-206430. (Illus.). 340p. (ENG & HEB.). 1987. Set. pap. 6,500.00 (*0-9624473-1-5*) Bet Alpha Editions.

Moss, David, jt. ed. see Misztal, Barbara A.

***Moss, David A.** Socializing Security: Progressive-Era Economists & the Origins of American Social Policy. 256p. (C). 1995. text ed. 39.95 (*0-674-81502-5*) HUP.

Moss, David J. Thomas Attwood: The Biography of a Radical. 400p. 1990. text ed. 55.00 (*0-7735-0708-6*, Pub. by McGill CN) U of Toronto Pr.

Moss, Deborah. Lee, the Rabbit with Epilepsy. LC 88-40249. (Illus.). 32p. (J). (gr. k-4). 1989. lib. bdg. 12.95 (*0-933149-32-8*) Woodbine House.

— Shelley, the Hyperactive Turtle. LC 88-40248. (Illus.). 24p. (J). (gr. k up). 1989. lib. bdg. 12.95 (*0-933149-31-X*) Woodbine House.

Moss, Dennis R. Pressure Vessel Design Manual: Illustrated Procedures for Solving Every Major Pressure Vessel Design Problem. LC 87-360. (Illus.). 236p. 1987. 79.00 (*0-87201-719-2*) Gulf Pub.

Moss, Donald G. Why Didn't They Tell Me. rev. ed. 50p. 1989. pap. 3.00 (*0-9623251-1-2*) Laryngectomee.

Moss, E. H. Flora of Alberta. 2nd ed. (Illus.). 704p. 1983. text ed. 60.00 (*0-8020-2508-0*) U of Toronto Pr.

***Moss, Edna J.** Basic Keyboarding for the Medical Office Assistant. LC 94-26242. 312p. 1994. pap. text ed. 24.95 (*0-8273-5798-2*) Delmar.

Moss, Edward. The Grammar of Consciousness: An Exploration of Tacit Knowing. LC 94-18454. 1994. write for info. (*0-312-12222-5*) St Martin.

Moss, Elaine. Part of the Pattern: A Personal Journey Through the World of Children's Books, 1960-1985. LC 85-30211. 224p. 1986. 11.75 (*0-688-04559-6*) Greenwillow.

— Polar. LC 89-2115. (Illus.). 32p. (J). (ps up). 1990. 13.95 (*0-688-09176-8*); lib. bdg. 13.88 (*0-688-09177-6*) Greenwillow.

Moss, Elizabeth. Domestic Novelists in the Old South: Defenders of Southern Culture. LC 91-40827. (Southern Literary Studies). 272p. (C). 1992. text ed. 130.00 (*0-8071-1730-7*) La State U Pr.

Moss, Eric O. Eric Owen Moss. (Architectural Monographs: No. 29). (Illus.). 144p. 1993. 55.00 (*1-85490-189-3*, Academy Edits); pap. 38.00 (*1-85490-190-7*, Academy Edits) St Martin.

Moss, Ezra H. & Packer, John G. Flora of Alberta: A Manual of Flowering Plants, Conifers, Ferns, & Fern Allies Found Growing Without Cultivation in the Province of Alberta, Canada. 2nd ed. LC 84-179310. (Illus.). 701p. reprint ed. pap. 180.00 (*0-8357-8132-1*, 2033988) Bks Demand.

Moss, Francis, jt. auth. see Pedersen, Ted.

Moss, Frank. How Anyone Can Prosper & Get Wealthy Trading Country Land. 4th ed. 120p. 1990. pap. 21.95 (*0-934311-67-6*) Intl Wealth.

— How Anyone Can Prosper & Get Wealthy Trading Country Land. 5th ed. 120p. 1992. pap. 21.95 (*1-56150-018-6*) Intl Wealth.

— How Anyone Can Prosper & Get Wealthy Trading Country Land. 6th ed. 120p. 1993. pap. 21.95 (*1-56150-068-2*) Intl Wealth.

— How Anyone Can Prosper & Get Wealthy Trading Country Land. 7th ed. 120p. 1994. pap. 21.95 (*1-56150-116-6*) Intl Wealth.

Moss, Frank, ed. Story of the Riot: Persecution of Negroes by Roughs & Policemen, in the City of New York, August, Nineteen Hundred. LC 73-90186. (Mass Violence in America Ser.). 1976. reprint ed. 21.95 (*0-405-01329-9*) Ayer.

Moss, Frank & McClintock, P. V., eds. Noise in Nonlinear Dynamical Systems, Vol. 2: Theory of Noise-Induced Processes in Special. (Illus.). 320p. (C). 1989. 110.00 (*0-521-35229-0*) Cambridge U Pr.

— Noise in Nonlinear Dynamical Systems, Vol. 3: Experiments & Simulation. (Illus.). 200p. (C). 1989. 110.00 (*0-521-35265-7*) Cambridge U Pr.

Moss, G. M., et al. Military Ballistics: A Basic Manual. (Land Warfare: Brassey's New Battlefield Weapons & Technology Ser.: Vol. 12). (Illus.). 200p. 1994. 40.00 (*1-85753-079-9*, Pub. by Brasseys UK); pap. 25.00 (*0-685-74738-7*, Pub. by Brasseys UK) Brasseys Inc.

Moss, Gene R. Healthcare Reform D. O. A. Why Politics Will Destroy Healthcare & How One Physician's Plan Can Prevent It. 206p. (Orig.). 1994. pap. 12.95 (*0-9639747-0-X*) Behav Med Assocs.

Moss, Geoffrey. Corporate Trainer's Quick Reference. 192p. 1993. text ed. 25.00 (*1-55623-905-X*) Irwin Prof Pubng.

Moss, George D. America in the Twentieth Century. 2nd ed. 544p. 1992. pap. text ed. write for info. (*0-13-031733-0*) P-H.

— Moving On: The American People since 1945. LC 93-27288. 432p. 1994. pap. text ed. write for info. (*0-13-606138-9*) P-H.

— The Rise of Modern America: A History of the American People, 1890-1945. LC 94-36595. 400p. 1994. pap. text ed. write for info. (*0-13-181587-3*) P-H.

— A Vietnam Reader: Sources & Essays. 352p. (C). 1990. pap. text ed. write for info. (*0-13-946625-8*) P-H.

Moss, George H., Jr. Double Exposure: Early Stereographic Views of Historic Monmouth County, New Jersey & Their Relationship to Pioneer Photography. LC 70-154560. (Illus.). 176p. 1971. 20.00 (*0-912396-00-8*) Ploughshare Pr.

— Steamboat to the Shore: A Pictorial History of the Steamboat Era in Monmouth County, New Jersey. (Illus.). 102p. 1972. 15.00 (*0-912396-02-4*) Ploughshare Pr.

Moss, Glenn & Obery, Ingrid, eds. South Africa Contemporary Analysis. 650p. 1990. lib. bdg. 82.00 (*0-905450-42-6*, Pub. by H Zell Pubs UK) Bowker-Saur.

— South African Review, No. 6: From "Red Friday" to Codesa. xxi, 508p. (C). 1993. pap. text ed. 24.95 (*0-86975-418-1*, Pub. by Ravan Pr ZA) Ohio U Pr.

Moss, Graveyard. Graveyard Moss Is Still Alive. 48p. (Orig.). (YA). (gr. 9). 1988. pap. 5.00 (*0-945237-00-6*) Morgan Virginia Pub.

Moss, H., jt. auth. see Domoryad, A.

Moss, Halina, tr. see Vorob'ev, Nikolai N.

Moss, Heather R. Kimfessions. LC 91-67748. 154p. (Orig.). 1993. pap. 6.95 (*1-56002-149-7*, Univ Edtns) Aegina Pr.

Moss, Helen. Silky, the Woods Cat. (Illus.). 80p. (J). (gr. 2-4). 1993. 10.95 (*0-89015-867-3*) Sunbelt Media.

Moss, Henry S. The Birth of the Middle Ages, 395-814. LC 80-24038. (Illus.). xvi, 291p. 1980. reprint ed. text ed. 69.50 (*0-313-22708-X*, MOBM, Greenwood Pr) Greenwood.

Moss, Howard. Instant Lives & More. (Illus.). 106p. 1985. reprint ed. pap. 6.50 (*0-88001-076-2*) Ecco Pr.

— Minor Monuments: Selected Essays. 352p. (C). 1986. 20.00 (*0-88001-089-4*); pap. 10.50 (*0-88001-104-1*) Ecco Pr.

Moss, Howard, jt. auth. see Kagan, Jerome.

Moss, Howard A., ed. see Hess, Robert, et al.

Moss, Hugh. By Imperial Command, 2 vols., Set. (Illus.). 272p. 1976. 225.00 (*0-905298-00-4*, Pub. by Bamboo Pub UK) Antique Collect.

— By Imperial Command: An Intro to Ch'ing Imperial Painted Enamels, 2 vols., Set. (Illus.). 250p. 1976. 350.00 (*0-87556-740-1*) Saifer.

Moss, Hugh, et al. The Art of the Chinese Snuff Bottle: The J & J Collection, 2 vols. LC 93-4947. (Illus.). 800p. 1994. boxed 250.00 (*0-8348-0289-9*) Weatherhill.

Moss, Hunter V., ed. see Compton, Eric N.

Moss, Ian S., ed. see Smith, Adam.

Moss, Irvin & Foster, Mark. Home Run in the Rockies: The History of Baseball in Colorado. 144p. 1994. text ed. write for info. (*0-9641818-0-0*) H I Moss.

***Moss, J., et al.** Handbook of Natural Toxins Vol. 8: Bacterial Toxins & Virulence Factors in Disease. 664p. 1995. 195.00 (*0-8247-9381-1*) Dekker.

Moss, James N., jt. ed. see Scott, Carl D.

Moss, Janice, jt. auth. see Southwestern Legal Foundation Staff.

Moss, Jean. Knits for All Seasons: Twenty-Seven Original Designs for All the Family. (Illus.). 160p. 1994. 29.95 (*0-943955-86-6*) Trafalgar.

Moss, Jean D. Novelties in the Heavens: Rhetoric & Science in the Copernican Controversy. LC 92-21608. 352p. (C). 1993. pap. text ed. 17.95 (*0-226-54235-1*) U Ch Pr.

— Novelties in the Heavens: Rhetoric & Science in the Copernican Controversy. LC 92-21608. 352p. (C). 1993. lib. bdg. 49.95 (*0-226-54234-3*) U Ch Pr.

Moss, Jean D., ed. Rhetoric & Praxis: The Contribution of Classical Rhetoric to Practical Reasoning. LC 85-25449. 184p. reprint ed. pap. 52.50 (*0-7837-4631-8*, 2044354) Bks Demand.

Moss, Jeff. Bob & Jack: A Boy & His Yak. LC 92-17458. (Illus.). 64p. (J). (gr. 4 up). 1992. 15.00 (*0-553-08931-5*) Bantam.

— Hieronymus White: A Bird Who Believed That He Always Was Right. LC 94-15566. (Illus.). 128p. 1994. 16.00 (*0-345-38590-X*) Ballantine.

— Other Side of the Door. (J). (gr. k up). 1991. 15.00 (*0-553-07259-5*) Bantam.

— The Sesame Street Book of Poetry. LC 90-8994. (Illus.). 48p. (J). (ps-3). 1992. 10.00 (*0-679-80774-8*) Random Bks Yng Read.

Moss, Jeffrey. The Butterfly Jar. (Illus.). (J). (ps up). 1989. 15.95 (*0-553-05704-9*) Bantam.

Moss, Joan. The Five-Minute Hors d'Oeuvres. LC 92-30667. 1993. 18.00 (*0-517-59265-7*, Crown) Crown Pub Group.

Moss, Joanna & Ravenhill, John. The Emerging Japanese Economic Influence in Africa: Implications for the United States. LC 84-82151. (Policy Papers in International Affairs Ser.: No. 21). (Illus.). xi, 150p. 1985. pap. 8.95 (*0-87725-521-0*) U of Cal IAS.

***Moss, Joel, ed.** ADP-Ribosylation: Metabolic Effects & Regulatory Functions. LC 94-21849. 256p. (C). 1994. lib. bdg. 190.00 (*0-7923-2951-1*) Kluwer Ac.

Moss, Joel & Vaughan, Martha, eds. ADP-Ribosylating Toxins & G Proteins: Insights into Signal Transduction. (Illus.). 585p. 1990. text ed. 59.00 (*1-55581-017-9*) Am Soc Microbio.

Moss, John. Introduction to Data Processing. 1978. 30.00 (*0-905897-25-0*) St Mut.

An Asterisk (*) at the beginning of an entry indicates that the title is appearing in BIP for the first time.

Moss, John, ed. The Canadian Novel: Beginnings, Vol. 2. (Illus.). 216p. Date not set. text ed. 17.95 (*0-920053-15-7*, Pub. by NC Press CN); pap. 12.95 (*0-920053-17-3*, Pub. by NC Press CN) U of Toronto Pr.
— The Canadian Novel: Here & Now, Vol. 1. (Illus.). 204p. Date not set. text ed. 17.95 (*0-920053-06-8*, Pub. by NC Press CN); pap. 12.95 (*0-920053-04-1*, Pub. by NC Press CN) U of Toronto Pr.
— The Canadian Novel: Modern Times, Vol. 3. (Illus.). 204p. Date not set. pap. 12.95 (*0-919601-90-1*, Pub. by NC Press CN) U of Toronto Pr.
— The Canadian Novel: Present Tense, Vol. 4. (Illus.). 224p. Date not set. text ed. 17.95 (*0-919601-67-7*, Pub. by NC Press CN); pap. 12.95 (*0-919601-65-0*, Pub. by NC Press CN) U of Toronto Pr.
— From the Heart of the Heartland: The Fiction of Sinclair Ross. (Reappraisals: Canadian Writers Ser.: No. 17). 139p. 1992. pap. 20.00 (*0-7766-0329-9*, Pub. by Univ Ottawa Pr CN) Paul & Co Pubs.
Moss, John R. & Ragsdale, Elizabeth S. Enhancing Self-Esteem for Exceptional Leaners. 1994. pap. 29.95 (*0-937660-18-3*) PIP.
Moss, John R. & Skelton, Louise. Developing Self-Concept for Exceptional Learners: A Handbook. rev. ed. (C). 1977. pap. 7.00 (*0-937660-05-1*) PIP.
Moss, John R., jt. ed. see Fielding, P. M.
Moss, John R., et al. A College Level Program for Learning Disabled Students. (C). 1980. pap. 15.95 (*0-937660-01-9*) PIP.
Moss-Jones, John. Automating Managers. 1991. text ed. 47. 50 (*0-86187-837-X*, Pub. by Pinter Pubs UK) St Martin.
Moss, Joseph. Manual of Classical Bibliography, 2 vols., Set. 2nd ed. LC 76-101049. reprint ed. lib. bdg. 190.00 (*0-8046-0714-1*) Irvington.
Moss, Joseph L. A Manual of Classical Bibliography, 2 vols., Set. 1973. 200.00 (*0-8490-0581-7*) Gordon Pr.
Moss, Joy. Literature in the Middle Grades: A Thematic Approach. 252p. (J). (gr. 3-8). 1994. text ed. 26.95 (*0-926842-38-2*) CG Pubs Inc.
Moss, Joy F. Focus on Literature: A Context for Literacy Learning. LC 89-22804. 272p. (Orig.). (C). 1990. pap. text ed. 17.95 (*0-913461-17-2*) R Owen Pubs.
Moss, Joyce & Wilson, George, eds. Peoples of the World: Africans South of the Sahara. 2nd ed. 450p. 1996. 42.00 (*0-8103-8895-2*, 101541) Gale.
— Peoples of the World: Latin Americans. 1989. 45.00 (*0-8103-7445-5*) Gale.
— Peoples of the World: North Americans, Vol. 2. 441p. 1990. 45.00 (*0-8103-7768-3*, 100732-M94800) Gale.
Moss, Joyce, jt. auth. see Wilson, George.
Moss, Judy, jt. auth. see Horrocks, Brian.
Moss, Julian V. Servicing & Supporting IBM PCs & Compatibles. 358p. (Orig.). 1992. pap. 47.50 (*1-85058-243-2*, Pub. by Sigma Press UK) Coronet Bks.
— Upgrading, Maintaining, & Servicing IBM PC's & Compatibles. Leventhal, Lance A., ed. LC 92-24227. (Lance A. Leventhal Microtrend Ser.). 400p. (Orig.). 1992. pap. 29.95 (*0-915391-70-8*, Microtrend) Slawson Comm.
Moss, Karen. Altered Egos. Boberg, Scott, ed. (Illus.). 84p. (Orig.). 1994. pap. 25.00 (*0-9624941-2-7*) SM Mus Art.
Moss, Karen, ed. see Drew, Nancy, et al.
Moss, Karen, ed. see Kohl, Jeanette, et al.
Moss, Kathlyn & Scherer, Alice. The New Beadwork. (Illus.). 112p. 1992. 29.95 (*0-8109-3670-4*) Abrams.
Moss, Kenneth B. Technology & the Future Strategic Environment. 194p. 1990. pap. text ed. 12.95 (*0-943875-24-2*, Johns Hopkins) W Wilson Ctr Pr.
Moss, Laurence S. Mountifort Longfield: Ireland's First Professor of Political Economy. LC 75-34003. 240p. 1976. 14.95 (*0-916054-02-0*) Green Hill.
Moss, Laurence S. & Ryan, Christopher, eds. Economic Thought in Spain: Selected Essays of Marjorie Grice-Hutchinson. 224p. 1993. 59.95 (*1-85278-868-2*, Pub. by E Elgar Pub UK) Ashgate Pub Co.
Moss, Leonard. Arthur Miller. rev. ed. (United States Authors Ser.: No. 115). 200p. 1980. text ed. 20.95 (*0-8057-7311-8*, Twayne) Macmillan.
— Henry Miller. (United States Authors Ser.: No. 115). 168p. 1990. text ed. 20.95 (*0-8057-7607-9*, Pub. by Royal Botanic Garden UK) Macmillan.
Moss, Lloyd. Zin! Zin! Zin! A Violin. LC 93-37902. (Illus.). (J). 1995. 15.00 (*0-671-88239-2*, S&S Bks Young Read) S&S Childrens.
Moss, M. E. Benedetto Croce Reconsidered: Truth & Error in Theories of Art, Literature & History. LC 86-22399. 164p. 1987. text ed. 20.00 (*0-87451-399-5*) U Pr of New Eng.
Moss, M. E., tr. Benedetto Croce: Essays on Literature & Literary Criticism. LC 89-4627. 244p. 1990. 59.50 (*0-7914-0200-2*); pap. 19.95 (*0-7914-0201-0*) State U NY Pr.
Moss, M. O., ed. see Smith, J. E.
***Moss, Maria.** We've Been Here Before: Women in Creation Myths & Contemporary Literature of the Native American Southwest. (North American Studies). (C). 1994. pap. text ed. 33.50 (*3-89473-928-2*) Westview.
Moss, Marion. Removing Your Mask: No More Hiding from Your Truth. Warden, Rosemary & Hubbard, Richard, eds. (Illus.). 320p. (Orig.). 1992. pap. 13.95 (*0-9631341-0-8*) Orion Pub.
Moss, Marissa. After-School Monster. LC 90-49416. (Illus.). 32p. (J). (gr. k up). 1991. 13.95 (*0-688-10116-X*); lib. bdg. 13.88 (*0-688-10117-8*) Lothrop.
— After-School Monster. 32p. (J). (ps-3). 1993. pap. 4.99 (*0-14-054829-7*, Puffin) Puffin Bks.
— Amelia's Notebook. LC 94-5382. (Illus.). 32p. (J). (gr. 2 up). 1995. 14.00 (*1-883672-18-X*) Tricycle Pr.
— But Not Kate. Donovan, Melanie, ed. LC 90-25751. (Illus.). 32p. (J). (ps-3). 1992. 14.00 (*0-688-10600-5*); lib. bdg. 13.93 (*0-688-10601-3*) Lothrop.
— In America. LC 93-26885. (Illus.). (J). 1994. 14.99 (*0-525-45152-8*, DCB) Dutton Child Bks.
— Knick Knack Paddywack. (Illus.). 32p. (J). (ps-3). 1992. 13.95 (*0-395-54701-6*) HM.
— Mel's Diner. LC 93-38683. (Illus.). 32p. (J). (gr. k-3). Date not set. pap. text ed. 3.95 (*0-8167-3461-5*) BrdgeWater.
— Mel's Diner. LC 93-38683. (Illus.). 32p. (J). (gr. k-3). 1994. lib. bdg. 13.95 (*0-8167-3460-7*) BrdgeWater.
— Regina's Big Mistake. (Illus.). 32p. (J). (gr. k-3). 1990. 13. 95 (*0-395-55330-X*) HM.
— Regina's Big Mistake. LC 90-32740. (J). (ps-3). 1995. pap. 4.95 (*0-395-70093-0*) HM.
Moss, Mark, ed. see Gillette, Steve.
Moss, Mark B., jt. ed. see Albert, Marilyn S.
Moss, Martha. Photography Books Index: A Subject Guide to Photo Anthologies, Vol. 1. LC 79-26938. 298p. 1980. lib. bdg. 25.00 (*0-8108-1283-5*) Scarecrow.
— Photography Books Index: A Subject Guide to Photo Anthologies, Vol. II. LC 84-23652. 276p. 1985. 23.50 (*0-8108-1773-X*) Scarecrow.
Moss, Marvin A. Designing for Minimal Maintenance Expense: The Practical Application of Reliability & Maintainability. (Quality & Reliability Ser.: Vol. 1). 184p. 1985. 65.00 (*0-8247-7314-4*) Dekker.
Moss, Matthew, tr. see O'Maolmorda, Sheila.
Moss, Maurice, tr. see Moreau, Claude.
Moss, Maurice O., jt. auth. see Smith, J. E.
Moss, Michael. An Invaluable Treasure: A History of the TSB. (Illus.). 336p. 1994. 55.00 (*0-297-81118-5*) Trafalgar.
Moss, Michael, jt. auth. see Jobert, Philippe.
Moss, Michael H., et al. Histology: A Text & Atlas. 3rd ed. (Illus.). 823p. 1994. 53.00 (*0-683-07369-9*) Williams & Wilkins.
Moss, Milton, ed. Measurement of Economic & Social Performance. (Studies in Income & Wealth: No. 38). 615p. 1973. 159.90 (*0-87014-259-3*) Natl Bur Econ Res.
Moss, Milton, ed. see Conference on the Measurement of Economic & Social Performance Staff.
Moss, Miriam. Be Positive. LC 92-26717. (Staying Healthy Ser.). (Illus.). 32p. (J). (gr. 6). 1993. text ed. 13.95 (*0-89686-786-2*, Crstwood Hse) Silver Burdett Pr.
— Eat Well. LC 92-28738. (Staying Healthy Ser.). (Illus.). 32p. (J). (gr. 6). 1993. text ed. 13.95 (*0-89686-785-4*, Crstwood Hse) Silver Burdett Pr.
— Eggs. Stefoff, Rebecca, ed. LC 91-18186. (Threads Ser.). (Illus.). 32p. (J). (gr. 3-5). 1991. lib. bdg. 15.93 (*1-56074-005-1*) Garrett Ed Corp.
— Fashion Designer. LC 90-48323. (Fashion World Ser.). (Illus.). 32p. (J). (gr. 5-6). 1991. text ed. 13.95 (*0-89686-610-6*, Crstwood Hse) Silver Burdett Pr.
— Fashion Model. LC 90-15082. (Fashion World Ser.). (Illus.). 32p. (J). (gr. 5-6). 1991. text ed. 13.95 (*0-89686-609-2*, Crstwood Hse) Silver Burdett Pr.
— Fashion Photographer. LC 90-15059. (Fashion World Ser.). (Illus.). 32p. (J). (gr. 5-6). 1991. text ed. 13.95 (*0-89686-608-4*, Crstwood Hse) Silver Burdett Pr.
— Forts & Castles. LC 93-11167. (Pointers Ser.). (Illus.). 32p. (J). (gr. 4-6). 1993. lib. bdg. 19.97 (*0-8114-6157-2*) Raintree Steck-V.
— Fruit. Stefoff, Rebecca, ed. (Threads Ser.). (Illus.). 28p. (J). (gr. 2-4). 1995. lib. bdg. 15.93 (*1-56074-059-0*) Garrett Ed Corp.
— Keep Fit. LC 92-13916. (Staying Healthy Ser.). (Illus.). 32p. (J). (gr. 6). 1993. text ed. 13.95 (*0-89686-788-9*, Crstwood Hse) Silver Burdett Pr.
— Street Fashion. LC 90-48913. (Fashion World Ser.). (Illus.). 32p. (J). (gr. 5-6). 1991. lib. bdg. 13.95 (*0-89686-611-4*, Crstwood Hse) Silver Burdett Pr.
Moss, N. Henry & Mayer, Jean, eds. Food & Nutrition in Health & Disease. (Annals Ser.: Vol. 300). 474p. 1977. 42.00 (*0-89072-046-0*) NY Acad Sci.
Moss, Nathaniel. Ron Kovic: Antiwar Activist. LC 93-16373. (Great Achievers: Lives of the Physically Challenged Ser.). (Illus.). (J). 1994. 18.95 (*0-7910-2076-2*, Am Art Analog); pap. write for info. (*0-7910-2089-4*, Am Art Analog) Chelsea Hse.
Moss, Norman. British-American Language Dictionary. 192p. 1984. 12.95 (*0-8442-9105-6*, Natl Textbk); pap. 7.95 (*0-8442-9104-8*, Natl Textbk) NTC Pub Grp.
— British-English Language Dictionary: For More Effective Communication Between Americans & Britons. 2nd ed. (Illus.). 192p. 1991. 14.95 (*0-8442-9115-3*, Natl Textbk); pap. 8.95 (*0-8442-9116-1*, Natl Textbk) NTC Pub Grp.
— Travel Guide to British-American English. 192p. 1984. pap. 3.95 (*0-8442-9512-4*, Passport Bks) NTC Pub Grp.
Moss, P. Buckley. The Etchings of P. Buckley Moss. Henderson, Malcolm & Henderson, Jaikie, eds. (Illus.). 114p. 1988. 58.00 (*0-9626627-0-4*) Shenandoah Pub.
— P. Buckley Moss, The People's Artist: An Autobiography. Henderson, Malcolm et al, eds. (Illus.). 103p. 1989. lib. bdg. 12.00 (*0-9626627-1-2*) Shenandoah Pub.
Moss, Paul, notes. Between Heaven & Earth. (Illus.). 160p. 1988. 49.95 (*0-89815-280-1*) Ten Speed Pr.
Moss, Peter & Melhuish, Edward. Current Issues in Day Care for Young Children. 140p. 1991. pap. 30.00 (*0-11-321337-9*, HM9733) UNIPUB.
Moss, Peter & Palmer, Thelma. France. LC 86-9628. (Enchantment of the World Ser.). (Illus.). 128p. (J). (gr. 5-9). 1986. lib. bdg. 20.55 (*0-516-02761-1*) Childrens.
***Moss, Peter & Pence, Alan, eds.** Valuing Quality in Early Childhood Services: New Approaches to Defining Quality. (Early Childhood Education Ser.). 192p. (C). 1994. pap. text ed. 19.95 (*0-8077-3431-4*) Tchrs Coll.
Moss, Peter, jt. auth. see McClusky, William.
Moss, Peter, jt. auth. see Melhuish, Edward.
Moss, Peter J., jt. ed. see Gupta, Ajaya K.
Moss, R., ed. Transport of Animals Intended for Breeding, Production & Slaughter. 1982. lib. bdg. 80.00 (*90-247-2679-4*) Kluwer Ac.
Moss, R. & Winkler, G. C. Victorian Interiors. 25.00 (*0-670-80612-9*) Viking Penguin.
Moss, R. P. & Morgan, W. B. Fuelwood & Rural Energy Production & Supply in Humid Tropics: Report for the UNU with Special Reference to Tropical Africa & South East Asia, Vol. 4. (Natural Resources & the Environment Ser.). (Illus.). 234p. 1981. text ed. 105.00 (*0-907567-03-7*, Tycooly Pub); write for info. (*0-685-13030-4*, Tycooly Pub) Weidner & Sons.
Moss, Ralph. Fire Bell in the Night. LC 93-61443. 112p. (Orig.). pap. 5.95 (*0-945383-53-3*) Teach Servs.
Moss, Ralph W. The Cancer Industry: The Classic Expose on the Cancer Establishment. pap. 14.95 (*1-55778-439-6*); pap. 19.95 (*1-881025-09-8*) Equinox Pr.
— Cancer Therapy: The Independent Consumer's Guide to Non-Toxic Treatment & Prevention. 1993. pap. 19.95 (*1-881025-06-3*) Equinox Pr.
— Questioning Chemotherapy: A Critique of the Use of Toxic Drugs in the Treatment of Cancer. LC 95-11440. 1995. write for info. (*1-881025-25-X*) Equinox Pr.
Moss, Ralph W., jt. auth. see Randolph, Theron G.
Moss, Ray, jt. ed. see Gabel, Detlaf.
Moss Rehabilitation Center Staff, jt. auth. see Kardon Institute Staff.
Moss, Richard. The Black Butterfly: An Invitation to Radical Aliveness. LC 86-11773. 320p. (Orig.). 1986. pap. 14.95 (*0-89087-475-1*) Celestial Arts.
— How Shall I Live: Where Spiritual Healing & Conventional Medicine Meet. LC 85-17468. 167p. (Orig.). 1985. pap. 8.95 (*0-89087-418-2*) Celestial Arts.
— The I That Is We: Awakening to Higher Energies Through Unconditional Love. LC 81-65713. 240p. 1981. pap. 8.95 (*0-89087-327-5*) Celestial Arts.
Moss, Richard, ed. see Muensterberg, Hugo.
Moss, Richard B., ed. Cystic Fibrosis: Infection, Immunopathology, & Host Response. 264p. 1990. 79.50 (*0-89603-192-6*) Humana.
***Moss, Richard J.** The Life of Jedidiah Morse: A Station of Peculiar Exposure. LC 94-28143. (Illus.). 192p. (C). 1995. text ed. 28.00x (*0-87049-868-1*) U of Tenn Pr.
Moss, Richard S. Slavery on Long Island: A Study in Local Institutional & Early Communal Life, 1609-1827. LC 92-44922. (Studies in African American History & Culture). 280p. 1993. 63.00 (*0-8153-1016-1*) Garland.
***Moss, Robert.** Capstone of Faith. 176p. 1995. pap. 10.95 (*1-55517-174-5*) CFI Dist.
— The Films of Carol Reed. LC 85-17512. 256p. 1987. text ed. 37.00 (*0-231-05984-1*) Col U Pr.
— Fire along the Sky. 416p. 1995. pap. 5.99 (*0-8125-3536-7*) Forge NYC.
— The Firekeeper. 512p. 1995. 24.95 (*0-312-85738-1*) Forge NYC.
Moss, Robert, jt. auth. see Mahler, Walter R.
Moss, Robert A. The Brain & the Bible: Is Psychology Compatible with Christianity? 108p. 1993. pap. 8.95 (*0-9638848-1-6*) R A Moss.
— Understanding Emptiness: The Think - Feel Conflict. 128p. 1993. pap. 9.95 (*0-9638848-0-8*) R A Moss.
Moss, Robert A. & Dunlap, Helen. Why Johnny Can't Concentrate: Coping with Attention Deficit Problems. 1990. pap. 11.95 (*0-553-34968-6*) Bantam.
Moss, Robert A. & Jones, Maitland, eds. Carbenes, 2 vols., Set. LC 80-11836. (Reactive Intermediates in Organic Chemistry Ser.). 368p. 1983. reprint ed. Vol. 1. lib. bdg. 72.50 (*0-89874-620-5*) Krieger.
— Carbenes, Vol. 1. LC 80-11836. (Reactive Intermediates in Organic Chemistry Ser.). 368p. 1983. reprint ed. Set. lib. bdg. 41.00 (*0-89874-216-1*) Krieger.
— Carbenes, Vol. 2. LC 80-11836. (Reactive Intermediates in Organic Chemistry Ser.). 390p. 1983. reprint ed. lib. bdg. 35.00 (*0-89874-160-2*) Krieger.
Moss, Robert D. The Art of Ship & Boat Handling. Kimel, Neal, ed. LC 93-206641. (Illus.). 150p. 1991. 49.95 (*1-883121-00-0*) Onboard Marine.
Moss, Robert F. Rudyard Kipling & the Fiction of Adolescence. LC 81-14561. 256p. 1982. text ed. 29.95 (*0-312-69549-7*) St Martin.
Moss, Robert H. The Covenant Coat. LC 85-81312. 174p. 1985. pap. 11.98 (*0-88290-311-X*, 1959) Horizon Utah.
— The Waters of Mormon. LC 86-81775. 176p. 1986. 11.98 (*0-88290-285-7*) Horizon Utah.
Moss, Roberta. Makin' Buckskin Clothes. 1982. 5.00 (*0-913150-48-7*) Pioneer Pr.
Moss, Roger W. Lighting for Historic Buildings. LC 87-36012. (Historic Interiors Ser.). (Illus.). 192p. 1988. pap. 14.95 (*0-89133-131-X*) Preservation Pr.
***Moss, Roger W., ed.** Paint in America: The Color of Historic Buildings. (Orig.). 1994. pap. 19.95 (*0-89133-263-4*) Preservation Pr.
— Paint in America: The Color of Historic Buildings. (Illus.). 318p. (Orig.). 1994. 34.95 (*0-89133-255-3*) Preservation Pr.
Moss, Roger W. & Winkler, Gail C. Victorian Exterior Decoration: How to Paint Your 19th Century American House Historically. LC 86-15014. (Illus.). 1992. pap. 19. 95 (*0-8050-2313-5*, Owl) H Holt & Co.
— Victorian Interior Decoration: American Interiors, 1830-1900. (Illus.). 272p. 1992. pap. 19.95 (*0-8050-2312-7*, Owl) H Holt & Co.
Moss, Roger W., jt. auth. see Tatman, Sandra L.
Moss, Roger W., jt. auth. see Winkler, Gail C.
***Moss, Rose.** The Schoolmaster. (Writers Ser.). 239p. 1995. reprint ed. pap. text ed. 12.95x (*0-86975-470-X*, Pub. by Ravan Pr ZA) Ohio U Pr.
Moss, S. E., ed. The Annexins. (Monograph Ser.: Vol. 2). 173p. 1992. 70.00 (*1-85578-008-9*, Pub. by Portland Pr Ltd UK) Ashgate Pub Co.
Moss, S. J. & Ledwith, A., eds. The Chemistry of the Semiconductor Industry. (Illus.). 352p. 1986. pap. text ed. 125.00 (*0-412-01321-5*, 9953, Chap & Hall NY) Chapman & Hall.
Moss-Salentijn, Letty & Hendricks-Klyvert, Marlene. Dental & Oral Tissues: An Introduction. 3rd ed. LC 89-13713. (Illus.). 327p. 1990. pap. text ed. 35.95 (*0-8121-1320-9*) Williams & Wilkins.
Moss, Sanford. Natural History of the Antarctic Peninsula. (Illus.). 256p. 1990. text ed. 50.00 (*0-231-06268-0*); pap. text ed. 18.00 (*0-231-06269-9*) Col U Pr.
Moss, Scott & Rae, John, eds. Artificial Intelligence & Economic Analysis: Prospects & Problems. 192p. 1992. 63.95 (*1-85278-685-X*, Pub. by E Elgar Pub UK) Ashgate Pub Co.
Moss, Sidney. Poe's Literary Battles: The Critic in the Context of His Literary Milieu. LC 63-9010. (Arcturus Books Paperbacks). 277p. 1969. pap. 2.85 (*0-8093-0351-5*) S Ill U Pr.
Moss, Sidney P. Charles Dickens' Quarrel with America. LC 82-50401. 333p. 1984. 28.50 (*0-87875-255-2*) Whitston Pub.
— Poe's Major Crisis: His Libel Suit & New York's Literary World. LC 74-100089. 256p. reprint ed. pap. 73.00 (*0-317-20452-1*, 2023424) Bks Demand.
Moss, Sidney P. & Moss, Carolyn J. Charles Dickens & His Chicago Relatives. LC 93-60503. (Illus.). 186p. 1994. 23. 50 (*0-87875-444-X*) Whitston Pub.
Moss, Stanley. A Guide to the Manuscripts & Special Collections. 76p. 1988. pap. write for info. (*1-882162-02-1*) Lynn Hist Soc.
— The Intelligence of Clouds. 81p. 1989. 13.95 (*0-15-144850-7*); pap. 7.95 (*0-15-644800-9*) HarBrace.
Moss, Stanley, ed. see Kunitz, Stanley.
Moss, Stephen. Growing up Cavity-Free: A Parent's Guide to Prevention. (Illus.). 180p. (Orig.). 1993. pap. 18.00 (*0-86715-256-7*) Quint Pub Co.
Moss, Stephen & Simons, Paul. Weather Watch. (Illus.). 112p. (Orig.). 1993. pap. 15.95 (*0-563-36486-6*, BBC-Parkwest) Parkwest Pubns.
Moss, Stirling. Fangio: A Pirelli Album. (Illus.). 168p. 1992. pap. 34.95 (*1-85145-872-7*, Pub. by Pavilion Bks Ltd UK) Motorbooks Intl.
***Moss, Susan.** Keep Your Breasts! Preventing Breast Cancer the Natural Way. LC 94-92245. (Illus.). 316p. (Orig.). 1994. pap. 19.95 (*0-9642329-0-1*) Res Pubns CA.
***Moss, Susan K. & Hopkins, William A., Jr.** Pharmacy Technician Certification Quick Study Guide. 100p. 1995. student ed 20.00 (*0-917330-72-2*) Am Pharm Assn.
***Moss, Sylvia.** Cities in Motion: Poems. LC 87-5003. (National Poetry Ser.). 69p. 1987. reprint ed. pap. 25.00 (*0-7837-8081-8*, 2047834) Bks Demand.
Moss, Sylvia, jt. auth. see Tubbs, Stewart L.
***Moss, T. S. & Balkanski, M., eds.** Optical Properties of Solids, Vol. 2. enl. rev. ed. (Handbook on Semiconductors Ser.: vol. 2). 872p. 1994. 308.75 (*0-444-89101-3*) Elsevier.
Moss, T. S. & Stenholm, S. Progress in Quantum Electronics, Vol. 6, Complete. (Illus.). 292p. 1981. 88.00 (*0-08-028387-X*, Pergamon Pr) Elsevier.
Moss, T. S., jt. auth. see Balkanski, M.
Moss, T. S., jt. ed. see Hilsum, C.
Moss, T. S., jt. auth. see Keller, S. P.
Moss, T. S., jt. ed. see Kneubuhl, Fritz K.
Moss, T. S., jt. ed. see Landsberg, Peter T.
Moss, T. S., jt. ed. see Paul, W.
Moss, T. S., jt. ed. see Schultz, G.
Moss, T. S., ed. see U. S. Specialty Group on Infrared Detectors.
Moss, T. S., et al, eds. Progress in Quantum Electronics, Vol. 8. (Illus.). 278p. 1985. 140.00 (*0-08-031718-9*, Pub. by PPL UK) Elsevier.
— Progress in Quantum Electronics, Vol. 9. (Illus.). 346p. 1999. 126.00 (*0-08-034010-5*, Pub. by PPL UK) Elsevier.
***Moss, Terry.** American History to the 1960s...the Final Exam. LC 94-77897. (Final Exam Ser.). 77p. 1994. pap. 5.49 (*1-885962-54-1*) Lincoln Lrning.
— Food & Drink...in a Nutshell. LC 94-77895. (Nutshell Ser.). 50p. 1994. pap. 4.95 (*1-885962-50-9*) Lincoln Lrning.
— Geography & Travel...in a Nutshell. LC 94-77901. (Nutshell Ser.). 60p. 1994. pap. 4.95 (*1-885962-53-3*) Lincoln Lrning.
— Literature...the Final Exam. LC 94-77900. (Final Exam Ser.). 68p. 1994. pap. 5.49 (*1-885962-57-6*) Lincoln Lrning.
— Nutty Poems for Nutty People. (Firelight Ser.). 60p. 1995. pap. 5.49 (*1-885962-62-2*) Lincoln Lrning.
— Photography, 35mm...in a Nutshell. LC 94-77896. (Nutshell Ser.). 52p. 1994. pap. 4.95 (*1-885962-51-7*) Lincoln Lrning.
— Poems for the Rhyming Impaired. (Firelight Ser.). 60p. 1995. pap. 5.49 (*1-885962-61-4*) Lincoln Lrning.
— Poems from the Hammock. (Firelight Ser.). 60p. 1995. pap. 5.49 (*1-885962-63-0*) Lincoln Lrning.
— Weight Training & Total Fitness...in a Nutshell. LC 94-77894. (Nutshell Ser.). 53p. 1994. pap. 4.95 (*1-885962-52-5*) Lincoln Lrning.
— World History to 1700...the Final Exam. LC 94-77898. (Final Exam Ser.). 60p. 1994. pap. 4.95 (*1-885962-56-8*) Lincoln Lrning.
— World History 1600 to 1960...the Final Exam. LC 94-77899. (Final Exam Ser.). 77p. 1994. pap. 5.49 (*1-885962-55-X*) Lincoln Lrning.
Moss, Thomas C. Fiscal Year Nineteen Seventy-Six Rating Factors: HUD Community Development Grant Program Non-Metropolitan Communities. 8p. (Orig.). 1975. pap. 1.00 (*1-55719-024-0*) U NE CPAR.

M

Moss, Thomas C. & O'Connor, Michael G. Community Development Needs in Rural Nebraska & Iowa. 16p. (Orig.). 1975. pap. 1.50 (*1-55719-026-7*) U NE CPAR.
Moss, Thomas H., jt. ed. see Lunstedt, Sven B.
***Moss, Thylia.** Somewhere Else Right Now. LC 94-37435. 1996. lib. bdg. write for info. (*0-8037-1747-4*); pap. write for info. (*0-8037-1746-6*) Dial Bks Young.
Moss, Thylias. At Redbones. (CSU Poetry Ser.: No. XXIX). 56p. (Orig.). 1990. pap. 7.00 (*0-914946-73-0*) Cleveland St Univ Poetry Ctr.
— Hosiery Seams on a Bowlegged Woman. (Orig.). pap. 4.50 (*0-318-18369-2*) League Bks.
— I Want to Be. LC 92-28965. (Illus.). 32p. (J). (ps-3). 1993. 14.99 (*0-8037-1286-3*); lib. bdg. 14.89 (*0-8037-1287-1*) Dial Bks Young.
— Pyramid of Bone. Rowell, Charles H., ed. LC 88-25855. (Callaloo Poetry Ser.). ix, 56p. 1989. pap. 9.95 (*0-8139-1202-4*) U Pr of Va.
— Rainbow Remnants in Rock Bottom Ghetto Sky: Poems. LC 90-23770. (National Poetry Ser.: 1990). 72p. (Orig.). 1991. pap. 9.95 (*0-89255-157-7*) Persea Bks.
— Small Congregations: New & Selected Poems. 1994. pap. 12.00 (*0-88001-363-X*) Ecco Pr.
— Small Congregations New & Selected Poems. 1993. 22.95 (*0-88001-289-7*) Ecco Pr.
Moss, Trevor S., et al. Semiconductor Opto-Electronics. LC 73-167813. 453p. reprint ed. pap. 129.20 (*0-317-41852-1*, 2025735) Bks Demand.
Moss, Troy, ed. see Reeder, Ellen D.
Moss, Troy, ed. see Zafran, Eric.
Moss, Veronica, jt. auth. see Sims, Ruth.
Moss, Veronica A., jt. auth. see Sims, Ruth.
Moss, Vladimir A. The Saints of Anglo-Saxon England. (Orig.). Date not set. pap. write for info. (*0-913026-33-6*) St Nectarios.
— The Saints of Anglo-Saxon England, Vol. I. LC 92-82557. (Illus.). 112p. (Orig.). 1992. pap. 8.50 (*0-913026-32-8*) St Nectarios.
— The Saints of Anglo-Saxon England, Vol. II. (Illus.). 128p. (Orig.). 1993. pap. 8.50 (*0-913026-34-4*) St Nectarios.
Moss, W. From Page to Screen: Children's Books on Film. 1992. 40.00 (*0-8103-7893-0*) Gale.
— Peoples of the World: Africa South Sahara 1, Vol. 3. 1991. 45.00 (*0-8103-7942-2*) Gale.
— Peoples of the World: Mid East, North Africa 1, Vol. 4. 1991. 45.00 (*0-8103-7941-4*) Gale.
Moss, W. & Wilson. People's of the World: ASNA & Pacific Islands 1, Vol. 7. 1993. 45.00 (*0-8103-8866-9*, 101508) Gale.
— People's of the World: Eastern Europeans & Russians, Vol. 5. 1992. 45.00 (*0-8103-8867-7*, 101509) Gale.
— People's of the World: Western Europeans 1, Vol. 6. 1993. 45.00 (*0-8103-8868-5*, 101510) Gale.
Moss, Wayne F. Know-It-All Guide to the Trinity Alps. 2nd ed. LC 81-80959. (Illus.). 144p. 1982. pap. 7.95 (*0-9606162-0-9*) Mossart.
Moss, William. Confederate Broadside Poems: An Annotated Descriptive Bibliography. (Illus.). 225p. 1988. text ed. 55.00 (*0-313-27704-4*) Greenwood.
— Corporation Report 2020. (Cyberpunk Ser.). (Illus.). 88p. (Orig.). 1991. pap. 10.00 (*0-614-02724-1*, CP3111) R Talsorian.
— Corporation Report 2020, Vol. 3. (Cyberpunk Ser.). (Illus.). 88p. (Orig.). 1992. pap. 10.00 (*0-937279-24-2*, CP3161) R Talsorian.
— Corporation Report 2020 Vol. 2. (Cyberpunk Ser.). (Illus.). 80p. (Orig.). 1992. pap. 10.00 (*0-937279-20-X*, CP3151) R Talsorian.
— Land of the Free. (Cyberpunk Ser.). (Illus.). 120p. (Orig.). 1994. boxed, pap. 18.00 (*0-937279-38-2*, CP3231) R Talsorian.
— Tales of the Forlorn Hope. (Cyberpunk Ser.). (Illus.). 104p. (Orig.). 1992. pap. 10.00 (*0-937279-21-8*, CP3121) R Talsorian.
— The Wisdom of Oat: An American Indian Philosophy. 100p. 1993. pap. 10.00 (*0-9637830-3-3*) Triangle Books.
***Moss, William A.** 10-Minute Card Games. LC 95-22505. (Illus.). 96p. 1995. pap. 4.95 (*0-8069-3847-1*) Sterling.
Moss, William M., jt. auth. see AVSC Staff.
Moss, William R. School Desegregation, Enough Is Enough. 216p. 1992. 19.95 (*0-9634115-0-0*) Danmo Pub Co.
Mossa, Joann, jt. auth. see Henry, James.
Mossava-Rahmani, Bijan, et al. Lower Oil Prices: Mapping the Impact. LC 87-83646. (International Energy Studies: No. 4). x, 109p. (Orig.). 1988. pap. 21.50 (*0-942781-03-1*) Harvard EEPC.
Mossavar-Rahmani, Bijan, ed. Natural Gas Trade in Transition. LC 87-81051. (International Energy Studies: No. 1). x, 91p. (Orig.). 1987. pap. 16.50 (*0-942781-00-7*) Harvard EEPC.
Mossavar-Rahmani, Bijan, et al. Natural Gas in Western Europe: Structure, Strategies, & Politics. LC 87-81459. viii, 68p. (Orig.). 1987. pap. 16.50 (*0-942781-01-5*) Harvard EEPC.
Mossberg, Barbara A. Emily Dickinson: When a Writer is a Daughter. LC 80-8633. 224p. reprint ed. pap. 63.90 (*0-7837-3721-1*, 2057899) Bks Demand.
Mossberg, Christer L. Scandinavian Immigrant Literature. (Western Writers Ser.: No. 47). (Illus.). 52p. (Orig.). 1981. pap. 3.95 (*0-88430-071-4*) Boise St U W Writ Ser.
Mossberg, O. F. Mossberg's Guide to Modern Slug Shooting . . . & More. Stoeger Industries Staff, ed. (Illus.). 96p. (Orig.). 1989. pap. text ed. write for info. (*0-318-65856-9*) O F Mossberg & Sons.
***Mossberg, Walter S.** The Wall Street Journal Book of Personal Technology. 1995. pap. 15.00 (*0-8129-2602-1*) Random.
— The Wall Street Journal on Personal Technology. LC 95-12196. 1995. pap. write for info. (*0-614-05424-9*, Times Bks) Random.
***Mosse, Claude.** Dictionnaire de la Civilisation Grecque. 512p. (FRE.). 1992. 125.00 (*0-7859-8173-X*, 2870274416) Fr & Eur.
— Fin de la Democratie Atheniennn: Aspects Sociaux et Politiques du Declin de la Cite Grecque au le Siecle avant J.-C. la Vie Economique d'Athenes au le Siecle: Crise ou Renouveau? Finley, Moses, ed. LC 79-4995. (Ancient Economic History Ser.). (FRE.). 1979. reprint ed. lib. bdg. 48.95 (*0-405-12382-5*) Ayer.
Mosse, Fernand. Handbook of Middle English. rev. ed. Walker, James A., tr. LC 68-17255. (Illus.). 519p. (C). 1969. reprint ed. 39.95 (*0-8018-0478-7*) Johns Hopkins.
Mosse, George L. Confronting the Nation: Jewish & Western Nationalism. LC 93-17227. (Tauber Institute for the Study of European Jewry Ser.: Vol. 16). 232p. 1993. text ed. 35.00 (*0-87451-635-8*); pap. 15.95 (*0-87451-636-6*) U Pr of New Eng.
— The Culture of Western Europe: The Nineteenth & Twentieth Centuries. 3rd ed. 430p. (C). 1988. pap. text ed. 26.50 (*0-8133-0623-X*) Westview.
— Fallen Soldiers: Reshaping the Memory of the World Wars. (Illus.). 272p. 1990. 24.95 (*0-19-506247-7*) OUP.
— Fallen Soldiers: Reshaping the Memory of the World Wars. (Illus.). 272p. 1991. reprint ed. pap. 10.95 (*0-19-507139-5*) OUP.
— German Jews Beyond Judaism. LC 84-42841. (Modern Jewish Experience Ser.). (Illus.). 112p. 1985. 25.00 (*0-253-32575-7*); pap. 7.95 (*0-253-20355-4*, MB-355) Ind U Pr.
— Germans & Jews: The Right, the Left, & the Search for a 'Third Force' in Pre-Nazi Germany. LC 68-9631. 1970. 35.00 (*0-86527-081-3*) Fertig.
— Germans & Jews: The Right, the Left & the Search for a "Third Force" in Pre-Nazi Germany. LC 87-6148. 270p. 1987. reprint ed. pap. 19.95 (*0-8143-1893-2*) Wayne St U Pr.
— Masses & Man: Nationalist & Fascist Perceptions of Reality. LC 80-15399. xi, 362p. 1980. 45.00 (*0-86527-334-0*) Fertig.
— Masses & Man: Nationalist & Fascist Perceptions of Reality. LC 87-6131. 374p. 1987. reprint ed. pap. 16.95 (*0-8143-1895-9*) Wayne St U Pr.
— Nationalism & Sexuality: Middle-Class Morality & Sexual Norms in Modern Europe. LC 88-5547. 250p. (C). 1988. reprint ed. pap. text ed. 14.50 (*0-299-11894-0*) U of Wis Pr.
— Nationalism & Sexuality: Respectabilty & Abnormal Sexuality in Modern Europe. LC 84-6082. (Illus.). 256p. 1985. 40.00 (*0-86527-350-2*) Fertig.
— The Nationalization of the Masses: Political Symbolism & Mass Movements in Germany, from the Napoleonic Wars Through the Third Reich. LC 91-55260. (Illus.). 272p. 1991. pap. 14.95 (*0-8014-9978-X*) Cornell U Pr.
— The Nationalization of the Masses: Political Symbolism & Mass Movements in Germany, from the Napoleonic Wars Through the Third Reich. LC 74-11105. (Illus.). xiv, 272p. 1975. 40.00 (*0-86527-140-2*) Fertig.
— Nazi Culture. LC 80-26608. 432p. 1981. reprint ed. pap. 15.16 (*0-8052-0668-X*) Schocken.
— The Reformation. rev. ed. (Illus.). 64p. (C). 1991. pap. text ed. 2.25 (*1-877891-02-9*) Paperbook Pr Inc.
— Toward the Final Solution: A History of European Racism. LC 77-24356. (Illus.). 1978. 40.00 (*0-86527-941-1*) Fertig.
— Toward the Final Solution: A History of European Racism. LC 84-40501. (Illus.). 324p. 1985. reprint ed. pap. text ed. 16.95 (*0-299-10184-3*) U of Wis Pr.
Mosse, George L., ed. Police Forces in History. LC 74-84258. 344p. reprint ed. pap. 98.10 (*0-317-29602-7*, 2021935) Bks Demand.
Mosse, George L., jt. auth. see Reinhartz, Jehuda.
Mosse, George L., jt. ed. see Vago, Bela.
Mosse, Hilde. You Can Prevent or Correct Learning Disorders: The Complete Handbook of Children's Reading Disorders. 732p. (C). 1989. reprint ed. pap. text ed. 34.95 (*0-8077-2983-3*) Tchrs Coll.
Mosse, Hilde L. The Complete Handbook of Children's Reading Disorders: You Can Prevent or Correct Learning Disorders. 2nd ed. (Illus.). 714p. (Orig.). 1987. pap. text ed. 34.95 (*0-942311-00-0*) Riggs Inst Pr.
Mosse, Julia & Heaton, Josephine. The Fertility & Contraception Book. (Illus.). 400p. (Orig.). 1991. pap. 13.95 (*0-571-15173-6*) Faber & Faber.
Mosse, Julia C. Half the World: Half the Chance: An Introduction to Gender & Development. 240p. (C). 1992. text ed. 100.00 (*0-85598-185-7*, Pub. by Oxfam Pubns UK); pap. text ed. 60.00 (*0-85598-186-5*, Pub. by Oxfam Pubns UK) St Mut.
— India: Paths to Development. (C). 1991. pap. text ed. 21.00 (*0-85598-153-9*, Pub. by Oxfam Pubns UK) St Mut.
Mosse, W. E. Alexander the Second & the Modernization of Russia. 200p. 1992. 39.50 (*0-685-51843-4*, Pub. by I B Tauris UK) St Martin.
— The German-Jewish Economic Elite, 1820-1935: A Socio-Cultural Profile. (Illus.). 384p. 1989. 78.00 (*0-19-822990-9*) OUP.
***Mosse, Werner E., et al, eds.** Second Chance. xii, 654p. 1991. 79.00 (*3-16-145741-2*, Pub. by J C B Mohr GW) Coronet Bks.
Mosse, Werner E., et al. Revolution & Evolution 1848 in German-Jewish History. 443p. 1981. lib. bdg. 79.50x (*3-16-743752-9*, Pub. by J C B Mohr GW) Coronet Bks.
Mossek, M. Palestine Immigration Policy under Sir Herbert Samuel: British, Zionist & Arab Attitudes. 197p. 1978. 35.00 (*0-7146-3096-9*, Pub. by F Cass Pubs UK) Intl Spec Bk.
Mossel, Bob. Atlas of South Australia. 148p. (C). 1989. text ed. 120.00 (*0-89771-032-0*, Pub. by Bob Mossel AT) St Mut.
— Learning & Other Things: The History of Education in South Australia. 496p. (C). 1989. pap. text ed. 60.00 (*0-89771-025-8*, Pub. by Bob Mossel AT) St Mut.
— Light Aircraft Adventure into PNG. (C). 1989. pap. text ed. 45.00 (*0-89771-019-3*, Pub. by Bob Mossel AT) St Mut.
— Where No Road Goes. 104p. (C). 1989. text ed. 75.00 (*0-89771-017-7*, Pub. by Bob Mossel AT) St Mut.
Mossel, Bob & Kuhne, D. Beyond Lake Eyre. 112p. (C). 1989. text ed. 75.00 (*0-89771-016-9*, Pub. by Bob Mossel AT) St Mut.
Mossel, Bob, jt. auth. see Kotwicki, V.
Mossel, Bob, et al. The Great Nineteen Seventy-Four Filling of Lake Eyre. 136p. (C). 1989. pap. text ed. 40.00 (*0-89771-034-7*, Pub. by Bob Mossel AT) St Mut.
Mossel, D. A., et al. Essentials of the Microbiology of Foods: A Textbook of Advanced Studies. 725p. 1994. text ed. 124.95 (*0-471-93036-9*) Wiley.
Mossell, N. F. The Work of the Afro-American Woman. LC 72-161270. (Black Heritage Library Collection). 1977. reprint ed. 27.95 (*0-8369-8829-9*) Ayer.
— The Work of the Afro-American Woman. (Schomburg Library of Nineteenth-Century Black Women Writers). 224p. 1988. reprint ed. 21.00 (*0-19-505265-X*) OUP.
— The Work of the Afro-American Woman. (Schomburg Library of Nineteenth-Century Black Women Writers). 224p. 1990. reprint ed. pap. 9.95 (*0-19-506326-0*) OUP.
Mossenbock, Hanspeter. Object-Oriented Programming in Oberon-2. Bach, Robert, tr. LC 93-10033. 278p. 1993. pap. text ed. 39.00 (*0-387-56411-X*) Spr-Verlag.
Mossenson, David. Hebrew, Israelite, Jew: The History of the Jews of Western Australia. 1991. 29.95 (*0-85564-314-5*, Pub. by Univ of West Aust Pr AT) Intl Spec Bk.
Mosser, David, jt. auth. see Laney, Joan.
Mosser, Marjorie. Good Maine Food. 424p. 1978. reprint ed. pap. 10.95 (*0-89272-038-7*) Down East.
Mosser, Monique & Teyssot, Georges. The Architecture of Western Gardens: A Design History from the Renaissance to the Present Day. (Illus.). 544p. 1991. 135.00x (*0-262-13264-8*) MIT Pr.
Mosses, Peter D. Action Semantics. (Tracts in Theoretical Computer Science Ser.: No. 26). 400p. (C). 1992. 54.95 (*0-521-40347-2*) Cambridge U Pr.
Mosses, Peter D., ed. see Sixth International Joint Conference on Theory & Practice of Software Development Staff, et al.
Mossetto, Gianfranco. Aesthetics & Economics. LC 93-15476. 232p. (C). 1993. Acid-free paper. lib. bdg. 104.00 (*0-7923-2296-7*) Kluwer Ac.
Mosshammer, Alden A. The Chronicle of Eusebius & Greek Chronographic Tradition. LC 76-1029. 366p. 1979. 40.00 (*0-8387-1939-2*) Bucknell U Pr.
Mossholder, Ray. Kids Are a Plus. 1995. pap. 9.99 (*0-88419-357-8*, Creation Hse) Strang Comms Co.
— Marriage Plus. LC 90-81609. 1990. pap. 9.99 (*0-88419-301-2*) Strang Comms Co.
— Singles Plus. LC 91-55230. 1991. pap. 9.99 (*0-88419-290-3*) Strang Comms Co.
Mossi, John & Toolan, Suzanne. Canticles & Gathering Prayers. 148p. 1989. spiral bd. 9.95 (*0-88489-228-X*) St Marys.
***Mossi, John P.** Prayers from the Cross: Solace for All Seasons. LC 94-34750. (Illus.). 80p. 1995. pap. 4.95 (*0-8091-3524-8*) Paulist Pr.
Mossiker, Frances. Madame de Sevigne: A Life & Letters. LC 85-4096. 560p. 1985. reprint ed. pap. text ed. 19.50 (*0-231-06153-6*) Col U Pr.
Mossin, Albert C. Selling Performance & Contentment in Relation to School Background. LC 79-177093. (Columbia University. Teachers College. Contributions to Education Ser.: No. 952). reprint ed. 37.50 (*0-404-55952-2*) AMS Pr.
***Mossinger, Rosemarie.** Woodleaf Legacy. rev. ed. Chapman, Jean, ed. LC 94-77982. (Illus.). 180p. (J). (gr. 5-8). 1994. 34.95 (*0-614-00309-1*); pap. 19.95 (*0-9621940-4-2*) C Mautz Pubng.
Mossinghoff, Michael J., jt. auth. see Blachman, Nancy R.
Mosslacher, Egon. Breeding & Caring for Chinchillas. (Illus.). 52p. 1989. 12.95 (*0-86622-118-2*, PS-850) TFH Pubns.
Mossle, Klaus P. Extraterritoriale Beweisbeschaffung im Internationalen Wirtschaftsrecht: Eine Vergleichende Untersuchung unter Besonderer Berucksichtigung des Amerikanischen & Deutschen Rechts. 533p. 1990. pap. 100.00 (*3-7890-1888-0*, Pub. by Nomos Verlags GW) Intl Bk Import.
Mossman, B. C. & Stark, M. W. Last Salute: Civil & Military Funerals, 1921-1969. (Illus.). 450p. 1990. reprint ed. per. 16.00 (*0-16-024685-7*, S/N 008-029-00086-5) USGPO.
Mossman, B. T. & Begin, R. O., eds. Effects of Mineral Dusts on Cells. (NATO ASI Series H: Vol. 30). (Illus.). 155p. 1989. 139.00 (*0-387-50422-2*, 3117) Spr-Verlag.
Mossman, Billy C. United States Army in the Korean War: Ebb & Flow, Nov. 1950-July 1951. LC 89-600137. (Illus.). 569p. 1990. boxed 31.00 (*0-16-023486-7*, S/N 008-029-00210-8); per. 28.00 (*0-16-023487-5*) USGPO.
Mossman, Carol A. The Narrative Matrix: Stendhal's "Le Rouge & le Noir" LC 84-80768. (French Forum Monographs: No. 53). 177p. (Orig.). 1984. pap. 13.45 (*0-917058-53-4*) French Forum.
— Politics & Narratives of Birth: Gynocolonization from Rousseau to Zola. (Cambridge Studies in French: No. 41). 264p. (C). 1993. 59.95 (*0-521-41586-1*) Cambridge U Pr.
Mossman, Harland W. Vertebrate Fetal Membranes Comparative Ontogeny & Morphology; Evolution; Phylogenetic Significance, Basic Functions; Research Opportunities. 400p. 1987. text ed. 100.00 (*0-8135-1132-1*) Rutgers U Pr.
Mossman, Harland W. & Duke, Kenneth L. Comparative Morphology of the Mammalian Ovary. LC 72-143765. (Illus.). 492p. 1975. pap. 20.00 (*0-299-05934-0*) U of Wis Pr.
Mossman, Jennifer. Acronyms Initialisms & Abbreviations Dictionary, 3 pts. 19th ed. 1994. write for info. (*0-318-68502-7*) Gale.
— Acronyms Initialisms & Abbreviations Dictionary, Pt. 1, A-F. 18th ed. 1993. write for info. (*0-8103-8204-0*) Gale.
— Acronyms Initialisms & Abbreviations Dictionary, Pt. 2, G-O. 18th ed. 1993. write for info. (*0-8103-8205-9*) Gale.
— Acronyms Initialisms & Abbreviations Dictionary, Pt. 3, P-Z. 18th ed. 1993. write for info. (*0-8103-8206-7*) Gale.
— Acronyms Initialisms & Abbreviations Dictionary, Vol. 1. 18th ed. 1993. 245.00 (*0-8103-8203-2*) Gale.
— Acronyms Initialisms & Abbreviations Dictionary, Vol. 1. 19th ed. 1994. 245.00 (*0-8103-5566-3*, 030045) Gale.
— New Acronyms Initialisms & Abbreviations, Vol. 2. 19th ed. 1994. 250.00 (*0-8103-5570-1*, 030047) Gale.
— Reverse Acronyms, Initialisms & Abbreviations Dictionary, Vol. 3. 19th ed. 1994. 250.00 (*0-8103-5562-0*) Gale.
— Reverse Acronyms, Initialisms & Abbreviations Dictionary, Vol. 3, 19th Pt. 2. 1994. write for info. (*0-8103-5564-7*) Gale.
— Reverse Acronyms, Initialisms & Abbreviations Dictionary, Vol. 3, 19th Pt. 3. 1994. write for info. (*0-8103-5565-5*) Gale.
— Reverse Acronyms, Initialisms & Abbreviations Dictionary, Vol. 3, Pt. 1. 19th ed. 1994. write for info. (*0-8103-5563-9*, 101359) Gale.
Mossman, Jennifer, ed. Encyclopedia of Geographic Information Sources. 4th ed. 428p. 1986. International Vol. 120.00 (*0-8103-0410-4*) Gale.
— Encyclopedia of Geographic Information Sources, 2 vols., Set. 4th ed. 1986. 250.00 (*0-8103-4253-7*, 009660-99584) Gale.
— Encyclopedia of Geographic Information Sources: International Volume. 4th ed. (Encyclopedia of Geographic Information Sources Ser.). 450p. 1987. 145.00 (*0-8103-0415-5*) Gale.
— Holidays & Anniversaries of the World. 2nd ed. 1080p. 1989. 95.00 (*0-8103-4870-5*, 004466-M94871) Gale.
— Pseudonyms & Nicknames Dictionary, 2 vols., Set. 3rd ed. 2207p. 1986. 235.00 (*0-8103-0541-0*) Gale.
— Reverse Acronyms, Initialisms & Abbreviations Dictionary, 3 Pts., Vol. 3. 18th ed. 3800p. 1993. 280.00 (*0-8103-8207-5*, 030044) Gale.
— Reverse International Acronyms, Initialisms & Abbreviations Dictionary. 3rd ed. 1300p. 1993. 205.00 (*0-8103-7367-X*, 009241) Gale.
Mossman, Jennifer & Ruffner, James A., eds. Eponyms Dictionaries Index: A Reference Guide to Persons, Both Real & Imaginary, & the Terms Derived from Their Names. suppl. ed. 248p. 1984. 94.00 (*0-8103-0689-1*) Gale.
***Mossman, Judith.** Wild Justice: A Study in Euripides' Hecuba. (Oxford Classical Monographs). (Illus.). 304p. 1995. text ed. 55.00 (*0-19-814789-9*) OUP.
Mossman, Lois Coffey. Changing Conception Relative to the Planning of Lessons. LC 72-177094. (Columbia University. Teachers College. Contributions to Education Ser.: No. 147). reprint ed. 37.50 (*0-404-55147-5*) AMS Pr.
Mossman, Marilyn. Introduction to Logo, Bk. 1. Schroeder, Bonnie, ed. 1989. pap. text ed. 5.95 (*1-56177-109-0*, 402-1) CES Compu-Tech.
— Introduction to Logo, Bk. 2. Schroeder, Bonnie, ed. (Illus.). 1989. pap. text ed. 5.95 (*1-56177-110-4*, 402-2) CES Compu-Tech.
— Introduction to Logo: Lab Pack 1. Schroeder, Bonnie, ed. (Illus.). student ed, teacher ed 199.95 (*1-56177-113-9*, L402-1); disk 15.95 (*1-56177-111-2*, D402-1) CES Compu-Tech.
— Introduction to Logo: Lab Pack 2. Schroeder, Bonnie, ed. (Illus.). student ed, teacher ed 199.95 (*1-56177-114-7*, L402-2); disk 15.95 (*1-56177-112-0*, D402-2) CES Compu-Tech.
— Introduction to Logo, Pt. 1: Teacher Edition. Schroeder, Bonnie, ed. (Illus.). 1989. 19.95 (*1-56177-115-5*, TE402-1) CES Compu-Tech.
— Introduction to Logo, Pt. 2: Teacher Edition. Schroeder, Bonnie, ed. (Illus.). 1989. 19.95 (*1-56177-116-3*, TE402-2) CES Compu-Tech.
— Introduction to Word Processing: Course Code 182-N. Schroeder, Bonnie, ed. (Illus.). 141p. (Orig.). (gr. 4). 1989. pap. text ed. 8.95 (*0-917531-59-0*) CES Compu-Tech.
— Introduction to Word Processing: Lab Pack. Schroeder, Bonnie, ed. (Illus.). student ed, teacher ed 179.95 (*1-56177-053-1*, L182); 5.25 hd 8.95 (*1-56177-052-3*, D-182) CES Compu-Tech.
— Skill Builders: Lab Pack 1. Schroeder, Bonnie, ed. (Illus.). teacher ed 19.95 (*1-56177-123-6*, TE492-1); student ed 5.95 (*1-56177-117-1*, 492-1); student ed, teacher ed 199.95 (*1-56177-121-X*, L492-1) CES Compu-Tech.
— Skill Builders: Lab Pack 2. Schroeder, Bonnie, ed. (Illus.). teacher ed 19.95 (*1-56177-124-4*, TE492-2); student ed 5.95 (*1-56177-118-X*); student ed, teacher ed 199.95 (*1-56177-122-8*, L492-2) CES Compu-Tech.
Mossman, Marilyn & Roberts, Diane. Introduction to Word Processing Teacher Edition: Course Code 182 N. Schroeder, Bonnie, ed. (Illus.). 150p. (Orig.). 1989. 19.95 (*0-917531-75-2*) CES Compu-Tech.
Mossman, Philip. Money of the American Colonies & Confederation: A Numismatic, Economic & Historical Correlation. (Numismatic Studies: No. 20). 100.00 (*0-89722-249-0*) Am Numismatic.

An Asterisk (*) at the beginning of an entry indicates that the title is appearing in BIP for the first time.

***Mossman, S. T. & Morris, P. J., eds.** The Development of Plastics. 120p. 1994. 65.00 (*0-85186-575-5*, R6575) CRC Pr.

Mossman, Tam, ed. Answers from a Grander Self. 221p. (Orig.). 1995. pap. 12.95 (*0-9632947-0-9*) Tiger Maple Pr.

Mossner, Ernest C. Bishop Butler & the Age of Reason. LC 69-13247. 1972. reprint ed. 18.95 (*0-405-08807-8*, Pub. by Blom Pubns UK) Ayer.

Mossner, Ernest C., ed. see Smith, Adam.

Mossner, Ernest G., ed. see Hume, David.

Mosston, Muska & Ashworth, Sara. Teaching Physical Education. 4th ed. 288p. (C). 1994. pap. write for info. (*0-02-384183-4*) Macmillan.

Most, Benjamin A. Changing Authoritarian Rule & Public Policy in Argentina, 1930-1970. LC 90-42342. (GSIS Monograph in World Affairs). 206p. 1990. lib. bdg. 25.00 (*1-55587-246-8*) Lynne Rienner.

Most, Benjamin A. & Starr, Harvey. Inquiry, Logic & International Politics. Kegley, Charles W., Jr. & Puchala, Donald J., eds. (Studies in International Relations). 244p. 1989. text ed. 39.95 (*0-87249-613-9*); pap. text ed. 21.95 (*0-87249-630-9*) U of SC Pr.

Most, Bernard. Can You Find It? LC 92-33691. (J). (ps-3). 1993. 13.95 (*0-15-292872-3*) HarBrace.

— Catbirds & Dogfish. LC 94-17839. (J). 1995. 13.00 (*0-15-292844-8*) HarBrace.

— Catbirds & Dogfish. LC 94-17839. (J). (ps-3). 1995. pap. 5.00 (*0-15-200779-2*) HarBrace.

— The Cow That Went Oink. (Illus.). 32p. (J). (ps-00). 1990. 10.00 (*0-15-220195-5*) HarBrace.

— Cow That Went Oink. (Big Bks.). 30p. (J). (ps-1). 1991. pap. 19.95 (*0-15-220196-3*, HB Juv Bks) HarBrace.

— Dinosaur Cousins? LC 86-18485. (Illus.). 40p. (J). (ps-3). 1987. 13.95 (*0-15-223497-7*, HB Juv Bks) HarBrace.

— Dinosaur Cousins? 32p. (J). (ps-3). 1990. pap. 4.95 (*0-15-223498-5*, Voyager Bks) HarBrace.

— A Dinosaur Named after Me. D'Andrade, Diane, ed. (Illus.). 32p. (J). (ps-3). 1991. 12.95 (*0-15-223494-2*) HarBrace.

— Dinosaur Named after Me. LC 90-36272. (J). (ps-2). 1995. pap. 5.00 (*0-15-223493-4*, Voyager Bks) HarBrace.

— Dinosaur Questions. LC 94-42630. (J). 1995. write for info. (*0-15-292885-5*) HarBrace.

— Four & Twenty Dinosaurs. LC 89-34472. (Illus.). 40p. (J). (ps-2). 1990. lib. bdg. 14.89 (*0-06-024377-5*) HarpC Child Bks.

— Happy Holidaysaurus! (J). 1992. 13.95 (*0-15-233386-X*, HB Juv Bks) HarBrace.

— Hippopotamus Hunt. LC 93-39988. (J). 1994. 14.95 (*0-15-234520-5*) HarBrace.

— How Big Were the Dinosaurs? LC 93-19152. (Illus.). (J). 1994. 15.00 (*0-15-236800-0*, HB Juv Bks) HarBrace.

— If the Dinosaurs Came Back. LC 77-23911. (Illus.). (J). (ps-2). 1978. 13.95 (*0-15-238020-5*, HB Juv Bks) HarBrace.

— If the Dinosaurs Came Back. LC 77-23911. (Illus.). 32p. (J). (ps-2). 1984. pap. 4.95 (*0-15-238021-3*, Voyager Bks) HarBrace.

— If the Dinosaurs Came Back. (Illus.). (J). (gr. k-3). 1991. audio 22.95 (*0-87499-237-0*); audio, pap. 14.95 (*0-87499-236-2*) Live Oak Media.

— If the Dinosaurs Came Back. (Big Bks.). (Illus.). 32p. (J). (ps-2). 1991. reprint ed. pap. 19.95 (*0-15-238022-1*) HarBrace.

— If the Dinosaurs Came Back, 4 bks., Set. (Illus.). (J). (gr. k-3). 1991. audio, pap. 31.95 (*0-87499-238-9*) Live Oak Media.

— The Littlest Dinosaurs. (Illus.). 30p. (J). (ps-3). 1989. 13.95 (*0-15-248125-7*) HarBrace.

— The Littlest Dinosaurs. (Illus.). (J). (gr. 4-6). 1993. audio, pap. 14.95 (*0-614-06494-5*) Live Oak Media.

— Littlest Dinosaurs. LC 88-30063. (J). (ps-3). 1993. pap. 5.95 (*0-15-248126-5*) HarBrace.

— My Very Own Octopus. D'Andrade, Diane, ed. (Illus.). 32p. (J). (ps-3). 1991. pap. 4.95 (*0-15-256345-8*, Voyager Bks) HarBrace.

— Pets in Trumpets & Other Word-Play Riddles. (J). (ps-3). 1991. 12.95 (*0-15-261210-6*, HB Juv Bks) HarBrace.

— There's an Ant in Anthony. LC 79-23089. (Illus.). 32p. (J). (gr. k-3). 1980. lib. bdg. 13.93 (*0-688-32226-3*); pap. 3.95 (*0-688-11513-6*, Mulberry) Morrow Jr Bks.

— La Vaca Que Decia Oink. Mlawrer, Teresa, tr. (Illus.). 32p. (SPA.). (J). Date not set. 12.95 (*1-880507-14-5*) Lectorum Pubns.

— Whatever Happened to the Dinosaurs? LC 84-3779. (Illus.). 30p. (J). (ps-3). 1984. 13.95 (*0-15-295295-0*, HB Juv Bks) HarBrace.

— Whatever Happened to the Dinosaurs? LC 84-37795. (Voyager Picture Bks.). (Illus.). 32p. (J). (ps-3). 1987. pap. 4.95 (*0-15-295296-9*, Voyager Bks) HarBrace.

— Where to Look for a Dinosaur. LC 92-19443. (J). 1993. 12.95 (*0-15-295616-6*, HB Juv Bks) HarBrace.

— Zoodles. (J). 1992. 13.95 (*0-15-299969-8*, HB Juv Bks) HarBrace.

— Zoodles. LC 91-33490. (J). (ps-3). 1994. pap. 19.95 (*0-15-200071-2*, HB Juv Bks) HarBrace.

Most, Bernard & Freeman, Don. Corduroy: (Edicion Espanola) (Illus.). (SPA.). (J). (gr. 4-6). 1993. reprint ed. audio 22.95 (*0-87499-192-7*) Live Oak Media.

— Corduroy: (Edicion Espanola), 4 bks., Set. (Illus.). (SPA.). (J). (gr. 4-6). 1993. reprint ed. audio, pap. 33.95 (*0-87499-193-5*) Live Oak Media.

Most, Clark F. Experimental Organic Chemistry. LC 87-21653. 586p. 1988. Net. text ed. write for info. (*0-471-82043-1*) Wiley.

Most, Glenn W., ed. see Conte, Gian B.

Most, Glenn W., tr. see Conte, Gian Biagio.

***Most, Howard H.** Our Fragile Planet. 280p. 1995. pap. 8.95 (*1-56901-871-5*) NW Pub.

Most, J. Science of Revolutionary Warfare: A Guide for Would-Be Anarchists. (Anarchists & Anarchism Ser.). 1990. lib. bdg. 79.95 (*0-87700-887-6*) Revisionist Pr.

Most, Johann. Science of Revolutionary Warfare. (Explosives, Incendiaries & Demolitions Ser.: No. 2). 1990. lib. bdg. 79.95 (*0-8490-3993-2*) Gordon Pr.

Most, John. Revolutionaire Kriegswissenschaft. Bd. with Beast of Property. (History of Political Violence Ser.). 1985. reprint ed. Set lib. bdg. 30.00 (*0-527-41194-9*) Periodicals Srv.

Most, Johnny. Feelings: Private Thoughts & Poems. LC 92-71501. (Illus.). 104p. (Orig.). 1992. pap. 13.95 (*0-9632856-0-2*) Charm Pub Co.

Most, Kenneth S. The Future of the Accounting Profession: A Global Perspective. LC 92-34945. 240p. 1993. text ed. 55.00 (*0-89930-726-4*, MUT, Quorum Bks) Greenwood.

Most, Kenneth S., ed. Advances in International Accounting, Vol. 2. 1988. 73.25 (*0-89232-694-8*) Jai Pr.

— Advances in International Accounting, Vol. 3. 249p. (-). 1990. 73.25 (*1-55938-078-0*) Jai Pr.

— Research in Accounting Regulation, Vol. 1. 1988. 73.25 (*0-89232-693-X*); write for info. (*0-317-58932-6*) Jai Pr.

Most, Kenneth S., tr. see Schmalenbach, Eugen.

***Most, Philippe.** Dictionnaire de Medecine du Sport. 274p. (FRE.). 1987. pap. 95.00 (*0-7859-7828-3*, 2225810176) Fr & Eur.

Most, Rachel, jt. ed. see Kelso, William M.

Most, Robert, jt. ed. see Zeidner, Moshe.

Most, Stephen, ed. see Sakharov, Alexander.

***Most, William.** The Thought of St. Paul: A Commentary on the Pauline Epistles. 301p. (Orig.). 1994. pap. 14.95 (*0-931888-56-5*) Christendom Pr.

Most, William G. Catholic Apologetics Today: Answers to Modern Critics: Does It Make Sense to Believe? LC 86-50853. 272p. (C). 1986. pap. 8.00 (*0-89555-305-8*) TAN Bks Pubs.

— The Consciousness of Christ. LC 80-68761. 232p. (Orig.). 1980. pap. text ed. 6.95 (*0-931888-03-4*) Christendom Pr.

— Free from All Error: Authorship, Inerrancy, Historicity of Scripture, Church Teaching, & Modern Scripture Scholars. 179p. (Orig.). 1985. pap. 11.95 (*0-913382-51-5*, 101-31) Prow Bks-Franciscan.

— The Heart Has Its Reasons: The Sacred Heart of Jesus & the Immaculate Heart of Mary. 35p. (Orig.). 1985. pap. 1.50 (*0-913382-50-7*, 105-40) Prow Bks-Franciscan.

— Our Father's Plan: God's Arrangements & Our Response. 276p. 1993. reprint ed. pap. 7.95 (*0-931888-50-6*) Christendom Pr.

***Mostacchi, Massimo.** A Dog's Best Friend. LC 95-8434. (Illus.). (J). 1995. write for info. (*1-55858-497-8*) North-South Bks NYC.

— A Dog's Best Friend. LC 95-8434. (Illus.). (J). 1995. lib. bdg. write for info. (*1-55858-498-6*) North-South Bks NYC.

***Mostacchi, Masssimo & Miceli, Monica.** The Beast & the Boy. LC 94-44060. Orig. Title: Marcolino und das Monster. (Illus.). 32p. (J). (gr. k-3). 1995. 14.95 (*1-55858-443-9*); lib. bdg. 14.88 (*1-55858-444-7*) North-South Bks NYC.

Mostaert, Antoine & Cleaves, Francis W., eds. Lettres De 1289 et 1305 Des Ilkhan Argun et Oljeitu A. Philippe Le Bel. LC 62-19219. (Harvard-Yenching Institute, Scripta Mongolica Ser.: No. 1). (Illus.). 111p. (FRE.). 1962. pap. 10.00 (*0-674-52850-6*) HUP.

Mostafa, Javed, et al. The Easy Internet Handbook. 130p. 1994. pap. text ed. 20.00 (*0-931510-50-3*) Hi Willow.

Mostafa, Sobhy M., ed. Anaesthesia for Ophthalmic Surgery. (Illus.). 352p. 1992. 85.00 (*0-19-261960-8*) OUP.

Mostafavi, Mohsen & Leatherbarrow, David. On Weathering: The Life of Buildings in Time. (Illus.). 150p. 1993. 31.50 (*0-262-13291-5*); pap. 14.95 (*0-262-63144-X*) MIT Pr.

Mostafavi, Mohsen, jt. auth. see Fardjadi, Homa.

Mostecky, Vaclav, jt. auth. see Ruggles, Melville J.

Mosteller, F. & Wallace, D. L. Applied Bayesian & Classical Inference: The Case of the Federalist Papers. 2nd ed. LC 84-5489. (Series in Statistics). (Illus.). 290p. 1984. 49.00 (*0-387-90991-5*) Spr-Verlag.

Mosteller, Frederick. Fifty Challenging Problems in Probability with Solutions. viii, 88p. 1987. reprint ed. pap. text ed. 3.95 (*0-486-65355-2*) Dover.

Mosteller, Frederick & Tukey, John W. Data Analysis & Regression: A Second Course in Statistics. LC 76-15465. (Behavioral Science Ser.). 608p. (C). 1977. text ed. 64.50 (*0-201-04854-X*, Adv Bk Prog) Addison-Wesley.

Mosteller, Frederick, jt. ed. see Bailar, John C., III.

Mosteller, Frederick, jt. ed. see Frazier, Howard S.

Mosteller, Frederick, jt. ed. see Lovie, A. D.

Mosteller, Frederick, jt. ed. see Warren, Kenneth S.

Mosteller, Lee. Survival English Three. 192p. 1994. pap. text ed. 11.25 (*0-13-878166-4*) P-H.

— Survival English 3A. Date not set. write for info. (*0-13-017005-4*) P-H.

— Survival English 3B. Date not set. pap. write for info. (*0-13-017013-5*) P-H.

Mosteller, Lee & Haight, Michele A. Survival English: English Through Conversations, Bk. 2A. (Illus.). 128p. 1988. pap. text ed. 5.25 (*0-13-879230-5*) P-H.

— Survival English: English Through Conversations, Bk. 2B. (Illus.). 128p. 1988. pap. text ed. 5.25 (*0-13-879263-1*) P-H.

Mosteller, Lee & Paul, Bobbi. Survival English. (Illus.). 200p. (C). 1985. pap. text ed. 8.50 (*0-13-879172-4*) P-H.

— Survival English: English Through Conversations, BK. 1B. (Illus.). 144p. 1988. pap. text ed. 5.25 (*0-13-879222-4*) P-H.

— Survival English 1. 2nd ed. 1993. pap. text ed. 11.25 (*0-13-016635-9*) P-H.

— Survival English 1A. 2nd ed. 1993. pap. text ed. 7.50 (*0-13-016593-X*) P-H.

— Survival English 1B. 2nd ed. 1993. pap. text ed. 7.50 (*0-13-016601-4*) P-H.

— Survival English 2. 2nd ed. 240p. 1994. pap. text ed. 11.25 (*0-13-016650-2*) P-H.

— Survival English 2A. 2nd ed. Date not set. pap. write for info. (*0-13-016619-7*) P-H.

— Survival English 2B. 2nd ed. Date not set. pap. write for info. (*0-13-016627-8*) P-H.

Mosteller, William S. Systems Programmer's Problem Solver. 280p. 1989. 34.95 (*0-471-58429-0*) Wiley.

— Systems Programmer's Problem Solver. 2nd ed. LC 88-31759. 280p. 1989. 34.95 (*0-89435-271-7*) Wiley.

Mosten, Doug, intro. The First Folio of Shakespeare, 1623. LC 94-15121. 1995. 250.00 (*1-55783-185-8*); pap. 45.00 (*1-55783-184-X*) Applause Theatre Bk Pubs.

Moster, Mary B. Living with Cancer. 2nd ed. 192p. 1985. pap. 8.99 (*0-8423-3679-6*) Tyndale.

Moster, Mary B., ed. see Lingeman, James E., et al.

***Mostert.** Dutch-English, English-Dutch Medical Dictionary. 3rd ed. 206p. (DUT & ENG.). 1990. 75.00 (*0-7859-7519-5*, 9031310786) Fr & Eur.

Mostert, F. J. Dutch-English, English-Dutch Medical Dictionary. 3rd rev. ed. 206p. 1990. 73.00 (*90-313-1078-6*, Pub. by Bohn Scheltema) IBD Ltd.

Mostert, Noel. Frontiers. 1992. pap. 34.50 (*0-679-40136-9*) McKay.

Mostert, Paul S., jt. auth. see Hofmann, Karl H.

Mosteshar, Sai'd. Mosteshar on Telecommunications: Regulation in the European Community. (European Business Law & Practice Ser.). 448p. (C). 1993. lib. bdg. 125.00 (*1-85333-756-0*, Pub. by Graham & Trotman UK) Kluwer Ac.

***Mosteshar, Said, ed.** Research & Invention in Outer Space: Liability & Intellectual Property Rights. LC 95-44. 1995. lib. bdg. 160.00 (*0-7923-2982-1*, Pub. by M Nijhoff) Kluwer Ac.

Mostofi, F. K. Atlas of Tumor Pathology: Tumors of the Male Genital System. (Second Ser.: Fascicle 8). (Illus.). 324p. 1990. reprint ed. per., pap. 15.00 (*0-16-001833-1*, S/N 008-023-000) USGPO.

Mostofsky, David I., ed. Stimulus Generalization. (Illus.). viii, 389p. 1965. 47.50 (*0-8047-0221-7*) Stanford U Pr.

Mostofsky, David I. & Loyning, Yngve, eds. The Neurobehavioral Treatment of Epilepsy. 352p. 1993. text ed. 69.95 (*0-8058-1106-0*) L Erlbaum Assocs.

Mostofsky, David I. & Piedmont, Ralph L. Therapeutic Practice in Behavioral Medicine: A Selective Guide to Assessment, Treatment, Clinical Issues, & Therapies for Specific Disorders. LC 84-43031. (Joint Publication in the Jossey-Bass Social & Behavioral Science Series & the Jossey-Bass Health Ser.). 380p. reprint ed. pap. 108.30 (*0-7837-2536-1*, 2042695) Bks Demand.

Mostoller, Dwight E., et al. Ready-to-Use Computer Literacy Activities Kits, Level I. 64p. (J). (gr. 4-6). 1987. student ed 5.95 (*0-317-66399-2*); teacher ed 24.95 (*0-13-762022-5*) P-H.

— Ready-to-Use Computer Literacy Activities Kits Level II. 64p. (J). (gr. 7-10). 1987. student ed 5.95 (*0-317-66401-8*); teacher ed 24.95 (*0-13-762048-9*) P-H.

Mostoller, Ed. Deer Hunting: The Guide to Doing It Right. (Illus.). 97p. 1994. 16.95 (*1-885018-00-2*); pap. 9.95 (*1-885018-01-0*) Logo Press.

Moston, Doug. Coming to Terms with Acting: An Instructive Glossary: What You Need to Know to Understand It, Discuss It, Deal with It, & Do It. 216p. (Orig.). 1993. pap. 16.95 (*0-89676-121-5*) Drama Bk.

Mostov, Julie. Power, Process & Popular Sovereignty. 256p. (C). 1992. 39.95 (*0-87722-970-8*) Temple U Pr.

Mostovych, Anna, jt. comp. see Liber, George O.

Mostow, jt. auth. see Gould, S. H.

Mostow, G. & Caldi, D., eds. Proceedings of the Gibbs Symposium, Yale University, May 15-17, 1989. LC 90-37667. 321p. 1990. 68.00 (*0-8218-0157-0*, GIBBS) Am Math.

Mostow, G. D. Strong Rigidity of Locally Symmetric Spaces. (Annals of Mathematics Studies: No. 78). 220p. 1974. 32.50 (*0-691-08136-0*) Princeton U Pr.

Mostow, G. D., ed. see Pure Mathematics Symposium Staff.

Mostow, G. Daniel, jt. auth. see Deligne, Pierre.

Mostow, Mark A. Continuous Cohomology of Spaces with Two Topologies. LC 76-25187. (Memoirs of the American Mathematical Society Ser.: No. 7/175). 142p. 1976. pap. 22.00 (*0-8218-2175-X*, MEMO 7/175) Am Math.

Mostowski, Andrej. Sentences Undecidable in Formalized Arithmetic: An Exposition of the Theory of Kurt Godel. LC 82-11886. (Studies in Logic & the Foundations of Mathematics). viii, 117p. 1982. reprint ed. text ed. 35.00 (*0-313-23151-6*, MOSU) Greenwood.

Mostrerd, W. L., jt. auth. see Hermans, G. P.

Mostwin, Danuta. The Transplanted Family: A Study of Social Adjustment of the Polish Immigrant Family to the United States after the Second World War. Cordasco, Francesco, ed. LC 80-881. (American Ethnic Groups Ser.). 1981. lib. bdg. 42.95 (*0-405-13442-8*) Ayer.

Mostyn, Trevor. Coming of Age in the Middle East. 256p. 1987. 35.00 (*0-7103-0208-8*, Pub. by Kegan Paul Intl UK) Routledge Chapman & Hall.

Mostyn, Trevor & Hourani, Albert, eds. The Cambridge Encyclopedia of the Middle East & North Africa. (Illus.). 456p. 1988. 64.95 (*0-521-32190-5*) Cambridge U Pr.

Moszkowski, Steven A., ed. see Proceedings of the International Conference, Los Angeles, 1972, et al.

Moszynska, Anna. Abstract Art. LC 89-51347. (World of Art Ser.). (Illus.). 1990. pap. 14.95 (*0-500-20237-0*) Thames Hudson.

Moszynska, W., jt. auth. see Chernetsov, Valeriui.

Moszynski, Jerzy R, ed. see American Society of Mechanical Engineers Staff.

Moszynski, Jerzy R.

Mota, A. Teixeira & Hair, P. E., eds. East of Mina: Afro-European Relations on the Gold Coast in the 1550s & 1560s. LC 90-146629. (Studies in African Sources: No. 3). 107p. (Orig.). 1989. pap. 22.00 (*0-942615-05-0*) U Wis African Stud.

Mota-Hernandez, F., ed. Seminar on Kidney Diseases in Children. (Journal: Paediatrician: Vol. 8, No. 5-6, 1979). 1979. pap. 53.00 (*3-8055-0344-X*) S Karger.

Mota, Miguel, jt. auth. see Tiessen, Paul.

Mota Oreja, Ignacio H. Diccionario de la Communicacion, Vol. 2. 368p. (SPA.). 1988. 59.95 (*0-7859-5856-8*, 8428316090) Fr & Eur.

Mota Soares, Carlos A., ed. Computer Aided Optimal Design: Structural & Mechanical Systems. (NATO Asi Series F: Vol. 27). 1045p. 1987. 171.00 (*0-387-17598-9*) Spr-Verlag.

Mota Soares, Carlos A., jt. ed. see Bendse, Martin P.

Motai, L. & Boone, Edgar J. Strategies in Reading: Developing Essential Reading Skills. 112p. 1988. pap. text ed. 13.95 (*0-8013-0515-2*, 78361) Longman.

— Strategies in Reading: Developing Essential Reading Skills. 112p. (YA). 1988. teacher ed 14.95 (*0-8013-0516-0*, 78362) Longman.

Motala, Ziyad. Constitutional Options for A Democratic South Africa: A Comparative Perspective. LC 94-6680. 1994. 39.95 (*0-88258-187-2*); pap. 19.95 (*0-88258-180-5*) Howard U Pr.

Motamed, Hosein A. Anatomy, Radiology, & Kinesiology of Hand-Unit. 8th ed. LC 81-90206. (Illus.). 344p. 1995. reprint ed. 150.00 (*0-910161-06-2*) Motamed Med Pub.

— Surgery of Hand-Unit in Adults & Children, 2 vols., I. 9th ed. LC 77-78228. (Illus.). 1614p. 1995. reprint ed. write for info. (*0-910161-03-8*) Motamed Med Pub.

— Surgery of Hand-Unit in Adults & Children, 2 vols., II. 9th ed. LC 77-78228. (Illus.). 1614p. 1995. reprint ed. write for info. (*0-910161-04-6*) Motamed Med Pub.

— Surgery of Hand-Unit in Adults & Children, 2 vols., Set. 9th ed. LC 77-78228. (Illus.). 1614p. 1995. reprint ed. 250.00 (*0-910161-02-X*) Motamed Med Pub.

Motamed-Nejad, Kazem, ed. Communication in-on the "Third World" National Development, Critical International Bibliography, Vol. I. 450p. Date not set. 35.00 (*0-88477-027-3*) Intl General.

Motamen, H., ed. Economic Modelling in the OECD Countries. 840p. 1988. lib. bdg. 199.00 (*0-412-29770-1*) Chapman & Hall.

Motamen, Homa, jt. auth. see Fayad, Marwan.

Motamen, Sima, jt. ed. see Res, Zannis.

Motard-Noar, Martine. Les Fictions d'Helene Cixous: Une Autre Langue de Femme. LC 91-70279. (French Forum Monographs: No. 73). 208p. (Orig.). (FRE.). 1991. pap. 14.95 (*0-917058-77-1*) French Forum.

Motard, Rudolphe L. & Joseph, Babu, eds. Wavelet Applications in Chemical Engineering. LC 94-13695. (International Series in Engineering & Computer Science, VLSI, Computer Architecture, & Digital Screen Processing: Vol. 272). 344p. (C). 1994. lib. bdg. 105.00 (*0-7923-9461-5*) Kluwer Ac.

Motazedi, Robert. Building & Flying RC Sailplanes & Electric Gliders. Emmerich, Michael, ed. LC 93-28719. (Illus.). 88p. (Orig.). 1993. pap. 11.95 (*0-89024-179-1*) Kalmbach.

Motchenbacher, C. D. & Connelly, J. A. Low Noise Electronic System Design. 448p. 1993. text ed. 79.95 (*0-471-57742-1*, Wiley-Interscience) Wiley.

Motchenbacher, C. D. & Fitchen, F. C. Low-Noise Electronic Design. LC 72-8713. 358p. 1973. text ed. 95.00 (*0-471-61950-7*, Wiley-Interscience) Wiley.

Mote, C. D., Jr. Skiing Trauma & Safety: International Symposium, STP 1104, 8th. LC 89-14984. (Special Technical Publication Ser.). (Illus.). 463p. 1991. pap. text ed. 113.00 (*0-8031-1405-2*, 04-011040-47) ASTM.

Mote, C. D., Jr. & Johnson, Robert J., eds. Skiing Trauma & Skiing Safety: Sixth International Symposium. LC 87-1826. (Special Technical Publication Ser.: No. 938). (Illus.). 378p. 1987. text ed. 79.00 (*0-8031-0936-9*, 04-938000-47) ASTM.

Mote, C. Daniel, Jr., jt. ed. see Johnson, Robert J.

Mote, Frederick W. Intellectual Foundations of China. 2nd ed. 144p. (C). 1989. pap. text ed. write for info. (*0-07-554030-4*) McGraw.

Mote, Frederick W. & Twitchett, Denis C., eds. The Cambridge History of China Vol. 7: The Ming Dynasty, 1368-1644. (Illus.). 752p. 1988. 155.00 (*0-521-24332-7*) Cambridge U Pr.

Moteka, Patricia, ed. see Brom, Elgar.

Motekaitis, Ramumas J., jt. auth. see Martell, Arthur E.

***Motekat, Ula.** Advanced Accounting. 7th ed. 1055p. (C). 1993. student ed, text ed. 24.95 (*0-256-12045-5*) Irwin.

***Moten, Abdul Rashid.** Political Science: An Islamic Perspective. LC 95-7827. 1995. write for info. (*0-312-12711-1*) St Martin.

Motet, Gilles & Marpinard, Alain. Design of Dependable ADA Software: The Use of Exception Mechanisms. 320p. 1993. pap. 38.00 (*0-13-204967-8*) P-H.

Mothander, Bjorn, et al. Farm Implements for Small-Scale Farmers in Tanzania. (Scandinavian Institute of African Studies). (Illus.). 214p. (Orig.). 1989. pap. 41.00 (*91-7106-290-4*, Pub. by Almqv & Wiksell SW) Coronet Bks.

Mother. Health & Healing in Yoga. 305p. 1989. pap. 6.00 (*81-7058-023-4*) Aurobindo Assn.

— The Lesson of Life. 180p. 1985. pap. 6.00 (*0-89071-322-7*, Pub. by SAA II) Aurobindo Assn.

— The Life Divine: The Mother's Talks. 154p. (Orig.). 1989. pap. 4.95 (*0-317-99972-9*, Pub. by Sri Aurob Ashram Trust II) Auromere.

M

An Asterisk (*) at the beginning of an entry indicates that the title is appearing in BIP for the first time.

— Mantras of the Mother. 1983. 5.00 (*0-89071-319-7*, Pub. by SAA II) Aurobindo Assn.

— The Sunlit Path. 194p. 1987. pap. 7.25 (*81-7058-025-0*, Pub. by SAA II) Aurobindo Assn.

— Tales of All Times. Orig. Title: Youth's Noble Path. (Illus.). 138p. (J). (gr. 3-8). 1983. pap. 4.95 (*0-89071-321-9*, Pub. by SAA II) Aurobindo Assn.

— Three Plays. 101p. (Orig.). 1989. pap. 3.95 (*0-317-99973-7*, Pub. by Sri Aurob Ashram Trust II) Auromere.

Mother & Satprem. Mother's Agenda, Vol. 2, 1961. LC 80-472990. 500p. (Orig.). 1981. pap. 12.50 (*0-938710-01-X*) Inst Evolutionary.

Mother, pseud. & Satprem, pseud. Mother's Agenda, Vol. 3, 1962. LC 80-472990. Orig. Title: L' Agenda De Mere 1962. 540p. (Orig.). 1982. pap. text ed. 12.50 (*0-938710-02-8*) Inst Evolutionary.

Mother & Satprem. Mother's Agenda 1963, Vol. 4. LC 80-472990. (Works of Satprem-Institute for Evolutionary Research). 485p. (Orig.). 1987. pap. 12.50 (*0-938710-09-5*) Inst Evolutionary.

— Mother's Agenda. 1964, Vol. 5. 450p. (Orig.). 1988. pap. text ed. 12.50 (*0-938710-10-9*) Inst Evolutionary.

— Mother's Agenda, 1972-73, Vol. 13. LC 80-472990. 460p. (Orig.). 1984. pap. text ed. 12.50 (*0-938710-07-9*) Inst Evolutionary.

Mother, jt. auth. see Aurobindo, Sri.

Mother & Satprem. Mother's Agenda - 1966, Vol. 7. LC 80-472990. 340p. 1991. pap. 12.50 (*0-938710-13-3*) Inst Evolutionary.

Mother Angelica. Mother Angelica Answers Not Promises. 1991. mass mkt. 5.99 (*0-671-74673-1*) PB.

Mother Columba Hart, tr. Hadewijch: The Complete Works. LC 80-84500. (Classics of Western Spirituality Ser.). 440p. 1981. 13.95 (*0-8091-0311-7*); pap. 10.95 (*0-8091-2297-9*) Paulist Pr.

Mother Earth News Editors. The Abundant Vegetable Garden: A Handbook for Success. (Illus.). 224p. (Orig.). 1985. pap. 19.95 (*0-938432-28-1*) Mother Earth.

— The Backcountry Handbook: An Illustrated Guide to the Techniques & Joys of the Wilderness Experience. 1989. pap. write for info. (*0-671-65795-X*, Fireside) S&S Trade.

— The Fresh Foods Country Cookbook. (Illus.). 196p. (Orig.). 1984. pap. 17.95 (*0-938432-23-0*) Mother Earth.

— How to Convert Your Vehicle to Propane. Hoffman, Robert, ed. 50p. (Orig.). 1981. pap. 7.50 (*0-938432-01-X*) Mother Earth.

— Living on Less. (Illus.). (Orig.). 1984. pap. 14.95 (*0-938432-07-9*) Mother Earth.

— Mother's Homebuilding & Shelter Guide. Miner, Robert, ed. (Illus.). 200p. 1983. pap. text ed. 15.95 (*0-938432-15-X*) Mother Earth.

— Mother's One Hundred & One Workshop Projects. (Illus.). 208p. 1984. pap. 14.95 (*0-938432-06-0*) Mother Earth.

— The Rural Living Handbook: An Illustrated Guide to Practical Country Skills. 1989. pap. write for info. (*0-671-65794-1*, Fireside) S&S Trade.

Mother Earth News Editors & Davis, William C. Mother's Energy Efficiency Book: Heat, Light, Power. (Illus.). 250p. 1983. 17.95 (*0-938432-22-2*) Mother Earth.

Mother Earth News Staff & Kerley, Michael R., eds. The Mother Earth News Alcohol Fuel Handbook. (Illus.). 120p. (Orig.). 1980. pap. 12.95 (*0-938432-00-1*) Mother Earth.

Mother Goof. The Sheep Who Was Allergic to Wool. LC 92-60096. (Illus.). 32p. (J). (gr. 3 up). 1992. 8.95 (*0-9623184-1-8*) Sunflower Hill.

Mother Goose. Mother Goose in Hieroglyphics. Bleiler, E. F., ed. 64p. pap. 2.95 (*0-486-20745-5*) Dover.

Mother Immaculata. Consecration & the Spirit of Carmel. LC 82-72203. (Living Meditation & Prayerbook Ser.). (Illus.). 270p. (Orig.). 1985. pap. text ed. 6.00 (*0-932406-08-4*) AFC.

***Mother Love & Church, Connie.** Listen Up, Girlfriends! Lessons on Life from the Queen of Advice. (Illus.). 256p. 1995. 18.95 (*0-312-11995-X*) St Martin.

Mother Maria. An Introduction to the Divine Liturgy. 1989. pap. 3.95 (*0-937032-66-2*) Light&Life Pub Co MN.

Mother Martha. Papa Nicholas Planas. Holy Transfiguration Monastery, ed. & tr. by. LC 80-85217. (Orig.). 1981. pap. 5.50 (*0-913026-18-2*) St Nectarios.

Mother Mary & Ware, Kallistos, trs. The Festal Menaion. 564p. 1990. reprint ed. 21.95 (*1-878997-00-9*) St Tikhons Pr.

Mother Mary Francis. Walled in Light: St. Colette. 1985. 9.50 (*0-8199-0889-4*, Frncscn Herld) Franciscan Pr.

Mother Mary Francis, tr. see St. Colette.

Mother Meera. Bringing down the Light: Journey of a Soul after Death. LC 89-13577. (Illus.). 64p. (ENG, FRE & GER.). 1990. 29.95 (*0-9622973-2-1*) Meeramma Pubns.

Mother Roux. Now You're Cooking...with Laughs! LC 81-17819. (Illus.). 81p. (Orig.). 1982. spiral bd. 6.95 (*0-88289-296-7*) Pelican.

Mother Teresa. The Best Gift Is Love: Meditations. LC 92-42958. Orig. Title: A Way of Love. (Illus.). 122p. 1993. reprint ed. 8.99 (*0-89283-814-0*, Charis) Servant.

— Heart of Joy: The Transforming Power of Self-Giving. 160p. (Orig.). 1987. pap. 5.99 (*0-89283-342-4*) Servant.

— Jesus, the Word to Be Spoken. 176p. (Orig.). 1986. 5.99 (*0-89283-304-1*) Servant.

— Jesus, the Word to Be Spoken. large type ed. (Large Print Inspirational Ser.). (Orig.). 1987. pap. 9.95 (*0-8027-2574-0*) Walker & Co.

— Love: A Fruit Always in Season: Daily Meditations from the Words of Mother Teresa of Calcutta. Hunt, Dorothy S., ed. LC 86-81472. (Illus.). 260p. (Orig.). 1987. pap. 10.95 (*0-89870-167-8*) Ignatius Pr.

— The Love of Christ: Spiritual Counsels. LC 81-48216. 128p. 1982. 10.95 (*0-06-068229-9*) Harper SF.

— Loving Jesus. 166p. 1991. pap. 5.99 (*0-89283-676-8*) Servant.

— One Heart Full of Love. Gonzalez-Balado, Jose L., ed. 170p. 1988. 5.99 (*0-89283-393-9*) Servant.

— Seeking the Heart of God. LC 92-54257. 112p. 1993. 12.00 (*0-06-068238-8*) Harper SF.

— A Simple Path. 288p. 1995. 20.00 (*0-345-39745-2*) Ballantine.

— Total Surrender. large type ed. DeVananda, Angelo, ed. LC 93-8541. (EasyRead Type Ser.). 162p. (Orig.). 1993. reprint ed. pap. text ed. 8.95 (*0-8027-2676-3*) Walker & Co.

— Total Surrender. rev. ed. Devananda, Bro. Angelo, ed. 140p. (Orig.). (C). 1989. pap. 5.99 (*0-89283-651-2*) Servant.

— Words to Love By. LC 82-73373. (Illus.). 80p. (Orig.). 1983. pap. 5.95 (*0-87793-261-1*) Ave Maria.

— Words to Love By. large type ed. 160p. (Orig.). 1985. reprint ed. pap. 6.95 (*0-8027-2478-7*) Walker & Co.

Mother Teresa of Calcutta. A Mother Teresa Treasury: Mother Teresa of Calcutta, 3 vols. Incl. Vol. 1. Gift for God. LC 85-42786. 96p. 1985. (*0-318-59241-X*); Vol. 2. Love of Christ. LC 85-42786. 128p. 1985. (*0-318-59242-8*); Vol. 3. Life in the Spirit. LC 85-42786. 96p. 1985. (*0-318-59243-6*); LC 85-42786. 1985. 32.95 (*0-06-068228-0*) Harper SF.

Mother Teresa of Calcutta & Roger of Taize. Meditations on the Way of the Cross. LC 86-9313. (Illus.). 64p. (Orig.). 1987. pap. 6.95 (*0-8298-0585-0*) Pilgrim OH.

Mother Thais. Zhitija Russkikh Svatikh, v 2 tom, 2 vols., 1. LC 82-81204. pap. 10.00 (*0-88465-012-X*) Holy Trinity.

— Zhitija Russkikh Svatikh, v 2 tom, 2 vols., 2. LC 82-81204. pap. 13.00 (*0-88465-020-0*) Holy Trinity.

Mother, The. Flowers & Their Messages. LC 92-70607. (Illus.). 330p. 1992. pap. 29.95 (*0-941524-68-X*) Lotus Light.

— The Soul & Its Powers. LC 92-70605. 147p. (Orig.). 1992. pap. 9.95 (*0-941524-67-1*) Lotus Light.

Mother, The, jt. auth. see Aurobindo, Sri.

Mother Thekla. The Blessing of Ikons. 1988. pap. 1.95 (*0-937032-60-3*) Light&Life Pub Co MN.

Mothering Magazine Editors. Being a Father: Family, Work & Self. (Illus.). 176p. (Orig.). 1990. pap. 12.95 (*0-945465-69-6*) John Muir.

— Schooling at Home: Parents, Kids & Learning. (Illus.). 258p. (Orig.). 1990. pap. 14.95 (*0-945465-52-1*) John Muir.

Mothering Magazine Staff. Circumcision: Rest of the Story. 1993. pap. 12.95 (*0-914257-11-0*) Mothering Magazine.

Mothering Magazine Staff, ed. see Pedersen, Anne.

Mothers & Others for a Livable Planet. Color the Rainforest. 48p. 1990. pap. 4.95 (*0-9626072-4-X*) Living Planet Pr.

Mothershead, Alice B. Dining Customs Around the World. LC 81-85930. (Illus.). 150p. (Orig.). (C). 1982. pap. text ed. 9.95 (*0-912048-29-8*) Garrett Pk.

Mothershead, John L., Jr., jt. ed. see Goheen, John D.

Mothersill, C. & Seymour, C., eds. New Developments in Fundamental & Applied Radiobiology. 460p. 1991. 95.00 (*0-7484-0020-6*, Pub. by Tay Francis Ltd UK) Taylor & Francis.

Mothersill, Mary. Beauty Restored. 438p. (C). 1991. reprint ed. pap. text ed. 19.95 (*0-937431-04-4*) Adams Bannister Cox.

Mothersole, Peter L. & White, Norman W. Broadcast Data Systems: Teletext & RDS. (Illus.). 158p. 1990. pap. 29.95 (*0-240-51354-1*, Focal) Buttrwrth-Heinemann.

Motherwell, Robert. The Collected Writings of Robert Motherwell. Terenzio, Stephania, ed. LC 92-13639. (Illus.). 448p. 1993. 45.00 (*0-19-507700-8*) OUP.

— The Collected Writings of Robert Motherwell. Terenzio, Stephanie, ed. (Illus.). 358p. 1994. reprint ed. pap. 21.95 (*0-19-509047-0*) OUP.

Motherwell, Robert, ed. The Dada Painters & Poets: An Anthology. 2nd ed. LC 88-10349. (Paperbacks in AA History Ser.). (Illus.). 464p. 1989. reprint ed. pap. 23.50 (*0-674-18500-5*) HUP.

Motherwell, W. B. & Crich, D. Free-Radical Chain Reactions in Organic Synthesis. (Best Synthetic Methods Ser.). (Illus.). 268p. 1991. text ed. 109.00 (*0-12-508760-8*) Acad Pr.

Motherwell, William, ed. Rob Stene's Dream, a Poem. LC 70-173003. (Maitland Club, Glasgow. Publications: No. 52). reprint ed. 37.50 (*0-404-53033-8*) AMS Pr.

Motherwool, W. Minstrelsy. 1972. 35.00 (*0-8490-0641-4*) Gordon Pr.

Mothes, R., jt. ed. see Schwenke, K. D.

Mothner, Carol, intro. Carol Mothner: Private Places. LC 90-61446. (Illus.). 24p. 1990. pap. 8.00 (*0-935037-32-2*) G Peters Gallery.

Motier, Donald. Just Friends: A Novel & Two Short Stories. LC 84-62218. 119p. 1984. 5.00 (*0-9614048-0-9*) Phaedrus.

Motil, John. Digital Systems Fundamentals. xx, 490p. (C). 1983. reprint ed. pap. text ed. 22.00 (*0-917930-65-7*) Ridgeview.

Motil, Rebecca. Readings in Life Science - Exercise Book. (C). 1990. pap. text ed. write for info. (*0-13-753674-7*) P-H.

— Readings in Physical Science - Exercise Book. (C). 1990. pap. text ed. write for info. (*0-13-753682-8*) P-H.

***Motion & Rodd.** New Writing Vol. 3. 508p. 1994. pap. 13.95 (*0-7493-9748-9*) Heinemann.

Motion, Andrew. Natural Causes. 57p. 1991. pap. 13.95 (*0-7011-3271-X*, Pub. by Chatto & Windus UK) Trafalgar.

— Philip Larkin: A Writer's Life. 1993. 35.00 (*0-374-23168-0*) FS&G.

— Philip Larkin: A Writer's Life. 1994. pap. 13.00 (*0-374-52407-6*) FS&G.

— The Price of Everything. 128p. (Orig.). 1995. pap. 10.95 (*0-571-16900-7*) Faber & Faber.

Motion Picture Producers & Distributors of America Staff, jt. auth. see National Conference on Motion Pictures Staff.

Motiska, Paul J., jt. auth. see Shilliff, Karl A.

Motiu, Enea, tr. see Barlea, Octavian.

Motiuk, I. L., ed. Environmental Risk in Real Estate Transactions: The Innocent Landowner Defense. LC 89-83362. 392p. 1989. pap. 74.95 (*0-89707-498-X*, 543-0302) Amer Bar Assn.

Motivational Dialogues Central Council Staff. How to Turn-on to Life: Reach Way Beyond Money. LC 85-61067. 148p. 1988. teacher ed 4.00 (*0-317-89801-9*); lib. bdg. 11.00 (*0-317-89799-3*); pap. 8.00 (*0-317-89800-0*) Mahon Pr.

Motizuki, Kazuko, ed. Structural Phase in Transitions in Layered Transition Metal Compounds. 1986. lib. bdg. 144.00 (*90-277-2171-8*) Kluwer Ac.

Motlagh, Cyrus K. Structuring Uncertainties in Long-Range Power Planning. LC 76-620019. (MSU Public Utilities Papers: No. 1976). 183p. reprint ed. pap. 52.20 (*0-7837-6267-4*, 2045979) Bks Demand.

Motlagh, Hushidar, comp. Unto Him Shall We Return: Selections from the Baha'i Writings on the Reality & Immortality of the Human Soul. 144p. 1985. pap. 12.50 (*0-87743-201-5*) Bahai.

Motlagh, Hushidar H. I Shall Come Again. 486p. 1992. 34.95 (*0-937661-00-7*); pap. 24.95 (*0-937661-01-5*) Global Persp.

Motley. Today's French Theatre. (Yale French Studies). 1954. 15.00 (*0-527-01722-1*); pap. 16.00 (*0-685-02866-6*) Periodicals Srv.

***Motley, Alice.** Close to Me & Closer...(The Language of Heaven) & Desamere. 1995. write for info. (*1-882022-26-2*) O Bks.

Motley, James B. Beyond the Soviet Threat: The U. S. Army in a Post Cold War Environment. (Low Intensity Conflict Ser.). 224p. 1991. text ed. 39.95 (*0-669-24986-6*) Free Pr.

— Protect Yourself, Your Family, Your Home: Checklists Against Crime. 192p. 1994. pap. 9.95 (*0-02-881074-0*) Brasseys Inc.

Motley, James B., jt. auth. see Bluhm, Raymond K.

Motley, John J. & Kelly, Philip R. Now Hear This! Histories of U. S. Ships in World War II. LC 79-18703. reprint ed. 19.95 (*0-89201-057-6*) Zenger Pub.

Motley, John L. Merry-Mount: A Romance of the Massachusetts Colony, 2 vols., Set. LC 78-64081. reprint ed. 75.00 (*0-404-17290-3*) AMS Pr.

— Morton's Hope; or, the Memoirs of a Provincial, 2 vols., Set. LC 78-64082. reprint ed. 75.00 (*0-404-17300-4*) AMS Pr.

— The Writings of John Lothrop Motley, 17 vols, Set. Curtis, George W., ed. Incl. 1. Rise of the Dutch Republic. 67.50 (*0-404-04521-9*); 2. Rise of the Dutch Republic. 67.50 (*0-404-04522-7*); 3. Rise of the Dutch Republic. 67.50 (*0-404-04523-5*); 4. Rise of the Dutch Republic. 67.50 (*0-404-04524-3*); 5. Rise of the Dutch Republic. 67.50 (*0-404-04525-1*); 6. History of the United Netherlands. 67.50 (*0-404-04526-X*); 7. History of the United Netherlands. 67.50 (*0-404-04527-8*); 8. History of the United Netherlands. 67.50 (*0-404-04528-6*); 9. History of the United Netherlands. 67.50 (*0-404-04529-4*); 10. History of the United Netherlands. 67.50 (*0-404-04530-8*); 11. History of the United Netherlands. 67.50 (*0-404-04531-6*); 12. Life & Death of John of Barneveld, Advocate of Holland, with a View of the Primary Causes & Movements of the Thirty Years' War. 67.50 (*0-404-04532-4*); 13. Life & Death of John of Barneveld, Advocate of Holland, with a View of the Primary Causes & Movements of the Thirty Years' War. 67.50 (*0-404-04533-2*); 14. Life & Death of John of Barneveld, Advocate of Holland, with a View of the Primary Causes & Movements of the Thirty Years' War. 67.50 (*0-404-04534-0*); 15. Correspondence. 67.50 (*0-404-04535-9*); 16. Correspondence. 67.50 (*0-404-04536-7*); 17. Correspondence. 67.50 (*0-404-04537-5*); reprint ed. 552.50 (*0-685-00418-X*) AMS Pr.

Motley, Lynne. Modem U. S. A. Low Cost & Free Online Sources for Information, Databases, & Electronic Bulletin Boards Via Personal Computer & Modem in 50 States. 2nd rev. ed. LC 93-73826. 401p. 1994. pap. 24.95 (*0-9631233-6-X*) Allium Pr.

Motley, Marion, ed. see Stone, Sarah H.

Motley, Mark. Becoming a French Aristocrat: The Education of the Court Nobility, 1580-1715. 262p. (C). 1990. text ed. 45.00 (*0-691-05547-5*) Princeton U Pr.

Motley, Mary P. Africa, Its Empires, Nations, & People: A Reader for Young Adults. LC 72-96720. (Illus.). 165p. reprint ed. pap. 47.10 (*0-7837-3592-8*, 2043456) Bks Demand.

Motley, Mary P., comp. The Invisible Soldier: The Experience of the Black Soldier, World War II. LC 87-26370. (Illus.). 364p. (C). 1987. pap. 17.95 (*0-8143-1961-0*) Wayne St U Pr.

Motley, Robert J. Student Applications Guide to Accompany Wolford-Vanneman, Business Communication. 378p. (C). 1993. student ed, pap. text ed. 18.75 (*0-15-500252-X*) Dryden Pr.

Motley, Warren. The American Abraham: James Fenimore Cooper & the Frontier Patriarch. (Cambridge Studies in American Literature & Culture: No. 27). 160p. 1988. 54.95 (*0-521-32782-2*) Cambridge U Pr.

Motley, Willard. Knock on Any Door. 515p. 1989. reprint ed. pap. text ed. 16.00 (*0-87580-543-4*) N Ill U Pr.

— We Fished All Night. LC 73-18875. reprint ed. 39.50 (*0-404-11370-2*) AMS Pr.

Motley, Wilma E. Ethics, Jurisprudence & History for the Dental Hygienist. 3rd ed. LC 82-23926. 227p. reprint ed. pap. 64.70 (*0-7837-2732-1*, 2043112) Bks Demand.

Motlhabi, Mokgethi B. Challenge to Apartheid: Toward a Morally Defensible Strategy. LC 88-7157. 255p. reprint ed. pap. 72.70 (*0-7837-0521-2*, 2040845) Bks Demand.

Motloch, J. L., jt. auth. see Landphair, H. C.

Motloch, John. Intro to Landscape Design. 1990. text ed. 39.95 (*0-442-23688-3*) Van Nos Reinhold.

Motlow, James. Bitter Melon: Inside America's Last Rural Chinese Town. 2nd ed. Gillenkirk, Jeff, ed. (Illus.). 144p. 1993. pap. 19.95 (*0-930588-58-4*) Heyday Bks.

Motlow, James, jt. auth. see Gillenkirk, Jeff.

Moto-Oka, T., ed. see International Conference on the Fifth Generation Computer Systems Staff.

Moto-Oka, T., jt. ed. see Koomen, C. J.

***Moto, Shoichi, ed.** Galleria-26: Shopping Centers in Europe. (Illus.). 232p. 1995. 89.95 (*4-7661-0792-6*, Pub. by Meisei Co Ltd JA) Bks Nippan.

Motoda, H., et al, eds. Knowledge Acquisition for Knowledge-Based Systems: Proceedings of the Japanese Workshop, JKAW '90. 447p. 1991. pap. 110.00 (*90-5199-044-8*, Pub. by IOS Pr NE) IOS Press.

Motohashi, Y. Sieve Methods & Prime Numbers Theory. (Tata Institute Lectures on Mathematics Ser.). xi, 205p. 1984. pap. 19.00 (*0-387-12281-8*) Spr-Verlag.

Motoki. Karate Girl. Verre, Tom, ed. (Eros Graphic Novel Ser.: No. 7). (Illus.). 96p. (Orig.). 1993. pap. 12.95 (*1-56097-206-8*) Fantagraph Bks.

Motoki, S. & Saito, T. The Chemistry of Thione S-Imides. 24p. 1984. pap. text ed. 23.00 (*3-7186-0271-7*) Gordon & Breach.

Motolinia, Toribio. History of the Indians of New Spain. Foster, Elizabeth A., tr. LC 73-8449. (Illus.). 294p. 1970. reprint ed. text ed. 35.00 (*0-8371-6977-1*, MONS, Greenwood Pr) Greenwood.

***Motomora.** Specs: The True Story of Baseball Player George Toporcer. (J). 1995. pap. text ed. (*0-8114-6746-5*) Raintree Steck-V.

Motomora, Mitchell. Happy Birthday! (Real Readers Ser.: Level Red). (Illus.). 32p. (J). (gr. 1-4). 1989. lib. bdg. 19.97 (*0-8172-3510-8*); pap. 3.95 (*0-8114-6706-6*) Raintree Steck-V.

— Lazy Jack & the Silent Princess. (Real Readers Ser.: Level Green). (Illus.). 32p. (J). (gr. 1-4). 1989. lib. bdg. 19.97 (*0-8172-3529-9*); pap. 3.95 (*0-8114-6726-0*) Raintree Steck-V.

— Momotaro. (Real Readers Ser.). (J). (ps). 1993. pap. 3.95 (*0-8114-6714-7*) Raintree Steck-V.

— Momotaro. (Real Readers Ser.). (J). (ps). 1993. lib. bdg. 19.97 (*0-614-05133-9*) Raintree Steck-V.

— Peach Boy. (Real Readers Ser.: Level Blue). (Illus.). 32p. (J). (gr. 1-3). 1989. lib. bdg. 12.33 (*0-8172-3513-2*) Raintree Steck-V.

— Specs: The True Story of Baseball Player George Toporcer. (Ready-Set-Read Ser.). (Illus.). 24p. (J). (ps-2). 1990. 17.84 (*0-8172-3585-X*); lib. bdg. 10.95 (*0-685-58557-3*) Raintree Steck-V.

***Motomura, Hiroshi.** Immigration & Nationality Laws of the United States, Selected Statutes, Regulations & Forms, 1995. 641p. (C). 1995. pap. text ed. 16.50 (*0-314-06817-1*) West Pub.

Motooka, Tohru & Kitsuregawa, Masaru. The Fifth Generation Computer: The Japanese Challenge. Apps, F. D., tr. LC 85-12290. (Illus.). 130p. reprint ed. pap. 37.10 (*0-8357-4603-8*, 2037536) Bks Demand.

Motor Vehicle Manufacturers Association of the U. S., Inc. Staff. Making the Car. (Illus.). 36p. 1987. write for info. (*0-943350-14-X*) Motor Veh Man.

Motor Vehicle Manufacturers Association of the U. S. Staff. America's Light Trucks. Brinley, Sheridan, ed. 36p. 1986. write for info. (*0-943350-13-1*) Motor Veh Man.

Motor Vehicle Manufacturers Association of the United States Staff. Automobiles of America: Milestones, Pioneers, Roll Call, Highlights. 4th rev. ed. LC 73-19838. 304p. reprint ed. pap. 86.70 (*0-8357-5919-9*, 2031016) Bks Demand.

Motor Vehicle Manufacturers Association of the U. S. Staff & American Vocational Association Industry Planning Council Staff. Guidelines for Vocational Automotive Service Instruction. 84p. 1985. write for info. (*0-943350-12-3*) Motor Veh Man.

Motorbooks International Staff. Datsun 311 1600-2000 Sports Car: Shop Manual. (Illus.). 392p. (Orig.). 1988. pap. 29.95 (*0-87938-294-5*) Motorbooks Intl.

— Warbirds Worldwide, No. 26. (Illus.). 48p. 1993. pap. 10.95 (*1-870601-33-5*, Pub. by Warbirds Worldwide) Motorbooks Intl.

***Motorbooks Staff.** Haynes Jeep Wrangler 1987-94. 1994. pap. text ed. 16.95 (*1-56392-120-0*) Haynes Pubns.

Motorcycle Mechanics Institute Staff. The Complete Guide to Motorcycle Mechanics. (Illus.). 416p. (C). 1984. text ed. 60.00 (*0-13-160549-6*) P-H.

— The Complete Guide to Motorcycle Mechanics. 2nd ed. LC 93-14849. 1993. text ed. 57.00 (*0-13-225889-7*) P-H Gen Ref & Trav.

Motorcycle Safety Foundation Staff. Motorcycle Journeys Through the Appalachians: Skills, Knowledge, & Strategies for Riding Right. (Illus.). 176p. 1995. pap. 24.95 (*1-884313-01-9*) Whitehorse MA.

Motorola Codex Staff. The Basics Book of Frame Relay. (Illus.). 176p. 1993. pap. 11.95 (*0-201-56377-0*) Addison-Wesley.

— Basics Book of Information Networking. 176p. 1992. pap. 15.95 (*0-201-56370-3*) Addison-Wesley.

— The Basics Book of OSI & Networking Management. (Illus.). 96p. 1993. pap. 11.95 (*0-201-56371-1*) Addison-Wesley.

— Basics Book of X.25 Packet Switching. (Illus.). 80p. 1992. pap. 11.95 (*0-201-56369-X*) Addison-Wesley.

An Asterisk (*) at the beginning of an entry indicates that the title is appearing in BIP for the first time.

Motorola, Inc. Staff. MC Sixty-Eight Eight Eighty-One & Eight Eighty-Two Floating-Point Coprocessor User's Manual. 2nd ed. 1989. pap. text ed. 27.00 (*0-13-567009-8*) P-H.
— MC 68020 32-Bit Microprocessor User's Manual. (Illus.). 448p. 1984. pap. 18.95 (*0-13-541467-9*) P-H.
— MC68000 8- 16- 32-Bit Microprocessor User's Manual. 368p. 1989. pap. 22.95 (*0-13-567074-8*) P-H.
— MC68020 32-Bit Microprocessor: User's Manual. 464p. 1986. 21.95 (*0-13-566860-3*) P-H.
— MC88100 Microprocessors User's Manual. 2nd ed. 1989. pap. text ed. 32.00 (*0-13-567090-X*) P-H.
— MC88200 Cache-Memory Management Unit User's Manual. 2nd ed. 1989. pap. text ed. 32.00 (*0-13-567033-0*) P-H.
— M68000 8-, 16-, 32-Bit Microprocessor's Programmer's Reference Manual. 5th ed. 240p. 1986. 26.95 (*0-13-541475-X*) P-H.
— M68000 8-16-32-Bit Microprocessor User's Manual. 8th ed. 214p. 1990. pap. text ed. 30.00 (*0-13-541665-5*, 330502) P-H.
— Programmer's Reference Manual. 560p. 1991. pap. text ed. 29.00 (*0-13-723289-6*, 330504) P-H.
Motorola, Inc. Staff & Spinks, Brian. Introduction to Integrated Circuit Layout. (Illus.). 192p. (C). 1984. pap. text ed. 51.00 (*0-13-485400-4*) P-H.
Motorola Museum of Electronics Staff. Motorola: A Journey Through Time & Technology. (Illus.). (Orig.). (SPA.). (YA). 1994. 50.00 (*1-56946-007-8*); 50.00 (*1-56946-006-X*); pap. 25.00 (*1-56946-010-8*) Motorola Univ.
— Motorola: A Journey Through Time & Technology. (Illus.). 100p. (Orig.). (YA). 1994. 50.00 (*1-56946-005-1*); 50.00 (*1-56946-008-6*); pap. 25.00 (*1-56946-011-6*) Motorola Univ.
— Motorola: A Journey Through Time & Technology. (Illus.). 96p. (Orig.). (MAN.). (C). 1995. pap. text ed. 25.00 (*1-56946-013-2*); pap. text ed. 25.00 (*1-56946-012-4*) Motorola Univ.
Motorola UNIX Staff. UNIX System V Release 4 Commands Reference Manual: Commands A-L for Motorola Processors, Vol. 1. 800p. (C). 1992. pap. text ed. 44.00 (*0-13-088832-X*) P-H.
— UNIX System V Release 4 Commands Reference Manual: Commands M-Z for Motorola Processors, Vol. 2. 784p. (C). 1992. pap. text ed. 44.00 (*0-13-088840-0*) P-H.
— UNIX System V Release 4 Device Driver-Kernel Interface Reference Manual for Motorola Processors. 320p. (C). 1992. pap. text ed. 35.00 (*0-13-088824-9*) P-H.
— UNIX System V Release 4 Master Permuted Index for Motorola Processors. 224p. (C). 1992. pap. text ed. 34.00 (*0-13-035833-9*) P-H.
— UNIX System V Release 4 System Calls & Library Functions Reference Manual for Motorola Processors. 1104p. (C). 1992. pap. text ed. 49.00 (*0-13-035841-X*) P-H.
— UNIX System V Release 4 System Files & Devices Reference Manual for Motorola Processors. 464p. (C). 1992. pap. text ed. 44.00 (*0-13-035874-6*) P-H.
Motovilova, jt. auth. see Mitrokhina, V. I.
Motoyama. Smith's Anesthesia for Infants & Children. 5th ed. (Illus.). 976p. 1989. 99.00 (*0-8016-3568-3*) Mosby Yr Bk.
Motoyama, Hiroshi. Karma & Reincarnation. 160p. (Orig.). 1993. pap. 10.00 (*0-380-77213-2*) Avon.
— Theories of the Chakras. LC 81-51165. 350p. (Orig.). 1982. pap. 12.00 (*0-8356-0551-5*, Quest) Theos Pub Hse.
Motoyama, Yukihiko, jt. auth. see Holzman, Donald.
Motoyoshi, Hiroko, tr. see Ogaki, Tetsuya.
Motsonelidze, N. S. Stability & Seismic Resistance of Buttress Dams. Kothekar, V. S., tr. 293p. (C). 1987. text ed. 90.00 (*90-6191-490-6*, Pub. by A A Balkema NE) Ashgate Pub Co.
— Stability & Seismic Resistance of Buttress Dams. 278p. (C). 1987. 30.00 (*81-204-0207-3*, Pub. by Oxford IBH II) S Asia.
Mott. Investment Appraisal for Managers. 2nd ed. 200p. 1987. text ed. 49.95 (*0-566-02704-6*, Pub. by Gower UK) Ashgate Pub Co.
— Sp-Etica Biblica y Cambio Soci. 1995. pap. text ed. (*0-8028-0923-5*) Eerdmans.
Mott, et al. Study Guide for Earth, Sea & Sky. 2nd ed. 132p. 1991. pap. text ed. 19.95 (*0-88725-149-8*) Hunter Textbks.
Mott, Albert J., see A. J. Barrowcliffe, pseud..
***Mott, Barbara & Mott, Elizabeth.** Mott Miniature Furniture Workshop Manual. 2nd rev. ed. (Illus.). 224p. 1995. pap. 19.95 (*1-56523-052-3*) Fox Chapel Pub.
Mott, Brian & Rion, Rosana. Harrap's Tintin Illustrated Spanish Dictionary: English-Spanish - Spanish-English. (Illus.). 448p. 1993. 25.00 (*0-671-84869-0*, Harraps) P-H Gen Ref & Trav.
Mott, Brian, et al. Harrap's Tintin Illustrated English-Spanish - Spanish-English Dictionary. (Illus.). 448p. 1992. 25.00 (*0-13-391152-7*, Harraps) P-H Gen Ref & Trav.
Mott, Carol Wilder & Weakland, John H. Rigor & Imagination: Essays on Human Communication from the Interactional View. LC 81-83995. 432p. 1981. text ed. 65.00 (*0-275-90741-4*, C0741, Praeger Pubs) Greenwood.
Mott, Donald R. & Saunders, Cheryl M. Stephen Spielberg. (Twayne's Filmmakers Ser.). 216p. 1988. pap. 14.95 (*0-8057-9311-9*, Pub. by Royal Botanic Garden UK) Macmillan.
— Steven Spielberg. (Twayne Filmmakers Ser.). 220p. (C). 1986. lib. bdg. 20.95 (*0-8057-9307-0*, Twayne) Macmillan.
Mott, Elizabeth, jt. auth. see Mott, Barbara.
Mott, Elliott. Cycling Possibilities, Vol. 1: Course Guide for the Salt Lake Bicyclist. (Illus.). 88p. 1990. pap. 8.95 (*0-9626322-1-X*) Roosevelt & Torrey.
Mott, Elliott R. Cycling Possibilities: Course Guides for the Wasatch Front Bicyclist. (Illus.). 114p. 1993. pap. 8.95 (*0-9626322-3-6*) Roosevelt & Torrey.
— Cycling Possibilities, Vol. 2: Course Guides for the Northern Utah Bicyclist. (Illus.). 96p. 1991. pap. 8.95 (*0-9626322-2-8*) Roosevelt & Torrey.
Mott, Evelyn C. Balloon Ride. (Illus.). 32p. (J). (ps-1). 1991. 13.95 (*0-8027-8124-1*); lib. bdg. 14.85 (*0-8027-8126-8*) Walker & Co.
— A Day at the Races with Austin & Kyle Petty. LC 92-10947. (Pictureback Ser.). 32p. (J). (ps-3). 1993. pap. 2.25 (*0-679-83258-0*) Random Bks Yng Read.
— Steam Train Ride. (Illus.). 32p. (J). (gr. 4-8). 1991. 13.95 (*0-8027-6995-0*); lib. bdg. 14.85 (*0-8027-6996-9*) Walker & Co.
— Steam Train Ride. LC 90-49223. 32p. (J). (gr. k-4). 1995. pap. 4.95 (*0-8027-7452-0*) Walker & Co.
Mott, Evelyn C., jt. auth. see Isaacs, Gwynne L.
Mott, Frank L. A History of American Magazines, Vol. 1: 1741-1850. LC 39-2823. 848p. reprint ed. Vol. 1, 1741-1850 - 848p. pap. 180.00 (*0-7837-4086-7*, 2057458) Bks Demand.
— A History of American Magazines, Vol. 2. LC 39-2823. (Illus.). 608p. reprint ed. pap. 173.30 (*0-7837-3069-1*, 2057458) Bks Demand.
— A History of American Magazines, Vol. 3. LC 39-2823. (Illus.). 683p. reprint ed. pap. 180.00 (*0-7837-3070-5*, 2057458) Bks Demand.
— A History of American Magazines, Vol. 4: 1885-1905. LC 39-2823. 890p. reprint ed. Vol. 4, 1885-1905 - 890p. pap. 180.00 (*0-7837-4087-5*) Bks Demand.
— A History of American Magazines, Vol. 5. LC 39-2823. 595p. reprint ed. pap. 174.80 (*0-7837-4088-3*) Bks Demand.
Mott, Frank L., ed. The Employment Revolution: Young American Women of the 1970's. 256p. 1982. 35.00 (*0-262-13186-2*) MIT Pr.
— Journalism in Wartime. LC 84-696. v, 216p. (C). 1984. reprint ed. text ed. 55.00 (*0-313-24458-8*, MOJW, Greenwood Pr) Greenwood.
Mott, George & Aall, Sally S. Follies & Pleasure Pavilions: England, Ireland, Scotland, Wales. (Illus.). 132p. 1989. 34.95 (*0-8109-1175-2*) Abrams.
Mott, George F. & Lambert, Richard D., eds. Urban Change & the Planning Syndrome. LC 72-93250. (Annals of the American Academy of Political & Social Science Ser.: No. 405). 250p. (C). 1973. 27.00 (*0-685-00185-7*, 87761); pap. 18.00 (*0-87761-157-2*) Am Acad Pol Soc Sci.
***Mott, Graham.** Accounting for Managers. 160p. (Orig.). 1994. pap. text ed. 25.95 (*0-7494-1216-X*, Pub. by Kogan Page UK) Nichols Pub.
— Management Accounting for Decision-Makers. 224p. (Orig.). 1991. pap. text ed. 43.50 (*0-273-03318-2*, Pub. by Pitman Pub Ltd UK); 43.50 (*0-273-03347-6*, Pub. by Pitman Pub Ltd UK) Trans-Atl Phila.
Mott, Graham M. Scams, Swindles, & Rip-Offs: How to Recognize & Avoid. rev. ed. (Illus.). 208p. 1993. pap. 14.95 (*0-9633155-0-1*) Gldn Shadows.
— Scams, Swindles, & Rip-Offs: How to Recognize & Avoid. rev. ed. (Illus.). 208p. 1994. pap. 14.95 (*0-9633155-1-X*) Gldn Shadows.
Mott, Harold. Antennas for Radar & Communications: A Polarimetric Approach. (Series in Microwave & Optical Engineering). 544p. 1992. text ed. 99.95 (*0-471-57538-0*) Wiley.
— Polarization in Antennas & Radar. LC 86-1349. 297p. 1986. text ed. 105.00 (*0-471-01167-3*) Wiley.
Mott, Helen, jt. ed. see Quinn, Brian.
Mott Hospital Staff. Ann Arbor's Cookin' Betz, Ann & Ronald McDonald House Staff, eds. 368p. (Orig.). 1985. pap. 12.00 (*0-9618208-0-2*) Ronald McDonald Hse.
Mott Iron Works Staff. Mott's Illustrated Catalog of Victorian Plumbing Fixtures for Bathrooms & Kitchens. (Illus.). 288p. 1987. reprint ed. pap. 15.95 (*0-486-25526-3*) Dover.
Mott, J. J., jt. ed. see Tothill, J. C.
Mott, Jack R. A., jt. ed. see Gogg, Thomas J.
Mott, Jacolyn A., ed. The American Paintings in the Pennsylvania Academy of the Fine Arts: An Illustrated Checklist. (Illus.). 204p. (Orig.). 1989. pap. 22.95 (*0-943836-11-5*) Penn Acad Art.
Mott, Jacolyn A., ed. see Danly, Susan.
Mott, Jacolyn A., ed. see Fresella-Lee, Nancy.
Mott, Joanna, tr. see Paris, Ginette.
Mott, John R. The Evangelization of the World in This Generation. LC 76-38457. (Religion in America, Ser. 2). 258p. 1972. reprint ed. 19.95 (*0-405-04078-4*) Ayer.
Mott, John R., et al. Student Mission Power: Report of the First International Convention of the Student Volunteer Movement for Foreign Missions, 1891. LC 79-92013. 235p. 1979. reprint ed. pap. 7.95 (*0-87808-736-2*) William Carey Lib.
Mott, Kenneth E., ed. Plant Molluscicides. LC 86-19045. 320p. 1987. pap. text ed. 112.00 (*0-471-91228-X*) Wiley.
Mott, Lawrence. To the Credit of the Sea. LC 78-150555. (Short Story Index Reprint Ser.). 1977. reprint ed. 21.95 (*0-8369-3852-6*) Ayer.
— White Darkness: & Other Stories of the Great Northwest. LC 74-150554. (Short Story Index Reprint Ser.). (Illus.). 1977. reprint ed. 23.95 (*0-8369-3851-8*) Ayer.
Mott, Lawrie & Snyder, Karen. Pesticide Alert: A Guide to Pesticides in Fruits & Vegetables. 128p. 1987. 6.95 (*0-318-39812-5*) Natl Resources Defense Coun.
— Pesticide Alert: A Guide to Pesticides in Fruits & Vegetables. LC 87-42965. (Illus.). 128p. 1988. pap. 6.95 (*0-87156-726-1*) Sierra.
Mott, Lewis F. System of Courtly Love. LC 65-26458. (Studies in Comparative Literature: No. 35). (C). 1969. reprint ed. lib. bdg. 75.00 (*0-8383-0599-7*) M S G Haskell Hse.
Mott-McDonald Associates Staff. Using Title XX to Serve Children & Youth. LC 76-357536. 80p. reprint ed. pap. 25.00 (*0-317-29896-8*, 2019375) Bks Demand.
Mott, Michael. Corday. 90p. 1987. lib. bdg. 13.95 (*0-933833-15-6*) Beacham Pub.
— Corday. rev. ed. (International-Visions Ser.). (Illus.). 84p. 1995. pap. 7.95 (*0-938872-21-4*) Black Buzzard.
— The Seven Mountains of Thomas Merton. 1993. pap. 17.95 (*0-15-680681-9*) HarBrace.
Mott, N. Atomic Structure & the Strength of Metals: ACC for Nonscientist Research in Understanding Charac Str & Duc. 1956. 40.00 (*0-08-013765-2*, Pub. by Pergamon Repr UK) Franklin.
Mott, N. F., jt. auth. see Alexandrov, A. S.
Mott, Nevill. A Life in Science. 180p. 1986. 49.00 (*0-85066-333-4*) Taylor & Francis.
— Metal-Insulator Transitions. 2nd rev. ed. 296p. 1990. 110.00 (*0-85066-783-6*) Taylor & Francis.
Mott, Nevill, ed. Can Scientists Believe? Some Examples of the Attitude of Scientists to Religion. vi, 182p. (Orig.). (C). 1991. 40.00 (*0-907383-54-8*, Pub. by J & J Sci Pubs UK) Bks Intl VA.
— Workshop on Oxidation Processes, Vol. 55, No. 6. (Philosophical Magazine Ser.). 1987. pap. 34.00 (*0-85066-930-8*) Taylor & Francis.
— Workshop on Oxidation Processes II, Vol. 55, No. 6. (Philosophical Magazine Ser.). 1987. pap. 34.00 (*0-85066-917-0*) Taylor & Francis.
Mott, Nevill F. & Jones, H. Theory of the Properties of Metals & Alloys. 1936. pap. 8.95 (*0-486-60456-X*) Dover.
Mott, Neville. Conduction in Non-Crystalline Materials. 2nd ed. LC 92-32384. (Illus.). 160p. 1993. 38.00 (*0-19-853979-7*, Clarendon Pr) OUP.
Mott, Richard D. Principles of Accounting I. (Academe Collections). 142p. (C). 1987. 7.95 (*0-944554-00-8*) Educ Images.
Mott, Robert L. Applied Fluid Mechanics. 4th ed. 704p. (C). 1994. text ed. write for info. (*0-02-384231-8*) Macmillan.
— Applied Strength of Materials. 2nd ed. 624p. 1989. text ed. 75.00 (*0-13-043415-9*) P-H.
— Machine Elements in Mechanical Design. 2nd ed. 880p. (C). 1992. text ed. write for info. (*0-675-22289-3*) Macmillan.
— Radio Sound Effects: Who Did It, & How, in the Era of Live Broadcasting. LC 92-50313. 303p. 1993. lib. bdg. 39.95 (*0-89950-747-6*) McFarland & Co.
— Sound Effects: Radio, TV & Film. (Illus.). 236p. 1990. 36.95 (*0-240-80029-X*, Focal) Buttrwrth-Heinemann.
Mott, Rodney L. Due Process of Law. LC 72-165604. (American Constitutional & Legal History Ser). 702p. 1973. reprint ed. lib. bdg. 85.00 (*0-306-70225-8*) Da Capo.
Mott, Sandra R. Handbook of Child Health Nursing. 1986. pap. text ed. 15.96 (*0-201-13699-6*) Addison-Wesley.
— Nursing Care of Children & Families. 2nd ed. Hunter, Debra, ed. 1907p. (C). 1990. teacher ed write for info. (*0-201-52923-8*); text ed. 70.95 (*0-201-12923-X*); Workbook. student ed write for info. (*0-201-12924-8*); write for info. (*0-201-52924-6*) Addison-Wesley.
Mott, Sandra R., jt. auth. see James.
***Mott, Sarah.** InService Education: Its Effect on the Ability of an Extended Care Facility to Meet the Outcome Standards. (Research Paper Ser.: No. 10). 1983. pap. 21.00 (*0-7300-2046-0*, Pub. by Deakin Univ AT) St Mut.
***Mott, Sarah & Riggs, Ann, eds.** Elderly People - Their Need for an Participation in Social Interactions (Dinroo) (Research Monograph Ser.: No. 5). 73p. 1993. pap. 33.00 (*0-7300-1521-1*, Pub. by Deakin Univ AT) St Mut.
Mott, Sheryl S. Ratio Analysis Workbook. Andover, James J., ed. LC 84-18977. 256p. 1984. student ed 22.95 (*0-934914-57-5*) NACM.
Mott-Smith, Geoffrey. Mathematical Puzzles for Beginners & Enthusiasts. 2nd ed. (Illus.). 248p. 1954. pap. 4.95 (*0-486-20198-8*) Dover.
Mott-Smith, Geoffrey, jt. auth. see Morehead, Albert H.
Mott-Smith, Geoffrey, jt. ed. see Morehead, Albert H.
Mott, Stephen C. Biblical Ethics & Social Change. 1982. pap. 14.95 (*0-19-502948-8*) OUP.
— Political Visions: A Christian Analysis. LC 92-25045. 1993. 59.00 (*0-19-507121-2*); pap. 29.95 (*0-19-508138-2*) OUP.
***Mott, Steve & Lutz, Susan.** The Original College Adventure Guide: 333 Secrets to the Art of College with Style & Imagination. 192p. 1995. pap. 6.95 (*0-9645383-0-X*) Vertigo Pr.
Mott, Thomas B. Myron T. Herrick, Friend of France. 1993. reprint ed. lib. bdg. 89.00 (*0-7812-5392-6*) Rprt Serv.
— Twenty Years as Military Attache. Kohn, Richard H., ed. LC 78-22390. (American Military Experience Ser.). 1980. reprint ed. lib. bdg. 25.95 (*0-405-11867-8*) Ayer.
Mott, Vincent, jt. auth. see Chirovsky, Nicholas.
Mott, Vincent L. How to Play Drums. (Self Improvement Ser.). 96p. (Orig.). 1985. pap. text ed. 7.95 (*0-8494-1550-0*, 85-10) Hansen Ed Mus.
Mott, Vincent V. The American Consumer: A Sociological Analysis, Pt. 3. 1981. pap. 3.50 (*0-912598-19-0*) Florham.
Mott, W. S. Printing Four Color Process on a Duplicator or Small Press: A How-to Guide from Graphic Services Publications. 48p. 1992. pap. 12.50 (*1-882602-01-3*) Graphic Srvs.
Mott, Wesley T. The Strains of Eloquence: Emerson & His Sermons. LC 88-28123. 288p. 1989. lib. bdg. 32.50 (*0-271-00660-9*) Pa St U Pr.
Mott, Wesley T. & Von Frank, Albert J., eds. The Complete Sermons of Ralph Waldo Emerson, Vol. 4. 448p. 1992. text ed. 44.95 (*0-8262-0859-2*) U of Mo Pr.
Mott, William P., Jr., jt. auth. see Weeks, George.
Motta, J. & Riley, K. Breakthrough to Literacy, 3 bks., Bk. 1. 1981. pap. write for info. (*0-318-50127-9*); teacher ed, pap. write for info. (*0-318-50128-7*) Addison-Wesley.
— Breakthrough to Literacy, 3 bks., Bk. 2. 1981. teacher ed write for info. (*0-318-50130-9*); Bk.2. write for info. (*0-318-50129-5*) Addison-Wesley.
— Breakthrough to Literacy, 3 bks., Bk. 3. 1981. write for info. (*0-318-50131-7*) Addison-Wesley.
— Impact! Adult Literacy & Language Skills, Bk. 1. 1982. pap. text ed. write for info. (*0-318-56708-3*) Addison-Wesley.
— Impact! Adult Literacy & Language Skills, Bk. 2. 1982. pap. text ed. write for info. (*0-318-56710-5*) Addison-Wesley.
— Impact! Adult Literacy & Language Skills, Bk. 3. 1982. write for info. (*0-318-56712-1*) Addison-Wesley.
— Impact! Adult Literacy & Language Skills, No. I. 1982. teacher ed write for info. (*0-318-56709-1*) Addison-Wesley.
— Impact! Adult Literacy & Language Skills, No. II. 1982. teacher ed write for info. (*0-318-56711-3*) Addison-Wesley.
— Impact! Adult Literacy & Language Skills, No. III. 1982. teacher ed write for info. (*0-318-56713-X*) Addison-Wesley.
Motta, Marcella. Brain Endocrinology. 2nd ed. Martini, Luciano, ed. (Comprehensive Endocrinology, Revised Ser.). 496p. 1991. 160.50 (*0-88167-768-X*) Raven.
***Motta, Marcella, ed.** The Endocrine Functions of the Brain. fac. ed. LC 77-84553. (Comprehensive Endocrinology Ser.). (Illus.). 492p. Date not set. pap. 140.30 (*0-7837-7292-0*, 2047014) Bks Demand.
***Motta, Marcella & Serio, Mario, eds.** Sex Hormones & Antihormones in Endocrine Dependent Pathology: Proceedings of an International Symposium, Milano, 10-14 April 1994. LC 94-32151. (International Congress Ser.: Vol. 1064). 1994. write for info. (*0-444-81879-0*) Elsevier.
Motta, Marcella, ed. see International Symposium on Androgens & Antiandrogens Staff.
Motta, P. Color Atlas of Microscopic Anatomy. 268p. 1990. text ed. 40.00 (*1-57235-011-3*) Piccin NY.
Motta, P. M. Basic, Clinical & Surgical Nephrology. DiDio, L. J., ed. LC 84-25483. (Developments in Nephrology Ser.). 1985. lib. bdg. 69.50 (*0-318-04536-2*) Kluwer Ac.
Motta, P. M., ed. Biopathology of the Liver: An Ultrastructural Approach. (C). 1988. lib. bdg. 168.00 (*0-7462-0049-8*) Kluwer Ac.
— Ultrastructure of Endocrine Cells & Tissues: Electron Microscopy in Biology & Medicine. 1983. lib. bdg. 160.50 (*0-89838-568-7*) Kluwer Ac.
Motta, P. M. & Didio, L. J., eds. Basic & Clinical Hepatology. 200p. 1981. lib. bdg. 126.50 (*90-247-2404-X*) Kluwer Ac.
Motta, P. M. & Fujita, Hisao, eds. Ultrastructure of the Digestive Tract. (Electron Microscopy in Biology & Medicine Ser.). (C). 1988. lib. bdg. 131.00 (*0-89838-893-7*) Kluwer Ac.
Motta, P. M. & Hafez, E. S., eds. Biology of the Ovary. (Developments in Obstetrics & Gynecology Ser.: No. 2). 345p. 1980. lib. bdg. 154.50 (*90-247-2316-7*) Kluwer Ac.
Motta, P. M., jt. ed. see Bonucci, E.
Motta, P. M., jt. ed. see Ruggeri, A.
Motta, P. M., et al, eds. Scanning Electron Microscopy of Vascular Casts: Methods & Applications. (Electron Microscopy in Biology & Medicine Ser.). 416p. (C). 1992. lib. bdg. 234.00 (*0-7923-1297-X*) Kluwer Ac.
Motta, Philip J. The Butterflyfishes: Success on the Coral Reef. (Developments in Environmental Biology of Fishes Ser.). (C). 1989. lib. bdg. 140.50 (*0-7923-0168-4*) Kluwer Ac.
Motta, Pietro M., ed. Ultrastructure of Smooth Muscle. (Electron Microscopy in Biology & Medicine Ser.). (C). 1990. lib. bdg. 162.00 (*0-7923-0480-2*) Kluwer Ac.
Motta, Pietro M., jt. ed. see Riva, Alessandro.
Motta, Pietro M., jt. ed. see Van Blerkom, Jonathan.
Mottahedeh, Roy. The Mantle of the Prophet: Religion & Politics in Iran. LC 86-42737. 416p. 1986. pap. 14.95 (*0-394-74865-4*) Pantheon.
Mottale, Morris M. The Arms Buildup in the Persian Gulf. 244p. (Orig.). (C). 1986. pap. text ed. 24.00 (*0-8191-5203-X*) U Pr of Amer.
— Iran: The Political Sociology of the Islamic Revolution. LC 94-35179. 1995. write for info. (*0-8191-9743-2*) U Pr of Amer.
Mottana, A. & Barragato, F., eds. Absorption Spectroscopy in Mineralogy: First European Meeting, Academia Nazionale del Lincei, Palazzo Corsini, Rome, Italy, 4-7 Oct., 1989. 294p. 1990. 89.75 (*0-444-88799-7*) Elsevier.
Mottana, Annibale. Guide to Minerals & Rocks: Guia de Minerales y Rocas. 6th ed. 608p. (SPA.). 1991. write for info. (*0-7859-4933-X*) Fr & Eur.
Mottaz, Jess H., ed. see Zelickson, Alvin S.
Motte, Andrew, tr. see Newton, Isaac.
Motte, Ganzague. Homilies for Sundays of the Year: Cycle A. 1974. 15.00 (*0-8199-0535-6*, Frncscn Herld) Franciscan Pr.
— Homilies for Sundays of the Year: Cycle A. Drury, John, tr. 312p. 1974. 15.00 (*0-8199-0461-9*, Frncscn Herld) Franciscan Pr.
Motte, Geoff A. & Stout, Thomas M. Chartwork & Marine Nagivation: For Fishermen & Boat Operators. LC 83-46037. (Illus.). 187p. reprint ed. pap. 53.30 (*0-7837-6296-8*, 2046011) Bks Demand.
***Motte, Warren.** Playtexts: Ludics in Contemporary Literature. LC 94-19827. 1995. text ed. 30.00 (*0-8032-3181-4*) U of Nebr Pr.

M

An Asterisk (*) at the beginning of an entry indicates that the title is appearing in BIP for the first time.

Motte, Warren & Prince, Gerald, eds. Alteratives. LC 93-76190. (French Forum Monographs: No. 82). 229p. (Orig.). 1993. pap. 17.95 (*0-917058-87-9*) French Forum.

***Motte, Warren F.** Questioning Edmond Jab Es. LC 89-14642. 202p. 1990. reprint ed. pap. 57.60 (*0-7837-8897-5*, 2049608) Bks Demand.

Motte, Warren F., Jr., ed. & tr. Oulipo: A Primer of Potential Literature. LC 85-8724. 223p. reprint ed. pap. 63.60 (*0-7837-6625-4*, 2046191) Bks Demand.

Motte, Warren F. Jr. The Poetics of Experiment: A Study of the Work of George Perec. LC 83-81599. (French Forum Monographs: No. 51). 163p. (Orig.). 1984. pap. 12.95 (*0-917058-51-8*) French Forum.

Mottelay, Paul F., ed. Bibliographical History of Electricity & Magnetism. LC 74-26277. (History, Philosophy & Sociology of Science Ser.). (Illus.). 1975. reprint ed. 52.95 (*0-405-06605-8*) Ayer.

Motteleta, L. Industrial Safety Is a Good Business. 1995. pap. 39.95 (*0-442-01842-8*) Van Nos Reinhold.

Mottelson, Ben R., jt. auth. see Bohr, Aage.

***Motter & Dupre.** The Heart of the Beast. Berger, K., ed. (Illus.). 96p. (Orig.). Date not set. pap. 14.95 (*1-56389-168-9*, Vertigo) DC Comics.

Motter & Steacy. The Sacred & the Profane. (Illus.). 1990. 25.00 (*0-913035-18-1*); pap. 14.95 (*0-913035-17-3*) Eclipse Bks.

Motter, Alton M., ed. Preaching about Death: Eighteen Sermons Dealing with the Experience of Death from the Christian Perspective. LC 74-26336. 94p. reprint ed. pap. 26.80 (*0-685-16043-2*, 2026862) Bks Demand.

Motter, Charlotte K. Theatre in High School: Planning, Teaching, Directing. (Illus.). 202p. 1984. pap. text ed. 20.50 (*0-8191-3791-X*) U Pr of Amer.

Motter, D. & Askwith, M. The Prisoner: Shattered Visage. Bruning, R. & Carlson, KC, eds. 208p. 1990. pap. 19.95 (*0-930289-53-6*) DC Comics.

Motter, Dean. The Prisoner: Shattered Visage. 1991. pap. 14.95 (*0-446-39245-6*) Warner Bks.

Motter, Dean, jt. auth. see Coleridge, Samuel Taylor.

Motter, Dean, ed. see Gilbert, Mario & Hernandez, Jaime.

Motter, Wendell & Foster, Charles A. Finite Mathematics with Applications: Florida Edition. (Illus.). 640p. 1990. write for info. (*0-912675-87-X*); pap. text ed. 44.95 (*0-912675-82-9*) Ardsley.

Mottern, Nicholas. Suffering Strong: The Journal of a Westerner in Ethiopia, the Sudan, Eritrea & Chad. (Current Issues Ser.: No. 3). (Illus.). 110p. 1987. 12.95 (*0-932415-30-X*); pap. 5.95 (*0-932415-31-8*) Red Sea Pr.

Mottershead, Allen. Electronic Devices & Circuits: An Introduction. LC 72-93687. 655p. reprint ed. pap. 180.00 (*0-685-09000-0*, 2007756) Bks Demand.

— Introduction to Electricity & Electronics: Electron Flow Version. 2nd ed. LC 85-26304. 716p. 1986. text ed. 49.50 (*0-471-80656-0*) P-H.

Mottershead, J. Suetonius: Claudius. 190p. 1986. 16.95 (*0-86292-080-9*, Pub. by Brstl Class Pr UK) Focus Info Gr.

Mottershead, J. E., ed. Modern Practice in Stress & Vibration Analysis. (Proceedings of Conference, University of Liverpool, 3-5 April 1989 Ser.). 350p. 1989. 145.00 (*0-08-037522-7*, Pub. by Pergamon Repr UK); pap. 40.00 (*0-08-037523-5*, Pub. by Pergamon Repr UK) Franklin.

Mottershead, J. E., jt. auth. see Friswell, M. I.

Mottesi, A. Atrevete a Dar Amor (Dare to Give Love) (SPA.). Date not set. 1.79 (*1-56063-099-X*, 498144) Editorial Unilit.

Mottesi, A. H. Calles Rectas, Sendero Torcido (Straight Sts, Crooked Path) (SPA.). Date not set. 1.79 (*0-685-74906-1*, 498505) Editorial Unilit.

— De Inspiracion (Of Inspiration) (SPA.). Date not set. 1.79 (*0-8423-6450-1*, 498508) Editorial Unilit.

— De Pleno Gozo (To Fill You with Joy) (SPA.). Date not set. 1.79 (*0-8423-6349-1*, 498507) Editorial Unilit.

— Dia Del Bien, Dia Del Mal (Good Day, Bad Day) (SPA.). Date not set. 1.79 (*0-685-74927-4*, 498506) Editorial Unilit.

— Escogiendo Caminos (Choosing a Path) (SPA.). Date not set. 1.99 (*0-685-74934-7*, 498502) Editorial Unilit.

— Eternidad, Tiempo, Vanidad (Eternity, Time, Vanity) (SPA.). Date not set. 1.99 (*0-685-74935-5*, 498504) Editorial Unilit.

— Frente a un Problema (Facing the Problem) (SPA.). Date not set. 1.79 (*0-685-74938-X*, 498503) Editorial Unilit.

— La Lus de la Casa (The Light of the Home) (SPA.). Date not set. 1.79 (*0-685-74950-9*, 498501) Editorial Unilit.

Mottesi, Alberto. America: Five Hundred Anos Despues. 164p. (Orig.). (SPA.). 1992. pap. 10.95 (*0-9633528-0-6*) A Mottesi Evang Assn.

— En Su Presencia (In His Presence) (SPA.). 1988. 8.99 (*0-945792-19-0*, 498509) Editorial Unilit.

Mottet, N. Karle, ed. Environmental Pathology. (Illus.). 1985. 60.00 (*0-19-503427-9*) OUP.

Motteux, Peter A. & Eccles, John. The Rape of Europa by Jupiter, a Masque; As It Is Sung at the Queens Theatre, in Dorset-Garden: And the Masque of Acis & Galatea... in a New Opera Call'd the Mad Lover. LC 92-24905. (Augustan Reprints Ser.: No. 208 (1981)). reprint ed. 12.00 (*0-404-70208-2*, M52.E27R3) AMS Pr.

Mottin, Marie-France, jt. auth. see Dumont, Rene.

Mottinger, Lyle D., et al. Appleseeds. 42p. (Orig.). 1987. pap. text ed. 7.00 (*0-937652-35-0*) Natl Art Ed.

Mottl, Felix, ed. see Wagner, Richard.

Mottla, Gabriel V. New York Evidence-Proof of Cases, 2 Vols. 2nd ed. LC 66-275456. 1658p. 180.00 (*0-317-00483-2*) Lawyers Cooperative.

— New York Evidence-Proof of Cases, 2 Vols. 2nd suppl. ed. LC 66-275456. 1658p. 1993. Suppl. 1993. 89.50 (*0-317-03184-8*) Lawyers Cooperative.

— Proof of Cases in Massachusetts, 2 vols. 2nd ed. LC 66-24570. 1780p. 220.00 (*0-317-00489-1*) Lawyers Cooperative.

— Proof of Cases in Massachusetts, 2 vols. 2nd suppl. ed. LC 66-24570. 1780p. 1993. Suppl. 1993. 60.00 (*0-317-03185-6*) Lawyers Cooperative.

Motto, Anna L. Seneca: Moral Epistles. LC 81-21252. (American Philological Association Textbook Ser.). (C). 1985. pap. 16.95 (*0-89130-897-0*) Scholars Pr GA.

Motto, Anna L. & Clark, John R. Senecan Tragedy. 367p. 1988. 86.00 (*90-256-0920-1*, Pub. by A M Hakkert NE) Benjamins North Am.

Motto, Anna L. & Clark, John R., eds. Seneca: A Critical Bibliography, 1900-1980: Scholarship on His Life, Thought, Prose, & Influence. 372p. (Orig.). 1989. pap. 67.00 (*90-256-0959-7*, Pub. by A M Hakkert NE) Benjamins North Am.

Motto, Jerome A., et al. Standards for Suicide Prevention & Crisis Centers. LC 73-17029. 114p. 1974. 32.95 (*0-87705-105-4*) Human Sci Pr.

Mottola, Anthony, tr. see St. Ignatius.

Mottola, H. A., ed. Henry Freisher: "Talanta" Issue. (Illus.). 160p. 1985. pap. 31.00 (*0-08-032639-0*, Pub. by PPL UK) Elsevier.

Mottola, Horacio A. Kinetic Aspects of Analytical Chemistry. LC 87-26344. (Chemical Analysis Ser.). 285p. 1988. text ed. 125.00 (*0-471-83676-1*) Wiley.

Mottola, Tony. Play the Guitar in Thirty Minutes. 1986. pap. 7.95 (*0-671-63297-3*) S&S Trade.

***Mottram.** Drugs in Sports. 2nd ed. 1995. (*0-419-18890-8*) Routledge Chapman & Hall.

Mottram, Bob. Salt-Water Salmon Angling. (Illus.). 160p. 1990. pap. 9.95 (*0-936608-89-7*) F Amato Pubns.

Mottram, D. R. Drugs in Sport. 192p. 1988. text ed. 29.00 (*0-87322-222-9*, BMOT0222) Human Kinetics.

Mottram, E. C., jt. auth. see Mottram, V. H.

Mottram, Eric. The Algebra of Need: William Burroughs & the Gods of Death. 2nd enl. ed. 320p. 1994. pap. 19.95 (*0-7145-2916-8*) M Boyars Pubs.

Mottram, R. A., jt. auth. see Woolman, J.

Mottram, R. F. Human Nutrition. 3rd ed. 179p. 1979. pap. 30.00 (*0-917678-09-5*) Food & Nut Pr.

Mottram, Ralph H. Armistice & Other Memories: Forming a Pendant to the 'Spanish Farm Trilogy' LC 79-160946. (Short Story Index Reprint Ser.). 1977. reprint ed. 19.95 (*0-8369-3925-5*) Ayer.

Mottram, Ron. The Danish Cinema Before Dreyer. LC 87-16125. 315p. 1988. 29.50 (*0-8108-2035-8*) Scarecrow.

Mottram, V. H. & Mottram, E. C. Sound Catering for Hard Times: How to Economize on Food Without Starving the Body. 1974. lib. bdg. 69.95 (*0-685-51375-0*) Revisionist Pr.

Mottram, William. The True Story of George Eliot. LC 72-3376. (English Literature Ser.: No. 33). 1972. reprint ed. lib. bdg. 65.95 (*0-8383-1508-9*) M S G Haskell Hse.

Mottu, A., jt. auth. see Kienzle, O.

Mottu, Philippe. The Story of Caux. (Illus.). 1989. 8.95 (*0-901269-03-4*) Grosvenor USA.

Mottweiler, Jack. Adults As Learners. (Christian Education Ministries Ser.). 95p. (Orig.). 1984. pap. 3.95 (*0-89367-098-7*) Light & Life.

Motulsky, A. G., jt. auth. see Vogel, F.

Motulsky, Arno G., jt. ed. see Goodman, Richard M.

***Motulsky, Harvey.** Intuitive Biostatistics. (Illus.). 384p. (C). 1995. 39.95 (*0-19-508606-6*); pap. text ed. 19.95 (*0-19-508607-4*) OUP.

Motum, John, ed. The Putnam Aeronautical Review, Vol. II. (Illus.). 256p. 1991. 45.00 (*1-55750-676-0*) Naval Inst Pr.

— The Putnam Aeronautical Review, Vol. 1. LC 89-61978. (Illus.). 256p. 1990. 45.00 (*0-87021-610-4*) Naval Inst Pr.

Motus, Cecile L. Hiligaynon Dictionary. LC 73-152469. (University of Hawaii, Honolulu. Pacific & Asian Linguistics Institute Ser.). 337p. reprint ed. pap. 96.10 (*0-317-10091-2*, 2007709) Bks Demand.

— Hiligaynon Lessons. LC 78-152470. (University of Hawaii, Honolulu. Pacific & Asian Linguistics Institute Ser.). 454p. reprint ed. pap. 129.40 (*0-317-10133-1*, 2017220) Bks Demand.

Motus, L. & Narita, S., eds. Distributed Computer Control Systems 1989. (IFAC Workshop Ser.: No. 9005). 200p. 1990. 77.00 (*0-08-037870-6*, Pergamon Pr) Elsevier.

***Motus, Leo & Rodd, Michael G.** Timing Analysis of Real-Time Software: A Practical Approach to the Specification & Design of Real-Time. LC 94-28551. 1994. text ed. 125.00 (*0-08-042026-5*, Pergamon Pr); pap. text ed. 51.00 (*0-08-042025-7*, Pergamon Pr) Elsevier.

Motus, Leo & Rodd, Mike G. Specification of Real-Time Distributed Systems. 350p. 1993. pap. text ed. 36.00 (*0-13-834060-9*) P-H.

Motwani, Jagat, et al. Global Indian Diaspora: Yesterday, Today & Tomorrow. 1993. write for info. (*0-9639318-6-5*) M Gosine.

Motwani, Prem. A Dictionary of Loanwords Usage: Katakana-English. 258p. (ENG & JPN.). 1991. 125.00 (*0-8288-7340-2*) Fr & Eur.

***Motwani, Rajeev & Raghavan, Prabhakar.** Randomized Algorithms. 500p. (C). 1995. 39.95 (*0-521-47465-5*) Cambridge U Pr.

Motycka, Thomas J., jt. auth. see Cobb, Tyson K.

Motyer, J. A. The Message of Amos. LC 74-14300. (Bible Speaks Today Ser.). 208p. (Orig.). 1988. pap. 12.99 (*0-87784-283-3*, 283) InterVarsity.

— The Message of James. Stott, John R., ed. LC 85-4316. (Bible Speaks Today Ser.). 156p. 1985. pap. 12.99 (*0-87784-292-2*, 292) InterVarsity.

— The Message of Philippians. Stott, John R., ed. LC 83-22684. (Bible Speaks Today Ser.). 252p. 1984. pap. 12.99 (*0-87784-310-4*, 310) InterVarsity.

— The Prophecy of Isaiah: An Introduction & Commentary. LC 93-17815. 512p. (Orig.). 1993. 29.99 (*0-8308-1424-8*, 1424) InterVarsity.

Motyer, J. A., ed. see Atkinson, David.

Motyer, J. A., ed. see Baldwin, Joyce G.

Motyer, J. A., ed. see Barnett, Paul.

Motyer, J. A., ed. see Brown, Raymond.

Motyer, J. A., ed. see Kidner, Derek.

Motyer, J. A., ed. see Lucas, R. C.

Motyer, J. A., ed. see Prior, David.

Motyer, J. A., ed. see Stott, John R.

Motyer, J. A., ed. see Wilcock, Michael.

Motyer, J. Alec. El Mensaje de Filipenses. Orig. Title: The Message of Philippians. 304p. (SPA.). 1993. pap. 8.99 (*0-8254-1486-5*) Kregel.

Motyka, W. Annotated Bibliography of Russian Language Publications on Accounting, 1736-1917, 2 vols. 848p. 1993. Vol. I, 1736-1900. write for info. (*0-318-70046-8*); Vol. II, 1901-1917. write for info. (*0-318-70047-6*) Garland.

— Annotated Bibliography of Russian Language Publications on Accounting, 1736-1917, 2 vols., Set. LC 93-2711. (New Works in Accounting History). 848p. 1993. 132.00 (*0-8153-1247-4*) Garland.

Motyl, Alexander J. Dilemmas of Independence: Ukraine after Totalitarianism. LC 93-16966. 200p. 1993. pap. 17.95 (*0-87609-131-1*) Coun Foreign.

— Sovietology, Rationality, Nationality: Coming to Grips with Nationalism in the U. S. S. R. 1990. text ed. 35.00 (*0-231-07326-7*) Col U Pr.

— Will the Non-Russians Rebel? State, Ethnicity, & Stability in the U. S. S. R. LC 86-24386. (Cornell Studies in Soviet History & Science). 224p. (C). 1987. 29.95 (*0-8014-1947-6*) Cornell U Pr.

Motyl, Alexander J., ed. The Post-Soviet Nations: Perspectives in the Demise of the U. S. S. R. 360p. 1992. text ed. 34.50 (*0-231-07894-3*) Col U Pr.

— Thinking Theoretically About Soviet Nationalities. 288p. 1992. text ed. 45.00 (*0-231-07512-X*) Col U Pr.

Motz, H., jt. auth. see Luchini, P.

Motz, Lloyd & Weaver, Jefferson H. The Concepts of Science: From Newton to Einstein. LC 87-38493. 446p. 1988. 23.50 (*0-306-42872-5*, Plenum Pr) Plenum.

— The Story of Astronomy. (Illus.). 385p. 1995. 28.95 (*0-306-45090-9*, Plenum Pr) Plenum.

— The Story of Mathematics. 355p. 1993. 25.95 (*0-306-44508-5*, Plenum Pr) Plenum.

— The Story of Mathematics. 1995. pap. 14.00 (*0-380-72458-8*) Avon.

— The Story of Physics. 432p. 1992. pap. 12.50 (*0-380-71725-5*) Avon.

— The Story of Physics. LC 88-33655. (Illus.). 428p. 1989. 24.50 (*0-306-43076-2*, Plenum Pr) Plenum.

— The Unfolding Universe: A Stellar Journey. (Illus.). 379p. 1989. 24.50 (*0-306-43264-1*, Plenum Pr) Plenum.

Motz, Lloyd & Weaver, Jefferson H., eds. Conquering Mathematics: From Arithmetic to Calculus. LC 91-9329. (Illus.). 292p. 1991. 23.50 (*0-306-43768-6*, Plenum Pr) Plenum.

Motz, Marilyn F. True Sisterhood: Michigan Women & Their Kin, 1820-1920. LC 82-19198. 199p. 1984. 64.50 (*0-87395-715-6*); pap. 21.95 (*0-87395-716-4*) State U NY Pr.

Motz, Marilyn F. & Browne, Pat, eds. Making the American Home: Middle-Class Women & Domestic Material Culture, 1840-1940. LC 88-70387. (Illus.). 212p. (C). 1988. text ed. 33.95 (*0-87972-433-1*); pap. text ed. 16.95 (*0-87972-434-X*) Bowling Green Univ.

Motz, Marilyn F., et al, eds. Eye on the Future. LC 94-70244. 294p. (C). 1994. text ed. 39.95 (*0-87972-655-5*) Bowling Green Univ.

Motzkin, Gabriel. Time & Transcendence: Secular History, the Catholic Reaction, & the Rediscovery of the Future. LC 92-10249. (Philosophical Studies in Contemporary Culture: Vol. 1). (C). 1992. lib. bdg. 115.00 (*0-7923-1773-4*) Kluwer Ac.

Motzkin, Linda, jt. auth. see Resnikoff, Irene.

Motzkin, T. S., ed. see Pure Mathematics Symposium Staff.

Motzo, Giovanni, et al, eds. Administrative Justice in Western Societies, Vol. 1. 1991. 125.00 (*0-929179-79-X*) Transnatl Juris Pubns.

Motzwadi, Stan. Soweto: Portrait of a City. 144p. (C). 1989. 130.00 (*0-685-32441-9*, Pub. by New Holland Pubs UK) St Mut.

Mou-Lam, Wong, jt. tr. see Price, A. F.

Mou-Tuan Huang, et al. Food Phytochemicals for Cancer Prevention: Fruits & Vegetables. LC 93-33775. (ACS Symposium Ser.: Vol. 546). 427p. 1994. 99.95 (*0-8412-2768-3*) Am Chemical.

Moua, Mitt, tr. see Smalley, William A., et al.

Mouat, et al, eds. Wordweavers. 93p. (Orig.). 1986. pap. write for info. (*0-917557-02-6*) Wyo Writers.

Mouat, Marty, jt. auth. see Petrino, Bob.

Moubray House Publishing Ltd. Staff. Daniel Defoe's Scotland. (Illus.). (C). 1991. pap. 90.00 (*0-948473-19-3*) St Mut.

— Scottish Interiors Series, 4 vols. (Illus.). 384p. (C). 1989. Scottish Renaissance Interiors. 35.00 (*0-948473-06-1*); Scottish Georgian Interiors. 35.00 (*0-948473-05-3*); Scottish Victorian Interiors. 35.00 (*0-948473-04-5*); Scottish Edwardian Interiors. 35.00 (*0-948473-07-X*) St Mut.

— Scottish Interiors Series, 4 vols., Set. (Illus.). 384p. (C). 1989. 140.00 (*0-685-40597-4*) St Mut.

Moubray, John. Reliability Centered Maintenance. 336p. 1992. 69.95 (*0-8311-3044-X*) Indus Pr.

***Mouchet, Jean-Paul & Mitchell, Alan.** Abnormal Pressure While Drilling. (Illus.). 264p. (C). 1989. pap. text ed. 32.00 (*2-901026-28-1*) Technip.

Moudgil, jt. auth. see Somasundaran.

Moudgil, B. & Somasundaran, P., eds. Dispersion & Aggregation: Fundamentals & Applications. Date not set. 150.00 (*0-939204-51-7*) Eng Found.

Moudgil, V. K., ed. Molecular Mechanism of Steroid Hormone Action: Recent Advances. (Illus.). xii, 824p. 1985. 223.10 (*0-89925-032-7*) De Gruyter.

— Molecular Mechanism of Steroid Hormone Action: Recent Advances. (Illus.). xii, 824p. 1985. 223.10 (*3-11-010118-1*) De Gruyter.

— Recent Advances in Steroid Hormone Action. 552p. (C). 1987. lib. bdg. 207.70 (*0-89925-313-X*) De Gruyter.

— Recent Advances in Steroid Hormone Action. 552p. (C). 1987. lib. bdg. 207.70 (*3-11-010762-7*) De Gruyter.

— Steroid Receptors in Health & Disease. LC 88-22477. (Serono Symposia U. S. A. Ser.). (Illus.). 346p. 1988. 95.00 (*0-306-42987-X*, Plenum Pr) Plenum.

Moudgil, Virinder K., ed. Receptor Phosphorylation. 400p. 1988. 294.00 (*0-8493-6318-7*, QP552) CRC Pr.

— Steroid Hormone Receptors: Basic & Clinical Aspects. LC 93-33850. (Hormones in Health & Disease Ser.). 1993. 94.50 (*0-8176-3694-3*) Birkhauser.

Moudon, Anne V., ed. Public Streets for Public Use. (Illus.). 352p. 1991. pap. text ed. 30.00 (*0-231-07599-5*) Col U Pr.

Moudry, Vladimir, jt. auth. see Nemec, Frantisek.

Moudud, Hasna J. Women in China. 94p. 1980. 17.95 (*0-7069-1084-2*) Asia Bk Corp.

Mouer, Ross E. & Sugimoto, Yoshio. Images of Japanese Society: A Study in the Structure of Social Reality. (Japanese Studies). 600p. 1985. 65.00 (*0-7103-0078-6*, Pub. by Kegan Paul Intl UK) Routledge Chapman & Hall.

— Images of Japanese Society: A Study in the Structure of Social Reality. 552p. 1990. pap. 25.00 (*0-7103-0379-3*, A4425, Pub. by Kegan Paul Intl UK) Routledge Chapman & Hall.

Mouer, Ross E. & Sugimoto, Yoshio, eds. Constructs for Understanding Japan. 250p. 1989. text ed. 69.50 (*0-7103-0209-6*) Routledge Chapman & Hall.

Mouer, Ross E., tr. see Nishikawa, Shunsaku, ed.

Moufang, Christoph, ed. Katholische Katechismen des 16 Jahrhunderts in Deutscher Sprache. l, 626p. 1964. reprint ed. write for info. (*0-318-71847-2*, Pub. by Georg Olms GW) Lubrecht & Cramer.

Mouffe, Barbara S., ed. see Hawthorne, Nathaniel.

Mouffe, Chantal. The Return of the Political. 240p. 1993. 59.95 (*0-86091-486-0*, B2508, Pub. by Verso UK); pap. 18.95 (*0-86091-651-0*, B2512, Pub. by Verso UK) Routledge Chapman & Hall.

Mouffe, Chantal, jt. auth. see Laclau, Ernesto.

Mougeon, Raymond & Beniak, Edouard. The Case of French in Ontario, Canada. (Oxford Studies in Language Contact). 256p. 1991. 69.00 (*0-19-824827-X*) OUP.

***Moughtin, Cliff, et al.** Urban Design: Ornament & Decoration. LC 94-47287. 1995. write for info. (*0-7506-0792-0*, Butterwrth Archit) Buttrwrth-Heinemann.

Moughtin, J. C. Urban Design: Street & Square. (Illus.). 224p. 1992. 64.95 (*0-7506-0416-6*) Buttrwrth-Heinemann.

Mouhot, Henri. Travels in Siam, Cambodia & Laos 1858-1860, Set, Vols. I & II. (Oxford in Asia Hardback Reprints Ser.). (Illus.). 632p. 1991. Set. 65.00 (*0-19-588951-7*) OUP.

Mouillesseaux, Claire & Seger, Doris. Devil-Kings & Cannibals. (Illus.). 52p. (J). (gr. k-4). 1962. pap. text ed. 8.99 (*1-55976-053-2*) CEF Press.

Mouilloron-Becar, jt. auth. see Bruno, A.

***Moukarim, Moustafa.** Al-Kiama (The Life after) 100p. Date not set. pap. 7.95 (*0-7610-0424-6*) NW Pub.

Moukwa, Mosongo, et al, eds. Cement-Based Materials: Present, Future, & Environmental Aspects. LC 93-33157. (Ceramic Transactions Ser.: No. 37). 202p. 1993. 69.00 (*0-944904-68-8*, TRANS037) Am Ceramic.

Moulaert, Frank & Salinas, Wilson. Regional Analysis & the New International Division of Labor. (Studies in Applied Regional Science). 1982. lib. bdg. 39.00 (*0-89838-107-X*) Kluwer Ac.

Moulaert, Frank, jt. ed. see Daniels, Peter W.

Moulakis, Athanasios. Beyond Utility: Liberal Education for a Technological Age. LC 93-27212. 184p. 1994. 21.95 (*0-8262-0929-7*) U of Mo Pr.

***Moulakis, Athanasios, ed.** Legitimacy-Legitimate: Proceedings of the Conference Held in Florence, June 3-4, 1982 (Actes de Colloque de Florence 3 et 4 June 1982) (European University Institute, Series C (Political & Social Science): No. 3). vi, 105p. 1985. 36.55 (*3-11-010063-0*) De Gruyter.

— Legitimacy-Legitimite: Proceedings of the Conference held in Florence, June 3-4, 1982 (Actes de Colloque de Florence 3 et 4 June 1982. (European University Institute, Series C (Political & Social Science): No. 3). vi, 105p. 1985. 36.55 (*0-89925-106-4*) De Gruyter.

— The Promise of History: Essays in Political Philosophy. (European University Institute, Series C (Political & Social Science): No. 2). vi, 206p. 1985. 69.25 (*0-89925-107-2*) De Gruyter.

— The Promise of History: Essays in Political Philosophy. (European University Institute, Series C (Political & Social Science): No. 2). vi, 206p. 1985. 69.25 (*3-11-010043-6*) De Gruyter.

— Technology & Responsibility: Essays Presented on the Occasion of the Centenary of the College of Engineering & Applied Science, University of Colorado, Boulder. LC 93-61149. (Illus.). 155p. 1993. 17.00 (*0-918714-39-7*) Intl Res Ctr Energy.

Moulard, Barbara L. & Wilson, Lee A. Within the Underworld Sky: Mimbres Art in Context. 190p. 1984. 65.00 (*0-942642-11-2*) Twelvetrees Pr.

***Mould, Alan.** Step-by-Step: Slam Bidding. 144p. 1995. 16.95 (*0-7134-7712-1*, Pub. by Batsford UK) Trafalgar.

An Asterisk (*) at the beginning of an entry indicates that the title is appearing in BIP for the first time.

Mould, Charles, ed. see Boalch, Donald H.
Mould, David H. Dividing Lines: Canals, Railroads & Urban Rivalry in Ohio's Hocking Valley, 1825-1875. 318p. (C). 1992. lib. bdg. 51.00 (*1-882090-06-3*) Wright State Univ Pr.
Mould, George. Manchester Memories. 132p. (C). 1988. 85.00 (*0-900963-41-7*, Pub. by T Dalton UK) St Mut.
Mould, Maurice C. Financial Information for Management of Development Finance Institutions: Some Guidelines. (Technical Paper Ser.: No. 63). 464p. 1987. 23.95 (*0-8213-0913-7*, 10913) World Bank.
Mould, Owen, ed. see Montana, Denby.
Mould, P. R., jt. auth. see Cotterill, P.
Mould, R. F. Cancer Statistics. (Medical Science Ser.). (Illus.). 302p. 1983. 76.00 (*0-85274-541-9*) IOP Pub.
— A Century of X-Rays & Radioactivity in Medicine with Emphasis on Photographic Records of the Early Years. (Illus.). 236p. 1993. 59.50 (*0-7503-0224-0*) IOP Pub.
— Chernobyl: The Real Story. 256p. 1988. text ed. write for info. (*0-08-035718-0*, Pub. by Pergamon Repr UK) Franklin.
— Introductory Medical Statistics. 2nd ed. (Medical Science Ser.). (Illus.). 208p. 1989. pap. 25.00 (*0-85274-382-3*) IOP Pub.
— Radiation Protection in Hospitals. (Medical Science Ser.). (Illus.). 224p. 1985. 70.00 (*0-85274-802-7*) IOP Pub.
Mould, R. F., ed. see Bewley, D. K.
Mould, R. F., ed. see International Conference on International Strategies for the Eradication of Carcinoma of the Cervix in Developing Areas (1987: Calcutta, India) Staff.
Mould, R. F., ed. see International Working Party for Treatment of Cancer of Cervix in Developing Areas, Meeting (8th: 1985: Ban Phattaya, Thailand) Staff.
Mould, R. F., ed. see Intl. Conf. on Intl. Strategies for the Eradication of Carcinoma of the Cervix in Dev. Areas Staff.
Mould, R. F., jt. ed. see Perry, J. A.
Mould, R. F., ed. see Workshop on the Use of Computers in Data Handling in Radiotherapy & Oncology in Europe (1984: World Health Organization) Staff.
Mould, Richard A. Basic Relativity. LC 93-38098. (Illus.). 416p. 1995. 49.95 (*0-387-94188-6*) Spr-Verlag.
Mould, William A., jt. ed. see Tappan, Donald W.
Moulden. Fundamentals of Transonic Flow. LC 84-7381. 332p. 1989. 54.50 (*0-471-04661-2*, Wiley-Interscience) Krieger.
Moulden, T. H. Fundamentals of Transonic Flow. 350p. (C). 1991. reprint ed. 59.50 (*0-89464-441-6*) Krieger.
Moulder, Bennett. A Guide to the Common Spiders of Illinois. (Popular Science Ser.: Vol. X). (Illus.). 125p. 1992. pap. 10.00 (*0-89792-135-6*) Ill St Museum.
Moulder, D. S. & Williamson, P., eds. Estuarine & Coastal Pollution: Detection, Research & Control: Proceedings of an IAWPRC Conference Held in Plymouth, 16-19 July 1985. 364p. 1986. pap. 105.00 (*0-08-033669-8*, Pergamon Pr) Elsevier.
Moulder, Evelina, ed. Compensation Ninety-Four: An Annual Report on Local Government Executive Salaries & Fringe Benefits. (Illus.). 404p. (Orig.). 1994. pap. text ed. 180.00 (*0-87326-095-3*) Intl City-Cnty Mgt.
— Compensation 93: An Annual Report on Local Government Executive Salaries & Fringe Benefits. 1993. per. 180.00 (*0-87326-982-9*) Intl City-Cnty Mgt.
— Compensation 95: An Annual Report on Local Government Executive Salaries & Fringe Benefits. (Illus.). 404p. (Orig.). 1995. pap. text ed. 180.00 (*0-87326-098-8*, 41000) Intl City-Cnty Mgt.
— Municipal Year Book, 1991. (Illus.). 416p. 1991. 77.50 (*0-87326-966-7*) Intl City-Cnty Mgt.
— Municipal Year Book, 1992. (Illus.). 416p. 1992. 77.50 (*0-87326-967-5*) Intl City-Cnty Mgt.
— Municipal Year Book, 1993. (Illus.). 416p. 1993. 79.95 (*0-87326-968-3*) Intl City-Cnty Mgt.
— Municipal Year Book, 1994. (Illus.). 416p. 1994. 79.95 (*0-87326-969-1*) Intl City-Cnty Mgt.
— Municipal Year Book 1995. (Illus.). 416p. 1995. text ed. 79.95 (*0-87326-970-5*, 41001) Intl City-Cnty Mgt.
Moulder, James W., ed. Intracellular Parasitism. 288p. 1989. 204.00 (*0-8493-5065-4*, QR171) CRC Pr.
Moulder, John F., et al. Handbook of X-ray Photoelectron Spectroscopy: A Reference Book of Standard Spectra for Identification & Interpretation of XPS Data. Chastain, Jill, ed. LC 92-61338. (Illus.). 275p. 1992. 290.00 (*0-9627026-2-5*) Perkin-Elmer.
Moulder, Rebecca, see O'Conner, Rebecca, pseud..
Moulder, Robert, jt. auth. see McCrory, Martin.
Moulds, A. J., et al. Emergencies in General Practice. 1983. lib. bdg. 25.00 (*0-318-00073-3*) Kluwer Ac.
— Emergencies in General Practice. 2nd ed. 1985. lib. bdg. 33.50 (*0-85200-926-7*) Kluwer Ac.
Moulds, JoAnn M. & Laird-Fryer, Barbara, eds. Blood Groups: Ch-Rg, Kn-McC-Yk, Cromer. LC 92-49706. 1992. 43.00 (*1-56395-009-X*) Am Assn Blood.
Moulds, JoAnn M. & Tregellas, Michael W., eds. Introductory Molecular Genetics. LC 86-17295. 1986. text ed. 7.00 (*0-915355-28-0*) Am Assn Blood.
Moulds, JoAnn M. & Woods, Laura L. Blood Groups: P, I, Sda & Pr. LC 91-4870. (Illus.). (C). 1991. text ed. 40.00 (*1-56395-002-2*) Am Assn Blood.
Moulds, JoAnn M., jt. auth. see Masouredis, Serafeim P.
Moulds, JoAnn M., et al. Scientific & Technical Aspects of the Major Histocompatibility Complex. LC 89-17881. (Illus.). (C). 1989. text ed. 28.00 (*0-915355-71-X*) Am Assn Blood.
Moulds, Maxwell. A Guide to Australian Cicadas. (Illus.). 217p. 1990. 39.95 (*0-86840-139-0*, Pub. by New South Wales Univ Pr AT) Intl Spec Bk.
Moulds, Tony, intro. National Conference on Engineering Heritage, 5th, 1990: Interpreting Engineering Heritage. (Illus.). 153p. (Orig.). 1990. pap. 72.00 (*0-909421-23-4*) Accents Pubns.
Moule, A. C. Christians in China Before the Year 1550. 1972. 59.95 (*0-87968-865-3*) Gordon Pr.
Moule, C. F., jt. ed. see Farmer, William R.
Moule, Charles F. Epistles of Paul the Apostle to the Colossians & to Philemon. (Cambridge Greek Testament Ser.). (C). 1957. pap. 21.95 (*0-521-09236-1*) Cambridge U Pr.
— Gospel According to Mark. (Cambridge Bible Commentary on the New English Bible, New Testament Ser.). (Orig.). (C). 1965. 15.50 (*0-521-04210-0*); pap. 19.95 (*0-521-09288-4*) Cambridge U Pr.
— Idiom Book of New Testament Greek. 2nd ed. (C). 1959. pap. 21.95 (*0-521-09237-X*) Cambridge U Pr.
— The Origin of Christology. LC 76-11087. 1979. pap. 21.95 (*0-521-29363-4*) Cambridge U Pr.
Moule, Charles F., jt. ed. see Bammel, E.
Moule, D. M. The Stars Shall Fall from Heaven: The Coming World Catastrophe. 1994. 16.95 (*0-533-10922-1*) Vantage.
Moule, H. C. Antiguo Evangelio Para Una Nueva Era: The Old Gospel for a New Age. (SPA.). 5.50 (*84-7645-015-X*, 223092, Pub. by Edit Clie SP) TSELF.
— Bosquejos de Doctrina Cristiana: Outlines of Christian Doctrine. (SPA.). 6.95 (*84-7228-901-X*, 220114, Pub. by Edit Clie SP) TSELF.
— The Classic New Testament Commentary: Romans. 437p. 1992. pap. 15.99 (*0-551-02592-1*) HarpC.
— Estudios sobre Colosenses: Lectures in Colossians. (SPA.). 4.95 (*84-7228-900-1*, 222323, Pub. by Edit Clie SP) TSELF.
— Estudios sobre Efesios: Studies in Ephesians. (SPA.). 5.50 (*84-7228-902-8*, 222333, Pub. by Edit Clie SP) TSELF.
— Estudios sobre Hebreos: Studies on Hebrews. (SPA.). 3.25 (*84-7645-092-3*, 223154, Pub. by Edit Clie SP) TSELF.
— Exposicion De la Epistola a Los: Paul's Letter to the Romans. (SPA.). 21.95 (*84-7645-200-4*, 223229, Pub. by Edit Clie SP) TSELF.
— La Santidad Que Es en Cristo: Holiness That Is in Christ. (SPA.). 3.25 (*84-7228-884-6*, 220800, Pub. by Edit Clie SP) TSELF.
— Studies in Colossians & Philemon. LC 77-79185. (Kregel Popular Commentary Ser.). 196p. 1977. kivar 6.99 (*0-8254-3217-0*) Kregel.
— Studies in Hebrews. LC 77-79181. (Kregel Popular Commentary Ser.). 120p. 1977. kivar 5.99 (*0-8254-3223-5*) Kregel.
— Studies in Second Timothy. LC 77-79182. (Kregel Popular Commentary Ser.). 180p. 1977. kivar 6.99 (*0-8254-3219-7*) Kregel.
Moule, Handley C. Colossians & Philemon. 1988. pap. 5.95 (*0-87508-361-7*) Chr Lit.
— Ephesians. 1982. pap. 5.95 (*0-87508-363-3*) Chr Lit.
— Philippians. 1975. pap. 5.95 (*0-87508-364-1*) Chr Lit.
— Second Corinthians. 1979. pap. 5.95 (*0-87508-359-5*) Chr Lit.
Moule, William R. God's Arms Around Us. LC 90-21982. (Illus.). 400p. 1990. reprint ed. 19.95 (*0-931892-60-0*) B Dolphin Pub.
— A Little Moule History: Eighteen Nineties - Nineteen Thirty-Seven. LC 90-22041. (Illus.). 624p. 1990. 24.95 (*0-931892-61-9*) B Dolphin Pub.
Moules, Joan. A Golden Flame. large type ed. (Linford Romance Library). 288p. 1987. pap. 11.95 (*0-7089-6378-1*, Linford) Ulverscroft.
— Passionate Enchantment. large type ed. (Linford Romance Library). 320p. 1989. pap. 11.95 (*0-7089-6648-9*, Linford) Ulverscroft.
— Precious Inheritance. large type ed. (Linford Romance Library). 240p. 1988. pap. 11.95 (*0-7089-6548-2*, Linford) Ulverscroft.
— Richer Than Diamonds. large type ed. 1990. pap. 12.95 (*0-7089-6931-3*, Trailtree Bookshop) Ulverscroft.
Moulijn, J. A. & Kapteijn, F., eds. Coal Characterisation for Conversion Processes, 1986: Proceedings of the First International Rolduc Symposium, Rolduc, The Netherlands, April 28-May 1, 1986. 440p. 1987. 154.00 (*0-444-42742-2*) Elsevier.
Moulijn, J. A., jt. ed. see Figueiredo, J. L.
Moulijn, J. A., et al, eds. Catalysis: An Integrated Approach to Homogeneous, Heterogeneous & Industrial Catalysis. (Studies in Surface Science & Catalysis: Vol. 79). 500p. 1993. 168.50 (*0-444-89229-X*) Elsevier.
Moulik, Achala, tr. see Mukherjee, Moni S.
Moulik, Moni. Twilight. 1976. 6.75 (*0-89253-830-9*) Ind-US Inc.
Moulik, T., ed. Food Energy Nexus & Ecosystems. (C). 1988. 47.50 (*81-204-0362-2*, Pub. by Oxford IBH II) S Asia.
Moulik, T. K. & Purushotham, P. Technology Transfer in Rural Industries: Cases & Analysis. 1986. 18.50 (*0-86132-124-3*, Pub. by Popular Prakashan II) S Asia.
Moulik, T. K., jt. ed. see Streefkerek, Hein.
Moulin, Annie. Peasantry & Society in France since 1789. Cleary, M. C. & Cleary, M. F., trs. (Illus.). 256p. (C). 1991. 59.95 (*0-521-39534-8*); pap. 17.95 (*0-521-39577-1*) Cambridge U Pr.
Moulin-Eckart, Richard D. Cosima Wagner, 2 vols., Set. Phillips, Catherine A., tr. LC 81-1500. (Music Ser.). (Illus.). 1981. reprint ed. lib. bdg. 110.00 (*0-306-76102-5*) Da Capo.
Moulin, Herve. Axioms of Cooperative Decision-Making. (Econometric Society Monographs: No. 15). (Illus.). 300p. 1988. 74.95 (*0-521-36055-2*) Cambridge U Pr.
— Axioms of Cooperative Decision-Making. (Econometric Society Monographs: No. 15). (Illus.). 400p. (C). 1991. pap. 27.95 (*0-521-42458-5*) Cambridge U Pr.
— Cooperative Microeconomics: A Game-Theoretic Introduction. LC 95-3606. 1995. write for info. (*0-691-03481-8*) Princeton U Pr.
Moulin, Herve, ed. Eighty-Nine Exercises with Solutions from Game Theory for the Social Sciences. 2nd rev. ed. LC 86-5315. 156p. 1986. 35.00x (*0-8147-5432-5*) NYU Pr.
Moulin, J. A., et al. Nineteen Eighty-Seven International Conference on Coal Science. (Coal Science & Technology Ser.: Vol. 11). 1987. 256.50 (*0-444-42893-3*) Elsevier.
Moulin, Pierre, et al. Pierre Deux's French Country. (Illus.). 1989. 45.00 (*0-517-54787-2*, C P Pubs) Crown Pub Group.
Moulin, Raymonde. The French Art Market: A Sociological Perspective. Goldhammer, Arthur, tr. 231p. 1987. text ed. 35.00 (*0-8135-1232-8*) Rutgers U Pr.
Moulin, Thomas, jt. auth. see DeNevi, Don.
Moulin, V., et al. Study of the Interactions Between Organic Matter & Transuranic Elements, No. EUR 13651. 46p. 1991. pap. 7.00 (*92-826-2909-0*, CD-NA-13651-EN-C) UNIPUB.
Moulinie, Henri. De Bonald: La Vie, la Carriere Politique, la Doctrine. Mayer, J. P., ed. LC 78-67373. (European Political Thought Ser.). (FRE.). 1980. reprint ed. lib. bdg. 35.95 (*0-405-11723-X*) Ayer.
Moulinier, Louis. Le Pur et l'Impur dans la Pensee des Grecs d'Homere a Aristote. LC 75-10642. (Ancient Religion & Mythology Ser.). (FRE.). 1976. reprint ed. 47.95 (*0-405-07260-0*) Ayer.
Moulinier, M. B. Haviland - Lounsbury - Moulinier Genealogy & Memoirs. 169p. 1994. reprint ed. lib. bdg. 35.00 (*0-8328-4123-4*); reprint ed. pap. 25.00 (*0-8328-4124-2*) Higginson Bk Co.
Moullade, M. & Nairn, Alan E. Phanerozoic Geology of the World 1. (Palaeozoic Ser.: Pt. A). 1991. 164.00 (*0-444-87384-8*) Elsevier.
Moullade, M. & Nairn, Alan E., eds. The Phanerozoic Geology of the World: The Mesozoic, Vol. 2A. 530p. 1978. 159.00 (*0-444-41671-4*) Elsevier.
— Phanerozoic Geology of the World: The Mesozoic, Vol. 2B. 450p. 1983. 154.00 (*0-444-41672-2*, I-343-83) Elsevier.
Moulnier, ed. see De Chateaubriand, Francois-Rene.
Moulson, A. J. & Herbert, J. M. Electroceramics: Materials, Properties, Applications. (Illus.). 464p. (C). 1992. pap. text ed. 49.95 (*0-412-47360-7*, A7044) Chapman & Hall.
Moulson, A. J., jt. auth. see Herbert, J.
Moulsworth, Martha. My Name Was Martha: A Renaissance Woman's Autobiographical Poem. Evans, Robert C. & Wiedemann, Barbara, eds. LC 93-27167. 117p. (C). 1993. lib. bdg. 22.50 (*0-933951-53-1*) Locust Hill Pr.
Moult, Thomas. The Best Poems of 1922. LC 78-74821. (Granger Poetry Library). (Illus.). 1979. reprint ed. 15.00 (*0-89609-140-6*) Roth Pub Inc.
Moult, Thomas, ed. The Best Poems of 1923. LC 78-74822. (Granger Poetry Library). (Illus.). 1979. reprint ed. 15.00 (*0-89609-141-4*) Roth Pub Inc.
— Best Poems of 1924. LC 79-50845. (Granger Poetry Library). (Illus.). 1979. reprint ed. 15.00 (*0-89609-163-5*) Roth Pub Inc.
— Best Poems of 1926. LC 79-50846. (Granger Poetry Library). (Illus.). 1979. reprint ed. 15.00 (*0-89609-164-3*) Roth Pub Inc.
— Best Poems of 1930. LC 77-94819. (Granger Poetry Library). (Illus.). 1978. reprint ed. 15.00 (*0-89609-090-6*) Roth Pub Inc.
— Best Poems of 1931. LC 78-73492. (Granger Poetry Library). (Illus.). 1979. reprint ed. 15.00 (*0-89609-118-X*) Roth Pub Inc.
— Best Poems of 1932. LC 78-73493. (Granger Poetry Library). (Illus.). 1979. reprint ed. 15.00 (*0-89609-119-8*) Roth Pub Inc.
Moulton, jt. auth. see Bellow.
***Moulton, A., et al, eds.** Centennial History of Harrison, Containing the Celebration of 1905 & Historical & Biographical Matter. (Illus.). 727p. 1995. reprint ed. lib. bdg. 75.00 (*0-8328-4595-7*) Higginson Bk Co.
Moulton, Anthony L., ed. Congenital Heart Surgery: Current Techniques & Controversies. LC 83-21342. (Illus.). 347p. 1984. text ed. 97.50 (*0-941022-00-5*) Appleton Davies.
Moulton-Barrett, Edward R., comp. Moulton-Barrett Family Trees. 1983. 4.50 (*0-911459-14-6*) Wedgestone Pr.
Moulton, Bea, jt. auth. see Bellow, Gary.
Moulton, Bruce. Our Honeymoon: A Journal of Romantic Memories. 1994. 7.95 (*0-9633573-1-X*) Lakeland Color.
— Vacation Getaway: A Journal of Your Travel Memories. 36p. 1992. 6.95 (*0-9633573-0-1*) Lakeland Color.
***Moulton, Bruce A.** Bridal Shower Journal. (Illus.). 22p. 1995. 16.95 (*0-9633573-2-8*) Lakeland Color.
Moulton, C., ed. see Moulton, H. W.
***Moulton, Candy.** Roadside History of Wyoming. Greer, Dan, ed. (Roadside History Ser.). (Illus.). 480p. 1995. 25.00 (*0-87842-315-X*); pap. 16.00 (*0-87842-316-8*) Mountain Pr.
Moulton, Candy V. Legacy of the Tetons: Homesteading in Jackson Hole. 237p. (Orig.). 1994. pap. 15.95 (*0-9634839-4-3*) Tamarack Bks.
Moulton, Candy V. & Moulton, Flossie. Steamboat, Legendary Bucking Horse: His Life & Times, & the Cowboys Who Tried to Tame Him. LC 92-8507. 1992. pap. 11.95 (*0-931271-19-3*) Hi Plains Pr.
Moulton, Charles A. Moulton's Library of Literary Criticism of English & American Authors Through the Beginning of the 20th Century, 4 vols. abr. ed. Tucker, Martin, ed. LC 65-16619. 2400p. 1966. 260.00 (*0-8044-3190-6*, F Ungar Bks) Continuum.
Moulton, Charles W. The Library of Literary Criticism of English & American Authors, 8 vols., Set. 276.00 (*0-8446-1318-5*) Peter Smith.
— The Library of Literary Criticism of English & American Authors, 8 vols., Set. (BCL1-PR English Literature Ser.). 1992. reprint ed. lib. bdg. 600.00 (*0-7812-7004-9*) Rprt Serv.
Moulton, Dwayne. The Mystery of the Pink Waterfall. LC 80-84116. (Illus.). 192p. (J). (gr. 3-8). 1980. 14.95 (*0-9605236-0-X*) Pandoras Treasures.
Moulton, Faye S. Adventuring into Vermont's Past. LC 90-80145. (Illus.). 84p. (Orig.). 1990. pap. 8.95 (*0-914960-81-4*) Academy Bks.
Moulton, Flossie, jt. auth. see Moulton, Candy V.
Moulton, Forest R. An Introduction to Celestial Mechanics. 437p. 1984. reprint ed. pap. 10.95 (*0-486-64687-4*) Dover.
Moulton, Gary. American Encounters: Lewis & Clark, the People, & the Land. (Illus.). 32p. (Orig.). 1991. pap. text ed. 10.00 (*0-938932-03-9*) U Nebr CFGPS.
— Lewis & Clark & the Route to the Pacific. Goetzmann, William H., ed. (World Explorers Ser.). (Illus.). 112p. (YA). (gr. 5 up). 1991. lib. bdg. 18.95 (*0-7910-1327-8*) Chelsea Hse.
Moulton, Gary, ed. see Lewis & Clark.
Moulton, Gary E. John Ross: Cherokee Chief. LC 76-1146. (Brown Thrasher Bks.). 292p. 1986. reprint ed. pap. 11.95 (*0-8203-0888-9*) U of Ga Pr.
Moulton, Gary E., ed. see Lewis, Meriwether & Clark, William.
Moulton, Gene A., ed. see Bryan, John L.
Moulton, Gene A., ed. see Jacobs, Don T.
Moulton, H. J. Houdini's History of Magic in Boston, 1792-1915. (Illus.). 176p. 1983. 35.00 (*0-916638-27-8*) Meyerbooks.
Moulton, H. W. Moulton Annals. Moulton, C., ed. (Illus.). 454p. 1989. reprint ed. lib. bdg. 76.00 (*0-8328-0888-1*); reprint ed. pap. 68.00 (*0-8328-0889-X*) Higginson Bk Co.
Moulton, Harland B. From Superiority to Parity: The United States & the Strategic Arms Race, 1961-1971. LC 79-140920. 333p. 1973. text ed. 55.00 (*0-8371-5822-2*, MNS/, Greenwood Pr) Greenwood.
Moulton, Harold G. Financial Organization & the Economic System. LC 75-2652. (Wall Street & the Security Market Ser.). 1975. reprint ed. 46.95 (*0-405-06977-4*) Ayer.
— The Financial Organization of Society. LC 75-2653. (Wall Street & the Security Market Ser.). 1975. reprint ed. 65.95 (*0-405-06978-2*) Ayer.
— The Formation of Capital. LC 75-2654. (Wall Street & the Security Market Ser.). 1975. reprint ed. 23.95 (*0-405-06979-0*) Ayer.
Moulton, Harold G. & Ko, Junichi. Japan: An Economic & Financial Appraisal. LC 77-97886. reprint ed. 49.50 (*0-404-04507-3*) AMS Pr.
Moulton, Harold G., et al. Capital Expansion, Employment & Economic Stability. LC 75-2655. (Wall Street & the Security Market Ser.). 1975. reprint ed. 35.95 (*0-405-06980-4*) Ayer.
— The Recovery Problem in the United States. LC 73-176337. (FDR & the Era of the New Deal Ser.). (Illus.). 1972. reprint ed. lib. bdg. 85.00 (*0-306-70421-8*) Da Capo.
***Moulton, Harper W.** The Evaluation Guide to Executive Programs. 500p. 1993. ring bd. 160.00 (*0-8095-8401-8*) Borgo Pr.
Moulton, Harper W. & Fickel, Arthur A. Executive Development: Preparing for the 21st Century. (Illus.). 224p. 1993. 32.00 (*0-19-507465-3*) OUP.
Moulton, J. H. Treasure of the Magi: A Study of Modern Zoroastrianism. 1973. lib. bdg. 59.95 (*0-8490-2759-4*) Gordon Pr.
Moulton, J. H. & Milligan, G. The Vocabulary of the Greek Testament: Illustrated from the Papyri & Other Non-Literary Sources, 2 vols. 1977. lib. bdg. 250.00 (*0-8490-2800-0*) Gordon Pr.
Moulton, Jack E. Tumors in Domestic Animals. 3rd enl. rev. ed. 1990. 125.00 (*0-520-05818-6*) U CA Pr.
Moulton, James H. Early Zoroastrianism. 1976. lib. bdg. 59.95 (*0-8490-1743-2*) Gordon Pr.
— Early Zoroastrianism: Lectures Delivered at Oxford & in London, February to May, 1912. LC 77-27517. (Hibbert Lectures). reprint ed. 55.00 (*0-404-60414-5*) AMS Pr.
— Grammar of New Testament Greek, Vol. I. 320p. 1906. 37.95 (*0-567-01011-2*, Pub. by T & T Clark UK) Bks Intl VA.
— Grammar of New Testament Greek, Vol. 4: Style. 184p. 1976. 33.95 (*0-567-01018-X*, Pub. by T & T Clark UK) Bks Intl VA.
— Treasure of the Magi: A Story of Modern Zoroastrianism. LC 73-173004. reprint ed. 41.50 (*0-404-04508-1*) AMS Pr.
Moulton, Janice & Robinson, George. Scaling the Dragon. LC 94-71584. 250p. (Orig.). 1994. pap. 19.95 (*0-940121-29-8*, P209, Cross Roads Bks) Cross Cultural Pubns.
Moulton, Jeanne M. Animation Rurale: Education for Rural Development. 249p. (Orig.). (C). 1977. pap. 6.00 (*0-932288-48-0*) Ctr Intl Ed U of MA.
Moulton, Jenni K., ed. The Random House Basic Dictionary: German. 1987. pap. 3.50 (*0-345-34600-9*) Ballantine.
Moulton, Jenni K., jt. auth. see Moulton, William G.
Moulton, Jenni K., jt. auth. see Moulton, William.
Moulton, Joy W. Genealogical Resources in English Repositories. LC 87-82876. (Illus.). 648p. 1988. 32.00 (*0-944485-00-6*) Hampton OH.
— Supplement to Genealogical Resources in English Repositories. (Orig.). (C). 1992. pap. text ed. 4.75 (*0-944485-01-4*) Hampton OH.

An Asterisk (*) at the beginning of an entry indicates that the title is appearing in BIP for the first time.

Moulton, LeArta. The Gluten Book. rev. ed. (Illus.). 165p. (Orig.). 1981. pap. 7.50 (*0-935596-11-9*) Nat Med Chest.
— The New Gluten Book: Complete Recipes & Instructions for Meats, Sweets, & Other Treats Made from Wheat Gluten. 12th ed. (Illus.). 97p. 1992. student ed 9.95 (*0-935596-12-7*) Nat Med Chest.

Moulton, Lynda W. Data Bases for Special Libraries: A Strategic Guide to Information Management. LC 91-11338. (Library Management Collection). 176p. 1991. text ed. 47.95 (*0-313-27369-3*, MOI/, Greenwood Pr) Greenwood.

Moulton, Margaret. Dog Dreams. 1993. pap. 4.95 (*0-8118-0422-4*) Chronicle Bks.

Moulton, Nancy. Dark Desires. 352p. 1988. pap. 3.95 (*0-380-75419-3*) Avon.
— Defiant Heart. 368p. (Orig.). 1989. pap. 3.95 (*0-380-75730-3*) Avon.
— Savage Heat. 384p. 1991. mass mkt. 4.25 (*0-8217-3405-9*) Zebra.

Moulton, Phillips, ed. Journal & Major Essays of John Woolman. LC 71-171970. 336p. 1989. pap. 10.95 (*0-944350-10-0*) Friends United.

Moulton, Phillips P. The Living Witness of John Woolman. LC 72-94969. 36p. (Orig.). 1973. 3.00 (*0-87574-187-8*) Pendle Hill.
— Violence, or Aggressive Nonviolent Resistance. LC 76-170019. (Orig.). 1971. pap. 3.00 (*0-87574-178-9*) Pendle Hill.

Moulton, Richard G. The Ancient Classical Drama. 1972. 59.95 (*0-87968-625-1*) Gordon Pr.
— The Literary Study of the Bible. 1972. 250.00 (*0-8490-0544-2*) Gordon Pr.
— The Literary Study of the Bible. LC 70-4534. 1898. 59.00 (*0-403-00113-7*) Scholarly.
— The Literary Study of the Bible. 1988. reprint ed. lib. bdg. 59.00 (*0-7812-0552-2*) Rprt Serv.
— Shakespeare As a Dramatic Artist. (BCL1-PR English Literature Ser.). 443p. 1992. reprint ed. lib. bdg. 99.00 (*0-7812-7303-X*) Rprt Serv.

Moulton, Rolf T. Computer Security Handbook: Strategies & Techniques for Preventing Data Loss or Theft. LC 85-19124. 246p. 1986. text ed. 39.95 (*0-13-165804-2*, Busn) P-H.

Moulton, W. F., et al, eds. A Concordance to the Greek Testament. 5th ed. 1120p. (GRE.). 1978. 59.95 (*0-567-01021-X*, Pub. by T & T Clark UK) Bks Intl VA.

Moulton, William & Moulton, Jenni K. German Vest Pocket Dictionary. (GER.). 1974. pap. 5.00 (*0-394-40056-9*) Random.

Moulton, William G. A Linguistic Guide to Language Learning. 2nd ed. xii, 140p. (Orig.). 1970. pap. 10.00 (*0-87352-027-0*, E30) Modern Lang.
— Swiss German Dialect & Romance Patois. (LD Ser.: No. 34). 1941. pap. 16.00 (*0-527-00780-3*) Periodicals Srv.

Moulton, William G. & Moulton, Jenni K. Spoken German. LC 76-416. (Spoken Language Ser.). 290p. 1971. audio 70.00 (*0-87950-096-4*); audio 80.00 (*0-87950-097-2*) Spoken Lang Serv.
— Spoken German, Units 1-12. LC 76-416. (Spoken Language Ser.). 290p. 1971. pap. 10.00 (*0-87950-091-3*) Spoken Lang Serv.

Moultrie, William. Memoirs of the American Revolution, So Far As It Related to the States of North & South Carolina & Georgia. LC 67-29045. (Eyewitness Accounts of the American Revolution Ser., No. 1). 1979. reprint ed. 36.95 (*0-405-01139-3*) Ayer.

Moultrup, David J. Husbands, Wives & Lovers: The Emotional System of the Extramarital Affair. LC 89-71492. (Guilford Family Therapy Ser.). 278p. 1990. lib. bdg. 32.50 (*0-89862-105-4*) Guilford Pr.

Mouly, Francoise, jt. auth. see Coe, Sue.

Mouly, Ruth W. The Religious Right & Israel: The Politics of Armageddon. (Midwest Research Monograph Ser.: No. 2). 47p. 1985. pap. 4.50 (*0-915987-01-5*) Political Rsch Assocs.

***Mouly, V. Suchitra & Sankaran, Jayaram K.** Organizational Ethnography: An Illustrative Application in the Study of Indian R & D Settings. LC 94-33425. 180p. 1995. text ed. 22.95 (*0-8039-9211-4*) Sage.

Moulyn, Adrian C. The Meaning of Suffering: An Interpretation of Human Existence from the Viewpoint of Time. LC 82-6171. (Contributions in Philosophy Ser.: No. 22). (Illus.). xiii, 336p. 1982. text ed. 59.95 (*0-313-22233-9*, MOS/, Greenwood Pr) Greenwood.
— Mind-Body: A Pluralistic Interpretation of Mind-Body Interaction under the Guidelines of Time, Space, & Movement. LC 90-47286. (Contributions in Philosophy Ser.: No. 46). 192p. 1991. text ed. 55.00 (*0-313-27351-0*, MMU/, Greenwood Pr) Greenwood.

***Mounce.** New International Commentary on the New Testament Revelation. 1994. (*0-8028-2519-2*) Eerdmans.

Mounce, Earl W., jt. auth. see Dawson, Townes L.

Mounce, H. O. Wittgenstein's Tractatus: An Introduction. LC 81-40474. viii, 136p. (C). 1989. reprint ed. pap. text ed. 13.95 (*0-226-54321-8*) U Ch Pr.

Mounce, Louis. Li'l Charley. LC 90-70285. 262p. (Orig.). 1990. pap. 9.95 (*0-935069-34-8*) White Oak Pr.

Mounce, Robert A. Matthew. (New International Biblical Commentary Ser.). 304p. 1990. pap. 9.95 (*0-943575-18-4*) Hendrickson MA.

Mounce, Robert H. The Book of Revelation. LC 77-7664. (New International Commentary on the New Testament Ser.). 1977. 24.99 (*0-8028-2348-3*) Eerdmans.
— What Are We Waiting For? A Commentary on Revelation. fac. ed. LC 91-45243. 151p. 1992. reprint ed. pap. 43.10 (*0-7837-7967-4*, 2047723) Bks Demand.

Mounce, William D. Analytical Lexicon to the Greek New Testament. 608p. 1993. 34.99 (*0-310-54210-3*) Zondervan.
— Basics of Biblical Greek: Grammar. 464p. (ENG & GRE.). 1993. Printed caseside. 24.99 (*0-310-59800-1*) Zondervan.
— Basics of Biblical Greek: Workbook. 242p. (ENG & GRE.). 1993. 12.99 (*0-310-40091-0*) Zondervan.
— The Morphology of Biblical Greek: A Companion to the Basics of Biblical Greek & Analytical Lexicon to the Greek New Testament. LC 93-34331. 368p. (ENG & GRE.). 1994. 39.99 (*0-310-41040-1*) Zondervan.

Mound, Laurence. Amazing Insects. LC 92-26735. (Eyewitness Juniors Ser.: Vol. 26). 32p. (Orig.). (J). (gr. 1-5). 1993. lib. bdg. 11.99 (*0-679-93925-3*) Knopf Bks Yng Read.
— Amazing Insects. LC 92-26735. (Eyewitness Juniors Ser.: Vol. 26). 32p. (Orig.). (J). (gr. 1-5). 1993. pap. 7.99 (*0-679-83925-9*) Knopf Bks Yng Read.
— Insect. LC 89-15603. (Eyewitness Bks.). (Illus.). 64p. (J). (gr. 5 up). 1990. 16.00 (*0-679-80441-2*); lib. bdg. 16.99 (*0-679-90441-7*) Knopf Bks Yng Read.

***Mound, Laurence & Brooks, Stephen.** Insects. LC 94-31842. (DK Pocket Ser.). (Illus.). 160p. (YA). (gr. 7 up). 1995. pap. 5.95 (*1-56458-887-4*) Dorling Kindersley.

Mound, Peggy E. The Art of Business Credit Investigation, Vol. I: When Red Flags Appear & "It Just Doesn't Feel Right" I N V E S T I G A T E. 152p. (Orig.). 1990. pap. 26.95 (*0-9627792-6-1*) Advanced Verification.

Mounfield, Peter R. World Nuclear Power: A Geographical Appraisal. (Illus.). 416p. (C). 1991. text ed. 117.50 (*0-415-00463-2*, A5086) Routledge.

Moungovan, Roy. Shop Savvy. LC 89-11386. (Illus.). 352p. (Orig.). 1989. pap. 17.95 (*0-8069-5800-6*) Sterling.
— Shop Savvy. (Illus.). 342p. (Orig.). (C). 1990. reprint ed. lib. bdg. 41.00x (*0-8095-7560-4*) Borgo Pr.

Mounier, Emmanuel. Personalism. Mairet, Philip, tr. LC 75-122050. 1970. reprint ed. pap. 6.95 (*0-268-00434-X*) U of Notre Dame Pr.

Mounier, Emmanuel, ed. see Maritain, Jacques.

Mounier, J. P., jt. ed. see Gomella, C.

Mounier, Jean J. On the Influence Attributed to Philosophers, Free-Masons, & to the Illuminati, on the Revolution of France. LC 74-13148. 280p. 1974. reprint ed. 50.00 (*0-8201-1135-X*) Schol Facsimiles.

Mounin. Diccionario De Linguistica. (SPA.). 32.95 (*0-7859-0895-1*, S-50062) Fr & Eur.

***Mounin, Georges.** Dictionnaire de la Linguistique. 346p. (FRE.). 1974. 105.00 (*0-7859-7741-4*, 2130331335) Fr & Eur.
— Dictionnaire de la Linguistique. 384p. (FRE.). 1993. pap. 31.95 (*0-7859-8625-1*, 213044881x) Fr & Eur.
— Semiotic Praxis: Studies in Pertinence & in the Means of Expression & Communication. Tihanyi, Catherine, tr. (Topics in Contemporary Semiotics Ser.). 226p. 1985. 54.50 (*0-306-41767-7*, Plenum Pr) Plenum.

Mounsey, Augustus H. Satsuma Rebellion: An Episode of Modern Japanese History. LC 79-65367. (Studies in Japanese History & Civilization). 294p. 1979. reprint ed. text ed. 65.00 (*0-313-26993-9*, U6993, Greenwood Pr) Greenwood.

Mount, Balfour M., jt. ed. see Ajemian, Ina.

***Mount, Charles M.** Designer Interiors. 1994. 29.95 (*0-86636-346-7*) PBC Intl Inc.
— Dining Design Two: Informal Restaurant Interiors. (Illus.). 200p. 1995. 50.00 (*0-86636-241-X*) PBC Intl Inc.

Mount, Ellis. Adaptation of Turnkey Computer Systems in Sci-Tech Libraries. LC 88-23593. (Science & Technology Libraries: Vol. 9, No. 1). (Illus.). 116p. 1989. text ed. 29.95 (*0-86656-859-X*) Haworth Pr.
— Creative Planning of Special Library Facilities. LC 88-24633. (Haworth Series in Special Librarianship: No. 1). 197p. 1988. text ed. 39.95 (*0-86656-697-X*); pap. text ed. 19.95 (*0-86656-804-2*) Haworth Pr.
— Milestones in Science & Technology: The Ready Reference Guide to Discoveries, Inventions, & Facts. 2nd ed. LC 93-25679. (Illus.). 216p. 1994. 34.50 (*0-89774-671-6*) Oryx Pr.
— Role of Standards in Sci-Tech Libraries. LC 90-4306. (Science & Technology Libraries: Vol. 10, No. 3). 127p. 1990. text ed. 29.95 (*1-56024-021-0*) Haworth Pr.
— Special Libraries & Information Centers: An Introductory Text. 2nd ed. 1991. 36.00 (*0-87111-354-6*) SLA.
— Special Libraries & Information Centers: An Introductory Text. 3rd ed. LC 95-10605. 1995. write for info. (*0-87111-437-2*) SLA.
— Special Libraries & Information Centers: An Introductory Text. LC 83-571. (Illus.). 200p. reprint ed. pap. 57.00 (*0-8357-6428-1*, 2035796) Bks Demand.
— University Science & Engineering Libraries. 2nd ed. LC 84-6530. (Contributions in Librarianship & Information Science Ser.: No. 49). (Illus.). x, 303p. 1985. text ed. 59.95 (*0-313-23949-5*, MOU/, Greenwood Pr) Greenwood.

Mount, Ellis, ed. Cataloging & Indexing in Sci-Tech Libraries. (Science & Technology Libraries: Vol. 2, No. 3). 86p. 1982. pap. text ed. 24.95 (*0-86656-204-4*) Haworth Pr.
— Collection Development in Sci-Tech Libraries. LC 83-22478. (Science & Technology Libraries: Vol. 4, No. 2). 138p. 1984. text ed. 29.95 (*0-86656-279-6*) Haworth Pr.
— Current Awareness Services in Sci-Tech Libraries. (Science & Technology Libraries: Vol. 2, No. 1). 80p. 1982. pap. 22.95 (*0-86656-113-7*) Haworth Pr.
— Data Manipulation in Sci-Tech Libraries. LC 85-5569. (Science & Technology Libraries: Vol. 5, No. 4). 131p. 1985. text ed. 29.95 (*0-86656-441-1*) Haworth Pr.
— Document Delivery for Sci-Tech Libraries. (Science & Technology Libraries: Vol. 2, No. 4). 127p. 1982. pap. text ed. 29.95 (*0-86656-200-1*) Haworth Pr.
— End-User Training for Sci-Tech Databases. LC 89-27971. (Science & Technology Libraries: Vol. 10, No. 1). (Illus.). 128p. 1990. text ed. 29.95 (*0-86656-963-4*) Haworth Pr.
— Fee-Based Services in Sci-Tech Libraries. LC 84-19186. (Science & Technology Libraries: Vol. 5, No. 2). 105p. 1985. text ed. 29.95 (*0-86656-326-1*) Haworth Pr.
— Management of Sci-Tech Libraries. LC 84-6615. (Science & Technology Libraries: Vol. 4, Nos. 3-4). 169p. 1984. text ed. 39.95 (*0-86656-280-X*) Haworth Pr.
— Monographs in Sci-Tech Libraries. LC 82-23435. (Science & Technology Libraries: Vol. 3, No. 3). 101p. 1983. text ed. 29.95 (*0-86656-218-4*) Haworth Pr.
— Networking in Sci-Tech Libraries & Information Centers. (Science & Technology Libraries: Vol. 1, No. 2). 119p. 1981. pap. text ed. 29.95 (*0-917724-72-0*) Haworth Pr.
— One Hundred Years of Sci-Tech Libraries: A Brief History. LC 87-34567. (Science & Technology Libraries: Vol. 8, No. 1). (Illus.). 193p. 1988. text ed. 39.95 (*0-86656-745-3*) Haworth Pr.
— Online vs. Manual Searching in Sci-Tech Libraries. (Science & Technology Libraries: Vol. 3, No. 1). 83p. 1982. pap. text ed. 19.95 (*0-86656-203-6*) Haworth Pr.
— Opening New Doors: Alternative Careers for Librarians. LC 92-38494. 1992. 36.00 (*0-87111-408-9*) SLA.
— Planning Facilities for Sci-Tech Libraries. LC 83-8570. (Science & Technology Libraries: Vol. 3, No. 4). 121p. 1983. text ed. 29.95 (*0-86656-237-0*) Haworth Pr.
— Planning for Online Search Services in Sci-Tech Libraries. (Science & Technology Libraries: Vol. 1, No. 1). 143p. 1981. pap. text ed. 29.95 (*0-917724-73-9*) Haworth Pr.
— Planning the Special Library: A Project of the New York Chapter, SLA. Blueprint for the '70s: A Seminar on Library Planning (1971: New York) LC 72-85956. (Special Libraries Association Monographs: No. 4). 128p. reprint ed. pap. 36.50 (*0-685-15575-7*, 2026756) Bks Demand.
— Preservation & Conservation of Sci-Tech Materials. LC 86-33540. (Science & Technology Libraries: Vol. 7, No. 3). 171p. 1987. text ed. 29.95 (*0-86656-650-3*) Haworth Pr.
— Relation of Sci-Tech Information to Environmental Studies. LC 89-71657. (Science & Technology Libraries: Vol. 10, No. 2). 154p. 1990. text ed. 29.95 (*0-86656-988-X*) Haworth Pr.
— Role of Computers in Sci-Tech Libraries. LC 86-7619. (Science & Technology Libraries: Vol. 6, No. 4). 145p. 1986. 29.95 (*0-86656-577-9*) Haworth Pr.
— Role of Maps in Sci-Tech Libraries. LC 84-27919. (Science & Technology Libraries: Vol. 5, No. 3). 122p. 1985. text ed. 29.95 (*0-86656-395-4*) Haworth Pr.
— Role of Patents in Sci-Tech Libraries. LC 82-2885. (Science & Technology Libraries: Vol. 2, No. 2). 97p. 1982. pap. text ed. 29.95 (*0-86656-114-5*) Haworth Pr.
— Role of Serials in Sci-Tech Libraries. LC 83-12682. (Science & Technology Libraries: Vol. 4, No. 1). 109p. 1983. text ed. 29.95 (*0-86656-260-5*) Haworth Pr.
— Role of Technical Reports in Sci-Tech Libraries. LC 81-7231. (Science & Technology Libraries: Vol. 1, No. 4). 82p. 1982. pap. 29.95 (*0-917724-74-7*) Haworth Pr.
— The Role of Trade Literature in Sci-Tech Libraries. LC 90-4806. (Science & Technology Libraries: Vol. 10, No. 4). 134p. 1990. text ed. 29.95 (*1-56024-038-5*) Haworth Pr.
— Role of Translations in Sci-Tech Libraries. LC 82-23353. (Science & Technology Libraries: Vol. 3, No. 2). 94p. 1983. 29.95 (*0-86656-217-6*) Haworth Pr.
— Sci-Tech Libraries in Museums & Aquariums. LC 85-16436. (Science & Technology Libraries: Vol. 6, Nos. 1-2). 204p. 1985. text ed. 32.95 (*0-86656-484-5*) Haworth Pr.
— Sci-Tech Library Networks Within Organizations. LC 88-540. (Science & Technology Libraries: Vol. 8, No. 2). (Illus.). 162p. 1988. text ed. 29.95 (*0-86656-747-X*) Haworth Pr.
— Serving End-Users in Sci-Tech Libraries. LC 84-10789. (Science & Technology Libraries: Vol. 5, No. 1). 122p. 1984. text ed. 29.95 (*0-86656-327-X*) Haworth Pr.
— Training of Sci-Tech Librarians & Library Users. LC 81-6975. (Science & Technology Libraries: Vol. 1, No. 3). 72p. 1981. pap. text ed. 22.95 (*0-917724-75-5*) Haworth Pr.
— Weeding of Collections in Sci-Tech Libraries. LC 85-27010. (Science & Technology Libraries: Vol. 6, No. 3). 164p. 1986. text ed. 29.95 (*0-86656-552-3*) Haworth Pr.

Mount, Ellis, intro. Libraries Serving Science-Oriented & Vocational High Schools. LC 88-6597. (Science & Technology Libraries: Vol. 8, No. 3). (Illus.). 134p. 1989. text ed. 29.95 (*0-86656-792-5*) Haworth Pr.
— Sci-Tech Archives & Manuscript Collections. LC 89-19779. (Science & Technology Libraries: Vol. 9, No. 4). (Illus.). 144p. 1989. text ed. 32.95 (*0-86656-950-2*) Haworth Pr.
— Sci-Tech Libraries Servng Zoological Gardens. LC 88-17548. (Science & Technology Libraries: Vol. 8, No. 4). (Illus.). 111p. 1989. text ed. 29.95 (*0-86656-837-9*) Haworth Pr.

Mount, Ellis & Kovacs, Beatrice. Using Science & Technology Information Sources. 200p. 1991. 26.95 (*0-89774-593-0*) Oryx Pr.

Mount, Ellis & Newman, Wilda B. Top Secret-Trade Secret: Accessing & Safeguarding Restricted Information. LC 85-19864. 214p. 1985. pap. text ed. 39.95 (*0-918212-90-1*) Neal-Schuman.

Mount, Eric, Jr. Professional Ethics in Context: Institutions, Images, & Empathy. 168p. (Orig.). 1990. pap. 15.99 (*0-664-25143-9*) Westminster John Knox.

Mount, Ferdinand. Of Love & Asthma. 336p. 1993. pap. 13.95 (*0-7493-1064-2*, Pub. by W Heinemann Ltd) Trafalgar.
— The Subversive Family: An Alternative History of Love & Marriage. LC 92-30779. 300p. 1992. text ed. 24.95 (*0-02-921992-2*) Free Pr.

Mount, Ferdinand, intro. Communism: A TLS Companion. LC 92-44913. (TLS Companions Ser.). xxviii, 322p. (C). 1993. lib. bdg. 45.00 (*0-226-54323-4*); pap. 14.95 (*0-226-54324-2*) U Ch Pr.

Mount, Graeme S. The Sudbury Region: An Illustrated History. LC 86-5653. (Illus.). 144p. 1986. 24.95 (*0-89781-177-1*) Preferred Mktg.

Mount, Guy. Coyote's Big Penis & Other Stories. 80p. 1989. pap. 5.95 (*0-9604462-5-7*) Sweetlight.
— How Steelhead Lost His Stripes: A Children's Story & Coloring Book. (Illus.). (J). (gr. k-6). 1984. pap. 3.00 (*0-9604462-1-4*) Sweetlight.
— Lady Ocean: A Love Story for Children. (Illus.). (J). (gr. k-6). 1986. pap. 3.00 (*0-9604462-2-2*) Sweetlight.
— The Marijuana Mystery: A Novel. 168p. 1993. pap. 9.95 (*0-9604462-8-1*) Sweetlight.

Mount, Guy, comp. The Peyote Book: A Study of Native Medicine. 3rd ed. 128p. 1993. per. 9.95 (*0-9604462-3-0*) Sweetlight.

Mount, Guy, ed. Earthsongs: A Visionary Journal. 2nd ed. (Annual Collection: Vol. 1). 1994. 4.95 (*0-9604462-6-5*) Sweetlight.
— Holy Smoke: For People Who Love Marijuana. 80p. Date not set. pap. 5.00 (*1-877714-06-2*) Sweetlight.
— Serrano Songs & Stories. 48p. 1993. 4.95 (*0-9604462-7-3*) Sweetlight.

Mount, Guy, jt. auth. see Modesto, Ruby.

Mount Holyoke College Staff. Those Having Torches. LC 68-57335. (Essay Index Reprint Ser.). 1977. 18.95 (*0-8369-0716-7*) Ayer.

Mount, J. A. Mount: History & Genealogy Record of the Mount & Flippin Families. 120p. 1991. reprint ed. lib. bdg. 31.00 (*0-8328-1820-8*); reprint ed. pap. 21.00 (*0-8328-1821-6*) Higginson Bk Co.

***Mount, Jeffrey F.** California Rivers & Streams: The Conflict Between Fluvial Process & Land Use. LC 95-10822. (Illus.). 1995. write for info. (*0-520-20192-2*); pap. write for info. (*0-520-22502-3*) U CA Pr.

Mount, Jenny, ed. see Harrison, John M.

Mount, Kay, jt. ed. see Salmon, Shirley.

Mount, L. E., ed. see Easter School of Agricultural Science (20th: 1973: University of Nottingham) Staff.

Mount, Marshall W. African Art: The Years Since 1920. (Quality Paperbacks Ser.). (Illus.). 254p. 1989. pap. 16.95 (*0-306-80373-9*) Da Capo.

Mount, Patti, jt. auth. see Mount, Tom.

Mount, Robert H. The Reptiles & Amphibians of Alabama. (Illus.). 356p. 1975. pap. 14.50 (*0-8173-0054-6*, Ag Experiment) U of Ala Pr.

Mount, Robert H., jt. auth. see Schwaner, Terry D.

Mount San Antonio College Philosophy Group Staff, ed. Plato's Cave, Vol. 1: Interviews with the Wise. 60p. (Orig.). 1992. pap. 9.95 (*1-56543-012-3*) Mt SA Coll Philos.

Mount, Steven R., jt. auth. see Lindmier, Thomas A.

Mount, Timothy, jt. auth. see In, Francis.

Mount, Tom. The Greatest Adventure: Photography. (Illus.). 200p. pap. 24.95 (*0-915539-01-2*) Sea-Mount Pub Co.

Mount, Tom & Gilliam, Bret. Mixed Gas Diving: The Ultimate Challenge for Technical Diving. 1992. pap. 24.95 (*0-922769-41-9*) Watersport Pub.

Mount, Tom & Ikehara, Akira J. The New Practical Diving: A Complete Manual for Compressed Air Divers. LC 79-52941. (Illus.). 200p. 1980. reprint ed. pap. 13.95 (*0-87024-300-4*) U of Miami Pr.

Mount, Tom & Mount, Patti. Tom & Patti Mount's Dive & Travel Haiti. (Illus.). 86p. pap. 9.95 (*0-915539-03-9*) Sea-Mount Pub Co.

Mount, Tom & Schaeffer, Patti. The Complete Guide to Underwater Modeling. (Illus.). 80p. pap. 10.95 (*0-915539-00-4*) Sea-Mount Pub Co.

Mount, Tom, et al. Tom & Patti Mount's Dive & Travel Florida's Gold Coast. (Illus.). 86p. pap. 9.95 (*0-915539-02-0*) Sea-Mount Pub Co.

Mountain Bike Magazine Editors, jt. auth. see Bicycling Magazine Editors.

Mountain, Lee. Bobby Bear & Uncle Sam's Riddle. (Bobby Bear Ser.). (Illus.). 32p. (J). (ps-1). 1988. lib. bdg. 11.45 (*0-87783-221-8*) Oddo.
— El Fuego del Dragon - Dragon Fire. (Illus.). 23p. (ENG & SPA.). (J). (gr. k-1). 1992. pap. 23.75 (*0-89061-720-1*) Jamestown Pubs.
— Jamestown Heritage Readers, Bk. G. 1995. pap. 15.40 (*0-89061-957-3*, 957) Jamestown Pubs.
— Jungle Trip. (Attention Span Stories Ser). (Illus.). 48p. (Orig.). (gr. 6-9). 1978. pap. text ed. 5.95 (*0-89061-148-3*, 584) Jamestown Pubs.
— Pelea con Dragon - Dragon Fight. (Illus.). 24p. (ENG & SPA.). (J). (gr. k-1). 1992. pap. 23.75 (*0-89061-719-8*) Jamestown Pubs.
— Sports Trip. (Attention Span Stories Ser). (Illus.). 48p. (Orig.). 1978. pap. text ed. 5.95 (*0-89061-147-5*, 583) Jamestown Pubs.
— Star Trip. (Attention Span Stories Ser). (Illus.). 48p. (Orig.). 1978. pap. text ed. 5.95 (*0-89061-149-1*, 585) Jamestown Pubs.
— Survival Trip. (Attention Span Stories Ser). (Illus.). 48p. (Orig.). 1978. pap. text ed. 5.95 (*0-89061-146-7*, 582) Jamestown Pubs.
— Time Trip. (Attention Span Stories Ser.). (Illus.). 48p. (Orig.). 1978. pap. text ed. 5.95 (*0-89061-145-9*, 581) Jamestown Pubs.
— Uncle Sam & the Flag. LC 77-83633. (Illus.). 32p. (J). (gr. 2-3). 1978. lib. bdg. 9.95 (*0-87783-145-9*) Oddo.
— Uncle Sam & the Flag. deluxe ed. LC 77-83633. (Illus.). 32p. (J). (gr. 2-3). 1978. pap. 3.94 (*0-87783-148-3*) Oddo.

***Mountain, Lee, ed.** Jamestown Heritage Readers, Bk. H. 1995. pap. 15.40 (*0-89061-958-1*, 958) Jamestown Pubs.

Mountain, Lee, jt. auth. see Crawley, Sharon J.

An Asterisk (*) at the beginning of an entry indicates that the title is appearing in BIP for the first time.

Mountain, Lee, et al. The Gingerbread Man. (Big Book Ser.). (Illus.). 20p. (J). (gr. k-1). 1991. pap. 18.75 (*0-89061-943-3*) Jamestown Pubs.
— The Gingerbread Man. (Little Book Ser.). (Illus.). 20p. (J). (gr. k-1). 1993. pap. 14.75 (*0-89061-740-6*) Jamestown Pubs.
— Goldilocks & the Three Bears. (Big Book Ser.). (Illus.). 16p. (J). (gr. k-1). 1991. pap. 18.75 (*0-89061-942-5*) Jamestown Pubs.
— Goldilocks & the Three Bears. (Little Book Ser.). (Illus.). 16p. (J). (gr. k-1). 1993. pap. 14.75 (*0-89061-739-2*) Jamestown Pubs.
— Jamestown Heritage Reader, Bk. C. 256p. (J). (gr. 3). 1991. 14.95 (*0-89061-712-0*); teacher ed 24.95 (*0-89061-963-8*); pap. 11.95 (*0-89061-953-0*) Jamestown Pubs.
— Jamestown Heritage Reader, Bk. D. 256p. (J). (gr. 4). 1991. 15.75 (*0-89061-713-9*); teacher ed 25.75 (*0-89061-964-6*); pap. 12.75 (*0-89061-954-9*) Jamestown Pubs.
— Jamestown Heritage Reader, Bk. A. (Illus.). 160p. (J). (gr. 1). 1991. 12.10 (*0-89061-710-4*); teacher ed 22.10 (*0-89061-961-1*); pap. 9.10 (*0-89061-951-4*) Jamestown Pubs.
— Jamestown Heritage Reader, Bk. AA. (Illus.). 120p. (J). (gr. 1). 1994. 11.50 (*0-89061-709-0*); pap. 8.50 (*0-89061-950-6*) Jamestown Pubs.
— Jamestown Heritage Reader, Bk. B. (Illus.). 226p. 1991. 13.50 (*0-89061-711-2*); teacher ed 23.50 (*0-89061-962-X*); pap. 10.50 (*0-89061-952-2*) Jamestown Pubs.
— Jamestown Heritage Reader, Bk. E. 256p. (J). (gr. 5). 1991. 16.50 (*0-89061-714-7*); teacher ed 26.50 (*0-89061-965-4*); pap. 13.50 (*0-89061-955-7*) Jamestown Pubs.
— Jamestown Heritage Reader, Bk. F. 246p. (J). (gr. 6). 1991. 17.20 (*0-89061-715-5*); teacher ed 27.20 (*0-89061-966-2*); pap. 14.20 (*0-89061-956-5*) Jamestown Pubs.
— Jamestown Heritage Reader: Pocketful of Posiers. (Illus.). 80p. (J). (gr. 1). 1994. pap. 6.50 (*0-89061-949-2*) Jamestown Pubs.
— The Little Red Hen. (Big Book Ser.). (Illus.). 12p. (J). (gr. k-1). 1991. pap. 18.75 (*0-89061-941-7*) Jamestown Pubs.
— The Little Red Hen. (Little Book Ser.). (Illus.). 12p. (J). (gr. k-1). 1993. pap. 14.75 (*0-89061-738-4*) Jamestown Pubs.
— Mother Goose Tea Party. (Big Book Ser.). (Illus.). 16p. (J). (gr. k-1). 1991. pap. 18.75 (*0-89061-944-1*) Jamestown Pubs.
— Mother Goose Tea Party. (Little Book Ser.). (Illus.). 16p. (J). (gr. k-1). 1993. pap. 14.75 (*0-89061-741-4*) Jamestown Pubs.
***Mountain Lion, Inc., Staff.** Angler's Guide & Calendar '96. Date not set. pap. write for info. (*0-679-76117-9*) Random.
Mountain Missionary Press Staff. Natural Healing Centers of America. Glen, Streimer, ed. (Illus.). 48p. 2.95 (*0-912145-07-2*) MMI Pr.
Mountain Top Historical Society Staff. Kaaterskill: From the Catskill Mountain House to the Hudson River School. (Illus.). 100p. (Orig.). 1939. pap. 13.95 (*0-9628523-8-4*) Blk Dome Pr.
Mountaine, Trevor. Eden's Guide: (Evidence for & Control of Our Miraculous Power) LC 92-74816. 256p. (Orig.). 1993. pap. 15.00 (*1-882478-00-2*) Heyberg Media.
Mountaingrove, Jean & Menefee, Christine, eds. WomanSpirit Index: A Comprehensive Guide to a Decade of Women's Spirituality, 1974-1984. (Illus.). 120p. (Orig.). 1989. spiral bd. 13.95 (*0-9621035-1-9*) WomanSpirit.
Mountainwater, Shekhinah. Ariadne's Thread: A Workbook of Goddess Magic. 250p. (Orig.). 1991. pap. 14.95 (*0-89594-475-8*) Crossing Pr.
Mountbatten, Marco L. An Introduction to Polo. 188p. (C). 1990. 100.00 (*0-85131-142-3*, Pub. by J A Allen & Co UK) St Mut.
***Mountbatten, Patricia, et al.** Proceedings of the International Churchill Societies 1990-1991. (Oral History Ser.: No. 4). (Illus.). 124p. 1993. per., pap. 10.00 (*0-943879-08-6*) Intl Churchill Soc.
Mountcastle, Maxine. Poems "From Deep Within" LC 94-96059. 56p. 1994. lib. bdg. 5.00 (*0-9639403-0-9*) Maish & Mountcastle.
Mountcastle, V. B., jt. ed. see Deecke, L.
Mountcastle, Vernon B. Medical Physiology, 2 vols., 1. 14th ed. LC 79-25943. (Illus.). 2192p. 1979. 52.95 (*0-8016-3562-4*) Mosby Yr Bk.
— Medical Physiology, 2 vols., 2. 14th ed. LC 79-25943. (Illus.). 2192p. 1979. 44.50 (*0-8016-3566-7*) Mosby Yr Bk.
— Medical Physiology, 2 vols., Set. 14th ed. LC 79-25943. (Illus.). 2192p. 1979. 75.95 (*0-8016-3560-8*) Mosby Yr Bk.
Mountcastle, William D., jt. auth. see McGee, Robert S.
***Mountfield, David.** Castles. (Illus.). 144p. 1995. 15.98 (*0-8317-1307-0*) Smithmark.
— Rossini. LC 95-5611. (Compact Companions Ser.). 1995. 17.50 (*0-684-81361-0*) S&S Trade.
Mountford, A. J., jt. ed. see Mackay, Ronald.
Mountford, Christine. Kids Can Type Too! 32p. (J). (gr. 3-7). 1987. pap. 6.95 (*0-8120-3780-4*) Barron.
***Mountford, Debra.** Guide Aran. & Fair Isle Knitting. Date not set. 17.00 (*0-517-88405-4*) Random.
— The Harmony Guide to Crocheting: Techniques & Stitches. 1993. pap. 16.00 (*0-517-88074-1*, Harmony) Crown Pub Group.
Mountford, Frances. A Commoner's Cottage: The Story of a Surrey Cottage. (Illus.). 160p. 1992. 30.00 (*0-7509-0118-7*) A Sutton Pub.
Mountford, J. F. Bradley's Arnold Latin Prose Composition. (College Classical Ser.). (gr. 11-12). 1992. reprint ed. 32.50 (*0-89241-344-1*); reprint ed. pap. text ed. 20.00 (*0-89241-119-8*) Caratzas.
Mountford, James F. & Schultz, Joseph T. Index Rerum et Nominum in Scholiis Servii et Aelii Donati Tractatorum. No. 23. 205p. 1963. reprint ed. write for info. (*0-318-71180-X*, Pub. by Georg Olms GW) Lubrecht & Cramer.
Mountfort & Orpin, eds. Anaerobic Fungi: Biology, Ecology & Function. (Mycology Ser.: Vol. 12). 312p. 1994. 135.00 (*0-8247-8948-2*) Dekker.
Mountfort, G. Wild India: The Wild Life & Scenery of India & Nepal. (C). 1991. 105.00 (*0-7855-0222-X*, Pub. by Ratna Pustak Bhandar) St Mut.
Mountfort, Guy. Wild India: The Wildlife & Scenery of India & Nepal. (Illus.). 208p. 1991. 39.95 (*0-262-13276-1*) MIT Pr.
Mountfort, Guy, jt. auth. see Peterson.
Mountfort, William. The Life & Death of Doctor Faustus, Made into a Farce. LC 92-22711. (Augustan Reprints Ser.: No. 157 (1972)). reprint ed. 12.00 (*0-404-70157-4*, PR3605) AMS Pr.
— Plays of William Mountfort. LC 77-21660. 1977. 50.00 (*0-8201-1292-5*) Schol Facsimiles.
Mountjoy-Pepka, Vincent. Democracy for Americans: A Real Plan to Reinvent the Government. 256p. (Orig.). 1994. pap. 12.00 (*0-9639883-8-7*) Kick Pr.
***Mountjoy, Richard D.** One Hundred Years of Bell Telephone. (Illus.). 176p. (Orig.). 1995. pap. text ed. 29.95 (*0-88740-872-9*) Schiffer.
Mountney, G. J., jt. auth. see Parkhurst, C. R.
Mountney, George J., pref. Poultry Products Technology. (Illus.). 368p. 1989. reprint ed. pap. 39.95 (*1-56022-001-5*) Haworth Jrnl Co-Edits.
Mountney, George J. & Gould, Wilbur A. Practical Food Microbiology & Technology. 3rd ed. 364p. (C). 1992. reprint ed. lib. bdg. 74.50 (*0-89464-673-7*) Krieger.
Mounts, Willard. The Pioneer & the Prairie Lawyer: Boone & Lincoln Family Historical & Biographical Heritage. Manuscripts International Staff, ed. LC 91-72847. (Illus.). 224p. (Orig.). 1992. pap. 14.95 (*0-9630038-0-1*) Ginwill Pub.
Mountziaris, T. J., et al, eds. Gas-Phase & Surface Chemistry in Electronic Materials Processing, Vol. 334: Materials Research Society Symposium Proceedings. 1994. text ed. 74.00 (*1-55899-233-2*) Materials Res.
Moura, Eduardo C. How to Determine Sample Size & Estimate Failure Rate in Life Testing, Vol. 15. (Illus.). 98p. 1991. pap. 23.95 (*0-87389-112-0*) ASQC Qual Pr.
Moura, Jose M., jt. ed. see Bucy, Richard S.
Moura, Josee M. & Lourtie, Isabel M., eds. Acoustic Signal Processing for Ocean Exploration: Proceedings of the NATO Advanced Study Institute on Acoustic Signal Processing for Ocean Exploration, Funchal, Madeira, Portugal, July 26-August 7, 1992. LC 92-43800. (NATO Advanced Study Institutes Series C, Mathematical & Physical Sciences: No. 388). 1993. lib. bdg. 250.00 (*0-7923-2133-2*) Kluwer Ac.
Mourad. American Nursing Review for NCLEX-PN. 1991. 22.95 (*0-87434-396-8*) Springhouse Pub.
— Nursing Care of Adults with Orthopaedic Conditions. 2nd ed. LC 87-279. 576p. 1988. text ed. 39.95 (*0-8273-4315-9*) Delmar.
— Orthopedic Disorders. (Illus.). 320p. 1991. 29.95 (*0-8016-3438-5*) Mosby Yr Bk.
Mourad, jt. auth. see Healy.
Mourad, Leona. Orthopaedic Nursing. LC 94-16955. (Plans of Care for Specialty Practice Ser.). 360p. 1994. pap. text ed. 28.95 (*0-8273-5944-6*) Delmar.
Mourad, Leona A. American Nursing Review for NCLEX-PN. 2nd ed. LC 93-45151. 1994. write for info. (*0-87434-709-2*) Springhouse Pub.
— American Nursing Review of NCLEX-PN. 3rd ed. LC 94-39452. 1995. write for info. (*0-87434-801-3*) Springhouse Pub.
Mourad, Leona A. & Droste, Millie M. The Nursing Process in the Care of Adults with Orthopaedic Conditions. 3rd ed. LC 92-22066. 558p. 1993. pap. text ed. 39.95 (*0-8273-4939-4*) Delmar.
Mourad, Samiha, jt. auth. see Chan, Pak K.
***Mouradian, George.** Armenian InfoText. (Illus.). 342p. (Orig.). 1995. pap. 15.00 (*0-9634509-2-1*) Bookshelf Pubs.
Mourant, A. E. Blood Relations: Blood Groups & Anthropology. (Illus.). 1985. pap. 15.95 (*0-19-857631-5*) OUP.
Mourant, Arthur E., et al. The Distribution of the Human Blood Groups, & Other Polymorphisms. 2nd ed. LC 76-364647. (Oxford Monographs on Medical Genetics). 1071p. reprint ed. pap. 180.00 (*0-685-15918-3*, 2027067) Bks Demand.
Mourant, John A., tr. see Augustine, St.
Mourant, John A., jt. auth. see Harshbarger, Luther H.
Mourareau, R. & Thomas, M., eds. Fire in Buildings. xi, 661p. 1985. 120.75 (*0-85334-381-0*, Pub. by Elsevier Applied Sci UK) Elsevier.
Mouravieff, A. N. A History of the Church of Russia. Blackmore, R. W., tr. 448p. (C). 1988. reprint ed. 16.95 (*1-878997-09-2*) St Tikhons Pr.
Mouravieff, Boris. Gnosis: Esoteric Cycle. Amis, Robin, ed. & tr. by. D'Oncieu, Manek, tr. (Studies & Commentary on the Esoteric Tradition of Eastern Orthodoxy: Vol. 3). (Illus.). 300p. (Orig.). (C). 1993. pap. text ed. 24.95 (*1-872292-12-7*) Praxis Inst.
— Gnosis, Vol. I, Exoteric Cycle: Study & Commentaries on the Esoteric Tradition of Eastern Orthodoxy. Amis, Robin & Wissa, S. A., trs. (Illus.). 274p. (Orig.). (C). 1990. pap. text ed. 14.97 (*1-872292-10-0*) Praxis Inst.
— Gnosis, Vol. II, Mesoteric Cycle: Study & Commentaries on the Esoteric Tradition of Eastern Orthodoxy. Amis, Robin, ed. & tr. by. D'Oncley, Manek, tr. (Illus.). 296p. (Orig.). (C). 1992. pap. text ed. 14.97 (*1-872292-11-9*) Praxis Inst.
***Mourdoukoutas, Panos.** The Experiment. 188p. (Orig.). 1995. pap. 11.99 (*0-87411-693-7*) Copley Pub.
— How to Compete in Japan. (Illus.). 153p. (C). 1995. lib. bdg. 39.00 (*1-56072-222-3*) Nova Sci Pubs.
— How to Compete in the Japanese Market: Adapt, Develop, Promote. 152p. (Orig.). (C). 1995. pap. text ed. 35.25 (*0-87411-771-2*) Copley Pub.
— Japan's Turn: The Interchange in Economic Leadership. LC 92-42461. (C). 1993. 49.50 (*0-8191-9036-5*) U Pr of Amer.
— Japan's Turn: The Interchange in Economic Leadership. 244p. (C). 1993. pap. text ed. 21.50 (*0-8191-9298-8*) U Pr of Amer.
— When to Buy Stocks, Bonds, & Gold. (Illus.). 151p. 1994. pap. 19.95 (*0-87411-657-0*) Copley Pub.
Moure, Erin. Domestic Fuel. 108p. (Orig.). 1985. pap. 8.95 (*0-88784-143-0*, Pub. by Hse of Anansi Pr CN) Genl Dist Srvs.
— Furious. 101p. (Orig.). 1988. pap. 11.95 (*0-88784-157-0*, Pub. by Hse of Anansi Pr CN) Genl Dist Srvs.
Moure, Gloria. Marcel Duchamp. LC 88-42716. (Twentieth Century Artists Ser.). (Illus.). 128p. 1988. 24.95 (*0-8478-0978-1*) Rizzoli Intl.
Moure, Kenneth. Managing the Franc Poincare, 1928-1936: Economic Understanding & Political Constraint in French Monetary Policy, 1928-1936. (Studies in Monetary & Financial History). 320p. (C). 1991. 74.95 (*0-521-39458-9*) Cambridge U Pr.
Moure, Nancy D. Los Angeles Painters of the Nineteen-Twenties. (Illus.). 40p. 1972. 2.00 (*0-915478-29-3*) Galleries Coll.
— William L. Sonntag, Artist of the Ideal. (Illus.). 157p. 1980. 35.00 (*0-318-01276-6*) Goldfld Pub.
— William Louis Sonntag: Artist of the Ideal. (Illus.). 157p. 1980. text ed. 35.00 (*0-686-35887-2*) Goldfld Pub.
— William Louis Sonntag: Artist of the Ideal. deluxe limited ed. (Illus.). 157p. 1980. 65.00 (*0-686-37195-X*) Goldfld Pub.
Moure, Nancy D., ed. Publications in Southern California Art 1, 2, 3 vols. in 1. rev. ed. Incl. Vol. 1. Index to the California Watercolor Society Exhibitions 1921-1954. 1984. (*0-318-59104-9*); Vol. 2. Index to Artists Clubs & Exhibitions in Los Angeles Before 1930. 1984. (*0-318-59105-7*); Vol. 3. Dictionary of Art & Artists in Southern California Before 1930. 1984. (*0-318-59106-5*); 525p. 1984. 80.00 (*0-9614622-0-5*) Dustin Pubns.
***Moure, Nancy D. & Goldfield, Edward.** Edgar Payne 1882-1947. (Illus.). 82p. 1987. 35.00 (*0-9617802-0-7*) Goldfld Pub.
Moureau, M. & Brace, G. French-English - English-French Comprehensive Dictionary of Petroleum Science & Technology. 2nd ed. 990p. 1993. 225.00 (*2-7108-0648-7*) IBD Ltd.
— French-English - English-French Dictionary of Drilling & Boreholes. 436p. 1990. 106.50 (*2-7108-0592-8*) IBD Ltd.
Moureau, Magdeleine. Dictionary of Drilling & Boreholes: English-French - French-English. 436p. 1990. 89.95 (*0-8288-3188-2*, 2710805928) Fr & Eur.
— Dictionary of Drilling & Boreholes: English-French, French-English. 436p. (ENG & FRE.). 1990. 175.00 (*0-7859-7936-0*, 2710805928) Fr & Eur.
— Dictionary of Petroleum Technology: English-French - French-English. 1991. lib. bdg. 325.00 (*0-8288-3189-0*) Fr & Eur.
***Moureau, Magdeleine & Brace, Gerald.** Comprehensive Dictionary of Petroleum Science & Technology: English-French, French-English. 1040p. (ENG & FRE.). 1993. 350.00 (*0-7859-7134-3*, 2710806487) Fr & Eur.
Moureau, Magdeleine & Rouge, Janine. Dictionnaire Technique des Termes Utilises dans l'Industrie du Petrole, Anglais-Francais, Francais-Anglais: English-French, French-English Dictionary of the Petroleum Industry. 914p. (ENG & FRE.). 1977. 325.00 (*0-8288-5394-0*, M6419) Fr & Eur.
Mourelatos, Alexander P., ed. The Pre-Socratics: A Collection of Critical Essays. 580p. 1993. pap. text ed. 19.95 (*0-691-02088-4*) Princeton U Pr.
***Mourell, M.** Butterworths Student Companions: Real Property. 1992. pap. 17.00 (*0-409-30396-8*, Austral) Butterworth Legal Pubs.
Mourelle, Don F. The Voyage of the Sonora in 1775. 150p. 1988. 32.50 (*0-87770-402-3*) Ye Galleon.
Mouret, Francois J., ed. see De Montaigne, Michel E.
***Mouret, Jean-Noel.** Knives of the World. 1994. 17.98 (*1-55521-993-4*) Bk Sales Inc.
— Rifles of the World. 1994. 17.98 (*1-55521-997-7*) Bk Sales Inc.
Mourey, Gabriel, et al. Art Nouveau Jewelry & Fans. (Illus.). 150p. 1973. reprint ed. pap. 8.95 (*0-486-22961-0*) Dover.
Mouri, Allahyar. The International Law of Expropriation As Reflected in the Work of the Iran-U. S. Claims Tribunal. LC 93-44433. (Developments in International Law Ser.: No. 17). 612p. (C). 1994. lib. bdg. 207.00 (*0-7923-2654-7*) Kluwer Ac.
***Mouriki, Doula, ed.** Byzantine East, Latin West: Art-Historical Studies in Honor of Kurt Weitzmann. LC 94-22518. 1995. write for info. (*0-691-04339-6*) Princeton A & A.
Mouriquand, Jacqueline, et al. Diagnosis of Non-Palpable Breast Lesions: Ultrasonographical Controlled Fine Needle Aspiration. LC 93-13055. (Illus.). x, 72p. 1993. 69.00 (*3-8055-5747-7*) S Karger.
Mouritsen, Laurie. The Passage Way. Date not set. pap. 9.98 (*1-55503-695-3*, 01111663) Covenant Comms.
Mouritsen, O. G. Computer Studies of Phase Transitions & Critical Phenomena. (Computational Physics Ser.). (Illus.). 210p. 1984. 69.00 (*0-387-13397-6*) Spr-Verlag.
Mouritsen, Ole G., jt. auth. see Mosekilde, Erik.
Mouritzen, Hans. Finlandization: Towards a General Theory of Adaptive Politics. 463p. 1988. text ed. 69.95 (*0-566-05656-9*, Pub. by Dartmth Pub UK) Ashgate Pub Co.
— The International Civil Service: A Study of Bureaucracy: International Organizations. 192p. 1990. text ed. 52.95 (*1-85521-163-7*, Pub. by Dartmth Pub UK) Ashgate Pub Co.
Mouritzen, Poul E., ed. Managing Cities in Austerity: Urban Fiscal Stress in Ten Western Countries. (Urban Innovation Ser.: Vol. 2). 256p. 1992. 59.95 (*0-8039-8632-7*) Sage.
Mourlot, Fernand & Sorlier, Charles. Chagall's Complete Lithographs, 1922-1985, 6 vols. in 3. (Illus.). 900p. 1987. boxed 2,200.00 (*1-55660-081-X*) A Wofsy Fine Arts.
Mourlot, Fernand, et al. Miro Litografo, 4 vols., Set. (Illus.). 926p. (SPA.). 1981. 1,900.00 (*1-55660-227-8*) A Wofsy Fine Arts.
Mourning Dove. Cogewea, the Half-Blood. LC 80-29687. xxx, 302p. 1981. 30.00 (*0-8032-3069-9*); pap. 9.95 (*0-8032-8110-2*) U of Nebr Pr.
— Coyote Stories. Guie, Heister D., ed. & illus. by. LC 76-43793. reprint ed. 27.50 (*0-404-15648-7*) AMS Pr.
— Coyote Stories. Guie, Heister D., ed. LC 89-28956. (Illus.). xviii, 246p. 1990. reprint ed. pap. 8.95 (*0-8032-8169-2*) U of Nebr Pr.
— Mourning Dove: A Salishan Autobiography. Miller, Jay, ed. LC 89-14780. (American Indian Lives Ser.). (Illus.). xl, 265p. 1990. 30.00 (*0-8032-3119-9*) U of Nebr Pr.
Mourois, Andre. Vie de Disraeli. (FRE.). 1978. pap. 11.95 (*0-7859-4494-X*, 207036884X) Fr & Eur.
Mourot, Jean, jt. auth. see De Chateaubriand, Rene.
Mourou, G. A., et al, eds. Picosescond Electronics & Optoelectronics. (Electrophysics Ser.: Vol. 21). (Illus.). x, 258p. 1985. 66.00 (*0-387-15884-7*) Spr-Verlag.
Mourrain, Jacques, tr. see Baudrillard, Jean.
Mourre, Michel. Dictionnaire Encyclopedique d'Histoire: Encyclopedic Dictionary of History, 8 vols., Set. 5480p. (FRE.). 1978. 595.00 (*0-8288-5194-8*, M6420) Fr & Eur.
— Le Petit Mourre: Dictionnaire de l'Histoire. (FRE.). 1990. lib. bdg. 125.00 (*0-7859-3953-9*) Fr & Eur.
— Universal Dictionary of History: Dictionnaire d'Histoire Universelle. (FRE.). 1981. 125.00 (*0-8288-1489-9*, F700) Fr & Eur.
Moursand, David G. & Duris, Charles S. Elementary Theory & Application of Numerical Analysis. 297p. 1988. pap. 7.95 (*0-486-65754-X*) Dover.
Moursund, Dave. Computer Integrated Instruction Inservice Notebook: Elementary School. 222p. 1989. teacher ed, disk 40.00 (*0-924667-57-5*) Intl Society Tech Educ.
— Computer Integrated Instruction Inservice Notebook: Secondary School Science. 290p. 1989. teacher ed, disk 40.00 (*0-924667-67-2*) Intl Society Tech Educ.
— Computer Integrated Instruction Inservice Notebook: Secondary School Social Studies. 314p. 1989. teacher ed, disk 40.00 (*0-924667-68-0*) Intl Society Tech Educ.
— Effective Inservice for Integrating Computer-As-Tool into the Curriculum. 180p. 1989. Incl. 1 disk. disk 25.00 (*0-924667-58-3*) Intl Society Tech Educ.
— High Tech - High Touch: A Computer Education Leadership Development Workshop. 200p. 1988. 18.00 (*0-924667-52-4*) Intl Society Tech Educ.
— The Technology Coordinator. (Illus.). 192p. 1992. pap. text ed. 23.95 (*1-56484-015-8*) Intl Society Tech Educ.
Moursund, Dave & Yoder, Sharon. LogoPLUS for Educators: A Problem Solving Approach. 155p. 1990. pap. text ed. 10.95 (*0-924667-73-7*) Intl Society Tech Educ.
— LogoWriter for Educators: A Problem Solving Approach. 115p. 1990. pap. text ed. 10.95 (*0-924667-72-9*) Intl Society Tech Educ.
— Problem Solving & Communication in a HyperCard Environment. (Illus.). 156p. 1993. pap. text ed. 12.95 (*1-56484-036-0*) Intl Society Tech Educ.
Moursund, David. Computer Integrated Instruction Inservice Notebook: Secondary School Mathematics. 300p. 1988. teacher ed 40.00 (*0-924667-51-6*) Intl Society Tech Educ.
Moursund, Janet. The Process of Counseling & Therapy. 3rd ed. LC 92-12024. 240p. 1992. pap. text ed. 21.00 (*0-13-720657-7*) P-H.
Moursund, Janet, jt. auth. see Erskine, Richard.
Moursund, Janet P., jt. auth. see Kranzler, Gerald D.
Mousa, Issam S. The Arab Image in the U. S. Press, Vol. 1. LC 83-49021. (American University Studies: Communications: Ser. XV). 201p. (Orig.). 1984. pap. text ed. 19.20 (*0-8204-0069-6*) P Lang Pubs.
Mousalimas, S. A. The Transition from Shamanism to Russian Orthodoxy in Alaska. LC 94-36777. 272p. (C). 1995. text ed. 49.95 (*1-57181-006-4*) Berghahn Bks.
***Mousalimas, S. A., ed.** Ecology & Identity: Examples from the Attic. 240p. 1995. 45.00 (*1-57181-864-2*) Berghahn Bks.
***Mouse, Stanley.** Excuse My Dust: Confessions of a Hot Rod Artist. Williams, Roger, ed. & frwd. by. (Illus.). 192p. (Orig.). (YA). 1995. pap. text ed. 15.00 (*0-943389-16-X*) Snow Lion-SLG Bks.
— Freehand: The Art of Stanley Mouse. Williams, Roger, ed. 128p. (Orig.). 1993. 39.95 (*0-943389-12-7*); pap. 24.95 (*0-943389-11-9*) Snow Lion-SLG Bks.
Mouse, Timothy D., tr. see Tudor, Tasha.
Mouser, Barbara, jt. auth. see Mouser, Bill.
***Mouser, Bill & Mouser, Barbara.** Aspects of a Man. (Illus.). 160p. 1995. 10.00 (*0-614-07437-1*) Wine Pr Pub.
— Aspects of a Woman. (Illus.). 450p. 1995. 10.00 (*1-883893-16-X*) Wine Pr Pub.

***Mouser, Bruce L., ed. & intro.** Journal of James Watt: Expedition to Timbo, Capital of the Fula Empire in 1794. 1994. write for info. (*0-942615-25-5*) U Wis African Stud.

Mouser, G. W., jt. auth. see Brown, Robert E.

Mouser, William. Proverbs: Learning to Live Wisely. (LifeGuide Bible Studies). 95p. 1990. 4.99 (*0-8308-1026-9*, 1026) InterVarsity.

Moushabeck, Michel, jt. ed. see Bennis, Phyllis.

Moushine, Naomi, jt. auth. see Friesem, Ricky.

Mousley, Judith & Marks, Genee. Discourses in Mathematics. 112p. (C). 1991. pap. 60.00x (*0-7300-1291-3*, ECT403, Pub. by Deakin Univ AT) St Mut.

Mousnier, Roland. Peasant Uprisings in Seventeenth-Century France, Russia, & China. Pearce, Brian, tr. LC 76-884549. (Great Revolutions Ser.: 1). 381p. reprint ed. pap. 108.60 (*0-317-20060-7*, 2023314) Bks Demand.

Mousnier, Roland E. The Institutions of France under the Absolute Monarchy, 1598 to 1789: Volume II, The Organs of State & Society. Goldhammer, Arthur, tr. LC 78-26857. (C). 1984. 55.00 (*0-226-54328-5*) U Ch Pr.

— The Institutions of France under the Absolute Monarchy, 1598-1789: Society & the State, Vol. 1. Pearce, Brian, tr. LC 78-26857. 1979. reprint ed. lib. bdg. 55.00 (*0-226-54327-7*) U Ch Pr.

Moussa, Effat A. Computer Integrated Probability & Mathematical Statistics for Science & Management. rev. ed. 924p. 1993. per. 70.95 (*0-8403-8753-9*) Kendall-Hunt.

Moussa-Mahmoud, Fatma, tr. see Mahfouz, Naguib.

Moussalli, Ahmad S. Radical Islamic Fundamentalism: The Ideological & Political Discourse of Sayyid Qutb. 326p. (C). 1993. pap. text ed. 20.00 (*0-8156-6089-8*) Syracuse U Pr.

Moussavi, Fakhreddin, comp. Guide to the Hanna Collection & Related Archival Materials at the Hoover Institution on War, Revolution & Peace on the Role of Education in Twentieth-Century Society. (Bibliographical Ser.: No. 64). 250p. 1982. lib. bdg. 19.95 (*0-8179-2641-0*) Hoover Inst Pr.

Mousseron-Canet, M. & Mani, J. C. Photochemistry of Molecular Reactions. 278p. 1972. text ed. 63.50x (*0-7065-1120-4*, Pub. by Keter Pub IS) Coronet Bks.

Mousset & Dupuis, Hector. Dictionnaire Francais-Tamoul; French-Tamil Dictionary. 1253p. (FRE & TAM.). 1990. 150.00 (*0-8288-1108-3*, M223) Fr & Eur.

Mousset-Jones, Pierre, ed. International Mine Ventilation Congress, 2nd: Proceedings. LC 80-52943. (Illus.). 864p. 1980. 5.00 (*0-89520-271-9*) SMM&E Inc.

Moussett-Jones, Pierre, ed. Mine Ventilation: U. S. Mine Ventilation Symposium, Reno, Nevada, 2nd, 23-25 September 1985, Vol. 1. (C). 1985. text ed. 145.00 (*90-6191-611-9*, Pub. by A A Balkema NE) Ashgate Pub Co.

Moussinac, L. Panoramique du Cinema. 1976. lib. bdg. 99.95 (*0-8490-2406-4*) Gordon Pr.

Moussinac, Leon, comp. New Movement in the Theatre. LC 65-19619. (Illus.). 1972. reprint ed. 82.95 (*0-405-08808-6*, Pub. by Blom Pubns UK) Ayer.

Moussiopoulos, N., et al, eds. Urban Air Pollution Vol. 1, Vol. 1. LC 94-68174. (Urban Air Pollution Ser.: Vol. 1). 300p. 1994. 145.00 (*1-56252-255-8*) Computational Mech MA.

Moussorgsky, Modest P. Pictures at an Exhibition & Other Works for Piano. 1990. pap. 11.95 (*0-486-26515-3*) Dover.

Moustafa, Laila, ed. see Faison, Brenda S.

***Moustakas, Clark.** Being-In, Being-For, Being-With. LC 95-7080. 1995. 35.00 (*1-56821-537-1*) Aronson.

— Existential Psychotherapy & the Interpretation of Dreams. LC 93-40807. 232p. 1994. 35.00 (*1-56821-180-5*) Aronson.

— Heuristic Research: Design, Methodology, & Applications. 160p. (C). 1990. 44.00 (*0-8039-3881-0*); pap. 19.95 (*0-8039-3882-9*) Sage.

— Individuality & Encounter: A Brief Journey into Loneliness & Sensitivity Groups. LC 68-25353. (C). 1968. pap. 4.50 (*0-87299-002-8*) Howard Doyle.

— Phenomenological Research Methods. LC 94-7355. 240p. 1994. 44.00 (*0-8039-5798-X*); pap. 21.95 (*0-8039-5799-8*) Sage.

Moustakas, Clark E. Loneliness. (Orig.). 1990. pap. 6.95 (*0-13-540378-2*) P-H.

— Psychotherapy with Children: The Living Relationship. reprint ed. pap. 11.95 (*0-9634031-0-9*) Carron CO.

Moustakas, T. D., et al, eds. Wide Band-Gap Semiconductors. (Symposium Proceedings Ser.: Vol. 242). 1992. text ed. 60.00 (*1-55899-136-0*) Materials Res.

Moustiers, Pierre. L' Hiver d'un Gentilhomme. (FRE.). 1975. pap. 11.95 (*0-7859-4046-4*) Fr & Eur.

— La Paroi. 224p. (FRE.). 1969. pap. 15.95 (*0-7859-3961-X*, 2070246590) Fr & Eur.

Moutafakis, Nicholas J. The Logics of Preference. (C). 1987. lib. bdg. 92.00 (*90-277-2591-8*) Kluwer Ac.

Moutafchieva, Vera P. Agrarian Relations in the Ottoman Empire in the Fifteenth & Sixteenth Centuries. (East European Monographs: No. 251). 200p. 1988. text ed. 34.50 (*0-88033-148-8*) East Eur Quarterly.

Moutal, Patrick. Comparative Study of Selected Hindustani Ragas on Contemporary Practice. (C). 1991. text ed. 38.00 (*0-685-50093-4*, Pub. by Munshiram Manoharial II) S Asia.

— Hindustani Ragas Index. (C). 1991. 27.50 (*0-685-50025-X*, Pub. by Munshiram Manoharial II) S Asia.

Moutaouakil, Ahmed. Pragmatic Functions in Functional Grammar of Arabic. (Functional Grammar Ser.: No. 8). xi, 156p. 1989. pap. 35.75 (*90-6765-271-7*) Mouton.

Moutet, Fernand. Golden Chord. Barkan, Stanley H., ed. Festinger, Nancy, tr. (Review Chapbook Ser.: No. 17: Provencal Poetry 1). 16p. 1981. 15.00 (*0-89304-840-2*, CCC144); pap. 5.00 (*0-89304-816-X*); audio 10.00 (*0-89304-841-0*) Cross-Cultrl NY.

Mouthany, J. R. English Without Teacher & Dictionary: English-Arabic. 1986. 14.95x (*0-86685-058-9*) Intl Bk Ctr.

***Mouthier, Annie.** Dictionnaire des Termes Juridiques et Commerciaux. 227p. (FRE.). 1991. pap. 39.95 (*0-7859-8645-6*, 273280102x) Fr & Eur.

— Encyclopedie de SARL. 260p. 1993. pap. 59.95 (*0-7859-5639-5*, 2732801070) Fr & Eur.

Moutinho, Luiz & Evans, Martin. Applied Marketing Research. LC 92-17238. 1992. 34.00 (*0-201-56504-8*) Addison-Wesley.

Moutinho, Luiz, jt. auth. see Witt, Stephen F.

Moutinho, Luiz, jt. ed. see Witt, Stephen F.

Moutinho, Luiz, et al. Computer Modelling & Expert Systems in Marketing. LC 94-7100. 224p. 1994. 65.00x (*0-415-08983-2*, B4539) Routledge.

Mouton, Boyce. Beyond the Veil. 158p. 1987. pap. 5.99 (*0-89900-314-1*) College Pr Pub.

— By This Shall All Men Know. LC 79-56541. 102p. 1980. pap. 5.99 (*0-89900-139-4*) College Pr Pub.

— Personal Vignettes. 264p. (Orig.). 1989. pap. 6.99 (*0-89900-321-4*) College Pr Pub.

— The Schoolmaster. LC 85-62798. 138p. 1985. pap. 5.99 (*0-89900-209-9*) College Pr Pub.

— These Two Commandments. 2nd ed. 112p. (Orig.). 1978. pap. 5.99 (*0-89900-138-6*) College Pr Pub.

Mouton, Boyce, ed. see Pratt, Michael C.

Mouton, Donald, ed. see De la Salle, John B.

Mouton, Jane S. & Blake, Robert R. Synergogy: A New Strategy for Education, Training, & Development. LC 83-23898. (Joint Publication in the Jossey-Bass Management Series & the Jossey-Bass Social & Behavioral Science Ser.). 206p. reprint ed. pap. 58.80 (*0-7837-2549-3*, 2042708) Bks Demand.

Mouton, Jane S., jt. auth. see Blake, Robert R.

Mouton, John, jt. auth. see Householder, Jerry.

Moutos, Thomas, jt. auth. see Hart, Robert A.

Moutoussamy-Ashe, Jeanne. Daddy & Me. LC 93-11513. (Illus.). 40p. (J). (ps-3). 1993. 13.00 (*0-679-85096-1*); lib. bdg. 14.99 (*0-679-95096-6*) Knopf Bks Yng Read.

— Viewfinders: Black Women Photographers. 1993. 39.95 (*0-86316-159-6*); pap. 19.95 (*0-86316-158-8*) Writers & Readers.

Moutran, Julia S. Elementary Science Activities for All Seasons. 224p. 1989. pap. 27.95 (*0-685-32916-X*) P-H.

— The Story of Punxsutawney Phil, "The Fearless Forecaster" LC 86-82950. (Adventures of Punxsutawney Phil Ser.). 64p. (J). (ps-5). 1987. 14.95 (*0-9617819-2-0*); pap. 8.95 (*0-9617819-0-4*); audio 10.95 (*0-9617819-3-9*) Lit Pubns.

— Will Spring Ever Come to Gobbler's Knob? A Punxsutawney Phil Adventure Story. (Illus.). 64p. (J). (ps-5). 1992. audio 10.95 (*0-685-48131-X*) Lit Pubns.

— Will Spring Ever Come to Gobbler's Knob? A Punxsutawney Phil Adventure Story, Incl. Phil's Field Guide to Woodland Animals. (Illus.). 64p. (J). (ps-5). 1992. pap. 9.95 (*0-9617819-4-7*) Lit Pubns.

— Will Spring Ever Come to Gobbler's Knob? A Punxsutawney Phil Adventure Story, Incl. Phil's Field to Woodland Animals. (Illus.). 64p. (J). (ps-5). 1992. Incl. Phil's Field Guide to Woodland Animals. 15.95 (*0-9617819-5-5*) Lit Pubns.

Moutran, Julie. Science Teacher's Almanac: Practical Ideas & Activities for Every Month of the School Year. 1992. pap. text ed. 27.95 (*0-87628-809-3*) Ctr Appl Res.

Moutron, Julia S. Collecting Bugs & Things: A Science Activity Storybook. (Illus.). 48p. (J). (gr. k up). 1988. pap. 2.95 (*0-8431-2226-9*) Price Stern.

***Moutsatson, Peter.** Management Fundamentals. 1995. pap. text ed. write for info. (*1-56226-232-7*) CT Pub.

Moutsatson, Peter & Straub, Joseph. Management Fundamentals. 1992. pap. 42.00 (*1-56226-109-6*) CT Pub.

Moutschen, Jean. Introduction to Genetic Toxicology. LC 84-11868. (Wiley-Interscience Publication Ser.). 202p. reprint ed. pap. 57.60 (*0-8357-6940-2*, 2037999) Bks Demand.

Moutsopoulos, Evanqhelos, jt. ed. see Gruender, C. David.

Moutzan-Martinengou, Elisavet. My Story. Kolias, Helen D., ed. & tr. by. LC 88-35102. 168p. 1989. 22.50 (*0-8203-1125-1*) U of Ga Pr.

Mouvet, Maurice. Maurice's Art of Dancing. (Ballroom Dance Ser.). 1986. lib. bdg. 79.95 (*0-8490-3362-4*) Gordon Pr.

— Maurice's Art of Dancing. (Ballroom Dance Ser.). 1985. lib. bdg. 78.85 (*0-87700-700-4*) Revisionist Pr.

Mouw, Gene H. The Bible Condensed: Written in Current American. Mouw, Lynne A., ed. LC 89-92099. 144p. (Orig.). (C). 1989. pap. 8.95 (*0-9624551-0-5*) Mouw.

Mouw, John T., jt. auth. see Lewis, Ernest L.

Mouw, Lynne A., ed. see Mouw, Gene H.

***Mouw, Richard.** Consulting the Faithful: What Christian Intellectuals Can Learn from Popular Culture. 96p. (Orig.). 1994. pap. text ed. 6.99 (*0-8028-0738-0*) Eerdmans.

Mouw, Richard J. The God Who Commands: A Study in Divine Command Ethics. LC 89-40385. (C). 1990. text ed. 24.95 (*0-268-01019-6*) U of Notre Dame Pr.

— The God Who Commands: A Study in Divine Command Ethics. LC 89-40385. (C). 1991. text ed. 10.95 (*0-268-01021-8*) U of Notre Dame Pr.

— Reasons Three, Objections to Christianity. 64p. (Orig.). (YA). (gr. 10-12). 1981. teacher ed 5.75 (*0-933140-28-2*); pap. text ed. 5.75 (*0-933140-27-4*) CRC Pubns.

— Uncommon Decency: Christian Civility in an Uncivil World. LC 92-5680. 192p. (Orig.). 1992. 16.99 (*0-8308-1826-X*); pap. 9.99 (*0-8308-1825-1*) InterVarsity.

Mouw, Richard J., jt. auth. see Griffioen, Sander.

Mouwen, J. M. & De Groot, E. C. Atlas of Veterinary Pathology. (Illus.). 160p. 1983. text ed. 142.00 (*0-7216-6577-2*) Saunders.

Mouy, Paul. Le Developpment de la Physique Cartesienne 1646-1712 (the Development of Cartesian Physics) Cohen, I. Bernard, ed. LC 80-2138. (Development of Science Ser.). 1981. reprint ed. lib. bdg. 33.95 (*0-405-13893-8*) Ayer.

Mouzannar, Ibrahim. Lebanese Cooking: Tabbakh Al-Lebanie. 1981. 16.95x (*0-86685-278-6*) Intl Bk Ctr.

***Mouzard, Francois.** Informatics Glossary. (Terminology Bulletin Ser.: No. 225). 209p. (Orig.). 1994. pap. 25.95x (*0-660-59112-X*, Pub. by Canada Commun Grp CN) Accents Pubns.

***Mouzelis, Nicos.** Sociological Theory: What Went Wrong?: Diagnosis & Remedies. LC 94-44296. 1995. 55.00 (*0-415-12720-3*, Routledge NY); pap. 16.95 (*0-415-07694-3*, Routledge NY) Routledge.

Mouzelis, Nicos P. Back to Sociological Theory: The Construction of Social Orders. LC 91-9240. 240p. 1991. text ed. 65.00 (*0-312-06175-7*) St Martin.

— Back to Sociological Theory: The Construction of Social Orders. LC 91-9240. 1993. pap. write for info. (*0-312-10361-1*) St Martin.

— Modern Greece: Facets of Underdevelopment. LC 78-312273. 222p. (C). 1980. 39.50 (*0-8419-0357-3*); pap. 17.95 (*0-8419-0523-1*) Holmes & Meier.

— Organisation & Bureaucracy: An Analysis of Modern Theories. LC 68-11361. 239p. 1967. pap. 22.95 (*0-202-30078-1*) Aldine de Gruyter.

Movat, H. Z. The Inflammatory Reaction. 368p. 1985. 160.00 (*0-444-80662-8*) Elsevier.

Movat, H. Z., ed. Leukocyte Emigration & Its Sequelae. (Illus.). vi, 186p. 1987. 111.25 (*3-8055-4489-8*) S Karger.

Movchan, A. Human Rights & International Relations. 245p. (C). 1988. 30.00 (*0-685-31555-X*, Pub. by Collets UK) Pro-Am Music.

***Movement for a Peoples Assembly Staff.** The Los Angeles Rebellion Against Racism. 1992. pap. 2.50 (*0-89567-104-2*) World View Forum.

Movenkamp, Herbert, jt. auth. see Kurtz, Sheldon F.

Movius, H. L., Jr., jt. auth. see Howe, B.

Movius, Hallam L. Early Man & Pleistocene Stratigraphy in Southern & Eastern Asia. (HU PMP Ser.). (Illus.). 1944. 23.00 (*0-527-01249-1*) Periodicals Srv.

Movsesian, Ara J. Love Poems for Cards & Letters. LC 88-81507. (Illus.). 90p. (Orig.). 1988. pap. 6.95 (*0-916919-60-9*) Electric Pr.

— Pearls of Love: How To Write Love Letters & Love Poems. LC 84-147625. (Illus.). 310p. (Orig.). 1983. pap. 12.95 (*0-916919-00-5*) Electric Pr.

Movshon, J. Anthony, jt. ed. see Landy, Michael S.

Movsovic, M. I. Technical & Vocational Education in the U.S.S.R. A Bibliographical Survey (UNESCO) (Education Studies & Documents: No. 30). 1974. reprint ed. pap. 15.00 (*0-8115-1354-8*) Periodicals Srv.

Mow. Biophysical Properties of Articular Cartilage. 1995. write for info. (*0-318-70404-8*) CRC Pr.

Mow, Anna B. Descubra Su Propia Fe: Find Out Your Own Faith. (SPA.). 4.95 (*84-7228-590-1*, 220258, Pub. by Edit Clie SP) TSELF.

— Tu Hijo, del Nacimiento Al Nuevo: Your Child: From Birth to Rebirth. (SPA.). 5.50 (*84-7228-140-X*, 220912, Pub. by Edit Clie SP) TSELF.

— Tu y Tu Hijo: Your Teenager & You. (SPA.). 3.25 (*84-7228-219-8*, 220915, Pub. by Edit Clie SP) TSELF.

Mow, Merrill. How Great Is Our God: Stories from the Bible. (Illus.). 95p. (Orig.). 1989. pap. text ed. 6.00 (*0-87486-509-3*) Plough.

— Torches Rekindled: The Bruderhof's Struggle for Renewal. 2nd ed. Brethren, Hutterian, ed. LC 89-8772. (Illus.). 345p. (Orig.). 1989. pap. 12.00 (*0-87486-024-5*) Plough.

— Torches Rekindled: The Bruderhof's Struggle for Renewal. 3rd rev. ed. Brethren, Hutterian, ed. LC 90-49626. (Illus.). 354p. (Orig.). (C). 1991. pap. 14.50 (*0-87486-032-6*) Plough.

Mow, Merrill, ed. see Arnold, Eberhard.

Mow, V. C., et al, eds. Biomechanics of Diarthrodial Joints, 2 vols., Vol. I. (Illus.). xix, 450p. 1990. 69.50 (*0-387-97378-8*) Spr-Verlag.

— Biomechanics of Diarthrodial Joints, 2 vols., Vol. II. (Illus.). xx, 464p. 1990. 69.50 (*0-387-97379-6*) Spr-Verlag.

Mow, Van C. & Hayes, Wilson C. Basic Orthopaedic Biomechanics. 464p. 1991. 76.50 (*0-88167-796-5*) Raven.

Mow, Van C., et al. Knee Meniscus: Basic & Clinical Foundations. 208p. 1992. 93.50 (*0-88167-895-3*) Raven.

Mowaljarlai, David & Malnic, Jutta. Yorro Yorro - Aboriginal Creation & the Regeneration of the World: The Art & Stories of the People of the Australian Kimberley. (Illus.). 248p. (Orig.). 1993. pap. 19.95 (*0-89281-460-8*) Inner Tradit.

Mowat, Alex P. Liver Disorders in Childhood. 2nd ed. 408p. 1987. text ed. 95.00 (*0-407-00480-7*) Buttrwrth-Heinemann.

— Liver Disorders in Childhood. 3rd ed. (Illus.). 432p. 1994. 125.00 (*0-7506-1039-5*) Buttrwrth-Heinemann.

Mowat, Alexander, jt. auth. see Mowat, William.

Mowat, Barbara A., ed. see Shakespeare, William.

***Mowat-Brown, George.** The Rover. 1989. pap. 25.00 (*0-7478-0154-1*, Pub. by Shire UK) St Mut.

Mowat, Charles. Britain Between the Wars, Nineteen Eighteen to Nineteen Forty. LC 55-5139. 704p. reprint ed. pap. 180.00 (*0-8357-7411-2*, 2024060) Bks Demand.

Mowat, David. Anna-Luse. (Orig.). 1988. pap. 7.95 (*0-7145-0644-3*) Riverrun NY.

Mowat, F. Owls in the Family. 1976. 19.95 (*0-89190-820-X*, Am Repr) Amereon Ltd.

Mowat, Farley. And No Birds Sang. 19.95 (*0-89190-821-8*, Am Repr) Amereon Ltd.

— And No Birds Sang. 208p. 1982. mass mkt. 5.99 (*0-7704-2237-3*) Bantam.

— The Boat That Wouldn't Float. (J). 1984. mass mkt. 3.99 (*0-553-27788-X*) Bantam.

— Born Naked. large type ed. LC 94-31743. 1994. pap. 19.95 (*1-56895-076-4*) Wheeler Pub.

— Born Naked: The Early Adventures of the Author of "Never Cry Wolf" LC 93-23702. 1994. 21.95 (*0-395-68927-9*) HM.

— Born Naked: The Early Adventures of the Author of Never Cry Wolf. 1995. pap. 10.95 (*0-395-73528-9*) HM.

— The Desperate People. 240p. 1984. mass mkt. 5.99 (*0-7704-2323-X*) Bantam.

— The Dog Who Wouldn't Be. 19.95 (*0-89190-819-6*, Am Repr) Amereon Ltd.

— The Dog Who Wouldn't Be. (J). 1984. mass mkt. 3.99 (*0-553-27928-9*) Bantam.

— The Dog Who Wouldn't Be. (Illus.). (J). (gr. 3-7). 1957. 18.95 (*0-316-58636-6*, Joy St Bks) Little.

— Grey Seas Under. 1976. pap. 1.95 (*0-345-25328-0*) Ballantine.

— Lost in the Barrens. 1985. pap. 3.95 (*0-553-27525-9*, Starfire) Bantam.

— Lost in the Barrens. (Illus.). (J). (gr. 7 up). 1956. 15.95 (*0-316-58638-2*, Joy St Bks) Little.

— My Father's Son: Memories of War & Peace. LC 92-31729. (Illus.). 352p. 1993. 24.95 (*0-395-65029-1*) HM.

— Never Cry Wolf. 17.95 (*0-89190-823-4*, Am Repr) Amereon Ltd.

— Never Cry Wolf. 176p. 1983. mass mkt. 4.99 (*0-553-27396-5*) Bantam.

— Never Cry Wolf. 1963. 18.95 (*0-316-58639-0*, Joy St Bks) Little.

— Owls in the Family. (J). (gr. 4-7). 1985. pap. 3.50 (*0-553-15585-7*) Bantam.

— People of the Deer. 23.95 (*0-89190-818-8*, Am Repr) Amereon Ltd.

— The People of the Deer. 304p. 1984. mass mkt. 5.99 (*0-7704-2254-3*) Bantam.

— The Serpent's Coil. 224p. 1981. mass mkt. 4.95 (*0-7704-2313-2*) Bantam.

— The Snow Walker. 224p. 1984. mass mkt. 4.99 (*0-7704-2209-8*) Bantam.

— A Whale for the Killing. 19.95 (*0-89190-822-6*, Am Repr) Amereon Ltd.

— Woman in the Mists: The Story of Dian Fossey & the Mountain Gorillas of Africa. LC 87-40166. 400p. 1988. pap. 10.95 (*0-446-38720-7*) Warner Bks.

Mowat, J. L., ed. Alphita, a Medico-Botanical Glossary. (Anecdota Oxoniensia Ser.: No. 2). 1988. reprint ed. 67.40 (*0-404-63952-6*) AMS Pr.

Mowat, J. L., ed. see Mirfeld, John.

Mowat, Keith, jt. ed. see Curtis, Mike.

Mowat, Linda. Casava & Chica: Bread & Beer of the Amazonian Indians. 1989. pap. 25.00 (*0-7478-0008-1*, Pub. by Shire UK) St Mut.

Mowat, Robert B. Americans in England. LC 79-99642. (Essay Index Reprint Ser.). 1977. 28.95 (*0-8369-1423-6*) Ayer.

— International Relations. LC 67-22105. (Essay Index Reprint Ser.). 1977. 17.95 (*0-8369-0725-6*) Ayer.

***Mowat, Susan.** The Port of Leith. 470p. (C). 1993. pap. 69.00x (*0-85976-403-6*) St Mut.

Mowat, William & Mowat, Alexander. A Treatise on Stairbuilding & Handrailing. LC 85-6916. (Illus.). 390p. 1985. reprint ed. pap. 24.95 (*0-941936-02-3*) Craftsman.

Mowatt, Anna C. Autobiography of an Actress. Baxter, Annette K., ed. LC 79-8807. (Signal Lives Ser.). (Illus.). 1980. reprint ed. lib. bdg. 50.95 (*0-405-12853-3*) Ayer.

Mowatt, D. G. & Secker, Hugh. The Nibelungenlied: An Interpretative Commentary. LC 68-83851. 152p. reprint ed. pap. 43.40 (*0-8357-4145-1*, 2036918) Bks Demand.

Mowatt, John J., ed. The Ukrainians in Rhode Island: Faith & Determination. (Rhode Island Ethnic Heritage Pamphlet Ser.). (Illus.). (Orig.). 1988. pap. 4.75 (*0-917012-90-9*) RI Pubns Soc.

Mowatt, Marian H. Divorce Counseling: A Practical Guide. 176p. 1987. text ed. 29.95 (*0-669-14573-4*); pap. 12.95 (*0-685-17564-2*) Free Pr.

Mowbray, Andrew, ed. see Campbell, Archibald.

Mowbray, Carol T, et al, eds. Women & Mental Health: New Directions for Change. LC 84-22454. (Women & Therapy Ser.: Vol. 3, Nos. 3 & 4). 202p. 1985. pap. text ed. 14.95 (*0-918393-13-2*) Harrington Pk.

Mowbray, Carol T., et al, eds. Women & Mental Health: New Directions for Change. LC 84-19228. (Women & Therapy Ser.: Vol. 3, Nos. 3-4). 202p. 1985. text ed. 49.95 (*0-86656-331-8*); pap. text ed. 14.95 (*0-86656-437-3*) Haworth Pr.

Mowbray, D. F., jt. ed. see Spera, D. A.

Mowbray, E. Andrew. The American Eagle Pommel Sword: The Early Years 1794-1830. LC 88-61132. (Illus.). 244p. 1988. 45.00 (*0-917218-36-1*) A Mowbray.

Mowbray, E. Andrew, jt. auth. see Dow, Richard A.

Mowbray, E. J. & Reeder, J. C. Basic Applied Math for the Trades. (C). 1984. pap. text ed. 41.95 (*0-8053-6760-8*) Addison-Wesley.

Mowbray, George, jt. auth. see Rutman, Leonard.

Mowbray, James F. Post-Viral Fatigue Syndrome. Jenkins, Rachel, ed. 463p. 1991. text ed. 189.95 (*0-471-92846-1*, Wiley-Liss) Wiley.

— Post-Viral Fatigue Syndrome. Jenkins, Rachel, ed. 463p. 1993. pap. text ed. 79.95 (*0-471-93879-3*, Wiley-Liss) Wiley.

An Asterisk (*) at the beginning of an entry indicates that the title is appearing in BIP for the first time.

Mowbray, John. Plot Pak: Precalculus Tutorials with Computer Graphics. (Software Ser.). 191p. (C). 1987. disk 39.95 (*0-534-07542-8*) PWS Pubs.

***Mowbray, Thomas & Zahavi, Ron.** System Integration with Corba. Date not set. text ed. 49.95 (*0-471-10611-9*) Wiley.

Mowbray, William W. The Eastern Shore Baseball League. LC 88-32224. (Illus.). 204p. 1989. 19.95 (*0-87033-394-1*, Tidewtr Pubs) Cornell Maritime.

— Powerboat Racing on the Chesapeake. (Illus.). 104p. (Orig.). 1995. pap. 19.95 (*0-87033-473-5*, Tidewtr Pubs) Cornell Maritime.

Mowdy, Sharon, ed. see Van Horn, Brian & Van Horn, Chris.

Mowe, Richard. Evaluating Computer Integration in the Elementary School: A Step by Step Guide. 80p. 1990. 15.00 (*0-924667-70-2*) Intl Society Tech Educ.

— Evaluating Technology Integration in the Elementary School: A Step by Step Guide. 50p. 1993. pap. text ed. 19.95 (*0-685-72760-2*) Intl Society Tech Educ.

Mowe, Richard & Mummaw, Ron. The Academic Commodore 64. LC 84-9978. 1984. pap. 16.95 (*0-8359-0017-7*, Reston) P-H.

Mowen, Carol & Mowen, Gregg. Focus on Independent Study. Romano, Louis G., ed. 16p. 1990. pap. text ed. write for info. (*0-318-72649-1*) MI Middle Educ.

Mowen, Gregg, jt. auth. see Mowen, Carol.

Mowen, John C. Consumer Behavior. 3rd ed. (Illus.). 848p. (C). 1992. text ed. write for info. (*0-02-384591-0*) Macmillan.

— Consumer Behavior. 4th ed. LC 94-6027. 832p. 1995. write for info. (*0-02-384611-9*) Macmillan.

— Judgement Calls. 1994. pap. 12.00 (*0-671-89883-3*, Fireside) S&S Trade.

— Judgment Calls: High-Stakes Decisions in a Risky World. LC 93-11011. 304p. 1993. 22.00 (*0-671-72838-5*) S&S Trade.

Mowen, Maryanne M. Accounting for Costs As Fixed & Variable. 75p. 10.95 (*0-86641-117-8*, 85180) Inst Mgmt Account.

Mowen, Maryanne M., jt. auth. see Hansen, Don R.

Mower, A. Glenn, Jr. The European Community & Latin America: A Case Study in Global Role Expansion. LC 81-7244. (Contributions in Economics & Economic History Ser.: No. 46). xii, 180p. 1982. text ed. 49.95 (*0-313-22550-8*, MEC/, Greenwood Pr) Greenwood.

— Human Rights & American Foreign Policy: The Carter & Reagan Experiences. LC 87-7528. (Studies in Human Rights: No. 7). 175p. 1987. text ed. 49.95 (*0-313-25082-0*, MFP/, Greenwood Pr) Greenwood.

— International Cooperation for Social Justice: Global & Regional Protection of Economic-Social Rights. LC 84-27954. (Studies in Human Rights: No. 6). (Illus.). x, 288p. 1985. text ed. 59.95 (*0-313-24702-1*, MIP/, Greenwood Pr) Greenwood.

— Regional Human Rights: A Comparative Study of the West European & Inter-American Systems. LC 91-28. (Studies in Human Rights: No. 12). 192p. 1991. text ed. 55.00 (*0-313-27235-2*, MRF, Greenwood Pr) Greenwood.

— The United States, the United Nations, & Human Rights: The Eleanor Roosevelt & Jimmy Carter Eras. LC 78-22134. (Studies in Human Rights: No. 4). xii, 215p. 1979. text ed. 49.95 (*0-313-21090-X*, MUH/, Greenwood Pr) Greenwood.

Mower, Anna L. & Hagerman, Robert L. Morristown Two Times: History of Morristown, Vermont & More About Morristown, 1935-1980. LC 81-84221. (Illus.). 575p. 1982. 16.95 (*0-9607288-0-5*) Morristown Hist Soc.

Mower, D. Arthur. Showdown at Duck Run. Ingram, tr. 178p. 1992. pap. 7.95 (*1-880416-11-5*) NW Pub.

Mower, Jerry & Mower, Tedi J. St. James United Church of Christ Church Register, Reformed Church: Loudoun County, Virginia, Sept. 17, 1789-August 23, 1823. 53p. 1993. pap. 7.00 (*1-55856-130-7*) Closson Pr.

Mower, Nancy. Tutu Kane & Granpa. (Illus.). 32p. (J). (ps). 1989. 8.95 (*0-916630-66-8*) Pr Pacifica.

Mower, Nancy A. I Visit My Tutu & Grandma. LC 84-3280. (Treasury of Children's Hawaiian Stories Ser.). (Illus.). (J). (ps). 1984. 8.95 (*0-916630-41-2*) Pr Pacifica.

***Mower, Otto A.** History of Art: General Review for Survey Courses & Advanced Placement Examinations. Date not set. 12.00 (*0-614-05140-1*) Rusco Pubs.

***Mower, Richard K.** Overcoming Depression. LC 85-29228. 1994. pap. 6.95 (*0-87579-946-9*) Deseret Bk.

Mower, Roland. Aviation Regulation Study Guide-Workbook (AS 254) 112p. (C). 1992. pap. text ed. 19.95 (*0-8403-8366-5*) Kendall-Hunt.

Mower, Tedi J., jt. auth. see Mower, Jerry.

Mower, Walter L. History of the Town of Greene, Androscoggin County, Maine, 1775-1900: With Some Matter Extending to a Later Date. (Illus.). xvi, 627p. 1991. reprint ed. pap. 35.00 (*1-55613-386-3*) Heritage Bk.

— Sesquicentennial History of the Town of Greene, Androscoggin Co., Me., 1775 to 1900, with Some Matter Extending to a Later Date. (Illus.). 578p. 1995. reprint ed. lib. bdg. 58.00 (*0-8328-4463-2*) Higginson Bk Co.

Mowery, Carlene, jt. auth. see Deitz, Dennis.

Mowery, David C. Science & Technology Policy in Interdependent Economies. LC 93-41058. 320p. (C). 1994. lib. bdg. 110.00 (*0-7923-9422-4*) Kluwer Ac.

***Mowery, David C., ed.** The International Computer Software Industry: A Comparative Study of Industry Evolution & Structure. (Illus.). 320p. 1995. 45.00 (*0-19-509410-7*) OUP.

Mowery, David C. & Rosenberg, Nathan. The Japanese Commercial Aircraft Industry Since 1945: Government Policy, Technical Development & Industrial Structure. (Occasional Paper of the Northeast Asia-United States Forum on International Policy, Stanford University). 34p. (Orig.). 1985. pap. 5.00 (*0-935371-12-5*) CFISAC.

— Technology & the Pursuit of Economic Growth. (C). 1989. 44.95 (*0-521-38033-2*) Cambridge U Pr.

— Technology & the Pursuit of Economic Growth. 352p. (C). 1991. pap. 17.95 (*0-521-38936-4*) Cambridge U Pr.

Mowery, David M., ed. see National Academy of Science, et al.

Mowforth, P., ed. BMVC 91: Proceedings of the British Machine Vision Conference, Organized for the British Machine Vision Association by the Turing Institute, 23-26 September 1991, University of Glasgow. (Illus.). 448p. 1991. pap. 79.00 (*0-387-19715-X*) Spr-Verlag.

Mowinkel, Sigmund. The Psalms in Israels Worship. (Biblical Seminar Ser.). 549p. (C). 1992. 20.00 (*1-85075-333-4*, Pub. by Sheffield Acad UK) CUP Services.

Mowitt, John. Text: The Genealogy of an Antidisciplinary Object. LC 92-11618. (Post-Contemporary Interventions Ser.). (Illus.). 256p. 1992. lib. bdg. 39.95 (*0-8223-1251-4*); pap. text ed. 15.95 (*0-8223-1273-5*) Duke.

Mowitz, Robert J. & Wright, Deil S. Profile of a Metropolis: A Case Book. LC 62-14069. (Illus.). 691p. reprint ed. pap. 180.00 (*0-7837-3604-5*, 2043469) Bks Demand.

Mowl, Mary, jt. auth. see Roppelt, Donna.

Mowl, Timothy. Elizabethan & Jacobean Style. (Illus.). 240p. (C). 1993. 49.95 (*0-7148-2882-3*, Pub. by Phaidon Press UK) Chronicle Bks.

***Mowl, Timothy & Earnshaw, Brian.** Architecture Without Kings: The Rise of Puritan Classicism under Cromwell. LC 94-43001. 1995. text ed. write for info. (*0-7190-4678-5*, Pub. by Manchester Univ Pr UK) St Martin.

Mowlana, Hamid, et al, eds. Triumph of the Image: The Media's War in the Persian Gulf, a Global Perspective. 269p. (C). 1992. pap. text ed. 21.50 (*0-8133-1610-3*) Westview.

Mowle, Frederic J. Systematic Approach to Digital Logic Design. LC 75-18156. (Electrical Engineering Ser.). 500p. (C). 1976. text ed. write for info. (*0-201-04920-1*); teacher ed write for info. (*0-201-04921-X*) Addison-Wesley.

Mowlem, Alan. Goat Farming. (Illus.). 192p. 1988. 27.95 (*0-85236-183-1*, Pub. by Farming Pr UK) Diamond Farm Bk.

Mowli, P. & Subbaya, N. V. Air Pollution & Control. (C). 1990. text ed. 135.00 (*0-685-63521-X*, Pub. by Scientific Pubs II) St Mut.

Mowli, P. Pratapa & Subbayya, V. Venkata. Air Pollution & Control. (C). 1988. 260.00 (*81-85312-02-8*, Scientific) St Mut.

Mowli, V. Chandra. B. R. Ambedkar: His Life, Mission & Vision. 144p. 1990. text ed. 22.50 (*81-207-1273-0*, Pub. by Sterling Pubs II) Apt Bks.

— Bridging the Gulf: India's Manpower Migrations to West Asia. xiii, 106p. 1992. 18.95 (*81-207-1416-4*, Pub. by Sterling Pubs II) Apt Bks.

— Jogin: Girl-Child Labour Studies. xiii, 98p. 1992. 18.95 (*81-207-1415-6*, Pub. by Sterling Pubs II) Apt Bks.

— Where the West Meets the East. 1993. 25.00 (*81-207-1459-8*, Pub. by Sterling Pubs II) Apt Bks.

Mowli, V. Chandra, ed. Labour Landscape: A Study of Industrial & Agrarian Relations in India. 400p. 1990. text ed. 50.00 (*81-207-1150-5*, Pub. by Sterling Pubs II) Apt Bks.

— Role of Voluntary Organisations. 104p. 1990. text ed. 18.95 (*81-207-1142-4*, Pub. by Sterling Pubs II) Apt Bks.

Mowoe, Isaac J. & Bjornson, Richard, eds. Africa & the West: The Legacies of Empire. LC 85-5618. (Contributions in Afro-American & African Studies: No. 92). (Illus.). 284p. 1986. text ed. 55.00 (*0-313-24109-0*, MOW/, Greenwood Pr) Greenwood.

Mowrer, David S. Costing Data for Fire Protection in Complex Industrial Occupancies. 1982. 4.65 (*0-686-37671-4*, TR 82-7) Society Fire Protect.

Mowrer, Donald E. Methods of Modifying Speech Behaviors: Learning Theory in Speech Pathology. 2nd ed. (Illus.). 464p. (C). 1988. reprint ed. pap. text ed. 22.95 (*0-88133-376-X*) Waveland Pr.

Mowrer, Ernest R. Family Disorganization: An Introduction to a Sociological Analysis. LC 74-169396. (Family in America Ser.). 322p. 1979. reprint ed. 20.95 (*0-405-03873-9*) Ayer.

Mowrer, Lilian T. I've Seen It Happen Twice: First Hand Reports on a World in Crisis. 1969. 9.95 (*0-8159-5822-6*) Devin.

— Journalist's Wife. (American Biography Ser.). 414p. 1991. reprint ed. lib. bdg. 89.00 (*0-7812-8291-8*) Rprt Serv.

Mowrer, O. H. The Quest for Community. LC 65-167. (Augustana College Library Occasional Papers, Wallin Lecture: No. 8). 15p. 1962. pap. 0.50 (*0-910182-38-8*) Augustana Coll.

Mowrer, O. Hobart. Learning Theory & Behavior. LC 59-15671. 576p. 1973. reprint ed. 39.50 (*0-88275-127-1*) Krieger.

— Leaves from Many Seasons: Selected Papers. LC 82-18977. 368p. 1983. text ed. 59.95 (*0-275-91047-4*, C1047, Praeger Pubs) Greenwood.

Mowrer, Robert R., jt. ed. see Klein, Stephen B.

Mowrey, Daniel B. Echinacea. 1993. pap. 2.95 (*0-87983-610-5*) Keats.

— Fat Management: The Thermogenic Factor. (Illus.). 359p. (Orig.). 1995. write for info. (*0-936261-08-0*); pap. text ed. 16.95 (*0-936261-07-2*) Victory Pubns.

— Next Generation Herbal Medicine: Guaranteed Potency Herbs. rev. ed. (Illus.). 157p. 1990. pap. 8.95 (*0-87983-532-X*) Keats.

— Proven Herbal Blends. rev. ed. 1990. pap. 6.95 (*0-87983-524-9*) Keats.

— Scientific Validation of Herbal Medicine. 336p. (Orig.). 1990. pap. 14.95 (*0-87983-534-6*) Keats.

Mowrey, Daniel H. Herbal Tonic Therapies. (Illus.). 416p. (Orig.). 1993. pap. 14.95 (*0-87983-565-6*) Keats.

Mowrey, Joe, aft. Unheard Voices - Sixteen Poets: Survivors of Incest & Sexual Abuse to: Sixteen Voices, Poets: Survivors of Incest & Sexual Abuse. rev. ed. 80p. (Orig.). (C). 1994. 12.00 (*0-933553-10-2*) Mariposa Print Pub.

Mowrey, Joe, ed. see Hayes, Joe.

Mowrey, Joe, ed. see Stevens, Reed.

Mowrey, Peter C. Award Winning Films: A Viewer's Reference to 2700 Acclaimed Motion Pictures. LC 92-56667. 560p. 1993. pap. 35.00 (*0-89950-783-2*) McFarland & Co.

Mowry, Elizabeth. Paint the Changing Seasons in Pastel. LC 94-11698. (Illus.). 144p. 1995. 28.99 (*0-89134-574-4*) North Light Bks.

Mowry, George E., ed. Twenties: Fords, Flappers & Fanatics. 19.25 (*0-8446-2624-4*) Peter Smith.

Mowry, Jess. Children of the Night. (Orig.). 1989. pap. 3.95 (*0-87067-575-3*) Holloway.

— Rats in the Trees. 176p. 1993. pap. 9.00 (*0-14-017873-2*, Penguin Bks) Viking Penguin.

— Rats in the Trees: Stories. LC 89-27909. 160p. (Orig.). (J). 1990. pap. 8.95 (*0-936784-81-4*) J Daniel.

— Six Out Seven. LC 93-15676. 1993. 22.00 (*0-374-22083-2*) FS&G.

— Six out Seven. LC 94-20252. 1994. 12.95 (*0-385-47534-9*, Anchor NY) Doubleday.

— Way Past Cool. 288p. 1992. 17.00 (*0-374-28669-8*) FS&G.

— Way Past Cool. 320p. 1993. pap. 11.00 (*0-06-097545-8*, PL) HarpC.

Mowry, Kathryn L., jt. auth. see Robinson, Ed.

Mowry, Robert D. China's Renaissance in Bronze: The Robert H. Clague Collection of Later Chinese Bronzes, 1100-1911. Brown, Claudia & Gully, Anne, eds. LC 93-20881. 256p. (Orig.). 1993. pap. 40.00 (*0-910407-29-0*) Phoenix Art.

Mowry, Robert D., jt. auth. see Brown, Claudia.

Mowry, Robert G., tr. see Lenero, Vicente.

Mowry, Sylvester. Arizona & Sonora: The Geography, History, & Resources of the Silver Region of North America. 3rd ed. LC 72-9460. (Far Western Frontier Ser.). (Illus.). 256p. 1980. reprint ed. 25.95 (*0-405-04988-9*) Ayer.

Mowry, Thomas A., jt. auth. see Johnson, David B.

Mowry, W. The Descendants of Nathaniel Mowry of Rhode Island. (Illus.). 343p. 1989. reprint ed. lib. bdg. 64.50 (*0-8328-0890-3*); reprint ed. pap. 54.50 (*0-8328-0891-1*) Higginson Bk Co.

Mowry, William A. Recollections of a New England Educator. LC 73-89207. (American Education: Its Men, Institutions & Ideas, Ser. 1). 1978. reprint ed. 21.95 (*0-405-01446-5*) Ayer.

Mowschenson, Peter M. Aids to Undergraduate Surgery. 4th ed. LC 93-34955. 1994. 19.95 (*0-443-04966-1*) Churchill.

Mowsesian, Richard. Golden Goals, Rusted Realities: Work & Aging in America. 1987. 18.95 (*0-88282-024-9*) New Horizon NJ.

Mowshowitz, Israel. A Rabbi's Rovings. 385p. 1985. 20.00 (*0-88125-069-4*) Ktav.

Mowvley, Harry. The Books of Amos & Hosea. 176p. pap. 14.95 (*0-7162-0475-4*, Epworth Pr) TPI PA.

Moxey, Keith. Peasants, Warriors, & Wives: Studies in the Popular Imagery of Reformation Nuremburg. LC 88-37668. (Illus.). 192p. 1989. 29.95 (*0-226-54391-9*) U Ch Pr.

— The Practice of Theory: Poststructuralism, Cultural Politics, & Art History. LC 93-27229. (Illus.). 208p. 1994. 32.50 (*0-8014-2933-1*); pap. 12.95 (*0-8014-8153-8*) Cornell U Pr.

Moxham, B. J., jt. auth. see Berkovitz, B.

Moxham, J., jt. ed. see Souhami, R. L.

Moxham, John. Assisted Ventilation. (Illus.). 93p. 1991. pap. 22.00 (*0-7279-0306-3*, Pub. by Brit Med Assn UK) Amer Coll Phys.

***Moxie, Stephen C.** Locked Within Time. 260p. 1995. pap. 8.95 (*1-56901-654-2*) NW Pub.

Moxley, Cynthia. Knoxville: A Bicentennial Portrait. 1990. 29.95 (*0-89781-357-X*) Preferred Mktg.

***Moxley, Cynthia & Martines, Melissa.** Knoxville: An American Enterprise Book. Gilreath, Lenita & Turner, James E., eds. (Illus.). 272p. 1995. 45.00 (*1-885352-15-8*) Community Comm.

Moxley, David P. The Practice of Case Management. (Human Services Guides Ser.: Vol. 58). 188p. (C). 1989. pap. text ed. 17.95 (*0-8039-3205-7*) Sage.

***Moxley, Joseph M.** Becoming an Academic Writer: A Modern Rhetoric. 384p. 1994. pap. text ed. write for info. (*0-669-24496-1*) Heath.

— Publish, Don't Perish: The Scholars Guide to Academic Writing & Publishing. LC 92-4885. 224p. 1992. text ed. 42.95 (*0-313-27735-4*, MUD, Praeger Pubs); pap. text ed. 14.95 (*0-275-94453-0*, B4453, Praeger Pubs) Greenwood.

***Moxley, Joseph M. & Lenker, Lagretta T.** The Politics & Processes of Scholarship. LC 95-16147. (Contributions to the Study of Education Ser.: No. 66). 1995. text ed. write for info. (*0-313-29572-7*, Greenwood Pr) Greenwood.

Moxley, Julia. From the Window. (Illus.). 128p. 1988. 14.95 (*0-9620184-0-6*) J Moxley.

***Moxley, Juliet.** Baby Crafts: Over 25 Projects to Make & Give. (Illus.). 96p. 1995. 19.95 (*0-09-178692-4*, Pub. by Ebury Pr UK) Trafalgar.

Moxley, Juliet B. Decoupage: Cut, Glue, Varnish to Make Decoupage. (Illus.). 96p. 1994. pap. 14.95 (*0-8050-2813-7*) H Holt & Co.

Moxley, Lucina B. All about Sam. LC 91-58050. 175p. 1991. pap. 13.95 (*1-878208-09-8*) Guild Pr IN.

— The Best Years. LC 91-58047. 510p. 1991. pap. 16.95 (*1-878208-10-1*) Guild Pr IN.

— Dandy Dollhouse: Twenty Years Later. 92p. 1994. write for info. (*1-878208-51-9*) Guild Pr IN.

— The Dandy Dollhouse Stories. (Illus.). 74p. 1993. 16.95 (*1-878208-30-6*) Guild Pr IN.

— For the Love of Music. 80p. 1992. pap. 8.95 (*1-878208-18-7*) Guild Pr IN.

Moxley, Ray. Building Management by Professionals: For Building Owners, Developers, Architects, & the Design & Construction Team. LC 92-2429. 144p. 1993. 49.95 (*0-7506-0443-3*, Butterwrth Archit) Buttrwrth-Heinemann.

Moxley, Richard T., jt. ed. see Griggs, Robert C.

Moxley, Robert, jt. ed. see Kalb, Gilbert.

Moxley, Roy. Writing & Reading in Early Childhood: A Functional Approach. LC 81-9686. (Illus.). 290p. 1982. 34.95 (*0-87778-180-X*) Educ Tech Pubns.

Moxley, Sheila, illus. The Arabian Nights. LC 94-9137. 160p. (YA). (gr. 5 up). 1994. 19.95 (*0-531-06868-4*) Orchard Bks Watts.

— The Christmas Story: A Lift-the-Flap Advent Calendar. LC 92-29520. 24p. (J). 1993. 15.99 (*0-8037-1351-7*) Dial Bks Young.

— Skip Across the Ocean: Nursery Rhymes from Around the World. LC 94-48739. 48p. (J). (ps-1). 1995. 15.95 (*0-531-09455-3*) Orchard Bks Watts.

Moxley, Susan. Play with Papier-Mache. LC 94-14247. (Play with Crafts Ser.). 24p. (J). (ps-2). 1995. lib. bdg. 18.95 (*0-87614-865-8*, Carolrhoda) Lerner Group.

Moxly, S. H. Coastal Tables: For Use in Sight of Land. (C). 1987. 40.00 (*0-85174-128-2*, Pub. by Brwn Son Ferg) St Mut.

Moxon-Brown, E. Political Change in Spain. 144p. 1990. 49.95 (*0-415-02322-X*, A3946) Routledge.

Moxon-Browne, Edward. Nation, Class & Creed in Northern Ireland. 224p. (Orig.). 1983. pap. 53.95 (*0-566-00607-3*) Ashgate Pub Co.

Moxon-Browne, Edward, ed. European Terrorism, Vol. 3. LC 93-6399. (International Library of Terrorism: No. 3). 501p. 1994. text ed. 45.00 (*0-8161-7335-4*) G K Hall.

Moxon, D., jt. auth. see Hedderman, C.

Moxon, D. Corkery & Hedderman, C. Developments in the Use of Compensation Orders in Magistrates' Courts Oct 88. (Home Office Research Study Ser.: No. 126). 58p. 1992. pap. 14.00 (*0-11-341042-5*, HM10425, Pub. by HMSO UK) UNIPUB.

Moxon, Geoffrey. The Raven's Wing. large type ed. (General Ser.). 416p. 1993. 21.95 (*0-7089-2883-8*) Ulverscroft.

— The Red Knight. large type ed. 1990. 21.95 (*0-7089-2286-4*) Ulverscroft.

— Spycracker. large type ed. 480p. 1988. 16.95 (*0-7089-1804-2*) Ulverscroft.

Moxon, I. S., et al, eds. Past Perspectives: Studies in Greek & Roman Historical Writing. 240p. 1986. 64.95 (*0-521-26625-4*) Cambridge U Pr.

Moxon, Joseph. Mechanick Exercises: Or the Doctrine of Handy- Works. (Illus.). 352p. 1989. reprint ed. 25.00 (*0-9618088-1-0*) Astragal Pr.

Moxon, Julian. How Jet Engines Are Made. LC 85-21049. (How It Is Made Ser.). (Illus.). 32p. (YA). (gr. 7 up). 12.95 (*0-8160-0037-9*) Facts on File.

Moxon, P. R. Training the Roughshooter's Dog. (Illus.). 176p. 1994. 25.00 (*1-85310-501-5*) Voyageur Pr.

Moxon, Peter. Building a Better Team: A Handbook for Managers & Facilitators. LC 93-20443. 208p. 1993. 55.95 (*0-566-07424-9*, Pub. by Gower UK) Ashgate Pub Co.

Moxon, Richard, jt. auth. see Isaacs, David.

Moxon, Richard W. Offshore Production in the Less Developed Countries: A Case Study of Multinationality in the Electronics Industry. (New York University, Institute of Finance, Bulletin Ser.: No. 98-99, July, 1974). 95p. reprint ed. pap. 27.10 (*0-685-20492-8*, 2029933) Bks Demand.

Moxon, Richard W., et al, eds. Research in International Business & Finance: International Business Strategies in the Asia-Pacific Region, Vol. 4. 1983. 113.00 (*0-89232-308-6*) Jai Pr.

Moy, Caryl, jt. auth. see Nunnally, Elam.

Moy, Doug H. Estate Planning Simplified, 2 vols. suppl. ed. 817p. 1993. 60.00 (*0-471-55427-8*); 75.00 (*0-471-57961-0*) Wiley.

— Estate Planning Simplified, 2 vols., Vol. 2. 817p. 1993. Set. 228.00 (*0-471-55340-9*) Wiley.

— Estate Planning Simplified: 1991 Supplement Current to January 31, 1991, 2 vols. 344p. 1991. ring bd. 65.00 (*0-471-55763-3*) Wiley.

— Estate Planning Simplified Coursebook. (Estate Planning Library). 128p. 1992. pap. 15.00 (*0-471-58300-6*) Wiley.

***Moy, Henry, intro.** Treasures of Beloit College: 100 Works from the Logan Museum of Anthropology & the Wright Museum of Art. (Illus.). 100p. (Orig.). 1995. pap. 12.95 (*1-884941-03-6*) Beloit Coll.

Moy, J. Erik, jt. auth. see Theodore, Louis.

Moy, James S. Marginal Sights: Staging the Chinese in America. LC 93-17415. (Studies in Theatre History & Culture). (Illus.). 172p. 1993. 29.95x (*0-87745-427-2*) U of Iowa Pr.

— Marginal Sights: Staging the Chinese in America. LC 93-17415. (Studies in Theatre History & Culture). (Illus.). 172p. 1994. reprint ed. pap. 12.95 (*0-87745-448-5*) U of Iowa Pr.

M

Moy, Jean O., tr. see Inoue, Yasushi.

Moy, Joan O., tr. see Inoue, Yasushi.

Moy, Juellen, jt. auth. see McCurtain, Margaret.

Moy, Ronald L. Atlas of Cutaneous Facial Flaps & Grafts: A Differential Diagnosis of Wound Closures. LC 89-13856. 224p. 1990. text ed. 98.50 (*0-8121-1313-6*) Williams & Wilkins.

Moy, Ronald L., jt. auth. see Lask, Gary P.

Moy, Tina. Chinese Americans. LC 94-12601. (Cultures of America Ser.). 1994. 19.95 (*1-85435-785-9*) Marshall Cavendish.

Moya. Philosophy of Action. 1991. pap. 14.95 (*0-7456-0747-0*) Blackwell Pubs.

Moyal, Georges J., ed. Rene Descartes: Critical Assessments, 4 vols., Set. 1600p. 1991. 610.00 (*0-415-02358-0*, A5795) Routledge.

Moyano, Daniel. The Devil's Trill. 128p. 1991. pap. 10.95 (*1-85242-122-3*) Serpents Tail.

— The Flight of the Tiger. DiGiovanni, Norman T., tr. (Masks Title Ser.). 224p. (Orig.). 1995. pap. 13.99 (*1-85242-174-6*) Serpents Tail.

***Moyano, Maria J.** Argentina's Lost Patrol: Armed Struggle, 1969-1979. LC 94-35509. 1995. 25.00 (*0-300-06122-6*) Yale U Pr.

Moyano, Pilar. Fernando Villalon: El Poeta y Su Obra. 1990. 46.50 (*0-916379-80-9*) Scripta.

Moybridge, Eadweard & Masterson, B. L. The Human Figure in Motion. (Illus.). 288p. 1989. 12.99 (*0-517-64107-0*) Random Hse Value.

Moyd, Olin P. Preaching & Practical Theology: An African American Perspective. LC 94-9198. 1994. 9.95 (*0-910683-23-9*) Townsnd-Pr.

Moye, H. Anson. Analysis of Pesticide Residues. LC 90-33710. 478p. (C). 1990. reprint ed. 89.50 (*0-89464-330-4*) Krieger.

Moye, John E. Colorado Corporate Forms, 2 vols. 1988. ring bd. 269.00 (*0-87189-055-0*) Butterworth Legal Pubs.

— Colorado Corporate Forms, 2 vols. suppl. ed. 1993. 85.00 (*0-685-74605-4*) Butterworth Legal Pubs.

— Colorado Corporate Forms, 2 vols., Set. 1878p. 1994. 5.25 hd, ring bd. 269.00 (*0-250-47236-8*) Michie Butterworth.

— The Law of Business Organizations. 3rd ed. Tubb, ed. 692p. (C). 1989. text ed. 54.75 (*0-314-47359-9*) West Pub.

— The Law of Business Organizations. 4th ed. Hannan, ed. LC 93-33053. 700p. (C). 1994. text ed. 57.50 (*0-314-01219-2*) West Pub.

Moyer, Albert E. A Scientist's Voice in American Culture: Simon Newcomb & the Rhetoric of Scientific Method. (C). 1992. 40.00 (*0-520-07689-3*) U CA Pr.

Moyer, Ann, ed. see Lewis, Laura.

Moyer, Ann E. Musica Scientia: Musical Scholarship in the Italian Renaissance. LC 91-55057. (Illus.). 336p. 1992. 45.95 (*0-8014-2426-7*) Cornell U Pr.

***Moyer, Bill.** Kitchener: Yesterday Revisited. Date not set. 19.95 (*0-89781-004-X*) Preferred Mktg.

Moyer, Charles R., et al. Financial Management with Lotus 1-2-3. (Illus.). 316p. 1986. pap. text ed. 47.25 (*0-314-99984-1*) West Pub.

***Moyer, Christine M.** Serenity to the End: A Collection of Photos & Verse. (Illus.). 50p. (Orig.). Date not set. pap. 9.95 (*1-886453-02-0*) Candleberry Pr.

— Simple Things to the Believer: A Collection of Photos & Verse. (Illus.). 53p. (Orig.). 1994. pap. 9.95 (*1-886453-00-4*) Candleberry Pr.

***Moyer, Christine M., ed. & photos.** The Journey to Deliverance: A Collection of Photos & Verse. (Illus.). 50p. (Orig.). Date not set. pap. 9.95 (*1-886453-01-2*) Candleberry Pr.

Moyer, Craig A. & Francis, Michael A. Hazard Communication Handbook: A Right-to-Know Compliance Guide, 1993. 1991. pap. 90.00 (*0-87632-888-5*) Clark Boardman Callaghan.

Moyer, Darienne, tr. see Bernard, Yves & Colli, Jean-Claude.

Moyer, Ellen. Arthritis: Questions You Have - Answers You Need. 1993. pap. 9.95 (*1-882606-01-9*) Peoples Med Soc.

— Vitamins & Minerals: Questions You Have - Answers You Need. 1993. pap. 9.95 (*1-882606-05-1*) Peoples Med Soc.

— Vitamins & Minerals Ques You H. 1994. 6.99 (*0-517-11932-3*) Random Hse Value.

Moyer, F. Special Forces Foreign Weapons Handbook. 1986. lib. bdg. 79.95 (*0-8490-3663-1*) Gordon Pr.

Moyer, Frank A. Special Forces Foreign Weapons Handbook. 1987. pap. 14.95 (*0-8065-1044-7*, Citadel Pr) Carol Pub Group.

Moyer, H. Wayne. Agricultural Policy Reform: Politics & Process in the EC & U. S. A. LC 89-48550. (Illus.). 256p. 1990. text ed. 29.95 (*0-8138-1371-9*) Iowa St U Pr.

Moyer, Homer E., Jr. & Mabry, Linda A. Export Controls As Instruments of Foreign Policy: The History, Legal Issues, & Policy Lessons of Three Recent Cases. LC 88-13606. 574p. (Orig.). (C). 1989. lib. bdg. 48.00 (*0-935328-32-7*) Intl Law Inst.

Moyer, Imogene. The Changing Roles of Women in the Criminal Justice System: Offenders, Victims, & Professionals. 2nd rev. ed. (Illus.). 367p. (C). 1992. pap. text ed. 19.95 (*0-88133-654-8*) Waveland Pr.

Moyer, Inez. Responding to Infants. LC 83-71345. 200p. (Orig.). (J). (ps). 1983. pap. 18.95 (*0-513-01769-0*) Denison.

Moyer, J. H., jt. auth. see Armstrong, T. E.

Moyer, J. W., jt. auth. see Clark, C. A.

Moyer, James M., jt. auth. see Evans, Thomas J.

Moyer, Janet L. The Landscape Lighting Book. 304p. 1992. text ed. 79.95 (*0-471-52726-2*) Wiley.

***Moyer, Jeff.** We're People First. 48p. (J). (gr. 1-8). 1995. pap. text ed. 29.95 (*1-57129-002-8*) Brookline Bks.

Moyer, Joan, et al. The Child-Centered Kindergarten. 1987. pap. 2.50 (*0-87173-115-0*) ACEI.

Moyer, Joan & Martin, Lucy P., eds. Selecting Educational Equipment & Materials for School & Home. 1986. rev. ed. LC 86-1116. (Illus.). (C). 1986. pap. 10.50 (*0-87173-111-8*) ACEI.

Moyer, Joan, ed. see Association for Childhood Education International.

Moyer, John W. Practical Taxidermy. 2nd ed. LC 92-4770. 158p. 1992. reprint ed. lib. bdg. 21.50 (*0-89464-743-1*) Krieger.

Moyer, K. E. You & Your Child: A Primer for Parents. LC 74-17316. 222p. 1974. 24.95 (*0-88229-156-4*) Nelson-Hall.

Moyer, Kermit. Tumbling. Stories. LC 87-34284. (Illinois Short Fiction Ser.). 144p. 1988. 14.95 (*0-252-01525-8*) U of Ill Pr.

Moyer, Larry & Abell, Cameron D. One Hundred Forty-Two Evangelism Ideas for Your Church. (Orig.). 1990. pap. 4.99 (*0-8010-6271-3*) Baker Bk.

***Moyer, Laurence.** Victory Must Be Ours: Germany in the Great War. (Illus.). 219p. 1995. 24.95 (*0-7818-0370-5*) Hippocrene Bks.

Moyer, Linda L. & Willes, Burl. Undiscovered Islands of the Mediterranean. 2nd rev. ed. (Illus.). 232p. 1992. pap. 13.95 (*1-56261-049-X*) John Muir.

— Undiscovered Islands of the U. S. & Canadian West Coast. 208p. (Orig.). 1991. pap. 12.95 (*1-56261-013-9*) John Muir.

Moyer, Lloyd K. The Holy Rosary of Mary, the Beloved: A Devotional to Mary Magdalene. LC 92-80734. (Illus.). 67p. (Orig.). 1992. pap. 16.95 (*0-9631507-0-7*) Sophia Pr VT.

Moyer, Mary P. & Poste, George H., eds. Colon Cell Cancer. (Cell Biology Ser.). 620p. 1989. text ed. 241.00 (*0-12-509375-6*) Acad Pr.

Moyer, Miriam W. Demands of Love. 1978. 6.15 (*0-686-24048-0*) Rod & Staff.

Moyer, Page E. The ABCs of a Really Good Speech: For Managers, Ministers, & Most of the Rest of Us Who Are Less Than Confident Speakers. LC 89-82274. (Illus.). 120p. (Orig.). 1990. pap. 12.95 (*0-9625294-0-0*) Circle NY.

Moyer, Patricia. How to Talk to Your Cat. LC 92-44737. (Illus.). 1993. 5.99 (*0-517-09296-4*, Pub. by Wings Bks) Random Hse Value.

Moyer, R. Charles, jt. auth. see McGuigan, James R.

Moyer, R. Charles, et al. Contemporary Financial Management. 5th ed. Schiller, ed. 841p. (C). 1992. text ed. 65.50 (*0-314-91348-3*) West Pub.

— Contemporary Financial Management. 6th ed. LC 94-21326. 850p. 1994. text ed. 64.25 (*0-314-04342-X*) West Pub.

— Managerial Economics: Readings, Cases & Exercises. 261p. 1979. pap. text ed. 35.50 (*0-8299-0157-4*); pap. text ed. write for info. (*0-314-43376-7*) West Pub.

Moyer, Reed. Competition in the Midwestern Coal Industry. (Economic Studies: No. 122). (Illus.). 238p. 1964. 16.50 (*0-674-15400-2*) HUP.

— International Business: Issues & Concepts. (International Business Ser.: 1-402). 454p. (C). 1989. 46.95 (*0-471-87411-6*) Krieger.

Moyer, Reed, et al. Macro Marketing. 2nd ed. LC 77-26816. (Wiley Hamilton Series in Marketing). (Illus.). 213p. reprint ed. pap. 60.80 (*0-317-09658-3*, 2020186) Bks Demand.

Moyer, Robert E., jt. auth. see Ayres, Frank, Jr.

Moyer, Robert M., jt. auth. see Bargmann, Dale.

Moyer, Ronald L. American Actors, Eighteen Sixty-One to Twelve Hundred & Ten: An Annotated Bibliography of Books Published in the United States in English from 1861 Through 1976. LC 79-64229. 268p. 1979. 18.00 (*0-87875-167-X*) Whitston Pub.

Moyer, Ruth, jt. auth. see Meyer, Louis.

Moyer, Susan L. Silk Painting: The Artist's Guide to Gutta & Wax Resist Techniques. (Illus.). 144p. 1991. pap. 24.95 (*0-8230-4828-4*, Watsn-Guptill) Watsn-Guptill.

***Moyer, Terry J.** Crescendo. (YA). 1995. 14.98 (*0-88290-527-9*, 1059) Horizon Utah.

Moyer, Thomas & Boeckx, Roger, eds. Applied TDM, Vol. II. LC 82-72107. 387p. 1984. 20.00 (*0-915274-23-X*) Am Assn Clinical Chem.

Moyer, Willard, et al. The Witchery of Sleep: An Anthology. 1977. lib. bdg. 59.95 (*0-8490-2828-0*) Gordon Pr.

Moyer, William. Guide to Equine Joint Injection. 1993. pap. text ed. 28.00 (*1-884254-12-8*) Vet Lrn Syst.

Moyer, William & Sigafoos, Robert D. A Guide to Equine Hoof Wall Repair. 1993. pap. 28.00 (*1-884254-11-X*) Vet Lrn Syst.

Moyers, et al. Standards of Human Occlusal Development. (Craniofacial Growth Ser.: Vol. 5). (Illus.). 371p. 1976. 55.00 (*0-929921-03-8*) UM CHGD.

Moyers, Bill. Healing & the Mind. Flowers, Betty S., ed. LC 92-31074. 1993. 25.00 (*0-385-46870-9*) Doubleday.

— Healing & the Mind. LC 92-31074. 1995. pap. 17.50 (*0-385-47687-6*) Doubleday.

— The Language of Life: A Festival of Poets. Haba, James & Grubin, David, eds. LC 95-10348. 1995. write for info. (*0-385-47917-4*) Doubleday.

— The Secret Government: The Constitution in Crisis. 2nd ed. Kytle, Calvin, ed. LC 89-70131. 131p. 1990. 16.95 (*0-932020-61-5*); pap. 9.95 (*0-932020-60-7*) Seven Locks Pr.

— A World of Ideas: Conversations with Thoughtful Men & Women about American Life Today & the Ideas Shaping Our Future. 1989. pap. 25.00 (*0-385-26346-5*) Doubleday.

Moyers, Bill, jt. auth. see Campbell, Joseph.

Moyers, Bill, jt. auth. see Center for Investigative Reporting Staff.

Moyers, Bill, et al. The Parabola Book of Healing. 256p. 1994. 22.95 (*0-8264-0633-5*) Continuum.

Moyers, J. Ralph. A Stranger at the Crucifixion. 1992. 7.95 (*0-533-09729-0*) Vantage.

Moyers, Penelope A. Substance Abuse: A Multidimensional Assessment & Treatment Approach. LC 88-43456. (Illus.). 216p. (C). 1992. pap. text ed. 24.00 (*1-55642-084-6*) SLACK Inc.

Moyers, R. E. & Krogman, W. M. Craniofacial Growth in Man. 1971. 157.00 (*0-08-016331-9*, Pub. by Pergamon Repr UK) Franklin.

***Moyers, Richard L., ed.** Nonprofit Governance Case Studies Vol. 1. 38p. 1994. 14.00 (*0-925299-38-3*) Natl Ctr Nonprofit.

Moyers, Richard L. & Butler, James C., eds. Accountability at the Crossroads: (A Special Edition to Board Member - a Member's Only Publication) (Nonprofit Governance Ser.: No. 58). 16p. (Orig.). (C). 1993. pap. text ed. 12.00 (*0-685-72370-4*) Natl Ctr Nonprofit.

— Executive Compensation: (A Special Edition of Board Member - a Member's Only Publication) (Nonprofit Governance Ser.: No. 55). 16p. (Orig.). (C). 1993. pap. text ed. 12.00 (*0-685-72369-0*) Natl Ctr Nonprofit.

Moyers, Robert. Handbook of Orthodontics. 4th ed. 600p. 1988. 59.00 (*0-8151-6003-8*, Yr Bk Med Pubs) Mosby Yr Bk.

Moyes. Johnny under Ground. (Black Dagger Crime Ser.). 16.50 (*0-86220-789-4*, C1029, Black Dagger) Chivers N Amer.

Moyes, Adrian. Common Ground. 98p. (C). 1987. pap. text ed. 21.00 (*0-85598-078-8*, Pub. by Oxfam Pubns UK) St Mut.

Moyes, Canon. Why Catholics Pray to the Blessed Virgin Mary: An Incident in Catholic Life. (Compact Study Ser.). 15p. (Orig.). 1993. pap. 1.95 (*0-935952-94-2*) Angelus Pr.

Moyes, Leah E. Of Chosen Few. Van Treese, James B., ed. 98p. (Orig.). 1994. pap. 6.95 (*1-880416-36-0*) NW Pub.

Moyes, Patricia. Angel Death. LC 80-1396. 240p. (Orig.). 1982. pap. 4.95 (*0-8050-0505-6*, Owl) H Holt & Co.

— Black Girl, White Girl. LC 89-7440. 224p. 1990. pap. 4.95 (*0-8050-1149-8*, Owl) H Holt & Co.

— Black Girl, White Girl. large type ed. (General Ser.). 326p. 1991. lib. bdg. 19.95 (*0-8161-5011-7*, Large Print Bks) Hall.

— Black Widower. LC 85-8493. 224p. 1985. pap. 4.95 (*0-8050-0243-X*, Owl) H Holt & Co.

— The Coconut Killings. LC 76-29910. 224p. 1985. pap. 5.95 (*0-8050-0754-7*, Owl) H Holt & Co.

— The Curious Affair of the Third Dog. LC 85-17610. 224p. 1986. pap. 4.95 (*0-8050-0503-X*, Owl) H Holt & Co.

— Dead Men Don't Ski. LC 84-6732. 288p. 1984. pap. 5.95 (*0-8050-0705-9*, Owl) H Holt & Co.

— Death & the Dutch Uncle. LC 82-23259. 256p. 1983. pap. 5.95 (*0-8050-0506-4*, Owl) H Holt & Co.

— Death on the Agenda. LC 84-6750. 192p. 1984. pap. 5.95 (*0-8050-0507-2*, Owl) H Holt & Co.

— Down among the Dead Men. (Black Dagger Crime Ser.). 16.50 (*0-86220-823-8*, BD022, Black Dagger) Chivers N Amer.

— Down among the Dead Men. LC 86-9834. 240p. 1986. pap. 5.95 (*0-8050-0117-4*, Owl) H Holt & Co.

— Down among the Dead Men. large type ed. 1994. 18.95 (*0-7451-6461-7*, Scarlet Dagger Lrg Print) Chivers N Amer.

— Falling Star. LC 81-7030. 256p. (Orig.). 1982. pap. 4.95 (*0-8050-0755-5*, Owl) H Holt & Co.

— How to Talk to Your Cat. (Illus.). 128p. (Orig.). 1991. pap. 6.95 (*0-8050-1645-7*, Owl) H Holt & Co.

— Johnny under Ground. large type ed. (Scarlet Dagger Ser.). 1993. 18.95 (*0-7451-6441-2*, Scarlet Dagger Lrg Print) Chivers N Amer.

— Johnny Underground: An Inspector Henry Tibbett Mystery. LC 66-10121. 256p. 1987. pap. 5.95 (*0-8050-0270-7*, Owl) H Holt & Co.

— Many Deadly Returns: An Inspector Henry Tibbett Mystery. 256p. 1987. pap. 5.95 (*0-8050-0598-6*, Owl) H Holt & Co.

— Murder a la Mode. LC 63-12604. 224p. 1983. pap. 5.95 (*0-8050-0706-7*, Owl) H Holt & Co.

— Murder Fantastical. LC 84-6752. 256p. 1984. pap. 5.95 (*0-8050-0504-8*, Owl) H Holt & Co.

— Night Ferry to Death. LC 85-5567. 192p. 1986. pap. 5.95 (*0-8050-0116-6*, Owl) H Holt & Co.

— Season of Snows & Sins. LC 74-155526. 224p. 1988. pap. 5.95 (*0-8050-0849-7*, Owl) H Holt & Co.

— A Six-Letter Word for Death. LC 82-18738. 252p. 1985. pap. 4.95 (*0-8050-0244-8*, Owl) H Holt & Co.

— A Six-Letter Word for Death. large type ed. 432p. 1984. 21.95 (*0-7089-1163-3*) Ulverscroft.

— To Kill a Coconut. large type ed. 336p. 1981. 12.00 (*0-7089-0632-X*) Ulverscroft.

— Twice in a Blue Moon. 1994. pap. 5.95 (*0-8050-2948-6*) H Holt & Co.

— Twice in a Blue Moon. large type ed. LC 93-47393. 1994. 19.95 (*0-7862-0168-1*) Thorndike Pr.

— Who Is Simon Warwick? LC 78-53951. 176p. 1982. pap. 5.95 (*0-8050-0719-9*, Owl) H Holt & Co.

***Moyes, Robert.** Island Pubbing Two: A Guide to Pubs on Vancouver Island & the Gulf Islands. 176p. (Orig.). 1991. pap. 12.95 (*0-920501-60-5*) Orca Bk Pubs.

Moykopf, jt. auth. see Delarue-Martini-Vogt.

Moylan. Surgical Critical Care. 600p. 1994. 89.95 (*1-55664-163-X*, Yr Bk Med Pubs) Mosby Yr Bk.

***Moylan, Bridget.** Glacier's Grandest: A Pictorial History of the Hotels & Chalets of Glacier National Park. LC 94-67154. (Illus.). 92p. 1995. pap. 9.95 (*0-929521-89-7*) Pictorial Hist.

Moylan, Charles E., Jr., jt. auth. see Gilbert, Richard P.

Moylan, Charles E.

Moylan, David J., jt. auth. see Coia, Lawrence R.

Moylan, John, jt. auth. see Means, R. S.

***Moylan, Margaret F.** Symphony in Counterpoint: An Overture to Hope. 7p. 1994. pap. 5.95 (*0-9642109-0-8*) Parkinsonian.

***Moylan, Terry, ed.** Johnny O'Leary of Sliabh Luachra: Dance Music from the Cork-Kerry Border. (Illus.). 232p. (Orig.). 1994. pap. 35.95 (*1-874675-42-2*, Pub. by Lilliput Pr Ltd IE) Irish Bks Media.

Moylan, Tom. Demand the Impossible: Science Fiction & the Utopian Imagination. 256p. 1987. 39.95 (*0-317-54027-0*, 1125); pap. 14.95 (*0-416-00022-3*, 1154) Routledge Chapman & Hall.

Moylan, Tom, jt. ed. see Daniel, Jamie O.

Moylan, William M. The Art of Recording. (Illus.). 300p. 1992. text ed. 49.95 (*0-442-00669-1*) Van Nos Reinhold.

Moyle, Evelyn W., jt. auth. see Moyle, John B.

Moyle, J. B. The Contract of Sale in the Civil Law: With References to the Laws of England Scotland & France. LC 93-79720. 292p. 1994. reprint ed. 70.00 (*1-56169-078-3*) W W Gaunt.

— Imperatoris Iustiniani Institutionum: Libri Quattuor, with Introductions, Commentary & Excuses. 4th ed. LC 93-79719. 690p. 1994. reprint ed. 150.00 (*1-56169-077-5*) W W Gaunt.

Moyle, Jeremy, tr. see Gerbi, Antonello.

Moyle, John B. & Moyle, Evelyn W. Northland Wild Flowers. LC 76-55173. (Illus.). 246p. 1977. text ed. 29.95 (*0-8166-0806-7*); pap. 18.95 (*0-8166-1355-9*) U of Minn Pr.

Moyle, Natalie. The Turkish Minstrel Tale Tradition. LC 90-3620. (Harvard Dissertations in Folklore & Oral Literature Ser.). 244p. 1990. reprint ed. lib. bdg. 64.00 (*0-8240-2673-X*) Garland.

Moyle, P. B., jt. ed. see Schreck, C. B.

Moyle, Peter B. Fish: An Enthusiast's Guide. (Illus.). 1993. 25.00 (*0-520-07977-9*) U CA Pr.

— Fish: An Enthusiast's Guide. (Illus.). 278p. 1995. pap. 12.00 (*0-520-20165-5*) U CA Pr.

Moyle, Peter B. & Cech, Joseph J., Jr. Fishes: An Introduction to Ichthyology. 2nd ed. (Illus.). 560p. 1988. text ed. 76.00 (*0-13-319211-3*) P-H.

***Moyle, Peter B., et al.** Distribution & Ecology of Stream Fishes of the Sacramento-San Joaquin Drainage System, California. LC 81-13072. (University of California Publications in Zoology: No. 115). 266p. 1982. pap. 75.90 (*0-7837-7495-8*, 2049217) Bks Demand.

Moyle, Richard. Polynesian Sound-Producing Instruments. (Ethnography Ser.). (Illus.). 64p. 1990. pap. text ed. 10.50 (*0-7478-0095-2*, Pub. by Shire Pubns UK) Lubrecht & Cramer.

— Traditional Samoan Music. (Illus.). 288p. 1989. 55.00 (*1-86940-027-5*) OUP.

***Moyles, Janet, ed.** Beginning Teaching, Beginning Learning in Primary Education. LC 95-1199. 1995. write for info. (*0-335-19436-2*, Open Univ Pr); pap. write for info. (*0-335-19435-4*, Open Univ Pr) Taylor & Francis.

Moyles, Janet R. Just Playing? The Role & Status of Play in Early Childhood Education. 192p. 1989. pap. 24.00 (*0-335-09564-X*, Open Univ Pr) Taylor & Francis.

— Organizing for Learning in the Primary Classroom: A Balanced Approach to Classroom Management. LC 92-5706. 1993. 80.00 (*0-335-15660-6*); pap. 24.00 (*0-335-15659-2*) Taylor & Francis.

Moyles, Janet R., ed. The Excellence of Play. LC 93-25317. 192p. 1994. 75.00 (*0-335-19069-3*, Open Univ Pr); pap. 25.00 (*0-335-19068-5*, Open Univ Pr) Taylor & Francis.

Moyles, Lois. Alleluia Chorus. LC 78-68471. 1979. 7.95 (*0-913506-10-9*) Woolmer-Brotherson.

Moyles, R. G. A Bibliography of Salvation Army Literature in English, 1865-1987: Mightier than the Sword. LC 88-8964. (Texts & Studies in Religion: Vol. 38). 250p. 1988. lib. bdg. 89.95 (*0-88946-827-3*) E Mellen.

— Complaints Is Many & Various, but the Odd Devil Likes It: Nineteenth Century Views of Newfoundland. (Illus.). 187p. 1977. pap. 4.95 (*0-88778-160-8*, Pub. by Stoddart Pubng CN) Genl Dist Srvs.

— Improved by Cultivation: An Anthology of English Canadian Prose to 1914. 400p. 1994. pap. 22.95 (*1-55111-049-0*) Broadview Pr.

— The Text of Paradise Lost: A Study in Editorial Procedure. 198p. 1985. 30.00 (*0-8020-5634-2*) U of Toronto Pr.

Moyles, R. G., ed. English-Canadian Literature to Nineteen Hundred: A Guide to Information Sources. LC 73-16986. (American Literature, English Literature, & World Literatures in English Information Guide Ser.: Vol. 6). 358p. 1976. 68.00 (*0-8103-1222-0*) Gale.

Moyles, R. G. & Owram, Doug. Imperial Dreams & Colonial Realities: British Views of Canada, 1880-1914. (Illus.). 278p. 1988. 29.95 (*0-8020-2675-3*) U of Toronto Pr.

Moyles, R. G., jt. ed. see Demers, R. A.

Moyles, R. G., jt. ed. see Djwa, Sandra.

Moynahan, Brian. Russian Century: Birth of a Nation, 1894-1994. 1994. 45.00 (*0-679-42075-4*) Random.

Moynahan, J. M. & Stewart, Earle K. The American Jail: Its Development & Growth. LC 79-19372. (Illus.). 200p. 1980. text ed. 26.95 (*0-88229-531-4*) Nelson-Hall.

Moynahan, John K. Designing an Effective Sales Compensation Program. LC 79-54844. 222p. reprint ed. pap. 63.30 (*0-317-26019-7*, 2023891) Bks Demand.

— The Sales Compensation Handbook. 400p. 1991. 69.95 (*0-8144-0110-4*) AMACOM.

Moynahan, Juliam. Anglo-Irish: The Literary Imagination in a Hyphenated Culture. LC 94-19545. 1995. 24.95 (*0-691-03757-4*) Princeton U Pr.

Moynahan, Julian. Pairing Off. 1979. reprint ed. pap. 1.75 (*0-8439-0642-1*) Dorchester Pub Co.

An Asterisk (*) at the beginning of an entry indicates that the title is appearing in BIP for the first time.

— Vladimir Nabokov. LC 71-633325. (University of Minnesota Pamphlets on American Writers Ser.: No. 96). 47p. (Orig.). reprint ed. pap. 25.00 (0-7837-2871-9, 2057584) Bks Demand.

Moynahan, Julian, ed. see Lawrence, D. H.

Moynahan, Michael E. God of Seasons. LC 79-93127. 64p. 1980. pap. text ed. 4.95 (0-89390-019-2) Resource Pubns.

— How the Word Became Flesh: Story Dramas for Religious Worship & Education. LC 80-54874. 140p. 1981. pap. 10.95 (0-89390-029-X) Resource Pubns.

Moynahan, Michael E. Once upon a Miracle: Drama for Worship & Religious Education. LC 92-41325. 224p. 1993. pap. 12.95 (0-8091-3361-X) Paulist Pr.

Moynahan, Michael E. Orphaned Wisdom: Meditations for Lent. 1990. pap. 5.95 (0-8091-3198-6) Paulist Pr.

Moyne, Ernest J. Raising the Wind: The Legend of Lapland & Finland Wizards in Literature. Kime, Wayne R., ed. (Illus.). 224p. 1981. 34.50 (0-87413-146-4) U Delaware Pr.

Moyne, Ernest J., ed. & tr. Alexandra Gripenberg's "A Half Year in the New World" Miscellaneous Sketches of Travel in the United States (1888) 225p. 20.00 (0-87413-100-6) U Delaware Pr.

Moyne, John, jt. tr. see Barks, Coleman.

Moyne, John, tr. see Rumi, Jelaluddin.

Moyne, John, tr. see Rumi, Mevlana J.

Moyne, John A. LISP: A First Language for Computing. (Illus.). 208p. 1991. pap. 44.95 (0-442-00426-5) Van Nos Reinhold.

— Understanding Language: Man or Machine. (Foundations of Computer Science Ser.). 374p. 1985. 75.00 (0-306-41970-X, Plenum Pr) Plenum.

Moyne, Ron. A Star of Honor. LC 89-273. 1990. 21.95 (0-87949-302-X) Ashley Bks.

Moynes, et al. Rehabilitation of Sports Injuries. (Illus.). 300p. 1989. 40.00 (0-8016-3580-2) Mosby Yr Bk.

Moynet, M. J. L' Envers du Theatre: Machines et Decorations. LC 76-174870. (Illus.). 1972. reprint ed. 26.95 (0-405-08809-4) Ayer.

Moynier, John. Avalanche Awareness: A Practical Guide to Safe Travel in Avalanche Terrain. (Illus.). 32p. (Orig.). 1993. pap. 4.95 (0-934641-72-2) Chockstone Pr.

— Backcountry Skiing in the High Sierra. (Illus.). 200p. (Orig.). 1993. pap. 12.95 (0-934641-44-7) Chockstone Pr.

— The Basic Essentials of Cross-Country Skiing. LC 90-41890. (Basic Essentials Ser.). (Illus.). 72p. (Orig.). 1990. pap. 5.99 (0-934802-49-1) ICS Bks.

— The Basic Essentials of Mountaineering. LC 90-26009. (Basic Essentials Ser.). (Illus.). 72p. (Orig.). 1991. pap. 5.99 (0-934802-65-3) ICS Bks.

Moynier, John & Fiddler, Claude. Sierra Classics: Best Routes in the Sierra Backcountry. (Illus.). 328p. (Orig.). 1993. pap. 25.00 (0-934641-60-9) Chockstone Pr.

***Moynihan.** EDI: A Guide for Integrating Electronic Data Interchange in Today's Healthcare Facility. 1995. 45.00 (1-55738-624-2) Probus Pub Co.

— Implementation Manual for the Healthcare Claim Payment Advice: Guidelines For... rev. ed. 1995. 95.00 (1-55738-625-0) Probus Pub Co.

Moynihan, Betty. Augusta Tabor: A Pioneering Woman. LC 88-14962. (Illus.). 160p. (Orig.). 1988. pap. 9.95 (0-917895-23-1) Cordillera CO.

Moynihan, Brendan, jt. auth. see Patch, Cecilia.

Moynihan, Brendan, jt. auth. see Paul, Jim.

Moynihan, C. T., jt. ed. see Frischat, G. H.

Moynihan, C. T., jt. ed. see Lucas, J.

Moynihan, Cornelius J. Property: Introduction to the Law. 2nd ed. 239p. (C). 1993. reprint ed. text ed. 24.00 (0-314-60555-X) West Pub.

Moynihan, Daniel P. Family & Nation. LC 85-27041. 160p. 1986. 12.95 (0-15-130143-3) HarBrace.

— Family & Nation. 1987. pap. 5.95 (0-15-630140-7, Harvest Bks) HarBrace.

— Loyalties. LC 83-22666. 112p. 1984. 9.95 (0-15-154748-3) HarBrace.

— Maximum Feasible Misunderstanding. LC 69-18005. 1970. pap. 16.95 (0-02-922010-6) Free Pr.

— On the Law of Nations. 211p. 1990. text ed. 28.50 (0-674-63575-2) HUP.

— On the Law of Nations. 224p. 1992. pap. text ed. 10.95 (0-674-63576-0) HUP.

— Pandaemonium: Ethnicity in International Politics. LC 92-41370. 240p. 1993. 22.00 (0-19-827787-3) OUP.

Moynihan, Daniel P., jt. ed. see Denton, James S.

Moynihan, Daniel P., jt. intro. see Galicich, Anne.

Moynihan, Daniel P., jt. auth. see Glazer, Nathan.

Moynihan, Daniel P., jt. ed. see Glazer, Nathan.

Moynihan, Daniel P., jt. auth. see Morrice, Polly.

Moynihan, Daniel P., jt. auth. see Shapiro, Ellen.

Moynihan, Eddie. Business Management & Systems Analysis. (Information Systems Ser.). (Illus.). 240p. 1993. write for info. (0-632-03168-9) Blackwell Sci.

— Business Management & Systems Analysis. 500p. Date not set. pap. 26.00 (1-872474-05-5, Pub. by Alfred Waller UK) Paul & Co Pubs.

Moynihan, James H. The Life of Archbishop John Ireland. LC 76-6358. (Irish Americans Ser.). (Illus.). 1976. reprint ed. 40.95 (0-405-09351-9) Ayer.

Moynihan, James J. EDI: A Guide for the Healthcare Professional. LC 93-16554. (Illus.). 98p. 1993. pap. 24.95 (1-882198-17-4) Hlthcare Fin Mgmt.

— Implementation Manual for the 835 Health Care Claim-Payment - Advice. 175p. 1992. 75.00 (0-930228-91-X) Hlthcare Fin Mgmt.

— Implementation Manual for the 835 Health Care Claim Payment-Advice Supplement. 40p. 1992. 50.00 (1-882198-12-3) Hlthcare Fin Mgmt.

Moynihan, Martin. Communication & Noncommunication by Cephalopods. LC 84-47821. (Animal Communication Ser.). (Illus.). 154p. 1985. 35.00 (0-253-31382-1) Ind U Pr.

— Geographic Variation in Social Behavior & In Adaptations to Competition among Andean Birds. (Publications of the Nuttall Ornithological Club: No. 18). (Illus.). 162p. (C). 1979. 17.50 (1-877973-28-9) Nuttall Ornith.

— The New World Primates: Studies of Adaptive Radiation & the Evolution of Social Behavior, Languages, & Intelligence. LC 75-3467. 1976. 49.50 (0-691-08168-9) Princeton U Pr.

Moynihan, Maurice, ed. Eamon De Valera: Speeches & Statements 1917-1973. LC 80-51761. 1980. text ed. 85.00 (0-312-22457-5) St Martin.

Moynihan, Michael. Global Manager: Recruiting, Developing, & Keeping World Class Executives. (Economist Intelligence Unit Ser.). 192p. 1993. text ed. 29.95 (0-07-009351-2) McGraw.

— People at War: Nineteen Thirty-Nine to Nineteen Forty-Five. 216p. (C). 1990. reprint ed. lib. bdg. 25.00x (0-8095-7576-0) Borgo Pr.

— War Correspondent. 256p. 1994. 42.50 (0-85052-413-X, Pub. by L Cooper Bks UK) Trans-Atl Phila.

Moynihan, Michael W. Attitudes of Americans on Coping with Interdependence: Findings of Opinion Research Organizations. 20p. 1976. pap. text ed. 10.50 (0-8191-5859-3, Aspen Inst for Humanistic Studies) U Pr of Amer.

Moynihan, P., et al. Diabetes Youth Curriculum: A Toolbox for Educators, Bk. 1: The Curriculum. LC 88-7111. (Illus.). 136p. (Orig.). 1988. pap. text ed. 95.00 (0-937721-49-2) Chronimed.

Moynihan, Patricia M. Diabetes Youth Curriculum: A Toolbox for Educators: Resource & Activities Guide - "The Toolbox", Bk. 2. Raab, Patricia B., ed. LC 88-7112. (Illus.). 260p. (Orig.). 1988. ring bd. 55.00 (0-937721-50-6) Chronimed.

Moynihan, Patricia M., jt. auth. see Haig, Broatch.

Moynihan, Patrick. Pandaemonium: Ethnicity in International Politics. 240p. 1994. reprint ed. pap. 8.95 (0-19-827946-9) OUP.

Moynihan, Robert, intro. The Necessary Learning: Liberal Arts & Sciences, Defense & Reform. LC 88-26185. 116p. (C). 1988. lib. bdg. 32.00 (0-8191-7204-9) U Pr of Amer.

Moynihan, Ruth B. Coming of Age: Four Centuries of Connecticut Women & Their Choices. Wilkie, Everett C., Jr., ed. (Illus.). 116p. (C). 1987. reprint ed. pap. write for info. (0-940748-99-1) Conn Hist Soc.

— Rebel for Rights: Abigail Scott Duniway. LC 83-1142. (Yale Historical Publications: No. 130). (Illus.). 320p. 1985. pap. 15.00 (0-300-03478-4) Yale U Pr.

— Second to None, Vol. 2: A Documentary History of American Women, from 1865-Present, Vol. 2. (C). 1994. 45.00 (0-8032-3166-0); pap. 20.00 (0-8032-8204-4) U of Nebr Pr.

Moynihan, Ruth B., et al, eds. Second to None: A Documentary History of American Women, Vol. 1: From the Sixteenth Century to 1865, Vol. 1. LC 93-14347. (Illus.). xx, 404p. 1994. 45.00 (0-8032-3165-2); pap. 20.00 (0-8032-8199-4) U of Nebr Pr.

— So Much to Be Done: Women Settlers on the Mining & Ranching Frontier. LC 89-22549. (Women in the West Ser.). (Illus.). xxii, 326p. 1990. 35.00 (0-8032-3134-2); pap. 12.95 (0-8032-8165-X) U of Nebr Pr.

Moynihan, T. P., jt. auth. see Smart, P.

Moyo, Ambrose, jt. ed. see Pero, Albert.

Moyo, Jonah & Holland, Grace. Acercando las Personas a Jesus. (SPA.). 1980. 8.50 (1-55955-054-6) CITE MI.

Moyo, Sam, et al. The Southern African Environment: Environmental Profiles of the SADC Countries. 416p. (Orig.). 1992. 55.00 (1-85383-171-9, Pub. by Erthscan Pubns UK) Island Pr.

***Moys, Alan.** Colloquial French: A Complete Language Course. LC 95-16104. (ENG & FRE.). 1995. write for info. (0-415-12089-6); audio write for info. (0-415-12091-8) Routledge.

Moys, Elizabeth M., ed. Manual of Law Librarianship: The Use & Organization of Legal Literature. 2nd ed. (Professional Librarian Ser.). 952p. 1987. text ed. 65.00 (0-8161-1854-X, Hall Reference) Macmillan.

— Moys Classification & Thesaurus for Legal Materials. 3rd ed. 400p. 1992. 110.00 (0-86291-903-7) Bowker-Saur.

***Moyse-Faurie, Claire.** Dictionnaire Futunien-Francais. 1993. write for info. (0-7859-8186-1, 2-87723-070-8) Fr & Eur.

***Moyse-Faurie, Claire & Joredie, Marie-Adele.** Dictionnaire Xaracuu-Francais (Nouvelle-Caledonie) 1986. write for info. (0-7859-8235-3, 2-906341-00-2) Fr & Eur.

Moyse, R. & Elsom-Cook, M. T., eds. Knowledge Negotiation: Multiple Viewpoints & Uncertainty in Intelligent Tutoring Systems Design. (Illus.). 363p. 1992. text ed. 85.00 (0-12-509378-0) Acad Pr.

Moyser, George, ed. Politics & Religion in the Modern World. 240p. 1991. 49.95 (0-415-02328-9, A5690) Routledge.

Moyser, George & Wagstaff, Margaret, eds. Research Methods for Elite Studies. (Contemporary Social Research Ser.: No. 14). 240p. (C). 1987. text ed. 55.00 (0-04-312035-0); pap. text ed. 19.95 (0-04-312036-9) Routledge Chapman & Hall.

Moyser, George H., jt. auth. see Medhurst, Kenneth H.

Moysie, David. Memoirs of the Affairs of Scotland. LC 75-193018. (Bannatyne Club, Edinburgh. Publications: No. 39). reprint ed. 22.00 (0-404-52925-9) AMS Pr.

Mozaffar, Mehdi, jt. ed. see Ferdinand, Klaus.

Mozaffar, Mehdi. Authority in Islam: From Muhammad to Kohmeini. LC 86-13070. 140p. 1987. 50.95 (0-87332-388-2) M E Sharpe.

Mozan. Racing Numerology: A Standard System of the Science of Numbers Applied to Horse Racing. 2nd ed. 103p. 1993. reprint ed. spiral bd. 16.50 (0-7873-0628-2) Mokelumne.

Mozan, R. Mozan's Racing Numerology: A System for Finding Winners of Horse Racing Based on the Science of Numbers. 1991. lib. bdg. 75.00 (0-8490-4377-8) Gordon Pr.

Mozans, H. J. Woman in Science. LC 90-50964. (C). 1991. reprint ed. pap. text ed. 14.95 (0-268-01946-0) U of Notre Dame Pr.

Mozart. My First Book of Classics: Mozart. (Easy Classics Ser.). 1990. 4.95 (0-685-32053-7, H701) Hansen Ed Mus.

Mozart & Russell. Magic Flute, Vol. 1. (Illus.). 1990. 4.95 (0-685-40982-1) Eclipse Bks.

— Magic Flute, Vol. 2. 1990. pap. 4.95 (1-56060-050-0) Eclipse Bks.

— Magic Flute, Vol. 3. 1990. pap. 4.95 (1-56060-051-9) Eclipse Bks.

Mozart, Leopold. A Treatise on the Fundamental Principles of Violin Playing. 2nd ed. Knocker, Editha, tr. (Early Music Ser.). (Illus.). (C). 1985. pap. 35.00 (0-19-318513-X) OUP.

Mozart, Wolfgang A. Complete Serenades in Full Score Series II. 1990. pap. 12.95 (0-486-26566-8) Dover.

— The Mozart Libretti: The Marriage of Figaro, Don Giovanni & Cosi Fan Tutte. LC 93-1233. 320p. (ENG & ITA.). 1993. reprint ed. pap. text ed. 8.95 (0-486-27726-7) Dover.

Mozart, Wolfgang Amadeus. Complete Serenades in Full Score Series I. 1990. pap. 12.95 (0-486-26565-X) Dover.

— Complete String Quartets. 277p. 1970. pap. 12.95 (0-486-22372-8) Dover.

— Complete String Quintets. 181p. 1978. reprint ed. pap. 8.95 (0-486-23603-X) Dover.

— Cosi Fan Tutte. John, Nicholas, ed. Browne, Marmaduke E., tr. (English National Opera Guide Series: Bilingual Libretto, Articles: No. 22). (Illus.). 128p. (Orig.). 1984. pap. 9.95 (0-7145-3882-5) Riverrun NY.

— Don Giovanni. 19.00 (0-8446-5069-2) Peter Smith.

— Don Giovanni. John, Nicholas, ed. Platt, Norman & Sarti, L., trs. (English National Opera Guide Series: Bilingual Libretto, Articles: No. 18). (Illus.). 128p. 1982. pap. 9.95 (0-7145-3853-1) Riverrun NY.

— Don Giovanni: Complete Orchestral & Vocal Score. Schunemann, Georg & Soldan, Kurt, eds. LC 73-91488. (Opera Libretto Ser.). 480p. 1974. reprint ed. pap. 16.95 (0-486-23026-0) Dover.

— Later Symphonies. 285p. 1974. pap. 11.95 (0-486-23052-X) Dover.

— Letters of Wolfgang Amadeus Mozart. Mersman, Hans, ed. Bozman, M. M., tr. (Illus.). 320p. 1972. pap. 5.95 (0-486-22859-2) Dover.

— The Magic Flute. John, Nicholas, ed. & tr. by. Beasch, Anthony, tr. (English National Opera Guide Series: Bilingual Libretto, Articles: No. 3). (Illus.). (Orig.). 1980. pap. 9.95 (0-7145-3768-3) Riverrun NY.

— The Magic Flute (Die Zauberflote) in Full Score. (Music Scores to Play & Study Ser.). 225p. 1985. reprint ed. pap. 10.95 (0-486-24783-X) Dover.

— The Marriage of Figaro. John, Nicholas, ed. Dent, Edward, tr. (English National Opera Guide Series: Bilingual Libretto, Articles: No. 17). (Illus.). (Orig.). 1982. pap. 9.95 (0-7145-3771-3) Riverrun NY.

— The Marriage of Figaro: Complete Orchestral Score. LC 78-67726. 1979. reprint ed. pap. 16.95 (0-486-23751-6) Dover.

— Melody Dicer. 32p. 1984. pap. 8.95 (0-935474-09-9) Carousel Pubns Ltd.

— Melody Dicer Manuscript Book. Mercuri, Carmela, ed. 32p. 1984. pap. text ed. 4.95 (0-935474-10-2) Carousel Pubns Ltd.

— Mozart - Twelve Songs (for High Voice) Paton, John G., ed. 72p. (Orig.). (C). 1992. pap. 8.95 (0-88284-497-0, 3389) Alfred Pub.

— Mozart - Twelve Songs (for Medium Voice) Paton, John G., ed. 72p. (Orig.). (C). 1992. pap. text ed. 8.95 (0-88284-498-9, 3390) Alfred Pub.

— Mozart Piano Concerto in C Major. Kerman, Joseph, ed. (Critical Scores Ser.). (Illus.). (C). 1970. pap. text ed. 10.95 (0-393-09890-7) Norton.

— Mozart, Symphony in G Minor, K.550. Broder, Nathan, ed. (Critical Scores Ser.). (Orig.). (C). 1967. pap. text ed. 6.95 (0-393-09775-7) Norton.

— Piano Concertos Seventeen - Twenty Two. pap. 14.95 (0-486-23599-8) Dover.

— Piano Concertos Twenty Three - Twenty Seven. pap. 11.95 (0-486-23600-5) Dover.

— Practical Elments of Thorough-Bass. LC 76-27136. 1976. reprint ed. pap. 3.00 (0-915282-04-6) J Patelson Mus.

— Seventeen Divertimenti for Various Instruments. 256p. 1979. reprint ed. pap. 10.95 (0-486-23862-8) Dover.

— Symphony No. Thirty-Five in D, K. 385: The Haffner Symphony. 1968. pap. 8.00 (0-19-385289-6) OUP.

— Works for Piano Four Hands & Two Pianos. 1990. pap. 9.95 (0-486-26501-3) Dover.

Mozatao. Plant Vitamins: Agronomic, Physiological & Nutr. Aspects. 1993. write for info. (0-8493-4734-3) CRC Pr.

Mozejko, Edward. Yordan Yovkov. 117p. 1984. pap. 12.95 (0-89357-117-2) Slavica.

Mozejko, Edward, et al, eds. Vasiliy Pavlovich Aksenov: A Writer in Quest of Himself. (Illus.). 272p. 1986. 23.95 (0-89357-141-5) Slavica.

Mozeleski, Paul M., ed. see Mozeleski, Peter A.

Mozeleski, Peter A. The Rubbers Bros. Comics, Vol 1, No. 1. Mozelski, Paul M. & Pinatti, Gloria J., eds. Pagan, Margarita, tr. (Illus.). 16p. (YA). (gr. 6-12). 1990. pap. write for info. (1-880058-01-4); pap. 0.85 (1-880058-13-8) Rubbers Bros Comics.

— The Rubbers Bros. Comics, Vol. 1, No. 2. Mozeleski, Paul M. & Pinatti, Gloria J., eds. Pagan, Margarita, tr. (Illus.). 16p. (YA). (gr. 6-12). 1991. pap. 0.85 (1-880058-02-2); pap. 0.85 (1-880058-14-6) Rubbers Bros Comics.

— The Rubbers Bros. Comics, Vol. 1, No. 3. Mozeleski, Paul M. & Pinatti, Gloria J., eds. Pagan, Margarita, tr. (Illus.). 16p. 1992. English. pap. text ed. 0.85 (1-880058-03-0); Spanish. pap. text ed. 0.85 (1-880058-15-4) Rubbers Bros Comics.

— The Rubbers Bros. Comics, Vol. 1, No. 4. Mozeleski, Paul M. & Pinatti, Gloria J., eds. Castalanas, Guadalupe, tr. (Illus.). 16p. 1992. pap. text ed. 0.85 (0-685-74434-5) Rubbers Bros Comics.

— The Rubbers Bros. Comics, Vol 1, No. 4. Mozeleski, Paul M. & Pinatti, Gloria J., eds. Castalanas, Guadalupe, tr. (Illus.). 16p. (SPA.). (YA). (gr. 6-12). 1992. pap. text ed. 0.85 (0-685-74435-3) Rubbers Bros Comics.

— The Rubbers Bros. Comics, Vol 1, Nos. 1-4. Mozeleski, Paul M. & Pinatti, Gloria J, eds. (Illus.). (YA). (gr. 6-12). 1992. pap. 5.00 (1-880058-00-6) Rubbers Bros Comics.

— When AIDS Strikes. Mozeleski, Paul M. & Pinatti, Gloria J., eds. (Illus.). 8p. (Orig.). 1991. pap. 0.55 (1-880058-85-5) Rubbers Bros Comics.

— When AIDS Strikes, Vol. 1, Nos. 1 & 2. Mozeleski, Paul M. & Pinatti, Gloria J., eds. (Illus.). 8p. (Orig.). 1991. pap. write for info. (1-880058-84-7) Rubbers Bros Comics.

Mozelle, Isaac. The Flowering Plants of Western India. 383p. 1989. 200.00 (81-7158-039-4, Pub. by Scientific Pubs II) St Mut.

Mozelle, Shirley. Zack's Alligator. LC 88-32069. (I Can Read Bk.). (Illus.). 64p. (J). (gr. k-3). 1989. lib. bdg. 14.89 (0-06-024310-4) HarpC Child Bks.

— Zack's Alligator. LC 88-32067. (I Can Read Bk.). (Illus.). 64p. (J). (ps-2). 1995. pap. 3.50 (0-06-444186-5) HarpC Child Bks.

— Zack's Alligator Goes to School. LC 92-29871. (I Can Read Bk.). (Illus.). 64p. (J). (gr. k-3). 1994. 14.00 (0-06-022887-3) HarpC Child Bks.

— Zack's Alligator Goes to School. LC 92-29871. (I Can Read Bk.). (Illus.). 64p. (J). (gr. k-3). 1994. lib. bdg. 13.89 (0-06-022888-1) HarpC Child Bks.

Mozelski, Paul M., ed. see Mozeleski, Peter A.

Mozena, James P. & Anderson, Debby L. Quality Improvement Handbook for Health Care Professionals. LC 92-48914. 120p. 1993. pap. 19.95 (0-87389-237-2) ASQC Qual Pr.

***Mozer, David.** Bicycling in Africa: The Place in Between. rev. ed. (Illus.). 196p. 1989. pap. 14.95 (0-9623052-0-0) IBF WA.

Mozer, Michael C. The Perception of Multiple Objects: A Connectionist Approach. (Bradford Neural Network Modeling & Connectionism Ser.). 165p. 1991. 27.50 (0-262-13270-2) MIT Pr.

Mozer, Michael C., et al, eds. Proceedings of the 1993 Connectionist Models Summer School. 424p. 1993. text ed. 89.95 (0-8058-1590-2) L Erlbaum Assocs.

Mozes, G. Paraffin Products: Properties, Technologies, Applications. (Developments in Petroleum Products Ser.: Vol. 14). 336p. 1983. 120.50 (0-444-99712-1) Elsevier.

Mozes, Nava, et al, eds. Microbial Cell Surface Analysis: Structural & Physico-Chemical Methods. 368p. 1991. lib. bdg. 95.00 (0-89573-783-3) VCH Pubs.

Mozes, T. E. Raw Wool Carbonizing, Vol. 17, No. 3. (C). 1988. pap. text ed. 90.00 (1-870812-01-8, Pub. by Textile Institue UK) St Mut.

***Mozeson, I. E. & Stavsky, Lois.** Jerusalem Mosaic: Voices from the Holy City. LC 94-21439. (J). (gr. 1-8). 1994. pap. text ed. write for info. (0-02-767651-X, Four Winds Pr) S&S Childrens.

Mozeson, I. E., jt. auth. see Stavsky, Lois.

Mozeson, Isaac E. The Word: Dictionary That Reveals the Hebrew Source of English. 1990. 29.95 (0-933503-44-X) Sure Sellers.

— The Word: The Dictionary That Reveals the Hebrew Sources of English. 1995. pap. write for info. (1-56821-615-7) Aronson.

Mozeson, Issac E. Word: The Dictionary That Reveals the Hebrew Source of English. 1995. pap. 19.99 (1-56171-088-1) Sure Sellers.

Mozeson, Leon M. Echoes of the Song of the Nightingale: The Torah As a Divine Document. 20.00 (0-88125-380-4) Ktav.

Mozga, Ilsa A., tr. see Goetz-Stankiewicz, Marketa, ed.

Mozgovoi, A. A. Ascaridata of Animals & Man, & Diseases Caused by Them, Pt. III. (C). 1986. 38.50 (81-205-0039-3, Pub. by Oxford IBH II) S Asia.

Mozheiko, I., jt. auth. see Chifrin, Gennadi.

Mozhin, V. Distribution of Productive Forces: Theory & Practice. 326p. (C). 1988. 70.00 (0-685-31521-5, Pub. by Collets UK) Pro-Am Music.

Mozina, Stane, jt. ed. see Kukovica, Anton.

Mozingo, David. Chinese Policy Toward Indonesia, 1949-1967. LC 75-14719. 303p. 1976. 39.95 (0-8014-0921-7) Cornell U Pr.

Mozingo, David, jt. ed. see Nee, Victor.

Mozingo, Hugh N. Shrubs of the Great Basin: A Natural History. LC 86-7070. (Great Basin Ser.: No. 4). 364p. (Orig.). 1987. pap. 34.95 (0-87417-112-1) U of Nev Pr.

Mozino, Jose M. Noticias de Nutka: An Account of Nootka Sound in 1792. 2nd ed. Engstrand, Iris H., ed. & tr. by. LC 90-50981. 200p. 1991. reprint ed. pap. 14.95 (0-295-97103-7) U of Wash Pr.

— Noticias de Nutka: An Account of Nootka Sound in 1792. LC 84-45542. (American Ethnological Society Monographs: No. 50). 1988. reprint ed. 35.00 (0-404-62948-2) AMS Pr.

Mozley & Whiteley. Mozley & Whitely's Law Dictionary. 10th rev. ed. 520p. 1988. U.K. pap. 18.00 (0-406-62526-3) Butterworth Legal Pubs.

M

Mozley, E. N. The Theology of Albert Schweitzer. LC 73-16630. 108p. 1974. reprint ed. text ed. 35.00 (*0-8371-7204-7*, SCTH, Greenwood Pr) Greenwood.
Mozley, E. N., ed. see Schweitzer, Albert.
***Mozley, Robert F.** Uranium Enrichment & Other Technical Problems Relating to Nuclear Weapons Proliferation. 64p. (Orig.). 1994. pap. 9.00 (*0-935371-30-3*) CFISAC.
Mozo, Segundo M. Salvadoran Migration to the United States: An Exploratory Study. 56p. (Orig.). 1988. pap. 7.50 (*0-924046-04-X*) Ctr EPRA.
***Mozolin, Viktor P.** Property Law in Contemporary Russia. 174p. 1993. 60.00 (*0-935328-75-0*) Intl Law Inst.
Mozolin, Viktor P., jt. auth. see Farnsworth, E. Allen.
Mozqovoi, A. A. Fundamentals of Nematology: Ascaridata of Animals & Men. (C). 1986. 17.50 (*0-8364-2112-4*, Pub. by Oxford IBH II) S Asia.
Mozsik, et al, eds. Oxygen Free Radicals & Scavengers in the Natural Sciences. 355p. 1993. text ed. 55.00 (*963-05-6589-7*, Pub. by A K HU) Intl Spec Bk.
Mozsik, G. & Javor, T. Progress in Peptic Ulcer. 774p. 1976. 254.00 (*0-569-08386-9*, Pub. by Collets UK) Pro-Am Music.
***Mozsik, Gy & Javor, T.** Progress in Peptic Ulcer. 774p. (C). 1976. 150.00x (*963-05-1210-6*) St Mut.
Mozsik, Gy, et al, eds. Cell Injury & Protection in the Gastrointestinal Tract: From Basic Science to Clinical Perspectives: Proceedings of Third International Symposium on Gastrointestinal Cytoprotection Held at Pecs, Hungary, October 7-8, 1991. 444p. 62.00 (*963-05-6633-8*, Pub. by A K HU) Intl Spec Bk.
Mozsik, Gy., et al, eds. Gastrointestinal Defence Mechanisms: Proceedings of a Satellite Symposium of the 28th International Congress of Physiological Sciences, Budapest, 1980. LC 80-41883. (Advances in Physiological Sciences Ser.: Vol. 29). (Illus.). 590p. 1981. 249.00 (*0-08-027350-5*, Pub. by Pergamon Repr UK) Franklin.
Mozumdar, A. K. Today & Tomorrow. 2nd ed. 1979. pap. 4.00 (*0-87516-066-2*) DeVorss.
Mozur, Joseph P., Jr. Parables from the Past: The Prose Fiction of Chingiz Aitmatov. (Russian & East European Studies Ser.). 224p. (C). 1994. 59.95 (*0-8229-3791-3*); pap. 22.95 (*0-8229-5531-8*) U of Pittsburgh Pr.
***Mozzillo, Mario.** Things Are Out of Joint. 225p. 1995. 21.95 (*0-9644443-0-5*) Windsor House.
Mphahlele, Es'kia. Afrika My Music: An Autobiography, 1957-1983. 260p. 1986. pap. 13.95 (*0-86975-237-5*, Pub. by Ravan Pr ZA) Ohio U Pr.
— Chirundu. 172p. (Orig.). 1994. pap. text ed. 14.95x (*0-86975-449-1*, Pub. by Ravan Pr ZA) Ohio U Pr.
— Renewal Time. LC 88-61391. (Readers International Ser.). 225p. (Orig.). (C). 1988. 16.95 (*0-930523-55-5*); pap. 8.95 (*0-930523-56-3*) Readers Intl.
Mphahlele, Ezekiel. Down Second Avenue. 222p. 1985. pap. 8.95 (*0-571-09716-2*) Faber & Faber.
— Down Second Avenue: Growing up in a South African Ghetto. 21.50 (*0-8446-4451-X*) Peter Smith.
***MPIF Standards Committee Staff.** Standard Test Methods for Metal Powders & Metallurgy Products, 1995. (Illus.). 1995. student ed 35.00 (*1-878954-55-5*) Metal Powder.
***Mpoza, Caroli L.** The Great Heroes of African Origin: Our Ancestors in the Faith. (Illus.). (Orig.). 1995. pap. 12.95 (*0-8062-5281-2*) Carlton.
M'Queen, James. Geographical Survey of Africa. 303p. reprint ed. 45.00 (*0-7146-1834-9*, Pub. by F Cass Pubs UK) Intl Spec Bk.
Mr. Fresh & the Supreme Rockers Staff. Breakdancing. 128p. 1984. pap. 2.95 (*0-380-88153-5*) Avon.
***Mr. George.** A Child's Coloring Book of Angels. (J). 1995. pap. 7.95 (*0-533-11437-3*) Vantage.
Mr. J. More of the World's Best Dirty Jokes. 224p. 1986. mass mkt. 4.95 (*0-345-34687-4*) Ballantine.
— More of the World's Dirty Jokes. 1980. pap. 5.95 (*0-8065-0710-1*, Citadel Pr) Carol Pub Group.
— Still More of the World's Best Dirty Jokes. 1985. mass mkt. 5.99 (*0-345-32622-9*) Ballantine.
— The World's Best Dirty Jokes. 1985. mass mkt. 4.95 (*0-345-33106-0*) Ballantine.
— The World's Best Dirty Jokes. (Illus.). 160p. 1976. 7.95 (*0-8184-0223-7*) Carol Pub Group.
— The World's Best Dirty Jokes. (Illus.). 1979. pap. 4.95 (*0-8065-0702-0*, Citadel Pr) Carol Pub Group.
Mr. P. World's Best Yiddish Dirty Jokes. (Illus.). 128p. 1984. pap. 4.95 (*0-8065-0887-6*, Citadel Pr) Carol Pub Group.
***Mr. X.** Fired? Fight Back! The No-Nonsense Guide for the Newly Fired, Downsized, Outplaced, Laid-off & Those Who Are Worried about It. 240p. 1995. 16.95 (*0-8144-7875-1*) AMACOM.
Mrabet, Mohammed. Big Mirror. Bowles, Paul, tr. 80p. 1990. pap. 10.95 (*0-7206-0730-2*, Pub. by P Owen Ltd UK) Dufour.
— The Boy Who Set the Fire & Other Stories. Bowles, Paul, tr. 144p. 1989. reprint ed. pap. 8.95 (*0-87286-230-5*) City Lights.
— The Chest. Bowles, Paul, tr. 120p. (ARA.). 1983. pap. 7.50 (*0-939180-18-9*) Tombouctou.
— The Chest. deluxe limited ed. Bowles, Paul, tr. 120p. (ARA.). 1983. 35.00 (*0-939180-21-9*) Tombouctou.
— Chocolate Creams & Dollars. Igliori, Paola, ed. Bowles, Paul, tr. (Illus.). 192p. 1993. 29.95 (*0-9625119-6-X*) Inanout Pr.
— The Lemon. Bowles, Paul, tr. 192p. (Orig.). 1986. reprint ed. pap. 8.95 (*0-87286-181-3*, Subterranean Co) City Lights.
— Look & Move On. Bowles, Paul, tr. 128p. 1989. 25.00 (*0-7206-0756-6*, Pub. by P Owen Ltd UK) Dufour.
— Love with a Few Hairs. Bowles, Paul, tr. 176p. reprint ed. pap. 8.95 (*0-87286-192-9*) City Lights.
— Marriage with Papers. Bowles, Paul, tr. LC 85-52107. 88p. (Orig.). 1986. pap. 6.00 (*0-939180-32-4*) Tombouctou.
— Marriage with Papers. deluxe ed. Bowles, Paul, tr. LC 85-52107. 88p. (Orig.). 1986. 35.00 (*0-939180-29-4*) Tombouctou.
— M'Hashish. Bowles, Paul, tr. LC 70-88228. (Orig.). 1969. pap. 7.95 (*0-87286-034-5*) City Lights.
Mracek, Jan. Technical Illustration & Graphics. (Illus.). 352p. (C). 1983. 34.00 (*0-685-05866-2*) P-H.
Mrachek, L. A., jt. auth. see Palmer, Claude I.
Mrachek, Leonard & Komschilies, Charles. Basic Technical College Mathematics. 2nd ed. 336p. 1993. pap. text ed. write for info. (*0-13-891995-X*) P-H.
Mrak, E. M. & Stewart, George F., eds. Advances in Food Research, Vol. 29. (Serial Publication Ser.). 1984. text ed. 114.00 (*0-12-016429-9*) Acad Pr.
Mrak, Robert E., ed. Muscle Membranes in Diseases of Muscle. 168p. 1985. 113.95 (*0-8493-5622-9*, RC925, CRC Reprint) Franklin.
Mrantz, Maxine. Hawaiian Monarchy: The Romantic Years. LC 74-175013. (Hawaiiana Ser.). (Illus.). 46p. (Orig.). 1974. pap. 5.95 (*0-941351-00-9*) Aloha.
— Hawaii's Tragic Princess. LC 87-125360. (Hawaiiana Ser.). (Illus.). 38p. (Orig.). 1980. pap. 5.95 (*0-941351-04-1*) Aloha.
— Hawaii's Whaling Days. LC 87-400678. (Hawaiiana Ser.). Orig. Title: Whaling Days in Old Hawaii. (Illus.). (Orig.). 1987. reprint ed. pap. 4.95 (*0-941351-10-6*) Aloha.
— Women of Old Hawaii. LC 87-125364. (Hawaiiana Ser.). (Illus.). 38p. (Orig.). pap. 4.95 (*0-941351-01-7*) Aloha.
Mraovitch, Sima. Kako da Saberem Korake. Maljkovic-Petkovic, Djero et al, eds. (Biblioteka Jugoslovenska Diaspora Ser.). (Illus.). 84p. (Orig.). (CRO & SER.). 1982. 5.95 (*0-943898-04-8*); pap. 4.95 (*0-943898-05-6*) Gospic Realty.
***Mraz, Bohumir.** Ingres: Dibujos. (Grandes Monografias). (Illus.). 200p. (SPA.). 1993. 150.00 (*84-343-0381-7*) Elliots Bks.
***Mraz, Charles.** Health & the Honeybee. LC 94-67746. (Illus.). 104p. (Orig.). 1994. pap. 12.95 (*0-9642485-0-6*) Queen City VT.
Mrazek, Rick, ed. Alternative Paradigms in Environmental Education Research. (Monograph Ser.: Vol. 9). (Illus.). 332p. (Orig.). 1993. pap. 20.00 (*1-884008-04-6*) NAAEE.
— Proceedings from NAAEE's 1993 Annual Conference in Big Sky, Montana: Pathways to Partnerships - Coalitions for Environmental Education. 536p. (Orig.). 1994. pap. 15.00 (*1-884008-19-4*) NAAEE.
Mrazek, Rudolf. Sjahrir: Politics & Exile in Indonesia. (Studies on Southeast Asia: No. 14). (Orig.). 1994. pap. text ed. 20.00 (*0-87727-713-3*) Cornell SE Asia.
Mrazkova & Remes, eds. The Russian War: Nineteen Forty One Nineteen Forty Five. 152p. 1987. 22.50 (*0-88029-084-6*) Dorset Pr.
Mrazkova, Daniela, ed. see Macijauskas, Aleksandras.
Mrkvicka, Edward F., Jr. The Bank Book. 3rd ed. LC 93-24924. (Illus.). 320p. 1994. pap. 12.00 (*0-06-273265-X*, Harper Ref) HarpC.
— How to Become Number One: A Crash Course for Career Success. LC 91-90115. (Orig.). 1991. pap. 8.95 (*0-9628726-0-1*) Reliance Enter.
***MRM Staff.** Pashto Newspaper Reader. 1984. digital audio 5.00 (*1-881265-22-6*) Dunwoody Pr.
— Pashto Newspaper Reader. LC 84-72437. iv, 246p. 1984. text ed. 39.00 (*0-931745-04-7*) Dunwoody Pr.
— Vietnamese-English Glossary of Commercial Terms. 1995. write for info. (*1-881265-10-2*) Dunwoody Pr.
M'Robert, P. Tour Through Part of the North Provinces of America. LC 67-29039. (Eyewitness Accounts of the American Revolution Ser., No. 1). 1979. reprint ed. 17.95 (*0-405-01136-9*) Ayer.
Mroczkowska-Brand, Katarzyna, tr. see Kapuscinski, Ryszard.
Mroczkowski, Tomasz. Topics in Clinical Dermatology: Sexually Transmitted Diseases. LC 89-26963. (Illus.). 408p. 1990. 110.00 (*0-89640-163-4*) Igaku-Shoin.
Mroczowski, P. J., ed. see Stephen, Baron.
Mrosovsky, Kitty, tr. see Flaubert, Gustave.
Mrosovsky, Nicholas. Rheostasis: The Physiology of Change. (Illus.). 192p. 1990. 49.95 (*0-19-506184-5*) OUP.
Mrowec, S. Defects & Diffusion in Solids: An Introduction. (Materials Science Monographs: Vol. 5). 466p. 1980. 105.25 (*0-444-99776-8*) Elsevier.
Mrowicki, Linda. Let's Work Safely! English Language Skills for Safety in the Workplace. (Illus.). 114p. (Orig.). 1984. pap. text ed. 7.50 (*0-916591-00-X*); 4.50 (*0-916591-01-8*) Linmore Pub.
— Practice with Your Partner: Dictation Activities for Student-Student Interaction. 46p. 1987. pap. text ed. 19.95 (*0-9655910-9-3*) Linmore Pub.
Mrowicki, Linda, ed. see Terdy, Dennis.
Mroz, John E. Beyond Security: Private Perceptions among Arabs & Israelis. LC 80-82857. (Illus.). 230p. 1981. text ed. 46.00 (*0-08-027517-6*, Pergamon Pr); pap. text ed. 20.00 (*0-08-027516-8*, Pergamon Pr) Elsevier.
— Beyond Security: Private Perceptions among Arabs & Israelis. 200p. 1980. 23.00 (*0-685-11730-8*); pap. 9.95 (*0-937722-00-6*) Intl Peace.
— Influence in Conflict: The Impact of Third Parties on the Arab-Israeli Dispute since 1973. 400p. 1987. text ed. 44.01 (*0-08-028797-2*, Pergamon Pr); pap. text ed. 16.51 (*0-08-028796-4*, Pergamon Pr) Elsevier.
Mroz, M. Divine Vengeance. LC 77-120130. (Studies in Shakespeare: No. 24). 1970. reprint ed. lib. bdg. 48.95 (*0-8383-1091-5*) M S G Haskell Hse.
Mroz, Ralph. The Beginners Guide to Self-Protection: Your Options & Choices in Martial Arts & Firearms Training. (Illus.). 54p. (Orig.). 1990. pap. 9.95 (*0-9619055-1-4*) Iris Development.
— The Marketing Formula: Four Steps of Four Steps to Marketing Success. 64p. (Orig.). 1988. pap. 8.95 (*0-9619055-0-6*) Iris Development.
Mroz, Z., ed. see International Union of Theoretical & Applied Mechanics Staff.
***Mroz, Zenon, et al, eds.** Inelastic Behaviour of Structures under Variable Loads. LC 95-410. (Solid Mechanics & Its Applications Ser.: Vol. 36). 516p. (C). 1995. lib. bdg. 211.00 (*0-7923-3397-7*) Kluwer Ac.
Mrozek, Donald J. Air Power & the Ground War in Vietnam: Ideas & Actions. LC 87-31931. (Orig.). 1988. pap. 9.00 (*0-16-002237-1*, S/N 008-070-00601-4) USGPO.
— Sport & American Mentality, 1880-1910. LC 83-3667. (Illus.). 304p. (C). 1983. text ed. 36.00x (*0-87049-394-9*); pap. text ed. 18.00x (*0-87049-395-7*) U of Tenn Pr.
Mrozek, Donald J., et al, eds. The Martin Marauder & the Franklin Allens: A Wartime Love Story. (Illus.). 544p. 1980. pap. 10.00 (*0-89745-007-8*) Sunflower U Pr.
Mrozek, John P. & Schafer, Marilyn E. Chiropractic Research Abstracts Collection (CRAC) 1990, Vol. 4. 130p. 1991. 38.00 (*0-683-01420-X*) Williams & Wilkins.
Mrozek, Slawomir. Three Plays: Striptease, Repeat Performance, the Prophets. Gruenthal, Lola et al, trs. 168p. (Orig.). 1986. pap. 5.95 (*0-936839-49-X*) Applause Theatre Bk Pubs.
— Vatzlav. Manheim, Ralph, tr. 92p. 1986. pap. 5.95 (*0-936839-50-3*) Applause Theatre Bk Pubs.
Mroziewicz, B., et al. Physics of Semiconductor Lasers. 480p. 1991. 160.00 (*0-444-98737-1*, North Holland) Elsevier.
Mrozinska, T. Suesswasserflora von Mitteleuropa, Vol. 14: Mrozinska, T. Chlorophyta VI. Oedogoniophyceae: Oedogoniales. Pascher, A., ed. (Illus.). (GER.). 1985. lib. bdg. 103.00 (*3-437-30413-5*) Lubrecht & Cramer.
Mrozinski, Ronald. Franciscan Prayer Life. 1983. 12.50 (*0-8199-0795-2*, Frncscn Herld) Franciscan Pr.
Mrozowski, S. & Walker, P. Proceedings of the Fifth Conference on Carbon, Vol. 2. LC 57-933. 1963. 279.00 (*0-08-009708-1*, Pub. by Pergamon Repr UK) Franklin.
Mrs. Alistair MacLean & Bowser, Milton. Mother Wore White, Mother Wore Black. Simmons, Jeffrey, ed. (Illus.). 300p. 1989. lib. bdg. 25.00 (*0-940178-24-9*) Sitare.
Mrs. Edward King Poor, ed. see Garden Club of America, Horticultural Committee Staff.
Mrs. Henry Wood. East Lynne. LC 93-29084. (Pocket Classic Ser.). 1993. 10.00 (*0-7509-0446-1*) A Sutton Pub.
MRS International Meeting on Advanced Materials, First, Tokyo, Japan Staff. Biosensors: May 31-June 1, 1988, Sunshine City, Ikebukuro, Tokyo, Japan. LC 90-174424. (Proceedings of the MRS International Meeting on Advanced Materials Ser.: No. 14). (Illus.). 268p. reprint ed. pap. 76.40 (*0-7837-1931-0*, 2042146) Bks Demand.
— Superconductivity: May 31-June 3, 1988, Sunshine City, Ikebukuro, Tokyo, Japan. LC 90-174207. (Proceedings of the MRS International Meeting on Advanced Materials Ser.: No. 6). (Illus.). 1055p. reprint ed. pap. 180.00 (*0-7837-1930-2*, 2042145) Bks Demand.
***Mrs. Kern's 1994-1995 Third Grade Class Staff.** The Joke Ghost: Big Book. (Wee Write Bks.: No. 14). (Illus.). 35p. (J). (ps-3). 1994. 32.95 (*1-884987-47-8*) WeWrite.
Mrs. Moose. Raymond Floyd Goes to Africa: or There Are No Bears in Africa. (Illus.). 32p. (J). (gr. 1-4). 1993. 14.95 (*0-86543-375-5*); pap. 6.95 (*0-86543-376-3*) Africa World.
***Mrs. Salisbury's 1994-1995 Third Grade Class Staff.** Our Cool Field Trip: Big Books. (Wee Write Bks.: No. 13). (Illus.). 35p. (J). (ps-3). 1994. 32.95 (*1-884987-44-3*) WeWrite.
Mrs. W. Reese Harris, ed. see Florida Federation of Garden Clubs Staff.
Mrstina, V. & Fejgl, F. Needle Punching Textile Technology. (Textile Science & Technology Ser.: No. 8). 290p. 1990. 100.00 (*0-444-98804-1*) Elsevier.
***Mrudula, R.** From Pain & Pleasure. 1994. 8.95 (*0-533-11081-5*) Vantage.
***Mruk, Chris.** Self-Esteem: Research, Theory, & Practice. (Illus.). 240p. 1995. 35.95 (*0-8261-8750-1*) Springer Pub.
***Mryglot, Gerard & Marks, Ted.** How to Say Fabulous in 8 Different Languages: A Multilingual Phrasebook for Gay Men. 120p. 1995. pap. 5.95 (*0-9646511-3-0*) Translator Network.
Ms. X. How to Beat the IRS. LC 83-21549. 134p. 1988. 50.00 (*0-88723-002-4*) Boardroom.
MSA Federated Womans Club Staff. Kit Carson County, Colorado. (Illus.). 862p. 1988. 65.00 (*0-88107-118-8*) Curtis Media.
***MSA Women's Committee.** Parents' Manual. 1990. pap. 4.00 (*0-89259-093-9*) Am Trust Pubns.
MSFC Staff, jt. auth. see NASA Staff.
Mshigeni, K. E. Biology & Ecology of Benthic Marine Algae with Special Reference to Hypnea (Rhodophyta, Gigartinales: A Review of the Literature. (Bibliotheca Phycologica Ser.: No. 37). 1978. pap. 26.80 (*3-7682-1166-5*) Lubrecht & Cramer.
Mshomba, Richard E. The Uncertainty of the International Coffee Agreement. (Pew Case Studies in International Affairs). 50p. (C). 1994. pap. 2.50 (*1-56927-159-3*) Geo U Inst Dplmcy.
Msika, Hangson, jt. auth. see Roscoe, Adrian.
Msimuko, jt. ed. see Achola.
Mstislavskii, Sergei. Five Days Which Transformed Russia. Zelensky, Elizabeth K., tr. LC 88-636. (Second World Ser.). (Illus.). 182p. (Orig.). 1988. 29.95 (*0-253-32482-3*) Ind U Pr.
MSU (Kovacs) Staff. Introductory Physics Experiments. 304p. (C). 1992. spiral bd. 18.95 (*0-8403-8377-0*) Kendall-Hunt.
Msukwa, Louis A., jt. auth. see Pelletier, David L.
Mswell, Seth & Crider, Donald. Trabajo del Pastor Evangelico. Tinoco, David, tr. & adapt. by. (SPA.). 1982. 7.90 (*1-55955-106-2*) CITE MI.
M&T Books Editors. Getting Graphic: Programming Fundamentals in C & C Plus Plus. (Illus.). 500p. (Orig.). 1992. pap. 39.95 (*1-55851-282-9*) M&T Bks.
Mt. Shasta, Peter, ed. see Ascended Masters.
Mtewa, Mekki. Malawi: Democratic Theory & Public Policy. 150p. 1986. 18.95 (*0-87047-004-3*); pap. 13.95 (*0-87047-005-1*) Schenkman Bks Inc.
Mtewa, Mekki, ed. International Science & Technology: Philosophy, Theory & Policy. 220p. 1990. text ed. 45.00 (*0-312-03688-4*) St Martin.
— Perspectives in International Development. 1987. 18.00 (*0-8364-2063-2*, Pub. by Allied II) S Asia.
***MTI Staff.** Experience Survey - Stress Corrosion Cracking of Austenitic Stainless Steels in Water Pub. No. 27. (Illus.). 31p. 1987. 24.00 (*0-614-02611-3*) NACE Intl.
— Furan Reinforced Thermoset Plastics for Chemical Process Equipment Pub. No. 21. (Illus.). 1986. 24.00 (*0-614-02613-X*) NACE Intl.
— Ultrasonic Inspection & Failure Analysis of Expansion Bellows Pub. No. 28. (Illus.). 36p. 1987. 24.00 (*0-614-02634-2*) NACE Intl.
***MTI Staff & Society of Plastics Industry Staff.** Quality Assurance Report - RTP Corrosion-Resistant Equipment. 131p. 1981. 71.00 (*0-614-02628-8*) NACE Intl.
Mtoro Mwinyi Bakarai. The Customs of the Swahili People: The "Desturi Za Waswahili" of Mtoro Bin Mwinyi Bakari & Other Swahili Persons. Allen, J. W., ed. & tr. by. LC 81-3387. (Hermeneutics: Studies in the History of Religions: No. 10). (Illus.). 350p. 1982. 45.00 (*0-520-04122-4*) U CA Pr.
Mtshali, Oswald. Fireflames. (Illus.). 72p. (Orig.). 1983. reprint ed. pap. 6.95 (*0-88208-203-5*) L Hill Bks.
Mtshali, Oswald J. & Gordimer, Nadine. Sounds of a Cowhide Drum. LC 73-183198. 96p. 1972. 15.95 (*0-89388-034-5*); pap. 9.95 (*0-89388-035-3*) Okpaku Communications.
MTU Staff & Hugine. PreCalculus: An Intuitive Approach-Michigan Technological University Customized Edition. 656p. (C). 1993. per. 39.95 (*0-8403-8939-6*) Kendall-Hunt.
Mtwa, Percy, et al. Woza Albert! 80p. 1988. pap. 9.95 (*0-413-53000-0*, A0323) Heinemann.
Mu. Memento. (Illus.). 24p. 1977. 3.00 (*0-929436-03-2*) Eyesburg Pr.
Mu Alpha Theta Staff. Mathematical Buds, Vol. II. 126p. 1981. 2.50 (*0-940790-02-5*) Mu Alpha Theta.
Mu, Ch'ien. Traditional Government in Imperial China: A Critical Analysis. LC 81-18460. 300p. 1982. text ed. 29.95 (*0-312-81232-9*) St Martin.
Mu, Rui & Guiguo, Wang, eds. Chinese Foreign Economic Law. 1990. 82.00 (*0-935328-62-9*) Intl Law Inst.
Muakasa, Sahar. Love Life Rhythm. LC 87-71849. 181p. (ARA & ENG.). 1987. 30.00 (*0-944025-00-5*) Advance Research.
Muakasa, Sahar, jt. auth. see Veenaskay.
Mu'Allakat. The Seven Poems Suspended in the Temple at Mecca. LC 73-12764. reprint ed. 27.50 (*0-404-11238-2*) AMS Pr.
Muammar Al Qathafi. The Green Book of Muammar Al Qathafi. 1982. lib. bdg. 250.00 (*0-87700-451-X*) Revisionist Pr.
Mu'asir, Nadwat I. & Al Haqq, Jad A. Abhath Nadwat Is'ham al Fikr al Islami fi al Iqtisad al Mu'asir: Proceedings of the Conference on the Contribution of Islamic Thought in Contemporary Economics. 2nd ed. (Silsilat Islamiyat al Ma'rifah: No. 11). 754p. 1993. 25.00 (*1-56564-149-3*); pap. 15.00 (*1-56564-155-8*) IIIT VA.
Muata. Egyptian Yoga, Volume I: Yoga of Wisdom & Action. 230p. 1993. pap. text ed. 12.95 (*1-884564-01-1*) Cruzian Mystic.
— Tem T Tchaas: Egyptian Proverbs. 160p. 1993. pap. 9.95 (*1-884564-00-3*) Cruzian Mystic.
Muazzam, M. Ghulam. Ramadan Fasting & Medical Science. (C). 1991. 35.00 (*0-685-54755-8*, Pub. by A H S Ltd UK); 40.00 (*0-7223-2545-2*, Pub. by A H S Ltd UK) St Mut.
Mubarak, Muhammad A. Nizam al Islam al 'Aqa'idi fi al 'Asr al Hadith: (The Credal System of Islam in the Modern Age) (Silsilat Rasa'il Islamiyat al Ma'rifah Ser.: No. 2). 44p. (Orig.). (ARA.). 1989. pap. 2.00 (*1-56564-161-2*) IIIT VA.
***Mubarek, Helena.** Trouble in Riddle City. 1992. pap. text ed. 9.97 (*0-937659-49-5*) GCT.
Mucci, Dallas. This Pair of Hands. 150p. (Orig.). 1988. pap. 6.95 (*0-8341-1239-6*) Beacon Hill.
Mucci, J. F., jt. auth. see March, Norman H.
Mucciaroni, Gary. The Political Failure of Employment Policy, 1945-1982. LC 90-31987. (Series in Policy & Institutional Studies). 328p. 1990. 49.95 (*0-8229-3648-8*) U of Pittsburgh Pr.
— The Political Failure of Employment Policy, 1945-1982. LC 90-31987. (Series in Policy & Institutional Studies). 336p. 1992. pap. 19.95 (*0-8229-5474-5*) U of Pittsburgh Pr.
— Reversals of Fortune: Public Policy & Private Interests. 225p. (C). 1995. 34.95x (*0-8157-5876-6*); pap. 14.95x (*0-8157-5875-8*) Brookings.
Mucciaroni, Gary, ed. Whither Public Policy? Liberalism, Conservatism, & Social Change. (Orig.). 1990. pap. 12.00 (*0-944285-21-X*) Pol Studies.

An Asterisk (*) at the beginning of an entry indicates that the title is appearing in BIP for the first time.

Muccigrosso, Lynne, et al. Double Jeopardy: Pregnant & Parenting Youth in Special Education. (Exceptional Children at Risk Ser.). 44p. 1991. 8.90 (*0-86586-217-6*, P360) Coun Exc Child.

Muccigrosso, Robert. Celebrating the New World: Chicago's Columbian Exposition of 1893. (American Ways Ser.). (Illus.). 224p. 1993. 24.95 (*1-56663-013-4*); pap. text ed. 11.95 (*1-56663-014-2*) I R Dee.

Muccigrosso, Robert, ed. Research Guide to American Historical Biography, 3 vols., Set. LC 88-19316. 1778p. 1988. lib. bdg. 189.00 (*0-933833-09-1*) Beacham Pub.

Muccigrosso, Robert, jt. ed. see Contosta, David R.

Muccini, Ugo. Palazzo Vecchio: Guide to the Building, the Apartments & the Collections. (Illus.). 128p. 1992. pap. 19.95 (*0-8161-0611-8*) G K Hall.

Muccino, R. R., ed. Synthesis & Applications of Isotopically Labeled Compounds, 1985. 558p. 1986. 195.00 (*0-444-42612-4*) Elsevier.

Muccio, E. A. Plastic Part Technology. (Illus.). 300p. 1991. 75.00 (*0-87170-432-3*) ASM.

Muccio, Edward A. Plastics Processing Technology. 1994. 75.00 (*0-87170-494-3*) ASM.

Muccio, Tom, jt. auth. see Marshall, Tom.

***Mucciolo, John M.** Shakespeare's Universe: Renaissance Ideas & Conventions: Essays for W. R. Elton. 400p. 1996. 68.95 (*1-85928-193-1*, Pub. by Scolar Pr UK) Ashgate Pub Co.

Mucciolo, Louis. Eighty Something: Interviews with Senior Citizens Who Stay Involved. large type ed. (Illus.). 256p. 1992. 18.95 (*1-55972-149-9*, Birch Ln Pr) Carol Pub Group.

Much, Fred. The Pass after Class. rev. ed. LC 86-90709. 104p. (Orig.). 1987. pap. 7.95 (*0-9618053-0-7*) Fred Much.

Mucha, Alphonse M. The Art Nouveau Style Book of Alphonse Mucha. (Illus.). 80p. 1980. pap. 9.95 (*0-486-24044-4*) Dover.

— Drawings of Mucha: Seventy Works. 1978. pap. 6.95 (*0-486-23672-2*) Dover.

— Full Color Art Nouveau Borders: Forty-Eight Plates by Alphonse Maia Mucha. (Fine Art Ser.). (Illus.). 48p. 1984. pap. 6.95 (*0-486-24542-X*) Dover.

— Mucha's Figures Decoratives. Orig. Title: Figure Decoratives. (Illus.). 48p. 1981. reprint ed. pap. 7.95 (*0-486-24234-X*) Dover.

— Mucha's Floral Borders: Thirty Full-Color Art Nouveau Designs. (Illus.). 32p. (Orig.). 1985. pap. 5.95 (*0-486-24916-6*) Dover.

Mucha, Alphonse M., et al. Art Nouveau Designs in Color. (Illus.). 90p. (Orig.). 1974. pap. 6.95 (*0-486-22885-1*) Dover.

Mucha, Janusz L., jt. auth. see Keen, Mike Forrest.

Mucha, Juanita, jt. auth. see Hanzak, Gary.

Muche, Helmut & Zimmermann, Harald. The Purification of Biogas. (GATE Ser.). 34p. (Orig.). (C). 1985. pap. 7.00 (*3-528-02015-6*, Pub. by Vieweg & Sohn GW) Ballen Bkslr.

Mucheix, ed. Fruit Phenolics. 1990. 240.00 (*0-8493-4968-0*, SB357) CRC Pr.

Muchembled, Robert. La Sorciere au Village. (FRE.). 1991. pap. 15.95 (*0-7859-3979-2*) Fr & Eur.

Muchenberg, B., et al, eds. The Symphony in Poland. (Symphony 1720-1840 Series F: Vol. 21). 398p. 1982. lib. bdg. 25.00 (*0-8240-3820-7*) Garland.

Muchene, Barbara S. & Muchene, Munene. Suzanne's African Adventure: A Visit to Cucu's Land. Wagner, Shirley L., ed. LC 92-75821. (Illus.). 90p. (Orig.). (J). (gr. 3-6). 1993. pap. 9.95 (*1-878398-18-0*) Blue Note Pubns.

Muchene, Munene, jt. auth. see Muchene, Barbara S.

Muchinsky, Paul. Psychology Applied to Work: An Introduction to Industrial & Organizational Psychology. 4th ed. 738p. (C). 1993. text ed. 54.95 (*0-534-16620-2*) Brooks-Cole.

Muchlberger, ed. Structure & Stratigraphy of Trans-Pecos Texas. (IGC Field Trip Guidebooks Ser.). 216p. 1989. 35.00 (*0-87590-574-9*, T317) Am Geophysical.

***Muchlinski, Peter.** Multinational Enterprises & the Law. 550p. (C). 1995. write for info. (*0-631-17311-0*); pap. write for info. (*0-631-19785-0*) Blackwell Pubs.

Muchmore, Clyde A. & Ellis, Harvey. Oklahoma Civil Procedure Forms, 2 vols. suppl. ed. 1993. 89.00 (*0-685-74633-X*) Butterworth Legal Pubs.

— Oklahoma Civil Procedure Forms, 2 vols., Set. 1000p. 1994. disk, ring bd. 239.00 (*0-87189-074-7*) Michie Butterworth.

***Muchmore, Jo Ann.** Johnny Rides Again. LC 94-19466. 128p. (J). (gr. 3-7). 1995. 14.95 (*0-8234-1156-7*) Holiday.

Muchmore, Lynn, jt. ed. see Beyle, Thad L.

***Muchmore, Pat.** Prairie Flower. 400p. (Orig.). 1995. mass mkt. 4.50 (*0-8439-3725-4*) Dorchester Pub Co.

Muchmore, Wes & Hanson, William. Coming along Fine. 149p. (Orig.). 1986. pap. 6.95 (*0-932870-92-9*) Alyson Pubns.

— Coming Out Right: A Handbook for the Gay Male. rev. ed. 228p. (Orig.). 1991. pap. 7.95 (*1-55583-021-8*) Alyson Pubns.

Muchnic, Suzanne, contrib. Paul Darrow: A Retrospective. (Illus.). 62p. 1992. 15.00 (*0-685-62731-4*) Galleries Coll.

Muchnic, Suzanne, text. Martha Alf: Retrospective. LC 83-83032. (Illus.). 79p. (Orig.). 1984. pap. 16.00 (*0-911291-09-1*) Fellows Cont Art.

Muchnic, Suzanne & Courtney, Julie. Mark Lere. (Illus.). 36p. (Orig.). 1986. pap. 4.00 (*0-939351-00-5*) Temple U Tyler Gal.

Muchnick. Clinical Medicine in Optometric Practice. 352p. 1994. 45.95 (*0-8016-6306-7*) Mosby Yr Bk.

Muchnick, Barbara. The Laughing Horse. 58p. write for info. (*0-318-58342-9*) Just Fun Horse.

Muchnick, S. S., jt. auth. see Jones, N. D.

Muchnick, S. S., ed. see Merritt, D.

Muchnick, S. S., ed. see Reisig, W.

***Muchnick, Steven.** RISC Compilers & Architectures. 1995. 65.95 (*1-55860-320-4*) Morgan Kaufmann.

Muchnick, Steven S. & Jones, Neil D. Program Flow Analysis: Theory & Application. (Software Ser.). (Illus.). 448p. (C). 1981. 50.00 (*0-13-729681-9*) P-H.

Muchnik, Michoel. The Cuckoo Clock Castle of Shir. LC 79-55560. (Illus.). (J). (ps-3). 1980. 8.95 (*0-8197-0476-8*) Bloch.

Muchnik, S. S. & Schnupp, P. An Integrated Approach to Software Engineering. (Compass International Ser.). (Illus.). xiv, 375p. 1994. 49.95 (*0-387-97561-6*) Spr-Verlag.

Muchnik, S. S., ed. see Lins, Charles.

Muchnik Staff. Diccionario de Americanismos. 740p. (SPA.). 1985. pap. 65.00 (*0-7859-3459-6*, S12121) Fr & Eur.

Mucho, Thomas P., et al. Room-&-Pillar Mining in Bump-Prone Conditions & Thin Pillar Mining As a Bump Mitigation Technique. 1993. write for info. (*0-318-71698-4*) US Interior.

***Muchoney, Douglas M., et al.** A Rapid Ecological Assessment of the Blue & John Crow Mountains National Park, Jamaica. Baker, Douglas S., ed. (Illus.). 80p. Date not set. pap. write for info. (*0-9624590-9-7*) Nature VA.

Muchow, Kenneth & Deem, Bill R. Microprocessors: Principles, Programming & Interfacing. 1983. teacher ed write for info. (*0-8359-4384-4*, Reston) P-H.

Muchow, Kenneth, et al. Digital Circuits. (Illus.). 480p. (C). 1987. 16.95 (*0-685-17183-3*) P-H.

Muchow, Russell C. & Bellamy, J. A., eds. Climatic Risk in Crop Production: Models & Management for the Semiarid Tropics & Subtropics. 550p. 1991. text ed. 94.00 (*0-85198-665-X*) CAB Intl.

Mucina, L. & Dale, M. B., eds. Numerical Syntaxology: Proceedings of Part of the Symposium "Numerical Syndynamics" Held in Unovce Near Galanta, Slovakia, May 18-23, 1983. (Advances in Vegetation Science Ser.). (C). 1989. reprint ed. lib. bdg. 175.50 (*0-7923-0388-1*) Kluwer Ac.

Muck, Terry C. The Mysterious Beyond: A Basic Guide to Studying Religion. LC 93-2852. 160p. (Orig.). 1993. pap. 9.99 (*0-8010-6303-5*) Baker Bk.

— World Religions in Your Neighborhood: Loving Your Neighbor When You Don't Know How. LC 92-14188. 176p. 1992. pap. 9.99 (*0-310-54041-0*) Zondervan.

Mucke, Burkhard, jt. auth. see Ferguson, John.

Mucke, Edith. Beginning in Triumph. LC 94-15569. 160p. 1994. 9.95 (*0-87839-086-3*) North Star.

Muckenhoupt, B. Transplantation Theorems & Multiplier Theorems for Jacobi Series. LC 86-22270. (Memoirs of the American Mathematical Society Ser.: Vol. 64/356). 86p. 1986. pap. text ed. 18.00 (*0-8218-2418-X*, MEMO 64/356) Am Math.

Muckenhoupt, Benjamin, jt. auth. see Chanillo, Sagun.

Muckenstrum-Chavin, Bernadette, jt. auth. see Chavin, Remy.

***Muckian, Bruce J.** Rush Limbaugh Said What? 1994. pap. 5.99 (*1-56171-380-5*, S P I Bks) Sure Sellers.

Muckle, James. The Class Act Reading Game. 2nd rev. ed. 16p. 1992. pap. 3.00 (*0-9620445-3-9*) KSJ Publishing.

— A Guide to the Soviet Curriculum: What the Russian Child Is Taught at School. 224p. 1988. lib. bdg. 57.50 (*0-7099-4667-8*) Routledge Chapman & Hall.

— PB: How to Find Jobs Teaching Overseas, 1992. 2nd ed. Conradson, Shari, ed. LC 91-76506. (Illus.). 89p. (Orig.). 1992. pap. 7.95 (*0-9620445-5-5*) KSJ Publishing.

— Portrait of a Soviet School under Glasnost. LC 90-31927. 225p. 1990. text ed. 39.95 (*0-312-04748-7*) St Martin.

Muckle, James E. An American Abroad. Conradson, Diane & Conradson, Shari, eds. LC 92-71705. (Illus.). 99p. (Orig.). 1992. pap. 7.95 (*0-9620445-6-3*) KSJ Publishing.

Muckle, Jim. A Self Publishing Success Story. Conradson, Shari, ed. (Illus.). 50p. (Orig.). 1990. pap. 5.00 (*0-9620445-4-7*) KSJ Publishing.

Muckle, W. C. Muckle's Naval Architecture. 2nd ed. (Marine Engineering Ser.). (Illus.). 400p. 1987. text ed. 97.95 (*0-408-00334-0*) Buttrwrth-Heinemann.

***Mucklow, William.** Islands of the Mist. 110p. Date not set. pap. 7.95 (*1-56901-813-8*) NW Pub.

Muclchandani, N. H. Five Thousand Legal Maxims & Phrases with Meaning & Citations. (C). 1990. 30.00 (*0-89771-129-7*) St Mut.

Mucnik, jt. auth. see Humbaraci.

Mud Circulation Subcommittee Staff & IADC Rotary Drilling Committee Staff. Mud Equipment Manual Binder. 1989. ring bd. 35.00 (*0-87201-624-2*, 9ME1) Gulf Pub.

Mud Flower Collective Staff. God's Fierce Whimsy: Christian Feminism & Theological Education. Heyward, Carter, ed. LC 84-26561. 240p. (Orig.). 1985. pap. 12.95 (*0-8298-0546-X*) Pilgrim OH.

Mudahar, M. S. & Hignett, T. P. Energy & Fertilizer: Policy Implications & Options for Developing Countries (Executive Brief) (Technical Bulletin Ser.: No. T-19). (Illus.). 25p. (Orig.). 1981. pap. 4.00 (*0-88090-018-0*) Intl Fertilizer.

— Energy & Fertilizer: Policy Implications & Options for Developing Countries (Executive Brief) LC 82-6084. (Technical Bulletin Ser.: No. T-20). (Illus.). 241p. (Orig.). 1982. pap. 15.00 (*0-88090-019-9*) Intl Fertilizer.

Mudahar, M. S., jt. auth. see Kanwar, J. S.

Mudahar, Mohinder S. & Kapusta, Edwin C. Fertilizer Marketing Systems & Policies in the Developing World. Roth, E. N., ed. LC 87-3152. (Technical Bulletin Ser.: No. T-33). 43p. (Orig.). 1987. pap. text ed. 4.00 (*0-88090-059-8*) Intl Fertilizer.

Mudahar, Mohinder S., jt. auth. see Johl, S. S.

Mudahar, Mohinder S., jt. auth. see Kanwar, J. S.

Mudallar, Chandra Y. Secular State & Religious Institutions in India: A Study of the Administration of Hindu Public Religious Trusts in Madras. 273p. (Orig.). 1974. pap. 57.50 (*3-515-01991-X*) Coronet Bks.

Mudassar, Imran & Barnes, Philip M. Energy Demand in the Developing Countries: Prospects for the Future. (Commodity Working Paper Ser.: No. 23). 96p. 1990. 7.95 (*0-8213-1628-1*, 11628) World Bank.

Mudd, Charles & Sillars, Malcolm. Public Speaking: Content & Communication. 6th ed. (Illus.). 424p. (Orig.). (C). 1991. pap. text ed. 20.95 (*0-88133-587-8*) Waveland Pr.

Mudd, Chris. Cholesterol & Your Health - the Great American Rip-Off!, Pt. 1. (Illus.). 170p. 1990. pap. write for info. (*0-9624515-1-7*) Am Lite Co.

— Cholesterol & Your Health - the Great American Ripoff, Pt. 1. 125p. 1990. pap. 13.00 (*0-685-29288-6*) Am Lite Co.

Mudd, Harvey. A European Education. LC 85-22840. 87p. (Orig.). 1986. 14.00 (*0-87685-659-8*); pap. 8.50 (*0-87685-658-X*) Black Sparrow.

— A European Education, signed ed. deluxe ed. LC 85-22840. 87p. (Orig.). 1986. 25.00 (*0-87685-660-1*) Black Sparrow.

— The Plain of Smokes. LC 82-14792. (Illus.). 98p. (Orig.). (C). 1982. 14.00 (*0-87685-567-2*); pap. 6.50 (*0-87685-566-4*) Black Sparrow.

— The Plain of Smokes, signed ed. deluxe ed. LC 82-14792. (Illus.). 98p. (Orig.). (C). 1982. 20.00 (*0-87685-568-0*) Black Sparrow.

Mudd, Joseph A. With Porter in North Missouri: A Chapter in the History of the War Between the States. LC 91-66906. (Illus.). 460p. 1992. reprint ed. 35.00 (*0-9628936-1-7*) Pr Camp Pope.

Mudd, Norman. In Defense of Aleister Crowley: An Open Letter to Lord Beaverbrook. 1993. pap. 4.95 (*1-55818-208-X*, Sure Fire) Holmes Pub.

***Mudd-Ruth, Maria.** The Ultimate Ocean Book: A Unique Introduction to the Amazing World under Water in Fabulous, Full-Color Pop-ups. (Illus.). 5p. (J). 1995. 19.95 (*0-307-17628-2*, Artsts Writrs) Western Pub.

Mudd, S. E., ed. Night Writers. 150p. (Orig.). 1989. pap. 3.95 (*0-9623686-5-2*) Castalia MN.

Mudd, Samuel. Briggs' Information-Processing Model of the Binary Classification Task. 152p. (C). 1983. text ed. 29.95 (*0-89859-291-7*) L Erlbaum Assocs.

Muddiman, Joseph G. King's Journalist 1659-1689: Studies in the Reign of Charles II. LC 74-125774. (English Book Trade Ser.). (Illus.). x, 294p. 1971. reprint ed. 39.50 (*0-678-00729-2*) Kelley.

Mudditt, B. Howard, ed. Christian Worship (Hymns) 716p. 1976. text ed. 19.50 (*0-85364-194-3*) Attic Pr.

Muddle, B. C., ed. Martensitic Transformations. 714p. (C). 1990. text ed. 190.00 (*0-87849-610-6*, Pub. by Trans Tech GW) LPS Dist Ctr.

Mudfoot, Judyl. Masked Ball: Dreams & Disguises. 36p. (Orig.). 1986. pap. 10.00 (*0-930012-47-X*) J Mudfoot.

Mudge, et al. Immunologic Disorders. 368p. 1992. 29.95 (*0-8016-2775-3*) Mosby Yr Bk.

Mudge, Arthur E. Innovative Change: One Hundred One Case Histories. 163p. 1989. text ed. 37.00 (*0-939332-19-1*) J Pohl Assocs.

— Successful Program Management: Sharpening the Competitive Edge. 216p. 1989. text ed. 37.00 (*0-939332-18-3*) J Pohl Assocs.

— Value Engineering: A Systematic Approach. 286p. 1989. reprint ed. text ed. 37.00 (*0-939332-17-5*) J Pohl Assocs.

Mudge, Bradford K. Sara Coleridge, a Victorian Daughter: Her Life & Essays. LC 88-37427. 312p. (C). 1989. text ed. 35.00 (*0-300-04443-7*) Yale U Pr.

Mudge, Bradford K., ed. British Romantic Novelists, 1789-1832, Vol. 116. LC 92-9153. (Dictionary of Literary Biography Ser.: Vol. 116). 1992. 128.00 (*0-8103-7593-1*) Gale.

Mudge, Eugene T. Social Philosophy of John Taylor of Carolina. LC 76-181960. reprint ed. 20.00 (*0-404-04515-4*) AMS Pr.

— The Social Philosophy of John Taylor of Caroline: A Study in Jeffersonian Democracy. (BCL1 - U. S. History Ser.). 227p. 1992. reprint ed. lib. bdg. 79.00 (*0-7812-6131-7*) Rprt Serv.

Mudge, Gilbert H., Jr. Manual Electr ISE, No. 2. 1986. 15.95 (*0-316-58919-5*) Little.

— Manual of Electrocardiography. (Little, Brown Spiral Manual Ser.). 1986. spiral bd. 32.95 (*0-316-58918-7*) Little.

Mudge, Isadore G. George Eliot Dictionary. LC 72-762. (Reference Ser.: No. 44). 1972. reprint ed. lib. bdg. 75.00 (*0-8383-1350-7*) M S G Haskell Hse.

— A George Eliot Dictionary. (BCL1-PR English Literature Ser.). 260p. 1992. reprint ed. lib. bdg. 79.00 (*0-7812-7526-1*) Rprt Serv.

Mudge, Jean M. Chinese Export Porcelain for the American Trade, 1785-1835. LC 61-16518. (Illus.). 284p. 40.00 (*0-87413-102-2*) U Delaware Pr.

— Chinese Export Porcelain for the American Trade, 1785-1835. rev. ed. LC 79-4713. (Illus.). 300p. 1980. 55.00 (*0-87413-166-9*) U Delaware Pr.

Mudge, John T. The White Mountains - Names, Places & Legends. (Illus.). 224p. 1992. pap. 13.95 (*0-9633560-0-3*) Durand Pr.

***Mudge, John T., ed. & comp.** The Old Man's Reader: History & Legends of Franconia Notch. (Illus.). 232p. (Orig.). 1995. pap. 13.95 (*0-9633560-3-8*) Durand Pr.

Mudge, Lewis S. The Sense of a People: Toward a Church for the Human Future. LC 92-7926. 272p. 1992. pap. 17.95 (*1-56338-040-4*) TPI PA.

Mudge, Lewis S., ed. see Ricoeur, Paul.

Mudge, Zachariah A. Sketches of Mission Life among the Indians of Oregon. 1983. 12.50 (*0-87770-308-6*) Ye Galleon.

Mudie, Colin, jt. auth. see Ellam, Patrick.

Mudie, Peter & Cottam, Angela. The Management & Marketing of Services. 250p. 1993. pap. 34.95 (*0-7506-0789-0*) Buttrwrth-Heinemann.

Mudimbe, V. Y. The Idea of Africa. LC 94-1183. (African Systems of Thought Ser.). 1994. 29.95 (*0-253-33898-0*) Ind U Pr.

— The Idea of Africa. (African Systems of Thought Ser.). 1994. pap. 11.95 (*0-253-20872-6*) Ind U Pr.

— The Invention of Africa: Gnosis, Philosophy, & the Order of Knowledge. LC 87-45324. (African Systems of Thought Ser.). 256p. 1988. 39.95 (*0-253-33126-9*); pap. 14.95 (*0-253-20468-2*, MB-468) Ind U Pr.

— Parables & Fables: Exegesis, Textuality & Politics in Central Africa. LC 91-12498. (Illus.). 260p. (Orig.). (C). 1991. lib. bdg. 47.50 (*0-299-13060-6*); pap. 19.95 (*0-299-13064-9*) U of Wis Pr.

— The Rift. De Jager, Marjolijn, tr. LC 92-44511. 128p. 1993. text ed. 16.95 (*0-8166-2312-0*) U of Minn Pr.

Mudimbe, V. Y., ed. The Surreptitious Speech: "Presence Africaine" & the Politics of Otherness, 1947-1987. (Illus.). 368p. 1992. lib. bdg. 65.00 (*0-226-54506-7*); pap. text ed. 22.50 (*0-226-54507-5*) U Ch Pr.

Mudlark, Ichabod. Gustave Dore's Primer on the Medical Profession. (Illus.). 164p. (C). 1991. 17.50 (*0-87527-298-3*) Green.

Mudliar, T. D. Property, a Constitutional Right. (C). 1988. 150.00 (*0-685-36469-0*) St Mut.

Mudore, John. Making Math Matter: A Math Resource - Methods Book for Experienced & Beginning Teachers. LC 93-77825. 144p. (Orig.). (YA). (gr. 7-12). 1994. pap. 17.95 (*0-9636514-8-X*) Infinity Pubs.

Mudra, Darrell & Scoles, Gordon. Freedom in the Huddle: The Creative Edge in Coaching Psychology. 144p. (Orig.). (C). 1986. pap. 10.95 (*0-932741-05-3*) Championship Bks & Vid Prodns.

Mudrak, Myroslava M. The New Generation & Artistic Modernism in the Ukraine. LC 86-7043. (Studies in the Fine Arts: The Avant-Garde: No. 50). (Illus.). 294p. reprint ed. pap. 83.80 (*0-8357-1687-2*, 2070514) Bks Demand.

***Mudroch, Alena & Azcue, Jose.** Manual of Aquatic Sediment Sampling. LC 94-26847. 1995. write for info. (*1-56670-029-9*) Lewis Pubs.

Mudroch, Alena & MacKnight, Scott D. Handbook of Techniques for Aquatic Sediments Sampling. (Illus.). 208p. 1991. 120.95 (*0-8493-3587-6*, GC380) CRC Pr.

Mudroch, Alena & MacKnight, Scott D., eds. Handbook of Techniques for Aquatic Sediments Sampling. 2nd ed. LC 94-14255. 1994. write for info. (*1-56670-027-2*) Lewis Pubs.

Mudrooroo, Narogin. Master of the Ghost Dreaming. 148p. (Orig.). 1993. pap. 10.00 (*0-207-16952-7*, Pub. by Angus & Robertson AT) HarpC.

***Mudry, Robert.** Serving the Web. 1995. pap. 34.99 (*1-883577-30-6*) Coriolis Grp.

Mudumbai, Srinivas. United States Foreign Policy Towards India, 1947-1954. 1985. 12.00 (*0-8364-1335-0*, Pub. by Manohar II) S Asia.

Mudur, S. P. & Pattanaik, S. N., eds. Graphics, Design, & Visualization: Proceedings of the International Conference on Computer Graphics, Bombay, India, 24-26 February 1993. LC 93-27999. (IFIP Transactions B: Applications in Technology Ser.: Vol. B-9). 1993. write for info. (*0-444-81564-3*, North Holland) Elsevier.

Muecke, ed. see Horace.

Muecke, Frances. Plautus: Menaechmi: A Companion to the Penguin Translation. 96p. 1987. 13.75 (*0-86292-239-9*, Pub. by Brstl Class Pr UK) Focus Info Gr.

Muecke, Stephen. Speaking into Space (Textual Spaces) Aboriginality & Cultural Studies. 1992. pap. 29.95 (*0-86840-101-3*, Pub. by New South Wales Univ Pr AT) Intl Spec Bk.

Muegge, Herman, jt. auth. see Stohr, Walter B.

Muego, Benjamin N. Spectator Society: The Philippines under Martial Rule. LC 88-25304. (Monographs in International Studies, Southeast Asia Ser.: No. 77). 201p. 1986. pap. text ed. 17.00x (*0-89680-138-1*, Ohio U Ctr Intl) Ohio U Pr.

Muehl, John. Flexible Spending Accounts: A Fact Sheet for Employees. 8p. 1993. pap. text ed. 0.95 (*0-87179-784-4*) BNA.

Muehl, John, jt. auth. see Wise, Val.

Muehl, Lois. Talkable Tales. (Illus.). 128p. 1993. 25.95 (*0-937857-44-0*, 1540) Speech Bin.

Muehl, Lois & Muehl, Siegmar. Trading Cultures in the Classroom: Two American Teachers in China. 288p. (Orig.). 1993. pap. 18.95 (*0-8248-1442-8*, Kolowalu Bk) UH Pr.

Muehl, Siegmar, jt. auth. see Muehl, Lois.

Muehlbauer, F. J. & Kaiser, W. J., eds. Expanding the Production & Use of Cool Season Food Legumes: Proceedings of the Second International Food Legume Research Conference on Pea, Lentil, Faba Bean, Chickpea, & Grasspea, Cairo, Egypt, 12-16 April 1992. LC 93-31539. (Current Plant Science & Biotechnology in Agriculture Ser.: Vol. 19). 1028p. (C). 1994. lib. bdg. 456.00 (*0-7923-2535-4*) Kluwer Ac.

Muehldorf, E. I., jt. auth. see Kim, J. C.

Muehlenberg, Ekkehard. Psalmenkommentare aus der Katenenueberlieferung, Vol. 1. LC 73-91808. (Patristische Texte und Studien Ser.: Band 15). (GER.). (C). 1974. 157.70 (*3-11-004182-0*) De Gruyter.

— Psalmenkommentare aus der Katenenueberlieferung: Untersuchungen zu den Psalmenkatenen, Vol. 3. (Patristische Texte und Studien Ser.: No. 19). (C). 1978. 108.50 (*3-11-006959-8*) De Gruyter.

— Psalmenkommentare aus Katenenveberlieferung, Vol. 2. (Patristische Texte und Studien Ser.: No. 16). (C). 1977. 157.70 (*3-11-005717-4*) De Gruyter.

Muehlman, Sandra. Word Processing Applications & Exercises. 2nd ed. 256p. (C). 1991. pap. text ed. write for info. (*0-13-963133-X*) P-H.

— Word Processing on Microcomputers: Applications & Exercises. 256p. (C). 1989. pap. text ed. write for info. (*0-13-964511-X*) P-H.

— Word Processing on Microcomputers: Applications & Exercises. alternate ed. 256p. (C). 1989. pap. text ed. write for info. (*0-13-964750-3*) P-H.

— Word Processing on Microcomputers: Legal Applications & Exercises. 256p. (C). 1989. pap. text ed. write for info. (*0-318-65463-6*) P-H.

Muehlman-Shortt, Sandra. Legal Word Processing Exercises. 192p. (C). 1991. pap. text ed. 13.00 (*0-13-964545-4*, 180101) P-H.

Muehlmann, Robert G. Berkeley's Ontology. LC 92-17820. 320p. 1992. lib. bdg. 37.95 (*0-87220-146-5*) Hackett Pub.

***Muehlmann, Robert G., ed.** Berkeley's Metaphysics: Structural, Interpretive, & Critical Essays. 288p. 1995. 45.00 (*0-271-01427-X*) Pa St U Pr.

Muehlmatt, Ernest, jt. auth. see Schroeder, Roger.

***Muehrcke, Jill, ed.** Accounting & Financial Management. (Leadership Ser.). 115p. 1993. spiral bd. 20.00 (*0-614-07095-3*) Soc Nonprofit Org.

— Board Leadership & Governance. (Leadership Ser.). 106p. 1993. spiral bd. 20.00 (*0-614-07092-9*) Soc Nonprofit Org.

— Computers & Information Systems. (Leadership Ser.). 106p. 1993. spiral bd. 20.00 (*0-614-07093-7*) Soc Nonprofit Org.

— Enterprise (for Profit) Endeavors. (Leadership Ser.). 124p. 1993. spiral bd. 20.00 (*0-614-07094-5*) Soc Nonprofit Org.

— Fundraising & Resource Development, Vol. 1. (Leadership Ser.). 164p. 1990. spiral bd. 20.00 (*0-614-07096-1*) Soc Nonprofit Org.

— Fundraising & Resource Development, Vol. 2. (Leadership Ser.). 128p. 1993. spiral bd. 20.00 (*0-614-07097-X*) Soc Nonprofit Org.

— Law & Taxation, Vol. 1. (Leadership Ser.). 100p. 1990. spiral bd. 20.00 (*0-614-07098-8*) Soc Nonprofit Org.

— Law & Taxation, Vol. 2. (Leadership Ser.). 81p. 1993. spiral bd. 20.00 (*0-614-07099-6*) Soc Nonprofit Org.

— Management & Planning, Vol. 1. (Leadership Ser.). 123p. 1990. spiral bd. 20.00 (*0-614-07100-3*) Soc Nonprofit Org.

— Management & Planning, Vol. 2. (Leadership Ser.). 130p. 1993. spiral bd. 20.00 (*0-614-07101-1*) Soc Nonprofit Org.

— Marketing. (Leadership Ser.). 90p. 1993. spiral bd. 20.00 (*0-614-07103-8*) Soc Nonprofit Org.

— Personnel & Human Resources Development, Vol. 1. (Leadership Ser.). 95p. 1990. spiral bd. 20.00 (*0-614-07105-4*) Soc Nonprofit Org.

— Personnel & Human Resources Development, Vol. 2. (Leadership Ser.). 72p. 1993. spiral bd. 20.00 (*0-614-07106-2*) Soc Nonprofit Org.

— PR & Communications. (Leadership Ser.). 93p. 1993. spiral bd. 20.00 (*0-614-07104-6*) Soc Nonprofit Org.

— Profiles in Excellence. (Leadership Ser.). 147p. 1993. spiral bd. 20.00 (*0-614-07102-X*) Soc Nonprofit Org.

— Volunteer Management. (Leadership Ser.). 75p. 1993. spiral bd. 20.00 (*0-614-07107-0*) Soc Nonprofit Org.

Muehrcke, Jill & Barry, Martha, eds. National Directory of Service & Product Providers to Nonprofit Organizations & Resource Center Catalog. 112p. 1988. pap. text ed. 18.50 (*0-945567-00-6*) Soc Nonprofit Org.

Muehrcke, Juliana O., jt. auth. see Muehrcke, Phillip C.

Muehrcke, Phillip C. Map Use: Reading, Analysis & Interpretation. 2nd ed. LC 78-70573. (Illus.). 525p. (C). 1986. pap. text ed. 25.00 (*0-9602978-2-0*) JP Pubns WI.

Muehrcke, Phillip C. & Muehrcke, Juliana O. Map Use: Reading, Analysis, & Interpretation. 3rd rev. ed. (Illus.). 600p. 1992. pap. text ed. 30.00 (*0-9602978-3-9*) JP Pubns WI.

Muehrcke, Robert C. & Micek, Joseph G., eds. Orchids in the Mud: Personal Accounts by Veterans of the 132nd Infantry Regiment. (Illus.). 460p. 1985. 19.50 (*0-9615127-0-9*) One Hund Thirty-Second Infantry.

Muelder, Walter G. The Ethical Edge of Christian Theology: Forty Years of Communitarian Personalism. LC 83-21935. (Toronto Studies in Theology: Vol. 13). 435p. 1983. lib. bdg. 109.95 (*0-88946-754-4*) E Mellen.

Muellbauer, John, jt. auth. see Deaton, Agnus.

Muellbauer, Lydia, ed. see Wangchen, Geshe N.

Mueller. Kurze Krimis. 163p. (GER.). (C). 1981. pap. text ed. 20.75 (*0-03-056719-X*) HB Coll Pubs.

***Mueller & Walsh.** CA-Visual Objects Interface Handbook. 1995. disk, pap. text ed. 44.95 (*0-07-912089-X*) McGraw.

Mueller, A. Perturbative QCD. (Advanced Series on Directions in Hep.: Vol. 5). 624p. 1989. text ed. 110.00 (*9971-5-0564-9*); pap. text ed. 40.00 (*9971-5-0565-7*) World Scientific Pub.

Mueller, A. & Diemann, E. Transition Metal Chemistry. (Illus.). 338p. 1981. pap. 90.00 (*0-89573-039-1*) VCH Pubs.

Mueller, A. C. My Good Shepherd Bible Story Book. LC 70-89876. (J). (gr. 3-5). 1969. bds. 15.99 (*0-570-03400-0*, 56-1126) Concordia.

Mueller, Amelia. Jeremy's Jack-O-Lantern. (Illus.). 24p. (Orig.). (J). (gr. k-3). 1995. pap. 5.95 (*0-945530-06-4*) Wordsworth KS.

— A Quiet Strength. LC 92-82738. 146p. (Orig.). 1992. pap. 9.95 (*0-87303-201-2*) Faith & Life.

Mueller, Arlene & Indelicato, Dorothy. Wine, Food & the Good Life. (Wine Cookbook Ser.). (Illus.). 144p. (Orig.). 1985. pap. 7.95 (*0-932664-47-4*) Wine Appreciation.

Mueller Associates, Inc. Staff. Waste Oil: Reclaiming Technology, Utilization & Disposal. LC 88-38438. (Pollution Technology Review Ser.: No. 166). (Illus.). 193p. 1989. 39.00 (*0-8155-1193-0*) Noyes.

Mueller, B. & Von Wichert, P., eds. Lung Surfactant: Basic Research in the Pathogenesis of Lung Disorders. (Progress in Respiration Research Ser.: Vol. 27). (Illus.). x, 266p. 1994. 192.00 (*3-8055-5837-6*) S Karger.

Mueller, B. Jeanne, jt. auth. see Reinoehl, Richard.

Mueller, Barbara R., ed. The Congress Book, 1990. LC 40-2870. (Illus.). 198p. 1990. text ed. 25.00 (*0-929333-16-0*) Am Philat Congr.

Mueller-Beilschmidt, Peter, jt. auth. see Richardson, Gail.

Mueller, Benito, ed. see Brentano, Franz.

Mueller, Bernard. A Statistical Handbook of the North Atlantic Area: Apercu Statisque De la Region Atlantique Nord. LC 65-26294. (Twentieth Century Fund Ser.). (ENG & FRE.). 1965. pap. 12.00 (*0-527-02830-4*) Periodicals Srv.

Mueller, Bertha, tr. see Goethe, Johann Wolfgang von.

Mueller, Betty, ed. Packrat Papers No. I: Tips on Equipment (& Other Stuff) for Hiker, Campers, & Those Who Travel Lightly. (Illus.). 1977. pap. 4.95 (*0-913140-14-7*) Signpost Bk Pub.

Mueller, C. Foundations of the Mathematical Theory of Electromagnetic Waves. rev. ed. Higgins, T. P., tr. LC 75-81586. (Grundlehren der Mathematischen Wissenschaften Ser.: Vol. 155). (Illus.). 1969. 79.00 (*0-387-04506-6*) Spr-Verlag.

Mueller, Carl R., tr. see Buchner, Georg.

Mueller, Carol. Marketing Today's Fashion. 3rd ed. 320p. 1994. pap. text ed. 50.00 (*0-13-043001-3*) P-H.

Mueller, Carol M., ed. The Politics of the Gender Gap: The Social Construction of Political Influence. (Yearbooks in Women's Policy Studies: Vol. 12). 320p. (C). 1988. text ed. 44.00 (*0-8039-2732-0*); pap. text ed. 21.95 (*0-8039-2733-9*) Sage.

— The Politics of the Gender Gap: The Social Construction of Political Influence. LC 87-22454. (Sage Yearbooks in Women's Policy Studies: No. 12). 316p. reprint ed. pap. 90.10 (*0-7837-6719-6*, 2046346) Bks Demand.

Mueller, Carol M., jt. ed. see Katzenstein, Mary F.

Mueller, Carol M., jt. ed. see Morris, Aldon.

Mueller, Carolyn, ed. Periodicals of the Mid-West & West. LC 85-60590. 1986. 35.00 (*0-87650-210-9*) Pierian.

Mueller, Charles. Almost Adult: Devotions for 9-12 Year Olds. LC 92-27014. 160p. (Orig.). (J). (gr. 4-7). 1993. pap. 6.99 (*0-570-04598-3*) Concordia.

— The Economics of Labor Migration: A Behavioral Analysis. LC 81-19046. (Studies in Urban Economics). 1981. text ed. 47.00 (*0-12-509580-5*) Acad Pr.

Mueller, Charles, jt. auth. see Kim, Jae-On.

Mueller, Charles S. Bible Reading for Teenagers. LC 81-52274. (Bible Readings Ser.). 112p. (Orig.). 1982. pap. 5.99 (*0-8066-1906-6*, 10-0681, Augsburg) Augsburg Fortress.

— Christian Family Prepares for Christmas. 1965. 5.99 (*0-570-03023-4*, 6-1092) Concordia.

— God Will Not Forget You. LC 83-72111. 80p. 1983. pap. 5.99 (*0-8066-2055-2*, 10-2650, Augsburg) Augsburg Fortress.

— The Parents Perspective. Bd. with Teenagers' Turn. (Let's Talk Ser.). 144p. 1987. Set pap. 6.99 (*0-570-09061-X*, 12-3028) Concordia.

— School-Dazed Parents. LC 94-13042. 1994. write for info. (*0-570-04667-X*) Concordia.

— Thank God I Have a Teenager. LC 84-24363. 128p. (Orig.). 1985. pap. 8.99 (*0-8066-2126-5*, 10-6239, Augsburg) Augsburg Fortress.

— Then Comes the Baby in the Baby Carriage. LC 94-25525. 1994. write for info. (*0-570-04666-1*) Concordia.

Mueller, Charles S. & Bardill, Donald R. Thank God, I'm a Teenager. rev. ed. LC 88-6215. (Illus.). 144p. (YA). (gr. 7-12). 1988. pap. 8.99 (*0-8066-2351-9*, 10-6242, Augsburg) Augsburg Fortress.

Mueller, Charles W., jt. auth. see Kim, Jae-On.

Mueller, Charles W., jt. auth. see Price, James L.

Mueller, Christine L. The Styrian Estates, 1740-1848: A Century of Transition. McNeill, William H. & Kraehe, Enno E., eds. (Modern European History Ser.). 448p. 1987. lib. bdg. 15.00 (*0-8240-8049-1*) Garland.

Mueller, Christopher B. & Kirkpatrick, Laird C. Federal Rules of Evidence with Advisory Committee Notes & Legislative History. 1988. pap. 14.00 (*0-316-58922-5*) Little.

Mueller, Christopher B., jt. auth. see Louisell, David W.

Mueller, Cookie. Garden of Ashes. 116p. (Orig.). 1990. pap. 5.95 (*0-937815-36-5*) Hanuman Bks.

— How to Get Rid of Pimples. (Illus.). 80p. (Orig.). 1984. pap. 6.00 (*0-917061-19-5*) Top Stories.

— Walking Through Clear Water in a Pool Painted Black. 150p. 1990. pap. 6.00 (*0-936756-61-6*) Autonomedia.

Mueller, Craig M. Fling Wide the Doors. 31p. (Orig.). 1992. pap. 4.00 (*0-929650-90-5*) Liturgy Tr Pubns.

Mueller, Daniel W., et al, eds. Controversies in Modern Geology: Evolution of Geologic Theories in Sedimentology, Earth History & Tectonics. (Illus.). 490p. 1991. text ed. 95.00 (*0-12-510340-9*) Acad Pr.

Mueller, David L. Foundation of Karl Barth's Doctrine of Reconciliation: Jesus Christ Crucified & Risen. LC 91-262. (Toronto Studies in Theology: Vol. 53). 510p. 1991. lib. bdg. 119.95 (*0-88946-583-5*) E Mellen.

Mueller, Delbert. A Guide for Curriculum Writers. 308p. (C). 1992. lib. bdg. 23.50 (*0-8191-8398-9*); pap. text ed. 20.50 (*0-8191-8399-7*) U Pr of Amer.

— An Interactive Guide to Educational Research: A Modular Approach. 192p. (C). 1991. pap. text ed. 19.00 (*0-205-13359-2*) Allyn.

***Mueller, Dennis.** Constitutional Democracy. 384p. 1995. 55.00 (*0-19-509588-X*) OUP.

Mueller, Dennis C. The Corporation: Growth, Diversification & Mergers. (Fundamentals of Pure & Applied Economics Ser.: Vol. 16). viii, 100p. 1987. pap. text ed. 26.00 (*3-7186-0357-8*) Gordon & Breach.

— The Dynamics of Company Profits. (Illus.). 250p. (C). 1990. 64.95 (*0-521-38372-2*) Cambridge U Pr.

— Profits in the Long Run. (Illus.). 352p. 1986. 69.95 (*0-521-30693-0*) Cambridge U Pr.

— The Public Choice Approach to Politics. (Economists of the Twentieth Century Ser.). 560p. 1993. 74.95 (*1-85278-805-4*, Pub. by E Elgar Pub UK) Ashgate Pub Co.

— Public Choice II. rev. ed. (Illus.). (C). 1989. pap. 22.95 (*0-521-37952-0*) Cambridge U Pr.

— Public Choice II. rev. ed. (Illus.). (C). 1989. 69.95 (*0-521-37083-3*) Cambridge U Pr.

Mueller, Dennis C., ed. The Political Economy of Growth. LC 81-15955. (Illus.). 292p. reprint ed. pap. 83.30 (*0-7837-5197-4*, 2057681) Bks Demand.

Mueller-Dombois, D., jt. ed. see Huettl, R. F.

***Mueller, E. W.** The Lost Land: E. W. Mueller's Vision for the Development of the Regional Community. Waldkoenig, Gilson A., ed. 248p. 1995. 24.95 (*1-884723-02-0*) Tyrone Pr.

***Mueller, Edward A.** Perilous Journeys: A History of Steamboating on the Chattahoochee, Apalachicola & Flint Rivers, 1828-1925. (Illus.). 489p. 1990. 24.95 (*0-945477-09-0*) Hist Chattahoochee.

— Upper Mississippi River Rafting Steamboats. (Illus.). 350p. 1995. text ed. 44.95x (*0-8214-1113-6*) Ohio U Pr.

Mueller, Edward C. & Cooper, Catherine R., eds. Process & Outcome in Peer Relationships. (Developmental Psychology Ser.). 1985. pap. text ed. 51.00 (*0-12-509561-9*) Acad Pr.

Mueller, Elaine A. Oh Boy! What Is It? Story Cookbook, Vol. 1. LC 85-61810. (Illus.). 128p. (Orig.). 1985. spiral bd. 14.95 (*0-934713-00-6*) Results Ent.

Mueller, Elizabeth F., tr. see Deforges, Regine.

Mueller, Eric & Schaul, Joe. I Once Knew an Indian. 1988. 15.00 (*0-317-90578-3*) Earnest Pubns.

Mueller, Erik T. Daydreaming in Humans & Machines: A Computer Model of the Stream of Thought. LC 89-6483. 416p. 1990. text ed. 65.00 (*0-89391-562-9*) Ablex Pub.

Mueller, Erwin & Nolte, Oliver, eds. American Subsidiaries of German Firms 1992-1993 (Tochtergesellschaften Deutscher Unternehmen in Den U. S. A. 1992-1993) 20th ed. 280p. (ENG & GER.). 1992. 100.00 (*0-86640-042-7*) Manhattan Pub Co.

— U. S. Firms in Germany 1993: Amerikanische Unternehmen in Deutschland. 140p. 1993. 75.00 (*0-86640-046-X*) German Am Chamber.

Mueller, Eva, et al. Technological Advance in an Expanding Economy: Its Impact on a Cross-Section of the Labor Force. LC 71-627965. 266p. reprint ed. pap. 75.90 (*0-685-23663-3*, 2029137) Bks Demand.

Mueller, F. von, jt. auth. see Bentham, G.

Mueller, Frank P. The Burdick Family Chronology. LC 82-72466. (Illus.). 560p. 1990. 45.00 (*0-685-46906-9*) Pan Prods.

Mueller, Franz H. Church & the Social Question. 158p. 1984. 33.25 (*0-8447-3567-1*) Am Enterprise.

Mueller, Frederick A., ed. see Spencer, William.

Mueller, Frederick O. & Ryan, Allan J., eds. Prevention of Athletic Injuries: The Role of the Sports Medicine Team. (Contemporary Exercise & Sports Medicine Ser.: Vol. 5). (Illus.). 275p. (C). 1991. text ed. 50.00 (*0-8036-6338-2*) Davis Co.

Mueller, Friedrich M. Anthropological Religion. LC 73-18822. (Gifford Lectures: 1891). 1975. reprint ed. 67.50 (*0-404-11428-8*) AMS Pr.

— Buddhist Texts from Japan, 3 pts. in 1 vol. LC 73-18824. (Illus.). reprint ed. 34.50 (*0-404-11430-X*) AMS Pr.

— A History of Ancient Sanskrit Literature. 2nd rev. ed. LC 73-18826. reprint ed. 76.50 (*0-404-11437-7*) AMS Pr.

— Last Essays. LC 73-18815. (Second Ser.). reprint ed. 55.00 (*0-404-11439-3*) AMS Pr.

— Last Essays, First Series: Essays on Language, Folklore & Other Subjects. LC 73-18828. reprint ed. 55.00 (*0-404-11438-5*) AMS Pr.

— Lectures on the Origin & Growth of Religion, as Illustrated by the Religions of India. LC 73-18816. reprint ed. 45.00 (*0-404-11440-7*) AMS Pr.

— Lectures on the Science of Religion: With a Paper on Buddhist Nihilism, & a Translation of the Dhammapada or Path of Virtue. LC 73-18818. reprint ed. 15.00 (*0-404-11444-X*) AMS Pr.

— The Life & Letters of the Right Honourable Friedrich Max Mueller, 2 vols., Set. LC 73-18820. (Illus.). reprint ed. 82.50 (*0-404-11445-8*) AMS Pr.

— Life & Religion. LC 73-18821. reprint ed. 39.50 (*0-404-11448-2*) AMS Pr.

— Natural Religion. LC 73-18810. (Gifford Lectures: 1888). reprint ed. 44.50 (*0-404-11450-4*) AMS Pr.

— Physical Religion. LC 73-18811. (Gifford Lectures: 1890). reprint ed. 34.00 (*0-404-11451-2*) AMS Pr.

— Ramakrishna, His Life & Sayings. LC 73-18812. reprint ed. 32.50 (*0-404-11452-0*) AMS Pr.

— Rig-Veda-Samhita: The Sacred Hymns of the Brahmans, 4 vols., 1. 2nd ed. LC 73-18831. 1892. write for info. (*0-404-11462-8*) AMS Pr.

— Rig-Veda-Samhita: The Sacred Hymns of the Brahmans, 4 vols., 2. 2nd ed. LC 73-18831. 1892. write for info. (*0-404-11463-6*) AMS Pr.

— Rig-Veda-Samhita: The Sacred Hymns of the Brahmans, 4 vols., 3. 2nd ed. LC 73-18831. 1892. write for info. (*0-404-11464-4*) AMS Pr.

— Rig-Veda-Samhita: The Sacred Hymns of the Brahmans, 4 vols., 4. 2nd ed. LC 73-18831. 1892. write for info. (*0-404-11465-2*) AMS Pr.

— Rig-Veda-Samhita: The Sacred Hymns of the Brahmans, 4 vols., Set. 2nd ed. LC 73-18831. 1892. 176.00 (*0-404-11461-X*) AMS Pr.

— The Science of Language, 2 vols. LC 73-18817. reprint ed. 155.00 (*0-404-11441-5*) AMS Pr.

— The Science of Thought. LC 73-18813. reprint ed. 69.50 (*0-404-11453-9*) AMS Pr.

— Selected Essays on Language, Mythology & Religion, 2 vols. LC 73-18814. reprint ed. 125.00 (*0-404-11456-3*) AMS Pr.

— The Six Systems of Indian Philosophy. LC 73-18829. reprint ed. 44.50 (*0-404-11459-8*) AMS Pr.

— Theosophy: Or, Psychological Religion. LC 73-18830. (Gifford Lectures: 1892). reprint ed. 62.50 (*0-404-14460-8*) AMS Pr.

Mueller, G. Mikroradiographische Untersuchungen zur Mineralisation der Knochen Fruehgeborener und junger Saeuglinge 1980. (Journal: Acta Anatomica: Vol. 108, Suppl. 64). (Illus.). iv, 44p. 1981. pap. 36.00 (*3-8055-1719-X*) S Karger.

Mueller, G., jt. ed. see Krause, G.

Mueller, G. J. & Sliney, D. H. Dosimetry of Laser Radiation in Medicine & Biology (Institute) 253p. 1989. 81.00 (*0-8194-0070-X*, IS05/HC); pap. 66.00 (*0-685-52035-8*, IS05) SPIE.

Mueller, G. O., jt. ed. see Adler, F.

Mueller, G. O., jt. tr. see Moreau, J. F.

Mueller, Gary & Hughes, Allison, eds. Vision, 1994, Vol. 2: Harvard Students Look Ahead. xiv, 137p. (Orig.). 1994. pap. 10.95 (*0-9641866-0-8*) Dipylon Pr.

Mueller, Gene & Denyer, Bob. Never Let a Skinny Guy Make Sandwiches. (Illus.). 1994. pap. 14.95 (*0-9640419-4-4*) B&G MD.

Mueller, Gene, jt. auth. see Mitcham, Samuel W., Jr.

Mueller, George. Answers to Prayer. (Moody Classics Ser.). Date not set. pap. 3.99 (*0-8024-0565-7*) Moody.

— God Answers Prayer. pap. 3.99 (*0-88019-031-0*) Schmul Pub Co.

Mueller, Gerhard, ed. Theologische Realenzyklopaedie: Teil I, Band 1-17 und Registerband, Set. (TRE Ser.). (Orig.). (GER.). (C). 1993. pap. text ed. 795.00 (*3-11-013898-0*) De Gruyter.

Mueller, Gerhard G. & Kelly, Lauren. Introductory Financial Accounting. 3rd ed. 416p. 1990. pap. text ed. 58.00 (*0-13-485616-3*) P-H.

Mueller, Gerhard G., jt. auth. see Choi, Frederick D.

Mueller, Gerhard G., jt. ed. see Choi, Frederick D.

Mueller, Gerhard G., et al. Accounting: An International Perspective. LC 93-3989. 180p. 1993. 28.00 (*0-7863-0007-8*) Irwin Prof Pubng.

— Accounting: An International Perspective. 2nd ed. 150p. (C). 1990. pap. text ed. 23.95 (*0-256-09089-0*) Irwin.

— Accounting: An International Perspective - A Supplement to Introductory Accounting Textbook. 3rd ed. LC 93-3990. 224p. (C). 1993. text ed. 23.95 (*0-256-12403-5*) Irwin.

Mueller, Gerhard O. Comparative Criminal Law in the United States. (New York University Criminal Law Education & Research Center Monograph: No. 4). (Illus.). 72p. 1970. pap. text ed. 8.50 (*0-8377-0827-3*) Rothman.

Mueller, Gerhard O., et al. Delinquency & Puberty: Examination of a Juvenile Delinquency Fad. (New York University Criminal Law Education & Research Center Monograph: No. 5). (Illus.). x, 123p. (Orig.). 1971. pap. text ed. 8.50 (*0-8377-0830-3*) Rothman.

Mueller-Goldingen, Christian. Untersuchungen Zu Xenophons Kyrupadie. Bd. 52. (GER.). Date not set. write for info. (*0-318-70631-8*, Pub. by Georg Olms GW) Lubrecht & Cramer.

Mueller, Gus. Successful Conference: Programming Methods. 90p. (Orig.). 1982. pap. 10.00 (*0-9614097-0-3*) Fern Pubns.

Mueller, Gustar E. Philosophy of Literature. LC 72-14195. (Essay Index Reprint Ser.). 1977. reprint ed. 21.95 (*0-518-10021-9*) Ayer.

Mueller, Gustav E. Philosophy of Our Uncertainties: A Comment on the Uncertainties of Our Philosophies. LC 36-17433. 251p. reprint ed. pap. 71.60 (*0-317-08112-8*, 2004834) Bks Demand.

Mueller, H. & Weber, W., eds. Familial Cancer. (Illus.). xx, 292p. 1985. 148.00 (*3-8055-4245-3*) S Karger.

Mueller, H., jt. ed. see Yakscht, Tony L.

***Mueller, H. Gustav & Geoffery, Virgina C., eds.** Communication Disorders in Aging: Assessment & Management. fac. ed. LC 87-21084. (Illus.). 528p. 1994. pap. 150.50 (*0-7837-7687-X*, 2047441) Bks Demand.

Mueller, H. Gustav, jt. ed. see Hall, James W., 3rd.

Mueller, H. Gustav, et al. Probe Microphone Measurements: Hearing Aid Selection & Assessment. (Illus.). 303p. (C). 1992. text ed. 57.50 (*1-879105-68-3*) Singular Publishing.

Mueller, H. N., III, jt. ed. see Steffens, Henry J.

Mueller, Hans-Peter, ed. Bibel und Alter Orient: Altorientische Beitrage zum Alten Testament von Wolfram von Soden. (Beiheft zur Zeitschrift fuer die Alttestamentliche Wissenschaft Ser.: Band 162). xii, 224p. 1985. 92.35x (*3-11-010091-6*) De Gruyter.

Mueller, Hans R. Schulkinder unter Stress: Theoretische Ueberlegungen zum Stressmodell. Ritzel, G., ed. (Sozialmedizinische und Paedagogische Jugendkunde Ser.: Band 12). 140p. 1976. 19.25 (*3-8055-2299-1*) S Karger.

Mueller, Heiner. Germania. Lotringer, Sylvere, ed. Schutze, Bernard & Schutze, Carolind, trs. (Foreign Agents Ser.). 256p. (Orig.). (C). 1990. pap. text ed. 6.00 (*0-936756-63-2*) Autonomedia.

Mueller, Heinz P., et al, eds. Law Librarianship: A Handbook, 2 vols. No. 19. 1983. Vol. 1, pgs. 1-498. write for info. (*0-318-57950-2*); Vol. 2, pgs. 499-896. write for info. (*0-318-57951-0*) Rothman.

An Asterisk (*) at the beginning of an entry indicates that the title is appearing in BIP for the first time.

— Law Librarianship: A Handbook, 2 vols., Set. (American Association of Law Libraries Publications Ser.: No. 19). 1983. text ed. 95.00 (*0-8377-0116-3*) Rothman.

Mueller, Helga. Hydrocarbons in the Freshwater Environment: A Literature Review. (Advances in Limnology Ser.: No. 24). (Illus.). 69p. 1987. pap. text ed. 30.00 (*3-510-47022-2*, Pub. by Schweitzerbart'sche GW) Lubrecht & Cramer.

Mueller, Henry R. Whig Party in Pennsylvania. LC 74-82233. (Columbia University. Studies in the Social Sciences: No. 230). reprint ed. 21.00 (*0-404-51230-5*) AMS Pr.

Mueller, Herbert C. Learning to Teach Through Playing: A Brass Method. (Illus.). 163p. 1991. pap. 27.50 (*1-56516-005-3*) Houston IN.

Mueller, Hilbert F. How to Cultivate Common Sense. rev. ed. LC 80-82006. (Illus.). 240p. 1980. pap. 5.00 (*0-937342-00-9*) Hawk-Island.

Mueller-Hillebrand, Burkhart H. German Armored Traffic Control During the Russian Campaign. (DA Pam 20-242 Center for Military History Publication Ser.: No. 104-17). (Illus.). 49p. 1989. reprint ed. pap. 2.00 (*0-16-001977-X*, S/N 008-029-00175-6) USGPO.

— German Tank Maintenance in World War II: An Historical Study. (Illus.). 52p. (Orig.). (C). 1994. pap. text ed. 30.00x (*0-7881-1169-8*) Diane Pub.

— German Tank Maintenance in World War 2. (Center for Military History Publication German Report Series, DA Pam: No. 104-7). 50p. 1988. reprint ed. pap. 1.50 (*0-16-001965-6*, S/N 008-029-00163-2) USGPO.

Mueller, Hugo. Deutsch: Intermediate German Lessons, 2 vols. 350p. 1967. Bk. 1, pt. 2. 25.50 (*0-87559-207-4*); Bk. 3, 246p., 1973 German Lessons for Advanced Students. 22.50 (*0-87559-208-2*) Shalom.

Mueller, I. I. & Zerbini, S., eds. The Interdisciplinary Role of Space Geodesy. (Lecture Notes in Earth Sciences Ser.: Vol. 22). xv, 300p. 1989. pap. 38.00 (*0-387-51161-X*) Spr-Verlag.

Mueller, I. I., jt. ed. see Colombo, Oscar.

Mueller, Ian. Philosophy of Mathematics & Deductive Structure in Euclid's "Elements" (Illus.). 400p. (C). 1981. 50.00 (*0-262-13163-3*) MIT Pr.

Mueller, Ilze, tr. see Reinig, Christa.

Mueller, Iris W. John Stuart Mill & French Thought. LC 68-58805. (Essay Index Reprint Ser.). 1977. 20.95 (*0-8369-0089-8*) Ayer.

Mueller, Ivan I. Introduction to Satellite Geodesy. LC 64-15693. (Illus.). 437p. reprint ed. pap. 124.60 (*0-317-07950-6*, 2051272) Bks Demand.

Mueller, Ivan I. & Kolaczek, Barbara, eds. Developments in Astrometry & Their Impact on Astrophysics & Geodynamics: Proceedings of the 156th Symposium of the International Astronomical Union Held in Shanghai, China, September 15-19, 1992. LC 93-16750. 1993. lib. bdg. 129.00 (*0-7923-2237-1*) Kluwer Ac.

Mueller, Ivan I., jt. auth. see Moritz, Helmut.

Mueller, Ivan J., ed. see Wyclif, John.

Mueller, J., ed. Neurology & Psychiatry: A Meeting of Minds. (Illus.). xiv, 290p. 1989. 179.25 (*3-8055-4712-9*) S Karger.

Mueller, J. J. Practical Discipleship: A United States Christology. 175p. (Orig.). 1992. pap. text ed. 14.95 (*0-8146-5012-0*) Liturgical Pr.

— What Are They Saying about Theological Method? LC 84-61031. (What Are They Saying about...Ser.). 88p. (Orig.). 1985. pap. 5.95 (*0-8091-2657-5*) Paulist Pr.

— What Is Theology? (Zacchaeus Studies). 103p. (Orig.). 1988. pap. 7.95 (*0-8146-5681-1*) Liturgical Pr.

Mueller, J. Theodore, tr. see Luther, Martin.

Mueller, James. The Workplace Workbook 2.0: An Illustrated Guide to Workplace Accommodation & Technology. 2nd ed. (Illus.). 148p. 1992. ring bd. 49.95 (*0-87425-200-8*) Human Res Dev Pr.

Mueller, James R., jt. auth. see Charlesworth, James H.

Mueller, James W. The Use of Sampling in Archaeological Survey. (Memoir Ser.: No. 28). 104p. 1974. 6.00 (*0-932839-07-X*) Soc Am Arch.

Mueller, James W., ed. Sampling in Archaeology. LC 74-26372. 300p. (C). 1975. pap. 15.95 (*0-8165-0482-2*) U of Ariz Pr.

Mueller, Janel M., ed. see Donne, John.

Mueller, Jerome F. Plumbing Design & Installation Details. 1987. text ed. 55.00 (*0-07-043963-X*) McGraw.

— Standard Application of Mechanical Details. 352p. 1985. text ed. 53.00 (*0-07-043962-1*) McGraw.

Mueller, Jerome F., jt. auth. see Hicks, Tyler G.

Mueller, Johannes. Elements of Physiology. Baly, William, tr. LC 78-72814. (Brainedness, Handedness, & Mental Abilities Ser.). reprint ed. 60.00 (*0-404-60884-1*) AMS Pr.

— Enzymatische Regulation des Fruchtkoerperwachstums bei Basidiomyceten: Entwicklung eines Modells am Beispiel des Pleurotus Ostreatus (Jacq. ex Fr.) Kummer. (Bibliotheca Mycologica Ser.: Vol. 106). (Illus.). 186p. (GER.). 1986. pap. text ed. 48.00 (*3-443-59007-1*) Lubrecht & Cramer.

Mueller, John. Astaire Dancing. (Illus.). 448p. 1991. reprint ed. 24.99 (*0-517-06075-2*) Random Hse Value.

— Astaire Dancing: The Musical Films. LC 84-47874. (Illus.). 448p. 1985. 45.00 (*0-394-51654-0*) Knopf.

— The Clipper Interface Handbook. 1992. pap. 27.95 (*0-07-155353-3*) McGraw.

— The Clipper Interface Handbook. 720p. 1992. pap. 27.95 (*0-8306-3532-7*, Windcrest) TAB Bks.

— Clipper Programmer's Guide. 1990. pap. 24.95 (*0-672-22734-7*, Bobbs) Michie Butterworth.

— Films on Ballet & Modern Dance. rev. ed. 102p. 1978. 3.25 (*0-318-12490-4*) Am Dance Guild.

— Films on Ballet & Modern Dance. 102p. 1978. reprint ed. 4.75 (*0-318-12489-0*) Am Dance Guild.

— Microsoft Certification Success Guide. LC 94-29630. 1994. pap. text ed. 29.95 (*0-07-043973-7*, Windcrest) TAB Bks.

— The Novell CNA-CNE Study Guide. LC 94-33619. 1994. disk, pap. text ed. 38.95 (*0-07-911904-2*, Windcrest) TAB Bks.

— Policy & Opinion in the Gulf War. LC 93-21226. 1994. pap. text ed. 19.95 (*0-226-54565-2*) U Ch Pr.

— Policy & Opinion in the Gulf War. LC 93-21226. 1994. lib. bdg. 55.00 (*0-226-54564-4*) U Ch Pr.

— Quiet Cataclysm: Reflections on the Recent Transformation of World Politics. LC 94-1948. (C). 1994. 15.50 (*0-673-99327-2*) HarpCollege.

— The Ultimate DOS Programmer's Manual. 2nd ed. 1993. text ed. 40.00 (*0-07-043965-6*); pap. text ed. 29.95 (*0-07-043966-4*) McGraw.

— The Ultimate DOS Programmer's Manual. 2nd ed. (Illus.). 880p. 1993. text ed. 39.95 (*0-8306-4114-9*, 4221, Windcrest); pap. text ed. 29.95 (*0-8306-4115-7*, 4221, Windcrest) TAB Bks.

— The Ultimate OS-2 Programmer's Manual. LC 93-43685. 1994. text ed. 50.00 (*0-07-043971-0*); pap. text ed. 36.95 (*0-07-043972-9*) TAB Bks.

Mueller, John & Wang, Wallace. Microsoft Macro Assembler 5.1: Programming in the 80386 Environment. (Illus.). 384p. (Orig.). 1989. pap. 34.95 (*0-8306-3179-8*, Windcrest) TAB Bks.

— Microsoft Macro 5.1. 1991. 24.95 (*0-8306-8691-6*) TAB Bks.

— Ultimate DOS Programmer's Manual. (Illus.). 800p. 1990. 36.95 (*0-8306-7534-5*, 3534, Windcrest); pap. 29.95 (*0-8306-3534-3*, Windcrest) TAB Bks.

— Ultimate DOS Programmers Manual. 1991. 29.95 (*0-8306-6752-0*); 29.95 (*0-8306-6753-9*) TAB Bks.

Mueller, John & Williams, Robert A. The Hands-On Guide to Network Management. 1993. text ed. 39.95 (*0-07-043967-2*); pap. text ed. 26.95 (*0-07-043968-0*) McGraw.

— The Hands-On Guide to Network Management. LC 92-47461. 1993. pap. 26.95 (*0-8306-4439-3*, Windcrest); pap. 26.45 (*0-8306-4440-7*, Windcrest) TAB Bks.

— Novell Certification Handbook. 1993. pap. text ed. 24.95 (*0-07-043970-2*) McGraw.

— Novell Certification Handbook. 1994. text ed. 39.95 (*0-07-043969-9*) McGraw.

— Novell Certification Handbook. 1993. 39.95 (*0-8306-4554-3*, Windcrest); pap. 24.60 (*0-8306-4555-1*, Windcrest) TAB Bks.

Mueller, John, jt. auth. see Bailes, Lenny.

Mueller, John A., jt. auth. see Thomann, Robert V.

Mueller, John E., ed. see National Center for State Courts Staff.

Mueller, John H. The American Symphony Orchestra: A Social History of Musical Taste. LC 76-8875. (Illus.). 437p. 1976. reprint ed. text ed. 79.50 (*0-8371-8915-2*, MUAS, Greenwood Pr) Greenwood.

***Mueller, John P. & Walsh, B. J.** The CA-Clipper Interface Handbook. 2nd ed. LC 95-2754. 1995. pap. text ed. 44.95 (*0-07-911919-0*) McGraw.

Mueller, John T. Great Missionaries to China. LC 73-38329. (Biography Index Reprint Ser.). 1977. reprint ed. 15.95 (*0-8369-8124-3*) Ayer.

— Great Missionaries to the Orient. LC 78-38330. (Biography Index Reprint Ser.). 1977. reprint ed. 18.95 (*0-8369-8125-1*) Ayer.

Mueller, Johnm & Wang, Wallace. Microsoft Macro Assembler 5.1: Programming in the 80386 Environment. (Orig.). 1989. pap. text ed. 34.95 (*0-07-156445-4*) McGraw.

***Mueller-Joseph, Laura & Petersen, Marie.** Dental Hygiene Process: Diagnosis & Care Planning. LC 94-32214. 192p. 1995. 24.95 (*0-8273-5678-1*) Delmar.

Mueller, Joseph N. Guadalcanal 1942. (Campaign Ser.: No. 18). (Illus.). 96p. pap. 14.95 (*1-85532-253-6*, 9517, Pub. by Osprey UK) Stackpole.

Mueller, Julianne, ed. see Piechowski, Carol.

Mueller, K. The Fragments of the Lost Historians of Alexander the Great. 162p. 1979. 50.00 (*0-89005-273-5*) Ares.

— Die Lebermoose: Musci Hepatici, 2 pts., Set. 3rd ed. 1990. reprint ed. 407.00 (*3-87429-295-9*) Koeltz Sci Bks.

Mueller, K. A. & Benedek, G. Phase Separation in Cuprate Superconductors: Proceedings of the 3rd Workshop. 392p. 1993. text ed. 109.00 (*981-02-1274-7*) World Scientific Pub.

Mueller, K. A. & Thomas, H., eds. Structural Phase Transitions, Vol. I. (Topics in Current Physics Ser.: Vol. 23). (Illus.). 190p. 1981. 40.00 (*0-387-10329-5*) Spr-Verlag.

Mueller, Karen. Beating Bully O'Brien. (J). (gr. 3-7). 1991. pap. 2.95 (*0-380-75935-7*, Camelot) Avon.

Mueller, Karl. Die Lebermoose Europas. 3rd ed. Herzog, T., ed. (Rabenhorst's Kryptogamenflora Ser.: No. 6/1). (Illus.). 1365p. (GER.). 1990. reprint ed. text ed. 299.00 (*81-211-0049-6*, Pub. by Mahendra Pal Singh II) Lubrecht & Cramer.

Mueller, Kate. Antimatter Universe. (Young Readers Ser.: No. 147). (J). (gr. 6 up). 1994. pap. 3.50 (*0-553-56391-2*) Bantam.

Mueller, Kate, ed. see McLure, John.

Mueller, Keith J. Health Care Policy in the United States. LC 93-15252. (Illus.). xi, 216p. 1993. 30.00 (*0-8032-3173-3*) U of Nebr Pr.

Mueller, Kenneth. Complete Guide to the Maintenance & Repair of Band Instruments. 288p. 1982. text ed. 29.95 (*0-13-160499-6*, Parker Publishing Co) P-H.

Mueller, Kimberly J. The Nuclear Power Issue: A Guide to Who's Doing What in the U. S. & Abroad. LC 79-52430. (Who's Doing What Ser.: No. 8). (Illus.). 106p. (Orig.). 1981. pap. 25.00 (*0-912102-44-6*) Cal Inst Public.

Mueller, Klaus A. & Hoppmann-Liecty, Susanne. Die Presse: A Reader & Workbook. 181p. (GER.). (C). 1976. pap. text ed. 16.00 (*0-669-92536-5*) Heath.

Mueller-Krumbhar, H., jt. ed. see Chernov, A. A.

Mueller, L., ed. Rock Mechanics. (CISM International Centre for Mechanical Sciences Ser.: Vol. 165). (Illus.). 390p. 1982. pap. 55.00 (*0-387-81301-2*) Spr-Verlag.

Mueller, L., et al. The Coins of Alexander the Great. Oikonomides, A., ed. (Illus.). 173p. 1981. pap. 15.00 (*0-89005-382-0*) Ares.

Mueller, L. Ann, jt. auth. see Ketcham, Katherine.

Mueller, L. W., ed. Modern Day Poets & Authors. LC 77-81769. 1977. 6.50 (*0-8187-0029-7*) Harlo Press.

Mueller, Larry. The Calculating Fisherman. (Illus.). 192p. 1975. 12.95 (*0-944383-05-X*) High-Lonesome.

— Speed Train Your Own Bird Dog. LC 89-39933. (Illus.). 256p. (Orig.). 1990. pap. 18.95 (*0-8117-2304-6*) Stackpole.

— Speed Train Your Own Retriever: The Quick, Efficient, Proven System for Training a Finished Dog. LC 86-23109. (Illus.). 192p. (Orig.). 1987. pap. 18.95 (*0-8117-2201-5*) Stackpole.

Mueller, Laura M. Collector's Encyclopedia of Compacts: Carryalls & Face Powder Boxes. 1993. 24.95 (*0-89145-562-0*) Collector Bks.

Mueller-Lauter, Wolfgang. Dostoevskijs Ideendialektik. 66p. (C). 1974. 11.55 (*3-11-005731-X*) De Gruyter.

Mueller-Lauter, Wolfgang & Pestalozzi, Karl, eds. Nietzsche Werke Two, Bd. 2-3: Kritische Gesamtausgabe, Bd. 2. xii, 446p. (GER.). (C). 1992. lib. bdg. 153.85 (*3-11-009922-5*) De Gruyter.

— Nietzsche Werke Two, Bd. 2-3: Kritische Gesamtausgabe, Bd. 3. vi, 441p. (GER.). (C). 1992. lib. bdg. 149.25 (*3-11-013915-4*) De Gruyter.

Mueller, Lavonne. Breaking the Prairie Wolf Code. 1986. pap. 4.75 (*0-8222-0148-8*) Dramatists Play.

— Little Victories. 1984. pap. 4.75 (*0-8222-0680-3*) Dramatists Play.

Mueller, Lavonne & Reynolds, Jerry D. Creative Writing: Forms & Techniques. 256p. 1990. 15.95 (*0-8442-5379-0*, Natl Textbk); pap. 10.95 (*0-8442-5365-0*, Natl Textbk) NTC Pub Grp.

Mueller, Lavonne, jt. ed. see Horvath, John.

Mueller, Lisel. Learning to Play by Ear. (W.N.J. Ser.: No. 26). (Illus.). 80p. (Orig.). 1990. 20.00 (*1-55780-137-1*); pap. 12.00 (*1-55780-138-X*) Juniper Pr WI.

— The Need to Hold Still. Poems. LC 79-20965. xii, 68p. 1980. pap. 8.95 (*0-8071-0670-4*) La State U Pr.

— The Private Life. Poems. LC 75-5350. 64p. 1976. text ed. 13.95 (*0-8071-0182-6*); pap. 6.95 (*0-8071-0171-0*) La State U Pr.

— Second Language. Poems. LC 86-7246. 72p. 1986. pap. 8.95 (*0-8071-1337-9*) La State U Pr.

— Voices from the Forest. (W.N.J. Ser.: No. 7). 1977. pap. 8.00 (*1-55780-056-1*) Juniper Pr WI.

— Waving from Shore. LC 89-12144. 64p. 1989. text ed. 14.95 (*0-8071-1575-4*); pap. 7.95 (*0-8071-1576-2*) La State U Pr.

Mueller, Lisel, tr. see Kaschnitz, Marie L.

Mueller, Lisel, tr. see Kaschnitz, Mary L.

Mueller, Lisel, et al. Primavera, IV. Heller, Janet R. et al, eds. LC 76-647540. (Illus.). (C). 1978. pap. 4.00 (*0-916980-04-9*) Primavera.

Mueller, Lothar W. How to Publish Your Own Book. LC 75-12222. (Illus.). 184p. 1976. 7.95 (*0-8187-0019-X*); pap. 5.95 (*0-8187-0017-3*) Harlo Press.

Mueller, Lothar W., ed. Harlo's Anthology of Modern-Day Poets & Authors - 1972. LC 72-95005. 128p. 1973. 6.00 (*0-8187-0010-6*) Harlo Press.

— Harlo's Anthology of Modern-Day Poets & Authors 1974. LC 74-27876. 152p. 1974. 6.00 (*0-8187-0016-5*) Harlo Press.

Mueller, Lucian. De Re Metrica Poetarum Latinorum Praeter Plautum et Terentium, Libri VII. xiv, 651p. (GER.). 1967. reprint ed. write for info. (*0-318-70573-7*, Pub. by Georg Olms GW) Lubrecht & Cramer.

— De Re Metrica Poetarum Latinorum Praeter Plautum et Terentium Libri VII. xiv, 651p. 1967. reprint ed. write for info. (*0-318-71182-6*, Pub. by Georg Olms GW) Lubrecht & Cramer.

Mueller-Lutz, H. L. Diccionario de Seguros. 282p. (ENG, FRE, GER & SPA.). 1977. pap. 15.75 (*0-7859-0901-X*, S-50035) Fr & Eur.

Mueller-Lyer, Franz C. The Evolution of Modern Marriage: A Sociology of Sexual Relations. LC 72-11292. reprint ed. 37.50 (*0-404-57484-X*) AMS Pr.

Mueller, M. Let's Color Korea: Traditional Games. 24p. (J). (gr. k-3). 1989. 8.50 (*0-930878-95-7*) Hollym Intl.

Mueller, M. E., et al. Manual of Internal Fixation. 2nd rev. ed. LC 78-20743. (Illus.). 1979. 230.00 (*3-540-92113-3*) Spr-Verlag.

Mueller, Magda, jt. ed. see Funk, Nanette.

Mueller, Marge & Mueller, Ted. The Essential San Juan Islands Guide. (Illus.). 272p. (Orig.). 1994. pap. 12.95 (*1-881409-08-2*) Jhnstn Assocs.

— Exploring Washington's Wild Areas: A Guide for Hikers, Backpackers, Climbers, XC Skiers, & Paddlers. (Illus.). 356p. 1994. pap. 14.95 (*0-89886-351-1*) Mountaineers.

— Middle Puget Sound & Hood Canal, Afoot & Afloat. LC 89-77763. (Illus.). 224p. (Orig.). 1990. pap. 12.95 (*0-89886-236-1*) Mountaineers.

— North Puget Sound: Afoot & Afloat. LC 88-1808. (Illus.). 224p. (Orig.). 1988. pap. 12.95 (*0-89886-149-7*) Mountaineers.

— The San Juan Islands: Afoot & Afloat. (Illus.). 224p. (Orig.). 1995. pap. 12.95 (*0-89886-435-6*) Mountaineers.

— The San Juan Islands Afoot & Afloat. 2nd ed. LC 88-12261. (Illus.). 240p. 1988. pap. 12.95 (*0-89886-157-8*) Mountaineers.

— The San Juan Islands, Afoot & Afloat. 3rd ed. LC 94-44878. 1995. pap. write for info. (*0-89886-434-8*) Mountaineers.

— South Puget Sound, Afoot & Afloat. 2nd ed. LC 90-48553. (Illus.). 240p. 1990. pap. 12.95 (*0-89886-256-6*) Mountaineers.

— Washington State Parks: A Complete Recreation Guide. LC 92-39612. (Illus.). 288p. (Orig.). 1993. pap. 14.95 (*0-89886-324-4*) Mountaineers.

Mueller, Marge, jt. auth. see Diamond, Lynnell.

Mueller, Mark, ed. Mr. Moon & Miss Sun. (Korean Folk Tales for Children Ser.: No. 2). (Illus.). 45p. (J). (gr. 2-5). 1990. lib. bdg. 9.95 (*0-930878-72-8*) Hollym Intl.

— The Woodcutter & the Heavenly Maiden. (Korean Folk Tales for Children Ser.: No. 1). (Illus.). 45p. (J). (gr. 2-5). 1990. lib. bdg. 9.95 (*0-930878-71-X*) Hollym Intl.

Mueller, Mark, jt. auth. see Vorhees, Duance.

Mueller, Marlies. Les Idees Politiques dans le Roman Heroique de 1630 a 1670. LC 84-81405. (Harvard Studies in Romance Languages: No. 40). 219p. 1984. pap. 15.00 (*0-940940-40-X*) Harvard U Romance Lang & Lit.

Mueller, Marnie. Green Fires: Assault on Eden: A Novel of the Ecuadorian Rainforest. LC 94-2426. 320p. 1994. 19.95 (*1-880684-16-0*) Curbstone.

Mueller, Martin. Children of Oedipus & Other Essays on the Imitation of Greek Tragedy, 1550-1800. LC 79-26018. 296p. reprint ed. pap. 84.40 (*0-8357-8068-6*, 2034070) Bks Demand.

— The Iliad. (Unwin Critical Library). 192p. (C). 1986. pap. text ed. 10.95 (*0-04-800087-6*) Routledge Chapman & Hall.

Mueller, Martin & Wertenschlag, Lukas. Los Emol, Schweizerdeutsch Verstehen. 112p. Lehr-und Arbeitschbuch, 112p. pap. 23.50 (*3-468-49840-3*); audio 46.00 (*3-468-84481-6*) Langenscheidt.

Mueller, Martin, et al, eds. The Science of Biological Specimen Preparation for Microscopy & Microanalysis, 1985. (Proceedings of the Pfefferkorn Conference Ser.: No. 4). (Illus.). xii, 308p. 1986. text ed. 46.00 (*0-931288-37-1*) Scanning Microscopy.

Mueller, Mary L., jt. auth. see Cove, Mary K.

Mueller, Mary M., tr. see Caesarius Of Arles, St.

Mueller, Mary M., tr. see Caesarius Of Arles.

Mueller, Michael. The Sinner's Return to God: Or, the Prodigal Son. LC 82-74244. 224p. 1983. reprint ed. pap. 9.00 (*0-89555-205-1*) TAN Bks Pubs.

Mueller, Mike. Chevelle, 1964-1972. LC 93-13164. (Muscle Car Color History Ser.). 1993. pap. 19.95 (*0-87938-761-0*) Motorbooks Intl.

— Chevy Muscle Cars. (Enthusiast Color Ser.). (Illus.). 96p. 1994. pap. 12.95 (*0-87938-864-1*) Motorbooks Intl.

— Chevy 55-56-57. LC 93-17024. (Enthusiast Color Ser.). 1993. 12.95 (*0-87938-816-1*) Motorbooks Intl.

— Chrysler Muscle Cars. LC 93-13064. (Enthusiast Color Ser.). 1993. pap. 12.95 (*0-87938-817-X*) Motorbooks Intl.

— Corvette Sting Ray 1963-1967. (Illus.). 128p. 1994. pap. 19.95 (*0-87938-788-2*) Motorbooks Intl.

— Fifties American Cars. (Enthusiast Color Ser.). (Illus.). 96p. 1994. pap. 12.95 (*0-87938-924-9*) Motorbooks Intl.

— Ford Muscle Cars. LC 93-13063. (Enthusiast Color Ser.). 1993. pap. 12.95 (*0-87938-815-3*) Motorbooks Intl.

— Ford Mustang. (Enthusiast Color Ser.). (Illus.). 96p. 1995. pap. 12.95 (*0-87938-990-7*) Motorbooks Intl.

— Muscle Cars of the Fifties. (Illus.). 128p. 1995. pap. text ed. 19.95 (*0-7603-0006-2*) Motorbooks Intl.

— Pontiac Muscle Cars. (Enthusiast Color Ser.). (Illus.). 96p. 1994. pap. 12.95 (*0-87938-863-3*) Motorbooks Intl.

Mueller, Mike, jt. auth. see Brownell, Tom.

Mueller, Mike, jt. auth. see Herd, Paul A.

Mueller, Mike, jt. auth. see Young, Anthony.

Mueller, Milton L. Telephone Companies in Paradise: A Case Study in Telecommunications Deregulation. 250p. (C). 1993. text ed. 39.95 (*1-56000-103-8*) Transaction Pubs.

Mueller, Norbert. Suedbayerische Parkrasen-Soziologie und Dynamik bei Unterschiedlicher Pflege. (Dissertationes Botanicae Ser.: Vol. 123). (Illus.). ii, 176p. (GER.). 1988. spiral bd. 45.50 (*3-443-64035-4*) Lubrecht & Cramer.

Mueller, P. & Boswell, J. Estates, Trusts, Wills & Probate. (Texas Legal Assistant Education Ser.). 1991. write for info. (*0-8205-0639-7*) Bender.

Mueller, P., jt. ed. see Werner, D.

Mueller, P. B. Vocal Re-Education Therapy: A Clinician's Guide to the Hyperkinetic Voice. 50p. 1989. ring bd. 35.00 (*0-930599-53-5*) Thinking Pubns.

Mueller, P. C. & Schiehlen, W. O. Forced Linear Vibrations. (CISM International Center for Mechanical Sciences, Courses & Lectures Ser.: Vol. 172). (Illus.). 1979. pap. 27.00 (*0-387-81487-6*) Spr-Verlag.

Mueller, P. Henry. Perspective on Credit Risk. LC 88-436. (Illus.). 76p. 1988. pap. 43.00 (*0-936742-48-8*, 34131) Robt Morris Assocs.

Mueller, P. S. The Spread of Terror: Plus Lots of Cartoons We Could Have Put on the Cover but Didn't. 122p. 1986. pap. 5.95 (*0-933893-15-9*) Bonus Books.

Mueller, P. S., jt. auth. see Schreiner, Dave.

Mueller, Paul & Mueller, Sage. The North Carolina Employment Guide, 1993. 153p. 1992. disk 69.95 (*0-685-61600-2*); pap. 34.95 (*1-881803-01-5*) Career Res.

Mueller, Peter. Diccionario Rioduero: Literatura, Vol. 1. 304p. (SPA.). 1977. 14.95 (*0-8288-5360-6*, S50164) Fr & Eur.

— Lexikon der Datenverarbeitung. (GER.). 1968. 55.00 (*0-7859-0836-6*, M-7265) Fr & Eur.

Mueller, Peter, jt. auth. see Loebel.

Mueller, Peter O. Wortbildung des Nuernberger Frueneuhochdeutsch, Bd. 1: Substantiv-Derivation in den Schriften Albrecht Duerers. xx, 532p. (GER.). (C). 1993. lib. bdg. 200.00 (*3-11-012815-2*) De Gruyter.

An Asterisk (*) at the beginning of an entry indicates that the title is appearing in BIP for the first time.

Mueller, Phyllis, ed. see Davis, Ren & Davis, Helen.

Mueller, Phyllis, ed. see Massengale, Dee.

Mueller, Phyllis, ed. see Massie, Mariam.

Mueller, Phyllis, ed. see Purdy, A. Jane.

Mueller-Pohle, Andrea, jt. ed. see Ammann, Jean C.

Mueller, R. F. & Saxena, Surendra K. Chemical Petrology: With Applications to the Terrestinal Planets & Meteorites. LC 76-26049. (Illus.). 1977. 109.00 (*0-387-90196-5*) Spr-Verlag.

Mueller, Ralph & Turk, Jerry. Report after Action: The Story of the 103rd Infantry Division. (Divisional Ser.: No. 1). (Illus.). 166p. 1978. reprint ed. 27.50 (*0-89839-010-9*) Battery Pr.

Mueller, Ralph A. Der Un teilbare Geist: Modularismus und Holismus in der Kognitionsforschung. (Foundations of Communication & Cognition Ser.). xix, 443p. (GER.). (C). 1991. lib. bdg. 152.35 (*3-11-012916-7*, 250-91) De Gruyter.

***Mueller, Ralph O.** Basic Principles of Structural Equation Modelling: An Introduction to LISREL & EQS. LC 95-15043. (Statistics Ser.). 1995. write for info. (*0-387-94516-4*) Spr-Verlag.

Mueller, Reinhold, jt. auth. see Lane, Frederic C.

Mueller, Reinhold C. The Procuratori Di San Marco & the Ventian Credit Market: A Study of the Development of Credit & Banking in the Trecento. Bruchey, Stuart, ed. LC 77-77181. (Dissertations in European Economic History Ser.). 1978. lib. bdg. 40.95 (*0-405-10794-3*) Ayer.

Mueller, Reinhold C., ed. see Lane, Frederic C.

Mueller, Richard. Ghostbusters. 256p. 1989. pap. 3.95 (*0-8125-0382-1*) Tor Bks.

Mueller, Richard J. Instructional Psychology: Principles & Practices. 294p. (C). 1992. pap. text ed. 18.80 (*0-87563-397-8*) Stipes.

Mueller, Robert. Air Force Bases, Vol. 1: Active Air Force Bases Within the United States on 17 September 1982. 1990. write for info. (*0-912799-53-6*) Off Air Force.

— Air Force Bases, Vol. 1: Active Air Force Bases Within the United States on 17 September 1982. LC 88-600231. (Illus.). 651p. 1989. 31.00 (*0-16-002261-4*, S/N 008-070-00027-8) USGPO.

— For People Just Like Us. Sherer, Michael L., ed. (Orig.). 1986. pap. 3.95 (*0-89536-834-X*, 6848) CSS OH.

Mueller, Robert, jt. auth. see Carter, Kit C.

Mueller, Robert, jt. ed. see Carter, Kit C.

Mueller, Robert, et al. The Lovers' Tarot. (Illus.). 320p. (Orig.). 1993. pap. 11.00 (*0-380-76886-0*) Avon.

Mueller, Robert A. Automated Microcode Synthesis. Stone, Harold, ed. LC 83-24095. (Computer Science: Computer Architecture & Design Ser.: No. 1). 134p. 1984. reprint ed. pap. 38.20 (*0-8357-1498-5*, 2070409) Bks Demand.

Mueller, Robert A. & Lundberg, Dag B. Manual of Drug Interactions for Anesthesiology. 2nd ed. (Illus.). 370p. 1992. pap. text ed. 42.00 (*0-443-08877-2*) Churchill.

— Manual of Drug Interactions for Anesthesiology. LC 88-20410. 384p. reprint ed. pap. 109.50 (*0-7837-2564-7*, 2042723) Bks Demand.

Mueller, Robert A. & Page, Rex L. Symbolic Computing with LISP & Prolog. 469p. 1988. Net. text ed. write for info. (*0-471-60771-1*) Wiley.

***Mueller, Robert F. & Young, Ian D.** Emery's Elements of Medical Genetics. 9th ed. LC 95-5827. Orig. Title: Elements of Medical Genetics. (Illus.). 1995. write for info. (*0-443-05175-5*) Churchill.

Mueller, Robert F., jt. auth. see Emery, Alan E.

Mueller, Robert J. Seven Tell Their Story. Sherer, Michael L., ed. (Orig.). 1988. pap. 3.40 (*1-55673-019-5*, 8803) CSS OH.

Mueller, Robert K. Corporate Networking: Building Channels of Communication. 176p. 1986. text ed. 32.95 (*0-02-922150-1*) Free Pr.

— The Director's & Officer's Guide to Advisory Boards. LC 89-32858. 289p. 1990. text ed. 65.00 (*0-89930-467-2*, MDJ/, Quorum Bks) Greenwood.

— Smarter Board Meetings: For Effective Nonprofit Governance. (Nonprofit Governance Ser.: No. 12). 22p. (Orig.). (C). 1993. reprint ed. pap. text ed. 10.00 (*0-925299-18-9*) Natl Ctr Nonprofit.

Mueller, Rolf R. Festival & Fiction in Heinrich Wittenwiler's "Ring" A Study of the Narrative in Its Relation to the Traditional Topoi of Marriage, Folly, & Play. (German Language & Literature Monographs: No 3). viii, 155p. 1977. 39.00x (*90-272-0963-4*) Benjamins North Am.

***Mueller, Rosawitha.** Valie Export - Fragments of the Imagination. LC 94-6589. 1994. pap. 24.95 (*0-253-20925-0*) Ind U Pr.

Mueller, Roseanna, tr. see De Montemayor, Jorge.

Mueller, Rosemary. Feeling of War 1991. (Illus.). 32p. (Orig.). 1992. pap. 11.95 (*0-9632214-0-X*) Piper-Davies.

Mueller, Roswitha. Bertolt Brecht & the Theory of Media. LC 88-33805. (Modern German Culture & Literature Ser.). (Illus.). xiv, 149p. 1989. 30.00 (*0-8032-3132-6*) U of Nebr Pr.

— Valie Export - Fragments of the Imagination. LC 94-6589. (Women Artists in Film Ser.). 1995. 49.95 (*0-253-33906-5*) Ind U Pr.

Mueller, Ruth. The Eye of the Child. 274p. 1985. 19.95 (*0-86571-046-5*); pap. 7.95 (*0-86571-039-2*) New Soc Pubs.

Mueller, Sage, jt. auth. see Mueller, Paul.

Mueller-Schwefe, Gerhard. William Shakespeare: Welt-Werk-Wirkung. (Sammlung Goeschen Ser.: Vol. 2208). (C). 1978. 15.85 (*3-11-007545-8*) De Gruyter.

Mueller, Scott. Mueller's Official Puppy Owner Manual. (Orig.). Date not set. pap. text ed. 4.95 (*0-9637183-0-4*) Bridgept Pub.

— Upgrading & Repairing PCs. 3rd ed. (Illus.). 1312p. 1993. pap. 34.95 (*1-56529-467-X*) Que.

— Upgrading & Repairing PC's. 4th ed. 1994. pap. 34.99 (*1-56529-932-9*) Que.

— Upgrading & Repairing PCs Quick Reference. 1994. pap. 19.95 (*1-56529-736-9*) Que.

Mueller, Scott, et al. Killer PC Utilities. (Illus.). 1120p. (Orig.). 1993. pap. 39.95 (*1-56529-328-2*) Que.

Mueller-Shore, Margaret. An Independent Study Guide to Anatomy & Physiology to Prepare for ACT - PEP Exams or Other Challenge Exams. 272p. (C). 1994. pap. text ed. write for info. (*0-697-24692-2*) Wm C Brown Pubs.

Mueller, Siegfried. Elektrische und Dieselelektrische Triebfahrzeuge. (Illus.). 204p. (GER.). 1979. 52.95 (*0-8176-1033-2*) Birkhauser.

Mueller, Ted, jt. auth. see Mueller, Marge.

Mueller, Theodore & Niedzielski, Henri. Basic French, 3 vols., Set. Incl. Premiers Pas. (FRE.). 1974. pap. text ed. 4.40 (*0-89197-670-1*); Pratique de la grammaire. (FRE.). 1974. pap. text ed. 8.20 (*0-89197-671-X*); Introduction a la culture. (FRE.). 1974. pap. text ed. 3.10 (*0-89197-672-8*); (FRE.). 1974. Set pap. text ed. 15.70 (*0-89197-673-6*) Irvington.

Mueller, Thomas. What a Beautiful Day! (J). (ps-3). 1992. 18.95 (*0-87614-739-2*, Carolrhoda) Lerner Group.

Mueller, Thomas J. & Ames, Charlotte A., eds. Father Theodore Hesburgh: Commitment, Compassion, Consecration. LC 88-63542. (Orig.). 1989. pap. 5.95 (*0-87973-430-2*, 430) Our Sunday Visitor.

Mueller, Tobin J. Danger, Dinosaurs! A Musical Comedy about the Evolution & Extinction of the Dinosaurs, Incl. audio tape. (Illus.). (J). (ps-8). 1990. Audio tape incl. audio, pap. 14.95 (*1-56213-003-X*) Ctr Stage Prodns.

— Music of the Planet: A Musical Journey about the World & Wonders of Our Solar System. (J). (ps-8). 1990. pap. 14.95 (*1-56213-017-X*) Ctr Stage Prodns.

— Say Yes! to Life: A Musical Drama about the Dangers Drugs Pose to the Joys of Living. (Illus.). (J). (gr. 4-9). 1990. Audio tape incl. pap. 14.95 (*1-56213-045-5*) Ctr Stage Prodns.

— The Sound of Money: A Musical Adventure about Economics & the Building of Community. (Illus.). (J). (ps-8). Audio tape incl. audio 14.95 (*1-56213-031-5*) Ctr Stage Prodns.

— To Save the Planet: A Musical Fable about the Global Environment & What We Can Do to Help. 54p. (J). (gr. 4-9). 1991. Inc. audio cass. audio 14.95 (*1-56213-078-1*) Ctr Stage Prodns.

Mueller, Tobin J., jt. auth. see Pulaski High School Drama Club Staff.

Mueller, U., jt. ed. see Franke, W. W.

Mueller, Udo. Diccionario Riodeuro Literatura, Vol. 2. 352p. (SPA.). 1978. 14.95 (*0-7859-5750-2*, 8422008602) Fr & Eur.

— Herder Literature Lexicon, Biographic Dictionary: Herder-Lexikon Literatur: Biographisches Woerterbuch, 2 vols. 574p. (GER.). 1981. 75.00 (*0-8288-1572-0*, M7442) Fr & Eur.

Mueller, Ulrich R. Insect Sting Allergy: Clinical Picture, Diagnosis & Treatment. 183p. 1990. pap. 40.00 (*0-89574-313-2*) G F Verlag.

Mueller, Virginia. A Halloween Mask for Monster. Fay, Ann, ed. LC 86-1569. (Monster Bks.). (Illus.). 24p. (J). (ps-1). 1986. 11.95 (*0-8075-3134-0*) A Whitman.

— A Halloween Mask for Monster. (Illus.). (J). (ps-1). 1988. pap. 4.99 (*0-14-050879-1*, Puffin) Puffin Bks.

— Jacob's Ladder. LC 59-1444. (Arch Bks.). (Illus.). 24p. (J). (ps-4). 1990. pap. 1.99 (*0-570-09021-0*) Concordia.

— Monster & the Baby. Fay, Ann, ed. LC 85-3127. (Illus.). 24p. (J). (ps-1). 1985. lib. bdg. 11.95 (*0-8075-5253-4*) A Whitman.

— Monster Can't Sleep. Fay, Ann, ed. LC 86-1568. (Monster Bks.). (Illus.). 24p. (J). (ps-1). 1986. lib. bdg. 11.95 (*0-8075-5261-5*) A Whitman.

— Monster Goes to School. Levine, Abby, ed. LC 90-29873. (Illus.). 24p. (J). (ps-1). 1991. 11.95 (*0-8075-5264-X*) A Whitman.

— Monster's Birthday Hiccups. Levine, Abby, ed. LC 91-2118. (Illus.). 24p. (J). (ps-1). 1991. 11.95 (*0-8075-5267-4*) A Whitman.

— A Playhouse for Monster. Fay, Ann, ed. LC 85-3144. (Illus.). 24p. (J). (ps-1). 1985. lib. bdg. 11.95 (*0-8075-6541-5*) A Whitman.

— A Playhouse for Monster. (Illus.). (J). (ps-1). 1988. pap. 3.95 (*0-14-050877-5*, Puffin) Puffin Bks.

— What Is Faith? Beegle, Shirley, ed. (Happy Day Bks.). (Illus.). 24p. (Orig.). (J). (ps-3). 1994. reprint ed. pap. 1.89 (*0-7847-0265-9*) Standard Pub.

Mueller-Vollmer, Kurt, ed. Herder Today: Contributions from the International Herder Conference, Nov. 5-8, 1987, Stanford, California. xxiv, 451p. (C). 1990. lib. bdg. 144.65 (*3-11-011739-8*) De Gruyter.

Mueller-Vollmer, Kurt, jt. ed. see Muller-Vollmer, Kurt.

Mueller, W. The Knee: Form, Function, & Ligament Reconstruction. (Illus.). 314p. 1985. 225.00 (*0-387-11716-4*) Spr-Verlag.

— Manifolds with Cusps of Rank One. (Lecture Notes in Mathematics Ser.: Vol. 1244). xi, 158p. 1987. pap. 31.30 (*0-387-17696-9*) Spr-Verlag.

Mueller, W., jt. ed. see Schattenkirchner, M.

Mueller, W. E. G., et al, eds. Progress in Molecular & Subcellular Biology: Molecular & Cellular Enzymology, Vol. 13. (Illus.). 1994. 136.00 (*0-387-57337-2*) Spr-Verlag.

***Mueller, Walt.** Understanding Today's Youth Culture. LC 94-26142. 448p. 1994. pap. 14.99 (*0-8423-7736-0*) Tyndale.

Mueller, Walter. Grammatical Aids for Students of New Testament Greek. 1972. pap. 6.99 (*0-8028-1447-6*) Eerdmans.

Mueller, Walter & Mayer, Karl U., eds. Social Stratification & Career Mobility. LC 72-88184. (Sociology Ser.). (Illus.). 1974. text ed. 33.35 (*90-279-7248-6*) Mouton.

Mueller, Walter W., jt. auth. see Jungraithmayr, Hermann.

Mueller, Werner, et al. Geometrie & Physik. Academy of Sciences & Technology in Berlin Staff, ed. (Akademie der Wissenschaften zu Berlin, Forschungsbericht Ser.: No. 8). (Illus.). vii, 192p. (Orig.). (GER.). (C). 1993. pap. text ed. 90.80 (*3-11-013944-8*) De Gruyter.

Mueller, Werner A. Nibelungenlied Today. LC 70-181961. (North Carolina. University. Studies in the Germanic Languages & Literatures: No. 34). reprint ed. 27.00 (*0-404-50934-7*) AMS Pr.

Mueller, Willard F. Primer on Monopoly & Competition. 1970. pap. text ed. 6.00 (*0-394-30738-0*) Random.

Mueller, Willard F. & Garoian, Leon. Changes in the Market Structure of Grocery Retailing. LC 86-18317. 240p. 1986. reprint ed. text ed. 65.00 (*0-313-25222-X*, MUCM, Greenwood Pr) Greenwood.

Mueller, Willard F., et al. The Sunkist Case: A Study in Legal-Economic Analysis. LC 86-46242. 288p. 1987. text ed. 39.95 (*0-669-15189-0*) Free Pr.

Mueller-Wille, Christopher. Natural Landscape Amenities & Suburban Growth: Metropolitan Chicago, 1970-1980. LC 90-10818. (Geography Research Papers). (Illus.). xii, 154p. 1991. pap. 12.00 (*0-89065-136-1*) U Ch Pr.

Mueller-Wille, Christopher, ed. Roads of Texas. (Illus.). 160p. 1988. pap. 12.95 (*0-940672-45-6*) Shearer Pub.

Mueller, William & Smith, David. EPA's Sampling & Analysis Methods Database, Vol. 1: Industrial Chemicals. Keith, Lawrence H., ed. (Illus.). 1990. 119.95 (*0-87371-375-3*, TD426) Lewis Pubs.

***Mueller, William A.** Battered Victory. 330p. 1994. 8.00 (*0-9643960-0-9*) Panhandle Jackie.

Mueller, William B. How to Grow All of Your Own Food: A Natural Step-by-Step Method. (Illus.). 1976. 5.95 (*0-940536-00-5*) Big Toad Pr.

Mueller, William J. & Aniskiewicz, Albert S. Psychotherapeutic Intervention in Hysterical Disorders. LC 85-15. 300p. 1986. 35.00 (*0-87668-913-6*) Aronson.

Mueller, William L. Ladner on Conveyancing in Pennsylvania, 2 vols. 4th rev. ed. LC 79-53058. 1994. ring bd. 125.00 (*0-318-41044-3*) Bisel Co.

Mueller, William M. & Shaw, Milton C., eds. Energetics in Metallurgical Phenomena, 4 vols, Vol. 1. 440p. 1965. text ed. 250.00 (*0-677-00570-9*) Gordon & Breach.

— Energetics in Metallurgical Phenomena, 4 vols, Vol. 2. 214p. 1965. text ed. 169.00 (*0-677-01010-9*) Gordon & Breach.

— Energetics in Metallurgical Phenomena, 4 vols, Vol. 3. 204p. 1967. text ed. 169.00 (*0-677-11120-7*) Gordon & Breach.

— Energetics in Metallurgical Phenomena, 4 vols, Vol. 4. 392p. 1968. text ed. 255.00 (*0-677-11680-2*) Gordon & Breach.

Mueller, William M., ed. see Conference on Application of X-Ray Analysis (10th, 1961, Denver).

Mueller, William M., ed. see Conference on Applications of X-Ray Analysis.

Mueller, William M., ed. see Conference on Applications of X-Ray Analysis (6th-1957-Denver).

Mueller, William M., ed. see Conference on Applications of X-Ray Analysis (7th: 1958).

Mueller, William M., ed. see Conference on Applications of X-Ray Analysis (12th: 1963, Denver).

Mueller, Wolfgang. Dichter-Helden in der DDR-Literatur der Siebziger Jahre. (DDR-Studien - East German Studies: Vol. 5). 220p. (C). 1989. text ed. 40.95 (*0-8204-0897-2*) P Lang Pubs.

Mueller, Wolfgang E. Albert Schweitzers Kulturphilosophie Im Horizont Saekularer Ethik. (Theologische Bibliothek Toepelmann Ser.: Vol. 59). ix, 331p. (GER.). (C). 1993. lib. bdg. 113.85 (*3-11-013966-9*) De Gruyter.

Muellner, Leonard, tr. see Bertin, Celia.

Muellner, Leonard, tr. see Detienne, Marcel.

Muellner, Leonard, tr. see Grmek, Mirko D.

Muellner, Mireille, tr. see Bertin, Celia.

Muellner, Mireille, tr. see Detienne, Marcel.

Muellner, Mireille, tr. see Grmek, Mirko D.

Muench, D., photos. National Parks of America. (Illus.). 1993. cd-rom 75.00 (*1-55868-194-9*) Gr Arts Ctr Pub.

***Muench, David.** Nature's America. rev. ed. 160p. 1995. pap. 24.95 (*1-57098-024-1*) R Rinehart.

— Portrait of Colorado. 1993. pap. 12.95 (*1-55868-102-7*) Gr Arts Ctr Pub.

— Uncommon Places. LC 91-65. (Illus.). 168p. 1991. 39.95 (*0-917953-40-1*) Appalachian Trail.

***Muench, David, illus.** David Muench in Texas. 128p. 1995. 39.95 (*1-56313-757-7*) BrownTrout Pubs Inc.

— Eternal Desert. 143p. 1990. 39.95 (*0-916179-22-2*) Ariz Hwy.

Muench, David, photos. American Landscape. LC 86-83243. (Illus.). 208p. 1987. 42.50 (*0-932575-30-7*) Gr Arts Ctr Pub.

— Colorado II. LC 86-83242. (Illus.). 160p. 1987. 39.95 (*0-932575-31-5*) Gr Arts Ctr Pub.

— National Parks of America. 208p. 1993. 50.00 (*1-55868-124-8*) Gr Arts Ctr Pub.

— New Mexico II. (Illus.). 160p. 1991. 39.95 (*1-55868-048-9*) Gr Arts Ctr Pub.

— Utah. LC 89-81615. (Illus.). 160p. 1990. 39.95 (*1-55868-024-1*) Gr Arts Ctr Pub.

***Muench, David & Muench, Marc.** American Portfolios: Three Wilderness Portfolios. (Illus.). 168p. 1994. 39.95 (*1-56313-441-1*) BrownTrout Pubs Inc.

Muench, David & Reynolds, Robert, photos. New Mexico & Rio Grande & Other Essays. (Illus.). 96p. 1992. 27.50 (*1-55868-093-4*) Gr Arts Ctr Pub.

***Muench, David & Schaafsma, Polly.** Images in Stone: Petroglyphs & Pictographs. (Illus.). 192p. 1995. 49.95 (*1-56313-442-X*) BrownTrout Pubs Inc.

Muench, David & Temple, David. Santa Barbara. (Illus.). 96p. 1988. 19.95 (*1-55652-046-8*) Chicago Review.

Muench, David & Whitmore, Jeff. Big Sur & the Central Coast. (Illus.). 96p. 1988. 19.95 (*1-55652-045-X*) Chicago Review.

Muench, David, jt. text see Ballard, Michael B.

Muench, David, jt. auth. see Pike, Donald G.

Muench, David, jt. auth. see Pike, Donald.

***Muench, David, et al.** Colorado: A Photographic Portfolio. 112p. 1995. 25.95 (*1-56313-616-3*); pap. 17.95 (*1-56313-758-5*) BrownTrout Pubs Inc.

— Michigan: A Photographic Portfolio. (Illus.). 112p. 1995. 25.95 (*1-56313-760-7*); pap. 17.95 (*1-56313-761-5*) BrownTrout Pubs Inc.

Muench, Karl. Genetic Medicine. (Illus.). 270p. 1987. text ed. 39.50 (*0-8385-3121-0*, A3121-9) Appleton & Lange.

Muench, Marc, photos. Ski the Rockies. 144p. 1994. 39.95 (*1-55868-196-5*) Gr Arts Ctr Pub.

Muench, Marc, jt. auth. see Muench, David.

Muench, Steve, et al. Oracle: Forms Developer's Companion. 596p. (Orig.). (C). 1994. pap. text ed. 44.50 (*0-9637526-5-0*) Maverick CA.

Muench, Teri & Pomerantz, Susan. ATTN: A&R: A Step-by-Step Guide into the Recording Industry. Feldstein, Sandy & Wilson, Patrick, eds. (Illus.). 120p. (Orig.). 1988. pap. 16.95 (*0-88284-361-3*, 2260) Alfred Pub.

Muenchner Rueckversicherungs-Gesellschaft Staff, jt. ed. see Allianz Versicherungs-AG Staff.

Muenchow, Charles, tr. see Westermann, Claus.

Muenchow, Susan, jt. auth. see Zigler, Edward F.

Muendel, Renate. George Meredith. (Twayne's English Authors Ser.: No. 434). 160p. 1986. text ed. 21.95 (*0-8057-6932-3*, Pub. by Royal Botanic Garden UK) Macmillan.

Muenger, Elizabeth. The British Military Dilemma in Ireland: Occupation Politics, 1886-1914. LC 91-11120. (Modern War Studies). 288p. 1991. 29.95 (*0-7006-0487-1*) U Pr of KS.

Muenscher, Walter C. Weeds. 2nd ed. LC 79-48017. (Comstock Book Ser.). (Illus.). 560p. 1987. pap. 18.95 (*0-8014-9417-6*) Cornell U Pr.

Muensterberg, Hugo. On the Witness Stand: Essays on Psychology & Crime. Moss, Richard, ed. LC 70-156030. reprint ed. 35.00 (*0-404-09180-6*) AMS Pr.

Muensterberg, M. A Harvest of German Verse. 1973. 59.95 (*0-8490-0284-2*) Gordon Pr.

Muensterberger, W. Vincent Van Gogh - Dessins, Pastels, Etudes. (Illus.). 106p. (FRE.). 1948. lib. bdg. 14.95 (*0-8288-3978-6*) Fr & Eur.

Muensterberger, W. & Axelrad, S., eds. Psychoanalysis & the Social Sciences, 4. LC 47-12480. reprint ed. pap. 73.80 (*0-317-10715-1*, 2010452) Bks Demand.

— Psychoanalysis & the Social Sciences, 5. LC 47-12480. reprint ed. pap. 76.80 (*0-317-10716-X*) Bks Demand.

Muensterberger, Warner, jt. ed. see Wilbur, George B.

Muensterberger, Werner. Collecting: An Unruly Passion: Psychological Perspectives. LC 93-2174. 203p. 1994. text ed. 29.95 (*0-691-03361-7*) Princeton U Pr.

Muensterberger, Werner, et al, eds. The Psychoanalytic Study of Society, Vol. 8. LC 61-486. (Illus.). 1979. text ed. 50.00 (*0-300-02257-3*) Yale U Pr.

Muensterberger, Werner L., et al, eds. The Psychoanalytic Study of Society, Vol. 10. (Muensterberger Ser.). 400p. 1984. text ed. 39.95 (*0-88163-004-7*) Analytic Pr.

Muenterberger, W., et al, eds. The Psychoanalytic Study of Society, 6 Vols., 1. reprint ed. pap. 96.00 (*0-317-11204-X*, 2010451) Bks Demand.

— The Psychoanalytic Study of Society, 6 Vols., 2. reprint ed. pap. 79.30 (*0-317-11205-8*) Bks Demand.

— The Psychoanalytic Study of Society, 6 Vols., 3. reprint ed. pap. 102.00 (*0-317-11206-6*) Bks Demand.

— The Psychoanalytic Study of Society, 6 Vols., 4. reprint ed. pap. 87.50 (*0-317-11207-4*) Bks Demand.

— The Psychoanalytic Study of Society, 6 Vols., 5. reprint ed. pap. 64.50 (*0-317-11208-2*) Bks Demand.

— The Psychoanalytic Study of Society, 6 Vols., 6. reprint ed. 80.00 (*0-317-11209-0*) Bks Demand.

Muentner, Carolyn. My Unicorn Thinks He Is Real: And Similar Confusions. 68p. 1982. reprint ed. 8.95 (*0-9606240-2-3*) Pearl-Win.

— The Wind Will Not Forget. 68p. 1983. 8.95 (*0-9606240-3-1*) Pearl-Win.

Muenzer, Clark S. Figures of Identity: Goethe's Novels & the Enigmatic Self. LC 83-43033. (Studies in German Literature). 176p. 1984. 30.00 (*0-271-00361-8*) Pa St U Pr.

Muer, Chuck. The Simply Great Cookbook: Recipes & the Experience of Fine Dining from the Kitchens of Chuck Muer. LC 92-15339. (Illus.). 166p. (Orig.). 1992. pap. 19.95 (*1-879094-13-4*) Momentum Bks.

Mues, R., jt. auth. see Zinsmeister, H. D.

Mueser, Anne M. & Liptay, Lynne. Talk & Toddle: A Commonsense Guide for the First Three Years. 160p. 1983. pap. 7.95 (*0-312-78430-9*) St Martin.

Mueser, Anne M., ed. see Russell, David, et al.

Mueser, Anne M., jt. auth. see Verrilli, George E.

***Mueser, Kim T. & Gingerich, Susan.** Coping with Schizophrenia: A Guide for Families. LC 94-67043. (Illus.). 355p. 1994. text ed. 24.95 (*1-879237-79-2*); pap. 13.95 (*1-879237-78-4*) New Harbinger.

Mueser, Kim T. & Glynn, Shirley M. Behavioral Family Therapy for Psychiatric Disorders. 1994. text ed. 39.95 (*0-205-16653-9*, Longwood Div) Allyn.

Muet, P. A., jt. auth. see Artus, P.

Muet, P. A., jt. auth. see Dagenais, M. G.

Muet, Pierre-Alain & Fonteneau, Alain. Reflation & Austerity: Economic Policy under Mitterand. Slater, Malcolm, tr. LC 89-28948. 335p. 1991. 76.00 (*0-85496-644-7*) Berg Pubs.

Muether, John J., jt. auth. see Kepple, Robert J.

Mueting, Donald, jt. auth. see Hawkins, Robert.

Muetterties, E. L., jt. auth. see Jesson, J. P.

Muetterties, Earl L. & Knoth, Walter H. Polyhedral Boranes. LC 68-11437. 205p. reprint ed. pap. 58.50 (*0-685-16233-8*, 2027109) Bks Demand.

Muetze. ABC der Optik. 960p. (GER.). 1991. 95.00 (*0-8288-6079-3*, M-7290) Fr & Eur.

Muezzino-Lu, A. & Williams, M. L., eds. Industrial Air Pollution: Assessment & Control. (NATO ASI Series G: Ecological Sciences: Vol. 31). x, 235p. 1992. 139.00 (*0-387-53098-3*) Spr-Verlag.

Mufarrij-Sherower, T. S., ed. see Sherower, Abbott W.

Mufassir, Sulaiman S. Jesus, a Prophet of Islam. 23p. (Orig.). (YA). (gr. 10-12). 1980. pap. 1.25 (*0-89259-089-0*) Am Trust Pubns.

Mufassir, Sulayman. Biblical Studies from a Muslim Perspective. Obaba, Al I., ed. 49p. (Orig.). (YA). 1991. pap. text ed. 2.00 (*0-916157-61-X*) African Islam Miss Pubns.

Muff, Janet. Socialization, Sexism & Stereotyping: Women's Issues in Nursing. (Illus.). 434p. (C). 1988. reprint ed. pap. text ed. 21.95 (*0-88133-372-5*) Waveland Pr.

Muffler, ed. South Cascades Arc Volcanism, California & Southern Oregon. (IGC Field Trip Guidebooks Ser.). 64p. 1989. 21.00 (*0-87590-563-3*, T312) Am Geophysical.

Muffler, L. J., jt. ed. see Rybach, L.

***Muffley, J. W., ed.** The Story of Our Regiment: A History of the 148th Pennsylvania Volunteers. (Army of the Potomac Ser.). (Illus.). 1200p. 1994. 55.00x (*0-935523-39-1*) Butternut & Blue.

Muffoletto, Robert & Knupfer, Nancy N. Computers in Education: Social, Political & Historical Perspectives. (Media, Education, Culture, Technology Ser.). 272p. 1993. text ed. 45.00 (*1-881303-59-4*); pap. text ed. 19.95 (*1-881303-60-8*) Hampton Pr NJ.

Muffs, Judith H. The Holocaust in Books & Films: A Selected Annotated List. 64p. 5.00 (*0-686-95068-2*) ADL.

***Muffs, Yochanan.** Love & Joy: Law, Language, & Religion in Ancient Israel. (Jewish Theological Seminary of America Ser.). 240p. (Orig.). (C). 1995. pap. text ed. 15.95 (*0-674-53932-X*) HUP.

— Love & Joy, Law, Language, & Religion in Ancient Israel. LC 92-11977. 1992. 29.95 (*0-674-53931-1*) Jewish Sem.

Mufson, Laura, et al. Interpersonal Psychotherapy for Depressed Adolescents. 211p. 1993. lib. bdg. 26.95 (*0-89862-686-2*) Guilford Pr.

Mufson, Steven. Fighting Years: Black Resistance & the Struggle for a New South Africa. LC 90-52515. (Illus.). 376p. 1991. pap. 14.00 (*0-8070-0213-5*) Beacon Pr.

Mufson, Susan & Kranz, Rachel. Straight Talk about Child Abuse. (Straight Talk Ser.). 128p. (YA). 1991. 16.95 (*0-8160-2376-X*) Facts on File.

— Straight Talk about Date Rape. Ryan, Elizabeth A., ed. (Straight Talk Ser.). 128p. (YA). (gr. 9-12). 1993. 16.95 (*0-8160-2863-X*) Facts on File.

Mufti, G. J. & Galton, D. A., eds. The Myelodysplastic Syndromes. (Illus.). 256p. 1992. text ed. 89.95 (*0-443-04083-4*) Churchill.

Mufti, G. J., jt. ed. see Schmalzi, F.

Mufti, Shawkat. Heroes & Emperors in Circassian History. (Arab Background Ser.). 1972. 15.00 (*0-86685-175-5*) Intl Bk Ctr.

Muftic, Sead, Jr., et al. Security Architecture for Open Distributed Systems. (Communication & Distributed Systems Ser.). 281p. 1993. text ed. 69.95 (*0-471-93472-0*) Wiley.

Mufwene, Salikoko & Moshi, Lioba, eds. Topics in African Linguistics. LC 93-5761. (Current Issues in Linguistic Theory Ser.: No. 100). x, 304p. 1993. 76.00x (*1-55619-553-2*) Benjamins North Am.

Mufwene, Salikoko S., ed. Africanisms in Afro-American Language Varieties. LC 92-8225. 576p. (C). 1993. 40.00 (*0-8203-1465-X*) U of Ga Pr.

Mugaas, John N., et al. Metabolic Adaptation to Climate & Distribution of the Raccoon Procyon Lotor & Other Procyonidae. LC 93-3119. (Smithsonian Contributions to Zoology Ser.: No. 542). (Illus.). 38p. reprint ed. pap. 25.00 (*0-7837-5897-9*, 2045688) Bks Demand.

Mugan, Daniel J., ed. & intro. Curriculum Guide on Argentina. (Curriculum Guides on Latin America Ser.: No. 4). (Illus.). 225p. 1986. teacher ed 14.50 (*0-938305-03-4*) Assn Tchrs Latin Amer.

— Curriculum Guide on Brazil. (Curriculum Guides on Latin America Ser.: No. 3). (Illus.). 230p. 1986. teacher ed 14.50 (*0-938305-02-6*) Assn Tchrs Latin Amer.

— Curriculum Guide on Chile. (Curriculum Guides on Latin America Ser.: No. 1). (Illus.). 195p. 1981. reprint ed. teacher ed 12.95 (*0-317-46209-1*) Assn Tchrs Latin Amer.

— Curriculum Guide on Ecuador. (Curriculum Guides on Latin America Ser.: No. 2). (Illus.). 350p. 1984. reprint ed. teacher ed 14.95 (*0-938305-01-8*) Assn Tchrs Latin Amer.

Mugan, Daniel J., ed. Curriculum Guide to Venezuela, No. 5. 185p. (Orig.). 1989. teacher ed 15.95 (*0-938305-04-2*) Assn Tchrs Latin Amer.

Mugerauer, Robert. Heidegger's Language & Thinking. LC 86-27188. 232p. (C). 1990. pap. 18.50 (*0-391-03667-X*) Humanities.

— Interpretations on Behalf of Place: Environmental Displacements & Alternative Responses. LC 93-11617. (SUNY Series in Environmental & Architectural Phenomenology). (Illus.). 237p. (C). 1994. 59.50x (*0-7914-1943-6*); pap. 19.95x (*0-7914-1944-4*) State U NY Pr.

— Interpreting Environments: Traditions, Deconstruction, Hermeneutics. LC 95-8156. 1996. write for info. (*0-292-75178-8*); pap. write for info. (*0-292-75189-3*) U of Tex Pr.

Mugerauer, Robert, jt. auth. see Seamon, David.

Mugerwa, M. N., jt. ed. see Blomen, L. J.

Mugford, Roger. Dr. Mugford's Casebook: Understanding Dogs - Their Companions. (Illus.). 224p. 1993. pap. 19.95 (*0-09-177163-3*, Pub. by Jonathan Cape UK) Trafalgar.

— Never Say No! The Complete Program for a Happier & More Cooperative Dog. LC 93-32929. (Illus.). 224p. (Orig.). 1994. 18.95 (*0-399-13947-8*, Putnam) Putnam Pub Group.

— Never Say No: The Complete Program for a Happier & More Cooperative Dog. LC 93-32929. 208p. (Orig.). 1994. 12.00 (*0-399-51884-3*) Putnam Pub Group.

***Muggamin.** Jewish Americans. 1995. (*0-7910-3365-1*) Chelsea Hse.

Mugge, Maximilian A. Friedrich Nietzsche. 1972. 250.00 (*0-8490-0201-X*) Gordon Pr.

Mugge-Meiburg, Beth L. Words Chiseled into Marble: Artworks in the Prose Narratives of Conrad Ferdinand Meyer. LC 90-49695. (North American Studies in Nineteenth-Century German Literature: Vol. 9). 236p. (C). 1991. text ed. 41.95 (*0-8204-1493-X*) P Lang Pubs.

Muggeridge, Anne R. Desolate City: Revolution in the Catholic Church. 1990. pap. 12.00 (*0-06-066046-5*) Harper SF.

Muggeridge, Malcolm. Chronicles of Wasted Time: An Autobiography. LC 88-38725. 558p. 1989. reprint ed. pap. 14.95 (*0-89526-762-4*) Regnery Pub.

— Earnest Atheist: A Study of Samuel Butler. LC 77-153491. (English Literature Ser.: No. 33). 1971. reprint ed. lib. bdg. 75.00 (*0-8383-1242-X*) M S G Haskell Hse.

— Jesus. LC 74-28794. 176p. 1976. reprint ed. pap. 14.00 (*0-06-066042-2*, RD149) Harper SF.

— Something Beautiful for God. LC 77-155106. (Illus.). 1971. 18.45 (*0-06-066041-4*, PL 4124); pap. 6.95 (*0-685-02073-8*) Harper SF.

— Something Beautiful for God: Mother Teresa of Calcutta. 1986. pap. 10.00 (*0-06-066043-0*) Harper SF.

— Something Beautiful for God: Mother Teresa of Calcutta. large type ed. (Large Print Inspirational Ser.). 186p. 1985. pap. 9.95 (*0-8027-2474-4*) Walker & Co.

Muggeridge, Malcolm, ed. see Ciano, Galeazzo.

Muggeridge, Thomas M. Winter in Moscow. LC 87-9170. 270p. reprint ed. pap. 77.00 (*0-7837-3170-1*, 2042808) Bks Demand.

Muggia, Franco M., et al. Anthracycline Antibiotics in Cancer Therapy. 1982. text ed. 69.50 (*0-686-37594-7*) Kluwer Ac.

Muggia, Franco M. Cancer Chemotherapy I. 1983. lib. bdg. 125.00 (*90-247-2713-8*) Kluwer Ac.

Muggia, Franco M., ed. Cancer Chemotherapy: Concepts, Clinical Investigations & Therapeutic Advances. (Cancer Treatment & Research Ser.). (C). 1988. lib. bdg. 107.00 (*0-89838-381-1*) Kluwer Ac.

— Concepts, Clinical Developments, & Therapeutic Advances in Cancer Chemotherapy. (Cancer Treatment & Research Ser.). (C). 1987. lib. bdg. 75.00 (*0-89838-875-9*) Kluwer Ac.

— Experimental & Clinical Progress in Cancer Chemotherapy. (Cancer Treatment & Research Ser.). 1985. lib. bdg. 98.00 (*0-89838-679-9*) Kluwer Ac.

— New Drugs, Concepts & Results in Cancer Chemotherapy. (Cancer Treatment & Research Ser.). 176p. (C). 1991. lib. bdg. 98.50 (*0-7923-1253-8*) Kluwer Ac.

Muggia, Franco M. & Rozencweig, Marcel, eds. Clinical Evaluation of Antitumor Therapy. (Developments in Oncology Ser.). 1986. lib. bdg. 93.50 (*0-89838-803-1*) Kluwer Ac.

— Lung Cancer: Progress in Therapeutic Research. fac. ed. LC 77-84552. (Progress in Cancer Research & Therapy Ser.: No. 11). (Illus.). 640p. Date not set. pap. 180.00 (*0-7837-7179-7*, 2047120) Bks Demand.

Muggia, Franco M., jt. ed. see Mathe, G.

Muggia, Franco M., et al, eds. Cancer Treatment & the Heart. LC 92-17266. (Johns Hopkins Series Hematology - Oncology). 432p. 1992. text ed. 125.00 (*0-8018-4526-2*) Johns Hopkins.

Muggler, Dixie M. Poisoning & Medicine: Guidebook for Reference & Research. LC 83-46109. 150p. 1985. 37.50 (*0-88164-152-9*); pap. 31.50 (*0-88164-153-7*) ABBE Pubs Assn.

***Mugglestone, Lynda.** Talking Proper: The Rise of Accent as Social Symbol. (Illus.). 368p. 1995. 55.00 (*0-19-823948-3*) OUP.

Mugglestone, Lynda, ed. see Eliot, George.

Muggleton, Pat, et al. The Complete St. Bernard. Nebenhaus, Kathy, ed. (Illus.). 160p. 1992. 25.95 (*0-87605-299-5*) Howell Bk.

Muggleton, Stephen, ed. Inductive Logic Programming. (APIC Ser.). (Illus.). 576p. 1992. text ed. 89.00 (*0-12-509715-8*) Acad Pr.

***Muggs.** Lady & Me. (Illus.). 48p. (J). (gr. 1-3). 1995. pap. 8.00 (*0-8059-3671-8*) Dorrance.

Mughabghab, S. F., et al, eds. Neutron Cross Sections, Vol. 1, Pt. B: Z - 61-100: Neutron Resonance Parameters & Thermal Cross Sections. 652p. 1984. text ed. 114.00 (*0-12-509711-5*) Acad Pr.

Mughan, A., jt. auth. see McKinlay, Robert D.

Mughan, Anthony. Party & Participation in British Elections. LC 85-22320. 250p. 1986. text ed. 35.00 (*0-312-59756-8*) St Martin.

Mughan, Anthony & Patterson, Samuel C., eds. Political Leadership in Democratic Societies. 500p. 1992. pap. text ed. 22.95 (*0-8304-1218-2*) Nelson-Hall.

Mughniyyah, Allamah M. The Hajj: According to the Five Schools of Islamic Jurisprudence. Qara'i, Ali Q., tr. 96p. (C). 1989. pap. text ed. 6.70 (*1-871031-09-5*) Abjad Bk.

Mughniyyah, Muhammad J. The Despotic Rulers: Ash Shiah Wa Hakimun. rev. ed. Wasi, S. M. & Aini, A. A., eds. Haq, M. Fazal, tr. 274p. reprint ed. pap. 8.00 (*0-941724-46-8*) Islamic Seminary.

Mugica Berrondo, Placido. Diccionario Castellano - Vasco. 1032p. (BAQ & SPA.). 1987. 95.00 (*0-7859-3346-8*) Fr & Eur.

Mugica, Jacques, jt. ed. see Barold, S. Serge.

Mugika, Placido. Diccionario Castellano-Vasco. 4th ed. 1027p. 95.00 (*0-8288-6235-4*, S-50441) Fr & Eur.

Mugler, Charles. Dictionnaire Historique de la Terminologie Optique des Grecs. 460p. (FRE.). 1964. pap. 150.00 (*0-8288-6767-4*, M-6421) Fr & Eur.

— Dictionnaire Historique de la Terminologie Optique des Grecs. 460p. (FRE.). 1964. pap. 165.00 (*0-7859-7845-3*, 2252001674) Fr & Eur.

Mugler, Dale H., ed. see Boas, Ralph P., Jr.

Muglia, V., ed. Enterprise Information Exchange: A Roadmap for Electronic Data Interchange for Manufacturing Companies. 188p. 1992. 42.00 (*0-87263-435-3*) SME.

Mugnai, D., ed. see Ranfagni, A.

Mugnaini, Joseph. Expressive Drawing. (Illus.). 224p. 1988. 24.95 (*0-87192-207-X*) Davis Mass.

Mugnaini, Joseph A. The Hidden Elements of Drawing. LC 73-3944. (Illus.). 211p. reprint ed. pap. 60.20 (*0-317-10410-1*, 2006340) Bks Demand.

Mugnal, Massimo. Leibniz's Theory of Relations. 291p. (Orig.). 1992. pap. 77.50x (*3-515-05895-8*) Coronet Bks.

Mugnier, Charlotte. The Paraprofessional & the Professional Job Structure. LC 80-12543. 163p. reprint ed. pap. 46.50 (*0-317-26564-4*, 2023951) Bks Demand.

***Mugno, Salvatore.** Io Ho Mangiato le Fragole: Italian Essays. 89p. (ITA.). 1988. 10.00 (*0-89304-526-8*) Cross-Cultrl NY.

Mugny, Gabriel. The Power of Minorities. (European Monographs in Social Psychology: No. 31). 1982. text ed. 83.00 (*0-12-509720-4*) Acad Pr.

Mugny, Gabriel & Carugati, Felice. Social Representations of Intelligence. (European Monographs in Social Psychology). (Illus.). 225p. (C). 1989. 69.95 (*0-521-33348-2*) Cambridge U Pr.

Mugny, Gabriel & Perez, Juan A. The Social Psychology of Minority Influence. Lamongie, Vivian E., tr. (European Monographs in Social Psychology). 216p. (C). 1991. 74.95 (*0-521-39054-0*) Cambridge U Pr.

Mugo, Phoebe, ed. Lodu's Escape: And Other Stories from Africa. (Illus.). 64p. (Orig.). (J). (gr. 3-5). 1994. pap. 6.95 (*0-377-00269-0*) Friendship Pr.

Mugrage, Bill. The Official Price Guide to Beer Cans. 5th ed. (Illus.). 400p. 1993. pap. 12.50 (*0-87637-873-4*, House of Collect) Ballantine.

Mugridge, Donald H. & Conover, Helen F. An Album of American Battle Art, 1755-1918. LC 72-6278. (Illus.). 340p. 1972. reprint ed. lib. bdg. 55.00 (*0-306-70523-0*) Da Capo.

Mugridge, Ian & Kaufman, David, eds. Distance Education in Canada. 336p. 1986. 39.95 (*0-7099-4619-8*, Pub. by Croom Helm UK) Routledge Chapman & Hall.

Mugridge, Ian, jt. ed. see Moran, Louise.

Mugridge, Larry R. Elementary Algebra. 600p. (C). 1990. text ed. 48.00 (*0-03-009409-7*) SCP.

— Elementary Algebra. annot. ed. 600p. (C). 1990. teacher ed write for info. (*0-03-031442-9*) SCP.

— Elementary Algebra. 2nd ed. LC 93-48371. (C). 1994. text ed. 55.75 (*0-03-072991-2*) SCP.

— Intermediate Algebra. 896p. (C). 1991. text ed. 47.00 (*0-03-009477-1*) SCP.

— Intermediate Algebra. annot. ed. 896p. (C). 1991. teacher ed write for info. (*0-03-031587-5*) SCP.

— Intermediate Algebra. 2nd ed. LC 93-42142. (C). 1994. text ed. 55.75 (*0-03-072943-2*) SCP.

***Muha, Thomas & Vernon, Maureen.** If Your Divorce Is the Pits, Stop Digging: A Parent's Handbook. 1996. write for info. (*0-614-06627-1*) Lookng Glass.

— If Your Divorce Is the Pits, Stop Digging: The Group Leader's Guide. 1996. write for info. (*0-614-06628-X*) Lookng Glass.

***Muhaiyaddeen, M. R.** Gems of Widsom No. IV: Come to Prayer. 65p. (Orig.). 1995. pap. 5.00 (*0-914390-48-1*) Fellowship Pr PA.

— Gems of Wisdom: Beyond Mind & Desire. LC 93-6734. (Gems of Wisdom Ser.). 80p. 1993. pap. 5.00 (*0-914390-36-8*) Fellowship Pr PA.

— Gems of Wisdom: The Value of Good Qualities. 80p. 1992. pap. 5.00 (*0-914390-34-1*) Fellowship Pr PA.

— Guidebook to the True Secret of the Heart, Vol. 1. (Illus.). 230p. reprint ed. pap. 6.00 (*0-914390-07-4*) Fellowship Pr PA.

— A Mystical Journey. LC 89-1102. 150p. 1990. 12.00 (*0-914390-28-7*); pap. 7.00 (*0-914390-29-5*) Fellowship Pr PA.

— Question of Life - Answers of Wisdom, Vol. 1. LC 90-3822. 350p. 1991. 20.00 (*0-914390-32-5*) Fellowship Pr PA.

— A Song of Muhammad. 275p. 1995. text ed. write for info. (*0-914390-49-X*); pap. write for info. (*0-914390-50-3*) Fellowship Pr PA.

— To Die Before Death: The Sufi Way of Life. 300p. 1994. text ed. 20.00 (*0-914390-37-6*); pap. 12.00 (*0-914390-39-2*) Fellowship Pr PA.

— Treasures of the Heart: Sufi Stories for Young Children. Steele, Christine, ed. Balamore, Usha, tr. (Illus.). 110p. (J). (ps). 1993. 10.00 (*0-914390-33-3*) Fellowship Pr PA.

— Wisdom of the Divine, 4 vols., Vols. 1-4. 90p. 1972. pap. 5.00 (*0-914390-00-7*) Fellowship Pr PA.

Muhaiyaddeen, M. R. Bawa. Come to the Secret Garden: Sufi Tales of Wisdom. LC 83-49210. (Illus.). 450p. (J). 1985. 20.00 (*0-914390-27-9*) Fellowship Pr PA.

— Golden Words of a Sufi Sheikh. LC 82-11854. 472p. 1983. 20.00 (*0-914390-24-4*) Fellowship Pr PA.

— Islam & World Peace. LC 87-11921. 150p. 1987. 16.00 (*0-914390-30-9*); pap. 7.95 (*0-914390-25-2*) Fellowship Pr PA.

— My Love You, My Children: One Hundred & One Stories for Children of All Ages. LC 81-9847. (Illus.). 425p. 1981. 20.00 (*0-914390-20-1*) Fellowship Pr PA.

— Sheikh & Disciple. LC 83-1565. (Illus.). 120p. 1983. 8.00 (*0-914390-26-0*) Fellowship Pr PA.

— A Tasty Economical Cookbook, Vol. 2. (Illus.). 166p. 1983. spiral bd. 5.00 (*0-914390-22-8*) Fellowship Pr PA.

Muhajir. Lessons from the Stories of the Quran. pap. 16.50 (*1-56744-120-3*) Kazi Pubns.

Muhajir, M. R. Islam in Practical Life. 14.50 (*1-56744-082-7*) Kazi Pubns.

Muhalyaddeen, M. R. Gem of Wisdom, No. 3: The Innermost Heart. 70p. (Orig.). 1994. pap. 5.00 (*0-914390-38-4*) Fellowship Pr PA.

***Muhamad, Jaafar.** Sales Success in Asia: Dealing with Customers in Malaysia. 150p. 1995. pap. 19.95 (*1-884015-67-0*) St Lucie Pr.

Muhammad. The Qur'an: A New Translation with a Critical Rearrangement of the Surahs, 2 vols. Bell, Richard, tr. write for info. (*0-318-50937-7*, Pub. by T & T Clark UK) Bks Intl VA.

— The Qur'an: A New Translation with a Critical Rearrangement of the Surahs, 2 vols., Vol. 1. Bell, Richard, tr. 348p. 33.95 (*0-567-02027-4*, Pub. by T & T Clark UK) Bks Intl VA.

— The Qur'an: A New Translation with a Critical Rearrangement of the Surahs, 2 vols., Vol. 2. Bell, Richard, tr. 352p. 33.95 (*0-567-02028-2*, Pub. by T & T Clark UK) Bks Intl VA.

Muhammad & Ali, Hazrat. Excellent Sayings of Muhammad & Ali. Campbell, Charles I., tr. 1978. pap. 7.50 (*0-917220-02-1*) Khaneghah & Maktab.

***Muhammad, Abdallah.** The First Three Days of Creation. (Illus.). 116p. 1995. pap. 6.95x (*1-886543-00-3*) Islamic Lights.

— The Likeness of Jesus to Adam... (Illus.). 1995. pap. text ed. 3.95x (*1-886543-01-1*) Islamic Lights.

— Reflections of Edgar A. Poe in the Light of the Holy Qur'an Pt. 1: A Quantitative Study. 98p. (Orig.). 1995. pap. 4.95 (*1-886543-02-X*) Islamic Lights.

— Reflections of Edgar A. Poe in the Light of the Holy Qur'an Pt. II: A Qualitative Study. 265p. 1995. pap. 9.95 (*1-886543-03-8*) Islamic Lights.

Muhammad Abdullah & Al-Buraey. Administrative Development: An Islamic Perspective. 420p. 1986. pap. 80.00 (*0-7103-0059-X*, A3186, Pub. by Kegan Paul Intl UK); pap. 22.50 (*0-685-24717-1*, A3186, Pub. by Kegan Paul Intl UK) Routledge Chapman & Hall.

Muhammad, Al-Hajj I. What Should You Do If You Are Arrested or Framed by the Cops? 32p. (Orig.). 1990. pap. 4.95 (*1-56411-034-6*) Untd Bros & Sis.

Muhammad, Al-Hajj W. Muslims in Georgia: A Chronology & Oral History, Vol. 1: 1771-1965. LC 93-73991. (Illus.). 80p. (Orig.). 1994. pap. text ed. 6.95 (*0-9638618-5-9*) Brandon Inst.

Muhammad al-Tijani al-Samawi. Then I Was Guided. LC 91-66698. 232p. 1993. pap. 6.00 (*1-879402-06-8*, OO) Tahrike Tarsile Quran.

Muhammad-'Aliy-Salmani, Ustad. My Memories of Baha'u'llah: Ustad Muhammad-'Aliy-Salmani, the Barber. Gail, Marzieh, tr. (Illus.). xii, 148p. 1982. 14.95 (*0-933770-21-9*) Kalimat.

Muhammad 'Ata Ur-Rahim. Jesus Prophet of Islam. LC 91-66699. 244p. (Orig.). (C). reprint ed. pap. 8.00 (*1-879402-07-6*, 45A) Tahrike Tarsile Quran.

Muhammad Aziz Shukri. International Terrorism: A Legal Critique. 200p. (Orig.). (C). 1991. pap. 12.50 (*0-915597-86-1*) Amana Bks.

Muhammad bin Uthman Adh-Shahabi. The Major Sins in Islam. 550p. 1993. text ed. 35.00 (*1-56744-489-X*) Kazi Pubns.

Muhammad, Elijah. Christianity vs. Islam. 37p. (Orig.). 1993. pap. text ed. 6.95 (*0-685-71988-X*) Untd Bros & Sis.

— The Fall of America. 265p. (Orig.). 1991. pap. 11.95 (*1-56411-107-5*) Untd Bros & Sis.

— How to Eat to Live, Bk. I. 123p. (Orig.). reprint ed. pap. 8.95 (*1-56411-019-2*) Untd Bros & Sis.

— Message to the Blackman in America. 356p. (Orig.). pap. text ed. 24.90 (*1-56411-005-2*) Untd Bros & Sis.

— Our Saviour Has Arrived. 226p. reprint ed. pap. 11.95 (*1-56411-021-4*) Untd Bros & Sis.

— The Supreme Wisdom, Vol. 2. 96p. 1957. pap. 6.95 (*1-56411-080-X*) Untd Bros & Sis.

— The Supreme Wisdom: Solution to the So-Called Negroes' Problem. 56p. 1957. pap. 4.95 (*1-56411-079-6*) Untd Bros & Sis.

— The Theology of Time. 551p. (Orig.). 1992. pap. 24.95 (*1-56411-025-7*) Untd Bros & Sis.

— The Theology of Time. 551p. (Orig.). 1992. 49.95 (*1-56411-032-X*) Untd Bros & Sis.

— The Theology of Time, Vol. I. 170p. (Orig.). 1992. pap. 10.00 (*1-56411-028-1*) Untd Bros & Sis.

— The True History of Jesus. 37p. (Orig.). 1992. pap. 6.95 (*1-56411-047-8*) Coal Remb Elijah.

— The True History of Jesus: Religion. 37p. 1992. pap. text ed. 6.95 (*0-9632728-0-2*) Coal Remb Elijah.

Muhammad Farah. The Legal Status of Israel & the Occupied Territories. (Information Papers: No. 15). 60p. (Orig.). (C). 1975. pap. 1.00 (*0-937694-31-2*) Assn Arab-Amer U Grads.

Muhammad Fazl ur-Rahman Ansari. Quranic Foundations & Structure of Muslim Society, Vol. I. 445p. 1993. text ed. 65.00 (*1-56744-485-7*) Kazi Pubns.

— Quranic Foundations & Structure of Muslim Society, Vol. II. 445p. 1993. text ed. 69.00 (*1-56744-486-5*) Kazi Pubns.

Muhammad Ibn-Jusuf Al-Herewi. The Buhr-ool Juwahir (Bahr al-Gewahir) Mujeed, Hukem A., ed. 294p. reprint ed. write for info. (*0-318-71535-X*, Pub. by Georg Olms GW) Lubrecht & Cramer.

M

An Asterisk (*) at the beginning of an entry indicates that the title is appearing in BIP for the first time.

Muhammad Ibn Musa, Al K. The Algebra of Mohammed Ben Musa, 2 pts. in 1. Rosen, Frederic, ed. & tr. by. xvi, 208p. 1986. reprint ed. lib. bdg. 63.70 (*3-487-07722-1*, Pub. by Georg Olms GW) Lubrecht & Cramer.

Muhammad Ibn Yusuf, Abu'Umar. History of the Governors of Egypt. Koenig, Nicholas A., ed. LC 70-180364. (Columbia University. Contributions to Oriental History & Philology Ser.: No. 2). reprint ed. 20.00 (*0-404-50532-5*) AMS Pr.

Muhammad Iqbal Siddiqi. Asharah Mubasharah. 200p. (Orig.). 1990. pap. 9.95 (*1-56744-223-4*) Kazi Pubns.

Muhammad, Isam. Give Yourself Good Credit: The 7 Easy Steps to Help You Repair Your Credit. 2nd ed. Harrell, Willie, ed. (Illus.). 175p. 1993. 29.95 (*0-9637870-0-4*) Credit-Master.

Muhammad Khan Kayani. Islamic Perspective of History. 112p. (Orig.). 1989. pap. 9.95 (*1-56744-310-9*) Kazi Pubns.

Muhammad, Lateef. Welfare: A Novocain. Muhammad, Sabir K., ed. 75p. (Orig.). (C). 1991. lib. bdg. 5.00 (*0-9627663-1-3*) Designer Comns.

— Welfare, a Novocaine. 80p. 1991. pap. write for info. (*0-9630973-0-X*) Lateefs Pubns.

Muhammad, S. A., jt. auth. see Tax Practioners Association Staff.

Muhammad, S. Ifetayo. The Goals of a Polygamous Woman. 16p. (Orig.). (J). 1987. pap. 0.50 (*0-916157-11-3*) African Islam Miss Pubns.

— Vitamin A Through Zinc: An Alphabet of Good Health. 16p. (Orig.). (J). 1985. pap. 1.00 (*0-916157-13-X*) African Islam Miss Pubns.

Muhammad, Sabir K. The Need for Logic in Religion among African Americans. (Orig.). 1990. pap. text ed. 5.00 (*0-9627663-0-5*) Designer Comns.

Muhammad, Sabir K., ed. see Muhammad, Lateef.

***Muhammad, Sayf A.** Bani Unveiled, al- 156p. (Orig.). (C). 1995. pap. text ed. 12.95 (*0-934905-55-X*) Kazi Pubns.

Muhammad, Shan. The Growth of Muslim Politics in India. (C). 1991. 28.00 (*81-7024-418-8*, Pub. by Ashish II) S Asia.

***Muhammad, Silis.** Reparations Petition: For United Nations Assistance under Resolution 1503 (XLVIII) on Behalf of African-Americans in the United States of America. 23p. (Orig.). Date not set. pap. 5.00 (*1-56411-083-4*) Untd Bros & Sis.

Muhammad Soaleh Korejo. Frontier Gandhi: His Place in History. 272p. (C). 1993. 35.00 (*0-19-577461-2*) OUP.

Muhammad, Yolanda. Egyptian Echoes: Contemporary Art Inspired by Ancient Monuments. 32p. 1993. 15.00 (*0-9635774-0-9*) Sun Cities Art.

Muhammad Zafrulla Khan, tr. Gardens of the Righteous: Riyadh As Salihin of Imam Nawawi. 2nd ed. LC 89-3225. 332p. 1989. reprint ed. 19.95 (*0-940793-27-X*, Olive Branch Pr) Interlink Pub.

Muhammad Zubayr Siddiqi. Hadith Literature. 191p. 1995. pap. 10.95 (*0-946621-38-1*, Pub. by Islamic Texts UK) Atrium Pubs.

Muhammad'Abduh. The Theology of Unity. LC 79-52560. (Islam Ser.). 1980. reprint ed. lib. bdg. 19.95 (*0-8369-9267-9*) Ayer.

Muhammed H. al-Tabataba'i. Shi'ite Islam. Nasr, Seyyed H., tr. LC 74-8289. 253p. 1979. 59.50 (*0-87395-272-3*); pap. 19.95 (*0-87395-390-8*) State U NY Pr.

Muhanji, Cherry. Her. LC 90-47570. 225p. 1990. lib. bdg. 19.95 (*1-879960-03-6*); pap. 9.95 (*1-879960-02-8*) Aunt Lute Bks.

Muhawi, Ibrahim & Kanaana, Sharif. Speak, Bird, Speak Again: Palestinian Arab Folktales. 512p. 1988. pap. 17.00 (*0-520-06292-2*) U CA Pr.

Muhawi, Ibrahim, tr. see Darwish, Mahmoud.

Muhl, Barbara M. Along the Royal Road. (Anatomy of Spirituality Ser.: Vol. 2). 338p. (Orig.). 1992. pap. 18.95 (*1-880863-02-2*) Christus Pub. This book is the second half of the Principles & Practices of The Infinite Way. No one should be without these books....They will lead you to the God Experience... Barbara was, & is, a beloved student of Joel S. Goldsmith... Her teaching & writings are not separate nor apart from the Infinite Way, but a part of the whole." --Geri McDonald, The Infinite Way, Peoria, Arizona. *Publisher Provided Annotation.*

— The Anatomy of Spirituality, 10 vols. Set. pap. write for info. (*1-880863-00-6*) Christus Pub.

—The Royal Road to Reality. (Anatomy of Spirituality Ser.: Vol. 1). 352p. (Orig.). 1994. pap. 18.95 (*1-880863-01-4*) Christus Pub. This book lays the foundation for spiritual development according to the Principles & Practices of The Infinite Way. Second printing 1994. *Publisher Provided Annotation.*

—Script, Kid & Fantasyland: The Truth That Makes You Free. 1995. 18.95 (*0-615-00767-8*) Christus Pub. This book is the culmination of the immensely successful workshop classes of the same name, taught by the author since 1986. The acceptance & practice of the Principles & Steps of the SCRIPT, KID, & FANTASYLAND work that the book encompasses has drastically improved the quality of life & relationships for hundreds of people. The work is designed to "break the chains" which keep us in "bondage" to the painful (& unproductive) reactions & emotions we experience as human beings & which actually "block" love & spiritual unfoldment. By "clearing away the wreckage of the past once & for all" we free ourselves to experience an "unhindered" spiritual growth & as a result, a harmonious & loving human experience. THE TRUTH THAT MAKES YOU "REAL," IS THE TRUTH THAT MAKES YOU "FREE". $18.95 *Publisher Provided Annotation.*

—This Pilgrim's Progress: A Correspondence with Joel Goldsmith. 364p. (Orig.). 1991. pap. 18.95 (*1-880863-25-1*) Christus Pub. Barbara Mary Muhl, Infinite Way Teacher & practitioner since 1962, has published a new book, THIS PILGRIM'S PROGRESS: A CORRESPONDENCE WITH JOEL GOLDSMITH. The book tells the warm, personal story of her spiritual growth under Joel's guidance, & affords an intimate glimpse into the way a valid teacher deals with a serious student--bringing her from being a beginner to spiritual maturity. COMMENTS FROM READERS: "I felt the love. I cried & I laughed. The book has changed me."--E.W., Newhall, CA "This wonderful book will put at ease the students like me who thought they had to be "good" to go to God."--T.H., New York, NY "Joel's consciousness was oozing off the pages. I understand him now in a way I would not have thought possible."--R.W., Rancho Mirage, CA. *Publisher Provided Annotation.*

Muhlbacher, Hans, jt. auth. see Dahringer, Lee D.

Muhlbauer, Alfred, jt. auth. see Keller, Wolfgang.

Muhlbauer, Gene & Dodder, Laura. The Losers: Gang Delinquency in an American Suburb. LC 82-25497. 154p. 1983. text ed. 65.00 (*0-275-91048-2*, C1048, Praeger Pubs) Greenwood.

Muhlbauer, W. Kent. Pipeline Risk Management Manual. 276p. 1992. 65.00 (*0-88415-035-6*) Gulf Pub.

Muhlberger, Detlef. Hitler's Followers: Studies in the Sociology of the Nazi Movement. (Illus.). 288p. (C). 1991. text ed. 49.95 (*0-415-00802-6*, A5095) Routledge.

Muhlberger, Detlef, ed. The Social Basis of European Fascist Movements. LC 87-14093. 384p. 1987. lib. bdg. 49.95 (*0-7099-3585-4*, Pub. by Croom Helm UK) Routledge Chapman & Hall.

Muhlberger, Richard. Bible in Art: Old Testament. 1991. 19.99 (*0-517-03746-7*) Random Hse Value.

Muhlberger, Richard, text. What Makes a Bruegel a Bruegel? (Illus.). 48p. (J). (gr. 5 up). 1993. 9.95 (*0-670-85203-1*) Viking Child Bks.

— What Makes a Degas a Degas? (Illus.). 48p. (J). (gr. 5 up). 1993. 9.95 (*0-670-85205-8*) Viking Child Bks.

— What Makes a Monet a Monet? (Illus.). 48p. (J). (gr. 5 up). 1993. 9.95 (*0-670-85200-7*) Viking Child Bks.

— What Makes a Raphael a Raphael? (Illus.). 48p. (J). (gr. 5 up). 1993. 9.95 (*0-670-85204-X*) Viking Child Bks.

— What Makes a Rembrandt a Rembrandt? (Illus.). 48p. (J). (gr. 5 up). 1993. 9.95 (*0-670-85199-X*) Viking Child Bks.

— What Makes a van Gogh a van Gogh? (Illus.). 48p. (J). (gr. 5 up). 1993. 9.95 (*0-670-85198-1*) Viking Child Bks.

Muhle, P., et al. Dictionary of Agriculture, Forestry, Horticulture. 732p. (ENG & GER.). 1990. 141.00 (*0-444-98782-7*) Elsevier.

Muhle, Peter. Agriculture-Forestry-Horticulture Dictionary: English-German. 144p. (ENG & GER.). 1990. lib. bdg. 150.00 (*0-8288-3597-7*, F92570) Fr & Eur.

— Agriculture-Forestry-Horticulture Dictionary: English-German. 732p. (ENG & GER.). 1990. 225.00 (*0-7859-8516-6*, 3861170124) Fr & Eur.

— Dictionary of Wood Science & Technology: English-German - German-English. 466p. 1992. 183.00 (*3-87097-157-6*, Pub. by O Brandstetter Verlag GW) IBD Ltd.

— German-English Dictionary of Agriculture, Forestry & Horticulture. 731p. (ENG & GER.). 1993. write for info. (*0-7859-8774-6*) Fr & Eur.

— Landwirtschaft - Forstwirtschaft - Gartenbau: Englisch - Deutsch. 1991. 150.00 (*0-8288-2481-9*) Fr & Eur.

— Woerterbuch der Holzwirtschaft: English-German, German-English. 466p. (ENG & GER.). 1992. 225.00 (*0-7859-7067-3*) Fr & Eur.

Muhle, Peter, ed. German-English Dictionary of Agriculture, Forestry & Horticulture. 731p. (ENG & GER.). 1993. 168.00 (*3-86117-025-6*, Pub. by Verlag A Hatier GW) IBD Ltd.

***Muhlebach, Richard F.** Managing & Leasing Commercial Properties: Complex Issues. 1994 Supplement. 1994. pap. text ed. 45.00 (*0-471-30546-4*) Wiley.

Muhlebach, Richard F., jt. auth. see Alexander, Alan A.

***Muhleisen, Martin.** Human Capital Decay & Persistance. (C). 1994. pap. text ed. 52.50 (*0-8133-2239-1*) Westview.

***Muhleitner, Elke.** Biographisches Lexikon der Psychoanalyse. 400p. (GER.). 1992. 125.00 (*0-7859-8542-5*, 3892955573) Fr & Eur.

Muhlemann, A. P., et al. Production & Operations Management. 6th ed. 576p. (Orig.). 1992. pap. 57.50 (*0-273-03235-6*, Pub. by Pitman Pub Ltd UK) Trans-Atl Phila.

Muhlemann, Hans R. Introduction to Oral Preventive Medicine. (Illus.). 253p. 1976. text ed. 32.00 (*3-87652-591-8*) Quint Pub Co.

***Muhlenburg, Heinrich M.** The Correspondence of Heinrich Melchior Muhlenberg Vol. 2: 1748-1752. Lehmann, Helmut T. & Kleiner, John W., trs. 400p. Date not set. write for info. (*0-89725-227-6*, 494) Picton Pr.

Muhlenfeld, Elisabeth. Mary Boykin Chesnut: A Biography. LC 80-26610. (Southern Biography Ser.). (Illus.). 302p. (C). 1981. pap. 11.95 (*0-8071-1804-4*) La State U Pr.

Muhlenfeld, Elisabeth, jt. ed. see Woodward, C. Vann.

Muhlgassner, Dietlinde, tr. see Lichtenberger, Elisabeth.

Muhlhaus, J., jt. auth. see Tyutyunov, I.

***Muhlhauser, Max, ed.** Cooperative Computer-Aided Authoring & Learning: A Systems Approach. 351p. (C). 1994. lib. bdg. 95.00 (*0-7923-9527-1*) Kluwer Ac.

Muhlhausler, Peter & Harre, Rom. Pronouns & People: The Linguistic Construction of Social & Personal Identity. (Language in Society Ser.). 320p. 1990. text ed. 49.95 (*0-631-16592-4*) Blackwell Pubs.

Muhlstein, ed. see Proust, Marcel.

Muhlstein, Anka. La Salle: Explorer of the North American Frontier. Wood, Willard, tr. LC 94-47991. (Illus.). 256p. 1994. 22.95 (*1-55970-219-2*) Arcade Pub Inc.

— La Salle: Explorer of the North American Frontier. Wood, Willard, tr. LC 94-47991. (Illus.). 256p. 1995. pap. 11.95 (*1-55970-294-X*) Arcade Pub Inc.

Muhly, James D. Copper & Tin: The Distribution of Mineral Resources & the Nature of the Metals Trade in the Bronze Age, Including Supplement. (Connecticut Academy of Arts & Sciences Ser., Trans.: Vol. 43). 380p. 1973. pap. 69.50 (*0-685-22879-7*) Elliots Bks.

Muhly, Paul S., jt. ed. see Jorgensen, Palle E.

Muhr, C., et al. Frontiers in European Radiology, Vol. 3. (Illus.). 140p. 1983. 70.00 (*0-387-11446-7*) Spr-Verlag.

Muhrer, Verle, jt. ed. see Whitehead, Fred.

***Muhs, Joachim F.** How to Choose the Right Yacht. (Illus.). 128p. Date not set. pap. 18.50 (*0-7136-3950-4*) Sheridan.

Muhsin, Amina W. Qur'an & Woman. 1993. 6.95 (*967-65-1976-6*) OUP.

Mui, Hoh-cheung & Mui, Lorna H. Shops & Shopkeeping in Eighteenth-Century England. 400p. 1989. 55.00 (*0-7735-0620-9*, Pub. by McGill CN) U of Toronto Pr.

***Mui, Linda.** When You Can't Find Your UNIX System Administrator. 140p. 1995. pap. text ed. 19.95 (*1-56592-104-6*) OReilly & Assocs.

Mui, Linda & Pearce, Eric. X Window System Administrator's Guide, Vol. 8. O'Reilly, Tim, ed. (X Window System Ser.). (Illus.). 372p. (Orig.). 1992. pap. text ed. 29.95 (*0-937175-83-8*) OReilly & Assocs.

***Mui, Linda & Quercia, Valerie.** X User Tools. O'Reilly, Tim, ed. (Illus.). 856p. (Orig.). 1994. cd-rom 49.95 (*1-56592-019-8*) OReilly & Assocs.

Mui, Lorna H., jt. auth. see Mui, Hoh-cheung.

Mui, Peter, ed. see Lunde, Ken.

Muia, Paul J. Esthetic Restorations: Improved Dentist-Laboratory Communication. LC 92-48524. (Illus.). 1993. text ed. 98.00 (*0-86715-226-5*) Quint Pub Co.

Muilenbery. Aerobiology. 1995. write for info. (*0-87371-724-4*) Lewis Pubs.

Muilenburg, Grace & Swineford, Ada. Land of the Post Rock: Its Origins, History & People. LC 74-23833. (Illus.). xiv, 210p. 1975. pap. 9.95 (*0-7006-0194-5*) U Pr of KS.

Muiler, R., ed. see Popa, Constantin M.

Muillo. Enciclopedia Juvenil, 10 vols., Set. 1500p. (SPA.). (J). 1974. 295.00 (*0-8288-6034-3*, S50472) Fr & Eur.

Muimhneachain, Aindrias O., tr. see Buckley, Timothy.

Muinzer, Genevieve. New to the U. K. A Guide to Your Life & Rights in the U. K. 224p. 1987. 35.00 (*0-7102-0852-9*, 08529, RKP) Routledge.

Muinzer, L. A., tr. see Carling, Finn.

Muinzer, Louis, tr. see Hauger, Torill Thorstad.

Muinzer, Louis A., tr. see Carling, Finn.

Muir & Hubbell. Equine Anesthesia: Monitoring & Emergency Therapy. (Illus.). 528p. 1991. 67.00 (*0-8016-3576-4*) Mosby Yr Bk.

Muir, et al. Handbook of Veterinary Anesthesia. (Illus.). 352p. 1988. pap. text ed. 44.00 (*0-8016-3583-7*) Mosby Yr Bk.

Muir, Ada. Healing Herbs & Health Foods of the Zodiac. LC 92-37676. (Illus.). 192p. 1993. pap. 3.99 (*0-87542-575-5*) Llewellyn Pubns.

Muir, Alexander. From Aberdeen to Ottawa in Eighteen Forty-Five: The Diary of Alexander Muir. Mackenzie, George A., ed. (Illus.). 116p. 1990. pap. text ed. 12.00 (*0-08-037983-4*, Pub. by Aberdeen U Pr) Macmillan.

Muir, Alison, jt. auth. see Sinclair-House, Elizabeth.

Muir, Andrew F., ed. Texas in 1837. (Illus.). 264p. 1988. reprint ed. pap. 9.95 (*0-292-78099-0*) U of Tex Pr.

Muir, B. J. Leod: Six Old English Poems: A Handbook. xxxvi, 162p. 1989. 26.00 (*2-88124-357-6*) Gordon & Breach.

Muir, Bernard J. A Pre-Conquest English Prayer-Book: BL MSS Cotton Galba A.xiv & Nero A.ii. (Publications of the Henry Bradshaw Society Ser. No. XCIV (94)). 1987. 50.00 (*0-9501009-5-1*) Boydell & Brewer.

Muir, Bernard J., jt. ed. see Manion, Margaret M.

Muir, Bernice L. Pathophysiology: An Introduction to the Mechanisms of Disease. 2nd ed. LC 87-25298. 685p. 1988. text ed. 42.50 (*0-8273-4317-5*) Delmar.

Muir, Bryce & Muir, Margaret. Lawn Wars: Lawn Ornaments (A Field Guide) (Illus.). 32p. (Orig.). 1988. pap. 8.95 (*0-942396-55-3*) Blackberry ME.

Muir, Calum S. & Wagner, G. Directory of On-Going Research in Cancer Epidemiology 1981. (IARC Scientific Publications: No. 38). 696p. 1986. pap. 26.95 (*0-19-723038-5*) OUP.

— Directory of On-Going Research in Cancer Epidemiology 1982. (IARC Scientific Publications: No. 46). 722p. 1986. pap. 32.00 (*0-19-723046-6*) OUP.

Muir, Calum S. & Wagner, G., eds. Directory of On-Going Research in Cancer Epidemiology, 1984. (IARC Scientific Publications: No. 62). 748p. 1985. pap. 26.50 (*0-19-723062-8*) OUP.

Muir, Calum S., ed. see Wagner, G.

Muir, Calum S., et al, eds. Cancer Incidence in Five Continents, Vol. V. (IARC Scientific Publications: No. 88). 1010p. 1988. 120.00 (*92-832-1188-X*) OUP.

Muir, Caroline, jt. auth. see Muir, Charles.

Muir, Charles & Muir, Caroline. Freeing the Female Orgasm: Awakening the Goddess. 1993. 29.95 (*1-882570-03-0*) HI Goddess.

— Tantra: The Art of Conscious Loving. LC 88-7854. (Illus.). 134p. 1989. pap. 11.50 (*0-916515-86-9*) Mercury Hse Inc.

Muir, Chaun & Haynes, J. H. Haynes Honda ATCR Owners Workshop Manual, M798: '81 thru '85. pap. 16.95 (*1-85010-220-1*) Haynes Pubns.

Muir, Chaun, jt. auth. see Haynes, J. H.

Muir, D. How to Dance. (Ballroom Dance Ser.). 1986. lib. bdg. 79.95 (*0-8490-3361-6*) Gordon Pr.

— How to Dance. (Ballroom Dance Ser.). 1985. lib. bdg. 74.00 (*0-87700-699-7*) Revisionist Pr.

Muir, Dan & Williams, Jon. Corporate Images: Photography & the Dupont Company, 1865-1972. 72p. 1984. pap. 5.00 (*0-914650-24-6*) Hagley Museum.

Muir, Dorothy T. Mount Vernon: The Civil War Years. 1993. pap. 10.95 (*0-931917-26-3*) Mt Vernon Ladies.

Muir, Douglas A. & Puzo, Michael J. Massachusetts Corporations. LC 79-92872. (Practice Systems Library Manual). ring bd. 120.00 (*0-317-03186-4*) Lawyers Cooperative.

— Massachusetts Corporations. suppl. ed. LC 79-92872. (Practice Systems Library Manual). 1993. 69.50 (*0-317-03187-2*) Lawyers Cooperative.

Muir, E. Politics of King Lear. LC 76-99171. (Studies in Shakespeare: No. 24). 1970. reprint ed. lib. bdg. 49.95 (*0-8383-0331-5*) M S G Haskell Hse.

Muir, Edward. Civic Ritual in Renaissance Venice. LC 80-8568. (Illus.). 376p. 1986. pap. 19.95 (*0-691-10200-7*) Princeton U Pr.

— The Leopold Von Ranke Manuscript Collection of Syracuse University: The Complete Catalogue. 240p. 1983. text ed. 70.00x (*0-8156-2294-5*) Syracuse U Pr.

— Mad Blood Stirring: Vendetta & Factions in Friuli During the Renaissance. LC 92-15211. 424p. 1993. text ed. 45.00 (*0-8018-4446-0*) Johns Hopkins.

Muir, Edward & Ruggiero, Guido, eds. History from Crime. Curry, Corrada B. et al, trs. LC 93-32009. (Selections from Quaderni Storici Ser.). 1994. 37.50 (*0-8018-4732-X*); pap. 14.95 (*0-8018-4733-8*) Johns Hopkins.

— Microhistory & the Lost Peoples of Europe. LC 90-27638. (Selections from Quaderni Storici Ser.). 240p. 1991. text ed. 35.00 (*0-8018-4182-8*); pap. text ed. 14.95x (*0-8018-4183-6*) Johns Hopkins.

— Sex & Gender in Historical Perspective. Gallucci, Margaret A. et al, trs. LC 90-31730. (Selections from Quaderni Storici Ser.). 264p. 1990. text ed. 35.00 (*0-8018-3991-2*); pap. text ed. 14.95x (*0-8018-4072-4*) Johns Hopkins.

Muir, Edwin. An Autobiography. (Memoir Ser.). 320p. (C). 1990. reprint ed. pap. 10.95 (*1-55597-128-8*) Graywolf.

— The Estate of Poetry. LC 92-39289. (Discovery Ser.). 144p. 1993. pap. 11.00 (*1-55597-182-2*) Graywolf.

— John Knox: Portrait of a Calvinist. LC 76-148892. (Select Bibliographies Reprint Ser.). 1977. reprint ed. 23.95 (*0-8369-5656-7*) Ayer.

— The Politics of King Lear. 1972. 200.00 (*0-87968-032-6*) Gordon Pr.

— The Story & the Fable: An Autobiography. LC 87-60854. 272p. 1987. reprint ed. pap. 13.95 (*0-937672-22-X*) Rowan Tree.

— Transition: Essays on Contemporary Literature. (BCL1-PR English Literature Ser.). 218p. 1992. reprint ed. lib. bdg. 79.00 (*0-7812-7061-8*) Rprt Serv.

Muir, Edwin, tr. see Broch, Hermann.

Muir, Edwin, tr. see Kafka, Franz.

***Muir, Elizabeth G. & Whiteley, Marilyn F., eds.** Changing Roles of Women Within the Christian Church in Canada. (Illus.). 376p. 1995. 60.00 (*0-8020-0669-8*) U of Toronto Pr.

— Changing Roles of Women Within the Christian Church in Canada. (Illus.). 376p. 1995. pap. 24.95 (*0-8020-7623-8*) U of Toronto Pr.

Muir, F. A., jt. auth. see Sharp, D.

Muir, Frank, ed. The Oxford Book of Humorous Prose. 200p. 1992. pap. 17.95 (*0-19-282959-9*) OUP.

An Asterisk (*) at the beginning of an entry indicates that the title is appearing in BIP for the first time.

— The Oxford Book of Humorous Prose: From William Caxton to P. G. Wodehouse. 1200p. 1990. 39.95 (0-19-214106-6) OUP.

Muir, Frank & Norden, Denis. Oh, My Word! 128p. 1981. 7.95 (0-416-00811-9, NO. 0235) Routledge Chapman & Hall.

Muir, Fredric J. A Reason for Hope: Liberation Theology Confronts a Liberal Faith. LC 93-86732. 160p. (Orig.). (C). 1994. pap. 10.00 (0-931104-39-4) Sunflower Ink.

Muir, Hazel, ed. Larousse Dictionary of Scientists. LC 94-75739. 608p. 1994. 35.00 (0-7523-0002-4) LKC.

***Muir, Helen.** Frost in Florida: A Memoir. Seibel, Mark, ed. (Illus.). 208p. 1995. 19.95 (0-9633461-6-4) Valiant Pr.

— Miami, U. S. A. 2nd ed. (Illus.). 360p. 1990. 39.95 (0-940495-19-8) Pickering Pr.

Muir, Holly J. Conducting a Preliminary Benchmarking Analysis: A Librarian's Guide. 32p. 1993. pap. text ed. 24.00 (1-884935-12-5) Lib Benchmarking.

— Conducting & Analyzing Benchmarking Data: A Librarian's Guide. 42p. 1994. pap. text ed. 31.50 (1-884935-15-X) Lib Benchmarking.

— Developing Benchmarking Metrics: A Librarian's Guide. 48p. 1993. pap. text ed. 36.00 (1-884935-13-3) Lib Benchmarking.

— Identifying Benchmarking Partners: Academic, Public & School Libraries. 35p. 1994. pap. text ed. 26.25 (1-884935-17-6) Lib Benchmarking.

— Identifying Benchmarking Partners: Special Libraries. 66p. 1993. pap. text ed. 49.50 (1-884935-14-1) Lib Benchmarking.

— Presenting Benchmarking Results: A Librarian's Guide. 44p. 1994. pap. text ed. 33.00 (1-884935-16-8) Lib Benchmarking.

Muir, I. D. The Four-Axis Universal Stage, Vol. 49. LC 80-83455. (Illus.). 1981. 20.00 (0-904962-08-3) Microscope Pubns.

Muir, I. F., et al. Burns & Their Treatment. 3rd ed. (Illus.). 192p. 1987. pap. text ed. 95.00 (0-407-00333-9) Buttrwrth-Heinemann.

Muir, Ian. Plastic Surgery in Pedeatrics. 1988. 116.00 (0-316-58944-6) Little.

Muir, J. E. & Roberts, Ronald. Recent Developments in Aquaculture, No. 4. (Illus.). 450p. 1993. 124.95 (0-632-02898-X) Blackwell Sci.

Muir, J. Gordon, ed. see Reisman, Judith A. & Eichel, Edward W.

Muir, J. Gordon, ed. see Reisman, Judith & Eichel, Edward.

Muir, J. V. Homer: Odyssey IX Text & Commentary. 80p. 1980. 16.95 (0-906515-61-0, Pub. by Brstl Class Pr UK) Focus Info Gr.

Muir, J. V., jt. ed. see Easterling, P. E.

***Muir, Janette.** Introduction to Oral Communication Handbook. 96p. (C). 1994. 12.95 (0-8403-9635-X) Kendall-Hunt.

Muir, Janette K. Introduction to Interpersonal & Small Group Communication Handbook. 176p. 1993. per. 17.95 (0-8403-8887-X) Kendall-Hunt.

Muir, Janette K., ed. C-SPAN in the Communication Classroom: Theories & Application. LC 92-61675. 112p. (C). 1992. pap. text ed. 17.95 (0-944811-09-4) Speech Commun Assn.

Muir, Janette K. & Muir, Star A. Foundations of Public Communication Workbook. 240p. 1993. per. 35.95 (0-8403-8920-5) Kendall-Hunt.

Muir, Jim. Little Girls Have to Sleep. LC 92-37456. (Illus.). (J). 1994. 16.00 (1-881320-03-0) Black Belt Pr.

Muir, John. The Cruise of the Corwin. LC 92-25139. (John Muir Library). (Illus.). 240p. (Orig.). 1993. pap. 10.00 (0-87156-523-4) Sierra.

— The Discovery of Glacier Bay (1879) Jones, William R., ed. (Illus.). 16p. 1978. reprint ed. pap. 3.95 (0-89646-045-2) Vistabooks.

— How to Keep Your Volkswagen Alive: A Manual of Step by Step Procedures for the Compleat Idiot. 15th ed. (Illus.). 464p. Date not set. pap. 21.95 (1-56261-070-8) John Muir.

— How to Keep Your Volkswagen Alive: A Manual of Step by Step Procedures for the Complete Idiot. 25th rev. ed. (Illus.). 464p. 1994. spiral bd. 25.00 (1-56261-190-9) John Muir.

— The Hummingbird of the California Waterfalls. Jones, William R., ed. (Illus.). 24p. 1977. reprint ed. pap. 3.95 (0-89646-019-3) Vistabooks.

— In the Heart of the California Alps. Jones, William R., ed. (Illus.). 24p. 1977. reprint ed. pap. 3.95 (0-89646-026-6) Vistabooks.

— Industrial Relations Procedures & Agreements. 200p. 1981. text ed. 61.95 (0-566-02275-3) Ashgate Pub Co.

— John Muir: The Eight Wilderness Discovery Books. LC 92-53740. 1056p. 1992. 35.00 (0-89886-335-X) Mountaineers.

— John of the Mountains: The Unpublished Journals of John Muir. (American Biography Ser.). 459p. 1991. reprint ed. lib. bdg. 89.00 (0-7812-8292-6) Rprt Serv.

— Letters from Alaska. Engberg, Robert & Merrell, Bruce, eds. LC 93-18845. (Illus.). 128p. (Orig.). (C). 1993. lib. bdg. 30.00 (0-299-13950-6); pap. 12.95 (0-299-13954-9) U of Wis Pr.

— Letters to a Friend: Written to Mrs. Ezra S. Carr, 1866-1879. 200p. 1990. reprint ed. 14.95 (0-87797-224-9) Cherokee.

— The Mountains of California. LC 88-16318. (Illus.). 1988. 22.95 (1-55591-034-3) Fulcrum Pub.

— The Mountains of California. LC 88-23938. (John Muir Library). (Illus.). 304p. 1989. pap. 10.00 (0-87156-663-X) Sierra.

— Mountains of California. (Reprints Ser.). (Illus.). 389p. 1989. 19.95 (0-88029-267-9) Dorset Pr.

— Mountains of California. (American Library). 272p. 1985. pap. 7.95 (0-14-039038-3, Penguin Classics) Viking Penguin.

— The Mountains of California. 1992. reprint ed. lib. bdg. 75.00 (0-7812-5067-6) Rprt Serv.

— The Mountains of California. (Illus.). 400p. 1977. reprint ed. pap. 9.95 (0-89815-446-4) Ten Speed Pr.

— Mountains of California. LC 90-47833. (Illus.). 406p. 1990. reprint ed. 29.95 (0-87797-191-9) Cherokee.

— My First Summer in the Sierra. 1992. 19.50 (0-8446-6523-1) Peter Smith.

— My First Summer in the Sierra. LC 89-6081. (Illus.). 208p. 1990. 35.00 (0-87156-600-1); pap. 10.00 (0-87156-748-2) Sierra.

— My First Summer in the Sierra. (Nature Library). 292p. 1987. pap. 9.95 (0-14-017001-4, Penguin Bks) Viking Penguin.

— My First Summer in the Sierra. LC 90-47834. (Illus.). 361p. 1990. reprint ed. 29.95 (0-87797-192-7) Cherokee.

— My First Summer in the Sierra. (BCL1 - United States Local History Ser.). 353p. 1991. reprint ed. lib. bdg. 89.00 (0-7812-6342-5) Rprt Serv.

— Our National Parks. LC 01-26282. 1901. 10.00 (0-403-00194-3) Scholarly.

— Our National Parks. LC 90-45254. (John Muir Library). (Illus.). 296p. 1991. pap. 10.00 (0-87156-626-5) Sierra.

— Our National Parks. LC 70-120568. reprint ed. 22.50 (0-404-04516-2) AMS Pr.

— Our National Parks. 1988. reprint ed. lib. bdg. 49.00 (0-7812-0771-1) Rprt Serv.

— Our National Parks. LC 80-53957. 394p. 1981. reprint ed. 29.50 (0-299-08590-2); reprint ed. pap. 10.95 (0-299-08594-5) U of Wis Pr.

— Our Yosemite National Park. Jones, William R., ed. (Illus.). 96p. (Orig.). 1980. reprint ed. pap. 5.95 (0-89646-061-4) Vistabooks.

— The Proposed Yosemite National Park: Treasures & Features. Jones, William R., ed. (Illus.). 64p. 1976. reprint ed. pap. text ed. 3.95 (0-89646-077-0) Vistabooks.

— Rambles of a Botanist among the Plants & Climates of California. (Illus.). 43p. 1974. 10.00 (0-87093-301-9) Dawsons.

— A Rival of the Yosemite: The Canon of the South Fork of King's River, California. Jones, William R., ed. (Illus.). 24p. 1977. reprint ed. pap. 3.95 (0-89646-010-X) Vistabooks.

— Sierra Big Trees. abr. ed. Jones, William R., ed. (Illus.). 80p. 1981. reprint ed. pap. 4.95 (0-89646-069-X) Vistabooks.

— Songs & Seeds: A Journal with John Muir. 150p. 1996. pap. 12.00 (0-945519-17-6) Mountn Meadw Pr.

— South of Yosemite: Selected Writings of John Muir. Gunsky, Frederic, ed. LC 88-40000. (Illus.). 144p. 1988. pap. 15.95 (0-89997-095-8) Wilderness Pr.

— Steep Trails. LC 93-25661. (John Muir Library). 304p. 1994. pap. 10.00 (0-87156-535-8) Sierra.

— Steep Trails. (BCL1 - United States Local History Ser.). 390p. 1991. reprint ed. lib. bdg. 89.00 (0-7812-6326-3) Rprt Serv.

— Stickeen. 1989. 8.95 (1-55709-112-9) Applewood.

— Stickeen. (Illus.). 96p. 1991. reprint ed. lib. bdg. 23.00x (0-8095-4961-1) Borgo Pr.

— Stickeen. LC 90-84443. (Illus.). 96p. 1990. reprint ed. pap. 6.95 (0-930588-48-7) Heyday Bks.

— Stickeen: An Adventure with a Dog & a Glacier. (Illus.). 1978. reprint ed. pap. 3.95 (0-89646-032-0) Vistabooks.

— Story of My Boyhood & Youth. (Illus.). 246p. 1965. reprint ed. pap. 12.95 (0-299-03654-5) U of Wis Pr.

— Thomas Carlyle's Apprenticeship. LC 79-116797. (English Biography Ser.: No. 31). 1970. reprint ed. lib. bdg. 49.95 (0-8383-1039-7) M S G Haskell Hse.

— A Thousand-Mile Walk to the Gulf. (Illus.). 256p. 1981. pap. 12.95 (0-395-31542-5) HM.

— A Thousand-Mile Walk to the Gulf. (BCL1 - United States Local History Ser.). 219p. 1991. reprint ed. lib. bdg. 79.00 (0-7812-6291-7) Rprt Serv.

— A Thousand-Mile Walk to the Gulf. LC 91-30471. (John Muir Library). (Illus.). 160p. 1992. reprint ed. pap. 10.00 (0-87156-591-9) Sierra.

— A Thousand-Mile Walk to the Gulf. (Nature Library). 240p. 1992. reprint ed. pap. 12.00 (0-14-017017-0, Penguin Bks) Viking Penguin.

— A Thousand Mile Walk to the Gulf. LC 90-47830. (Illus.). 246p. 1990. reprint ed. 24.95 (0-87797-193-5) Cherokee.

— Travels in Alaska. LC 77-19358. (Illus.). reprint ed. 32.50 (0-404-16075-1) AMS Pr.

— Travels in Alaska. LC 77-19358. 1979. reprint ed. pap. 11.95 (0-395-28522-4) HM.

— Travels in Alaska. 1988. reprint ed. lib. bdg. 49.00 (0-7812-0154-3) Rprt Serv.

— Travels in Alaska. (BCL1 - United States Local History Ser.). 326p. 1991. reprint ed. lib. bdg. 89.00 (0-7812-6345-X) Rprt Serv.

— Travels in Alaska. LC 70-145196. 1915. reprint ed. 59.00 (0-403-01120-5) Scholarly.

— Travels in Alaska. LC 87-26311. (John Muir Library). 352p. 1988. reprint ed. pap. 10.00 (0-87156-783-0) Sierra.

— The Wild Sheep. Jones, William R., ed. (Illus.). 32p. 1977. reprint ed. pap. 3.95 (0-89646-017-7) Vistabooks.

— Yellowstone National Park. (Illus.). 1978. pap. 4.95 (0-89646-079-7) Vistabooks.

— The Yosemite. 1992. reprint ed. lib. bdg. 75.00 (0-7812-5068-4) Rprt Serv.

— The Yosemite. LC 87-23573. (John Muir Library). (Illus.). 288p. 1988. reprint ed. pap. 10.00 (0-87156-782-2) Sierra.

Muir, John & Sierra Club Staff. The Story of My Boyhood & Youth. LC 88-23988. (John Muir Library). (Illus.). 176p. 1989. pap. 10.00 (0-87156-749-0) Sierra.

Muir, John, jt. auth. see Austin, Mary.

Muir, John G. Classroom Clangers. 64p. (C). 1989. 20.00 (0-903065-49-5, Pub. by G Wright Pub Ltd) St Mut.

— More Classroom Clangers. 64p. (C). 1989. 20.00 (0-903065-54-1, Pub. by G Wright Pub Ltd) St Mut.

Muir, Karen L. The Strongest Part of the Family: A Study of Lao Refugee Women in Columbus, Ohio. LC 87-45782. (Immigrant Communities & Ethnic Minorities in the U. S. & Canada Ser.: No. 17). 1988. 38.50 (0-404-19427-3) AMS Pr.

Muir, Kenneth. Last Periods of Shakespeare, Racine, Ibsen. LC 60-9132. 126p. reprint ed. pap. 36.00 (0-7837-3677-0, 2043551) Bks Demand.

— Shakespeare: Contrasts & Controversies. LC 85-40473. 208p. 1985. 29.95 (0-8061-1940-3) U of Okla Pr.

— Shakespeare Survey, 40 vols., Set. 1986. 1,600.00 (0-317-52152-7, Pub. by S Chand II) St Mut.

Muir, Kenneth, comp. Richard II. 1988. pap. 3.50 (0-451-52217-6, Sig Classics) NAL-Dutton.

Muir, Kenneth, ed. Elizabethan Lyrics. LC 79-75715. (Granger Index Reprint Ser.). 1977. 19.95 (0-8369-6032-7) Ayer.

Muir, Kenneth & O'Loughlin, Sean. The Voyage to Illyria: A New Study of Shakespeare. LC 79-128891. (Select Bibliographies Reprint Ser.). 1977. reprint ed. 19.95 (0-8369-5511-0) Ayer.

Muir, Kenneth & Wells, Stanley, eds. Aspects of King Lear: Articles Reprinted from Shakespeare Survey. LC 82-4344. (Illus.). 111p. reprint ed. pap. 31.70 (0-8357-5797-8, 2030611) Bks Demand.

Muir, Kenneth, tr. see Calderon de la Barca, Pedro.

Muir, Kenneth, ed. see Shakespeare, William.

Muir, Kenneth, et al, eds. Shakespeare: Man of the Theater. LC 82-40346. (Illus.). 272p. 1983. 38.50 (0-87413-217-7) U Delaware Pr.

***Muir, Kerry, ed.** Childsplay: A Collection of Scenes & Monologues for Children. (Illus.). 200p. (Orig.). (J). 1995. pap. 10.00 (0-87910-188-1) Limelight Edns.

Muir-Leresche, Kay, jt. ed. see Valdes, Alberto.

Muir, Lucy. Highland Rivalry. (Regency Romance Ser.: No. 43). 1991. pap. 2.75 (0-373-31143-5) Harlequin Bks.

***Muir, Lynette R.** The Biblical Drama of Medieval Europe. (Illus.). 368p. (C). 1995. 59.95 (0-521-41291-9) Cambridge U Pr.

Muir, M. M. A History of Chemical Theories & Laws. LC 74-26279. (History, Philosophy & Sociology of Science Ser.). 1975. reprint ed. 41.95 (0-405-06606-6) Ayer.

— The Story of Alchemy & the Beginnings of Chemistry. 208p. 1992. reprint ed. pap. 18.95 (1-56459-019-4) Kessinger Pub.

***Muir, M. M. P.** The Alchemical Essence: An Episode in the Quest for the Unchanging. 1994. pap. 8.95 (1-55818-291-8) Holmes Pub.

***Muir, Malcolm, Jr.** Black Shoes & Blue Water: Surface Warfare in the United States Navy, 1945-1975. LC 95-2964. (Contributions to Naval History Ser.: No. 6). 1995. pap. write for info. (0-945274-31-9) Naval Hist Ctr.

Muir, Marcie & White, Kerry. Australian Children's Books: A Bibliography 1788-1988, 2 vols., Set. 1993. 220.00 (0-522-84431-6) Intl Spec Bk.

Muir, Margaret, jt. auth. see Muir, Bryce.

Muir, Marie A. The Environmental Contexts of AIDS. LC 90-7705. 232p. 1991. text ed. 49.95 (0-275-93618-X, C3618, Praeger Pubs) Greenwood.

Muir, Matthew M. The Story of Alchemy & the Beginnings of Chemistry. LC 79-8618. reprint ed. 27.50 (0-404-18482-0) AMS Pr.

Muir, Michael. Fantastic Journey Through Minds & Machines, 2 disks, Set. (YA). (gr. 9-12). 1990. 5.25 hd, pap. text ed. 19.95 (0-924667-74-5) Intl Society Tech Educ.

Muir, Pamela B. NATARS II: Airline Reservations Systems Training. LC 93-25895. 1993. pap. text ed. 52.00 (0-13-613514-5) P-H.

Muir, Percy. Minding My Own Business: An Autobiography. (Illus.). 256p. 1991. reprint ed. 35.00 (0-938768-28-X) Oak Knoll.

Muir, R. M., jt. ed. see Addis, T. R.

Muir, Rachel. Lisa: The Story of a Young Jewish Girl in a Siberian Labor Camp During World War Two. LC 90-83109. 224p. (Orig.). 1991. pap. 14.95 (1-55618-088-8) Brunswick Pub.

Muir, Ramsay. America the Golden. LC 73-13145. (Foreign Travelers in America, 1810-1935 Ser.). 156p. 1974. reprint ed. 15.95 (0-405-05469-6) Ayer.

Muir, Richard. The Villages of England. LC 91-66265. (Illus.). 224p. 1992. 27.50 (0-500-01529-5) Thames Hudson.

Muir, Richard & Paddison, Ronan. Politics, Geography & Behavior. 1981. pap. 13.95 (0-416-31340-X, NO. 3460) Routledge Chapman & Hall.

Muir, Roy & May, Jerry. Developing an Effective Major Gift Program: From Managing Staff to Soliciting Gifts. 1993. pap. 37.00 (0-89964-302-7) Coun Adv & Supp Ed.

Muir, Star A., jt. auth. see Muir, Janette K.

Muir, Theda, ed. see Baxter, Ellen.

Muir, Vic. Lawn Bowls Straight from the Shoulder. 140p. (C). 1990. pap. 36.00 (0-9589209-0-7, Pub. by Boolarong Pubns AT) St Mut.

Muir, Virginia, jt. auth. see Taylor, Ken.

Muir, Virginia J. The One Year Bible Story Book. (Illus.). 384p. (J). (gr. 5 up). 1988. 12.99 (0-8423-2631-6) Tyndale.

Muir, Virginia J., jt. auth. see Talbot, Carol T.

Muir, W. The Caliphate. 624p. 1984. 280.00 (1-85077-014-X, Darf Pubs Ltd) St Mut.

— Mahomet & Islam. 256p. 1986. 220.00 (1-85077-085-9, Darf Pubs Ltd) St Mut.

Muir, W. M. & Hubbell, John. Handbook of Veterinary Anesthesia. 2nd ed. LC 94-24404. 425p. 1994. pap. 39.95 (0-8016-7656-8) Mosby Yr Bk.

Muir, Warren & Underwood, Joanna. Promoting Hazardous Waste Reduction: Six Steps States Can Take. 24p. 1987. pap. 3.50 (0-918780-45-4) INFORM NY.

Muir, Willa, tr. see Broch, Hermann.

Muir, Willa, tr. see Kafka, Franz.

Muir, William. Annals of the Early Caliphate from Original Sources. 1977. lib. bdg. 59.95 (0-8490-1434-4) Gordon Pr.

— The Caliphate: Its Rise, Decline, & Fall. LC 74-180365. reprint ed. 52.50 (0-404-56305-8) AMS Pr.

— The Life of Mohammad from Original Sources. rev. ed. Weir, Thomas H., ed. LC 78-180366. reprint ed. 57.50 (0-404-56306-6) AMS Pr.

— The Mameluke or, Slave Dynasty of Egypt, 1260-1517. LC 71-180367. reprint ed. 28.50 (0-404-56307-4) AMS Pr.

Muir, William, ed. Notices from the Local Records of Dysart. LC 73-164819. (Maitland Club, Glasgow. Publications: No. 73). reprint ed. 12.50 (0-404-53110-5) AMS Pr.

Muir, William & Kraus, Bernard. Marion: A History of the United States Watch Company. Fuller, Eugene T., ed. LC 85-61588. (Illus.). 218p. 1985. 24.15 (0-9614984-0-4) Natl Assn Watch & Clock.

Muir, William A. Christmas Traditions. LC 89-29237. 179p. 1992. reprint ed. lib. bdg. 42.00 (1-55888-895-0) Omnigraphics Inc.

Muir, William K. The Bully Pulpit: The Presidential Leadership of Ronald Reagan. 275p. 1992. 22.95 (1-55815-167-2) ICS Pr.

Muir, William K., Jr. Police: Streetcorner Politicians. LC 76-8085. (Illus.). 1979. 11.95 (0-226-54632-2); pap. text ed. 14.95 (0-226-54633-0, P825) U Ch Pr.

Muir Wood, A. M. Coastal Hydraulics. 200p. 1969. text ed. 169.00 (0-677-61680-5) Gordon & Breach.

Muira, Ayako. Shiokari Pass. 1968. 4.95 (9971-972-23-9) OMF Bks.

***Muirden.** How Do We Know about the Universe? 1995. 22.80 (0-8114-4884-3) Raintree Steck-V.

Muirden, B. M. Puzzled Patriots: The Story of the Australia First Movement. 1968. 27.50 (0-522-83907-X) Intl Spec Bk.

***Muirden, James.** About the Universe? LC 94-27356. (How Do We Know Ser.). (J). (gr. 1-8). 1995. lib. bdg. write for info. (0-8114-3884-8) Raintree Steck-V.

— How to Use an Astronomical Telescope: A Beginner's Guide to Observing the Cosmos. 1988. pap. 14.00 (0-671-66404-2, Fireside) S&S Trade.

— Planets. LC 93-51250. (Little Library). (Illus.). 32p. (J). (gr. 2-5). 1994. 3.95 (1-85697-507-X, Kingfisher LKC) LKC.

— Stars & Planets. LC 93-20104. (Visual Factfinders Ser.). (Illus.). 96p. (J). (gr. 5 up). 1993. 15.95 (1-85697-852-4, Kingfisher LKC); pap. 9.95 (1-85697-851-6, Kingfisher LKC) LKC.

Muirden, James, ed. The Sky Watcher's Handbook: The Expert Reference Source for the Non-Professional Astronomer. LC 92-32996. 1995. text ed. write for info. (0-7167-4502-X) W H Freeman.

Muirhead, B. W. The Development of Postwar Canadian Trade Policy: The Failure of the Anglo-European Option. 224p. 1992. 42.95 (0-7735-0922-4, Pub. by McGill CN) U of Toronto Pr.

Muirhead, C. Diary of a Bomb Aimer. 160p. (C). 1991. 65.00 (0-946771-75-8, Pub. by Spellmount UK) St Mut.

***Muirhead, Desmond & Rando, Guy L.** Golf Course Development & Real Estate. 192p. 1994. pap. text ed. 39.95 (0-87420-762-2, G03) Urban Land.

Muirhead, H. Notes on Elementary Particle Physics. 264p. (C). 1971. 113.00 (0-08-016550-8, Pub. by Pergamon Repr UK) Franklin.

— Physics of Elementary Particles. LC 64-15737. 1965. 303.00 (0-08-010674-9, Pub. by Pergamon Repr UK) Franklin.

Muirhead, James. Historical Introduction to the Private Law of Rome. 2nd ed. Goudy, Henry, ed. (Illus.). xxv, 457p. 1985. reprint ed. lib. bdg. 37.50 (0-8377-0821-4) Rothman.

— The Institutes of Gaius & Rules of Ulpian: The Former from Studemund's Apograph of the Verona Codex. LC 93-79718. 658p. 1994. reprint ed. 140.00 (1-56169-076-7) W W Gaunt.

Muirhead, James F. America, the Land of Contrasts: A Briton's View of His American Kin. LC 74-87430. (American Scene Ser.). Orig. Title: Bodley Head. 1970. reprint ed. lib. bdg. 37.50 (0-306-71576-7) Da Capo.

Muirhead, John H. Rule & End in Morals. LC 74-99665. (Select Bibliographies Reprint Ser.). 1977. 19.95 (0-8369-5094-1) Ayer.

Muirhead, Robb J. Aspects of Multivariate Statistical Theory. LC 82-1912. (Probability & Mathematical Statistics Ser.). 673p. 1982. text ed. 144.00 (0-471-09442-0, Wiley-Interscience) Wiley.

***Muirhead, Sara.** I Was a Country Girl. (American Autobiography Ser.). 211p. 1995. reprint ed. lib. bdg. 79.00 (0-7812-8598-4) Rprt Serv.

Muirhead, Thomas, jt. auth. see Maxwell, Robert.

Muirhead-Thomson, E. C. Behaviour Patterns of Blood-Sucking Flies. LC 81-21019. (Illus.). 240p. 1982. 102.00 (0-08-025497-7, Pub. by Pergamon Repr UK) Franklin.

Muirhead-Thomson, R. C. Pesticide Impact on Stream Fauna: With Special Reference to Macroinvertebrates. LC 86-20696. (Illus.). 288p. 1987. 69.95 (0-521-30967-0) Cambridge U Pr.

Muirhead-Thomson, R. C., ed. Trap Responses of Flying Insects: The Influence of Trap Design on Capture Efficiency. (Illus.). 287p. 1991. text ed. 77.00 (0-12-509755-7) Acad Pr.

Muise, D. A., ed. A Reader's Guide to Canadian History, No. 1: Beginnings to Confederation. 256p. 1982. pap. 14.95 (0-8020-6442-6) U of Toronto Pr.

Muise, D. A., jt. ed. see Forbes, E. R.

Muise, O., tr. see Walter, H.

Muise, Richard. R-C Car Painting & Finishing Techniques. 30p. (Orig.). 1992. pap. 7.95 (*0-911295-19-4*) Air Age.

Muise, Roxana. The Fourth Sign: A New Image. 25p. (Orig.). 1989. pap. text ed. 4.00 (*0-939625-01-6*) S West Astrology Cnfrnce.

Muisener, Philip P. Understanding & Treating Adolescent Substance Abuse. LC 93-32463. (Sourcebooks for the Human Services Ser.: Vol. 27). (C). 1993. text ed. 49.95 (*0-8039-4275-3*); pap. text ed. 24.00 (*0-8039-4276-1*) Sage.

Mujahid, Abdulmalik. Conversion to Islam: Untouchables Strategy for Protest in India. LC 88-2445. 1989. 16.95 (*0-89012-050-1*) Anima Pubns.

***Mujahid, Sharif A.** Quaid-I-Azam Jinnah: Studies in Interpretation. (C). 1993. 22.00x (*81-85557-04-7*, Pub. by Low Price II) S Asia.

Mujal-Leon, Eusebio. Communism & Political Change in Spain. LC 81-48616. 288p. 1983. 35.00 (*0-253-31389-9*) Ind U Pr.

— The Cuban University under the Revolution. (Occasional Paper Ser.: No. 25). 70p. (Orig.). (C). 1988. pap. 5.00 (*0-317-90486-8*) Cuban Amer Natl Fndtn.

— The Cuban University under the Revolution. 70p. (Orig.). 1988. pap. 14.95 (*0-935501-14-2*) U Miami N-S Ctr.

— European Socialism & the Conflict in Central America. LC 88-35952. (Washington Papers: No. 138). 144p. 1989. text ed. 45.00 (*0-275-93238-9*, C3238, Praeger Pubs); pap. text ed. 12.95 (*0-275-93239-7*, B3239, Praeger Pubs) Greenwood.

Mujal-Leon, Eusebio, ed. The U. S. S. R. & Latin America: A Developing Relationship. 288p. 1989. text ed. 39.95 (*0-04-445165-2*) Routledge Chapman & Hall.

Mujal-Leon, Eusebio M., jt. ed. see Penniman, Howard R.

Mujeed, Hukem A., ed. see Muhammad Ibn-Jusuf Al-Herewi.

***Mujica.** Antologia de la Literatura Espanola, from Seventeen Hundred Siglos Eighteen & Nineteen 2 Vol. Set. Date not set. pap. text ed. write for info. (*0-471-54535-X*) Wiley.

Mujica, Barbara. Antologia de la Literatura Espanola: Edad Media. 260p. 1991. Net. text ed. write for info. (*0-471-53693-8*) Wiley.

— Antologia de la Literatura Espanola: Renacimiento y Siglo de Oro, Vol. 2. 640p. 1991. Net. text ed. write for info. (*0-471-53694-6*) Wiley.

— Antologia de la Literature Espanola - to 1681, 2 vols., 2. 864p. 1991. text ed. 56.96 (*0-471-89027-8*) Wiley.

— Antologia de la Literature Espanola - to 1681, 2 vols., Vol. 1. 864p. 1991. text ed. write for info. (*0-471-89028-6*) Wiley.

— Aqui y Ahora. (SPA.). (C). 1979. text ed. 21.50 (*0-03-042396-1*) HB Coll Pubs.

— The Deaths of Don Bernardo. (Mujer Latina Ser.). 365p. (Orig.). 1990. pap. 19.95 (*0-685-45619-6*) Floricanto Pr.

— Entrevista. (SPA.). (C). 1982. text ed. 37.25 (*0-03-058947-9*) HB Coll Pubs.

— Iberian Pastoral Characters. 33.00 (*0-916379-17-5*) Scripta.

— Texto y Vida: Introduccion a la Literatura Espanola. Vardy, Katherine L., ed. 608p. (C). 1990. pap. text ed. 40.00 (*0-03-013164-2*) HB Coll Pubs.

— Texto y Vida: Introduccion a la Litteratura Hispano Americana. (Illus.). 608p. (SPA.). (C). 1992. pap. text ed. 41.75 (*0-03-026237-2*) HB Coll Pubs.

Mujica, Barbara, ed. Texto y Espectaculo: Selected Proceedings of the Symposium on Spanish Golden Age Theatre, March 11, 12, 13, 1987 the University of Texas at El Paso. LC 88-37834. 172p. (C). 1989. lib. bdg. 34. 50 (*0-8191-7312-6*) U Pr of Amer.

Mujica, Barbara, et al, eds. Looking at the Comedia in the Year of the Quincentennial: Proceedings of the 1992 Symposium on Golden Age Drama at the University of Texas, El Paso, March 18-21. LC 93-2619. (ENG & SPA.). 1993. 59.00 (*0-8191-9249-X*); pap. 26.00 (*0-8191-9357-7*) U Pr of Amer.

Mujica, Barbara L., et al. Pasaporte: First-Year Spanish. 2nd ed. LC 84-125653. (Illus.). 472p. (ENG & SPA.). reprint ed. pap. 134.60 (*0-7837-3500-6*, 2057833) Bks Demand.

Mujica, Francisco. History of the Skyscraper. LC 76-57764. (Architecture & Decorative Art Ser.). 1977. reprint ed. lib. bdg. 125.00 (*0-306-70862-0*) Da Capo.

Mujica, J. Complex Analysis in Banach Spaces: Holomorphic Functions & Domains of Holomorphy in Finite & Infinite Dimensions. (Mathematics Studies: Vol. 120). 434p. 1986. 84.75 (*0-444-87886-6*, North Holland) Elsevier.

Mujica, J., ed. Complex Analysis, Functional Analysis & Approximation Theory: Proceedings of a Conference on Complex Analysis & Approximation Theory, Univesidade Estadual de Campinas, Brazil, 23-27 July 1984. (North Holland Mathematics Studies: Vol. 125). 298p. 1986. 64.00 (*0-444-87997-8*) Elsevier.

Mujica, K., jt. auth. see Oudijk, G.

Mujumdar. Advances in Transplant Procedure, Vol. 8. 1993. write for info. (*0-8493-9320-5*) CRC Pr.

— Handbook of Industrial Drying, Vol. 1. 2nd expanded rev. ed. 146p. 1995. 295.00 (*0-8247-8996-2*) Dekker.

— Handbook of Industrial Drying, Vol. 2. 2nd expanded rev. ed. 146p. 1995. 295.00 (*0-8247-9644-6*) Dekker.

Mujumdar, A. S. Advances in Drying, Vol. 1. 1980. 55.00 (*0-07-043975-3*) McGraw.

— Drying of Solids. 536p. 1992. 95.00 (*1-881570-03-7*) Intl Sci Pub.

Mujumdar, A. S. & Mashelkar, R. A., eds. Advances in Transport Processes IX. 586p. 1993. 340.00 (*0-444-89737-2*) Elsevier.

Mujumdar, Arun S. Advances in Drying, Vol. 4. 421p. 1987. 136.00 (*0-89116-408-1*) Hemisp Pub.

— Drying Eighty-Two. 1982. text ed. 95.00 (*0-07-043982-6*) McGraw.

— Drying of Solids. 342p. 1986. text ed. 64.95 (*0-470-20754-X*) Wiley.

— Handbook of Industrial Drying. 968p. 1987. 250.00 (*0-8247-7606-2*) Dekker.

Mujumdar, Arun S., ed. Advances in Drying, Vol. 3. LC 80-10432. (Advances in Drying Ser.). (Illus.). 361p. 1984. text ed. 93.00 (*0-89116-297-6*) Hemisp Pub.

— Advances in Drying, Vol. 5. 350p. 1991. 87.50 (*0-685-40759-4*) Hemisp Pub.

— Advances in Drying, Vol. 5. 375p. 1992. 99.50 (*0-89116-109-0*) Hemisp Pub.

— Drying Nineteen '87. 237p. 1987. 152.00 (*0-89116-722-6*) Hemisp Pub.

— Drying 'Ninety-Two: Proceedings of the 8th International Drying Symposium (IDS '92), Montreal, Quebec, Canada, August 2-5, 1992. LC 92-19924. 1992. write for info. (*0-444-89393-8*) Elsevier.

— Drying of Solids. (C). 1992. 72.50 (*81-204-0706-7*, Pub. by Oxford IBH II) S Asia.

— Drying '86, 2 vols., Set. 919p. 1986. 205.00 (*0-89116-566-5*) Hemisp Pub.

Mujumdar, Arun S. & Mashelkar, R. A., eds. Advances in Transport Processes, Vol. 8. 280p. 1991. 84.00 (*0-89116-987-3*) Elsevier.

Mujumdar, Arun S. & Roques, Marlo, eds. Drying '89. (Illus.). 550p. 1990. 152.00 (*0-89116-749-8*) Hemisp Pub.

Mujumdar, Arun S., jt. ed. see Doraiswamy, L. K.

Mukai, Shigeru, jt. ed. see Mabuchi, Toshiki.

Mukai, Tsuyoshi, jt. ed. see Suzuki, Takashi.

Mukaiyama. Organic Chemistry, Vol. 4. (Organic Synthesis--Today & Tomorrow Ser.). 1979. 48.00 (*0-08-022038-X*, Pub. by Pergamon Repr UK) Franklin.

Mukaiyama, Teruaki. Challenges in Synthetic Organic Chemistry. Baldwin, J. E., ed. (International Series of Monographs on Chemistry: No. 20). (Illus.). 240p. 1994. reprint ed. pap. 29.95 (*0-19-855855-4*) OUP.

Mukamel, S., jt. ed. see Lefebvre, R.

***Mukamel, Shaul.** Principles of Nonlinear Optical Spectroscopy. (Illus.). 480p. 1995. text ed. 95.00 (*0-19-509278-3*) OUP.

Mukand, Jon. Rehabilitation for Patients with HIV Disease. 320p. 1991. pap. text ed. 50.00 (*0-07-043993-1*) Hlth Prof Div.

Mukand, Jon, ed. Articulations: The Body & Illness in Poetry. LC 94-16528. 452p. (Orig.). 1994. pap. 19.95 (*0-87745-478-7*) U of Iowa Pr.

Mukandala, Rwekaza, jt. auth. see Grosh, Barbara.

Mukarovsky, J. On Poetic Language. Steiner, P. & Burbank, J., trs. 88p. 1976. pap. 21.00x (*90-316-0080-6*) Benjamins North Am.

Mukarovsky, Jan. Structure, Sign, & Function: Selected Essays. Burbank, John & Steiner, Peter, eds. Steiner, Peter, tr. LC 77-76310. (Yale Russian & East European Studies: No. 14). 309p. reprint ed. pap. 88.10 (*0-8357-8336-7*, 2033836) Bks Demand.

— The Word & Verbal Art: Selected Essays by Jan Mukarovsky. Burbank, John & Steiner, Peter, eds. Steiner, Peter, tr. LC 76-49733. (Yale Russian & East European Studies: No. 13). 256p. reprint ed. pap. 73.00 (*0-8357-8378-2*, 2033837) Bks Demand.

Mukasa, Ham. Uganda's Katikiro in England. Millar, Ernest, tr. LC 74-152926. (Black Heritage Library Collection). 1977. 22.95 (*0-8369-8770-5*) Ayer.

Mukerhjee, Hirendra N. The Great Tibetologist: Alexander Csoma de Koros. 112p. 1984. text ed. 17.95 (*0-86590-263-1*, Pub. by Sterling Pubs II) Apt Bks.

Mukerjee, jt. auth. see Chaudhuri.

Mukerjee, M. Commentary on Customs Act with Rules & Notifications. (C). 1990. 275.00 (*0-89771-224-2*) St Mut.

Mukerjee, M. K., tr. The Pomegranate Princess & Other Tales from India. LC 90-47284. (Illus.). 136p. 1991. text ed. 29.95 (*0-8143-2329-4*); pap. text ed. 14.95 (*0-8143-2330-8*) Wayne St U Pr.

Mukerjee, R., jt. auth. see Gupta, S.

Mukerji, A. B. The Chamars of Uttar Pradesh: A Study in Social Geography. 155p. 1980. 12.95 (*0-318-36868-4*) Asia Bk Corp.

Mukerji, A. P. Doctrine & Practice of Yoga. 9.00 (*0-911662-23-5*) Yoga.

— Yoga Lessons for Developing Spiritual Consciousness. 9.00 (*0-911662-24-3*) Yoga.

Mukerji, B., jt. auth. see Chen, K.

Mukerji, Bithika. The Hindu Tradition. 128p. 1990. pap. 13. 95 (*0-916349-48-9*) Element MA.

Mukerji, Chandra. A Fragile Power: Scientists & the State. (Illus.). 322p. (C). 1989. text ed. 32.50 (*0-691-08538-2*) Princeton U Pr.

Mukerji, Chandra & Schudson, Michael, eds. Rethinking Popular Culture: Contemporary Perspectives in Cultural Studies. LC 90-39009. 512p. 1991. 50.00 (*0-520-06892-0*); pap. 17.00 (*0-520-06893-9*) U CA Pr.

Mukerji, D. Textbook of Zoology, 2 vols. 1985. text ed. 95. 00 (*0-317-38806-1*, Current Dist) St Mut.

Mukerji, D. G. Chitra, The Story of a Pigeon. 225p. (C). 1988. 39.00 (*1-85219-040-X*, Pub. by Bishopsgate Pr Ltd UK) St Mut.

Mukerji, Dhan G. Gay-Neck: The Story of a Pigeon. LC 68-13419. (Illus.). 192p. (J). (gr. 4 up). 1968. 15.00 (*0-525-30400-2*, DCB) Dutton Child Bks.

— Gay-Neck: The Story of a Pigeon. braille ed. 190p. (J). 1991. vinyl bd. 15.20 (*1-56956-238-5*, BR8403) W A T Braille.

Mukerji, Jatin N., jt. ed. see Surles, Richard H., Jr.

Mukerji, K. G. & Garg, K. L., eds. Biocontrol of Plant Diseases. 1988. write for info. (*0-318-62925-9*, SB732) CRC Pr.

— Biocontrol of Plant Diseases, Vol. I. 224p. 1988. 204.00 (*0-8493-4595-2*, SB732) CRC Pr.

— Biocontrol of Plant Diseases, Vol. II. 224p. 1988. 121.00 (*0-8493-4596-0*, SB732, CRC Reprint) Franklin.

Mukerji, K. G., jt. auth. see Bhandari, N. N.

Mukerji, K. G., jt. auth. see Lakhanpal, T. N.

Mukerji, P. N., tr. see Hariharananda, S. Aranya.

Mukerji, Rose, jt. auth. see Lasky, Lila.

Mukerji, Vanita S. Ivo Andric: A Critical Biography. LC 89-43661. (Illus.). 224p. 1990. lib. bdg. 43.50x (*0-89950-504-X*) McFarland & Co.

Mukes, Martin J. & Miles, Daniel J. Miles Chart Display of Popular Music, Vol. 3. 400p. 1981. lib. bdg. 40.00 (*0-913920-04-5*) Convex Indus.

Mukh, Firma K. & Dastidar, Sachi G. Regional Disparities & Regional Development: Planning of West Bengal. (C). 1991. 24.00 (*0-8364-2645-2*, Pub. by Firma KLM) S Asia.

Mukhachev, Iu. Classes & the Class Struggle in the U. S. S. R. 1920's-1930's. 150p. (C). 1988. 30.00 (*0-685-31477-4*) St Mut.

Mukhametshin, Boris. Anti-Posters: Soviet Icons in Reverse. LC 86-28104. 164p. 1987. reprint ed. lib. bdg. 20.00x (*0-89370-842-9*); reprint ed. pap. 10.00x (*0-89370-942-5*) Borgo Pr.

— Gorbyshow: Anti-Posters for Our Time. (Illus.). xx, 160p. 1991. 29.95 (*1-879378-02-7*); pap. 14.95 (*1-879378-01-9*) Xenos Riverside.

— Gorbyshow: Anti-Posters for Our Time. 180p. 1991. reprint ed. lib. bdg. 31.00x (*0-8095-6116-6*) Borgo Pr.

— Gorbyshow: Anti-Posters for Our Time. 180p. 1991. reprint ed. pap. 15.00x (*1-879278-01-4*) Borgo Pr.

Mukhanov, M. S. Kazakh Domestic Handicrafts. 76p. 1979. 55.00 (*0-317-14242-9*, Pub. by Collets UK) Pro-Am Music.

Mukharjee, B. N. Mass Media & Political Modernity. 168p. 1971. 15.95 (*0-318-37278-9*) Asia Bk Corp.

Mukharjee, M., ed. Considerations. 153p. 1977. 10.95 (*0-318-36945-1*) Asia Bk Corp.

Mukharjee, R. K. Society & Community in India. 155p. 1979. 12.95 (*0-318-36864-1*) Asia Bk Corp.

Mukharji, D. P. Sociology of Indian Culture. 239p. 1979. 18.95 (*0-318-36974-5*) Asia Bk Corp.

Mukharji, P. Hindu Women. 118p. 1980. 11.95 (*0-318-37062-X*) Asia Bk Corp.

Mukharji, Sumana. Teach Yourself Bengali. (Language Ser.). 176p. 1990. pap. 6.95 (*0-87052-619-7*) Hippocrene Bks.

Mukherjea, A. & Pothoven, K. Real & Functional Analysis, Part A: Real Analysis. 2nd ed. (Mathematical Concepts & Methods in Science & Engineering Ser.: Vol. 27). 352p. 1984. 85.00 (*0-306-41557-7*, Plenum Pr) Plenum.

— Real & Functional Analysis, Pt B: Functional Analysis. 2nd ed. (Mathematical Concepts & Methods in Science & Engineering Ser.: Vol. 28). 276p. 1985. 75.00 (*0-306-41558-5*, Plenum Pr) Plenum.

Mukherjea, A., jt. auth. see Hognas, G.

Mukherjea, Sushil. Historicity of Lord Jagannatha: A Socio-Historical Study. (C). 1989. 14.00 (*81-85195-17-X*, Pub. by Minerva II) S Asia.

Mukherjee. From the Man Human to Man Divine. 250p. 1991. pap. 9.00 (*81-7058-232-6*) Aurobindo Assn.

— Handbook of Chromatography, Lipids, Vol. III. 1993. 169.95 (*0-8493-3039-4*, QP751) CRC Pr.

Mukherjee, jt. auth. see Allen.

Mukherjee, A. Accountancy Problems. 1985. 85.00 (*0-317-38745-6*, Current Dist) St Mut.

— Towards a Non-Static Theory of Profit Maximization. 1990. 34.00 (*81-7017-274-8*, Pub. by Abhinav II) S Asia.

Mukherjee, A. B., ed. Biochemistry, Molecular Biology, & Physiology of Phospholipase A2 & Its Regulatory Factors. (Advances in Experimental Medicine & Biology Ser.: Vol. 279). (Illus.). 270p. 1990. 85.00 (*0-306-43699-X*, Plenum Pr) Plenum.

Mukherjee, A. K. Flora of Pachmarhi & Bori Reserves. (Flora of India Ser.: No. 3). 407p. 1984. text ed. 40.00 (*0-945345-54-2*, Pub. by Mahendra Pal Singh II) Lubrecht & Cramer.

Mukherjee, A. K., ed. see International Symposium on Rate Processes in Plastic Deformation Staff.

Mukherjee, A. L. A Short Textbook of Otolaryngology. 1985. 59.00 (*0-317-39560-2*, Current Dist) St Mut.

Mukherjee, Amar. Introduction to NMOS & CMOS VLSI Systems Design. (Illus.). 416p. (C). 1985. text ed. 105.00 (*0-13-490947-X*) P-H.

Mukherjee, Amitabha. Structural Adjustment Programme & Food Security: Hunger & Poverty in India. 373p. 1994. 72.95 (*1-85628-595-2*, Pub. by Avebury Pub UK) Ashgate Pub Co.

Mukherjee, Amitava. Studies in Multilevel Planning, Vol. I: Researches in Decentralisation with Special Reference to District Planning in India. Yugandhar, B. N., ed. 1990. 48.50 (*81-7026-158-9*, Pub. by Heritage IA) S Asia.

***Mukherjee, Amitava & Agnihotri, V. K., eds.** Environment & Development: Views from the East & the West. (C). 1993. 68.00x (*81-7022-788-7*, Pub. by Concept II) S Asia.

Mukherjee, Aparna. British Colonial Policy in Burma: An Aspect of Colonialism in South East Asia, 1840-1885. 1988. 50.00 (*0-8364-2290-2*, Pub. by Abhinav II) S Asia.

— British Colonial Policy in Burma: An Aspect of Colonialism in South-East Asia, 1840-1885. LC 88-61303. 557p. 1988. 34.00 (*0-913215-37-6*) Riverdale Co.

Mukherjee, Arun. The Gospel of Wealth in the American Novel: The Rhetoric of Dreiser & Some of His Contemporaries. 240p. (C). 1987. 59.50 (*0-389-20681-4*, N8239) B&N Imports.

Mukherjee, B., ed. Traditional Medicine. 419p. (C). 1993. text ed. 45.00 (*1-881570-32-0*) Intl Sci Pub.

Mukherjee, B., jt. ed. see Tyson, W.

***Mukherjee, B. N.** Coins & Currency Systems of Post-Gupta Bengal: (c. AD 550-700) (C). 1993. 19.50x (*81-215-0563-1*, Pub. by Munshiram Manoharlal II) S Asia.

— External Trade of Early North-Eastern India. 124p. 1992. text ed. 18.95 (*0-7069-6164-1*, Pub. by Vikas II) S Asia.

— Mathura & Its Society: The Saka Pahlava Phase. 1981. 14.00 (*0-8364-1589-2*, KL Mukhopadhyay) S Asia.

— The Rise & Fall of the Kushana Empire. (C). 1988. 96.00 (*0-8364-2393-3*, Pub. by Firma KLM) S Asia.

Mukherjee, B. N., ed. East Indian Art Styles. 1985. 20.00 (*0-8364-1483-7*, Pub. by KP Bagchi IA) S Asia.

Mukherjee, Bhabananda. Structure & Kinship in Tribal India. 1981. 10.00 (*0-8364-0769-5*, Pub. by Minerva II) S Asia.

Mukherjee, Bharati. Darkness. 1992. 5.99 (*0-449-22099-0*, Crest) Fawcett.

— The Holder of the World. 304p. 1994. reprint ed. pap. 12. 00 (*0-449-90966-2*) Fawcett.

— The Holder of the World: A Novel. LC 93-22066. 1993. 22.00 (*0-394-58846-0*) Knopf.

— Jasmine. 244p. 1990. mass mkt. 5.99 (*0-449-21923-2*, Crest) Fawcett.

— The Middleman & Other Stories. 1989. mass mkt. 4.99 (*0-449-21718-3*, Crest) Fawcett.

— Political Culture & Leadership in India. (C). 1991. 36.00 (*81-7099-320-2*, Pub. by Mittal II) S Asia.

— Regionalism in Indian Perspective. 1992. 13.00 (*81-7074-123-8*, Pub. by KP Bagchi IA) S Asia.

— The Tiger's Daughter. 1991. mass mkt. 5.99 (*0-449-22100-8*, Crest) Fawcett.

— Wife. 1992. reprint ed. mass mkt. 5.99 (*0-449-22098-2*, Crest) Fawcett.

Mukherjee, Bharati, jt. auth. see Blaise, Clark.

Mukherjee, D., ed. Applied Many-Body Methods in Spectroscopy & Electronics. (Illus.). 292p. (C). 1992. 89. 50 (*0-306-44193-4*, Plenum Pr) Plenum.

— Aspects of Many-Body Effects in Molecules & Extended Systems. (Lecture Notes in Chemistry Ser.: Vol. 50). viii, 565p. 1989. pap. 83.00 (*0-387-50765-5*) Spr-Verlag.

Mukherjee, Dhurjati. Youth: Change & Challenge - India. 1977. 7.50 (*0-8364-0481-5*) S Asia.

Mukherjee, H. Plant Groups. (C). 1989. 100.00 (*0-89771-410-5*, Current Dist) St Mut.

***Mukherjee, Hena.** The Early History of the East Indian Railway: 1845-1879. (C). 1994. text ed. 28.50 (*81-7102-003-8*, Pub. by Firma KLM) S Asia.

Mukherjee, Jaya. Tagore & Radhakrishnan: A Study in Religious Perspective. 120p. 1992. 12.00 (*81-85078-79-3*, Pub. by Janaki Prakashan II) Nataraj Bks.

Mukherjee, K. & Mazumder, J., eds. Lasers in Metallurgy: Proceedings of a Symposium. LC 81-85419. (Conference Proceedings Ser.). (Illus.). 309p. reprint ed. pap. 88.10 (*0-8357-7502-X*, 2032600) Bks Demand.

Mukherjee, K. K., tr. see Bauer, Karl M.

Mukherjee, K. N., jt. ed. see Mazumder, J.

Mukherjee, Kalyan K. Numerical Analysis. (C). 1989. 50.00 (*0-89771-396-6*, Current Dist) St Mut.

Mukherjee, M. A Passage to Medicine Practice. (C). 1990. 75.00 (*0-685-36207-8*, Current Dist) St Mut.

— Prescription Writing. 2nd ed. (C). 1989. 24.00 (*0-685-36202-7*, Current Dist) St Mut.

Mukherjee, Meenakshi. Jane Austen. Figes, Eva & King, Adele, eds. LC 90-48428. (Women Writers Ser.). 180p. 1991. text ed. 29.95 (*0-312-05794-6*) St Martin.

— Realism & Reality: The Novel & Society in India. 232p. 1994. reprint ed. pap. 7.95 (*0-19-563434-9*) OUP.

Mukherjee, Meenakshi, ed. Considerations: Twelve Studies in Indo-Anglian Writings. (C). 1977. 8.00 (*0-8364-0082-8*) S Asia.

Mukherjee, Meenakshi, tr. see Bhattacharya, Lokenath.

Mukherjee, Meenakshi, tr. see Chakrabarti, Nirendranath.

Mukherjee, Meenakshi, tr. see Tagore, Rabindranath.

Mukherjee, Moni S. Sankar Company Limited: A Novel. Moulik, Achala, tr. 162p. 1977. pap. text ed. 5.95 (*0-86125-336-1*, Pub. by Orient Longman Ltd II) Apt Bks.

Mukherjee, Neela. Dynamics of India's Invisible Trade. 94p. 1985. text ed. 17.95 (*0-86590-692-0*, Pub. by Sterling Pubs II) Apt Bks.

Mukherjee, P. K. & Constance, Lincoln. Umbelliferae (Apiaceae) of India. 287p. (C). 1993. text ed. 59.00 (*1-881570-26-6*) Intl Sci Pub.

Mukherjee, Prabhat. The History of Jagannath Temple. 1977. 14.50 (*0-8364-0414-9*) S Asia.

— The History of Medieval Vaishnavism in Orissa. 200p. 1986. reprint ed. 14.00 (*0-8364-1754-2*, Pub. by Manohar II) S Asia.

— History of the Chaitanya Faith in Orissa. 1979. 14.00 (*0-8364-0547-1*) S Asia.

Mukherjee, Prabhat K. Life of Rabindranath Tagore. 1976. lib. bdg. 10.00 (*0-89253-024-3*) Ind-US Inc.

Mukherjee, Prabhati. Beyond the Four Varnas: The Untouchables in India. (C). 1988. 14.00 (*81-208-0459-7*, Pub. by Motilal Banarsidass II) S Asia.

Mukherjee, R. The Culture & Art of India. (Illus.). 1984. text ed. 48.00 (*0-685-13648-5*) Coronet Bks.

— Family & Planning in India. 90p. 1976. 5.95 (*0-318-36834-X*) Asia Bk Corp.

Mukherjee, R. R. Long Vegetable Fibres, Vol. 4, No. 4. 81p. (C). 1972. pap. text ed. 85.00 (*0-685-36085-7*, Pub. by Textile Institue UK) St Mut.

Mukherjee, R. R. & Radhakrishnan, T. Long Vegetable Fibres. 81p. 1972. 90.00 (*0-686-63771-2*) St Mut.

Mukherjee, Ramkrishna. Classification in Social Research. LC 82-682. 255p. (C). 1984. 64.50 (*0-87395-607-9*); pap. 21.95 (*0-87395-608-7*) State U NY Pr.

— The Quality of Life: Valuation in Social Research. 240p. (C). 1989. text ed. 24.00 (*0-8039-9587-3*) Sage.

— The Rise & Fall of the East India Company: A Sociological Appraisal. LC 73-90082. 461p. reprint ed. pap. 131.40 (*0-7837-3919-2*, 2043767) Bks Demand.

— Society, Culture, & Development. 272p. 1992. 29.95 (*0-8039-9102-9*) Sage.

An Asterisk (*) at the beginning of an entry indicates that the title is appearing in BIP for the first time.

— Sociology of Indian Sociology. 1980. write for info. (*0-8364-1453-5*, Pub. by Allied II) S Asia.

— Systemic Sociology. (Illus.). 256p. (C). 1993. text ed. 26.00 (*0-8039-9126-6*) Sage.

MukherJee, Ramkrishna. Uganda: An Historical Accident? Class, Nation, State Formation. LC 85-71370. 290p. 1985. 35.00 (*0-86543-015-2*); pap. 14.95 (*0-86543-016-0*) Africa World.

Mukherjee, Ramkrishna. What Will It Be? Explorations in Inductive Sociology. LC 78-54441. 266p. 1978. 18.75 (*0-89089-094-3*) Carolina Acad Pr.

***Mukherjee, Rudrangshu, ed.** The Penguin Gandhi Reader. 320p. 1995. pap. 10.95 (*0-14-023686-4*, Penguin Bks) Viking Penguin.

Mukherjee, S. Boundary Element Methods in Creep & Fracture. (Illus.). 224p. 1983. 56.00 (*0-85334-163-X*, I-430-82, Pub. by Elsevier Applied Sci UK) Elsevier.

Mukherjee, S., jt. auth. see Banerjee, P. K.

Mukherjee, S. B. Population Growth & Urbanization in South & Southeast Asia. 176p. 1988. text ed. 25.00 (*81-207-0844-X*, Pub. by Sterling Pubs II) Apt Bks.

Mukherjee, S. D., ed. Advanced Processing of Semiconductor Devices. 376p. 1987. 57.00 (*0-89252-832-X*, 797) SPIE.

Mukherjee, S. K. Orchids. (C). 1988. 20.00 (*0-685-22333-7*, Scientific) St Mut.

Mukherjee, S. N. Sir William Jones: A Study in Eighteenth-Century British Attitudes to India. 184p. 1987. text ed. 22.50 (*0-86131-581-2*, Pub. by Orient Longman Ltd II) Apt Bks.

Mukherjee, S. N. & Waghmare, Y. R. Physics of Rotating Nuclei. LC 93-36009. 1994. text ed. 31.95 (*0-470-23358-3*) Wiley.

Mukherjee, Sadhan. Internationalism in a Changing World. v, 129p. 1989. text ed. 20.00 (*81-207-0998-5*, Pub. by Sterling Pubs II) Apt Bks.

— South Asia Media Handbook. (C). 1990. 19.50 (*81-7023-305-4*, Pub. by Allied II) S Asia.

Mukherjee, Samir, jt. ed. see Tray, Amita.

Mukherjee, Sampat. Methods of Economic Investigation. (C). 1989. 55.00 (*0-89771-424-5*, Current Dist) St Mut.

Mukherjee, Sampat, ed. Economic Environment of Business. (C). 1989. 60.00 (*0-89771-428-8*, Current Dist) St Mut.

Mukherjee, Sandeep. Commentaries on Prevention of Corruption Act. (C). 1990. 65.00 (*0-89771-173-4*) St Mut.

Mukherjee, Sanjib K., jt. auth. see Goldman, Robert L.

Mukherjee, Santilal. Basic Economics. Mukhopadhyaya, Sampat, ed. 1985. 75.00 (*0-317-38748-0*, Current Dist) St Mut.

— Managerial Economics. 1985. 75.00 (*0-317-38783-9*, Current Dist) St Mut.

***Mukherjee, Sipra.** Indian Administration of Lord William Bentinck. (C). 1995. 18.00x (*81-7074-142-4*, Pub. by KP Bagchi IA) S Asia.

Mukherjee, Subrata. Gandhian Thought: Marxist Interpretation. (C). 1991. 21.50 (*0-685-50011-X*, Pub. by Deep) S Asia.

Mukherjee, Sujit, tr. see Chakrabarti, Nirendranath.

Mukherjee, Sujit, tr. see Tagore, Rabindranath.

Mukherjee, Sushil K. The Story of the Calcutta Theatre, 1753-1980. 1983. 32.00 (*0-8364-0994-9*, Pub. by KP Bagchi IA) S Asia.

Mukherji, A. A Passage to Medicine Practical. (C). 1989. 75.00 (*0-89771-357-5*, Current Dist) St Mut.

— Prescription Writing. (C). 1989. 40.00 (*0-89771-356-7*, Current Dist) St Mut.

Mukherji, A. K. Analytical Chemistry of Zirconium & Hafnium. LC 71-109236. 1970. 146.00 (*0-08-006886-3*, Pub. by Pergamon Repr UK) Franklin.

Mukherji, Anjan. Walrasian & Non-Walrasian Equilibria: An Introduction to General Equilibrium Analysis. (Illus.). 256p. 1990. pap. 29.95 (*0-19-877289-0*) OUP.

Mukherji, Arandita. Socio Economic Backwardness in Women. (C). 1987. 9.00 (*81-7024-096-4*, Pub. by Ashish II) S Asia.

***Mukherji, B. C.** Vendanta & Tagore. 89p. (C). 1994. 30.00x (*81-85880-42-5*, Pub. by Print Hse II) St Mut.

Mukherji, Dhan G. The Face of Silence: A Biography of Rama Krishna. LC 85-22355. 255p. 1985. reprint ed. lib. bdg. 27.00x (*0-89370-584-5*) Borgo Pr.

Mukherji, M. & Roychowdhury, R. Advanced Cost & Management Accountancy. (C). 1989. 135.00 (*0-89771-437-7*, Current Dist) St Mut.

Mukherji, Nirmal, jt. ed. see Arora, Balveer.

Mukherji, P. N., jt. ed. see Oomen, T. K.

Mukherji, Partha N. From Left Extremism to Electoral Politics. 1984. 22.50 (*0-8364-1096-3*, Pub. by Manohar II) S Asia.

Mukherji, Runi B., jt. auth. see Adler, Leonore L.

Mukherji, S. K. College Botany, Vol. III. (C). 1989. 75.00 (*0-89771-415-6*, Current Dist) St Mut.

Mukherji, S. M., et al. Organic Chemistry, Set, Vols. I & II. (C). 1985. Set. pap. 36.00 (*0-685-25151-9*, Pub. by Wiley Eastern II) S Asia.

Mukherji, Santi L. The Philosophy of Man-Making. (C). 1989. 40.00 (*0-89771-452-0*, Current Dist) St Mut.

***Mukhia, Harbans.** Perspectives on Medieval History. (C). 1993. 32.00x (*0-7069-6387-3*, Pub. by Vikas II) S Asia.

Mukhia, Harbans, jt. ed. see Aymard, Maurice.

Mukhia, Harbans, tr. see Aymard, Maurice & Mukhia, Harbans, eds.

Mukhia, Harbans, jt. ed. see Aymard, Maurice.

Mukhia, Harbans, jt. ed. see Byres, T. J.

Mukhin, K. N. Experimental Nuclear Physics, Vols. 1-2. 1032p. (C). 1987. 235.00 (*0-685-46640-X*, Pub. by Collets) St Mut.

Mukhina, A. M., jt. auth. see Balog, G. P.

Mukhopadhaya, M. A Guide to Employees Providence Fund. (C). 1988. 95.00 (*0-685-27894-8*) St Mut.

Mukhopadhyay, A., jt. auth. see Randhawa, G. S.

Mukhopadhyay, A. N. Handbook of Diseases of Sugar Beet, 2 Vols., Set. 467p. 1987. 240.00 (*0-8493-3130-7*, SB608) CRC Pr.

Mukhopadhyay, A. N., et al. Plant Diseases of International Importance, Vol. 1: Diseases of Cereals & Pulses. 544p. 1992. text ed. 99.00 (*0-13-678582-4*) P-H.

— Plant Diseases of International Importance, Vol. 2: Diseases of Vegetables & Oil Seed Crops. 416p. 1992. text ed. 99.00 (*0-13-678558-1*) P-H.

— Plant Diseases of International Importance, Vol. 3: Diseases of Fruit Crops. 544p. 1992. text ed. 99.00 (*0-13-678566-2*) P-H.

— Plant Diseases of International Importance, Vol. 4: Diseases of Sugar, Forest, & Plantation Crops. 512p. 1992. text ed. 99.00 (*0-13-678574-3*) P-H.

***Mukhopadhyay, Amal K. & Raizada, Mohan K., eds.** Tissue Renin-Angiotensin Systems: Current Concepts of Local Regulators in Reproductive & Endocrine Organs. (Advances in Experimental Medicine & Biology Ser.: Vol. 377). 440p. 1995. 120.00 (*0-306-45077-1*) Plenum.

***Mukhopadhyay, B.** Motivation in Education Management: Issues & Strategies. (C). 1995. 20.00x (*81-207-1621-3*, Pub. by Sterling Plns Pvt II) S Asia.

Mukhopadhyay, B., jt. auth. see Barki, B. G.

Mukhopadhyay, Carol C. & Seymour, Susan. Women, Education, & Family Structure in India. LC 93-35560. 246p. (C). 1993. text ed. 54.85 (*0-8133-8511-3*) Westview.

Mukhopadhyay, Durgadas. Culture, Performance & Communication. (C). 1989. 29.50 (*81-7018-565-3*, Pub. by BR Pub II) S Asia.

— Religion, Philosophy & Literature of Bengal Vaishnavism. 1990. 17.50 (*81-7018-597-1*, Pub. by BR Pub II) S Asia.

Mukhopadhyay, Durgadas, ed. & tr. In Praise of Krishna. (C). 1990. text ed. 18.50 (*81-7018-546-7*, Pub. by BR Pub II) S Asia.

Mukhopadhyay, M. Structures: Matrix & Finite Element. 3rd ed. 423p. 1993. 70.00 (*90-5410-234-9*, Pub. by A A Balkema NE) Ashgate Pub Co.

Mukhopadhyay, Nitis & Solanky, Tumulesh K. Multistage Selection & Ranking Procedures: Second-Order Asymptotics. LC 93-47524. (Statistics: Vol. 142). 424p. 1994. 125.00 (*0-8247-9078-2*) Dekker.

Mukhopadhyay, P., ed. Theory of Probability - an Introduction. (C). 1989. 60.00 (*0-89771-399-0*, Current Dist) St Mut.

Mukhopadhyay, P. K. Organic Petrography & Organic Geochemistry of Texas Tertiary Coals in Relation to Depositional Environment & Hydrocarbon Generation. (Report of Investigations Ser.: RI 188). (Illus.). 118p. 1989. 9.00 (*0-317-03121-X*) Bur Econ Geology.

Mukhopadhyay, Pradyot K. Nyaya Theory of Linguistic Performance: A New Interpretation of Tattvacintamani. (Jadavpur Studies in Philosophy, Second Ser.). 1992. 25.00 (*81-7074-095-9*, Pub. by KP Bagchi IA) S Asia.

***Mukhopadhyay, Prasanta K. & Dow, Wallace G.** Vitrinite Reflectance As a Maturity Parameter: Applications & Limitations. LC 94-34670. (Symposium Ser.: No. 570). (Illus.). 306p. 1994. 79.95 (*0-8412-2994-5*) Am Chemical.

Mukhopadhyay, Purnachandra. Journey of the Upanishads to the West. 1987. 32.50 (*0-8364-2025-X*, KL Mukhopadhyay) S Asia.

Mukhopadhyay, S. K. The Structure & Properties of Typical Metal Spun Fibres, Vol. 18, No. 4. 116p. (C). 1989. pap. text ed. 95.00 (*1-870812-11-5*, Pub. by Textile Institue UK) St Mut.

Mukhopadhyay, Samir, ed. Advances in Fibre Science. 218p. 1993. 395.00 (*1-870812-37-9*, Pub. by Textile Institue UK) St Mut.

***Mukhopadhyay, Samir K.** Permanent Settlement to Operation Barga. (C). 1994. text ed. 16.00 (*0-614-04131-7*, Pub. by Minerva II) S Asia.

Mukhopadhyay, Sampat. Corporate Planning & Policy. (C). 1989. 45.00 (*0-89771-438-5*, Current Dist) St Mut.

Mukhopadhyay, Satya N. & Das, Dipak K. Oxygen Responses, Reactivities, & Measurements in Biosystems. LC 94-6561. 1994. write for info. (*0-8493-4730-0*) CRC Pr.

***Mukhopadhyay, Subrata K.** Cult of Goddess Sitala in Bengal: An Enquiry into Folk Culture. (C). 1994. text ed. 19.50 (*81-7102-001-1*, Pub. by Firma KLM) S Asia.

***Mukhopadhyay, Tapas, et al.** P53 Suppressor Gene. LC 95-4045. (Molecular Biology Intelligence Unit Ser.). 160p. 1995. 69.00 (*1-57059-212-8*) R G Landes.

Mukhopadhyay, Tarun K. Feroze Gandhi: A Crusader in Parliament. (C). 1992. 18.00 (*81-7023-335-6*, Pub. by Allied II) S Asia.

Mukhopadhyaya, Sampat, ed. see Mukherjee, Santilal.

Mukhopadyay, M. Vibration, Dynamics & Structural Systems. (C). 1989. 20.00 (*81-204-0421-1*) S Asia.

Mukhopakhyaya, Mihir M. Sculptures of the Ganga-Yamuna Valley. 1986. 40.00 (*0-8364-1627-9*, Pub. by Abhinav II) S Asia.

Mukhtar. Skin Cancer: Mechanisms & Human Relevance. 1995. write for info. (*0-8493-7358-1*) CRC Pr.

Mukhtar, Hasan. Pharmacology of the Skin. (Illus.). 440p. 1991. 92.00 (*0-8493-7292-5*, RL801) CRC Pr.

Mukhtar us-Sihah & Ar'Rhazi. Arabic-Arabic Dictionary. 1990. 24.95 (*0-86685-375-8*) Intl Bk Ctr.

Mukjika, P. Diccionario Vasco-Castellano: Basque-Spanish Dictionary, 2 vols. Set. (BAQ & SPA.). 1991. 195.00 (*0-8288-7253-8*, 8427112696) Fr & Eur.

Muklewicz, Chet & Bender, Michael. Competitive Job-Finding Guide for Persons with Handicaps. LC 90-21685. 197p. 1988. pap. text ed. 31.00 (*0-89079-402-2*, 1749) PRO-ED.

— Job-Finder's Workbook, Set of 10. 64p. 1988. 37.00 (*0-318-35159-5*) PRO-ED.

Mukoda, Kuniko. The Name of the Flower: Stories. Matsumoto, Tomone, tr. LC 93-6309. (Rock Spring Collection). 152p. (Orig.). 1993. pap. 10.95 (*1-880656-09-4*) Stone Bridge Pr.

Mukohata, Yasuo, ed. New Era in Bioenergetics. (Illus.). 308p. 1992. text ed. 64.95 (*0-12-509854-5*) Acad Pr.

Mukonoweshuro, Eliphas G. Colonialism, Class Formation & Underdevelopment in Sierra Leone. 268p. (Orig.). (C). 1991. lib. bdg. 45.00 (*0-8191-8282-6*); pap. text ed. 23.50 (*0-8191-8283-4*) U Pr of Amer.

Muksian, Robert. Financial Mathematics Handbook. LC 83-13963. 486p. 1984. text ed. 59.95 (*0-13-316406-3*, Busn) P-H.

***Mukta, Parita.** Upholding the Common Life: The Community of Mirabai. (Illus.). 272p. 1995. 24.00 (*0-19-563115-3*) OUP.

***Muktananda.** Does Death Really Exist? LC 95-14439. 1995. write for info. (*0-911307-36-2*) SYDA Found.

Muktananda, Swami. En Busca del Ser. LC 81-50917. 140p. 1981. pap. 5.00 (*0-914602-71-3*) SYDA Found.

— En Compania de un Siddha. LC 81-84263. 1981. pap. 6.00 (*0-914602-81-0*) SYDA Found.

— From the Finite to the Infinite, 2 vols., Set. Scott, Sarah, ed. LC 87-63526. (Illus.). 1990. 44.95 (*0-911307-00-1*) SYDA Found.

— From the Finite to the Infinite, 2 vols., Vol. 1. Scott, Sarah, ed. LC 87-63526. (Illus.). 312p. 1990. 19.95 (*0-911307-01-X*) SYDA Found.

— From the Finite to the Infinite, 2 vols., Vol. 2. Scott, Sarah, ed. LC 87-63526. (Illus.). 352p. 1990. 19.95 (*0-911307-02-8*) SYDA Found.

— God Is with You. (Illus.). 40p. (Orig.). 1978. pap. 2.00 (*0-914602-57-8*) SYDA Found.

— I Am That. rev. ed. LC 92-35416. 69p. 1992. reprint ed. 6.95 (*0-914602-27-6*) SYDA Found.

— I Welcome You All with Love. 40p. (Orig.). 1978. pap. 2.00 (*0-914602-59-4*) SYDA Found.

— Meditate. 128p. (JPN.). 1991. 11.00 (*0-911307-19-2*) SYDA Found.

— Meditate: With a New Chapter by Gurumayi Chidvilasananda. 2nd ed. LC 91-3641. (SUNY Series in Transpersonal & Humanistic Psychology). 99p. 1991. pap. 7.95 (*0-7914-0978-3*) State U NY Pr.

— Mukteshwari: Aphorism. 2nd ed. LC 95-15966. 1995. write for info. (*0-911307-35-4*) SYDA Found.

— Perfect Relationship. Swami Chidvilasananda, tr. LC 80-54457. 222p. 1980. pap. 8.95 (*0-914602-53-5*) SYDA Found.

— Play of Consciousness. 400p. 1991. 21.95 (*0-911307-20-6*) SYDA Found.

— Play of Consciousness. 2nd ed. LC 78-62769. 1978. pap. 9.95 (*0-914602-37-3*) SYDA Found.

— Play of Consciousness: A Spiritual Autobiography. 4th ed. LC 94-40709. (ENG & HIN.). 1994. write for info. (*0-911307-33-8*) SYDA Found.

— La Relacion Perfecta. LC 81-84261. 218p. 1982. pap. 7.00 (*0-914602-84-5*) SYDA Found.

— Satsang with Baba, 5 vols., Set. LC 76-1384. 1978. 22.95 (*0-914602-40-3*) SYDA Found.

— Satsang with Baba, Vol. 2. LC 76-1384. 382p. 1976. pap. 8.95 (*0-914602-31-4*) SYDA Found.

— Satsang with Baba, Vol. 3. LC 76-670008. 1977. pap. 8.95 (*0-914602-38-1*) SYDA Found.

— Satsang with Baba, Vol. 4. LC 76-1384. 1978. pap. 8.95 (*0-914602-32-2*) SYDA Found.

— Satsang with Baba, Vol. 5. LC 76-1384. 1978. pap. 8.95 (*0-914602-33-0*) SYDA Found.

— Secret of the Siddhas. LC 80-53590. 256p. 1980. pap. 9.95 (*0-914602-52-7*) SYDA Found.

— The Self Is Already Attained. 40p. 1981. pap. 2.00 (*0-914602-77-2*) SYDA Found.

Mukund, Lath, ed. Ardhoka Thanaka: Half a Tale. 1983. 28.50 (*0-8364-1087-4*) S Asia.

***Mukunda, N.** World of Bohr & Dirac: Images of Twentieth Century Physics. (C). 1993. reprint ed. 10.00x (*81-224-0483-9*, Pub. by Wiley Eastern II) S Asia.

Mukundan, Monisha, ed. The Namaste Book of Indian Short Stories, Vol. 1. (C). 1992. 14.00 (*81-85674-02-7*, Pub. by UBS Pubs Dist II) S Asia.

— Namaste Book of Indian Short Stories Vol. II. (C). 1994. 9.00 (*81-85944-85-7*, Pub. by UBS Pubs Dist II) S Asia.

Mukurasi, Laeticia. Post Abolished: One Woman's Struggle for Employment Rights in Tanzania. (Cornell International Industrial & Labor Relations Reports: No. 19). 144p. 1991. 24.00 (*0-87546-702-4*); pap. 12.95 (*0-87546-703-2*) ILR Pr.

Mulac, Jim, jt. ed. see Sklar, Morty.

***Mulak, Steven.** Pointing Dogs Made Easy: How to Train, Nurture, & Appreciate Your Bird Dog. limited ed. Traux, Doug & DeLaurier, Art, Jr., eds. (Illus.). 208p. Date not set. 25.00 (*0-924357-54-1*) Countrysport Pr.

Mulanax, Richard B. The Boer War in American Politics & Diplomacy. 248p. (Orig.). (C). 1994. lib. bdg. 46.50 (*0-8191-9356-9*) U Pr of Amer.

Mular, Andrew L. & Anderson, Mark A., eds. Design & Installation of Concentration & Dewatering Circuits. LC 85-63667. (Illus.). 852p. reprint ed. pap. 180.00 (*0-8357-6643-8*, 2035310) Bks Demand.

Mular, Andrew L. & Bhappu, Roshan B., eds. Mineral Processing Plant Design. LC 77-26531. 897p. reprint ed. pap. 180.00 (*0-317-29751-1*, 2017420) Bks Demand.

Mular, Andrew L. & Jergensen, Gerald V., eds. Design & Installation of Comminution Circuits. LC 82-71992. (Illus.). 1032p. reprint ed. pap. 180.00 (*0-8357-6642-X*, 2035309) Bks Demand.

Mular, Andrew L., ed. see Mineral Processing Plant Design Symposium Staff.

Mulari, Mary. Adventure in Applique. (Illus.). 44p. (Orig.). 1989. pap. 8.95 (*0-9613569-6-0*) Mary Prodns.

— Applique Design Collection. (Illus.). 56p. (Orig.). 1984. pap. 8.95 (*0-9613569-3-6*) Mary Prodns.

— Country Style Appliques. (Illus.). 42p. (Orig.). 1987. pap. 7.95 (*0-9613569-5-2*) Mary Prodns.

— Deluxe Designs: Designing with Ultrasuede & Other Special Fabrics. (Illus.). 48p. (Orig.). 1992. pap. 12.95 (*0-9613569-9-5*) Mary Prodns.

— Designer Sweatshirts. (Illus.). 44p. (Orig.). 1989. pap. 7.95 (*0-9613569-1-X*) Mary Prodns.

— Mary Mulari's Garments with Style: Adding Flair to Tops, Jackets, Vests, Dresses & More! LC 94-23783. (StarWear Ser.). 160p. 1995. pap. 17.95 (*0-8019-8640-0*) Chilton.

— More Designer Sweatshirts. (Illus.). 60p. (Orig.). 1986. pap. 8.95 (*0-9613569-4-4*) Mary Prodns.

— Sweatshirts with Style. LC 93-8197. (Illus.). 124p. 1993. pap. 15.95 (*0-8019-8392-4*) Chilton.

Mulase, Motohico, tr. see Kuga, Michio.

***Mulathino.** Origami. 1995. (*0-7858-0262-2*) Bk Sales Inc.

Mulawka, E. J. African Grey Parrots. (Illus.). 128p. 19.95 (*0-86622-975-2*, PS-780) TFH Pubns.

Mulawka, Edward J. Blue-Fronted Amazon Parrots. (Illus.). 128p. 1983. 16.95 (*0-87666-834-1*, PS-782) TFH Pubns.

— Taming & Training Parrots. (Illus.). 1981. 19.95 (*0-86622-098-4*, H-1019) TFH Pubns.

Mulay, Regina. Mass Media, International Relations & Non-Alignment. 536p. 1987. 48.50 (*0-8364-2030-6*, Pub. by Deep) S Asia.

Mulbagala, K. V. The Popular Practice of Yoga. 238p. 1995. pap. 17.00 (*0-89540-295-5*, SB-295) Sun Pub.

***Mulberg, Jon.** Social Limits to Economic Theory. LC 94-47651. (Modern Economics Ser.). 1995. pap. write for info. (*0-415-09298-1*); pap. write for info. (*0-415-12386-0*) Routledge.

Mulcahy, D. L., et al, eds. Biotechnology & Ecology of Pollen. (Illus.). 700p. 1986. 96.00 (*0-387-96267-0*) Spr-Verlag.

Mulcahy, David E. Warehouse Distribution & Operations Handbook. 544p. 1993. text ed. 89.50 (*0-07-044002-6*) McGraw.

***Mulcahy, Greg.** Out of Work. 1994. pap. 3.99 (*0-517-13071-8*) Random.

— Out of Work: Novella & Stories. LC 92-54799. 1993. 21.00 (*0-679-41967-5*) Knopf.

***Mulcahy, Katie V.** Pot of Gold Caper. 40p. (J). 1995. pap. 9.95 (*0-7610-0031-3*) NW Pub.

Mulcahy, Kevin, jt. auth. see Crabb, Cecil V., Jr.

Mulcahy, Kevin V., jt. auth. see Crabb, Cecil V.

Mulcahy, Kevin V., jt. ed. see Pankratz, David B.

Mulcahy, Kevin V., et al, eds. America's Commitment to Culture: Government & the Arts. 235p. 1994. text ed. 49.95 (*0-8133-0692-2*) Westview.

***Mulcahy, Lucille.** Dark Arrow. LC 94-39582. (Illus.). 224p. (J). 1995. pap. 7.95 (*0-8032-8220-6*, Bison Books) U of Nebr Pr.

Mulcahy, Pat, ed. see Hirsch, E. D., Jr.

Mulcahy, Richard, jt. auth. see Langley, Aidan.

Mulcahy, Risteard. The Longterm Care of the Coronary Patient. (Illus.). 124p. (Orig.). 1991. text ed. 27.95 (*0-443-04673-5*) Churchill.

Mulcahy, Robert F., et al, eds. Enhancing Learning & Thinking. LC 91-15556. 304p. 1991. text ed. 65.00 (*0-275-93666-X*, C3666, Praeger Pubs) Greenwood.

Mulcahy, Robert W. & Smith, Marion C. Strike Prevention & Control Handbook. 1983. pap. 29.95 (*0-88057-065-2*) Exec Ent Pubns.

— Strike Prevention & Control Handbook. 1994. pap. text ed. 19.95 (*0-471-11285-2*) Wiley.

Mulcahy, Rosemarie. The Decoration of the Royal Basilica of El Escorial. LC 93-6504. 368p. (C). 1994. 95.00 (*0-521-41344-3*) Cambridge U Pr.

Mulcahy, Sylvia, tr. see Verdi, Giuseppe.

Mulcaster, Richard. Positions Concerning the Training up of Children. Barker, William, ed. 696p. 1993. 80.00 (*0-8020-2987-6*) U of Toronto Pr.

Mulchow & Mogel. Law of Energy Trans, 5 vols. 1990. Updates. ring bd. write for info. (*0-8205-1336-9*) Bender.

***Mulcrone, Patricia, ed.** Current Perspectives on Administration of Adult Education Programs. LC 85-644750. (New Directions for Adult & Continuing Education Ser.: No. 60). 115p. (Orig.). 1993. pap. 16.95 (*1-55542-714-6*) Jossey-Bass.

Mulder. Imported Foundation Stock of North American Arabian Horses, Vol. 1. limited rev. ed. 1991. 45.00 (*0-87505-360-2*) Borden.

— Imported Foundation Stock of North American Arabian Horses, Vol. 1. rev. ed. 1991. 30.00 (*0-87505-361-0*) Borden.

— Imported Foundation Stock of North American Arabian Horses, Vol. 2. 1993. 39.00 (*0-87505-111-1*) Borden.

Mulder, A. C., jt. ed. see Knyn, T.

***Mulder-Bakker, Anneke B., ed.** Sanctity & Motherhood: Essays on Holy Mothers in the Middle Ages. LC 95-13824. (Medieval Casebooks Ser.: Vol. 14). (Illus.). 368p. 1995. 50.00 (*0-8153-1425-6*, H1767) Garland.

Mulder, C. L. & De Bruin, E. J., eds. Psychosocial Interventions in Patients with Cancer & Coronary Heart Disease: Examples of Field Studies & Methodological Considerations. LC 93-19354. 1993. 24.50 (*90-265-1349-6*, Pub. by Swets Pub Serv NE) Taylor & Francis.

Mulder, Chris J. & Tytgat, N. J., eds. Is Crohn's Disease a Mycobacterial Disease? 1992. lib. bdg. 58.00 (*0-7923-2026-3*) Kluwer Ac.

Mulder, Clara H. Migration Dynamics: A Life Course Approach. 251p. 1993. pap. 26.50 (*90-5170-236-1*, Pub. by Thesis Pubs NE) IBD Ltd.

Mulder, David. The Alchemy of Revolution: Gerrard Winstanley's Occultism & Seventeenth-Century English Communism. LC 89-34745. (American University Studies: History: Ser. IX, Vol. 77). 364p. 1990. text ed. 60.95 (*0-8204-1173-6*) P Lang Pubs.

Mulder, Dwayne, jt. auth. see Moser, Paul.

Mulder, G. J., et al, eds. Sulfate Metabolism & Sulfate Conjugation. 312p. 1982. 85.00 (*0-8002-3665-3*) Taylor & Francis.

Mulder, Gerald J. Sulfation of Drugs & Related Compounds. 248p. 1981. 99.00 (*0-8493-5920-1*, RM301, CRC Reprint) Franklin.

Mulder, Gerard J., ed. Conjugation Reactions in Drug Metabolism: An Integral Approach. 300p. 1990. 135.00 (*0-85066-738-0*) Taylor & Francis.

Mulder, Henk L. & Van de Velde-Schlick, Barbara, eds. Moritz Schlick: Philosophical Papers, Vol. 2, 1925-1936. (Vienna Circle Collection Ser.: No. 11). 1980. lib. bdg. 145.50 (*90-277-0941-6*) Kluwer Ac.

Mulder, Henk L. & Van De Velde-Schlick, Barbara, eds. Moritz Schlick: Philosophical Papers, Vol. 1, 1909-1922. (Vienna Circle Collection: No. 11). 1978. lib. bdg. 126. 50 (*90-277-0314-0*) Kluwer Ac.

Mulder, Henk L., ed. see Menger, Karl.

Mulder, Henk L., ed. see Schlick, Moritz.

Mulder, J. W. & Hervey, S. G. Theory of the Linguistic Sign. (Janua Linguarum, Ser. Minor: No. 136). 70p. (Orig.). 1972. pap. text ed. 14.70 (*90-279-2187-3*) Mouton.

Mulder, Jan. Foundations of Axiomatic Linguistics. (Trends in Linguistics, Studies & Monographs: No. 40). xii, 475p. (C). 1989. lib. bdg. 121.95 (*0-89925-323-7*) Mouton.

Mulder, Jean G. Ergativity in Coast Tsimshian. LC 94-9526. (Publications in Linguistics Ser.: Vol. 124). 1994. 28.00x (*0-520-09788-2*) U CA Pr.

Mulder, John, et al, eds. The Diversity of Discipleship: Presbyterians & Twentieth-Century Christian Witness. (Presbyterian Presene Ser.). 372p. (Orig.). 1991. pap. 16. 99 (*0-664-25196-X*) Westminster John Knox.

— The Presbyterian Predicament: Six Perspectives. (Presbyterian Presence Ser.). 168p. (Orig.). 1990. pap. 12.99 (*0-664-25097-1*) Westminster John Knox.

Mulder, John M. Woodrow Wilson: The Years of Preparation. LC 77-72128. (Supplementary Volumes to the Papers of Woodrow Wilson). (Illus.). 334p. reprint ed. pap. 95.20 (*0-8357-6548-2*, 2035912) Bks Demand.

Mulder, John M., et al, eds. The Organizational Revolution: Presbyterians & American Denominationalism. (Presbyterian Presence Ser.). 300p. (Orig.). 1991. pap. 16.99 (*0-664-25197-8*) Westminster John Knox.

Mulder, John R. Temple of the Mind: Education & Literary Taste in Seventeenth-Century England. LC 79-79059. 1969. 27.50 (*0-672-53602-1*) Irvington.

Mulder, John T., jt. ed. see Kerr, Hugh T.

Mulder-Krieger, T. & Verpoorte, R. Anthocyanins As Flower Pigments: Feasibilities for Flower Colour Modification. LC 93-11838. 164p. (C). 1993. pap. text ed. 0.01 (*0-7923-2465-X*) Kluwer Ac.

Mulder, L. J., et al, eds. Computers in Psychology: Application in Education, Research & Psychodiagnostics. 240p. 1991. 48.00 (*90-265-1170-1*, Pub. by Swets Pub Serv NE) Taylor & Francis.

Mulder, Linnea. Sarah & Puffle: A Story for Children about Diabetes. LC 92-25638. (Illus.). 32p. (J). 1992. pap. 8.95 (*0-945354-42-8*) Magination Pr.

Mulder, M., et al. Strategic Human Resource Management. 180p. 1990. 36.00 (*90-265-1092-6*, Pub. by Swets Pub Serv NE) Taylor & Francis.

Mulder, M. J. The Old Testament in Syriac According to the Peshitta Version, Pt. III, Fasc. 3: Ezekiel. LC 78-339247. xxxvi, 113p. 1993. reprint ed. 60.75 (*90-04-07314-0*) E J Brill.

Mulder, M. J., jt. ed. see Dirksen, P. B.

Mulder, Mark. Group Structure, Motivation & Group Performance. (Psychology Ser.). (Illus.). 1963. text ed. 14.65 (*3-10-800280-5*) Mouton.

Mulder, Martin J., ed. Mikra: Text, Translation, Reading, & Interpretation of the Hebrew Bible in Ancient Judaism & Early Christianity. LC 88-7163. (Compendia Ser.: No. II). 850p. 1989. text ed. 86.00 (*0-8006-0604-3*, 1-604, Fortress Pr) Augsburg Fortress.

Mulder, Mary J. & Coyle, Richard. Come, Sing & Celebrate! (Orig.). 1988. pap. 3.65 (*1-55673-074-8*, 8871) CSS OH.

Mulder, Mauk. The Daily Power Game. (Quality of Working Life Ser.: No. 6). 1977. lib. bdg. 33.00 (*90-207-0707-8*) Kluwer Ac.

***Mulder, Niels.** Psycho-Immunology & HIV Infection. 176p. 1994. pap. 25.00 (*90-5170-300-7*, Pub. by Thesis Pubs NE) IBD Ltd.

Mulder, Rev. Imported Foundation Stock of North American Arabian Horses, Vol. 2. 1993. 39.00 (*0-685-72639-8*) Borden.

— Imported Foundation Stock of North American Arabian Horses, Vol. 2. limited ed. 1993. 47.00 (*0-685-72640-1*) Borden.

Mulder, W. C., jt. ed. see Brasser, L. J.

Mulder, William. The Mormons in American History. LC 80-27308. (University of Utah Frederick William Reynolds Lecture Ser.: No. 21). 1981. reprint ed. 4.95 (*0-87480-184-2*) U of Utah Pr.

***Mulderig, Gerald P.** The Heath Guide to Grammar & Usage. 160p. (C). 1994. pap. write for info. (*0-669-35378-7*) Heath.

— The Heath Guide to Writing the Research Paper. 216p. (C). 1992. pap. text ed. write for info. (*0-669-27704-5*) Heath.

— The Heath Guide to Writing the Research Paper. 2nd ed. 224p. (C). 1995. pap. text ed. write for info. (*0-669-35377-9*) Heath.

— The Heath Handbook. 13th ed. 800p. (C). 1995. text ed. write for info. (*0-669-34131-2*) Heath.

Mulderig, Gerald P. & Elsbree, Langdon. The Heath Handbook. 12th ed. LC 89-85074. 771p. (C). 1990. text ed. 14.50 (*0-669-17859-4*); Wkbk. student ed 11.00 (*0-669-17861-6*); Instr.'s guide. teacher ed 14.50 (*0-669-17860-8*); Transparency masters. trans. write for info. (*0-318-66918-8*); Diagnostic tests. 2.00 (*0-669-17864-0*); Answer key. 2.00 (*0-669-17862-4*) Heath.

Mulders, M. A. Remote Sensing in Soil Science. (Developments in Soil Science Ser.: No. 15). 378p. 1987. 105.25 (*0-444-42783-X*) Elsevier.

Muldner, Tomasz & Steele, Peter W. C As a Second Language: A Text for Pascal Programmers. LC 86-28837. (A-W Computer Science Ser.). (Illus.). 456p. (C). 1988. pap. text ed. 37.75 (*0-201-19210-1*) Addison-Wesley.

Muldoon, James. The Americas in the Spanish World Order: The Justification for Conquest in the Seventeenth Century. LC 93-50529. 256p. (C). 1994. text ed. 32.95 (*0-8122-3245-3*) U of Pa Pr.

Muldoon, James B. You Have No Courts with Any Sure Rule of Law: The Saga of the Supreme Judicial Court of Massachusetts. (Illus.). 353p. (Orig.). 1992. pap. 16.95 (*0-9632270-0-9*) Lookout Hill.

***Muldoon, James P., ed.** A Guide to Delegate Preparation, 1994-95. 185p. 1994. pap. 10.00 (*1-880632-26-8*) UNA-USA.

Muldoon, John F. & Furlong, Thomas F., eds. Essays on Blindness Rehabilitation in Honor of Thomas J. Carroll: A Festschrift. LC 89-18277. 160p. 1990. 24.95 (*0-89128-164-9*); audio 24.95 (*0-89128-165-7*) Am Foun Blind.

Muldoon, Joseph A. The Facilitator's Guide for the Insight Class Program. 112p. 1988. teacher ed 24.95 (*0-9613416-8-8*) Comm Intervention.

— Nobody's Fault, Everybody's Responsibility: What Parents Can Do When a Child Is Using Alcohol & Other Drugs. 48p. (Orig.). 1989. pap. 3.95 (*0-945485-09-3*) Comm Intervention.

Muldoon, Joseph A. & Crowley, James F. One Step Ahead: Early-Intervention Strategies for Adolescent Drug Problems. LC 85-73646. (Illus.). 180p. (Orig.). 1986. pap. 14.95 (*0-9613416-1-0*) Comm Intervention.

Muldoon, Kathleen M. Princess Pooh. Mathews, Judith, ed. LC 88-33978. (Illus.). 32p. (J). (gr. 2-5). 1989. lib. bdg. 13.95 (*0-8075-6627-6*) A Whitman.

Muldoon, Katie. Catalog Marketing. 2nd ed. 608p. 1988. 75. 00 (*0-8144-5922-6*) AMACOM.

— How to Profit Through Catalog Marketing. Knudsen, Anne, ed. 1995. 89.95 (*0-8442-3572-5*, NTC Busn Bks) NTC Pub Grp.

Muldoon, Marilynn C., ed. see Muldoon, Virginia.

Muldoon, Maureen. The Abortion Debate in the United States & Canada: A Source Book. LC 91-3658. 256p. 1991. 34.00 (*0-8240-5260-9*, SS648) Garland.

Muldoon, Maureen, ed. Abortion: An Annotated Indexed Bibliography. LC 79-91622. (Studies in Women & Religion: Vol. 3). 167p. 1980. lib. bdg. 79.95 (*0-88946-972-5*) E Mellen.

***Muldoon, Paul.** The Annals of Chile. 191p. Date not set. 10.00 (*0-374-52456-4*) FS&G.

— The Annals of Chile. LC 94-10874. 1994. 21.00 (*0-374-10518-9*) FS&G.

— Madoc: A Mystery. 1991. 19.95 (*0-374-19557-9*) FS&G.

— Madoc: A Mystery. 272p. 1992. pap. 12.00 (*0-374-52344-4*) FS&G.

— Meeting the British. LC 87-50181. 64p. (Orig.). 1987. pap. 6.95 (*0-916390-26-8*) Wake Forest.

— Mules & Early Poems. 72p. 1986. pap. 6.95 (*0-916390-22-5*) Wake Forest.

— The Prince of the Quotidian. 40p. 1994. pap. 5.95 (*0-916390-63-2*) Wake Forest.

— Quoof. LC 83-50028. 64p. 1983. pap. 5.95 (*0-916390-19-5*) Wake Forest.

— Selected Poems, 1968-1986. 128p. 1987. 16.50 (*0-88001-154-8*) Ecco Pr.

— Selected Poems, 1968-1986. 1993. pap. 12.00 (*0-374-52374-6*, Noonday) FS&G.

— Shining Brow. 80p. (Orig.). 1993. pap. 8.95 (*0-571-16789-6*) Faber & Faber.

— Why Brownlee Left. LC 80-50846. 48p. 1981. pap. 5.95 (*0-916390-13-6*) Wake Forest.

Muldoon, Paul, ed. The Faber Book of Contemporary Irish Poetry. 416p. 1986. pap. 14.95 (*0-571-13761-X*) Faber & Faber.

Muldoon, Paul, sel. The Essential Byron. (Essential Poets Ser.). 128p. 1989. pap. 6.00 (*0-88001-181-5*) Ecco Pr.

Muldoon, Paul, tr. see Nuala Ni Dhomhnaill.

Muldoon, Robert L., jt. auth. see Jackson, George G.

Muldoon, Sylvan & Carrington, Hereward. Projection of the Astral Body. (Illus.). 336p. 1968. reprint ed. pap. 10.95 (*0-87728-069-X*) Weiser.

Muldoon, Sylvan J. & Carrington, Hereward. The Projection of the Astral Body. (Collector's Library of the Unknown). 242p. 1990. reprint ed. write for info. (*0-8094-8062-X*); reprint ed. lib. bdg. write for info. (*0-8094-8063-8*) Time-Life.

Muldoon, Virginia. When Nancy Lived on Chestnut Street. Muldoon, Marilynn C., ed. (Illus.). 52p. 1982. pap. 3.95 (*0-940930-00-5*) Forsythe & Cromwell.

Muldowney, Mary S., tr. see Augustine.

Muldowny, John, jt. auth. see McDonald, Michael J.

Muldrew, Jessie. Focus on Creative Playmaking. Romano, Louis G., ed. 17p. 1989. pap. text ed. write for info. (*0-318-72650-5*) MI Middle Educ.

Muldrey, Mary H. Abounding in Mercy - Mother Austin Carroll. (Illus.). 452p. (Orig.). 1988. 23.50 (*0-944784-00-3*); pap. 9.00 (*0-944784-01-1*) Habersham.

Muldron, Diane. Walt Disney's Bambi: Count to Five. (Golden Board Bks.). (Illus.). (J). (ps-00). 1991. bds. write for info. (*0-307-06114-0*, Golden Pr) Western Pub.

Muldrow, Diane. Dearest Baby. (Golden Sturdy Shape Bks.). (Illus.). 14p. (J). (ps). 1993. bds. 3.95 (*0-307-12394-4*, 12394, Golden Pr) Western Pub.

— Disney's Aladdin: Action Words. (J). (ps). 1994. 3.95 (*0-307-12495-9*, Golden Pr) Western Pub.

— Walt Disney's Dumbo the Circus Baby. (J). (ps). 1993. 4.95 (*0-307-12397-9*, Golden Pr) Western Pub.

Muldrow, George M. Milton & the Drama of the Soul: A Study of the Theme of the Restoration of Man in Milton's Later Poetry. LC 76-89796. (Studies in English Literature: Vol. 51). 1970. text ed. 38.75 (*90-279-0530-4*) Mouton.

Muldrow, George M., jt. auth. see Donker, Marjorie.

Mule, Barbara, jt. auth. see Kaiser, Geoffrey.

Mule, Marty. Rolling Green: A Century of Tulane Football. (Illus.). 101p. 1993. 24.95 (*0-9639795-0-7*) Tulane U Athletic.

Mule, Marty & Remy, Bob. Louisiana Athletes: The Top Twenty. LC 81-4601. (Illus.). 160p. (J). (gr. 6 up). 1981. 11.95 (*0-88289-282-7*) Pelican.

Mule, S. J. & Brill, Henry. Chemical & Biological Aspects of Drug Dependence. LC 72-191695. (Drug Dependence Ser.). 576p. 1972. 55.00 (*0-87819-011-2*, CRC Reprint) Franklin.

Mule, S. Joseph, ed. Behavior in Excess: An Examination of the Volitional Disorders. LC 81-65506. (Illus.). 480p. 1981. text ed. 45.00 (*0-02-922220-6*) Free Pr.

***Mulfinger, Dale.** The Architecture of Edwin Lundie. LC 95-15039. 1995. write for info. (*0-87351-313-4*); pap. write for info. (*0-87351-314-2*) Minn Hist.

Mulfinger, George, ed. Design & Origins in Astronomy. (Creation Research Society Monograph Ser.: No. 2). (Illus.). 152p. (Orig.). 1984. pap. 8.95 (*0-940384-03-5*) Creation Research.

Mulfinger, George, Jr., ed. see Rusch, Wilbert H., Sr.

Mulford. H. C. & Eagle's Brood. 1976. 22.95 (*0-88411-206-3*) Amereon Ltd.

— H. C. & Eagle's Brood. large type ed. 1976. 22.95 (*0-88411-235-7*) Amereon Ltd.

— H. C. Returns. 1976. 22.95 (*0-88411-218-7*) Amereon Ltd.

— H. C. Serves Writ. 1976. 21.95 (*0-88411-220-9*) Amereon Ltd.

— H. C. Takes Cards. 1976. 21.95 (*0-88411-221-7*) Amereon Ltd.

— H. C.'s Protege. 1976. 23.95 (*0-88411-219-5*) Amereon Ltd.

— Johnny Nelson. 1976. 24.95 (*0-88411-222-5*) Amereon Ltd.

— Me an' Shorty. 1976. 21.95 (*0-88411-223-3*) Amereon Ltd.

— Mesquite Jenkins. 1976. 22.95 (*0-88411-208-X*) Amereon Ltd.

— Mesquite Jenkins. large type ed. 1976. 22.95 (*0-88411-236-5*) Amereon Ltd.

— Mesquite Jenkins, Tumbleweed. 1976. 22.95 (*0-88411-224-1*) Amereon Ltd.

— On Trail Tumbling T. 1976. 22.95 (*0-88411-209-8*) Amereon Ltd.

— Round-Up. 1976. 22.95 (*0-88411-210-1*) Amereon Ltd.

— Trail Dust. large type ed. 1976. 22.95 (*0-88411-240-3*) Amereon Ltd.

Mulford, A. C. Boundaries & Landmarks. 1977. reprint ed. pap. 15.00 (*0-686-18920-5*, 611) CARBEN Survey.

Mulford, Beverley M. The Mulford Method: A Preschool Teaching Program. (Illus.). 96p. (C). Date not set. teacher ed write for info. (*0-9639125-0-X*) Mulford School.

Mulford, Carla, ed. see Stockton, Annis B.

Mulford, Charles. Interorganizational Relations: Implications for Community Development. (Center for Policy Research Monographs: Vol. 4). 227p. 1984. 34.95 (*0-89885-147-5*) Human Sci Pr.

Mulford, Clarence. Bar Twenty. (Hopalong Cassidy Ser.). 382p. 1974. reprint ed. lib. bdg. 25.95 (*0-88411-213-6*, Aeonian Pr) Amereon Ltd.

— Bar Twenty Days. (Hopalong Cassidy Ser.). 412p. 1974. reprint ed. lib. bdg. 25.95 (*0-88411-214-4*, Aeonian Pr) Amereon Ltd.

— Bar Twenty Three. (Hopalong Cassidy Ser). 1976. reprint ed. lib. bdg. 23.95 (*0-88411-227-6*, Aeonian Pr) Amereon Ltd.

— Coming of Cassidy. (Hopalong Cassidy Ser.). 438p. 1974. reprint ed. lib. bdg. 27.95 (*0-88411-216-0*, Aeonian Pr) Amereon Ltd.

— Corson of the J. C. (Hopalong Cassidy Ser.). 340p. 1974. reprint ed. lib. bdg. 22.95 (*0-685-00358-2*, Aeonian Pr) Amereon Ltd.

— Cottonwood Gulch. large type ed. (Hopalong Cassidy Ser.). 348p. 1974. reprint ed. lib. bdg. 23.95 (*0-88411-233-0*, Aeonian Pr) Amereon Ltd.

— Hopalong Cassidy. 1976. reprint ed. lib. bdg. 25.95 (*0-88411-217-9*, Aeonian Pr) Amereon Ltd.

— Hopalong Cassidy Series. large type ed. Incl. Black Buttes. 1976. reprint ed. 16.95 (*0-685-29615-6*); Corson of the J. C. 1976. reprint ed. 17.95 (*0-685-29616-4*); Cottonwood Gulch. 1976. reprint ed. 17.95 (*0-685-29617-2*); Deputy Sheriff. 1976. reprint ed. 15.95 (*0-685-29618-0*); Hopalong Cassidy & the Eagle's Brood. 1976. reprint ed. 16.95 (*0-685-29619-9*); Mesquite Jenkins. 1976. reprint ed. 16.95 (*0-685-29620-2*); On the Trail of the Tumbling T. 1976. reprint ed. 22.95 (*0-88411-237-3*); Round-Up. 1976. reprint ed. 16.95 (*0-685-29621-0*); Rustler's Valley. 1976. reprint ed. 17. 95 (*0-685-29622-9*); Trail Dust. 1976. reprint ed. 16.95 (*0-685-29623-7*); 1976. write for info. (*0-318-66020-2*) Amereon Ltd.

— The Man from Bar Twenty. (Hopalong Cassidy Ser.). 1976. reprint ed. lib. bdg. 22.95 (*0-88411-229-2*, Aeonian Pr) Amereon Ltd.

— Man from the Bar-20. 1995. pap. 4.99 (*0-8125-5050-1*) Forge NYC.

— Orphan. 308p. 1974. reprint ed. lib. bdg. 25.95 (*0-88411-225-X*, Aeonian Pr) Amereon Ltd.

— Tex. (Hopalong Cassidy Ser.). 1976. reprint ed. lib. bdg. 22.95 (*0-88411-226-8*, Aeonian Pr) Amereon Ltd.

Mulford, Clarence E. Bar-Twenty Days. 256p. 1993. mass mkt. 4.99 (*0-8125-3003-9*) Tor Bks.

— Bar-20. 288p. 1992. mass mkt. 4.99 (*0-8125-2290-7*) Tor Bks.

— Bring Me His Ears. (Hopalong Cassidy Ser.). 1976. reprint ed. 24.95 (*0-88411-228-4*, Aeonian Pr) Amereon Ltd.

— Buck Peters, Ranchman. 320p. 1993. mass mkt. 4.99 (*0-8125-2499-3*) Tor Bks.

— Buck Peters, Ranchman. 1973. reprint ed. lib. bdg. 24.95 (*0-88411-202-0*, Aeonian Pr) Amereon Ltd.

— Coming of Cassidy. (Hopalong Cassidy Ser.: No. 1). 1992. mass mkt. 4.99 (*0-8125-2291-5*) Tor Bks.

— Cottonwood Gulch. 1976. 23.95 (*0-88411-204-7*) Amereon Ltd.

— Hopalong Cassidy. 320p. 1992. mass mkt. 4.99 (*0-8125-2242-7*) Tor Bks.

— The Round-Up. large type ed. 1973. reprint ed. lib. bdg. 22.95 (*0-88411-238-1*, Aeonian Pr) Amereon Ltd.

— Rustler's Valley. large type ed. reprint ed. lib. bdg. 23.95 (*0-88411-239-X*, Aeonian Pr) Amereon Ltd.

Mulford, Elisha. Nation: The Foundations of Civil Order & Political Life in the United States. LC 71-120327. xiv, 418p. 1971. reprint ed. 45.00 (*0-678-00705-5*) Kelley.

Mulford, Judy. Decorative Marshallese Baskets. LC 91-90213. (Illus.). 82p. 1991. pap. text ed. 8.95 (*0-8248-1477-0*) UH Pr.

***Mulford, Karen.** Arizona's Historic Restaurants & Their Recipes. (Illus.). 1995. 14.95 (*0-89587-132-7*) Blair.

Mulford, Karen, jt. auth. see O'Brien, Dawn.

Mulford, Philippa G. Everything I Hoped For. 192p. (Orig.). (YA). (gr. 8-12). 1990. pap. 2.95 (*0-380-76074-6*, Flare) Avon.

— Keys to Successful Stepmothering. LC 95-13018. (Parenting Keys Ser.). 1996. write for info. (*0-8120-9330-5*) Barron.

— Making Room for Katherine. LC 93-32268. 192p. (J). (gr. 5-9). 1994. text ed. 14.95 (*0-02-767652-8*, Mac Bks Young Read) S&S Childrens.

Mulford, Prentice. Gift of the Spirit. 1981. 300.00 (*0-8490-0235-4*) Gordon Pr.

— Gift of the Spirit. 267p. 1993. pap. 22.00 (*0-89540-261-0*, SB-261) Sun Pub.

— The Gift of Understanding. 288p. 1994. pap. text ed. 24. 00 (*0-89540-296-3*) Sun Pub.

— Thought Forces. 172p. 1984. pap. 17.00 (*0-89540-144-4*, SB-144) Sun Pub.

— Thoughts Are Things. 1991. lib. bdg. 79.95 (*0-8490-4293-3*) Gordon Pr.

— Thoughts Are Things. 171p. 1993. pap. 16.00 (*0-89540-232-7*, SB-232) Sun Pub.

— Thoughts Are Things. 171p. 1977. reprint ed. spiral bd. 5.50 (*0-7873-0629-0*) Mokelumne.

Mulford, Wendy. Love Poems by Women. 1991. pap. 10.00 (*0-449-90538-1*, Columbine) Fawcett.

Mulgan, G. J. Communication & Control: Networks & the New Economies of Communication. LC 90-40759. (Guilford Communication Ser.). 302p. 1991. text ed. 36. 95 (*0-89862-311-1*) Guilford Pr.

— Politics in an Antipolitical Age. 220p. 1994. 49.95 (*0-7456-0812-4*); pap. 19.95 (*0-7456-0813-2*) Blackwell Pubs.

Mulgan, John, jt. auth. see Bolitho, Hector.

Mulgan, Richard. Politics in New Zealand. (Auckland University Press Book Ser.). 250p. 1994. 33.00 (*1-86940-093-3*) OUP.

Mulgrave, Norman & Nitko, Anthony J. Educational Tests & Measurement: An Introduction. 674p. (C). 1983. Also by Norman Mulgrave. student ed, pap. text ed. 16.50 (*0-15-520911-6*) HB Coll Pubs.

Mulgrew, Bernard & Cowan, Colin F. Adaptive Filters & Equalisers. (C). 1988. lib. bdg. 67.00 (*0-89838-285-8*) Kluwer Ac.

Mulhall, A., jt. ed. see Hardey, M.

Mulhall, Brian E., jt. auth. see Parkinson, David H.

Mulhall, Michael G. Dictionary of Statistics. 1972. 300.00 (*0-8490-0046-7*) Gordon Pr.

— The English in South America. Wilkins, Mira, ed. LC 76-29753. (European Business Ser.). (Illus.). 1977. reprint ed. lib. bdg. 57.95 (*0-405-09769-7*) Ayer.

Mulhall, Stephen. Liberals & Communitarians: An Introduction. 1992. pap. 19.95 (*0-631-18378-7*) Blackwell Pubs.

— On Being in the World: Wittgenstein & Heidegger on Seeing Aspects. 208p. 1990. 52.50 (*0-415-04416-2*, A4252) Routledge.

— Stanley Cavell: Philosophy's Recounting of the Ordinary. 376p. 1994. 52.00 (*0-19-824074-0*) OUP.

***Mulhausen, Harold L. & Alexander, James E.** Korea: Memories of a U. S. Marine. (Illus.). 80p. 1995. pap. 7.50 (*0-939965-11-9*) Macedon Prod.

Mulhauser, Ruth. Maurice Sceve. LC 76-28722. (Twayne's World Authors Ser.). 138p. (C). 1977. lib. bdg. 17.95 (*0-8057-6264-7*) Irvington.

Mulhearn, Daniel & Taibi, John. General Motors F Units the Locos: That Revolutionized Railroading. 1982. pap. 11.95 (*0-915276-39-9*) Quadrant Pr.

Mulhearn, Henry J. Graphing & Charting Simplified. 105p. 1976. pap. 11.95 (*0-87526-221-X*) Gould.

— Police Science Fundamentals. 1,973th ed. 220p. pap. 11. 95 (*0-87526-160-4*) Gould.

Mulherin, Jennifer. As You Like It: Shakespeare for Everyone. LC 90-478. (Illus.). 32p. (J). (gr. 3-7). 1990. lib. bdg. 12.95 (*0-87226-339-8*) P Bedrick Bks.

An Asterisk (*) at the beginning of an entry indicates that the title is appearing in BIP for the first time.

— Little Book of Christmas. 1991. 4.99 (*0-517-06537-1*) Random Hse Value.
— The Macmillan Treasury of Spices & Natural Flavorings. 160p. 1988. text ed. 17.95 (*0-02-587850-6*) Macmillan.
Mulherin, Jenny. Presentation Techniques for the Graphic Artist. (Illus.). 144p. 1987. 24.95 (*0-89134-213-3*, 30008) North Light Bks.
Mulherin, Jenny, jt. auth. see Barrett, Norman S.
Mulherin, Tim. Behind Bars: A Guidebook for Successful Bartending & Bar-Attending. (Illus.). 256p. (Orig.). 1994. pap. 10.95 (*0-9639648-0-1*) White River.
Mulhern, Chieko. Koda Rohan. LC 76-50541. (Twayne's World Authors Ser.). 178p. (C). 1977. lib. bdg. 17.95 (*0-8057-6272-8*) Irvington.
Mulhern, Chieko, tr. see Arai, Shinya.
Mulhern, Chieko I., ed. Heroic with Grace: Legendary Women of Japan. LC 90-28750. 344p. (C). 1991. 48.95 (*0-87332-527-3*); pap. text ed. 20.95 (*0-87332-552-4*) M E Sharpe.
— Japanese Women Writers: A Bio-Critical Sourcebook. LC 94-617. 536p. 1994. text ed. 95.00 (*0-313-25486-9*) Greenwood.
Mulhern, Francis. Contemporary Marxist Literary Criticism. 280p. (C). 1993. pap. text ed. 18.50 (*0-582-05976-3*, 79363) Longman.
Mulhern, Gerry, jt. ed. see Greer, Brian.
Mulhern, James. History of Secondary Education in Pennsylvania. LC 77-89208. (American Education: Its Men, Institutions & Ideas, Ser. 1). 1970. reprint ed. 30. 95 (*0-405-01447-3*) Ayer.
Mulhern, Raymond K., jt. ed. see Bearison, David J.
Mulhern, Tom, ed. Bass Heroes: Styles, Stories & Secrets of 30 Great Bass Players. (Illus.). 208p. pap. 17.95 (*0-87930-274-7*) Miller Freeman.
Mulhern, Tom, jt. auth. see Dellavalle, Charles.
Mulholland, Ann, ed. Oral Education: Today & Tomorrow. 560p. (Orig.). (C). 1981. pap. 19.95 (*0-88200-144-2*, D2153) Alexander Graham.
Mulholland, Catherine. The Owensmouth Baby: The Making of a San Fernando Valley Town. (Illus.). 212p. 1987. text ed. 40.00 (*0-937048-42-9*) CSUN.
Mulholland, David H. A Reading Guide to the Book of Mormon. v, 119p. 1989. student ed. pap. 6.95 (*0-87579-183-2*) Deseret Bk.
— A Reading Guide to the Old Testament. iv, 261p. 1989. pap. 9.95 (*0-87579-283-9*) Deseret Bk.
Mulholland, J. Derral, ed. Scientific Applications of Lunar Laser Ranging. (Astrophysics & Space Science Library: No. 62). 1977. lib. bdg. 94.00 (*90-277-0790-1*) Kluwer Ac.
Mulholland, J. Derral, jt. auth. see Evans, David S.
***Mulholland, J. F.** It's Okay to be Happy. 160p. 1994. pap. 5.95 (*1-884621-00-7*) Tipperary Pr.
Mulholland, J. R. Heating, Ventilation & Air Conditioning Plant. 142p. 1970. 28.00 (*0-8464-1468-6*) Beekman Pubs.
Mulholland, James. The Drama of Worship: Worship Enhancers for Traditional Services & Special Occasions. 1988. 8.50 (*0-685-68705-8*, MP-650) Lillenas.
— No Compromise & the Fool: Two Life-Centered Plays That Relate Biblical Themes to Contemporary Life. 1987. 8.50 (*0-8341-9243-8*, MP-638) Lillenas.
Mulholland, Joan. Handbook of Persuasive Tactics: A Handbook of Strategies for Influencing Others Through Communication. LC 93-17210. 600p. 1994. 55.00 (*0-415-08930-1*, B0737) Routledge.
— Language of Negotiation: A Handbook of Practical Strategies for Improving Communication. 1992. pap. 17. 95 (*0-415-06041-9*, Pub. by Tavistock UK); pap. 57.50 (*0-415-06040-0*, Pub. by Tavistock UK) Routledge Chapman & Hall.
Mulholland, John. Beware Familiar Spirits. LC 75-7388. (Perspectives in Psychical Research Ser.). 1975. reprint ed. 29.95 (*0-405-07036-5*) Ayer.
Mulholland, Kenneth, jt. auth. see Hulbert, Terry C.
Mulholland, Leslie A. Kant's System of Rights. 464p. 1990. text ed. 49.00 (*0-231-06874-3*) Col U Pr.
Mulholland, M. Robert, Jr. Invitation to a Journey: A Road Map for Spiritual Formation. LC 93-3529. 173p. (Orig.). 1993. pap. 9.99 (*0-8308-1386-1*, 1386) InterVarsity.
— Revelation. 21.99 (*0-310-51741-9*) Zondervan.
Mulholland, M. Robert. Shaped by the Word. LC 85-51241. (Orig.). 1985. pap. 8.95 (*0-8358-0519-0*) Upper Room Bks.
Mulholland, Michael, jt. auth. see Phillips, Sidney.
Mulholland, Michael W. Review of Surgery. 1992. text ed. 29.95 (*0-397-51313-5*) Lippincott.
Mulholland, Michael W., ed. see Greenfield, Lazar J., et al.
Mulholland, Paul, ed. see Middleton, Thomas & Dekker, Thomas.
***Mulholland, R. D.** Introduction to the New Zealand Legal System. 7th ed. 352p. 1990. pap. 90.00 (*0-409-78895-3*, NZ) Butterworth Legal Pubs.
Mulholland, S. C., jt. ed. see Rapp, G., Jr.
***Mulholland, St. Clair A.** The Story of the 116th Regiment Pennsylvania Infantry. 422p. Date not set. 35.00 (*1-56013-005-9*) Olde Soldier Bks.
Mulholland, T. B., jt. ed. see Evans, C. R.
Mulholland, W. D. Adirondack Campsites. 42p. 1993. reprint ed. lib. bdg. 69.00 (*0-7812-5258-X*) Rprt Serv.
— Catskill Campsites. 14p. 1993. reprint ed. lib. bdg. 69.00 (*0-7812-5259-8*) Rprt Serv.
— Catskill Trails. 34p. 1993. reprint ed. lib. bdg. 69.00 (*0-7812-5260-1*) Rprt Serv.
— Lake Placid Trails. 22p. 1993. reprint ed. lib. bdg. 69.00 (*0-7812-5261-X*) Rprt Serv.
Mulica, Barbara, jt. auth. see Damiani, Bruno.
Mulick, James, ed. Parent-Professional Partnerships in Developmental Disability Services. 1983. 19.95 (*0-938550-06-3*) Acad Guild.
Mulick, James & Antonak, Richard, eds. Transitions in Mental Retardation: The Community Imperative Revisited, Vol. 3. (Transitions in Mental Retardation Ser.). 272p. 1987. text ed. 65.00 (*0-89391-408-8*) Ablex Pub.
Mulick, James & Mallory, Bruce L. Transitions in Mental Retardation, Vol. I. (Transitions in Mental Retardation Ser.). 320p. 1985. 65.00 (*0-89391-236-0*) Ablex Pub.
Mulick, James, jt. ed. see Antonak, Richard.
Mulick, James, jt. ed. see Pueschel, Siegfried.
Mulick, James A., jt. ed. see Matson, Johnny L.
Mulisch, Harry. The Assault. White, Claire, tr. LC 84-22623. 162p. 1986. pap. 13.00 (*0-394-74420-9*) Pantheon.
— What Poetry Is. Barkan, Stanley H., ed. White, Claire Nicolas, tr. (Cross-Cultural Review Chapbook Ser.: No. 9:). 40p. (DUT & ENG.). 1981. 15.00 (*0-89304-875-5*, CCC133); pap. 5.00 (*0-89304-808-9*) Cross-Cultrl NY.
Mulk-Raj, Anand. Author to Critic: The Letters of Mulk Raj Anand to Saros Cowasjee. Cowasjee, Saros, ed. (Writers Workshop Greybird Ser.). 128p. 1973. 8.00 (*0-317-42430-0*) Ind-US Inc.
— Bubble. 604p. 1984. 19.90 (*0-86578-243-1*) Ind-US Inc.
Mulk Raj Anand. Coolie. 320p. (gr. 10-12). 1981. reprint ed. pap. 4.00 (*0-86578-005-6*) Ind-US Inc.
Mulkay, Michael. Sociological Pilgrimage. 1990. 65.00 (*0-335-09409-0*, Open Univ Pr); pap. 21.00 (*0-335-09404-X*, Open Univ Pr) Taylor & Francis.
— Sociology of Science: A Sociological Pilgrimage. LC 90-5275. (Science, Technology, & Society Ser.). (Illus.). 248p. 1991. 39.95 (*0-253-33933-2*) Ind U Pr.
— The Word & the World: Explorations in the Form of Sociological Analysis. 240p. (C). 1985. text ed. 49.95 (*0-04-301196-9*); pap. text ed. 19.95 (*0-04-301197-7*) Routledge Chapman & Hall.
Mulkay, Michael, ed. see Larrain, Jorge.
Mulkay, Michael, jt. ed. see Outhwaite, William.
Mulkearn, Lois, ed. see Pownall, Thomas.
Mulkeen, et al. Issues of Professional Preparation & Practice. Wendel, Frederick C., ed. 79p. (Orig.). (C). 1992. pap. text ed. 7.00 (*1-55996-149-X*) Univ Council Educ Admin.
Mulkeen, Anne. Wild Thyme, Winter Lightning: The Symbolic Novels of L. P. Hartley. LC 73-18047. 209p. reprint ed. pap. 59.60 (*0-318-39794-3*, 2033197) Bks Demand.
Mulkeen, Thomas A., et al. Administrative Decision Making in Schools: A Case Study Approach to Strategic Planning. LC 85-31084. 170p. 1986. pap. text ed. 16.00 (*0-379-20692-7*) Oceana.
Mulkeen, Thomas A., et al, eds. Democratic Leadership: The Changing Context of Administrative Preparation. LC 93-42751. (Interpretive Perspectives on Education & Policy Ser.). 1993. 49.50 (*0-89391-912-8*); pap. 22.50 (*1-56750-049-8*) Ablex Pub.
Mulkerin, Mary T. The Carolinas. (Road Atlas Ser.). (Illus.). 64p. 1992. pap. 5.95 (*0-13-117722-2*, H M Gousha) P-H Gen Ref & Trav.
Mulkern, John R. The Know-Nothing Party in Massachusetts: The Rise & Fall of a People's Party. (New England Studies). 300p. 1990. text ed. 40.00 (*1-55553-071-0*) NE U Pr.
Mulkerne, D. D. & Andrews, M. E. Civil Service, Business & Industry Tests: Clerical & Stenographic. 2nd ed. 1983. text ed. 14.56 (*0-07-043987-7*) McGraw.
Mulkerne, Donald J., Jr. Perfect Term Paper: Step-by-Step. LC 87-12630. 168p. 1988. mass mkt. 8.95 (*0-385-24794-X*, Anchor NY) Doubleday.
Mulkerns, Val. A Time Outworn. 9.95 (*0-8159-6905-8*) Devin.
Mulkers, Anne. Live Data Structures in Logic Programs. LC 93-19196. (Lecture Notes in Computer Science Ser.: Vol. 675). 1993. 39.00 (*0-387-56694-5*) Spr-Verlag.
Mulkey, David, jt. ed. see Beaulieu, Lionel J.
***Mulkey, Lynn M.** Seeing & Unseeing Social Structure: Sociology's Essential Insights. LC 94-49567. 1995. pap. text ed. 10.00 (*0-205-14881-6*) Allyn.
— Sociology of Education: Theoretical & Empirical Investigations. 450p. (C). 1993. text ed. 46.75 (*0-03-032343-6*) HB Coll Pubs.
Mulkey, Michael, jt. ed. see Gardiner, John.
Mulkey, S. Wayne, jt. auth. see Cassell, Jack L.
***Mulkey, Stephen S., et al, eds.** Tropical Forest Plant Ecophysiology. LC 95-6750. 1995. write for info. (*0-412-03571-5*) Chapman & Hall.
Mulkey, Young J., ed. see Character Education Institute Staff.
Mulky, M. J., et al. Research in Industry. (C). 1987. 20.00 (*81-204-0273-1*, Pub. by Oxford IBH II) S Asia.
Mulky, M. J., et al, eds. Industrial Research. (C). 1988. 36. 00 (*0-8364-2432-8*, Pub. by Oxford IBH II); 36.00 (*81-204-0286-3*, Pub. by Oxford IBH II) S Asia.
Mull, C. G., jt. auth. see Kelly, K. D.
Mull, Carol. Seven Hundred Fifty Over-the-Counter Stocks. LC 84-71342. 438p. 1986. 30.00 (*0-86690-279-1*, M2614-014) Am Fed Astrologers.
— Standard & Poor's 500. LC 83-72385. 100p. 1984. 30.00 (*0-86690-261-9*, M2400-014) Am Fed Astrologers.
***Mull, David K.** The Death of Old Man Hanson. 77p. (Orig.). (J). (gr. 5-8). 1995. lib. bdg. 15.00 (*0-88092-119-6*) Royal Fireworks.
— The Death of Old Man Hanson. 77p. (Orig.). (J). (gr. 5-9). 1995. pap. 5.00 (*0-88092-118-8*) Royal Fireworks.
Mull, Gary & Feldman, Martin. Good Food, Good Mood. 208p. 1991. pap. 10.95 (*0-312-06985-5*) St Martin.
Mull, J. Alexander & Boger, Gordon. Recollections of the Catawba Valley. LC 82-20721. 1983. 6.50 (*0-913239-05-4*) Appalach Consortium.
Mull, J. Dennis, jt. ed. see Coreil, Jeannine.
Mull, Kayla & Boldrick, Lorrie. Pot-Bellied Pet Pigs: Mini-Pig Care & Training Manual. (Illus.). 154p. (Orig.). 1989. pap. 9.95 (*0-9624531-0-2*) All Pub.
***Mull, Martin.** Martin Mull: Paintings, Drawings & Words. (Illus.). 144p. 1995. 45.00 (*1-885203-19-5*) Jrny Editions.
Mull, Robert W., jt. auth. see Sanger, S. L.
Mull, William P., jt. auth. see Howarth, Francis G.
Mulla, B., jt. auth. see Pollock, T.
Mulla, M. Code of Civil Procedure. (C). 1990. 100.00 (*0-89771-242-0*) St Mut.
— Code of Civil Procedure, 3 vols., Set. (C). 1990. 300.00 (*0-89771-241-2*) St Mut.
— The Indian Contract Act. (C). 1990. 50.00 (*0-89771-223-4*) St Mut.
— Principles of Hindu Law. (C). 1990. 100.00 (*0-89771-144-0*) St Mut.
— Principles of Mohammedan Law. (C). 1990. 60.00 (*0-89771-143-2*) St Mut.
Mulla Sadra. The Metaphysics of Mulla Sadra. Morewedge, Parviz, tr. (Islamic Philosophy Translation Ser.). 240p. (C). 1992. 30.00 (*0-9633277-1-2*) Inst Global Cultl.
— The Wisdom of the Throne: An Introduction to the Philosophy of Mulla Sadra. Morris, James W., tr. LC 81-47153. (Library of Asian Translations). 300p. 1981. 45. 00 (*0-691-06493-8*) Princeton U Pr.
Mullahy, Catherine M. The Case Manager's Handbook. 464p. 1994. 49.00 (*0-8342-0537-8*, 20537) Aspen Pub.
***Mullahy, Patrick, ed.** The Contributions of Harry Stack Sullivan. 242p. 1995. pap. 30.00 (*1-56821-560-6*) Aronson.
Mullahy, Patrick & Melinek, Menachem, eds. Interpersonal Psychiatry. LC 82-23045. 232p. 1983. text ed. 25.00 (*0-88331-152-6*) Luce.
Mullaley, Michael P. Fireside: Poems of Life, Love, & Laughter. 1990. 7.95 (*0-533-08750-3*) Vantage.
Mullaley, Robert C. History of the Mullaleys: A Twelve Hundred Year Journey from County Galway to Iowa. LC 93-91767. (Illus.). 214p. 1993. 45.00 (*0-9639174-0-4*) R C Mullaley.
Mullally, Evelyn. The Artist at Work: Narrative Technique in Chretien de Troyes. LC 88-71547. (Transactions Ser.: Vol. 78, Pt. 4). 240p. (Orig.). (C). 1988. pap. 30.00 (*0-87169-784-X*, T784-MUE) Am Philos.
***Mullally, Frederic.** Primo: The Story of 'Man Mountain' Carnera World Heavyweight Champion. (Illus.). 210p. 1995. 25.95 (*0-86051-745-4*, Robson-Parkwest) Parkwest Pubns.
Mullally, Frederick. Amanda: First American Edition Series. Dakin, John, ed. (Illus.). 64p. (Orig.). 1984. pap. 5.95 (*0-912277-03-3*) K Pierce Inc.
Mullally, Joseph, tr. Peter of Spain: Tractatus Syncategorematum. Bd. with Selected Anonymous TreatisesLC 64-17335. LC 64-17335. (Medieval Philosophical Texts in Translation Ser.). Set pap. 15.00 (*0-87462-213-1*) Marquette.
Mullally, Margaret L. The Competition for U. S. Banking Markets. 320p. 1989. 1,700.00 (*0-945235-18-6*) Lead Edge Reports.
— A Competitive Analysis of Hazardous Waste Management. 158p. 1990. 1,950.00 (*0-945235-40-2*) Lead Edge Reports.
— A Competitive Analysis of the U. S. Sensor Industry. 226p. 1988. 1,500.00 (*0-945235-10-0*) Lead Edge Reports.
— Construction Aggregates: Crushed Stone, Sand & Gravel. 296p. 1990. 2,000.00 (*0-945235-32-1*) Lead Edge Reports.
— Electronic Filters: Competitive Strategies & Markets. 173p. 1990. 1,700.00 (*0-945235-27-5*) Lead Edge Reports.
— Industrial Ceramics: Current Markets & Future Opportunities. 125p. 1988. 1,600.00 (*0-945235-03-8*) Lead Edge Reports.
— U. S. Regional Outlook for Cement & Ready Mix Concrete Markets. 369p. 1990. 2,150.00 (*0-945235-35-6*) Lead Edge Reports.
Mullaly, Edward J. Archibald MacLeish: A Checklist. LC 72-619620. (Serif Series: Bibliographies & Checklists: No. 26). 109p. reprint ed. pap. 31.10 (*0-8357-5576-2*, 2035203) Bks Demand.
Mullaly, Margaret L. Recycling Opportunities. 160p. 1990. 2,500.00 (*0-945235-23-2*) Lead Edge Reports.
Mullaly, Paula A. Index to New Jersey School Law Decisions. write for info. (*0-318-61246-1*) NJ Schl Bds.
Mullan, Bob. Are Mothers Really Necessary? 224p. 1988. 60.00 (*1-85283-200-2*, Pub. by Boxtree Ltd UK); pap. 30.00 (*1-85283-210-X*, Pub. by Boxtree Ltd UK) St Mut.
— The Enid Blyton Story. 160p. 1988. 40.00 (*1-85283-201-0*, Pub. by Boxtree Ltd UK) St Mut.
— Mad to Be Normal: Conversations with R. D. Laing. 406p. 1995. pap. 22.95 (*1-85343-395-0*) NYU Pr.
Mullan, Brendan, ed. see Grummon, Phyllis T.
Mullan, C. S. Census of India, 1931 Vol. 3: Assam, 2 Vols., Part 1-Report, Part 2-Tables, Set. (C). 1992. reprint ed. 140.00 (*81-85425-93-0*, Pub. by Manohar II) S Asia.
Mullan, D., et al, eds. Astrophysics in Antarctica. LC 89-46421. (AIP Conference Proceedings Ser.: No. 198). 288p. 1989. lib. bdg. 80.00 (*0-88318-398-6*) Am Inst Physics.
Mullan, D. J., jt. ed. see Byrne, P. B.
Mullan, E. H. Mentality of the Arriving Immigrant. LC 77-129408. (American Immigration Collection, Ser. 2). (Illus.). 1970. reprint ed. 14.95 (*0-405-00562-8*) Ayer.
Mullan, Harry. Great Book of Boxing. 1990. 24.99 (*0-517-02893-X*) Random Hse Value.
Mullan, John. Miners & Travelers Guide. Brown, Kimberly R. & Adams, Glen, eds. (Illus.). 178p. 1991. reprint ed. 18.95 (*0-87770-502-X*) Ye Galleon.
— Miner's & Travelers' Guide to Oregon, Washington, Idaho, Montana, Wyoming, & Colorado. LC 72-9461. (Far Western Frontier Ser.). (Illus.). 158p. 1978. reprint ed. 18.95 (*0-405-04989-7*) Ayer.
— Report on the Construction of a Military Road from Fort Walla Walla to Fort Benton. (Illus.). 183p. 1994. 24.95 (*0-87770-102-4*) Ye Galleon.
***Mullane, Deirdre, ed.** Words to Make My Dream Children Live: An African Book of Quotations. LC 94-32710. 1995. 14.95 (*0-385-42244-X*, Anchor NY) Doubleday.
Mullane, Deirdre, intro. Crossing the Danger Water: Four Hundred Years of African-American Writing. LC 93-17194. 1993. 16.00 (*0-385-42243-1*, Anchor NY) Doubleday.
Mullane, Janet, ed. Nineteenth-Century Literature Criticism, Vol. 18. 600p. 1988. 122.00 (*0-8103-5818-2*) Gale.
Mullane, Janet, et al, eds. Nineteenth-Century Literary Criticism, Vol. 23. 600p. 1989. 122.00 (*0-8103-5823-9*) Gale.
Mullane, Janet & Sherman, Laurie, eds. Nineteenth-Century Literature Criticism, Vol. 27. LC 84-643008. (Illus.). 511p. 1990. text ed. 122.00 (*0-8103-5827-1*) Gale.
Mullane, Janet & Wilson, Bob, eds. Nineteenth-Century Literary Criticism, Vol. 25. 1990. 122.00 (*0-8103-5825-5*) Gale.
— Nineteenth-Century Literature Criticism, Vol. 19. 600p. 1988. 122.00 (*0-8103-5819-0*) Gale.
— Nineteenth-Century Literature Criticism, Vol. 22. 1989. 122.00 (*0-8103-5822-0*) Gale.
— Nineteenth-Century Literature Criticism: Archives, Vol. 20. 1988. 122.00 (*0-8103-5820-4*) Gale.
Mullane, Janet & Wilson, Robert, eds. Nineteenth-Century Literature Criticism, Vol. 21. 1989. 122.00 (*0-8103-5821-2*) Gale.
Mullane, Janet & Wilson, Robert T., eds. Nineteenth-Century Literature Criticism, Vol. 26. LC 84-643008. (Illus.). 511p. 1990. text ed. 122.00 (*0-8103-5826-3*) Gale.
Mullane, Janet, jt. ed. see Abbey, Cherie D.
Mullane, Janet, et al. Nineteenth-Century Literary Criticism, Vol. 24. 1989. 122.00 (*0-8103-5824-7*) Gale.
Mullane, Mike. Red Sky: A Novel of Love, Space, War. Van Treese, James B., ed. 480p. 1993. 21.95 (*1-56901-111-7*) NW Pub.
Mullane, R. Mike. Lift Off! An Astronaut's Dream. LC 94-18122. (Illus.). (J). 1994. 13.95 (*0-382-24663-2*); pap. 4.95 (*0-382-24664-0*) Silver Burdett Pr.
Mullaney, Aidan, tr. see Pazzelli, Raffaele.
Mullaney, Charles P., jt. auth. see Buccini, Eugene P.
Mullaney, Dean, ed. see Englehart, Steve & Rogers, Marshall.
Mullaney, Marie M. Bibliographic Directory of the Governors of the United States, 1983-1988. LC 89-2273. 408p. 1989. text ed. 75.00 (*0-313-28083-5*, MGX/, Greenwood Pr) Greenwood.
— Biographical Directory of the Governors of the United States, 1988-1993. LC 93-37875. 425p. 1994. text ed. 75.00 (*0-313-28312-5*, Greenwood Pr) Greenwood.
Mullaney, Marie M., comp. American Governors & Gubernatorial Elections, 1979-1987. LC 88-13248. 104p. 1988. text ed. 47.95 (*0-313-28092-4*, MGZ/, Greenwood Pr) Greenwood.
***Mullans, Constance J.** Workbook for Military Careers in Transition. 73p. 1992. 15.00 (*0-9641795-0-4*) Military Careers.
Mullany, N. & Handford, P. Tort Liability for Psychiatric Damage. 1993. write for info. (*0-455-21175-2*, Pub. by Law Bk Co) W W Gaunt.
Mullany, Peter. Monarch Notes on Marlowe's Dr. Faustus & Other Writings. (Orig.). (C). pap. 3.95 (*0-671-00717-3*, Arco Test) P-H Gen Ref & Trav.
Mullard, Chris. Black Britain: With an Account of Recent Events at the Institute of Race Relations by Alexander Kirby. LC 73-331041. 194p. reprint ed. pap. 55.30 (*0-8357-7284-5*, 2023187) Bks Demand.
— Race, Power & Resistance. 256p. 1985. 42.50 (*0-7100-9774-3*, RKP) Routledge.
***Mullard, Maurice.** Policy Making in Britain: An Introduction. LC 94-48178. 240p. 1995. 79.95x (*0-415-10849-7*, C0051); pap. 17.95 (*0-415-10850-0*, C0052) Routledge.
— Understanding Economic Policy. (Illus.). 288p. 1991. 85. 00 (*0-415-06881-9*, A6575) Routledge.
Mullard Technical Service Dept. Staff. Circuits for Audio Amplifiers. (Illus.). 144p. (Orig.). 1993. reprint ed. pap. 16.95 (*1-882580-03-6*) Audio Amateur.
Mullarkey, Barbara A. Bittersweet Aspartame: A Diet Delusion. 88p. (Orig.). 1992. pap. 11.00 (*0-944366-00-7*) Hlth Watch Bk.
— Bittersweet Aspartame, a Diet Delusion. 2nd ed. (Illus.). 86p. 1993. pap. 11.00 (*0-944366-01-5*) Hlth Watch Bk.
Mulleady, Geraldine. Counselling Drug Users about HIV & AIDS. (Illus.). 192p. 1992. pap. 36.95 (*0-632-02939-0*) Blackwell Sci.
Mullen. Black American African American: Vietnam Through the Gulf War. 1991. 17.35 (*0-536-58069-3*) Ginn Pr.
Mullen, Ann. Twin Justice...Shattered Dreams: A Mother Tells of the Heartbreaking Events That Preceded the Death of Her Twin Sons. Smith, Kathleen, ed. 128p. (Orig.). 1992. pap. 9.95 (*0-943135-14-1*, Grn Briar Patch) Gallagher Jordan.
Mullen, B. Advanced BASIC Meta-Analysis, 1989. 29.95 (*0-685-48947-7*); 3.5 ld 79.95 (*1-56321-036-3*); 5.25 ld 79.95 (*1-56321-035-5*) LEA S&AM.
Mullen, B. & Geothals, G. R., eds. Theories of Group Behavior. (Social Psychology Ser.). (Illus.). 255p. 1986. 72.00 (*0-387-96351-0*) Spr-Verlag.

Mullen, Barbara D. & McGinn, Kerry A. Ostomy Book: Living Comfortably with Colostomies, Ileostomies, & Urostomies. 2nd rev. ed. 1991. pap. 14.95 (*0-923521-12-7*) Bull Pub.

Mullen, Brian. Advanced BASIC Meta-Analysis: Version 1. 10. 184p. (C). 1989. text ed. 29.95 (*0-8058-0502-8*) L Erlbaum Assocs.

— The Phenomenology of Being in a Group: Meta-Analytic Integrations of Social Cognition & Group Processes. (International Library of Psychology). 200p. 1991. 74.50 (*0-415-04353-0*, A6285) Routledge.

Mullen, Brian & Johnson, Craig. The Psychology of Consumer Behavior. 232p. 1990. 29.95 (*0-89859-857-5*); teacher ed write for info. (*0-8058-1165-6*) L Erlbaum Assocs.

Mullen, Denise, jt. auth. see Altman, Kimberly D.

Mullen, Dore. All We Know of Heaven. large type ed. 608p. 1985. 15.95 (*0-7089-1339-3*) Ulverscroft.

Mullen, E. Theodore, Jr. Narrative History & Ethnic Boundaries: The Deuteronomistic Historian & the Creation of the Israelite National Identity. LC 93-12315. (Society of Biblical Literature Semeia Studies). 344p. 1993. 49.95 (*1-55540-846-X*, 06 06 24); pap. 34.95 (*1-55540-847-8*, 060624) Scholars Pr GA.

Mullen, Edward J. Carlos Pellicer. LC 77-1959. (Twayne's World Authors Ser.). 173p. (C). 1977. lib. bdg. 17.95 (*0-8057-6288-4*) Irvington.

— Critical Essays on Langston Hughes. (Critical Essays on American Literature Ser.). 211p. (C). 1986. text ed. 45. 00 (*0-8161-8697-9*) G K Hall.

Mullen, Edward J. & Darst, David H. Sendas Literarias: Hispanoamerica. 256p. (C). 1988. pap. text ed. write for info. (*0-07-554129-7*) McGraw.

Mullen, Edward J. & Garganigo, John F., eds. El Cuento Hispanico: A Graded Literary Anthology. 4th ed. 1993. pap. text ed. write for info. (*0-07-043955-9*) McGraw.

Mullen, Edward J., jt. ed. see Hess, Peg M.

***Mullen, Edwin.** Short Bike Rides in Connecticut. 5th ed. (Short Bike Rides Ser.). (Illus.). 144p. 1995. pap. 9.95 (*1-56440-641-5*) Globe Pequot.

Mullen, Edwin & Griffith, Jane. Short Bike Rides on Cape Cod, Nantucket, & the Vineyard. 5th ed. LC 93-40253. (Short Bike Rides Ser.). (Illus.). 160p. 1994. pap. 9.95 (*1-56440-392-0*) Globe Pequot.

Mullen, Francis. Drug Enforcement Agent. (Illus.). 256p. 1988. pap. 15.00 (*0-13-220997-7*) P-H.

Mullen, G. L., jt. auth. see Lidl, R.

Mullen, Gail S. & Bothmer, Richard. The Quiz Book: 1729 Academic Questions to Challenge the Mind. 104p. 1990. pap. 14.95 (*0-936386-55-X*) Creative Learning.

Mullen, Gary L. & Shiue, Peter J., eds. Finite Fields, Coding Theory, & Advances in Communications & Computing. LC 92-23503. (Lecture Notes in Pure & Applied Mathematics Ser.: Vol. 141). 480p. 1992. 160.00 (*0-8247-8805-2*) Dekker.

Mullen, Gary L. & Shiue, Peter J. S., eds. Finite Fields - Theory, Applications & Algorithms: Proceedings of the Second International Conference on Finite Fields - Theory, Applications & Algorithms, August 17-21, 1993, Las Vegas, Nevada. LC 94-19971. (Contemporary Mathematics Ser.: Vol. 168). 1994. write for info. (*0-8218-5183-7*) Am Math.

Mullen, George. The Jew & the Arab: a Puzzle Solved! A Realistic Proposal for Peace in the Mideast. Thomson, T. L., ed. (Illus.). 140p. 1994. 19.95 (*0-912495-25-1*) San Diego Pub Co.

***Mullen, George D.** Peace in the Middle East: Israeli-Palestinian Peace Proposal. (C). 1994. 19.95 (*1-881116-46-8*) Black Forrest Pr.

***Mullen, Harris. 10 Incredible Mistakes Made at Gettysburg: A Review of the Battle & How Blunders by the Generals Shaped the Outcome. (Illus.). 32p. (Orig.). 1995. pap. text ed. 5.95 (*0-9646629-0-6*) High Water Pr.**
A condensed review of The Battle of Gettysburg explains how blunders by the generals of both armies shaped the outcome. Battle maps for each day of the three-day battle explain the performance of each army in non-technical terms. There is a photograph of each general & a description of his mistake. A roster of the 19 West Point officers of both armies who participated shows how they compared as cadets, age & rank. Covers the lost tactical opportunities of both armies, especially the Confederates. Excellent FOR LIVELY CLASSROOM USE which allows students to research individual generals. Among those accused of critical blunders are the commanding officers of both armies, Gen. Robert E. Lee, CSA & Maj. Gen. George G. Meade, USA. Order from: High Water Press, 315 S. Arrawana, Tampa, FL 33609, (813) 876-9786, FAX (813) 877-1627. *Publisher Provided Annotation.*

***Mullen, Harryette.** Muse & Drudge. 80p. (Orig.). 1995. pap. 12.50 (*0-935162-15-1*) Singing Horse.

— S PeRM K T. 48p. (Orig.). 1992. pap. 6.00 (*0-935162-12-7*) Singing Horse.

Mullen, I. Blunders & Brilliancies. 1989. pap. 9.95 (*0-08-037136-1*, Pergamon Pr) Elsevier.

Mullen, Inga E. German Realism in the United States: The American Reception of Meyer, Storm, Raabe, Keller & Fontane. (Studies in Modern German Literature: Vol. 6). 206p. (C). 1988. text ed. 36.50 (*0-8204-0424-1*) P Lang Pubs.

Mullen, J., jt. auth. see Harrison, W.

Mullen, Jack B. The Practitioner's Guide to EDP Auditing. 1990. 98.00 (*0-13-691262-1*) NY Inst Finance.

***Mullen, James X.** The Simple Art of Greatness: Building, Managing, & Motivating a Kick-Ass Work Force. 200p. 1995. 19.95 (*0-670-85211-2*, Viking) Viking Penguin.

Mullen, Jean. Outsiders: American Short Stories for Students of English as a Second Language. (Illus.). 275p. (C). 1984. pap. text ed. 19.25 (*0-13-645366-X*) P-H.

***Mullen, Jena K. Intro to Managed Care. (Step One Products Ser.). 120p. (Orig.). 1995. pap. text ed. 27.00 (*0-939921-68-5*) LOMA.**
This introductory-level text/workbook is an excellent resource for anyone who works in or with managed care coverages or who is interested in learning about managed care plans. In a single source it provides up-to-date information on all the basics, including: the changing environment of group health insurance, managed care concepts, health maintenance organizations (HMOs), preferred provider organizations (PPOs), point of service plans (POSs) operational aspects of health care coverage, funding health care coverage, & regulation of group health care coverage. INTRO TO MANAGED CARE is a complete package designed for self-directed learning. It is clear & inviting to read. Real-life examples, a glossary of terms & helpful figures & graphics enhance your learning experience. The text concludes with a quiz that allows you to gauge your knowledge. LOMA has been the internationally- recognized leader in life & health insurance education for more than half a century. To order: call 1-800-848-0773 or contact LOMA 404-984-3761. *Publisher Provided Annotation.*

Mullen, Jena K., jt. auth. see Huggins, Kenneth.

Mullen, Jena K., jt. auth. see Jones, Harriett.

Mullen, Jim, jt. auth. see Rubenstein, Hal.

Mullen, Jo. Aspects: Beginner's Notebook. LC 85-71464. 90p. 1986. 7.50 (*0-86690-297-X*, M2357-014) Am Fed Astrologers.

— Astrology Beginner's Notebook. LC 83-73608. 80p. 1984. 7.50 (*0-86690-269-4*, M2531-014) Am Fed Astrologers.

Mullen, Joe. Strength Training for Women Only: Using Nautilus Equipment. 115p. 1986. 19.95 (*0-935783-05-9*) Fitness Ctr Info.

***Mullen, John D.** Hard Thinking: The Reintroduction of Logic to Everyday Life. 328p. 1995. lib. bdg. 64.50 (*0-8476-8002-9*); pap. text ed. 24.50 (*0-8476-8003-7*) Rowman.

— Kierkegaard's Philosophy: Self-Deception & Cowardice in the Present Age. (Orig.). 1988. pap. 7.95 (*0-452-00908-1*, Mer) NAL-Dutton.

— Kierkegaard's Philosophy: Self-Deception & Cowardice in the Present Age. LC 95-7348. 1995. pap. write for info. (*0-8191-9803-X*) U Pr of Amer.

Mullen, John D., jt. auth. see Roth, Byron M.

Mullen, Joseph. The Fitness Center Owners Manual (Emphasis on Nautilus) 200p. 1986. 29.95 (*0-935783-01-6*) Fitness Ctr Info.

— The Fitness Instructors Manual (Emphasis on Nautilus) How to Earn Money & Respect As a Fitness Instructor. 165p. 1986. 19.95 (*0-935783-06-7*) Fitness Ctr Info.

— The Nautilus Fitness Center Management Manual. 150p. 1982. 19.95 (*0-935783-00-8*) Fitness Ctr Info.

— Secrets of Advanced Nautilus Training. 150p. 1986. 19.95 (*0-935783-04-0*) Fitness Ctr Info.

— The Ultimate Workout Journal (for Nautilus Enthusiasts) A Personal Workout Guide. 2nd ed. 150p. 1986. 12.95 (*0-935783-03-2*) Fitness Ctr Info.

***Mullen, Joseph, ed.** Rural Poverty Alleviation: International Development Perspectives. 200p. 57.95 (*1-85628-864-1*, Pub. by Avebury Pub UK) Ashgate Pub Co.

Mullen, Karin, jt. auth. see Ianni, Marilyn.

Mullen, Kathleen D., et al. Connections for Health. (C). 1990. student ed write for info. (*0-697-07611-3*) Brown & Benchmark.

— Connections for Health. 3rd ed. 624p. (C). 1993. student ed write for info. (*0-697-10129-0*); pap. write for info. (*0-697-20948-2*); pap. text ed. write for info. (*0-697-10127-4*); write for info. (*0-697-17345-3*) Brown & Benchmark.

Mullen, Kathy, jt. auth. see Barkeley, Mary B.

Mullen, Kenneth. Healthy Balance: A Qualitative Study of Men's Health Beliefs. 200p. 1993. 59.95 (*1-85628-548-0*, Pub. by Avebury Pub UK) Ashgate Pub Co.

Mullen, Kevin J. Let Justice Be Done: Crime & Politics in Early San Francisco. LC 89-4750. (Wilbur S. Shepperson Series in History & Humanities). (Illus.). 336p. 1989. 24. 95 (*0-87417-146-6*) U of Nev Pr.

Mullen, Laura. The Surface. 88p. (Orig.). 1991. pap. 10.95 (*0-252-06187-X*) U of Ill Pr.

Mullen, Margaret. An Arkansas Childhood: Growing up in the Athens of the Ozarks. (Illus.). 1989. 14.95 (*0-943099-06-4*) M&M Pr.

— Safe for Now. 88p. (Orig.). 1993. pap. 11.95 (*0-9627007-1-1*) Monday Pr CA.

Mullen, Marjorie, jt. auth. see Graham, Earl C.

Mullen, Mary C., jt. auth. see Shield, Jo E.

***Mullen, Mary J.** Wavelength. 240p. 1995. pap. 5.95 (*0-9645523-0-2*) Custom Media Design.

***Mullen, Michael.** The First Christmas. 182p. (J). (gr. 4-7). 1994. pap. 6.95 (*1-85371-296-5*, Pub. by Poolbeg Pr IE) Dufour.

— The Four Masters. 153p. (YA). (gr. 5 up). 1992. pap. 9.95 (*1-85371-204-3*, Pub. by Poolbeg Pr IE) Dufour.

— Sea Wolves from the North. (Illus.). 112p. (J). (gr. 3-9). 1989. 10.95 (*0-905473-94-9*, Pub. by Wolfhound Pr IE); pap. 7.95 (*0-86327-023-9*, Pub. by Wolfhound Pr IE) Dufour.

Mullen, Mike, jt. auth. see Ratermann, Dale.

Mullen, Nina A., jt. auth. see Olsen, Laurie.

Mullen, Norma D. & Brown, P. Charles. English for Computer Science. 2nd ed. 1988. teacher ed 3.95 (*0-19-437657-5*); pap. 12.95 (*0-19-437655-9*) OUP.

Mullen, Patricia. The Stone Movers. 368p. (Orig.). 1995. mass mkt. 5.50 (*0-446-60106-3*, Aspect) Warner Bks.

Mullen, Patrick B. The Heart of the Lion Tamer. 80p. (Orig.). 1993. pap. 9.95 (*0-9628594-7-8*) Wintergrn-Orchard Hse.

— I Heard the Old Fishermen Say: Folklore of the Texas Gulf Coast. 2nd ed. 183p. 1988. reprint ed. pap. text ed. 17.95 (*0-87421-139-5*) Utah St U Pr.

— Listening to Old Voices: Folklore, Life Stories, & the Elderly. (Folklore & Society Ser.). (Illus.). 312p. 1992. text ed. 30.95 (*0-252-01808-7*) U of Ill Pr.

Mullen, Patrick B., jt. auth. see Lloyd, Timothy C.

Mullen, Paul E., jt. auth. see White, Gregory L.

Mullen, Paul M. Some Things I Have Learned on the Way. Van Treese, James B., ed. 150p. 1994. 7.95 (*1-56901-208-3*) NW Pub.

***Mullen, Peg.** Unfriendly Fire: A Mother's Memoir. LC 94-48108. (Singular Lives: The Iowa Series in North American Autobiography). (Illus.). 175p. 1995. 22.95 (*0-87745-506-6*); pap. 12.95 (*0-87745-507-4*) U of Iowa Pr.

Mullen, R., jt. auth. see Grimes, G.

Mullen, R. D., et al, eds. Philip K. Dick: Forty Articles on Philip K. Dick from Science-Fiction Studies. 320p. 1992. 24.95 (*0-9633169-0-7*); pap. 14.95 (*0-9633169-1-5*) SF-TH.

Mullen, Richard. Anthony Trollope: A Victorian in His World. LC 91-16912. 767p. 1991. 45.00 (*0-913720-77-1*) Beil.

— Birds of Passage: Five Englishwomen in Search of America. LC 94-14200. 1994. text ed. 45.00 (*0-312-12228-4*) St Martin.

Mullen, Robert. Choosing & Using Your First CD-ROM Drive. LC 94-66140. 232p. 1994. cd-rom, pap. 19.99 (*0-7821-1526-8*) Sybex.

— Ten Minute Guide to Approach. 160p. 1994. 10.99 (*1-56761-407-8*) Alpha Bks IN.

Mullen, Robert, jt. auth. see Wempen, Faithe.

Mullen, Robert J. The Architecture & Sculpture of Oaxaca. (Monographs). (Illus.). 456p. (Orig.). (C). 1995. per. 60. 00 (*0-87918-079-X*) ASU Lat Am St.

Mullen, Robert W. Blacks in America's Wars: The Shift in Attitudes from the Revolutionary War to Vietnam. LC 73-89091. (Illus.). 96p. 1991. reprint ed. 30.00 (*0-913460-30-3*); reprint ed. pap. 8.95 (*0-913460-29-X*) Pathfinder NY.

Mullen, Ruth, ed. see AVSC International Staff.

Mullen, Samuel. Emergency Planning Guide for Utilities. LC 93-49432. 250p. 1994. 72.95 (*0-87814-413-7*, S4529) PennWell Bks.

Mullen, Sherry, jt. auth. see Anderson, Mark.

Mullen, Sidney, jt. ed. see Jensen, Ferne.

Mullen, Sue. Creole Cooking. 1993. 12.98 (*1-55521-908-X*) Bk Sales Inc.

Mullen, Thomas. Laughing Outloud & Other Religious Experiences. LC 83-3643. 130p. 1989. pap. 5.50 (*0-944350-11-9*) Friends United.

Mullen, Thomas, jt. ed. see Tverdohlebou, Stanislav.

Mullen, Thomas P., jt. auth. see Stumpf, Stephen A.

Mullen, Tom. Middle Age & Other Mixed Blessings. LC 91-9653. 160p. (Orig.). 1991. pap. 8.99 (*0-8007-5399-2*) Revell.

— Where Two or Three Are Gathered, Someone Spills the Milk. LC 86-14322. 126p. 1986. reprint ed. pap. 4.50 (*0-913408-95-6*) Friends United.

***Mullen, Tom, ed.** Witness in Washington. 310p. 1994. 14. 99 (*0-944350-34-8*) Friends United.

Mullen, Tom J., ed. Butterworths Scottish Housing Law Handbook. 800p. 1992. U.K. pap. 130.00 (*0-406-11551-6*) Butterworth Legal Pubs.

Mullen, Victor. Tree House. 1989. pap. 3.95 (*0-8217-2706-0*) Zebra.

Mullen, W. Frank, et al, eds. The Government & Politics of Washington State. LC 79-101175. (Illus.). 228p. reprint ed. pap. 65.00 (*0-8357-4566-X*, 2037475) Bks Demand.

***Mullen, Wendell D.** How to Model Your Ministry after the New Testament. (Illus.). 311p. 1994. pap. 12.95 (*0-9622191-5-0*) McElroy Pub.

Mullen, William. Choreia: Pindar & Dance. LC 81-47936. 280p. 1982. 39.50 (*0-691-06500-4*) Princeton U Pr.

Mullen, William J., III, jt. auth. see Brownlee, Romie L.

Mullen, Yvonne. Computer Applications Calc - Spreadsheet Planner: Course Code 394-3. Schroeder, Bonnie, ed. (Illus.). 100p. (gr. 8). 1989. reprint ed. 19.95 (*0-917531-80-9*) CES Compu-Tech.

— Word Processing Teacher Edition: Course Code S04-2. Schroeder, Bonnie, ed. (Illus.). 80p. 1989. reprint ed. 15. 00 (*0-917531-77-9*) CES Compu-Tech.

Mullen, Yvonne & Schroeder, Bonnie. BASIC Programming 1. (Illus.). 120p. 1989. reprint ed. teacher ed 19.95 (*0-685-45805-9*, T303-1) CES Compu-Tech.

— Basic Programming 1: Lab Pack, Pt. 1. Doheny, Catherine, ed. (Illus.). 179.95 (*1-56177-074-4*, L303-1); teacher ed 19.95 (*0-685-45806-7*, T303-1) CES Compu-Tech.

— Basic Programming 1: Lab Pack, Pt. 2. Doheny, Catherine, ed. (Illus.). 179.95 (*0-685-45807-5*, L303-2); 19.95 (*1-56177-077-9*, T303-2) CES Compu-Tech.

— Basic Programming 1: Lab Pack, Pt. 2, No. 1. Doheny, Catherine, ed. (Illus.). disk 6.95 (*1-56177-072-8*, D303-1) CES Compu-Tech.

— Basic Programming 1: Lab Pack, Pt. 2, No. 2. Doheny, Catherine, ed. (Illus.). disk 6.95 (*1-56177-073-6*, D303-2) CES Compu-Tech.

— Word Processing: Lab Pack. (Illus.). 1990. 149.95 (*1-56177-135-X*, L404) CES Compu-Tech.

Mullen, Yvonne & Weinman, Susan. Programming with Logo: Lab Pack. Schroeder, Bonnie, ed. (Illus.). 97p. 1990. teacher ed 19.95 (*1-56177-100-7*, TE394-6); student ed, teacher ed 149.95 (*1-56177-099-X*, L394-6); disk 15.95 (*1-56177-098-1*, D394-6) CES Compu-Tech.

Mullen, Yvonne, jt. auth. see Weinman, Susan.

Mullenax, Foster. Capasheea's Leadmine: A Novel. 200p. (Orig.). 1989. pap. 9.95 (*0-87012-484-6*) McClain.

Mullenax, Michelle, ed. see Ashcraft, Howard D.

Mullender, Audrey & Morley, Becky, eds. Children Living with Domestic Violence. 212p. 1994. 67.50 (*1-871177-71-5*, Pub. by Whiting & Birch UK); pap. 29. 95 (*1-871177-72-3*, Pub. by Whiting & Birch UK) Paul & Co Pubs.

Mullender, Audrey & Ward, Dave. Self-Directed Groupwork: Users Take Action for Empowerment. 194p. 1992. pap. text ed. 17.95 (*1-871177-11-1*, Pub. by Whiting & Birch UK) Paul & Co Pubs.

Mullender, Sape. Distributed Systems. 2nd ed. (C). 1993. text ed. 49.50 (*0-201-62427-3*) Addison-Wesley.

Mullendore, Richard H., jt. ed. see Bryan, William A.

Mullens, Joseph. The Religious Aspects of Hindu Philosophy. (C). 1991. reprint ed. 32.00 (*81-7054-123-9*, Pub. by Classical Pub II) S Asia.

Mullens, Leonard. Lord Teach Us to Pray. 1963. pap. 1.00 (*0-686-75248-1*) Firm Foun Pub.

— Unity in Christ. 1958. 3.00 (*0-88027-053-5*) Firm Foun Pub.

Mullens, Robert L., jt. ed. see Rencis, Joseph J.

Muller. Breve Diccionario de Filosofia: Brief Dictionary of Philosophy. 464p. (SPA.). 1977. 29.95 (*0-8288-5292-8*, S50199) Fr & Eur.

— Diccionario Aleman-Espanol, Espanol-Aleman. 900p. (GER & SPA.). 24.25 (*0-7859-0883-8*, S-50384) Fr & Eur.

— Duden Woerterbuch Vol. 8: Sinnverwandte. 2nd ed. 800p. (GER.). 1986. 59.95 (*0-7859-7224-2*, 3411209089) Fr & Eur.

— Long-Haired Cats. (Pet Care Ser.). 1984. pap. 5.95 (*0-8120-2803-1*) Barron.

— Physical Geography of the Global Environment. 2nd ed. Date not set. pap. text ed. write for info. (*0-471-03917-9*) Wiley.

***Muller & Roche.** Safe Passage into the Twenty-First Century: The United Nations' Quest for Peace, Equality, Justice & Development. 120p. 1995. pap. text ed. 11.95 (*0-8264-0866-4*) Continuum.

Muller, jt. auth. see Reina.

Muller, et al. Autonomes und Partnerschaftliches Lernen. 208p. 1989. 24.50 (*3-468-49439-4*) Langenscheidt.

Muller, A., ed. International Association of Logopaedics & Phoniatrics, 19th Congress, Edinburgh 1983: Main Papers. (Journal: Folia Phoniatrica: Vol. 35, No. 1-2). 96p. 1983. pap. 29.00 (*3-8055-3729-8*) S Karger.

Muller, A. & Krebs, B., eds. Sulfur: Its Significance for Chemistry, for the Geo-, Bio- & Cosmosphere & Technology. (Studies in Organic Chemistry: Vol. 5). 512p. 1984. 169.25 (*0-444-42355-9*) Elsevier.

Muller, A., jt. auth. see Morcay, Raoul.

Muller, A., jt. ed. see Sumer, B. Mutlu.

Muller, A., et al, eds. Electron & Proton Transfer in Chemistry & Biology. LC 92-14464. (Studies in Physical & Theoretical Chemistry: Vol. 78). 1992. write for info. (*0-444-88862-4*) Elsevier.

Muller, A. S., et al, eds. Health Disease in East Africa: A Bibliography. 340p. 1988. 128.25 (*0-444-80931-7*) Elsevier.

Muller, Alberto. Todos Heridos por el Norte y por el Sur. LC 80-70474. (Coleccion Caniqui Ser.). 63p. (Orig.). (SPA.). 1982. pap. 5.00 (*0-89729-282-0*) Ediciones.

Muller, Alberto & Suarez, Manuel L. Tierra Metalizada (Poemas) LC 85-82279. 62p. (Orig.). (SPA.). 1986. pap. 6.95 (*0-89729-385-1*) Ediciones.

***Muller, Alexander.** I: Western Civilization SG. 192p. (C). 1995. per., pap. text ed. 12.82 (*0-7872-0964-3*) Kendall-Hunt.

Muller, Alexander V., ed. Soloview, the Character of Old Russia, Vol. 24. 1987. pap. 15.00 (*0-87569-095-5*) Academic Intl.

Muller, Alexander V., ed. & tr. The Spiritual Regulation of Peter the Great. LC 74-4590. (Publications on Russia & Eastern Europe of the School of International Studies: No. 3). 188p. 1972. 20.00 (*0-295-95237-7*) U of Wash Pr.

Muller, Andre, jt. auth. see Jones, Stuart.

Muller, Andreas, ed. Discharge & Velocity Measurements: Proceedings of a Short Course, Zurich, 26-27 August 1987. 280p. (C). 1988. text ed. 95.00 (*90-6191-782-4*, Pub. by A A Balkema NE) Ashgate Pub Co.

An Asterisk (*) at the beginning of an entry indicates that the title is appearing in BIP for the first time.

Muller, Ann. Parents Matter: Parents' Relationships with Lesbian Daughters & Gay Sons. (Illus.). 240p. 1987. pap. 9.95 (*0-930044-91-6*) Naiad Pr.

***Muller, Antal.** Interaction & Determination Attempt at Elaborating an Up-to-Date Theory of Determinancy in Natural Philosophy. 234p. (C). 1991. 90.00x (*963-05-5552-2*, Pub. by Akad Kiado HU) St Mut.

— Quantum Mechanics: A Physical World Picture. LC 73-18062. 1974. 51.00 (*0-08-017936-3*, Pub. by Pergamon Repr UK) Franklin.

Muller Associates Inc. Staff, et al, comps. Handbook of Radon in Buildings: Detection, Safety, & Control. 266p. 1988. 67.00 (*0-89116-823-0*) Hemisp Pub.

Muller, B. The Physics of the Quark-Gluon Plasma. (Lecture Notes in Physics Ser.: Vol. 225). vii, 142p. 1985. pap. 17.00 (*0-387-15211-3*) Spr-Verlag.

Muller, B. & Fried, H. M. QCD Vacuum Structure: Proceedings of the Workshop on QCD Vacuum Structure & Its Applications. 388p. 1993. text ed. 95.00 (*981-02-1280-1*) World Scientific Pub.

Muller, B. & Reinhardt, J. Neural Networks: An Introduction. Domany, E. et al, eds. (Physics of Neural Networks Ser.). (Illus.). xiii, 266p. 1991. reprint ed. text ed., 5.25 hd 49.00 (*0-387-52380-4*) Spr-Verlag.

Muller, B., jt. auth. see Fried, H. M.

Muller, B., jt. ed. see Fried, H. M.

Muller, Barbara. Florentine Embroidery. (Illus.). 96p. 1993. pap. 18.00 (*0-916896-54-4*) Lacis Pubns.

Muller, Baron. The Adventures of a San Francisco Newsman. 100p. 1991. pap. 8.95 (*0-917583-21-3*) Lexikos.

Muller-Bergh, Klaus, jt. auth. see Gonzalez Echevarria, Roberto.

Muller, Berghaus G., ed. Workshop on Disseminated Intravascular Coagulation. LC 93-41243. 1993. 187.50 (*0-444-81647-X*) Elsevier.

Muller-Berghaus, G., et al, eds. Fibrinogen & Its Derivatives--Biochemistry, Physiology & Pathophysiology. 356p. 1987. 117.50 (*0-444-80847-7*, Excerpta Medica) Elsevier.

Muller, Bernhardt, jt. auth. see Greiner, Walter.

Muller-Bierl, Maja. The Professional's Book of Budgerigars. T. F. H. Publications, Editorial Staff, tr. (Illus.). 144p. 1991. lib. bdg. 14.95 (*0-86622-076-3*, TS-138) TFH Pubns.

Muller, Birgit. Toward an Alternative Culture of Work: Political Idealism & Economic Practices in West Berlin Collective Enterprises. (Illus.). 212p. (C). 1991. pap. text ed. 37.50 (*0-8133-8079-0*) Westview.

Muller, Brenda, jt. auth. see Muller, Carrel.

Muller-Brettel, Marianne, ed. Bibliography on Peace Research & Peaceful International Relations: The Contributions of Psychology 1900-1991. 384p. 1993. lib. bdg. 85.00 (*3-598-11072-3*) K G Saur.

***Muller, Brigitte & Gunther, Horst H.** A Complete Reiki Healing Book: Heal Yourself, Others, & the World Around You. LC 94-47299. 1995. 12.95 (*0-940795-16-7*) LifeRhythm.

Muller, Brunhild. Painting with Children. 48p. 1990. pap. 8.95 (*0-86315-048-9*, 1192, Pub. by Floris Books UK) Anthroposophic.

— Painting with Children. (J). 1988. pap. 8.50 (*0-86315-052-7*, 20240) Gryphon Hse.

Muller, Bruno J., jt. auth. see Mohamed, Saad M.

Muller, C., ed. Ecology & Mental Health. (Journal: Psychiatria Clinica: Vol. 7, Nos. 4 & 5). 100p. 1974. 45.00 (*3-8055-2212-6*) S Karger.

Muller, C., ed. see Metochites, Theodorus.

Muller, C. F. Nachtrage zur Plautinischen Prosodie. xvi, 159p. (GER.). 1973. reprint ed. write for info. (*0-318-70442-0*, Pub. by Georg Olms GW) Lubrecht & Cramer.

Muller, Carl F. Nachtrage Zur Plautinischen Prosodie. xvi, 159p. 1973. reprint ed. write for info. (*0-318-71181-8*, Pub. by Georg Olms GW) Lubrecht & Cramer.

— Plautinische Prosodie. 800p. (GER.). 1971. reprint ed. write for info. (*3-487-04085-9*, Pub. by Georg Olms GW) Lubrecht & Cramer.

Muller, Carrel & Jacques, Ethel M. Dinosaur Discovery. (Illus.). 32p. (J). (gr. 4-6). 1987. student ed 5.00 (*0-915785-02-1*) Bonjour Books.

Muller, Carrel & Muller, Brenda. Explore Louisiana. (Illus.). 32p. (J). (gr. 4 up). 1984. 5.50 (*0-915785-00-5*) Bonjour Books.

— Louisiana Indians. (Illus.). 64p. (J). (gr. 3 up). 1985. 7.50 (*0-915785-01-3*) Bonjour Books.

Muller, Ch. The Art & Antiques Dictionary, Vol. 1. 376p. (ENG, FRE & GER.). 1982. 125.00 (*0-8288-0950-X*, M14333) Fr & Eur.

Muller, Charles R. & Rieman, Timothy D. The Shaker Chair. LC 91-40646. (Illus.). 268p. (C). 1992. reprint ed. pap. 26.95 (*0-87023-795-0*) U of Mass Pr.

Muller, Charlotte, et al. Costs & Effectiveness of Cervical Cancer Screening in Elderly Women. (Illus.). 93p. 1990. pap. 4.25 (*0-16-019038-X*, S/N 052-003-01176-0) USGPO.

Muller, Charlotte F. Health Care & Gender. LC 90-8383. 272p. 1990. text ed. 45.00 (*0-87154-610-8*) Russell Sage.

— Health Care & Gender. (Illus.). 258p. 1992. pap. 14.95 (*0-87154-611-6*) Russell Sage.

— Light Metals Monopoly. LC 68-58611. (Columbia University. Studies in the Social Sciences: No. 519). reprint ed. 22.50 (*0-404-51519-3*) AMS Pr.

Muller, Christian, jt. auth. see Hecker, Stephen.

Muller, Claude, jt. ed. see Attal, Pierre.

Muller, Curt-Christian, ed. Diekholzen - Eine Ortschronik. xi, 162p. (GER.). 1992. write for info. (*3-487-09683-8*, Pub. by Georg Olms GW) Lubrecht & Cramer.

Muller, Cynthia, et al. Apples for Teachers Series, 5 bks. (J). (ps). 1988. Letters A-Z. pap. write for info. (*0-8224-0456-7*); Numbers 0-10. pap. write for info. (*0-8224-0457-5*); Time. pap. write for info. (*0-8224-0458-3*); Colors & Shapes. pap. write for info. (*0-8224-0459-1*) Fearon Teach Aids.

— Apples for Teachers Series, 5 bks. (J). (ps-00). 1988. pap. 10.95 (*0-685-18080-8*) Fearon Teach Aids.

Muller, D. Dictionary of Microprocessor Systems. 2nd rev. ed. 448p. (ENG, FRE, GER & RUS.). 1990. 154.00 (*0-685-47417-8*) Elsevier.

Muller, D., ed. Dictionary of Microprocessor Systems. 312p. (ENG, FRE, GER & RUS.). 1984. 100.00 (*0-444-99645-1*, I-401-83) Elsevier.

Muller, D. E. A Goya Oil Sketch for an Officer's Portrait. 1984. 1.50 (*0-87535-136-0*) Hispanic Soc.

***Muller, Daniel & Groves, David I.** Potassic Igneous Rocks & Associated Gold-Copper Mineralization. LC 95-10058. (Lecture Notes in Earth Sciences: Vol. 56). 1995. write for info. (*0-387-59116-8*) Spr-Verlag.

Muller, Dave. Colorado Mountain Hikes for Everyone: Routes & Maps to 105 Named Summits. LC 87-92198. (Illus.). 196p. (Orig.). 1987. pap. 10.95 (*0-9619666-0-2*) D J Muller.

— Colorado Mountain Ski Tours & Hikes: A Year Round Guide. (Illus.). 224p. (Orig.). 1993. pap. 14.95 (*0-9619666-1-0*) D J Muller.

Muller, Dave, jt. auth. see Taylor, Jayne.

Muller, Dave J., jt. auth. see Code, Chris.

Muller, Dave J., jt. ed. see Code, Chris.

Muller, Dave J., et al. Nursing Children: Psychology, Research, & Practice. 2nd ed. LC 92-20109. 1992. write for info. (*1-56593-023-1*) Singular Publishing.

Muller, Dave J., et al, eds. Psychology & Law: Topics from an International Conference. LC 83-21684. 472p. 1984. text ed. 165.00 (*0-471-90336-1*) Wiley.

— Psychology & Law: Topics from an International Conference. LC 83-21684. 494p. reprint ed. pap. 140.80 (*0-7837-5204-0*, 2044932) Bks Demand.

***Muller, David.** Whitey. (Writers Ser.). 120p. 1995. reprint ed. pap. text ed. 12.95x (*0-86975-468-8*, Pub. by Ravan Pr ZA) Ohio U Pr.

Muller, Detlef, et al, eds. The Rise of the Modern Educational System: Structural Change & Social Reproduction, 1870-1920. 280p. 1990. pap. 19.95 (*0-521-36685-2*) Cambridge U Pr.

Muller, Dieter. Dictionary of Microprocessor Systems. 4th ed. 448p. (ENG, FRE, GER & RUS.). 1990. 175.00 (*0-8288-0270-X*, M 13124) Fr & Eur.

— Dictionary of Microprocessor Systems: English-German-French-Russian. rev. ed. 448p. (ENG, FRE, GER & RUS.). 1990. 75.00 (*3-86117-013-2*, Pub. by A Hatier GW) IBD Ltd.

Muller, Donna. Handwoven Laces. LC 91-18696. (Illus.). 152p. (Orig.). 1991. pap. 16.95 (*0-934026-66-1*) Interweave.

Muller, E., ed. see Come, B., et al.

Muller, E. E., ed. Neuroactive Drugs in Endocrinology. (Developments in Endocrinology Ser.: Vol. 9). 406p. 1980. 93.50 (*0-444-80222-3*) Elsevier.

Muller, E. E. & Agnoli, A., eds. Neuroendocrine Correlates in Neurology & Psychiatry. (Developments in Neurology Ser.: Vol. 2). 1979. 74.50 (*0-444-80121-9*, North Holland) Elsevier.

Muller, E. E. & MacLeod, R. M., eds. Neuroendocrine Perspectives, Vol. 1. 406p. 1982. 151.00 (*0-444-80365-3*) Elsevier.

— Neuroendocrine Perspectives, Vol. 2. 380p. 1983. 137.50 (*0-444-80449-8*, I-336-83) Elsevier.

— Neuroendocrine Perspectives, Vol. 8. (Illus.). xiv, 182p. 1990. 87.00 (*0-387-97365-6*) Spr-Verlag.

— Neuroendocrine Perspectives, Vol. 9. (Illus.). xiv, 246p. 1991. 108.00 (*0-387-97524-1*) Spr-Verlag.

— Neuroendocrine Perspectives: Proceedings of the 2nd Meeting of the European Neuroendocrine Association, Milan, Italy, 15-17 Oct. 1985, Vol. 5. 360p. 1986. 111.50 (*0-444-80787-X*) Elsevier.

Muller, E. E., et al, eds. Neuroendocrine Perspectives, Vol. 4. 301p. 1985. 132.50 (*0-444-80665-2*) Elsevier.

Muller, Earl C. Trinity & Marriage in Paul: The Establishment of a Communitarian Analogy of the Trinity Grounded in the Theological Shape of Pauline Thought. (American University Studies: Theology & Religion: Ser. VII, Vol. 60). 553p. (C). 1989. text ed. 81.50 (*0-8204-0914-6*) P Lang Pubs.

Muller-Eberhard, H. J. & Miescher, P A., eds. Complement. (Illus.). vi, 480p. 1985. pap. 93.00 (*0-387-15075-7*) Spr-Verlag.

Muller, Edith A., ed. Highlights of Astronomy, 2 pts., Pt. 1. (International Astronomical Union Highlights Ser.). 1977. lib. bdg. 94.00 (*90-277-0849-5*) Kluwer Ac.

— Highlights of Astronomy, 2 pts., Pt. 1. (International Astronomical Union Highlights Ser.). 1977. pap. text ed. 64.00 (*90-277-0830-4*) Kluwer Ac.

— Highlights of Astronomy, 2 pts., Pt. 2. (International Astronomical Union Highlights Ser.). 1977. lib. bdg. 103.00 (*90-277-0850-9*) Kluwer Ac.

— Highlights of Astronomy, 2 pts., Pt. 2. (International Astronomical Union Highlights Ser.). 1977. pap. text ed. 70.00 (*90-277-0832-0*) Kluwer Ac.

— Reports on Astronomy, 3 pts., Pt. 1. (Transactions of the International Astronomical Union Ser.: Vol. XVII A). 1979. lib. bdg. 64.00 (*90-277-1005-8*) Kluwer Ac.

— Reports on Astronomy, 3 pts., Pt. 2. (Transactions of the International Astronomical Union Ser.: Vol. XVII A). 1979. lib. bdg. 64.00 (*90-277-1006-6*) Kluwer Ac.

Muller, Edith A., ed. see International Astronomical Union Staff.

Muller, Edmund & Bhattacharjee, Arun. India Wins Independence: A History of Modern India, 1707-1947: A Connected Historical Narration of India's Freedom Struggle. (C). 1988. 34.00 (*0-8364-2437-9*, Pub. by Ashish II) S Asia.

— Subhas Chandra Bose & Indian Freedom Struggle. 1985. 17.50 (*0-8364-1452-7*, Pub. by Ashish II) S Asia.

Muller, Eduard, ed. see Muller, Karl O.

Muller, Edward, ed. see Buddhaghosa.

***Muller, Edward J.** Reading Architectural Working Drawings Vol. 1: Basics, Residential & Light Construction. 4th ed. LC 95-16326. (Illus.). 1995. pap. text ed. 58.00 (*0-13-440108-5*) P-H.

— Reading Architectural Working Drawings, Vol. I: Basics, Residential, a Light Construction. 3rd ed. (Illus.). 380p. 1988. pap. text ed. 61.00 (*0-13-755778-7*) P-H.

Muller, Edward J. & Fausett, James G. Architectural Drawing & Light Construction. 4th ed. 592p. 1993. text ed. 60.00 (*0-13-045477-X*) P-H.

Muller, Edward J. & Myatt, Robert L., Jr. Reading Architectural Working Drawings: Commercial Construction, Vol. II. 3rd ed. (Illus.). 1988. pap. text ed. 70.00 (*0-13-755794-9*) P-H.

Muller, Edward K., ed. A Concise Historical Atlas of Pennsylvania. 1989. pap. 29.95 (*0-87722-672-5*) Temple U Pr.

Muller, Edward N. Aggressive Political Participation. LC 78-70309. 1979. 47.50 (*0-691-07605-7*) Princeton U Pr.

— Aggressive Political Participation. LC 78-70309. Date not set. reprint ed. pap. 90.10 (*0-7837-9396-0*, 2060141) Bks Demand.

Muller, Emilio. Cada Celebracion. LC 89-50924. 72p. 1989. 5.95 (*0-88177-078-7*, DR078) Discipleship Res.

Muller, Engenio E. & Nistico, Giuseppe. Brain Messengers & the Pituitary. 711p. 1989. text ed. 201.00 (*0-12-510310-7*) Acad Pr.

Muller, Eric. Opening Arguments: A Brief Rhetoric with Readings. LC 93-22960. 1993. write for info. (*0-15-501189-8*) HarBrace.

Muller, Eric & Koehler, Barbara. Frailing the Five-String Banjo. 1993. 7.95 (*0-87166-878-5*, 93335); audio 9.98 (*0-87166-756-8*, 93335) Mel Bay.

Muller, Erich H., ed. see Handel, George F.

Muller, Erich M., ed. see Schutz, Heinrich.

Muller, Erwin & Neuneck, Gotz. Abrustung & Konventionelle Stabilitat in Europa. 203p. 1990. pap. 36.00 (*3-7890-1974-7*, Pub. by Nomos Verlags GW) Intl Bk Import.

***Muller, Eugene W.** Job Analysis Comparing the Tasks in State-Local Government Purchasing & Institutional Purchasing. Ketchum, Carol, ed. 40p. (Orig.). (C). 1994. pap. text ed. write for info. (*0-945968-16-7*) Ctr Advanced Purchasing.

— Job Analysis Identifying the Tasks of Purchasing. Ketchum, Carol, ed. 68p. (Orig.). (C). 1992. pap. text ed. 20.00 (*0-945968-10-8*) Ctr Advanced Purchasing.

***Muller, Eugenio E. & Genazzani, Andrea R., eds.** Central & Peripheral Endorphins: Basic & Clinical Aspects. fac. ed. LC 83-42986. (Frontiers in Neuroscience Ser.). (Illus.). 389p. Date not set. pap. 110.90 (*0-7837-7534-2*, 2046970) Bks Demand.

Muller, Eugenio E., et al, eds. Growth Hormone & Somatomedins During Lifespan. LC 93-19508. 1993. 149.00 (*0-387-56690-2*) Spr-Verlag.

Muller, F. Atheneum Worterbuch: Aleman-Espanol, Espanol-Aleman. 383p. (GER & SPA.). 1979. pap. 9.95 (*0-8288-4719-3*, S35066) Fr & Eur.

Muller, F. M. Seedlings of the North-Western European Lowland. 1978. lib. bdg. 147.00 (*90-6193-588-1*) Kluwer Ac.

— Vedanta Philosophy. 182p. 1984. text ed. 27.00 (*0-685-14047-4*) Coronet Bks.

Muller, F. Max. Collected Works of Max Muller, 4 Vols. 1986. 140.00 (*0-685-14469-0*, Pub. by Manohar II) S Asia.

— India: What Can It Teach Us? 2nd ed. (C). 1991. reprint ed. 14.00 (*81-215-0394-9*, Pub. by Munshiram Manoharial II) S Asia.

— My Indian Friends. (Auld Lang Syne Second Ser.). (C). 1993. reprint ed. 18.50 (*81-206-0839-9*, Pub. by Asian Educ Servs II) S Asia.

— Three Introductory Lectures on the Science of Thought. (C). 1988. reprint ed. 11.50 (*81-206-0423-7*, Pub. by Asian Educ Servs II) S Asia.

— The Upanishads, 2 vols. 1974. lib. bdg. 500.00 (*0-8490-1252-X*) Gordon Pr.

— Upanishads, 2 Vols, 1. 1963. reprint ed. text ed. 8.95 (*0-486-20993-8*) Dover.

— Upanishads, 2 Vols, 2. 1963. reprint ed. text ed. 8.95 (*0-486-20992-X*) Dover.

Muller, F. Max, ed. The Texts of Taoism, 2 vols, 1. Legge, James, tr. 396p. 1891. pap. 7.95 (*0-486-20990-3*) Dover.

— The Texts of Taoism, 2 vols, 2. Legge, James, tr. 396p. 1891. pap. 7.95 (*0-486-20991-1*) Dover.

Muller, F. Max & Oldenberg, H. Vedic Hymns, 2 vols. 1974. lib. bdg. 500.00 (*0-685-01976-4*) Gordon Pr.

Muller, F. Max, ed. see Arya-Sura.

Muller, F. Max, ed. see Kasawara, Kenju.

Muller, Fabiola, jt. auth. see O'Rahilly, Ronan.

***Muller-Fahrenholz.** Gods Spirit. 1995. (*0-8264-0824-9*) Continuum.

Muller-Fahrenholz, Geiko, ed. Partners in Life: The Handicapped & the Church. LC 80-473412. (Faith & Order Paper Ser.: No. 89). 188p. reprint ed. pap. 53.60 (*0-7837-6005-1*, 2045815) Bks Demand.

Muller, Florencia & Hopkins, Barbara. A Guide to Mexican Ceramics. (Illus.). 128p. 1974. pap. 6.50 (*0-912434-17-1*) Ocelot Pr.

Muller, Francis J. De Paroecia Domui Religiosae Commissa. 1956. 3.50 (*0-686-11580-5*) Franciscan Inst.

***Muller, Frank G.** The Aldobrandini Wedding. (Iconological Studies in Roman Art: Vol. 3). (Illus.). xii, 208p. 1994. lib. bdg. 49.00x (*90-5063-266-1*, Pub. by Gieben NE) Benjamins North Am.

— The So-Called Peleus & Thetis Sarcophagus in the Villa Albani. (Iconological Studies in Roman Art: Vol. 1). (Illus.). xii, 208p. 1994. lib. bdg. 49.00x (*90-5063-246-7*, Pub. by Gieben NE) Benjamins North Am.

— The Wall Paintings from the Oecus of the Villa of Publius Fannius Synistor in Boscoreale. (Iconological Studies in Roman Art: Vol. 2). (Illus.). x, 156p. 1994. lib. bdg. 49.00x (*90-5063-256-4*, Pub. by Gieben NE) Benjamins North Am.

Muller, Frank G., jt. ed. see Ahmad, Yusuf J.

Muller, Franz. Chemistry & Biochemistry of Flavoenzymes, II. (Illus.). 512p. 1991. 225.00 (*0-8493-4394-1*, QP552) CRC Pr.

— Chemistry & Biochemistry of Flavoenzymes, Vol. I. (Illus.). 528p. 1991. 251.00 (*0-8493-4393-3*, QP552) CRC Pr.

— Chemistry & Biochemistry of Flavoenzymes, Vol. III. (Illus.). 512p. 1991. 230.00 (*0-8493-4395-X*, QP552) CRC Pr.

Muller, Frederick. La Comida: The Foods, Cooking & Traditions of the Upper Rio Grande. LC 94-42423. 196p. (Orig.). 1995. pap. 18.95 (*0-87108-842-8*) Pruett.

Muller, Frederik. Energy & Environment in Interregional Input-Output Models. (Studies in Applied Regional Science: Vol. 15). 1979. lib. bdg. 49.50 (*0-89838-002-2*) Kluwer Ac.

Muller, Friedrich A. Der Islam Im Morgen-und Abendland, 2 vols. (Illus.). 1331p. reprint ed. write for info. (*0-318-71534-1*, Pub. by Georg Olms GW) Lubrecht & Cramer.

Muller, Friedrich M. Biographies of Words & the Home of the Aryas. (C). 1987. reprint ed. 22.00 (*81-206-0299-4*, Pub. by Asian Educ Servs II) S Asia.

— Comparative Mythology: An Essay. rev. ed. Dorson, Richard M., ed. LC 77-70612. (International Folklore Ser.). 1979. reprint ed. lib. bdg. 24.95 (*0-405-10111-2*) Ayer.

— Introduction to the Science of Religion. Bolle, Kees W., ed. LC 77-79145. (Mythology Ser.). 1978. lib. bdg. 35.95 (*0-405-10554-1*) Ayer.

Muller, G. Convection & Inhomogeneities in Crystal Growth from the Melt. (Crystals - Growth, Properties & Applications Ser.). 140p. 1988. 98.00 (*0-387-18603-4*) Spr-Verlag.

— Se Puede Confiar En Dios (God Can Be Trusted) large type ed. (SPA.). Date not set. 2.99 (*1-56063-341-7*, 494026) Editorial Unilit.

Muller, G., jt. ed. see Kruger, G.

Muller, G. H. & Richter, M. M., eds. Models & Sets, Pt. 1. (Lecture Notes in Mathematics Ser.: Vol. 1103). viii, 484p. 1984. pap. 53.80 (*0-387-13900-1*) Spr-Verlag.

Muller, G. H., ed. see Proof Theory Symposium Staff.

Muller, Georg. Comparative World Data: A Statistical Handbook for Social Science. LC 88-45391. 504p. (C). 1989. text ed. 60.00 (*0-8018-3734-0*); 3.5 hd 95.00 (*0-8018-3805-3*); 5.25 hd 95.00 (*0-8018-3770-7*) Johns Hopkins.

Muller, George. The Autobiography of George Muller. 300p. 1984. pap. 5.99 (*0-88368-159-5*) Whitaker Hse.

— Faith in Action. Setran, David P., ed. & intro. by. (Collection of Classics Ser.). 74p. (Orig.). 1994. pap. text ed. 1.95 (*1-879089-19-X*) B Graham Ctr.

Muller, Gerald. Gentle Giants. LC 87-24537. (Illus.). (J). (gr. 6-9). 1988. pap. 7.95 (*0-8198-3045-3*) Pauline Bks.

Muller, Gerda. Around the Oak. LC 93-32310. (J). (gr. 3 up). 1994. 14.99 (*0-525-45239-7*, DCB) Dutton Child Bks.

— Circle of Seasons. LC 95-10382. (J). 1995. write for info. (*0-525-45394-6*, DCB) Dutton Child Bks.

— The Garden in the City. (Illus.). 40p. (J). (gr. k-5). 1992. 13.50 (*0-525-44697-4*, DCB) Dutton Child Bks.

Muller, Gerda, illus. The Adventures of Tom Thumb. 48p. (J). (gr. 2-6). 1991. 2.99 (*0-517-02418-7*) Random Hse Value.

— Jack & the Beanstalk. 48p. (J). (gr. 2-6). 1991. 2.99 (*0-517-02421-7*) Random Hse Value.

— The Ugly Duckling. 48p. (J). (gr. 2-6). 1991. 2.99 (*0-517-02422-5*) Random Hse Value.

***Muller, Gerhard.** Lexikon Technoloie Metallverarbeitende Industri. 2nd ed. 699p. (GER.). 1992. 125.00 (*0-7859-8694-4*, 380855102x) Fr & Eur.

Muller, Gerhard F. Bering's Voyages: The Reports From Russia. Urness, Carol, ed. & tr. by. LC 86-51585. (Rasmuson Library Historical Translation Ser.: Vol. III). (Illus.). 221p. (Orig.). 1986. pap. 15.00 (*0-912006-22-6*) U of Alaska Pr.

Muller, Gerhard J., ed. Medical Optical Tomography: Functional Imaging & Monitoring. LC 93-5546. 1993. write for info. (*0-8194-1380-1*); pap. write for info. (*0-8194-1379-8*) SPIE.

***Muller, Gerhard J. & Roggan, Andre, eds.** Laser-Induced Interstitial Thermotherapy. LC 95-12212. (Institute Ser.: Vol. IS13). 1995. write for info. (*0-8194-1859-5*) SPIE.

Muller, Gerhard M., jt. auth. see Viswanath, V. S.

***Muller, German.** Lexikon Elektrotechnik. (GER.). 1994. 195.00 (*0-7859-8416-X*, 3527281541) Fr & Eur.

Muller, Gilbert & Wiener, Harvey S. The Short Prose Reader. 6th ed. 1991. pap. text ed. write for info. (*0-07-044135-9*) McGraw.

Muller, Gilbert H. Chester Himes. (Twayne's United States Authors Ser.: No. 553). 184p. 1989. text ed. 20.95 (*0-8057-7545-5*, Twayne) Macmillan.

— The McGraw-Hill Introduction to Literature. 1124p. 1985. text ed. write for info. (*0-07-043989-3*) McGraw.

— The McGraw-Hill Introduction to Literature. 1124p. 1985. Instr's. manual. teacher ed, pap. text ed. write for info. (*0-07-043990-7*) McGraw.

Muller, Gilbert H., ed. The McGraw-Hill Reader: Themes in the Disciplines. 5th ed. LC 93-20824. 1993. pap. text ed. write for info. (0-07-044254-1) McGraw.

Muller, Gilbert H. & Wiener, Harvey S. The Short Prose Reader. (Illus.). 1979. pap. text ed. write for info. (0-07-043991-5) McGraw.

Muller, Gilbert H. & Williams, John A. Ways in Approaches to Reading & Writing about Literature. LC 93-1666. 1993. pap. text ed. write for info. (0-07-044203-7) McGraw.

Muller, Gilbert H. & Williams, John A., comps. Bridges: Literature Across Cultures. LC 93-3954. 1993. pap. text ed. write for info. (0-07-044216-9) McGraw.

Muller, Gilbert H. & Williams, John A., intros. The McGraw-Hill Introduction to Literature. LC 94-17019. 1995. write for info. (0-07-044246-0) McGraw.

Muller-Goldingen, Christian, ed. see Aristoteles.

Muller-Gotama, Franz. Grammatical Relations: A Cross-Linguistic Perspective on Their Syntax & Semantics. LC 94-3344. (Empirical Approaches to Language Typology Ser.: Vol. 11). x, 171p. 1994. 75.40 (3-11-013737-2) Mouton.

Muller, Gottfried H., jt. auth. see Bootz, Friedrich.

Muller, Gunther. Woerterbuecher der Biologie, Mikrobiologie: Dictionary of Biology, Microbiology. 25p. (GER.). 1980. 35.00 (0-8288-1221-7, M15333) Fr & Eur.

Muller, H. Jet. (Gem Bks.). (Illus.). 176p. 1987. text ed. 39.95 (0-408-03110-7) Buttrwrth-Heinemann.

Muller, H., jt. auth. see Gachter, R.

Muller, H. G. An Introduction to Tropical Food Science. (Illus.). 295p. 1988. pap. 37.95 (0-521-33686-4) Cambridge U Pr.

— An Introduction to Tropical Food Science. (Illus.). 295p. 1989. 99.95 (0-521-33488-8) Cambridge U Pr.

Muller, H. G. & Tobin, G. Nutrition & Food Processing. (C). 1980. pap. 30.95 (0-87055-363-1) AVI.

Muller, H. H. Fiscal Policies in a General Equilibrium Model with Persistent Unemployment. (Lecture Notes in Economics & Mathematical Systems Ser.: Vol. 216). 92p. 1983. pap. 28.00 (0-387-12316-4) Spr-Verlag.

Muller, H. J., ed. see Seneca, L. Annaei.

Muller, H. Nicholas, III. From Ferment to Fatigue? 1870-1900: A New Look at the Neglected Winter of Vermont. (Occasional Papers: No. 7). 28p. (Orig.). 1984. pap. text ed. 2.50 (0-944277-12-8, M8) U VT Ctr Rsch VT.

Muller, H. Nicholas, III, jt. auth. see Duffy, John J.

Muller, Hanns. Pocket Dictionary of Horseman's Terms in English, German, French & Spanish. (FRE.). 1971. 9.95 (0-685-00343-4) Transatl Arts.

Muller, Hans. Diccionario Lexicon, Aleman-Espanol, Espanol-Aleman: German-Spanish, Spanish-German Dictionary Lexicon. 384p. (GER & SPA.). 1977. pap. 14.95 (0-8288-5350-9, S31392) Fr & Eur.

Muller, Hans A. Farm Animals. (Mini Fact Finders Ser.). (Illus.). 64p. (Orig.). 1992. pap. 4.95 (0-8120-4775-3) Barron.

— Sheep: An Owner's Manual. (Illus.). 1989. pap. 5.95 (0-8120-4091-0) Barron.

Muller, Hans-Peter. Mythos-Kerygma-Wahrheit: Gesammelte Aufsatze Zum Alten Testament in Seiner Umwelt und Zur Biblischen Theologie. (Beihefte zur Zeitschrift fuer die Alttestamentliche Wissenschaft Ser.: Band 200). xiv, 319p. (GER.). (C). 1991. lib. bdg. 101.55 (3-11-012885-3) De Gruyter.

Muller, Hans W., jt. auth. see Lloyd, Seton.

Muller, Harald. How Western Nuclear Policy Is Made: Deciding on the Atom. 248p. 1991. text ed. 69.95 (0-312-05354-1) St Martin.

Muller, Harald, ed. A Survey of European Nuclear Policy, 1985-87. 240p. 1989. text ed. 55.00 (0-312-02796-6) St Martin.

Muller-Hartmann, E., et al, eds. Valence Fluctuations. 620p. 1986. 136.00 (0-444-87000-8, North Holland) Elsevier.

Muller, Heiner. The Battle: Plays, Prose, Poems. 176p. 1989. pap. 12.95x (1-55554-049-X) PAJ Pubns.

— Explosion of a Memory: And Other Writings. Weber, Carl, ed. & tr. by. (Illus.). 1989. 28.00 (1-55554-040-6); pap. 12.95x (1-55554-041-4) PAJ Pubns.

— Hamletmachine & Other Texts for the Stage. Weber, Carl, tr. LC 83-61193. 140p. 1984. pap. 12.95x (0-933826-45-1) PAJ Pubns.

***Muller, Heiner & Schmidt, Jochen.** Pina Bausch: Photographs by Detlef Erler. 152p. 1995. 55.00 (3-905514-18-4) Dist Art Pubs.

Muller, Heinrich. Juggernaut. (Orig.). 1981. pap. 2.75 (0-89083-854-2) Zebra.

— Lovis Corinth: The Late Graphic Work, Die Spate Graphik. rev. ed. (Illus.). 224p. (ENG & GER.). 1994. 150.00 (1-55660-171-9) A Wofsy Fine Arts.

— Panzer Grenadiers. 288p. (Orig.). 1980. pap. 2.50 (0-89083-697-3) Zebra.

Muller, Heinz. Langenscheidt Spanish-German, German-Spanish Pocket Dictionary: Langenscheidt Handwoerterbuch Spanisch-Deutsch-Spanisch. 1400p. (GER & SPA.). 1987. 110.00 (0-8288-0352-8, S39871) Fr & Eur.

Muller, Heinz & Haensch, Gunther. Langenscheidt Spanish-German Pocket Dictionary: Langenscheidt Handwoerterbuch Spanisch-Deutsch. 656p. (GER & SPA.). 1987. 69.95 (0-8288-0351-X, F19592) Fr & Eur.

Muller, Helen. Jet Jewellery & Ornaments. 1989. pap. 25.00 (0-85263-503-6, Pub. by Shire UK) St Mut.

Muller, Helen D., jt. auth. see McGovern, Edythe M.

Muller, Helen J. & Ventriss, Curtis. Public Health in a Retrenchment Era: An Alternative to Managerialism. LC 84-16432. (SUNY Series in Public Administration). 162p. 1985. 59.50 (0-87395-985-X); pap. 19.95 (0-87395-986-8) State U NY Pr.

Muller, Henry F. & Taylor, Pauline. A Chrestomathy of Vulgar Latin: With a Detailed Glossary & Bibliography. xvii, 315p. 1990. reprint ed. 54.60 (3-487-09378-2, Pub. by Georg Olms GW) Lubrecht & Cramer.

Muller, Herbert J. The Children of Frankenstein: A Primer of Modern Technology & Human Values. LC 76-103926. 447p. reprint ed. pap. 127.40 (0-317-08704-5, 2017633) Bks Demand.

— Thomas Wolfe. 1976. 19.95 (0-8488-1435-5) Amereon Ltd.

Muller, Herbert W. Epicyclic Drive Trains: Analysis, Synthesis, & Applications. Glover, John H., ed. Mannhardt, Werner G., tr. LC 81-114220. (Illus.). 373p. 1982. 75.00 (0-8143-1663-8) Wayne St U Pr.

Muller, Herman J. Bishop East of the Rockies: The Life & Letters of John Baptist Miege, S.J. LC 93-42171. 198p. 1994. pap. 13.95 (0-8294-0780-4) Loyola Univ Pr.

Muller, Hermann. The Fertilisation of Flowers. Egerton, Frank N., 3rd, ed. Thompson, D'Arcy W., tr. LC 77-74241. (History of Ecology Ser.). (Illus.). 1978. reprint ed. lib. bdg. 57.95 (0-405-10410-3) Ayer.

Muller, Hermann J. & Carlson, Elof A., eds. Man's Future Birthright: Essays on Science & Humanity. LC 79-171215. 164p. 1973. 39.50 (0-87395-097-6) State U NY Pr.

— The Modern Concept of Nature: Essays on Theoretical Biology & Evolution. LC 74-170884. (Illus.). 272p. 1973. 39.50 (0-87395-096-8) State U NY Pr.

Muller, Hermann J., jt. ed. see Weissenborn, Wilhelm.

Muller, Herta. The Passport. 96p. 1992. pap. 7.95 (1-85242-139-8) Serpents Tail.

Muller-Hillebrand, Burkhart. Germany & Its Allies in World War II. LC 79-67365. 304p. 1980. text ed. 45.00 (0-313-27066-X, U7066, Greenwood Pr) Greenwood.

Muller, Horst M. Sprache und Evolution: Grundlagen der Evolution und Ansatze einer Evolutionstheoretischen Sprachwissenschaft. (Grundlagen der Kommunikation & Kognition (Foundations of Communication & Cognition) Ser.). (Illus.). x, 137p. (C). 1990. lib. bdg. 98.50 (3-11-011041-5) De Gruyter.

Muller-Idzerda, A. C. One Hundred Indoor Plants. (Illus.). 1959. 7.95 (0-87523-114-4) Emerson.

Muller, Ingo. Hitler's Justice: The Courts of the Third Reich. Schneider, Deborah L., tr. LC 90-39068. 368p. 1991. 37.00 (0-674-40418-1, MULHIT) HUP.

— Hitler's Justice: The Courts of the Third Reich. Schneider, Deborah L., tr. 208p. 1992. pap. 16.95 (0-674-40419-X) HUP.

Muller, Ingo & Ruggeri, Tommaso. Extended Thermodynamics. LC 92-26754. (Tracts in Natural Philosophy Ser.: Vol. 37). 230p. 1993. 69.00 (0-387-97922-0); write for info. (3-540-97922-0) Spr-Verlag.

Muller, J. Regulation of Aldosterone Biosynthesis. 2nd rev. ed. (Monographs on Endocrinology: Vol. 29). (Illus.). 300p. 1987. 133.00 (0-387-17907-0) Spr-Verlag.

Muller, J. P., ed. Digital Image Processing in Remote Sensing. 280p. 1988. 99.00 (0-85066-314-8) Taylor & Francis.

Muller, J. P., jt. ed. see Demazeau, Yves.

Muller, J. R., jt. ed. see Baker, John R.

Muller, J. W. European Collaboration in Advanced Technology. 424p. 1990. 165.75 (0-444-88418-1) Elsevier.

Muller, Jacobus J. Epistles of Paul to the Philippians. (New International Commentary on the New Testament Ser.). 1985. 22.99 (0-8028-2188-X) Eerdmans.

Muller, James A., ed. see Gardiner, Stephen.

***Muller, James W.** The Revival of Constitutionalism. LC 87-30177. 276p. 1988. reprint ed. pap. 78.70 (0-7837-8908-4, 2049619) Bks Demand.

***Muller, Jean.** Dictionnaire Abrege des Imprimateurs/Editeurs Francais du 16 Siecle. 150p. (FRE.). 1970. pap. 125.00 (0-7859-8525-5, 3873200309) Fr & Eur.

— Dictionnaire Abrege des Imprimeurs/Editeurs Francais Du. 16th ed. 1970. write for info. (0-7859-8670-7, 3873200309) Fr & Eur.

***Muller, Jean-Claude, et al, eds.** GIS & Generalisation: Methodology & Practice. (GISDATA Ser.: No. 1). 224p. 1995. 85.00 (0-7484-0318-3, Pub. by Tay Francis Ltd UK) Taylor & Francis.

— GIS & Generalisation: Methodology & Practice. (GISDATA Ser.: No. 1). 224p. 1995. pap. 34.95 (0-7484-0319-1, Pub. by Tay Francis Ltd UK) Taylor & Francis.

Muller, Jeffrey M. Rubens: The Artist As Collector. (Illus.). 330p. 1992. text ed. 80.00 (0-691-04064-8); pap. text ed. 24.95 (0-691-00298-3) Princeton U Pr.

Muller, Jerry Z. Adam Smith in His Time & Ours: Designing the Decent Society. 180p. 1992. text ed. 24.95 (0-02-922234-6) Free Pr.

— Adam Smith in His Time & Ours: Designing the Decent Society. LC 95-13210. 1995. write for info. (0-691-00161-8) Princeton U Pr.

— The Other God that Failed: Hans Freyer & the Deradicalization of German Conservatism. 472p. 1988. text ed. 65.00 (0-691-05508-4); pap. text ed. 18.95 (0-691-00823-X) Princeton U Pr.

Muller, Jim. One-Two-Three My Computer & Me: A LOGO Funbook for Kids. (J). (gr. 3 up). 1984. Commodore 64. pap. 15.95 (0-8359-5244-4, Reston) P-H.

Muller, Joachim W. The Reform of the United Nations: A Report, 2 vols., Set. LC 91-50824. 1992. lib. bdg. 120.00 (0-379-20671-4) Oceana.

***Muller, Joan.** Under the Cloak of Justice: The Work of Ned Cartledge. High, Steven, ed. (Illus.). 24p. 1994. 9.00 (0-935519-19-X) Anderson Gal.

Muller, Johann G. Des Flavius Josephus Schrift Gegen Den Apion. 394p. 1969. reprint ed. write for info. (0-318-70978-3, Pub. by Georg Olms GW) Lubrecht & Cramer.

Muller, Johannes. Die Wissenschaftlichen Vereine und Gesellschaften Deutschlands Im 19 Jahrhundert, 3 vols., Set. 1965. reprint ed. write for info. (0-318-71848-0, Pub. by Georg Olms GW) Lubrecht & Cramer.

***Muller, John P.** Beyond the Psychoanalytic Dyad: Developmental Semiotics in Freud, Peirce, & Lacan. LC 95-14600. 1995. write for info. (0-415-91068-4, Routledge NY); pap. write for info. (0-415-91069-2, Routledge NY) Routledge.

Muller, John P. & Richardson, William J. Lacan & Language: A Reader's Guide to Ecrits. LC 81-23681. 433p. 1982. 50.00 (0-8236-2945-7) Intl Univs Pr.

— Lacan & Language: A Reader's Guide to "Ecrits" 443p. 1994. pap. text ed. 29.95 (0-8236-8129-7) Intl Univs Pr.

Muller, John P. & Richardson, William J., eds. The Purloined Poe: Lacan, Derrida, & Psychoanalytic Reading. LC 87-2760. 424p. 1988. text ed. 58.00x (0-8018-3292-6); pap. text ed. 14.95 (0-8018-3293-4) Johns Hopkins.

Muller, Jon. Archaeology of the Lower Ohio River Valley. LC 85-15050. (New World Archaeological Record Ser.). 1986. pap. text ed. 58.00 (0-12-510331-X) Acad Pr.

Muller, Jorg. The Changing City. LC 76-46646. (Illus.). 8p. (J). (gr. 4 up). 1977. pap. 18.95 (0-689-50084-X, McElderry) S&S Childrens.

— The Changing Countryside. LC 76-46647. (Illus.). 8p. (J). (ps up). 1977. pap. 18.95 (0-689-50085-8, McElderry) S&S Childrens.

Muller, Joseph. The Star-Spangled Banner: Words & Music Issued Between 1814-1864. LC 79-169653. (Music Ser.). (Illus.). 1973. reprint ed. lib. bdg. 35.00 (0-306-70263-0) Da Capo.

Muller, Julia. Words & Music in Henry Purcell's First Semi-Opera, Dioclesian: An Approach to Early Music Through Early Theatre. LC 90-5676. (Studies in History & Interpretation of Music: Vol. 28). 520p. 1990. lib. bdg. 119.95 (0-88946-495-2) E Mellen.

Muller, Julian P., jt. auth. see West, Jessamyn.

Muller, Jurgen, jt. ed. see Foreman-Peck, James.

Muller, K., ed. Coastal Research in the Gulf of Bothnia. (Monographiae Biologicae: No. 45). 480p. 1982. lib. bdg. 186.50 (90-6193-098-7) Kluwer Ac.

Muller, K. A. & Thomas, H., eds. Structural Phase Transitions Two. (Topics in Current Physics Ser.: Vol. 45). (Illus.). 192p. 1991. text ed. 44.00 (0-387-52238-7) Spr-Verlag.

Muller, K. A., jt. ed. see Bednorz, J. G.

Muller, K. A., jt. auth. see Sigmund, E.

Muller, K A., ed. see Sigmund, E.

Muller, K. H., jt. ed. see Hierholzer, G.

Muller, K. R., et al, eds. Chemical Waste. (Illus.). 370p. 1985. 208.00 (0-387-13246-5) Spr-Verlag.

Muller, Kal. Bali. 1990. pap. 15.95 (0-8442-9900-6, Passport Bks) NTC Pub Grp.

— East of Bali: From Lombok to Timor. 1991. pap. 15.95 (0-8442-9905-7, Passport Bks) NTC Pub Grp.

— Indonesia in Color. (Illus.). 80p. 1992. pap. 9.95 (0-945971-26-5) Periplus.

— Indonesia in Colour. (Illus.). 1993. pap. 9.95 (0-945971-97-4); pap. 9.95 (0-945971-93-1); pap. text ed. 9.95 (0-945971-95-8) Periplus.

— Indonesian New Guinea: Irian Jaya. 2nd ed. Pickell, David, ed. (Indonesia Travel Guides Ser.). (Illus.). 208p. 1994. pap. 19.95 (0-945971-06-0) Periplus.

— Indonesie. (Oog op de Wereld Ser.). (Illus.). (DUT.). 1990. pap. text ed. 9.95 (0-945971-27-3) Periplus.

— Irian Jaya: Nieuw-Guinea. Oey, Eric, ed. Wassing, Rene & Wassing, Rita, trs. (Indonesie Reisbibliotheek Ser.). 175p. (DUT.). 1991. 19.95 (0-945971-19-2) Periplus.

— Kalimantan: Borneo. Pickell, David, ed. Keers, Francien et al, trs. (Indonesie Reisbibliotheek Ser.). 206p. (DUT.). 1991. pap. 19.95 (0-945971-37-0) Periplus.

— Kalimantan: Indonesian Borneo. Pickell, David, ed. 203p. 1995. pap. 19.95 (962-593-045-0) Periplus.

— Maluku: De Molukken. Pickell, David, ed. Pattiruhu, Maureen, tr. (Indonesie Reisbibliotheek Ser.). 175p. (DUT.). 1991. pap. 19.95 (0-945971-18-4) Periplus.

— Spice Islands: Exotic Eastern Indonesia. 1990. pap. 12.95 (0-8442-9902-2, Passport Bks) NTC Pub Grp.

— Spice Islands: The Moluccas. Pickell, David, ed. (Indonesia Travel Guides Ser.). (Illus.). 200p. 1993. pap. 19.95 (0-945971-07-9) Periplus.

— Underwater Indonesia: A Guide to the World's Greatest Diving. 2nd ed. Pickell, David, ed. 326p. 1995. pap. 19.95 (962-593-029-9) Periplus.

Muller, Kal, ed. Irian Jaya. 176p. 1991. pap. 37.50 (0-945971-34-6) Periplus.

— Maluku. 176p. 1991. pap. 37.50 (0-945971-33-8) Periplus.

— Nusa Tenggara. 296p. 1991. pap. 37.50 (0-945971-36-2) Periplus.

Muller, Karen, ed. Authority Control Symposium. (Occasional Papers: No. 6). (Illus.). 144p. (Orig.). 1987. pap. 20.00 (0-942740-05-X) Art Libs Soc.

Muller, Karl O. Die Dorier, 2 vols., Set. (Geschichten Hellenischer Stamme und Stadte Ser.: Bd. II und III). xxiii, 1110p. 1989. reprint ed. write for info. (3-487-09261-1, Pub. by Georg Olms GW) Lubrecht & Cramer.

— Introduction to a Scientific System of Mythology. Bolle, Kees W., ed. LC 77-79144. (Mythology Ser.). 1978. reprint ed. lib. bdg. 33.95 (0-405-10553-3) Ayer.

— Kleine Deutsche Schriften Uber Religion, Kunst, Sprache und Literatur, Leben und Geschichte Des Alterthums, 2 vols., Set. Muller, Eduard, ed. xlix, 1321p. 1979. reprint ed. write for info. (3-487-06757-9, Pub. by Georg Olms GW) Lubrecht & Cramer.

***Muller-Karpe, H.** Historia de la Edad de Piedra. 414p. (SPA.). 1993. 100.00 (84-249-0332-3) Elliots Bks.

Muller, Kaspar, jt. auth. see Koechlin, Dominik.

Muller, Katherine K., et al. Trees of Santa Barbara. (Illus.). 1974. 10.00 (0-916436-00-4) Santa Barb Botanic.

Muller, Kathleen, ed. San Jose: City with a Past. (Illus.). 112p. 1988. write for info. (0-914139-07-X) San Jose His Mus Assn.

Muller, Kathleen, jt. auth. see Douglas, Jack.

Muller, Kathleen, ed. see Loomis, Patricia.

Muller, Kathleen, ed. see McEnery, Thomas.

Muller, Kathleen, ed. see Peyton, Wes.

Muller, Kathleen, ed. see Yu, Connie Y.

Muller, Kenneth J., et al, eds. Neurobiology of the Leech. LC 81-68893. 320p. (C). 1981. 55.00 (0-87969-146-8) Cold Spring Harbor.

Muller-Kirsten, H. & Wiedemann, A., eds. Supersymmetry: An Introduction with Conceptual & Calculational Details. (Lecture Notes in Physics Ser.: Vol. 7). 608p. 1987. text ed. 104.00 (9971-5-0354-9); pap. text ed. 51.00 (9971-5-0355-7) World Scientific Pub.

***Muller, Klaus-Jurgen, et al, eds.** The Military in Politics & Society in France & Germany in the 20th Century. LC 94-46596. (German Historical Perspectives Ser.: Vol. 9). 168p. 1995. 36.95 (0-85496-812-1) Berg Pubs.

Muller, Kurt E. Language Competence: Implications for National Security. LC 85-31240. (Washington Papers: No. 119). 181p. 1986. text ed. 49.95 (0-275-92213-8, C2213, Praeger Pubs); pap. text ed. 9.95 (0-275-92214-6, B2214, Praeger Pubs) Greenwood.

Muller, Kurt E., ed. Languages As Barrier & Bridge. (Papers of the Center for Research & Documentation on World Language Problems). 140p. (Orig.). (C). 1992. lib. bdg. 42.50 (0-8191-8670-8) U Pr of Amer.

— Languages in Elementary Schools. 232p. 1989. pap. 10.00 (0-614-03013-7) Amer Forum.

Muller, Kurt E., jt. auth. see Benya, Rosemarie.

Muller, L., et al. The Coinage of Ancient Africa: (Numismatique De L'Ancienne Afrique) (Illus.). 1977. 80.00 (0-916710-35-1) Obol Intl.

***Muller, Lauren, ed.** June Jordan's Poetry for the People: A Revolutionary Blueprint. LC 95-8470. 1995. write for info. (0-415-91167-2, Routledge NY); pap. write for info. (0-415-91168-0, Routledge NY) Routledge.

Muller, Leonard, tr. see Cohen, Marcel.

Muller, Leonard R., tr. see Cohen, Marcel.

Muller, Liguori G., tr. see Augustinius, Aurelius.

***Muller, Lillian & Coleman, John.** Feels Great, Be Beautiful over 40: Inside Tips on How to Look Better, Be Healthier & Slow the Aging Process. Pirch, Sarah, ed. (Illus.). 256p. 1995. pap. 17.95 (1-881649-61-X) Genl Pub Grp.

Muller, Linda L. & Hamer, Jan. One, Two-Cycloaddition Reactions: The Formation of Three- & Four-Membered Heterocycles. LC 67-20265. 372p. reprint ed. pap. 106.10 (0-7837-3459-X, 2057785) Bks Demand.

Muller-Lutz. Insurance Dictionary. 304p. (ENG, FRE, GER & SPA.). 1990. pap. 61.00 (3-88487-210-9, Pub. by V Versich) IBD Ltd.

Muller-Lutz, H. L. Insurance Dictionary. 3rd ed. 281p. (ENG, FRE, GER & SPA.). 1981. pap. 39.95 (0-8288-0969-0, M 7807) Fr & Eur.

Muller-Lux, William & Roltgen, Ingrid. Muller-Lux Drawings, 1958-1963. (Illus.). 184p. 1988. 65.00 (0-9621943-0-1) Sunrise AZ.

Muller, M. Consistent Classical Supergravity Theories. (Lecture Notes in Physics Ser.: Vol. 336). vi, 125p. 1989. 31.00 (0-387-51427-9, 3358) Spr-Verlag.

Muller, M., ed. see Scherer, W.

Muller, M. E. & Ganz, R., eds. Total Hip Prostheses. 1976. ring bd. 221.00 (0-387-92103-6) Spr-Verlag.

Muller, M. E., et al. The Comprehensive Classification of Fractures of Long Bones. (Illus.). 220p. 1994. pap. 89.00 (0-387-18165-2) Spr-Verlag.

Muller, M. E., et al, eds. Manual of Internal Fixation. 3rd rev. ed. (Illus.). 792p. 1991. 198.00 (0-387-52523-8) Spr-Verlag.

Muller, M. J., et al, eds. Hormones & Nutrition in Obesity & Cachexia. (Illus.). 160p. 1990. pap. 38.00 (0-387-51637-9) Spr-Verlag.

Muller, Manfred J. Selected Climatic Data for a Global Set of Standard Stations for Vegetation Science. 1982. lib. bdg. 186.50 (90-6193-945-3) Kluwer Ac.

Muller, Marcel. Prefiguration et Structure Romanesque dans A la Recherche du Temps Perdu. LC 78-73096. (French Forum Monographs: No. 14). (Illus.). 95p. (Orig.). 1979. pap. 9.95 (0-917058-13-5) French Forum.

Muller, Marcel N., ed. see Chambers, Ross, et al.

Muller, Marcia. Ask the Cards a Question. 224p. 1990. reprint ed. mass mkt. 5.50 (0-445-40849-X, Mysterious Paperbk) Warner Bks.

— The Cavalier in White. 1993. mass mkt. 3.99 (0-373-83304-0, 1-83304-5) Harlequin Bks.

— The Cheshire Cat's Eye. 224p. 1990. reprint ed. mass mkt. 5.50 (0-445-40850-2, Mysterious Paperbk) Warner Bks.

— Dark Star. 1993. mass mkt. 3.99 (0-373-83308-3, 1-83308-6) Harlequin Bks.

— Edwin of the Iron Shoes. (Black Dagger Crime Ser.). 184p. 1993. 16.50 (0-7451-8617-3, Black Dagger) Chivers N Amer.

— Edwin of the Iron Shoes. 224p. 1990. reprint ed. mass mkt. 5.50 (0-445-40902-9, Mysterious Paperbk) Warner Bks.

— Eye of the Storm. 1988. 15.95 (0-89296-269-0) Mysterious Pr.

— Eye of the Storm. 256p. 1989. mass mkt. 5.50 (0-445-40625-9, Mysterious Paperbk) Warner Bks.

— Games to Keep the Dark Away. 256p. 1990. reprint ed. mass mkt. 5.50 (0-445-40851-0, Mysterious Paperbk) Warner Bks.

An Asterisk (*) at the beginning of an entry indicates that the title is appearing in BIP for the first time.

— Games to Keep the Dark Away: A Sharon McCone Mystery. 160p. 1984. 10.95 (*0-312-31620-8*) St Martin.

— Leave a Message for Willie. 224p. 1990. mass mkt. 5.50 (*0-445-40900-2*, Mysterious Paperbk) Warner Bks.

— The Legend of Slain Soldiers. 1996. mass mkt. write for info. (*0-446-40421-7*, Mysterious Paperbk) Warner Bks.

— Pennies on a Dead Woman's Eyes. 304p. 1993. 18.95 (*0-89296-454-5*) Mysterious Pr.

— Pennies on a Dead Woman's Eyes. 336p. 1993. mass mkt. 5.50 (*0-446-40033-5*, Mysterious Paperbk) Warner Bks.

— The Shape of Dread. 1989. 16.95 (*0-89296-271-2*) Mysterious Pr.

— The Shape of Dread. 288p. 1990. mass mkt. 5.50 (*0-445-40916-9*, Mysterious Paperbk) Warner Bks.

— There Hangs the Knife. 1993. mass mkt. 3.99 (*0-373-83307-5*, 1-83307-8) Harlequin Bks.

— There's Nothing to be Afraid Of. 224p. 1990. mass mkt. 5.50 (*0-445-40901-0*, Mysterious Paperbk) Warner Bks.

— There's Something in a Sunday. 1989. 15.95 (*0-89296-270-4*) Mysterious Pr.

— There's Something in a Sunday. 224p. 1990. mass mkt. 5.50 (*0-445-40865-0*, Mysterious Paperbk) Warner Bks.

— Till the Butchers Cut Him Down. 352p. 1994. 18.95 (*0-89296-455-3*) Mysterious Pr.

— Till the Butchers Cut Him Down. 1995. pap. write for info. (*0-446-40034-3*, Mysterious Paperbk) Warner Bks.

— Till the Butchers Cut Him Down. 336p. 1995. mass mkt. 5.99 (*0-446-60302-3*, Mysterious Paperbk) Warner Bks.

— The Tree of Death. 240p. 1996. mass mkt. 5.99 (*0-446-40420-9*, Mysterious Paperbk) Warner Bks.

— Trophies & Dead Things. 272p. 1990. 16.95 (*0-89296-417-0*) Mysterious Pr.

— Trophies & Dead Things. 272p. 1991. mass mkt. 5.50 (*0-446-40039-4*, Mysterious Paperbk) Warner Bks.

— Trophies & Dead Things. large type ed. (General Ser.). 379p. 1991. text ed. 19.95 (*0-8161-5134-2*, Large Print Bks) Hall.

— Where Echoes Live. 1991. 17.95 (*0-89296-418-9*) Mysterious Pr.

— Where Echoes Live. 368p. 1992. mass mkt. 5.50 (*0-446-40161-7*, Mysterious Paperbk) Warner Bks.

— A Wild & Lonely Place. 300p. 1995. 19.95 (*0-89296-526-6*) Mysterious Pr.

— A Wild & Lonely Place. 1996. mass mkt. write for info. (*0-446-60328-7*) Warner Bks.

— Wolf in the Shadows. 368p. 1993. 18.95 (*0-89296-525-8*) Mysterious Pr.

— Wolf in the Shadows. 384p. 1994. mass mkt. 5.50 (*0-446-40383-0*) Warner Bks.

— Wolf in the Shadows: A Sharon McCone Mystery. large type ed. LC 93-37404. (Cloak & Dagger Ser.). 1993. 20. 95 (*0-7862-0087-1*) Thorndike Pr.

Muller, Marcia & Pronzini, Bill. Beyond the Grave. (Mystery Scene Book Ser.). 240p. 1991. pap. 3.95 (*0-88184-731-3*) Carroll & Graf.

— Beyond the Grave. 224p. 1986. 15.95 (*0-8027-5651-4*) Walker & Co.

— The Lighthouse. (Mystery Scene Book Ser.). 304p. 1992. pap. 4.50 (*0-88184-885-9*) Carroll & Graf.

Muller, Marcia & Prozini, Bill. Double. 288p. 1995. mass mkt. 5.50 (*0-446-40413-6*, Mysterious Paperbk) Warner Bks.

***Muller, Marianne.** Grosse Lexikon der Gastronomie. 2nd ed. 680p. (GER.). 1991. 150.00 (*0-7859-8558-1*, 3925673393) Fr & Eur.

Muller, Marianne, et al. Great Napkin Folding & Table Decorations. LC 90-36204. (Illus.). 96p. (Orig.). 1990. pap. 12.95 (*0-8069-7384-6*) Sterling.

Muller, Mary. Cloud Across the Moon. large type ed. 388p. 1981. 12.00 (*0-7089-0676-1*) Ulverscroft.

— Encounter at Dawn. large type ed. 512p. 1983. 15.95 (*0-7089-1030-0*) Ulverscroft.

— Flagdown. large type ed. 401p. 1981. 12.00 (*0-7089-0566-8*) Ulverscroft.

— Tree in the Wind. large type ed. 394p. 1981. 12.00 (*0-7089-0606-0*) Ulverscroft.

Muller, Mary B. & Neeld, Elizabeth H. Sister Bernadette: Cowboy Nun from Texas. (Illus.). 256p. (Orig.). 1991. pap. 14.95 (*0-937897-98-1*) Centerpoint Pr.

Muller, Mary L. Imagery of Dissent. (Illus.). 1989. pap. 10. 00 (*0-932900-20-8*) Elvejhem Mus.

Muller, Max. Chips from a German Workshop: Volume I: Essays on the Science of Religion. (Reprints & Translations Ser.). 1985. pap. 16.95 (*0-89130-890-3*, 00-07-10) Scholars Pr GA.

— History of Ancient Sanskrit Literature: So Far As It Illustrates the Primitive Religion of the Brahmans. (C). 1993. reprint ed. 27.50 (*81-206-0554-3*, Pub. by Asian Educ Servs II) S Asia.

— Life & Religion: An Aftermath from the Writings of the Right Honourable Professor F. Max Muller. 2nd ed. 237p. (Orig.). 1995. reprint ed. pap. 14.95 (*1-885395-10-8*) Book Tree.

— Philosophisches Woerterbuch. (GER.). Date not set. 39. 95 (*0-7859-8369-4*, 3451041510) Fr & Eur.

Muller, Max, ed. Sacred Book of the East: Vedic Hymns, 2 vols, Set. 1975. 600.00 (*0-8490-3963-0*) Krishna Pr.

— Sacred Books of China: Text of Taoism, 2 vols, Set. 1975. lib. bdg. 600.00 (*0-87968-298-1*) Krishna Pr.

Muller, Max, tr. The Upanishads, 2 vols, Set. 1975. lib. bdg. 600.00 (*0-87968-548-4*) Krishna Pr.

Muller, Max & Halder, Alois. Small Dictionary of Philosophy: Kleines Philosophisches Woerterbuch. 12th ed. 343p. (GER.). 1985. pap. 19.95 (*0-8288-2279-4*, M7506) Fr & Eur.

Muller, Max F. The Vedanta Philosophy. 173p. 1985. 29.95 (*0-318-37034-4*) Asia Bk Corp.

***Muller, Michael.** The Blessed Eucharist: Our Greatest Treasure. LC 93-61595. 297p. 1994. pap. 9.00 (*0-89555-507-7*) TAN Bks Pubs.

— Blessed Eucharist: Our Greatest Treasure. LC 79-112490. 1973. reprint ed. pap. 13.00 (*0-89555-040-7*) TAN Bks Pubs.

— The Holy Sacrifice of the Mass. LC 90-71853. 599p. 1992. reprint ed. pap. 20.00 (*0-89555-437-2*) TAN Bks Pubs.

— Prayer-the Key to Salvation. LC 85-52207. 226p. 1985. reprint ed. pap. 7.00 (*0-89555-287-6*) TAN Bks Pubs.

Muller, Michael, jt. auth. see Bentmann, Reinhard.

Muller, Nancy C. Paintings & Drawings at the Shelburne Museum. (Forge Ahead Ser.: No. 2). (Illus.). (Orig.). 1976. pap. 12.50 (*0-939384-06-X*) Shelburne.

Muller, Nathan, jt. auth. see Davidson, Robert.

Muller, Nathan J. Computerized Document Imaging Systems: Technology & Applications. LC 92-37800. (Telecommunications Ser.). 395p. 1993. text ed. 79.00 (*0-89006-661-2*) Artech Hse.

— Focus on OpenView: A Guide to Hewlett-Packard's Network & Systems Management Platforms. (Illus.). 350p. (C). 1995. pap. text ed. 40.00 (*1-878956-48-5*) CBM Bks.

— Intelligent Hubs. LC 93-6111. 336p. 1993. 75.00 (*0-89006-698-1*) Artech Hse.

— Minimum Risk Strategy for Acquiring Communications Equipment & Services. (Telecommunications Management Library). 457p. 1989. text ed. 49.00 (*0-89006-304-4*) Artech Hse.

— Wireless Data Networking. LC 94-23116. 1994. 69.00 (*0-89006-753-8*) Artech Hse.

Muller, Nathan J. & Davidson, Robert P. LANs to WANs: Network Management in the 1990s. (Artech House Telecom Engineering Library). 520p. 1990. text ed. 79. 00 (*0-89006-410-5*) Artech Hse.

Muller, Nathan J., jt. auth. see Davidson, Robert P.

Muller, Nicole, jt. auth. see Ball, Martin J.

Muller, Norbert. Civilization Dynamics: Fundamentals of a Model-Oriented Description, No. 1. (Illus.). 239p. 1989. text ed. 68.95 (*0-566-05516-3*, Pub. by Avebury Pub UK) Ashgate Pub Co.

— Civilization Dynamics, Vol. II: Nine Simulation Models. 435p. 1991. text ed. 68.95 (*1-85628-234-1*, Pub. by Avebury Pub UK) Ashgate Pub Co.

Muller-Oerlinghausen, B., jt. ed. see Kielholz, P.

Muller-Ortega, Paul, jt. auth. see Singh, Jaideva.

Muller-Ortega, Paul E. The Triadic Heart of Siva: Kaula Tantricism of Abhinavagupta in the Non-Dual Shaivism of Kashmir. LC 87-30953. (SUNY Series in the Chaiva Traditions of Kashmir). 330p. 1988. 44.50 (*0-88706-786-7*); pap. 14.95 (*0-88706-787-5*) State U NY Pr.

Muller, P. Economy & Ecological Equilibrium. 100p. (C). 1975. pap. 23.00 (*0-08-019681-0*, Pergamon Pr) Elsevier.

Muller, P. & Rathjens, C., eds. Landscape Ecology: In Honor of Prof. Dr. J. Schmithusen. (Biogeographica Ser.: No. 16). 1979. lib. bdg. 103.00 (*90-6193-217-3*) Kluwer Ac.

Muller, P., jt. ed. see Werner, D.

Muller, P., et al. Investigation of Irradiation Damage in Glass Specimens by Thermoluminescence, EUR 13613. 216p. 1900. pap. 25.00 (*92-826-3644-5*, CD-NA-13613-EN-C, Pub. by Europ Com) UNIPUB.

Muller, P. C. & Schiehlen, W. O. Linear Vibrations. LC 59-1296. 1985. lib. bdg. 154.00 (*90-247-2983-1*) Kluwer Ac.

Muller, P. F. & Schachermayer, W., eds. Geometry of Banach Spaces: Proceedings of the Conference Held in Linz, 1989. (London Mathematical Society Lecture Note Ser.: No. 158). 250p. (C). 1991. pap. 39.95 (*0-521-40850-4*) Cambridge U Pr.

Muller, P. M. & Lamparsky, D., eds. Perfumes: Art, Science & Technology. 668p. 1991. 190.00 (*1-85166-573-0*) Elsevier.

Muller, Paul, ed. Ecosystem Research in South America. (Biogeographica Ser.: Vol. 8). 1977. lib. bdg. 62.00 (*90-6193-209-2*) Kluwer Ac.

Muller, Paul J., jt. auth. see Mochmann, Ekkehard.

Muller, Peter. The Music Business: A Legal Perspective. LC 93-18523. (Music & Live Performances Ser.). 376p. 1993. Alk. paper. text ed. 59.95 (*0-89930-702-7*, MRQ, Quorum Bks) Greenwood.

— Show Business Law: Motion Pictures, Television, Videos. LC 90-40699. 280p. 1990. text ed. 55.00 (*0-89930-493-1*, MBC, Quorum Bks) Greenwood.

Muller, Peter, jt. auth. see Kraus, Wolfgang.

Muller, Peter O., jt. auth. see De Blij, Harm J.

Muller, Peter O., jt. auth. see Wheeler, James O.

Muller, Phil K. The Army, Politics & Society in Germany, 1933-45: Studies in the Army's Relation to Nazism. LC 87-16333. 130p. 1987. text ed. 35.00 (*0-312-00918-6*) St Martin.

Muller, Pricilla A., ed. Goya's Black Paintings Truth & Reason in Light & Liberty. 1985. 85.00 (*0-87535-135-2*) Hispanic Soc.

Muller, Priscilla E. Jewels in Spain, 1500-1800. (Illus.). 260p. 1972. 30.00 (*0-87535-121-2*) Hispanic Soc.

Muller, R. Bibliography of Onchocerciasis. 292p. (Orig.). 1987. pap. text ed. 69.00 (*0-85198-604-8*) CAB Intl.

— Unsolved Problems Related to Smarandache Function. (Illus.). 66p. (Orig.). 1993. pap. text ed. 9.85 (*1-879585-37-5*) Xiquan Pubng.

Muller, R. & Lloyd, R. Sublethal & Chronic Toxic Effects of Pollutants on Freshwater Fish. 371p. 1994. 125.00 (*0-85238-207-3*) Blackwell Sci.

Muller, R., ed. see Dumitrescu, C. & Smarandache, F.

Muller, R., ed. see Dumitrescu, C.

Muller, R., jt. auth. see Gray, W. A.

Muller, R., ed. see Mitroiescu, Ilie.

Muller, R., ed. see Smarandache, Florentin.

Muller, R., ed. see Soare, Ion.

Muller, R., ed. see Vasiliu, Florin.

Muller, R. A. & Willis, J. E. New Orleans Weather, 1961-1980: A Climatology by Means of Synoptic Weather Types. LC 83-80108. (Miscellaneous Publication Ser.: No. 83-1). 70p. 1983. pap. 8.00 (*0-938909-29-0*) Geosci Pubns LSU.

Muller, R. S., et al, eds. Microsensors. LC 90-4745. 480p. 1991. 59.95 (*0-87942-245-9*, PC02576) Inst Electrical.

Muller, Ralph, jt. ed. see Baker, John R.

Muller-Rappard, Ekkehart, ed. European Inter-State Cooperation in Criminal Matters - La Cooperation Inter-Etatique Europeene en Matiere Penale, the Council of Europe's Legal Instruments - les Instruments: Juridiques du Conseil de l'Europe. 2nd rev. ed. 1824p. (C). 1992. lib. bdg. 875.50 (*0-7923-2096-4*) Kluwer Ac.

Muller-Rappard, Ekkehart & Bassiouni, M. Cherif. European Inter-State Co-operation in Criminal Matters: The Council of Europe's Legal Instruments. LC 86-28640. 1988. ring bd. 146.00 (*90-247-3465-7*) Kluwer Ac.

***Muller, Reiner F.** Dominoes: Basic Rules & Variations. (Illus.). 96p. 1995. pap. 5.95 (*0-8069-3880-3*) Sterling.

Muller, Rene F., jt. auth. see Heise, Edward T.

Muller, Rene J. Alembics: Baltimore Sketches, Etc. LC 92-85558. 80p. 1993. pap. 6.95 (*0-944806-05-8*) Icarus Books.

— Anatomy of a Splitting Borderline: Description & Analysis of a Case History. LC 94-16995. 240p. 1994. text ed. 65.00 (*0-275-94975-3*, Praeger Pubs) Greenwood.

Muller-Reuter, Theodor. Lexikon der Deutschen Konzertliteratur, 2 vols., Set. LC 70-171079. (Music Ser.). (GER.). 1972. reprint ed. lib. bdg. 110.00 (*0-306-70274-6*) Da Capo.

Muller, Richard A. Christ & the Decree: Christology & Predestination in Reformed Theology from Calvin to Perkins. LC 88-6296. 240p. 1988. pap. 12.99 (*0-8010-6231-4*) Baker Bk.

— Christ & the Decree: Christology & Predestination in Reformed Theology from Calvin to Perkins. LC 84-20117. (Studies in Historical Theology: Vol. 2). 244p. (C). 1986. lib. bdg. 30.00 (*0-939464-39-X*) Labyrinth Pr.

— A Dictionary of Latin & Greek Theological Terms. LC 85-70795. 1985. 27.99 (*0-8010-6185-7*) Baker Bk.

— God, Creation, & Providence in the Thought of Jacob Arminius: Sources & Directions of Scholastic Protestantism in the Era of Early Orthodoxy. LC 91-6417. 320p. (Orig.). 1991. pap. text ed. 15.99 (*0-8010-6279-9*) Baker Bk.

— Post Reformation Reformed Dogmatics: Prolegomena to Theology, Vol. I. 292p. 1987. pap. 12.99 (*0-8010-6214-4*) Baker Bk.

— Post-Reformation Reformed Dogmatics: The Cognitive Foundation of Theology, Vol. 2. 672p. (C). 1993. pap. text ed. 24.99 (*0-8010-6299-3*) Baker Bk.

— Study of Theology. 1991. 18.99 (*0-310-41001-0*) Zondervan.

Muller, Richard A., jt. auth. see Bradley, James E.

Muller, Richard A., jt. ed. see Bradley, James E.

Muller, Richard R. The German Air War in Russia. LC 92-53806. 260p. 1992. 24.95 (*1-877853-13-5*) Nautical & Aviation.

Muller, Richard S. & Kamins, Theodore I. Device Electronics for Integrated Circuits. 2nd ed. LC 85-22774. 524p. (C). 1986. Net. text ed. write for info. (*0-471-88758-7*) Wiley.

Muller, Robert. First Lady of the World. 208p. (Orig.). (C). 1991. pap. 7.95 (*1-880455-01-3*) Wrld Happiness.

— Great Book of Math Teasers. LC 90-9882. (Illus.). 96p. 1990. pap. 4.95 (*0-8069-6953-9*) Sterling.

— A Plants of Hope. (Chrysalis Bks.). (Illus.). 128p. 1986. pap. 7.95 (*0-916349-04-7*) Amity Hse Inc.

— A Testament to the Earth. (Chrysalis Bks.). 176p. 1988. pap. 9.95 (*0-317-65997-9*) Amity Hse Inc.

Muller, Robert A. & Faiers, Gregory E., eds. A Climatic Perspective of Louisiana Floods, 1982-1983. (Illus.). 56p. (C). 1984. pap. text ed. 4.00 (*0-938909-62-2*) Geosci Pubns LSU.

Muller, Robert A. & Oberlander, Theodore M. Physical Geography Today. 3rd ed. 608p. (C). 1984. text ed. write for info. (*0-07-554435-0*) McGraw.

Muller, Robert A., jt. auth. see Oberlander, Theodore M.

Muller, Robin. Hickory, Dickory, Dock. LC 92-37588. (Illus.). 32p. (J). (ps-6). 1994. 15.95 (*0-590-47278-X*) Scholastic Inc.

— The Magic Paintbrush. (YA). 1992. mass mkt. 8.50 (*0-385-25373-7*) Doubleday.

— The Magic Paintbrush. LC 89-51265. (Illus.). 32p. (J). 1990. pap. 13.95 (*0-670-83167-0*) Viking Child Bks.

***Muller, Rolf-Dieter & Ueberschar, Gerd R.** Hitler's War in the East, 1941-1945: A Critical Assessment. Little, Bruce, tr. (Library of Contemporary History: Vol. 1). 256p. 1995. 45.00 (*1-57181-068-4*) Berghahn Bks.

***Muller-Rommel, Ferdinand & Poguntke, Thomas, eds.** New Politics. LC 95-7762. (International Library of Politics & Comparative Government). (Illus.). 500p. 1995. text ed. 129.95 (*1-85521-374-5*) Ashgate Pub Co.

Muller-Rommel, Ferdinand & Pridham, Geoffrey, eds. Small Parties in Western Europe: Comparative & National Perspectives. (Illus.). 240p. 1991. 55.00 (*0-8039-8261-5*); pap. 19.95 (*0-8039-8262-3*) Sage.

Muller-Rommel, Ferdinand, jt. ed. see Blondel, Jean.

Muller, Sam & Mijs, Wim, eds. The Flame Rekindled: New Hopes for International Arbitration. LC 93-44432. 232p. (C). 1994. lib. bdg. 89.00 (*0-7923-2659-8*) Kluwer Ac.

Muller-Schwarze, Dietland. The Behavior of Penguins: Adapted to Ice & Tropics. LC 83-18020. (Animal Behavior Ser.). (Illus.). 193p. 1985. 64.50 (*0-87395-866-7*); pap. 22.95 (*0-87395-867-5*) State U NY Pr.

Muller-Schwarze, Dietland, jt. ed. see Doty, Richard L.

Muller-Schwarze, Dietland, jt. ed. see Silverstein, Robert M.

Muller, Sheila D. Charity in the Dutch Republic: Pictures in Rich & Poor for Charitable Institutions. LC 84-8775. (Studies in the Fine Arts - Art Patronage: No. 3). (Illus.). 317p. reprint ed. pap. 90.40 (*0-8357-1518-3*, 2070565) Bks Demand.

Muller, Steven. From Occupation to Cooperation: The United States & United Germany in a Changing World Order. (C). 1992. pap. text ed. 10.95 (*0-393-96254-7*) Norton.

***Muller, Steven, ed.** Universities in the Twenty-First Century. (International Political Currents Ser.: Vol. 2). 192p. 1995. 29.95 (*1-57181-026-9*) Berghahn Bks.

Muller, Steven & Schweigler, Gebhard, eds. From Occupation to Cooperation: The U. S. & United Germany in a Changing World Order. 384p. 1992. 24.95 (*0-393-03359-7*) Norton.

Muller, Theodor. Sculpture in the Netherlands, Germany, France, & Spain: 1400-1500. (Pelican History of Art Ser.). (Illus.). 262p. (C). 1976. reprint ed. text ed. 55.00 (*0-300-05309-6*) Yale U Pr.

Muller, Theresa G. Fundamentals of Psychiatric Nursing. (Quality Paperback Ser.: No. 308). 226p. 1974. reprint ed. pap. 11.00 (*0-8226-0308-X*) Littlefield.

Muller, Thomas. Immigrants & the American City. 1993. pap. 16.95 (*0-8147-5506-2*) NYU Pr.

Muller, Thomas & Espenshade, Thomas J. The Fourth Wave: California's Newest Immigrants. LC 85-22646. (Illus.). 217p. (Orig.). 1994. lib. bdg. 54.00 (*0-87766-349-1*); pap. text ed. 22.50 (*0-87766-375-0*) Urban Inst.

Muller, Thomas E. Immigrants & the American City. LC 92-8934. (C). 1993. 45.00 (*0-8147-5479-1*) NYU Pr.

Muller, Ulrich. Inorganic Structural Chemistry. LC 92-25227. 264p. 1993. text ed. 98.00 (*0-471-93379-1*); pap. text ed. 39.95 (*0-471-93717-7*) Wiley.

Muller, Ulrich, et al, eds. Wagner Handbook. (Illus.). 711p. 1992. text ed. 45.00 (*0-674-94530-1*) HUP.

Muller, Ulrike. New Cat Handbook: Everything about the Care, Nutrition, Diseases, & Breeding of Cats. 1984. pap. 8.95 (*0-8120-2922-4*) Barron.

***Muller, Ulrike, et al.** Healthy Cat, Happy Cat: A Complete Guide to Cat Diseases & Their Treatment. Katze, Kranke, tr. LC 95-9792. (ENG & GER.). 1995. write for info. (*0-8120-9136-1*) Barron.

Muller, V. English-Russian Dictionary. 864p. (C). 1985. 180. 00 (*0-569-09287-6*, Pub. by Collets) St Mut.

Muller, V. A. English-Russian Dictionary. 912p. (C). 1988. 17.95 (*0-8285-0588-8*) Firebird NY.

Muller, V. K. English-Russian Dictionary. 888p. (ENG & RUS.). 1988. 49.95 (*0-8288-4005-9*, M9007) Fr & Eur.

Muller, Virginia L. The Idea of Perfectibility. 230p. (Orig.). (C). 1986. lib. bdg. 49.50 (*0-8191-5026-6*); pap. text ed. 23.00 (*0-8191-5027-4*) U Pr of Amer.

Muller, Vladimir K. English-Russian Dictionary. 6th ed. (ENG & RUS.). 39.50 (*0-685-20186-4*, 066-6X) Saphrograph.

Muller-Vollmer, Kurt & Mueller-Vollmer, Kurt, eds. The Hermeneutics Reader: Texts of the German Tradition from the Enlightenment to the Present. rev. ed. 600p. (C). 1988. pap. text ed. 19.95 (*0-8264-0402-2*) Continuum.

Muller, W. Dictionary of the Graphic Arts Industry. 1020p. (ENG, FRE, GER, HUN, POL, RUS, SLO & SPA.). 1981. 295.00 (*0-8288-9284-9*) Fr & Eur.

— Technical Dictionary of Automotive Engineering: Containing about Ten Thousand Terms. LC 63-23053. 1964. 416.00 (*0-08-010153-4*, Pub. by Pergamon Repr UK) Franklin.

— Technical Dictionary of Printing. 1020p. (C). 1981. 195. 00 (*0-685-37160-3*, Pub. by Collets) St Mut.

Muller, W., ed. Dictionary of the Graphic Arts Industry. 1020p. (ENG, FRE, GER, HUN, POL, RUS, SLO & SPA.). 1981. 156.50 (*0-444-99745-8*) Elsevier.

Muller, W. & Blank, H., eds. Heavy Element Properties: Proceedings of the Joint Session of the Baden Meetings, Sept. 1975. LC 75-44241. (Illus.). 1976. 18.00 (*0-444-11048-8*, North Holland) Elsevier.

Muller, W. & Hackenbruch, W., eds. Surgery & Arthroscopy of the Knee. (Illus.). 800p. 1988. 199.00 (*0-387-17982-8*) Spr-Verlag.

Muller, W. & Lindner, R., eds. Transplutonium Nineteen Seventy-Five: Proceedings. 1976. 48.75 (*0-444-11049-6*, North Holland) Elsevier.

Muller, W. A. & Ebert, H. G. Biological Effects of 224 Ra. 1978. lib. bdg. 84.00 (*90-247-2081-8*) Kluwer Ac.

Muller, W. E., ed. Progress in Molecular & Subcellular Biology, Vol. II. (Illus.). 215p. 1990. 99.00 (*0-387-51832-0*) Spr-Verlag.

Muller, W. E. G., et al, eds. Progress in Molecular & Subcellular Biology: Biological Response Modifiers Interferone, Double-Stranded RNA & 2-5 Adenylate, Vol. 14. (Illus.). 1994. 136.00 (*0-387-57285-6*) Spr-Verlag.

Muller, W. G., et al, eds. Model Oriented Data-Analysis. (Contributions to Statistics Ser.). (Illus.). 287p. 1993. pap. 62.00 (*0-387-91457-9*) Spr-Verlag.

Muller, W. H. Early History of the Supreme Court. xii, 117p. 1982. reprint ed. lib. bdg. 22.50 (*0-8377-0845-1*) Rothman.

Muller, W. Max. Egyptian Mythology & Indochinese Mythology. Bd. with LC 63-19097. LC 63-19097. (Mythology of All Races Ser.: Vol. 12). (Illus.). reprint ed. 40.00 (*0-8154-0160-4*) Cooper Sq.

Muller, Walter E. The Benzodiazepine Receptor: Drug Acceptor Only or a Physiologically Relevant Part of Our Central Nervous System. (Scientific Basis of Psychiatry Ser.: No. 3). (Illus.). 225p. 1987. 64.95 (*0-521-30418-0*) Cambridge U Pr.

Muller, Walter H. Botany: A Functional Approach. 4th ed. (C). 1979. write for info. (0-02-384700-X) Macmillan.

Muller-Warmuth, W. & Schollhorn, R., eds. Progress in Intercalation Research. LC 93-4586. (Physics & Chemistry of Materials with Low-Dimensional Structures Ser.: Vol. 17). 544p. 1993. lib. bdg. 225.50 (0-7923-2357-2) Kluwer Ac.

Muller, Wayne. Legacy of the Heart: The Spiritual Advantages of a Painful Childhood. 224p. 1993. pap. 11.00 (0-671-79784-0, Fireside) S&S Trade.

— Legacy of the Heart: The Spiritual Advantages of a Painful Childhood. 224p. 1992. pap. 20.00 (0-671-76119-6) S&S Trade.

— Programming Using VAX Basic. 320p. 1985. pap. text ed. 18.95 (0-317-38895-9) P-H.

***Muller, Werner, et al.** German 20MM Flak in World War II: 1935-1945. Force, Edward, tr. (Illus.). 48p. (Orig.). 1995. pap. 8.95 (0-88740-758-7) Schiffer.

Muller, Wenzel. Das Sonnenfest Der Braminen: Vienna, 1790. Bauman, Thomas, ed. (German Opera Ser., 1770-1800). 516p. 1986. lib. bdg. 15.00 (0-8240-8865-4) Garland.

Muller, Werner. The Eighty-Eight Millimeter Flak. Force, Edward, tr. LC 91-62751. (Illus.). 48p. 1991. pap. 7.95 (0-88740-360-3) Schiffer.

— German Medium Flak in Combat: Twenty Millimeter - Eighty-Eight Millimeter Flak. Force, Edward, tr. LC 91-62749. (Illus.). 48p. 1991. pap. 7.95 (0-88740-351-4) Schiffer.

— Heavy Flak Guns, 1930-1945. Force, Edward, tr. LC 90-61169. (Illus.). 140p. 1990. 24.95 (0-88740-263-1) Schiffer.

Muller, Werner E. & Rohen, Johannes W., eds. Biochemical & Morphological Aspects of Ageing. (Research in Molecular Biology Ser.: No. 10). (Illus.). 226p. (Orig.). 1981. pap. text ed. 67.50 (3-515-03457-9) Coronet Bks.

Muller-Wieland, Marcel. Sehende Liebe. (Illus.). xiv, 230p. (GER.). 1992. write for info. (3-487-09502-5, Pub. by Georg Olms GW) Lubrecht & Cramer.

***Muller-Wille, Michael.** Death & Burial in Medieval Europe. (Illus.). 71p. (Orig.). 1993. pap. 29.00x (91-22-01575-2, Pub. by Almqv & Wiksell SW) Coronet Bks.

Muller, William A. Fishing for Weakfish & Seatrout. 2nd rev. ed. Barrett, Linda, ed. (Fisherman Library). (Illus.). 136p. 1985. 9.95 (0-923155-04-X) Fisherman Lib.

— Fishing for Winter Flounder. 2nd rev. ed. Barrett, Pete, ed. (Fisherman Library). (Illus.). 120p. (Orig.). 1988. 9.95 (0-923155-08-2) Fisherman Lib.

— Secrets of Surf Fishing at Night. 140p. (Orig.). 1993. pap. 11.95 (0-9625187-6-X) Wavecrest Comns.

— Smallboat Fishing with the Experts. (With the Experts Ser.). (Illus.). 213p. 1988. text ed. 16.95 (0-9625187-2-7) Wavecrest Comns.

— Surf Fishing for Stripers & Blues. (Illus.). 100p. 1991. 10.95 (0-9625187-4-3) Wavecrest Comns.

Muller, William A., ed. & illus. Science Manual: The Process & Communication. 78p. 1991. pap. text ed. 10.95 (0-9625187-3-5) Wavecrest Comns.

Muller, William A., jt. auth. see Reina, Richard.

Muller, William D. International Register of Research on British Politics, 1988. 7th ed. LC 88-27181. 336p. 1988. 99.95 (0-88946-980-6) E Mellen.

Muller, William D., ed. International Register of Research on British Politics. 8th ed. LC 89-640687. 472p. 1992. lib. bdg. 109.95 (0-685-54715-9) E Mellen.

Muller, Wolfgang, ed. Printing: Technical Dictionary Of. 1020p. (C). 1981. 330.00 (0-685-36912-9, Pub. by Collets) St Mut.

Muller, Wolfgang, jt. ed. see Cosentino, Christine.

***Muller, Wolfgang C. & Wright, Vincent, eds.** The State in Western Europe: Retreat or Redefinition? LC 94-22208. 199p. 1994. 27.50 (0-7146-4594-X, Pub. by F Cass Pubs UK) Intl Spec Bk.

Muller, Wolfgang C., jt. ed. see Luther, Kurt R.

Muller, Wolfgang P. Huguccio: The Life, Works, & Thought of a Twelfth-Century Jurist. LC 93-1896. (Studies in Medieval & Early Modern Canon Law: Vol. 3). 1994. 59.95 (0-8132-0787-8) Cath U Pr.

Muller, Wulf, jt. auth. see Wunderli, Peter.

Mullerson, Rein. International Law, Rights & Politics: Developments in Eastern Europe & the CIS. LC 93-46093. (New International Relations Ser.). 1994. 59.95 (0-415-10687-7, Routledge NY); pap. 17.95 (0-415-11134-X, Routledge NY) Routledge.

Mullerus, Carolus, ed. Geographi Graeci Minores, 3 vols., Bd. 1 & 2. ccviii, 1242p. (GER.). 1990. reprint ed. write for info. (0-318-70586-9, Pub. by Georg Olms GW) Lubrecht & Cramer.

— Geographi Graeci Minores, 3 vols., Bd. 3. ccviii, 1242p. (GER.). 1990. reprint ed. write for info. (0-318-70587-7, Pub. by Georg Olms GW) Lubrecht & Cramer.

— Geographi Graeci Minores, 3 vols., Set. ccviii, 1242p. (GER.). 1990. reprint ed. write for info. (3-487-09217-4, Pub. by Georg Olms GW) Lubrecht & Cramer.

Mullery, Virginia. Lake County, Illinois: This Land of Lakes & Rivers: An Illustrated History. 160p. 1989. 25.95 (0-89781-267-0, 5262) Preferred Mktg.

Mullet, J. Five Years Whaling Voyage, Eighteen Forty-Eight to Eighteen Forty-Three. 1977. 12.00 (0-87770-182-2) Ye Galleon.

***Mullet, Kevin.** Designing Visual Interfaces: Communication Oriented Techniques. 304p. 1994. pap. text ed. 46.00 (0-13-303389-9) P-H.

Mullet, Rosa K. Fall & Winter in N. C. Forests. 241p. 1982. pap. 6.45 (0-686-35754-X) Rod & Staff.

— Spring & Summer in N.C. Forests. 238p. 1982. pap. 6.45 (0-686-35755-8) Rod & Staff.

Mullet, Rosa M. God's Marvelous Work, Bk. 1. 1980. teacher ed write for info. (0-686-11150-8) Rod & Staff.

— God's Marvelous Work, Bk. 1. 1980. reprint ed. write for info. (0-686-11149-4) Rod & Staff.

— God's Marvelous Work, Bk. 2. 1981. write for info. (0-686-25256-X); teacher ed write for info. (0-686-25257-8) Rod & Staff.

Mullett, G. M. Spider Woman Stories. LC 78-11556. 142p. 1979. pap. 9.95 (0-8165-0621-3) U of Ariz Pr.

Mullett, Gary M., jt. auth. see Noddings, Charles R.

Mullett, Glen, jt. auth. see Curran, Anne.

Mullett, Michael. Calvin. 80p. 1989. pap. 7.95 (0-415-00057-2, A3843) Routledge.

— James II & English Politics, 1678-1688. LC 93-23857. (Lancaster Pamphlets Ser.). 80p. 1993. pap. 9.95 (0-415-09042-3, B2465) Routledge.

— Popular Culture & Popular Protest in Late Medieval & Early Modern Europe. 256p. 1987. lib. bdg. 49.95 (0-7099-3566-8, Pub. by Croom Helm UK) Routledge Chapman & Hall.

Mulley, Athol, jt. auth. see Sigley, Bill.

Mulley, Graham, ed. Everyday Aids & Appliances. (Illus.). 111p. 1989. pap. text ed. 18.00 (0-7279-0241-5, Pub. by British Med Jrnl UK) Amer Coll Phys.

Mulley, Graham P. Practical Management of Stroke. 174p. 1985. pap. 33.95 (0-87489-613-4) Med Economics.

Mulley, Raymond. Control System Documentation: Applied Instrumentation Symbols & Identification. LC 93-30757. 232p. 1994. 65.00 (1-55617-490-X) Instru Soc.

***Mullholland, Clair.** Story of the 116th Regiment: Pennsylvania Volunteers in the War of Rebellion. Kohl, Lawrence F., ed. (Irish in the Civil War Ser.: 5). (Illus.). 512p. 1995. 27.50 (0-8232-1606-3) Fordham.

Mullica, Karyn, jt. auth. see Ausberger, Carolyn.

***Mullican, Judith.** Under the Sea. (Little Bks.). 8p. (J). (ps-k). 1995. pap. text ed. 10.95 (1-57332-012-9) HighReach Lrning.

***Mullican, Judy.** Apples, Apples. (HRL Little Book Ser.). (Illus.). 8p. (J). (ps-k). 1995. pap. 10.95 (1-57332-020-X) HighReach Lrning.

— Bonnie's Beach Towel. (HighReach Learning Big Bks.). 8p. (J). (ps-k). 1994. pap. text ed. 10.95 (1-57332-008-0) HighReach Lrning.

— The Day the Dinosaur Came to the Library. (HighReach Learning Big Bks.). 8p. (J). (ps-k). 1994. pap. text ed. 10.95 (1-57332-005-6) HighReach Lrning.

— The Jungle Band. (HighReach Learning Big Bks.). 8p. (J). (ps-k). 1994. pap. text ed. 10.95 (1-57332-009-9) HighReach Lrning.

— Let's Go to the Balloon Show! (HighReach Learning Big Bks.). 8p. (J). (ps-k). 1994. pap. text ed. 10.95 (1-57332-004-8) HighReach Lrning.

— Marsha Gets Mad. (Illus.). 8p. (J). (ps-k). 1995. pap. text ed. 10.95 (1-57332-013-7) HighReach Lrning.

— My Forest Friends. (HighReach Learning Big Bks.). 8p. (J). (ps-k). 1994. pap. text ed. 10.95 (1-57332-003-X) HighReach Lrning.

— Our Very Own Rocket. (HighReach Learning Big Bks.). 8p. (J). (ps-k). 1994. pap. text ed. 10.95 (1-57332-010-2) HighReach Lrning.

— Riding the Range. (Little Bks.). 8p. (J). (ps-k). 1995. pap. text ed. 10.95 (1-57332-014-5) HighReach Lrning.

— What Will We Play Today? (Big Book Ser.). (Illus.). 8p. (J). (ps-k). 1995. pap. text ed. 10.95 (1-57332-019-6) HighReach Lrning.

— Who Am I? (Little Book Ser.). (Illus.). 8p. (J). (ps-k). 1995. pap. text ed. 10.95 (1-57332-017-X) HighReach Lrning.

— Who Am I? (Little Book Ser.). (Illus.). 8p. (J). (ps-k). 1995. pap. text ed. 10.95 (1-57332-018-8) HighReach Lrning.

— Who Can? (HighReach Learning Big Bks.). 8p. (J). (ps-k). 1994. pap. text ed. 10.95 (1-57332-001-3) HighReach Lrning.

Mullican, Matt. Matt Mullican. 1994. 75.00 (3-88375-189-8, Pub. by Walther Konig GW) Dist Art Pubs.

— Matt Mullican World Frame. (Illus.). 222p. (Orig.). 1992. pap. text ed. 35.00 (1-879293-04-8) Contemp Art Mus.

Mullican, W. F. & Senger, R. K. Hydrogeologic Investigations of Deep Ground-Water Flow in the Chihuahuan Desert, Texas. (Illus.). 60p. 1992. pap. 5.00 (0-317-05172-5, RI 205) Bur Econ Geology.

Mullick, M. & Bhattacharyya, B. Technology of Machining Systems. (C). 1989. 50.00 (0-89771-381-8, Current Dist) St Mut.

Mullick, Promatha N. History of the Vaisyas of Bengal. 169p. 1986. reprint ed. 22.00 (0-8364-1633-3, Pub. by Usha II) S Asia.

Mullie, Sozef L. The Structural Principles of the Chinese Language, 3 vols. 1976. lib. bdg. 300.00 (0-8490-2698-9) Gordon Pr.

Mulligan, Allan. The Complete Guide to Developing & Marketing Your Own Seminar. 164p. 1984. pap. 14.95 (0-912551-00-3) Independence House.

Mulligan, Brian O., ed. see Grant, John & Grant, Carol.

Mulligan, E. Jeanne. Pencil Playground: A Creative Writing Curriculum. (Illus.). 1991. student ed 29.95 (0-9608502-0-1) Estella Graphics.

Mulligan, Eileen J. Physiology: PSAAR. 7th ed. (Basic Sciences PreTest Ser.). (Illus.). 224p. 1993. pap. text ed. 16.95 (0-07-051997-8) Hlth Prof Div.

Mulligan-Ennis, Carla, jt. auth. see Gates, Ronda.

Mulligan, Frank. A Lector's Guide to the Episcopal Eucharistic Lectionary. (Orig.). 1987. pap. 12.25 (0-9618112-0-X) St Marks Pr.

— Reading at Mass. 140p. 1989. text ed. 7.95 (0-8146-1907-X) Liturgical Pr.

Mulligan, Gerald & Agriculture Canada Staff. Common Weeds of Canada. (Illus.). 140p. (Orig.). 1987. pap. 16.95 (0-920053-59-9, Pub. by NC Press CN) U of Toronto Pr.

Mulligan, J. P. Agricultural Planning Handbook. (Illus.). 400p. 1986. text ed. write for info. (0-408-10797-9) Buttrwrth-Heinemann.

Mulligan, James. The Riddle of Justice: A Monograph Together with Suggestions for Much-Needed New Laws. xvi, 155p. 1983. reprint ed. lib. bdg. 20.00 (0-8377-0849-4) Rothman.

Mulligan, James A. The Hanoi Commitment. LC 81-90096. (Illus.). 298p. 1981. 15.00 (0-9606000-0-0) RIF Mktg.

— The Hanoi Commitment. 5th ed. (Illus.). 298p. 1981. lib. bdg. 20.00 (0-685-45814-8) RIF Mktg.

Mulligan, James G. Managerial Economics: Strategy for Profit. 592p. 1989. teacher ed write for info. (0-318-63858-4, H1973-0) Allyn.

Mulligan, James J. Choose Life. 383p. 1991. pap. text ed. 17.95 (0-935372-31-8) Pope John Ctr.

— Theologians & Authority Within the Living Church. 139p. (Orig.). 1987. pap. 13.95 (0-935372-18-0) Pope John Ctr.

Mulligan, Jean, tr. The Lute: Kao Ming's P'i-P'a chi. LC 79-26082. (Translations from the Asian Classics Ser.). 1980. text ed. 53.50 (0-231-04760-6); pap. text ed. 18.50 (0-231-04761-4) Col U Pr.

Mulligan, John & Griffin, Colin, eds. Empowerment Through Experiential Learning: Explorations of Good Practice. 200p. 1992. 69.00 (0-7494-0680-1, Pub. by Kogan Page Educ UK) Taylor & Francis.

***Mulligan, Joseph E.** The Jesuit Martyrs of El Salvador: Celebrating the Anniversaries. (Illus.). 200p. (Orig.). (C). 1994. pap. 17.95 (1-879175-15-0) Fortkamp.

— The Nicaraguan Church & the Revolution. LC 90-63486. 320p. (Orig.). (C). 1991. pap. 17.95 (1-55612-411-2, LL1411) Sheed & Ward MO.

Mulligan, Joseph F. Introductory College Physics. 2nd ed. 1991. text ed. write for info. (0-07-044057-3) McGraw.

Mulligan, Joseph F., ed. see Hertz, Heinrich R.

Mulligan, Kevin, ed. Language, Truth & Ontology. (Philosophical Studies in Philosophy Ser.). 224p. (C). 1992. lib. bdg. 97.00 (0-7923-1509-X) Kluwer Ac.

— Mind, Meaning & Metaphysics: The Philosophy & Theory of Language of Anton Marty. (C). 1990. lib. bdg. 126.50 (0-7923-0578-7) Kluwer Ac.

Mulligan, Mark. Ghost of Black's Island: The Screenplay. (Illus.). 121p. (Orig.). (YA). (gr. 6-8). 1993. pap. 9.95 (1-882444-01-9) Blvd Bks FL.

— Manatee: The Screenplay. (Illus.). 121p. (Orig.). (YA). (gr. 9-12). 1993. pap. 9.95 (1-882444-00-0) Blvd Bks FL.

***Mulligan, Mary E.** Wine for Dummies. 1995. pap. 16.99 (1-56884-390-9) IDG Bks.

Mulligan, Patrick J. Dented Rose. 75p. 1993. pap. 5.95 (0-9636104-0-6) P J Mulligan.

Mulligan, R. W., tr. see Aquinas, Thomas.

Mulligan, Robert W., tr. see Aquinas, Thomas.

Mulligan, Robert W., tr. see St. Thomas Aquinas.

***Mulligan, Steve, photos.** Living Landscapes of Kansas. (Illus.). 144p. (C). 1995. 29.95x (0-7006-0727-7) U Pr of KS.

***Mulligan, Therese, et al.** For My Best Beloved Sister Mia: An Album of Photographs by Julia Margaret Cameron. 68p. 1995. pap. 24.00 (0-8263-1610-7); pap. 24.00 (0-944282-17-2) U of NM Pr.

Mulligan, Tim. Hudson River Valley: A Historical Guide. 1985. pap. 8.95 (0-394-73099-2) Random.

— The Hudson River Valley: A History & Guide: 1992-93 Edition. LC 91-52659. (Illus.). 240p. 1991. pap. 12.00 (0-679-73737-5) Random.

— The Traveler's Guide to the Hudson River Valley. 3rd ed. 1995. 14.00 (0-679-76175-6) Random.

— Traveler's Guide to Western New England & the Connecticut River: Vermont, New Hampshire, Western Massachusetts & Connecticut. 1994. pap. 13.00 (0-679-74413-4) Random.

— Virginia. 1986. pap. 12.95 (0-394-74648-1) Random.

— Virginia: A History & Guide. 1986. pap. write for info. (0-394-73321-5) Random.

Mulligan, Timothy P. Lone Wolf: The Life & Death of U-Boat Ace Werner Henke. LC 93-20128. 288p. 1993. text ed. 22.95 (0-275-93677-5, C3677, Praeger Pubs) Greenwood.

— Lone Wolf: The Life & Death of U-boat Ace Werner Henke. LC 95-15838. 1995. pap. write for info. (0-8061-2780-5) U of Okla Pr.

— The Politics of Illusion & Empire: German Occupation Policy in the Soviet Union, Nineteen Forty-Two to Nineteen Forty Three. LC 87-32702. 220p. 1988. text ed. 55.00 (0-275-92837-3, C2837, Praeger Pubs) Greenwood.

Mulligan, William C. The Adventurous Gardener's Sourcebook of Rare & Unusual Plants. LC 92-12060. (Illus.). 1993. 40.00 (0-671-75104-2) S&S Trade.

— Complete Guide to North American Gardens: The Northeast. 1991. pap. 15.95 (0-316-58907-1) Little.

— Complete Guide to North American Gardens: The Northeast, Vol. 1. 1991. pap. 15.95 (0-316-59807-0) Little.

— Complete Guide to North American Gardens: The West Coast. 1991. pap. 15.95 (0-316-58909-8) Little.

— The Lattice Gardener. LC 95-8158. (Illus.). 1995. write for info. (0-02-587885-9) Macmillan.

Mulligan, William G. Expert Witnesses: Direct & Cross Examination. (Trial Practice Library). 750p. 1987. text ed. 138.00 (0-471-63387-9) Wiley.

— Expert Witnesses: Direct & Cross Examination. suppl. ed. (Trial Practice Library). 256p. 1987. pap. 65.00 (0-471-58855-5) Wiley.

Mulligan, William H., Jr., ed. A Historical Dictionary of American Industrial Language. LC 87-37544. 320p. 1988. text ed. 79.50 (0-313-24171-6, MAI/, Greenwood Pr) Greenwood.

Mulliken, Frances H. The Widowed. 1983. pap. 6.50 (0-8309-0361-5) Herald Hse.

Mulliken, R. S. Life of a Scientist. (Illus.). 180p. 1989. 79.00 (0-387-50375-7) Spr-Verlag.

Mulliken, Robert S. Selected Papers of Robert S. Mulliken. Hinze, J. & Ramsay, D. A., eds. LC 74-11633. xvi, 1128p. 1975. lib. bdg. 55.00 (0-226-54847-3) U Ch Pr.

Mulliken, Robert S. & Person, Willis B. Molecular Complexes: A Lecture & Reprint Volume. LC 71-84970. 516p. reprint ed. pap. 147.10 (0-317-09073-9, 2007666) Bks Demand.

***Mullin, Ann & Clough, Jan.** Drawing. 175p. (C). 1995. per., pap. text ed. 32.95 (0-7872-1049-8) Kendall-Hunt.

Mullin, B., jt. ed. see Lovold, S.

Mullin, Bernard J., et al. Sport Marketing. LC 92-36331. (Illus.). 312p. 1993. text ed. 42.00x (0-87322-449-3, BMUL0449) Human Kinetics.

Mullin, Chris. Error of Judgement: The Truth about the Birmingham Bombings. 1990. pap. 11.95 (1-85371-090-3, Pub. by Poolbeg Pr IE) Dufour.

Mullin, Christopher A. & Scott, Jeffrey G., eds. Molecular Mechanisms of Insecticide Resistance: Diversity among Insects. LC 92-28366. (Symposium Ser.: No. 505). (Illus.). 321p. 1992. 74.95 (0-8412-2474-9) Am Chemical.

Mullin, Donald, comp. Victorian Actors & Actresses in Review: A Dictionary of Contemporary Views of Representative British & American Actors & Actresses, 1837-1901. LC 83-1407. (Illus.). xxxvi, 571p. 1983. text ed. 65.00 (0-313-23316-0, MVA/) Greenwood.

— Victorian Plays: A Record of Significant Productions on the London Stage, 1837-1901. LC 86-25718. (Bibliographies & Indexes in the Performing Arts Ser.: No. 4). 460p. 1987. text ed. 69.50 (0-313-24211-9, MVP/) Greenwood.

Mullin, Gerald W. Flight & Rebellion: Slave Resistance in 18th Century Virginia. LC 73-173327. 1974. reprint ed. pap. 8.95 (0-19-501788-9) OUP.

Mullin, Glenn, tr. see Dalai Lama.

Mullin, Glenn H. Death & Dying: The Tibetan Tradition. 272p. 1988. pap. 11.95 (0-14-019013-9, Arkana) Viking Penguin.

— Mystical Verses of a Mad Dalai Lama. 250p. (Orig.). 1994. pap. 14.00 (0-8356-0700-3, Quest) Theos Pub Hse.

— Path of the Bodhisattva Warrior. LC 88-18300. 387p. 1988. pap. 14.95 (0-937938-55-6) Snow Lion Pubns.

— The Practice of Kalachakra. 348p. (Orig.). 1991. pap. 16.95 (0-937938-95-5) Snow Lion Pubns.

— Training the Mind in the Great Way. 1993. pap. 12.95 (0-937938-96-3) Snow Lion Pubns.

Mullin, Glenn H., et al. Selected Works of the Dalai Lama Three: Essence of Refined Gold. rev. ed. LC 85-8359. (Teachings of the Dalai Lamas Ser.). Orig. Title: Essence of Refined Gold. 264p. (TIB.). (C). 1985. pap. 12.95 (0-937938-29-7) Snow Lion Pubns.

— Selected Works of the Dalai Lama Two: The Tantric Yogas of the Sister Niguma. LC 85-40081. (Teachings of the Dalai Lamas Ser.). (Illus.). 240p. (Orig.). (TIB.). (C). 1985. pap. 12.95 (0-937938-28-9) Snow Lion Pubns.

Mullin, J. B. & Stradling, R. A., eds. Narrow Gap Semiconductors, 1992: Proceedings of the 6th International Conference, University of Southampton, U. K., 19-23 July, 1992. (Illus.). 455p. 1993. 183.00 (0-7503-0249-6) IOP Pub.

Mullin, J. B., jt. auth. see Heinrich, H.

Mullin, J. B., jt. ed. see Miller, L. S.

Mullin, J. W. Crystallization. 3rd ed. (Illus.). 528p. 1993. 125.00 (0-7506-1129-4) Buttrwrth-Heinemann.

Mullin, James, ed. see Shotwell, James M.

Mullin, James J., jt. auth. see Smith, Henry C.

Mullin, Jim T., jt. auth. see Bushnell, Ian W.

Mullin, Joan A. & Wallace, Ray, eds. Intersections: Theory-Practice in the Writing Center. 196p. (C). 1994. pap. 19.95 (0-8141-2331-7) NCTE.

Mullin, John. Reports to the Hon. George Stoneman, Governor of California, on Certain Claims of the State of California Against the United States, November 1, 1878, to November 1, 1886. Bruchey, Stuart, ed. LC 78-56670. (Management of Public Lands in the U. S. Ser.). (Illus.). 1979. reprint ed. lib. bdg. 44.95 (0-405-11345-5) Ayer.

— Stay with Us. (Spirit Life Ser.). 48p. (Orig.). Date not set. pap. 3.95 (1-878718-28-2) Resurrection.

Mullin, Karen, jt. ed. see Barteck, Lynn.

***Mullin, Kathy.** ABC's of Home Schooling. (Illus.). 180p. (Orig.). 1994. pap. 14.95 (1-57327-001-6, M Pr CA) Busn Concepts.

Mullin, Lenore M., ed. Arrays, Functional Languages & Parallel Systems. 336p. (C). 1991. lib. bdg. 91.00 (0-7923-9213-2) Kluwer Ac.

Mullin, M., jt. auth. see ICSID Staff.

Mullin, Mark. Educating for the Twenty-First Century: The Challenge for Parents & Teachers. LC 91-635. 1993. 17.95 (0-685-71892-1); pap. 14.95 (1-56833-012-X) Madison Bks UPA.

Mullin, Mark. Object Oriented Program Design. 1989. pap. 24.95 (0-201-51722-1) Addison-Wesley.

— Rapid Prototyping for Object. 1990. pap. 22.95 (0-201-55024-5) Addison-Wesley.

Mullin, Mark H. Headmaster Looks Toward the Year 2000. 1991. 17.95 (0-8191-8062-9) Madison Bks UPA.

***Mullin, Michael.** Africa in America: Slave Acculturation & Resistance in the American South & the British. 1994. pap. 15.95 (0-252-06446-1) U of Ill Pr.

— Africa in America: Slave Acculturation & Resistance in the American South & the British Caribbean, 1736-1831. (Blacks in the New World Ser.). 432p. (C). 1992. 37.50 (0-252-01889-3) U of Ill Pr.

— Design by Motley. LC 94-42667. 1995. write for info. (0-87413-569-9) U Delaware Pr.

An Asterisk (*) at the beginning of an entry indicates that the title is appearing in BIP for the first time.

— Theatre at Stratford-Upon-Avon: First Supplement, A Catalogue-Index to Productions of the Royal Shakespeare Company, 1979-1993. LC 94-22456. (Bibliographies & Indexes in the Performing Arts Ser.: Vol. 17). 352p. 1994. text ed. 95.00 (*0-313-25028-6*, Greenwood Pr) Greenwood.

Mullin, Michael, comp. Theatre at Stratford-Upon-Avon: A Catalogue-Index to Productions of the Shakespeare Memorial-Royal Shakespeare Theatre, 1879 to 1978, 2 vols., 1. LC 79-8578. 1980. text ed. 85.00 (*0-313-22169-3*, MSH/1) Greenwood.

— Theatre at Stratford-Upon-Avon: A Catalogue-Index to Productions of the Shakespeare Memorial-Royal Shakespeare Theatre, 1879 to 1978, 2 vols., Set. LC 79-8578. 1980. text ed. 150.00 (*0-313-22126-X*, MSH/) Greenwood.

— Theatre at Stratford-Upon-Avon: A Catalogue-Index to Productions of the Shakespeare Memorial-Royal Shakespeare Theatre, 1879 to 1978, 2 vols., Vol. 2. LC 79-8578. 1980. text ed. 85.00 (*0-313-22170-7*, MSH/2) Greenwood.

Mullin, Michael M. Webs & Scales: Physical & Ecological Processes in Marine Fish Recruitment. LC 93-10188. (Washington Sea Grant Ser.). 144p. 1993. 25.00 (*0-295-97244-0*); pap. 15.00 (*0-295-97245-9*) U of Wash Pr.

Mullin, Molly A. Merriweather's Reign. LC 94-2416. 1995. 6.00 (*0-88734-239-6*) Players Pr.

Mullin, Molly A., jt. auth. see Blu, Susan.

Mullin, Penn. Ghosts of Black Point. Kratoville, Betty L., ed. (Meridian Bks.). (Illus.). 64p. (J). (gr. 3-9). 1989. lib. bdg. 4.95 (*0-87879-653-3*) High Noon Bks.

— High-Five Series: Whale Summer, Spirits of the Canyon & Trail to Danger, 3 bks. (Orig.). (J). (gr. 6-11). 1991. student ed 9.00 (*0-87879-924-9*) High Noon Bks.

— High-Five Series: Whale Summer, Spirits of the Canyon & Trail to Danger, 3 bks., Set. (Orig.). (J). (gr. 6-11). 1991. pap. text ed. 11.00 (*0-87879-913-3*) High Noon Bks.

— Message from Outer Space. Kratoville, Betty L., ed. (Meridian Bks.). (Illus.). 64p. (J). (gr. 3-9). 1989. lib. bdg. 4.95 (*0-87879-616-9*) High Noon Bks.

— Postcards from America Series: The White House Mystery, High Time in New York, Windy City Whirl, Trouble in the Black Hills, San Francisco Adventure. Kratoville, B. L., ed. (Illus.). (Orig.). (J). (gr. 4-12). 1992. pap. 17.00 (*0-87879-957-5*, 957-5) High Noon Bks.

— Postcards from Europe Series, 5 bks. Kratoville, B. L., ed. (Illus.). 48p. (J). (gr. 6-10). 1994. pap. text ed. 17.00 (*0-87879-976-1*) High Noon Bks.

Mullin, Ray C. Electrical Wiring: Residential Plans. 11th ed. (Illus.). 1993. 12.95 (*0-8273-5774-5*) Delmar.

— Electrical Wiring - Residential. 11th ed. 1993. teacher ed 12.00 (*0-8273-5096-1*); text ed. 34.95 (*0-8273-5795-8*); trans. 89.95 (*0-8273-5652-8*) Delmar.

— Electrical Wiring-Residential. 10th ed. 304p. 1989. teacher ed 10.00 (*0-8273-3491-5*); pap. text ed. 30.95 (*0-8273-3490-7*) Delmar.

— Electrical Wiring, Residential. 11th ed. 1992. pap. text ed. 29.95 (*0-8273-5095-3*) Delmar.

— Electrical Wiring, Residential. 12th ed. 1995. write for info. (*0-8273-6841-0*) Delmar.

***Mullin, Ray C. & Smith, Robert L.** Electrical Wiring: Commercial. LC 95-13501. 1996. write for info. (*0-8273-6655-8*) Delmar.

— Electrical Wiring: Commercial. 7th ed. 256p. 1991. teacher ed 14.00 (*0-8273-4093-1*); pap. text ed. 28.95 (*0-8273-4092-3*) Delmar.

— Electrical Wiring: Commercial. 8th ed. LC 92-12939. 1992. pap. text ed. 28.95 (*0-8273-5093-7*) Delmar.

— Electrical Wiring - Commercial. 8th ed. 1993. teacher ed 10.00 (*0-8273-5094-5*) Delmar.

Mullin, Ray C., jt. auth. see Sanders, Melvin K.

Mullin, Ray C., jt. auth. see Stauffer, H. Brooke.

Mullin-Rindler, Nancy & Twombly, Susan. Child Care Resource & Referral Counselors & Trainers Manual. LC 89-5233. 112p. (Orig.). 1989. pap. 14.95 (*0-934140-54-5*) Redleaf Pr.

Mullin, Rita, ed. see Sinclair, Upton.

Mullin, Robert, jt. auth. see Sosinsky, Barry.

Mullin, Robert B. Episcopal Vision-American Reality: High Church Theology & Social Thought in Evangelical America. 1986. 32.00 (*0-300-03487-3*) Yale U Pr.

— Moneygripe's Apprentice: The Personal Narrative of Samuel Seabury III. LC 88-26182. 259p. (C). 1989. text ed. 30.00 (*0-300-04379-1*) Yale U Pr.

Mullin, Robert B. & Richey, Russell E., eds. Reimagining Denominationalism: Interpretive Essays. LC 93-31858. (Religion in America Ser.). 320p. 1994. 35.00 (*0-19-508778-X*) OUP.

Mullin, Robert B., jt. auth. see Ahlstrom, Sydney E.

Mullin, Robert N. Stagecoach Pioneers of the Southwest. (Southwestern Studies: No. 71). 64p. 1983. pap. 10.00 (*0-87404-131-7*) Tex Western.

Mullin, Ronald C., jt. auth. see Blake, Ian F.

Mullin, Ronald C., jt. auth. see Gao, XuHong.

Mullin, Sue. Nuevo Cubano Cooking. 1993. 12.98 (*1-55521-906-3*) Bk Sales Inc.

Mullin, Timothy J. The One Hundred Greatest Combat Pistols: Hands-on Tests & Evaluations of Handguns from Around the World. (Illus.). 424p. 1994. pap. 40.00 (*0-87364-781-5*) Paladin Pr.

Mullin, Tom, ed. The Nature of Chaos. LC 92-41598. 1993. pap. 24.95 (*0-19-853954-1*, Clarendon Pr) OUP.

Mullin, Virginia L. Chemistry Experiments for Children. LC 68-9306. (Illus.). (J). (gr. 3-10). 1968. reprint ed. pap. 3.50 (*0-486-22031-1*) Dover.

Mullineaux, Philip M., jt. ed. see Foyer, Christine H.

***Mulliner Box & Planing Co. Staff.** Turn-of-the-Century Doors, Windows & Decorative Millwork: The Mulliner Catalog of 1893. LC 94-23833. Orig. Title: Combined Book of Sash, Doors, Blinds, Mouldings, Stair Work, Mantels & All Kinds of Interior & Exterior Finish. (Illus.). 336p. 1995. pap. text ed. 12.95 (*0-486-28514-6*) Dover.

Mulliner, John D. The Seed Carriers. 176p. 1993. 15.95 (*0-8059-3370-0*) Dorrance.

Mulliner, K. & The-Mulliner, Lian. Historical Dictionary of Singapore. LC 91-35697. (Asian Historical Dictionaries Ser.: No. 7). (Illus.). 285p. 1991. 32.50 (*0-8108-2504-X*) Scarecrow.

Mulliner, Kent, jt. ed. see Lent, John A.

***Mullineux.** Financial Reform in Central & Eastern Europe. 314p. 1995. lib. bdg. 77.00 (*1-56072-231-2*) Nova Sci Pubs.

— Financial Reform in Central & Eastern Europe: Lessons from the 'West', Poland & Further East. 264p. 1995. lib. bdg. 73.00 (*1-56072-233-9*) Nova Sci Pubs.

Mullineux, A. W. The Business Cycle after Keynes: A Contemporary Analysis. LC 83-27160. 132p. 1984. 45.00 (*0-389-20453-6*, 08014) B&N Imports.

— Business Cycles & Financial Crisis. 200p. 1990. reprint ed. text ed. 42.50 (*0-472-10181-1*) U of Mich Pr.

Mullineux, Andy. U. K. Banking after Deregulation. 192p. 1987. lib. bdg. 55.00 (*0-7099-4689-9*, Pub. by Croom Helm UK) Routledge Chapman & Hall.

Mullineux, Andy, et al. Business Cycles: Theory & Evidence. LC 92-26627. 208p. 1993. 44.95 (*0-631-18566-6*); pap. 19.95 (*0-631-18567-4*) Blackwell Pubs.

Mullinex, Phyllis. Testing Programs for Behavior Toxicology Test Guides: Methodology & Interpretation of Data. 1989. 58.00 (*0-911131-21-3*) Princeton Sci Pubs.

Mullings, Pal M. Euphemistic: A Jamaican Way of Life. 1992. 18.95 (*0-533-09693-6*) Vantage.

Mullins, A. F., Jr. Born Arming: Development & Military Power in New States. LC 86-23043. (ISIS Studies in International Security & Arms Control: Vol. 2). 168p. 1987. 32.50 (*0-8047-1375-8*) Stanford U Pr.

Mullins, A. L., jt. auth. see Drake, W. Homer, Jr.

Mullins, Alma J. Contests & Legends Eighteen Ninety-Five. LC 92-91195. 72p. (Orig.). 1994. pap. 9.00 (*1-56002-287-6*, Univ Edtns) Aegina Pr.

***Mullins, Andrea.** Women on Mission Guide. Hansen, Susan, ed. 44p. (Orig.). 1995. pap. text ed. 3.95 (*1-56309-109-7*) Womans Mission Union.

***Mullins, Anne & Saunders, Cheryl.** Economic Union in Federal Systems. 283p. 1994. 64.00 (*1-86287-123-X*, Pub. by Federation Pr AU) W W Gaunt.

Mullins, B. Edward. Alice Waynewright & More. 65p. (Orig.). 1989. pap. 4.95 (*0-929880-00-5*) Gall Pr Intl.

Mullins, B. P., ed. see Shtern, V. Y.

Mullins, C. Daniel, jt. auth. see Hartzema, Abraham G.

Mullins, Carolyn J. A Guide to Writing & Publishing in the Social & Behavioral Sciences. LC 83-12014. 448p. (C). 1983. reprint ed. text ed. 38.50 (*0-89874-643-4*) Krieger.

Mullins, Cecil J. Seining the Air for Sparrows. LC 88-31434. (Illus.). viii, 44p. (Orig.). 1988. pap. 5.95 (*0-936015-15-2*) Pocahontas Pr.

Mullins, Charles E. & Mayer, David C. Congenital Heart Disease: A Diagrammatic Atlas. (Illus.). 1991. pap. text ed. 99.95 (*0-471-58817-2*, Wiley-Liss) Wiley.

Mullins, Craig S. DB2 Developer's Guide. 2nd ed. 1200p. 1994. 49.99 (*0-672-30512-7*) Sams.

— DB2 Developer's Guide. (Illus.). 400p. (Orig.). 1992. pap. 59.95 (*0-672-30191-1*) Sams.

***Mullins, Denvil.** The Cornfields of Coaley Creek: Tales from Southwest Virginia. 224p. (Orig.). 1994. pap. 9.95 (*1-57072-011-8*) Overmountain Pr.

— Times of Used to Be. 188p. 1993. pap. 9.95 (*1-57072-001-0*) Overmountain Pr.

Mullins, E. J. & McKnight, T. S., eds. Canadian Woods: Their Properties & Uses. 3rd ed. 400p. 1981. 40.00 (*0-8020-2430-0*) U of Toronto Pr.

Mullins, E. L. Texts & Calendars II: An Analytical Guide to Serial Publications, 1957-1982. (Royal Historical Society Guides & Handbooks Ser.: No.12). 324p. 1983. 30.00 (*0-86193-100-9*) Boydell & Brewer.

Mullins, E. Y. Manual de Evidencias Cristianas: Christian Evidence Manual. (SPA.). 8.95 (*84-7645-181-4*, 223226, Pub. by Edit Clie SP) TSELF.

Mullins, Edgar Y. Baptist Beliefs. 1987. pap. 8.50 (*0-8170-1014-9*) Judson.

— La Religion Cristiana En Su Expresion Doctrinal. Hale, Sara A., tr. Orig. Title: The Christian Religion in Its Doctrinal Expression. 522p. 1983. reprint ed. pap. 8.50 (*0-311-09042-7*) Casa Bautista.

Mullins, Edmund. Cornish Primitive: Alfred Wallis. (Illus.). 64p. 1994. 24.95 (*1-85793-274-9*, Pub. by Pavilion UK) Trafalgar.

Mullins, Edwin, comment. Tapestry: Henry Moore & West Dean. (Illus.). 49p. (Orig.). 1980. pap. 5.00 (*0-88397-032-5*) Art Srvc Intl.

Mullins, Elaine. Electronic Office Equipment Users Handbook: An Operating Guide for Students. 192p. (Orig.). 1987. pap. 30.00 (*0-273-02354-3*, Pub. by Pitman Pub Ltd UK) Trans-Atl Phila.

Mullins, Eustace C. This Difficult Individual: Ezra Pound. LC 78-64049. (Des Imagistes: Literature of the Imagist Movement Ser.). reprint ed. 31.00 (*0-404-17081-1*) AMS Pr.

Mullins, Gene. Dog Bark. Ingram, tr. 212p. 1994. pap. 7.95 (*1-56901-340-3*) NW Pub.

Mullins, Henry. Utopia. abr. ed. 420p. 1994. pap. 12.95 (*0-685-72781-5*) NW Pub.

Mullins, Henry T. Carbonate Depositional Environments-Modern & Ancient: Pt. 4: Periplatform Carbonates. Warme, John E. & Shanley, Keith W., eds. LC 85-22384. (Colorado School of Mines Quarterly Ser.: Vol. 81, No. 2, 1986). (Illus.). 63p. 1986. pap. text ed. 20.00 (*0-918062-69-1*) Colo Sch Mines.

Mullins, Hilary. The Cat Came Back. 224p. 1993. pap. 9.95 (*1-56280-040-X*) Naiad Pr.

Mullins, Hugh A. Marine Insurance Digest. LC 59-15426. 308p. reprint ed. 87.80 (*0-8357-9073-8*, 2019105) Bks Demand.

Mullins, I. J. Management & Organisational Behaviour. 546p. (C). 1989. 195.00 (*0-685-39849-8*, Inst Pur & Supply) St Mut.

***Mullins, John D.** An Escort of P-38s: The 1st Fighter Group in World War II. Lambert, John W., ed. LC 94-65588. (Illus.). (C). Date not set. 32.95 (*1-883809-03-7*) Phalanx Pub.

Mullins, Johnny. City of Love. 213p. 1984. 7.45 (*0-89697-134-1*) Intl Univ Pr.

Mullins, Joleen W. Let's Cook, America: Traditional American Cooking. LC 91-91371. 265p. (Orig.). 1992. pap. text ed. 14.95 (*0-9631418-0-5*) W Mullins Pubs.

Mullins, Joseph. Hawaii U. S. A. A Different State Racial Mixtures & Cultures. LC 87-125358. (Hawaiiana Ser.). (Illus.). 38p. 1986. pap. 3.95 (*0-941351-08-4*) Aloha.

— Hawaii's Greatest Moments. LC 87-123092. (Hawaiiana Ser.). (Illus.). 38p. (Orig.). 1977. pap. 4.95 (*0-941351-02-5*) Aloha.

— Hawaii's Volcanoes, Legends & Fact. LC 87-123116. (Hawaiiana Ser.). Orig. Title: The Goddess Pele. (Illus.). 35p. (Orig.). 1985. pap. 4.95 (*0-941351-09-2*) Aloha.

Mullins, Joseph G. Hawaiian Journey. (Illus.). 128p. 1984. pap. 11.95 (*0-935180-04-4*) Mutual Pub HI.

Mullins, L. J. Ion Transport in Heart. 144p. 1981. 45.00 (*0-89004-645-X*) Raven.

— Management & Organizational Behaviour. 546p. (C). 1989. 175.00 (*0-685-36137-3*, Inst Pur & Supply) St Mut.

Mullins, L. J., et al, eds. Annual Review of Biophysics & Bioengineering, Vol. 2. LC 79-188446. (Illus.). 1973. 55.00 (*0-8243-1802-1*) Annual Reviews.

— Annual Review of Biophysics & Bioengineering, Vol. 3. LC 79-188446. (Illus.). 1974. 55.00 (*0-8243-1803-X*) Annual Reviews.

— Annual Review of Biophysics & Bioengineering, Vol. 4. LC 79-188446. (Illus.). 1975. 55.00 (*0-8243-1804-8*) Annual Reviews.

— Annual Review of Biophysics & Bioengineering, Vol. 5. LC 79-188446. (Illus.). 1976. 55.00 (*0-8243-1805-6*) Annual Reviews.

— Annual Review of Biophysics & Bioengineering, Vol. 6. LC 79-188446. (Illus.). 1977. 55.00 (*0-8243-1806-4*) Annual Reviews.

— Annual Review of Biophysics & Bioengineering, Vol. 7. LC 79-188446. (Illus.). 1978. 55.00 (*0-8243-1807-2*) Annual Reviews.

— Annual Review of Biophysics & Bioengineering, Vol. 8. LC 79-188446. (Illus.). 1979. 55.00 (*0-8243-1808-0*) Annual Reviews.

— Annual Review of Biophysics & Bioengineering, Vol. 9. LC 79-188446. (Illus.). 1980. 55.00 (*0-8243-1809-9*) Annual Reviews.

— Annual Review of Biophysics & Bioengineering, Vol. 10. LC 79-188446. (Illus.). 1981. 55.00 (*0-8243-1810-2*) Annual Reviews.

— Annual Review of Biophysics & Bioengineering, Vol. 11. LC 79-188446. (Illus.). 1982. 55.00 (*0-8243-1811-0*) Annual Reviews.

— Annual Review of Biophysics & Bioengineering, Vol. 12. LC 79-188446. (Illus.). 1983. 55.00 (*0-8243-1812-9*) Annual Reviews.

Mullins, Larry. Goal Setting for Women Only! (Illus.). 64p. 1984. pap. 3.95 (*0-912137-03-7*) Actionizing.

— Immature People With Power: How to Handle Them! LC 82-73202. (Illus.). 256p. 1983. 17.95 (*0-912137-00-2*); pap. 9.95 (*0-912137-01-0*) Actionizing.

— Sixty-Two Minutes That Will Change Your Life. (Illus.). 40p. 1983. pap. 2.50 (*0-912137-02-9*) Actionizing.

***Mullins, Larry, illus.** God's Bible: The Life & Teachings of Jesus, Pt. IV. 436p. 1994. pap. 9.95 (*0-9644586-0-8*) Pathways NJ.

Mullins, Laurie. Hospitality: A Human Resources Approach. 352p. (Orig.). 1992. pap. 46.50 (*0-273-03395-6*, Pub. by Pitman Pub Ltd UK) Trans-Atl Phila.

Mullins, Laurie J. Management & Organisational Behaviour. 3rd ed. 624p. 1993. pap. 52.50 (*0-273-60039-7*, Pub. by Pitman Pub Ltd UK) Trans-Atl Phila.

Mullins, Leith, ed. Cities in the United States: Studies in Urban Anthropology. LC 87-5218. 368p. 1987. pap. text ed. 19.50 (*0-231-05001-1*) Col U Pr.

***Mullins, Linda.** American Teddy Bear Encyclopedia. 144p. 1995. 29.95 (*0-87588-432-6*) Hobby Hse.

— Raikes Bear & Doll Story. 2nd rev. ed. 1993. 22.95 (*0-87588-412-1*) Hobby Hse.

— Teddy Bear & Friends Price Guide. 4th ed. 192p. 1992. pap. 12.95 (*0-87588-399-0*) Hobby Hse.

— Teddy Bears Past & Present, Vol. I. (Illus.). 305p. 1986. 29.95 (*0-87588-264-1*, 3120) Hobby Hse.

— Teddy Bears Past & Present, Vol. II. (Illus.). 256p. 1991. 25.00 (*0-87588-384-2*) Hobby Hse.

— Tribute to Teddy Bear Artists. 1995. 29.95 (*0-87588-427-X*) Hobby Hse.

Mullins, Linda, jt. auth. see Simmons, Patricia L.

Mullins, Lisa C., ed. Blueprints for America's Past. (Architectural Treasures of Early America Ser.). (Illus.). 224p. 1988. 19.95 (*0-918678-33-1*) Natl Hist Soc.

— Colonial Architecture of the Mid-Atlantic. (Architectural Treasures of Early America Ser.). (Illus.). 246p. 1987. 19.95 (*0-918678-23-4*) Natl Hist Soc.

— Early American Community Structures. (Architectural Treasures of Early America Ser.). 248p. 1988. 19.95 (*0-918678-29-3*) Natl Hist Soc.

— Early American Southern Homes. (Architectural Treasures of Early America Ser.). 248p. 1987. 19.95 (*0-918678-27-7*) Natl Hist Soc.

— Early Architecture of Rhode Island. (Architectural Treasures of Early America Ser.). 248p. 1987. 19.95 (*0-918678-25-0*) Natl Hist Soc.

— The Evolution of Colonial Architecture. (Architectural Treasures of Early America Ser.). 248p. 1988. 19.95 (*0-918678-28-5*) Natl Hist Soc.

— The Georgian Heritage. (Architectural Treasures of Early America Ser.). (Illus.). 224p. 1988. 19.95 (*0-918678-37-4*) Natl Hist Soc.

— Grandeur of the South. (Architectural Treasures of Early America Ser.). (Illus.). 224p. 1988. 19.95 (*0-918678-36-6*) Natl Hist Soc.

— Homes of New York & Connecticut. (Architectural Treasures of Early America Ser.). (Illus.). 245p. 1987. 19.95 (*0-918678-24-2*) Natl Hist Soc.

— New England by the Sea. (Architectural Treasures of Early America Ser.). (Illus.). 245p. 1987. 19.95 (*0-918678-22-6*) Natl Hist Soc.

— Regional Architecture of the Early South. (Architectural Treasures of Early America Ser.). (Illus.). 245p. 1987. 19.95 (*0-918678-21-8*) Natl Hist Soc.

— The Southern Tradition. (Architectural Treasures of Early America Ser.). (Illus.). 224p. 1988. 19.95 (*0-918678-34-X*) Natl Hist Soc.

— Styles of the Emerging Nation. (Architectural Treasures of Early America Ser.). (Illus.). 224p. 1988. 19.95 (*0-918678-35-8*) Natl Hist Soc.

— Survey of Early American Design. (Architectural Treasures of Early America Ser.). (Illus.). 248p. 1987. 19.95 (*0-918678-20-X*) Natl Hist Soc.

— Village Architecture of Early New England. (Architectural Treasures of Early America Ser.). 248p. 1987. 19.85 (*0-918678-26-9*) Natl Hist Soc.

Mullins, M., jt. auth. see Bary, N.

Mullins, Marion Day. The First Census of Texas, Eighteen Twenty-Nine to Eighteen Thirty-Six. 63p. 9.25 (*0-915156-22-9*, 22) Natl Genealogical.

***Mullins, Mark.** Business, Loan & Real Property Forms, 3 vols., Set. 1994. 375.00 (*1-55834-140-4*) Michie Butterworth.

— Religion & Society in Modern Japan. LC 93-23877. (Nanzan Studies in Asian Religions: Vol. 5). 256p. (C). 1993. text ed. 60.00 (*0-89581-935-X*, Asian Human Pr); pap. text ed. 22.00 (*0-89581-936-8*, Asian Human Pr) Jain Pub Co.

— Religious Minorities in Canada: A Sociological Study of the Japanese Experience. LC 88-1703. (Canadian Studies: Vol. 4). 220p. 1989. lib. bdg. 89.95 (*0-88946-195-3*) E Mellen.

Mullins, Mary V., ed. see Wright, Ronald & Wright, Bonnie.

Mullins, Michael. Called to Be Saints: Christian Living in First Century Rome. 576p. 1989. 60.00 (*1-85390-177-6*, Pub. by Veritas IE) St Mut.

Mullins, Michael & Reed, Rowena. The Union Bookshelf: A Selected Civil War Bibliography. LC 82-71852. (Illus.). 100p. 1982. pap. text ed. 25.00 (*0-916107-12-4*) Broadfoot.

Mullins, Michael A. & Winschel, Terence J. Vicksburg: A Self-Guiding Tour of the Battlefield. (Illus.). 32p. (Orig.). 1992. pap. 3.95 (*0-916107-88-4*) Broadfoot.

Mullins, Michael G., et al. Biology of the Grapevine. (Biology of Horticultural Crops Ser.). (Illus.). 250p. (C). 1992. 69.95 (*0-521-30507-1*) Cambridge U Pr.

Mullins, Nicholas. Science: Some Sociological Perspectives. LC 72-12826. (Studies in Sociology). 42p. (C). 1973. pap. text ed. write for info. (*0-672-61205-4*, Bobbs) Macmillan.

Mullins, Nicholas C. Social Networks among Biological Scientists. Zuckerman, Harriet & Merton, Robert K., eds. LC 79-6270. (Dissertations on Sociology Ser.). 1980. lib. bdg. 25.95 (*0-405-12983-1*) Ayer.

Mullins, Patricia. V for Vanishing: An Alphabet of Endangered Animals. LC 93-8181. (Illus.). 32p. (J). (ps-2). 1994. 15.00 (*0-06-023556-X*) HarpC Child Bks.

— V for Vanishing: An Alphabet of Endangered Animals. LC 93-8181. (Illus.). 32p. (J). (ps-2). 1994. lib. bdg. 14.89 (*0-06-023557-8*) HarpC Child Bks.

Mullins, Patricia, jt. auth. see Vaughan, Marcia.

Mullins, Patrick. Retreat from Africa. 115p. (C). 1989. text ed. 49.00 (*1-872795-37-4*, Pub. by Pentland Pr UK) St Mut.

Mullins, Patty, ed. see Benke, Adrian.

Mullins, Reuben B. Pulling Leather: Being the Early Recollections of a Cowboy on the Wyoming Range, 1884-1889. Clayton, Lawrence, ed. LC 88-16491. (Illus.). xvi, 219p. (Orig.). 1988. pap. 10.95 (*0-931271-10-X*) Hi Plains Pr.

Mullins, Shirley S. Teaching Music: The Human Experience. 115p. (Orig.). 1985. pap. text ed. 9.95 (*0-9616262-0-8*) Media Servs.

***Mullins, Terry W.** Staff Development Programs: A Guide to Evaluation. LC 94-21623. (Program Evaluation Guides for Schools Ser.). 1994. pap. 19.95 (*0-8039-6045-X*) Corwin Pr.

Mullins, Tom, ed. Irish Stories for Children. 111p. (YA). (gr. 5 up). 1993. pap. 11.95 (*1-85635-027-4*, Pub. by Mercier Pr IE) Dufour.

Mullins, W. & Shaw, M. C. Metal Transformations. 320p. 1968. text ed. 241.00 (*0-677-10900-8*) Gordon & Breach.

***Mullins, Walter G.** Strike Defense Manual. fac. ed. LC 80-14961. 152p. Date not set. pap. 43.40 (*0-7837-7418-4*, 2047213) Bks Demand.

An Asterisk (*) at the beginning of an entry indicates that the title is appearing in BIP for the first time.

Mullins, Wayman C. Nineteen Forty-Two: Issue in Doubt. LC 94-5234. 1994. 29.95 (0-89015-968-8) Sunbelt Media.
— Terrorist Organizations in the United States: An Analysis of Issues, Organizations, Tactics & Responses. (Illus.). 246p. 1988. pap. 33.95 (0-398-06300-1) C C Thomas.
— Terrorist Organizations in the United States: An Analysis of Issues, Organizations, Tactics & Responses. (Illus.). 246p. (C). 1988. text ed. 55.95x (0-398-05505-X) C C Thomas.
Mullins, William & Allen, Phyllis. Student Housing: Architectural & Social Aspects. LC 76-159965. (Illus.). 1971. 94.50 (0-89197-955-7) Irvington.
Mullins, William H. The Depression & the Urban West Coast, 1929-1933: Los Angeles, San Francisco, Seattle, & Portland. LC 90-4752. (American West in the Twentieth Century Ser.). 192p. 1991. 35.00 (0-253-33935-9) Ind U Pr.
Mullins, William J., jt. auth. see Brehm, John J.
Mullis, Clifford T., jt. auth. see Roberts, Richard A.
Mullis, Garnette. Some Days: Poems by Garnette Mullis. LC 93-32772. 72p. 1994. 18.00 (1-55728-299-4); pap. 12.00 (1-55728-300-1) U of Ark Pr.
***Mullis, Ina V., et al.** The State of Mathematics Achievement: Executive Summary NAEP's 1990 Assessment of the Nation & the Trial Assessment of the States. (Illus.). 51p. (Orig.). (C). 1993. pap. text ed. 35. 00x (0-7881-0106-4) Diane Pub.
— The State of Mathematics Achievement: NAEP's 1990 Assessment of the Nation & the Trial Assessment of the States. (Illus.). 532p. (Orig.). (C). 1993. pap. text ed. 95. 00x (0-7881-0107-2) Diane Pub.
***Mullis, K. B.** Polymerase Chain Reaction. 1994. pap. 45.00 (0-8176-3750-8) Birkhauser.
Mullis, Kary B. & Gibbs, R., eds. The Polymerase Chain Reaction: A Textbook. xxii, 458p. (C). 1994. 79.00 (0-8176-3607-2) Birkhauser.
Mullish, H. Basics: A Guide to the Timex-Sinclair 1000 (2k) 160p. 1983. pap. text ed. 9.95 (0-07-044041-7, BYTE Bks) McGraw.
Mullish, H. & Kruger, D. Programming the Apple IIc. 384p. 1985. pap. text ed. 10.95 (0-07-044042-5, BYTE Bks) McGraw.
Mullish, H., jt. auth. see Chiu, Y.
Mullish, Henry. A Basic Approach to Structured BASIC. LC 89-7975. 394p. (C). 1989. reprint ed. lib. bdg. 42.50 (0-89464-397-5) Krieger.
— Introduction to Computer Programming. (Notes on Mathematics & Its Applications Ser.). 256p. 1966. text ed. 62.00 (0-677-01165-2); pap. 48.00 (0-685-57731-7) Gordon & Breach.
— Modern Programming: FORTRAN IV. LC 68-3217. 144p. reprint ed. pap. 41.10 (0-317-08706-1, 2012591) Bks Demand.
Mullish, Henry & Cooper, Herbert. The Spirit of "C" An Introduction to Modern Programming. 527p. (C). 1987. pap. text ed. 52.75 (0-314-28500-8); teacher ed, pap. text ed. write for info. (0-314-35228-7) West Pub.
Mullivan, M. J., et al, eds. Directory of Biotechnology Companies: U. S. Companies, Western Region I. 2nd ed. 95p. 1992. pap. 23.95 (1-880343-06-1) A Gee.
Mulla, M. S., et al. Distribution, Transport, & Fate of the Insecticides: Malathion & Parathion in the Environment. Gunther, Francis A., ed. (Residue Reviews Ser.: Vol. 30). (Illus.). 172p. 1981. 54.00 (0-387-90634-7) Spr-Verlag.
Mullner, Ross M., jt. ed. see Brehm, Henry P.
Mullock, B., jt. ed. see Snell, Keith.
Mullock, Philip, jt. auth. see Aqvist.
Mullooly, Patrick. The Signet Ultimate Basketball Quiz Book. 176p. (Orig.). 1993. pap. 3.99 (0-451-17764-9, Sig) NAL-Dutton.
Mulloy, Barbara & Thomas, Adrian, eds. Microscopy, Optical Spectroscopy & Macroscopic Techniques. LC 93-23977. (Methods in Molecular Biology Ser.: Vol. 22). (Illus.). 264p. 1993. spiral bd. 59.50 (0-89603-232-9) Humana.
Mulloy, John J., ed. see Dawson, Christopher.
Mulloy, William & Figueroa, Gonzalo. A Kivi-Vai Teka Complex & Its Relationship to Easter Island Architectural Prehistory. (Asian & Pacific Archaeology Ser.: No. 8). (Illus.). 226p. 1978. pap. text ed. 9.00 (0-8248-0652-2) UH Pr.
Mulls, Kathi. Confessions from the Far Side of Thirty. 208p. (Orig.). 1993. pap. 1.80 (1-56476-095-2, Victor Books) SP Pubns.
Mullvihill, Sharon T., ed. see Nystul, Mike & Smith, Lester.
Mulmuley, Ketan. Full Abstraction & Semantic Equivalence. (ACM Doctoral Dissertation Award Ser.). (Illus.). 150p. 1987. 30.00x (0-262-13227-3) MIT Pr.
Mulock, Dinah M. A Life for a Life, 3 vols. in 2, 1. LC 79-8179. reprint ed. write for info. (0-404-62069-8) AMS Pr.
— A Life for a Life, 3 vols. in 2, 2. LC 79-8179. reprint ed. write for info. (0-404-62070-1) AMS Pr.
— A Life for a Life, 3 vols. in 2, Set. LC 79-8179. reprint ed. 84.50 (0-404-62068-X) AMS Pr.
— Little Lame Prince, Adventures of Brownie. (J). 1976. 18. 95 (0-8488-1109-7) Amereon Ltd.
Mulock, Miss. The Little Lame Prince. (Illus.). 116p. 1991. reprint ed. lib. bdg. 14.95 (0-89966-762-7) Buccaneer Bks.
Mulongey, K., et al, eds. Biological Nitrogen Fixation & Sustainability of Tropical Agriculture. 488p. 1992. text ed. 165.00 (0-471-93560-3) Wiley.
Mulongoy, K. & Merckx, R., eds. Soil Organic Matter Dynamics & the Sustainability of Tropical Agriculture. 392p. 1993. text ed. 115.00 (0-471-93915-3) Wiley.
Mulpeter, Virginia A. & Rosenfield, Judith F. Program for the Assessment & Instruction of Swallowing (PAIS) 24p. (Orig.). (C). 1993. teacher ed 55.00 (0-937857-39-4, 1529) Speech Bin.
Mulqueen, Jack & Chatton, Ray. God's Mother Is My Mother. (Illus.). 28p. (Orig.). (J). (gr. 1-3). 1978. pap. 2.50 (0-913382-49-3, 103-13) Prow Bks-Franciscan.
Mulqueen, Maggie. On Our Own Terms: Redefining Competence & Femininity. LC 91-12245. 221p. 1992. 64.50x (0-7914-0951-1); pap. 21.95 (0-7914-0952-X) State U NY Pr.
Mulready, Sally, jt. auth. see Callaghan, Hugh.
Mulrenin, Paul E., ed. Marauder Memoirs: History of the 455th Bombardment Squadron in World War II (1942-1945) (Illus.). 300p. (C). 1987. write for info. (0-9619535-1-9); pap. 25.00 (0-9619535-2-7) Four Fifty Fifth.
Mulrine, Stephen, ed. Scottish Stories from MacGregor's Gathering. 63p. 1992. pap. 6.95 (0-563-20739-6, BBC-Parkwest) Parkwest Pubns.
Mulrine, Stephen, tr. see Petrushevskaya, Ludmila.
Mulroney, Catherine, jt. auth. see Babad, Michael.
Mulrow, P. J, jt. ed. see Ganten, D.
Mulrow, Patrick J. & Schrier, Robert W., eds. Atrial Hormones & Other Natriuretic Factors. (American Physiological Society Book). (Illus.). 186p. 1988. 44.50 (0-19-520687-8) OUP.
Mulroy, David. Horace's Odes & Epodes. 230p. (C). 1994. text ed. 37.50 (0-472-10531-0) U of Mich Pr.
Mulroy, David, tr. & comment. Early Greek Lyric Poetry. LC 91-42973. 230p. (C). 1992. text ed. 34.50 (0-472-10296-6) U of Mich Pr.
Mulroy, David D. Comites Catulli: Structured Vocabulary Lists for Catullus 1-60. LC 86-10984. 112p. (Orig.). (C). 1986. pap. text ed. 17.00 (0-8191-5449-0) U Pr of Amer.
— Picturing the Tale: Chapters in the Study of the Use of Classical Myths by Painters & Sculptors. 96p. (C). 1992. pap. text ed. 14.50 (0-8403-7761-4) Kendall-Hunt.
***Mulroy, Elizabeth A.** The New Uprooted: Single Mothers in Urban Life. LC 95-2084. 200p. 1995. text ed. 55.00 (0-86569-038-3, Auburn Hse); pap. text ed. 16.95 (0-86569-039-1, Auburn Hse) Greenwood.
Mulroy, Elizabeth A., ed. Women As Single Parents: Confronting Institutional Barriers in the Courts, the Workplace, & the Housing Market. LC 88-11920. 228p. 1988. text ed. 49.95 (0-86569-176-2, Auburn Hse) Greenwood.
Mulroy, Kevin. Freedom on the Border: The Seminole Maroons in Florida, the Indian Territory, Coahuila & Texas. LC 92-29135. (Illus.). 278p. 1993. 29.00 (0-89672-250-3) Tex Tech Univ Pr.
Mulry, Terrence J., jt. auth. see Church, F. Forrester.
Mulryan, John, ed. Milton & the Middle Ages. LC 81-694400. 192p. 1982. 29.50 (0-8387-5036-2) Bucknell U Pr.
Mulryne, J. R. & Shewring, Margaret, eds. Italian Renaissance Festivals & Their European Influence. LC 92-1736. (Illus.). 364p. 1992. text ed. 99.95 (0-7734-9608-4) E Mellen.
— Theatre & Government under the Early Stuarts. LC 92-33796. 264p. (C). 1993. 59.95 (0-521-40159-3) Cambridge U Pr.
— Theatre of the English & Italian Renaissance. LC 91-21021. 268p. 1991. text ed. 49.95 (0-312-06771-2) St Martin.
— War, Literature & the Arts in 16th Century Europe. LC 88-36592. (Illus.). 208p. 1989. text ed. 45.00 (0-312-03107-6) St Martin.
Mulryne, J. R., ed. see Dessen, Alan C.
Mulryne, J. R., ed. see Kyd, Thomas.
Mulryne, J. R., ed. see Middleton, Thomas.
Mulryne, J. R., ed. see Warren, Roger.
Mulryne, J. R., ed. see Webster, John.
Mulsoon, Paul. Ireland: A Troubled Mirror. (Illus.). 1994. pap. 14.95 (0-89381-566-7) Aperture.
Multani, M. S. & Gupta, L. C. Selected Topics in Superconductivity. LC 92-43565. (Frontiers in Solid State Sciences Ser.). 676p. 1993. text ed. 135.00 (981-02-1201-1); pap. write for info. (981-02-1202-X) World Scientific Pub.
Multani, M. S., jt. auth. see Gupta, L. C.
***Multatuli.** Max Havelaar: Or the Coffee Auctions of the Dutch Trading Company. Edwards, Roy, tr. & notes by. 352p. 1995. 12.95 (0-14-044516-1, Penguin Classics) Viking Penguin.
Multatuli, pseud. Max Havelaar: Or the Coffee Auctions of the Dutch Trading Company. Edwards, Roy, tr. LC 82-2043. (Library of the Indies). 400p. 1982. lib. bdg. 37. 50x (0-87023-359-9); pap. 18.95x (0-87023-360-2) U of Mass Pr.
Multer, Barbara. The Dr. Ruth Phenomenon. 240p. 1988. reprint ed. pap. 3.95 (0-8439-2589-2) Dorchester Pub Co.
Multer, Susan D. Singing Your Own Song: Using the Mind-Body Connection to Enhance Your Health. LC 94-23113. (Illus.). 96p. (Orig.). 1995. pap. 7.95 (0-942963-51-2) Distinctive Pub.
Multhauf, Robert O. Neptune's Gift: A History of Common Salt. LC 77-8668. (Johns Hopkins Studies in the History of Technology; New Ser.: No. 2). (Illus.). 344p. reprint ed. pap. 98.10 (0-8357-4033-1, 2036725) Bks Demand.
Multhauf, Robert P. The Origins of Chemistry. Vol. 13. 1993. write for info. (0-318-70031-X) Gordon & Breach.
Multi - AMP Institute Staff. Test Equipment. LC 93-20199. 241p. 1994. 28.95 (0-8273-4923-8) Delmar.
Multi-Amp Institute Staff. Basic Electricity for Electricians. 256p. 1992. text ed. 26.95 (0-8273-4917-3) Delmar.
— Industrial Instrumentation. Rader, Billie T., ed. (Illus.). (Orig.). (C). 1989. write for info. (0-318-66525-5) Multi-Amp Inst.
— Motors, Generators & Transformers. LC 94-20840. 512p. 1995. text ed. 33.95 (0-8273-4920-3); Instr's. manual. teacher ed 12.00 (0-8273-4921-1) Delmar.
Multi Conference Attendees Staff. Annual Technical Session Proceedings, 1991: Inelastic Behavior & Design of Frames. Gu, Yixian, ed. 500p. (Orig.). 1991. pap. text ed. 55.00 (1-879749-51-3) Structural Stability.
Multi-Phase Flow & Heat Transfer Symposium Staff. Multiphase Transport: Fundamentals, Reactor Safety, Applications: Proceedings of the Multi-Phase Flow & Heat Transfer Symposium, 2nd, Miami Beach, April 16-18, 1979, 5 vols., Set. Veziroglu, T. Nejat, ed. LC 80-11157. (Illus.). 3932p. 1980. text ed. 625.00 (0-89116-159-7) Hemisp Pub.
Multilateral Church Conversation in Scotland Staff. Deacons for Scotland. 88p. 1993. pap. 22.00 (0-86153-125-6) St Mut.
Multilateral Trade Negotiations, the Uruguay Trade Negotiations Committee. The Dunkel Draft from the GATT Secretariat: Multilateral Trade Negotiations - The Uruguay Round Track Negotiations Committee Draft Final Act Embodying the Results of the Uruguay Round of Multilateral Trade Negotiations. Institute for International Legal Information Staff, ed. LC 92-17248. 547p. 1992. 75.00 (0-89941-799-X, 307560) W S Hein.
***Multimedia Development Serivces Staff.** Process Chemistry, Vol. II, Module II. (Plant Fundamentals Ser.). (Illus.). (Orig.). 1995. teacher ed 45.00 (1-57431-045-3) Tech Trng Systs.
***Multimedia Development Services Ser.** Plant Fundamentals: A Performance-Based Training Series for the Process Industries, 12 vols., Set. (Illus.). (Orig.). 1995. student ed 960.00 (1-57431-000-3) Tech Trng Systs.
***Multimedia Development Services Staff.** Basic Electrical Equipment. (Plant Fundamentals Ser.: Vol. XI, Module II). (Illus.). 1995. teacher ed 45.00 (1-57431-075-5); student ed 30.00 (1-57431-035-6) Tech Trng Systs.
— Basic Electricity. (Plant Fundamentals Ser.). (Illus.). (Orig.). 1995. student ed 30.00 (1-57431-007-0) Tech Trng Systs.
— Basic Electricity Vol., Vol. II, Module IV. (Plant Fundamentals Ser.). (Illus.). (Orig.). 1995. teacher ed 45. 00 (1-57431-047-X) Tech Trng Systs.
— Communication. (Plant Fundamentals Ser.). (Illus.). (Orig.). 1995. student ed 30.00 (1-57431-002-X) Tech Trng Systs.
— Communication, Vol. 1, Module 11. (Plant Fundamentals Ser.). (Illus.). (Orig.). 1995. teacher ed 45.00 (1-57431-042-9) Tech Trng Systs.
— Compressors Vol. IV, Module II. (Plant Fundamentals Ser.). (Illus.). (Orig.). 1995. teacher ed 45.00 (1-57431-053-4); student ed 30.00 (1-57431-013-5) Tech Trng Systs.
— Continuous Improvement. (Plant Fundamentals Ser.: Vol. X, Module I). (Illus.). 1995. teacher ed 45.00 (1-57431-071-2); student ed 30.00 (1-57431-031-3) Tech Trng Systs.
— Cooling Towers. (Plant Fundamentals Ser.). (Illus.). 50p. (Orig.). 1995. student ed 30.00 (1-57431-016-X) Tech Trng Systs.
— Cooling Towers, Vol. V, Module II. (Plant Fundamentals Ser.). (Illus.). (Orig.). 1995. teacher ed 45.00 (1-57431-056-9) Tech Trng Systs.
— Crushing & Milling. (Plant Fundamentals Ser.). (Illus.). (Orig.). 1995. student ed 30.00 (1-57431-018-6) Tech Trng Systs.
— Crushing & Milling, Vol. VI, Module I. (Plant Fundamentals Ser.). (Illus.). (Orig.). 1995. teacher ed 45. 00 (1-57431-058-5) Tech Trng Systs.
— Distillation. (Plant Fundamentals Ser.: Vol. VII, Module IV). (Illus.). 1995. teacher ed 45.00 (1-57431-064-X); student ed 30.00 (1-57431-024-0) Tech Trng Systs.
— Distributed Control Systems. (Plant Fundamentals Ser.: Vol. VIII, Module III). (Illus.). 1995. teacher ed 45.00 (1-57431-067-4); student ed 30.00 (1-57431-027-5) Tech Trng Systs.
— Fired Equipment, Vol. V, Module III. (Plant Fundamentals Ser.). (Illus.). (Orig.). 1995. teacher ed 45. 00 (1-57431-057-7); student ed 30.00 (1-57431-017-8) Tech Trng Systs.
— Heat Exchangers, Vol. V, Module I. (Plant Fundamentals Ser.). (Illus.). (Orig.). 1995. teacher ed 45.00 (1-57431-055-0); student ed 30.00 (1-57431-015-1) Tech Trng Systs.
— Instrumentation. (Plant Fundamentals Ser.: Vol. VIII, Module II). (Illus.). 1995. teacher ed 45.00 (1-57431-066-6); student ed 30.00 (1-57431-026-7) Tech Trng Systs.
— ISO 9000. (Plant Fundamentals Ser.: Vol. X, Module III). (Illus.). 1995. teacher ed 45.00 (1-57431-073-9); student ed 30.00 (1-57431-033-X) Tech Trng Systs.
— Lubrication. (Plant Fundamentals Ser.: Vol. XI, Module III). (Illus.). 1995. teacher ed 45.00 (1-57431-076-3); student ed 30.00 (1-57431-036-4) Tech Trng Systs.
— Mixing. (Plant Fundamentals Ser.: Vol. VII, Module III). (Illus.). 1995. teacher ed 45.00 (1-57431-063-1); student ed 30.00 (1-57431-023-2) Tech Trng Systs.
— Piping, Vol. III, Module II. (Plant Fundamentals Ser.). (Illus.). (Orig.). 1995. teacher ed 45.00 (1-57431-049-6) Tech Trng Systs.
— Piping V, Vol. III, Module II. (Plant Fundamentals Ser.). (Illus.). 46p. (Orig.). 1995. student ed 30.00 (1-57431-009-7) Tech Trng Systs.
— Plant Fundamentals Instructor's Guides: A Performance-Based Training Series for the Process Industries, 12 Vols., Set. (Plant Fundamentals Ser.). (Illus.). (Orig.). 1995. teacher ed 1,500.00 (1-57431-040-2) Tech Trng Systs.
— Prime Movers Vol. IV, Module III. (Plant Fundamentals Ser.). (Illus.). (Orig.). 1995. teacher ed 45.00 (1-57431-054-2); student ed 30.00 (1-57431-014-3) Tech Trng Systs.
— Problem Solving. (Plant Fundamentals Ser.). (Illus.). (Orig.). 1995. student ed 30.00 (1-57431-003-8) Tech Trng Systs.
— Problem Solving, Vol. 1, Module III. (Plant Fundamentals Ser.). (Illus.). (Orig.). 1995. teacher ed 45.00 (1-57431-043-7) Tech Trng Systs.
— Process Chemistry. (Plant Fundamentals Ser.: Vol. II, Module II). (Illus.). 80p. 1995. student ed 30.00 (1-57431-005-4) Tech Trng Systs.
— Process Control. (Plant Fundamentals Ser.: Vol. VIII, Module I). (Illus.). 1995. teacher ed 45.00 (1-57431-065-8); student ed 30.00 (1-57431-025-9) Tech Trng Systs.
— Process Math, Vol. II, Module I. (Plant Fundamentals Ser.). (Illus.). 92p. (Orig.). 1995. student ed 30.00 (1-57431-004-6) Tech Trng Systs.
— Process Math Vol., Vol. II, Module I. (Plant Fundamentals Ser.). (Illus.). (Orig.). 1995. teacher ed 45. 00 (1-57431-044-5) Tech Trng Systs.
— The Process Operator. (Plant Fundamentals Ser.). (Illus.). (Orig.). 1995. student ed 30.00 (1-57431-001-1) Tech Trng Systs.
— The Process Operator Vol., Vol. 1, Module 1. (Plant Fundamentals Ser.). (Illus.). (Orig.). 1995. teacher ed 45. 00 (1-57431-041-0) Tech Trng Systs.
— Process Physics. (Plant Fundamentals Ser.). (Illus.). 64p. (Orig.). 1995. student ed 30.00 (1-57431-006-2) Tech Trng Systs.
— Process Physics Vol., Vol. II, Module III. (Plant Fundamentals Ser.). (Illus.). (Orig.). 1995. teacher ed 45. 00 (1-57431-046-1) Tech Trng Systs.
— Pumps. (Plant Fundamentals Ser.). (Illus.). 54p. (Orig.). 1995. student ed 30.00 (1-57431-012-7) Tech Trng Systs.
— Pumps, Vol. IV, Module I. (Plant Fundamentals Ser.). (Illus.). (Orig.). 1995. teacher ed 45.00 (1-57431-052-6) Tech Trng Systs.
— Quality Principles. (Plant Fundamentals Ser.: Vol. XII, Module I). (Illus.). 1995. teacher ed 45.00 (1-57431-077-1); student ed 30.00 (1-57431-037-2) Tech Trng Systs.
— Quality Teams. (Plant Fundamentals Ser.: Vol. XII, Module III). (Illus.). 1995. teacher ed 45.00 (1-57431-079-8); student ed 30.00 (1-57431-039-9) Tech Trng Systs.
— Quality Tools. (Plant Fundamentals Ser.: Vol. XII, Module II). (Illus.). 1995. teacher ed 45.00 (1-57431-078-X); student ed 30.00 (1-57431-038-0) Tech Trng Systs.
— Reacting. (Plant Fundamentals Ser.: Vol. VII, Module I). (Illus.). 1995. teacher ed 45.00 (1-57431-061-5); student ed 30.00 (1-57431-021-6) Tech Trng Systs.
— Reading Drawings. (Plant Fundamentals Ser.: Vol. IX, Module I). (Illus.). 1995. teacher ed 45.00 (1-57431-068-2); student ed 30.00 (1-57431-028-3) Tech Trng Systs.
— Separation. (Plant Fundamentals Ser.: Vol. VII, Module II). (Illus.). 1995. teacher ed 45.00 (1-57431-062-3); student ed 30.00 (1-57431-022-4) Tech Trng Systs.
— Solid Materials Handling. (Plant Fundamentals Ser.: Vol. VI, Module III). (Illus.). 1995. teacher ed 45.00 (1-57431-060-7); student ed 30.00 (1-57431-020-8) Tech Trng Systs.
— Solid Materials Transporting. (Plant Fundamentals Ser.: Vol. VI, Module II). (Illus.). 1995. teacher ed 45.00 (1-57431-059-3); student ed 30.00 (1-57431-019-4) Tech Trng Systs.
— Statistical Process Control. (Plant Fundamentals Ser.: Vol. X, Module II). (Illus.). 1995. teacher ed 45.00 (1-57431-072-0); student ed 30.00 (1-57431-032-1) Tech Trng Systs.
— Steam Traps. (Plant Fundamentals Ser.). (Illus.). 62p. (Orig.). 1995. student ed 30.00 (1-57431-011-9) Tech Trng Systs.
— Steam Traps, Vol. III, Module IV. (Plant Fundamentals Ser.). (Illus.). (Orig.). 1995. teacher ed 45.00 (1-57431-051-8) Tech Trng Systs.
— Tanks & Vessels. (Plant Fundamentals Ser.). (Illus.). 68p. (Orig.). 1995. student ed 30.00 (1-57431-008-9) Tech Trng Systs.
— Tanks & Vessels Vol., Vol. III, Module I. (Plant Fundamentals Ser.). (Illus.). (Orig.). 1995. teacher ed 45. 00 (1-57431-048-8) Tech Trng Systs.
— Total Productive Maintenance. (Plant Fundamentals Ser.: Vol. XI, Module I). (Illus.). 1995. teacher ed 45.00 (1-57431-074-7); student ed 30.00 (1-57431-034-8) Tech Trng Systs.
— Using Procedure Information. (Plant Fundamentals Ser.: Vol. IX, Module III). (Illus.). 1995. teacher ed 45.00 (1-57431-070-4); student ed 30.00 (1-57431-030-5) Tech Trng Systs.
— Using Process Safety Information. (Plant Fundamentals Ser.: Vol. IX, Module II). (Illus.). 1995. teacher ed 45.00 (1-57431-069-0); student ed 30.00 (1-57431-029-1) Tech Trng Systs.
— Valves. (Plant Fundamentals Ser.). (Illus.). 90p. (Orig.). 1995. student ed 30.00 (1-57431-010-0) Tech Trng Systs.
— Valves, Vol. III, Module III. (Plant Fundamentals Ser.). (Illus.). (Orig.). 1995. teacher ed 45.00 (1-57431-050-X) Tech Trng Systs.
***Multimedia Ventures Staff, ed.** International Multimedia Yearbook 1995-96. 1000p. 1995. cd-rom 150.00 (0-614-06190-3) Fitzroy Dearborn.
Multinational Communications Inc. Staff. Global Telecommunications Guide. 1987. pap. 15.00 (0-931000-27-0) Suburban Pub CT.

An Asterisk (*) at the beginning of an entry indicates that the title is appearing in BIP for the first time.

Multinational Executive Inc. Staff. Nineteen Eighty-Eight Multinational Executive Travel Companion. rev. ed. 1988. pap. 60.00 (*0-931000-28-9*) Suburban Pub CT.

***Multon, J. L., ed.** Quality Control: General Principles & Legal Aspects. LC 94-39865. 1995. 125.00 (*1-56081-698-8*) VCH Pubs.

Multon, J. L., jt. ed. see Simatos, D.

***Multon, J. L., et al, eds.** Analysis & Control Methods for Foods & Agricultural Products. LC 95-7026. Orig. Title: Techniques d'Analyse et de Controle Dans les Industries Agro-Alimentaires. 1995. write for info. (*1-56081-673-2*) VCH Pubs.

***MuLuhan, T. C.** The Way of the Earth: Encounters with Nature in Ancient & Contemporary Thought. 1995. pap. 17.50 (*0-684-80157-4*, Touchstone Bks) S&S Trade.

***Mulukutla, P. S., ed.** Reagents for Better Metallurgy. fac. ed. LC 93-86997. (Illus.). 373p. 1994. reprint ed. pap. 107.80 (*0-7837-8205-5*, 2047963) Bks Demand.

Mulvaney. Growth & Developmental Biology of Meat Animals. 1995. write for info. (*0-8493-8758-2*) CRC Pr.

Mulvaney, D. J., ed. Commandant of Solitude: Journals of Captain Collet Barker 1784-1831. 1992. 44.95 (*0-522-84472-3*) Intl Spec Bk.

Mulvaney, John. Analysis Bar Charting. LC 77-670112. 100p. (Orig.). 1980. 10.00 (*0-317-17178-X*, Mgmt Planning & Control) Kumarian Pr.

Mulvaney, Rebekah M. & Nelson, Carlos I. Rastafari & Reggae: A Dictionary & Sourcebook. LC 90-3591. 272p. 1990. text ed. 49.95 (*0-313-26071-0*, MVR/, Greenwood Pr) Greenwood.

Mulvaney, Robert, ed. see Simon, Yves.

Mulvany, M. J., ed. Fourth International Symposium on Resistance Arteries, Warren, Vermont, January 1994: Abstracts. (Journal: Vol. 31, Suppl. 1, 1994). ii, 60p. 1994. pap. 24.00 (*3-8055-5919-4*) S Karger.

— International Symposium on Resistance Arteries, 3rd, Rebild, Skrping, Denmark, May 1991 Abstracts. (Journal: Blood Vessels: Vol. 28, No. 4, 1991). 80p. 1991. pap. 50.50 (*3-8055-5409-5*) S Karger.

Mulvany, M. J., et al, eds. Resistance Vessels: Physiology, Pharmacology & Hypertensive Pathology. (Mikrozirkulation in Forschung und Klinik; Progress in Applied Microcirculation Ser.: Vol. 8). (Illus.). x, 236p. 1985. pap. 112.00 (*3-8055-4052-3*) S Karger.

Mulvany, Nancy C. Indexing Books. (Illus.). 352p. 1994. 29.95 (*0-226-55014-1*) U Ch Pr.

Mulvany, Nancy C., ed. Indexing, Providing Access to Information: Looking Back, Looking Ahead: The Proceedings of the 25th Annual Meeting of the American Society of Indexers. LC 93-25136. 161p. 1993. pap. text ed. 35.00 (*0-936547-19-7*) Am Soc Index.

***Mulvey.** We Had Everything But Money. 1995. 14.99 (*0-517-12393-2*) Random Hse Value.

Mulvey, Charles. The Economic Analysis of Trade Unions. LC 78-9094. 1978. text ed. 29.95 (*0-312-22684-5*) St Martin.

Mulvey, Christopher. Anglo-American Landscapes: A Study of Nineteenth-Century Anglo-American Travel Literature. LC 82-4380. (Illus.). 300p. 1983. 49.95 (*0-521-23755-6*) Cambridge U Pr.

— Transatlantic Manners: Social Patterns in Nineteenth-Century Anglo-American Travel Literature. (Illus.). 260p. (C). 1990. 59.95 (*0-521-30366-4*) Cambridge U Pr.

Mulvey, Deb, ed. We Had Everything but Money. LC 92-60979. 164p. 1992. 14.98 (*0-89821-099-2*) Reiman Pubns.

— We Pulled Together & Won! LC 93-84612. (Illus.). 160p. 1994. 14.95 (*0-89821-112-3*) Reiman Pubns.

— When Families Made Memories Together. 160p. 1994. 14.98 (*0-89821-124-7*) Reiman Pubns.

Mulvey, J. M., jt. ed. see Klingman, Darwin.

Mulvey, Janemarie, jt. auth. see Moon, Marilyn.

Mulvey, Kathleen A. Let's Pray Together: Thirty-Two Complete Prayer Services. LC 87-83384. 64p. (Orig.). 1988. pap. 6.95 (*0-937997-08-0*) Hi-Time Pub.

Mulvey, Laura. Citizen Kane. (BFI Film Classics Ser.). (Illus.). 1993. pap. 9.95 (*0-85170-339-9*, Pub. by British Film Inst UK) Ind U Pr.

— Jimmie Durham. (Contemporary Artists Ser.). (Illus.). 160p. (Orig.). 1995. pap. 29.95 (*0-7148-3348-7*, Pub. by Phaidon Press UK) Chronicle Bks.

— Visual & Other Pleasures. LC 88-9627. (Theories of Representation & Difference Ser.). 218p. (Orig.). 1989. 35.00 (*0-253-36226-1*); pap. 12.95 (*0-253-20494-1*, MB-494) Ind U Pr.

Mulvey, Mary D. French Catholic Missionaries in the Present United States (1604-1791) LC 73-3578. (Catholic University of America. Studies in Romance Languages & Literatures: No. 23). reprint ed. 32.50 (*0-404-57773-3*) AMS Pr.

Mulvey, Michael, ed. Formation & Communion - Priests of the Future. 128p. 1991. 7.95 (*0-911782-89-3*) New City.

Mulvey, T., ed. see Institute of Physics, Great Britain, Electron Microscopy & Analysis Group Staff.

Mulvey, Tom & Sheppard, Colin, eds. Advances in Optical & Electron Microscopy, Vol. 11. (Serial Publication Ser.). 220p. 1989. text ed. 97.00 (*0-12-029911-9*) Acad Pr.

— Advances in Optical & Electron Microscopy, Vol. 12. 363p. 1991. text ed. 116.00 (*0-12-029912-7*) Acad Pr.

— Advances in Optical & Electron Microscopy, Vol. 13. (Illus.). 320p. 1994. text ed. 99.00 (*0-12-029913-5*) Acad Pr.

— Advances in Optical & Electron Microscopy, Vol. 14. (Illus.). 320p. 1994. text ed. 99.00 (*0-12-029914-3*) Acad Pr.

Mulvihill, Donna C. Flexography Primer. LC 85-70601. (Illus.). 112p. 1985. 40.00 (*0-88362-076-6*, 1330) Graphic Arts Tech Found.

Mulvihill, Edward R., ed. see Sanchez-Silva, Jose M.

Mulvihill, James. Thomas Love Peacock. (Twayne's English Authors Ser.: No. 456). 152p. 1987. lib. bdg. 26.95 (*0-8057-6957-9*, Twayne) Macmillan.

Mulvihill, James E., jt. ed. see Greenwald, Robert A.

Mulvihill, John J., et al, eds. Genetics of Human Cancer. LC 75-44924. (Progress in Cancer Research & Therapy: No. 3). (Illus.). 541p. reprint ed. pap. 154.20 (*0-7837-7094-4*, 2046919) Bks Demand.

***Mulvihill, Margaret.** St. Patrick's Daughter. 252p. 1995. pap. 10.95 (*0-340-59774-7*, Pub. by H & S UK) Trafalgar.

Mulvihill, Margaret, ed. People in the Past. LC 92-54483. (Picturepedia Ser.). (Illus.). (J). 1993. write for info. (*1-56458-217-5*) Dorling Kindersley.

Mulvihill, Mary L. Human Diseases: A Systemic Approach. 4th ed. LC 94-8977. 1994. 34.95 (*0-8385-3928-9*) Appleton & Lange.

Mulvihill, Maureen, ed. see Ephelia.

***Mulvihill, Peggy.** Letters to Mead: A Mother's Extraordinary Gift to Her Son. 224p. 1995. 14.95 (*1-57071-052-X*) Sourcebks.

Mulvihill, Robert F., jt. auth. see Farren, Sean.

Mulvihill, S. Somatostatin Analog. (Medical Intelligence Ser.). 95p. 1993. text ed. 89.95 (*1-879702-15-0*, LN0215) R G Landes.

Mulvihill, Sharon T., ed. see Dowd, Tom & Kubasik, Christopher.

Mulvihill, Sharon T., ed. see Findley, Nigel D.

Mulvihill, Sharon T., ed. see McGregor, Philip.

Mulvihill, Sharon T., ed. see Sargent, Carl.

Mulvihill, William. Sands of the Kalahari. 18.95 (*0-89190-869-2*, Am Repr) Amereon Ltd.

Mulville, Frank. Dear Dolphin: Iskra's Atlantic Adventures. (Illus.). 192p. (Orig.). 1992. pap. 14.95 (*0-924486-26-0*) Sheridan.

— The Death of the Schooner Integrity. (Illus.). 169p. 1981. 12.95 (*0-89182-032-9*); pap. 7.95 (*0-89182-033-7*) Charles River Bks.

— In Gramma's Wake: Girl Stella's Voyage to Cuba. 330p. 1970. pap. 12.50 (*0-87556-439-9*) Saifer.

— Rustler on the Beach. 160p. 1982. 12.95 (*0-89182-047-7*) Charles River Bks.

— Schooner Integrity. (Illus.). 184p. 1992. pap. 14.95 (*0-85036-425-6*, Pub. by Seafarer Bks UK) Sheridan.

— Single-Handed Sailing. (Illus.). 192p. (Orig.). 1990. pap. 17.50 (*0-85036-410-8*) Sheridan.

Mulvoy, Mark. Sports Illustrated Golf. 1988. pap. 9.95 (*1-56800-036-7*, Pub. by Sports Illus Bks) Natl Bk Netwk.

— Sports Illustrated Golf: Play Like a Pro. 1993. pap. 12.95 (*1-56800-007-3*, Pub. by Sports Illus Bks) Natl Bk Netwk.

Muly, James D., jt. auth. see Wertime, Theodore A.

Mulys, jt. auth. see Detaille, Georges.

Mulzer, Johann & Berger, Eberhard. Chiral Auxiliaries: Application in Organic Synthesis. 500p. 1993. 100.00 (*3-528-06463-3*, Pub. by Vieweg & Sohn GW) Ballen Bkslr.

Mulzer, Johann, et al. Organic Synthesis Highlights. 410p. 1991. lib. bdg. 70.00 (*0-89573-918-6*) VCH Pubs.

Muma, John R. Language Handbook: Concepts, Assessment, Intervention. (Illus.). 1978. text ed. write for info. (*0-13-522755-0*) P-H.

Muma, Richard D., et al. HIV Manual for Health Care Professionals. (Illus.). 300p. 1994. pap. text ed. 25.95 (*0-8385-0170-2*, A0170-9) Appleton & Lange.

***Mumau.** Dean Smith: A Biography. 1994. pap. 5.99 (*0-517-13435-7*) Random.

Mumau, Thad. Go Wolfpack: North Carolina State Football. LC 80-54310. (College Sports Book Ser.). (Illus.). 250p. 1981. 10.95 (*0-87397-179-5*) Strode.

Mumaw, Catherine & Voran, Marilyn. The Whole Thing. 24p. (J). (gr. 6-11). 1981. pap. 1.50 (*0-8361-1962-2*) Herald Pr.

***Mumaw, Evelyn K.** More Like Jesus: You Can Grow in Your Christian Life. LC 88-32001. (Illus.). reprint ed. pap. 43.40 (*0-7837-9052-X*, 2049803) Bks Demand.

Mumaw, John R. Answers to Anxiety. 1993. pap. 6.95 (*0-87813-551-0*) Christian Light.

— Assurance of Salvation. 1989. pap. 4.95 (*0-87813-955-9*) Christian Light.

— Preach the Word: Expository Preaching from the Book of Ephesians. LC 87-23763. 288p. (Orig.). 1987. pap. 14.95 (*0-8361-3452-4*) Herald Pr.

Mumaw, Laura, ed. see Ling, Shao-Wen.

***Mumba, Nevers.** Integrity with Fire. 1994. per. 8.95 (*0-927936-55-0*) Christ for the Nations.

Mumby, Dennis K. Communication & Power in Organizations. Thayer, Lee, ed. LC 88-3356. (People, Communication, Organization Ser.). 208p. 1988. text ed. 39.50 (*0-89391-480-0*) Ablex Pub.

— Narrative & Social Control: Critical Perspectives. (Annual Reviews of Communication Research Ser.: Vol. 21). (Illus.). 304p. (C). 1993. text ed. 52.00 (*0-8039-4931-6*); pap. text ed. 24.00 (*0-8039-4932-4*) Sage.

***Mumcuoglu, Madeleine.** Sambuco Black Elderberry Extract: A Breakthrough in the Treatment of Influenza Viruses. 16p. 1995. 2.50 (*0-9646056-0-0*) RSS Pub.

Mumenthaler, M. & Schliack, H., eds. Peripheral Nerve Lesions: Diagnosis & Therapy. (Illus.). 464p. 1990. text ed. 99.00 (*0-86577-361-0*) Thieme Med Pubs.

Mumenthaler, Mark. Neurologic Differential Diagnosis. 2nd ed. Appenzeller, Otto, tr. (Illus.). 192p. (GER.). (C). 1992. pap. text ed. 39.00 (*0-86577-432-3*) Thieme Med Pubs.

— Neurology. 3rd ed. (Flexibook Ser.). (Illus.). 551p. (Orig.). 1990. text ed. 27.00 (*0-86577-317-3*) Thieme Med Pubs.

***Mumey, Jack.** The New Joy of Being Sober: A Book for Recovering Alcoholics & Those who love them. rev. ed. LC 94-28358. 1994. pap. 11.95 (*0-925190-31-4*) Fairview Press.

— Recharging Your Relationship: Finding the Fun Again. 1995. pap. 10.95 (*0-925190-34-9*) Fairview Press.

— Sex & Sobriety: Facing the Fear & Building a New Sexual Life. 208p. (Orig.). 1993. pap. 9.00 (*0-671-76835-2*, Fireside) S&S Trade.

Mumey, Jack & Tinsley, Cynthia. Age Different Relationships: The Pleasures, the Pitfalls. 192p. 1993. 9.95 (*0-925190-65-9*) Fairview Press.

Mumey, Nolie. Life of Jim Baker. 1976. 22.95 (*0-8488-0246-2*) Amereon Ltd.

Mumford & Jedynakiewicz. Principles of Endodontics. 1988. pap. text ed. 52.00 (*1-85097-006-8*, 1569) Quint Pub Co.

Mumford, jt. auth. see Smith.

Mumford, Alan. Gower Handbook of Management Development. 4th ed. 600p. 1995. 93.95 (*0-566-07445-1*, Pub. by Gower UK) Ashgate Pub Co.

— How Managers Can Develop Managers. 240p. 1993. 49.95 (*0-566-07403-6*, Pub. by Gower UK) Ashgate Pub Co.

— Learning at the Top. LC 95-790. 1995. 19.95 (*0-07-709066-7*) McGraw.

— Management Development: Strategies for Action. 256p. (C). 1989. 125.00 (*0-685-34646-3*, Pub. by IPM Hse UK); 110.00 (*0-85292-426-7*, Pub. by IPM Hse UK) St Mut.

— Management Development: Strategies for Action. 248p. (C). 1993. pap. text ed. 79.00 (*0-85292-518-2*, Pub. by IPM Hse UK) St Mut.

Mumford, Amy R. It Hurts to Lose a Special Person. (Accent Expressions Ser.). (Illus.). 24p. (Orig.). 1982. 4.99 (*0-89636-093-8*, LifeJourney) Chariot Family.

— It Only Hurts Between Paydays: A Handbook for Personal Money Management. rev. ed. LC 80-70679. 160p. 1992. pap. 8.99 (*0-89636-067-9*, LifeJourney) Chariot Family.

Mumford, Anne & Henderson, Loften. The CGM Handbook. (Illus.). 480p. 1993. text ed. 59.95 (*0-12-510560-6*) Acad Pr.

***Mumford, Bob.** Fifteen Steps Out. 137p. 1969. 3.95 (*0-88270-106-1*) Bridge Pub.

— Take Another Look at Guidance: Proven Methods to Help You Sail Through Life's Tough Choices. 192p. 1993. pap. 7.95 (*1-884004-01-6*) Lifechangers.

Mumford, C. J., jt. auth. see Carson, P. A.

Mumford, C. J., jt. auth. see Carson, P.

Mumford, Claire, illus. The Nile. (Butterfly Bks.). 32p. (J). (gr. 3-5). 1983. 7.95 (*0-86685-447-9*) Intl Bk Ctr.

Mumford, Clive, jt. auth. see Carson, Phillip.

Mumford, D. The Red Book of Varieties & Schemes. (Lecture Notes in Mathematics Ser.: Vol. 1358). v, 309p. 1994. pap. 35.00 (*0-387-50497-4*) Spr-Verlag.

Mumford, D., jt. ed. see Artin, M.

Mumford, D., jt. ed. see Hironaka, H.

Mumford, D., jt. auth. see Nitzberg, M.

Mumford, D., et al. Geometric Invariant Theory. 3rd enl. ed. (Ergebnisse der Mathematik und Ihrer Grenzgebiete Ser.: Vol. 2). 320p. 1993. write for info. (*3-540-56963-4*) Spr-Verlag.

— Geometric Invariant Theory. 3rd enl. ed. (Ergebnisse der Mathematik und Ihrer Grenzgebiete Ser.: Vol. 34). 320p. 1995. 98.00 (*0-387-56963-4*) Spr-Verlag.

— Tata Lectures on Theta III. (Progress in Mathematics Ser.: Vol. 97). vii, 202p. 1991. 49.50 (*0-8176-3440-1*) Spr-Verlag.

***Mumford, David.** Algebraic Geometry I: Complex Projective Varieties. 2nd ed. LC 94-39113. (Classics in Mathematics Ser.). 1994. write for info. (*3-540-58657-1*) Spr-Verlag.

— An Atlas of Kleinian Groups. (Illus.). 120p. 1994. write for info. (*0-521-35253-3*) Cambridge U Pr.

— Tata Lecture Notes on Theta Functions, Vol. 1. (Progress in Mathematics Ser.: Vol.43). 220p. 1994. text ed. 34.50 (*0-8176-3109-7*) Birkhauser.

— Tata Lecture Notes on Theta Functions, Vol. 2. (Progress in Mathematics Ser.: Vol.43). 200p. 1993. text ed. 36.50 (*0-8176-3110-0*) Birkhauser.

Mumford, David, jt. ed. see Artin, Michael.

Mumford, E., ed. see IFIP Conference Staff.

Mumford, E., jt. auth. see Legge, K.

Mumford, E., et al, eds. Research Methods in Information Systems: Proceedings of the IFIP WG 8.2 Colloquium, Manchester Business School, 1-3 September 1984. 320p. 1985. 72.00 (*0-444-87807-6*, North Holland) Elsevier.

Mumford, Enid & Macdonald, Bruce. Xsel's Progress: The Continuing Journey of an Expert System. (Series in Information Systems). 241p. 1989. text ed. 64.95 (*0-471-92322-2*) Wiley.

Mumford, Enid & Ward, T. B. Computers: Planning for People. (Modern Management Ser.). (Illus.). 176p. (C). 1968. text ed. 25.00 (*0-8464-1177-6*) Beekman Pubs.

Mumford, Enid, jt. ed. see Cooper, Cary L.

Mumford, Erika. Willow Water. 120p. (Orig.). 1988. pap. 7.95 (*0-9619960-1-3*) Every Other Thursday.

— Words for Myself. 48p. (Orig.). 1992. pap. 8.95 (*0-9619960-2-1*) Every Other Thursday.

Mumford, Esther H. Calabash: A Guide to the History, Culture, & Art of African Americans in Seattle & King County, Washington. (Illus.). 158p. (Orig.). 1993. pap. 9.95 (*0-9605670-7-0*) Ananse Pr.

— The Man Who Founded a Town. (Washington Biography Ser.). (Illus.). 32p. (Orig.). (J). (gr. 2-5). 1990. 8.95 (*0-9605670-2-X*); pap. 4.95 (*0-9605670-3-8*) Ananse Pr.

— Seattle's Black Victorians: Eighteen Fifty-Two to Nineteen One. (Illus.). 253p. (Orig.). 1980. pap. 7.95 (*0-9605670-0-3*) Ananse Pr.

— Seven Stars & Orion: Reflections of the Past. (Illus.). 112p. (Orig.). 1986. pap. 7.95 (*0-9605670-1-1*) Ananse Pr.

Mumford, J. Endodontics: Diagnosis & Treatment of Pulp Disease & Its Sequelae. LC 66-17269. (Series on Dentistry: No. 4). 1966. 76.00 (*0-08-011739-2*, Pub. by Pergamon Repr UK) Franklin.

Mumford, J., jt. auth. see Norton, G.

***Mumford, John.** A Chakra & Kundalini Workbook: Psycho-Spiritual Techniques for Health Rejuvenation, Psychic Powers & Spiritual Realization. 2nd enl. rev. ed. LC 94-41231. 1994. pap. 15.00 (*1-56718-474-X*) Llewellyn Pubns.

Mumford, Jonn. Ecstasy Through Tantra. 3rd ed. LC 87-45734. (Tantra & Sexual Arts Ser.). (Illus.). 208p. 1987. pap. 12.95 (*0-87542-494-5*) Llewellyn Pubns.

***Mumford, Laura S.** Plotting Patriarchy: Soap Opera, Women, & Television Genre. LC 94-44239. (Arts & Politics of the Everyday Ser.). 1995. write for info. (*0-253-32879-9*); pap. write for info. (*0-253-20965-X*) Ind U Pr.

Mumford, Lewis. Art & Technics. LC 52-1930. (Bampton Lectures in America: No. 4). 62p. 1972. text ed. 34.00 (*0-231-01903-3*); pap. text ed. 14.00 (*0-231-08509-5*) Col U Pr.

— Brown Decades. 266p. 1993. reprint ed. lib. bdg. 79.00 (*0-7812-5302-0*) Rprt Serv.

— The Brown Decades: A Study of the Arts in America, 1865-1895. 2nd ed. 1955. pap. 4.95 (*0-486-20200-3*) Dover.

— The City in History: Its Origins, Its Transformations & Its Prospects. LC 61-7689. 1968. reprint ed. pap. 22.95 (*0-15-618035-9*, Harvest Bks) HarBrace.

— The Condition of Man. LC 72-91160. (Illus.). 467p. 1973. reprint ed. pap. 9.95 (*0-15-621550-0*, Harvest Bks) HarBrace.

— Conduct of Life. LC 51-12387. 342p. 1960. pap. 7.95 (*0-15-621600-0*, Harvest Bks) HarBrace.

— The Culture of Cities. LC 80-23130. (Illus.). xviii, 586p. 1981. reprint ed. text ed. 52.50 (*0-313-22746-2*, MUCC, Greenwood Pr) Greenwood.

— The Culture of Cities. LC 32-27277. 586p. 1970. reprint ed. pap. 19.95 (*0-15-623301-0*, Harvest Bks) HarBrace.

— From the Ground Up: Observations on Contemporary Architecture, Housing, Highway Building, & Civic Design. LC 56-13736. 243p. (Orig.). 1956. pap. 12.95 (*0-15-634019-4*, Harvest Bks) HarBrace.

— The Future of Technics & Civilization. 184p. 1986. reprint ed. pap. 9.00 (*0-900384-32-8*) Left Bank.

— Herman Melville. (BCL1-PS American Literature Ser.). 377p. 1992. reprint ed. lib. bdg. 89.00 (*0-7812-6797-8*) Rprt Serv.

— Herman Melville. 377p. 1993. reprint ed. lib. bdg. 89.00 (*0-7812-5280-6*) Rprt Serv.

— The Highway & the City. LC 80-22641. viii, 246p. 1981. reprint ed. text ed. 38.50 (*0-313-22747-0*, MUHC, Greenwood Pr) Greenwood.

— The Human Way Out. (C). 1958. pap. 3.00 (*0-87574-097-9*) Pendle Hill.

— Interpretations & Forecasts Nineteen Twenty-Two to Nineteen Seventy-Two: Studies in Literature, History, Biography, Technics, & Contemporary Society. LC 79-10266. 522p. 1979. pap. 5.95 (*0-15-644903-X*, Harvest Bks) HarBrace.

— Myth of the Machine, 2 vols. Incl. Vol. 1. Technics & Human Development. 1971. reprint ed. pap. 19.95 (*0-15-662341-2*, Harvest Bks); Vol. 2. Myth of the Machine. 496p. 1974. reprint ed. pap. 19.95 (*0-15-671610-0*, Harvest Bks); (Illus.). Set pap. write for info. (*0-318-52958-0*, Harvest Bks) HarBrace.

— Pentagon of Power: The Myth of the Machine, Vol. 2. LC 70-124836. (Illus.). 496p. 1970. 12.95 (*0-15-163974-4*) HarBrace.

— Roots of Contemporary American Architecture. LC 75-171490. 1972. reprint ed. pap. text ed. 8.95 (*0-486-22072-9*) Dover.

— South in Architecture. LC 67-27462. (Architecture & Decorative Art Ser.). 1967. reprint ed. lib. bdg. 25.00 (*0-306-70972-4*) Da Capo.

— Sticks & Stones. rev. ed. (Illus.). 1955. pap. 4.95 (*0-486-20202-X*) Dover.

— Sticks & Stones. 247p. 1993. reprint ed. lib. bdg. 79.00 (*0-7812-5301-2*) Rprt Serv.

— The Story of Utopias. 23.50 (*0-8446-1319-3*) Peter Smith.

— Technics & Civilization. LC 63-19641. (Illus.). 495p. 1963. pap. 18.95 (*0-15-688254-X*, Harvest Bks) HarBrace.

— The Transformations of Man. 20.75 (*0-8446-4590-7*) Peter Smith.

— Values for Survival: Essays, Addresses, & Letters on Politics & Education. LC 79-167387. (Essay Index Reprint Ser.). 1977. reprint ed. 22.95 (*0-8369-2704-4*) Ayer.

Mumford, Lewis, et al. Arts in Renewal. LC 70-84296. (Essay Index Reprint Ser.). 1977. 18.95 (*0-8369-1121-0*) Ayer.

***Mumford, Lloyd R., Jr.** Computer Consulting 101: A Beginner's How-To Guide to Becoming a Computer Consultant. Kaplan, Gale, ed. (Illus.). 104p. (C). 1995. write for info. (*0-9644847-2-2*) Lloyds Bridges.

Mumford, M. D., et al, eds. Patterns of Life History: The Ecology of Human Individuality. 512p. (C). 1990. text ed. 99.95 (*0-8058-0225-8*) L Erlbaum Assocs.

Mumford, M. J. Philosophical Perspectives on Accounting: Essays in Honour of Edward Stamp. 256p. 1992. 87.50 (*0-415-08093-2*, A9718) Routledge.

Mumford, Marilyn R., jt. ed. see Swartzlander, Susan.

Mumford, Monica G., jt. ed. see Fowler, Sandra M.

Mumford, Richard L. An American History Primer. 396p. (C). 1989. pap. text ed. 17.50 (*0-15-502344-6*) HB Coll Pubs.

M

An Asterisk (*) at the beginning of an entry indicates that the title is appearing in BIP for the first time.

Mumford, Russell E. & Keller, Charles E. The Birds of Indiana. LC 83-49454. (Illus.). 400p. 1984. 59.95 (*0-253-10736-9*) Ind U Pr.

Mumford, S. D. Vasectomy: The Decision-Making Process. (Illus.). 1978. pap. 12.50 (*0-911302-33-6*) San Francisco Pr.

— Vasectomy Counseling. (Illus.). 1977. 10.00 (*0-911302-31-X*); pap. 6.00 (*0-317-58585-1*) San Francisco Pr.

Mumford, S. R. Himalayan Dialogue - Tibetan Lamas & Gurung Shamans in Nepals. (C). 1991. text ed. 60.00 (*0-7855-0141-X*, Pub. by Ratna Pustak Bhandar) St Mut.

Mumford, Stanley R. Himalayan Dialogue: Tibetan Lamas & Gurung Shamans in Nepal. LC 88-40440. 352p. 1989. pap. text ed. 21.75 (*0-299-11984-X*) U of Wis Pr.

— Himalayan Dialogue: Tibetan Lamas & Gurung Shamans in Nepal. LC 88-40440. 352p. (C). 1990. text ed. 40.00 (*0-299-11980-7*) U of Wis Pr.

Mumford, Stephen D. American Democracy & the Vatican: Population Growth & National Security. LC 84-72500. 268p. (Orig.). 1984. 11.95 (*0-931779-00-6*); pap. 7.95 (*0-931779-01-4*) Humanist Pr.

— The Life & Death of NSSM Zoo: How the Destruction of Political Will Doomed a U.S. Population Policy. 384p. 1994. 24.95 (*0-937307-02-5*); pap. 18.95 (*0-937307-03-3*) CRPS.

— The Pope & the New Apocalypse: The Holy War Against Family Planning. (Illus.). 82p. (Orig.). 1986. 6.95 (*0-937307-00-9*); pap. 3.95 (*0-937307-01-7*) CRPS.

Mumford, Susan. Sensual Massage: The Joy of Touch. LC 93-38649. Orig. Title: Sensual Touch. 128p. 1994. pap. 14.95 (*0-8069-0479-8*) Sterling.

Mumford, Thomas F., Jr., jt. auth. see Cheney, Daniel P.

Mumford, Thomas M. Horizontal Harmony of the Four Gospels in Parallel Columns: (King James Version) LC 90-6346. xiii, 169p. 1982. pap. 5.99 (*0-87747-942-9*) Deseret Bk.

Mumford, William W., et al. Noise Performance Factors in Communication Systems. LC 68-5234. (Illus.). 97p. reprint ed. pap. 27.70 (*0-317-09124-7*, 2010075) Bks Demand.

Mu'Min, Ridgely A. Amen: The Secret Waters of the Great Pyramid. (Illus.). 196p. (Orig.). 1988. lib. bdg. 29.95 (*0-317-93344-2*); pap. 16.95 (*0-317-93345-0*) AM Distributors.

Mumm, Debbie. More Quick Country Quilting: Over Sixty New Fast & Fun Projects from the Author of Quick Country Quilting. (Illus.). 256p. 1994. 26.95 (*0-87596-627-6*) Rodale Pr Inc.

— Quick Country Christmas Quilts. LC 95-9830. Date not set. 27.95 (*0-87596-653-5*) Rodale Pr Inc.

— Quick Country Quilting: Over 80 Projects Featuring Easy, Timesaving Techniques. LC 91-27283. (Illus.). 256p. 1991. 27.95 (*0-87857-984-2*, 11-314-0) Rodale Pr Inc.

***Mumm, Robert C.** Photometrics Handbook. 245p. (Orig.). (C). Date not set. pap. 15.00 (*0-614-07059-7*) Broadway Pr.

***Mumma, Albert.** Environmental Law: Meeting U. K. & E. C. Requirements. LC 95-5091. 1995. write for info. (*0-07-707952-3*) McGraw.

Mumma, Barbara J. Two to Tango. (Silver Skates Ser.: No. 4). (J). (gr. 6 up). 1989. pap. 2.95 (*0-449-13466-0*) Fawcett.

***Mumma, George.** A Cowboy's First Christmas. (Illus.). 24p. (Orig.). (J). (ps-6). Date not set. pap. write for info. (*0-9645687-0-5*) New Wine Pub.

Mumma, Michael J. & Smith, Harlan J., eds. Astrophysics from the Moon. LC 90-55582. (Conference Proceeding Ser.: No. 207). (Illus.). 696p. 1990. 85.00 (*0-88318-770-1*) Am Inst Physics.

Mumma, Ralph O., jt. ed. see Von Emon, Jeanette M.

Mummah, Hazel & Smith, Marsella. The Geriatric Assistant. (Illus.). 320p. 1980. text ed. 24.95 (*0-07-044015-8*) McGraw.

Mummaw, Ron, jt. auth. see Mowe, Richard.

Mumme, jt. auth. see Balchen, Jens G.

Mumme, I. A. The Emerald. 158p. (C). 1989. text ed. 40.00 (*0-89771-023-1*, Pub. by Bob Mossel AT) St Mut.

— The World of Sapphires. 212p. (C). 1989. pap. text ed. 70.00 (*0-89771-027-4*, Pub. by Bob Mossel AT) St Mut.

Mumme, Patricia Y. The Srivaisnava Theological Dispute - Manavalamamuni & Bedanta Desika. (C). 1988. 25.00 (*0-8364-2453-0*, Pub. by New Era Pubns) S Asia.

Mumme, Patricia Y., jt. ed. see Fort, Andrew O.

Mumme, Ronald L., jt. auth. see Koenig, Walter D.

Mumme, Stephen P. Apportioning Groundwater Beneath the U. S.-Mexico Border. (Research Report Ser.: No. 45). 54p. 1988. ring bd. 5.00 (*0-935391-79-7*, RR-45) UCSD Ctr US-Mex.

Mummert, J. Abiding in Christ. 1991. 6.95 (*0-937032-79-4*) Light&Life Pub Co MN.

Mummert, John R. & Bach, Jeff. Refugee Ministry in the Local Congregation. 128p. (Orig.). 1992. pap. 9.95 (*0-8361-3580-6*) Herald Pr.

Mummery, A. F. & Hobson, John A. Physiology of Industry: Being an Exposure of Certain Fallacies in Existing Theories of Economics. LC 87-17943. (Reprints of Economic Classics Ser.). xvii, 215p. reprint ed. 29.50 (*0-678-00673-3*) Kelley.

Mummery, W. Kerry, jt. auth. see Sefton, Judy M.

***Mumper, Michael.** Removing College Price Barriers: What Government Has Done & Why It Hasn't Worked. (SUNY Series). 320p. 1995. 74.50x (*0-7914-2703-X*) State U NY Pr.

— Removing College Price Barriers: What Government Has Done & Why It Hasn't Worked. (SUNY Series). 320p. (C). 1995. pap. 24.95x (*0-7914-2704-8*) State U NY Pr.

Mumpower, Carl. Intraactive Therapy: A Practical Approach to Effective Short-Term Treatment. 164p. (Orig.). (C). 1992. lib. bdg. 21.50 (*0-89464-611-7*) Krieger.

— Vietnam: Coming All the Way Home. (Illus.). 112p. (Orig.). 1992. pap. 9.95 (*1-56664-008-3*) WorldComm.

Mumpower, J., et al, eds. Expert Judgement & Expert Systems. (NATO Asi Series F: Vol. 35). viii, 361p. 1987. 71.00 (*0-387-17986-0*) Spr-Verlag.

Mumpower, Jeryl L. & Ilchman, Warren F., eds. New York State in the Year 2000. LC 87-6486. 572p. 1988. 69.50 (*0-88706-602-X*) State U NY Pr.

MUMPS Development Committee Staff. American National Standards for Information System - Programming Languages - MUMPS. 1990. 30.00 (*0-918118-37-9*) M Technol.

MUMPS Users' Group Staff. Proceedings of the MUMPS Users' Group Meeting. Faulkner, Judith R., ed. 1979. 20. 00 (*0-918118-06-9*) M Technol.

— Proceedings of the MUMPS Users' Group Meeting, 1973. Zimmerman, Joan, ed. 20.00 (*0-918118-00-X*) M Technol.

— Proceedings of the MUMPS Users' Group Meeting, 1974. Zimmerman, Joan, ed. 20.00 (*0-918118-01-8*) M Technol.

— Proceedings of the MUMPS Users' Group Meeting, 1978. Zimmerman, Pat, ed. 1978. pap. 20.00 (*0-918118-05-0*) M Technol.

Mumpton, F. A., jt. ed. see Mackinnon, I. D.

Mumpton, F. A., jt. ed. see Pevear, D. R.

Mumpton, F. A., jt. ed. see Sand, L. B.

Mumtamayee, C. Rural Ecology. (C). 1989. 34.00 (*81-7024-231-2*, Pub. by Ashish II) S Asia.

Mumtaz Ali Khan. Scheduled Castes & Their Status in India. 276p. 1980. 23.50 (*0-940500-23-X*) Asia Bk Corp.

Mumy, et al. Dreamwalker. 64p. 1988. 6.95 (*0-87135-550-7*) Marvel Entmnt.

Mun, J. & M'Baye, A. A., eds. Gallium Arsenide Technology in Europe. LC 94-15890. (Research Reports ESPRIT, Project Group Microelectronic Ser.: Vol. 1). viii, 388p. 1994. pap. 53.00 (*0-387-57906-0*) Spr-Verlag.

Mun, Joseph. Gallium Arsenide Integrated Circuits. 352p. 1988. text ed. 70.00 (*0-07-044025-5*) McGraw.

Mun, Thomas. A Discourse of Trade. LC 30-21325. 39p. 1988. reprint ed. pap. 5.00 (*0-942153-22-7*) Entropy Conserv.

— A Discourse of Trade, from England unto the East-Indies. LC 68-30534. (Reprints of Economic Classics Ser.). 58p. 1971. reprint ed. 17.50 (*0-678-00873-6*) Kelley.

— A Discourse of Trade Unto the East Indies. LC 72-6257. (English Experience Ser.: No. 85). 58p. 1969. reprint ed. 11.50 (*90-221-0085-5*) Walter J Johnson.

— England's Treasure by Forraign Trade. LC 86-7467. (Reprints of Economic Classics Ser.). vii, 88p. 1986. reprint ed. 19.50 (*0-678-06274-9*) Kelley.

Munakata, Kiyohiko. Sacred Mountains in Chinese Art. (Illus.). 208p. (Orig.). 1991. pap. 39.95 (*0-252-06188-8*) U of Ill Pr.

Munakata, Shiko & Kodansha International Staff. The Woodblock & the Artist: The Life & Work of Shiko Munakata. (Illus.). 144p. 1992. 35.00 (*4-7700-1612-3*) Kodansha.

Munakata, Toshinori. Matrices & Linear Programming with Business Applications. LC 78-54198. 1979. text ed. 36. 95 (*0-8162-6166-0*); 6.00 (*0-8162-6167-9*) Holden-Day.

Munan, Heidi. Culture Shock: Malaysia. (Illus.). 1991. pap. 10.95 (*1-55868-070-5*) Gr Arts Ctr Pub.

— Malaysia. LC 89-25464. (Cultures of the World Ser.: Group 1: Asia). (Illus.). 128p. (YA). (gr. 5-9). 1991. lib. bdg. 21.95 (*1-85435-296-2*) Marshall Cavendish.

Munashinge, Mohan, ed. Environmental Economics & Natural Resource Management in Developing Countries. 326p. 1993. 17.95 (*0-8213-2670-8*, 12670) World Bank.

Munasingh, M. Energy Economic Demand: Management & Conservation Policy. 35.95 (*0-685-19116-8*) Van Nos Reinhold.

Munasinghe, Mohan. The Economics of Power System Reliability & Planning: Theory & Case Study. LC 79-2182. (World Bank Book Ser.). 344p. 1980. pap. text ed. 14.95 (*0-8018-2277-7*) Johns Hopkins.

— Electric Power Economics. (Illus.). 323p. 1990. text ed. 110.00 (*0-408-05622-3*) Buttrwrth-Heinemann.

— Energy Analysis & Policy. (Illus.). 320p. 1990. text ed. 110.00 (*0-408-05634-7*) Buttrwrth-Heinemann.

— Environmental Economics & Sustainable Development. LC 92-42952. (Environment Paper Ser.: No. 3). 120p. 1993. 7.95 (*0-8213-2352-0*, 12352) World Bank.

***Munasinghe, Mohan, ed.** Environmental Impacts of Macroeconomic Policies. LC 95-13305. 1995. write for info. (*0-8213-3225-2*) World Bank.

***Munasinghe, Mohan & Cruz, Wilfrido.** Economywide Policies & the Environment: Lessons from Experience. LC 94-45027. (World Bank Environment Paper Ser.: No. 10). 96p. 1995. 7.95 (*0-8213-3153-1*, 13153) World Bank.

***Munasinghe, Mohan & McNeely, Jeffrey A.** Protected Area Economics & Policy: Linking Conservation & Sustainable Development. LC 94-45272. 372p. 1995. 21. 95 (*0-8213-3132-9*, 13132) World Bank.

Munasinghe, Mohan & Meier, Peter. Energy Policy Analysis & Modelling. (Studies in Energy & the Environment). 320p. (C). 1993. 59.95 (*0-521-36326-8*) Cambridge U Pr.

Munasinghe, Mohan & Warford, Jeremy J. Electricity Pricing: Theory & Case Studies. LC 81-47613. 400p. reprint ed. pap. 114.00 (*0-7837-4405-6*, 2044145) Bks Demand.

Munasinghe, Mohan, jt. ed. see Guarnizo, Caroline.

Munasinghe, Mohan, jt. auth. see Meier, Peter.

Munasinghe, Mohan, et al, eds. Conservation of West & Central African Rainforests: Conservation de la Foret Dense en Afrique Centrale et de l'Ouest. LC 92-26870. (Technical Paper, 1253-7494 Environment Ser.: No. 1). 366p. (ENG & FRE.). 1992. 21.95 (*0-8213-2256-7*, 12256) World Bank.

— Defining & Measuring Sustainability: The Biophysical Foundation. LC 95-2865. 1995. write for info. (*0-8213-3134-5*) World Bank.

Munavvar, Mohamed. Ocean States: Archipelagic Regimes in the Law of the Sea. LC 94-13947. (Publications on Ocean Development: Vol. 22). 240p. (C). 1995. lib. bdg. 110.00 (*0-7923-2882-5*) Kluwer Ac.

Munawar, M., ed. Limnology & Fisheries of Georgian Bay & the North Channel Ecosystems. (Developments in Hydrobiology Ser.). 1988. lib. bdg. 162.00 (*90-6193-653-5*) Kluwer Ac.

— The Phycology of Large Lakes of the World: Proceedings of an International Symposium Held at St. John's, Newfoundland, Canada. (Ergebnisse der Limnologie Ser.: No. 25). (Illus.). 256p. 1987. pap. text ed. 68.00 (*3-510-47023-0*) Lubrecht & Cramer.

— Symposium on the Phycology of Large Lakes of the World. (Limnology Report: No. 22). (Illus.). (Orig.). 1985. pap. text ed. 87.50 (*0-317-63452-6*, Pub. by E Schweizerbartsche GW) Lubrecht & Cramer.

Munawar, M. & Edsall, T., eds. Environmental Assessment & Habitat Evaluation of the Upper Great Lakes Connecting Channels. (Developments in Hydrobiology Ser.). (C). 1991. lib. bdg. 193.50 (*0-7923-1206-6*) Kluwer Ac.

Munawar, M. & Talling, J. F., eds. Seasonality of Freshwater Phytoplankton. (Developments in Hydrobiology Ser.). 1986. lib. bdg. 147.00 (*90-6193-577-6*) Kluwer Ac.

Munawar, M., et al, eds. Environmental Bioassay Techniques & Their Application: Proceedings of the First International Conference Held in Lancaster, England, 11-14 July 1988. (C). 1990. lib. bdg. 307.00 (*0-7923-0498-5*) Kluwer Ac.

Munawwar, Muhammad. Dimensions of Pakistan Movement. 367p. 1987. 39.95 (*1-56744-261-7*) Kazi Pubns.

Munby, Denys. Road Passenger Transport & Road Goods Transport. Manunder, W. F., ed. LC 77-30558. 1978. 63. 00 (*0-08-022449-0*, Pub. by Pergamon Repr UK) Franklin.

Munby, Denys L. God & the Rich Society: A Study of Christians in a World of Abundance. LC 85-21886. v, 218p. 1985. reprint ed. text ed. 55.00 (*0-313-24925-3*, MGRS, Greenwood Pr) Greenwood.

Munby, Hugh, jt. ed. see Russell, Tom.

Munby, Hugh, et al, eds. Seeing Curriculum in a New Light: Essays from Science Education. 190p. 1984. reprint ed. pap. text ed. 20.50 (*0-8191-4238-7*) U Pr of Amer.

Munby, John. Communicative Syllabus Design: A Sociolinguistic Model for Defining the Content of Purpose-Specific Language Programmes. 232p. 1981. pap. 17.95 (*0-521-28294-2*) Cambridge U Pr.

Muncaster, Alice L. & Sawyer, Ellen Y. The Black Cat Made Me Buy It! (Illus.). 96p. 1988. pap. 12.95 (*0-517-56891-8*, Crown) Crown Pub Group.

— The Cat Sold It! The Feline Stars of the Advertising World. (Illus.). 96p. 1987. pap. 14.00 (*0-517-56303-7*, Crown) Crown Pub Group.

Muncaster, Alice L. & Yanow, Ellen. The Cat Made Me Buy It: A Collection of Cats Who Sold Yesterday's Products. (Illus.). 1984. pap. 12.00 (*0-517-55338-4*, Crown) Crown Pub Group.

Muncaster, Alice L., et al. The Baby Made Me Buy It! A Treasury of Babies Who Sold Yesterday's Products. (Illus.). 96p. 1991. pap. 14.00 (*0-517-58206-6*, Crown) Crown Pub Group.

Muncaster, Alice M. Dog Made Me Buy It. 1990. pap. 12. 95 (*0-517-57453-5*, Crown) Crown Pub Group.

Muncaster, Barbara & Prescott, Susan. Computer Calculator. LC 93-4198. 1994. pap. 8.95 (*0-538-62332-2*) S-W Pub.

Muncaster, R. A-Level Physics. (C). 1989. text ed. 140.00 (*0-7487-0050-1*, Pub. by S Thornes Pubs UK) St Mut.

— A Level Physics. (C). 1987. text ed. 40.00 (*0-85950-815-3*, Pub. by S Thornes Pubs UK) St Mut.

Muncaster, R. G., jt. auth. see Cohen, H.

***Muncaster, Roger.** A-Level Physics. 960p. (C). 1994. pap. 57.00x (*0-7478-1584-4*, Pub. by S Thornes Pubs UK) St Mut.

Munce, Howard. Sounds from the Bullpen. 80p. 1983. pap. 17.95 (*0-942604-01-6*) Madison Square.

Munce, R. H. Ruth. 117p. 1971. 3.95 (*0-914674-00-5*) Freelandia.

Munce, Robert. Grace Livingston Hill. 176p. 1986. pap. 8.95 (*0-8423-1179-3*) Tyndale.

Munce, Robert L. Grace Livingston Hill Story. 1990. pap. 3.99 (*0-8423-1172-6*) Tyndale.

Muncey, Jim, jt. auth. see Ainscow, Mel.

Muncey, R. W. Heat Transfer Calculations for Buildings. (Illus.). vii, 110p. 1979. 41.50 (*0-85334-852-9*, Pub. by Elsevier Applied Sci UK) Elsevier.

Munch, Christopher H., jt. auth. see Dorr, Robert C.

Munch, Christopher H., jt. ed. see Dorr, Robert C.

Munch, Edvard. Graphic Works of Edvard Munch. (Illus.). 1979. pap. 8.95 (*0-486-23765-6*) Dover.

Munch, Freidrich, tr. see Boernstein, Henry.

Munch, Helen, ed. see Brookes, Gay & Withrow, Jean.

Munch, Helen, ed. see Haverson, Wayne W. & Haverson, Susan.

Munch, Helen, ed. see Kuntz, Laurie.

Munch, Helen, jt. auth. see Kunz, Linda A.

Munch, James C., Jr. Financial & Estate Planning with Life Insurance Products. 750p. 1989. 125.00 (*0-316-58941-1*) Little.

— Financial Planning Set. 1990. 125.00 (*0-316-58947-0*) Little.

— Life Insurance in Estate Planning. suppl. ed. LC 80-84027. (C). 1981. text ed. 80.00 (*0-316-58932-2*) Little.

Munch, Peter A. Norse Mythology, Legends of Gods & Heroes. Hustvedt, Sigurd B., tr. LC 74-112002. 1970. reprint ed. 49.50 (*0-404-04538-3*) AMS Pr.

— Sociology of Tristan da Cunha: Results of the Norwegian Scientific Expedition to Tristan da Cunha, 1937-1938. LC 77-87549. reprint ed. 30.00 (*0-404-16511-7*) AMS Pr.

Munch-Petersen, Agnete, ed. Metabolism of Nucleotides, Nucleosides & Nucleobases in Microorganisms. 1983. text ed. 125.00 (*0-12-510580-0*) Acad Pr.

Munch-Petersen, Thomas, tr. see Nissen, Henrik S., ed.

Munch, R., jt. ed. see Murthy, T. K.

Munch, Richard. Sociological Theory, Set, Vols. 1-3. 1088p. 1994. Set. text ed. 51.95 (*0-8304-1394-4*) Nelson-Hall.

— Sociological Theory I: From the 1850s to the 1920s, 2 vols., I. LC 92-39833. (Sociology Ser.). 1994. pap. text ed. 22.95 (*0-8304-1255-7*) Nelson-Hall.

— Sociological Theory III: Development since the 1960s. (Sociology Ser.). 400p. 1994. pap. text ed. 24.95 (*0-8304-1342-1*) Nelson-Hall.

— Theory of Action: Towards a New Synthesis Going Beyond Parsons. 358p. (C). 1988. text ed. 67.50 (*0-7102-1218-6*, RKP) Routledge.

— Understanding Modernity: Towards a New Perspective Going Beyond Durkheim & Webber. (International Library of Sociology). 356p. 1988. text ed. 75.00 (*0-415-01283-X*) Routledge.

Munch, Richard & Smelser, Neil, eds. Theory of Culture. 435p. 1994. 50.00 (*0-520-07598-6*); pap. 17.00 (*0-520-07599-4*) U CA Pr.

Munch, Richard W. Harry G. Travers: Legends of Terror. Hershey, Richard & Bush, Lee, eds. (Roller Coaster Designers Ser.). (Illus.). 175p. (C). 1982. pap. 19.95 (*0-935408-02-9*) Amusement Pk Bks.

Munch, William H., Jr. Homeless Mind. 288p. 1992. pap. 12.95 (*1-880977-03-6*) Watusi.

Muncheryan, Hrand M. Laser & Optoelectronic Engineering. 336p. 1991. 116.00 (*1-56032-062-1*) Hemisp Pub.

— Laser Systems & Devices Handbook. 1988. 49.95 (*0-8306-9339-4*, TAB/TPR) TAB Bks.

— Principles & Practice of Laser Technology. (Illus.). 294p. 1983. 15.95 (*0-8306-0129-5*) TAB Bks.

Munchow, L. & Reif, R. Recent Developments in the Nuclear Many Body Problems. 152p. (C). 1985. 60.00 (*0-685-36856-4*, Pub. by Collets) St Mut.

Munchow, Michael, jt. ed. see Shamdasani, Sonu.

Muncie, John & Sparks, Richard, eds. Imprisonment: European Perspectives. LC 91-33872. 280p. 1991. text ed. 49.95 (*0-312-07482-4*) St Martin.

***Muncie, John, et al, eds.** Understanding the Family. 320p. 1995. 65.00 (*0-8039-7954-1*) Sage.

— Understanding the Family. 320p. 1995. pap. 21.95 (*0-8039-7955-X*) Sage.

Munck, J. L. The Kornilov Revolt: A Critical Examination of Sources & Research. Schmidt, T. K., tr. (Illus.). 175p. (Orig.). 1987. pap. 35.00x (*87-7288-040-6*) Coronet Bks.

Munck, L., jt. ed. see Hill, R. D.

Munck, Lars, jt. ed. see Pomeranz, Y.

Munck, Ronaldo. The Difficult Dialogue: Marxism & Nationalism. 192p. (C). 1986. pap. 15.00 (*0-86232-494-7*, Pub. by Zed Books UK) Humanities.

— Latin America: The Transition of Democracy. LC 89-36323. 224p. (C). 1989. text ed. 49.95 (*0-86232-818-7*, Pub. by Zed Books UK); pap. 17.50 (*0-86232-819-5*, Pub. by Zed Books UK) Humanities.

— The New International Labour Studies: An Introduction. LC 88-27566. 256p. (C). 1988. text ed. 49.95 (*0-86232-586-2*, Pub. by Zed Books UK); pap. 17.50 (*0-86232-587-0*, Pub. by Zed Books UK) Humanities.

Munck, Ronaldo, et al. Argentina from Anarchism to Peronism: Workers, Unions & Politics, 1855-1985. (Illus.). 276p. (C). 1987. text ed. 45.00 (*0-86232-570-6*, Pub. by Zed Books UK); pap. 17.50 (*0-86232-571-4*, Pub. by Zed Books UK) Humanities.

Munck, Ronnie. The Irish Economy: Results and Prospects. LC 92-45632. 256p. (C). 1993. text ed. 63.00 (*0-7453-0673-X*); pap. text ed. 19.95 (*0-7453-0674-8*) Westview.

Munck, Ronnie & Rolston, Bill. Belfast in the Thirties: An Oral History. LC 85-18395. 256p. 1987. text ed. 39.95 (*0-312-07424-7*) St Martin.

Munck, Thomas. Seventeenth Century Europe: State, Conflict & the Social Order in Europe 1598-1700. LC 89-10893. 480p. 1990. text ed. 45.00 (*0-312-04011-3*); pap. 14.95 (*0-312-04012-1*) St Martin.

Munck, Thomas, jt. auth. see Mawdsley, Evan.

Muncy, Harold W., ed. Asphalt Emulsions, No. 1079. LC 89-49641. (Special Technical Publication Ser.). (Illus.). 122p. 1990. text ed. 32.00 (*0-8031-1457-5*, 04-010790-08) ASTM.

Muncy, Lysbeth W. The Junker in the Prussian Administration under William II, 1888-1914. LC 70-80574. 1970. reprint ed. 40.00 (*0-86527-112-7*) Fertig.

Muncy, Pat. The Reading Teacher's Almanack: Hundreds of Practical Ideas, Games, Activities, Bulletin Boards, & Reproducibles for Every Month of the Year. 272p. 1991. 27.95 (*0-87628-791-7*) P-H.

Muncy, Patricia T. Complete Book of Illustrated K-3 Alphabet Games & Activities. 1980. 24.95 (*0-87628-230-3*) Ctr Appl Res.

— Hooked on Books! Activities & Projects That Make Kids Want to Read. LC 94-31460. 1994. pap. text ed. 27.95 (*0-87628-411-X*) Ctr Appl Res.

— Springboards to Creative Thinking. LC 85-11389. 237p. 1985. pap. 27.95 (*0-87628-775-5*) Ctr Appl Res.

Muncy, Robyn. Creating a Female Dominion in American Reform, 1890-1935. 240p. 1994. reprint ed. pap. 13.95 (*0-19-508924-3*) OUP.

Mund, Ed, ed. see Birkland, Barbara J., et al.

Mund, Edward L., ed. see Fish, Harriet U.

An Asterisk (*) at the beginning of an entry indicates that the title is appearing in BIP for the first time.

Mund, Vernon A., jt. auth. see Wolf, Ronald H.
Munda, D. T. Fizits. (Illus.). 48p. 1993. 14.95 (*0-8048-1970-X*) C E Tuttle.
— Zen Munchkins: Little Wisdoms. (Illus.). 104p. (Orig.). 1991. pap. 12.95 (*0-8048-1640-9*) C E Tuttle.
Munda, I. M. Survey of the Benthis Algal Vegetation of the Dyrafjordur, Northwest Iceland. (Offprint from Nova Hedwigia Ser.: No. 29). (Illus.). 1978. pap. text ed. 24.00 (*3-7682-1201-7*) Lubrecht & Cramer.
Munda, Ramdayal, tr. see Bhattacarya, Jagadishvara.
Mundahl, John. Tales of Courage, Tales of Dreams: A Multicultural Reader. LC 92-42252. 1993. 11.56 (*0-201-53962-4*) Addison-Wesley.
***Mundale Communications Staff.** Investing in the Future: A Century of IDS. (Illus.). 91p. (Orig.). 1994. pap. 10.00 (*0-9640319-0-6*) IDS Finan Srvs.
Mundale, Susan, ed. see Otis, Caroline H.
Munday, A., tr. The Defence of Contraries. LC 72-188. (English Experience Ser.: No. 175). 1969. reprint ed. 13.00 (*90-221-0175-4*) Walter J Johnson.
Munday, A. R., jt. auth. see Peckett, C. W.
Munday, Anthony. John-A-Kent & John-A-Cumber. LC 70-133714. (Tudor Facsimile Texts. Old English Plays Ser.: No. 58). reprint ed. 49.50 (*0-404-53358-2*) AMS Pr.
— Sir Thomas More. Gabrieli, Vittorio et al, eds. LC 89-2528. (Revels Plays Ser.). 240p. 1990. text ed. 17.95 (*0-7190-1544-8*, Pub. by Manchester Univ Pr UK) St Martin.
Munday, Anthony & Chettle, Henry. Death of Robert Earl of Huntington. LC 73-133712. (Tudor Facsimile Texts. Old English Plays Ser.: No. 95). reprint ed. 49.50 (*0-404-53395-7*) AMS Pr.
— Downfall of Robert Earl of Huntington. LC 77-133713. (Tudor Facsimile Texts. Old English Plays Ser.: No. 94). reprint ed. 49.50 (*0-404-53394-9*) AMS Pr.
Munday, Anthony & Shakespeare, William. Sir Thomas More. LC 74-133715. (Tudor Facsimile Texts. Old English Plays Ser.: No. 65). reprint ed. 49.50 (*0-404-53365-5*) AMS Pr.
Munday, C. W., ed. see IFAC Symposium, 8th, Oxford, UK, 2-6 July 1979.
Munday, Godfrey B. The Life & Correspondence of the Late Admiral Lord Rodney, 2 vols., Set. LC 72-8677. (American Revolutionary Ser.). 970p. reprint ed. lib. bdg. 119.00 (*0-8398-1271-X*) Irvington.
Munday, J. G., jt. auth. see Dhir, R. K.
***Munday, John & Wohlenhaus-Munday, Frances.** Surviving the Death of a Child. 96p. (Orig.). 1995. pap. 9.99 (*0-664-25566-3*) Westminster John Knox.
Munday, K. & Kerkut, G. A. Studies in Comparative Biochemistry. LC 64-7813. (International Series of Monographs on Pure & Applied Mathematics: No. 23). 1965. 95.00 (*0-08-011018-5*, Pub. by Pergamon Repr UK) Franklin.
Munday, Laurie D. & Curren, Anna M. Instructor Testbank: Dosages & Solutions. 160p. 1986. teacher ed 16.95 (*0-918082-04-8*) WI Pubns Inc.
Munday, Laurie D., jt. auth. see Curren, Anna M.
Munday, Marianne. Opportunities in Crafts Careers. LC 93-17351. (Opportunities in...Ser.). 1994. 13.95 (*0-8442-4068-0*, VGM Career Bks); pap. 10.95 (*0-8442-4069-9*, VGM Career Bks) NTC Pub Grp.
Munday, Marianne F. Opportunities in Crafts Careers. (Illus.). 160p. 1988. 13.95 (*0-8442-6015-0*, VGM Career Bks); pap. 10.95 (*0-8442-6017-7*, VGM Career Bks) NTC Pub Grp.
— Opportunities in Word Processing Careers. rev. ed. LC 90-50735. (Opportunities in...Ser.). 160p. (YA). (gr. 7 up). 1991. 13.95 (*0-8442-8164-6*, VGM Career Bks); pap. 10.95 (*0-8442-8165-4*, VGM Career Bks) NTC Pub Grp.
Munday, R. J., jt. auth. see Markesinis, B. S.
Munday, Talbot. Black Light. 288p. 1991. 10.95 (*0-89804-157-0*) Ariel GA.
Munde, Alan, jt. auth. see Carr, Joe.
Munde, Gail, jt. auth. see Leonard, Susan.
Mundel, August B. Ethics in Quality. 232p. 1991. 75.00 (*0-8247-8513-4*) Dekker.
***Mundel, Marvin E.** Measuring & Enhancing the Productivity of Service & Government Organizations. 3rd ed. (Illus.). 296p. 1980. pap. text ed. 22.25 (*92-833-1030-6*, 310306, Pub. by APO JA) Qual Resc.
— Measuring the Productivity of Commercial Banks: Algorithms & PC Programs. 100p. 1987. pap. 23.95 (*0-527-91641-2*, 916412, Pub. by APO JA) Qual Resc.
— Measuring Total Productivity in Manufacturing Organization: Algorithms & PC Programs. 155p. 1987. pap. 27.95 (*0-527-91625-0*, 916250, Pub. by APO JA) Qual Resc.
— The White-Collar Knowledge Worker: Measuring & Improving Productivity & Effectiveness. 355p. 1989. pap. text ed. 36.00 (*0-685-45554-8*, 92-833-1092-0) Qual Resc.
***Mundel, Marvin E., ed.** Operational Level Productivity Measurement Analysis & Improvement. (Illus.). 213p. 1985. pap. text ed. 15.00 (*92-833-2026-3*, 320263, Pub. by APO JA) Qual Resc.
Mundel, Marvin E. & Danner, David L. BASIC-A Personal Computer Language. 322p. 1986. pap. 14.00 (*92-833-1089-6*, 310890, Pub. by APO JA) Qual Resc.
— Motion & Time Study: Improving Productivity. 7th ed. LC 93-23108. 1994. text ed. 72.00 (*0-13-588369-5*) P-H Gen Ref & Trav.
Mundell, Bryan, jt. ed. see Bacharach, Samuel B.
Mundell, E. H. Erle Stanley Gardner: A Checklist. LC 70-97619. (Serif Series: Bibliographies & Checklists: No. 6). 104p. reprint ed. pap. 29.70 (*0-8357-5577-0*, 2035204) Bks Demand.
— A List of the Original Appearances of Dashiell Hammett's Magazine Work. LC 75-97620. (Serif Series: Bibliographies & Checklists: No. 13). 52p. 1968. text ed. 15.00 (*0-87338-033-9*) Boulevard.
Mundell, E. H., comp. A List of the Original Appearances of Dashiell Hammett's Magazine Work. LC 75-97620. (Serif Series Bibliographies & Checklists: No. 13). 60p. reprint ed. pap. 25.00 (*0-317-55821-8*, 2029408) Bks Demand.
Mundell, E. H., Jr. & Rausch, G. Jay. The Detective Short Story: A Bibliography & Index. 1974. 15.00 (*0-318-22157-8*) KSU.
Mundell Mango, Marlia. Silver Treasure from Early Byzantium: The Kaper Karaon & Related Treasures. LC 86-50138. (Illus.). 125p. (Orig.). 1986. pap. 35.00 (*0-911886-32-X*) Walters Art.
Mundell, Matt. Country Diary. 208p. (C). 1989. 45.00 (*0-903065-33-9*, Pub. by G Wright Pub Ltd) St Mut.
Mundell, Matt, jt. auth. see Templeton, John.
Mundell, Robert A. & Polak, Jacques J., eds. The New International Monetary System. LC 77-10485. 244p. 1977. text ed. 46.50 (*0-231-04368-6*) Col U Pr.
Mundell, Sue & DeLario, Karen. Practical Portfolios: Reading, Writing, Math, & Life Skills, Grades 3-6. (Illus.). 160p. 1994. pap. text ed. 22.00 (*1-56308-197-0*) Teacher Ideas Pr.
Munden, D. L. & Dorkin, C. M. Developments in the Clothing Industry. 56p. 1973. 95.00 (*0-686-63760-7*) St Mut.
— Developments in the Clothing Industry, Vol. 5, No. 1. (C). 1973. pap. text ed. 85.00 (*0-685-46407-5*, Pub. by Textile Institue UK) St Mut.
Munden, Kenneth W. & Beers, Henry P. The Union: A Guide to Federal Archives Relating to the Civil War. LC 86-8363. 721p. 1986. reprint ed. text ed. 25.00 (*0-911333-46-0*, 100050) National Archives & Recs.
Munder, Barbara, jt. auth. see Barrow, Joe Louis, Jr.
Munder, Carole. Fierce Power Bad Fate. 1987. 15.00 (*0-317-61771-0*) Nexus Pr.
***Mundere, Sylvestre, et al, eds.** Guide des Responsables des Programmes de Planifaction Familiale: Aptitudes et Outils Essentiels pour la Conduite des Programmes de Planification Familiale. (Library of Management for Development). (Illus.). 420p. (Orig.). (FRE.). 1994. pap. 34.95 (*1-56549-033-9*) Kumarian Pr.
Mundfrom, Gerald F. Baptism, a Covenant. (Illus.). 130p. (Orig.). 1985. pap. text ed. 4.00 (*0-9615494-0-8*) Mercy & Truth.
— The Depressed Christian. 110p. (Orig.). 1983. 2.50 (*0-318-19335-3*) Mercy & Truth.
— Depression & What to Do about It. rev. ed. 221p. (YA). 1994. pap. 6.00x (*0-9615494-4-0*) Mercy & Truth.
— My Experience with Clinical Depression. rev. ed. Orig. Title: Purged. (Illus.). 191p. 1990. reprint ed. pap. 7.50 (*0-685-45389-8*) Mercy & Truth.
— The Threat of False Doctrine. 144p. (Orig.). 1988. pap. 5.00 (*0-9615494-2-4*) Mercy & Truth.
Mundi, Carta. Transition Tarot. 30p. 1983. 16.00 (*0-88079-057-1*) US Games Syst.
Mundie, Edward. Go Country: A Troubleshooter's Guide to Successful Country Living. 231p. Date not set. pap. 24.95 (*1-875657-17-7*, Pub. by Hyland Hse AT) Intl Spec Bk.
Mundinger, F., ed. see Stereoencephalotomy Symposium Staff.
Mundis, Hester. One Hundred One Ways to Avoid Reincarnation. LC 88-40606. 160p. 1989. pap. 6.95 (*0-89480-383-2*, 1383) Workman Pub.
Mundis, Jerrold. Break Writer's Block Now. 1991. 13.95 (*0-312-05394-0*) St Martin.
— How to Cope with Credit Cards. (Money Talks Ser.). 72p. 1993. pap. 1.95 (*1-55874-273-5*) Health Comm.
— How to Create Savings. (Money Talks Ser.). 72p. 1993. pap. 1.95 (*1-55874-272-7*) Health Comm.
— How to Free Yourself from Debt. (Money Talks Ser.). 72p. 1993. pap. 1.95 (*1-55874-274-3*, 2816) Health Comm.
— How to Get out of Debt, Stay out of Debt, & Live Prosperously. 1990. mass mkt. 5.99 (*0-553-28396-0*) Bantam.
— How to Make Friends with Money. (Money Talks Ser.). 72p. 1993. pap. 1.95 (*1-55874-271-9*) Health Comm.
— Prospering: How to Stop Underearning & Start Thriving. LC 94-10329. 1995. 19.95 (*0-553-08968-4*) Bantam.
***Mundis, Jerrold J. & Leonard, Robert E.** King of the Ice Cream Mountain. 1968. write for info. (*0-87129-437-0*, K14) Dramatic Pub.
Mundkur, Balaji. The Cult of the Serpent: An Interdisciplinary Survey of Its Manifestations & Origins. LC 82-19394. (Illus.). 363p. 1983. 69.50 (*0-87395-631-1*); pap. 24.95 (*0-87395-632-X*) State U NY Pr.
Mundlak, Yair, jt. auth. see Coeymans, Juan E.
Mundo, Philip A. Interest Groups: Cases & Characteristics. (Political Science Ser.). 350p. (C). 1992. pap. text ed. 19.95 (*0-8304-1214-X*) Nelson-Hall.
Mundry, E. & Homilius, J. Three Layer Model Curves for Geoelectrical Curves for Geoelectrical Measurements: Schlumberger Array Log Cycle 83,33mm. (Illus.). (ENG & GER.). 1980. spiral bd. 110.50 (*0-945345-07-0*, Pub. by Schweitzerbart'sche GW) Lubrecht & Cramer.
Mundsack, Allan. How to Prepare for the ELM - California Entry Level Mathematics Test. 480p. 1992. pap. 11.95 (*0-8120-4904-7*) Barron.
Mundt. Occupational Surveillance. 1995. write for info. (*0-87371-602-7*) Lewis Pubs.
Mundt, C., jt. ed. see Gerbaldo, H.
***Mundt, Robert J.** Historical Dictionary of Cote d'Ivoire (the Ivory Coast) 2nd ed. LC 95-10313. (African Historical Dictionaries Ser.: Vol. 41). 1995. write for info. (*0-8108-3015-9*) Scarecrow.
— Historical Dictionary of the Ivory Coast (Cote D'Ivoire) LC 87-12724. (African Historical Dictionaries Ser.: No. 41). (Illus.). 246p. 1987. 29.50 (*0-8108-2029-3*) Scarecrow.
Mundus, Frank. Monster Man. 1976. 20.95 (*0-8488-0407-4*); pap. 12.95 (*0-8488-0408-2*) Amereon Ltd.
Mundwiler. Michael Ondaatje. (NFS Canada Ser.). 1993. pap. 11.95 (*0-88922-216-9*, Pub. by Talonbooks CN) InBook.
Mundy. Om - Secret of Ahbor Valley. 1976. 25.95 (*0-8488-1110-0*) Amereon Ltd.
— Story of Music. (Fine Arts Ser.). (J). (gr. 6-9). 1980. lib. bdg. 13.96 (*0-88110-031-5*, Usborne); pap. 6.95 (*0-86020-443-X*, Usborne) EDC.
Mundy, A. R. Current Operative Surgery: Urology. (Current Operative Surgery Ser.). (Illus.). 255p. 1988. text ed. 115.00 (*0-7020-1141-X*) Saunders.
— Urodynamic & Reconstructive Surgery: The Practice of Surgery. (Illus.). 348p. 1993. text ed. 235.00 (*0-443-03348-X*) Churchill.
Mundy, A. R., jt. auth. see Borzyskowski, M.
Mundy, A. R., et al. Urodynamics. 2nd ed. 1994. pap. 149.95 (*0-443-04005-2*) Churchill.
Mundy, B. Concepts of Organic Chemistry. (Studies in Organic Chemistry: Vol. 8). 408p. 1979. 115.00 (*0-8247-7448-5*) Dekker.
Mundy, Bradford & Ellerd, Michael G. Name Reactions & Reagents in Organic Synthesis. 546p. 1988. text ed. 69.95 (*0-471-83626-5*) Wiley.
***Mundy, Bradford P. & Ellerd, Michael G.** Organic Chemistry - An Alphabetical Guide. Date not set. text ed. 44.95 (*0-471-52445-X*) Wiley.
Mundy, E. F. Mundy: Nicholas Mundy & Descendants Who Settled in NJ in 1665. (Illus.). 160p. 1991. reprint ed. lib. bdg. 35.00 (*0-8328-1697-3*); reprint ed. pap. 25.00 (*0-8328-1698-1*) Higginson Bk Co.
Mundy, E. J. Renaissance into Baroque: Italian Master Drawings by the Zuccari, 1550-1600. (Illus.). 240p. (C). 1990. 95.00 (*0-685-74173-7*) Cambridge U Pr.
Mundy, E. James & Ourusoff de Fernandez-Gimenez, Elizabeth. Renaissance into Baroque: Italian Master Drawings by the Zuccari 1550-1600. LC 89-12920. (Illus.). 315p. (Orig.). 1989. write for info. (*0-944110-01-0*) Milwauk Art Mus.
Mundy, Gregory R. Calcium Homeostasis: Hypercalcemia & Hypocalcemia. 2nd ed. (Illus.). 284p. 1990. 80.00 (*0-19-520894-3*) OUP.
Mundy, Gregory R. & Martin, T. John, eds. Physiology & Pharmacology of Bone. LC 92-42565. (Handbook of Experimental Pharmacology Ser.: Vol. 107). 1993. 398.00 (*0-387-56293-1*) Spr-Verlag.
Mundy, James. Hidden Treasures: Wisconsin Collects Painting & Sculpture. (Illus.). 126p. (Orig.). 1987. pap. 14.00 (*0-944110-04-5*) Milwauk Art Mus.
Mundy, James H. Hard Times, Hard Men: Maine & the Irish, 1830-1860. (Illus.). 210p. 1991. 29.95 (*0-9626389-0-0*) Harp Pubns.
— No Rich Mens Sons: The Sixth Maine Volunteer Infantry. (Illus.). 220p. 1994. 39.95 (*0-9626389-4-3*) Harp Pubns.
— Second to None: The Story of the Second Maine Volunteer Infantry. (Illus.). 1992. 34.95 (*0-9626389-2-7*) Harp Pubns.
Mundy, Jane. Sydney Wildflower Bushwalks. (Illus.). 96p. pap. 13.95 (*0-86417-335-0*, Pub. by Kangaroo Pr AT) Seven Hills Bk.
***Mundy, Jennifer.** Georges Braque: Printmaker. (Illus.). 80p. 1993. pap. 35.00 (*1-85437-117-7*) U of Wash Pr.
Mundy, Jennifer, jt. auth. see Cowling, Elizabeth.
Mundy, John H. Europe in the High Middle Ages, 1150-1309. 2nd ed. (General History of Europe Ser.). (Illus.). 448p. (C). 1991. pap. text ed. 17.95 (*0-582-49395-1*, 78833) Longman.
Mundy, John H. & Riesenberg, Peter. The Medieval Town. LC 79-9718. (Anvil Ser.). 192p. 1979. reprint ed. pap. 10.50 (*0-88275-906-X*) Krieger.
Mundy, John H., et al. Essays in Medieval Life & Thought. LC 65-25472. 1955. 25.00 (*0-8196-0159-4*) Biblo.
Mundy, Jon. Awaken to Your Own Call: Exploring a Course in Miracles. 192p. (Orig.). 1994. pap. 11.95 (*0-8245-1387-8*) Crossroad NY.
— Listening to Your Inner Guide. 176p. (Orig.). 1995. pap. 12.95 (*0-8245-1498-X*) Crossroad NY.
Mundy, Joseph L. & Zisserman, Andrew, eds. Geometric Invariance in Computer Vision. (Artificial Intelligence - Bobrow, Brody & Davis Ser.). (Illus.). 560p. 1992. 57.50 (*0-262-13285-0*) MIT Pr.
Mundy, Joseph L., jt. ed. see Kapur, Deepak.
Mundy, Linus. Keep Life Simple Therapy. LC 90-75341. 1993. pap. 3.95 (*0-87029-257-9*) Abbey.
— Prayer-Walking. LC 93-72446. 55p. 1994. pap. 4.95 (*0-87029-264-1*) Abbey.
— Prayer-Walking: A Simple Path to Body & Soul Fitness. 55p. (Orig.). 1994. pap. 4.95 (*0-614-04665-3*, 201772) Abbey.
— Slow-down Therapy. LC 90-81236. (Illus.). 72p. (Orig.). 1990. pap. 3.95 (*0-87029-229-3*) Abbey.
Mundy, Marianne. Opportunities in Word Processing. (Illus.). 160p. 1987. 13.95 (*0-8442-6200-5*, VGM Career Bks); pap. 10.95 (*0-8442-6201-3*, VGM Career Bks) NTC Pub Grp.
***Mundy, Martha.** Domestic Government: Kinship, Community, & Polity in North Yemen. (Society & Culture in the Modern Middle East Ser.). 256p. 1995. text ed. 59.50 (*1-85043-918-4*) St Martin.
Mundy, Paul, jt. auth. see Fredericks, Marcel A.
Mundy, Peter, et al. The Vultures of Africa. (Illus.). 450p. 1992. text ed. 99.95 (*0-12-510585-1*) Acad Pr.
Mundy, S. P. A Key to the British & European Freshwater Bryozoans. 1980. 40.00 (*0-900386-39-8*) St Mut.
Mundy, Simon. Elgar. (Illustrated Lives of the Great Composers Ser.). (Illus.). 138p. 1984. pap. 14.95 (*0-7119-0263-1*, OP42498) Omnibus NY.
Mundy, Talbert. Jimgrim. reprint ed. lib. bdg. 20.95 (*0-89190-488-3*, Rivercity Pr) Amereon Ltd.
Mundy, Talbot. Avenging Liafail. (Tros of Samothrace Ser.: No. 2). 1978. pap. 2.25 (*0-89083-378-8*) Zebra.
— I Say Sunrise. 1969. pap. 7.95 (*0-87516-068-9*) DeVorss.
— King-of the Khyber Rifles. (Illus.). 1978. 15.00 (*0-937986-14-3*) D M Grant.
— King of the Khyber Rifles. 1976. 25.95 (*0-8488-0837-1*) Amereon Ltd.
— King of the Khyber Rifles. 256p. 1985. pap. 3.95 (*0-88184-169-2*) Carroll & Graf.
— King of the Khyber Rifles. 461p. 1983. reprint ed. lib. bdg. 17.95 (*0-89966-458-X*) Buccaneer Bks.
— Lud of Lunden, Vol. 1. (Tros of Samothrace Ser.). 1978. pap. 2.25 (*0-89083-372-9*) Zebra.
— Om: The Secret of Ahbor Vallet. reprint ed. lib. bdg. 24.95 (*0-89190-490-5*, Rivercity Pr) Amereon Ltd.
— Om, the Secret of Ahbor Valley. 400p. 1984. pap. 3.95 (*0-88184-045-9*) Carroll & Graf.
— Om, the Secret of Ahbor Valley. 392p. 1980. pap. 10.95 (*0-913004-39-1*) Point Loma Pub.
Mundy, Wanda M. & Passmore, Gregory, eds. Curriculum Guide for Nuclear Medicine Technologists. 2nd ed. 200p. 1993. 19.95 (*0-932004-42-3*) Soc Nuclear Med.
Munem & Yizze, James P. Precalculus. 5th ed. 1989. text ed. 57.95x (*0-87901-418-0*); student ed, pap. 11.95x (*0-87901-419-9*) Worth.
Munem, M. A. & Foulis, D. J. Calculus. 2nd ed. LC 83-50583. (Illus.). 1048p. 1984. text ed. 69.95x (*0-87901-236-6*); Brief ed., 738p. text ed. 59.95x (*0-87901-254-4*) Worth.
— Calculus, 1. 2nd ed. LC 83-50583. (Illus.). 1984. student ed 11.95x (*0-87901-237-4*) Worth.
— Calculus, 2. 2nd ed. LC 83-50583. (Illus.). 1984. student ed 11.95x (*0-87901-253-6*) Worth.
— College Trigonometry with Applications. LC 81-52995. 1982. student ed 11.95x (*0-87901-175-0*); text ed. 49.95x (*0-87901-171-8*) Worth.
Munem, M. A. & Foulis, David. Algebra & Trigonometry with Applications. 3rd ed. (Illus.). 738p. 1991. text ed. 55.95x (*0-87901-498-9*); student ed, pap. 11.95x (*0-87901-513-6*) Worth.
— College Algebra with Applications. 3rd ed. 452p. 1991. student ed 11.95x (*0-87901-515-2*); text ed. 53.95x (*0-87901-499-7*) Worth.
Munem, M. A. & Tschirhart, W. Algebra for College Students. 2nd ed. 609p. (C). 1988. text ed. 49.95x (*0-87901-384-2*); student ed, pap. 11.95x (*0-87901-386-9*) Worth.
— Beginning Algebra. 4th ed. 404p. (C). 1988. text ed. 48.95x (*0-87901-378-8*); student ed 11.95x (*0-87901-380-X*) Worth.
— College Trigonometry. (Illus.). (C). 1974. student ed 11.95x (*0-87901-029-0*); text ed. 49.95x (*0-87901-028-2*) Worth.
— Intermediate Algebra. 4th ed. 612p. (C). 1988. text ed. 49.95x (*0-87901-377-X*); student ed 11.95x (*0-87901-379-6*) Worth.
Munenori, Yagyu. The Sword & the Mind. Sato, Hiroaki, tr. LC 85-8899. (Illus.). 144p. 1986. 16.95 (*0-87951-209-1*) Overlook Pr.
— The Sword & the Mind. Sato, Hiroaki, tr. 144p. 1988. pap. 11.95 (*0-87951-256-3*) Overlook Pr.
Munenori, Yagyu, tr. see Musashi, Miyamoto.
Muneo Saito, et al, eds. Fractionation by Packed-Column SFE & SFC: Principles & Applications. LC 93-44145. 1994. 115.00 (*1-56081-591-4*) VCH Pubs.
Munevar, Gonzalo. Radical Knowledge: A Philosophical Inquiry into the Nature & Limits of Science. LC 81-4258. 135p. (C). 1981. 25.00 (*0-915145-17-0*); pap. 12.50 (*0-915145-16-2*) Hackett Pub.
Munevar, Gonzalo, ed. Beyond Reason: Essays on the Philosophy of Paul Feyerabend. 548p. (C). 1991. lib. bdg. 161.50 (*0-7923-1272-4*) Kluwer Ac.
Muney, Julia, jt. auth. see Van Liere, Eldon N.
Munford, Alan, ed. Management Development: Strategies for Action. 240p. (C). 1991. pap. 95.00 (*0-85292-476-3*, Pub. by IPM Hse UK) St Mut.
Munford, Christopher. River Night. 50p. (Orig.). 1989. pap. 3.00 (*0-945085-09-5*) Sub Rosa.
— Sermons in Stone. (Illus.). 92p. (Orig.). 1993. pap. 8.95 (*0-913559-22-9*) Birch Brook Pr.
Munford, Clarence J. The Black Ordeal of Slave Trading & Slavery in the French West Indies, 1625-1715, 3 vols., 1. LC 91-22009. 300p. 1991. lib. bdg. 89.95 (*0-7734-9741-2*) E Mellen.
— The Black Ordeal of Slave Trading & Slavery in the French West Indies, 1625-1715, 3 vols., 2. LC 91-22009. 300p. 1991. lib. bdg. 89.95 (*0-7734-9431-6*) E Mellen.
— The Black Ordeal of Slave Trading & Slavery in the French West Indies, 1625-1715, 3 vols., 3. LC 91-22009. 300p. 1991. lib. bdg. 89.95 (*0-7734-9433-2*) E Mellen.
Munford, J. Kenneth, ed. see Nash, Wallis.
Munford, Luther T. Mississippi Supreme Court Practice. rev. ed. LC 87-24834. 250p. 1993. reprint ed. 165.00 (*0-9619323-0-9*) On Point Pr.
— Mississippi Appellate Practice. 450p. 1995. 170.00 (*0-9619323-1-7*) On Point Pr.
Munford, Robert. The Plays of Robert Munford. 105p. 1992. 5.95 (*0-929408-06-3*) Amer Eagle Pubns Inc.
Munford, Tony. Victorian Rotherham: A Pictorial History. (Illus.). 80p. (C). 1989. pap. 50.00 (*1-85563-003-6*, Pub. by Quoin Pub Ltd UK) St Mut.
Mungall, Constance. Probate Guide for British Columbia: A Step-by-Step Guide to Probating an Estate - Canadian Edition. 14th ed. (Legal Ser.). 12.95 (*0-88908-470-X*); 14.95 (*0-88908-469-6*) Self-Counsel Pr.

M

Mungall, Constance & Amer, Elizabeth. Taking Action: Working Together for Positive Change in Your Community. (Reference Ser.). (Illus.). 200p. (Orig.). 1992. Canadian Edition. pap. 10.95 (*0-88908-532-3*) Self-Counsel Pr.

Mungall, Constance & McLaren, Digby, eds. Planet under Stress: The Challenge of Global Change. (Illus.). 360p. 1990. pap. 24.95 (*0-19-540731-8*) OUP.

***Mungall, Dennis R., ed.** Applied Clinical Pharmacokinetics. fac. ed. LC 83-565. (Illus.). 458p. Date not set. pap. 130.60 (*0-7837-7530-X*) Bks Demand.

Mungall, E. C., ed. Ungulate Behavior & Management: Proceedings of the Conference College Station, TX, 23-27 May, 1988. 540p. 1991. reprint ed. 185.50 (*0-444-88995-7*) Elsevier.

Mungall, Elizabeth C. The Indian Blackbuck Antelope: A Texas View. (Kleberg Studies in Natural Resources). (Illus.). 184p. 1978. pap. 8.95x (*0-89096-197-2*) Tex A&M Univ Pr.

Mungall, Elizabeth C. & Sheffield, William J. Exotics on the Range: The Texas Example. LC 93-24131. (Louise Lindsey Merrick Natural Environment Ser.: No. 16). (Illus.). 286p. 1994. 49.50 (*0-89096-399-1*) Tex A&M Univ Pr.

Mungazi, Dickson. The Struggle for Social Change in Southern Africa: Visions of Liberty. (Illus.). 180p. (C). 1989. text ed. 58.00 (*0-8448-1594-2*); pap. text ed. 32.00 (*0-8448-1595-0*) Taylor & Francis.

Mungazi, Dickson A. The Challenge of Educational Innovation & National Development in Southern Africa. LC 91-38677. (American University Studies: Education: Ser. XIV, Vol. 36). 200p. (C). 1992. text ed. 41.95 (*0-8204-1713-0*) P Lang Pubs.

— Colonial Education for Africans: George Stark's Policy in Zimbabwe. LC 91-2273. 176p. 1991. text ed. 45.00 (*0-275-94029-2*, C4029, Praeger Pubs) Greenwood.

— Colonial Policy & Conflict in Zimbabwe: A Study of Cultures in Collision, 1890-1979. 200p. 1991. 47.00 (*0-8448-1703-1*, Crane Russak) Taylor & Francis.

— Education & Government Control in Zimbabwe: A Study of the Commissions of Inquiry, 1908-1974. LC 89-3655. 150p. 1990. text ed. 45.00 (*0-275-93170-6*, C3170, Praeger Pubs) Greenwood.

— Educational Policy & National Character: Africa, Japan, the United States, & the Soviet Union. LC 92-31842. 248p. 1993. text ed. 49.95 (*0-275-94423-9*, C4423, Praeger Pubs) Greenwood.

— The Fall of the Mantle: The Educational Policy of the Rhodesia Front Government & Conflict in Zimbabwe. LC 92-36435. (American University Studies: Regional Studies: Ser. XX, Vol. 7). 259p. (Orig.). (C). 1993. pap. text ed. 29.95 (*0-8204-2109-X*) P Lang Pubs.

Mungazi, Dickson a. Gathering Under the Mango Tree: Values in Traditional Culture in Africa. LC 93-35796. (American University Studies: Regional Studies: Ser. XX, Vol. 9). 1994. write for info. (*0-8204-2336-X*) P Lang Pubs.

Mungazi, Dickson A. To Honor the Sacred Trust of Civilization. 320p. 1983. 24.95 (*0-87073-454-7*); pap. 18.95 (*0-87073-455-5*) Schenkman Bks Inc.

— Where He Stands: Albert Shanker of the American Federation of Teachers. 256p. 1995. text ed. 49.95 (*0-275-94929-X*, Praeger Pubs) Greenwood.

Mungekar, B. L. The Political Economy of Terms of Trade. 1992. 25.00 (*81-7040-457-6*, Pub. by Himalaya II) Apt Bks.

Mungello, D. E. The Forgotten Christians of Hangzhou. LC 93-36553. (Illus.). 240p. (C). 1994. text ed. 36.00 (*0-8248-1540-8*) UH Pr.

Mungello, David E. Curious Land: Jesuit Accommodation & the Origins of Sinology. LC 88-27874. (Illus.). 408p. 1989. reprint ed. pap. text ed. 17.00 (*0-8248-1219-0*) UH Pr.

— Leibniz & Confucianism: The Search for Accord. LC 77-4053. 1977. text ed. 14.00 (*0-8248-0545-3*) UH Pr.

Munger, Anne R. The Not-So-Witchy Witch. (Illus.). 32p. (J). (gr. 1-3). 1991. pap. 2.99 (*0-87406-583-6*) Willowisp Pr.

Munger, Asahel & Munger, Eliza. Diary of Asahel Munger & Wife: Travel to the Marcus Whitman Mission, May 4, 1839-September 3, 1839. LC 92-19319. 1992. 4.95 (*0-87770-508-9*) Ye Galleon.

Munger, Carol V. Billy Groat. LC 87-71679. (Illus.). 23p. (Orig.). (J). 1990. pap. 4.00 (*0-916383-45-8*) Aegina Pr.

Munger, Donna B. Pennsylvania Land Records: A History & Guide for Research. LC 90-21384. 240p. 1991. 75.00 (*0-8420-2377-1*); pap. 29.95 (*0-8420-2497-2*) Scholarly Res Inc.

Munger, Edwin S. Touched by Africa. 1983. 12.50 (*0-934912-00-9*) Munger Africana Lib.

Munger, Eliza, jt. auth. see Munger, Asahel.

Munger, Elizabeth M. A History of the Trail Creek Region. (Little Bit of History Ser.: Bk. 2). 24p. 1988. 2.00 (*0-935549-11-0*) MI City Hist.

Munger, Evelyn M. & Bowdon, Susan J. The New Beyond Peek-A-Boo & Pat-a-Cake: Activities for Baby's First 24 Months. 3rd ed. LC 93-1421. 256p. 1993. spiral bd. 15.95 (*0-8329-0504-6*) New Win Pub.

Munger, Fredi, jt. auth. see Droegkamp, Janis.

Munger, George & Munger, Piret. Piret's: The George & Piret Munger Cookbook. LC 85-10871. 321p. 1985. 18.95 (*0-317-37982-8*); pap. 12.95 (*0-317-37983-6*) HM.

Munger, Guy, ed. see Rogers, Dennis.

Munger, Guy, ed. see Snow, A. C.

Munger, J. P., jt. auth. see Michie Butterworth Editorial Staff.

Munger, James. Two Years in the Pacific & Arctic Oceans & China, Being a Journal of Events Peculiar to a Whaling Voyage. 82p. 1987. 14.95 (*0-87770-401-5*) Ye Galleon.

Munger, James I., jt. auth. see Miller, Erston V.

Munger, Jeffrey, jt. auth. see Zafran, Eric.

***Munger, Mark A.** November One. 360p. (Orig.). Date not set. pap. 9.95 (*0-7610-0184-0*) NW Pub.

Munger, Michael, jt. auth. see Hinich, Melvin.

Munger, Piret, jt. auth. see Munger, George.

Munger, Richard. Changing Children's Behavior Quickly. (Illus.). 230p. (Orig.). 1993. pap. 13.95 (*1-56833-001-4*) Madison Bks UPA.

Munger, Richard L. Child Mental Health Practice from the Ecological Perspective. 426p. (Orig.). (C). 1991. lib. bdg. 60.50 (*0-8191-8318-0*); pap. 38.00 (*0-8191-8319-9*) U Pr of Amer.

***Munger, Robert.** My Heart Christ's Home. 1989. pap. 3.99 (*0-529-07007-3*, Meridian IA) World Bible.

Munger, Robert B. Commitment. (Christian Basics Bible Studies). 64p. (Orig.). 1994. pap. 4.99 (*0-8308-2005-1*, 2005) InterVarsity.

— My Heart - Christ's Home. LC 92-5678. (Stories for Old & Young Ser.). (Illus.). 48p. 1992. reprint ed. 12.99 (*0-8308-1842-1*, 1842) InterVarsity.

Munger, Robert T. The Architecture of Exclusion: Professional Self-Regulation: Fountainhead of the Pseudo-Elite. (Illus.). 168p. (Orig.). 1992. pap. 12.95 (*0-9633812-0-2*) Nova Arch Pub.

Munger, Susan H. The International Business Communications Desk Reference. 250p. 1993. pap. 25.95 (*0-8144-7786-0*) AMACOM.

Mungin, Horace. Sleepy Willie. Orange, Charlotte, ed. LC 90-82440. 128p. (Orig.). (YA). (gr. 8-12). 1991. pap. 8.95 (*0-936026-24-3*) R&M Pub Co.

Mungkandi, Wiwat, jt. ed. see Jackson, Karl D.

Mungkandi, Wiwat, jt. ed. see Neher, Clark.

Mungkandi, Wiwat, jt. ed. see Ramsay, Ansil.

Mungo, P. & Clough, B. Approaching Zero. 1993. 22.00 (*0-679-40938-6*) McKay.

Mungo, Ray. Famous Long Ago. 1990. pap. 14.95 (*0-8065-1204-0*, Citadel Pr) Carol Pub Group.

— The Learning Annex Guide to Getting Successfully Published: From Typewriter to Royalty Checks: All You Need to Know! 256p. 1992. pap. 10.95 (*0-8065-1371-3*, Citadel Pr) Carol Pub Group.

— Liberace. LC 94-10201. (Lives of Notable Gay Men & Lesbian Women Ser.). (YA). (gr. 9 up). 1995. write for info. (*0-7910-2850-X*) Chelsea Hse.

— Liberace. Duberman, Martin, ed. (Lives of Notable Gay Men & Lesbians Ser.). (Illus.). 168p. (YA). (gr. 9 up). 1995. pap. 9.95 (*0-7910-2885-2*) Chelsea Hse.

— Palm Springs Babylon: Sizzling Stories from the Desert Playground of the Stars. (Illus.). 256p. (Orig.). 1993. pap. 14.95 (*0-312-06438-1*) St Martin.

— San Francisco Confidential: Tales of Scandal & Excess from the Town That's Seen Everything. LC 94-12615. 1994. 19.95 (*1-55972-246-0*) Carol Pub Group.

— Your Autobiography: More Than Three Hundred Questions to Help You Write Your Personal History. 132p. (Orig.). 1994. pap. 8.00 (*0-02-029545-6*, Collier S&S) S&S Trade.

Mungo, Ray & Yamaguchi, Robert H. No Credit Required: How to Buy a House When You Don't Qualify for a Mortgage. 192p. (Orig.). 1993. pap. 4.99 (*0-451-17564-6*, Sig) NAL-Dutton.

Mungoshi, Charles. The Setting Sun & the Rolling World: Selected Short Stories. LC 89-42588. 208p. (Orig.). 1989. pap. 11.00 (*0-8070-8321-6*) Beacon Pr.

Mungovan. Competition Law: A Legal Handbook for Business. 104p. 1990. pap. 25.00 (*0-409-89648-9*) Butterworth Legal Pubs.

— Contracts: A Legal Handbook for Business. 104p. 1990. pap. 25.00 (*0-409-89659-4*) Butterworth Legal Pubs.

Munguia, E., Jr., tr. see Azuelo, Mariano.

Munguia, Juan C. Supervision of Bilingual Programs. Cordasco, Francesco, ed. LC 77-90555. (Bilingual-Bicultural Education in the U. S. Ser.). 1978. lib. bdg. 26.95 (*0-405-11093-6*) Ayer.

Munhall, Edgar, ed. Ange-Laurent de la Live de Jully: A Facsimile Reprint of the Catalogue Historique (1764) & the Catalogue Raisonne des Tableaux (1770) (Reprint Series of Historical Auction Catalogues). (Illus.). 318p. 1988. reprint ed. text ed. 50.00 (*0-317-93171-7*) Acanthus Pr.

Munhall, Edgar, ed. see Davilier, Charles.

***Munhall, Patricia, ed.** In Women's Experience, Vol. I. 1994. pap. 37.95 (*0-88737-610-X*) Natl League Nurse.

— In Women's Experience, Vol. II. 1995. pap. 37.95 (*0-88737-647-9*) Natl League Nurse.

Munhall, Patricia L. Nursing & Health Science Research: A Phenomenological Perspective. LC 94-1454. 1994. 37.95 (*0-88737-597-9*) Natl League Nurse.

Munhall, Patricia L. & Boyd, Carolyn O., eds. Nursing Research: A Qualitative Perspective. 2nd ed. LC 93-20494. 1993. 35.95 (*0-88737-590-1*) Natl League Nurse.

Munholland, John K. & Betts, Raymond F., eds. French Colonial Studies-Etudes Coloniales Francaises, Vol. III. LC 76-644752. 118p. (Orig.). (C). 1986. 39.00 (*0-8191-5072-X*, French Colonial Hist Soc); pap. text ed. 17.00 (*0-8191-5073-8*, French Colonial Hist Soc) U Pr of Amer.

Muni, Matanga. Brhaddesi of Sri Matanga Muni, Vol. 1. Sharma, Prem L. & Vatsyayan, Kapila, eds. (Kalamulasastra Series Eight: Vol. 1). (C). 1995. 28.50x (*81-208-1031-7*, Pub. by Motilal Banarsidass II) S Asia.

— Brhaddesi of Sri Matanga Muni, Vol. 2. Kata, Oren & Sharma, Prem L., eds. (C). 1995. 28.50x (*81-208-1032-5*, Pub. by Motilal Banarsidass II) S Asia.

Muni, Narada, ed. see Kripalvananda, Svami.

Muni, P. K., jt. auth. see Padhy, K. S.

Muni, Rajarshi. Awakening the Life Force: The Philosophy & Psychology of Spontaneous Yoga. LC 93-40373. (Illus.). 224p. 1994. pap. 15.00 (*0-87542-581-X*) Llewellyn Pubns.

Muni, S. D. India & Nepal: A Changing Relationship. (C). 1992. 48.00 (*0-7855-0185-1*, Pub. by Ratna Pustak Bhandar) St Mut.

— India & Nepal: Erosion of a Relationship. 308p. 1992. text ed. 30.00 (*81-220-0181-5*, Pub. by Konark Pubs Pvt Ltd II) Advent Bks Div.

— Pangs of Proximity: India & Sri Lanka's Ethnic Crisis. LC 93-12317. (Peace Research Institute Ser.). (Illus.). 256p. (C). 1993. 33.50 (*0-8039-9112-6*) Sage.

***Muni, S. D., ed.** Understanding South Asia: Essays in the Memory of Late Professor (Mrs.) Urmila Phadnis. (C). 1994. 28.00x (*81-7003-173-7*, Pub. by S Asia Pubs II) S Asia.

Muni Shri Nagraj Ji. Agama & Tripitaka Eka Anusilana (A Critical Comparative Study of the Jaina & Buddhist Canonical Literature), Vol. 1: History & Tradition. 900p. 1986. 85.00 (*1-55528-024-2*, Pub. by Today & Tomorrows P & P II) Scholarly Pubns.

— The Contemporaneity & the Chronology of Mahavira & Buddha. 188p. 1975. 4.00 (*0-88065-163-6*, Messers Today & Tomorrow) Scholarly Pubns.

Muniain, J., jt. auth. see Baez, J.

Munich, Adrienne. Andromeda's Chains: Gender & Interpretation in Victorian Literature & Art. (Illus.). 222p. (C). 1993. text ed. 35.50 (*0-231-06872-7*); pap. 14.00 (*0-231-06873-5*) Col U Pr.

Munich, Adrienne, jt. auth. see Bloom, Harold.

Munich, Adrienne A., jt. ed. see Maynard, John.

***Munich, C. Hammer, et al, eds.** Transplant International: Proceedings of the 6th ESOT Congress, Rodos, October 25-28, 1993. (Official Journal of the European Society for Organ Transplantation). 705p. 1994. pap. text ed. 129.00 (*0-387-57835-8*) Spr-Verlag.

***Municio, A. M. & Miras-Portugal, M. T., eds.** Cell Signal Transduction, Second Messengers, & Protein Phosphorylation in Health & Disease. (Illus.). 258p. 1994. 79.50 (*0-306-44814-9*, Plenum Pr) Plenum.

Municipal Analysis Services, Inc., ed. Governments of Alabama 1987. (Governments of Your State Ser.). 1987. text ed. 150.00 (*1-55507-131-7*) Municipal Analysis.

— Governments of Alabama 1987. (Expert Edition Ser.). 1987. text ed. 325.00 (*1-55507-174-0*) Municipal Analysis.

— Governments of Alabama 1988. (Governments of Your State Ser.). 1988. text ed. 150.00 (*1-55507-220-8*) Municipal Analysis.

— Governments of Alabama 1988. (Expert Edition Ser.). 1988. text ed. 325.00 (*1-55507-264-X*) Municipal Analysis.

— Governments of Arkansas 1987. (Expert Edition Ser.). 1987. text ed. 325.00 (*1-55507-175-9*) Municipal Analysis.

— Governments of Arkansas 1988. (Governments of Your State Ser.). 1988. text ed. 150.00 (*1-55507-221-6*) Municipal Analysis.

— Governments of Arkansas 1988. (Expert Edition Ser.). 1988. text ed. 325.00 (*1-55507-265-8*) Municipal Analysis.

— Governments of California 1987. (Expert Edition Ser.). 1987. text ed. 325.00 (*1-55507-176-7*) Municipal Analysis.

— Governments of California 1987. (Governments of Your States Ser.). 1988. text ed. 150.00 (*1-55507-133-3*) Municipal Analysis.

— Governments of California 1988. (Governments of Your State Ser.). 1988. text ed. 150.00 (*1-55507-222-4*) Municipal Analysis.

— Governments of California 1988. (Expert Edition Ser.). 1988. text ed. 325.00 (*1-55507-266-6*) Municipal Analysis.

— Governments of Colorado 1987. (Governments of Your State Ser.). 1987. text ed. 150.00 (*1-55507-134-1*) Municipal Analysis.

— Governments of Colorado 1987. (Expert Edition Ser.). 1987. text ed. 325.00 (*1-55507-177-5*) Municipal Analysis.

— Governments of Colorado 1988. (Governments of Your State Ser.). 1988. text ed. 150.00 (*1-55507-223-2*) Municipal Analysis.

— Governments of Colorado 1988. (Expert Edition Ser.). 1988. text ed. 325.00 (*1-55507-267-4*) Municipal Analysis.

— Governments of Connecticut 1987. (Governments of Your State Ser.). 1987. text ed. 150.00 (*1-55507-135-X*) Municipal Analysis.

— Governments of Connecticut 1987. (Expert Edition Ser.). 1987. text ed. 325.00 (*1-55507-178-3*) Municipal Analysis.

— Governments of Connecticut 1988. (Governments of Your State Ser.). 1988. text ed. 150.00 (*1-55507-224-0*) Municipal Analysis.

Municipal Analysis Services, Inc, ed. Governments of Connecticut 1988. (Expert Edition Ser.). 1988. text ed. 325.00 (*1-55507-268-2*) Municipal Analysis.

Municipal Analysis Services, Inc., ed. Governments of Florida, 1987. (Governments of Your State Ser.). 1987. text ed. 150.00 (*1-55507-136-8*) Municipal Analysis.

— Governments of Florida 1987. (Expert Edition Ser.). 1987. text ed. 325.00 (*1-55507-179-1*) Municipal Analysis.

— Governments of Florida 1988. (Governments of Your State Ser.). 1988. text ed. 150.00 (*1-55507-225-9*) Municipal Analysis.

— Governments of Florida 1988. (Expert Edition Ser.). 1988. text ed. 325.00 (*1-55507-269-0*) Municipal Analysis.

— Governments of Georgia 1987. (Governments of Your State Ser.). 1987. text ed. 150.00 (*1-55507-137-6*) Municipal Analysis.

— Governments of Georgia 1987. (Expert Edition Ser.). 1988. text ed. 325.00 (*1-55507-180-5*) Municipal Analysis.

— Governments of Georgia 1988. (Governments of Your State Ser.). 1988. text ed. 150.00 (*1-55507-226-7*) Municipal Analysis.

— Governments of Georgia 1988. (Expert Edition Ser.). 1988. text ed. 325.00 (*1-55507-270-4*) Municipal Analysis.

— Governments of Illinois 1987. (Governments of Your State Ser.). 1987. text ed. 150.00 (*1-55507-138-4*) Municipal Analysis.

— Governments of Illinois, 1987. (Expert Edition Ser.). 1987. text ed. 325.00 (*1-55507-181-3*) Municipal Analysis.

— Governments of Illinois, 1988. (Governments of Your State Ser.). 1988. text ed. 150.00 (*1-55507-227-5*) Municipal Analysis.

— Governments of Illinois, 1988. (Expert Edition Ser.). 1988. text ed. 325.00 (*1-55507-271-2*) Municipal Analysis.

— Governments of Indiana 1987. (Governments of Your State Ser.). 1987. text ed. 150.00 (*1-55507-139-2*) Municipal Analysis.

— Governments of Indiana 1987. (Expert Edition Ser.). 1987. text ed. 325.00 (*1-55507-182-1*) Municipal Analysis.

— Governments of Indiana 1988. (Governments of Your State Ser.). 1988. text ed. 150.00 (*1-55507-228-3*) Municipal Analysis.

— Governments of Indiana 1988. (Expert Edition Ser.). 1988. text ed. 325.00 (*1-55507-272-0*) Municipal Analysis.

— Governments of Iowa 1987. (Governments of Your State Ser.). 1987. text ed. 150.00 (*1-55507-140-6*) Municipal Analysis.

— Governments of Iowa, 1987. (Expert Edition Ser.). 1987. text ed. 325.00 (*1-55507-183-X*) Municipal Analysis.

— Governments of Iowa 1988. (Governments of Your State Ser.). 1988. text ed. 150.00 (*1-55507-229-1*) Municipal Analysis.

— Governments of Iowa, 1988. (Expert Edition Ser.). 1988. text ed. 325.00 (*1-55507-273-9*) Municipal Analysis.

— Governments of Kansas 1987. (Governments of Your State Ser.). 1987. text ed. 150.00 (*1-55507-141-4*) Municipal Analysis.

— Governments of Kansas 1987. (Expert Edition Ser.). 1987. text ed. 325.00 (*1-55507-184-8*) Municipal Analysis.

— Governments of Kansas 1988. (Governments of Your State Ser.). 1988. text ed. 150.00 (*1-55507-230-5*) Municipal Analysis.

— Governments of Kansas 1988. (Expert Edition Ser.). 1988. text ed. 325.00 (*1-55507-274-7*) Municipal Analysis.

— Governments of Kentucky 1987. (Expert Edition Ser.). 1987. text ed. 325.00 (*1-55507-185-6*) Municipal Analysis.

— Governments of Kentucky 1987. (Governments of Your State Ser.). 1987. text ed. 150.00 (*1-55507-142-2*) Municipal Analysis.

Municipal Analysis Services, Inc, ed. Governments of Kentucky 1988. (Governments of Your State Ser.). 1988. text ed. 150.00 (*1-55507-231-3*) Municipal Analysis.

Municipal Analysis Services, Inc., ed. Governments of Kentucky 1988. (Expert Edition Ser.). 1988. text ed. 325.00 (*1-55507-275-5*) Municipal Analysis.

— Governments of Louisana 1987. (Expert Edition Ser.). 1987. text ed. 325.00 (*1-55507-186-4*) Municipal Analysis.

— Governments of Louisiana 1987. (Governments of Your State Ser.). 1987. text ed. 150.00 (*1-55507-143-0*) Municipal Analysis.

— Governments of Louisiana 1988. (Governments of Your State Ser.). 1988. text ed. 150.00 (*1-55507-232-1*) Municipal Analysis.

— Governments of Louisiana 1988. (Expert Edition Ser.). 1988. text ed. 325.00 (*1-55507-276-3*) Municipal Analysis.

— Governments of Maine 1987. (Governments of Your State Ser.). 1987. text ed. 150.00 (*1-55507-144-9*) Municipal Analysis.

— Governments of Maine 1987. (Expert Edition Ser.). 1987. text ed. 325.00 (*1-55507-187-2*) Municipal Analysis.

— Governments of Maine 1988. (Governments of Your State Ser.). 1988. text ed. 150.00 (*1-55507-233-X*) Municipal Analysis.

— Governments of Maine 1988. (Expert Edition Ser.). 1988. text ed. 325.00 (*1-55507-277-1*) Municipal Analysis.

— Governments of Massachusetts 1987. (Governments of Your State Ser.). 1987. text ed. 150.00 (*1-55507-145-7*) Municipal Analysis.

— Governments of Massachusetts 1987: Expert Edition. (Expert Edition 1987 Ser.). 1987. text ed. 325.00 (*1-55507-188-0*) Municipal Analysis.

— Governments of Massachusetts 1988. (Governments of Your State Ser.). 1988. text ed. 150.00 (*1-55507-234-8*) Municipal Analysis.

— Governments of Massachusetts 1988. (Expert Edition Ser.). 1988. text ed. 325.00 (*1-55507-278-X*) Municipal Analysis.

— Governments of Michigan 1987. (Governments of Your State Ser.). 1987. text ed. 150.00 (*1-55507-146-5*) Municipal Analysis.

— Governments of Michigan 1987. (Expert Edition Ser.). 1987. text ed. 325.00 (*1-55507-189-9*) Municipal Analysis.

— Governments of Michigan 1988. (Governments of Your State Ser.). 1988. text ed. 150.00 (*1-55507-235-6*) Municipal Analysis.

An Asterisk (*) at the beginning of an entry indicates that the title is appearing in BIP for the first time.

— Governments of Michigan 1988. (Expert Edition Ser.). 1988. text ed. 325.00 (*1-55507-279-8*) Municipal Analysis.
— Governments of Minnesota 1987. (Governments of Your State Ser.). 1987. text ed. 150.00 (*1-55507-147-3*) Municipal Analysis.
— Governments of Minnesota 1987. (Expert Edition Ser.). 1987. text ed. 325.00 (*1-55507-190-2*) Municipal Analysis.
— Governments of Minnesota 1988. (Governments of Your State Ser.). 1988. text ed. 150.00 (*1-55507-236-4*) Municipal Analysis.
— Governments of Minnesota 1988. (Expert Edition Ser.). 1988. text ed. 325.00 (*1-55507-280-1*) Municipal Analysis.
— Governments of Mississippi 1987. (Governments of Your State Ser.). 1987. text ed. 150.00 (*1-55507-148-1*) Municipal Analysis.
— Governments of Mississippi 1987. (Expert Edition Ser.). 1987. text ed. 325.00 (*1-55507-191-0*) Municipal Analysis.
— Governments of Mississippi 1988. (Governments of Your State Ser.). 1988. text ed. 150.00 (*1-55507-237-2*) Municipal Analysis.
— Governments of Mississippi 1988. (Expert Edition Ser.). 1988. text ed. 325.00 (*1-55507-281-X*) Municipal Analysis.
— Governments of Missouri 1987. (Governments of Your State Ser.). 1987. text ed. 150.00 (*1-55507-149-X*) Municipal Analysis.
— Governments of Missouri 1987. (Expert Edition Ser.). 1987. text ed. 325.00 (*1-55507-192-9*) Municipal Analysis.
— Governments of Missouri 1988. (Governments of Your State Ser.). 1988. text ed. 150.00 (*1-55507-238-0*) Municipal Analysis.
— Governments of Missouri 1988. (Expert Edition Ser.). 1988. text ed. 325.00 (*1-55507-282-8*) Municipal Analysis.
— Governments of Nebraska 1987. (Governments of Your State Ser.). 1987. text ed. 150.00 (*1-55507-150-3*) Municipal Analysis.
— Governments of Nebraska 1987. (Expert Edition Ser.). 1987. text ed. 325.00 (*1-55507-193-7*) Municipal Analysis.
— Governments of Nebraska 1988. (Governments of Your State Ser.). 1988. text ed. 150.00 (*1-55507-239-9*) Municipal Analysis.
— Governments of Nebraska 1988. (Expert Edition Ser.). 1988. text ed. 325.00 (*1-55507-283-6*) Municipal Analysis.
— Governments of New Jersey 1987. (Governments of Your States Ser.). 1987. text ed. 150.00 (*1-55507-151-1*) Municipal Analysis.
— Governments of New Jersey 1987. (Expert Edition Ser.). 1987. text ed. 325.00 (*1-55507-194-5*) Municipal Analysis.
— Governments of New Jersey 1988. (Governments of Your State Ser.). 1988. text ed. 150.00 (*1-55507-240-2*) Municipal Analysis.
— Governments of New Jersey 1988. (Expert Edition Ser.). 1988. text ed. 325.00 (*1-55507-284-4*) Municipal Analysis.
— Governments of New York 1987. (Governments of Your State Ser.). 1987. text ed. 150.00 (*1-55507-152-X*) Municipal Analysis.
— Governments of New York 1987. (Expert Edition Ser.). 1987. text ed. 325.00 (*1-55507-195-3*) Municipal Analysis.
— Governments of New York 1988. (Governments of Your State Ser.). 1987. text ed. 150.00 (*1-55507-241-0*) Municipal Analysis.
— Governments of New York 1988. (Expert Edition Ser.). 1988. text ed. 325.00 (*1-55507-285-2*) Municipal Analysis.
— Governments of North Dakota 1987. (Governments of Your State Ser.). 1987. text ed. 150.00 (*1-55507-153-8*) Municipal Analysis.
— Governments of North Dakota 1987. (Expert Edition Ser.). 1987. text ed. 325.00 (*1-55507-196-1*) Municipal Analysis.
— Governments of North Dakota 1988. (Governments of Your State Ser.). 1988. text ed. 150.00 (*1-55507-242-9*) Municipal Analysis.
— Governments of North Dakota 1988. (Expert Edition Ser.). 1988. text ed. 325.00 (*1-55507-286-0*) Municipal Analysis.
— Governments of Ohio 1987. (Governments of Your State Ser.). 1987. text ed. 150.00 (*1-55507-154-6*) Municipal Analysis.
— Governments of Ohio 1987. (Expert Edition Ser.). 1987. text ed. 325.00 (*1-55507-197-X*) Municipal Analysis.
— Governments of Ohio 1988. (Governments of Your State Ser.). 1988. text ed. 150.00 (*1-55507-243-7*) Municipal Analysis.
— Governments of Ohio 1988. (Expert Edition Ser.). 1988. text ed. 325.00 (*1-55507-287-9*) Municipal Analysis.
— Governments of Oklahoma 1987. (Governments of Your State Ser.). 1987. text ed. 150.00 (*1-55507-155-4*) Municipal Analysis.
— Governments of Oklahoma 1987. (Expert Edition Ser.). 1987. text ed. 325.00 (*1-55507-198-8*) Municipal Analysis.
— Governments of Oklahoma 1988. (Governments of Your State Ser.). 1988. text ed. 150.00 (*1-55507-244-5*) Municipal Analysis.
— Governments of Oklahoma 1988. (Expert Edition Ser.). 1988. text ed. 325.00 (*1-55507-288-7*) Municipal Analysis.
— Governments of Pennsylvania 1987. (Governments of Your State Ser.). 1987. text ed. 150.00 (*1-55507-156-2*) Municipal Analysis.
— Governments of Pennsylvania 1987. (Expert Edition Ser.). 1987. text ed. 325.00 (*1-55507-199-6*) Municipal Analysis.
— Governments of Pennsylvania 1988. (Governments of Your State Ser.). 1988. text ed. 150.00 (*1-55507-245-3*) Municipal Analysis.
— Governments of Pennsylvania 1988. (Expert Edition Ser.). 1988. text ed. 325.00 (*1-55507-289-5*) Municipal Analysis.
— Governments of South Dakota 1987. (Governments of Your State Ser.). 1987. text ed. 150.00 (*1-55507-157-0*) Municipal Analysis.
— Governments of South Dakota 1987. (Expert Edition Ser.). 1987. text ed. 325.00 (*1-55507-200-3*) Municipal Analysis.
— Governments of South Dakota 1988. (Governments of Your State Ser.). 1988. text ed. 150.00 (*1-55507-246-1*) Municipal Analysis.
— Governments of South Dakota 1988. (Expert Edition Ser.). 1988. text ed. 325.00 (*1-55507-290-9*) Municipal Analysis.
— Governments of Tennessee 1987. (Governments of Your State Ser.). 1987. text ed. 150.00 (*1-55507-158-9*) Municipal Analysis.
— Governments of Tennessee 1987. (Expert Edition Ser.). 1987. text ed. 325.00 (*1-55507-201-1*) Municipal Analysis.
— Governments of Tennessee 1988. (Governments of Your State Ser.). 1988. text ed. 150.00 (*1-55507-247-X*) Municipal Analysis.
— Governments of Tennessee 1988. (Expert Edition Ser.). 1988. text ed. 325.00 (*1-55507-291-7*) Municipal Analysis.
— Governments of Texas 1987. (Governments of Your State Ser.). 1987. text ed. 150.00 (*1-55507-159-7*) Municipal Analysis.
— Governments of Texas 1987. (Expert Edition Ser.). 1987. text ed. 325.00 (*1-55507-202-X*) Municipal Analysis.
— Governments of Texas 1988. (Governments of Your State Ser.). 1988. text ed. 150.00 (*1-55507-248-8*) Municipal Analysis.
— Governments of Texas 1988. (Expert Edition Ser.). 1988. text ed. 325.00 (*1-55507-292-5*) Municipal Analysis.
— Governments of the Carolinas 1987. (Governments of Your State Ser.). 1987. text ed. 150.00 (*1-55507-165-1*) Municipal Analysis.
— Governments of the Carolinas 1987. (Expert Edition Ser.). 1987. text ed. 325.00 (*1-55507-208-9*) Municipal Analysis.
— Governments of the Carolinas 1988. (Governments of Your State Ser.). 1988. text ed. 150.00 (*1-55507-254-2*) Municipal Analysis.
— Governments of the Carolinas 1988. (Expert Edition Ser.). 1988. text ed. 325.00 (*1-55507-298-4*) Municipal Analysis.
— Governments of the Northeast 1987. (Governments of Your State Ser.). 1987. text ed. 150.00 (*1-55507-168-6*); text ed. 150.00 (*1-55507-166-X*) Municipal Analysis.
— Governments of the Northeast 1987. (Expert Edition Ser.). 1987. text ed. 325.00 (*1-55507-211-9*) Municipal Analysis.
— Governments of the Northeast 1988. (Governments of Your State Ser.). 1988. text ed. 150.00 (*1-55507-257-7*) Municipal Analysis.
— Governments of the Northeast 1988. (Expert Edition Ser.). 1988. text ed. 325.00 (*1-55507-301-8*) Municipal Analysis.
— Governments of the Northwest 1987. (Expert Edition Ser.). 1987. text ed. 325.00 (*1-55507-209-7*) Municipal Analysis.
— Governments of the Northwest 1988. (Governments of Your State Ser.). 1988. text ed. 150.00 (*1-55507-255-0*) Municipal Analysis.
— Governments of the Northwest 1988. (Expert Edition Ser.). 1988. text ed. 325.00 (*1-55507-299-2*) Municipal Analysis.
— Governments of the West. (Governments of Your State Ser.). 1987. text ed. 150.00 (*1-55507-167-8*) Municipal Analysis.
— Governments of the West 1987. (Expert Edition Ser.). 1987. text ed. 325.00 (*1-55507-210-0*) Municipal Analysis.
— Governments of the West 1988. (Governments of Your State Ser.). 1988. text ed. 150.00 (*1-55507-256-9*) Municipal Analysis.
— Governments of the West 1988. (Expert Edition Ser.). 1988. text ed. 325.00 (*1-55507-300-X*) Municipal Analysis.
— Governments of Vermont 1987. (Governments of Your State Ser.). 1987. text ed. 150.00 (*1-55507-160-0*) Municipal Analysis.
— Governments of Vermont 1987. (Expert Edition Ser.). 1987. text ed. 325.00 (*1-55507-203-8*) Municipal Analysis.
— Governments of Vermont 1988. (Governments of Your State Ser.). 1988. text ed. 150.00 (*1-55507-249-6*) Municipal Analysis.
— Governments of Vermont 1988. (Expert Edition Ser.). 1988. text ed. 325.00 (*1-55507-293-3*) Municipal Analysis.
— Governments of Virginia 1987. (Governments of Your State Ser.). 1987. text ed. 150.00 (*1-55507-161-9*) Municipal Analysis.
— Governments of Virginia 1987. (Expert Edition Ser.). 1987. text ed. 325.00 (*1-55507-204-6*) Municipal Analysis.
— Governments of Virginia 1988. (Governments of Your State Ser.). 1988. text ed. 150.00 (*1-55507-250-X*) Municipal Analysis.
— Governments of Virginia 1988. (Expert Edition Ser.). 1988. text ed. 325.00 (*1-55507-294-1*) Municipal Analysis.
— Governments of Washington 1987. (Governments of Your State Ser.). 1987. text ed. 150.00 (*1-55507-162-7*) Municipal Analysis.
— Governments of Washington 1987. (Expert Edition Ser.). 1987. text ed. 325.00 (*1-55507-205-4*) Municipal Analysis.
— Governments of Washington 1988. (Governments of Your State Ser.). 1988. text ed. 150.00 (*1-55507-251-8*) Municipal Analysis.
— Governments of Washington 1988. (Expert Edition Ser.). 1988. text ed. 325.00 (*1-55507-295-X*) Municipal Analysis.
— Governments of West Virginia 1987. (Governments of Your State Ser.). 1987. text ed. 150.00 (*1-55507-163-5*) Municipal Analysis.
— Governments of West Virginia 1987. (Expert Edition Ser.). 1987. text ed. 325.00 (*1-55507-206-2*) Municipal Analysis.
— Governments of West Virginia 1988. (Governments of Your State Ser.). 1988. text ed. 150.00 (*1-55507-252-6*) Municipal Analysis.
— Governments of West Virginia 1988. (Expert Edition Ser.). 1988. text ed. 325.00 (*1-55507-296-8*) Municipal Analysis.
— Governments of Wisconsin 1987. (Governments of Your State Ser.). 1987. text ed. 150.00 (*1-55507-164-3*) Municipal Analysis.
— Governments of Wisconsin 1987. (Expert Edition Ser.). 1987. text ed. 325.00 (*1-55507-207-0*) Municipal Analysis.
— Governments of Wisconsin 1988. (Governments of Your State Ser.). 1988. text ed. 150.00 (*1-55507-253-4*) Municipal Analysis.
— Governments of Wisconsin 1988. (Expert Edition Ser.). 1988. text ed. 325.00 (*1-55507-297-6*) Municipal Analysis.

Municipal Finance Officers Association, Government Finance Research Center Staff. State & Local Government Finance & Financial Management: A Compendium of Current Research. LC 78-70328. 690p. 1978. 18.00 (*0-686-84363-0*) Municipal.
Municipal Finance Officers Association Staff. A Capital Improvement Programming Handbook for Small Cities & Other Governmental Units. LC 78-71712. (Illus.). 80p. 1978. 15.00 (*0-686-84280-4*) Municipal.
— Community Development Block Grant Budgetary & Financial Management. 134p. 1978. 14.95 (*0-686-84366-5*) Municipal.
— A Debt Management Handbook for Small Cities & Other Governmental Units. LC 78-71726. (Debt Administration Ser.). (Illus.). 69p. 1978. 15.00 (*0-686-84294-4*) Municipal.
— Governmental Accounting, Auditing, & Financial Reporting. LC 80-84747. (Illus.). 314p. 1980. 35.00 (*0-686-84252-9*) Municipal.
— Guidelines for the Preparation of a Public Employee Retirement System Comprehensive Annual Financial Report. (Illus.). 66p. 1980. pap. 10.00 (*0-686-84368-1*) Municipal.
— Is Your City Heading for Financial Difficulty? A Guidebook for Small Cities & Other Governmental Units. (Illus.). 43p. 1978. 6.00 (*0-686-84361-4*) Municipal.
— Official Statements for Offerings of Securities by Local Governments - Examples & Guidelines. 64p. 1981. 12.00 (*0-686-84334-7*); 10.00 (*0-686-84335-5*) Municipal.
— State & Local Government Fiscal Almanac 1982-MFOA Membership Directory. 400p. 1982. pap. 50.00 (*0-686-84339-8*); pap. 35.00 (*0-686-84340-1*) Municipal.
— A Treasury Management Handbook for Small Cities & Other Governmental Units. LC 78-71725. (Illus.). 93p. 1978. 15.00 (*0-686-84374-6*) Municipal.
Municipal Finance Officers Association Staff & Miller, Girard. Systems That Work: Government Financial Manuals, Analyses & Operating Procedures. (Illus.). ix, 273p. write for info. (*0-318-60754-9*) Municipal.
Municipal Finance Officers Association Staff & United States, Bureau of the Census Staff. State Supervision of Local Finance: Proceedings of a Conference, December 4, 5, 6, 1941. 127p. write for info. (*0-318-59326-2*) Municipal.
Municipal Research & Services Center, Washington Staff & Association of Washington Cities Staff. Handbook for City Officials of Washington Municipal Code Cities. (Illus.). ix, 232p. 1985. pap. write for info. (*0-318-60205-9*) Muni Res WA.
Municipality of Anchorage Department of Economic Development & Planning Staff. Anchorage Indicators: A Socioeconomic Review. (Orig.). 1989. pap. text ed. 10.00 (*0-685-28889-7*) Municipality Anchorage.
***Munier, Bertrand, ed.** Models & Experiments in Risk & Rationality. (Theory & Decision Library B). 450p. (C). 1994. lib. bdg. 114.00 (*0-7923-3031-5*) Kluwer Ac.
Munier, Bertrand R., ed. Markets, Risk & Money: Essays in Honor of Maurice Allais. LC 93-36635. (Theory & Decision Library Series B: Vol. 26). 388p. (C). 1993. lib. bdg. 165.50 (*0-7923-2578-8*) Kluwer Ac.
Munier, Charles. Authorite' Episcopale et Sollicitude Pastorale. (Collected Studies: No. CS341). 320p. (FRE.). 1991. text ed. 91.95 (*0-86078-296-4*, Pub. by Variorum UK) Ashgate Pub Co.
— Vie Conciliaire et Collections Canoniques en Occident, IVe-XIIe Siecles. (Collected Studies: No. CS265). 318p. (FRE.). (C). 1987. reprint ed. text ed. 95.00 (*0-86078-213-1*, Pub. by Variorum UK) Ashgate Pub Co.
Muniesa, David. Una Fe Contra un Imperio: Samuel Vila: Faith Against an Empire: Samuel Vila. (SPA.). 8.95 (*84-7228-444-1*, 220795, Pub. by Edit Clie SP) TSELF.
Munif, Abdelrahman. Cities of Salt. Theroux, Peter, tr. LC 87-40078. (International Ser.). 464p. (Orig.). 1989. pap. 16.00 (*0-394-75526-X*, Vin) Random.
— The Trench. Theroux, Peter, tr. LC 92-50609. (Cities of Salt Trilogy Ser.: Vol. 2). 1993. pap. 14.00 (*0-679-74533-5*, Vin) Random.
— Variations on Night & Day. Theroux, Peter, tr. LC 92-50786. 1993. 24.00 (*0-394-57673-X*) Pantheon.
— Variations on Night & Day. 1994. pap. 12.00 (*0-679-75551-9*, Vin) Random.
Munion, Michael, jt. ed. see Zeig, Jeffrey K.
Munir, Edward. Fisheries after Factortame. 265p. 1991. pap. 180.00 (*0-406-00298-3*, U.K.) Butterworth Legal Pubs.
Munir, Z. A. & Holt, J. B., eds. Combustion & Plasma Synthesis of High-Temperature Materials: Proceedings of the First International Symposium on Combustion & Plasma Synthesis of High-Temperature Material, October 23-26, 1988, San Francisco, CA. 501p. 1990. lib. bdg. 100.00 (*0-89573-756-6*) VCH Pubs.
Muniraj, R. Farm Finance for Development. 1987p. (C). 1987. 10.50 (*81-204-0223-5*, Pub. by Oxford IBH II) S Asia.
Munis, G. & Zerzan, J. Unions Against Revolution. 1975. pap. 1.25 (*0-934868-12-3*) Black & Red.
Munishi, G. K., jt. auth. see Mhina, A. K.
Munitz, Milton, jt. ed. see Keifer, Howard.
Munitz, Milton K. Cosmic Understanding: Philosophy & Science of the Universe. 296p. (Orig.). 1990. text ed. 45.00 (*0-691-07312-0*) Princeton U Pr.
— Does Life Have a Meaning? 114p. 1993. 22.95x (*0-87975-860-0*) Prometheus Bks.
— The Question of Reality. 221p. 1992. text ed. 39.50 (*0-691-07362-7*); pap. text ed. 14.95 (*0-691-02091-4*) Princeton U Pr.
— The Ways of Philosophy. (C). 1979. text ed. write for info. (*0-02-384850-2*) Macmillan.
Munitz, Milton K., ed. Theories of the Universe: From Babylonian Myth to Modern Science. LC 57-6746. 438p. 1965. pap. 16.95 (*0-02-922270-2*) Free Pr.
Munitz, Milton K., ed. see International Philosophy Year Conferences, Brockport.
Munitz, Milton K., tr. see Kant, Immanuel.
Munitz, Milton K., jt. ed. see Kiefer, Howard E.
***Muniz, Castro.** English-Spanish, Spanish-English Legal Dictionary. 613p. (ENG & SPA.). 1992. 105.00 (*0-7859-7520-9*, 8476951086) Fr & Eur.
Muniz Castro, E. Spanish-English - English-Spanish Dictionary of Legal Terms. 613p. (ENG & SPA.). 1992. 100.00 (*84-7695-108-6*, Pub. by La Ley SP) IBD Ltd.
Muniz, Dora Nevares. Derecho de Menores. 128p. (Orig.). (SPA.). (C). 1987. pap. text ed. write for info. (*0-914939-03-3*) Instituto Desarrollo.
Muniz-Huberman, Angelina. Enclosed Garden. Miller, Yvette E., ed. Zamora, Lois P., tr. LC 87-3643. 104p. 1988. pap. 11.50 (*0-935480-29-3*) Lat Am Lit Rev Pr.
***Muniz, Mirta, ed.** Elecciones en Cuba: Farsa o Democracia? (Illus.). 172p. 1993. pap. 9.95 (*1-875284-71-0*, Pub. by Ocean Pr AT) Talman.
Muniz, Peter & Chasnoff, Robert. Conflict & Confrontation: A Training Program. 26p. (C). 1981. pap. text ed. 7.00 (*0-943300-01-0*) LABS.
Muniz, Peter, jt. auth. see Chasnoff, Robert.
Munjal, M. L. Acoustics of Ducts & Mufflers. 328p. 1987. text ed. 115.00 (*0-471-84738-0*) Wiley.
Munk, Arthur W. A Synoptic Approach to the Riddle of Existence: Toward an Adequate World View for a World Civilization. LC 77-818. 264p. 1977. 12.75 (*0-87527-165-0*) Green.
— Whither America: Will There be a Tricentennial? 1984. 9.75 (*0-8158-0419-9*) Chris Mass.
Munk, E. Call of the Torah: Bamidbar. 1993. 20.95 (*0-89906-046-3*); 17.95 (*0-89906-047-1*) Mesorah Pubns.
— Call of the Torah: Bereishis - Genesis. 1994. 20.95 (*0-89906-040-4*); pap. 17.95 (*0-89906-041-2*) Mesorah Pubns.
— Call of the Torah: Shimos - Exodus. 1994. 20.95 (*0-89906-042-0*); pap. 17.95 (*0-89906-043-9*) Mesorah Pubns.
— Call of the Torah: Vayikra. 1992. 20.95 (*0-89906-044-7*); pap. 17.95 (*0-89906-045-5*) Mesorah Pubns.
Munk, Elie. The World of Prayer, 2 vols. pap. 22.95 (*0-685-73248-7*) Feldheim.
— The World of Prayer, 2 vols., Set. 29.95 (*0-87306-080-6*) Feldheim.
Munk, G. The Canadian Pacific Line. 1990. 75.00 (*0-9516038-5-X*, Pub. by Ship Pictorial Pubng UK) St Mut.
Munk, K. Virologie in Deutschland: Die Entwicklung eines Fachgebietes. (Illus.). x, 170p. 1994. 40.00 (*3-8055-6004-4*) S Karger.
Munk, K., ed. see Hofschneider, P. H.
Munk, K., et al, eds. Oncogenes in Cancer Diagnostics. (Beitraege zur Onkologie, Contributions to Oncology Ser.: Vol. 39). (Illus.). viii, 198p. 1990. 63.25 (*3-8055-5231-9*) S Karger.
Munk, Linda. The Trivial Sublime: Theology & American Poetics. LC 92-19511. 1992. text ed. 59.95 (*0-312-08561-3*) St Martin.
Munk, Michael L. The Wisdom in the Hebrew Alphabet: The Sacred Letters As a Guide to Jewish Deed & Thought. (ArtScroll Mesorah Ser.). (Illus.). 240p. 1983. 21.95 (*0-89906-193-1*); pap. 18.95 (*0-89906-194-X*) Mesorah Pubns.
Munk, Michael L., et al, eds. Shechita: Religious & Historical Research on the Method of Slaughter. (Illus.). 1976. 10.95 (*0-87306-992-7*) Feldheim.

M

Munk, Peter L. & Helms, Clyde A. MRI of the Knee. (Clinical Diagnostic Imaging Ser.). 250p. 1991. 93.50 (*0-8342-0246-8*) Raven.

Munk, Petr. Introduction to Macromolecular Science. 544p. 1989. text ed. 69.95 (*0-471-83212-X*) Wiley.

Munk, Robert J. & Lovett, Marc. Hospitalwide Education & Training. LC 77-13675. (Illus.). 1977. boxed 12.00 (*0-87914-045-3*, 549615) Hosp Res & Educ.

Munk, S. Philosophy & Philosophical Authors of the Jews: A Historical Sketch with Explanatory Notes. Kalisch, Isidor, tr. (Reprints in Philosophy Ser.). reprint ed. lib. bdg. 26.50 (*0-697-00012-5*) Irvington.

Munk, Salomon. Melanges Philosophie Juive et Arabe. Katz, Steven, ed. LC 79-7148. (Jewish Philosophy, Mysticism & History of Ideas Ser.). 1980. reprint ed. lib. bdg. 56.95 (*0-405-12278-0*) Ayer.

***Munk, Walter, et al.** Ocean Acoustic Tomography. (Monographs on Mechanics). (Illus.). 450p. (C). 1995. write for info. (*0-521-47095-1*) Cambridge U Pr.

Munk, William. Euthanasia: Or, Medical Treatment in Aid of an Easy Death. Kastenbaum, Robert, ed. LC 76-19584. (Death & Dying Ser.). 1979. reprint ed. lib. bdg. 21.95 (*0-405-09580-5*) Ayer.

Munk, Zelda V. Deodorants: Index of New Information & Medical Research Bible. 150p. 1994. 44.50 (*0-7883-0118-7*); pap. 39.50 (*0-7883-0119-5*) ABBE Pubs Assn.

Munkacsi, Bernat, jt. ed. see Kunos, Ignacz.

Munkasey, Michael. The Astrological Thesaurus, Vol. 1. LC 92-34334. (Llewellyn's Modern Astrology Library). 490p. 1992. 19.95 (*0-87542-579-8*) Llewellyn Pubns.

— Midpoints: Unleashing the Power of the Planets. 414p. (Orig.). 1991. pap. 19.95 (*0-935127-11-9*) ACS Pubns.

Munkelt, Margarete. Buehnenanweisung und Dramaturgie. Hinweise zu Interpretation und Inszenierung in Shakespeare's First Folio und den Quartoversionen. (Bochum Studies in English: No. 12). x, 346p. (Orig.). (GER.). 1981. pap. 37.00 (*90-6032-206-1*) Benjamins North Am.

Munker, Dona, jt. auth. see Farmaian, Sattareh F.

Munkirs, John R. The Transformation of American Capitalism: From Competitive Market Structures to Centralized Private Sector Planning. LC 83-27093. 246p. 1985. pap. 25.95 (*0-87332-270-3*) M E Sharpe.

Munkman, J. Employers Liability (At Common Law) (C). 1985. 480.00 (*0-685-32825-2*, Pub. by Witherby & Co UK) St Mut.

Munkman, John. Damages for Personal Injuries & Death. 9th ed. 304p. 1993. boxed 80.00 (*0-406-01481-7*, U.K.) Butterworth Legal Pubs.

— Munkman: The Technique of Advocacy. 1991. reprint ed. 30.00 (*0-406-00264-9*) Butterworth Legal Pubs.

Munkman, John, ed. Employer's Liability. 11th ed. 1990. 144.00 (*0-406-18100-4*, U.K.) Butterworth Legal Pubs.

Munkres, James. Topology: A First Course. (Illus.). 448p. 1974. text ed. 68.00 (*0-13-925495-1*) P-H.

Munkres, James R. Analysis on Manifolds. (Illus.). 384p. (C). 1991. 49.95 (*0-201-51035-9*, Adv Bk Prog) Addison-Wesley.

Munkres, Robert L. Saleratus & Sagebrush: The Oregon Trail Through Wyoming. 2nd ed. (Illus.). 156p. 1974. reprint ed. pap. 3.50 (*0-943398-02-9*) Wyoming St Mus.

Munley, Joan. Self Care Deficit Theory of Nursing. 128p. (C). 1984. pap. text ed. write for info. (*0-910973-03-2*) Arrowhead AZ.

Munman, Robert. Optical Corrections in the Sculpture of Donatello. LC 84-71080. (Transactions Ser.: Vol. 75, Pt. 2). 1985. pap. 18.00 (*0-87169-752-1*, T752-MUR) Am Philos.

— Sienese Renaissance Tomb Monuments. LC 92-85343. (Memoirs Ser.: Vol. 205). (Illus.). 295p. (C). 1993. 25.00 (*0-87169-205-8*, M205-MUR) Am Philos.

***Munn.** Precious Love. 1995. mass mkt. 4.99 (*0-7860-0124-0*, Pinnacle NY) Windsor NY.

Munn, David. The Joy of Pastry. (Illus.). 224p. 1985. 15.95 (*0-8120-5670-1*) Barron.

— The Joy of Pastry. (Joy of Cookbook Ser.). 240p. 1990. pap. 10.95 (*0-8120-4517-3*) Barron.

Munn, Debra D. Big Sky Ghosts. LC 93-3176. (Eerie True Tales of Montana Ser.: Vol. 1). 146p. 1993. pap. 14.95 (*0-87108-838-X*) Pruett.

— Big Sky Ghosts, Vol. 2: Eerie True Tales of Montana. LC 93-3176. 131p. 1994. pap. 14.95 (*0-87108-839-8*) Pruett.

— Ghosts on the Range: Eerie True Tales of Wyoming. LC 89-39754. 190p. (Orig.). 1989. pap. 14.00 (*0-87108-771-5*) Pruett.

Munn, Debra D., ed. see Krause, Danna J.

Munn, Felicity. Two to Twenty-Two Days in Eastern Canada: The Itinerary Planner, 1994. (Two to Twenty-Two Days Ser.). (Orig.). 1993. pap. 10.95 (*1-56261-096-1*) John Muir.

— Two to Twenty-Two Days in Eastern Canada, 1995 Edition. (Two to Twenty-Two Days Itinerary Planner Ser.). (Illus.). 240p. 1995. pap. 12.95 (*1-56261-204-2*) John Muir.

Munn, Geoffrey C. The Triumph of Love: Amatory Jewelry from the Renaissance to Art Deco. LC 93-60429. (Illus.). 112p. 1993. 29.95 (*0-500-23661-5*) Thames Hudson.

Munn, Geoffrey C., jt. auth. see Gere, Charlotte.

Munn, Glenn G., et al, eds. Encyclopedia of Banking & Finance, 3 vols. 9th ed. (Illus.). 1161p. 1993. lib. bdg. 235.00 (*0-89356-496-6*) Salem Pr.

Munn, Heidi, ed. Culture Shock! Borneo. (Illus.). 250p. 1991. pap. 10.95 (*1-55868-075-6*) Gr Arts Ctr Pub.

***Munn, Jarod.** One Bullet Short: A Deer-Hunting Story. 1994. 12.95 (*0-533-10978-7*) Vantage.

Munn, Kenneth. Three-Minute Bible Stories with Cut & Paste Projects. (Three-Minute Bible Story Ser.). (Illus.). 96p. (J). (gr. k-3). 1994. 9.95 (*0-86653-776-7*, SS3809, Shining Star Pubns) Good Apple.

Munn, Mark H. Defense of Attica: The Dema Wall & the Boiotian War of 378-375 B.C. (C). 1994. 40.00 (*0-520-07685-0*) U CA Pr.

Munn, Michael. Clint Eastwood: Hollywood's Loner. (Illus.). 258p. 1993. 24.95 (*0-86051-790-X*, Robson-Parkwest) Parkwest Pubns.

— Hollywood Bad. 1993. mass mkt. 4.99 (*0-312-92984-6*) St Martin.

— Hollywood Murder Case Book. 1990. mass mkt. 4.50 (*0-312-92362-7*) St Martin.

— Hollywood Rogues: The Off-Screen Antics of Hollywood's Hellraisers. large type ed. (Illus.). 283p. 1992. 23.95 (*1-85089-581-3*, Pub. by ISIS UK) Transaction Pubs.

— Trevor Howard. LC 90-41123. (Illus.). 196p. 1990. 19.95 (*0-8128-4006-2*, Scrbrough Hse) Madison Bks UPA.

Munn, Michael, jt. auth. see Sparks, William.

Munn, Nancy D. The Fame of Gawa: A Symbolic Study of Value Transformation in a Massim (Papua New Guinea) Society. LC 92-9614. (Henry Louis Morgan Lecture Ser.). (Illus.). 352p. 1992. pap. text ed. 16.95 (*0-8223-1270-0*) Duke.

Munn, Pamela, ed. Parents & Schools: Customers, Managers or Partners? LC 92-28832. (Educational Management Ser.). 256p. 1993. 57.50 (*0-415-07692-7*, A7705, Routledge NY); pap. 22.50 (*0-415-08926-3*, B0246, Routledge NY) Routledge.

Munn, Pamela & Jonstone, Margaret. Effective Discipline in Primary Schools & Classrooms. 160p. 1992. pap. 29.95 (*1-85396-174-4*, Pub. by Paul Chapman UK) Taylor & Francis.

— Effective Discipline in Secondary Schools & Classrooms. 160p. 1992. pap. 29.95 (*1-85396-175-2*, Pub. by Paul Chapman UK) Taylor & Francis.

Munn, R. E., ed. Boundary Layer Studies & Applications: A Special Issue of Boundary-Layer Meteorology in Honor of Dr. Hans A. Panofsky (1917-1988) (C). 1989. lib. bdg. 172.00 (*0-7923-0277-X*) Kluwer Ac.

Munn, R. W. & Ironside, C. N., eds. Principles & Applications of Nonlinear Optical Materials. 1993. 96.50 (*0-8493-7109-0*, QC446) CRC Pr.

Munn, R. W., jt. auth. see Rohleder, J. W.

Munn, Raymond S., ed. Computer Modeling in Corrosion. LC 92-12525. (Special Technical Publication Ser.: Vol. 1154). (Illus.). 300p. 1992. 86.00 (*0-8031-1473-7*, 04-011540-27) ASTM.

Munn, Robert F. Coal Industry in America: Bibliography & Guide to Studies. 2nd ed. LC 77-77913. 351p. 1977. 30.00 (*0-930284-00-3*) West Va U Pr.

— Strip Mining: An Annotated Bibliography. LC 72-96636. 110p. 1973. 22.50 (*0-937058-09-2*) West Va U Pr.

Munn, Robert W., jt. auth. see Hinchliffe, Alan.

Munn, Sheldon A. Freemasons at Gettysburg. (Illus.). 92p. (C). 1993. pap. text ed. 8.95 (*0-939631-68-7*) Thomas Publications.

Munn, Sherrill. Beacon Small-Group Bible Studies, Luke: Lessons on Discipleship, Vol. 2. 68p. (Orig.). 1981. pap. 3.95 (*0-8341-0689-2*) Beacon Hill.

Munn, Vella. Daughter of the Forest. 416p. 1995. mass mkt. 5.99 (*0-8125-3499-9*) Forge NYC.

— Daughter of the Mountain. 416p. (Orig.). 1994. mass mkt. 5.99 (*0-8125-2325-3*) Tor Bks.

— The Eagles' Daughter. (Orig.). 1996. mass mkt. write for info. (*0-614-05517-2*) Forge NYC.

— Midnight Sun. 224p. (Orig.). 1993. pap. 2.95 (*1-56597-050-0*, Kismet) Meteor Pub.

— Navajo Nights. 1995. mass mkt. 3.50 (*0-373-27058-5*, 1-27058-6) Silhouette.

— Precious Love. 288p. 1995. pap. 4.99 (*0-8217-0124-X*) Zebra.

— The River's Daughter. 416p. (Orig.). 1993. mass mkt. 4.99 (*0-8125-1930-2*) Tor Bks.

— Song of Silence. 224p. (Orig.). 1993. pap. 2.95 (*1-56597-090-X*, Kismet) Meteor Pub.

— Winter Legacy. 320p. 1992. mass mkt. 3.99 (*0-8217-3841-0*) Zebra.

Munn, W. D., et al. Semigroups with Applications: Proceedings of the Conference. 276p. 1992. text ed. 81.00 (*981-02-1121-X*) World Scientific Pub.

Munna, Raymond J. As I See It: Radial Keratotomy Before, During & After Surgery. (Illus.). 110p. 1986. pap. 9.95 (*0-935669-07-8*) A Granite Pubs.

— Franchise Selection: Separating Fact from Fiction. 216p. (Orig.). 1988. pap. 19.95 (*0-935669-12-4*) A Granite Pubs.

— Legal Power for Small Business Owners & Managers. LC 91-8838. 309p. (Orig.). 1991. pap. 19.95 (*0-935669-10-8*) A Granite Pubs.

Munneke, Gary. Careers in Law. 160p. 1992. 16.95 (*0-8442-8554-4*, VGM Career Bks); pap. 12.95 (*0-8442-8555-2*, VGM Career Bks) NTC Pub Grp.

Munneke, Gary A. How to Succeed in Law School. 1989. pap. 9.95 (*0-8120-4261-1*) Barron.

— How to Succeed in Law School. 2nd ed. 280p. 1994. pap. 9.95 (*0-8120-1449-9*) Barron.

— Law Practice Management: Materials & Cases. (American Casebook Ser.). 634p. 1992. reprint ed. text ed. 44.50 (*0-314-83688-8*) West Pub.

— Law Practice Management, Materials & Cases, Teacher's Manual. (American Casebook Ser.). 123p. (C). 1991. pap. text ed. write for info. (*0-314-00055-0*) West Pub.

— Opportunities in Law Careers. (Illus.). 160p. 1986. 13.95 (*0-8442-6174-2*, VGM Career Bks); pap. 10.95 (*0-8442-6175-0*, VGM Career Bks) NTC Pub Grp.

— Opportunities in Law Careers. LC 93-25120. 1994. 13.95 (*0-8442-4086-9*, VGM Career Bks); pap. 10.95 (*0-8442-4087-7*, VGM Career Bks) NTC Pub Grp.

Munnell. Retirement & Public Policy. 272p. 1991. boxed 39.95 (*0-8403-6477-6*) Kendall-Hunt.

Munnell, Alicia H. The Economics of Private Pensions. LC 82-4223. (Studies in Social Economics). 240p. 1982. 28.95 (*0-8157-5894-4*); pap. 10.95 (*0-8157-5893-6*) Brookings.

— The Future of Social Security. LC 76-51883. (Studies in Social Economics). 1977. pap. 12.95 (*0-8157-5895-2*) Brookings.

Munnell, Alicia H. & Connolly, Ann M. Pensions for Public Employees. LC 79-89303. 128p. 1979. 7.00 (*0-89068-048-5*) Natl Planning.

Munnell, Alicia H., jt. ed. see Bodie, Zvi.

Munnell, Michael D., ed. American Indian Marriage Record Directory for Ashland County, Wisconsin, 1874-1907. 279p. (Orig.). 1993. pap. 35.00 (*0-9638897-4-5*) Chippewa Heritage.

Munnich, F. E., jt. ed. see Abshagen, U.

Munnichs, J. M. Old Age & Finitude: A Contribution to Psychogerontology. Stein, Leon, ed. LC 79-8676. (Growing Old Ser.). 1980. reprint ed. lib. bdg. 18.95 (*0-405-12792-8*) Ayer.

Munnichs, Joep, et al, eds. Life-Span & Change in a Gerontological Perspective. 1985. pap. text ed. 47.00 (*0-12-510261-5*) Acad Pr.

Munnichs, Joep M., et al. Dependency or Interdependency in Old Age. 1976. lib. bdg. 51.50 (*90-247-1895-3*) Kluwer Ac.

Munnick, Adrian R., ed. & illus. Catholic Church Records of the Pacific Northwest: St. Ann, Walla Walla & Frenchtown. LC 88-63227. 328p. 1989. 25.00 (*0-8323-0466-2*) Binford Mort.

Munnick, Harriet D. Catholic Church Records of the Pacific Northwest: Oregon City, Salem & Jacksonville. LC 84-70844. (Illus.). 400p. 1984. 25.00 (*0-8323-0429-8*) Binford Mort.

— Catholic Church Records of the Pacific Northwest: St. Louis, Gervais & Brooks. LC 72-71955. (Illus.). 528p. 1982. 25.00 (*0-8323-0408-5*) Binford Mort.

— Catholic Church Records of the Pacific Northwest: St. Paul, Oregon 1839-1898. LC 79-3575. (Illus.). 832p. 1980. 25.00 (*0-8323-0348-8*) Binford Mort.

— Catholic Church Records of the Pacific Northwest: Vancouver & Stellamaris Mission. LC 72-83958. (Illus.). 444p. 1972. 25.00 (*0-8323-0375-5*) Binford Mort.

— Priest's Progress: The Journey of Frances Norbert Blanchet from the Atlantic Ocean to the Pacific in Three Parishes. LC 89-62677. (Illus.). 100p. 1989. 15.00 (*0-8323-0474-3*) Binford Mort.

Munnick, Harriet D., comp. Catholic Church Records of the Pacific Northwest: Roseburg & Portland. LC 85-63221. (Illus.). 440p. 1986. 25.00 (*0-8323-0447-6*) Binford Mort.

Munnick, Harriet D. & Beckman, Stephan D., eds. Catholic Church Records of the Pacific Northwest: Grand Ronde. (Illus.). 312p. 1987. 25.00 (*0-8323-0455-7*); Register I, 1860-1885. write for info. (*0-318-61703-X*); Register II, 1885-1898. write for info. (*0-318-61704-8*) Binford Mort.

Munnik, Josha & Oostendorp, Eric. The Sound Blaster Book. LC 93-87420. 534p. 1994. pap. 27.99 (*0-7821-1320-6*) Sybex.

Munniksma, F. Dictionary of Economics: Oekonomisches Woerterbuch. 764p. (ENG & GER.). 1980. 95.00 (*0-8288-0099-5*, M 15199) Fr & Eur.

— Dictionnaire International du Commerce et de L'Economie: French, English, Esperanto, German, Spanish, Italian, Portuguese, Swedish, Japanese, Chinese. 1990. 75.00 (*0-685-48811-X*, M15696) Fr & Eur.

— International Dictionary of Commerce & Economics: Dictionnaire International du Commerce et de L'Economie: French, English, Esperanto, German, Spanish, Italian, Portuguese, Swedish, Japanese, Chinese. 1991. 75.00 (*0-8288-4041-5*, M15696) Fr & Eur.

***Munniksma, F., ed.** Dictionnaire International du Commerce et de l'Economie. 1990. write for info. (*0-7859-8704-5*, 7505200259) Fr & Eur.

Munning, K. A., jt. ed. see Taylor, Robert B.

Munns, Dencie. The Storms of Love. LC 90-7513. 238p. 1990. 15.75 (*0-930950-23-2*); pap. 9.75 (*0-930950-24-0*) Nopoly Pr.

Munns, Frank, ed. George Tsutakawa & Morris Graves: Paintings, Drawings, & Sculpture. (Illus.). 14p. (Orig.). (C). 1978. pap. 10.00 (*1-880269-03-1*) D H Sheehan.

Munns, Frank & Lynx, David, eds. The Columbia & Plateau: The Roger J. Bounds Foundation, Inc. Collection Exhibition. (Illus.). 8p. (Orig.). (C). 1990. pap. 6.95 (*1-880269-06-6*) D H Sheehan.

***Munns, Jessica.** Restoration Politics & Drama: The Plays of Thomas Otway, 1675-1683. LC 95-10377. 1996. write for info. (*0-87413-548-6*) U Delaware Pr.

Munns, Ron R., jt. auth. see Marsh, W. Jeffrey.

Muno-Faure, Lesley & Muno-Faure, Malcolm. TQM: A Primer for Implementation. 300p. 1994. text ed. 30.00 (*0-7863-0138-4*) Irwin Prof Pubng.

Muno-Faure, Malcolm, jt. auth. see Muno-Faure, Lesley.

Muno, Jean. Glove of Passion, Voice of Blood. Connell, Kim, tr. 127p. (Orig.). 1986. pap. 8.00 (*0-937669-22-9*) Owl Creek Pr.

Munonye, John. Obi. (African Writers Ser.). 210p. 1969. pap. 8.95 (*0-435-90045-5*) Heinemann.

— The Only Son. (African Writers Ser.). 152p. 1966. pap. 8.95 (*0-435-90021-8*) Heinemann.

Munowitz, M. Coherence & NMR. LC 88-10605. 289p. 1988. text ed. 74.95 (*0-471-61523-4*) Wiley.

Munoz. La Musica En Puerto Rico. 1966. 12.95 (*0-87751-012-1*) E Torres & Sons.

Munoz, A. Lopez. Programas para Dias Especiales Tomo I. 107p. 1986. reprint ed. pap. 3.50 (*0-311-07005-1*) Casa Bautista.

— Programas para Dias Especiales Tomo II. 64p. 1984. reprint ed. pap. 3.50 (*0-311-07006-X*) Casa Bautista.

Munoz, Alejandra, et al. Sensory Evaluation in Quality Control. (Illus.). 268p. 1991. text ed. 54.95 (*0-442-00459-1*) Chapman & Hall.

Munoz, Alfred M. Days Before the Tube in Plainfield. LC 83-70391. 1983. pap. 9.95 (*0-89754-033-6*) Dan River Pr.

Munoz, Alfredo N. & Ongkeko, Lourdes A., eds. Anthology of Philippine Writing in America. (Illus.). 260p. 1989. 19.00 (*0-685-26955-8*) Filipino Amer Pr Club.

Munoz, Antonio J. Forgotten Legions: Obscure Combat Formations of the Waffen-SS. (Illus.). 424p. 1991. text ed. 59.95 (*0-87364-646-0*) Paladin Pr.

Munoz, Arthur. From a Cops Journal & Other Poems. LC 84-70035. 64p. (Orig.). 1984. pap. 6.95 (*0-931722-32-2*) Corona Pub.

Munoz, Braulio. Sons of the Wind: The Search for Identity in Spanish American Indian Literature. LC 81-15403. 335p. (Orig.). reprint ed. pap. 95.50 (*0-7837-5678-X*, 2059106) Bks Demand.

— Tensions in Social Theory: Groundwork for a Future Moral Sociology. LC 92-26436. (Values & Ethics Ser.). 384p. 1993. 39.95 (*0-8294-0739-1*) Loyola Univ Pr.

Munoz, Carlos. Youth, Identity, Power: The Chicano Movement. (Haymarket Ser.). 320p. 1989. 50.00 (*0-86091-197-7*, Pub. by Verso UK); pap. 14.95 (*0-86091-913-7*, Pub. by Verso UK) Routledge Chapman & Hall.

Munoz-Cobo, J. L. & Difilippo, F. C., eds. Noise & Nonlinear Phenomena in Nuclear Systems. (NATO ASI Series B, Physics: Vol. 192). (Illus.). 482p. 1989. 115.00 (*0-306-43102-5*, Plenum Pr) Plenum.

***Munoz, E.** Spanish Dictionary of Uncommon Words. (SPA.). 1992. pap. 30.00 (*0-7859-8922-6*) Fr & Eur.

— Spanish Dictionary of Uncommon Words - Diccionario de Palabras Olvidadas. 409p. (SPA.). 1992. pap. 30.00 (*84-283-1986-3*, Pub. by Paraninfo) IBD Ltd.

Munoz, Elias M. Crazy Love. LC 88-6394. 180p. (Orig.). 1989. pap. 9.50 (*0-934770-83-2*) Arte Publico.

— The Greatest Performance. LC 91-9216. (Orig.). 1991. pap. 9.50 (*1-55885-038-4*) Arte Publico.

— Los Viajes de Orlando Cachumbambe. LC 83-81356. (Coleccion Caniqui Ser.). 143p. (Orig.). (SPA.). 1984. pap. 7.95 (*0-89729-332-0*) Ediciones.

Munoz-Furlong, Anne. The Food Allergy News Cookbook. LC 92-97152. 156p. 1992. text ed. 15.00 (*1-882541-00-6*) Food Allergy.

Munoz, Gabriel T. Permanent Work: Poems 1981-1992. Irby, Patricia L. et al, trs. (Baja California Literature in Translation Ser.). 96p. 1993. pap. 12.50 (*1-879691-13-2*) SDSU Press.

Munoz, Gabriela, tr. see Maultsby, Maxie C., Jr.

Munoz, Hector, jt. auth. see Alessio, Luis.

Munoz, Heraldo, ed. Environment & Diplomacy in the Americas. LC 92-4480. 149p. 1992. pap. text ed. 9.95 (*1-55587-390-1*) Lynne Rienner.

— Latin American Views of U. S. Policy: Politics of Latin America. LC 85-19365. (Hoover Institute Ser.). 162p. 1985. text ed. 49.95 (*0-275-92048-8*, C2048, Praeger Pubs) Greenwood.

Munoz, Heraldo & Rosenberg, Robin, eds. Difficult Liaison: Trade & the Environment in the Americas. LC 93-17922. 304p. (C). 1993. pap. 21.95 (*1-56000-679-X*, U Miami North-South Ctr) Transaction Pubs.

Munoz, Heraldo & Tulchin, Joseph S., eds. Latin American Nations in World Politics. 2nd ed. (C). 1929. text ed. 50.00 (*0-8133-0872-0*); pap. text ed. 18.95 (*0-8133-0873-9*) Westview.

Munoz, Heraldo & Vaky, Viron P. The Future of the Organization of American States. LC 93-31243. 1993. 9.95 (*0-87078-348-3*) TCFP-PPP.

Munoz, James L., jt. auth. see Nordstrown, Kirk.

Munoz, John J. & Bergman, R. K. Bordetella Pertussis: Immunological & Other Biological Activities. LC 76-26453. (Immunology Ser.: No. 4). (Illus.). 249p. reprint ed. pap. 71.00 (*0-7837-0815-7*, 2041130) Bks Demand.

Munoz, Jose & Sampayo, Carlos. Nicaragua. Thompson, Kim, ed. Bonner, Deborah, tr. (Sinner Ser.). (Illus.). 80p. (Orig.). 1988. pap. 8.95 (*0-930193-37-7*) Fantagraph Bks.

***Munoz, Juan & Rothenberg, Susan.** Parkett 43. 200p. 1995. pap. 19.50 (*3-907509-93-5*, Pub. by Parkett Pubs SZ) Dist Art Pubs.

Munoz, Luis, ed. see Fielding, Henry.

Munoz-Marin, Luis. Mensajes al Pueblo Puertorriqueno: Pronunciados ante las Camaras Legislativas, 1949-1964. LC 80-24258. (Illus.). 358p. 1980. 12.50 (*0-913480-47-9*); pap. 6.95 (*0-913480-48-7*); mass mkt. 4.95 (*0-913480-49-5*) Inter Am U Pr.

Munoz, Mary E., jt. auth. see Pyle, Michael A.

Munoz, Miguel M. Complete Works of Miguel Melendez Munoz, 3 vols., Set. (Puerto Rico Ser.). 1979. lib. bdg. 350.00 (*0-8490-2899-X*) Gordon Pr.

Munoz, N., et al, eds. Epidemiology of Cervical Cancer & Human Papillomavirus. (IARC Scientific Publications: No. 119). 308p. 1993. pap. 60.00 (*92-832-2119-2*) OUP.

— Human Papillomavirus & Cervical Cancer. (IARC Scientific Publications: No. 94). (Illus.). 176p. 1989. pap. 40.00 (*92-832-1194-4*) OUP.

Munoz, Olivia, jt. auth. see Lipton, Gladys C.

Munoz, Oscar, ed. Economic Reforms in Chile. 97p. 1992. write for info. (*0-940602-56-3*) IADB.

— Reformas Economicas En Chile. 1992. write for info. (*0-940602-49-0*) IADB.

Munoz, Rafael A. & Mantione, Anthony J. The Health of the Foot. Van Treese, James B., ed. 172p. 1992. pap. 9.95 (*1-880416-84-0*) NW Pub.

Munoz, Ricardo F., ed. Depression Prevention: Research Directions. 301p. 1987. 68.00 (*0-89116-452-9*) Hemisp Pub.

An Asterisk (*) at the beginning of an entry indicates that the title is appearing in BIP for the first time.

Munoz, Ricardo F., et al. The Prevention of Depression: Research & Practice. LC 92-49536. (Series in Psychiatry & Neuroscience). (Illus.). 360p. 1993. text ed. 65.00 (*0-8018-4496-7*) Johns Hopkins.

— Social & Psychological Research in Community Settings. LC 79-88107. (Jossey-Bass Social & Behavioral Science Ser.). 416p. reprint ed. pap. 118.60 (*0-8357-6881-3*, 2037933) Bks Demand.

Munoz, Rodrigo, jt. auth. see Morrison, James.

Munoz, Rodrigo A., ed. Treating Anxiety Disorders. LC 85-81896. (New Directions for Mental Health Services Ser.: No. MHS 32). (Orig.). 1986. pap. 17.95 (*1-55542-989-0*) Jossey-Bass.

Munoz, Ronaldo. The God of Christians. LC 90-25461. (Theology & Liberation Ser.). 1991. 39.95 (*0-88344-696-0*) Orbis Bks.

***Munoz, Roni & Pitty, Abelino.** Guia Fotografioa Para la Identification de Malezas, Pt. I. (Illus.). 124p. (Orig.). (SPA.). (C). 1994. pap. 5.00 (*1-885995-13-X*) Escuela Agricola.

Munoz, Rony, jt. auth. see Pitty, Abelino.

Munoz Seca, Pedro. La Venganza de Don Mendo. (Nueva Austral Ser.: Vol. 30). (SPA.). 1991. pap. text ed. 24.95x (*84-239-1830-0*) Elliots Bks.

Munoz, Sharon R. The Afro-American Griot Speaks: Afro-American Names. LC 93-61423. 140p. 1994. pap. 6.95 (*1-55523-671-5*) Winston-Derek.

Munoz, Silverio. Amanecer en Manhattan. 76p. (Orig.). 1985. pap. text ed. 5.00 (*0-937985-00-7*) Ediciones Arauco.

— Post-Coup Chilean Poetry: A Bilingual Anthology. Acevedo, Mary E. & Paska, Jocelyn, trs. LC 86-80932. (Illus.). 88p. 1986. pap. text ed. 7.50 (*0-937985-01-5*) Ediciones Arauco.

— Relatos. 250p. (Orig.). (SPA.). 1991. pap. text ed. 15.00 (*0-937985-06-6*) Ediciones Arauco.

— Tenure-Track: Historia de Profesores. 427p. (Orig.). (SPA.). 1993. pap. 21.50 (*0-937985-07-4*) Ediciones Arauco.

— Vivir en Madrid. 140p. (Orig.). (SPA.). 1991. text ed. 13.00 (*0-937985-05-8*) Ediciones Arauco.

Munoz, Silverio & Stok, Ana L. Benedictina: Relatos de Silverio Munoz - Dibujos de Ana Luisa Stok. (Illus.). 122p. (Orig.). (SPA.). 1991. pap. text ed. 12.50 (*0-937985-03-1*) Ediciones Arauco.

Munoz, Tisziji. The Beginner's Book, Vol. 1: The Holy Ground Discourse. 127p. (Orig.). (C). 1981. pap. 15.00 (*0-945174-00-4*) Illum Soc Pubns.

— The Facts of Light, Bk. 1. 25p. (Orig.). (C). 1987. pap. text ed. 10.00 (*0-945174-05-5*) Illum Soc Pubns.

— The Facts of the Process, Bk. 1: Free-Master Consciousness. 35p. (Orig.). (C). 1987. pap. text ed. 10.00 (*0-945174-04-7*) Illum Soc Pubns.

— Once Is for Always. (Orig.). 1991. pap. 10.00 (*0-945174-24-1*) Illum Soc Pubns.

— The Song of the Free Self: The Song of Who I Am. 43p. (Orig.). (C). 1981. pap. text ed. 10.00 (*0-945174-03-9*) Illum Soc Pubns.

— Time Mastery: The Beginner's Book, Vol. 5. (Illus.). (Orig.). (C). 1987. pap. 15.00 (*0-945174-02-0*) Illum Soc Pubns.

Munoz, Tizsiji. The Beginners Book, Vol. 2: Satsang Talks & Readings. 169p. (Orig.). (C). 1987. pap. text ed. 15.00 (*0-945174-01-2*) Illum Soc Pubns.

***Munoz-Tunon, C.** The Formation & Evolution of Galaxies. Sanchez, F., ed. (Illus.). 553p. (C). 1995. 64.95 (*0-521-49575-X*) Cambridge U Pr.

Munoz, V. Alberto Ghiraldo: A Chronology. Johnson, W. Scott, tr. (Libertarian & Anarchist Chronology Ser.). 1979. lib. bdg. 59.95 (*0-8490-3033-1*) Gordon Pr.

— Anarchists: A Biographical Encyclopedia. Johnson, Scott, tr. (History of Anarchism Ser.). 1980. lib. bdg. 300.00 (*0-8490-3101-X*) Gordon Pr.

— Anselmo Lorenzo: A Chronology. Johnson, W. Scott, tr. (Libertarian & Anarchist Chronology Ser.). 1979. lib. bdg. 59.95 (*0-8490-3052-8*) Gordon Pr.

— Bakunin: A Chronology. Johnson, W. Scott, tr. (Libertarian & Anarchist Chronology Ser.). 1979. lib. bdg. 59.95 (*0-8490-3025-0*) Gordon Pr.

— E. Armand: A Chronology. Johnson, W. Scott, tr. (Libertarian & Anarchist Chronology Ser.). 1979. lib. bdg. 59.95 (*0-8490-3048-X*) Gordon Pr.

— Eliseo Reclus: A Chronology. Johnson, W. Scott, tr. (Libertarian & Anarchist Chronology Ser.). 1979. lib. bdg. 59.95 (*0-8490-3023-4*) Gordon Pr.

— Federico Urales: A Chronology. (Libertarian & Anarchist Chronology Ser.). 1980. lib. bdg. 59.95 (*0-8490-3089-7*) Gordon Pr.

— Fermin Salvochea: A Chronology. Johnson, W. Scott, tr. (Libertarian & Anarchist Chronology Ser.). 1979. lib. bdg. 59.95 (*0-8490-3039-0*) Gordon Pr.

— Florencio Sanchez: A Chronology. Johnson, W. Scott, tr. (Libertarian & Anarchist Chronology Ser.). 1979. lib. bdg. 59.95 (*0-8490-3041-2*) Gordon Pr.

— Francisco Ferrer: A Chronology. Johnson, W. Scott, tr. (Libertarian & Anarchist Chronology Ser.). 1979. lib. bdg. 59.95 (*0-8490-3044-7*) Gordon Pr.

— Francisco Piy Margall: A Chronology. Johnson, W. Scott, tr. (Libertarian & Anarchist Chronology Ser.). 1979. lib. bdg. 59.95 (*0-8490-3030-7*) Gordon Pr.

— Giovanni Rossi: A Chronology. Johnson, W. Scott, tr. (Libertarian & Anarchist Chronology Ser.). 1979. lib. bdg. 59.95 (*0-8490-3056-0*) Gordon Pr.

— Gustav Landauer: A Chronology. Johnson, W. Scott, tr. (Libertarian & Anarchist Chronology Ser.). 1979. lib. bdg. 59.95 (*0-8490-3029-3*) Gordon Pr.

— Han Ryner: A Chronology. Johnson, W. Scott, tr. (Libertarian & Anarchist Chronology Ser.). 1979. lib. bdg. 59.95 (*0-8490-3024-2*) Gordon Pr.

— Hem Day: A Chronology. Johnson, W. Scott, tr. (Libertarian & Anarchist Chronology Ser.). 1979. lib. bdg. 59.95 (*0-8490-3049-8*) Gordon Pr.

— Henrik Ibsen: A Chronology. Johnson, W. Scott, tr. (Libertarian & Anarchist Chronology Ser.). 1979. lib. bdg. 59.95 (*0-8490-3031-5*) Gordon Pr.

— Johann Most: A Chronology. Johnson, W. Scott, tr. (Libertarian & Anarchist Chronology Ser.). 1979. lib. bdg. 59.95 (*0-8490-3027-7*) Gordon Pr.

— Joseph Ishill: A Chronology. Johnson, W. Scott, tr. (Libertarian & Anarchist Chronology Ser.). 1979. lib. bdg. 59.95 (*0-8490-3035-8*) Gordon Pr.

— Josiah Warren: A Chronology. Johnson, W. Scott, tr. (Libertarian & Anarchist Chronology Ser.). 1979. lib. bdg. 59.95 (*0-8490-3047-1*) Gordon Pr.

— Juan Grave: A Chronology. Johnson, W. Scott, tr. (Libertarian & Anarchist Chronology Ser.). 1979. lib. bdg. 59.95 (*0-8490-3043-9*) Gordon Pr.

— Kropotkin: A Chronology. Johnson, W. Scott, tr. (Libertarian & Anarchist Chronology Ser.). 1979. lib. bdg. 59.95 (*0-8490-3022-6*) Gordon Pr.

— Leo Tolstoy: A Chronology. Johnson, W. Scott, tr. (Libertarian & Anarchist Chronology Ser.). 1979. lib. bdg. 59.95 (*0-8490-3034-X*) Gordon Pr.

— Li Pei Kan & Chinese Anarchism: A Chronology. 1976. 250.00 (*0-87700-242-8*) Revisionist Pr.

— Louis Lecoin: A Chronology. Johnson, W. Scott, tr. (Libertarian & Anarchist Chronology Ser.). 1979. lib. bdg. 59.95 (*0-8490-3051-X*) Gordon Pr.

— Luigi Fabbri: A Chronology. Johnson, W. Scott, tr. (Libertarian & Anarchist Chronology Ser.). 1979. lib. bdg. 59.95 (*0-8490-3040-4*) Gordon Pr.

— Luisa Michel: A Chronology. Johnson, W. Scott, tr. (Libertarian & Anarchist Chronology Ser.). 1979. lib. bdg. 59.95 (*0-8490-3028-5*) Gordon Pr.

— Manuel Gonzalez Prada: A Chronology. Johnson, W. Scott, tr. (Libertarian & Anarchist Chronology Ser.). 1979. lib. bdg. 59.95 (*0-8490-3046-3*) Gordon Pr.

— Maria Lacerda De Moura: A Chronology. Johnson, W. Scott, tr. (Libertarian & Anarchist Chronology Ser.). 1979. lib. bdg. 59.95 (*0-8490-3053-6*) Gordon Pr.

— Max Nettlau Chronology. 1973. 250.00 (*0-87700-179-0*) Revisionist Pr.

— Max Stirner: A Chronology. Johnson, W. Scott, tr. (Libertarian & Anarchist Chronology Ser.). 1979. lib. bdg. 59.95 (*0-8490-3045-5*) Gordon Pr.

— P. J. Proudhon: A Chronology. Johnson, W. Scott, tr. (Libertarian & Anarchist Chronology Ser.). 1979. lib. bdg. 59.95 (*0-8490-3038-2*) Gordon Pr.

— Panait Musoiu: A Chronology. (Libertarian & Anarchist Chronology Ser.). 1980. lib. bdg. 59.95 (*0-8490-3088-9*) Gordon Pr.

— Paul Robin: A Chronology. Johnson, W. Scott, tr. (Libertarian & Anarchist Chronology Ser.). 1979. lib. bdg. 59.95 (*0-8490-3055-2*) Gordon Pr.

— Pedro Vallina: A Chronology. Johnson, W. Scott, tr. (Libertarian & Anarchist Chronology Ser.). 1979. lib. bdg. 59.95 (*0-8490-3057-9*) Gordon Pr.

— Ramon de la Sagra: A Chronology. Johnson, W. Scott, tr. (Libertarian & Anarchist Chronology Ser.). 1979. lib. bdg. 59.95 (*0-8490-3042-0*) Gordon Pr.

— Ricardo Flores Magon: A Chronology. Johnson, W. Scott, tr. (Libertarian & Anarchist Chronology Ser.). 1979. lib. bdg. 59.95 (*0-8490-3050-1*) Gordon Pr.

— Ricardo Mella: A Chronology. Johnson, W. Scott, tr. (Libertarian & Anarchist Chronology Ser.). 1979. lib. bdg. 59.95 (*0-8490-3037-4*) Gordon Pr.

— Robert Owen: A Chronology. Johnson, W. Scott, tr. (Libertarian & Anarchist Chronology Ser.). 1979. lib. bdg. 59.95 (*0-8490-3054-4*) Gordon Pr.

— Rodolfo Gonzalez Pacheco: A Chronology. Johnson, W. Scott, tr. (Libertarian & Anarchist Chronology Ser.). 1979. lib. bdg. 59.95 (*0-8490-3032-3*) Gordon Pr.

— Thoreau: A Chronology. Johnson, W. Scott, tr. (Libertarian & Anarchist Chronology Ser.). 1979. lib. bdg. 59.95 (*0-8490-3021-8*) Gordon Pr.

— Voltairine de Cleyre: A Chronology. Johnson, W. Scott, tr. (Libertarian & Anarchist Chronology Ser.). 1979. lib. bdg. 59.95 (*0-8490-3036-6*) Gordon Pr.

— William Godwin: A Chronology. Johnson, W. Scott, tr. (Libertarian & Anarchist Chronology Ser.). 1979. lib. bdg. 59.95 (*0-8490-3026-9*) Gordon Pr.

Munoz-Vazquez, Marya & Fernandez-Bauzo, Edwin. El Divorcio en la Sociedad Puertorriquena. LC 88-80390. (Huracan Academia Ser.). 175p. (SPA.). 1988. pap. 6.75 (*0-940238-96-9*) Ediciones Huracan.

***Munoz, Victoria I.** Where "Something Catches" Work, Love, & Identity in Youth. (Identities in the Classroom Ser.). 224p. (C). 1995. text ed. 49.50x (*0-7914-2685-8*); pap. 16.95x (*0-7914-2686-6*) State U NY Pr.

Munro. Statistical Methods for Health Care Research. 1993. 33.95 (*0-397-54982-2*) Lippincott.

Munro & Scott. Reproductive Seasonality in Teleosts: Environmental Influence. 1990. 205.00 (*0-8493-6875-8*, QL) CRC Pr.

Munro, Alice. The Beggar Maid. (Fiction Ser.). 224p. 1984. mass mkt. 6.95 (*0-14-006011-1*, Penguin Bks) Viking Penguin.

— Beggar Maid. 1991. 10.00 (*0-679-73271-3*) McKay.

— Dance of the Happy Shades & Other Stories. 240p. (J). 1990. pap. 10.00 (*0-14-012408-X*) Viking Child Bks.

— Friend of My Youth. 1990. 18.95 (*0-394-58442-2*) Knopf.

— Friend of My Youth. LC 90-50495. 288p. 1991. pap. 11.00 (*0-679-72957-7*, Publishers Media) Random.

— Lives of Girls & Women. 1974. pap. 4.95 (*0-451-15352-9*, Sig) NAL-Dutton.

— Lives of Girls & Women. LC 83-50575. 244p. 1983. pap. 10.95 (*0-452-26184-8*, Plume) NAL-Dutton.

— Lives of Girls & Women. 1989. pap. 7.95 (*0-452-25975-4*) NAL-Dutton.

— The Moons of Jupiter. LC 82-48734. 233p. 1983. 13.95 (*0-394-52952-9*) Knopf.

— Moons of Jupiter. 1991. pap. 10.00 (*0-679-73270-5*, Villard Bks) Random.

— Open Secrets: Stories. LC 94-2099. 1994. 23.00 (*0-679-43575-1*) Knopf.

— The Progress of Love. 1986. 16.95 (*0-394-55272-5*) Knopf.

— The Progress of Love. 320p. 1987. mass mkt. 6.95 (*0-14-009879-8*, Penguin Bks) Viking Penguin.

— Something I've Been Meaning to Tell You. 208p. 1983. pap. 2.95 (*0-451-14343-4*, Sig) NAL-Dutton.

— Something I've Been Meaning to Tell You: Thirteen Stories. 256p. 1984. pap. 9.95 (*0-452-26021-3*, Plume) NAL-Dutton.

— A Wilderness Station: Stories. 1995. pap. 13.00 (*0-679-75562-4*) Knopf.

Munro, Barry G. Smart Salespeople Sometimes Wear Plaid: Dare to Be Extraordinary in a Mediocre World. LC 93-34369. 1994. pap. 12.95 (*1-55958-422-X*) Prima Pub.

Munro, Bob. Aircraft. LC 93-19868. (Pointers Ser.). (Illus.). 32p. (J). (gr. 4-6). 1993. lib. bdg. 19.97 (*0-8114-6161-0*) Raintree Steck-V.

Munro, Charles, ed. see Whiddon, Debra.

Munro, Colin R. Studies in Constitutional Law. 1987. pap. 28.00 (*0-406-26145-8*) Butterworth Legal Pubs.

Munro, Craig. Inky Stephensen: Wild Man of Letters. (Orig.). pap. 29.95 (*0-7022-2389-1*, Pub. by Univ Queensland Pr AT) Intl Spec Bk.

Munro, Craig, ed. see Stephensen, P. R.

Munro, D., jt. auth. see Bradley, R. S.

Munro, D. G. The Five Republics of Central America. 1976. lib. bdg. 59.95 (*0-8490-1842-0*) Gordon Pr.

Munro, Dana C. A Syllabus of Medieval History, Three Hundred Ninety-Five to Thirteen Hundred. 1980. lib. bdg. 49.95 (*0-8490-3193-1*) Gordon Pr.

Munro, Dana G. Intervention & Dollar Diplomacy in the Caribbean, 1900-1921. LC 80-14089. (Illus.). ix, 553p. 1980. reprint ed. text ed. 85.00 (*0-313-22510-9*, MUIN, Greenwood Pr) Greenwood.

— A Student in Central America, 1914-1916. LC 83-60479. (Publication Ser.: No. 51). 75p. 1983. pap. 10.00 (*0-939238-77-2*) Tulane MARI.

— The United States & the Caribbean Republics, 1921-1933. LC 73-2471. 400p. 1974. 62.50x (*0-691-04623-9*) Princeton U Pr.

— The United States & the Caribbean Republics, 1921-1933. LC 73-16767. Date not set. reprint ed. pap. 115.50 (*0-7837-9397-9*, 2060142) Bks Demand.

Munro, David. The Four Horsemen: The Flames of War in the Third World. (Illus.). 288p. 1987. 29.95 (*0-8184-0441-8*) Carol Pub Group.

— The Oxford Dictionary of the World. (Illus.). 640p. 1995. 25.00 (*0-19-866184-3*) OUP.

Munro, David, ed. World Record of Major Conflict Areas. 600p. 1990. lib. bdg. 85.00 (*1-55862-066-4*) St James Pr.

Munro, David, jt. auth. see Jacobs, Peter.

Munro, David, jt. auth. see Wood, Jenny.

Munro, Donald, jt. ed. see Pieterse, Cosmo.

Munro, Donald J. The Concept of Man in Early China. LC 68-21288. xiv, 224p. 1969. 32.50 (*0-8047-0682-4*); pap. 11.95 (*0-8047-0829-0*) Stanford U Pr.

— Images of Human Nature: A Sung Portrait. 307p. 1988. 47.50 (*0-691-07330-9*) Princeton U Pr.

Munro, Donald J., ed. Individualism & Holism: Studies in Confucian & Taoist Values. (Michigan Monographs in Chinese Studies: No. 52). 399p. 1985. pap. 12.50 (*0-89264-058-8*) Ctr Chinese Studies.

Munro, Eleanor. Originals: American Women Artists. 1982. pap. 19.00 (*0-671-42812-8*, Touchstone Bks) S&S Trade.

— Wedding Readings: Centuries of Writing & Rituals on Love & Marriage. braille ed. 415p. 1992. vinyl bd. 33.20 (*1-56956-102-8*, BR8743) W A T Braille.

Munro, Eleanor, intro. & sel. Wedding Readings. LC 88-40334. 256p. 1989. 22.50 (*0-670-81088-6*) Viking Penguin.

***Munro-Faure, Lesley, et al.** Achieving Quality Standards: A Step by Step Guide to BS5750 - ISO 9000. 224p. 1993. pap. 45.00 (*0-273-60164-4*, Pub. by Pitman Pubng UK) St Mut.

Munro, George E., jt. ed. see Griffiths, David.

Munro, George E., tr. see Griffiths, David & Munro, George E., eds.

Munro, H. H. The Open Window. 1964. 2.50 (*0-87129-288-2*, O17) Dramatic Pub.

Munro, H. H., ed. Complete Works of Saki. (Reprints Ser.). 960p. 1989. 19.95 (*0-88029-259-8*) Dorset Pr.

Munro, H. H., see Saki, pseud..

Munro, H. N. & Danford, D. E., eds. Human Nutrition: A Comprehensive Treatise, Vol. 6: Nutrition, Aging, & the Elderly. LC 88-39816. (Illus.). 414p. 1989. 85.00 (*0-306-43047-9*, Plenum Pr) Plenum.

Munro, H. S., jt. ed. see Feast, W. I.

Munro, Hamish N. & Schlierf, Gunter. Nutrition of the Elderly. (Nestle Nutrition Workshop Ser.: Vol. 29). 248p. 1992. 63.00 (*0-88167-874-0*) Raven.

Munro, Hamish N., jt. auth. see Hutchinson, Martha L.

***Munro-Hay, S. C.** The Coinage of Aksum. 168p. 1994. 150.00 (*0-9511308-0-3*, Pub. by R C Senior UK) St Mut.

Munro-Hay, Stuart. An African Civilization: The Aksumite Kingdom of Northern Ethiopia. 256p. 1989. 45.00 (*0-7486-0106-6*, Pub. by Edinburgh U Pr UK) Col U Pr.

— Aksum: An African Civilization of Late Antiquity. 288p. 1992. pap. 29.50 (*0-7486-0209-7*, Pub. by Edinburgh U Pr UK) Col U Pr.

Munro, Hector H. Novels & Plays of Saki. 1988. reprint ed. lib. bdg. 49.00 (*0-7812-0544-1*) Rprt Serv.

— Novels & Plays of Saki. LC 71-145199. 1971. reprint ed. 39.00 (*0-403-01123-X*) Scholarly.

Munro, Hector H., see Saki, pseud..

Munro, I., jt. auth. see Borodin, Allan.

Munro, I., jt. ed. see Greaves, N.

Munro, Ian R., jt. auth. see Farkas, Leslie G.

Munro, Ion S. Through Fascism to World Power: A History of the Revolution in Italy. 1976. lib. bdg. 50.00 (*0-8490-2748-9*) Gordon Pr.

— Through Fascism to World Power: A History of the Revolution in Italy. LC 73-164618. (Select Bibliographies Reprint Ser.). 1977. reprint ed. 36.95 (*0-8369-5912-4*) Ayer.

Munro, Irmtraut. Untersuchengen zu den Totenbuch-Papyri der 18 Dyn. 300p. (GER.). 1988. lib. bdg. 125.00 (*0-7103-0288-6*) Routledge Chapman & Hall.

Munro, J. Discrete Mathematics for Computing. (Illus.). 306p. 1992. pap. 25.00 (*0-412-45650-8*, A9584) Chapman & Hall.

Munro, J. Alex. At Christmas Time. 80p. 1982. write for info. (*0-9601670-4-8*) J Alex Munro.

— Lines from Lincoln Land. (Illus.). 80p. 1981. pap. 3.75 (*0-9601670-3-X*) J Alex Munro.

Munro, J. G. Movement Education: A Program for Young Children. (J). (gr. 2-7). 1985. 13.95 (*0-9611820-0-8*) M D E A.

Munro, J. J., ed. see Broke, Arthur.

Munro, J. L., ed. Caribbean Coral Reef Fishery Resources. 2nd ed. (ICLARM Studies & Reviews: No. 7). (Illus.). 276p. 1983. text ed. 37.00 (*971-10-2200-1*, Pub. by ICLARM PH); pap. text ed. 33.00 (*971-10-2201-X*, Pub. by ICLARM PH) Intl Spec Bk.

Munro, J. L. & Nash, W. J., eds. A Bibliography of the Giant Clams. (Bibliographies Ser.: No. 5). 26p. 1986. pap. 4.50 (*971-10-2222-2*, Pub. by ICLARM PH) Intl Spec Bk.

Munro, J. M., jt. ed. see Bushrui, S. B.

Munro, James. Homeland. large type ed. (General Fiction Ser.). 624p. 1992. 23.95 (*0-7089-8641-2*) Ulverscroft.

***Munro, Jane.** British Landscape Watercolors. (Illus.). 160p. 1994. pap. text ed. 28.00 (*1-56131-063-8*) New Amsterdam Bks.

Munro, Jane, ed. see Donald, Mary Ellen.

Munro, John. A Trip to Venus: A Novel. LC 75-10655. (Classics of Science Fiction Ser.). 254p. 1976. reprint ed. 15.00 (*0-88355-360-0*); reprint ed. pap. 10.00 (*0-88355-460-7*) Hyperion Conn.

Munro, John, ed. Caton's History of Jason. (EETS, ES Ser.: No. 111). 1972. reprint ed. 32.00 (*0-527-00314-X*) Periodicals Srv.

Munro, John & Edwards, Christopher, eds. Macleod's Clinical Examination. 8th ed. (Illus.). 432p. 1990. pap. text ed. 32.95 (*0-443-04079-6*) Churchill.

Munro, John A., Associates, Inc. Staff, ed. see Munro, Robert A.

Munro, John F. & Ford, Michael J., eds. Introduction to Clinical Examination. 6th ed. LC 92-48188. 144p. 1993. pap. text ed. 19.95 (*0-443-04787-1*) Churchill.

Munro, John H. Bullion Flows & Monetary Policies in England & the Low Countries, 1350-1500. (Collected Studies: No. CS355). 336p. 1992. text ed. 89.95 (*0-86078-312-X*, Pub. by Variorum UK) Ashgate Pub Co.

— Textiles, Towns & Trades: Essays in the Economic History of Late-Medieval England & the Low Countries. LC 94-4405. (Collected Studies: Vol. 442). 350p. 1994. 89.95 (*0-86078-404-5*, Pub. by Variorum UK) Ashgate Pub Co.

Munro, John J., jt. auth. see Furnivall, Frederick J.

Munro, John M. Arthur Symons. Bowman, Sylvia E., ed. LC 68-17234. (Twayne's English Authors Ser.). 174p. (C). 1969. lib. bdg. 17.95 (*0-8290-1721-6*) Irvington.

— James Elroy Flecker. LC 75-46531. (Twayne's English Authors Ser.). 143p. (C). 1976. lib. bdg. 17.95 (*0-8057-6656-1*) Irvington.

— A Mutual Concern: The Story of the American University of Beirut. LC 77-22003. 1977. 25.00 (*0-88206-014-7*) Caravan Bks.

— Nairn Way: Desert Bus to Baghdad. LC 80-11875. 1980. 35.00 (*0-88206-035-X*) Caravan Bks.

— The Royal Aquarium: Failure of a Victorian Compromise. 1971. 10.00 (*0-8156-6033-2*, Am U Beirut) Syracuse U Pr.

Munro, John M., ed. Decadent Poetry of the Eighteen Nineties. (Illus.). 1967. 11.95 (*0-8156-6018-9*, Am U Beirut) Syracuse U Pr.

— Selected Poems of Theo. Marzials. 1973. 10.00 (*0-8156-6040-5*, Am U Beirut) Syracuse U Pr.

Munro, John M., jt. ed. see Beckson, Karl.

Munro, Joyce H., jt. ed. see Paciorek, Karen M.

Munro, June G. Movement Education: A Program for Young Children Ages 2-7. 2nd ed. (Illus.). 150p. (C). 1991. pap. text ed. 13.95 (*0-685-63072-2*) M D E A.

Munro, Kate & Elder-Woodward, Jim. Independent Living. (Skills for Caring Ser.). (Illus.). 40p. (Orig.). 1992. pap. text ed. 12.00 (*0-443-04533-X*) Churchill.

Munro, Kathy. Bringing Typesetting In-House. 176p. 1991. pap. 51.95 (*0-948905-16-6*) Chapman & Hall.

Munro, Kenneth J. The Political Career of Sir Adolphe Chapleau, Premier of Quebec, 1879-1882. LC 92-4338. 244p. 1992. lib. bdg. 89.95 (*0-7734-9494-4*) E Mellen.

Munro, Mackenzie. Wildflower. 183p. (C). 1990. 90.00 (*0-86439-149-8*, Pub. by Boolarong Pubns AT) St Mut.

Munro, Malcolm G., jt. auth. see Gomel, Victor.

Munro, Mary. The Bargain. large type ed. 1991. pap. 13.95 (*0-7089-6982-8*) Ulverscroft.

— A Dream Came True. large type ed. 336p. 1988. 16.95 (*0-7089-1839-5*) Ulverscroft.

— From March to September. large type ed. 1990. 21.95 (*0-7089-2254-6*) Ulverscroft.

— The Honey Pot. large type ed. 368p. 1987. 16.95 (*0-7089-1645-7*) Ulverscroft.

— The Hotel by the Loch. large type ed. (Linford Romance Library). 1989. pap. 11.95 (*0-7089-6786-8*, Trailtree Bookshop) Ulverscroft.

— Second Love. large type ed. 352p. 1986. 21.95 (*0-7089-1464-0*) Ulverscroft.
— Shadow Across the Desert. large type ed. 1989. 17.95 (*0-7089-2094-2*) Ulverscroft.
— The Singing House. large type ed. 336p. 1985. 21.95 (*0-7089-1340-7*) Ulverscroft.
— The Wheel of Life. large type ed. 330p. 1989. 17.95 (*0-7089-1964-2*) Ulverscroft.
— Whispering Sands. large type ed. 400p. 1988. 16.95 (*0-7089-1869-7*) Ulverscroft.

Munro, Mary Lynn, jt. auth. see Meyer, Annie.

Munro, Mike. Northwest Landscaping: A Practical Guide to Creating the Garden You've Always Wanted. (Illus.). 192p. (Orig.). 1992. pap. 16.95 (*0-88240-393-1*) Alaska Northwest.

Munro, N., ed. Modern Approaches to Control System Design. LC 80-479861. (IEE Control Engineering Ser.: Vol. 9). (Illus.). 431p. reprint ed. pap. 122.90 (*0-685-23330-8*, 2032256) Bks Demand.

Munro, Neil. John Splendid: The Tale of a Poor Gentleman & the Little Wars of Lorn. LC 79-8180. reprint ed. 44.50 (*0-404-62072-8*) AMS Pr.
— The Quick & the Dead: Electronic Combat & Modern Warfare. 290p. 1991. 29.95 (*0-312-04802-5*) St Martin.

Munro, Nev. Exiled to Parkinson's Domain. Van Treese, James B., ed. 332p. 1994. pap. 9.95 (*1-56901-044-7*) NW Pub.

Munro, Pamela. Slang U. 1991. pap. 10.00 (*0-517-58243-0*, Harmony) Crown Pub Group.

Munro, Pamela & Willmond, Catherine. Chickasaw: An Analytical Dictionary. LC 94-12872. 608p. 1994. 39.95 (*0-8061-2662-0*) U of Okla Pr.

Munro, Pamela, jt. ed. see Haiman, John.

Munro, Pamela, jt. auth. see Sauvel, Katherine S.

Munro, R. W., ed. Monro's Western Isles of Scotland & Genealogies of the Clans, 1549. 181p. 1993. reprint ed. pap. 18.50 (*0-685-69973-0*, 9114) Clearfield Co.

Munro, Robert A. Real Estate Periodicals Index, 1981, Vol. 1. Munro, John A., Associates, Inc. Staff et al, eds. 118p. (Orig.). 1982. pap. text ed. 60.00 (*0-911553-00-2*) Munro Assocs.
— Real Estate Periodicals Index, 1982, Vol. 2. Munro, John A., Associates, Inc. Staff, ed. 135p. (Orig.). 1983. pap. 60.00 (*0-911553-01-0*) Munro Assocs.

Munro, Robert J. International Environmental Law. (Collection of Bibliographic & Research Resources). 121p. 1990. pap. text ed. 50.00 (*0-379-20919-5*) Oceana.

Munro, Robert J., jt. auth. see Baldwin, Fletcher N., Jr.

Munro, Robert J., jt. auth. see Taylor, Betty W.

Munro, Roberta, ed. see Hayes, Doven.

Munro, Robin, jt. auth. see Black, George.

Munro, Robin, tr. see Erjin, Chen.

Munro, Roxie. Blimps. LC 88-18138. (Illus.). 32p. (J). (gr. 2-7). 1988. 12.95 (*0-525-44441-6*, DCB) Dutton Child Bks.
— Blimps. (Illus.). 32p. (J). (gr. 2-5). 1994. pap. 4.99 (*0-14-055292-8*, Puff Unicorn) Puffin Bks.
— Christmastime in New York City. (Illus.). 32p. (J). (ps-3). 1994. pap. 5.99 (*0-14-050462-1*) Puffin Bks.
— The Inside-Outside Book of London. LC 89-12023. (Illus.). 48p. (J). (ps up). 1989. 13.95 (*0-525-44522-6*, DCB) Dutton Child Bks.
— The Inside-Outside Book of New York City. (Illus.). 32p. (J). (ps-3). 1994. pap. 4.99 (*0-14-050454-0*) Puffin Bks.
— The Inside-Outside Book of Paris. LC 91-29318. (Inside-Outside Ser.). (Illus.). 48p. (J). (ps up). 1992. 15.00 (*0-525-44863-2*, DCB) Dutton Child Bks.
— The Inside-Outside Book of Washington, D. C. (Illus.). 48p. (J). 1993. pap. 4.99 (*0-14-054940-4*, Puff Unicorn) Puffin Bks.
— Inside Outside Book of Washington D.C. LC 86-24267. (Illus.). 48p. (J). (ps up). 1987. 13.95 (*0-525-44298-7*, DCB) Dutton Child Bks.

Munro, Roxie, illus. Architects Make Zigzags: Looking at Architecture from A to Z. LC 84-9679. 64p. (Orig.). (J). (gr. 3 up). 1986. pap. 9.95 (*0-89133-121-2*) Preservation Pr.
— The Great American Landmarks Adventure. LC 92-31806. (J). 1992. 3.25 (*0-16-038003-0*) USGPO.

Munro, S. Ethiopia. (World Bibliographical Ser.). 1993. lib. bdg. 70.00 (*1-85109-111-4*) ABC-CLIO.

Munro Saki, H. H. Beasts & Superbeasts. large type ed. (Mainstream Ser.). 168p. 1988. reprint ed. lib. bdg. 18.95 (*1-85089-193-1*, Pub. by ISIS UK) Transaction Pubs.

Munro, Sandra H., jt. auth. see Shelley, Mary V.

Munro, Stanley R. Genesis of a Revolution: An Anthology of Modern Chinese Short Stories. (Writing in Asia Ser.). 202p. (C). 1979. pap. 7.00 (*0-685-62992-9*, 00206) Heinemann.

Munro, Susan. Music Therapy in Palliative Hospice Care. 112p. (Orig.). (C). 1984. pap. 12.95x (*0-918812-37-2*) MMB Music.

Munro, W. H. The History of Bristol: The Story of the New Hope Lands from the Visit of the Northmen to the Present Time. (Illus.). 396p. 1989. reprint ed. lib. bdg. 42.00 (*0-8328-0579-3*) Higginson Bk Co.

Munro, Wilfred H., ed. see Prescott, William H.

Munro, William B. Crusaders of New France: A Chronicle of the Fleur-de-Lis in the Wilderness. (BCL1 - History - Canada Ser.). 237p. 1991. reprint ed. text ed. 79.00 (*0-7812-6352-2*) Rprt Serv.
— The Invisible Government & Personality in Politics, 2 vols. in 1. LC 73-19162. (Politics & People Ser.). 308p. 1974. reprint ed. 23.95 (*0-405-05884-5*) Ayer.
— The Makers of the Unwritten Constitution: The Fred Morgan Kirby Lectures Delivered at Lafayette College, 1929. 156p. 1982. reprint ed. lib. bdg. 20.00 (*0-8377-0842-7*) Rothman.

Munro, William B., ed. Documents Relating to the Seigniorial Tenure in Canada, 1598-1854, Vol. 3. LC 68-28598. 380p. 1969. reprint ed. text ed. 75.00 (*0-8371-5042-6*, MUDS, Greenwood Pr) Greenwood.

Munroe, Alexandra. Japanese Art after 1945: Scream Against the Sky. LC 94-4557. 1994. write for info. (*0-8109-3512-0*) Abrams.

***Munroe, Andrew A.** Caribbean Stories: Supernatural Tales of Guyana. 145p. (Orig.). 1994. pap. 9.95 (*0-9643010-0-8*) Golden Grove.

Munroe-Blum, Heather, jt. auth. see Marziali, Elsa.

Munroe, Clark C. The Second United States Infantry Division in Korea, 1950-1951. (Divisional Ser.: No. 40). (Illus.). 256p. reprint ed. 39.95 (*0-89839-171-7*) Battery Pr.

Munroe, Enid. An Artist in the Garden: A Guide to Creating Small & Natural Gardens. LC 92-30053. 1994. 25.00 (*0-8050-2718-1*) H Holt & Co.

Munroe, Eugene. The Moths of America North of Mexico, Fascicle 13.1A: Pyraloidea - Scopariinae, Nymphulinae. Dominick et al, eds. LC 78-149292. (Illus.). 134p. (Orig.). (C). 1972. pap. text ed. 22.00 (*0-900848-53-7*) Wedge Entomological.
— The Moths of America North of Mexico, Fascicle 13.1B: Pyraloidea, Pyralidae: Odontiinae, Glaphyriinae. LC 78-149292. (Illus.). 250p. (Orig.). (C). 1972. pap. text ed. 22.00 (*0-900848-54-5*) Wedge Entomological.
— The Moths of America North of Mexico, Fascicle 13.1C: Pyraloidea, Pyralidae: Evergestinae. LC 78-149292. (Illus.). 304p. (Orig.). (C). 1973. pap. text ed. 44.00 (*0-900848-63-4*) Wedge Entomological.
— The Moths of America North of Mexico, Fascicle 13.2A: Pyraloidea, Pyralidae: Pyraustinae, Pyraustini (Part) LC 78-149292. (Illus.). viii, 78p. (C). 1976. pap. text ed. 38.00 (*0-900848-79-0*) Wedge Entomological.
— The Moths of America North of Mexico, Fascicle 13.2B: Pyraloidea, Pyralidae: Pyraustinae, Pyraustini (Conclusion) LC 78-149292. (Illus.). xviii, 150p. (C). 1976. pap. text ed. 38.00 (*0-900848-96-0*) Wedge Entomological.

Munroe, J. B. A List of Alien Passengers: Bonded from January 1, 1847 to January 1, 1851. 99p. 1991. reprint ed. pap. 12.50 (*0-685-60508-6*, 3940) Clearfield Co.

Munroe, J. P. Munro: A Sketch of the Munro Clan, Also of William Munro Who, Deported from Scotland, Settled in Lexington, Mass., & Some of His Posterity. 80p. 1992. reprint ed. lib. bdg. 26.00 (*0-8328-2692-8*); reprint ed. pap. 16.00 (*0-8328-2693-6*) Higginson Bk Co.

Munroe, John A. Colonial Delaware: A History. LC 78-18738. (History of the American Colonies Ser.). 292p. 1978. lib. bdg. 35.00 (*0-527-18711-9*) Kraus Intl.
— History of Delaware. 3rd ed. LC 92-32067. (Illus.). 304p. (C). 1993. 29.50 (*0-87413-493-5*) U Delaware Pr.

Munroe, Kirk. Derrick Sterling: A Story of the Mines. 1993. reprint ed. lib. bdg. 89.00 (*0-7812-5496-5*) Rprt Serv.

Munroe, M. International Encyclopaedia of Education, 10 pts. in 5 vols., Set. (C). 1988. 995.00 (*0-7855-0050-2*, Pub. by Print Hse II) St Mut.

Munroe, Mary H. & Banja, Judith. The Birthday Book: A Birthdate & Birthplace Index to Biographies of American Children's Authors. 500p. (Orig.). (C). 1991. text ed. 49.95 (*1-55570-051-9*) Neal-Schuman.

Munroe, Myles. In Pursuit of Purpose. 168p. (Orig.). 1992. pap. 8.99 (*1-56043-103-2*) Destiny Image.
— Liberando Su Potencial - Releasing Your Potential. 224p. (Orig.). 1994. pap. 8.99 (*1-56043-108-3*) Destiny Image.
— Releasing Your Potential. 182p. (Orig.). 1992. pap. 8.99 (*1-56043-072-9*) Destiny Image.
— Releasing Your Potential Workbook. 48p. 1993. pap. 6.99 (*1-56043-093-1*) Destiny Image.
— Single Married Separated. 128p. (Orig.). 1992. pap. 7.99 (*1-56043-094-X*) Destiny Image.
— Understanding Your Potential. 48p. (Orig.). 1992. student ed, pap. 6.99 (*1-56043-092-3*) Destiny Image.
— Understanding Your Potential. 168p. (Orig.). 1992. pap. 8.99 (*1-56043-046-X*) Destiny Image.

Munroe, Myles, ed. Single Married Separated Workbook. 48p. (Orig.). 1993. student ed, pap. 6.99 (*1-56043-115-6*) Destiny Image.

Munroe, Ng. Coins of Japan. 1990. reprint ed. lib. bdg. 40.00 (*0-942666-49-6*) S J Durst.

Munroe, R., tr. see Dolci, Danilo.

***Munroe, Robert L. & Munroe, Ruth H.** Cross-Cultural Human Development. rev. ed. (Illus.). 181p. (C). 1994. pap. text ed. 9.95x (*0-88133-804-4*) Waveland Pr.

Munroe, Ruth H., jt. auth. see Munroe, Robert L.

Munroe, Tapan & Zimmerman, Andrew. The Future of Oil: Managing Risk & Uncertainty. 20p. 1986. pap. 10.00 (*0-918714-12-5*) Intl Res Ctr Energy.

***Muns, J. B.** Musical Autographs: A Comparative Guide. Incl. Musical Autographs: A Comparative Guide. suppl. ed. (Illus.). (Orig.). 1992. pap. 15.00 (*1-881858-01-4*); Musical Autographs: A Comparative Study. (Illus.). 32p. (Orig.). 1989. pap. 15.00 (*1-881858-00-6*); Musical Autographs 2nd Supplement: A Comparative Guide. (Illus.). 32p. (Orig.). 1994. pap. 15.00x (*1-881858-02-2*); 15.00 (*1-881858-03-0*) J B Muns.
— Musical Autographs: A Comparative Guide. suppl. ed. (Musical Autographs). (Illus.). (Orig.). 1992. pap. 15.00 (*1-881858-01-4*) J B Muns.

Muns, Joaquin, ed. Adjustment, Conditionality, & International Financing. xi, 214p. 1985. reprint ed. English. pap. 10.00 (*0-939934-28-0*); reprint ed. Span. pap. 10.00 (*0-939934-29-9*) Intl Monetary.

Muns, Ron. The Help Desk Handbook: The Help Desk Institute Guide to Help Desk Operations & Problem Management. Bultema, Patrick et al, eds. (Illus.). (Orig.). (C). Date not set. pap. write for info. (*1-57125-000-X*) Help Desk Inst.

Munsart, Craig A. Investigating Science with Dinosaurs. (Illus.). 200p. (Orig.). 1993. pap. 23.00 (*1-56308-008-7*) Teacher Ideas Pr.

Munsart, Craig A. & Gundy, Karen A. Primary Dinosaur Investigations. (Illus.). 175p. 1994. pap. text ed. 21.00 (*1-56308-246-2*) Teacher Ideas Pr.

Munsat, Theodore L. Post-Polio Syndrome. (Illus.). 224p. 1990. pap. text ed. 60.00 (*0-409-90153-9*) Buttrwrth-Heinemann.
— Quantification of Neurologic Deficit. (Illus.). 372p. 1989. text ed. 74.95 (*0-409-90152-0*) Buttrwrth-Heinemann.

Munsat, Theodore L., et al. Neuromuscular Disease, Clinical Neurophysiology, Neuro-Otology, & Neuro-Ophthalmology, Neurologic Rehabilitation. (Current Opinion in Neurology, 1993 Ser.). (Illus.). 150p. (Orig.). 1993. pap. text ed. 49.95 (*1-85922-009-6*) Current Science.

Munsch, Bob. Get Me Another One! 1992. mass mkt. 6.50 (*0-385-25337-0*) Doubleday.

Munsch, Robert. Agu, Agu, Agu: Murmel, Murmel, Murmel. (Illus.). 32p. (SPA.). (J). (ps-2). 1991. pap. 5.95 (*1-55037-095-2*, Pub. by Annick CN) Firefly Bks Ltd.
— Angela's Airplane. (Annikin Ser.: Series 3). (Illus.). 24p. (J). (ps-1). 1986. pap. 0.99 (*0-920236-75-8*, Pub. by Annick CN) Firefly Bks Ltd.
— Angela's Airplane. 24p. (J). (gr. k-3). 1988. lib. bdg. 14.95 (*1-55037-027-8*, Pub. by Annick CN); pap. 4.95 (*1-55037-026-X*, Pub. by Annick CN) Firefly Bks Ltd.
— El Avion de Angela: (Angela's Airplane) Langer, Shirley, tr. (Illus.). 32p. (SPA.). (J). 1991. pap. 5.95 (*1-55037-189-4*, Pub. by Annick CN) Firefly Bks Ltd.
— Boy in the Drawer. 32p. (J). (gr. k-3). 1982. lib. bdg. 14.95 (*0-920236-34-0*, Pub. by Annick CN); pap. 4.95 (*0-920236-36-7*, Pub. by Annick CN) Firefly Bks Ltd.
— The Boy in the Drawer. (Annikin Ser.: Series 5). (Illus.). 24p. (J). (ps-1). 1987. pap. 0.99 (*0-920303-50-1*, Pub. by Annick CN) Firefly Bks Ltd.
— Los Cochinos: (Pigs) Langer, Shirley, tr. (Illus.). 32p. (SPA.). (J). 1991. pap. 5.95 (*1-55037-191-6*, Pub. by Annick CN) Firefly Bks Ltd.
— El Cumpleanos de Mariela: Moira's Birthday. (Illus.). 32p. (SPA.). (J). (ps-1). 1992. pap. 5.95 (*1-55037-269-6*, Pub. by Annick CN) Firefly Bks Ltd.
— The Dark. 32p. (J). (gr. k-3). 1984. pap. 4.95 (*0-920236-85-5*, Pub. by Annick CN) Firefly Bks Ltd.
— The Dark. (Annikin Ser.: Series 5). (Illus.). 24p. (J). (ps-1). 1987. pap. 0.99 (*0-920303-47-1*, Pub. by Annick CN) Firefly Bks Ltd.
— David's Father. 32p. (J). (gr. k-3). 1983. lib. bdg. 14.95 (*0-920236-62-6*, Pub. by Annick CN); pap. 4.95 (*0-920236-64-2*, Pub. by Annick CN) Firefly Bks Ltd.
— David's Father. (Annick Press Ser.: Series 7). (Illus.). 24p. (J). (ps-2). 1989. pap. 0.99 (*1-55037-011-1*, Pub. by Annick CN) Firefly Bks Ltd.
— La Estacion de Bomberos: The Fire Station. (Illus.). 32p. (SPA.). (J). (ps-1). 1992. pap. 5.95 (*1-55037-268-8*, Pub. by Annick CN) Firefly Bks Ltd.
— Fifty Below Zero. 24p. (J). (gr. k-3). 1986. lib. bdg. 14.95 (*0-920236-86-3*, Pub. by Annick CN); pap. 4.95 (*0-920236-91-X*, Pub. by Annick CN) Firefly Bks Ltd.
— The Fire Station. (Annikin Ser.: Series 3). (Illus.). 24p. (J). (ps-1). 1986. pap. 0.99 (*0-920236-77-4*, Pub. by Annick CN) Firefly Bks Ltd.
— The Fire Station. (Illus.). 24p. (Orig.). (J). (gr. k-3). 1991. lib. bdg. 14.95 (*1-55037-170-3*, Pub. by Annick CN); pap. 4.95 (*1-55037-171-1*, Pub. by Annick CN) Firefly Bks Ltd.
— Giant. 32p. (J). (gr. k-3). 1989. lib. bdg. 15.95 (*1-55037-071-5*, Pub. by Annick CN); pap. 5.95 (*1-55037-070-7*, Pub. by Annick CN) Firefly Bks Ltd.
— I Have to Go! 24p. (J). (gr. k-2). 1987. lib. bdg. 14.95 (*0-920303-77-3*, Pub. by Annick CN); pap. 4.95 (*0-920303-74-9*, Pub. by Annick CN) Firefly Bks Ltd.
— I Have to Go! (Annikin Ser.: Series 5). (Illus.). 24p. (J). (ps-1). 1987. pap. 0.99 (*0-920303-51-X*, Pub. by Annick CN) Firefly Bks Ltd.
— Jonathan Cleaned Up. (Annikin Ser.: Series 1). (Illus.). 24p. (J). (ps-1). 1986. pap. 0.99 (*0-920236-21-9*, Pub. by Annick CN) Firefly Bks Ltd.
— Jonathan Cleaned-up: Then He Heard a Sound. 32p. (J). (gr. 4-7). 1981. lib. bdg. 14.95 (*0-920236-22-7*, Pub. by Annick CN); pap. 4.95 (*0-920236-20-0*, Pub. by Annick CN) Firefly Bks Ltd.
— Love You Forever. (Illus.). 32p. (J). (gr. 4-10). 1986. 12.95 (*0-920668-36-4*); pap. 4.95 (*0-920668-37-2*) Firefly Bks Ltd.
— Love You Forever: A Big Book. (Illus.). 32p. (J). (ps-3). 1994. pap. 19.95 (*1-895565-37-5*) Firefly Bks Ltd.
— Mais, Ou Est Donc Gah-Ning? (Illus.). 32p. (Orig.). (FRE.). (J). (ps-1). 1994. pap. 4.95 (*1-55037-984-4*, Pub. by Annick CN) Firefly Bks Ltd.
— Mateo y la Grua de Medianoche: (Matthew & the Midnight Tow Truck) Langer, Shirley, tr. (Illus.). 32p. (SPA.). (J). 1991. pap. 5.95 (*1-55037-190-8*, Pub. by Annick CN) Firefly Bks Ltd.
— Millicent & the Wind. 32p. (J). (gr. k-3). 1984. lib. bdg. 14.95 (*0-920236-98-7*, Pub. by Annick CN); pap. 4.95 (*0-920236-93-6*, Pub. by Annick CN) Firefly Bks Ltd.
— Millicent & the Wind. (Annick Press Ser.: Series 7). (Illus.). 24p. (J). (ps-2). 1989. pap. 0.99 (*1-55037-010-3*, Pub. by Annick CN) Firefly Bks Ltd.
— Moira's Birthday. 32p. (J). (gr. k-3). 1987. lib. bdg. 14.95 (*0-920303-85-4*, Pub. by Annick CN); pap. 4.95 (*0-920303-83-8*, Pub. by Annick CN) Firefly Bks Ltd.
— Moira's Birthday. Martchenko, Michael, ed. (Annikin Ser.). (Illus.). 1995. pap. 0.99 (*1-55037-389-7*, Pub. by Annick CN) Firefly Bks Ltd.
— Mortimer. 24p. (J). (gr. k-3). 1985. lib. bdg. 14.95 (*0-920303-12-9*, Pub. by Annick CN); pap. 4.95 (*0-920303-11-0*, Pub. by Annick CN) Firefly Bks Ltd.
— Mortimer. (Annikin Ser.: Series 3). (Illus.). 24p. (J). (ps-1). 1986. pap. 0.99 (*0-920236-68-5*, Pub. by Annick CN) Firefly Bks Ltd.
— El Muchacho en la Gaveta: The Boy in the Drawer. (Illus.). 32p. (SPA.). (J). (ps-2). 1989. pap. 5.95 (*1-55037-097-9*, Pub. by Annick CN) Firefly Bks Ltd.
— Mud Puddle. 32p. (J). (gr. k-3). 1982. pap. 4.95 (*0-920236-28-6*, Pub. by Annick CN) Firefly Bks Ltd.
— Mud Puddle. (Annikin Ser.: Series 1). (Illus.). 24p. (J). (ps-1). 1986. pap. 0.99 (*0-920236-23-5*, Pub. by Annick CN) Firefly Bks Ltd.
— Murmel, Murmel, Murmel. 32p. (J). (gr. k-3). 1982. lib. bdg. 14.95 (*0-920236-29-4*, Pub. by Annick CN); pap. 4.95 (*0-920236-31-6*, Pub. by Annick CN) Firefly Bks Ltd.
— Murmel, Murmel, Murmel. (Annick Press Ser.: Series 7). (Illus.). 24p. (J). (ps-2). 1989. pap. 0.99 (*1-55037-012-X*, Pub. by Annick CN) Firefly Bks Ltd.
— El Papa de David: David's Father. (Illus.). 32p. (SPA.). (J). (ps-2). 1991. pap. 5.95 (*1-55037-096-0*, Pub. by Annick CN) Firefly Bks Ltd.
— Paper Bag Princess. 32p. (J). (gr. k-3). 1980. lib. bdg. 14.95 (*0-920236-82-0*, Pub. by Annick CN); pap. 4.95 (*0-920236-16-2*, Pub. by Annick CN) Firefly Bks Ltd.
— The Paper Bag Princess. (Annikin Ser.: Series 1). (Illus.). 24p. (J). (ps-1). 1986. pap. 0.99 (*0-920236-25-1*, Pub. by Annick CN) Firefly Bks Ltd.
— Pigs. 24p. (J). (gr. k-2). 1989. lib. bdg. 14.95 (*1-55037-039-1*, Pub. by Annick CN); pap. 4.95 (*1-55037-038-3*, Pub. by Annick CN) Firefly Bks Ltd.
— Pigs. (Illus.). 32p. (CHI.). (J). 1993. pap. 5.95 (*1-55037-304-8*, Pub. by Annick CN) Firefly Bks Ltd.
— Pigs: Annikind. Martchenko, Michael, ed. (Illus.). 1995. pap. 0.99 (*1-55037-388-9*, Pub. by Annick CN) Firefly Bks Ltd.
— La Princesa Vestida Con Una Bolsa De Papel: The Paperbag Princess. (Illus.). 32p. (SPA.). (J). (ps-2). 1991. pap. 5.95 (*1-55037-098-7*, Pub. by Annick CN) Firefly Bks Ltd.
— Purple, Green & Yellow. (Illus.). 32p. (J). (ps-2). 1992. lib. bdg. 14.95 (*1-55037-255-6*, Pub. by Annick CN); pap. 4.95 (*1-55037-256-4*, Pub. by Annick CN) Firefly Bks Ltd.
— Siempre Te Querre (Love You Forever) (Illus.). 32p. (J). 1992. pap. 4.95 (*1-895565-01-4*) Firefly Bks Ltd.
— Something Good. (Illus.). 24p. (J). (ps-2). 1990. lib. bdg. 14.95 (*1-55037-099-5*, Pub. by Annick CN); pap. 4.95 (*1-55037-100-2*, Pub. by Annick CN) Firefly Bks Ltd.
— Something Good. (Annikin Ser.). (Illus.). 1995. pap. 0.99 (*1-55037-390-0*, Pub. by Annick CN) Firefly Bks Ltd.
— Thomas' Snowsuit. 24p. (J). (gr. k-3). 1985. lib. bdg. 14.95 (*0-920303-32-3*, Pub. by Annick CN); pap. 4.95 (*0-920303-33-1*, Pub. by Annick CN) Firefly Bks Ltd.
— Verde, Violeta y Amarillo (Purple, Green & Yellow) (Illus.). 32p. (J). 1994. pap. 5.95 (*1-55037-971-2*, Pub. by Annick CN) Firefly Bks Ltd.
— Violet, Vert et Jaune: Purple, Green & Yellow in French. 32p. (J). 1992. pap. 5.95 (*1-55037-272-6*, Pub. by Annick CN) Firefly Bks Ltd.
— Where Is Gah-Ning? (Illus.). 32p. (J). (gr. 3 up). 1994. lib. bdg. 14.95 (*1-55037-983-6*, Pub. by Annick CN); pap. 4.95 (*1-55037-982-8*, Pub. by Annick CN) Firefly Bks Ltd.

Munsch, Robert & Kusugak, M. A Promise Is a Promise. 32p. (J). (gr. k-3). 1988. lib. bdg. 14.95 (*1-55037-009-X*, Pub. by Annick CN); pap. 4.95 (*1-55037-008-1*, Pub. by Annick CN) Firefly Bks Ltd.

***Munsch, Robert & Kusugak, Michael.** A Promise Is a Promise. 1995. write for info. (*0-87129-493-1*, P72) Dramatic Pub.

Munsch, Robert & Martchenko, Michael. Show & Tell. (J). (ps-2). 1991. 14.95 (*1-55037-195-9*, Pub. by Annick CN); pap. 4.95 (*1-55037-197-5*, Pub. by Annick CN) Firefly Bks Ltd.
— Wait & See. 24p. (J). 1993. lib. bdg. 14.95 (*1-55037-335-8*, Pub. by Annick CN); pap. 4.95 (*1-55037-334-X*, Pub. by Annick CN) Firefly Bks Ltd.

Munschauer, John L. Jobs for English Majors & Other Smart People. 3rd ed. LC 91-208. 176p. (Orig.). 1991. pap. 11.95 (*1-56079-050-4*) Petersons Guides.

Munse, W. H. Fatigue of Welded Steel Structures. 1964. 20.00 (*0-318-18646-2*) Welding Res Coun.

Munsell & Clough. Practical Guide for Advanced Writers. 1984. teacher ed 5.00 (*0-8384-3280-8*) Heinle & Heinle.

Munsell, F. Darrell. The Unfortunate Duke: Henry Pelham, Fifth Duke of Newcastle, 1811-1864. LC 84-20882. (Illus.). 344p. 1985. text ed. 30.00 (*0-8262-0456-2*) U of Mo Pr.
— The Victorian Controversy Surrounding the Wellington War Memorial: The Archduke of Hyde Park Corner. LC 91-22672. (Illus.). 125p. 1991. lib. bdg. 69.95 (*0-7734-9735-8*) E Mellen.

Munsell, Joel. Chronology & Process of Papermaking, 1876-1990. 263p. 1992. pap. 25.00 (*0-87556-813-0*) Saifer.
— Origin, Progress & Vicissitudes of the Mohawk & Hudson Railroad. 20p. 1993. reprint ed. lib. bdg. 69.00 (*0-7812-5218-0*) Rprt Serv.

Munsell, Paul, jt. auth. see Lee, Hans.

Munsell, W. Keith, jt. auth. see Vanderwerf, Pieter A.

Munsen, Sylvia. Cooking the Norwegian Way. LC 82-259. (Easy Menu Ethnic Cookbooks Ser.). (Illus.). 48p. (J). (gr. 5 up). 1982. lib. bdg. 14.95 (*0-8225-0901-6*, Lerner Publctns) Lerner Group.

Munsey, Brenda, ed. Moral Development, Moral Education, & Kohlberg. LC 80-50. 457p. (Orig.). 1980. pap. 19.95 (*0-89135-020-9*) Religious Educ.

Munsey, Terence. The Flight of the Stoneman's Son. LC 93-93660. (Stoneman Ser.). 208p. (Orig.). (YA). (gr. 7 up). 1993. pap. 4.99 (*0-9697066-0-X*, 70660) Munsey Music.

M

An Asterisk (*) at the beginning of an entry indicates that the title is appearing in BIP for the first time.

— The Keeper of Three. LC 93-86550. (Stoneman Ser.: Bk. 2). 230p. (J). (gr. 4 up). 1995. pap. 4.99 (*0-9697066-1-8*) Munsey Music.

— Labyrinths of Light. LC 95-94007. (Stoneman Ser.: Bk. 3). 248p. (Orig.). (YA). (gr. 7 up). 1995. pap. 4.99 (*0-9697066-2-6*) Munsey Music.

Munshaw, Nancy, jt. ed. see Nagel, Stuart.

Munshi, A. H. & Javeid, G. N. Systematic Studies in Polygonaceae of Kashmir Himalaya. 215p. (C). 1986. 275.00 (*81-85046-32-8*, Scientific) St Mut.

Munshi, Carol. Baby Bunny Sticker Paper Doll. (Illus.). (J). (gr. k-3). 1994. pap. 1.00 (*0-486-27925-1*) Dover.

Munshi, Iskander. History of Shah Abbas the Great, 2 Vols., Vol. 1. LC 78-20663. 1400p. 1979. 55.00 (*0-89158-296-7*) Mazda Pubs.

— History of Shah Abbas the Great, 2 Vols., Vol. 2. LC 78-20663. 1400p. 1979. 65.00 (*0-685-05860-3*) Mazda Pubs.

***Munshi, J. S. & Dutta, Hiran M., eds.** Horizon of New Research on Fish Morphology in the 21st Century. 350p. 1995. text ed. 99.00 (*1-886106-31-2*) Science Pubs.

Munshi, Jamal. Stock Exchange Automation. LC 94-483. (Financial Sector of the American Economy Ser.). 104p. 1994. 32.00 (*0-8153-1702-6*) Garland.

Munshi, M. Z. A. & Prasad, P. S. S. Handbook of Solid State Batteries & Capacitors. 800p. 1995. text ed. 177.00 (*981-02-1794-3*) World Scientific Pub.

Munshi, Usha. An Integrated Approach to Pollution Control. LC 90-43712. (Environment: Problems & Solutions Ser.: Vol. 24). 216p. 1990. 53.00 (*0-8240-9786-6*) Garland.

Munshi, Vijay. Silences. (Redbird Ser.). 24p. 1975. 8.00 (*0-88253-846-2*); pap. text ed. 4.80 (*0-88253-715-6*) Ind-US Inc.

Munshower, Frank F. Practical Handbook of Disturbed Land Revegetation. LC 93-21625. 1993. 75.00 (*1-56670-026-4*, S627) Lewis Pubs.

Munshower, Susan S., ed. All the World's a Stage... Art & Pageantry in the Renaissance & Baroque, 2 pts. (Papers in Art History: Vol. VI). (Illus.). 575p. (Orig.). 1990. boxed, pap. 45.00 (*0-915773-05-8*) Penn St Univ Dept Art Hist.

— Projects & Monuments in the Period of the Roman Baroque. LC 83-43269. (Papers in Art History: Vol. I). (Illus.). 168p. (Orig.). 1984. pap. 20.00 (*0-915773-00-7*) Penn St Univ Dept Art Hist.

Munshower, Susan S., jt. ed. see Fleischer, Roland.

Munshower, Susan S., jt. ed. see Hager, Hellmut.

Munshower, Susan S., jt. ed. see Millon, Henry A.

Munshower, Susan S., jt. ed. see Zabel, Craig.

***Munshower, Suzanne.** Simply Sophisticated: What Every Wordly Person Needs to Know. Towle, Mike, ed. (Illus.). 178p. 1994. pap. 12.95 (*1-56530-148-X*) Summit TX.

Munsie, Lynne, jt. auth. see Cairney, Trevor H.

Munsil, Janet. Dinner at Auntie Rose's. (Annick Press Ser.: Series 8). (Illus.). 24p. (J). (ps-2). 1989. pap. 0.99 (*1-55037-047-2*, Pub. by Annick CN) Firefly Bks Ltd.

— Donde Hay Huomo (Where There's Smoke) (Illus.). 24p. 1994. pap. 5.95 (*1-55037-968-2*, Pub. by Annick CN) Firefly Bks Ltd.

— Il N'y a Pas de Fumee - Where There's Smoke. (Illus.). 24p. (ENG & FRE.). (J). 1992. lib. bdg. 14.95 (*1-55037-291-2*, Pub. by Annick CN); English ed. pap. 4.95 (*1-55037-290-4*, Pub. by Annick CN) Firefly Bks Ltd.

— Il N'y a Pas de Fumee - Where There's Smoke. (Illus.). 24p. (ENG & FRE.). (J). 1993. French ed. pap. 4.95 (*1-55037-311-0*, Pub. by Annick CN) Firefly Bks Ltd.

Munsil, Ritchie. Dinner at Auntie Rose's. (Illus.). 24p. (J). (ps-8). 1984. 12.95 (*0-920236-66-9*, Pub. by Annick CN); pap. 4.95 (*0-920236-63-4*, Pub. by Annick CN) Firefly Bks Ltd.

Munsing, Stephanie A., ed. Made in America: Printmaking, 1760-1860. LC 73-161317. (Illus.). 59p. (Orig.). 1973. pap. 3.50 (*0-914076-52-3*) Lib Co Phila.

Munsinger, Lynn, illus. A Zooful of Animals. 96p. (J). (ps-8). 1992. 17.95 (*0-395-52278-1*) HM.

***Munske.** The Two Plus Four Negotiations from a German-German Perspective: An Analysis of Perception. (Studies in Peace Research). (C). 1995. pap. text ed. 32.00 (*3-8258-2071-8*) Westview.

Munske, Horst H. Der Germanische Rechtswortschatz im Bereich der Missetaten, Philologische & Sprachgeographische Untersuchungen: Die Terminologie der Aelteren Westgermanischen Rechtsquellen, Vol. 1. LC 72-76055. (Studia Linguistica Germanica: Vol. 8). 335p. (C). 1973. 96.95 (*3-11-003578-2*) De Gruyter.

Munslow, Alan. Discourse & Culture: The Creation of American Society 1870-1920. LC 91-46120. 224p. 1992. 59.95 (*0-415-08234-X*, A7608) Routledge.

***Munslow, Alun & Ashton, Owen R., eds.** Henry Demarest Lloyd's Critiques of American Capitalism, 1881-1903. LC 95-18559. 268p. 1996. text ed. 89.95 (*0-7734-8916-9*) E Mellen.

Munslow, Barry. Mozambique: The Revolution & Its Origins. LC 82-16204. 207p. reprint ed. pap. 59.00 (*0-8357-6226-2*, 2034468) Bks Demand.

— Southern African Annual Review, 1987-88, 2 vols., Set. 1100p. 1989. 170.00 (*0-905450-02-7*, Pub. by H Zell Pubs UK) Bowker-Saur.

— Southern African Annual Review, 1987-88, 2 vols., Vol. 1, Country Reviews. 550p. 1990. 85.00 (*0-905450-03-5*, Pub. by H Zell Pubs UK) Bowker-Saur.

— Southern African Annual Review, 1987-88, 2 vols., Vol. 2, Regional Review. 550p. 1990. 85.00 (*0-905450-04-3*, Pub. by H Zell Pubs UK) Bowker-Saur.

Munso, J. Diccionario Turistico de Cataluna, Baleares y Andora. deluxe ed. 693p. (SPA.). 1975. 125.00 (*0-8288-5835-7*, S32722) Fr & Eur.

Munson, Bruce R., et al. Fundamentals of Fluid Mechanics. 2nd ed. 893p. 1993. Net. text ed. write for info. (*0-471-57958-0*) Wiley.

Munson, Carlton E. Clinical Social Work Supervision. 2nd ed. LC 92-1462. (Illus.). 478p. 1993. lib. bdg. 59.95 (*1-56024-284-1*) Haworth Pr.

— Family of Origin Applications in Clinical Supervision. LC 84-9017. (Clinical Supervisor Ser.: Vol. 2, No. 2). 86p. (C). 1984. text ed. 29.95 (*0-86656-287-7*) Haworth Pr.

— An Introduction to Clinical Social Work Supervision. LC 83-62. 376p. 1983. text ed. 44.95 (*0-86656-196-X*, B196); pap. text ed. 29.95 (*0-86656-197-8*, B197) Haworth Pr.

— Social Work with Families: Theory & Practice. LC 79-7851. 1980. 24.95 (*0-02-922300-8*); pap. 19.95 (*0-02-922310-5*) Free Pr.

Munson, Carlton E., ed. Social Work Supervision: Classic Statements & Critical Issues. LC 78-72149. 1979. pap. 21.95 (*0-02-922280-X*) Free Pr.

— Supervising Student Internships in Human Services. LC 83-26393. (Clinical Supervisor Ser.: Vol. 2, No. 1). 84p. 1984. text ed. 29.95 (*0-86656-301-6*) Haworth Pr.

Munson, Carol J. Postcranial Descriptions of Ilaria & Ngapakaldia, Vombatiformes, Marsupialia, & the Phylogeny of the Vombatiforms Based on Postcranial Morphology. (Publications in Zoology: Vol. 125). (C). 1992. pap. 11.00 (*0-520-09772-6*) U CA Pr.

Munson, Cheryl A., jt. auth. see Sieber, Ellen.

Munson, Danni, ed. Lesbian & Gay Almanac & events of 1990: Gay Games Edition. (Illus.). 160p. (Orig.). 1989. pap. 9.95 (*0-945043-02-3*) Envoy Enter.

Munson, Don. The Illustrated History of McLean County. Wyckoff, Martin & Koos, Greg, eds. LC 82-14833. (Illus.). 392p. 1982. 29.95 (*0-943788-00-5*) McLean County.

Munson, Doug, ed. Eckankar, Ancient Wisdom for Today: How Past Lives, Dreams, & Soul Travel Help You Find God. 134p. 1994. pap. 4.95 (*1-57043-095-0*) ECKANKAR.

Munson, Douglas A. Hostile Witness. 288p. 1992. reprint ed. mass mkt. 4.50 (*1-55817-640-3*, Pinnacle NY) Windsor NY.

Munson, Eric M., ed. see Ferguson, John H. & McHenry, Dean E.

Munson, Fred C. Labor Relations in the Lithographic Industry. LC 63-10872. (Wertheim Publications in Industrial Relations). (Illus.). 290p. 1963. 14.95 (*0-674-50850-5*) HUP.

Munson, Gorham. Aladdin's Lamp: The Wealth of the American People. (Social Credit Ser.). 420p. 1982. lib. bdg. 75.00 (*0-8490-3222-9*) Gordon Pr.

— Awakening Twenties: A Memoir-History of a Literary Period. LC 84-14316. (Illus.). 317p. 1985. 35.00 (*0-8071-1201-1*) La State U Pr.

Munson, Gorham B. Destinations: A Canvass of American Literature since 1900. LC 70-131784. 1971. 7.00 (*0-403-00671-6*) Scholarly.

— Destinations: A Canvass of American Literature since 1900. (BCL1-PS American Literature Ser.). 218p. 1992. reprint ed. lib. bdg. 79.00 (*0-7812-6621-1*) Rprt Serv.

— Robert Frost: A Study in Sensibility & Good Sense. LC 72-10857. (Studies in Poetry: No. 38). 1969. reprint ed. lib. bdg. 75.00 (*0-8383-0788-4*) M S G Haskell Hse.

— Twelve Decisive Battles of the Mind: The Story of Propaganda During the Christian Era, with Abridged Versions of Texts That Have Shaped History. LC 72-167388. (Essay Index Reprint Ser.). 1977. reprint ed. 20.95 (*0-8369-2705-2*) Ayer.

Munson, H. Lee. Mortimer Gunmakers 1753-1923. (Illus.). 320p. 1994. 65.00 (*0-917218-52-3*) A Mowbray.

Munson, Henry, Jr. The House of Si Abd Allah: The Oral History of a Moroccan Family. (Illus.). 280p. (C). 1991. reprint ed. pap. text ed. 17.00 (*0-300-05029-1*) Yale U Pr.

— Islam & Revolution in the Middle East. 180p. (C). 1989. reprint ed. pap. 11.00 (*0-300-04604-9*) Yale U Pr.

— Religion & Power in Morocco. LC 92-40202. (Illus.). 256p. 1993. 25.00 (*0-300-05376-2*) Yale U Pr.

Munson, Howard R. Science Activities with Simple Things. (J). (gr. 4-8). 1972. pap. 7.99 (*0-8224-6320-2*) Fearon Teach Aids.

— Science Experiences with Everyday Things. (J). (gr. 4-8). 1988. pap. 9.99 (*0-8224-6846-8*) Fearon Teach Aids.

Munson, James D. Alexandria, Virginia, Vol. 1: Alexandria Hustings Court Deeds, 1783-1797. 274p. (Orig.). 1990. pap. 20.00 (*1-55613-329-4*) Heritage Bk.

— Alexandria, Virginia, Vol. 2: Alexandria Hustings Court Deeds 1797-1801. x, 287p. (Orig.). 1991. pap. 21.50 (*1-55613-448-7*) Heritage Bk.

Munson, James W., ed. Pharmaceutical Analysis: Modern Methods, Pt. B. LC 81-15171. (Drugs & the Pharmaceutical Sciences Ser.: No. 11). 512p. reprint ed. pap. 146.00 (*0-7837-2772-0*, 2043163) Bks Demand.

***Munson, John W.** Reminiscences of a Mosby Guerilla. (Illus.). 277p. Date not set. 35.00 (*1-56013-012-1*) Olde Soldier Bks.

— Reminiscenses of a Mosby Guerilla. 1983. reprint ed. 21.95 (*0-89201-109-2*) Zenger Pub.

Munson, K., jt. auth. see Hooten, T.

Munson, Kenneth. Texas Playparty: A LaVaca County Life 1906 to Today. 175p. 1992. 15.95 (*1-878208-15-2*) Guild Pr IN.

— World Unmanned Aircraft. (Illus.). 208p. 1988. 40.00 (*0-7106-0401-7*) Janes Info Group.

Munson, Lawrence S. How to Conduct Training Seminars: A Complete Reference Guide for Training Managers. 2nd ed. 1992. text ed. 34.95 (*0-07-044201-0*) McGraw.

Munson, Lillian S., jt. auth. see Munson, Voyle L.

Munson, M. A. The Munson Record, 1637-1887: A Genealogical & Biographical Account of Captain Thomas Munson (Pioneer of Hartford & New Haven) & His Descendants, 2 vols. in 1. (Illus.). 1263p. 1989. reprint ed. lib. bdg. 197.00 (*0-8328-0892-X*); reprint ed. pap. 189.00 (*0-8328-0893-8*) Higginson Bk Co.

Munson, Michael J., jt. auth. see Tashman, Leonard J.

Munson, Patrick J. & Harn, Alan D. An Archaeological Survey of the American Bottoms & Adjacent Bluffs, Illinois, 2 pts. (Reports of Investigations Ser.: No. 21). (Illus.). 123p. 1971. pap. 3.00 (*0-89792-046-5*) Ill St Museum.

***Munson, Paul L., et al, eds.** Principals of Pharmacology: Basic Concepts & Clinical Applications. LC 94-41659. 1994. write for info. (*0-412-04701-2*) Chapman & Hall.

— Vitamins & Hormones, Vol. 37. LC 43-10535. 1980. text ed. 165.00 (*0-12-709837-2*) Acad Pr.

— Vitamins & Hormones, Vol. 38. (Serial Publication Ser.). 1981. text ed. 165.00 (*0-12-709838-0*) Acad Pr.

Munson, Philip E., et al. Glancing Back at - Clinton & Neighboring Communities: The Way It Used to Be. Searles, George et al, eds. LC 93-20997. (Illus.). 112p. 1993. 24.95 (*1-879511-13-4*); pap. 16.95 (*1-879511-14-2*) Vestal.

Munson, R., jt. auth. see Neary, G.

Munson, R. D. Potassium in Agriculture. (Illus.). 1123p. 1985. 58.00 (*0-89118-086-9*) Am Soc Agron.

Munson, R. W., Jr. Hemerocallis: The Daylily. LC 89-5025. (Illus.). 160p. 1989. 44.95 (*0-88192-140-8*) Timber.

— Hemerocallis: The Daylily. LC 89-5025. (Illus.). 160p. 1993. pap. 19.95 (*0-88192-240-4*) Timber.

***Munson, Richard, ed.** Retaining Natural Resource Subsidies: Saving Money & the Environment. 200p. (Orig.). (C). Date not set. pap. 23.00 (*1-882061-38-1*) Northeast-Midwest.

Munson, Robert D. Potassium, Calcium, & Magnesium in the Tropics & Subtropics. Brosheer, J. C., ed. LC 82-11944. (Technical Bulletin Ser.: No. T-23). (Illus.). 70p. (Orig.). 1982. pap. text ed. 4.00 (*0-88090-041-5*) Intl Fertilizer.

Munson, Robert S. Favorite Hobbies & Pastimes: A Sourcebook of Leisure Pursuits. (Illus.). 366p. (Orig.). 1994. pap. 55.00 (*0-8389-0638-9*) ALA.

Munson, Ronald. Fan Mail. 432p. 1994. reprint ed. pap. 5.99 (*0-451-40482-3*, Onyx) NAL-Dutton.

— Intervention & Reflection: Basic Issues in Medical Ethics. 4th ed. 669p. (C). 1992. text ed. 46.95 (*0-534-16326-2*) Intl Thomson.

— Night Vision. LC 94-3264. 384p. 1995. 21.95 (*0-525-93781-1*, Dutton) NAL-Dutton.

Munson, Ronald, jt. auth. see Conway, David A.

Munson, Rosaria V., tr. see Comotti, Giovanni.

Munson, Russell. Skyward: Why Flyers Fly. Valenzi, Kathleen D., ed. LC 89-84490. (Illus.). 208p. 1989. 45.00 (*0-943231-23-X*) Howell Pr VA.

Munson, Sammye. Hej Texas, Goodbye Sweden. LC 93-38928. (J). 1994. 12.95 (*0-89015-948-3*) Sunbelt Media.

— Our Tejano Heroes: Outstanding Mexican-Americans. Eakin, Edwin M., ed. (Illus.). 96p. (J). (gr. 4-6). 1989. 10.95 (*0-89015-691-3*) Sunbelt Media.

Munson, Sheryl M. Siege of the Heart. 224p. (Orig.). 1990. pap. 2.75 (*1-878702-12-2*, Kismet) Meteor Pub.

Munson, Shirley & Nelson, Jo. Apple-Lovers' Cook Book. LC 89-23639. 120p. (Orig.). 1989. spiral bd. 6.95 (*0-914846-43-4*) Golden West Pub.

Munson, Steven C., ed. The State of the Nation: A Conference of the Committee for the Free World. LC 84-23444. 126p. (Orig.). 1985. lib. bdg. 27.00 (*0-8191-4390-1*); pap. text ed. 11.50 (*0-8191-4391-X*) U Pr of Amer.

Munson, Thomas N. The Challenge of Religion: A Philosophical Appraisal. LC 85-10297. 238p. 1985. text ed. 21.00x (*0-8207-0179-3*); pap. text ed. 12.00x (*0-8207-0181-5*) Duquesne.

— The Essential Wisdom of George Santayana. LC 62-10453. 236p. reprint ed. pap. 67.30 (*0-317-09240-5*, 2006116) Bks Demand.

Munson, Voyle L. & Munson, Lillian S. A Gift of Faith: Elias H. Blackburn. (Illus.). 1991. 27.95 (*0-9617133-2-1*); pap. 17.95 (*0-9617133-1-3*) Basin-Plateau Pr.

Munson, Wayne. All Talk: The Talkshow in Media Culture. LC 92-9389. (Culture & the Moving Image Ser.). 232p. (C). 1994. pap. 18.95 (*1-56639-194-6*) Temple U Pr.

Munson, Will. How Lucky Can You Get? How You Can Attract Good Luck by Responding to Everyday Opportunities. Briggs, Charlie, ed. LC 89-81422. 192p. (Orig.). 1990. 16.95 (*0-923485-22-8*); pap. 9.95 (*0-923485-23-6*) Eden Hse.

Munson-Williams-Proctor Institute Staff. The Olympics in Art: An Exhibition of Works Related to Olympic Sports. LC 80-65038. (Illus.). 168p. (C). 1980. pap. 15.00 (*0-295-96399-9*) U of Wash Pr.

***Munster, Andrew.** Severe Burns: A Family Guide to Medical & Emotional Recovery. Date not set. 24.95 (*0-614-06541-0*) Phoenix Soc.

Munster, Andrew, jt. auth. see Haponik, Edward F.

Munster, Andrew M., jt. auth. see Baltimore Regional Burn Center Staff.

Munster, Arnold. Classical Thermodynamics. Halberstadt, E. S., tr. LC 71-122348. 401p. reprint ed. pap. 114.30 (*0-317-12980-5*, 2020834) Bks Demand.

Munster, Bill, ed. Sudden Fear: The Horror & Dark Suspense Fiction of Dean R. Koontz. enl. rev. ed. (I. O. Evans Studies in the Philosophy & Criticism of Literature). 208p. 1995. pap. 20.00 (*1-55742-144-7*) Borgo Pr.

— Sudden Fear: The Horror & Dark Suspense Fiction of Dean R. Koontz. 2nd enl. rev. ed. (I. O. Evans Studies in the Philosophy & Criticism of Literature). 208p. 1995. 30.00 (*1-55742-145-5*) Borgo Pr.

Munster, Gernot, jt. auth. see Montvay, Istvan.

Munsterberg, Hugo. American Patriotism, & Other Social Studies. LC 68-22934. (Essay Index Reprint Ser.). 1977. 19.95 (*0-8369-0726-4*) Ayer.

— American Problems from the Point of View of a Psychologist. LC 75-84328. (Essay Index Reprint Ser.). 1977. 19.95 (*0-8369-1098-2*) Ayer.

— Chinese Buddhist Bronzes. LC 87-80393. (Illus.). 191p. 1988. reprint ed. lib. bdg. 50.00 (*0-87817-324-2*) Hacker.

— The Japanese Print: A Historical Guide. LC 81-16195. (Illus.). 232p. 1982. 29.95 (*0-8348-0167-1*) Weatherhill.

— On the Witness Stand: Essays on Psychology & Crime. 269p. 1981. reprint ed. lib. bdg. 26.00 (*0-8377-0840-0*) Rothman.

— Photoplay: A Psychological Study. LC 79-124021. (Literature of Cinema, Ser. 1). 1970. reprint ed. 14.95 (*0-405-01628-X*) Ayer.

— Psychology & Industrial Efficiency. LC 73-2979. (Classics in Psychology Ser.). 1974. reprint ed. 23.95 (*0-405-05151-4*) Ayer.

— A Short History of Chinese Art. LC 70-88990. (Illus.). 227p. 1969. reprint ed. text ed. 55.00 (*0-8371-2117-5*, MUCA, Greenwood Pr) Greenwood.

— Symbolism in Ancient Chinese Art. LC 84-82430. (Illus.). 250p. 1986. lib. bdg. 50.00 (*0-87817-303-X*) Hacker.

— Unspoken Bequest: The Contribution of German Jews to German Culture. (Illus.). 224p. (YA). (gr. 10 up). 1995. 20.00 (*1-878352-10-5*) McPherson & Co.

— Zen & Oriental Art. (Illus.). 158p. 1993. pap. 9.95 (*0-8048-1902-5*) C E Tuttle.

Munsterberg, Hugo, ed. Harvard Psychological Studies, Vol. 1. (Psychological Monographs General & Applied: Vol. 4). 1969. reprint ed. pap. 35.00 (*0-8115-1403-X*) Periodicals Srv.

Munsterberg, Peggy. Beastly Feasts: Tasty Treats for Animal Appetites. LC 94-2951. (Illus.). (J). Date not set. write for info. (*0-8037-1481-5*); pap. write for info. (*0-8037-1482-3*) Dial Bks Young.

Munsterberg, Rudolf. Die Beamtennamen Auf den Griechischen Munzen, Geographisch und Alphabetisch Geordnet. (Subsidia Epigraphica Ser.: Vol. III). 338p. (GER.). 1985. reprint ed. write for info. (*3-487-05059-5*, Pub. by Georg Olms GW) Lubrecht & Cramer.

Munsterer, Hans O. The Young Brecht. Kuhn, Tom & Leeder, Karen, trs. (Illus.). 220p. 1992. 35.00 (*1-870352-73-4*, Pub. by Libris UK) Paul & Co Pubs.

Munsterman, Janice & Grimm, Claire. Child Support Guidelines Summary. 139p. 1990. 9.00 (*0-685-38116-1*, WPO-015) Natl Ctr St Courts.

Munsterman, Janice & Henderson, Thomas. Child Support Guidelines Summary. 139p. 1988. 9.00 (*0-685-33611-5*, WPO-003) Natl Ctr St Courts.

Munsterman, Janice & Munsterman, Thomas. Microcomputer Applications for Jury Systems Support. 106p. 1989. 7.00 (*0-685-33624-7*, WPO-009) Natl Ctr St Courts.

Munsterman, Janice, et al. Child Support Guidelines: A Compendium. 1016p. 1991. pap. text ed. 95.00 (*0-89656-101-1*, R-119) Natl Ctr St Courts.

— Child Support Guidelines: A Compendium, 1991 Supplement. 1230p. 1991. 50.00 (*0-685-55343-4*, R126) Natl Ctr St Courts.

— Relationship of Juror Fees & Terms of Service to Jury System Performance. 186p. 1991. 11.50 (*0-685-55338-8*, WPO029) Natl Ctr St Courts.

Munsterman, Thomas, jt. auth. see Munsterman, Janice.

Munsterman, Tom, et al. Comparison of the Performance of Eight- & Twelve-Person Juries. 155p. 1990. 9.50 (*0-685-38114-5*, WPO-014) Natl Ctr St Courts.

Munsters & the Addams Family Fan Club Staff, ed. The Munsters & the Addams Family Reunion. (Munsters & the Addams Family Television Shows Ser.). (Illus.). 95p. (Orig.). 1988. pap. 20.00 (*0-317-05621-2*) Fan Club.

Munt, Sally, ed. New Lesbian Criticism: Literary & Cultural Readings. (Between Men - Between Women Ser.). 256p. 1992. text ed. 40.00 (*0-231-08018-2*); pap. 15.00 (*0-231-08019-0*) Col U Pr.

Munt, Sally R. & Munt, Sally R. Murder by the Book? Crime Fiction & Feminism. LC 93-49588. (Narrative Forms & Social Formations Ser.). 264p. 1994. 55.00 (*0-415-10918-3*, B4240, Routledge NY); pap. 16.95 (*0-415-10919-1*, B4244, Routledge NY) Routledge.

Munt, Sally R., jt. auth. see Munt, Sally R.

Muntarbhorn, Vitit, ed. The Status of Refugees in Asia. 226p. 1992. 49.95 (*0-19-825668-X*) OUP.

***Muntean.** Imagine...Big Bird Goes to the Moon: Sesame Street Imagine Book. (J). 1995. pap. text ed. 2.50 (*0-307-13132-7*, Golden Pr) Western Pub.

Muntean, Michaela. All about Me. (Illus.). 48p. (J). (ps-3). 1984. 5.95 (*0-8193-1123-5*) Parents.

— Baby Fozzie Goes Camping. (Muppet Magic Ser.). (Illus.). 26p. (J). (ps up). 1987. 12.95 (*1-55578-604-9*) Worlds Wonder.

— Bert & the Magic Lamp & Other Good-Night Stories. (Big Golden Book Ser.). (Illus.). 24p. (J). (ps-1). 1989. write for info. (*0-307-12073-2*, Golden Bks) Western Pub.

— Bicycle Bear. LC 93-15458. (Parents Magazine Read Aloud Original Ser.). (Illus.). (J). 1994. lib. bdg. 14.60 (*0-8368-0963-7*) Gareth Stevens Inc.

— Bicycle Bear. LC 83-3980. (Illus.). 48p. (J). (ps-3). 1983. 5.95 (*0-8193-1103-0*); lib. bdg. 5.95 (*0-8193-1104-9*) Parents.

— Bicycle Bear Rides Again. LC 93-15470. (Parents Magazine Read Aloud Original Ser.). (Illus.). (J). 1995. 14.60 (*0-8368-0964-5*) Gareth Stevens Inc.

— Bicycle Bear Rides Again. LC 89-27823. (Illus.). 48p. (J). (ps-3). 1989. 5.95 (*0-8193-1193-6*) Parents.

— Cookie Soup & Other Good-night Stories. (Big Golden Book Ser.). (J). (ps-3). 1990. write for info. (*0-307-12114-3*) Western Pub.

— A Garden for Miss Mouse. LC 82-2135. (Illus.). 48p. (J). (ps-3). 1982. 5.95 (*0-8193-1083-2*); lib. bdg. 5.95 (*0-8193-1084-0*) Parents.

— Grouchs Christmas. (J). (ps). 1990. write for info. (*0-307-12049-X*) Western Pub.

— I Want to Be a Veterinarian. (Sesame Street Ser.). (Illus.). 24p. (J). (ps-00). 1992. pap. write for info. (*0-307-13116-5*, 13116, Golden Pr) Western Pub.

— I Want to Be President. (Sesame Street I Want to Be Book Ser.). (Illus.). 24p. (J). (ps-00). 1993. pap. 1.95 (*0-307-13118-1*, 13118, Golden Pr) Western Pub.

— Imagine: Ernie Is King. (J). (ps-3). 1993. pap. 2.25 (*0-307-13123-8*, Golden Pr) Western Pub.

— Imagine: Grover's Magic Carpet Ride. (J). (ps-3). 1993. pap. 2.25 (*0-307-13120-3*, Golden Pr) Western Pub.

— Kermit & Robin's Scary Story. (Illus.). 32p. (J). (gr. k-3). 1995. 11.99 (*0-670-86106-5*) Viking Child Bks.

— Kermit & Robin's Scary Story. (Easy-to-Read Program, Level 2 (Red) Ser.). (Illus.). 32p. (J). (gr. k-3). 1995. 3.50 (*0-14-037555-4*) Puffin Bks.

— The Little Engine That Could & the Big Chase. (Illus.). 32p. (J). (ps-2). 1988. pap. 1.95 (*0-448-19095-8*, Platt & Munk Pubs) Putnam Pub Group.

— The Old Man & the Afternoon Cat. LC 81-11047. (Illus.). 48p. (J). (ps-3). 1982. 5.95 (*0-8193-1071-9*); lib. bdg. 5.95 (*0-8193-1072-7*) Parents.

— Sesame Street: Ernie & His Merry Monsters & Other Good-Night Stories. (Big Golden Book Ser.). (Illus.). 24p. (J). (ps-3). 1992. write for info. (*0-307-12336-7*, 12336, Golden Pr) Western Pub.

— The Very Bumpy Bus Ride. LC 93-13042. (Parents Magazine Read Aloud Original Ser.). (Illus.). (J). 1993. lib. bdg. 14.60 (*0-8368-0980-7*) Gareth Stevens Inc.

— The Very Bumpy Bus Ride. LC 81-16905. (Illus.). 48p. (J). (ps-3). 1982. 5.95 (*0-8193-1079-4*); 5.95 (*0-8193-1080-8*) Parents.

— We're Counting on You, Grover! (Sesame Street Growing-up Bks.). (Illus.). (J). (ps-00). 1991. write for info. (*0-307-12050-3*, Golden Pr) Western Pub.

— What's in Oscar's Trash Can? And Other Good-Night Stories. (Sesame Street Good-Night Stories Ser.). (Illus.). (J). (ps-1). 1991. 3.25 (*0-307-12342-1*, Golden Pr) Western Pub.

Munteanu, Basil. Ante Saeclvm: Fantezii Panteiste. Lozovan, Eugen & Shelden, R. D., eds. (Illus.). 256p. (Orig.). (ROM.). 1993. pap. 19.99 (*1-883300-00-2*) R D Shelden.

— Permanente Romanesti: De la Origini la Exil. Shelden, R. D., ed. 250p. (Orig.). (ROM.). 1993. pap. 14.99 (*1-883300-01-0*) R D Shelden.

— Permanente Romanesti: Discursuri Si Portrete. Shelden, Ruxandra D. & Lozovan, Eugen, eds. 302p. (Orig.). Date not set. pap. 19.99 (*1-883300-02-9*) R D Shelden.

Munter, Carol, jt. auth. see Hirschmann, Jane R.

Munter, Mary. Business Communication: Strategy & Skill. (Illus.). 448p. 1987. text ed. write for info. (*0-13-091919-5*) P-H.

— Guide to Managerial Communication. 3rd ed. 192p. 1991. pap. text ed. write for info. (*0-13-365990-9*) P-H.

Munter, Pam. Almost Famous: Personal Growth & Other Adventures In & Out of Show Biz. LC 85-13621. (Illus.). 275p. 1985. 16.95 (*0-9614926-0-0*) Westgate Oregon.

Munter, Paul. Corporate Accounting Deskbook. 1990. pap. 59.95 (*1-55840-443-0*) Exec Ent Pubns.

— Corporate Accounting Deskbook 1991. 1994. pap. text ed. 59.95 (*0-471-11233-X*) Wiley.

Munter, Paul & Ratcliffe, Thomas A. Applying GAAP & GAAS, 2 vols. LC 84-72343. 1985. Looseleaf updates avail. ring bd. write for info. (*0-8205-1012-2*) Bender.

— A Guide to Financial Statement Disclosures. LC 85-9603. (Illus.). 282p. 1986. text ed. 65.00 (*0-89930-032-4*, MUF/, Quorum Bks) Greenwood.

Munter, Preston K. Counseling Students: Lessons from Northfield, Echoes from Fountain Valley. LC 87-35130. 220p. 1988. text ed. 45.00 (*0-86569-172-X*, Auburn Hse) Greenwood.

Munter, Robert. A Dictionary of the Print Trade in Ireland, 1550-1775. LC 88-80279. 351p. reprint ed. pap. 100.10 (*0-7837-5615-1*, 2045522) Bks Demand.

Munter, Robert & Grose, Clyde L. Englishmen Abroad: Being an Account of Their Travels in the Seventeenth Century. LC 87-1547. (Studies in British History: Vol. 3). 496p. 1986. lib. bdg. 109.95 (*0-88946-453-7*) E Mellen.

Munter, Robert L. The History of the Irish Newspaper, 1685-1760. LC 66-21653. 231p. reprint ed. pap. 65.90 (*0-317-20627-3*, 2024581) Bks Demand.

Munthe, Axel. Story of San Michele. 351p. 1984. pap. 10.95 (*0-88184-109-9*) Carroll & Graf.

— The Story of San Michele. 425p. 1990. reprint ed. lib. bdg. 25.95 (*0-89966-676-0*) Buccaneer Bks.

Munthe, Elaine, jt. ed. see Roland, Erling.

***Munthe, Jens.** Miocene Mammals of the Split Rock Area, Granite Mountains Basin, & Central Wyoming. (UC Publications in Geological Sciences). 1989. pap. 25.00 (*0-520-09706-8*) U CA Pr.

Munthe, Kathleen. The Skeleton of the Boraphaginae (Carnivora, Canidae) Morphology & Function. 1990. pap. 20.00 (*0-520-09724-6*) U CA Pr.

Munting, Abraham. Fantastic Floral Engravings. Menten, Theodore, ed. (Pictorial Archive Ser.). (Illus.). 128p. 1975. reprint ed. pap. 6.95 (*0-486-23117-8*) Dover.

Munting, Roger. Hedges & Hurdles. 144p. 1990. 52.00 (*0-85131-424-4*, Pub. by J A Allen & Co UK) St Mut.

Munting, Roger & Holderness, B. A. Crisis, Recovery & War: An Economic History of Continental Europe, 1918-1945. LC 91-28931. 270p. 1991. text ed. 65.00 (*0-312-07195-7*) St Martin.

Munton, Ann. Robert Kroetsch & His Works (Poetry) (Canadian Author Studies). 118p. (C). 1992. pap. text ed. 9.95 (*1-55022-072-1*, Pub. by ECW Press CN) Genl Dist Srvs.

Munton, Anthony G., et al. Job Relocation: Managing People on the Move. LC 92-23725. 168p. 1993. pap. text ed. 34.95 (*0-471-93728-2*) Wiley.

Munton, R. & Stott, J. R. Refrigeration at Sea. 2nd ed. (Illus.). 238p. 1978. 79.25 (*0-85334-766-2*, Pub. by Elsevier Applied Sci UK) Elsevier.

Munts, Raymond. Bargaining for Health: Labor Unions, Health Insurance & Medical Care. LC 67-13555. 330p. reprint ed. pap. 94.10 (*0-8357-5966-0*, 2023716) Bks Demand.

Muntz, E. P., et al. Rarefied Gas Dynamics, Vol. 1: Space-Related Studies. Campbell, D. H., ed. (PAAS Ser.: Vol. 116). 570p. 1989. 75.95 (*0-930403-53-3*) AIAA.

Muntz, E. P., et al, eds. Rarefied Gas Dynamics, Vol. 2: Physical Phenomena. (PAAS Ser.: Vol. 117). 522p. 1989. 75.95 (*0-930403-54-1*) AIAA.

— Rarefied Gas Dynamics, Vol. 3: Theoretical & Computational Techniques. (PAAS Ser.: Vol. 118). 616p. 1989. 75.95 (*0-930403-55-X*) AIAA.

Muntz, E. Phillip, jt. auth. see Logan, Wende W.

Muntz, Eugene. Les Arts A la Cour Des Papes Pendant le Fifteenth et le Sixteenth Siecle, 3 vols., Set. (Bibliotheque Des Ecoles Francaises d'Athenes et De Rome Ser.: Nos. 4, 9, 28). 997p. 1983. reprint ed. write for info. (*3-487-07306-4*, Pub. by Georg Olms GW) Lubrecht & Cramer.

Muntzing, L. Manning. International Instruments of Nuclear Technology Transfer. LC 78-67158. 1978. 56.00 (*0-89448-016-2*, 690001) Am Nuclear Soc.

Muntzing, L. Manning, ed. Nuclear Power & Its Regulation in the United States, Vol. 7, Pt. 2. (Illus.). 125p. 1981. pap. 36.00 (*0-08-027139-1*, Pergamon Pr) Elsevier.

Muntzing, L. Manning, jt. auth. see Muntzing, William H., II.

Muntzing, William H., II & Muntzing, L. Manning. The Muntzings & Their Related Families: Five Centuries of Ancestors. 224p. 1991. 40.00 (*0-9629967-0-X*) McClain.

Munyan, Arthur C., ed. Polar Wandering & Continental Drift. LC 64-6318. (Society of Economic Paleontologists & Mineralogists, Special Publication Ser.: No. 10). 175p. reprint ed. pap. 49.90 (*0-317-27161-X*, 2024736) Bks Demand.

Munyon, Paul G. A Reassessment of New England Agriculture in the Last Thirty Years of the Nineteenth Century: New Hampshire, a Case History. LC 77-14783. (Dissertations in American Economic History Ser.). 1978. 33.95 (*0-405-11051-0*) Ayer.

Munz, Ludwig & Haak, Bob. Rembrandt. (Masters of Art Ser.). 164p. 1984. 22.95 (*0-8109-1594-4*) Abrams.

Munz, Peter. Our Knowledge of the Growth of Knowledge: Popper or Wittgenstein? (International Library of Philosophy). 341p. 1985. 42.50 (*0-7102-0460-4*, RKP) Routledge.

— Philosophical Darwinism: On the Origin of Knowledge by Means of Natural Selection. LC 92-19364. 272p. 1993. 49.95 (*0-415-08602-7*, B0295) Routledge.

— The Shapes of Time: A New Look at the Philosophy of History. LC 77-2459. 394p. reprint ed. pap. 112.30 (*0-8357-3533-8*, 2034661) Bks Demand.

Munz, Peter, tr. see Fichtenau, Heinrich.

Munz, Peter, tr. see Garin, Eugenio.

Munz, Philip A. California Desert Wildflowers. (Illus.). (Orig.). 1962. pap. 10.00 (*0-520-00899-5*) U CA Pr.

— California Mountain Wildflowers. (Orig.). 1963. pap. 10.00 (*0-520-00901-0*) U CA Pr.

— California Spring Wildflowers: From the Base of the Sierra Nevada & Southern Mountains to the Sea. (Orig.). 1961. pap. 12.00 (*0-520-00896-0*) U CA Pr.

— A Flora of Southern California. (Illus.). 1974. 60.00 (*0-520-02146-0*) U CA Pr.

— Shore Wildflowers of California, Oregon, & Washington. (Illus.). (Orig.). 1965. pap. 11.00 (*0-520-00903-7*) U CA Pr.

— Supplement to a "California Flora" 1968. 30.00 (*0-520-00904-5*) U CA Pr.

Munz, Philip A. & Keck, David D. A California Flora & Supplement. 1973. 55.00 (*0-520-02405-2*) U CA Pr.

Munz, Rainer, jt. ed. see Fassman, Heinz.

Munzberg, Olav. Step Human into This World: Travel Poems. Cohen, Mitch, tr. LC 90-81862. (Illus.). 125p. (Orig.). 1991. pap. 21.00 (*0-948259-53-1*, Pub. by Forest Bks UK) Dufour.

Munzenrider, Robert F., jt. auth. see Golembiewski, Robert T.

Munzer, Friedrich. Beitrage Zur Quellenkritik der Naturgeschichte Des Plinius. xii, 432p. 1988. write for info. (*3-615-00040-4*, Pub. by Georg Olms GW) Lubrecht & Cramer.

Munzer, Stephen R. A Theory of Property. (Cambridge Studies in Philosophy & Law). (Illus.). 450p. (C). 1990. pap. 29.95 (*0-521-37886-9*) Cambridge U Pr.

Munzert. Test Your I. Q. 3rd ed. 1994. pap. 7.00 (*0-671-87459-4*) P-H Gen Ref & Trav.

Munzert, Alfred W. Poor Richard's Economic Survival Manual. Pepper, Christina A., ed. (Illus.). 272p. (C). 1982. 11.95 (*0-917292-03-0*) H-U Public.

— Self-Scoring I.Q. Test. Elskamp, Karen K., ed. 1977. pap. 1.95 (*0-917292-00-6*) H-U Public.

— Symbol Communication Technique (SCT) A Self-Motivating Method of Learning to Write. rev. ed. Elskamp, Karen K., ed. LC 70-134719. 88p. 1987. pap. 8.95 (*0-917292-04-9*) H-U Public.

— Teacher Handbook for Symbol Communications Technique (SCT) rev. ed. 8p. pap. write for info. (*0-917292-30-8*) H-U Public.

Muolo, Paul, jt. auth. see Pizzo, Stephen.

Muoneke, Romanus O. Art, Rebellion & Redemption: A Reading of the Novels of Chinua Achebe, Vol. 5. LC 92-43155. (American University Studies: African Literature: Ser. XVIII, Vol. 5). 176p. (C). 1994. text ed. 37.95 (*0-8204-2049-2*) P Lang Pubs.

Muppet Workshop Staff & Henson, Cheryl. The Muppets Make Puppets. Kovalchick, Sally, ed. (Illus.). 112p. (Orig.). (J). 1994. pap. 15.95 (*1-56305-708-5*) Workman Pub.

Muqiao, Xue, ed. see Economic Research Centre Staff, et al.

Mur, Frank X., ed. see Moran, Pablo.

Mur, L., jt. ed. see Barica, J.

Mura, David. The Colors of Desire: Poems. LC 94-6587. 1995. mass mkt. 10.00 (*0-385-47461-X*, Anchor NY) Doubleday.

— A Male Grief: Notes on Pornography & Addiction. LC 87-42896. (Thistle Series of Chapbooks). 24p. (C). 1987. pap. 4.00 (*0-915943-27-1*) Milkweed Ed.

— Turning Japanese. 1992. pap. 12.00 (*0-385-42344-6*, Anchor NY) Doubleday.

Mura Editors Staff & Kodbov, Tonci. AIDS World in Nineteen Ninety-Nine: A Modern Plague That May Destroy the World if We Stay Naive, Passive, Unaware,... 250p. (Orig.). (ENG & JPN.). 1989. pap. write for info. (*0-929602-02-1*) Mura Pub Co.

Mura, R. & Rhemtulla, A., eds. Orderable Groups. (Lecture Notes in Pure & Applied Mathematics Ser.: Vol. 27). 176p. 1977. 110.00 (*0-8247-6579-6*) Dekker.

Mura, Toshio. Micromechanics of Defects in Solids. 1982. lib. bdg. 210.00 (*90-247-2560-7*) Kluwer Ac.

— Micromechanics of Defects in Solids. 2nd rev. ed. 1987. lib. bdg. 254.00 (*90-247-3343-X*); pap. text ed. 99.50 (*90-247-3256-5*) Kluwer Ac.

Mura, Toshio, et al. Variational Methods in Mechanics. (Illus.). 336p. (C). 1992. text ed. 39.95 (*0-19-506830-0*, 230) OUP.

Mura, Toshio, ed. Mathematical Theory of Dislocations. LC 70-88019. 215p. reprint ed. pap. 61.30 (*0-317-08725-8*, 2004722) Bks Demand.

***Muraca, Maurizio, ed.** Methods in Biliary Research. 336p. 1994. 189.95 (*0-8493-8701-9*, 8701) CRC Pr.

Murach, Joel. The Least You Need to Know about WordPerfect for DOS. LC 92-33846. (Illus.). 380p. 1992. pap. 15.00 (*0-911625-66-6*) M Murach & Assoc.

— The WordPerfect Tutorial for DOS. LC 93-11990. 132p. 1993. Alk. paper. pap. 10.00 (*0-911625-77-1*) M Murach & Assoc.

Murach, Joel & Murach, Tom. WordPerfect 6.0 for DOS. LC 94-2216. (Essential Guide Ser.). (Illus.). 498p. 1994. pap. 25.00 (*0-911625-81-X*) M Murach & Assoc.

— WordPerfect 6.0 for Windows. LC 94-10557. (Essential Guide Ser.). (Illus.). 600p. 1994. pap. 25.00 (*0-911625-83-6*) M Murach & Assoc.

Murach, Joel, jt. auth. see Bultema, Patrick.

Murach, Mike. Write Better with a PC. LC 89-60556. 410p. 1989. pap. 19.95 (*0-911625-51-8*) M Murach & Assoc.

Murach, Mike & Noll, Paul. How to Design & Develop COBOL Programs. LC 84-61556. (Illus.). 536p. 1985. pap. 34.50 (*0-911625-20-8*) M Murach & Assoc.

— Structured ANS COBOL, Pt. 1: A Course for Novices Using 1974 or 1985 ANS COBOL. 2nd ed. LC 86-61654. 408p. (C). 1986. teacher ed, ring bd. 75.00 (*0-911625-39-9*) M Murach & Assoc.

— Structured ANS COBOL, Pt. 1: A Course for Novices Using 1974 or 1985 ANS COBOL, Pt. 1. 2nd ed. LC 86-61654. 438p. (C). 1986. pap. 31.00 (*0-911625-37-2*) M Murach & Assoc.

— Structured ANS COBOL, Pt. 2: An Advanced Course Using 1974 or 1985 ANS COBOL. 2nd ed. LC 86-61654. 462p. (C). 1987. teacher ed, ring bd. 75.00 (*0-911625-40-2*) M Murach & Assoc.

— Structured ANS COBOL, Pt. 2: An Advanced Course Using 1974 or 1985 ANS COBOL, Pt. 2. 2nd ed. LC 86-61654. 498p. (C). 1987. pap. 31.00 (*0-911625-38-0*) M Murach & Assoc.

Murach, Mike, jt. auth. see Prince, Anne.

Murach, Tom, jt. auth. see Murach, Joel.

Murad, jt. auth. see Sellers.

Murad, Adel. Animal Farm: The Next Generation. LC 93-73346. x, 135p. 1994. 19.95 (*0-9638643-7-8*); pap. 7.00 (*0-9638643-9-4*) Child War Trust.

Murad, Anatol. Franz Joseph I of Austria & His Empire. LC 68-17233. (Illus.). 259p. 1968. text ed. 29.50 (*0-8290-0172-7*) Irvington.

— What Keynes Means. 1962. pap. 15.95x (*0-8084-0320-6*, B18) NCUP.

Murad, Khurram, ed. see Nadwi, Abul H.

Murad, Marcela. Put on a Happy Face: Mama Clown's Complete Guide to Face Painting. (Illus.). 96p. 1993. pap. 24.95 (*1-878853-26-0*) Venture Pr FL.

Murad, Mounir. Axioms: In Search of a Comprehensive Philosophy of Life. (Illus.). 80p. (Orig.). 1992. pap. 7.50 (*0-9633519-6-6*) Murad Pub.

— Daheshism & the Journey of Life. LC 93-91483. (Illus.). 128p. 1993. 20.00 (*0-9633519-1-5*); pap. 10.00 (*0-9633519-2-3*) Murad Pub.

***Murad, Richard D.** To the Fallen Angels: Man's Spiritual Heritage, Earthly Missing, & Evolutionary Destiny. LC 94-92105. 104p. 1994. pap. 11.45 (*1-885384-00-9*) Soldier Mystic.

Muradian, Khachik K., jt. auth. see Frolkis, Vladimir V.

Murado, Miguelanxo. A Bestiary of Discontent: Bestiario dos Descontentos. Evans-Corrales, Carys, tr. LC 93-32609. (Hispanic Literature Ser.: Vol. 21). (Illus.). 144p. 1993. 69.95 (*0-7734-9338-7*) E Mellen.

Murail, Marie-Aude. Mystere. (Folio - Cadet Bleu Ser.: No. 217). (Illus.). 64p. (FRE.). (J). (gr. 1-5). 1987. pap. 9.95 (*2-07-031217-8*) Schoenhof.

— Uncle Giorgio. (I Love to Read Ser.). (Illus.). 48p. (J). (gr. 3-8). 1990. 12.79 (*0-89565-809-7*) Childs World.

Murakami, H. & Shirahata, S., eds. Animal Cell Technology: Basic & Applied Aspects: Proceedings of the Fourth Annual Meeting of the Japanese Association for Animal Cell Technology, Fukuoka, Japan, 13-15 November 1991. LC 92-23657. 600p. (C). 1992. lib. bdg. 225.00 (*0-7923-1882-X*) Kluwer Ac.

***Murakami, Haruki.** Dance Dance Dance. 1995. pap. 13.00 (*0-679-75379-6*, Vin) Random.

— Dance Dance Dance: A Novel. Luke, Elmer, ed. Birnbaum, Alfred, tr. LC 93-14098. 384p. 1994. 22.00 (*4-7700-1683-2*) Kodansha.

— The Elephant Vanishes. LC 92-54277. 1993. 21.00 (*0-679-42057-6*) Knopf.

— The Hard-Boiled Wonderland & the End of the World. Birnbaum, Alfred, tr. 416p. 1991. 21.95 (*4-7700-1544-5*) Kodansha.

— Hard-Boiled Wonderland & the End of the World: A Novel. Birnbaum, Alfred, tr. LC 92-56345. 1993. pap. 12.00 (*0-679-74346-4*) Vintage NY.

— A Wild Sheep Chase: A Novel. Birnbaum, Alfred, tr. 272p. (YA). 1989. 18.95 (*0-87011-905-2*) Kodansha.

Murakami, Hiroki, ed. Trends in Animal Cell Culture Technology: Proceedings of Annual Meeting of the Japanese Association for Animal Cell Technology, 2nd, Tsukuba, Ibaraki, Japan, Nov. 20-22, 1989. 342p. 1991. lib. bdg. 95.00 (*0-89573-999-2*) VCH Pubs.

Murakami, Hiroshi, jt. tr. see Gibson, Morgan.

Murakami, Hisayo, ed. Catalogue of Kanagawa Prefecture Magazines: 1945-1949. LC 91-34018. 133p. 1991. 35.00 (*1-880223-00-7*) G W Prange Collect.

Murakami, K., et al, eds. Recent Advances in Pediatric Nephrology: Proceedings of the Seventh International Congress, Tokyo, Japan, September 7-12, 1986. (International Congress Ser.: No. 733). 676p. 1987. 190.25 (*0-444-80888-4*) Elsevier.

***Murakami, Linda, et al.** Environmental Restoration & Waste Management: A Guide to the Issues. 115p. 1995. 15.00 (*1-55516-427-7*, 4643) Natl Conf State Legis.

Murakami, Linda K., jt. auth. see Mahoney, Katherine.

Murakami, M. Melt Processed High Temperature Superconductors. 380p. 1993. text ed. 121.00 (*981-02-1244-5*) World Scientific Pub.

Murakami, Naojiro, ed. see MacDonald, Ranald.

Murakami, Paul, jt. auth. see Hanson, Handt.

Murakami, Ryu. Almost Transparent Blue. Shaw, ed. Andrew, Nancy, tr. LC 77-75959. 128p. 1992. reprint ed. pap. 8.00 (*0-87011-469-7*) Kodansha.

— Coin Locker Babies. Snyder, Stephen, tr. 400p. 1995. 23.00 (*4-7700-1590-9*) Kodansha.

— Sixty-Nine. Shaw, ed. 184p. 1993. 20.00 (*4-7700-1736-7*) Kodansha.

— 69. McCarthy, Ralph F., tr. LC 93-28815. 192p. 1995. pap. 10.00 (*4-7700-1951-3*) Kodansha.

Murakami, S., ed. Computational Wind Engineering One: Proceedings of the 1st International Symposium on Computational Wind Engineering (CWE92), Tokyo, Japan, August 21-23, 1992. LC 93-31564. 1993. 468.75 (*0-444-81688-7*) Elsevier.

Murakami, Shigeyoshi. Japanese Religion in the Modern Century. Earhart, H. Byron, tr. 186p. 1979. 24.50 (*0-86008-260-1*, Pub. by U of Tokyo JA) Col U Pr.

Murakami, Sumio, jt. ed. see Fan, Jinghong.

Murakami, T. High Temperature Superconductors: A Special Issue of the Journal Phase Transitions, Section B. 90p. 1989. pap. text ed. 182.00 (*0-677-25820-8*) Gordon & Breach.

***Murakami, T. & Ewing, R. C., eds.** Scientific Basis for Nuclear Waste Management: Materials Research Society Symposium Proceedings, Vol. XVIII. 1995. 80.00 (*1-55899-253-7*, 353K4) Materials Res.

Murakami, Y. New Developments in Applied Superconductivity. (Progress in High Temperature Super Conductivity Ser.: Vol. 15). 828p. (C). 1989. pap. 61.00 (*9971-5-0834-6*) World Scientific Pub.

— The Rainflow Method in Fatigue. (Illus.). 240p. 1992. 160.00 (*0-7506-0504-9*) Buttrwrth-Heinemann.

Murakami, Y., jt. auth. see Tsukui, J.

Murakami, Y., et al, eds. New Developments in Zeolite Science & Technology: Proceedings of the 7th International Zeolite Conference, Tokyo, Japan, August 17-22, 1986. (Studies in Surface Science & Catalysis: No. 28). 1092p. 1986. 295.00 (*0-444-98981-1*) Elsevier.

Murakami, Yasusuke & Kosai, Yutaka, eds. Japan in the Global Community: Its Role & Contribution on the Eve of the 21st Century. (Illus.). 186p. (Orig.). 1987. pap. 22.50 (*0-86008-405-1*, Pub. by U of Tokyo JA) Col U Pr.

Murakawa, S., jt. auth. see Kiya, F.

Muraki, Eiji & Bock, R. Darrell. PARSCALE: IRT Based Test Scoring & Item Analysis for Graded Open-Ended Exercises & Performance Tasks. 1993. ring bd. 30.00 (*0-89498-032-7*) Sci Ware.

Murakovic, Antun. Overcome Shyness from Inside & Succeed in Life: New Approach to Shyness Control Without Medication or Boring Treatment. 200p. (Orig.). (ENG & JPN.). 1989. pap. write for info. (*0-929602-01-3*) Mura Pub Co.

Mural, T. A Real Variable Method for the Cauchy Transform, & Analytic Capacity. (Lecture Notes in Mathematics Ser.: Vol. 1307). viii, 133p. 1988. pap. 28.90 (*0-387-19091-0*) Spr-Verlag.

Muraleedharan, N., jt. auth. see Ananthakrishnan, T. N.

Muralidhar, A., jt. ed. see Patanjali, V.

Muralidhar, A., tr. see Patanjali, V. & Muralidhar, A., eds.

Muralidhara, H. S., ed. Advances in Solid Liquid Separation. LC 86-26569. 494p. 1986. 79.50 (*0-85186-363-9*) Battelle.

— Advances in Solid-Liquid Separation: Supplement. 180p. 1986. pap. 26.50 (*0-685-40037-9*) Battelle.

— Solid-Liquid Separations: Waste Management & Productivity Enhancement. LC 89-17828. 584p. 1990. 87.50 (*0-935470-54-9*) Battelle.

An Asterisk (*) at the beginning of an entry indicates that the title is appearing in BIP for the first time.

Muramaru, N. Japanese Folktales. (Illus.). 160p. (J). (gr. 4-9). 1993. pap. 11.95 (4-89684-228-6, Pub. by Yohan Pubns JA) Weatherhill.

Muramatsu, Mitsuo, jt. ed. see Evans, E. Anthony.

Muramatsu, R. & Dudley, N. A., eds. Production & Industrial Systems: Proceedings of the 4th International Conference on Production Research, Tokyo, 1977. 1340p. 1978. 187.00 (0-85066-138-2) Taylor & Francis.

Muramatsu, T. Cell Surface & Differentiation. (Illus.). 160p. 1990. text ed. 69.95 (0-412-30850-9, A4750) Chapman & Hall.

Muramatsu, Takashi, ed. Handbook of Endoglycosidases & Glycoamidases. 362p. 1992. 156.95 (0-8493-3618-X, QP 609) CRC Pr.

Muramoto, Naboru. Healing Ourselves. (Illus.). 160p. 1976. pap. 12.50 (0-380-00900-5) Avon.

Muramoto, Noboru B. Natural Immunity: Insights on Diet & AIDS. LC 88-81555. 1988. pap. 12.95 (0-918860-48-2) G Ohsawa.

Murano, Genesio. Protease Inhibitors of Human Plasma-Biochemistry & Pathophysiology, Vol. II. (Reviews of Hematology: Vol. II). 1985. 69.95 (0-915340-14-3) PJD Pubns.

Murano, Genesio & Bick, Rodger L., eds. Basic Concepts of Hemostasis & Thrombosis. 304p. 1980. 132.00 (0-8493-5393-9, RC633, CRC Reprint) Franklin.

Murano, Vincent & Hammer, Richard. The Thursday Club. Rubenstein, Julie, ed. 288p. 1994. reprint ed. mass mkt. 5.50 (0-671-73864-X) PB.

Murano, Vincent & Hoffer, William. Cop Hunter. 320p. 1991. reprint ed. mass mkt. 4.95 (0-671-66959-1, Pocket Star Bks) PB.

Murao, S., ed. see Hiromi, K., et al.

Murao, Tadahiro, jt. auth. see Welch, Graham.

Muraoka, Kageo & Okamura, Kichiemon. Folk Arts & Crafts of Japan. Stegmaier, Daphne, tr. LC 72-78600. (Heibonsha Survey of Japanese Art Ser.: Vol. 26). Orig. Title: Mingei. (Illus.). 168p. 1973. 20.00 (0-8348-1009-3) Weatherhill.

Muraoka, Takamitsu, ed. The Melbourne Symposium on Septuagint Lexicography. (Society of Biblical Literature Septuagint & Cognate Studies Ser.). 154p. 1990. 19.95 (1-55540-486-3); pap. 14.95 (1-55540-487-1) Scholars Pr GA.

Muraoka, Tsunetsugu. Studies in Shinto Thought, 10 vols., Set. Brown, Delmer M. & Araki, James T., trs. (Documentary Reference Collections). 293p. 1988. 395. 00 (0-318-35981-2, CMJ05, Greenwood Pr) Greenwood.

— Studies in Shinto Thought, 10 vols., Vol. 5. Brown, Delmer M. & Araki, James T., trs. LC 88-21311. (Documentary Reference Collections). 243p. 1988. text ed. 49.95 (0-313-26555-0, CNJ05, Greenwood Pr) Greenwood.

Murari, G., jt. ed. see Villa, A.

Murarka, S. P., et al, eds. Advanced Metallization for Devices & Circuits - Science, Technology, & Manufacturability, No. Three: Materials Research Society Symposium Proceedings, Vol. 337. 1994. text ed. 57.00 (1-55899-237-5) Materials Res.

— Interface Control of Electrical, Chemical, & Mechanical Properties, Vol. 318: Materials Research Society Symposium Proceedings. 1994. text ed. 80.00 (1-55899-217-0) Materials Res.

Murarka, Shyam P. Metallization: Theory & Practice for VLSI & ULSI. 288p. 1992. 54.95 (0-7506-9001-1) Buttrwrth-Heinemann.

Murarka, Shyam P., ed. Silicides for VLSI Applications. 1983. text ed. 55.00 (0-12-511220-3) Acad Pr.

Murarka, Shyam P. & Peckerar, Martin C. Electronic Materials: Science & Technology. 622p. 1989. text ed. 79.00 (0-12-511120-7) Acad Pr.

Muraro, M. & Grabar, A. Venice. 39.95 (0-517-62645-4) Random Hse Value.

Muraro, Michelangelo. Paolo da Venezia. LC 77-84667. (Illus.). 1970. With a Catalogue Raisonne of the 14th century founder of the Venetian School. 95.00 (0-271-00098-8) A Wofsy Fine Arts.

Murasaki, Lady. The Tale of Genji. Seidensticker, Edward G., tr. LC 76-13680. 1978. pap. 25.00 (0-394-73530-7) Knopf.

— The Tale of Genji. Waley, Arthur, tr. LC 60-52014. 1977. 16.95 (0-394-60405-9, Modern Lib) Random.

Murase, Masatoshi. Dynamics of Cellular Motility. (Nonlinear Science: Theory & Applications Ser.). 376p. 1992. text ed. 229.00 (0-471-93576-X) Wiley.

Murase, Miyeko. Masterpieces of Japanese Screen Painting: The American Collections. (Braziller Library of Far Eastern Art). (Illus.). 232p. 1990. 150.00 (0-8076-1230-8) Braziller.

Murase, Miyeko, et al. Court & Samurai in an Age of Transition: Medieval Paintings & Blades from the Gotoh Museum, Tokyo. LC 89-63130. (Illus.). 128p. 1990. 36. 00 (0-913304-28-X) Japan Soc.

— Court & Samurai in an Age of Transition: Medieval Paintings & Blades from the Gotoh Museum, Tokyo. LC 89-63130. (Illus.). 127p. 1995. pap. 25.00 (0-913304-29-8, 298) Japan Soc.

— Jewel Rivers: Japanese Art from the Burke Collection. West, Rosalie A., ed. (Illus.). 287p. (Orig.). 1994. pap. 35.00 (0-917046-35-8) Va Mus Arts.

Murashkevich, A. M. English-Russian Aviation & Space Abbreviations Dictionary. 622p. (ENG & RUS.). 1981. 39.95 (0-8288-0005-7, M15483) Fr & Eur.

Murashkevich, A. M. & Vladimirov, O. N. English-Russian Aviation & Space Abbreviations Dictionary. 622p. (ENG & RUS.). 1981. 70.00 (0-686-44706-9, Pub. by Collets UK) St Mut.

Muraski, Michel L., jt. auth. see Zimmerman, Donald E.

Muraskin, Roslyn, ed. Issues in Justice: Exploring Policy Issues in the Criminal Justice System. LC 90-50420. xi, 175p. (C). 1990. text ed. 39.95 (1-55605-169-7); pap. text ed. 29.95 (1-55605-168-9) Wyndhall Pr.

Muraskin, Roslyn & Alleman, Ted. It's a Crime: Women & Justice. 448p. 1993. pap. text ed. 44.00 (0-13-962051-6) P-H.

***Muraskin, William.** The War Against Hepatitis B. A History of the International Task Force on Hepatitis B Immunization. LC 94-43276. (Illus.). 256p. 1995. text ed. 29.95 (0-8122-3267-4) U of Pa Pr.

Murasugi, Kunio. On Closed Three-Braids. LC 74-17176. (Memoirs Ser.: No. 1/151). 114p. 1974. pap. 18.00 (0-8218-1851-1, MEMO 1/151) Am Math.

Murasugi, Kunio & Przytycki, Jozef H. An Index of a Graph with Applications to Knot Theory. LC 93-27284. (Memoirs of the American Mathematical Society Ser.: No. 508). 120p. 1993. pap. 29.00 (0-8218-2570-4) Am Math.

Murat, Achille. The United States of North America. 1977. text ed. 23.95 (0-8369-9231-8, 9085) Ayer.

Murat, Felix. The Last Days of the U. S. A., 1971. 25.00 (0-9600356-1-3) F Murat.

Murat, Ines. Colbert. Cook, Robert F. & Van Asselt, Jeannie, trs. LC 84-2194. (Illus.). 308p. reprint ed. pap. 87.80 (0-8357-3134-0, 2039397) Bks Demand.

Murat, J., tr. see Rimbaud, Arthur & Verlaine, Paul.

Murat, Laure, jt. auth. see Schezen, Roberto.

Murata. Handbook of Optical Fibers & Cables. (Optical Engineering Ser.: Vol. 15). 480p. 1988. 140.00 (0-8247-7694-1) Dekker.

Murata, H. Development of Optical Fibers in Japan. xii, 156p. 1989. pap. text ed. 66.00 (2-88124-372-X) Gordon & Breach.

Murata, K. & Harrison, Alan. How to Make Japanese Management Methods Work Best in the West. 93p. 1991. text ed. 39.95 (0-566-09085-6, Pub. by Gower UK) Ashgate Pub Co.

Murata, Keinosuke, et al. Sakura: Cherry Blossom Paintings by Yoshiko Ishikawa. LC 92-62884. (Illus.). 104p. 1993. pap. text ed. 21.95 (0-940979-22-5) Natl Museum Women.

Murata, Kiyoaki. An Enemy among Friends. 241p. 1991. 19.95 (4-7700-1609-3) Kodansha.

Murata, Kiyoji, ed. An Industrial Geography of Japan. LC 80-13404. 1980. text ed. 39.95 (0-312-41428-5) St Martin.

Murata Kyuzo. Four Seasons of Bonsai. (Illus.). 168p. 1991. 24.95 (4-7700-1498-8) Kodansha.

Murata, Margaret, ed. Marc'Antonio Pasqualini (1614-1691), Vol. 3. (Italian Cantata in the Seventeenth Century Ser.). 300p. 1986. lib. bdg. 25.00 (0-8240-8877-8) Garland.

Murata, Michinori. Water & Light: Looking Through Lenses. LC 92-19969. (Illus.). (J). (gr. 1-3). 1993. 18.95 (0-8225-2904-1, Lerner Publctns) Lerner Group.

Murata, Norio, ed. Research in Photosynthesis: Proceedings of the IXth International Congress on Photosynthesis, Nagoya, Japan, August 30-September 4, 1992. LC 92-39162. 3512p. (C). 1993. lib. bdg. 0.01 (0-7923-2073-5) Kluwer Ac.

Murata, Sachiko. The Tao of Islam: A Sourcebook on Gender Relationships in Islamic Thought. LC 91-2610. 397p. (C). 1992. 59.50 (0-7914-0913-9); pap. 19.95 (0-7914-0914-7) State U NY Pr.

Murata, Sachiko & Chittick, William C. The Vision of Islam: Reflecting on the Hadith of Gabriel. LC 94-16064. (Visions of Reality Ser.). (Illus.). 320p. (Orig.). (C). 1994. pap. text ed. 18.95x (1-55778-516-3) Paragon Hse.

Murata, Yasuo. Optimal Control Methods for Linear Discrete-Time Economic Systems. (Illus.). 175p. 1982. 76.00 (0-387-90709-2) Spr-Verlag.

Muratake, Miki, tr. see Thomas, Kenneth L.

Muratore, Carol. Scooter Goes to the Hospital. (Illus.). (Orig.). 1992. pap. text ed. 3.75 (0-9628084-2-3) Hlth Mgmnt Pubns.

Muratore, Joseph R. The Remains of Christopher Columbus. (Illus.). 91p. 1973. pap. 3.00 (0-686-09021-7) Muratore.

Muratore, Mary J. Cornelian Theater: The Metadramatic Dimension. LC 90-70978. 117p. 1990. lib. bdg. 23.95 (0-917786-84-X) Summa Pubns.

Muratorio, Blanca. Culture & History in Ecuadorian Upper Amazon: The Life & Times of Grandfather Alonso. (Illus.). 320p. (C). 1991. text ed. 45.00 (0-8135-1684-6); pap. text ed. 15.00 (0-8135-1685-4) Rutgers U Pr.

Murauchi, Sadanori & Asanuma, Toshio, comps. Seismic Reflection Profiles in the Western Pacific, 1965-74. 232p. 1977. 57.50 (0-86008-193-1, Pub. by U of Tokyo JA) Col U Pr.

Murav, Harriet. Holy Foolishness: Dostoevsky's Novels & the Poetics of Cultural Critique. (Illus.). 272p. (C). 1993. 37.50 (0-8047-2059-2) Stanford U Pr.

Muravchick. The Anesthetic Plan. 440p. 1990. 55.00 (0-8151-6241-3, Yr Bk Med Pubs) Mosby Yr Bk.

— Geriatric Anesthesia. 350p. 1995. 65.00 (0-8016-7238-4) Mosby Yr Bk.

Muravchik, Joshua. Exporting Democracy: Fulfilling America's Destiny. 276p. 1991. 24.95 (0-8447-3733-X, AEI Pr) Am Enterprise.

— Exporting Democracy: Fulfilling America's Destiny. 276p. 1992. pap. 12.95 (0-8447-3734-8, AEI Pr) Am Enterprise.

— Nicaragua's Slow March to Communism. 1986. 3.00 (0-317-90495-7) Cuban Amer Natl Fndtn.

Murav'Ev, Andrei N. A History of the Church of Russia. LC 76-133816. reprint ed. 49.50 (0-404-04541-3) AMS Pr.

Muravina, Nina. Vstrechi s Pasternakom. LC 90-4742. 223p. (Orig.). (RUS.). 1990. pap. 15.00 (1-55779-036-1) Hermitage.

Muravyova, L. Verbs of Motion in Russian. 238p. (C). 1986. 60.00 (0-569-08976-X, Pub. by Collets UK) Pro-Am Music.

Murawski, Elisabeth. Moon & Mercury. LC 90-11915. 72p. (Orig.). 1990. pap. 8.00 (0-931846-37-4) Wash Writers Pub.

Murawski, Frank. U. S. Secondary Telecom Industry - Markets & Opportunities: 1989-1995 Analysis. (Illus.). 320p. 1989. pap. text ed. 2,400.00 (1-878218-24-7) World Info Tech.

Murawski, Frank, jt. auth. see Bender, Amadee.

Murawski, H., jt. ed. see Dennis, J. G.

***Murawski, Hans.** Geologisches Woerterbuch. (GER.). Date not set. 39.95 (0-7859-8352-X, 3423030380) Fr & Eur.

— Geology Dictionary: Geologisches Woerterbuch. 9th ed. 254p. (GER.). 1992. pap. 29.95 (0-8288-1470-8, M7418) Fr & Eur.

Muray, Julius J., jt. auth. see Brodie, Ivor.

Muray, Les. An Introduction to the Process Understanding of Science, Society, & the Self: A Philosophy for Modern Man. LC 88-9319. (Symposium Ser.: Vol. 26). 200p. 1988. lib. bdg. 79.95 (0-88946-336-0) E Mellen.

Muray, Nickolas. Muray's Celebrity Portraits of the Twenties & Thirties. LC 77-87448. (Illus.). 1978. pap. 7.95 (0-486-23578-5) Dover.

Murayama, Milton. All I Asking for Is My Body. LC 88-6967. 120p. 1988. reprint ed. pap. 5.95 (0-8248-1172-0, Kolowalu Bk) UH Pr.

— Five Years on a Rock. LC 94-9806. 144p. (C). 1994. 18. 00 (0-8248-1647-1, Kolowalu Bk); pap. 9.95 (0-8248-1677-3, Kolowalu Bk) UH Pr.

Murayama, Yoshimasa, jt. ed. see Ezawa, Hiroshi.

Murburg, Michele, ed. Catecholamine Function in Posttraumatic Stress Disorder: Emerging Concepts. LC 93-5677. (Progress in Psychiatry Ser.: Vol. 42). 352p. 1994. text ed. 35.00 (0-88048-473-X) Am Psychiatric.

Murcava, L. O., ed. see Dinneen, Patrick S.

Murch, A. E., ed. see Pavese, Cesare.

Murch, A. E., tr. see Pavese, Cesare.

Murch, Alma E. Development of the Detective Novel. LC 69-10138. 272p. 1969. reprint ed. text ed. 35.00 (0-8371-0581-1, MUDN, Greenwood Pr) Greenwood.

Murch, Alma E., ed. see Dumas, Alexandre.

Murch, Arvin. Black Frenchmen: The Political Integration of the French Antilles. 184p. 1971. 18.95 (0-87073-034-7) Schenkman Bks Inc.

Murch, Gerald M. Visual & Auditory Perception. LC 74-172349. (Illus.). (C). 1973. pap. write for info. (0-672-60779-4, Bobbs) Macmillan.

Murch, Gerald M., ed. Studies in Perception. LC 74-8398. (C). 1976. pap. text ed. write for info. (0-672-61189-9, Bobbs) Macmillan.

Murch, Graeme, ed. Diffusion in Solids: Unsolved Problems. 294p. 1992. text ed. 72.00 (0-87849-631-9, Pub. by Trans Tech GW) LPS Dist Ctr.

Murch, Graeme E. & Nowick, Arthur S., eds. Diffusion in Solids II. (Materials Science & Technology Ser.). 1984. text ed. 140.00 (0-12-522662-4) Acad Pr.

***Murch, Walter.** In the Blink of an Eye: A Perspective on Film Editing. 108p. (Orig.). 1995. pap. 12.95 (1-879505-23-1) Silman James Pr.

Murchie-Beyma, Tia A. An Analytic Profile of Hispanic Organizations of the Washington Area, Vol. O8. 1991. 6.50 (0-317-04774-4) GWU CWAS.

— An Annotated Directory of Hispanic Organizations of the Washington Area, Vol. O9. 1991. 6.50 (0-317-04775-2) GWU CWAS.

Murchie, Guy. Music of the Spheres: The Material Universe from Atom to Quasar, Simply Explained, 2 Vols, 1. rev. ed. (Illus.). (YA). (gr. 7-12). pap. 8.95 (0-486-21809-0) Dover.

— Music of the Spheres: The Material Universe from Atom to Quasar, Simply Explained, 2 Vols, 2. rev. ed. (Illus.). (YA). (gr. 7-12). pap. 6.95 (0-486-21810-4) Dover.

— The Seven Mysteries of Life: An Exploration in Science & Philosophy. 1981. pap. 14.95 (0-395-30537-3) HM.

— The Soul School: Confessions of a Passenger on Planet Earth. (Illus.). 672p. 1994. pap. 14.95 (1-56474-105-2) Fithian Pr.

Murchison, Bill. Nacogdoches - Past & Present: A Legacy of Texas Pride. Murchison, Cynthia H., ed. LC 86-72139. 100p. (Orig.). 1986. pap. 21.95 (0-9617381-0-3) B & C Pub Odessa.

Murchison, Carl. The Case for & Against Psychical Belief. LC 75-7389. (Perspectives in Psychical Research Ser.). (Illus.). 1975. reprint ed. 33.95 (0-405-07037-3) Ayer.

— Criminal Intelligence. (Historical Foundations of Forensic Psychiatry & Psychology Ser.). 291p. 1983. reprint ed. lib. bdg. 29.50 (0-306-76183-1) Da Capo.

Murchison, Carl, ed. Psychologies of 1930. LC 73-2980. (Classics in Psychology Ser.). 1976. reprint ed. 34.95 (0-405-05152-2) Ayer.

Murchison, Claudius T. Resale Price Maintenance. LC 68-56673. (Columbia University. Studies in the Social Sciences: No. 192). reprint ed. 20.00 (0-404-51192-9) AMS Pr.

Murchison, Cynthia H., ed. see Murchison, Bill.

Murchison, D. G., ed. see Stach, E., et al.

Murchison, Kenneth M. Federal Criminal Law Doctrines: The Forgotten Influence of National Prohibition. 288p. 1994. text ed. 42.95 (0-8223-1510-6) Duke.

Murchison, Myles. The Deathless. 368p. 1989. pap. 3.95 (0-345-35378-1) Ballantine.

Murchland, Bernard. The Dream of Christian Socialism: An Essay on Its European Origins. LC 81-14919. (AEI Studies: No. 343). 88p. reprint ed. pap. 25.10 (0-7837-1081-X, 2041611) Bks Demand.

— Humanism & Capitalism: A Survey of Thought on Morality. LC 83-11785. (AEI Studies: No. 387). 76p. reprint ed. pap. 25.00 (0-8357-4489-2, 2037342) Bks Demand.

— Voices in America: Bicentennial Conversations. LC 86-63412. 250p. 1987. pap. 14.95 (0-911168-70-2) Prakken.

Murchland, Bernard, comp. Voices in American Education: Conversations with Fourteen Major Educators & Public Figures. 219p. (Orig.). 1990. pap. 11.95 (0-911168-77-X) Prakken.

***Murchland, Bernard, ed. & intro.** Higher Education & the Practice of Democratic Politics: A Political Education Reader. (Kettering Political Education Ser.). 251p. (Orig.). (C). 1991. pap. text ed. write for info. (0-923993-01-0) Kettering Found.

Murchland, Bernard, ed. Noble Achievements: Ohio Wesleyan from 1942-1992. (Illus.). 316p. 1992. 20.00 (0-9630909-1-7) OH Wesleyan U.

Murcia, Andy. Helping the Woman You Love Recover from Breast Cancer, Vol. 1. 1991. mass mkt. 4.99 (0-312-92191-8) St Martin.

— Man to Man: When the Woman You Love Has Breast Cancer. 1990. pap. 10.95 (0-312-04347-3) St Martin.

Murcia, Eligia. Record Keeping for Small Rural Businesses. (Technical Notes Ser.: No. 26). (Illus.). 25p. (Orig.). pap. text ed. 2.00 (0-932288-75-8) Ctr Intl Ed U of MA.

Murck, Alfreda & Fong, Wen C. Words & Images: Chinese Poetry, Calligraphy, & Painting. (Illus.). 616p. 1991. 75. 00 (0-691-04096-6) Princeton U Pr.

Murck, Christian, jt. ed. see Bush, Susan.

Murcko, Terry, jt. auth. see Peffer, George.

Murcott, Anne, ed. Sociology of Food & Eating. 208p. 1983. text ed. 59.50 (0-566-00580-8) Ashgate Pub Co.

Murcott, Susan. First Buddhist Women. LC 91-10819. 219p. 1992. pap. 15.00 (0-938077-42-2) Parallax Pr.

Murcray, David G., ed. Handbook of High Resolution Infrared Laboratory Spectra of Gases of Atmospheric Interest. 288p. 1981. 79.00 (0-8493-2950-7, QC879, CRC Reprint) Franklin.

Murd, M. A. Intellectual Modernism of Shibli Nu'mani: An Exposition of His Religious & Political Ideas. pap. 19.95 (1-56744-060-6) Kazi Pubns.

Murday, R., jt. ed. see Harrison, M. L.

***Murden, Simon.** Emergent Regional Powers & International Relations in the Gulf: 1988-1991. 250p. 1995. 85.00 (0-86372-193-1, Pub. by Ithaca UK) Paul & Co Pubs.

Murdick, Kent. Jazz Comping for Fingerstyle Guitar. 1993. 6.95 (0-685-64276-3, 94021); audio 9.98 (0-685-64277-1, 94021) Mel Bay.

Murdick, Robert, jt. auth. see Karger, Delmar.

Murdick, Robert G. MIS: Concepts & Design. 2nd ed. (Illus.). 672p. 1986. text ed. 50.00 (0-13-586322-8) P-H.

Murdick, Robert G. & Ross, Joel E. Information Systems for Modern Management. 2nd ed. (Illus.). 640p. 1975. 29.95 (0-685-03873-4) P-H.

— Introduction to Management Information Systems. (Illus.). 1977. text ed. 35.40 (0-13-486233-3) P-H.

Murdick, Robert G., et al. Information Systems for Modern Management. 3rd ed. (Illus.). 432p. 1984. text ed. 46.00 (0-13-464736-X) P-H.

— Services Operations Management. 650p. 1990. teacher ed write for info. (0-318-66339-2, H22510); text ed. 74.00 (0-205-12250-7, H2250-2) Allyn.

Murdie, Alan. Environmental Law Citizen Action. 176p. (Orig.). 1992. 17.95 (1-85383-156-5, Pub. by Erthscan Pubns UK) Island Pr.

Murdin, Leslie, jt. auth. see Murdin, Paul.

Murdin, P., jt. ed. see Beers, P.

Murdin, Paul. End in Fire: The Supernova in the Large Magellanic Cloud. (Illus.). 250p. (C). 1990. 32.95 (0-521-37495-2) Cambridge U Pr.

Murdin, Paul & Murdin, Leslie. Supernovae. 260p. 1985. 29.95 (0-521-30038-X) Cambridge U Pr.

Murdocca, Miles. Principles of Computer Architecture. 656p. (C). 1996. text ed. write for info. (0-8053-5460-3) Benjamin-Cummings.

Murdocca, Miles J. A Digital Design Methodology for Optical Computing. (Illus.). 225p. 1990. 30.00x (0-262-13251-6) MIT Pr.

Murdocca, Sal. Baby Wants the Moon. LC 94-14517. (Illus.). 32p. (J). (ps up). 1994. 15.00 (0-688-13664-8); lib. bdg. 14.93 (0-688-13665-6) Lothrop.

— Christmas Bear. (J). (gr. k-3). 1990. pap. 3.95 (0-671-70849-X, Litl Simon S&S) S&S Childrens.

***Murdoch.** Amputation: Surgical Practice & Patient Management. 1995. text ed. write for info. (0-7506-0843-9, Focal) Buttrwrth-Heinemann.

— Basic Behaviour Therapy. 190p. 1991. 32.95 (0-632-02322-8) Blackwell Sci.

— Clinical Gastroenterology in the Dog & Cat. 1991. write for info. (0-632-01402-4) Mosby Yr Bk.

— Ideas for Environmental Education in the Elementary Classroom. LC 94-11803. 194p. 1994. pap. text ed. 18. 50 (0-435-08347-3) Heinemann.

Murdoch, A. I., jt. ed. see Kosinski, W.

Murdoch, Anna. Coming to Terms. 1992. mass mkt. 4.99 (0-06-109949-X, Harp PBks) HarpC.

— Coming to Terms. large type ed. (General Ser.). 304p. 1993. 21.95 (0-7089-2790-4) Ulverscroft.

— In Her Own Image. large type ed. 432p. 1986. 23.95 (0-7089-8334-0, Charnwood) Ulverscroft.

Murdoch, Anna K. Stories from the Motherland. (Illus.). 80p. 1994. 7.00 (1-86371-228-3, Pub. by Collins Dove AT) Harper SF.

Murdoch, Anne. In Her Own Image. 1986. pap. 3.50 (0-449-21162-2) Fawcett.

Murdoch, Beamish. Epitome of the Laws of Nova Scotia, 4 vols, Set. LC 73-26626. 1034p. 1971. reprint ed. lib. bdg. 168.00 (0-912004-04-5) W W Gaunt.

Murdoch, Brian. Cornish Literature. 192p. (C). 1993. text ed. 45.00 (0-85991-364-3) Boydell & Brewer.

— Fighting Songs & Warring Words: Popular Lyrics of Two World Wars. 272p. 1990. 67.50 (0-415-03184-2, A3953) Routledge.

Murdoch, Brian O. Im Western Nichts Neues, Remarque: Critical Monographs in English. 68p. 1993. pap. 32.00 (*0-85261-322-9*, Pub. by Univ of Glasgow UK) St Mut.

Murdoch, Bruce E., ed. Acquired Neurological Speech-Language Disorders in Childhood. (Brain Damage, Behavior & Cognition Ser.). 360p. 1990. 79.95 (*0-86377-190-4*); pap. 39.95 (*0-86377-191-2*) L Erlbaum Assocs.

Murdoch, Bruce E., jt. auth. see Sitkin, Lesley A.

Murdoch, Christopher W., et al. Transferring Technologies for the Hardwood Industry: Wetwood Detection, Biocides, Cutting Optimization & Value-Added Wood Products. (Illus.). 70p. (Orig.). (C). 1994. pap. text ed. 60.00 (*0-7881-0547-7*) Diane Pub.

Murdoch, D. R. Niels Bohr's Philosophy of Physics. (Illus.). 280p. 1989. pap. 32.95 (*0-521-37927-X*) Cambridge U Pr.

Murdoch, David H. Cowboy. LC 93-12768. (Eyewitness Bks.). (Illus.). 64p. (J). (gr. 5 up). 1993. 16.00 (*0-679-84014-1*); lib. bdg. 16.99 (*0-679-94014-6*) Knopf Bks Yng Read.

Murdoch, Derrick. The Agatha Christie Mystery. (Illus.). 192p. 1976. 19.95 (*0-88932-034-9*) Boulevard.

Murdoch, Dugald, tr. see Descartes, Rene, et al.

Murdoch, Eugene C., jt. auth. see Kavanaugh, Jack.

Murdoch, Frank. The Quiet Place. (Illus.). 128p. 1990. 45.00 (*0-9625635-0-1*) Sea Quest Pub.

Murdoch, Iris. Acastos. 144p. 1988. mass mkt. 5.95 (*0-14-008696-X*, Penguin Bks) Viking Penguin.

— An Accidental Man. 448p. 1988. pap. 11.00 (*0-14-003611-3*, Penguin Bks) Viking Penguin.

— The Bell. 342p. 1987. pap. 10.95 (*0-14-001688-0*, Penguin Bks) Viking Penguin.

— The Black Prince. 224p. 1983. pap. 12.95 (*0-14-003934-1*, Penguin Bks) Viking Penguin.

— The Book & the Brotherhood. 624p. 1989. pap. 10.95 (*0-14-010470-4*, Penguin Bks) Viking Penguin.

— Bruno's Dream. 320p. 1976. pap. 10.95 (*0-14-003176-6*, Penguin Bks) Viking Penguin.

— Les Cloches. 416p. (FRE.). 1985. pap. 17.95 (*0-7859-4222-X*, 2070376508) Fr & Eur.

— A Fairly Honourable Defeat. 1979. pap. 10.95 (*0-14-003332-7*, Penguin Bks) Viking Penguin.

— The Flight from the Enchanter. 316p. 1987. mass mkt. 10.00 (*0-14-001770-4*, Penguin Bks) Viking Penguin.

— The Good Apprentice. 528p. 1987. pap. 10.95 (*0-14-009815-1*, Penguin Bks) Viking Penguin.

— The Green Knight. LC 93-30618. 480p. 1994. 23.95 (*0-670-85229-5*, Viking) Viking Penguin.

— The Green Knight. 480p. 1995. pap. 12.95 (*0-14-024337-2*, Penguin Bks) Viking Penguin.

— Henry & Cato. 1977. pap. 10.00 (*0-14-004569-4*, Penguin Bks) Viking Penguin.

— The Italian Girl. 1979. mass mkt. 10.95 (*0-14-002559-6*, Penguin Bks) Viking Penguin.

— The Message to the Planet. 640p. 1991. pap. 11.00 (*0-14-012664-3*) Viking Penguin.

— Metaphysics as a Guide to Morals. braille ed. 1292p. 1994. text ed. 103.36 (*1-56956-509-0*, BR9233) W A T Braille.

— Metaphysics As a Guide to Morals: Philosophical Reflections. LC 92-53533. 784p. 1992. 35.00 (*0-670-84666-X*, Viking) Viking Penguin.

— Metaphysics As a Guide to Morals: Philosophical Reflections. 784p. 1994. pap. 15.00 (*0-14-017232-7*, Penguin Bks) Viking Penguin.

— The Nice & the Good. 1978. mass mkt. 11.00 (*0-14-003034-4*, Penguin Bks) Viking Penguin.

— Nuns & Soldiers. 1982. mass mkt. 6.95 (*0-14-006143-6*, Penguin Bks) Viking Penguin.

— The Philosopher's Pupil. (Fiction Ser.). 592p. 1984. pap. 7.95 (*0-14-007614-X*, Penguin Bks) Viking Penguin.

— The Red & the Green. 288p. 1988. pap. 10.95 (*0-14-002756-4*, Penguin Bks) Viking Penguin.

— The Sacred & Profane Love Machine. 368p. 1984. pap. 11.95 (*0-14-004111-7*, Penguin Bks) Viking Penguin.

— Sandcastle. 1978. pap. 11.00 (*0-14-001474-8*, Penguin Bks) Viking Penguin.

— The Sea, the Sea. 1980. pap. 11.95 (*0-14-005199-6*, Penguin Bks) Viking Penguin.

— A Severed Head. 1976. pap. 10.95 (*0-14-002003-9*, Penguin Bks) Viking Penguin.

— Sous le Filet. (FRE.). 1985. pap. 15.95 (*0-7859-4221-1*) Fr & Eur.

— The Time of the Angels. 240p. 1988. mass mkt. 10.00 (*0-14-002848-X*, Penguin Bks) Viking Penguin.

— Under the Net. 1977. pap. 10.95 (*0-14-001445-4*, Penguin Bks) Viking Penguin.

— Under the Net. large type ed. 379p. 1990. 22.95 (*1-85089-359-4*, Pub. by ISIS UK) Transaction Pubs.

— Une'Tete Coupee. 316p. (FRE.). 1988. pap. 15.95 (*0-7859-4303-X*, 2070380777) Fr & Eur.

— The Unicorn. 312p. 1987. pap. 10.95 (*0-14-002476-X*, Penguin Bks) Viking Penguin.

— An Unofficial Rose. 334p. 1987. pap. 10.95 (*0-14-002154-X*, Penguin Bks) Viking Penguin.

— A Word Child. 392p. 1987. mass mkt. 12.00 (*0-14-008153-4*, Penguin Bks) Viking Penguin.

Murdoch, J. Review of Caste in India. 110p. 1977. 14.95 (*0-318-36811-0*) Asia Bk Corp.

Murdoch, J. M. Portrait of Obedience: The Biography of Robert T. Ketcham. 328p. 1979. kivar 8.95 (*0-87227-070-X*) Reg Baptist.

Murdoch, James E. Stage; or, Recollections of Actors & Acting. LC 79-81213. 1972. 24.95 (*0-405-08810-8*) Ayer.

Murdoch, John. Ethnological Results of the Point Barrow Expedition. (Classics of Smithsonian Anthropology Ser.: No. 6). (Illus.). 450p. 1987. reprint ed. pap. 27.50 (*0-87474-665-5*, MUERP) Smithsonian.

— Hindu & Muhammadan Festivals: Compiled from Wilson, Wilkins, Crooke, Sell, Hughes & Other Writers. (C). 1991. reprint ed. 9.00 (*81-206-0708-2*, Pub. by Asian Educ Servs II) S Asia.

— The Mahabharata. 160p. 1986. reprint ed. 14.00 (*0-8364-1762-3*, Pub. by Manohar II) S Asia.

Murdoch, John, ed. The Mahabharata, An English Abridgement with Introduction, Notes & Review. 1987. reprint ed. 12.00 (*0-8364-2042-X*, Pub. by Usha II) S Asia.

Murdoch, John B., tr. see Sananikone, Oun.

Murdoch, John B., tr. see Wyatt, David K., ed.

Murdoch, John E. Album of Science, Vol. 1: Antiquity & the Middle Ages. LC 84-1400. (Illus.). 375p. 1984. text ed. 85.00 (*0-684-15496-X*, Scribners) S&S Trade.

Murdoch, John E., jt. ed. see Grant, Edward.

***Murdoch, Jonathan & Marsden, Terry.** Reconstituting Rurality: The Changing Countryside in an Urban Context. (Reconstructing Rural Areas Ser.: No. 2). 192p. 1994. 59.95x (*1-85728-041-5*, Pub. by UCL Pr UK) Taylor & Francis.

Murdoch, Joseph, jt. auth. see Tunell, George.

***Murdoch, Joseph P.** Illumination Engineering: From Edison's Lamp to the Laser. LC 94-30117. 1994. write for info. (*1-885750-00-5*) Visions Communs.

Murdoch, Joseph S., jt. auth. see Donovan, Richard E.

Murdoch, Joyce, jt. auth. see Price, Deb.

Murdoch, Kathleen, jt. auth. see Ray, Stephen.

***Murdoch, Larry & Wilson, David.** Alternative Methods for Fluid Delivery & Recovery. (Illus.). 87p. (Orig.). (C). 1995. pap. text ed. 45.00 (*0-7881-1616-9*) Diane Pub.

Murdoch, Norman H. Origins of the Salvation Army. LC 94-9334. (Illus.). 256p. (C). 1995. text ed. 32.00 (*0-87049-858-4*) U of Tenn Pr.

Murdoch, Robert, ed. see Pitteway, Les.

Murdoch, Royal. The Disrobing: Sex & Satire. 112p. (Orig.). 1982. pap. 5.95 (*0-917342-96-8*) Gay Sunshine.

— The Disrobing: Sex & Satire. limited ed. 112p. (Orig.). 1982. 30.00 (*0-917342-95-X*) Gay Sunshine.

Murdoch, Tessa, ed. Boughton House: The English Versailles. (Illus.). 304p. 1993. 150.00 (*0-571-16338-6*) Faber & Faber.

Murdoch, Tessa, jt. auth. see Gilbert, Christopher.

Murdoch, Walter L. Seventy-Two Essays: A Selection. LC 76-90665. (Essay Index Reprint Ser.). 1977. reprint ed. 23.95 (*0-8369-1813-4*) Ayer.

Murdoch, William D. Brahms. LC 74-24161. reprint ed. 37.50 (*0-404-13056-9*) AMS Pr.

— Chopin: His Life. LC 70-136077. (Illus.). 410p. 1971. reprint ed. 65.00 (*0-8371-5227-5*, MUCH, Greenwood Pr) Greenwood.

Murdoch, William W. The Poverty of Nations: The Political Economy of Hunger & Population. LC 80-16201. 400p. 1981. pap. 16.95 (*0-8018-2462-1*) Johns Hopkins.

***Murdock.** Making of a Man. 1995. pap. text ed. 5.95 (*1-56292-091-X*) Honor Bks OK.

— Suffer the Children. 1994. 3.99 (*0-517-13563-9*) Random Hse Value.

Murdock & Kelly. History of Oceana County (Michigan) 1990. write for info. (*0-917231-11-2*) Ferguson Comns Pubs.

Murdock, Alexander & Scutt, Carol. Personal Effectiveness. 244p. 1993. pap. 25.95 (*0-7506-0665-7*) Buttrwrth-Heinemann.

Murdock, Barbara S., ed. Environmental Issues in Primary Care. (Illus.). 76p. (Orig.). (C). 1994. pap. text ed. 50.00 (*0-7881-0819-0*) Diane Pub.

***Murdock, Carol V.** Writing Skills. Evento, Susan, ed. (Macmillan Early Skills Program - Conversion Ser.). 64p. (J). (ps-2). Date not set. pap. text ed. 9.95 (*1-56784-511-8*) Newbridge Comms.

Murdock, Denis R. What Shape Is Your Parachute In? The Fastest Way to Land a Better Job. 272p. (Orig.). 1989. 39.95 (*0-9623774-0-6*) Mountainwest.

***Murdock, Dick.** Bill Knapke - a Railroad Legend: Sketches from the Life of an Oldtime Boomer. Rockefeller, Ruth & Gibbs, Joyce, eds. LC 95-6797. (Illus.). 144p. (Orig.). (YA). (gr. 8-10). 1996. pap. 12.95 (*0-932916-18-X*) May-Murdock.

— Hogheads & Highballs: Railroad Lore & Humor. 2nd ed. Murdock, Jayne, ed. LC 79-89177. (Illus.). 64p. (Orig.). 1979. pap. 5.00 (*0-932916-04-X*) May-Murdock.

— Lime Point to Lawson's Landing: Outdoors in Marin Sixty-One More Places to Visit. Murdock, Jayne, ed. & photos by. LC 91-20154. (Illus.). 160p. (Orig.). 1992. pap. 10.95 (*0-932916-15-5*) May-Murdock.

— Love Affair with Steam. Murdock, Jayne M., ed. (Illus.). 40p. (Orig.). 1985. pap. 3.00 (*0-932916-09-0*) May-Murdock.

— Point Bonita to Point Reyes: Outdoors in Marin - 61 Places to Visit. 2nd ed. LC 88-26633. (Illus.). 160p. (Orig.). 1989. reprint ed. pap. 9.95 (*0-932916-14-7*) May-Murdock.

— Smoke in the Canyon: My Steam Days in Dunsmuir. Murdock, Jayne, ed. LC 85-90443. (Illus.). 144p. (Orig.). 1986. 25.95 (*0-932916-11-2*); pap. 15.95 (*0-932916-10-4*) May-Murdock.

Murdock, Dick, jt. auth. see May, Jayne.

Murdock, Dick, ed. see Murdock, Jayne M.

Murdock, Dick, ed. see Shannon, Wayne.

Murdock, Dick, ed. see Wurm, Ted.

Murdock, Eugene. Patriotism Limited, Eighteen Sixty-Two to Eighteen Sixty-Five: The Civil War Draft & the Bounty System. LC 67-64665. 296p. reprint ed. 84.40 (*0-8357-9372-9*, 2010413) Bks Demand.

— Tom Johnson of Cleveland. 379p. (C). 1992. lib. bdg. 56.00 (*1-882090-05-5*) Wright State Univ Pr.

Murdock, Eugene C. Ban Johnson: Czar of Baseball. LC 81-20336. (Contributions to the Study of Popular Culture Ser.: No. 3). xii, 294p. 1982. text ed. 55.00 (*0-313-23459-0*, MBJ/, Greenwood Pr) Greenwood.

— Mighty Casey: All-American. LC 83-16338. (Contributions to the Study of Popular Culture Ser.: No. 7). xii, 164p. 1984. text ed. 45.00 (*0-313-24075-2*, MMC/, Greenwood Pr) Greenwood.

— Ohio: The Buckeye Empire: An Illustrated History of Ohio Enterprise. 320p. (YA). (gr. 7 up). 1988. 34.95 (*0-89781-250-6*) Preferred Mktg.

— One Million Men: The Civil War Draft in the North. LC 80-14431. (Illus.). xi, 366p. 1980. reprint ed. text ed. 55.00 (*0-313-22502-8*, MUOM, Greenwood Pr) Greenwood.

Murdock, Everett E. Computers Today! 160p. (C). 1995. write for info. (*0-697-20403-0*) Bus & Educ Tech.

— DOS the Easy Way: A Complete Guide to Microsoft's MS-DOS. 350p. (Orig.). (C). 1988. pap. text ed. 18.50 (*0-923178-00-7*) HOT Pr.

— DOS 5: The Easy Way. 224p. (C). 1993. spiral bd. write for info. (*0-697-16800-X*) Bus & Educ Tech.

— Hypercard: The Easy Way. 2nd ed. 208p. (C). 1993. spiral bd. write for info. (*0-697-16563-9*) Bus & Educ Tech.

Murdock, Everett E. & Sudbury, Susan. School & Home Guide to Apple Macintosh Computer. LC 85-530. (Illus.). 204p. 1985. pap. 15.95 (*0-13-793605-2*) P-H.

— School & Home Guide to IBM Compatible Personal Computers. LC 84-24786. 292p. 1985. pap. 18.95 (*0-13-793662-1*) P-H.

— School & Home Guide to the IBM PCjr. (Illus.). 224p. 1985. text ed. 29.00 (*0-13-793654-0*); pap. text ed. 15.95 (*0-13-793647-8*) P-H.

***Murdock, George P.** Atlas of World Cultures. LC 80-53030. 157p. 1981. pap. 44.80 (*0-7837-8551-8*, 2049366) Bks Demand.

— Outline of World Cultures. 6th rev. ed. LC 83-80510. (HRAF Manuals Ser.). 259p. 1983. pap. 25.00 (*0-87536-664-3*) HRAFP.

— Social Structure. 1965. pap. 16.95 (*0-02-922290-7*) Free Pr.

— Theories of Illness: A World Survey. LC 80-5257. 142p. 1980. pap. 40.50 (*0-7837-8545-3*, 2049360) Bks Demand.

Murdock, George P. & O'Leary, Timothy. Ethnographic Bibliography of North America, Vol. 4: Eastern United States. LC 75-17091. (Behavior Science Bibliographies Ser.). (Illus.). 293p. reprint ed. pap. 73.30 (*0-7837-1765-2*, 2015592) Bks Demand.

Murdock, George P. & O'Leary, Timothy J. Ethnographic Bibliography of North America. 4th ed. Incl. Vol. 1. General North America. 4th ed. LC 75-17091. 494p. 1975. text ed. 35.00 (*0-87536-205-2*); Vol. 2. Arctic & Subarctic. 4th ed. LC 75-17091. 294p. 1975. text ed. 35.00 (*0-87536-207-9*); Vol. 3. 4th ed. LC 77-1665. 304p. 1975. text ed. 35.00 (*0-685-73345-9*); Vol. 4. Eastern United States. 4th ed. LC 75-17091. 292p. 1975. text ed. 35.00 (*0-87536-211-7*); Vol. 5. 4th ed. LC 75-17091. 444p. 1975. text ed. 35.00 (*0-87536-213-3*); LC 75-17091. (Bibliographies Ser.). 1975. write for info. (*0-318-53458-4*) HRAFP.

— Ethnographic Bibliography of North America, Vol. 2: Arctic & Subarctic. 4th ed. LC 75-17091. (Behavior Science Bibliographies Ser.). (Illus.). 296p. reprint ed. pap. 74.00 (*0-8357-2802-1*, 2015592) Bks Demand.

Murdock, George P., et al. Outline of Cultural Materials. 5th rev. ed. LC 81-83836. (HRAF Manuals Ser.). 273p. 1982. pap. 25.00 (*0-87536-654-6*) HRAFP.

Murdock, Harold. Bunker Hill: Notes & Queries on a Famous Battle, Notes & Queries on a Famous Battle. LC 68-58328. (Illus.). 1969. reprint ed. 15.00 (*0-87152-054-0*) Reprint.

— The Nineteenth of April, Seventeen Seventy-Five: Concord & Lexington. LC 68-58327. (Illus.). 1969. reprint ed. 15.00 (*0-87152-053-2*) Reprint.

Murdock, Hy. Jack & the Beanstalk. (First Fairy Tales Ser.: No. S852-4). (J). 1989. pap. 3.95 (*0-7214-5061-X*) Ladybird Bks.

Murdock, J. E. Words from the Heart. 80p. (C). 1991. text ed. 10.95 (*1-56394-001-9*) Wisdom Intl.

Murdock, J. W. & Smith, L. T., eds. ASME Text Booklet, SI Units in Thermodynamics: SI-4. 55p. 1976. 6.50 (*0-317-33430-1*, E00084); 3.25 (*0-317-33431-X*) ASME.

Murdock, James A. Perturbations Theory & Methods. LC 90-12944. 504p. 1991. text ed. 91.95 (*0-471-61294-4*) Wiley.

Murdock, James W. Fundamental Fluid Mechanics for the Practicing Engineer. (Mechanical Engineering Ser.: Vol. 82). 448p. 1993. 110.00 (*0-8247-8808-7*) Dekker.

Murdock, Jayne, ed. see Murdock, Dick.

Murdock, Jayne, ed. see Murdock, Jayne M.

Murdock, Jayne, ed. see Shannon, Wayne.

Murdock, Jayne, ed. see Wurm, Ted.

Murdock, Jayne M. Brief Infinity: A Love Story in Haiku. Murdock, Dick, ed. LC 80-83998. (Illus.). 64p. (Orig.). 1981. pap. 4.00 (*0-932916-06-6*) May-Murdock.

— I Painted on a Bright Red Mouth: The War Years, 1941-1945. Murdock, Dick, ed. LC 81-90168. (Illus.). 64p. (Orig.). 1981. pap. 5.00 (*0-932916-07-4*) May-Murdock.

— Until Death & After: How to Live with a Dying Intimate. Murdock, Dick & Murdock, Jayne, eds. LC 79-90348. (Illus.). 64p. 1979. pap. 4.00 (*0-932916-05-8*) May-Murdock.

Murdock, Jayne M., ed. see Murdock, Dick.

Murdock, Jayne R. Wind Chimes: The Story of a Family. LC 93-33526. (Illus.). 256p. (Orig.). 1993. pap. 14.95 (*0-932916-17-1*) May-Murdock.

Murdock, John E., ed. see International Colloquium on Philosophy, Science Theology in the Middle Ages Staff.

***Murdock, Jos. B.** Murdock Genealogy: Robert Murdock of Roxbury, MA & Some of His Descendants, with Notes on the Descendants of John Munro of Plymouth; George Murdock of Plainfield, CT; Peter Murdock of Saybrook, CT; William Murdock of Philadelphia & Others. (Illus.). 274p. 1994. reprint ed. lib. bdg. 54.00 (*0-8328-4347-4*); reprint ed. pap. 44.00 (*0-8328-4348-2*) Higginson Bk Co.

Murdock, Kenneth B. Increase Mather, the Foremost American Puritan. (BCL1 - United States Local History Ser.). 442p. 1991. reprint ed. text ed. 99.00 (*0-7812-6267-4*) Rprt Serv.

— Literature & Theology in Colonial New England. LC 78-104247. xi, 235p. 1970. reprint ed. text ed. 35.00 (*0-8371-3990-2*, MUCN, Greenwood Pr) Greenwood.

Murdock, Kenneth B., ed. see Mather, Cotton.

Murdock, Kenneth B., jt. ed. see Matthiessen, F. O.

Murdock, L. J., et al. Concrete Materials & Practice. 6th ed. (Illus.). 480p. 1991. 95.00 (*0-7131-3653-7*, A7294, Pub. by E Arnold UK) Routledge Chapman & Hall.

Murdock, M. S. Armageddon off Vesta. LC 88-51716. (Buck Rogers: Martian Wars Trilogy Ser.: Bk. 3). (Illus.). 288p. (Orig.). (J). 1989. pap. 3.95 (*0-88038-761-0*) TSR Inc.

— Rebellion 2456. LC 88-51714. (Buck Rogers: Martian Wars Trilogy Ser.: Bk. 1). 288p. (Orig.). (J). 1989. pap. 3.95 (*0-88038-728-9*) TSR Inc.

— Web of the Romulans. (Star Trek Ser.: No. 10). 1989. mass mkt. 5.50 (*0-671-70093-6*) PB.

Murdock, Maureen. Heroine's Journey. LC 89-43513. (Illus.). 160p. 1990. pap. 11.00 (*0-87773-485-2*, Sham Pocket Class) Shambhala Pubns.

— The Hero's Daughter. LC 94-7245. 304p. 1994. 23.00 (*0-449-90962-X*, Columbine) Fawcett.

— Spinning Inward: Using Guided Imagery with Children. enl. rev. ed. LC 87-9740. (Illus.). 158p. 1987. pap. 22.50 (*0-87773-422-4*) Shambhala Pubns.

Murdock, Michael D. The God-Book. Loy, Joy A., ed. 250p. (Orig.). (YA). 1991. pap. text ed. 4.95 (*1-56394-004-3*) Wisdom Intl.

— The Jesus Book. Loy, Joy A., ed. (Orig.). 1991. pap. text ed. 4.95 (*1-56394-002-7*) Wisdom Intl.

— Jesus Was a Double Diamond. Loy, Joy A., ed. 175p. (Orig.). 1991. pap. text ed. 4.95 (*1-56394-000-0*) Wisdom Intl.

— The Teenager's One Minute Bible. Loy, Joy A., ed. 365p. (Orig.). (YA). 1991. pap. text ed. 5.95 (*1-56394-003-5*) Wisdom Intl.

— The Widow's Topical Bible. Loy, Joy A., ed. 165p. (Orig.). 1991. pap. text ed. 4.95 (*1-56394-005-1*) Wisdom Intl.

Murdock, Michael L. Writing Clearly & Effectively. 2nd ed. 166p. (Orig.). 1981. pap. 7.25 (*0-930124-01-4*) Transemantics.

Murdock, Mike. Dream-Seeds. 169p. (Orig.). 1986. pap. 4.95 (*1-56292-392-7*) Honor Bks OK.

— God Book. 1990. pap. 6.95 (*0-926775-45-6*) Sensible Des.

— One-Minute Businessman's Devotional. 1994. pap. 9.95 (*1-56292-025-1*) Honor Bks OK.

— One-Minute Businesswoman's Devotional. 1994. pap. 9.95 (*1-56292-026-X*) Honor Bks OK.

— The Winner's Daily Word. (Orig.). 0.98 (*1-56292-419-2*) Honor Bks OK.

— Wisdom for Winning. 300p. (Orig.). 1988. pap. 7.95 (*1-56292-398-6*, HB398) Honor Bks OK.

Murdock, Robert. Bill Freeland. (Illus.). 52p. (Orig.). 1989. pap. 15.00 (*0-944751-02-4*) Maxwells Busn.

Murdock, Robert M. Ceroli Pistoletto. (Illus.). (Orig.). 1969. pap. 1.50 (*0-685-07680-6*) Buffalo Acad.

Murdock, Rosamond L. & Hartley, Mariette. Suffer the Children: A Pediatrician's Reflections on Abuse. LC 91-35371. 220p. 1992. 19.95 (*0-929173-09-0*) Health Press.

***Murdock, Steve H.** An America Challenged: Population Change & the Future of the United States. LC 94-29676. (C). 1995. text ed. 49.95 (*0-8133-1808-4*) Westview.

Murdock, Steve H. & Ellis, David. Applied Demography: An Introduction to Basic Concepts, Methods, & Data. 299p. (C). 1991. pap. text ed. 37.00 (*0-8133-8372-2*) Westview.

Murdock, Steve H. & Leistritz, F. Larry. Energy Development in the Western United States: Impact on Rural Areas. LC 79-18478. 384p. 1979. text ed. 65.00 (*0-275-90397-4*, C0397, Praeger Pubs) Greenwood.

***Murdock Travel Systems Staff.** Travel Reservations. 309p. (C). 1992. pap. text ed. 35.00 (*1-879982-11-0*) Educ Systs.

Murdock, William D. Chopin: His Life. 1988. reprint ed. lib. bdg. 59.00 (*0-7812-0495-X*) Rprt Serv.

— Chopin: His Life. LC 73-181213. 410p. 1935. reprint ed. 59.00 (*0-403-01625-8*) Scholarly.

Murdy, Kay. Ninety Days: Daily Reflections for Lent & Easter. LC 94-33529. 224p. (Orig.). 1995. pap. 8.95 (*0-89390-306-X*) Resource Pubns.

Murdza, Peter J., Jr., ed. Immigrants to Liberia, 1865-1904: An Alphabetical Listing. (Liberian Studies Research Working Papers: No. 4). 1975. 8.00 (*0-686-17780-0*) Arden Assocs.

Murdzek, Benjamin P. Emigration in Polish Social & Political Thought, 1870-1914. (East European Monographs: No. 33). 396p. 1977. text ed. 54.00 (*0-914710-26-5*) East Eur Quarterly.

Mure, Geoffrey R. Aristotle. LC 75-17199. 282p. 1975. reprint ed. text ed. 38.50 (*0-8371-8298-0*, MUAR, Greenwood Pr) Greenwood.

— An Introduction to Hegel. LC 82-15853. xviii, 180p. 1982. reprint ed. text ed. 45.00 (*0-313-23741-7*, MUIH, Greenwood Pr) Greenwood.

— A Study of Hegel's Logic. LC 83-26391. viii, 375p. 1984. reprint ed. text ed. 69.50 (*0-313-24397-2*, MUSH, Greenwood Pr) Greenwood.

Mure, Mary, jt. auth. see Barber, Nicola.

An Asterisk (*) at the beginning of an entry indicates that the title is appearing in BIP for the first time.

Mure, William. Selections from the Family Papers Preserved at Caldwell, 2 pts. in 3 vols., Set. LC 70-173006. (Maitland Club, Glasgow. Publications: No. 71). reprint ed. 105.00 (*0-404-53091-5*) AMS Pr.

Muren, Nancy L., jt. illus. see Somerville, Sheila.

Murena, Hector E. Ensayos Sobre Subversion. 105p. 1963. 2.00 (*0-8477-2413-1*); pap. 1.00 (*0-8477-2414-X*) U of PR Pr.

Murer, Esther G., tr. see Bjorneboe, Jens.

Murer, H., ed. The Molecules of Transport: Carriers. (Journal: Cellular Physiology & Biochemistry: Vol. 4, Nos. 5-6, 1994). (Illus.). 140p. 1994. pap. 69.75 (*3-8055-5972-0*) S Karger.

Murer, Jos. Saemtliche Dramen, 2 vols. Adomatis, Hans-Joachim et al, eds. LC 73-78235. (Ausgaben Deutscher Literatur des XV bis XVIII Jahrhunderts Ser.: Reihe Drama 4). (C). 1974. 634.60 (*3-11-003865-X*) De Gruyter.

Muresan, George C., tr. see Barlea, Octavian.

***Muret, Eduard & Sanders, Daniel.** Langenscheidt's Encyclopedic Dictionary of English & German Vol. 1: English-German A-M. 883p. (ENG & GER.). 1992. 395.00 (*0-7859-8385-6*, 3468011202) Fr & Eur.

— Langenscheidt's Encyclopedic Dictionary of English & German Vol. 2: English-German N-Z. 956p. (ENG & GER.). 1992. 395.00 (*0-7859-8386-4*, 346801129) Fr & Eur.

— Langenscheidt's Encyclopedic Dictionary of English & German Vol. 3: German-English A-K. 973p. (ENG & GER.). 1992. 395.00 (*0-7859-8387-2*, 3468011245) Fr & Eur.

— Langenscheidt's Encyclopedic Dictionary of English & German Vol. 4: German-English L-Z. 1046p. (ENG & GER.). 1992. 395.00 (*0-7859-8388-0*, 3468011261) Fr & Eur.

Muret, M. The Twilight of the White Races. 1976. lib. bdg. 59.95 (*0-8490-2780-2*) Gordon Pr.

Murez, Diane. A Day on the Boat with Captain Betty. LC 92-11428. (Illus.). 32p. (J). (gr. 2 up). 1993. text ed. 14.95 (*0-02-767430-4*, Mac Bks Young Read) S&S Childrens.

Murfett, Malcolm H. The First Sea Lords: From Fisher to Mountbatten. LC 94-17009. 328p. 1995. text ed. 59.95 (*0-275-94231-7*, Praeger Pubs) Greenwood.

— Hostage on the Yangtze: Britain, China, & the Amethyst Crisis of 1949. LC 90-42359. (Illus.). 416p. 1991. 36.95 (*0-87021-289-3*) Naval Inst Pr.

— In Jeopardy: The Royal Navy & British Far Eastern Defence Policy 1945-1951. (South-East Asian Historical Monographs). (Illus.). 184p. 1995. 38.00 (*967-65-3058-1*) OUP.

Murfett, Malcolm H., jt. ed. see Hattendorf, John B.

Murff, Samuel J. Occupational Safety & Health Comprehensive Compliance Checklist Manual for Safety-Health Professionals. 72p. (Orig.). 1991. 75.00 (*0-9623315-1-1*) CTSC Pub.

— Occupational Safety & Health Model Policy & Procedure Manual. (Illus.). 210p. (Orig.). 1989. 150.00 (*0-685-26268-5*) CTSC Pub.

— Occupational Safety & Health Model Policy & Procedure Manual. rev. ed. (Illus.). 312p. (Orig.). 1990. 199.00 (*0-9623315-0-3*) CTSC Pub.

Murfield, Jeff. Shadow Creek. abr. ed. 180p. 1995. pap. 7.95 (*1-56901-363-2*) NW Pub.

Murfin, Andy, jt. auth. see Fine, Ben.

Murfin, James. Eastern National Parks. 1991. 19.99 (*0-517-64417-7*) Random Hse Value.

Murfin, James & National Flag Foundation Staff. National Park & America's Wit. (Illus.). 432p. 1992. 19.95 (*0-317-91090-6*, 34526) Interp Mktg Prods.

Murfin, James, jt. auth. see Gibson, William.

Murfin, James V. Battlefields of the Civil War. 1988. 17.99 (*0-517-62371-4*) Random Hse Value.

— The Gleam of Bayonets: The Battle of Antietam & Robert E. Lee's Maryland Campaign, Sept 1862. LC 65-11502. (Illus.). 456p. 1982. pap. 12.95 (*0-8071-0990-8*) La State U Pr.

— National Parks of the Rockies. 1988. 17.99 (*0-517-64418-5*) Random Hse Value.

— National Parks of the U. S. A. 1988. 7.99 (*0-517-64946-2*) Random Hse Value.

***Murfin, James V. & Pavitt, Irene, eds.** The Sierra Club Guides to the National Parks of the Desert Southwest. rev. ed. LC 95-11448. (Sierra Club Guides to the National Parks Ser.). 1995. pap. write for info. (*0-679-76493-3*) Random.

Murfin, Marjory E. & Whitlatch, Jo B., eds. Research in Reference Effectiveness: Proceedings of a Preconference. (RASD Occasional Papers: No. 16). 129p. (Orig.). 1993. pap. 25.00 (*0-8389-7704-9*) ALA.

Murfin, Patrick, jt. auth. see Thompson, Fred.

Murfin, Robert, ed. see Miller, Judith & Miller, Martin.

Murfin, Ross C. Lord Jim: After the Truth. (Masterwork Studies: No. 88). 160p. (C). 1992. text ed. 21.95 (*0-8057-8094-7*, Twayne); pap. 12.95 (*0-8057-8560-4*, Twayne) Macmillan.

— The Poetry of D. H. Lawrence: Texts & Contexts. LC 82-10940. 281p. reprint ed. pap. 80.10 (*0-7837-4661-X*, 2044386) Bks Demand.

— Sons & Lovers: A Novel of Division & Desire. (Twayne's Masterwork Studies: No. 7). 176p. 1987. text ed. 21.95 (*0-8057-7967-1*, Pub. by Royal Botanic Garden UK) Macmillan.

Murfin, Ross C., ed. Conrad Revisited: Essays for the Eighties. LC 83-17937. 200p. 1985. 22.50 (*0-8173-0205-0*) U of Ala Pr.

Murfin, Ross C., ed. see Conrad, Joseph.

Murfin, Ross C., ed. see Hawthorne, Nathaniel.

***Murfitt.** Children's Party Food. 1995. pap. text ed. 8.95 (*0-316-54807-3*) Little.

— Chocolate. 1995. pap. text ed. 8.95 (*0-316-54806-5*) Little.

Murfitt, Janice. Book of Christmas Foods. (Illus.). 120p. (Orig.). 1989. pap. 10.95 (*0-89586-821-0*) Price Stern.

— Book of Dressings & Marinades. (Illus.). 120p. (Orig.). 1989. pap. 10.95 (*0-89586-819-9*) Price Stern.

— Essential Cake Decorator. (Illus.). 128p. 1995. 14.98 (*0-8317-6226-8*) Smithmark.

— Essential Cake Decorator: A Course in Decorating Techniques. 1994. 14.98 (*0-8317-6509-7*) Smithmark.

— Savory to Sweet: Pies & Tarts. LC 93-37195. (Creative Cook Ser.). 1993. 16.95 (*1-56426-651-6*) Cole Group.

— Step by Step Christmas Treats. 96p. 1994. 9.98 (*0-8317-7843-1*) Smithmark.

Murfree, Mary N. Bushwhackers & Other Stories. LC 73-90588. (Short Story Index Reprint Ser., Vol. 1). 1977. 20.95 (*0-8369-3071-1*) Ayer.

— Frontiersmen. LC 79-116963. (Short Story Index Reprint Ser.). 1977. 24.95 (*0-8369-3467-9*) Ayer.

— In the Tennessee Mountains. LC 78-100406. 360p. reprint ed. 102.60 (*0-685-16056-4*, 2027560) Bks Demand.

— In the Tennessee Mountains. (BCL1-PS American Literature Ser.). 322p. 1992. reprint ed. lib. bdg. 89.00 (*0-7812-6803-6*) Rprt Serv.

— The Mystery of Witch-Face Mountain & Other Stories. 1972. reprint ed. lib. bdg. 29.00 (*0-8422-8099-5*) Irvington.

— The Phantoms of the Footbridge & Other Stories. (C). 1973. reprint ed. lib. bdg. 29.50 (*0-8422-8100-2*) Irvington.

— The Phantoms of the Footbridge & Other Stories. (C). 1986. reprint ed. pap. text ed. 9.50 (*0-8290-1942-1*) Irvington.

— Prophet of the Great Smoky Mountains. LC 76-110350. reprint ed. 34.50 (*0-404-04542-1*) AMS Pr.

— The Prophet of the Great Smoky Mountains. (BCL1-PS American Literature Ser.). 308p. 1992. reprint ed. lib. bdg. 89.00 (*0-7812-6804-4*) Rprt Serv.

— Raid of the Guerilla, & Other Stories. LC 71-150556. (Short Story Index Reprint Ser.). (Illus.). 1977. reprint ed. 23.95 (*0-8369-3853-4*) Ayer.

— The Story of Old Fort Loudon. LC 73-104531. (Illus.). 409p. reprint ed. lib. bdg. 36.00 (*0-8398-1269-8*) Irvington.

— The Story of Old Fort Loudon. (C). 1986. reprint ed. pap. text ed. 10.95 (*0-8290-1941-3*) Irvington.

— Young Mountaineers. LC 70-98588. (Short Story Index Reprint Ser.). 1977. 20.95 (*0-8369-3162-9*) Ayer.

***Murgatroyd, Francis D. & Camm, A. John, eds.** Atrial Fibrillation for the Clinician. LC 95-176. (Clinical Approaches to Tachyarrhythmias Ser.: Vol. 4). (Illus.). 152p. 1995. 19.00 (*0-87993-614-2*) Futura Pub.

Murgatroyd, Paul. A Collection of Translations into Latin & Neo-Latin Poetry - Original Compositions. LC 91-31508. 120p. 1991. lib. bdg. 59.95 (*0-7734-9750-1*) E Mellen.

— Melpome: Translations of Selected Greek Lyrics with Notes. 92p. (Orig.). 1989. pap. 12.00 (*90-256-0986-4*, Pub. by A M Hakkert NE) Benjamins North Am.

Murgatroyd, Paul, ed. Ovid with Love: Selection from the Ars Amatoria, Books I & II. 228p. 1982. pap. text ed. 16.00 (*0-86516-015-5*) Bolchazy-Carducci.

Murgatroyd, Stephen, ed. Helping the Troubled Child: Interprofessional Case Studies. 196p. 1980. pap. 27.00 (*0-335-09818-5*, Open Univ Pr) Taylor & Francis.

Murgatroyd, Stephen & Morgan, Colin. Total Quality Management & the School. LC 92-17386. 1992. 90.00 (*0-335-15723-8*, Open Univ Pr); pap. 29.00 (*0-335-15722-X*, Open Univ Pr) Taylor & Francis.

Murgatroyd, Stephen & Woole, Ray. Coping with Crisis: Understanding & Helping People in Need. 180p. 1982. pap. 29.00 (*0-335-09819-3*, Open Univ Pr) Taylor & Francis.

Murgatroyd, Stephen & Woolfe, Ray, eds. Helping Families in Distress: An Introduction to Family Focussed Helping. 192p. 1985. pap. 29.00 (*0-335-09822-3*, Open Univ Pr) Taylor & Francis.

Murgatroyd, Stephen, jt. auth. see Morgan, Colin.

Murgatroyd, Stephen J., jt. auth. see Mills, Albert J.

Murger, Henri. Latin Quarter: Scenes De la Vie De Boheme. Hughes, Elizabeth W., tr. LC 76-48444. (Library of World Literature Ser.). 1988. reprint ed. 30.00 (*0-88355-584-0*) Hyperion Conn.

Murger, Henry. Scenes de la Vie de Boheme. (Folio Ser.: No. 1968). 476p. (FRE.). 1988. pap. 13.95 (*2-07-038055-6*) Schoenhof.

Murguia, Al. LAN Management, Vol. 1: Network Primer. (Illus.). 236p. (C). 1993. lib. bdg. 35.00 (*0-9632193-0-8*) A Murguia.

Murguia, Alejandro. Southern Front. LC 89-7336. 128p. 1990. pap. 10.00 (*0-916950-97-2*) Biling Rev-Pr.

Murguia, Alejandro & Paschke, Barbara, eds. Volcan: Poems from Central America. LC 83-20936. 159p. 1984. pap. 6.95 (*0-87286-153-8*) City Lights.

Murguia, Alejandro, tr. see Murillo, Rosario.

Murguia, Edward. Chicano Intermarriage: A Theoretical & Empirical Study. 134p. 18.00 (*0-911536-93-0*); pap. 11.00 (*0-911536-94-9*) Trinity U Pr.

***Murhphy, John.** Irish Shopfronts & Pubs. (Illus.). 1995. 7.95 (*0-8118-0413-5*) Chronicle Bks.

Muri, Donna, ed. see Boloz, Sigmund A.

Murickan, J. Religion & Power Structure in Rural India: (A Study of Two Fishing Villages in Kerala) Poovar-Sakthikulangara. (C). 1991. 18.00 (*81-7033-117-X*, Pub. by Rawat II) S Asia.

Muricy, Carmen M. The Brazilian Amazon: Institutions & Publications. (Bibliography & Reference Ser.: No. 28). vii, 50p. 1991. pap. 26.00 (*0-685-53178-3*) SALALM.

Murie, Adolph. The Grizzlies of Mount McKinley. LC 84-52203. (Illus.). 272p. 1984. reprint ed. pap. 10.95 (*0-295-96204-6*) U of Wash Pr.

— Mammals of Denali. rev. ed. LC 94-14061. 1994. write for info. (*0-930931-12-2*) Alaska Natural.

— A Naturalist in Alaska. LC 89-20671. 302p. 1990. reprint ed. pap. 16.95 (*0-8165-1168-3*) U of Ariz Pr.

— The Wolves of Mount McKinley. LC 84-22017. (Illus.). (Orig.). 1985. reprint ed. pap. 12.95 (*0-295-96203-8*) U of Wash Pr.

Murie, Alan, jt. auth. see Birrell, Derek.

Murie, Alan, jt. auth. see Forrest, Ray.

Murie, Alan, jt. ed. see Forrest, Ray.

Murie, James R. Ceremonies of the Pawnee. Parks, Douglas R., ed. LC 88-28290. (Studies in the Anthropology of North American Indians). (Illus.). xiv, 497p. 1989. reprint ed. 46.00 (*0-8032-3138-5*); reprint ed. pap. 19.95 (*0-8032-8162-5*) U of Nebr Pr.

***Murie, Jan O. & Michener, Gail R., eds.** The Biology of Ground-Dwelling Squirrels: Annual Cycles, Behavioral Ecology, & Sociality. LC 83-26035. (Illus.). 475p. 1984. reprint ed. pap. 135.40 (*0-7837-8909-2*, 2049620) Bks Demand.

Murie, Margaret & Murie, Olaus. Wapiti Wilderness: The Life of Olaus & Margaret Murie in Jackson Hole, Wyoming. (Illus.). 302p. 1985. pap. 11.95 (*0-87081-155-X*) Univ Pr Colo.

Murie, Margaret E. Grand Teton. LC 83-600157. (Handbook Ser.: No. 122). (Illus.). 96p. (Orig.). 1984. pap. 4.50 (*0-912627-19-0*) Natl Park Serv.

— Island Between. LC 76-62991. (Illus.). 228p. 1977. 9.95 (*0-912006-04-8*) U of Alaska Pr.

— Two in the Far North. 2nd ed. LC 78-16407. (Illus.). 396p. 1978. reprint ed. pap. 12.95 (*0-88240-111-4*) Alaska Northwest.

Murie, Margaret E., jt. auth. see Schreier, Carl.

Murie, Martin. Sage Hen. LC 94-77619. 256p. (Orig.). 1994. pap. 12.95 (*0-943972-34-5*) Homestead WY.

Murie, Michael. Macintosh Multimedia Workshop. (Macintosh Library). (Illus.). 384p. (Orig.). 1993. Incl. CD. cd-rom 39.95 (*1-56830-018-2*) Hayden.

— Macintosh Multimedia Workshop. 2nd ed. (Orig.). 1994. Incl. CD-ROM. cd-rom 30.00 (*1-56830-113-8*) Hayden.

Murie, Michael, jt. auth. see Drucker, David.

Murie, Olaus, jt. auth. see Murie, Margaret.

Murie, Olaus J. Elk of North America. LC 79-83649. (Illus.). 376p. (gr. 7-12). 1990. 15.98 (*0-933160-02-X*); pap. 10.95 (*0-933160-03-8*) Teton Bkshop.

— Field Sketches of a Naturalist. (Illus.). 8p. 1986. pap. 6.95 (*0-931895-10-3*) Grand Teton NHA.

— Nature Guide to Jackson Hole. (Illus.). 60p. (Orig.). (gr. 6-12). 1980. pap. 2.95 (*0-933160-05-4*) Teton Bkshop.

Muriedas, Mercedes. Anos De Ofun: Recuerdos, Relatos y Anotaciones. LC 92-75279. (Coleccion Caniqui Ser.). (Illus.). 85p. (Orig.). (SPA.). 1993. pap. 9.95 (*0-89729-667-2*) Ediciones.

Muriel, Amador, jt. auth. see Chiu Hone-Yee.

Muriell, Christopher. An Answer unto the Catholiques Supplication, Presented unto the Kings Maiestie, for a Tolleration of Popish Religion in England...Annexed the Supplication of the Papists. LC 74-28874. (English Experience Ser.: No. 753). 1975. reprint ed. 15.00 (*90-221-0753-1*) Walter J Johnson.

Murihead, James P. Life of James Watt. (Industrial Antiquities Ser.). (Illus.). 608p. (C). 1989. reprint ed. 135.00 (*1-85297-016-2*, Pub. by Archival Facs UK) St Mut.

***Murillo, Beatriz.** Manual de Laboratorio de Nutricion Animal. 110p. (C). 1993. 4.50 (*1-885995-08-3*) Escuela Agricola.

Murillo-Castano, Gabriel. Migrant Workers in the Americas: A Comparative Study of Migration Between Colombia & Venezuela & Between Mexico & the United States. Del Castillo, Sandra, tr. (Monograph Ser.: No. 13). 78p. (Orig.). (C). 1984. pap. 7.50 (*0-935391-51-7*, MN-13) UCSD Ctr US-Mex.

Murillo, L. A. A Critical Introduction to Don Quixote. 270p. (C). 1988. pap. 29.95 (*0-685-44145-8*) P Lang Pubs.

Murillo, Luis. Instrument Pilot All-Figures Rapid-Training Manual. Video Books Staff, ed. (Illus.). 340p. (Orig.). 1988. pap. 22.95 (*0-923444-00-9*) Video Bks.

— The Noriega Mess. (Illus.). 1100p. 1995. 32.00 (*0-923444-02-5*) Video Bks.

— Private Pilot All-Figures Rapid-Training Manual. Video Books Staff, ed. (Illus.). 160p. (Orig.). 1988. pap. 14.95 (*0-923444-01-7*) Video Bks.

Murillo, Mario. Critical Mass. 96p. 1985. pap. text ed. 5.00 (*0-9639982-0-X*) A Douglas.

— Fresh Fire. 160p. 1991. pap. 7.00 (*0-9639982-1-8*) A Douglas.

— Fresh Impact. 1995. pap. 9.99 (*0-88419-379-9*, Creation Hse) Strang Comms Co.

Murillo, Rosario. Angel in the Deluge. Murguia, Alejandro, tr. (Pocket Poets Ser.: No. 50). 120p. (Orig.). 1993. pap. 6.95 (*0-87286-274-7*) City Lights.

Murimuth, Adam. Chronica Sui Temporis, Nunc Primum per Decem Annos Aucta, 1303-1346: Cum Eorundem Contunuantione AD 1380 a Quodam Anonymo. (English Historical Society Publications Ser.: Vol. 9). 1972. reprint ed. 25.00 (*0-8115-1534-6*) Periodicals Srv.

Murin, William J. & Pryor, Judith. Delivering Government Services: An Annotated Bibliography. (Public Affairs & Administration Ser.). 352p. 1988. lib. bdg. 51.00 (*0-8240-6618-9*) Garland.

Murina, T. M., ed. YAG-Er3 Plus Lasers. (Proceedings of the Institute of General Physics of the Academy of Sciences of the U. S. S. R. Ser.: Vol. 19). 205p. (C). 1994. text ed. 144.00 (*0-941743-82-9*) Nova Sci Pubs.

Murinde, Victor. Macroeconomic Policy Modelling for Developing Countries. 462p. 1993. 78.95 (*1-85628-448-4*, Pub. by Avebury Pub UK) Ashgate Pub Co.

Murio, Diego A. The Mollification Method & the Numerical Solution of Ill-Posed Problems. LC 93-163. 272p. 1993. text ed. 74.95 (*0-471-59408-3*) Wiley.

Muris, Jean & Starmans, Richard. Non Acute Abdominal Complaints: Diagnostic Studies in General Practice & Outpatient Clinic. 213p. 1993. pap. 23.50 (*90-5170-237-X*, Pub. by Thesis Pubs NE) IBD Ltd.

Muris, Timothy J., jt. auth. see Beales, J. Howard.

Muris, Timothy J., et al. Strategy, Structure, & Antitrust in the Carbonated Soft Drink Industry. LC 92-34944. 272p. 1993. text ed. 59.95 (*0-89930-788-4*, MYJ, Quorum Bks) Greenwood.

Murison, Charles L. Galba, Otho & Vitellius: Careers & Controversies. Bd. 52. (GER.). Date not set. write for info. (*0-318-70630-X*, Pub. by Georg Olms GW) Lubrecht & Cramer.

— Gallah, Otho & Vitellius: Careers & Controversies. (Spudasmata Ser.: Vol. 52). 179p. 1993. pap. 29.95 (*3-487-09756-7*, Pub. by Georg Olms GW) Lubrecht & Cramer.

Murison, David. The Guid Scots Tongue. 64p. (C). 1989. pap. 29.00 (*0-901824-78-X*, Pub. by Mercat Pr Bks UK) St Mut.

Murison, David, ed. Robert Henryson: Selected Poems. 58p. 1989. 29.00 (*0-85411-010-0*, Pub. by Saltire Soc) St Mut.

Murison, David A., jt. auth. see Grant, William.

Murison, Hamish S. & Lea, John P. Housing in Third World Countries: Perspectives on Policy & Practice. LC 79-20565. 1980. text ed. 32.50 (*0-312-39350-4*) St Martin.

Murison, R., jt. ed. see Ursin, H.

Murison, W., ed. see Burke, Edmund.

***Murith, J.** Dictionary of Initials of Scientific, Technical & Commercial Organization. 2nd ed. 471p. 1993. write for info. (*0-7859-8800-9*) Fr & Eur.

— Dictionary of Initials of Scientific, Technical & Commercial Organizations. 2nd ed. 471p. 1993. 180.00 (*2-85206-384-0*) IBD Ltd.

— Dictionary of Scientific, Technical & Economic Abbreviations & Acronyms. 2nd rev. ed. 949p. (ENG & FRE.). 1992. 395.00 (*0-7859-4637-7*) Fr & Eur.

***Murith, Jean.** Dictionnaire des Sigles Scientifiques, Techniques et Economiques. 2nd ed. 470p. (FRE.). 1987. 250.00 (*0-7859-8071-7*, 2852063840) Fr & Eur.

Murkes, J. & Carlsson, C. G. Cross Flow Filtration: Theory & Practice. 133p. 1989. text ed. 195.00 (*0-471-92097-5*) Wiley.

Murkherjee, Sujit. Forster & Further: The Tradition of Anglo-Indian Fiction. 1993. 30.00 (*0-86311-289-7*, Pub. by Orient Longman Ltd II) Apt Bks.

Murkovic, Antun. Blood Transfusion ID Card & Book: For Safer Blood at the Time of AIDS, Hepatitis, VDs, etc. 120p. (Orig.). (ENG & JPN.). 1989. pap. write for info. (*0-929602-00-5*) Mura Pub Co.

Murkute, S. R. Castes & Tribes of India Series 2: Socio-Cultural Study of Scheduled Tribes. 1990. 29.00 (*0-317-99725-4*, Pub. by Ashish II) S Asia.

— Socio-Cultural Study of Scheduled Tribes: The Pardhans of Maharastra. (Castes & Tribes of India Ser.: Vol. II). 1990. 28.00 (*81-7022-262-1*, Pub. by Concept II) S Asia.

Murless, Dick & Stallings, Constance. Hiker's Guide to the Smokies. LC 72-83981. (Totebook Ser.). (Illus.). 374p. 1973. pap. 12.95 (*0-87156-068-2*); 2.95 (*0-87156-095-X*) Sierra.

Murley, Clare & Murley, Fred. Waterside: A Pictorial Past. (C). 1989. 50.00 (*1-85455-068-3*, Pub. by Ensign Pubns & Print UK) St Mut.

Murley, Fred, jt. auth. see Murley, Clare.

Murley, John A., et al, eds. Law & Philosophy: The Practice of Theory: Essays in Honor of George Anastaplo, 2 vols., Vol. 1. LC 91-42908. 617p. (C). 1992. 150.00 (*0-8214-1013-X*) Ohio U Pr.

— Law & Philosophy: The Practice of Theory: Essays in Honor of George Anastaplo, Vol. 2. 553p. (C). 1992. write for info. (*0-318-68853-0*) Ohio U Pr.

Murli, Almerico, jt. ed. see Messina, Paul.

Murlin, Bill, ed. see Guthrie, Woody.

Murlis, Helen, jt. auth. see Armstrong, Michael.

Murmann-Kristen, Luise. Die Vegetationsmosaik im Nordschwarzwaelder Waldgebiet. (Dissertationes Botanicae Ser.: Vol. 104). (Illus.). 290p. (GER.). 1987. pap. 100.00 (*3-443-64016-8*) Lubrecht & Cramer.

Murnaghan, Sheila. Disguise & Recognition in the Odyssey. LC 87-2296. 215p. 1987. text ed. 37.50 (*0-691-06716-3*) Princeton U Pr.

***Murname.** Rescuing Robinson Crusoe: Reconnecting Schools with the Changing Economy. 1996. 25.95 (*0-02-874066-1*) Free Pr.

Murnane, Lynne, ed. see ISFTA Committee Staff.

Murnane, Lynne C., ed. see IFSTA Committee Staff.

Murnane, Lynne C., ed. see IFSTA Committee.

Murnane, Lynne C., ed. see Walker, Susan S.

Murnane, Mary, jt. auth. see Daniels, Kay.

Murnane, Richard J., ed. see National Research Council.

Murnane, Richard J., et al. Who Will Teach? Policies That Matter. 182p. (C). 1991. 28.00 (*0-674-95192-1*) HUP.

Murnane, William J. The Penguin Guide to Ancient Egypt. (Illus.). 336p. 1983. pap. 12.95 (*0-14-046326-7*, Penguin Bks) Viking Penguin.

— The Road to Kadesh: A Historical Interpretation of the Battle Reliefs of King Sety I at Karnak. 2nd rev. ed. LC 90-63725. (Studies in Ancient Oriental Civilization: No. 42). (Illus.). 157p. (C). 1990. pap. 25.00 (*0-918986-67-2*) Orientl Inst Pr IT.

— Texts from the Amarna Period in Egypt. Meltzer, Edmund S., ed. LC 94-5147. (Writings from the Ancient World Ser.: Vol. 5). 1994. write for info. (*1-55540-965-2*); pap. write for info. (*1-55540-966-0*) Scholars Pr GA.

Murnane, William J. & Van Siclen, Charles C., III. The Boundary Stelae of Akhenaten. LC 93-7007. (Studies in Egyptology). 1993. write for info. (*0-7103-0464-1*, Pub. by Kegan Paul Intl UK) Routledge Chapman & Hall.

Murnane, William J., ed. see Nelson, Harold H.

Murnen, George J., jt. auth. see Botwin, Michael R.

Murner, Thomas. Deutsche Schriften mit den Holzschnitten der Erstdrucke, 9 vols. Schultz, Franz, ed. (C). 1969. reprint ed. 1,107.70 (*3-11-000276-0*) De Gruyter.

Murnighan, J. Keith. Bargaining Games: A New Approach to Strategic Thinking in Negotiations. 1993. pap. 12.00 (*0-688-12837-8*, Quill) Morrow.

— The Dynamics of Bargaining Games. 240p. 1991. pap. text ed. 25.40 (*0-13-222118-7*, 140107) P-H.

— Social Psychology in Organizations: Advances in Theory & Research. 416p. (C). 1992. text ed. write for info. (*0-13-374059-5*) P-H.

Murnighan, Keith. Bargaining Games: A New Approach to Strategic Thinking in Negotiations. 1992. 20.00 (*0-688-10905-5*) Morrow.

Murnion, Philip & Wenzel, Anne. The Crisis of the Church in the Inner City: Pastoral Options for Inner City Parishes. (Illus.). 83p. (Orig.). 1990. pap. 9.95 (*1-881307-00-X*) Natl Pastoral LC.

Murnion, Philip J. The Catholic Priest & the Changing Structure of Pastoral Ministry. 1978. 44.95 (*0-405-10845-1*, 11822) Ayer.

— New Parish Ministers: Laity & Religious on Parish Staffs. (Illus.). (Orig.). 1992. pap. 11.95 (*1-881307-01-8*) Natl Pastoral LC.

Muro, Amado. Collected Stories. 1979. 10.00 (*0-914476-82-3*) Thorp Springs.

Muro, Ernest A. Automation Services for Libraries: A Resource Handbook. rev. ed. (Library Management Ser.). (C). 1991. pap. 47.50 (*1-879491-00-1*) Vendor Rltns.

— Automation Services for Libraries: A Resource Handbook of Marketing & Sales. (C). 1991. pap. 47.50 (*1-879491-01-X*) Vendor Rltns.

— Automation Services for Libraries: LATINET '91. Lau, Jesus & Allan, Martha, eds. Allan, Martha & Covitz, Barbara, trs. (Library Management Ser.). (Illus.). 347p. (ENG & SPA.). 1992. pap. 67.50 (*1-879491-03-6*) Vendor Rltns.

Muro, Ernest A., ed. Automation Services for Libraries: A Resource Handbook of Marketing & Sales - 92. 2nd ed. (Illus.). 1995. pap. 57.50 (*1-879491-05-2*) Vendor Rltns.

Muro, Ernest A., intro. Automation Services for Libraries: A Resource Handbook - 92. 2nd ed. (Library Management Ser.). 1992. pap. 57.50 (*1-879491-04-4*) Vendor Rltns.

Muro, James J. Creating & Funding Educational Foundations: A Guide for Local School Districts. 1994. 39.95 (*0-205-15573-1*, Longwood Div) Allyn.

Muro, James J. & Kottman, Terry A. Guidance & Counseling in the Elementary & Middle Schools: A Practical Approach. 528p. (C). 1995. boxed write for info. (*0-697-20560-6*) Brown & Benchmark.

Muroff, Melvin, jt. ed. see Rosenbaum, Max.

Muroga, Saburo. Logic Design & Switching Theory. 636p. (C). 1990. reprint ed. 67.50 (*0-89464-463-7*) Krieger.

Muromtsev, A. M. The Principal Hydrological Features of the Pacific Ocean. 424p. 1963. text ed. 97.75 (*0-7065-0216-7*, Pub. by Keter Pub IS) Coronet Bks.

Muron, A., tr. see Schmirler, Otto.

***Muroni, Jean-Marc.** Petit Dictionnaire Bantou du Gabon: Francais-Ndjabi, Ndjabi-Francais. 207p. (FRE.). 1989. pap. 55.00 (*0-7859-8014-8*, 2738402658) Fr & Eur.

Murooka & Imanaka, eds. Recombinant Microbes for Industrial & Agricultural Applications. (Bioprocess Technology Ser.: Vol. 19). 904p. 1994. 195.00 (*0-8247-9141-X*) Dekker.

Murota, K. Structural Solvability & Controllability. (Algorithms & Combinatorics Ser.: Vol. 3). (Illus.). 295p. 1987. pap. 54.00 (*0-387-17659-4*) Spr-Verlag.

Murotsu, Y., jt. auth. see Thoft-Christensen, P.

Murov, Steven & Stedjee, Brian. Experiments in Basic Chemistry. 383p. 1989. Net. pap. text ed. write for info. (*0-471-62138-2*) Wiley.

Murov, Steven L. Handbook of Photochemistry. LC 73-89496. (Illus.). 290p. reprint ed. pap. 82.70 (*0-8357-6137-1*, 2034553) Bks Demand.

Murov, Steven L., et al. Handbook of Photochemistry. 2nd exp. rev. ed. LC 93-4764. 432p. 1993. 140.00 (*0-8247-7911-8*) Dekker.

Murowchick, Robert E., ed. China: Ancient Culture, Modern Land. LC 94-13366. (Cradles of Civilization Ser.: Vol. 2). (Illus.). 192p. 1994. 34.95 (*0-8061-2683-3*) U of Okla Pr.

Murphet, H. Sai Baba, Man of Miracles. 224p. (Orig.). 1977. pap. 8.95 (*0-87728-335-4*) Weiser.

Murphet, Howard. Beyond Death: The Undiscover'd Country. 240p. (Orig.). (C). 1990. pap. 9.95 (*0-8356-0654-6*, Quest) Theos Pub Hse.

— Sai Baba Avatar: A New Journey into Power & Glory. LC 77-83643. 1977. pap. 6.30 (*0-9600958-3-7*) Birth Day.

— Walking the Path with Sai Baba. (Illus.). 208p. (Orig.). 1993. pap. 12.95 (*0-87728-781-3*) Weiser.

— When Daylight Comes. LC 74-18958. (Orig.). 1987. pap. 7.50 (*0-8356-0459-4*) Theos Pub Hse.

— Where the Road Ends: From Self Through Sai to Self. 228p. 1994. reprint ed. pap. 12.00 (*0-9629835-3-5*) Leela Pr.

— Yankee Beacon of Buddhist Light: The Life of Colonel Henry S. Olcott. rev. ed. LC 88-40133. Orig. Title: Hammer on the Mountain. (Illus.). 350p. (Orig.). 1988. reprint ed. pap. 8.75 (*0-8356-0638-4*, Quest) Theos Pub Hse.

Murphey. History of Asia. (C). 1992. text ed. 36.00 (*0-06-044663-3*) HarpCollege.

Murphey, Cecil. Day to Day: Spiritual Help When Someone You Love Has Alzheimer's. deluxe ed. 140p. 1987. 9.00 (*0-664-24074-7*, Westminster) Westminster John Knox.

Murphey, Cecil, jt. auth. see Carson, Benjamin S.

Murphey, Cecil B., ed. The Encyclopedia of Christian Marriage. LC 83-13780. 416p. 1994. reprint ed. pap. 19.99 (*0-8007-5541-3*) Revell.

Murphey, Cecil B., jt. auth. see Vaughan, Norman D.

Murphey, Cecil R., jt. auth. see Vaughan, Norman D.

Murphey, Dwight D. Liberalism in Contemporary America. (Journal of Social, Political & Economic Studies Monograph Ser.: No. 22). 320p. (Orig.). (C). 1992. pap. 25.00 (*0-930690-50-8*) Coun Soc Econ.

Murphey, Joseph C. A Return to the Landscape. Oliphant, Dave, ed. (Illus.). 1979. 8.00 (*0-933384-02-5*); pap. 5.00 (*0-933384-01-7*) Prickly Pear.

Murphey-Lenahan, B. J. Colorado Trivia. LC 91-33797. 192p. (Orig.). 1991. pap. 5.95 (*1-55853-135-1*) Rutledge Hill Pr.

Murphey, Murray G. Development of Peirce's Philosophy. LC 61-13739. (Illus.). 440p. reprint ed. pap. 125.40 (*0-8357-9155-6*, 2006013) Bks Demand.

— The Development of Peirce's Philosophy. LC 93-2777. 448p. (C). 1993. reprint ed. lib. bdg. 38.95 (*0-87220-231-3*); reprint ed. pap. text ed. 19.95 (*0-87220-183-X*) Hackett Pub.

— Our Knowledge of the Historical Past. LC 72-80408. 215p. (C). 1980. 24.95 (*0-87220-097-3*); pap. 6.95 (*0-87220-096-5*) Hackett Pub.

— Philosophical Foundations of Historical Knowledge. LC 93-5321. 344p. (C). 1994. text ed. 73.50x (*0-7914-1919-3*); pap. text ed. 24.95x (*0-7914-1920-7*) State U NY Pr.

Murphey, Murray G. & Berg, Ivar, eds. Values & Value Theory in Twentieth Century America: Essays in Honor of Elizabeth Flower. LC 87-33675. 308p. (C). 1988. 39.95 (*0-87722-557-5*) Temple U Pr.

Murphey, Murray G., jt. auth. see Flower, Elizabeth.

Murphey, Rhoads. Fifty Years of China to Me: Personal Recollections of 1942-1992. LC 93-50528. (Monographs & Occasional Papers). 1994. 5.00 (*0-924304-17-0*) Assn Asian Studies.

— Fifty Years of China to Me: Personal Recollections 1942-1992. LC 93-50528. (Occasional Papers). 125p. (Orig.). 1994. 5.00 (*0-924304-27-8*) Assn Asian Studies.

— A History of Asia. 464p. 1995. reprint ed. pap. 36.00 (*1-886746-48-6*) Talman Pub.

— Scope of Geography. 3rd ed. 228p. 1982. pap. 13.95 (*0-416-33410-5*, NO. 6354) Routledge Chapman & Hall.

***Murphey, Sallyann J.** Bean Blossom Dreams. 320p. (Orig.). 1995. pap. 5.99 (*0-425-15018-6*) Berkley Pub.

— Bean Blossom Dreams: A City Family's Search for a Simple Country Life. large type ed. LC 94-32217. 1994. pap. 17.95 (*0-7838-1127-6*, Large Print Bks) Hall.

— Bean Blossom Dreams: A City Family's Search for Simple Country Gifts. LC 93-33502. 1994. 19.00 (*0-688-12325-2*) Hearst Bks.

Murphey, Wayne K. & Jorgensen, Richard. Wood As an Industrial Arts Material. 1974. 72.00 (*0-08-017906-1*, Pub. by Pergamon Repr UK) Franklin.

Murphey, Wesley. Blacktail Deer Hunting Adventures: A Refreshingly Candid Account Valuable for Hunters Everywhere. LC 94-76671. (Illus.). 176p. 1995. pap. 12.95 (*0-9641320-4-4*) Lost Creek.

Murphree, Dorothy R. The Mask. 1967. 2.50 (*0-87129-231-9*, M22) Dramatic Pub.

Murphree, Jon T. The Love Motive: A Practical Psychology of Sanctification. LC 89-82275. 114p. (C). 1990. pap. 8.99 (*0-87509-422-8*) Chr Pubns.

— Responsible Evangelism: Relating Theory to Practice. 153p. (Orig.). (C). 1994. pap. write for info. (*1-885729-00-6*) Toccoa Falls.

— Road to Sifat. 208p. (Orig.). 1990. pap. text ed. write for info. (*0-932281-06-0*) Quill Pubns GA.

Murphree, Julie J., ed. see Murphree, Pennee.

Murphree, Mabel M., ed. see Tupelo Symphony League Staff.

***Murphree, Pennee.** The Adventures of 100% Happy Shirt. Murphree, Julie J., ed. (Illus.). 28p. (Orig.). (J). (gr. 1-3). 1995. pap. 10.00 (*0-9646188-0-X*) Murphree Pr.

Murphree, Wallace A. Numerically Exceptive Logic: A Reduction of the Classical Syllogism. LC 90-23023. (American University Studies: Philosophy: Ser. V, Vol. 112). 222p. (C). 1991. text ed. 32.95 (*0-8204-1449-2*) P Lang Pubs.

Murphy. Decision Making in Pediatric Nursing. (Illus.). 216p. (C). 1988. 29.50 (*0-941158-85-3*) Mosby Yr Bk.

— Decision Making in Pediatric Nursing, No. 2. 2nd ed. Date not set. 44.00 (*1-55664-354-3*) Mosby Yr Bk.

— Electronic Devices Tutor. 1995. pap. text ed. 25.00 (*0-02-385151-1*) P-H.

— Farberware Turbo Conventional Oven Cookbook. 1981. 12.95 (*0-916752-44-5*) Dorison Hse.

— Fly Like an Eagle. 1995. mass mkt. 3.99 (*0-440-21948-5*) Dell.

— In-Process Measurement & Control. (Manufacturing Engineering & Materials Processing Ser.: Vol. 32). 352p. 1990. 125.00 (*0-8247-8130-9*) Dekker.

— Literary Books of Days. 1994. pap. 20.00 (*0-517-59432-3*) Random.

— Murphy: Plays Three. 1994. pap. 15.95 (*0-413-68350-8*, Pub. by Methuen UK) Heinemann.

— Numerical Analysis Algorithm. 1990. pap. write for info. (*0-318-68279-6*) P-H.

— One - Ten Pop-up Surprise. (Illus.). (J). 1995. 12.95 (*0-671-89908-2*, Litl Simon S&S) S&S Childrens.

— Operational Amplifiers Tutor. 1995. pap. text ed. 25.00 (*0-02-385146-5*) P-H.

— Roman Enigma. 1981. 13.95 (*0-02-588250-3*) Macmillan.

— Study Guide to Accompany Essentials of Pediatric Nursing. 4th ed. 230p. 1992. pap. 17.95 (*0-8016-7415-8*) Mosby Yr Bk.

— Urogenital Pathology. 560p. 1989. pap. text ed. 155.00 (*0-7216-2417-0*) Saunders.

Murphy & Dehkarghani, Fereydoun, eds. Handbook of Pediatric Epilepsy. LC 92-49814. (Neurological Disease & Therapy Ser.: Vol. 14). 392p. 1992. 140.00 (*0-8247-8725-0*) Dekker.

Murphy & Parker. Handbook of EDP Auditing, No. 3314. rev. ed. 1328p. 1989. boxed 149.00 (*0-7913-0411-6*) Warren Gorham & Lamont.

— Handbook of EDP Auditing, No. 3314. rev. suppl. ed. 1328p. 1991. Supplemented annually; write for info. 60.25 (*0-685-56163-1*) Warren Gorham & Lamont.

Murphy & Pelton. ECG Essentials: A Pocket Reference for Systematic Interpretation. 1991. pap. text ed. 24.00 (*0-86715-222-2*) Quint Pub Co.

***Murphy & Rogan.** Closing the Shop: Conversion from Sheltered to Integrated Work. 240p. 1995. pap. 26.00 (*1-55766-153-7*) P H Brookes.

Murphy, jt. auth. see Jenkins.

Murphy, jt. auth. see Jenne.

Murphy, jt. auth. see McKenna.

Murphy, jt. auth. see Uohara.

Murphy, et al. Angeles National Forest. (Illus.). 80p. (Orig.). 1991. pap. 9.95 (*0-9615421-4-4*) Big Santa Hist.

— Captive Management Conservation of Amphibians & Reptiles. 1994. write for info. (*0-916984-33-8*) SSAR.

Murphy, A. & James, C. Aspectival Usage in Russian. LC 64-66364. (Pergamon Oxford Russian Ser.). 1965. 72.00 (*0-08-010360-X*, Pub. by Pergamon Repr UK) Franklin.

Murphy, A. A., jt. ed. see Azziz, R.

Murphy, A. B., ed. see Chekhov, Anton.

Murphy, Agnes. Melba: A Biography. LC 77-8029. (Music Reprint Ser.). (Illus.). 1977. reprint ed. lib. bdg. 45.00 (*0-306-77428-3*) Da Capo.

Murphy, Agnes G. Melba: A Biography. LC 74-24162. (Illus.). reprint ed. 22.50 (*0-404-13057-7*) AMS Pr.

Murphy-Aivazian, Mary K. The Post-Robot Age(1994-?) As More of Us "Get a Life," Work Becomes Personal. 259p. 1995. 29.95 (*1-881705-25-0*) Antilles Pub.

Murphy, Albert T. & Fitzsimons, Ruth M. Stuttering & Personality Dynamics: Play Therapy, Projective Therapy, & Counseling. LC 60-14180. 527p. reprint ed. pap. 150.20 (*0-317-07907-7*, 2012382) Bks Demand.

Murphy, Albert T., jt. auth. see FitzSimons, Ruth M.

Murphy, Alexander B. The Regional Dynamics of Language Differentiation in Belgium: A Study in Cultural-Political Geography. (Research Papers Ser.: No. 227). 1988. pap. 12.00 (*0-89065-132-9*) U Chicago Comm Geo.

Murphy, Alexander B., ed. Brussels. (World Cities Ser.). 224p. 1993. text ed. 49.95 (*0-470-22010-4*) Halsted Pr.

Murphy, Alexandra & Giese, Lucretia K. Monet in the Museum of Fine Arts, Boston. 2nd rev. ed. Spear, Judy, ed. LC 85-61990. (Illus.). 60p. (Orig.). pap. 12.95 (*0-87846-256-2*) Mus Fine Arts Boston.

Murphy, Alexandra, jt. auth. see Department of Paintings Museum of Fine Arts.

Murphy, Alexandra L. Graced by Pines: The Ponderosa Pine in the American West. Ort, Kathleen, ed. (Illus.). 128p. 1994. per. 10.00 (*0-87842-307-9*) Mountain Pr.

Murphy, Alexandra R. Winslow Homer in the Clark Collection. LC 86-61315. (Illus.). 76p. (Orig.). 1986. pap. 14.95 (*0-931102-19-7*) S & F Clark Art.

Murphy, Alexandra R., jt. auth. see Fernandez, Rafael.

Murphy, Allan, jt. auth. see Campbell, Colin.

Murphy, Andrew. Cultural Encounters in the U. S. A. Cross-Cultural Dialogues & Mini-Dramas. 128p. 1991. pap. 9.95 (*0-8442-0715-2*, Natl Textbk) NTC Pub Grp.

***Murphy, Andrew, ed. & intro.** The Tragedy of Othello, the Moore of Venice. LC 94-42994. (Shakespearean Originals--First Edition Ser.). 1995. write for info. (*0-13-355488-0*) P-H.

***Murphy, Andy.** Bloodless. LC 94-72730. 1995. write for info. (*0-944435-33-5*) Glenbridge Pub.

Murphy, Ann. Deja Vu. 120p. (Orig.). 1994. pap. 10.00 (*1-56002-304-X*, Univ Edtns) Aegina Pr.

Murphy, Ann & Murphy, John. God's Gift of Life: A Child's First Book about Life. (Illus.). 32p. (Orig.). (J). (gr. 1-3). 1994. pap. 4.95 (*0-8198-3070-4*) Pauline Bks.

— God's Gift of Life Parents' Guide. (Illus.). 24p. (Orig.). 1994. pap. 2.75 (*0-8198-3071-2*) Pauline Bks.

— Sex Education & Successful Parenting. LC 94-4980. 1994. write for info. (*0-8198-6960-0*) Pauline Bks.

Murphy, Anne. Working with Elderly People. 1995. pap. 14.95 (*0-285-63151-9*, Pub. by Souvenir UK) Atrium Pubs.

Murphy, Anne, jt. auth. see Murphy, Chuck.

Murphy, Annie & De Rosa, Peter. Forbidden Fruit: The True Story of My Secret Love Affair with Ireland's Most Powerful Bishop. 408p. 1994. mass mkt. 5.99 (*0-446-36523-8*) Warner Bks.

— Forbidden Fruit: The True Story of My Secret Love Affair with the Bishop of Ireland. 1993. 21.95 (*0-316-59090-8*) Little.

Murphy, Arthur. The Englishman from Paris. (Augustan Reprints Ser.: No. 137 (1969)). reprint ed. 12.00 (*0-404-70137-X*) AMS Pr.

— Life of Garrick, 2 Vols. in 1. LC 76-84521. 1972. 42.95 (*0-405-08811-6*, Pub. by Blom Pubns UK) Ayer.

— Lives of Henry Fielding & Samuel Johnson, with Essays from Gray's Inn Journal, 1752-1792. LC 68-24212. 1968. 95.00 (*0-8201-1035-3*) Schol Facsimiles.

Murphy, Arthur D. & Stepick, Alex. Social Inequality in Oaxaca: A History of Resistance & Change. (Conflicts in Urban & Regional Development Ser.). (Illus.). 300p. (Orig.). (C). 1993. 44.95 (*0-87722-868-X*); pap. 19.95 (*0-87722-869-8*) Temple U Pr.

Murphy, Arthur E., ed. see Mead, George H.

Murphy, Arthur W., et al. The Law of Product Liability, Problems & Policies. LC 81-84335. 174p. (C). 1982. text ed. 39.50 (*0-89834-048-9*); pap. 24.50 (*0-685-05675-9*) Natl Chamber Foun.

Murphy, Arthur W., ed. The Nuclear Power Controversy. LC 76-40017. (American Assembly Guides Ser.). 1976. 9.95 (*0-13-625582-5*); pap. 3.95 (*0-13-625574-4*) Am Assembly.

Murphy, Arthur W., ed. see American Assembly Staff.

Murphy, Ashton. On the Wallaby. (C). 1990. pap. 21.00 (*0-86439-108-0*, Pub. by Boolarong Pubns AT) St Mut.

Murphy, Audie. To Hell & Back. (Military Classics Ser.). (Illus.). 304p. 1988. 21.95 (*0-8306-4002-9*, 40002) TAB Bks.

Murphy, Austin. The Last Year of a Country That Never Existed. 202p. 1995. pap. 8.95 (*1-56901-224-5*) NW Pub.

— Scientific Investment Analysis. 588p. 1994. disk 74.95 (*0-914061-51-8*) Orchises Pr.

Murphy, Avon J., ed. Annual Conference Proceedings of the Society for Technical Communication, 41st. Date not set. per., pap. text ed. 50.00 (*0-914548-79-4*); ring bd. 50.00 (*0-914548-80-8*) Soc Tech Comm.

Murphy, B. Greener Pastures on Your Side of the Fence: Better Farming with Voisin Management Intensive Grazing. 3rd ed. (Illus.). 353p. 1994. pap. 24.95 (*0-9617807-2-X*) Arriba Pub.

Murphy, B., jt. auth. see Kutten, L. J.

Murphy, Barbara, jt. auth. see Hoover, Rosalie.

Murphy, Barbara B. Eagles in Their Flight. LC 93-11438. (YA). (gr. 6 up). 1994. 14.95 (*0-385-32035-3*) Delacorte.

— One Another. LC 91-15651. 160p. (YA). (gr. 7 up). 1991. reprint ed. pap. 3.95 (*0-02-042015-3*, Collier Bks Young) S&S Childrens.

Murphy, Beatrice M., ed. Ebony Rhythm. LC 68-57062. (Granger Index Reprint Ser.). 1977. 20.95 (*0-8369-6033-5*) Ayer.

Murphy, Betty S. & Azoff, Elliot S. Practice & Procedure Before the National Labor Relations Board. 2nd ed. (Corporate Practice Ser.: No. 41). 1989. 95.00 (*1-55871-104-X*) BNA.

Murphy, Bill. In Pursuit of Giant Bass. Prorok, Paul, ed. (Illus.). 376p. (Orig.). 1992. pap. 16.95 (*0-9633120-0-6*) Giant Bass Pub.

— Lifetime Treasury of Tested Tennis Tips: Secrets of Winning Play. 1981. pap. text ed. 9.95 (*0-13-536433-7*) P-H.

— Presentations: For Professional Communicators. (Illus.). 96p. 1995. 34.95 (*0-7134-7172-7*, Pub. by Batsford UK) Trafalgar.

Murphy, Bill, jt. auth. see Culver, Bruce.

Murphy, Blakely M., ed. Conservation of Oil & Gas: A Legal History, 1948. LC 72-2858. (Use & Abuse of America's Natural Resources Ser.). 776p. 1972. reprint ed. 57.95 (*0-405-04522-0*) Ayer.

Murphy, Bob. Desert Shadows: A True Story of the Charles Manson Family in Death Valley. LC 93-93688. (Illus.). 144p. 1993. pap. 9.95 (*0-930704-29-0*) Sagebrush Pr.

Murphy, Brenda. American Realism & American Drama: 1800-1940. (Cambridge Studies in American Literature & Culture: No. 22). 272p. 1987. 54.95 (*0-521-32711-3*) Cambridge U Pr.

— Clarinet Fingering Chart. (Illus.). 1984. pap. 3.95 (*0-8256-2383-9*, AM35700) Music Sales.

— Flute Fingering Chart. (Illus.). 1984. pap. 3.95 (*0-8256-2381-2*, AM35718) Music Sales.

— Miller: "Death of a Salesman" (Plays in Production Ser.). (Illus.). 245p. (C). 1995. 54.95 (*0-521-43451-3*); pap. 16.95 (*0-521-47865-0*) Cambridge U Pr.

— Saxophone Fingering Chart. (Illus.). 1984. pap. 3.95 (*0-8256-2384-7*, AM35742) Music Sales.

— Tennessee Williams & Elia Kazan: A Collaboration in the Theatre. (Illus.). 224p. (C). 1992. 44.95 (*0-521-40095-3*) Cambridge U Pr.

— Trumpet Fingering Chart. (Illus.). 1984. pap. 3.95 (*0-8256-2385-5*, AM35759) Music Sales.

Murphy, Brenda, ed. Every Musician's Handbook. (Illus.). 64p. 1984. pap. 4.95 (*0-8256-2339-1*, AM37391) Music Sales.

Murphy, Brenda, intro. A Realist in the American Theatre: Selected Drama Criticism of William Dean Howells. LC 92-14195. 270p. (C). 1992. text ed. 34.95 (*0-8214-1036-9*) Ohio U Pr.

Murphy, Brendan. Turncoat: The Strange Case of British Traitor Sergeant Harold Cole, "The Worst Traitor of the War" (Illus.). 1987. 19.95 (*0-15-191410-9*) HarBrace.

Murphy, Brian. International Politics of New Information Technology. LC 86-13046. 256p. 1986. text ed. 39.95 (*0-312-42304-7*) St Martin.

— The Other Australia: Experiences of Migration. LC 92-42536. (Illus.). 272p. (C). 1993. 59.95 (*0-521-44194-3*) Cambridge U Pr.

— Teach Yourself Management Accounting. (Teach Yourself Ser.). 1978. pap. 3.95 (*0-679-10477-1*) McKay.

Murphy, Bruce. Portraits in American Politics: A Reader. (C). 1991. write for info. (*0-395-55385-7*) HM Soft Schl Col Div.

— Sing Sing Sing. 112p. 1990. 30.00 (*0-8147-5460-0*); pap. 13.50 (*0-8147-5461-9*) NYU Pr.

Murphy, Bryan. Experiment with Air. (Science Experiments Ser.). 32p. (J). (gr. 2-5). 1991. lib. bdg. 17.50 (*0-8225-2452-X*, Lerner Publctns) Lerner Group.

— Experiment with Light. (Science Experiments Ser.). 32p. (J). (gr. 2-5). 1991. lib. bdg. 17.50 (*0-8225-2454-6*, Lerner Publctns) Lerner Group.

An Asterisk (*) at the beginning of an entry indicates that the title is appearing in BIP for the first time.

— Experiment with Movement. (Science Experiments Ser.). 32p. (J). (gr. 2-5). 1991. lib. bdg. 17.50 (*0-8225-2451-1*, Lerner Publctns) Lerner Group.

— Experiment with Water. (Science Experiments Ser.). 32p. (J). (gr. 2-5). 1991. lib. bdg. 17.50 (*0-8225-2453-8*, Lerner Publctns) Lerner Group.

Murphy, C. Edward, ed. see Foundation Center Staff.

Murphy, Campbell. David & I Talk to God Series. (J). (ps-2). 1983. pap. 2.95 (*0-686-45018-3*, Chariot Bks) Chariot Family.

Murphy, Carol. Christopher Columbus. (Famous People Ser.). (Illus.). (J). (gr. k-6). 1991. 11.95 (*0-89868-228-2*); pap. 20.00 (*0-89868-229-0*) ARO Pub.

— A Deeper Faith. (C). 1958. pap. 3.00 (*0-87574-099-5*) Pendle Hill.

— The Examined Life. (C). 1955. pap. 3.00 (*0-87574-085-5*) Pendle Hill.

— The Faith of An Ex-Agnostic. (C). 1949. pap. 3.00 (*0-87574-046-4*) Pendle Hill.

— Four Women: Four Windows on Light. Mather, Eleanore P., ed. LC 81-80220. 26p. 1981. pap. 3.00 (*0-87574-236-X*) Pendle Hill.

— Holy Morality. LC 71-110286. (Orig.). (C). 1970. pap. 3.00 (*0-87574-169-X*) Pendle Hill.

— Martin Luther King, Jr. (Famous People Ser.). (Illus.). (J). (gr. k-6). 1991. 11.95 (*0-89868-230-4*); pap. 20.00 (*0-89868-231-2*) ARO Pub.

— Milestone 70. (Orig.). 1989. pap. 3.00 (*0-87574-287-4*) Pendle Hill.

— The Ministry of Counseling. (C). 1952. pap. 3.00 (*0-87574-067-7*) Pendle Hill.

— Nurturing Contemplation. LC 88-62745. (C). 1983. pap. 3.00 (*0-87574-251-3*) Pendle Hill.

— Religion & Mental Illness. (C). 1955. pap. 3.00 (*0-87574-082-0*) Pendle Hill.

Murphy, Carol, ed. see Boulding, Kenneth E. & Mayer, Milton.

Murphy, Carol J. Alienation & Absence in the Novels of Marguerite Duras. LC 82-82426. (French Forum Monographs: No. 37). 172p. (Orig.). 1982. pap. 13.95 (*0-917058-36-4*) French Forum.

— The Allegorical Impulse in the Works of Julien Gracq: History As Rhetorical Enactment in le Rivage des Syrtes & un Balcon en Foret. LC 95-2416. (Studies in the Romance Languages & Literatures: No. 250). 1995. write for info. (*0-8078-9254-8*) U of NC Pr.

Murphy, Carol R. The Available Mind. LC 73-94186. (Orig.). 1974. pap. 3.00 (*0-87574-193-2*) Pendle Hill.

— Man: The Broken Image. LC 68-30960. (Orig.). 1968. pap. 3.00 (*0-87574-158-4*) Pendle Hill.

— Many Religions: One God. LC 66-30689. (Orig.). 1966. pap. 3.00 (*0-87574-150-9*) Pendle Hill.

— O Inward Traveller. LC 77-91637. 31p. (Orig.). 1977. pap. 3.00 (*0-87574-216-5*) Pendle Hill.

— Revelation & Experience. LC 64-22765. (Orig.). 1964. pap. 3.00 (*0-87574-137-1*) Pendle Hill.

— The Roots of Pendle Hill. LC 78-1768. (Orig.). 1979. pap. 3.00 (*0-87574-223-8*) Pendle Hill.

— The Sound of Silence: Moving with T'ai Chi. LC 75-41548. (Orig.). 1976. pap. 3.00 (*0-87574-205-X*) Pendle Hill.

— The Valley of the Shadow. LC 72-80095. 24p. (Orig.). 1972. pap. 3.00 (*0-87574-184-3*) Pendle Hill.

Murphy, Carol W. Smashed Potatoes & Other Thanksgiving Disasters. LC 94-15001. 128p. (J). (gr. 3-6). 1994. pap. 2.95 (*0-8167-3518-2*, Rainbow NJ) Troll Assocs.

Murphy, Carole. Annie's Night Out. Zarucci, Roy & Page, Carolyn, eds. (Chapbook Ser.). 28p. (Orig.). 1990. pap. 5.00 (*0-9623862-5-1*) Nightshade Pr.

Murphy, Caroline, tr. see Schebera, Jurgen.

Murphy, Carolyn, jt. auth. see Murphy, Jim.

Murphy, Carolyn H. Carolina Rocks! The Geology of South Carolina. Tiger Creek Productions Staff, ed. LC 94-20979. (Illus.). 250p. (Orig.). 1995. pap. 19.95 (*0-87844-121-2*) Sandlapper Pub Co.

Murphy, Catherine. Automating School Library Catalogs: A Reader. 211p. 1992. lib. bdg. 27.00 (*0-87287-771-X*) Libs Unl.

— CD-ROMs for School Libraries: An Evaluative Guide to Collection Building. 200p. 1994. pap. text ed. 45.00 (*0-88736-897-2*) Learned Info.

Murphy, Catherine F. Alice Dodd & the Spirit of Truth. LC 92-32039. 176p. (J). (gr. 3-7). 1993. text ed. 14.95 (*0-02-767702-8*, Mac Bks Young Read) S&S Childrens.

— Songs in the Silence. LC 93-26947. 192p. (J). (gr. 3-7). 1994. text ed. 14.95 (*0-02-767730-3*, Mac Bks Young Read) S&S Childrens.

Murphy, Catherine P. & Hunter, Howard. Ethical Problems in the Nurse-Patient Relationship. 276p. (C). 1982. text ed. 29.95 (*0-205-07762-5*, H77621) Allyn.

Murphy Center for Liturgical Research Staff. Made, Not Born: New Perspectives on Christian Initiation & the Catechumenate. LC 75-19874. 192p. 1976. pap. 10.95 (*0-268-01337-3*) U of Notre Dame Pr.

Murphy, Charles H. Handbook of Particle Sampling & Analysis Methods. LC 83-18970. 354p. 1984. lib. bdg. 80.00 (*0-89573-116-9*) VCH Pubs.

Murphy, Charles M. At Home on Earth: Foundations for a Catholic Ethic of the Environment. 200p. 1989. 15.95 (*0-8245-0966-8*) Crossroad NY.

Murphy, Chester W. Advanced Tennis. 4th ed. 136p. (C). 1988. pap. write for info. (*0-697-07274-6*) Brown & Benchmark.

Murphy, Chet. A Parents' Guide to Teaching Kids to Play. LC 81-85622. (Illus.). 144p. (Orig.). 1983. pap. text ed. 15.00 (*0-918438-91-8*, PMUR0091) Human Kinetics.

— Tennis for Thinking Players. 2nd ed. (Illus.). 176p. (C). 1985. pap. 15.00 (*0-88011-251-4*, PMUR0251) Human Kinetics.

Murphy, Christina. Ann Beattie. (Twayne's United States Authors Ser.: No. 510). 168p. 1986. text ed. 19.95 (*0-8057-7474-2*, Twayne) Macmillan.

***Murphy, Christina & Law, Joe, eds.** Landmark Essays on Writing Centers. (Landmark Essays Ser.: Vol. 9). xxx, 272p. (C). 1995. pap. text ed. 15.95 (*1-880393-22-0*) Hermagoras Pr.

Murphy, Christine & Murphy, Michael, eds. Radiology for Anesthesia & Critical Care. (Illus.). 273p. 1988. 64.00 (*0-443-08306-1*) Churchill.

Murphy, Christopher. Dance for a Diamond. 272p. 1986. 16.95 (*0-8027-0925-7*) Walker & Co.

— Dance for a Diamond. large type ed. 576p. 1988. 15.95 (*0-7089-1775-5*) Ulverscroft.

— I, Said the Sparrow. large type ed. 464p. 1986. 15.95 (*0-7089-1406-3*) Ulverscroft.

— The Jericho Rumble. 1987. 16.95 (*0-8027-0996-6*) Walker & Co.

— The Jericho Rumble. large type ed. 464p. 1985. 15.95 (*0-7089-1286-9*) Ulverscroft.

— Scream at the Sea. large type ed. 432p. 1985. 15.95 (*0-7089-1241-9*) Ulverscroft.

***Murphy, Chuck.** My First Book of Animal Sounds. (Lift-the-Flap Concept Bks.). (Illus.). 10p. (J). (ps-k). 1995. bds. 6.95 (*0-590-20301-0*, Cartwheel) Scholastic Inc.

— My First Book of Colors. (J). (ps). 1991. 6.95 (*0-590-44481-6*) Scholastic Inc.

— My First Book of Counting. (J). (ps). 1991. 6.95 (*0-590-44471-9*) Scholastic Inc.

— My First Book of Shapes. (Illus.). 12p. (J). 1993. 6.95 (*0-590-46303-9*) Scholastic Inc.

— My First Book of the Alphabet. (Illus.). 12p. (J). 1993. 6.95 (*0-590-46304-7*) Scholastic Inc.

— My First Book of the Body. (Lift-the-Flap Concept Bks.). (Illus.). 10p. (J). (ps-k). 1995. bds. 6.95 (*0-590-20315-0*, Cartwheel) Scholastic Inc.

Murphy, Chuck & Murphy, Anne. When the Saints Go Marching Out. LC 87-4525. 1987. pap. 5.99 (*0-8007-9101-0*) Chosen Bks.

Murphy, Claire R. A Child's Alaska. LC 93-48164. (Illus.). 48p. (J). (gr. 4-10). 1994. 14.95 (*0-88240-457-1*) Alaska Northwest.

— Gold Star Sister. LC 94-48135. 224p. (J). (gr. 5-9). 1994. 14.99 (*0-525-67492-6*, Lodestar Bks) Dutton Child Bks.

Murphy, Clare M., et al, eds. Miscellanea Moreana: Essays for Germain Marc'hadour. (Medieval & Renaissance Texts & Studies: Vol. 61). 608p. 1989. 18.00 (*0-86698-045-8*) MRTS.

Murphy, Cliona. The Women's Suffrage Movement & Irish Society in the Early Twentieth Century. LC 89-4705. 240p. (C). 1989. 34.95 (*0-87722-636-9*) Temple U Pr.

Murphy, Cliona, jt. auth. see Luddy, Maria.

Murphy, Clive, ed. At the Dog in Dulwich. 200p. 1987. 30.95 (*0-436-29671-3*, Pub. by Seck & Warburg UK) Trafalgar.

Murphy, Corinne. Exploring the Hand Arts: For Juniors, Cadettes, Seniors, & Leaders. 112p. (J). (gr. 4-12). 1955. pap. 5.00 (*0-88441-140-0*, 19-994) Girl Scouts USA.

Murphy, Cornelius F. Beyond Feminism: Towards a Dialogue on Difference. LC 93-47404. 300p. (C). 1995. 24.95 (*0-8132-0806-8*); pap. 14.95 (*0-8132-0807-6*) Cath U Pr.

— Cases & Materials on Introduction to Law: Legal Process & Procedure. (American Casebook Ser.). 772p. 1977. text ed. 42.50 (*0-314-32845-9*) West Pub.

— Descent into Subjectivity: Rawls, Dworkin & Unger in the Context of Modern Thought. LC 90-6005. 1990. 30.00 (*0-89341-620-7*, Longwood Academic); pap. 14.95 (*0-89341-621-5*, Longwood Academic) Hollowbrook.

Murphy, Cornelius F., Jr. The Search for World Order. 1985. lib. bdg. 93.00 (*90-247-3188-7*) Kluwer Ac.

Murphy, Craig, jt. auth. see Augelli, Enrico.

Murphy, Craig N. International Organization & Industrial Change: Global Governance since 1850. (Europe & the International Order Ser.). (Illus.). 352p. (C). 1994. 39.95 (*0-19-521070-0*); pap. 17.95 (*0-19-521071-9*) OUP.

Murphy, Craig N. & Tooze, Roger, eds. The New International Political Economy. LC 90-19266. (International Political Economy Yearbook Ser.: Vol. 6). 240p. 1991. pap. text ed. 16.95 (*1-55587-261-1*) Lynne Rienner.

Murphy, Cullen. Just Curious. 256p. 1995. 21.95 (*0-395-70099-X*) HM.

Murphy, Cullen, jt. auth. see Rathie, William.

Murphy, Cullen, jt. auth. see Rathje, William.

Murphy, D. J. Customers & Thieves. 200p. 1985. text ed. 75.00 (*0-566-00882-3*) Ashgate Pub Co.

— T. J. Ryan: A Political Biography. 1990. pap. 24.95 (*0-7022-2289-5*, Pub. by Univ Queensland Pr AT) Intl Spec Bk.

Murphy, D. J., ed. The Big Strikes: Queensland 1889-1965. LC 82-23881. (Illus.). 303p. 1983. pap. 18.95 (*0-7022-1721-2*) Intl Spec Bk.

Murphy, Dale & Patton, Curtis. Ask Dale Murphy. (Illus.). 112p. 1987. pap. 8.95 (*0-912697-59-8*) Algonquin Bks.

Murphy, Dallas. Apparent Wind. Chelias, Jane, ed. 320p. (Orig.). 1991. mass mkt. 4.99 (*0-671-68554-6*) PB.

— Lover Man. 1988. mass mkt. 4.99 (*0-671-66188-4*) PB.

— Lush Life. 288p. (Orig.). 1993. mass mkt. 4.99 (*0-671-68556-2*) PB.

— Stormy Weather. LC 95-8887. 1996. write for info. (*0-671-86687-7*) PB.

Murphy, Dan. The Guadalupe Mountains National Park. Houk, Rose & Peters, Robert, eds. (Illus.). 32p. 1984. pap. 3.00 (*0-916907-00-7*) Carlsbad His.

— Lewis & Clark: Voyage of Discovery. LC 76-57451. (Illus.). 64p. 1977. pap. 6.95 (*0-916122-50-6*) KC Pubns.

— Oregon Trail: Voyage of Discovery. LC 92-70247. (Illus.). 64p. 1992. pap. 6.95 (*0-88714-064-5*) KC Pubns.

— Powell, John Wesley: Voyage of Discovery. LC 91-60044. (Illus.). 64p. 1991. 6.95 (*0-88714-059-9*) KC Pubns.

— Santa Fe Trail: Voyage of Discovery. LC 94-75107. (Illus.). 64p. 1994. pap. 6.95 (*0-88714-086-6*) KC Pubns.

Murphy, Dan, ed. see Dodge, Natt N.

Murphy, Dan, ed. see Dosch, Donald F.

Murphy, Dan J., tr. see Sicardo, Joseph A.

Murphy, Daniel. Imagination & Religion in Anglo-Irish Literature, 1930-80. 228p. 1987. 39.50 (*0-7165-2400-7*, Pub. by Irish Acad Pr IE) Intl Spec Bk.

— Martin Buber's Philosophy of Education. 240p. 1991. 39.50 (*0-7165-2427-9*, Pub. by Irish Acad Pr IE) Intl Spec Bk.

— Tolstoy & Education. 302p. 1992. text ed. 39.50 (*0-7165-2484-8*, Pub. by Irish Acad Pr IE) Intl Spec Bk.

Murphy, Daniel, jt. auth. see Ehrlich, Eugene H.

Murphy, Daniel J., jt. auth. see Ehrlich, Eugene H.

Murphy, Daniel O. El Morro National Monument. Priehs, T. J., ed. LC 88-63877. (Illus.). 16p. (Orig.). 1989. pap. 2.95 (*0-911408-81-9*) SW Pks Mnmts.

— Salinas Pueble Missions: Abo Quarai, & Gran Quivira. Jorgen, Randolph & Foreman, Ronald, eds. LC 91-60459. (Illus.). 64p. (YA). 1993. pap. 9.95 (*0-911408-98-3*) SW Pks Mnmts.

Murphy, Danny W., jt. auth. see Dolecheck, Carolyn C.

Murphy, Daryl. Carrera Panamericana: The Mexican Road Race, 1950-54. LC 92-33694. (Illus.). 160p. 1993. 49.95 (*0-87938-734-3*) Motorbooks Intl.

— Generalities, Truths, & Assorted Fables: Aviation Anecdotes & Adventures. Hamilton, Frank et al, eds. (Illus.). 89p. (Orig.). 1995. pap. 14.95 (*1-879825-15-5*) Jones Publish.

Murphy, Daryl E. Flying VFR in Marginal Weather. 3rd ed. 1991. text ed. 28.95 (*0-07-157676-2*); pap. text ed. 16.95 (*0-07-157675-4*) McGraw.

— Flying VFR in Marginal Weather. 3rd ed. (Practical Flying Ser.). (Illus.). 224p. 1991. 26.95 (*0-8306-8699-1*, 3699, TAB-Aero); pap. 16.95 (*0-8306-7699-6*, TAB-Aero) TAB Bks.

Murphy, David. The Stalker Affair & the Press. 276p. (C). 1990. text ed. 49.95 (*0-04-445411-2*); pap. text ed. 17.95 (*0-04-445412-0*) Routledge Chapman & Hall.

Murphy, David & Carter, David A., eds. Transgenesis Techniques: Principles & Protocols. LC 93-6775. (Methods in Molecular Biology Ser.: Vol. 18). (Illus.). 480p. 1993. spiral bd. 69.50 (*0-89603-245-0*) Humana.

Murphy, David, jt. ed. see Evans, Terry.

Murphy, David, jt. auth. see Franklin, Bob.

Murphy, David G. Debates on God & Experience in the Netherlands, 1965-1989. 250p. 1993. 64.95 (*1-883255-09-0*, Cath Scholar Pr); pap. 44.95 (*1-883255-02-3*, Cath Scholar Pr) Intl Scholars.

Murphy, David S., et al. Personal Computing: Level 1. (Easy Way Ser.). 170p. 1993. pap. 29.95 (*1-57048-000-1*) Trning Express.

— WordPerfect for Windows: Level 1. (Easy Way Ser.). 197p. 1993. pap. 29.95 (*1-57048-100-8*) Trning Express.

Murphy, David S. & Goodman, Margaret E. WordPerfect 6.0: Level 1. (Easy Way Ser.). 150p. 1993. pap. 29.95 (*1-57048-340-X*) Trning Express.

Murphy, David S., et al. WordPerfect 5.1: Level 1. (Easy Way Ser.). 155p. 1993. pap. 29.95 (*1-57048-040-0*) Trning Express.

Murphy, Dawes, ed. Designing an Effective Compliance Program, 11 vols. (Corporate Compliance Ser.). 1993. 990.00 (*0-685-68839-9*) Clark Boardman Callaghan.

***Murphy, Dean A.** Fishing Tackle Made in Missouri: History & Identification. 1993. 17.95 (*0-9636800-1-3*) Dammo Pub.

***Murphy, Deborah A., et al.** Exceptions: A Handbook of Inclusion Activities for Teachers of Students at Grades 6-12 with Mild Disabilities. 2nd ed. (Illus.). 166p. 1994. teacher ed 14.95 (*1-57035-023-X*, 10EXCPT) Sopris.

Murphy, Denis. The Pope's Confessor & Other Stories. 115p. (Orig.). 1985. pap. 7.50 (*971-10-0188-8*, Pub. by New Day Pub PH) Cellar.

Murphy, Denis, et al. The Premiers of Queensland: Revised Edition of Queensland Political Portraits 1859-1952. rev. ed. 1990. pap. 34.95 (*0-7022-2249-6*, Pub. by Univ Queensland Pr AT) Intl Spec Bk.

***Murphy, Denis J.** Designer Oil Crops: Breeding, Processing & Biotechnology. 1994. 120.00 (*1-56081-827-1*) VCH Pubs.

Murphy, Dennis, jt. ed. see Coccaro, Emil.

Murphy, Dennis E. & Johnson, Marilyn C. Getting Ahead. 96p. (Orig.). 1988. pap. 7.50 (*1-877948-09-8*) Prof Train TX.

Murphy, Dennis G. The Business Management of Interior Design. (Orig.). (C). 1988. pap. text ed. write for info. (*0-938614-05-3*) Stratford Hse.

— The Fabric Estimator. (Calculating Wheel for Draperies & Upolstered Furniture Yardage Ser.). (Illus.). 1981. pap. 12.95 (*0-938614-02-9*) Stratford Hse.

— The Materials of Interior Design. Murphy, Gladys N., ed. (Interior Furnishings & Products Ser.). (Illus.). 208p. (Orig.). (C). 1978. 14.00 (*0-938614-00-2*, 211-196) Stratford Hse.

Murphy, Dennis J. Safety & Health for Production Agriculture. LC 92-74464. 256p. 1992. 39.00 (*0-929355-32-6*, M0792) Am Soc Ag Eng.

— Supervisory Handbooks, 3 vols. rev. ed. (Speaking from Experience Ser.). Successful Time Management for Supervisors: How to Get More Done, Improve Quality, Meet Deadlines &. pap. 7.50 (*1-877948-07-1*); Effective Supervision Skills: How to Lead Effectively, Prevent Problems, Praise Genuinely & Get Resu. pap. 7.50 (*1-877948-06-3*) Prof Train TX.

— Supervisory Handbooks, 3 vols. rev. ed. (Speaking from Experience Ser.). 47p. 1986. Increasing Employee Motivation: A Guide for Supervisors, 1986, 47p. pap. 7.50 (*1-877948-05-5*) Prof Train TX.

— Supervisory Handbooks, 3 vols., Set. rev. ed. (Speaking from Experience Ser.). pap. 15.00 (*1-877948-08-X*) Prof Train TX.

Murphy, Dervla. Cameroon with Egbert. (Illus.). 282p. 1991. 21.95 (*0-87951-415-9*) Overlook Pr.

— Cameroon with Egbert. (Illus.). 282p. 1992. pap. 13.95 (*0-87951-476-0*) Overlook Pr.

— Eight Feet in the Andes. 288p. 1989. 16.95 (*0-87951-245-8*); pap. 10.95 (*0-87951-262-8*) Overlook Pr.

— Full Tilt: Ireland to India with a Bicycle. LC 85-13759. 288p. 1987. reprint ed. 17.95 (*0-87951-236-9*); reprint ed. pap. 10.95 (*0-87951-248-2*) Overlook Pr.

— Muddling Through in Madagascar. LC 88-22512. (Illus.). 276p. 1989. 18.95 (*0-87951-342-X*) Overlook Pr.

— Muddling Through in Madagascar. 276p. 1990. pap. 9.95 (*0-87951-360-8*) Overlook Pr.

— On a Shoestring to Coorg: A Travel Memoir of India. LC 89-8830. 272p. 1990. 19.95 (*0-87951-372-1*); pap. 9.95 (*0-87951-381-0*) Overlook Pr.

— A Place Apart. 1980. 15.00 (*0-8159-6516-8*) Devin.

— Transylvania & Beyond. 256p. 1993. 21.95 (*0-87951-472-8*) Overlook Pr.

— Transylvania & Beyond. 256p. 1995. pap. 13.95 (*0-87951-603-8*) Overlook Pr.

— Transylvania & Beyond. large type ed. (Charnwood Library). 400p. 1993. 23.95 (*0-7089-8730-3*, Trail West Pubs) Ulverscroft.

— The Ukimwi Road: From Kenya to Zimbabwe. 290p. 1995. 22.95 (*0-87951-556-2*) Overlook Pr.

— The Waiting Land: A Spell in Nepal. LC 85-5736. 216p. 1987. 17.95 (*0-87951-251-2*) Overlook Pr.

— The Waiting Land: A Spell in Nepal. 216p. 1989. pap. 10.95 (*0-87951-305-5*) Overlook Pr.

***Murphy, Desmond.** The Death & Rebirth of Religious Life. 1995. pap. 14.95 (*0-85574-126-0*, Pub. by E J Dwyer AT) Morehouse Pub.

Murphy, Dianne, jt. auth. see Murphy, Thomas.

Murphy, Dolores A. In Red Hats, Beads, & Bags: 1908 Graduates Sharing Their Lives Through Letters. LC 90-80014. (Illus.). 320p. 1990. 18.95 (*0-9625596-0-1*) Cassiopeia Pr.

Murphy, Donald J. Agriculture in the U. S. A. Today. LC 92-3516. (Illus.). 156p. 1992. pap. text ed. 49.95 (*0-7734-9910-5*) E Mellen.

— Honest Medicine: Shattering Myths about Aging & Health Care. 320p. 1995. 22.00 (*0-87113-587-6*) Grove-Atltic.

Murphy, Donald W., jt. ed. see Interrante, Leonard V.

Murphy, Donn B. & Moore, Stephen. Helen Hayes: A Bio-Bibliography. LC 93-83. (Bio-Bibliographies in the Performing Arts Ser.: No. 38). 392p. 1993. Alk. paper. text ed. 49.95 (*0-313-27793-1*, MHV, Greenwood Pr) Greenwood.

Murphy, Doris, ed. see Williams, Glenn R.

***Murphy, Dudley & Edmisten, Rick.** Fishing Lure Collectibles. 336p. 1995. 24.95 (*0-89145-541-8*, 3968) Collector Bks.

Murphy, E. F., ed. Nature, Bureaucracy & the Rules of Property. 336p. 1977. 56.50 (*0-7204-0700-1*, North Holland) Elsevier.

Murphy, E. Jefferson. African Mythology: Old & New. (Occasional Papers Ser.). 11p. 1973. 2.00 (*0-317-65383-0*) I N Thut World Educ Ctr.

— Schooling for Servitude: Some Aspects. 38p. 1972. 4.50 (*0-317-65386-5*) I N Thut World Educ Ctr.

— Tradition & Change in Modern Morocco. (Instructional Unit Based on Film Study). 12p. 1974. 2.50 (*0-317-65384-9*) I N Thut World Educ Ctr.

Murphy, E. Louise. The History of Winston-Salem State University, 1892-1992. rev. ed. Allen, Simona A. & Turner, William H., eds. LC 92-28011. 1992. write for info. (*0-89865-849-7*) Donning Co.

Murphy, Eamon. Unions in Conflict: A Comparative Study Four South Indian Textile Centres, 1918-1939. 1982. 18.00 (*0-8364-0874-8*) S Asia.

Murphy, Earl F. Energy & Environmental Balance. (Policy Studies). 1980. 96.00 (*0-08-025082-3*, Pergamon Pr) Elsevier.

Murphy, Edmond A. Biostatistics in Medicine. LC 81-48191. (Illus.). 560p. (C). 1982. text ed. 60.00x (*0-8018-2727-2*) Johns Hopkins.

— A Companion to Medical Statistics. LC 84-21806. 288p. (C). 1985. text ed. 45.00 (*0-8018-2612-8*) Johns Hopkins.

— Probability in Medicine. LC 78-10611. 320p. 1979. text ed. 47.50x (*0-8018-2135-5*) Johns Hopkins.

— Skepsis, Dogma, & Belief: Uses & Abuses in Medicine. LC 80-8870. 176p. 1981. text ed. 30.00x (*0-8018-2510-5*) Johns Hopkins.

Murphy, Edmond A. & Chase, Gary A. Principles of Genetic Counseling. LC 75-16020. 409p. reprint ed. pap. 116.60 (*0-317-26170-3*, 2024267) Bks Demand.

Murphy, Edna. ESL: A Handbook for Teachers & Administrators in International Schools. 220p. 1990. 69.00 (*1-85359-090-8*, Pub. by Multilingual Matters UK) Taylor & Francis.

Murphy, Edna, ed. ESL: A Handbook for Teachers & Administrators in International Schools. 192p. 1990. pap. 24.95 (*1-85359-157-2*, Pub. by Multilingual Matters UK) Taylor & Francis.

***Murphy, Edward.** Dakto: 173d Airborne Brigade in South Vietnam's Central Highlands, June-November 1967. Grad, Doug, ed. 400p. (Orig.). 1995. pap. 6.99 (*0-671-52268-X*) PB.

Murphy, Edward F. Dak To: The 173d Airborne Brigade in South Vietnam's Central Highlands, June-November 1967. LC 93-4142. 355p. 1993. 24.95 (*0-89141-429-0*) Presidio Pr.

— Heroes of World War II. 1990. 24.95 (*0-89141-367-7*) Presidio Pr.

M

An Asterisk (*) at the beginning of an entry indicates that the title is appearing in BIP for the first time.

— Heroes of WW II. 1991. mass mkt. 5.99 (0-345-37545-9) Ballantine.

— Korean War Heroes. 1992. 24.95 (0-89141-404-5) Presidio Pr.

— The Tenth Man. LC 72-4647. (Black Heritage Library Collection). 1977. reprint ed. 29.95 (0-8369-9114-1) Ayer.

— Two Thousand Seven Hundred Fifteen One-Line Quotations for Speakers, Writers & Raconteurs. 1989. 6.99 (0-517-68236-2) Random Hse Value.

Murphy, Edward J. & Speidel, Richard E. Studies in Contract Law. 3rd ed. LC 84-6083. (University Casebook Ser.). 1376p. 1988. reprint ed. text ed. 33.00 (0-88277-177-9) Foundation Pr.

— Studies in Contract Law. 4th ed. (University Casebook Ser.). 1401p. 1991. text ed. 45.50 (0-88277-875-7) Foundation Pr.

— Studies in Contract Law, Teaching Notes. 4th ed. (University Casebook Ser.). 150p. (C). 1991. pap. text ed. write for info. (0-88277-938-9) Foundation Pr.

Murphy, Edward J., jt. auth. see Trai Le, Tang T.

***Murphy, Edwin.** After the Funeral: The Posthumous Adventures of Famous Corpses. LC 94-45464. 256p. 1995. pap. 9.95 (0-8065-1599-6, Citadel Pr) Carol Pub Group.

— The Antiquities of Egypt: A Translation, with Notes, of Book I of the Library of History of Diodorus Siculus. 178p. 1989. 39.95 (0-88738-303-3) Transaction Pubs.

Murphy, Edwin W. The Antiquities of Asia: A Translation, with Commentary, of the Library of History, Book II, by Diodorus Siculus. 117p. 1989. 39.95 (0-88738-272-X) Transaction Pubs.

Murphy, Eileen. Healthy Living. (Skills for Caring Ser.). (Illus.). 40p. (Orig.). 1992. pap. text ed. 12.00 (0-443-04529-1) Churchill.

Murphy, Eileen M. The Original Dictionary of Modern Hairstyling for Beauty Salons. (Illus.). 67p. 1981. spiral bd. 12.95 (0-9609792-0-4) Eileens Beautique.

***Murphy, Elaineshwar & Alexopoulos, George, eds.** Geriatric Psychology: Key Search Topics for Clinicians. LC 94-21812. 1995. text ed. 59.95 (0-471-95168-4) Wiley.

Murphy, Elizabeth. The Developing Child: Using Jungian Type to Understand Children. LC 92-29717. 168p. 1992. pap. 12.95 (0-89106-060-X) Consulting Psychol.

— Effective Writing: Plain English at Work. 176p. (Orig.). 1991. pap. 23.50 (0-273-03482-0, Pub. by Pitman Pub Ltd UK) Trans-Atl Phila.

— There Is a Season. 384p. 1992. 24.95 (0-7472-0336-9, Pub. by Headline UK) Trafalgar.

— To Give & Take All. large type ed. 754p. 1992. 21.95 (0-7505-0099-9) Ulverscroft.

Murphy, Elizabeth R. The Assistant: New Tasks, New Opportunities. LC 81-69370. 191p. reprint ed. pap. 54.50 (0-8357-5811-7, 2023532) Bks Demand.

Murphy, Elspeth C. Barney Wigglesworth & the Birthday Surprise. LC 88-4346. (Little Epistles for Kids Ser.). (Illus.). 32p. (J). (ps-2). 1988. 9.99 (1-55513-696-6, Chariot Bks) Chariot Family.

— Barney Wigglesworth & the Church Flood. LC 88-5008. (Little Epistles for Kids Ser.). (Illus.). 32p. (J). (ps-2). 1988. 9.99 (1-55513-685-0, Chariot Bks) Chariot Family.

— Barney Wigglesworth & the Party That Almost Wasn't. LC 88-4342. (Little Epistles for Kids Ser.). (Illus.). 32p. (J). (ps-2). 1988. 9.99 (1-55513-684-2, Chariot Bks) Chariot Family.

— Barney Wigglesworth & the Smallest Christmas Pageant. LC 88-5009. (Little Epistles for Kids Ser.). (Illus.). 32p. (J). (ps-2). 1989. 9.99 (1-55513-686-9, Chariot Bks) Chariot Family.

— Becky Garcia. LC 86-8877. (Apple Street Church Ser.). 108p. (J). (gr. 3-7). 1986. pap. 4.99 (1-55513-029-1, Chariot Bks) Chariot Family.

— Chalkdust: Prayer Meditations for a Teacher. 1978. 6.99 (0-8010-6065-6) Baker Bk.

— Do You See Me God? LC 88-27445. (Illus.). 32p. (J). (ps). 1989. text ed. 9.99 (1-55513-457-2, Chariot Bks) Chariot Family.

— It's My Birthday, God: Psalm 90. (David & I Talk to God Ser.). (Illus.). (J). (ps-2). 1983. 3.99 (0-89191-580-X, Chariot Bks) Chariot Family.

— Julie Chang. LC 85-27989. (Kids from Apple Street Church Ser.). 107p. (J). (gr. 3-7). 1986. 4.99 (0-89191-720-9, 57208, Chariot Bks) Chariot Family.

— Kids Can Be Wise Too. LC 87-35539. (Proverbs to Grow on Ser.). 24p. (J). (ps-2). 1988. pap. 4.99 (1-55513-893-4, Chariot Bks) Chariot Family.

— Make Way for the King: Psalm 145 & 24. (David & I Talk to God Ser.). (Illus.). (J). (ps-2). 1983. 3.99 (0-89191-581-8, Chariot Bks) Chariot Family.

— Mary Jo Bennett. LC 85-17059. (Kids from Apple Street Church Ser.). 107p. (Orig.). (J). (gr. 3-7). 1985. pap. 4.99 (0-89191-711-X, 57117, Chariot Bks) Chariot Family.

— Le Mystere De l'Idole Muette. 48p. (FRE.). 1990. 2.95 (0-8297-1532-0) Life Pubs Intl.

— Le Mystere Du Cadeau Fantome. 48p. (FRE.). 1991. 2.95 (0-8297-1534-7) Life Pubs Intl.

— Le Mystere Du Deuxieme Plan. 48p. (FRE.). 1991. 2.95 (0-8297-1531-2) Life Pubs Intl.

— Mystere Due Perroquet Bavard. 48p. (FRE.). 1990. 2.95 (0-8297-1533-9) Life Pubs Intl.

— The Mystery of the Carousel Horse. LC 87-16722. (Ten Commandment Mysteries Ser.). (J). (gr. 2-4). 1988. pap. 3.99 (1-55513-163-8, Chariot Bks) Chariot Family.

— The Mystery of the Clumsy Juggler. LC 89-39821. (Beatitudes Mysteries Ser.). 48p. (J). (gr. 2-4). 1991. pap. 3.99 (1-55513-897-7, 38976, Chariot Bks) Chariot Family.

— The Mystery of the Dancing Angels. (Three Cousins Detective Club Ser.: No. 4). 64p. (J). 1995. pap. 3.99 (1-55661-408-X) Bethany Hse.

— The Mystery of the Double Trouble. LC 87-26461. (Ten Commandment Mysteries Ser.). (J). (gr. 2-4). 1988. pap. 3.99 (1-55513-545-5, Chariot Bks) Chariot Family.

— The Mystery of the Gravestone Riddle. LC 87-16721. (Ten Commandment Mysteries Ser.). (J). (gr. 2-4). 1988. pap. 3.99 (1-55513-800-4, Chariot Bks) Chariot Family.

— The Mystery of the Hidden Egg. LC 89-29863. (Beatitudes Mysteries Ser.). 48p. (J). (gr. 2-4). 1991. pap. 3.99 (1-55513-915-9, 39156, Chariot Bks) Chariot Family.

— Mystery of the Hobo's Message. (Three Cousins Detective Club Ser.: No. 5). 64p. (J). 1995. pap. 3.99 (1-55661-409-8) Bethany Hse.

— The Mystery of the Laughing Cat. LC 87-16719. (Ten Commandment Mysteries Ser.). (J). (gr. 2-4). 1988. pap. 3.99 (1-55513-649-4, Chariot Bks) Chariot Family.

— Mystery of the Messed-Up Wedding. LC 87-16720. (Ten Commandment Mysteries Ser.). (J). (gr. 2-4). 1988. pap. 3.99 (1-55513-687-7, Chariot Bks) Chariot Family.

— The Mystery of the Second Map. LC 87-24919. (Ten Commandment Mysteries Ser.). (J). (gr. 2-4). 1988. pap. 3.99 (1-55513-526-9, Chariot Bks) Chariot Family.

— The Mystery of the Silent Idol. LC 87-24285. (Ten Commandment Mysteries Ser.). (J). (gr. 2-4). 1988. pap. 3.99 (1-55513-527-7, Chariot Bks) Chariot Family.

— Mystery of the Silent Nightingale. (Three Cousins Detective Club Ser.). (J). (ps-3). 1994. pap. 2.99 (1-55661-406-3) Bethany Hse.

— The Mystery of the Silver Dolphin. LC 87-24285. (Ten Commandment Mysteries Ser.). (J). (gr. 2-4). 1988. pap. 3.99 (1-55513-515-3, Chariot Bks) Chariot Family.

— Mystery of the Tattletale Parrot. LC 87-26460. (Ten Commandment Mysteries Ser.). (J). (gr. 2-4). 1988. pap. 3.99 (1-55513-528-5, Chariot Bks) Chariot Family.

— The Mystery of the Vanishing Present. LC 87-20852. (Ten Commandment Mysteries Ser.). (J). (gr. 2-4). 1988. pap. 3.99 (1-55513-364-9, Chariot Bks) Chariot Family.

— Mystery of the White Elephant. (Three Cousins Detective Club Ser.). (J). (ps-3). 1994. pap. 2.99 (1-55661-405-5) Bethany Hse.

— Mystery of the Wrong Dog. (Three Cousins Detective Club Ser.). (J). (ps-3). 1994. pap. 2.99 (1-55661-407-1) Bethany Hse.

— Pug McConnell. LC 85-26922. (Kids from Apple Street Church Ser.). 107p. (J). (gr. 3-7). 1986. 4.99 (0-89191-728-4, Chariot Bks) Chariot Family.

— Recess: Prayer Meditations for Teachers. (Orig.). 1988. 6.99 (0-8010-6244-6) Baker Bk.

— Sometimes Everything Feels Just Right. LC 86-2256. (David & I Talk to God Ser.). (Illus.). (J). (ps-2). 1987. pap. 3.99 (1-55513-038-0, Chariot Bks) Chariot Family.

— Sometimes I Get Lonely. LC 80-70251. (David & I Talk to God Ser.). (Illus.). 24p. (J). (ps-2). 1981. pap. 3.99 (0-89191-367-X, 53678, Chariot Bks) Chariot Family.

— Sometimes I Get Mad. LC 81-67739. (David & I Talk to God Ser.). (J). (ps-2). 1981. pap. 3.99 (0-89191-493-5, 54932, Chariot Bks) Chariot Family.

— Sometimes I Get Scared. (David & I Talk to God Ser.). (Illus.). (J). (ps-2). 1980. pap. 3.99 (0-89191-275-4, 52753, Chariot Bks) Chariot Family.

— Sometimes I Have to Cry. (David & I Talk to God Ser.). (Illus.). (J). (ps-2). 1981. pap. 3.99 (0-89191-494-3, 54940, Chariot Bks) Chariot Family.

— Sometimes I Need to Be Hugged. LC 81-67740. (David & I Talk to God Ser.). (Illus.). (J). (ps-2). 1981. pap. 3.99 (0-89191-492-7, 54924, Chariot Bks) Chariot Family.

— Sometimes I'm Good, Sometimes I'm Bad. (David & I Talk to God Ser.). (Illus.). 24p. (J). (ps-2). 1981. pap. 3.99 (0-89191-368-8, 53686, Chariot Bks) Chariot Family.

— What Can I Say to You, God? (David & I Talk to God Ser.). (Illus.). (J). (ps-2). 1980. pap. 3.99 (0-89191-276-2, Chariot Bks) Chariot Family.

Murphy, Elspeth C. & Hanna, Wayne. My First Books About Jesus, 4 bks. Incl. Bk. 1. Jesus Does Good Things. 1981. 2.95 (0-89191-334-3); Bk. 2. Jesus Is God's Son. 1981. 2.95 (0-89191-332-7); Bk. 3. Jesus Loves Children. 1981. 2.95 (0-89191-333-5); Bk. 4. Jesus Tells Us About God. 1981. 2.95 (0-89191-335-1); (Illus.). 1981. write for info. (0-318-51433-8) Cook.

Murphy, Emalee G., ed. see Kleinfeld, Vincent A., et al.

Murphy, Emma, jt. ed. see Niblock, Timothy C.

***Murphy, Emmett C. & Snell, Michael.** Forging the Heroic Organization: A Daring Blueprint for Revitalizing American Business. LC 94-34165. 1994. 22.95 (0-13-100793-9) P-H.

— The Genius of Sitting Bull: Thirteen Heroic Strategies for Today's Business Leaders. LC 92-30240. 1992. 18.95 (0-13-349226-5) P-H.

Murphy, Emmy L. Who Made God. (J). (ps-3). 1978. pap. 2.50 (0-915374-07-2, 07-2) Rapids Christian.

Murphy, Erin, ed. see Eddington, Patrick & Makov, Susan.

Murphy, Erin, ed. see Frederick, Joan.

Murphy, Erin, ed. see Jacka, Lois E.

Murphy, Erin, ed. see Moroney, Lynn.

Murphy, Erin, ed. see Nez, Redwing T.

Murphy, Erin, ed. see Raczek, Linda T.

Murphy, Erin, ed. see Rogers, W. Lane.

Murphy, Erin, ed. see Rossi, Joyce.

Murphy, Erin, ed. see Secakuku, Alph H. & Heard Museum Staff.

Murphy, Erin, ed. see Walker, Judy.

***Murphy, Eslpeth C.** Mystery of the Magi's Treasure. (Three Cousins Detective Club Ser.: No. 6). 64p. (J). 1995. pap. 3.99 (1-55661-410-1) Bethany Hse.

Murphy, Esther. How to Make a Wedding Cake. 2nd rev. ed. Carnes, Del, ed. (Illus.). 1987. pap. 9.95 (0-937016-00-4) Deco-Pr Pub.

— Mrs. Mayo's Book of Creative Foods: A Complete Guide to Fancy Food Decorating Anyone Can Do. rev. ed. Carnes, Del, ed. (Illus.). 176p. (Orig.). 1987. pap. text ed. 6.95 (0-937016-01-2) Deco-Pr Pub.

Murphy, Eva, ed. see Good Grief Program Volunteers Staff.

Murphy, F., jt. auth. see Gijlstra, D. J.

Murphy, F. A., jt. auth. see International Committee on Taxonomy of Viruses.

Murphy, Florence. Sugarless Cookery. 64p. 1978. pap. 3.95 (0-8323-0306-2) Binford Mort.

Murphy, Frances J. Life Is a Symphony. (Illus.). 36p. (Orig.). 1992. pap. 5.00 (1-878149-21-0) Counterpoint Pub.

Murphy, Francis. J. Francis Murphy: The Landscape Within. LC 82-80992. (Illus.). 30p. (Orig.). 1982. pap. 3.25 (0-943651-18-2) Hudson Riv.

Murphy, Francis, ed. Whitman: The Complete Poems. (Poets Ser.). 1977. pap. 12.95 (0-14-042222-6, Penguin Classics) Viking Penguin.

Murphy, Francis, ed. see Bradford, William.

Murphy, Francis C. Regulating Flood-Plain Development. LC 59-16022. (University of Chicago, Department of Geography, Research Paper Ser.: No. 56). 216p. reprint ed. pap. 61.60 (0-7837-0383-X, 2040703) Bks Demand.

Murphy, Francis J. Communists & Catholics in France, 1936-1939: The Politics of the Outstretched Hand. (University of Florida Social Sciences Monographs: No. 76). (Illus.). 168p. 1989. pap. text ed. 17.95 (0-8130-0936-7) U Press Fla.

Murphy, Francis X. The Christian Way of Life. (Fathers of the Church Ser.: Vol. 18). 1986. 15.95 (0-8146-5358-8); pap. 11.95 (0-8146-5329-4) Liturgical Pr.

***Murphy, Frank J.** A Cold Clear Day: The Athletic Biography of Buddy Edelen. 2nd ed. LC 91-9113. (Illus.). 200p. (Orig.). 1995. pap. 11.95 (0-614-06930-0) Wind Sprint.

Murphy, Fred. Radio-Controlled Action Cars. (Photo-Fact Book). (Illus.). 24p. (Orig.). (J). 1990. pap. 2.50 (0-942025-87-3) Kidsbks.

Murphy, Frederick J. Bilingual Homilies for Feast Days & Other Occasions. LC 91-40302. 96p. (Orig.). 1992. pap. 4.95 (0-8189-0622-7) Alba.

— Pseudo-Philo: Rewriting the Bible. LC 92-44041. 1993. 49.95 (0-19-507622-2) OUP.

— Religious World of Jesus. LC 90-21922. 1991. pap. 21.95 (0-687-36049-8) Abingdon.

— The Structure & Meaning of Second Baruch. (C). 1985. 23.95 (0-89130-844-X, 06-01-78); pap. 15.95 (0-89130-845-8) Scholars Pr GA.

Murphy, G. Ovid: Metamorphoses XI. 144p. 1979. reprint ed. 15.95 (0-906515-40-8, Pub. by Brstl Class Pr UK) Focus Info Gr.

Murphy, G. I., jt. ed. see Pauly, D.

Murphy, G. J. Transport & Distribution. 200p. 1972. 32.00 (0-8464-1437-6) Beekman Pubs.

Murphy, G. P., ed. Transplantation in Primates. (Primates in Medicine Ser.: Vol. 7). 1972. 47.25 (3-8055-1408-5) S Karger.

Murphy, G. P. & Oelschlager, H., eds. Fosfestrol, HONVANr, ST 52r, HONVOLr, A Review of New Pharmacokinetic & Clinical Data. (Journal: Urologia Internationalis: Vol. 42, Suppl., 1988). iv, 60p. 1988. 19.25 (3-8055-4903-2) S Karger.

Murphy, G. Ronald. Brecht & the Bible: A Study of Religious Nihilism & Human Weakness in Brecht's Plays. LC 80-20207. (Germanic Languages & Literatures Ser.: No. 96). xi, 107p. 1980. 17.50 (0-8078-8096-5) U of NC Pr.

— The Saxon Savior: The Germanic Transformation of the Gospel in the Ninth-Century Heliand. 144p. (C). 1995. pap. text ed. 13.95 (0-19-509720-3) OUP.

Murphy, G. Ronald, tr. The Heliand: The Saxon Gospel. 248p. (C). 1992. pap. 15.95 (0-19-507376-2) OUP.

Murphy, G. W., tr. see Schmalenbach, Eugen.

Murphy, Gael, ed. Directory of Foodservice Distribution, 1992. 852p. 1992. pap. 249.00 (0-86730-564-9, CSG Info Servs) Lebhar Friedman.

— Directory of Wholesale Grocers, 1993. 672p. 1992. pap. 260.00 (0-86730-578-9, CSG Info Servs) Lebhar Friedman.

Murphy, Gardner & Dale, Laura A. Challenge of Psychical Research: A Primer of Parapsychology. LC 78-31335. (World Perspectives Ser.: Vol. 26). (Illus.). 297p. 1979. reprint ed. text ed. 59.75 (0-313-20944-8, MUCP, Greenwood Pr) Greenwood.

Murphy, Gardner & Kuhlen, Raymond G. Psychological Needs of Adults: A Symposium. (Notes & Essays on Education for Adults Ser.: 12). 27p. reprint ed. pap. 25.00 (0-317-08265-5, 2000410) Bks Demand.

Murphy, Gene, jt. auth. see Lawson, Robert.

Murphy, George. Dermatopathology. LC 94-6843. (Illus.). 480p. 1995. text ed. 125.00 (0-7216-2418-9) Saunders.

Murphy, George, ed. Tendril, No. 14-15. 256p. 1983. pap. 5.95 (0-937504-03-3) Tendril.

— Tendril, No. 16. 182p. 1983. pap. 5.95 (0-937504-04-1) Tendril.

— Tendril, No. 17. 212p. 1984. pap. 5.95 (0-937504-05-X) Tendril.

— Tendril, Nos. 19-20. 440p. 1985. pap. 10.95 (0-937504-07-6) Tendril.

Murphy, George, jt. auth. see Zimmerman, Oscar G.

***Murphy, George E.** It Didn't Happen on My Watch. LC 95-68646. Date not set. 19.95 (1-884570-31-3) Research Triangle.

— Rounding Ballast Key. 1987. 5.50 (0-935331-01-8) Ampersand RI.

— Suicide in Alcoholism. (Monographs in Psychiatry: No. 1). 304p. 1992. 49.95 (0-19-507153-0) OUP.

Murphy, George E., Jr., ed. The Poet's Choice: One Hundred American Poets' Favorite Poems. 176p. 1980. 12.95 (0-937504-01-7); pap. 5.95 (0-937504-00-9) Tendril.

***Murphy, George F. & Hurtzberg, Arlene.** Atlas of Dermatopathology. LC 95-1014. (Illus.). 312p. 1995. text ed. write for info. (0-7216-4886-X) Saunders.

Murphy, George J. The Evolution of Canadian Corporate Reporting Practices, 1900-1970. Brief, Richard P., ed. (Foundations of Accounting Ser.: No. 13). 240p. 1988. 15.00 (0-8240-6119-5) Garland.

Murphy, George J., ed. A History of Canadian Accounting Thought & Practice. LC 93-9763. (New Works in Accounting History). 664p. 1993. reprint ed. 97.00 (0-8153-1248-2) Garland.

Murphy, George L. The Trademark of God. LC 86-5402. 138p. (Orig.). 1986. pap. 6.95 (0-8192-1382-9) Morehouse Pub.

Murphy, George M., ed. see AEC Technical Information Center Staff.

Murphy, Gerald. Copper Mandarina: A Memoir. 144p. 1984. 34.00 (0-7212-0674-3, Pub. by Regency Press) St Mut.

Murphy, Gerald, jt. auth. see Stewart, Rick.

***Murphy, Gerald P., et al, eds.** American Cancer Society Textbook of Clinical Oncology. 2nd ed. LC 95-132. 1995. write for info. (0-944235-10-7) Am Cancer NY.

Murphy, Gerard. Managing Persons with Mental Disabilities: A Curriculum Guide for Police Trainers. 91p. (Orig.). (C). 1989. pap. text ed. 10.00 (1-878734-13-X) Police Exec Res.

— Special Care: Improving the Police Response to the Mentally Disabled. LC 85-62557. (Illus.). 292p. (Orig.). (C). 1986. pap. text ed. 15.00 (1-878734-16-4) Police Exec Res.

Murphy, Gerard J. C-Algebras & Operator Theory. 286p. (C). 1990. text ed. 54.95 (0-12-511360-9) Acad Pr.

Murphy, Geri. Underwater Photography Camera Basics Equipment Care. Shreeves, Karl et al, eds. (Underwater Photography Ser.). (Illus.). 87p. (Orig.). 1989. pap. text ed. 9.95 (1-878663-03-8) PADI.

— Underwater Photography Macro. Hurrell, Mary E. et al, eds. (Underwater Photography Ser.). (Illus.). 59p. (Orig.). 1990. pap. text ed. 12.95 (1-878663-04-6) PADI.

Murphy, Gladys N., ed. see Murphy, Dennis G.

Murphy, Glenn, et al. Engineering Analogies. LC 63-16671. (Illus.). 256p. 1963. pap. 14.95 (0-8138-2225-4) Iowa St U Pr.

Murphy, Gloria. Bloodties. LC 86-46383. 252p. 1987. 17.95 (1-55611-036-7) D I Fine.

— Down Will Come Baby. 1991. 18.95 (1-55611-196-7) D I Fine.

— Down Will Come Baby. 288p. 1993. mass mkt. 4.99 (0-515-11098-1) Jove Pubns.

— Nightshade. LC 86-82116. 256p. 1987. 16.95 (1-55611-004-9) D I Fine.

— The Playroom. LC 87-45108. 256p. 1988. 17.95 (1-55611-043-X) D I Fine.

— A Shadow on the Stair. 400p. 1993. pap. 4.99 (0-451-17716-9, Sig) NAL-Dutton.

— Simon Says. 416p. (Orig.). 1994. pap. 4.99 (0-451-18140-9) NAL-Dutton.

— A Stranger in the House. 416p. 1995. pap. 5.99 (0-451-18586-2, Sig) NAL-Dutton.

— A Whisper in the Attic. 352p. 1992. 4.99 (0-451-17315-5, Sig) NAL-Dutton.

Murphy, H., jt. auth. see Crosling, G.

Murphy, Hank. Assembler for COBOL Programmers: MVS, VM. (Ranade IBM Ser.). 1991. text ed. 40.00 (0-07-044129-4) McGraw.

— MVS Control Blocks. 1994. text ed. 59.00 (0-07-044309-2) McGraw.

Murphy, Harold. Murphy Moments. LC 87-92229. (Illus.). 127p. (Orig.). 1988. pap. 6.00 (0-9620017-7-5) H Murphy.

Murphy, Harry J., ed. see California State University at Northridge, Office of Disabled Student Services Staff.

Murphy, Haughton. Murder for Lunch. large type ed. 1990. 21.95 (0-7089-2225-2) Ulverscroft.

— Murder Keeps a Secret. 240p. 1990. mass mkt. 4.99 (0-449-21788-4, Crest) Fawcett.

— Murder Takes a Partner. large type ed. 1990. 21.95 (0-7089-2158-2) Ulverscroft.

— Murder Takes a Partner. 288p. 1987. reprint ed. pap. 3.50 (0-449-21434-6) Fawcett.

— Murders & Acquisitions. 1989. pap. 3.95 (0-449-21643-8) Fawcett.

— A Very Venetian Murder. 1993. mass mkt. 4.50 (0-449-22066-4, Crest) Fawcett.

Murphy, Helen M. & Reilly, James R. Marriages in the Roman Catholic Diocese of Tuam, Ireland, 1821-1829. x, 192p. (Orig.). 1993. pap. text ed. 28.50 (1-55613-812-1) Heritage Bk.

Murphy, Henry C. Voyage of Verrazzano. LC 72-126244. (Select Bibliographies Reprint Ser.). 1977. 25.95 (0-8369-5471-8) Ayer.

Murphy, Henry C., ed. Anthology of New Netherland or Translations from Early Dutch Poetry of New York. 1972. reprint ed. 12.00 (0-8422-8101-0); reprint ed. pap. text ed. 6.50 (0-8290-0651-6) Irvington.

Murphy, Henry T., jt. auth. see Kerker, Ann E.

Murphy, Herta A. & Hildebrandt, Herbert W. Effective Business Communications. 4th ed. 1984. Instr's. manual. teacher ed write for info. (0-07-044092-1) McGraw.

— Effective Business Communications. 6th ed. 880p. 1991. text ed. write for info. (0-07-044157-X) McGraw.

Murphy, J. Feelings. (Illus.). 24p. (J). (ps-8). 1985. pap. 4.95 (0-88753-129-6, Pub. by Black Moss Pr CN) Firefly Bks Ltd.

Murphy, J., jt. auth. see Stern, Robert A.

Murphy, J., jt. auth. see Swan, A.

An Asterisk (*) at the beginning of an entry indicates that the title is appearing in BIP for the first time.

***Murphy, J. A.** Ireland in the Twentieth Century. 180p. 1975. 9.95 (*0-8159-5832-3*) Devin.

Murphy, J. Austin. Research Solutions to the Financial Problems of Depository Institutions. LC 91-47641. 168p. 1992. text ed. 55.00 (*0-89930-705-1*, MRX, Quorum Bks) Greenwood.

Murphy, J. C., jt. auth. see Rubottom, Richard R.

Murphy, J. C., et al, eds. Photoacoustic & Photothermal Phenomena II. (Optical Sciences Ser.: Vol. 62). (Illus.). 544p. 1990. 83.00 (*0-387-52367-7*) Spr-Verlag.

***Murphy, J. David.** Plunder & Preservation: Cultural Property Law & Practice in the People's Republic of China. (Illus.). 280p. 1996. 59.00 (*0-19-586874-9*) OUP.

Murphy, J. F. Pictorial History of New Earswick. (C). 1988. 58.00 (*0-685-37105-0*, Pub. by W Sessions UK) St Mut.

— Pictorial History of New Earswick: Illustrating Daily Life in the Model Village Near York During the Past 80 Years. (C). 1988. 39.95 (*1-85072-098-3*, Pub. by W Sessions UK) St Mut.

Murphy, J. F., ed. Pictorial History of New Earswick. (C). 1990. 65.00 (*0-685-37379-7*, Pub. by W Sessions UK) St Mut.

Murphy, J. L., jt. auth. see Harnett, Donald L.

Murphy, J. M., ed. Branding: A Key Marketing Tool. 272p. 1987. text ed. 24.95 (*0-07-044055-7*) McGraw.

Murphy, J. M. & Turnbull, F. G. Power Semiconductor Control of AC Motor Drives. (Illus.). 220p. 1988. 222.00 (*0-08-022683-3*, CRC Reprint) Franklin.

Murphy, J. P., ed. see Avienus, Lucius Festus.

Murphy, J. P., jt. ed. see Stalker, H. T.

Murphy, J. Palmer & Murphy, Margaret. Paterson & Passaic County: An Illustrated History. LC 87-13262. 216p. 1987. 24.95 (*0-89781-203-4*) Preferred Mktg.

Murphy, J. Patrick. Visions & Values in Catholic Higher Education. LC 90-64033. 256p. (Orig.). (C). 1991. pap. 14.95 (*1-55612-421-X*) Sheed & Ward MO.

Murphy, J. W., jt. ed. see Pardech, J. T.

Murphy, J. W., jt. auth. see Pardeck, J. T.

Murphy, J. W., et al, eds. Fungal Infections & Immune Responses. (Infectious Agents & Pathogenesis Ser.). (Illus.). 550p. 1993. 110.00 (*0-306-44075-X*, Plenum Pr) Plenum.

Murphy, Jack. History of the U. S. Marines. 1987. 14.98 (*0-671-06982-9*) S&S Trade.

Murphy, Jack, jt. auth. see Murphy, Wendy.

Murphy, Jacqueline S., jt. ed. see Goeliner, Ellen W.

Murphy, Jacquelyn, ed. Photo Directory of the United States Catholic Hierarchy. (Illus.). (Orig.). 1993. pap. 19.95 (*0-685-67865-2*, 7001) Our Sunday Visitor.

Murphy, James. Laws, Courts, & Lawyers: Through the Years in Arizona. LC 79-89656. 261p. reprint ed. pap. 74.40 (*0-317-26800-7*, 2024320) Bks Demand.

Murphy, James, tr. see Planck, Max K.

Murphy, James, tr. see Planck, Max.

Murphy, James B. The Moral Economy of Labor: Aristotelian Themes in Economic Theory. LC 92-45689. 256p. 1993. 25.00 (*0-300-05406-8*) Yale U Pr.

Murphy, James B. & Armstrong, Barry L. Maintenance of Rattlesnakes in Captivity. (Special Publication Ser.: No.3). (Illus.). 40p. 1978. pap. 3.00 (*0-89338-006-7*) U of KS Mus Nat Hist.

Murphy, James B. & Collins, Joseph T. A Review of the Diseases & Treatments of Captive Turtles. LC 82-73100. pap. text ed. 16.00 (*0-685-19240-7*) Meseraule Prnting.

Murphy, James B., jt. auth. see Armstrong, Barry L.

Murphy, James F., et al. Leisure Service Delivery System: A Modern Perspective. LC 73-7851. (Health Education, Physical Education, & Recreation Ser.). 224p. reprint ed. pap. 63.90 (*0-317-26692-6*, 2056004) Bks Demand.

Murphy, James F. Miracle of Mind Dynamics. 1972. pap. text ed. 8.95 (*0-13-585398-2*, Reward) P-H.

— The Proletarian Moment: The Controversy over Leftism in Literature. 240p. 1991. 27.50 (*0-252-01788-9*) U of Ill Pr.

Murphy, James F. & Howard, Dennis R. Delivery of Community Leisure Services: A Holistic Approach. LC 76-41372. 227p. reprint ed. pap. 64.70 (*0-317-26690-X*, 2056003) Bks Demand.

Murphy, James F., et al. Leisure Systems: Critical Concepts & Applications. LC 91-60386. 400p. 1991. 37.95 (*0-915611-17-1*) Sagamore Pub.

Murphy, James J. Medieval Rhetoric: A Select Bibliography. 2nd ed. (Medieval Bibliographies Ser.). 80p. 1989. text ed. 37.50 (*0-8020-5750-0*); pap. text ed. 18.95 (*0-8020-6659-3*) U of Toronto Pr.

— Rhetoric in the Middle Ages: A History of Rhetorical Theory from Saint Augustine to the Renaissance. 1974. 60.00 (*0-520-02439-7*); pap. 15.00 (*0-520-04406-1*) U CA Pr.

Murphy, James J., ed. Arguments in Rhetoric Against Quintilian: Translation & Text of Peter Ramus's Rhetoricae Distinctiones in Quintilianum. LC 85-15462. 235p. 1986. 27.00 (*0-87580-113-7*) N Ill U Pr.

— Demosthenes' on the Crown: A Critical Case Study of a Masterpiece of Ancient Oratory. Keaney, John J., tr. 209p. (Orig.). (C). 1983. reprint ed. pap. text ed. 9.50 (*0-9611800-1-3*) Hermagoras Pr.

— Quintilian on the Teaching of Speaking & Writing: Translations from Books One, Two, & Ten of the Institutio Oratoria. LC 87-4655. (Landmarks in Rhetoric & Public Address Ser.). 200p. 1987. text ed. 19.95 (*0-8093-1377-4*); pap. text ed. 12.95 (*0-8093-1378-2*) S Ill U Pr.

— A Short History of Writing Instruction from Ancient Greece to Twentieth-Century America. (Illus.). vi, 241p. (Orig.). (C). 1990. text ed. 19.50 (*0-9611800-7-2*); pap. text ed. 9.95 (*0-9611800-6-4*) Hermagoras Pr.

— Three Medieval Rhetorical Arts. LC 72-132416. 1971. pap. 15.00 (*0-520-05632-9*) U CA Pr.

Murphy, James J., ed. see Byron, William J., et al.

Murphy, James J., et al. The Rhetorical Tradition & Modern Writing. LC 82-2103. vii, 149p. 1982. 37.50 (*0-87352-097-1*); pap. 19.75 (*0-87352-098-X*) Modern Lang.

— A Synoptic History of Classical Rhetoric. 2nd ed. 336p. (C). 1995. pap. text ed. 17.95 (*1-880393-19-0*) Hermagoras Pr.

Murphy, James L. An Archaeological History of the Hocking Valley. rev. ed. LC 73-92906. (Illus.). 390p. (C). 1989. pap. 21.95 (*0-8214-0920-4*) Ohio U Pr.

Murphy, James L., jt. auth. see Harnett, Donald L.

Murphy, James S. The Condom Industry in the United States. LC 90-52637. (Illus.). 174p. 1990. lib. bdg. 32.50x (*0-89950-533-3*) McFarland & Co.

Murphy, James T. Skip Bombing in Rabaul Harbor. LC 92-43434. 200p. 1993. text ed. 45.00 (*0-275-94540-5*, C4540, Praeger Pubs) Greenwood.

Murphy, Jamie. What Every Parent Should Know about Childhood Immunization. White, Carol, ed. 192p. (Orig.). 1993. pap. 13.95 (*0-9630373-0-7*) Earth Healing.

Murphy, Jane. My Pet Tyrannosaurus. LC 88-81468. (Illus.). 32p. (Orig.). (J). (ps-2). 1988. pap. 8.95 (*0-937124-17-6*) Kimbo Educ.

Murphy, Jay. For Palestine. 1992. pap. 12.00 (*0-86316-092-1*) Writers & Readers.

Murphy, Jeannette, et al, eds. Dialogues & Debates in Social Psychology. 368p. 1985. pap. 19.95 (*0-86377-020-7*) L Erlbaum Assocs.

Murphy, Jeffrey G. Kant: The Philosophy of Right. LC 94-4605. 1994. 20.00 (*0-86554-441-7*); pap. 14.00 (*0-86554-443-3*) Mercer Univ Pr.

Murphy, Jeffrie & Hampton, Jean. Forgiveness & Mercy. (Studies in Philosophy & Law). 208p. (C). 1990. pap. 14.95 (*0-521-39567-4*) Cambridge U Pr.

Murphy, Jeffrie G. Evolution, Morality & the Meaning of Life. LC 82-9782. (Philosophy & Society Ser.). 170p. 1982. 34.50 (*0-8476-7147-X*) Rowman.

— Punishment & Rehabilitation. 3rd ed. LC 94-11228. 313p. 1995. pap. 19.95 (*0-534-24600-1*) Intl Thomson.

— Retribution, Justice & Therapy. 1979. lib. bdg. 65.50 (*90-277-0998-X*); pap. text ed. 32.50 (*90-277-0999-8*) Kluwer Ac.

— Retribution Reconsidered: More Essays in the Philosophy of Law. LC 92-16624. (Philosophical Studies in Philosophy Ser.: Vol. 54). 244p. (C). 1992. lib. bdg. 87.50 (*0-7923-1815-3*) Kluwer Ac.

Murphy, Jeffrie G., ed. Punishment & Rehabilitation. 2nd ed. 233p. (C). 1985. pap. 18.95 (*0-534-04614-2*) Intl Thomson.

Murphy, Jeffrie G. & Coleman, Jules L. Philosophy of Law: An Introduction to Jurisprudence. 2nd rev. ed. 240p. (C). 1989. pap. text ed. 21.50 (*0-8133-0848-8*) Westview.

Murphy, Jenny & Welch, Wayne. Turning Global Competition into Local Economic Development. Poole, Kenneth, ed. 30p. (Orig.). 1990. pap. 19.00 (*0-317-04870-8*) Natl Coun Econ Dev.

Murphy, Jenny, ed. see Anderson, Eric.

Murphy, Jenny, ed. see Bartsch, Charles.

Murphy, Jenny, ed. see Boyle, M. Ross.

Murphy, Jenny, ed. see Breagy, James.

Murphy, Jenny, jt. auth. see Breagy, James.

Murphy, Jenny, ed. see Dobson, Eric.

Murphy, Jenny, ed. see Eilers, Sarah.

Murphy, Jenny, ed. see Gillen, Lori.

Murphy, Jenny, ed. see Gregerman, Alan.

Murphy, Jenny, ed. see Grossman, Howard.

Murphy, Jenny, ed. see Mayer, Virginia.

Murphy, Jenny, ed. see McClean, Mary.

Murphy, Jenny, ed. see McCrea, Nancy.

Murphy, Jenny, ed. see Patrylick, Carol.

Murphy, Jenny, ed. see Poole, Kenneth.

Murphy, Jenny, ed. see Purcell, Mia.

Murphy, Jenny, ed. see Tompros, Jody.

Murphy, Jenny, ed. see Unger, James.

Murphy, Jenny, ed. see Welch, Wayne.

Murphy, Jerome T. State Leadership in Education: On Being a Chief State School Officer. 144p. 1980. 12.00 (*0-318-03017-9*); pap. 7.00 (*0-318-03018-7*) Inst Educ Lead.

Murphy, Jerre C. The Comical History of Montana: A Serious Story for Free People... McCurry, Dan C. & Rubenstein, Richard E., eds. LC 74-30644. (American Farmers & the Rise of Agribusiness Ser.). 1975. reprint ed. 33.95 (*0-405-06814-X*) Ayer.

Murphy, Jill. Bad Spell for the Worst Witch. (J). (gr. 4-7). 1991. pap. 3.95 (*0-14-031446-6*, Puffin) Puffin Bks.

— A Bad Spell for the Worst Witch. large type ed. (Illus.). (J). 1993. 16.95 (*0-7451-1809-7*, Galaxy Child Lrg Print) Chivers N Amer.

— Five Minutes' Peace: Miniature Edition. (Illus.). 32p. (J). (ps-3). 1989. 4.95 (*0-399-21938-2*, Putnam) Putnam Pub Group.

— Jeffrey Strangeways. LC 91-71844. (Illus.). 144p. (J). (gr. 3-6). 1992. 14.95 (*1-56402-018-5*) Candlewick Pr.

— Jeffrey Strangeways. LC 91-71844. (Illus.). 144p. (J). (gr. 3-6). 1994. pap. 4.50 (*1-56402-283-8*) Candlewick Pr.

— The Last Noo-Noo. LC 94-48927. 1995. 14.95 (*1-56402-581-0*) Candlewick Pr.

— Peace at Last. LC 80-66743. (Pied Piper Bks.). (Illus.). 32p. (J). (ps-2). 1982. pap. 3.95 (*0-8037-6964-4*) Dial Bks Young.

— A Quiet Night In. LC 93-875. (Illus.). 32p. (J). (ps up). 1994. 12.95 (*1-56402-248-X*) Candlewick Pr.

— What Next, Baby Bear! LC 83-7316. (Pied Piper Bks.). (Illus.). 32p. (J). (ps-2). 1986. pap. 3.95 (*0-685-37306-1*) Dial Bks Young.

— What Next, Baby Bear! LC 83-7316. (Illus.). 32p. (J). (ps-3). 1992. pap. 17.99 (*0-14-054539-5*, Puff Pied Piper) Puffin Bks.

— The Worst Witch. (Illus.). 80p. (J). (gr. 3-7). 1982. pap. 2.50 (*0-380-60665-8*, Camelot) Avon.

— The Worst Witch at Sea. LC 95-10319. (Illus.). (J). 1995. write for info. (*1-56402-421-0*) Candlewick Pr.

— The Worst Witch Strikes Again. 80p. (J). (gr. 3-7). 1982. pap. 2.50 (*0-380-60673-9*, Camelot) Avon.

Murphy, Jim. Across America on an Emigrant Train. LC 92-38650. 160p. (J). 1993. 16.95 (*0-395-63390-7*, Clarion Bks) HM.

— Backyard Bear. LC 92-15479. (Illus.). 32p. (J). (gr. k-3). 1993. 15.95 (*0-590-44375-5*) Scholastic Inc.

— The Boys' War: Confederate & Union Soldiers Talk about the Civil War. (Illus.). 128p. (J). (gr. 4-9). 1990. 15.95 (*0-89919-893-7*, Clarion Bks) HM.

— The Boys' War: Confederate & Union Soldiers Talk about the Civil War. (Illus.). 128p. (J). (gr. 4-7). 1993. pap. 7.95 (*0-395-66412-8*, Clarion Bks) HM.

— The Call of the Wolves. (J). (ps-3). 1994. pap. 4.95 (*0-590-41940-4*) Scholastic Inc.

— Dinosaur for a Day. (Illus.). (J). 1992. 15.95 (*0-590-42866-7*, Scholastic Hardcover) Scholastic Inc.

— The Great Fire. LC 94-9963. (J). 1995. 16.95 (*0-590-47267-4*) Scholastic Inc.

— Guess Again: More Weird & Wacky Inventions. LC 85-24320. (Illus.). 64p. (J). (gr. 3-6). 1986. text ed. 13.95 (*0-02-767720-6*, Bradbury S&S) S&S Childrens.

— Into the Deep Forest. LC 94-11791. (J). 1995. 14.95 (*0-395-60522-9*, Clarion Bks) HM.

— The Last Dinosaur. LC 87-3008. (Illus.). 32p. (J). (gr. 1-3). 1988. pap. 14.95 (*0-590-41097-0*, Scholastic Hardcover) Scholastic Inc.

— The Last Dinosaur. (Illus.). (J). 1991. pap. 3.95 (*0-590-44875-7*, Blue Ribbon Bks) Scholastic Inc.

— The Long Road to Gettysburg. (Illus.). 128p. (J). (gr. 4-7). 1992. 15.95 (*0-395-55965-0*, Clarion Bks) HM.

— Managing Conflict at Work. LC 93-11509. (Business Skills Express Ser.). 112p. 1993. pap. 10.00 (*1-55623-890-8*) Irwin Prof Pubng.

— Managing Conflict at Work. LC 94-72157. (Illus.). 80p. (Orig.). 1994. per., pap. 9.95 (*1-884926-25-8*) Amer Media.

— Napoleon Lajoic: Modern Baseball's First Superstar. 1988. (Illus.). 88p. 1988. pap. 8.00 (*0-910137-31-5*) Soc Am Baseball Res.

— Night Terrors. LC 92-27102. 1993. 13.95 (*0-590-45341-6*) Scholastic Inc.

— Night Terrors. (YA). 1994. pap. 3.50 (*0-590-45342-4*) Scholastic Inc.

— Sanctions. (Adelphi Papers). 1995. pap. 23.00 (*0-19-828057-2*) OUP.

— A Young Patriot: The American Revolution As Experienced by One Boy. LC 93-38789. (J). 1995. write for info. (*0-395-60523-7*, Clarion Bks) HM.

Murphy, Jim & Murphy, Carolyn. How to Defeat Demons: An International Manual. LC 91-77501. (Illus.). 224p. (Orig.). 1992. pap. 8.95 (*0-9624398-7-8*) Abel II Pub.

Murphy, Jo. Keys to Fitness over Fifty. 1991. pap. 5.95 (*0-8120-4514-9*) Barron.

— Keys to Nutrition over Fifty. (Retirement Keys Ser.). 160p. 1991. pap. 5.95 (*0-8120-4512-2*) Barron.

***Murphy, Joel.** How to Care for Your Pet Bird: Practical Advice from Dr. Joel Murphy. 336p. Date not set. 65.00 (*0-9643838-0-2*); pap. 45.00 (*0-9643838-1-0*) MABH Pubng.

***Murphy, Joelle.** Quick, Go Peek! 2nd ed. (Let Me Read, Level 3, Ser.). (Illus.). (J). 1995. bds. 2.95 (*0-673-36273-6*) GdYrBks.

Murphy, John. A Cheyenne Moon. large type ed. (Western Ser.). 208p. 1994. pap. 14.95 (*0-7089-7583-6*, Trailtree Bookshop) Ulverscroft.

— Dorset at War: Nineteen Thirty-Nine to Nineteen Forty-Five. 300p. 1988. 40.00 (*0-686-75654-1*) Dorset Pr.

— Harvest of Fear: A History of Australia's Vietnam War. 335p. (C). 1993. pap. text ed. 24.95 (*0-8133-2039-9*) Westview.

— Irish Shopfronts. (Illus.). 96p. 1981. pap. 8.95 (*0-86281-448-0*, Pub. by Appletree Pr IE) Irish Bks Media.

— A Little Irish Cookbook. (Illus.). 60p. 1986. 7.95 (*0-87701-400-0*) Chronicle Bks.

Murphy, John & Rowe, Michael. How to Design Trademarks & Logos. (Illus.). 144p. 1991. pap. 19.95 (*0-89134-400-4*, 30335) North Light Bks.

Murphy, John & Schiller, Jeffry. Transforming America's Schools: An Administrators' Call to Action. LC 92-21020. 319p. 1992. text ed. 32.95 (*0-8126-9203-9*) Open Court.

— Transforming America's Schools: An Administrators' Call to Action. LC 92-21020. 319p. 1995. pap. text ed. 17.95 (*0-8126-9255-1*) Open Court.

Murphy, John, jt. ed. see Fletcher, Pauline.

Murphy, John, jt. auth. see Longino, Charles.

Murphy, John, jt. auth. see Murphy, Ann.

Murphy, John D. Azerbaijani Newspaper Reader. LC 93-71726. 113p. 1993. text ed. 42.00 (*1-881265-01-3*); audio 5.00 (*1-881265-04-8*) Dunwoody Pr.

— Luganda-English Dictionary. 651p. 1972. 75.00 (*0-7859-3733-1*, M591) Fr & Eur.

Murphy, John D. & Somay, Metin. Turkish Newspaper Reader. LC 88-70934. 330p. 1988. text ed. 44.00 (*0-931745-35-7*); audio 15.00 (*0-931745-44-6*) Dunwoody Pr.

Murphy, John D., ed. see Feghali, Habaka J.

Murphy, John D., jt. auth. see Sowhagyalakshmi Vaidyanathan.

Murphy, John E., intro. Clinical Pharmacokinetics: Pocket Reference. (Illus.). 400p. (Orig.). 1993. pap. 30.00 (*1-879907-31-3*) Am Soc Hlth-Syst.

Murphy, John E., jt. ed. see Moore, John A., Jr.

Murphy, John F. Legal Aspects of International Terrorism: Summary Report of an International Conference, No. 19. (Studies in Transnational Legal Policy). 80p. 1980. 4.00 (*0-318-13186-2*) Am Soc Intl Law.

— Punishing International Terrorists: The Legal Framework for Policy Initiatives. LC 85-15845. 152p. 1985. 43.00 (*0-8476-7449-5*) Rowman.

— The United Nations & the Control of International Violence: A Legal & Political Analysis. LC 81-69989. 224p. 1983. text ed. 48.25 (*0-86598-079-9*) Rowman.

Murphy, John H. & Cunningham, Isabella C. Advertising & Marketing Communication Management. LC 92-43667. 528p. (C). 1993. text ed. 49.00 (*0-03-051069-4*) Dryden Pr.

— Instructor's Manual to Accompany Advertising & Marketing Communication Management. 275p. (C). 1994. pap. text ed. 28.00 (*0-03-097021-0*) Dryden Pr.

***Murphy, John J.** Agent of Change: Leading a Cultural Revolution. 265p. (Orig.). 1994. pap. 12.00 (*0-9639013-1-1*) Venture Mgmt.

— Intermarket Technical Analysis: Trading Strategies for the Global Stock, Bond, Commodity & Currency Markets. (Finance Editions Ser.). 282p. 1991. text ed. 55.00 (*0-471-52433-6*) Wiley.

— My Antonia: The Road Home. (Masterwork Studies: No. 31). 136p. (C). 1989. text ed. 21.95 (*0-8057-7986-8*, MWS-31, Twayne); pap. 12.95 (*0-8057-8035-1*, Twayne) Macmillan.

— Pulling Together: The Power of Teamwork. 200p. 1993. pap. 12.00 (*0-9639013-0-3*) Venture Mgmt.

— Technical Analysis of the Futures Markets: A Comprehensive Guide to Trading Methods & Applications. 1986. 49.95 (*0-13-898008-X*) NY Inst Finance.

— Technical Analysis of the Futures Markets: Study Guide. LC 87-10991. (Illus.). 160p. (Orig.). 1987. pap. text ed. 27.95 (*0-13-858747-7*) NY Inst Finance.

Murphy, John J., ed. Critical Essays on Willa Cather. (Critical Essays on American Literature Ser.). 344p. (C). 1984. text ed. 45.00 (*0-8161-8676-6*) G K Hall.

Murphy, John L. Darkness & Devils: Exorcism & King Lear. LC 83-22055. xii, 267p. 1984. 26.95 (*0-8214-0732-5*) Ohio U Pr.

Murphy, John M. Brand Strategy. 208p. 1990. pap. text ed. 69.00 (*0-13-084161-7*) P-H.

— Confederate Carbines & Musketoons. (Illus.). 224p. 1986. 45.00 (*0-9616425-0-5*); 125.00 (*0-9616425-1-3*) J M Murphy.

Murphy, John M. & Madaus, Howard M. Confederate Rifles & Muskets. LC 92-75534. 700p. Date not set. 99.95 (*1-882824-01-6*) Graphic Pubs.

Murphy, John P. Pragmatism: From Peirce to Davidson. 152p. (C). 1990. pap. text ed. 17.95 (*0-8133-7810-9*) Westview.

Murphy, John P., ed. Jesuit Latin Poets of the Seventeenth & Eighteenth Centuries: An Anthology of Neo-Latin Poetry. Mertz, James J., tr. LC 88-62698. (Illus.). 200p. (Orig.). (ENG & LAT.). (C). 1989. text ed. 39.00 (*0-86516-214-X*); pap. 24.00 (*0-86516-215-8*) Bolchazy-Carducci.

***Murphy, John S. & Hudson, Frederic M.** The Joy of Old: A Guide to Successful Elderhood. LC 96-94012. (Illus.). 160p. (Orig.). 1995. pap. 16.95 (*1-886851-44-1*) Geode Pr.

Murphy, John V. The Dark Angel: Gothic Elements in Shelley's Works. LC 73-8304. 199p. 1975. 32.50 (*0-8387-1407-2*) Bucknell U Pr.

Murphy, John W. Postmodern Social Analysis & Criticism. LC 88-35774. (Contributions in Sociology Ser.: No. 79). 185p. 1989. text ed. 45.00 (*0-313-26683-2*, MMS/, Greenwood Pr) Greenwood.

Murphy, John W. & Dison, Jack E., eds. Are Prisons Any Better: Twenty Years of Correctional Reform. (Criminal Justice System Annuals Ser.: Vol. 26). (Illus.). 240p. (C). 1990. 49.95 (*0-8039-3569-2*); pap. 24.00 (*0-8039-3570-6*) Sage.

Murphy, John W. & Pardeck, John T. The Computerization of Human Service Agencies: A Critical Appraisal. LC 90-22750. 184p. 1991. text ed. 45.00 (*0-86569-023-5*, T023, Auburn Hse) Greenwood.

Murphy, John W. & Pardeck, John T., eds. Technology & Human Productivity: Challenges for the Future. LC 85-23237. 256p. 1986. text ed. 55.00 (*0-89930-194-0*, PTH/, Quorum Bks) Greenwood.

Murphy, John W. & Peck, Dennis L., eds. Open Institutions: The Hope for Democracy. LC 92-20048. 224p. 1992. text ed. 55.00 (*0-275-94028-4*, C4028, Praeger Pubs) Greenwood.

Murphy, John W., jt. auth. see Choi, Jung M.

Murphy, John W., jt. auth. see Vega, William A.

Murphy, John W., et al, eds. The Underside of High-Tech: Technology & the Deformation of Human Sensibilities. LC 85-27265. (Contributions in Sociology Ser.: No. 59). 226p. 1986. text ed. 55.00 (*0-313-24612-2*, Greenwood Pr) Greenwood.

Murphy, Jonne. Handbook of Radio Advertising. LC 79-8395. 252p. reprint ed. pap. 71.90 (*0-317-55806-4*, 2029388) Bks Demand.

Murphy, Joseph. The Amazing Laws of Cosmic Mind Power. 1989. 6.95 (*0-13-023888-0*) P-H.

— Collected Essays of Joseph Murphy. LC 87-70783. (Mentors of New Thought Ser.). 192p. (Orig.). 1987. pap. 8.95 (*0-87516-592-3*) DeVorss.

— The Cosmic Power Within You. 203p. 1988. pap. 7.95 (*0-13-179128-1*) P-H.

— Cosmic Power Within You. 1986. 5.95 (*0-13-179176-1*, Reward) P-H.

— Great Bible Truths for Human Problems. 1976. pap. text ed. 8.00 (*0-87516-214-2*) DeVorss.

— How to Attract Money. 13th ed. 75p. 1975. reprint ed. pap. 3.50 (*0-87516-204-5*) DeVorss.

M

— How to Pray with a Deck of Cards. 1958. pap. 1.50 (0-87516-335-1) DeVorss.

— How to Use the Laws of Mind. LC 80-68548. 271p. 1981. pap. 9.50 (0-87516-426-9) DeVorss.

— How to Use Your Healing Power. 158p. 1973. reprint ed. pap. 7.50 (0-87516-186-3) DeVorss.

— The Landscape of Leadership Preparation: Reframing the Education of School Administrators. 272p. 1993. 42.95 (0-8039-6027-1); pap. 21.95 (0-8039-6028-X) Corwin Pr.

— Living Without Strain. 157p. 1973. pap. 7.50 (0-87516-187-1) DeVorss.

— Miracle Power for Infinite Riches. 1974. pap. 6.95 (0-13-585612-4, Parker Publishing Co) P-H.

— Peace Within Yourself. 300p. 1972. pap. 9.00 (0-87516-188-X) DeVorss.

— The Power of the Subconscious. 1982. mass mkt. 5.99 (0-553-27043-5) Bantam.

— The Power of Your Subconscious Mind. 224p. 1988. 6.95 (0-13-687972-1) P-H.

— Power of Your Subconscious Mind. 1963. pap. 5.95 (0-685-03917-X, Reward) P-H.

— Pray Your Way Through It. 171p. 1973. pap. 7.50 (0-87516-190-1) DeVorss.

— Prayer Is the Answer. 190p. 1973. pap. 7.50 (0-87516-189-8) DeVorss.

— Quiet Moments with God. 1958. pap. 4.50 (0-87516-276-2) DeVorss.

— Restructuring Schools: Capturing & Assessing the Phenomena. 144p. (C). 1991. text ed. 35.95 (0-8077-3112-9); pap. text ed. 16.95 (0-8077-3111-0) Tchrs Coll.

— Secrets of the I Ching. 1989. pap. 7.95 (0-13-798083-3) P-H.

— Songs of God. LC 79-52353. (Orig.). 1979. pap. 8.00 (0-87516-379-3) DeVorss.

— Special Meditations for Health, Wealth, Love. 1952. pap. 2.50 (0-87516-336-X) DeVorss.

— Telepsychics: The Magic Power of Perfect Living. LC 73-6775. 230p. 1988. reprint ed. pap. 11.00 (0-87516-598-2) DeVorss.

— These Truths Can Change Your Life. 280p. 1982. pap. 8.50 (0-87516-476-5) DeVorss.

— Windows. 1985. pap. 20.95 (0-8384-1302-1) Heinle & Heinle.

— Within You Is the Power. LC 77-86026. 1978. pap. 8.50 (0-87516-247-9) DeVorss.

— Your Infinite Power to Be Rich. 1968. pap. text ed. 8.95 (0-13-979591-X, Reward) P-H.

Murphy, Joseph, ed. The Educational Reform Movement of the 1980s: Perspectives & Cases. LC 89-63476. 364p. (C). 1990. 33.50 (0-8211-1261-9); text ed. write for info. (0-685-45504-1) McCutchan.

*Murphy, Joseph & Beck, Lynn G. School-Based Management As School Reform: Taking Stock. (Illus.). 248p. 1995. 46.95 (0-8039-6175-8); pap. 23.95 (0-8039-6176-6) Corwin Pr.

Murphy, Joseph & Hallinger, Philip. Restructuring Schooling: Learning from Ongoing Efforts. 296p. 1993. 46.95 (0-8039-6060-3); pap. 23.95 (0-8039-6061-1) Corwin Pr.

Murphy, Joseph & Hallinger, Philip, eds. Approaches to Administrative Training in Education. LC 86-14579. (Educational Leadership Ser.). 291p. 1987. 64.50 (0-88706-433-7); pap. 24.95 (0-88706-434-5) State U NY Pr.

Murphy, Joseph & Louis, Karen S., eds. Reshaping the Principalship: Insights from Transformational Reform Efforts. 312p. 1994. 46.95 (0-8039-6079-4); pap. 23.95 (0-8039-6080-8) Corwin Pr.

Murphy, Joseph, jt. auth. see Beck, Lynn G.

Murphy, Joseph E. Stock Market Probability: Using Statistics to Predict & Optimize Investment Outcomes. rev. ed. 1994. 37.50 (1-55738-564-5) Probus Pub Co.

Murphy, Joseph E., jt. ed. see Sigler, Jay A.

*Murphy, Joseph F., Jr. Maryland Evidence Handbook. 2nd ed. 1009p. 1993. 90.00 (1-55834-124-2) Michie Butterworth.

Murphy, Joseph H. Murphy's Will Clauses: Annotations & Forms with Tax Effects, 4 vols. 1960. Updates. ring bd. write for info. (0-8205-1441-1) Bender.

Murphy, Joseph M. Santeria: African Spirits in America. LC 92-8590. 224p. 1993. pap. 14.00 (0-8070-1021-9) Beacon Pr.

— Santeria: An African Religion in America. 1989. pap. 10.95 (0-942272-22-6) Original Pubns.

— Working the Spirit: Ceremonies of the African Diaspora. LC 93-3929. 288p. 1993. 25.00 (0-8070-1220-3) Beacon Pr.

— Working the Spirit: Ceremonies of the African Diaspora. LC 93-3929. 280p. 1994. pap. 14.00 (0-8070-1221-1) Beacon Pr.

Murphy, Joseph P. But, Daddy, Did You See Shoshoni? Pebbles, Rocks, & Steppingstones. 256p. 1991. pap. 17.95 (0-9631361-0-0) An Tostal Pr.

Murphy, Joseph P., jt. auth. see Rumney, Jay.

Murphy, Joseph P., jt. auth. see Sigler, Jay A.

Murphy, Joseph S., II. Deck Officer Study Guide, 5 vols., Set. 1000p. (C). 1990. teacher ed 85.00 (0-685-38551-5); pap. 125.00 (0-685-38550-7) Academy Pub.

— Deck Officer Study Guide, 5 vols., Set. 2nd ed. 1000p. (C). 1990. lib. bdg. 85.00 (0-9625393-0-9) Academy Pub.

— Deck Officer Study Guide, Vol. 1: Deck General. 2nd ed. 200p. (C). 1990. lib. bdg. write for info. (0-9625393-1-7) Academy Pub.

— Deck Officer Study Guide, Vol. 2: Navigation General. 2nd ed. 175p. (C). 1990. lib. bdg. write for info. (0-9625393-2-5) Academy Pub.

— Deck Officer Study Guide, Vol. 3: Deck Safety. 2nd ed. 250p. (C). 1990. lib. bdg. write for info. (0-9625393-3-3) Academy Pub.

— Deck Officer Study Guide, Vol. 4: Rules of the Road. 2nd ed. 175p. (C). 1990. lib. bdg. write for info. (0-9625393-4-1) Academy Pub.

— Deck Officer Study Guide, Vol. 5: Navigation Problems. 2nd ed. 300p. (C). 1990. lib. bdg. write for info. (0-9625393-5-X) Academy Pub.

Murphy, Joseph S., II, ed. Deck Officer Study Guide. 800p. (C). 1989. teacher ed 85.00 (0-685-32261-0); pap. 125.00 (0-685-32260-2) Academy Pub.

*Murphy, Josette & Marchant, Tim J. Monitoring & Evaluation in Extension Agencies. (Technical Paper Ser.: No. 79). 96p. (FRE.). 1988. 7.95 (0-614-02821-3, 11079) World Bank.

— Monitoring & Evaluation in Extension Agencies: World Bank Technical Paper, No. 79. (Monitoring & Evaluation Ser.). 96p. 1988. 7.95 (0-8213-1000-3, 11000) World Bank.

Murphy, Josette, et al. Estimations des Agriculteurs Comme Source de Donnees Sur la Production. (Technical Paper Ser.: No. 132). 80p. (FRE.). 1991. French. 7.95 (0-8213-2068-8, 12068) World Bank.

*Murphy, Josette L. Gender Issues in World Bank Lending. LC 95-6965. (Operations Evaluation Study Ser.). 146p. 1995. 9.95 (0-8213-3213-9, 13213) World Bank.

Murphy, Judith A. Preparation of Biological Specimens for Scanning Electron Microscopy. Roomans, Godfried M., ed. (Illus.). 352p. (Orig.). (C). 1984. pap. text ed. 32.00 (0-931288-33-9) Scanning Microscopy.

Murphy, Judith A., jt. auth. see Burke, Laura J.

Murphy, Judy, jt. ed. see Burke, Laura.

Murphy, Judy, ed. see Zaleski, Karol.

Murphy-Judy, Kathy, tr. see Zumthor, Paul.

Murphy, Julia, jt. auth. see Murphy, Roy.

*Murphy, Julien S. AIDS, Reproductive Technology, & Ethics. 160p. (C). 1995. text ed. 44.50x (0-7914-2517-7); pap. text ed. 14.95 (0-7914-2518-5) State U NY Pr.

*Murphy, K. J., et al, eds. The Ecology of Loch Lomond. LC 94-34275. (Developments in Hydrobiology Ser.: Vol. 101). 1994. lib. bdg. 144.00 (0-7923-3168-0) Kluwer Ac.

Murphy, Kathleen, jt. ed. see Alward, Edgar C.

Murphy, Kathleen, ed. see Brogan, Isabel.

Murphy, Kathleen E., tr. see Bellarmino, Roberto F.

Murphy, Kay. The Autopsy. 64p. 1985. pap. 3.95 (0-933180-78-0) Spoon Riv Poetry.

Murphy, Kenneth. Andre Malraux: Man's Fate, Man's Hope. 680p. 1993. 29.95 (0-02-922319-9) Free Pr.

— Conceived in Liberty: The Rise & Transformation of Modern Conservatism. 350p. 1994. text ed. 22.95 (0-02-922317-2) Free Pr.

— Retreat from the Finland Station: Moral Odysseys in the Breakdown of Communism. 288p. 1992. text ed. 27.95 (0-02-922315-6) Free Pr.

Murphy, Kenneth H., jt. auth. see Feinstein, Irwin K.

Murphy, Kevin. Honesty in the Workplace. LC 92-13136. 180p. (C). 1993. pap. 23.95 (0-534-15492-1) Brooks-Cole.

— Training Your Parrot. (Illus.). 192p. 1983. 19.95 (0-87666-872-4, H-1056) TFH Pubns.

*Murphy, Kevin & LeVert, Suzanne. Out of the Fog: Treatment Options & Coping Strategies for Adult Attention Deficit Disorder. 320p. 1995. pap. 12.95 (0-7868-8087-2) Hyperion.

Murphy, Kevin, jt. contrib. see Moore, James.

Murphy, Kevin D. & Giffen, Sarah L., eds. A Noble & Dignified Stream: The Piscataqua River Region in the Colonial Revival, 1860-1930. 272p. 1992. 50.00 (0-9631955-0-6) Old York Hist Soc.

Murphy, Kevin E. Concepts in Federal Taxation: 1995 Edition. Leyh, ed. LC 93-40131. 450p. (C). 1994. text ed. 61.50 (0-314-02595-2) West Pub.

— Concepts in Federal Taxation: 1995 Edition. LC 93-47062. 766p. 1994. text ed. 63.00 (0-314-03653-9) West Pub.

Murphy, Kevin J. Back-to-Basics Management: Business Philosophies That Build a Proud & Successful Company. (Back-To-Basics Ser.: No. 1). 64p. 1993. pap. 6.95 (1-879501-10-4) Effect Listen Inst.

— Back-to-Basics Selling: Responsive Actions That Show Customers You Care about Their Business. (Back-To-Basics Ser.: No. 2). 64p. 1993. pap. 6.95 (1-879501-05-8) Effect Listen Inst.

— Effective Listening: How to Profit by Tuning into the Idea. 2nd rev. ed. 220p. reprint ed. 21.95 (1-879501-02-3) Effect Listen Inst.

— How to Keep Employees & Customers Faithful to Your Company. (Back-to-Basics Loyalty Ser.). 64p. 1993. pap. 6.95 (1-879501-16-3) Effect Listen Inst.

— How to Minimize Conflicts & Confusion by Hearing What Is Really Being Said. (Back-to-Basics Listening Ser.). 64p. 1993. pap. 6.95 (1-879501-14-7) Effect Listen Inst.

— Profit Builders. (Back-To-Basics Ser.). (Orig.). (C). 1993. pap. 22.95 (1-879501-17-1) Effect Listen Inst.

— See Spot Run: How to Profit by Tuning into the Ideas & Suggestions of Others. 208p. 1992. 18.95 (1-879501-01-5) Effect Listen Inst.

Murphy, Kevin J., jt. auth. see Pieterse, Arnold H.

*Murphy, Kevin R. & Cleveland, Jeanette. Understanding Performance Appraisal: Social, Organizational, & Goal-Based Perspectives. 500p. 1995. text ed. 55.00 (0-8039-5474-3); pap. text ed. 27.95 (0-8039-5475-1) Sage.

Murphy, Kevin R. & Cleveland, Jeannette N. Performance Appraisal: An Organizational Perspective. 300p. 1990. pap. text ed. 44.00 (0-205-12343-0, H23435) Allyn.

Murphy, Kevin R. & Davidshofer, Charles O. Psychological Testing: Principles & Applications. 3rd ed. LC 92-41594. 1993. text ed. write for info. (0-13-226994-5) P-H.

Murphy, Kevin R. & Saal, Frank E., eds. Psychology in Organizations: Integrating Science & Practice. 304p. (C). 1990. text ed. 39.95 (0-8058-0477-3) L Erlbaum Assocs.

Murphy, Kristin, ed. Who's Who in Foreign Trade. 150p. 1995. pap. 25.00 (0-318-14134-5) Foreign Trade.

Murphy, L. M., ed. Solar Engineering, 1983. 632p. 1983. pap. text ed. 25.00 (0-317-02649-6, H00253) ASME.

Murphy, L. S., et al, eds. Moving up the Yield Curve: Advances & Obstacles. (Illus.). 103p. 1980. pap. 5.50 (0-89118-064-8) Am Soc Agron.

Murphy, Lamar R. Enter the Physician: The Transformation of Domestic Medicine, 1760-1860. 336p. 1991. 38.95 (0-8173-0514-9) U of Ala Pr.

Murphy, Larry G., et al, eds. Encyclopedia of African-American Religions. LC 93-7224. (Religious Information Systems Ser.: Vol. 9). 1008p. 1993. 125.00 (0-8153-0500-1, SS721) Garland.

Murphy, Laura, jt. auth. see Murphy, Michael.

Murphy, Lawrence R. The American University in Cairo, 1919-1986. (Illus.). 256p. 1987. 50.00 (977-424-156-8, Pub. by Am Univ Cairo Pr UA) Col U Pr.

— Anti-Slavery in the Southwest. Antone, E. H., ed. (Southwestern Studies: No. 54). (Illus.). 55p. 1978. pap. text ed. 10.00 (0-87404-112-0) Tex Western.

— Frontier Crusader - William F. M. Arny. LC 73-184712. 313p. 1972. pap. 5.95 (0-8165-0390-7) U of Ariz Pr.

— Lucien Bonaparte Maxwell: The Napoleon of the Southwest. LC 82-40454. (Illus.). 280p. 1983. 28.95 (0-8061-1807-5) U of Okla Pr.

— Philmont: A History of New Mexico's Cimarron Country. 2nd ed. LC 72-76828. (Illus.). 283p. 1972. pap. 11.95 (0-8263-0244-0) U of NM Pr.

Murphy, Lawrence R., ed. Perverts by Official Order: The Campaign Against Homosexuals by the United States Navy. LC 90-4451. (Journal of Homosexuality: No. 1). (Illus.). 340p. 1988. text ed. 49.95 (0-86656-708-9) Haworth Pr.

Murphy, Lawrence R., ed. & intro. Perverts by Official Order: The Campaign Against Homosexuals by the United States Navy. LC 87-33452. (Journal of Homosexuality Ser.: No. 1). (Illus.). 340p. 1988. pap. text ed. 14.95 (0-918393-44-2) Harrington Pk.

Murphy, Lawrence R. & Schoenborn, Theodore F., eds. Stress Management in Work Settings. LC 88-32439. 183p. 1989. text ed. 49.95 (0-275-93271-0, C3271, Praeger Pubs) Greenwood.

— Stress Management in Work Settings. 198p. 1987. per. 9.50 (0-16-002528-1, S/N 017-033-00428-5) USGPO.

Murphy, Lawrence R., jt. ed. see Rocco, Thomas M.

Murphy, Leona S. Using the Power of Prayer. 143p. (Orig.). 1987. pap. 5.95 (0-937580-06-6) LeSEA Pub Co.

Murphy, Leonard J. The History of Urology. (Illus.). 548p. 1972. 86.95x (0-398-02366-2) C C Thomas.

Murphy, Lester F. Indiana Medical Malpractice. LC 87-82668. 1991. 115.00 (0-318-33008-3) Lawyers Cooperative.

— Indiana Medical Malpractice, Suppl. 1992. LC 87-82668. 1991. 55.00 (0-318-33009-1) Lawyers Cooperative.

Murphy, Linda U., jt. ed. see Impara, James C.

Murphy, Linda U., et al, eds. Tests in Print No. IV, 2 vols., Set. 1473p. (C). 1994. text ed. 325.00 (0-910674-53-1) Buros Inst Mental.

Murphy, Linnea S. Mrs. Murphy's Swedish Cook Book. (Illus.). 156p. 1987. 12.98 (0-9618520-0-3) J & L Pub.

Murphy, Lois. Story Clay. (Illus.). 8p. (J). (gr. 1-8). 1990. pap. write for info. (0-9620672-0-2) Dragon Studio.

Murphy, Lois B. On Coping & Change. 17p. (Orig.). pap. 2.50 (0-918374-19-7) City Coll Wk.

Murphy, Lois B. & Moriarty, Alice E. Vulnerability, Coping, & Growth: From Infancy to Adolescence. LC 75-2772. 484p. reprint ed. pap. 138.00 (0-7837-5303-9, 2080316) Bks Demand.

Murphy, Lorraine. The Prize. 192p. (J). (gr. 8). 1993. pap. text ed. 7.95 (1-883511-02-X) Veritas Pr CA.

Murphy, Lorraine M., jt. auth. see Farrell, James P.

Murphy, Louise S. The Marriage Triangle: Man, Woman & God. 66p. (Orig.). 1984. pap. text ed. 1.95 (0-937580-40-6) LeSEA Pub Co.

— A Teenager Who Dared Obey God. 97p. (Orig.). (YA). 1985. pap. text ed. 3.95 (0-937580-44-9) LeSEA Pub Co.

Murphy, Lula K. Thoughts on Culture. LC 86-50664. 65p. 1986. 5.95 (1-55523-021-0) Winston-Derek.

*Murphy, Lyle. Lyle Murphy's System of Horizontal Composition Based on Equal Intervals, 2 bks. in 1, Set. Mitacek, Lynn, ed. (Illus.). 107p. (C). 1993. pap. text ed. 24.95 (1-882597-00-1) E I S Pubns.

Murphy, Lyle P. Good News for Every Catholic. LC 90-85848. 1991. pap. 1.95 (0-89636-302-3, MB 332) Accent CO.

Murphy, M. Father of the Submarine. (C). 1986. text ed. 140.00 (0-685-38779-8, Pub. by Maritime Bks UK) St Mut.

— Guidelines in Art. (C). 1989. 70.00 (0-685-37697-4, Pub. by S Thornes Pubs UK) St Mut.

Murphy, M., jt. auth. see Harrison, T.

Murphy, M., jt. auth. see Schmid, Michael.

Murphy, M. Gertrude. St. Basil & Monasticism. LC 70-144661. reprint ed. 29.50 (0-404-04543-X) AMS Pr.

Murphy, M. M. Understanding Phrasal Verbs. (C). 1983. 55.00 (0-7175-1011-5, Pub. by S Thornes Pubs UK) St Mut.

Murphy, Mabel A. When America Was Young. LC 72-38326. (Biography Index Reprint Ser.). (Illus.). 1977. reprint ed. 22.95 (0-8369-8126-X) Ayer.

Murphy, Madeline W. Madeline Murphy Speaks. LC 88-63313. (Illus.). 388p. (Orig.). 1988. pap. 15.95 (0-935132-12-0) C H Fairfax.

Murphy Manning, Maryann & Manning, Gary L. Improving Spelling in the Middle Grades. 2nd ed. 48p. 1986. 7.95 (0-8106-1695-5) NEA.

Murphy, Marcy. The Managerial Competencies of Twelve Corporate Librarians: A Validation Study of New Directions in Library & Information Science Education. LC 88-138233. (SLA Research Ser.: No. 2). 43p. reprint ed. pap. 25.00 (0-7837-6300-X, 2046015) Bks Demand.

Murphy, Marcy & Johns, Claude J. Handbook of Library Regulations. LC 76-19994. (Books in Library & Information Science: No. 20). 176p. reprint ed. pap. 50.20 (0-318-35007-6, 2030867) Bks Demand.

Murphy, Marcy, jt. auth. see Jobin, Pamela.

Murphy, Margaret, jt. auth. see Murphy, J. Palmer.

Murphy, Margaret, ed. see Session, Irie L.

Murphy, Margaret D. The Boston Globe Cookbook: A Collection of Classic New England Specialties. 3rd ed. LC 90-39525. (Illus.). 336p. 1990. pap. 15.95 (0-87106-535-5) Globe Pequot.

— A Cape Cod Seafood Cookbook. (Illus.). 172p. 1985. 14.95 (0-940160-30-7) Parnassus Imprints.

— Farberware Convection Turbo-Oven Cookbook. LC 78-72950. (Illus.). 144p. 1980. 10.95 (0-318-33059-8) Dorison Hse.

— Hamilton Beach Food Processor Cookery. LC 78-72950. (Illus.). 144p. 1978. 9.95 (0-318-33058-X) Dorison Hse.

Murphy, Margaret M., jt. auth. see Dreyfus, Daniel A.

Murphy, Marge. Monsters. 11p. (J). (gr. 1). 1989. pap. text ed. 2.50 (1-882225-07-4) Tott Pubns.

— Work. 9p. (J). (gr. 1). 1988. pap. text ed. 2.50 (1-882225-08-2) Tott Pubns.

Murphy, Margueritte S. A Tradition of Subversion: The Prose Poem in English from Wilde to Ashbery. LC 91-40282. 264p. (C). 1992. lib. bdg. 27.50 (0-87023-781-0) U of Mass Pr.

Murphy, Marie. Authorizing Fictions: Jose Donoso's "Casa de Campo" (Monografias Ser.: No. A 152). 160p. (C). 1992. text ed. 63.00 (1-85566-020-2, Pub. by Tamesis Bks Ltd UK) Boydell & Brewer.

— Betrayed in Paradise. Robertson, Jon, ed. 240p. 1995. pap. 14.95 (0-87604-345-7, 417) ARE Pr.

Murphy, Marie A., jt. auth. see Schechter, Leslie F.

Murphy, Marilyn. Are You Girls Traveling Alone? Adventures in Lesbianic Logic. 235p. (Orig.). 1991. pap. 10.95 (1-878533-03-7) Clothespin Fever Pr.

Murphy, Marion F., jt. auth. see Murphy, Raymond E.

Murphy, Marjorie. Blackboard Unions: The AFT & the NEA, 1900-1980. LC 89-46175. (Illus.). 304p. 1991. 35.00 (0-8014-2365-1) Cornell U Pr.

— Blackboard Unions: The AFT & the NEA, 1900-1980. LC 89-46175. (Illus.). 304p. 1992. pap. 14.95 (0-8014-8076-0) Cornell U Pr.

Murphy, Marjorie M., jt. ed. see Forsten, D. I.

Murphy, Mark C., jt. auth. see Solomon, Robert C.

Murphy, Marsha A. Secrets of Making A's the Easy SpeedLearning Way: Powerful Learning Tools & Study Techniques Revealed. LC 92-75555. (Illus.). (Orig.). (YA). 1993. Incl. audio tape. pap. 39.95 (0-9635508-0-2) DataQuest VA.

Murphy, Martha W. The Bed & Breakfast Cookbook: Great American B & Bs & Their Recipes from All Fifty States. (Illus.). 288p. 1991. 35.00 (0-88045-046-0) Stemmer Hse.

— How to Start & Operate Your Own Bed-&-Breakfast: Down-to-Earth Advice from an Award-Winning B&B Owner. LC 93-37836. (Illus.). 1994. pap. 14.95 (0-8050-2903-6) H Holt & Co.

Murphy, Martin. Blanco White: Self-Banished Spaniard. LC 88-26139. 152p. (C). 1989. text ed. 37.00 (0-300-04458-5) Yale U Pr.

Murphy, Martin F. Dominican Sugar Plantations: Production & Foreign Labor Integration. LC 90-44147. 200p. 1991. text ed. 55.00 (0-275-93113-7, C3113, Praeger Pubs) Greenwood.

*Murphy, Martin F. & Margolis, Maxine L., eds. Science, Materialism & the Study of Culture. (Illus.). 256p. (C). 1995. lib. bdg. 49.95 (0-8130-1413-1) U Press Fla.

Murphy, Martin J., Jr., ed. Blood Cell Growth Factors: Their Present & Future Use in Hematology & Oncology. 225p. (C). 1991. pap. text ed. 89.00 (1-880854-00-7) AlphaMed Pr.

— Concise Reviews in Clinical & Experimental Hematology. LC 92-17634. 1992. 60.00 (1-880854-01-5) AlphaMed Pr.

— Polyfunctionality of Hemopoietic Regulators: The Metcalf Forum. (Illus.). 325p. (C). 1994. text ed. 145.00 (1-880854-19-8) AlphaMed Pr.

— Polyfunctionality of Hemopoietic Regulators: The Metcalf Forum. (Illus.). 325p. (C). 1994. pap. text ed. 99.00 (1-880854-20-1) AlphaMed Pr.

Murphy-Martin, Mary. Planning Your Cosmetology Career. LC 93-28878. 1993. pap. text ed. 17.20 (0-13-605999-6) P-H.

Murphy, Marvin L. & Bone, Roger C., eds. Cor Pulmonale in Chronic Bronchitis & Emphysema. LC 84-80453. (Illus.). 296p. 1984. 37.50 (0-87993-226-0) Futura Pub.

Murphy, Mary. Empowered for Worship. (C). 1988. 39.00 (0-85439-123-1, Pub. by St Paul Pubns UK) St Mut.

— Mary Had a Baby. Amen! 16p. (Orig.). (J). (ps-8). 1991. pap. text ed. 14.95 (0-89243-339-6); pap. text ed. 1.00 (0-89243-340-X) Liguori Pubns.

— The Way We Feel Inside: With the Song "How I'm Made" (Illus.). 48p. (J). (gr. k-4). 1990. pap. 9.00 (0-89486-618-4) Hazelden.

Murphy, Mary K., ed. Building Bridges: Fund Raising for Deans, Faculty, & Development Officers. 131p. 1992. pap. 37.00 (0-89964-291-8) Coun Adv & Supp Ed.

— Cultivating Foundation Support for Education. 210p. 1989. 37.00 (0-89964-263-2) Coun Adv & Supp Ed.

Murphy, Mary-Kate & Knoll, Jean. International Adoption: Sensitive Advice for Prospective Parents. LC 93-41422. 192p. (Orig.). 1994. pap. 12.95 (1-55652-211-8) Chicago Review.

An Asterisk (*) at the beginning of an entry indicates that the title is appearing in BIP for the first time.

Murphy, Mary L. Barnaby: The Struggle of a Word Blind Child. 74p. 1968. pap. 1.95 (*0-85225-535-7*) Ed Solutions.

— Creative Writing: A Log-Book of Teaching 1st Graders. (Illus.). 104p. 1966. 6.35 (*0-87825-254-1*) Ed Solutions.

— Douglas Can't Read. 52p. 1968. pap. 1.95 (*0-85225-531-4*) Ed Solutions.

— To Perceive & to Write. 144p. 1970. pap. 4.35 (*0-85225-536-5*) Ed Solutions.

Murphy, Matthew F. & O'Connor, John C. Betraying the Bishops: How the Pastoral Letter on War & Peace Is Being Taught. LC 87-32932. 146p. (Orig.). (C). 1988. lib. bdg. 33.50 (*0-89633-121-0*); pap. text ed. 14.25 (*0-89633-122-9*) Ethics & Public Policy.

Murphy, Maud K., tr. see Warcollier, Rene.

Murphy, Maureen, jt. ed. see Ben-Merre, Diana A.

Murphy, Maureen O. & MacKillop, James, eds. Irish Literature: A Reader. (Irish Studies). 288p. (Orig.). 1987. pap. text ed. 24.95 (*0-8156-2405-0*) Syracuse U Pr.

Murphy, May. For the Good of Others. 16.95 (*0-318-03970-2*); pap. 10.95 (*0-318-03971-0*) U Wisc-River Falls Pr.

***Murphy, Melvin E.** Desire: The Emotional Appetite for Success. Starks, Carol et al, eds. LC 95-94334. (Illus.). 180p. (YA). 1995. 20.00 (*0-9646799-0-6*) M Murphy.

***Murphy, Merilene.** Under Peace Rising No. A1. 64p. 1995. pap. write for info. (*0-934172-38-2*) Win Pubns.

***Murphy, Merilene M.** A Book of Cards, 4 vols., Set. (Illus.). (Orig.). 1995. pap. text ed. 19.95 (*0-9644606-5-3*) Telepoetics.

— A Book of Cards, Vol. 2. (Illus.). (Orig.). 1995. pap. text ed. 7.50 (*0-9644606-7-X*) Telepoetics.

— A Book of Cards, Vol. 3. (Illus.). (Orig.). 1995. pap. text ed. 7.50 (*0-9644606-8-8*) Telepoetics.

— A Book of Cards Vol. 1. (Illus.). (Orig.). 1995. pap. text ed. 7.50 (*0-9644606-6-1*) Telepoetics.

— Just People-Just People: Here You Are: A Multimedia Poetic Odyssey. (Illus.). 64p. (Orig.). (FRE & SPA.). (C). 1995. 19.95 (*0-9644606-1-0*); pap. 9.95 (*0-9644606-2-9*); vhs 19.95 (*0-9644606-4-5*); cd-rom 15. 95 (*0-9644606-3-7*) Telepoetics.

***Murphy, Merilene M. & Moreta, Andes.** A Book of Cards. (Illus.). (Orig.). 1995. pap. text ed. 7.50 (*0-9644606-9-6*) Telepoetics.

Murphy, Michael. The Appalachian Dulcimer Book. LC 75-35427. (Illus.). 110p. 1976. pap. 8.95 (*0-916454-01-0*) Folksay Pr.

— The Appalachian Dulcimer Book. (Illus.). 102p. 1987. pap. 14.95 (*0-8256-2677-3*, AM41278) Music Sales.

— The Future of the Body: Explorations into the Further Evolution of Human Nature. 800p. 1992. 30.00 (*0-87477-686-4*) J P Tarcher.

— The Future of the Body: Explorations into the Further Evolution of Human Nature. 800p. 1993. pap. 17.95 (*0-87477-730-5*, J P T-Putnam) Putnam Pub Group.

— Future of the Body: Explorations into the Further Evolution of Human Nature. 800p. 1993. pap. 17.95 (*0-685-74799-9*) J P Tarcher.

— Golf in the Kingdom. 202p. 1993. 15.95 (*0-914178-95-4*) Golf Digest.

— Golf in the Kingdom. 224p. 1972. 19.95 (*0-670-34529-6*, Arkana) Viking Penguin.

— Golf in the Kingdom. 224p. 1992. pap. 11.00 (*0-14-019450-9*, Arkana) Viking Penguin.

— My Brother Sam Is Dead - Study Guide. Friedland, Joyce & Kessler, Rikki, eds. (Novel-Ties Ser.). (YA). (gr. 5-8). 1993. pap. text ed. 15.95 (*0-88122-119-8*) Lrn Links.

— Names of Ireland. (International Library of Names). 250p. text ed. write for info. (*0-8290-1286-9*) Irvington.

— Working Together in Child Protection: An Exploration of the Multi-Disciplinary Task & System. 1995. 59.95 (*1-85742-197-3*); pap. 21.95 (*1-85742-198-1*, Pub. by Ashgate UK) Ashgate Pub Co.

Murphy, Michael, ed. Geoffrey Chaucer: The Canterbury Tales: The General Prologue & Twelve Major Tales in Modern Spelling. 414p. (Orig.). (C). 1991. lib. bdg. 55.75 (*0-8191-8148-X*) U Pr of Amer.

Murphy, Michael & Donovan, Steven. The Physical & Psychological Effects of Meditation: A Review of Contemporary Meditation Research with a Comprehensive Bibliography, 1931-1988. 187p. (Orig.). (C). 1988. pap. 17.95 (*0-9621232-0-X*) Esalen Inst.

***Murphy, Michael & Murphy, Laura.** Guide to Vacation Rentals in Europe: Villas, Apartments, Cottages, Chalets, Farmhouses, & Condos. LC 94-23035. (Illus.). 336p. 1994. pap. 14.95 (*1-56440-493-5*) Globe Pequot.

Murphy, Michael & White, Rhea. Psychic Side of Sports. (Illus.). 1978. 10.95 (*0-201-04728-4*) Addison-Wesley.

***Murphy, Michael & White, Rhea A.** Transcendent Experience in Sports. LC 94-44134. 288p. 1995. pap. 11. 95 (*0-14-019492-4*, Arkana) Viking Penguin.

Murphy, Michael, jt. auth. see Leonard, George.

Murphy, Michael, jt. ed. see Murphy, Christine.

Murphy, Michael A. & Matti, Jonathan C. Lower Devonian Conodonts (Hesperius-Kindlei Zones), Central Nevada. LC 82-8638. (University of California Publications in Social Welfare: No. 123). (Illus.). 97p. reprint ed. pap. 27.70 (*0-8357-6863-5*, 2035561) Bks Demand.

Murphy, Michael C. How to Buy a Home While You Can Still Afford To. exp. rev. ed. LC 88-34927. 160p. 1989. pap. 8.95 (*0-8069-6974-1*) Sterling.

— How to Buy a Home While You Can Still Afford To. rev. ed. 160p. (C). 1989. reprint ed. lib. bdg. 27.00x (*0-8095-7534-5*) Borgo Pr.

— How to Sell Your Home in Good or Bad Times. LC 91-22130. (Illus.). 160p. 1991. pap. 8.95 (*0-8069-7366-8*) Sterling.

Murphy, Michael J. Cambridge Newspapers & Opinion, 1780-1850. (Cambridge Town, Gown & County Ser.: Vol. 12). (Illus.). 1977. 21.95 (*0-900891-15-7*) Oleander Pr.

— The Mountain Biking Guide to Vail, Colorado. Giuiland, Mary E., ed. & illus. by. 72p. (Orig.). 1990. pap. text ed. 8.95 (*0-9626114-0-9*) M Murphy & Assocs.

— Mountain Year. 73p. 1987. pap. 8.95 (*0-85640-382-2*, Pub. by Blackstaff Pr IE); pap. 5.95 (*0-685-25951-X*, Pub. by Blackstaff Pr IE) Dufour.

— Mountain Year: Life on the Slopes of Slieve Gullion. LC 64-25512. 1964. 12.95 (*0-8023-1079-6*) Dufour.

— My Man Jack: Bawdy Tales from Irish Folklore. 126p. 1989. pap. 8.95 (*0-86322-104-1*) Irish Bks Media.

— Poverty in Cambridgeshire. (Cambridge Town, Gown & County Ser.: Vol. 23). (Illus.). 1978. pap. 4.95 (*0-900891-29-7*) Oleander Pr.

***Murphy, Michael P. & O'Neill, Luke, eds.** What Is Life? The Next Fifty Years: Speculations on the Future of Biology. (Illus.). 170p. (C). 1995. 24.95 (*0-521-45509-X*) Cambridge U Pr.

Murphy, Michael R., jt. auth. see Veit, E. Theodore.

Murphy, Mike & Russo, Douglas. Springfield, IL: Building on the Legacy. (American Enterprise Ser.). (Illus.). 136p. 1993. 32.95 (*0-89781-465-7*) Preferred Mktg.

Murphy, M'Layne & Ungerman, Jill. Historic North Carolina Inns. (Illus.). 160p. 1989. 17.95 (*0-940672-47-2*) Shearer Pub.

Murphy-Muth, Susan M. Medical Records: Management in a Changing Environment. (Health Care Administration Ser.). 224p. 1987. 55.00 (*0-87189-872-1*) Aspen Pub.

Murphy, Nancey. Theology in the Age of Scientific Reasoning. LC 89-39375. (Cornell Studies in the Philosophy of Religion). (Illus.). 232p. 1990. 33.50 (*0-8014-2400-3*) Cornell U Pr.

— Theology in the Age of Scientific Reasoning. LC 89-39375. (Cornell Studies in the Philosophy of Religion). 232p. 1993. pap. 12.95 (*0-8014-8114-7*) Cornell U Pr.

Murphy, Nancey C. Reasoning & Rhetoric in Religion. 224p. (Orig.). (C). 1994. pap. 16.00 (*1-56338-098-6*) TPI PA.

— Reasoning & Rhetoric in Religion: Key to the Exercises. 1994. pap. 5.00 (*1-56338-099-4*) TPI PA.

Murphy, Nancy. The House at Brawmon's Landing. 1994. 16.95 (*0-533-10676-1*) Vantage.

Murphy, Nicy. The Flip Side: Workin' for the Lord Ain't All That Dull. LC 89-60969. 128p. 1989. pap. 9.95 (*0-88100-062-0*) Natl Writ Pr.

Murphy, Norma J., jt. ed. see Cunningham, Rita.

Murphy, Norman. True & Faithful Account. (Illus.). 73p. 1995. 25.00 (*0-87008-074-1*) JAS Heineman.

Murphy, O. J., et al, eds. Electrochemistry in Transition. (Illus.). 730p. (C). 1992. 125.00 (*0-306-43946-8*, Plenum Pr) Plenum.

Murphy-O'Connor. Corinthians. 1989. pap. 21.00 (*0-86217-014-1*, Pub. by Veritas IE) St Mut.

Murphy-O'Connor, Jerome. Becoming Human Together: The Pastoral Anthropology of St. Paul. LC 77-84373. (Good News Studies: Vol. 2). 224p. 1982. pap. 14.95 (*0-8146-5075-9*) Liturgical Pr.

— First Corinthians. LC 79-53891. (New Testament Message Ser.: Vol. 10). 168p. 1980. pap. 11.95 (*0-8146-5133-X*) Liturgical Pr.

— The Holy Land: An Archaeological Guide from Earliest Times to 1700. 3rd ed. (Illus.). 496p. 1992. pap. 15.95 (*0-19-285269-8*) OUP.

— St. Paul's Corinth: Texts & Archaeology. LC 83-80110. (Good News Studies: Vol. 6). 192p. 1983. pap. 14.95 (*0-8146-5303-0*) Liturgical Pr.

— The Theology of the Second Letter to the Corinthians. (New Testament Theology Ser.). 168p. (C). 1991. 44.95 (*0-521-35379-3*); pap. 15.95 (*0-521-35898-1*) Cambridge U Pr.

Murphy, Oliver F., tr. see Chekhov, Anton.

Murphy, Orville T. Charles Gravier, Comte de Vergennes: French Diplomacy in the Age of Revolution, 1719-1787. LC 81-2281. 607p. (C). 1983. 74.50 (*0-87395-482-3*); pap. 24.95 (*0-87395-483-1*) State U NY Pr.

Murphy, Owen, jt. auth. see Owen, Lyla H.

Murphy, P. Blackstone's Criminal Practice. (C). 1991. text ed. 350.00 (*1-85431-200-6*, Pub. by Blackstone Pr UK) W W Gaunt.

— Blackstone's Criminal Practice. 1995. 169.00 (*1-85431-402-5*, Pub. by Blackstone Pr UK) W W Gaunt.

Murphy, P. J. Reconstructing Beckett: Language & Being in Samuel Beckett's Fiction. 256p. 1990. 40.00 (*0-8020-5868-X*) U of Toronto Pr.

Murphy, P. J., et al. A Critique of Beckett Criticism: A Guide to Research in English, French, & German. (Literary Criticism in Perspective Ser.). 200p. 1994. 57. 95 (*1-879751-93-3*) Camden Hse.

Murphy, P. M. & Kupshik, G. A. Loneliness, Stress & Well-Being: A Helper's Guide. 160p. (Orig.). 1992. 59.95 (*0-415-01450-6*, A6455, Tavistock); pap. 15.95 (*0-415-07032-5*, A6459, Tavistock) Routledge.

Murphy, Pat. By Nature's Design: An Exploratorium Book. Dunham, Judith, ed. LC 92-41313. (Illus.). 120p. 1993. 29.95 (*0-8118-0444-5*); pap. 18.95 (*0-8118-0329-5*) Chronicle Bks.

— The Falling Woman. 288p. 1993. pap. 9.95 (*0-312-85406-4*) Orb NYC.

— Pigasus. LC 93-32214. (J). (gr. 3 up). 1995. write for info. (*0-8037-1587-0*); lib. bdg. write for info. (*0-8037-1588-9*) Dial Bks Young.

Murphy, Pat & McCafferty, Mell. Women in Focus: Contemporary Irish Women's Lives. 132p. (Orig.). (C). 1987. pap. 19.95 (*0-946211-30-2*, Pub. by Attic IE) InBook.

Murphy, Pat, jt. auth. see Fairfield, Gail.

Murphy, Pat, et al. Bending Light: An Exploratorium Toolbook. LC 92-20336. (Illus.). (J). 1993. 15.95 (*0-316-25851-2*) Little.

Murphy, Patricia. Making the Connections: Women, Work, & Abuse. LC 92-75487. 244p. 1993. pap. 29.95 (*1-878205-65-X*) GR Press.

— My Angel & Me. JPM Publishers Staff, ed. 224p. (Orig.). Date not set. lib. bdg. 9.95 (*0-925589-05-5*) JPM Pubs.

Murphy, Patricia, jt. auth. see Gipps, Caroline.

***Murphy, Patricia, et al, eds.** Subject Learning in the Primary Curriculum: Issues in English, Science & Mathematics. 272p. 1995. pap. 22.95x (*0-415-12537-5*, C0423) Routledge.

Murphy, Patrick. An Introduction to Unified Field Astrology. 110p. 1993. pap. 19.95 (*0-9636106-0-0*) Nirvana Pr.

Murphy, Patrick, jt. auth. see Bailey, Bill.

Murphy, Patrick, jt. auth. see Barsky, Ivy.

Murphy, Patrick, jt. ed. see Hoffman, Michael J.

Murphy, Patrick, et al. Football on Trial: Spectator Violence in the Football World. 224p. 1990. pap. 17.95 (*0-415-05024-3*, A4826) Routledge.

Murphy, Patrick A. Creditors' Rights in Bankruptcy. LC 79-25731. 784p. 1980. text ed. 90.00 (*0-07-044060-3*) Shepards-McGraw.

— Creditors' Rights in Bankruptcy. 2nd ed. 1058p. 1988. text ed. 90.00 (*0-07-172186-X*) Shepards-McGraw.

Murphy, Patrick D. Literature, Nature, & Other: Ecofeminist Critiques. LC 94-8733. 226p. 1995. 59.50x (*0-7914-2277-1*); pap. 19.95x (*0-7914-2278-X*) State U NY Pr.

— Understanding Gary Snyder. Bruccoli, Matthew J., ed. LC 91-46461. (Understanding Contemporary American Literature Ser.). 224p. 1992. text ed. 34.95 (*0-87249-821-2*) U of SC Pr.

Murphy, Patrick D., ed. Gary Snyder. (Critical Essays on American Literature Ser.). 1990. text ed. 45.00 (*0-8161-8900-5*) G K Hall.

— Staging the Impossible: The Fantastic Mode in Modern Drama. LC 92-10678. (Contributions to the Study of Science Fiction & Fantasy Ser.: No. 54). 256p. 1992. text ed. 55.00 (*0-313-27270-0*, MIJ/, Greenwood Pr) Greenwood.

Murphy, Patrick D. & Hyles, Vernon, eds. The Poetic Fantastic: Studies in an Evolving Genre. LC 89-11930. (Contributions to the Study of Science Fiction & Fantasy Ser.: No. 40). 226p. 1989. text ed. 55.00 (*0-313-26160-1*, MYT/, Greenwood Pr) Greenwood.

Murphy, Patrick D., jt. ed. see Wu, Dingbo.

Murphy, Patrick E. & Wilkie, William L., eds. Marketing & Advertising Regulation: The Federal Trade Commission in the 1990s. LC 90-70855. 496p. (C). 1990. text ed. 34. 95 (*0-268-01382-9*); pap. text ed. 16.95 (*0-268-01383-7*) U of Notre Dame Pr.

Murphy, Patrick E., ed. see American Marketing Association Staff.

Murphy, Patrick E., jt. auth. see Laczniak, Gene R.

***Murphy, Patrick J.** Way Below E. 1994. pap. 14.00 (*1-877727-42-3*) White Pine.

Murphy, Patrick M. A History of Oklahoma State University Student Life & Services. Hanneman, Carolyn, ed. LC 88-25283. (Centennial Histories Ser.). (Illus.). 472p. 1989. 17.95 (*0-914956-34-5*) Okla State Univ Pr.

Murphy, Paud, jt. ed. see Zhiri, Abdelwahed.

Murphy, Paul. The Meaning of Freedom of Speech. LC 72-133500. (Contributions in American History Ser.: No. 15). 401p. 1972. text ed. 39.95 (*0-8371-5176-7*, MCLB, Greenwood Pr) Greenwood.

Murphy, Paul E. Triadic Mysticism. 1986. 23.00 (*0-685-17541-3*, Pub. by Motilal Banarsidass II) S Asia.

Murphy, Paul L. The Constitution in the Twentieth Century. LC 86-70475. (Bicentennial Essays on the Constitution Ser.). 70p. 1985. pap. 7.00 (*0-87229-036-0*) Am Hist Assn.

— World War I & the Origin of Civil Liberties in the United States. (Essays in American History Ser.). (C). 1979. pap. text ed. 9.95 (*0-393-95012-3*) Norton.

Murphy, Paul L., ed. The Bill of Rights & the States. (Bill of Rights & American Legal History Ser.). 540p. 1990. reprint ed. 69.00 (*0-8240-5866-6*) Garland.

— Criminal Procedure, 4 vols. (Bill of Rights & American Legal History Ser.). 2768p. 1990. reprint ed. 440.00 (*0-8240-5865-8*) Garland.

— Free Press, 3 vols. (Bill of Rights & American Legal History Ser.). 2328p. 1990. reprint ed. 378.00 (*0-8240-5861-5*) Garland.

— Free Speech, 4 vols. (Bill of Rights & American Legal History Ser.). 2544p. 1990. reprint ed. 412.00 (*0-8240-5860-7*) Garland.

— The Historic Background of the Bill of Rights. (Bill of Rights & American Legal History Ser.). 600p. 1990. reprint ed. 103.00 (*0-8240-5858-5*) Garland.

— Pre-Nineteen Sixty Developments in the Bill of Rights Area, 2 vols. (Bill of Rights & American Legal History Ser.). 1472p. 1990. reprint ed. 241.00 (*0-8240-5859-3*) Garland.

— Religious Freedom: Separation & Free Exercise, 2 vols. (Bill of Rights & American Legal History Ser.). 952p. 1990. reprint ed. 154.00 (*0-8240-5862-3*) Garland.

— The Right to Privacy & the Ninth Amendment, 2 vols. (Bill of Rights & American Legal History Ser.). 824p. 1990. reprint ed. 137.00 (*0-8240-5864-X*) Garland.

— Rights of Assembly, Petition, Arms & Just Compensation. (Bill of Rights & American Legal History Ser.). 764p. 1990. reprint ed. 126.00 (*0-8240-5863-1*) Garland.

Murphy, Paul R., tr. see Herbert, George.

***Murphy, Paul T.** Toward a Working-Class Canon: Literary Criticism in British Working-Class Periodicals 1816-1858. (Studies in Victorian Life & Literature). 208p. 1995. text ed. 39.50 (*0-8142-0654-9*) Ohio St U Pr.

Murphy, Paul W., jt. ed. see Schuster, Reinhart.

***Murphy, Peter.** Murphy on Evidence. 5th ed. 566p. 1995. pap. 44.00 (*1-85431-373-8*, Pub. by Blackstone Pr UK) W W Gaunt.

— A Practical Approach to Evidence. 637p. 1992. pap. 48. 00 (*1-85431-223-5*, Pub. by Blackstone Pr UK) W W Gaunt.

Murphy, Peter, ed. Blackstone's Criminal Practice. 2550p. 1993. 194.00 (*1-85431-255-3*, Pub. by Blackstone Pr UK) W W Gaunt.

— Blackstone's Criminal Practice. 4th ed. 2446p. 1994. 194. 00 (*1-85431-325-8*) W W Gaunt.

Murphy, Peter & Barnard, David. Evidence & Advocacy. 236p. (C). 1986. 110.00 (*0-906322-96-0*, Pub. by Blackstone Pr UK) St Mut.

— Evidence & Advocacy. 4th ed. 275p. 1994. pap. 30.00 (*1-85431-281-2*, Pub. by Blackstone Pr UK) W W Gaunt.

Murphy, Peter & Barnard, David, eds. Evidence & Advocacy. 3rd ed. 236p. text ed. 26.00 (*0-685-65117-7*, Pub. by Blackstone Pr UK) W W Gaunt.

Murphy, Peter & Beaumont, John. Evidence: Materials for Discussion. 546p. 1987. pap. 40.00 (*0-906322-97-9*, Pub. by Blackstone Pr UK) W W Gaunt.

Murphy, Peter & Broukal, Milada. All about the U. S. A. 96p. 1991. pap. text ed. 12.95 (*0-8013-0637-X*, 78572) Longman.

Murphy, Peter, jt. auth. see Broukal, Milada.

Murphy, Peter E. Tourism: A Community Approach. 260p. 1986. 42.50 (*0-416-39790-5*, 9612); pap. 19.95 (*0-415-04506-1*, 9613) Routledge Chapman & Hall.

Murphy, Peter F., ed. Fictions of Masculinity: Crossing Cultures, Crossing Sexualities. LC 93-44104. 1994. 45.00 (*0-8147-5497-X*); pap. 18.95 (*0-8147-5498-8*) NYU Pr.

Murphy, Peter T. Poetry As an Occupation & an Art in Britain, 1760-1830. LC 92-33949. (Studies in Romanticism: No. 3). 268p. (C). 1993. 54.95 (*0-521-44085-8*) Cambridge U Pr.

***Murphy, Philip.** Party Politics & Decolonization: The Conservative Party & British Colonial Policy in Tropical Africa 1951-1964. (Oxford Historical Monographs). 304p. 1995. 55.00 (*0-19-820505-8*) OUP.

Murphy, Philip, jt. auth. see Domberger, Simon.

Murphy, Phyllis, jt. auth. see Michels, Jeanne.

Murphy, Quillian R., ed. Metabolic Aspects of Transport Across Cell Membranes. LC 57-9808. 406p. reprint ed. pap. 115.80 (*0-317-30078-4*, 2021143) Bks Demand.

Murphy, R. A., et al, eds. Annotated Bibliography on Laboratory Animal Welfare. LC 91-67379. 91p. 1991. 15.00 (*0-685-59679-6*) Scientists Ctr.

Murphy, R. C. Mass Spectrometry of Lipids. (Handbook of Lipid Research Ser.: Vol. 7). (Illus.). 240p. (C). 1993. 65. 00 (*0-306-44361-9*, Plenum Pr) Plenum.

Murphy, R. J., ed. see Vogelsang, Dieter.

Murphy, R. Patrick, ed. Immigration & Nationality Law Handbook, 2 vols. 1300p. (Orig.). (C). 1993. pap. text ed. 129.00 (*1-878677-54-3*) Amer Immi Law Assn.

— Immigration & Nationality Law Handbook, 1992-1993, 2 vols., Set, Vols. 1-2. 1344p. (C). 1992. Set. pap. text ed. 125.00 (*1-878677-37-3*) Amer Immi Law Assn.

— Immigration & Nationality Law Handbook, 1992-1993, Vol. 1: Immigration Basics. 640p. (C). 1992. pap. text ed. 100.00 (*1-878677-35-7*) Amer Immi Law Assn.

— Immigration & Nationality Law Handbook, 1992-1993, Vol. 2: Advanced Practice. 704p. (C). 1992. pap. text ed. 100.00 (*1-878677-36-5*) Amer Immi Law Assn.

— Immigration & Nationality Law Handbook, 1993-1994, Vol. II: Advance Practice. 700p. (Orig.). (C). 1993. pap. text ed. 105.00 (*1-878677-53-5*) Amer Immi Law Assn.

— Immigration & Nationality Law 1991 Annual, 3 vols., Set. 1700p. (Orig.). 1992. pap. write for info. (*1-878677-30-6*) Amer Immi Law Assn.

— Immigration & Nationality Law 1991 Annual, 3 vols., Vol. I: Fundamentals. 1700p. (Orig.). 1992. Vol. I, Fundamentals. pap. write for info. (*1-878677-20-9*) Amer Immi Law Assn.

— Immigration & Nationality Law 1991 Annual, 3 vols., Vol. II: Advanced Topics. 1700p. (Orig.). 1992. Vol. II, Advanced Topics. pap. write for info. (*1-878677-21-7*) Amer Immi Law Assn.

— Immigration & Nationality Law 1991 Annual, 3 vols., Vol. III: Regulatory Overview. 1700p. (Orig.). 1992. Vol. III, Regulatory Overview. pap. 64.00 (*1-878677-29-2*) Amer Immi Law Assn.

— Immigration & Nationality Law, 1993-1994, Vol. I: Immigration Basics. 600p. (Orig.). (C). 1993. pap. text ed. 105.00 (*1-878677-52-7*) Amer Immi Law Assn.

Murphy, R. Patrick, et al, eds. Immigration & Nationality Law Handbook, 1991-92, 2 vols., Set. 1363p. 1991. pap. text ed. 125.00 (*1-878677-22-5*) Amer Immi Law Assn.

***Murphy, R. Taggart.** The Real Price of Japanese Money. 320p. 1996. 25.00 (*0-393-03832-7*) Norton.

Murphy, R. W. The Nation Reunited. Time-Life Books Staff & Flaherty, Thomas, eds. (Civil War Ser.). 176p. 1987. 14.95 (*0-8094-4792-4*); lib. bdg. 25.93 (*0-8094-4793-2*) Time-Life.

Murphy, Ray. If You Felt Like I Did...You'd Start Running. LC 89-91634. 109p. 1990. pap. write for info. (*0-9626835-1-5*) Stethophonics.

Murphy, Raymond. Basic Grammar in Use: Reference & Practice for Students of English. (Illus.). 240p. (C). 1993. Student's Book. student ed, pap. 14.95 (*0-521-42606-5*) Cambridge U Pr.

— Basic Grammar in Use: Reference & Practice for Students of English. (Illus.). 48p. (C). 1993. Teacher's Answer Key. teacher ed, pap. 3.95 (*0-521-42607-3*) Cambridge U Pr.

— Grammar in Use: Reference & Practice for Intermediate Students of American English. (Illus.). 288p. (C). 1989. pap. 15.95 (*0-521-34843-9*) Cambridge U Pr.

— Grammar in Use: Reference & Practice for Intermediate Students of American English. (Illus.). 48p. (C). 1989. Answer key, 48 pgs. pap. 3.95 (*0-521-35701-2*) Cambridge U Pr.
— Rationality & Nature: A Sociological Inquiry into a Changing Relationship. LC 94-25665. 1994. text ed. 55.00 (*0-8133-2168-9*) Westview.
— Rationality & Nature: A Sociological Inquiry into a Changing Relationship. LC 94-25665. (C). 1994. pap. text ed. 21.95 (*0-8133-2169-7*) Westview.
— Social Closure: The Theory of Monopolization & Exclusion. 256p. 1988. 65.00 (*0-19-827268-5*) OUP.
Murphy, Raymond E. & Murphy, Marion F. Pennsylvania Landscapes: A Geography of the Commonwealth. LC 73-77560. (J). (gr. 8-10). 1974. 7.95 (*0-931992-19-2*) Penns Valley.
Murphy, Remington. Fear of Vision: A Book of Poems. Probstein, Ian E. & Gluck, Karl, eds. 64p. (Orig.). 1993. pap. text ed. 5.00 (*1-882725-01-8*) Arch-Arcada.
Murphy, Rhoda J., jt. auth. see House Beautiful Magazine Editors.
***Murphy, Ricardo L., ed.** Fiscal Decentralization in Latin America. 250p. (Orig.). 1995. pap. text ed. 18.50x (*0-940602-94-6*) IADB.
Murphy, Richard. Carlo Scarpa & the Castelvecchio. (Illus.). 224p. 1991. text ed. 99.95 (*0-408-50052-2*, Butterwrth Archit) Butrwrth-Heinemann.
— Imaginary Worlds: Notes on a New Curriculum. 110p. (Orig.). 1974. pap. 9.95 (*0-915924-00-5*) Tchrs & Writers Coll.
— The Mirror Wall. 64p. 1989. 13.95 (*0-916390-36-5*); pap. 7.95 (*0-916390-35-7*) Wake Forest.
— Querini Stampalia Foundation: Venice 1961-3 Carlo Scarpa. (Architecture in Detail Ser.). (Illus.). 60p. (C). 1993. pap. 29.95 (*0-7148-2848-3*, Pub. by Phaidon Press UK) Chronicle Bks.
— Reflections on the Sunday Readings. 210p. (Orig.). 1991. pap. 7.99 (*0-89283-716-0*) Servant.
Murphy, Richard C. Guestworkers in the German Reich. 1983. text ed. 46.00 (*0-88033-034-1*, 143) Col U Pr.
Murphy, Richard J., Jr. The Calculus of Intimacy: A Teaching Life. LC 93-2555. 208p. 1993. 29.50 (*0-8142-0611-5*) Ohio St U Pr.
Murphy, Richard T. Hume & Husserl: Towards Radical Subjectivism. 156p. 1980. lib. bdg. 65.50 (*90-247-2172-5*) Kluwer Ac.
Murphy, Robert, Jr. Psychotherapy Based on Human Longing. LC 60-14173. (Orig.). 1960. pap. 3.00 (*0-87574-111-8*) Pendle Hill.
Murphy, Robert. Realism & Tinsel: Cinema & Society in Britain, 1989-48. (Cinema & Society Ser.). 288p. 1989. 49.50 (*0-415-02982-1*, A3176) Routledge.
— Robert M. Lowie. 1978. text ed. 40.50 (*0-231-03375-3*) Col U Pr.
— Sixties British Cinema. (Illus.). 320p. 1992. text ed. 59.95 (*0-85170-309-7*, Pub. by British Film Inst UK); pap. 25.95 (*0-85170-324-0*, Pub. by British Film Inst UK) Ind U Pr.
— Smash & Grab: The Rise of the British Gangster in London's Underworld. (Illus.). 224p. 1993. 24.95 (*0-571-15442-5*) Faber & Faber.
— The Stream. (Illus.). 208p. 1989. reprint ed. pap. 12.95 (*1-55821-026-1*) Lyons & Burford.
Murphy, Robert C. Fish Shape Paumanok. 1976. 14.95 (*0-8488-1111-9*) Amereon Ltd.
— Fish-Shape Paumanok: Nature & Man on Long Island. (Illus.). 88p. 1991. reprint ed. pap. 9.95 (*0-9628492-0-0*) Waterline Bks.
Murphy, Robert D. AC Circuit Tutor: A Software Tutorial Using Animated Hypertext. (C). 1996. pap. write for info. (*0-02-385144-9*) Macmillan.
— DC Tutor: A Software Tutorial Using Animated Hypertext. 32p. (C). 1994. pap. write for info. (*0-02-385141-4*) Macmillan.
— Diplomat Among Warriors. LC 75-42364. (Illus.). 470p. 1976. reprint ed. lib. bdg. 65.00 (*0-8371-7693-X*, MUDW, Greenwood Pr) Greenwood.
Murphy, Robert F. Body Silent. 1990. pap. 9.95 (*0-393-30702-6*) Norton.
— Cultural & Social Anthropology. 3rd ed. 256p. (C). 1988. pap. text ed. write for info. (*0-13-195273-0*) P-H.
— The Trumai Indians of Central Brazil. LC 84-45523. (American Ethnological Society Monographs: No. 24). 1988. reprint ed. 22.00 (*0-404-62923-7*) AMS Pr.
Murphy, Robert F., ed. Selected Papers from the "American Anthropologist" 1946-1970. 424p. 1976. text ed. 9.00 (*0-913167-06-1*); pap. 5.00 (*0-685-10030-8*) Am Anthro Assn.
Murphy, Robert F., jt. auth. see Murphy, Yolanda.
Murphy, Robert F., ed. see Steward, Julian.
Murphy, Robert T. Postal History-Cancellation Study of the U.S. Pacific Islands: Including the Trust Territories. (Illus.). 361p. 1983. 46.00 (*0-933580-11-8*) Am Philatelic Society.
***Murphy, Robin.** Homeopathic Medical Repertory: A Modern Alphabetical Repertory. 1600p. (C). Date not set. text ed. 80.00 (*0-9635764-0-2*) Hahnemann Acad.
Murphy, Roger & Torrance, Harry. The Changing Face of Educational Assessment. 128p. 1988. 80.00 (*0-335-15827-7*, Open Univ Pr); pap. 27.00 (*0-335-15826-9*, Open Univ Pr) Taylor & Francis.
Murphy, Roger, jt. auth. see Pennycuick, David.
***Murphy, Roger, et al.** Effective Assessment & the Improvement of Education: A Tribute to Desmond Nuttall. 180p. 1995. 75.00x (*0-7507-0374-1*, Falmer Pr) Taylor & Francis.
— Effective Assessment & the Improvement of Education: A Tribute to Desmond Nuttall. 180p. 1995. pap. 24.95 (*0-7507-0375-X*, Falmer Pr) Taylor & Francis.
Murphy, Roland. WBC, Vol. 23A: Ecclesiastes. 1992. 24.99 (*0-8499-0222-3*) Word Inc.
Murphy, Roland E. The Psalms Are Yours. LC 93-15639. 160p. 1993. pap. 10.95 (*0-8091-3411-X*) Paulist Pr.
— The Song of Songs. LC 89-16891. (Hermeneia Ser.). 176p. 1990. 26.00 (*0-8006-6024-2*, 1-6024) Augsburg Fortress.
— Wisdom Literature: Ruth, Esther, Job, Proverbs, Ecclesiastes, Canticles. (Forms of the Old Testament Literature Ser.). (Orig.). 1981. pap. 19.99 (*0-8028-1877-3*) Eerdmans.
Murphy, Roland E., ed. & intro. Medieval Exegesis of Wisdom Literature: Essays by Beryl Smalley. LC 86-6689. (Reprints & Translations Ser.). (C). 1986. 15.95 (*1-55540-026-4*, 00 07 16) Scholars Pr GA.
***Murphy, Ronald E.** Responses to One Hundred One Questions on the Psalms & Other Writings. LC 94-3739. 144p. 1995. pap. 8.95 (*0-8091-3526-4*) Paulist Pr.
***Murphy, Rosalea.** In the Pink: Southwestern Menus from the World-Famous Pink Abode Restaurant. 1995. pap. 11.95 (*0-440-50667-0*) Dell.
— The Pink Adobe Cookbook. (Orig.). 1988. pap. 11.95 (*0-440-56972-9*, Dell Trade Pbks) Dell.
Murphy, Rosalie, ed. see Hawthorne, Nathaniel.
***Murphy, Roseanne.** Julie Billiart: Woman of Courage: The Story of the Foundress of the Sisters of Notre Dame. LC 94-25230. 240p. (Orig.). (C). 1995. pap. 17.95 (*0-8091-3535-3*) Paulist Pr.
Murphy, Roy & Murphy, Julia. The San Gabriel Mountains. (Illus.). 88p. 1985. 25.00 (*0-9615421-0-1*) Big Santa Hist.
Murphy, S. Wind Child. (J). 1996. 15.00 (*0-06-024351-1*); lib. bdg. 14.89 (*0-06-024352-X*) HarpC Child Bks.
Murphy, Sandra. Reckoning the Earth: Some Lessons from the Land. LC 94-13180. 136p. (Orig.). 1994. pap. 12.95 (*0-87358-590-9*) Northland AZ.
Murphy, Sandra & Smith, Mary A. Writing Portfolios: A Bridge from Teaching to Assessment. (Illus.). 96p. Date not set. pap. text ed. 10.50 (*0-685-63055-2*, 00707) Heinemann.
***Murphy, Sandra & Smith, Mary Ann.** Writing Portfolios: A Bridge from Teaching to Assessment. (Illus.). 96p. 1995. pap. text ed. 13.00 (*0-88751-044-2*, 00707) Heinemann.
Murphy, Sandra, jt. auth. see Ruth, Leo.
Murphy, Scott B., jt. auth. see Wetzel, Edward D.
Murphy, Sean. Astrocytes: Pharmacology & Function. (Illus.). 457p. 1993. text ed. 99.00 (*0-12-511370-6*) Acad Pr.
Murphy, Sean, et al. No Fire, No Thunder: The Threat of Chemical & Biological Weapons. LC 84-20579. 160p. 1984. 23.00 (*0-85345-661-5*); pap. 7.50 (*0-85345-662-3*) Monthly Rev.
Murphy, Sean P., jt. auth. see Mann, Robert W.
Murphy, Shane M., ed. Sport Psychology Interventions. LC 94-10390. (Illus.). 392p. 1995. text ed. 42.00x (*0-87322-659-3*, BMUR0659) Human Kinetics.
***Murphy, Sharon, ed.** Celebrate Life! A Guide for Planning All Night Alcohol & Drug-Free Celebrations for Teens: A Guide for Planning All Night Alcohol - Drug-Free Celebrations for Teens. 4th ed. (Illus.). 179p. (Orig.). (C). (gr. 12 up). 1994. pap. text ed. 20.00 (*0-7881-0865-4*) Diane Pub.
Murphy, Sharon M., jt. auth. see Schilpp, Madelon G.
***Murphy, Shawn J.** Becoming a Real Estate Professional. 1995. pap. 19.95 (*0-533-11243-5*) Vantage.
Murphy, Sheila. A Delicate Dance: Sex, Celibacy, & Relationships Among Catholic Clergy & Religous. 128p. 1992. pap. 14.95 (*0-8245-1159-X*) Crossroad NY.
— Teth. 88p. (Orig.). 1990. pap. 9.00 (*0-925904-05-8*) Chax Pr.
Murphy, Sheila, et al, eds. The Literature of Work: Short Stories, Essays, & Poems by Men & Women of Business. LC 91-67284. 314p. 1991. 24.95 (*1-880708-00-0*) U Phoenix Pr.
***Murphy, Sheila E.** Heat a Form of Privacy Like Snow. 64p. 1994. pap. 7.95 (*1-884106-01-3*) Jumping Cholla.
— Tommy & Neil. 12.95 (Illus.). 96p. (Orig.). 1993. 20.00 (*0-933313-17-9*); 30.00 (*0-933313-16-0*); pap. 12.95 (*0-933313-18-7*) SUN Gemini Pr.
Murphy, Sheila E. & Sollfrey, Stacey. A Rich Timetable & Appendices; Feeling the Roof of a Mouth That Hangs Open, 2 bks. in 1. 1991. 3.00 (*0-935350-30-6*); write for info. (*0-935350-31-4*) Luna Bisonte.
***Murphy, Sheila E., et al.** Pavement Saw. 40p. 1994. pap. 3.50 (*1-886350-00-0*) Pavement Saw.
Murphy, Shirley R. The Catswold Portal. 400p. 1992. 22.00 (*0-451-45146-5*, ROC) NAL-Dutton.
— The Catswold Portal. 432p. 1993. pap. 5.50 (*0-451-45275-5*, ROC) NAL-Dutton.
— Nightpool. LC 85-42626. (Trophy Starwanderer Bk.). 256p. (YA). (gr. 7 up). 1987. pap. 2.95 (*0-06-447041-5*, Trophy) HarpC Child Bks.
— Silver Woven in My Hair. LC 91-23144. (Illus.). 128p. (J). (gr. 3-7). 1992. reprint ed. pap. 3.95 (*0-689-71525-0*, Aladdin Paperbacks) S&S Childrens.
— The Song of the Christmas Mouse. LC 89-19744. (Illus.). 96p. (J). (gr. 2-5). 1990. 13.95 (*0-06-024357-0*); lib. bdg. 13.89 (*0-06-024358-9*) HarpC Child Bks.
— Wind Child. LC 94-13861. (J). 1995. 15.00 (*0-06-024903-X*); lib. bdg. 14.89 (*0-06-024904-8*) HarpC.
Murphy, Siobhan M., jt. auth. see Birchall, Martin A.
***Murphy, Stephanie & Thuma, Cynthia.** Insiders' Guide to Boca Raton & the Palm Beaches. 1995. 14.95 (*0-912367-77-6*) Insiders Guide.
Murphy, Stephen. The Carnival Caper: Teenage Mutant Ninja Turtles. (Sound Doodles Ser.). 16p. (J). (ps-2). 1994. write for info. (*1-883366-49-6*) YES Ent.
— Het Mysterie Van De Verdwenen Pizza: Teenage Mutant Ninja Turtles. DigiPro Staff, tr. (Comes to Life Bks.). 16p. (DUT.). (J). (ps-2). 1994. write for info. (*1-883366-91-7*) YES Ent.
— I Mostri Sono Tra Noi: Teenage Mutant Ninja Turtles. DigiPro Staff, tr. (Comes to Life Bks.). 16p. (ITA.). (J). (ps-2). 1994. write for info. (*1-883366-97-6*) YES Ent.
— Ignite Your Inner Genius. 1993. pap. 12.00 (*1-883077-07-9*, Am Capital Fnd) Am Capital Invest.
— Il Mistero della Pizza Scomparsa: Teenage Mutant Ninja Turtles. DigiPro Staff, tr. (Comes to Life Bks.). 16p. (ITA.). (J). (ps-2). 1994. write for info. (*1-883366-96-8*) YES Ent.
— Il Mistero delle Pizze Scomparse: Teenage Mutant Ninja Turtles. DigiPro Staff, tr. (Comes to Life Bks.). 16p. (SPA.). (J). (ps-2). 1994. write for info. (*1-57234-008-8*) YES Ent.
— Monsters among Us: Teenage Mutant Hero Turtles. (Comes to Life Bks.). 16p. (J). (ps-2). 1994. write for info. (*1-883366-76-3*) YES Ent.
— Monsters among Us: Teenage Mutant Ninja Turtles. (Comes to Life Bks.). 16p. (J). (ps-2). 1993. write for info. (*1-883366-09-7*) YES Ent.
— Monstruos Entre Nosotros: Teenage Mutant Ninja Turtles. DigiPro Staff, tr. (Comes to Life Bks.). 16p. (SPA.). (J). (ps-2). 1994. write for info. (*1-57234-009-6*) YES Ent.
— Le Mystere de la Pizza Disparue: Teenage Mutant Ninja Turtles. DigiPro Staff, tr. (Comes to Life Bks.). 16p. (FRE.). (J). (ps-2). 1994. write for info. (*1-883366-66-6*) YES Ent.
— The Mystery of the Missing Pizza: Teenage Mutant Hero Turtles. (Comes to Life Bks.). 16p. (J). (ps-2). 1994. write for info. (*1-883366-75-5*) YES Ent.
— The Mystery of the Missing Pizza: Teenage Mutant Ninja Turtles. (Comes to Life Bks.). 16p. (J). (ps-2). 1993. write for info. (*1-883366-08-9*) YES Ent.
— One up on Trump. 250p. Date not set. pap. 12.00 (*1-883077-00-1*) Am Capital Invest.
Murphy, Stephen, et al. Developing Natural Supports in the Workplace: A Practitioner's Guide. LC 94-6930. 109p. (Orig.). 1994. pap. 20.00 (*1-883302-06-4*) Trning Res.
Murphy, Stephen T. On Being L. D. Perspectives & Strategies of Young Adults. (Special Education Ser.). 200p. (C). 1992. text ed. 41.00 (*0-8077-3170-6*); pap. text ed. 18.95 (*0-8077-3169-2*) Tchrs Coll.
Murphy, Steven. Leonardo, the Wilderness Adventure. (Teenage Mutant Ninja Turtles Ser.). (J). (ps-3). 1993. pap. 3.50 (*0-440-40866-0*) Dell.
***Murphy, Stuart J.** The Best Bug Parade. LC 94-49316. (Illus.). (J). 1996. 15.00 (*0-06-025871-3*); lib. bdg. 14.89 (*0-06-025872-1*) HarpC Child Bks.
Murphy, Susan. Romantic Atlanta. (Romantic Guide Ser.). (Illus.). 296p. (Orig.). 1993. pap. 10.95 (*1-879244-45-4*) Windom Bks.
— Romantic L. A. (Romantic Guide Ser.). (Illus.). 296p. (Orig.). 1994. pap. 10.95 (*1-879244-49-7*) Windom Bks.
— Romantic New York. (Romantic Guide Ser.). (Illus.). 296p. (Orig.). 1994. pap. 10.95 (*1-879244-48-9*) Windom Bks.
Murphy, Susan A. An Etymological Glossary for El Libro del Cauallero Zifar. (American University Studies: Romance Languages & Literature: Ser. II, Vol. 115). 200p. (ENG & SPA.). (C). 1989. text ed. 30.00 (*0-8204-1092-6*) P Lang Pubs.
***Murphy, Susan S.** Legal Handbook of Texas Nurses. LC 94-27848. 256p. 1995. text ed. 35.00x (*0-292-75161-3*); pap. 17.95x (*0-292-75176-1*) U of Tex Pr.
Murphy, T. Classic Cocktails. 234p. pap. 6.95 (*0-507-46050-2*, 217) Am Bartenders.
— Tropical Cocktails. 233p. 6.95 (*0-507-46051-0*, 214) Am Bartenders.
Murphy, T., et al. Statistical Methods for Textile Technologists. 107p. 1979. 40.00 (*0-686-63797-6*) St Mut.
— Statistical Methods for Textile Technologists. 107p. (C). 1979. pap. text ed. 70.00 (*0-685-36068-7*, Pub. by Textile Institue UK) St Mut.
***Murphy, Ted.** Secrets of Belltown. LC 95-6476. (Belltown Mystery Ser.: No. 1). (J). 1995. write for info. (*0-382-39114-4*); pap. write for info. (*0-382-39115-2*) Silver Burdett Pr.
***Murphy, Terence & Hardy, C. Thompson.** Hospital-Physician Integration: Strategies for Success. LC 94-27666. 1994. 57.50 (*1-55648-124-1*, 145159) AHPI.
Murphy, Terence R., jt. auth. see MacDonald, Michael.
Murphy, Teresa A. Ten Hours' Labor: Religion, Reform, & Gender in Early New England. LC 91-55534. 248p. 1992. 31.50 (*0-8014-2683-9*) Cornell U Pr.
Murphy, Terrence & Stortz, Gerald, eds. Creed & Culture: The Place of English-Speaking Catholics in Canadian Society, 1750-1930. (Illus.). 304p. 1993. 44.95 (*0-7735-0954-2*, Pub. by McGill CN) U of Toronto Pr.
Murphy, Terrence V. Tenth Virginia Infantry. (Virginia Regimental Histories Ser.). (Illus.). 186p. 1989. 19.95 (*0-930919-74-2*) H E Howard.
Murphy, Therese, jt. ed. see Mills, Elizabeth.
***Murphy, Thomas.** Change of Allegiance. 390p. (Orig.). Date not set. pap. 19.95 (*0-7610-0219-7*) NW Pub.
Murphy, Thomas & Murphy, Dianne. The Wellness for Life Workbook. 2nd ed. 80p. 1982. 8.95 (*0-9611482-0-9*) Fitness Pubns.
— The Wellness for Life Workbook. 3rd ed. 80p. 1982. 8.95 (*0-9611482-2-5*) Fitness Pubns.
— The Wellness for Life Workbook. 4th ed. 80p. 1982. 8.95 (*0-9611482-3-3*) Fitness Pubns.
Murphy, Thomas, jt. auth. see Christen, William.
***Murphy, Thomas J. & Snyder, Kenneth.** What! I Have to Give a Speech? LC 94-37438. 224p. (Orig.). (YA). (gr. 7-12). 1995. pap. 12.95 (*1-883790-10-7*, EDINFO Pr) Grayson Bernard Pubs.
Murphy, Thomas J., jt. auth. see Petersen, Kristen A.
Murphy, Timothy. Manual for Managing Notorious Cases. 196p. (Orig.). 1992. pap. text ed. 8.50 (*0-89656-110-0*, R130) Natl Ctr St Courts.
Murphy, Timothy & James, James R. Indigent Defense Services: Appointed Counsel & Its Alternatives, Galveston County, Texas. 81p. 1988. 5.00 (*0-685-33620-4*, SERO-050) Natl Ctr St Courts.
Murphy, Timothy F. Ethics in an Epidemic: AIDS, Morality & Culture. LC 94-8248. 1994. 32.00 (*0-520-08636-8*) U CA Pr.
— Writing Aids. 1994. pap. 14.50 (*0-231-07865-X*) Col U Pr.
Murphy, Timothy F., ed. & intro. Gay Ethics: Controversies in Outing, Civil Rights, & Sexual Science. LC 94-14155. (Journal of Homosexuality Ser.: Vol. 27, Nos. 3-4). (Illus.). 220p. 1994. lib. bdg. 39.95 (*1-56024-671-5*) Harrington Pk.
— Gay Ethics: Controversies in Outing, Civil Rights, & Sexual Science. LC 94-14155. (Journal of Homosexuality Ser.: Vol. 27, Nos. 3-4). (Illus.). 220p. 1994. pap. text ed. 17.95 (*1-56023-056-8*) Harrington Pk.
Murphy, Timothy F. & Lappe, Marc, eds. Justice & the Human Genome Project. LC 93-18094. 1994. 28.00 (*0-520-08363-6*) U CA Pr.
Murphy, Timothy F. & Poirier, Suzanne, eds. Writing AIDS: Gay Literature, Language, & Analysis. LC 92-20373. (Between Men - Between Women Ser.). 352p. (C). 1993. 29.50 (*0-231-07864-1*) Col U Pr.
Murphy, Timothy S., jt. auth. see Stein, Elias M.
Murphy, Tom. The Gigli Concert. (Methuen Modern Plays Ser.). 86p. (Orig.). 1991. pap. 9.95 (*0-413-65930-5*, A0591, Pub. by Methuen UK) Heinemann.
— Harley-Davidson Big Twin Performance Handbook. (Illus.). 192p. 1995. pap. text ed. 18.95 (*0-7603-0009-7*) Motorbooks Intl.
— Murphy: Plays One. (Methuen World Dramatists Ser.). 231p. 1992. pap. 13.95 (*0-413-66570-4*, A0660, Pub. by Methuen UK) Heinemann.
— Murphy: Plays Two. (C). 1993. pap. 15.95 (*0-413-67560-2*, A0670, Pub. by Methuen UK) Heinemann.
— Too Late for Logic. (Methuen Modern Plays Ser.). 54p. 1990. pap. 9.95 (*0-413-63220-2*, A0484, Pub. by Methuen UK) Heinemann.
Murphy, Tom & Cloud, Barbara. Media Law in Nevada. (State Law Ser.). 74p. (C). 1992. pap. text ed. 7.95 (*0-913507-28-8*) New Forums.
Murphy, Tom, ed. see Hopkins, Tom.
Murphy, Tommy. Elegant Wine Cocktails: One Hundred Eleven Recipes for Delicious Wine Drinks. 256p. 1985. mass mkt. 6.95 (*0-446-38313-9*) Warner Bks.
Murphy, V., jt. auth. see Baker, J.
Murphy, Vincent, tr. see Yoshimura, Akira.
Murphy, Virginia R. Across the Plains in the Donner Party: 1846-47. Jones, William R., ed. (Illus.). 64p. 1980. pap. 6.95 (*0-89646-063-0*) Vistabooks.
Murphy, Vreni, jt. auth. see Baker, Joseph T.
Murphy, Vreni, jt. ed. see Baker, Joseph T.
Murphy, Walter F. Elements of Judicial Strategy. LC 64-24973. 1973. pap. text ed. 15.95 (*0-226-55370-1*) U Ch Pr.
— Upon This Rock: A Life of St. Peter. 1988. mass mkt. 4.95 (*0-345-35761-2*) Ballantine.
— The Vicar of Christ. 1985. mass mkt. 5.95 (*0-345-32039-5*) Ballantine.
Murphy, Walter F. & Pritchett, Charles H. Courts, Judges & Politics: An Introduction to the Judicial Process. 4th ed. 544p. 1986. pap. text ed. write for info. (*0-07-554829-1*) McGraw.
Murphy, Walter F., jt. auth. see Danielson, Michael N.
***Murphy, Walter F., et al.** American Constitutional Interpretation. 2nd ed. 1410p. (C). 1995. text ed. 49.95 (*1-56662-240-9*) Foundation Pr.
— American Constitutional Interpretations. LC 86-6240. (University Casebook Ser.). 1262p. 1986. text ed. 40.95 (*0-88277-321-6*) Foundation Pr.
***Murphy, Walter L.** New Hampshire Civil Jury Instructions. 3rd ed. 456p. 1994. ring bd. 89.00 (*0-250-40748-5*) Michie Butterworth.
Murphy, Walter L. & Pope, Daniel C. New Hampshire Civil Jury Instructions. 2nd ed. 400p. 1992. ring bd. 75.00 (*1-56257-310-1*) Butterworth Legal Pubs.
— New Hampshire Civil Jury Instructions. 2nd suppl. ed. 400p. 1993. 27.00 (*0-685-74472-8*) Butterworth Legal Pubs.
Murphy, Warren. Acid Rock. (Destroyer Ser.: No. 13). 1989. pap. 3.50 (*1-55817-195-9*, Pinnacle NY) Windsor NY.
— Assassin's Play-Off. (Destroyer Ser.: No. 20). 1989. pap. 3.50 (*1-55817-211-4*, Pinnacle NY) Windsor NY.
— Bay City Blast. (Destroyer Ser.: No. 38). 1990. pap. 3.50 (*1-55817-443-5*, Pinnacle NY) Windsor NY.
— Bottom Line. (Destroyer Ser.: No. 37). 1990. pap. 3.50 (*1-55817-419-2*, Pinnacle NY) Windsor NY.
— Brain Drain. (Destroyer Ser.: No. 22). (Orig.). 1989. pap. 3.50 (*1-55817-247-5*, Pinnacle NY) Windsor NY.
— Child's Play. (Destroyer Ser.: No. 23). 1989. pap. 3.50 (*1-55817-258-0*, Pinnacle NY) Windsor NY.
— Chinese Puzzle. (Destroyer Ser.: No. 3). (Orig.). 1988. pap. 3.50 (*1-55817-038-3*, Pinnacle NY) Windsor NY.
— Created, the Destroyer. (Destroyer Ser.: No. 1). 1988. pap. 3.50 (*1-55817-036-7*, Pinnacle NY) Windsor NY.
— Dangerous Games. (Destroyer Ser.: No. 40). 192p. (Orig.). 1991. pap. 3.50 (*1-55817-468-0*, Pinnacle NY) Windsor NY.
— Deadly Seed. (Destroyer Ser.: No. 21). 1989. pap. 3.50 (*1-55817-237-8*, Pinnacle NY) Windsor NY.
— Death Check. (Destroyer Ser.: No. 2). 1988. pap. 3.50 (*1-55817-037-5*, Pinnacle NY) Windsor NY.
— Death Therapy. (Destroyer Ser.: No. 6). 1988. pap. 3.50 (*1-55817-041-3*, Pinnacle NY) Windsor NY.

An Asterisk (*) at the beginning of an entry indicates that the title is appearing in BIP for the first time.

— Destroyer, No. 29: The Final Death. 1990. pap. 3.50 (*1-55817-319-6*, Pinnacle NY) Windsor NY.
— Destroyer, No. 32: Killer Chromosomes. 1990. pap. 3.50 (*1-55817-355-2*, Pinnacle NY) Windsor NY.
— Destroyer, No. 33: Voodoo Die. 1990. pap. 3.50 (*1-55817-370-6*, Pinnacle NY) Windsor NY.
— Destroyer No. 34: Chained Reaction. 1990. pap. 3.50 (*1-55817-383-8*, Pinnacle NY) Windsor NY.
— Destroyer, No. 35: Last Call. 1990. pap. 3.50 (*1-55817-395-1*, Pinnacle NY) Windsor NY.
— Destroyer, No. 36: Power Play. 1990. pap. 3.50 (*1-55817-406-0*, Pinnacle NY) Windsor NY.
— Digger Smoked Out. 256p. 1994. 4.95 (*0-7867-0177-3*) Carroll & Graf.
— Dr. Quake. (Destroyer Ser.: No. 5). 1988. pap. 3.50 (*1-55817-040-5*, Pinnacle NY) Windsor NY.
— Firing Line. (Destroyer Ser.: No. 41). 192p. (Orig.). 1991. pap. 3.50 (*1-55817-483-4*, Pinnacle NY) Windsor NY.
— Funny Money. (Destroyer Ser.: No. 18). 1989. pap. 3.50 (*1-55817-200-9*, Pinnacle NY) Windsor NY.
— The Head Men. (Destroyer Ser.: No. 31). 1990. pap. 3.50 (*1-55817-343-9*, Pinnacle NY) Windsor NY.
— Holy Terrors. (Destroyer Ser.: No. 19). 1989. pap. 3.50 (*1-55817-210-6*, Pinnacle NY) Windsor NY.
— Honor among Thieves. 448p. 1992. mass mkt. 5.99 (*1-55817-614-4*, Pinnacle NY) Windsor NY.
— In Enemy Hands. (Destroyer Ser.: No. 26). 1989. pap. 3.50 (*1-55817-285-8*, Pinnacle NY) Windsor NY.
— Jericho Day. 1991. mass mkt. 4.95 (*0-06-100150-3*, Harp PBks) HarpC.
— King's Curse. (Destroyer Ser.: No. 24). 1989. pap. 3.50 (*1-55817-268-8*, Pinnacle NY) Windsor NY.
— The Last Temple. (Destroyer Ser.: No. 27). 1989. pap. 3.50 (*1-55817-295-5*, Pinnacle NY) Windsor NY.
— Last War Dance. (Destroyer Ser.: No. 17). 1989. pap. 3.50 (*1-55817-199-1*, Pinnacle NY) Windsor NY.
— Mafia Fix. (Destroyer Ser.: No. 4). 1988. pap. 3.50 (*1-55817-039-1*, Pinnacle NY) Windsor NY.
— Missing Link. (Destroyer Ser.: No. 39). 1990. pap. 3.50 (*1-55817-457-5*, Pinnacle NY) Windsor NY.
— Mugger Blood. (Destroyer Ser.: No. 30). 1990. pap. 3.50 (*1-55817-328-5*, Pinnacle NY) Windsor NY.
— Murder Ward. (Destroyer Ser.: No. 15). 1989. pap. 3.50 (*1-55817-197-5*, Pinnacle NY) Windsor NY.
— Oil Slick. (Destroyer Ser.: No. 16). 1989. pap. 3.50 (*1-55817-198-3*, Pinnacle NY) Windsor NY.
— Scorpion's Dance. 1990. mass mkt. 4.95 (*1-55817-333-1*, Pinnacle NY) Windsor NY.
— Ship of Death. (Destroyer Ser.: No. 28). 1990. pap. 3.50 (*1-55817-310-2*, Pinnacle NY) Windsor NY.
— The Sure Thing. 448p. 1988. mass mkt. 4.50 (*1-55817-129-0*, Pinnacle NY) Windsor NY.
— Sweet Dreams. (Destroyer Ser.: No. 25). 1989. pap. 3.50 (*1-55817-276-9*, Pinnacle NY) Windsor NY.
— Trace & Forty-Seven Miles of Rope. (Trace Ser.: No. 2). 1984. pap. 2.95 (*0-317-00847-1*, Sig) NAL-Dutton.

Murphy, Warren & Cochran, Molly. Grandmaster. 1988. mass mkt. 4.50 (*1-55817-101-0*, Pinnacle NY) Windsor NY.
— The Hand of Lazarus. 480p. 1988. mass mkt. 4.50 (*1-55817-100-2*, Pinnacle NY) Windsor NY.
— The Temple Dogs. 416p. 1989. 18.95 (*0-318-40988-7*) NAL-Dutton.

Murphy, Warren & Sapik, Richard. High Priestess. 1994. mass mkt. 4.99 (*0-373-63210-X*) Harlequin Bks.

Murphy, Warren & Sapir, Richard. Blood Ties. (Destroyer Ser.: No. 69). 1987. pap. 3.95 (*0-451-14879-7*, Sig) NAL-Dutton.
— The Destroyer: Kill or Cure, No. 11. 1988. pap. 3.50 (*1-55817-148-7*, Pinnacle NY) Windsor NY.
— The Destroyer: Murder's Shield, No. 9. 1988. pap. 3.50 (*1-55817-146-0*, Pinnacle NY) Windsor NY.
— The Destroyer: Slave Safari, No. 12. 1988. pap. 3.50 (*1-55817-149-5*, Pinnacle NY) Windsor NY.
— The Destroyer: Summit Chase, No. 8. 1988. pap. 3.50 (*1-55817-145-2*, Pinnacle NY) Windsor NY.
— The Destroyer: Terror Squad, No. 10. 1988. pap. 3.50 (*1-55817-147-9*, Pinnacle NY) Windsor NY.
— The Destroyer: Union Bust, No. 7. pap. 3.50 (*1-55817-144-4*, Pinnacle NY) Windsor NY.
— The Ultimate Death. (Destroyer Ser.: No. 88). 256p. (Orig.). 1992. pap. 4.50 (*0-451-17115-2*, Sig) NAL-Dutton.

Murphy, Warren & Sapir, Richard, creators. Arabian Nightmare. (Destroyer Ser.: No. 86). 256p. 1991. pap. 4.50 (*0-451-17060-1*, Sig) NAL-Dutton.

Murphy, Warren, jt. auth. see Cochran, Molly.

Murphy, Wendy. Frank Lloyd Wright. (Genius Ser.). (Illus.). 128p. (J). (gr. 7-9). 1990. 7.95 (*0-382-24033-2*); lib. bdg. 12.95 (*0-382-09905-2*) Silver Burdett Pr.

Murphy, Wendy & Murphy, Jack. Hong Kong. (Great Cities Library). (Illus.). 64p. (J). (gr. 3-7). 1991. lib. bdg. 14.95 (*1-56711-021-5*) Blackbirch.
— Nuclear Medicine. Garell, Dale C. & Snyder, Solomon H., eds. (Medical Disorders & Their Treatment Ser.). (Illus.). (YA). (gr. 6-12). 1994. 19.95 (*0-7910-0070-2*, Am Art Analog); pap. write for info. (*0-7910-0497-X*, Am Art Analog) Chelsea Hse.
— Toronto. (Great Cities Library). (Illus.). 64p. (J). (gr. 3-7). 1992. lib. bdg. 14.95 (*1-56711-025-8*) Blackbirch.

Murphy, Wendy B. Beds & Borders: Traditional & Original Garden Designs. (Illus.). 166p. 1993. pap. 18.95 (*0-395-66078-5*) HM.
— Science & Serendipity. LC 93-74286. Date not set. write for info. (*0-87502-249-9*) Benjamin Co.

***Murphy, William A., Jr., et al.** Musculoskeletal Disease Test & Syllabus. (Professional Self-Evaluation & Continuing Education Program Ser.: Vol. 37). (Illus.). 900p. 1994. 200.00 (*1-55903-036-4*) Am Coll Radiology.

***Murphy, William D. & Barbaree, Howard E.** Assessments of Sex Offenders by Measures of Erectile Response: Psychometric Properties & Decision Making. rev. ed. 90p. (C). Date not set. pap. text ed. 10.00 (*1-884444-14-8*) Safer Soc.

Murphy, William D., jt. auth. see Dattilo, John.

Murphy, William F. The Tactics of Psychotherapy: An Application of Psychoanalytic Theory to Psychotherapy. LC 65-19462. 1965. text ed. 65.00 (*0-8236-6360-4*) Intl Univs Pr.

Murphy, William F., jt. auth. see Deutsch, Felix.

Murphy, William J. R & D Cooperation among Marketplace Competitors. LC 90-8919. 272p. 1990. text ed. 55.00 (*0-89930-489-3*, MRD/, Quorum Bks) Greenwood.

Murphy, William L. A Birder's Guide to Trinidad & Tobago. (Illus.). v, 124p. (Orig.). 1986. pap. 12.95 (*0-941475-01-8*) Peregrine Enter.
— Duplin County Wills, Genealogical Abstracts Of, 1730-1860. 280p. 1986. reprint ed. 27.50 (*0-89308-597-9*, NC 32) Southern Hist Pr.
— Ten-Day Checklist of the Birds of Trinidad & Tobago. 10p. (Orig.). (C). 1988. 2.00 (*0-318-50102-3*) Peregrine Enter.

Murphy, William M. Atlas of Bladder Carcinoma. (Illus.). 150p. 1986. text ed. 75.00 (*0-89189-211-7*, 16-1-035-00); sl. 85.00 (*0-89189-212-5*) Am Soc Clinical.
— Family Secrets: William Butler Yeats & His Relatives. LC 94-19006. (Irish Studies). (Illus.). 464p. 1995. 39.95 (*0-8156-0301-0*) Syracuse U Pr.
— Prodigal Father: The Life of John Butler Yeats, 1839-1922. LC 77-3122. (Illus.). 688p. 1978. pap. 22.95 (*0-8014-9179-7*) Cornell U Pr.

Murphy, William M., jt. auth. see Cullen, Fintan.

Murphy, Yolanda & Murphy, Robert F. Women of the Forest. 2nd ed. LC 85-14969. 275p. 1985. text ed. 39.50 (*0-231-06088-2*); pap. text ed. 15.50 (*0-231-06089-0*) Col U Pr.

Murr, et al. Metallurgical Applications of Shock-Wave & High-Strain Rate Phenomena. (Mechanical Engineering Ser.: Vol. 52). 1136p. 1986. 235.00 (*0-8247-7612-7*) Dekker.

Murr, George G. The Lebanese Village: An Old Culture in a New Era. 1987. 24.95x (*0-86685-419-3*) Intl Bk Ctr.

Murr, L. Solid-State Electronics. (Electrical Engineering & Electronics Ser.: Vol. 4). 432p. 1978. 110.00 (*0-8247-6676-8*) Dekker.

Murr, L. E. Interfacial Phenomena in Metals & Alloys. (Illus.). 376p. (C). reprint ed. text ed. 45.00 (*1-878907-12-3*) TechBooks.

Murr, Lawarence E. Electron & Ion Microscopy & Microanalysis: Principles & Applications. 2nd rev. ed. (Optical Engineering Ser.: Vol. 29). 856p. 1991. 165.00 (*0-8247-8556-8*) Dekker.

Murr, Lawrence E., ed. Shock Waves for Industrial Applications. LC 88-27516. (Illus.). 533p. 1989. 78.00 (*0-8155-1170-1*) Noyes.

Murr, Lawrence E. & Stein, Charles, eds. Frontiers in Materials Science: Distinguished Lectures. LC 75-39870. (Monographs & Textbooks in Material Science: No. 8). (Illus.). 610p. reprint ed. pap. 173.90 (*0-7837-0973-0*, 2041279) Bks Demand.

Murr, Lawrence E., jt. auth. see Staudhammer, Karl P.

Murr, Muhammed A. Dubai Tales. Clark, Peter, tr. 160p. (Orig.). 1990. pap. 26.00 (*0-948259-86-8*, Pub. by Forest Bks UK) Dufour.

Murra, John V. The Economic Organization of the Inca State. Dalton, George, ed. (Research in Economic Anthropology Ser.: Suppl. 1). 214p. 1980. 73.25 (*0-89232-118-0*) Jai Pr.

Murra, John V., jt. ed. see Urioste, George L.

Murrah, David J. Oil, Taxes, & the Cats: A History of the Devitt Family & the Mallet Ranch. LC 93-33654. (Illus.). 247p. 1994. 25.00 (*0-89672-332-1*) Tex Tech Univ Pr.

Murrah, Judy. Jacket Jazz. Weiland, Barbara, ed. LC 93-7120. (Illus.). 88p. (Orig.). 1993. pap. 21.95 (*1-56477-021-4*, B153) That Patchwork.
— Jacket Jazz Encore. Weiland, Barbara, ed. LC 94-29985. (Illus.). 136p. (Orig.). 1994. pap. 21.95 (*1-56477-069-9*, B190) That Patchwork.

Murranka, Patricia, et al. Readings & Materials for Managerial Communication. 315p. 1991. pap. 25.00 (*0-536-57984-9*) Ginn Pr.

Murrant, Jim. The Boating Bible: The Essential Handbook for Every Sailor. (Illus.). 320p. 1991. 24.95 (*0-924486-13-9*) Sheridan.

***Murray.** Andrew Murray Collection, No. 2. 1995. 9.97 (*1-55748-636-0*) Barbour & Co.
— Caught in the Web of Words: James A. H. Murray & the "Oxford English Dictionary" 1995. pap. text ed. 16.00 (*0-300-06310-5*) Yale U Pr.
— Covenants & Blessings. 176p. pap. 4.99 (*0-88368-136-6*) Whitaker Hse.
— Educating Adults in the Workplace. 1995. write for info. (*0-89464-751-2*) Krieger.
— Handlist to Howard Carters Catalogue of Objects in Tutankhamuns Tomb, Vol. 1: Tutankhamuns Tomb. 1963. 34.00 (*0-900416-06-8*, Pub. by Aris & Phillips UK) David Brown.
— Hero & the Blues. pap. 9.00 (*0-679-76220-5*) Random.
— History of the Bellingham Rotary Club: 1917-1981. (Occasional Papers: No. 16). 1986. pap. 4.95 (*0-318-23334-7*) WWU CPNS.
— Nuclear Energy: Solutions Manual. 4th ed. 1994. pap. text ed. write for info. (*0-08-042127-X*, Pergamon Pr) Elsevier.
— Prayer: A 31-Day Plan to Enrich Your Prayer Life. (Little Library). 1995. pap. text ed. 0.99 (*1-55748-646-8*) Barbour & Co.
— Reindeer & Gold. 1988. pap. 10.95 (*1-882008-02-2*) WWU CPNS.
— Street in Petra. 1940. 5.50 (*0-85668-110-5*, Pub. by Aris & Phillips UK) David Brown.

Murray & Birnbaum. Wall Street Journal. 1987. write for info. (*0-318-61167-8*) Random.

Murray & Fox. Fisher-Price (an ID & Value Guide) 222p. 1991. 24.95 (*0-89689-086-4*) Bks Americana.

Murray, jt. auth. see Carr.

Murray, jt. auth. see Olsen.

Murray, et al. Medical Microbiology. (Illus.). 736p. 1990. 44.95 (*0-8016-3586-1*) Mosby Yr Bk.
— The Works - One of Everything: Psychological Type & Temperament Training & Counseling Materials. 124p. 1990. 87.50 (*1-878287-17-6*) Type & Temperament.

Murray, A. D., ed. John Ludlow: The Autobiography of a Christian Socialist. (Illus.). 354p. 1981. 30.00 (*0-7146-3085-3*, Pub. by F Cass Pubs UK) Intl Spec Bk.

Murray, A. T., tr. see Homer.

Murray, Alan & Tarassenko, Lionel. Analogue Neural VLSI: A Pulse Stream Approach. LC 93-32970. 1993. write for info. (*0-412-45060-7*, Chap & Hall NY) Chapman & Hall.

***Murray, Alan F.** Applications of Neural Networks. LC 94-43161. 336p. (C). 1994. lib. bdg. 110.00 (*0-7923-9442-9*) Kluwer Ac.

Murray, Alan F. & Reekie, H. Martin. Integrated Circuit Design. LC 87-12935. 147p. 1987. 42.00 (*0-387-91303-3*) Spr-Verlag.

Murray, Alan I. & Siehl, Caren. Joint Ventures & Other Alliances: Creating a Successful Cooperative Linkage. LC 89-85781. (Illus.). 100p. 1990. pap. 12.00 (*0-910586-76-4*, 086-89) Finan Exec.

Murray, Alan P. Depreciation. LC 74-172243. (Tax Technique Handbook Ser.). (Illus.). 138p. (Orig.). 1971. pap. 5.00 (*0-915506-12-2*) Harvard Law Intl Tax.

Murray, Alan S., jt. auth. see Birnbaum, Jeffrey H.

***Murray, Alber.** The Seven League Boots: A Novel. 384p. 1995. 24.00 (*0-679-43986-2*) Pantheon.

Murray, Albert. The Omni-Americans: Black Experience & American Culture. (Quality Paperbacks Ser.). 227p. 1990. reprint ed. pap. 10.95 (*0-306-80395-X*) Da Capo.
— Reflections Behind the Wheel of a Taxi: The Autobiography of a 30-Year Dropout. 258p. (Orig.). 1990. pap. 19.95 (*1-877586-01-3*) Braimanna Pubs.
— Reflections on Logic, Politics & Reality: A Challenge to the Sacred Consensus of Contemporary American Thinking. 256p. (C). 1989. 24.95 (*1-877586-00-5*) Braimanna Pubs.
— South to a Very Old Place. 1992. 19.50 (*0-8446-6630-0*) Peter Smith.
— South to a Very Old Place. LC 91-50214. 240p. 1991. pap. 9.00 (*0-679-73695-6*, Vin) Random.
— South to a Very Old Place. LC 94-32198. 1995. 13.50 (*0-679-60147-3*, Modern Lib) Random.
— The Spyglass Tree. LC 92-50077. 1992. 10.00 (*0-679-73085-0*, Vin) Random.
— Stomping the Blues. (Quality Paperbacks Ser.). (Illus.). 272p. 1989. pap. 11.95 (*0-306-80362-3*) Da Capo.
— Train Whistle Guitar. (Northeastern Library of Black Literature). 183p. 1989. reprint ed. pap. text ed. 10.95 (*1-55553-051-6*) NE U Pr.

Murray, Albert, jt. auth. see Basie, Count.

Murray, Albert V. The State & the Church in a Free Society. LC 77-27134. (Hibbert Lectures: 1957). reprint ed. 37.50 (*0-404-60433-1*) AMS Pr.

Murray, Alex, jt. ed. see Fallis, George.

Murray, Alex L. & Wilkinson, Paul F. Integrated Camping & the Retarded, Nos. 949-950. 1976. 12.50 (*0-686-20381-X*) CPL Biblios.

Murray, Alexander S. Who's Who in Mythology. 1988. 7.99 (*0-517-01741-5*) Random Hse Value.

Murray, Alexander V. The Manual of Mythology: Greek & Roman, Norse & Old German, Hindoo & Egyptian Mythology. Gross, Gina R., ed. (Illus.). 368p. 1993. reprint ed. pap. 12.95 (*0-87877-182-4*) Newcastle Pub.

Murray, Alice E. A History of the Commercial & Financial Relations Between England & Ireland from the Period of the Restoration. LC 70-133529. (Select Bibliographies Reprint Ser.). 1977. reprint ed. 28.95 (*0-8369-5561-7*) Ayer.

Murray, Allison J. No Money, No Honey: A Study of Street Traders & Prostitutes in Jakarta. (Illus.). 190p. 1991. 37.00 (*0-19-588991-6*) OUP.

Murray, Amanda, ed. Breads. 100p. 1992. pap. 5.95 (*1-882232-02-X*) Kitchen Collect.
— Chicken. 100p. 1992. pap. 5.95 (*1-882232-06-2*) Kitchen Collect.
— Desserts. 100p. 1992. pap. 5.95 (*1-882232-07-0*) Kitchen Collect.
— Meats. 96p. Date not set. spiral bd. 5.95 (*1-882232-08-9*) Kitchen Collect.
— Salads. 100p. 1992. pap. 5.95 (*1-882232-01-1*) Kitchen Collect.
— Seafood. 100p. 1992. pap. 5.95 (*1-882232-05-4*) Kitchen Collect.
— Soups. 100p. 1992. pap. 5.95 (*1-882232-00-3*) Kitchen Collect.
— Vegetables. 100p. 1992. spiral bd. 5.95 (*1-882232-03-8*) Kitchen Collect.

Murray, Andrew. Abide in Christ. 1992. pap. 3.97 (*1-55748-298-5*) Barbour & Co.
— Abide in Christ. 1992. pap. 4.95 (*0-87508-370-6*) Chr Lit.
— Abide in Christ. (Kregel Large Print Inspirational Classics Ser.). 283p. 9.99 (*0-8254-5314-3*) Kregel.
— Abide in Christ. 208p. 1980. pap. 3.99 (*0-88368-091-2*) Whitaker Hse.
— Abide in Christ. 1992. pap. 5.99 (*0-7208-0752-2*) Zondervan.
— Abide in Christ. (Christian Library). 1985. reprint ed. text ed. 7.99 (*0-916441-10-5*) Barbour & Co.
— Absolute Surrender. 7.99 (*0-916441-04-0*, Christian Lib) Barbour & Co.
— Absolute Surrender. pap. 4.50 (*0-8024-0560-6*) Moody.
— Absolute Surrender. 128p. 1981. pap. 3.99 (*0-88368-093-9*) Whitaker Hse.
— Acerquemonos Al Senor: Let Us Draw Nigh. (SPA.). 3.25 (*84-7228-890-0*, 220011, Pub. by Edit Clie SP) TSELF.
— Andrew Murray Collection. (Collector's Edition Ser.). 1994. 9.97 (*1-55748-528-3*) Barbour & Co.
— Apostles Inner Life. 1989. pap. 5.99 (*0-310-56132-9*) Zondervan.
— The Believer's Absolute Surrender. LC 85-447. 150p. 1985. pap. 5.99 (*0-87123-827-6*) Bethany Hse.
— The Believer's Call to Commitment. LC 83-3819. 101p. 1983. reprint ed. pap. 5.99 (*0-87123-289-8*) Bethany Hse.
— Believer's Daily Renewal. LC 81-6143. 125p. 1981. pap. 5.99 (*0-87123-147-6*) Bethany Hse.
— The Believer's Full Blessing of Pentecost. LC 84-12301. 112p. 1984. reprint ed. pap. 5.99 (*0-87123-597-8*) Bethany Hse.
— The Believer's New Covenant. LC 83-21408. 128p. 1983. reprint ed. pap. 5.99 (*0-87123-406-8*) Bethany Hse.
— The Believer's New Life. LC 83-3006. 208p. 1984. pap. 6.99 (*0-87123-431-9*) Bethany Hse.
— The Believer's Prayer Life. CRM Staff, tr. 187p. (CHI.). 1991. pap. 5.00 (*1-56582-033-9*) Christ Renew Min.
— The Believer's Prayer Life. rev. ed. LC 83-12254. (Andrew Murray Prayer Library). 141p. 1983. pap. 5.99 (*0-87123-277-4*) Bethany Hse.
— The Believer's School of Prayer. rev. ed. LC 82-4401. 201p. 1982. pap. 6.99 (*0-87123-195-6*) Bethany Hse.
— The Believer's Secret of a Perfect Heart. LC 83-22490. 176p. 1984. reprint ed. pap. 5.99 (*0-87123-425-4*) Bethany Hse.
— The Believer's Secret of Holiness. LC 84-2973. 208p. 1984. reprint ed. pap. 6.99 (*0-87123-432-7*) Bethany Hse.
— The Believer's Secret of Living Like Christ. LC 85-26683. 176p. (Orig.). 1985. pap. 6.99 (*0-87123-445-9*) Bethany Hse.
— Believer's Secret of Obedience. LC 82-14603. (Andrew Murray Christian Maturity Library). 88p. 1982. reprint ed. pap. 5.99 (*0-87123-279-0*) Bethany Hse.
— The Believer's Secret of the Master's Indwelling. rev. ed. LC 86-6814. 192p. 1986. pap. 6.99 (*0-87123-653-2*, 210653) Bethany Hse.
— The Believer's Secret of Waiting on God. LC 85-32068. 169p. 1986. pap. 5.99 (*0-87123-886-1*) Bethany Hse.
— Las Bendiciones De Pentecostes: The Blessings of Pentecost. (SPA.). 3.95 (*84-7228-747-5*, 222221, Pub. by Edit Clie SP) TSELF.
— The Best of Andrew Murray. (Best Ser.). 256p. 1991. reprint ed. pap. 7.99 (*0-8010-6281-0*) Baker Bk.
— The Blessings of Obedience. Orig. Title: School of Obedience; Believer's Secret of Obedience. 107p. 1984. pap. text ed. 3.99 (*0-88368-155-2*) Whitaker Hse.
— Blood of the Cross. 1992. pap. 5.50 (*0-87508-374-9*) Chr Lit.
— The Blood of the Cross. 144p. 1981. reprint ed. pap. 4.50 (*0-88368-103-X*) Whitaker Hse.
— Como Criar a los Hijos Para Cristo: How to Raise Children for Christ. (SPA.). 6.95 (*84-7228-682-7*, 220227, Pub. by Edit Clie SP) TSELF.
— Como Ser Libres Del Egoismo: Freedom from Self. (SPA.). 4.95 (*84-7228-623-1*, 220199, Pub. by Edit Clie SP) TSELF.
— Como Vivir En la Voluntad De Dios: How to Live in the Will of God. (SPA.). 5.50 (*84-7228-914-1*, 222236, Pub. by Edit Clie SP) TSELF.
— Confesion y Perdon: Confession & Forgiveness. (SPA.). 4.95 (*84-7228-536-7*, 220187, Pub. by Edit Clie SP) TSELF.
— Confession: The Road to Forgiveness. Orig. Title: Have Mercy Upon Me. 160p. 1983. pap. text ed. 4.99 (*0-88368-134-X*) Whitaker Hse.
— La Consagracion Total: Absolute Surrender. (SPA.). 4.25 (*84-7228-633-9*, 220210, Pub. by Edit Clie SP) TSELF.
— Crecimiento En Cristo: Growing in Christ. (SPA.). 3.25 (*84-7228-595-2*, 220197, Pub. by Edit Clie SP) TSELF.
— The Deeper Christian Life. large type ed. (Large Print Inspirational Ser.). 1987. pap. 8.95 (*0-8027-2589-9*) Walker & Co.
— El Dinero: Money. (SPA.). 2.95 (*84-7228-824-2*, 220286, Pub. by Edit Clie SP) TSELF.
— Divine Healing. 1993. pap. 4.50 (*0-87508-375-7*) Chr Lit.
— Divine Healing. 1980. pap. 2.99 (*0-88019-019-1*) Schmul Pub Co.
— Divine Healing. 160p. 1982. reprint ed. pap. text ed. 3.99 (*0-88368-112-9*) Whitaker Hse.
— En Cristo y Con Cristo: The Master's Indwelling. (SPA.). 4.25 (*84-7228-696-7*, 220352, Pub. by Edit Clie SP) TSELF.
— La Escuela de la Obediencia. Orig. Title: The School of Obedience. 112p. (SPA.). 1984. pap. 4.50 (*0-8254-1498-9*) Kregel.
— La Escuela De la Oracion: With Christ in the School of Prayer. (SPA.). 5.95 (*84-7228-736-X*, 220388, Pub. by Edit Clie SP) TSELF.
— Esperando En Dios: Waiting on God. (SPA.). 3.95 (*84-7228-634-7*, 220384, Pub. by Edit Clie SP) TSELF.
— Full Blessing of Pentecost. 1979. pap. 4.95 (*0-87508-376-5*) Chr Lit.
— The Geographical Distribution of Mammals. Sterling, Keir B., ed. LC 77-81073. (Biologists & Their World Ser.). (Illus.). 1978. reprint ed. lib. bdg. 59.95 (*0-405-10642-4*) Ayer.
— God's Best Secrets. LC 93-39325. 376p. 1994. pap. 12.99 (*0-8254-3277-4*) Kregel.
— God's Will Our Dwelling Place. 176p. 1982. pap. 4.99 (*0-88368-119-6*) Whitaker Hse.
— Helps to Intercession. 1979. pap. 2.50 (*0-87508-377-3*) Chr Lit.

M

An Asterisk (*) at the beginning of an entry indicates that the title is appearing in BIP for the first time.

— Holiest of All: An Exposition of the Epistle to the Hebrews. 576p. 1993. reprint ed. pap. 18.99 (*0-8007-5472-7*) Revell.

— How to Be Perfect. 144p. 1982. reprint ed. pap. text ed. 2.99 (*0-88368-113-7*) Whitaker Hse.

— How to Bring Your Children to Christ. 320p. 1984. pap. 5.99 (*0-88368-135-8*) Whitaker Hse.

— How to Raise Your Children for Christ. LC 75-29344. 288p. 1975. pap. 8.99 (*0-87123-224-3*) Bethany Hse.

— How to Work for God. 144p. 1983. pap. 2.99 (*0-88368-129-3*) Whitaker Hse.

— Humildad: Humility. (SPA.). 2.95 (*84-7228-520-0*, 220474, Pub. by Edit Clie SP) TSELF.

— Humility. 1993. pap. 4.95 (*0-87508-383-8*) Chr Lit.

— Humility. 112p. 1982. reprint ed. pap. text ed. 3.99 (*0-88368-110-2*) Whitaker Hse.

— In Search of Spiritual Excellence. Orig. Title: The Full Blessing of Pentecost. 125p. 1984. pap. text ed. 4.99 (*0-88368-163-3*) Whitaker Hse.

— The Inner Life. 224p. 1984. pap. text ed. 4.99 (*0-88368-138-2*) Whitaker Hse.

— Jesucristo: Profeta y Sacerdote: Jesus Christ, Prophet & Priest. (SPA.). 3.25 (*84-7228-638-X*, 220504, Pub. by Edit Clie SP) TSELF.

— Let Us Draw Nigh. 1979. pap. 4.95 (*0-87508-379-X*) Chr Lit.

— Like Christ. 240p. 1981. reprint ed. pap. 4.99 (*0-88368-099-8*) Whitaker Hse.

— Living the New Life. 256p. 1982. reprint ed. pap. text ed. 4.99 (*0-88368-108-0*) Whitaker Hse.

— Living to Please God. 100p. 1985. pap. text ed. 4.99 (*0-88368-166-8*) Whitaker Hse.

— Lord's Table. 1985. pap. 4.95 (*0-87508-424-9*) Chr Lit.

— The Master's Indwelling. 176p. 1983. pap. 4.99 (*0-88368-121-8*) Whitaker Hse.

— Mighty Is Your Hand: A Forty-Day Journey in the Company of Andrew Murray. 1993. pap. 6.99 (*1-55661-369-5*) Bethany Hse.

— Ministerio de la Oracion Intercesora. 176p. (Orig.). (SPA.). 1985. pap. 4.95 (*0-88113-207-1*) Edit Betania.

— The Ministry of Intercession. 208p. 1982. reprint ed. pap. text ed. 4.99 (*0-88368-114-5*) Whitaker Hse.

— The Ministry of Intercessory Prayer. rev. ed. LC 81-18011. 1982. pap. 6.99 (*0-87123-353-3*) Bethany Hse.

— La Nueva Vida Del Cristiano. 2nd ed. 240p. (SPA.). (C). 1989. pap. 4.95 (*0-88113-221-7*) Edit Betania.

— Permaneced en Cristo: Abide in Christ. (SPA.). 5.50 (*84-7228-524-3*, 220684, Pub. by Edit Clie SP) TSELF.

— Poder de la Sangre de Jesus: Power of the Blood of Jesus. (SPA.). 3.95 (*84-7228-823-4*, 220693, Pub. by Edit Clie SP) TSELF.

— Por Que No Crees? Why Do You Not Believe? (SPA.). 3.25 (*84-7228-705-X*, 220709, Pub. by Edit Clie SP) TSELF.

— Power of the Blood. 1993. pap. 5.95 (*0-87508-428-1*) Chr Lit.

— Power of the Blood of Jesus. 192p. 1993. pap. 4.99 (*0-88368-234-6*) Whitaker Hse.

— The Prayer Life. 160p. 1981. reprint ed. pap. 4.99 (*0-88368-102-1*) Whitaker Hse.

— Prayer Topics. 80p. 1993. pap. 3.99 (*0-88368-235-4*) Whitaker Hse.

— Prayers Inner Chamber. 1989. pap. 5.99 (*0-310-56112-4*) Zondervan.

— Principios para Ministerio: Key to the Missionary Problem. (SPA.). 4.25 (*84-7228-849-8*, 222711, Pub. by Edit Clie SP) TSELF.

— Promise of the Spirit. 1990. pap. 4.99 (*0-7208-0748-4*) Zondervan.

— Revival. 144p. (Orig.). 1990. pap. 7.99 (*1-55661-123-4*) Bethany Hse.

— Sangre de la Cruz: Blood of the Cross. (SPA.). 4.25 (*0-317-04299-8*, 220797, Pub. by Edit Clie SP) TSELF.

— Secret of Adoration. (Secret Ser.). 1992. pap. 2.50 (*0-87508-384-6*) Chr Lit.

— The Secret of Adoration. 65p. Date not set. pap. text ed. write for info. (*0-614-02760-8*) Christ Stewards.

— The Secret of Believing Prayer. LC 80-69320. 80p. 1980. pap. 5.99 (*0-87123-590-0*) Bethany Hse.

— Secret of Brotherly Love. (Secret Ser.). 1992. pap. 2.50 (*0-87508-390-0*) Chr Lit.

— Secret of Christ Our Life. (Secret Ser.). 1992. pap. 2.50 (*0-87508-385-4*) Chr Lit.

— Secret of Fellowship. (Secret Ser.). 1990. pap. 2.50 (*0-87508-388-9*) Chr Lit.

— Secret of Inspiration. (Secret Ser.). 1990. pap. 2.50 (*0-87508-386-2*) Chr Lit.

— Secret of Intercession. (Secret Ser.). 1990. pap. 2.50 (*0-87508-391-9*) Chr Lit.

— The Secret of Intercession. 65p. Date not set. pap. text ed. write for info. (*0-614-02759-4*) Christ Stewards.

— Secret of Power from on High. (Secret Ser.). 1992. pap. 2.50 (*0-87508-392-7*) Chr Lit.

— Secret of the Abiding Presence. (Secret Ser.). 1990. pap. 2.50 (*0-87508-382-X*) Chr Lit.

— Secret of the Cross. (Secret Ser.). 1990. pap. 2.50 (*0-87508-389-7*) Chr Lit.

— Secret of the Faith Life. (Secret Ser.). 1990. pap. 2.50 (*0-87508-387-0*) Chr Lit.

— The Secret of the Faith Life. 65p. Date not set. pap. text ed. write for info. (*0-614-02758-6*) Christ Stewards.

— Secret of the Throne of Grace. (Secret Ser.). 1992. pap. 2.50 (*0-87508-393-5*) Chr Lit.

— Secret of United Prayer. (Secret Ser.). 1979. pap. 2.50 (*0-87508-394-3*) Chr Lit.

— Secretos de la Oracion de Fe: Secret of Believing Prayer. (SPA.). 2.95 (*84-7228-817-X*, 220803, Pub. by Edit Clie SP) TSELF.

— The Spirit of Christ. rev. ed. LC 79-51335. 288p. 1983. pap. 8.99 (*0-87123-589-7*) Bethany Hse.

— The Spirit of Christ. 2nd ed. 240p. 1984. reprint ed. pap. 5.99 (*0-88368-126-9*) Whitaker Hse.

— State of the Church. (Orig.). 1989. pap. 4.95 (*0-87508-407-9*) Chr Lit.

— The True Vine. 112p. 1983. pap. text ed. 3.99 (*0-88368-118-8*) Whitaker Hse.

— Two Covenants. 1992. pap. 4.95 (*0-87508-396-X*) Chr Lit.

— Vid Verdadera: True Vine. (SPA.). 3.25 (*84-7228-619-3*, 220945, Pub. by Edit Clie SP) TSELF.

— Waiting on God. 1992. pap. 5.95 (*0-87508-399-4*) Chr Lit.

— Waiting on God. 160p. 1981. reprint ed. pap. 4.99 (*0-88368-101-3*) Whitaker Hse.

— With Christ in the School of Prayer. large type ed. (Large Print Inspirational Ser.). 1987. pap. 9.95 (*0-8027-2600-3*) Walker & Co.

— With Christ in the School of Prayer. (Christian Libarary). 274p. 1986. reprint ed. 7.99 (*0-916441-57-1*) Barbour & Co.

— With Christ in the School of Prayer. 288p. 1981. reprint ed. pap. 4.99 (*0-88368-106-4*) Whitaker Hse.

— With Wings As Eagles. 96p. 1993. pap. 4.99 (*0-88368-262-1*) Whitaker Hse.

— Working for God. 1980. pap. 4.95 (*0-87508-404-4*) Chr Lit.

Murray, Andrew & Choy, Leona. Key to the Missionary Problem. 1993. pap. 5.95 (*0-87508-401-X*) Chr Lit.

Murray, Andrew & Edwards, Jonathan. The Believer's Secret of Christian Love. Parkhurst, L. G., Jr., ed. 144p. (Orig.). 1990. pap. 5.99 (*1-55661-129-3*) Bethany Hse.

Murray, Andrew & Finney, Charles G. The Believer's Secret of Spiritual Power. rev. ed. Parkhurst, L. G., ed. LC 87-16838. 160p. 1987. pap. 5.99 (*0-87123-983-3*) Bethany Hse.

***Murray, Andrew & Hunt, Tim.** The Cell Cycle: An Introduction. (Illus.). 264p. (C). 1993. pap. text ed. 23.95 (*0-19-509529-4*) OUP.

Murray, Andrew & Spurgeon, Charles. Believer's Secret of Intercession. Parkhurst, L. G., ed. LC 87-34145. 160p. (Orig.). (C). 1988. pap. 5.99 (*0-87123-992-2*) Bethany Hse.

Murray, Andrew, ed. see Law, William.

Murray, Andrew, et al. The Believer's Secret of the Abiding Presence. rev. ed. LC 86-28307. (Andrew Murray Devotional Library). 144p. 1987. pap. 5.99 (*0-87123-899-3*) Bethany Hse.

— Healing: The Three Great Classics on Divine Healing. Graf, Jonathan L., ed. LC 92-90119. 375p. 1992. 14.99 (*0-87509-491-0*) Chr Pubns.

Murray, Andrew D., ed. see Katchmer, George A., Jr.

Murray, Anna. My Christmas Craft Book. (J). 1993. 9.99 (*0-307-16750-X*) Western Pub.

Murray, Annabel. Island of Turmoil. large type ed. 1990. lib. bdg. 18.95 (*0-263-12349-9*, Pub. by Mills & Boon UK) Thorndike Pr.

— A Man for Christmas. 1993. mass mkt. 2.99 (*0-373-11613-6*, 1-11613-6) Harlequin Bks.

Murray, Arthur. Arthur Murray's Dance Secrets. (Ballroom Dance Ser.). 1986. lib. bdg. 79.95 (*0-8490-3371-3*) Gordon Pr.

— Arthur Murray's Dance Secrets. (Ballroom Dance Ser.). 1985. lib. bdg. 100.00 (*0-87700-698-9*) Revisionist Pr.

— Down Memory Lane. (Ballroom Dance Ser.). 1986. lib. bdg. 79.95 (*0-8490-3370-5*) Gordon Pr.

— Down Memory Lane. (Ballroom Dance Ser.). 1985. lib. bdg. 120.00 (*0-87700-697-0*) Revisionist Pr.

— How to Become a Good Dancer. (Ballroom Dance Ser.). 1986. lib. bdg. 79.95 (*0-8490-3369-1*) Gordon Pr.

— How to Become a Good Dancer. (Ballroom Dance Ser.). 1985. lib. bdg. 120.00 (*0-87700-696-2*) Revisionist Pr.

— The Modern Dances. (Ballroom Dance Ser.). 1986. lib. bdg. 79.95 (*0-8490-3338-1*) Gordon Pr.

— The Modern Dances. (Ballroom Dance Ser.). 1985. lib. bdg. 79.95 (*0-87700-695-4*) Revisionist Pr.

— Social Dancing. (Ballroom Dance Ser.). 1986. lib. bdg. 79.95 (*0-8490-3255-5*) Gordon Pr.

— Social Dancing. (Ballroom Dance Ser.). 1985. lib. bdg. 79.95 (*0-87700-694-6*) Revisionist Pr.

Murray, Arthur, et al. Down Memory Lane: A Pictorial History of Ballroom & Social Dancing. (Ballroom Dance Ser.). 1989. lib. bdg. 79.95 (*0-8490-3966-5*) Gordon Pr.

Murray, Barbara A., jt. auth. see Murray, Kenneth T.

Murray, Beth. Gifts Children Can Make: Creative Presents for Family & Friends. LC 93-73301. (Illus.). 32p. (J). (ps-5). 1994. pap. 4.95 (*1-56397-324-3*) Boyds Mills Pr.

— Highlights Book of Travel Fun: Crafts & Activities for the Car, Plane, Bus, or Train. LC 94-72625. (Illus.). 32p. (J). (gr. 2-7). 1995. 3.95 (*1-56397-405-3*, Wordsong) Boyds Mills Pr.

— Kitchen Fun: A Hearty Helping of Things to Make, Play, & Eat. LC 93-70872. (Illus.). 32p. (J). (ps-5). 1994. pap. 4.95 (*1-56397-317-0*) Boyds Mills Pr.

— Puppet & Theater Activities: Theatrical Things to Do & Make. 32p. (J). (ps-2). 1995. pap. 4.95 (*1-56397-333-2*) Boyds Mills Pr.

— Thanksgiving Fun: A Bountiful Harvest of Crafts, Recipes, & Games. (Illus.). 32p. (Orig.). (J). (gr. 2-7). 1993. pap. 3.95 (*1-56397-280-8*) Boyds Mills Pr.

Murray, Beth, ed. Animal Craft Fun: Indoor & Outdoor Animal Crafts Projects. (Illus.). 32p. (J). (gr. k-5). 1994. pap. 3.95 (*1-56397-314-6*) Boyds Mills Pr.

Murray, Betty. Carved in Stone: Heffington Cemetery, Faulkner Co., Arkansas, Vol. 1. Vanaman, Henryetta, ed. (Illus.). 64p. 1992. 22.95 (*1-56869-006-1*); pap. 14.95 (*1-56869-007-X*) Oldbuck Pr.

— Eighteen Sixty U. S. Federal Census, Conway Co., Arkansas. 314p. 1993. 27.95 (*1-56869-022-3*); pap. 19.95 (*1-56869-023-1*) Oldbuck Pr.

***Murray, Bill.** Soccer: The World's Game. LC 95-13742. (Illinois History of Sports Ser.). (Illus.). 1996. write for info. (*0-252-01748-X*) U of Ill Pr.

***Murray-Blunt, Kathryn J.** The Universe Would Have No Reason to Exist Without Man to Comprehend It. (Illus.). 56p. (Orig.). Date not set. pap. text ed. 19.95 (*1-887401-06-7*) Essence Immort.

Murray-Blunt, Kathryn L., jt. auth. see Blunt, John E.

***Murray, Bob & Fortinberry, Alicia.** Maud of Llangibbi. 376p. (Orig.). 1996. pap. 9.95 (*1-885610-02-5*) European Amer.

Murray, Bob, ed. see Ati.

Murray, Brian. Charles Dickens. (Literature & Life Ser.). 192p. (C). 1994. 19.95 (*0-8264-0565-7*) Continuum.

Murray, Bruce. Film & the German Left in the Weimar Republic: From Caligari to Kuhle Wampe. (Film Studies). (Illus.). 303p. (C). 1990. text ed. 32.50 (*0-292-72464-0*); pap. 16.95 (*0-292-72465-9*) U of Tex Pr.

Murray, Bruce A. & Wickham, Christopher J., eds. Framing the Past: The Historiography of German Cinema & Television. LC 91-39848. (Illus.). 384p. (C). 1992. 34.95 (*0-8093-1756-7*) S Ill U Pr.

Murray, Bruce C. Journey into Space: The First Thirty Years of Space Exploration. (Illus.). 1989. 19.95 (*0-393-02675-2*) Norton.

— Journey Into Space: The First Thirty Years of Space Exploration. 1990. pap. 14.95 (*0-393-30703-4*) Norton.

Murray, Bruce C. & Burgess, Eric. Flight to Mercury. LC 76-25017. (Illus.). 162p. 1977. text ed. 43.00 (*0-231-03996-4*) Col U Pr.

Murray, Bruce C., jt. auth. see Davies, Merton.

Murray, C., jt. auth. see Lubbe, G.

Murray, C. A. Vectorial Astrometry. (Illus.). 368p. 1983. 103.00 (*0-85274-372-6*) IOP Pub.

Murray, C. H. & Murray, M. S. A Drugless Treatment for Deafness & Partial Deafness: Osteopathic, Somapathic, Naturopathic, Chiropractic & Mechano-Therapic. (Alternative Medicine Ser.). 1991. lib. bdg. 69.95 (*0-8490-4263-1*) Gordon Pr.

Murray, Carmin R., jt. auth. see Larmouth, Thomas E.

Murray, Carol. Women with & Without. (American Dust Ser.: No. 14). 200p. 1984. 10.95 (*0-913218-81-2*) Dustbooks.

Murray, Carol, jt. auth. see Shalhoub, Judy.

Murray, Carolyn K. Walking the Spiritual Walk: A Successful Search for Purpose & Partner. LC 94-18154. 244p. 1994. pap. 14.95 (*0-87604-324-4*, 391) ARE Pr.

Murray, Catherine T. A Taste of Memories from the Old "Bush", Vol. II: Recipes, Memories & Photographs of the Old Greenbush Neighborhood. (Illus.). 554p. (Orig.). 1990. spiral bd. 18.50 (*0-9626346-1-1*) Greenbush Remembered.

Murray, Catherine T., intro. A Taste of Memories from Columbus Park, Vol. III: Recipes, Memories & Photographs of the Old West Side Neighborhood in Kenosha, Wisconsin. (Illus.). 535p. (Orig.). 1992. spiral bd. 19.95 (*0-9626346-2-X*) Greenbush Remembered.

Murray, Charles. Hamewith: The Complete Poems of Charles Murray. Shepherd, Nan, ed. (Illus.). 180p. 1982. 15.00 (*0-08-024522-6*, Pergamon Pr); pap. 7.00 (*0-08-024521-8*, Pergamon Pr) Elsevier.

— In Pursuit of Happiness & Good Government. 1994. pap. 16.95 (*1-55815-297-0*) ICS Pr.

— Losing Ground: American Social Policy, 1950-1980. (Illus.). 352p. 1994. pap. 16.00 (*0-465-04233-3*) Basic.

Murray, Charles, jt. auth. see Herrnstein, Richard J.

Murray, Charles A. Travels in North America, During the Years 1834-36, Including a Summer with the Pawnees. 2nd ed. LC 68-54845. (American Scene Ser.). 878p. 1974. reprint ed. lib. bdg. 85.00 (*0-306-71021-8*) Da Capo.

Murray, Charles S. Blues on CD: The Essential Guide. 432p. 1993. pap. 22.95 (*1-85626-084-4*) Trafalgar.

— Crosstown Traffic: Jimi Hendrix & the Post-War Rock 'n' Roll Revolution. (Illus.). 256p. 1991. pap. 9.95 (*0-312-06324-5*) St Martin.

Murray, Chas H. & Murray, M. S. A Drugless Treatment for Partial Deafness & Deafness. 39p. 1966. reprint ed. spiral bd. 4.40 (*0-7873-0630-4*) Mokelumne.

***Murray, Chris.** Butter Thief. (Illus.). 32p. (J). Date not set. pap. write for info. (*0-89213-274-4*) Bhaktivedanta.

***Murray, Christina.** Gender & the New South African Legal Order. 255p. 1994. pap. 34.00 (*0-7021-3316-7*, Pub. by Juta SA) W W Gaunt.

Murray, Christopher, jt. ed. see Hayley, Barbara.

Murray, Christopher, ed. see Robinson, Lennox.

Murray, Christopher, jt. auth. see Sekine, Masaru.

***Murray, Cindy C.** Planning a Tradeshow from Z to A Guidebook. Lingham, Gretchen, ed. 24p. (Orig.). 1995. pap. text ed. 14.95 (*0-9645468-0-9*) Staicer & Assocs.

— Planning a Tradeshow from Z to A Worksheets. Lingham, Gretchen, ed. 54p. (Orig.). 1995. 14.95 (*0-9645468-1-7*) Staicer & Assocs.

Murray-Clark, Ian. Night & Day. 1989. 1.98 (*0-945603-02-9*) Dinnerman Bks.

— Windows. 1989. 1.98 (*0-945603-05-3*) Dinnerman Bks.

Murray, Cleitus O. Stories of the Southern Mountains & Swamps. (Illus.). 192p. (Orig.). (YA). 1992. pap. 9.95 (*0-9632132-0-2*) Murray Pubns.

Murray, Colin. Black Mountain: Land, Class, & Power in the Eastern Orange Free State, 1880s to 1980s. LC 92-60159. (Illus.). 368p. (C). 1992. text ed. 49.95 (*1-56098-227-6*) Smithsonian.

— Celtic Tree Oracle. 1988. 27.50 (*0-312-02032-5*) St Martin.

Murray, Corinne, ed. Accessible Art: A Layman's Look at Seattle's Public Art. LC 90-82681. (Illus.). (Orig.). 1990. pap. text ed. 12.95 (*0-9626878-0-4*, 72920) At Your Fingertips.

Murray, Craig. Benjamin Vaughan, Seventeen Fifty-One to Eighteen Thirty-Five: The Life of an Anglo-American Intellectual. 1981. 66.95 (*0-405-14101-7*) Ayer.

Murray, D., jt. auth. see Allen, W.

Murray, D. A., ed. see International Symposium on Chironomidae Staff.

Murray, D. Duncan, jt. auth. see Burke, David C.

Murray, D. M. & Wong, T. W. Noodle Words: An Introduction to Chinese & Japanese Characters. LC 79-147179. (Illus.). 96p. (YA). (gr. 9 up). 1971. pap. 6.95 (*0-8048-0948-8*) C E Tuttle.

Murray, Dave. House-Training Your VCR: A Help Manual for Humans. 120p. 1992. pap. 9.95 (*0-931011-39-6*) Grapevine Pubns.

Murray, David. Chapters in the History of Bookkeeping, Accountancy & Commercial Arithmetic. Brief, Richard P., ed. LC 77-87281. (Development of Contemporary Accounting Thought Ser.). 1978. reprint ed. lib. bdg. 44.95 (*0-405-10909-1*) Ayer.

— Poems. LC 70-144428. (Bannatyne Club, Edinburgh. Publications: No. 2). reprint ed. 27.50 (*0-404-52702-7*) AMS Pr.

Murray, David, ed. Forked Tongues: Speech, Writing & Representation in North American Indian Texts. LC 90-49156. 188p. 1991. 39.95 (*0-253-33942-1*); pap. 14.50 (*0-253-20650-2*, MB-650) Ind U Pr.

— Seed Dispersal. LC 86-72353. 322p. 1987. text ed. 83.00 (*0-12-511900-3*) Acad Pr.

Murray, David, jt. auth. see Gigerenzer, Gerd.

Murray, David J. A History of Western Psychology. 2nd ed. 464p. (C). 1988. text ed. 56.00 (*0-13-392580-3*) P-H.

Murray, David L. Pragmatism. LC 75-3292. reprint ed. 22.50 (*0-404-59278-3*) AMS Pr.

— Scenes & Silhouettes. LC 68-16959. (Essay Index Reprint Ser.). 1977. reprint ed. 20.95 (*0-8369-0727-2*) Ayer.

Murray, David R. Biology of Food Irradiation. 270p. 1990. text ed. 99.95 (*0-471-92621-3*) Wiley.

— Nutrition of the Angiosperm Embryo. 246p. 1989. text ed. 145.00 (*0-471-92153-X*) Wiley.

— Odious Commerce: Britain, Spain & the Abolition of the Cuban Slave Trade. LC 79-52835. (Cambridge Latin American Studies: No. 37). 435p. 1981. 79.95 (*0-521-22867-0*) Cambridge U Pr.

Murray, David R., ed. Advanced Methods in Plant Breeding & Biotechnology. (Biotechnology in Agriculture Ser.: No. 4). 365p. 1991. 95.00 (*0-85198-706-0*) CAB Intl.

Murray, David W. & Buxton, Bernard F. Experiments in the Machine Interpretation of Visual Motion. (Artificial Intelligence Ser.). 250p. 1990. 40.00 (*0-262-13263-X*) MIT Pr.

***Murray, Denise E.** Knowledge Machines: Language & Information in a Technological Society. LC 95-6900. (Language in Social Life Ser.). (C). 1995. pap. text ed. 21.95 (*0-582-07131-3*, Pub. by Longman UK) Longman.

— Knowledge Machines: Language & Information in a Techonological Society. LC 95-6900. (Language in Social Life Ser.). (C). 1995. text ed. 51.95 (*0-582-07132-1*, Pub. by Longman UK) Longman.

Murray, Denise E., ed. Diversity As Resource: Redefining Cultural Literacy. LC 92-61747. 326p. 1992. pap. 22.95 (*0-939791-42-0*) Tchrs Eng Spkrs.

Murray, Dennis, jt. intro. see Williams, William J.

***Murray, Dennis J.** The Guaranteed Fund-Raising System: A Systems Approach to Developing Fund-Raising Plans. 2nd ed. LC 93-74528. 368p. 1994. ring bd. 187.00 (*0-935517-03-0*) Amer Inst Mgnt.

— How to Evaluate Your Fund-Raising Program: A Performance Audit System. LC 84-71530. 215p. 1985. ring bd. 187.00 (*0-935517-00-6*) Amer Inst Mgnt.

Murray, Dennis J., jt. ed. see Keller, Peter A.

Murray, Derik, photos. Hockey Hall of Fame Legends: The Official Book. (Illus.). 200p. 1994. 34.95 (*0-670-85258-9*, Viking Studio) Studio Bks.

Murray, Dian H. Pirates of the South China Coast, 1790-1810. LC 87-10049. (Illus.). 256p. 1987. 37.50 (*0-8047-1376-6*) Stanford U Pr.

***Murray, Diane.** Nature Leanings. 1995. 8.95 (*0-8062-5092-5*) Carlton.

Murray, Dick. Teaching the Bible to Adults & Youth. rev. ed. LC 93-20102. 176p. 1993. Alk. paper. pap. 11.95 (*0-687-41084-3*) Abingdon.

— Teaching the Bible to Adults & Youth: Korean Edition. 176p. 1995. pap. 12.50 (*0-687-00785-2*) Abingdon.

Murray, Donal. The Church Guardian of Freedom. 1989. pap. 15.00 (*0-86217-257-8*, Pub. by Veritas IE) St Mut.

— The Future of Faith. 1989. pap. 15.00 (*0-86217-210-1*, Pub. by Veritas IE) St Mut.

— On the Road to Emmaus: Eucharist Renewal Today. 1989. pap. 15.00 (*1-85390-111-3*, Pub. by Veritas IE) St Mut.

— A Question of Morality: Christian Morality & In Vitro Fertilization. 1989. pap. 22.00 (*0-86217-230-6*, Pub. by Veritas IE) St Mut.

Murray, Donald M. The Craft of Revision. 185p. (C). 1991. pap. text ed. 7.50 (*0-03-070692-0*) HB Coll Pubs.

— The Craft of Revision. 2nd ed. (Illus.). 256p. (C). 1994. pap. text ed. write for info. (*0-15-501636-9*) HB Coll Pubs.

— Expecting the Unexpected: Teaching Myself - & Others - to Read & Write. LC 88-8490. xi, 276p. (Orig.). (C). 1989. pap. text ed. 17.50 (*0-86709-243-2*, 0243) Boynton Cook Pubs.

— Learning by Teaching: Selected Articles on Writing & Teaching. LC 82-20558. 184p. (C). 1982. pap. text ed. 17.50 (*0-86709-025-1*) Boynton Cook Pubs.

— Literature of Tomorrow: An Anthology of Student Fiction, Poetry, & Drama. (C). 1990. teacher ed write for info. (*0-03-032919-1*); text ed. 14.00 (*0-03-032903-5*) HB Coll Pubs.

An Asterisk (*) at the beginning of an entry indicates that the title is appearing in BIP for the first time.

— Read to Write. 3rd ed. (Illus.). 608p. 1993. pap. text ed. 21.50 (*0-15-500190-6*); Instructor's edition. teacher ed write for info. (*0-15-500191-4*) HarBrace.
— Read to Write: A Writing Process Reader. 2nd rev. ed. 457p. (C). 1990. pap. text ed. 19.75 (*0-03-030797-X*) HB Coll Pubs.
— Shoptalk: Learning to Write with Writers. 207p. (Orig.). 1990. pap. text ed. 12.95 (*0-86709-258-0*) Boynton Cook Pubs.
— Write to Learn. 3rd ed. 272p. (C). 1990. teacher ed write for info. (*0-03-033124-2*); pap. text ed. 20.75 (*0-03-033123-4*) HB Coll Pubs.
— Write to Learn. 4th ed. (Illus.). 240p. (C). 1993. pap. text ed. 21.50 (*0-15-500203-1*); Instructor's edition. teacher ed write for info. (*0-15-500204-X*) HB Coll Pubs.
— A Writer Teaches Writing, 2 Vols. 2nd ed. LC 84-81981. 304p. (C). 1984. pap. 31.56 (*0-395-35441-2*) HM.
Murray, Donna, jt. ed. see Seward, Melea L.
Murray, Donnaphee & Kunz, Carol. Celebrating Our Heritage: Kendall, Wisconsin 1894-1994. (Illus.). 152p. 1994. pap. 25.00 (*0-938627-21-X*) New Past Pr.
***Murray, Dorothy I.** Dear Teddy Bear. 12p. 1994. pap. 5.99 (*0-925037-19-2*) Great Lks Poetry.
— Two Bullies Meet. 12p. 1994. pap. 5.99 (*0-925037-20-6*) Great Lks Poetry.
Murray, Doug. The War, No. 4. 48p. 1989. 3.50 (*0-87135-551-5*) Marvel Entmnt.
Murray, Doug & Heath, Russ. Hearts & Minds. 64p. 1990. 8.95 (*0-87135-699-6*) Marvel Entmnt.
Murray, Doug, et al. The 'Nam Vol. 1. (Illus.). 96p. 1987. pap. 6.95 (*0-87135-284-2*) Marvel Entmnt.
— The 'Nam Vol. 2. (Illus.). 96p. 1988. pap. 6.95 (*0-87135-352-0*) Marvel Entmnt.
— The 'Nam Vol. 3. (Illus.). 96p. 1989. pap. 6.95 (*0-87135-543-4*) Marvel Entmnt.
Murray, Douglas. Freedom to Reform: The "Articles Declaratory" of the Church of Scotland, 1921. 121p. 1993. pap. text ed. 17.95 (*0-567-29216-9*, Pub. by T & T Clark UK) Bks Intl VA.
— Gentle Rain. LC 95-60131. 158p. 1995. pap. 16.95 (*0-9632825-1-4*) Tigermoon Ent.
Murray, Douglas, ed. see Austen, Jane.
Murray, Douglas J. & Viotti, Paul R., eds. The Defense Policies of Nations: A Comparative Study. 3rd ed. LC 93-20958. (Orig.). 1994. text ed. 65.00 (*0-8018-4793-1*); pap. text ed. 25.95 (*0-8018-4794-X*) Johns Hopkins.
— The Defense Policies of Nations: A Comparative Study. LC 81-3790. (Illus.). 541p. (Orig.). reprint ed. pap. 154.20 (*0-8357-7886-X*, 2036305) Bks Demand.
***Murray, Douglas L.** Cultivating Crisis: The Human Cost of Pesticides. 3rd ed. (Illus.). 208p. (C). 1995. text ed. 35.00x (*0-292-75168-0*); pap. 12.95 (*0-292-75169-9*) U of Tex Pr.
Murray, Douglas M., jt. ed. see Forrester, Duncan B.
Murray, E. B., contrib. Bodleian Manuscript Shelley, 2 vols., Set. LC 87-25710. (Bodleian Shelley Manuscripts: Vol. IV). 800p. 1988. 217.00 (*0-8240-6980-3*) Garland.
Murray, E. Patrick, pseud. Ten Little Indians. 432p. 1988. pap. 3.95 (*0-8217-2452-5*) Zebra.
***Murray, Earl.** Flaming Sky. 352p. 1995. 23.95 (*0-312-85915-5*) Forge NYC.
— Free Flows the River. 416p. 1995. mass mkt. 4.99 (*0-8125-1102-6*) Tor Bks.
— Ghosts of the Old West. 256p. 1994. mass mkt. 4.99 (*0-8125-3527-8*) Tor Bks.
— Mountain Sheriff. 384p. 1987. pap. 3.50 (*0-8217-2237-9*) Zebra.
— Mountain Sheriff, No. 3: The Canyon Mountain War. 256p. 1988. pap. 2.95 (*0-8217-2413-4*) Zebra.
— Mountain Sheriff, No. 4: Wild Stallion. 256p. 1988. pap. 3.50 (*0-8217-2493-2*) Zebra.
— Song of the Horse. 1995. 20.95 (*0-685-75361-1*) Tor Bks.
— Song of Wovoka. 416p. (Orig.). 1992. pap. 10.99 (*0-8125-2091-2*) Tor Bks.
— Song of Wovoka. 416p. (Orig.). 1993. mass mkt. 4.99 (*0-8125-1318-5*) Tor Bks.
— Thunder in the Dawn. LC 93-11522. 416p. 1993. 21.95 (*0-312-85675-X*) Forge NYC.
— Thunder in the Dawn. 416p. 1994. mass mkt. 4.99 (*0-8125-1319-3*) Tor Bks.
Murray, Earl, see E. Patrick Murray, pseud..
Murray, Earl P. High Freedom. 480p. 1988. mass mkt. 4.99 (*0-8125-8596-8*) Tor Bks.
Murray, Edward. Varieties of Dramatic Structure: A Study of Theory & Practice. 158p. (Orig.). (C). 1990. lib. bdg. 38.00 (*0-8191-7785-7*); pap. text ed. 19.00 (*0-8191-7786-5*) U Pr of Amer.
Murray, Edward J., ed. Methods in Molecular Biology, Vol. 7: Gene Transfer & Expression Protocols. LC 84-15696. (Illus.). 456p. 1991. 79.50 (*0-89603-178-0*); spiral bd. 45.00 (*0-89603-216-7*) Humana.
Murray, Edward L. Imaginative Thinking & Human Existence. LC 85-27368. 287p. (C). 1986. pap. text ed. 18.95 (*0-8207-0213-7*) Duquesne.
Murray, Edward L., ed. Imagination & Phenomenological Psychology. LC 87-13437. 230p. 1987. text ed. 27.00 (*0-8207-0195-5*) Duquesne.
Murray, Elaine. A Layman's Guide to New Age & Spiritual Terms. LC 92-41892. 208p. (Orig.). 1993. pap. 12.95 (*0-931892-53-8*) B Dolphin Pub.
Murray, Eleanor B. Cherokee County Summer. (Illus.). 48p. (Orig.). (YA). (gr. 9-12). 1981. pap. 3.98 (*1-879313-01-4*) Murrays Leprechaun Bks.
— God's Green Valley: And Its People. (Illus.). 28p. 1983. pap. 2.98 (*1-879313-03-0*) Murrays Leprechaun Bks.
Murray, Eleanor H. Bend Like the Bamboo. 91p. (Orig.). (YA). (gr. 9-12). 1982. pap. 8.95 (*1-879313-02-2*) Murrays Leprechaun Bks.
— Growing up in Aunt Molly's Omaha, 1920-1965: And Facing the World Beyond. (Illus.). 140p. (Orig.). (YA). (gr. 9-12). 1990. pap. 8.95 (*1-879313-00-6*) Murrays Leprechaun Bks.
Murray, Elizabeth. Essential Annuals. (Essential Gardening Ser.). 1989. 14.99 (*0-517-66177-2*) Random Hse Value.
— Monet's Passion: Ideas, Inspiration & Insights from the Painter's Gardens. LC 89-61640. (Illus.). 115p. 1989. 26.95 (*0-87654-443-X*) Pomegranate Calif.
— Painterly Photography: Awakening the Artist Within. LC 92-62862. (Illus.). 88p. 1993. 16.95 (*1-56640-601-3*) Pomegranate Calif.
***Murray, Elizabeth & Fell, Derek.** Creative Landscaping: Ideas, Designs & Blueprints. LC 94-26765. 1995. write for info. (*1-56799-156-4*, Friedman-Fairfax) M Friedman Pub Grp Inc.
Murray, Elizabeth M. Trips: New York City & Out-of-Town. rev. ed. (Illus.). 112p. 1980. pap. 3.95 (*0-936426-10-1*) Play Schs.
Murray, Ellen. Peace & Adventure. (C). 1990. 20.00 (*0-9501351-6-X*, Pub. by Wild Goose Pubns UK) St Mut.
Murray, Elwood, et al. Speech: Science-Art. LC 79-77823. (C). 1969. text ed. write for info. (*0-672-60863-4*, Bobbs) Macmillan.
Murray, Emily, jt. auth. see Murray, J. B.
Murray, F. W. Astronomy Simply Explained for Beginners. (C). 1987. 45.00 (*0-85174-485-0*, Pub. by Brwn Son Ferg) St Mut.
Murray, Frances. The Belchamber Scandal. large type ed. 448p. 1986. 15.95 (*0-7089-1558-2*) Ulverscroft.
— Payment for the Piper. large type ed. 596p. 1987. 16.95 (*0-7089-1590-6*) Ulverscroft.
Murray, Francis. World's Wildest Animal Jokes. LC 91-47701. (Illus.). 96p. (J). (gr. 3-8). 1992. 13.95 (*0-8069-8538-0*) Sterling.
Murray, Francis J. Introduction to Linear Transformations in Hilbert Space. (Annals of Mathematics Studies). 1941. 15.00 (*0-527-02720-0*) Periodicals Srv.
Murray, Francis J. & Miller, Kenneth S. Existence Theorems for Ordinary Differential Equations. LC 54-10566. 164p. reprint ed. pap. 46.80 (*0-317-08535-2*, 2050206) Bks Demand.
— Existence Theorems for Ordinary Differential Equations. LC 75-12685. 164p. 1976. reprint ed. 19.50 (*0-88275-320-7*) Krieger.
***Murray, Frank.** The Big Family Guide to all the Minerals. Barilla, Jean, ed. 1995. 24.95 (*0-87983-670-9*) Keats.
— Happy Feet. 370p. 1990. pap. 11.95 (*0-87983-476-5*) Keats.
Murray, Frank B., ed. Critical Features of Piaget's Theory of the Development of Thought. LC 72-6359. 196p. 1972. pap. text ed. 9.95 (*0-8422-0244-7*) Irvington.
— The Teacher Educator's Handbook: Building a Knowledge Base for the Preparation of Teachers. (Education Ser.). 1995. 75.00 (*0-7879-0121-0*) Jossey-Bass.
Murray, Frank B., ed. see Danks, Joseph H. & Pezdek, Kathy.
Murray, Frank B., ed. see Waterhouse, Lynn H., et al.
Murray, Frank S. All Israel Restored. 293p. 1992. 10.00 (*0-910840-21-0*) Kingdom.
— The Sublimity of Faith. LC 81-81770. (Illus.). 952p. 1982. 25.00 (*0-910840-20-2*) Kingdom.
Murray, Frank S., ed. Standard, 20 vols., Vols. 15-35. Incl. Vol. 15. Standard 1963. LC 49-3353. 1963. 3.00 (*0-910840-63-6*); Vol. 16. Standard 1964. 1964. 3.00 (*0-910840-64-4*); Vol. 17. Standard 1965. 1965. 3.00 (*0-910840-65-2*); Vol. 18. Standard 1966. 1966. 3.00 (*0-910840-66-0*); Vol. 19. Standard 1967. 1967. 3.00 (*0-910840-67-9*); Vol. 20. Standard 1968. 1968. 3.00 (*0-910840-68-7*); Vol. 21. Standard 1969. 1969. 3.00 (*0-910840-69-5*); Vol. 22. Standard 1970. 1970. 3.00 (*0-910840-70-9*); Vol. 23. Standard 1971. 1971. 3.00 (*0-910840-71-7*); Vol. 24. Standard 1972. 4p. 1995. pap. 3.00 (*0-910840-72-5*); Vol. 25. Standard 1973. 4p. 1995. pap. 3.00 (*0-910840-73-3*); Vol. 26. Standard 1974. 4p. 1995. pap. 3.00 (*0-910840-74-1*); Vol. 27. Standard 1975. 4p. 1995. pap. 3.00 (*0-910840-75-X*); Vol. 28. Standard 1976. 4p. 1995. pap. 3.00 (*0-910840-76-8*); Vol. 29. Standard 1977. 4p. 1995. pap. 3.00 (*0-910840-77-6*); Vol. 30. Standard 1978. 4p. 1995. pap. 3.00 (*0-910840-78-4*); Vol. 31. Standard 1979. 4p. 1995. pap. 3.00 (*0-910840-79-2*); Vol. 32. Standard 1980. 4p. 1995. pap. 3.000-*910840-80-6*); Vol. 33. Standard 1981. 4p. 1995. pap. 3.00 (*0-910840-81-4*); Vol. 34. Standard 1982. 4p. 1995. pap. 3.00 (*0-910840-82-2*); Vol. 35. Standard 1983. 1995. pap. 3.00 (*0-910840-83-0*); Vol. 26. Standard 1974. 4p. 1995. pap. 3.00 (*0-910840-74-1*); Vol. 24. Standard 1972. 4p. 1995. pap. 3.00 (*0-910840-72-5*); write for info. (*0-318-53986-1*) Kingdom.
***Murray, Fred & Murray, Jody L.** God Loves Even Cowboys. LC 94-96344. (Illus.). 177p. (Orig.). (J). (gr. 4 up). 1994. pap. 11.95 (*0-9642685-4-X*) F Murray Pubng.
Murray, Frederic W. The Aesthetics of Contemporary Spanish American Social Protest Poetry. LC 90-19948. (Hispanic Literature Ser.: Vol. 9). 224p. 1990. lib. bdg. 89.95 (*0-88946-591-6*) E Mellen.
Murray, Frederick G., jt. auth. see Murray, Janette S.
Murray, Freeman H. Emancipation & the Freed in American Sculpture. LC 70-38016. (Black Heritage Library Collection). 1977. reprint ed. 28.95 (*0-8369-8983-X*) Ayer.
Murray, G., jt. auth. see Davies, B.
Murray, G., tr. see Wilamowitz & Moellendorff, U.
Murray, G. E. Gasoline Dreams. 1978. per. 3.00 (*0-88031-046-4*) Invisible-Red Hill.
— Oils of Evening: Journeys in the Art Trade. Spelius, ed. 155p. (Orig.). 1995. pap. 12.95 (*0-941363-36-8*) Lake Shore Pub.
— Repairs: Poems. LC 79-5379. (Devins Award Breakthrough Ser.). 96p. 1979. text ed. 14.95 (*0-8262-0290-X*) U of Mo Pr.
— Walking the Blind Dog: Poems by G. E. Murray. 112p. (Orig.). 1992. pap. 10.95 (*0-252-06231-0*) U of Ill Pr.
Murray, G. G. Gobi or Shamo: A Story of Three Songs. Reginald, R. & Melville, Douglas, eds. LC 77-84259. (Lost Race & Adult Fantasy Ser.). 1978. reprint ed. lib. bdg. 34.95 (*0-405-11002-2*) Ayer.
Murray, G. T. Introduction to Engineering Materials: Behavior, Properties, & Selection. LC 93-12660. (Engineering Materials Ser.: Vol. 2). 688p. 1993. 150.00 (*0-8247-8965-2*) Dekker.
Murray, G. W. English-Nubian Comparative Dictionary. Hooton, E. A. & Bates, Natica I., eds. (Harvard African Studies: Vol. 4). (ENG & NUB.). 1923. 49.00 (*0-527-01027-8*) Periodicals Srv.
Murray, Gale B. Toulouse-Lautrec: A Retrospective. (Illus.). 384p. 1992. 75.00 (*0-88363-492-9*) H L Levin.
Murray, Geoffrey. Doing Business in China: The Last Great Market. 240p. 1994. text ed. 80.00 (*1-873410-28-X*, Pub. by Curzon Pr UK); pap. 29.95 (*1-873410-29-8*, Pub. by Curzon Pr UK) St Martin.
— Doing Business in China: The Last Great Market. LC 94-13029. 1994. text ed. 20.00 (*0-312-11683-7*) St Martin.
— Doing Business in China: The Last Great Market. LC 94-13029. 1994. write for info. (*0-312-11682-9*) St Martin.
Murray, George, ed. see Marlborough, John C.
Murray, George B., jt. ed. see Fisher, Alden L.
Murray, George W. Sons of Ishmael: A Study of the Egyptian Bedouin. LC 74-15071. reprint ed. 49.50 (*0-404-12115-2*) AMS Pr.
Murray, Gerard M. Career Angel: Female Version. 1945. pap. 13.00 (*0-8222-0183-6*) Dramatists Play.
— Career Angel: Male Version. 1944. pap. 4.75 (*0-8222-0182-8*) Dramatists Play.
Murray, Gilbert. Aeschylus, the Creator of Tragedy. LC 77-18893. 242p. 1978. reprint ed. text ed. 35.00 (*0-8371-9919-0*, MUAE, Greenwood Pr) Greenwood.
— Euripides & His Age. LC 79-4184. 132p. 1979. reprint ed. text ed. 35.00 (*0-313-20989-8*, MUEA, Greenwood Pr) Greenwood.
— Five Stages of Greek Religion. LC 76-27675. 276p. 1976. reprint ed. text ed. 35.00 (*0-8371-9080-0*, MUFS, Greenwood Pr) Greenwood.
— Five Stages of Greek Religion: Studies Based on a Course of Lectures Delivered in April 1912 at Columbia University. LC 75-41202. reprint ed. 30.00 (*0-404-14577-9*) AMS Pr.
— From the League to U. N. LC 87-14934. 232p. 1948. reprint ed. text ed. 59.75 (*0-313-26080-X*, MLUN, Greenwood Pr) Greenwood.
— Liberality & Civilization: Lectures Given at the Invitation of the Hibbert Trustees in the Universities of Bristol, Glasgow & Birmingham. LC 77-27139. (Hibbert Lectures). reprint ed. 30.00 (*0-404-60430-7*) AMS Pr.
— Stoic, Christian & Humanist. LC 75-99712. (Essay Index Reprint Ser.). 1977. 19.95 (*0-8369-1363-9*) Ayer.
— Tradition & Progress. LC 68-20323. (Essay Index Reprint Ser.). 1977. 19.95 (*0-8369-0728-0*) Ayer.
— Tradition & Progress. LC 68-20323. (Essay Index Reprint Ser.). 221p. reprint ed. lib. bdg. 16.00 (*0-8290-0490-4*) Irvington.
***Murray, Glenn E.** Collateral Consequences of Criminal Conduct. LC 92-61678. 346p. (Orig.). 1992. pap. 50.00 (*0-942954-53-X*) NYS Bar.
Murray, Gordon, jt. contrib. see Sloan, Audrey.
***Murray-Graham, Sylvia A.** Living in Eternity: Channeled Wisdom on Life, the Hereafter, & the Reality of It All. 225p. (Orig.). Date not set. pap. write for info. (*0-9643806-0-9*) CandleLght TX.
Murray, H. A. Tennis for Beginners. 1980. pap. 2.00 (*0-87980-263-4*) Wilshire.
***Murray, H. H., et al, eds.** Kaolin Genesis & Utilization. No. 1. 341p. 1993. 20.00 (*0-614-00501-9*) Clay Minerals.
Murray, H. J. A History of Chess. (Illus.). 936p. 1985. reprint ed. 39.95 (*0-936317-01-9*) Benjamin Pr.
Murray, Harold D. & Leonard, A. B. Handbook of Unionid Mussels in Kansas. (Miscellaneous Publications: No. 28). 184p. 1962. pap. 8.00 (*0-686-79811-2*) U of KS Mus Nat Hist.
Murray, Harry. Do Not Neglect Hospitality: The Catholic Worker & the Homeless. 304p. 1991. 34.95 (*0-87722-726-8*) Temple U Pr.
— Fly Fishing for Smallmouth Bass. (Illus.). 160p. 1989. 22.95 (*0-941130-85-1*) Lyons & Burford.
Murray, Harry W. Trout Fishing in the Shenandoah National Park. (Illus.). 100p. (Orig.). 1989. pap. 10.95 (*0-9622555-0-5*) Shenandoah Edinburg.
Murray, Haydn, et al, eds. Kaolin Genesis & Utilization, No. 1. (Special Publication). (Illus.). 341p. (C). 1993. text ed. 20.00 (*1-881208-05-2*) Clay Minerals.
Murray, Heather. Double Lives: Women in the Stories of Katherine Mansfield. 1990. pap. 19.95 (*0-908569-56-4*, Pub. by U Otago Pr NZ) Intl Spec Bk.
Murray, Helen. African Love Song. (Orig.). 1980. pap. 1.75 (*0-8439-8010-9*) Dorchester Pub Co.
— Doctor of the Isles. (Orig.). 1981. pap. 1.75 (*0-8439-8026-5*) Dorchester Pub Co.
— Doctor of the Isles. large type ed. (Orig.). 1991. 18.95 (*0-7927-0896-2*, CH0139, Curley Lrg Print) Chivers N Amer.
— Heart of a Nurse. (Orig.). 1980. pap. 1.75 (*0-8439-8001-X*) Dorchester Pub Co.
— Heart of a Nurse. large type ed. (Orig.). 1991. 18.95 (*0-7927-0696-X*, CH011, Curley Lrg Print); pap. 16.95 (*0-7927-0697-8*, CS0115, Curley Lrg Print) Chivers N Amer.
— Island of Desire. (Orig.). 1981. pap. 1.75 (*0-8439-8032-X*) Dorchester Pub Co.
— Prescription for Love. (Orig.). 1981. pap. 1.95 (*0-8439-8039-7*) Dorchester Pub Co.
— Prescription for Love. large type ed. (Orig.). 1990. pap. 16.95 (*0-7927-0430-4*, C0487, Curley Lrg Print) Chivers N Amer.
— Ski Lift to Love. 1980. pap. 1.75 (*0-8439-8003-6*) Dorchester Pub Co.
— To Love Again. (Orig.). pap. 1.75 (*0-8439-8014-1*) Dorchester Pub Co.
— To Love Again. large type ed. (Orig.). 1990. 12.95 (*0-7927-0327-8*, C0278, Curley Lrg Print) Chivers N Amer.
Murray, Helen & Leavens, Donald C. When Your Child Flies Alone: A Guide for Parents. 44p. 1990. pap. text ed. 6.95 (*1-879668-00-9*) Info Finders.
Murray, Henry A. Thematic Apperception Test. LC 43-3797. 20p. 1943. Manual with cards. student ed 25.00 (*0-674-87720-9*); pap. 3.95 (*0-674-87721-7*) HUP.
Murray, Henry A., ed. see Melville, Herman.
Murray, Henry V. & Sluder, Troy B. Fixed Restorative Techniques. enl. rev. ed. Barton, Roger E., ed. LC 88-39479. (Dental Laboratory Technology Manuals Ser.). (Illus.). viii, 364p. 1989. reprint ed. pap. 45.00 (*0-8078-4250-8*) U of NC Pr.
Murray, Hilda, ed. Erthe upon Erthe: All Known Texts. (EETS, OS Ser.: Vol. 141). 1972. reprint ed. 15.00 (*0-8115-3371-9*) Periodicals Srv.
Murray, Holly L. The Anatomy of a Woman. (Illus.). 55p. (Orig.). (C). 1989. pap. 5.95 (*0-9623358-0-0*, TXU 329-044) Pegasus Print.
Murray, Hugh. Dr. Evelyn's York: Illustrations of Bygone York 1891-1935. (Illus.). (C). 1988. 110.00 (*0-900657-85-5*, Pub. by W Sessions UK) St Mut.
— Historical Account of Discoveries & Travels in Asia, from the Earliest Ages to the Present Time, 3 Vols, 1. LC 77-153625. reprint ed. lib. bdg. 18.50 (*0-404-09571-2*) AMS Pr.
— Historical Account of Discoveries & Travels in Asia, from the Earliest Ages to the Present Time, 3 Vols, 2. LC 77-153625. reprint ed. lib. bdg. 18.50 (*0-404-09572-0*) AMS Pr.
— Historical Account of Discoveries & Travels in Asia, from the Earliest Ages to the Present Time, 3 Vols, 3. LC 77-153625. reprint ed. lib. bdg. 18.50 (*0-404-09573-9*) AMS Pr.
— Historical Account of Discoveries & Travels in Asia, from the Earliest Ages to the Present Time, 3 Vols, Set. LC 77-153625. reprint ed. lib. bdg. 55.00 (*0-404-09570-4*) AMS Pr.
— The History of York Cemetery: The Garden of Death. (C). 1988. 45.00 (*0-9517737-0-4*, Pub. by W Sessions UK) St Mut.
— Opportunity of Leisure: The History of the York Railway Institute 1889-1989. (C). 1989. 30.00 (*0-9514452-0-0*, Pub. by W Sessions UK) St Mut.
— Photographs & Photographers of York 1844-1879. (C). 1988. 80.00 (*0-9503519-4-6*, Pub. by W Sessions UK) St Mut.
Murray, Hugh, jt. ed. see Trist, Eric.
Murray, I. Progress in Mathematics 5G Answer Book. (C). 1988. 65.00 (*0-85950-268-6*, Pub. by S Thornes Pubs UK) St Mut.
Murray, I., ed. Progress in Mathematics 5-E: Copymasters. (C). 1990. 230.00 (*0-85950-748-3*, Pub. by S Thornes Pubs UK) St Mut.
Murray, I. & Murray, T. The Modern Scottish Novels. 224p. 1984. 19.00 (*0-685-09404-9*, Pergamon Pr); pap. text ed. 15.90 (*0-08-028493-0*, Pergamon Pr) Elsevier.
***Murray, I. P. & Ell, P. J., eds.** Nuclear Medicine in Clinical Diagnosis & Treatment, SET. LC 94-34613. 1994. write for info. (*0-443-04710-3*) Churchill.
Murray, Iain. The Invitation System. 1984. pap. 1.95 (*0-85151-171-6*) Banner of Truth.
— Spurgeon un Principe Olividado. 2nd ed. 156p. (SPA.). 1984. reprint ed. pap. 3.95 (*0-85151-439-1*) Banner of Truth.
Murray, Iain, ed. see Houghton, S. M.
Murray, Iain H. Australian Christian Life From 1788: An Introduction & an Anthology. 347p. 1988. 25.95 (*0-85151-524-X*) Banner of Truth.
— The Forgotten Spurgeon. 256p. 1988. pap. 8.95 (*0-85151-156-2*) Banner of Truth.
— Jonathan Edwards: A New Biography. 503p. 1992. 29.95 (*0-85151-494-4*) Banner of Truth.
— The Life of A. W. Pink. (Illus.). 272p. (Orig.). 1981. pap. 8.95 (*0-85151-332-8*) Banner of Truth.
— The Life of D. M. Lloyd-Jones: The First Forty Years: 1899-1939. (Illus.). 408p. 1983. 26.95 (*0-85151-353-0*) Banner of Truth.
— Life of D. M. Lloyd-Jones, Vol. 2: The Fight of Faith, 1939-1981. 862p. 1990. 39.95 (*0-85151-564-9*) Banner of Truth.
— The Puritan Hope. 1975. pap. 9.95 (*0-85151-247-X*) Banner of Truth.
— Revival & Revivalism: The Making & Marring of American Evangelicalism 1750-1858. 455p. 1994. 27.95 (*0-85151-660-2*) Banner of Truth.
Murray, Iain H., ed. Diary of Kenneth Macrae. (Illus.). 535p. 1980. 29.95 (*0-85151-297-6*) Banner of Truth.
Murray, Iain H., ed. see Spurgeon, Charles H.
Murray, Ian. Houseplants & Bottle Gardens: Step by Step to Growing Success. (Crowood Gardening Guides Ser.). (Illus.). 128p. 1992. pap. 16.95 (*1-85223-504-7*, Pub. by Crowood Pr UK) Trafalgar.
— Practical Bedding Plants. (Illus.). 64p. 1994. pap. 8.95 (*1-85223-780-5*, Pub. by Crowood Pr UK) Trafalgar.
— Practical Clematis Growing. (Illus.). 64p. 1993. pap. 8.95 (*1-85223-656-6*, Pub. by Crowood Pr UK) Trafalgar.
— Practical Greenhouse Gardening. (Illus.). 64p. 1993. pap. text ed. 8.95 (*1-85223-739-2*, Pub. by Crowood Pr UK) Trafalgar.

— Practical Pruning. (Illus.). 64p. 1992. pap. 8.95 (*1-85223-657-4*, Pub. by Crowood Pr UK) Trafalgar.
— Practical Small Gardening. (Illus.). 64p. 1995. pap. 8.95 (*1-85223-869-0*, Pub. by Crowood Pr UK) Trafalgar.
Murray, Ian & Cowe, Ian A., eds. Making Light Work: Advances in Near Infrared Spectroscopy: the 4th International Conference on Near Infrared Spectroscopy, August 19-23, 1991, Aberdeen, Scotland. LC 92-11232. 652p. 1992. 180.00 (*1-56081-264-8*) VCH Pubs.
Murray, Ian, jt. auth. see Miller, Sheila.
Murray, Ian H. The Reformation of the Church: A Collection of Reformed & Puritan Documents on Church Issues. 416p. (C). 1987. reprint ed. 16.95 (*0-85151-118-X*) Banner of Truth.
Murray, Isobel, ed. see Wilde, Oscar.
Murray, Isobel M., ed. see Wilde, Oscar.
Murray, J. Avifauna of British India & Its Dependencies, Set. 1984. reprint ed. 750.00 (*81-7089-020-9*, Pub. by Intl Bk Distr II) St Mut.
— Lord Byron & His Detractors. LC 77-119079. (Studies in Byron: No. 5). 1970. reprint ed. lib. bdg. 59.95 (*0-8383-1075-3*) M S G Haskell Hse.
— Vertebrate Zoology of Sind. 424p. (C). 1988. 260.00 (*81-7089-058-6*, Pub. by Intl Bk Distr II) St Mut.
Murray, J., ed. Transgenesis: Applications of Gene Transfer. 331p. 1992. text ed. 99.95 (*0-471-93294-9*, Wiley-Liss) Wiley.
Murray, J. A., ed. The Complaynt of Scotlande, Pts. 1 & 2. (EETS, ES Ser.: Nos. 17, 18). 1972. reprint ed. 40.00 (*0-527-00231-3*) Periodicals Srv.
Murray, J. B. & Murray, Emily. And Say What He Is: The Life of a Special Child. LC 75-5810. 304p. 1975. pap. 5.95 (*0-262-63069-9*) MIT Pr.
Murray, J. D. Asymptotic Analysis. 2nd ed. (Applied Mathematical Sciences Ser.: Vol. 48). Orig. Title: Introduction to Asymptotic Analysis. (Illus.). 160p. 1992. reprint ed. 39.00 (*0-387-90937-0*) Spr-Verlag.
— Mathematical Biology. (Biomathematics Ser.: Vol. 19). (Illus.). 760p. 1989. 59.00 (*0-387-19460-6*) Spr-Verlag.
— Mathematical Biology. 2nd rev. ed. Levin, S. A., ed. (BIOMED Ser.: Vol. 19). xiv, 767p. 1993. pap. 39.95 (*0-387-57204-X*) Spr-Verlag.
Murray, J. Dennis & Keller, Peter A., eds. Innovations in Rural Community Mental Health. 285p. (Orig.). (C). 1986. pap. text ed. 19.95 (*0-940299-00-3*) Manfld U Rural.
Murray, J. J. & Rugg-Gunn, R. J. Fluorides in Caries Prevention. 3rd ed. (Dental Practitioners' Handbook Ser.: No. 20). (Illus.). 272p. 1991. text ed. 120.00 (*0-7236-2363-5*, Pub. by John Wright UK) Buttrwrth-Heinemann.
Murray, J. L., intro. Phase Diagrams of Binary Titanium Alloys. (Monograph Series on Alloy Phase Diagrams). (Illus.). 345p. (C). 1990. reprint ed. text ed. 256.00 (*0-87170-248-7*) ASM.
Murray, J. Middleton, tr. see Dostoyevsky, Fyodor.
Murray, J. Ross. Influence of Italian Upon English Literature During the Sixteenth & Seventeenth Centuries. LC 70-138743. reprint ed. 29.50 (*0-404-04544-8*) AMS Pr.
Murray, Jack. The Landscapes of Alienation: Ideological Subversion in Kafka, Celine, & Onetti. LC 90-20976. 288p. 1991. 32.50 (*0-8047-1868-7*) Stanford U Pr.
Murray, Jacqueline, ed. see Firenzuola, Agnolo.
Murray, Jacqueline, tr. see Firenzuola, Agnolo.
Murray, James. Letters of James Murray, Loyalist. (American Biography Ser.). 324p. 1991. reprint ed. lib. bdg. 79.00 (*0-7812-8293-4*) Rprt Serv.
Murray, James A. Antisense RNA & DNA. (Modern Cell Biology Ser.: No. 1916). 410p. 1992. text ed. 104.95 (*0-471-56130-4*, Wiley-Liss) Wiley.
Murray, James A., ed. Thomas of Erceldoune. (EETS, OS Ser.: No. 61). 1974. reprint ed. 29.00 (*0-527-00055-8*) Periodicals Srv.
Murray, James C. Spanish Chronicles of the Indies: Sixteenth Century. LC 93-29499. (Twayne's World Authors Series: Spanish Literature: No. 847). 188p. 1994. text ed. 25.95 (*0-8057-4306-5*, Pub. by Royal Botanic Garden UK) Macmillan.
Murray, James D. & vanRyper, William. Encyclopedia of Graphics File Formats. (Illus.). 928p. (Orig.). 1994. cd-rom, pap. 59.95 (*1-56592-058-9*) OReilly & Assocs.
Murray, James M. Fifty Things You Can Do about Guns. LC 94-17633. 100p. 1994. pap. 7.95 (*1-885003-00-5*) R D Reed Pubs.
Murray, James W., jt. ed. see Izdar, Erol.
***Murray, Jane E.** Fear of Filing - Musical. 1995. write for info. (*0-87129-429-X*, F03) Dramatic Pub.
Murray, Janet H. & Stark, Myra, eds. The Englishwoman's Review of Social & Industrial Questions, 40 Vols. 1979. 20.00 (*0-318-52457-0*) Garland.
— The Englishwoman's Review of Social & Industrial Questions, 40 Vols., Set. 1979. lib. bdg. 800.00 (*0-8153-0258-4*) Garland.
***Murray, Janette S. & Murray, Frederick G.** The Story of Cedar Rapids. (Illus.). 284p. 1995. reprint ed. lib. bdg. 35.00 (*0-8328-4665-1*) Higginson Bk Co.
Murray, Jean, jt. auth. see Darin, Bobby.
Murray, Jean W. Starting & Operating a Word Processing Service. LC 83-2229. 32p. 1983. pap. 3.50 (*0-87576-102-X*) Pilot Bks.
***Murray, Jeff.** For Big Bucks Only. LC 87-63364. (Hunter's Information Ser.). 216p. 1989. write for info. (*0-914697-17-X*) N Amer Outdoor Grp.
Murray, Jeff & Mcclelland, Mike. How to Win the Walleye Game: Walleye Game. (Illus.). 220p. (Orig.). (C). 1988. write for info. (*0-9622571-0-9*); lib. bdg. write for info. (*0-9622571-1-7*); pap. write for info. (*0-9622571-3-3*) Fishing Enterprises.
Murray, Jerome. From Uptight to All Right: A Twelve Step Program for Stress Prevention. LC 87-7762. 187p. (Orig.). 1987. pap. 12.95 (*0-942383-06-0*) Manor Hse Pub.
— Murray on Marriage: A Guide for Lawyers & Lovers. 220p. 1990. pap. 12.95 (*0-685-27058-0*) Manor Hse Pub.
Murray, Jerome T. & Murray, Marilyn J. Expert Systems in Data Processing: A Professional's Guide. (Illus.). 288p. 1988. text ed. 43.00 (*0-07-044088-3*) McGraw.
Murray, Jill. Arrow to the Heart. large type ed. (Linford Romance Library). 1990. pap. 12.95 (*0-7089-6824-4*, Linford) Ulverscroft.
— My Cousin Mandy. large type ed. 1989. 17.95 (*0-7089-2107-8*) Ulverscroft.
— Nurse from Newstone. large type ed. 1991. 21.95 (*0-7089-2522-7*) Ulverscroft.
— Nurse in Izbah. large type ed. (Linford Romance Library). 320p. 1985. pap. 11.95 (*0-7089-6070-7*, Linford) Ulverscroft.
— The Other Margaret. large type ed. 1990. 21.95 (*0-7089-2255-4*) Ulverscroft.
— The Relentless Tide. large type ed. (Linford Romance Library). 240p. 1984. pap. 11.95 (*0-7089-6009-X*, Trailtree Bookshop) Ulverscroft.
Murray, Jim. Comprehensive Study Questions for the EMI-A: Basic Life Support. (C). 1982. pap. text ed. 22.00 (*0-8359-0895-X*, Reston) P-H.
— Jim Murray: An Autobiography. 256p. 1993. text ed. 20.00 (*0-02-588151-5*) Macmillan.
— Weight Lifting & Progressive Resistance Exercise. 95p. reprint ed. pap. 27.10 (*0-317-28592-0*, 2055167) Bks Demand.
***Murray, Jim, intro.** Casey Stengel. LC 94-36778. (Baseball Legends Ser.). (Illus.). 64p. (YA). (gr. 3 up). 1995. lib. bdg. 14.95 (*0-7910-2172-6*) Chelsea Hse.
Murray, Jimm. Comprehensive Study Questions for the EMT-A: Basic Life Support. 151p. 1982. pap. 13.95 (*0-317-58940-7*) P-H.
Murray, Joan. The Last Buffalo: The Story of Frederick Arthur Verner, Painter of the Northwest, 2 vols. (Illus.). 192p. 1985. 130.00 (*0-87951-232-6*) Overlook Pr.
— Poems by Joan Murray, 1917-1942. Code, Grant, ed. LC 71-144751. (Yale Series of Younger Poets: No. 45). reprint ed. 18.00 (*0-404-53845-2*) AMS Pr.
— The Same Water: Poems. LC 89-33954. (Wesleyan New Poets Ser.). 64p. 1990. 22.50 (*0-8195-2181-7*, Wesleyan Univ Pr); pap. 10.95 (*0-8195-1183-8*, Wesleyan Univ Pr) U Pr of New Eng.
Murray, Joan, ed. Off the Shelf: A Marketing & Distribution Guide for Independent Literary & Artist Book Publishers. (Illus.). 160p. (Orig.). 1989. pap. 10.95 (*0-9618487-0-7*) Writers & Bks.
Murray, Joan & Abramson, Paul R. Bias in Psychotherapy. 398p. 1983. text ed. 65.00 (*0-275-91050-4*, C1050, Praeger Pubs) Greenwood.
Murray, Joan, ed. see Bruce, William B.
Murray, Joan, ed. see Macleod, Pegi N.
Murray, Jocelyn. Africa. (Cultural Atlas for Young People Ser.). 96p. (J). 1990. 17.95 (*0-8160-2209-7*) Facts on File.
— Cultural Atlas of Africa. (Cultural Atlas Ser.). (Illus.). 240p. 1981. 45.00 (*0-87196-558-5*) Facts on File.
Murray, Jocelyn, ed. see Shank, David A.
Murray, Jody L., jt. auth. see Murray, Fred.
Murray, John. Atlas of Invertebrate Macrofossils. LC 84-6699. 235p. 1985. pap. text ed. 59.95 (*0-470-20084-7*) Wiley.
— Calvin on Scripture & Divine Sovereignty. 1960. pap. 5.99 (*0-85234-118-0*, Pub. by Evangel Pr UK) Presby & Reformed.
— Christian Baptism. 1974. pap. 5.99 (*0-87552-343-9*) Presby & Reformed.
— The Collected Writings of John Murray, 4 vols., Set. 1976. 139.95 (*0-85151-396-4*) Banner of Truth.
— Collected Writings of John Murray, Vol. 1: Claims of Truth. 374p. 1976. 37.95 (*0-85151-241-0*) Banner of Truth.
— The Collected Writings of John Murray, Vol. 2: Lectures in Systematic Theology. 1978. 37.95 (*0-85151-242-9*) Banner of Truth.
— Collected Writings of John Murray, Vol. 4: Studies in Theology. 390p. 1983. 37.95 (*0-85151-340-9*) Banner of Truth.
— A Comparative View of the Huttonian & Neptunian Systems of Geology: In Answer to the Illustrations of the Huttonian Theory of the Earth. Albritton, Claude C., Jr., ed. LC 77-6533. (History of Geology Ser.). 1978. reprint ed. lib. bdg. 26.95 (*0-405-10453-7*) Ayer.
— Covenant of Grace: A Biblico-Theological Study. LC 87-29117. 32p. 1987. reprint ed. pap. 2.50 (*0-87552-363-3*) Presby & Reformed.
— Divorce. 1961. pap. 5.99 (*0-87552-344-7*) Presby & Reformed.
— Epistle of Paul to the Romans. (New International Commentary on the New Testament Ser.). 1960. 29.99 (*0-8028-2506-0*) Eerdmans.
— Imputation of Adam's Sin. LC 59-10078. 1977. pap. 4.99 (*0-87552-341-2*) Presby & Reformed.
— Lake Superior, Wow! A Kid's Guide to 99 Fun Things to Do in Duluth, Superior, & along Lake Superior's North Shore. (Illus.). 96p. (J). 1993. pap. 7.95 (*0-943400-73-2*) Marlor Pr.
— The Media Law Dictionary. LC 78-63257. 1978. pap. text ed. 18.50 (*0-8191-0616-X*) U Pr of Amer.
— Modern Monologues for Young People. rev. ed. 150p. (J). (gr. 7-12). 1982. pap. 12.00 (*0-8238-0255-8*) Plays.
— Mystery Plays for Young Actors. (Orig.). (J). (gr. 5-12). 1984. pap. 13.95 (*0-8238-0265-5*) Plays.
— Principles of Conduct: Aspects of Biblical Ethics. 280p. 1991. pap. 12.99 (*0-8028-1144-2*) Eerdmans.
— Redemption: Accomplished & Applied. 1955. pap. 9.99 (*0-8028-1143-4*) Eerdmans.
— The Russian Press from Brezhnev to Yeltsin: Behind the Paper Curtain. LC 93-49830. (Studies in Communism in Transition). 288p. 1994. 67.95 (*1-85278-885-2*, Pub. by E Elgar Pub UK) Ashgate Pub Co.
— Selections from the Report on the Scientific Results of the Voyage of H.M.S. Challenger During the Years 1872-76. Egerton, Frank N., 3rd, ed. LC 77-74242. (History of Ecology Ser.). (Illus.). 1978. reprint ed. lib. bdg. 21.95 (*0-405-10411-1*) Ayer.
— X-Stat: Statistical Experiment Design, Data Analysis, & Non-Linear Optimization, Verson 2.0. LC 92-28868. 200p. 1992. 595.00 (*0-471-52444-1*) Wiley.
***Murray, John, ed.** American Nature Writing 1995. 1995. pap. 12.00 (*0-87156-438-6*) Sierra.
Murray, John & Morrison, Catherine. Bi-Lingual Education in the Western Isles, Scotland 1975-81. 1985. 65.00 (*0-86152-036-X*, Pub. by Acair Ltd UK) St Mut.
Murray, John & Pullar, Laurence. Bathymetrical Survey of the Scottish Fresh Water Lochs, Vol. 1. Egerton, Frank N., 3rd, ed. LC 77-74243. (History of Ecology Ser.). (Illus.). 1978. reprint ed. lib. bdg. 71.95 (*0-405-10412-X*) Ayer.
Murray, John A. The Gila Wilderness Area: A Hiking Guide. LC 87-35753. (Coyote Books Ser.). (Illus.). 260p. (Orig.). 1988. pap. 14.95 (*0-8263-1067-2*) U of NM Pr.
— Grizzly Bears: An Illustrated Field Guide. (Illus.). 160p. (Orig.). 1995. pap. 14.95 (*1-57098-029-2*) R Rinehart.
— Out among the Wolves: Contemporary Writings on the Wolf. LC 93-10971. (Illus.). 248p. 1993. pap. 14.95 (*0-88240-439-3*) Alaska Northwest.
— A Republic of Rivers: Three Centuries of Nature Writing from Alaska & the Yukon. (Illus.). 368p. 1990. 25.00 (*0-19-506102-0*) OUP.
— The Sierra Club Nature Writing Handbook: A Creative Guide. LC 95-5601. 208p. (Orig.). 1995. pap. 14.00 (*0-87156-436-X*) Sierra.
— Wild Africa: Three Centuries of Nature Writing from Africa. LC 92-10672. (Illus.). 256p. 1993. 25.00 (*0-19-507377-0*) OUP.
Murray, John A., ed. American Nature Writing, 1994. 288p. (Orig.). 1994. pap. 12.00 (*0-87156-479-3*) Sierra.
— American Nature Writing, 1994. 1995. 21.00 (*0-8446-6858-3*) Peter Smith.
— The Great Bear: Contemporary Writings on the Grizzly. 248p. (Orig.). 1992. pap. 14.95 (*0-88240-392-3*) Alaska Northwest.
— Nature's New Voices. LC 92-53030. 256p. (Orig.). 1992. pap. 15.95 (*1-55591-117-X*) Fulcrum Pub.
— A Republic of Rivers: Three Centuries of Nature Writing from Alaska & the Yukon. (Illus.). 322p. 1992. pap. 9.95 (*0-19-507605-2*) OUP.
Murray, John A., sel. A Thousand Leagues of Blue: The Sierra Club Book of the Pacific. LC 93-23196. 488p. (Orig.). 1994. pap. 16.00 (*0-87156-452-1*) Sierra.
Murray, John A., jt. ed. see Brown, David E.
Murray, John C. Bridging the Sacred & the Secular: Selected Writings. Hooper, J. Leon, ed. LC 94-9698. 1994. 55.00 (*0-87840-561-5*) Georgetown U Pr.
— Eye of the Needle. (Illus.). 42p. (Orig.). 1992. pap. text ed. 6.95 (*1-56315-058-1*) Sterling Hse.
— Morality & Modern War. (Ethics & Foreign Policy Ser.). 1959. pap. 1.00 (*0-87641-102-2*) Carnegie Ethics & Intl Affairs.
— Problem of God: Yesterday & Today. (St. Thomas More Lectures Ser.: No. 1). (Orig.). (C). 1965. pap. 9.00 (*0-300-00171-1*, Y138) Yale U Pr.
— Religious Liberty: Catholic Struggles with Pluralism. Hooper, J. Leon, ed. LC 92-17829. (Library of Theological Ethics). 256p. (Orig.). 1993. pap. 15.99 (*0-664-25360-1*) Westminster John Knox.
— Visions of a Harp Player. (Illus.). 24p. (Orig.). 1990. pap. text ed. 5.95 (*1-56315-017-4*) Sterling Hse.
Murray, John C. & Burghardt, Walter. We Hold These Truths: Catholic Reflections on the American Proposition. LC 60-12876. 350p. 1985. reprint ed. 19.95 (*0-934134-83-9*); reprint ed. pap. 15.95 (*0-934134-50-2*) Sheed & Ward MO.
Murray, John E., Jr. Commercial Law, Problems & Materials. 366p. 1986. reprint ed. pap. text ed. 21.00 (*0-314-28310-2*) West Pub.
— Contracts: Cases & Materials. 4th ed. 1037p. 1991. 44.00 (*0-87473-801-6*) Michie Butterworth.
— Murray on Contracts. 3rd ed. 1202p. 1990. 42.00x (*0-87473-613-7*) Michie Butterworth.
Murray, John E. & Flechtner, Harry M. Sales & Leases: Problems & Materials on National & International Transactions. (American Casebook Ser.). 255p. 1994. pap. text ed. write for info. (*0-314-03487-0*) West Pub.
Murray, John E., Jr. & Fletcher, Harry M. Sales & Leases: Problems & Materials on National & International Transactions. LC 93-11497. (American Casebook Ser.). 399p. 1993. pap. text ed. 29.00 (*0-314-02457-3*) West Pub.
Murray, John F., ed. Pulmonary Complications of Systemic Disease. LC 92-18424. (Lung Biology in Health & Disease Ser.: Vol. 59). 708p. 1992. 199.00 (*0-8247-8707-2*) Dekker.
Murray, John F. & Nadel, Jay A., eds. Textbook of Respiratory Medicine, 2 vols., Set. 2nd ed. LC 92-48497. (Illus.). 2816p. 1994. text ed. 279.00 (*0-7216-3890-2*) Saunders.
Murray, John J. Amsterdam in the Age of Rembrandt. (Centers of Civilization Ser.: No. 21). 203p. reprint ed. 57.90 (*0-8357-9719-8*, 2016242) Bks Demand.
— Behind a Frowning Providence. 30p. 1990. pap. 1.75 (*0-85151-572-X*) Banner of Truth.
— The Prevention of Dental Disease. 2nd ed. (Illus.). 520p. 1989. 95.00 (*0-19-261807-5*) OUP.
— The Prevention of Dental Disease. 2nd ed. (Illus.). 520p. 1989. pap. 49.95 (*0-19-261806-7*) OUP.
— Senior Citizens on Stage. 1980. pap. 3.00 (*0-686-30558-2*) Eldridge Pub.
Murray, John J., Jr. Yes, You Can Beat City Hall. 372p. 1994. 18.95 (*0-89914-039-4*) Third Party Pub.
***Murray, John J., ed.** Prevention of Oral Disease. 3rd ed. (Illus.). 350p. 1995. pap. 52.00 (*0-19-262457-1*) OUP.
Murray, John J., ed. see Walpole, Horatio.
Murray, John L., jt. auth. see Lenz, Heinz.
Murray, John O. Catholic Heros & Heroines of America. 1972. 35.00 (*0-87968-818-1*) Gordon Pr.
— Catholic Pioneers of America. 1972. 35.00 (*0-87968-819-X*) Gordon Pr.
— Little Lives of the Great Saints. LC 82-50593. 495p. 1985. reprint ed. pap. 16.50 (*0-89555-190-X*) TAN Bks Pubs.
Murray, John P. Status Offenders: A Sourcebook. 135p. 1983. pap. text ed. 7.50 (*0-938510-03-7*) Boys Town Pr.
— Television & Youth: Twenty-Five Years of Research & Controversy. 278p. (Orig.). 1980. pap. text ed. 10.00 (*0-938510-00-2*, 010-TV) Boys Town Pr.
Murray, John R. The Normal Lung. 2nd ed. (Illus.). 377p. 1986. text ed. 40.50 (*0-7216-6613-2*) Saunders.
Murray, John S., et al. Dispute Resolution, Processes of, The Role of Lawyers. (University Casebook Ser.). 761p. 1988. text ed. 37.00 (*0-88277-688-6*) Foundation Pr.
Murray, Jon. Bangladesh: A Travel Survival Kit. 2nd ed. (Illus.). 168p. 1991. pap. 10.95 (*0-86442-108-7*) Lonely Planet.
— Cape Town: City Guide. (Illus.). 240p. 1996. pap. 9.95 (*0-86442-325-X*) Lonely Planet.
— New South Wales: Australia Guide. (Illus.). 576p. 1994. pap. 16.95 (*0-86442-223-7*) Lonely Planet.
— Sydney: City Guide. 2nd ed. (Illus.). 280p. 1994. pap. 9.95 (*0-86442-227-X*) Lonely Planet.
Murray, Jon & O'Hair, Madalyn. All the Questions You Ever Wanted to Ask American Atheists with All the Answers. 2nd ed. 248p. (Orig.). 1986. pap. 9.00 (*0-910309-24-8*, 5356) Am Atheist.
Murray, Jon & Wheeler, Tony. Papua New Guinea: A Travel Survival Kit. 5th ed. (Illus.). 380p. 1993. pap. 15.95 (*0-86442-190-7*) Lonely Planet.
Murray, Jon, jt. auth. see Everist, Richard.
Murray, Jon G. Essays on American Atheism, 2 vols., Set. (Orig.). pap. 19.00 (*0-910309-39-6*, 5351) Am Atheist.
— Essays on American Atheism, Vol. I. 350p. (Orig.). 1986. pap. 10.00 (*0-910309-28-0*, 5349) Am Atheist.
— Essays on American Atheism, Vol. II. 284p. (Orig.). 1986. pap. 10.00 (*0-910309-29-9*, 5350) Am Atheist.
Murray, Joseph. Training for Student Leaders. 224p. (C). 1994. per. 24.95 (*0-8403-9436-5*) Kendall-Hunt.
Murray, Joseph P. Selective English Old-French Glossary As a Basis for Studies in Old French Onomatology & Synonymics. LC 77-128932. (Catholic University of America. Studies in Romance Languages & Literature: No. 40). (ENG & FRE.). reprint ed. 37.50 (*0-404-50340-3*) AMS Pr.
Murray, J.S., jt. ed. see Politzer, P.
Murray, Judith. Mars. 64p. (Orig.). 1986. write for info. (*0-9617376-0-3*) Murpubco.
Murray, Judith S. The Gleaner: A Miscellany. (C). 1993. text ed. 37.95 (*0-912756-26-8*) Syracuse U Pr.
— Selected Writings of Judith Sargent Murray. Harris, Sharon M., ed. (Women Writers in English 1350-1850 Ser.). 320p. 1995. 35.00 (*0-19-507883-7*); pap. 18.95 (*0-19-510038-7*) OUP.
Murray, Judy. The Soft Sighs of If. (Illus.). 24p. (Orig.). 1992. pap. 3.00 (*0-926935-75-5*) Runaway Spoon.
***Murray, Julia.** Master of Herringham. large type ed. 1994. 21.95 (*0-7089-3152-9*) Ulverscroft.
Murray, Julia K. A Decade of Discovery: Selected Acquisitions, 1970-1980. LC 79-55426. (Illus.). 1979. pap. 18.50 (*0-934686-36-X*) Freer.
— Last of the Mandarins: Calligraphy & Painting from the F.Y. Chang Collection. (Illus.). 104p. 1995. pap. 14.95 (*0-916724-63-8*, 463-8) Harvard Art Mus.
— Ma Hezhi & the Illustration of the Book of Odes. (Illus.). 300p. (C). 1993. 100.00 (*0-521-41787-2*) Cambridge U Pr.
Murray, K. My Husband, Arthur Murray. (Ballroom Dance Ser.). 1986. lib. bdg. 74.00 (*0-8490-3254-7*) Gordon Pr.
— My Husband, Arthur Murray. (Ballroom Dance Ser.). 1985. lib. bdg. 74.00 (*0-87700-693-8*) Revisionist Pr.
Murray, K. M. Caught in the Web of Words: James A. H. Murray & the "Oxford English Dictionary" LC 77-76309. (Illus.). 1977. 45.00 (*0-300-02131-3*) Yale U Pr.
Murray, Katharine, ed. see Medved, Robert.
Murray, Katherine. Homeward Bound: A Collection of Short Stories. Croy, Greg, ed. LC 91-65827. 131p. (Orig.). 1991. pap. 9.95 (*0-9629914-0-6*) ReVisions Plus.
— Introduction to Personal Computers. 3rd ed. (Illus.). 1992. pap. 19.95 (*1-56529-029-1*) Que.
— Mastering Freelance Grahics Release X for Windows 95. 1995. 29.99 (*0-7821-1770-8*) Sybex.
— Mastering Powerpoint 4.0 for Windows. LC 94-65378. 402p. 1994. pap. 24.99 (*0-7821-1385-0*) Sybex.
— SOS for DOS. 256p. 1993. pap. 12.95 (*1-56884-043-8*) IDG Bks.
— SOS for Windows. 256p. 1993. pap. 12.95 (*1-56884-045-4*) IDG Bks.
— SOS for WordPerfect. 256p. 1994. pap. 12.95 (*1-56884-053-5*) IDG Bks.
— Understanding Freelance Graphics for Windows. LC 92-83944. 507p. 1993. 26.95 (*0-7821-1231-5*) Sybex.
Murray, Katherine & Sabotin, Doug. Ten Minute Guide to Lotus 1-2-3. 160p. 1991. pap. 9.95 (*0-672-22809-2*) Macmillan.
— Ten Minute Guide to WordPerfect 5.1. 160p. 1991. pap. 9.95 (*0-672-22808-4*) Alpha Bks IN.

An Asterisk (*) at the beginning of an entry indicates that the title is appearing in BIP for the first time.

— Ten Minute Guide to 1-2-3, Release 2.4. (Ten Minute Guides Ser.). (Illus.). (Orig.). 1992. pap. 10.95 (0-672-30117-2) Alpha Bks IN.

Murray, Kathryn J., jt. auth. see Blunt, John E.

Murray, Kathryn L., jt. auth. see Blunt, John E.

Murray, Kathy. Using Microsoft Publisher 2. 2nd ed. (Using Ser.). (Illus.). 350p. (Orig.). pap. 19.99 (1-56529-284-7) Que.

Murray, Keith A. The Modocs & Their War. LC 59-7488. (Civilization of the American Indian Ser.: Vol. 52). (Illus.). 358p. 1976. pap. 14.95 (0-8061-1331-6) U of Okla Pr.

Murray, Keith, Publishing Staff. Memories of Aberdeen a Hundred Years Ago. (C). 1990. reprint ed. 50.00 (0-685-41003-X, K Murray Pub) St Mut.

— No State in Earth. (C). 1990. pap. 39.00 (1-870978-26-9) St Mut.

Murray, Keith, Publishing Staff & Bold, Alan. The Malfeasance. 1990. pap. text ed. 30.00 (1-870978-27-7, K Murray Pub) St Mut.

Murray, Kelly A. Caught in the Middle. 1993. 10.95 (0-8062-4730-4) Carlton.

Murray, Ken, ed. see White, Steve & White, Ruth B.

Murray, Kenneth. Footsteps of the Mountain Spirits: Appalachia. (Illus.). 96p. 1992. pap. 14.95 (0-932807-78-X) Overmountain Pr.

— Highland Trails: A Guide to Scenic Walking & Riding Trails in Northeast Tennessee, Western North Carolina & Southwest Virginia. rev. ed. (Illus.). 208p. 1992. pap. 10.95 (0-932807-71-2) Overmountain Pr.

— Paths of the Ancients...Appalachia. (Illus.). 128p. 1993. 22.95 (0-932807-94-1) Overmountain Pr.

***Murray, Kenneth T. & Murray, Barbara A.** School Law for the Florida Educator. 246p. (C). 1995. pap. text ed. 46. 50x (0-9644512-0-4) IntraCoast Pub.

***Murray, Kevin.** Inside El Salvador. 1995. pap. text ed. 11. 95 (0-911213-53-8) Interhemisp Res Ctr.

— A Survey of Organism Form & Function Laboratory Manual. 128p. (C). 1994. per., pap. text ed. 19.96 (0-8403-9873-5) Kendall-Hunt.

Murray, Kevin, ed. The Judgement of Paris. 192p. (Orig.). 1992. pap. text ed. 19.95 (1-86373-055-9, Pub. by Allen Unwin AT) Paul & Co Pubs.

Murray, L. Progress in Mathematics 3-E Answer Book. (C). 1989. 65.00 (0-85950-741-6, Pub. by S Thornes Pubs UK) St Mut.

Murray, Lawrence. The Celluloid Persuasion: Movies & the Liberal Arts. LC 79-16764. 181p. reprint ed. 51.60 (0-685-07746-2, 2019346) Bks Demand.

Murray, Les. The Boys Who Stole the Funeral: A Novel Sequence. 80p. 1992. 20.00 (0-374-11603-2) FS&G.

— The Daylight Moon & Other Poems. LC 87-7918. 120p. 1988. 17.95 (0-89255-125-9); pap. 9.95 (0-89255-138-0) Persea Bks.

— Dog Fox Field: Poems. LC 92-16860. 1993. 19.00 (0-374-14314-5) FS&G.

— Translations from the Natural World: Poems. LC 93-11183. 1994. 21.00 (0-374-27870-9) FS&G.

— The Vernacular Republic. 1982. pap. 8.95 (0-89255-063-5) Persea Bks.

Murray, Les A. The Rabbiter's Bounty: Collected Poems. 300p. 1992. 25.00 (0-374-12622-4) FS&G.

Murray, Les A., ed. The New Oxford Book of Australian Verse. enl. ed. 420p. 1992. pap. 19.95 (0-19-553362-3) OUP.

Murray, Linda. High Renaissance & Mannerism: Italy, the North & Spain, 1500-1600. (World of Art Ser.). (Illus.). 288p. 1985. pap. 14.95 (0-500-20162-5) Thames Hudson.

— How to Draw Pets. LC 94-47279. (Illus.). (J). 1995. write for info. (0-8167-2742-2); pap. write for info. (0-8167-2743-0) Troll Assocs.

— How to Draw Prehistoric Animals. LC 93-23058. (How to Draw Ser.). (Illus.). 32p. (J). (gr. k-6). 1993. lib. bdg. 10.65 (0-8167-3287-6); pap. text ed. 1.95 (0-8167-3288-4) Troll Assocs.

— Michelangelo. (World of Art Ser.). (Illus.). 216p. 1985. pap. 14.95 (0-500-20174-9) Thames Hudson.

— Michelangelo. (World of Art Ser.). (Illus.). 216p. 1985. 19.95 (0-500-18175-6) Thames Hudson.

Murray, Linda & Richardson, John, eds. Intelligent Systems in a Human Context: Development, Implications, & Applications. (Illus.). 192p. 1989. 39.95 (0-19-853736-0) OUP.

Murray, Linda, tr. see Chastel, Andre.

Murray, Linda, jt. auth. see Murray, Peter.

Murray, Lindley. English Grammar. LC 81-9062. (American Linguistics Ser.). 1982. reprint ed. 50.00 (0-8201-1369-7) Schol Facsimiles.

— Narratives of Colored Americans. LC 70-170702. (Black Heritage Library Collection). 1977. reprint ed. 28.95 (0-8369-8892-2) Ayer.

***Murray, Louise G., comp.** The Dogs of Our Lives: Heartwarming Celebrity Reminiscences of Canine Companions. (Illus.). 256p. 1995. 17.95 (1-55972-289-4, Birch Ln Pr) Carol Pub Group.

Murray, Louise W. A History of Old Tioga Point & Early Athens, Pennsylvania. (Illus.). 656p. 1994. reprint ed. lib. bdg. 65.00 (0-8328-3878-0) Higginson Bk Co.

Murray, Lyn. Musician. 384p. 1987. 17.95 (0-8184-0432-9) Carol Pub Group.

Murray, M., jt. auth. see Gilbert, J.

Murray, M., et al. Smoking among Young Adults. 1988. text ed. 63.95 (0-566-05467-1, Pub. by Avebury Pub UK) Ashgate Pub Co.

Murray, M. J. Cases in Managerial Finance. 1994. pap. 20. 00 (1-878975-43-9) Kolb Pub.

Murray, M. Mary, jt. auth. see Yesner, Bernice L.

Murray, M. S., jt. auth. see Murray, C. H.

Murray, M. S., jt. auth. see Murray, Chas H.

Murray, M. V., jt. auth. see Clarke, D.

Murray, Maggie P. Changing Styles In Fashion: Who, What, Why. (Illus.). 280p. (C). 1988. text ed. 25.00 (0-87005-585-2) Fairchild.

Murray, Malcolm G., Jr. Alignment Manual for Horizontal, Flexibly-Coupled Rotating Machines. 3rd ed. LC 83-90158. (Illus.). 200p. (C). 1983. 36.00 (0-9611896-0-6) Murray & Garig.

Murray, Marcella M. Goal Performance System: A Complete Guide to Achieving Strategic Goals. 2nd ed. 110p. 1991. student ed 35.00 (0-9630252-0-1) Ctr Human Work.

— Making Positive Change: An Interactive Training Program. 88p. 1993. teacher ed 2,400.00 (0-9630252-1-X) Ctr Human Work.

Murray, Margaret. God of the Witches. (Illus.). 1970. reprint ed. pap. 10.95 (0-19-501270-4) OUP.

Murray, Margaret, tr. see Orff, Carl.

Murray, Margaret A. The Divine King of England: A Study in Anthropology. LC 79-8115. reprint ed. 29.50 (0-404-18428-6) AMS Pr.

— Egyptian Religious Poetry. Cranmer-Byng, J. L., ed. LC 79-8714. (Wisdom of the East Ser.). 120p. 1980. reprint ed. text ed. 35.00 (0-313-21012-8, MUER, Greenwood Pr) Greenwood.

— Egyptian Sculpture. LC 74-109802. 207p. 1970. reprint ed. text ed. 45.00 (0-8371-4293-8, MUEG, Greenwood Pr) Greenwood.

— Egyptian Temples. LC 75-41203. reprint ed. 27.50 (0-404-14719-4) AMS Pr.

— Genesis of Religion. 1963. 49.50 (0-614-00159-5) Elliots Bks.

Murray, Margaret A. M., jt. auth. see Lewis, John L.

Murray, Margo. Beyond the Myths & Magic of Mentoring: How to Facilitate an Effective Mentoring Program. LC 90-25580. (Management Ser.). 236p. 1991. 29.95 (1-55542-333-7) Jossey-Bass.

Murray, Marian. Circus: From Rome to Ringling. LC 74-171420. (Illus.). 354p. 1973. reprint ed. text ed. 49.75 (0-8371-6259-9, MUCI, Greenwood Pr) Greenwood.

Murray, Marilyn J., jt. auth. see Murray, Jerome T.

Murray, Marjorie D. Saturday with Little Rabbit. LC 91-48362. (Illus.). 48p. (J). (gr. k-3). 1993. text ed. 12.95 (0-02-767753-2, Mac Bks Young Read) S&S Childrens.

Murray, Mark F. International Business. LC 92-46094. (Management Ser.). 1993. 9.50 (0-87051-132-7) Am Inst CPA.

Murray, Martin. South Africa: Time of Agony, Time of Destiny. 1994. pap. 18.95 (0-86091-577-8, Pub. by Verso UK) Routledge Chapman & Hall.

— South Africa: Time of Agony, Time of Destiny. 1994. 59. 95 (0-86091-365-1, Pub. by Verso UK) Routledge Chapman & Hall.

— Time of Agony, Time of Destiny: The Upsurge of Popular Protest in South Africa. 272p. 1987. 39.95 (0-86091-146-2, Pub. by Verso UK); pap. 14.95 (0-86091-857-2, Pub. by Verso UK) Schocken.

Murray, Mary. Artwork of the Mind. Farr, Marcia, ed. (Written Language Ser.). 172p. 1995. text ed. 42.50 (1-881303-63-2); pap. text ed. 17.95 (1-881303-64-0) Hampton Pr NJ.

— Cruel & Unusual Punishment: The U. S. Blockade of Cuba. 117p. 1993. pap. 9.95 (1-875284-78-8, Pub. by Ocean Pr AT) Talman.

— The Law of the Father? Patriarchy in the Transition from Feudalism to Capitalism. LC 94-12147. 176p. 1995. 59. 95x (0-415-04256-9, B4195); pap. 16.95 (0-415-04257-7, B4199) Routledge.

Murray, Mary E. & Atkinson, Leslie D. Understanding the Nursing Process: The Next Generation. 5th ed. LC 93-1938. (Illus.). 192p. 1994. pap. 23.00 (0-07-105458-8) Hlth Prof Div.

Murray, Mary E., jt. auth. see Atkinson, Leslie D.

Murray, Mary E., jt. auth. see Beesch, Ruth K.

Murray, Matthew N. Economic Development Incentives & the Tennessee Valley Economy. 95p. (Orig.). (C). 1990. pap. text ed. write for info. (0-940191-16-4) Univ TN Ctr Bus Econ.

***Murray, Maureen.** All about Beads: A Guide to Beads & Bead Jewelery. (Illus.). 144p. 1995. 29.95 (0-7134-7863-2, Pub. by Batsford UK) Trafalgar.

Murray, Meg M., ed. Face to Face: Fathers, Mothers, Masters, Monsters--Essays for a Nonsexist Future. LC 82-11708. (Contributions in Women's Studies: No. 36). xxiv, 344p. 1983. text ed. 59.95 (0-313-23044-7, MFF/, Greenwood Pr) Greenwood.

Murray, Melba L., ed. see Murray, Raymond L.

Murray, Melba W. & Hay-Roe, Hugh. Engineered Writing. 2nd ed. 304p. 1986. 54.95 (0-87814-293-2, P4397) PennWell Bks.

Murray, Melissa. Changelings. 160p. (Orig.). (C). 1987. pap. 9.95 (0-946211-41-8, Pub. by Attic IE) InBook.

Murray, Melissa, jt. auth. see Mahoney, Mick.

Murray, Melvin L. Fostoria, Ohio Glass II. LC 90-93415. (Illus.). 186p. (Orig.). 1992. pap. 20.00 (0-9634864-0-3) M L Murray.

Murray, Michael. Albert Schweitzer, Musician. 176p. 1994. 44.95 (1-85928-031-5, Pub. by Scolar Pr UK) Ashgate Pub Co.

— Healing Power of Herbs: The Enlightened Person's Guide to the Wonders of Medicinal Plants. (Illus.). 256p. (Orig.). 1992. pap. 12.95 (1-55958-138-7) Prima Pub.

— Politics & Pragmatism of Urban Containment of Belfast since 1940. 224p. 1991. 68.95 (1-85628-245-7, Pub. by Avebury Pub UK) Ashgate Pub Co.

— The Saw Palmetto Story. rev. ed. 14p. Date not set. reprint ed. pap. 2.95 (0-9647080-2-7) Healing Wisdom.

Murray, Michael, ed. Heidegger & Modern Philosophy: Critical Essays. LC 77-21684. (Yale Paperbound Ser.). 397p. reprint ed. pap. 113.20 (0-7837-3304-6, 2057706) Bks Demand.

Murray, Michael & Greer, John, eds. Rural Development in Ireland: A Challenge for the 1990s. 278p. 1993. 68.95 (1-85628-408-5, Pub. by Avebury Pub UK) Ashgate Pub Co.

Murray, Michael & Pizzorno, Joseph. Encyclopedia of Natural Medicine. 609p. (Orig.). 1991. pap. 18.95 (1-55958-091-7) Prima Pub.

Murray, Michael & Rice, John. Differential Geometry & Statistics. LC 93-12009. (Monographs on Statistics & Applied Probability: Vol. 48). 1993. write for info. (0-412-39860-5) Chapman & Hall.

Murray, Michael, jt. auth. see Swan, Anthony V.

Murray, Michael, jt. auth. see Trillium Health Products Nutritionists Staff.

Murray, Michael D. The Political Performers: CBS Broadcasts in the Public Interest. LC 93-30985. 272p. 1994. text ed. 55.00 (0-275-94490-5, Praeger Pubs) Greenwood.

Murray, Michael D. & Ferri, Anthony J., eds. Teaching Mass Communication: A Guide to Better Instruction. LC 91-28831. 288p. 1992. text ed. 49.95 (0-275-94156-6, C4156, Praeger Pubs) Greenwood.

Murray, Michael J. A Tear to Remember. LC 85-62296. (Illus.). (Orig.). 1985. pap. 3.95 (0-9614642-0-8, 927-1) Media Arts.

— Washington, D. C. A Prospice (The Political Socialization of Community) LC 78-61328. 300p. 1987. text ed. 26.50 (0-9614642-1-6) Media Arts.

Murray, Michael P. Subsidizing Industrial Location: A Conceptual Framework with Application to Korea. LC 88-45375. (World Bank Occasional Papers, New Ser.: No. 3). 160p. (Orig.). 1988. pap. text ed. 14.95 (0-8018-3752-9) Johns Hopkins.

Murray, Michael T. Arthritis: How You Can Benefit from Diet, Vitamins, Minerals, Herbs, Exercise, & Other Natural Methods. LC 93-50095. (Getting Well Naturally Ser.). 1994. write for info. (1-55958-491-2) Prima Pub.

— Chronic Fatigue Syndrome: How You Can Benefit from Diet, Vitamins, Minerals, Herbs, Exercise, & Other Natural Methods. LC 94-7471. (Getting Well Naturally Ser.). 1994. write for info. (1-55958-490-4) Prima Pub.

— The Complete Book of Juicing: Your Delicious Guide to Healthful Living. (Illus.). 250p. (Orig.). 1992. pap. 12.95 (1-55958-268-5) Prima Pub.

— Diabetes & Hypoglycemia. LC 93-36307. (Getting Well Naturally Ser.). 1994. pap. 9.95 (1-55958-426-2) Prima Pub.

— The Healing Power of Foods: Nutrition Secrets for Vibrant Health & Long Life. LC 93-16251. 500p. (Orig.). 1993. pap. 16.95 (1-55958-317-7) Prima Pub.

— The Healing Power of Foods Cookbook: Over 150 Delicious Recipes for Vibrant Health. 300p. (Orig.). 1993. pap. 12.95 (1-55958-318-5) Prima Pub.

— The Healing Power of Herbs: The Enlightened Person's Guide to the Wonders of Medicinal Plants. 2nd expanded rev. ed. 1995. 12.95 (1-55958-700-8) Prima Pub.

— Male Sexual Vitality. LC 93-29270. (Getting Well Naturally Ser.). 1994. 8.95 (1-55958-428-9) Prima Pub.

— Menopause: Getting Well Naturally. 1994. pap. 8.95 (1-55958-427-0) Prima Pub.

— Natural Alternatives to Over-the-Counter & Prescription Drugs. LC 93-14152. 1994. 25.00 (0-688-12358-9) Morrow.

— Stress, Anxiety & Insomnia. 1994. pap. 9.95 (1-55958-489-0) Prima Pub.

Murray, Michael T., jt. auth. see Werbach, Melvyn R.

Murray, Michael V., tr. see Giles of Rome.

***Murray, Michelle L.** Antepartal & Intrapartal Fetal Monitoring. 2nd ed. (Illus.). 260p. (C). 1995. pap. text ed. 48.00 (0-942835-01-8) Lrning Res Intl.

***Murray, Milton.** Words of Wisdom: For Writers, Speakers, & Leaders. Scoggins, Jeff & Fox, Randy, eds. LC 93-84878. (Illus.). 212p. (Orig.). 1993. pap. write for info. (0-9643585-0-6) Philanthropic Srv.

Murray, Mitch. The Mitch Murray Book of One-Liners for Wedding Speeches & How to Use Them. (Orig.). 1994. pap. 11.95 (0-572-01896-7, Pub. by W Foulsham UK) Trans-Atl Phila.

Murray, Muz. Sharing the Quest. (Illus.). 272p. 1990. pap. 13.95 (1-85230-087-6) Element MA.

Murray, Nancy. Palestinians: Life under Occupation. LC 91-66234. (Illus.). 100p. (Orig.). 1991. pap. text ed. 12.95 (0-9630674-0-0) Mddle East Just.

Murray, Nancy, jt. auth. see Goodsell, Charles T.

Murray, Nancy, jt. auth. see Sorenson, Joyce.

Murray, Nancy A. Revision of Cymbopetalum & Porcelia (Annonaceae) Anderson, Christiane, ed. (Systematic Botany Monographs: Vol. 40). (Illus.). 121p. 1993. pap. 16.00 (0-912861-40-1) Am Soc Plant.

Murray, Nancy R., jt. auth. see Wall, Jennifer A.

Murray, Natalia D., jt. auth. see Flanner, Janet.

Murray, Nicholas. Bruce Chatwin. (Illus.). 139p. 1993. 32.00 (1-85411-079-9, Pub. by Seren Bks UK); pap. 15.95 (1-85411-080-2, Pub. by Seren Bks UK) Dufour.

— Letters to the Right Rev. John Hughes, Roman Catholic Bishop of New York. Grob, Gerald, ed. LC 76-46091. (Anti-Movements in America Ser.). 1977. reprint ed. 31. 95 (0-405-09964-9) Ayer.

— Notes Historical & Biographical, Concerning Elizabeth-Town, New Jersey: Its Eminent Men, Churches & Ministers. xviii, 179p. 1991. reprint ed. pap. 17.50 (1-55613-392-8) Heritage Bk.

***Murray, Nick.** Bicycling Around Galena: A Guide to the Backroads. (Illus.). 76p. (Orig.). 1994. pap. write for info. (0-9644209-0-2) Omnivore Pr.

— Serious Money: The Art of Marketing Mutual Funds. Stanger, Robert A., ed. 300p. 1991. write for info. (0-943570-11-5) R A Stanger.

Murray, Noel W. Introduction to the Theory of Thin-Walled Structures. (Oxford Engineering Science Ser.: No. 13). (Illus.). 465p. 1986. pap. 35.00 (0-19-856186-5) OUP.

— When It Comes to the Crunch: The Mechanics of Car Collections. (Series on Engineering Machines). 180p. 1995. text ed. 43.00 (981-02-2096-0) World Scientific Pub.

Murray, Noel W. & Thierauf, Georg. Tables for the Design & Analysis of Stiffened Steel Plates. 197p. 1981. 54.00 (3-528-08673-4, Pub. by Vieweg & Sohn GW) Ballen Bkslr.

Murray-Oliver, C. M., jt. auth. see Vaughan, Thomas.

Murray, Oswyn. Early Greece. LC 83-42539. (Illus.). 320p. 1980. pap. 12.95 (0-8047-1185-2) Stanford U Pr.

— Early Greece. 2nd ed. LC 93-15040. 359p. 1993. pap. 13. 95 (0-674-22132-X) HUP.

— Sympotica. (A Symposium on the Sumposion). (Illus.). 368p. 1995. pap. 39.95 (0-19-815004-0) OUP.

Murray, Oswyn & Price, Simon, eds. The Greek City: From Homer to Alexander. 400p. 1991. reprint ed. pap. 34.00 (0-19-814791-0) OUP.

Murray, Oswyn, jt. ed. see Godman, Peter.

Murray, Pamela. The New Success: Redefining, Creating & Surviving Your Own Success. 200p. 1993. pap. 12.95 (0-9638021-0-0) Many Waters.

Murray, Patricia. Let's Learn the Hawaiian Alphabet Coloring & Activity Book. 1988. pap. 2.95 (0-89610-022-7) Island Heritage.

Murray, Patricia, ed. Choosing Childcare: Solving Your Childcare Problems. 1992. 31.00 (1-85549-062-5, Pub. by Attic Pr IE) St Mut.

Murray, Patricia, tr. see Yoshitake, Oka.

Murray, Patricia A. Let's Learn the Hawaiian Alphabet. (Illus.). 24p. (J). (ps-00). 1987. 7.95 (0-89610-075-8) Island Heritage.

— Let's Learn the Hawaiian Alphabet. (Illus.). 24p. (J). (ps-00). 1988. audio 11.95 (0-89610-079-0) Island Heritage.

Murray, Patricia H. Choosing Childcare: Solving Your Childcare Problems. 144p. (Orig.). 1993. pap. 15.99 (1-85594-062-0, Pub. by Attic IE) InBook.

Murray, Patrick. Marx's Theory of Scientific Knowledge. LC 86-3052. 270p. (C). 1990. pap. 18.50 (0-391-03662-9) Humanities.

— Mary: A Marian Anthology. 192p. 1989. pap. 22.00 (0-905092-85-6, Pub. by Veritas IE) St Mut.

***Murray, Patrick, et al, eds.** Manual of Clinical Microbiology. 6th ed. 1995. 98.00 (1-55581-086-1) Am Soc Microbio.

Murray, Patrick R., et al. Medical Microbiology. 2nd ed. LC 93-11644. 755p. 1993. pap. 44.95 (0-8016-7634-7) Mosby Yr Bk.

***Murray, Patrick S.** All-in-1 User's Guide. 550p. 1995. pap. 44.95 (1-55558-138-2, Digital DEC) Buttrwrth-Heinemann.

— All-in-1 User's Handbook. 336p. 1995. pap. 27.95 (0-614-00829-8) Buttrwrth-Heinemann.

Murray, Patrick T. Friedrich Schiller's Philosophy of Aesthetic Education. LC 92-10126. (Studies in German Language & Literature: Vol. 12). 444p. 1993. lib. bdg. 109.95 (0-7734-9511-8) E Mellen.

— Hegel's Philosophy of Mind & Will. LC 91-10314. (Studies in the History of Philosophy: Vol. 21). 145p. 1991. lib. bdg. 69.95 (0-7734-9773-0) E Mellen.

Murray, Paul. The Absent Fountain. 72p. (C). 1991. 24.00 (0-948268-99-9, Pub. by Dedalus Pr IE); pap. 15.00 (0-948268-98-0, Pub. by Dedalus Pr IE) St Mut.

— A Fantastic Journey: The Life & Literature of Lafcadio Hearn. (Japan Library). 240p. (C). 1993. text ed. 39.95 (1-873410-23-9, Pub. by Curzon Pr UK) Humanities.

— The Mysticism Debate. 1978. 1.95 (0-8199-0722-7, Frncscn Herld) Franciscan Pr.

— Rites & Meditations. 1982. pap. 9.95 (0-85105-393-9, Pub. by Colin Smythe Ltd UK) Dufour.

Murray, Paul T. The Civil Rights Movement: References & Resources. (G. K. Hall Reference Ser.). 280p. 1993. text ed. 40.00 (0-8161-1837-X) G K Hall.

Murray, Pauli. The Autobiography of a Black Activist, Feminist, Lawyer, Priest, & Poet. LC 88-20728. Orig. Title: Song in a Weary Throat; an American Pilgrimage. 464p. 1989. reprint ed. pap. 18.95 (0-87049-596-8) U of Tenn Pr.

— Proud Shoes: The Story of An American Family. 280p. 1992. 20.75 (0-8446-6627-0) Peter Smith.

— Proud Shoes: The Story of an American Family. LC 77-11807. (Illus.). 304p. 1987. reprint ed. pap. 13.00 (0-06-091398-3, PL 1398, PL) HarpC.

Murray, Peggy. Child Abuse. 3rd ed. LC 94-60264. (Illus.). 272p. (C). 1993. pap. 49.95 (1-878025-59-7) Western Schls.

Murray, Peggy, ed. see Karpen, Maxine, et al.

Murray, Penelope, ed. Genius: The History of an Idea. (Illus.). 242p. 1989. text ed. 29.95 (0-631-15785-9) Blackwell Pubs.

***Murray, Peter.** The Amazon. LC 93-7617. (ENG & SPA.). (J). (gr. 2-6). 1993. lib. bdg. 22.79 (1-56766-039-8) Childs World.

— The Amazon. LC 93-7617. (ENG & SPA.). (J). (gr. 2-6). 1993. lib. bdg. 22.79 (1-56766-021-5) Childs World.

— The Architecture of the Italian Renaissance. rev. ed. LC 85-26243. (Illus.). 252p. 1986. 16.00 (0-8052-0807-0) Schocken.

— Beavers. (Nature Books Ser.). (J). (gr. 2-6). 1992. lib. bdg. 22.79 (0-89565-844-5) Childs World.

— Beetles. LC 92-29742. (J). (gr. 2-6). 1993. lib. bdg. 22.79 (1-56766-000-2) Childs World.

— Black Widows. (Nature Books Ser.). (J). (gr. 2-6). 1992. lib. bdg. 22.79 (0-89565-845-3) Childs World.

— Cactus. (Nature Bks.). (Illus.). 32p. (J). (gr. 2-6). 1995. lib. bdg. 22.79 (1-56766-191-2) Childs World.

M

— Chameleons. LC 92-41543. (Naturebook Ser.). (J). (gr. 2-6). 1993. lib. bdg. 22.79 (*1-56766-016-9*) Childs World.

— Dirt, Wonderful Dirt! LC 92-42741. (Umbrella Bks.). (Illus.). (J). (gr. 2-6). 1996. lib. bdg. 21.36 (*1-56766-079-7*) Childs World.

— Dogs. (Nature Books Ser.). (J). (gr. 2-6). 1992. lib. bdg. 22.79 (*0-89565-848-8*) Childs World.

— Earthquakes. (Nature Bks.). (Illus.). 32p. (J). (gr. 2-6). 1995. lib. bdg. 22.79 (*1-56766-198-X*) Childs World.

— The Everglades. LC 92-37962. (Vision Book Ser.). (ENG & SPA.). (J). 1993. lib. bdg. 22.79 (*1-56766-012-6*) Childs World.

— The Everglades. LC 92-37962. (Vision Bks.). (ENG & SPA.). (J). 1993. lib. bdg. 22.79 (*1-56766-036-3*) Childs World.

— Frogs. LC 92-32499. (Naturebooks Ser.). (J). (gr. 2-6). 1993. lib. bdg. 22.79 (*1-56766-010-X*) Childs World.

— How to Make Kites. LC 93-49604. (Umbrella Bks.). (Illus.). 24p. (J). (gr. 2-6). 1996. lib. bdg. 21.36 (*1-56766-083-5*) Childs World.

— How to Make Pizza. LC 93-4032. (Umbrella Bks.). (Illus.). 24p. (J). (gr. 2-6). 1996. lib. bdg. 21.36 (*1-56766-080-0*) Childs World.

— Hummingbirds. LC 92-32320. (Naturebooks Ser.). (J). (gr. 2-6). 1993. 22.79 (*1-56766-011-8*) Childs World.

— Hurricanes. (Nature Bks.). (Illus.). 32p. (J). (gr. 2-6). 1995. lib. bdg. 22.79 (*1-56766-196-3*) Childs World.

— La Lanzadera Espacial. LC 93-17916. (Visionbooks Ser.). 32p. (J). (gr. 2-6). 1993. lib. bdg. 22.79 (*1-56766-038-X*) Childs World.

— Mushrooms. (Nature Bks.). (Illus.). 32p. (J). (gr. 2-6). 1995. lib. bdg. 22.79 (*1-56766-193-9*) Childs World.

— Orchids. (Nature Bks.). (Illus.). 32p. (J). (gr. 2-6). 1995. lib. bdg. 22.79 (*1-56766-194-7*) Childs World.

— Parrots. LC 92-44265. (Naturebooks Ser.). (Illus.). (J). (gr. 2-6). 1993. lib. bdg. 22.79 (*1-56766-015-0*) Childs World.

— Planet Earth. LC 92-8412. (Nature Books Ser.). (J). (gr. 2-6). 1992. lib. bdg. 22.79 (*0-89565-854-2*) Childs World.

— The Planets. LC 92-20016. (Umbrella Bks.). (Illus.). (J). (gr. 2-6). 1992. lib. bdg. 21.36 (*0-89565-975-1*) Childs World.

— Porcupines. LC 93-22833. (Illus.). (J). (gr. 2-6). 1993. lib. bdg. 22.79 (*1-56766-019-3*) Childs World.

— Professor Solomon Snickerdoodle Looks at Air. (Umbrella Bks.). (Illus.). 32p. (J). (gr. 2-6). 1996. lib. bdg. 14.95 (*1-56766-082-7*) Childs World.

— Professor Solomon Snickerdoodle Looks at Light. (Umbrella Bks.). (Illus.). 32p. (J). (gr. 2-6). 1996. lib. bdg. 14.95 (*1-56766-148-3*) Childs World.

— Professor Solomon Snickerdoodle Looks at Water. LC 93-1322. (Umbrella Bks.). (Illus.). (J). (gr. 2-6). 1996. lib. bdg. 14.95 (*1-56766-081-9*) Childs World.

— Renaissance Architecture. LC 82-62749. (History of World Architecture Ser.). (Illus.). 220p. pap. 29.95 (*0-8478-0474-7*) Rizzoli Intl.

— Roses. (Nature Bks.). (Illus.). (J). (gr. 2-6). 1995. lib. bdg. 15.95 (*0-614-04747-1*) Childs World.

— The Sahara. LC 93-25782. (Vision Bks.). (ENG & SPA.). (J). (gr. 2-6). 1993. lib. bdg. 22.79 (*1-56766-023-1*) Childs World.

— The Sahara. LC 93-25782. (Vision Bks.). (ENG & SPA.). (J). (gr. 2-6). 1993. lib. bdg. 22.79 (*1-56766-040-1*) Childs World.

— Saturn. LC 92-41542. (Vision Bks.). (ENG & SPA.). (J). (gr. 2-6). 1993. lib. bdg. 22.79 (*1-56766-037-1*) Childs World.

— Saturn. LC 92-41542. (Vision Bks.). (ENG & SPA.). (J). (gr. 2-6). 1993. lib. bdg. 22.79 (*1-56766-014-2*) Childs World.

— Sea Otters. LC 93-42. (J). (gr. 2-6). 1993. lib. bdg. 22.79 (*1-56766-007-X*) Childs World.

— Silly Science Tricks. LC 92-18903. (J). (gr. 2-6). 1992. lib. bdg. 21.36 (*0-89565-976-X*) Childs World.

— Snakes. (Nature Books Ser.). (J). (gr. 2-6). 1992. lib. bdg. 22.79 (*0-89565-849-6*) Childs World.

— Spiders. (Nature Books Ser.). (J). (gr. 2-6). 1992. lib. bdg. 22.79 (*0-89565-847-X*) Childs World.

— Tarantulas. (Naturebooks Ser.). (J). (gr. 2-6). 1993. lib. bdg. 22.79 (*1-56766-060-6*) Childs World.

— Tornadoes. (Nature Bks.). (Illus.). 32p. (J). (gr. 2-6). 1995. lib. bdg. 21.36 (*1-56766-195-5*) Childs World.

— Volcanos. (Nature Bks.). (Illus.). 32p. (J). (gr. 2-6). 1995. lib. bdg. 22.79 (*1-56766-197-1*) Childs World.

— Wildflowers. (Nature Bks.). (Illus.). 32p. (J). (gr. 2-6). 1995. lib. bdg. 22.79 (*1-56766-192-0*) Childs World.

— World's Greatest Chocolate Chip Cookies. (Umbrella Bks.). (Illus.). (J). (gr. 2-6). 1992. lib. bdg. 21.36 (*0-89565-892-5*) Childs World.

— World's Greatest Paper Airplanes. (Umbrella Bks.). (Illus.). (J). (gr. 2-6). 1992. lib. bdg. 21.36 (*0-89565-963-8*) Childs World.

— You Can Juggle. LC 92-9504. (J). (gr. 2-6). 1992. lib. bdg. 21.36 (*0-89565-966-2*); Resale. 21.35 (*0-89565-906-9*) Childs World.

— Your Bones: An Inside Look at Skeletons. LC 92-7460. (Umbrella Bks.). (Illus.). (J). (gr. 1-8). 1992. lib. bdg. 21.36 (*0-89565-968-9*) Childs World.

Murray, Peter, ed. Contemporary British Architecture. (Illus.). 240p. 1994. 65.00 (*3-7913-1349-5*, Pub. by Prestel) TeNeues.

Murray, Peter & Murray, Linda. Art of the Renaissance. LC 84-51305. (World of Art Ser.). (Illus.). 288p. 1985. pap. 12.95 (*0-500-20008-4*) Thames Hudson.

— Diccionario de Artes y Artistas: Dictionary of Arts & Artists. 600p. (SPA.). 1978. 29.95 (*0-8288-4880-7*, S50013) Fr & Eur.

— A Dictionary of Art & Artists. rev. ed. (Reference Ser.). 1984. pap. 8.95 (*0-14-051133-4*, Penguin Bks) Viking Penguin.

Murray, Peter, ed. see Burckhardt, Jacob.

Murray, Peter, tr. see Chastel, Andre.

Murray, Peter L. & Field, Richard H. Maine Evidence. 3rd ed. 670p. 1994. ring bd. 115.00 (*1-56257-198-2*) Michie Butterworth.

Murray, Philip, jt. auth. see Cooke, Morris L.

Murray, Placid. One Hundred Liturgical Homilies. 128p. (Orig.). 1988. pap. 7.95 (*0-948183-55-1*, Pub. by Columba Pr IE) Twenty-Third.

Murray, Placid, tr. see Holzherr, George.

Murray, Placid, ed. see Newman, John H.

Murray, R. B., jt. auth. see Tallarida, R. J.

***Murray, R. L.** The Redemption of the 11th & 126th New York Cowards" The Story of the 111th & 126th New York Volunteer Regiments at Gettysburg. 178p. 1994. pap. write for info. (*0-9646261-0-X*) R L Murray NY.

Murray, R. L. & Cobb, G. C. Physics: Concepts & Consequences. (American Nuclear Society Textbook Ser.). 710p. 1970. text ed. 13.95 (*0-13-672501-5*, 350004) Am Nuclear Soc.

Murray, R. M. & Turner, T. H., eds. Lectures on the History of Psychiatry. (Squibb Ser.). 236p. 1990. write for info. (*0-88048-601-5*, Pub. by Royal Coll Psych UK) Am Psychiatric.

— Lectures on the History of Psychiatry: The Squibb Series. LC 91-46193. 235p. reprint ed. pap. 67.00 (*0-7837-4059-X*, 2044009) Bks Demand.

Murray, Raymond. Images in the Dark: An Encyclopedia of Gay & Lesbian Film & Video. LC 94-60358. (Orig.). 1994. pap. 19.95 (*1-880707-01-2*) TLA Vid Mgt.

— The SAS in Ireland. (Illus.). 501p. (Orig.). 1991. pap. 21.00 (*0-85342-991-X*, Pub. by Mercier Pr IE) Dufour.

— The SAS in Ireland, 1969-1989. (Illus.). 500p. 1991. 34.00 (*0-85342-938-3*, Pub. by Mercier Pr IE) Dufour.

Murray, Raymond C. & Tedrow, John C. Forensic Geology. 176p. 1991. text ed. 75.00 (*0-13-327453-5*) P-H.

Murray, Raymond C., jt. ed. see Pray, Lloyd C.

Murray, Raymond L. Grandpa Saw It Happen - WWII: Normandy Beach to Elbe River. Murray, Melba L., ed. (Illus.). 250p. 1993. 19.95 (*0-9640671-0-2*) R L Murray.

— Nuclear Energy. LC 74-8685. 296p. 1975. text ed. 28.00 (*0-685-04008-9*, Pergamon Pr); pap. text ed. 16.50 (*0-685-04009-7*, Pergamon Pr) Elsevier.

— Nuclear Energy. 3rd ed. (Unified Engineering Ser.: No. 22). (Illus.). 350p. 1988. text ed. 90.00 (*0-08-031628-X*, Pergamon Pr); pap. text ed. 38.00 (*0-08-031629-8*, Pergamon Pr) Elsevier.

— Nuclear Energy: An Introduction to the Concepts, Systems, & Applications of Nuclear Processes. 4th ed. LC 93-17144. 1993. text ed. 104.00 (*0-08-042126-1*, Pergamon Pr); pap. text ed. 48.00 (*0-08-042125-3*, Pergamon Pr) Elsevier.

— Nuclear Energy: In SI Metric Units. 2nd ed. 1980. text ed. 52.00 (*0-08-024751-2*, Pergamon Pr); pap. text ed. 22.00 (*0-08-024750-4*, Pergamon Pr) Elsevier.

— Understanding Radioactive Waste. 4th ed. Powell, Judith A., ed. (Illus.). 200p. 1994. pap. text ed. 12.50 (*0-935470-79-4*) Battelle.

Murray, Regina W. The Last One up the Hill: A Biography of Thomas F. Waldron. (Illus.). 150p. 1993. 19.95 (*0-9636918-0-5*) R W Murray.

***Murray, Ric, photos.** John Dunnigan: New Work. (Illus.). 5p. (Orig.). 1993. pap. text ed. 10.00 (*0-614-02572-9*) P J Gallery.

Murray, Richard D., ed. see Society of Photographic Scientists & Engineers Staff.

Murray, Richard N., jt. auth. see Zimmer, Jim L.

***Murray, Richard P.** Basic Guide to Understanding Clinical Laboratory Tests. LC 93-77871. 110p. 1993. 14.95 (*1-882657-01-2*) Health Hope.

Murray, Richard W., jt. auth. see Thomas, Robert D.

Murray, Robert. The Cosmic Covenant. (Illus.). 260p. (Orig.). (C). 1992. pap. 24.95 (*0-7220-2750-8*) Chr Classics.

— Harper's Biochemistry. 23th ed. 816p. (C). 1993. pap. text ed. 31.95 (*0-8385-3562-3*, A3562-4) Appleton & Lange.

— High Cockalorum. 1964. pap. 4.75 (*0-8222-0518-1*) Dramatists Play.

Murray, Robert & White, Kate. Research for Writers. 152p. (C). 1985. 59.00 (*0-7300-0302-7*, Pub. by Deakin Univ AT) St Mut.

Murray, Robert, jt. ed. see Lamb, David R.

Murray, Robert B. C Plus Plus Strategies & Tactics. 1993. pap. 33.95 (*0-201-56382-7*) Addison-Wesley.

Murray, Robert D. Thunder over the Door: The Ships, Shores, & Woods of Wisconsin's Door Peninsula. LC 91-16418. (Illus.). (Orig.). 1991. 19.95 (*0-940473-22-4*) Wm Caxton.

Murray, Robert D., et al. The Natural Coumarins: Occurrence, Chemistry & Biochemistry. LC 81-14776. 714p. reprint ed. pap. 180.00 (*0-685-44057-5*, 2030429) Bks Demand.

Murray, Robert F., jt. auth. see Bowman, James E.

Murray, Robert H. Erasmus & Luther: Their Attitude to Toleration. LC 83-45659. (Zodiac Club Ser.). reprint ed. 57.50 (*0-404-19809-0*) AMS Pr.

— Group Movements Throughout the Ages. LC 72-301. (Essay Index Reprint Ser.). 1977. reprint ed. 24.95 (*0-8369-2810-5*) Ayer.

— The Only Way Home. (Illus.). 159p. 1987. 24.00 (*0-9617970-0-2*) Robert H Murray.

Murray, Robert K. The Harding Era: Warren G. Harding & His Administration. LC 74-91797. 654p. reprint ed. pap. 180.00 (*0-8357-3333-5*, 2039558) Bks Demand.

Murray, Robert K. & Blessing, Tim H. Greatness in the White House: Rating the Presidents. rev. ed. LC 93-20451. 192p. (C). 1993. pap. 14.95 (*0-271-01090-8*) Pa St U Pr.

— Greatness in the White House: Rating the Presidents. 2nd rev. ed. LC 93-20451. 192p. (C). 1993. 30.00 (*0-271-01089-4*) Pa St U Pr.

— Greatness in the White House: Rating the Presidents, Washington Through Carter. LC 88-28124. (Penn State Studies: No. 50). 153p. (Orig.). 1988. pap. text ed. 10.00 (*0-271-00659-5*) Pa St U Pr.

Murray, Robert K. & Brucker, Roger W. Trapped! The Story of Floyd Collins. LC 82-40177. (Illus.). 344p. 1982. reprint ed. pap. 18.00 (*0-8131-0153-0*) U Pr of Ky.

***Murray, Robert M.** Fountain of Guilt: Survivors Guide to the Nuclear Family. 256p. (Orig.). 1996. pap. 11.95 (*1-885610-03-3*) European Amer.

Murray-Robertson, J. Ways into Work. Waller, R., ed. (C). 1986. 35.00 (*0-09-165541-2*, Pub. by S Thornes Pubs UK) St Mut.

Murray-Robertson, J., ed. Ways into Work. (C). 1989. 30.00 (*0-09-165531-5*, Pub. by S Thornes Pubs UK) St Mut.

Murray, Robin, ed. see Royal College of Psychiatrists Staff.

Murray, Robin, jt. ed. see Swanson, Meg.

Murray, Robin M., jt. ed. see McGuffin, Peter.

Murray, Roger F. Economic Aspects of Pensions: A Summary Report. (General Ser.: No. 85). 148p. 1968. 38.50 (*0-87014-473-1*) Natl Bur Econ Res.

— Economic Aspects of Pensions: A Summary Report. LC 68-20444. (National Bureau of Economic Research. General Ser.: No. 85). 148p. reprint ed. pap. 42.20 (*0-8357-2602-9*, 2015980) Bks Demand.

Murray, Roger N. Wordsworth's Style: Figures & Themes in the Lyrical Ballads of 1800. LC 67-13152. xii, 166p. 1967. 19.95 (*0-8032-0127-3*) U of Nebr Pr.

Murray, Ronald J. Memories Never Die. 90p. (Orig.). 1993. pap. 10.00 (*0-9641018-0-7*) R J Murray.

Murray, Ronald O., et al. The Radiology of Skeletal Disorders, 4 vols., Set. 3rd ed. (Illus.). 2368p. 1990. text ed. 495.00 (*0-443-01980-0*) Churchill.

Murray, Rosalie R., jt. auth. see Murray, William D.

Murray, Rose. Astro-Numerology. 48p. 1991. 6.00 (*0-86690-400-X*, M3172-014) Am Fed Astrologers.

— When Will You Marry? Your Romantic Destiny Through Astrology. LC 95-2101. 240p. 1995. pap. 12.95 (*1-56718-479-0*) Llewellyn Pubns.

Murray, Royce. Molecular Design of Electrode Surfaces. (Techniques of Chemistry Ser.: Vol. 22). 448p. 1992. text ed. 175.00 (*0-471-55773-0*) Wiley.

Murray, Ruth B. & Huelskoetter, M. Psychiatric - Mental Health Nursing: Giving Emotional Care. 3rd ed. (Illus.). 160p. (C). 1991. write for info. (*0-8385-7994-9*, A7994-5); boxed 52.95 (*0-8385-7993-0*, A7993-7) Appleton & Lange.

Murray, Ruth B. & Zentner, Judy. Nursing Assessment & Health Promotion Strategies Through the Life Span. 5th ed. (Illus.). 796p. (C). 1993. pap. text ed. 39.95 (*0-8385-6637-5*, A6637-1) Appleton & Lange.

Murray, Ruth L. Your Chihuahua. LC 66-22308. (Your Dog Bk.). (Illus.). 1966. 8.95 (*0-87714-019-7*); pap. 4.95 (*0-87714-020-0*) Denlingers.

Murray, S. G., jt. auth. see Bailey, A.

***Murray, Scott.** Australian Cinema. 1994. pap. 16.95 (*1-86373-311-6*) IPG Chicago.

Murray, Scott, ed. Australian Film Nineteen Seventy-Eight to Nineteen Eighty-Two, Vol. 2. (Illus.). 352p. 1994. pap. 27.00 (*0-19-553584-7*) OUP.

— Australian Film 1978-1994. (Illus.). 464p. 1995. pap. 25.00 (*0-19-553777-7*) OUP.

Murray, Shirley E., et al. In Every Corner Sing: The Hymns of Shirley Erena Murray. Schrader, Jack, ed. LC 92-73734. 200p. (Orig.). 1992. 11.95 (*0-916642-48-8*) Hope Pub.

Murray-Smith, D., et al, eds. Proceedings of the Third European Simulation Congress. 846p. 1989. 90.00 (*0-911801-60-X*, EURO-89) Soc Computer Sim.

Murray-Smith, Stephen & Dare, Anthony J. The Tech: A Centenary History of the Royal Melbourne Institute of Technology. 248p. 1987. 49.95 (*0-947062-06-8*, Pub. by Hyland Hse AT) Intl Spec Bk.

Murray, Sonia. Season of Growth. York, Sherri, ed. LC 87-42911. 290p. 1990. pap. 3.95 (*1-55523-114-4*) Winston-Derek.

Murray, Spence, ed. see Peterson's Staff.

Murray, Spencer. Pitcairn Island: The First Two Hundred Years. LC 92-81932. (Illus.). 192p. 1992. pap. 19.95 (*0-9633229-0-7*) Bounty Sagas.

Murray, Spencer, jt. auth. see Crow, James T.

Murray, Stephen. Beauvais Cathedral: Architecture of Transcendence. (Illus.). 352p. (C). 1989. text ed. 65.00 (*0-691-04236-5*) Princeton U Pr.

— Building Troyes Cathedral: The Late Gothic Campaigns. LC 85-45744. (Illus.). 278p. 1987. 50.00 (*0-253-31277-9*) Ind U Pr.

— Fatal Opinions. 256p. 1992. 18.95 (*0-312-08193-6*) St Martin.

Murray, Stephen O. Life in Angkor. (Illus.). 176p. (Orig.). 1995. write for info. (*0-942777-15-8*) Bua Luang Pub. Sociologist Stephen O. Murray, drawing on a variety of ancient sources, summarized what is known about the Angkor-era Khmer society. Subjects include jurisprudence, dress & rank, slaves, conjugal duties, defloration ceremonies & weddings, elite women intellectuals, funeral practices, bathing, health care, festivals & entertainment, the Khmer army, Khmer religious traditions, rice growing, & peasant exhaustion. Appendices include the kings of Angkor & an extensive glossary. To order: International Wavelength Inc., 2215-R Market St., #829, San Francisco, CA 94114, (415) 864-6522 FAX (415) 864-6615.** ***Publisher Provided Annotation.

— Theory Groups & the Study of Language in North America: A Social History. LC 93-34835. (Studies in the History of the Language Sciences: No. 69). x, 550p. 1993. 110.00x (*1-55619-364-5*) Benjamins North Am.

***Murray, Stephen O., ed.** Latin American Male Homosexualities. 256p. 1995. pap. 24.95x (*0-8263-1658-1*) Free Spirit Pub.

— Latin American Male Homosexualities. LC 95-4349. 256p. 1995. 45.00 (*0-8263-1646-8*) U of NM Pr.

Murray, Stephen O. & Hong, Keelung. Taiwanese Culture, Taiwanese Society: A Critical Review of Social Science Research Done on Taiwan. LC 93-48342. 250p. (Orig.). (C). Date not set. lib. bdg. 49.50 (*0-8191-9433-6*); pap. text ed. 28.50 (*0-8191-9434-4*) U Pr of Amer.

Murray, Sterling E. Anthologies of Music: An Annotated Index. 2nd ed. LC 92-34086. (Detroit Studies in Music Bibliography: No. 68). 1992. 35.00 (*0-89990-061-5*) Info Coord.

Murray, Steve, tr. see Davidsen, Leif.

Murray, Steve, tr. see Lindgren, Babro.

Murray, Steve, tr. see Newth, Mette.

Murray, Steve, tr. see Rifbjerg, Klaus.

Murray, Steve, tr. see Sorensen, Villy.

Murray, Steven T., tr. see Andersen Nexo, Martin.

Murray, Steven T., tr. see Nexo, Martin A.

Murray, Steven T., tr. see Rifbjerg, Klaus.

Murray, Stuart. Go for the Goal. 1994. pap. 12.00 (*0-671-88232-5*, Fireside) S&S Trade.

— The Shaker Heritage Guidebook: Exploring the Historic Sites, Museums & Collections. LC 93-79992. (Illus.). 261p. (Orig.). 1994. pap. 15.95 (*0-9614876-6-6*) Golden Hl Pr NY.

Murray, Stuart & McCabe, James. Norman Rockwell's Four Freedoms: Images That Inspired a Nation. 1993. 24.95 (*0-936399-43-0*); pap. 14.95 (*0-936399-42-2*) Berkshire Hse.

Murray, Sue & Monash University Staff. Bibliography of Australian Poetry: 1935-55. 274p. 1991. 45.00 (*1-875589-00-7*) D W Thorpe.

Murray, Susan. Birds of a Feather. 192p. 1994. 17.95 (*0-8034-9057-7*, Avalon Bks) Bouregy.

— Birds of Paradise. 192p. 1994. 17.95 (*0-8034-9065-8*, Avalon Bks) Bouregy.

— Love Birds. 1995. 17.95 (*0-8034-9091-7*, 094622) Bouregy.

Murray, Susan M. & Taylor, Barbara. Going-to-Work-Book. 96p. 1987. spiral bd. 18.95 (*0-8403-4339-6*) Kendall-Hunt.

Murray, Suzanne P. The Joseph Veach Noble Collection. LC 85-52166. (Illus.). 56p. (Orig.). (C). 1985. pap. 6.00 (*1-878293-00-1*) Tampa Mus Art.

Murray, T., jt. auth. see Murray, I.

Murray, T. P. & Horn, R. C. Organic Nitrogen Compounds for Use As Fertilizers. (Technical Bulletin Ser.: No. T-14). 64p. (Orig.). 1979. pap. 4.00 (*0-88090-013-X*) Intl Fertilizer.

Murray, Tania C., tr. see Camporesi, Piero.

Murray, Teresa G., Sr. Vocational Guidance in Catholic Secondary Schools: A Study of Developments & Present Status. LC 77-177098. (Columbia University. Teachers College. Contributions to Education Ser.: No. 754). reprint ed. 37.50 (*0-404-55754-6*) AMS Pr.

Murray, Terry. The I. U. Cookbook. 125p. 1993. 18.95 (*1-878208-33-0*); pap. 14.95 (*1-878208-28-4*) Guild Pr IN.

Murray, Thom & Wiley, Linda. Staying Power: How to Get the B.S. Out of College or the B.A. or the Degree of Your Choice. LC 93-35802. (Practical Guide Ser.: No. 2). 185p. (Orig.). 1994. pap. 18.95 (*0-929398-65-3*) UNTX Pr.

Murray, Thomas. His Truth Keeps Marching On. (Orig.). 1992. pap. 6.50 (*1-55673-411-5*) CSS OH.

— Pitcairn's Island. LC 72-281. (World History Ser.: No. 48). 1972. reprint ed. lib. bdg. 75.00 (*0-8383-1410-4*) M S G Haskell Hse.

— Reclaiming Christian Piety. 1993. pap. 6.95 (*1-55673-548-0*, 7972) CSS OH.

Murray, Thomas B. Par Choix: The Remarkable Life Story of Philippe. 192p. (Orig.). 1994. pap. 10.95 (*1-56474-069-2*) Fithian Pr.

***Murray, Thomas C.** License Plate Book '95. (Illus.). 128p. 1995. pap. 12.95 (*0-9629962-9-7*) Inter Directory.

Murray, Thomas D. Tire Tracks Back. LC 89-81149. 266p. (Orig.). 1990. pap. 14.95 (*0-916383-96-2*) Aegina Pr.

Murray, Thomas E. The Language of St. Louis, Missouri: Variations in the Gateway City. (American University Studies: Linguistics: Ser. XIII, Vol. 4). 276p. 1986. text ed. 36.00 (*0-8204-0324-5*) P Lang Pubs.

— The Structure of English: Phonetics, Phonology, Morphology. LC 94-188. 1994. pap. text ed. 15.75 (*0-205-16053-0*) Allyn.

Murray, Thomas E. & Murrell, Thomas R. The Language of Sadomasochism: A Glossary & Linguistic Analysis. LC 88-25099. 208p. 1989. text ed. 65.00 (*0-313-26481-3*, MYD/, Greenwood Pr) Greenwood.

Murray, Thomas H., ed. The Journal of the American-Irish Historical Society, Vol. 1, 1898. (Illus.). 140p. 1991. reprint ed. pap. 15.00 (*1-55613-432-0*) Heritage Bk.

— The Journal of the American-Irish Historical Society, Vol. 5: 1905. 216p. 1992. reprint ed. pap. 18.00 (*1-55613-567-X*) Heritage Bk.

— The Journal of the American-Irish Historical Society, 1900, Vol. 3. (Illus.). 243p. 1991. reprint ed. pap. 19.00 (*1-55613-484-3*) Heritage Bk.

An Asterisk (*) at the beginning of an entry indicates that the title is appearing in BIP for the first time.

Murray, Thomas H. & Caplan, Arthur L., eds. Which Babies Shall Live? LC 85-18058. (Contemporary Issues in Biomedicine, Ethics, & Society Ser.). 240p. 1985. 39.95 (*0-89603-086-5*) Humana.

Murray, Thomas H., et al, eds. Feeling Good & Doing Better. LC 84-4552. (Contemporary Issues in Biomedicine, Ethics, & Society Ser.). 232p. 1984. 39.50 (*0-89603-061-X*) Humana.

Murray, Thomas J., ed. The Journal of the American-Irish Historical Society, Vol. 6: 1906. 174p. 1992. reprint ed. pap. 15.50 (*1-55613-568-8*) Heritage Bk.

Murray, Thomas J. & Robertson, Donald W. Understanding & Handling the Back & Neck Injury Case. (Personal Injury Library). 371p. 1991. pap. text ed. 55.00 (*0-471-55325-5*) Wiley.

Murray, Thomas J., jt. auth. see Bryson, Reid A.

Murray, Thomas M. & Hymer, David M. Real Property & Commercial Transactions Deadlines, Pt. 6: Summer 1992, Action Guide. Stein, Carolyn J., ed. (Meeting Statutory Deadlines Ser.). 78p. 1992. pap. text ed. 47.00 (*0-88124-557-7*, RE-11412) Cont Ed Bar-CA.

Murray, Thompson C. License Plate Book. 1993. 5.99 (*0-517-08802-9*) Random Hse Value.

— License Plate Games. 1993. pap. 3.95 (*0-87131-749-4*) M Evans.

— Road Sign Games. 1993. pap. 3.95 (*0-87131-750-8*) M Evans.

— Truck Games. 1993. pap. 3.95 (*0-87131-748-6*) M Evans.

Murray, Thomson C. License Plate Book: How to Read & Decode Plates from All 50 States. Wiener, Michael, ed. (Illus.). 128p. (J). (gr. 2-12). 1993. reprint ed. 14.95 (*0-9629962-1-1*); reprint ed. pap. 12.95 (*0-87131-710-9*) Inter Directory.

Murray, Timothy. Like a Film: Ideological Fantasy on Screen, Camera, & Canvas. LC 93-17147. (Illus.). 272p. 1993. 49.95 (*0-415-07733-8*, A7257); pap. 17.95 (*0-685-66551-8*, A7261) Routledge.

— Theatrical Legitimation: Allegories of Genius in 17th-Century England & France. (Illus.). 304p. 1987. 45.00 (*0-19-504268-9*) OUP.

Murray, Tom. Estimation Exploration. (J). (gr. 3-8). 1994. pap. text ed. 7.95 (*1-882293-02-9*) Activity Resources.

— Waterfront Supercargo. (Little Bks.). 59p. (Orig.). 1980. pap. 2.25 (*0-917300-10-6*) Singlejack Bks.

Murray, Toni, ed. see Spencer, Ernest.

Murray, Tracy, Associates Staff, jt. ed. see Walter, Ingo.

Murray, Venetia. Shadows from the Past. (C). 1988. 75.00 (*1-85219-060-4*, Pub. by Bishopsgate Pr Ltd UK) St Mut.

Murray, Vic. Improving Corporate Donations: New Strategies for Grantmakers & Grantseekers. LC 91-23755. (Nonprofit Sector-Public Administration Ser.). 200p. 1991. 29.95 (*1-55542-394-9*) Jossey-Bass.

Murray, W., ed. Numerical Methods for Unconstrained Optimization. (Institute of Mathematics & Its Applications Conference Series, New Ser.). 1972. text ed. 91.00 (*0-12-512250-0*) Acad Pr.

Murray, W. Cotter. Irish Fictions. 128p. 1994. 14.95 (*0-944266-18-5*) Maecenas Pr.

***Murray, W. H.** Holiday Tales: Christmas in the Adirondacks. (Illus.). 118p. 1995. pap. 25.00 (*0-925168-02-5*) North Country.

Murray, W. J., jt. ed. see Gilchrist, W.

Murray, Wayne A., ed. see Valenti, Vince & Jaeger, Jag.

Murray, William. Automatic Program Debugging for Intelligent Tutoring Systems. (Research Notes in Artificial Intelligence Ser.). 347p. 1989. Research Monograph. 29.95 (*0-934613-98-2*) Morgan Kaufmann.

— The Last Italian: Portrait of a People. (Illus.). 272p. 1992. pap. 10.00 (*0-671-77999-0*, Touchstone Bks) S&S Trade.

— My Life Without God. enl. rev. ed. LC 92-10586. 1992. mass mkt. 5.99 (*1-56507-029-1*) Harvest Hse.

— Now You See Her, Now You Don't. LC 94-13433. 1994. 22.00 (*0-8050-2971-0*) H Holt & Co.

— Picture Dictionary. (Read with Me Ser.). (Illus.). 28p. (J). (ps-2). 1991. 3.50 (*0-7214-1416-8*, 9112-1) Ladybird Bks.

— Picture Word Cards. (Read with Me Ser.). (J). (ps-2). 1991. 9.95 (*0-7214-3232-8*, 9113) Ladybird Bks.

— A Slick Italian Hand. 1995. 22.50 (*0-8050-2972-9*) H Holt & Co.

— Using Visual Basic Writing Windows Applications. 1992. pap. 34.95 (*0-201-58145-0*) Addison-Wesley.

— The Wrong Horse: An Odyssey Through the American Racing Scene. LC 94-5206. 1994. pap. 10.95 (*0-316-59131-9*) Little.

— The Wrong Horse: An Odyssey Through the American Racing Scene. LC 92-15250. 1992. pap. 20.00 (*0-671-76774-7*) S&S Trade.

Murray, William, ed. Automatic Program Debugging for Intelligent Tutoring Systems. 248p. (C). 1988. pap. text ed. 200.00 (*0-273-08795-9*, Pub. by Pitman Pubng UK) St Mut.

Murray, William & Millett, Allan R., eds. Calculations: Net Assessment & the Coming of World War II. 350p. 1992. text ed. 35.00 (*0-02-921585-4*) Free Pr.

Murray, William C. Michael Joe: A Novel of Irish Life. 320p. 1991. reprint ed. pap. 11.95 (*0-86322-128-9*, Pub. by Brandon Bk Pubs IE) Irish Bks Media.

Murray, William D. And You Didn't Think You Had a Prayer. 1993. pap. write for info. (*1-878287-03-6*) Type & Temperament.

— Give Yourself the Unfair Advantage. 1993. pap. write for info. (*1-878287-02-8*) Type & Temperament.

Murray, William D. & Murray, Rosalie R. Introduction to Psychological Type: An Introduction to Yourself. 145p. 1988. 119.95 (*1-878287-10-9*, KTAA) Type & Temperament.

— Oppositeness: How Opposite Personalities Interact. 115p. 1988. 119.95 (*1-878287-12-5*, KTAC) Type & Temperament.

— Opposites: When ENFP & ISTJ Interact. (When Types Interact Ser.). 104p. 1988. pap. 9.95 (*1-878287-01-X*, BTAB) Type & Temperament.

— Thinkers & Feelers Mini Seminar. (Type & Temperament Seminar Kits Ser.). 83p. 1989. 99.95 (*1-878287-13-3*, KTAF) Type & Temperament.

— Type & Your Career Seminar Kit: Using Type in Career Selection. 1991. 159.95 (*1-878287-15-X*, KTAD) Type & Temperament.

— Type Communications Seminar Kit: Using Type to Enhance Organizational & Interpersonal Communication. 130p. 1988. 139.95 (*1-878287-11-7*, KTAB) Type & Temperament.

— When ENFP & INFJ Interact. (When Types Interact Ser.). 56p. 1987. pap. text ed. 9.95 (*1-878287-00-1*, BTAA) Type & Temperament.

Murray, William D. & Rigney, Francis J. Paper Folding for Beginners. (Illus.). (J). (gr. 1 up). pap. 2.95 (*0-486-20713-7*) Dover.

Murray, William D. & Walsh, Peter. Type & Team Development Seminar Kit: Using Type to Unleash the Power of Your Team. (Type & Temperament Seminar Kits Ser.). 160p. 1990. 159.95 (*1-878287-14-1*, KTAE) Type & Temperament.

Murray, William G., jt. ed. see Timmons, John F.

Murray, William G., et al. Farm Appraisal & Valuation. 6th ed. LC 83-8408. (Illus.). 304p. 1983. text ed. 26.95 (*0-8138-0570-8*) Iowa St U Pr.

Murray, William H. Adventures in the Wilderness. Verner, William K., ed. LC 72-132972. (Illus.). 332p. 1989. reprint ed. text ed. 13.95 (*0-8156-2466-2*) Syracuse U Pr.

Murray, William H., III. Application Programming for Windows NT. 1993. text ed. 39.95 (*0-07-881933-4*) Osborne-McGraw.

Murray, William H. Borland C ++ Handbook, Fourth Edition. 4th ed. 1993. pap. text ed. 34.95 (*0-07-881960-1*) Osborne-McGraw.

— Turbo Pascal for Windows Programming: The Complete Guide to Developing Windows Applications. 1994. pap. write for info. (*0-201-58118-3*) Addison-Wesley.

— Window's Programming: An Introduction. 1990. pap. text ed. 28.95 (*0-07-881536-3*) Osborne-McGraw.

Murray, William H. & Pappas, Chris H. Manual de Microprocesador 80386. 1991. pap. text ed. 19.95 (*0-07-104084-6*) McGraw.

Murray, William H., III & Pappas, Chris H. Microsoft C-C Plus Plus 7: The Complete Reference. 1008p. 1992. text ed. 29.95 (*0-07-881664-5*) Osborne-McGraw.

— OLE Wizardry: Programming OLE Applications & Custom Controls Using Wizards. 1995. cd-rom, pap. text ed. 39.95 (*0-07-882102-9*) Osborne-McGraw.

— The Visual C++ Handbook, Second Edition. 2nd ed. Date not set. pap. text ed. 34.95 (*0-07-882125-8*) Osborne-McGraw.

Murray, William J. Anarchic Harmony. LC 91-78422. 144p. (Orig.). 1992. pap. 11.95 (*1-55950-082-4*, 94187) Loompanics.

— The Complete Constitution of the United States of America. (Orig.). 1986. pap. 4.95 (*0-940917-01-7*) MFM Publish.

— Football: A History of the World Game. LC 94-15190. 297p. 1994. 49.95 (*1-85928-091-9*, Pub. by Scolar Pr UK) Ashgate Pub Co.

— Nicaragua: Portrait of a Tragedy. 128p. 1987. pap. 6.95 (*0-940917-03-3*) MFM Publish.

— The Right-Wing Press in the French Revolution: 1789-1792, No. 44. (Royal Historical Society Ser.). 349p. 1986. 63.00 (*0-86193-201-3*) Boydell & Brewer.

— Uncommon Sense: The Real American Manifesto. LC 94-27822. 383p. (Orig.). 1994. pap. text ed. 6.95 (*0-922356-95-5*) Amer West Pubs.

— Unconditional Freedom: Social Revolution Through Individual Empowerment. LC 93-78631. 260p. (Orig.). (C). 1993. pap. 15.95 (*1-55950-103-0*, 94222) Loompanics.

Murray, William M. Octavian's Campsite Memorial for the Actian War. LC 89-84932. (Transactions Ser.: Vol. 79, Pt. 4). (Illus.). 161p. 1989. pap. 18.00 (*0-87169-794-7*, T794-MUW) Am Philos.

Murray, William M., Jr. Thomas W. Martin: A Biography. LC 77-85483. (Illus.). 276p. 1978. 6.50 (*0-940824-01-9*) S Res Inst.

Murray, William M. & Miller, William R. The Bonded Electrical Resistance Strain Gage. (Illus.). 432p. 1992. text ed. 75.00 (*0-19-507209-X*) OUP.

Murray, William S. Making of the Balkan States. LC 10-17934. (Columbia University. Studies in the Social Sciences: No. 102). reprint ed. 24.50 (*0-404-51102-3*) AMS Pr.

***Murray, Williamson.** Air War in the Persian Gulf. 1994. 28.95 (*1-877853-36-4*) Nautical & Aviation.

— The Change in the European Balance of Power, 1938-1939: The Path to Ruin. LC 83-43085. (Illus.). 408p. 1984. pap. 23.95 (*0-691-10161-2*) Princeton U Pr.

— The Change in the European Balance of Power, 1938-1939: The Path to Ruin. LC 83-43085. reprint ed. pap. 146.80 (*0-7837-9280-8*, 2060019) Bks Demand.

— German Military Effectiveness. 264p. 1992. 29.95 (*1-877853-11-9*) Nautical & Aviation.

— Luftwaffe. LC 84-22735. (Illus.). 380p. 1985. reprint ed. 24.95 (*0-933852-45-2*) Nautical & Aviation.

Murray, Williamson, jt. ed. see Millett, Allan R.

Murray, Williamson, et al, eds. The Making of Strategy: Rulers, States, & War. (Illus.). 656p. (C). 1994. 34.95 (*0-521-45389-5*) Cambridge U Pr.

Murray, Winifred. A Socio-Cultural Study of 118 Mexican Families Living in a Low-Rent Public Housing Project in San Antonio, Texas. Cortes, Carlos E., ed. LC 76-1275. (Chicano Heritage Ser.). 1977. reprint ed. lib. bdg. 17.95 (*0-405-09515-5*) Ayer.

Murray-Wooley, Carolyn & Raitz, Karl. Rock Fences of the Bluegrass. LC 91-22584. (Illus.). 240p. 1992. text ed. 35.00 (*0-8131-1762-3*) U Pr of Ky.

Murre, Jacob. Learning & Categorization in Modular Neural Networks. 250p. 1992. text ed. 49.95 (*0-8058-1337-3*); pap. 24.95 (*0-8058-1338-1*) L Erlbaum Assocs.

Murrel, Thomas. A New Reputation: A Novel. 1992. text ed. 18.95 (*0-533-10122-0*) Vantage.

***Murrell.** Democracy: A Play. 1993. per. 10.95 (*0-921368-28-3*, Pub. by Blizzard Pub CN) InBook.

Murrell, Dan & Dwyer, William. Constitutional Law & Liability for Agents, Deputies & Police Officers. LC 92-73633. 1992. pap. 15.00 (*0-89089-521-X*) Carolina Acad Pr.

— Constitutional Law & Liability for Public-Sector Police. 1992. pap. 15.00 (*0-89089-502-3*) Carolina Acad Pr.

Murrell, Dan S. & Dwyer, William O. Constitutional Law & Liability for Park Law Enforcement Officers. 3rd ed. 192p. (C). 1991. pap. text ed. 15.00 (*0-89089-474-4*) Carolina Acad Pr.

Murrell, George, et al. Research in Medicine: A Guide to Writing a Thesis in the Medical Sciences. (Illus.). 120p. (C). 1990. 49.95 (*0-521-39043-5*); pap. 16.95 (*0-521-39925-4*) Cambridge U Pr.

Murrell, J. C. & Dalton, H., eds. Methane & Methanol Utilizers. (Biotechnology Handbooks Ser.: Vol. 5). (Illus.). 270p. 1992. 69.50 (*0-306-43878-X*, Plenum Pr) Plenum.

Murrell, J. N. & Bosanac, S. D. Introduction to the Theory of Atomic & Molecular Collisions. 199p. 1989. text ed. 155.00 (*0-471-92365-6*) Wiley.

Murrell, J. N. & Jenkins, A. D. Properties of Liquids & Solutions. 2nd ed. LC 93-46721. 1994. text ed. 79.95 (*0-471-94418-1*); pap. text ed. 34.95 (*0-471-94419-X*) Wiley.

Murrell, John. Memoir. 124p. 1990. 10.00 (*0-317-91357-3*) Playsmith.

— The Seagull: A New Version. 57p. (Orig.). 1989. 7.95 (*0-317-91355-7*) Playsmith.

— Waiting for the Parade. 112p. (Orig.). Date not set. pap. 10.95 (*0-88922-183-9*, Pub. by Talonbooks CN) InBook.

Murrell, John, tr. Uncle Vanya: A New Version. 57p. (Orig.). 1990. 7.95 (*0-317-91358-1*) Playsmith.

Murrell, John, et al. Heroines. Doolittle, Joyce, ed. LC 92-54101. 192p. (Orig.). 1992. pap. 13.00 (*0-88734-624-3*) Players Pr.

Murrell, John N. & Boucher, E. A. Properties of Liquids & Solutions. LC 81-21921. 298p. reprint ed. pap. 85.00 (*0-8357-6983-6*, 2052360) Bks Demand.

Murrell, John N. & Harget, A. J. Semi-Empirical Self-Consistent-Field Molecular Orbital Theory of Molecules. LC 71-172470. (Illus.). 190p. reprint ed. pap. 54.20 (*0-685-20751-X*, 2030392) Bks Demand.

Murrell, John N., et al. The Chemical Bond. 2nd ed. LC 85-6383. (Illus.). 345p. reprint ed. pap. 98.40 (*0-7837-1875-6*, 2042076) Bks Demand.

— The Chemical Bond. 2nd ed. LC 85-6383. 333p. 1985. pap. text ed. 34.95 (*0-471-90760-X*) Wiley.

— Valence Theory. 2nd ed. LC 70-129161. 444p. reprint ed. pap. 126.60 (*0-685-15458-0*, 2026688) Bks Demand.

Murrell, Kenneth L., jt. auth. see Vogt, Judith F.

Murrell, Larry L., jt. ed. see Baker, R. Terry.

Murrell, M. Teach Yourself Romanian. (Teach Yourself Ser.). 1972. pap. 8.95 (*0-679-10222-1*) McKay.

Murrell, Patricia H., jt. auth. see Claxton, Charles S.

Murrell, Patricia H., jt. auth. see Davis, Todd M.

Murrell, Peter. Nature of Socialist Economics: Lessons from Eastern European Foreign Trade. (Illus.). 320p. 1990. text ed. 50.00 (*0-691-04246-2*) Princeton U Pr.

Murrell, Sandra & Olsen, Paul. Mathematics for the Health Sciences. (Developmental & Precalculus Math Ser.). (Illus.). 432p. 1981. pap. text ed. write for info. (*0-201-04647-4*) Addison-Wesley.

Murrell, Shirley. Perilous Rock. large type ed. 1978. 15.95 (*0-7089-0116-6*) Ulverscroft.

— The Sin Flood. large type ed. 1978. 15.95 (*0-7089-0102-6*) Ulverscroft.

Murrell, Thomas R., jt. auth. see Murray, Thomas E.

Murrell, William G. & Kennedy, Ivan R., eds. Microbiology in Action. 356p. 1988. text ed. 299.95 (*0-471-91827-X*) Wiley.

Murrells, Joseph. Million Selling Records from the Nineteen Hundreds to the Nineteen Eighties: An Illustrated Directory. (Illus.). 528p. 1985. pap. 9.95 (*0-685-09767-6*, Arco Test) P-H Gen Ref & Trav.

Murren, Doug. The Baby Boomerang: Catching Baby Boomers As They Return to Church. Roe, Earl, ed. LC 90-46029. 200p. 1990. pap. 9.99 (*0-8307-1395-6*, 5419951) Regal.

— Keeping Your Dreams Alive When They Steal Your Coat. 1993. pap. 8.99 (*0-88419-268-7*, Creation Hse) Strang Comms Co.

— Leadershift: How to Lead Your Church into the 21st Century by Managing Change. Woodward, Virginia, ed. LC 94-34881. 216p. 1994. 15.99 (*0-8307-1594-0*, 5112256) Regal.

Murrer, B. A., jt. ed. see Abrams, M. J.

Murri, L., jt. ed. see Giannitrapani, D.

Murrieta Foundation Staff. Murrieta Hot Springs Vegetarian Cookbook. LC 87-21881. (Illus.). 232p. 1987. pap. 9.95 (*0-913990-54-X*) Book Pub Co.

Murrill, Cynthia A., et al. Primary Care of the Cataract Patient. (Illus.). 254p. 1994. text ed. 85.00 (*0-8385-7899-3*, A7899-6) Appleton & Lange.

Murrill, Paul W. Application Concepts of Process Control. LC 88-4557. (Independent Learning Module Ser.). 287p. 1988. 55.00 (*1-55617-080-7*, A080-7) Instru Soc.

— Fundamentals of Process Control Theory. 2nd ed. LC 80-84764. (Independent Learning Module Ser.). 256p. 1991. text ed. 65.00 (*1-55617-297-4*, A297-4) Instru Soc.

— Fundamentals of Process Control Theory. LC 80-84764. (Illus.). 253p. reprint ed. pap. 72.20 (*0-7837-1799-7*, 2042000) Bks Demand.

Murrill, Paul W. & Smith, Cecil L. FORTRAN IV Programming for Engineers & Scientists. 2nd ed. LC 73-1689. (Illus.). 322p. (C). 1973. pap. text ed. 6.95 (*0-06-044684-6*); 6.95 (*0-06-364697-8*) HarpCollege.

Murrill, Rupert I. Cranial & Postcranial Skeletal Remains from Easter Island. LC 67-10609. (Illus.). 113p. reprint ed. pap. 32.30 (*0-8357-8854-7*, 2033274) Bks Demand.

Murrill, W. A. Tropical Polypores. 1973. reprint ed. 21.00 (*3-7682-0914-8*) Lubrecht & Cramer.

Murrin, John M. Beneficiaries of Catastrophe: The English Colonies in America. (New American History Essays Ser.). 1991. reprint ed. 5.00 (*0-87229-051-4*) Am Hist Assn.

Murrin, John M., jt. ed. see Sheridan, Eugene R.

Murrin, Michael. The Allegorical Epic: Essays in Its Rise & Decline. LC 79-20832. 1980. lib. bdg. 23.00 (*0-226-55402-3*) U Ch Pr.

— History & Warfare in Renaissance Epic. (Illus.). 352p. 1994. 32.50 (*0-226-55403-1*) U Ch Pr.

Murris, Roelef J., jt. ed. see Demaison, Gerard.

***Murro, Jonathan.** The Divine Image. (Illus.). 477p. 1990. 14.95 (*0-917189-08-6*) Colton Found.

— God-Realization Journal. 337p. 1975. 10.00 (*0-917187-16-4*) A R Colton Fnd.

Murro, Jonathan, jt. auth. see Colton, Ann R.

Murro, Jonathan, jt. auth. see Colton, Ann-Ree.

Murro, Jonathon. The Path of Virtue. LC 79-54382. (Illus.). 487p. 1980. 14.95 (*0-917189-00-0*) Colton Found.

***Murrow, Bobbi.** Natural Acts: A Collection of Poems by Bobbi Murrow. Helfrich, Peter, ed. (Illus.). (Orig.). (YA). 1994. pap. 18.00 (*0-938055-00-3*) Emerald People.

Murrow, Gene, jt. auth. see Lang, Serge A.

Murrow, Liza K. Allergic to My Family. LC 91-31529. (Illus.). 160p. (J). (gr. 2-6). 1992. 13.95 (*0-8234-0959-7*) Holiday.

— Dancing on the Table. MacDonald, Pat, ed. (Illus.). 128p. (J). 1993. reprint ed. pap. 2.99 (*0-671-73829-1*, Minstrel Bks) PB.

— Fire in the Heart. 255p. (J). (gr. 5-9). 1990. pap. 2.95 (*0-8167-2261-7*) Troll Assocs.

— The Ghost of Lost Island. LC 90-47671. 176p. (J). (gr. 3-7). 1991. 14.95 (*0-8234-0874-4*) Holiday.

— The Ghost of Lost Island. MacDonald, Pat, ed. 176p. (J). (gr. 3-6). 1993. reprint ed. pap. 3.50 (*0-671-75368-1*, Minstrel Bks) PB.

— Good-Bye, Sammy. LC 88-17011. (Illus.). 32p. (J). (ps-3). 1989. lib. bdg. 13.95 (*0-8234-0726-8*) Holiday.

— Twelve Days in August. 192p. (YA). 1995. reprint ed. mass mkt. 3.99 (*0-380-72353-0*, Flare) Avon.

— Twelve Days in August: A Novel. LC 92-54489. 160p. (J). (gr. 7 up). 1993. 15.95 (*0-8234-1012-9*) Holiday.

— West Against the Wind. LC 87-45337. 240p. (YA). (gr. 7 up). 1987. 15.95 (*0-8234-0668-7*) Holiday.

— West Against the Wind. 240p. (YA). (gr. 7 up). 1988. reprint ed. pap. 2.50 (*0-8167-1324-3*) Troll Assocs.

Murry, Calvin. Prisoner on Board the S. S. Beagle. (Prison Writing Ser.). 1983. spiral bd. 5.00 (*0-912678-53-4*, Greenfld Rev Pr) Greenfld Rev Lit.

Murry, J. M. & Mansfield, K., eds. Blue Review May-July, 1913, Nos. 1-3. (Illus.). 220p. 1968. 65.00 (*0-7146-2103-X*, BHA-02103, Pub. by F Cass Pubs UK) Intl Spec Bk.

Murry, John M. Aspects of Literature. LC 79-128280. (Essay Index Reprint Ser.). 1977. 18.95 (*0-8369-1838-X*) Ayer.

— The Betrayal of Christ by the Churches. 1972. 59.95 (*0-87968-724-X*) Gordon Pr.

— Countries of the Mind: Essays in Literary Criticism, 1st Series. LC 68-22111. (Essay Index Reprint Ser.). 1980. 18.95 (*0-8369-0729-9*) Ayer.

— Countries of the Mind: Essays in Literary Criticism, 2nd Series. LC 68-22112. (Essay Index Reprint Ser.). 1977. 18.95 (*0-8369-0730-2*) Ayer.

— Evolution of an Intellectual. LC 67-28738. (Essay Index Reprint Ser.). 1977. 19.95 (*0-8369-0731-0*) Ayer.

— Keats & Shakespeare: A Study of Keats Poetic Life from 1816-1820. LC 78-15430. 248p. 1978. reprint ed. text ed. 35.00 (*0-313-20581-7*, MUKS, Greenwood Pr) Greenwood.

— Pencillings. LC 70-90666. (Essay Index Reprint Ser.). 1977. 21.95 (*0-8369-1229-2*) Ayer.

— The Problem of Style. LC 80-21463. x, 133p. 1980. reprint ed. text ed. 45.00 (*0-313-22523-0*, MUPR, Greenwood Pr) Greenwood.

— Reminiscences of D. H. Lawrence. LC 75-157349. (Select Bibliographies Reprint Ser.). 1977. reprint ed. 19.95 (*0-8369-5810-1*) Ayer.

— Selected Criticism, Nineteen Sixteen to Nineteen Fifty-Seven. LC 86-18339. 320p. 1986. reprint ed. text ed. 69.50 (*0-313-25219-X*, MUSE, Greenwood Pr) Greenwood.

— Studies in Keats. LC 78-185023. (Studies in Keats: No. 19). 1969. reprint ed. lib. bdg. 75.00 (*0-8383-0671-3*) M S G Haskell Hse.

— Things to Come. LC 70-93364. (Essay Index Reprint Ser.). 1977. 21.95 (*0-8369-1337-X*) Ayer.

— William Blake. LC 71-173845. (Studies in Blake: No. 3). 1971. reprint ed. lib. bdg. 75.00 (*0-8383-1344-2*) M S G Haskell Hse.

Murry, John Middleton, jt. auth. see Mantz, R.

Murry, L. Progress in Mathematics 5-C Answer Book. (C). 1988. 65.00 (*0-85950-280-5*, Pub. by S Thornes Pubs UK) St Mut.

Murry, R. Joshua. Why We're Here. LC 88-51384. 56p. 1989. 5.95 (*1-55523-198-5*) Winston-Derek.

Murse. The Whirlwind in Culture: Frontiers in Theology. LC 88-42731. 288p. (Orig.). 1988. pap. 22.95 (*0-940989-39-5*) Meyer Stone Bks.

M

An Asterisk (*) at the beginning of an entry indicates that the title is appearing in BIP for the first time.

— The Whirlwind in Culture: Frontiers in Theology. Musser, Donald W. & Price, Joseph L., eds. LC 88-42731. 288p. (Orig.). 1988. 33.95 (0-940989-43-1) Meyer Stone Bks.

***Mursell, Gordon, intro. & text.** The Meditations of Guigo I, Prior of the Charterhouse. LC 94-21178. (Cistercian Studies Ser.: No. 155). 1994. write for info. (0-87907-555-4); pap. write for info. (0-87907-655-0) Cistercian Pubns.

Mursell, James. Psychology of Music. 1988. reprint ed. lib. bdg. 25.00 (0-317-90101-X) Rprt Serv.

Mursell, James L. Psychology of Music. 1991. lib. bdg. 45. 00 (0-403-01750-5) Scholarly.

— The Psychology of Music. LC 77-110274. (Illus.). 389p. 1971. reprint ed. text ed. 65.00 (0-8371-4500-7, MUPM, Greenwood Pr) Greenwood.

Murshed, S. Mansoob. Economic Aspects of North-South Interaction: Analytical Macroeconomic Issues. (Illus.). 208p. 1992. text ed. 75.00 (0-12-512070-2) Acad Pr.

Murshed, S. Mansoob & Raffer, Kunibert, eds. Trade, Transfers & Development: Problems & Prospects for the 21st Century. (Illus.). 272p. 1994. 69.95 (1-85278-796-1, Pub. by E Elgar Pub UK) Ashgate Pub Co.

Mursi Saad El Din, ed. see Mahfouz, Naguib.

Murstein, Bernard. Paths to Marriage. (Family Studies Text Ser.). (Illus.). 160p. (Orig.). (C). 1986. pap. text ed. 16. 95 (0-8039-2383-X) Sage.

Murtagh, F., jt. ed. see Heck, Andre.

Murtagh, F. Reed, jt. auth. see Schnitzlein, H. N.

Murtagh, Fionn & Heck, Andre. Multivariate Data Analysis. (C). 1986. lib. bdg. 88.00 (90-277-2425-3) Kluwer Ac.

— Multivariate Data Analysis. (C). 1988. disk 49.50 (90-277-9154-6) Kluwer Ac.

Murtagh, Fionn, jt. ed. see Heck, Andre.

Murtagh, James J. How to Prepare for the Fire Fighter Examinations. 2nd ed. 384p. 1990. pap. 11.95 (0-8120-4372-3) Barron.

Murtagh, John. Cautionary Tales. 220p. 1992. pap. 39.00 (0-07-452806-8) Hlth Prof Div.

— General Practice. 750p. 1994. text ed. 79.00 (0-07-452807-6) Hlth Prof Div.

— Practice Tips. (Illus.). 200p. 1995. pap. 39.00 (0-07-452805-X) Hlth Prof Div.

— Practice Tips. 2nd ed. (Illus.). 224p. 1995. pap. text ed. write for info. (0-07-470180-0) Hlth Prof Div.

Murtagh, Peter, jt. auth. see Joyce, Joe.

Murtagh, Steven J. Staffing, Scheduling, & Workforce Planning: A Help Desk Institute White Paper. Bultema, Patrick et al, eds. (Illus.). (Orig.). (C). Date not set. pap. write for info. (1-57125-002-6) Help Desk Inst.

Murtagh, Terence, jt. auth. see Ridpath, Ian.

Murtagh, William J. Keeping Time: The History & Theory of Preservation in America. (Illus.). 240p. 1993. pap. 19. 95 (0-8069-0516-6, Sterling-Main St) Sterling.

Murtaugh, Daniel M. Piers Plowman & the Image of God. LC 77-25544. 137p. reprint ed. pap. 39.10 (0-7837-4909-0, 2044574) Bks Demand.

Murtaugh, Frank M. Cavour & the Economic Modernization of the Kingdom of Sardinia. LC 91-28338. (Modern European History Ser.: No. 2). 368p. 1991. 76.00 (0-8153-0671-7) Garland.

***Murtaugh, James J.** Barron's How to Prepare for Fire Fighter Examinations. 3rd ed. LC 94-46425. 1995. write for info. (0-8120-9086-1) Barron.

Murtaugh, Kristen O. Aristo & the Classical Smile. (Studies in Romance Languages: No. 36). 206p. (C). 1981. 12.50 (0-674-04487-8) HUP.

Murtaugh, Melinda. Italian Labor in Protest, 1904-1914: Political General Strikes to Protest Eccidi. LC 91-3268. (Modern European History Outstanding Studies & Dissertations). 352p. 1991. 72.00 (0-8153-0416-1) Garland.

Murtaugh, Michael P., jt. ed. see Myers, Michael J.

Murtaugh, Paul A. Tobacco Scare Found Faked: Revealing the Biggest Science Scandal in History. 200p. 1992. 16. 95 (0-9633367-0-3) Am Rights Coun.

Murtaugh, Robert J. & Kaplan. Veterinary Emergency & Critical Care Medicine. 685p. 1991. 69.00 (0-8016-6399-7) Mosby Yr Bk.

Murtaza, Mutahhery, jt. auth. see Sadr, Muhammad B.

Murth, D. N., jt. auth. see Osaki, S.

Murtha, James A., jt. auth. see Cress, David.

Murtha, Philly. Blank Books Series, 8 bks., Set. (Illus.). (J). 1986. 2.55 (0-88682-117-7, 31196-098) Creative Ed.

— Creative Reading: You Can Be a Free Reader. Redpath, Ann, ed. (Skills for Living Ser.). 32p. 1984. lib. bdg. 11. 95 (0-87191-997-4) Creative Ed.

— Library: Your Teammate. Redpath, Ann, ed. (Skills for Living Ser.). 32p. (J). (gr. 4 up). 1984. lib. bdg. 11.95 (0-87191-999-0) Creative Ed.

— Reading Fast: You Can Be a Reading Athlete. Redpath, Ann, ed. (Skills for Living Ser.). 32p. (J). (gr. 4 up). 1984. lib. bdg. 11.95 (0-87191-996-6) Creative Ed.

— Writing: You Can Be an Author. Redpath, Ann, ed. (Skills for Living Ser.). 32p. (J). (gr. 4 up). 1984. lib. bdg. 11.95 (0-87191-998-2) Creative Ed.

Murtha, Steve, jt. auth. see Matthews, David A.

***Murtha, Theresa & Wolden, Kathy, eds.** Peterson's International Guide to MBA Programs. 736p. (Orig.). 1995. pap. 16.95 (1-56079-366-X, Petersons Pacesetter) Petersons Guides.

Murthi, R. K. Historic Assassinations. ix, 158p. 1992. text ed. 25.00 (81-220-0249-8, Pub. by Konark Pubs Pvt Ltd II) Advent Bks Div.

Murthi, R. K. & Parashar, Rajan. Jawaharlal Nehru: Glimpses of Greatness. x, 270p. 1990. text ed. 35.00 (81-85047-48-0, Pub. by Reliance Pub Hse II) Apt Bks.

Murthi, V. K. & Sharma, G. Rajiv Gandhi: Challenges & Choices. 1985. 22.95 (81-7027-089-8) Asia Bk Corp.

Murthy, jt. ed. see Blischke.

Murthy, A. S. & Mohle, R. Henry. Transportation Engineering Basics. LC 93-15229. 52p. 1993. 16.00 (0-87262-881-7) Am Soc Civil Eng.

Murthy, A. V., ed. Studies in South Indian Customs, Vol. 2. (C). 1992. 19.50 (0-8364-2765-3, Pub. by New Era Pubns) S Asia.

Murthy, Anjneya N. & Pandey, D. P. Ayurvedic Cure for Common Diseases. 2nd rev. ed. 200p. 1983. pap. 4.95 (0-86578-126-5) Ind-US Inc.

Murthy, B. S. International Relations & Organisation for Law Students. (C). 1991. text ed. 55.00 (0-89771-501-2) St Mut.

Murthy, B. Srinivasa. Mother Teresa & India. LC 82-80522. (Illus.). 144p. (Orig.). 1983. pap. 6.95 (0-941910-00-8) Long Beach Pubns.

Murthy, B. Srinivasa, tr. The Bhagavad Gita: Translated with Introduction & Notes. 2nd rev. ed. LC 90-82501. 156p. 1991. 11.95 (0-941910-05-9) Long Beach Pubns.

Murthy, B. Srinivasa, ed. see Gandhi, M. K. & Tolstoy, Leo.

Murthy, Belur N. & Mann, Alfred N. Economics of Present & Future Fossil-Based Electricity Generation: A Comparison of Available & Emerging Fuel & Technology Options. LC 84-23180. (Series of Special Reports: No. 12). (Illus.). 133p. reprint ed. pap. 38.00 (0-7837-0686-3, 2041019) Bks Demand.

Murthy, G. V., jt. ed. see Kadekodi, G. K.

Murthy, H. V. History of India, Pt. 1: For Law Students. 1993. 60.00 (81-7012-525-1) St Mut.

Murthy, J. Y., jt. ed. see Kececioglu, I.

Murthy, K. & Murthy, P. K. Dictionary of Archeo-Zoology. (C). 1990. 28.00 (81-202-0287-2, Pub. by Ajanta II) S Asia.

Murthy, K. Krishna. Buddhism in Japan. (C). 1989. 34.00 (81-85067-25-2, Pub. by Sundeep II) S Asia.

— Buddhism in Tibet. (C). 1989. 28.50 (81-85067-16-3, Pub. by Sundeep Prakashan II) S Asia.

— Dictionary of Buddhist Literature & Literary Personalities. (C). 1994. 34.00x (81-85067-88-0, Pub. by Sundeep II) S Asia.

— Dictionary of Buddhist Terms & Terminologies. 1991. 37. 00 (81-85067-67-8, Pub. by Sundeep II) S Asia.

— Mirros of Indian Buddhism. (C). 1991. text ed. 28.50 (81-85067-72-4, Pub. by Sundeep Prakashan II) S Asia.

— Sculptures of Vajrayana Buddhism. (C). 1989. 32.50 (81-85132-06-2, Pub. by Classics India Pubns II) S Asia.

Murthy, Keshava S. National Environmental Policy (NEPA) Process. 224p. 1988. 130.00 (0-8493-6746-8, KF3775, CRC Reprint) Franklin.

Murthy, Krishna. Iconography of Buddhist Deity Heruka. (C). 1988. 20.00 (81-85067-12-0, Pub. by Sundeep II) S Asia.

Murthy, M. K. & Spagnolo, S., eds. Nonlinear Hyperbolic Equations & Field Theory. (Pitman Research Notes in Mathematics Ser.). 227p. 1992. pap. text ed. 52.95 (0-470-21853-3) Halsted Pr.

Murthy, M. V., et al, eds. Current Research in Heat & Mass Transfer: A Compendiem & Festschrift for Professor Arcot Ramachandran. 283p. 1988. 89.00 (0-89116-578-9) Hemisp Pub.

Murthy, Mukunda S., jt. auth. see Ruggles, William S.

Murthy, N. A. & Pandey, D. P. Ayurvedic Cures for Common Diseases. 200p. 1985. 11.95 (0-318-36354-2) Asia Bk Corp.

Murthy, P. G., jt. auth. see Pavella, M.

Murthy, P. K., jt. auth. see Murthy, K.

Murthy, Poolla V. & Wolfendale, Arnold W. Gamma-Ray Astronomy. 2nd ed. LC 92-16465. (Astrophysics Ser.: Vol. 22). (Illus.). 275p. (C). 1993. 69.95 (0-521-42081-4) Cambridge U Pr.

Murthy, S. Laxmana. The Novels of William Styron. 204p. 1988. text ed. 27.50 (81-85218-03-X, Pub. by Prestige II) Advent Bks Div.

Murthy, S. N. & Paynter, G. C., eds. Numerical Methods for Engine-Airframe Integration. LC 86-10920. (PAAS Ser.: Vol. 102). (Illus.). 544p. 1986. 79.95 (0-930403-09-6) AIAA.

Murthy, S. N., jt. ed. see Borghi, R. P.

Murthy, S. N., jt. ed. see Curran, E. T.

***Murthy, S. R.** Glimpses of Hindu Astrology & Some Aspects of Indology. (C). 1993. 28.00x (81-7030-383-4, Pub. by Sri Satguru Pubns II) S Asia.

Murthy, Satya M. & Scanlon, Edward F. Injury & Tumor Implantation. LC 93-37851. (Medical Intelligence Unit Ser.). 1993. 89.95 (1-879702-82-7) R G Landes.

Murthy, Srikanata K., tr. see Sarngadhara.

Murthy, T. & Ram, Manatha. Law of Adverse Possession. (C). 1988. 100.00 (0-685-25688-X) St Mut.

Murthy, T. K., ed. Advances in Ice Technology: Proceedings of the Third International Conference on Ice Technology (ITC 92) Held in Cambridge, Massachusetts, August 11-13, 1992. LC 92-81588. (ITC Ser.: Vol. 3). 376p. 1992. 159.00 (1-56252-104-7) Computational Mech MA.

— Computational Methods in Hypersonic Aerodynamics. LC 91-77003. (Computational Methods in Aerodynamics Ser.). 510p. 1992. 159.00 (1-56252-083-0) Computational Mech MA.

— Computer Methods in Marine & Offshore Engineering. LC 90-85217. (CADMO Ser.: Vol. 3). 432p. 1991. 169. 00 (1-56252-054-7) Computational Mech MA.

Murthy, T. K. & Alaez, J. A., eds. Design of Marine & Offshore Structures: Proceedings of the Fourth International Conference on Computer Aided Design, Manufacture & Operation in the Marine & Offshore Industries (CADMO 92) Held in Madrid, Spain, October 27-29, 1992. LC 92-82811. (CADMO Ser.). 828p. 1992. 324.00 (1-56252-107-1) Computational Mech MA.

Murthy, T. K. & Brebbia, C. A., eds. Computers in Design, Construction & Operation of Automobiles. 1987. 72.00 (0-931215-69-2) Computational Mech MA.

— Marine Engineering: Design & Operation of Ships & Offshore Structures: Proceedings of the NEVA Conference Held in Russia, in September, 1993. LC 93-71027. 276p. 1994. 134.00 (1-56252-172-1) Computational Mech MA.

— Structural Design & Crashworthiness of Automobiles. 1987. 72.00 (0-931215-21-8) Computational Mech MA.

— Supercomputing in Fluid Flow: Proceedings of the First International Seminar on Supercomputers in Fluid Flow, Held in Lowell, Massachusetts, October 3-5, 1989. LC 90-84998. (Computational Engineering Ser.). 368p. 1992. 198.00 (0-945824-59-9) Computational Mech MA.

Murthy, T. K. & Brebbia, Carlos A., eds. Advances in Computer Technology & Applications in Japan. (Lecture Notes in Engineering Ser.: Vol. 69). (Illus.). xiv, 158p. 1991. pap. 34.00 (0-387-54072-5) Spr-Verlag.

— Computational Methods in Viscous Aerodynamics. 384p. 1990. 133.25 (0-444-88669-9) Elsevier.

— Structural Design & Crashworthiness of Automobiles. 240p. 1987. 75.00 (0-387-17504-0) Spr-Verlag.

Murthy, T. K. & Dern, J. C., eds. Marine & Offshore Computer Applications. 810p. 1988. 173.00 (0-387-50172-X) Spr-Verlag.

Murthy, T. K. & Fielding, J. P., eds. Computer Applications in Aircraft Design & Operation. 254p. 1987. 72.00 (0-931215-56-0) Computational Mech MA.

— Computer Applications in Aircraft Design & Operation. 285p. 1987. 83.00 (0-387-17749-3) Spr-Verlag.

Murthy, T. K. & Keramidas, G. A., eds. Computer Aided Design, Manufacture & Operation in the Marine & Offshore Industries. (CADMO Ser.). 657p. 1986. 130.00 (0-931215-34-X) Computational Mech MA.

Murthy, T. K. & Munch, R., eds. Computer Applications in Spacecraft Design & Operation. 198p. 1987. 51.00 (0-931215-75-7) Computational Mech MA.

Murthy, T. K. & Young, F. E., eds. Computers in Railway Installations, Track, & Signalling. LC 87-70872. (COMPRAIL Ser.: Vol. 1). 324p. 1987. 79.00 (0-931215-78-1) Computational Mech MA.

Murthy, T. K., et al, eds. Computers in Railway Installations, Track, & Signalling. 480p. 1987. 119.00 (0-387-17933-X) Spr-Verlag.

— Computers in Railway Management. LC 87-70871. (COMPRAIL Ser.: Vol. 1). 254p. 1987. 66.00 (0-931215-58-7) Computational Mech MA.

— Computers in Railway Management & Technology: Proceedings of the Third International Conference on Computer Aided Design, Manufacture & Operation in Railway & Other Advanced Mass Transit Systems Held in Washington, DC, August 18-20, 1992, 2 vols., Set. LC 91-81589. (COMPRAIL Ser.: Vol. 3). 1992. 378.00 (1-56252-105-5) Computational Mech MA.

— Computers in Railway Management & Technology: Proceedings of the Third International Conference on Computer Aided Design, Manufacture & Operation in Railway & Other Advanced Mass Transit Systems, Vol. 1: Management. LC 91-81589. (COMPRAIL Ser.: Vol. 3). 632p. 1992. 235.00 (1-56252-132-2) Computational Mech MA.

— Computers in Railway Operations. LC 87-70870. (COMPRAIL Ser.: Vol. 1). 344p. 1987. 84.00 (0-931215-79-X) Computational Mech MA.

— Computers in Railways III: Proceedings of the Third International Conference on Computer Aided Design, Manufacture & Operation in Railway & Other Advanced Mass Transit Systems, Vol. 2: Technology. LC 91-81589. (COMPRAIL Ser.: Vol. 3). 498p. 1992. 186.00 (1-56252-133-0) Computational Mech MA.

— Ice Technology. (ITC Ser.: Vol. 1). 1986. 125.00 (0-931215-27-7) Computational Mech MA.

— Ice Technology for Polar Operations. LC 90-83758. (ITC Ser.: Vol. 9). 436p. 1990. 149.00 (0-945824-74-2) Computational Mech MA.

— Marine & Offshore Computer Applications. LC 88-71664. (CADMO Ser.: Vol. 2). 812p. 1988. 149.00 (0-945824-05-X) Computational Mech MA.

— Marine, Offshore & Ice Technology: Proceedings of CADMO 94 & ITC 94. LC 94-72458. (CADMO Ser.: Vol. 4). 416p. 1994. text ed. 188.00 (1-56252-268-X) Computational Mech MA.

Murthy, T. S. Life & Teaching of Sri Ramana Maharshi. LC 90-81266. (Basket of Tolerance Ser.). 272p. 1990. pap. 12.95 (0-918801-19-2) Dawn Horse Pr.

— Maharaj. rev. ed. 246p. 1986. pap. 8.95 (0-913922-17-X) Dawn Horse Pr.

Murthy, T. S., ed. Snake Book of India with Many Plates & Diagrams. (C). 1987. 150.00 (81-7089-049-7, Pub. by Intl Bk Distr II) St Mut.

Murthy, U. R. Awasthe, A Novel. 1990. 16.00 (81-7023-298-8, Pub. by Allied II) S Asia.

— Samskara: A Rite for a Dead Man. Ramnujan, A. K., tr. 1979. pap. 8.95 (0-19-561079-2) OUP.

Murthy, V. A. & Ananthakrishnan, T. N. Studies on Indian Chelonethi. (Oriental Insects Monograph Ser.: No. 4). 1977. pap. 45.00 (1-877711-10-1) Assoc Pubs FL.

Murthy, V. K., jt. auth. see Krishnamurthy, E. V.

***Murthy, V. R., et al, eds.** Microwave Materials. VII,257p. 1994. 69.00 (0-387-58075-1) Spr-Verlag.

Murthy, V. Rama, jt. ed. see Pollack, H. N.

Murti, K. V. Kohinoor in the Crown. 180p. 1987. text ed. 25.00 (81-207-0644-7, Pub. by Sterling Pubs II) Apt Bks.

Murti, Kamakshi P. Die Reinkarnation des Lesers als Autor: Ein Rezeptionsgeschichtlicher Versuch Uber den Einfluss der Altindischen Literatur auf Deutsche Schriftsteller um 1900. (Quellen und Forschungen zur Sprach und Kulturgeschichte der Germanischen Voelker Ser.: NF 96 (220)). vi, 156p. (C). 1990. lib. bdg. 60.00 (3-11-012371-1) De Gruyter.

Murti, V., jt. ed. see Pulmano, V. A.

Murti, V. G. Budgeting: A Guide for Practising Managers. 188p. 1984. text ed. 27.50 (0-86590-560-6, Pub. by Sterling Pubs II) Apt Bks.

Murtiashaw, Sherer M. Behind Closed Doors: A Consumer's Guide to Psychiatric Hospitals. 128p. 1994. pap. text ed. 9.95 (0-9639267-9-9) HRS.

Murto, Nancy, jt. auth. see Parnes, Beatrice.

Murton, M. Phyllis. How to Get the Teaching Position You Want! Teacher Candidate Guide. 104p. (Orig.). 1993. pap. write for info. (0-9636749-0-0) Educ Ent.

***Murton, Nancy.** The Busy Woman's Guide to the Stock Market. 52p. 1994. pap. 7.95 (0-9641711-0-4) N Murton.

Murtonen, A. Hebrew in Its West Semitic Setting: A Comparative Survey of Non-Masoretic Hebrew Dialects & Traditions, Pt. 1: A Comparative Lexicon, Sect. Bb-E. (Studien in Semitic Languages & Linguistics: Vol. 13-3). x, 516p. 1990. 168.75 (90-04-08899-7) E J Brill.

— Hebrew in its West Semitic Setting: A Comparative Survey of Non-Masoretic Hebrew Dialects & Traditions. Pt. One: A Comparative Lexicon, Section A: Proper Names. (Studies in Semitic Languages & Linguistics: No. 13). xxxii, 341p. 1986. 109.75 (90-04-07245-4) E J Brill.

— Hebrew in Its West Semitic Setting: Pt. 2 - Phonetics & Phonology, Pt. 3 - Morphosyntactics. LC 87-32287. (Studies in Semitic Languages & Linguistics: No. 16). (Illus.). 1990. Pt. 2: xii, 187; Pt. 3: xxxix, 113. 151.50 (90-04-09309-5) E J Brill.

***Murtuza, Athar.** The New Accounting Manual: Guide to the Documentation Process. 1995. text ed. 95.00 (0-471-30370-4) Wiley.

Murty, A. S., ed. Toxicity of Pesticides to Fish, Vol. I. 1986. 168.00 (0-8493-6058-7, SH174) CRC Pr.

— Toxicity of Pesticides to Fish, Vol. II. 192p. 1986. 156.00 (0-8493-6059-5, SH174) CRC Pr.

Murty, A. V., jt. ed. see Reddy, J. N.

Murty, B. S. The International Law of Propaganda. (C). 1989. lib. bdg. 158.00 (0-89838-904-6) Kluwer Ac.

— International Relations & Organisation. (C). 1991. 65.00 (0-685-54754-X) St Mut.

Murty, C. Satyanarayana. Design of Minor Irrigation & Canal Structures. (C). 1991. pap. 16.00 (81-224-0280-1, Pub. by Wiley Eastern II) S Asia.

Murty, K. S. Vedic Hermeneutics. (C). 1993. 14.00 (81-208-1105-4, Pub. by Motilal Banarsidass II) S Asia.

Murty, K. Satchidananda. The Quest for Peace. 1986. 17.50 (81-202-0165-5, Pub. by Ajanta II) S Asia.

***Murty, K. Satchidananda & DasGupta, Amit, eds.** Divine Peacock: Understanding Contemporary India. (C). 1994. text ed. 24.00 (81-224-0699-8, Pub. by Wiley Eastern II) S Asia.

Murty, K. Satchidananda & Vohra, Ashok. Radhakrishnan. (His Life & Ideas Ser.). (C). 1989. 44.00 (81-202-0253-8, Pub. by Ajanta II) S Asia.

— Radhakrishnan: His Life & Ideas. LC 89-39718. 239p. 1990. 49.50 (0-7914-0343-2); pap. 16.95 (0-7914-0344-0) State U NY Pr.

Murty, K. Satya. Handbook of Indian Architecture. 1991. 22.50 (81-7024-389-0, Pub. by Ashish II) S Asia.

— Indian Heritage & Culture. (C). 1988. 26.00 (81-7024-205-3, Pub. by Ashish II) S Asia.

— Textbook of Indian Epigraphy. (C). 1992. text ed. 14.00 (81-85418-88-8, Pub. by Low Price II) S Asia.

Murty, Katta. Linear & Combinatorial Programming. LC 85-8867. 592p. 1985. reprint ed. lib. bdg. 59.50 (0-89874-852-6) Krieger.

Murty, Katta B. Network Programming. 1992. text ed. 72. 00 (0-13-615493-X) P-H.

Murty, Katta G. Linear Programming. LC 83-7012. 482p. (C). 1983. Net. text ed. write for info. (0-471-09725-X) Wiley.

— Linear Programming. LC 83-7012. 231p. (C). 1984. teacher ed 20.00 (0-471-89249-1) Wiley.

— Operations Research: Deterministic Optimization Models. LC 94-19150. 1994. text ed. 59.00 (0-13-056517-2) P-H.

Murty, Komanduri S., jt. auth. see Roebuck, Julian B.

Murty, M. Ram, ed. Theta Functions. LC 93-15008. (CRM Proceedings & Lecture Notes Ser.: Vol. 1). 174p. 1993. 58.00 (0-8218-6997-3) Am Math.

Murty, M. Ram, jt. ed. see Kisilevsky, Hershy.

Murty, Mantha R. Special Marriage Act. (C). 1990. 138.00 (0-89771-142-4) St Mut.

Murty, Ram, jt. ed. see Groves, Michael J.

Murty, Ram, tr. see Levin, L. I.

Murty, T. R. Studies in Indian Thought: The Collected Papers of Professor TRV Murti. Coward, Harold, ed. 1983. 25.00 (0-8364-0866-7); text ed. 17.00 (0-8364-0984-1) S Asia.

Murty, T. S. India-China Boundary: India's Options. 143p. 1987. 24.95 (0-318-37245-2) Asia Bk Corp.

Murty, T. S., jt. ed. see El-Sabh, M. I.

Murty, T. S., jt. auth. see Kowalik, Z.

Murty, T. V. Studies in Earth Sciences. 614p. 1971. 25.00 (0-88065-164-4, Messers Today & Tomorrow) Scholarly Pubns.

Murty, U. S., jt. auth. see Bondy, J. Adrian.

Murty, V. Kumar. Introduction to Abelian Varieties. LC 93-14570. (CRM Monograph Ser.: No. 3). 138p. 1993. 49. 00 (0-8218-6995-7) Am Math.

Murty, Y. V. & Mollard, F. R., eds. Continuous Casting of Small Cross Sections: Proceedings of a Symposium. LC 81-85418. (Conference Proceedings Ser.). (Illus.). 211p. reprint ed. pap. 60.20 (0-685-23391-X, 2032595) Bks Demand.

Murtz, Harold A., ed. Gun Digest Book of Exploded Handgun Drawings. LC 92-81889. (Illus.). 512p. (Orig.). 1992. pap. 20.95 (0-87349-146-7) DBI.

— Gun Digest Book of Exploded Long Gun Drawings. LC 92-81890. (Illus.). 512p. (Orig.). 1993. pap. 20.95 (0-87349-147-5) DBI.

An Asterisk (*) at the beginning of an entry indicates that the title is appearing in BIP for the first time.

— Gun Digest Treasury. 7th ed. LC 61-9610. (Illus.). 320p. (Orig.). 1994. pap. 16.95 (*0-87349-156-4*) DBI.
— Guns Illustrated, 1996. 28th ed. LC 69-11342. 336p. (Orig.). 1995. pap. 19.95 (*0-87349-171-8*, G196) DBI.
Murugiah, R. T. German-English Economic Dictionary. 603p. 1993. 185.00 (*3-349-00597-7*) IBD Ltd.
Murugkar, Lata. Dalit Panther Movement in Magarashtra: A Sociological Appraisal. (C). 1990. 32.00 (*0-86132-246-0*, Pub. by Popular Prakashan II) S Asia.
Murumba, S. K. Commercial Exploitation of Personality. xvii, 184p. 1986. 64.50 (*0-455-20692-9*, Pub. by Law Bk Co) W W Gaunt.
Murvar, Vatro. The Balkan Vlachs: A Typological Study. LC 77-87535. reprint ed. 23.50 (*0-404-16588-5*) AMS Pr.

—Nation & Religion in Central Europe & the Western Balkans, Vol. 1 - the Muslims in Bosnia, Hercegovina & Sandzak: A Sociological Analysis. 180p. 1990. 30.00 (*0-931633-04-4*); pap. 15.00 (*0-931633-05-2*) Fnd Soc Stdy.
This work presents some culture case studies reflecting the validity of the propositions of Ernest Renan in the 19th century & Max Weber in this century on nationalism & religion. Some (sub) chapters' titles are: Pre-Islamic Ancestors. Voluntary Islamization. Western Anti-Ottoman Bias. Islamic Egalitarianism & New Sacred Universal Imperium. Croat & Albanian Great Viziers of the Ottoman Empire. Documentation from Western, Eastern & Domestic sources. Common Origin & Cultural Heritage of the Catholics & Muslims. Absence of Eastern Orthodox Christianity before the 16th century. When the Patriotic Mythology Becomes History. Eastern Orthodox Croats. Crvena Hrvatska, (Red Croatia) - an Ancient Territory at the convergence of three nations: Albania, Croatia & Montenegro. Northern Albania. National Identity & Sovereignty of Montenegro, (Crna Gora). The Vlachs & their major types of social structure: Pastoral-Nomadic, Military & Semi-Military & Urban Merchant. The Celebrated Old Vlach: the Facts vs. Myths. The Eastern Orthodox Croats of Vlach Origin & Their Bishops. Conclusions & Continuity of Research. A Russian Diplomat's Travelogue. A Politically Innocent Franciscan priest & an Imperialist government. A Famous Sculptor, Some Politicians & a Prime Minister. A Native Muslim Witness with the Rank of a Commissar. Extensive & Detailed References. Index. ***Publisher Provided Annotation.***

— Submerged Nations: An Introduction to Theory & Bibliography on One Major Case Study. 93p. 1982. pap. 7.50 (*0-931633-01-X*) Fnd Soc Stdy.
— The Vlachs of the Balkans: A Submerged Nation Existing Throughout the Millennia. 155p. 30.00 (*0-931635-02-0*); pap. 16.00 (*0-931635-03-9*) Fnd Soc Stdy.
Murvar, Vatro, ed. & contrib. Theory of Liberty, Legitimacy & Power: New Directions in the Intellectual & Scientific Legacy of Max Weber. (International Library of Sociology). 224p. 1985. 39.95 (*0-7102-0355-1*, RKP) Routledge.
Murvar, Vatro, intro. Max Weber Today-An Introduction to a Living Legacy: Selected Bibliography. 159p. 1983. pap. 9.00 (*0-931633-00-1*) Fnd Soc Stdy.
Murvar, Vatro, jt. ed. see Glassman, Ronald M.
Murvin, H. L. Architect's Responsibilities in the Project Delivery Process. 3rd ed. (Illus.). 375p. 1989. pap. 44.50 (*0-9608498-3-1*) H L Murvin.
— Computer Aided Drafting on the Bausch & Lomb Producer Drafting System (Beginning Level) (Illus.). 84p. 1983. pap. 11.95 (*0-9608498-1-5*) H L Murvin.
— Pre-Columbian Architecture, Art, & Artifacts Slide Catalog. 99p. 1988. pap. 3.95 (*0-9608498-2-3*) H L Murvin.
Murvin, Harry J. & Price, Richard L. Micro-Ledger: Financial Accounting Student Workbook Manual & Computer Applications for IBM--Version 2.2. 158p. 1990. pap. text ed. 10.95 (*1-57094-039-8*); pap. text ed. 5.95 (*1-57094-040-1*) S E Warner Sftware.
Murwin, Susan A. & Payne, Suzzy C. The Quick & Easy Giant Dahlia Quilt on the Sewing Machine: Step-By-Step Instructions & Full Size Templates for Three Quilt Sizes. (Illus.). 80p. (Orig.). 1983. pap. 4.95 (*0-486-24501-2*) Dover.
— Quick & Easy Patchwork on the Sewing Machine: Instructions & Full-Size Templates for 12 Quilts. LC 78-74751. (Illus.). 1979. pap. 4.95 (*0-486-23770-2*) Dover.
Murzin, Howy, jt. auth. see Schiff, Irwin A.
Mus, David. Wall to Wall Speaks. (Contemporary Poets Ser.). 112p. 1988. text ed. 21.95 (*0-691-06728-7*); pap. text ed. 10.95 (*0-691-01444-2*) Princeton U Pr.
Mus, Paul. Barabudur: Esquisse d'une histoire du bouddhisme fondee sur la critique archeologique des textes, 2 vols. in 1. Bolle, Kees W., ed. LC 77-79146. (Mythology Ser.). (FRE.). 1978. reprint ed. lib. bdg. 90.95 (*0-405-10555-X*) Ayer.
Musa, Adam, ed. Letters & Lectures of Idries Shah. 40p. 1981. pap. 7.00 (*0-86304-010-1*, Pub. by Octagon Pr UK) ISHK Bk Service.
Musa, Dalal, intro. Guide to Gas-Fueled Cogenerators. 174p. (Orig.). 1990. pap. write for info. (*0-935453-31-8*) Pasha Pubns.
Musa, Dalal, et al, eds. Space Station Directory & Program Guide: 1990 Edition. 3rd rev. ed. (Illus.). 300p. 1990. pap. 200.00 (*0-935453-34-2*) Pasha Pubns.
Musa, John D. Software Reliability: Measurement, Prediction, Application. 688p. 1987. text ed. write for info. (*0-07-044093-X*) McGraw.
— Software Reliability: Professional Edition. 1990. text ed. 50.00 (*0-07-044119-7*) McGraw.
Musa, John D., et al. Software Reliability. 688p. 1987. write for info. (*0-318-62006-5*) McGraw.
***Musa, M.** Machiavelli's the Prince. (C). Date not set. pap. text ed. 20.03 (*0-7870-0002-7*) Digital Print.
Musa, Mahmoud N., ed. Pharmacokinetics & Therapeutic Monitoring of Psychiatric Drugs. LC 92-48220. (Illus.). 226p. 1993. text ed. 49.95 (*0-398-05841-5*) C C Thomas.
— Pharmacokinetics & Therapeutic Monitoring of Psychiatric Drugs. LC 92-48220. (Illus.). 226p. 1993. pap. 29.95 (*0-398-06301-X*) C C Thomas.
Musa, Mark. Advent at the Gates: Dante's Comedy. LC 72-21243. 185p. reprint ed. pap. 52.80 (*0-8357-5199-6*, 2056048) Bks Demand.
Musa, Mark, ed. see Boccaccio, Giovanni.
Musa, Mark, tr. see Boccaccio, Giovanni.
Musa, Mark, jt. tr. see Bondanella, Peter E.
Musa, Mark, tr. see Dante Alighieri.
Musa, Mark, ed. see Dante Alighieri.
Musa, Mark, tr. see Dante Alighieri.
Musa, Mark, ed. see Dante Alighieri.
Musa, Mark, ed. see Dantee Alighieri.
Musa, Mark, tr. see Machiavelli, Niccolo.
Musa, Mark, ed. see Pavese, Cesare.
Musa, Mark, ed. see Petrarch, Francesco.
Musacchio, Donald J., jt. auth. see Gilson, Robert J.
Musacchio, George. Milton's Adam & Eve: Fallible Perfection. LC 90-49694. (American University Studies: English Language & Literature: Ser. IV, Vol. 118). 214p. (C). 1991. text ed. 37.95 (*0-8204-1326-7*) P Lang Pubs.
Musaelyan, S. A. Barrier Waves in the Atmosphere. 120p. 1964. text ed. 40.00 (*0-7065-0289-2*, Pub. by Keter Pub IS) Coronet Bks.
Musaeus. Musaei Lexicon. Bo, Domenico, ed. Bd. V. 96p. 1966. write for info. (*0-318-70979-1*, Pub. by Georg Olms GW) Lubrecht & Cramer.
Musaios. Lion Path: You Can Take It with You. 4th ed. (Illus.). 176p. 1989. pap. 14.95 (*0-685-27023-8*) Golden Sceptre.
Musaph, H. & Mettrop, P. J., eds. The Role of Aggression in Human Pathology. (Psychotherapy & Psychosomatics Journal: Vol. 20, No. 5). (Illus.). 1972. pap. 14.50 (*3-8055-1562-6*) S Karger.
Musaph, H., ed. see Congress of International College of Psychosomatic Medicine, 2nd, Amsterdam, June 18-21, 1973.
Musaph, H., jt. ed. see Money, J.
Musashi, Miyamoto. A Book of Five Rings. Harris, Victor, tr. LC 73-83986. 1982. 18.95 (*0-87951-018-8*); pap. 10.95 (*0-87951-153-2*) Overlook Pr.
— Book of Five Rings. 1982. mass mkt. 5.99 (*0-553-27096-6*) Bantam.
— Book of Five Rings. 1992. pap. 9.95 (*0-553-35170-2*) Bantam.
— Book of Five Rings. 1988. 8.99 (*0-517-41528-3*) Random Hse Value.
— The Book of Five Rings. Cleary, Thomas & Munenori, Yagyu, trs. LC 92-56443. 136p. (Orig.). 1993. pap. 9.00 (*0-87773-868-8*, Sham Dragon Edits) Shambhala Pubns.
— The Book of Five Rings. Cleary, Thomas, tr. LC 93-36271. (Pocket Classics Ser.). (Orig.). 1994. 6.00 (*0-87773-998-6*) Shambhala Pubns.
— The Martial Artist's Book of Five Rings: A New Interpretation of Miyamoto Musashi's Classic Book of Strategy. Kaufman, Hanshi S., tr. LC 94-7394. 128p. (Orig.). 1994. pap. 14.95 (*0-8048-3020-7*) C E Tuttle.
Musavi, Sayyed M. Western Civilization Through Muslim Eyes. Goulding, F. J., tr. 146p. 1977. 14.95 (*0-941722-20-1*); pap. 7.95 (*0-941722-06-6*) Book Dist Ctr.
Musberger, R., jt. ed. see Lechter, Michael.
Musburger. Electronic News Gathering: A Guide to ENG. (Electronic Media Guide Ser.). 96p. 1991. pap. 15.95 (*0-240-80079-6*, Focal) Buttrwrth-Heinemann.
Musburger, Robert B. Single Camera Video Production. LC 92-13909. (Illus.). 176p. 1992. pap. 12.95 (*0-240-80034-6*, Focal) Buttrwrth-Heinemann.
Muscara, Calogero, jt. auth. see Agnew, John.
Muscarella. Phrygian Fibulae from Gordion. (Colt Monograph Ser.: Vol. 4). 1967. 15.00 (*0-85668-064-8*, Pub. by Aris & Phillips UK) David Brown.
Muscarella, Anthony. Iwo Jima - The Young Heroes. Goodman, Charles, ed. (American Heroes Ser.). (Illus.). 104p. (Orig.). 1989. pap. 9.95 (*0-916693-13-9*) Castle Bks.
Muscarella, O. W. Unexcavated Objects & Ancient Near Eastern Art: Addenda. (Occasional Papers: No. 1-1). 19p. (C). 1979. pap. text ed. 5.25 (*0-685-65599-7*) Undena Pubns.
Muscarella, Oscar W. Bronze & Iron: Ancient Near Eastern Artifacts in the Metropolitan Museum of Art. 1994. 75.00 (*0-8109-6450-3*) Abrams.
— Bronze & Iron: Ancient Near Eastern Artifacts in the Metropolitan Museum of Art. (Illus.). 504p. 1989. 75.00 (*0-87099-525-1*) Metro Mus Art.
— The Catalogue of Ivories from Hasanlu, Iran. Dyson, Robert H., Jr., ed. (University Museum Monographs: Hasanlu Special Studies: Nos. 40 & 2). (Illus.). xi, 231p. (Orig.). (C). 1980. pap. 30.00 (*0-934718-33-4*) U PA Mus Pubns.
***Muscarella, T.** Through the Eyes of Two Enemies. 120p. (Orig.). 1995. pap. 12.00 (*0-9641970-1-4*) Freedom Press.
***Muscarella, Tony.** Iwo Jima: The Young Heroes. 105p. 1994. pap. 12.00 (*0-9641970-0-6*) Freedom Press.
Muscari, Ann & Marrone, Wenda W. Child Care That Works: How Families Can Share Their Lives with Child Care & Thrive. braille ed. 433p. 1991. vinyl bd. 34.64 (*1-56956-209-1*, BR8441) W A T Braille.
Muscat, Colette A. Alone with the One. (Illus.). 100p. (Orig.). 1994. write for info. (*1-883148-00-6*); pap. write for info. (*1-883148-01-4*) ACMI Pr.
Muscat, Eugene J. & Lorton, Paul, Jr. Information Processing Microcomputer Applications. 2nd ed. 64p. 1990. pap. text ed. 3.96 (*0-07-044123-5*) McGraw.
— Microcomputer Applications for the Data Processing Work Kit TRS-80 Diskette. (Microcomputer Software Program Ser.). 1983. 120.00 (*0-07-044107-3*); Apple II Plus Version. 120.00 (*0-07-044108-1*); 6.25 (*0-07-044109-X*) McGraw.
Muscat, Robert J. The Fifth Tiger: A Study of Thai Development Policy. LC 93-25775. 360p. (C). 1994. text ed. 59.95 (*1-56324-323-7*, East Gate Bk); pap. text ed. 22.50 (*1-56324-324-5*, East Gate Bk) M E Sharpe.
— Thailand & the United States: Development, Security, & Foreign Aid. (Studies of the East Asian Institute). 352p. 1990. text ed. 40.00 (*0-231-07144-2*) Col U Pr.
Muscat, Robert J. & Stromseth, Jonathan. Cambodia: Post-Settlement Reconstruction & Development. (Occasional Papers of the East Asian Institute). 143p. 1989. pap. 9.00 (*0-913418-04-8*) Columbia U E Asian Inst.
Muscatine, Charles. Chaucer & the French Tradition: A Study in Style & Meaning. (C). 1957. pap. 14.00 (*0-520-00908-8*) U CA Pr.
— The Old French Fabliaux. LC 85-17992. 224p. 1986. 32.00 (*0-300-03527-6*) Yale U Pr.
Muscatine, Charles & Griffith, Marlene. Borzoi College Reader. 6th ed. 848p. (C). 1988. pap. text ed. write for info. (*0-07-555587-5*) McGraw.
Muscatine, Charles & Griffith, Marlene, eds. The Borzoi College Reader. 7th ed. 1992. pap. text ed. write for info. (*0-07-044166-9*) McGraw.
— The Borzoi College Reader. 7th ed. 1992. pap. text ed. write for info. (*0-07-044199-5*) McGraw.
Muscatine, Doris, et al, eds. University of California Sotheby Book of California Wine. LC 83-47666. (Illus.). 640p. 1984. 25.00 (*0-520-05085-1*) U CA Pr.
Musch, Don, jt. ed. see Swindler, William F.
Musch, Donald J., jt. auth. see Holbein, James R.
Musch, Donald J., jt. ed. see Holbein, James R.
Muschamp, Herbert. Man about Town: Frank Lloyd Wright in New York City. (Illus.). 224p. 1985. reprint ed. pap. 9.95x (*0-262-63100-8*) MIT Pr.
Muschamp, Herbert, et al. The Once & Future Park. Karasov, Deborah & Waryan, Stephen, eds. LC 92-40464. (Illus.). 58p. (Orig.). 1993. pap. 19.95 (*1-878271-76-8*) Princeton Arch.
Muschell, David. Mixed Emotions. 24p. (Orig.). 1990. pap. 2.50 (*0-87129-010-3*, M77) Dramatic Pub.
Muschik, W. Aspects of Non-Equilibrium Thermodynamics. (Series in Theoretical & Applied Mechanics: Vol. 9). 112p. 1989. text ed. 28.00 (*981-02-0087-0*) World Scientific Pub.
Muschik, W., ed. Non-Equilibrium Thermodynamics with Application to Solids: Dedicated to the Memory of Professor Theodor Lehmann. (CISM International Centre for Mechanical Sciences Ser.: No. 336). ix, 329p. 1994. pap. 60.00 (*0-387-82453-7*) Spr-Verlag.
Muschik, W. & Ebeling, W. Statistical Physics & Thermodynamics of Nonlinear Equilibrium Systems. 268p. 1993. text ed. 95.00 (*981-02-1134-1*) World Scientific Pub.
Muschik, W., jt. ed. see Axelrad, D. R.
Muschla, Gary. Writing Resource Activities Kit: Ready-to-Use Worksheets & Enrichment Lessons for Grades 4-9. 272p. 1989. spiral bd. 27.95 (*0-87628-970-7*) Ctr Appl Res.
— Writing Workshop Teacher's Survival Kit. 288p. 1993. pap. 28.95 (*0-87628-972-3*) Ctr Appl Res.
Muschla, Gary R. English Teacher's Great Books Activities Kit: Sixty Ready-to-Use Activity Packets Featuring Classic, Popular, & Current Literature. LC 93-44779. 1994. pap. 27.95 (*0-87628-854-9*) Ctr Appl Res.
— The Writing Teacher's Book of Lists: With Ready-to-Use Activities & Worksheets. 256p. 1991. pap. 24.95 (*0-13-971169-4*, 710302) P-H.
***Muschla, Gary R. & Muschla, Judith.** Math Teacher's Book of Lists. LC 94-36753. 1994. pap. 29.95 (*0-13-180357-3*) P-H.
Muschla, Judith, jt. auth. see Muschla, Gary R.
Muschler, R. A Manual Flora of Egypt, 2 vols. in one. (Illus.). 1971. reprint ed. 180.00 (*3-7682-0678-5*) Lubrecht & Cramer.
Muschlitz, Beverly, jt. auth. see Michener, Dorothy.
***Muscia, Jorge.** El Filete: Popular Art of Buenos Aires. (Illus.). 56p. 1995. pap. 10.95 (*1-883675-09-X*) J Shaw Studio.
Musciano, Walter. Eagles of the Black Cross. (Illus.). 1965. 27.95 (*0-8392-1144-9*) Astor-Honor.
— Warbirds of the Sea: A History of Aircraft Carriers & Carrier-Based Aircraft. (Illus.). 336p. 1994. 49.95 (*0-88740-583-5*) Schiffer.
Musciano, Walter A. Building & Flying Model Airplanes. LC 84-28445. (Illus.). 224p. 1901. pap. 10.95 (*0-668-05933-8*) P-H Gen Ref & Trav.
— Messerschmitt Aces. (Orig.). 1989. pap. 17.95 (*0-07-156446-2*) McGraw.
— Messerschmitt Aces. (Illus.). 304p. (Orig.). 1989. pap. 17.95 (*0-8306-8379-8*, TAB-Aero) TAB Bks.
— Warbirds of the Sea: Part One, 1911-1945. (Illus.). 304p. 1992. 29.95 (*0-8306-4235-8*, 4281, TAB-Aero) TAB Bks.
Muscle Shoals District Service League Staff. Cooks & Company: A Collection of Recipes from Muscle Shoals District Service League. 320p. 1988. pap. 11.95 (*0-9620209-0-7*) Muscle Shoals.
Muscular Dystrophy Symposium Staff. Muscular Dystrophy 1976: Proceedings of the Symposium, Jerusalem, 1976. Robin, Gordon C. & Falewski de Leon, George, eds. (Illus.). 1977. 39.25 (*3-8055-2680-6*) S Karger.
Muse, Benjamin. American Negro Revolution. 1970. pap. 2.95 (*0-8065-0003-4*, Citadel Pr) Carol Pub Group.
— American Negro Revolution: From Nonviolence to Black Power, 1963-1967. LC 68-27350. 359p. reprint ed. 102.40 (*0-8357-9194-7*, 2015831) Bks Demand.
— Virginia's Massive Resistance. 12.00 (*0-8446-0816-5*) Peter Smith.
Muse, Charles L. How to Deal Like a Millionaire & Get Rich on Borrowed Money. 1981. pap. 7.95 (*0-13-404640-4*) P-H.
Muse, Charlotte. The Comfort Teacher. (Flowering Quince Poetry Ser.: No. 5). (Illus.). 24p. (Orig.). 1985. pap. 7.50 (*0-940592-17-7*) Heyeck Pr.
Muse, Dan T. The Song of Songs. pap. 5.95 (*0-911866-78-7*) LifeSprings Res.
***Muse, Daphne, ed.** Prejudice: Stories about Hate, Ignorance, Revelation, & Transformation. LC 94-35187. 256p. (YA). (gr. 7 up). 1995. 16.95 (*0-7868-0024-0*) Hyprn Child.
Muse, David, jt. auth. see Muse, Kenneth.
***Muse, Eben J.** The Land of Nam: The Vietnam War in American Film. LC 94-34912. 1995. write for info. (*0-8108-2952-5*) Scarecrow.
Muse, Kenneth. Photo One. 2nd ed. (Illus.). 240p. 1987. pap. text ed. 42.00 (*0-13-665340-5*) P-H.
— The Total Cartoonist. (Illus.). 240p. (C). 1986. 21.00 (*0-13-925263-0*) P-H.
Muse, Kenneth & Muse, David. Home Video Made Easy. (Illus.). 224p. 1986. 20.50 (*0-13-393042-4*) P-H.
Muse, Mark, et al. Exercise for the Chronic Pain Patient. 1984. pap. 14.95 (*0-932392-19-9*) Mouvement Pubns.
Muse, Meeka. Between You & Me. 101p. 1992. pap. 10.00 (*0-9639774-0-7*) Meeka Muse.
Muse, Nina J. Depression & Suicide in Children & Adolescents. (Child Guidance Mental Health Ser.). 1990. pap. text ed. 8.00 (*0-89079-264-X*, 1508) PRO-ED.
Muse, Vance. The Smithsonian Guide to Historic America: Northern New England: Maine, Vermont, New Hampshire. Kennedy, Roger G., ed. LC 88-33092. (Smithsonian Guide to Historic America Ser.). (Illus.). 294p. 1989. 24.95 (*1-55670-049-0*); pap. 18.95 (*1-55670-066-0*) Stewart Tabori & Chang.
— We Bombed in Burbank: A Joyride to Primetime. 279p. 1994. 21.15 (*0-201-62223-8*) Addison-Wesley.
Muse, Vance, jt. auth. see Logan, William B.
Musee d'Orsay Staff. Van Gogh a Paris. (Illus.). 280p. (FRE.). 1988. pap. 39.95 (*0-295-97048-0*) U of Wash Pr.
Musee en Herbe Staff. Livre de la Tour Eiffel. (Gallimard - Decouverte Cadet Ser.: No. 2). 96p. (FRE.). (J). (gr. 4-9). 1983. 14.95 (*2-07-039502-2*) Schoenhof.
Musee Picasso Staff. Les Demoiselles d'Avignon, 2 vols., Set. (Illus.). 712p. (FRE.). 1988. pap. 75.00 (*0-295-97046-4*) U of Wash Pr.
Musej. Ivan Mestrovich. 138p. 1983. 20.00 (*0-918660-43-2*) Ragusan Pr.
Musek, Matjaz, et al, comps. Bibliography of ICPE: 1985-1986. 139p. 1987. pap. 20.00 (*92-9038-103-5*, Pub. by Intl Ctr Pub Ent XV) Kumarian Pr.
Museley, David & Nichol, Catherine. Aurally Coded English Spelling Dictionary: ACE. 1989. pap. 70.00 (*0-317-58012-4*) St Mut.
Musell, R. Mark, jt. auth. see Belasco, Amy.
Musella, Donald, jt. ed. see Leithwood, Kenneth A.
Musella, Donald F. Selecting School Administrators. LC 83-191790. (Informal Ser.: No. 54). 181p. reprint ed. pap. 51.60 (*0-7837-0554-9*, 2040895) Bks Demand.
Musello, Damian. Mystic Lakes. LC 87-45106. 304p. 1988. 17.95 (*1-55611-046-4*) D I Fine.
Musemeche & Ellis. Pete Maravich: Basketball Whiz. 1969. 2.95 (*0-685-00420-1*) Claitors.
Musen, Mark. Automated Generation of Model-Based Knowledge-Acquisition Tools. (Research Notes in Artificial Intelligence Ser.). 1989. 29.95 (*1-55860-090-6*) Morgan Kaufmann.
Musen, Mark A. Automated Generation of Model Based Knowledge Acquisition Tools. 300p. (C). 1989. pap. text ed. 200.00 (*0-273-08812-2*, Pub. by Pitman Pubng UK) St Mut.
***Museo del Prado Staff, ed.** Museo del Prado Inventario General de Pinturas Vol. 1: La Coleccion Real. (Illus.). 840p. (SPA.). 1993. 500.00x (*84-239-4311-9*) Elliots Bks.
— Museo del Prado Inventario General de Pinturas Vol. 2: El Museo de la Trinidad. (Illus.). 514p. (SPA.). Date not set. 400.00x (*84-239-4312-7*) Elliots Bks.
Musere, Jonathan. African Sleeping Sickness: Political Ecology, Colonialism, & Control in Uganda. LC 90-44199. (Studies in African Health & Medicine: Vol. 5). 224p. 1990. lib. bdg. 89.95 (*0-88946-280-1*) E Mellen.

Muses, Charles. Destiny & Control in Human Systems: Studies in the Interactive Connectedness of Time (Chronotopology) 1984. lib. bdg. 68.00 (*0-89838-156-8*) Kluwer Ac.

Museum of American Folk Art Staff, jt. auth. see Ketchum, William C., Jr.

Museum of Art & Archaeology, University of Missouri-Columbia Staff. The Art of the July Monarchy: France 1830 to 1848. LC 89-4864. (Illus.). 336p. 1990. text ed. 49.00 (*0-8262-0721-9*) U of Mo Pr.

Museum of Art, Rhode Island School. Pattern & Poetry: No-Robes from the Lucy Truman Aldrich Collection. 1993. pap. 45.00 (*1-55859-641-0*) Abbeville Pr.

Museum of Arts & Sciences Macon, Georgia Staff. George Bellows: The Personal Side. (Illus.). 56p. (Orig.). 1984. pap. 8.50 (*0-916769-01-1*) Museum Art GA.

***Museum of Church History & Art Staff, et al.** Images of Faith: Art of the Latter-Day Saints. (Illus.). 1995. write for info. (*0-87579-912-4*) Deseret Bk.

Museum of Fine Arts, Boston & Harvard College Library. The Artist & the Book in Western Europe & the United States, Eighteen Sixty to Nineteen Sixty. LC 81-81721. (Illus.). 332p. 1982. reprint ed. lib. bdg. 65.00 (*0-87817-277-7*) Hacker.

***Museum of Fine Arts Boston Staff.** Deluxe Wedding Gift Set: Wedding Planner & Guest Book. 1992. 45.00 (*0-8478-5680-1*) Rizzoli Intl.

Museum of Fine Arts, Boston Staff. An Illustrated Handbook: The Museum of Fine Arts, Boston. rev. ed. LC 75-21769. (Illus.). 438p. 1984. pap. 8.99 (*0-87846-092-6*) Mus Fine Arts Boston.

Museum of Fine Arts, Boston Staff, jt. auth. see Boucher, Norman.

Museum of Fine Arts Curatorial Staff. Art for Boston: A Decade of Acquisitions under the Directorship of Jan Fontein. Purvis, Cynthia, ed. LC 87-61094. (Illus.). 216p. (Orig.). 1987. 35.00 (*0-87846-290-2*); pap. 24.95 (*0-87846-291-0*) Mus Fine Arts Boston.

Museum of Fine Arts, Research Laboratory Staff. Applications of Science in Examination of Works of Art: Proceedings of the Museum of Fine Arts, Research Laboratory Seminar, Boston, 1958. LC 78-99280. 1960. 19.95 (*0-405-00070-7*) Ayer.

Museum of Fine Arts Staff. And the Angels Sing. 1991. 19. 95 (*0-8478-1408-4*) Rizzoli Intl.

— Guest Book. 80p. 1992. 19.95 (*0-8478-5636-4*); (*0-8478-5647-X*) Rizzoli Intl.

— Mother's Journal: A Book of Days. (Illus.). 128p. 1991. 15.95 (*0-8212-1886-7*) Bulfinch Pr.

— Tidings of Comfort & Joy: A Family Christmas Album. (Illus.). 80p. 1992. 18.95 (*0-8478-5643-7*) Rizzoli Intl.

— Wedding Planner. (Illus.). 96p. 1992. 29.95 (*0-8478-5637-2*) Rizzoli Intl.

Museum of Fine Arts Staff, ed. And the Angels Sing: A Songbook of Classic Christmas Carols. LC 91-17327. 80p. 1991. 19.99 (*0-8010-0224-9*) Baker Bk.

— Rembrandt: Experimental Etcher. LC 87-80024. 1988. reprint ed. lib. bdg. 60.00 (*0-87817-320-X*) Hacker.

Museum of Modern Art, Film Department Staff, ed. Circulating Film Library Catalog. (Illus.). 304p. (Orig.). 1984. pap. 15.95 (*0-87070-327-7*, 0-8109-6021-4) Mus of Modern Art.

Museum of Modern Art Library Staff. Annual Bibliography of Modern Art: Nineteen-Hundred Ninety-One. 600p. 1992. text ed. 225.00 (*0-8161-0557-X*) G K Hall.

— Annual Bibliography of Modern Art: 1992. 700p. 1993. lib. bdg. 225.00 (*0-8161-0597-9*, Hall Reference) Macmillan.

— Annual Bibliography of Modern Art, 1989: The Museum of Modern Art Library, New York. (Monograph Ser.). 700p. (C). 1990. lib. bdg. 215.00 (*0-8161-0508-1*) G K Hall.

— Annual Bibliography of Modern Art, 1990: The Museum of Modern Art, New York. annuals 700p. 1991. text ed. 225.00 (*0-8161-0517-0*) G K Hall.

— Annual Bibliography of the Museum of Modern Art Library, 1988 Edition. (Library Catalogs Ser.). 525p. 1989. lib. bdg. 190.00 (*0-8161-0487-5*) G K Hall.

Museum of Modern Art Library Staff, et al. Arp. 1981. 19. 95 (*0-405-12886-X*) Ayer.

Museum of Modern Art Library Staff. Art in Progress: A Survey Prepared for the Fifteenth Anniversary of the Museum of Modern Art, New York Staff. 1981. 35.95 (*0-405-12882-7*) Ayer.

— Bulletin of the Museum of Modern Art, 1933-1963, 7 Vols. LC 38-43. 1967. reprint ed. 35.00 (*0-685-06505-7*) Ayer.

— Bulletin of the Museum of Modern Art, 1933-1963, 7 Vols. LC 38-43. 1967. reprint ed. 203.95 (*0-405-01500-3*) Ayer.

— Vincent Van Gogh. Barr, Alfred H., Jr., ed. LC 78-109811. (Illus.). 193p. 1971. reprint ed. text ed. 49.75 (*0-8371-4302-0*, NYVG, Greenwood Pr) Greenwood.

Museum of Modern Art Library Staff, ed. Catalog of the Library of the Museum of Modern Art, New York, 14 vols., Set. 1976. lib. bdg. 1,310.00 (*0-8161-0015-2*, Hall Library) G K Hall.

Museum of Modern Art Library Staff & Ritchie, Andrew C. Masters of British Painting, Eighteen Hundred to Nineteen Fifty. 1981. 24.95 (*0-405-12884-3*) Ayer.

***Museum of Modern Art Oxford Staff.** Art from Argentina. 144p. 1994. pap. 80.00 (*0-905836-76-6*, Pub. by Museum Modern Art UK) St Mut.

— Fisher, Joel. (Illus.). 1977. pap. 21.00 (*0-905836-02-2*, Pub. by Museum Modern Art UK) St Mut.

— Logan, Andrew: An Artistic Adventure. 1991. pap. 24.00 (*0-905836-73-1*, Pub. by Museum Modern Art UK) St Mut.

— Soviet Film Posters of the Silent Cinema: Colour Poster of Alexander Ilyich Naumov's "Bella Donna" (Illus.). 1987. pap. 20.00 (*0-905836-59-6*, Pub. by Museum Modern Art UK) St Mut.

***Museum of Modern Art Oxford Staff, ed.** Signs of the Times: A Decade of Video, Film & Slide-Tape Installation in Britain 1980-1990. 87p. 1990. pap. 48.00 (*0-905836-72-3*, Pub. by Museum Modern Art UK) St Mut.

***Museum of Natural History, Roger Williams Park Staff.** All Things Connected: Native American Creations. 65p. 1995. pap. 14.95x (*0-9646544-0-7*) Mus Nat Hist.

Museum of Oxford Staff, ed. The Story of Oxford. 2nd rev. ed. (Illus.). 48p. 1992. pap. 6.00 (*0-7509-0097-0*) A Sutton Pub.

Museum Practice Program, Graduate Students Staff. Art a la Carte: Decorative Imagery in Maps, 1600-1900. (Illus.). 22p. 1979. pap. 2.00 (*0-912303-17-4*) Michigan Mus.

— John Mix Stanley: A Traveller in the West. (Illus.). 40p. 1970. pap. 3.00 (*0-317-99609-6*) Michigan Mus.

— Pompeii As Source & Inspiration: Reflections in Eighteenth & Nineteenth Century Art. (Illus.). 58p. 1977. pap. 4.00 (*0-912303-13-1*) Michigan Mus.

Museum Practice Program Graduate Students. Margaret Watson Parker: A Collector's Legacy. (Illus.). 30p. 1982. pap. 3.00 (*0-912303-26-3*) Michigan Mus.

***Museum Senior Curators.** The Mauritshuis Museum. (Illus.). 128p. 1994. 29.95 (*1-85759-031-7*, Pub. by P Wilson Pubs) Sothebys Pubns.

Museum Store Association, Inc. Staff. MSA Data Banque Report 1990. 215p. (Orig.). 1990. pap. text ed. 50.00 (*0-9616104-1-7*) Museum Store.

— The New Store Workbook: MSA's Guide to Remodeling, Expanding & Opening the Museum Store. (Illus.). 107p. (Orig.). 1994. student ed, spiral bd. 49.95 (*0-9616104-3-3*) Museum Store.

Museum Store Association Staff. The Manager's Guide: Basic Guidelines for the New Store Manager. (Illus.). 144p. 1992. spiral bd. 55.00 (*0-9616104-2-5*) Museum Store.

Museum Studies Class, et al. Arnoldi: Just Bronze. Glenn, Constance W., ed. (Illus.). 56p. (Orig.). (C). 1987. pap. 20.00 (*0-936270-26-8*) CA St U LB Art.

— A Collective Vision: Clarence H. White & His Students. Barnes, Lucinda, ed. LC 85-16558. (Illus.). 72p. (Orig.). 1985. pap. 35.00 (*0-936270-24-1*) CA St U LB Art.

Museum Studies Class of Nineteen Seventy-Eight Staff. Selections from the Frederick Weisman Co. Collection of Southern California. (Illus.). 64p. (Orig.). (C). 1978. pap. text ed. 35.00 (*0-936270-11-X*) CA St U LB Art.

Museum Studies Class Staff. Bryan Hunt: A Decade of Drawings. (Illus.). 61p. 1983. pap. 20.00 (*0-936270-20-9*) CA St U LB Art.

— Doumani House. (Illus.). 11p. 1981. pap. 15.00 (*0-685-42743-9*) CA St U LB Art.

— Vapor Dreams in L.A. Terry Schoonhaven's Empty Stage. (Illus.). 40p. 1982. pap. 20.00 (*0-936270-19-5*) CA St U LB Art.

Museum Studies Graduate Certificate Program Staff. In Praise of Nature: The Landscapes of William Wendt. Glenn, Constance & Taylor-Winter, Sue, eds. (Illus.). 64p. (Orig.). (C). 1989. pap. text ed. 17.50 (*0-936270-29-2*) CA St U LB Art.

Museums & Galleries Commission Staff, jt. auth. see Conservation Unit Staff.

Museums at Stony Brook Staff. The Carriage Collection. LC 86-12594. (Illus.). 127p. (Orig.). 1986. pap. 8.00 (*0-943924-09-X*) Mus Stony Brook.

— The Museums at Stony Brook: Highlights of the Collection. LC 82-81912. (Illus.). 72p. (Orig.). 1982. pap. 5.00 (*0-943924-04-9*) Mus Stony Brook.

— Nineteenth Century American Carriages: Their Manufacture, Decoration & Use. LC 87-12282. (Illus.). 112p. (Orig.). 1987. pap. 8.00 (*0-943924-10-3*) Mus Stony Brook.

— Nineteenth-Century American Music & Dance in the Art of William Sidney Mount. (Illus.). 64p. (Orig.). 1986. 95. 00 (*0-943924-11-1*); audio (*0-318-60984-3*) Mus Stony Brook.

Museums for a New Century Commission. Museums for a New Century. LC 84-72051. (Illus.). 144p. (Orig.). 1984. pap. 17.95 (*0-931201-08-X*) Am Assn Mus.

Musey, Charles W., ed. see Nelson, William J.

Musgrave, Alan E. Commonsense, Science, & Scepticism: A Historical Introduction to the Theory of Knowledge. LC 92-12657. (Illus.). 310p. (C). 1993. 59.95 (*0-521-43040-2*); pap. 18.95 (*0-521-43625-7*) Cambridge U Pr.

Musgrave, Alan E., jt. ed. see Currie, Gregory.

Musgrave, Anthony. Studies in Political Economy. LC 67-18581. (Reprints of Economic Classics Ser.). viii, 185p. 1968. reprint ed. 29.50 (*0-678-00337-8*) Kelley.

Musgrave, Beatrice. Change & Choice: Women & Middle Age. Menell, Zoe, ed. 186p. 1980. 19.95 (*0-685-18790-X*, Pub. by P Owen Ltd UK) Dufour.

Musgrave, Beatrice & Menell, Zoe, eds. Change & Choice. 1980. text ed. 29.95 (*0-7206-0539-3*) Dufour.

Musgrave, Daniel D, jt. auth. see Nelson, Thomas B.

Musgrave, Frank. School & the Social Order. LC 79-40738. 210p. reprint ed. pap. 59.90 (*0-685-20598-3*, 2030532) Bks Demand.

Musgrave, G., ed. see Symposium, Brussels Staff.

Musgrave, Gerald & Goodman, John C. State Health Care Reform Under the Clinton Administration. 1992. pap. 10.00 (*0-943802-76-8*, 173) Natl Ctr Pol.

Musgrave, Gerald, jt. auth. see Goodman, John C.

Musgrave, Gerald L., jt. auth. see Goodman, John C.

Musgrave, Jan. Patchwork Projects: With Full Size Patterns & Easy to Follow Step by Step Instructions. 1984. write for info. (*0-914169-00-9*, Patchwrk Orig) Econ America.

Musgrave, John & Thompson, Fred. How to Plan & Design Additions. Burke, Ken, ed. LC 86-71057. (Illus.). 96p. (Orig.). 1986. pap. 9.95 (*0-89721-074-3*) Ortho Info.

Musgrave, John B. UFO Occupants & Critters. 64p. 1979. reprint ed. spiral bd. 7.50 (*0-7873-1266-5*) Mokelumne.

Musgrave, Kate. Womb with Views: A Contradictionary of the English Language. LC 88-63760. (Illus.). 182p. 1989. pap. 8.95 (*0-941300-12-9*) Mother Courage.

Musgrave, Michael. The Music of Brahms. (Illus.). 352p. 1994. pap. 18.95 (*0-19-816401-7*) OUP.

— The Music of Brahms. (Companions to the Great Composers Ser.). (Illus.). 320p. 1985. 39.95 (*0-7100-9776-X*, RKP) Routledge.

— The Musical Life of the Crystal Palace. (Illus.). 270p. (C). 1995. 54.95 (*0-521-37562-2*) Cambridge U Pr.

Musgrave, Michael, ed. Brahms 2: Biographical, Documentary & Analytical Studies. (Illus.). 240p. 1987. 69.95 (*0-521-32606-0*) Cambridge U Pr.

Musgrave, P. W. Curricular Decisions in Their Administrative Contexts. 122p. (C). 1985. 48.00 (*0-7300-0187-3*, Pub. by Deakin Univ AT) St Mut.

— Knowledge, Curriculum & Change. (Second Century in Australian Education Ser.). 112p. 1973. pap. 14.95 (*0-522-84052-3*) Intl Spec Bk.

— Socialising Contexts. 200p. 1987. pap. text ed. 21.95 (*0-04-176011-5*) Routledge Chapman & Hall.

Musgrave, Peggy B. United States Taxation of Foreign Investment Income: Issues & Arguments. LC 68-58098. (Illus.). 186p. (Orig.). 1969. pap. 6.00 (*0-915506-10-6*) Harvard Law Intl Tax.

Musgrave, Peggy B., jt. auth. see Musgrave, Richard A.

Musgrave, Percy. Musgrave: Notes on the Ancient Family of Musgrave of Musgrave, Westmorland, England, & Its Various Branches in Cumberland, Yorkshire, Northumberland. (Illus.). 351p. 1993. reprint ed. lib. bdg. 59.50 (*0-8328-3723-7*); reprint ed. pap. 49.50 (*0-8328-3724-5*) Higginson Bk Co.

Musgrave, Peter. Land & Economy in Baroque Italy: Valpolicella, 1630-1797. LC 92-14244. 1992. 65.00 (*0-7185-1368-1*) St Martin.

Musgrave, Peter W. From Humanity to Utility: Melbourne University & Public Examinations, 1856-1964. (C). 1992. 95.00 (*0-86431-118-4*, Pub. by Aust Council Educ Res AT) St Mut.

***Musgrave, Richard.** Memoirs of the Different Rebellions in Ireland, from the Arrival of the English: Also, a Particular Detail of That Which Broke Out the 23rd of May 1798. (1798 Collection: Vol. 1). 1000p. 1995. 49.95 (*0-9643925-0-X*) Round Tower.

Musgrave, Richard A. Fiscal Reform for Colombia: Final Report & Staff Papers of the Colombian Commission on Tax Reform. Gillis, Malcolm, ed. LC 75-148648. (Illus.). 876p. 1971. pap. 15.00 (*0-915506-11-4*) Harvard Law Intl Tax.

— Fiscal Reform in Bolivia: Final Report of the Bolivian Mission on Tax Reform. LC 80-14943. (Illus.). 604p. 1981. pap. text ed. 18.00 (*0-915506-22-X*) Harvard Law Intl Tax.

— Fiscal Systems. LC 80-29652. (Studies in Comparative Economics). (Illus.). xix, 397p. (ps-3). 1981. reprint ed. text ed. 35.00 (*0-313-22431-5*, MUFC, Greenwood Pr) Greenwood.

— Strengthening the Progressive Income Tax: The Responsible Answer to America's Budget Problem. 1989. 10.00 (*0-944826-07-5*) Economic Policy Inst.

Musgrave, Richard A., ed. Broad-Based Taxes: New Options & Sources. 302p. 1973. 3.00 (*0-317-33984-2*, 238) Comm Econ Dev.

— Essays in Fiscal Federalism. LC 76-49481. (Brookings Institution, Studies of Government Finance Ser.). (Illus.). 301p. 1977. reprint ed. text ed. 35.00 (*0-8371-9366-4*, MUEFF, Greenwood Pr) Greenwood.

Musgrave, Richard A. & Musgrave, Peggy B. Public Finance in Theory & Practice. 5th ed. (Illus.). 736p. 1989. text ed. write for info. (*0-07-044127-8*) McGraw.

Musgrave, Richard A. & Peacock, Alan T., eds. Classics in the Theory of Public Finance. LC 94-1158. 1994. text ed. 69.95 (*0-312-12162-8*) St Martin.

Musgrave, Richard A., et al, eds. Taxation & Economic Development among Pacific Asian Countries. 290p. (C). 1994. text ed. 69.95 (*0-8133-8751-5*) Westview.

Musgrave, Ruth & Stein, Mary A. State Wildlife Laws Handbook: Center for Wildlife Law at the Institute of Public Law, University of New Mexico, Albuquerque, New Mexico. LC 93-23418. 840p. 1993. text ed. 89.00 (*0-86587-357-7*) Gov Insts.

Musgrave, Thea. Music for Horn & Piano. Date not set. pap. 24.50 (*0-685-69098-9*, Chester Music) Music Sales.

Musgrove, A. Data Response for GCSE Geography. (C). 1988. 60.00 (*0-7487-0190-7*, Pub. by S Thornes Pubs UK) St Mut.

***Musgrove, Clive L. & Fox, Michael J.** Quality Costs: Their Impact on Company Strategy & Profitability. (C). 1994. 150.00 (*0-946655-43-X*, Pub. by S Thornes Pubs UK) St Mut.

Musgrove, Frank & Fielden, Sarah. Ecstacy & Holiness: Counter Culture & the Open Society. (Modern Revivals in Sociology Ser.). 250p. (C). 1993. text ed. 59.95 (*0-7512-0289-4*, Pub. by Gregg Revivals UK) Ashgate Pub Co.

Musgrove, Gerald L., jt. auth. see Goodman, John C.

Musgrove, John, ed. A History of Architecture: Sir Banister Fletcher's. 19th ed. (Illus.). 1621p. 1987. 85.00 (*0-408-01587-X*) Buttrwrth-Heinemann.

— Sir Banister Fletcher's a History of Architecture. (Illus.). 1664p. 1987. text ed. 94.95 (*0-7506-0262-7*) Buttrwrth-Heinemann.

***Musgrove, Margaret.** Ashanti to Zulu: African Traditions. (Illus.). (J). 1992. pap. 4.99 (*0-14-054604-9*) Puffin Bks.

Musgrove, Margaret W. Ashanti to Zulu: African Traditions. Dillon, Leo D., ed. LC 76-6610. (Pied Piper Bks.). (Illus.). (J). (gr. k-4). 1976. 17.00 (*0-8037-0357-0*); lib. bdg. 15.89 (*0-8037-0358-9*) Dial Bks Young.

— Ashanti to Zulu: African Traditions. LC 76-6610. (Pied Piper Bks.). (Illus.). 32p. (J). (gr. k up). 1980. pap. 4.95 (*0-8037-0308-2*, Puff Pied Piper) Puffin Bks.

Musgrove, Mary L., jt. ed. see Miller, Juliet V.

Musgrove, Mary R. Beaded Dream Catchers. (Illus.). 4p. 1993. pap. 3.95 (*0-932255-05-1*) Promenade Pub.

Musgrove, Peggy. Pleasing God: A Self-Directed Bible Study for Living the Christian Life. 80p. 1991. pap. text ed. 3.95 (*0-88243-651-1*, 02-0651) Gospel Pub.

— Praying Always: A Self-Directed Bible Study for Christian Service. 80p. 1993. pap. text ed. 3.95 (*0-88243-684-8*, 02-0684) Gospel Pub.

— Who's Who among Bible Women. LC 81-81126. (Radiant Life Ser.). 128p. (Orig.). 1981. 2.95 (*0-88243-883-2*, 02-0883); teacher ed 4.50 (*0-88243-193-5*, 32-0193) Gospel Pub.

Musgrove, Peter J., ed. Wind Energy Conversion, 1983: Proceedings of the Fifth BWEA Wind Energy Conference. LC 83-20878. 384p. 1984. 89.95 (*0-521-26250-X*) Cambridge U Pr.

Musgrove, Philip. Consumer Behavior in Latin America: Income & Spending of Families in Ten Andean Cities. LC 77-1108. 1978. 36.95 (*0-8157-5914-2*) Brookings.

— United States Household Consumption, Income, & Demographic Changes, 1975-2025. LC 81-86060. (Illus.). 263p. reprint ed. pap. 75.00 (*0-8357-4684-4*, 2037631) Bks Demand.

Musgrove, Philip, jt. auth. see Grunwald, Joseph.

Musgrove, S. Shakespeare & Jonson: The Macmillan Brown Lectures. LC 76-38501. reprint ed. 20.00 (*0-404-04545-6*) AMS Pr.

— T. S. Eliot & Walt Whitman. 1972. 200.00 (*0-87968-012-1*) Gordon Pr.

— T. S. Eliot & Walt Whitman. LC 72-100773. (Studies in Comparative Literature: No. 35). (C). 1970. reprint ed. lib. bdg. 49.95 (*0-8383-0332-3*) M S G Haskell Hse.

Musha, T. & Sawada, Y. Physics of the Living State. LC 93-80960. 289p. 1994. 69.50 (*90-5199-147-9*, Pub. by IOS Pr NE) IOS Press.

Musha, T., et al, eds. Noise & Clutter Rejection in Radars & Imaging Sensors, 1984: Proceedings of the 1984 International Symposium Held in Tokyo, Japan, October 22-24, 1984. 750p. 1985. 179.50 (*0-444-87674-X*, North Holland) Elsevier.

— Noise in Physical Systems & 1-f Fluctuations: Proceedings of the International Conference, ICNF 1991, November 24-27, 1991, Kyoto, Japan. LC 92-52686. 800p. 1992. 170.00 (*90-5199-083-9*, Pub. by IOS Pr NE) IOS Press.

Mushaben, Joyce. Post-Postwar Generations: Changing Attitudes Toward Nationalism & Security in West Germany. 288p. 1996. text ed. 29.95 (*0-8133-1152-7*) Westview.

Musham, J. F., jt. auth. see Sheppard, T.

Mushaski, Myamoto. A Book of Five Rings. 1985. 42.50 (*0-911156-99-2*) Bern Porter.

Musher, Daniel M., jt. ed. see Schell, Ronald F.

Mushin, William W. & Rendell-Baker, Leslie. Origins of Thoracic Anaesthesia. Orig. Title: Principles of Thoracic Anaesthesia. (Illus.). xx, 172p. 1991. reprint ed. write for info. (*0-9614932-2-4*) Wood Lib-Mus.

Mushiru, Hasan. Nationalism & Communal Politics in India. 1979. 18.50 (*0-8364-0198-0*) S Asia.

Mushirul, Hasan. A Nationalist Conscience: M. A. Ansari, the Congress & the Raj. (C). 1987. 25.00 (*0-317-66950-8*, Pub. by Manohar II) S Asia.

Mushkat, Jerome. Aaron Burr: Controversial Politician of Early America. Rahmas, D. Steve & Kurland, Gerald, eds. (Outstanding Personalities Ser.: No. 71). 32p. (YA). (gr. 7-12). 1974. lib. bdg. 4.95 (*0-87157-571-X*) SamHar Pr.

— Fernando Wood: A Political Biography. LC 90-4486. (Illus.). 334p. 1990. 35.00 (*0-87338-413-X*) Kent St U Pr.

— The Reconstruction of the New York Democracy, 1861-1874. LC 78-16826. 328p. 1981. 33.50 (*0-8386-3002-2*, 3002) Fairleigh Dickinson.

Mushkat, Marian. Philo-Semitic & Anti-Jewish Attitudes in Post-Holocaust Poland. LC 92-37136. (Symposium Ser.: Vol. 33). 456p. 1992. text ed. 109.95 (*0-7734-9176-7*) E Mellen.

Mushkat, Marion. The Third World & Peace: Some Aspects of Problems of the Inter-Relationship of Interdevelopment & International Security. LC 82-774. 356p. 1983. text ed. 32.50 (*0-312-80039-8*) St Martin.

Mushkatel, Alvin, jt. ed. see Pijawka, David.

Mushkatel, Alvin H., jt. ed. see Herzik, Eric B.

Mushkatel, Alvin H., jt. auth. see Perry, Ronald W.

Mushkin, Selma J., ed. Proposition Thirteen & Its Consequences for Public Management. 186p. (C). 1984. reprint ed. lib. bdg. 41.00 (*0-8191-4116-X*) U Pr of Amer.

— Public Prices for Public Products. 460p. (Orig.). 1972. lib. bdg. 22.50x (*0-87766-010-7*, 90010) Urban Inst.

Mushlin, Michael B. Rights of Prisoners. 2nd ed. Kramer, Donald T., ed. LC 93-36644. (Individual Rights Ser.). 1993. text ed. 150.00 (*0-07-172514-8*) Shepards-McGraw.

Mushrafi, Mokhdum E. Pakistan & Bangladesh: Political Culture & Political Parties. (C). 1992. 54.00 (*81-85565-17-1*, Pub. by Uppal Pub Hse II) S Asia.

***Mushrush, George W. & Speight, James G.** Petroleum Products: Instability & Incompatibility. 300p. 1995. 69. 50 (*1-56032-297-7*) Taylor & Francis.

An Asterisk (*) at the beginning of an entry indicates that the title is appearing in BIP for the first time.

*__Mushtaq, Q. & Tan, A. L.__ Complete Bibliography of the Works of Seyyed Hossein Nasr: From 1958 Through April 1993. Aminrazavi, Mehdi & Moris, Zailan, eds. (Orig.). 1995. pap. text ed. 14.95 (*0-934905-60-6*) Kazi Pubns.
— Mathematics: The Islamic Legacy. 1995. pap. text ed. 12.95 (*0-934905-59-2*) Kazi Pubns.
Mushtari, Kh M. & Galimou, K. Z. Non-Linear Theory of Thin Elastic Shells. LC 61-62238. 383p. reprint ed. pap. 109.20 (*0-317-08780-0*, 2002333) Bks Demand.
Mushtukov, V. & Tikhonov, L. Museums of Leningrad. (Illus.). 170p. (C). 1982. 40.00 (*0-685-37514-5*, Pub. by Collets) St Mut.
Musial, Kathy, ed. see Chandler, Philip E.
Musial, W. D., et al, eds. Wind Energy 1994, Vol. 15. 288p. 1994. pap. 52.50 (*0-7918-1187-5*) ASME.
*__Musial, Walter D., et al, eds.__ Wind Energy: The Energy & Environmental Expo '95 - The Energy-Sources Technology Conference & Exhibition, Houston, Texas - January 29-February 1, 1995. (SED Ser.: Vol. 16). 300p. 1995. 105.00 (*0-7918-1294-4*, H00926) ASME.
Music, David H., jt. auth. see Book, Beverley C.
Music Education Research Council Staff. Bibliography of Research Studies in Music Education, 1932-48. 119p. 1993. reprint ed. lib. bdg. 69.00 (*0-7812-9685-4*) Rprt Serv.
Music Educators National Conference Southern Division Special Committee. Beyond the Classroom: Informing Others. 85p. 1987. 18.00 (*0-940796-52-X*, 1007) Music Ed Natl.
Music Educators Staff. Arts in Schools: State by State. rev. ed. 104p. 1988. reprint ed. 17.50 (*0-940796-57-0*, 1005) Music Ed Natl.
Music Educators Staff & American String Teachers Association Staff. The Complete String Guide: Standards, Programs, Purchase, & Maintenance. 52p. 1988. 11.00 (*0-940796-38-4*, 1009) Music Ed Natl.
Music Forum Staff. Music Forum, Vol. 4. 1977. text ed. 50.00 (*0-231-03934-4*) Col U Pr.
*__Music, Jennifer.__ Against the Sickle Moon. 320p. 1995. pap. 9.95 (*0-7610-0092-5*) NW Pub.
Music Library Association Committee, ed. A Survey of Musical Instrument Collections in the United States & Canada. 135p. 1974. 8.50 (*0-318-14925-7*); pap. 6.50 (*0-318-14927-3*) Music Library Assn.
Music Trade Board, U. S. A. Staff. Complete Catalogue of Sheet Music & Musical Works. LC 69-1666. 575p. 1973. reprint ed. lib. bdg. 95.00 (*0-306-71401-9*) Da Capo.
Music Video Productions Staff, jt. auth. see Christiansen, Michael.
Musical Lynn. Cave Man Talk. 6p. (C). 1990. pap. 6.95 (*1-880718-06-5*); pap. text ed. 6.95 (*1-880718-01-4*) Genius New.
— The Early Poems. 5p. (Orig.). (YA). (gr. 12). 1990. pap. 7.95 (*1-880718-05-7*) Genius New.
— Musical Lynn Essays, Vol. 1: A Baker's Dozen. 13p. (Orig.). (YA). (gr. 12). 1991. pap. 8.95 (*1-880718-02-2*); pap. text ed. 8.95 (*1-880718-03-0*) Genius New.
— Universal Genius Letter, Vol. I. (Illus.). 22p. (Orig.). (C). 1992. pap. 12.95 (*1-880718-04-9*) Genius New.
Musicant, Ivan. Battleship at War. 376p. 1988. mass mkt. 4.95 (*0-380-70487-0*) Avon.
— Divided Waters. 496p. 1995. 30.00 (*0-06-016482-4*, HarpT) HarpC.
*__Musich, Patty.__ Focus: Orange County. (Illus.). 92p. 1986. lib. bdg. 9.95 (*0-942581-00-8*) Metro Lifestyles.
— Focus: Orange County, 1988. (Illus.). 104p. 1988. lib. bdg. 9.95 (*0-942581-01-6*) Metro Lifestyles.
— Focus: Orange County, 1990. rev. ed. (Illus.). 144p. 1990. lib. bdg. 9.95 (*0-942581-02-4*) Metro Lifestyles.
— Focus: Orange County 1991/1992. rev. ed. (Illus.). 144p. 1991. lib. bdg. 9.95 (*0-942581-04-0*) Metro Lifestyles.
— Focus: Orange County '95. Harrison, Dan, ed. (Illus.). 144p. 1994. lib. bdg. 10.95 (*0-942581-12-1*) Metro Lifestyles.
— Focus: Riverside County. Harrison, Dan, ed. (Illus.). 128p. 1994. lib. bdg. 9.95 (*0-942581-06-7*) Metro Lifestyles.
— Focus: Riverside County '95. Harrison, Dan, ed. (Illus.). 128p. 1995. lib. bdg. 10.95 (*0-942581-14-8*) Metro Lifestyles.
— Focus: San Diego County. Harrison, Dan, ed. (Illus.). 120p. 1994. lib. bdg. 9.95 (*0-942581-10-5*) Metro Lifestyles.
— Focus: San Diego County '95. Harrison, Dan, ed. (Illus.). 120p. 1994. lib. bdg. 10.95 (*0-942581-13-X*) Metro Lifestyles.
Musick, David. An Introduction to the Sociology of Juvenile Delinquency. 352p. (C). 1995. 64.50x (*0-7914-2351-4*) State U NY Pr.
— An Introduction to the Sociology of Juvenile Delinquency. 352p. (C). 1995. pap. 21.95x (*0-7914-2352-2*) State U NY Pr.
Musick, J. A., et al, eds. The Biology of Latimeria Chalumnae & Evolution of Coelacanths. (Developments in Environmental Biology of Fishes Ser.). 424p. 1991. lib. bdg. 226.00 (*0-7923-1224-4*) Kluwer Ac.
Musick, Judith, jt. ed. see Weissbourd, Bernice.
Musick, Judith S. Young, Poor, & Pregnant: The Psychology of Teenage Motherhood. LC 92-34612. 256p. (C). 1993. text ed. 30.00 (*0-300-05353-3*) Yale U Pr.
— Young, Poor, & Pregnant: The Psychology of Teenage Motherhood. 1995. 15.00 (*0-300-06195-1*) Yale U Pr.
Musick, Michael P. Sixth Virginia Cavalry. (Virginia Regimental Histories Ser.). (Illus.). 177p. 1990. 19.95 (*0-685-57636-1*) H E Howard.
Musick, Phil. Reflections on Roberto. 138p. 1994. pap. 14.95 (*0-9641355-0-7*) Pitts Pirates.
Musick, Ruth A. Coffin Hollow & Other Ghost Tales. LC 76-51157. (Illus.). 216p. 1977. pap. 11.00 (*0-8131-1416-0*) U Pr of Ky.
— Green Hills of Magic: West Virginia Folktales from Europe. 320p. 1989. reprint ed. pap. 9.95 (*0-8131-1191-9*) McClain.
— The Telltale Lilac Bush & Other West Virginia Ghost Tales. LC 64-14000. (Illus.). 208p. 1965. reprint ed. pap. 11.00 (*0-8131-0136-0*) U Pr of Ky.
Musiek, David, jt. auth. see Turner, Jonathan H.
Musiek, Frank E., et al. Neuroaudiology: Case Studies. LC 93-9066. (Illus.). 320p. (Orig.). (C). 1993. pap. text ed. 65.00 (*1-56593-217-X*, 0577) Singular Publishing.
Musielak, J. Orlicz Spaces & Modular Spaces. (Lecture Notes in Mathematics Ser.: Vol. 1034). 222p. 1983. pap. 27.00 (*0-387-12706-2*) Spr-Verlag.
Musielak, J., ed. see Mathematical Institute of the Polish Academy of Sciences Staff & Institute of Mathematics of the Adam Mickiewicz University Staff.
Musikant. Optical Materials: An Introduction to Selection & Application. (Optical Engineering Ser.: Vol. 6). 272p. 1985. 115.00 (*0-8247-7309-8*) Dekker.
Musikant, ed. Advances in Nonlinear Polymers & Inorganic Crystals, Liquid Crystals, & Laser Media. 1987. 45.00 (*0-89252-859-1*, 824) SPIE.
— Infrared Optical Materials, No. IV. 1988. 38.00 (*0-89252-964-4*, 929) SPIE.
— Optical Materials, Vol. 1: A Series of Advances. 424p. 1990. 150.00 (*0-8247-8131-7*) Dekker.
Musikant, S. Optical Surfaces Resistant to Severe Environments, Vol. 1330. 1990. 42.00 (*0-8194-0391-1*) SPIE.
Musikant, Solomon. WEESKA Ceramics. (What Every Engineer Should Know Ser.: Vol. 28). 224p. 1991. 55.00 (*0-8247-8498-7*) Dekker.
Musil, Alois. Arabia Deserta. LC 77-87085. (American Geographical Society Oriental Explorations & Studies: No. 2). (Illus.). reprint ed. 74.50 (*0-404-60232-0*) AMS Pr.
— Arabia Petraea: Reisebericht, 3 vols. (Illus.). xxxix, 1636p. 1989. reprint ed. Vol. I: Moab. write for info. (*0-318-71536-8*, Pub. by Georg Olms GW) Lubrecht & Cramer.
— Arabia Petraea: Reisebericht, 3 vols., Set. (Illus.). xxxix, 1636p. 1989. reprint ed. write for info. (*3-487-06480-4*, Pub. by Georg Olms GW) Lubrecht & Cramer.
— Arabia Petraea: Reisebericht, 3 vols., Vol. II. (Illus.). xxxix, 1636p. 1989. reprint ed. write for info. (*0-318-71537-6*, Pub. by Georg Olms GW) Lubrecht & Cramer.
— Arabia Petraea: Reisebericht, 3 vols., Vol. III. (Illus.). xxxix, 1636p. 1989. reprint ed. write for info. (*0-318-71538-4*, Pub. by Georg Olms GW) Lubrecht & Cramer.
— The Manners & Customs of the Rwala Bedouins. LC 77-87091. (American Geographical Society Oriental Explorations & Studies: No. 6). reprint ed. 74.50 (*0-404-60236-3*) AMS Pr.
— The Middle Euphrates: A Topographical Itinerary. LC 77-87086. (American Geographical Society Oriental Explorations & Studies: No. 3). reprint ed. 74.50 (*0-404-60233-9*) AMS Pr.
— Northern Arabia, According to the Original Investigations of Alois Musil. LC 77-87092. (American Geographical Society Oriental Explorations & Studies: Map Vol.). reprint ed. 49.50 (*0-404-60237-1*) AMS Pr.
— The Northern Hegaz: A Topographical Itinerary. LC 77-87084. (American Geographical Society Oriental Explorations & Studies: No. 1). reprint ed. 55.00 (*0-404-60231-2*) AMS Pr.
— Northern Negd: A Topographical Itinerary. LC 77-87090. (American Geographical Society Oriental Explorations & Studies: No. 5). reprint ed. 55.00 (*0-404-60235-5*) AMS Pr.
— Palmyrena: A Topographical Itinerary. LC 77-87087. (American Geographical Society Oriental Explorations & Studies: No. 4). reprint ed. 55.00 (*0-404-60234-7*) AMS Pr.
Musil, Caryn M., ed. The Courage to Question. 224p. 1992. 15.00 (*0-911696-55-5*) Assn Am Coll.
— Students at the Center: Feminist Assessment. 80p. 1992. 12.00 (*0-911696-56-3*) Assn Am Coll.
Musil, J. & Zacek, F. Microwave Measurements of Complex Permittivity by Free Space Methods & Their Applications. (Studies in Electrical & Electronic Engineering: No. 22). 276p. 1986. 97.50 (*0-444-99536-6*) Elsevier.
*__Musil, Jirl, ed.__ The End of Czechoslovakia. (Central European University Press Book Ser.). (Illus.). 288p. 1995. 59.00 (*1-85866-019-X*); pap. 21.00 (*1-85866-020-3*) OUP.
Musil, Robert. Five Women. LC 66-12663. 224p. 1987. pap. 10.95 (*0-87923-603-5*) Godine.
— Man Without Qualities. 1965. pap. 9.00 (*0-399-50152-5*, Perigree Bks) Berkley Pub.
— The Man Without Qualities. Wilkins, Sophie & Pike, Burton, trs. LC 92-37943. 1994. 60.00 (*0-394-51052-6*) Knopf.
— Posthumous Papers of a Living Author. Wortsman, Peter, tr. LC 87-83298. 145p. 1987. pap. 12.00 (*0-941419-01-0*, Eridanos Library) Marsilio Pubs.
— Precision & Soul: Essays & Addresses. Pike, Burton & Luft, David S., eds. Luft, David S., tr. LC 90-10828. 376p. 1990. 29.95 (*0-226-55408-2*) U Ch Pr.
— Precision & Soul: Essays & Addresses. Pike, Burton & Luft, David S., eds. Luft, David S., tr. xxviii, 301p. 1994. pap. 16.95 (*0-226-55409-0*) U Ch Pr.
— Selected Writings. (German Library: Vol. 72). 320p. 1986. 29.50 (*0-8264-0305-0*); pap. text ed. 14.95 (*0-8264-0304-2*) Continuum.
Musil, Rosemary G. The Ghost of Mr. Penny. (J). 1940. 5.00 (*0-87602-129-1*) Anchorage.
Musk, Denise. Machine Knitting: The Technique of Pattern Card Design. (Illus.). 144p. 1992. 39.95 (*0-7134-7044-5*, Pub. by Batsford UK) Trafalgar.
Musk, Leslie F., et al. Weather Systems. (Cambridge Topics in Geography Ser.). (Illus.). 160p. 1988. pap. 18.50 (*0-521-27874-0*) Cambridge U Pr.
Muska, Arlene, ed. Vegetarian Creations. (Illus.). 272p. (Orig.). 1992. pap. 17.00 (*0-918224-26-8*) S K Pubns.
Muskat, Beth T. & Neeley, Mary A. The Way It Was: Eighteen Fifty to Nineteen Thirty Photographs of Montgomery & Her Central Alabama Neighbors. LC 85-50334. (Illus.). 185p. 1985. 20.00 (*0-9614653-0-1*) Landmarks Found.
Muske, Carol. Applause. LC 88-29086. (Poetry Ser.). 64p. 1989. 19.95 (*0-8229-3613-5*); pap. 10.95 (*0-8229-5417-6*) U of Pittsburgh Pr.
— Red Trousseau. 96p. 1993. pap. 12.00 (*0-14-058686-5*, Penguin Bks) Viking Penguin.
— Wyndmere. LC 84-19565. (Poetry Ser.). 59p. 1985. 19.95 (*0-8229-3503-1*); pap. 10.95 (*0-8229-5365-X*) U of Pittsburgh Pr.
Muske, L. E., ed. The Neurobiology of Reproductive Behavior. (Journal: Brain, Behavior & Evolution: Vol. 42, No. 4-5, 1993). (Illus.). 84p. 1993. pap. 39.00 (*3-8055-5852-X*) S Karger.
Muskeg Research Conference Staff. Muskeg & the Northern Environment in Canada. Radforth, N. W. & Brawner, C. O., eds. LC 76-54734. (Illus.). 417p. reprint ed. pap. 118.90 (*0-8357-8238-7*, 2033980) Bks Demand.
Muskens, George & Gruppelaar, Jacob. Global Telecommunication Networks: Strategic Considerations. (C). 1988. lib. bdg. 86.50 (*90-277-2682-5*) Kluwer Ac.
*__Muskett, John.__ Site Surveying. 2nd ed. LC 95-1472. 1995. 15.99 (*0-632-03848-9*) Blackwell Sci.
Muskett, Netta. The Flickering Lamp. large type ed. 512p. 1983. 15.95 (*0-7089-0950-7*) Ulverscroft.
— Golden Harvest. large type ed. 544p. 1983. 21.95 (*0-7089-1059-9*) Ulverscroft.
— Light from One Star. large type ed. 1974. 16.95 (*0-85456-242-7*) Ulverscroft.
— Love & Deborah. large type ed. 382p. 1982. 21.95 (*0-7089-0776-8*) Ulverscroft.
— The Open Window. large type ed. 528p. 1983. 21.95 (*0-7089-1019-X*) Ulverscroft.
— Wide & Dark. large type ed. 480p. 1981. 12.00 (*0-7089-0664-8*) Ulverscroft.
Muskhelishvili, N. I. Singular Integral Equations: Boundary Problems of Function Theory & Their Application to Mathematical Physics. 2nd ed. 447p. 1992. reprint ed. pap. 12.95 (*0-486-66893-2*) Dover.
Muskie, Edmund S. Exploring Cambodia: Issues & Reality in a Time of Transition. (Illus.). 88p. (C). 1991. pap. 19.95 (*0-944237-33-9*) Ctr National Policy.
Muskie, Edmund S., ed. The U. S. in Space: Issues & Policy Choices for a New Era. 94p. 1988. 19.75 (*0-944237-23-1*); pap. 8.50 (*0-944237-24-X*) Ctr National Policy.
Muskie, Edmund S., jt. auth. see Bundy, McGeorge.
Muskrat, Bruce, tr. see McKinney, James C.
*__Muskrat, Nancy, des.__ Only the Best: Sacred Arrangements for the Advanced Pianist. 1995. 7.95 (*0-8341-9259-4*, MB-692) Lillenas.
Musladin, Judith M. & Lueke, Ada. The New Beagle. (Illus.). 288p. 1990. 25.95 (*0-87605-025-9*) Howell Bk.
Musleh-ud-Din, Muhammad. Crime & the Islamic Doctrine of Preventive Measures. 9.95 (*0-685-67613-7*) Kazi Pubns.
— Islamic Education, Its Forms & Features. 7.50 (*1-56744-094-0*) Kazi Pubns.
— Islamic Jurisprudence & the Rule of Necessity & Need. 9.95 (*1-56744-097-5*) Kazi Pubns.
Muslehuddin. Insurance & Islamic Law. pap. 4.95 (*1-56744-058-4*) Kazi Pubns.
Muslehuddin, Mohammad. Islamic Socialism: What It Implies. 100p. (C). 1985. pap. text ed. 4.50 (*1-56744-314-1*) Kazi Pubns.
— Sociology & Islam. 295p. 1985. pap. 4.00 (*1-56744-388-5*) Kazi Pubns.
Muslehuddin, Muhammad. Philosophy of Islamic Law & Orientalists. 300p. 1985. 19.95 (*1-56744-353-2*) Kazi Pubns.
Muslih, Muhammad. Toward Coexistence: An Analysis of the Resolutions of the Palestine National Council. LC 90-81685. (IPS Papers). 56p. (Orig.). (C). 1990. pap. text ed. 3.95 (*0-88728-210-5*) Inst Palestine.
Muslih, Muhammad & Norton, Augustus R. Political Tides in the Arab World. Hoepli, Nancy L., ed. LC 91-78231. (Headline Ser.: No. 296). (Illus.). 72p. (Orig.). 1992. pap. 5.95 (*0-87124-142-0*, 296) Foreign Policy.
Muslih, Muhammad Y. The Origins of Palestinian Nationalism. (Institute for Palestine Studies). 288p. 1989. text ed. 43.00 (*0-231-06508-6*); pap. text ed. 16.00 (*0-231-06509-4*) Col U Pr.
Muslim-Christian Research Group, GRIC Staff. The Challenge of the Scriptures: The Bible & the Qur'an. Brown, Stuart A., tr. LC 89-8828. (Faith Meets Faith Ser.). 112p. 1989. pap. 14.95 (*0-88344-650-2*) Orbis Bks.
Muslim, M. Sahih Muslim. Siddiqui, tr. 1613p. 1982. 80.00 (*0-318-37192-8*) Asia Bk Corp.
Muslim Students' Association Staff. Contemporary Aspects of Economic Thinking in Islam. 1976. pap. 2.75 (*0-89259-003-3*) Am Trust Pubns.
Muslim Student's Association Staff. The Educational Guide: A Handbook for Foreign Muslim Applicants to U. S. & Canadian Universities. 124p. (Orig.). Date not set. pap. 4.50 (*0-89259-150-1*) Am Trust Pubns.
Muslin, H. L. Lyndon Johnson: The Tragic Self - A Psychohistorical Portrait. LC 91-210. (Illus.). 250p. 1990. 23.95 (*0-306-43563-2*, Plenum Insight) Plenum.
Muslin, Hyman L. The Psychotherapy of the Elderly Self. LC 91-43419. 240p. 1992. 27.95 (*0-87630-657-1*) Brunner-Mazel.
Muslin, Hyman L. & Lewis, Jonathan D. The Art & Science of Patient Care. 140p. 1990. per. 28.95 (*0-8403-6299-4*) Kendall-Hunt.
Muslin, Hyman L. & Val, Eduardo R. The Psychotherapy of the Self. LC 87-6356. 232p. 1987. 27.95 (*0-87630-464-1*) Brunner-Mazel.
Musll, Thomas. Minnesota Supplement For Modern Real Estate Practice. 6th ed. 1990. pap. 12.95 (*0-7931-0101-8*, 1510-22) Dearborn Finan.
Musmann, Klaus. Technological Innovations in Libraries, 1860-1960: An Anecdotal History. LC 93-18143. (Contributions in Librarianship & Information Science Ser.: No. 73). 272p. 1993. text ed. 55.00 (*0-313-28015-0*, MTV, Greenwood Pr) Greenwood.
Musmanno, Michael A. Proposed Amendments to the Constitution: A Monograph on the Resolutions Introduced in Congress Proposing Amendments to the Constitution of the United States of America. LC 75-35374. (U. S. Government Documents Program Ser.). 253p. 1976. reprint ed. text ed. 59.75 (*0-8371-8610-2*, MUPAC) Greenwood.
Muso, Mark & Bondanella, Julia C. The Italian Renaissance Reader. 1987. pap. 9.95 (*0-452-00873-5*, Mer) NAL-Dutton.
Muson, Howard. Triumph of the American Spirit: Johnstown, Pennsylvania. (Johnstown Flood Museum Ser.). 1989. 43.00 (*0-8026-0032-8*) Univ Pub Assocs.
Musopole, Augustine C. Being Human in Africa: Toward an African Christian Anthropology. LC 93-14315. (Am. Univ. Studies, XI: Vol. 65). 261p. (Orig.). (C). 1994. text ed. 34.95 (*0-8204-2304-1*) P Lang Pubs.
Muss-Arnolt, William. A Concise Dictionary of the Assyrian Languages, 2 vols., Set. LC 78-72752. (Ancient Mesopotamian Texts & Studies). (AKK.). reprint ed. 97.50 (*0-404-18195-3*) AMS Pr.
Mussa, Michael L. Exchange Rates in Theory & in Reality. Riccardi, Margaret B., ed. LC 90-27127. (Essays in International Finance Ser.: No. 179). 46p. (Orig.). 1990. pap. text ed. 8.00 (*0-88165-086-2*) Princeton U Int Finan Econ.
Mussa, Michael L., jt. ed. see Frenkel, Jacob A.
Mussalam, Sami. The PLO-The Palestine Liberation Organization: Its Function & Structure. 70p. (Orig.). (C). 1988. pap. 6.95 (*0-915597-72-1*) Amana Bks.
Mussari, Mark. The Danish Americans. (Peoples of North America Ser.). (Illus.). 112p. (J). (gr. 5 up). 1988. lib. bdg. 17.95 (*0-87754-871-4*) Chelsea Hse.
— Suzanne De Passe: Motown's Boss Lady. Young, Richard G., ed. LC 91-28541. (Wizards of Business Ser.). (Illus.). 64p. (J). (gr. 4-8). 1992. lib. bdg. 17.26 (*1-56074-026-4*) Garrett Ed Corp.
*__Musschenga.__ Does Religion Matter Morally? 1993. pap. text ed. (*0-8028-6177-6*) Eerdmans.
Musse, jt. auth. see Eareckson, Joni.
*__Mussell, Barry D.__ The Roof Framers Bible: The Complete Pocket Reference to Roof Framing. LC 94-96225. (Illus.). 216p. (C). 1994. 18.95 (*0-9643354-0-9*) M E I.
Mussell, Harry & Staples, Richard C., eds. Stress Physiology in Crop Plants. 526p. (C). 1990. reprint ed. lib. bdg. 67.50 (*0-471-03809-1*) Krieger.
Mussell, Kay. Fantasy & Reconciliation: Contemporary Formulas of Women's Romance Fiction. LC 83-12731. (Contributions in Women's Studies: No. 46). 217p. 1984. text ed. 55.00 (*0-313-23915-0*, MFR/, Greenwood Pr) Greenwood.
— Women's Gothic & Romantic Fiction: A Reference Guide. LC 80-28683. (American Popular Culture Ser.). 176p. 1981. text ed. 42.95 (*0-313-21402-6*, MGF/, Greenwood Pr) Greenwood.
Mussell, Kay, jt. ed. see Brown, Linda K.
Musselman, Don, ed. O Ye Jigs & Juleps! (J). 1992. pap. 6.00 (*0-87602-315-4*) Anchorage.
Musselman, Eric P., jt. auth. see Anderson, Christian S.
Musselman, Homer D. Caroline, Light, Parker & Stafford Light Virginia Artillery. (Virginia Regimental Histories Ser.). (Illus.). 144p. 1992. 19.95 (*1-56190-036-2*) H E Howard.
— Forty-Seventh Virginia Infantry. (Virginia Regimental Histories Ser.). (Illus.). 172p. 1991. 19.95 (*1-56190-012-5*) H E Howard.
Musselman, James. Cadillac the Heartbreak of America: Fifteen Years of Consumer Disillusionment. 140p. (Orig.). 1988. pap. 12.95 (*0-9621259-0-3*) Essential Info Inc.
Musselman, L. Parasitic Weeds in Agriculture Striga, Vol. 1. LC 86-6139. 1986. 191.00 (*0-8493-6272-5*) CRC Pr.
Musselman, Vernon A., et al. Methods of Teaching Accounting, 2nd ed. (Illus.). (C). 1978. text ed. 31.00 (*0-07-044132-4*) McGraw.
Musselman, Vernon A., jt. auth. see Jackson, John H.
Musselwhite, Brian, jt. ed. see Burton, Lesley.
Musselwhite, Caroline R. Adaptive Play for Special Needs Children: Strategies to Enhance Communication & Learning. LC 90-52761. (Illus.). 249p. (C). 1986. pap. text ed. 27.00 (*0-89079-303-4*, 1751) PRO-ED.
Musselwhite, Caroline R. & St. Louis, Karen W. Communication Programming for Persons with Severe Handicaps: Vocal & Augmentative Strategies. 2nd ed. LC 90-21220. 395p. 1988. pap. text ed. 34.00 (*0-89079-388-3*, 1752) PRO-ED.
Musselwhite, Charlie, jt. auth. see Duncan, Phil.
Musselwhite, David. Partings Welded Together: Politics & Desire in the Nineteenth Century English Novel. 304p. 1987. text ed. 57.50 (*0-416-06162-1*); pap. text ed. 14.95 (*0-416-06172-9*) Routledge Chapman & Hall.
Mussen, Eric C. Beekeeping in California. LC 87-71574. (Illus.). 72p. (Orig.). 1987. pap. 3.50 (*0-931876-79-6*, 21422) ANR Pubns CA.

M

An Asterisk (*) at the beginning of an entry indicates that the title is appearing in BIP for the first time.

Mussen, Eric C., jt. ed. see Humphrey, Shirley.

Mussen, Paul & Rosenzweig, Mark R., eds. Annual Review of Psychology, Vol. 22. 1971. text ed. 40.00 (*0-8243-0222-2*) Annual Reviews.

— Annual Review of Psychology, Vol. 23. 1972. text ed. 40.00 (*0-8243-0223-0*) Annual Reviews.

Mussen, Paul, ed. see Eisenberg, Nancy.

Mussen, Paul, et al. Child Development & Personality. 7th ed. 688p. (C). 1989. text ed. 57.50 (*0-06-044695-1*) HarpCollege.

— Psychology: An Introduction, Brief Edition. (Illus.). 506p. (C). 1979. text ed. 28.00 (*0-669-01672-1*); Study guide. student ed 9.00 (*0-669-01681-0*); Instr.'s guide. teacher ed 2.00 (*0-669-01680-2*); Transparencies. trans. write for info. (*0-669-01682-9*) Heath.

Mussen, Paul H. Psychological Development of the Child. 3rd ed. (Foundations of Modern Psychology Ser.). (Illus.). 1979. text ed. 17.95 (*0-13-732420-0*) P-H.

Mussen, Paul H. & Rosenzweig, Mark R., eds. Annual Review of Psychology, Vol. 24. LC 50-13143. (Illus.). 1973. text ed. 40.00 (*0-8243-0224-9*) Annual Reviews.

Musser & Dick, eds. Precalculus Activities for the HP 28S. (Illus.). (Orig.). 1989. pap. text ed. 18.95 (*0-685-48358-4*, 2198) EduCALC Pubns.

Musser, Benjamin F. Franciscan Poets. LC 67-26768. (Essay Index Reprint Ser.). 1977. 19.95 (*0-8369-0732-9*) Ayer.

Musser, Charles. Before the Nickelodeon: Edwin S. Porter & the Edison Manufacturing Company. LC 90-11045. 1990. 65.00 (*0-520-06080-6*); pap. 32.00 (*0-520-06986-2*) U CA Pr.

— The Emergence of Cinema: The American Screen to 1907. LC 93-40205. 1994. 20.00 (*0-520-08533-7*) U CA Pr.

— History of the American Cinema, Vol. 1: The Emergence of Cinema: The American Screen to 1907. Harpole, Charles H. et al, eds. LC 90-48307. 613p. 1990. text ed. 65.00 (*0-684-18413-3*, Scribners) S&S Trade.

— Thomas A. Edison & His Kinetographic Motion Pictures. LC 93-96. 1993. Alk. paper. pap. 12.95 (*0-9634879-0-6*) Frnds of Edison.

— Thomas A. Edison & His Kinetoscopic Motion Pictures. (Illus.). 70p. (C). 1995. pap. 14.95 (*0-8135-2210-2*) Rutgers U Pr.

Musser, Charles & Nelson, Carol. High-Class Moving Pictures: Lyman H. Howe & the Forgotten Era of Traveling Exhibition, 1880-1920. (Illus.). 351p. 1991. text ed. 45.00 (*0-691-04781-2*) Princeton U Pr.

Musser, Charles, jt. ed. see Sklar, Robert.

Musser, David R. ADA Generic Library. 1989. 49.00 (*0-387-97133-5*, 3398) Spr-Verlag.

Musser, Donald W. & Price, Joseph L., eds. A New Handbook of Christian Theology. 544p. (Orig.). 1992. pap. 19.95 (*0-687-27802-3*) Abingdon.

Musser, Donald W., ed. see Murse.

***Musser, Edward G.** Designing Offsite Facilities by Use of Routing Diagrams. fac. ed. LC 83-5608. (Illus.). 78p. 1983. reprint ed. pap. 25.00 (*0-7837-8146-6*, 2047954) Bks Demand.

Musser, Frederic O. The History of Goucher College, 1930-1985. LC 89-35238. (Goucher College Ser.). (Illus.). 352p. 1990. text ed. 35.00x (*0-8018-3902-5*) Johns Hopkins.

Musser, Gary & Burger, William. Mathematics for Elementary Teachers. 3rd ed. 1120p. (C). 1994. text ed. write for info. (*0-02-385452-9*) Macmillan.

Musser, Gary L. & Trimpe, Lynn E. College Geometry: A Problem-Solving Approach with Applications. LC 93-39365. 592p. (C). 1994. text ed. write for info. (*0-02-385450-2*) Macmillan.

Musser, Guy G., jt. auth. see Robertson, Paul B.

Musser, Joe. Dilema De un Esceptico: A Skeptics Quest. (SPA.). 6.95 (*84-7645-315-9*, 223381, Pub. by Edit Clie SP) TSELF.

Musser, Joe, jt. auth. see Eareckson, Joni.

Musser, Joe, jt. auth. see Tada, Joni E.

Musser, John M. The Establishment of Maximilian's Empire in Mexico. 1976. lib. bdg. 59.95 (*0-8490-1789-0*) Gordon Pr.

Musser, Linda. God Is a Birdwatcher. Johnson, Joy, ed. (Illus.). 60p. 1991. pap. 6.50 (*1-56123-020-0*) Centering Corp.

Musser, Paul H. James Nelson Barker, Seventeen Eighty-Four to Eighteen Fifty-Eight: With a Reprint of His Comedy, Tears & Smiles. LC 71-94313. reprint ed. 29.50 (*0-404-04546-4*) AMS Pr.

— James Nelson Barker, 1784-1858: With a Reprint of His Comedy Tears & Smiles. LC 73-131785. 1971. 14.00 (*0-403-00672-4*) Scholarly.

— James Nelson Barker, 1784-1858: With a Reprint of His Comedy, Tears & Smiles. (BCL1-PS American Literature Ser.). 230p. 1992. reprint ed. lib. bdg. 79.00 (*0-7812-6673-4*) Rprt Serv.

Musser, Sandra K. I Would Have Searched Forever. Verica, Thomas, ed. LC 79-64955. 160p. 1992. reprint ed. pap. 11.95 (*0-934896-00-3*) Adopt Aware Pr.

— To Prison with Love: The True Story of Sandy Musser's Indecent Indictment & America's Adoption Travesty. Pesatrice, Terri, ed. (Illus.). 276p. (Orig.). 1995. pap. 14.95 (*0-934896-37-2*) Adopt Aware Pr.

— What Kind of Love Is This. Zimmerman, Steve, ed. LC 82-84236. (Orig.). 1982. pap. 7.95 (*0-934896-43-7*) Adopt Aware Pr.

Musset, Alfred. Comedies et Proverbes. Gastinel, Francis, ed. 376p. (FRE.). 1957. pap. 28.95 (*0-7859-4694-2*); pap. 28.95 (*0-7859-4695-0*) Fr & Eur.

— Comedies et Proverbes, Vol. 1. Gastinel, Francis, ed. 376p. (FRE.). 1957. pap. 28.95 (*0-7859-4696-9*) Fr & Eur.

— Comedies et Proverbes, Vol. 2: On ne Badine pas avec l'Amour, Lorenzaccio. (FRE.). 1985. pap. 8.95 (*0-7859-4699-3*) Fr & Eur.

— Comedies et Proverbes, Vol. 3: Le Chandelier, Il ne Faut Jurer de Rein. 2nd ed. 127p. (FRE.). 1985. pap. 8.95 (*0-7859-4700-0*) Fr & Eur.

— Comedies et Proverbes, Vol. 4: Louison, on ne Saurait Penser a Tout. 128p. (FRE.). 1985. pap. 8.95 (*0-7859-4698-5*) Fr & Eur.

— Lorenzaccio. (Illus.). (FRE.). 1964. pap. 10.95 (*0-8288-9647-X*, M2487) Fr & Eur.

— Oeuvres Completes, 12 vols., Set. (Illus.). 300p. (FRE.). 1969. 1,995.00 (*0-8288-9648-8*, F69130) Fr & Eur.

— On ne Badine Pas avec l'Amour. 159p. (FRE.). 1992. Text plus 2 cassettes. audio 49.95 (*0-7859-0582-0*); pap. 10.95 (*0-7859-1258-4*, 2038713448) Fr & Eur.

— Premieres Poesies 1829-1835. Allem, Maurice, ed. 338p. (FRE.). 1958. 29.95 (*0-8288-9649-6*, F69060) Fr & Eur.

— Theatre, Vol. 3. 512p. (FRE.). 1964. 10.95 (*0-8288-9650-X*, FC1473) Fr & Eur.

— Theatre, Vol. 1: Avec: Les Marrons de feu, La Nuit Ventienne, La Coup et les Levres, A quoi revent les Jeunes Filles, Andre del Sorto, Les Caprices de Marianne. 448p. (FRE.). 1964. 10.95 (*0-8288-9652-6*, FC1471) Fr & Eur.

— Theatre, Vol. 2: Avec: Le Quenouille de Barberine, Le Chandelier, Il Ne Faut Jurer de Rein, Un Caprice, Il Faut Qu'Une Port Soit Ouverte ou Fermee. Rat, Maurice, ed. 448p. (FRE.). 1964. 10.95 (*0-8288-9651-8*, FC1472) Fr & Eur.

Musset, Alfred de. Oeuvres Completes, Vol. 1. Allem, Maurice, ed. 972p. (FRE.). 1933. lib. bdg. 105.00 (*0-7859-3770-6*, 2070103870) Fr & Eur.

— Oeuvres Completes, Vol. 3. Allem, Maurice, ed. 1344p. (FRE.). 1938. lib. bdg. 105.00 (*0-7859-3771-4*, 2070103897) Fr & Eur.

Mussett, A. E., jt. auth. see Brown, Geoffrey C.

Mussett, Alan E., jt. auth. see Brown, Geoffrey C.

Mussey, Robert D., Jr., ed. The First American Furniture Finisher's Manual: A Reprint of "The Cabinetmaker's Guide" of 1827. 160p. 1987. reprint ed. pap. 4.95 (*0-486-25530-1*) Dover.

Mussiett, Salomon, ed. Musica para Ocasiones Especiales - Music for Special Occasions. 48p. (Orig.). (SPA.). 1993. pap. 4.25 (*0-311-32219-0*) Casa Bautista.

Mussiett, Salomon C., tr. see Nelson, Edward W.

Mussiett, Salomon R., ed. Cancionero para Preescolares. 54p. (SPA.). (J). (ps). 1989. pap. 3.50 (*0-311-32226-3*) Casa Bautista.

Mussinan, Cynthia J. & Keelan, Mary E., eds. Sulfur Compounds in Foods. LC 94-20826. (ACS Symposium Ser.: Vol. 564). 1994. 79.95 (*0-8412-2943-0*) Am Chemical.

Mussington, David. Arms Unbound: The Globalization of Defense Production. (CSIA Studies in International Security Ser.). 150p. 1994. pap. 14.95x (*0-02-881089-9*) Brasseys Inc.

Mussini, Gianni, jt. ed. see Marchione, Margherita.

Mussman, Robert B. The Candle of the Lord. 1992. pap. 5.99 (*0-88019-292-5*) Schmul Pub Co.

Mussmann, Linda. Room - Raum. Schelbert, Tarcisi & Rappolt, Hedwig, trs. LC 81-51013. 107p. (Orig.). 1981. pap. 6.00 (*0-939858-00-2*) T S L Pr.

Musso, Louis, III. Theodore Roosevelt, Soldier, Statesman & President. Rahmas, Sigurd C., ed. (Outstanding Personalities Ser.: No. 90). 32p. (gr. 7-12). 1982. 4.95 (*0-87157-590-6*) SamHar Pr.

Musso, Van A. How to Retire Rich & Stay Rich: A Financial Road Map to Success. (Illus.). 248p. (Orig.). 1994. 24.95 (*0-9639484-1-5*); pap. 14.95 (*0-9639484-0-7*) V Musso Ent.

***Mussolini.** My Autobiography. 1928. 15.25 (*0-8371-4294-6*) Greenwood.

Mussolini, Benito. The Corporate State. 1976. lib. bdg. 59.95 (*0-8490-1675-4*) Gordon Pr.

— Memoirs, Nineteen Forty-two to Nineteen Forty-three. Klibansky, Raymond, ed. Lobb, Frances, tr. xxviii, 320p. 1975. reprint ed. 45.00 (*0-86527-126-7*) Fertig.

— The Political & Social Doctrine of Fascism. 1976. 250.00 (*0-87968-434-8*) Gordon Pr.

— Talks with Mussolini. Paul, Eden & Paul, Cedar, trs. LC 78-63699. (Studies in Fascism: Ideology & Practice). (Illus.). 256p. reprint ed. 32.00 (*0-404-16968-6*) AMS Pr.

Musson, A. E. The Growth of British Industry. LC 78-178. 396p. 1978. 45.00 (*0-8419-0367-0*) Holmes & Meier.

Musson, A. E. & Robinson, E., eds. Science & Technology in the Industrial Revolution. xii, 534p. 1969. pap. text ed. 46.00 (*2-88124-382-7*) Gordon & Breach.

Musson, Albert E. Enterprise in Soap & Chemicals: Joseph Crosfield & Sons, Ltd., 1815-1865. LC 68-431. (Illus.). xi, 384p. 1967. 45.00 (*0-678-06763-5*) Kelley.

Musson, Cyril D., jt. auth. see Musson, Gloria J.

Musson, David, jt. ed. see Eve, Martin.

Musson, Gloria J. & Musson, Cyril D. RAPmetic, the Arithmetic Rap. (Illus.). 48p. (Orig.). (J). (gr. 3 up). 1988. pap. text ed. 3.50 (*0-9619321-0-4*); audio 6.50 (*0-9619321-1-2*) Sq One Pubns.

Musson, H. E. Trade Union & Social History. 224p. 1974. 37.50 (*0-7146-3031-4*, Pub. by F Cass Pubs UK) Intl Spec Bk.

***Musson, Jean.** A Distant Dream. large type ed. (Romance Ser.). 1994. pap. 14.95 (*0-7089-7620-4*, Linford) Ulverscroft.

— Silk Domino. (Rainbow Romances Ser.). 160p. 1993. 14.95 (*0-7090-4924-2*, Hale-Parkwest) Parkwest Pubns.

— Silk Domino. large type ed. (Romance Ser.). 1994. pap. 14.95 (*0-7089-7609-3*, Linford) Ulverscroft.

Musson, John. Evil - Is It Real? A Theological Analysis. LC 91-34921. (Toronto Studies in Theology: Vol. 61). 168p. 1991. lib. bdg. 79.95 (*0-7734-9654-8*) E Mellen.

Musson, Steve & Gibbons, Maurice. The New Youth Challenge: A Model for Working with Older Children in School-Age Child Care. (Illus.). 107p. (Orig.). (C). 1988. pap. text ed. 12.95 (*0-917505-02-6*) School Age.

Mussorgsky, Modeste. Boris Godunov. John, Nicholas, ed. Lloyd-Jones, David, tr. (English National Opera Guide Series: Bilingual Libretto, Articles: No. 11). (Illus.). 128p. (Orig.). 1982. pap. 9.95 (*0-7145-3922-8*) Riverrun NY.

— Boris Godunov: Full Score in Three Languages. Lloyd-Jones, David, ed. & tr. by. Hube, Max, tr. (ENG, GER & RUS.). 1976. boxed 250.00 (*0-19-337699-7*) OUP.

— Boris Godunov: Full Score in Three Languages. Lloyd-Jones, David, ed. & tr. by. Hube, Max, tr. (ENG, GER & RUS.). 1976. pap. 125.00 (*0-19-337700-4*) OUP.

Must, Art, ed. Why We Still Need Public Schools: Church - State Relations & Visions of Democracy. 311p. (Orig.). (C). 1992. pap. 17.95 (*0-87975-758-2*) Prometheus Bks.

Mustacchi, Marianna M. & Archambault, Paul J., eds. A Renaissance Woman: Helisenne's Personal & Invective Letters. Arcambault, Paul J., tr. 96p. (Orig.). 1986. text ed. 29.95 (*0-8156-2347-X*) Syracuse U Pr.

Mustachio, Thomas, jt. auth. see Dyches, Richard.

Mustacich, Suzanne. Nutshell Classics: A Doll's House. 1988. pap. text ed. 40.00 (*0-938735-50-0*) Classic Theatre Schl.

— Nutshell Classics: Cyrano de Bergerac, Set. 1988. Regular set. pap. text ed. 150.00 (*0-938735-52-7*); Small set. pap. text ed. 100.00 (*0-938735-53-5*) Classic Theatre Schl.

Mustafa. Plastics Waste Management: Disposal, Recycling, & Reuse. (Environmental Science & Pollution Ser.: Vol. 5). 432p. 1993. 150.00 (*0-8247-8920-2*) Dekker.

Mustafa, D. & Glover, K. Minimum Entropy H Control. Thoma, M. & Wyner, A., eds. (Lecture Notes in Control & Information Sciences Ser.: Vol. 146). (Illus.). ix, 144p. 1990. pap. 34.00 (*0-387-52947-0*) Spr-Verlag.

***Mustafa, Fawzia.** V. S. Naipaul. (Studies in African & Caribbean Literature: No. 4). 245p. (C). Date not set. write for info. (*0-521-40378-2*) Cambridge U Pr.

— V. S. Naipaul. (Studies in African & Caribbean Literature: No. 4). 245p. (C). 1995. write for info. (*0-521-48359-X*) Cambridge U Pr.

Mustafa, Husain. Postal Technology & Management. LC 73-165579. (Illus.). 240p. 1971. 23.50 (*0-912338-01-6*); fiche 9.50 (*0-912338-02-4*) Lomond.

***Mustafa, M. A.** Microcomputer Interfacing & Applications. 2nd ed. (Illus.). 432p. 1995. pap. 47.95 (*0-7506-1752-7*) Buttrwrth-Heinemann.

Mustafi, C. K. Operations Research Method & Practice. (C). 1988. pap. 20.00 (*81-224-0054-X*, Pub. by Wiley Eastern II) S Asia.

Mustain, Gene, jt. auth. see Capeci, Jerry.

Mustajoki, A. & Nikkila, E. Venajaa Opiskelevan Sanakirja Venaja-Suomi. 534p. (FIN & RUS.). 1982. 49.95 (*0-8288-1076-1*, F 85800) Fr & Eur.

Mustapha, Samina, ed. see Ghazi, Tasneema.

Mustard, Andrews G. James White & SDA Organization: Historical Development 1844-1881. (Andrews University Seminary Doctoral Dissertation Ser.: Vol. 12). 328p. 1988. pap. 19.99 (*0-943872-46-4*) Andrews Univ Pr.

Mustard, Helen M. & Merwin, W. S., trs. Medieval Epics. LC 63-7651. 1978. 14.95 (*0-394-60455-5*, Modern Lib) Random.

Mustard, J. Fraser, jt. ed. see Yamazaki, Hiroh.

Mustard, W. P. Classical Echoes in Tennyson. LC 72-116798. (Studies in Tennyson: No. 27). 1970. reprint ed. lib. bdg. 49.95 (*0-8383-1040-0*) M S G Haskell Hse.

Mustarde, John C., ed. Repair & Reconstruction in the Orbital Region. 3rd ed. (Illus.). 565p. 1991. text ed. 175.00 (*0-443-04023-0*) Churchill.

***Mustazza, Leonard.** The Critical Response to Kurt Vonnegut. LC 94-29147. (Critical Responses Ser.). 384p. 1994. text ed. 59.95 (*0-313-28634-5*) Greenwood.

— Forever Pursuing Genesis: The Myth of Eden in the Novels of Kurt Vonnegut. LC 89-46407. 224p. 1991. 37.50 (*0-8387-5176-8*) Bucknell U Pr.

— Such Prompt Eloquence: Language As Agency & Character in Milton's Epics. LC 86-48007. 176p. 1988. 32.50 (*0-8387-5121-0*) Bucknell U Pr.

Mustazza, Leonard, jt. auth. see Petkov, Steven.

Muste, A. J. Of Holy Disobedience. 23p. (Orig.). 1964. pap. 1.25 (*0-934676-09-7*) Greenlf Bks.

— Of Holy Disobedience. LC 52-1568. (Orig.). 1952. pap. 3.00 (*0-87574-064-2*) Pendle Hill.

— Saints for This Age. LC 62-21962. (Orig.). 1962. pap. 3.00 (*0-87574-124-X*) Pendle Hill.

— War is the Enemy. (C). 1942. pap. 3.00 (*0-87574-015-4*) Pendle Hill.

— The World Task of Pacifism. (C). 1942. pap. 3.00 (*0-87574-013-8*) Pendle Hill.

Musteata, Boris. How to Use CICS to Create On-Line Applications: Methods & Solutions. 546p. 1993. pap. text ed. 39.95 (*0-471-58434-7*) Wiley.

Musteikus, Antanas. The Reformation in Lithuania: Religious Fluctuations in the Sixteenth Century. (East European Monographs: No. 246). 160p. 1988. text ed. 30.00 (*0-88033-143-7*) East Eur Quarterly.

Mustelier, Evelio, pseud. Kid Tunero: Veinte Anos de Ring.. .y Fuera. (Illus.). 119p. (Orig.). (SPA.). 1987. pap. 5.00 (*84-359-0390-7*, Pub. by Editorial Playor SP) Ediciones.

Mustelin, Tomas. Src Family of Tyrosine Kinases in Leukocytes. (Molecular Biology Intelligence Unit Ser.). 118p. 1994. 89.95 (*1-57059-113-X*, LN9113) R G Landes.

Muster, D., ed. Interfaces in Biomaterials Sciences: Proceedings of Symposium E, European-Materials Research Society Symposia, Strasbourg, France, 30 May-2 June, 1989, No. 13. 220p. 1990. 97.25 (*0-444-88836-5*, North Holland) Elsevier.

Muster, D., et al, eds. Biomaterials: Hard Tissue Repair & Replacement. LC 92-22652. 1992. write for info. (*0-444-88350-9*, North Holland) Elsevier.

Muster, John. UNIX Made Easy. 1990. pap. text ed. 24.95 (*0-07-881576-2*) Osborne-McGraw.

Musterman, Jack L., jt. auth. see Eckenfelder, W. W.

Mustill, Lord & Boyd, Stewart C. Commercial Arbitration. 2nd ed. 836p. 1989. boxed 220.00 (*0-406-31124-2*, UK) Butterworth Legal Pubs.

Mustill, Norman O. Twinpak. (Nova Broadcast Ser.: No. 6). (Illus.). (Orig.). 1969. 4.50 (*0-89366-021-3*) Ultramarine Pub.

Mustin, Bob. The Children of Light. (Illus.). 32p. (Orig.). 1992. pap. text ed. 6.95 (*1-56315-065-4*) Sterling Hse.

Mustin, Henry C. Surveying Fiberglass Sailboats: A Step-by-Step Guide for Buyers & Owners. 1993. pap. text ed. 17.95 (*0-87742-347-4*) Intl Marine.

— Surveying Fiberglass Sailboats: A Step by Step Guide for Buyers & Owners. 1994. pap. text ed. 17.95 (*0-07-044248-7*) McGraw.

Musto, David F. The American Disease: Origins of Narcotic Control. enl. ed. 400p. 1988. pap. 14.95 (*0-19-505211-0*) OUP.

— The American Disease: Origins of Narcotic Control. LC 72-75204. 368p. reprint ed. pap. 104.90 (*0-8357-8018-X*, 2033838) Bks Demand.

Musto, Frederick W., jt. auth. see Goehlert, Robert U.

Musto, Ken. Breaking into Advertising: Making Your Portfolio Work for You. (Illus.). 144p. 1988. pap. 19.95 (*0-442-26432-1*) Van Nos Reinhold.

Musto, Michael. Downtown. 1986. 10.95 (*0-317-53541-2*, Vin) Random.

Musto, Ronald G. Liberation Theologies: A Research Guide. annot. ed. LC 90-29156. 632p. 1991. 70.00 (*0-8240-3624-7*, SS507) Garland.

Musto, Ronald G., ed. Catholic Peacemakers: A Collection of Readings, 2 vols. LC 92-42658. (Illus.). 864p. 1993. Vol. 2, From the Renaissance to the Twentieth Century, 450p. 95.00 (*0-8153-0605-9*, H1372) Garland.

— Catholic Peacemakers: A Collection of Readings, 2 vols., Set. LC 92-42658. (Illus.). 864p. 1993. 170.00 (*0-8240-7388-6*) Garland.

— Catholic Peacemakers: A Collection of Readings, 2 vols., Vol. 1: From the Bible to the Crusades. LC 92-42658. (Illus.). 350p. 1993. Vol. 1, From the Bible to the Crusades, 350p. 95.00 (*0-8153-0604-0*, H1346) Garland.

Musto, Ronald G., jt. ed. see Monfasani, John.

Musto, Ronald G., ed. see Petrarca, Francisco.

Musto, Stefan A. & Pinkele, Carl F. Europe at the Crossroads. LC 82-16658. 368p. 1985. text ed. 65.00 (*0-275-90147-5*, C0147, Praeger Pubs) Greenwood.

Mustoe, Julian E. An Atlas of Renewable Energy Resources: In the United Kingdom & North America. LC 83-10301. 202p. 1984. text ed. 162.95 (*0-471-10293-8*, Wiley-Interscience) Wiley.

Mustoe, L. R. Worked Examples in Advanced Engineering Mathematics. LC 88-2058. 137p. 1988. pap. text ed. 42.95 (*0-471-91951-9*) Wiley.

Mustoe, M. Myles. Shortwave Goes to School: A Teacher's Guide to Using Shortwave in the Classroom. 60p. (Orig.). 1989. pap. 24.95 (*0-936653-17-5*) Tiare Pubns.

Muston, Alexis. The Israel of the Alps: A Complete History of the Waldenses & Their Colonies, 2 vols. Montgomery, John, tr. LC 77-84718. reprint ed. 84.50 (*0-404-16140-5*) AMS Pr.

Mustoo, Terence. Sherlock Holmes in The Deerstalker: Chameleons' Dramascripts. 50p. (Orig.). 1991. pap. 8.00 (*0-86025-886-6*) Players Pr.

Mustric, Florence, jt. auth. see Becker, Hal.

Musu-Boy, R. Dizionario Italiano-Inglese, Inglese-Italiano: Italian-English, English-Italian Dictionary. deluxe ed. 463p. (ENG & ITA.). 1979. 9.95 (*0-8288-4732-0*, M9177) Fr & Eur.

Musumeci, D. Il Carciofo: Strategie di Lettura e Proposte di Attivia. 1990. pap. text ed. write for info. (*0-07-557836-0*) McGraw.

Musun, Chris. Peeps & Freaks. LC 85-73404. 446p. (Orig.). 1986. pap. 3.95 (*0-936729-01-5*) Dare Co.

— The White House Sucks. (Orig.). 1986. pap. 8.95 (*0-936729-00-7*) Dare Co.

Musurillo, Herbert A. Symbol & Myth in Ancient Poetry. LC 77-2395. 220p. 1977. reprint ed. text ed. 55.00 (*0-8371-9554-3*, MUSM, Greenwood Pr) Greenwood.

Musurillo, Herbertus, ed. Gregorii Nysseni De Vita Moysis. LC 90-21633. (Gregorius Nyssenus Opera Ser.: No. VII,1). xx, 145p. (GRE & LAT.). 1991. reprint ed. 68.75 (*90-04-00747-4*) E J Brill.

Musvosvi, Joel N. Vengeance in the Apocalypse. (Andrews University Seminary Doctoral Dissertation Ser.: Vol. 17). 305p. 1993. pap. 16.95 (*0-943872-48-0*) Andrews Univ Pr.

Musyoki, Agnes. An Elementary Swahili Newspaper Reader. LC 85-70271. viii, 201p. 1985. text ed. 39.00 (*0-931745-07-1*); audio 15.00 (*0-931745-15-2*) Dunwoody Pr.

Muszynska, J., jt. auth. see Fraga, S.

Muta, T. Foundations of Quantum Chromodynamics: An Introduction to Perturbative Methods in Theories. 424p. 1987. text ed. 97.00 (*9971-950-40-5*); pap. text ed. 44.00 (*9971-950-41-3*) World Scientific Pub.

Muta, T. & Yamawaki, K. Strong Coupling Gauge Theories & Beyond: The 2nd International Workshop. 500p. 1991. text ed. 118.00 (*981-02-0424-8*) World Scientific Pub.

Mutaftschiev, B. Interfacial Aspects of Phase Transformation. 1982. lib. bdg. 172.50 (*90-277-1440-1*) Kluwer Ac.

Mutahaba, Gelase. Reforming Public Administration for Development: Experiences from Eastern Africa. LC 89-24550. (Library of Management for Development). xv, 183p. 1989. pap. 24.50 (*0-931816-93-9*) Kumarian Pr.

An Asterisk (*) at the beginning of an entry indicates that the title is appearing in BIP for the first time.

Mutahaba, Gelase & Balogun, M. Jide, eds. Enhancing Policy Management Capacity in Africa. LC 91-47066. (Library of Management for Development; New Directions in Development management). (Illus.). xi, 194p. 1992. pap. 15.95 (*1-56549-007-X*) Kumarian Pr.

Mutahaba, Gelase, ed. see Alfani, Mohamed.

Mutahaba, Gelase, jt. ed. see Balogun, M. Jide.

Mutahhari, Ayatullah M. Fundamentals of Islamic Thought: God, Man & the Universe. Algar, Hamid, ed. Campbell, R., tr. LC 85-15446. (Contemporary Islamic Thought, Persian Ser.). Orig. Title: Per. 231p. (Orig.). 1985. pap. 9.95 (*0-933782-15-2*) Mizan Pr.

— Social & Historical Change: An Islamic Perspective. Algar, Hamid, ed. Campbell, R., tr. LC 85-28554. (Contemporary Islamic Thought, Persian Ser.). 156p. (C). 1986. 19.95 (*0-933782-18-7*); pap. 9.95 (*0-933782-19-5*) Mizan Pr.

Mutahhari, Morteza. The Martyr. Yasin, A., tr. 28p. pap. 2.00 (*0-941722-07-4*) Book Dist Ctr.

Mutahhari, Murtaza. Islamic Hijab Modest Dress. Bakhtiar, Laleh, tr. 112p. (C). 1993. pap. 9.95 (*1-871031-15-X*) Abjad Bk.

— The Islamic Modest Dress. Bukhtiar, Laleh, tr. 1990. 12.00 (*0-685-66737-5*, 42) Tahrike Tarsile Quran.

— Islamic Mysticism (Irfan) An Introduction. Qara'i, Ali Q., tr. 64p. 1989. pap. text ed. 4.50 (*1-871031-34-6*) Abjad Bk.

— The Universal Prototype: An Islamic Perspective. Bakhtiar, Laleh, tr. 112p. (Orig.). (C). 1989. pap. 10.00 (*1-871031-04-4*) Abjad Bk.

Mutahheri, Murtaza. Man & His Destiny. rev. ed. Islamic Seminary Staff, tr. 124p. (C). 1985. reprint ed. pap. 4.00 (*0-941724-39-5*) Islamic Seminary.

— Man & Universe: Mugaddamai Bar Jahan Bin'i Islami. rev. ed. Islamic Seminary Staff, tr. 663p. (C). reprint ed. text ed. 18.00 (*0-941724-52-2*) Islamic Seminary.

Mutahhery, Murtaza. Master & Mastership: Wila Wa Wilayat. rev. ed. Islamic Seminary Staff & Ansari, M. A., trs. 131p. (C). 1983. reprint ed. pap. 4.00 (*0-941724-15-8*) Islamic Seminary.

Mutahhery, Murtaza, et al. Rationality of Islam. rev. ed. Islamic Seminary Staff & Ansari, M. A., trs. 182p. (C). 1990. reprint ed. pap. 7.00 (*0-941724-17-4*) Islamic Seminary.

Mutalib, Hussin. Islam & Ethnicity in Malay Politics. (South-East Asian Social Science Monographs). (Illus.). 230p. 1990. 38.00 (*0-19-588935-5*) OUP.

Mutalib, Hussin & Hashmi, Taj U., eds. Islam, Muslims, & the Modern State. LC 93-24000. 1994. text ed. 69.95 (*0-312-10300-X*) St Martin.

Mutalik-Desai, A. A., jt. ed. see Kamath, P. M.

Mutambirwa, James A. The Rise of Settler Power in Southern Rhodesia (Zimbabwe) 1898-1923. LC 78-75181. 248p. 1970. 34.50 (*0-8386-2267-4*) Fairleigh Dickinson.

Mutatkar, R. K. Caste Dimensions in Village. 189p. 1978. 9.95 (*0-318-36799-8*) Asia Bk Corp.

Mutawakil, G. Business & Law in Saudi Arabia. 220p. (C). 1990. 125.00 (*0-907151-18-3*, Pub. by IMMEL Pubng UK) St Mut.

Mutch, Robert E. Campaigns, Congress & the Courts: The Making of Federal Campaign Finance Laws. LC 87-30874. 237p. 1988. text ed. 49.95 (*0-275-92784-9*, C2784, Praeger Pubs) Greenwood.

***Mutch, Thomas A.** Geology of the Moon: A Stratigraphic View. rev. ed. LC 70-39387. Date not set. pap. 114.90 (*0-7837-9398-7*, 2060143) Bks Demand.

— Geology of the Moon: A Stratigraphic View. rev. ed. LC 79-83687. 1973. 85.00x (*0-691-08110-7*) Princeton U Pr.

Mutch, Thomas A., et al. The Geology of Mars. LC 75-30199. (Illus.). 436p. 1976. 90.00 (*0-691-08173-5*) Princeton U Pr.

— The Geology of Mars. LC 75-30199. (Illus.). 410p. reprint ed. pap. 116.90 (*0-7837-1943-4*, 2042158) Bks Demand.

Mutch, William A., ed. Film Goers Annual of 1932. 1976. lib. bdg. 88.95 (*0-8490-1833-1*) Gordon Pr.

Mutchler, Augusta. Five Acres & Dementia. LC 82-73293. (Illus.). 96p. 1983. pap. 8.95 (*0-931722-18-7*) Corona Pub.

Mutchler, David G. The Deeper Reaches of Love & Fear: The Birth of a New Psychology. 250p. 1989. 18.95 (*0-922639-00-0*) Lakeshore Counsel.

Mutchler, David G., jt. auth. see Bleech, James M.

***Mutchnick, Robert J. & Berg, Bruce L.** Research Methods for the Social Sciences: Practice & Applications. LC 95-11824. 1995. write for info. (*0-02-385451-0*) Allyn.

Mutel, C. F. & Donham, K. J. Medical Practice in Rural Communities. (Illus.). 168p. 1983. 58.00 (*0-387-91224-X*) Spr-Verlag.

Mutel, Cornelia F. Fragile Giants: A Natural History of the Loess Hills. LC 89-35497. (Bur Oak Original Ser.). (Illus.). 304p. 1989. pap. 17.95 (*0-87745-257-1*) U of Iowa Pr.

— Tropical Rain Forests: Our Endangered Planet. (J). (gr. 4 up). 1993. pap. 8.95 (*0-8225-9629-6*, Lerner Publctns) Lerner Group.

***Mutel, Cornelia F. & Rodgers, Mary M.** Nuestro Planeta en Peligro: Las Selvas Tropicales. (Illus.). 64p. (SPA.). (YA). (gr. 5 up). 1994. 21.50 (*0-8225-2005-2*, Carolrhoda) Lerner Group.

Mutel, Cornelia F. & Swander, Mary, eds. Land of the Fragile Giants: Landscapes, Environments, & Peoples of the Loess Hills. LC 94-14909. (Bur Oak Original Ser.). (Illus.). 168p. (Orig.). 1994. pap. 24.95 (*0-87745-477-9*) U of Iowa Pr.

Mutel, Cornelia F., et al. From Grassland to Glacier: The Natural History of Colorado and the Surrounding Region. rev. ed. LC 84-80539. (Illus.). 280p. 1992. pap. 12.95 (*1-55566-089-4*) Johnson Bks.

Muten, Burleigh, ed. Return of the Great Goddess. LC 94-6189. 1994. 20.00 (*1-57062-034-2*) Shambhala Pubns.

Muterthies. Esthetic Approach to Metal Ceramic Restorations for the Mandibular Anterior Region. (Illus.). 94p. 1990. text ed. 54.00 (*1-85097-016-5*) Quint Pub Co.

Muterthies, Klaus. Replication of Anterior Teeth in the Four Seasons of Life. (Illus.). 92p. 1991. text ed. 62.00 (*1-85097-023-8*) Quint Pub Co.

Muth, jt. auth. see DeMatteis, J. M.

Muth, James. The Why of Life: Answers Beyond Organized Religion. Westheimer, Mary, ed. 112p. (Orig.). 1994. pap. 6.95 (*1-885001-02-9*) Via Press.

Muth, John F., jt. auth. see Groff, Gene K.

Muth, Jon, jt. auth. see Lang, Fritz.

Muth, Jon J. Dracula: A Symphony in Moonlight & Nightmares. (Illus.). 80p. 1986. 7.95 (*0-87135-171-4*) Marvel Entmnt.

— Dracula: A Symphony in Moonlight & Nightmares. 80p. 1993. 45.00 (*1-56163-060-8*); pap. 11.95 (*1-56163-059-4*) NBM.

— Mythology of an Abandoned City. Baisden, Greg, ed. (Illus.). 56p. 1992. reprint ed. 9.95 (*1-879450-56-9*) Tundra MA.

Muth, K. Denise, ed. Children's Comprehension of Text: Research into Practice. LC 88-34806. 288p. reprint ed. pap. 82.10 (*0-7837-5990-8*, 2045799) Bks Demand.

Muth, K. Denise & Alvermann, Donna E. Teaching & Learning in the Middle Grades. 448p. (C). 1992. text ed. 54.00 (*0-205-13302-9*) Allyn.

Muth, Marcia. How to Paint & Sell Your Art. LC 83-18252. 76p. (Orig.). 1984. pap. 8.95 (*0-86534-019-6*) Sunstone Pr.

— Indian Pottery of the Southwest: A Selected Bibliography. LC 90-9870. (Illus.). 64p. (Orig.). 1991. pap. 6.95 (*0-86534-067-6*) Sunstone Pr.

— Is It Safe to Drink the Water? A Guide to Santa Fe. LC 83-9212. 32p. 1983. pap. 2.95 (*0-86534-036-6*) Sunstone Pr.

— Kachinas: A Selected Bibliography. LC 83-18302. 32p. (Orig.). 1984. pap. 4.95 (*0-86534-031-5*) Sunstone Pr.

— Sticks & Stones & Other Poems. 32p. (Orig.). 1994. pap. 4.95 (*0-86534-214-8*) Sunstone Pr.

— Thin Ice & Other Poems. LC 85-27958. 48p. (Orig.). 1987. pap. 4.95 (*0-86534-081-1*) Sunstone Pr.

— Writing & Selling Poetry, Fiction, Articles, Plays & Local History. LC 85-490. 96p. (Orig.). 1985. pap. 8.95 (*0-86534-048-X*) Sunstone Pr.

Muth, Marcia, ed. see Boyce, George A.

Muth, R. F., jt. auth. see Goodman, A. C.

Muth, Rodney, et al, eds. Harold D. Lasswell: An Annotated Bibliography. (C). 1990. lib. bdg. 144.00 (*0-7923-0018-1*) Kluwer Ac.

Muth, Thomas A. State Interest in Cable Communications. Sterling, Christopher H., ed. LC 78-21728. (Dissertations in Broadcasting Ser.). 1980. lib. bdg. 30.95 (*0-405-11767-1*) Ayer.

Muthe, Norma C. Endocrinology: A Nursing Approach. 1981. pap. 13.00 (*0-316-59160-2*) Little.

Muthen, Bengt O. Liscomp: Analysis of Linear Structural Equations with a Comprehensive Measurement Model. 2nd ed. 1988. ring bd. 30.00 (*0-89498-016-5*) Sci Ware.

Muther, et al. Consultation in Nephrology. 336p. (C). 1990. 32.00 (*1-55664-048-X*) Mosby Yr Bk.

Muther, Richard. Creating Personal Success. LC 86-60274. 1986. 10.00 (*0-933684-05-3*) Mgmt & Indus Res Pubns.

— Leaders Guide & Casebook for Simplified S.L.P. (Supporting Simplified Systematic Layout Planning Ser.). (Illus.). 130p. (C). 1994. ring bd. 236.00 (*0-933684-10-X*) Mgmt & Indus Res Pubns.

— Systematic Layout Planning (SLP) 2nd ed. (Illus.). 485p. (C). 1987. reprint ed. pap. 37.75 (*0-933684-06-1*) Mgmt & Indus Res Pubns.

Muther, Richard & Haganas, Knut. Systematic Handling Analysis (SHA) 1988. reprint ed. 26.95 (*0-933684-03-7*) Mgmt & Indus Res Pubns.

Muther, Richard & Hales, Lee. Systematic Planning of Industrial Facilities, 2 vols, Vol. I. LC 79-84256. 1979. Vol I, 1979. 18.00 (*0-933684-01-0*) Mgmt & Indus Res Pubns.

Muther, Richard & Wheeler, J. D. Simplified Systematic Layout Planning. 1962. 8.00 (*0-933684-04-5*) Mgmt & Indus Res Pubns.

— Simplified Systematic Layout Planning. 3rd ed. (Illus.). 36p. (C). 1994. pap. 12.00 (*0-933684-09-6*) Mgmt & Indus Res Pubns.

Muther, Richard, et al. High Performance Planning: A Guide to Planning Anything. 2nd ed. Orig. Title: Planning in a Nutshell. (Illus.). 135p. (Orig.). 1988. pap. text ed. 18.00 (*0-933684-08-8*) Mgmt & Indus Res Pubns.

— Simplified Systematic Handling Analysis. 3rd ed. (Illus.). 24p. (C). 1994. pap. 12.00 (*0-933684-11-8*) Mgmt & Indus Res Pubns.

Mutherich, Florentine & Gaehde, J. E. Carolingian Painting. LC 76-15908. 127p. 1977. pap. 11.95 (*0-8076-0852-1*) Braziller.

Muthesius, Hermann. Style-Architecture & Building-Art: Transformations of Architecture in the Nineteenth Century & Its Present Condition. Anderson, Stanford, tr. LC 94-14964. (Texts & Documents Ser.). (Illus.). 208p. 1994. 29.95 (*0-89236-282-0*); pap. 19.95 (*0-89236-283-9*) J P Getty Trust.

Muthesius, Stefan. The English Terraced House. LC 82-50442. (Illus.). 288p. 1982. 55.00 (*0-300-02871-7*) Yale U Pr.

— The English Terraced House. LC 82-50442. (Illus.). 288p. 1984. reprint ed. pap. 25.00 (*0-300-03176-9*) Yale U Pr.

Muthesius, Stefan & Glendinning, Miles. Tower Block: Modern Public Housing in England, Scotland, Wales, & Northern Ireland. (Illus.). 288p. Date not set. 65.00 (*0-300-05444-0*) Yale U Pr.

Muthesius, Stefan, jt. auth. see Dixon, Roger.

Muthiah, S. Splendour of South India. (C). 1992. 20.00 (*81-85273-56-1*, Pub. by UBS Pubs Dist II) S Asia.

— Words in Indian English: A Readers Guide. (C). 1991. text ed. 14.00 (*81-7223-000-1*, Pub. by Indus Pub II) S Asia.

Muthien, Yvonne. State & Resistance in South Africa, 1939-1965. (Making of Modern Africa Ser.). 233p. 1994. 68.95 (*1-85628-501-4*, Pub. by Avebury Pub UK) Ashgate Pub Co.

Muthu, S. K. Probability & Errors: For the Physical Sciences. 568p. 1982. text ed. 35.00 (*0-86131-137-X*, Pub. by Orient Longman Ltd II) Apt Bks.

Muthukumar, M. Polymer Physics: Concepts, Methods & Open Problems. (Lecture Notes in Physics Ser.: Vol. 22). 250p. (C). 1995. text ed. 61.00 (*9971-5-0594-0*); pap. text ed. 38.00 (*9971-5-0595-9*) World Scientific Pub.

***Muthusami, I. J.** Implementation of Education Projects: An Ethiopian Experience. LC 92-91192. 104p. (Orig.). 1994. pap. 8.00 (*1-56002-283-3*) Aegina Pr.

Mutibwa, Phares. Uganda since Independence. LC 92-53941. 150p. 1992. 49.95 (*0-86543-356-9*); pap. 16.95 (*0-86543-357-7*) Africa World.

Mutis, Alvaro. Adventures of Maqroll. 320p. 1995. 24.00 (*0-06-017004-2*, HarpT) HarpC.

— Maqroll: Three Novellas. Grossman, Edith, tr. LC 92-52571. 288p. 1993. reprint ed. pap. 10.00 (*0-06-092444-6*, PL) HarpC.

***Mutis, Alvaro & Grossman, Edith.** The Adventures of Maqroll: Four Novellas. 369p. Date not set. 24.00 (*0-615-00587-X*) HarpC.

Mutizwa-Mangiza, N. D. & Helmsing, A. H. Rural Development & Planning in Zimbabwe. 491p. 1991. text ed. 85.95 (*1-85628-142-6*, Pub. by Avebury Pub UK) Ashgate Pub Co.

Mutizwa, Tasiyana C. EC 'Ninety-Two Opportunities. 150p. 1991. 1,950.00 (*0-945235-50-X*) Lead Edge Reports.

— The Market for Converted Flexible Packaging Products & Materials in U. S. & Canada. 224p. 1995. 1,995.00 (*0-945235-53-4*) Lead Edge Reports.

— The Market for Home Entertainment Equipment. 150p. 1992. 1,750.00 (*0-945235-60-7*) Lead Edge Reports.

— Market Trends for Advanced Paints & Coatings. 150p. 1990. 1,700.00 (*0-945235-33-X*) Lead Edge Reports.

— Mini-Marts: Markets for Convenience, Products & Services. 100p. 1990. 1,750.00 (*0-945235-38-0*) Lead Edge Reports.

— Outlook for the Precious Metals Market. 118p. 1991. 1,950.00 (*0-945235-44-5*) Lead Edge Reports.

— Transportation Equipment Lighting. 100p. 1990. 1,600.00 (*0-945235-29-1*) Lead Edge Reports.

— U. S. Market for Small Household Appliances. 178p. 1992. 1,750.00 (*0-945235-58-5*) Lead Edge Reports.

Mutka, Norman E. The Degenerates. 175p. (Orig.). 1994. pap. 8.95 (*0-9637082-0-1*) N E Mutka.
THE DEGENERATES is the story of family life as it existed in the 1950s & 1960s. It highlights a time when people lived by values, whether they were spiritual, family, etc., or a combination of all of them. The following is a review of the book as seen through the eyes of a book critic. This novel is also under consideration for the possibility of a motion picture. "THE DEGENERATES is a thought-provoking tale that traces Kelly Waterman's spiritual growth as he develops into a responsible young man. The compelling plot also details intimacies regarding the Waterman family & relays the activities concerning the quaint but aged Soapwood Church located in Stapleton, Oregon. The story line deals with the morality taught through religious beliefs, the significance of seeking redemption, & the beauty of love. Colloquial dialogue & vivid descriptions enhance this story's endearing theme while your unique character development adds to the overall quality of this work." To order, write to Norman E. Mutka, 5214 Great View Ave. N., Brooklyn Center, MN 55429. Or call (612) 537-5727 collect.
Publisher Provided Annotation.

Mutke, Peter H. Selective Awareness. 197p. (C). 1984. pap. 8.95 (*0-930298-07-1*) Westwood Pub Co.

— Selective Awareness: The New Mind-Body Answer to Self Healing. rev. ed. Mikesell, Suzanne, ed. 193p. 1987. pap. 7.95 (*0-914629-50-6*, St Martin) Prima Pub.

Mutlak, I., jt. auth. see Elsasser, H. H.

Mutlak, Suheil. In Memory of Kahil Gibran. (ARA.). 1982. 14.95 (*0-86685-295-6*) Intl Bk Ctr.

Mutloatse, Mothobi, ed. Reconstruction: Ninety Years of Black Historical Literature. (Staffrider Ser.: No. 8). 320p. (C). 1981. pap. text ed. 8.95 (*0-86975-207-3*, Pub. by Ravan Pr ZA) Ohio U Pr.

Mutnick, Alan H., et al, eds. Comprehensive Pharmacy Review Practice Exams. 2nd rev. ed. LC 93-47687. 1994. 19.95 (*0-683-06255-7*) Williams & Wilkins.

Mutnick, Barbara, ed. see Lenin, Vladimir I. & Trotsky, L.

Muto, Albert. The University of California Press: The Early Years, 1893-1953. LC 92-20506. (C). 1993. 30.00 (*0-520-07732-6*) U CA Pr.

***Muto, Lisa M. & Bohlmann, Paul A.** The Harvard College Guide to Grants. rev. ed. 302p. 1994. pap. 13.00 (*0-943747-14-7*) Harvard OCS.

Muto, Susan. The Ascent. LC 90-84357. (John of the Cross for Today Ser.). 200p. (Orig.). 1991. pap. 6.95 (*0-87793-439-8*) Ave Maria.

— Blessings That Make Us Be. (C). 1988. 39.00 (*0-85439-219-X*, Pub. by St Paul Pubns UK) St Mut.

— Blessings That Make Us Be: Living the Beatitudes. LC 82-13102. 176p. 1982. 8.95 (*0-8245-0516-6*) Crossroad NY.

— The Dark Night. LC 94-71727. (John of the Cross for Today Ser.). 360p. (Orig.). 1994. pap. 9.95 (*0-87793-532-7*) Ave Maria.

— Womanspirit: Reclaiming the Deep Feminine in Our Human Spirituality. 180p. 1993. reprint ed. pap. 10.95 (*0-8245-1212-X*) Crossroad NY.

— Words of Wisdom for Our World: The Precautions & Counsels of St. John of the Cross. Kavanaugh, Kieran, tr. & pref. by. LC 94-47484. Date not set. pap. write for info. (*0-935216-52-9*) ICS Pubns.

Muto, Susan & Van Kaam, Adrian. Commitment: Key to Christian Maturity. 1989. pap. 8.95 (*0-8091-3069-6*) Paulist Pr.

— Divine Guidance: Learn to Listen & Discern the Will of God. 180p. 1994. pap. 8.99 (*0-89283-857-4*, Charis) Servant.

— Divine Guidance: Seeking to Find & Follow the Will of God. 208p. 1994. 39.00 (*0-85439-498-2*, Pub. by St Paul Pubns UK) St Mut.

— Harnessing Stress: A Spiritual Quest. (Spirit Life Ser.). 64p. (Orig.). 1993. pap. 3.95 (*1-878718-18-5*) Resurrection.

Muto, Susan & VanKaam, Adrian. Healthy & Holy under Stress. (Spirit Life Ser.). 64p. (Orig.). 1993. pap. 3.95 (*1-878718-19-3*) Resurrection.

— Practicing the Prayer of Presence. rev. ed. LC 93-83751. 190p. 1993. pap. 7.95 (*1-878718-14-2*) Resurrection.

— Stress & the Search for Happiness. (Spirit Life Ser.). 64p. (Orig.). 1993. pap. 3.95 (*1-878718-17-7*) Resurrection.

Muto, Susan, jt. auth. see Van Kaam, Adrian.

Muto, Susan, et al, des. A Workbook & Guide for Commitment: Key to Christian Maturity. 1990. 14.95 (*0-8091-3189-7*) Paulist Pr.

Muto, Susan A. Blessings That Make Us Be: A Formative Approach to Living the Beatitudes. LC 82-13102. 137p. 1991. reprint ed. pap. 7.95 (*0-932506-88-7*) St Bedes Pubns.

— Celebrating the Single Life. 192p. 1989. pap. 11.95 (*0-8245-0954-4*) Crossroad NY.

— Pathways of Spiritual Living. 2nd ed. LC 84-1564. 191p. 1988. reprint ed. pap. 6.95 (*0-932506-65-8*) St Bedes Pubns.

— A Practical Guide to Spiritual Reading. rev. ed. LC 94-19939. 328p. 1994. reprint ed. pap. 19.95 (*1-879007-09-6*) St Bedes Pubns.

Muto, Susan A., jt. auth. see Van Kaam, Adrian.

Mutoh, H., et al, eds. Industrial Policies for Pacific Economic Growth. 280p. (C). 1987. text ed. 44.95 (*0-04-330381-1*, Pub. by Allen Unwin AT) Paul & Co Pubs.

Mutoh, Nancy W., jt. auth. see Pifer, George W.

Mutoh, Y., et al, eds. Medicine & Science in Aquatic Sports. (Medicine & Sport Science Ser.: Vol. 39). (Illus.). xii, 236p. 1994. 5.25 hd 198.50 (*3-8055-5981-X*) S Karger.

Mutschler, Charles V., et al. Spokane's Street Railways: An Illustrated History. 208p. (Orig.). 1987. 30.00 (*0-943181-01-1*) IERHS.

***Mutschler, Ernst.** Woerterbuch der Pharmazie Vol. 2: Pharmakologie. 536p. (GER.). 1985. write for info. (*0-7859-8487-9*, 3804706673) Fr & Eur.

Mutschler, Ernst & Derendorf, Hartmut. Basic & Applied Principles of Drug Actions. LC 93-36069. 1994. write for info. (*0-8493-7774-9*) CRC Pr.

Mutschmann, Heinrich. Milton's Eyesight & the Chronology of His Works. LC 75-163458. (Studies in Milton: No. 22). 1971. reprint ed. lib. bdg. 39.95 (*0-8383-1325-6*) M S G Haskell Hse.

— Studies Concerning the Origins of Milton's Paradise Lost. LC 79-163459. (Studies in Milton: No. 22). 1971. reprint ed. lib. bdg. 49.95 (*0-8383-1324-8*) M S G Haskell Hse.

***Mutsu, Iso.** Kamakura: Fact & Legend. rev. ed. (Illus.). 248p. 1995. pap. 14.95 (*0-8048-1968-8*) C E Tuttle.

Mutswairo, Solomon. Mapondera: Soldier of Zimbabwe. LC 77-90992. (Orig.). 1978. pap. 7.00 (*0-914478-20-6*) Three Continents.

Mutswairo, Solomon T. Chaminuka: Prophet of Zimbabwe. Herdeck, Donald, tr. LC 77-71232. (Illus.). 120p. 1983. 15.00 (*0-89410-002-5*); pap. 8.00 (*0-89410-003-3*) Three Continents.

Mutt, V., jt. ed. see Jorpes, T. E.

Mutt, Viktor, et al, eds. Advances in Metabolic Disorders, Vol. 11. (Serial Publication Ser.). 545p. 1988. text ed. 158.00 (*0-12-027311-X*) Acad Pr.

Mutt, Viktor, et al. Neuropeptide Y. (Karolinska Institute Nobel Conference Ser.). 378p. 1989. 138.50 (*0-88167-556-3*) Raven.

Muttalib, M. A. Child Development: A Study in Health Culture of a Low Income Urban Settlement. 1989. text ed. 30.00 (*81-207-0448-7*, Pub. by Sterling Pubs II) Apt Bks.

Muttalib, M. A., ed. Voluntary Action in Education. 256p. 1989. text ed. 27.50 (*81-207-0956-X*, Pub. by Sterling Pubs II) Apt Bks.

Muttenaere, C., jt. ed. see Desmet, G.

Mutter, Letitia, jt. ed. see Kalb, Mary.

Mutter, Reg, ed. see Fielding, Henry.

M

An Asterisk (*) at the beginning of an entry indicates that the title is appearing in BIP for the first time.

Mutter, Scott, photos. Surrational Images. (Illus.). 96p. (C). 1992. 27.50 (*0-252-01935-0*) U of Ill Pr.

Mutti, E. Turbidites of the Northern Apennines: Introduction to Facies Analysis. Ricci Lucchi, F., ed. (AGI Reprint Ser.: No. 3). 46p. 1978. 6.95 (*0-913312-18-5*) Am Geol.

Mutti, John. Taxes, Subsidies & Competitiveness Internationally. LC 81-86163. (Committee on Changing International Realities Ser.). 76p. 1982. pap. 7.00 (*0-89068-062-0*) Natl Planning.

Mutti, John & Morici, Peter. Changing Patterns of U. S. Industrial Activity & Comparative Advantage. LC 83-62893. (Committee on Changing International Realities Ser.). 72p. 1983. pap. 8.00 (*0-89068-069-8*, NPA 201) Natl Planning.

Mutton, Alice F. Western Europe in Color. (Illus.). 279p. 1972. pap. 12.00 (*0-7137-0555-8*) Transatl Arts.

Mutton, J. L., jt. ed. see Bureau, G.

Muttukumaru, Anton. The Military History of Ceylon: An Outline. 227p. (C). 1987. 36.00 (*81-7013-046-8*, Pub. by Navrang) S Asia.

Mutual Fund Public Co., Ltd. Staff. The MFC Investment Handbook: Thailand 1994. 404p. reprint ed. pap. 46.95 (*974-89094-9-2*, Pub. by Mutual Fund TH) Ref Press.

Muturana, Humberto & Varela, Francisco J. Autopoiesis & Cognition: The Realization of the Living. (Boston Studies in the Philosophy of Science: No. 42). 140p. (C). 1980. lib. bdg. 75.00 (*90-277-1015-5*); pap. text ed. 29.50 (*90-277-1016-3*) Kluwer Ac.

***Mutwa, Credo.** Song of Stars. Larsen, Stephen, ed. LC 95-12499. 1995. write for info. (*1-886449-01-5*) Barrytown Ltd.

***Mutza, Wayne.** Bent & Battered Rotors. (Aircraft Specials Ser.). (Illus.). 56p. 1993. pap. 9.95 (*0-89747-306-X*) Squad Sig Pubns.

— C-7 Caribou in Action. (Aircraft in Action Ser.). (Illus.). 50p. Date not set. pap. 8.95 (*0-89747-292-6*, 1132) Squad Sig Pubns.

— H-13 Sioux "Mini" in Action. (Mini in Action Ser.). (Illus.). 50p. 1995. pap. 5.95 (*0-89747-345-0*) Squad Sig Pubns.

— UH-1 Huey in Color. (Fighting Colors Ser.). (Illus.). 32p. 1992. pap. 9.95 (*0-89747-279-9*, 6564) Squad Sig Pubns.

Mutzell, Julius, ed. see Curtius Rufus, Quintus.

Muus, L. T., et al, eds. Chemically Induced Magnetic Polarization. (Nato Advanced Study Institutes Ser. C: No. 34). 1977. lib. bdg. 103.00 (*90-277-0845-2*) Kluwer Ac.

Muuss, Rolf E. Adolescent Behavior & Society: A Book of Readings. 4th ed. 1990. pap. text ed. write for info. (*0-07-044164-2*) McGraw.

— Theories of Adolescence. 5th ed. 512p. (C). 1988. pap. text ed. write for info. (*0-07-553752-4*) McGraw.

Muvandi, Ityai, jt. auth. see Duncan, Thomas.

Muvdi, B. B. & McNabb, J. W. Engineering Mechanics of Materials. 3rd ed. (Illus.). 704p. 1990. text ed. 49.50 (*0-387-97338-9*) Spr-Verlag.

Muxworthy, D. T. Programming for Software Sharing. 1983. pap. text ed. 56.50 (*90-277-1547-5*) Kluwer Ac.

Muxworthy, Peter, jt. auth. see Gwynn, David.

Muybridge, Eadweard. Animals in Motion. Brown, Lewis S., ed. (Illus.). 1957. 26.95 (*0-486-20203-8*) Dover.

— Horses & Other Animals in Motion: Forty-Five Classic Photographic Sequences. (Illus.). 91p. (Orig.). 1985. pap. 8.95 (*0-486-24911-5*) Dover.

— Human Figure in Motion. (Illus.). 1955. 24.95 (*0-486-20204-6*) Dover.

— The Male & Female Figure in Motion: Sixty Classic Photographic Sequences. 128p. 1984. pap. 9.95 (*0-486-24745-7*) Dover.

— Muybridge's Complete Human & Animal Locomotion: All 781 Plates from the 1887 Animal Locomotion, 3 vols., Set. Incl. Vol. 1. LC 77-1665. 55.00 (*0-486-23792-3*); Vol. 2. LC 77-1665. 55.00 (*0-486-23793-1*); Vol. 3. LC 77-1665. 55.00 (*0-486-23794-X*); (Illus.). 1979. reprint ed. 165.00 (*0-685-01500-9*) Dover.

***Muyerson, George.** Rhetoric, Reason, & Society: Rationality as Dialogue. 160p. 1995. text ed. 65.00 (*0-8039-7866-9*); pap. text ed. 21.95 (*0-8039-7867-7*) Sage.

Muysken, Joan, ed. Measurement & Analysis of Job Vacancies: An International Comparison. LC 94-9578. 1994. 63.95 (*1-85628-617-7*, Pub. by Avebury Pub UK) Ashgate Pub Co.

Muysken, P. & Van Riemsdyk, H., eds. Features & Projections. (Studies in Generative Grammar). xviii, 254p. 1986. pap. 57.70 (*90-6765-144-3*) Mouton.

Muysken, Pieter & Smith, Norval, eds. Substrata versus Universals in Creole Genesis. LC 86-18856. (Creole Language Library: No. 1). vii, 311p. 1986. 97.00x (*0-915027-90-9*) Benjamins North Am.

Muysken, Pieter, jt. auth. see Appel, Rene.

Muysken, Pieter, jt. auth. see Lefebvre, Claire.

Muysken, Pieter, jt. ed. see Maracz, Laszlo K.

Muysken, Pieter, jt. ed. see Milroy, Lesley.

Muyskens, Dirk. Cleaning Compounds, No. YC-174: Highlighting Additives to Surfactants in These Compounds. (Illus.). 179p. 1993. 2,650.00 (*1-56965-003-9*) BCC.

Muyskens, James L. The Sufficiency of Hope: Conceptual Foundations of Religion. LC 79-18714. (Philosophical Monographs: Third Annual Ser.: 3rd Annual Ser.). 186p. 1979. 27.95 (*0-87722-162-6*) Temple U Pr.

Muyskens, Judith A., et al. Bravo! Communication et Grammaire. 2nd ed. LC 92-38753. 1993. student ed, pap. 28.95 (*0-8384-4418-0*) Heinle & Heinle.

— Bravo! Communication et Grammaire. 2nd ed. LC 92-38753. 1993. pap. 30.95 (*0-8384-4422-9*) Heinle & Heinle.

— Bravo! Communication et Grammaire. 2nd ed. LC 92-38753. 1993. 34.95 (*0-8384-4427-X*) Heinle & Heinle.

— Rendez-Vous: An Invitation to French. 1990. teacher ed write for info. (*0-07-540871-6*) McGraw.

— Rendez-Vous: An Invitation to French. 3rd ed. 1990. text ed. write for info. (*0-07-540867-8*) McGraw.

— Rendez-Vous: An Invitation to French. 3rd ed. 1990. student ed, pap. text ed. 13.03 (*0-07-540869-4*) McGraw.

— Rendez-Vous: An Invitation to French. 3rd ed. 1990. student ed, pap. text ed. 13.03 (*0-07-540868-6*); audio write for info. (*0-07-540878-3*); write for info. (*0-07-540877-5*) McGraw.

— Rendez-Vous: An Invitation to French. 4th ed. LC 93-35951. 1994. text ed. write for info. (*0-07-044337-8*) McGraw.

— Rendez-Vous: An Invitation to French. 4th ed. LC 93-35951. 1994. Wkbk. student ed, pap. text ed. write for info. (*0-07-044339-4*) McGraw.

— Rendez-Vous: An Invitation to French. 4th ed. LC 93-35951. 1994. Lab manual. student ed, pap. text ed. write for info. (*0-07-044340-8*) McGraw.

— Rendez-Vous: An Invitation to French. 4th ed. LC 93-35951. 1994. Tapescript. text ed. write for info. (*0-07-044342-4*) McGraw.

— Rendezvous: An Invitation to French. 2nd ed. 608p. (C). 1982. write for info. (*0-394-32638-5*) Random.

Muzaffaruddin, Syed. Comparative Study of Islam & Other Religions. 125p. (Orig.). 1987. pap. 7.50 (*1-56744-254-4*) Kazi Pubns.

Muzbek, ed. Hemostasis & Cancer. 1987. 259.00 (*0-8493-5754-3*, RC262, CRC Reprint) Franklin.

Muzik, Katy. At Home in the Coral Reef. (Illus.). 32p. (J). (ps-3). 1992. 14.95 (*0-88106-487-4*) Charlesbridge Pub.

— At Home in the Coral Reef. 32p. Date not set. pap. 6.95 (*0-88106-486-6*) Charlesbridge Pub.

— Dentro del Arrecife de Coral (At Home in the Coral Reef) (Illus.). 32p. (J). (ps-3). 1993. lib. bdg. 15.88 (*0-88106-642-7*); pap. 6.95 (*0-88106-422-X*) Charlesbridge Pub.

Muzinga. The Computer Book for Beginners: Level I. 190p. 1992. lib. bdg. 29.95 (*1-882938-00-3*); pap. 24.95 (*1-882938-02-X*) AmaZulu Pr.

— The Computer Book for Beginners: Level I. deluxe ed. 190p. 1992. 65.95 (*1-882938-01-1*) AmaZulu Pr.

Muzj, Maria G. Transfiguration: Introduction to the Contemplation of Icons. Whitehead, Kenneth D., tr. LC 91-2341. (Illus.). 179p. 1991. 19.95 (*0-8198-7350-0*) Pauline Bks.

Muzny, Charles C. The Vietnamese in Oklahoma City: A Study of Ethnic Change. LC 88-35115. (Immigrant Communities & Ethnic Minorities in the U. S. & Canada Ser.: No. 37). 1989. 45.00 (*0-404-19447-8*) AMS Pr.

Muzorewa, Gwinyai H. An African Theology of Mission. LC 89-78555. (Studies in History of Missions: Vol. 5). (Illus.). 256p. 1990. lib. bdg. 89.95 (*0-88946-073-6*) E Mellen.

— The Origins & Development of African Theology. LC 84-14769. 160p. (Orig.). reprint ed. pap. 45.60 (*0-8357-4068-4*, 2036758) Bks Demand.

Muzumdar, Haridas T. India's Contributions to World Civilization: Swaraj Quintet II: A Cultural History of India, 5 vols. 230p. (C). 1989. write for info. (*0-318-64789-3*) Gandhi Institute.

Muzzarelli, Riccardo, et al, eds. Chitin in Nature & Technology. LC 85-28088. 594p. 1986. 135.00 (*0-306-42211-5*, Plenum Pr) Plenum.

Muzzarelli, Riccardo A. Chitin. LC 76-52421. 365p. 1977. 147.00 (*0-08-020367-1*, Pub. by Pergamon Repr UK) Franklin.

— Natural Chelating Polymers. 260p. 1973. 116.00 (*0-08-017235-0*, Pub. by Pergamon Repr UK) Franklin.

Muzzey, D. S. The Spiritual Franciscans. 1972. 59.95 (*0-8490-1113-2*) Gordon Pr.

Muzzio, Douglas. Watergate Games: Strategies, Choices, Outcomes. LC 81-16964. 176p. 1984. 30.00x (*0-8147-5384-1*) NYU Pr.

Muzzio, John. Astrological Life Scripts: Mythological Archtypes in the Natal Horoscope. 190p. 1986. pap. 7.95 (*0-930706-17-X*) Seek-It Pubns.

MVA - SME Staff, ed. MVA - SME University - Industry Outreach Directory, 1992. LC 91-67595. 75p. 1991. pap. text ed. 18.00 (*0-87263-415-9*) SME.

Mvula, Enoch T. Tukumba Pounding Songs: A Device for Resolving Familial Conifict. (Graduate Student Term Paper Ser.). 19p. 1984. pap. text ed. 2.00 (*0-941934-45-4*) Indiana Africa.

Mwadilifu, Mwalimu I. A Bibliographical & Pictorial Curriculum Guide to Egypt: From Abu Simbel to the Egyptian Museum of Antiquities. LC 89-81781. (Monograph Ser.: No. 5). 64p. 1989. 4.95 (*0-938818-20-1*, Alkebulan Hist Res Soc) ECA Assoc.

— European Scholars on the African Origins of the Africans of Antiquity. LC 91-93121. (Monograph Ser.: No. 6). 85p. 1991. 11.95 (*0-938818-47-3*) ECA Assoc.

— How to Plan African Heritage Book Fairs. 1993. 11.95 (*0-938818-84-8*) ECA Assoc.

— Selected Speeches, Sermons & Writings of Adam Clayton Powell Jr., 1935-1971. LC 89-81785. 150p. pap. 10.95 (*0-938818-17-1*) ECA Assoc.

Mwadilifu, Mwalimu I., ed. Who's Who in African Heritage Book Publishing, 1989-90. 2nd ed. LC 89-647142. 300p. 1990. 24.95 (*0-938818-16-3*) ECA Assoc.

— Who's Who in African Heritage Book Publishing, 1990-1991. 3rd ed. LC 89-647142. 1990. 25.95 (*0-938818-51-1*) ECA Assoc.

— Who's Who in African Heritage Book Publishing, 1991-1992. 4th ed. LC 89-647142. 325p. 1992. spiral bd. 34.95 (*0-938818-95-3*) ECA Assoc.

Mwale, Genevieve & Burnard, Philip. Women & AIDS in Rural Africa: Rural Women's Views of AIDS in Zambia. 135p. 1992. 55.95 (*1-85628-396-8*, Pub. by Avebury Pub UK) Ashgate Pub Co.

Mwamula-Lubandi, E. D. Clan Theory in African Development Studies: Reconsidering African Development Promotive Bases. 240p. (C). 1992. lib. bdg. 44.50 (*0-8191-8427-6*) U Pr of Amer.

Mwangi, Meja. Cockroach Dance. (C). 1988. pap. text ed. 9.95 (*0-582-00392-X*, 76410) Longman.

— Cockroach Dance. 1990. pap. 9.95 (*0-582-64276-0*) Longman.

— Going down River Road. (African Writers Ser.). 215p. 1976. pap. 8.95 (*0-435-90176-1*) Heinemann.

— Striving for the Wind. (African Writers Ser.). 199p. 1992. pap. 8.95 (*0-435-90979-7*, 90979) Heinemann.

Mwangudza, Johnson A. Mijikenda. (Kenya People Ser.). (Illus.). 37p. (YA). (gr. 6-9). 1991. pap. 4.95 (*0-237-50490-1*, Pub. by Evans Bros Ltd UK) Trafalgar.

Mwaniki, Nyaga. Pastoral Societies & Resistance to Change: A Re-evaluation. (Graduate Student Paper Competition Ser.: No. 3). 40p. (Orig.). 1980. pap. text ed. 2.00 (*0-941934-32-2*) Indiana Africa.

Mwansasu, Bismarck & Pratt, Cranford, eds. Towards Socialism in Tanzania. LC 78-10350. 1979. pap. 11.95 (*0-8020-6433-7*) U of Toronto Pr.

Mwansasu, Bismarck U. & Pratt, Cranford, eds. Towards Socialism in Tanzania. LC 78-10350. (Illus.). 253p. reprint ed. pap. 72.20 (*0-8357-3662-8*, 2036389) Bks Demand.

MWPS Engineers. House Planning Handbook. 2nd ed. MWPS Staff, ed. LC 88-9305. (Illus.). 84p. 1988. pap. 7.00 (*0-89373-073-4*, MWPS-16) MidWest Plan Serv.

MWPS Engineers & Staff, ed. see MWPS Engineers Staff.

MWPS Engineers Staff. Farm & Home Concrete, MWPS-35. MWPS Engineers & Staff, ed. LC 89-14021. (Illus.). 44p. 1989. pap. 6.00 (*0-89373-079-3*, MWPS-35) MidWest Plan Serv.

— Mechanical Ventilating Systems for Livestock Housing. LC 89-77073. (Illus.). 70p. 1990. pap. 6.00 (*0-89373-075-0*, MWPS-32) MidWest Plan Serv.

MWPS Staff, ed. see Midwest Plan Service Engineers Staff.

MWPS Staff, ed. see MWPS Engineers.

Mya Than & Tan, Joseph L., eds. Vietnam's Dilemmas & Options: The Challenge of Economic Transition in the 1990s. 306p. 1993. 28.00 (*981-3016-40-X*, Pub. by Inst SE Asian Studies SI); pap. 22.00 (*981-3016-38-8*, Pub. by Inst SE Asian Studies SI) Ashgate Pub Co.

Myachina, E. N. The Swahili Language: A Descriptive Language. (Languages of Asia & Africa Ser.). 96p. (Orig.). (C). 1981. pap. 19.95 (*0-7100-0849-X*, RKP) Routledge.

Myakishev, G., jt. auth. see Grigoryev, V.

Myall, Carolynne, jt. auth. see Chambers, Sydney.

Myamlin, Viktor & Pleskov, Yurii V. Electrochemistry of Semiconductors. LC 66-12887. 452p. reprint ed. pap. 128.90 (*0-317-27893-2*, 2055790) Bks Demand.

Myanmar Pitaka Associates Staff, ed. Twenty-five Suttas from Uparipannasa: Suttanta Pitaka. Majjhima Nikaya Medium Length Discourses of the Buddha. (C). 1991. 23.00 (*81-7030-294-3*) S Asia.

Myant, Martin. Transforming Socialist Economies: The Case of Poland & Czechoslovakia. LC 93-2692. (Studies of Communism in Transition). 304p. 1993. 59.95 (*1-85278-786-4*, Pub. by E Elgar Pub UK) Ashgate Pub Co.

Myant, Martin, jt. ed. see Waller, Michael.

Myant, Martin R. Socialism & Democracy in Czechoslovakia, 1945-1948. LC 80-41951. (Soviet & East European Studies). 312p. reprint ed. pap. 89.00 (*0-318-34842-X*, 2031697) Bks Demand.

Myant, Nicholas B. Cholesterol Metabolism, LDL, & the LDL Receptor. 465p. 1990. text ed. 88.00 (*0-12-512300-0*) Acad Pr.

Myasnikov, A. Atherosclerosis & Thrombosis. (Illus.). 229p. 1967. 25.00 (*0-8464-1078-8*) Beekman Pubs.

Myasnikova, A. V., et al. Handbook of Food Products: Grain & its Products. 408p. 1968. text ed. 99.00 (*0-7065-0664-2*, Pub. by Keter Pub IS) Coronet Bks.

Myasnikova, L. & Marikhin, V. A., eds. Orientational Phenomena in Polymers. (Progress in Colloid & Polymer Science Ser.). 142p. 1994. 72.00 (*0-387-91453-6*) Spr-Verlag.

Myasoedov, B. F. Transplutonium Elements. (Analytical Chemistry of the Elements Ser.). 380p. 1970. text ed. 94.00 (*0-7065-1375-4*, Pub. by Keter Pub IS) Coronet Bks.

Myatt, Dana. A Physician's Diary, Case Histories of Hope & Healing with Edgar Cayce's & Other Natural Remedies. 242p. 1993. pap. 13.95 (*0-87604-316-3*, 393) ARE Pr.

Myatt, Frederick. British Sieges of the Peninsular War, 1811-1813. 200p. (C). 1991. 95.00 (*0-946771-59-6*, Pub. by Spellmount UK) St Mut.

— Illustrated Encyclopedia of Nineteenth Century Firearms. 1994. 19.99 (*0-517-27786-7*) Random Hse Value.

Myatt, Frederick & Ridefort, Gerard. Modern Rifles & Sub-Machines. (New Illustrated Guide Ser.). (Illus.). 160p. 1992. 5.98 (*0-8317-5055-3*) Smithmark.

Myatt, G., jt. auth. see Cashmore, R. J.

Myatt, John. Effective Skippering: A Comprehensive Guide to Yacht Mastery. (Illus.). 256p. 1992. 29.95 (*0-924486-32-5*) Sheridan.

Myatt, L. J. Symmetrical Components. LC 68-26942. 1968. 83.00 (*0-08-012979-X*, Pub. by Pergamon Repr UK) Franklin.

Myatt, Robert L., Jr., jt. auth. see Muller, Edward J.

Mycielski, J., et al. A Lattice of Chapters of Mathematics: (Interpretations Between Theorems) LC 89-18632. 70p. 1990. pap. 18.00 (*0-8218-2488-0*, MEMO 84/426) Am Math.

Mycko, David, et al. Vintage American & European, Bk. 3. (Illus.). 224p. (Orig.). 1989. pap. text ed. 25.00 (*0-913902-57-8*) Heart Am Pr.

***Mycock, John C., et al, eds.** Handbook of Air Pollution Control Engineering & Technology. LC 95-7041. 416p. 1995. 79.95 (*1-56670-106-6*, L1106) Lewis Pubs.

Mycoff, David, tr. see Maurus, Rhabanus.

Mycological Society of America, Mycology Guidebook Committee. Mycology Guidebook. rev. ed. Stevens, Russell B., ed. LC 81-14738. (Illus.). 736p. (C). 1981. 50.00 (*0-295-95841-3*) U of Wash Pr.

Mycoskie, Pam. Butter Busters. 1993. pap. 19.95 (*0-9633507-0-6*) Butter Busters.

— Butter Busters. 496p. 1994. pap. 19.99 (*0-446-67040-5*) Warner Bks.

— I'm Listening! The Butter Busters Cookbook Companion. 320p. (Orig.). 1995. pap. 16.99 (*0-446-67189-4*) Warner Bks.

Mycue, Edward. Damage Within the Community. (Illus.). 72p. 1973. pap. 6.00 (*0-915572-11-7*) Panjandrum.

— Night Boats. (Illus.). 64p. (Orig.). 1994. pap. 10.00 (*1-879457-38-5*) Norton Coker Pr.

Mycue, Edward, ed. see Albert, Gwen & Sparling, Kent.

Mycue, Edward, ed. see Albert, Gwendolyn.

Mycue, Edward, ed. see Bellm, Dan.

Mycue, Edward, ed. see Blevins, Richard.

Mycue, Edward, ed. see Bove, Robert.

Mycue, Edward, ed. see Bunch, Richard A.

Mycue, Edward, ed. see Bunse, Lois.

Mycue, Edward, ed. see Cannarozzi, Sam.

Mycue, Edward, ed. see Erickson, Ann.

Mycue, Edward, ed. see Farnsworth, Vincent.

Mycue, Edward, ed. see Foley, Jack.

Mycue, Edward, ed. see Ford, Betsy.

Mycue, Edward, ed. see Foster, Edward.

Mycue, Edward, ed. see Gallegos, Frances.

Mycue, Edward, ed. see Gigiorno, Geri.

Mycue, Edward, ed. see Gove, Chris M.

Mycue, Edward, ed. see Gove, Jim.

Mycue, Edward, jt. auth. see Gove, Jim.

Mycue, Edward, ed. see Hamill, Tom.

Mycue, Edward, ed. see Hill, Crag.

Mycue, Edward, ed. see Hill, Owen.

Mycue, Edward, ed. see Hurst, Elizabeth.

Mycue, Edward, ed. see Jameson, Carol.

Mycue, Edward, ed. see Jensen, Dale.

Mycue, Edward, ed. see Johnson, Honor.

Mycue, Edward, ed. see Johnson, Wayne.

Mycue, Edward, ed. see Kennelly, Laura B.

Mycue, Edward, ed. see King, Martha.

Mycue, Edward, ed. see Leigh, Julianne.

Mycue, Edward, ed. see Mann, Jules.

Mycue, Edward, ed. see McPherson, D. Jayne.

Mycue, Edward, ed. see Neville, Mark.

Mycue, Edward, ed. see Powell, Douglas A., et al.

Mycue, Edward, ed. see Powell, Douglas.

Mycue, Edward, ed. see Retecki, Richard.

Mycue, Edward, ed. see Selawsky, John.

Mycue, Edward, ed. see Stedman, Judy.

Mycue, Edward, ed. see Sventitsky, Helen.

Mycue, Edward, ed. see Talcott, William.

Mycue, Edward, ed. see Taylor, Ruth.

Mycue, Edward, et al. The Whispering Surgeon. 2nd ed. Uphoff, Joseph A., Jr., ed. (Illus.). 32p. 1986. pap. text ed. 2.00 (*0-943123-01-1*) Arjuna Lib Pr.

Mydans, Carl. Carl Mydans: Photojournalist. LC 84-24349. (Illus.). 208p. 1993. 39.95 (*0-8109-1323-2*) Abrams.

Myddelton, D. R., jt. auth. see Reid, Walter.

***Myddelton, David.** The Essence of Financial Management. LC 94-35311. (Essence of Management Ser.). 1995. pap. 19.95 (*0-13-284787-6*) P-H.

Mydosh, John A. Spin Glasses: An Experimental Introduction. 280p. 1993. 85.00 (*0-7484-0038-9*) Taylor & Francis.

Myeers. Theology of the Letter to Hebrews. 1992. pap. write for info. (*0-521-35778-0*) Cambridge U Pr.

***Myer.** Silent Witness. 1995. mass mkt. 4.99 (*0-312-95481-6*) St Martin.

Myer, Bruce. Dybbuk. 48p. (Orig.). 1990. 7.95 (*0-317-91356-5*) Playsmith.

***Myer, Charles M., 3rd.** Pediatric Otolaryngology. (Current Opinion in Otolaryngology & Head & Neck Surgery Ser.). (Illus.). 548p. 1994. pap. text ed. write for info. (*1-85922-635-3*) Current Science.

Myer, Charles M., ed. A Practical Approach to Pediatric Otolaryngology. (Illus.). 250p. 1987. 49.95 (*0-8151-1865-1*, QMW-1, Yr Bk Med Pubs) Mosby Yr Bk.

Myer, Charles M. & Cotton, Robin T. The Pediatric Airway: An Interdisciplinary Approach. (Illus.). 400p. 1994. 99.50 (*0-397-51415-8*) Lippincott.

Myer, Charles M., III, jt. auth. see Goodwin, W. Jarrad, Jr.

Myer, Dillon S. Uprooted Americans: The Japanese Americans & the War Relocation Authority During World War II. LC 76-125169. (Illus.). 390p. reprint ed. pap. 111.20 (*0-317-58772-2*, 2029656) Bks Demand.

Myer, Donna. Answers to Your Mushroom Questions Plus Recipes. LC 77-87780. (Illus.). 1977. pap. 3.95 (*0-9601516-1-3*) Mushroom Cave.

Myer, Edwin C., jt. auth. see Pellock, John M.

Myer, Isaac. Qabbalah: The Philosophical Writings of Solomon Ben Yehudah Ibn Gabirol. 1975. 250.00 (*0-8490-0922-7*) Gordon Pr.

— Qabbalah: The Philosophy of IBN Gebirol, Qabbalah & the Zohar. LC 85-52064. (Secret Doctrine Reference Ser.). (Illus.). 528p. 1988. 28.00 (*0-913510-57-2*) Wizards.

Myer, John N. Accounting for Non-Accountants. 2nd rev. ed. 1979. 14.95 (*0-8015-0026-5*, 01451-440, Dutton) NAL-Dutton.

An Asterisk (*) at the beginning of an entry indicates that the title is appearing in BIP for the first time.

***Myer, Laura, illus.** Ecology: Christian Reflections. 48p. (Orig.). 1994. pap. 2.95 (0-88028-152-9, 1273) Forward Movement.

Myer, Phillip C. Creative Paint Finishes for the Home. (Illus.). 144p. 1992. 27.95 (0-89134-433-0, 30426) North Light Bks.

— Painting Styles Mix Media Painting Techniques. (Designer Ser.). (Illus.). 32p. 1986. pap. 6.95 (0-917121-15-5, 50-102) M F Weber Co.

Myer, Phillip C., ed. see Hauser, Priscilla.

Myer, Rick, jt. auth. see Ottens, Allen.

Myer, Suzzanne N. & Enslin, Teresa K. Nutrition in Kitchen: A Cookbook. (Illus.). (Orig.). 1988. pap. 7.95 (0-317-91385-9) Cooking Concepts.

Myer, Valerie G. Margaret Drabble: A Reader's Guide. LC 91-10737. (Critical Studies of Key Texts). 224p. 1991. text ed. 29.95 (0-312-06104-8) St Martin.

— Ten Great English Novelists. LC 89-77771. 160p. 1990. text ed. 39.95 (0-312-03564-0) St Martin.

Myer, Valerie G., ed. Samuel Richardson: Passion & Prudence. LC 86-10809. 224p. 1986. 50.00 (0-389-20650-4, N8208) B&N Imports.

Myerburg, R. J., ed. Sudden Cardiac Death. (Journal: Cardiology: Vol. 74, Suppl. 2, 1987). (Illus.). iv, 72p. 1987. pap. 21.75 (3-8055-4629-7) S Karger.

Myerhoff, Barbara. Number Our Days. 1980. pap. 10.95 (0-671-25430-8, Touchstone Bks) S&S Trade.

— Number Our Days: Culture & Community among Elderly Jews in an American Ghetto. LC 93-45422. 318p. 1994. pap. 11.95 (0-452-01122-1, Mer) NAL-Dutton.

— Remembered Lives: The Work of Ritual, Storytelling, & Growing Older. 250p. (C). 1992. text ed. 42.50 (0-472-10317-2); pap. 18.95 (0-472-08177-2) U of Mich Pr.

Myerhoff, Barbara, jt. ed. see Tufte, Virginia.

Myerhoff, Barbara G. Peyote Hunt: The Sacred Journey of the Huichol Indians. LC 73-16923. (Symbol, Myth & Ritual Ser.). (Illus.). 288p. 1976. pap. 11.95 (0-8014-9137-1) Cornell U Pr.

Myerhoff, Barbara G. & Simic, Andrei, eds. Life's Career; Aging: Cultural Variations on Growing Old. (Cross-Cultural Research & Methodology Ser.: Vol. 4). 252p. 1979. 32.50 (0-8039-0867-9); pap. 18.95 (0-8039-6000-X) Sage.

Myerly, Marilyn. Wild about Fudge. 96p. 1989. spiral bd. 7.95 (0-8120-4161-5) Barron.

Myerovich, Marcy. Rabbits: Look & Learn. (Illus.). 64p. 1993. write for info. (0-7938-0073-0, KD004) TFH Pubns.

Myerowitz, Molly. Ovid's Games of Love. LC 85-8927. 255p. 1985. 32.50 (0-8143-1746-4) Wayne St U Pr.

Myerowitz, P. David, ed. Heart Transplantation. (Illus.). 416p. 1987. 59.00 (0-87993-308-9) Futura Pub.

Myers. Advances in Otolaryngology, Vol. 4. 206p. 1990. 69.95 (0-8151-6262-6, Yr Bk Med Pubs) Mosby Yr Bk.

— Advances in Otolaryngology: Head & Neck, Vol. 3. 368p. 1989. 69.95 (0-8151-6261-8, Yr Bk Med Pubs) Mosby Yr Bk.

— Advances in Otolaryngology: Head & Neck Surgery, Vol. 5. 215p. 1991. 69.95 (0-8151-6263-4) Mosby Yr Bk.

— C-Set Kit. (C). 1995. pap. text ed. write for info. (0-7167-2117-1) W H Freeman.

— Cluttering: A Clinical Perspective. 146p. 1992. pap. 38.25 (1-56593-543-8, 0488) Singular Publishing.

— Compensation Management. 832p. 1989. 75.00 (0-685-67123-2, 5109) Commerce.

— Digital Signal Processing: Efficient Convolution & Fourier Transform Techniques. 320p. 1990. boxed 45.00 (0-13-211814-9) P-H.

— Exploring Psychology. 2nd ed. 1992. text ed. 43.95x (0-87901-578-0); pap. 39.95x (0-87901-577-2); student ed, pap. 11.95x (0-87901-605-1) Worth.

— Head & Neck Oncology: Diagnosis, Treatment, & Rehabilitation. 1991. 115.00 (0-316-59317-6) Little.

— Human Resources Management Principles & Practice. 2nd ed. 1120p. 1992. 74.50 (0-685-67136-4, 4821) Commerce.

— Safe at Home. 1982. pap. 3.95 (0-915936-10-0) Armstrong Pub.

— Social Security. 2nd ed. (C). 1981. 44.95 (0-256-02585-1) Irwin Prof Pubng.

Myers & Well. Research Design & Statistical Analysis. (C). 1991. text ed. 44.00 (0-673-46414-8) HarpCollege.

Myers, jt. auth. see Beare.

Myers, jt. ed. see Rose.

Myers, et al. Advances in Otolaryngology: Head & Neck Surgery. 320p. 1995. 69.95 (0-8151-6267-7, Yr Bk Med Pubs) Mosby Yr Bk.

— Advances in Otolaryngology: Head & Neck Surgery, Vol. 6. 290p. 1992. 69.95 (0-8151-6264-2) Mosby Yr Bk.

— Advances in Otolaryngology - Head & Neck Surgery. 320p. 1993. 69.95 (0-8151-6265-0, Yr Bk Med Pubs) Mosby Yr Bk.

— Advances in Otolaryngology - Head & Neck Surgery. 320p. 1994. 69.95 (0-8151-6266-9, Yr Bk Med Pubs) Mosby Yr Bk.

— Advances in Otolaryngology - Head & Neck Surgery. 320p. 1996. 69.95 (0-8151-6268-5, Yr Bk Med Pubs) Mosby Yr Bk.

Myers, A. L., jt. auth. see Valenzuela, D. P.

Myers, A. R. Crown, Household & Parliament in Fifteenth-Century England. Clough, Cecil H., ed. 400p. 1985. text ed. 60.00 (0-907628-63-X) Hambledon Press.

— England in the Late Middle Ages. (Orig.). 1952. mass mkt. 5.95 (0-14-020234-X, Penguin Bks) Viking Penguin.

— London in the Age of Chaucer. LC 73-177342. (Centers of Civilization Ser.: Vol. 31). (Illus.). 256p. 1972. reprint ed. pap. 9.95 (0-8061-2111-4) U of Okla Pr.

Myers, Alan, tr. An Age Ago: A Selection of Nineteenth-Century Russian Poetry. 1988. pap. 9.95 (0-374-52084-4) FS&G.

Myers, Alan, tr. see Brodsky, Joseph.

Myers, Alan, tr. see Bykov, Vasil.

Myers, Alan, tr. see Dostoevsky, Fyodor.

Myers, Alan A. & Giller, Paul S., eds. Analytical Biogeography: An Integrated Approach to the Study of Animal & Plant Distributions. (Illus.). 584p. 1991. pap. 35.00 (0-412-40050-2, A5330) Chapman & Hall.

Myers, Albert. Blueprint for Success: The Complete Guide to Starting a Business after Fifty. 1990. pap. 12.95 (0-87877-166-2) Newcastle Pub.

Myers, Albert C. Hannah Logan's Courtship. 1993. reprint ed. lib. bdg. 89.00 (0-7812-5497-3) Rprt Serv.

— Narratives of Early Pennsylvania, West New Jersey & Delaware, 1630-1707. (Illus.). xvi, 476p. 1989. reprint ed. pap. 25.00 (1-55613-176-3) Heritage Bk.

Myers, Albert C., ed. William Penn's Own Account of Lenni Lenape or Delaware Indians. (Illus.). 96p. (J). (gr. 7 up). 1986. pap. 6.95 (0-912608-13-7) Mid Atlantic.

Myers, Albert C., ed. see Wister, Sally.

Myers, Alfred S. Letters for All Occasions. (Orig.). 1994. mass mkt. 5.99 (0-06-109283-5, Harp PBks) HarpC.

— Letters for All Occasions. rev. ed. Ferrari, Lynn, ed. LC 92-34472. 208p. (Orig.). 1993. pap. 10.00 (0-06-273177-7, HarpT) HarpC.

Myers, Allen C., ed. Eerdmans' Bible Dictionary. rev. ed. (Illus.). 1116p. 1987. 34.99 (0-8028-2402-1) Eerdmans.

Myers, Allen R., ed. Medicine. 2nd ed. LC 93-16370. (National Medical Series for Independent Study). (Illus.). 600p. 1994. 26.00 (0-683-06233-6) Williams & Wilkins.

Myers, Alonzo F. A Teacher-Training Program for Ohio. LC 70-177049. (Columbia University. Teachers College. Contributions to Education Ser.: No. 266). reprint ed. 37.50 (0-404-55266-8) AMS Pr.

Myers, Amy. Murder at Plum's. 224p. (Orig.). 1993. mass mkt. 4.50 (0-380-76586-1) Avon.

— Murder at Plum's. large type ed. (General Ser.). 432p. (Orig.). 1993. 21.95 (0-7089-2847-1) Ulverscroft.

— Murder at the Masque. 256p. (Orig.). 1993. mass mkt. 4.99 (0-380-76584-5) Avon.

— Murder in Pug's Parlour. 256p. (Orig.). 1992. mass mkt. 4.50 (0-380-76587-X) Avon.

— Murder in Pugs Parlour. large type ed. 432p. 1993. 21.95 (0-7089-2732-7) Ulverscroft.

— Murder in the Limelight. 224p. (Orig.). 1992. mass mkt. 4.50 (0-380-76585-3) Avon.

— Murder in the Limelight. large type ed. (General Ser.). (Orig.). 1993. 21.95 (0-7089-2435-2) Ulverscroft.

Myers, Andrew B., ed. see Irving, Washington.

Myers, Andrew B., jt. ed. see Lenehan, William.

Myers, Anna. Red-Dirt Jessie. 107p. (YA). 1992. 13.95 (0-8027-8172-1) Walker & Co.

— Red-Dirt Jessie. 112p. (J). (gr. 3-6). 1994. pap. 4.95 (0-8027-7435-0) Walker & Co.

— Rosie's Tiger. LC 94-50814. (J). 1994. 14.95 (0-8027-8305-8) Walker & Co.

Myers, Anna & Sherman, Josepha. Windleaf. LC 93-615. 136p. (J). (gr. 2-6). 1995. 14.95 (0-8027-8260-4) Walker & Co.

Myers, Antoinette & Hansen, Christine. Experimental Psychology. 3rd ed. 448p. (C). 1993. text ed. 53.95 (0-534-16758-6) Brooks-Cole.

***Myers, Arthur.** Drugs & Emotions. LC 95-13902. (Drug Abuse Prevention Library). (J). 1995. write for info. (0-8239-2143-3) Rosen Group.

— Drugs & Peer Pressure. LC 94-37885. (Drug Abuse Prevention Library). 1995. 15.95 (0-8239-2066-6) Rosen Group.

— The Ghosthunter's Guide: To Haunted Landmarks, Parks, Churches, & Other Public Places. LC 92-10505. 336p. 1993. pap. 13.95 (0-8092-4288-5) Contemp Bks.

— Ghostly American Places. LC 94-44788. 1995. text ed. 8.99 (0-517-12391-6) Random Hse Value.

— The Ghostly Gazetteer: America's Most Fascinating Haunted Landmarks. 304p. (Orig.). 1990. pap. 12.95 (0-8092-4204-4) Contemp Bks.

— Ghostly Register: A Guide to Haunted America. (Illus.). 378p. 1990. 17.95 (0-88029-472-8) Marboro Bks.

— The Ghostly Register: Haunted Dwellings, Active Spirits--a Journey to America's Strangest Landmarks. LC 86-13416. (Illus.). 256p. (Orig.). 1986. pap. 14.95 (0-8092-5081-0) Contemp Bks.

— The Pawnee. LC 93-18369. (First Bks.). (Illus.). 64p. (J). (gr. 4-6). 1993. lib. bdg. 13.93 (0-531-20165-1) Watts.

— The Pawnee. (First Bks.). (Illus.). 64p. (J). (gr. 5-8). 1994. pap. 5.95 (0-685-70385-1) Watts.

— World's Most Terrifying "True" Ghost Stories. LC 95-12612. (Illus.). 96p. 1995. pap. 3.95 (0-8069-1350-9) Sterling.

Myers-Avis, Judith, jt. auth. see Crowder, Adrienne.

Myers, Barbara K. & Myers, William R. Engaging in Transcendence: The Church's Ministry & Covenant with Young Children. LC 92-22223. 192p. (Orig.). 1992. pap. 13.95 (0-8298-0932-5) Pilgrim OH.

Myers, Barry. Raiders. (Preacher's Law Ser.: No. 7). 176p. (Orig.). 1989. pap. 2.75 (0-8439-2741-0) Dorchester Pub Co.

— Rebel. (Preacher's Law Ser.: No. 6). 176p. (Orig.). 1988. pap. 2.75 (0-8439-2715-1) Dorchester Pub Co.

Myers, Bernard. History of Art. 1988. 29.98 (0-671-07208-0) S&S Trade.

Myers, Bernice. Ding-a-Ling-a-Ling. (Whole-Language Big Bks.). 16p. (J). (ps-2). 1992. pap. 14.95 (1-56784-055-8) Newbridge Comms.

— The Flying Shoes. LC 91-335. (J). (ps up). 1992. 15.00 (0-688-10695-1); lib. bdg. 14.93 (0-688-10696-X) Lothrop.

— Sidney Rella & the Glass Sneaker. LC 85-3044. (Illus.). 32p. (J). (gr. k-3). 1985. text ed. 14.95 (0-02-767790-7, Mac Bks Young Read) S&S Childrens.

Myers, Betty, jt. auth. see Mager, Gerald M.

Myers, Bill. Christ B. C. Becoming Closer Friends with the Hidden Christ of the Old Testament. Parrish, Annette, ed. LC 90-35816. 120p. (Orig.). 1990. pap. 6.99 (0-8307-1304-2, 5184459) Regal.

— The Deceived. (Forbidden Doors Ser.: No. 2). 176p. (YA). 1994. pap. 4.99 (0-8423-1352-4) Tyndale.

— The Experiment. (Journeys to Fayrah Ser.: Bk. 2). (Illus.). 160p. (Orig.). (J). (gr. 3 up). 1991. pap. 5.99 (1-55661-214-1) Bethany Hse.

— Hot Topics, Tough Questions. 144p. 1987. pap. 5.99 (0-89693-517-5, Victor Books) SP Pubns.

— My Life As a Broken Bungee Cord. (J). (gr. 4-7). 1993. pap. 4.99 (0-8499-3404-4) Word Inc.

— My Life As a Human Hockey Puck. (The/Incredible Worlds of Wally McDoogle Ser.: No. 7). (J). (gr. 4-7). 1994. pap. 4.99 (0-8499-3601-2) Word Inc.

— My Life As a Smashed Burrito with Extra Hot Sauce. (Incredible Worlds of Wally McDougle Ser.). (J). 1993. pap. 4.99 (0-8499-3402-8) Word Inc.

— My Life as a Tornado Test Target. (J). (gr. 4-7). 1994. pap. 4.99 (0-8499-3538-5) Word Inc.

— My Life As Alien Monster Bait. (Incredible Worlds of Wally McDougle Ser.). (J). (gr. 3-7). 1993. pap. 4.99 (0-8499-3403-6) Word Inc.

— My Life as an Afterthought Astronaut. LC 94-45373. (Incredible Worlds of Wally McDoogle Ser.: Bk. 8). (J). 1995. pap. 4.99 (0-8499-3602-0) Word Pub.

— My Life As Crocodile Junk Food. (Incredible Worlds of Wally McDougle Ser.). (J). (gr. 3-7). 1993. pap. 4.99 (0-8499-3405-2) Word Inc.

— My Life as Dinosaur Dental Floss. (J). (gr. 4-7). 1994. pap. 4.99 (0-8499-3537-7) Word Inc.

— The Portal. (Journeys to Fayrah Ser.: Bk. 1). (Illus.). 160p. (Orig.). (J). (gr. 3 up). 1991. pap. 5.99 (1-55661-163-3) Bethany Hse.

— The Society. LC 94-7014. (Forbidden Doors Ser.: Vol. 1). 1994. 4.99 (0-8423-5922-2) Tyndale.

— The Tablet. LC 92-34301. (Journeys to Fahrah Ser.). (Illus.). 160p. (Orig.). (J). (gr. 3 up). 1992. pap. 5.99 (1-55661-299-0) Bethany Hse.

— The Whirlwind. (Journeys to Fayrah Ser.). 160p. (Orig.). (J). (gr. 4-8). 1992. pap. 5.99 (1-55661-258-3) Bethany Hse.

Myers, Bill & Johnson, Ken. McGee & Me: The Big Lie. (J). 1989. pap. 4.99 (0-8423-4169-2) Tyndale.

— McGee & Me! No. 2: Star in the Breaking. (J). 1989. pap. 4.99 (0-8423-4168-4); vhs 14.99 (0-8423-4153-6) Tyndale.

— McGee & Me! No. 3: Not-So-Great Escape. (McGee & Me! Ser.). (J). 1989. vhs 14.99 (0-8423-4154-4) Tyndale.

— McGee & Me! No. 4: Skate Expectations. (McGee & Me! Ser.). (J). 1989. pap. 4.99 (0-8423-4165-X); vhs 14.99 (0-8423-4155-2) Tyndale.

Myers, Bill & West, Robert. The Blunder Years. LC 93-964. (Illus.). (J). 1993. 4.99 (0-8423-4117-X) Tyndale.

Myers, Bill & West, Robert E. Beauty in the Least. LC 93-14026. (J). 1993. 4.99 (0-8423-4124-2) Tyndale.

***Myers, Bob & Myers, Robin.** Making the Connection: Finding Romance in the Personal Ads. (Illus.). 72p. (Orig.). 1994. pap. 9.95 (0-9645308-0-5) Benchtree Pub.

Myers, Brad A. Creating User Interfaces by Demonstration. (Perspectives in Computing Ser.). 276p. 1988. text ed. 61.00 (0-12-512305-1) Acad Pr.

Myers, Brad A., ed. Languages for Developing User Interfaces. LC 92-3677. (Illus.). 480p. (C). 1992. text ed. 59.95 (0-86720-450-8) AK Peters.

Myers, Brian. Han Sorya & North Korean Literature. (Cornell East Asia Ser.: No. 69). 224p. (C). 1994. lib. bdg. 18.00 (0-939657-84-8); pap. 12.00 (0-939657-69-4) Cornell East Asia Pgm.

Myers, Brian & Hamer, E. Mastering Windows NT Programming. LC 93-60631. 1236p. 1993. disk, pap. 44.99 (0-7821-1264-1) Sybex.

Myers, Bryant L. The Changing Shape of World Mission. 52p. 1993. pap. write for info. (0-912552-83-2) MARC.

Myers, C. Roger, jt. ed. see Wright, Mary J.

Myers, Candice E., jt. auth. see Myers, Stanley E.

Myers, Carol A. & Weiner, Ronald G. Coping with Tax Reform. LC 87-406325. 51p. reprint ed. pap. 25.00 (0-7837-6626-2, 2046208) Bks Demand.

Myers, Carol F. Women in Literature: Criticism of the Seventies. LC 75-35757. 263p. 1976. 19.50 (0-8108-0885-4) Scarecrow.

Myers, Catherine. Delay Learning in Artificial Neural Networks. LC 92-19237. (Neural Computing Ser.). 1992. write for info. (0-442-31627-5) Chapman & Hall.

***Myers, Celia.** Stoma Care Nursing: A Patient-Centered Approach. 240p. 1995. pap. 38.25 (1-56593-597-7, 1222) Singular Publishing.

***Myers, Charles.** Memoirs of a Hunter. (American Autobiography Ser.). 309p. 1995. reprint ed. lib. bdg. 89.00 (0-7812-8599-2) Rprt Serv.

Myers, Charles A. The Role of the Private Sector in Manpower Development. LC 72-152912. (Policy Studies in Employment & Welfare: No. 13). 111p. reprint ed. pap. 31.70 (0-317-19898-X, 2023134) Bks Demand.

Myers, Charles A., ed. Wages, Prices, Profits & Productivity. LC 59-12574. 1959. 4.00 (0-936904-07-0) Am Assembly.

Myers, Charles B. & Myers, Lynn K. Introduction to Teaching & Schools. 692p. (C). 1990. text ed. 46.75 (0-03-002513-3) HB Coll Pubs.

— The Professional Educator: A New Introduction to Teaching & Schools. rev. ed. LC 94-23321. 1995. text ed. 47.95 (0-534-20574-7) Intl Thomson.

Myers, Charles E. A Connecticut Yankee in Penn's Woods: The Life & Times of Thomas Bennet. LC 93-60796. (Illus.). 220p. (Orig.). Date not set. pap. 14.95 (0-912975-03-2) Upshur Pr.

Myers, Charles F. & Dolson, Edward M. Missouri Corporate Forms, 2 vols. suppl. ed. 1993. 89.00 (0-685-74599-6) Butterworth Legal Pubs.

— Missouri Corporate Forms, 2 vols., Set. 1100p. 1994. disk, ring bd. 239.00 (0-87189-067-4) Michie Butterworth.

Myers, Charles N. U. S. University Activity Abroad: Implications of the Mexican Case. 1968. pap. 1.50 (0-89192-245-8) Interbk Inc.

Myers, Charles S. Industrial Psychology. Stein, Leon, ed. LC 77-70519. (Work Ser.). (Illus.). 1977. reprint ed. lib. bdg. 19.95 (0-405-10188-0) Ayer.

Myers, Ched. Binding the Strong Man: A Political Reading of Mark's Story of Jesus. LC 88-39205. 512p. 1988. pap. 19.95 (0-88344-620-0, 620-0) Orbis Bks.

— Who Will Roll Away This Stone? Discipleship Queries for First World Christians. LC 94-4445. 425p. (Orig.). 1994. pap. 18.95 (0-88344-947-1) Orbis Bks.

Myers, Ched & Aldridge, Robert. Resisting the Serpent: Palau's Struggle for Self-Determination. (Illus.). 211p. (Orig.). 1990. pap. 9.95 (1-879175-05-3) Fortkamp.

Myers, Christopher A. & Myers, Lynne B. Forest of the Clouded Leopard. LC 93-350. (J). (gr. 4 up). 1994. 13.95 (0-395-67408-5) HM.

— McCrephy's Field. (Illus.). 32p. (J). (gr. 2-5). 1991. 14.95 (0-395-53807-6, Sandpiper) HM.

Myers, Christopher A., jt. auth. see Myers, Lynne B.

Myers, Cindy, ed. see Walkow, Richard A. & O'Brien, Kevin J.

Myers, Coco, ed. see Gibson, Cynthia.

***Myers, Colin, ed.** Professional Awareness in Software Engineering: Or Should a Software Engineer Wear a Suit? LC 94-45888. 1995. write for info. (0-07-707837-3) McGraw.

Myers, Constance A. The Prophet's Army: Trotskyists in America 1928-1941. LC 76-15330. (Contributions in American History Ser.: No. 56). 281p. 1977. text ed. 59.95 (0-8371-9030-4, MPA/, Greenwood Pr) Greenwood.

Myers, Cynthia, ed. Specialty & Minor Crops Handbook. (Illus.). 144p. 1991. ring bd. 30.00 (1-879906-00-7, 3346) ANR Pubns CA.

Myers, Cynthia L., jt. ed. see Madden, Carolyn G.

Myers, D. A., et al. Geology of the Late Paleozoic Horseshoe Atoll in West Texas. (Publication Ser.: PUB 5607). (Illus.). 113p. 1956. 2.00 (0-686-29360-6) Bur Econ Geology.

***Myers, D. G.** The Elephants Teach: Creative Writing since 1880. LC 95-15224. (Studies in Writing & Culture). 1995. pap. text ed. 23.00 (0-13-324013-4) P-H.

Myers, Darlene. Computer Science Resources: A Guide to Professional Literature. LC 81-559. 346p. 1981. pap. 59.50 (0-313-25774-4, Greenwood Pr) Greenwood.

Myers, Dave, jt. auth. see Forman, Jeffrey W.

Myers, Dave, jt. auth. see Jones, Mimi.

***Myers, David.** Exploring Psychology. 548p. 1995. text ed. 43.95x (1-57259-083-1) Worth.

— Exploring Psychology. 3rd ed. 548p. 1995. pap. text ed. 39.95x (1-57259-069-6) Worth.

— Social Psychology. 2nd ed. 270p. 1987. pap. text ed. write for info. (0-07-044277-0) McGraw.

Myers, David & Jeeves, Malcolm. Psychology: Through the Eyes of Faith. 176p. 1987. pap. text ed. 12.00 (0-06-065557-7) Harper SF.

Myers, David, jt. auth. see PC World Editors.

Myers, David, jt. auth. see Plemmons, Patrick.

Myers, David B. Marx & Nietzsche: The Record of an Encounter-the Reminiscences & Transcripts of a Nineteenth Century Journalist. (Illus.). 186p. (Orig.). (C). 1986. pap. text ed. 21.00 (0-8191-5102-5) U Pr of Amer.

— New Soviet Thinking & U.S. Nuclear Policy. 304p. 1990. 44.95 (0-87722-710-1) Temple U Pr.

Myers, David G. Exploring Social Psychology. LC 93-17347. (Series in Social Psychology). 1993. pap. text ed. write for info. (0-07-044296-7); Study guide. student ed, pap. text ed. write for info. (0-07-044303-3) McGraw.

— Psychology. 3rd ed. 636p. 1992. text ed. 56.95x (0-87901-506-3); student ed, pap. 11.95x (0-87901-507-1) Worth.

— Psychology, 1995. 4th ed. 1995. 56.95x (0-87901-644-2); student ed, pap. 13.95 (0-87901-645-0) Worth.

— The Pursuit of Happiness: Discovering the Pathway to Fulfillment, Well-Being, & Enduring Personal Joy. 336p. 1993. reprint ed. pap. 10.00 (0-380-71522-8) Avon.

— Pursuit of Happiness: What Makes a Person Happy - & Why. 1992. 20.00 (0-688-10550-5) Morrow.

— Social Psychology. 3rd ed. 1990. 13.16 (0-07-044284-3) McGraw.

— Social Psychology. 4th ed. LC 92-16358. 1992. text ed. write for info. (0-07-044292-4) McGraw.

— Social Psychology. 4th ed. LC 92-16358. 1992. Study guide. student ed, pap. text ed. 10.36 (0-07-044298-3) McGraw.

Myers, David J. Venezuela's Pursuit of Caribbean Basin Interests: Implications for United States National Security. LC 83-19144. 1985. 4.00 (0-8330-0527-8, R-2994-AF) Rand Corp.

Myers, David J., jt. ed. see Martz, John D.

Myers, David L., jt. auth. see Wilcox, Howard J.

Myers, David L., jt. auth. see Wilcox, Howard.

***Myers, David N.** Re-inventing the Jewish Past: European Jewish Intellectuals & the Zionist Return to History. (Studies in Jewish History). 272p. 1995. 49.95 (0-19-509842-0) OUP.

***Myers, Dawn.** Angels, Angels Everywhere. 128p. (Orig.). (J). 1994. pap. 3.99 (0-380-77935-8, Camelot) Avon.

An Asterisk (*) at the beginning of an entry indicates that the title is appearing in BIP for the first time.

Myers, Dennis & Lamb, Annette. HyperCard Creativity Tool. Schach, Mickey, ed. 704p. 1992. 49.95 (*0-89262-329-2*); 50.00 (*0-89262-371-3*) Career Pub.
— Hypercard (Mac) Authoring Tool 2.0. Schach, Mickey, ed. 800p. 1993. 49.95 (*0-89262-362-4*); 50.00 (*0-89262-364-0*) Career Pub.
Myers, Dennis, jt. auth. see Lamb, Annette.
Myers, Denys P. Historic Architecture of Maine: The Maine Catalog-HABS. LC 74-84742. (Illus.). 1975. 8.95 (*0-913764-05-1*) Maine St Mus.
Myers, Denys. Gaslighting in America: A Pictorial Survey, 1815-1910. 1990. pap. 16.95 (*0-486-26482-3*) Dover.
Myers, Desaix B., et al. U. S. Business in South Africa: The Economic, Political, & Moral Issues. LC 79-3638. 389p. reprint ed. pap. 111.50 (*0-685-44452-X*, 2056713) Bks Demand.
Myers, Diana & Roberts, Bennett. A Slice of Mid-Life. abr. ed. 106p. 1994. pap. 7.95 (*1-56901-312-8*) NW Pub.
Myers, Diana, ed. see Brodsky, Joseph, et al.
***Myers, Diana K. & Bean, Susan S.** From the Land of the Thunder Dragon: Textile Arts of Bhutan. (Illus.). 248p. 1994. pap. 29.95 (*0-906026-33-4*) Peabody Essex Mus.
***Myers, Diana K. & Bean, Susan S., eds.** From the Land of the Thunder Dragon: Textile Arts of Bhutan. (Illus.). 248p. 1995. 44.95 (*0-906026-31-8*, Pub. by Serindia UK) Weatherhill.
Myers, Diana K., et al. Temple Household Horseback: Rugs of the Tibetan Plateau. LC 84-52139. (Illus.). 112p. 1984. pap. 27.50 (*0-87405-024-3*) Textile Mus.
— Temple, Household, Horseback: Rugs of the Tibetan Plateau. (Illus.). 112p. 1984. pap. 27.50 (*0-295-96979-2*) U of Wash Pr.
Myers, Donald J. ERISA Class Exemptions, with Supplements. LC 90-36108. 814p. 1991. text ed. 115.00 (*0-87179-621-X*, 0621) BNA.
— ERISA Class Exemptions, 1994 Supplement: Current Through May 2, 1994. 189p. 1994. pap. 50.00 (*0-87179-817-4*) BNA.
Myers, Donald W. Establishing & Building Employee Assistance Programs. LC 83-21168. (Illus.). xx, 335p. 1984. text ed. 59.95 (*0-89930-044-8*, MYE/, Quorum Bks) Greenwood.
Myers, Donald W., ed. Employee Problem Prevention & Counseling: A Guide for Professionals. LC 84-26499. xiii, 338p. 1985. text ed. 55.00 (*0-89930-084-7*, MEM/, Quorum Bks) Greenwood.
Myers, Doris T. C. S. Lewis in Context. LC 94-7537. 264p. 1994. 28.00x (*0-87338-497-0*) Kent St U Pr.
Myers, Dowell. Analysis with Local Census Data: Portraits of Change. (Illus.). 369p. 1992. pap. text ed. 44.95 (*0-12-512308-6*) Acad Pr.
Myers, Dowell, ed. Housing Demography: Linking Demographic Structure & Housing Markets. LC 90-50094. (Social Demography Ser.). 320p. (Orig.). (C). 1991. text ed. 45.00 (*0-299-12550-5*); pap. text ed. 18.25 (*0-299-12554-8*) U of Wis Pr.
Myers, Drew. Surfaces, Interfaces, & Colloids: Principles & Applications. 433p. 1991. lib. bdg. 49.50 (*1-56081-033-5*) VCH Pubs.
— Surfactant Science & Technology. 2nd ed. 360p. 1992. text ed. 49.50 (*1-56081-586-8*) VCH Pubs.
Myers, E. & Dodge, A. J. Preserving the Dead. 1984. reprint ed. pap. 9.95 (*0-917914-24-4*) Lindsay Pubns.
Myers, E. N., ed. New Dimensions in Otorhinolaryngology Head & Neck Surgery, 2 vols., Vol. 1. (International Congress Ser.: No. 680). 780p. 1986. 245.25 (*0-444-80729-2*, Excerpta Medica) Elsevier.
— New Dimensions in Otorhinolaryngology Head & Neck Surgery, 2 vols., Vol. 2. (International Congress Ser.: No. 680). 1180p. 1986. 229.75 (*0-444-80730-6*, Excerpta Medica) Elsevier.
Myers, E. R. & Kingon, A. I., eds. Ferroelectric Thin Films. (MRS Symposium Proceedings Ser.: Vol. 200). 1990. text ed. 40.00 (*1-55899-089-5*) Materials Res.
Myers, E. R., et al, eds. Ferroelectric Thin Films III. (Symposium Proceedings Ser.: Vol. 310). 1993. text ed. 68.00 (*1-55899-206-5*) Materials Res.
Myers, Edith. The Mysteries of the Rosary. (Illus.). 41p. 1977. reprint ed. 3.00 (*0-912414-13-8*) Stella Maris Bks.
Myers, Edward. The Chosen Few: Surviving the Nuclear Holocaust. LC 82-72604. 180p. (Orig.). 1982. pap. 7.95 (*0-89708-107-2*) And Bks.
— Climb or Die. LC 93-44861. 192p. (J). (gr. 5-9). 1995. 14.95 (*0-7868-0026-7*) Hyprn Child.
— Fire & Ice. 432p. (Orig.). 1992. pap. 4.99 (*0-451-45211-9*, ROC) NAL-Dutton.
— Forri the Baker. LC 93-2468. (J). 1995. 14.99 (*0-8037-1396-7*, MR-291-AF); lib. bdg. 14.89 (*0-8037-1397-5*) Dial Bks Young.
— The Mountain Made of Light. 424p. 1992. pap. 4.99 (*0-451-45136-8*, ROC) NAL-Dutton.
— A Study of Angels. rev. ed. 97p. (Orig.). 1993. pap. 7.95 (*1-878990-00-4*) Howard Pub LA.
— The Summit. 432p. (Orig.). 1994. pap. 5.99 (*0-451-45419-7*, ROC) NAL-Dutton.
— When Parents Die: A Guide for Adults. 224p. 1987. pap. 11.95 (*0-14-009211-0*, Penguin Bks) Viking Penguin.
***Myers, Edward C.** Children of the Thunderbird. 160p. 1994. pap. 9.95 (*0-88839-264-8*) Hancock House.
Myers, Edward P. If I Had One More Sermon to Preach. 1987. pap. 7.50 (*0-89137-328-4*) Quality Pubns.
— The Problem of Evil & Suffering. 132p. (Orig.). 1978. pap. 7.95 (*1-878990-07-1*) Howard Pub LA.
Myers, Edwards, jt. auth. see Turner, J. J.
Myers, Elaine, ed. The Soup Collection. 1995. write for info. (*0-944943-55-1*, 25272-8) Current Inc.
Myers, Elaine, ed. see Brummett, Nancy P. & McConnell, Nancy P.
Myers, Elaine, ed. see Lynch, Linda.
Myers, Elaine M., ed. The Farmer's Market Cookbook. 40p. 1993. pap. 5.40 (*0-944943-36-5*, 21348-7) Current Inc.
— Favorite Bar Cookies from Current. 62p. 1993. pap. 7.10 (*0-944943-21-7*, 20974-0) Current Inc.
— Homemade for the Holidays. (Illus.). 32p. 1993. pap. 7.20 (*0-944943-37-3*, 21327-2) Current Inc.
— Snacks 'n Stuff: Recipes for Kids. (Illus.). 48p. (Orig.). 1993. pap. 5.40 (*0-944943-27-6*, CODE 21154-0) Current Inc.
— Tasty Tidbits-Easy Appetizers & Hors D'Oeuvres. 48p. 1993. pap. 7.20 (*0-944943-38-1*, 21328-1) Current Inc.
Myers, Elaine M., ed. see Spangler, Steven D.
Myers, Elizabeth L. The Upper Places: Nazareth, Gnadenthal & Christian's Spring. 10p. (Orig.). 1978. reprint ed. pap. text ed. 3.00 (*1-877701-04-1*) NCH&GS.
Myers, Eric, jt. auth. see Mandelbaum, Howard.
Myers, Ernest R., ed. Challenges for a Changing America: Perspectives on Immigration & Multiculturalism in the United States. LC 93-42350. 1994. 54.95 (*1-880921-71-5*); pap. 34.95 (*1-880921-70-7*) Austin & Winfield.
Myers, Esther S. Roses in December. (Illus.). 164p. 1979. 13.00 (*0-931068-01-0*) Purcells.
Myers, Eugene N. & Suen, James Y., eds. Cancer of the Head & Neck. 2nd ed. (Illus.). 1132p. 1989. text ed. 179.00 (*0-443-08597-8*) Churchill.
Myers, Eugene N., jt. ed. see Suen, James Y.
Myers, Eugene N., et al, eds. Tracheotomy. (Illus.). 318p. 1985. text ed. 49.95 (*0-443-08381-9*) Churchill.
Myers, Eunice & Adamson, Ginette, eds. Continental, Latin-American & Francophone Women Writers: Selected Papers from the Wichita State University Conference on Foreign Literature, 1984-1985. (Illus.). 224p. (C). 1987. lib. bdg. 42.50 (*0-8191-6290-6*) U Pr of Amer.
Myers, Eunice, jt. ed. see Adamson, Ginette.
Myers, F. J., jt. auth. see Harring, H. K.
Myers, F. M. The Comanches. 1976. 37.50 (*0-934085-00-5*, J M C & Co) Amereon Ltd.
Myers, F. W. Essays, Classical & Modern, 2 vols. in 1. LC 72-13467. (Essay Index Reprint Ser.). 1977. reprint ed. 30.95 (*0-8369-8170-7*) Ayer.
Myers, Florence, jt. auth. see Wall, Meryl J.
Myers, Forrest D. & Clouse, Jerry A. Briner Family History: A Genealogy of George Michael Breiner & Anna Catharina Loy. LC 82-63190. (Illus.). 704p. (Orig.). 1984. 18.00 (*0-9602156-2-X*) A E Myers.
Myers, Frank. Soldiering in Dakota: Among the Indians in 1863-5. LC 77-160983. (Select Bibliographies Reprint Ser.). 1977. reprint ed. 15.95 (*0-8369-5851-9*) Ayer.
Myers, Fred. The Cumberland River Cruise Guide. (Illus.). 88p. (Orig.). 1993. pap. 14.95 (*0-9632005-1-8*) F Myers.
— The Tenn-Tom Nitty-Gritty Cruise Guide. (Illus.). 91p. (Orig.). 1994. pap. 16.95 (*0-9632005-2-6*) F Myers.
— The Tennessee River Cruise Guide. rev. ed. (Illus.). 232p. 1991. pap. 18.95 (*0-9632005-4-2*) F Myers.
— The Tennessee River Cruise Guide. 2nd ed. (Illus.). 1995. pap. 18.95 (*0-9632005-3-4*) F Myers.
Myers, Fred, jt. auth. see Brenneis, Donald.
Myers, Fred R. Pintupi Country, Pintupi Self: Sentiment, Place, & Politics among Western Desert Aborigines. (Illus.). 334p. 1991. pap. 15.00 (*0-520-07411-4*) U CA Pr.
Myers, Fred R., jt. ed. see Marcus, George E.
Myers, Frederic W. Human Personality & Its Survival of Bodily Death, 2 Vols. LC 75-7391. (Perspectives in Psychical Research Ser.). 1975. reprint ed. 132.95 (*0-405-07038-1*) Ayer.
— The Subliminal Consciousness. LC 75-37305. (Occult Ser.). 1976. reprint ed. 58.95 (*0-405-07952-4*) Ayer.
Myers, Gail A. A World of Sports for Girls. LC 81-10440. (Illus.). 160p. (J). (gr. 5-9). 1981. 11.00 (*0-664-32683-8*, Westminster) Westminster John Knox.
Myers, Gail E. & Myers, Michele T. Dynamics of Human Communication. 5th ed. 464p. (C). 1988. pap. text ed. write for info. (*0-07-044223-1*) McGraw.
— The Dynamics of Human Communication: A Laboratory Approach. 6th ed. 480p. 1992. pap. text ed. write for info. (*0-07-044231-2*) McGraw.
Myers, Gail E., jt. auth. see Myers, Michele T.
Myers, Garry C. Creative Thinking Activities. rev. ed. 32p. (J). (gr. 2-6). 1980. pap. 2.95 (*0-87534-113-6*) Highlights.
Myers, Garry C., Jr., jt. auth. see Gessow, Alfred.
Myers, Gary. The House of the Worm. LC 75-2523. (Illus.). 1975. 7.95 (*0-87054-071-8*) Arkham.
***Myers, Gary E.** Do You Hear That Beat: Wisconsin Pop/Rock in the 50s & 60s. LC 94-96410. (Illus.). 385p. 1994. pap. 27.90 (*0-9643073-9-1*) Hummngbrd Pub.
Myers, Gene. LeaderTrip: A Lesson in Organizational Transformation. Beauchemin, Tim et al, eds. (Illus.). 320p. (Orig.). 1993. text ed. 47.77 (*1-884332-00-5*); pap. text ed. 27.77 (*1-884332-01-3*) Netwrk Pr TX.
Myers, Gene, ed. see Otto, Helen T.
Myers, Geoffrey, tr. see Giono, Jean.
Myers, Geoffrey M., et al, eds. Les Chetifs. LC 79-2565. (Old French Crusade Cycle Ser.: Vol. V). 416p. 1981. 39.50 (*0-8173-0023-6*) U of Ala Pr.
Myers, George, Jr. Bodies of Water. (Ohio Writers Ser.: No. 7). (Illus.). 40p. (Orig.). 1987. pap. 4.95 (*0-317-55078-0*) Bottom Dog Pr.
— Nairobi. LC 77-99271. 1978. pap. 3.00 (*0-917976-01-0*, White Ewe Pr) Thunder Baas Pr.
Myers, George. Piranhas. 9.95 (*0-87666-771-X*, M539) TFH Pubns.
Myers, George, Jr. Worlds Without End. LC 90-80551. 98p. 1990. pap. 8.95 (*0-929968-12-3*) Another Chicago Pr.
Myers, Gerald, jt. auth. see Irani, K. S.
Myers, Gerald, jt. ed. see Rosenberg, Alan.
Myers, Gerald E. Insurance Manual for Libraries. LC 77-24524. 78p. reprint ed. pap. 25.00 (*0-685-16431-4*, 2027359) Bks Demand.
— William James: His Life & Thought. 633p. (C). 1988. reprint ed. 22.00 (*0-300-04211-6*) Yale U Pr.
Myers, Gerald E., ed. Writings, 1878-1899: William James: Includes: Psychology; Briefer Course; The Will to Believe; Talks to Teachers; Essays. 1212p. 1992. 35.00 (*0-940450-72-0*) Library of America.
Myers, Gerald E., jt. ed. see Rosenberg, Alan.
Myers, Gerry. Targeting the New Professional Woman: How to Market & Sell to Today's 57 Million Working Women. 1993. 32.50 (*1-55738-549-1*) Probus Pub Co.
Myers, Glen E. Analytical Methods in Conduction Heat Transfer. LC 87-8790. (Illus.). 508p. 1987. reprint ed. text ed. 55.00 (*0-931690-24-2*) Genium Pub.
Myers, Glenford J. Advances in Computer Architecture. LC 77-19001. (Illus.). 329p. 1978. pap. 94.70 (*0-7837-3529-4*, 2057865) Bks Demand.
— Advances in Computer Architecture. 2nd ed. LC 81-11374. 545p. 1982. text ed. 139.00 (*0-471-07878-6*) Wiley.
— The Art of Software Testing. LC 78-12923. (Business Data Processing Ser.). 177p. 1979. text ed. 53.95 (*0-471-04328-1*, Wiley-Interscience) Wiley.
— Software Reliability: Principles & Practices. LC 76-22202. (Business Data Processing Ser.). 360p. 1976. text ed. 55.00 (*0-471-62765-8*, Wiley-Interscience) Wiley.
Myers, Glenford J. & Budde, David L. The 80960 Microprocessor Architecture. 255p. 1988. text ed. 79.95 (*0-471-61857-8*) Wiley.
Myers, Glenn. World Christian Starter Kit. rev. ed. 126p. reprint ed. pap. text ed. 3.99 (*0-9630908-5-2*) O M Lit.
***Myers, Gordon.** Singing Teachers Wear Many Hats. (Illus.). 86p. (Orig.). (C). 1992. pap. 10.00 (*1-878617-02-8*) Leyerle Pubns.
— Twenty-Four Songs of Early Americans - For Church: A Thanksgiving Celebration. (Orig.). (C). Date not set. pap. 12.95 (*1-878617-06-0*) Leyerle Pubns.
Myers, Gordon B. & Wolfson, William Q. Corticotropin: Its Pharmacologic Effects in Man & Practical Therapeutic Utilization. LC 55-7773. (Illus.). 83p. reprint ed. pap. 25.00 (*0-7837-3823-4*, 2043643) Bks Demand.
***Myers, Greg.** Words in Ads. 224p. 1994. pap. 14.95 (*0-340-61444-7*, B4707, Pub. by E Arnold UK) Routledge Chapman & Hall.
— Writing Biology: Texts in the Social Construction of Scientific Knowledge. LC 89-40263. (Science & Literature Ser.). (Illus.). 256p. (Orig.). (C). 1990. text ed. 37.50 (*0-299-12230-1*); pap. text ed. 15.75 (*0-299-12234-4*) U of Wis Pr.
Myers, Gustavus. Ending of Hereditary American Fortunes. LC 68-20528. (Reprints of Economic Classics Ser.). vi, 395p. 1969. reprint ed. 45.00 (*0-678-00454-4*) Kelley.
— The History of American Idealism. LC 74-26126. (Labor Movement in Fiction & Non-Fiction Ser.). reprint ed. 32.50 (*0-404-58506-X*) AMS Pr.
— History of Canadian Wealth. LC 68-9159. 1968. reprint ed. 20.00 (*0-87266-024-9*) Argosy.
— History of Public Franchises in New York City: Manhattan, Bronx, March, 1900. LC 73-19163. (Politics & People Ser.). 136p. 1974. reprint ed. 13.95 (*0-405-05885-3*) Ayer.
— History of the Great American Fortunes, Vol. I. 296p. text ed. 60.00 (*0-88286-068-2*) C H Kerr.
***Myers, H. Ann.** Fifty Ways to Leave Your Love Handles: Your Guide to Healthier Eating & More Enjoyable Exercise in 50 Quick Tips. (Think Fit Ser.). (Illus.). (Orig.). 1995. pap. 4.95 (*1-887011-02-1*) Fresh Aer Hlth.
— Fifty Ways to Leave Your Love Handles: Your Guide to Healthier Eating & More Enjoyable Exercise in 50 Quick Tips, Set. (Illus.). (Orig.). 1995. audio 19.95 (*1-887011-03-X*) Fresh Aer Hlth.
***Myers, H. D.** Brandi. LC 93-86270. 1994. pap. 12.95 (*1-885487-03-7*) Brownell & Carroll.
Myers, H. M. Fluorides & Dental Fluorosis. (Monographs in Oral Science: Vol. 7). (Illus.). 1978. 31.25 (*3-8055-1412-3*) S Karger.
Myers, H. M, comp. Reprinted Selected Top Articles Published 1977, No. 1. (Karger Highlights, Oral Science One Ser.). 1979. 12.00 (*3-8055-3028-5*) S Karger.
Myers, H. M., ed. New Biotechnology in Oral Research. (Illus.). x, 170p. 1989. 117.75 (*3-8055-4916-4*) S Karger.
Myers, H. M., ed. see Levy, Barnet M., et al.
Myers, Hector F., et al, comps. Black Child Development in America, 1927-1977: An Annotated Bibliography. LC 78-20028. 470p. 1979. text ed. 49.95 (*0-313-20719-4*, FBC/, Greenwood Pr) Greenwood.
— Research in Black Child Development: Doctoral Dissertation Abstracts, 1927-1979. LC 81-13425. (Illus.). xxi, 737p. 1982. text ed. 59.95 (*0-313-22631-8*, FRC/, Greenwood Pr) Greenwood.
Myers, Hector F., et al, eds. Ethnic Minority Perspectives on Clinical Training & Services in Psychology. 208p. (Orig.). 1991. pap. 24.00 (*1-55798-120-5*) Am Psychol.
Myers, Helen & Sadie, Stanley, eds. Ethnomusicology. (Grove Handbooks in Music Ser.). (Illus.). 300p. 1992. 55.00 (*0-393-03377-5*) Norton.
— Ethnomusicology: Historical & Regional Studies. (Illus.). 400p. 1993. 40.00 (*0-393-03378-3*) Norton.
Myers, Helen, jt. auth. see Nettl, Bruno.
Myers, Helen R. A Father's Promise. (Silhouette Romance Ser.). 1994. pap. 2.75 (*0-373-19002-6*, 5-19002-0) Harlequin Bks.
— A Father's Promise. (Silhouette Romance Ser.). 1994. pap. 2.75 (*0-373-91002-9*, 5-91002-1) Silhouette.
— Forbidden Passion. large type ed. LC 93-20047. 1993. Alk. paper. pap. 16.95 (*1-56054-683-2*) Thorndike Pr.
— Jake. (Silhouette Desire Ser.). 1993. mass mkt. 2.99 (*0-373-05797-0*, 5-05797-1) Silhouette.
— The Law Is No Lady. (Montana Mavericks Ser.). 1995. mass mkt. 3.99 (*0-373-50172-2*, 1-50172-5) Harlequin Bks.
— The Merry Matchmakers. 1995. pap. 2.99 (*0-373-19121-9*, 1-19121-2) Silhouette.
— Night Mist. (Shadows Ser.: No. 6). 1993. mass mkt. 3.50 (*0-373-27006-2*) Silhouette.
— The Rebel & the Hero. (Desire Ser.). 1995. mass mkt. 3.25 (*0-373-05941-8*, 1-05941-9) Silhouette.
— Through My Eyes. large type ed. 214p. 1992. reprint ed. lib. bdg. 17.95 (*1-56054-308-6*) Thorndike Pr.
— To Wed at Christmas: (Under the Mistletoe) (Sil Romance Ser.). 1994. pap. 2.75 (*0-373-19049-2*, 1-19049-5) Silhouette.
— Watching for Willa. (Shadows Ser.). 1995. mass mkt. 3.50 (*0-373-27049-6*, 1-27049-5) Silhouette.
— Whispers in the Woods. (Shadows Ser.). 1994. mass mkt. 3.50 (*0-373-27023-2*, 5-27023-6) Silhouette.
Myers, Henry, jt. auth. see Holbik, Karel.
Myers, Henry A. Medieval Kingship. LC 81-11050. 520p. (C). 1981. text ed. 39.95 (*0-88229-633-7*) Nelson-Hall.
Myers, Henry S, Jr. Fundamentally Speaking. LC 77-3072. (Orig.). 1977. pap. 4.95 (*0-89407-007-X*) Strawberry Hill.
Myers, Howard & Pudlow, Jan. The Trial: A Procedural Description & Case Study. Hannan, ed. 234p. (C). 1991. pap. text ed. 28.25 (*0-314-82441-3*) West Pub.
Myers, Hugh E. Nimzovich Defense to 1.e4. 2nd ed. (Openings Ser.). (Illus.). 171p. 1993. pap. text ed. 16.00 (*0-939433-11-7*) Caissa Edit.
Myers, Iris, ed. see Collier, R. B.
Myers, Irma. Destiny. 404p. (Orig.). 1993. pap. 16.95 (*1-880365-29-4*) Prof Pr NC.
Myers, Isabel B. Murder Yet to Come. LC 93-49476. 311p. 1994. reprint ed. 14.95 (*0-935652-22-1*) Ctr Applications Psych.
Myers, Isabel B. & Myers, Peter B. Gifts Differing. 256p. (Orig.). 1990. reprint ed. 22.95 (*0-89106-015-4*, 7271R) Consulting Psychol.
— Gifts Differing: Understanding Personality Type. 3rd ed. LC 95-4184. 256p. 1995. pap. 14.95 (*0-89106-074-X*) Davies-Black.
— Gifts Differing: Understanding Personality Type. LC 93-13087. 1993. reprint ed. pap. 14.95 (*0-89106-064-2*) Consulting Psychol.
Myers, J. Arthur. Captain of All These Men of Death. 300p. 1977. 14.80 (*0-87527-160-X*) Green.
— Masters of Medicine: An Historical Sketch of the College of Medical Sciences of the University of Minnesota, 1888-1966. LC 68-8890. (Illus.). 942p. 1968. 19.10 (*0-87527-058-1*); pap. 14.80 (*0-87527-140-5*) Green.
Myers, J. E., jt. auth. see Bennett, C. O.
Myers, J. Jay. Altered Brand. LC 92-45715. 142p. 1993. 19.95 (*0-8027-1271-1*) Walker & Co.
Myers, J. Martin. Cures by Psychotherapy: What Effects Change? LC 83-21195. 176p. 1984. text ed. 45.00 (*0-275-91445-3*, C1445, Praeger Pubs) Greenwood.
Myers, J. P., Jr., et al, eds. Constructivity in Computer Science: Summer Symposium, San Antonio, TX, June 19-22, 1991, Proceedings. LC 92-19519. (Lecture Notes in Computer Science Ser.: Vol. 613). x, 247p. 1992. 47.00 (*0-387-55631-1*); pap. 43.00 (*3-540-55631-1*) Spr-Verlag.
Myers, J. Wilson, et al, eds. An Aerial Atlas of Ancient Crete. LC 91-20649. (Centennial Book Ser.). (C). 1992. 110.00 (*0-520-07382-7*) U CA Pr.
Myers, Jack. Adbashing: Surviving the Attacks on Advertising. 325p. (Orig.). (C). 1993. pap. text ed. 17.95 (*0-9635864-0-8*) Amer Media Coun.
— As Long As You're Happy. LC 85-82575. (National Poetry Ser.). 96p. 1986. 15.00 (*0-915308-81-9*); pap. 8.00 (*0-915308-82-7*) Graywolf.
— Blindsided. 96p. 1993. pap. 12.95 (*0-87923-956-5*) Godine.
— Can Birds Get Lost? And Other Questions about Animals. LC 90-85911. (Illus.). 64p. (J). (gr. 1-5). 1991. 12.95 (*1-878093-32-0*) Boyds Mills Pr.
— Can Birds Get Lost? And Other Questions about Animals. (Illus.). 64p. (J). (gr. 1-7). 1994. 7.95 (*1-56397-401-0*) Boyds Mills Pr.
— Do Cats Really Have Nine Lives? And Other Questions about Your World. LC 91-77713. (J). (gr. 4-7). 1993. 12.95 (*1-56397-089-9*) Boyds Mills Pr.
— Do Cats Really Have Nine Lives? And Other Questions about Your World. LC 91-77713. (Illus.). 64p. (J). (gr. 1-7). 1994. pap. 7.95 (*1-56397-215-8*) Boyds Mills Pr.
— Highlights Book of Science Questions That Children Ask. LC 94-79501. (Illus.). 256p. (J). (gr. 1-5). 1995. 10.95 (*1-56397-478-9*, Wordsong) Boyds Mills Pr.
— How Do We Dream? And Other Questions about Your Body. (Illus.). 64p. (J). (gr. 1-5). 1992. 12.95 (*1-56397-091-0*) Boyds Mills Pr.
— How Do We Dream? And Other Questions about Your Body. (Illus.). 64p. (J). (gr. 1-7). 1994. pap. 7.95 (*1-56397-400-2*) Boyds Mills Pr.
— I'm Amazed That You're Still Singing. LC 81-8452. 69p. 1981. text ed. 9.95 (*0-934332-35-5*); pap. text ed. 4.25 (*0-934332-34-7*) LEpervier Pr.
— What Makes Popcorn Pop? And Other Questions about the World Around Us. LC 90-85912. (Illus.). 64p. (J). (gr. 1-5). 1991. 12.95 (*1-878093-33-9*) Boyds Mills Pr.
— What Makes Popcorn Pop? And Other Questions about the World Around Us. (Illus.). 64p. (J). (gr. 1-7). 1994. pap. 7.95 (*1-56397-402-9*) Boyds Mills Pr.
Myers, Jack & Simms, Michael. Longman Dictionary of Poetic Terms. Orig. Title: Longman Dictionary & Handbook of Poetry. 366p. (C). 1989. pap. text ed. 27.95 (*0-8013-0344-3*, 78119) Longman.
Myers, Jack & Weingarten, Roger, eds. New American Poets of the Eighties. 480p. 1984. pap. 12.95 (*0-931694-35-3*) Wampeter Pr.
— New American Poets of the Nineties. 464p. 1991. pap. 18.95 (*0-87923-907-7*) Godine.
Myers, Jack & Wojahn, David, eds. A Profile of Twentieth-Century American Poetry. LC 90-37757. 336p. (C). 1991. text ed. 16.95 (*0-8093-1349-9*) S Ill U Pr.

An Asterisk (*) at the beginning of an entry indicates that the title is appearing in BIP for the first time.

Myers, Jack D., ed. see Ryan, Will G.

Myers, Jack F. The Language of Visual Art: Perception as a Basis for Design. 368p. (C). 1989. pap. text ed. 35.25 (*0-03-012604-5*) HB Coll Pubs.

Myers, Jacob M. Esdras One & Two. 1974. pap. 18.00 (*0-385-00426-5*) Doubleday.

Myers, Jacob M., ed. Chronicles Two. (Anchor Bible Ser.: Vol. 13). 1965. pap. 18.00 (*0-385-03757-0*, Anchor NY) Doubleday.

Myers, James. Broom Hilda Comic Strip Tease. (Illus.). 1982. pap. 1.95 (*0-449-14459-3*) Fawcett.

— Never Trust Short Green People. 1985. pap. 1.95 (*0-449-12429-0*) Fawcett.

— Sore Loser. (Broomhilda Ser.: No. 11). (Illus.). 1987. pap. 2.25 (*0-449-12991-8*) Fawcett.

***Myers, James C., ed.** Science & Technology of Building Seals, Sealants, Glazing & Waterproofing Vol. 3. (Special Technical Publication: No. 1254). (Illus.). 106p. 1994. text ed. 59.00 (*0-8031-1993-3*, 04-012540-10) ASTM.

Myers, James E. The Great American Liar: A Treasury of Tall Tales. 375p. (Orig.). 1987. pap. 9.95 (*0-942936-13-2*) Lincoln-Herndon Pr.

— Jones. LC 82-81241. 216p. 1982. 12.95 (*0-942936-03-5*) Lincoln-Herndon Pr.

— A Treasury of Farm & Ranch Humor. (Illus.). 325p. 1989. pap. 10.95 (*0-942936-15-9*) Lincoln-Herndon Pr.

Myers, James E., ed. America's Phunniest Phellow - Josh Billings. 275p. 1985. 14.95 (*0-942936-05-1*); pap. 7.95 (*0-942936-07-8*) Lincoln-Herndon Pr.

— Grandpa's Rib Ticklers & Knee-Slappers. 1984. 15.95 (*0-942936-02-7*); pap. 8.95 (*0-942936-01-9*) Lincoln-Herndon Pr.

— A Treasury of Hunting & Fishing Humor. (Illus.). 320p. 1990. pap. 10.95 (*0-942936-19-1*) Lincoln-Herndon Pr.

— A Treasury of Husband & Wife Humor. 350p. (Orig.). 1993. pap. 10.95 (*0-942936-22-1*) Lincoln-Herndon Pr.

— A Treasury of Medical Humor. 350p. (Orig.). 1992. pap. 10.95 (*0-942936-21-3*) Lincoln-Herndon Pr.

Myers, James E., Sr., ed. A Treasury of Religious Humor. (Illus.). 300p. 1994. pap. 10.95 (*0-942936-24-8*) Lincoln-Herndon Pr.

Myers, James E., ed. A Treasury of Senior Humor. 350p. (Orig.). 1992. pap. 10.95 (*0-942936-20-5*) Lincoln-Herndon Pr.

Myers, James E., ed. see Benton, Frank.

Myers, James E., jt. ed. see Lehmann, Arthur C.

Myers, James E., ed. see Whiting, Robert R.

Myers, James E., et al, eds. A Treasury of Military Humor. (Illus.). 350p. (Orig.). 1989. pap. 10.95 (*0-942936-16-7*) Lincoln-Herndon Pr.

***Myers, James G.** Mastering Psychology: A Computer Assisted Laboratory Manual. 2nd ed. (Illus.). 278p. (C). 1994. reprint ed. pap. text ed. 32.00 (*1-879972-00-X*, NW Innovations) Chemeketa Coll.

Myers, James P., Jr., ed. see Davies, John.

Myers, James T. Enemies Without Guns: The Catholic Church in China. LC 90-23647. (Illus.). 334p. (C). 1991. 29.95 (*0-943852-90-0*) Prof World Peace.

Myers, James T. & Lin, Bih-Jaw, eds. Contemporary China & the Changing International Community. LC 94-11684. 1994. write for info. (*1-57003-024-3*) U of SC Pr.

Myers, James T., jt. auth. see Lin, Bih-Jaw.

Myers, James T., et al. Chinese Politics: Documents & Analysis, Vol. 1: Cultural Revolution to 1969. LC 85-22466. 433p. 1986. text ed. 69.95 (*0-87249-475-6*) U of SC Pr.

— Chinese Politics: Documents & Analysis, Vol. 2: Ninth Party Congress (1969) to the Death of Mao (1976) 467p. (C). 1989. text ed. 69.95 (*0-87249-601-5*) U of SC Pr.

***Myers, James T., et al, eds.** Chinese Politics: Documents & Analysis: The Death of Mao (1976) to the Fall of Hua Kuo-feng (1980), Vol. 3. Date not set. 69.95 (*1-57003-062-6*) U of SC Pr.

— Chinese Politics: Documents & Analysis: The Fall of Hua Kuo-feng (1980) to the Twelfth Party Congress (1982), Vol. 4. Date not set. 69.95 (*1-57003-063-4*) U of SC Pr.

Myers, Jamie. You Can Encourage Your High School Student to Read. 24p. 1989. pap. 1.75 (*0-87207-162-6*) Intl Reading.

Myers, Jane & Ayres, Linda. George Bellows: The Artist & His Lithographs, 1916-1924. LC 88-70703. (Illus.). 212p. 1988. 39.95 (*0-88360-059-5*) Amon Carter.

Myers, Jane, jt. auth. see Ayres, Linda.

Myers, Jane, jt. auth. see Brown, Jill.

Myers, Jane, jt. auth. see Riker, Harold C.

Myers, Jane, et al. Stuart Davis: Graphic Work & Related Paintings with a Catalogue Raisonne of the Prints. LC 86-70931. (Illus.). 100p. 1986. 29.95 (*0-88360-054-4*); pap. 14.95 (*0-88360-055-2*) Amon Carter.

Myers, Jane E. Adult Children & Aging Parents. 216p. 1989. 19.95 (*0-8403-5448-7*) Am Coun Assn.

— Empowerment for Later Life. 1990. pap. write for info. (*1-56109-029-8*) ERIC Clearinghouse.

Myers, Jane E., ed. Developing & Directing Counselor Education Laboratories: Proceedings of an ACES National Conference Think Tank. LC 94-3946. 1994. 27.95 (*1-55620-137-0*) Am Coun Assn.

Myers, Jane E., jt. ed. see Schwiebert, Valerie L.

Myers, Janet L. Productive Bankers & Profitable Banks: The Grand Slam of Banking. LC 91-61867. (Illus.). 176p. 1992. 49.95 (*1-880023-44-X*) Dearborn Busn Pr.

Myers, Jay A. Fighters of Fate. LC 79-84329. (Essay Index Reprint Ser.). 1977. 21.95 (*0-8369-1099-0*) Ayer.

— Tuberculosis: A Half-Century of Study & Conquest. LC 75-96989. (Illus.). 378p. 1970. 14.80 (*0-87527-059-X*) Green.

Myers, Jean M., jt. auth. see Myers, Joseph A.

Myers, Jeffrey R. Shakespeare's Mannerist Canon: Ut Picturas Poemata. (Literature & the Visual Arts: New Foundations Ser.: Vol. 2). 224p. (C). 1989. text ed. 52.00 (*0-8204-0891-3*) P Lang Pubs.

***Myers, Jerome L. & Well, Arnold D.** Research Design & Statistical Analysis. LC 95-8542. 752p. 1995. reprint ed. 49.95 (*0-8058-2067-1*) L Erlbaum Assocs.

Myers, Jess. Winnipeg Jets. LC 93-48451. (NHL Today Ser.). 32p. (J). 1995. 14.95 (*0-88682-692-6*) Creative Ed.

Myers, Joan, photos & contrib. Santiago: Saint of Two Worlds: Published in Observance of the 500th Anniversary of Spain's First Encounter with the New World. LC 91-6498. (Illus.). 207p. 1991. 45.00 (*0-8263-1273-X*); pap. 27.50 (*0-8263-1274-8*) U of NM Pr.

***Myers, John.** Bravos of the West. 480p. 1995. pap. 15.00 (*0-8032-8222-2*, Bison Books) U of Nebr Pr.

— The Eucharist: Sacrifice of Love. 1992. 0.50 (*1-56036-025-9*) AMI Pr.

— Prospering in the Nineties: Essays from "The Quiet Corner" 137p. 1991. 14.95 (*0-9630380-0-1*) Myers Fin.

— Voices from the Edge of Eternity. 1994. 9.97 (*1-55748-548-8*) Barbour & Co.

Myers, John & Monson, Luetta. Involving Families in Middle Level Education. 48p. (C). 1992. pap. text ed. 10.00 (*1-56090-065-2*) Natl Middle Schl.

Myers, John, jt. auth. see Church, David.

Myers, John, jt. auth. see Digby, Christine.

Myers, John, ed. see Finnerty, Margaret.

Myers, John, ed. see King, Jean B.

Myers, John, jt. auth. see Koprowicz, Constance.

Myers, John A., Jr. A Manual of Usage. 1986. teacher ed 6.96 (*0-88334-076-3*, 75752); student ed 7.50 (*0-8013-0088-6*, 75752) Longman.

Myers, John B. Legal Issues in Child Abuse & Neglect Practice. (Interpersonal Violence Practice Ser.: Vol. 1). (Illus.). 184p. (C). 1992. 42.95 (*0-8039-4231-1*); pap. 18.95 (*0-8039-4232-X*) Sage.

Myers, John D. Solar Applications in Industry & Commerce. (Illus.). 432p. (C). 1984. text ed. 43.00 (*0-13-822404-8*) P-H.

Myers, John E. The Backlash: Child Protection under Fire. 176p. 1994. 38.00 (*0-8039-5403-4*); pap. 17.95 (*0-8039-5404-2*) Sage.

— Evidence in Child Abuse & Neglect Cases, 2 vols., Vol. 2. 2nd ed. LC 92-15816. (Trial Practice Library Ser.). 896p. 1992. Set. text ed. 218.00 (*0-471-55664-5*, Pub. by Wiley Law Pubns) Wiley.

— The Way of the Pipa: Structure & Imagery in Chinese Lute Music. LC 91-33965. (World Music Ser.). (Illus.). 152p. 1992. lib. bdg. 35.00 (*0-87338-455-5*) Kent St U Pr.

Myers, John G., jt. auth. see Aaker, David A.

Myers, John L. Holy Family. 231p. (Orig.). 1992. pap. 8.95 (*1-55583-200-8*) Alyson Pubns.

Myers, John L. & Gryder, Robert. The Salt-River Pima-Maricopa Indians. (Illus.). 176p. (Orig.). (C). 1988. write for info. (*0-929690-01-X*); pap. write for info. (*0-929690-00-1*) Herit Pubs AZ.

Myers, John L. & Kroman, Karen K. Your Life Story: A Step-by-Step Workbook. Gryder, Robert, ed. (C). 1989. student ed 19.50 (*0-929690-06-0*) Herit Pubs AZ.

Myers, John L., et al. The History of the University of Nevada, Las Vegas Athletic Department: The First Thirty Years, 1959-1989. 225p. (C). 1990. 29.95 (*0-929690-08-7*) Herit Pubs AZ.

Myers, John L., et al, eds. The Arizona Governors, 1912-1990. LC 89-80719. 208p. (C). 1989. 29.95 (*0-929690-05-2*) Herit Pubs AZ.

Myers, John M. The Alamo. LC 48-5208. (Illus.). 240p. 1973. reprint ed. pap. 8.95 (*0-8032-5779-1*) U of Nebr Pr.

— Doc Holliday. LC 55-5528. 224p. 1973. reprint ed. pap. 8.95 (*0-8032-5781-3*, Bison Books) U of Nebr Pr.

— The Saga of Hugh Glass: Pirate, Pawnee, & Mountain Man. LC 75-38613. viii, 237p. 1976. reprint ed. pap. 8.95 (*0-8032-5834-8*) U of Nebr Pr.

— Silverlock. (Orig.). 1993. reprint ed. lib. bdg. 18.95 (*0-89968-409-2*, Lghtyr Pr) Buccaneer Bks.

— Tombstone's Early Years. LC 94-41319. 272p. 1995. pap. 10.00 (*0-8032-8215-X*, Bison Books) U of Nebr Pr.

Myers, John W. Writing to Learn Across the Curriculum. LC 84-61203. (Fastback Ser.: No. 209). 50p. (Orig.). 1984. pap. 1.25 (*0-87367-209-7*) Phi Delta Kappa.

Myers, Johnnie J. Texas Electric Railway: Bulletin No. 121. King, LeRoy O., Jr., ed. LC 82-71474. (Illus.). 256p. 1982. 36.00 (*0-915348-21-7*) Central Electric.

Myers, Joseph A. & Myers, Jean M. Nine Lives: The Reincarnation Story. rev. ed. 220p. 1994. pap. 14.95 (*0-913911-08-9*) Akashic Pr.

Myers, Joseph A., ed. see American Indian Lawyer Training Program, Inc., Staff.

Myers, Judith L. Quick Medication Administration Reference. 64p. 1991. spiral bd. 8.95 (*0-8016-6583-3*) Mosby Yr Bk.

Myers, Judith L., jt. ed. see Beare, Patricia G.

Myers, Julie. Dream Builder. (Superromance Ser.). 1993. mass mkt. 3.39 (*0-373-70535-2*, 1-70535-9) Harlequin Bks.

Myers, K., jt. auth. see Emery, D.

Myers, K. H. & Danner, R. P. Prediction Methods for Organo-Metallic Compounds: Supplements. 186p. 1991. spiral bd. 105.00 (*0-8169-0560-6*) Am Inst Chem Eng.

Myers, K. Sara. Ovid's Causes: Cosmogony & Aetiology in the Metamorphoses. 180p. 1994. text ed. 34.50 (*0-472-10459-4*) U of Mich Pr.

Myers, Karen. Harmonious Companions, Vol. 1: Being a Compendium of One Hundred Dramatic, Romantic, Convivial, Sporting, Seasonal, Martial & Celebratory Songs. LC 92-85278. (Illus.). 272p. (Orig.). 1993. pap. 19.95 (*0-9635384-7-0*) Perkunas Pr.

Myers, Karen, jt. auth. see Porat, Frieda.

Myers, Kathy. Understains: The Sense & Seduction of Advertising. (Comedia Bks.). 160p. 1988. pap. text ed. 13.95 (*0-906890-98-5*, Pub. by Comedia NY) Routledge Chapman & Hall.

Myers, Ken. All God's Children & Blue Suede Shoes: Christians & Popular Culture. LC 87-71899. (Turning Point Christian Worldview Ser.). 224p. 1989. pap. 12.99 (*0-89107-538-0*) Crossway Bks.

Myers, Kenneth A., ed. see Berger, Peter L., et al.

***Myers, Kenneth D.** False Security: Greed & Deception in America's Multibillion-Dollar Insurance Industry. 225p. (C). 1995. 24.95 (*0-87975-928-3*) Prometheus Bks.

Myers, Kenneth H. Marketing Policy Determination by a Major Firm in a Capital Goods Industry. LC 75-41773. (Companies & Men: Business Enterprises in America Ser.). 1976. 47.95 (*0-405-08087-5*) Ayer.

Myers, Kenneth N. Total Contingency Planning for Disasters: Managing Risk...Minimizing Loss...Ensuring Business Continuity. 288p. 1993. text ed. 65.00 (*0-471-57418-X*) Wiley.

***Myers, Kirk.** When Old Town Was Young: The Early Decades of Old Pasadena. 24p. 1994. pap. 6.95 (*0-9642429-0-7*) K Myers.

Myers, Kurtz, comp. Index to Record Reviews, 5 vols. 2000p. 1978. lib. bdg. 420.00 (*0-8161-0087-X*) G K Hall.

— Index to Record Reviews, 1978-1983: First Supplement. (Library Catalogs & Supplements). 1985. lib. bdg. 165.00 (*0-8161-0435-2*, Hall Library) G K Hall.

Myers, L. Create a Computer Bulletin Board System. 1991. 30.50 (*0-8306-6225-1*) TAB Bks.

Myers, L. H. The Root & the Flower. (Twentieth-Century Classics Ser.). 583p. 1986. pap. 7.95 (*0-19-281911-9*) OUP.

Myers, L. Rex. Daviess County, Indiana, Vol. II. LC 88-50352. 336p. 1991. 45.00 (*0-685-50370-4*) Turner Pub KY.

— Daviess County, Indiana History. LC 88-50352. 336p. 1988. 50.00 (*0-938021-66-4*) Turner Pub KY.

Myers, Larry. Training with Cerutty. LC 77-85323. (Illus.). 176p. 1978. pap. 6.95 (*0-89037-081-8*) Anderson World.

***Myers, Larry E.** Hungry for God: Are the Poor Really Unspiritual. LC 94-77740. 208p. 1994. pap. 10.99 (*1-56384-075-8*) Huntington Hse.

Myers, Larry T. Stories from Latin America: An ESL-EFL Reader. (Illus.). 96p. (C). 1987. pap. text ed. write for info. (*0-318-61593-2*) P-H.

***Myers, Lary.** Amazing 3-D Games Adventure Set. 1995. pap. 39.99 (*1-883577-15-2*) Coriolis Grp.

Myers, Laura G., jt. auth. see Landau, Lois.

Myers, Laurie. Earthquake in the Third Grade. LC 92-26609. (J). 1993. 13.95 (*0-395-65360-6*, Clarion Bks) HM.

— Garage Sale Fever. LC 92-40342. (Illus.). 80p. (J). (gr. 2-5). 1993. 13.95 (*0-06-022905-5*); lib. bdg. 12.89 (*0-06-022908-X*) HarpC.

— Guinea Pigs Don't Talk. LC 93-39642. (Illus.). (YA). 1994. 13.95 (*0-395-68967-8*, Clarion Bks) HM.

Myers, Laurie A., jt. ed. see Thomas, John A.

Myers, Lawrence. Smart Bombs: Improvised Sensory Detonation Techniques & Advanced Weapons System. (Illus.). 112p. 1990. pap. 12.00 (*0-87364-548-0*) Paladin Pr.

Myers, Lawrence W. Counterbomb: Protecting Yourself Against Car, Mail, & Area-Emplaced Bombs. (Illus.). 96p. 1991. pap. 14.00 (*0-87364-608-8*) Paladin Pr.

— Improvised Radio Detonation Techniques. (Illus.). 80p. 1988. pap. 12.00 (*0-87364-479-4*) Paladin Pr.

— Improvised Radio Jamming Techniques: Electronic Guerrilla Warfare. (Illus.). 256p. 1989. pap. 19.95 (*0-87364-520-0*) Paladin Pr.

— Spycomm: Covert Communication Techniques of the Underground. (Illus.). 256p. 1991. pap. 19.95 (*0-87364-643-6*) Paladin Pr.

Myers, Lena W. Black Women - Do They Cope Better? rev. ed. LC 91-32935. 96p. 1991. reprint ed. lib. bdg. 49.95 (*0-685-56377-4*); reprint ed. pap. 19.95 (*0-7734-9854-0*) E Mellen.

***Myers, Leo O.** Debtor-Creditor Relations: Manual & Forms. (Business Practice Library). 1994. text ed. 118.00 (*0-471-11225-9*) Wiley.

— Debtor-Creditor Relations: Manual & Forms. LC 86-7179. 734p. 1986. text ed. 95.00 (*0-07-044266-5*) Shepards-McGraw.

Myers, Leopold H. Clio. 1971. reprint ed. 29.00 (*0-403-00673-2*) Scholarly.

— Orissers. 1971. reprint ed. 59.00 (*0-403-01125-6*) Scholarly.

Myers, Linda, ed. Approaches to Computer Writing Classrooms: Learning from Practical Experience. LC 92-32896. (SUNY Series, Literacy, Culture, & Learning: Theory & Practice). (Illus.). 225p. (C). 1993. 59.50 (*0-7914-1567-8*); pap. 19.95 (*0-7914-1568-6*) State U NY Pr.

Myers, Linda J. Understanding of Afrocentric World View: Introduction to an Optimal Psychology. 128p. 1992. per. 15.96 (*0-8403-8342-8*) Kendall-Hunt.

Myers, Loicy, jt. auth. see Tatam, Robert D.

Myers, Lois, jt. auth. see Pelton, Charles L.

Myers, Lois E. Letters by Lamplight: A Woman's View of Everyday Life in South Texas, 1873-1883. LC 90-85476. (Illus.). 222p. (Orig.). 1991. 23.95 (*0-918954-53-3*) Baylor Univ Pr.

Myers, Lonny & Leggitt, Hunter. Adultery & Other Private Matters: Your Right to Personal Freedom in Marriage. LC 75-4701. (Illus.). 221p. 1975. 26.95 (*0-911012-51-6*) Nelson-Hall.

Myers, Loretta C. The Socialization of Neophyte Nurses. LC 82-7014. (Studies in Nursing Management: No. 1). (Illus.). 156p. reprint ed. pap. 44.50 (*0-685-20336-0*, 2070022) Bks Demand.

Myers, Lynda. Becoming an Effective Tutor. Gerould, Phil, ed. LC 89-82096. (Fifty-Minute Ser.). 80p. (Orig.). 1990. pap. 9.95 (*1-56052-028-0*) Crisp Pubns.

Myers, Lynn K., jt. auth. see Myers, Charles B.

Myers, Lynn R., jt. auth. see Horton, Laurel.

Myers, Lynn R., jt. auth. see Terry, George D.

***Myers, Lynne B. & Myers, Christopher A.** Galapagos: Islands of Change. LC 94-26173. (Illus.). 48p. (J). (gr. 4-7). 1995. 16.95 (*0-7868-0074-7*); lib. bdg. 16.89 (*0-7868-2061-6*) Hyprn Child.

— Turnip Soup. (Illus.). 32p. (J). (ps-2). 1994. 13.95 (*1-56282-445-7*); lib. bdg. 13.89 (*1-56282-446-5*) Hyprn Child.

Myers, Lynne B., jt. auth. see Myers, Christopher A.

Myers, M., ed. Ann Eliza Bleecker: An Anthology in Memoriam (1752-1783) LC 93-71851. 251p. (Orig.). 1993. pap. text ed. 24.95 (*1-879183-21-8*) Bristol Banner.

— Celia Thaxter: An Anthology in Memoriam (1835-1894) LC 93-74631. (Orig.). 1994. pap. 24.95 (*1-879183-23-4*) Bristol Banner.

— Charles Warren Stoddard: An Anthology in Memioriam (1843-1909) 160p. (Orig.). 1993. pap. text ed. 24.95 (*1-879183-18-8*) Bristol Banner.

— Edna St. Vincent Millay: The Rebirth (1892-1950) LC 92-71523. (Orig.). 1992. pap. text ed. 14.95 (*1-879183-16-1*) Bristol Banner.

— Eugene Field: An Anthology in Memoriam (1850-1895) LC 94-73734. 184p. (Orig.). 1995. pap. text ed. 24.95 (*1-879183-25-0*) Bristol Banner.

— Rose Terry Cooke: Am Anthology in Memoriam (1827-1892) LC 92-82713. 202p. (Orig.). 1992. pap. text ed. 24.95 (*1-879183-17-X*) Bristol Banner.

— Sorin of Notre Dame: A Centennial Celebration in Poetry on the Anniversary of the Death of Edward Sorin, C. S. C. 1814-1893. LC 91-75432. 211p. (Orig.). 1991. pap. text ed. 14.95 (*1-879183-07-2*) Bristol Banner.

Myers, M., ed. see McNeely, Marian G.

Myers, M., ed. see Poole, Laura.

Myers, M. A., ed. see Borrege, Jose X.

Myers, M. A., ed. see Flandorf, Vera.

Myers, M. A., ed. see Scott, Helen E.

Myers, M. Bert, jt. ed. see Grabb, William C.

Myers, M. Scott. Every Employee a Manager. 3rd ed. LC 90-21040. (Illus.). 354p. 1991. 34.95 (*0-88390-259-1*) Pfeiffer & Co.

—Rhymes of the Ancient Manager: Leadership in the New Age. (Illus.). 192p. (Orig.). 1994. 19.95 (*0-9639930-0-3*); pap. 14.95 (*0-9639930-1-1*) Choctaw Pubng.
Management principles succinctly stated & illustrated. Humorous but serious guidelines for leadership, communication, industrial engineering, & personal effectiveness. Easy reading but powerful message, for wageroll & managerial staff. Interesting to general public & useful as training aid in business & secondary education. What reviewers say: TOM PETERS: "FABULOUS! JOYOUS! PRACTICAL! SUCCINCT!" PHIL ENSOR (Eaton & Goodyear): "WOW! What I learned during a 30-year career with two Fortune 500 companies, Scott Myers has presented & illustrated in this concise & fascinating publication. I have not run across anything remotely like it." J.M. JURAN: "Thanks for the opportunity to scan your new manuscript. This is a brilliant concept indeed -- managers seem to like their lessons served with a dash of drollery." To order contact: Ingram 800-937-8000 or Choctaw Publishing, P.O. Box 1315 B, Fort Walton Beach, FL 32549. 904-664-5666; 800-664-5667. FAX 904-664-5667. MasterCard & Visa accepted.
Publisher Provided Annotation.

***Myers, M. Scott & Howard, Jennifer. Countering Sexual Harassment: A Handbook for Self Defense. (Illus.). 142p. 1995. 18.00 (*0-9639930-2-X*) Choctaw Pubng.**
This book defines principles & techniques to empower women to deal with sexual harassment & gender bias on the job. It explains the difference between male & female perceptions of the other gender & why harassment occurs. Unlike most books on the subject, it recommends avoidance of litigation, EEOC intervention, & female coalitions to counter harassment. "You've tackled a highly sensitive issue & share a practical analysis through a 'how-to' handbook. It is a rare text when issues are handled in practical real world context, unencumbered by

legalese & philosophical projections. We need more, keep them coming. Enjoyable! Thanks." Marian Schultz, Ph.D., Professor of Management, The University of West Florida. "This book offers hope that there is a way to counter sexual harassment while preserving your dignity & career. It is readable & refreshing! Reading this book & taking the time to develop your own personal responses to sexual harassment can help you develop another of the many skills women must master in today's workplace." Deborah Wachob, CPA. Order from: Choctaw Publishing, P.O. Box 1315, Fort Walton Beach, FL 32549, Visa, MasterCard, Check, Purchase Order, (800) 664-5667, (904) 664-5666, FAX (904) 664-5667.

Publisher Provided Annotation.

Myers, Marcia J. & Jirjees, Jassim M. The Accuracy of Telephone Reference-Information Services in Academic Libraries: Two Studies. LC 82-10785. 282p. 1983. 25.00 (*0-8108-1584-2*) Scarecrow.

Myers, Margaret. Blowing Her Own Trumpet: European Ladies' Orchestras & Other Women Musicians in Sweden, 1870-1950. (Goteborg Univ. Dept. of Musicology Ser.: No. 30). 411p. (Orig.). 1993. pap. 93.00x (*91-85974-22-6*, Pub. by Almqv & Wiksell SW) Coronet Bks.

— Monetary Proposals for Social Reform. LC 71-110574. 1970. reprint ed. 20.00 (*0-404-04548-0*) AMS Pr.

Myers, Margaret & Scarborough, Mayra, eds. Women in Librarianship: Melvil's Rib Symposium. (Issues in Library & Information Sciences Ser.: No. 2). 1975. pap. text ed. 15.00 (*0-8135-0807-X*) Rutgers U SICLS.

Myers, Margaret, jt. auth. see Heim, Kathleen.

Myers, Margaret E. Meyersville, Md., Lutheran Baptisms. Russell, Donna V., ed. (Illus.). 70p. 1986. pap. 10.00 (*0-914385-04-6*) Catoctin Pr.

Myers, Margaret G. A Financial History of the United States. LC 70-104900. (Illus.). 463p. reprint ed. pap. 132.00 (*0-317-09327-4*, 2019888) Bks Demand.

Myers, Marguerite, jt. auth. see Goffin, Stacie G.

Myers, Marilyn. Economic Planning & Political Process Altering Urban Open Space: Selected References with a Case Study. (CPL Bibliographies Ser.: No. 56). 72p. 1981. 11.00 (*0-86602-056-X*) Coun Plan Librarians.

Myers, Marilyn, jt. auth. see Myers, Richard.

Myers, Martha A., jt. ed. see Bridges, George S.

Myers, Mary, jt. ed. see Heron, Alastair.

Myers, Mary L. French Architectural & Ornament Drawings of the Eighteenth Century. (Illus.). 256p. 1991. 60.00 (*0-8109-6411-2*, Abrams); pap. 30.00 (*0-87099-626-6*, Abrams) Metro Mus Art.

Myers, Mary R. Ice Hot. 1986. pap. write for info. (*0-345-32988-0*) Macmillan.

— Insights. (Love & Life Romance Ser.). 176p. 1983. pap. 1.75 (*0-345-30966-9*) Ballantine.

***Myers, MaryAnn.** Call Me Lydia. 580p. (Orig.). 1995. pap. 12.95 (*1-56901-617-8*) NW Pub.

Myers, Marye, ed. see Grieco, Joseph.

Myers, Matt. Art Nouveau Tarot. 24p. 1989. 14.00 (*0-88079-375-9*) US Games Syst.

Myers, Max A. & LaChat, Michael R., eds. Studies in the Theological Ethics of Ernst Troeltsch. LC 90-33012. (Toronto Studies in Theology: Vol. 49). 264p. 1991. lib. bdg. 89.95 (*0-88946-923-7*) E Mellen.

Myers, Max H., ed. see American Joint Committee on Cancer.

***Myers, Melvin L., et al, eds.** Papers & Proceedings of the Surgeon General's Conference on Agricultural Safety & Health. (Illus.). 645p. (Orig.). (C). 1994. pap. text ed. 95.00x (*0-7881-1225-2*) Diane Pub.

Myers, Michael. Fuer den Buerger: The Role of Christian Schubart's Deutsche Chronik in the Development of a Political Public Sphere. LC 89-37984. (German Life & Civilization Ser.: Vol. 6). 302p. (C). 1990. text ed. 46.50 (*0-8204-1168-X*) P Lang Pubs.

— Proverbs. 1994. 5.95 (*0-681-00430-4*) Longmeadow Pr.

Myers, Michael, ed. Passages for Consolation. (Illus.). 64p. 1993. 5.95 (*0-681-41891-5*) Longmeadow Pr.

— Proverbs for Today. (Illus.). 64p. 1993. 5.95 (*0-681-41442-1*) Longmeadow Pr.

— Psalms for Today. (Illus.). 64p. 1993. 5.95 (*0-681-41443-X*) Longmeadow Pr.

— Reflections of Jesus. (Illus.). 64p. 1993. 5.95 (*0-681-41890-7*) Longmeadow Pr.

Myers, Michael F. Doctors' Marriages: A Look at the Problems & Their Solutions. LC 87-36054. 254p. 1988. 32.50 (*0-306-42754-0*, Plenum Med Bk) Plenum.

— Men & Divorce. LC 88-35101. 286p. 1989. lib. bdg. 32.95 (*0-89862-386-3*) Guilford Pr.

***Myers, Michael J. & Murtaugh, Michael P., eds.** Cytokines in Animal Health & Disease. LC 95-13663. 1995. write for info. (*0-8247-9435-4*) Dekker.

Myers, Michele T. & Myers, Gail E. Managing by Communication: An Organizational Approach. (Illus.). 512p. 1982. text ed. write for info. (*0-07-044235-5*) McGraw.

Myers, Michele T., jt. auth. see Myers, Gail E.

***Myers, Mike & Ruzan, Robin.** Coffee Talk. 96p. 1997. pap. 8.95 (*0-7868-8085-6*) Hyperion.

Myers, Mildred S. Writing Skills for Bankers. (Illus.). 1992. student ed 49.00 (*0-685-62688-1*) Am Bankers.

Myers, Minor, Jr. Liberty Without Anarchy: A History of the Society of the Cincinnati. LC 83-5764. 280p. 1983. 29.50 (*0-8139-0993-7*) U Pr of Va.

Myers-Moro, Pamela. Thai Music & Musicians in Contemporary Bangkok. LC 93-32327. (Monograph - Center for Southeast Asia Studies: No. 34). 1993. 22.50 (*0-944613-20-9*) UC Berkeley Ctrs SE Asia.

Myers, N. A. & Angerpointner, T. A., eds. Paediatric Thoracic Surgery. (Progress in Pediatric Surgery Ser.: Vol. 27). (Illus.). 272p. 1991. 185.00 (*0-387-52525-4*) Spr-Verlag.

Myers, Nancy. Mathematics for Electronics. Pullins, ed. LC 92-25704. 450p. (C). 1993. pap. text ed. 55.50 (*0-314-01266-4*) West Pub.

Myers, Nancy, intro. Evelyn Madsen Miles: a Teacher's Perspective of Austin, Nevada: 1932-1936. (Illus.). 86p. 1983. lib. bdg. 24.00 (*1-56475-232-1*); fiche write for info. (*1-56475-233-X*) U NV Oral Hist.

Myers, Neil. All That, So Simple. LC 78-71637. 72p. 1980. pap. 7.95 (*0-911198-56-3*) Purdue U Pr.

— The Blade of Manjusri. 64p. 1989. pap. 15.00 (*0-9620634-1-X*) Sun Moon Bear Pr.

— The Blade of Manjusri. deluxe limited ed. 64p. 1989. 40.00 (*0-9620634-2-8*) Sun Moon Bear Pr.

Myers, Nicholas G. My Memoirs of World War Two. Harris, Paul N., ed. (Illus.). 144p. (Orig.). 1988. pap. 8.95 (*0-915180-31-6*) Harrowood Bks.

Myers, Norma & Scobey, Joan. Gifts from the Kitchen. LC 79-8914. 320p. 1980. reprint ed. pap. 9.95 (*0-672-52631-X*, Bobbs) Macmillan.

Myers, Norman. Not Far Afield: U. S. Interests & the Global Environment. LC 87-50723. 84p. (Orig.). 1987. pap. text ed. 10.00 (*0-915825-24-4*) World Resources Inst.

— The Primary Source: Tropical Forests & Our Future. (Illus.). 448p. 1992. Updated for the 1990s. pap. 10.95 (*0-393-30828-6*) Norton.

— Ultimate Security: How Environmental Concerns Affect Global Political Stability. LC 92-43499. 1993. 25.00 (*0-393-03545-X*) Norton.

Myers, Norman, ed. Gaia, an Atlas of Planet Management. rev. ed. LC 92-18126. 1993. 23.00 (*0-385-42626-7*) Doubleday.

— Rainforests. LC 92-46131. (Illustrated Library of the Earth). 1993. 35.00 (*0-87596-597-0*) Rodale Pr Inc.

Myers, Norman & Simon, Julian L. Scarcity or Abundance? A Debate on the Environment. 160p. 1994. 21.00 (*0-393-03590-5*) Norton.

Myers, Patricia, ed. see Marenzio, Luca.

Myers, Patricia A. A Glossary for Radiologic Technologists. LC 80-20917. 206p. 1981. text ed. 59.95 (*0-275-91351-1*, C1351, Praeger Pubs) Greenwood.

Myers, Patricia I. & Hammill, Donald D. Learning Disabilities: Basic Concepts, Assessment Practices, & Instructional Strategies. 4th ed. LC 89-29044. (Illus.). 593p. (Orig.). 1990. text ed. 41.00 (*0-89079-225-9*, 1499) PRO-ED.

Myers, Patrick R. Succession Between International Organizations. LC 92-2353. (Publication of the Graduate Institute of International Studies, Geneva). 200p. 1993. 89.95 (*0-7103-0457-9*, B0088, Pub. by Kegan Paul Intl UK) Routledge Chapman & Hall.

Myers, Paul, jt. auth. see Williams, Richard A.

Myers, Paul W. Lawrence County, PA Soldiers. 91p. 1988. pap. text ed. 9.00 (*0-933227-86-8*) Closson Pr.

— Mercer County, PA Soldiers. 78p. 1988. pap. text ed. 8.50 (*0-933227-84-1*) Closson Pr.

— Pennsylvania Soldiers of the Revolutionary War. 30p. 1987. lib. bdg. 5.00 (*0-933227-64-7*) Closson Pr.

— Revolutionary War Veterans Who Settled in Butler County, Pennsylvania. 30p. 1987. per. 5.00 (*0-933227-69-8*) Closson Pr.

— Venango County, PA Soldiers. 73p. 1988. pap. text ed. 8.50 (*0-933227-83-3*) Closson Pr.

— Washington County Frontier Rangers. 1988. pap. text ed. 7.00 (*0-933227-85-X*) Closson Pr.

— Westmoreland County, PA in the American Revolution. 263p. (Orig.). 1989. pap. text ed. 24.00 (*1-55856-001-7*) Closson Pr.

Myers-Pelton, Lois, jt. auth. see Pelton, Charles L.

***Myers, Pennie & Nance, Don.** Tactful Toughness Workbook. (Orig.). 1994. pap. text ed. write for info. (*0-9620723-5-4*) Mid Am Consult.

— The Upset Book: A Guide for Dealing with Upset People. (Illus.). 222p. (Orig.). 1986. pap. 8.95 (*0-937647-01-2*) Academic Pubns.

— The Upset Book: How to Deal with Upset People. rev. ed. 218p. (Orig.). 1991. pap. 12.95 (*0-9620723-4-6*) Mid Am Consult.

— The Upset Workbook: Client Service Edition for Insurance Companies & Agencies. 118p. 1989. student ed 50.00 (*0-9620723-1-1*) Mid Am Consult.

— The Upset Workbook: Health Care Edition. 118p. 1989. 50.00 (*0-9620723-2-X*) Mid Am Consult.

— The Upset Workbook: Insurance Claims Edition. 132p. (Orig.). 1988. student ed 50.00 (*0-9620723-0-3*) Mid Am Consult.

— The Upset Workbook: Patient Representative Edition. 130p. 1990. 50.00 (*0-9620723-3-8*) Mid Am Consult.

Myers, Peter B., jt. auth. see Myers, Isabel B.

Myers, Peter C. Your Senior Year & Beyond. 172p. 1991. per. 21.95 (*0-8403-7152-7*) Kendall-Hunt.

Myers, Philip. Patterns of Reproduction of Four Species of Vespertilionid Bats in Paraguay. LC 76-3878. (University of California Publications in Social Welfare: No. 107). (Illus.). 71p. reprint ed. pap. 25.00 (*0-685-23995-0*, 2031578) Bks Demand.

Myers, Philip E. Aboveground Storage Tanks. 1995. text ed. 80.00 (*0-07-044272-X*) McGraw.

Myers, Phyllis. Lessons from the States: Strengthening Land Conservation Programs Through Grants to Nonprofit Land Trusts. LC 92-16663. 76p. (Orig.). 1992. pap. 17.00 (*0-943915-08-2*) Land Trust DC.

— State Parks in a New Era Vol. 2: Future Directions in Funding, 3 vols. LC 89-9732. 75p. (Orig.). 1989. pap. 25.00 (*0-685-44944-0*) World Wildlife Fund.

— State Parks in a New Era Vol. 3: Strategies for Tourism & Economic Development, 3 vols., Set. LC 89-9732. 79p. (Orig.). 1989. pap. 25.00 (*0-685-44946-7*) World Wildlife Fund.

Myers, Poochie. Knit Like Crazy. 62p. 1993. student ed 19.95 (*1-881571-04-1*) Letters Etcetera.

Myers, R. B. & Cantino, E. C. The Gamma Particle: A Study of Cell-Organelle Interactions in the Development of the Water Mold Blastocladiella Emersonii. (Monographs in Developmental Biology: Vol. 8). 150p. 1974. 53.75 (*3-8055-1735-1*) S Karger.

Myers, R. David, intro. Toward a History of the New Left: Essays from Within the Movement. LC 89-25472. 210p. 1989. 50.00 (*0-926019-23-6*) Carlson Pub.

Myers, R. E. & Torrance, E. P. Wondering: Invitations to Think about the Future for Primary Grades. (Orig.). 1984. pap. 14.95 (*0-936386-22-3*) Creative Learning.

Myers, Ralph G. Mabuhay: Sentimental Journey World War II Experience. (Illus.). 62p. (Orig.). (C). 1989. pap. 7.95 (*0-9625571-0-2*) R E Myers.

Myers, Ramon, ed. Last Chance in Manchuria: The Diary of Chang Kia-ngau. Zen, Dolores, tr. (Publication Series: Archival Documentaries: No. 379). 350p. 1989. text ed. 36.95 (*0-8179-8791-6*) Hoover Inst Pr.

Myers, Ramon H. The Chinese Peasant Economy: Agricultural Development in Hopei & Shantung, 1890-1949. LC 79-115189. (Harvard East Asian Ser.: No. 47). 410p. reprint ed. pap. 116.90 (*0-317-09167-0*, 2005498) Bks Demand.

— Thoughts on U.S. Foreign Policy Toward the People's Republic of China. LC 94-5583. (Essays in Public Policy Ser.: No. 47). 1994. 5.00 (*0-8179-5522-4*) Hoover Inst Pr.

Myers, Ramon H., ed. The Storm Clouds Clear over China: The Memoir of Ch'en Li-fu, 1900-1993. LC 93-23214. (Studies in Economic, Social, & Political Change, the Republic of China Ser.: Vol. 419). (Illus.). 359p. 1993. text ed. 39.95 (*0-8179-9271-5*); pap. text ed. 24.95 (*0-8179-9272-3*) Hoover Inst Pr.

— Two Societies in Opposition: The Republic of China & the People's Republic of China after Forty Years, No. P 401. 500p. (C). 1991. text ed. 38.95 (*0-8179-9091-7*); pap. text ed. 25.95 (*0-8179-9092-5*) Hoover Inst Pr.

— A Unique Relationship: The United & the Republic of China under the Taiwan Relations Act. 176p. 1989. 25.95 (*0-8179-8871-8*); pap. 15.95 (*0-8179-8872-6*) Hoover Inst Pr.

Myers, Ramon H. & Peattie, Mark R., eds. The Japanese Colonial Empire: 1895-1945. LC 83-42571. (Illus.). 560p. 1987. pap. text ed. 24.95 (*0-691-10222-8*) Princeton U Pr.

Myers, Ramon H., jt. auth. see Kuo, Tai-chun.

Myers, Ramon H., jt. ed. see Mo, Jongryn.

Myers, Rawley. American Women of Faith. LC 89-61665. (Orig.). 1989. pap. 4.95 (*0-87973-435-3*, 435) Our Sunday Visitor.

— Lent: A Journey to Resurrection Prayers & Reflections for the Penitential Season. LC 83-63084. 192p. 1984. pap. 5.95 (*0-87973-605-4*) Our Sunday Visitor.

Myers, Rawleyq, ed. Daily Reflections with Mary. (Illus.). 95p. 1988. pap. 3.95 (*0-89942-372-8*, 372-04) Catholic Bk Pub.

Myers, Raymond H. & Milton, J. S. A First Course in the Theory of Linear Statistical Models. 352p. (C). 1991. text ed. 57.95 (*0-534-91645-7*) Intl Thomson.

Myers, Raymond H., jt. auth. see Montgomery, Douglas C.

Myers, Raymond H., jt. auth. see Walpole, Ronald E.

Myers, Raymond M. & Kramer, Bruce M. Law of Pooling & Utilization: Voluntary, Compulsory, 3 vols. 1957. Updates. ring bd. write for info. (*0-8205-1455-1*) Bender.

Myers, Raymond R. & Long, J. S., eds. Characterization of Coatings, Pt. 1: Physical Techniques. (Treatise on Coatings Ser.: No. 2). 680p. reprint ed. pap. 180.00 (*0-317-08360-0*, 2055321) Bks Demand.

— Characterization of Coatings, Pt. 2: Physical Techniques. LC 67-21701. (Treatise on Coatings Ser.: No. 2). (Illus.). 677p. reprint ed. pap. 180.00 (*0-7837-4303-3*, 2043994) Bks Demand.

— Film Forming Compositions, Pt. 2. LC 67-21701. (Treatise on Coatings Ser.: No. 1). 446p. pap. 127.20 (*0-7837-0016-4*, 2027097) Bks Demand.

— Film Forming Compositions, Pt. 3. LC 67-21701. (Treatise on Coatings Ser.: Vol. 1). 606p. reprint ed. pap. 172.80 (*0-685-16150-1*, 2027097) Bks Demand.

— Formulations, Pt. 1. LC 67-21701. (Treatise on Coatings Ser.: No. 4). (Illus.). 607p. reprint ed. pap. 173.00 (*0-8357-6119-3*, 2034554) Bks Demand.

— Pigments, Pt. 1. LC 67-21701. (Treatise on Coatings Ser.: No. 3). (Illus.). 590p. reprint ed. pap. 168.20 (*0-7837-0885-8*, 2041191) Bks Demand.

— Treatise on Coatings, Vol. 2, Part 1. LC 67-21701. reprint ed. pap. 160.00 (*0-685-16095-5*, 2026411) Bks Demand.

Myers, Rex C., ed. Lizzie: The Letters of Elizabeth Chester Fisk, 1864-1893. LC 88-39998. 176p. 1989. 24.95 (*0-87842-241-2*); pap. 12.95 (*0-87842-226-9*) Mountain Pr.

Myers, Rex C. & Ashby, Norma B. Symbols of Montana. 32p. (Orig.). reprint ed. pap. 3.50 (*0-917298-26-8*, 4537) MT Hist Soc.

Myers, Reyburn W., jt. auth. see Marcum, Richard.

Myers, Reyburn W., jt. auth. see Wills, Donald H.

Myers, Richard & Myers, Marilyn. Best Guide to Florida Golf. 2nd ed. 150p. 1993. pap. 14.95 (*0-9631786-1-X*) SwainMyer Pubn.

Myers, Richard, jt. auth. see Benjamin, Hugh.

Myers, Richard, jt. auth. see Yorgason, Brenton G.

Myers, Richard, jt. auth. see Yorgason, Brenton.

***Myers, Richard B.** The Best of the Peter Island Morning Sun: Excerpts from Peter Island Resort's Daily Newspaper. LC 94-37959. 128p. (Orig.). 1994. pap. 12.95 (*0-9639905-2-7*) Two Thous-Three Assocs.

Myers, Richard D., ed. The Cowboy Humor of Alfred Henry Lewis. 350p. 1987. pap. 9.95 (*0-942936-12-4*) Lincoln-Herndon Pr.

Myers, Richard L. Immunology: A Laboratory Manual. 112p. (C). 1989. spiral bd. write for info. (*0-697-05378-4*) Wm C Brown Pubs.

— Immunology: A Laboratory Manual. 2nd ed. 128p. (C). 1994. spiral bd. write for info. (*0-697-11313-2*) Wm C Brown Pubs.

Myers, Richard L., jt. auth. see Berndt, Robert J.

Myers, Richmond E. Northampton County in the American Revolution. (Publications of the Northampton County Historical & Genealogical Society: No. 6). (Illus.). vi, 90p. 1976. 10.00 (*1-877701-12-2*) NCH&GS.

***Myers, Robert.** Never Such Innocence Again. 520p. 1995. pap. 12.95 (*0-7610-0019-4*) NW Pub.

— The Professional Wrestling Trivia Book. (Illus.). 120p. 1989. pap. 7.95 (*0-8283-1920-0*) Branden Pub Co.

— Solstice Points. 1988. pap. write for info. (*0-87500-022-3*) RKM Pub Co.

Myers, Robert A. Dominica. (World Bibliographical Ser.: No. 82). 190p. 1987. lib. bdg. 55.00 (*1-85109-031-2*) ABC-CLIO.

— Excuses! Excuses! How to Explain Your Way Out of Any Situation. 1979. pap. 5.95 (*0-8065-0824-8*, Citadel Pr) Carol Pub Group.

— Ghana. (World Bibliographical Ser.). 1991. lib. bdg. 108.50 (*1-85109-135-1*) ABC-CLIO.

Myers, Robert A., ed. Encyclopedia of Astronomy & Astrophysics. 770p. 1988. text ed. 85.00 (*0-12-226690-0*) Acad Pr.

— Nigeria. (World Bibliographical Ser.: No. 100). (Illus.). 400p. 1989. lib. bdg. 80.00 (*1-85109-083-5*, Pub. by Clio Pr UK) ABC-CLIO.

***Myers, Robert E.** Facing the Issues: Creative Strategies for Probing Social Concerns. LC 94-28032. 1995. write for info. (*1-56976-009-8*) Zephyr Pr AZ.

— The Intersection of Science Fiction & Philosophy: Critical Studies. LC 82-25162. (Contributions to the Study of Science Fiction & Fantasy Ser.: No. 4). (Illus.). xvi, 262p. 1983. text ed. 49.95 (*0-313-22493-5*, MYS/, Greenwood Pr) Greenwood.

Myers, Robert E. & Torrance, E. Paul. What Would You Do? Scenarios for Creative Problem Solving & Decision Making. LC 94-3990. 1994. write for info. (*1-56976-001-2*) Zephyr Pr AZ.

Myers, Robert F. Micronesian Reef Fishes: A Practical Guide to the Identification of the Coral Reef Fishes of the Tropical Central & Western Pacific. (Illus.). iv, 288p. 1989. text ed. 46.00 (*0-9621564-1-8*); pap. text ed. 33.00 (*0-9621564-0-X*) Coral Graphics.

— Micronesian Reef Fishes: A Practical Guide to the Identification of the Coral Reef Fishes of the Tropical Central & Western Pacific. 2nd ed. (Illus.). 442p. 1991. 46.00 (*0-9621564-3-4*); pap. 33.50 (*0-9621564-2-6*) Coral Graphics.

Myers, Robert J. Social Security. 4th ed. LC 92-30848. (Pension Research Council Publications). (Illus.). 968p. (C). 1993. text ed. 59.95 (*0-8122-3191-0*) U of Pa Pr.

— Speaking Truth to Power. (Eleventh Morgenthau Memorial Lecture Ser.). 23p. 1991. pap. 4.00 (*0-87641-116-2*) Carnegie Ethics & Intl Affairs.

Myers, Robert J., ed. Religion & the State: The Struggle for Legitimacy & Power. LC 85-72100. (Annals of the American Academy of Political & Social Science Ser.: Vol. 483). 1986. text ed. 26.00 (*0-8039-2538-7*); pap. text ed. 17.00 (*0-8039-2539-5*) Sage.

***Myers, Robert J. & Rosenthal, Joel H., eds.** Ethics & International Affairs, Vol. 1. 223p. 1987. pap. 10.00 (*0-614-05438-9*) Carnegie Ethics & Intl Affairs.

— Ethics & International Affairs, Vol. 2. 239p. 1988. pap. 10.00 (*0-614-05439-7*) Carnegie Ethics & Intl Affairs.

— Ethics & International Affairs, Vol. 3. 301p. 1989. pap. 10.00 (*0-614-05440-0*) Carnegie Ethics & Intl Affairs.

— Ethics & International Affairs, Vol. 4. 177p. 1990. pap. 10.00 (*0-614-05441-9*) Carnegie Ethics & Intl Affairs.

— Ethics & International Affairs, Vol. 5. 249p. 1991. pap. 10.00 (*0-614-05442-7*) Carnegie Ethics & Intl Affairs.

— Ethics & International Affairs, Vol. 6. 191p. 1992. pap. 10.00 (*0-614-05443-5*) Carnegie Ethics & Intl Affairs.

— Ethics & International Affairs, Vol. 7. 251p. 1993. pap. 10.00 (*0-614-05444-3*) Carnegie Ethics & Intl Affairs.

— Ethics & International Affairs, Vol. 8. 225p. 1994. pap. 10.00 (*0-614-05445-1*) Carnegie Ethics & Intl Affairs.

— Ethics & International Affairs, Vol. 9. 251p. 1995. pap. 10.00 (*0-614-05446-X*) Carnegie Ethics & Intl Affairs.

Myers, Robert J. & Vernaci, Richard L. Within the System: My Half Century in Social Security. (Illus.). 263p. 1992. 19.50 (*0-936031-12-3*) Actex Pubns.

Myers, Robert J., jt. auth. see Detlefs, Dale R.

Myers, Robert J., jt. ed. see Sung-joo, Han.

Myers, Robert J., jt. ed. see Thompson, Kenneth.

Myers, Robert L. Racine's La Thebaide: Political, Moral, & Aesthetic Dimensions. LC 81-51476. (Rice University Studies: Vol. 67, No. 2). 51p. (Orig.). (C). 1981. pap. 5.50 (*0-89263-249-6*) Rice Univ.

Myers, Robert M. The Children of Pride. LC 83-10377. 688p. 1987. reprint ed. pap. 20.00 (*0-300-04053-9*, Y-675) Yale U Pr.

— From Beowulf to Virginia Woolf: An Astounding & Wholly Unauthorized History of English Literature. 2nd ed. LC 84-5974. (Illus.). 112p. 1984. 14.95 (*0-252-01126-0*); pap. 7.95 (*0-252-01150-3*) U of Ill Pr.

An Asterisk (*) at the beginning of an entry indicates that the title is appearing in BIP for the first time.

— Handel's Messiah, a Touchstone of Taste: Music Book Index. 338p. 1993. reprint ed. lib. bdg. 89.00 (*0-7812-9600-5*) Rprt Serv.
— Quintet: A Five-Play Cycle Drawn from The Children of Pride. 256p. 1991. 29.95 (*0-252-01751-X*) U of Ill Pr.
— Reluctant Expatriate: The Life of Harold Frederic. LC 94-39267. (Contributions to the Study of World Literature: Vol. 59). 216p. 1995. text ed. 49.95 (*0-313-29256-6*, Greenwood Pr) Greenwood.

Myers, Robin. Boat Ride to Destiny. LC 93-93512. 200p. (Orig.). 1994. pap. 7.95 (*1-56002-366-X*, Univ Edtns) Aegina Pr.
— Dictionary of Literature in the English Language, 2 vols. LC 68-18529. 1978. From Chaucer to 1970. 842.00 (*0-08-023684-7*, Pub. by Pergamon Repr UK) Franklin.
— Dictionary of Literature in the English Language, 2 vols, 1. LC 68-18529. 1978. 400.00 (*0-08-012079-2*, Pub. by Pergamon Repr UK) Franklin.
— Dictionary of Literature in the English Language, 2 vols, 2. LC 68-18529. 1978. 224.00 (*0-08-016142-1*, Pub. by Pergamon Repr UK) Franklin.
— Dictionary of Literature in the English Language, 2 vols, Set. LC 68-18529. 1978. 623.00 (*0-08-016143-X*, Pub. by Pergamon Repr UK) Franklin.
— A Dictionary of Literature in the English Language, Vol. 3: From 1940-1970. 1978. 265.00 (*0-08-018050-7*, Pergamon Pr) Elsevier.

Myers, Robin & Harris, Michael, eds. Aspects of Printing from 1600. (Illus.). 174p. 1987. pap. text ed. 28.00 (*0-902692-36-4*) Oak Knoll.
— Censorship & the Control of Print in England & France, 1600-1910. 154p. 1992. 27.50 (*1-873040-16-4*) Oak Knoll.
— Maps & Prints: Aspects of the English Booktrade. (Publishing History Occasional Ser.). (Illus.). 130p. 1984. pap. 49.00 (*0-902692-33-X*) Chadwyck-Healey.
— A Millennium of the Book: Production, Design & Illustration in Manuscript & Print 900-1900. LC 94-30712. (Publishing Pathways Ser.: No. 8). (Illus.). 192p. 1995. 30.00 (*1-884718-07-8*) Oak Knoll Pr.
— Pioneers in Bibliography. 117p. 1988. 24.00 (*0-906795-69-9*) Oak Knoll.
— Property of a Gentleman: The Formation, Organisation & Dispersal of the Private Library, 1620-1920. 164p. 1991. 26.00 (*0-906795-99-0*) Oak Knoll.
— Serials & Their Readers, 1620-1914. 192p. 1993. 30.00 (*1-873040-20-2*) Oak Knoll.
— Spreading the Word: Distribution Networks of Print 1550-1850. 241p. 1990. lib. bdg. 28.00 (*0-906795-87-7*) Oak Knoll.
— Stationers' Company Archive: An Account of the Records 1554-1984. 376p. 1990. lib. bdg. 60.00 (*0-906795-71-0*) Oak Knoll.

Myers, Robin, jt. auth. see Myers, Bob.

Myers, Roger, comp. Guide to Archival Materials of the Center for Creative Photography. 136p. 25.00 (*0-938262-13-0*) Ctr Creat Photog.

Myers, Rollie J., jt. auth. see Mahan, Bruce M.

Myers, Rollo. Modern French Music. LC 82-7249. (Music Reprint Ser.). (Illus.). 209p. 1984. reprint ed. lib. bdg. 29.50 (*0-306-76158-0*) Da Capo.

Myers, Rollo, ed. Strauss-Rolland Correspondence. 1987. pap. 11.95 (*0-7145-0503-X*) Riverrun NY.

Myers, Rollo, tr. see Chailley, Jacques.

Myers, Rollo H. Debussy. LC 78-66912. (Encore Music Editions Ser.). (Illus.). 1985. reprint ed. 16.50 (*0-88355-752-5*) Hyperion Conn.
— Debussy: Music Book Index. 125p. 1993. reprint ed. lib. bdg. 89.00 (*0-7812-9592-0*) Rprt Serv.
— Erik Satie. (Illus.). (Orig.). 1968. pap. 4.95 (*0-486-21903-8*) Dover.
— Erik Satie. (Orig.). 1988. reprint ed. lib. bdg. 49.00 (*0-7812-0772-X*) Rprt Serv.
— Erik Satie. LC 73-181217. 150p. (Orig.). 1948. reprint ed. 59.00 (*0-403-01628-2*) Scholarly.
— Music in the Modern World: Music Book Index. 211p. 1993. reprint ed. lib. bdg. 79.00 (*0-7812-9576-9*) Rprt Serv.
— Ravel: His Life & Works. LC 73-2340. (Illus.). 239p. 1973. reprint ed. text ed. 59.75 (*0-8371-6841-4*, MYRA, Greenwood Pr) Greenwood.

Myers, Ron, jt. auth. see Voth, Eric R.

Myers, Ronald L. & Ewel, John J., eds. Ecosystems of Florida. 765p. (C). 1990. lib. bdg. 75.00 (*0-8130-1012-8*); pap. text ed. 34.95 (*0-8130-1022-5*) U Press Fla.

Myers, Rose S. Saunders Manual of Physical Therapy Practice. LC 94-452. (Illus.). 1072p. 1995. text ed. 75.00 (*0-7216-3671-3*) Saunders.

***Myers, Roy & Myers, Stephanie.** The Rescue of Robby Robo. (The Robby Robo Ser.: No. 1). (Illus.). 24p. (Orig.). (J). (gr. k-6). 1995. pap. write for info. (*1-884108-00-8*) R J Myers Pub.

Myers, Roy E. Microcomputer Graphics. (Illus.). 304p. 1984. pap. text ed. write for info. (*0-318-56714-8*) Addison-Wesley.
— Microcomputer Graphics for the IBM PC. 1438p. 1984. pap. 14.95 (*0-201-05158-3*); Apple II write for info. (*0-201-05312-8*) Addison-Wesley.

Myers, Roy E., jt. auth. see Finley, Clarence W., Jr.

Myers, Russell. Open at Your Own Risk. (Broom Hilda Ser.: No. 2). 128p. (Orig.). 1981. pap. 1.50 (*0-449-14418-6*, GM) Fawcett.
— Rotten Apple. (Broom Hilda Ser.: No. 1). (Illus.). 1986. pap. 2.25 (*0-449-13095-9*) Fawcett.

Myers, Ruth. A-Worming We Did Go. (Illus.). (Orig.). 1968. pap. 5.00 (*0-9600102-1-1*) Shields.
— ABCs of the Earthworm Business. (Orig.). 1969. pap. 5.00 (*0-9600102-2-X*) Shields.
— Thirty One Days of Praise. 120p. 1994. Spiral bdg. spiral bd. 7.99 (*0-88070-634-1*, Multnomah Bks) Questar Pubs.

Myers, S. Myers' History of West Virginia, 2 vols., Set. 1993. reprint ed. lib. bdg. 105.00 (*0-8328-3087-9*) Higginson Bk Co.

Myers, S. E. The Ohio State University: Where an Economics Degree Means Unemployment: An Unflattering Portrayal of Indifference, Callousness & Ineptitude. 65p. 1992. pap. text ed. 67.95 (*1-895583-98-5*) MAYA Pubs.
— Ohio State University's Korean Connection. 1992. pap. text ed. 67.95 (*1-895583-99-3*) MAYA Pubs.

Myers, Sally L. & Woolls, Blanche M. Substance Abuse: A Resource Guide for Secondary Schools. 300p. 1991. lib. bdg. 28.50 (*0-87287-805-8*) Libs Unl.

Myers, Samuel L., Sr., ed. Desegregation in Higher Education. LC 88-39407. (Illus.). 98p. (Orig.). (C). 1989. pap. text ed. 13.50 (*0-8191-7291-X*, NAEOHE) U Pr of Amer.

Myers, Samuel L., ed. Economic Issues & Black Colleges. (NAFEO Conference Ser.). 60p. 1987. pap. text ed. 6.95 (*0-695-60053-2*) Follett Pr.

Myers, Samuel L., Jr. & Simms, Margaret C., eds. The Economics of Race & Crime. 220p. (Orig.). 1988. pap. 18.95 (*0-88738-755-1*) Transaction Pubs.

Myers, Sarah K. Language Shift Among Migrants to Lima, Peru. LC 73-78730. (Research Papers Ser.: No. 147). (Illus.). 203p. 1973. pap. 12.00 (*0-89065-054-3*) U Chicago Comm Geo.

Myers-Scotton, Carol. Duelling Languages: Grammatical Structure in Codeswitching. LC 92-39655. 1993. 49.95 (*0-19-824059-7*, Clarendon Pr) OUP.
— Social Motivations for Codeswitching: Evidence from Africa. LC 92-26242. (Oxford Studies in Language Contact). (Illus.). 192p. 1993. 35.00 (*0-19-823905-X*, Old Oregon Bk Store) OUP.
— Social Motivations for Codeswitching: Evidence from Africa. (Oxford Studies in Language Contact). (Illus.). 192p. 1995. pap. 19.95 (*0-19-823923-8*) OUP.

***Myers, Selma.** Team-Building for Diverse Work Groups: A Practical Guide to High-Performance & Diverse Teams. (Workplace Diversity Ser.). (Illus.). 120p. 1995. pap. 12. 95 (*1-883553-68-7*) R Chang Assocs.

Myers, Selma & Filner, Barbara. Mediation Across Cultures: A Handbook about Culture & Conflict. 81p. 1994. 27.50 (*1-883998-13-1*) Amherst Educ.

***Myers, Selma & Harris, Anthony W.** Tools for Valuing Diversity: A Practical Guide to Techniques to Capitalize in Team Diversity. (Workplace Diversity Ser.). (Illus.). 120p. 1995. pap. 12.95 (*1-883553-70-9*) R Chang Assocs.

Myers, Selma & Lambert, Joanna. Diversity Icebreakers: A Guide for Diversity Training. 56p. 1994. pap. text ed. 55.00 (*1-883998-11-5*) Amherst Educ.

***Myers, Selma & Lambert, Jonamay.** Customer Relations & the Diversity Challenge: A Trainer's Guide. 55p. 1995. 69.95 (*1-883998-16-6*) Amherst Educ.
— Diversity Icebreaker: A Trainer's Guide. 60p. 1994. 55.00 (*1-883998-12-3*) Amherst Educ.

Myers, Selma, jt. auth. see Lambert, Jonamay.

Myers, Sherrill, jt. auth. see O'Connor, Sara.

Myers, Sherrill M., jt. auth. see Beckley, Robert M.

Myers, Sondra, jt. auth. see Rittner, Carol.

***Myers, Sophia, illus.** Beginning from the Middle: A Collection of Fiction, Poetry, & Essays by the Kansas City Writers' Group. 128p. (Orig.). 1994. pap. 9.95 (*0-9644170-0-6*) Whispering Prairie.

Myers, Stanley E. RPG II with Business Applications. (Illus.). 1979. teacher ed write for info. (*0-8359-6304-7*, Reston); text ed. write for info. (*0-8359-6303-9*, Reston) P-H.
— RPG Two, RPG Three & RPG - 400 with Business Applications. 2nd ed. 896p. 1991. pap. text ed. 53.00 (*0-13-783077-7*, 260301) P-H.

Myers, Stanley E. & Myers, Candice E. RPG-400 Programming on the AS-400. LC 94-25819. 1995. pap. text ed. 60.00 (*0-13-096736-X*) P-H.

Myers, Stephan, jt. auth. see Dunn, Barbara.

Myers, Stephanie, jt. auth. see Myers, Roy.

Myers, Stephen W. Yeat's Book of the Nineties: Poetry, Politics, & Rhetoric. LC 92-17894. (American University Studies: English Language & Literature: Ser. IV, Vol. 150). 186p. (C). 1993. text ed. 35.95 (*0-8204-1957-5*) P Lang Pubs.

Myers, Stewart, jt. ed. see Miller, Deborah H.

***Myers, Stuart.** Between the Worlds: Witchcraft & the Tree of Life: a Program of Spiritual Development. (Illus.). 256p. 1995. pap. 17.95 (*0-87542-480-5*) Llewellyn Pubns.

Myers, Sylvia H. The Bluestocking Circle: Women, Friendship, & the Life of the Mind in Eighteenth-Century England. (Illus.). 360p. 1990. 69.00 (*0-19-811767-1*) OUP.

Myers, Talarico. The Social Contexts of Criminal Sentencing. LC 87-4771. (Research in Criminology Ser.). 245p. 1987. 85.00 (*0-387-96483-5*) Spr-Verlag.

***Myers, Tamar.** Parsley, Sage, Rosemary & Crime. LC 95-14704. 1995. write for info. (*0-385-47140-8*) Doubleday.
— Too Many Crooks Spoil the Broth. 256p. 1995. mass mkt. 4.99 (*0-451-18296-0*, Sig) NAL-Dutton.
— Too Many Crooks Spoil the Broth: A Pennsylvania-Dutch Mystery with Recipes. LC 93-13424. 1994. 17.00 (*0-385-47139-4*) Doubleday.

Myers, Ted. Faith & Survival: Ethiopian Jewish Life, 1983-1992. LC 92-60746. (Illus.). 8p. (Orig.). 1992. pap. write for info. (*0-943376-51-3*) Magnes Mus.

Myers, Teresa S. How to Keep Control of Your Life after 50: A Guide for Your Legal, Medical, & Financial Well-Being. LC 88-45305. 448p. 1989. pap. 19.95 (*0-669-19457-3*) Free Pr.

Myers, Terry, et al, eds. Reasoning & Discourse Processes. (Cognitive Science Ser.). 312p. 1986. text ed. 137.00 (*0-12-512320-5*); pap. text ed. 58.00 (*0-12-512321-3*) Acad Pr.

Myers, Theresa F., ed. see Anthony, Edd & Setticase, Christine E.

Myers, Theresa F., ed. see Heffernan, Anne E.

***Myers, Thomas, et al.** Florida Retirement Guide: 1995 Edition. (State Retirement Guides Ser.). (Illus.). 320p. (Orig.). 1995. pap. 19.95 (*1-886429-01-4*) Retirement Info.

***Myers, Thomas, Jr., et al.** State Retirement Guides Series. Bowman, William L. & Wilson, David A., eds. (Orig.). 1995. pap. 39.90 (*1-886429-02-2*) Retirement Info.

Myers, Thomas. Walking Point: American Narratives of Vietnam. (Illus.). 272p. 1988. 39.95 (*0-19-505351-6*) OUP.

***Myers, Thomas, et al.** North Carolina Retirement Guide: 1995 Edition. (State Retirement Guides Ser.). (Illus.). 320p. (Orig.). 1994. pap. 19.95 (*1-886429-00-6*) Retirement Info.

Myers, Thomas A. The Problem Loan Action Plan: A Uniform System for Managing Problem Assets. 512p. 1989. text ed. 80.00 (*1-55623-226-8*) Irwin Prof Pubng.
— Real Estate Problem Loans: Workout Strategies & Procedures. 500p. 1989. text ed. 80.00 (*1-55623-148-2*) Irwin Prof Pubng.

Myers, Thomas G. Census Index - Bucks County, PA, 1900. LC 93-80295. 183p. (Orig.). 1993. pap. text ed. 13.00 (*0-9637799-1-5*) T G Myers.
— Nineteen Twenty Census Index: Bucks Counnty, PA. LC 93-91749. 190p. 1993. spiral bd. 13.00 (*0-9637799-0-7*) T G Myers.

Myers, Thomas J. Equations, Models & Programs: A Mathematical Introduction to Computer Science. (Illus.). 528p. (C). 1988. text ed. 60.00 (*0-13-283474-X*) P-H.

Myers, Tim. Let's Call Him Lau-Wili-Wili-Humu-Humu-Nukunuku-Nukunuku-Apuaa-Oioi. LC 93-72767. (Illus.). 24p. (J). (ps-3). 1993. 12.95 (*1-880188-67-8*); pap. 6.95 (*1-880188-66-X*) Bess Pr.

Myers, Vivian F. Shafer: Swamp to Village. (Illus.). 227p. (Orig.). 1980. pap. 15.50 (*0-933565-04-6*) Porter Pub Co.

Myers, W. D., jt. auth. see Hasse, R. W.

Myers, W. S., ed. Woodrow Wilson: Some Princeton Memories. 1946. 29.95x (*0-691-04580-1*) Princeton U Pr.

Myers-Walls, Judith, jt. auth. see Fry-Miller, Kathleen.

Myers, Walter D. Brown Angels: An Album of Pictures & Verse. LC 92-36792. (Illus.). 40p. (J). (gr. 2 up). 1993. 16.00 (*0-06-022917-9*); lib. bdg. 15.89 (*0-06-022918-7*) HarpC Child Bks.
— Darnell Rock Reporting. LC 94-8666. (J). 1994. 14.95 (*0-385-32096-5*) Delacorte.
— The Dragon Takes a Wife. LC 93-26877. (Illus.). (J). 1995. 14.95 (*0-590-46693-3*) Scholastic Inc.
— Fallen Angels. 336p. (YA). (gr. 8 up). 1988. pap. 13.95 (*0-590-40942-5*) Scholastic Inc.
— Fallen Angels. (YA). (gr. 8 up). 1989. pap. 3.95 (*0-590-40943-3*) Scholastic Inc.
— Fashion by Tasha. (Eighteen Pine Street Ser.: No. 6). (YA). 1993. pap. 3.50 (*0-553-29724-4*) Bantam.
— Fast Sam, Cool Clyde & Stuff. (J). (gr. 5-9). 1988. pap. 3.99 (*0-14-032613-8*, Puffin) Puffin Bks.
— Fast Sam, Cool Clyde, & Stuff. 1995. 17.25 (*0-8446-6798-6*) Peter Smith.
— Glorious Angels: An Album of Pictures & Verse. LC 94-49699. (Illus.). 48p. (J). (gr. 1 up). 1995. 15.95 (*0-06-024822-X*); lib. bdg. 15.89 (*0-06-024823-8*) HarpC Child Bks.
— The Glory Field. LC 93-43520. (YA). (gr. 6 up). 1994. 14.95 (*0-590-45897-3*) Scholastic Inc.
— Hoops. 192p. (YA). (gr. 7 up). 1983. mass mkt. 3.99 (*0-440-93884-8*, LFL) Dell.
— How Mr. Monkey Saw the Whole World. LC 94-31976. (Illus.). (J). 1996. write for info. (*0-385-32057-4*) Doubleday.
— Intensive Care. (Eighteen Pine Street Ser.: No. 7). (YA). 1993. 3.50 (*0-553-56268-1*) Bantam.
— The Legend of Tarik. 180p. (YA). (gr. 7 up). 1991. pap. 2.95 (*0-590-44426-3*) Scholastic Inc.
— Un Lugar En las Sombras: Somewhere in the Darkness. (YA). 1994. pap. 3.25 (*0-590-47701-3*) Scholastic Inc.
— Malcolm X: By Any Means Necessary. (YA). 1994. pap. 3.95 (*0-590-48109-6*) Scholastic Inc.
— Me, Mop & the Moondance Kid. (J). (gr. k-6). 1991. reprint ed. pap. 3.50 (*0-440-40396-0*, Yearling Classics) Dell.
— Mop, Moondance, & the Nagasaki Knights. LC 91-36824. 160p. (J). (gr. 3-7). 1992. 14.00 (*0-385-30687-3*) Delacorte.
— Mop, Moondance, & the Nagasaki Knights. (J). (gr. 4-7). 1994. pap. 3.50 (*0-440-40914-4*) Dell.
— Motown & Didi. (J). (gr. k-12). 1987. mass mkt. 3.99 (*0-440-95762-1*, LFL) Dell.
— The Mouse Rap. LC 89-36419. 192p. (J). (gr. 5-9). 1990. lib. bdg. 14.89 (*0-06-024344-9*) HarpC Child Bks.
— Now Is Your Time! The African-American Struggle for Freedom. LC 91-314. (Illus.). 304p. (J). (gr. 6 up). 1991. lib. bdg. 17.89 (*0-06-024371-6*) HarpC Child Bks.
— Now Is Your Time! The African-American Struggle for Freedom. LC 91-314. (Trophy Nonfiction Bk.). (Illus.). 320p. (J). (gr. 6 up). 1992. pap. 10.95 (*0-06-446120-3*, Trophy) HarpC Child Bks.
— Now Is Your Time! The African-American Struggle for Freedom. braille ed. 391p. (J). 1993. vinyl bd. 31.28 (*1-56956-381-0*, BR9071) W A T Braille.
— One More River to Cross: An African Photograph Album. LC 95-3839. (Illus.). 1996. write for info. (*0-15-200089-5*) HarBrace.
— The Outside Shot. (J). (gr. 7 up). 1993. 17.25 (*0-8446-6674-2*) Peter Smith.
— The Outside Shot. (J). (gr. k-12). 1987. reprint ed. mass mkt. 3.99 (*0-440-96784-8*, LFL) Dell.
— A Place Called Heartbreak: A Story of Vietnam. LC 92-14428. (Stories of America Ser.). (Illus.). 71p. (J). (gr. 2-5). 1992. lib. bdg. 22.13 (*0-8114-7237-X*) Raintree Steck-V.
— The Righteous Revenge of Artemis Bonner. LC 91-42401. 144p. (J). (gr. 5-9). 1992. lib. bdg. 14.89 (*0-06-020846-5*) HarpC Child Bks.
— The Righteous Revenge of Artemis Bonner. LC 91-42401. (Trophy Bk.). 144p. (J). (gr. 5-9). 1994. pap. 3.95 (*0-06-440462-5*, Trophy) HarpC Child Bks.
— Scorpions. LC 85-45815. 160p. (YA). (gr. 7 up). 1988. 14. 95 (*0-06-024364-3*); lib. bdg. 14.89 (*0-06-024365-1*) HarpC Child Bks.
— Scorpions. LC 85-45815. (Trophy Keypoint Bk.). (Illus.). 224p. (YA). (gr. 7 up). 1990. pap. 3.95 (*0-06-447066-0*, Trophy) HarpC Child Bks.
— Shadow of the Red Moon. LC 94-42298. (J). 1995. write for info. (*0-590-45895-7*) Scholastic Inc.
— Somewhere in the Darkness. 224p. (J). 1992. 14.95 (*0-590-42411-4*, Scholastic Hardcover) Scholastic Inc.
— Somewhere in the Darkness. (J). (gr. 10 up). 1993. pap. 3.25 (*0-590-42412-2*) Scholastic Inc.
— The Story of the Three Kingdoms. LC 94-2685. (Illus.). 32p. (J). (gr. 1-4). 1995. 14.95 (*0-06-024286-8*); lib. bdg. 14.89 (*0-06-024287-6*) HarpC Child Bks.
— Sweet Illusions. 146p. (Orig.). (YA). 1987. 14.95 (*0-915924-14-5*); pap. 7.95 (*0-915924-15-3*) Tchrs & Writers Coll.
— The Test. (Eighteen Pine Street Ser.: No. 4). (YA). 1993. pap. 3.50 (*0-553-29722-8*) Bantam.
— Won't Know Till I Get There. LC 87-7340. (J). (gr. 3 up). 1988. pap. 3.99 (*0-14-032612-X*, Puffin) Puffin Bks.
— Won't Know Till I Get There. large type ed. 188p. (J). (gr. 6-9). reprint ed. 52.98 (*0-317-01969-4*, 4-27630-00) Am Printing Hse.
— The Young Landlords. (YA). (gr. 6-10). 1992. 17.75 (*0-8446-6569-X*) Peter Smith.
— The Young Landlords. (ALA Notable Bk.). 208p. (J). (gr. 5-9). 1989. pap. 4.99 (*0-14-034244-3*, Puffin) Puffin Bks.
— Young Martin's Promise. LC 92-18070. (Stories of America Ser.). (Illus.). 32p. (J). (gr. 2-5). 1992. lib. bdg. 19.97 (*0-8114-7210-8*) Raintree Steck-V.

Myers, Walter Dean. Malcolm X: By Any Means Necessary. LC 92-13480. 224p. (J). (gr. 5 up). 1993. 13. 95 (*0-590-46484-1*) Scholastic Inc.

Myers, Walter L. The Later Realism: A Study of Characterization in the British Novel. LC 73-2801. (Select Bibliographies Reprint Ser). 1977. reprint ed. 20. 95 (*0-8369-7166-3*) Ayer.

Myers, Warren, et al, eds. Topical Memory System: Life Issues. 10.00 (*0-685-72515-4*) NavPress.

Myers, Wayne A. Dynamic Therapy of the Older Patient. LC 83-25772. 270p. 1984. 30.00 (*0-87668-623-4*) Aronson.
— New Techniques in the Psychotherapy of Older Patients. LC 90-14490. 270p. 1991. text ed. 39.95 (*0-88048-352-0*) Am Psychiatric.
— Shrink Dreams. 256p. 1993. pap. 11.00 (*0-671-86677-X*, Touchstone Bks) S&S Trade.

Myers, Wayne A., jt. ed. see Fogel, Gerald I.

Myers, Wayne A., jt. auth. see Ross, John M.

Myers, William. Evelyn Waugh & the Problem of Evil. 192p. 1991. 24.95 (*0-571-14094-7*) Faber & Faber.
— Milton & Freewill: An Essay in Criticism & Philosophy. 256p. 1987. 65.00 (*0-7099-4620-1*) Routledge Chapman & Hall.
— Theological Themes of Youth Ministry. LC 87-18493. 128p. 1987. pap. 9.95 (*0-8298-0756-X*) Pilgrim OH.

Myers, William, ed. see Farquhar, George.

Myers, William A. Replacing the Warrior: Cultural Ideals & Militarism. LC 85-81253. 32p. (Orig.). 1985. pap. 3.00 (*0-87574-263-7*) Pendle Hill.

Myers, William A., jt. auth. see Donaldson, Stephen E.

***Myers, William C.** Environmental Legislation: The Increasing Costs of Regulatory Compliance to the City of Columbus (Ohio) (Illus.). 135p. (Orig.). (C). 1995. pap. text ed. 30.00x (*0-7881-1657-6*) Diane Pub.

Myers, William E., ed. Protecting Working Children. LC 91-13767. 192p. (C). 1991. text ed. 49.95 (*1-85649-006-8*, Pub. by Zed Books UK); pap. 19.95 (*1-85649-007-6*, Pub. by Zed Books UK) Humanities.

Myers, William F. The Brightness of His Presence: Theological Dissertation. LC 82-90351. 64p. 1982. 6.95 (*0-87948-049-1*) Beatty.

Myers, William H. God's Yes Was Louder Than My No: Rethinking the African American Call to Ministry. 300p. (Orig.). (C). 1994. 49.95 (*0-86543-426-3*); pap. 16.95 (*0-86543-427-1*) Africa World.
— God's Yes Was Louder Than My No: Rethinking the African American Call to Ministry. LC 93-46991. 240p. (Orig.). (C). 1994. pap. 19.99 (*0-8028-0109-9*) Eerdmans.

Myers, William R. Black & White Styles of Youth Ministry: Two Congregations in America. LC 90-43961. 240p. (Orig.). 1990. pap. 12.95 (*0-8298-0868-X*) Pilgrim OH.
— Research in Ministry: A Primer for the Doctor of Ministry Program. LC 93-72091. (Studies in Ministry & Parish Life). 87p. (C). 1993. pap. text ed. 10.95 (*0-913552-51-8*) Exploration Pr.

Myers, William R., ed. Becoming & Belonging: A Practical Design for Confirmation. LC 93-23349. 184p. 1993. pap. 12.95 (*0-8298-0942-2*) Pilgrim OH.

Myers, William R., jt. auth. see Modley, Rudol F.

Myers, William R., jt. auth. see Modley, Rudolf.

Myers, William R., jt. auth. see Myers, Barbara K.

Myers, William S. The Mexican War Diary of General George B. McClellan. LC 71-87641. (American Scene Ser.). 98p. 1972. reprint ed. lib. bdg. 22.50 (*0-306-71789-1*) Da Capo.

***Myers, William S., ed.** Woodrow Wilson: Some Princeton Memories - George McLean Harper, Robert K. Root, Edward S. Corwin et al. LC 47-266. Date not set. reprint ed. pap. 28.80 (*0-7837-9399-5*, 2060144) Bks Demand.

Myers, William S. & Newton, Walter H. Hoover Administration: A Documented Narrative. LC 79-145202. 1971. reprint ed. 69.00 (*0-403-01126-4*) Scholarly.

Myerscough, P. R. Munro Kerr's Operative Obstetrics. 10th ed. (Illus.). 1982. text ed. 68.95 (*0-7020-0904-0*, Bailliere-Tindall) Saunders.

Myerscough, Philip R. Talking with Patients. 2nd ed. (Illus.). 160p. 1992. 59.95 (*0-19-262288-9*); pap. 26.95 (*0-19-262185-8*) OUP.

Myerscough, Thomas R. A Photographic Study Guide for Oriental Rugs. LC 84-90640. 45.00 (*0-318-04446-3*) Persian Rug Ctr.

Myerson. Current Therapy in Foot & Ankle Surgery. 305p. 1993. 79.00 (*1-55664-389-6*) Mosby Yr Bk.

Myerson, Abraham. The Inheritance of Mental Diseases. LC 75-16724. (Classics in Psychiatry Ser.). 1976. reprint ed. 28.95 (*0-405-07448-4*) Ayer.

— The Nervous Housewife. LC 72-2616. (American Women Ser.: Images & Realities). 278p. 1974. reprint ed. 21.95 (*0-405-04470-4*) Ayer.

— Speaking of Man. Grob, Gerald N., ed. LC 78-22577. (Historical Issues in Mental Health Ser.). 1980. reprint ed. lib. bdg. 23.95 (*0-405-11929-1*) Ayer.

Myerson, Allan S. Handbook of Industrial Crystallization. LC 92-14704. (Series in Chemical Engineering). 342p. 1992. 110.00 (*0-7506-9155-7*) Buttrwrth-Heinemann.

Myerson, Allan S. & Toyokura, Ken, eds. Crystallization As a Separations Process. LC 90-1162. (Symposium Ser.: No. 438). (Illus.). 405p. 1990. 99.95 (*0-8412-1864-1*) Am Chemical.

Myerson, George. The Argumentative Imagination: Wordsworth, Dryden, Religious Dialogues. 208p. 1992. text ed. 69.95 (*0-7190-3676-3*, Pub. by Manchester Univ Pr UK) St Martin.

Myerson, George, jt. auth. see Leith, Dick.

Myerson, J. Technology - Systems Approach. (C). 1989. 60.00 (*0-09-173089-9*, Pub. by S Thornes Pubs UK) St Mut.

***Myerson, Jeremy.** Beware Wet Paint: Designs by Alan Fletcher. (Illus.). 266p. 1995. 55.00 (*0-7148-3354-1*, Pub. by Phaidon Press UK) Chronicle Bks.

— Gordon Russell - Designer of Furniture, 1892-1992. 144p. (C). 1992. text ed. 100.00 (*0-85072-306-X*) St Mut.

Myerson, Joel. Critical Essays on Henry David Thoreau's Walden. (Critical Essays Ser.). 240p. 1988. text ed. 45.00 (*0-8161-8885-8*) G K Hall.

— Emily Dickinson: A Descriptive Bibliography. LC 83-21678. (Series in Bibliography). (Illus.). 226p. 1984. 100.00 (*0-8229-3491-4*) U of Pittsburgh Pr.

— Margaret Fuller: A Descriptive Bibliography. LC 78-4203. (Series in Bibliography). (Illus.). 1978. 100.00 (*0-8229-3381-0*) U of Pittsburgh Pr.

— New England Transcendentalists & the DIAL: A History of the Magazine & Its Contributors. LC 78-66814. 400p. 1970. 45.00 (*0-8386-2294-1*) Fairleigh Dickinson.

— Ralph Waldo Emerson: A Descriptive Bibliography. LC 81-11502. (Series in Bibliography). (Illus.). 830p. 1982. 110.00 (*0-8229-3452-3*) U of Pittsburgh Pr.

— Studies in the American Renaissance 1995. (Illus.). 400p. (C). 1995. text ed. 50.00 (*0-8139-1631-3*) U Pr of Va.

— Walt Whitman: A Descriptive Bibliography. LC 92-25927. (Series in Bibliography). (Illus.). 1128p. (C). 1993. text ed. 250.00 (*0-8229-3739-5*) U of Pittsburgh Pr.

Myerson, Joel, ed. The American Renaissance in New England. LC 77-82803. (Dictionary of Literary Biography Ser.: Vol. 1). (Illus.). 240p. 1978. 128.00 (*0-8103-0913-0*) Gale.

— Antebellum Writers in New York & the South, Vol. 3. LC 79-15481. (Dictionary of Literary Biography Ser.: Vol 3.). (Illus.). 400p. 1979. 128.00 (*0-8103-0915-7*) Gale.

— The Cambridge Companion to Henry David Thoreau. (Cambridge Companions to Literature Ser.). 304p. (C). 1995. 59.95 (*0-521-44037-8*); pap. 16.95 (*0-521-44594-9*) Cambridge U Pr.

— Emerson & Thoreau: The Contemporary Reviews. (American Critical Archives Ser.). (Illus.). 500p. (C). 1992. 94.95 (*0-521-38336-6*) Cambridge U Pr.

— Emerson Centenary Essays. LC 81-18516. 230p. 1982. 19.95 (*0-8093-1023-6*) S Ill U Pr.

— Studies in the American Renaissance, 1983. (Illus.). x, 417p. 1983. 50.00 (*0-8139-0997-X*) U Pr of Va.

— Studies in the American Renaissance, 1984. (Illus.). vii, 458p. (C). 1984. 50.00 (*0-8139-1021-8*) U Pr of Va.

— Studies in the American Renaissance, 1985. (Illus.). x, 410p. 1985. 50.00 (*0-8139-1060-9*) U Pr of Va.

— Studies in the American Renaissance 1986. (Illus.). x, 450p. 1986. 40.00 (*0-8139-1106-0*) U Pr of Va.

— Studies in the American Renaissance, 1987. (Illus.). x, 416p. 1987. text ed. 50.00 (*0-8139-1114-1*) U Pr of Va.

— Studies in the American Renaissance, 1988. (Illus.). 475p. 1989. text ed. 50.00 (*0-8139-1164-8*) U Pr of Va.

— Studies in the American Renaissance, 1989. (Illus.). 400p. 1990. lib. bdg. 50.00 (*0-8139-1230-X*) U Pr of Va.

— Studies in the American Renaissance, 1991. 15th ed. (Illus.). 436p. (C). 1992. text ed. 50.00 (*0-8139-1337-3*) U Pr of Va.

— Studies in the American Renaissance, 1992. (Illus.). 350p. (C). 1992. text ed. 50.00 (*0-8139-1389-6*) U Pr of Va.

— Studies in the American Renaissance, 1993. 400p. 1993. 50.00 (*0-8139-1453-1*) U Pr of Va.

— Studies in the American Renaissance 1994. (Illus.). 370p. (C). 1994. text ed. 50.00 (*0-8139-1292-X*) U Pr of Va.

— The Transcendentalists: A Review of Research & Criticism. LC 83-19442. (Reviews of Research Ser.: No. 7). xix, 534p. 1984. 37.50 (*0-87352-260-5*); pap. 25.00 (*0-87352-261-3*) Modern Lang.

— The Walt Whitman Archive: A Facsimile of the Poet's Manuscripts, Vol. 2: Whitman Manuscripts at Duke University & the Humanities Research Center of the University of Texas. LC 93-13839. (Illus.). 742p. 1993. 370.00 (*0-8153-1111-7*) Garland.

— Whitman in His Own Time: A Biographical Chronicle of His Life, Drawn from Recollections, Memoirs, Interviews by His Friends & Associates. (Writers in Their Own Time Ser.). (Illus.). 1991. lib. bdg. 65.00 (*1-55888-424-6*) Omnigraphics Inc.

***Myerson, Joel & Shealy, Daniel, eds.** The Selected Letters of Louisa May Alcott. 1995. pap. 19.95 (*0-8203-1740-3*) U of Ga Pr.

Myerson, Joel, jt. auth. see Burkholder, Robert E.

Myerson, Joel, jt. contrib. see Burkholder, Robert E.

Myerson, Joel, ed. see Cranch, Christopher P.

Myerson, Joel, ed. see Emerson, Ralph Waldo.

Myerson, Joel, jt. auth. see Whitman, Walt.

Myerson, Joel, ed. see Whitman, Walt.

Myerson, Joel, et al, eds. The Journals of Louisa May Alcott. (Illus.). 352p. 1989. 24.95 (*0-316-59362-1*) Little.

Myerson, Joel M., jt. auth. see Foose, Robert A.

Myerson, Julie. Sleepwalking. LC 94-9475. 1995. 20.00 (*0-385-47506-3*) Doubleday.

Myerson, Kathleen, et al. Introduction to Data Processing. 1978. text ed. 12.00 (*0-89433-036-5*); pap. text ed. 9.95 (*0-89433-035-7*); 15.00 (*0-89433-037-3*) Petrocelli.

Myerson, Michael, jt. auth. see Abt, John.

Myerson, Paul G. Childhood Dialogues & the Lifting of Repression: Character Structure & Psychoanalytic Technique. 192p. (C). 1991. text ed. 26.00 (*0-300-04928-5*) Yale U Pr.

***Myerson, Ralph M.** How Your Heart Works. 200p. 1994. 19.95 (*1-56276-238-9*) Ziff-Davis.

Myerson, Richard J. Is Selling for You? It's a Great Job & Somebody's Got to Do It. 112p. (Orig.). 1992. pap. 12.95 (*0-9631841-9-9*) Pine Pubns.

Myerson, Roger B. Game Theory: Analysis of Conflict. (Illus.). 568p. 1991. 50.00 (*0-674-34115-5*, MYEGAM) HUP.

Myes, M., ed. John Trumbull: An Anthology in Memoriam (1756-1843) LC 93-70706. 109p. (Orig.). 1993. pap. 24.95 (*1-879183-19-6*) Bristol Banner.

Mygak, Joe, jt. auth. see Mavlin, George J.

Mygatt, Emmie & Cheney, Roberta. Hans Kleiber: Artist of the Big Horn Mountains. LC 74-28285. (Illus.). 1975. boxed 17.95 (*0-87004-247-5*) Caxton.

Mygind. Allergic & Vasometer Rhinitic Pathological Aspects. 1988. 37.00 (*0-685-65099-5*) Mosby Yr Bk.

Mygind & Naclerio. Allergic & Non-Allergic Rhinits: Clinical Aspects. 250p. 1993. 59.00 (*87-16-10911-2*) Mosby Yr Bk.

Mygind, Holger. Deafmutism. 1976. 300.00 (*0-8490-0008-4*) Gordon Pr.

Mygind, N. & Naclerio, R., eds. Rhinoconjunctivitis: New Perspectives in Topical Treatment. LC 89-1681. 64p. (C). 1989. text ed. 22.00 (*0-920887-54-6*) Hogrefe & Huber Pubs.

***Mygind, Niels, et al.** Essential Allergy. 2nd rev. ed. LC 95-14201. 1995. text ed. write for info. (*0-632-03645-1*) Blackwell Sci.

Myhammad, Maulana. Manual of Hadith. 1987. 10.95 (*0-913321-15-X*) Ahmadiyya Anjuman.

Myhill, John. Typological Discourse Analysis: Quantitative Approaches to the Study of Linguistic Function. 1992. text ed. 54.95 (*0-631-17614-4*) Blackwell Pubs.

Myhre, Dick, intro. Lives in Focus: Profiles of Struggle & Strength. 112p. (Orig.). 1988. pap. 2.95 (*0-939159-15-5*) Cityhill Pub.

Myhre, Helen & Vold, Mona. Farm Recipes & Other Secrets from the Norske Nook: The Midwest's Number One Roadside Cafe. LC 92-12628. 320p. 1993. 24.00 (*0-517-58550-2*, Crown) Crown Pub Group.

Myhre, M., ed. see McManus, Dorothy.

Myhrhaug, B. & Wilson, D. R., eds. Advances in Microprocessing & Microprogramming: Tenth EUROMICRO Symposium on Microprocessing & Microprogramming. 434p. 1985. 97.50 (*0-444-87591-3*, North Holland) Elsevier.

Myhrman, David V. Babylonian Hymns & Prayers. 1972. 59.95 (*0-87968-691-X*) Gordon Pr.

— Sumerian Administrative Documents Dated in the Reigns of the Kings of the Second Dynasty of the Ur from the Temple Archives of Nippur Preserved in Philadelphia. LC 11-1230. (University of Pennsylvania, Babylonian Expedition, Series A: Cuneiform Texts: Vol. 3, Pt. 1). 242p. reprint ed. pap. 69.00 (*0-317-29805-4*, 2052013) Bks Demand.

Myhrman, Matts, jt. auth. see MacDonald, S. O.

Myint, S. & Cann, Alan, eds. Molecular Biology of Opportunistic Infections in AIDS. (Molecular & Cell Biology of Human Diseases Ser.). (Illus.). 320p. 1992. 79.95 (*0-412-45330-4*, A7991) Chapman & Hall.

Myint-U, T. Ordinary Differential Equations. 296p. 1977. 45.75 (*0-444-00233-2*, North Holland) P-H.

Myint-U, T. & Debnath, L. Partial Differential Equations for Scientists & Engineers. 3rd ed. 620p. 1987. 45.75 (*0-444-01173-0*) P-H.

***Myka, Frank P.** Decline of Indigenous Populations: The Case of the Andaman Islanders. (C). 1993. 18.00x (*81-7033-208-7*, Pub. by Rawat II) S Asia.

Mykel, A. W. Luxus Conspiracy. 1992. mass mkt. 5.99 (*0-312-92775-4*) St Martin.

Mykian, M. Numerology Made Easy. 1979. pap. 5.00 (*0-87980-376-2*) Wilshire.

Mykitiuk, Roxanne. The Public Nature of Private Violence. Fineman, Martha A., ed. LC 94-4591. 1994. write for info. (*0-415-90844-2*); pap. write for info. (*0-415-90845-0*) Routledge.

Mykkanen, Donald L., jt. auth. see Lee, Jonathan A.

Mykkeltveit, S., jt. auth. see Husebye, E. S.

Myklebust, Helmer R. Understanding Ourselves as Adults: The Meaning of Emotional Maturity. LC 93-37825. 1994. pap. write for info. (*0-89876-198-0*) Gardner Pr.

Myklebust, Helmer R., jt. auth. see Johnson, Doris J.

Myklebust, Joel B., et al, eds. Neural Stimulation, 2 vols. 1985. 124.95 (*0-318-58963-X*, RC350, CRC Reprint) Franklin.

— Neural Stimulation, 2 vols., Vol. I. 168p. 1985. 144.00 (*0-8493-5253-3*, RC350, CRC Reprint) Franklin.

— Neural Stimulation, 2 vols., Vol. II. 176p. 1985. 144.00 (*0-8493-5254-1*, RC350, CRC Reprint) Franklin.

Myklestad, J. Meyer & Soras, H. English-Norwegian, Norwegian-English Dictionary, Norwegian-English Dictionary. (ENG & NOR.). 42.50 (*0-87557-054-2*, 054-2) Saphrograph.

Myklevoll, Martinus. Martinus Myklevolls Sjfartsminner. (Orig.). (NOR.). 1989. pap. 8.95 (*0-9621657-0-0*) Jest Pubns.

Mykoff, Moshe, ed. The Empty Chair: Finding Hope & Joy - Timeless Wisdom from a Hasidic Master, Rebbe Nachman of Breslov. LC 94-6763. 128p. 1994. 9.95 (*1-879045-16-8*); 59.70 (*1-879045-38-9*) Jewish Lights.

Mykoff, Moshe, ed. see Kramer, Chaim.

Mykoff, Moshe, ed. see Nachman.

Mykoff, Moshe, ed. see Nachman & Nathan.

Mykoff, Moshe, ed. see Rabbe Nachman.

Mykoff, Moshe, tr. see Rabbi Nachman of Breslov.

Mykoff, Moshe, ed. see Starret, Yehoshua & Kramer, Chaim.

Mykoff, Moshe, tr. see Yerushalmi, Shmuel.

Mykrantz, John R. Garden Design Kit: Flowering Perennials. (Illus.). 20p. 1993. student ed 24.95 (*1-880301-02-4*) Gardeners.

— Garden Planning Kit: Vegetable Garden Planner. (Illus.). 7p. 1993. student ed 24.95 (*1-880301-00-8*) Gardeners.

Mykura, W., jt. auth. see Johnstone, G. S.

Mykytka, Edward F., ed. see Stephens, Kenneth S.

Mykytyns. Micro Mainframe Connection. 1985. text ed. write for info. (*0-442-26419-4*) Van Nos Reinhold.

Mylan, Sheryl, jt. auth. see Meyer, Russell.

Myland, Jan C., jt. auth. see Oldham, Keith B.

Mylander, Charles. Secrets for Growing Churches. LC 79-1764. 1979. pap. 4.95i (*0-06-066055-4*, RD 302) Harper SF.

Mylander, Charles, jt. auth. see Anderson, Neil T.

Mylander, Maureen, jt. auth. see Adams, Patch.

***Mylar, Isaac L.** Early Days at the Mission San Juan Bautista: Portrayal of an Historic California Town by an Early Settler. (Illus.). 204p. 1994. pap. 9.95 (*1-884995-02-0*) Word Dancer.

Myler, Harley R. Handbook of Image Processing Algorithms in C. 1993. text ed. 30.00 (*0-13-642240-3*) P-H.

Myler, Harley R. & Weeks, Arthur R. Computer Imaging Recipes in C. LC 92-23501. 304p. 1992. boxed, disk 56.00 (*0-13-189879-5*) P-H.

Myler, Randal. Adventures of Huckleberry Finn. 1990. 4.95 (*0-87129-141-X*, A50) Dramatic Pub.

Myles, Anita. Doris Lessing: A Novelist with Organic Sensibility. 1990. text ed. 22.50 (*81-7045-068-3*, Pub. by Associated Pub Hse II) Advent Bks Div.

Myles, Bruce. Night Witches: The Amazing Story of Russia's Women Pilots in WW II. (Illus.). 272p. 1990. pap. 7.95 (*0-89733-288-1*) Academy Chi Pubs.

Myles, Carolyn, jt. auth. see Day, Anne L.

Myles, Colette G., ed. The Butterflies Carried Him Home & Other Indian Tales. LC 80-70506. (Illus.). 73p. 1981. 4.95 (*0-9605468-1-2*) Artmans Pr.

Myles, Eileen. Bread & Water. 208p. (Orig.). 1987. pap. 5.95 (*0-937815-02-0*) Hanuman Bks.

— Chelsea Girls. LC 94-9895. 276p. (Orig.). 1994. 25.00 (*0-87685-933-3*); pap. 14.00 (*0-87685-932-5*) Black Sparrow.

— Maxfield Parrish: Early & New Poems. LC 95-8852. 200p. (Orig.). (C). 1995. 25.00 (*0-87685-975-9*); pap. 13.50 (*0-87685-974-0*) Black Sparrow.

— Maxfield Parrish: Early & New Poems, signed ed. deluxe ed. LC 95-8852. 200p. (Orig.). (C). 1995. 35.00 (*0-87685-976-7*) Black Sparrow.

— Not Me. 202p. 1991. pap. 6.00 (*0-936756-67-5*) Autonomedia.

Myles, Eileen, text. Martha Diamond: New Paintings. (Illus.). 1990. pap. 10.00 (*0-944680-06-2*) R Miller Gal.

Myles, G. D., ed. Measurement & Modelling in Economics. (Contributions to Economic Analysis Ser.: No. 195). 462p. 1990. 75.00 (*0-444-88515-3*, North Holland) Elsevier.

***Myles, Gareth D.** Public Economics. LC 94-44774. 568p. (C). 1995. write for info. (*0-521-49721-3*); pap. write for info. (*0-521-49769-8*) Cambridge U Pr.

Myles, Glenn. Down & Country. LC 74-82249. (Bebop Drawing Club Book Ser.). (Illus.). 58p. 1974. pap. 4.95 (*0-9605468-0-4*) Artmans Pr.

Myles, Glenn, ed. see Lehman, Yvette K.

***Myles, Janet.** L. N. Cottingham (1787-1857) Architect of the Gothic Revival. (Illus.). 176p. Date not set. write for info. (*0-85331-678-3*, Pub. by Lund Humphries UK) Antique Collect.

Myles, Jeanette. Change of Heart. large type ed. (Linford Romance Library). 1991. pap. 13.95 (*0-7089-7057-5*) Ulverscroft.

— Dreams of Yesterday. (Rainbow Romances Ser.). 160p. 1993. 14.95 (*0-7090-4903-X*, Hale-Parkwest) Parkwest Pubns.

— Images of Clover. large type ed. (Linford Romance Library). 272p. 1992. pap. 14.95 (*0-7089-7288-8*, Traitree Bookshop) Ulverscroft.

Myles, Jeffery L. Yoga Ala Carte: Yogacise. (Illus.). (Orig.). 1988. pap. 9.95 (*0-9621800-0-9*) J L Myles.

Myles, John & Quadgano, Jill, eds. States, Labor Markets & the Future of Old Age Policy. 340p. 1991. 49.95 (*0-87722-790-X*) Temple U Pr.

Myles, John, jt. auth. see Clement, Wallace.

Myles, Myrtle. Nevada's Governors from Territorial Days to the Present. (Illus.). 310p. 1972. 19.95 (*0-685-34729-X*) Nevada Pubns.

Myles, Robert. Chaucerian Realism. LC 94-5852. (Chaucer Studies: Vol. XX). 224p. (C). 1994. text ed. 53.00 (*0-85991-409-7*, DS Brewer) Boydell & Brewer.

Myles, W. C. Transition to Manhood: Through Rites of Passage. Cook, Edward, tr. (Illus.). 165p. (C). 1993. pap. write for info. (*0-9638582-0-3*) Stud Ninety.

Mylet, Trish. Children, Today's Joy & Tomorrow's Hope, 8 bks., Set 2. (Illus.). 224p. (J). (ps-3). 1991. Set. pap. text ed. 16.00 (*0-945590-62-8*); Pals 1, Pals 2, Pals 3, Pals 4, Pals 5, Pals 6, Pals 7, Pals 8. write for info. (*0-318-68375-X*) Sizzy Bks.

— Fun with Phonics, 19 bks. (Illus.). 448p. (J). (ps-3). 1991. Set 1 & 2. pap. text ed. 32.00 (*1-881754-70-7*) Dolphin Pubng.

— Phonetic Readers for the Short Vowels, 11 bks., Set. (Illus.). 224p. (J). (ps-2). 1988. pap. text ed. 16.00 (*0-945590-00-8*) Sizzy Bks.

Mylett, Howard. Jimmy Page: Tangents Within a Framework. (Illus.). 96p. 1983. pap. 12.95 (*0-7119-0265-8*, OP42514) Omnibus NY.

Mylin, Barbara K., jt. auth. see Fulton, Eleanore J.

Mylin, Barbara K., jt. ed. see Fulton, Eleanore J.

Mylius, K. Sanskrit-German Dictionary: Woerterbuch Sanskrit-Deutsch. 3rd ed. 583p. (GER & SAN.). 1987. 150.00 (*0-8288-1157-1*, F60923) Fr & Eur.

***Mylius, Klaus.** Woerterbuch Deutsch-Sanskrit. 2nd ed. 322p. (GER & SAN.). 1992. 135.00 (*0-7859-8305-8*, 3324003377) Fr & Eur.

— Woerterbuch Sanskrit-Deutsch. 4th ed. 583p. (GER & SAN.). 1992. 150.00 (*0-7859-8300-7*, 3324002451) Fr & Eur.

Myll, Nancy. The Dropout Prevention Handbook: A Guide for Administrators, Counselors & Teachers. 224p. 1988. text ed. 29.95 (*0-13-220799-0*) P-H.

Myller, Rolf. How Big Is a Foot? (J). 1991. pap. 3.50 (*0-440-40495-9*) Dell.

— Sweet & Sour: Uncle Rolf's Guide to Eating in New York's Chinatown. 48p. 1991. pap. 5.95 (*0-9631810-3-3*) Cato Pub.

Mylls, Robert. Information Engineering: Case, Practices & Techniques. (New Dimensions in Engineering Ser.). 440p. 1993. text ed. 69.95 (*0-471-58711-7*) Wiley.

Myllylae, G., jt. ed. see Lane, T. A.

Myllymaki, Theodora & Akerson, James. Comprehensive Guide to Cosmetic Sources. 225p. 1992. pap. text ed. 24.95 (*1-56253-102-6*) Milady Pub.

Mylnarczyk, Rebecca & Haber, Steven B. In Our Own Words: A Guide with Readings for Student Writers. LC 89-63920. 384p. (Orig.). (C). 1990. pap. text ed. 18.50 (*0-312-02482-7*); write for info. (*0-312-05601-X*) St Martin.

Mylne, Alexander. Vitae Dunkeldensis Ecclesiae Episcoporum, a Prima Sedis Foundatione, Ad Annum MDXV Ab Alexandro Myln, Eiusdem Ecclesiae Canonica Conscriptae, Repr. Of 1823 Ed. Thomson, Thomas, ed. Bd. with Compotum Magistri Fabrice Pontis Dunkeldensis, MDXIII-MDXVI. LC 78-173008. LC 78-173008. 20.00 (*0-404-52701-9*) AMS Pr.

Mylnikov, V., et al. Photoconducting Polymers & Metal-Containing Polymers. (Advances in Polymer Science Ser.: Vol. 115). (Illus.). 145p. 1994. 88.00 (*0-387-57476-X*) Spr-Verlag.

Mylonas, Anastassios D. Perception of Police Power: A Study in Four Cities. (New York University Criminal Law Education & Research Center Monograph: No. 8). (Illus.). x, 131p. (Orig.). 1974. pap. text ed. 8.50 (*0-8377-0418-9*) Rothman.

Mylonas, George E. Mycenae & the Mycenaean Age. LC 65-17154. (Illus.). 340p. reprint ed. pap. 96.90 (*0-8357-6229-7*, 2034285) Bks Demand.

— Mycenae Rich in Gold. (Illus.). 75.00 (*0-89241-441-3*) Caratzas.

Mylopoulos, J., jt. ed. see Brodie, M. L.

Mylopoulos, John & Brodie, Michael, eds. Readings in Artificial Intelligence & Databases. 650p. (C). 1988. pap. text ed. 44.95 (*0-934613-53-2*) Morgan Kaufmann.

Mylott, Thomas R., III. Computer Law for Computer Professionals. write for info. (*0-318-58179-5*) P-H.

— Computer Outsourcing: Managing the Transition of Information Systems. LC 94-42556. 1995. pap. 24.95 (*0-13-127614-X*) P-H.

Mylroi, M. G. & Calvert, G. Measurement & Instrumentation for Control. (IEE Control Engineering Ser.: No. 26). 296p. 1984. boxed 69.00 (*0-86341-024-3*, CE026) Inst Elect Eng.

Mylroie, John, ed. Proceedings of the Fourth Symposium on the Geology of the Bahamas. (Illus.). 381p. (Orig.). (C). 1989. pap. text ed. 20.00 (*0-935909-31-1*) Bahamian.

***Mylroie, John E. & Carew, James L.** A Field Trip Guide Book of Lighthouse Cave, San Salvador Island, Bahamas. (Illus.). 10p. (Orig.). (C). 1994. pap. text ed. 6.00 (*0-935909-48-6*) Bahamian.

Mylroie, John E., jt. auth. see Carew, James L.

Mymer, Stephen, jt. ed. see Kay, Geoffrey.

***Mynatt, Daniel S.** The Sub Loco Notes in the Torah of Biblia Hebraica Stuttgartensia. LC 95-6988. (Dissertation Ser.: No. 2). 288p. 1995. pap. 18.95 (*0-941037-33-9*) BIBAL Pr.

Mynatt, Elizabeth B., ed. see Brown, Alma C.

An Asterisk (*) at the beginning of an entry indicates that the title is appearing in BIP for the first time.

Myneni, R. B. & Ross, J., eds. Photon-Vegetation Interactions: Applications in Optical Remote Sensing & Plant Ecology. (Illus.). 560p. 1991. 193.00 (0-387-52108-9) Spr-Verlag.
Mynors, R. A., tr. see Bietenholz, Peter G., ed.
Mynors, R. A., tr. see Erasmus, Desiderius.
Mynors, R. A., tr. see Erasmus.
Mynors, R. A., ed. see Virgil.
Mynors, Roger, ed. see Bede.
Mynors, Roger, tr. see Bede.
Mynors, Roger, ed. see Erasmus, Desiderius.
Mynors, Roger, tr. see Erasmus, Desiderius.
Mynors, Roger A., ed. XII Panegyrici Latini. (Oxford Classical Texts Ser.). 1964. 39.95 (0-19-814647-7) OUP.
Mynors, Roger A., ed. see Catullus, Gaius V.
Mynors, Roger A., ed. see Pliny.
Mynors, Roger A., ed. see Virgil.
Myo-Bong, Master & Hye-Am Choi. Gateway to Patriarchal Son (Zen) Venerable Master Hye-Am's Dharma Talks. LC 86-50754. 524p. (Orig.). (CHI & KOR.). 1986. 14.95 (0-938647-01-6) Western Son Acad.
Myong-Won Cho, Litt D. Landscape, Peoplescape & Self-Escape. (C). 1989. pap. text ed. 49.00 (1-85821-032-1, Pub. by Pentland Pr UK) St Mut.
Myopia International Conference Staff. Proceedings of the Myopia International Conference, 3rd, Copenhagen, 1980. Fledelius, H. C. et al, eds. (Documenta Ophthalmologica Proceedings Ser.: No. 28). 266p. 1981. lib. bdg. 126.50 (90-6193-725-6) Kluwer Ac.
Myra, Anne & Benjamin, Goodman. Decadence in Thirteenth Century Provencial & Hebrew Poetry. (Medieval & Renaissance Monograph: No. VIII). 249p. (Orig.). 1987. pap. 10.00 (0-941107-01-9) MARC Pub Co.
Myra, Harold. Children in the Night. 350p. 1991. pap. 9.99 (0-310-57251-7) Zondervan.
— The Choice: The First Man, the First Woman - The Story of Innocence Lost. 208p. 1992. pap. 9.99 (0-310-58601-1) Zondervan.
— Debe un Cristiano Ir a la Guerra? Should a Christian Go to War? (SPA.). 3.25 (84-7228-259-7, 220256, Pub. by Edit Clie SP) TSELF.
— Living by God's Surprises. 156p. 1988. 11.99 (0-8499-0631-8) Word Inc.
— The Shining Face: A Novel. 256p. 1993. pap. 9.99 (0-310-58771-9) Zondervan.
Myra, Harold L. The New You: Answers to Your First Questions As a New Christian. 80p. 1992. pap. 7.99 (0-310-57581-8) Zondervan.
Myrabo, Leik. Future of Flight. 1985. pap. 7.95 (0-671-55941-9) S&S Trade.
Myrad, Ferid, et al, eds. Advances in Pharmacology Vol. 29A: DNA Topoisomerases. (Illus.). 320p. 1994. text ed. 79.00 (0-12-032929-8) Acad Pr.
— Advances in Pharmacology, Vol. 29B: DNA Topoisomerases. (Illus.). 315p. 1994. text ed. 74.95 (0-12-032930-1) Acad Pr.
Myrberg, Mats. Towards an Ergonomic Theory of Text Design & Composition. (Upsala Studies in Education: No. 5). 175p. (Orig.). 1978. pap. 29.50x (91-554-0762-5) Coronet Bks.
Myrdal, A., jt. auth. see Sorsa, K.
Myrdal, Alva, et al. America's Role in International Social Welfare. 11.25 (0-8446-1320-7) Peter Smith.
— Dynamics of European Nuclear Disarmament. 1982. 35.00 (0-85124-320-7, Pub. by Spkesman UK); pap. 13.95 (0-85124-321-5, Pub. by Spkesman UK) Dufour.
Myrdal, Gunnar. Beyond the Welfare State: Economic Planning & Its International Implications. LC 82-15819. xiii, 287p. 1982. reprint ed. text ed. 38.50 (0-313-23697-6, MYBW, Greenwood Pr) Greenwood.
— An International Economy: Problems & Perspectives. LC 77-25683. 381p. 1978. reprint ed. text ed. 35.00 (0-313-20078-5, MYIC, Greenwood Pr) Greenwood.
— Monetary Equilibrium. LC 65-23216. (Reprints of Economic Classics Ser.). xi, 214p. 1965. reprint ed. 29.50 (0-678-00092-1) Kelley.
— Objectivity in Social Research. 125p. 1983. reprint ed. pap. 35.70 (0-7837-8198-9, 2047903) Bks Demand.
— The Political Element in the Development of Economic Theory. 311p. (C). 1990. pap. 19.95 (0-88738-827-2) Transaction Pubs.
Myrdal, Jan. Another World. LC 93-41239. 1994. 19.95 (1-884468-00-4) Ravenswood Bks.
— Childhood. Swanson, Christine, tr. LC 91-26744. 192p. (SWE.). 1991. 18.95 (0-941702-29-4) Lake View Pr.
— China Notebook, Nineteen Seventy-Five to Nineteen Seventy-Eight. Von Dorp, Rolf, tr. LC 79-88412. (Illus.). 1982. lib. bdg. 12.95 (0-930720-59-8) Lake View Pr.
— Confessions of a Disloyal European. 216p. 1990. 25.00 (0-941702-27-8); pap. 9.95 (0-941702-26-X) Lake View Pr.
— India Waits. Bernstein, Alan, tr. LC 86-20069. (Illus.). 364p. (Orig.). 1986. 29.95 (0-941702-06-5); pap. 12.95 (0-941702-07-3) Lake View Pr.
— Twelve Going on Thirteen. Swanson, Christine, tr. 200p. 1995. 19.95 (1-884468-01-2) Ravenswood Bks.
Myrdal, Jan & Kessle, Gun. Albania Defiant. LC 74-21469. 249p. reprint ed. pap. 71.00 (0-8357-5294-1, 2030764) Bks Demand.
Myren, Richard A. Law & Justice: An Introduction. LC 87-11792. 287p. (C). 1988. pap. 22.95 (0-534-08112-6) Intl Thomson.
Myren, Richard A. & Garcia, Carol H. Investigation for Determination of Fact: A Primer on Proof. LC 88-3770. 240p. (C). 1989. text ed. 31.95 (0-534-09348-5) Intl Thomson.
***Myrent, Glenn, et al.** Henri Langlois, First Citizen of Cinema. LC 94-27336. (Filmmakers Ser.). (Illus.). 300p. 1995. text ed. 29.95x (0-8057-4522-X, Twayne); pap. 18.95 (0-8057-4521-1, Twayne) Macmillan.
Myrer, Anton. A Green Desire. 720p. 1983. pap. 3.95 (0-380-61580-0) Avon.
— The Last Convertible. 1993. reprint ed. lib. bdg. 37.95x (1-56849-240-5) Buccaneer Bks.
— Once an Eagle. 1976. 47.95 (0-8488-1438-X) Amereon Ltd.
— Once an Eagle. 800p. 1991. reprint ed. lib. bdg. 49.95 (0-89966-789-9) Buccaneer Bks.
Myres, J. L., ed. see Pitt-Rivers, Augustus H.
Myres, J. N. The English Settlements. (Oxford History of England Ser.: Vol. IB). (Illus.). 288p. 1986. 39.95 (0-19-821719-6) OUP.
— The English Settlements. (Oxford History of England Ser.: Vol. 18). (Illus.). 290p. 1989. reprint ed. pap. 17.95 (0-19-282235-7) OUP.
Myres, J. N., jt. auth. see Collingwood, R. G.
Myres, John L. Handbook of the Cesnola Collection of Antiquities from Cyprus. LC 77-168425. (Metropolitan Museum of Art Publications in Reprint). (Illus.). 656p. 1974. reprint ed. 60.95 (0-405-02263-8) Ayer.
— The Political Ideas of the Greeks. 436p. 1927. 25.00 (0-8196-1163-8) Biblo.
— Political Ideas of the Greeks. LC 71-137278. reprint ed. 22.50 (0-404-04549-9) AMS Pr.
Myres, Samuel D. Education of a West Texan: A Personal Account 1899-1985. LC 85-50377. 250p. 1985. 10.00 (0-87404-085-X) Tex Western.
Myres, Sandra L. Native Americans of Texas. (Texas History Ser.). (Illus.). 46p. 1981. pap. text ed. 3.95x (0-89641-083-8) American Pr.
— Westering Women & the Frontier Experience, 1800-1915. LC 82-6956. (Histories of the American Frontier Ser.). (Illus.). 385p. 1982. pap. 16.95 (0-8263-0626-8) U of NM Pr.
Myres, Sandra L., ed. Ho for California: Women's Overland Diaries from the Huntington Library. LC 79-28115. (Illus.). 314p. 1986. pap. 14.95 (0-87328-119-5) Huntington Lib.
Myres, Sandra L., ed. see Alexander, Eveline M.
Myres, Sandra L., jt. ed. see Morris, Margaret F.
Myrfors, Jesper. Castle Skye. (Pandevelopment Ser.). 128p. 1993. pap. 11.95 (1-880992-14-0) Wizards Coast.
— The Compleat Necromancer. (Pandevelopment Ser.). 72p. 1994. pap. 10.95 (1-880992-18-3) Wizards Coast.
Myrhaug, B., jt. ed. see Waldschmidt, K.
Myrianthopoulos, Ntinos C., ed. External Ear Malformations: Epidemiology, Genetics & Natural History. LC 79-2501. (Alan R. Liss Ser.: Vol. 15, No. 9). 1979. 22.00 (0-685-03287-6) March of Dimes.
Myrianthopoulos, Ntinos C. & Bergsma, Daniel, eds. Recent Advances in the Developmental Biology of Central Nervous System Malformations. LC 79-4947. (Alan R. Liss Ser.: Vol. 15, No. 3). 1979. 19.00 (0-685-03296-5) March of Dimes.
Myrick, David F. Montecito & Santa Barbara, Vol. 2. LC 87-30188. (Illus.). 320p. (YA). (gr. 11). 1991. 54.95 (0-87046-100-1, Trans-Anglo) Interurban.
— New Mexico's Railroads: A Historical Survey. rev. ed. LC 89-27309. (Illus.). 297p. 1990. pap. 18.95 (0-8263-1185-7) U of NM Pr.
Myrick-Harris, Clarissa, jt. ed. see Harris, Norman.
Myrick-Harris, Clarissa, et al. Mainstreaming African-American Studies: A Resource Guide for Middle & High School Teachers. 240p. (Orig.). 1990. pap. text ed. write for info. (1-878531-02-6) Black Res Ctr.
Myrick, Linda S., jt. auth. see Myrick, Robert D.
Myrick, Mildred. Secret Three. LC 63-13323. (Harper I Can Read Bk.). (Illus.). 64p. (J). (gr. k-3). 1963. lib. bdg. 14.89 (0-06-024356-2) HarpC Child Bks.
Myrick, N., ed. Heritage Seventy Six. (Illus.). 117p. (C). 1976. 5.00 (0-686-81380-4) Ridgefield Bicen Com.
Myrick, R., ed. World Litigation Law & Practice, 5 vols., Ea. 1989. 165.00 (0-318-72426-X) Transnatl Juris Pubns.
— World Litigation Law & Practice, 5 vols., Set. 1989. 625.00 (0-685-70529-3) Transnatl Juris Pubns.
— World Litigation Law & Practice: Belgium. 1989. ring bd. 165.00 (0-929179-03-X) Transnatl Juris Pubns.
— World Litigation Law & Practice: Canada. 1989. ring bd. 165.00 (0-929179-08-0) Transnatl Juris Pubns.
— World Litigation Law & Practice: England & Wales. 1989. ring bd. 165.00 (0-929179-06-4) Transnatl Juris Pubns.
— World Litigation Law & Practice: Italy. 1989. ring bd. 165.00 (0-929179-11-0) Transnatl Juris Pubns.
Myrick, Richard. Deer Isle Sketches. (Illus.). 72p. (Orig.). 1990. pap. 9.50 (0-9625851-0-6) R Myrick.
Myrick, Robert D. Developmental Guidance & Counseling: A Practical Approach. 2nd ed. LC 93-70231. 390p. (C). 1993. pap. text ed. 29.95 (0-932796-53-2) Ed Media Corp.
Myrick, Robert D. & Bowman, Robert P. Becoming a Friendly Helper: A Handbook for Student Facilitators. Sorenson, Don L., ed. LC 81-82899. (Illus.). 120p. (Orig.). (gr. 5-6). 1981. pap. 5.95 (0-932796-08-7) Ed Media Corp.
— Children Helping Children: Teaching Students to Become Friendly Helpers. Sorenson, Don L., ed. LC 81-82900. (Illus.). 280p. 1991. pap. text ed. 10.95 (0-932796-09-5) Ed Media Corp.
Myrick, Robert D. & Erney, Tom. Caring & Sharing: Becoming a Peer Facilitator. Sorenson, Don L., ed. LC 78-70543. (Illus.). 224p. (YA). (gr. 9-12). 1984. pap. text ed. 8.95x (0-932796-01-X) Ed Media Corp.
— Youth Helping Youth: A Handbook for Training Peer Facilitators. Sorenson, Don L., ed. LC 78-70544. (Illus.). 224p. 1985. pap. text ed. 8.95 (0-932796-02-8) Ed Media Corp.
Myrick, Robert D. & Folk, Betsy E. Peervention: Training Peer Facilitators for Prevention Education. LC 90-86235. (Illus.). 210p. (Orig.). (YA). (gr. 9-12). 1991. pap. text ed. 13.95 (0-932796-35-4) Ed Media Corp.
— The Power of Peervention: A Manual for the Trainers of Peer Facilitators. LC 90-86234. (Illus.). 226p. (C). 1991. teacher ed, ring bd. 79.95x (0-932796-36-2) Ed Media Corp.
Myrick, Robert D. & Myrick, Linda S. The Teacher Advisor Program: An Innovative Approach to School Guidance. 117p. 1990. pap. 16.95 (1-56109-003-4) ERIC Clearinghouse.
Myrick, Robert D. & Sorenson, Don L. Helping Skills for Middle School Students. LC 92-70820. (Illus.). 160p. (Orig.). (J). (gr. 6-8). 1992. pap. text ed. 7.95 (0-932796-40-0) Ed Media Corp.
— Peer Helping: A Practical Guide. (Illus.). 160p. (Orig.). 1988. pap. 7.95 (0-932796-24-9) Ed Media Corp.
— Teaching Helping Skills to Middle School Students: Program Leader's Guide. LC 92-70804. (Illus.). 128p. (Orig.). (J). (gr. 6-8). 1992. teacher ed, pap. 8.95x (0-932796-41-9) Ed Media Corp.
Myrick, Robert D., jt. auth. see Sabella, Russell A.
Myrick, Robert D., jt. auth. see Wittmer, Joe.
Myrick, Ronald, ed. World Litigation Law & Practice: Germany. 1990. ring bd. 165.00 (0-929179-05-6) Transnatl Juris Pubns.
Myrick, Susan. White Columns in Hollywood: Reports from the GWTW Sets. LC 82-18881. (Illus.). 345p. 1982. pap. 14.95 (0-86554-245-7, P37) Mercer Univ Pr.
Myring. First Guide to the Universe. (Explainers Ser.). (J). (gr. 2-5). 1982. 11.95 (0-86020-611-4, Usborne) EDC.
— Rockets & Spaceflight. (Explainers Ser.). (J). (gr. 2-5). 1982. pap. 4.50 (0-86020-584-3, Usborne) EDC.
Myring, Lynn. Sun, Moon & Planets. (Explainers Ser.). (J). (gr. 2-5). 1982. pap. 4.50 (0-86020-580-0, Usborne) EDC.
Myrivilis, Stratis. Life in the Tomb. Bien, Peter, tr. LC 86-40519. (Illus.). 349p. 1977. pap. 15.95 (0-87451-391-X) U Pr of New Eng.
Myrman, M. B., jt. auth. see Collin, P. H.
Myrna, Harold. Morning Child: A Novel. (Children of the Night Ser.: Vol. 3). 256p. 1994. pap. 9.99 (0-310-46221-5) Zondervan.
Myrna, John W. One Hundred Quick Tips for Business Success. Taylor, Don, ed. 112p. (Orig.). 1994. pap. 3.95 (0-9637314-1-6) QuickStudy.
Myron. Art History. (Barron's E Z 101 Study Keys Ser.). 144p. 1991. pap. 5.95 (0-8120-4595-5) Barron.
Myron, Marie-Rose & Smetana, Josette. Nouvelles Perspectives. 3rd ed. (Illus.). 240p. (FRE.). (C). 1988. pap. text ed. 22.75 (0-03-022817-4) HB Coll Pubs.
Myron, Marie-Rose, jt. auth. see Smetana, Josette.
Myrowitz, Catherine H. Finding a Home for the Soul: Interviews with Converts to Judaism. LC 94-32903. 424p. 1995. pap. 27.50 (1-56821-322-0) Aronson.
Myrsiades, Kostas, ed. Approaches to Teaching Homer's Iliad & Odyssey. LC 86-31167. (Approaches to Teaching World Literature Ser.: No. 13). 158p. 1987. 37.50 (0-87352-499-3, AP13C); pap. 18.00x (0-87352-500-0, AP13P) Modern Lang.
Myrsiades, Kostas, tr. The Karagiozis Heroic Performance in Greek Shadow Theater. LC 87-40508. (Illus.). 258p. 1988. text ed. 35.00 (0-87451-429-0) U Pr of New Eng.
***Myrsiades, Kostas & McGuire, Jerry, eds.** Order & Partialities: Theory, Pedagogy & the "Postcolonial" LC 94-41282. (Interruptions). 320p. (C). 1995. text ed. 59.50x (0-7914-2639-4); pap. text ed. 19.95x (0-7914-2640-8) State U NY Pr.
Myrsiades, Kostas & Myrsiades, Linda S. Karagiozis: Culture & Comedy in Greek Puppet Theater. LC 92-9927. (Illus.). 248p. (C). 1992. text ed. 35.00 (0-8131-1795-X) U Pr of Ky.
Myrsiades, Kostas & Myrsiades, Linda S., eds. Margins in the Classroom: Teaching Literature. LC 93-8692. (Pedagogy & Cultural Practice Ser.: Vol. 2). 1994. text ed. 44.95 (0-8166-2319-8); pap. 17.95 (0-8166-2320-1) U of Minn Pr.
Myrsiades, Kostas, tr. see Papatsonis, Takis.
Myrsiades, Kostas, tr. see Ritsos, Yannis.
Myrsiades, Kostas, ed. see Ritsos, Yannis.
Myrsiades, Kostas, tr. see Ritsos, Yannis.
Myrsiades, Linda S., jt. auth. see Myrsiades, Kostas.
Myrsiades, Linda S., jt. ed. see Myrsiades, Kostas.
Myrtle, Robert C., jt. auth. see Siegel, Gilbert B.
Myrus, Joyce. Angel's Ecstasy. 512p. 1988. pap. 3.95 (0-8217-2347-2) Zebra.
— Beyond Surrender. 1988. pap. 3.95 (0-8217-2525-4) Zebra.
— Desperado's Kiss. 448p. 1991. mass mkt. 4.50 (0-8217-3443-1) Zebra.
— Island Enchantress. 1990. mass mkt. 4.50 (0-8217-3139-4) Zebra.
— Love & Glory. 400p. 1993. mass mkt. 4.50 (0-8217-4090-3) Zebra.
— Master of Moonlight. 384p. 1995. mass mkt. 4.99 (0-8217-4900-5) Windsor NY.
— Sweet Fierce Fires. 576p. 1984. pap. 3.95 (0-8217-1401-5) Zebra.
— Temptation. 448p. 1994. mass mkt. 4.50 (0-8217-4525-5) Zebra.
— Tender Torment. 576p. 1985. pap. 3.95 (0-8217-1550-X) Zebra.
Myrvang, June C. & Myrvang, Steve. The Home Design Handbook: The Essential Planning Guide for Building, Buying, or Remodeling a Home. (Illus.). 256p. (Orig.). 1992. pap. 14.95 (0-8050-1833-6, Owl) H Holt & Co.
Myrvang, Steve, jt. auth. see Myrvang, June C.
Myrvik, Quentin N. & Weiser, Russell S. Fundamentals of Medical Bacteriology & Mycology. 2nd ed. LC 87-2866. 611p. reprint ed. pap. 174.20 (0-7837-2733-X, 2043113) Bks Demand.
Myrvik, Quentin N., jt. auth. see Kucera, Louis S.
Mysak, L. A., jt. auth. see LeBond, P. H.
Myscofski, Carol A. When Men Walk Dry: Portuguese Messianism in Brazil. LC 88-24015. (American Academy of Religion Academy Ser.). 211p. 1989. pap. 15.95 (1-55540-257-7, 01-01-61) Scholars Pr GA.
Mysel, Ruth A. Circle of Love. LC 92-60128. (Illus.). 1992. 12.95 (0-9627974-6-4) Tabby Hse Bks.
Mysell, Bella, tr. see Yablokoff, Herman.
Mysels, Karol J. Introduction to Colloid Chemistry. LC 77-13916. (Illus.). 475p. 1978. 20.00 (0-317-64214-6) Theorex.
Mysels, Karol J., jt. ed. see Fort, Tomlinson.
Mysels, Karol J., jt. auth. see Van Olphen, H.
Mysen, B. O. Structure & Properties of Silicate Melts. (Developments in Geochemistry Ser.: Vol. 4). 368p. 1988. 82.00 (0-444-42959-X) Elsevier.
Mysen, B. O., ed. Magmatic Processes: Physicochemical Principles. LC 86-83155. (Special Publication: No. 1). 490p. 1987. 65.00 (0-941809-00-5) Geochemical Soc.
— Phase Diagrams for Ceramists: High-Pressure Systems, Vol. VIII. 416p. 1990. 150.00 (0-944904-23-8, PHASE8) Am Ceramic.
Mysheeta, Azinna. Support Your Light Body Handbook. 110p. (Orig.). 1993. pap. 9.95 (0-9628328-2-0) Starlite Inc.
Myshkis, A., jt. auth. see Kolmanovski, V. B.
Myshkis, A. D., et al, eds. Low-Gravity Fluid Mechanics: Mathematical Theory of Capillary Phenomena. Wadhwa, R. S., tr. (Illus.). 610p. 1987. text ed. 142.00 (0-387-16189-9) Spr-Verlag.
Myshlyaeva, L. V. Silicon. (Analytical Chemistry of the Elements Ser.). 236p. 1970. text ed. 79.00 (0-7065-1402-5, Pub. by Keter Pub IS) Coronet Bks.
Mysiewicz, Thomas. Bio 1000, 1990-1991. LC 78-12345. 300p. 1990. pap. 495.00 (0-936451-04-1, 987A) D Mysiewicz.
Mysiewicz, Thomas, ed. Bio 1000, 1989-1990. LC 78-12345. (Bio 1000 Ser.). 295p. 1989. pap. write for info. (0-936451-03-3, 987A) D Mysiewicz.
— BioEngineering News: Bio1000 1992-93: World Biotechnology Company Directory. 189p. 1992. spiral bd. 6.95 (0-936451-08-4) D Mysiewicz.
— Bio1000, World Biotechnology Company Directory 1987-88. (BioEngineering News World Biotechnology Company Directory Ser.). 221p. 1987. pap. write for info. (0-936451-01-7) D Mysiewicz.
— Bio1000, 1988-1989. LC 78-12345. 304p. 1988. pap. write for info. (0-936451-02-5, 987A) D Mysiewicz.
Mysiewicz, Thomas, intro. Bio1000 1991-1992: World Biotechnology Company Directory. LC 78-12345. 255p. 1991. pap. write for info. (0-936451-06-8, 987A) D Mysiewicz.
Mysina, S. D., jt. auth. see Knorre, D. K.
Myslenski, Skip, jt. auth. see Henson, Lou.
Myslivec, A. & Kysela, Z. Bearing Capacity of Building Foundations. (Developments in Geotechnical Engineering Ser.: Vol. 21). 1978. 97.50 (0-444-99794-6) Elsevier.
***Myslivecek, Milan.** Erbovnik: 1152 Cost-of-Arms in Color. (CZE.). 1993. 52.00 (0-614-02657-1) Szwede Slavic.
Mysliwski, Wieslaw. The Palace. Phillips, Ursula, tr. 208p. 1991. 32.00 (0-7206-0790-6, Pub. by P Owen Ltd UK) Dufour.
Myslobodsky, Michael S. & Mirsky, Allan F., eds. Elements of Petit Mal Epilepsy: Basic Mechanisms. 419p. (C). 1988. text ed. 81.95 (0-8204-0369-5) P Lang Pubs.
Mysnyk, Mark, et al. Winning Wrestling Moves. LC 93-42161. (Illus.). 208p. 1994. pap. 19.95 (0-87322-482-5, PMYS0482) Human Kinetics.
Myss, Caroline M, jt. auth. see Shealy, C. Norman.
Myss, Caroline M.
Mysse, Janet W. Affordable Furs: Combining Fur & Leather with Knitting. LC 83-62505. (Illus.). 150p. 1983. spiral bd. 16.50 (0-934318-21-2) Falcon Pr MT.
— Cabbage Soup: Knitting Patterns for Soft-Sculptured Dolls. (Illus.). Date not set. spiral bd., pap. 6.95 (0-9623098-0-X) Janknits.
— The Classics: Fisherman Knits. (Illus.). 206p. 1984. spiral bd. 14.50 (0-934318-43-3) Falcon Pr MT.
— Knitting for All Seasons: A Collection of Thirty Knit Classics, Bk. I. (Illus.). (Orig.). Date not set. spiral bd., pap. 6.95 (0-9623098-2-6) Janknits.
— Knitting for All Seasons: A Collection of Thirty Knit Classics, Bk. II. (Illus.). (Orig.). Date not set. spiral bd., pap. 6.95 (0-9623098-3-4) Janknits.
— Knitting for All Seasons: A Collection of Thirty Knit Classics, Bk. II. Hay, Richard, ed. (Illus.). (Orig.). 1989. pap. 9.95 (0-685-29410-2) Janknits.
— Knitting for All Seasons: A Collection of Thirty Knit Classics, Bk. III. (Illus.). (Orig.). Date not set. spiral bd., pap. 6.95 (0-9623098-4-2) Janknits.
— Knitting for All Seasons: A Collection of Thirty Knit Classics, Bk. IV. (Illus.). (Orig.). Date not set. spiral bd., pap. 6.95 (0-9623098-5-0) Janknits.
Mystery Scene Editors. The Fine Art of Murder: The Mystery Reader's Indispensable Companion. (Illus.). 208p. 1993. pap. 17.95 (0-88184-972-3) Carroll & Graf.
Mystery Scene Magazine Staff, ed. The Year's Twenty-Five Finest Crime & Mystery Stories. 3rd ed. 352p. 1994. 20.00 (0-7867-0141-2) Carroll & Graf.
Mystery Scene Staff. The Year's Twenty-Five Finest Crime & Mystery Stories. 320p. 1992. 21.00 (0-88184-903-0) Carroll & Graf.
— The Year's 25 Finest Crime & Mystery Stories. 4th ed. 368p. 1995. 21.95 (0-7867-0251-6) Carroll & Graf.
Mystery Scene Staff, ed. The Year's Twenty-Five Finest Crime & Mystery Stories. 352p. 1994. pap. 12.95 (0-7867-0018-1) Carroll & Graf.
— The Year's Twenty Five Finest Crime & Mystery Stories. 2nd ed. 352p. 1993. 20.00 (0-88184-999-5) Carroll & Graf.

***Mystery Writers of America Staff.** The Crown Crime Companion. 1995. 12.00 (*0-517-88115-2*) Random.

Mystic Jhamom Publishers Staff, ed. Is Man a Free Agent Illustrations Booklet: Supplement. (Conversations with a Mystic Ser.: No. 1). 12p. 1985. pap. 1.75 (*0-933961-02-2*) Mystic Jhamom.

Mystic Jhamon Publishers Staff, ed. Free Agent Horoscope Charts: Supplement. (Conversations with a Mystic Ser.: No. 1). 12p. 1985. pap. 1.25 (*0-933961-03-0*) Mystic Jhamom.

— Is Man a Free Agent? (Conversations with a Mystic Ser.: No. 1). (Illus.). 128p. (J). (gr. 6 up). 1985. pap. 9.95 (*0-933961-01-4*) Mystic Jhamom.

— Jhamom's Story of Creation. (Conversations with a Mystic Ser.: No. 3). (Illus.). 136p. 1986. pap. 9.95 (*0-933961-07-3*) Mystic Jhamom.

— Jhamom's Story of Creation Illustration Booklet: Supplement. (Conversations with a Mystic Ser.: No. 3). (Illus.). 16p. 1986. pap. 2.00 (*0-933961-08-1*) Mystic Jhamom.

— The Phenomena of Life. (Conversations with a Mystic Ser.: No. 4). (Illus.). 1986. pap. write for info. (*0-933961-09-X*) Mystic Jhamom.

— The Phenomena of Life Illustrations Booklet: Supplement. (Conversations with a Mystic Ser.: No. 4). (Illus.). 24p. 1986. pap. write for info. (*0-933961-10-3*) Mystic Jhamom.

— Why? Psychic Development & How! (Conversations with a Mystic Ser.: No. 2). (Illus.). 176p. 1985. pap. 11.75 (*0-933961-05-7*) Mystic Jhamom.

— Why? Psychic Development & How! Illustration Booklet, Supplement. (Conversations with a Mystic Ser.: No. 2). (Illus.). 12p. 1985. pap. 1.75 (*0-933961-06-5*) Mystic Jhamom.

Mystic Seaport Museum Staff, jt. auth. see Gourley, Catherine.

***Myszkowski, Eugene.** The Remington-Lee Rifle. (Illus.). 104p. (Orig.). 1994. pap. 22.95 (*1-880677-04-0*) Excalibur NY.

Mytelka, Lynn K., ed. Strategic Partnerships: States, Firms & International Competition. LC 90-49475. 1991. 45.00 (*0-8386-3445-1*) Fairleigh Dickinson.

Mythen, John. Claude M. Sing Around: Fighting Against Multiple Sclerosis. 1990. 14.95 (*0-9694457-0-9*) Gordon Soules Bk.

Myung, H. C., ed. Hadronic Mechanics & Nonpotential Interactions - 5, Pt. II: Mathematics. 421p. (C). 1992. text ed. 145.00 (*1-56072-043-3*) Nova Sci Pubs.

— Hadronic Mechanics & Nonpotential Interactions - 5, Pt. 1: Physics. 293p. (C). 1992. text ed. 139.00 (*1-56072-035-2*) Nova Sci Pubs.

Myung, H. C., jt. ed. see Gonzalez, S.

Myung, H. C., et al, eds. Applications of Lie-Admissible Algebras in Physics, Vol. 2. 595p. 1978. reprint ed. pap. text ed. 55.00 (*0-911767-04-5*) Hadronic Pr Inc.

Myung, Hyo C. Lie Algebras & Flexible Lie-Admissible Algebras. (Monographs in Mathematics). 351p. (Orig.). (C). 1983. pap. text ed. 50.00 (*0-911767-00-2*) Hadronic Pr Inc.

— Malcev-Admissible Algebras. (Progress in Mathematics Ser.: Vol. 64). 376p. 1986. 68.50 (*0-8176-3345-6*) Birkhauser.

Myung, Hyo C., jt. auth. see Elduque, Alberto.

Myung-Ki Kim. The Korean War & International Law. 280p. 1991. 26.95 (*0-941690-44-X*, Paige Pr) Regina Bks.

Myung Mi Kim. Under Flag. Dienstfrey, Patricia & Rosenwasser, Rena, eds. LC 91-23726. (Illus.). 56p. (Orig.). 1991. pap. 9.00 (*0-932716-27-X*) Kelsey St Pr.

Myzk, William R. The History & Origins of the Virginia Gold Cup. Woolfe, Raymond, Jr., ed. LC 88-9993. (Illus.). 300p. (C). 1988. 485.00 (*0-929129-00-8*) Piedmont VA.

MZ Media Group, Inc. Staff. Agora Services Guide. Date not set. 14.95 (*1-885313-01-2*) MZ Group.

— Top One Hundred Guide. 1994. 14.95 (*1-885313-00-4*) MZ Group.

***Mzamane, Mbulelo.** Mtzala. (Writers Ser.). 185p. 1995. reprint ed. pap. text ed. 12.95x (*0-86975-465-3*, Pub. by Ravan Pr ZA) Ohio U Pr.

Mzimela, Sipo E. Marching to Slavery: South Africa's Descent into Communism. Wheeler, Dennis, ed. 258p. (Orig.). (C). 1993. pap. 12.50 (*0-9626646-8-5*) Soundview Pubns.

N

N. A. D. A. Official Used Car Guide Co. Staff. N. A. D. A. Retail Consumer Edition. Weaver, Lynn A., ed. 320p. 1992. pap. 9.95 (*1-881406-00-8*) NADA VA.

N. C. Poetry Society Staff. Here's to the Land: A Celebration of Sixty Years. (Periodic Anthologies Ser.). 216p. 1992. text ed. 15.00 (*0-9633529-0-3*); pap. text ed. 10.00 (*0-9633529-1-1*) NC Poetry Soc.

***N. E. Thing Enterprises Staff.** Do You See What I See? 3D Christmas Surprises from Magic Eye. (Illus.). 32p. (J). 1994. pap. 6.95 (*0-8362-7018-5*) Andrews & McMeel.

— Garfield's Magic Eye. (Illus.). 32p. 1995. pap. 6.95 (*0-8362-7054-1*) Andrews & McMeel.

— Looney Tunes' Magic Eye. (Illus.). 32p. 1995. 12.95 (*0-8362-7053-3*) Andrews & McMeel.

— Magic Eye: A Book of Postcards. (Illus.). 30p. 1994. pap. 8.95 (*0-8362-3201-1*) Andrews & McMeel.

— The Vision of Nostradamus: A Magic Eye Book. (Illus.). 34p. 1995. 12.95 (*0-8362-7056-8*) Andrews & McMeel.

***N. E. Thing Enterprises Staff, et al.** Magic Eye: The 3D Guide. (Illus.). 64p. 1995. 9.95 (*0-8362-0467-0*) Andrews & McMeel.

***N. E. Think Enterprises Staff.** Magic Eye: A New Bag of Tricks. (Illus.). 32p. 1995. 12.95 (*0-8362-0768-8*) Andrews & McMeel.

N. E. Wildflower Society Staff, jt. auth. see Hunken, Jorie.

Na, T. Y. Computational Methods in Engineering: Boundary Value Problems. LC 79-51682. (Mathematics in Science & Engineering Ser.). 1979. text ed. 107.00 (*0-12-512650-6*) Acad Pr.

Na, T. Y., jt. auth. see Seshadri, R.

Na, Tsung, jt. auth. see Aziz, A.

NAA Forty-Third Staff. Arbitration, 1990: New Perspectives on Old Issues - 43rd Annual Meeting. Gruenberg, Gladys, ed. (National Academy of Arbitrators Proceedings of the Annual Meetings, 1948-1992 Ser.). 320p. 1991. text ed. 40.00 (*0-87179-692-9*) BNA.

Naab, Maxine, jt. auth. see Green, Mimi.

***Naabe, William.** Richard's Story. 330p. 1995. pap. 9.95 (*1-56901-905-3*) NW Pub.

NAACP Legal Defense & Educational Fund Staff. Death Row U. S. A. Reporter 1975-1988 & 1989-1993. LC 89-81793. 1990. ring bd. 300.00 (*0-89941-708-6*, 306050) W S Hein.

NAACP Staff. The Crisis - a Record of the Darker Races 1910-60: Journal of the National Association for the Advancement of Colored People, 50 vols, Set. LC 70-84750. 1,985.50 (*0-405-01001-X*) Ayer.

Naake, John T. Slavonic Fairy Tales: From the Russian, Polish, Serbian & Bohemian. 1972. 59.95 (*0-8490-1062-4*) Gordon Pr.

Naaman, A. E., jt. ed. see Reinhardt, H. W.

Naaman, A. E., et al. High Early Strength Fiber-Reinforced Concrete. 297p. (Orig.). (C). 1993. pap. text ed. 15.00 (*0-309-05618-7*, SHRP-C-366) SHRP.

Naaman, Antoine E. Prestressed Concrete: Analysis & Design. (Illus.). 736p. 1982. text ed. write for info. (*0-07-045761-1*) McGraw.

Naaman, Antoine Y., jt. auth. see Flaubert, Gustave.

Na'aman, N. Borders & Districts in Biblical Historiography. (Jerusalem Biblical Studies: Vol. 4). 275p. 1986. pap. text ed. 28.00 (*0-685-74281-4*, Pub. by Simor Ltd IS) Eisenbrauns.

Naaman, R. & Vager, Z., eds. The Structure of Small Molecules & Ions. (Illus.). 354p. 1988. 95.00 (*0-306-43016-9*, Plenum Pr) Plenum.

Naamani, Houda. I Was a Point, I Was a Circle. (Dual Arabic-English Texts Ser.). 192p. 1994. pap. 16.00 (*0-89410-723-2*) Three Continents.

Naar, J., jt. auth. see Skurka, N.

Naar, Jon. Design for a Livable Planet: The Eco-Action Guide to Positive Energy. LC 89-45697. (Illus.). 320p. 1990. pap. 15.00 (*0-06-096387-5*, PL) HarpC.

— This Land Is Your Land: A Field Guide to North America's Native Ecosystems. LC 91-50508. 320p. 1993. pap. 15.00 (*0-06-096882-6*, PL) HarpC.

Naar, M. D. The Law of Suffrage & Elections: Being a Compendium of Cases & Decisions, Showing the Origin of the Elective Franchise. (Illus.). xiii, 317p. 1985. reprint ed. lib. bdg. 30.00 (*0-8377-0910-5*) Rothman.

Naar, Maria E. Colloquial Portugese. (Trubner's Colloquial Manuals Ser.). 192p. 1983. pap. 14.95 (*0-7100-7450-6*, RKP) Routledge.

Naar, Ray. A Primer of Group Psychotherapy. LC 81-4244. 215p. 1982. 35.95 (*0-89885-027-4*); pap. 22.95 (*0-89885-289-7*) Human Sci Pr.

Naarden, Bruno. Socialist Europe & Revolutionary Russia: Perception & Prejudice, 1848-1923. 424p. (C). 1993. 74.95 (*0-521-41473-3*) Cambridge U Pr.

Naas, Jayni, jt. auth. see Carey, Frank.

Naas, Lucille, jt. ed. see McAllister, Donald.

Naas, Michael. Turning - From Persuasion to Philosophy: A Reading of Homer's Iliad. LC 93-20211. (Philosophy & Literary Theory Ser.). 344p. (C). 1995. text ed. 55.00 (*0-391-03821-4*) Humanities.

Naas, Michael, tr. see Derrida, Jacques.

Naas, Michael B., tr. see Derrida, Jacques.

Naatanen, Risto. Attention & Brain Function. 494p. 1991. text ed. 89.95 (*0-8058-0984-8*) L Erlbaum Assocs.

Naats, I. E., jt. auth. see Zuev, V. E.

Naava. The Golden Goose. LC 93-11681. (J). Date not set. write for info. (*0-688-11302-8*, Tambourine Bks); lib. bdg. write for info. (*0-688-11303-6*, Tambourine Bks) Morrow.

Nab. Catholic Book of Bible Promises. 1990. pap. 4.95 (*1-55748-061-3*) Barbour & Co.

NAB Staff. Careers in Radio. rev. ed. (Illus.). 32p. (Orig.). 1991. 3.50 (*0-89324-106-7*) Natl Assn Broadcasters.

— NAB Guide for Broadcast Station Chief Operators. 82p. 1991. 60.00 (*0-89324-105-9*) Natl Assn Broadcasters.

— NAB Guide to Advanced Television Systems: 1991. 2nd ed. (Illus.). 150p. (Orig.). 1991. 60.00 (*0-89324-111-3*) Natl Assn Broadcasters.

Nabakov, Ilya. The Fly with the Wings, Vol. 1. (Illus.). 244p. 1993. pap. 85.00 (*0-8109-2535-4*) Abrams.

— Mental Institution, or, Institute of Creative Research, Vol. 2. (Illus.). 248p. 1993. pap. 85.00 (*0-8109-2537-0*) Abrams.

— The Red Wagon, Vol. 3. (Illus.). 60p. 1993. pap. 65.00 (*0-8109-2539-7*) Abrams.

— We Are Leaving Here Forever!, Vol. 4. (Illus.). 326p. 1993. pap. 95.00 (*0-8109-2541-9*) Abrams.

Nabakov, Vladimir. Eugene Onegin: A Commentary. (Bollingen Ser.: No. LXXII). 1152p. (C). 1990. pap. text ed. 19.95 (*0-691-01904-5*) Princeton U Pr.

Nabakov, Vladimir, tr. see Pushkin, Aleksandr.

***Nabar, Vrinda.** Endless Female Hungers: A Study of Kamala Das. (C). 1994. 15.00x (*81-207-1282-X*, Pub. by Sterling Plns Pvt II) S Asia.

Nabarro, F. R. Dislocations in Solids: Applications & Recent Advances. (Dislocations in Solids Ser.: Vol. 6). 552p. 1984. 159.00 (*0-444-86490-3*, I-004-84, North Holland) Elsevier.

— Moving Dislocations. (Dislocations in Solids Ser.: Vol. 3). 354p. 1980. 105.25 (*0-444-85015-5*, North Holland) Elsevier.

— Theory of Crystal Dislocations. (Illus.). 864p. 1987. reprint ed. pap. 19.95 (*0-486-65488-5*) Dover.

***Nabarro, F. R., ed.** Dislocations & Disclinations. (Dislocations in Solids Ser.: Vol. 9). x, 424p. 1992. 208.50 (*0-444-89560-4*) Elsevier.

— Dislocations in Crystals. (Dislocations in Solids Ser.: Vol. 2). 562p. 1979. 172.00 (*0-444-85004-X*, North Holland) Elsevier.

— Dislocations in Metallurgy. (Dislocations in Solids Ser.: Vol. 4). 464p. 1980. 154.00 (*0-444-85025-2*, North Holland) Elsevier.

— Dislocations in Solids, Vol. 7. 440p. 1987. pap. 125.75 (*0-444-87011-3*, North Holland) Elsevier.

— Dislocations in Solids: Basic Problems & Applications, Vol. 8. 842p. 1989. 169.25 (*0-444-70515-5*, North Holland) Elsevier.

— The Elastic Theory. LC 78-10507. (Dislocations in Solids Ser.: Vol. 1). 364p. 1979. 105.25 (*0-7204-0756-7*, North Holland) Elsevier.

— Other Effects of Dislocations: Disclinations. (Dislocations in Solids Ser.: Vol. 5). 420p. 1980. 128.25 (*0-444-85050-3*, North Holland) Elsevier.

Nabarro, F. R. & Filmer, H. Physics of Creep & Creep-Resistant Alloys. 200p. 1993. 75.00 (*0-85066-852-2*) Taylor & Francis.

Nabarro, Rupert, jt. auth. see Healey, Patsey.

Nabb, Magdalen. The Enchanted Horse. LC 93-18423. (Illus.). 96p. (J). (gr. 3-7). 1993. 14.95 (*0-531-06805-6*); lib. bdg. 14.99 (*0-531-08655-0*) Orchard Bks Watts.

— The Enchanted Horse. LC 95-3785. (Illus.). 96p. (J). (gr. 2-5). 1995. pap. 3.95 (*0-7868-1029-7*) Hyprn Ppbks.

— Josie Smith. LC 88-8301. (Illus.). 80p. (J). (gr. 1-4). 1989. text ed. 12.95 (*0-689-50485-3*, McElderry) S&S Childrens.

— Josie Smith & Eileen. LC 91-31848. (Illus.). 96p. (J). (gr. 1-5). 1992. text ed. 12.95 (*0-689-50534-5*, McElderry) S&S Childrens.

— Josie Smith & Eileen. large type ed. (J). 1995. 16.95 (*0-7451-2672-3*, Pub. by Chivers Lrg Print UK) Chivers N Amer.

— Josie Smith at School. LC 91-10970. (Illus.). 112p. (J). (gr. 1-5). 1991. text ed. 12.95 (*0-689-50533-7*, McElderry) S&S Childrens.

— Josie Smith at School. large type ed. (Illus.). (J). 1994. write for info. (*0-7451-2090-3*, Galaxy Child Lrg Print) Chivers N Amer.

— Josie Smith at the Seashore. LC 89-8168. (Illus.). 96p. (J). (gr. 1-5). 1990. text ed. 12.95 (*0-689-50492-6*, McElderry) S&S Childrens.

— Josie Smith at the Seaside. large type ed. (Illus.). (J). 1993. 16.95 (*0-7451-1808-9*, Galaxy Child Lrg Print) Chivers N Amer.

— The Marshal at the Villa Torrini. 192p. 1994. 20.00 (*0-06-016915-X*) HarpC.

Nabbes, Thomas. Works of Thomas Nabbes, 2 Vols. in 1. Bullen, Arthur H., ed. LC 68-24818. 1972. reprint ed. 36.95 (*0-405-08812-4*) Ayer.

Nabe, Clyde. Mystery & Religion: Newman's Epistemology of Religion. 76p. (Orig.). (C). 1988. pap. text ed. 13.00 (*0-8191-6712-6*) U Pr of Amer.

Naber, Gregory L. The Geometry of Minkowski Spacetime: An Introduction to the Mathematics of the Special Theory of Relativity. LC 92-12652. (Applied Mathematical Sciences Ser.: Vol. 92). (Illus.). 280p. 1992. 49.95 (*0-387-97848-8*) Spr-Verlag.

— Methods of Topology in Euclidean Spaces. LC 79-7225. (Illus.). 1980. 47.95 (*0-521-22746-1*) Cambridge U Pr.

— Spacetime & Singularities: An Introduction. (London Mathematical Society Student Texts Ser.: No. 10). (Illus.). 176p. 1989. pap. 21.95 (*0-521-33612-0*) Cambridge U Pr.

Naber, Robert J., jt. ed. see Hearn, Gregory K.

Nabers & Stalker. Periodontal Therapy. (Illus.). 200p. (C). 1990. 84.00 (*1-55664-219-9*) Mosby Yr Bk.

Nabeshima, Masakazu. Introduction to Expressing Textures in Oil Painting. (Easy Start Guide Ser.). (Illus.). 112p. 1994. 36.95 (*4-7661-0718-7*, Pub. by Graphic Sha JA) Bks Nippan.

Nabet, jt. auth. see Pinter.

Nabet, Bahram & Pinter, Robert B. Sensory Neural Networks: Lateral Inhibition. 1991. 79.95 (*0-8493-4278-3*, QA) CRC Pr.

Nabeya, K., ed. see Fifth World Congress of the International Society for Diseases of the Esophagus Staff.

Nabham, Marty. Skateboarding. LC 93-23317. (Pro-Am Sports Ser.). (J). 1993. write for info. (*0-86593-346-4*) Rourke Corp.

Nabhan. Cy Young Winners. (Baseball Heroes Ser.). (J). 1991. 12.50 (*0-86593-133-X*) Rourke Corp.

Nabhan, Gary. Desert Legends. (J). 1995. 45.00 (*0-8050-3100-6*) H Holt & Co.

— Songbirds, Truffles & Wolves: An American Naturalist in Italy. LC 92-50783. 208p. 1993. 22.00 (*0-679-41585-8*) Pantheon.

Nabhan, Gary P. The Desert Smells Like Rain: A Naturalist in Papago Indian Country. LC 81-81505. 192p. 1987. pap. 10.95 (*0-86547-050-2*, North Pt Pr) FS&G.

— Enduring Seeds: Native American Agriculture & Wild Plant Conservation. 250p. 1991. pap. 11.95 (*0-86547-344-7*, North Pt Pr) FS&G.

— Gathering the Desert. LC 85-13933. (Illus.). 209p. 1985. 24.95 (*0-8165-0935-2*); pap. 17.95 (*0-8165-1014-8*) U of Ariz Pr.

— Saguaro: A View of Saguaro National Monument & the Tucson Basin. Priehs, T. J. & Dodson, Carolyn, eds. LC 86-61422. (Illus.). 76p. (Orig.). 1986. pap. 4.95 (*0-911408-69-X*) SW Pks Mnmts.

— Songbirds, Truffles & Wolves: An American Naturalist in Italy. 256p. 1994. reprint ed. pap. 10.95 (*0-14-023972-3*, Penguin Bks) Viking Penguin.

Nabhan, Gary P., ed. Counting Sheep: Twenty Ways of Seeing Desert Bighorn. LC 93-12477. (Southwest Center Ser.). 260p. (Orig.). 1993. lib. bdg. 29.95 (*0-8165-1385-6*); pap. 16.95 (*0-8165-1398-8*) U of Ariz Pr.

***Nabhan, Gary P. & Carr, John L., eds.** Ironwood: An Ecological & Cultural Keystone of the Sonoran Desert. LC 94-70016. 92p. 1994. pap. 10.00 (*1-881173-07-0*) Conser Intl.

Nabhan, Gary P. & Trimble, Stephen. The Geography of Childhood: Why Children Need Wild Places. LC 93-31484. (Concord Library). 216p. 1994. 22.00 (*0-8070-8524-3*) Beacon Pr.

— The Geography of Childhood: Why Children Need Wild Places. 216p. 1995. pap. 12.00 (*0-8070-8525-1*) Beacon Pr.

***Nabhan, Gary P. & Wilson, Caroline.** Canyons of Color: Utah's Slickrock Wildland. (Genesis Ser.). 1995. 37.50 (*0-06-258571-1*, HarpT); pap. 25.00 (*0-06-258560-6*, HarpT) HarpC.

Nabhan, Martin. Australia. (World Partners Ser.). (Illus.). 64p. (YA). (gr. 7 up). 1990. lib. bdg. 17.27 (*0-86593-088-0*); lib. bdg. 12.95 (*0-685-36362-7*) Rourke Corp.

— White Water Rafting. (Action Sports Ser.). 48p. (J). (gr. 3-4). 1991. lib. bdg. 11.95 (*1-56065-053-2*) Capstone Pr.

Nabhan, Martin, et al. World Partners, 6 bks., Set. (Illus.). 384p. (YA). (gr. 7 up). 1990. lib. bdg. 95.58 (*0-86593-087-2*); lib. bdg. 77.70 (*0-685-36361-9*) Rourke Corp.

Nabhan, Marty. Fabulous Forwards. LC 92-9479. (Basketball Heroes Ser.). (YA). 1992. lib. bdg. 17.26 (*0-86593-161-5*); lib. bdg. 12.95 (*0-685-59298-7*) Rourke Corp.

Nabhi, N. Exporter's Manual, 1991. (C). 1990. 75.00 (*0-89771-312-5*) St Mut.

— Labour Laws: One Should Know 1991. (C). 1990. 55.00 (*0-89771-309-5*) St Mut.

— Manual for One Hundred Percent Export Units, Free Trade & Export Processing Zones, 1991. (C). 1990. 110.00 (*0-89771-311-7*) St Mut.

Nabholtz, John R. My Reader, My Fellow-Labourer: A Study of English Romantic Prose. LC 85-20118. 144p. 1986. text ed. 22.00 (*0-8262-0491-0*) U of Mo Pr.

Nabholtz, John R., ed. see Hazlitt, William.

Nabholtz, John R., ed. see Lamb, Charles.

Nabholz, A., jt. ed. see Folsch, D. W.

Nabi, Ijaz, jt. ed. see Lele, Uma.

Nabi, Malik B. The Quranic Phenomenon. Kirkari, Abu B., tr. LC 82-70460. (Illus.). 187p. (Orig.). 1982. pap. 7.00 (*0-89259-023-8*) Am Trust Pubns.

Nabighian, Misac N., ed. Electromagnetic Methods in Applied Geophysics, Vols. 1 & 2: Theory & Applications, Vol. 1. LC 87-6330. (Investigations in Geophysics Ser.: No. 3). (Illus.). 528p. 47.00 (*0-931830-51-6*, 443) Soc Expl Geophys.

— Electromagnetic Methods in Applied Geophysics, Vols. 1 & 2: Theory & Applications, Vol. 2. LC 87-6330. (Investigations in Geophysics Ser.: No. 3). (Illus.). 992p. 1991. 82.00 (*1-56080-022-4*, 449) Soc Expl Geophys.

Nabil, M. K., jt. ed. see Nugent, J. B.

Nable. New Catholic Picture Bible. 1988. 8.25 (*0-89942-435-X*) Catholic Bk Pub.

Nablo, S. Progress in Radiation Processing: Proceedings of the International Meeting, 5th, San Diego, California, October 24-26, 1984. 916p. 1985. pap. 205.00 (*0-08-032620-X*, Pub. by PPL UK) Elsevier.

Nablow, Ralph A. The Addisonian Tradition in France: Passion & Objectivity in Social Observation. LC 89-45404. (Illus.). 280p. 1990. 42.50 (*0-8386-3379-X*) Fairleigh Dickinson.

Nabney, Janet. Designing Garments on the Knitting Machine. (Illus.). 192p. 1992. 45.00 (*0-7134-6164-0*, Pub. by Batsford UK) Trafalgar.

— Machine Knitted Fabrics: Felting Techniques. (Illus.). 160p. 1993. 39.95 (*0-7134-6505-0*, Pub. by Batsford UK) Trafalgar.

Nabney, Peter. Marketing Opportunities in Ireland. 246p. 1985. 450.00 (*0-903706-75-X*, Pub. by Euromonitor Pubns UK) St Mut.

Nabokov. Speak Memory. Date not set. pap. 17.00 (*0-679-43318-X*) Random.

Nabokov, Dmitri & Bruccoli, Matthew J., eds. The Nabokov Letters. 1989. 29.95 (*0-685-26632-X*) HarBrace.

— Vladimir Nabokov: Selected Letters, 1940-1977. (Illus.). 608p. 1990. pap. 14.95 (*0-15-693610-0*, Harvest Bks) HarBrace.

Nabokov, Dmitri, tr. see Lermontov, Mikhail.

Nabokov, Dmitri, ed. see Nabokov, Vladimir.

Nabokov, Dmitri, tr. see Nabokov, Vladimir.

Nabokov, P. Who Spirits This Place? Date not set. 20.00 (*0-06-250646-3*, HarpT); pap. 10.00 (*0-06-250722-2*, PL) HarpC.

Nabokov, Peter. Indian Running: Native American History & Tradition. 2nd ed. LC 87-71658. (Illus.). 208p. 1987. reprint ed. pap. 14.95 (*0-941270-41-6*) Ancient City Pr.

— Two Leggings: The Making of a Crow Warrior. LC 82-6979. (Illus.). xxx, 242p. 1982. reprint ed. pap. 9.95 (*0-8032-8351-2*, Bison Books) U of Nebr Pr.

Nabokov, Peter, ed. Native American Testimony: A Chronicle of Indian-White Relations from Prophecy to the Present, 1492-1992. (Illus.). 512p. 1992. reprint ed. pap. 15.00 (*0-14-012986-3*, Penguin Bks) Viking Penguin.

Nabokov, Peter & Easton, Robert. Native American Architecture. (Illus.). 432p. 1988. 65.00 (*0-19-503781-2*) OUP.

An Asterisk (*) at the beginning of an entry indicates that the title is appearing in BIP for the first time.

— Native American Architecture. (Illus.). 432p. 1990. pap. 29.95 (*0-19-506665-0*) OUP.

Nabokov, Vera, tr. see Nabokov, Vladimir.

Nabokov, Vladimir. Ada, or Ardor. 1989. pap. 10.95 (*0-685-26529-3*, Vin) Random.

— ADA or Ardor. LC 89-40107. (Vintage International Ser.). 608p. 1990. pap. 16.00 (*0-679-72522-9*, Vin) Random.

— Annotated Lolita. LC 90-50264. 544p. 1991. pap. 19.00 (*0-679-72729-9*, Vin) Random.

— Bend Sinister. LC 89-40559. (Vintage International Ser.). 256p. 1990. pap. 13.00 (*0-679-72727-2*, Vin) Random.

— Blednii Ogon' Nabokov, Vera, tr. (RUS.). 1983. 27.50 (*0-88233-602-9*); pap. 15.00 (*0-88233-603-7*) Ardis Pubs.

— Defense. LC 89-40546. (Vintage International Ser.). 256p. 1990. pap. 11.00 (*0-679-72722-1*, Vin) Random.

— Despair. (International Ser.). 1989. pap. 11.00 (*0-679-72343-9*, Vin) Random.

— The Enchanter. LC 90-55704. 128p. 1991. pap. 10.00 (*0-679-72886-4*, Vin) Random.

— Eye. LC 90-50265. (Vintage International Ser.). 128p. 1990. pap. 10.00 (*0-679-72723-X*, Vin) Random.

— Gift. 1991. 11.00 (*0-679-72725-6*) Random.

— Glory. LC 91-50488. (Vintage International Ser.). 224p. 1991. pap. 10.00 (*0-679-72724-8*, Vin) Random.

— Le Guetteur. (FRE.). 1984. pap. 10.95 (*0-7859-4209-2*) Fr & Eur.

— Invitation to a Beheading. 1989. pap. 10.00 (*0-679-72531-8*, Vin) Random.

— Invitations au Supplice. (FRE.). 1980. pap. 10.95 (*0-7859-4129-0*) Fr & Eur.

— King, Queen, Knave. (International Ser.). 1989. pap. 11.00 (*0-679-72340-4*, Vin) Random.

— Laughter in the Dark. (Vintage International Ser.). 1989. pap. 11.00 (*0-679-72450-8*, Vin) Random.

— Laughter in the Dark. LC 91-18665. (Revived Modern Classics Ser.). 296p. 1991. reprint ed. pap. 10.95 (*0-8112-1186-X*, NDP729) New Directions.

— Lectures on Don Quixote. LC 83-18550. 240p. 1984. pap. 7.95 (*0-15-649540-6*, Harvest Bks) HarBrace.

— Lectures on Literature. LC 79-3690. 416p. 1982. pap. 14.00 (*0-15-649589-9*, Harvest Bks) HarBrace.

— Lectures on Literature: British, French & German Writers. LC 79-3690. 416p. 1980. 19.95 (*0-15-149597-1*) HarBrace.

— Lectures on Russian Literature. Bowers, Fredson, ed. LC 81-47315. (Illus.). 416p. 1982. pap. 11.95 (*0-15-649591-0*, Harvest Bks) HarBrace.

— Lectures on Ulysses: A Facsimile of the Manuscript. limited ed. 1980. 85.00 (*0-89723-027-2*) Bruccoli.

— The Letters of Vladimir Nabokov 1940-1977. Nabokov, Dmitri & Bruccoli, Matthew J., eds. 1989. 29.95 (*0-15-164190-0*) HarBrace.

— Lolita. LC 92-52931. 368p. 1993. 17.00 (*0-679-41043-0*, Everymans Lib) Knopf.

— Lolita. (FRE.). 1973. pap. 13.95 (*0-7859-4075-8*) Fr & Eur.

— Lolita. (International Ser.). 1989. pap. 10.00 (*0-679-72316-1*, Vin) Random.

— Lolita. adapted ed. 1983. pap. 4.75 (*0-8222-0683-8*) Dramatists Play.

— Lolita. 300p. 1991. reprint ed. lib. bdg. 22.95 (*0-89966-860-7*) Buccaneer Bks.

— Look at the Harlequins. LC 89-40553. (Vintage International Ser.). 272p. 1990. pap. 12.00 (*0-679-72728-0*, Vin) Random.

— The Man from the U. S. S. R. & Other Plays. Nabokov, Dmitri, tr. 352p. 1985. pap. 9.95 (*0-15-656945-0*, Harvest Bks) HarBrace.

— The Man from U. S. S. R. & Other Plays. Nabokov, Dmitri, tr. 342p. 1986. 75.60 (*0-317-40746-5*, Pub. by Collets UK) St Mut.

— Mary. (Vintage International Ser.). 1989. pap. 10.00 (*0-679-72620-9*, Vin) Random.

— Nikolai Gogol. LC 44-8135. 1961. pap. 8.95 (*0-8112-0120-1*, NDP78) New Directions.

— Pale Fire. 1992. pap. 17.00 (*0-679-41077-5*) McKay.

— Pale Fire. (International Ser.). 1989. pap. 11.00 (*0-679-72342-0*, Vin) Random.

— Pale Fire. limited ed. 288p. 1994. 600.00 (*0-318-72983-0*) Arion Pr.

— P'esy. (Sobranie Sochinenii v 15 Tomakh Ser.: Vol. 9). 228p. 1996. 30.00 (*0-88233-979-6*) Ardis Pubs.

— Pnin. Barabtarlo, G., tr. 175p. (RUS.). 1983. 25.00 (*0-88233-737-8*); pap. 12.50 (*0-88233-738-6*) Ardis Pubs.

— Pnin. (International Ser.). 1989. pap. 10.00 (*0-679-72341-2*, Vin) Random.

— Pnin. LC 82-1208. 192p. 1982. reprint ed. 16.00 (*0-8376-0465-6*) Bentley.

— Real Life of Sebastian Knight. LC 59-9489. 1959. 16.00 (*0-8112-0327-1*); pap. 8.95 (*0-8112-0644-0*, NDP432) New Directions.

— The Real Life of Sebastian Knight. 1992. 11.00 (*0-679-72726-4*, Vin) Random.

— Roi, Dame, Valet. (FRE.). 1975. pap. 11.95 (*0-7859-4045-6*) Fr & Eur.

— A Russian Beauty. 1976. 20.95 (*0-8488-0838-X*) Amereon Ltd.

— Sobranie Sochinenii, Vol. 10: Lolita. (Collected Works Ser.). 312p. (RUS.). 1989. 25.00 (*0-88233-535-9*) Ardis Pubs.

— Speak, Memory: An Autobiography Revisited. (International Ser.). 1989. pap. 13.00 (*0-679-72339-0*, Publishers Media) Random.

— Strong Opinions. (Vintage International Ser.). 1990. pap. 12.00 (*0-679-72609-8*, Vin) Random.

— Transparent Things. (Vintage International Ser.). 1989. pap. 10.00 (*0-679-72541-5*, Vin) Random.

Nabokov, Vladimir, tr. The Song of Igor's Campaign. 135p. 1989. reprint ed. pap. 7.95 (*0-87501-061-X*) Ardis Pubs.

Nabokov, Vladimir, tr. see Carroll, Lewis.

Nabokov, Vladimir, tr. see Lermontov, Mikhail.

Nabokov, Vladimir, tr. see Pushkin, Aleksandr.

Nabokov, Vladimir D. V. D. Nabokov & the Russian Provisional Government, 1917. Medlin, Virgil D. & Parsons, Steven L., eds. LC 75-18177. 196p. reprint ed. pap. 55.90 (*0-8357-8363-4*, 2033823) Bks Demand.

Nabokov, Vladimir V. Nabokov's Dozen. LC 75-91138. (Short Story Index Reprint Ser.). 1977. 18.95 (*0-8369-3078-9*) Ayer.

Nabors, Gary S. Remnants: The R. E. M. Collector's Handbook & Price Guide. LC 93-70503. (Illus.). 271p. (Orig.). 1993. pap. 17.95 (*0-9636241-4-8*) Eclipse PA.

Nabors, Murray W. A Romantic Old West Christmas. (Orig.). 1993. pap. write for info. (*0-9639523-3-1*) Associates CO.

***Nabours, Robert E.** Forensic Electrical Engineering & Liability. LC 94-32203. (Illus.). 144p. 1994. 49.00 (*0-913875-07-4*, 0993) Lawyers & Judges.

Nabrink, G. Bibliografie Van, Over en In Verband met Ferdinand Domela Nieuwenhuis. 917p. 1985. 171.50 (*90-04-07572-0*) E J Brill.

Nabseth, Lars & Ray, G. F., eds. The Diffusion of New Industrial Processes: An International Study. LC 73-88309. (National Institute of Economic & Social Research Occasional Papers: No. 29). 346p. reprint ed. pap. 98.70 (*0-317-27314-0*, 2024504) Bks Demand.

Nabuco, Carolina. The Life of Joaquim Nabuco. Hilton, Ronald, ed. LC 50-8549. 120p. reprint ed. pap. 30.00 (*0-317-27234-9*, 2025084) Bks Demand.

Nabwire, Constance. Cooking the African Way. (YA). (gr. 5 up). 1990. pap. 5.95 (*0-8225-9564-8*, Lerner Publctns) Lerner Group.

Nabwire, Constance, jt. auth. see Montgomery, Bertha.

Naby, Eden, jt. auth. see Magnus, Ralph H.

Nacca, Rick, ed. see Finch, John.

Naccache, Paul H., ed. G Proteins & Calcium Signaling. 160p. 1989. text ed. 144.00 (*0-8493-4572-3*, QP55) CRC Pr.

Naccarelli, Gerald V., ed. Cardiac Arrhythmias: A Practical Approach. (Clinical Cardiovascular Therapeutics Ser.: Vol. 2). (Illus.). 600p. 1991. 70.00 (*0-87993-373-9*) Futura Pub.

Naccarelli, Gerald V. & Veltri, Enrico P. Implantable Cardioverter-Defibrillators. LC 93-21732. (Interventional Cardiology Ser.). 1993. 75.00 (*0-86542-270-2*) Blackwell Sci.

Nace, Edgar P. Achievement & Addiction: A Guide to the Treatment of Professionals. 272p. 1995. 32.95 (*0-87630-753-5*) Brunner-Mazel.

— The Treatment of Alcoholism. LC 87-11691. 304p. 1987. 38.95 (*0-87630-468-4*) Brunner-Mazel.

***NACE Staff.** Atmospheric Corrosion of Control Equipment Pub. No. 38. (Illus.). 77p. 1993. 91.00 (*1-877914-52-5*) NACE Intl.

— Development of Controlled Hydrodynamic Techniques for Corrosion Testing. (MTI Publication: No. T-3). (Illus.). 188p. 1992. 96.00 (*1-877914-43-6*) NACE Intl.

— Guidelines for Assessing Fire & Explosion Damage Pub. No. 30. (Illus.). 142p. 1990. 74.00 (*1-877914-16-9*) NACE Intl.

— Guidelines for the Mothballing of Process Plants Pub. No. 34. LC 89-63607. (MTI Publication Ser.: No. 34). 128p. 1989. 53.00 (*1-877914-00-2*) NACE Intl.

— Hydrodynamic Modeling of Corrosion of Carbon Steels & Cast Irons in Sulfuric Acid. (MTI Publication Ser.: No. T-2). (Illus.). 272p. 1992. 96.00 (*1-877914-40-1*) NACE Intl.

— Inspection Guidelines for Pressure Vessels & Piping Vol. 1: New Fabrication, Pub. No. 40. (Illus.). 136p. 1994. 115.00 (*1-877914-64-9*) NACE Intl.

— Prediction of Service Performance of Equipment Made of or Lined with Polymeric Materials. (MTI Publication Ser.: No. T-4). (Illus.). 102p. 1993. 120.00 (*1-877914-44-4*) NACE Intl.

— Pyrophoric Behavior & Combustion of Reactive Metals Pub. No. 32. LC 88-61124. (MTI Publication Ser.: No. 32). (Illus.). 21p. 1988. 33.00 (*0-915567-35-0*) NACE Intl.

— Thermal Spray Coating Applications in the Chemical Process Industries Pub. No. 42. (Illus.). 252p. 1994. 85.00 (*1-877914-59-2*) NACE Intl.

Nace, Ted, jt. auth. see Felici, James.

Nacfaire, H., ed. Grid-Connected Wind Turbines: Proceedings of a Contractors' Meeting on Wind Demonstration Projects, Organized by the Commision of the European Communities, Directorate-General for Energy, Alghero, Italy, 11-12 June 1987. 128p. 1988. 45.00 (*1-85166-185-9*) Elsevier.

Nachalo, Sophia & Vochek, Yarostan. Letters of Insurgents. 1976. pap. 7.50 (*0-934868-13-1*) Black & Red.

Nachamkin, Irving, et al, eds. Campylobacter Jejuni: Current Status & Future Trends. (Illus.). 312p. 1992. text ed. 79.00 (*1-55581-042-X*) Am Soc Microbio.

Nachazel, Karel. Estimation Theory in Hydrology & Water Systems. LC 92-9199. (Developments in Water Science Ser.: Vol. 42). 1993. write for info. (*0-444-98726-6*) Elsevier.

Nachbin, A. Modelling of Water Waves in Shallow Channels. LC 92-75036. (Topics in Engineering Ser.: Vol. 13). 160p. 1993. 86.00 (*1-56252-062-8*) Computational Mech MA.

Nachbin, L. Topology in Spaces of Holomorphic Mappings. LC 68-29710. (Ergebnisse der Mathematik und Ihrer Grenzgebiete Ser.: Vol. 47). 1969. 54.00 (*0-387-04470-1*) Spr-Verlag.

Nachbin, Leopoldo. Elements of Approximation Theory. LC 76-48. 131p. reprint ed. pap. 37.40 (*0-8357-8869-5*, AU00370) Bks Demand.

— Elements of Approximation Theory. LC 76-48. 132p. 1976. reprint ed. 13.50 (*0-88275-388-6*) Krieger.

— Holomorphic Functions, Domains of Holomorphy & Local Properties. LC 78-134642. (North-Holland Mathematics Studies: Vol. 1). 130p. reprint ed. pap. 37.10 (*0-318-39710-2*, AU00368) Bks Demand.

— Introduction to Functional Analysis, Banach Spaces, & Differential Calculus. LC 80-24382. (Monographs & Textbooks in Pure & Applied Mathematics: No. 60). 182p. reprint ed. pap. 51.90 (*0-7837-5886-3*, 2045606) Bks Demand.

— Topology & Order. Bechtolsheim, Lulu, tr. LC 76-59. (Illus.). 128p. reprint ed. pap. 36.50 (*0-8357-7057-5*, AU00369) Bks Demand.

— Topology & Order. LC 76-59. 128p. 1976. reprint ed. 14.00 (*0-88275-387-8*) Krieger.

***Nachel, Marty.** Beer Across America: A Regional Guide to Brewpubs & Microbreweries. (Illus.). 192p. 1995. pap. 14.95 (*0-88266-902-8*, Storey Pub) Storey Comm Inc.

Nachemson. Back Pain. 1993. write for info. (*0-397-51202-3*) Lippincott.

Nachfigall, P. E. & Moore, P. W., eds. Animal Sonar: Processes & Performance. LC 88-28886. (NATO ASI Series A, Life Sciences: Vol. 156). (Illus.). 878p. 1988. 165.00 (*0-306-43031-2*, Plenum Pr) Plenum.

Nachi-Fujikoshi, ed. Training for TPM: A Manufacturing Success Story. LC 90-40276. (Illus.). 274p. 1990. 65.00 (*0-915299-34-8*) Prod Press.

Nachinkin. Polymeric Microfilters. 212p. 1992. text ed. 82.00 (*0-13-647041-6*) P-H.

Nachlas, jt. auth. see Papel, Ira D.

Nachman. Likutey Moharan, Vol. 10: Lessons 109-200. Mykoff, Moshe & Bergman, Ozer, eds. (Illus.). 500p. 1992. 18.00 (*0-930213-85-8*) Breslov Res Inst.

— Likutey Moharan, Vol. 4: Lessons 23-32. Mykoff, Moshe & Bergman, Ozer, eds. (Illus.). 520p. 1992. 18.00 (*0-930213-79-3*) Breslov Res Inst.

— Le Tikoun Haklali. rev. ed. Dimermanas, A., ed. & tr. by. 115p. (FRE.). 1989. pap. text ed. 7.00 (*0-930213-34-3*) Breslov Res Inst.

Nachman & Nathan. Mayim. Mykoff, Moshe, ed. 64p. (Orig.). 1987. pap. 3.00 (*0-930213-28-9*) Breslov Res Inst.

Nachman, Elana. Riverfinger Women. 192p. 1992. reprint ed. pap. 8.95 (*1-56280-013-2*) Naiad Pr.

Nachman, Gerald. The Fragile Bachelor. (Illus.). 192p. (Orig.). 1989. pap. 8.95 (*0-89815-289-5*) Ten Speed Pr.

Nachman, Joseph F. & Lundin, C. E., eds. Rare Earth Research, Vol. 1. 370p. 1962. text ed. 320.00 (*0-677-10490-1*) Gordon & Breach.

Nachman, Louis J. Fundamental Mathematics. LC 77-17239. 677p. reprint ed. pap. 180.00 (*0-317-09173-5*, 2051297) Bks Demand.

Nachman of Breslov. Advice. Greenbaum, Avraham, tr. LC 83-70202. 522p. 1983. 16.00 (*0-930213-04-1*) Breslov Res Inst.

— Les Contes. Regnot, Franz, tr. 180p. (Orig.). (FRE.). 1981. pap. 7.00 (*0-930213-22-X*) Breslov Res Inst.

— The Fixer. Succot, Miriam & Succot, Eliyah, trs. (Illus.). (J). (gr. 3-12). 1977. pap. 1.95 (*0-917246-04-7*) Maimes.

— The Gems of Rabbi Nachman. Rosenfeld, Tzvi A., ed. Kaplan, Ayreh, tr. (Illus.). 186p. (Orig.). 1980. pap. 3.00 (*0-930213-10-6*) Breslov Res Inst.

— Hitbodedouth: Ou La Porte du Ciel. 110p. (Orig.). (FRE.). 1982. pap. 2.00 (*0-930213-27-0*) Breslov Res Inst.

— Rabbi Nachman's Stories. Kaplan, Aryeh, tr. LC 83-70201. 552p. 1983. 21.00 (*0-930213-02-5*) Breslov Res Inst.

— Rabbi Nachman's Stories: Skazocnniji Histori Rabbi Nechman iz Bratzlav. Avni, Baruch, tr. (Illus.). 332p. (Orig.). (C). 1987. pap. 10.00 (*0-930213-29-7*) Breslov Res Inst.

— Rabbi Nachman's Tikkun: The Comprehensive Remedy. Greenbaum, Avraham, tr. 256p. 1984. 12.00 (*0-930213-06-8*) Breslov Res Inst.

— Rabbi Nachman's Wisdom. Rosenfeld, Zvi A., ed. Kaplan, Aryeh, tr. (Illus.). 510p. 1984. reprint ed. 16.00 (*0-930213-00-9*) Breslov Res Inst.

Nachman of Breslov & Nathan of Breslov. Ayeh? (Where)? Greenbaum, Avraham, tr. 64p. (Orig.). 1985. pap. 3.00 (*0-930213-12-2*) Breslov Res Inst.

— Azamra (I Will Sing) Greenbaum, Avraham, tr. 64p. (Orig.). 1984. pap. 3.00 (*0-930213-11-4*) Breslov Res Inst.

— Courage! 119p. (Orig.). 1983. pap. 3.00 (*0-930213-23-8*) Breslov Res Inst.

— Outpouring of the Soul. Kaplan, Aryeh, tr. 96p. (Orig.). 1980. reprint ed. pap. 4.00 (*0-930213-14-9*) Breslov Res Inst.

— Restore My Soul. Greenbaum, Avraham, tr. 128p. (Orig.). 1980. pap. 4.00 (*0-930213-13-0*) Breslov Res Inst.

Nachman, Rebbe. Azamra. Dimermanas, A., ed. & tr. by. 64p. (FRE.). 1989. pap. text ed. 3.00 (*0-930213-33-5*) Breslov Res Inst.

Nachman, Resi. Seven Poems. 1971. reprint ed. pap. 1.00 (*0-918230-01-2*) Barnstable.

Nachmani, Amikam. Great Power Discord in Palestine: The Anglo-American Committee of Inquiry into the Problems of European Jewry & Palestine, 1945-1946. (Illus.). 296p. 1986. 47.50 (*0-7146-3298-8*, Pub. by F Cass Pubs UK) Intl Spec Bk.

— International Intervention in the Greek Civil War: The United Nations Special Committee on the Balkans, 1947-1952. LC 89-26544. 224p. 1990. text ed. 49.95 (*0-275-93367-9*, C3367, Greenwood Pr) Greenwood.

— Israel, Turkey, Greece: Uneasy Relations in the East Mediterranean. 1987. 35.00 (*0-7146-3321-6*, Pub. by F Cass Pubs UK) Intl Spec Bk.

Nachmanovitch, Stephen. Free Play: The Power of Improvisation in Life & the Arts. (Illus.). 224p. 1991. pap. 8.95 (*0-87477-631-7*) J P Tarcher.

Nachmanson, Eva, ed. see Kemp-Slaughter, James.

Nachmias, Carolyn S. & Nasuti, James F. Joint Ventures: Structuring Alternatives. 1162p. 1988. text ed. 90.00 (*0-07-172113-4*) Shepards-McGraw.

Nachmias, Chara F. & Nachmias, David. Research Methods in the Social Sciences. 4th ed. LC 90-63540. 592p. (C). 1991. text ed. write for info. (*0-312-06275-3*); pap. text ed. 11.50 (*0-312-06254-0*); pap. text ed. 1.50 (*0-312-06758-5*) St Martin.

Nachmias, David & Rosenbloom, David H. Bureaucratic Government: U. S. A. 269p. (Orig.). 1980. pap. text ed. 16.00 (*0-312-10806-0*) St Martin.

Nachmias, David, jt. auth. see Nachmias, Chara F.

Nachmias, Nitza. Transfer of Arms, Leverage, & Peace in the Middle East. LC 88-17777. (Contributions in Military Studies: No. 83). 208p. 1988. text ed. 49.95 (*0-313-26300-0*, NAT/, Greenwood Pr) Greenwood.

Nachod, E. C., tr. see Steudel, Ralf.

Nachowitz, Todd. Alternative Directory of Nongovernmental Organizations in South Asia. rev. ed. (Foreign & Comparative Studies Program, South Asian Ser.: No. 14). 1990. pap. text ed. 15.00 (*0-915984-41-5*) Syracuse U Foreign Comp.

Nachowitz, Todd, ed. An Alternative Directory of Non-Governmental Organizations in South Asia. LC 89-83678. (Orig.). (C). 1989. pap. 15.00 (*0-9622716-0-8*) Fourth Wrld Pr.

Nachshoni, Yehuda. Studies in the Weekly Parashah, Vol. I: Bereishis. Himelstein, Shmuel, tr. (ArtScroll Judaica Classics Ser.). 320p. 1988. 21.95 (*0-89906-933-9*); pap. 18.95 (*0-89906-934-7*) Mesorah Pubns.

— Studies in the Weekly Parashah, Vol. II: Sh'mos. Himelstein, Shmuel, tr. (ArtScroll Judaica Classics Ser.). 296p. 1988. 21.95 (*0-89906-935-5*); pap. 18.95 (*0-89906-936-3*) Mesorah Pubns.

— Studies in the Weekly Parashah, Vol. III: Vayikra. Himelstein, Shmuel, tr. (ArtScroll Judaica Classics Ser.). 278p. 1989. 21.95 (*0-89906-937-1*); pap. 18.95 (*0-89906-938-X*) Mesorah Pubns.

— Studies in the Weekly Parashah, Vol. IV: Bamidbar. Blumberg, Raphael, tr. (ArtScroll Judaica Classics Ser.). 296p. 1989. 21.95 (*0-89906-939-8*); pap. 18.95 (*0-89906-940-1*) Mesorah Pubns.

— Studies in the Weekly Parashah, Vol. V: Devarim. Himelstein, Shmuel, tr. (ArtScroll Judaica Classics Ser.). 256p. 1989. 21.95 (*0-89906-941-X*); pap. 18.95 (*0-89906-942-8*) Mesorah Pubns.

Nacht, Michael. The Age of Vulnerability: Threats to the Nuclear Stalemate. LC 84-45849. 209p. 1985. 12.95 (*0-8157-5964-9*); pap. 12.95 (*0-8157-5963-0*) Brookings.

— The War in Vietnam: The Influence of Concepts on Policy. (CISA Working Paper Ser.: No. 26). 28p. (Orig.). Date not set. pap. 10.00 (*0-86682-025-6*) Ctr Intl Relations.

Nacht, Michael, jt. auth. see Goodwin, Craufurd D.

Nachtigal, Chester & Martin, Marvin D. Instrumentation & Control: Fundamentals & Applications. 890p. 1990. text ed. 145.00 (*0-471-88045-0*) Wiley.

***Nachtigall, Lila & Heilman, Joan R.** Estrogen. 2nd ed. 1995. pap. 11.00 (*0-06-092602-3*, PL) HarpC.

Nachtigall, Lila, et al. What Every Woman Should Know: Staying Healthy after 40. 416p. 1995. 22.95 (*0-446-51731-3*) Warner Bks.

— What Every Woman Should Know: Staying Healthy after 40. 1996. pap. write for info. (*0-446-67214-9*) Warner Bks.

Nachtigall, W. Temperature Relations in Animals & Man. (BIONA Report Ser.: No. 4). 229p. 1986. pap. 19.00 (*0-89574-226-8*, Pub. by Gustav Fischer Verlag) VCH Pubs.

Nachtigall, W., ed. Biona Report Five - Bat Flight. 1987. pap. text ed. 40.00 (*0-89574-239-X*) VCH Pubs.

***Nachtigall, Werner.** Exploring with the Microscope: A Book of Discovery & Learning. LC 94-23844. (Illus.). 160p. (ENG & GER.). (J). 1995. 19.95 (*0-8069-0866-1*) Sterling.

Nachtigall, Werner, ed. The Flying Honeybee: Aspects of Energetics. (BIONA Report Ser.: No. 6). 148p. (ENG & GER.). 1989. pap. text ed. 20.00 (*0-89574-289-6*, Pub. by Gustav Fischer Verlag) VCH Pubs.

Nachtigall, Werner, et al, eds. Three-D SEM-Atlas of Insect Morphology, Vol. 1: Heteroptera, Report 7. 1991. pap. text ed. 45.00 (*1-56081-310-5*) G F Verlag.

Nachtman & Kalpakjian. Lubricants & Lubrication in Metalworking Operations. (Manufacturing Engineering & Materials Processing Ser.: Vol. 14). 288p. 1985. 125.00 (*0-8247-7401-9*) Dekker.

Nachtmann, Francis W. Exercises in French Phonics. 79p. (C). 1981. reprint ed. pap. text ed. 5.95 (*0-87563-215-7*) Stipes.

Nachtmann, O. Elementary Particle Physics. (Texts & Monographs in Physics). (Illus.). 592p. 1989. 98.00 (*0-387-50496-6*, 2466); pap. 49.00 (*0-387-51647-6*) Spr-Verlag.

Nachtrieb, Norman H., jt. auth. see Oxtoby, David W.

Nachwalter, Elliott & Poole, Fred. The Pipemaker's Book: A Step-by-Step Guide to Making & Appreciating Fine Pipes. pap. write for info. (*0-671-60724-3*) S&S Trade.

Nacianceno, Natividad T. & Waterman, Floyd. Land Use & Housing in the City of Manila. 48p. (Orig.). 1985. pap. 3.50 (*1-55719-110-7*) U NE CPAR.

Nacianceno, Natividad T. & Waterman, Floyd T. The Trail of Education in Two Cities Omaha & Manila. 100p. (Orig.). 1985. pap. 6.00 (*1-55719-057-7*) U NE CPAR.

Nack, James M. Writings of James M. Nack: The Deaf & Dumb Poet. 1972. 59.95 (*0-8490-1339-9*) Gordon Pr.

Nack, William. Secretariat: The Making of a Champion. (Quality Paperbacks Ser.). 342p. 1988. reprint ed. pap. 11.95 (*0-306-80317-8*) Da Capo.

Nackenoff, Carol. The Fictional Republic: Horatio Alger & American Political Discourse. (Illus.). 384p. 1994. 35.00 (*0-19-507923-X*) OUP.

An Asterisk (*) at the beginning of an entry indicates that the title is appearing in BIP for the first time.

Nackerud, Larry G. The Central American Refugee Issue in Brownsville, Texas: Seeking Understanding of Public Policy Formulation from Within a Community Setting. LC 93-24044. 236p. 1993. text ed. 89.95 (*0-7734-2240-4*) E Mellen.

Nackley, Jeffrey V. Primer on Workers' Compensation. 2nd ed. 200p. 1989. pap. text ed. 45.00 (*0-87179-596-5*, 0596) BNA.

Nackman, Lee R., jt. auth. see Barton, John J.

***NACLA Staff.** Haiti: Dangerous Crossroads. 200p. 1995. 35.00 (*0-89608-506-6*); pap. 15.00 (*0-89608-505-8*) South End Pr.

Naclerio, jt. auth. see Mygind.

Naclerio, Emil A., et al. Understanding Pacemakers. LC 80-22912. (Illus.). 176p. 1982. 24.95 (*0-935576-04-5*); pap. 14.95 (*0-935576-05-3*) Kesend Pub Ltd.

Naclerio, R., jt. ed. see Mygind, N.

Naclerio, Ron, jt. auth. see Valenti, John.

Nacogdoches Genealogical Society Staff, ed. History of Nacogdoches County, Texas. (Illus.). 752p. 1985. 57.50 (*0-88107-036-X*) Curtis Media.

Nacos, Brigitte L. The Press, Presidents, & Crises. 288p. 1990. text ed. 35.00 (*0-231-07064-0*) Col U Pr.

— Terrorism & the Media: From the Iran Hostage Crisis to the World Trade Center Bombing. LC 94-4602. 224p. 1994. 32.50 (*0-231-10014-0*) Col U Pr.

Nacozy, Paul E. & Ferraz-Mello, Sylvio, eds. Natural & Artificial Satellite Motion. (Illus.). 450p. 1979. text ed. 27.50 (*0-292-75514-7*) U of Tex Pr.

Nacpil, Emerito P., ed. see All-Asia Consultation on Theological Education for Christian Ministry Staff.

Naczk, Marion, jt. auth. see Shahidi, Fereidoon.

Nada-Yolanda. Angels & Man. LC 73-90881. 138p. 1974. 15.00 (*0-912322-03-9*) Mark-Age.

— Evolution of Man: Two Hundred Six Million Years on Earth. 2nd ed. LC 88-61526. 161p. 1988. 15.00 (*0-912322-06-3*) Mark-Age.

— MAPP to Aquarius: Mark Age Period & Program. LC 85-62167. (Illus.). 351p. 1985. 20.00 (*0-912322-05-5*); pap. 15.00 (*0-912322-53-5*) Mark-Age.

— Visitors from Other Planets. LC 73-90880. 334p. 1974. 15.00 (*0-912322-04-7*) Mark-Age.

Nadakavukaren, Anne. Man & Environment: A Health Perspective. 3rd ed. (Illus.). 530p. (C). 1990. pap. text ed. 24.95 (*0-88133-445-6*); student ed 9.50 (*0-88133-489-8*) Waveland Pr.

— Our Global Environment: A Health Perspective. 4th rev. ed. (Illus.). 711p. (C). 1995. pap. text ed. 29.95x (*0-88133-831-1*) Waveland Pr.

— Study Guide to Accompany Our Global Environment: A Health Perspective. 4th rev. ed. 196p. (C). 1995. pap. text ed. 9.95x (*0-88133-832-X*) Waveland Pr.

***Nadal, David Arhtur.** Consulting by "The Book" 250p. 1994. reprint ed. spiral bd. 49.50 (*0-9632383-4-5*) Intl Mgmt FL.

— Multinational Consulting by "The Book" 420p. 1994. spiral bd. 60.00 (*0-9632383-8-8*) Intl Mgmt FL.

Nadal, David Arthur. Agenda for MultiNational Networking. 390p. (C). 1994. 60.00 (*0-9632383-2-9*) Intl Mgmt FL.

— MultiNational Networking. 410p. (C). 1993. text ed. 49.50 (*0-9632383-0-2*) Intl Mgmt FL.

Nadal, Ehrman S. Virginian Village, & Other Papers. LC 68-20324. (Essay Index Reprint Ser.). 1977. 20.95 (*0-8369-0733-7*) Ayer.

Nadal, Jean-Pierre, jt. ed. see Grassberger, Peter.

Nadal, Rafael M. Lorca's the Public: A Study of His Unfinished Play el Publico & of Love & Death in the Work of Federico Garcia Lorca. 247p. (C). 1981. pap. 9.95 (*0-7145-2752-1*) M Boyars Pubs.

Nadan, Corinne J. & Blue, Rose. Jerry Rice. LC 94-4596. (Football Legends Ser.). (Illus.). 64p. (J). (gr. 3 up). 1994. lib. bdg. 14.95 (*0-7910-2456-3*) Chelsea Hse.

Nadaner, Dan, jt. ed. see Egan, Kieran.

Nadar, Gaspard F. Quand J'etais Photographie. Sobieszek, Robert A. & Bunnell, Peter C., eds. LC 76-24657. (Sources of Modern Photography Ser.). (FRE.). 1979. reprint ed. lib. bdg. 18.95 (*0-405-09636-4*) Ayer.

***Nadarajah, Devapoopathy.** Love in Sanskrit & Tamil Literature: A Study of Characters & Nature. (C). 1995. 26.00x (*81-208-1215-8*, Pub. by Motilal Banarsidass II) S Asia.

Nadaraya, E. A. Nonparametric Estimation of Probability Densities & Regression Curves. (C). 1988. lib. bdg. 122.00 (*90-277-2757-0*) Kluwer Ac.

***Nadas, John.** Journey Toward Energy. 260p. (Orig.). 1995. pap. 11.95 (*0-9644756-0-X*) J Nadas.

Nadasdy, Dean. Tough Days & Talks with God. LC 89-429. (Prayers for Young Teen Boys Ser.). 112p. (Orig.). 1989. pap. 5.99 (*0-8066-2399-3*, 10-6680, Augsburg) Augsburg Fortress.

Nadasdy, Dean, jt. auth. see Schroeder, Theodore W.

***Nadaus, Roland.** Dictionnaire Initiatique de L'Orant. 1993. write for info. (*0-7859-8190-X*, 2-87744-154-7) Fr & Eur.

Nadawi, Abul H. Islam & the World. Kidwai, Mohammad A., tr. 218p. (Orig.). 1977. pap. 5.95 (*0-939830-04-3*, Pub. by IIFSO KW) New Era Publns MI.

Naddaf, Gerard. L' Origine et l'Evolution Du Concept Crec De Phusis. LC 92-43280. 616p. (FRE.). 1993. text ed. 129.95 (*0-7734-9937-7*) E Mellen.

Naddaka, V. I., et al, eds. Telluranes: Synthesis, Structure & Reactivity. (Sulfur Report Ser.: Vol. 8, Pt. 2). 44p. 1988. pap. text ed. 44.00 (*3-7186-4834-2*) Gordon & Breach.

***Nadeau, Alyce.** Making & Selling Herbal Crafts: Tips, Techniques, Projects. LC 95-12428. (Illus.). 128p. 1995. 24.95 (*0-8069-3174-4*, Lark Bks) Sterling.

Nadeau, Claude H., ed. see North American Society for the Psychology of Sport & Physical Activity Staff.

Nadeau, Gene A. Highway to Paradise: A Pictorial History of the Roadway to Mount Rainier. (Illus.). 148p. (Orig.). 1983. pap. 14.95 (*0-9613891-0-9*) Nadeau Pub.

Nadeau, Hugues W., jt. auth. see Black, Bernard.

Nadeau, Kathleen G. Survival Guide for College Students with ADD or LD. LC 94-15724. (Illus.). 64p. 1994. pap. 9.95 (*0-945354-63-0*) Magination Pr.

Nadeau, Kathleen G., ed. A Comprehensive Guide to Attention Deficit Disorder in Adults: Research, Diagnosis, & Treatment. 426p. 1995. 38.95 (*0-87630-760-8*) Brunner-Mazel.

***Nadeau, Lynn.** Haggadah: The Promised Land. (Illus.). 22p. (Orig.). 1995. pap. text ed. 5.00 (*0-9646074-9-2*) Anagogala.

Nadeau, M. & Levesque, D. English-French Lexicon of Childhood Problems: Lexique Anglais-Francais de l'Enfant en Difficulte. 454p. (ENG & FRE.). 1982. pap. 35.00 (*0-8288-0938-0*, M8670) Fr & Eur.

Nadeau, Maurice. The History of Surrealism. Howard, Richard, tr. LC 88-39354. (Paperbacks in AA History Ser.). (Illus.). 376p. 1989. reprint ed. pap. 19.95 (*0-674-40345-2*) HUP.

Nadeau, Michael. Byte Guide to CD ROM. 1994. cd-rom, pap. text ed. 39.95 (*0-07-881982-2*) Osborne-McGraw.

— Byte Guide to CD-ROM, Second Edition. 2nd ed. 1995. cd-rom, pap. text ed. 39.95 (*0-07-882104-5*) Osborne-McGraw.

Nadeau, R., jt. auth. see Kafatos, M.

Nadeau, Ray, et al. Speaking Effectively in Public Settings: A Modern Rhetoric with a Traditional Base. 296p. (Orig.). (C). 1993. pap. text ed. 24.50 (*0-8191-9122-1*) U Pr of Amer.

Nadeau, Remi. Ghost Towns & Mining Camps of California: A History & Guide. 4th rev. ed. (Illus.). 335p. (Orig.). 1992. pap. 13.95 (*0-9627104-2-3*) Crest Pubs.

— The Real Joaquin Murieta: California's Gold Rush Bandit; Truth-Myth. 2nd ed. (Illus.). 160p. 1992. reprint ed. pap. 11.95 (*0-9627104-3-1*) Crest Pubs.

— Stalin, Churchill, & Roosevelt Divide Europe, Vol. 3. LC 90-7413. 272p. 1990. text ed. 59.95 (*0-275-93450-0*, C3450, Praeger Pubs) Greenwood.

— The Water Seekers. 3rd rev. ed. (Illus.). 286p. 1993. pap. 14.95 (*0-9627104-4-X*) Crest Pubs.

Nadeau, Richard. Outdoor Journal-Book. 48p. 1993. pap. text ed. 4.95 (*1-881857-02-6*) Moose Riv Trading.

Nadeau, Richard P. Historical Post Cards of the Adirondacks, Vol. I. 24p. 1993. pap. text ed. 9.95 (*1-881857-04-2*) Moose Riv Trading.

Nadeau, Robert L. Nature Talks Back: Surviving in the Nuclear Age. LC 84-3574. (Illus.). 128p. (Orig.). 1984. pap. 6.00 (*0-914061-01-1*) Orchises Pr.

— Readings from the New Book on Nature: Physics & Metaphysics in the Modern Novel. LC 81-2625. 224p. 1981. lib. bdg. 27.50 (*0-87023-331-9*) U of Mass Pr.

Nadeau, Tom, jt. auth. see Stein, Peter.

Nadejda Gorodetzky. St. Tikhon of Zadonsk: Inspirer of Dostoevsky. LC 76-49919. 320p. 1977. pap. 9.95 (*0-913836-32-X*) St Vladimirs.

Nadel. Leonard Cohen: A Life in Art. (NFS Canada Ser.). 1994. pap. 9.95 (*1-55022-210-4*, Pub. by ECW Pr CN) InBook.

Nadel, ed. see Bulwer-Lytton, Edward G.

Nadel, Alan. Invisible Criticism: Ralph Ellison & the American Canon. LC 87-25071. 197p. 1988. text ed. 26.95x (*0-87745-190-7*) U of Iowa Pr.

— Invisible Criticism: Ralph Ellison & the American Canon. LC 87-25071. 197p. 1991. reprint ed. pap. 12.95x (*0-87745-321-7*) U of Iowa Pr.

Nadel, Alan, ed. May All Your Fences Have Gates: Essays on the Drama of August Wilson. LC 93-34628. (Illus.). 282p. 1993. text ed. 34.95x (*0-87745-428-0*); pap. 14.95 (*0-87745-439-6*) U of Iowa Pr.

Nadel, David A. Consulting by "The Book" 227p. 1992. 43.00 (*0-685-54729-9*) Intl Mgmt FL.

Nadel, Eric. The Night Wilt Scored One Hundred: Tales from Basketball's Past. LC 90-34641. 192p. 1990. pap. 9.95 (*0-87833-662-1*) Taylor Pub.

Nadel, Eric & Wright, Craig R. The Man Who Stole First Base. LC 88-26706. 184p. (Orig.). 1989. pap. 9.95 (*0-87833-633-8*) Taylor Pub.

Nadel, Harold, ed. see Anderson, Alex.

Nadel, Harold, ed. see Laury, Jean R.

Nadel, Harold, ed. see McClun, Diana & Nownes, Laura.

Nadel, Harold, ed. see McDowell, Ruth B.

Nadel, Harold, ed. see Montano, Judith B.

Nadel, Harold, ed. see Peters, Margaret.

Nadel, Harold, ed. see Porcella, Yvonne.

Nadel, Harold, ed. see Quilt San Diego Staff.

Nadel, Harold, ed. see Speckmann, Doreen.

Nadel, Harold, ed. see Wells, Jean.

Nadel, Harold, ed. see Wolfrom, Joen.

Nadel, Ira B. Joyce & the Jews: Culture and Texts. LC 88-50767. 302p. 1989. text ed. 34.95x (*0-87745-221-0*) U of Iowa Pr.

Nadel, Ira B. & Fredeman, William E., eds. Victorian Novelists after Eighteen Eighty-Five, Vol. 18. (Dictionary of Literary Biography Ser.: Vol. 18). (Illus.). 410p. 1983. 128.00 (*0-8103-1143-7*) Gale.

Nadel, Ira B. & Oberlander, Cornelia H. Trees in the City. LC 77-1713. 1978. 46.00 (*0-08-021489-4*, Pub. by Pergamon Repr UK) Franklin.

Nadel, Ira B., jt. ed. see Buitenhuis, Peter.

Nadel, Ira B., jt. ed. see Fredeman, William E.

Nadel, Ira B., jt. ed. see Neuman, Shirley.

Nadel, Ira B., ed. see Pound, Ezra.

Nadel, Ira B., et al, eds. Victorian Novelists Before Eighteen Eighty-Five, Vol. 21. LC 83-8848. (Dictionary of Literary Biography Ser.: Vol. 21). 432p. 1983. 128.00 (*0-8103-1701-X*) Gale.

Nadel, J. A., jt. ed. see Olivieri, D.

Nadel, Jack. How to Succeed in Business Without Lying, Cheating or Stealing. Peters, Sally, ed. 160p. (Orig.). 1993. pap. 7.00 (*0-671-79543-0*) S&S Trade.

— Passport to Prosperity. 246p. 1989. pap. 9.95 (*0-922658-00-5*) Nadel Wrldwide.

Nadel, Jacqueline & Camaioni, Luigia, eds. New Perspectives in Early Communicative Development. LC 92-40459. (International Library of Psychology). 256p. 1993. 62.50 (*0-415-07639-0*, B0707, Routledge NY) Routledge.

Nadel, Jay A., ed. Physiology & Pharmacology of the Airways. LC 80-16046. (Lung Biology in Health & Disease Ser.: No. 15). (Illus.). 371p. reprint ed. pap. 105.80 (*0-7837-0863-7*, 2041171) Bks Demand.

Nadel, Jay A., jt. ed. see Murray, John F.

Nadel, Jennifer. Sara Thornton. (Illus.). 256p. 1994. pap. 15.95 (*0-575-05581-2*, Pub. by V Gollancz UK) Trafalgar.

Nadel, Joel & Wright, J. R. Special Men & Special Missions: Inside American Special Operations Forces, 1945 to the Present. LC 93-41727. (Illus.). 256p. 1994. 29.95 (*1-85367-159-2*, 5593) Stackpole.

Nadel, Laurie. Corazon Aquino: Journey to Power. LC 86-33266. 93p. (J). (gr. 6 up). 1987. lib. bdg. 13.98 (*0-671-63950-1*, Julian Messner) Silver Burdett Pr.

— The Great Stream of History: A Biography of Richard M. Nixon. LC 90-920. (Illus.). 256p. (J). (gr. 5-9). 1991. text ed. 14.95 (*0-689-31559-7*, Atheneum Bks Young) S&S Childrens.

— The Kremlin Coup. LC 91-36892. (Headliners Ser.). (Illus.). 64p. (J). (gr. 5-8). 1992. lib. bdg. 15.90 (*1-56294-170-4*) Millbrook Pr.

— Kremlin Coup. (YA). 1992. pap. 5.00 (*0-395-62468-1*) HM.

— Kremlin Coup. LC 91-36892. 1992. pap. 6.95 (*1-878841-94-7*) Millbrook Pr.

Nadel, Laurie, et al. Sixth Sense. 304p. 1992. reprint ed. mass mkt. 4.99 (*0-380-71503-1*) Avon.

Nadel, Lynn, ed. The Psychobiology of Down Syndrome. (Issues in the Biology of Language & Cognition Ser.). 300p. 1988. 37.50 (*0-262-14043-8*, Bradford Bks) MIT Pr.

Nadel, Lynn & Cooper, Lynn A., eds. Neural Connections: Mental Computation. (Illus.). 368p. 1992. reprint ed. pap. 24.95 (*0-262-64029-5*, Bradford Bks) MIT Pr.

Nadel, Lynn & Epstein, Charles J., eds. Down Syndrome & Alzheimer Disease. LC 92-18114. 334p. 1992. text ed. 121.95 (*0-471-58841-5*) Wiley.

***Nadel, Lynn & Rosenthal, Donne, eds.** Down Syndrome: Living & Learning in the Community. 1995. text ed. 49.95 (*0-471-02192-X*); pap. text ed. 17.95 (*0-471-02201-2*) Wiley.

Nadel, Lynn & Stein, Daniel. Lectures in Complex Systems 1992. (Illus.). (C). 1993. 49.95 (*0-201-62498-2*) Addison-Wesley.

Nadel, Lynn & Stein, Daniel L. Lectures in Complex Systems, 1990. (Santa Fe Institute Ser.). (Illus.). 500p. (C). 1991. 49.95 (*0-201-52575-5*, Adv Bk Prog) Addison-Wesley.

— 1993 Lectures in Complex Systems. 639p. (C). 1995. 55.95 (*0-201-48368-8*) Addison-Wesley.

Nadel, Lynn, et al, eds. Neural Connections, Mental Computation. (Computational Models of Cognition & Perception Ser.). 320p. 1989. 45.00 (*0-262-14042-X*, Bradford Bks) MIT Pr.

Nadel, Mark, ed. Consumer Protection Policy. (Orig.). (C). 1983. pap. 12.00 (*0-918592-60-7*) Pol Studies.

Nadel, Mark V. Corporations & Political Accountability. 265p. (C). 1976. pap. text ed. 13.00 (*0-669-93013-X*) Heath.

Nadel, Max & Sherrer, Arthur, Jr. How to Prepare for the Advanced Placement Test - AP, English. 5th ed. 420p. 1992. pap. 11.95 (*0-8120-4887-3*) Barron.

***Nadel, S. F.** Black Byzantium: The Kingdom. (Classics in African Anthropology Ser.). (C). 1996. text ed. 64.50 (*3-89473-691-7*); pap. text ed. 25.50 (*3-89473-873-1*) Westview.

Nadel, Semen N. Contemporary Capitalism & the Middle Classes. LC 82-1046. 448p. reprint ed. pap. 127.70 (*0-7837-0586-7*, 2040930) Bks Demand.

Nadel, Siegfried. Black Byzantium: The Kingdom of Nupe in Nigeria. 1976. lib. bdg. 59.95 (*0-8490-1510-3*) Gordon Pr.

Nadel, Siegfried F. The Nuba: An Anthropological Study of the Hill Tribes in Kordofan. LC 76-44768. reprint ed. 67.50 (*0-404-15957-5*) AMS Pr.

Nadel, Stanley. Little Germany: Ethnicity, Religion & Class in New York City, 1845-80. LC 89-20684. (Illus.). 264p. 1990. 37.50 (*0-252-01677-7*) U of Ill Pr.

Nadel, Steven, et al. Energy-Efficient Motor Systems: A Handbook on Technology, Programs & Policy Opportunities. (Illus.). 379p. (C). 1991. pap. 27.00 (*0-918249-10-4*) Am Coun Energy.

Nadel, Steven M., et al, eds. Regulatory Incentives for Demand-Side Management. LC 92-28968. (Illus.). 302p. (Orig.). 1992. pap. 28.00 (*0-918249-16-3*) Am Coun Energy.

Nadelhaft, Jerome J. The Disorders of War: The Revolution in South Carolina. 310p. 1981. reprint ed. 27.50 (*0-89101-048-3*); reprint ed. pap. 12.95 (*0-89101-049-1*) U Maine Pr.

Nadelhoffer, Hans. Cartier: Jewelers Extraordinary. LC 83-26646. (Illus.). 312p. 1984. 60.00 (*0-8109-0770-4*) Abrams.

Nadell, James. Bob Marley, Jimi Hendrix, & Black Music: Profiles in Fanonist National Culture. LC 94-60448. 591p. 1995. pap. 17.95 (*1-55523-695-2*) Winston-Derek.

Nadell, Judith, jt. auth. see Langan, John.

***Nadell, Judith, et al.** The Macmillan Reader. LC 95-10133. 1995. pap. write for info. (*0-02-385890-7*) Allyn.

— The Macmillan Reader. 3rd ed. (Illus.). 768p. (C). 1992. teacher ed write for info. (*0-318-69337-2*) Macmillan.

— The Macmillan Reader. 3rd ed. (Illus.). 768p. (C). 1993. pap. write for info. (*0-02-385882-6*) Macmillan.

— Macmillan Writer: Rhetoric, Reader, Handbook. 2nd ed. LC 93-20314. 642p. (C). 1994. pap. write for info. (*0-02-386031-6*) Macmillan.

— Macmillan Writer: Rhetoric, Reader, Handbook, Brief Edition. 2nd ed. LC 93-20315. 575p. (C). 1993. pap. write for info. (*0-02-386011-1*) Macmillan.

Nadell, Pamela S. Conservative Judaism in America: A Biographical Dictionary & Sourcebook. LC 87-31782. (Jewish Denominations in America Ser.). 436p. 1988. text ed. 79.50 (*0-313-24205-4*, NCJ, Greenwood Pr) Greenwood.

***Nadelman, Barry M. & Solomon, Lewis D.** Estate Planning: Complete Guide & Workbook. 450p. 1994. ring bd. 125.00 (*1-886035-06-7*) Pro Tax & Business.

Nadelmann, Ethan A. Cops Across Borders: The Internationalization of U. S. Criminal Law Enforcement. LC 93-1305. 480p. 1993. 55.00 (*0-271-01094-0*); pap. 16.95 (*0-271-01095-9*) Pa St U Pr.

Nadelson, C., jt. ed. see Guggenheim.

Nadelson, Carol, jt. auth. see Bachrach, Leona.

Nadelson, Carol, jt. ed. see Notman, Malkah.

Nadelson, Carol C. & Marcotte, David B., eds. Treatment Interventions In Human Sexuality. LC 83-4078. (Critical Issues in Psychiatry Ser.). 502p. 1983. 89.50 (*0-306-41082-6*, Plenum Pr) Plenum.

Nadelson, Carol C. & Polonsky, Derek C., eds. Marriage & Divorce: A Contemporary Perspective. LC 83-1567. (Guilford Family Therapy Ser.). 273p. 1984. lib. bdg. 32.00 (*0-89862-047-3*) Guilford Pr.

Nadelson, Carol C. & Robinowitz, Carolyn B., eds. Training Psychiatrists for the, 90s: Issues & Recommendations. (Issues in Psychiatry Ser.). 144p. 1987. pap. text ed. 21.00 (*0-88048-142-0*) Am Psychiatric.

Nadelson, Carol C., jt. ed. see Costa e Silva, Jorge A.

Nadelson, Carol C., jt. auth. see Dickstein, Leah J.

Nadelson, Carol C., jt. ed. see Dickstein, Leah J.

Nadelson, Carol C., jt. ed. see Notman, Malkah T.

Nadelson, Carol C., et al, eds. The Woman Patient Vol. 2: Concepts of Femininity & the Life Cycle. LC 82-5326. (Women in Context Ser.). 216p. 1982. 45.00 (*0-306-40846-5*, Plenum Pr) Plenum.

Nadelstern, Paula. Color Design in Patchwork: With Plastic Templates for 10 Pairs of Blocks. (Needlecraft Ser.). (Illus.). 32p. (Orig.). 1991. pap. 4.50 (*0-486-26736-9*) Dover.

Nadelstern, Paula & Hancock, LynNell. Quilting Together: How to Organize, Design, & Make Group Quilts. (Illus.). 256p. 1988. 14.99 (*0-517-05433-7*) Random Hse Value.

Naden, C. J. Cycle Chase. LC 79-64638. (Illus.). 32p. (J). (gr. 4-9). 1980. lib. bdg. 10.79 (*0-89375-249-5*); pap. 2.95 (*0-89375-263-0*) Troll Assocs.

— I Can Read About All Kinds of Giants. LC 78-65833. (Illus.). (J). (gr. 2-4). 1979. pap. 2.50 (*0-89375-201-0*) Troll Assocs.

— I Can Read About Caves. LC 78-66271. (Illus.). (J). (gr. 2-5). 1979. pap. 2.50 (*0-89375-205-3*) Troll Assocs.

— I Can Read About Creepy Crawly Creatures. LC 78-68469. (Illus.). (J). (gr. 3-6). 1979. pap. 2.50 (*0-89375-207-X*) Troll Assocs.

— I Can Read About Elephants. LC 78-65834. (Illus.). (J). (gr. 2-5). 1979. pap. 2.50 (*0-89375-208-8*) Troll Assocs.

— I Can Read About Motorcycles. LC 78-74657. (Illus.). (J). (gr. 3-6). 1979. pap. 2.50 (*0-89375-212-6*) Troll Assocs.

— I Can Read About Pioneers. LC 78-65835. (Illus.). (J). (gr. 3-6). 1979. pap. 2.50 (*0-89375-214-2*) Troll Assocs.

— I Can Read About Racing Cars. LC 78-74658. (Illus.). (J). (gr. 3-6). 1979. pap. 2.50 (*0-89375-216-9*) Troll Assocs.

— I Can Read About Sharks. LC 78-73736. (Illus.). (J). (gr. 2-6). 1979. pap. 2.50 (*0-89375-218-5*) Troll Assocs.

— I Can Read about Sharks. LC 95-5942. (Illus.). 48p. (J). (gr. k-3). 1995. lib. bdg. 11.89 (*0-8167-3646-4*); pap. text ed. 4.95 (*0-8167-3647-2*) Troll Assocs.

— John Henry, the Steeldriving Man. LC 79-66317. (Illus.). 48p. (J). (gr. 3-6). 1980. lib. bdg. 9.89 (*0-89375-304-1*); pap. 3.50 (*0-89375-303-3*) Troll Assocs.

— Motorcycle Challenge, Trials & Races. LC 79-52178. (Illus.). 32p. (J). (gr. 4-9). 1980. lib. bdg. 10.79 (*0-89375-252-5*); pap. 2.95 (*0-89375-253-3*) Troll Assocs.

— Rough Rider. LC 79-52177. (Illus.). 32p. (J). (gr. 4-9). 1980. lib. bdg. 10.79 (*0-89375-250-9*); pap. 2.95 (*0-89375-251-7*) Troll Assocs.

Naden, C. J., adapt. Pegasus, the Winged Horse. LC 80-50069. (Illus.). 32p. (J). (gr. 4-8). 1980. lib. bdg. 11.79 (*0-89375-361-0*); pap. 2.95 (*0-89375-365-3*) Troll Assocs.

Naden, Corinne. Ronald McNair. (Black Americans of Achievement Ser.). (Illus.). 112p. (YA). (gr. 5 up). 1991. lib. bdg. 17.95 (*0-7910-1133-X*) Chelsea Hse.

— Ronald McNair. (J). (gr. 4-7). 1993. pap. 7.95 (*0-7910-1158-5*) Chelsea Hse.

Naden, Corinne, jt. auth. see Blue, Rose.

Naden, Corinne J. John Muir: Saving the Wilderness. (J). (gr. 4-7). 1992. pap. 5.00 (*0-395-63569-1*) HM.

***Naden, Corinne J. & Blue, Rose.** The Black Sea. LC 94-40912. (Wonders of the World Ser.). (J). 1995. 24.26 (*0-8114-6371-0*) Raintree Steck-V.

— Christa McAuliffe: Teacher in Space. (Gateway Biographies Ser.). (Illus.). 48p. (J). (gr. 2-4). 1991. lib. bdg. 12.90 (*1-56294-046-5*) Millbrook Pr.

— John Muir: Saving the Wilderness. LC 91-18106. (Gateway Biographies Ser.). (Illus.). 48p. (J). (gr. 2-4). 1992. lib. bdg. 13.40 (*1-56294-110-0*); pap. 5.95 (*1-56294-797-4*) Millbrook Pr.

— The U. S. Coast Guard. LC 92-31042. (Defending Our Country Ser.). (Illus.). 64p. (J). (gr. 3-6). 1993. lib. bdg. 15.40 (*1-56294-321-9*) Millbrook Pr.

An Asterisk (*) at the beginning of an entry indicates that the title is appearing in BIP for the first time.

— The U. S. Navy. LC 92-13430. (Defending Our Country Ser.). (Illus.). 64p. (J). (gr. 3-6). 1993. lib. bdg. 15.40 (*1-56294-216-6*); pap. 5.95 (*1-56294-753-2*) Millbrook Pr.

Naden, Corinne J., jt. auth. see Blue, Rose.

Naden, Corinne J., jt. auth. see Gillespie, John T.

Naden, Corinne J., jt. ed. see Gillespie, John T.

Naden, Corrine J. Christa McAuliffe: A Teacher in Space. (J). (gr. 4-7). 1992. pap. 4.95 (*1-878841-58-0*) Millbrook Pr.

Naden, Corrine J., jt. auth. see Blue, Rose.

Naden, D., jt. ed. see Streat, M.

***Nader.** Human Physiology. 1995. 75.00 (*1-895958-06-7*) Atrium Pubs.

***Nader & Smith.** Collision Course: The Truth about Airline Safety. 1995. pap. text ed. 14.95 (*0-07-045987-8*) TAB Bks.

***Nader, Edith.** Cooking Without No-No's. 200p. 1994. pap. 14.95 (*0-9643513-0-7*) E G Nader.

***Nader, George.** Chrome. 380p. 1995. pap. 5.95 (*1-55583-606-2*, AlyCat) Alyson Pubns.

Nader, Helen. Liberty in Absolutist Spain: The Habsburg Sale of Towns, 1516-1700. (Johns Hopkins University Studies in Historical & Political Science). 400p. (C). 1993. reprint ed. pap. text ed. 19.95 (*0-8018-4731-1*) Johns Hopkins.

— The Mendoza Family in the Spanish Renaissance, 1350-1550. LC 79-9945. 291p. reprint ed. pap. 83.00 (*0-8357-7949-1*, 2057024) Bks Demand.

***Nader, Helen & Formisano, Luciano, eds.** Book of Privileges Issued to Christopher Columbus by King Fernando & Queen Isabel, 1492-1502. (Repertorium Columbianum Ser.: Vol. 2). (Illus.). 434p. 1995. 55.00 (*0-520-08897-2*) U CA Pr.

Nader, Iyad A. Kangaroo Rats: Intraspecific Variation in Dipodomys Spectabilis Merriam & Dipodomys Deserti Stephens. LC 78-9317. (Illinois Biological Monographs: No. 49). 128p. reprint ed. pap. 36.50 (*0-8357-9686-8*, 2019004) Bks Demand.

Nader, Jerry. The Complete Traffic Engineering Handbook. 1991. 59.50 (*0-685-61696-7*) Telecom Lib.

***Nader, Jonah.** Prentice Hall Illustrated Dictionary of Computing. 2nd ed. LC 94-47617. 1995. pap. 24.95 (*0-13-205725-5*) P-H.

Nader, Jonar. Prentice Hall's Illustrated Dictionary of Computing. LC 92-19637. 544p. 1992. pap. 30.00 (*0-13-719998-8*) P-H.

Nader, Laura. Harmony Ideology: Justice & Control in a Zapotec Mountain Village. LC 89-78333. 366p. 1990. 45.00 (*0-8047-1809-1*); pap. 15.95 (*0-8047-1810-5*) Stanford U Pr.

Nader, Laura, ed. No Access to Law: Alternatives to the American Judicial System. LC 80-526. 1980. pap. text ed. 51.00 (*0-12-513562-9*) Acad Pr.

Nader, Laura & Todd, Harry F., Jr., eds. The Disputing Process in Ten Societies. LC 78-8729. 372p. 1978. pap. text ed. 21.50 (*0-231-04537-9*) Col U Pr.

Nader, Nathra, jt. auth. see Nader, Rose B.

Nader, Ralph. Canada Firsts. LC 91-77176. 165p. 1992. pap. 12.00 (*0-936758-25-2*) Country Rds.

Nader, Ralph & Blackwell, Kate. You & Your Pension. 215p. 1973. pap. 1.65 (*0-686-36546-1*) Ctr Responsive Law.

Nader, Ralph & Ditlow, Clarence. The Lemon Book: Auto Rights. 3rd ed. 352p. 1990. 22.50 (*1-55921-019-2*); pap. 12.95 (*1-55921-020-6*) Moyer Bell.

Nader, Ralph & Fortun, Michael, eds. Eating Clean: Food Safety & the Chemical Harvest. 294p. 1982. 6.50 (*0-936758-05-8*) Ctr Responsive Law.

Nader, Ralph & Smith, Wesley J. Collision Course: The Truth About Airline Safety. LC 93-8266. 1993. 21.95 (*0-8306-4271-4*) TAB Bks.

— Collision Course: The Truth about Airline Safety. 1993. text ed. 21.95 (*0-07-045937-1*) McGraw.

Nader, Ralph, jt. auth. see Vaughn, Robert G.

Nader, Ralph, et al. Case Against "Free Trade" GATT, NAFTA, & the Globalization of Corporate Power. 230p. (Orig.). 1993. pap. 10.00 (*1-55643-169-4*) North Atlantic.

— What to Do with Your Bad Car. 175p. 1971. pap. 2.95 (*0-686-36552-6*) Ctr Responsive Law.

Nader, Rose B. & Nader, Nathra. It Happened in the Kitchen: Recipes for Food & Thought. LC 91-70432. 180p. (Orig.). 1991. pap. 9.00 (*0-936758-29-5*) Ctr Responsive Law.

***Nader, Sam.** The River of Years: Looking Back on My Life As a Methodist Minister. 208p. (Orig.). 1995. pap. 9.95 (*0-925854-14-X*) Defiant Pr.

Nadezhda, Kramova. Poka Nas Pomniat. LC 89-20107. (Illus.). 175p. (Orig.). (RUS.). 1989. pap. 8.50 (*1-55779-020-5*) Hermitage.

Nadezhin, D. K., jt. auth. see Imshennik, V. S.

Nadgorny, Boris E., jt. auth. see Cahn, Sidney B.

***Nadi, Aldo.** The Living Sword: A Fencer's Autobiography. Lobo, Lance C., ed. (Illus.). 416p. 1995. pap. 17.95 (*1-884528-20-1*) Laureate Pr.

— On Fencing. LC 93-80473. (Illus.). 300p. 1994. reprint ed. pap. 19.95 (*1-884528-04-X*) Laureate Pr.

Nadich, Judah. The Legends of the Rabbis Vol. 1: Jewish Legends of the Second Commonwealth. LC 94-208. 512p. 1994. pap. 25.00 (*1-56821-130-9*) Aronson.

— The Legends of the Rabbis, Vol. 2: The First Generation after the Destruction of the Temple & Jerusalem. LC 94-209. 264p. 1994. pap. 20.00 (*1-56821-131-7*) Aronson.

Nadich, Judah, ed. The Legends of the Rabbis, 2 vol. set. LC 94-1942. 776p. 1994. pap. 45.00 (*1-56821-129-5*) Aronson.

Nadien, Margot B. The Child's Psychosocial Development: From Birth to Early Adolescence. 164p. (Orig.). 1980. pap. 11.95 (*0-89529-115-0*) Avery Pub.

Nadin, Mihai & Zakia, Richard D. Creating Effective Advertising: Using Semiotics. LC 94-4481. 268p. 1994. 39.95 (*0-913069-46-5*) Consultant Pr.

Nadin, Peter, et al. Peter Nadin: Recent Work & Notes on Six Series. limited ed. (Illus.). 72p. (Orig.). 1992. pap. 24.95 (*0-685-63223-7*) Yale Ctr Brit Art.

Nadin, V., jt. ed. see Hill, L.

Nadin, Vincent & Doak, Joe. Town Planning Responses to City Change. 252p. 1991. text ed. 63.95 (*1-85628-161-2*, Pub. by Avebury Pub UK) Ashgate Pub Co.

Nadin, Vincent, jt. auth. see Collingworth, J. B.

Nadiri, M. Ishaq & Rosen, Sherwin. Disequilibrium Model of Demand for Factors of Production. (General Ser.: No. 99). 226p. 1974. 58.80 (*0-87014-261-5*) Natl Bur Econ Res.

Nadiri, M. Ishaq, jt. ed. see Labys, Walter C.

***Nadja.** Little Nina & the Radio. 1993. pap. 2.99 (*0-517-10488-1*) Random.

— Little Nina Plays Ball. 1993. pap. 2.99 (*0-517-10518-7*) Random.

Nadji, Mehrzad, jt. auth. see Harris, Curtis C., Jr.

Nadkarni, K. M., ed. Dr. K. M. Nadkarni's Indian Materia Medica. (C). 1988. 70.00 (*0-8364-2337-2*, Pub. by Popular Prakashan II) S Asia.

— Indian Materia Medica, 2 vols., Set. 1989. 74.00 (*0-8364-2572-3*, Pub. by Popular Prakashan II) S Asia.

Nadkarni, M. V. Marketable Surplus & Market Dependence: A Study of a Millet Region. 176p. 1980. 24.95 (*0-940500-80-9*, Pub. by Allied Pubs II) Asia Bk Corp.

Nadkarni, M. V., jt. ed. see Bharadwaj, R.

Nadkarni, M. V., et al. The Political Economy of Forest Use & Management. 184p. (C). 1989. text ed. 22.50 (*0-8039-9591-1*) Sage.

Nadkarni, M. V., et al, eds. India - The Emerging Challenges: Essays in Honour of Professor V. K. R. V. Rad. 400p. (C). 1991. 38.00 (*0-8039-9665-9*) Sage.

***Nadkarni, Mahan.** Bhimsen Joshi: A Biography. (C). 1995. 22.50x (*81-7223-126-1*, Pub. by Indus Pub II) S Asia.

Nadkarni, Nalini M., jt. ed. see Lowman, Margaret D.

Nadkarni, R. A., ed. Analysis of Petroleum Products & Lubricants. LC 91-10488. (Special Technical Publication Ser.: No. STP 1109). (Illus.). 165p. 1991. text ed. 55.00 (*0-8031-1416-8*, 04-011090-12) ASTM.

Nadkarnia, M. V. Marketable Surplus & Market Dependence in a Millet Region. 176p. 1980. 24.95 (*0-318-37333-5*) Asia Bk Corp.

Nadler, ed. Continuum Theory: An Introduction. (Pure & Applied Mathematics Ser.: Vol. 158). 352p. 1992. 140.00 (*0-8247-8659-9*) Dekker.

Nadler, Allan. A Religion of Limits: The Theology of Mitnaggedism According to Pinchas, Maggid of Polotsk. write for info. (*0-88125-400-2*) Ktav.

***Nadler, Beth.** The Magic School Bus Inside Ralphie: A Book about Germs. LC 94-44655. (Illus.). (J). 1995. write for info. (*0-590-40025-8*) Scholastic Inc.

Nadler, Bob. Advanced B&W Darkroom Book. LC 79-9934. (Illus.). 80p. 1979. pap. 8.95 (*0-933596-00-6*) F-Twenty-Two.

— Basic B&W Darkroom Book. LC 78-56969. (Illus.). 96p. 1978. pap. 8.95 (*0-933596-02-2*) F-Twenty-Two.

— Computing for Cheapskates. 250p. 1994. 12.95 (*1-56276-293-1*) Ziff-Davis.

— The Illustrated B&W Darkroom Book. LC 79-9933. (Illus.). 176p. 1979. 21.95 (*0-933596-01-4*) F-Twenty-Two.

Nadler, Burton J. Liberal Arts Jobs: What They Are & How to Get Them. 2nd ed. LC 89-38153. 153p. (Orig.). 1989. pap. 9.95 (*0-87866-879-9*) Petersons Guides.

— Liberal Arts Power! What It Is & How to Sell It on Your Resume. 2nd ed. LC 89-23099. 174p. (Orig.). 1989. pap. 9.95 (*0-87866-880-2*) Petersons Guides.

— Naked at the Interview: Tips & Quizzes to Prepare You for Your First Real Job. 256p. 1994. pap. text ed. 10.95 (*0-471-59449-0*) Wiley.

Nadler, Charles. Spelling Dynamics for Typing Speed. 90p. 10.00 (*0-936862-10-6*, STD-1) DDC Pub.

Nadler, David A. Feedback & Organization Development: Using Data-Based Methods. (Illus.). (C). 1977. pap. text ed. 26.95 (*0-201-05006-4*) Addison-Wesley.

Nadler, David A., jt. auth. see Kearns, David T.

***Nadler, David A., et al.** Discontinuous Change: Leading Organizational Transformation. LC 94-30752. (Management Ser.). 388p. 1994. 28.95 (*0-7879-0042-7*) Jossey-Bass.

— Organizational Architecture: Designs for Changing Organizations. LC 92-4071. (Management Ser.). 304p. 1992. 29.95 (*1-55542-443-0*) Jossey-Bass.

Nadler, Dru, jt. auth. see Hare, Deborah.

Nadler, Ellis. The Bee's Sneeze. LC 92-32470. (Illus.). 32p. (J). (ps-1). 1993. pap. 12.00 (*0-671-86575-7*, S&S Bks Young Read) S&S Childrens.

— Tiny Tippy Truck. (J). (ps). 1994. 14.95 (*0-316-59688-4*) Little.

Nadler, Ellis, jt. auth. see Porritt, Jonathon.

Nadler, Gerald & Hibino, Shozo. Breakthrough Thinking. 1989. 22.95 (*1-55958-004-6*) Prima Pub.

— Breakthrough Thinking. 2nd rev. ed. LC 93-23559. 1994. 24.95 (*1-55958-421-1*) Prima Pub.

— Conceptual Problem Solving. LC 94-19879. 1994. pap. text ed. write for info. (*1-55958-567-6*) Prima Pub.

Nadler, Gerald, jt. auth. see Hoffherr, Glen D.

***Nadler, Holly M.** Haunted Island: True Ghost Stories from Martha's Vineyard. LC 94-72609. (Illus.). 144p. (Orig.). 1994. pap. 10.95 (*0-89272-353-X*) Down East.

Nadler, James. Dover Electronic Clip Art: PC Edition. 1993. pap. 49.95 (*0-679-79097-7*) Random.

— Dover Electronic Clip Art, Vol. 1: Macintosh Edition. 1993. pap. 49.95 (*0-679-79098-5*) Random.

— How to Keep Your Novell Network Alive. 1993. pap. 26.95 (*0-679-79109-4*) Random.

— Microsoft Publisher Made Easy. 1992. disk, pap. text ed. 29.95 (*0-07-881811-7*) McGraw.

— Netware Answers: Certified Tech Support. 1994. pap. text ed. 16.95 (*0-07-882044-8*) Osborne-McGraw.

Nadler, L. Designing Training Programs: The Critical Events Model. 1982. 25.95 (*0-201-05168-0*) Addison-Wesley.

Nadler, Lawrence B., et al, eds. Advances in Gender & Communication Research. LC 87-13350. 428p. (Orig.). 1987. pap. text ed. 34.00 (*0-8191-6478-X*) U Pr of Amer.

Nadler, Leonard. Corporate Human Resources Development: A Management Tool. 217p. 16.95 (*0-318-13267-2*, NACB); 13.50 (*0-318-13268-0*) Am Soc Train & Devel.

— Employee Training in Japan. LC 65-22294. (Illus.). 49p. (C). 1965. text ed. 10.00 (*0-87657-117-8*) Ed & Training.

— Human Resource Development: The Perspective of Business & Industry. 42p. 1983. 4.25 (*0-318-22128-4*, IN259) Ctr Educ Trng Employ.

Nadler, Leonard & Nadler, Zeace. The Conference Book. LC 76-52238. 266p. 1977. 19.00 (*0-87201-140-2*) Gulf Pub.

— Designing Training Programs: The Critical Events Model. 2nd ed. LC 94-637. 280p. 1994. 32.50 (*0-88415-100-X*) Gulf Pub.

— Developing Human Resources: Concepts & a Model. 3rd ed. LC 88-46096. (Management Ser.). 328p. 1989. 29.95 (*1-55542-155-5*) Jossey-Bass.

— Every Manager's Guide to Human Resource Development. LC 91-36300. (Management Ser.). 187p. 1992. 27.95 (*1-55542-421-X*) Jossey-Bass.

Nadler, Leonard & Nadler, Zeace, eds. The Handbook of Human Resource Development. 2nd ed. 832p. 1990. text ed. 124.95 (*0-471-50653-2*) Wiley.

Nadler, Leonard & Wiggs, Garland D. Managing Human Resource Development: A Practical Guide. LC 86-7339. (Management Ser.). 213p. 1986. 28.95x (*1-55542-006-0*) Jossey-Bass.

Nadler, Leonard, jt. auth. see Reynolds, Angus.

Nadler, M., ed. see Conant, Charles A.

Nadler, M., jt. auth. see Fradin, A.

Nadler, M. P., et al, eds. Glare & Contrast Sensitivity for Clinicians. (Illus.). 248p. 1989. 84.00 (*0-387-97009-6*) Spr-Verlag.

Nadler, Marcus, jt. auth. see Bogen, Jules I.

Nadler, Marcus, jt. auth. see Madden, John T.

Nadler-Moodie, Marlene. Psychiatric Aspects of General Patient Care. 2nd ed. LC 94-60363. 208p. (Orig.). (C). 1993. pap. text ed. 49.95 (*1-878025-44-9*) Western Schls.

Nadler, Morton & Smith, Eric P. Pattern Recognition Engineering. 608p. 1993. text ed. 84.95 (*0-471-62293-1*, Wiley-Interscience) Wiley.

Nadler, Myra, ed. How to Start an Audiovisual Collection. LC 78-1993. 1978. 22.50 (*0-8108-1124-3*) Scarecrow.

Nadler, Sam B. Hyperspaces of Sets: A Text with Research Questions. (Pure & Applied Mathematics Ser.: Vol. 49). 728p. 1978. 175.00 (*0-8247-6768-3*) Dekker.

Nadler, Sam B., Jr. & Quinn, J. Embeddability & Structure Properties of Real Curves. LC 72-4343. (Memoirs Ser.: No. 1/125). 74p. 1972. pap. 17.00 (*0-8218-1825-2*, MEMO 1/125) Am Math.

Nadler, Steven, ed. Causation in Early Modern Philosophy: Cartesianism, Occasionalism, & Preestablished Harmony. 232p. (C). 1993. 32.50 (*0-271-00863-6*) Pa St U Pr.

Nadler, Steven M. Arnauld & the Cartesian Philosophy of Ideas. 220p. 1989. text ed. 39.50 (*0-691-07340-6*) Princeton U Pr.

— Malebranche & Ideas. 216p. 1992. 42.00 (*0-19-507724-5*) OUP.

Nadler, Susan. Good Girls Gone Bad: American Women in Crime. LC 86-29155. 288p. 1987. 17.95 (*0-88191-048-1*) Freundlich.

Nadler, Zeace, jt. auth. see Nadler, Leonard.

Nadler, Zeace, jt. ed. see Nadler, Leonard.

Nadol, Joseph B., Jr., ed. Meniere's Disease. LC 89-19868. (Illus.). 568p. 1989. lib. bdg. 140.00 (*0-685-54898-8*, Pub. by Kugler NE) Kugler Pubns.

Nadol, Joseph B., Jr. & Schuknecht, Harold F., eds. Surgery of the Ear & Temporal Bone. (Illus.). 494p. 1993. 194.50 (*0-88167-803-1*, 2287); sl. 315.00 (*0-88167-935-6*) Raven.

Nadol, Joseph B., Jr., jt. auth. see Pensak, Myles L.

Nadolney. Handbook of Toxicology in Vitro. 1994. write for info. (*0-8493-2956-6*) CRC Pr.

Nadolny & Young. Regulatory Management & Compliance Audit Deskbook. 2nd ed. 550p. 1992. 195.00 (*1-55738-364-2*) Probus Pub Co.

***Nadolny, Nancy Z., et al.** Bank Internal Audit Vol. II: Conducting the Internal Audit Program. 430p. 1993. 155.00 (*1-55738-375-8*) Probus Pub Co.

Nadolny, Paul R., jt. auth. see Rosenberg, Marc L.

Nadolski, Dieter. Old Household Pewterware: Its Appearance & Function in the Course of Six Centuries. Stanton, M. O., tr. (Illus.). 328p. 1987. 65.00 (*0-8419-1088-X*) Holmes & Meier.

Nadon, John M. & Gelmine, Bert J. Industrial Electricity. 2nd ed. 1984. teacher ed. 12.00 (*0-8273-3569-5*); text ed. 37.95 (*0-8273-3568-7*) Delmar.

Nadon, John M., et al. Industrial Electricity. 5th ed. LC 93-20198. 658p. 1994. text ed. 37.95 (*0-8273-6074-6*) Delmar.

— Industrial Electricity: Instructor's Guide. 5th ed. 111p. 1994. 14.00 (*0-8273-6075-4*) Delmar.

Nadotti, Maria, jt. ed. see Bruno, Giuliana.

Nadramia, Peggy, ed. Narcopolis & Other Poems. (Illus.). 64p. (Orig.). (C). 1989. pap. 4.00 (*0-9623286-1-8*) Hells Kitchen.

Nadrchal, J. & De Groot, Roy A. Computational Physics: Proceedings of the Computational Physica 1992 Europhysics Conference. 540p. 1993. text ed. 121.00 (*981-02-1245-3*) World Scientific Pub.

Nadrchial, J., ed. Microcomputers & Graphics in Physics: Proceedings of the 7th European Summer School on Computing Techniques in Physics, Bechyne Castle, Czechoslovakia. 288p. 1989. 82.00 (*0-444-87111-X*, North Holland) Elsevier.

Nadui, A. H. Islam: The Perfect Religion & a Way of Life. pap. 1.00 (*1-56744-085-1*) Kazi Pubns.

Nadui, S. Heroic Deeds of Muslim Women. pap. 3.50 (*1-56744-037-1*) Kazi Pubns.

Nadvi, A. H. Four Pillars of Islam. 16.95 (*1-56744-015-0*) Kazi Pubns.

— A Geographical History of the Qur'an. 14.50 (*1-56744-020-7*) Kazi Pubns.

— Glory of Iqbal. 19.95 (*1-56744-025-8*) Kazi Pubns.

— Islam & the World. 1988. 9.95 (*1-56744-076-2*) Kazi Pubns.

— Qadianism: A Critique. pap. 2.00 (*1-56744-201-3*) Kazi Pubns.

— Religion & Civilization. 4.00 (*0-933511-34-5*) Kazi Pubns.

— Western Civilization, Islam & Muslims. 18.50 (*0-933511-87-6*) Kazi Pubns.

Nadvi, S. Arab Navigation. 15.95 (*0-935782-39-7*) Kazi Pubns.

Nadvi, S. S. Muhammad, the Ideal Prophet. 1988. 9.95 (*1-56744-151-3*) Kazi Pubns.

Nadwi, Abul H. Muslims in the West: The Message & the Mission. Murad, Khurram, ed. 191p. (Orig.). 1983. pap. 6.95 (*0-86037-130-1*) New Era Publns MI.

Nadworny, Laura. JP Rufio, Entrepreneur: An American Success Story. (Illus.). 128p. (Orig.). 1983. pap. text ed. 5.95 (*0-9612658-0-9*, 83-62817) Rufio Ent.

Nadzieja, jt. ed. see Biler.

Nadzo, Nancy R. Sun Days, Moon Days: When the Miracles Begin. LC 88-83597. 153p. 1989. pap. 10.50 (*0-937226-04-1*) Laugh Cat.

Nadzo, Nancy R., jt. auth. see Nadzo, Stefan C.

Nadzo, Stefan C. Being Who You Are. LC 82-84415. 140p. 1983. pap. 6.95 (*0-937226-02-5*) Laugh Cat.

— In the Beginning: The Eden Conspiracy Unveiled. LC 89-83895. 100p. 1989. pap. 10.95 (*0-937226-06-8*) Laugh Cat.

— Take off Your Shoes: A Guide to the Nature of Reality. LC 81-66185. 140p. (Orig.). 1981. pap. 5.95 (*0-937226-01-7*) Laugh Cat.

— There Is a Way: Meditations for a Seeker. LC 80-66831. (Illus.). 129p. (Orig.). 1980. pap. 5.95 (*0-937226-00-9*) Laugh Cat.

Nadzo, Stefan C. & Nadzo, Nancy R. Hear the Wind, See the Wind. LC 87-82954. 113p. (Orig.). 1987. pap. 8.50 (*0-937226-03-3*) Laugh Cat.

Nae, Randolph. Decapitated Head of a Dog: Baroque Outhouse. 64p. (Orig.). 1991. pap. 7.00 (*0-916397-16-5*) Manic D Pr.

Naeb, Yuli, tr. see Lehman, Yvette K.

Naeem, Muhammad. Muslim Military History: A Preliminary Bibliography. (Orig.). 1992. pap. 14.50 (*1-56744-460-1*) Kazi Pubns.

Naef, A. P. The Story of Thoracic Surgery: Milestones & Pioneers. LC 89-71619. 160p. 1990. 19.80 (*0-920887-79-1*) Hogrefe & Huber Pubs.

***Naef, Weston.** The J. Paul Getty Museum Handbook of the Photographs Collection. LC 94-22516. (Illus.). 1995. 12.95 (*0-89236-316-9*, J P Getty Museum) J P Getty Trust.

Naef, Weston, et al. Pioneers of Landscape Photography: Gustave LeGray & Carelton E. Watkins. (Illus.). 128p. 1993. 45.00 (*0-89236-299-5*) J P Getty Trust.

Naef, Weston J., jt. auth. see Ferrez, Gilberto.

Naegele, Bede. Minute Meditations for Each Day. 1982. pap. 4.95 (*0-89942-190-3*) Catholic Bk Pub.

Naegele, Timothy D. A Tapestry of Life. (Illus.). 1400p. 1990. write for info. (*0-9625131-7-2*) Sotweed Pr.

Naegeli, Bruce A., jt. auth. see Gara, Otto G.

Naegeli, K. Die Neuren Algensysteme & Versuch zur Begruendung eines eigenen Systems der Algen & Florideen. (Illus.). 1970. reprint ed. 77.00 (*90-6123-204-X*) Lubrecht & Cramer.

Naegelin, Lanny. Getting Started in Oral Interpretation. 128p. (YA). (gr. 7-12). 1993. teacher ed. 10.60 (*0-8442-5404-5*, Natl Textbk); pap. text ed. 13.25 (*0-8442-5403-7*, Natl Textbk) NTC Pub Grp.

Naegle, Madeline, ed. Substance Abuse Education for Nursing: A Model Curriculum, 3 vols. 1992. pap. write for info. (*0-685-56350-2*) Natl League Nurse.

— Substance Abuse Education for Nursing: A Model Curriculum, 3 vols., Vol. I. 624p. 1992. pap. 39.95 (*0-88737-523-5*) Natl League Nurse.

— Substance Abuse Education for Nursing: A Model Curriculum, 3 vols., Vol. II. 688p. 1992. pap. 49.95 (*0-88737-545-6*) Natl League Nurse.

— Substance Abuse Education for Nursing: A Model Curriculum, 3 vols., Vol. III. 544p. 1992. pap. 49.95 (*0-88737-546-4*) Natl League Nurse.

Naehring, Douglas, jt. auth. see Emerson, Howard.

Naeim, Faramarz. Pathology of Bone Marrow. LC 91-35311. (Illus.). 376p. 1992. 175.00 (*0-89640-209-6*) Igaku-Shoin.

***Naeim, Farzad & Anderson, James C.** Classification & Evaluation of Earthquake Records for Design. (Illus.). 288p. (Orig.). (C). 1994. pap. text ed. 75.00 (*0-7881-0877-8*) Diane Pub.

Naeim, Farzed, ed. The Seismic Design Handbook. (Illus.). 576p. 1989. text ed. 95.00 (*0-442-26922-6*) Chapman & Hall.

Naenna, Patricia C. Costume & Culture: Vanishing Textiles of Some of the Tai Groups in Laos P. D. R. (Illus.). 48p. 1992. pap. text ed. 20.00 (*0-8248-1454-1*) UH Pr.

N

An Asterisk (*) at the beginning of an entry indicates that the title is appearing in BIP for the first time.

Naert, P. A. & Leeflang, P. S. Building Implementable Marketing Models. 1974. pap. text ed. 44.50 (*90-207-0436-2*) Kluwer Ac.

Naes, Tormod, jt. auth. see Martens, Harold.

Naeser, Margaret A. Outline Guide to Chinese Herbal Patent Medicines in Pill Form - with Sample Pictures of the Boxes: An Introduction to Chinese Herbal Medicines. 2nd ed. LC 90-80264. (Illus.). 370p. (Orig.). 1990. pap. 24.95 (*0-9625651-1-3*) Boston Chinese Med.

Naeser, Margaret A. & Xiu-Bing Wei. Laser Acupuncture, an Introductory Textbook for Treatment of Pain, Paralysis, Spasticity & Other Disorders: Clinical & Research Uses of Laser Acupuncture from Around the World. (Illus.). 218p. 1994. spiral bd. 30.00 (*0-9625651-2-1*) Boston Chinese Med.

Naeser, N. D. & McCullogh, T. H., eds. Thermal History of Sedimentary Basins: Methods & Case Histories. (Illus.). 320p. 1988. 93.00 (*0-387-96702-8*) Spr-Verlag.

Naeseth, Henriette C. The Swedish Theatre of Chicago, 1868-1950. LC 51-14886. (Augustana College Library Publication Ser.: No. 22). 390p. 1951. 4.95 (*0-910182-17-5*) Augustana Coll.

— The Swedish Theatre of Chicago, 1869-1950. LC 51-14886. (Augustana Historical Society Publication Ser.: Vol. 12). 390p. 1951. 4.95 (*0-910184-12-7*) Augustana.

Naess, Arne. Ecology, Community & Lifestyle: Outline of an Ecosophy. Rothenberg, David, tr. (Illus.). 240p. (C). 1990. pap. 24.95 (*0-521-34873-0*) Cambridge U Pr.

Naess, Harald & McFarlane, James, eds. Knut Hamsun: Selected Letters: Vol. I: 1879-98. LC 89-81771. (Norvik Press Series A: No. 7). 300p. (Orig.). 1990. pap. 45.00 (*1-870041-13-5*, Pub. by Norvik Pr UK) Dufour.

Naess, Harald & Stafford, Kate. On Both Sides of the Ocean: The Memoirs of Per Hagen. Lovoll, Odd S., ed. (Travel & Description Ser.). (Illus.). 70p. 1984. 10.00 (*0-87732-069-1*) Norwegian-Am Hist Assn.

Naess, Harald S., ed. A History of Norwegian Literature. LC 92-20990. (History of Scandinavian Literature Ser.: Vol. 2). (Illus.). xviii, 435p. (C). 1993. 50.00 (*0-8032-3317-5*) U of Nebr Pr.

Naess, Tor. A New Generation Floating Production Facility. 1989. 150.00 (*90-6314-505-5*, Pub. by Lorne & MacLean Marine) St Mut.

— A New Generation Floating Production Facility. (C). 1989. 95.00 (*0-89771-732-5*, Pub. by Lorne & MacLean Marine) St Mut.

Naess, Tor, jt. ed. see Andenaes, Olav.

Naeth, Marie-Luise. Chinas Weg in die Weltpolitik: Die Nationalen und Aussenpolitischen Konzeptionen Sun Yat-Sens, Chiang Kaisheks und Mao Tse-Tungs. (Beitraege zur Auswaertigen und Internationalen Politik Ser.: Vol. 7). (C). 1976. pap. 93.85 (*3-11-004737-3*) De Gruyter.

Naether, Carl. Pigeons. (Illus.). 1989. 9.95 (*0-86622-778-4*, KW-148) TFH Pubns.

Naether, Carl & Vriends, Matthew M. Building an Aviary. (Illus.). 160p. (J). (gr. 8 up). 1989. lib. bdg. 12.95 (*0-685-28494-8*, PS-763) TFH Pubns.

Naeve, Milo. Identifying American Furniture: A Pictorial Guide to Styles & Terms, Colonial to Contemporary. LC 81-3524. (Illus.). 102p. 1981. 10.95 (*0-910050-96-1*) AASLH.

Naeve, Milo M. Identifying American Furniture: A Pictorial Guide to Styles & Terms, Colonial to Contemporary. (Illus.). 1989. pap. 10.95 (*0-393-30580-5*) Norton.

— John Lewis Krimmel: An Artist in Federal America. LC 83-40480. (Illus.). 208p. 1988. 85.00 (*0-87413-232-0*) U Delaware Pr.

Naeve, Milo M., ed. Winterthur Portfolio, No. 3. (Winterthur Bk.). (Illus.). 1978. lib. bdg. 19.95 (*0-226-92127-1*) U Ch Pr.

Naeve, Peter, jt. ed. see Buning, Herbert.

Naeve, Robert A. Maintaining a Drug-Free Workplace: The Management Primer on the Major Legal Issues Surrounding Drugs & Alcohol in the Workplace. Johnson, Margaret L., ed. 199p. (Orig.). 1990. pap. 38.00 (*0-932823-03-3*) Am Somerset.

Naeve, Robert A. & Cowan, Ari. Managing ADA: The Complete Compliance Guide, 2 vols. suppl. ed. LC 92-15445. 944p. 1993. ring bd. write for info. (*0-471-59238-2*) Wiley.

— Managing ADA: The Complete Compliance Guide, 2 vols., Vol. 2. LC 92-15445. 944p. 1992. Set. ring bd. 238.00 (*0-471-58275-1*) Wiley.

Naeye. Diseases of the Placenta, Fetus & Neonate: Clinical Correlations & Medical - Diagnos. (Illus.). 375p. 1991. 79.00 (*0-8016-3352-4*) Mosby Yr Bk.

NAF Legal Clearinghouse Staff. The First Amendment Book: A Guide for Abortion Providers & Their Attorneys. rev. ed. 1992. pap. text ed. 15.00 (*0-9601326-9-4*) Natl Abort Fed.

***Naff.** Lebonese Christian Americans. 1995. (*0-7910-3370-8*) Chelsea Hse.

Naff, Alixa. The Arab Americans. (Peoples of North America Ser.). (Illus.). 112p. (J). (gr. 5 up). 1988. lib. bdg. 17.95 (*0-87754-861-7*) Chelsea Hse.

— Becoming American: The Early Arab Immigrant Experience. LC 92-33848. 392p. 1993. pap. 16.95 (*0-8093-1896-2*) S Ill U Pr.

Naff, Clayton. About-Face: How I Stumbled onto Japan's Social Revolution. Turner, Philip, ed. 320p. 1994. 23.00 (*1-56836-041-X*) Kodansha.

Naff, Thomas. Paths to the Middle East: Ten Scholars Look Back. 360p. (C). 1993. 59.50 (*0-7914-1883-9*); pap. 19.95 (*0-7914-1884-7*) State U NY Pr.

Naff, Thomas, ed. The Middle East Challenge: 1980-1985. LC 81-5651. 192p. (Orig.). 1981. pap. 15.95 (*0-8093-1042-2*) S Ill U Pr.

Naff, William E., tr. see Shimazaki, Toson.

Naff, William E., tr. see Shimazaki, Toson.

Naffah, N. Office Information Systems. 656p. 1982. 102.75 (*0-444-86398-2*, North Holland) Elsevier.

Naffah, N., jt. auth. see Ellis, C.

Naffine, Ngaire. Female Crime: The Construction of Women in Criminology. LC 87-14372. 1988. text ed. 44.95 (*0-04-302004-6*, Pub. by Allen Unwin AT); pap. text ed. 18.95 (*0-04-330393-5*, Pub. by Allen Unwin AT) Paul & Co Pubs.

— Law & the Sexes: Explorations in Feminist Jurisprudence. 184p. 1991. pap. text ed. 19.95 (*0-04-442210-5*, Pub. by Allen Unwin AT) Paul & Co Pubs.

***Naffine, Ngaire, ed.** Feminism & Modern Criminology. (International Library of Criminology, Criminal Justice & Penology). (Illus.). 500p. 1995. text ed. 112.95 (*1-85521-543-8*, Pub. by Dartmth Pub UK) Ashgate Pub Co.

Naffziger, Douglas W. Hodgetts & Kuratko Management. 3rd ed. 218p. (C). 1990. student ed, pap. text ed. 17.00 (*0-15-554632-5*) HB Coll Pubs.

Nafi. Economic & Social Development in Quatar. 1992. text ed. 55.00 (*0-86187-389-0*, Pub. by Pinter Pubs UK) St Martin.

Naficie, Said. French-Persian Dictionary: Dictionnaire Francais-Persan, 2 vols., Set. 2300p. (FRE & PER.). 1985. 150.00 (*0-8288-1123-7*, F126574) Fr & Eur.

Naficy, Hamid. The Making of Exile Cultures: Iranian Television in Los Angeles. LC 93-13428. 302p. 1993. text ed. 44.95 (*0-8166-2084-9*); pap. text ed. 18.95 (*0-8166-2087-3*) U of Minn Pr.

Naficy, Hamid, comp. Iran Media Index. LC 84-6572. (Bibliographies & Indexes in World History Ser.: No. 1). xxxiii, 264p. 1984. text ed. 65.00 (*0-313-23895-2*, NIR/, Greenwood Pr) Greenwood.

Naficy, Hamid & Gabriel, Teshome, eds. Otherness & the Media: The Ethnography of the Imagined & the Imaged. 1993. pap. text ed. 18.00 (*3-7186-0569-4*) Gordon & Breach.

Nafie, L. A., jt. auth. see Birge, R. R.

Naftali, Timothy J., jt. auth. see Doran, Cahrles F.

Naftali, Timothy J., jt. auth. see Doran, Charles F.

Naftalin, Ethan S., jt. auth. see Turnbull, Bruce H.

***Naftalin, M., et al, eds.** FME '94: Industrial Benefit of Formal Methods: Proceedings of the Second International Symposium of Formal Methods Europe, Barcelona, Spain, October 24-28, 1994. (Lecture Notes in Computer Science: Vol. 873). xi, 723p. 1994. 96.00 (*3-540-58555-9*) Spr-Verlag.

Naftalin, Maurice, ed. see International Symposium of Formal Methods Europe.

Naftalis, Gary P., ed. White Collar Crimes. LC 80-65258. 389p. 1980. 15.00 (*0-686-28718-5*, B188) Am Law Inst.

Naftchi, N. E., ed. Spinal Cord Injury. LC 81-8573. (Illus.). 306p. 1982. text ed. 45.00 (*0-88331-202-6*) Luce.

Naftolin, F., jt. ed. see Lobo, R. A.

***Naftolin, Frederick & Stubblefield, Phillip G., eds.** Dilatation of the Uterine Cervix: Connective Tissue Biology & Clinical Management. fac. ed. LC 78-19621. 406p. Date not set. pap. 115.80 (*0-7837-7509-1*, 2046996) Bks Demand.

Nafy-al-Nazzam. Encyclopedie De l'Islam, 2 vols., Set. 1903p. 1993. pap. 95.00 (*0-7859-6440-1*, 9004097589) Fr & Eur.

Nafziger, E. Wayne. Class, Caste, & Entrepreneurship: A Study of Indian Industrialists. LC 78-16889. 198p. 1978. text ed. 14.00 (*0-8248-0575-5*, Eastwest Ctr Pr) UH Pr.

— The Debt Crisis in Africa. LC 92-23735. 288p. 1993. text ed. 38.50 (*0-8018-4476-2*) Johns Hopkins.

— Learning from the Japanese: Japan's Pre-War Development & the Third World. LC 94-27010. 240p. (C). 1994. text ed. 55.00 (*1-56324-485-3*, East Gate Bk); pap. text ed. 22.50 (*1-56324-486-1*, East Gate Bk) M E Sharpe.

— Poverty & Wealth: Comparing Afro-Asian Development. (Contemporary Studies in Economic & Financial Analysis: Vol. 75). 1994. write for info. (*1-55938-761-0*) Jai Pr.

Nafziger, E. Wayne, ed. Essays in Entrepreneurship, Equity & Economic Development. LC 86-20151. (Contemporary Studies in Economic & Financial Analysis: Vol. 53). 308p. 1986. 73.25 (*0-89232-601-8*) Jai Pr.

Nafziger, Elfrieda T. A Man of His Word: A Biography of John A Toews. (Illus.). 200p. (Orig.). 1992. pap. 11.50 (*1-895432-18-9*) Kindred Prods.

Nafziger, George. Litzen & Bautzen: Napoleon's Spring Campaign of 1813. 1994. 38.00 (*0-9626655-6-8*) Emperors Pr.

Nafziger, George, et al. Poles & Saxons of the Napoleonic Wars. (Illus.). 266p. 1991. 35.00 (*0-9626655-3-3*) Emperors Pr.

Nafziger, George F. Napoleon's Invasion of Russia. (Illus.). 704p. 1988. 45.00 (*0-89141-322-7*) Presidio Pr.

Nafziger, James A. International Sports Law. 300p. 1988. lib. bdg. 55.00 (*0-941320-52-9*) Transnatl Pubs.

Nafziger, Ralph O., comp. International News & the Press: An Annotated Bibliography. LC 72-4675. (International Propaganda & Communications Ser.). 223p. 1980. reprint ed. 17.95 (*0-405-04759-2*) Ayer.

Nafziger, Wayne. Inequality in Africa: Political Elites, Proletariat, Peasants & the Poor. (African Society Today Ser.). (Illus.). 240p. 1988. pap. 15.95 (*0-521-31703-7*) Cambridge U Pr.

Nag, A. Management Refresher. 1993. 30.00 (*0-7069-6818-2*, Pub. by Vikas II) S Asia.

Nag, B. R. Electron Transport in Compound Semiconductors. (Solid-State Sciences Ser.: Vol. 11). (Illus.). 470p. 1980. 56.00 (*3-540-09845-3*) Spr-Verlag.

— Theory of Electrical Transport in Semi-Conductors. 238p. 1972. 102.00 (*0-08-016802-7*, Pub. by Pergamon Repr UK) Franklin.

Nag, Chitta R. Mizo Society in Transition. (C). Date not set. 28.00 (*0-7069-6963-4*, Pub. by Vikas II) S Asia.

Nag, Moni. Factors Affecting Human Fertility in Nonindustrial Societies: A Cross-Cultural Study. LC 68-22204. (Yale University Publications in Anthropology Reprints Ser.: No. 66). 227p. 1968. pap. 20.00x (*0-87536-514-0*) HRAFP.

Nag, Moni, ed. Population & Social Organization. (World Anthropology Ser.). x, 368p. 1975. 35.40 (*90-279-7589-2*) Mouton.

Nag, N. K. Business Mathematics. 1985. 75.00 (*0-317-38752-9*, Current Dist) St Mut.

— Business Statistics. Maity, J. C., ed. 1985. 79.00 (*0-317-38754-5*, Current Dist) St Mut.

— Elements of Mathematics. 1985. 69.00 (*0-317-38764-2*, Current Dist) St Mut.

Nag, Prithvish. Population, Settlement & Development in Zambia. 1990. 34.00 (*0-685-34761-3*, Pub. by Concept II) S Asia.

Nag, Prithvish, ed. Thematic Cartography & Remote Sensing. (C). 1992. 38.00 (*81-7022-410-1*, Pub. by Concept II) S Asia.

Nag Raj, T. R. & DiCosmo, F. A Monograph of Herknessia & Mastigospoella with Notes on Associated Teleomorphs. (Bibliotheca Mycologica Ser.: Vol. 80). (Illus.). 160p. 1981. text ed. 30.00 (*3-7682-1300-5*) Lubrecht & Cramer.

Nag, Subhashis. The Complex Analytic Theory of Teichmuller Spaces. LC 87-28037. (Canadian Mathematical Society Series of Mnongraphs & Advanced Texts). 427p. 1988. text ed. 132.00 (*0-471-62773-9*) Wiley.

Nag, Subir. High Dose Rate Brachytherapy: A Textbook. LC 94-5083. (Illus.). 480p. 1994. 69.00 (*0-87993-588-X*) Futura Pub.

Nagahara Yoshiaki, Six-Dan. Strategic Concepts of Go. 1972. pap. 13.95 (*4-87187-006-5*, G6) Ishi Pr Intl.

Nagahara Yoshiaki, Six-Dan, jt. auth. see Haruyama Isamu, Eight-Dan.

Nagai. Central Regulation of Energy Metabolism. 1992. 110.00 (*0-8493-6657-7*, QP356) CRC Pr.

— Linear Circuits, Systems & Signal Processing: Advanced Theory & Applications. (Electrical Engineering & Electronics Ser.: Vol. 62). 456p. 1990. 125.00 (*0-8247-8185-6*) Dekker.

Nagai, Althea K., et al. Giving for Social Change: Foundations, Public Policy & the American Political Agenda. LC 93-25060. 218p. 1994. text ed. 55.00 (*0-275-94697-5*, C4697, Praeger Pubs) Greenwood.

Nagai, Gayle A., jt. auth. see Johnson, Betty S.

***Nagai, H. & Kamiya, K., eds.** Intracranial Pressure IX: Proceedings of the Ninth International Symposium on Intracranial Pressure Held in Nagoya, Japan 16-19, 1994. 685p. 1995. 171.00 (*0-387-70146-X*) Spr-Verlag.

Nagai-ha, Ng L., et al, eds. Historical Traces of Sun Yat-Sen's Activities in Hong Kong, Macao & Overseas. xvii, 182p. (Orig.). (CHI & ENG.). 1987. pap. text ed. 32.50x (*962-201-386-4*) Coronet Bks.

Nagai, Jun, jt. auth. see Adachi, Hideo.

***Nagai, K. & Mattaj, I., eds.** RNA-Protein Interactions: Frontiers in Molecular Biology. (Frontiers in Molecular Biology Ser.). (Illus.). 272p. 1995. text ed. 98.00 (*0-19-963505-6*, IRL Pr); pap. text ed. 53.00 (*0-19-963504-8*, IRL Pr) OUP.

Nagai, Michio, ed. Development in the Non-Western World. (United Nations Global Community Lecture Ser.: No. 1). 243p. 1985. 37.50 (*0-86008-363-2*, Pub. by U of Tokyo JA) Col U Pr.

— Higher Education in Japan: Its Take-off & Crash. Dusenberry, Jerry, tr. 264p. 1971. 24.50 (*0-86008-067-6*, Pub. by U of Tokyo JA) Col U Pr.

Nagai, Mona, tr. see Tanaka, Yukiko & Hanson, Elizabeth, eds.

Nagai, Noriko, jt. ed. see Mazuka, Reiko.

Nagai, Takashi. The Bells of Nagasaki. Shaw, ed. 118p. 1994. pap. 9.00 (*4-7700-1845-2*) Kodansha.

Nagakura. Physical Chemistry, Vol. 2. (Organic Synthesis--Today & Tomorrow Ser.). 1979. 48.00 (*0-08-022036-3*, Pub. by Pergamon Repr UK) Franklin.

Nagakura, Mieko, jt. ed. see Lowrie, Jean E.

Nagal, Robert F. Judicial Power & American Character: Censoring Ourselves in an Anxious Age. LC 93-41891. 224p. 1994. 29.95 (*0-19-508901-4*) OUP.

Nagamachi, Mitsuo, jt. ed. see Helander, Martin.

Nagamatsu, Ernest T., ed. see Friedman, Dave.

Nagamine, S. Essence of Okinawan Karate Do. 1976. 29.95 (*0-685-83525-1*) Wehman.

Nagamine, Shoshin. The Essence of Okinawan Karate-Do. LC 75-28717. (Illus.). 278p. 1976. 29.95 (*0-8048-1163-6*) C E Tuttle.

Nagan, Robert, jt. ed. see Arregui, Maurice E.

Nagano, M. & Takahara, F., eds. Astrophysical Aspects of the Most Energetic Cosmic Rays. 516p. (C). 1991. text ed. 118.00 (*981-02-0686-0*) World Scientific Pub.

Nagano, Makoto & Dhalla, Naranjan S. The Diabetic Heart. 560p. 1991. 115.00 (*0-88167-743-4*) Raven.

Nagano, Makoto, et al. The Adapted Heart. 560p. 1994. 99.00 (*0-7817-0167-8*) Raven.

Nagano, Makoto, et al, eds. The Cardiomyopathic Heart. LC 93-4656. 480p. 1994. 100.00 (*0-7817-0092-2*) Raven.

— Cardiovascular Disease in Diabetes. (Developments in Cardiovascular Medicine Ser.). 416p. (C). 1992. lib. bdg. 125.00 (*0-7923-1554-5*) Kluwer Ac.

Nagano, Paul. Shepherd God: The 23rd Psalm for Today. Mau, Rennie, ed. 30p. (Orig.). 1989. pap. write for info. (*0-318-66304-X*); audio write for info. (*0-318-66305-8*) Media Bridge.

Nagano, Tadashi. Homotopy Invariants in Differential Geometry. LC 52-42839. (Memoirs Ser.: No. 1/100). 41p. 1992. 16.00 (*0-8218-1800-7*, MEMO 1/100) Am Math.

Naganuma, N. Practical Japanese, a Basic Course. 363p. 1962. pap. 39.00 (*0-87040-319-2*) IBD Ltd.

— Practical Japanese, a Basic Course. 363p. 1976. audio 83.00 (*0-88431-688-2*) IBD Ltd.

Nagao, F., et al, eds. Gastrointestinal Function: Regulation & Disturbances, Vol. 7: Proceedings of the 7th Symposium on the Regulation & Disturbances of Gastrointestinal Function, Tokyo, Japan, 5 Nov., 1988. (International Congress Ser.: No. 874). 136p. 1990. 82.25 (*0-444-81104-4*, Excerpta Medica) Elsevier.

Nagao, Gadjin M. The Foundational Standpoint of Madhyamika Philosophy. Keenan, John P., tr. LC 88-16077. (SUNY Series in Buddhist Studies). 183p. 1989. 64.50 (*0-88706-952-5*); pap. 21.95 (*0-88706-953-3*) State U NY Pr.

— Madhyamika & Yogacara: A Study of Mahayana Philosophies. Kawamura, Leslie S., ed. LC 89-4278. (SUNY Series in Buddhist Studies). 318p. 1991. 64.50 (*0-7914-0186-3*); pap. 21.95 (*0-7914-0187-1*) State U NY Pr.

Nagao, Hirosi & Tsushima, Yukio. Representations of Finite Groups. 424p. 1989. text ed. 109.00 (*0-12-513660-9*) Acad Pr.

Nagao, Makoto. Knowledge & Inference. Weyrauch, Richard & Kitajima, Yasuko, trs. 304p. 1990. text ed. 61.00 (*0-12-513662-5*) Acad Pr.

— Machine Translation: How Far Can It Go? Cook, Norman D., tr. (Illus.). 168p. 1989. 45.00 (*0-19-853739-5*) OUP.

Nagao, Makoto & Matsuyama, Takashi, eds. A Structural Analysis of Complex Aerial Photographs. (Advanced Applications in Pattern Recognition Ser.). 224p. 1980. 65.00 (*0-306-40571-7*, Plenum Pr) Plenum.

***Nagao, Masanori.** Impressions of Edentulous Patients. (Dental Technique Ser.: No. 4). (Illus.). 51p. 1994. per. 25.00 (*1-56386-028-7*) Ishiyaku Euro.

Nagao, Yoshimi, ed. Coastlines of Japan 2. LC 93-2250. (Coastlines of the World Ser.). 352p. 1993. 29.00 (*0-87262-957-0*) Am Soc Civil Eng.

Nagao, Yoshimi & Magoon, Orville T., eds. Coastlines of Japan. (Coastlines of the World Ser.). 472p. 1991. pap. text ed. 43.00 (*0-87262-838-8*) Am Soc Civil Eng.

Nagaoka, Megumi, jt. ed. see Owens, Jessie A.

Nagaoka, Y. & Fukuyama, H., eds. Anderson Localization, Kyoto, Japan, 1981: Proceedings. (Solid-State Sciences Ser.: Vol. 39). (Illus.). 225p. 1982. 61.00 (*0-387-11518-8*) Spr-Verlag.

Nagar, A., ed. Fracture & Damage. (AD Ser.: Vol. 27). 148p. 1992. 45.00 (*0-7918-1074-7*, G00718) ASME.

Nagar, A. & Kuo, A. Y., eds. Fatigue & Fracture of Aerospace Structural Materials. LC 93-73600. 225p. Date not set. pap. 60.00 (*0-7918-1049-6*) ASME.

Nagar, A., jt. ed. see Basu, P. K.

Nagar, Amritial. Face Behind Seven Veils: English Translation of Famous Hindi Novel Saat Ghunghat Wala Mukhada. (New World Literature Ser.: No. 55). (C). 1992. 5.00 (*81-7018-712-5*, Pub. by BR Pub II) S Asia.

Nagar, K. S. & Sharma, Gautam, eds. India's Security: Super Power Threat. xv, 220p. 1990. text ed. 30.00 (*81-85047-63-4*, Pub. by Reliance Pub Hse II) Apt Bks.

Nagar, Murari L. Bilhana's Vikramankadevacarita: And Its Neo-Expounders. 2nd ed. (Illus.). 339p. (Orig.). 1992. pap. 55.00 (*0-943913-23-3*) Intl Lib Ctr.

— First American Library Pioneer in India: An Immortal Contribution of William Alanson Borden. 251p. 1986. 22.50 (*0-943913-15-2*); Beautifully bound. write for info. (*0-318-68831-X*) Intl Lib Ctr.

— Indian Library Scene as Seen at the Dawn of Independence. LC 90-4736. 225p. (Orig.). 1990. pap. 25.00 (*0-943913-13-6*) Intl Lib Ctr.

— Indo-American Library Cooperation, 2 pts. Nagar, Sarla D., ed. LC 91-32130. (Spectrum of Alpha: America's Library Promotional Heritage in Asia). 89p. (Orig.). 1991. pap. 20.00 (*0-943913-22-5*) Intl Lib Ctr.

— Indo-American Library Cooperation, Pt. 1: The Inspirer. Nagar, Sarla D., ed. 89p. (Orig.). 1991. Pt 1: The Inspirer. write for info. (*0-318-68714-3*) Intl Lib Ctr.

— Indo-American Library Cooperation, Pt. 2: What They Say. Nagar, Sarla D., ed. 89p. (Orig.). 1991. Pt 2: What They Say. write for info. (*0-318-68715-1*) Intl Lib Ctr.

— Shri Sayajirao Gaikwad, Maharaja of Baroda: The Prime Promoter of Public Libraries. Nagar, Sarla D., ed. LC 92-2528. (Spectrum of Alpha: America's Library Promotional Heritage in Asia: No. 5). 72p. (Orig.). 1992. pap. 18.00 (*0-943913-24-1*) Intl Lib Ctr.

— Test: The Eternal Saga of Tulip. Nagar, Sarla D., ed. LC 87-173017. 268p. (Orig.). 1986. pap. 25.00 (*0-943913-11-X*) Intl Lib Ctr.

— Tulsi: The Union Lists of Serials: History; Literature; Philosophy. Nagar, Sarla D., ed. LC 87-173042. 230p. (Orig.). 1986. pap. 23.00 (*0-943913-12-8*) Intl Lib Ctr.

— William Alanson Borden: An Apostle of International Librarianship. Nagar, Sarla D., ed. LC 91-29463. (Spectrum of Alpha: America's Library Promotional Heritage in Asia). 211p. (Orig.). 1992. 40.00 (*0-943913-25-X*) Intl Lib Ctr.

Nagar, Murari L. & Nagar, Sarla D. Tulip: The Universal - Union List of Indian Periodicals, Vol. 1. 186p. (Orig.). 1986. pap. 45.00 (*0-943913-00-4*) Intl Lib Ctr.

— Tulip: The Universal - Union List of Indian Periodicals, Vol. 1. 208p. (Orig.). 1988. pap. 45.00 (*0-943913-04-7*) Intl Lib Ctr.

— Tulip: The Universal - Union List of Indian Periodicals, Vol. 1. 215p. (Orig.). 1989. pap. 45.00 (*0-943913-07-1*); pap. 45.00 (*0-943913-08-X*) Intl Lib Ctr.

— Tulip: The Universal - Union List of Indian Periodicals, Vol. 1, Set, Vols. 1-10 (1986-1991) LC 87-26291. (Orig.). 1991. Set. pap. 450.00 (*0-943913-01-2*) Intl Lib Ctr.

An Asterisk (*) at the beginning of an entry indicates that the title is appearing in BIP for the first time.

— Tulip: The Universal - Union List of Indian Periodicals, Vol. 1, Subject Index I. xxx, 150p. (Orig.). 1991. pap. 45.00 (*0-943913-19-5*) Intl Lib Ctr.
— Tulip: The Universal - Union List of Indian Periodicals, Vol. 1, Suject Index II. 201p. (Orig.). 1991. pap. 45.00 (*0-943913-20-9*) Intl Lib Ctr.
— Tulip: The Universal - Union List of Indian PERIodicals, Vol. 6. LC 87-26291. 214p. (Orig.). 1989. pap. 45.00 (*0-943913-06-3*) Intl Lib Ctr.
— Tulip: The Universal List of Indian Periodicals, Vol. 2. 207p. (Orig.). 1986. pap. 45.00 (*0-943913-02-0*) Intl Lib Ctr.
— Tulip: The Universal List of Indian Periodicals, Vol. 3. 221p. (Orig.). 1987. pap. 45.00 (*0-943913-03-9*) Intl Lib Ctr.

Nagar, Murari L., et al. Tulip: The Universal - Union List of Indian Periodicals, Vol. 1. 215p. (Orig.). 1989. pap. 45.00 (*0-943913-05-5*) Intl Lib Ctr.

Nagar, S. L. Temples of Himachal Pradesh. (C). 1990. 120.00 (*81-85179-48-4*, Pub. by Aditya Prakashan II) S Asia.

Nagar, Sarla D. Gandharan Sculpture: A Catalogue of the Collection in the Museum of Art & Archaeology, University of Missouri-Columbia. (Illus.). 72p. (Orig.). 1981. pap. 6.00 (*0-910501-02-5*) U of Missouri Mus Art Arch.

Nagar, Sarla D., ed. see Nagar, Murari L.

Nagar, Sarla D., jt. auth. see Nagar, Murari L.

Nagar, Sarla D., ed. see Nagar, Murari L.

Nagar, Shanti L. Cult of Vinayaka. (Illus.). 270p. (C). 1992. 59.00 (*81-7076-044-5*) Nataraj Bks.
— Indian Monoliths. (Illus.). xv, 142p. (C). 1992. 39.00 (*81-7076-043-7*) Nataraj Bks.
— Mahishasuramardini in Indian Art. (C). 1988. 74.00 (*81-85179-09-3*, Pub. by Aditya Prakashan II) S Asia.
— Siva in Art, Literature & Thought. (C). 1995. 125.00x (*81-7387-019-5*, Pub. by Indus Pub II) S Asia.
— Varaha in Indian Art, Culture & Literature. (C). 1993. 60.00 (*81-7305-030-9*, Pub. by Aryan Bks Intl IA) S Asia.

Nagara, Susumu. Japanese for Everyone: Teacher's Manual. 136p. (Orig.). 1993. pap. 29.00 (*0-87040-922-0*) Japan Pubns USA.
— Japanese Pidgin English in Hawaii: A Bilingual Description. LC 70-184352. (Oceanic Linguistics Special Publication Ser.: No. 9). 341p. reprint ed. pap. 97.20 (*0-685-17127-2*, 2027031) Bks Demand.

Nagaraj, T. S. Principles of Testing Soils, Rock, & Concrete. LC 92-25238. 1992. write for info. (*0-444-88911-6*) Elsevier.

Nagarajan, ed. Glycopeptide Antibiotics. LC 94-585. (Drugs & the Pharmaceutical Sciences Ser.: Vol. 63). 432p. 1994. 165.00 (*0-8247-9193-2*) Dekker.

Nagarajan, Nilakantan. Testbank to Accompany Systems Analysis & Design: An Organizational Approach, by R. McLeod. 176p. (C). 1994. pap. text ed. 28.50 (*0-03-076683-4*) Dryden Pr.

Nagarajan, S. & Viswanathan, S. Shakespeare in India. 128p. 1987. 18.95 (*0-685-21573-3*) Asia Bk Corp.

Nagarajan, S., ed. see Shakespeare, William.

Nagarathna, R., et al. Yoga for Common Ailments. (Illus.). 96p. (Orig.). 1991. pap. 10.95 (*0-671-70528-8*, Fireside) S&S Trade.

Nagaratnam, R. Criminal Procedure: Principles & Precedents. (C). 1990. 150.00 (*0-89771-164-5*) St Mut.

***Nagare, Masayuki.** Nagare: The Life of a Samurai Artist. LC 94-21603. (Illus.). 324p. 1995. 125.00 (*0-8348-0325-9*) Weatherhill.

Nagarjuna. She-rab Dong-bu, or Prajnya Danda: A Metrical Translation in Tibetan of a Sanskrit Ethical Work. Campbell, W. L., ed. LC 78-70103. reprint ed. 22.00 (*0-404-17354-3*) AMS Pr.

Nagarjuna & Pandit, Sakya. Elegant Sayings. LC 77-23433. (Tibetan Translation Ser.: Vol. 6). 1977. 18.95 (*0-913546-12-7*); pap. 12.95 (*0-913546-13-5*) Dharma Pub.

***Nagarkar, Kiran.** Seven Sixes Are Forty-Three. (Asian Writers Ser.). 1995. pap. 10.95 (*0-435-95088-6*) Heinemann.

Nagarkatte, Umesh, jt. auth. see Berebom, Joshua.

Nagarwalla, Arati. The Bait. (Writers Workshop Bluebird Ser.). 33p. 1975. 5.00 (*0-88253-506-4*); pap. text ed. 4.00 (*0-88253-505-6*) Ind-US Inc.

Nagasaka, K., et al, eds. Prospects of Mathematical Science. 284p. (C). 1988. pap. 40.00 (*9971-5-0465-0*) World Scientific Pub.

Nagasaka, Kenji. Analytic Number Theory & Related Topics: Proceedings of the Conference. 190p. 1993. text ed. 53.00 (*981-02-1499-5*) World Scientific Pub.

Nagasawa, H. & Abe, K., eds. Hormone-Related Tumors. 380p. 1981. 79.00 (*0-387-10925-0*) Spr-Verlag.

Nagasawa, Hiroshi, ed. Prolactin Lesions in Breasts, Uterus, Prostate. 272p. 1988. 138.00 (*0-8493-6836-7*, RC280, CRC Reprint) Franklin.

Nagasawa, Hiroshi, jt. ed. see Mori, Takao.

Nagasawa, Kimiko & Condon, Camy. Eating Cheap in Japan: The Gaijin Gourmet's Guide to Ordering in Non-Tourist Restaurants. (Illus.). 104p. (Orig.). 1972. pap. 9.95 (*4-07-971548-X*, Pub. by Shufunomoto Co Ltd JA) C E Tuttle.

Nagasawa, M., ed. Molecular Conformation & Dynamics of Macromolecules in Condensed Matter. (Studies in Polymer Science). 370p. 1988. 141.00 (*0-444-42993-X*) Elsevier.

Nagasawa, Masao. Schrodinger Equations & Diffusion Theory. LC 93-1170. xii, 319p. 1993. 99.00 (*0-8176-2875-4*) Birkhauser.

Nagasawa, Richard. Summer Wind: The Story of an Immigrant Chinese Politician. LC 86-50080. 19.95 (*0-87026-063-4*) Westernlore.

Nagase, Michihiro, tr. see Kumano-Go, Hitoshi.

Nagashima, Kei, jt. auth. see Watanabe, Masahiro.

Nagashima, Soichiro. One Hundred Management Charts. 2nd ed. 344p. 1987. reprint ed. text ed. 38.00 (*92-833-1043-8*, Pub. by APO JA); reprint ed. pap. text ed. 32.75 (*92-833-1044-6*, Pub. by APO JA) Qual Resc.

Nagaswamy, R. Masterpieces of Early South Indian Bronzes. 172p. 1983. 52.95 (*0-940500-90-6*, Pub. by Natl Museum II) Asia Bk Corp.

Nagata, C., et al, eds. Biomolecules: Electronic Aspects. (Studies in Physical & Theoretical Chemistry: No. 36). 300p. 1985. 110.25 (*0-444-99551-X*) Elsevier.

Nagata, Donna K. Legacy of Injustice: Exploring the Cross-Generational Impact of the Japanese-American Internment. (Critical Issues in Social Justice Ser.). (Illus.). 277p. (C). 1993. 39.50 (*0-306-44425-9*, Plenum Pr) Plenum.

Nagata, J. Modern General Topology. 3rd rev. ed. (Mathematical Library: Vol. 33). 500p. 1985. 133.50 (*0-444-87655-3*, North Holland) Elsevier.

Nagata, J., jt. ed. see Morita, K.

Nagata, Judith, jt. ed. see Matthews, Bruce.

Nagata, Judith A. Continuity & Change among the Old Order Amish of Illinois. LC 87-45783. (Immigrant Communities & Ethnic Minorities in the U. S. & Canada Ser.: No. 18). 1988. 59.50 (*0-404-19428-1*) AMS Pr.

Nagata, Kenneth. The Story of Pineapple in Hawaii. (Illus.). 32p. (Orig.). 1990. pap. 4.95 (*0-89610-165-7*) Island Heritage.

Nagata, M. Polynomial Rings & Affine Spaces. LC 78-8264. (CBMS Regional Conference Series in Mathematics: No. 37). 33p. 1980. reprint ed. 17.00 (*0-8218-1687-X*, CBMS 37) Am Math.

Nagata, M. & Matsumura, Hideyuki, eds. Commutative Algebra & Combinatorics. (Advanced Studies in Pure Mathematics: Vol. 11). 360p. 1988. 159.00 (*0-444-70314-4*) Elsevier.

Nagata, Masayoshi. Theory of Commutative Fields. LC 93-6503. (Translations of Mathematical Monographs: Vol. 125). 280p. 1993. 125.00 (*0-8218-4572-1*) Am Math.

***Nagata, Seiji.** Hokusai: Genius of the Japanese Ukiyo-e. (Illus.). 96p. 1995. 40.00 (*4-7700-1928-9*) Kodansha.

Nagata, Yoshimi. Stone Cats. LC 93-18223. (Illus.). 48p. 1993. 14.95 (*0-8348-0279-1*) Weatherhill.

***Nagataki, Shigenobu, ed.** Chernobyl Update & in the Future. LC 94-35040. (International Congress Ser.: No. 1074). 1994. write for info. (*0-444-81953-3*) Elsevier.

Nagataki, Shigenobu & Torizuka, Kanji, eds. The Thyroid Nineteen Eighty-Eight: Proceedings of the International Thyroid Symposium, Tokyo, Japan, 13-15 July, 1988. (International Congress Ser.: No. 796). 696p. 1989. 184.75 (*0-444-81054-4*, Excerpta Medica) Elsevier.

Nagataki, Shigenobu, et al, eds. Eighty Years of Hashimoto Disease: Proceedings of the International Hashimoto Symposium, 2-5 December, 1992, Fukuoka, Japan. LC 93-26274. (International Congress Ser.: No. 1028). 721p. 1993. 237.25 (*0-444-89671-6*) Elsevier.
— Prevention of Type One Diabetes & Autoimmune Thyroid Disease. (Current Clinical Practice Ser.: Vol. 49). 158p. 1988. 65.75 (*0-685-20122-8*) Elsevier.
— Thyroid Research in Japan & China: Proceedings of the 1st Conference, Nagasaki, Japan, October 18, 1988. (Current Clinical Practice Ser.: No. 54). 102p. 1990. 46.25 (*90-219-1732-7*, Excerpta Medica) Elsevier.

Nagatani, Keizo. Macroeconomic Dynamics. LC 80-28883. (Illus.). 250p. 1981. 47.95 (*0-521-23515-4*) Cambridge U Pr.
— Political Macroeconomics. (Illus.). 288p. 1990. 64.00 (*0-19-828642-2*) OUP.

Nagatani, Patrick, photos. Nuclear Enchantment. LC 91-3523. (Illus.). 144p. 1991. 45.00 (*0-8263-1271-3*); pap. 32.50 (*0-8263-1272-1*) U of NM Pr.

Nagatani, T., tr. see Bloom, Alred.

Nagatomi, Masatoshi, et al, eds. Sanskrit & Indian Studies: Essays in Honour of Daniel H. H. Ingalls. (Studies in Classical India: No. 2). 1980. lib. bdg. 84.00 (*90-277-0991-2*) Kluwer Ac.

***Nagatomo, Kazuhiko.** Talk Japanese Gambatte! (Illus.). 156p. 1995. pap. 15.00 (*4-7700-1932-7*) Kodansha.
— Talk Japanese Gambatte! Hirowatari, Taro & Hulbert, Paul, eds. 1995. audio 20.00 (*4-7700-1933-5*) Kodansha.

***Nagatomo, Kazuhiko & Steinburg, Miho.** Do-It-Yourself Japanese Through Comics: An Introduction to Japanese in Twelve Lessons. (Illus.). 156p. 1995. pap. 15.00 (*4-7700-1935-1*) Kodansha.

Nagatomo, Shigenori. Attunement Through the Body. LC 91-39372. (SUNY Series, The Body in Culture, History, & Religion). 305p. 1992. 59.50 (*0-7914-1231-8*); pap. 19.95 (*0-7914-1232-6*) State U NY Pr.
— A Philosophical Foundation of Miki Kiyoshi's Concept of Humanism. LC 94-39460. (Studies in Asian Thought & Religion: Vol. 15). 130p. 1995. text ed. 69.95 (*0-7734-9145-7*) E Mellen.

Nagatomo, Shigenori, tr. see Yuasa, Yasuo.

Nagatsu, T. Senile Neurodegeneration & Neurotransmitters. (International Congress Ser.: Vol. 964). 1991. 77.25 (*0-444-81437-X*) Elsevier.

Nagatsu, T. & Hayaishi, O., eds. Aging of the Brain: Cellular & Molecular Aspects of Brain Aging & Alzheimer's Disease. (Taniguchi Symposia on Brain Sciences Ser.: Vol. 13). (Illus.). x, 302p. 1991. 134.50 (*3-8055-5334-X*) S Karger.

Nagatsu, T., et al, eds. Basic, Clinical, & Therapeutic Aspects of Alzheimer's & Parkinson's Disease, Vol. 1. (Advances in Behavioral Biology Ser.: Vol. 38A). (Illus.). 780p. 1990. 145.00 (*0-306-43680-9*, Plenum Pr) Plenum.
— Basic, Clinical, & Therapeutic Aspects of Alzheimer's & Parkinson's Diseases, Vol. 2. (Advances in Behavioral Biology Ser.: Vol. 38B). (Illus.). 600p. 1990. 125.00 (*0-306-43681-7*, Plenum Pr) Plenum.
— Parkinson's Disease: From Clinical Aspects to Molecular Basis. (Key Topics in Brain Research Ser.). (Illus.). 240p. 1992. pap. 69.00 (*0-387-82272-0*) Spr-Verlag.

Nagda, N. L. & Harper, J. P., eds. Design & Protocol for Monitoring Indoor Air Quality. LC 88-37486. (Special Technical Publication Ser.: No. STP 1002). (Illus.). 310p. 1989. text ed. 53.00 (*0-8031-1176-2*) ASTM.

Nagda, Niren L., ed. Modeling of Indoor Air Quality & Exposure. LC 93-31561. (Special Technical Publication Ser.: No. 1205). (Illus.). 310p. 1993. 65.00 (*0-8031-1875-9*, 0401205017) ASTM.
— Radon: Prevalence, Measurements, Health Risks, & Control. LC 94-11665. (ASTM Manual Ser.: MNL 15). (Illus.). 170p. 1994. text ed. 59.00 (*0-8031-2057-5*, 28-015094-17) ASTM.

Nagdi, Khairi. Rubbers As an Engineering Material: How to Design Rubber Components. 280p. (C). 1992. text ed. 89.95 (*1-56990-067-1*) Hanser-Gardner.

Nagdi, P. M., et al, eds. Non-Linear Elasticity & Theoretical Mechanics: In Honour of A. E. Green. (Illus.). 256p. 1994. 75.00 (*0-19-853486-8*) OUP.

Nagdy, jt. auth. see Gray.

Nagel. Encyclopedia of Policy Studies. 2nd expanded rev. ed. (Public Administration & Public Policy Ser.: Vol. 53). 952p. 1994. 195.00 (*0-8247-9142-8*) Dekker.
— Nagel's Guide to Sweden. 1989. 39.95 (*0-8442-9782-8*, Passport Bks) NTC Pub Grp.

Nagel, A. & Stein, E. M. Lectures on Pseudo-Differential Operators: Regularity Theorems & Applications to Non-Elliptic Problems. LC 79-19388. (Mathematical Notes Ser.: No. 24). 1980. 29.95 (*0-691-08247-2*) Princeton U Pr.

***Nagel, Alexander.** Cherubs: Angels of Love, Vol. 1. (Illus.). 128p. 1994. 29.95 (*0-8212-2122-1*) Bulfinch Pr.

Nagel, Alexander & Stout, Edgar L., eds. The Madison Symposium on Complex Analysis: (Proceedings of the Symposium on Complex Analysis Held June 2-7, 1991 at the University of Wisconsin-Madison) LC 92-23702. (Contemporary Mathematics Ser.: Vol. 137). 478p. 1992. 49.00 (*0-8218-5147-0*) Am Math.

Nagel, David C., jt. ed. see Wiener, Earl L.

Nagel, Ed. Cheez! Uncle Sam. 1978. 8.95 (*0-9603096-0-8*) Santa Fe Comm Sch.

***Nagel, Edward A.** No Entry. LC 94-37598. 300p. 1995. 20.00 (*1-56858-025-8*) FWEW.

Nagel, Ernest. The Structure of Science. LC 60-15504. 640p. (C). 1979. reprint ed. lib. bdg. 37.95 (*0-915144-72-7*); reprint ed. pap. text ed. 16.50 (*0-915144-71-9*) Hackett Pub.
— Teleology Revisited & Other Essays in the Philosophy & History of Science. LC 78-1437. 368p. 1982. pap. text ed. 18.50 (*0-231-04505-0*) Col U Pr.

Nagel, Ernest & Newman, James R. Godel's Proof. LC 58-5610. 1958. pap. 9.50 (*0-8147-0325-9*) NYU Pr.

Nagel, Ernest, jt. auth. see Cohen, Morris R.

Nagel, Ernest, ed. see International Congress of Logic, Methodology & Philosophy of Science Staff.

Nagel, Ernest, ed. see Wesleyan Conference on Induction Staff.

Nagel, Fritz. Fritz: The World War I Memoirs of a German Lieutenant. Baumgartner, Richard A., ed. (Illus.). 160p. (Orig.). 1980. pap. 6.95 (*0-9604770-0-4*) RMR Bks.
— Fritz: The World War I Memoirs of a German Lieutenant. 2nd ed. Baumgartner, Richard A., ed. (Illus.). 160p. (Orig.). 1995. 20.00 (*1-885033-15-X*) Blue Acorn Pr.

Nagel, G., ed. see Brade, W., et al.

Nagel, G. A., jt. ed. see Burkert, H.

Nagel, G. A., et al, eds. Plasmapheresis in Immunology & Oncology: Beitraege zur Onkologie. Contributions to Oncology, Vol. 10. (Illus.). viii, 266p. 1982. pap. 46.50 (*3-8055-3467-1*) S Karger.

Nagel, Greta K. The Tao of Teaching: The Special Meaning of the Tao Te Ching As Related to the Art of Teaching. LC 94-71108. 240p. 1994. 21.95 (*1-55611-416-8*); pap. 10.95 (*1-55611-415-X*) D I Fine.

Nagel, Gwen L. Critical Essays on Sarah Orne Jewett. (Critical Essays on American Literature Ser.). 264p. 1984. lib. bdg. 40.00 (*0-8161-8422-4*) G K Hall.

Nagel, H. H., jt. ed. see Orban, G. A.

Nagel, H. T., et al. An Introduction to Computer Logic. (Illus.). 544p. 1974. text ed. 22.00 (*0-13-480012-5*) P-H.

Nagel, Hildegard, tr. see Jung, Emma.

Nagel, Hildegard, et al, trs. The Place of Creation Vol. 3: Essays of Erich Neumann. (Bollingen Ser.). 280p. 1989. text ed. 49.50 (*0-691-09965-0*) Princeton U Pr.

Nagel, Ivan. Autonomy & Mercy: Reflections on Mozart's Operas. Faber, Marion, tr. LC 90-22827. 149p. 1974. 26.00 (*0-674-05477-6*, NAGAUT) HUP.

Nagel, Jack H. The Descriptive Analysis of Power. LC 74-14087. 214p. reprint ed. pap. 61.00 (*0-8357-8092-9*, 2033839) Bks Demand.

***Nagel, James.** Critical Essays on Hemingway's The Sun Also Rises. LC 94-34994. (Critical Essays on American Literature Ser.). 1995. lib. bdg. 45.00x (*0-8161-7312-5*, Twayne) Macmillan.
— Stephen Crane & Literary Impressionism. LC 80-16051. 200p. (C). 1980. 30.00 (*0-271-00267-0*) Pa St U Pr.

Nagel, James, ed. American Fiction: Historical & Critical Essays. LC 77-88848. 216p. 1977. 30.00 (*0-8057-9006-3*) NE U Pr.
— Ernest Hemingway: The Writer in Context. LC 83-40268. 264p. 1984. 27.50 (*0-299-09740-4*) U of Wis Pr.

Nagel, James, ed. see Pizer, Donald.

Nagel, James, jt. auth. see Villard, Henry S.

Nagel, Jeff. The Blind Date Survival Guide: A Practical & Funny (Well, Practically Funny) Step-by-Step Guide to Meeting the Person of Your Dreams. (Illus.). 128p. (Orig.). 1988. pap. 5.95 (*0-923032-00-2*) Blockbuster Pubns Inc.

***Nagel, Joane.** American Indian Ethnic Renewal: Red Power & the Resurgence of Identity & Culture. (Illus.). 320p. 1995. 45.00 (*0-19-508053-X*) OUP.

Nagel, Joane, jt. auth. see Olzak, Susan.

***Nagel, Jon W.** Glimpses, a Novel. 384p. 1994. text ed. 24.95 (*0-9642850-0-2*) Delphic Pubns.

Nagel, Karen. Two Crazy Pigs. (Illus.). 32p. (J). 1992. pap. 2.95 (*0-590-44972-9*, Cartwheel) Scholastic Inc.

Nagel, Karen B. Norfin Trolls Campout Adventure. (J). (ps-3). 1993. pap. 2.50 (*0-590-46630-5*) Scholastic Inc.

Nagel, Kurt. Lexikon EDV und Rechnungswesen. (GER.). 1977. 59.95 (*0-8288-5493-9*, M7203) Fr & Eur.

Nagel, Molli E. Two Hundred Fifty Reasons to Quit Smoking. Bacci, Andrea, ed. 78p. (Orig.). (C). 1994. pap. 8.95 (*1-56550-021-0*) Vis Bks Intl.

Nagel, Muska. Elements. 135p. (Orig.). 1990. pap. 10.95 (*0-913006-44-0*) Puckerbrush.
— Things That Surround Us. Hunting, Constance, ed. 68p. (Orig.). 1987. pap. 8.95 (*0-913006-39-4*) Puckerbrush.

Nagel, Muska, tr. see Bobrowski, Johannes.

Nagel, Myra B. Talking with Your Child about Prayer. LC 89-39927. (Growing Together Ser.). (Orig.). 1990. pap. 1.95 (*0-8298-0845-0*) Pilgrim OH.

Nagel, Norman, tr. see Sasse, Herman.

Nagel, Norman, tr. see Sasse, Hermann.

Nagel, Patrick. Nagel: The Art of Patrick Nagel. LC 89-45324. (Illus.). 160p. 1989. reprint ed. pap. 25.00 (*0-06-097269-6*, PL) HarpC.

Nagel, Paul C. The Adams Women: Abigail & Louisa Adams, Their Sisters & Daughters. (Illus.). 320p. 1987. 30.00 (*0-19-503874-6*) OUP.
— The Adams Women: Abigail & Louisa Adams, Their Sisters & Daughters. (Illus.). 324p. 1989. reprint ed. pap. 10.95 (*0-19-505920-4*) OUP.
— Descent from Glory: Four Generations of the John Adams Family. (Galaxy Bks.). (Illus.). 1983. 30.00 (*0-19-503172-5*) OUP.
— Descent from Glory: Four Generations of the John Adams Family. (Galaxy Bks.). (Illus.). 1984. pap. 12.95 (*0-19-503445-7*) OUP.
— The Lees of Virginia: Seven Generations of an American Family. (Illus.). 352p. 1990. 24.95 (*0-19-505385-0*) OUP.
— The Lees of Virginia: Seven Generations of an American Family. 368p. 1992. pap. 14.95 (*0-19-507478-5*) OUP.
— Missouri: A History. LC 88-27761. xiv, 210p. 1988. pap. 7.95 (*0-7006-0386-7*) U Pr of KS.
— Missouri: A History. (States & the Nation Ser.). (Illus.). 1977. 14.95 (*0-393-05633-3*) Norton.
— One Nation Indivisible: The Union in American Thought, 1776 to 1861. LC 80-36682. vii, 328p. 1980. reprint ed. text ed. 35.00 (*0-313-22656-3*, NAON, Greenwood Pr) Greenwood.

Nagel, R., et al, eds. Aspects of Positivity in Functional Analysis. (North Holland Mathematics Studies: Vol. 122). 274p. 1986. 59.00 (*0-444-87959-5*, North Holland) Elsevier.

Nagel, Rob & Commire, Anne, eds. World Leaders: People Who Shaped the World, Set. LC 94-20544. 1994. write for info. (*0-8103-9768-4*, UXL) Gale.

Nagel, Robert F. Constitutional Cultures: The Mentality & Consequences of Judicial Review. 1989. pap. 13.00 (*0-520-08278-8*) U CA Pr.

***Nagel, Robert F., ed.** Intellect & Craft: Writings. (New Perspectives on Law, Culture, & Society Ser.). (C). 1995. text ed. 49.95 (*0-8133-8576-8*) Westview.

Nagel, Roland & Loskill, R., eds. Bioaccumulation in Aquatic Systems: Contributions to the Assessment. (Illus.). 237p. 1992. text ed. 93.00 (*1-56081-201-X*) VCH Pubs.

Nagel, Ronald L., ed. Genetically Abnormal Red Cells, 2 vols., Vol. I. 192p. 1988. 105.00 (*0-8493-6826-X*, RC647, CRC Reprint) Franklin.
— Genetically Abnormal Red Cells, 2 vols., Vol. II. 208p. 1988. 113.00 (*0-8493-6827-8*, RC647, CRC Reprint) Franklin.

Nagel, Stephan, ed. see Newland, Mary R.

Nagel, Stephan, ed. see Stoutzenberger, Joseph.

Nagel, Steve, ed. see Ahlers, Julia, et al.

Nagel, Stuart, ed. Basic Facilities & Institutions in Policy Studies. (C). 1972. pap. 12.00 (*0-918592-01-1*) Pol Studies.
— Basic Issues & References in Policy Studies. (C). 1972. pap. 12.00 (*0-918592-00-3*) Pol Studies.
— Environmental Policy & Political Science Fields. (C). 1973. pap. 12.00 (*0-918592-03-8*) Pol Studies.
— Interdisciplinary Approaches to Policy Studies. (C). 1973. pap. 12.00 (*0-918592-04-6*) Pol Studies.
— Policy Studies & the Social Sciences. (Organization Ser.). 329p. 1975. pap. 12.00 (*0-317-35632-1*) Pol Studies.
— Policy Studies Around the World. 1973. pap. 12.00 (*0-918592-02-X*) Pol Studies.

Nagel, Stuart & Mills, Miriam. Developing Nations & Super-Optimum Policy Analysis. (Political Science Ser.). 275p. 1994. 32.95 (*0-8304-1274-3*) Nelson-Hall.

Nagel, Stuart & Munshaw, Nancy, eds. Policy Studies Personnel Directory. 1979. pap. 12.00 (*0-918592-33-X*) Pol Studies.

Nagel, Stuart & Neef, Marian. Policy Studies Directory. 1976. pap. 12.00 (*0-918592-18-6*) Pol Studies.
— Political Science Utilization Directory. 1975. pap. 12.00 (*0-918592-19-4*) Pol Studies.

Nagel, Stuart & Neef, Marian, eds. Policy Grants Directory. 1977. pap. 12.00 (*0-918592-25-9*) Pol Studies.
— Policy Research Centers Directory. 1978. pap. 12.00 (*0-918592-30-5*) Pol Studies.

Nagel, Stuart & Palumbo, Dennis, eds. Cross National Policy Studies Directory. (Orig.). 1984. pap. 12.00 (*0-918592-72-0*) Pol Studies.

Nagel, Stuart S. Causation, Prediction & Legal Analysis. LC 86-8142. 298p. 1986. text ed. 55.00 (*0-89930-180-0*, NCP/, Quorum Bks) Greenwood.

N

An Asterisk (*) at the beginning of an entry indicates that the title is appearing in BIP for the first time.

— Computer-Aided Judicial Analysis: Predicting, Prescribing, & Administering. LC 91-33090. 392p. 1992. text ed. 79.50 (*0-89930-670-5*, NJP/, Quorum Bks) Greenwood.

— Contemporary Public Policy Analysis. 192p. 1984. pap. 10.50 (*0-8173-0163-1*) U of Ala Pr.

— Decision-Aiding Software. LC 90-32087. (Policy Studies Organization). 315p. 1991. text ed. 45.00 (*0-312-04212-4*) St Martin.

— Decision-Aiding Software & Legal Decision-Making: A Guide to Skills & Applications Throughout the Law. LC 88-39911. 272p. 1989. text ed. 69.50 (*0-89930-382-X*, NLD, Quorum Bks) Greenwood.

— Evaluative & Explanatory Legal Reasoning. LC 91-32381. 232p. 1992. text ed. 59.95 (*0-89930-445-1*, NEE/, Quorum Bks) Greenwood.

— Higher Goals for America: Doing Better Than the Best. LC 88-31498. (Illus.). 246p. (Orig.). (C). 1989. lib. bdg. 45.00 (*0-8191-7306-1*); pap. text ed. 22.50 (*0-8191-7307-X*) U Pr of Amer.

— Law, Policy & Optimizing Analysis. LC 86-8140. 347p. 1986. text ed. 65.00 (*0-89930-181-9*, NLP/, Quorum Bks) Greenwood.

— Legal Scholarship, Microcomputers, & Super-Optimized Decision-Making. LC 92-44684. 232p. 1993. text ed. 59.95 (*0-89930-444-3*, NLA, Quorum Bks) Greenwood.

— Microcomputers As Decision Aids in Law Practice. LC 86-16873. 394p. 1987. text ed. 79.50 (*0-89930-197-5*, NLU/, Quorum Bks) Greenwood.

— Policy-Analysis Methods & Super-Optimum Solutions. 274p. 1994. lib. bdg. 59.00 (*1-56072-134-0*) Nova Sci Pubs.

— Policy Evaluation: Making Optimum Decisions. LC 81-12123. 352p. 1982. text ed. 49.95 (*0-275-90866-6*, C0866, Praeger Pubs) Greenwood.

— The Policy Process & Super-Optimum Solutions. 227p. 1994. lib. bdg. 59.00 (*1-56072-135-9*) Nova Sci Pubs.

— Policy Studies: Integration & Evaluation. LC 88-3122. (Contributions in Political Science Ser.: No. 216). 320p. 1988. text ed. 59.95 (*0-313-26256-X*, NSP/, Greenwood Pr) Greenwood.

— Policy Studies: Integration & Evaluation. LC 88-4148. 320p. 1989. pap. text ed. 16.95 (*0-275-93007-6*, B3007, Praeger Pubs) Greenwood.

— Professional Developments in Policy Studies. LC 91-38209. (Contributions in Political Science Ser.: No. 297). 288p. 1993. text ed. 59.95 (*0-313-28429-6*, NPV, Greenwood Pr) Greenwood.

— Public Policy: Goals, Means & Methods. 546p. (C). 1983. teacher ed write for info. (*0-318-57732-1*) St Martin.

— Public Policy: Goals, Means & Methods. 480p. (C). 1990. reprint ed. pap. text ed. 39.00 (*0-8191-7912-4*) U Pr of Amer.

— Research in Public Policy Analysis & Management, Vol. 4. 1987. 73.25 (*0-89232-663-8*) Jai Pr.

Nagel, Stuart S., ed. Africa, Development & Public Policy. LC 93-26989. 1994. text ed. 69.95 (*0-312-10383-2*) St Martin.

— Applications of Decision-Aiding Software. LC 91-25429. 280p. 1992. text ed. 59.95 (*0-312-06811-5*) St Martin.

— Asia, Development & Public Policy. LC 93-31946. (Policy Studies Organization). 1994. text ed. 69.95 (*0-312-10649-1*) St Martin.

— Computer-Aided Decision Analysis: Theory & Applications. LC 92-38003. 304p. 1993. text ed. 79.50 (*0-89930-771-X*, NCK/, Quorum Bks) Greenwood.

— East Europe, Development & Public Policy. LC 93-31947. (Policy Studies Organization). 1994. text ed. 69.95 (*0-312-10648-3*) St Martin.

— Global Policy Studies: International Interaction Toward Improving Public Policy. LC 90-43257. 184p. 1991. text ed. 49.95 (*0-312-05309-6*) St Martin.

— Latin America, Development & Public Policy. LC 93-31948. (Policy Studies Organization). 1994. text ed. 69.95 (*0-312-10650-5*) St Martin.

— Law, Decision-Making, & Microcomputers: A Cross-National Perspective. LC 90-8918. 376p. 1991. text ed. 75.00 (*0-89930-503-2*, NLM/, Quorum Bks) Greenwood.

— Policy Studies & the Social Sciences. LC 77-82859. 315p. 1979. reprint ed. pap. text ed. 21.95 (*0-87855-641-9*) Transaction Pubs.

— Policy Studies in America & Elsewhere. (Organization Ser.). 229p. 1975. 12.00 (*0-317-35633-X*) Pol Studies.

— Policy Studies Review Annual, Vol. 1. 704p. 1977. text ed. 69.95 (*0-8039-0848-2*) Transaction Pubs.

— Public Administration & Decision-Aiding Software: Improving Procedure & Substance. LC 90-36737. (New Directions in Information Management Ser.: No. 23). 280p. 1990. text ed. 59.95 (*0-313-27518-1*, NPA, Greenwood Pr) Greenwood.

— Research in Law & Policy Studies, Vol. 1. 1987. 73.25 (*0-89232-525-9*) Jai Pr.

— Research in Law & Policy Studies, Vol. 2. 1988. 73.25 (*0-89232-662-X*) Jai Pr.

— The Rights of the Accused in Law & Action. LC 72-84052. (Sage Criminal Justice System Annuals Ser.: No. 1). 320p. reprint ed. pap. 83.20 (*0-8357-8500-9*, 2034776) Bks Demand.

Nagel, Stuart S. & Bievenue, Lisa A. Social Science, Law, & Public Policy. 344p. (C). 1992. lib. bdg. 47.50 (*0-8191-8428-4*); pap. text ed. 24.50 (*0-8191-8429-2*) U Pr of Amer.

— Teach Yourself Decision-Aiding Software. LC 92-11135. 318p. (Orig.). (C). 1992. lib. bdg. 37.50 (*0-8191-8738-0*) U Pr of Amer.

Nagel, Stuart S. & Dunn, William N., eds. Policy Theory & Evaluation Concepts, Knowledge, Causes & Norms. LC 89-25784. (Contributions in Political Science Ser.: No. 258). 256p. 1990. text ed. 59.95 (*0-313-27356-1*, NPT/, Greenwood Pr) Greenwood.

Nagel, Stuart S. & Mills, Miriam K. Multi-Criteria Methods in Alternative Dispute Resolution: With Microcomputer Software Applications. LC 90-8416. 288p. 1990. text ed. 75.00 (*0-89930-520-2*, NMC, Quorum Bks) Greenwood.

Nagel, Stuart S. & Mills, Miriam K., eds. Public Policy in China. LC 92-37519. (Contributions in Political Science Ser.: No. 318). 176p. 1993. text ed. 55.00 (*0-313-28848-8*, GM8848) Greenwood.

— Systematic Analysis in Dispute Resolution. LC 90-22125. 304p. 1991. text ed. 69.50 (*0-89930-623-3*, NSA, Quorum Bks) Greenwood.

Nagel, Stuart S. & Neef, Marian. Operations Research Methods. LC 76-25693. (Quantitative Applications in the Social Sciences Ser.: Vol. 2). 76p. 1976. pap. 9.95 (*0-8039-0651-X*) Sage.

— Policy Analysis in Social Science Research. 242p. 1985. reprint ed. pap. text ed. 22.50 (*0-8191-4795-8*) U Pr of Amer.

Nagel, Stuart S., jt. ed. see Holzer, Marc.

Nagel, Stuart S., jt. ed. see Mills, Miriam K.

Nagel, Susan. The Influence of the Novels of Jean Giraudoux on the Hispanic Language Novels of the 1920s-1930s. LC 90-55650. 152p. 1991. 32.50 (*0-8387-5201-2*) Bucknell U Pr.

Nagel, Suzanne R., ed. see Materials Research Society Staff.

Nagel, Thomas. Equality & Partiality. 208p. 1991. 22.00 (*0-19-506967-6*) OUP.

— Equality & Partiality. 224p. 1995. pap. 14.95 (*0-19-509839-0*) OUP.

— Mortal Questions. (Canto Book Ser.). (Illus.). 240p. (C). 1991. pap. 10.95 (*0-521-40676-5*) Cambridge U Pr.

— Other Minds: Critical Essays, 1969-1994. 208p. 1995. 24.95 (*0-19-509008-X*) OUP.

— The Possibility of Altruism. LC 78-4323. 1979. pap. 12.95 (*0-691-02002-7*) Princeton U Pr.

— The View from Nowhere. 256p. 1986. reprint ed. text ed. 36.00 (*0-19-503668-9*) OUP.

— The View from Nowhere. 256p. 1989. reprint ed. pap. 16.95 (*0-19-505644-2*) OUP.

— What Does It All Mean? A Very Short Introduction to Philosophy. 120p. 1987. 16.95 (*0-19-505292-7*); pap. 10.95 (*0-19-505216-1*) OUP.

Nagel, Thomas, ed. Experimental & Theoretical Studies of Consciousness: Ciba Foundation Symposium. (CIBA Foundation Symposia Ser.: No. 174). 316p. 1993. text ed. 72.00 (*0-471-93866-1*) Wiley.

***Nagel, Walter, et al.** Leading U. S. Supreme Court Tax Cases: Official Syllabi, Notes, & Indices. LC 94-41031. 1994. write for info. (*1-55871-312-3*) Tax Mgmt.

Nagel, Walter H. & Ndyajunwoha, Gaston Z. Export Marketing Handbook. LC 87-82237. 149p. 1988. text ed. 49.95 (*0-275-92949-3*, C2949, Praeger Pubs) Greenwood.

Nagele, Rainer. Reading after Freud: Essays on Goethe, Holderlin, Habermas, Nietzsche, Brecht, Celan, & Freud. LC 86-20730. 216p. 1987. text ed. 42.00 (*0-231-06286-9*) Col U Pr.

— Theater, Theory, Speculation: Walter Benjamin & the Scenes of Modernity. LC 90-45358. 208p. 1991. text ed. 37.50x (*0-8018-4123-2*) Johns Hopkins.

Nagele, Rainer, ed. Benjamin's Ground: New Readings of Walter Benjamin. LC 88-14300. 190p. 1988. reprint ed. 27.95 (*0-8143-2040-6*); reprint ed. pap. 15.95 (*0-8143-2041-4*) Wayne St U Pr.

Nageleisen, John A. Charity for the Suffering Souls. LC 82-83797. 375p. 1982. reprint ed. pap. 15.00 (*0-89555-200-0*) TAN Bks Pubs.

***Nageley, Jack R.** The Dissolution of Society. 112p. 1994. pap. text ed. 6.90 (*0-9642631-0-6*) J R Nageley.

Nagell, Trygve. Introduction to Number Theory. 309p. 1981. 19.95 (*0-8284-0163-2*) Chelsea Pub.

Nagelschmidt, Joseph S., ed. The Public Affairs Handbook. LC 82-6710. 319p. reprint ed. pap. 91.00 (*0-317-26318-8*, 2055750) Bks Demand.

Nagem, Monique, tr. see Chawaf, Chantal.

Nagem, Monique F., tr. see Chawaf, Chantal.

Nagenda, John. The Seasons of Thomas Tebo. (African Writers Ser.). 156p. (Orig.). 1986. pap. 8.95 (*0-435-90824-3*) Heinemann.

Nagengast, Bernard, jt. auth. see Kamin, John V.

Nagengast, Carole. Reluctant Socialists, Rural Entrepreneurs: Class, Culture & the Polish State. (Studies in Ethnographic Imagination). 239p. (C). 1993. pap. text ed. 21.50 (*0-8133-1932-3*) Westview.

Nager, George T. Pathology of the Ear & Temporal Bone. LC 93-27739. (Illus.). 1408p. 1994. 295.00 (*0-683-63049-0*) Williams & Wilkins.

Nager, Norman R. & Allen, T. Harrell. Public Relations: Management by Objectives. (Illus.). 416p. (C). 1991. reprint ed. pap. text ed. 24.50 (*0-8191-8330-X*) U Pr of Amer.

Nager, Norman R. & Truitt, Richard H. Strategic Public Relations Counseling: Models from the Counselors Academy. 392p. (C). 1991. reprint ed. pap. 32.50 (*0-8191-8331-8*) U Pr of Amer.

Nager, Sandra, ed. see Millinary Institute Staff.

Nagera, Humberto. Early Childhood Disturbances, the Infantile Neurosis, & the Adult Disturbances. LC 66-17526. (Psychoanalytic Study of the Child Monographs: No. 2). 96p. 1966. text ed. 25.00 (*0-8236-1520-0*) Intl Univs Pr.

— Obsessional Neuroses: Developmental Psychopathology. LC 84-45012. 240p. 1993. pap. 27.50 (*1-56821-151-1*) Aronson.

— Vincent Van Gogh Psychological. (Illus.). 182p. 1990. pap. 24.95 (*0-685-02649-3*, BN 26741) Intl Univs Pr.

Nagera, Humberto, ed. The Hampstead Clinic Psychoanalytic Library, Vol. I: Basic Psychoanalytic Concepts on the Libido Theory. 200p. 1990. reprint ed. pap. 21.95 (*0-9507146-3-1*, Pub. by Karnac Bks UK) Brunner-Mazel.

— The Hampstead Clinic Psychoanalytic Library, Vol. II: Basic Psychoanalytic Concepts on the Theory of Dreams. 126p. 1990. reprint ed. pap. 21.95 (*0-9507146-4-X*, Pub. by Karnac Bks UK) Brunner-Mazel.

— The Hampstead Clinic Psychoanalytic Library, Vol. III: Basic Psychoanalytic Concepts on Metapsychology, Conflicts, Anxiety, & Other Subjects. 240p. 1990. reprint ed. pap. 21.95 (*0-9507146-6-6*, Pub. by Karnac Bks UK) Brunner-Mazel.

— The Hampstead Clinic Psychoanalytic Library, Vol. IV: Basic Psychoanalytic Concepts on the Theory of Instincts. 212p. 1990. reprint ed. pap. 21.95 (*0-9507146-5-8*, Pub. by Karnac Bks UK) Brunner-Mazel.

Nageswara Rao, N. Studies in Urban Public Sector, India. 1985. 30.00 (*0-8364-1386-5*, Pub. by Ashish II) S Asia.

Naggar. Dictionnaire des Photographes. rev. ed. 567p. (FRE.). 1982. write for info. (*0-8288-7909-5*, 8185243077) Fr & Eur.

Naggar, Carole & Ritchin, Fred, eds. Mexico Through Foreign Eyes: Photographs, 1850-1990. LC 92-36919. (Illus.). 304p. 1993. 50.00 (*0-393-03473-9*) Norton.

Nagi, Dennis L. The Albanian-American Odyssey: A Pilot Study of the Albanian Community of Boston, Massachusetts. LC 87-45791. (Immigrant Communities & Ethnic Minorities in the U. S. & Canada Ser.: No. 26). 1988. 37.50 (*0-404-19436-2*) AMS Pr.

Nagi, R. ASEAN: The Association of South-East Asian Nations 20 Years. (C). 1988. 28.50 (*81-7095-008-2*, Pub. by Lancers Books II) S Asia.

— Big Powers & South-East Asian Security. xiv, 220p. 1986. 12.50 (*0-685-67632-3*, Pub. by Lancers Books II) Nataraj Bks.

Nagi, Saad Z. Child Maltreatment in the United States: A Challenge to Social Institutions. LC 77-22121. 1977. text ed. 36.50 (*0-231-04394-5*) Col U Pr.

Nagiev, M. & Hardbottle, R. Theory of Recycle Processes in Chemical Engineering. LC 63-16865. (International Series of Monographs on Chemistry: Vol. 3). 1964. 120.00 (*0-08-010154-2*, Pub. by Pergamon Repr UK) Franklin.

***Nagin, Paul & Impagliazzo, John.** Computer Science: A Breadth-First Approach with Pascal. 1995. pap. text ed. write for info. (*0-471-31198-7*) Wiley.

Nagin, Paul, jt. auth. see Impagliazzo, John.

Naginski, Isabelle. George Sand: Writing for Her Life. 280p. (C). 1994. reprint ed. pap. text ed. 17.00 (*0-8135-1674-9*) Rutgers U Pr.

Naginski, Isabelle H. George Sand: Writing for Her Life. LC 90-42140. 280p. (C). 1991. text ed. 40.00 (*0-8135-1640-4*) Rutgers U Pr.

Nagl, A., et al. Nuclear Pion Photoproduction. (Tracts in Modern Physics Ser.: Vol. 120). viii, 174p. 1991. 98.00 (*0-387-50671-3*) Spr-Verlag.

Nagl, M., ed. Graph-Theoretic Concepts in Computer Science. (Lecture Notes in Computer Science Ser.: Vol. 411). vii, 374p. 1990. pap. 38.60 (*0-387-52292-1*) Spr-Verlag.

Nagla, B. K. Development & Transformation: Themes & Variations in Indian Society. (C). 1993. 36.00 (*81-7033-189-7*, Pub. by Rawat II) S Asia.

— Women Crime & Law. (C). 1991. 14.00 (*0-685-66147-4*, Pub. by Rawat II) S Asia.

Nagle & Staff. Differential Equations. rev. ed. Moller, Lisa, ed. 750p. (C). 1993. teacher ed 8.95 (*0-8053-5057-8*) Addison-Wesley.

— Differential Equations. 3rd rev. ed. Moller, Lisa, ed. 750p. (C). 1993. text ed. 62.50 (*0-8053-5056-X*) Addison-Wesley.

***Nagle, Ami.** Dollars & Sense: A Guide to Spending on Children & Families in Illinois. (C). 1995. pap. 15.00 (*1-886008-01-9*) Voices IL Chdrn.

***Nagle, Ami, et al.** Illinois Kids Count, 1994: Raising the Grade. (Orig.). 1994. pap. 15.00 (*1-886008-00-0*) Voices IL Chdrn.

Nagle, Barbara A., ed. see Gurdak, John A.

Nagle, Barbara T., jt. auth. see Hitner, Henry.

Nagle, Betty R., tr. see Ovid.

Nagle, D. B. & Burstein, Stanley M., eds. The Ancient World: Readings in Social & Cultural History. LC 94-18200. 323p. 1994. pap. text ed. write for info. (*0-13-756222-5*) P-H.

Nagle, D. Brendan. The Ancient World. 2nd ed. 464p. (C). 1989. pap. text ed. write for info. (*0-13-036419-3*) P-H.

— The Ancient World: A Social & Cultural History. 3rd ed. LC 95-6482. 1995. pap. text ed. write for info. (*0-13-310806-6*) P-H.

Nagle, Elizabeth N. Legacy of Grace. LC 85-96921. 1986. 10.00 (*0-87212-191-7*) Libra.

Nagle, Evelyn M. Winning with Astrology. 18p. 1988. 3.00 (*0-86690-358-5*, N2834-014) Am Fed Astrologers.

Nagle, Geraldine. The Arts: World Themes. 368p. (C). 1993. pap. text ed. write for info. (*0-697-12048-1*) Brown & Benchmark.

Nagle, H. Troy, Jr., jt. auth. see Phillips, Charles L.

Nagle, Jack. Power Pattern Offenses for Winning Basketball. LC 85-32072. 185p. 1986. 19.95 (*0-13-687708-7*, Parker Publishing Co) P-H.

Nagle, James F. Federal Construction Contracting. (Construction Law Library: No. 1815). 608p. 1992. text ed. 138.00 (*0-471-52871-4*) Wiley.

— A History of Government Contracting. 400p. 1992. pap. 35.00 (*0-935165-21-5*) GWU Gov Contracts.

Nagle, John. Art Metalwork. LC 78-730845. 1977. student ed 9.00 (*0-8064-0233-4*, 508); audio 279.00 (*0-8064-0234-2*) Bergwall.

— Basic Offset Press. 1977. student ed 9.00 (*0-8064-0047-1*, 305); audio 139.00 (*0-8064-0048-X*) Bergwall.

— Sheet Metalwork. LC 79-730773. 1977. student ed 9.00 (*0-8064-0231-8*, 507); audio 359.00 (*0-8064-0232-6*) Bergwall.

— Woodworking Hand Tools Explained. LC 78-730852. 1979. student ed 6.00 (*0-8064-0263-6*, 703); audio 289.00 (*0-8064-0264-4*) Bergwall.

Nagle, John D. Introduction to Comparative Politics: Challenges of Conflict & Change in a New Era. 4th ed. 400p. 1995. pap. text ed. 24.95 (*0-8304-1408-8*) Nelson-Hall.

— The National Democratic Party: Right Radicalism in the Federal Republic of Germany. LC 78-101340. 231p. reprint ed. pap. 65.90 (*0-318-34922-1*, 2031443) Bks Demand.

Nagle, Judy. Instructor's Manual to The Responsive Arts. (C). 1982. teacher ed, pap. write for info. (*0-87484-101-1*) Mayfield Pub.

— The Responsive Arts. LC 79-24450. 428p. (C). 1982. pap. text ed. 40.95 (*0-87484-627-7*) Mayfield Pub.

Nagle, Kent R. & Saff, Edward B. Fundamentals of Differential Equations. 2nd ed. (Illus.). 820p. (C). 1989. teacher ed 10.75 (*0-8053-0255-7*); text ed. 60.25 (*0-8053-0254-9*); pap. text ed. 10.75 (*0-8053-0256-5*) Addison-Wesley.

Nagle, Mary D., jt. ed. see Harpole, Patricia C.

Nagle, P. Michael. Guide to Annual Meeting, Special Meetings, & Elections. (GAP Report Ser.: Vol. 21). (C). 1992. pap. 14.50 (*0-944715-22-2*) CAI.

***Nagle, R. Kent & Saff, Edward B.** Fundamentals of Differential Equations. 4th ed. LC 95-9799. (C). 1996. text ed. write for info. (*0-201-80875-7*) Addison-Wesley.

— Fundamentals of Differential Equations & Boundary Value Problems. 2nd ed. LC 95-10162. (C). 1996. text ed. write for info. (*0-201-80879-X*) Addison-Wesley.

— Fundamentals of Differential Equations with Boundary Value Problems. (Illus.). 864p. (C). 1992. write for info. (*0-318-69246-5*) Addison-Wesley.

Nagle, S. D., jt. auth. see Colclaser, R. A.

Nagle, Thomas T. Strategy & Tactics of Pricing: A Guide to Profitable Decision Making. 2nd ed. (C). 1994. pap. text ed. 29.95 (*0-13-669060-2*) P-H.

Nagle, Tim, et al. Conceptual Structures: Current Research & Practice. LC 92-18180. (Ellis Horwood Workshop Ser.). 500p. 1992. 63.00 (*0-13-175878-0*, Tavistock-E Horwood) Routledge Chapman & Hall.

Nagle, Timothy E. & Pfeiffer, Heather D., eds. Conceptual Structures - Theory & Implementation: Proceedings of the Seventh Annual Workshop, Las Cruces, New Mexico, U. S. A., July 1992. LC 93-39736. (Lecture Notes in Computer Science, Lecture Notes in Artificial Intelligence Ser.: Vol. 754). 1993. 50.00 (*0-387-57454-9*) Spr-Verlag.

Nagle, Troy, jt. auth. see Phillips, Charles L.

Naglee, David. Sons of Eli. (Illus.). 400p. 1993. pap. 14.95 (*0-938991-82-5*) Colonial Pr AL.

Naglee, David I. From Everlasting to Everlasting: John Wesley on Eternity & Time, 2 vols., 1. LC 90-47316. (American University Studies: Theology & Religion: Ser. VII, Vols. 65 & 66). 651p. (C). 1991. text ed. 103.80 (*0-8204-1113-2*) P Lang Pubs.

Nagler, A. M. Theatre Festivals of the Medici, 1539-1637. LC 76-8447. (Music Reprint Ser.). 190p. 1976. reprint ed. lib. bdg. 32.50 (*0-306-70779-9*) Da Capo.

Nagler, Alois M. The Medieval Religious Stage: Shapes & Phantoms. Schoolfield, George C., tr. LC 75-43328. (Illus.). 120p. reprint ed. pap. 34.20 (*0-8357-8220-4*, 2033840) Bks Demand.

— Source Book in Theatrical History. Orig. Title: Sources of Theatrical History. (Illus.). 1952. pap. 9.95 (*0-486-20515-0*) Dover.

Nagler, Barney, jt. auth. see Brenner, Teddy.

Nagler, Ellen. Integrating Windows Applications. (Illus.). 590p. (Orig.). 1992. disk 34.95 (*1-56205-083-4*) New Riders Pub.

Nagler, Eric P. Learning C: A Hands-on Approach. Mixter, ed. LC 93-16017. 650p. (C). 1994. pap. text ed. 37.25 (*0-314-02464-6*) West Pub.

Nagler, Harris M., jt. auth. see Thomas, Anthony J., Jr.

Nagler, Harris M., jt. ed. see Whitehead, E. Douglas.

Nagler, Jorg, jt. ed. see Hoerder, Dirk.

Nagler, Mark, ed. Perspectives on Disability: Text & Readings on Disability. 2nd ed. 460p. (C). 1993. text ed. 45.00 (*0-9627640-3-5*) Hlth Mrkts Res.

***Nagler, Michael & Swanson, William, eds.** Stolen Moments: Stories of Men, Women & Desire. 340p. (Orig.). (C). Date not set. pap. 14.50 (*0-88739-112-5*) Creat Arts Bk.

Nagler, Monte. How to Improve Your Photographic Vision. Farrar, Bev, ed. 1988. pap. 14.95 (*0-9620829-1-0*) Suburb Comns.

— How to Improve Your Photographic Vision. limited ed. Farrar, Bev, ed. 1988. 250.00 (*0-9620829-0-2*) Suburb Comns.

***Nagler, Richard.** Oakland Rhapsody: The Secret Soul of an American Downtown. (Illus.). 112p. (Orig.). (C). 1995. 35.00 (*1-55643-197-X*); pap. 22.95 (*1-55643-196-1*) North Atlantic.

Nagler, William & Androff, Anne. Dirty Half Dozen: Six Radical Rules to Make Relationships Last. 1991. 14.95 (*0-446-51604-X*) Warner Bks.

— The Dirty Half Dozen: Six Radical Rules to Make Relationships Last. 1992. reprint ed. mass mkt. 6.99 (*0-446-39408-4*) Warner Bks.

An Asterisk (*) at the beginning of an entry indicates that the title is appearing in BIP for the first time.

Nagodawithana, Tilak & Reed, Gerlad, eds. Enzymes in Food Processing. 3rd ed. (Food Science & Technology Ser.). (Illus.). 480p. 1993. text ed. 110.00 (0-12-513630-7) Acad Pr.

***Nagodawithana, Tilak W.** Savory Flavors. (Illus.). 480p. (C). 1995. write for info. (0-9646172-3-4) Esteekay Assocs.

Nagorny, N. M., jt. auth. see Markov, A. A.

***Nagorsen, D. W. & Brigham, R. Mark.** Bats of British Columbia. LC 94-153386. (Mammals of British Columbia Ser.: Vol. 1). 164p. 1994. pap. 15.95 (0-7748-0482-3) U BC Pr.

Nagorski, Andrew. The Birth of Freedom: Shaping Lives & Societies in the New Eastern Europe. LC 93-1750. 336p. 1993. 23.00 (0-671-78225-8) S&S Trade.

Nagorski, R. T., jt. auth. see Mazurkiewicz, Z. E.

***Nagpal, B. N. & Sharma, V. P.** Indian Anophelines. 440p. 1995. text ed. 88.00 (1-886106-09-6) Science Pubs.

Nagpal, R. & Sell, H. Subjective Well-Being. (SEARO Regional Health Papers: No. 7). 161p. 1985. pap. 3.60 (92-9022-176-3) World Health.

Nagpal, R. C. Modern Hindu Law. 815p. (HIN.). 1984. 225. 00 (0-317-54701-1) St Mut.

Nagpall, J. C. Mural Paintings in India. 1988. 64.00 (81-212-0149-7, Pub. by Gian Publng Hse II) S Asia.

Nagrin, Daniel. Dance & the Specific Image: Improvisation. (Illus.). 256p. (C). 1993. text ed. 49.95 (0-8229-3776-X); pap. text ed. 19.95 (0-8229-5520-2) U of Pittsburgh Pr.

— How to Dance Forever: Surviving Against the Odds. Williams, Jennifer, ed. LC 88-1421. (Illus.). 320p. (Orig.). 1988. pap. 14.95 (0-688-07479-0, Quill) Morrow.

Naguib, Mohammed. Egypt's Destiny: A Personal Statement by Mohammed Naguib. LC 84-1516. 256p. 1984. reprint ed. text ed. 59.75 (0-313-24433-2, NAED/, Greenwood Pr) Greenwood.

Nagumo, Mitio. Collected Papers. Yamaguti, Masaya et al, eds. LC 93-9561. (ENG, FRE & GER.). 1993. 132.00 (0-387-70112-5) Spr-Verlag.

Nagurney, Anna. Network Economics: A Variational Inequality Approach. LC 92-36524. (Advances in Computational Economics Ser.). 384p. (C). 1992. lib. bdg. 103.00 (0-7923-9293-0) Kluwer Ac.

NAGWS Staff. NAGWS Volleyball Guide, 1991. 240p. 1991. pap. text ed. 5.95 (0-8403-6666-3) Kendall-Hunt.

Nagy & Verakis. Development & Control of Dust Explosions. (Occupational Safety & Health Ser.: Vol. 8). 296p. 1983. 110.00 (0-8247-7004-8) Dekker.

Nagy, et al. Adulteration of Fruit Juice Beverages. (Food Science & Technology Ser.: Vol. 30). 568p. 1988. 189.00 (0-8247-7912-6) Dekker.

Nagy, Alexander G., jt. ed. see Cuesta, Miguel A.

Nagy, Andrea. Princeton Review Student Access Guide to the Best Medical Schools: Everything You Need to Know About the 126 Best Medical Schools. 1994. pap. 20.00 (0-679-75347-8, Villard Bks) Random.

***Nagy, Andrea & Princeton Review Staff.** The Princeton Review Student Access Guide to the Best Medical Schools '96. 1995. pap. 20.00 (0-679-76149-7, Villard Bks) Random.

Nagy, B. S. & Foias, Ciprian. Harmonic Analysis of Operators on Hilbert Space. LC 78-97933. 390p. 1971. 51.00 (0-7204-2035-0, North Holland) Elsevier.

Nagy, B. S. & Szabado, S. J. Functions, Series, Operators, 2 vols., Set. (Colloquia Mathematica Societatis Janos Bolyai Ser.: Vol. 35). 1984. 195.00 (0-444-86508-X, I-107-84) Elsevier.

***Nagy, Caroline S.** Introduction to Dialogue, for Flute & Keyboard (Harpsichord) (Contemporary Instrumental Ser.: No. 9). 8p. 1995. 10.00 (1-56571-123-8) PRB Prods.

Nagy, D. Radiological Anatomy. 1965. 219.00 (0-08-010675-7, Pub. by Pergamon Repr UK) Franklin.

Nagy, E. English-Hungarian Technical Dictionary. 5th ed. 791p. (ENG & HUN.). 1980. 65.00 (0-8288-0674-8, M 8433) Fr & Eur.

— English-Hungarian Technical Dictionary. 7th ed. 789p. 1990. 63.00 (963-05-5709-6) IBD Ltd.

— English-Hungarian Technical Dictionary. 7th ed. (ENG & HUN.). 1990. 63.00 (0-7859-8957-9) Fr & Eur.

— Hungarian English Technical Dictionary. 752p. (ENG & HUN.). 1993. 85.00 (0-7859-7153-X) Fr & Eur.

— Hungarian-English Technical Dictionary. 6th ed. 752p. 1990. 63.00 (963-05-5708-8) IBD Ltd.

— Hungarian-English Technical Dictionary. 6th ed. (ENG & HUN.). 1990. 63.00 (0-7859-8963-3) Fr & Eur.

***Nagy, E. & Klaar, J.** German-Hungarian Technical Dictionary. 1392p. 1992. 120.00x (963-05-5981-1, Pub. by Akad Kiado HU) St Mut.

***Nagy, E. & Klar, J.** Hungarian-German Technical Dictionary. 1300p. 1992. 120.00x (963-05-5982-X, Pub. by Akad Kiado HU) St Mut.

Nagy, E. & Klar, J., eds. English-Hungarian Technical Dictionary. 792p. (ENG & HUN.). 1980. 70.00 (0-686-72096-2, Pub. by Collets UK) St Mut.

Nagy, F. & Klar, J. Hungarian-German Technical Dictionary. 4th ed. 1300p. (GER & HUN.). 1987. 125. 00 (0-8288-2147-X, M8438) Fr & Eur.

Nagy, Gabor O. Abriss Einer Funktionellen Semantik. (Janua Linguarum, Series Minor: No. 137). 1973. 61.55 (90-279-2519-4) Mouton.

***Nagy, Gloria.** Marriage: A Novel. LC 94-43191. 448p. 1995. 22.95 (0-316-59675-2) Little.

Nagy, Gregory. The Best of the Achaeans: Concepts of the Hero in Archaic Greek Poetry. LC 79-9907. 416p. 1981. pap. 15.95 (0-8018-2388-9) Johns Hopkins.

— Comparative Studies in Greek & Indic Meter. LC 73-90339. (Studies in Comparative Literature: No. 33). 360p. 1974. 34.00 (0-674-15275-1) HUP.

— Greek Dialects & the Transformation of an Indo-European Process. LC 69-12730. (Loeb Classical Monographs). 214p. reprint ed. 61.00 (0-8357-9160-2, 2016732) Bks Demand.

— Greek Mythology & Poetics. LC 89-17447. (Myth & Poetics Ser.). 384p. 1990. 41.50 (0-8014-1985-9) Cornell U Pr.

— Greek Mythology & Poetics. LC 89-17447. (Myth & Poetics Ser.). 384p. 1992. pap. 15.95 (0-8014-8048-5) Cornell U Pr.

— Pindar's Homer: Lyric Possession of an Epic Past. LC 89-19938. 552p. 1990. text ed. 50.00x (0-8018-3932-7) Johns Hopkins.

— Pindar's Homer: The Lyric Possession of an Epic Past. (Softshell Bks.). 552p. (C). 1994. reprint ed. pap. text ed. 19.95 (0-8018-4847-4) Johns Hopkins.

Nagy, Gregory, jt. ed. see Figueira, Thomas J.

Nagy, Gregory, jt. auth. see Householder, Fred W.

Nagy, I. & Kertai, A. Technical Dictionary of Water Management. 516p. (C). 1988. 100.00 (0-569-09157-8, Pub. by Collets) St Mut.

Nagy, Imre & Kiraly, Bela, eds. A Magyar Nep Vedelmeben: Vitairatok es beszedek, 1955-1956. xix, 265p. (Orig.). 1984. pap. 10.00 (0-930888-27-8, Pub. by Dialogues Europeennes FR) Puski-Corvin.

Nagy, Janet R., ed. Good Health Guides Library, 7 vols., Set. (Illus.). 1990. lib. bdg. 355.00 (0-931013-79-8) Moonbeam Pubns.

— Healing & Herbs Library. (Good Health Guides Library: Vol. 6). (Illus.). 1990. lib. bdg. 50.00 (0-931013-85-2) Moonbeam Pubns.

— Healthy Foods & Recipes Library. (Good Health Guides Library: Vol. 4). (Illus.). 1990. lib. bdg. 50.00 (0-931013-83-6) Moonbeam Pubns.

— Nutrients Library. (Good Health Guides Library: Vol. 3). (Illus.). 1990. lib. bdg. 50.00 (0-931013-82-8) Moonbeam Pubns.

— Nutrition Library. (Good Health Guides Library: Vol. 7). (Illus.). 1990. lib. bdg. 50.00 (0-931013-86-0) Moonbeam Pubns.

— Prevention Guides Library, Pt. 1. (Good Health Guides Library: Vol. 1). (Illus.). 1990. lib. bdg. 55.00 (0-931013-80-1) Moonbeam Pubns.

— Prevention Guides Library, Pt. 2. (Good Health Guides Library: Vol. 2). (Illus.). 1990. lib. bdg. 50.00 (0-931013-81-X) Moonbeam Pubns.

— Vitamins & Minerals Library. (Good Health Guides Library: Vol. 5). (Illus.). 1990. lib. bdg. 50.00 (0-931013-84-4) Moonbeam Pubns.

Nagy, Jean. Brown Bagging It: A Guide to Fresh Food Cooking in the Wilderness. (Illus.). 1976. pap. 2.50 (0-917296-00-1) Marty-Nagy.

Nagy, Jill, ed. see Lee, Harry O., et al.

Nagy, Jill, ed. see Lee, Harry O. & LaForester, Wilford A.

Nagy, Jill, jt. auth. see Lee, Harry O.

***Nagy, K. R. & Blum, A. E., eds.** Scanning Probe Microscopy of Clay Minerals. (CMS Workshop Lectures: Vol. 7). (Illus.). 256p. (Orig.). (C). 1994. pap. text ed. 18.00 (1-881208-08-7) Clay Minerals.

Nagy, Karoly, ed. see Bibo, Istvan.

***Nagy, Kenneth A. & Peterson, Charles C.** Scaling of Water Flux Rate in Animals. LC 88-10791. (University of California Publications in Zoology: No. 120). 186p. 1988. pap. 53.10 (0-7837-7496-6, 2049218) Bks Demand.

Nagy, L. The Socialist Collective Agreement. 257p. (C). 1984. 54.00x (963-05-3368-5, Pub. by Akad Kiado HU) St Mut.

Nagy, Laszlo, jt. auth. see Molnar, Miklos.

Nagy, Laszlo, jt. auth. see Molnar, Niklos.

Nagy, Marilyn. Philosophical Issues in the Psychology of C. G. Jung. LC 89-26319. 252p. (C). 1991. 64.50 (0-7914-0451-X); pap. 21.95 (0-7914-0452-8) State U NY Pr.

Nagy, Moses M. Christopher Columbus in World Literature: An Annotated Bibliography. LC 93-24541. (Reference Library of the Humanities: Vol. 1629). (Illus.). 378p. 1994. 57.00 (0-8153-0927-9, H1629) Garland.

— A Journey into History: Essays on Hungarian Literature. LC 89-27320. (American University Studies: General Literature: Ser. IXX, Vol. 25). 240p. 1990. text ed. 44.50 (0-8204-1201-5) P Lang Pubs.

***Nagy, P.** English-Hungarian Banking & Finance Directory. (ENG & HUN.). 1993. 150.00 (0-7859-8883-1) Fr & Eur.

Nagy, P. & Tarjan, G. Elsevier's Dictionary of Information Processing. (ENG, FRE, GER, ITA, JPN & SPA.). 1993. write for info. (0-8288-9241-5) Fr & Eur.

— Elsevier's Dictionary of Microelectronics in English, German, French, Spanish & Japanese. 944p. (ENG, FRE, GER, JPN & SPA.). 1988. 350.00 (0-8288-0314-5, M1655) Fr & Eur.

Nagy, P. & Tarjan, G., eds. Elsevier's Dictionary of Microelectronics: In English, German, French, Spanish, & Japanese. 944p. 1988. 192.50 (0-444-42659-0) Elsevier.

***Nagy, P. & Trutz, S.** English-Hungarian Banking & Finance Dictionary. 900p. 1993. 90.00x (963-05-6593-5, Pub. by Akad Kiado HU) St Mut.

Nagy, Paul. Sadisfactions. 1977. pap. 5.00 (0-918406-08-0) Future Pr.

***Nagy, Phyllis.** Trip's Cinch. 1995. 3.00 (0-87129-512-1, T39) Dramatic Pub.

Nagy, Silvia. Historia de la Cancion Folklorica en los Andes. (American University Studies: Romance Languages & Literature: Ser. II, Vol. 73). 210p. (C). 1989. text ed. 32.95 (0-8204-0597-3) P Lang Pubs.

Nagy, Steven & Attaway, John, eds. Citrus Nutrition & Quality. LC 80-22562. (ACS Symposium Ser.: No. 143). 1980. 54.95 (0-8412-0595-7) Am Chemical.

Nagy, Steven & Attaway, John A., eds. Citrus Nutrition & Quality: Based on a Symposium Sponsored by the Division of Agricultural & Food Chemistry at the 179th Meeting of the American Chemical Society, Houston, TX, March 26, 1980. LC 80-22562. (ACS Symposium Ser.: No. 143). 464p. reprint ed. pap. 132.30 (0-8357-2530-8, 2052409) Bks Demand.

***Nagy, Steven & Wade, Robert L., eds.** Methods to Detect Adulteration of Fruit Juice Beverages, 1 of 3 vols., Vol. 1. LC 94-40210. (Illus.). 452p. (C). 1995. text ed. 78.00x (0-9631397-3-8) AgScience.

Nagy, Steven, et al, eds. Fruit Juice Processing Technology. LC 92-38443. (Illus.). 724p. (C). 1993. text ed. 109.00 (0-9631397-1-1) AgScience.

— Fruits of Tropical & Subtropical Origin: Composition, Properties, Uses. LC 89-92429. (Illus.). 391p. (C). 1990. text ed. 70.00 (0-944961-00-2) FL Sci Source.

Nagy, T. Hungarian-English Technical Dictionary. 752p. (ENG & HUN.). 1980. 99.00 (0-569-00731-3, Pub. by Collets UK) Pro-Am Music.

Nagy, William E. Teaching Vocabulary to Improve Reading Comprehension. 52p. 1988. pap. 6.25 (0-87207-151-0) Intl Reading.

Nagy, Z. Iron & Steel Production: Technical Dictionary of. 686p. (C). 1987. 125.00 (0-89771-921-2, Pub. by Collets) St Mut.

Nagy, Zoltan, ed. Electrochemical Synthesis of Inorganic Compounds: A Bibliography. LC 85-3642. 488p. 1985. 110.00 (0-306-41938-6, Plenum Pr) Plenum.

Nagylaki, T. Introduction to Theoretical Population Genetics. Levin, S. A., ed. (Biomathematics Ser.: Vol. 21). (Illus.). 384p. 1992. 59.00 (0-387-53344-3) Spr-Verlag.

— Selection in One-&-Two-Locus Systems. (Lecture Notes in Biomathematics Ser.: Vol. 15). 1977. 27.00 (0-387-08247-6) Spr-Verlag.

Nagyszalanczy, Sandor. Woodshop, Jigs & Fixtures. Albert, Helen, ed. (Illus.). (Orig.). 1994. pap. write for info. (1-56158-073-2) Taunton.

Nahai, Foad, jt. auth. see Mathes, Stephen J.

Nahal, Chaman. Azadi. 364p. 1979. reprint ed. pap. 4.00 (0-86578-111-7) Ind-US Inc.

— The Bhagavad-Gita. 64p. (C). 1989. 60.00 (81-209-0733-7, Pub. by Pitambar Pub II); pap. 20.00 (81-209-0032-4, Pub. by Pitambar Pub II) St Mut.

— The Bhagavad-Gita. 1990. 60.00 (81-209-0753-1, Pub. by Pitambar Pub II) St Mut.

— The Narrative Pattern in Ernest Hemingway's Fiction. 245p. 1975. 27.50 (0-8386-7795-9) Fairleigh Dickinson.

— The New Literatures in English. 225p. 1986. 24.00 (81-7023-056-X, Pub. by Allied II) S Asia.

— Sunrise in Fiji. (C). 1988. 21.00 (0-8364-2367-4, Pub. by Allied II) S Asia.

Nahale-a, Kihei, tr. see Kelly, Susan & Kelly, Thomas.

Nahar, Chand. Jainism: Precepts & Practice, 2 vols., Set. (C). 1988. 105.00 (81-85066-18-3) S Asia.

Nahar, Sujata. Mirra. (Mother's Chronicles Ser.: Bk. 1). 162p. 12.00 (0-685-65588-1) Aurobindo Assn.

— Mirra the Artist. (Mother's Chronicles Ser.: Bk. 2). 182p. 12.00 (2-902776-20-9) Aurobindo Assn.

— Mirra the Occultist. (Mother's Chronicles Ser.: Bk. 3). 319p. 12.00 (2-902776-21-7) Aurobindo Assn.

Nahar, Umed R., jt. auth. see Lal, Sheo K.

Nahas. Handbook of Toxicology of Controlled Substances. 1995. write for info. (0-8493-7939-3) CRC Pr.

— Houston. 1980. 19.95 (0-02-620900-4) Macmillan.

Nahas, Dominique & Perreault, John. Public Mind: Les Levine's Media Sculpture & Mass Ad Campaigns. Piche, Thomas, ed. LC 90-84035. (Illus.). 128p. (Orig.). 1990. text ed. write for info. (0-914407-14-7) Everson Mus.

Nahas, Gabriel G. Cannabis: Physiopathology, Epidemiology, Detection, Proceedings of the Second International Symposium, Paris, April 8-9, 1992. Latour, Colette, ed. 1992. 99.95 (0-8493-8310-2, QP801) CRC Pr.

— Cocaine: The Great White Plague. 320p. 1989. 19.95 (0-8397-1700-8) Eriksson.

— Keep off the Grass. 5th rev. ed. LC 90-3658. (Illus.). 400p. 1990. reprint ed. pap. 12.95 (0-8397-4384-X) Eriksson.

— A Manual on Drug Dependence. (Illus.). 268p. (Orig.). 1992. pap. 12.95 (0-929240-46-4) Essential Med Info Syst Inc.

Nahas, Gabriel G., ed. see International Congress of Pharmacology Staff.

Nahas, Gabriel G., et al. Marihuana in Science & Medicine. 324p. 1984. text ed. 95.50 (0-88167-014-6) Raven.

Nahas, M. Y. El, jt. auth. see Pau, Louis F.

Nahata, Milap C. & Hipple, Thomas F. Pediatric Drug Formulations. LC 89-52176. xv, 82p. (Orig.). 1990. pap. text ed. 17.50 (0-929375-00-9) H W Bks.

Nahata, Milap C., jt. auth. see Bates, Richard D.

Nahavandi, Afsaneh & Malekzadeh, Ali R. Organizational Culture in the Management of Mergers. LC 92-44685. 200p. 1993. text ed. 52.95 (0-89930-669-1, NAU, Quorum Bks) Greenwood.

Nahaylo, Dohdan. Soviet Disunion: A History of the Nationalities Problem in the USSR. 448p. 1990. text ed. 32.95 (0-02-922401-2) Macmillan.

NAHB Research Center. A Comprehensive Approach to Retrofitting Homes for a Lifetime. 82p. 1991. pap. 10.00 (0-685-69259-0) Home Builder.

NAHB Research Center Staff. Building with Alternatives to Lumber & Plywood. LC 93-41672. 72p. (Orig.). 1994. pap. 16.00 (0-86718-392-6) Home Builder.

— Residential Concrete. 2nd rev. ed. LC 93-36745. (Illus.). 96p. 1994. pap. 20.00 (0-86718-389-6) Home Builder.

NAHB Research Foundation Staff. Off Center Spliced Floor Joists, Vol. 4. (Research Report Ser.). 58p. 1982. pap. 9.00 (0-86718-143-5) Home Builder.

— Performance of Nominal Five-Eighths Inch Plywood Over Joists Spaced 24 Inches on Center, Vol. 1. (Research Report Ser.). 11p. 1981. pap. 5.50 (0-86718-114-1) Home Builder.

— Plywood Headers for Residential Construction, Vol. 5. (Research Report Ser.). 48p. 1983. pap. 8.00 (0-86718-200-8) Home Builder.

— Stress & Deflection Reduction in 2x4 Studs Spaced 24 Inches on Center Resulting from the Addition of Interior & Exterior Surfaces, Vol. 3. (Research Report Ser.). 46p. 1981. pap. 6.50 (0-86718-117-6) Home Builder.

Nahem, Joseph. Psychology & Psychiatry Today: A Marxist View. LC 81-680. 264p. reprint ed. pap. 75.30 (0-7837-0580-8, 2040924) Bks Demand.

Nahemov, Licille, ed. Humor & Aging. 1986. pap. text ed. 51.00 (0-12-513791-5) Acad Pr.

Nahfouz, Naguib. Maramar. (ARA.). 1980. 8.95 (0-86685-159-3) Intl Bk Ctr.

Nahikian, Howard M. Modern Algebra for Biologists. LC 64-13948. 248p. reprint ed. 70.70 (0-8357-9650-7, 2015760) Bks Demand.

Nahin, Paul J. Oliver Heaviside: Sage in Solitude. LC 87-26044. 344p. 1988. 39.95 (0-87942-238-6, PCO2279) Inst Electrical.

— Time Machines: Time Travel in Physics, Metaphysics, & Science Fiction. LC 92-75255. 1993. 40.00 (0-88318-935-6) Am Inst Physics.

— Time Machines: Time Travel in Physics, Metaphysics, & Science Fiction. LC 92-75255. (Illus.). 408p. 1994. pap. 15.95 (1-56396-371-X) Am Inst Physics.

Nahirny, Vladimir. The Russian Intelligentsia: From Torment to Silence. LC 82-4796. 192p. 1982. 32.95 (0-87855-463-7) Transaction Pubs.

Nahkosteen, J. A., jt. ed. see Allegra, G.

Nahle, Gerhard. Dictionary of Pharmaceutical Medicine. LC 94-11648. 1994. 25.00 (0-387-82557-6) Spr-Verlag.

Nahm, Andrew C. Historical Dictionary of the Republic of Korea. LC 93-3033. (Asian Historical Dictionaries Ser.: No. 11). (Illus.). 336p. 1993. 39.50 (0-8108-2603-8) Scarecrow.

— Introduction to Korean History & Culture. (Illus.). 352p. (C). 1993. 24.50 (0-930878-08-6) Hollym Intl.

— Korea: Tradition & Transformation; A History of the Korean People. LC 86-81681. 583p. 1988. 44.50 (0-930878-56-6) Hollym Intl.

— A Panorama of Five Thousand Years: Korean History. 2nd rev. ed. LC 81-84202. (Illus.). 123p. 1989. reprint ed. 24.50 (0-930878-23-X) Hollym Intl.

Nahm, Andrew C., et al, eds. I Love Korea! (Illus.). 86p. (YA). 1992. 22.50 (0-930878-87-6) Hollym Intl.

Nahm, M. C., jt. auth. see Clarke, F. P.

Nahm, W. Conformally Invariant Quantum Field Theories in Two Dimensions. (Advanced Series in Mathematical Physics: Vol. 6). 250p. 1995. text ed. 61.00 (9971-5-0649-1); pap. text ed. 40.00 (9971-5-0650-5) World Scientific Pub.

Nahm, W., et al. Topological Methods in Quantum Field Theories. 184p. 1991. text ed. 68.00 (981-02-0496-5); pap. 28.00 (981-02-0497-3) World Scientific Pub.

Nahmad, Claire. Catspells: A Collection of Enchantments for You & Your Feline Companion. LC 93-83533. (Illus.). 96p. 1993. 12.95 (1-56138-292-2) Running Pr.

— Dreamspells: Victorian Spells to Reveal the Magical Wisdom of Dreams. 1994. 12.95 (1-56138-410-0) Running Pr.

— Earth Magic: A Wisewoman's Guide to Herbal, Astrological, & Other Folk Wisdom. (Illus.). 224p. (Orig.). 1993. pap. 12.95 (0-89281-424-1) Inner Tradit.

— Gardenspells. LC 93-85513. (Illus.). 96p. 1994. 12.95 (1-56138-191-8) Running Pr.

— Lovespells. LC 92-50794. (Illus.). 96p. 1993. 12.95 (1-56138-243-4) Running Pr.

Nahmad, H. M., jt. auth. see Haywood, J. A.

Nahmanides. The Holy Letter: A Study in Jewish Sexual Morality. Cohen, Seymour J., tr. & intro. by. LC 93-22582. 192p. 1994. 25.00 (1-56821-086-8) Aronson.

Nahmias, Andre J. & O'Reilly, Richard, eds. Immunology of Human Infection. Incl. Pt. 1, Bacteria, Mycoplasmae, Chlamydiae, & Fungi. LC 79-9162. 678p. 1981. 120.00 (0-306-40257-2); Pt. 2, Viruses & Parasites; Immunodiagnosis & Prevention of Infectious Disease. LC 79-9162. 632p. 1982. 120.00 (0-306-40258-0); LC 79-9162. (Comprehensive Immunology Ser.: Vols. 8 & 9). write for info. (0-318-55323-6, Plenum Med Bk) Plenum.

Nahmias, Steven. Production & Operations Analysis. 2nd ed. LC 92-23790. 800p. (C). 1992. text ed. 68.95 (0-256-10664-9) Irwin.

Nahmlos, John. Survivors. (Orig.). 1982. pap. 3.25 (0-8217-1071-0) Zebra.

Nahmod, Sheldon, ed. A Section Nineteen Eighty-Three Civil Rights Anthology. LC 93-19309. 1993. write for info. (0-87084-135-1) Anderson Pub Co.

Nahmod, Sheldon H. Civil Rights & Civil Liberties Litigation: The Law of Section 1983. 2nd ed. LC 86-26080. (Individual Rights Ser.). 1050p. 1991. text ed. 170.00 (0-07-172311-0) Shepards-McGraw.

***Nahmod, Sheldon H., et al.** Constitutional Torts Casebook. LC 94-43425. 1995. text ed. write for info. (0-87084-903-4) Anderson Pub Co.

Nahon, Daniel. Introduction to the Petrology of Soils & Chemical Weathering. (Basic Topics in Geology Ser.). 313p. 1991. text ed. 84.95 (0-471-50861-6) Wiley.

Nahon, Gerard, ed. see Ben-Israel, Menasseh.

Nahon, Marco. Birkenau, The Camp of Death. Bowman, Steven, ed. Bowers, Jacqueline H., tr. LC 89-4661. (Judaic Studies). (Illus.). 176p. 1989. 24.95 (0-8173-0449-5) U of Ala Pr.

Nahorski, S. R., ed. Transmembrane Signalling, Intracellular Messengers & Implications for Drug Development. 248p. 1990. text ed. 137.95 (0-471-92432-6) Wiley.

Nahorski, Z., et al. Optimization of Discrete Time Systems: The Upper Boundary Approach. (Lecture Notes in Control & Information Sciences Ser.: Vol. 51). 137p. 1983. pap. 17.00 (0-387-12258-3) Spr-Verlag.

Nahoum, Aldo. The Art of Israeli Cooking. (International Cooking Classics Ser.). 274p. 1992. pap. 8.95 (0-7818-0096-X) Hippocrene Bks.

Nahouraii, Ez & Petry, Fred. Object-Oriented Databases. LC 90-86086. 256p. 1991. 50.00 (0-8186-8929-3, 1929) IEEE Comp Soc.

Nahser, F. Byron & Mehrtens, Susan E. Executive Summary What's Really Going On? A Pragmatic Method for Achieving Success Through Self-Doubt. 33p. 1993. pap. text ed. 5.00 (1-884670-00-8) Corporantes.

Nahum, Alan & Melvin, John, eds. Accidental Injury: Biomechanics & Prevention. LC 92-2381. 1993. 110.00 (0-387-97881-X) Spr-Verlag.

Nahum, Andrew. Alec Issigonis. 100p. (C). 1988. pap. text ed. 50.00 (0-85072-172-5) St Mut.

— Flying Machine. LC 90-4007. (Eyewitness Bks.: No. 22). (Illus.). 64p. (J). (gr. 5 up). 1990. 16.00 (0-679-80744-6); lib. bdg. 16.99 (0-679-90744-0) Knopf Bks Yng Read.

Nahum, Lucien. Shadow Eighty-One. large type ed. 1981. 12.00 (0-7089-0556-0) Ulverscroft.

Nahum-Valensi, Maya. Mom's Sore Throat. (I Love to Read Collection). (Illus.). 48p. (J). (gr. 3-8). 1990. lib. bdg. 12.79 (0-89565-807-0) Childs World.

Nahumck, Nadia C. & Nahumck, Nicholas. Isadora Duncan: The Dances Choreographed in Labanotation. LC 93-43279. 532p. 1993. 165.00 (0-940979-23-3) Natl Museum Women.

Nahumck, Nicholas, jt. auth. see Nahumck, Nadia C.

Nahvi, Mahmood, jt. auth. see Edminister, Joseph.

Nai, Xia. Jade & Silk of Han China. Li, Chu-tsing, tr. LC 83-50538. (Franklin D. Murphy Lectures: No. 3). (Illus.). 88p. 1983. 12.00 (0-913689-10-6) Spencer Muse Art.

Naiad Press Authors Staff. The Romantic Naiad: Love Stories. Forrest, Katherine V. & Grier, Barbara, eds. 320p. 1993. pap. 14.95 (1-56280-054-X) Naiad Pr.

Nai'an, Shi & Guanzhong, Luo. Outlaws of the Marsh, 4 vols. Shapiro, Sidney, tr. (Illus.). 4144p. (Orig.). (YA). (gr. 12 up). 1988. pap. 29.95 (0-8351-2289-1) China Bks.

***Naib, Zuher M.** Cytopathology. 4th ed. LC 95-2408. 1995. 79.75 (0-316-59674-4) Little.

— Exfoliative Cytopathology. 3rd ed. 648p. 1985. 95.00 (0-316-59673-6, Little Med Div) Little.

Naidich, David P., et al. Computed Tomography & Magnetic Resonance of the Thorax. 2nd ed. (Illus.). 624p. 1991. 142.00 (0-88167-567-9) Raven.

Naiditch, David. Rendezvous with Ada: A Programmer's Introduction. 477p. 1989. pap. text ed. 44.95 (0-471-61654-0) Wiley.

— Rendezvous with Ada 94. 2nd ed. LC 94-32049. 1995. pap. text ed. 44.95 (0-471-01276-9) Wiley.

Naidoo, Beverley. Chain of Fire. LC 89-27551. (Illus.). 256p. (J). (gr. 6 up). 1990. lib. bdg. 14.89 (0-397-32427-8, Lipp Jr Bks) HarpC Child Bks.

— Chain of Fire. LC 89-27551. (Trophy Bk.). 256p. (J). (gr. 6 up). 1993. pap. 3.95 (0-06-440468-4, Trophy) HarpC Child Bks.

— Journey to Jo'burg: A South African Story. LC 85-45508. (Illus.). 96p. (J). (gr. 4-7). 1986. lib. bdg. 14.89 (0-397-32169-4, Lipp Jr Bks) HarpC Child Bks.

— Journey to Jo'burg: A South African Story. LC 85-45508. (Trophy Bk.). (Illus.). 96p. (J). (gr. 4-7). 1988. reprint ed. pap. 3.95 (0-06-440237-1, Trophy) HarpC Child Bks.

Naidoo, S., jt. auth. see Pringle, M.

Naidoo, Sandhya, jt. auth. see Haynes, Corinne.

Naidoo, Thillayvel. Arya Samaj Movement in South Africa. (C). 1992. 18.00 (81-208-0769-3, Pub. by Motilal Banarsidass II) S Asia.

Naidu, C. M. Nationalism in South India: Its Economic & Social Background, 1885-1918. 216p. (C). 1988. 31.00 (81-7099-043-2, Pub. by Mittal II) S Asia.

— Salt Satyagraha in Coastal Andhra. 238p. 1986. 13.50 (0-8364-2033-0, Pub. by Mittal II) S Asia.

Naidu, D. S. Singular Perturbation Methodology in Control Systems. (Control Engineering Ser.: No. 34). 1987. 94.00 (0-86341-107-X, CE034) Inst Elect Eng.

Naidu, D. S. & Rao, A. K. Singular Perturbation Analysis of Discrete Control Systems. (Lecture Notes in Mathematics Ser.: Vol. 1154). 195p. 1985. pap. 34.10 (0-387-15981-9) Spr-Verlag.

Naidu, D. Subbaram. Aeroassisted Orbital Transfer: Guidance & Control Strategies. LC 93-38670. 1993. 44.00 (0-387-19819-9) Spr-Verlag.

Naidu, D. Suran. The Congress Party in Transition. (C). 1991. 22.50 (81-85135-64-9, Pub. by Natl Bk Org II) S Asia.

Naidu, K. M. Rural Development & Planning Perspective. 1993. 40.00 (0-685-65107-X, Pub. by Reliance Pub Hse II) Apt Bks.

Naidu, K. Munirathna. Rural Economy Through Transportation. 130p. 1991. text ed. 25.00 (0-685-40676-8, Pub. by Reliance Pub Hse II) Apt Bks.

Naidu, L. K. Bank Finance for Rural Artisans. (C). 1988. 31.00 (81-7024-170-7, Pub. by Ashish II) S Asia.

— Bank Finance for Rural Development. (C). 1988. 34.00 (81-7024-174-X, Pub. by Ashish II) S Asia.

Naidu, Leela. New Housewife's First Cookbook. (C). 1992. pap. 16.00 (81-85846-00-6, Pub. by UBS Pubs Dist II) S Asia.

Naidu, Prema M. In Love with Life: Memoirs of a Lady Doctor. 96p. 1990. text ed. 15.95 (81-207-1200-5, Pub. by Sterling Pubs II) Apt Bks.

Naidu, Ratna. Old Cities, New Predicaments: A Study of Hyderabad. 178p. 1991. text ed. 27.50 (0-8039-9658-6) Sage.

Naidus, Beverly. One Size Does Not Fit All. LC 93-30780. 1993. reprint ed. 35.00 (1-883930-01-4); reprint ed. pap. 15.00 (1-883930-00-6) AIGIS Pubns.

Naier, Jeffrey. New York International Chess: Tournament 1984. 1985. 17.50 (0-911971-11-4) Effect Pub.

Naierman, Naomi, et al. Community Mental Health Centers: A Decade Later. 178p. 1984. reprint ed. lib. bdg. 49.50 (0-8191-4096-1) U Pr of Amer.

***Naifeh, Steven & Smith, Gregory W.** The Best Doctors in America 1994-1995. Stec, Lucienne P. et al, eds. 1130p. (C). Date not set. 76.00 (0-614-04589-4) Woodward-White.

— The Best Lawyers in America: 1989-1990. 3rd ed. 720p. 1989. lib. bdg. 89.00 (0-913391-03-4) Woodward-White.

— The Best Lawyers in America 1995-1996: 1995 - 1996. Greame, Christopher J. et al, eds. (Biennial Ser.). 1313p. (C). Date not set. 88.00 (0-913391-11-5) Woodward-White.

— Final Justice: The True Story of the Richest Man Ever Tried for Murder. 528p. 1994. pap. 5.99 (0-451-40513-7, Onyx) NAL-Dutton.

— The Mormon Murders. 528p. 1989. pap. 5.95 (0-451-40152-2, Onyx) NAL-Dutton.

— The Mormon Murders. 528p. (Orig.). 1995. mass mkt. 5.99 (0-451-40512-9, Onyx) NAL-Dutton.

— A Stranger in the Family: A True Story of Murder, Madness, & Unconditional Love. LC 94-48847. 1995. 24.95 (0-525-93973-3, Dutton) NAL-Dutton.

Naifeh, Steven & Smith, Gregory W., eds. The Best Doctors in America 1992-1993. 500p. 1992. lib. bdg. 65.00 (0-913391-05-0) Woodward-White.

— The Best Lawyers in America: Directory of Experts, 1990. 275p. 1990. lib. bdg. 80.00 (0-913391-07-7) Woodward-White.

— The Best Lawyers in America, 1993-1994. 5th ed. 1000p. 1993. write for info. (0-913391-09-3) Woodward-White.

Naifeh, Steven & White Smith, Gregory. The Best Lawyers in America: 1991-1992. 4th ed. 1000p. 1991. lib. bdg. 95.00 (0-913391-04-2) Woodward-White.

Naifeh, Steven, ed. see Smith, Gregory W.

Naigeon, Jacques A. La Militaire Philosophe. 200p. 1978. reprint ed. write for info. (3-487-06568-1, Pub. by Georg Olms GW) Lubrecht & Cramer.

Naigh, Marshall. A Beginner's Guide to Parrots. (Beginner's Guide Ser.). (Illus.). 61p. 1986. 3.95 (0-86622-312-6, T-109) TFH Pubns.

Naik, D. Murahari. Agrarian Unrest in Karnataka. (Sociological Publications in Honour of Dr. K. Ishwaran: No. 4). xiv, 134p. 1990. text ed. 25.00 (81-85047-45-6, Pub. by Reliance Pub Hse II) Apt Bks.

***Naik, J. A.** Death or Resurrection: A Story of the Hindus. (C). 1995. 14.00x (0-8364-2909-5, Pub. by Ajanta II) S Asia.

— India in Asia & Africa, 1976-78: Documents. 686p. (C). 1981. 140.00 (0-685-31703-X, Pub. by Collets UK) Pro-Am Music.

— India in Asia & Africa, 1979: Documents. 247p. (C). 1982. 95.00 (0-685-31702-1, Pub. by Collets UK) Pro-Am Music.

— India in Asia & Africa, 1980: Documents. 408p. (C). 1983. 170.00 (0-685-31701-3, Pub. by Collets UK) Pro-Am Music.

— India in Asia & Africa, 1981: Documents. 366p. (C). 1985. 180.00 (0-685-31700-5, Pub. by Collets UK) Pro-Am Music.

— Indian Politics: Documents, Events & Figures, 1979. 359p. (C). 1982. 170.00 (0-685-31697-1, Pub. by Collets) St Mut.

— Indian Politics: Documents, Events & Figures, 1980. 321p. (C). 1985. 180.00 (0-685-31698-X, Pub. by Collets) St Mut.

— The Opposition in India & the Future of Democracy. 236p. 1988. 35.00 (0-317-52148-9, Pub. by S Chand II) St Mut.

Naik, M. K. Dimensions of Indian English Literature. v, 208p. 1984. text ed. 20.00 (0-86590-230-5) Apt Bks.

— A History of Indian English Literature. 1982. 11.00 (0-8364-1595-7, Pub. by National Sahitya Akademi) S Asia.

— Mulk Raj Anand. (Indian Writers Ser.). 1976. 8.50 (0-89253-507-5) Ind-US Inc.

Naik, M. K., ed. Indian-English Short Story: A Representative Anthology. 280p. 1984. 12.00 (0-86578-269-5) Ind-US Inc.

— Perspectives on Indian Fiction in English. 1985. 20.00 (0-8364-1412-8, Pub. by Abhinav II) S Asia.

— Selected Short Stories of Mulk Raj Anand. 296p. 1984. 12.00 (0-86578-233-4) Ind-US Inc.

Naik, Niranjan. Woven Fabric Composites. LC 93-60363. 200p. 1993. pap. 65.00 (0-87762-990-0) Technomic.

Naik, Sandra, jt. auth. see Pennington, G. W.

Naik, T. B. Impact of Education on the Bhils. 337p. 1977. 14.95 (0-318-36824-2) Asia Bk Corp.

Naik, Tarun R., ed. Temperature Effect on Concrete - STP 858. LC 84-70335. (Illus.). 180p. 1985. text ed. 28.00 (0-8031-0435-9, 04-858000-07) ASTM.

Naik, Vijay K. Multiprocessing: Trade-Offs in Computation & Communication. LC 93-17930. (International Series in Engineering & Computer Science, VLSI, Computer Architecture, & Digital Screen Processing: Vol. 236). 224p. (C). 1993. lib. bdg. 87.50 (0-7923-9370-8) Kluwer Ac.

Naikar, Basavaraj S. Shakespeare's Last Plays. 1993. text ed. 30.00 (81-85231-10-9, Pub. by Creative Pubs II) Advent Bks Div.

***Nail, Frances.** When Pears & Lilacs Bloomed. (Illus.). 120p. 1995. 18.95 (1-885340-19-2) Coming Age Pr.

Nail, Gene, ed. see Minns, Michael L.

Nail, James T. Whose Tracks Are These? A Clue Book of Familiar Forest Animals. LC 94-65087. (Illus.). 32p. (J). (gr. k-4). 1994. lib. bdg. 13.95 (1-879373-89-0) R Rinehart.

Nail, Simonne & Caillot, Simonne. How to Get Your Child to Read. LC 81-71138. (Illus.). 122p. 1982. pap. 9.00 (0-942010-00-0) Famous Pr Pub.

Nailen, R. L. & Haight, James S. Beertown Blazes. 2nd rev. ed. 1982. 20.00 (0-932476-01-5) Renaiss Bks.

Nailen, Richard L. Managing Motors: The Complete Book of Electric Motor Application & Maintenance. rev. ed. Orig. Title: The Plant Engineer's Guide to Industrial Electric Motors. (Illus.). 432p. 1991. text ed. 64.95 (0-943876-04-4) Barks Pubns.

Nailor, P. The Nassau Connection: The Organisation & Management of the British POLARIS Project. 144p. 1988. 9.95 (0-11-772526-9, HM3585, Pub. by HMSO UK) UNIPUB.

***Nails, Debra.** Agora, Academy, & the Conduct of Philosophy. (Philosophical Studies Ser.). 284p. (C). 1995. lib. bdg. 130.00 (0-7923-3543-0) Kluwer Ac.

Naim, Bertha. Stories of Wonder. 1994. 12.95 (0-533-10879-9) Vantage.

***Naim, Moises.** Latin America's Journey to the Market: From Macroeconomic Shocks to Institutional Therapy. LC 94-42487. (Occasional Papers: No. 62). 1994. pap. 6.95 (1-55815-457-4) ICS Pr.

— Paper Tigers & Minotaurs: The Politics of Venezuela's Economic Reforms. LC 92-35295. 1992. 24.95 (0-87003-025-6); pap. 8.95 (0-87003-026-4) Carnegie Endow.

Naim, Patrick, jt. auth. see Davalo, Eric.

Naima. Annals of the Turkish Empire from 1591 to 1659 of the Christian Era. Fraser, Charles, tr. LC 73-6294. (Middle East Ser.). 1973. reprint ed. 33.95 (0-405-05352-5) Ayer.

Naiman, Anatoly. Stikhotvoreniia. LC 89-19817. 96p. (Orig.). (RUS.). 1989. pap. 8.00 (1-55779-014-0) Hermitage.

Naiman, Arnold, et al. Understanding Statistics. 3rd ed. (Illus.). 368p. (C). 1983. text ed. write for info. (0-07-045863-4) McGraw.

Naiman, Arthur. Every Goy's Guide to Common Jewish Expressions. 192p. 1985. pap. 3.95 (0-345-33598-8) Ballantine.

Naiman, Arthur, jt. ed. see Aker, Sharon Z.

Naiman, Arthur, ed. see Zepezauer, Mark.

Naiman, Arthur, et al, eds. This Is the Mac: It's Supposed to Be Fun! (Illus.). 354p. (Orig.). 1993. pap. 15.00 (1-56609-082-2) Peachpit Pr.

Naiman, Charles S., ed. Proceedings of the Associations of the Association of Orthodox Jewish Scientists, Vols. 8-9. (Illus.). 304p. (Orig.). 1987. pap. 14.95 (0-87203-125-X) Hermon.

Naiman, Doris. Curriculum for Multiply Handicapped Deaf Students. 196p. (C). 1982. pap. 4.95 (0-913072-47-8) Natl Assn Deaf.

Naiman, Doris, jt. auth. see Schein, Jerome.

Naiman, R., ed. The Ecology & Management of Aquatic-Terrestrial Ecotones. (Man & the Biosphere Ser.). 350p. 1990. 82.00 (92-3-102668-2, U6682) UNIPUB.

Naiman, R. J., ed. Watershed Management: Balancing Sustainability & Environmental Change. (Illus.). 542p. 1992. 79.00 (0-387-97790-2) Spr-Verlag.

— Watershed Management: Balancing Sustainability & Environmental Change. (Illus.). 560p. 1994. pap. 39.00 (0-387-94232-7) Spr-Verlag.

Naiman, R. J. & Decamps, H., eds. The Ecology & Management of Aquatic-Terrestrial Ecotones. (Man & the Biosphere Ser.: Vol. 4). (Illus.). 316p. 1990. 65.00 (1-85070-271-3) Prthnon Pub.

Naiman, Robert, jt. auth. see Soltz, David L.

Naiman, Robert J. & Soltz, David L. Fishes in North American Deserts. LC 81-202. 564p. 1985. 56.95 (0-471-08523-5) Wiley.

Naiman, Robert J., jt. auth. see Soltz, David L.

***Naiman, Robert J., et al.** The Freshwater Imperative: A Research Agenda. LC 94-39852. 200p. 1995. text ed. 35.00 (1-55963-406-5) Island Pr.

— The Freshwater Imperative: A Research Agenda. LC 94-39852. 200p. (C). 1995. pap. 19.95 (1-55963-407-3) Island Pr.

Naimark, Dana W., jt. ed. see McGuire, Therese J.

Naimark, George M. Communications on Communication. 3rd ed. 135p. 1987. 19.95 (0-911204-03-2) Rajah.

Naimark, M. & Swinfen, A. Linear Representations of the Lorentz Group. LC 63-10025. (International Series of Monographs on Pure & Applied Mathematics: Vol. 63). 1964. 186.00 (0-08-010155-0, Pub. by Pergamon Repr UK) Franklin.

Naimark, M. A. Theory of Group Representations. (Illus.). 576p. 1982. 109.00 (0-387-90602-9) Spr-Verlag.

Naimark, Norman M. A History of the "Proletariat" The Emergence of Marxism in the Kingdom of Poland, 1870-1887. (East European Monographs: No. 54). 329p. 1979. text ed. 56.50 (0-914710-50-8) East Eur Quarterly.

— The Russians in Germany: A History of the Soviet Zone of Occupation, 1945-1949. LC 95-7725. (Illus.). 608p. (C). 1995. text ed. 35.00 (0-674-78405-7) Belknap Pr.

— Terrorists & Social Democrats: The Russian Revolutionary Movement under Alexander III. (Russian Research Center Studies: No. 82). 328p. 1983. 37.00 (0-674-87464-1) HUP.

Naime, A. K. The Flowering Plants of Western India. 401p. (C). 1976. text ed. 160.00 (0-89771-608-6, Pub. by Intl Bk Distr II) St Mut.

Naimer, Lucille, jt. auth. see Hyman, Claire.

Naimy, Mikhail. The Book of Mirdad: A Lighthouse & a Haven. 192p. 1994. pap. 11.00 (0-14-019332-4, Arkana) Viking Penguin.

— El Libro de Mirdad. 248p. (SPA.). Date not set. pap. 15.00 (84-404-1600-8) Rosycross Pr.

Naimy, Nadeem. The Lebanese Prophets of New York. 112p. 1986. text ed. 19.95 (0-8156-6073-1, Am U Beirut) Syracuse U Pr.

Naimy, Nadeem, jt. auth. see Hawi, Khalil.

Naimy, Nadeem N. Mikhail Naimy, an Introduction. 1967. pap. 15.95 (0-8156-6028-6, Am U Beirut) Syracuse U Pr.

Naipaul, V. S. Among the Believers: An Islamic Journey. LC 82-40048. 448p. 1982. pap. 14.00 (0-394-71195-5, Vin) Random.

— An Area of Darkness. 1993. 20.50 (0-8446-6680-7) Peter Smith.

— An Area of Darkness. 288p. 1992. pap. 10.00 (0-14-002895-1, Penguin Bks) Viking Penguin.

— A Bend in the River. 1992. 21.00 (0-8446-6631-9) Peter Smith.

— A Bend in the River. (International Ser.). 1989. pap. 10.00 (0-679-72202-5, Vin) Random.

— Bend in the River. 1980. pap. 5.95 (0-394-74314-8) Random.

— The Enigma of Arrival. LC 87-45937. 368p. 1988. reprint ed. pap. 13.00 (0-394-75760-2, Vin) Random.

— A Flag on the Island. 224p. 1993. pap. 10.00 (0-14-002939-7, Penguin Bks) Viking Penguin.

— Guerrillas. LC 90-50147. (Vintage International Ser.). 256p. 1990. pap. 12.00 (0-679-73174-1, Publishers Media) Random.

— A House for Mr. Biswas. 576p. 1993. 12.95 (0-14-018604-2, Penguin Classics) Viking Penguin.

— In a Free State. 1984. pap. 8.00 (0-394-72205-1, Vin) Random.

— India: A Million Mutinies Now. 480p. 1992. pap. 14.00 (0-14-015680-1, Penguin Bks) Viking Penguin.

— India: A Wounded Civilization. (Departures Ser.). 1977. pap. 10.00 (0-394-72463-1, Vin) Random.

— Miguel Street. (Caribbean Writers Ser.). (C). 1974. pap. 7.95 (0-435-98645-7) Heinemann.

— Miguel Street. 1977. pap. 10.00 (0-14-003302-5, Penguin Bks) Viking Penguin.

— Mimic Men. 1976. pap. 10.95 (0-14-002940-0, Penguin Bks) Viking Penguin.

— The Mystic Masseur. (Caribbean Writers Ser.). 214p. (C). 1971. pap. 8.95 (0-435-98646-5) Heinemann.

— The Mystic Masseur. 1977. pap. 10.00 (0-14-002156-6, Penguin Bks) Viking Penguin.

— The Overcrowded Barracoon: Essays. 1984. pap. 6.95 (0-394-72207-8, Vin) Random.

— The Suffrage of Elvira. 1976. pap. 10.00 (0-14-002938-9, Penguin Bks) Viking Penguin.

— Three Novels. LC 82-47819. 1982. 18.95 (0-394-52847-6) Knopf.

— A Turn in the South. 1990. pap. 11.00 (0-679-72488-5, Vin) Random.

— A Way in the World. Date not set. pap. write for info. (0-679-76166-7) Random.

— Way in the World: A Sequence. 1994. 23.00 (0-394-56478-2) Knopf.

***Nair & Brody.** Macro Practice: A Generalist Approach. 215p. 1995. 28.00 (0-911541-32-2) Gregory Pub.

Nair, Adoor. Slavery in Kerala. 1986. 18.00 (0-8364-1914-6, Pub. by Mittal II) S Asia.

Nair, B. R., ed. see ASME-CSME Montreal Pressure Vessel & Piping Conference Staff.

***Nair, C. Sankaran.** Gandhi & Anarchy. (C). 1995. reprint ed. 28.50x (0-614-07150-X, Pub. by Motilal Banarsidass II) S Asia.

***Nair, D. Appukuttan & Paniker, K. Ayyappa, eds.** Kathakali: The Art of the Non-Wordly. (C). 1993. 72.00 (81-85026-22-X, Pub. by Marg) S Asia.

Nair, Gopinathan. Primary Education, Population Growth & Socio-Economic Change. 1981. 15.00 (0-8364-0760-1, Pub. by Allied II) S Asia.

Nair, Gwyneth, et al, eds. Highley. (C). 1989. 39.00 (0-947712-13-5, Pub. by S A Baldwin UK) St Mut.

Nair, Indira, tr. see Novozhilov, K. V., ed.

Nair, K. K., pseud. A Profile of Indian Culture. (India Library Ser.: Vol. 1). 202p. 1975. 8.95 (0-88253-774-1) Ind-US Inc.

Nair, K. M., et al, eds. Dielectric Ceramics: Processing, Properties, & Applications. LC 93-10030. (Ceramic Transactions Ser.: No. 32). 357p. 1993. 69.00 (0-944904-60-2, TRANS032) Am Ceramic.

Nair, K. N., jt. ed. see Doornbos, Martin.

Nair, K. N., et al. Ecology or Economics in Cardamom Development. (C). 1989. 14.00 (81-204-0426-2, Pub. by Oxford IBH II) S Asia.

Nair, Ken. Discovering the Heart of a Man. rev. ed. 227p. 1992. pap. 8.95 (0-9635458-0-9) K Nair.

— Discovering the Mind of a Woman. 123p. 1982. pap. 6.95 (0-937929-00-X) K Nair.

Nair, Keshavan. Beyond Winning. LC 87-62803. 105p. (Orig.). 1988. 14.95 (0-945150-19-9); pap. 9.95 (0-945150-22-9) Paradox AZ.

— A Higher Standard of Leadership: Lessons from the Life of Gandhi. LC 94-26927. (Illus.). 150p. 1994. 21.95 (1-881052-58-3) Berrett-Koehler.

Nair, Kusum. In Defense of the Irrational Peasant: Indian Agriculture after the Green Revolution. LC 78-26707. 1979. 17.00 (0-226-56798-2) U Ch Pr.

Nair, M. B. Politics in Bangladesh: A Study of Awami Leauge, 1949-1958. 1990. 40.00 (81-85119-79-1, Pub. by Northern Bk Ctr II) S Asia.

Nair, M. C. & Balakrisma, S. Beneficial Fungi & Their Utilisation. 196p. (C). 1986. 150.00 (81-85046-31-X, Scientific) St Mut.

Nair, M. K. Advances in Coconut Research & Development: Proceedings of the International Symposium on Coconut Research & Development. 780p. (C). 1993. text ed. 118.00 (1-881570-27-4) Intl Sci Pub.

Nair, P. K. Advances in Palynology. 500p. (C). 1981. text ed. 400.00 (0-89771-603-5, Pub. by Intl Bk Distr II) St Mut.

An Asterisk (*) at the beginning of an entry indicates that the title is appearing in BIP for the first time.

— Advances in Pollen Spore Research, Vol. XII. 170p. 1984. 20.00 (*1-55528-061-7*, Pub. by Today & Tomorrows P & P II) Scholarly Pubns.
— Essentials of Palynology. 129p. 1985. 19.00 (*1-55528-030-7*, Pub. by Today & Tomorrows P & P II) Scholarly Pubns.
— Essentials of Palynology. 150p. (C). 1991. text ed. 160.00 (*0-685-52012-9*, Pub. by Intl Bk Distr II) St Mut.
— Plantation & Agri-Horticultural Resources of Kerala. (Aspects of Plant Sciences Ser.: Vol. 7). 120p. 1984. 19. 00 (*1-55528-165-6*, Pub. by Today & Tomorrows P & P II) Scholarly Pubns.
— Progress in Palynology: Cumulation of Journal of Palynology, 2 vols. in 4 pts., Vols. 1-20. 3500p. 1986. 300.00 (*1-55528-077-3*, Pub. by Today & Tomorrows P & P II) Scholarly Pubns.
— The Prospects for Agroforestry in the Tropics. (Technical Paper Ser.: No. 131). 90p. 1990. 7.95 (*0-8213-1702-4*, 11702) World Bank.
Nair, P. K., ed. Advances in Pollen Spore Research, Vol. 1. 167p. 1975. 12.00 (*0-88065-165-2*, Messers Today & Tomorrow) Scholarly Pubns.
— Advances in Pollen Spore Research, Vol. II. 160p. 1977. 12.00 (*0-88065-166-0*, Messers Today & Tomorrow) Scholarly Pubns.
— Advances in Pollen Spore Research, Vol. IV. 160p. 1979. 12.00 (*0-88065-168-7*, Messers Today & Tomorrow) Scholarly Pubns.
— Advances in Pollen Spore Research, Vols. V - VII. 160p. 1980. 30.00 (*0-88065-169-5*, Messers Today & Tomorrow) Scholarly Pubns.
— Agroforestry Systems in the Tropics. (Forestry Sciences Ser.). (C). 1989. lib. bdg. 211.50 (*90-247-3790-7*) Kluwer Ac.
— Aspects of Plant Sciences, Vol. I. 210p. 1976. 15.00 (*0-88065-170-9*, Messers Today & Tomorrow) Scholarly Pubns.
— Aspects of Plant Sciences, Vol. II. 164p. 1979. 15.00 (*0-88065-171-7*, Messers Today & Tomorrow) Scholarly Pubns.
— Cytological Research Monographs. (Glimpses in Plant Research Ser.: Vol. VIII). (Illus.). 250p. 1988. 69.00 (*1-55528-164-8*, Pub. by Today & Tomorrows P & P II) Scholarly Pubns.
— Glimpses in Plant Research, Vol. VII. 202p. 1986. 39.00 (*1-55528-104-4*, Pub. by Today & Tomorrows P & P II) Scholarly Pubns.
— Glimpses in Plant Research, Vol. VIII. (Illus.). 250p. 1988. 69.00 (*0-685-24663-9*, Pub. by Today & Tomorrows P & P II) Scholarly Pubns.
— Pollen Morphology of Angiosperms: A Historical & Phylogenetic Study. 200p. (C). 1991. text ed. 200.00 (*0-89771-607-8*, Pub. by Intl Bk Distr II) St Mut.
Nair, P. K. & Achar, K. Prabhakar. A Textbook of Cell Biology. 224p. 1990. text ed. 25.00 (*81-220-0123-8*, Pub. by Konark Pubs Pvt Ltd II) Advent Bks Div.
— A Textbook of Genetics & Evolution. (Illus.). 356p. 1990. text ed. 30.00 (*81-220-0127-0*, Pub. by Konark Pubs Pvt Ltd II) Advent Bks Div.
Nair, P. K. & Kothari, Sushma. Studies in the Pollen Morphology of Indian Heteromerae. (Advances in Pollen Spore Research Ser.: Vol. 13). xii, 90p. 1985. 15. 00 (*1-55528-055-2*, Messers Today & Tomorrow) Scholarly Pubns.
Nair, P. K. & Lawrence, R. Pollen Morphology of Indian Compositae. (Advances in Pollen Spore Research Ser.: Vol. XIV). (Illus.). 176p. 1985. 25.00 (*1-55528-043-9*, Messers Today & Tomorrow) Scholarly Pubns.
Nair, P. K., ed. see Katiyar, Kamlesh.
Nair, P. K., jt. ed. see Khoshoo, T. N.
Nair, P. K., ed. see Srivastava, D.
Nair, P. K., jt. auth. see Yunus, Durdana.
Nair, P. K., et al, eds. Agroforestry Education & Training: Present & Future. (Forestry Sciences Ser.). (C). 1990. lib. bdg. 65.00 (*0-7923-0864-6*) Kluwer Ac.
Nair, P. P. & Kritchevsky, David, eds. The Bile Acids: Chemistry, Physiology & Metabolism. Incl. Chemistry. LC 71-138520. 384p. 1971. 65.00 (*0-306-37131-6*); Physiology & Metabolism. LC 71-138520. 330p. 1973. 65.00 (*0-306-37132-4*); Vol. 3. Pathophysiology. LC 71-138520. 242p. 1976. 55.00 (*0-306-37133-2*); LC 71-138520. write for info. (*0-318-55308-2*, Plenum Pr) Plenum.
Nair, P. Ramachandran. An Introduction to Agroforestry. LC 92-46550. 1993. lib. bdg. 175.00 (*0-7923-2134-0*) Kluwer Ac.
Nair, P. T., ed. Bruton's Visit of Lord Jagannath 350 Years Ago: British Beginnings in Orissa. 1986. 14.00 (*0-8364-1610-4*, Pub. by Minerva II) S Asia.
Nair, P. Thankappan. British Beginnings in Bengal. (C). 1991. text ed. 54.00 (*81-85094-36-5*, Pub. by Punthi Pus II) S Asia.
— Calcutta in the Eighteenth Century. 1984. 22.50 (*0-8364-1232-X*, Pub. by Mukhopadhyaya II) S Asia.
— Calcutta in the Seventeenth Century. 1986. 38.00 (*0-8364-1619-8*, KL Mukhopadhyay) S Asia.
— A History of Calcutta's Streets: A Tercentenary History of Calcutta. 992p. 1987. 72.00 (*0-8364-1934-0*, KL Mukhopadhyay) S Asia.
— Indian National Songs & Symbols. (C). 1987. 16.50 (*0-8364-2128-0*, KL Mukhopadhyay) S Asia.
Nair, S. V., et al, eds. Fracture Mechanics: Microstructure & Micromechanisms. (Illus.). 400p. 1988. 139.00 (*0-87170-342-4*) NACE Intl.
Nair, Sadanandan K. & White, Shirley A., eds. Perspectives on Development Communication. LC 93-25691. 256p. 1994. text ed. 36.00 (*0-8039-9132-0*); pap. text ed. 16.50 (*0-8039-9133-9*) Sage.
Nair, Sami, et al, eds. Perspectives on Europe. (Contemporary European Affairs Ser.: No. JCEA 4). 272p. 1992. pap. 30.00 (*0-08-041923-2*, Pergamon Pr) Elsevier.
***Nair, Shanti V. & Jakus, Karl.** High Temperature Mechanical Behavior of Ceramic Composites. 560p. 1995. 120.00 (*0-7506-9399-1*, Focal) Buttrwrth-Heinemann.
Nair, Sobha B. Social Security & the Weaker Sections. 1990. 17.50 (*81-85199-38-8*, Pub. by Renaiss Publng Hse II) S Asia.
Nair, Sreekantan S. On Certain Priority Queues. LC 78-132638. 171p. 1969. 22.00 (*0-403-04521-5*) Scholarly.
***Nair, V. Balakrishnan, ed.** Social Development & Demographic Changes in South India: Focus on Kerala 1994. (C). 1994. 60.00x (*81-85880-50-6*, Pub. by Print Hse II) St Mut.
Nair, V. Sankaran. Role of Students in Freedom Movement: With Special Reference to Madras Presidency. 248p. 1991. text ed. 30.00 (*81-220-0197-1*, Pub. by Konark Pubs Pvt Ltd II) Advent Bks Div.
Nair, V. Sukumaran. Swami Vivekananda: The Educator. 1987. text ed. 11.95 (*81-207-0610-2*, Pub. by Sterling Pubs II) Apt Bks.
Nairn, Alan E. & Stehli, Francis G., eds. Ocean Basins & Margins. Incl. Vol. 1, The South Atlantic. LC 72-83046. 600p. 1973. (*0-306-37771-3*); Vol. 2, The North Atlantic. LC 72-83046. 662p. 1974. (*0-306-37772-1*); Vol. 3, The Gulf of Mexico & The Caribbean. LC 72-83046. 722p. 1975. (*0-306-37773-X*); Vol. 4A, The Eastern Mediterranean. LC 72-83046. 520p. 1977. (*0-306-37774-8*); Vol. 4B, The Western Mediterranean. LC 72-83046. 462p. 1978. (*0-306-37779-9*); Vol. 5, The Arctic Ocean. LC 72-83046. 686p. 1981. (*0-306-37775-6*); LC 72-83046. (Illus.). 125.00 (*0-685-04080-1*, Plenum Pr) Plenum.
— The Ocean Basins & Margins, Vol. 6: The Indian Ocean. LC 72-83046. 794p. 1982. 125.00 (*0-306-37776-4*, Plenum Pr) Plenum.
— The Ocean Basins & Margins, Vol. 7A: The Pacific Ocean. 720p. 1985. 125.00 (*0-306-37777-2*, Plenum Pr) Plenum.
Nairn, Alan E., jt. auth. see Moullade, M.
Nairn, Alan E., jt. ed. see Moullade, M.
Nairn, Alan E., et al, eds. The Ocean Basins & Margins, Vol. 7B: The Pacific Ocean. (Illus.). 621p. 1988. 125.00 (*0-306-37778-0*, Plenum Pr) Plenum.
Nairn, Allan & Associates Staff, ed. The Reign of ETS: The Corporation That Makes up Minds. LC 80-107761. (Ralph Nader Report on the Educational Testing Service Ser.). 554p. (Orig.). 1980. pap. 30.00 (*0-936486-00-7*) R Nader.
Nairn, Angus C., jt. auth. see Shenolikar, Shirish.
Nairn, Bede. The Big Fella: Jack Lang & the Australian Labor Party, 1891-1949. (Illus.). 369p. 1987. 35.00 (*0-522-84329-8*) Intl Spec Bk.
— Civilizing Capitalism: The Beginnings of the Australian Labor Party. 1989. reprint ed. pap. 24.95 (*0-522-84382-4*) Intl Spec Bk.
Nairn, Bede, ed. Australian Dictionary of Biography, Vol. 6: 1851-1890, R-Z. 1976. 59.95 (*0-522-84108-2*) Intl Spec Bk.
Nairn, Bede & Serle, Geoffrey, eds. Australian Dictionary of Biography, Vol. 10: 1891-1939 Lat-ner. (Australian Dictionary of Biography Ser.). 680p. 1986. 59.95 (*0-522-84327-1*) Intl Spec Bk.
— Australian Dictionary of Biography, Vol. 9: 1891-1939, Gil-Las. 677p. 1983. 59.95 (*0-522-84273-9*) Intl Spec Bk.
Nairn, Ronald C. International Aid to Thailand: The New Colonialism? 1966. 59.50 (*0-685-45681-1*) Elliots Bks.
— Wealth of Nations in Crisis. LC 79-90284. 289p. 1979. 12.95 (*0-934018-00-6*, Houston Metropolitan Mag) ARC Comms.
Nairn, Thom, jt. ed. see Crawford, Robert.
Nairne, Alexander K. History of Konkan. (C). 1988. reprint ed. 17.00 (*81-206-0275-7*, Pub. by Asian Educ Servs II) S Asia.
Nairne, Carolina O. The Life & Songs of the Baroness Nairne, with a Memoir & Poems of Caroline Oliphant the Younger. LC 70-144571. (Illus.). reprint ed. 21.50 (*0-404-08577-6*) AMS Pr.
Nairne, Thomas. Nairne's Muskhogean Journals: The 1708 Expedition to the Mississippi River. Moore, Alexander, ed. LC 87-27683. (Illus.). 92p. 1988. 18.50 (*0-87805-346-8*) U Pr of Miss.
Nairon, Kevin. Building a Robot: A Straightforward Approach. 152p. 1993. spiral bd., pap. 19.95 (*0-9635636-1-0*) Humanform Robot.
Naisawald, L. Van Loan. Grape & Canister: Field Artillery of Army Potomac. 1983. reprint ed. 29.95 (*0-89201-102-5*) Zenger Pub.
***Naisawald, L. VanLoan.** Grape & Canister, the Story of the Field Artillery of the Army of the Potomac. 593p. Date not set. 35.00 (*1-56013-007-5*) Olde Soldier Bks.
Naisbitt Group. Small Business in America: The Year 2000 & Beyond. (Illus.). 20p. (Orig.). 1986. pap. 6.00 (*0-940791-00-5*) NFIB Found.
Naisbitt Group Staff & Naisbitt, John. The Year Ahead - 1987. (Orig.). 1999. mass mkt. 6.95 (*0-446-38342-2*) Warner Bks.
***Naisbitt, J.** Megatrends 2000. Date not set. pap. 5.98 (*0-8317-4372-7*) Smithmark.
***Naisbitt, John.** Global Paradox. 400p. 1995. mass mkt. 6.50 (*0-380-72489-8*) Avon.
— Global Paradox: The Bigger the World Econmy, the More Powerful Its Smallest Players. 1994. 23.00 (*0-688-12791-6*) Morrow.
— Megatrends. 1988. mass mkt. 6.50 (*0-446-35681-6*) Warner Bks.
Naisbitt, John & Aburdene, Patricia. Megatrends Two Thousand: Ten New Directions for the 1990's. 448p. 1991. mass mkt. 5.95 (*0-380-70437-4*) Avon.
Naisbitt, John & Auburdene, Patricia. Megatrends Two Thousand. LC 89-13301. 288p. 1990. 21.95 (*0-688-07224-0*) Morrow.
Naisbitt, John, jt. auth. see Aburdene, Patricia.
Naisbitt, John, jt. auth. see Naisbitt Group Staff.
Naish, Camille. Death Comes to the Maiden: Sex & Execution, 1431-1933. 304p. 1991. 45.00 (*0-415-05585-7*, A6227) Routledge.
— A Genetic Approach to Structures in the Work of Jean Genet. LC 78-7059. (Studies in Romance Languages: No. 34). 219p. 1978. 14.00 (*0-674-34581-9*) HUP.
Naish, Camille, tr. see Le Brun, Annie.
Naish, G. P., ed. Nelson's Letters to His Wife & Other Documents. 1989. 80.00 (*0-317-44199-X*) St Mut.
Naish, L. Negation & Control in Prology. (Lecture Notes in Computer Science Ser.: Vol. 238). ix, 119p. 1988. pap. 26.00 (*0-387-16815-X*) Spr-Verlag.
Naish, Michael, ed. Geography & Education: National & International Perspectives. 368p. 1992. pap. 37.50 (*0-85473-329-9*, Pub. by Kogan Page Educ UK) Taylor & Francis.
Naish, Michael, jt. ed. see Harnett, Anthony.
Naish, Peter L., ed. What Is Hypnosis? Current Theories & Research. 224p. 1987. 95.00 (*0-335-15338-0*, Open Univ Pr); pap. 39.00 (*0-335-15337-2*, Open Univ Pr) Taylor & Francis.
Naish, Reginald. Spiritual Aritmetic. Colson, Lynn G., ed. 125p. 1994. pap. write for info. (*0-318-72815-X*) Peace Pub Co.
Naishan, Cheng. The Banker. Dean, Britten, tr. & intro. by. 1993. 19.95 (*0-8351-2492-4*) China Bks.
— The Blue House. 400p. (Orig.). 1989. pap. 7.95 (*0-8351-2065-1*) China Bks.
Naismith, Archibald. Two Thousand Four Hundred Outlines, Notes, Quotes, & Anecdotes for Sermons, 2 vols. in 1. 536p. 1991. pap. 24.99 (*0-8010-6786-3*) Baker Bk.
Naismith, Helen. One Hundred American Festivals & Their Foods. 232p. 1990. write for info. (*0-87651-989-3*) Southern U Pr.
— Walking Cape Ann. (Illus.). 254p. (Orig.). 1994. pap. 11. 95 (*0-938459-08-2*) Ten Pound Isl Bk.
Naismith, Helen, comp. One Hundred Famous American Festivals & Their Foods. LC 75-30398. (Illus.). 1979. pap. 12.95 (*0-933718-30-6*) Browning Pubns.
Naismith, James. Basketball's Origins: Creative Problem-Solving in the Gilded Age. Cheney, Robert et al, eds. (Illus.). (C). (gr. 7 up). 1976. reprint ed. pap. 1.95 (*0-912934-03-4*) Bear.
Naison, Mark. Communists in Harlem During the Depression. LC 84-48112. 384p. 1985. pap. 9.95 (*0-8021-5183-3*) Grove-Atltic.
— Communists in Harlem During the Depression. LC 82-10848. (Blacks in the New World Ser.). 384p. 1983. 34. 95 (*0-252-00644-5*) U of Ill Pr.
Naithani, B. D. Flora of Chamoli, Vols. 1 & 2. (C). 1988. text ed. 50.00 (*0-685-74017-X*, Scientific); text ed. 40.00 (*0-685-74018-8*, Scientific) St Mut.
Naithani, H. B. Flowering Plants of India, Nepal & Bhutan. (C). 1990. 252.00 (*0-7855-0180-0*, Pub. by Ratna Pustak Bhandar) St Mut.
Naito, Akira. Katsura: A Princely Retreat. Terny, Charles S., tr. (Illus.). 182p. 1994. 150.00 (*4-7700-0542-3*) Kodansha.
Naito, H., ed. Nutrition & Heart Disease. (Monographs of the American College of Nutrition: Vol. 5). 365p. 1982. text ed. 37.50 (*0-88331-168-2*) Luce.
Naito, Hatsuho. Thunder Gods: The Kamikaze Pilots Tell Their Stories. Ichikawa, Mayumi, tr. LC 88-81848. 216p. 1989. 18.95 (*0-87011-909-5*) Kodansha.
Naito, Hideharu. Dinosaur Carton Craft. (Illus.). 68p. (Orig.). 1992. pap. 10.95 (*0-87040-911-5*) Japan Pubns USA.
***Naito, Hisamoto, ed.** Steven Arnold: Cabinet De Curiosite. (Illus.). 180p. (JPN.). 1994. write for info. (*4-946436-32-4*) Res Art Media.
Naito, T., jt. auth. see Ninomiya, I.
Naitoh, Hideharu. Animal Carton Craft. (Illus.). 70p. (Orig.). 1993. pap. 12.00 (*0-87040-919-0*) Japan Pubns USA.
— Whale Carton Craft. (Illus.). 70p. (Orig.). 1993. pap. 13. 00 (*0-87040-920-4*) Japan Pubns USA.
Naj, Amal. Peppers: A Story of Hot Pursuits. 1992. 23.00 (*0-394-57077-4*) Knopf.
— Peppers: A Story of Hot Pursuits. LC 92-50625. 1993. pap. 11.00 (*0-679-74427-4*, Vin) Random.
Najafi, S. Iraj, ed. Glass Integrated Optics & Optical Fiber Devices. LC 94-11385. (Critical Reviews of Optical Science & Technology Ser.: Vol. CR53). 1994. write for info. (*0-8194-1386-0*); pap. write for info. (*0-8194-1385-2*) SPIE.
— Introduction to Glass Integrated Optics. (Optoelectronics Library). 208p. 1992. text ed. 74.00 (*0-89006-547-0*) Artech Hse.
Najam, Adil, jt. ed. see Moomaw, William.
Najarian. Liver, Biliary & Pancreatic Surgery. 640p. 1990. 95.00 (*0-8151-6304-5*, Yr Bk Med Pubs) Mosby Yr Bk.
Najarian & Delaney. Progress in Cancer Surgery. 428p. 1991. 99.00 (*0-8016-3625-6*) Mosby Yr Bk.
Najarian, Haig H. Sex Lives of Animals Without Backbones. LC 75-4447. 125p. (Orig.). 1976. lib. bdg. 9.50 (*0-684-14613-4*) Krieger.
Najarian, John S. & Delaney, John P., eds. Progress in Trauma & Critical Care. LC 92-8466. 475p. 1992. 99.95 (*0-8016-6551-5*) Mosby Yr Bk.
Najarian, John S. & Simmons, Richard L. Transplantation. LC 73-135689. (Illus.). 811p. reprint ed. 180.00 (*0-8357-9424-5*, 2014566) Bks Demand.
Najarian, John S., et al, eds. Transplantation Today: Proceedings of the Tenth International Congress of the Transplantation Society, Vol. VIII. LC 79-3077. 1684p. 1985. text ed. 230.00 (*0-8089-1734-X*, 793077, Grune) Saunders.
Najarian, Peter. Daughters of Memory. LC 85-63859. (Illus.). 176p. (Orig.). 1986. pap. 8.95 (*0-933944-13-6*) City Miner Bks.
— Daughters of Memory. deluxe ed. LC 85-63859. (Illus.). 176p. (Orig.). 1986. 20.00 (*0-685-12079-1*) City Miner Bks.
— Voyages. LC 79-23722. 1980. 8.95 (*0-933706-12-X*); pap. 4.95 (*0-933706-13-8*) Ararat Pr.
— Wash Me on Home Mama. 86p. (Orig.). 1978. pap. 5.95 (*0-917658-10-8*) BPW & P.
Najavits, Joseph. How to Trash Our Young via Public Education: A Practical Guide. LC 93-86162. 182p. 1993. pap. 12.95 (*0-9638307-5-9*) Open Vistas.
Najbaro, Phyllis. Latvian Folk Tales. 1976. 2.50 (*0-913714-44-5*) Legacy Books.
Najder, Zdzislaw. Joseph Conrad: A Chronicle. (Illus.). 671p. 1983. pap. 18.95 (*0-8135-0945-9*) Rutgers U Pr.
***Najean, Y., et al, eds.** Safety Problems Related to Chloramphenicol & Thiamphenicol. LC 80-5838. (Monographs of the Mairo Negri Institute for Pharmacological Research, Milan). (Illus.). Date not set. reprint ed. pap. 36.50 (*0-7837-9562-9*, 2060311) Bks Demand.
Najee-Ullah, Deborah, jt. auth. see Hart, Lynn.
Najem, R., jt. auth. see Wedemeyer, C.
Najemy, John M. Between Friends: Discourses of Power & Desire in the Machiavelli-Vettori Letters of 1513-1515. LC 93-9737. 392p. 1993. text ed. 39.50 (*0-691-03262-9*) Princeton U Pr.
— Corporation & Consensus in Florentine Electoral Politics 1280 to 1400. LC 81-16481. 358p. reprint ed. pap. 102. 10 (*0-8357-4407-8*, 2037227) Bks Demand.
Najera, Jose A., et al. Malaria: New Patterns & Perspectives. Hammer, Jeffrey, ed. LC 92-49338. (Technical Paper Ser.: No. 183). 37p. 1992. 6.95 (*0-8213-2250-8*, 12250) World Bank.
Najim. Process Modeling & Control in Chemical Engineering. (Chemical Industries Ser.: Vol. 38). 504p. 1989. 170.00 (*0-8247-8204-6*) Dekker.
Najim, K. & Dufour, E., eds. Advanced Control of Chemical Processes (ADCHEM '91) Selected Papers from the IFAC Symposium, Toulouse, France, 14-16 October 1991. LC 92-2270. (IFAC Symposia Ser.: Vol. 1992, No. 8). 1992. 130.00 (*0-08-041267-X*, Pergamon Pr) Elsevier.
Najim, Kaddour. Control of Liquid-Liquid Extraction Columns. Hughes, R., ed. (Topics in Chemical Engineering Ser.: Vol. 5). 259p. 1988. text ed. 105.00 (*2-88124-703-2*) Gordon & Breach.
Najim, Kaddour & Poznyak, Alexandr S. Learning Automata: Theory Applications. LC 94-19346. 1994. text ed. 105.00 (*0-08-042024-9*, Pergamon Pr) Elsevier.
Najim, M. & Abdel-Fettah, Y. M., eds. System Approach for Development: Proceedings of the IFAC-IFIP-IFORS Conference, 3rd, Rabat, Morocco, Nov., 1980. LC 80-41530. 592p. 1980. 249.00 (*0-08-025670-8*, Pub. by Pergamon Repr UK) Franklin.
Najimy, Kathy & Gaffney, Mo. Parallel Lives. 1993. pap. 4.75 (*0-8222-1308-7*) Dramatists Play.
Najita, Tetsuo. Hara Kei in the Politics of Compromise, 1905-1915. LC 67-27090. (Harvard East Asian Ser.: No. 31). 331p. reprint ed. pap. 96.40 (*0-7837-2302-4*, 2057390) Bks Demand.
— Japan: The Intellectual Foundations of Modern Japanese Politics. LC 79-23710. 1980. reprint ed. pap. text ed. 11. 95 (*0-226-56803-2*, P883) U Ch Pr.
— Visions of Virtue in Tokugawa Japan: The Kaitokudo Merchant Academy of Osaka. LC 86-19825. 344p. (C). 1987. pap. text ed. 18.95 (*0-226-56805-9*) U Ch Pr.
Najita, Tetsuo, ed. see Koschmann, Victor.
Najita, Tetsuo, ed. see Scheiner, Irwin.
Najjar. Law Dictionary French-Arabic: Dictionnaire Juridique. (ARA & FRE.). 1983. 40.00 (*0-86685-303-0*) Intl Bk Ctr.
Najjar, A. Majid. Khilafat al Insan Bayna al Wahy wa al 'Aql: Bahth fi Jadaliyat al Nass wa al 'Aql wa al Waqi' - (Man's Vicegenerency Between Revelation & Reason) 2nd ed. LC 91-38923. (Silsilat al Manhajiyah al Islamiyah Ser.: No. 5). 141p. (ARA.). 1993. pap. 5.00 (*1-56564-001-2*) IIIT VA.
Najjar, Abdallah E., ed. see Najjar, Abdallah M.
Najjar, Abdallah M. The Druze. Najjar, Abdallah E., ed. Massey, Fred I., tr. & intro. by. 215p. 1973. write for info. (*0-9600800-1-5*) A E Najjar.
Najjar, Ibrahim. Legal Dictionary: Dictionnaire Juridique. 292p. (ARA & FRE.). 1983. 75.00 (*0-8288-0971-2*, F48378) Fr & Eur.
Najjar, Matthew F. Clinical Chemistry Profile Data for Hispanics, 1982-84. LC 92-48934. (Vital & Health Statistics Ser. 11: Data from the National Health Survey: No. 241). 1992. write for info. (*0-8406-0467-X*) Natl Ctr Health Stats.
Najjar, Matthew F. & Kuczmarski, Robert J., trs. Anthropometric Data & Prevalence of Overweight for Hispanics, 1982-84. (DHHS Publication PHS Ser., No. 89-1689: Vital & Health Statistics, Ser. 11: No. 239). (Illus.). 110p. (Orig.). 1989. pap. 5.50 (*0-16-002379-3*, S/N 017-022-01070-4) USGPO.
Najjar, Orayb A. Portraits of Palestinian Women. LC 91-51099. (Illus.). 304p. (C). 1992. 24.95 (*0-87480-385-3*) U of Utah Pr.
— Portraits of Palestinian Women. (Illus.). 328p. 1993. reprint ed. pap. 14.95 (*0-87480-441-8*) U of Utah Pr.
Najjar, Victor A. The Biological Effects of Glutamic Acid & Its Derivatives. 1982. lib. bdg. 183.00 (*90-6193-841-4*) Kluwer Ac.

An Asterisk (*) at the beginning of an entry indicates that the title is appearing in BIP for the first time.

— Immunologically Active Peptides. 1982. lib. bdg. 117.00 (*90-6193-842-2*) Kluwer Ac.

Najjar, Victor A., ed. Enzyme Induction & Modulation. 1983. lib. bdg. 139.00 (*0-89838-583-0*) Kluwer Ac.

Najjar, Victor A. & Fridkin, Mati, eds. Antineoplastic, Immunogenic & Other Effects of the Tetrapeptide Tuftsin, Vol. 419. 55.00 (*0-89766-232-6*); pap. 55.00 (*0-89766-233-4*) NY Acad Sci.

Najjar, Victor A. & Lorand, Laszlo, eds. Transglutaminase. (Developments in Molecular & Cellular Bio-Chemistry Ser.). 1984. lib. bdg. 94.50 (*0-89838-593-8*) Kluwer Ac.

Najlis, Elena. Lengua Abipona, 2 vols., Set. 1966. 60.00 (*0-7859-0703-3*, S-33069) Fr & Eur.

Najmabadi, Afsaneh. Land Reform & Social Change in Iran. LC 87-31630. 256p. reprint ed. pap. 73.00 (*0-7837-6870-2*, 2046700) Bks Demand.

Najmabadi, Afsaneh, ed. Women's Autobiographies in Contemporary Iran. (Middle Eastern Monographs: No. 26). 64p. 1991. pap. 9.95 (*0-685-38745-3*, NAJWOM) HUP.

Najmabadi, Afsansh, ed. see Astarabadi, Bibi W.

Najman, A., et al, eds. The Inhibitors of Hematopoiesis. (Colloquim Ser.: No. 162). 364p. (Orig.). 1987. pap. 65.00 (*2-85598-340-1*) S M P F Inc.

Najman, Dragoljub, jt. auth. see D'Orville, Hans.

Najman, Jake, jt. ed. see Lupton, Gillian.

Najmee, S. A. Islamic Legal Theory & the Orientalists. 25.00 (*1-56744-101-7*) Kazi Pubns.

Najock, D., ed. see Felix, Minucius.

Najock, D., jt. ed. see Kytzler, B.

Najock, Dietmar, jt. ed. see Fischer, Klaus-Dietrich.

Najock, Dietmar, jt. ed. see Morgenroth, Hermann.

Najock, Dietmar, ed. see Plinius Secundus, C.

Najock, Dietmar, jt. ed. see Rapsch, Jurgen.

Najock, Dietmar, jt. ed. see Rosumek, Peter.

Najock, Dietmar, ed. see Secundus, C. Plinius.

Najock, Dietmar, ed. see Secundus, Plinius.

Naka, Y., et al, eds. Introduction to VLSI Process Engineering for Chemical Engineers. McGreavy, C., tr. 224p. 1992. 85.00 (*0-412-39550-9*, A9488) Chapman & Hall.

Nakadate, Neil, ed. Robert Penn Warren: Critical Perspectives. LC 79-57569. 336p. 1981. 35.00 (*0-8131-1425-X*) U Pr of Ky.

Nakadhe, Stephanie, tr. see Liebes, Yehuda.

Nakae, Kiyose. Jiu Jitsu Complete. 10.95 (*0-685-21995-X*); pap. 6.95 (*0-686-66565-1*) Wehman.

Nakae, Kiyose & Yeager, Charles. Jiu Jitsu Complete. (Illus.). 176p. 1995. pap. 9.95 (*0-8065-0418-8*, Citadel Pr) Carol Pub Group.

Nakagaki, M., jt. ed. see Drioli, E.

Nakagawa, jt. ed. see Osada.

***Nakagawa, Allen S.** LIMS: Implementation Management. 180p. 1994. 59.95 (*0-85186-824-X*, R6824) CRC Pr.

Nakagawa, George. Seki-nin (Duty Bound) 1989. 19.95 (*0-930046-10-2*) CSUF Oral Hist.

Nakagawa, Kathryn, jt. auth. see Lewis, Dan A.

Nakagawa, Keiichiro, ed. The International Conferences on Business History: Government & Business, No. 5. 239p. 1980. 42.50 (*0-86008-265-2*, Pub. by U of Tokyo JA) Col U Pr.

— The International Conferences on Business History: Social Order & Entrepreneurship, No. 2. 330p. 1977. 42.50 (*0-86008-195-8*, Pub. by U of Tokyo JA) Col U Pr.

— The International Conferences on Business History: Strategy & Structure of Big Business, No. 1. 312p. 1976. 49.50 (*0-86008-170-2*, Pub. by U of Tokyo JA) Col U Pr.

Nakagawa, Keiichiro & Yui, Tsunehiko, eds. Business History of Shipping. 300p. 1985. 37.50 (*0-86008-367-5*, Pub. by U of Tokyo JA) Col U Pr.

Nakagawa, Keiichiro, jt. ed. see Yui, Tsunehiko.

Nakagawa, Ryoichi. From Aircraft to Automobiles and Automotive Electronics: Remembrances of an Internal Combustion Engineer. 52p. 1990. lib. bdg. 15.00 (*1-56091-040-2*, SP826) Soc Auto Engineers.

Nakagawa, T., jt. auth. see Akaike, H.

Nakagawara, Michio, jt. ed. see Kariya, Tetsuhiko.

Nakagoshi, N. & Golley, F. B., eds. Coniferous Forest Ecology, from an International Perspective. (Illus.). 182p. 1991. pap. 45.00 (*90-5103-065-7*, Pub. by SPB Acad Pub NE) Koeltz Sci Bks.

Nakahara, David, jt. auth. see Carradine, David.

Nakahara, David, ed. see Eng, Paul.

Nakahara, H., jt. ed. see Suga, S.

Nakahara, M. Geometry, Topology & Physics. (Graduate Student Series in Physics). (Illus.). 520p. (C). 1990. 172.00 (*0-85274-094-8*); pap. 55.00 (*0-85274-095-6*) IOP Pub.

Nakahara, Yasuo. Japanese Joinery: A Handbook for Joiners & Carpenters. Nii, Koichi P., tr. 240p. (Orig.). 1983. pap. 14.95 (*0-88179-001-X*, Cloudburst Press Bk) Hartley & Marks.

Nakai, Hiroshi & Yoo, Chai H. Analysis & Design of Curved Steel Bridges. 688p. 1988. text ed. 72.00 (*0-07-045866-9*) McGraw.

Nakai, Kate W. Shogunal Politics: Arai Hakuseki & the Premises of Tokugawa Rule. LC 87-30517. (East Asian Monographs: No. 134). 400p. 1988. 28.00 (*0-674-80653-0*) HUP.

Nakai, M., jt. auth. see Sario, L.

Nakai, S., jt. ed. see Sim, J. S.

Nakai, Shuryo & Li-Chan, Eunice. Hydrophobic Interaction in Food Systems. 224p. 1988. 118.00 (*0-8493-6044-7*, QP551, CRC Reprint) Franklin.

Nakaike, Toshiyuki. Enumeratio Pteridophytarum Japonicarum. 1975. 64.50 (*0-86008-135-4*, Pub. by U of Tokyo JA) Col U Pr.

Nakaike, Toshiyuki, jt. auth. see Kurata, Satoru.

Nakaike, Toshiyuki, jt. ed. see Kurata, Satoru.

Nakajima. Introduction to Bioprogressive Therapy. (Illus.). 166p. 1987. text ed. 78.00 (*1-85097-007-6*) Quint Pub Co.

— Macromolecular Chemistry, Vol. 5. (Organic Synthesis--Today & Tomorrow Ser.). 1979. 60.00 (*0-08-022039-8*, Pub. by Pergamon Repr UK) Franklin.

Nakajima, A., jt. ed. see Kono, Reisaku.

Nakajima, A., jt. ed. see Tsuruta, T.

Nakajima, Akihiko, jt. auth. see Otsuka, Akira.

Nakajima, C. Subjective Equilibrium Theory of the Farm Household. 302p. 1986. 87.25 (*0-444-42646-9*) Elsevier.

Nakajima, Caroline. Connecting Cultures & Literature. Miriani, Patricia, ed. (Curriculum Connections Ser.). (Illus.). 144p. (Orig.). (gr. k-3). 1992. student ed 12.95 (*1-55734-347-0*) Tchr Create Mat.

— In the Year of the Boar & Jackie Robinson: A Literature Unit. (Literature Units Ser.). (Illus.). 48p. (Orig.). 1992. student ed 6.95 (*1-55734-417-5*) Tchr Create Mat.

— Journey to Topaz: A Literature Unit. (Literature Units Ser.). (Illus.). 48p. (Orig.). 1993. student ed, pap. 6.95 (*1-55734-430-2*) Tchr Create Mat.

— Roald Dahl. (Favorite Authors Ser.). (Illus.). 1994. 10.95 (*1-55734-453-1*) Tchr Create Mat.

— Tuck Everlasting: A Literature Unit. Miriani, Patricia, ed. (Illus.). 48p. (Orig.). 1992. student ed, pap. 6.95 (*1-55734-408-6*) Tchr Create Mat.

Nakajima, F. Sanseido's New Concise Japanese-English Dictionary. 1362p. (ENG & JPN.). 1985. 49.95 (*0-8288-0465-6*, M9989) Fr & Eur.

Nakajima, H. & Ogawa, H. Compact Disc Technology. 228p. 1991. 60.00 (*90-5199-066-9*, Pub. by IOS Pr NE) IOS Press.

Nakajima, Heizo, ed. Current English Linguistics in Japan. LC 91-22180. (Trends in Linguistics, State-of-the-Art Reports: No. 16). vi, 544p. (C). 1991. lib. bdg. 198.50 (*3-11-011781-9*, 151-91) Mouton.

Nakajima, John M., jt. auth. see Francis, Carolyn B.

Nakajima, Kimiko, jt. auth. see Young, John.

Nakajima-Okano, Kimiko, jt. auth. see Young, John.

Nakajima, R. & Yuasa, T., eds. The IOTA Programming System. (Lecture Notes in Computer Science Ser.: Vol. 160). 217p. 1983. pap. 28.00 (*0-387-12693-7*) Spr-Verlag.

Nakajima, S. The Physics of Elementary Excitations. (Solid-State Sciences Ser.: Vol. 12). (Illus.). 340p. 1980. 75.00 (*0-387-09921-2*) Spr-Verlag.

Nakajima, Seiichi. Introduction to TPM: Total Productive Maintenance. LC 88-61394. (Illus.). 149p. 1988. 45.00 (*0-915299-23-2*) Prod Press.

— TPM Development Program: Implementing Total Productive Maintenance. LC 88-43566. (Illus.). 427p. 1989. 85.00 (*0-915299-37-2*) Prod Press.

***Nakajima, Tsuyoshi, ed.** Fluorine-Carbon & Fluoride-Carbon Materials: Chemistry, Physics, & Applications. LC 94-24904. 1994. pap. text ed. write for info. (*0-89579-305-9*) Dekker.

Nakajima, Tsuyoshi & Watanabe, Nobuatsu. Graphite Fluorides & Carbon-Fluorine Compounds. (Illus.). 168p. 1990. 144.00 (*0-8493-5605-9*, QD181, CRC Reprint) Franklin.

Nakakuki, Teruo, ed. Oligosaccharides: Production, Properties & Applications. (Japanese Technology Reviews, Section E. Ser.). 1993. pap. text ed. 75.00 (*2-88124-890-X*) Gordon & Breach.

Nakamoto, Kazuo. Infrared & Raman Spectra of Inorganic & Coordination Compounds. 4th ed. LC 86-1345. 484p. 1986. text ed. 120.00 (*0-471-01066-9*) Wiley.

Nakamoto, Kazuo, jt. ed. see Ferraro, John R.

Nakamura. Japanese-English-Japanese Glossary of Social Welfare & Related Sciences. 246p. (ENG & JPN.). 1981. 49.95 (*0-8288-2364-2*, M 10061) Fr & Eur.

Nakamura, A., et al, eds. Parallel Image Analysis: Second International Conference, ICPIA '92, Ube, Japan, December 1992: Proceedings. LC 92-39674. (Lecture Notes in Computer Science Ser.: Vol. 654). 1992. 52.00 (*0-387-56346-6*) Spr-Verlag.

Nakamura, Alice & Nakamura, Masao. Second Paycheck: An Analysis of the Employment & Earnings of Wives Compared with Unmarried Women & Men. 1985. text ed. 81.00 (*0-12-513820-2*) Acad Pr.

Nakamura, Alice O., jt. ed. see Diewert, W. Erwin.

Nakamura, Eiji. Flying Origami. LC 70-188761. (Illus.). 64p. 1972. pap. 11.00 (*0-87040-023-1*) Japan Pubns USA.

— Quick & Easy Flying Origami. (Illus.). 60p. 1993. pap. 17.00 (*0-87040-925-5*) Japan Pubns USA.

Nakamura, George, ed. Arizona Visitor's Guide for Japanese, Vol. 1. 104p. (JPN.). 1991. pap. 7.50 (*0-9629581-0-7*) ACE Japan.

Nakamura, Glenn V., et al, eds. Psychology of Learning & Motivation- Advances in Research & Theory: Categorization by Human & Machines, Vol. 29. (Illus.). 552p. 1993. text ed. 84.95 (*0-12-543329-8*) Acad Pr.

Nakamura, Hajima. History of Early Vedanta Philosophy, Pt. 2. 1990. 32.50 (*81-208-0651-4*, Pub. by Motilal Banarsidass II) S Asia.

Nakamura, Hajime. A Comparative History of Ideas. 580p. 1986. lib. bdg. 65.00 (*0-7103-0122-7*, Pub. by Kegan Paul Intl UK) Routledge Chapman & Hall.

— A Comparative History of Ideas. 572p. 1993. pap. 29.95 (*0-7103-0384-X*, A4717, Pub. by Kegan Paul Intl UK) Routledge Chapman & Hall.

— Comparative History of Ideas. (C). 1986. text ed. 30.00 (*81-208-1004-X*, Pub. by Motilal Banarsidass II) S Asia.

— Gotama Buddha. LC 77-8589. 1977. 12.95 (*0-914910-05-1*); pap. 10.95 (*0-914910-06-X*) Buddhist Bks.

— The Ways of Thinking of Eastern Peoples, 10 vols., Set. (Documentary Reference Collections). 1988. 395.00 (*0-318-35983-9*, CMJ/, Greenwood Pr) Greenwood.

— The Ways of Thinking of Eastern Peoples, 10 vols., Vol. 1. LC 88-21947. (Documentary Reference Collections). 657p. 1988. text ed. 69.50 (*0-313-26556-9*, CMJ01, Greenwood Pr) Greenwood.

— Ways of Thinking of Eastern Peoples: India, China, Tibet, Japan. rev. ed. Wiener, Philip P., ed. 732p. (C). 1964. pap. text ed. 16.95 (*0-8248-0078-8*, Eastwest Ctr Pr) UH Pr.

— Ways of Thinking of Eastern Peoples: India-Tibet-China-Japan. 1991. 27.00 (*81-208-0764-2*, Pub. by Motilal Banarsidass II) S Asia.

Nakamura, Hijime. Buddhism in Comparative Light. 1986. 15.00 (*0-685-35378-8*, Pub. by Motilal Banarsidass II) S Asia.

— Indian Buddhism: A Survey with Bibliographical Notes. xii, 423p. 1992. 32.00 (*0-317-56404-8*, Pub. by Motilal Banarsidass II) S Asia.

Nakamura, Hiroshi. Spirulina: Food for a Hungry World; A Pioneer's Story in Aquaculture. Hills, Christopher, ed. Wargo, Robert, tr. LC 82-4816. (Illus.). 224p. (Orig.). 1982. pap. 10.95 (*0-916438-47-3*) Univ of Trees.

— Tuna: Distribution & Migration. 1978. 125.00 (*0-685-63462-0*) St Mut.

Nakamura, Hiroshi, jt. auth. see Hills, Christopher.

Nakamura, I., et al. Emerging Nuclear Energy Systems - Icenes 1993: Proceedings of the Seventh International Conference. 580p. 1994. text ed. 122.00 (*981-02-1719-6*) World Scientific Pub.

Nakamura, Joyce. Applied Numerical Methods with Software. 464p. 1990. text ed. 79.00 (*0-13-041047-0*) P-H.

— Contemporary Authors, Vol. 19. (Autobiography Ser.). 1994. 122.00 (*0-8103-4516-1*, 002902) Gale.

— Contemporary Authors, Vol. 20. (Autobiography Ser.). 1994. 122.00 (*0-8103-4517-X*, 002903) Gale.

— High-Interest Books for Teens. 2nd ed. (Illus.). 300p. 1987. 99.00 (*0-8103-1830-X*) Gale.

— An Inter-Industry Translog Model of Prices & Technical Change for the West German Economy. (Lecture Notes in Economics & Mathematical Systems Ser.: Vol. 221). 290p. 1983. pap. 41.00 (*0-387-12709-7*) Spr-Verlag.

— Major Authors & Illustrated Children, Vol. 5. 1992. write for info. (*0-8103-8495-7*, 101444) Gale.

— Major Authors & Illustrated Children, Vol. 6. 1992. write for info. (*0-8103-8496-5*, 101445) Gale.

— Major Authors & Illustrators Children - Young Adult 1, Vol. 1. 1992. write for info. (*0-8103-7382-3*) Gale.

— Major Authors & Illustrators Children - Young Adult 1, Vol. 2. 1992. write for info. (*0-8103-7383-1*) Gale.

— Major Authors & Illustrators Children - Young Adult 1, Vol. 4. 1992. write for info. (*0-8103-7769-1*) Gale.

— SATA Autobiography Series, Vol. 14. 1992. 87.00 (*0-8103-4463-7*) Gale.

— SATA Autobiography Series, Vol. 15. 1992. 87.00 (*0-8103-4464-5*) Gale.

— SATA Autobiography Series, Vol. 18. 1994. 87.00 (*0-8103-4467-X*) Gale.

— SATA Autobiography Series, Vol. 19. 1994. 87.00 (*0-8103-4468-8*) Gale.

Nakamura, Joyce, ed. Children's Authors & Illustrators: An Index to Biographical Dictionaries. 4th ed. 1000p. 1986. 156.00 (*0-8103-2525-X*) Gale.

— Contemporary Authors, Vol. 12. LC 84-647879. (Autobiography Ser.). (Illus.). 400p. 1990. text ed. 122.00 (*0-8103-4511-0*) Gale.

— Contemporary Authors Autobiography Series, Vol. 21. 400p. 1995. 122.00 (*0-8103-4518-8*) Gale.

— Something about the Author, Vol. 6. (Autobiography Ser.). 1988. 87.00 (*0-8103-4455-6*) Gale.

— Something about the Author, Vol. 7. (Autobiography Ser.). 1988. 87.00 (*0-8103-4456-4*) Gale.

— Something about the Author, Vol. 8. (Autobiography Ser.). 1989. 87.00 (*0-8103-4457-2*) Gale.

— Something about the Author, Vol. 9. (Autobiography Ser.). 400p. 1989. 87.00 (*0-8103-4458-0*) Gale.

— Something about the Author, Vol. 10. LC 86-641293. (Autobiography Ser.). (Illus.). 384p. 1990. text ed. 87.00 (*0-8103-4459-9*, 002713) Gale.

— Something about the Author Autobiography Series Vol. 20. 1995. text ed. 85.00 (*0-8103-4469-6*) Gale.

Nakamura, Joyce, jt. ed. see Collier, Laurie.

Nakamura, Joyce, jt. ed. see Gottfries, C. G.

Nakamura, K., ed. Brain & Blood Pressure Control. (International Congress Ser.: No. 695). 464p. 1986. 139.00 (*0-444-80810-8*) Elsevier.

***Nakamura, Kaicho T.** One Day-One Lifetime: An Illustrated Guide to the Spirit, Practice, & Philosophy of Seido Karate Meditation. (Illus.). 210p. 1995. 25.00 (*0-8048-3064-9*) C E Tuttle.

NaKamura, Kaiko, tr. see Chijiiwa, Hideaki.

Nakamura, Katsuhiro. Quantum Chaos: A New Paradigm of Nonlinear Dynamics. (Nonlinear Science Ser.: No. 3). (Illus.). 180p. (C). 1993. 64.95 (*0-521-39249-7*) Cambridge U Pr.

— Quantum Chaos: A New Paradigm of Nonlinear Dynamics. (Cambridge Nonlinear Science Ser.: No. 3). (Illus.). 208p. (C). 1994. pap. 24.95 (*0-521-46746-2*) Cambridge U Pr.

Nakamura, Koichiro & Child, C. Allan. Pycnogonida from Waters Adjacent to Japan. LC 91-1984. (Smithsonian Contributions to Zoology Ser.: No. 512). 80p. reprint ed. pap. 25.00 (*0-7837-0268-X*, 2040577) Bks Demand.

— Shallow-Water Pycnogonida from the Izu Peninsula, Japan. LC 83-10183. (Smithsonian Contributions to Zoology Ser.: No. 386). 76p. reprint ed. pap. 25.00 (*0-317-29735-X*, 2022202) Bks Demand.

Nakamura, M. & Vanhoutte, Paul M., eds. Coronary Circulation in Physiological & Pathophysiological States. (Illus.). xiii, 178p. 1991. 69.00 (*0-387-70053-6*) Spr-Verlag.

Nakamura, Margaret, jt. auth. see Osborne, Larry N.

Nakamura, Masao, jt. auth. see Nakamura, Alice.

Nakamura, Matazo. Kabuki - Backstage, Onstage. Oshima, Mark, tr. (Illus.). 176p. 1990. 18.95 (*0-87011-985-0*) Kodansha.

Nakamura, N., jt. auth. see Chihara, H.

Nakamura, Norio, et al, eds. Recent Advances in Neurotraumatology. LC 92-48234. 1993. 145.00 (*0-387-70115-X*) Spr-Verlag.

Nakamura, R., et al, eds. Wrist Disorders: Current Concepts & Challenges. LC 92-29763. 1993. 198.00 (*0-387-70102-8*) Spr-Verlag.

Nakamura, Robert M., ed. see Ito, Kiichi, et al.

Nakamura, Robert M., jt. auth. see Yoshitsugi, Hokama.

Nakamura, Robert M., et al. Autoantibodies to Nuclear Antigens: Advances in Laboratory Tests & Significance in Systemic Rheumatic Diseases. 2nd ed. LC 85-5992. 1985. 25.00 (*0-89189-188-9*) Am Soc Clinical.

Nakamura, Robert M., et al, eds. Immunochemical Assays & Biosensor Technology for the 1990s. (Illus.). 421p. 1992. text ed. 51.00 (*1-55581-040-3*) Am Soc Microbio.

Nakamura, Robert T. & Smallwood, Frank. The Politics of Policy Implementation. 201p. (C). 1980. pap. text ed. 16.00 (*0-312-62780-7*) St Martin.

Nakamura, Robert T., jt. auth. see Church, Thomas W.

Nakamura, Sadao. The Color Source Book for Graphic Designers. (Illus.). 116p. (Orig.). (C). 1992. pap. 19.95 (*4-8381-0110-4*, Pub. by Mitsumura Suiko Shoin JA) Weatherhill.

Nakamura, Shigehiro. The New Standardization: Keystone of Continuous Improvement in Manufacturing. Talbot, Bruce, tr. (Illus.). 286p. 1993. 75.00 (*1-56327-039-0*) Prod Press.

Nakamura, Shoichiro. Applied Numerical Methods in C. LC 92-19039. 576p. 1992. text ed. 60.00 (*0-13-042052-2*) P-H Gen Ref & Trav.

— Computational Methods in Engineering & Science. LC 85-9737. 472p. 1986. reprint ed. lib. bdg. 48.95 (*0-89874-867-4*) Krieger.

— Numerical Methods Software: Computational Software Library (CSL) 178p. (Orig.). (C). 1990. pap. text ed. 35.00 (*0-9626943-8-X*) Compu Methods.

Nakamura, Shoichiro & Carswell, Peter. Scientific Computer Graphics in C. 1993. text ed. write for info. (*0-13-795790-4*) P-H.

Nakamura, T. & Nosay, G. Decorative Hand-Guards for Japanese Swords. (Legends in Japanese Ser.). (Illus.). 100p. 1983. pap. 17.50 (*0-87556-578-6*) Saifer.

— Decorative Hand-Guards for Japanese Swords. (Legends in Japanese Ser.). (Illus.). 100p. 1983. pap. 17.50 (*0-87556-660-X*) Saifer.

***Nakamura, Tadashi.** Karate: Technique & Spirit. (Illus.). 168p. 1986. 24.95 (*4-07-974179-0*, Pub. by Shufunomoto Co Ltd JA) C E Tuttle.

Nakamura, Takafusa. The Postwar Japanese Economy: Its Development & Structure. 292p. (Orig.). 1984. 30.00 (*0-86008-284-9*, Pub. by U of Tokyo JA); pap. 22.50 (*0-86008-355-1*, Pub. by U of Tokyo JA) Col U Pr.

— The Postwar Japanese Economy: Its Development & Structure. 300p. 1994. pap. 29.50 (*0-86008-514-7*) Col U Pr.

Nakamura, Takashi. Oriental Breathing Therapy. LC 79-91515. (Illus.). 160p. 1981. pap. 12.95 (*0-87040-478-4*) Japan Pubns USA.

Nakamura, Tomoko, tr. see Shohno, Naomi.

Nakamura, Toshikazu & Matsumoto, Kunio, eds. Growth Factors: Cell Growth, Morphogenesis & Transformation. LC 94-7003. (Gann Monograph on Cancer Research: No. 42). 1994. write for info. (*0-8493-7775-7*) CRC Pr.

Nakamura, Toshio, ed. Cesar Pelli. (Illus.). 232p. (ENG & JPN.). 1985. 150.00 (*0-685-63203-2*); pap. 100.00 (*0-685-63204-0*) Elliots Bks.

Nakamura, Tsuneo. Gentle Giant: At Sea with the Humpback Whale. LC 87-35310. (Illus.). 1988. pap. 12.95 (*0-87701-506-6*) Chronicle Bks.

Nakamura, Y. & Taketani, Y., eds. New Aspects of Pathophysiology & Treatment of Polycycstic Ovary Syndrome: Journal: Hormone Research, Vol. 33. (Illus.). vi, 50p. 1990. 22.50 (*3-8055-5262-9*) S Karger.

Nakamura, Yorinaga. Shoot Wrestling: Shoot Wrestling Training Guide. (Shoot Wrestling Training Ser.: Vol. I). 52p. 1993. pap. 14.99 (*0-9633592-2-3*) Third Eye Pub.

Nakamura, Yoshihiko. Theory of Robotic Manipulators. (Illus.). 224p. (C). 1991. text ed. 74.25 (*0-201-15198-7*) Addison-Wesley.

Nakamura, Zentaro, jt. auth. see Senju, Shizuo.

Nakan, Hiroshige, jt. ed. see Shiratori, Tsuneo.

Nakane, Chie. Garo & Khasi: A Comparative Study in Matrilineal Systems. 1967. pap. text ed. 30.80 (*3-10-800106-X*) Mouton.

— Japanese Society. LC 71-100021. (Center for Japanese & Korean Studies, UC Berkeley: No. 4). (C). 1970. pap. 12.00 (*0-520-02154-1*) U CA Pr.

Nakane, Chie & Oishi, Shinsaburo. Tokugawa Japan: The Social & Economic Antecedents of Modern Japan. Totman, Conrad, tr. 248p. 1992. 42.50 (*0-86008-447-7*, Pub. by U of Tokyo JA); pap. 19.50 (*0-86008-490-6*, Pub. by U of Tokyo JA) Col U Pr.

Nakanishi, Akira. Writing Systems of the World: Alphabets, Syllabaries, Pictograms. LC 79-64826. (Illus.). 122p. 1980. 29.95 (*0-8048-1293-4*); pap. 14.95 (*0-8048-1654-9*) C E Tuttle.

Nakanishi, Don T. & Nishida, Tina Y., eds. The Asian American Educational Experience: A Sourcebook for Teachers & Students. LC 94-16361. 352p. 1994. 55.00 (*0-415-90871-X*, B2999) Routledge.

Nakanishi, Donald T. & Nishida, Tina Y., eds. The Asian American Educational Experience: A Sourcebook for Teachers & Students. LC 94-16361. 416p. 1994. pap. 18.95 (*0-415-90872-8*, B3003) Routledge.

N

An Asterisk (*) at the beginning of an entry indicates that the title is appearing in BIP for the first time.

***Nakanishi, Himeko, ed.** Poems of Liberty, Vol. 1. (Illus.). 96p. 1995. pap. 29.95 (4-7636-3242-6, Pub. by Kyoto Shoin JA) Bks Nippan.
— Poems of Liberty, Vol. 2. (Illus.). 96p. 1995. pap. 29.95 (4-7636-3243-4, Pub. by Kyoto Shoin JA) Bks Nippan.
— Poems of Liberty, Vol. 3. (Illus.). 96p. 1995. pap. 29.95 (4-7636-3244-2, Pub. by Kyoto Shoin JA) Bks Nippan.
***Nakanishi, Koji.** Changing Trends in Structural Natural Products Chemistry: Selected Papers of Koji Nakanishi. (Series on 20th Century Chemistry). 600p. 1995. text ed. 109.00 (981-02-1827-3) World Scientific Pub.
Nakanishi, Koji, et al. Circular Dichroism: Principles & Applications. LC 93-39221. 1994. write for info. (1-56081-618-X) VCH Pubs.
Nakanishi, Koji. One Dimensional & Two Dimensional NMR Spectra by Modern Pulse Technique. (Illus.). 336p. (C). 1990. pap. text ed. 38.50 (0-935702-63-6) Univ Sci Bks.
— A Wandering Natural Products Chemist. Seeman, Jeffrey I., ed. LC 90-45062. (Profiles, Pathways, & Dreams Ser.). (Illus.). 200p. 1991. 24.95 (0-8412-1775-0) Am Chemical.
Nakanishi, Koji & Harada, Nobuyuki. Circular Dichroic Spectroscopy: Exciton Coupling in Organic Stereochemistry. LC 81-51270. (Illus.). 460p. (C). 1984. text ed. 46.50 (0-935702-09-1) Univ Sci Bks.
Nakanishi, Koji & Solomon, Philippa H. Infrared Absorption Spectroscopy. 2nd ed. LC 76-27393. 1977. pap. 36.95 (0-8162-6251-9) Holden-Day.
Nakanishi, Koji, et al. Natural Products Chemistry, Vol. III. LC 74-6431. (Illus.). 700p. 1984. 110.00 (0-935702-14-8) Univ Sci Bks.
Nakanishi, Kunio, ed. Switching Phenomena in High-Voltage Circuit Breakers. (Electrical Engineering & Electronics Ser.: Vol. 75). 296p. 1991. 125.00 (0-8247-8543-6) Dekker.
Nakanishi, N. Graph Theory & Feynman Integrals. (Mathematics & Its Applications Ser.). 236p. 1971. text ed. 152.00 (0-677-02950-0) Gordon & Breach.
Nakanishi, N & Ojima, I. Covariant Operator Formalism of Gauge Theories & Quantum Gravity. 452p. 1990. text ed. 85.00 (9971-5-0238-0); pap. text ed. 39.00 (9971-5-0239-9) World Scientific Pub.
Nakanishi, T., ed. Long Term Clinical Care of Parkinson's Disease: Journal: European Neurology, Vol. 30, Suppl. 1, 1990. vi, 42p. 1990. pap. text ed. 19.25 (3-8055-5161-4) S Karger.
— Long Term Clinical Care of Parkinson's Disease: 3rd Symposium, Tokyo, April 1988. (Journal: European Neurology: Vol. 29, Suppl. 1, 1988). 38p. 1989. pap. 17.75 (3-8055-4969-5) S Karger.
— Long Term Clinical Care of Parkinson's Disease, Tokyo, April 1987: Second Symposium. (Journal: European Neurology: Vol. 28, Suppl. 1, 1988). vi, 42p. 1988. pap. 13.75 (3-8055-4833-8) S Karger.
— Long Term Clinical Care of Parkinson's Disease, 5th Symposium, Tokyo, April 1990. (Journal: European Neurology: Vol. 31, Suppl. 1, 1991). (Illus.). iv, 60p. 1991. pap. 25.75 (3-8055-5401-X) S Karger.
— Long-Time Clinical Care of Parkinson's Disease, Symposium, Tokyo, April 1986: Journal: European Neurology, Vol. 26, Suppl. 1, 1987. (Illus.). iv, 56p. 1987. pap. 17.00 (3-8055-4590-8) S Karger.
— Sixth Symposium on a Long Term Clinical Care of Parkinson's Disease, Tokyo, October 1991. (Journal: European Neurology: Vol. 32, Suppl. 1, 1992). (Illus.). vi, 54p. 1992. pap. 24.00 (3-8055-5664-0) S Karger.
Nakano. Projective Modules over Lie Algebras of Cartan Type. 84p. 1992. 24.00 (0-8218-2530-5) Am Math.
Nakano, Dokuihtei. Easy Origami. Kenneway, Eric, tr. (Illus.). 64p. (J). (gr. 2-5). 1994. pap. 4.99 (0-14-036525-7) Puffin Bks.
Nakano, Dokuotei. Origami Classroom, Vol. I. (Illus.). 24p. 1993. pap. 12.95 (0-87040-912-3) Japan Pubns USA.
— Origami Classroom, Vol. 2. (Illus.). 24p. 1994. boxed 12.95 (0-87040-938-7) Japan Pubns USA.
— Origami Classroom Two. (Illus.). 24p. 1994. bds. 12.95 (0-87040-913-1) Japan Pubns USA.
Nakano, Hidegoreo. Linear Lattices. 2nd abr. ed. LC 66-24169. 157p. reprint ed. pap. 44.80 (0-7837-3774-2, 2043592) Bks Demand.
Nakano, Hidegoro. Uniform Spaces & Transformation Groups. LC 68-13935. 269p. reprint ed. pap. 76.70 (0-7837-3776-9, 2043595) Bks Demand.
Nakano, Hiroshi, jt. auth. see Hayashi, Susumu.
Nakano, Hismatsu. Helical & Spiral Antennas: A Numerical Approach. LC 87-16667. (Electromagnetic Applications Ser.). 261p. 1987. text ed. 195.00 (0-471-91736-2) Wiley.
Nakano, Jiro. Parker Ranch Paniolo: Yutaka Kimura. (Illus.). 192p. 1992. pap. 14.95 (0-8248-1432-0) UH Pr.
Nakano, Jiro, ed. see Soga, Keiho, et al.
Nakano, Kay, ed. see Soga, Keiho, et al.
Nakano, Mei T. Japanese American Women: Three Generations, 1890-1990. LC 89-91580. (Illus.). 256p. (Orig.). 1990. 21.95 (0-942610-05-9) Mina Pr.
— Japanese American Women: Three Generations, 1890-1990. LC 89-91580. (Illus.). 256p. (Orig.). 1995. pap. write for info. (0-942610-06-7) Mina Pr.
— Riko Rabbit. LC 82-81737. (J). (gr. 2-5). 1982. pap. 5.95 (0-942610-00-8) Mina Pr.
Nakano, Tomio. Ordinance Power of the Japanese Emperor. LC 71-173009. reprint ed. 31.50 (0-404-04650-9) AMS Pr.
Nakano, Toru. Trekking in Nepal. rev. ed. Ooka, Dianne, tr. (Illus.). 232p. 1990. pap. 29.95 (0-89346-251-9) Heian Intl.
Nakano, Yuichi, ed. Cholesteatoma & Mastoid Surgery: Proceedings of the Fourth International Conference, Nigata, Japan, September 8-12, 1993. LC 93-41769. (Illus.). 1994. lib. bdg. 216.00 (90-6299-102-5, Pub. by Kugler NE) Kugler Pubns.
Nakanose, Shigeyuki. Josiah's Passover: Sociology & the Liberating Bible. LC 93-18286. (Bible & Liberation Ser.). 250p. (Orig.). 1993. pap. 19.95 (0-88344-850-5) Orbis Bks.
***Nakao, Seigo.** Random House Japanese-English English-Japanese Dictionary. (JPN.). 1995. 22.00 (0-679-44149-2, Random Ref) Random.
***Nakao, Shigeo.** The Political Economy of Japanese Money. 215p. 1995. 39.50 (0-86008-507-4, Pub. by U of Tokyo JA) Col U Pr.
Nakarada, Radmila & Oberg, Jan, eds. Surviving Together: The Olaf Palme Lectures on Common Security, 1988. 214p. 1989. text ed. 49.95 (1-85521-067-3, Pub. by Dartmth Pub UK) Ashgate Pub Co.
Nakarai, Toyozo W. The Study of the Impact of Buddhism Upon Japanese Life As Revealed in the Order of Kokin-Shu. 1972. 59.95 (0-8490-1156-6) Gordon Pr.
Nakas, James P. & Hagedorn, Charles. Biotechnology of Plant-Microbe Interactions. 336p. 1990. text ed. 65.00 (0-07-045867-7) McGraw.
Nakas, James P., jt. ed. see Mitchell, Myron J.
Nakasa, Nat, jt. auth. see Patel, Essop.
Nakash, Yitzhak. The Shiis of Iraq. LC 93-31786. 1994. 35.00 (0-691-03431-1) Princeton U Pr.
Nakashima, George. The Soul of a Tree: A Woodworker's Reflections. LC 88-80298. 224p. 1988. pap. 45.00 (0-87011-903-6) Kodansha.
Nakashima, Masahiro, jt. auth. see Teerink, John R.
***Nakashima, Signe E.** The Cardinal Mine: A Ghost of the Past. 120p. 1995. pap. text ed. 9.95 (0-9646928-0-5) S E Nakashima.
Nakashima, T. English-Japanese. 605p. 1991. reprint ed. 39.00 (0-88431-078-7) IBD Ltd.
Nakashima, T. & Kojiro, M. Hepatocellular Carcinoma. (Illus.). 280p. 1987. 261.00 (0-387-70018-8) Spr-Verlag.
Nakasone, K. K. Cultural Studies & Identification of Wood-inhabiting Corticiaceae & Selected Hymenomycetes from North America. (Mycologia Memoirs Ser.: No. 15). (Illus.). 412p. 1990. lib. bdg. 105.00 (3-443-76005-8, Pub. by Cramer-Borntraeger GW) Lubrecht & Cramer.
Nakasone, Riri. Shiki: Four Seasons in the Eden. (Illus.). 20p. (ENG & JPN.). 1988. pap. 25.00 (0-944290-02-7) Light Speed.
Nakasone, Ronald Y. Ethics of Enlightenment: Essays & Sermons in Search for a Buddhist Ethic. 200p. (Orig.). 1990. 30.00 (0-9623086-0-9); pap. 12.00 (0-9623086-1-7) Dharma Cloud Pubs.
Nakasone, Yasuhiro. Beyond the Horizon of the Pacific. (CISA Working Paper Ser.: No. 63). 21p. (Orig.). Date not set. pap. 10.00 (0-86682-080-9) Ctr Intl Relations.
Nakata, I., et al, eds. Software Science & Engineering: Selected Papers from the Kyoto Symposia. (Computer Science Ser.: Vol. 31). 280p. (C). 1991. text ed. 74.00 (981-02-0776-X) World Scientific Pub.
Nakata, John K., jt. auth. see Nielson, Jane E.
Nakata, Kazuo, jt. ed. see Saito, Shuzo.
Nakata, M. & Wei, Stephen H. Occlusal Guidance in Pediatric Dentistry. (Illus.). 100p. 1988. 30.00 (0-912791-63-2) Ishiyaku Euro.
Nakata, T., ed. Three-D Electromagnetic Field Analysis. (Illus.). 322p. (Orig.). (C). 1990. 110.00 (0-907383-51-3, Pub. by J & J Sci Pubs UK) Bks Intl VA.
Nakata, Yujiro. The Art of Japanese Calligraphy. LC 72-92096. (Heibonsha Survey of Japanese Art Ser.: Vol. 27). (Illus.). 176p. 1973. 20.00 (0-8348-1013-1) Weatherhill.
Nakata, Yujiro, et al. Chinese Calligraphy. Hunter, Jeffrey, tr. LC 83-3490. (History of the Art of China Ser.: Vol. 1). Orig. Title: Chugoku no bijutsu-shoseki. (Illus.). 240p. (C). 1983. 65.00 (0-8348-1526-5) Weatherhill.
Nakatani, Alan I., ed. see American Chemical Society, Division of Polymeric Materials: Science & Engineering Staff.
Nakatani, Herbert Y. Photosynthesis. Head, J. J., ed. LC 84-45838. (Carolina Biology Readers Ser.: No. 193). (Illus.). 16p. (Orig.). (YA). (gr. 10 up). 1988. pap. text ed. 2.75 (0-89278-109-2, 45-9793) Carolina Biological.
Nakatani, Iwao. Japanese Firm in Transition. 102p. 1988. 21.75 (92-833-1097-7, Pub. by APO JA); pap. 17.25 (92-833-1098-5) Qual Resc.
Nakawa, Keiko, jt. ed. see Chatani, Masahiro.
Nakawatari, Harutaka. The Sea & I. (Illus.). 32p. (J). (ps-3). 1992. 15.00 (0-374-36428-1) FS&G.
— The Sea & I. Matsui, Susan, tr. (Illus.). 32p. (J). (ps-3). 1994. pap. 4.95 (0-374-46454-5, Sunburst Bks) FS&G.
Nakayama. Best Karate: Bassai Sho, Kaiku Sho Chintei. LC 77-74829. (Best Karate Ser.: Vol. 9). (Illus.). 1986. pap. 15.00 (0-87011-680-0) Kodansha.
***Nakayama, Akira.** PC-Aided Numerical Heat Transfer & Convective Flow. LC 95-7112. 320p. 1995. 99.00 (0-8493-7656-4, 7656) CRC Pr.
Nakayama, J. The Chemistry of 2-Alkoxy-1,3-Benzodithioles & 1,3-Benzodithiolium Salts, Reactions & Synthetic Applications. 35p. 1985. pap. text ed. 26.00 (3-7186-0288-1) Gordon & Breach.
Nakayama, M. Dynamic Karate. (Illus.). 1966. 22.95 (0-685-21935-6) Wehman.
Nakayama, Masatoshi. Best Karate, Vol. 11: Goiushiho, Sho, Meikyo. LC 77-74829. (Best Karate Ser.). (Illus.). 1990. pap. 15.00 (0-87011-758-0) Kodansha.
— Best Karate: Comprehensive. LC 77-74829. (Best Karate Ser.: Vol. 1). (Illus.). 1977. pap. 15.00 (0-87011-317-8) Kodansha.
— Best Karate: Fundamentals. LC 77-74829. (Best Karate Ser.: Vol. 2). (Illus.). 1978. pap. 15.00 (0-87011-324-0) Kodansha.
— Best Karate: Kata: Bassai & Kanku. LC 77-74829. (Best Karate Ser.: Vol. 6). (Illus.). (Orig.). 1980. pap. 15.00 (0-87011-383-6) Kodansha.
— Best Karate: Kata: Gankaku, Jion. LC 77-74829. (Best Karate Ser.: Vol. 8). (Illus.). 144p. (Orig.). 1981. pap. 15.00 (0-87011-402-6) Kodansha.
— Best Karate: Kata: Heian & Tekki. LC 77-74829. (Best Karate Ser.: Vol. 5). 1979. pap. 15.00 (0-87011-379-8) Kodansha.
— Best Karate: Kata: Jutte, Hangetsu, Empi. LC 77-74829. (Best Karate Ser.: Vol. 7). (Illus.). 144p. 1981. pap. 15.00 (0-87011-390-9) Kodansha.
— Best Karate: Kumite 1. LC 77-74829. (Best Karate Ser.: Vol. 3). (Illus.). 1978. pap. 15.00 (0-87011-332-1) Kodansha.
— Best Karate: Kumite 2. LC 77-74829. (Best Karate Ser.: Vol. 4). (Illus.). 1979. pap. 15.00 (0-87011-359-3) Kodansha.
— Dynamic Karate: Introduction by the Master. LC 66-28954. (Illus.). 308p. 1987. pap. 25.00 (0-87011-788-2) Kodansha.
Nakayama, Randall S., ed. The Life & Death of Mrs. Mary Frith: Commonly Called Moll Cutpurse, 1662, with a Facsimile of the Original Edition. LC 93-16326. (Renaissance Imagination Ser.). (Illus.). 320p. 1993. 71.00 (0-8153-1089-7) Garland.
Nakayama, Shigeru. History of Japanese Astronomy: Chinese Background & Western Impact. LC 68-21980. (Harvard-Yenching Institute Monograph: No. 18). (Illus.). 324p. 1969. 22.50 (0-674-39725-8) HUP.
— Science, Technology & Society in Postwar Japan. (Japanese Studies). 296p. 1992. 89.95 (0-7103-0428-5, A6701, Pub. by Kegan Paul Intl UK) Routledge Chapman & Hall.
Nakayama, Shigeru & Dusenberry, Jerry. Academic & Scientific Traditions in China, Japan, & the West. 251p. 1984. 37.50 (0-86008-339-X, Pub. by U of Tokyo JA) Col U Pr.
Nakayama, Wataru & Yang, Kwang-Tzu, eds. Computers & Computing in Heat Transfer Science & Engineering. LC 92-38379. 1992. 188.95 (0-8493-9935-1, TJ260) CRC Pr.
Nakayama, Yoshihiro, jt. ed. see Gray, John E.
***Nakazato, Nariaki.** Agrarian System in Eastern Bengal C 1870-1910. (C). 1994. 27.50x (81-7074-145-9, Pub. by KP Bagchi IA) S Asia.
Nakazawa, Akira, jt. auth. see Haga, Michio.
Nakazawa, Hiromu. Principles of Precision Engineering. LC 93-43452. (Illus.). 288p. (C). 1994. 98.00 (0-19-856266-7) OUP.
Nakazawa, K., jt. auth. see Ide, Y.
Nakazawa, Keiji. Barefoot Gen: Life after the Bomb. (Barefoot Gen Ser.: Vol. 3). (Illus.). 180p. (Orig.). 1988. 39.95 (0-86571-147-X); pap. 11.95 (0-86571-148-8) New Soc Pubs.
— Barefoot Gen Boxed Set: Vol. 1-2-3-4. 1993. 45.95 (0-86571-290-5) New Soc Pubs.
— Barefoot Gen, Vol. 1: A Cartoon Story of Hiroshima. (Illus.). 300p. 1987. 39.95 (0-86571-094-5); pap. 14.95 (0-86571-095-3) New Soc Pubs.
— Barefoot Gen, Vol. 2: The Day After. Project Gen Staff & Dadakai, trs. (Illus.). 192p. (Orig.). 1988. 39.95 (0-86571-122-4); pap. 9.95 (0-86571-123-2) New Soc Pubs.
— Barefoot Gen, Vol. 4: Out of the Ashes. (Illus.). 1993. pap. 39.95 (0-86571-280-8); pap. 12.95 (0-86571-281-6) New Soc Pubs.
***Nakazawa, Keiko.** Pop-up Best Greeting Cards. (Illus.). 92p. (Orig.). 1995. pap. 14.00 (0-87040-964-6) Japan Pubns USA.
Nakazawa, Keiko, jt. auth. see Chatani, Masahiro.
Nakazawa, M., jt. ed. see Imai, S.
Nakazawa, T., ed. Biological Basis of Schizophrenic Disorders. (Taniguchi Symposia on Brain Sciences Ser.: Vol. 14). (Illus.). x, 248p. 1991. 134.50 (3-8055-5503-2) S Karger.
Nakell, Barry & Hardy, Kenneth A. The Arbitrariness of the Death Penalty. LC 86-5931. 1987. lib. bdg. 49.95 (0-87722-443-9) Temple U Pr.
Nakhimovsky, Alexander D. & Leed, Richard L. Advanced Russian. 2nd rev. ed. 262p. (C). 1987. pap. text ed. 19.95 (0-89357-178-4) Slavica.
Nakhimovsky, Alice S. Russian-Jewish Literature & Identity: Jabotinsky, Babel, Grossman, Galich, Roziner, Markish. LC 90-15804. (Jewish Studies). 240p. 1991. text ed. 39.50x (0-8018-4205-0) Johns Hopkins.
Nakhimovsky, L. A., et al. Handbook of Low Temperature Electronic Spectra of Polycyclic Aromatic Hydrocarbons. (Physical Sciences Data Ser.: No. 40). 508p. 1989. 254.00 (0-444-87404-6) Elsevier.
Nakhjavani, Bahiyyih. Asking Questions: A Challenge to Fundamentalism. 190p. (Orig.). 1990. pap. 11.25 (0-85398-314-3) G Ronald Pub.
— Four on an Island. 144p. 1983. 13.50 (0-85398-173-6); pap. 7.25 (0-85398-174-4) G Ronald Pub.
— Response. 144p. 1981. pap. 8.95 (0-85398-107-8) G Ronald Pub.
— When We Grow Up. 120p. 1979. 11.50 (0-85398-085-3); pap. 6.00 (0-85398-086-1) G Ronald Pub.
Nakhla, Fayek & Jackson, Grace. Picking up the Pieces: Two Accounts of a Psychoanalytic Journey. LC 93-1304. 192p. 1993. 20.00 (0-300-05653-2) Yale U Pr.
Nakhleh, Emile A. The Gulf Cooperation Council: Policies, Problems & Prospects. LC 86-8186. 147p. 1986. text ed. 55.00 (0-275-92152-2, C2152, Praeger Pubs) Greenwood.
— Persian Gulf & American Policy. LC 82-13125. 172p. 1982. text ed. 45.00 (0-275-90867-4, C0867, Praeger Pubs) Greenwood.
— The West Bank & Gaza: Toward the Making of a Palestian State. LC 79-536. (AEI Studies: No. 232). (Illus.). 73p. reprint ed. pap. 25.00 (0-8357-4544-9, 2037442) Bks Demand.
Nakhleh, Emile A., ed. A Palestinian Agenda for the West Bank & Gaza. LC 80-15596. (AEI Studies: No. 277). 143p. reprint ed. pap. 40.80 (0-8357-4520-1, 2037379) Bks Demand.
Nakhleh, I. Encyclopedia of the Palestine Problem, 2 vols., Set, Vols. I & II. (Illus.). 1131p. Set. 48.00 (0-685-53439-1) Morning NY.
— Encyclopedia of the Palestine Problem, Set, Vols. I & II. (Illus.). 1131p. 1991. Set. 48.00 (0-685-50253-8) Morning NY.
Nakhleh, Issa. The True History of the Land of Canaan. 112p. 1989. pap. 4.00 (0-9622881-1-X) Morning NY.
Nakhleh, K. & Zureik, Elia. The Sociology of the Palestinians. LC 79-12706. 1980. text ed. 35.00 (0-312-74073-5) St Martin.
Nakhleh, Khalil. Palestinian Dilemma: Nationalist Consciousness & University Education in Israel. (Monograph Ser.: No. 10). 134p. (Orig.). 1979. pap. text ed. 6.00 (0-937694-04-5) Assn Arab-Amer U Grads.
— The Two Galilees. (Occasional Papers: No. 7). 27p. 1982. pap. text ed. 1.00 (0-937694-57-6) Assn Arab-Amer U Grads.
Nakhre, Amrut. Social Psychology of Nonviolent Action: A Study of Three Satyagrahas. 1982. 15.00 (0-8364-0897-7, Pub. by Chanakya II) S Asia.
Nakhshabi, Ziya'u'd-din. The Cleveland Museum of Art's Tuti-Nama: Tales of a Parrot. Simsar, Muhammed A., tr. LC 76-55714. (Illus.). 362p. 1978. 35.00 (0-910386-29-3) Cleveland Mus Art.
Nakicenovic, N. & Grubler, A., eds. Diffusion of Technologies & Social Behavior. (Illus.). xxvi, 605p. 1991. 149.00 (0-387-53846-1) Spr-Verlag.
Nakielny, Richard, jt. auth. see Chapman, Stephen.
Nakken, Craig. Addictive Personality: Roots, Rituals, & Recovery. 125p. (Orig.). 1989. pap. 9.00 (0-89486-489-0, 5149A) Hazelden.
— The Addictive Personality: Understanding Compulsion in Our Lives. LC 88-45140. 128p. (Orig.). 1988. pap. 10.00 (0-06-255488-3) Harper SF.
Nakken, Han, et al, eds. Research on Intervention in Special Education. LC 92-7742. 452p. 1992. lib. bdg. 109.95 (0-7734-9514-2) E Mellen.
Nakken, Jane. Enabling Change-When Your Child Returns from Treatment. 24p. 1985. pap. 1.55 (0-89486-264-2, 1271B) Hazelden.
— Step Two for Young Adults. (Step Pamphlets for Young Adults Ser.). 20p. (Orig.). 1986. pap. 3.00 (0-89486-351-7) Hazelden.
— Straight Back Home: To the Young Person Leaving Treatment. 16p. (Orig.). 1984. pap. 1.55 (0-89486-250-2, 1401B) Hazelden.
Nakken, Jane, jt. auth. see Van Dyke, Della.
Nakleushev, Yevgeny. Towards Integral Knowledge: An Outline of Metaphilosophy, Metascience, Metareligion. 296p. (Orig.). 1984. pap. 15.00 (0-914265-01-6) New Eng Pub MA.
Nakoa, Sarah, jt. tr. see Mookini, Esther T.
Nakon, Robert. Chemical Problem Solving Using Dimensional Analysis. 3rd ed. 416p. (C). 1990. pap. text ed. write for info. (0-13-131392-4) P-H.
Nakoryakov, V. E., et al, eds. Wave Propagation in Gas-Liquid Media. LC 93-15417. 1993. 129.00 (0-8493-9906-8, QC153) CRC Pr.
Nakosteen, Mehdi. History of Islamic Origins of Western Education. 362p. (C). 1964. 25.00 (0-936347-32-5) Iran Bks.
— Mulla's Donkey & Other Friends. LC 74-620109. (Illus.). 150p. 1988. 20.00 (0-936347-49-X) Iran Bks.
— Sufism & Human Destiny & Sufi Thought in Persian Literature. 236p. 1977. 25.00 (0-936347-17-1) Iran Bks.
Nakosteen, Mehdi, ed. Return Ties of Existence. 50p. (ENG & PER.). 1975. lib. bdg. 20.00x (0-936347-46-5) Iran Bks.
Nakosteen, Mehdi, tr. see Khawju of Kirman.
Nakosteen, Mehdi, tr. see Khayyam, Omar.
Nakosteen, Mehdi, tr. see Oryan, Baba T.
Nakosteen, Mehdi, tr. see Saadi of Shiraz.
Nakosteen, Mehdi, tr. see Zakani, Obeyd.
Nakosteen, Mehdi K. The History & Philosophy of Education. LC 65-12757. (Illus.). 758p. reprint ed. pap. 180.00 (0-317-07910-7, 2022244) Bks Demand.
Nakuina, Emma M. Nanaue the Shark Man & Other Hawaiian Shark Stories. Kaivaharadu, Dennis & Kawahanado, Dennis, eds. LC 93-83814. 96p. (Orig.). 1994. pap. 7.95 (0-9623102-4-7) Kalamaku Pr.
Nalbandian, John. Professionalism in Local Government: Transformations in the Roles, Responsibilities, & Values of City Managers. LC 91-9408. (Public Administration Ser.). 151p. 1991. 27.95 (1-55542-372-8) Jossey-Bass.
Nalbandian, John, jt. auth. see Klinger, Donald.
Nalbandov, Andrew V. Advances in Neuroendocrinology. LC 63-7252. 537p. reprint ed. pap. 153.10 (0-8357-5174-0, 2022260) Bks Demand.
Nalbandov, Sergei, tr. see Babel, Isaak E.
Nalbandov, Sergei, tr. see Briusov, Valerii I.
Nalbandov, Sergei, tr. see Leonov, Leonid M.
Nalbant. Switching Power Supplies & Power Factor. 1993. write for info. (0-07-045824-3) McGraw.
Nalbantian, Haig. Incentives, Cooperation & Risk Sharing: Economic & Psychological Perspectives on Employment Contracts. 256p. (C). 1988. text ed. 68.50 (0-8476-7464-9) Rowman.
Nalbantian, Suzanne. Aesthetic Autobiography: From Life to Art in Marcel Proust, James Joyce, Virginia Woolf, & Anais Nin. LC 94-9925. 1994. text ed. 35.00 (0-312-12170-9) St Martin.

N

An Asterisk (*) at the beginning of an entry indicates that the title is appearing in BIP for the first time.

— The Symbol of the Soul from Holderlin to Yeats: A Study in Metonymy. LC 76-25550. 151p. 1977. text ed. 37.00 (*0-231-04148-9*) Col U Pr.

— The Symbol of the Soul from Holderlin to Yeats: A Study in Metonymy. LC 76-25550. 159p. reprint ed. pap. 45.40 (*0-8357-4574-0*, 2037483) Bks Demand.

Nalco Chemical Co. Staff, et al. The Nalco Guide to Cooling-Water System Failure Analysis. LC 92-22428. 1992. text ed. 60.00 (*0-07-028400-8*) McGraw.

NALCO Chemical Company Staff. The NALCO Guide to Boiler Failure Analysis. 272p. 1991. text ed. 54.00 (*0-07-045873-1*) McGraw.

— The NALCO Water Handbook. 2nd ed. 1056p. 1988. text ed. 83.50 (*0-07-045872-3*) McGraw.

Nalder, Eric. Tankers Full of Trouble: The Perilous Journey of Alaskan Crude. LC 93-31198. 320p. 1994. 24.00 (*0-8021-1458-X*) Grove-Atltic.

Naldi, G. J. The Organization of African Unity: An Analysis of Its Role. 328p. 1989. text ed. 100.00 (*0-7201-2006-3*, Mansell Pub) Cassell.

Naldi, Gino J. Documents of the Organization of African Unity. 256p. 1992. text ed. 100.00 (*0-7201-2136-1*, Mansell Pub) Cassell.

Naldrett, Anthony J. Magmatic Sulfide Deposits. (Oxford Monographs on Geology & Geophysics: No. 14). (Illus.). 200p. 1989. 69.95 (*0-19-505119-X*) OUP.

Nalebuff, Barry J., jt. auth. see Dixit, Avinash.

Nalecz, M., ed. Control Aspects of Biomedical Engineering. (IFAC Publication Ser.). (Illus.). 334p. 1987. 72.00 (*0-08-032553-X*, Pergamon Pr) Elsevier.

***Naleid, James C.** Celebrating a Century As the Genuine Article: The Story of Oshkosh B'Gosh. Robbins, Ceila D., ed. (Illus.). 60p. 1995. write for info. (*0-944641-10-5*) Greenwich Pub Group.

Nalepa, B. H., jt. auth. see Blendon, E. G.

Nalepa, Christine A., jt. ed. see Hunt, James H.

Nalepa, Thomas F. & Schloesser, Don, eds. Zebra Mussels: Biology, Impacts, & Control. 1992. 69.95 (*0-87371-696-5*, QL430) Lewis Pubs.

Nalepka, James. Capsized. 1993. mass mkt. 5.50 (*0-06-109090-5*, Harp PBks) HarpC.

Nalepka, James & Callahan, Steven. Capsized. large type ed. LC 92-47254. 1993. 24.95 (*0-7927-1544-6*, Curley Lrg Print); pap. 22.95 (*0-7927-1543-8*, Curley Lrg Print) Chivers N Amer.

Naletov, Igor. Alternatives to Positivism: Criticism of Bourgeois Ideology & Revisionism. 470p. 1984. 30.00 (*0-685-17082-9*) St Mut.

Nalilmov, V. & Basu, Prabir. Application of Math Statistics to Chemical Analysis. LC 61-11161. 1963. 124.00 (*0-08-009916-5*, Pub. by Pergamon Repr UK) Franklin.

Nalin, David R. Medieval Sculpture from Eastern India: Selections from the Nalin Collection. Casey, Jane A., ed. (Illus.). 108p. (Orig.). 1985. pap. 45.00 (*0-9614416-0-7*) Nalini Intl Pubs.

Nalin, Y. & Nikolayev, A. Soviet Union & European Security. 141p. 1975. 19.95 (*0-8464-0875-9*) Beekman Pubs.

Nalivkin, D. Hurricanes, Storms & Tornadoes: Geographic Characteristics & Geological Activity. Bhattacharya, B. B., tr. 609p. (ENG.). (C). 1983. text ed. 130.00 (*90-6191-408-6*, Pub. by A A Balkema NE) Ashgate Pub Co.

Nalivkin, D. & Tomkeieff, S. I. Geology of the U. S. S. R. Short Outline. LC 60-14944. (International Series of Monographs on Earth Sciences: Vol. 8). 1960. 76.00 (*0-08-009410-4*, Pub. by Pergamon Repr UK) Franklin.

Nalivkin, Dmitrii V. Geology of the U. S. S. R. Rast, N. & Westoll, T. S., eds. LC 75-317194. 905p. reprint ed. pap. 180.00 (*0-685-16099-8*, 2056138) Bks Demand.

Nall, Barry T. & Dill, Ken A., eds. Conformations & Forces in Protein Folding. LC 91-7369. (AAAS Publication Ser.: No. 91-05S). (Illus.). 234p. (Orig.). reprint ed. pap. 66.70 (*0-7837-6740-4*, 2046368) Bks Demand.

***Nall, Beth.** Peter Pea & His Garden Friends. DHP, Inc. Staff, ed. (Illus.). 26p. (Orig.). (J). (ps-1). 1994. pap. write for info. (*1-885531-09-5*) Doghouse Pubng.

Nall, Bruce N. Model Railroading's Guide to Model Photography. Lee, Randall B., ed. (Illus.). 64p. 1993. pap. 8.95 (*0-9612692-8-6*) Rocky Mntn Pub Co.

Nall, C. Van, jt. auth. see Kerckhove, Michael G.

***Nall, James R.** Free-Born Slave: Diary of a Black Man in America. 96p. 1995. 12.95 (*1-881548-28-7*) Crane Hill AL.

Nall, Lexie, jt. auth. see Jacobs, Paul H.

Nall, S. E., jt. auth. see Day, P. D.

Nall, Van C., jt. auth. see Kerckhove, Michael C.

Nallari, Raj, jt. auth. see Gulhati, Ravi.

Nallari, Raj, jt. auth. see Mills, Cadman A.

Nalle, Sara T. God in La Mancha: Religious Reform & the People of Cuenca, 1500-1650. (Studies in Historical & Political Science). 288p. 1992. text ed. 38.50x (*0-8018-4384-7*) Johns Hopkins.

Nalluri, C., jt. auth. see Featherstone, R. E.

Nally, Robert V., ed. Human Resources & Compensation Management: CEBS Study Manual - Course Eight. 272p. 1993. 65.00 (*0-89154-461-5*) Intl Found Employ.

Nally, Susan. How to Say Yes! to All the Best Choices: And Really Mean It. 1994. pap. 7.99 (*0-8054-5363-6*) Broadman.

— How to Stay Way Cool! When Things Are Tough (& Really Like It) 208p. (J). (gr. 5-7). 1994. pap. 7.99 (*0-8054-4010-0*, 4240-10) Broadman.

Nally, Susan & Lee, Liz. How to Feel Most Excellent! About Who You Are (& Really Enjoy It) LC 93-48685. (Spending Prime Time with God Ser.). (J). (gr. 6 up). 1994. 7.99 (*0-8054-4008-9*) Broadman.

Nalman, Arthur, ed. see Chomsky, Noam.

Nalty, Bernard C. Air Power & the Fight for Khe Sanh. (Illus.). 134p. 1986. reprint ed. pap. write for info. (*0-912799-20-X*) Off Air Force.

— Strength for the Fight: A History of Black Americans in the Military. 424p. 1986. text ed. 29.95 (*0-02-922410-1*) Free Pr.

— Strength for the Fight: A History of Black Americans in the Military. 1989. pap. 14.95 (*0-02-922411-X*) Free Pr.

— War in the Pacific. 1991. 29.98 (*0-8317-6788-X*) Smithmark.

Nalty, Bernard C. & MacGregor, Morris J., eds. Blacks in the Military: Essential Documents. LC 80-54664. 367p. 1981. lib. bdg. 50.00 (*0-8420-2183-3*) Scholarly Res Inc.

Nalty, Bernard C., et al. With Courage: The U.S. Army Air Forces in World War II. Beck, Alfred M., ed. LC 94-4716. (General Histories Ser.). 1994. write for info. (*0-16-036396-9*) USGPO.

Nalty, Bernard C., et al, eds. Wrecks, Rescues & Investigations: Selected Documents of the U. S. Coast Guard & Its Predecessors. LC 78-12312. (Illus.). 473p. 1978. lib. bdg. 65.00 (*0-8420-2130-2*) Scholarly Res Inc.

Nalven, Joseph. Impacts & Undocumented Persons: The Quest for Useable Data in San Diego County. (Border Issue Ser.). 1989. 5.00 (*0-317-93039-7*) SDSU Inst Reg Studies.

Nalven, Nancy. The Famous Mister Ed: The Unbridled Truth about America's Favorite Talking Horse. 1991. pap. 9.99 (*0-446-39296-0*) Warner Bks.

Nalwa, Hari S. Nonlinear Optics of Org Molec & Polymeric Materials. 1995. write for info. (*0-8493-8923-2*) CRC Pr.

***Nalwa, Hari Singh.** Ferroelectric Polymers. (Plastics Engineering Ser.: vol. 28). 946p. 1995. write for info. (*0-8247-9468-0*) Dekker.

Nalwa, Vishvjit S. A Guided Tour of Computer Vision. LC 92-10896. (Illus.). (C). 1993. text ed. 34.95 (*0-201-54853-4*) Addison-Wesley.

***Nam.** Ways of Exile, Vol. 1. (Skoob Pacifica Ser.). 1995. pap. 11.95 (*1-871438-09-8*) Atrium Pubs.

Nam, Charles B. Nationality Groups & Social Stratification: A Study of the Socioeconomic Status & Mobility of Selected European Nationality Groups in America. Cordasco, Francesco, ed. LC 80-882. (American Ethnic Groups Ser.). 1981. lib. bdg. 30.95 (*0-405-13443-6*) Ayer.

— Our Population: The Changing Face of America. LC 87-21601. 1988. pap. 5.95 (*0-8027-6754-0*) Walker & Co.

— Understanding Population Change. LC 93-71269. 600p. 1994. 44.00 (*0-87581-377-1*) Peacock Pubs.

Nam, Charles B. & Powers, Mary G. The Socioeconomic Approach to Status Measurement: With a Guide to Occupational & Socioeconomic Status Scores. LC 82-73819. 166p. (C). 1984. text ed. 26.95 (*0-88105-011-3*) Cap & Gown.

Nam, Charles B., jt. auth. see Folger, John K.

Nam, Charles B., et al, eds. International Handbook on Internal Migration. LC 89-7487. 453p. 1990. text ed. 99.50 (*0-313-25858-9*, NIH/, Greenwood Pr) Greenwood.

Nam, Inja & Schmidt, Arno. Art of Garnishing. LC 93-7905. (Illus.). 1994. text ed. 34.95 (*0-442-01084-2*) Van Nos Reinhold.

Nam, Joo-Hong. America's Commitment to South Korea: The First Decade of the Nixon Doctrine. (London School of Economics Monographs in International Studies). (Illus.). 256p. 1986. 59.95 (*0-521-26765-X*) Cambridge U Pr.

Nam, Koon W. South Korean Politics: The Search for Political Consensus & Stability. 384p. (C). 1989. lib. bdg. 56.00 (*0-8191-7507-2*) U Pr of Amer.

Nam Ngoc Nguyen. Nguoi Viet Dau Tu Luat Thue Vu 1986 Cua Hoa Ky ("The Vietnamese & the Tax Reform Act of 1986") 135p. (Orig.). 1987. pap. 8.00 (*0-9614634-1-4*) N N Nguyen.

— Nguoi Viet Dau Tu ("The Vietnamese Investor") 267p. (Orig.). 1985. pap. 15.00 (*0-9614634-0-6*) N N Nguyen.

Nam, Park B., jt. auth. see Miller, Dan.

Nam-Sun Song. Thematic Relations & Transitivity in English, Japanese, & Korean. LC 93-29693. (Center for Korean Studies Monograph: No. 17). 1994. pap. text ed. 15.00 (*0-8248-1580-7*) UH Pr.

Nama, H. S. Cestods, Parasites of Indian Animals. (C). 1990. text ed. 150.00 (*81-85046-97-2*, Pub. by Scientific Pubs II) St Mut.

Nama, P. G., et al. Breast Self Examination & You. 1995. pap. 6.00 (*0-318-37463-3*) Budlong.

Nama, Prabharathie G., jt. auth. see Tetzleff, Judith.

***NAMA Staff.** IG: Refrigeration. 48p. 1995. pap. text ed., spiral bd. 16.90 (*0-7872-0991-0*) Kendall-Hunt.

— The Professional Vending Mechanic: Electrical Training Manual. 2nd ed. 240p. 1993. spiral bd. 78.00 (*0-8403-7978-1*) Kendall-Hunt.

— The Professional Vending Mechanic: Job Fundamentals Manual, Instructor's Guide. 2nd ed. 48p. (C). 1993. spiral bd. 32.50 (*0-8403-7977-3*) Kendall-Hunt.

— Refrigeration: Vending Mechanic. 140p. 1995. pap. text ed., spiral bd. 33.50 (*0-7872-0989-9*) Kendall-Hunt.

— Refrigeration: Vending Mechines. 140p. 1993. spiral bd. 78.00 (*0-8403-7974-9*) Kendall-Hunt.

Namachchivaya, N. S., jt. ed. see Paidoussis, M. P.

Naman, Anne A. The Jew in the Victorian Novel: Some Relationships Between Prejudice & Art. LC 79-8634. (Studies in the Nineteenth Century: No. 1). 1980. 34.50 (*0-404-18023-X*) AMS Pr.

Namartha-nirnaya of Kaundabhatta. The Meaning of Nouns: Semantic Theory in Classical & Medieval India. LC 92-17009. (Studies of Classical India: Vol. 13). 308p. (C). 1992. lib. bdg. 181.50 (*0-7923-1847-1*) Kluwer Ac.

Namazi, Nader M. New Algorithms for Variable Time Delay & Nonuniform Image Estimation. Zobrist, George W., ed. (Computer Engineering & Computer Science Ser.). 160p. (C). 1994. text ed. 39.50 (*0-89391-847-4*) Ablex Pub.

Namba, M. & Kaiya, H., eds. Psychobiology of Schizophrenia, In Memory of C. & O. Vogt & M. Hayashi: Proceedings of a Satellite Symposium to the 8th International Congress of Pharmacology, Gifu, Japan, June 27-29, 1981. (Advances in the Biosciences Ser.: Vol. 39). 342p. 1982. 146.00 (*0-08-028007-2*, Pub. by Pergamon Repr UK) Franklin.

Namba, M., ed. see Seventh International Symposium Staff.

Namba, S., et al, eds. Science & Technology of Mesoscopic Structures. LC 92-30098. 1993. write for info. (*4-431-70090-0*); write for info. (*3-540-70090-0*); 199.00 (*0-387-70090-0*) Spr-Verlag.

Namban, Akahige. Shogun's Agents. 1989. pap. 4.50 (*0-929654-07-2*, 49) Blue Moon Bks.

— Yakuza Perfume. 1992. pap. 5.95 (*0-929654-85-4*, 119) Blue Moon Bks.

Nambiar, A. C. Rural Poverty: Problems & Prospects. (Illus.). xiv, 134p. (C). 1992. 18.00 (*81-7024-510-9*, Pub. by Ashish Pub Hse II) Nataraj Bks.

Nambiar, E. K., jt. auth. see Bowen, Glyn D.

Nambisan, K. M. Design Elements of Landscape Gardening. (C). 1992. 36.00 (*81-204-0683-4*, Pub. by Oxford IBH II) S Asia.

Namboodiri, Krishnan. Demographic Analysis: A Stochastic Approach. 370p. 1990. text ed. 68.00 (*0-12-513830-X*) Acad Pr.

— Matrix Algebra: An Introduction. (Quantitative Applications in the Social Sciences Ser.: Vol. 38). 96p. (Orig.). (C). 1984. pap. text ed. 9.95 (*0-8039-2052-0*) Sage.

— Methods for Macrosociological Research. (Illus.). 293p. 1994. text ed. 69.00 (*0-12-513345-6*) Acad Pr.

Namboodiri, Krishnan, ed. Survey Sampling & Measurement. (Quantitative Studies in Social Relations). 1978. text ed. 58.00 (*0-12-513350-2*) Acad Pr.

Namboodiri, Krishnan & Corwin, Ronald G. The Logic & Method of Macro Sociology: An Input-Output Approach to Organizational Networks. LC 93-20302. 192p. 1993. text ed. 55.00 (*0-275-94529-4*, C4529, Praeger Pubs) Greenwood.

Namboodiri, Krishnan & Suchindran, C. M., eds. Life Table Techniques & Their Applications. (Studies in Population). 1987. text ed. 65.00 (*0-12-513930-6*) Acad Pr.

Namboodiri, P. K., jt. auth. see Mirchandani, G. G.

Namboodiri, P. K., et al. Intervention in the Indian Ocean. 361p. 1982. 35.95 (*0-940500-81-7*, Pub. by ABC Pub Hse II) Asia Bk Corp.

Namboodiripad. Kerala: Society & Politics-an Historical Survey. 1985. 10.00 (*0-8364-1495-0*) S Asia.

Namboodiripad, E. M. Crisis Into Chaos: Political India 1981. 172p. 1981. pap. text ed. 4.25 (*0-86131-279-1*, Pub. by Orient Longman Ltd II) Apt Bks.

Nambooripad, K. S. Structure of Regular Semigroups, No. 1. LC 79-21160. (Memoirs of the American Mathematical Society Ser.: No. 224). 132p. reprint ed. pap. 37.70 (*0-7837-7001-4*, 2046814) Bks Demand.

— Structure of Regular Semigroups - I. K. S. Nambooripad. LC 79-21160. (Memoirs Ser.: No. 22/224). 117p. 1985. reprint ed. pap. 18.00 (*0-8218-2224-1*, MEMO 22/224) Am Math.

Nambu, John, tr. see Transnational College of Lex Staff.

Nambu, Y. Quarks: Frontiers in Elementary Particle Physics. 240p. 1985. text ed. 47.00 (*9971-966-65-4*); pap. text ed. 14.00 (*9971-966-66-2*) World Scientific Pub.

Nambudiri, P. P. Aryans in South India. (C). 1992. 32.00 (*81-210-0266-4*, Pub. by Inter-India Pubns) S Asia.

Nambudripad, Devi S. Say Goodbye to Illness. 300p. 1993. pap. text ed. 21.00 (*0-9637570-0-8*) Delta Pubng CA.

— You Can Reprogram Your Brain to Perfect Health: Unsolved Health Problems Solved. (Illus.). 140p. (Orig.). 1990. pap. 47.60 (*0-685-29804-3*) Singer Pub.

Namburu, R. R., jt. ed. see Tamma, K. K.

Namdak, Lopon T. Heart Drops of Dharmakaya. Dixey, Richard, ed. 1993. pap. 15.95 (*1-55939-012-3*) Snow Lion Pubns.

Name Game Staff. Hanukkah Alphabet. (Shulsinger Spell & Learn Ser.). (Illus.). (J). (ps-5). 1977. pap. 2.50 (*0-914080-63-6*) Shulsinger Sales.

Namekata, Tsukasa & Du V Florey, Charles, eds. Health Effects of Air Pollution & the Japanese Compensation Law. LC 87-14548. 188p. 1987. text ed. 37.50 (*0-935470-38-7*) Battelle.

Nameroff, Rochelle. Body Prints. LC 73-155607. 54p. 1972. 2.95 (*0-87886-022-3*, Greenfld Rev Pr) Greenfld Rev Lit.

Nameroff, Steven, jt. auth. see O'Brien, Stephen K.

Names, Larry. Twice Dead. 1978. pap. 1.75 (*0-8439-0601-4*) Dorchester Pub Co.

***Names, Larry D.** Ironclads: Man-of-War. 384p. (Orig.). 1995. mass mkt. 5.99 (*0-380-77619-7*) Avon.

Names, Larry D., ed. see Hollatz, Tom.

Namey, Rick, jt. auth. see Limburgher, Rush N.

Namias, Jerome. Thirty-Day Forcasting: A Review of a Ten-Year Experiment. (Meteorological Monograph Ser.: Vol. 2, No. 6). (Illus.). 83p. (Orig.). 1953. pap. 17.00 (*0-933876-01-7*) Am Meteorological.

Namias, June. First Generation: In the Words of Twentieth-Century American Immigrants. 2nd ed. (Illus.). 304p. 1992. pap. 17.95 (*0-252-06170-5*) U of Ill Pr.

— White Captives: Gender & Ethnicity on the American Frontier. LC 92-31235. (Illus.). xxii, 378p. (C). 1993. 39.95 (*0-8078-2079-2*); pap. text ed. 16.95 (*0-8078-4408-X*) U of NC Pr.

Namias, June, ed. see Seaver, James E.

Namier, Lewis. Eighteen Forty-Eight: The Revolution of the Intellectuals. 138p. 1992. pap. 14.95 (*0-19-726111-6*) OUP.

Namier, Lewis & Brooke, John, eds. The House of Commons 1754-1790, 3 vols., Set. (History of Parliament Ser.). 1974p. 1993. text ed. 176.00 (*0-436-30420-1*) A Sutton Pub.

Namier, Lewis B. Conflicts. LC 73-90667. (Essay Index Reprint Ser.). 1977. 20.95 (*0-8369-1230-6*) Ayer.

— Crossroads of Power. LC 77-119604. (Essay Index Reprint Ser.). 1977. 18.95 (*0-8369-1690-5*) Ayer.

— Europe in Decay Nineteen Thirty-Six to Nineteen Forty. 11.75 (*0-8446-1322-3*) Peter Smith.

— In the Margin of History. LC 69-18934. (Essay Index Reprint Ser.). 1977. 20.95 (*0-8369-0050-2*) Ayer.

— Skyscrapers, & Other Essays. LC 68-22113. (Essay Index Reprint Ser.). 1977. 18.95 (*0-8369-0734-5*) Ayer.

— Vanished Supremacies, Vol. 1. Collected Essays Of Sir Lewis Namier. LC 73-119603. (Select Bibliographies Reprint Ser.). 1977. 15.95 (*0-8369-5195-6*) Ayer.

Namikawa, A. Cleavage Lines of the Skin. Bd. with Developmental Modulation of Neuronal Cell Surface Determinants. (Bibliotheca Anatomica Ser.: No. 27). (Illus.). viii, 140p. 1986. 71.25 (*3-8055-4202-X*) S Karger.

Namikawa, Y., et al, eds. Algebraic Geometry & Related Topics. (Series in Algebraic Geometry). 208p. 1994. 22.00 (*1-57146-013-6*) Intl Pr Boston.

Namiki, Mikio, et al. Stochastic Quantization. Beiglbock, W. et al, eds. LC 92-17584. (Lecture Notes in Physics, New Series, Monographs: Vol. M9). (Illus.). x, 217p. 1992. 47.00 (*0-387-55563-3*) Spr-Verlag.

Namikoshi, Ti. Shiatsu Therapy: Theory & Practice. pap. 18.95 (*0-685-70705-9*) Wehman.

Namikoshi, Tokujiro. Shiatsu: Japanese Finger-Pressure Therapy. LC 68-19983. (Illus.). 84p. 1994. pap. 9.95 (*0-87040-169-6*) Japan Pubns USA.

Namikoshi, Toru. The Complete Book of Shiatsu Therapy: Health & Vitality at Your Fingertips. LC 79-1963. (Illus.). 256p. 1994. pap. 19.00 (*0-87040-461-X*) Japan Pubns USA.

— Shiatsu Way to Health: Relaxation & Relief at a Touch. McCandless, Susan K., tr. LC 87-81676. (Illus.). 160p. 1988. pap. 22.00 (*0-87011-796-3*) Kodansha.

Namioka, Aki, jt. ed. see Schuler, Douglas.

Namioka, Isaac. Partially Ordered Linear Topological Spaces. LC 52-42389. (Memoirs Ser.: No. 1/24). 50p. 1990. reprint ed. pap. 22.00 (*0-8218-1224-6*, MEMO 1/24) Am Math.

Namioka, Lensey. April & the Dragon Lady. LC 93-27958. (J). 1994. 10.95 (*0-15-276644-8*, Browndeer Pr) HarBrace.

— The Loyal Cat. LC 94-10937. (Illus.). (J). 1995. write for info. (*0-15-200092-5*, Browndeer Pr) HarBrace.

— Valley of the Broken Cherry Trees. 176p. (YA). (gr. 6 up). reprint ed. pap. 8.95 (*0-936085-32-0*) Blue Heron.

— Village of the Vampire Cat. 192p. (YA). 1995. pap. 8.95 (*0-936085-29-0*) Blue Heron OR.

— Yang the Third & Her Impossible Family. LC 94-30110. (Illus.). (J). 1995. 15.95 (*0-316-59726-0*) Little.

— Yang the Youngest & His Terrible Ear. (J). (gr. 4-7). 1994. pap. 3.50 (*0-440-40917-9*) Dell.

— Yang the Youngest & His Terrible Ear. (Illus.). 112p. (J). (gr. 3-7). 1992. 15.95 (*0-316-59701-5*, Pub. by H K Lewis UK) Little.

Namir, L., jt. auth. see Schlesinger, I. M.

***Namjestnik, Kenneth J.** Trust Audit Manual: Fiduciary Audit Practices, Policies & Regulations. rev. ed. 250p. 1995. 60.00 (*1-55738-782-6*) Probus Pub Co.

— The Trust Risk Management Manual: A Hands-on Guide to Assessing & Monitoring Trust Operations. 200p. 1995. 125.00 (*1-55738-772-9*) Probus Pub Co.

Namjoshi, Sarojini, tr. see Govindagraj.

Namjoshi, Suniti. The Blue Donkey Fables. 1990. pap. 7.95 (*0-7043-4115-8*, Pub. by Womens Pr UK) Interlink Pub.

— Cyclone in Pakistan. (Writers Workshop Redbird Ser.). 1971. 8.00 (*0-89253-708-6*); 4.00 (*0-89253-709-4*) Ind-US Inc.

— More Poems. 8.00 (*0-89253-706-X*) Ind-US Inc.

— The Mother of Maya Diip. (Illus.). 160p. (Orig.). 1993. pap. 9.95 (*0-7043-4200-6*, Pub. by Womens Pr UK) Interlink Pub.

— Poems. 5.00 (*0-89253-704-3*); 4.00 (*0-89253-705-1*) Ind-US Inc.

— Saint Suniti & the Dragon: And Other Fables. 144p. 1995. pap. 11.95 (*1-85381-659-0*, Pub. by Virago Pr UK) Trafalgar.

Namjoshi, Suniti, tr. see Govindagraj.

***Namka, Lynne.** The Mad Family Gets Their Mads Out: Fifty Things Your Family Can Say & Do to Express Anger Constructively. LC 94-60804. (Illus.). 48p. (Orig.). 1994. pap. 10.95 (*0-9642167-0-1*) Talk Trust & Feel.

Namkoong, G., et al. A Philosophy of Strategy for Breeding Tropical Forest Trees. 1980. 40.00 (*0-85074-034-7*) St Mut.

— Tree Breeding: Principles & Strategies. (Monographs on Theoretical & Applied Genetics: Vol. 11). (Illus.). 190p. 1988. 96.00 (*0-387-96747-8*) Spr-Verlag.

Namkung, Johsel. Johsel Namkung: An Artist's View of Nature. (Illus.). 36p. 1978. pap. 5.95 (*0-295-95626-7*) U of Wash Pr.

Namm, D. Little Bear. (My First Reader Ser.). (Illus.). 28p. (J). (ps-2). 1990. lib. bdg. 10.50 (*0-516-05356-6*); pap. 3.95 (*0-516-45356-4*) Childrens.

— Monsters! (My First Reader Ser.). (Illus.). 28p. (J). (ps-2). 1990. lib. bdg. 10.50 (*0-516-05358-2*); pap. 3.95 (*0-516-45358-0*) Childrens.

Namm, Diane. First Love. LC 94-14502. (Kisses Ser.: No. 1). (Illus.). 224p. (YA). (gr. 6 up). 1994. pap. text ed. 3.50 (*0-8167-3440-2*) Troll Assocs.

— Good-Bye Kiss. LC 94-16883. (Kisses Ser.: No. 2). (Illus.). 224p. (YA). (gr. 6 up). 1994. pap. text ed. 3.50 (*0-8167-3441-0*) Troll Assocs.

An Asterisk (*) at the beginning of an entry indicates that the title is appearing in BIP for the first time.

— Senior Kisses. LC 94-25436. (Kisses Ser.: No. 3). 224p. (YA). (gr. 6 up). 1994. pap. text ed. 3.50 (0-8167-3442-9, WestWind) Troll Assocs.

Nammacher, Scott A., jt. auth. see Altman, Edward I.

Namoika, Lensey. April & the Dragon Lady. LC 93-27958. (YA). 1994. pap. 3.95 (0-15-200886-1) HarBrace.

Namoodiri, Neelakantan, ed. see Amritanadamayi, Mata.

Namorato, Michael V. Rexford G. Tugwell: A Biography. LC 88-2397. 202p. 1988. text ed. 55.00 (0-275-92961-2, C2961, Praeger Pubs) Greenwood.

Namorato, Michael V., ed. The Diary of Rexford G. Tugwell: The New Deal, 1932-1935. LC 92-1166. (Contributions in Economics & Economic History Ser.: No. 136). 544p. 1992. text ed. 65.00 (0-313-28017-7, NDY/, Greenwood Pr) Greenwood.

— Have We Overcome? Race Relations Since Brown. LC 78-31357. (Chancellor's Symposium on Southern History Ser.). (Illus.). 232p. 1979. text ed. 27.50 (0-87805-099-X) U Pr of Miss.

Namorato, Michael V., jt. ed. see Cobb, James C.

Namos, Larry D. Bury My Heart at Wrigley Field: When the Cubs Were the White Socks. (History of the Chicago Cubs Ser.: Pt. 1). (Illus.). 280p. 1989. 18.95 (0-9621684-0-8) G K Scott Pub.

Namovicz-Peat, Susan, ed. Medical Utilization Review Directory: 1994 Edition. 624p. 1993. 345.00 (1-881393-16-X) Faulkner & Gray.

Namovicz, Susan, jt. ed. see Vibbert, Spencer.

Namoyo, Veronica. A Memory for Wonders: A True Story. LC 92-74110. 189p. (Orig.). 1993. pap. 9.95 (0-89870-430-8) Ignatius Pr.

Namson, J., jt. ed. see Davis, T.

Namson, Jay S., jt. ed. see Davis, Thomas L.

Namsrai, Khavtgain. Nonlocal Quantum Theory & Stochastic Quantum Mechanics. 1985. lib. bdg. 182.00 (90-277-2001-0) Kluwer Ac.

Namuth, Hans. Pollock Painting. Rose, Barbara, ed. LC 79-57621. (Illus.). 112p. 1980. 25.00 (0-9601068-6-3); pap. 14.95 (0-9601068-5-5) Agrinde Pubns.

— Twenty-Five Artists. Bujese, Arlene, ed. 108p. 1982. text ed. 75.00 (0-313-27081-3, U7081, Greenwood Pr) Greenwood.

Nan Huai-Chin. To Realize Enlightenment: Practice of the Cultivation Path. Cleary, J. C., tr. 320p. (Orig.). 1994. pap. 14.95 (0-87728-802-X) Weiser.

Nan, Huai-Chin. Working Toward Enlightenment: The Cultivation of Practice. 304p. (Orig.). 1993. pap. 14.95 (0-87728-776-7) Weiser.

Nan, Huai-Chin, jt. auth. see Chu, Wen Kuan.

***Nan, Mistress.** My Private Life: Real Experiences of a Dominant Woman. Bean, Joseph, ed. LC 94-69814. 196p. (Orig.). 1995. pap. 14.95 (1-881943-11-9) Daedalus Pub.

Nanamoli, Bhikkhu, tr. see Bodhi, Bhikkhu, ed. & tr.

Nanamoli, Bhikkhu, tr. see Buddhaghosa, Acaeiya.

Nanamoli, Ven, tr. The Guide. (C). 1962. 41.90 (0-86013-024-X) Wisdom MA.

— The Minor Readings & the Illustrator of Ultimate Meaning. (C). 1960. 31.00 (0-86013-023-1, Pub. by Pali Text) Wisdom MA.

Nanamoli, Ven., tr. Pitaka Disclosure. (C). 1964. 40.00 (0-86013-026-6, Pub. by Pali Text) Wisdom MA.

Nanamoli, Ven & Warder, A K., trs. The Path of Discrimination. (C). 1982. 52.00 (0-86013-074-6, Pub. by Pali Text) Wisdom MA.

***Nananukool, Surasak, et al.** Productivity Improvement Through QC Circles in Service Industry. (Productivity Ser.: No. 21). (Illus.). 27p. 1987. pap. text ed. 7.50 (92-833-1711-4, 317114, Pub. by APO JA) Qual Resc.

Nanao, Jun. Life of the Ant. Pohl, Kathy, ed. LC 85-28198. (Nature Close-Ups Ser.). (Illus.). 32p. (J). (gr. 3-7). 1986. lib. bdg. 10.95 (0-8172-2539-0) Raintree Steck-V.

Nanassy, Louis C. & Fancher, C. General Business & Economic Understandings. 4th ed. 1973. text ed. 25.00 (0-13-348946-9); 8.96 (0-13-348953-1); 8.96 (0-13-348961-2) P-H.

Nanassy, Louis C. & Selden, William. The Prentice Hall Word Book. 1992. pap. 11.00 (0-13-697029-X) P-H.

Nanassy, Louis C., jt. auth. see Selden, William.

Nanassy, Louis C., et al. Principles & Trends in Business Education. LC 76-57995. 1977. text ed. write for info. (0-672-97092-9) Macmillan.

Nanavati, Manilal B. & Vakil, Chandulal N. Group Prejudices in India: A Symposium. LC 79-98783. 223p. 1970. reprint ed. text ed. 59.75 (0-8371-3132-4, NAGP, Greenwood Pr) Greenwood.

Nanavaty, Jal J. Educational Thought, Vol. 1. 1973. pap. 10.00 (0-89744-150-8) Auromere.

Nanavaty, Mahesh. Silk Production, Processing & Marketing. (C). 1990. 52.00 (81-224-0282-8, Pub. by Wiley Eastern II) S Asia.

Nanay, Julia. Transylvania: The Hungarian Minority in Romania. LC 76-19730. (Behind the Iron Curtain Ser.: No. 11). 1976. pap. 5.00 (0-87934-014-2) Danubian.

***Nanayakkara, Vesak.** Return to Kandy. (C). 1994. 58.00 (81-7013-121-9, Pub. by Navrang) S Asia.

Nancarrow, Paula R., et al, comps. Word Processors & the Writing Process: An Annotated Bibliography. LC 83-22749. xi, 146p. 1984. text ed. 45.00 (0-313-23995-9, NAW/, Greenwood Pr) Greenwood.

***Nance, Barry.** Client Server Lan Programming. 1994. disk, pap. 49.99 (1-56529-924-8) Que.

— Connecting with LAN Server. (Illus.). (Orig.). 1995. pap. 29.95 (1-56276-270-2) Ziff-Davis.

— Introduction to Networking. 2nd ed. (Illus.). 512p. (Orig.). 1993. pap. 34.95 (1-56529-297-9) Que.

— Introduction to Networking. 3rd ed. (Orig.). 1994. pap. 24.99 (1-56529-824-1) Que.

— Killer OS - 2 Utilities. (Illus.). 928p. (Orig.). 1993. pap. 45.00 (1-56529-294-4) Que.

— Network Programming in C. (Illus.). 648p. (Orig.). 1990. pap. text ed. 49.95 (0-88022-569-6, 1118) Que.

— Networking Windows for Workgroups. 320p. 1993. pap. text ed. 22.95 (0-471-59583-7) Wiley.

— OS-2-2.0 Quick Reference. (Quick Reference Ser.). (Illus.). (Orig.). 1992. pap. 9.95 (1-56529-068-2) Que.

— Que's Speed up Your Computer Book. (Illus.). (Orig.). 1992. pap. 19.95 (0-88022-761-3) Que.

— Using OS 2 2.1. 3rd ed. 1994. pap. 29.95 (1-56529-635-4) Que.

— Using Personal OS-2, Special Edition. (Illus.). 672p. (Orig.). 1995. pap. 29.99 (0-7897-0088-3) Que.

— Your Windows 4.0 Networking Consultant. 1994. pap. text ed. 24.95 (0-471-02026-5) Wiley.

Nance, Barry & Halliday, Caroline. Using OS-2 2.1 Special Edition. (Illus.). 1000p. 1993. pap. 29.95 (1-56529-118-2) Que.

Nance, C. Roger. The Archaeology of la Calsada: A Rockshelter in the Sierra Madre Oriental, Mexico. LC 91-41040. (Texas Archaeology & Ethnography Ser.). (Illus.). 256p. 1992. text ed. 35.00x (0-292-70427-5) U of Tex Pr.

***Nance, Cheryl E. & Irby, G. E.** Modern Real Estate Practice in Texas. 7th rev. ed. 518p. (C). 1994. pap. text ed. 38.95 (0-7931-1129-3, 1510-067A, Real Estate Ed) Dearborn Finan.

— Modern Real Estate Practice in Texas. 7th rev. ed. LC 92-41749. (Illus.). 512p. 1993. pap. 38.95 (0-7931-0621-4, 1510-06, Real Estate Ed) Dearborn Finan.

***Nance, Dale A.** Law & Justice: Cases & Readings on the American Legal System. LC 94-71947. 768p. (C). 1994. lib. bdg. 60.00 (0-89089-600-3) Carolina Acad Pr.

Nance, Don, jt. auth. see Myers, Pennie.

***Nance, Don W.** How Therapists ACT: Combining Major Approaches to Psychotherapy & the Adaptive Counseling & Therapy Model. 232p. 1995. 49.95x (1-56032-410-4); pap. 24.95x (1-56032-390-6) Taylor & Francis.

Nance, Douglas W. Pascal: Introduction to Programming & Problem Solving. (Illus.). 639p. (YA). (gr. 9-12). 1989. reprint ed. text ed. 34.25 (0-314-93206-2) West Pub.

— Pascal: Understanding Programming & Problem Solving. 2nd alternate ed. Westby, ed. 596p. (Orig.). (C). 1992. reprint ed. pap. text ed. 50.75 (0-314-93304-2) West Pub.

— Pascal: Understanding Programming & Problem Solving. 2nd ed. Westby, ed. 750p. (Orig.). (C). 1989. pap. text ed. 47.00 (0-314-43051-2) West Pub.

— Pascal: Understanding Programming & Problem Solving. 3rd ed. Westby, ed. 716p. (Orig.). (C). 1992. pap. text ed. 49.50 (0-314-90877-3) West Pub.

— Pascal: Understanding Programming & Problem Solving. 3rd ed. LC 94-37681. 600p. 1994. pap. text ed. 51.75 (0-314-04361-6) West Pub.

— Pascal: Understanding Programming & Problem Solving. 4th ed. LC 94-43063. 600p. 1994. pap. text ed. 51.50 (0-314-04306-3) West Pub.

— Understanding Turbo Pascal: Programming & Problem Solving. Westby, ed. LC 93-28875. 650p. (C). 1994. pap. text ed. 48.00 (0-314-02812-9) West Pub.

Nance, Douglas W. & Naps, Thomas L. Introduction to Computer Science: Programming, Problem Solving, & Data Structures. 2nd ed. Westby, ed. 900p. (C). 1992. text ed. 65.25 (0-314-93306-9) West Pub.

— Introduction to Computer Science: Programming Problem Solving & Data Structures. 3rd ed. LC 94-44474. 1200p. 1995. text ed. 65.75 (0-314-04556-2) West Pub.

Nance, Douglas W., jt. auth. see Naps, Thomas L.

Nance, E. Paul, et al. Emergency Radiology of the Pelvis & Lower Extremities. (Advanced Exercises in Diagnostic Radiology Ser.). (Illus.). 176p. 1983. pap. text ed. 44.95 (0-7216-6653-1) Saunders.

Nance, Frank. Blossoms from the Desert. 94p. (Orig.). 1981. pap. 5.00 (0-9615739-0-2) F Nance.

— Footprints in the Grass. 159p. (Orig.). 1990. pap. text ed. 6.00 (0-9615739-2-9) F Nance.

— Warm Memories. 106p. (Orig.). 1985. pap. text ed. 5.00 (0-9615739-1-0) F Nance.

Nance, Guinevera, jt. auth. see Jones, Judith.

Nance, Harold W., jt. auth. see Crossan, Richard M.

Nance, Harold W., jt. auth. see Heyel, Carl.

Nance, Herschel G. Contracting to Build Your Home. Smith, James C., Jr., ed. LC 91-32694. 160p. (Orig.). 1992. pap. 12.95 (0-86534-160-5) Sunstone Pr.

Nance, Joanne L. Charlotte County, Virginia, 1816-1850: Marriage Bonds & Ministers' Returns (with Additions to Marriages, 1764-1815) LC 87-81976. 176p. 1987. per. 22.00 (0-944334-00-8) N W Lapin.

Nance, Joanne L., comp. Charlotte County, Virginia, 1765-1771, Deed Bks. 1 & 2. LC 90-6208. (Illus.). viii, 102p. 1990. per. 18.00 (0-944334-01-6) N W Lapin.

Nance, John. Lobo of the Tasaday: A Stone Age Boy Meets the Modern World. LC 81-14113. (Illus.). 56p. (J). (gr. 3-7). 1982. 9.95 (0-394-85077-7) Pantheon.

Nance, John J. Blind Trust. Cady, Howard, ed. LC 86-22502. (Illus.). 416p. 1987. pap. 15.00 (0-688-06967-3, Quill) Morrow.

— Final Approach. 1992. mass mkt. 5.99 (0-449-45257-3, Crest) Fawcett.

— Final Approach. 1994. mass mkt. 5.99 (0-449-45450-9) Fawcett.

— On Shaky Ground. 448p. 1989. mass mkt. 4.95 (0-380-70743-8) Avon.

— Pandora's Clock. LC 95-8409. 336p. 1995. 23.50 (0-385-47944-1) Doubleday.

— Phoenix Rising. 1995. mass mkt. 6.99 (0-449-18290-8, GM) Fawcett.

— Scorpion Strike. 1993. mass mkt. 5.99 (0-449-22221-7, Crest) Fawcett.

Nance, John L. Scorpion Strike. 1992. 20.00 (0-517-58565-0, Crown) Crown Pub Group.

Nance, Joseph M. After San Jacinto: The Texas-Mexican Frontier, 1836-1841. LC 62-9789. (Illus.). 681p. reprint ed. pap. 180.00 (0-8357-5246-1, 2027908) Bks Demand.

***Nance, Kimi.** Advanced Training for WordPerfect 6.1 for Windows. Young, Natalie B., ed. 1995. pap. text ed. 195.00 (1-56562-065-8) OneOnOne Comp Trng.

— How to Use WordPerfect 6.1 for Windows. Young, Natalie B., ed. 1995. pap. text ed. 175.00 (1-56562-064-X) OneOnOne Comp Trng.

Nance, R. Morton. A New Cornish-English, English-Cornish Dictionary. 438p. (C). 1989. reprint ed. 100.00x (1-85022-055-7, Pub. by Dyllansow Truran UK) St Mut.

Nance, Sandra J. Clinical & Basic Science Aspects of Immunohematology. LC 91-31709. (Illus.). (C). 1991. text ed. 45.00 (1-56395-006-5) Am Assn Blood.

— Immune Destruction of Red Blood Cells. LC 89-17611. (C). 1989. text ed. 30.00 (0-915355-73-6) Am Assn Blood.

Nance, Sandra T., ed. Alloimmunity: 1993 & Beyond. 1993. text ed. 35.00 (1-56395-025-1) Am Assn Blood.

— Blood Safety: Current Challenges. LC 92-49346. 1992. 49.00 (1-56395-015-4) Am Assn Blood.

— Blood Supply: Risks, Perceptions & Prospects for the Future. (Illus.). (C). 1994. text ed. 50.00 (1-56395-033-2) Am Assn Blood.

— Transfusion Medicine in the 1990's. (C). 1990. text ed. 42.00 (0-915355-89-2) Am Assn Blood.

Nance, Scott. Bloodsuckers: Vampires at the Movies. 1992. pap. 14.95 (1-55698-317-4) Movie Pubs Servs.

— Exposing Northern Exposure. 1992. pap. 14.95 (1-55698-324-7) Movie Pubs Servs.

— Forty Years at Night: The Tonight Show Story. 1991. pap. 14.95 (1-55698-308-5) Movie Pubs Servs.

— Genesis of Phil Collins. 1991. pap. 9.95 (1-55698-306-9) Movie Pubs Servs.

— Making a Quantum Leap. 1992. pap. 14.95 (1-55698-312-3) Movie Pubs Servs.

— Music You Can See: The MTV Story. 1993. pap. 14.95 (1-55698-355-7) Movie Pubs Servs.

— Seinfeld: The Man, the Series. 1993. pap. 12.95 (1-55698-357-3) Movie Pubs Servs.

— Spirit of Trek. 1993. pap. 14.95 (1-55698-373-5) Movie Pubs Servs.

— Trek: Deep Space Nine. 1993. pap. 14.95 (1-55698-354-9) Movie Pubs Servs.

— Trek: The Printed Adventures. 1993. pap. 14.95 (1-55698-356-5) Movie Pubs Servs.

— Trekking to the Stars: The Patrick Stewart Story. 1993. pap. 14.95 (1-55698-358-1) Movie Pubs Servs.

— ZZ Top: Recycling the Blues. 1991. pap. 9.95 (1-55698-297-6) Movie Pubs Servs.

***Nance, Stephen W.** Sing to the Lord: Christian Hymnody. 208p. (Orig.). 1995. pap. 16.95 (0-942597-89-3) White Mane Pub.

Nance, Tabbie, jt. auth. see White, Sherry.

Nance, Tabbie, jt. auth. see Williams, Janis.

Nance, Terry. God's Armorbearer. 80p. (Orig.). 1990. pap. 3.95 (0-89274-723-4, HH723) Harrison Hse.

Nance, Virginia L. & McMahon, Kay E. Golf. 7th ed. 144p. 1994. pap. write for info. (0-697-12656-0) Brown & Benchmark.

Nance, Wayne E. Eating for a Lifetime: A Fourteen-Day Lowfat Eating Plan That Works! 92p. (Orig.). Date not set. pap. text ed. 14.95 (1-885182-00-7) Liten Up.

Nancollas, G. H., et al. Biological Mineralization & Demineralization: Report on the Dahlemn Workshop Berlin 1981. (Dahlem Workshop Reports: Vol. 23). (Illus.). 420p. 1982. 39.00 (0-387-11521-8) Spr-Verlag.

***Nancy, Ashis.** Alternative Sciences: Creativity & Authenticity in Two Indian Scientists. 172p. 1995. text ed. 15.95 (0-19-563198-6) OUP.

Nancy, E. Once I Was a Child & There Was Much Pain . . . A Glimpse into the Soul of an Incest Survivor. LC 88-28281. (Illus.). 104p. (Orig.). 1989. pap. 6.95 (0-9603628-7-8) Frog in Well.

Nancy, Jean-Luc. The Birth to Presence. Holmes, Brian et al, trs. LC 92-30596. 440p. 1993. 47.50 (0-8047-2060-6) Stanford U Pr.

— Birth to Presence. 440p. (C). 1993. pap. 15.95 (0-8047-2189-0) Stanford U Pr.

— The Experience of Freedom. McDonald, Bridget, tr. LC 93-16348. (Meridian: Crossing Aesthetics Ser.). 248p. 1993. Alk. paper. 37.50 (0-8047-2175-0); pap. 12.95 (0-8047-2190-4) Stanford U Pr.

— The Inoperative Community, Vol. 76. (Theory & History of Literature Ser.). 217p. (Orig.). 1991. text ed. 39.95 (0-8166-1923-9); pap. 14.95 (0-8166-1924-7) U of Minn Pr.

Nancy, Jean-Luc & Lacoue-Labarthe, Philippe. The Title of the Letter: A Reading of Lacan. Pettigrew, David & Raffoul, Francois, trs. LC 91-15114. (SUNY Series in Contemporary Continental Philosophy). 151p. 1992. 49.50 (0-7914-0961-9); pap. 16.95 (0-7914-0962-7) State U NY Pr.

Nancy, Jean-Luc, jt. auth. see Lacoue-Labarthe, Philippe.

Nancy, John J. Phoenix Rising. LC 93-31528. 1994. 22.00 (0-517-58566-9, Crown) Crown Pub Group.

Nand, Nitya & Kumar, Kamlesh. The Holy Himalaya: A Geographical Interpretation of Garwal. 1989. 86.00 (81-7035-055-7, Pub. by Daya Pub Hse II) S Asia.

Nand, Sucha, jt. auth. see Schumacher, Harold R.

Nanda. Classification of Nursing Diagnoses: Proceedings of the Ninth Conference. (Illus.). 488p. 1991. pap. 39.95 (0-397-54812-5) Lippincott.

— Classification of Nursing Diagnosis: Proceedings of the Eighth Conference. (Illus.). 612p. 1989. text ed. 37.50 (0-397-54736-6) Lippincott.

Nanda, B. R. Gandhi: Pan-Islamism, Imperialism, & Nationalism. (Illus.). 464p. 1990. 19.95 (0-19-562299-5) OUP.

— Gandhi & His Critics. (Oxford India Paperbacks). 188p. 1994. reprint ed. pap. 7.95 (0-19-563363-6) OUP.

— Gokhale: The Indian Moderates & the British Raj. LC 77-72129. (Illus.). 1977. 80.00 (0-691-03115-0) Princeton U Pr.

— In Gandhi's Footsteps: The Life & Times of Jamnalal Bajaj. (Illus.). 428p. 1990. 29.95 (0-19-562550-1) OUP.

— Jawaharlal Nehru: Rebel & Statesman. (Illus.). 320p. 1995. 29.95 (0-19-563684-8) OUP.

— Mahatma Gandhi: A Biography. 541p. 1989. 34.95 (0-318-36657-6) Asia Bk Corp.

Nanda, B. R., ed. Indian Women: From Purdah to Modernity. 175p. 1990. text ed. 27.50 (81-7027-146-0, Pub. by Radiant Pubs II) S Asia.

— Science & Technology in India. 1978. 9.00 (0-8364-0170-0) S Asia.

— Selected Works of Govind Ballabh Pant, Vol. 2. 392p. 1994. 24.95 (0-19-563463-2) OUP.

— Selected Works of Govind Ballabh Pant, Vol. 3. 400p. 1995. 24.00 (0-19-563464-0) OUP.

Nanda, B. R., ed. see Pant, Govind B.

Nanda, B. S., et al. Aging Pigment: Current Research, Vol. 1. 191p. 1974. text ed. 25.50 (0-8422-7197-X) Irvington.

Nanda, Bal R. Gokhale: The Indian Moderates & the British Raj. LC 77-72129. 540p. reprint ed. pap. 153.90 (0-7837-1415-7, 2041769) Bks Demand.

***Nanda, Bikram N. & Islamia, Jamia M.** Contours of Continuity & Change: The Story of the Bonda Highlanders. LC 94-31771. 200p. 1995. text ed. 24.95 (0-8039-9193-2) Sage.

NANDA Conference Attendees Nurse Theorist Group, Taxonomy & Diagnosis Review Committee Staff, et al. NANDA Nursing Diagnoses: Definitions & Classification, 1992-1993. 95p. 1992. pap. text ed. 10.00 (0-9637042-0-6) N Am Nursing.

Nanda-Gramiak. Clinical Echocardiography. 2nd ed. Date not set. pap. write for info. (0-8016-3727-9) Mosby Yr Bk.

Nanda, J. N. Development of the Resources of the Sea: India. (C). 1988. 22.00 (81-7022-220-6, Pub. by Concept II) S Asia.

Nanda, Jyotir M. Yoga Wisdom of the Upanishads: Kena.. Mundaka..Prashna..Ishavasya. (Illus.). 1974. pap. 6.99 (0-934664-36-6) Yoga Res Foun.

***Nanda, K. K.** Conquering Kashmir-A Pakistani Obsession. (C). 1995. 36.00x (81-7095-045-7, Pub. by Lancers Bks II) S Asia.

Nanda, Maya, jt. auth. see Swami, Jyotir.

Nanda, N. C., ed. Advances in Echo Imaging Using Contrast Enhancement. LC 92-46545. 408p. (C). 1993. lib. bdg. 122.00 (0-7923-2137-5) Kluwer Ac.

Nanda-Nandana, Sri. The Secret Teachings of the Vedas: The Ancient Knowledge of the East. LC 86-51209. 320p. (Orig.). 1987. pap. 14.95 (0-9617410-0-7) World Relief.

Nanda, Navin. Doppler Echocardiography. 2nd ed. (Illus.). 700p. 1992. text ed. 129.00 (0-8121-1588-0) Williams & Wilkins.

Nanda, Navin C. Textbook of Color Doppler Echocardiography. LC 88-32597. (Illus.). 347p. 1989. text ed. 130.00 (0-8121-1199-0) Williams & Wilkins.

Nanda, Navin C., ed. Atlas of Color Doppler Echocardiography. LC 88-8994. (Illus.). 544p. 1989. 149.00 (0-8121-1078-1) Williams & Wilkins.

Nanda, Rajni. Early History of Gold in India. (C). 1992. 27.00 (81-215-0548-8, Pub. by Munshiram Manoharial II) S Asia.

Nanda, Ravi. Evolution of National Strategy of India. 1987. 27.00 (81-7095-000-7, Pub. by Lancer II) S Asia.

— Indo-Pak Detente. 1989. 36.00 (81-7095-013-9, Pub. by Lancer II) S Asia.

— National Security: Perspective Policy & Planning. (C). 1991. text ed. 32.00 (81-7095-026-0, Pub. by Lancer International II) S Asia.

Nanda, Ravinder & Browne, James J. Introduction to Employee Scheduling. (Illus.). 352p. 1992. text ed. 64.95 (0-442-00495-8) Van Nos Reinhold.

Nanda, Ravindra & Burstone, Charles J., eds. Retention & Stability in Orthodontics. (Illus.). 176p. 1993. text ed. 68.50 (0-7216-4342-6) Saunders.

Nanda, Serena. Cultural Anthropology. 4th ed. 457p. (C). 1991. pap. 40.95 (0-534-13956-6) Intl Thomson.

— Cultural Anthropology. 5th ed. LC 93-5967. 506p. 1994. pap. 42.95 (0-534-21438-X) Intl Thomson.

— Neither Man nor Woman: The Hijras of India. 170p. (C). 1990. pap. 17.95 (0-534-12204-3) Intl Thomson.

Nanda, Serena, jt. auth. see Norgren, Jill.

NANDA Staff. Classification of Nursing Diagnoses: Proceedings of the Tenth Conference. Carroll-Johnson, Rose M. & Paquette, Mary, eds. 592p. (C). 1993. pap. 44.95 (0-397-55011-1, Lippincott Nursing) Lippincott.

Nanda, Ved P. The Law of Transnational Business Transactions, 3 vols., Set. LC 81-2392. (International Business & Law Ser.). 1981. ring bd. 375.00 (0-87632-342-5) Clark Boardman Callaghan.

***Nanda, Ved P., ed.** Hindu Law & Legal Theory. (International Library of Essays in Law & Legal Theory). 500p. 1996. 150.00x (0-8147-5772-3) NYU Pr.

— Refugee Law & Policy: International & U. S. Responses. LC 89-11901. (Studies in Human Rights: No. 9). 238p. 1989. text ed. 55.00 (0-313-26870-3, NRP/, Greenwood Pr) Greenwood.

Nanda, Ved P. & Carver, John A., Jr. International Environmental Law. 400p. 1994. lib. bdg. 95.00 (0-941320-59-6) Transnatl Pubs.

N

Nanda, Ved P. & Pansius, David K. Litigation of International Disputes in U. S. Courts. LC 86-13667. (International Business & Law Ser.). 1986. ring bd. 145.00 (*0-87632-509-6*) Clark Boardman Callaghan.

Nanda, Ved P., jt. ed. see Sheperd, George W.

Nanda, Ved P., et al, eds. World Debt & the Human Condition: Structural Adjustments & the Right to Development. LC 92-9329. (Studies in Human Rights: No. 14). 272p. 1992. text ed. 59.95 (*0-313-28531-4*, NWD, Greenwood Pr) Greenwood.

Nandakumar, Prema. The Mother of Sri Aurobindo Ashram. (National Biography Ser.). 1979. pap. 2.25 (*0-89744-198-2*) Auromere.

— Sri Aurobindo: A Critical Introduction. 128p. 1989. text ed. 18.95 (*81-207-0765-6*, Pub. by Sterling Pubs II) Apt Bks.

Nandakumar, Prema, jt. auth. see Iyengar, K. R.

Nandan, Anshu P. Nicobarese of Great Nicobar: An Ethnography. 1993. 14.00 (*81-212-0403-8*, Pub. by Gian Publng Hse II) S Asia.

Nandan, Deoki. Hindu Law: Marriage & Divorce. (C). 1989. 325.00 (*0-685-27911-1*) St Mut.

Nandan, Deoki, ed. see Monir, M.

Nandan, Yash, comp. The Durkheimian School: A Systematic & Comprehensive Bibliography. LC 77-12. 457p. 1977. text ed. 59.95 (*0-8371-9532-2*, NAD/, Greenwood Pr) Greenwood.

Nandan, Yash, ed. Emile Durkheim: Contributions to L'Annee Sociologique. LC 79-54670. 1980. text ed. 35.00 (*0-02-907980-2*) Free Pr.

Nandell, Bob. A Certain Longing: The Photography of Bob Nandell. LC 94-72899. (Illus.). 96p. (Orig.). 1994. pap. 10.00 (*1-883477-01-8*) Lone Oak MN.

Nandgopal, Choodamani. Dance & Music in the Temple Architecture. 1990. 135.00 (*81-7186-000-1*, Pub. by Agam II) S Asia.

Nandi, Jean. Playing with the Elements of Music: A Guide to Music Theory. LC 88-92717. (Illus.). 153p. (Orig.). (C). 1989. pap. 22.95 (*0-9622023-1-2*) Bon Gout Pub.

— Skill & Style on the Harpsichord: A Reference Manual for the Developing Harpsichordist. LC 88-92719. (Illus.). 147p. (Orig.). (C). 1990. pap. 22.95 (*0-9622023-2-0*) Bon Gout Pub.

Nandi, Jean & Anderson, Rica, eds. Recollections of Judy Greenwood. (Illus.). 92p. (Orig.). 1990. pap. 10.00 (*0-9622023-3-9*) Bon Gout Pub.

N

Nandi, Jean & Jenkins, Leonie. Starting on the Harpsichord: A First Book for the Beginner. LC 88-92718. (Illus.). 212p. (Orig.). (C). 1989. pap. 22.95 (*0-9622023-0-4*) Bon Gout Pub.

Nandi, N. Civil Ready Referencer, 2 vols. 4th ed. (C). 1989. 250.00 (*0-685-46480-6*) St Mut.

Nandi, Ramendra N. Social Roots of Religion in Ancient India. 218p. (C). 1987. 22.00 (*81-7074-009-6*) S Asia.

Nandris, Grigore. Old Church Slavonic Grammar: Handbook of Old Church Slavonic, Pt. 1. LC 88-3481. (London East European Ser.). (C). 1965. pap. 39.95 (*0-485-17520-7*, Pub. by Athlone Pr UK) Humanities.

Nandris, Mabel. Folktales from Roumania. 1976. lib. bdg. 59.95 (*0-8490-1853-6*) Gordon Pr.

Nandu. The Mobile Scheduled Castes: Rise of a New Middle Class. (C). 1988. 27.50 (*81-7075-007-5*, Pub. by Hindustan IA) S Asia.

Nandy, Ashis. The Illegitimacy of Nationalism: Rabindrath Tagore & the Politics of Self. 106p. 1994. pap. 8.95 (*0-19-563298-2*) OUP.

— The Intimate Enemy: Loss & Recovery of Self Under Colonialism. 142p. 1989. pap. 7.95 (*0-19-562237-5*) OUP.

— The Savage Freud & Other Essays on Possible & Retrievable Selves. LC 94-46626. (Studies in Culture/Power/History). 1995. 49.50 (*0-691-04411-2*); pap. 15.95 (*0-691-04410-4*) Princeton U Pr.

— Traditions, Tyranny & Utopias: Essays in the Politics of Awareness. (Oxford India Paperbacks Ser.). 190p. 1993. pap. 7.95 (*0-19-563067-X*) OUP.

Nandy, Ashis, ed. Science, Hegemony & Violence: A Requiem for Modernity. (Oxford India Paperbacks Ser.). (Illus.). 314p. 1990. reprint ed. pap. 11.95 (*0-19-562580-3*) OUP.

Nandy, Pritish. On Either Side of Arrogance. (Redbird Ser.). 1975. 4.80 (*0-88253-596-X*); pap. text ed. 4.00 (*0-88253-595-1*) Ind-US Inc.

— Riding the Midnight River: Selected Poems of Pritish Nandy. (Indian Poetry Ser.). 144p. 1975. 9.00 (*0-89253-013-8*) Ind-US Inc.

— Rites for a Plebian Statue. 4.80 (*0-89253-655-1*) Ind-US Inc.

— Some Friends. 104p. 1983. pap. 6.00 (*0-86578-238-5*) Ind-US Inc.

Nandy, Pritish, ed. Indian Poetry in English Today. (Indian Poetry Ser.). 140p. (Orig.). (C). 1974. reprint ed. 2.95 (*0-88253-312-6*) Ind-US Inc.

Nandy, Pritish, tr. see Sen, Samar.

Nanen, Elinor, ed. Diamonds Are a Girl's Best Friend: Women Writers on Baseball. 295p. 1995. pap. 12.95 (*0-571-19853-8*) Faber & Faber.

Nanes, Allan, jt. auth. see Alexander, Yonah.

Nanetti, Rafaella Y. Growth & Territorial Policies: The Italian Model of Social Capitalism. 220p. 1992. 47.50 (*0-86187-651-2*, Pub. by Pinter Pubs UK) St Martin.

Nanetti, Rafaella Y. & Leonardi, Robert, eds. Italian Politics, Vol. 2: A Review. 220p. 1988. text ed. 42.50 (*0-86187-955-4*, Pub. by Pinter Pubs UK) St Martin.

Nanetti, Rafaella Y., jt. ed. see Leonardi, Robert.

Nanez Falcon, Guillermo, ed. & pref. The Favrot Family Papers: Sixteen Ninety - Seventeen Eighty-Two, 2 vols., Vol. 2. LC 88-590. (Illus.). xliv, 286p. (FRE & SPA.). 1988. 15.00 (*0-87409-002-4*) Tulane Univ.

— The Favrot Family Papers: Sixteen Ninety - Seventeen Eighty-Two, 2 vols., Vol. 3. LC 88-590. (Illus.). xlii, 328p. (FRE & SPA.). 1988. 15.00 (*0-87409-003-2*) Tulane Univ.

Nanez-Falcon, Guillermo, ed. The Rosemonde E. & Emile Kuntz Collection: A Catalogue of the Manuscripts & Printed Ephemera. LC 81-13168. 1981. pap. 20.00 (*0-9603212-3-3*) Tulane Univ.

Nanfara, Frank. The CNC Workbook: Computer Numerical Control Programming Made Easy. (Illus.). 320p. (C). 1995. pap. text ed. 32.25 (*0-201-65600-0*) Addison-Wesley.

Nanfeng, Bai, jt. auth. see Xiaoquiang, Wang.

Nanfito, Kenneth L., ed. see Foster, Monica M.

Nange, Scott. The New Kids Book. 1990. pap. 9.95 (*1-55698-242-9*) Movie Pubs Servs.

Nangia, Sudesh, jt. ed. see Sundram, K. V.

Nangini, Mary A. My Ontario Beautiful. LC 94-5676. 64p. 1995. pap. 12.95 (*0-7734-2726-0*, Mellen Poetry Pr) E Mellen.

Nangle, Clint. Some Things Harvard Never Taught Me. LC 92-97522. 160p. (Orig.). 1993. pap. 14.95 (*0-9635615-2-9*) Blue Horiz Pr.

Nani, Daniel. Dictionary of Vitamins: Dictionnaire des Vitamines. 1986. 24.95 (*0-8288-1820-7*, M2330) Fr & Eur.

— Dictionnaire des Vitamines. 155p. (FRE.). 1993. pap. 12.95 (*0-7859-7985-9*, 2732841870) Fr & Eur.

Nania, G. A. Technical Dictionary of Computer Science: Hardware-Software. 808p. (ENG, FRE, ITA, POR & SPA.). 1983. 113.00 (*2-903988-01-3*) IBD Ltd.

Nania, George A. Computers Dictionary: Dictionnaire D'Informatique. 1000p. (ENG, FRE, ITA, POR & SPA.). 1983. 150.00 (*0-8288-3917-4*) Fr & Eur.

— Dictionnaire d'Informatique. 1000p. (ENG, FRE, ITA, POR & SPA.). 1983. 150.00 (*0-8288-0272-6*, M 14464) Fr & Eur.

— Spanish, English & French Computers Dictionaries: Diccionario de Informatica. 783p. (ENG, FRE & SPA.). 1985. 95.00 (*0-8288-0271-8*, S16405) Fr & Eur.

***Nania, Georges.** Dictionary of Computer Science Terminology: English-Spanish-French. 2nd ed. (ENG, FRE & SPA.). 1990. 64.00 (*0-7859-8949-8*) Fr & Eur.

Nania, Georges A. Dictionary of Computer Science Terminology English-Spanish-French. 2nd ed. 783p. (C). 1990. 64.00 (*84-283-1413-6*, Pub. by Paraninfo) IBD Ltd.

***Naniewicz, Z. & Panagiotopoulos, P. D.** Mathematical Theory of Hemivariational Inequalities & Applications. LC 94-35419. (Pure & Applied Mathematics Ser.: Vol. 188). 267p. 1994. 120.00 (*0-8247-9330-7*) Dekker.

Nanji, Aisha. Black Celebrations. Nanji, Taji & Mills, Joyce, eds. 62p. (Orig.). 1987. pap. 6.00 (*0-929003-00-4*) Prgrssv Pubs.

Nanji, Azim. The Nizari Ismaili Tradition in the Indo-Pakistan Subcontinent. LC 78-12990. (Monographs in Islamic Religion & Theology). 1979. 35.00 (*0-88206-020-1*) Caravan Bks.

Nanji, Taji, ed. see Nanji, Aisha.

Nanjiani, Max. Fluorescein Angiography: Technique, Interpretation, & Application. (Illus.). 160p. 1992. 75.00 (*0-19-261932-2*) OUP.

Nanjing Hydraulic Research Institute, ed. Coastal & Port Engineering in Developing Countries 1987: Proceedings, 2 vols. 2250p. (C). 1987. pap. 98.00 (*7-5027-0052-8*, Pub. by A A Balkema NE) Ashgate Pub Co.

Nanjio, Bunyiu, comp. A Short History of the Twelve Japanese Buddhist Sects. LC 78-70104. reprint ed. 23.00 (*0-404-17355-1*) AMS Pr.

Nanjio, Bunyiu, tr. Short History of the Twelve Buddhist Sects. LC 79-52924. (Studies in Japanese History & Civilization). 172p. 1979. reprint ed. text ed. 55.00 (*0-313-26989-0*, U6989, Greenwood Pr) Greenwood.

Nankani, Helen. Techniques of Privatization of State-Owned Enterprises, Vol. II: Selected Country Case Studies. (Technical Paper Ser.: No. 89). 168p. 1988. 10.95 (*0-8213-1112-3*, 11112) World Bank.

Nankin, Fran, ed. see McCall, Edith.

Nankivell, John H. History of the Twenty-Fifth Regiment: United States Infantry 1869-1926. (Illus.). 1972. pap. 7.95 (*0-88342-220-4*) Old Army.

Nanko, Heroki & Cote, Wilfred A. Bark Structure: Hardwoods Grown on Southern Pine Sites. 1980. pap. 19.95x (*0-8156-2234-1*) Syracuse U Pr.

Nann, Hermann, ed. Nuclear Structure at High Spin, Excitation, & Momentum Transfer. LC 86-70837. (AIP Conference Proceedings Ser.: No. 142). 488p. 1986. lib. bdg. 70.00 (*0-88318-341-2*) Am Inst Physics.

Nann, Hermann & Stephenson, Edward J., eds. Particle Production Near Threshold. (Conference Proceeding Ser.: No. 221). (Illus.). 488p. 1991. 95.00 (*0-88318-829-5*) Am Inst Physics.

Nann, Richard C. Uprooting & Surviving: Adaptation & Resettlement of Migrant Families. 1982. lib. bdg. 70.00 (*90-277-1339-1*) Kluwer Ac.

Nann, W. N., tr. see Lloyd, G. E., ed.

Nannenga-Bremekamp, N. E. A Guide to Temperate Myxomycetes. Feest, A. & Burggraaf, Y., trs. (Illus.). 400p. 1991. pap. 120.00 (*0-948737-12-3*, Pub. by Biopress Ltd UK) Lubrecht & Cramer.

Nannes, Caspar H. Politics in the American Drama. LC 60-50101. 272p. reprint ed. pap. 77.60 (*0-685-17811-0*, 2029495) Bks Demand.

Nannestad, Peter. Danish Design or British Disease? Danish Economic Crisis Policy 1974-1979 in a Comparative Perspective. (Acta Jutlandica LXVII: 2 Humanities Ser.). 285p. (Orig.). 1991. pap. 37.50 (*87-7288-399-5*, Pub. by Aarhus Univ Pr DK) Coronet Bks.

— Reactive Voting in Danish General Elections, 1971-1979. 208p. (Orig.). 1989. pap. 50.00x (*87-7288-243-3*, Pub. by Almqv & Wiksell SW) Coronet Bks.

***Nanney.** Environmental Risks in Real Estate Transanctions: A Practical Guide. 2nd ed. 1994. text ed. 69.95 (*0-471-12594-6*); pap. text ed. 49.95 (*0-471-12593-8*) Wiley.

Nanney, Donald C. Environmental Risks in Real Estate Transactions: A Practical Guide. 2nd ed. 1992. text ed. 60.00 (*0-07-046000-0*) McGraw.

— Real Estate Transactions & Environmental Risks: A Practical Guide. 2nd ed. 429p. 1992. 79.95 (*0-7816-0255-6*, P7420) Exec Ent Pubns.

Nanney, J. Louis & Cable, John L. Beginning Algebra. 512p. (C). 1991. student ed write for info. (*0-697-12086-4*) Wm C Brown Pubs.

— Beginning Algebra. 512p. (C). 1991. pap. write for info. (*0-697-11652-2*) Wm C Brown Pubs.

— Developing Skills in Algebra, Vol. I: A Lecture Worktext. 4th ed. 264p. (C). 1987. pap. write for info. (*0-697-06768-8*) Wm C Brown Pubs.

— Intermediate Algebra. 688p. (C). 1990. pap. write for info. (*0-697-11653-0*) Wm C Brown Pubs.

— Intermediate Algebra. 688p. (C). 1991. teacher ed write for info. (*0-697-12078-3*) Wm C Brown Pubs.

— PreAlgebra: College Preparatory Mathematics. 448p. (C). 1989. pap. write for info. (*0-697-06428-X*) Wm C Brown Pubs.

— Preparation for Algebra. 544p. (C). 1992. pap. text ed. write for info. (*0-697-12801-6*) Wm C Brown Pubs.

Nanney, J. Louis & Shaffer, Richard D. Arithmetic: A Review. LC 75-93297. 316p. reprint ed. pap. 90.10 (*0-8357-5736-6*, 2023213) Bks Demand.

Nanni, Antonio, ed. Fibre Reinforcing Plastic for Concrete Structures: Properties & Applications. LC 93-25585. (Developments in Civil Engineering Ser.: Vol. 42). 450p. 1993. 194.25 (*0-444-89689-9*) Elsevier.

Nannini, Roger, illus. Josephine's Toy Shop: A Look-&-Play Book with a Special Fold-Out Toy Shop. (J). (ps-2). 1991. 15.95 (*0-8037-1004-6*) Dial Bks Young.

Nannipieri, Paolo, jt. ed. see Alef, Kassem.

Nannis, Ellen D. & Cowan, Philip A., eds. Developmental Psychopathology & Its Treatment. LC 85-644581. (New Directions for Child Development Ser.: No. CD 39). 1988. 17.95 (*1-55542-914-9*) Jossey-Bass.

Nanopoulos, D. V., ed. Astroparticle Physics. 500p. (C). 1991. text ed. 128.00 (*981-02-0582-1*); pap. 46.00 (*981-02-0583-X*) World Scientific Pub.

Nanopoulos, D. V., jt. auth. see Lopez, J. L.

Nanovic, John L., see Henry Lysing, pseud..

Nansen, Fridtjof. Adventure, & Other Papers. LC 67-23251. (Essay Index Reprint Ser.). 1977. 15.95 (*0-8369-0735-3*) Ayer.

— Armenia & the Near East. LC 76-25120. (Middle East in the 20th Century Ser.). 1976. reprint ed. lib. bdg. 37.50 (*0-306-70760-8*) Da Capo.

— Eskimo Life. LC 74-5856. (Illus.). reprint ed. 26.50 (*0-404-11664-7*) AMS Pr.

— In Northern Mists: Arctic Exploration in Early Times, 2 Vols, Set. Chater, Arthur G., tr. LC 75-94314. (Illus.). reprint ed. 94.50 (*0-404-01955-2*) AMS Pr.

— Through Siberia: The Land of the Future. Chater, A. G., tr. LC 73-115568. (Russia Observed Ser.). (Illus.). 1971. reprint ed. 39.95 (*0-405-03087-8*) Ayer.

Nansen, Fridtjof, ed. Norwegian North Polar Expedition, 1893-96: Scientific Results, 6 Vols, 1. LC 68-55205. (Illus.). 1971. reprint ed. text ed. 95.00 (*0-8371-3877-9*, NANP) Greenwood.

— Norwegian North Polar Expedition, 1893-96: Scientific Results, 6 Vols, Set. LC 68-55205. (Illus.). 1971. reprint ed. text ed. 495.00 (*0-8371-3852-3*, NANO) Greenwood.

— Norwegian North Polar Expedition, 1893-96: Scientific Results, 6 Vols, Vol. 2. LC 68-55205. (Illus.). 1971. reprint ed. text ed. 95.00 (*0-8371-3881-7*, NANQ) Greenwood.

— Norwegian North Polar Expedition, 1893-96: Scientific Results, 6 Vols, Vol. 3. LC 68-55205. (Illus.). 1971. reprint ed. text ed. 95.00 (*0-8371-3882-5*, NANR) Greenwood.

— Norwegian North Polar Expedition, 1893-96: Scientific Results, 6 Vols, Vol. 4. LC 68-55205. (Illus.). 1971. reprint ed. text ed. 95.00 (*0-8371-3883-3*, NANS) Greenwood.

— Norwegian North Polar Expedition, 1893-96: Scientific Results, 6 Vols, Vol. 5. LC 68-55205. (Illus.). 1971. reprint ed. text ed. 95.00 (*0-8371-3884-1*, NANT) Greenwood.

— Norwegian North Polar Expedition, 1893-96: Scientific Results, 6 Vols, Vol. 6. LC 68-55205. (Illus.). 1971. reprint ed. text ed. 95.00 (*0-8371-3885-X*, NANU) Greenwood.

Nansen, P., et al, eds. Epidemiology & Control of Nematodiasis in Cattle: Current Topics in Veterinary Medicine & Animal Science, No. 9. 616p. 1981. lib. bdg. 164.50 (*90-247-2502-X*) Kluwer Ac.

***Nansen, Ralph.** Sun Power: The Global Solution for the Coming Energy Crisis. 264p. 1995. pap. 14.95 (*0-9647021-1-8*) Ocean Pr WA.

Nantambu, Kwame, pseud. Decoding European Geo-Politics: Afrocentric Perspectives. expanded ed. 128p. (Orig.). (C). 1994. pap. 11.95 (*0-9613067-2-6*) L A Hoskins.

Nantell, Judith. The Poetry of Francisco Brines: The Deconstructive Effects of Language. LC 93-30378. 1994. write for info. (*0-8387-5277-2*) Bucknell U Pr.

Nantier, T., tr. see Pratt, Hugo.

Nantier, Terry, tr. see Pratt, Hugo.

Nanton, Isabel. British Columbia. (Discover Canada Ser.). (Illus.). 144p. (J). (gr. 4 up). 1993. lib. bdg. 20.55 (*0-516-06619-6*) Childrens.

Nanton, Isabel & Simpson, Mary. Adventuring in British Columbia. LC 91-10193. (Adventure Travel Guide Ser.). (Illus.). 368p. 1992. reprint ed. pap. 15.00 (*0-87156-674-5*) Sierra.

***Nanu.** Thimble Thoughts: A Collection of Thimble Size Writings on Inspirational, Thought, Feeling & Fun Subjects. (Illus.). 154p. 1995. pap. 12.95 (*0-9645049-0-1*, 31870634, Easy Chair Bks) Easy Chair Pub.

Nanus, Bert, jt. auth. see Bennis, Warren G.

***Nanus, Burt.** Leading the Way to Organizational Renewal. (Management Master Ser.). (Illus.). 50p. 1995. 15.95 (*1-56327-099-4*) Prod Press.

— Visionary Leadership: Creating a Compelling Sense of Direction for Your Organization. LC 92-18435. (Management Ser.). 263p. 1992. 27.00 (*1-55542-460-0*) Jossey-Bass.

— Visionary Leadership: Creating a Compelling Sense of Direction for Your Organization. LC 92-18435. (Management Ser.). 1995. pap. 18.50 (*0-7879-0114-8*) Jossey-Bass.

Nanxe, Aline de. Diccionario del Amor. 122p. (SPA.). 1969. pap. 9.95 (*0-8288-6572-8*, S-50136) Fr & Eur.

Nanyenya-Takirambudde, Peter. Technology Transfer & International Law. LC 79-23571. 190p. 1980. text ed. 36.95 (*0-275-90529-2*, C0529, Praeger Pubs) Greenwood.

Nanzig, Thomas P. Third Virginia Cavalry. (Virginia Regimental Histories Ser.). (Illus.). 142p. 1989. 19.95 (*0-930919-85-8*) H E Howard.

Naock, Ruth. How to Play the Piano. LC 86-51471. 83p. 1988. 34.95 (*0-942229-02-9*); spiral bd. 5.95 (*0-942229-01-0*) Video Album.

Naoi, M. & Parvez, S. H., eds. Tyrosine Hydroxylase: A Tribute to Toshiharu Nagatsu. x, 312p. 1993. 163.50 (*90-6764-154-5*) Coronet Bks.

Naor, Bezalel. Lights of Prophecy: Orot Ha-Nevuah. 96p. (Orig.). (C). 1990. pap. 4.95 (*1-879016-00-1*) UOJC Amer.

Naor, Bezalel, tr. see Kook, Abraham I.

Naor, David, ed. Immunosuppression & Human Malignancy. LC 89-7474. (Contemporary Immunology Ser.). 1990. 99.50 (*0-89603-149-7*) Humana.

Naoroji, Dadabhai. Poverty & Un-British Rule in India. 1990. reprint ed. 20.00 (*81-85395-87-X*, Pub. by Low Price II) S Asia.

Naosherwan, Anzar, ed. The Ancient One: A Disciple's Memoirs of Meher Baba. (Illus.). 280p. (Orig.). 1985. 16.95 (*0-685-10268-8*); pap. 12.00 (*0-685-10269-6*) Beloved Bks.

Naosuke Itoigawa, et al, eds. Current Topics in Primatology, Vol. 2: Behavior, Ecology, & Conservation. 300p. 1992. 57.50 (*0-86008-484-1*, Pub. by U of Tokyo JA) Col U Pr.

Naoya, Shiga. Paper Door. Dunlop, Lane, tr. 192p. 1993. pap. 9.95 (*0-8048-1893-2*) C E Tuttle.

Napa, Amy. Dealing with Disappointment. (Active Bible Curriculum Ser.). (Illus.). 48p. 1992. pap. 9.99 (*1-55945-139-4*) Group Pub.

Napaljarri, Peggy R. & Cataldi, Lee, trs. Warlpiri Dreamings & Other Narratives: Yimikirli. LC 93-34863. (Sacred Literature Ser.). 224p. 1994. 20.00 (*0-06-066125-9*) Harper SF.

Napalkov, N. P. & Eckhardt, S. Cancer Control in the Countries of the Council of Mutual Economic Assistance. 742p. 1982. 177.00 (*0-569-08718-X*) St Mut.

***Napalkov, N. P. & Eckhardt, S., eds.** Cancer Control in the Countries of the Council of Mutual Economic Assistance. 741p. (C). 1982. 105.00x (*963-05-3036-8*) St Mut.

Napalkov, N. P., ed. see International Agency for Research on Cancer Staff.

Napalkov, N. P., et al, eds. Perinatal & Multigeneration Carcinogenesis. (IARC Scientific Publications: No. 96). (Illus.). 462p. 1989. pap. 110.00 (*92-832-1196-0*) OUP.

Naparstak, Arthur J., jt. auth. see Biegel, David.

Naparsteck, M. J. War Song. (Orig.). 1980. pap. 1.75 (*0-8439-0729-0*) Dorchester Pub Co.

Naparstek, Arthur J., et al. Neighborhood Networks for Humane Mental Health Care. 238p. 1982. 42.50 (*0-306-41051-6*, Plenum Pr) Plenum.

Naparstek, Belleruth. Staying Well with Guided Imagery. 240p. 1994. 19.95 (*0-446-51821-2*) Warner Bks.

— Staying Well with Guided Imagery. 1995. pap. write for info. (*0-446-67159-2*); pap. 10.99 (*0-446-67134-7*) Warner Bks.

***Naparstek, Nathan.** The Learning Solution: What to Do If Your Child Has Trouble with Schoolwork. LC 94-32742. 160p. (Orig.). 1995. pap. 10.00 (*0-380-77629-4*) Avon.

Napheys, George H., jt. auth. see Brinton, D. G.

Napier & Judd. Mastering & Using Lotus 1-2-3, Release 2.2. 648p. 1990. 26.50 (*0-87835-462-X*) Boyd & Fraser.

— Mastering & Using Lotus 1-2-3, Release 2.4. 640p. 1993. per. write for info. (*0-87709-068-8*) Boyd & Fraser.

— Mastering & Using WordPerfect 5.1. 720p. 1991. 24.00 (*0-87835-494-8*) Boyd & Fraser.

Napier & Judd, Inc. Staff & Judd, Philip J. Mastering & Using Lotus 1-2-3, Release 3.4. (C). 1994. pap. 32.95 (*0-87709-299-0*, BF2990) S-W Pub.

— Mastering & Using Microsoft EXCEL, Version 5.0. 471p. (C). 1994. text ed. 38.50 (*0-87709-308-3*, BF3083) S-W Pub.

Napier, A. David. Foreign Bodies: Performance, Art, & Symbolic Anthropology. (C). 1992. 38.00 (*0-520-06583-2*) U CA Pr.

— Masks, Transformation, & Paradox. 1986. pap. 17.00 (*0-520-04533-5*) U CA Pr.

Napier, A. Kam, jt. auth. see Chenoweth, Candace A.

Napier, A. S., jt. ed. see Ker, William P.

Napier, Albert & Judd, Philip J. Mastering & Using Lotus 1-2-3 for Windows: Release 4.0. LC 94-4202. 1994. write for info. (*0-87709-532-9*) Boyd & Fraser.

Napier, Alexander, ed. see Barrow, Isaac.

An Asterisk (*) at the beginning of an entry indicates that the title is appearing in BIP for the first time.

Napier, Arthur S., ed. The Crawford Collection of Early Charters & Documents Now in the Bodleian Library. (Anecdota Oxoniensia Ser.: No. 7). 1988. reprint ed. 59. 50 (*0-404-63957-7*) AMS Pr.
— History of the Holy Rood-Tree. (EETS, OS Ser.: No. 103). 1969. reprint ed. 35.00 (*0-527-00104-X*) Periodicals Srv.
— Old English Glosses, Chiefly Unpublished. (Anecdota Oxoniensia Ser.: No. 11). 1988. reprint ed. 76.50 (*0-404-63961-5*) AMS Pr.
— Old English Glosses Chiefly Unpublished. (Anecdota Oxoniensia Ser.: Vol. IV, Pt. XI). xxxix, 302p. 1969. reprint ed. 50.70 (*0-685-66495-3*, 05102254, Pub. by Georg Olms GW) Lubrecht & Cramer.
Napier, Augustus Y. The Fragile Bond: In Search of an Equal, Intimate, & Enduring Marriage. 416p. 1990. reprint ed. pap. 13.00 (*0-06-091598-6*, PL) HarpC.
Napier, Augustus Y. & Whitaker, Carl A. The Family Crucible: The Intense Experience of Family Therapy. LC 74-1872. 320p. 1988. pap. 13.00 (*0-06-091489-0*, PL-1489, PL) HarpC.
Napier, Bill, jt. auth. see Clube, Victor.
Napier, Charles J. Colonization: Particularly in South Australia, with Some Remarks on Small Farms & Overpopulation. LC 68-56551. (Reprints of Economic Classics Ser.). xxxii, 269p. 1969. reprint ed. 39.50 (*0-678-00575-3*) Kelley.
***Napier, Charles J., comment.** Life in Napoleon's Army: The Memoirs of Captain Elzear Blaze. (Napoleonic Library: Vol. 28). (Illus.). 208p. 1995. 35.00 (*1-85367-196-7*, Pub. by Greenhill Bks UK) Stackpole.
Napier, David, jt. auth. see Williams, Tom.
Napier, Davie. The Best of Davie Napier. 272p. (Orig.). 1992. pap. 9.95 (*0-687-02827-2*) Abingdon.
Napier, Elizabeth R. The Failure of Gothic: Problems of Disjunction in an Eighteenth-Century Literary Form. 224p. 1987. 55.00 (*0-19-812860-6*) OUP.
Napier, H. Albert & Judd, Philip J. Mastering & Using Lotus 1-2-3 for Windows. LC 92-18825. 642p. 1992. write for info. (*0-87835-890-0*) Boyd & Fraser.
— Mastering & Using Lotus 1-2-3 Release 3. 814p. 1990. 28.50 (*0-87835-332-1*) Boyd & Fraser.
— Mastering & Using Microsoft Word for Windows 2.0. LC 93-3285. 662p. 1994. pap. 34.95 (*0-87709-071-8*, BF0718) S-W Pub.
— Mastering & Using Microsoft Word for Windows 6.0. LC 94-23822. 1995. write for info. (*0-7895-0010-8*) Boyd & Fraser.
— Mastering & Using WordPerfect 5.1 for Windows. (Illus.). 720p. (Orig.). (C). 1993. pap. 30.95 (*0-87835-816-1*) Boyd & Fraser.
— Mastering & Using WordPerfect 5.2 for Windows. LC 93-14839. 659p. (C). 1994. pap. 34.95 (*0-87709-278-8*, BF2788) S-W Pub.
— Mastering & Using WordPerfect 6.0. LC 93-34938. 1993. pap. 33.25 (*0-87709-426-8*) Boyd & Fraser.
— Mastering & Using WordPerfect 6.0 for Windows. LC 94-14819. 751p. 1995. pap. 36.00 (*0-87709-536-1*) Boyd & Fraser.
— Mastering Lotus 1-2-3. 350p. 1988. pap. 26.50 (*0-87835-310-0*) Boyd & Fraser.
Napier, H. Albert & Judd, Phillip J. Mastering & Using Lotus 1-2-3, Release 2.3. (Illus.). 658p. (C). 1992. per., pap. text ed. 27.50 (*0-87835-800-5*) Boyd & Fraser.
— Mastering & Using Wordperfect 5.1. 556p. (C). 1990. pap. text ed. write for info. (*0-538-91222-7*, BF4948) S-W Pub.
Napier, J. A. Blood Transfusion Therapy: A Problem Oriented Approach. 430p. 1987. text ed. 130.00 (*0-471-91283-2*, A R Liss) Wiley.
Napier, J. R. Primates & Their Adaptations. 3rd ed. Head, J. J., ed. LC 87-70405. (Carolina Biology Readers Ser.: No. 28). (Illus.). 16p. (gr. 10 up). 1987. pap. 2.75 (*0-89278-228-5*, 45-9628) Carolina Biological.
Napier, J. R. & Napier, P. H. The Natural History of the Primates. (Illus.). 200p. 1994. 19.95 (*0-262-64033-3*) MIT Pr.
Napier, James. Folklore: Or, Superstitious Beliefs in the West of Scotland. 1977. lib. bdg. 59.95 (*0-8490-1852-8*) Gordon Pr.
Napier, Jane R., see Lady Lawrence, pseud..
Napier, John. De Arte Logistica Joannis Naperi Merchistonii, Baronis Libri Qui Supersunt. LC 76-173010. (Maitland Club, Glasgow. Publications: No. 47). reprint ed. 27.50 (*0-404-52773-6*) AMS Pr.
— Hands. rev. ed. Tuttle, Russell H., ed. LC 92-14513. (Science Library). (Illus.). 194p. (C). 1993. pap. 10.95 (*0-691-02547-9*) Princeton U Pr.
— Rabdology. Richardson, William F., tr. (Charles Babbage Institute Reprint Series for the History of Computing). 138p. 1991. 40.00 (*0-262-14046-2*) MIT Pr.
Napier, John H. Air Force Officer's Guide. 29th ed. LC 86-644873. (Illus.). 424p. 1992. pap. 19.95 (*0-8117-3020-4*) Stackpole.
***Napier, John H., 3rd.** Air Force Officer's Guide. 30th ed. (Illus.). 376p. 1995. pap. 19.95 (*0-8117-2410-7*) Stackpole.
Napier, Kristine. How Nutrition Works. (Illus.). (Orig.). 1995. pap. 19.95 (*1-56276-254-0*) Ziff-Davis.
Napier, L. A., ed. Brassey's Armed Services Careers Yearbook 1987-88. 344p. 1986. 57.75 (*0-08-033598-5*, T120, K122, Pergamon Pr) Elsevier.
Napier, Mark, ed. Memorials of Montrose & His Times, 2 Vols, Set. LC 73-173012. (Maitland Club, Glasgow. Publications: No. 66). reprint ed. 85.00 (*0-404-53075-3*) AMS Pr.
Napier, Mark, ed. see Spottiswood, John.
Napier, Miles. The Racing Men of TV. 128p. 1990. pap. 21. 00 (*0-85131-301-9*, Pub. by J A Allen & Co UK) St Mut.
— Thoroughbred Pedigrees Simplified. 76p. 1990. pap. 21.00 (*0-85131-351-5*, Pub. by J A Allen & Co UK) St Mut.
Napier, Miles, ed. Treasures of the Bloodstock Breeder's Review. 700p. 1990. 100.00 (*0-85131-502-X*, Pub. by J A Allen & Co UK) St Mut.
Napier, Nancy J. Getting Through the Day: Strategies for Adults Hurt As Children. 304p. 1994. pap. 12.00 (*0-393-31242-9*) Norton.
— Recreating Your Self: Building Self-Esteem Through Imaging & Self-Hypnosis. pap. 10.95 (*0-393-31243-7*) Norton.
— Recreating Your Self: Help for Adult Children of Dysfunctional Families. 1990. 19.95 (*0-393-02842-9*) Norton.
— Recreating Your Self: Help for Adult Children of Dysfunctional Families. 388p. 1991. pap. 10.95 (*0-393-30804-9*) Norton.
***Napier, Nancy K. & Taylor, Sully.** Western Women Working in Japan: Breaking Corporate Barriers. LC 95-9841. 248p. 1995. text ed. 59.95 (*0-89930-901-1*, Quorum Bks) Greenwood.
Napier, Nancy K., jt. ed. see Ofsanko, Frank J.
Napier, P. H., jt. auth. see Napier, J. R.
***Napier, Priscilla.** Barbarian Eye: Lord Napier in China, 1834: The Prelude to Hong Kong. (Illus.). 250p. 1995. 37.00 (*1-85753-116-7*, Pub. by Brasseys UK) Brasseys Inc.
— Imperial Winds. 1984. pap. 3.95 (*0-8217-1324-8*) Zebra.
Napier, Rick. Information Engineering & Application Development Using Knowledge's Case Tool Set. (Information Management Ser.). 304p. 1991. pap. text ed. 47.00 (*0-13-457565-2*, 270510) P-H.
Napier, Susan. The Cruellest Lie. (Presents Ser.). 1994. mass mkt. 2.99 (*0-373-11674-8*, 1-11674-8) Harlequin Bks.
— The Cruellest Lie. large type ed. (Traditional Romance Ser.). 1994. 17.95 (*0-263-13823-2*, Pub. by Mills & Boon Ltd UK) Chivers N Amer.
— Deal of a Lifetime. large type ed. 1991. reprint ed. lib. bdg. 16.95 (*0-263-12687-0*, Pub. by Mills & Boon UK) Thorndike Pr.
— The Hawk & the Lamb. large type ed. (Romance Ser.). 1993. 17.95 (*0-263-13458-X*, Pub. by Mills & Boon Ltd UK) Chivers N Amer.
— The Hawk & the Lamb Presents Plus. (Presents Ser.). 1994. mass mkt. 2.99 (*0-373-11616-0*, 1-11616-9) Harlequin Bks.
— The Love Conspiracy. large type ed. LC 94-28429. 1994. 19.95 (*0-7927-2174-8*) Chivers N Amer.
— No Reprieve. large type ed. 1991. reprint ed. lib. bdg. 18. 95 (*0-263-12624-2*, Pub. by Mills & Boon UK) Thorndike Pr.
— Phantom Lover. (Presents Ser.). 1994. mass mkt. 2.99 (*0-373-11707-8*, 1-11707-6) Harlequin Bks.
— Phantom Lover. large type ed. 1995. 18.95 (*0-263-13938-7*) Thorndike Pr.
— Savage Courtship. (Presents Ser.). 1995. mass mkt. 3.25 (*0-373-11744-2*, 1-11744-9) Harlequin Bks.
— Savage Courtship. large type ed. (Harlequin Romance Ser.). 1995. 18.95 (*0-263-14102-0*, Pub. by Mills & Boon UK) Thorndike Pr.
— Secret Admirer. (Presents Ser.). 1993. pap. 2.89 (*0-373-11554-7*, 1-11554-2) Harlequin Bks.
— Secret Admirer. large type ed. 1993. 17.95 (*0-263-13357-5*, Pub. by Mills & Boon Ltd UK) Chivers N Amer.
— Tempt Me Not. (Presents Ser.). 1993. pap. 2.89 (*0-373-11531-8*, 1-11531-0) Harlequin Bks.
— True Enchanter. large type ed. (Magna Large Print Ser.). 1994. 18.95 (*0-7505-0745-4*, Pub. by Magna Print Bks) Ulverscroft.
— Winter of Dreams. large type ed. 1993. reprint ed. lib. bdg. 18.95 (*0-263-13199-8*, Pub. by Mills & Boon UK) Thorndike Pr.
Napier, Susan J. Escape from the Wasteland: Romanticism & Realism in the Fiction of Mishima Yukio & Oe Kenzaburo. (Harvard-Yenching Institute Monograph: Vol. No. 33). 258p. (C). 1991. 28.00 (*0-674-26180-1*) HUP.
Napier, T. C., et al, eds. The Basal Forebrain: Anatomy to Function. (Advances in Experimental Medicine & Biology Ser.: Vol. 295). (Illus.). 396p. 1991. 125.00 (*0-306-43932-8*, Plenum Pr) Plenum.
Napier, Ted L., pref. Implementing the Conservation Title of the Food Security Act of 1985. 355p. 1990. 18.00 (*0-935734-22-8*) Soil & Water Conserv.
Napier, Ted L., jt. ed. see Lovejoy, Stephen B.
Napier, Ted L., et al, eds. Adopting Conservation on the Farm: An International Perspective of the Socioeconomics of Soil & Water Conservation. 530p. 1994. pap. text ed. 40.00 (*0-935734-31-7*) Soil & Water Conserv.
— Water Resources Research: Problems & Potentials for Agriculture & Rural Communities. LC 83-4821. 247p. 1983. 7.00 (*0-935734-10-4*) Soil & Water Conserv.
Napier, William. History of the War in the Peninsula & in the South of France, 5 Vols, Set. LC 77-118946. (Illus.). reprint ed. 345.00 (*0-404-04660-6*) AMS Pr.
Napierala, Susanna. A Midwife's Perspective. 1994. write for info. (*0-89789-284-4*, Bergin & Garvey) Greenwood.
— A Midwife's Prespective. LC 93-49703. 256p. 1994. pap. text ed. 16.95 (*0-89789-285-2*, Bergin & Garvey) Greenwood.
Naples Community Hospital, Hospital Service League Staff. A Slice of Paradise. LC 93-72352. 1993. write for info. (*0-87197-385-5*) Favorite Recipes.
Naples, Gary J. By the Numbers: Principles of Automotive Parts Management. 200p. 1994. 29.00 (*1-56091-520-X*, R140) Soc Auto Engineers.
Naples-Marco Philharmonic League Staff. Naples-Marco Philharmonic League Cookbook: Fantastic Foods of the Philharmonic. 324p. (Orig.). 1989. pap. text ed. 12.50 (*0-685-29164-2*) Naples Marco.
Naples, Marge. A Step-by-Step Book about Siamese Cats. (Step-by-Step Ser.). (Illus.). 64p. (YA). (gr. 9-12). 1988. pap. 3.95 (*0-86622-473-4*, SK-021) TFH Pubns.
Naples, Marie, ed. see Johnson, Lois M. & Stinnett, Hester.
Naples, Michael J. Effective Frequency: The Relationship Between Frequency & Advertising Effectiveness. 146p. 1987. pap. 14.95 (*0-8442-3132-0*, NTC Busn Bks) NTC Pub Grp.
Napodano, Rudolph J. Values in Medical Practice: A Statement of Philosophy for Physicians & Model for Teaching a Healing Science. LC 85-19742. 144p. 1986. 32.95 (*0-89885-268-4*) Human Sci Pr.
Napoleani, Claudio. Diccionario de Economia Politica, Vol. 1. 3rd ed. 832p. 1988. 95.00 (*0-7859-6193-3*, 8471891646) Fr & Eur.
— Diccionario de Economia Politica, Vol. 2. 3rd ed. 836p. 1988. 95.00 (*0-7859-6194-1*, 8471891654) Fr & Eur.
Napoleon. Forever Yours: Letters of Love. 1991. 9.95 (*0-312-05430-0*) St Martin.
Napoleon, 3rd. The Second Empire & Its Downfall. Wilson, Herbert, tr. LC 74-126266. (Select Bibliographies Reprint Ser.). 1977. reprint ed. 18.95 (*0-8369-5464-5*) Ayer.
Napoleon, Davi R. Chelsea on the Edge: The Adventures of an American Theater. (Illus.). 318p. 1991. text ed. 29.95 (*0-8138-1713-7*) Iowa St U Pr.
Napoleon First. Correspondance de Napoleon Ier, Supplement: Lettres Curieuses Omises par le Comite de Publication, Rectifications. LC 77-173013. 1975. reprint ed. 96.00 (*0-404-07148-1*) AMS Pr.
Napoleon, Harold. Yuuyaraq: The Way of the Human Being. Madsen, Eric, ed. (Illus.). 65p. (Orig.). (C). 1991. pap. 7.00 (*1-877962-21-X*) Univ AK Ctr CCS.
Napoleon I. Correspondance de Napoleon Ier; Publiee par Ordre de l'empereur Napoleon III, 32 vols., 26. Incl. Set. 3,060.00 (*0-404-07400-6*); 40.00 (*0-685-73117-0*); 1. 95. 65 (*0-404-07401-4*); 2. 95.65 (*0-404-07402-2*); 3. 95.65 (*0-404-07403-0*); 4. 95.65 (*0-404-07404-9*); 5. 95.65 (*0-404-07405-7*); 6. 95.65 (*0-404-07406-5*); 7. 95.65 (*0-404-07407-3*); 8. 95.65 (*0-404-07408-1*); 9. 95.65 (*0-404-07409-X*); 10. 95.65 (*0-404-07410-3*); 11. 95.65 (*0-404-07411-1*); 12. 95.65 (*0-404-07412-X*); 13. 95.65 (*0-404-07413-8*); 14. 95.65 (*0-404-07414-6*); 15. 95.65 (*0-404-07415-4*); 16. 95.65 (*0-404-07416-2*); 17. 95.65 (*0-404-07417-0*); 18. 95.65 (*0-404-07418-9*); 19. 95.65 (*0-404-07419-7*); 20. 95.65 (*0-404-07420-0*); 21. 95.65 (*0-404-07421-9*); 22. 95.65 (*0-404-07422-7*); 23. 95.65 (*0-404-07423-5*); 24. 95.65 (*0-404-07424-3*); 25. 95.65 (*0-404-07425-1*); reprint ed. 95.65 (*0-404-07426-X*) AMS Pr.
— Correspondance de Napoleon Ier; Publiee par Ordre de l'empereur Napoleon III, 32 vols., 27. Incl. Set. 3,060.00 (*0-404-07400-6*); 40.00 (*0-685-73117-0*); 1. 95.65 (*0-404-07401-4*); 2. 95.65 (*0-404-07402-2*); 3. 95.65 (*0-404-07403-0*); 4. 95.65 (*0-404-07404-9*); 5. 95.65 (*0-404-07405-7*); 6. 95.65 (*0-404-07406-5*); 7. 95.65 (*0-404-07407-3*); 8. 95.65 (*0-404-07408-1*); 9. 95.65 (*0-404-07409-X*); 10. 95.65 (*0-404-07410-3*); 11. 95.65 (*0-404-07411-1*); 12. 95.65 (*0-404-07412-X*); 13. 95.65 (*0-404-07413-8*); 14. 95.65 (*0-404-07414-6*); 15. 95.65 (*0-404-07415-4*); 16. 95.65 (*0-404-07416-2*); 17. 95.65 (*0-404-07417-0*); 18. 95.65 (*0-404-07418-9*); 19. 95.65 (*0-404-07419-7*); 20. 95.65 (*0-404-07420-0*); 21. 95.65 (*0-404-07421-9*); 22. 95.65 (*0-404-07422-7*); 23. 95.65 (*0-404-07423-5*); 24. 95.65 (*0-404-07424-3*); 25. 95.65 (*0-404-07425-1*); reprint ed. 95.65 (*0-404-07427-8*) AMS Pr.
— Correspondance de Napoleon Ier; Publiee par Ordre de l'empereur Napoleon III, 32 vols., 28. Incl. Set. 3,060.00 (*0-404-07400-6*); 40.00 (*0-685-73117-0*); 1. 95.65 (*0-404-07401-4*); 2. 95.65 (*0-404-07402-2*); 3. 95.65 (*0-404-07403-0*); 4. 95.65 (*0-404-07404-9*); 5. 95.65 (*0-404-07405-7*); 6. 95.65 (*0-404-07406-5*); 7. 95.65 (*0-404-07407-3*); 8. 95.65 (*0-404-07408-1*); 9. 95.65 (*0-404-07409-X*); 10. 95.65 (*0-404-07410-3*); 11. 95.65 (*0-404-07411-1*); 12. 95.65 (*0-404-07412-X*); 13. 95.65 (*0-404-07413-8*); 14. 95.65 (*0-404-07414-6*); 15. 95.65 (*0-404-07415-4*); 16. 95.65 (*0-404-07416-2*); 17. 95.65 (*0-404-07417-0*); 18. 95.65 (*0-404-07418-9*); 19. 95.65 (*0-404-07419-7*); 20. 95.65 (*0-404-07420-0*); 21. 95.65 (*0-404-07421-9*); 22. 95.65 (*0-404-07422-7*); 23. 95.65 (*0-404-07423-5*); 24. 95.65 (*0-404-07424-3*); 25. 95.65 (*0-404-07425-1*); reprint ed. 95.65 (*0-404-07428-6*) AMS Pr.
— Correspondance de Napoleon Ier; Publiee par Ordre de l'empereur Napoleon III, 32 vols., 29. Incl. Set. 3,060.00 (*0-404-07400-6*); 40.00 (*0-685-73117-0*); 1. 95.65 (*0-404-07401-4*); 2. 95.65 (*0-404-07402-2*); 3. 95.65 (*0-404-07403-0*); 4. 95.65 (*0-404-07404-9*); 5. 95.65 (*0-404-07405-7*); 6. 95.65 (*0-404-07406-5*); 7. 95.65 (*0-404-07407-3*); 8. 95.65 (*0-404-07408-1*); 9. 95.65 (*0-404-07409-X*); 10. 95.65 (*0-404-07410-3*); 11. 95.65 (*0-404-07411-1*); 12. 95.65 (*0-404-07412-X*); 13. 95.65 (*0-404-07413-8*); 14. 95.65 (*0-404-07414-6*); 15. 95.65 (*0-404-07415-4*); 16. 95.65 (*0-404-07416-2*); 17. 95.65 (*0-404-07417-0*); 18. 95.65 (*0-404-07418-9*); 19. 95.65 (*0-404-07419-7*); 20. 95.65 (*0-404-07420-0*); 21. 95.65 (*0-404-07421-9*); 22. 95.65 (*0-404-07422-7*); 23. 95.65 (*0-404-07423-5*); 24. 95.65 (*0-404-07424-3*); 25. 95.65 (*0-404-07425-1*); reprint ed. 95.65 (*0-404-07429-4*) AMS Pr.
— Correspondance de Napoleon Ier; Publiee par Ordre de l'empereur Napoleon III, 32 vols., 30. Incl. Set. 3,060.00 (*0-404-07400-6*); 40.00 (*0-685-73117-0*); 1. 95.65 (*0-404-07401-4*); 2. 95.65 (*0-404-07402-2*); 3. 95.65 (*0-404-07403-0*); 4. 95.65 (*0-404-07404-9*); 5. 95.65 (*0-404-07405-7*); 6. 95.65 (*0-404-07406-5*); 7. 95.65 (*0-404-07407-3*); 8. 95.65 (*0-404-07408-1*); 9. 95.65 (*0-404-07409-X*); 10. 95.65 (*0-404-07410-3*); 11. 95.65 (*0-404-07411-1*); 12. 95.65 (*0-404-07412-X*); 13. 95.65 (*0-404-07413-8*); 14. 95.65 (*0-404-07414-6*); 15. 95.65 (*0-404-07415-4*); 16. 95.65 (*0-404-07416-2*); 17. 95.65 (*0-404-07417-0*); 18. 95.65 (*0-404-07418-9*); 19. 95.65 (*0-404-07419-7*); 20. 95.65 (*0-404-07420-0*); 21. 95.65 (*0-404-07421-9*); 22. 95.65 (*0-404-07422-7*); 23. 95.65 (*0-404-07423-5*); 24. 95.65 (*0-404-07424-3*); 25. 95.65 (*0-404-07425-1*); reprint ed. 95.65 (*0-404-07430-8*) AMS Pr.
— Correspondance de Napoleon Ier; Publiee par Ordre de l'empereur Napoleon III, 32 vols., 31. Incl. Set. 3,060.00 (*0-404-07400-6*); 40.00 (*0-685-73117-0*); 1. 95.65 (*0-404-07401-4*); 2. 95.65 (*0-404-07402-2*); 3. 95.65 (*0-404-07403-0*); 4. 95.65 (*0-404-07404-9*); 5. 95.65 (*0-404-07405-7*); 6. 95.65 (*0-404-07406-5*); 7. 95.65 (*0-404-07407-3*); 8. 95.65 (*0-404-07408-1*); 9. 95.65 (*0-404-07409-X*); 10. 95.65 (*0-404-07410-3*); 11. 95.65 (*0-404-07411-1*); 12. 95.65 (*0-404-07412-X*); 13. 95.65 (*0-404-07413-8*); 14. 95.65 (*0-404-07414-6*); 15. 95.65 (*0-404-07415-4*); 16. 95.65 (*0-404-07416-2*); 17. 95.65 (*0-404-07417-0*); 18. 95.65 (*0-404-07418-9*); 19. 95.65 (*0-404-07419-7*); 20. 95.65 (*0-404-07420-0*); 21. 95.65 (*0-404-07421-9*); 22. 95.65 (*0-404-07422-7*); 23. 95.65 (*0-404-07423-5*); 24. 95.65 (*0-404-07424-3*); 25. 95.65 (*0-404-07425-1*); reprint ed. 95.65 (*0-404-07431-6*) AMS Pr.
— Correspondance de Napoleon Ier; Publiee par Ordre de l'empereur Napoleon III, 32 vols., 32. Incl. Set. 3,060.00 (*0-404-07400-6*); 40.00 (*0-685-73117-0*); 1. 95.65 (*0-404-07401-4*); 2. 95.65 (*0-404-07402-2*); 3. 95.65 (*0-404-07403-0*); 4. 95.65 (*0-404-07404-9*); 5. 95.65 (*0-404-07405-7*); 6. 95.65 (*0-404-07406-5*); 7. 95.65 (*0-404-07407-3*); 8. 95.65 (*0-404-07408-1*); 9. 95.65 (*0-404-07409-X*); 10. 95.65 (*0-404-07410-3*); 11. 95.65 (*0-404-07411-1*); 12. 95.65 (*0-404-07412-X*); 13. 95.65 (*0-404-07413-8*); 14. 95.65 (*0-404-07414-6*); 15. 95.65 (*0-404-07415-4*); 16. 95.65 (*0-404-07416-2*); 17. 95.65 (*0-404-07417-0*); 18. 95.65 (*0-404-07418-9*); 19. 95.65 (*0-404-07419-7*); 20. 95.65 (*0-404-07420-0*); 21. 95.65 (*0-404-07421-9*); 22. 95.65 (*0-404-07422-7*); 23. 95.65 (*0-404-07423-5*); 24. 95.65 (*0-404-07424-3*); 25. 95.65 (*0-404-07425-1*); reprint ed. 95.65 (*0-404-07432-4*) AMS Pr.
Napoleon Third. Oeuvres de Napoleon III, 5 vols., 1. LC 74-173015. reprint ed. 30.00 (*0-404-07381-6*) AMS Pr.
— Oeuvres de Napoleon III, 5 vols., 2. LC 74-173015. reprint ed. 30.00 (*0-404-07382-4*) AMS Pr.
— Oeuvres de Napoleon III, 5 vols., 3. LC 74-173015. reprint ed. 30.00 (*0-404-07383-2*) AMS Pr.
— Oeuvres de Napoleon III, 5 vols., 4. LC 74-173015. reprint ed. 30.00 (*0-404-07384-0*) AMS Pr.
— Oeuvres de Napoleon III, 5 vols., 5. LC 74-173015. reprint ed. 30.00 (*0-404-07386-7*) AMS Pr.
— Oeuvres de Napoleon III, 5 vols., Set. LC 74-173015. reprint ed. 150.00 (*0-404-07380-8*) AMS Pr.
Napoleone, Mary A., et al. Spirits & Seasons. (Illus.). 83p. 1982. pap. 3.95 (*0-9610038-0-4*) Heatherdown Pr.
Napoleoni, Claudio. Diccionario de Economia Politica, 2 vols. 3rd ed. 1668p. (SPA.). 1988. 175.00 (*0-7859-3361-1*) Fr & Eur.
Napoles, V. Corporative Identity Design. 1988. pap. 24.95 (*0-442-26844-0*) Van Nos Reinhold.
Napoli, D. & Kegl, J., eds. Bridges Between Psychology & Linguistics: A Swarthmore Festschrift for Lila Gleitman. 312p. (C). 1991. text ed. 59.95 (*0-8058-0783-7*) L Erlbaum Assocs.
Napoli, Dede & Reynolds, Bill. The Starving Students' Cookbook. 144p. 1984. mass mkt. 6.95 (*0-446-38145-4*) Warner Bks.
***Napoli, Donna J.** The Bravest Thing. LC 94-48347. (J). 1995. 14.99 (*0-525-45397-0*, DCB) Dutton Child Bks.
— Jimmy, the Pickpocket of the Palace. LC 94-26089. (Illus.). 176p. (J). 1995. 14.99 (*0-525-45357-1*, DCB) Dutton Child Bks.
— The Magic Circle. LC 92-27008. 112p. (J). (gr. 7 up). 1993. 14.99 (*0-525-45127-7*, DCB) Dutton Child Bks.
— The Magic Circle. 128p. (YA). (gr. 7 up). 1995. pap. 3.99 (*0-14-037439-6*) Puffin Bks.
— Predication Theory: A Case-Study for Indexing Theory. (Cambridge Studies in Linguistics: No. 50). (Illus.). 400p. 1989. 79.95 (*0-521-35298-3*); pap. 32.95 (*0-521-36820-0*) Cambridge U Pr.
— Prince of the Pond. LC 91-40340. (Illus.). 112p. (J). (gr. 2-5). 1992. 13.99 (*0-525-44976-0*, DCB) Dutton Child Bks.
— The Prince of the Pond. (Illus.). 160p. (J). (gr. 3-7). 1994. pap. 3.99 (*0-14-037151-6*) Puffin Bks.
— Shark Shock. LC 93-43975. (Illus.). 192p. (J). (gr. 3-7). 1994. 13.99 (*0-525-45267-2*, DCB) Dutton Child Bks.
— Soccer Shock. LC 91-20706. (Illus.). 192p. (J). (gr. 4-7). 1991. 13.95 (*0-525-44827-6*, DCB) Dutton Child Bks.
— Soccer Shock. LC 93-7483. (Illus.). 192p. (J). (gr. 3-7). 1993. pap. 3.99 (*0-14-036482-X*, Puffin) Puffin Bks.
— Syntax: Theory & Problems. (Illus.). 416p. (C). 1993. pap. text ed. 35.00 (*0-19-507946-9*) OUP.
— When the Water Closes over My Head. LC 93-14486. (Illus.). 60p. (J). (gr. 2-5). 1994. 13.99 (*0-525-45083-1*) Dutton Child Bks.
Napoli, Donna J. & Rando, Emily N. Syntactic Argumentation, Vol. 1: Text. LC 79-17605. 430p. reprint ed. pap. 122.60 (*0-7837-6334-4*, 2046047) Bks Demand.

— Syntactic Argumentation, Vol. 2: Teacher's Guide. LC 79-17605. 45p. reprint ed. pap. 25.00 (0-7837-6335-2, 2046047) Bks Demand.

Napoli, Donna J. & Rando, Emily N., eds. Lingua Franca: An Anthology of Poetry by Linguists. ii, 157p. (Orig.). 1990. pap. 12.00 (0-933104-29-4) Jupiter Pr.

Napoli, Joseph. A Dying Cadence: Memories of a Sicilian Childhood. 107p. 1986. 15.00 (0-9617151-0-3) Marna Pr.

Napoli, Maryann. Health Facts: A Critical Evaluation of the Major Problems, Treatments & Alternatives Facing Medical Consumers. LC 81-2127. 400p. 1984. 22.95 (0-87951-132-X); pap. 8.95 (0-87951-196-6) Overlook Pr.

***Napoli, Maryann, ed.** The Center for Medical Consumers Ultimate Medical Answerbook. LC 95-60. 1995. 23.00 (0-688-12753-3) Hearst Bks.

Napoli, Tony, ed. Stephen Crane: Great American Short Stories II. LC 94-75023. (Classic Short Stories Ser.). (Illus.). 80p. 1994. pap. 4.50 (1-56103-015-5) Lake Pub Co.

Napoli, Vince, jt. auth. see Jenrette, Mardee S.

Napoli, Vince, jt. auth. see Mendoza, Manuel G.

Napoli, Vince, et al. Adjustment & Growth in a Changing World. 4th ed. Marshall, ed. 514p. (C). 1992. pap. text ed. 48.00 (0-314-93372-7) West Pub.

— Adjustment & Growth in a Changing World. 5th ed. LC 94-32602. 575p. 1995. text ed. write for info. (0-314-04557-0) West Pub.

Napoli, Vincent, jt. auth. see Mendoza, Manuel.

Napoliello, Mike. Pop Poems & Selections. 120p. Date not set. pap. text ed. 4.50 (0-9640052-0-4) US Mrkting.

— Suicide Poems. 58p. (Orig.). Date not set. pap. text ed. 4.50 (0-9640052-1-2) US Mrkting.

Napolitane, Catherine & Pelligrino, Victoria. Living & Loving after Divorce. 1978. pap. 4.99 (0-451-14988-2, AE2705, Sig) NAL-Dutton.

Napolitano, Anna M. From the Desert. 32p. write for info. (0-938631-29-2) Pennywhistle Pr.

Napolitano, Annamaria & Devine, Maria T. Manuale Di Grammatica Italiana. (C). 1979. pap. text ed. 27.50 (0-915838-98-2) Anma Libri.

***Napolitano, George.** This Is Wrestling. (Illus.). 64p. 1995. 9.98 (0-8317-8016-9) Smithmark.

Napolitano, L. G. Microgravity Sciences & Processes. 1983. pap. 37.00 (0-08-029985-7, Pergamon Pr) Elsevier.

— Space: Mankind's Fourth Environment, Vol. II. 1983. pap. 75.00 (0-08-029986-5, Pergamon Pr) Elsevier.

— Using Space, Today & Tomorrow, Vol. 2: Communications Satellite Symposium. 1978. 68.00 (0-08-023232-9, Pub. by Pergamon Repr UK) Franklin.

Napolitano, L. G., ed. Space Developments: Applications of Space & Energy: Selected Proceedings of the XXXI International Astronautical Congress, Tokyo, Japan, 21-28 September 1980. LC 81-81909. 360p. 1981. 152.00 (0-08-026729-7, Pub. by Pergamon Repr UK) Franklin.

— Space Developments for the Future of Mankind II: Proceedings of the Thirtieth International Astronautical Congress, Munich, FRG. September 16-23 1979. 228p. 1980. pap. 58.00 (0-08-026159-0, Pergamon Pr) Elsevier.

— Space Two Thousand-Activities to Be Performed for the Next Decade: Selected Papers from the 33rd IAF Congress, Paris, France, 27 September - 2 October 1982. 150p. 1983. pap. 91.00 (0-08-031106-7, Pergamon Pr) Elsevier.

Napolitano, L. G., ed. see Congress of the International Astronautical Federation, 22nd, Brussels, Sept. 1971.

Napolitano, L. G., jt. auth. see International Astronautical Congress Staff.

Napolitano, L. G., ed. see International Astronautical Congress Staff.

Napolitano, Louise. An American Story: Pietro DiDonato's Christ in Concrete. LC 93-36534. (Studies in Southern Italian & Italian-American Culture: Vol. 4). 1994. write for info. (0-8204-2094-8) P Lang Pubs.

Napolitano, Luigi G., ed. International Developments in Space Station & Space Technologies. LC 85-19955. (Illus.). 377p. 1985. 94.50 (0-930403-06-1) AIAA.

— Space Two Thousand. LC 83-8795. 709p. 1983. 59.50 (0-915928-73-6) AIAA.

— Spacecraft & Technologies Advanced Missions: International Highlights. LC 84-12295. (Illus.). 740p. 1984. 69.50 (0-915928-83-3) AIAA.

Napolitano, Luigi G. & International Astronautical Congress, 28th, Prague, 1977. Using Space--Today & Tomorrow: Proceedings, Vol. 1. 1978. 117.00 (0-08-023231-0, Pub. by Pergamon Repr UK) Franklin.

Napolitano, Luigi G., et al, eds. Astronautical Research: International Astronautical Congress. Incl. Proceedings, 1975 - Space & Energy. 1976. (0-318-55139-X); write for info. (0-318-55138-1, Pub. by Pergamon Repr UK) Franklin.

Napolitano, M., et al, eds. Thirteenth International Conference on Numerical Methods in Fluid Dynamics: Proceedings of the Conference Held at the Consiglio Nazionale Delle Ricerche, Rome, Italy, 6-10 July 1992. (Lecture Notes in Physics Ser.: Vol. 414). xiv, 541p. 1993. 92.00 (0-387-56394-6) Spr-Verlag.

Napolitano, Pete. Produce Pete's Farmacopeia: From Apples to Zucchini, & Everything In Between: Hints, Tips, & Delicious Recipes for Selecting & Using the Very Best Produce. LC 94-16421. 1994. 16.95 (0-688-12847-5) Hearst Bks.

Napolski, Max von. Leben und Werke Des Trobadors Ponz De Capduoill. LC 80-2183. (GER.). reprint ed. 26.50 (0-404-19009-X) AMS Pr.

Napora, Joe. 'STo Recognize This Dying. Gogol, John M. & Davies, Robert A., eds. (Poetry Chapbook Ser.). 48p. (Orig.). 1987. pap. 10.00 (0-932191-09-6) Mr Cogito Pr.

— Walam Olum. 1994. pap. 12.95 (0-912678-82-8) Greenfld Rev Lit.

Napora, Paul E. The Teachings of Oscar Camille, Vols. 1 & 2. Costa, Gwen, ed. LC 91-32254. 1992. 21.95 (0-87949-354-2); 21.95 (0-87949-362-3) Ashley Bks.

Napp, John L. United States History, Bk. I: To 1877. (Illus.). 344p. (YA). (gr. 7-12). 1988. teacher ed 12.99 (0-86601-693-7); student ed 4.99 (0-86601-694-5); text ed. 18.49 (0-86601-692-9) Media Materials.

Nappa, Amy. Love or Infatuation? (Active Bible Curriculum Ser.). (Illus.). 48p. 1992. pap. 9.99 (1-55945-128-9) Group Pub.

Nappa, Amy, jt. auth. see Nappa, Mike.

Nappa, Amy, ed. see Wilger, Jennifer.

Nappa, Mike. Accepting Others: Beyond Barriers & Stereotypes. (Active Bible Curriculum Ser.). (Illus.). 48p. 1992. pap. 9.99 (1-55945-126-2) Group Pub.

***Nappa, Mike, ed.** Clip-Art Cartoons for Churches. (Illus.). 176p. 1995. pap. 19.99 (1-55945-791-0) Group Pub.

— Group's Singable Songs for Children's Ministry: Accompaniment & Leaders Guide. (Illus.). 240p. 1995. spiral bd. 24.99 (1-55945-464-4) Group Pub.

— Group's Singable Songs for Children's Ministry Vol. 1: Lyrics Big Book for Group Singing. (Illus.). 64p. 1995. 29.99 (1-55945-465-2) Group Pub.

— Group's Singable Songs for Children's Ministry Vol. 2: Lyrics Big Book for Group Singing. (Illus.). 64p. 1995. 29.99 (1-55945-466-0) Group Pub.

— Videotaping Your Church Members' Faith Stories. (Projects with a Purpose for Youth Ministry Ser.). 40p. 1994. pap. 9.99 (1-55945-239-0) Group Pub.

***Nappa, Mike & Lessard, Paul N., eds.** Super Plays for Worship & Special Occasions. (Illus.). 140p. 1994. pap. 15.99 (1-55945-254-4) Group Pub.

***Nappa, Mike & Nappa, Amy.** Bore No More! (For Every Pastor, Teacher, Speaker) 70 Creative Ways to Involve Your Audience in Unforgettable Bible Teaching. LC 94-24039. 1995. 12.99 (1-55945-266-8) Group Pub.

— Fifty-Two Fun Family Devotions: Exploring & Discovering God's Word. LC 93-47945. 1994. 6.99 (0-8066-2698-4, 9-2698, Augsburg) Augsburg Fortress.

Nappa, Mike, ed. see Yount, Christine.

Napper, Elizabeth. Dependent Arising & Emptiness: A Tibetan Buddhist Interpretation of Madhyamika Philosophy Emphasizing the Compatability of Emptiness & Convential Phenomena. LC 89-40013. (Advanced Book - Blue Ser.). (Illus.). 848p. (Orig.). 1989. 37.50 (0-86171-057-6) Wisdom MA.

Napper, Elizabeth, ed. see Rinbochay, Lati.

Napper, Elizabeth, ed. see Tenzin Gyatso, the Fourteenth Dalai Lama.

Napper, Elizabeth, ed. see Wangyal, Geshe.

Napper, Elizabeth S., jt. auth. see Magee, William A.

Nappholz, Carol, tr. Unsung Women: The Anonymous Female Voice in Troubadour Poetry. LC 93-37317. (Studies in the Humanities: Literature-Politics-Society: Vol. 13). 140p. (C). 1994. text ed. 39.95 (0-8204-2376-9) P Lang Pubs.

Nappi, G., jt. ed. see Gerber, W. D.

Nappi, Giuseppe, et al. Headache & Depression: Serotonin Pathways As a Common Clue. 329p. 1991. 136.50 (0-88167-861-9) Raven.

— Stress & the Aging Brain: Integrative Mechanisms. (Aging Ser.: Vol. 37). 240p. 1990. 83.00 (0-88167-700-0, 2183) Raven.

Nappi, Giuseppe, et al, eds. Neurodegenerative Disorders: The Role Played by Endotoxins & Xenobiotics. 344p. 1988. text ed. 101.00 (0-88167-450-8) Raven.

Naprawa, Andrew, ed. see Lesko, Matthew.

Naprawa, Andrew, jt. auth. see Lesko, Matthew.

Naprawa, Andrew, ed. see Lesko, Matthew & Martello, Mary Ann.

Naprawa, Andrew, ed. see Lesko, Matthew.

Naps, Thomas L. Introduction to Data Structures & Algorithm Analysis. 2nd ed. Westby, ed. 640p. (C). 1992. text ed. 56.00 (0-314-93309-3) West Pub.

— Introduction to Program Design & Data Structures. Westby, ed. LC 92-14933. 500p. (C). 1993. pap. text ed. 55.50 (0-314-93308-5) West Pub.

***Naps, Thomas L. & Nance, Douglas W.** Introduction to Computer Science: Programming, Problem Solving & Data Structures, Alternate. 3rd ed. LC 94-44472. 1200p. 1995. text ed. 65.75 (0-314-04565-1) West Pub.

— Introduction to Computer Science: Programming, Problem Solving, & Data Structures, 2nd Alternate Edition. Westby, ed. 900p. (C). 1992. text ed. 65.25 (0-314-93307-7) West Pub.

Naps, Thomas L. & Pothering. Introduction to Data Structures & Algorithm Analysis with Pascal. 2nd ed. Westby, ed. 679p. (C). 1992. text ed. 56.00 (0-314-93305-0) West Pub.

Naps, Thomas L. & Singh, Bhagat. Advanced Programming & Data Structures with Pascal. 493p. (C). 1988. text ed. 50.75 (0-314-62540-2) West Pub.

— Introduction to Data Structure with Pascal. (Illus.). 464p. (C). 1986. text ed. 51.75 (0-314-93207-0) West Pub.

***Naps, Thomas L. & Wilson, Carol.** Laboratory Manual for Program Design & Introductory Data Structures (CS2) Pascal Version. 2nd ed. 250p. 1995. spiral bd. 20.50 (0-314-04679-8) West Pub.

Naps, Thomas L., jt. auth. see Nance, Douglas W.

Naps, Thomas L., jt. auth. see Pothering, George J.

Naps, Thomas L., jt. auth. see Singh, Bhagat.

Naps, Thomas L., jt. auth. see Wilson, Carol.

Napuk, Kerry. The Strategy-Led Business: Step by Step Planning for Your Company's Future. LC 93-982. 1994. pap. text ed. 34.95 (0-07-707775-X) McGraw.

***Naqash, Nasir A.** SAARC: Challenges & Opportunities. ix, 175p. (C). 1995. 22.00x (81-7024-611-3, Pub. by Ashish II) S Asia.

Naqash, Nasir A., jt. auth. see Wani, Gull M.

Naqui, Tahira, tr. see Chughtai, Ismat.

Naquin, Susan. Millenarian Rebellion in China: The Eight Trigrams Uprising of 1813. LC 75-18180. (Yale Historical Publications: Miscellany: No. 108). (Illus.). 398p. reprint ed. pap. 113.50 (0-8357-8224-7, 2033841) Bks Demand.

— Shantung Rebellion: The Wang Lun Uprising of 1774. LC 81-1268. (Illus.). 256p. (C). 1981. text ed. 30.00 (0-300-02638-2) Yale U Pr.

Naquin, Susan & Rawski, Evelyn S. Chinese Society in the Eighteenth Century. LC 86-29007. 320p. (C). 1987. text ed. 32.00 (0-300-03848-8) Yale U Pr.

— Chinese Society in the Eighteenth Century. 270p. (C). 1989. reprint ed. pap. 15.00 (0-300-04602-2) Yale U Pr.

Naquin, Susan & Yu, Chun-Fang, eds. Pilgrims & Sacred Sites in China. LC 91-20671. (Studies on China: Vol. 15). 456p. (C). 1992. 50.00 (0-520-07567-6) U CA Pr.

Naqvi, A. Mahmood. Precambrian Geology of India. (Oxford Monographs on Geology & Geophysics). (Illus.). 240p. 1987. 85.00 (0-19-503653-0) OUP.

Naqvi, Haider, jt. auth. see Nawab, Syed N.

Naqvi, S. M., ed. Precambrian Continental Crust & Its Economic Resources: Developments in Precambrian Geology, No. 13. 690p. 1990. 123.00 (0-444-88310-X) Elsevier.

Naqvi, Syed N. H. Ethics & Economics: An Islamic Synthesis. 176p. (Orig.). 1981. 17.25 (0-86037-079-8); pap. 9.95 (0-86037-080-1) New Era Publns MI.

— Islam, Economics, & Society. LC 93-2443. 220p. 1994. 56.50 (0-7103-0470-6, Pub. by Kegan Paul Intl UK) Routledge Chapman & Hall.

***Naqvi, Tahina, tr.** Attar of Roses: Stories from Pakistan. 192p. 1996. pap. 12.00 (0-89410-809-3) Three Continents.

***Naqvi, Tahira, tr.** Attar of Roses: Stories from Pakistan. 192p. 1995. 22.00 (0-89410-808-5) Three Continents.

Nar, jt. auth. see McMakin, Jacqueline.

Nar Narayan Das, jt. ed. see Kesavan, K. V.

Nara, Andrew R., et al. Blood Pressure. Pramik-Holdaway, Mary J., ed. (Biophysical Measurement Ser.). 109p. (Orig.). (C). 1989. 28.00 (0-9627449-0-5) SpaceLabs.

Nara, I. S. Safarnama & Zafarnama. 327p. 1986. 25.00 (0-8364-1793-3, Pub. by Minerva II) S Asia.

Nara, Robert O. & Kemppainen, Rudolph C. Building the One Hundred Thousand Dollar Dental Practice. LC 81-8550. 268p. 1981. 44.50 (0-13-086256-8, Busn) P-H.

Nara, Robert O. & Mariner, Steven A. How to Become Dentally Self-Sufficient. LC 79-90865. pap. write for info. (0-933420-01-3) Oramedics Intl.

— Money - By the Mouthful! LC 79-91111. 1979. pap. write for info. (0-933420-00-5) Oramedics Intl.

— The One Hundred Eighty Degree Theory: How to Become Mentally Self-Sufficient. LC 79-90866. 194p. 1979. pap. write for info. (0-933420-02-1) Oramedics Intl.

Narabayashi, H., ed. see International Symposium on Stereoencephalotomy Research Staff.

Narabayashi, H., et al, eds. Use of Microphysiological Recordings During Stereotactic Neurosurgery Journal: Stereotactic & Functional Neurosurgery, 1989, Vol. 52, No. 2-4. (Illus.). 200p. 1989. pap. 84.00 (3-8055-5039-1) S Karger.

Narabayashi, Hirotaro, et al. Parkinson's Disease: From Basic Research to Treatment. (Advances in Neurology Ser.: Vol. 60). 800p. 1994. 157.50 (0-88167-967-4) Raven.

Narada. The Bhakti Sutras of Narada. Sinha, Nandalal, tr. & intro. by. LC 73-3792. (Sacred Books of the Hindus: No. 7, Pt. 1). reprint ed. 17.50 (0-404-57807-1) AMS Pr.

— Narada Bhakti Sutras: The Gospel of Divine Love. Tyagisananda, Swami, tr. 1949. Bilingual ed. pap. 4.95 (0-87481-427-8) Vedanta Pr.

— Narada's Way of Divine Love: The Bhakti Sutras. Prabhavananda, Swami, tr. LC 75-161488. 1971. pap. 4.95 (0-87481-508-8) Vedanta Pr.

***Narada Media Staff.** A Guide to Odin's Rune Cards (TM) Commentary by Cheryl Barnes. Maris, Mariann & Aufderheide, Anne, eds. (Illus.). 64p. (Orig.). 1995. pap. 6.98 (0-934245-35-5) Narada Prodns.

— A Guide to Odin's Rune Cards (TM) Commentary by Cheryl Barnes, Book & Card Set. Maris, Mariann & Aufderheide, Anne, eds. (Illus.). 64p. 1995. pap. 20.98 (0-934245-36-3) Narada Prodns.

Narada Records Staff. Narada New Age Piano Sampler. 80p. 1990. pap. 10.95 (0-7935-0016-8, 00490211) H Leonard.

Narada, U. Guide to Conditional Relations: Being a Guide to Pages 1-12 of "Conditional Relations" Patthana, Pt. 1. (Pali Text Society Ser.). 321p. (C). 1979. 41.90x (0-7100-0280-7, RKP) Routledge.

Narada, Ven U., tr. Conditional Relations, 2 vols., 1. (C). 1981. 55.00 (0-86013-028-2, Pub. by Pali Text) Wisdom MA.

— Conditional Relations, 2 vols., 2. (C). 1981. 66.00 (0-86013-264-1, Pub. by Pali Text) Wisdom MA.

— Conditional Relations, 2 vols., Set. (C). 1981. 115.00 (0-86013-257-9, Pub. by Pali Text) Wisdom MA.

— Discourse on Elements. (C). 1962. 24.00 (0-86013-025-8, Pub. by Pali Text) Wisdom MA.

Naradamuni. Sri Radha-Krsna-Sahasra-Nama: A Thousand Names of Sri Radha-Krsna from Sri Narada Purana. Kusakrathadasa, tr. (Krsna Library: Vol. 140). 78p. (C). 1991. pap. text ed. 6.00 (1-56130-047-0) Krsna Inst.

— Sri Radha-Sahasra-Nama-Stotra: A Thousand Names of Sri Radha. Kusakrathadasa, tr. (Krsna Library: Vol. 105). 84p. (Orig.). 1990. pap. text ed. 6.00 (1-56130-014-4) Krsna Inst.

Naradamuni & Sivadeva. Sri Satvata Tantra: The Devotees of the Lord, 2 vols., Set. Kusakrathadasa, tr. (Krsna Library: Vols. 109-110). 330p. (Orig.). 1990. pap. text ed. 20.00 (1-56130-025-X) Krsna Inst.

— Sri Satvata Tantra: The Devotees of the Lord, Vol. 1. Kusakrathadasa, tr. (Krsna Library: Vol. 109). 170p. (Orig.). 1990. pap. text ed. 10.00 (1-56130-018-7) Krsna Inst.

— Sri Satvata Tantra: The Devotees of the Lord, Vol. 2. Kusakrathadasa, tr. (Krsna Library: Vol. 110). 160p. (Orig.). 1990. pap. text ed. 10.00 (1-56130-019-5) Krsna Inst.

Naraghi, Ehsan. From Palace to Prison: Inside the Iranian Revolution. Mobasser, Nilou, tr. LC 93-13873. 304p. 1994. 28.95 (1-56663-033-9) I R Dee.

Narahari, Y., jt. auth. see Viswanadham, N.

Narahashi, Keiko. I Have a Friend. LC 86-27628. (Illus.). 32p. (J). (ps-3). 1987. text ed. 13.95 (0-689-50432-2, McElderry) S&S Childrens.

— Is That Josie. (J). 1994. 14.95 (0-689-50606-6, McElderry) S&S Childrens.

Narahashi, T., ed. Ion Channels, Vol. 1. (Illus.). 348p. 1988. 85.00 (0-306-42655-2, Plenum Pr) Plenum.

— Ion Channels, Vol. 2. LC 88-647703. (Illus.). 302p. 1990. 75.00 (0-306-43352-4, Plenum Insight) Plenum.

— Ion Channels, Vol. 3. (Illus.). 340p. (C). 1992. 85.00 (0-306-44166-7, Plenum Pr) Plenum.

Narahashi, T. & Chambers, J. E., eds. Insecticide Action: From Molecule to Organism. LC 89-26592. (Illus.). 283p. 1989. 85.00 (0-306-43406-7, Plenum Pr) Plenum.

Narahashi, Toshio, ed. Cellular & Molecular Neurotoxicology. 320p. 1984. text ed. 107.50 (0-88167-028-6) Raven.

Narahashi, Toshio & Conn, P. Michael, eds. Methods in Neurosciences, Vol. 19: Ion Channels of Excitable Cells. (Illus.). 387p. 1994. text ed. 85.00 (0-12-185287-3) Acad Pr.

Narain, A. K. Studies in Buddhist Art of South Asia. (Illus.). 140p. 1986. 48.00 (0-8364-1852-2, Pub. by Usha II) S Asia.

Narain, A. K., ed. Studies in Buddhist Art of South Asia. (Illus.). vi, 139p. 1985. 31.50 (0-685-58199-3) Nataraj Bks.

Narain, Aditya, jt. auth. see Khurelblat, B.

Narain, Brij. Indian Economic Life Past & Present. 1990. reprint ed. 22.00 (81-85395-81-0, Pub. by BR Pub II) S Asia.

Narain, Dharm. Studies on Indian Agriculture. Raj, K. N. et al, eds. 264p. 1990. 16.95 (0-19-562106-9) OUP.

Narain, I. Literature, Social Consciousness & Polity. Lutze, L., ed. (C). 1987. 17.00 (81-85054-21-5, Pub. by Manohar II) S Asia.

Narain, Igbal & Atal, Yogesh. Social Sciences & the Government: The Asian Scene. (C). 1987. 20.00 (81-7062-032-5, Pub. by Lancer II) S Asia.

Narain, Iqbal. Pages from a Vice-Chancellor's Diary. 1990. 21.50 (81-7001-080-2, Pub. by Chanakya II) S Asia.

— Political Dimensions of Development. (C). 1994. 18.50x (81-7033-253-2, Pub. by Rawat II) S Asia.

Narain, Iqbal, ed. Development, Politics & Social Theory: Essays in Honour of S P Varma, the Doyen of Political Scientists in India. 400p. 1989. text ed. 40.00 (81-207-0850-4, Pub. by Sterling Pubs II) Apt Bks.

Narain, Iqbal & Mathur, P. C. Politics in Changing India. (C). 1994. text ed. 34.00 (81-7033-227-3, Pub. by Rawat II) S Asia.

Narain, K. An Outline of Madhva Philosophy. 241p. 1986. 39.95 (0-318-37015-8) Asia Bk Corp.

Narain, K. S., jt. auth. see Gava, E.

Narain, Lakshmi, jt. auth. see Ball, Andrew.

Narain, Laxmi. Parliament & Public Enterprise in India. 1979. text ed. 20.00 (0-685-14088-1) Coronet Bks.

Narain, N. V., jt. ed. see Chakravarty, S. R.

Narain, R. B. Buddhist Remains in Afghanistan. 68p. 1991. 12.00 (0-685-62631-8, Pub. by Kala Prakashan) Nataraj Bks.

Narain, Sanjai, jt. auth. see Rothenberg, Jeff.

Narain, Udai. Reagan's Nuclear Terrorism. 1985. 18.50 (0-8364-1312-1, Pub. by Deep) S Asia.

Narain, Virendra, jt. ed. see Chakravarty, S. R.

Naraine, Bishnu, jt. auth. see Miller, Don.

Naraine, Rabina, jt. auth. see Friedland, Patricia A.

Narang, A. S. Democracy, Development & Distortion: Punjab Politics in National Perspective. 1986. 22.00 (0-8364-1537-X, Pub. by Gitanjali Prakashan) S Asia.

— Punjab Accord & Elections Retrospect & Prospect. 1986. pap. 8.50 (0-8364-1796-8, Pub. by Minerva II) S Asia.

— Storm over the Sutlej: The Sikhs & Akali Politics. 1983. 24.00 (0-8364-1079-3) S Asia.

Narang, C. L. History of Punjabi: Literature. 210p. 1987. 26.50 (0-8364-2076-4, Pub. by Usha II) S Asia.

Narang, Gopi C. Rajinder Singh Bedi: Selected Short Stories. (C). 1989. 12.50 (0-8364-2620-7, Pub. by Sahitya Akademi II) S Asia.

— Urdu: Readings in Literary Urdu Prose. LC 70-2757. 396p. reprint ed. pap. 112.90 (0-317-10097-1, 2004657) Bks Demand.

— Urdu Language & Literature: A Critical Perspective. 224p. 1991. text ed. 27.95 (81-207-1124-6, Pub. by Sterling Pubs II) Apt Bks.

Narang, Harish, jt. auth. see Mehta, Gurleena.

Narang, Harish, ed. see Rahman, Tariq.

Narang, Prem K., jt. ed. see Cutler, Neal R.

Narang, Rajanini, ed. see Barber, Ezekiel.

Narang, S. Karl, et al, eds. Applications of Genetics to Arthropods of Biological Control Significance. LC 93-44973. 1994. write for info. (0-8493-2607-9) CRC Pr.

Narang, Saloni. The Coloured Bangles & Other Stories. LC 83-50208. 78p. (C). 1984. 17.00 (0-89410-403-9); pap. 8.00 (0-89410-404-7) Three Continents.

— Khadi & the Bullet. 1991. text ed. 30.00 (0-7069-5603-6, Pub. by Vikas II) S Asia.

N

An Asterisk (*) at the beginning of an entry indicates that the title is appearing in BIP for the first time.

Narang, Saran A. Protein Engineering: Approaches to the Manipulation of Protein Engineering. (Biotechnology Ser.). (Illus.). 262p. 1990. text ed. 30.00 (*0-409-90116-4*) Buttrwrth-Heinemann.

Narang, Saran A., ed. Synthesis & Applications of DNA & RNA. 1987. text ed. 73.00 (*0-12-514030-4*) Acad Pr.

Narang, Satya P., jt. ed. see Kulshreshtha, Sushma.

Narang, Satyapal, jt. auth. see Kulshreshtha, Sushma.

Narang, V. P. & Batra, V. K. Ayakar Vidhi ke Tatva (Elements of Income Tax Law in Hindi) 852p. 1980. 90.00 (*0-317-54689-9*) St Mut.

— Elements of Income Tax Law. 817p. 1979. 75.00 (*0-317-54691-0*) St Mut.

Naranjo, C. A. & Jones, J. K., eds. Idiosyncratic Adverse Drug Reactions: Impact on Drug Development & Clinical Use after Marketing: Proceedings of the Satellite Symposium to the IV World Conference on Clinical Pharmacology & Therapeutics, Mannheim-Heidelberg, 29-30 July, 1989. (International Congress Ser.: No. 878). 222p. 1990. 92.50 (*0-444-81118-4*, Excerpta Medica) Elsevier.

Naranjo, C. A. & Sellers, E. M., eds. Novel Pharmacological Interventions for Alcoholism. (Illus.). xv, 378p. 1991. 55.00 (*0-387-97741-4*) Spr-Verlag.

— Research Advances in New Psychopharmacological Treatments for Alcoholism. (International Congress Ser.: No. 664). 296p. 1985. 122.75 (*0-444-80692-X*, Excerpta Medica) Elsevier.

Naranjo, Carmen. There Never Was a Once upon a Time. Miller, Yvette E., ed. Britt, Linda, tr. & intro. by. LC 80-12822. (Illus.). 96p. 1989. pap. 11.50 (*0-935480-41-2*) Lat Am Lit Rev Pr.

Naranjo, Claudio. Character & Neurosis: An Integrative View. LC 94-21263. 352p. (Orig.). 1994. pap. 18.95 (*0-89556-066-6*) Gateways Bks & Tapes.

— The End of Patriarchy: And the Dawning of a Tri-Une Society. 175p. (Orig.). 1994. pap. 14.95 (*1-56937-065-6*) Amber Lotus.

— Enneatypes in Psychotherapy. LC 94-77115. 150p. (Orig.). (C). 1995. pap. 12.95 (*0-934252-47-5*) Hohm Pr.

— Gestalt Therapy: The Attitude & Practice of an Atheoretical Experientialism. 352p. 1993. 29.95 (*0-89556-090-9*) Gateways Bks & Tapes.

Naranjo, Efren. Lucha Obrera De Cuba. LC 91-75690. (Coleccion Cuba y Sus Jueces Ser.). 80p. (Orig.). (SPA.). 1992. pap. 9.95 (*0-89729-621-4*) Ediciones.

Naranjo-Morse, Nora. Mud Woman: Poems from the Clay. LC 91-16611. (Sun Tracks Ser.: Vol. 20). (Illus.). 125p. (Orig.). 1992. 35.00 (*0-8165-1248-5*); pap. 15.95 (*0-8165-1281-7*) U of Ariz Pr.

Naranjo, N. Venezuela & Its Ruler. 1976. lib. bdg. 59.95 (*0-8490-2794-2*) Gordon Pr.

Naranjo, Rafael S. Great Animal Refuges. LC 93-3437. (World Heritage Ser.). (Illus.). 36p. (J). (gr. 3 up). 1993. lib. bdg. 15.00 (*0-516-08385-6*); pap. 6.95 (*0-516-48385-4*) Childrens.

Naranjo, Ralph. Boatyards & Marinas: A Boatowner's Guide to Smart Shopping. (Illus.). 180p. 1988. pap. text ed. 17.95 (*0-87742-962-6*) Intl Marine.

— Boatyards & Marinas: Boatowner's Guide to Smart Shopping. 1988. pap. text ed. 17.95 (*0-07-155638-9*) McGraw.

Naranjo, Tito. Native Americans of the Southwest. (Discovery Kit Ser.). (Illus.). 64p. (Orig.). (J). (gr. 2 up). 1993. pap. 17.95 (*1-56138-241-8*) Running Pr.

Narasaiah, P. V. Sericulture in India. (C). 1992. 34.00 (*81-7024-508-7*, Pub. by Ashish II) S Asia.

Narashima, R., jt. ed. see Liepmann, Hans W.

Narasimaiah, C. D. Raja Rao. (Indian Writers Ser.). 8.50 (*0-89253-511-3*) Ind-US Inc.

Narasimha, N. S. & Babaji, Ramananda. The Way of Vaisnava Sages: A Medieval Story of South Indian Sadhus. LC 86-28251. (Sanskrit Notes of Visnu-vijay Swami Ser.). 422p. (Orig.). 1987. lib. bdg. 59.50 (*0-8191-6060-1*) U Pr of Amer.

Narasimhacharya. History of Kannada Literature: Readership Lectures. 1988. reprint ed. 8.00 (*81-206-0303-6*, Pub. by Asian Educ Servs II) S Asia.

Narasimhaiah, C. D. Indian Critical Scene: Controversial Essays. 1990. 36.00 (*81-7018-599-8*, Pub. by BR Pub II) S Asia.

Narasimhaiah, C. D., ed. see Kohli, Devindra.

Narasimhaiah, C. D., ed. see Sastri, P. S.

Narasimham, M. World Economic Environment & Prospects for India. 190p. 1988. text ed. 27.50 (*81-207-0769-9*, Pub. by Sterling Pubs II) Apt Bks.

Narasimhamurthy, P. An, jt. ed. see Shrivastava, B. K.

Narasimhamurty, T. S. Photoelastic & Electro-Optic Properties of Crystals. LC 79-409. (Illus.). 544p. 1981. 95.00 (*0-306-31101-1*, Plenum Pr) Plenum.

Narasimhan, jt. auth. see Melnyk.

Narasimhan, C. R. Rajagopalachari: A Biography. 260p. 1992. 35.00 (*81-7027-156-8*, Pub. by Radiant Pubs II) S Asia.

Narasimhan, Chakravarthi V., tr. The Mahabharata. LC 64-10347. 254p. 1973. reprint ed. pap. text ed. 15.00 (*0-231-08321-1*) Col U Pr.

Narasimhan, Mysore N. Principles of Continuum Mechanics. LC 92-12205. 584p. 1992. text ed. 89.95 (*0-471-54000-5*) Wiley.

Narasimhan, Raghavan. Analysis of Real & Complex Manifolds. 2nd rev. ed. (North-Holland Mathematical Library: Vol. 25). 246p. 1986. 79.50 (*0-444-87776-2*, North Holland) Elsevier.

— Compact Riemann Surfaces. LC 92-19717. (Lectures in Mathemtics ETH Zurich Ser.). v, 120p. 1992. write for info. (*3-7643-2742-1*); pap. 26.50 (*0-8176-2742-1*) Birkhauser.

— Complex Analysis of One Variable. (C). 1985. text ed. 46.50 (*0-8176-3237-9*) Birkhauser.

— Several Complex Variables. LC 75-166949. (Chicago Lectures in Mathematics Ser.). (Orig.). 1974. pap. text ed. 22.00 (*0-226-56817-2*) U Ch Pr.

Narasimhan, Raghavan, ed. A Perspective in Theoretical Computer Science. 456p. (C). 1989. pap. 37.00 (*9971-5-0926-1*) World Scientific Pub.

Narasimhan, Raji. The Heart of Standing Is You Cannot Fly. (Writers Workshop Greenbird Ser.). 131p. 1975. pap. text ed. 6.75 (*0-88253-557-9*) Ind-US Inc.

— The Sky Changes: A Novel. 1991. 8.00 (*81-7018-664-1*, Pub. by BR Pub II) S Asia.

Narasimhan, Ram, jt. auth. see Carter, Joseph R.

Narasimhan, Ram, jt. auth. see Melnyk, Steven A.

Narasimhan, Sakuntala. Sati: Widow Burning in India. LC 92-10840. 1992. pap. 12.00 (*0-385-42317-9*, Anchor NY) Doubleday.

***Narasimhan, Seetharama L., et al.** Production Planning & Inventory Control. 2nd ed. LC 94-22418. 1994. text ed. write for info. (*0-13-186214-6*) P-H.

Narasimhan, T. N., ed. Recent Trends in Hydrogeology. LC 82-2872. (Geological Society of America, Special Paper Ser.: No. 189). (Illus.). 456p. reprint ed. pap. 130.00 (*0-7837-1850-0*, 2042050) Bks Demand.

Narasin, Rochelle M., jt. auth. see Yang, Sunny.

Narasinga, Rao. Kisamwar Glossary of Kannada Words. (ENG & KAN.). 1985. 24.95 (*0-8288-1768-5*, M7860) Fr & Eur.

Narasinga Rao. Kisamwar Glossary of Kannada Words: Classified by Subjects. 224p. 1985. 16.00 (*0-88431-101-5*) IBD Ltd.

Narasu, P. Lakshmi. The Essence of Buddhism with an Introduction by Anagarika H. Dharmmapals. 212p. 1986. reprint ed. 15.00 (*0-8364-1748-8*, Pub. by Manohar II) S Asia.

— A Study of Caste. (C). 1988. reprint ed. 15.00 (*81-206-0411-3*, Pub. by Asian Educ Servs II) S Asia.

Naravane, V. S. Sarojini Naidu: An Introduction to Her Life, Work & Poetry. 160p. 1980. 20.00 (*0-86131-253-8*, Pub. by Orient Longman Ltd II) Apt Bks.

Naravane, Vishwanath S. A Cultural History of Modern India. (C). 1991. 23.00 (*81-85119-92-9*, Pub. by Northern Bk Ctr II) S Asia.

Naray-Szabo, G. Steric Effects in Biomolecules: Proceedings International Symposium, Eger, Hungary, October 5-8, 1981. (Studies in Physical & Theoretical Chemistry: Vol. 18). 418p. 1982. 123.00 (*0-444-99693-1*) Elsevier.

Naray-Szabo, G., ed. Theoretical Chemistry of Biological Systems. (Studies in Physical & Theoretical Chemistry: No. 41). 504p. 1986. 164.00 (*0-444-42597-7*) Elsevier.

Naray-Szabo, G. & Simon, K., eds. Steric Aspects of Biomolecular Interactions. 386p. 1987. 155.00 (*0-8493-6840-5*, QP517, CRC Reprint) Franklin.

Naray-Szabo, Gabor, et al. Applied Quantum Chemistry. (C). 1987. lib. bdg. 194.50 (*90-277-1901-2*) Kluwer Ac.

Narayaman, V. K., jt. auth. see Fahey, Liam.

Narayan, jt. ed. see Craighead.

Narayan, B. K. Mohammad the Prophet of Islam. 205p. 1978. 29.95 (*0-318-37191-X*) Asia Bk Corp.

— Pan-Islamism. 232p. 1988. 35.00 (*0-317-52149-7*) St Mut.

— Saint Shah Waris Ali & Sai Baba. (C). 1995. 14.00x (*0-7069-8755-1*, Pub. by Vikas II) S Asia.

Narayan, C. Giri. Group Invariance in Statistical Inference. 250p. 1995. text ed. 48.00 (*981-02-1875-3*) World Scientific Pub.

***Narayan, Deepa.** The Contribution of People's Participation: Evidence from 121 Rural Water Supply Projects. LC 94-34109. (Environmentally Sustainable Development Occasional Papers: No. 1). 1994. write for info. (*0-8213-3043-8*) World Bank.

— Evaluation Participative: Outils De Gestion Du Changement Dans l'Approvisionnement En Eau et l'Assainissement. (Technical Paper Ser.: No. 207). 136p. (FRE.). 1994. 9.95 (*0-8213-2782-8*, 12782) World Bank.

— Participatory Evaluation: Tools for Managing Change in Water & Sanitation. LC 93-4478. (Technical Paper Ser.: No. 207). 136p. 1993. 9.95 (*0-8213-2477-2*, 12477) World Bank.

***Narayan, Deepa & Srinivasan, Lyra.** Participatory Development Tool Kit: Materials to Facilitate Community Empowerment. 1994. 39.95 (*0-8213-2687-2*, 12687) World Bank.

Narayan, J., ed. Laser - Optical Processing of Electronic Materials. 209p. 1990. 53.00 (*0-8194-0226-5*, VOL. 1190) SPIE.

Narayan, J., et al. Progress in High-Temperature Superconducting Transistors & Other Devices, Vol. 1394. 1991. 53.00 (*0-8194-0463-2*) SPIE.

Narayan, J., et al, eds. High Temperature Superconductors: Fundamental Properties & Novel Materials Processing: Materials Research Society Symposium Proceedings, Vol. 169. 1990. text ed. 49.00 (*1-55899-057-7*) Materials Res.

— Laser-Solid Interactions & Transient Thermal Processing of Materials. 782p. 1983. 150.75 (*0-444-00788-1*, North Holland) Elsevier.

Narayan, J. P. Towards Total Revolution: Writings of Jayaprakash Narayan, 4 vols., Set. (C). 1978. 34.00 (*0-8364-2547-2*, Pub. by Popular Prakashan II) S Asia.

Narayan, Joshi. Direct Instruction: Handicapped Children in Nepal. 53p. 1983. pap. 9.00 (*0-318-03448-4*) Am-Nepal Ed.

***Narayan, Kirin.** Love, Stars, & All That. Rosenman, Jane, ed. 320p. 1995. pap. 10.00 (*0-671-79396-9*) PB.

— Storytellers, Saints, & Scoundrels: Folk Narrative in Hindu Religious Teaching. LC 89-31363. (Publications of the American Folklore Society, Bibliographical & Special Ser.). (Illus.). 296p. (C). 1989. pap. text ed. 14.95 (*0-8122-1269-X*) U of Pa Pr.

Narayan, Perin. The New Dalda Cook Book. (Illus.). 200p. 1978. 11.95 (*0-7069-0377-3*) Asia Bk Corp.

Narayan, R. K. An Astrologer's Day & Other Stories. 229p. 1981, reprint ed. 4.95 (*0-88253-105-0*) Ind-US Inc.

— The Bachelor of Arts. 1980. pap. 10.95 (*0-226-56833-4*) U Ch Pr.

— Critical Perspectives. McLeod, A. L., ed. (C). 1994. 21.00x (*81-207-1623-X*, Pub. by Sterling Plns Pvt II) S Asia.

— The Dark Room. LC 80-39930. iv, 210p. (C). 1981. pap. 10.95 (*0-226-56837-7*) U Ch Pr.

— The Emerald Route. 115p. 1980. pap. 4.95 (*0-86578-075-7*) Ind-US Inc.

— The English Teacher. LC 80-16374. 184p. 1980. lib. bdg. 9.95 (*0-226-56834-2*); pap. 9.95 (*0-226-56835-0*) U Ch Pr.

— The Financial Expert. LC 81-3020. 224p. (C). 1981. pap. 9.95 (*0-226-56841-5*) U Ch Pr.

— Gods, Demons, & Others. LC 92-43997. (Illus.). 248p. (C). 1993. pap. 12.95 (*0-226-56825-3*) U Ch Pr.

— The Grandmother's Tale & Other Stories. LC 94-4581. 320p. 1994. 24.95 (*0-670-85220-1*, Viking) Viking Penguin.

— Guide. 1988. mass mkt. 5.95 (*0-14-009657-4*, Penguin Bks) Viking Penguin.

— The Guide. 1980. mass mkt. 5.95 (*0-14-005453-7*, Penguin Bks) Viking Penguin.

— The Guide. 224p. 1992. 10.95 (*0-14-018547-X*, Penguin Classics) Viking Penguin.

— The Mahabharata. (C). 1989. reprint ed. 8.00 (*81-7094-001-X*, Pub. by Vision) S Asia.

— Malgudi Days. (Fiction Ser.). 240p. 1985. mass mkt. 6.95 (*0-14-006910-0*, Penguin Bks) Viking Penguin.

— Malgudi Days. 1994. pap. 9.95 (*0-14-018543-7*, Penguin Classics) Viking Penguin.

— Malgudi Days II. 1999. write for info. (*0-670-80632-3*) Viking Penguin.

— The Man-Eater of Malgudi. 176p. 1983. mass mkt. 5.95 (*0-14-006257-2*, Penguin Bks) Viking Penguin.

— The Man-Eater of Malgudi. 176p. 1993. 8.95 (*0-14-018548-8*, Penguin Classics) Viking Penguin.

— Mr. Sampath: The Printer of Malgudi. LC 80-27352. 220p. (C). 1981. pap. 10.95 (*0-226-56839-3*) U Ch Pr.

— My Dateless Diary. 1960. reprint ed. pap. 3.25 (*0-86578-118-4*) Ind-US Inc.

— My Days: A Memoir. 192p. 1990. mass mkt. 6.95 (*0-14-011207-3*, Penguin Bks) Viking Penguin.

— The Painter of Signs. 1983. mass mkt. 5.95 (*0-14-006259-9*, Penguin Bks) Viking Penguin.

— The Painter of Signs. 144p. 1993. pap. 7.95 (*0-14-018549-6*, Penguin Classics) Viking Penguin.

— The Ramayana. (Illus.). 1977. pap. 7.00 (*0-14-004428-0*, Penguin Bks) Viking Penguin.

— The Ramayana. 190p. 1993. 8.95 (*0-14-018700-6*, Penguin Classics) Viking Penguin.

— A Story-Teller's World: Stories, Essays, Sketches. 224p. 1990. pap. 8.95 (*0-14-012844-1*, Penguin Bks) Viking Penguin.

— Swami & Friends. LC 80-16119. 192p. 1980. pap. 10.95 (*0-226-56831-8*) U Ch Pr.

— Talkative Man. 1988. mass mkt. 5.95 (*0-14-010134-9*, Penguin Bks) Viking Penguin.

— Talkative Man. 128p. 1994. 9.95 (*0-14-018546-1*, Penguin Classics) Viking Penguin.

— A Tiger for Malgudi. 160p. 1994. 8.95 (*0-14-018545-3*, Penguin Classics) Viking Penguin.

— Under the Banyan Tree. 256p. 1987. mass mkt. 6.95 (*0-14-008012-0*, Penguin Bks) Viking Penguin.

— Under the Banyan Tree. 1993. pap. 8.95 (*0-14-018544-5*, Penguin Bks) Viking Penguin.

— The Vendor of Sweets. 144p. 1983. mass mkt. 5.95 (*0-14-006258-0*, Penguin Bks) Viking Penguin.

— Waiting for the Mahatma. LC 81-3075. 256p. (C). 1981. reprint ed. lib. bdg. 15.00 (*0-226-56826-1*); reprint ed. pap. 10.95 (*0-226-56828-8*) U Ch Pr.

— The World of Nagaraj: A Novel of Malgudi. 192p. 1991. pap. 8.95 (*0-14-012979-0*, Penguin Bks) Viking Penguin.

Narayan, Rom. Data Dictionary: Implementation, Use, & Maintenance. (Illus.). 608p. (C). 1988. text ed. 73.00 (*0-13-197351-7*) P-H.

Narayan, S., ed. Buddhism in World Peace. 1990. 21.50 (*81-210-0251-6*, Pub. by Inter-India Pubns) S Asia.

— Jharkhand Movement: Origin & Evolution. (Tribal Studies of India Series T: No. 157). (C). 1992. 23.50 (*81-210-0290-7*, Pub. by Inter-India Pubns) S Asia.

Narayan, S. A. Sudhin N. Ghose. (Indian Writers Ser.). 8.50 (*0-89253-557-1*) Ind-US Inc.

Narayan, Shyamala A. Raja Rao: Man & His Works. viii, 143p. 1989. text ed. 22.50 (*81-207-0963-2*, Pub. by Sterling Pubs II) Apt Bks.

Narayan, Vijay. Venereal Diseases: A Social Dilemma. (Illus.). 345p. (C). 1985. 32.95 (*0-317-66157-4*) Asia Bk Corp.

Narayana. Animal Fables of India. Hutchins, F. G., tr. & aft. by. LC 85-71820. (Illus.). 269p. 1985. 26.00 (*0-935100-03-2*); pap. 12.00 (*0-935100-04-0*) Amarta Pr.

Narayana, A. V., et al. The Operation of Modvat. 1990. text ed. 35.00 (*0-7069-5326-6*, Pub. by Vikas II) S Asia.

Narayana, Asha, jt. auth. see Singer, Daniel R.

Narayana, Dhruva, et al. Analog Computer Simulation of the Runoff Characteristics of an Urban Watershed. LC 77-141023. 88p. 1969. 19.00 (*0-403-04522-3*) Scholarly.

Narayana, G. & Kantner, John F. Doing the Needful: The Dilemma of India's Population Policy. 187p. (C). 1992. pap. text ed. 37.00 (*0-8133-8432-X*) Westview.

Narayana, N. S., et al. Agriculture, Growth & Redistribution of Income. (Contributions to Economic Analysis Ser.: Vol. 190). 1991. 72.50 (*0-444-88667-2*, CEA 190) Elsevier.

Narayana, P. S. Commentaries on Indian Easements Act, 1882. (C). 1988. 100.00 (*0-685-36513-1*) St Mut.

— The Consumer Protection Act. (C). 1990. 75.00 (*0-89771-193-9*) St Mut.

Narayana, P. S., ed. Law of Specific Relief. (C). 1990. 100.00 (*0-89771-240-4*) St Mut.

Narayana, P. S., jt. auth. see Rao, V. S.

Narayana Rao, K. V. The Emergence of Andhra Pradesh. 350p. 1974. lib. bdg. 12.50 (*0-88253-472-6*) Ind-US Inc.

Narayana Reddy, G. Women & Child Development: Some Contemporary Issues. (C). 1987. 22.00 (*0-317-68214-8*, Pub. by Chugh Pubns II) S Asia.

Narayana, T. R. Bheesma. (Illus.). (J). (gr. 1-8). 1979. pap. 3.00 (*0-89744-151-6*) Auromere.

Narayanan, Ajit & Bennun, Mervyn, eds. Law, Computer Science & Artificial Intelligence. LC 90-870. 288p. (C). 1991. text ed. 45.00 (*0-89391-599-8*) Ablex Pub.

Narayanan, Ajit, jt. auth. see Asady, Raad A.

Narayanan, Gomathi. The Sahibs & the Natives. 174p. 1986. 18.50 (*81-7001-016-0*, Pub. by Chanakya II) S Asia.

Narayanan, Leila. Ethnicity in Urban Context. (C). 1989. 32.00 (*81-7033-071-8*, Pub. by Rawat II) S Asia.

***Narayanan, N. Hari.** Diagrammatic Reasoning: Cognitive & Computational Perspectives. Glasgow, Janice et al, eds. LC 95-14683. (AAAI Press Ser.). 500p. (C). 1995. pap. 39.95x (*0-262-57112-9*) MIT Pr.

Narayanan, R., ed. Aluminium Structures-Advances, Design & Construction: Proceedings of the International Conference on Steel & Aluminium Structures, Cardiff, U. K., 8-10 July, 1987. 202p. 1987. 59.50 (*1-85166-121-2*, Pub. by Elsevier Applied Sci UK) Elsevier.

— Axially Compressed Structures: Stability & Strength. (Illus.). 316p. 1982. 90.00 (*0-85334-139-7*, I-302-82, Pub. by Elsevier Applied Sci UK) Elsevier.

— Beams & Beam Columns: Stability & Strength. (Illus.). 252p. 1983. 97.25 (*0-85334-205-9*, Pub. by Elsevier Applied Sci UK) Elsevier.

— Composite Steel Structures: Proceedings of the International Conference on Steel Aluminium Structures Cardiff, U. K., 8-10 July, 1987. 178p. 1987. 54.00 (*1-85166-122-0*, Pub. by Elsevier Applied Sci UK) Elsevier.

— Concrete Framed Structures: Stability & Strength. 290p. 1986. 81.00 (*1-85166-014-3*, Pub. by Elsevier Applied Sci UK) Elsevier.

— Plated Structures: Stability & Strength. (Illus.). 272p. 1984. 84.75 (*0-85334-218-0*, I-340-83, Pub. by Elsevier Applied Sci UK) Elsevier.

— Shell Structures: Stability & Strength. 360p. 1985. 110.00 (*0-85334-343-8*, Pub. by Elsevier Applied Sci UK) Elsevier.

— Steel-Concrete Composite Structures: Stability & Strength. 347p. 1988. 102.75 (*1-85166-134-4*) Elsevier.

— Steel-Framed Structures: Stability & Strength. 352p. 1985. 106.25 (*0-85334-329-2*, Pub. by Elsevier Applied Sci UK) Elsevier.

— Steel Structures-Advances, Design & Construction: Proceedings of the International Conference on Steel & Aluminum Structures, Cardiff, U. K., 8-10 July, 1987. 860p. 1987. 180.00 (*1-85166-120-4*, Pub. by Elsevier Applied Sci UK) Elsevier.

— Structural Connections: Stability & Strength. (Illus.). 269p. 1989. 117.00 (*1-85166-288-X*) Elsevier.

— Structures Subjected to Repeated Loading: Stability & Strength. 286p. 1991. 130.00 (*1-85166-567-6*) Elsevier.

Narayanan, R. & Roberts, T., eds. Structures Subjected to Dynamic Loading: Stability & Strength. 342p. 1991. 136.00 (*1-85166-582-X*) Elsevier.

Narayanan, S., jt. auth. see Asopa, V. N.

Narayanan, Sheshadri. Principles & Applications of Laboratory Instrumentation. LC 89-17595. (Illus.). 218p. 1989. student ed 40.00 (*0-89189-273-7*) Am Soc Clinical.

Narayanan, T. K. Nyayasara of Bhasarvajna: A Critical Study. (C). 1992. text ed. 20.00 (*81-7099-391-1*, Pub. by Mittal II) S Asia.

Narayanan, V. K. & Nath, Raghu. Organization Theory: A Strategic Approach. LC 92-31180. 608p. (C). 1993. text ed. 66.95 (*0-256-08778-4*) Irwin.

Narayanan, Vasudha. The Vernacular Veda: Revelation, Recitation, & Ritual. LC 93-44400. 260p. (C). 1994. text ed. 42.95 (*0-87249-965-0*) U of SC Pr.

Narayanan, Vasudha & Creel, Austin B., eds. Monastic Life in the Christian & Hindu Traditions: A Comparative Study. LC 90-30951. (Studies in Comparative Religion: Vol. 3). (Illus.). 608p. 1990. lib. bdg. 129.95 (*0-88946-502-9*) E Mellen.

Narayanan, Vasudha, jt. auth. see Carman, John.

Narayanananda, Swami. The Primal Power in Man: The Kundalini Shakti. 155p. 1971. reprint ed. spiral bd. 7.70 (*0-7873-0631-2*) Mokelumne.

Narayanaswamy, K. R. Unreal Past & Other Poems. 6.75 (*0-89253-710-8*); 3.00 (*0-89253-711-6*) Ind-US Inc.

Narayanaswamy, M. Commentary on Law Relating to Insecticides in India. (C). 1988. 175.00 (*0-685-36519-0*) St Mut.

***Narayman, Raj K., et al.** Neurotrauma. (Illus.). 1312p. 1995. text ed. 225.00 (*0-07-045662-3*) Hlth Prof Div.

Narazaki, Muneshige. Sharaku. Abiko, Bonnie F., tr. LC 83-80220. (Great Japanese Art Ser.). (Illus.). 1983. 24.95 (*0-87011-603-7*) Kodansha.

— Sharaku: The Enigmatic Ukiyo-e Master. (Illus.). 96p. 1995. 40.00 (*4-7700-1910-6*) Kodansha.

— Ukiyo-E Masterpieces in Europe Collections, Vol. 2. LC 87-81680. (Illus.). 278p. 1988. 300.00 (*0-87011-869-2*) Kodansha.

— Ukiyo-E Masterpieces in European Collections, Vol. 8: Bibliotheque Nationale, Paris Ser. (UKIYO-E Ser.). (Illus.). 284p. 1990. 300.00 (*0-87011-879-X*) Kodansha.

— Ukiyo-E Masterpieces in European Collections, Vol. 6: Musee Guimet One, Paris. (UKIYO-E Ser.). (Illus.). 280p. 1990. 300.00 (*0-87011-877-3*) Kodansha.

N

— Ukiyo-E Masterpieces in European Collections, Vol. 10: Museo d'Arte Orientale, Genoa I, Vol. 10. LC 87-81680. (Ukiyo-E Masterpieces Ser.). (Illus.). 232p. 1988. 300.00 (*0-87011-856-0*) Kodansha.

Narazaki, Muneshige, contrib. Ukiyo-E Masterpieces in European Collections: Museum fur Ostasiatische Kunst, Berlin, Vol. 12. LC 87-81680. 260p. 1988. 300.00 (*0-87011-882-X*) Kodansha.

— Ukiyo-E Masterpieces in European Collections: Victor & Albert Museum, I, Vol. 4. LC 87-81680. 280p. 1989. 300.00 (*0-87011-875-7*) Kodansha.

— Ukiyo-E Masterpieces in European Collections, Vol. 9: Musees Royaux d'Art et Histoire, Brussels, Belgium. (Illus.). 272p. 1989. 300.00 (*0-87011-880-3*) Kodansha.

Narazaki, Muneshige, ed. Ukiyo-e Masterpieces in European Collections, Vol. XI: Museo d'Arte Orientale, Genoa II. 260p. 1989. 300.00 (*0-87011-881-1*) Kodansha.

— Ukiyo-E Masterpieces in European Collections, Vol. III: British Museum III. LC 87-81680. 278p. 1989. 300.00 (*0-87011-874-9*) Kodansha.

Narbeth, Colin. Collecting Paper Money. (Illus.). 168p. (Orig.). 1986. pap. 19.95 (*0-900652-89-6*, Pub. by Seaby UK) Trafalgar.

Narbeth, Colin, ed. Admiral Seymour's Expedition & Taku Forts, 1900. 88p. (C). 1987. 60.00 (*0-902633-69-4*, Pub. by Picton UK) St Mut.

Narboni, Jean, ed. see Godard, Jean-Luc.

Narcejac, jt. auth. see Boileau.

Narcejac, Thomas, jt. auth. see Boileau, Pierre.

Narcisco, John, jt. auth. see Burkett, David.

Narciso, John. How to Make Eighty to One Hundred Thousand Dollars Per Year in Data Processing. 64p. (Orig.). 1991. pap. write for info. (*1-879797-00-3*) Redman-Wright.

Narciso, John & Burkett, David. Relating Redefined: Discovering the New Language for Living. rev. ed. (Illus.). 127p. (C). 1994. pap. text ed. 12.95 (*1-879797-01-1*) Redman-Wright.

*__Narciss, Georg.__ Knaurs Woerterbuch der Medizin. 2nd ed. 574p. (GER.). 1988. 59.95 (*0-7859-8358-9*, 3426263610) Fr & Eur.

Narcowich, F. J., jt. ed. see Fulling, S. A.

Nardamuni & Bhaktivinodathakura. Sri Bala-Krsna-Sahasra-Nama: A Thousand Names of Child Krsna Taken by Srila Bhaktivinoda Thakura from Sri Narada-Pancaratra. Kusakrathadasa, tr. (Krsna Library: Vol. 97). 64p. (Orig.). 1990. pap. text ed. 8.00 (*1-56130-004-7*) Krsna Inst.

Nardantonio, Dennis N. Sound Studio Production Techniques. 1990. text ed. 29.95 (*0-07-157232-5*); pap. text ed. 21.95 (*0-07-157239-2*) McGraw.

— Sound Studio Production Techniques. (Illus.). 288p. 1989. 28.95 (*0-8306-9250-9*); pap. 19.95 (*0-8306-3250-6*) TAB Bks.

Nardella, Gino & Dougherty, Keith. Wine & Wine Service. (Catering Ser.). (Illus.). 160p. 1987. pap. 24.95 (*0-7134-4825-3*, Pub. by Batsford UK) Trafalgar.

Nardelli, G. F., jt. ed. see Maradudin, A. A.

Narden, Joyce C. Imaginative Activities for Today's Students. 29p. (Orig.). 1991. spiral bd. 3.50 (*0-939507-16-1*, B307) Amer Classical.

*__Nardi, Bonnie A.__ Context & Consciousness: Activity Theory & Human-Computer Interaction. (Illus.). 376p. (C). 1995. 40.00x (*0-262-14058-6*) MIT Pr.

— A Small Matter of Programming: Perspectives on End User Computing. (Illus.). 257p. 1993. pap. 30.00 (*0-262-14053-5*) MIT Pr.

Nardi, D., jt. ed. see Maes, P.

Nardi, G. L., jt. auth. see Cordiano, C.

Nardi, James B. Once upon a Tree: Life from Treetop to Root Tips. LC 92-36444. (Illus.). 104p. (J). (gr. 5-10). 1993. 16.95 (*0-8138-0917-7*) Iowa St U Pr.

Nardi, Jim. Close Encounters with Insects & Spiders. LC 87-26284. (Illus.). 204p. (Orig.). 1988. 17.95 (*0-8138-1978-4*) Iowa St U Pr.

Nardi, Peter, et al, eds. Growing up Before Stonewall: Life Stories of Some Gay Men. LC 93-20939. 1994. 50.95 (*0-415-10151-4*, Routledge NY); pap. 14.95 (*0-415-10152-2*, Routledge NY) Routledge.

Nardi, Peter M., ed. Men's Frendships. (Research on Men & Masculinities Ser.: Vol. 2). (Illus.). 320p. 1992. 49.95 (*0-8039-3773-3*); pap. 24.00 (*0-8039-3774-1*) Sage.

Nardi, R. V., jt. auth. see Cocchetto, David M.

Nardi, William A. How to Solve Algebra Word Problems. 2nd ed. 1991. pap. 10.00 (*0-13-425216-0*, Arco Test) P-H Gen Ref & Trav.

Nardin, Daya, jt. auth. see Goldberg, Jay.

Nardin, Jane. Barbara Pym. LC 85-774. (English Authors Ser.: No. 406). 1985. text ed. 19.95 (*0-8057-6897-1*, Twayne) Macmillan.

— He Knew She Was Right: The Independent Woman in the Novels of Anthony Trollope. LC 88-15785. (Ad Feminam Ser.). 254p. (C). 1988. text ed. 27.95 (*0-8093-1484-3*) S Ill U Pr.

— Those Elegant Decorums: The Concept of Propriety in Jane Austen's Novels. LC 73-4821. 168p. 1973. 49.50 (*0-87395-236-7*) State U NY Pr.

Nardin, Terry & Mapel, David R., eds. Traditions of International Ethics. (Studies in International Relations: No. 17). 342p. (C). 1993. pap. 19.95 (*0-521-45757-2*) Cambridge U Pr.

Nardine, Arlene. In Search of the Yellow Submarine. 222p. 1985. pap. write for info. (*0-88144-065-5*) Christian Pub.

Nardine, Frank E., et al. How Involved are State Education Agencies in Parent Involvement? (IRE Report: No. 17). 26p. (Orig.). 1989. pap. 5.00 (*0-685-60815-8*, 17P) Inst Responsive.

Nardinelli, Clark. Child Labor & the Industrial Revolution. LC 89-46001. (Illus.). 208p. 1990. 25.00 (*0-253-33971-5*) Ind U Pr.

Nardini, Robert F. Asbestos: An Annotated Bibliography. (CompuBibs Ser.: No. 14). 1986. pap. 15.00 (*0-914791-13-3*) Vantage Info.

Nardini, William, ed. see Caldwell, Robert G.

Nardo, Anna K. The Ludic Self in Seventeenth-Century English Literature. LC 90-44797. (SUNY Series, The Margins of Literature). 263p. 1991. 59.50 (*0-7914-0721-7*); pap. 19.95 (*0-7914-0722-5*) State U NY Pr.

— Milton's Sonnets & the Ideal Community. LC 79-17221. 227p. reprint ed. pap. 64.70 (*0-7837-1824-1*, 2042024) Bks Demand.

Nardo, Don. Ancient Greece. LC 93-6904. (World History Ser.). (J). (gr. 6-9). 1994. 16.95 (*1-56006-229-0*) Lucent Bks.

— Animation: Drawings Spring to Life. LC 92-5151. (Encyclopedia of Discovery & Invention Ser.). (Illus.). 96p. (J). (gr. 5-8). 1992. lib. bdg. 17.95 (*1-56006-218-5*) Lucent Bks.

— Anxiety & Phobias. (Psychological Disorders & Their Treatment Ser.). (Illus.). 112p. (YA). (gr. 6-12). 1992. 18.95 (*0-7910-0041-9*) Chelsea Hse.

— The Battle of Marathon. LC 95-11710. (Battles of the Ancient World Ser.). (J). 1995. lib. bdg. write for info. (*1-56006-412-9*) Lucent Bks.

— The Battle of Zama. LC 95-11760. (Battles of the Ancient World Ser.). (J). 1996. lib. bdg. write for info. (*1-56006-420-X*) Lucent Bks.

— Braving the New World, 1619-1784: From the Arrival of the Enslaved Africans to the End of the American Revolution. LC 94-2963. (Milestones in Black American History Ser.). (YA). (gr. 7 up). 1994. write for info. (*0-7910-2259-5*); pap. write for info. (*0-7910-2685-X*) Chelsea Hse.

— Caesar's Conquest of Gaul. LC 95-16225. (World History Ser.). 1996. lib. bdg. write for info. (*1-56006-301-7*) Lucent Bks.

— Charles Darwin. (Library of Biography). (Illus.). 112p. (J). (gr. 5 up). 1993. 18.95 (*0-7910-1729-X*, Am Art Analog); pap. write for info. (*0-7910-1730-3*, Am Art Analog) Chelsea Hse.

— Chernobyl. LC 90-33567. (World Disasters Ser.). (Illus.). 64p. (J). (gr. 5-8). 1990. lib. bdg. 14.95 (*1-56006-008-5*) Lucent Bks.

— Cleopatra. LC 93-11079. (Importance of Ser.). (J). (gr. 5-8). 1994. 16.95 (*1-56006-023-9*) Lucent Bks.

— Computers: Mechanical Minds. LC 90-6648. (Encyclopedia of Discovery & Invention Ser.). (Illus.). 96p. (J). (gr. 5-8). 1990. lib. bdg. 17.95 (*1-56006-206-1*) Lucent Bks.

— Death Penalty. LC 92-20366. (Overview Ser.). (Illus.). 112p. (J). (gr. 5-8). 1992. lib. bdg. 16.95 (*1-56006-132-4*) Lucent Bks.

— Democracy. LC 93-4912. (Overview Ser.). (J). (gr. 5-8). 1994. 16.95 (*1-56006-147-2*) Lucent Bks.

— Dinosaurs. LC 93-4314. (Exploring the Unknown Ser.). (J). (gr. 5 up). 1994. 17.95 (*1-56510-154-5*) Lucent Bks.

— Dinosaurs: Unearthing the Secrets of Ancient Beasts. (Encyclopedia of Discovery & Invention Ser.). (Illus.). (J). (gr. 5-8). 1994. 17.95 (*1-56006-253-3*) Lucent Bks.

— Drugs & Sports. LC 90-6686. (Overview Ser.). (Illus.). 112p. (J). (gr. 5-8). 1990. lib. bdg. 16.95 (*1-56006-112-X*) Lucent Bks.

— Eating Disorders. LC 91-15563. (Overview Ser.). (Illus.). 112p. (J). (gr. 5-8). 1991. lib. bdg. 16.95 (*1-56006-129-4*) Lucent Bks.

— Exercise. (Healthy Body Ser.). (Illus.). 112p. (YA). (gr. 6-12). 1992. 18.95 (*0-7910-0017-6*) Chelsea Hse.

— The Extinction of the Dinosaurs. LC 93-4314. (Exploring the Unknown Ser.). (J). (gr. 3-5). 1995. 17.95 (*1-56006-154-5*) Lucent Bks.

— Germs: Mysterious Microorganisms. LC 91-15569. (Encyclopedia of Discovery & Invention Ser.). (Illus.). 96p. (J). (gr. 5-8). 1991. lib. bdg. 17.95 (*1-56006-214-2*) Lucent Bks.

— Gravity: The Universal Force. LC 90-6413. (Encyclopedia of Discovery & Invention Ser.). (Illus.). 96p. (J). (gr. 5-8). 1990. lib. bdg. 17.95 (*1-56006-204-5*) Lucent Bks.

— Greek & Roman Theatre: World History Ser. LC 94-6459. (Illus.). 128p. (YA). (gr. 5 up). 1995. pap. 16.95 (*1-56006-249-5*) Lucent Bks.

— H. G. Wells. LC 92-19870. (Importance of Ser.). (Illus.). 112p. (J). (gr. 5-8). 1992. lib. bdg. 16.95 (*1-56006-025-5*) Lucent Bks.

— Hygiene. LC 92-32086. (Encyclopedia of Health Ser.). (J). 1993. pap. write for info. (*0-7910-0460-0*) Chelsea Hse.

— Hygiene. (Healthy Body Ser.). (Illus.). (YA). (gr. 7-12). 1994. 19.95 (*0-7910-0020-6*, Am Art Analog) Chelsea Hse.

— The Indian Wars. LC 91-23068. (America's Wars Ser.). (Illus.). 112p. (J). (gr. 5-8). 1991. lib. bdg. 19.95 (*1-56006-403-X*) Lucent Bks.

— The Irish Potato Famine. LC 90-6246. (World Disasters Ser.). (Illus.). 64p. (J). (gr. 5-8). 1990. lib. bdg. 14.95 (*1-56006-012-3*) Lucent Bks.

— Jim Thorpe. LC 93-41138. (Importance of Ser.). (J). (gr. 5-8). 1994. 16.95 (*1-56006-045-X*) Lucent Bks.

— John Wayne. LC 94-17328. (Pop Culture Legends Ser.). (J). 1994. write for info. (*0-7910-2348-6*); pap. write for info. (*0-7910-2373-7*) Chelsea Hse.

— Krakatoa. LC 90-6003. (World Disasters Ser.). (Illus.). 64p. (J). (gr. 5-8). 1990. lib. bdg. 14.95 (*1-56006-011-5*) Lucent Bks.

— Lasers: Humanity's Magic Light. LC 90-6269. (Encyclopedia of Discovery & Invention Ser.). (Illus.). 96p. (J). (gr. 5-8). 1990. lib. bdg. 17.95 (*1-56006-200-2*) Lucent Bks.

— Medical Diagnosis. (Medical Disorders & Their Treatment Ser.). (Illus.). (YA). (gr. 6-12). 1993. 18.95 (*0-7910-0067-2*) Chelsea Hse.

— The Mexican-American War. LC 91-16728. (America's Wars Ser.). (Illus.). 112p. (J). (gr. 5-8). 1991. lib. bdg. 19.95 (*1-56006-402-1*) Lucent Bks.

— Modern Japan. (World History Ser.). (Illus.). 128p. (J). (gr. 5-9). 1995. lib. bdg. 16.95 (*1-56006-281-9*, 2819) Lucent Bks.

— Oil Spills. LC 90-23524. (Overview Ser.). (Illus.). 112p. (J). (gr. 5-8). 1991. lib. bdg. 16.95 (*1-56006-151-0*) Lucent Bks.

— Ozone. LC 91-6275. (Overview Ser. Our Endangered Planet). (Illus.). 112p. (J). (gr. 5-8). 1991. lib. bdg. 16.95 (*1-56006-101-4*) Lucent Bks.

— The Persian Gulf War. LC 91-23064. (America's Wars Ser.). (Illus.). 112p. (J). (gr. 5-8). 1991. lib. bdg. 16.95 (*1-56006-411-0*) Lucent Bks.

— Population. LC 90-23525. (Overview Ser.). (Illus.). 112p. (J). (gr. 5-8). 1991. lib. bdg. 16.95 (*1-56006-123-5*) Lucent Bks.

— The Punic Wars. LC 95-11713. (World History Ser.). (J). 1996. lib. bdg. write for info. (*1-56006-417-X*) Lucent Bks.

— Recycling. LC 92-27849. (Overview Ser.: Our Endangered Planet). (Illus.). 112p. (J). (gr. 5-8). 1992. lib. bdg. 16.95 (*1-56006-135-9*) Lucent Bks.

— The Roman Empire. LC 93-6906. (World History Ser.). (J). (gr. 6-9). 1994. 16.95 (*1-56006-231-2*) Lucent Bks.

— The Roman Republic. LC 93-6905. (World History Ser.). (J). (gr. 6-9). 1994. 16.95 (*1-56006-230-4*) Lucent Bks.

— Franklin D. Roosevelt. (Great Achievers Ser.). (J). 1995. 18.95 (*0-7910-2406-7*) Chelsea Hse.

— Thomas Jefferson. LC 92-43913. (Importance of Ser.). (Illus.). 111p. (J). (gr. 5-8). 1993. lib. bdg. 16.95 (*1-56006-037-9*) Lucent Bks.

— Traditional Japan. LC 94-8376. (World History Ser.). (Illus.). 128p. (J). (gr. 6-9). 1995. 16.95 (*1-56006-244-4*) Lucent Bks.

— The U. S. Congress. LC 93-41137. (Overview Ser.). (J). (gr. 5-8). 1994. 16.95 (*1-56006-155-3*) Lucent Bks.

— The U. S. Presidency. (Lucent Overview Ser.). (Illus.). (J). (gr. 5-8). 1995. 16.95 (*1-56006-157-X*) Lucent Bks.

— Vitamins & Minerals. (Healthy Body Ser.). (Illus.). (YA). (gr. 7-12). 1994. 19.95 (*0-7910-0032-X*, Am Art Analog); pap. write for info. (*0-7910-0472-4*, Am Art Analog) Chelsea Hse.

— The War of 1812. LC 91-29501. (America's Wars Ser.). (Illus.). 112p. (J). (gr. 5-8). 1991. lib. bdg. 19.95 (*1-56006-401-3*) Lucent Bks.

— World War Two: The War in the Pacific. LC 91-16727. (America's Wars Ser.). (Illus.). 112p. (J). (gr. 5-8). 1991. lib. bdg. 19.95 (*1-56006-408-0*) Lucent Bks.

Nardo, Don & Belgum, Erik. Voodoo: Opposing Viewpoints. LC 91-14497. (Great Mysteries Ser.). (Illus.). 112p. (J). (gr. 5-8). 1991. lib. bdg. 16.95 (*0-89908-089-8*) Greenhaven.

Nardo, Paolo Di, jt. ed. see Claycomb, William C.

Nardo, Valentino W. & Landry, Anthony J. Americans with Disabilities Act - 1990: Title I Employment - A Practical Guide for Employers. LC 92-3975. 150p. 1991. student ed 79.95 (*0-9632679-0-6*) LanNar Pub.

— Americans with Disabilities Act 1990: Title I Employment - a Practical Guide for Employers. rev. ed. 190p. 1993. student ed 39.95 (*0-9632679-2-2*) LanNar Pub.

— The Disabled Person's Job Search Organizer: PLUS... Things You Need to Know about ADA Title I & Now You're Not Afraid to Ask!! LC 92-3975. 94p. 1992. pap. 7.95 (*0-9632679-1-4*) LanNar Pub.

Nardocchio, Elaine F., ed. Reader Response to Literature: The Empirical Dimension. LC 92-35778. (Approaches to Semiotics Ser.: No. 108). xiv, 313p. (C). 1993. lib. bdg. 115.90 (*3-11-012764-4*) Mouton.

*__Nardon, J. David.__ Bridge & Structure Estimating. 1995. text ed. 75.00 (*0-07-045669-0*) McGraw.

Nardone, Georgio & Watzlawick, Paul. The Art of Change: Strategic Therapy & Hypnotherapy Without Trance. Davis, Sally & Wyatt, Michael, trs. LC 92-32436. (Social & Behavioral Science Ser.). 164p. 1993. 30.95 (*1-55542-499-6*) Jossey-Bass.

Nardone, M. A., ed. Accounting. 428p. (C). 1990. pap. 50.00 (*1-85352-582-0*, Pub. by HLT Pubns UK); pap. 50.00 (*1-85352-020-9*, Pub. by HLT Pubns UK) St Mut.

— Accounts. 150p. (C). 1990. 60.00 (*0-685-52525-2*, Pub. by HLT Pubns UK) St Mut.

— Solicitors' Accounts. 204p. (C). 1990. pap. 40.00 (*1-85352-897-8*, Pub. by HLT Pubns UK) St Mut.

Nardone, Nancy K., jt. ed. see Frankel, Walter A.

Nardone, Richard M. The Story of the Christian Year. 1991. pap. 9.95 (*0-8091-3277-X*) Paulist Pr.

Narducci, L. M. & Abraham, N. B. Laser Physics & Laser Instabilities. 320p. (C). 1988. text ed. 71.00 (*9971-5-0062-0*); pap. text ed. 37.00 (*9971-5-0063-9*) World Scientific Pub.

Narducci, L. M., jt. ed. see Machado, M. A.

Nardulli, Peter F., ed. The Constitution & American Political Development: An Institutional Perspective. 344p. 1992. 39.95 (*0-252-01787-0*); pap. 14.95 (*0-252-06174-8*) U of Ill Pr.

— Diversity, Conflict, & State Politics: Regionalism in Illinois. LC 88-18719. 352p. 1989. 34.95 (*0-252-01576-2*); pap. 19.95 (*0-252-06036-9*) U of Ill Pr.

Nardulli, Peter F., et al. The Tenor of Justice: Criminal Courts & the Guilty Plea Process. LC 87-10772. 480p. (C). 1988. 39.95 (*0-252-01463-4*) U of Ill Pr.

Narduzzi, James L. Mental Health among Elderly Native Americans. LC 93-34972. (Studies on Elderly in America). 248p. 1993. 58.00 (*0-8153-1568-6*) Garland.

*__Narell, Irena.__ History's Choice: A Writer's Journey from Poland to America. Browning, Peter, ed. 160p. (Orig.). 1995. pap. 10.95 (*0-934764-03-4*) Akiba Pr.

— Joshua: Fighter for Bar Kochba. LC 78-55959. (J). (gr. 6-12). 1979. pap. 5.95 (*0-934764-01-8*) Akiba Pr.

— Our City: The Jews of San Francisco. 1981. 15.00 (*0-317-61576-9*) Akiba Pr.

Naremore, James. Acting in the Cinema. 316p. 1988. pap. 14.00 (*0-520-07194-8*) U CA Pr.

— Acting in the Cinema. (C). 1988. 35.00 (*0-520-06228-0*) U CA Pr.

— The Films of Vincente Minnelli. LC 92-39912. (Cambridge Film Classics Ser.). (Illus.). 208p. (C). 1993. 47.95 (*0-521-38366-8*); pap. 11.95 (*0-521-38770-1*) Cambridge U Pr.

— The Magic World of Orson Welles. LC 89-42895. (Illus.). 328p. 1989. reprint ed. pap. 14.95 (*0-87074-299-X*) SMU Press.

— The World Without a Self: Virginia Woolf & the Novel. LC 72-91315. 272p. 1973. 35.00 (*0-300-01594-1*) Yale U Pr.

Naremore, James, ed. Treasure of Sierra Madre. LC 78-53298. (Screenplay Ser.). (Illus.). 206p. 1979. 19.95 (*0-299-07680-6*); pap. 9.95 (*0-299-07684-9*) U of Wis Pr.

Naremore, James & Brantlinger, Patrick, eds. Modernity & Mass Culture. LC 90-41881. (Illus.). 288p. 1991. 37.50 (*0-253-33968-5*); pap. 14.95 (*0-253-20627-8*, MB-627) Ind U Pr.

Naremore, James, ed. see Hitchcock, Alfred.

*__Naremore, Rita C.__ Language Intervention with School-Aged Children: Conversation Narrative, & Text. (Illus.). 304p. (Orig.). (C). 1994. pap. text ed. 34.95 (*1-56593-222-6*, 0582) Singular Publishing.

Narendra, Kumpati S., ed. Adaptive & Learning Systems: Theory & Applications. LC 86-4962. 426p. 1986. 95.00 (*0-306-42263-8*, Plenum Pr) Plenum.

Narendra, Kumpati S. & Monopoli, Richard, eds. Applications of Adaptive Control. 1980. text ed. 114.00 (*0-12-514060-6*) Acad Pr.

Narendra, Kumpati S., et al, eds. Advances in Adaptive Control. LC 91-16922. (Illus.). 424p. (C). 1991. text ed. 69.95 (*0-87942-278-5*, PC0272-5) Inst Electrical.

Narens, Louis. Abstract Measurement Theory. 400p. 1985. 45.00 (*0-262-14037-3*) MIT Pr.

Nares, J. G. Seamanship, Eighteen Sixty-Two. 368p. 1984. 49.00 (*0-905418-37-9*, Pub. by Gresham Bks UK) St Mut.

Nares, Robert. A Glossary of Words, Phrases, & Allusions to English Authors, Particularly Shakespeare. 1972. 59.95 (*0-8490-0240-0*) Gordon Pr.

Nargi, Ben J. Are You He Who Is to Come. LC 88-51027. 138p. (J). 1989. pap. 6.95 (*1-55523-177-2*) Winston-Derek.

Nargolkar, Vasant, ed. see Bhave, Vinoba.

Narai, K. & Matsui, Y. Fundamentals of Practical Aberration Theory - Fundamental Knowledge & Techniques. 192p. 1993. text ed. 61.00 (*981-02-1349-2*) World Scientific Pub.

Narici & Beckenstein. Topological Vector Spaces. (Pure & Applied Mathematics Ser.: Vol. 95). 432p. 1985. 140.00 (*0-8247-7315-2*) Dekker.

Narici, Lawrence, et al. Functional Analysis & Valuation Theory. (Pure & Applied Mathematics Ser.: Vol. 5). 200p. 1971. 110.00 (*0-8247-1484-9*) Dekker.

Narikawa, Hirotoshi & Takimoto, Teruko. Purr-fect Shiatsu: Tender Touches for the Nineties Cat. (Illus.). 96p. (Orig.). 1993. pap. 9.95 (*1-881267-07-5*) Intercultural.

Nariman, G. K., tr. see Harshadeva.

Nariman, Gushtaspshah K. Literary History of Sanskrit Buddhism. LC 78-70106. reprint ed. 37.50 (*0-404-17356-X*) AMS Pr.

Nariman, Heidi N. Soap Operas for Social Change: Toward a Methodology for Entertainment-Education Television. LC 92-36547. (Media & Society Ser.). 184p. 1993. text ed. 49.95 (*0-275-94389-5*, C4389, Praeger Pubs) Greenwood.

Nariman, J. K. Literary History of Sanskrit Buddhism: From Winternitz, Sylvain Levi, Huber. (C). 1992. reprint ed. text ed. 15.00 (*81-208-0795-2*, Pub. by Motilal Banarsidass II) S Asia.

Narine, Dalton, ed. see Douglas, Bobb.

Narins, Robert G. Diagnostic Techniques in Renal Disease. (Contemporary Issues in Nephrology Ser.). (Illus.). 384p. 1992. text ed. 85.00 (*0-443-08806-3*) Churchill.

— Maxwell & Kleeman's Clinical Disorders of Fluid & Electrolyte Metabolism. 5th ed. (Illus.). 1440p. 1994. text ed. 185.00 (*0-07-041008-9*) Hlth Prof Div.

Narish, Frances A. Crusade Against Communism. 1992. 16.95 (*0-533-10185-9*) Vantage.

Narison, S. QCD Spectral Sum Rules. (Lecture Notes in Physics Ser.: Vol. 26). 544p. 1990. text ed. 48.00 (*9971-5-0653-X*) World Scientific Pub.

Narita, Katsuya. Systems of Higher Education: Japan. (Systems of Higher Education Ser.). 154p. (Orig.). 1978. pap. text ed. 5.50 (*0-89192-202-4*) Interbk Inc.

Narita, S., jt. ed. see Motus, L.

Narita, Shigehira, et al. The Kodansha Japanese-English Dictionary. 1250p. 1984. pap. 35.00 (*0-87011-671-1*) Kodansha.

Narita, Shigehisa, et al, eds. The Kodansha Japanese-English Dictionary. 1250p. (C). 1980. 43.00 (*0-87011-421-2*) Kodansha.

Narke, Rob. Succeed. LC 83-71420. (Illus.). 336p. (Orig.). 1983. pap. 7.95 (*0-9611336-0-0*) Dreaming.

Narkiewicz, O. Eurocommunism, 1968-1986: A Select Bibliography. 200p. 1987. text ed. 90.00 (*0-7201-1801-8*, Mansell Pub) Cassell.

Narkiewicz, Olga A. Eastern Europe Nineteen Sixty-Eight to Nineteen Eighty-Four. LC 85-22985. 288p. (C). 1986. 57.00 (*0-389-20607-5*, N8166) B&N Imports.

— Petrification & Progress: Communist Leaders in Eastern Europe, 1956-1988. LC 90-41333. 192p. 1990. text ed. 45.00 (*0-312-05287-1*) St Martin.

— Soviet Leaders: From the Cult of Personality to Collective Rule. LC 86-75516. 320p. 1986. text ed. 45.00 (*0-312-74857-4*) St Martin.

An Asterisk (*) at the beginning of an entry indicates that the title is appearing in BIP for the first time.

Narkiewicz, Olga A., jt. auth. see Hayward, Jack.

Narkiewicz, Olga N. The End of the Bolshevik Dream: Western European Communist Parties in the Late Twentieth Century. 208p. 1990. 45.00 (*0-415-02510-9*, A4132) Routledge.

Narkiewicz, Robert D. The Outplacement of Older Psychiatric Patients into the Community. LC 91-37479. (Studies on Elderly in America). 96p. 1992. 36.00 (*0-8153-0520-6*) Garland.

Narkiewicz, W. Elementary & Analytic Theory of Algebraic Numbers. 850p. 1990. 94.00 (*0-387-51250-0*, 3310) Spr-Verlag.

— Number Theory. Kanemitsu, S., tr. 371p. 1984. text ed. 54.00 (*9971-950-13-8*); pap. text ed. 30.00 (*9971-950-26-X*) World Scientific Pub.

— Uniform Distribution of Sequences of Integers in Residue Classes. (Lecture Notes in Mathematics Ser.: Vol. 1087). vii, 125p. 1984. pap. 28.10 (*0-387-13872-2*) Spr-Verlag.

***Narkis, M. & Rosenzweig, N., eds.** Polymer Powder Technology. LC 95-3061. 1995. text ed. 88.00 (*0-471-93872-6*) Wiley.

Narkiss, Bezalel, ed. Picture History of Jewish Civilization. (Tudor Book Ser.). (Illus.). 1974. 19.95 (*0-685-02932-8*) L Amiel Pub.

Narkiss, Bezalel, intro. Journal of Jewish Art, 2 vols., Set, Vols. III-IV. (Illus.). 143p. (Orig.). (C). 1977. Set. pap. 22.95 (*0-935982-32-9*, JJA-03) Spertus Coll.

— Journal of Jewish Art, Vol. I. (Illus.). 96p. (Orig.). (C). 1974. pap. 22.95 (*0-935982-30-2*, JJA-01) Spertus Coll.

— Journal of Jewish Art, Vol. II. (Illus.). 96p. (Orig.). (C). 1975. pap. 22.95 (*0-935982-31-0*, JJA-02) Spertus Coll.

— Journal of Jewish Art, Vol. V. 115p. (Orig.). (C). 1978. pap. 22.95 (*0-935982-33-7*) Spertus Coll.

Narkiss, Uzi. The Liberation of Jerusalem. 2nd ed. 285p. 1992. text ed. 22.50 (*0-85303-209-2*, Pub. by Vallentine Mitchell UK) Intl Spec Bk.

Narla, V. R. Gods, Goblins & Men. 1979. 12.00 (*0-8364-0559-5*, Pub. by Minerva II) S Asia.

Narlikar, A., ed. Studies of High Temperature Superconductors, Vol. 11. (Illus.). 467p. 1993. lib. bdg. 98.00 (*1-56072-132-4*) Nova Sci Pubs.

— Studies of High Temperature Superconductors, Vol. 10: Advances in Research & Applications. 345p. (C). 1992. lib. bdg. 125.00 (*1-56072-087-5*) Nova Sci Pubs.

Narlikar, A. V., ed. Studies of High Temperature Superconductors, Vol. 1. (Illus.). 382p. 1989. text ed. 125.00 (*0-941743-54-3*) Nova Sci Pubs.

— Studies of High Temperature Superconductors, Vol. 5. (Illus.). 413p. (C). 1990. text ed. 125.00 (*0-941743-87-X*) Nova Sci Pubs.

— Studies of High Temperature Superconductors, Vol. 6. (Illus.). 413p. (C). 1990. text ed. 125.00 (*0-941743-88-8*) Nova Sci Pubs.

— Studies of High Temperature Superconductors, Vol. 7. 398p. (C). 1991. text ed. 125.00 (*1-56072-007-7*) Nova Sci Pubs.

— Studies of High Temperature Superconductors, Vol. 2: Advances in Research & Applications. (Illus.). 370p. 1989. text ed. 125.00 (*0-941743-55-1*) Nova Sci Pubs.

— Studies of High Temperature Superconductors, Vol. 3: Advances in Research & Applications. (Illus.). 413p. 1989. text ed. 125.00 (*0-941743-56-X*) Nova Sci Pubs.

— Studies of High Temperature Superconductors, Vol. 4: Advances in Research & Applications. (Illus.). 402p. 1989. text ed. 125.00 (*0-941743-57-8*) Nova Sci Pubs.

***Narlikar, Anant, ed.** Electron Microscopy & Channeling Studies of High Temperature Superconductors. (Studies of High Temperature Superconductors: Vol. 15). (Illus.). 302p. (C). 1995. lib. bdg. 95.00 (*1-56072-219-3*) Nova Sci Pubs.

— Studies of High Temperature Superconductors, Vol. 9. 331p. 1992. 125.00 (*1-56072-061-1*) Nova Sci Pubs.

— Studies of High Temperature Superconductors, Vol. 14: Field Penetration & Magnetization of High Temperature Superconductors. (Illus.). 445p. (C). 1994. lib. bdg. 97.00 (*1-56072-182-0*) Nova Sci Pubs.

— Studies of High Temperature Superconductors, Vol. 12: High Tc Squids & Related Studies. (Illus.). 212p. (C). 1994. lib. bdg. 95.00 (*1-56072-184-7*) Nova Sci Pubs.

— Studies of High Temperature Superconductors, Vol. 13: HTSC Thin Films. (Illus.). 212p. (C). 1994. lib. bdg. 95.00 (*1-56072-183-9*) Nova Sci Pubs.

Narlikar, Anant V., ed. Studies of High Temperature Superconductors, Vol. 8. 414p. (C). 1991. text ed. 125.00 (*1-56072-019-0*) Nova Sci Pubs.

***Narlikar, J. V.** From Black Cloud to Black Hole. 2nd ed. 180p. 1995. text ed. 53.00 (*981-02-2032-4*); pap. text ed. 28.00 (*981-02-2033-2*) World Scientific Pub.

— From Black Clouds to Black Holes. LC 85-3334. 160p. 1985. text ed. 52.00 (*9971-978-13-X*); pap. text ed. 23.00 (*9971-978-15-6*) World Scientific Pub.

Narlikar, Jayant V. Introduction to Cosmology. (Illus.). 484p. 1983. boxed 48.75 (*0-86720-015-4*) Jones & Bartlett.

— Introduction to Cosmology. 2nd ed. (Illus.). 416p. (C). 1993. 79.95 (*0-521-41250-1*); pap. 29.95 (*0-521-42352-X*) Cambridge U Pr.

— The Return of Vaman. (C). 1989. 10.00 (*0-685-35373-7*, Pub. by Classics India Pubns II) S Asia.

Narlock, Lori, ed. see Diamond, Wendy.

NARMIC-AFSC Staff, ed. see Lamperti, John.

Narmour, Eugene. The Analysis & Cognition of Basic Melodic Structures: The Implication-Realization Model. LC 90-35357. (Illus.). 480p. 1990. lib. bdg. 60.00 (*0-226-56845-8*) U Ch Pr.

— The Analysis & Cognition of Melodic Complexity: The Implication-Realization Model. LC 91-37919. (Illus.). 384p. 1992. 49.95 (*0-226-56842-3*) U Ch Pr.

Narmour, Eugene & Solie, Ruth, eds. Explorations in Music, the Arts, & Ideas: Essays in Honor of Leonard B. Meyer. LC 87-32858. (Festschrift Ser.: No. 7). (Illus.). 470p. 1989. lib. bdg. 48.00 (*0-918728-94-0*) Pendragon NY.

Narney, Dean. The Christmas Tree That Ate My Mother. (J). 1992. 2.95 (*0-590-44881-1*, Apple Paperbacks) Scholastic Inc.

Narode, Ronald, et al. Teaching Thinking Skills: Science. 48p. 1987. 7.95 (*0-8106-0202-4*) NEA.

Naroditsky, V., jt. ed. see Lam, Lui.

Narodny, Ivan. American Artists. LC 74-93365. (Essay Index Reprint Ser.). 1977. 20.95 (*0-8369-1311-6*) Ayer.

Narogin, Mudrooroo. Writing from the Fringe. 192p. (C). 1990. pap. 19.95 (*0-947062-55-6*, Pub. by Hyland Hse AT) Intl Spec Bk.

Naroll, Raoul. The Moral Order: An Introduction to the Human Situation. LC 82-19204. 498p. reprint ed. pap. 142.00 (*0-7837-1129-8*, 2041659) Bks Demand.

Naroll, Raoul, et al. Worldwide Theory Testing. LC 76-48559. (HRAF Manuals Ser.). 139p. 1976. pap. 15.00 (*0-87536-662-7*) HRAFP.

Naroth. The Awataguchi Shinto School of Sword Making. 1986. reprint ed. pap. 4.95 (*0-910704-55-4*) Hawley.

Narottamadasa. Srila Narottama Dasa Thakura's Sri Prarthana: Prayers. Kusakrathadasa, tr. (Krsna Library: Vol. 128). 152p. (Orig.). 1991. pap. text ed. 10.00 (*1-56130-039-X*) Krsna Inst.

— Srila Narottama Dasa Thakura's Sri Prema-Bhakti-Candrika: The Moonlight of Loving Devotion. Kusakrathadasa, tr. (Krsna Library: Vol. 129). 76p. (Orig.). 1991. pap. text ed. 8.00 (*1-56130-040-3*) Krsna Inst.

Narovlyanskii, G. Y. Aviation Climatology. 224p. 1970. text ed. 58.00 (*0-7065-0731-2*, Pub. by Keter Pub IS) Coronet Bks.

Narramore. Guia De Educacion Infantil: A Guide to Child Rearing. (SPA.). 4.95 (*84-7228-289-9*, 220435, Pub. by Edit Clie SP) TSELF.

— Por Que Se Portan Mal los Ninos? Why Children Misbehave? (SPA.). 4.95 (*84-7228-647-9*, 220708, Pub. by Edit Clie SP) TSELF.

Narramore, Bruce. Adolescence Is Not an Illness. LC 91-23784. 224p. 1991. pap. 8.99 (*0-8007-5416-6*) Revell.

— Ayudenme, Soy Padre: Help, I'm a Parent. (SPA.). 5.95 (*84-7228-128-0*, 220068, Pub. by Edit Clie SP) TSELF.

— Como Criar a los Hijos Con Amor Y: Parenting with Love & Care. (SPA.). 5.50 (*84-7228-558-8*, 220164, Pub. by Edit Clie SP) TSELF.

— Help! I'm a Parent. rev. ed. 192p. 1995. pap. 9.99 (*0-310-46211-8*) Zondervan.

— The Help! I'm a Parent Handbook. 96p. 1995. pap. 5.99 (*0-310-30323-0*) Zondervan.

— Usted es Algo Especial: You Are Someone Special. (SPA.). 5.50 (*84-7228-530-8*, 220926, Pub. by Edit Clie SP) TSELF.

— Vale Mas Prevenir Que Curar: Ounce of Prevention. (SPA.). 5.50 (*84-7228-314-3*, 220931, Pub. by Edit Clie SP) TSELF.

— Your Child's Hidden Needs: Build Healthy Relationships Through Preventative Parenting. LC 90-33098. (Illus.). 219p. 1990. pap. 8.99 (*0-8007-5337-2*) Revell.

Narramore, Bruce & Lewis, Vern. Parenting Teens. rev. ed. 355p. 1992. pap. 9.99 (*0-8423-5012-8*) Tyndale.

Narramore, Bruce S. You're Someone Special. 2nd ed. 176p. 1980. pap. 7.99 (*0-310-30331-1*, 11038P) Zondervan.

Narramore, Bruce S. & Carter, John. The Integration of Psychology & Theology: An Introduction. (Rosemead Ser.). (Orig.). 1979. 10.99 (*0-310-30341-9*, 11190P) Zondervan.

Narramore, Clyde. Como Tener Exito En Relaciones: How to Succeed in Family Living. (SPA.). 3.95 (*84-7228-163-9*, 220174, Pub. by Edit Clie SP) TSELF.

— Enciclopedia-Problemas Psicologicos (Encyclopedia-Phychological Problems) (SPA.). 1990. 7.99 (*1-56063-000-0*, 497701) Editorial Unilit.

— Psicologia De la Felicidad (This Way to Happiness) (SPA.). 1990. 3.79 (*0-945792-82-4*, 497702) Editorial Unilit.

Narramore, Clyde & Narramore, Ruth. Como Dominar la Tension Nerviosa. Ward, Rhode, tr. 216p. (SPA.). pap. 6.25 (*0-89922-129-7*) Edit Caribe.

Narramore, Clyde M. La Disciplina en el Hogar. Zorzoli, Ruben O., tr. 32p. 1986. reprint ed. 1.95 (*0-311-46051-8*) Casa Bautista.

— Psychology of Counseling. 1960. 16.99 (*0-310-29930-6*, 10409) Zondervan.

Narramore, Kevin. Personality on the Job. 240p. (Orig.). 1994. pap. 8.99 (*0-89283-819-1*, Vine Bks) Servant.

Narramore, Robert E., jt. auth. see Nolen, Ben M.

Narramore, Ruth, jt. auth. see Narramore, Clyde.

Narrett, David, jt. ed. see Francaviglia, Richard.

Narrett, David E. Inheritance & Family Life in Colonial New York City. LC 92-7680. 264p. 1992. 42.50 (*0-8014-2517-4*) Cornell U Pr.

Narrett, David E. & Goldberg, Joyce S., eds. Essays on Liberty & Federalism: The Shaping of the U. S. Constitution. LC 88-2105. (Walter Prescott Webb Memorial Lectures: No. 22). 152p. 1988. 17.50 (*0-89096-341-X*) Tex A&M Univ Pr.

Narrett, David E., ed. see Jones, William R., et al.

Narrett, Eugene. Henry Schwartz. (Illus.). 28p. 1990. 10.00 (*0-934358-26-5*) Fuller Mus Art.

Narrow, Barbara & Buschl, Kay. Fundamentals of Nursing Practice. 2nd ed. 1024p. 1987. teacher ed 14.00 (*0-8273-4320-5*); text ed. 46.50 (*0-8273-4319-1*); 14.00 (*0-8273-4322-1*) Delmar.

Narsavage, Robert J., Jr., jt. auth. see Kimbler, Frank S.

Nartov, P. S., ed. Disk Soil-Working Implements. Sivaramakrishnan, M. M., tr. 156p. (C). 1985. text ed. 95.00 (*90-6191-443-4*, Pub. by A A Balkema NE) Ashgate Pub Co.

NARUC Staff Subcommittee on Water. Model Record-Keeping Manual for Small Water Companies. 95p. 1978. 5.00 (*0-317-01666-0*) NARUC.

Naruda, Pablo. Heaven Stones (Las Piedras del Cielo) Barkan, Stanley H., ed. Jacketti, Maria, tr. (Review International Writers Ser.: No. 2). 80p. (ENG & SPA.). 1992. 30.00 (*0-89304-746-5*); pap. 15.00 (*0-89304-747-3*) Cross-Cultrl NY.

***Narula.** Ceramic Precursor Technology & Its Applications. 308p. 1995. write for info. (*0-8247-9310-2*) Dekker.

Narula, D. D. & Sharma, R. R. Asian Dimension of Soviet Policy. 1986. 25.00 (*0-317-56324-6*, Patriot) S Asia.

Narula, Karen S. Voyage of the Emerald Buddha. (Images of Asia Ser.). (Illus.). 120p. 1994. 16.95 (*967-65-3057-3*) OUP.

Narula, Uma & Pearce, W. Barnett. Development As Communication: A Perspective on India. LC 85-2088. 240p. 1986. text ed. 19.95 (*0-8093-1223-9*) S Ill U Pr.

Narula, Uma & Pearce, W. Barnett, eds. Cultures, Politics & Research Programs: An International Assessment of Practical Problems in Field Research. 264p. (C). 1990. text ed. 59.95 (*0-8058-0134-0*) L Erlbaum Assocs.

Narula, Uma, jt. auth. see Hanson, Jarice.

Narum, William G. Design Your Own Model A Ford. 1990. pap. 5.95 (*0-486-26516-1*) Dover.

Narvaez, C., et al. A Model for Preacquisition Audits of Financial Institutions. Holman, Richard, ed. (IIA Monograph). 80p. 1984. pap. text ed. 15.00 (*0-89413-113-3*) Inst Inter Aud.

Narvaez, Darcia F., jt. ed. see Rest, James R.

Narvaez, Leon O., ed. see Narvaez, Ricardo A.

Narvaez, Peter, ed. The Good People: New Fairylore Essays. LC 91-8853. 534p. 1991. 70.00 (*0-8240-7100-X*, H1376) Garland.

Narvaez, Ricardo A. Morfologia Flexional del Espanol. Narvaez, Leon O., ed. LC 85-1208. (Illus.). 184p. (Orig.). (C). 1985. pap. text ed. 11.95 (*0-930795-00-8*) Editorial AI.

Narveson, Jan. The Libertarian Idea. LC 88-15986. (Ethics & Action Ser.). 382p. (C). 1989. 34.95 (*0-87722-569-9*) Temple U Pr.

— Libertarian Idea. LC 88-15986. (Ethics & Action Ser.). 382p. (C). 1992. pap. 19.95 (*1-56639-008-7*) Temple U Pr.

— Moral Matters. 256p. 1993. pap. 16.95 (*1-55111-011-3*) Broadview Pr.

— Morality & Utility. LC 66-29908. 313p. reprint ed. pap. 89.30 (*0-317-08990-0*, 2003889) Bks Demand.

Narveson, Jan, ed. Moral Issues. 1983. pap. 18.95 (*0-19-540426-2*) OUP.

Narveson, Jan, jt. auth. see Friedman, Marilyn.

Narwekar, Sanjit, comp. Directory of Indian Film-Makers & Films. LC 93-44642. 576p. 1994. text ed. 85.00 (*0-313-29284-1*, Greenwood Pr) Greenwood.

Nary, Rhoda, jt. auth. see McMakin, Jacqueline.

Naryanana Reddy, G. Rural Elite & Community Work. 1986. 31.00 (*81-85076-03-0*, Pub. by Chugh Pubns II) S Asia.

Nas. Bible-Ryrie Study Bible, New American Standard. 1986. 35.99 (*0-8024-7425-X*) Moody.

Nas, Peter J., ed. Urban Symbolism. LC 93-16885. (Studies in Human Society: No. 8). (Illus.). 393p. 1993. pap. 71.50 (*90-04-09855-0*) E J Brill.

Nas, Tevfik F. & Odekon, Mehmet, eds. Economics & Politics of Turkish Liberalization. LC 91-60583. (Illus.). 200p. 1992. 38.50 (*0-934223-19-X*) Lehigh Univ Pr.

— Liberalization & the Turkish Economy. LC 88-9755. (Contributions in Economics & Economic History Ser.: No. 86). 231p. 1988. text ed. 55.00 (*0-313-26031-1*, NLZ/, Greenwood Pr) Greenwood.

NASA, Jet Propulsion Lab Staff. Space Images. LC 81-84668. (Illus.). 100p. 1982. 27.95 (*0-912810-37-8*); pap. 15.95 (*0-912810-36-X*) Lustrum Pr.

NASA Johnson Space Center Staff & Gose, W. Journal of the Geochemical Society & Meteorcritical Society: Supplement 5, 3 vols., Set. LC 74-23095. 1974. 1,328.00 (*0-08-018318-2*, Pub. by Pergamon Repr UK) Franklin.

NASA Public Affairs Staff. The Kennedy Space Center Story. rev. ed. (Illus.). 208p. (Orig.). 1991. pap. text ed. 8.95 (*0-9610648-5-4*) Graphic Hse.

— NASA Kennedy Space Center's Spaceport U. S. A. Tour Book. Delavega, tr. (Illus.). 48p. (Orig.). (FRE, GER, ITA & SPA.). 1991. reprint ed. pap. 4.45 (*0-9610648-6-2*) Graphic Hse.

NASA Space Center Staff, jt. auth. see LBJ Space Center Staff.

NASA Staff & MSFC Staff. Standards for Epoxies Used in Microelectronics. 115p. 1990. reprint ed. pap. 58.00 (*0-938648-17-9*) T-C Pubns CA.

NASA, Technology Utilization Div., Office of Commercial Programs Staff & Haggerty, James J. Spinoff, 1990. (Illus.). 156p. 1990. per. 11.00 (*0-16-026321-2*) USGPO.

Nasa'i, Ahmad S. Kitab al 'Ilm: (The Book of Knowledge) Hamadah, Faruq, ed. LC 92-31589. (Silsilat Taysir al Turath al Islami Ser.: No. 4). 222p. (Orig.). (ARA.). 1993. pap. 7.75 (*1-56564-005-5*) IIIT VA.

***Nasar.** Electric Energy Systems. 1995. 62.00 (*0-02-386111-8*) P-H.

— Vector Control of AC Drives. 1992. 99.95 (*0-8493-4408-5*, TK2791) CRC Pr.

Nasar & Boldea, I. Electric Machines: Steady State Operation. 250p. 1990. 63.00 (*0-89116-991-1*) Hemisp Pub.

— Electric Machines, Vol. 2: Dynamics & Control. 250p. 1991. write for info. (*0-89116-992-X*) CRC Pr.

Nasar, Jack L., ed. Environmental Aesthetics: Theory, Research, & Application. (Illus.). 560p. (C). 1992. pap. 29.95 (*0-521-42916-1*) Cambridge U Pr.

***Nasar, S. A.** Electric Machines & Power Systems. LC 94-32717. (Electrical & Computer Engineering, Power & Energy Ser.: Vol. 1). 1994. pap. text ed. write for info. (*0-07-045958-4*) McGraw.

Nasar, S. A. & Boldea, I. Linear Motion Electromagnetic Systems. LC 84-25772. 504p. 1985. text ed. 52.50 (*0-471-87451-5*) Krieger.

NASAR Staff. High Angle Rescue Techniques. 2nd ed. 272p. 1992. per. 23.95 (*0-8403-7363-5*) Kendall-Hunt.

Nasar, Syed A. Electric Energy Conversion & Transmission. 431p. (C). 1985. text ed. write for info. (*0-02-385960-1*) Macmillan.

— Handbook of Electric Machines. 608p. 1987. text ed. 72.50 (*0-07-045888-X*) McGraw.

— Permanent Magnet, Reluctance & Self-Synchronous Motors. 1993. 89.95 (*0-8493-9313-2*, TK2787) CRC Pr.

— Schaum's Outline of Electric Machines & Electromechanics. (Schaum's Outline Ser.). (Illus.). 208p. (C). 1981. pap. text ed. 11.95 (*0-07-045886-3*) McGraw.

— Two Thousand Solved Problems in Electromagnetics. (Schaum's Solved Problems Ser.). 1992. pap. text ed. 18.95 (*0-07-045902-9*) McGraw.

Nasar, Syed A. & Boldea, I. Linear Electric Motors: Theory, Design & Practical Applications. 304p. 1987. text ed. 39.95 (*0-13-536863-4*) P-H.

Nasar, Syed A. & Boldea, Ion. Electric Machines: Dynamics & Control. 1992. 99.95 (*0-8493-9312-4*, TK2781) CRC Pr.

Nasar, Syed A. & Paul, Clayton R. Essential Engineering Equations. 175p. 1991. 19.95 (*0-8493-4263-5*, TA330) CRC Pr.

Nasar, Syed A., jt. auth. see Cathey, J. J.

Nasar, Syed A., jt. auth. see Paul, Clayton R.

Nasatir, A. P., ed. Before Lewis & Clark: Documents Illustrating the History of the Missouri, 1785-1804, Vol. II. LC 89-25080. (Illus.). xvii, 478p. 1990. reprint ed. 42.50 (*0-8032-3321-3*); reprint ed. pap. 12.95 (*0-8032-8362-8*) U of Nebr Pr.

— Before Lewis & Clark: Documents Illustrating the History of the Missouri, 1785-1804, Vol. II, Vol. I. LC 89-25080. (Illus.). xxii, 375p. 1990. reprint ed. 42.50 (*0-8032-3320-5*); reprint ed. pap. 11.95 (*0-8032-8361-X*) U of Nebr Pr.

Nasatir, Abraham P. Borderland in Retreat: From Spanish Louisiana to the Far Southwest. LC 75-21183. 187p. reprint ed. pap. 53.30 (*0-8357-7351-5*, 2031005) Bks Demand.

Nasatir, Abraham P. & Monell, Gary E. British Activities in California & the Pacific Coast of North America to 1860: An Archival Calendar Guide. 1224p. 1990. 175.00 (*0-916304-85-X*) SDSU Press.

Nasatir, Abraham P., jt. auth. see Din, Gilbert C.

Nasatir, Abraham P., ed. see Douglas, Walter B.

***Nasaw.** Shakedown Street. 1995. mass mkt. 3.99 (*0-440-21930-2*) Dell.

Nasaw, David. Children of the City: At Work & at Play. (Illus.). 256p. 1986. pap. 10.95 (*0-19-504015-5*) OUP.

— Going Out: The Rise & Fall of Public Amusements. LC 92-54515. (Illus.). 320p. 1993. 25.00 (*0-465-07030-2*) Basic.

— Going Out: The Rise & Fall of Public Amusements. (Illus.). 320p. 1994. pap. 14.00 (*0-465-02654-0*) Basic.

— Schooled to Order: A Social History of Public Schooling in the United States. 1981. pap. 11.95 (*0-19-502892-9*) OUP.

Nasby, David P., jt. auth. see Denton, Bob C.

Nasca, Don. Evaluating Gifted Programs: Formative Evaluation. (Illus.). 40p. 1983. pap. 8.00 (*0-88047-017-8*, 8221) DOK Pubs.

Nasca, Robert A. Testing Fluid Power Components. (Illus.). 352p. 1990. 49.95 (*0-8311-3002-4*) Indus Pr.

Nascentes, A. Dicionario de Sinonimos: Dictionary of Synonyms. 3rd ed. 485p. (POR.). 1981. 22.50 (*0-8288-1995-5*, M14429) Fr & Eur.

Nascher, Ignatz L. Geriatrics: The Diseases of Old Age & Their Treatment. Kastenbaum, Robert, ed. LC 78-22212. (Aging & Old Age Ser.). (Illus.). 1979. reprint ed. lib. bdg. 40.95 (*0-405-11825-2*) Ayer.

Naschold, Frieder & De Vroom, Bert, eds. Regulating Employment & Welfare: Company & National Policies of Labour Force Participation at the End of Worklife in Industrial Countries. LC 93-35001. (Studies in Organization: No. 53). x, 496p. (C). 1993. lib. bdg. 98.95 (*3-11-013513-2*) De Gruyter.

***Nascimbene, Yan.** A Day in September. LC 94-45649. (Illus.). (J). 1995. write for info. (*1-56846-112-7*) Creative Ed.

Nascimento, Abdias do. Brazil: Mixture or Massacre? Essays in the Genocide of a Black People. rev. ed. Nascimento, Elisa L., tr. xviii, 214p. (Orig.). 1989. reprint ed. pap. text ed. 12.95 (*0-912469-26-9*) Majority Pr.

Nascimento, C. A., ed. see Burnham, Forbes.

Nascimento, Elisa L., tr. see Nascimento, Abdias do.

Nascimento, M. A. C. Molecular Modeling - the Chemistry of the 21st Century. 172p. 1994. text ed. 81.00 (*981-02-1620-3*) World Scientific Pub.

NASDTEC Staff. NASDTEC Manual on Certification & Preparation of Educational Personnel in the U. S. 464p. 1994. pap. text ed., spiral bd. 74.95 (*0-8403-9235-4*) Kendall-Hunt.

— NASDTEC Outcome Based Standards & Portfolio Assessments. 64p. 1992. pap. 12.95 (*0-8403-8208-1*) Kendall-Hunt.

Nase, Eckart. Oskar Pfisters Analytische Seelsorge: Theorie & Praxis des Ersten Pastoralpsychologen, Dargestellt an Zwei Fallstudien. (Arbeiten zur Praktischen Theologie Ser.: Bd. 3). (Illus.). xviii, 622p. (GER.). (C). 1993. lib. bdg. 167.70 (*3-11-013235-4*) De Gruyter.

NASE Staff. Train America! Achieving Peak Performance & Fitness. 256p. 1988. per. 21.00 (*0-8403-4688-3*) Kendall-Hunt.

Naseef, A., ed. Today's Problems, Tomorrow's Solutions: The Future Structure of Muslim Societies. 190p. 1988. text ed. 80.00 (*0-7201-1991-X*, Mansell Pub) Cassell.

Nasenauer, Jim & Langton, Mark. Mountain Biking the Coast Range, Guide 7: Santa Monica Mountains. 1993. 9.95 (*0-938665-10-3*) Fine Edge Prods.

Naser, Joseph, ed. Expert Systems Applications for the Electric Power Industry, 2 vols., Set. 1450p. 1990. 226.00 (*1-56032-102-4*) Hemisp Pub.

Naser, Kamal H. M. Creative Financial Accounting: Its Nature & Use. LC 93-4009. 1993. pap. text ed. 45.00 (*0-13-061763-6*) P-H.

Nasgowitz, David, jt. auth. see Oriental Institute Staff.

Nash. Clinical Examination of the Dog & Cat. 1994. 35.00 (*0-8151-6317-7*, Yr Bk Med Pubs) Mosby Yr Bk.

— Health At School. (Illus.). 303p. 1985. pap. text ed. 45.00 (*0-433-23051-7*) Buttrwrth-Heinemann.

— Pocket Book of Ogden Nash. 1990. mass mkt. 5.50 (*0-671-72789-3*) PB.

***Nash & Graves.** From These Beginnings, Vol. 2. (C). 1994. text ed. 19.50 (*0-673-99206-3*) HarpCollege.

Nash & Said. Pathology of HIV Infection & AIDS. (Illus.). 224p. 1991. text ed. 69.95 (*0-7216-1540-6*) Saunders.

Nash, jt. auth. see Berry.

Nash, Al. Ruskin College: A Challenge to Adult & Labor Education. LC 81-1231. 144p. 1981. pap. 7.95 (*0-87546-084-4*) ILR Pr.

Nash, Alan E., ed. Human Rights & the Protection of Refugees under International Law. 338p. 1989. pap. text ed. 29.95 (*0-88645-080-2*, Pub. by Inst Res Pub CN) Ashgate Pub Co.

Nash, Alanna. Behind Closed Doors: Talking with the Legends of Country Music. LC 87-46321. (Illus.). 576p. 1988. pap. 14.95 (*0-679-72102-9*) Knopf.

***Nash, Alanna, et al.** Elvis Aaron Presley. 416p. 1995. 25.00 (*0-06-017619-9*) HarpC.

Nash, Alec. Structural Design for Architects. (Illus.). 240p. 1991. 57.50 (*0-87683-619-8*) GP Pub.

Nash, Alice. Collector's Handbook. (Illus.). 40p. (Orig.). 1982. pap. 5.00 (*0-911431-00-4*) Harmon-Meek Gal.

Nash, Allan. Managerial Compensation. (Studies in Productivity: Highlights of the Literature Ser.: Vol. 15). 56p. 1980. pap. 55.00 (*0-89361-022-4*) Work in Amer.

— Managerial Compensation, Vol. 15. LC 80-21044. (Work in America Institute Studies in Productivity). 1982. pap. 35.00 (*0-685-05448-9*, Pergamon Pr) Elsevier.

Nash, Amy. North Korea. (Let's Visit Places & Peoples of the World Ser.). (Illus.). 128p. (J). (gr. 5 up). 1990. 14.95 (*0-7910-0157-1*) Chelsea Hse.

Nash, Andrea. Talking Shop. 1992. pap. write for info. (*0-13-884503-4*) P-H.

Nash, Andrea, et al. Talking Shop: A Curriculum Sourcebook for Participatory Adult ESL. Keenan, Fran, ed. (Language in Education Ser.). (Illus.). 70p. (Orig.). 1992. pap. text ed. 10.50 (*0-937354-78-3*) Delta Systems.

Nash, Ann E., tr. see Bouyer, Louis.

Nash, Anne. Prize of Fear. (Orig.). 1980. pap. 1.75 (*0-8439-8006-0*) Dorchester Pub Co.

— Prize of Fear. large type ed. (General Ser.). 336p. (Orig.). 1993. 21.95 (*0-7089-2848-X*) Ulverscroft.

***Nash, Anne E., tr.** The Complete Works of Elizabeth of the Trinity, Vol. 2. LC 84-3748. 400p. (Orig.). 1995. pap. 12.95 (*0-935216-54-5*) ICS Pubns.

Nash, Arnold S., ed. Protestant Thought in the Twentieth Century: Whence & Whither? LC 78-5860. 296p. 1978. reprint ed. text ed. 59.75 (*0-313-20484-5*, NAPT, Greenwood Pr) Greenwood.

***Nash, Artemis D.** Soft Tissue Sarcomas: Histological Diagnosis. LC 88-26490. (Biopsy Interpretation Ser.). 285p. 1989. reprint ed. pap. 81.30 (*0-7837-8354-X*, 2049144) Bks Demand.

***Nash, Aubrey.** Hollywood Gorillas. 1995. 14.95 (*0-8062-5202-2*) Carlton.

Nash, Bartleby. Mother Nature's Greatest Hits. 176p. (Orig.). 1993. pap. 4.50 (*0-425-13652-3*) Berkley Pub.

— Mother Nature's Greatest Hits: The Top 40 Wonders of the Animal World. (Illus.). 144p. (Orig.). (J). 1991. pap. 5.95 (*0-9626072-7-4*) Living Planet Pr.

Nash, Bradley D., et al. Organizing & Staffing the Presidency, Vol. III. (Proceedings Ser.). (Orig.). 1980. 11.00 (*0-938204-01-7*) Ctr Study Presidency.

Nash, Bruce. Fishing Hall of Fame. 1991. mass mkt. 9.99 (*0-440-50318-3*) Dell.

— Little Big Leaguers: Amazing Boyhood Stories of Today's Baseball Stars. (J). (gr. 4-7). 1990. pap. 7.95 (*0-671-69360-3*, Litl Simon S&S) S&S Childrens.

— Runner's Weight Control Book. 1982. pap. 9.95 (*0-02-499640-8*) Macmillan.

— Runner's Weight Control Book. 1984. 9.95 (*0-02-499650-5*) Macmillan.

Nash, Bruce & Zullo, Allan. Amazing but True Cat Tales. (Illus.). 104p. (Orig.). 1993. pap. 6.95 (*0-8362-8034-2*) Andrews & McMeel.

— Amazing but True Elvis Facts. LC 94-45515. (Illus.). 96p. 1995. pap. 6.95 (*0-8362-7028-2*) Andrews & McMeel.

— Amazing but True Fishing Stories. LC 92-34622. 104p. 1993. pap. 6.95 (*0-8362-8022-9*) Andrews & McMeel.

— Amazing but True Golf Facts. 104p. 1992. pap. 6.95 (*0-8362-7994-8*) Andrews & McMeel.

— The Baseball Hall of Shame, Vol. 4. 192p. 1991. pap. 8.95 (*0-671-74609-X*) PB.

— The Baseball Hall of Shame: Young Fans' Edition. Clancy, Lisa, ed. 144p. 1990. pap. 2.99 (*0-671-69354-9*, Archway) PB.

— Baseball Hall of Shame Two: Young Fans' Edition. Clancy, Lisa, ed. 144p. (Orig.). (J). 1991. pap. 2.99 (*0-671-73533-0*, Archway) PB.

— Baseball Hall of Shame 3: Young Fans' Edition. Clancy, Lisa, ed. 144p. (Orig.). (J). 1992. pap. 2.99 (*0-671-75355-X*) PB.

— The Baseball Hall of Shame's Funtastic Trivia & Sticker Book. (Illus.). 24p. (J). (gr. 1 up). 1992. pap. 3.95 (*0-671-74439-9*, Litl Simon S&S) S&S Childrens.

— Baseball Hall of Shame's Warped Record Book. (Hall of Shame Ser.). 288p. (Orig.). 1991. pap. 8.95 (*0-02-029485-9*, Collier S&S) S&S Trade.

— Basketball Hall of Shame. Grad, Doug, ed. 192p. (Orig.). 1991. pap. 9.00 (*0-671-69414-6*) PB.

— The Basketball Hall of Shame: Young Fans' Edition. Clancy, Lisa, ed. 160p. (Orig.). (YA). 1993. pap. 2.99 (*0-671-75356-8*, Archway) PB.

— The Football Hall of Shame. (Orig.). 1991. pap. 8.95 (*0-671-74551-4*) PB.

— The Football Hall of Shame, Vol. 2. Vezeris, Olga, ed. 192p. (Orig.). 1990. pap. 7.95 (*0-671-69413-8*) PB.

— The Football Hall of Shame: Young Fans' Edition. (Illus.). 144p. (J). (gr. 5 up). 1990. pap. 2.95 (*0-671-72922-5*, Archway) PB.

— The Football Hall of Shame Two: Young Fans' Edition. Clancy, Lisa, ed. 160p. (Orig.). (J). (gr. 3-6). 1991. pap. 2.99 (*0-671-73534-9*, Archway) PB.

— Freebies for Sports Fans. (Illus.). 96p. (J). (gr. 1 up). 1990. pap. 4.95 (*0-671-70339-0*, S&S Bks Young Read) S&S Childrens.

— The Golf Hall of Shame. 224p. 1991. pap. 10.00 (*0-671-74583-2*) PB.

— The Golf Nut's Book of Amazing Feats & Records. 192p. 1994. pap. 8.95 (*0-8092-3790-3*) Contemp Bks.

— Golf's Most Outrageous Quotes: An Official BGA Book. (Illus.). 96p. 1995. pap. 6.95 (*0-8362-1789-6*) Andrews & McMeel.

— The Greatest Sports Stories Never Told. LC 92-15352. (J). 1993. pap. 13.00 (*0-671-79527-9*); pap. 8.95 (*0-671-75938-8*) S&S Trade.

— Gutter Humor: Amazing but True Bowling Stories. LC 94-1676. 1994. pap. 6.95 (*0-8362-1745-4*) Andrews & McMeel.

— The Hole Truth: Inside the Ropes of the PGA Tour. (Illus.). 1995. pap. 8.95 (*0-8362-7029-0*) Andrews & McMeel.

— The Hollywood Walk of Shame: The Wackiest, Funniest, & Most Outrageous Moments in Show Business History. (Illus.). 104p. (Orig.). 1993. pap. 6.95 (*0-8362-8035-0*) Andrews & McMeel.

— The Insider's Guide to Baseball Autographs. LC 93-49371. 1994. 7.95 (*0-8362-8050-4*) Andrews & McMeel.

— Little Basketball Big Leaguers: Amazing Boyhood Stories of Today's Basketball Stars. (Illus.). 96p. (J). (gr. 1 up). 1991. pap. 7.95 (*0-671-73445-8*, Litl Simon S&S) S&S Childrens.

— More Little Big Leaguers: Amazing Boyhood Stories of Today's Baseball Stars. (Illus.). 96p. (J). (gr. 1 up). 1991. pap. 7.95 (*0-671-73394-X*, Litl Simon S&S) S&S Childrens.

— Soap Dish. 112p. 1995. pap. 6.95 (*0-8362-7030-4*) Andrews & McMeel.

— Spooky Kids: Strange but True Tales. LC 93-44029. (Illus.). 128p. (J). (gr. 1-6). 1994. pap. 2.95 (*0-8167-3447-X*) Troll Assocs.

— The Sports Hall of Shame. 1987. write for info. (*0-318-62709-4*) PB.

— The Sports Hall of Shame: Young Fans Edition. MacDonald, Patricia, ed. 176p. (J). 1990. reprint ed. pap. 2.95 (*0-671-69355-7*, Archway) PB.

— The Sports Hall of Shame's Funtastic Trivia & Sticker Book. (Illus.). 24p. (J). (gr. 1 up). 1992. pap. 3.95 (*0-671-74438-0*, Litl Simon S&S) S&S Childrens.

— Tele-Visions: Words to the Wise from TV's Greatest Characters. 112p. 1995. pap. 6.95 (*0-8362-0561-8*) Andrews & McMeel.

— Totally Haunted Kids: True Ghost Stories. LC 94-18862. 128p. (J). (gr. 3-5). 1994. pap. 2.95 (*0-8167-3538-7*) Troll Assocs.

— Wacky Top Forty: The Most Annoying, Outrageous, & Unforgettable Hit Songs in Pop History. (Illus.). 204p. (Orig.). 1993. pap. 7.95 (*1-55850-302-1*) Adams Pubng.

Nash, Bruce & Zullo, Allen. Freebies for Cat Lovers. (Illus.). 128p. 1986. pap. 5.95 (*0-668-06267-3*) P-H.

***Nash, Bruce, et al.** Amazing but True Dog Tales. LC 94-25535. (J). 1994. pap. 6.95 (*0-8362-8066-0*) Andrews & McMeel.

— Haunted Kids: True Ghost Stories. LC 93-14489. (Illus.). (J). (gr. 4-9). 1993. pap. 2.95 (*0-8167-3266-3*) Troll Assocs.

— Life's Simple Pleasures. 12p. 1993. 8.95 (*1-56530-029-7*) Summit TX.

Nash, C. Relativistic Quantum Fields. 1979. text ed. 134.00 (*0-12-514350-8*) Acad Pr.

Nash, C. A., jt. auth. see Fowkes, A. S.

Nash, C. E., ed. Production of Aquatic Animals: Crustaceans, Molluscs, Amphibians & Reptiles. (World Animal Science Ser.: No. C4). 256p. 1991. 154.50 (*0-444-88312-6*) Elsevier.

***Nash, C. E. & Novotny, A. J., eds.** Production of Aquatic Animals: Fishes. 424p. 1995. 235.25 (*0-444-81950-9*) Elsevier.

Nash, C. Robert, jt. auth. see Nash, T. M.

Nash, Charles. Differential Topology & Quantum Field Theory. (Illus.). 386p. 1992. reprint ed. pap. text ed. 54.00 (*0-12-514076-2*) Acad Pr.

Nash, Charles & Sen, Siddartha. Topology & Geometry for Physicists. 1983. text ed. 97.00 (*0-12-514080-0*) Acad Pr.

Nash, Charles & Sen, Siddharta. Topology & Geometry for Physicists. 311p. 1988. reprint ed. pap. text ed. 49.00 (*0-12-514081-9*) Acad Pr.

Nash, Charles E. Biographical Sketches of Gen. Pat Cleburne & T.C. Hindman. (Illus.). 1977. 17.50 (*0-89029-039-3*) Morningside Bkshop.

Nash, Christopher. World Games: The Tradition of Anti-realist Revolt. 440p. 1988. text ed. 42.50 (*0-416-34710-X*) Routledge Chapman & Hall.

— World's Postmodern Fiction: A Guide. LC 92-39356. (C). 1993. pap. text ed. 32.50 (*0-582-20910-2*, 79761) Longman.

Nash, Christopher, ed. Narrative in Culture. 208p. 1990. 57.50 (*0-415-04156-2*, A3715) Routledge.

Nash, Christopher, jt. ed. see Nash, Cristopher.

Nash, Christopher A. Economics of Public Transport. LC 81-215543. (Modern Economics Ser.). (Illus.). 206p. reprint ed. pap. 58.80 (*0-8357-6588-1*, 2035983) Bks Demand.

Nash, Claude H., jt. ed. see Underkofler, Leland A.

Nash, Colin E., jt. auth. see Insull, David.

Nash, Constance & Oakey, Virginia. Screenwriter's Handbook: What to Write, How to Write It, Where to Sell It. LC 77-76031. 160p. 1978. pap. 10.00 (*0-06-463454-X*, EH 454) HarpC.

Nash, Corey. Jesse Willcox Smith's Mother Goose. (Illus.). 192p. 1991. 9.99 (*0-517-60357-8*, Derrydale Bks) Random Hse Value.

— Little Treasury of Beatrix Potter, 6 vols. in 1. (J). 1988. boxed 5.99 (*0-517-46667-8*) Random Hse Value.

— Little Treasury of Mother Goose, 6 vols. in 1, No. 6. (J). 1988. boxed 5.99 (*0-517-38571-6*) Random Hse Value.

— Little Treasury of Nursery Rhymes, 6 vols. in 1. (J). 1988. pap. 5.99 (*0-517-49203-2*) Random Hse Value.

— Little Treasury of Walt Disney: Mickey & Friends. (J). 1988. 5.99 (*0-517-61639-4*) Random Hse Value.

Nash, Cristopher & Nash, Christopher, eds. Narrative in Culture: Storytelling in the Sciences, Philosophy & Literature. LC 94-18539. (Warwick Studies in Philosophy & Literature). 1994. pap. 15.95 (*0-415-10344-4*, B4640) Routledge.

Nash, Daphne. Coinage in the Celtic World. (Illus.). 153p. 1987. 39.95 (*0-900652-85-3*, Pub. by Seaby UK) Trafalgar.

Nash, Daphne, tr. see Brunaux, Jean-Louis.

Nash, David. Secularism, Art & Freedom. 224p. 1992. text ed. 54.00 (*0-7185-1417-3*, Pub. by Pinter Pubs UK) St Martin.

Nash, David, jt. auth. see Goldfield, Norbert.

Nash, David, jt. auth. see Pchiluk, William.

Nash, David, ed. see Pochiluk, William R.

Nash, David, jt. auth. see Pochiluk, William R.

Nash, David, jt. auth. see Pochiluk, William.

Nash, David, et al, eds. Leicester in the Twentieth Century. LC 93-5298. 1993. 16.00 (*0-7509-0487-9*) A Sutton Pub.

Nash, David B., ed. Future Practice Alternatives in Medicine. 2nd ed. LC 93-14635. 1993. pap. 24.50 (*0-89640-236-3*) Igaku-Shoin.

— The Physician's Guide to Managed Care. 272p. 1993. 65.00 (*0-8342-0393-6*, 20393) Aspen Pub.

Nash, David B., jt. ed. see Goldfield, Norbert.

Nash, Dennison. A Little Anthropology. 2nd ed. LC 92-10343. 204p. 1993. pap. text ed. 24.40 (*0-13-532896-9*) P-H.

Nash, Dephne, jt. auth. see Allen, Derek.

Nash, Diane & Treffinger, Don. The Mentor. 76p. 1993. pap. 29.95 (*1-882664-06-X*) Prufrock Pr.

Nash, Dominie. Warp Painting: A Manual for Weavers. (Illus.). 32p. (Orig.). 1990. pap. 7.95 (*0-9623468-2-9*) Stellar Pub Hse.

***Nash, Douglas.** The Politics of Space: Architecture, Painting, & Theater in Postmodern Germany. LC 94-36388. (American University Studies, Series I, Germanic Languages & Literature: Vol. 107). 1995. write for info. (*0-8204-2599-0*) P Lang Pubs.

***Nash, E.** Corporate Directory of U. S. Public Companies, 1994. 1994. cd-rom 595.00 (*1-879346-16-8*) Walkers Western.

Nash, E. B. Leaders in Homoeopathic Therapeutics. 1981. 5.95 (*0-685-76565-2*) Formur Intl.

Nash, Edward. Allahu Akbar. (Illus.). 500p. (Orig.). 1988. 29.95 (*0-918266-21-1*); pap. 15.00 (*0-918266-20-3*) Smyrna.

Nash, Edward L. Database Marketing: The Ultimate Marketing Tool. 1993. text ed. 39.95 (*0-07-046063-9*) McGraw.

— Direct Marketing: Strategy, Planning, Execution. 3rd ed. 1994. text ed. 44.95 (*0-07-046032-9*) McGraw.

— The Direct Marketing Handbook. 2nd ed. 832p. 1992. text ed. 69.50 (*0-07-046027-2*) McGraw.

Nash, Elizabeth. The Luminous Ones: A History of the Great Actresses. LC 91-19225. (American University Studies: Theatre Arts: Ser. XXVI, Vol. 10). 224p. 1992. 43.95 (*0-8204-1577-4*) P Lang Pubs.

— Pieces of Rainbow. LC 93-33450. (American University Studies, XX, Fine Arts: Vol. 22). 136p. (C). 1994. text ed. 34.95 (*0-8204-2413-7*) P Lang Pubs.

— Plaisirs d'Amour: An Erotic Guide to the Senses. LC 94-23173. 1995. pap. 20.00 (*0-06-251149-1*) Harper SF.

Nash, Elizabeth T. One Hundred & One Legends of Flowers. 1977. lib. bdg. 59.95 (*0-8490-2375-0*) Gordon Pr.

Nash, Eugene A. History of the Forty-Fourth New York Volunteer Infantry. (Illus.). 484p. 1988. 40.00 (*0-89029-095-4*) Morningside Bkshop.

Nash, Franklin R. Estimating Device Reliability: Assessment of Credibility. LC 92-34878. (International Series in Engineering & Computer Science, VLSI, Computer Architecture, & Digital Screen Processing: Vol. 206). 1992. lib. bdg. 70.50 (*0-7923-9304-X*) Kluwer Ac.

Nash, Fred. Meta-Imperialism: A Study in Political Science. (Avebury Series in Philosophy). 534p. 1994. 88.95 (*1-85628-694-0*, Pub. by Avebury Pub UK) Ashgate Pub Co.

Nash, Gary. Quakers & Politics: Pennsylvania, 1681-1726. rev. ed. 384p. 1993. pap. text ed. 14.95 (*1-55553-166-0*) NE U Pr.

Nash, Gary B. American People Brief Edition, 2 vols., I. (C). 1991. 12.50 (*0-06-500433-7*) HarpCollege.

— American People Brief Edition, 2 vols., I. (C). 1991. text ed. 22.00 (*0-06-500262-8*) HarpCollege.

— American People Brief Edition, 2 vols., II. (C). 1991. 12.50 (*0-06-500434-5*) HarpCollege.

— American People Brief Edition, 2 vols., II. (C). 1991. text ed. 22.00 (*0-06-500263-6*) HarpCollege.

— American People Brief Edition, 2 vols., Vols. I-II. (C). 1991. Set. text ed. 31.50 (*0-06-044748-6*) HarpCollege.

— Forging Freedom: The Formation of Philadelphia's Black Community, 1720-1840. 368p. 1991. pap. 16.95 (*0-674-30933-2*, NASFOX) HUP.

— From These Beginnings, Vol. I. 4th ed. (C). 1990. pap. text ed. 19.00 (*0-06-044746-X*) HarpCollege.

— From These Beginnings, Vol. 2. 4th ed. (C). 1990. pap. text ed. 19.75 (*0-06-044747-8*) HarpCollege.

— Race & Revolution. 224p. 1990. 29.95 (*0-945612-11-7*); pap. 15.95 (*0-945612-21-4*) Madison Hse.

— Race, Class, & Politics: Essays on American Colonial & Revolutionary Society. 400p. 1986. pap. 15.95 (*0-252-01313-1*) U of Ill Pr.

— Red, White & Black: The Peoples of Early North America. 3rd ed. 352p. (C). 1991. pap. text ed. write for info. (*0-13-769878-X*) P-H.

— The Urban Crucible: The Northern Seaports & the Origins of the American Revolution. (Illus.). 300p. 1986. pap. 15.95 (*0-674-93059-2*) HUP.

Nash, Gary B. & Schultz. Retracing the Past, 2 Vols., I. 3rd ed. (C). 1993. text ed. 28.00 (*0-06-501060-4*) HarpCollege.

— Retracing the Past, 2 Vols., II. 3rd ed. (C). 1993. text ed. 28.00 (*0-06-501061-2*) HarpCollege.

Nash, Gary B. & Soderlund, Jean R. Freedom by Degrees: Emancipation in Pennsylvania & Its Aftermath. (Illus.). 272p. 1991. 35.00 (*0-19-504583-1*) OUP.

Nash, Gary B., jt. ed. see Sweet, David G.

Nash, Gary B., et al. The American People. 3rd ed. (C). 1993. Set. text ed. 58.00 (*0-06-501055-8*); Vol. I Study guide. 19.50 (*0-06-501058-2*); Vol. II Study guide. 19.50 (*0-06-501059-0*) HarpCollege.

— The American People, I. 3rd ed. (C). 1993. text ed. 43.50 (*0-06-501056-6*) HarpCollege.

— The American People, II. 3rd ed. (C). 1993. text ed. 43.50 (*0-06-501057-4*) HarpCollege.

— The American People: Creating a Nation & a Society, 2 vols. 2nd abr. ed. Incl. American People Vol. 1: Creating a Nation & a Society. 2nd abr. ed. LC 95-8877. (C). 1995. (*0-673-99527-5*); Vol. 2. American People Vol. 2: Creating a Nation & a Society. 2nd abr. ed. LC 95-8877. (C). 1995. (*0-673-99528-3*); LC 95-8877. write for info. (*0-673-99526-7*) HarpCollege.

— Private Side of American History: Readings in Everyday Life, Vol. 1: To 1877. 4th ed. 459p. (C). 1987. pap. text ed. 18.75 (*0-15-571960-2*) HB Coll Pubs.

— Private Side of American History: Readings in Everyday Life, Vol. 2: Since 1865. 4th ed. 462p. (C). 1987. pap. text ed. 19.50 (*0-15-571961-0*) HB Coll Pubs.

Nash, Geoffrey. The Phoenix & the Ashes. 160p. 1985. pap. 8.25 (*0-85398-199-X*) G Ronald Pub.

Nash, George. Do-It-Yourself Housebuilding: The Complete Handbook. LC 94-2371. (Illus.). 640p. 1995. pap. 24.95 (*0-8069-0424-0*) Sterling.

— Herbert Hoover & Stanford University. 224p. 1988. 24.95 (*0-8179-8691-X*); pap. text ed. 18.95 (*0-8179-8692-8*) Hoover Inst Pr.

— Old Houses: A Rebuilder's Manual. (Illus.). 1979. pap. 12.95 (*0-686-96841-7*) P-H.

— Renovating Old Houses. Beneke, Jeff, ed. 320p. (C). 1992. 37.95 (*0-942391-65-9*) Taunton.

Nash, George H. The Life of Herbert Hoover: The Engineer, 1874-1914. 768p. 1983. 25.00 (*0-685-32951-8*) Hoover Lib.

— The Life of Herbert Hoover: The Engineer, 1874-1914. (Illus.). 1983. 25.00 (*0-393-01634-X*) Norton.

— The Life of Herbert Hoover: The Humanitarian, 1914-1917. 497p. 1988. 25.00 (*0-685-32952-6*) Hoover Lib.

— The Life of Herbert Hoover: The Humanitarian, 1914-1917, Vol. 2. (Illus.). 1988. 25.00 (*0-393-02550-0*) Norton.

Nash, Gerald D. A. P. Giannini & the Bank of America. LC 92-54131. (Oklahoma Western Biographies Ser.: Vol. 5). (Illus.). 160p. 1992. 24.95 (*0-8061-2461-X*) U of Okla Pr.

— The American West Transformed: The Impact of the Second World War. LC 83-49524. (Illus.). 316p. 1985. 35.00 (*0-253-30649-3*) Ind U Pr.

— The American West Transformed: The Impact of the Second World War. LC 89-24957. xii, 320p. 1990. reprint ed. pap. 12.50 (*0-8032-8360-1*, Bison Books) U of Nebr Pr.

— Creating the West: Historical Interpretations, 1890-1990. LC 91-8584. (Calvin P. Horn Lectures in Western History & Culture). (Illus.). 384p. 1991. pap. 18.95 (*0-8263-1267-5*) U of NM Pr.

— The Crucial Era: The Great Depression & WWII, 1929-1945. 2nd ed. LC 90-63553. (Twentieth Century United States History Ser.). 224p. (C). 1991. pap. text ed. 14.50 (*0-312-03631-0*) St Martin.

— State Government & Economic Development. Bruchey, Stuart, ed. LC 78-56676. (Management of Public Lands in the U. S. Ser.). 1979. reprint ed. lib. bdg. 31.95 (*0-405-11346-3*) Ayer.

An Asterisk (*) at the beginning of an entry indicates that the title is appearing in BIP for the first time.

— World War II & the West. LC 89-4935. (Illus.). xiv, 312p. 1990. 35.00 (*0-8032-3303-5*) U of Nebr Pr.

Nash, Gerald D., ed. see Davies, Richard O.

Nash, Gerald R. Why God Allows Trials & Disappointments. (Uplook Ser.). 31p. 1972. pap. 0.99 (*0-8163-0082-8*, 23618-2) Pacific Pr Pub Assn.

Nash, Gerallt D. Victorian Schooldays in Wales. 38p. 1991. pap. 8.00 (*0-7083-1110-5*, Pub. by U of Wales UK) Bks Intl VA.

Nash, Gilbert. Humphreys Families in America: (Dorchester & Weymouth Families) (Illus.). 275p. 1992. reprint ed. lib. bdg. 49.00 (*0-8328-2388-0*); reprint ed. pap. 39.00 (*0-8328-2389-9*) Higginson Bk Co.

Nash, Grace C. Creative Approaches to Child Development with Music, Language & Movement: Incorporating the Philosophies & Techniques of Orff, Kodaly, & Laban. LC 73-93672. (Illus.). 176p. 1974. pap. text ed. 16.95 (*0-88284-014-2*, 1405) Alfred Pub.

— That We Might Live. De Mente, Boye, ed. LC 84-62031. (Illus.). 255p. 1985. pap. 9.95 (*0-914778-58-7*) Shano Pubs.

Nash, Grace C. & Rapley, Janice. Holidays & Special Days. Feldstein, Sandy et al, eds. (Illus.). 260p. (J). (gr. k-6). 1988. teacher ed 24.95 (*0-88284-368-0*, 3517); student ed 9.95 (*0-88284-369-9*, 3516) Alfred Pub.

Nash, Grace C., et al. Do It My Way: A Handbook for Building Creative Teaching Experiences. 172p. (Orig.). 1977. pap. text ed. 19.95 (*0-88284-055-X*, 1442) Alfred Pub.

Nash, Helen. Challenging Cryptograms. LC 93-39591. 128p. 1994. pap. 5.95 (*0-8069-0594-8*) Sterling.

— Helen Nash's Kosher Kitchen: Healthful & Nutritious Recipes for Everyday Eating & Entertaining. LC 88-42668. (Illus.). 320p. 1988. 25.00 (*0-394-57026-X*) Random.

— Kosher Cuisine. 352p. 1995. write for info. (*1-56821-611-4*) Aronson.

— Kosher Cuisine. LC 83-43183. 320p. 1984. 17.95 (*0-394-52788-7*) Random.

— Kosher Cuisine: Over Two Hundred Fifty Gourmet Recipes for the Modern Home. (Illus.). 319p. 1988. 12.95 (*0-944007-26-0*) Sure Sellers.

— The Pond Doctor: Planning & Maintaining a Healthy Water Garden. LC 94-19956. (Illus.). 144p. 1994. 27.95 (*0-8069-0686-3*) Sterling.

— The Pond Doctor: Planning & Maintaining a Healthy Water Garden. (Illus.). 160p. (Orig.). 1995. pap. 17.95 (*0-8069-0687-1*) Sterling.

***Nash, Helen & Masterson, Dorothy.** Humorous Cryptograms. LC 95-12624. 128p. 1995. pap. 5.95 (*0-8069-3982-6*) Sterling.

Nash, Henry T. American Foreign Policy: Changing Perspectives on National Security. rev. ed. LC 77-91308. (Dorsey Series in Political Science). 395p. reprint ed. pap. 112.60 (*0-8357-5370-0*, 2024232) Bks Demand.

Nash, Howard P., Jr. Andrew Johnson: Congress & Reconstruction. LC 72-248. 170p. 1972. 18.00 (*0-8386-1129-X*) Fairleigh Dickinson.

— Stormy Petrel: The Life & Times of General Benjamin F. Butler, 1818-1893. LC 71-81498. 335p. 1975. 35.00 (*0-8386-7383-X*) Fairleigh Dickinson.

Nash, Hugh O., Jr. Electrical Systems for Health Care Facilities. (Management & Compliance Ser.: Vol. 7). (Illus.). 144p. 1992. ring bd. 110.00 (*0-87258-608-1*, 055206) Am Hospital.

Nash, J. & Ross, S., eds. Motion Picture Annual 1988: The Films of 1987. (Illus.). 320p. (Orig.). 1988. pap. 19.95 (*0-933997-17-5*) CineBks.

Nash, J. M., ed. see American Society of Mechanical Engineers Staff.

Nash, J. P., et al. Road-Building Materials in Texas. (Bulletin Ser.: BULL 1839). (Illus.). 159p. 1918. 0.50 (*0-686-29341-X*) Bur Econ Geology.

Nash, J. Robert. Almanac of World Crime. (Illus.). 464p. 1988. 7.99 (*0-517-62530-X*) Random Hse Value.

— Makers & Breakers of Chicago. (Illus.). 265p. 1985. pap. 10.00 (*0-89733-133-8*) Academy Chi Pubs.

Nash, J. Thomas, et al. Geology & Geochemistry of Tertiary Volcanic Hosts Rocks, Sleeper Gold-Silver Deposit, Humboldt County, Nevada. 1995. write for info. (*0-318-72736-6*) US Geol Survey.

Nash, Jacob, et al, eds. Cev'armiut Qanemciit Qulirait-llu: Eskimo Narratives & Tales from Chevak, Alaska. (Illus.). 88p. (C). 1984. pap. 9.00 (*0-933769-09-1*); audio 4.00 (*0-933769-10-5*) Alaska Native.

Nash, James A. Loving Nature: Ecological Integrity & Christian Responsibility. 1991. pap. 16.95 (*0-687-22824-7*) Abingdon.

Nash, James H. & Nash, Mary F. A Nash-Allen Genealogy: Zachariah H. Nash, Lawson Allen, & Their Descendants. LC 83-62562. (Illus.). 1984. 22.00 (*0-9612498-0-3*) J H Nash.

Nash, Jane C. Veiled Images: Titian's Mythological Paintings for Philip II. LC 83-45949. (Illus.). 120p. 1986. 35.00 (*0-87982-511-1*) Art Alliance.

Nash, Jay R. Bloodletters & Badmen: A Narrative Encyclopedia of American Criminals from the Pilgrims to the Present. LC 72-95977. (Illus.). 640p. 1992. 16.95 (*0-87131-113-5*); pap. 17.95 (*0-87131-200-X*) M Evans.

— Bloodletters & Badmen: A Narrative Encyclopedia of American Criminals from the Pilgrims to the Present. expanded rev. ed. LC 94-49585. 1995. pap. 19.95 (*0-87131-777-X*) M Evans.

— Citizen Hoover: A Critical Study of the Life & Times of J. Edgar Hoover & His FBI. LC 72-76266. (Illus.). 304p. 1972. 26.95 (*0-911012-60-5*) Nelson-Hall.

— Darkest Hours: A Narrative Encyclopedia of Worldwide Disasters from Ancient Times to the Present. LC 76-7390. (Illus.). 826p. 1976. 63.95 (*0-88229-140-8*) Nelson-Hall.

— Dictionary of Crime. 1994. 39.95 (*1-56924-873-7*) Marlowe & Co.

— The Dillinger Dossier. LC 83-72087. (Illus.). 312p. 1983. pap. 19.95 (*0-913204-16-1*) December Pr.

— Encyclopedia of Western Lawmen. 1994. 49.95 (*1-56924-897-4*) Marlowe & Co.

— Encyclopedia of Western Lawmen & Outlaws. (Illus.). 581p. 1994. reprint ed. pap. 24.95 (*0-306-80591-X*) Da Capo.

— Encyclopedia of World Crime: Criminal Justice, Criminology & Law Enforcement, 6 vols., Set. (Illus.). 5500p. (C). 1990. boxed 600.00 (*0-685-24083-5*) CrimeBooks Inc.

— Encyclopedia of World Crime: Criminal Justice, Criminology, & Law Enforcement, 6 vols., Set. (Illus.). 4500p. 1990. 500.00 (*0-923582-00-2*) CrimeBooks Inc.

— Hustlers & Con Men: An Anecdotal History of the Confidence Man & His Games. LC 75-38602. (Illus.). 384p. 1975. 14.95 (*0-87131-188-7*) M Evans.

— Jay Robert Nash's Crime Chronology: A Worldwide Record, 1900-1983. LC 83-14046. (Illus.). 230p. reprint ed. pap. 65.60 (*0-7837-5344-6*, 2045087) Bks Demand.

— On All Fronts. LC 74-81911. (Illus.). 147p. (C). 1974. pap. 12.50 (*0-913204-03-X*) December Pr.

— World Encyclopedia of Organized Crime. 1994. 49.95 (*1-56924-898-2*) Marlowe & Co.

— World Encyclopedia of Organized Crime. (Illus.). 634p. 1993. reprint ed. pap. 25.00 (*0-306-80535-9*) Da Capo.

— World Encyclopedia of 20th Century Murder. 1994. 49.95 (*1-56924-872-9*) Marlowe & Co.

Nash, Jay R. & Ross, Stanley R. The Motion Picture Guide, 12 vols. 1986. Dist. by R.R. Bowker to libraries only. text ed. 750.00 (*0-685-14532-8*, CineBooks) Baseline Bks.

— The Motion Picture Guide, 12 vols., Set. LC 85-71145. (Complete Film Resource Center Ser.). 1987. 600.00 (*0-933997-00-0*) CineBooks.

— The Motion Picture Guide Annual, 1986 (The Films of 1985) (Illus.). 450p. 1987. text ed. 50.00 (*0-933997-14-0*) CineBks.

— The Motion Picture Guide Index, 2 vols. LC 85-71145. 3170p. 1987. 100.00 (*0-933997-11-6*) CineBks.

Nash, Jay R. & Ross, Stanley R., eds. The Motion Picture Guide Annual, 1986 (Films of 1985) 450p. 1986. Dist. by R.R. Bowker to libraries only. 119.95 (*0-685-43814-7*, CineBooks) Baseline Bks.

— The Motion Picture Guide Annual, 1987 (Films of 1986) 500p. 1987. Dist. by R.R. Bowker to libraries only. 119.95 (*0-685-18231-2*, CineBooks) Baseline Bks.

— Motion Picture Guide Annual, 1988 (Films of 1987) Dist. by R.R. Bowker to libraries only. 119.95 (*0-685-30164-8*, CineBooks) Baseline Bks.

— Motion Picture Guide Annual, 1989 (Films of 1988) Dist. by R.R. Bowker to libraries only. 119.95 (*0-685-30165-6*, CineBooks) Baseline Bks.

— The Motion Picture Guide Annual 1990 (the Films of 1989) (Illus.). 700p. 1990. Dist. by R.R. Bowker to libraries only. 124.95 (*0-685-60084-X*, CineBooks) Baseline Bks.

Nash, Jay Robert & Ross, Stanley Ralph, eds. Motion Picture Guide Annual, 1987: The Films of 1986. (Illus.). 726p. 1987. 119.95 (*0-933997-15-9*) CineBooks.

— Motion Picture Guide Annual 1988: The Films of 1987. (Illus.). 799p. 1988. 119.95 (*0-933997-16-7*) CineBooks.

— The Motion Picture Guide Annual 1989. (Films of 1988 Ser.). (Illus.). 665p. 1989. 119.95 (*0-933997-20-5*) CineBooks.

— The Motion Picture Guide Annual, 1990: The Films of 1989. (Illus.). 480p. 1990. 124.95 (*0-933997-29-9*) CineBooks.

Nash, Jean. The Silver Web. (Last of the Lattimers Ser.). 352p. (Orig.). 1984. pap. 3.50 (*0-8439-2064-5*) Dorchester Pub Co.

Nash, Jeffrey E. Social Psychology: Society & Self. (Illus.). 425p. (C). 1985. text ed. 49.25 (*0-314-85281-6*) West Pub.

Nash, Jeffrey E. & Calonico, James M. Institutions in Modern Society: Meanings, Forms, & Character. 1993p. 1990. text ed. 34.95 (*0-930390-07-5*); pap. text ed. 18.95 (*0-930390-06-7*) Gen Hall.

Nash, Jeffrey E., jt. ed. see Higgins, Paul C.

Nash, Jennie. Altared States: Portrait of a Fiancee. 1992. 16.00 (*0-517-58497-2*, Crown) Crown Pub Group.

Nash, Jerry C. The Love Aesthetics of Maurice Sceve: Poetry & Struggle. (Cambridge Studies in French: No. 34). 224p. (C). 1991. 59.95 (*0-521-39412-0*) Cambridge U Pr.

Nash, Jerry C., ed. Pre-Pleiade Poetry. LC 84-81851. (French Forum Monographs: No. 57). 148p. (Orig.). 1985. pap. 12.95 (*0-917058-57-7*) French Forum.

— A Sceve Celebration: Delie, 1544-1994. (Stanford French & Italian Studies: No. 77). 200p. 1993. pap. 46.50 (*0-915838-93-1*) Anma Libri.

Nash, Jerry C., jt. ed. see Bowen, Barbara C.

Nash, Jerry C., jt. ed. see Lacy, Norris J.

Nash, Jesse W. The Myth of Warmth. LC 93-72178. 78p. (Orig.). 1994. pap. 12.95 (*0-9625762-4-7*) Art Review Pr.

— Vietnamese Catholicism. LC 93-56459. (Illus.). xix, 184p. (Orig.). (C). 1994. pap. 9.95 (*0-9625762-1-2*) Art Review Pr.

Nash, Jesse W. & Nguyen, Elizabeth T. The L. S. A. T. Study Companion: Logical Reasoning. LC 93-72179. 200p. (Orig.). (C). 1994. pap. 14.95 (*0-9625762-3-9*) Art Review Pr.

Nash, Jesse W. & Nguyen, Elizabeth T., eds. Romance, Gender, & Religion in a Vietnamese-American Community: Tales of God & Beautiful Women. LC 94-16411. 192p. 1995. text ed. 79.95 (*0-7734-9087-6*) E Mellen.

Nash, John. Vermeer. (Illus.). 128p. 1991. 25.00 (*1-870248-62-7*) Scala Books.

— Views of the Royal Pavilion. (Illus.). 128p. 1992. 19.98 (*1-55859-340-3*) Abbeville Pr.

Nash, John, jt. ed. see Thomas, Vinod.

Nash, John C. Compact Numerical Methods for Computers: Linear Algebra & Function Minimisation. 2nd ed. (Illus.). 292p. 1990. 140.00 (*0-85274-318-1*); pap. 43.00 (*0-85274-319-X*); disk write for info. (*0-7503-0036-1*) IOP Pub.

— Effective Scientific Problem Solving with Small Computers. (Illus.). 272p. 26.95 (*0-8359-1594-8*, Reston) P-H.

Nash, John F. & Heagy, Cynthia D. Accounting Information Systems. 3rd ed. LC 92-32937. 1993. text ed. 58.95 (*0-538-82484-0*) S-W Pub.

Nash, Jonell. Essence Brings You Cooking. LC 93-25624. (Illus.). 465p. 1994. 29.95 (*1-56743-033-3*) Amistad Pr.

Nash, Joyce. Taking Charge of Your Smoking. 124p. (Orig.). 1981. student ed 14.95 (*0-915950-50-2*) Bull Pub.

Nash, Joyce D. Maximize Your Body Potential: Sixteen Weeks to a Lifetime of Weight Management. 554p. 1986. pap. 18.95 (*0-915950-69-3*) Bull Pub.

— Now That You've Lost It: How to Maintain Your Best Weight. 350p. (Orig.). 1992. pap. 16.95 (*0-923521-19-4*) Bull Pub.

— What Your Doctor Can't Tell You about Cosmetic Surgery. 200p. (Orig.). 1995. text ed. 24.95 (*1-57224-033-4*); pap. 12.95 (*1-57224-032-6*) New Harbinger.

Nash, June. I Spent My Life in the Mines: The Story of Juan Rojas, Bolivian Tin Miner. (Illus.). 416p. 1992. text ed. 49.00 (*0-231-07936-2*); pap. text ed. 18.50 (*0-231-07937-0*) Col U Pr.

— In the Eyes of the Ancestors: Belief & Behavior in a Mayan Community. (Illus.). 374p. (C). 1985. reprint ed. pap. text ed. 13.95 (*0-88133-142-2*) Waveland Pr.

— We Eat the Mines & the Mines Eat Us: Dependency & Exploitation in Bolivian Tin Mines. LC 79-11623. 1982. pap. text ed. 19.50 (*0-231-04711-8*) Col U Pr.

— We Eat the Mines & the Mines Eat Us: Dependency & Exploitation in Bolivian Tin Mines. (Illus.). 384p. 1992. text ed. 45.00 (*0-231-08050-6*); pap. 18.50 (*0-231-08051-4*) Col U Pr.

Nash, June & Safa, Helen I., eds. Women & Change in Latin America: New Directions in Sex & Class. LC 85-18563. (Illus.). 384p. 1985. text ed. 47.95 (*0-89789-069-8*, Bergin & Garvey); pap. text ed. 19.95 (*0-89789-070-1*, Bergin & Garvey) Greenwood.

Nash, June, et al, eds. Ideology & Social Change in Latin America. 312p. 1977. text ed. 63.00 (*0-677-04170-5*) Gordon & Breach.

— Popular Participation in Social Change: Cooperatives, Collectives, & Nationalized Industry. (World Anthropology Ser.). xviii, 622p. 1976. 63.35 (*90-279-7849-2*) Mouton.

Nash, June C. From Tank Town to High Tech: The Clash of Community & Industrial Cycles. LC 88-15378. (SUNY Series in the Anthropology of Work). (Illus.). 368p. 1989. 74.50 (*0-88706-938-X*); pap. 24.95 (*0-88706-939-8*) State U NY Pr.

Nash, June C., ed. Crafts in the World Market: The Impact of Global Exchange on Middle American Artisans. LC 91-21308. (SUNY Series in the Anthropology of Work). 264p. (C). 1993. 59.50 (*0-7914-1061-7*); pap. 19.95 (*0-7914-1062-5*) State U NY Pr.

Nash, June C. & Fernandez-Kelly, Maria P., eds. Women, Men, & the International Division of Labor. LC 82-10447. (SUNY Series in the Anthropology of Work). (Illus.). 463p. (C). 1984. 49.50 (*0-87395-683-4*); pap. 16.95 (*0-87395-684-2*) State U NY Pr.

Nash, K. Kennedy & Diefenbaker. (Illus.). 320p. 1990. 19.95 (*0-7710-6705-4*, Pub. by McClelland & Stewart CN) Firefly Bks Ltd.

Nash, Kathy, jt. auth. see Edwards, Diana.

***Nash, Kenneth L. & Choppin, Gregory R., eds.** Separations of f Elements: Proceedings of an ACS Symposium of f Elements Separations Held in San Diego, California, March 13-17, 1994. 270p. 1995. 95.00 (*0-306-45070-4*) Plenum.

Nash, Kermit B., ed. Psychosocial Aspects of Sickle Cell Disease: Past, Present, & Future Directions of Research. LC 94-12367. (Journal of Health & Social Policy: Vol. 5, Nos. 3 & 4). (Illus.). 282p. 1994. 39.95 (*1-56024-578-6*) Haworth Pr.

Nash, Kwame M. Cologne: The History & Anthropology of a Rural Texas African American Community. (Illus.). 100p. (Orig.). (C). 1990. pap. 10.00 (*0-9623350-0-2*) M C Nash Pubns.

Nash, Laura L. The Aggelia in Pindar. (Harvard Dissertations in the Classics Ser.). 250p. 1990. reprint ed. 25.00 (*0-8240-3307-8*) Garland.

— Good Intentions Aside: A Manager's Guide to Resolving Ethical Problems. 1990. text ed. 24.95 (*0-07-103259-2*) McGraw.

— Good Intentions Aside: A Manager's Guide to Resolving Ethical Problems. 1993. pap. text ed. 14.95 (*0-07-103431-5*) McGraw.

— Good Intentions Aside: A Manager's Guide to Resolving Ethical Problems. LC 93-14788. 288p. 1993. reprint ed. pap. 14.95 (*0-87584-429-4*) Harvard Busn.

Nash, Laura L., jt. ed. see Heuberger, Frank W.

Nash, Lee. North Cove Yacht Harbor. Brady, Maxine, ed. (Illus.). 50p. write for info. (*0-318-64708-7*) Watermark Assocs.

Nash, Lee, ed. Understanding Herbert Hoover: Ten Perspectives. 196p. 1988. 21.95 (*0-8179-8541-7*) Hoover Inst Pr.

Nash, Lee, ed. see Victor, Frances F.

Nash, Leonard K. The Atomic-Molecular Theory. LC 50-12355. (Harvard Case Histories in Experimental Science Ser.: Case 4). 163p. reprint ed. pap. 46.50 (*0-8357-5857-5*, 2006426) Bks Demand.

— ChemThermo: A Statistical Approach to Thermodynamics. (C). 1972. pap. text ed. write for info. (*0-201-05237-7*) Addison-Wesley.

— Elements of Statistical Thermodynamics. 2nd ed. 1974. pap. text ed. 16.25 (*0-201-05229-6*) Addison-Wesley.

Nash, Linda J. & Kampen, Martha G. Surviving in the Jungle: What You Really Need to Know to Market Your Business Without Losing Your Shirt. (Illus.). 153p. (Orig.). 1993. pap. 12.95 (*0-9636702-0-4*) PRISM MO.

Nash, M., et al. Better Baby Care: A Book for Family Day Care Providers. rev. ed. 164p. 1993. pap. text ed. 15.95 (*1-884093-03-5*) Chldrns Fnd.

— Mejor Cuidado Infantil: Un Libro Para Proveedoras de Cuidado Para Ninos En el Hogar. 184p. (SPA.). 1993. pap. text ed. 19.95 (*1-884093-04-3*) Chldrns Fnd.

Nash, M. A., pseud. How to Save a Fortune Using Refunds & Coupons. 32p. (Orig.). 1983. pap. 6.95 (*0-934650-03-9*) Sunnyside.

Nash, Manning. The Cauldron of Ethnicity in the Modern World. LC 88-29522. 152p. 1989. lib. bdg. 24.95 (*0-226-56866-0*); pap. text ed. 9.95 (*0-226-56867-9*) U Ch Pr.

Nash, Manning, ed. Essays on Economic Development & Cultural Change: In Honor of Bert F. Hoselitz. 1977. pap. text ed. 14.95 (*0-226-56865-2*) U Ch Pr.

Nash, Margaret & Brodley, Sue. Josh's Expedition. (Illus.). 32p. (J). (ps-1). 1993. 17.95 (*0-370-31572-3*, Pub. by Bodley Head UK) Trafalgar.

Nash, Marian L. Digest of United States Practice in International Law, 1979. (State Department Publications: No. 9374). 1955p. 1983. 22.00 (*0-16-004393-X*, S/N 044-000-01937-0) USGPO.

Nash, Mary. Women in the Spanish Civil War. (Women & Modern Revolutions Ser.). (Illus.). 220p. (Orig.). (C). 1995. text ed. 28.00 (*0-912869-15-1*); pap. text ed. 18.95 (*0-912869-16-X*) Arden Pr.

Nash, Mary F., jt. auth. see Nash, James H.

Nash, Mary H. Skulls Are Forever: A Book of Secret Truths. (Illus.). (Orig.). 1986. pap. 12.95 (*0-9618893-0-6*) Ichthys VA.

Nash, Michael. Computers, Automation, & Cybernetics at the Hagley Museum & Library. (Illus.). (Orig.). 1989. pap. 7.50 (*0-914650-27-0*) Hagley Museum.

— Managing Organizational Performance. LC 82-49040. (Management Ser.). 380p. 1983. 39.95 (*0-87589-561-1*) Jossey-Bass.

— Runner's World Weight Control Book. (Runner's World Instructional Ser.). (Illus.). 200p. (Orig.). 1981. spiral bd. 11.95 (*0-89037-087-7*) Anderson World.

Nash, Michael, et al. Pennsylvania Power & Light Co., A Guide to Records. 226p. 1985. 10.00 (*0-914650-22-X*) Hagley Museum.

Nash, Michael H. Conflict & Accommodation: Coal Miners, Steel Workers & Socialism, 1890 to 1920. LC 81-6691. (Contributions in Labor History Ser.: No. 11). (Illus.). xiv, 197p. 1982. text ed. 49.95 (*0-313-22838-8*, NCO/, Greenwood Pr) Greenwood.

Nash, Michael M. Managing Organizational Performance. LC 82-49049. (Joint Publication in the Jossey-Bass Management Series & the Jossey-Bass Social & Behavioral Science Ser.). 382p. 1983. reprint ed. pap. 108.90 (*0-7837-2545-0*, 2042704) Bks Demand.

Nash, Michael R., jt. ed. see Fromm, Erika.

Nash, Mildred J. Beyond Their Dreams. LC 89-37565. 104p. (Orig.). 1989. pap. 5.95 (*0-936015-16-0*) Pocahontas Pr.

Nash, N. Richard. Rouge Atomique. 1955. pap. 2.75 (*0-8222-0972-1*) Dramatists Play.

— The Young & Fair. 1948. pap. 4.75 (*0-8222-1289-7*) Dramatists Play.

Nash, Nancy, jt. auth. see Malmstrom, Karin.

Nash, Nancy S. & Hawthorne, Elizabeth M. Formal Recognition of Employer-Sponsored Instruction: Conflict & Collegiality in Postsecondary Education. Fife, Jonathan D., ed. & frwd. by. LC 87-71299. (ASHE-ERIC Higher Education Report Ser.: No. 3, 1987). 132p. (Orig.). (C). 1987. pap. text ed. 10.00 (*0-913317-37-3*) GWU Schl E&HD.

Nash, Newlyn. The Affair at Claife Manor. large type ed. (Linford Romance Library). 272p. 1988. pap. 11.95 (*0-7089-6576-8*, Linford) Ulverscroft.

— Beach of Dreams. large type ed. (Linford Romance Library). 288p. 1989. pap. 11.95 (*0-7089-6665-9*, Linford) Ulverscroft.

— Dance of Destiny. large type ed. (Linford Romance Library). 1990. pap. 12.95 (*0-7089-6825-2*, Trailtree Bookshop) Ulverscroft.

— Magic of Love. large type ed. (Linford Romance Library). 1989. pap. 11.95 (*0-7089-6784-1*, Linford) Ulverscroft.

— The Pearl. large type ed. 1990. pap. 12.95 (*0-7089-6885-6*, Linford) Ulverscroft.

— Wild Garlic. large type ed. (Linford Romance Library). 272p. 1987. pap. 11.95 (*0-7089-6432-X*, Linford) Ulverscroft.

Nash, Nicholas & Culbertson, Jack, eds. Linking Processes in Educational Improvement - Concepts & Applications. 316p. (Orig.). (C). 1977. pap. text ed. 10.95 (*1-55996-139-2*, W-133) Univ Council Educ Admin.

Nash, Ogden. The Adventures of Isabel. (Illus.). (J). (ps-3). 1991. 14.95 (*0-316-59874-7*) Little.

— Adventures of Isabel. (J). (ps-3). 1994. 4.95 (*0-316-59883-6*) Little.

— The Animal Garden. LC 65-21772. (Illus.). 48p. (YA). (gr. 10 up). 1988. pap. 5.95 (*0-87131-568-8*) M Evans.

— The Cruise of the Aardvark. LC 67-27296. (Illus.). 48p. (J). (ps up). 1989. pap. 5.95 (*0-87131-570-X*) M Evans.

— Custard & Company. (Illus.). 128p. (J). (gr. 2-6). 1985. mass mkt. 6.95 (*0-316-59855-0*) Little.
— Custard the Dragon. (Illus.). (J). (gr. k-3). 1973. lib. bdg. 14.95 (*0-316-59841-0*) Little.
— Custard the Dragon & the Wicked Knight. LC 95-9719. (Illus.). (J). 1996. write for info. (*0-316-59882-8*) Little.
— I Wouldn't Have Missed It: Selected Poems of Ogden Nash. Eberstadt, Isabel, ed. 416p. 1975. 29.95 (*0-316-59830-5*) Little.
— I'm a Stranger Here Myself. (Orig.). 1994. lib. bdg. 21.95x (*1-56849-468-8*) Buccaneer Bks.
— Ogden Nash's Zoo. LC 86-23173. (Illus.). 84p. 1987. 10.95 (*0-941434-95-8*) Stewart Tabori & Chang.
— A Penny Saved Is Impossible. (Illus.). 132p. 1983. reprint ed. pap. 9.95 (*0-316-59806-2*) Little.
— Pocket Book of Ogden Nash. 1976. 17.95 (*0-8488-1439-8*) Amereon Ltd.
— The Pocket Book of Ogden Nash. 200p. 1991. reprint ed. lib. bdg. 18.95 (*0-89966-867-4*) Buccaneer Bks.
— The Take of Custard the Dragon. (Illus.). (J). (ps-3). 1995. 14.95 (*0-316-59880-1*) Little.
— You Can't Get There from Here. (Illus.). 208p. 1984. mass mkt. 6.95 (*0-316-59854-2*) Little.
Nash, P. Systems Modelling & Optimisation. (Control Engineering Ser.: No. 16). 224p. 1981. boxed 73.00 (*0-906048-63-X*, CE016) Inst Elect Eng.
Nash, P., ed. Phase Diagrams of Binary Nickel Alloys. (Monograph Series on Alloy Phase Diagrams). (Illus.). 394p. (C). 1991. text ed. 284.00 (*0-87170-365-3*) ASM.
Nash, Padder. Grass. large type ed. 1991. pap. 13.95 (*0-7089-7026-5*) Ulverscroft.
— Grass & Supergrass. large type ed. (Linford Romance Library). 1989. pap. 11.95 (*0-7089-6756-6*, Trailtree Bookshop) Ulverscroft.
— Grass in Idleness. large type ed. (Linford Mystery Library). 304p. 1994. pap. 14.95 (*0-7089-7484-8*, Linford) Ulverscroft.
— Grass Makes Hay. large type ed. (Mystery Ser.). 304p. 1994. pap. 14.95 (*0-7089-7558-5*, Trailtree Bookshop) Ulverscroft.
— Grass's Fancy. large type ed. (Linford Mystery Library). 304p. 1993. pap. 14.95 (*0-7089-7346-9*, Trailtree Bookshop) Ulverscroft.
— Wayward Seeds of Grass. large type ed. (Linford Mystery Library). 1991. pap. 13.95 (*0-7089-7131-8*) Ulverscroft.
Nash, Paul. Authority & Freedom in Education: An Introduction to the Philosophy of Education. LC 66-17624. 352p. reprint ed. pap. 100.40 (*0-8357-5900-8*, 2012614) Bks Demand.
— Colossal Constructions. Young, Richard G., ed. LC 89-11714. (Illus.). 32p. (J). (gr. 3-5). 1989. lib. bdg. 13.26 (*0-944483-35-6*) Garrett Ed Corp.
— Models of Man: Explorations in the Western Educational Tradition. LC 83-8369. 484p. 1983. reprint ed. text ed. 47.00 (*0-89874-634-5*) Krieger.
— Super Structures. Harris, Peter, ed. LC 89-12009. (Illus.). 32p. (J). (gr. 2-4). 1989. lib. bdg. 13.26 (*0-944483-37-2*) Garrett Ed Corp.
Nash, Paul, jt. auth. see Flavell, A. J.
Nash, Paul W. The Gilded Fly: Short Stories. (Illus.). 40p. 1993. 28.00 (*0-930126-42-4*) Typographeum.
***Nash, Peggy N. & Nash, R.** Mr. McCamey-- Claude W. Brown: Life of a West Texas Oil Man. LC 94-37570. 1995. 15.96 (*0-89015-976-9*, Eakin Pr) Sunbelt Media.
Nash, Peggy W. Dinner for One. 188p. 1991. per. 22.95 (*0-8403-6721-X*) Kendall-Hunt.
Nash, Petra. All of Heaven. large type ed. (Masquerade Historical Romance Ser.). 1993. 18.95 (*0-263-13753-8*, Pub. by Mills & Boon Ltd UK) Chivers N Amer.
— Country Mouse. large type ed. (Historical Romance Ser.). 1994. 18.95 (*0-263-14009-1*, Pub. by Mills & Boon Ltd UK) Chivers N Amer.
— Mr. Ravensworth's Ward. (Regency Romance Ser.). 1993. mass mkt. 2.99 (*0-373-31193-1*, 1-31193-5) Harlequin Bks.
Nash, Petra, jt. auth. see Edmonds, Janet.
Nash-Price, Barbara. Inside Story: Real Estate Agent Manual, Vol. 1. (Illus.). 264p. (Orig.). 1994. student ed, pap. 29.95 (*0-9634419-0-6*) Nash-Price Pubs.
— Life Awareness Manual. (Illus.). 98p. (Orig.). 1995. pap. 8.95 (*0-9634419-1-4*) Nash-Price Pubs.
Nash, R., ed. Environment & Americans: The Problem of Priorities. LC 79-4177. (American Problem Studies). 126p. 1979. reprint ed. pap. text ed. 8.50 (*0-88275-936-1*) Krieger.
Nash, R., jt. auth. see Nash, Peggy N.
Nash, Ralph, tr. see Sannazaro, Jacopo.
Nash, Ralph, tr. see Tasso, Torquato.
Nash, Ralph C. Government Contract Changes & Supplement. 2nd ed. (Illus.). 600p. 1989. 175.00 (*0-317-03297-6*) Fed Pubns Inc.
Nash, Ralph C., Jr. & Cibinic, John, Jr. Competitive Negotiation: The Source Selection Process. LC 93-44517. 1000p. 1993. 60.00 (*0-935165-25-8*); pap. write for info. (*0-935165-29-0*) GWU Gov Contracts.
— Federal Procurement Law, 2 vols., Set. 3rd ed. 2436p. 100.00 (*0-935165-22-3*) GWU Gov Contracts.
— Federal Procurement Law, 2 vols., Vol. 1. 3rd ed. 2436p. 1977. 55.00 (*0-685-74402-7*) GWU Gov Contracts.
— Federal Procurement Law, 2 vols., Vol. 2. 3rd ed. 2436p. 1980. 55.00 (*0-685-74403-5*) GWU Gov Contracts.
— Federal Procurement Law, Vol. 1: Contract Formation, Vol. 1. 3rd ed. 946p. 1977. 50.00 (*0-935165-00-2*) GWU Gov Contracts.
— Federal Procurement Law, Vol. 2: Contract Performance. 3rd ed. 1490p. 1980. 60.00 (*0-935165-01-0*) GWU Gov Contracts.
Nash, Ralph C., Jr. & Rawicz, Leonard. Patents & Technical Data. 643p. 1983. 40.00 (*0-935165-09-6*) GWU Gov Contracts.
Nash, Ralph C., Jr. & Schooner, Stephen L. The Government Contracts Reference Book. 350p. 1992. pap. 40.00 (*0-935165-19-3*) GWU Gov Contracts.
Nash, Ralph C., Jr., jt. auth. see Cibinic, John, Jr.
Nash, Ralph G. & Leslie, Anne R., eds. Groundwater Residue Sampling Design. LC 91-15752. (ACS Symposium Ser.: No. 465). (Illus.). 395p. 1991. 84.95 (*0-8412-2091-3*) Am Chemical.
Nash, Ray. American Penmanship Eighteen Hundred to Eighteen Fifty: A History of Writing & a Bibliography of Copybooks from Jenkins to Spencer. LC 78-106556. 303p. 1969. 27.50 (*0-912296-10-0*, U Pr of Va) Am Antiquarian.
Nash, Ray, et al. Education in the Graphic Arts. 1969. 5.00 (*0-89073-025-3*) Boston Public Lib.
***Nash, Renea.** Coping As a Biracial-Biethnic Teen. LC 94-22140. (YA). 1994. 14.95 (*0-8239-1838-6*) Rosen Group.
Nash, Renea D. Coping with Interracial Dating. LC 93-6895. (YA). 1994. 15.95 (*0-8239-1606-5*) Rosen Group.
— Everything You Need to Know about Being a Biracial/Biethnic Teen. LC 94-34644. (Need to Know Library). (Illus.). 64p. (YA). (gr. 7-12). 1994. 15.95 (*0-8239-1871-8*) Rosen Group.
Nash, Richard. John Craige's "Mathematical Principles of Christian Theology" LC 89-39678. (Journal of the History of Philosophy Monograph Ser.). 156p. (C). 1991. pap. 15.95 (*0-8093-1662-5*) S Ill U Pr.
Nash, Roderick. The American Environment: Readings in the History of Conservation. 398p. (C). 1987. text ed. 12.00 (*0-394-37398-7*, KnopfC) Knopf.
— American Environmentalism: Reading in Conservation History. 3rd ed. 398p. (C). 1990. pap. text ed. write for info. (*0-07-046059-0*) McGraw.
— Big Drops: Ten Legendary Rapids of the American West. rev. ed. LC 89-63129. 240p. 1989. pap. 10.95 (*1-55566-051-7*) Johnson Bks.
— The Nervous Generation: American Thought 1917-1930. 192p. 1990. pap. 7.95 (*0-929587-21-9*, Elephant Paperbacks) I R Dee.
— The Rights of Nature: A History of Environmental Ethics. (History of American Thought & Culture Ser.). 320p. (C). 1989. text ed. 35.00 (*0-299-11840-1*); pap. text ed. 14.95 (*0-299-11844-4*) U of Wis Pr.
— Wilderness & the American Mind. 3rd rev. ed. LC 82-4874. 380p. 1982. pap. 16.00 (*0-300-02910-1*, Y-440) Yale U Pr.
***Nash, Roderick & Graves, Gregory.** From These Beginnings, Vol. 1. 5th ed. (Biographical Approach to American History Ser.). 304p. 1995. reprint ed. pap. 25.95 (*1-886746-01-X*) Talman Pub.
— From These Beginnings, Vol. 2. 5th ed. (Biographical Approach to American History Ser.). 288p. 1995. reprint ed. pap. 25.95 (*1-886746-02-8*) Talman Pub.
— From These Beginnings: A Biographical Approach to American History, Vol. 1. 5th ed. LC 94-6453. (C). 1994. 19.50 (*0-673-99205-5*) HarpCollege.
Nash, Roger. Settlement in a School of Whales & Other Poems. (C). 1989. 45.00 (*0-907839-26-6*, Pub. by Brynmill Pr Ltd UK) St Mut.
***Nash, Ronald.** Faith & Reason: Searching for a Rational Faith. 296p. 1994. pap. 18.99 (*0-310-29401-0*) Zondervan.
— Great Divides: Ten Controversies That Come Between Christians. LC 92-40957. 240p. (Orig.). 1993. pap. 10.00 (*0-89109-696-5*) NavPress.
***Nash, Ronald & Baldwin, J. F.** The Summit Ministries Guide to Choosing a College. 1995. pap. write for info. (*0-936163-34-8*) Summit Pr CO.
Nash, Ronald, jt. auth. see Belli, Humberto.
Nash, Ronald H. Christian Faith & Historical Understanding. 2nd ed. LC 89-48471. 169p. (C). 1989. reprint ed. pap. 11.99 (*0-945241-07-0*) Probe Bks.
— Closing of the American Heart: What's Really Wrong with America's Schools. LC 90-30823. 1990. 14.99 (*0-945241-11-9*) Probe Bks.
— The Concept of God. 1983. pap. 14.99 (*0-310-45141-8*, 12381P) Zondervan.
— Freedom, Justice, & the State. LC 80-8145. 243p. 1980. pap. text ed. 22.00 (*0-8191-1196-1*) U Pr of Amer.
— The Gospel & the Greeks: Did the New Testament Borrow from Pagan Thought? LC 91-40299. Orig. Title: Christianity & the Hellenistic World Ser. 318p. (C). 1992. pap. 14.99 (*0-945241-09-7*) Probe Bks.
— Is Jesus the Only Savior? 176p. 1994. pap. 12.99 (*0-310-44391-1*) Zondervan.
— The Light of the Mind: St. Augustine's Theory of Knowledge. LC 69-19765. 159p. reprint ed. 45.40 (*0-8357-9790-2*, 2016099) Bks Demand.
— Poverty & Wealth: Why Socialism Doesn't Work. LC 92-14204. 224p. (C). 1992. reprint ed. pap. 14.99 (*0-945241-16-X*) Probe Bks.
— Social Justice & the Christian Church. 180p. (C). 1990. reprint ed. pap. text ed. 15.75 (*0-8191-7732-6*) U Pr of Amer.
— The Word of God & the Mind of Man. 137p. 1992. reprint ed. pap. 7.99 (*0-87552-354-4*) Presby & Reformed.
— Worldviews in Conflict: Choosing Christianity in the World of Ideas. 144p. 1992. pap. 9.99 (*0-310-57771-3*) Zondervan.
Nash, Rose. Comparing English & Spanish: Patterns in Phonology & Orthography. (C). 1977. pap. text ed. 10.95 (*0-88345-297-9*, 18448); audio 25.00 (*0-685-79303-6*, 58449) Prentice ESL.
— Multilingual Lexicon of Linguistics & Philology: English-Russian-German-French. (Miami Linguistic Ser.). 52.50 (*0-685-36678-2*) Fr & Eur.
— Multilingual Lexicon of Linguistics & Philology: English, Russian, German, French. LC 68-31044. (Miami Linguistics Ser.: No. 3). (ENG, FRE, GER & RUS.). 1968. 15.95 (*0-87024-095-1*) U of Miami Pr.
— Turkish Intonation: An Instrumental Study. LC 71-120351. (Janua Linguarum, Series Practica: No. 114). (Illus.). 190p. (Orig.). 1973. pap. text ed. 48.00 (*90-279-2369-8*) Mouton.
Nash, Rose, ed. Readings in Spanish-English Contrastive Linguistics, Vol. I. LC 73-85939. 249p. 1973. pap. 4.50 (*0-913480-20-7*) Inter Am U Pr.
Nash, Rose & Alleyne, M. Lexique Multiligue De la Linguistique et De la Philogie: Anglais-Russe-Allemand-Francais. 416p. (ENG, FRE, GER & RUS.). 1968. pap. 99.50 (*0-8288-6654-6*, M-6422) Fr & Eur.
Nash, Rose & Belaval, Domitila, eds. Readings in Contrastive Spanish Linguistics, Vol II. LC 73-85939. 265p. 1980. pap. 7.95 (*0-913480-41-X*) Inter Am U Pr.
— Readings in Spanish-English Contrastive Linguistics, Vol. III. LC 73-85939. 270p. (C). 1982. pap. text ed. 9.95 (*0-913480-42-8*) Inter Am U Pr.
Nash, Roy. Conquest of Brazil. LC 67-29550. 1926. 25.00 (*0-8196-0207-8*) Biblo.
— Intelligence & Realism: A Materialist Critique of IQ. LC 90-31922. 192p. 1990. text ed. 45.00 (*0-312-04736-3*) St Martin.
Nash, S. Nash Family: or Records of the Descendants of Thomas Nash of New Haven, Connecticut, 1640. (Illus.). 304p. 1989. reprint ed. lib. bdg. 53.50 (*0-8328-0896-2*); reprint ed. pap. 45.50 (*0-8328-0897-0*) Higginson Bk Co.
— Paul Valery's "Album des Vers Anciens" A Past Transfigured. 1982. 47.00 (*0-691-06526-8*) Princeton U Pr.
Nash, Scott, ed. Interpreting Galatians for Teaching & Preaching. (Kerygna & Church Ser.). 192p. (Orig.). 1994. pap. 11.95 (*1-880837-87-0*) Smyth & Helwys.
— The Sermon on the Mount: Studies & Sermons. LC 92-42137. (Kerygma & Church Ser.). 192p. 1992. pap. 8.95 (*1-880837-06-4*) Smyth & Helwys.
Nash, Seymour C., jt. auth. see Meyer, Sylvan.
Nash, Stanley D. Prostitution in Great Britain, 1485-1901: An Annotated Bibliography. LC 94-331. 267p. 1994. 32.50 (*0-8108-2734-4*) Scarecrow.
Nash, Stephen G. A History of Scientific Computing. (ACM Press History Ser.). (Illus.). 304p. (C). 1990. text ed. 50.50 (*0-201-50814-1*) Addison-Wesley.
***Nash, Stephen G., et al, eds.** The Impact of Emerging Technologies on Computer Science & Operations Research. LC 94-41217. (Operations Research - Computer Science Interface Ser.). 328p. (C). 1995. lib. bdg. 92.50 (*0-7923-9542-5*) Kluwer Ac.
***Nash, Steven A.** Arneson & Politics: A Commemorative Exhibition. LC 93-73198. (Illus.). 56p. 1995. pap. 14.95 (*0-88401-077-5*) Fine Arts Mus.
— Ben Nicholson: Fifty Years of His Art. LC 78-62949. (Illus.). 1978. 14.00 (*0-914782-21-5*) Buffalo Acad.
***Nash, Steven A., ed.** Facing Eden: 100 Years of Landscape Art in the Bay Area. (Illus.). 250p. 1995. 50.00 (*0-520-20362-3*); pap. 29.95 (*0-520-20363-1*) U CA Pr.
Nash, Steven A. & Albright-Knox Art Gallery Staff. Painting & Sculpture from Antiquity to Nineteen Forty-Two. LC 77-79651. (Illus.). 1979. pap. 25.00 (*0-914782-17-7*) Buffalo Acad.
Nash, Steven A. & Merkert, Joern, eds. Naum Gabo: Sixty Years of Constructivism. (Illus.). 272p. 1985. 60.00 (*3-7913-0742-8*, Pub. by Prestel) TeNeues.
Nash, Steven A., jt. auth. see Albright-Knox Art Gallery Staff.
Nash, Steven A., jt. auth. see Eitner, Lorenz E.
Nash, Sue, jt. auth. see Khdir, Kate.
***Nash, Susan S.** A Half-Dozen Eclairs. 60p. Date not set. pap. 10.00 (*0-9641837-3-0*) Texture Pr.
— Liquid Babylon. 55p. (Orig.). Date not set. pap. 8.00 (*1-884438-07-5*) Epiphany AR.
— Liquid Babylon. limited ed. 60p. (Orig.). 1994. pap. 18.00 (*0-937013-50-1*) Potes Poets.
— A Paleontologist's Notebook. (Illus.). 96p. 1995. pap. 9.00 (*1-880516-16-0*) Left Hand Bks.
— Pornography. (Chapbook Ser.). 24p. 1992. pap. 4.00 (*0-945112-15-7*) Generator Pr.
***Nash, Susan S., ed.** Texture: Journal of Writing & Art, No. 6. 200p. (Orig.). 1995. pap. 10.00 (*0-9641837-2-2*) Texture Pr.
Nash, Suzanne. Les Contemplations of Victor Hugo: An Allegory of the Creative Process. LC 76-3273. 239p. reprint ed. pap. 68.20 (*0-8357-6188-6*, 2034297) Bks Demand.
— Paul Valery's Album de Vers Anciens: A Past Transfigured. LC 82-47606. 339p. reprint ed. pap. 96.70 (*0-7837-1934-5*, 2042149) Bks Demand.
Nash, Suzanne, ed. Home & Its Dislocations in Nineteenth-Century France. LC 92-31575. (SUNY Series, The Margins of Literature). 345p. (C). 1993. 64.50 (*0-7914-1549-X*); pap. 21.95 (*0-7914-1550-3*) State U NY Pr.
***Nash, T. H., 3rd, et al.** A Revision of the Lichen Genus Xanthoparmelia in South America. (Bibliotheca Lichenologica Ser.: Vol. 56). (Illus.). 156p. 1995. pap. 64.00x (*3-443-58035-1*, Pub. by Cramer-Borntraeger GW) Lubrecht & Cramer.
Nash, T. M. & Nash, C. Robert. Quick Reference Guide to WordStar. (Opposing Viewpoints Sources Ser.). 82p. 1985. student ed 19.95 (*0-934569-99-1*) Nash Group.
Nash, Theodore E. Love & Vengeance, or Little Viola's Victory. LC 78-173016. reprint ed. 16.45 (*0-404-00095-9*) AMS Pr.
Nash, Thomas. Pierce Penilesse. (BCL1-PR English Literature Ser.). 137p. 1992. reprint ed. lib. bdg. 69.00 (*0-7812-7217-3*) Rprt Serv.
Nash, Thomas, jt. auth. see Marlowe, Christopher.
***Nash, Thomas H., 3rd, ed.** Lichen Biology. (Illus.). 320p. (C). 1995. write for info. (*0-521-45368-2*); pap. write for info. (*0-521-45974-5*) Cambridge U Pr.
***Nash, Tom.** The Christian Communicator's Handbook. 240p. 1995. 17.99 (*1-56476-384-6*, 6-3384, Victor Books) SP Pubns.
Nash, Tom & Scofield, Twilo. The Well-Traveled Casket: A Collection of Oregon Folklife. LC 92-53609. (Illus.). 176p. (Orig.). 1992. pap. 24.95 (*0-87480-390-X*) U of Utah Pr.
Nash, Tony. Farewell Mum & Dad: The Diary of a London Evacuee. 114p. 1991. pap. 4.50 (*0-9630676-0-5*) T Nash.
Nash, Valery. The Narrows. (CSU Poetry Ser.: No. 7). 62p. (Orig.). 1980. pap. 3.50 (*0-914946-16-1*) Cleveland St Univ Poetry Ctr.
Nash, Vincent, tr. see Durckheim, Karlfried G.
Nash, W. G. Bricklaying. (Illus.). 128p. (Orig.). 1991. pap. 24.00 (*0-7487-1292-5*, Pub. by Stanley Thornes UK) Trans-Atl Phila.
— Brickwork, Vol. 1. 152p. (C). 1983. pap. 30.00x (*0-7487-0266-0*, Pub. by S Thornes Pubs UK) St Mut.
— Brickwork, Vol. 2. rev. ed. 204p. (C). 1988. pap. 33.00x (*0-7487-0310-1*, Pub. by S Thornes Pubs UK) St Mut.
— Brickwork 2. 224p. (C). 1988. pap. 30.00x (*0-7487-0265-2*, Pub. by S Thornes Pubs UK) St Mut.
Nash, W. J. A Bibliography of Trouchus (Trochus Niloticus L.) (Bibliographies Ser.: No. 7). 1987. pap. 3.00 (*971-10-2232-X*, Pub. by ICLARM PH) Intl Spec Bk.
Nash, W. J., jt. ed. see Munro, J. L.
Nash, Wallis. Oregon: There & Back in 1877. Munford, J. Kenneth, ed. LC 76-9770. (Illus.). 348p. 1976. reprint ed. 19.95 (*0-87071-077-X*) Oreg St U Pr.
Nash, Walter. Jargon: Its Uses & Abuses. LC 92-36120. (Language Library). 1993. 24.95 (*0-631-18063-X*) Blackwell Pubs.
— Language in Popular Fiction. (Interface Ser.). 256p. 1990. 45.00 (*0-415-04047-7*, A4183); pap. 14.95 (*0-415-02944-9*, A4187) Routledge.
— The Language of Humor. (English Language Ser.). (C). 1985. pap. text ed. 18.95 (*0-582-29127-5*, 71754) Longman.
— An Uncommon Tongue: The Uses & Resources of English. LC 91-30397. 192p. (Orig.). 1992. 69.95 (*0-415-06360-4*, A6693); pap. 16.95 (*0-415-06361-2*, A6697) Routledge.
Nash, Walter, ed. The Writing Scholar: Language & Conventions of Academic Disclosure. (Written Communication Annual Ser.: Vol. 3). (Illus.). 320p. (C). 1990. 52.00 (*0-8039-3692-3*) Sage.
Nash, Walter, jt. auth. see Carter, Ronald.
Nash, Walter F. Under the Skin of the Road. 1993. pap. 9.00 (*0-9639407-0-8*) W F Nash.
Nash, Wanda. At Ease with Stress. LC 91-65006. 224p. (Orig.). 1991. pap. 9.95 (*0-89622-482-1*, C55) Twenty-Third.
Nash, William A. Schaum's Outline of Strength of Materials. 3rd ed. 1994. pap. text ed. 14.95 (*0-07-045903-7*) McGraw.
— Statics & Mechanics of Materials: Including 400 Solved Problems. 1992. pap. text ed. 13.95 (*0-07-045896-0*) McGraw.
Nash-Williams, A. H. Legenda. 88p. (C). 1982. pap. text ed. 39.00 (*0-900269-18-9*, Pub. by Old Vicarage UK) St Mut.
Nashabe, Hisham. Muslim Educational Institutions. 1989. 16.95 (*0-86685-470-3*) Intl Bk Ctr.
Nashabe, Hisham, ed. Studia Palaestina: Studies in Honour of Constantine K. Zurayk. xviii, 477p. (ARA, ENG & FRE.). 1989. 29.95 (*0-88728-202-4*) Inst Palestine.
Nashashibi. Jerusalem's Other Voice. 1991. 49.95 (*0-86372-117-6*, Pub. by Ithaca UK) Paul & Co Pubs.
Nashashibi, Adib Y., et al. Measurement & Modeling Millimeter-Wave Response from Soil Surfaces. (University of Michigan Report Ser.: No. 029721-2-T). 60p. reprint ed. pap. 25.00 (*0-7837-6779-X*, 2046609) Bks Demand.
Nashashibi, Karim. The Fiscal Dimensions of Adjustment in Low-Income Countries. (Occasional Paper Ser.: No. 95). vi, 59p. 1992. pap. 15.00 (*1-55775-229-X*) Intl Monetary.
***Nashashibi, Salwa M., et al.** Forces of Change: Artists of the Arab World. 146p. 1994. 39.95 (*0-940979-27-6*) Natl Museum Women.
— Forces of Change: Artists of the Arab World. LC 93-47447. 146p. 1994. pap. 29.95 (*0-940979-26-8*) Natl Museum Women.
Nashat, Guity, ed. Middle Eastern History. (Selected Reading Lists & Course Outlines from Leading American Colleges & Universities Ser.). 300p. (Orig.). 1988. pap. 16.95 (*0-910129-70-3*) Wiener Pubs Inc.
Nashe, Thomas. A Concordance to the Works of Thomas Nashe, 2 vols., Set. Ule, Louis, ed. (Elizabethan Concordance Ser.). 1000p. write for info. (*3-487-09704-4*, Pub. by Georg Olms GW) Lubrecht & Cramer.
— The Unfortunate Traveller & Other Stories. Steanie, J. B., ed. (English Library). 512p. 1972. pap. 11.95 (*0-14-043067-9*, Penguin Classics) Viking Penguin.
Nashed, Fred. Time-Saving Techniques for Architectural Construction Drawings. LC 92-18922. 1993. text ed. 49.95 (*0-442-00951-8*) Van Nos Reinhold.
Nashed, N. Mokhtar, ed. see Alexander, L. D. & Thorpe, A. Dale.
Nashed, Z., ed. see Morozov, V. A.
Nashelsky, Louis. Introduction to Digital Technology. 4th ed. LC 93-6084. 448p. 1994. text ed. write for info. (*0-13-497785-8*) Prentice ESL.
Nashelsky, Louis & Boylestad, Robert L. IBM-PC-XT: BASIC Programming & Applications. (Illus.). 304p. 1986. 41.95 (*0-13-448341-3*); pap. 22.50 (*0-13-448325-1*); student ed, disk (*0-318-57914-6*) P-H.

An Asterisk (*) at the beginning of an entry indicates that the title is appearing in BIP for the first time.

Nashelsky, Louis, jt. auth. see Boylestad, Robert L.

Nashif, Ahid D., et al. Vibration Damping. LC 84-17247. 453p. 1985. text ed. 95.00 (*0-471-86772-1*, Wiley-Interscience) Wiley.

Nashif, Taysir. Nuclear Warfare in the Middle East: Dimensions & Responsibilities. (Leaders, Politics, & Social Change in the Islamic World Ser.: Vol. 3). 142p. 1984. 15.00 (*0-940670-20-8*) Kingston Pr.

Nashman, Honey W., jt. auth. see Hoare, Carol H.

***Nashoba, Nuchi.** Ben Nighthorse Campbell, Senator & Artist. (Illus.). (J). (gr. 1-4). 1995. lib. bdg. 9.95 (*0-8136-5757-1*); pap. 4.95 (*0-8136-5763-6*) Modern Curr.

Nashofer, Rachelle. The Eyes of Tomorrow. LC 86-72868. 125p. (Orig.). 1987. pap. 7.00 (*0-916383-22-9*) Aegina Pr.

Nashold, B. S., Jr., et al, eds. International Symposium Dorsal Root Entry Zone (DREZ) Lesions, Durham, N. C., 2nd, April 1987. (Journal: Applied Neurophysiology: Vol. 51, Nos. 2-5, 1988). (Illus.). 204p. 1988. pap. 144.00 (*3-8055-4747-1*) S Karger.

Nashold, Blaine S., Jr., ed. see Ovelmen-Levitt, Janice.

Nashone. Grandmother Stories of the Northwest: Northwestern Indian Tales. (Illus.). (J). (gr. 5-12). 1987. pap. 6.95 (*0-940113-06-6*) Sierra Oaks Pub.

— Where Indians Live: American Indian Houses. (Illus.). 37p. (Orig.). (J). (gr. k-6). 1989. pap. 6.95 (*0-940113-16-3*) Sierra Oaks Pub.

NASI Staff. Security for America's Children: Proceedings of the Fourth Annual Conference of NASI. 176p. 1992. pap. text ed. 34.95 (*0-8403-8250-2*) Kendall-Hunt.

— Social Insurance Issues '90s. 240p. 1992. boxed 34.95 (*0-8403-7409-7*) Kendall-Hunt.

Nasibova, A. Faceted Chamber in the Moscow Kremlin. (Illus.). 228p. (C). 1978. text ed. 130.00 (*0-685-40307-6*, Pub. by Collets) St Mut.

Nasibova, Aida. Art Treasures of the Moscow Kremlin. (Illus.). 238p. (C). 1988. text ed. 300.00 (*0-685-40303-3*, Pub. by Collets) St Mut.

Nasibova, Aida & Mendeleyev, William. Art Treasures of the Moscow Kremlin. 200p. 1984. 275.00 (*0-317-61218-2*, Pub. by Collets) St Mut.

Nasim, Anjum. Financing Pakistan's Development in the 1990s. 631p. 1993. 38.00 (*0-19-577459-0*) OUP.

Nasim, Anwar, jt. ed. see Hurst, A.

Nasim, Anwar, et al, eds. Molecular Biology of the Fission Yeast. (Cell Biology Ser.). 545p. 1989. text ed. 140.00 (*0-12-514085-1*) Acad Pr.

Nasipuri, D. Stereochemistry of Organic Compounds: Principles & Applications. (C). 1991. 55.00 (*0-685-51528-1*, Pub. by Wiley Eastern II) S Asia.

Nasir, Jamal, ed. The Status of Women under Islamic Law: And under Modern Arab Islamic Legislation. (C). 1990. pap. text ed. 58.00 (*1-85333-280-1*, Pub. by Graham & Trotman UK) Kluwer Ac.

Nasir, Jamal J. The Islamic Law of Personal Status. 2nd ed. 1986. lib. bdg. 108.00 (*0-86010-825-2*); lib. bdg. 179.00 (*0-86010-826-0*) G & T Inc.

Nasiruddin, Al-Amir. Ar-Rafed: Arabic-Arabic Dictionary. 1971. 19.95 (*0-86685-101-1*) Intl Bk Ctr.

Nasiruddin, Emir. Characteristics & Peculiarities of the Arabic Language. (ARA.). 1971. 25.00 (*0-86685-056-2*) Intl Bk Ctr.

Nasisse, Andy & Wahlam, Maude. Baking in the Sun: Visionary Images from the South. (Illus.). 136p. (Orig.). 1987. pap. 20.00 (*0-936819-02-0*) USL Art Museum.

Nasisse, Andy, jt. auth. see Wahlman, Maude S.

Nasjleti, Maria, jt. auth. see James, Beverly.

Naske, Claus M. Bob Bartlett of Alaska...a Life in Politics. LC 79-65321. (Illus.). 247p. 1979. 12.95 (*0-912006-05-6*) U of Alaska Pr.

— A History of Alaska Statehood. LC 84-29123. 322p. (Orig.). 1985. pap. text ed. 28.00 (*0-8191-4556-4*) U Pr of Amer.

— Paving Alaska'a Trails: The Work of the Alaska Road Commission. LC 86-15850. (Illus.). 354p. (Orig.). (C). 1986. lib. bdg. 62.00 (*0-8191-5576-4*) U Pr of Amer.

Naske, Claus M. & Rowinski, Ludwig J. Anchorage: A Pictorial History. Friedman, Donna R., ed. LC 80-28128. (Illus.). 208p. 1982. pap. 13.95 (*0-89865-106-9*) Donning Co.

Naske, Claus M. & Slotnick, Herman E. Alaska: A History of the 49th State. 2nd ed. LC 87-40215. (Illus.). 368p. 1994. pap. 16.95 (*0-8061-2573-X*) U of Okla Pr.

Naslain, R. & Harris, B., eds. Ceramic Matrix Composites: Components, Preparation, Microstructure & Properties. 346p. 1990. reprint ed. 171.00 (*1-85166-460-2*) Elsevier.

Nasledov, Dmitrii N. & Goryunova, N. A., eds. Soviet Research in New Semiconductor Materials. Tybulewicz, A., tr. LC 65-11956. 126p. reprint ed. pap. 36.00 (*0-317-09195-6*, 2020668) Bks Demand.

Naslin, P. Dynamics of Linear & Non-Linear Systems. 614p. 1965. text ed. 372.00 (*0-677-10710-2*) Gordon & Breach.

***Naslund, Agneta.** Curacao, a Cat & Her Friends. 1995. 11.95 (*0-285-63164-0*, Pub. by Souvenir UK) Atrium Pubs.

Naslund, Sena J. The Animal Way to Love. LC 92-75262. 1993. pap. 12.00 (*0-935331-14-X*) Ampersand RI.

— Ice Skating at the North Pole. 120p. 1989. pap. 10.00 (*0-935331-08-5*) Ampersand RI.

— Sherlock in Love. 232p. 1993. 21.95 (*0-87923-977-8*) Godine.

Naslund, Willard E. NATO Airpower: Organizing For Uncertainty. LC 93-38717. 1994. write for info. (*0-8330-1474-9*, MR-215-AF) Rand Corp.

Nasman, Leonard O. Beginning Cadkey Light. 240p. (Orig.). Date not set. pap. text ed. 29.95 (*1-880544-12-1*) Micro Educ.

— Beginning Cadkey 6. (Illus.). 440p. (C). 1993. pap. 36.95 (*1-880544-18-0*, CAD6-1) Micro Educ.

— Beginning DataCAD. LC 91-66358. 165p. (C). 1991. pap. 29.95 (*1-880544-00-8*) Micro Educ.

— The Cadkey Seven Workbook. (Illus.). 110p. 1994. student ed 19.95 (*1-880544-49-0*, CAD7-1) Micro Educ.

— Cadkey 107: The Complete Cadkey 7 Textbook. (Illus.). 330p. 1995. pap. text ed. 43.95 (*1-880544-51-2*, CAD7-2) Micro Educ.

— An Introduction to Datacad 5. (Illus.). 302p. (C). 1994. pap. 34.95 (*1-880544-34-2*, DCAD5-1) Micro Educ.

— El Libro de Datacad 5 en Espanol. Herrera, Raul, tr. (Illus.). 120p. (SPA.). 1994. student ed 15.95 (*1-880544-37-7*, DCAD5-2) Micro Educ.

— The Mastercam 4 Design Workbook. (Illus.). 100p. 1994. student ed 24.95 (*1-880544-48-2*) Micro Educ.

Nasmith, David. Institutes of English Adjective Law (Procedure in Court) Embracing an Outline of the Law of Evidence & Measure of Damages. xxi, 355p. 1980. reprint ed. lib. bdg. 30.00 (*0-8377-0904-0*) Rothman.

— Institutes of English Private Law: Embracing an Outline of the Substantive Branch of the Law of Persons & Things, 2 vols., Set. 720p. 1980. reprint ed. lib. bdg. 57.50 (*0-8377-0903-2*) Rothman.

— Institutes of English Public Law: Embracing an Outline of General Jurisprudence, the Development of the British Constitution, Public International Law, & the Public Municipal Law of England. vi, 455p. 1980. reprint ed. lib. bdg. 35.00 (*0-8377-0905-9*) Rothman.

Nasmyth, Spike, jt. auth. see Nasmyth, Virginia.

Nasmyth, Virginia & Nasmyth, Spike. Hanoi Release John Nasmyth. Behar, June, ed. (Illus.). 345p. 1984. 15.95 (*0-9613991-0-4*) V Parr Pub.

Nason, Arthur H. Heralds & Heraldry in Ben Jonson's Plays, Masques & Entertainments. LC 68-59042. 173p. (C). 1968. reprint ed. 45.00 (*0-87752-076-3*) Gordian.

— James Shirley, Dramatist. LC 67-23860. (Illus.). 1972. reprint ed. 30.95 (*0-405-08813-2*, Pub. by Blom Pubns UK) Ayer.

Nason, E. Howe Family Gathering, Harmony Grove, S. Framingham, Massachusetts, 1871. 46p. 1994. reprint ed. pap. 9.00 (*0-8328-4128-5*) Higginson Bk Co.

Nason, Elias. A History of the Town of Dunstable, Mass., from Its Earliest Settlement to the Year 1873. (Illus.). 316p. 1989. reprint ed. lib. bdg. 32.00 (*0-8328-0824-5*, MA0045) Higginson Bk Co.

Nason, James D., jt. auth. see Marshall, Mac.

Nason, Janet. Little Women Paper Dolls. 8p. (J). (gr. 8-12). 1982. pap. 4.00 (*0-914510-13-4*) Evergreen.

Nason, Jerry, et al. Famous American Athletes of Today, Seventh Series. LC 70-93348. (Essay Index Reprint Ser.: Famous Leaders Ser). 1977. reprint ed. 30.95 (*0-8369-2250-6*) Ayer.

Nason, John. Foundation Trusteeship: Service in the Public Interest. LC 88-38128. (Orig.). 1989. pap. 19.95 (*0-87954-285-3*) Foundation Ctr.

Nason, John W. Board Assessment of the Chief Executive: A Responsibility Essential to Good Governance. (Nonprofit Governance Ser.). 16p. 1990. pap. text ed. 10.00 (*0-925299-04-9*) Natl Ctr Nonprofit.

— The Nature of Trusteeship. 136p. 1982. 16.00 (*0-318-17378-6*) Assn Gov Bds.

— The Nature of Trusteeship: The Role & Responsibilities of College & University Boards. LC 83-174535. 102p. 1982. 9.95 (*0-318-03585-5*) Assn Gov Bds.

— Presidential Assessment. 86p. 1980. 18.00 (*0-318-17382-4*) Assn Gov Bds.

— Presidential Search. 92p. 1982. 18.00 (*0-318-17380-8*) Assn Gov Bds.

— Trustees & the Future of Foundations. LC 77-76677. 112p. 1977. pap. 12.00 (*0-913892-00-9*) Coun Found.

***Nason, Joseph G. & Holt, Robert L.** Horio, You Next Die! LC 86-62760. 264p. 1987. 14.95 (*0-930926-11-0*) Calif Fin Pubns.

Nason, Norman, jt. intro. see Doyle, William.

Nason, Richard. A Modern Dunciad. LC 77-92992. 114p. 1978. pap. 8.00 (*0-912292-49-0*) The Smith.

— Old Soldiers. LC 88-90815. (Illus.). 68p. (Orig.). 1988. pap. 8.95 (*0-912292-80-6*) The Smith.

— The Wedding at Touisset. LC 75-538. (Illus.). 56p. 1975. pap. 6.00 (*0-912292-37-7*) The Smith.

Nason, Richard W. Boiled Grass & the Broth of Shoes: Reconstructing Literary Deconstruction. LC 91-52758. 176p. 1991. lib. bdg. 31.50x (*0-89950-643-7*) McFarland & Co.

— Two Radicals: Unpublished Essays on Jean Genet & Ezra Pound Plus Selected Reviews on Sundry Subjects. LC 92-75617. 112p. 1993. pap. 25.00 (*0-9635297-5-7*) Black Spruce.

Nason, Tema. Full Moon. LC 93-25035. 39p. (Orig.). 1993. 7.95 (*0-9619111-5-8*) Chicory Blue.

Nason, Thelma C. A Stranger Here, Myself. Hunting, Constance, ed. 1980. pap. 3.50 (*0-913006-11-4*) Puckerbrush.

Nason, Thelma C., tr. see Ulibarri, Sabine R., et al.

Naspitz & Tinkelman. Childhood Rhinitis & Sinusitis: Pathophysiology & Treatment. (Allergic Disease & Therapy Ser.: Vol. 3). 304p. 1990. 99.75 (*0-8247-8228-3*) Dekker.

Naspitz, Charles K., jt. ed. see Tinkelman, David G.

Nasr Al-Din. Tales of Nasr-ed-Din Khoja. Barnham, Henry D., tr. LC 77-87632. 1977. reprint ed. 23.00 (*0-404-16457-9*) AMS Pr.

Nasr, H. & Sadiadi, F., eds. Signal & Image Processing Systems Performance Evaluation. 1990. 53.00 (*0-8194-0361-X*, VOL. 1310) SPIE.

Nasr, H. N., ed. Image Understanding for Aerospace Applications. 1991. 53.00 (*0-8194-0649-X*, VOL. 1521) SPIE.

Nasr, H. N., jt. auth. see Bazakos, M. E.

Nasr, H. N., jt. ed. see Larson, R. M.

Nasr, Hatem, ed. Selected Papers on Model-Based Vision. LC 92-42878. (Milestone Ser.: Vol. MS 72). 1993. write for info. (*0-8194-1164-7*); pap. write for info. (*0-8194-1165-5*) SPIE.

Nasr, Hatem N., ed. Automatic Object Recognition. (Institute Ser.: Vol. IS07). 254p. 1991. 62.00 (*0-8194-0467-5*) SPIE.

Nasr, Julinda A., et al, eds. Women, Employment & Development in the Arab World. LC 84-9935. (New Babylon Studies in the Social Sciences: No. 41). xi, 146p. 1985. 33.35 (*90-279-3380-4*) Mouton.

Nasr, Kameel. Bicycle Touring International: The Complete Book on Adventure Cycling. LC 92-75117. (Illus.). 256p. 1992. 18.95 (*0-933201-53-2*) Bicycle Books.

Nasr, Khatib. Al Mufid: Learner's English-Arabic Dictionary. 1983. 28.00 (*0-86685-376-6*) Intl Bk Ctr.

Nasr, Louise H. Geothermal Loan Guaranty Program & Its Impact on Exploration & Development. 207p. 1979. pap. 1.00 (*0-918062-05-5*) Colo Sch Mines.

Nasr, Mohammed. Arabic Standard Atlas Book. (ARA.). 1983. pap. 14.95 (*0-86685-164-X*) Intl Bk Ctr.

Nasr, Raja. Colloquial Arabic: An Oral Approach. (ARA.). 1968. 16.95 (*0-86685-044-9*) Intl Bk Ctr.

— English Colloquial Arabic Dictionary. 1972. pap. 6.95x (*0-86685-079-1*) Intl Bk Ctr.

— Intermediate Colloquial Arabic Course. 1974. 17.95 (*0-86685-046-5*) Intl Bk Ctr.

— Learn to Read Arabic. 1977. pap. 5.50x (*0-917062-02-7*); audio 20.00x (*0-86685-631-5*) Intl Bk Ctr.

— Structure of Arabic: From Sound to Sentence. 1968. 17.95 (*0-86685-045-7*) Intl Bk Ctr.

— Teaching of Arabic As a Foreign Language. 12.95 (*0-86685-047-3*) Intl Bk Ctr.

Nasr, Raja T. Communicate in Colloquial Arabic. 1989. 12.00x (*0-86685-457-6*) Intl Bk Ctr.

— A First English Dictionary: For ESL Students. 276p. 1994. lib. bdg. 44.50 (*0-8191-9730-0*) U Pr of Amer.

— A First English Dictionary: For ESL Students. 276p. (C). 1994. pap. text ed. 19.95 (*0-8191-9731-9*) U Pr of Amer.

— Ten International Short Stories: For ESL Students. LC 94-48840. 1995. write for info. (*0-8191-9865-X*) U Pr of Amer.

— Thirty International Short Stories: For ESL Students. LC 94-48843. 1995. pap. write for info. (*0-8191-9864-1*) U Pr of Amer.

— Twenty International Short Stories: For ESL Students. LC 94-48839. 1995. pap. write for info. (*0-8191-9866-8*) U Pr of Amer.

— Whole Education: A New Direction to Fill the Relevance Gap. LC 94-21380. 138p. (Orig.). (C). reprint ed. lib. bdg. 39.50 (*0-8191-9609-6*); reprint ed. pap. text ed. 24.50 (*0-8191-9610-X*) U Pr of Amer.

Nasr, S. H. Muhammad: Man of God. 96p. 1994. pap. 7.95 (*1-56744-501-2*) Kazi Pubns.

Nasr, Sayyed H., tr. see Tabatabai, Muhammad.

Nasr, Seyyed H. Ideals & Realities of Islam. 1994. reprint ed. pap. 14.00 (*1-85538-409-4*, Pub. by Aquarian Pr UK) Thorsons SF.

— An Introduction to Islamic Cosmological Doctrines. LC 92-25842. 322p. (C). 1993. 49.50 (*0-7914-1515-5*); pap. 16.95 (*0-7914-1516-3*) State U NY Pr.

— Islamic Art & Spirituality. LC 85-14737. (Illus.). 213p. 1987. 59.50 (*0-88706-174-5*); pap. 19.95 (*0-88706-175-3*) State U NY Pr.

— Islamic Intellectual Tradition in Persia. Aminrazavi, Mehdi, ed. 360p. (C). 1995. text ed. 70.00 (*0-7007-0314-4*, Pub. by Curzon Pr UK) Humanities.

— Islamic Life & Thought. LC 81-4723. 232p. (C). 1981. 59.50 (*0-87395-490-4*); pap. 19.95 (*0-87395-491-2*) State U NY Pr.

— Islamic Science: An Illustrated Study. (Illus.). 320p. (C). 1995. pap. text ed. 29.95 (*1-56744-502-0*) Kazi Pubns.

— Knowledge & the Sacred. LC 89-31177. 341p. 1989. 49.50 (*0-7914-0176-6*); pap. 16.95 (*0-7914-0177-4*) State U NY Pr.

— Science & Civilization in Islam. LC 68-25616. 384p. reprint ed. pap. 109.50 (*0-7837-4122-7*, 2057945) Bks Demand.

— The Soviet Union & Arab Nationalism. 320p. 1987. text ed. 65.00 (*0-7103-0213-4*, Pub. by Kegan Paul Intl UK) Routledge Chapman & Hall.

— Sufi Essays. 2nd ed. LC 91-20958. 184p. 1991. 49.50 (*0-7914-1051-X*); pap. 16.95 (*0-7914-1052-8*) State U NY Pr.

— Three Muslim Sages. LC 75-14430. 192p. (C). 1976. reprint ed. pap. text ed. 15.00x (*0-88206-500-9*) Caravan Bks.

— Traditional Islam in the Modern World. 320p. 1987. text ed. 49.50 (*0-7103-0177-4*) Routledge Chapman & Hall.

— Traditional Islam in the Modern World. 200p. 1989. pap. 19.95 (*0-7103-0332-7*) Routledge Chapman & Hall.

Nasr, Seyyed H., ed. The Essential Writings of Frithjof Schuon. (Roots of Wisdom Bks.). 552p. 1986. 34.95 (*0-916349-05-5*) Amity Hse Inc.

— The Essential Writings of Frithjof Schuon. 552p. 1991. pap. 29.95 (*1-85230-260-7*) Element MA.

— Islamic Spirituality I. (World Spirituality Ser.). (Illus.). 496p. 1987. 49.50 (*0-8245-0767-3*) Crossroad NY.

— Islamic Spirituality I: Foundations. (World Spirituality: An Encyclopedic History of the Religious Quest Ser.: Vol. 19). (Illus.). 480p. 1991. reprint ed. pap. 19.95 (*0-8245-1131-X*) Crossroad NY.

***Nasr, Seyyed H. & Leaman, Oliver, eds.** History of Islamic Philosophy. LC 95-6053. (Library of Philosophy: No. 1). 1995. write for info. (*0-415-05667-5*) Routledge.

Nasr, Seyyed H. & O'Brien, Katherine, eds. In Quest of the Sacred. 220p. (Orig.). 1994. pap. 14.95 (*0-9629984-2-7*) Foun Trad Studies.

Nasr, Seyyed H. & Stoddart, William, eds. Religion of the Heart: Essays Presented to Frithjof Schuon on His Eightieth Birthday. 1991. pap. 23.95 (*0-9629984-0-0*) Foun Trad Studies.

Nasr, Seyyed H., tr. see Muhammed H. al-Tabataba'i.

Nasr, Seyyed H., tr. see Omar, Khayyam.

Nasr, Seyyed H., et al, eds. Expectation of the Millennium: Shi'ism in History. LC 87-35326. 460p. (C). 1989. 74.50 (*0-88706-843-X*); pap. 24.95 (*0-88706-844-8*) State U NY Pr.

***Nasr, Seyyed V.** Mawlana Mawdudi & the Making of Islamic Revivalism. (Illus.). 256p. 1995. 45.00 (*0-19-509695-9*) OUP.

— The Vanguard of Islamic Revolution: The Jamaat-I Islami of Pakistan. LC 93-5403. (Comparative Studies on Muslim Societies: No. 19). 1994. 50.00 (*0-520-08368-7*); pap. 20.00 (*0-520-08369-5*) U CA Pr.

Nasr, Seyyed V. R., jt. ed. see Dabashi, Hamid.

Nasr, Zacharia. A Dictionary of Economics & Commerce. 320p. (ARA, ENG & FRE.). 1980. write for info. (*0-8288-0151-7*, M15757) Fr & Eur.

Nasrallah. A House Not Her Own: Stories from Beirut. (NFS Canada Ser.). Date not set. pap. 12.95 (*0-921881-19-3*, Pub. by Gynergy-Ragweed CN) InBook.

Nasrallah, H. A. & Weinberger, D. R., eds. Handbook of Schizophrenia Vol. 1: The Neurology of Schizophrenia. 430p. 1986. 228.25 (*0-444-90415-8*) Elsevier.

***Nasrallah, Hassan A. & Balling, Robert C., Jr.** The Heated Debate: Greenhouse Predictions vs. Climate Reality, Middle Eastern Edition. LC 94-46524. 1995. write for info. (*0-936488-68-9*) PRIPP.

***Nasrallah, Henry A. & Pettegrew, Jay W., eds.** NMR Spectroscopy in Psychiatric Brain Disorders. LC 94-34269. (Progress in Psychiatry Ser.: No. 47). 1995. boxed 32.50 (*0-88048-483-7*, 8483) Am Psychiatric.

Nasrallah, Henry A., jt. ed. see Henn, Fritz A.

Nasrallah, Henry A., jt. ed. see Shriqui, Christian L.

Nasrallah, Ibrahim. Prairies of Fever. Jayyusi, M. & Reed, J., trs. LC 92-23386. (Emerging Voices: New International Fiction Ser.). 160p. 1993. 22.95 (*1-56656-103-5*); pap. 9.95 (*1-56656-106-X*) Interlink Pub.

Nasri, William Z. Crisis in Copyright. LC 75-43046. (Books in Library & Information Science: No. 18). (Illus.). 190p. reprint ed. pap. 54.20 (*0-8357-6082-0*, 2034555) Bks Demand.

***Nasrin, Taslima.** The Game in Reverse: Poems & Essays. Wright, Carolyne et al, trs. 128p. 1995. pap. 14.95 (*0-8076-1392-4*) Braziller.

— The Game in Reverse: Poems & Essays. Wright, Carolyne et al, trs. 64p. 1995. 25.00 (*0-8076-1391-6*) Braziller.

Nasrudin, Mullah. The Pleasantries of the Incredible Mullah Nasrudin. 224p. 1993. pap. 11.95 (*0-14-019357-X*, Penguin Bks) Viking Penguin.

Nass & Heiberger. Encyclopedia of PVC, Vol. 1. 2nd exp. rev. ed. 720p. 1986. 199.00 (*0-8247-7427-2*) Dekker.

— Encyclopedia of PVC, Vol. 2. 2nd expanded rev. ed. 696p. 1987. 199.00 (*0-8247-7695-X*) Dekker.

— Encyclopedia of PVC, Vol. 3. 2nd rev. ed. 608p. 1992. 199.00 (*0-8247-7822-7*) Dekker.

Nass, David, ed. Holiday: Minnesotans Remember the Farmers' Holiday Association. 221p. (Orig.). 1984. pap. 5.95 (*0-918461-00-6*) Plains Press.

Nass, Elyse. Avenue of Dream. 1970. pap. 2.75 (*0-8222-0083-X*) Dramatists Play.

Nass, G., ed. Modified Nucleosides & Cancer: Workshop, Freiburg, FRG, 1981. (Recent Results in Cancer Research Ser.: Vol. 84). (Illus.). 440p. 1983. 86.00 (*0-387-12024-6*) Spr-Verlag.

Nass, Gilbert D., et al. Sexual Choices: An Introduction to Human Sexuality. LC 83-25951. 650p. (C). 1984. reprint ed. pap. text ed. 25.00 (*0-86720-392-7*) Jones & Bartlett.

Nass, Gilbert D. & Fisher, Mary P. Sexuality Today. 488p. (C). 1988. teacher ed 10.00 (*0-86720-414-1*); boxed 38.75 (*0-86720-408-7*) Jones & Bartlett.

Nass, Herbert E. Wills of the Rich & Famous. 1991. pap. 9.95 (*0-446-39218-9*) Warner Bks.

Nass, Leonard I., ed. Encyclopedia of PVC, Vol. 1. LC 76-3336. 616p. reprint ed. pap. 175.60 (*0-685-23523-8*, 2029005) Bks Demand.

Nass, Thomas. Life of Faith According to the Psalms: Teacher's Guide. 6.50 (*0-8100-0398-8*) WELS Board.

Nass, Ulla. Harness Lace. (Illus.). 52p. (C). 1977. pap. 8.95 (*0-9606468-0-9*) Nass.

— Weaves of the Incas. (Illus.). 108p. 1980. pap. 16.95 (*0-9606468-1-7*) Nass.

***Nassal, U.** Intelligent Autonomous Systems. LC 94-74249. 1995. 130.00 (*90-5199-213-0*) IOS Press.

Nassaney, Louie, et al. I Am Not a Victim: One Man's Triumph over Fear & AIDs. LC 88-84105. (Illus.). 128p. (Orig.). 1990. pap. 9.00 (*0-937611-47-6*, 111) Hay House.

***Nassaney, Michael S. & Sassaman, Kenneth E., eds.** Native American Interactions: Multiscalar Analyses & Interpretations in the Eastern Woodlands. LC 94-18772. 1995. write for info. (*0-87049-895-9*) U of Tenn Pr.

Nassaney, Michael S., et al. The Nineteen Eighty-Two Excavations at the Cahokia Interpretive Center Tract, St. Clair County, Illinois. (Center for Archaeological Investigations Research Paper Ser.: No. 37). (Illus.). ix, 132p. 1983. pap. 7.50 (*0-88104-010-X*) Center Archaeo.

Nassar, Eugene P. Essays Critical & Metacritical. LC 81-70955. 192p. 1983. 29.50 (*0-8386-3128-2*) Fairleigh Dickinson.

— Illustrations to Dante's "Inferno" LC 90-56173. (Illus.). 416p. 1994. 95.00 (*0-8386-3426-5*) Fairleigh Dickinson.

— Wallace Stevens: An Anatomy of Figuration. LC 64-24495. 229p. reprint ed. pap. 65.30 (*0-317-28693-5*, 2055280) Bks Demand.

Nassar, Eugene P., jt. auth. see Moses, John G.

Nassar, Jamal R. The Palestinian Liberation Organization: From Armed Struggle to the Declaration of Independence. LC 90-44335. (Illus.). 256p. 1991. text ed. 55.00 (0-275-93779-8, C3779, Praeger Pubs) Greenwood.

Nassar, Jamal R. & Heacock, Roger, eds. Intifada: Palestine at the Crossroads. LC 89-22879. 360p. 1990. text ed. 65.00 (0-275-93411-X, C3411, Greenwood Pr) Greenwood.

***Nassar, Nagla.** Sanctity of Contracts Revisited: A Study in the Theory & Practice of International Commercial Transactions. LC 94-30594. 1994. lib. bdg. 118.50 (0-7923-3079-X) Kluwer Ac.

Nassar, Noble J. One Jerusalem Is Not Enough. LC 83-61430. (New American Plays Ser.). (Illus.). 46p. 1983. 18.00 (0-918266-18-1) Smyrna.

Nassar, Syed. Schaum's Three Thousand Solved Problems in Electrical Circuits. (Illus.). 1992. pap. text ed. 21.95 (0-07-045936-3) McGraw.

Nassau County, Board of Cooperative Education Services Staff. Two Hundred Ways to Help Children Learn While You're at It. 1976. text ed. 30.00 (0-87909-845-7, Reston) P-H.

Nassau, E. How to Combat Psychic Attack. 39p. 1962. reprint ed. spiral bd. 3.30 (0-7873-0632-0) Mokelumne.

Nassau, Kurt. Gems Made by Man. 1980. 39.95 (0-87311-016-1) Gemological.

— Gemstone Enhancement. (Illus.). 296p. 1984. text ed. 47.95 (0-408-01447-4) Buttrwrth-Heinemann.

— Gemstone Enhancement: History, Science, & State of the Art. 2nd ed. LC 93-29282. (Illus.). 272p. 1994. pap. 54.95 (0-7506-1797-7) Buttrwrth-Heinemann.

— The Physics & Chemistry of Color: The Fifteen Causes of Color. LC 83-10580. (Pure & Applied Optics Ser.). 454p. 1983. text ed. 113.00 (0-471-86776-4, 1-349) Wiley.

Nassau, Mabel L. Old Age Poverty in Greenwich Village: A Neighborhood Study. Stein, Leon, ed. LC 79-8696. (Growing Old Ser.). 1980. reprint ed. lib. bdg. 17.95 (0-405-12793-6) Ayer.

Nassau, Robert H. Fetishism in West Africa: Forty Years' Observation of Native Customs & Superstitions. LC 69-18995. (Illus.). 389p. 1970. reprint ed. text ed. 38.50 (0-8371-0977-9, NAF&, Negro U Pr) Greenwood.

Nassauer, Rudolph. Kramer's Goats. LC 87-60979. (Illus.). 188p. 1987. 19.95 (0-7206-0659-4, Pub. by P Owen Ltd UK) Dufour.

Nassberg, Richard T. The Lender's Handbook. 316p. 1986. 88.00 (0-8318-0480-7, B480) Am Law Inst.

Nassberg, Richard T., ed. Resource Materials: Banking & Commercial Lending Law, Vol. V. 466p. (Orig.). 1984. pap. 25.00 (0-8318-0145-X, R145) Am Law Inst.

— Resource Materials: Banking & Commercial Lending Law, Vol. VI. 449p. (Orig.). 1985. pap. 25.00 (0-8318-0152-2, R152) Am Law Inst.

— Resource Materials: Banking & Commercial Lending Law, Vol. VII. 447p. (Orig.). 1986. pap. 25.00 (0-8318-0157-3, R157) Am Law Inst.

— Resource Materials: Banking & Commercial Lending Law, Vol. X. 641p. (Orig.). 1989. pap. text ed. 25.00 (0-8318-0169-7, R169) Am Law Inst.

— Resource Materials: Banking & Commercial Lending Law, Vol. XII. xiii, 545p. (Orig.). 1991. pap. text ed. 30.00 (0-8318-0172-7, R174) Am Law Inst.

— Resource Materials: Banking & Commercial Lending Law, Vol. XIV. 564p. (Orig.). 1993. pap. text ed. 80.00 (0-8318-0177-8, R179) Am Law Inst.

Nassberg, Richard T., ed. & intro. Resource Materials: Banking & Commercial Lending Law, Vol. VIII. 328p. (Orig.). 1987. pap. 25.00 (0-8318-0162-X, R161) Am Law Inst.

Nassberg, Richard T., pref. Resource Materials: Banking & Commercial Lending Law, Vol. XV. (Resource Materials Ser.). 610p. 1994. pap. text ed. 80.00 (0-8318-0182-4, R182) Am Law Inst.

— Resource Materials: Banking & Commercial Lending Law, Vol. XI. 656p. (Orig.). 1990. pap. 25.00 (0-8318-0171-9, R171) Am Law Inst.

Nasse, Erwin. On the Agricultural Community of the Middle Ages, & Inclosures of the 16th Century in England. Ouvray, H. A., tr. LC 79-1586. 1980. reprint ed. 15.00 (0-88355-891-2) Hyperion Conn.

Nasser, Essam. Fundamentals of Gaseous Ionization & Plasma Electronics. LC 77-125275. (Wiley Series in Plasma Physics). 470p. reprint ed. pap. 134.00 (0-317-08904-8, 2055184) Bks Demand.

Nasser, Fred N. & Giuliani, Emilio R. Clinical Two-Dimensional Echocardiography. LC 82-20215. (Illus.). 274p. reprint ed. pap. 78.10 (0-8357-7625-5, 2056948) Bks Demand.

Nasser, Hoda G. Britain & the Egyptian Nationalist Movement, 1936-1952. 1994. 65.00 (0-86372-177-X, Pub. by Ithaca UK) Paul & Co Pubs.

Nasser, Nemat S. Theoretical Foundation for Large-Scale Computations for Nonlinear Material Behavior. 1984. lib. bdg. 136.50 (90-247-3092-9) Kluwer Ac.

Nassib, Selim & Tisdall, Caroline. Beirut: Frontline Story. (Illus.). 160p. 1983. pap. 6.95 (0-86543-000-4) Africa World.

Nassif, Janet Z. Handbook of Health Careers: A Guide to Employment Opportunities. LC 79-23027. 354p. 1980. 45.95 (0-87705-489-4); pap. 24.95 (0-87705-413-4) Human Sci Pr.

Nassif, R. E. & Thaddeus, J. D., eds. Education for Health Manpower in the Middle East. 1967. pap. 12.95 (0-8156-6006-5, Am U Beirut) Syracuse U Pr.

Nassimbene, Raymond, jt. auth. see Carmichael, Fitzhugh L.

Nassit, Ramses. U Thant in New York. 180p. 1988. 24.95 (0-685-20013-2) St Martin.

Nasson, Bill. Abraham Esau's War: A Black South African War in the Cape, 1899-1902. (African Studies: No. 68). (Illus.). 272p. (C). 1991. 64.95 (0-521-38512-1) Cambridge U Pr.

Nassour, Ellis. Honky Tonk Angel: The Intimate Story of Patsy Cline. LC 92-43646. 1993. 22.95 (0-312-08870-1) St Martin.

— Honky Tonk Angel: The Intimate Story of Patsy Cline. 1994. mass mkt. 5.99 (0-312-95158-2) St Martin.

NASSP Curiculum Council Staff. Rethinking Reform: The Principal's Dilemma. 80p. (Orig.). 1986. pap. 9.00 (0-88210-193-5) Natl Assn Principals.

NASSP Middle Level Council Staff. Developing a Mission Statement for the Middle Level School. 40p. (Orig.). 1987. pap. text ed. 7.00 (0-88210-204-4) Natl Assn Principals.

NASSP Staff. GED Study Skills Coggeshop Kit. (Orig.). 1986. pap. 16.50 (0-88210-199-4) Natl Assn Principals.

NASSP staff. Workshop Leaders Handbook. (Orig.). 1985. pap. text ed. 39.95 (0-88210-169-2) Natl Assn Principals.

***Nassr, Donald.** In the Shadows of the Cross. 410p. 1994. 24.95x (0-9642463-0-9) ICAM Pub Co.

Nasstrom, Britt-Mari. The Abhorrence of Love: Studies in Rituals & Mystic Aspects in Catullus' Poem of Attis. (Uppsala Women's Studies, Women in Religion: No. 3). 98p. (Orig.). 1989. pap. 29.50x (91-554-2492-9, Pub. by Almqv & Wiksell SW) Coronet Bks.

Nassutti, Colette P., ed. The Marketing Advantage: How to Get & Keep the Clients You Want. LC 93-47895. 1993. write for info. (0-87051-146-7) Am Inst CPA.

Nast, Jo Anne, jt. auth. see Coggeshall, John M.

Nast, Lenora H., et al, eds. Baltimore: A Living Renaissance. LC 82-80490. (Illus.). 336p. 1982. 12.95 (0-942460-00-6) Hist Balt Soc.

Nast, Thomas. Thomas Nast's Christmas Drawings. (Illus.). 1978. pap. 5.95 (0-486-23660-9) Dover.

Nast, Thomas, jt. auth. see Webster, George P.

Nasta, Cynthia V. Peter & His Pick-up Truck: A Southwestern Children's Tale. LC 89-80351. (Illus.). 24p. (J). (ps-8). 1989. pap. 6.95 (0-9622064-0-7) Little Buckaroo.

— Peter & His Pick-up Truck: An Arizona Children's Tale. LC 89-80352. (Illus.). 24p. (J). (ps-8). 1989. lib. bdg. 6.95 (0-9622064-1-5); pap. 6.95 (0-9622064-2-3) Little Buckaroo.

Nasta, Phyllis. Aaron Goes to the Shelter: A Story about Abuse, Placement & Protective Services. 29p. (ENG & SPA.). (J). (gr. k-6). 1994. pap. 6.95 (1-880702-00-2) Whole Child.

— Aaron Goes to the Shelter: A Story & Workbook Guide about Abuse, Placement & Protective Services. (Illus.). 37p. (Orig.). (J). (gr. k-6). 1992. pap. text ed. 5.95 (1-880702-01-0) Whole Child.

Nasta, Susheila, ed. Critical Perspectives on Sam Selvon. LC 81-51645. (Critical Perspectives Ser.). 280p. 1988. 25.00 (0-89410-238-9); pap. 15.00 (0-89410-239-7) Three Continents.

— Motherlands: Black Women's Writings from Africa, the Caribbean, & South Asia. LC 91-30110. 365p. 1992. text ed. 40.00 (0-8135-1781-8); pap. text ed. 15.00 (0-8135-1782-6) Rutgers U Pr.

Nasta, Tony. Change Through Networking in Vocational Education. (New Developments in Vocational Education Ser.). 220p. 1994. 60.00x (0-7494-0679-8, Pub. by Kogan Page Educ UK) Taylor & Francis.

— Change Through Networking in Vocational Education. (New Developments in Vocational Education Ser.). 220p. 1994. pap. 34.00x (0-7494-1450-2, Pub. by Kogan Page Educ UK) Taylor & Francis.

Nastase, Ilie. The Net. Schwartz, Ros, tr. 1988. pap. 3.95 (0-317-70084-7) St Martin.

Nastasescu, Constantin & Van Oystaeyen, Freddy. Dimensions of Ring Theory. 1987. lib. bdg. 124.50 (90-277-2461-X) Kluwer Ac.

— Graded Ring Theory. (Mathematical Library: Vol. 28). 340p. 1982. 66.75 (0-444-86489-X, I-348-82, North Holland) Elsevier.

Nastasi, Bonnie K. & Dezolt, Denise. School Interventions for Children of Alcoholics. LC 94-853. (Guilford School Practitioner Ser.). 275p. 1994. text ed. 25.00 (0-89862-367-7) Guilford Pubns.

Nastasi, M. A., et al, eds. Beam-Solid Interactions - Fundamentals & Applications. (Materials Research Society Symposium Proceedings Ser.: Vol. 279). 1993. text ed. 67.00 (1-55899-174-3) Materials Res.

***Nastasi, Michael, et al.** Ion-Solid Interactions: Fundamentals & Applications. (Cambridge Solid State Science Ser.). (Illus.). 400p. (C). 1992. write for info. (0-521-37376-X) Cambridge U Pr.

Nastasi, Michael A., ed. see NATO Advanced Study Institute on Mechanical Properties & Deformation Behavior of Materials Having Ultra-Fine Microstructures.

Naster, P., et al, eds. A Survey of Numismatic Research, 1966-71, 3 vols. 1133p. 1973. 20.00 (0-89722-069-2) Am Numismatic.

Nastiuk, Virginia. Personal Patterns by Jinni: A Manual for Perfect Patternmaking. rev. ed. (Illus.). 281p. 1991. lib. bdg. 36.95 (0-942003-03-9) Personal Patterns.

Nastiuk, Virginia M. Personal Patterns by Jinni, 2 vols., Set. (Illus.). (C). 1988. 82.50 (0-942003-04-7) Personal Patterns.

— Personal Patterns by Jinni, 2 vols., Vol. 1. (Illus.). (C). 1988. write for info. (0-318-62738-8) Personal Patterns.

— Personal Patterns by Jinni, 2 vols., Vol. 2. (Illus.). (C). 1988. write for info. (0-318-62739-6) Personal Patterns.

— Personal Patterns by Jinni: A Manual for Flat Pattern Design, Vol. 2. (Illus.). 280p. (C). 1988. Series. write for info. (0-942003-05-5); lib. bdg. 39.95 (0-942003-07-1) Personal Patterns.

— Personal Patterns by Jinni: A Manual for Perfect Patternmaking, 2 vols., Vol. 1. (Illus.). 281p. (C). 1987. reprint ed. 42.95 (0-942003-02-0); reprint ed. pap. 36.95 (0-942003-01-2) Personal Patterns.

— Personal Patterns by Jinni: Choosing a Pattern. (Illus.). 82p. 1987. pap. 7.90 (0-942003-10-1) Personal Patterns.

— Personal Patterns by Jinni: Fitting Problems & Their Corrections. (Illus.). 101p. 1987. lib. bdg. 14.95 (0-942003-16-0) Personal Patterns.

— Personal Patterns by Jinni: Fitting Problems & Their Corrections. (Illus.). 101p. (C). 1987. pap. 14.95 (0-942003-15-2) Personal Patterns.

— Personal Patterns by Jinni: Introduction to Design. (Illus.). 110p. 1987. pap. 7.90 (0-942003-20-9) Personal Patterns.

— Personal Patterns by Jinni: Knitting to Your Personal Pattern. (Illus.). 250p. (Orig.). (C). 1988. pap. 32.95 (0-942003-35-7) Personal Patterns.

— Personal Patterns by Jinni: Pants - Fit & Design. (Illus.). 100p. 1987. lib. bdg. 16.50 (0-942003-27-6) Personal Patterns.

— Personal Patterns by Jinni: Pants - Fit & Design. (Illus.). 100p. 1987. pap. 14.95 (0-942003-25-X) Personal Patterns.

— Personal Patterns by Jinni: Skirts - Fit & Design. (Illus.). 110p. 1987. pap. 7.90 (0-942003-30-6) Personal Patterns.

Nastuk, William L., jt. auth. see Baker, Carleton H.

Nasty, Mack. Take No Prisoners. LC 90-62143. 128p. (Orig.). 1990. pap. 10.00 (1-55950-043-3, 19169) Loompanics.

***Nasu, Masakazu.** Textile Systems for Endomorphisms & Automorphisms of the Shift. LC 94-43210. (Memoirs Ser.: Vol. 546). 1995. write for info. (0-8218-2606-9) Am Math.

Nasu, Masamoto. Children of the Paper Crane: The Story of Sadako Sasaki & Her Struggle with the A-Bomb Disease. Baldwin, Elizabeth W. et al, trs. 232p. 1991. 45.00 (0-87332-715-2) M E Sharpe.

— Children of the Paper Crane: The Story of Sadako Sasaki & Her Struggle with the A-Bomb Disease. Baldwin, Elizabeth W. & Leeper, Steven L., trs. 232p. 1994. pap. 18.95 (0-87332-716-0) M E Sharpe.

Nasu, N. & Honjo, S., eds. New Directions of Oceanographic Research & Development. LC 92-32507. 1993. write for info. (4-431-70113-3) Spr-Verlag.

— New Directions of Oceanographic Research & Development. (Illus.). 232p. 1993. 140.00 (0-387-70113-3) Spr-Verlag.

Nasu, N., et al, eds. Formation of Active Fault Margins. 1986. lib. bdg. 309.00 (90-277-2302-8) Kluwer Ac.

Nasu, Shiroshi. Aspects of Japanese Agriculture: A Preliminary Survey. LC 75-30073. (Institute of Pacific Relations Ser.). reprint ed. 24.50 (0-404-59575-8) AMS Pr.

Nasuti, Harry P. Tradition History & the Psalms of Asaph. LC 86-25232. (Society of Biblical Literature Dissertation Ser.). 230p. 1989. 21.95 (0-89130-970-5, 06 01 88); pap. 14.95 (0-89130-971-3, 06 01 88) Scholars Pr GA.

Nasuti, James F. & Rotwitt, Jeffrey B. The Pennsylvania Corporation: Legal Aspects of Corporation & Operation. (Corporate Practice Ser.: No. 30). 1982. 92.00 (1-55871-260-7) BNA.

Nasuti, James F., jt. auth. see Nachmias, Carolyn S.

NASW Encyclopedia Supplement Committee Staff. Encyclopedia of Social Work Supplement. 18th ed. LC 30-30498. 348p. 1990. 26.95 (0-87101-178-6) Natl Assn Soc Wkrs.

NASW Legislative Affairs Department Staff. Social Workers & Social Work Services As Defined in Medicare Law & Regulation. 2nd ed. 420p. 1992. 65.00 (0-87101-216-2) Natl Assn Soc Wkrs.

— Social Worker's Guide to the Family Support Act Of 1988. 30p. 1989. pap. 6.95 (0-87101-173-5) Natl Assn Soc Wkrs.

NASW Professional Symposium on Social Work Staff. Social Work in a Turbulent World: Seventh NASW Symposium: Selected Papers, Seventh NASW Professional Symposium on Social Work, November 18-21, 1981, Philadelphia, PA. Dinerman, Miriam, ed. LC 82-8216. 220p. reprint ed. pap. 62.70 (0-7837-6548-7, 2045685) Bks Demand.

NASW Staff, ed. Social Work Speaks: NASW Policy Statements. 3rd ed. 304p. (C). 1994. pap. text ed. 28.95 (0-87101-234-0, 2340) Natl Assn Soc Wkrs.

***NATA Board of Certification Staff.** Role Delineation Study of the Entry-Level Athletic Trainer Certification Examination. 3rd ed. 62p. (C). 1994. pap. text ed. 25.00 (0-8036-6504-0) Davis Co.

— Study Guide for the Nata Board of Certification, Inc. Entry-Level Athletic Trainer Certification Examination. 2nd ed. (Illus.). (C). 1993. pap. text ed. 29.95 (0-8036-6501-6) Davis Co.

Natachee, Allan, tr. see Beier, Ulli, ed.

Nataf, Andre. The Occult. (Compact Reference Ser.). (Illus.). 256p. (Orig.). 1992. pap. 9.95 (0-550-17003-0, Chambers LKC) LKC.

***Nataf, Daniel.** Democratization & Social Settlements: The Politics of Change in Contemporary Portugal. LC 94-33690. 288p. 1995. text ed. 64.50x (0-7914-2589-4); pap. 21.95x (0-7914-2590-8) State U NY Pr.

***Nataga.** Bohr Maker. 1995. mass mkt. 4.99 (0-553-56925-2, Spectra) Bantam.

***Natale, Frank.** Trance Dance: The Dance of Life. LC 95-12177. 1995. pap. 22.95 (1-85230-702-1) Element MA.

***Natale, Leo.** When Soul & Spirit Agree: Anchoring the Soul to the Spirit to Achieve Ultimate Success & Prosperity. 115p. (Orig.). 1994. pap. 6.95 (0-88270-683-7) Bridge Pub.

Natale, Robert. Fast Stocks, Fast Money: How to Invest in New Issues & Quickly Growing Small Companies. 1995. text ed. 24.95 (0-07-045980-0) McGraw.

Natale, Samuel M. Ethics & Morals in Business. 2nd ed. LC 87-9424. 209p. (C). 1987. pap. text ed. 16.95 (0-89135-063-2) Religious Educ.

— Loneliness & Spiritual Growth. LC 86-10012. 171p. (Orig.). 1986. pap. 12.95 (0-89135-055-1) Religious Educ.

Natale, Samuel M., ed. Psychotherapy & the Lonely Patient. LC 86-12108. (Psychotherapy Patient Ser.: Vol. 2, No. 3). 120p. (C). 1986. text ed. 29.95 (0-86656-517-5) Haworth Pr.

— Psychotherapy & the Lonely Patient. LC 86-12101. (Psychotherapy Patient Ser.: Vol. 2, No. 3). 120p. (C). 1986. reprint ed. pap. 14.95 (0-918393-26-4) Harrington Pk.

Natale, Samuel M. & Wilson, John B., eds. The Ethical Contexts for Business Conflicts, Vol. 1. LC 89-22762. (Ethical Conflict Ser.). (Illus.). 202p. (Orig.). 1990. pap. text ed. 23.00 (0-8191-7598-6) U Pr of Amer.

Natale, Samuel M., jt. auth. see Wilson, John B.

***Natali, Alan.** Woody's Boys. (Illus.). 500p. 1995. text ed. 30.00 (1-882203-04-6) Orange Frazer.

Natali, Enrico & Sandrof, Mark. American Landscapes: 1968-1990. (Illus.). 104p. (Orig.). 1991. pap. 29.00 (0-945149-02-6) Panopticon Pr.

Natali, F. Socci, jt. ed. see Martino, Antonio A.

Natali, Louis M. United States v. Benjamin R. Darby. 59p. 1986. 13.75 (1-55681-106-3, FBA0106) Natl Inst Trial Ad.

Natali, Louis M., jt. auth. see Bocchino, Anthony J.

Natali, Patricia, jt. auth. see Chambers, Kate.

***Natalia.** The Victorious Queen of the World: The Spiritual Diary of Sr. Natalia of Hungary. Foglein, Stephen, tr. 159p. 1992. pap. 7.50 (1-884722-01-6) Two Hrts Bks.

Natalie, Andrea. The Night Audrey's Vibrator Spoke: A Stonewall Riots Collection. (Illus.). 108p. (Orig.). 1992. pap. 8.95 (0-939416-64-6) Cleis Pr.

— Rubyfruit Mountain: A Stonewall Riots Collection. (Illus.). 84p. (Orig.). 1993. pap. 9.95 (0-939416-74-3) Cleis Pr.

— Stonewall Riots. (Stonewall Riots Cartoons Ser.). (Illus.). 74p. (Orig.). 1990. pap. 4.95 (0-9628027-0-0, VA 154-987) A Natalie Pub.

— Stonewall Riots. (Illus.). 76p. (Orig.). 1990. reprint ed. pap. 4.95 (0-9628027-1-9, VA154987) A Natalie Pub.

Natambu, Kofi. The Melody Never Stops. 72p. (Orig.). 1991. pap. 8.00 (0-9622474-3-X) Past Tents Pr.

Natanson, I. Summation of Infinitesimal Quantities. (Russian Tracts on the Physical Sciences Ser.). 74p. 1962. text ed. 68.00 (0-677-20450-7) Gordon & Breach.

Natanson, Maurice. Anonymity: A Study in the Philosophy of Alfred Schutz. LC 85-45989. (Studies in Phenomenology & Existential Philosophy). 192p. 1986. 25.00 (0-253-30746-5) Ind U Pr.

— A Critique of Jean-Paul Sartre's Ontology. LC 72-8367. (Studies in Philosophy: No. 40). 136p. 1972. reprint ed. lib. bdg. 75.00 (0-8383-1412-0) M S G Haskell Hse.

— Edmund Husserl: Philosopher of Infinite Tasks. (Studies in Phenomenology & Existential Philosophy). 227p. 1973. 39.95 (0-8101-0425-3); pap. 17.95 (0-8101-0456-3) Northwestern U Pr.

Natanson, Maurice, ed. Phenomenology & the Social Sciences, I. LC 79-91001. (Studies in Phenomenology & Existential Philosophy). 1066p. (C). 1973. pap. 17.95 (0-8101-0616-7) Northwestern U Pr.

Natanson, Nicholas. The Black Image in the New Deal: The Politics of FSA Photography. LC 91-14344. (Illus.). 320p. (C). 1992. text ed. 45.00x (0-87049-723-5); pap. 18.95 (0-87049-724-3) U of Tenn Pr.

Natapoff, Janet & Wieczorek, Ruth, eds. Maternal-Child Health Policy: A Nursing Perspective. LC 90-9464. 360p. 1990. 39.95 (0-8261-6050-6) Springer Pub.

Natarajan. DNA Repair: Chromosome Alterations & Chromatin Structure. (Progress in Mutation Research Ser.: Vol. 4). 390p. 1982. 145.75 (0-444-80367-X) Elsevier.

Natarajan, A. T., jt. ed. see Obe, G.

Natarajan, B., tr. see Tirumulav.

Natarajan, Balas K. Machine Learning: A Theoretical Approach. 250p. 1991. 42.95 (1-55860-148-1) Morgan Kaufmann.

Natarajan, C., tr. see Shul'man, S. G., ed.

Natarajan, G., jt. auth. see Viswanath, D. S.

Natarajan, K. & Raman, N. South Indian Agaricales, Preliminary Study of Some Dark Spored Species. (Bibliotheca Mycologica Ser.: No. 89). (Illus.). 204p. 1983. text ed. 60.00 (3-7682-1344-7) Lubrecht & Cramer.

***Natarajan, K. V. & Rakoczy, Sharon.** General Biology Laboratory Manual. (Illus.). 167p. (Orig.). (C). 1994. student ed 22.00 (1-878045-66-0) Whittier Pubns.

Natarajan, N., jt. ed. see Vajpeyi, Dhirendra.

Natarajan, R. Institutional Finance for Small Scale Industries. 1989. 32.00 (81-202-0256-2, Pub. by Ajanta II) S Asia.

Natarajan, S. Introduction to Economics of Education. 88p. 1990. text ed. 15.95 (81-207-1239-0, Pub. by Sterling Pubs II) Apt Bks.

Natarajan, S. & Miang, Tan J. The Impact of MNC Investments in Malaysia, Singapore & Thailand. 70p. 1992. 23.50 (981-3016-29-9, Pub. by Inst SE Asian Studies SI) Ashgate Pub Co.

Natarajan, Sundaram. Theory & Design of Linear Active Networks. 464p. 1987. write for info. (0-317-53615-X) Macmillan.

— Theory & Design of Linear Active Networks. 1987. 50.00 (0-07-045911-8) McGraw.

***Natarajan, Swaminathan, ed.** Imprecise & Approximate Computation. LC 95-15532. (International Series in Engineering & Computer Science). 200p. (C). 1995. lib. bdg. 85.00 (0-7923-9579-4) Kluwer Ac.

Natarajan, T., jt. auth. see Ahmed, Nasir.

N

An Asterisk (*) at the beginning of an entry indicates that the title is appearing in BIP for the first time.

Natchez, Gladys. Personality Patterns & Oral Reading: A Study of Overt Behavior in the Reading Situation As It Reveals Reactions of Dependence, Aggression, & Withdrawal in Children. LC 60-6043. 112p. reprint ed. pap. 32.00 (*0-317-10337-7*, 2050322) Bks Demand.

Natella, Arthur, Jr. The New Theatre of Peru. LC 81-84037. (Senda de Estudios y Ensayos Ser.). 132p. (Orig.). (C). 1982. pap. text ed. 9.95 (*0-918454-28-X*) Senda Nueva.

Natella, Arthur A., Jr. Anacronismos De la Nueva Literatura Latinoamericana. LC 89-83446. (Coleccion Polymita Ser.). 64p. (Orig.). (SPA.). 1991. pap. 10.00 (*0-89729-527-7*) Ediciones.

Natella, Arthur A., Jr., jt. auth. see McKinnis, Candace B.

Natelson, B. H. Tomorrow's Doctors: The Path to Successful Practice in the 1990's. LC 89-26563. (Illus.). 302p. 1990. 19.95 (*0-306-43195-5*, Plenum Insight) Plenum.

Natelson, Jonathan D., jt. auth. see Cumpiano, William R.

Natelson, Nina, ed. Future Medical Research Without the Use of Animals: Facing the Challenge - May 15-16, 1990, Tel Aviv, Israel. (Illus.). (Orig.). 1991. pap. write for info. (*0-9631596-0-7*) CFH Animals IS.

Natelson, Robert G. Law of Property Owners Associations. 784p. 1989. 125.00 (*0-316-59865-8*) Little.

— Modern Law of Deeds to Real Property. 640p. 1992. 125.00 (*0-316-59876-3*) Little.

— Property Ownership Set. 1990. 125.00 (*0-316-59871-2*) Little.

Natelson, Samuel, et al. Amniotic Fluid: Physiology, Biochemistry, & Clinical Chemistry. LC 74-4444. (Current Topics in Clinical Chemistry Ser.: Vol. 1). 406p. reprint ed. 115.80 (*0-8357-5415-4*, 2055093) Bks Demand.

— Clinical Immunochemistry: Chemical & Cellular Bases & Applications in Disease. LC 78-72879. 505p. 1978. 25.00 (*0-915274-07-8*) Am Assn Clinical Chem.

***Natelson, Stephen E.** Die Ganze Mispoche: An Account of the Author's Family Notes, Oujevolk, Rosenfeld, Natelson, Winick, Bershansky, Movitz, Siegel, Brody, Burden, Melnick, Notkin, Tkotch, Schulman & Kuznitz Are Some of the Families Included. 280p. 1995. write for info. (*0-9645349-0-8*) S E Natelson.

Nateman, David. Introduction to Art. 1994. pap. text ed. 9.95 (*0-07-045912-6*) McGraw.

Natemeyer, Walter & Gilberg, Jay. Classics of Organizational Behavior. 370p. (Orig.). 1989. 21.95 (*0-8134-2814-9*) Interstate.

Natenberg, Sheldon. Option Volatility & Pricing: Advanced Trading Strategies & Techniques. rev. ed. 1994. 49.95 (*1-55738-486-X*) Probus Pub Co.

***Nater, S.** Rebounding to Win. 1994. pap. 13.95 (*0-915611-63-5*) Sagamore Pub.

Naterop, B. J. & Revel, R. Telephoning in English. 1987. pap. 11.95 (*0-521-26975-X*); Cassette. pap. 29.95 (*0-521-26429-4*) Cambridge U Pr.

Natesa Sastri, Pandit & Kingscote. Folklore of Southern India or Tales of the Sun. 320p. 1986. 17.50 (*0-8364-1711-9*, Pub. by Usha II) S Asia.

Natesa Sastri, Pandit, jt. auth. see Kingscote, Georgiana.

Natesa Sastri, Sangendi M. Folklore in Southern India, 3 vols. in 1. LC 78-63212. (Folktale Ser.). reprint ed. 26.50 (*0-404-16148-0*) AMS Pr.

— Indian Folk Tales. LC 78-63218. (Folktale Ser.). reprint ed. 38.50 (*0-404-16149-9*) AMS Pr.

Natesan, K., ed. see Metallurgical Society of AIME Staff.

Natesh, R., ed. see American Society for Metals Staff.

Natesh, S., et al. Biotechnology in Agriculture. 1987. 47.50 (*81-204-0241-3*, Pub. by Oxford IBH II) S Asia.

Nath & Thind, S. K. Staff. Unrolithiasis Research. (C). 1989. 34.00 (*81-7024-244-4*, Pub. by Ashish II) S Asia.

Nath, Aloke. Guide to SQL Server. 2nd ed. 1995. pap. 32.95 (*0-201-62631-4*) Addison-Wesley.

Nath, Aman & Wacziarg, Francis, eds. The Arts & Crafts of Rajasthan. (Illus.). 228p. 1987. 45.00 (*0-295-96465-0*) Mapin International Inc.

Nath, B. Commentaries on Mental Health Act, 1987. (C). 1989. 60.00 (*0-685-25671-5*) St Mut.

Nath, B. & Malik, P. L. Cases & Materials on Code of Criminal Procedure, 1973. (C). 1987. 260.00 (*0-685-25179-9*) St Mut.

Nath, B., jt. auth. see Chakravarti, S.

Nath, B., et al, eds. Environmental Management, Vol. One: The Compartmental Approach. (Illus.). 340p. 1994. pap. 45.00 (*90-5487-033-8*) Paul & Co Pubs.

— Environmental Management, Vol. Three: Instruments for Implementation. 295p. 1994. pap. 45.00 (*90-5487-035-4*) Paul & Co Pubs.

— Environmental Management, Vol. Two: The Ecosystems Approach. (Illus.). 252p. 1994. pap. 45.00 (*90-5487-034-6*) Paul & Co Pubs.

Nath, Bholeshwar. Cases & Materials on Code of Civil Procedure. (C). 1990. write for info. (*0-318-67354-1*) St Mut.

— Cases & Materials on Criminal Procedure Code, 1987: With Supplement 1989. 3rd ed. (C). 1989. 275.00 (*0-685-36421-6*) St Mut.

— Cases & Materials on Law of Evidence. 578p. 1983. 240.00 (*0-317-54684-8*) St Mut.

— Cases & Materials on Law of Evidence. 2nd ed. (C). 1991. 95.00 (*0-685-39713-0*) St Mut.

— Cases & Materials on Transfer of Property Act, 1882: 1987 Edition. (C). 1987. 175.00 (*0-685-36409-7*) St Mut.

— Civil Referencer. 1733p. (C). 1989. 350.00x (*0-685-37464-5*); 175.00 (*0-685-38612-0*) St Mut.

— Commentaries on Mental Health Act, 1987: With Supplement. (C). 1991. 70.00 (*0-685-39626-6*) St Mut.

Nath, Bholeshwar & Malik, P. L. Cases & Materials on Criminal Procedure Code. (C). 1991. 285.00 (*0-89771-778-3*, Pub. by Eastern Book II) St Mut.

— Cases & Materials on Criminal Procedure Code. 3rd ed. (C). 1990. 275.00 (*0-685-37416-5*) St Mut.

— Cases & Materials on Criminal Procedure Code. 1199p. 1984. reprint ed. 390.00 (*0-317-54686-4*) St Mut.

***Nath, D. Smith.** Apocalypses. 40p. 1994. pap. 5.95 (*1-886134-02-2*) Miraculous Fngerprnt.

—Flight into Infinity. 258p. Date not set. write for info. (*1-886134-04-9*) Miraculous Fngerprnt.
FLIGHT INTO INFINITY is exciting science fiction insight into man's destiny. After years in space mapping the galaxies Admiral Bernard Benadesky returns to find a genetically changed world. He is asked to choose one gorgeous woman out of five that matches his own DNA perfection for man's evolving progress in the 21st Century. The book offers a new "force" that propels man out of his old world into a new one. A drama unfolds with shocking events & hidden mystery that holds the reader spellbound. It portrays man defying gravity & being lifted from his earthbound sanctuary to inherit the universe that has been his all along. A mind-expanding experience awaits the reader. A divine urge to excellence calls our hero into a universe that grips his imagination beyond his wildest dreams. The decaying & doubting age has declined & died. A newer, stronger age is born. Man arises & courageously transfigures himself into a new dimension of humanhood. The reader will identify a new understanding of man's relationship to the Cosmos & his place in it as he learns to "power beam" his FLIGHT INTO INFINITY. The story gives insight into an enlightened, mystical, spiritual society pictured a colorful & dramatic way. Order from Miraculous Fingerprint Publishers, 74565 Dillon Rd. No. H-15, Desert Hot Springs, CA 92241. ***Publisher Provided Annotation.***

— Seeking. 50p. 1994. pap. 5.95 (*1-886134-01-4*) Miraculous Fngerprnt.

— She, the Tale of a Sail. 30p. (J). (gr. k-2). Date not set. pap. 5.95 (*1-886134-03-0*) Miraculous Fngerprnt.

Nath, Lala B., tr. see Puranas, Brahmandapurana.

Nath, M. Reflections of an Industrialist: From Mudhouse to Millionaire. 187p. (C). 1992. text ed. 25.00 (*0-7069-6026-2*, Pub. by Vikas II) S Asia.

Nath, Marie-Luise, ed. see Ladany, Laszlo.

Nath, N., et al, eds. Cases & Materials on Criminal Procedure Code, with Supplement. 3rd ed. (C). 1990. text ed. 275.00 (*0-89771-502-0*) St Mut.

Nath, N. C., ed. Transfer of Technology in Indian Agriculture: Experience of Agricultural Universities. (C). 1992. 18.00 (*81-85182-70-1*, Pub. by Indus Pub II) S Asia.

Nath, P. Fisheries of Eastern India, Vol. 1: (Arunachal Pradesh) 350p. (C). 1991. text ed. 350.00 (*0-89771-609-4*, Pub. by Intl Bk Distr II) St Mut.

— Supersymmetry & Unification of Fundamental Interaction (Susy 93) Proceedings of the International Workshop. 644p. 1993. text ed. 121.00 (*981-02-1593-2*) World Scientific Pub.

Nath, Pandit S. Speaking Of: Yoga: A Practical Guide to Better Living. 192p. 1989. text ed. 22.50 (*81-207-0684-6*, Pub. by Sterling Pubs II) Apt Bks.

— Stress Management through Yoga & Meditation. 1993. pap. 7.95 (*81-207-1514-4*, Pub. by Sterling Pubs II) Apt Bks.

Nath, Pashupati & Nath, Siddha. Environmental Pollution, Conservation & Planning, 2 vols., Set. 1990. 78.50 (*81-85076-86-3*) S Asia.

Nath, Pran & Reucroff, Stephen, eds. Particles, Strings & Cosmology: Proceedings of the Second International Symposium, Northeastern Univ., Boston, 25-30 March 1991. 800p. 1992. text ed. 121.00 (*981-02-0971-1*) World Scientific Pub.

Nath, Pran & Reucroft, S., eds. Particles, Strings & Cosmology - 90: Proceedings of the First International Symposium on Particles, Strings & Cosmology, Boston, U. S. A., March 27-31, 1990. 716p. 1991. text ed. 167.00 (*981-02-0392-6*); pap. 55.00 (*981-02-0393-4*) World Scientific Pub.

Nath, Pran, et al. Applied N Equals One Supergravity. (ICIP Lecture Series in Theoretical Physics Lectures: Vol. 1). 116p. 1984. text ed. 36.00 (*9971-966-48-4*); pap. text ed. 15.00 (*9971-966-49-2*) World Scientific Pub.

Nath, Prem, ed. Fresh Reflections on Samuel Johnson: Essays in Criticism. LC 86-51632. 420p. 1987. 38.50 (*0-87875-337-0*) Whitston Pub.

Nath, Prithvi. The Japanese Offensive. 112p. 1991. text ed. 18.95 (*81-207-1234-X*, Pub. by Sterling Pubs II) Apt Bks.

— Wingate: His Relevance to Contemporary Warfare. 1990. text ed. 15.95 (*81-207-1165-3*, Pub. by Sterling Pubs II) Apt Bks.

Nath, R. The Art of Khajuraho. 1980. 90.00 (*0-8364-0608-7*, Pub. by Abhinav II) S Asia.

— Environmental Pollution of Cadmium Biological, Physiological & Health Effects. 166p. (C). 1986. 150.00 (*81-85017-24-7*, Pub. by Interprint II) St Mut.

— History of Mughal Architecture, Vol. III. (C). 1994. 155.00 (*81-7017-159-8*, Pub. by Abhinav II) S Asia.

— History of Mughal Architecture, Vol. 2: Akbar. 1986. 125.00 (*0-8364-1628-7*, Pub. by Abhinav II) S Asia.

— History of Sultanate Architecture. 1978. 44.00 (*0-8364-0176-X*) S Asia.

— Some Aspects of Mughal Architecture. LC 76-902803. 1976. 38.50 (*0-88386-825-3*) S Asia.

— Tajmahal & Its Incarnation. 232p. 1985. 79.95 (*0-318-36975-3*) Asia Bk Corp.

Nath, R., ed. Electrical & Optical Behaviour of Solids. (C). 1989. 72.50 (*81-7099-097-1*, Pub. by Mittal II) S Asia.

— National Conference on Electrical & Optical Properties of Solids. (C). 1989. 78.00 (*0-685-29304-1*, Pub. by Mittal II) S Asia.

Nath, R., et al. Molecular Aspects of Idiopathic Urolithiasis. (Illus.). 176p. 1984. pap. 59.00 (*0-08-031697-2*, Pergamon Pr) Elsevier.

Nath, Raghu, jt. auth. see Narayanan, V. K.

Nath, Rajendra. Military Leadership in India: Vedic Period to Indo-Pak Wars. 1990. 72.50 (*81-7095-018-X*, Pub. by Lancer II) S Asia.

Nath, Rakhal. New Hindu Movement, Eighteen Sixty-Six to Nineteen Eleven. 1982. 14.50 (*0-685-59382-7*) S Asia.

Nath, Ramendra. The Ethical Philosophy of Bertrand Russell. 1994. 13.95 (*0-533-09424-0*) Vantage.

Nath, S. K. Reappraisal of Welfare Economics. LC 70-80108. vii, 247p. 1969. 29.50 (*0-678-06507-1*) Kelley.

Nath, Sanjiva, jt. auth. see Kahn, Philippe.

Nath, Shaileshwar. Terrorism in India. 350p. 1980. 25.95 (*0-940500-27-2*) Asia Bk Corp.

Nath, Shyam. Measuring Tax Burden in India: A Case Study of Rajasthan State. 1987. 28.50 (*81-7024-072-7*, Pub. by Ashish II) S Asia.

Nath, Siddha, jt. auth. see Nath, Pashupati.

Nath, Surinder, jt. ed. see Mahajan, Anil.

***Nath, Tribhuvan & Gupta, Madan M.** On the Yeti Trail: The Search for the Elusive Snowman. (C). 1995. 7.00x (*81-86112-29-4*, Pub. by UBS Pubs Dist II) S Asia.

Nath, Trilok. Indian Police Administration: A Guide for Police Officers. 232p. 1984. text ed. 27.50 (*0-86590-218-6*, Pub. by Sterling Pubs II) Apt Bks.

Nath, Vijay. Dana: Gift System in Ancient India: A Socio-economic Perspective. 1988. 33.50 (*81-215-0054-0*, Pub. by Munshiram Manoharial II) S Asia.

Nathan. Practical Approach to Assessment of Liability & Damages in Tort. 1986. 113.00 (*9971-70-051-4*) Butterworth Legal Pubs.

— Le Sagesse de Rebbe Nachman. Dimermanas, A., ed. & tr. by. 334p. (FRE.). 1989. text ed. 15.00 (*0-930213-31-9*); pap. text ed. 13.00 (*0-930213-32-7*) Breslov Res Inst.

— Tefilin: A Chassidic Discourse. Greenbaum, Avraham, ed. & tr. by. (Illus.). 96p. 1989. pap. text ed. 7.00 (*0-930213-38-6*) Breslov Res Inst.

Nathan & Gurewich, Ori. Paradox 4.5 for Windows Unleashed. 1993. disk 34.95 (*0-672-30410-4*) Sams.

Nathan, jt. auth. see Nachman.

Nathan, A. W., jt. auth. see Timmis, A. D.

Nathan, Adele G. First Transatlantic Cable. (Landmark Ser.: No. 88). (Illus.). (J). (gr. 5-9). 1963. lib. bdg. 8.99 (*0-394-90388-9*) Random Bks Yng Read.

Nathan Adelson Hospice Staff. Best Bets: Las Vegas Cooking at Its Best. LC 93-72353. 1993. write for info. (*0-87197-383-9*) Favorite Recipes.

Nathan, Amy. Fruit. (Illus.). 144p. 1988. 29.95 (*0-87701-556-2*); pap. 16.95 (*0-87701-444-2*) Chronicle Bks.

— Salad. LC 84-28519. (Illus.). 120p. (Orig.). 1985. pap. 17.95 (*0-87701-348-9*) Chronicle Bks.

Nathan, Andrew J. China's Crisis: Dilemmas of Reform & Prospects for Democracy. (Studies of the East Asian Institute). 256p. 1990. text ed. 26.00 (*0-231-07284-8*) Col U Pr.

— China's Crisis: Dilemmas of Reform & Prospects for Democracy. 1990. pap. 12.95 (*0-231-07285-6*) Col U Pr.

— Chinese Democracy. LC 85-40163. (Illus.). 336p. 1985. 22.95 (*0-394-51386-X*) Knopf.

— Chinese Democracy. 313p. (C). 1986. pap. 13.00 (*0-520-05933-6*) U CA Pr.

— History of the China International Famine Relief Commission. LC 65-5839. (East Asian Monographs: No. 17). 114p. 1965. pap. 11.00 (*0-674-40200-6*) HUP.

Nathan, Andrew J., jt. auth. see Edwards, Randle.

Nathan, Barbara. Gambling Times Guide to Basketball Handicapping. 253p. 1984. pap. 5.95 (*0-89746-023-5*) Gambling Times.

Nathan, Barry R., jt. auth. see Decker, Phillip J.

Nathan, Brian. The Platinum Yearbook 1991. 160p. 1991. 40.00 (*1-85573-045-6*, Pub. by Woodhead Pubng UK) St Mut.

Nathan, Carl F. Plague Prevention & Politics in Manchuria, 1910-1931. LC 67-8500. (East Asian Monographs: No. 23). 111p. (Orig.). 1967. pap. 11.00 (*0-674-67050-7*) HUP.

***Nathan, Cheryl.** Bugs & Beasties ABC. (Illus.). 32p. (Orig.). (J). (gr. 1-4). 1995. pap. 5.50 (*1-56790-515-3*) Cool Hand Comms.

***Nathan, Cheryl, et al.** Bugs & Beasties ABC. LC 95-11534. 32p. (Orig.). (J). (gr. 1-4). 1995. 15.95 (*1-56790-516-1*, Cool Kids Pr) Cool Hand Comms.

***Nathan, David G.** Genes, Blood, & Courage: A Boy Called Immortal Sword. LC 95-6080. (Illus.). 288p. (C). 1995. 24.95 (*0-674-34473-1*) Belknap Pr.

Nathan, David H., comp. Baseball Quotations: The Wisdom & Wisecracks of Players, Managers, Owners, Umpires, Announcers, Writers & Fans on the Great American Pastime. LC 90-53512. 231p. 1991. lib. bdg. 27.50x (*0-89950-562-7*) McFarland & Co.

Nathan, David H., ed. Baseball Quotations: The Wisdom & Wisecracks of Players, Manager, Owners, Umpires, Announcers, Writers & Fans on the Great American Pastime. 1994. mass mkt. 4.99 (*0-345-90324-2*) Ballantine.

— Baseball Quotations: The Wisdom & Wisecracks of Players, Managers, Owners, Umpires, Announcers, Writers & Fans on the Great American Pastime. LC 90-53512. 1995. mass mkt., pap. 4.99 (*0-345-38123-8*, Del Rey) Ballantine.

Nathan, Debbie. Women & Other Aliens: Essays from the U. S. - Mexico Border. LC 90-85078. 168p. 1991. pap. 10.95 (*0-938317-08-3*) Cinco Puntos.

Nathan, Dev, jt. auth. see Kelkar, Govind.

Nathan, George J. The American Credo: A Contribution Toward Interpretation of the National Mind. enl. rev. ed. (BCL1 - U. S. History Ser.). 266p. 1991. reprint ed. lib. bdg. 79.00 (*0-7812-6016-7*) Rprt Serv.

— Art of the Night. LC 75-120099. 296p. 1975. 25.00 (*0-8386-7965-X*) Fairleigh Dickinson.

— Autobiography of an Attitude. LC 76-145204. 1971. reprint ed. 39.00 (*0-403-00758-5*) Scholarly.

— Bottoms Up. LC 70-148843. (Select Bibliographies Reprint Ser.). 1977. 15.95 (*0-8369-5657-5*) Ayer.

— Critic & the Drama. LC 75-120099. 152p. 1975. 20.00 (*0-8386-7964-1*) Fairleigh Dickinson.

— Entertainment of a Nation. LC 75-120099. 290p. 1975. 26.50 (*0-8386-7887-4*) Fairleigh Dickinson.

— Materia Critica. LC 75-120099. 242p. 1975. 24.50 (*0-8386-7966-8*) Fairleigh Dickinson.

— Mister George Jean Nathan Presents. LC 70-145205. 1971. reprint ed. 18.00 (*0-403-03648-8*) Scholarly.

— Morning after the First Night. LC 75-120099. 282p. 1975. 25.00 (*0-8386-7779-7*) Fairleigh Dickinson.

— Mr. George Jean Nathan Presents. LC 75-120099. 310p. 1975. 25.00 (*0-8386-7967-6*) Fairleigh Dickinson.

— My Very Dear Sean: George Jean Nathan on Sean O'Casey, Letters & Articles. Angelin, Patricia & Lowery, Robert, eds. LC 82-48549. 192p. 1985. 32.50 (*0-8386-3166-5*) Fairleigh Dickinson.

— Passing Judgments. LC 71-86774. (Essay Index Reprint Ser.). 1977. 18.95 (*0-8369-1150-4*) Ayer.

— Passing Judgments: The Theatre World of George Jean Nathan. LC 75-120099. 271p. 1975. 25.00 (*0-8386-7722-3*) Fairleigh Dickinson.

— Popular Theatre. LC 75-120099. 236p. 1975. 25.00 (*0-8386-7945-5*) Fairleigh Dickinson.

— The Theater Book of the Year 1947-1948. 350p. 29.50 (*0-8386-1176-1*) Fairleigh Dickinson.

— Theatre Book of the Year, 1942-1943. LC 75-120099. (Illus.). 350p. 1975. 29.50 (*0-8386-7946-3*) Fairleigh Dickinson.

— Theatre Book of the Year, 1943-1944. LC 75-120099. 350p. 1975. 29.50 (*0-8386-7962-5*) Fairleigh Dickinson.

— Theatre Book of the Year, 1944-1945. LC 75-120099. 350p. 1975. 29.50 (*0-8386-7961-7*) Fairleigh Dickinson.

— The Theatre Book of the Year 1945-1946. LC 75-120099. (Theatre World of George Jean Nathan Ser.). 350p. 1974. 29.50 (*0-8386-1174-5*) Fairleigh Dickinson.

— The Theatre Book of the Year 1946-1947. LC 75-120099. (Theatre World of George Jean Nathan Ser.). 350p. 1975. 29.50 (*0-8386-1175-3*) Fairleigh Dickinson.

— Theatre of the Moment. LC 75-120099. (Theatre World of George Jean Nathan Ser.). 310p. 1975. 25.00 (*0-8386-7775-4*) Fairleigh Dickinson.

— The World in Falseface. LC 75-120099. 326p. 1975. 29.50 (*0-8386-7963-3*) Fairleigh Dickinson.

Nathan, George J. & Mencken, H. L., eds. The American Mercury: Facsimile Edition of Vol. One: The Original Issues of Jan., Feb., March & April, 1924. 600p. 1984. reprint ed. lib. bdg. 50.00 (*0-8334-1005-9*, Freedeeds Libr) Garber Comm.

Nathan Hale Institute Staff, ed. see McNamara, Francis J.

Nathan Hale Institute Staff, ed. see Sulc, Lawrence B.

Nathan, Hans. William Billings: Data & Documents. LC 75-33593. (Bibliographies in American Music Ser.: No. 2). 69p. 1976. 10.00 (*0-911772-67-7*) Info Coord.

Nathan, Hans, ed. see Billings, William.

***Nathan, Harold D.** Chemistry Quick Review. 1993. pap. 7.95 (*0-614-07038-4*) Cliffs.

— Chemistry Quick Review. (Cliffs Quick Reviews Ser.). (Illus.). 174p. (C). 1993. pap. text ed. 6.95 (*0-8220-5318-7*) Cliffs.

Nathan, Harriet. Critical Choices in Interviews: Conduct, Use, & Research Role. LC 86-10523. 137p. (Orig.). 1986. pap. 9.95 (*0-87772-309-5*) UCB IGS.

Nathan, Harriet & Scott, Stanley, eds. Emerging Issues in Public Policy: Research Reports & Essays, 1960-1965. LC 73-8712. 184p. reprint ed. pap. 52.50 (*0-7837-2126-9*, 2042408) Bks Demand.

— Emerging Issues in Public Policy: Research Reports & Essays, 1966-1972. LC 73-8711. 218p. reprint ed. pap. 62.20 (*0-7837-2127-7*, 2042409) Bks Demand.

— Emerging Issues in Public Policy: Research Reports & Essays, 1973-1976. LC 77-6469. 178p. reprint ed. pap. 50.80 (*0-7837-2128-5*, 2042410) Bks Demand.

— Experiment & Change in Berkeley: Essays on City Politics, 1950-1975. LC 78-26636. 501p. 1979. pap. 14.95 (*0-87772-261-7*) UCB IGS.

— Politics, Government, & Related Policy Issues, 1977-1982. LC 83-26374. (Emerging Issues in Public Policy: Research Reports & Essays). 45p. reprint ed. pap. 25.00 (*0-7837-2129-3*, 2042411) Bks Demand.

Nathan, Harriet, jt. auth. see Kreinberg, Nancy.

Nathan, Harriet, ed. see Kroeger, Louis J.

Nathan, Harvey K., jt. auth. see Lage, Gustavo A.

N

Nathan, Isaac. Memoirs of Madame Malibran De Beriot. LC 80-2291. reprint ed. 18.50 (*0-404-18860-5*) AMS Pr.

Nathan, James A. Cuban Missile Crisis Revisited. LC 91-47951. 304p. 1992. text ed. 39.95 (*0-312-06069-6*) St Martin.

Nathan, James A., ed. The Cuban Missile Crisis Revisited. 304p. 1993. text ed. 17.95 (*0-312-09725-5*) St Martin.

Nathan, James A. & Oliver, James K. Foreign Policy Making & the American Political System. 3rd ed. LC 94-7530. 1994. text ed. 45.00x (*0-8018-4771-0*); pap. text ed. 14.95x (*0-8018-4772-9*) Johns Hopkins.

— Foreign Policy Making in the American Political System. 2nd ed. (C). 1987. pap. text ed. 24.00 (*0-673-39467-0*) HarpCollege.

— The Future of United States Naval Power. LC 78-9512. 255p. reprint ed. pap. 72.70 (*0-685-16277-X*, 2056247) Bks Demand.

— United States Foreign Policy & World Order. 4th ed. (C). 1989. pap. text ed. 39.00 (*0-673-39689-4*) HarpCollege.

Nathan, Jay, jt. auth. see Ellis, Dennis.

Nathan, Jay, jt. ed. see Latona, Joseph C.

Nathan, Joan. The Children's Jewish Holiday Kitchen. LC 86-22016. (Illus.). 144p. 1987. spiral bd. 14.00 (*0-8052-0827-5*) Schocken.

— Jewish Cooking in America. LC 93-38581. 1994. 30.00 (*0-394-58405-8*) Knopf.

— Jewish Holiday Kitchen. enl. rev. ed. LC 88-42765. (Illus.). 336p. 1988. pap. 19.00 (*0-8052-0900-X*) Schocken.

Nathan, Joe. Free to Teach: Achieving Equity & Excellence in Schools. 2nd rev. ed. LC 91-12785. 256p. 1991. pap. 16.95 (*0-8298-0905-8*) Pilgrim OH.

Nathan, Joe, ed. Public Schools by Choice: Expanding Opportunities for Parents, Students & Teachers. LC 89-80266. 266p. (Orig.). 1989. pap. 6.95 (*0-9622302-0-0*) Inst Learn Teach.

Nathan, John, tr. see Oe, Kenzaburo.

Nathan, Kurt, jt. auth. see Strom, Steven.

Nathan, Laura E., jt. auth. see Kiecolt, K. Jill.

Nathan, Laurie, jt. ed. see Cock, Jacklyn.

Nathan, Leonard. Carrying On: New & Selected Poems. LC 85-40339. (Poetry Ser.). 160p. 1985. 29.95 (*0-8229-3525-2*); pap. 12.95 (*0-8229-5375-7*) U of Pittsburgh Pr.

— The Likeness: Poems Out of India. LC 75-12734. (Illus.). 48p. (Orig.). 1975. lib. bdg. 7.00 (*0-914476-47-5*); pap. 3.50 (*0-914476-40-8*) Thorp Springs.

— The Poets Work: An Introduction to Czeslaw Milosz. 1991. pap. 12.95 (*0-674-68970-4*) HUP.

— Returning Your Call: Poems. LC 75-3485. (Contemporary Poets Ser.). 76p. 1975. 19.95 (*0-691-06296-X*); pap. 8.95 (*0-691-01321-7*) Princeton U Pr.

— The Teachings of Grandfather Fox. LC 76-57990. 49p. 1976. 3.50 (*0-87886-079-7*, Greenfld Rev Pr) Greenfld Rev Lit.

Nathan, Leonard & Larson, James, trs. Songs of Something Else: Selected Poems of Gunnar Ekelof. LC 81-47915. (Lockert Library of Poetry in Translation). 344p. 1982. 29.95 (*0-691-06511-X*); pap. 12.95 (*0-691-01389-6*) Princeton U Pr.

Nathan, Leonard & Quinn, Arthur. The Poet's Work: An Introduction to Czeslaw Milosz. (C). 1991. pap. 9.95 (*0-685-48477-7*) HUP.

Nathan, Leonard, tr. see Wat, Aleksander.

Nathan, Leonard E. The Tragic Drama of William Butler Yeats: Figures in a Dance. LC 65-16513. 319p. reprint ed. pap. 91.00 (*0-8357-4570-8*, 2037480) Bks Demand.

Nathan, M. B., jt. ed. see Doxey, D. L.

Nathan, M. C. Franks of Western Expresses. (Illus.). 281p. 1973. 35.00 (*0-318-41002-8*) Collectors Club IL.

Nathan, Marvin, jt. auth. see Chandler, Arthur.

Nathan, Maud. Once upon a Time & Today. LC 74-3964. (Women in America Ser.). (Illus.). 360p. 1974. reprint ed. 31.95 (*0-405-06113-7*) Ayer.

— Once Upon a Time & Today. (American Biography Ser.). 327p. 1991. reprint ed. lib. bdg. 79.00 (*0-7812-8294-2*) Rprt Serv.

Nathan, Max, Jr. & Neff, Carole C. Louisiana Estate Planning, Will Drafting, & Estate Administration, 3 vols. suppl. ed. 1994. 85.00 (*0-685-74479-5*) Butterworth Legal Pubs.

— Louisiana Estate Planning, Will Drafting, & Estate Administration, 3 vols., Set. 1800p. 1992. ring bd. 240.00 (*1-56257-952-5*) Michie Butterworth.

Nathan, Michael & Galloway, Jeff. Runners Log Two Thousand. (Illus.). 80p. (Orig.). 1988. spiral bd. write for info. (*0-318-63185-7*) Nathan & Co.

Nathan, Michele. Nahuatl Sources in the Tulane University Latin American Library. 50p. 1978. pap. 3.50 (*0-317-43424-1*) Tulane Lat Am Lib.

Nathan, N. M. Evidence & Assurance. LC 79-50505. (Cambridge Studies in Philosophy). 1980. 44.95 (*0-521-22517-5*) Cambridge U Pr.

Nathan, Norma. Boston's Most Eligible Bachelors, 1989. (Illus.). 200p. (Orig.). 1988. pap. 8.95 (*0-9621200-0-6*) N Nathan.

Nathan, Norman. Prince William B. The Philosophical Conceptions of William Blake. (Studies in English Literature: No. 100). 164p. 1975. pap. text ed. 30.70 (*90-279-3117-8*) Mouton.

Nathan of Breslov, jt. auth. see Nachman of Breslov.

Nathan, Otto. Nazi War Finance & Banking. (Occasional Papers). 100p. 1944. reprint ed. 27.60 (*0-87014-335-2*); reprint ed. mic. film 20.00 (*0-685-61254-6*) Natl Bur Econ Res.

Nathan, P. E., jt. ed. see Marlatt, G. Alan.

Nathan, Paul. No Good Deed. LC 94-10137. 202p. 1995. 22.00 (*1-877946-56-7*) Permanent Pr.

— Protocol for Murder. 176p. 1994. pap. 16.00 (*1-877946-64-8*) Permanent Pr.

Nathan, Paul S., tr. see Gor'kii, Maksim.

Nathan, Paul S., tr. see Gorky, Maxim.

Nathan, Peter. The Nervous System. 3rd ed. (Illus.). 400p. 1988. pap. 14.95 (*0-19-282152-0*) OUP.

Nathan, Peter E., jt. ed. see Hay, William H.

Nathan, Peter E., jt. ed. see Howard, George S.

Nathan, Peter E., ed. see Weissbourd, Katherine.

***Nathan, R. K.** A Practical Approach to Evidence in Malaysia & Singapore. 500p. 1993. 160.00 (*0-409-99646-7*, SI) Butterworth Legal Pubs.

— Quantum of Damages. 455p. 1991. boxed 160.00 (*0-409-99598-3*, SI) Butterworth Legal Pubs.

Nathan, Rabbi. Tzaddik. Greenbaum, Avraham, tr. Orig. Title: Chayey Moharan. 1988. 17.00 (*0-930213-17-3*) Breslov Res Inst.

Nathan, Rhoda B., ed. Critical Essays on Katherine Mansfield. LC 93-2963. (Critical Essays on British Literature Ser.). 300p. 1993. text ed. 45.00 (*0-8161-8868-8*, Hall Reference) Macmillan.

— Nineteenth-Century Women Writers of the English-Speaking World. LC 85-27250. (Contributions in Women's Studies: No. 69). 304p. 1986. text ed. 49.95 (*0-313-25170-3*, NWW/, Greenwood Pr) Greenwood.

***Nathan, Rich & Wilson, Ken.** Renewed Evangelicals: Open to the Spirit, Rooted in the Word. 190p. 1995. pap. 8.99 (*0-89283-929-5*, Vine Bks) Servant.

Nathan, Richard A., ed. Fuels from Sugar Crops: Systems Study for Sugarcane, Sweet Sorghum, & Sugar Beets. LC 78-19127. (DOE Critical Review Ser.). 151p. 1978. pap. 11.75 (*0-87079-111-7*, TID-22781); fiche 9.00 (*0-87079-212-1*, TID-22781) DOE.

Nathan, Richard D., ed. Cardiac Muscles: The Regulation of Excitation & Contraction. 352p. 1986. text ed. 115.00 (*0-12-514370-2*) Acad Pr.

Nathan, Richard P. The Administrative Presidency. LC 82-21712. 180p. (C). 1983. pap. write for info. (*0-02-386210-6*) Macmillan.

— Turning Promises into Performance: The Management Challenge of Implementing Workfare. LC 92-42821. 160p. (C). 1993. text ed. 42.50 (*0-231-07962-1*); pap. 15.00 (*0-231-07963-X*) Col U Pr.

Nathan, Richard P. & Adams, Charles F., Jr. Revenue Sharing: The Second Round. LC 76-51884. 286p. reprint ed. pap. 81.60 (*0-317-26739-6*, 2025391) Bks Demand.

Nathan, Richard P. & Doolittle, Fred C. Reagan & the States. LC 87-45529. (Illus.). 344p. 1987. text ed. 55.00 (*0-691-07748-7*) Princeton U Pr.

Nathan, Richard P. & Webman, Jerry A. The Urban Development Action Grant Program. 125p. 1980. pap. text ed. 16.95 (*0-938882-01-5*) Transaction Pubs.

Nathan, Richard P., jt. ed. see DiIulio, John J., Jr.

Nathan, Richard P., ed. see Heller, Walter, et al.

Nathan, Richard P., jt. auth. see Schill, Michael H.

Nathan, Richard P., et al. The Consequences of Cuts: The Effects of the Reagan Domestic Program on State & Local Governments. LC 83-60542. (Illus.). 221p. (Orig.). 1983. pap. 7.95 (*0-938882-06-6*) Woodrow Wilson Schl.

— Monitoring Revenue Sharing. LC 74-28124. 416p. reprint ed. pap. 118.60 (*0-317-20852-7*, 2025392) Bks Demand.

— Public Service Employment: A Field Evaluation. LC 81-4596. 121p. 1981. pap. 12.95 (*0-8157-5987-8*) Brookings.

— Reagan & the States. LC 87-45529. Date not set. reprint ed. pap. 111.80 (*0-7837-9400-2*, 2060145) Bks Demand.

Nathan, Robert. The Barly Fields. 1976. 31.95 (*0-8488-0099-0*, Amereon Hse) Amereon Ltd.

— The Enchanted Voyage. LC 86-22753. 187p. 1987. reprint ed. text ed. 49.75 (*0-313-25270-X*, NAEN, Greenwood Pr) Greenwood.

— Portrait of Jennie. 1949. 19.95 (*0-394-44093-5*) Knopf.

— Portrait of Jennie. 1976. 17.95 (*0-8488-1096-1*) Amereon Ltd.

— Portrait of Jennie. 293p. (J). 1981. reprint ed. lib. bdg. 21.95x (*0-89966-356-7*) Buccaneer Bks.

— Portrait of Jennie. 234p. (J). 1981. reprint ed. lib. bdg. 16.95 (*0-89967-030-X*) Harmony Raine.

— Sir Henry. LC 79-12787. vi, 187p. 1979. reprint ed. lib. bdg. 27.00x (*0-89370-136-X*); reprint ed. pap. 17.00x (*0-89370-236-6*) Borgo Pr.

Nathan, Robert & Hill, Linda. Career Counselling in Practice. (Counselling in Practice Ser.). (Illus.). 160p. (C). 1992. 44.00 (*0-8039-8695-5*); pap. 19.95 (*0-8039-8696-3*) Sage.

Nathan, Robert L. The Dreamtime. LC 74-21584. 280p. 1975. 22.50 (*0-87951-028-5*) Overlook Pr.

Nathan, Robert T. Portrait of Jennie. large type ed. LC 91-32790. 151p. 1991. reprint ed. lib. bdg. 18.95 (*1-56054-264-0*) Thorndike Pr.

Nathan, Ronald G. Doctor's Guide to Instant Stress Relief. 288p. 1989. mass mkt. 4.95 (*0-345-35622-5*) Ballantine.

Nathan, Ronald G. & Charlesworth, Edward A. Stress Management: A Conceptual & Procedural Guide. LC 80-70400. (Illus.). 119p. (Orig.). 1980. pap. text ed. 19.95 (*0-938176-01-3*) Biobehavioral Pr.

Nathan, Ronald G. & Stuart, Marian R. Coping with the Stressed-out People in Your Life. 288p. (Orig.). 1994. pap. 10.00 (*0-345-38186-6*) Ballantine.

Nathan, Ronald G., jt. auth. see Charlesworth, Edward A.

Nathan, Ruth, ed. Writers in the Classroom. 288p. (J). (gr. k-12). 1990. text ed. 25.95 (*0-926842-05-6*) CG Pubs Inc.

Nathan, S. S., jt. ed. see Gupta, B. M.

Nathan Staff. Anglais Banque. 141p. (ENG & FRE.). 1992. 18.95 (*0-7859-0971-0*, 2098866011) Fr & Eur.

— Anglais Hotellerie. 125p. (ENG & FRE.). 1992. 18.95 (*0-7859-0972-9*, 2098866046) Fr & Eur.

— Anglais Restauration. 125p. (ENG & FRE.). 1992. 18.95 (*0-7859-0973-7*, 2098866070) Fr & Eur.

Nathan, Theodore R. Hotelmanship: A Guide to Hospitality Industry Marketing & Management. LC 81-7051. 264p. 1981. 49.50 (*0-685-05973-1*, Inst Busn Plan) P-H.

Nathan, Vasantha, ed. see Global Engineering Documents Staff.

Nathanail, Paul. Greek Dictionary: Greek-English & English-Greek Pocket Dictionary. (ENG & GRE.). 1985. pap. 16.95 (*0-7100-0625-X*) Routledge Chapman & Hall.

Nathanielsz, P. W., ed. Animal Models in Fetal Medicine (I) LC 80-17292. (Monographs in Fetal Physiology). (Illus.). 368p. 1985. reprint ed. 80.00 (*0-916859-14-2*) Perinatology.

— Animal Models in Fetal Medicine (II) (Monographs in Fetal Physiology). (Illus.). 339p. 1982. 80.00 (*0-444-80425-0*) Perinatology.

— Animal Models in Fetal Medicine (III) (Monographs in Fetal Physiology). (Illus.). 226p. 1984. 70.00 (*0-916859-00-2*) Perinatology.

— Animal Models in Fetal Medicine (IV) Intrauterine Growth. (Monographs in Fetal Physiology). (Illus.). 222p. 1984. 70.00 (*0-916859-01-0*) Perinatology.

— Animal Models in Fetal Medicine (V) Parturition. (Monographs in Fetal Physiology). (Illus.). 330p. 1986. 80.00 (*0-916859-09-6*) Perinatology.

— Animal Models in Fetal Medicine (VI) Metabolism. (Monographs in Fetal Physiology). 1987. 80.00 (*0-916859-15-0*) Perinatology.

Nathanielsz, P. W., jt. auth. see Jones, C. T.

Nathanielsz, Peter W. Life Before Birth & a Time to Be Born. LC 92-26052. (Illus.). 250p. 1992. 25.00 (*0-916859-55-X*) Promethean Pr.

Nathanielsz, Peter W. & Parer, Julian T., eds. Research in Perinatal Medicine. (Research in Perinatal Medicine Ser.: No. I). (Illus.). 246p. 1984. 67.50 (*0-916859-03-7*) Perinatology.

Nathans, Sydney. Daniel Webster & Jacksonian Democracy. LC 72-10779. (Johns Hopkins University Studies in Historical & Political Science: Series 91, No. 1). 263p. reprint ed. pap. 75.00 (*0-685-23508-4*, 2027899) Bks Demand.

Nathans, Sydney, ed. see Clayton, Thomas H.

Nathans, Sydney, ed. see Fenn, Elizabeth A. & Wood, Peter H.

Nathans, Sydney, ed. see Watson, Harry L.

***Nathanson, Bernard.** The Hand of God: A Journey from Death to Life by the Abortion Doctor Who Changed His Mind. 288p. 1995. 23.95 (*0-89526-463-3*) Regnery Pub.

Nathanson, Bernard N. & Ostling, Richard N. Aborting America. 320p. (C). 1981. reprint ed. pap. 6.95 (*0-919225-00-4*) Life Cycle Bks.

Nathanson, Carol, jt. auth. see Rosenberg, Barry A.

Nathanson, Constance. Dangerous Passage: The Social Control of Sexuality in Women's Adolescence. (Health, Society, & Policy Ser.). 350p. 1991. 44.95 (*0-87722-824-8*) Temple U Pr.

Nathanson, Constance A. Dangerous Passage: The Social Control of Sexuality in Women's Adolescence. 304p. 1993. pap. 18.95 (*1-56639-077-X*) Temple U Pr.

Nathanson, Donald L. Shame & Pride: Affect, Sex, & the Birth of the Self. (Illus.). 480p. 1992. 24.95 (*0-393-03097-0*) Norton.

— Shame & Pride: Affect, Sex & the Birth of the Self. 496p. 1994. pap. 14.95 (*0-393-31109-0*) Norton.

Nathanson, Donald L., ed. The Many Faces of Shame. LC 86-31937. 370p. 1987. lib. bdg. 42.00 (*0-89862-705-2*) Guilford Pr.

***Nathanson, E. M. & Bank, Aaron.** Knight's Cross. 448p. 1995. mass mkt. 5.99 (*0-8439-3724-6*) Dorchester Pub Co.

— Knight's Cross: A Novel. LC 92-35891. 1993. 19.95 (*1-55972-168-5*, Birch Ln Pr) Carol Pub Group.

Nathanson, Fred E. Radar Design Principles. 2nd ed. 1991. 70.00 (*0-07-046052-3*) McGraw.

— Radar Design Principles: Signal Processing & the Environment. (Illus.). 1969. text ed. 85.00 (*0-07-046047-7*) McGraw.

Nathanson, Irwin D. How to Start & Operate Your Own Profitable Consulting Business: The Successful Consultant's Course. (Illus.). 294p. 1990. 79.00 (*1-878614-02-9*) Worldwide Mktg.

Nathanson, J. & Kissam, Philip. Surveying Practice. 4th ed. 608p. 1987. text ed. 37.95 (*0-07-034903-7*) McGraw.

Nathanson, J. A. & Kobabian, J. W., eds. Cyclic Nucleotides, Part I: Biochemistry. (Handbook of Experimental Pharmacology Ser.: Vol. 58, Pt. I). (Illus.). 736p. 1982. 287.00 (*0-387-10786-X*) Spr-Verlag.

Nathanson, Jerry & Kissam, Philip C. Surveying Practice. 4th ed. 1988. text ed. write for info. (*0-07-046062-0*) McGraw.

Nathanson, L., et al. Small Group Problem Solving: An Aid to Organizational Effectiveness. 1981. pap. write for info. (*0-201-05203-2*) Addison-Wesley.

Nathanson, Larry, ed. Basic & Clinical Aspects of Malignant Melanoma. 240p. (C). 1987. lib. bdg. 101.50 (*0-89838-856-2*) Kluwer Ac.

— Current Research & Clinical Management of Melanoma, Alk. paper. LC 93-9325. (Cancer Treatment & Research Ser.: Vol. 65). 400p. (C). 1993. lib. bdg. 195.00 (*0-7923-2152-9*) Kluwer Ac.

— Malignant Melanoma: Biology, Diagnosis, & Therapy. (Cancer Treatment & Research Ser.). (C). 1988. lib. bdg. 100.00 (*0-89838-384-6*) Kluwer Ac.

— Management of Advanced Melanoma. (Contemporary Issues in Clinical Oncology Ser.: Vol. 6). (Illus.). 272p. 1986. text ed. 41.50 (*0-685-17326-7*); write for info. (*0-443-08463-7*) Churchill.

— Management of Advanced Melanoma. fac. ed. LC 86-17154. (Contemporary Issues in Clinical Oncology Ser.: No. 6). (Illus.). 286p. 1986. reprint ed. pap. 81.60 (*0-7837-7901-1*, 2047657) Bks Demand.

— Melanoma Research: Genetics, Growth Factors, Metastases & Antigens. (Cancer Treatment & Research Ser.). (C). 1991. lib. bdg. 115.00 (*0-7923-0895-6*) Kluwer Ac.

***Nathanson, Laura W.** Kid Shapes: A Guide to Helping Your Kids Control Their Weight. LC 95-1797. 240p. 1995. 17.50 (*0-06-270135-5*, HarpT) HarpC.

— The Portable Pediatrician. LC 93-24395. (Illus.). 624p. 1994. pap. 20.00 (*0-06-273176-9*, Harper Ref) HarpC.

Nathanson, Leonard. The Strategy of Truth: A Study of Sir Thomas Browne. LC 67-18216. 253p. reprint ed. pap. 72.20 (*0-317-08080-6*, 2020135) Bks Demand.

Nathanson, M. B., tr. see Karatsuba, A. A.

Nathanson, Martha D. Home Health Care Answer Book: Legal Issues for Providers. 200p. 1995. text ed. 69.00 (*0-8342-0575-0*, 20575) Aspen Pub.

Nathanson, Melvyn B., ed. see Freiman, Grigori.

Nathanson, Neil M. & Harden, T. Kendall, eds. G Proteins & Signal Transduction. (Society of General Physiologists Ser.). 211p. 1990. pap. 50.00 (*0-87470-046-9*) Rockefeller.

Nathanson, Paul. Over the Rainbow: The Wizard of Oz As a Secular Myth of America. LC 90-10163. (McGill Studies in the History of Religions). (Illus.). 432p. (C). 1991. 64.50 (*0-7914-0709-8*); pap. 21.95 (*0-7914-0710-1*) State U NY Pr.

Nathanson, Stephen. An Eye for an Eye: The Morality of Punishing by Death. LC 87-9579. (C). 1987. text ed. 41.00 (*0-8476-7561-0*) Rowman.

— Eye for an Eye? The Morality of Punishing by Death. 1992. pap. 14.95 (*0-8476-7725-7*) Rowman.

— The Ideal of Rationality: A Defense, Within Reason. 272p. 1994. 44.95 (*0-8126-9261-6*); pap. 18.95 (*0-8126-9262-4*) Open Court.

— Patriotism, Morality, & Peace. LC 92-32412. (Studies in Social & Political Philosophy). 1993. write for info. (*0-8476-7799-0*); pap. write for info. (*0-8476-7800-8*) Rowman.

— Should We Consent to Be Governed? A Short Introduction to Political Philosophy. 134p. (C). 1992. pap. 16.95 (*0-534-16746-2*) Intl Thomson.

Nathanson, Susan N. & Lerman, Dan, eds. Outpatient Cancer Centers: Implementation & Management. LC 88-8182. 287p. (Orig.). 1988. pap. 45.00 (*1-55648-026-1*, 016141) AHPI.

Nathanson, Tenney. The Book of Death. 1975. pap. 5.00 (*0-87924-024-5*) Membrane Pr.

— Whitman's Presence: Body, Voice, & Writing in Leaves of Grass. 528p. (C). 1992. text ed. 60.00 (*0-8147-5770-7*) NYU Pr.

— Whitman's Presence: Body, Voice & Writing in Leaves of Grass. 1994. pap. 18.50 (*0-8147-5779-0*) NYU Pr.

Nathenson, Michael B., jt. ed. see Henderson, Euan S.

Nather, Gunther. Bibliothekswesen in Italien. 96p. (GER.). 1991. pap. text ed. 22.00 (*3-598-10759-5*) K G Saur.

Nather, Wolfgang. Effective Observation of Random Fields. 184p. (C). 1985. 60.00 (*0-685-36898-X*, Pub. by Collets) St Mut.

Nather, Wolfgang, jt. auth. see Bandemer, Hans.

Natiello, Loretta, ed. see Foley, Raymond P.

Natiional Center for State Courts Staff. Security Analysis of the Hamilton County (OH) Courthouse & Justice Complex, South Building, First Floor. 48p. 1986. 3.00 (*0-685-15439-4*, NERO-183) Natl Ctr St Courts.

Nation. Teaching & Learning Vocabulary. 1990. pap. 20.95 (*0-8384-2863-0*) Heinle & Heinle.

Nation, Allan. Grass Farmers. (Illus.). 192p. (C). 1993. pap. 23.50 (*0-9632460-1-1*) Green Park.

— Pasture Profits with Stocker Cattle. 192p. (C). 1992. pap. text ed. 24.95 (*0-9632460-0-3*) Green Park.

— Quality Pasture: How to Create It, Manage It & Profit from It. (Illus.). (C). 1995. pap. write for info. (*0-9632460-3-8*) Green Park.

Nation, Daryl, jt. ed. see Evans, Terry.

Nation, Earl F., ed. Men & Books. (Illus.). x, 67p. 1987. reprint ed. 20.00 (*0-937543-01-2*) Sacrum Pr.

Nation, Edna. Caring Enough to Discipline: A Guide for Parents & Teachers of Children & Teens. 128p. (Orig.). 1987. pap. 5.95 (*0-9614669-3-6*) Edna Nation.

— Emotional Healing: A Guide for Hurting Women. 128p. (Orig.). 1987. pap. 4.95 (*0-9614669-4-4*) Edna Nation.

— More Than a Fig Leaf: A Guide for Christian Clothing, Clarification of Women's Clothing, Men's Clothing & the Distinction Between the Two. 128p. (Orig.). 1986. pap. 4.95 (*0-9614669-2-8*) Edna Nation.

Nation, Edna & Lamb, Joyce. Joyce: "Roaring Rorie", Ward of the State, Victim of Divorce, Alcoholism, & Neglect. (Illus.). 128p. (Orig.). 1985. pap. 4.95 (*0-9614669-0-1*) Edna Nation.

Nation, J. D. & Eaton, J. G., eds. Stratigraphy, Depositional Environments & Sedimentary Tectonics of the Western Margin, Cretaceous Western Seaway. (Special Paper Ser.: No. 260). (Illus.). 240p. 1991. pap. 42.50 (*0-8137-2260-8*) Geol Soc.

Nation, Jack, jt. auth. see LeUnes, Arnold.

Nation, James E. & Aram, Dorothy M. Diagnosis of Speech & Language Disorders. 2nd ed. (Illus.). (C). 1991. reprint ed. pap. text ed. 45.00x (*1-879105-05-5*, A055) Singular Publishing.

Nation, Joseph E., ed. The De-Escalation of Nuclear Crises. LC 91-20553. 210p. 1992. text ed. 59.95 (*0-312-05245-6*) St Martin.

Nation, Lindsay, jt. auth. see Johnson, Susan.

Nation Magazine Staff. View of the Nation: 1955-1959. Christman, Henry M., ed. LC 79-111853. (Essay Index Reprint Ser.). 1977. 21.95 (*0-8369-1620-4*) Ayer.

Nation Muzzle Loading Rifle Association Staff. Muzzle Blasts: Early Years Plus Vol. I & II 1939-41. LC 74-11637. 352p. 1974. pap. 20.00 (*0-87387-069-7*) Shumway.

Nation, Nyle. The Pine Nut Chronicle: The History & Adventures of Mining in Douglas County, Nevada. 300p. 1991. pap. 12.95 (*0-9630420-0-9*) Triple N Ent.

Nation, Nyle N. Pine Nut Chronicle: The History & Adventures of Mining in Douglas County Nevada. 2nd ed. Parkhurst, Sue, ed. 250p. 1992. reprint ed. pap. 12.95 (*0-9630420-1-7*) Triple N Ent.

Nation of Islam Staff. The Secret Relationship Between Blacks & Jews, Vol. 1. 334p. 1991. pap. text ed. 24.95 (*0-9636877-0-0*) Hist Res Dept.

Nation, Pat. Bouquet of Roses. LC 89-83522. (Illus.). 110p. 1989. lib. bdg. 12.95 (*0-944419-09-7*) Everett Cos Pub.

***Nation, Paul, ed.** New Ways in Teaching Vocabulary. 232p. 1994. pap. 22.95 (*0-939791-51-X*) Tchrs Eng Spkrs.

Nation, R. Craig. Black Earth, Red Star: A History of Soviet Security Policy, 1917-1991. LC 92-3717. (Illus.). 360p. 1993. 35.00 (*0-8014-2725-8*); pap. 14.95 (*0-8014-8007-8*) Cornell U Pr.

— War on War: Lenin, the Zimmerwald Left, & the Origins of Communist Internationalism. LC 89-35744. 304p. 1989. lib. bdg. 48.00 (*0-8223-0944-0*) Duke.

Nation, Terry, jt. auth. see Peel, John.

National & Provincial Building Society Staff. The National & Provincial Guide to House Restoration. 96p. (Orig.). 1989. pap. 17.95 (*0-8464-1400-7*) Beekman Pubs.

National Academic Recognition Information Center Staff. International Guide to Qualifications in Education. 3rd ed. LC 91-27610. 880p. 1991. 200.00 (*0-7201-2085-3*) Weidner & Sons.

National Academy of Arbitrators Staff. Arbitration Today: Proceedings of the 8th Annual Meeting, Boston Massachusetts, January 27-28, 1955. McKelvey, Jean T., ed. 219p. reprint ed. pap. 62.50 (*0-8357-5709-9*, 2026788) Bks Demand.

— Critical Issues in Labor Arbitration: Proceedings of the Tenth Annual Meeting. McKelvey, Jean T., ed. (National Academy of Arbitrators: Proceedings of the Annual Meeting Ser.: No. 10). 227p. reprint ed. pap. 64.70 (*0-685-43696-9*, 2056175) Bks Demand.

— Management Rights & the Arbitration Process: Proceedings of the Ninth Annual Meeting. McKelvey, Jean T., ed. (National Academy of Arbitrators: Proceedings of the Annual Meeting Ser.: Vol. 9). 245p. reprint ed. pap. 69.90 (*0-685-16014-9*, 2056176) Bks Demand.

National Academy of Design Staff. Artists by Themselves: Artists' Portraits from the National Academy of Design. LC 83-62156. (Illus.). 176p. 1983. pap. 20.00 (*0-295-96143-0*) U of Wash Pr.

National Academy of Early Childhood Programs Staff. Guide to Accreditation. LC 85-60990. 226p. 1985. pap. text ed. 37.00 (*0-912674-93-8*, NAEYC #916) Natl Assn Child Ed.

National Academy of Engineering. Cities & Their Vital Systems: Infrastructure Past, Present & Future. 368p. 1988. pap. text ed. 35.00 (*0-309-03786-7*) Natl Acad Pr.

— Design & Analysis of Integrated Manufacturing Systems. 248p. 1988. text ed. 29.50 (*0-309-03844-8*) Natl Acad Pr.

— Globalization of Technology: International Perspectives. 224p. 1988. pap. text ed. 22.50 (*0-309-03842-1*) Natl Acad Pr.

National Academy of Engineering & the Institute of Medicine. New Medical Devices: Invention, Development & Use. 204p. 1988. 34.50 (*0-309-03847-2*); pap. text ed. 24.50 (*0-309-03846-4*) Natl Acad Pr.

National Academy of Engineering, Committee on Engineering as an International Enterprise Staff. National Interests in an Age of Global Technology: National Interests in an Age of Global Technology. Lee, Thomas H. & Reid, Proctor R., eds. (Prospering in a Global Economy Ser.). 176p. 1991. pap. 27.95 (*0-309-04329-8*) Natl Acad Pr.

National Academy of Engineering Staff. Application of Technology to Improve Productivity in the Service Sector of the National Economy: Summary Report & Recommendations Based on a Symposium & Workshops Held on the Occasion of the Eighth Annual Meeting, November 1 & 2, 1971, at the National Academy of Engineering. LC 72-83855. 376p. reprint ed. pap. 107.20 (*0-8357-7695-6*, 2036047) Bks Demand.

— The Competitive Status of the U. S. Auto Industry: A Study of the Influences of Technology in Determining International Industrial Competitive Advantage. LC 82-12506. 217p. 1982. pap. 61.90 (*0-7837-7450-8*, 2049172) Bks Demand.

— Education for the Manufacturing World of the Future. 136p. 1985. pap. text ed. 16.75 (*0-309-03584-8*) Natl Acad Pr.

— Engineering & the Advancement of Human Welfare: Ten Outstanding Achievements, 1964-1989. 48p. 1989. pap. text ed. 8.95 (*0-309-04185-6*) Natl Acad Pr.

— Engineering Within Ecological Constraints. Schulze, Peter, ed. 200p. (Orig.). (C). 1995. text ed. 29.95 (*0-309-05198-3*) Natl Acad Pr.

— The Future of Aerospace. 88p. (Orig.). (C). 1993. pap. text ed. 23.00 (*0-309-04881-8*) Natl Acad Pr.

— Hazards: Technology & Fairness. (Series on Technology & Social Priorities). 240p. 1986. pap. text ed. 24.95 (*0-309-03644-5*) Natl Acad Pr.

— Improving Aircraft Safety. 118p. 1980. pap. text ed. 12.95 (*0-309-03091-9*) Natl Acad Pr.

— Information Technologies & Social Transformation. 184p. 1985. pap. text ed. 19.95 (*0-309-03529-5*) Natl Acad Pr.

— Keeping Pace with Science & Engineering: Case Studies in Environmental Regulation. LC 93-5530. 296p. 1993. 39.95 (*0-309-04938-5*) Natl Acad Pr.

— Lasers: Invention to Application. 144p. 1987. pap. text ed. 14.95 (*0-309-03776-X*) Natl Acad Pr.

— Mastering a New Role: Shaping Technology Policy for National Economic Performance. (Prospering in a Global Economy Ser.). 144p. 1993. pap. 22.95 (*0-309-04646-7*) Natl Acad Pr.

— Memorial Tributes: National Academy of Engineering, Vol. 3. 388p. 1989. text ed. 27.95 (*0-309-03939-8*) Natl Acad Pr.

— Memorial Tributes: National Academy of Engineering, Vol. 4. 356p. (C). 1991. text ed. 42.00 (*0-309-04349-2*) Natl Acad Pr.

— Memorial Tributes: National Academy of Engineering, Vol. 5. 312p. (C). 1992. text ed. 36.00 (*0-309-04689-0*) Natl Acad Pr.

— Memorial Tributes, Vol. 1: National Academy of Engineering. 303p. 1979. 24.95 (*0-309-02889-2*) Natl Acad Pr.

— Memorial Tributes, Vol. 2: National Academy of Engineering. 318p. 1984. text ed. 24.95 (*0-309-03482-5*) Natl Acad Pr.

— Memorial Tributes, Vol. 7: National Academy of Engineering. 256p. 1994. 46.00 (*0-309-05146-0*) Natl Acad Pr.

— People & Technology in the Workplace. 336p. 1991. 29.95 (*0-309-04583-5*) Natl Acad Pr.

— Product Liability & Innovation: Managing Risk in an Uncertain Environment. 216p. (C). 1994. text ed. 37.95 (*0-309-05130-4*) Natl Acad Pr.

— Technology & Economics. 140p. 1991. pap. text ed. 19.00 (*0-309-04397-2*) Natl Acad Pr.

— Technology & Environment. Ausubel, Jesse H. & Slodevich, Hedy E., eds. 236p. (C). 1991. pap. text ed. 25.95 (*0-309-04426-X*) Natl Acad Pr.

National Academy of Engineering Staff. Technology & Global Industry: Companies & Nations in the World Economy. 280p. 1987. pap. text ed. 34.95 (*0-309-03736-0*) Natl Acad Pr.

National Academy of Engineering Staff. Technology in Services: Policies for Growth, Trade, & Employment. Guile, Bruce R. & Quinn, James B., eds. 256p. 1988. pap. 24.95 (*0-309-03887-1*) Natl Acad Pr.

— Time Horizons & Technology Investments. 120p. 1992. pap. 19.00 (*0-309-04647-5*) Natl Acad Pr.

National Academy of Engineering Staff, et al. Science & Technology in the Academic Enterprise: Status, Trends, & Issues. 120p. 1989. pap. text ed. 15.00 (*0-309-04175-9*) Natl Acad Pr.

— Technological Trajectories & the Human Environment. 230p. (C). 1995. text ed. 34.95 (*0-309-05133-9*) Natl Acad Pr.

National Academy of Science, et al. Technology & Employment: Innovation & Growth in the U. S. Economy. Cyert, Richard M. & Mowery, David M., eds. 244p. 1987. pap. 16.95 (*0-309-03744-1*) Natl Acad Pr.

National Academy of Science Staff. Biodiversity. 538p. 1988. 24.50 (*0-309-03739-5*) Natl Acad Pr.

National Academy of Science Staff, jt. auth. see Institute of Medicine Staff.

National Academy of Science Staff, et al. The Academic Research Enterprise Within the Industrialized Nations: Comparative Perspectives. 124p. (C). 1990. pap. text ed. 15.00 (*0-309-04249-6*) Natl Acad Pr.

— Policy Implications of Greenhouse Warming: Mitigation, Adaptation, & the Science Base. 944p. (C). 1992. text ed. 89.95 (*0-309-04386-7*) Natl Acad Pr.

National Academy of Science (U. S.) Staff. High Schools & the Changing Workplace: The Employer's View: Report of the Panel on Secondary School Education for the Changing Workplace. 64p. reprint ed. pap. 25.00 (*0-8357-7711-1*, 2036067) Bks Demand.

National Academy of Sciences. Biographical Memoirs, Vol. 57. (Illus.). 560p. 1987. text ed. 29.50 (*0-309-03729-8*) Natl Acad Pr.

— Reykjavik & Beyond: Deep Reductions in Strategic Nuclear Arsenals & the Future Direction of Arms Control. 80p. 1988. pap. text ed. 12.95 (*0-309-03799-9*) Natl Acad Pr.

National Academy of Sciences, et al. Research Briefings 1987. 80p. 1988. pap. text ed. 9.95 (*0-309-03828-6*) Natl Acad Pr.

National Academy of Sciences, Academy Industry Program Staff, et al. Corporate Restructuring & Industrial Research & Development. 180p. 1990. pap. text ed. 18.00 (*0-309-04186-4*) Natl Acad Pr.

National Academy of Sciences, Committee on Linking Trade & Technology Policies Staff. Linking Trade & Technology Policies: An International Comparison of the Policies of Industrialized Nations. Moore, Gordon E. & Harris, Martha C., eds. LC 92-29614. (Prospering in a Global Economy Ser.). 176p. (C). 1992. pap. 21.00 (*0-309-04645-9*) Natl Acad Pr.

National Academy of Sciences, National Academy of Engineering, Institute of Medicine, Panel on Scientific Responsibility & the Conduct of Research Sta. Responsible Science Vol. II: Background Papers & Resource Documents. 288p. 1993. pap. text ed. 33.00 (*0-309-04788-9*) Natl Acad Pr.

National Academy of Sciences, Office of the Home Secretary Staff. Biographical Memoirs, Vol. 65. 500p. 1994. 59.00 (*0-309-05037-5*) Natl Acad Pr.

National Academy of Sciences, Office of International Affairs Staff. Biotechnology in China. 116p. 1989. 15.00 (*0-309-03988-6*) Natl Acad Pr.

National Academy of Sciences, Panel on Advanced Technology Competition & the Industrialized Allies Staff. International Competition in Advanced Technology: Decisions for America. 69p. (C). 1983. pap. text ed. 12.95 (*0-309-03379-9*) Natl Acad Pr.

National Academy of Sciences Panel on NSF Decisionmaking for Major Awards, et al. Major Award Decisionmaking at the National Science Foundation. 174p. (Orig.). (C). 1994. pap. text ed. 35.00 (*0-309-05029-4*) Natl Acad Pr.

National Academy of Sciences Staff, et al. Balancing the National Interest: U. S. National Security Export Controls & Global Economic Competition. 368p. 1987. 29.95 (*0-309-03738-7*) Natl Acad Pr.

National Academy of Sciences Staff. Biographical Memoirs, Vol. 44. xii, 370p. 1974. 29.50 (*0-309-02238-X*) Natl Acad Pr.

— Biographical Memoirs, Vol. 45. vii, 465p. 1974. 29.50 (*0-309-02239-8*) Natl Acad Pr.

— Biographical Memoirs, Vol. 46. 435p. 1975. 29.50 (*0-309-02240-1*) Natl Acad Pr.

— Biographical Memoirs, Vol. 47. 551p. 1975. 29.50 (*0-309-02245-2*) Natl Acad Pr.

— Biographical Memoirs, Vol. 50. 416p. 1979. text ed. 29.50 (*0-309-02549-4*) Natl Acad Pr.

— Biographical Memoirs, Vol. 51. 418p. 1980. text ed. 29.50 (*0-309-02888-4*) Natl Acad Pr.

— Biographical Memoirs, Vol. 53. 400p. 1982. text ed. 29.50 (*0-309-03287-3*) Natl Acad Pr.

— Biographical Memoirs, Vol. 54. 448p. 1983. text ed. 29.50 (*0-309-03391-8*) Natl Acad Pr.

— Biographical Memoirs, Vol. 55. LC 05-26629. 636p. reprint ed. pap. 180.00 (*0-7837-2594-9*, 2042757) Bks Demand.

— Biographical Memoirs, Vol. 56. 640p. 1987. text ed. 29.50 (*0-309-03693-3*) Natl Acad Pr.

— Biographical Memoirs, Vol. 58. 556p. 1989. text ed. 29.50 (*0-309-03938-X*) Natl Acad Pr.

— Biographical Memoirs, Vol. 59. 500p. (C). 1990. text ed. 29.50 (*0-309-04198-8*) Natl Acad Pr.

— Biographical Memoirs, Vol. 60: 1991. LC 05-26629. 429p. reprint ed. pap. 122.30 (*0-7837-3573-1*, 2043432) Bks Demand.

— Ecological Risks: Perspectives from Poland & the United States. Grodzinski, Wladyslaw et al, eds. 428p. 1990. pap. text ed. 35.00 (*0-309-04293-3*) Natl Acad Pr.

— Infectious Diseases in an Age of Change: The Impact of Human Ecology & Behavior on Disease Transmission. 250p. (Orig.). (C). 1995. text ed. 44.95 (*0-309-05136-3*) Natl Acad Pr.

— Reinventing Schools: The Technology Is Now. 32p. (Orig.). (C). 1995. pap. text ed. 5.00 (*0-309-05138-X*) Natl Acad Pr.

— Science at the Frontier, Vol. 1. (Illus.). 288p. (C). 1992. text ed. 24.95 (*0-309-04592-4*) Natl Acad Pr.

— Scientific Communication & National Security. 188p. (C). 1982. 19.95 (*0-309-03332-2*) Natl Acad Pr.

National Academy of Sciences Staff & Dreyfus, B. Proceedings Fifth Biennial International Codata Conference, Boulder 6-7, 1976. LC 77-78339. 1977. 99.00 (*0-08-021291-3*, Pub. by Pergamon Repr UK) Franklin.

National Academy of Sciences Staff & True, Frederick W. A History of the First Half-Century of the National Academy of Sciences, 1863-1913, Vol. 1. 1980. 26.95 (*0-405-12698-0*) Ayer.

— A History of the First Half-Century of the National Academy of Sciences, 1863-1913, Vol. 2. 1980. 26.95 (*0-405-12699-9*) Ayer.

National Academy of Sciences Staff, jt. auth. see Lewin, Walter H.

National Academy of Sciences Staff, jt. auth. see National Research Council Staff.

***National Academy of Sciences Staff, et al.** On Being a Scientist: Responsible Conduct in Research. 2nd rev. ed. 40p. (C). 1995. pap. text ed. 5.00 (*0-309-05196-7*) Natl Acad Pr.

— A Positron Named Priscilla: Scientific Discovery at the Frontier. 360p. (C). 1994. 29.95 (*0-309-04893-1*) Natl Acad Pr.

— Responsible Science, Vol. I: The Ensuring Integrity of the Research Process. 224p. 1992. pap. 24.95 (*0-309-04731-5*) Natl Acad Pr.

— Science & Technology Leadership in America Government: Ensuring the Best Presidential Appointments. 104p. (C). 1992. pap. text ed. 12.95 (*0-309-04727-7*) Natl Acad Pr.

— Science, Medicine, & Animals. 40p. 1991. pap. 5.00 (*0-309-04439-1*) Natl Acad Pr.

National Academy of Sciences, U. S. Committee on International Security & Arms Control. Nuclear Arms Control: Background & Issues. LC 84-62287. 378p. 1985. pap. text ed. 24.95 (*0-309-03491-4*) Natl Acad Pr.

National Academy of Sciences (U.S.), Institute of Medicine Staff. Aging & Medical Education: Report of a Study. LC 81-600911. (Publication IOM Ser.: No. 78-04). 82p. reprint ed. pap. 25.00 (*0-8357-7691-3*, 2036042) Bks Demand.

National Academy of Television Arts & Sciences Staff, ed. TV Dinners & Other Media Munchies. (Illus.). 176p. (Orig.). 1986. pap. 7.95 (*0-87491-816-2*) Acropolis.

National Academy of the Avant Garde Staff. Proceedings of the National Academy of the Avant Garde. Korn, Henry, ed. 1975. pap. 5.00 (*0-915066-62-9*) Assembling Pr.

National Accounts Review Committee. The National Economic Accounts of the United States: Review, Appraisal, & Recommendations. (General Ser.: No. 64). 206p. 1958. reprint ed. 53.60 (*0-87014-063-9*); reprint ed. mic. film 26.80 (*0-685-61315-1*) Natl Bur Econ Res.

National Advertising Company Staff. America's Advertisers: Who They Are, Where They Are, How They Have Developed, & What They Are Doing at the Present Time. LC 75-22830. (America in Two Centuries Ser.). 1976. reprint ed. 65.95 (*0-405-07702-5*) Ayer.

National Advisory Committee on Criminal Justice Standards & Goals Staff. Disorders & Terrorism: Report of the Task Force on Disorders & Terrorism, 1976, 1 vol. LC 77-601645. 1978. reprint ed. lib. bdg. 58.00 (*0-89941-530-X*, 200420) W S Hein.

National Advisory Council on Bilingual Education. Bilingual Education. Cordasco, Francesco, ed. LC 77-90411. (Bilingual-Bicultural Education in the U. S. Ser.). 1978. reprint ed. lib. bdg. 19.95 (*0-405-11080-4*) Ayer.

National Aeronautics & Space Administration, Lyndon B. Johnson Space Center Staff, ed. Engineering & Configurations of Space Stations & Platforms. LC 85-18737. (Illus.). 773p. 1986. 64.00 (*0-8155-1044-6*) Noyes.

National Aeronautics & Space Administration, Space Station Task Force Staff. Space Station Program: Description, Applications & Opportunities. LC 85-4963. (Illus.). 754p. 1985. 67.00 (*0-8155-1024-1*) Noyes.

National Aeronautics & Space Administration Staff & National Aeronautics & Space Administration, Lyndon B. Johnson Space Center Staff, eds. Nasa Space Plans & Scenarios to 2000 & Beyond. LC 85-31989. (Illus.). 239p. 1986. 36.00 (*0-8155-1071-3*) Noyes.

National Aeronautics & Space Administration, Lyndon B. Johnson Space Center Staff, jt. ed. see National Aeronautics.

National Agriculture Statistics Service Staff, jt. auth. see U. S. Department of Agriculture Staff.

National Air & Space Museum Library Staff, ed. The International Handbook of Aerospace Awards & Trophies. LC 77-25053. (Illus.). 252p. 1978. pap. text ed. 32.00 (*0-87474-670-1*, NAAH) Smithsonian.

***National Air & Space Museum Staff & Harwit, Martin O.** Treasures of the National Air & Space Museum. LC 94-41496. (Illus.). 320p. 1995. 11.95 (*1-55859-822-7*) Abbeville Pr.

National Air & Space Museum Staff & Smithsonian Institution Staff. Aerospace Periodical Index: 1973 to 1982. 1983. lib. bdg. 110.00 (*0-8161-0428-X*, Hall Library) G K Hall.

National Air & Space Museum Staff, jt. auth. see Watters, Thomas R.

National Alliance for Business Staff. Basic Skills for Job Performance: PICs & Workplace Literacy. 38p. 1991. pap. 5.95 (*0-88713-652-4*) Nat Alliance.

National Alliance for the Mentally Ill Staff & Public Citizen's Health Research Group Staff. Criminalizing the Seriously Mentally Ill: The Abuse of Jails As Mental Hospitals. (Illus.). (Orig.). 1992. pap. text ed. 10.00 (*0-937188-97-2*) Pub Citizen Inc.

National Alliance of Business Staff. Job Performance Learning: High Performance Workforce Training Systems. 41p. 1993. pap. 7.95 (*0-88713-656-7*) Nat Alliance.

National Alliance to End Homelessness Staff. Open House: Recipes & Food Memories from the Culinary Community. Rolfes, Ellen, ed. LC 93-60535. 256p. (C). 1993. Comb bdg. 15.95x (*1-879958-15-5*) Tradery Hse.

National Archives & Records Administration, Office of the Federal Register Staff. Code of Federal Regulations, List of Sections Affected, 1973-1985, Vol. 2, Titles 17-27. 629p. 1990. text ed. 25.00 (*0-16-022729-1*) USGPO.

— Code of Federal Regulations, List of Sections Affected, 1973-1985, Vol. 3, Titles 28-41. 737p. 1990. text ed. 28.00 (*0-16-025406-X*) USGPO.

— Code of Federal Regulations, List of Sections Affected, 1973-1985, Vol. 4, Titles 42-50. 648p. 1991. text ed. 25.00 (*0-16-026920-2*) USGPO.

National Archives & Records Administration Staff. Black Studies: A Select Catalog of National Archives Microfilm Publications. LC 83-15134. 97p. (Orig.). 1984. pap. text ed. 2.00 (*0-911333-08-8*, 200011) National Archives & Recs.

— Federal Court Records: A Select Catalog of National Archives Microfilm Publications. LC 87-5769. 64p. 1987. pap. text ed. 2.00 (*0-911333-44-4*, 200043) National Archives & Recs.

— Federal Population Census 1790 to 1890. 96p. 1979. pap. 2.00 (*0-911333-63-0*, 200032) National Archives & Recs.

— Gerald R. Ford. (Presidential Perspectives from the National Archives Ser.). (Illus.). 32p. 1994. pap. 3.50 (*1-880875-04-7*) National Archives & Recs.

— Guide to Cartographic Records in the National Archives. LC 76-611061. (Illus.). 444p. 1971. 25.00 (*0-911333-19-3*, 100005) National Archives & Recs.

— A Guide to Civil War Maps in the National Archives. rev. ed. LC 86-5132. (Illus.). 140p. 1986. text ed. 30.00 (*0-911333-36-3*, 100040) National Archives & Recs.

— Guide to Genealogical Research in the National Archives. rev. ed. LC 82-21040. (Illus.). 304p. 1985. reprint ed. pap. 25.00 (*0-911333-01-0*, 200001); reprint ed. boxed 35.00 (*0-911333-00-2*, 100001) National Archives & Recs.

— Milestone Documents of American History. rev. ed. LC 93-23047. Orig. Title: The Written Word Endures. Date not set. write for info. (*0-911333-98-3*) National Archives & Recs.

— Military Service Records: A Select Catalog of National Archives Microfilm Publications. 330p. 1985. pap. text ed. 2.00 (*0-911333-07-X*, 200028) National Archives & Recs.

— National Archives Microfilm Resources for Research: A Comprehensive Catalog. rev. ed. LC 85-15242. 136p. 5.00 (*0-911333-34-7*, 200033) National Archives & Recs.

National Archives & Records Service Staff, comp. Guide to Federal Archives Relating to Africa. (Archival & Bibliographic Ser.). 556p. 1977. 40.00 (*0-918456-07-X*, Crossroads) African Studies Assn.

N

National Archives of Canada Staff. Treasures of the National Archives. (Illus.). 368p. 1992. 50.00 (0-8020-5022-0) U of Toronto Pr.

National Archives of Canada Staff, ed. Documents That Move & Speak: Audiovisual Archives in the New Information Age; Proceedings of a Symposium Organized for the International Council of Archives by the National Archives of Canada, Ottawa, Canada, April 30, 1990-May 3, 1990. 318p. (ENG & FRE.). 1992. 55.00 (3-598-11043-X) K G Saur.

— Proceedings of the International Symposium: Conservation in Archives. 1990. lib. bdg. 27.00 (3-598-07564-2) K G Saur.

National Archives of Finland, Norway & Sweden Staff, ed. Guide to the Sources for the History of Nations, 3rd Series, Vol. 3: Sources of the History of North Africa, Asia & Oceania in Scandinavia, Pt. 2: Sources of the History of North Africa, Asia & Oceania in Finland, Norway & Sweden. 233p. 1981. lib. bdg. 95.00 (3-598-21475-8) K G Saur.

National Archives of Hungary Staff, jt. ed. see International Council on Archives Staff.

National Archives Staff. Teaching with Documents. LC 89-12602. (Illus.). 225p. (C). 1989. 15.00 (0-911333-79-7, 200047) National Archives & Recs.

National Archives Staff, ed. The Cuban Missile Crisis: President Kennedy's Address to the Nation, October 22, 1962. LC 88-600062. (Milestone Documents Ser.). (Illus.). 38p. 1988. pap. text ed. 3.50 (0-911333-59-2, 200113) National Archives & Recs.

— Federal Population Census 1910. LC 72-610891. 44p. (Orig.). 1982. pap. text ed. 2.00 (0-911333-15-0, 200009) National Archives & Recs.

— Federal Population Census 1920. LC 91-3417. (Orig.). 1991. pap. text ed. 2.00 (0-911333-86-X) National Archives & Recs.

— Japan Surrenders, 1945. LC 88-33031. (Milestone Documents Ser.). (Illus.). 36p. 1990. pap. text ed. 3.50 (0-911333-16-9, 200006) National Archives & Recs.

— Kennedy's Inaugural Address of 1961. LC 86-600367. (Milestone Documents Ser.). (Illus.). 30p. (Orig.). (YA). 1987. pap. text ed. 3.50 (0-911333-53-3, 200110) National Archives & Recs.

National Archives Trust Fund Board Staff. The Internment of the Japanese Americans. 48p. 1992. 5.95 (0-8403-7403-8) Kendall-Hunt.

— Watergate. 48p. 1992. 5.95 (0-8403-7401-1) Kendall-Hunt.

— Women in Industry in World War II. 48p. 1992. 5.95 (0-8403-7402-X) Kendall-Hunt.

National Art Education Association, Commission on Art Education, ed. Report of the NAEA Commission on Art Education. (C). 1977. 3.00 (0-937652-22-9) Natl Art Ed.

National Art Education Association Staff. Careers in Art. rev. ed. (C). 1971. pap. 2.00 (0-937652-14-8) Natl Art Ed.

National Art Education Association Staff, ed. see Lowenfeld, Viktor.

National Association Colonial Dames of America Staff. The Register Book for the Parish Prince Frederick Winyaw: Anno Domini 1713. (Illus.). 270p. 1982. reprint ed. 25.00 (0-89308-299-6) Southern Hist Pr.

National Association for Chicano Studies Staff & Garcia, J., eds. The Chicano Struggle: Analysis of Past & Present Efforts. LC 84-70569. 213p. 1984. pap. 16.00 (0-916950-50-6) Biling Rev-Pr.

National Association for Childbirth Education Staff. Cuidado Prenatal y Preparacion. (Avery's Childbirth Education Ser.). (Illus.). 104p. (SPA.). 1984. spiral bd. 7.95 (0-89529-238-6) Avery Pub.

National Association for Equal Opportunity in Higher Education Staff. A Resource Guide on Blacks in Higher Education. 66p. (Orig.). (C). 1988. pap. text ed. 10.50 (0-8191-6949-8) NAEOHE.

National Association for Legal Training & Testing Staff. Mastering the CLA: The N.A.L.T.T. Review. 418p. (Orig.). 1993. pap. 99.00 (1-884232-06-X) Nat Assn LT&T.

National Association for Preservation & Perpetuation of Storytelling Staff, ed. More Best-Loved Stories Told at the National Storytelling Festival. 224p. 1992. 24.95 (1-879991-09-8); pap. 14.95 (1-879991-08-X) Natl Assn Preserv & Perpet Storytelling.

National Association for Teaching of the Deaf Staff. A Second Reader for Deaf Children. 1973. 59.95 (0-8490-1009-8) Gordon Pr.

National Association for the Advancement of Colored People Staff. Thirty Years of Lynching in the United States, 1889-1918. LC 73-94142. (American Negro: His History & Literature, Ser. No. 3). 1970. reprint ed. 18.95 (0-405-01932-7) Ayer.

— Thirty Years of Lynching in the United States, 1889-1918. LC 72-89046. (Illus.). 105p. 1970. reprint ed. text ed. 35.00 (0-8371-1950-2, LYU&, Greenwood Pr) Greenwood.

National Association for the Advancement of Colored People Staff, et al. Beyond the Rodney King Story: An Investigation of Police Conduct in Minority Communities. 224p. 1994. text ed. 24.95 (1-55553-202-0) NE U Pr.

National Association for the Education of Young Children Staff. Early Childhood Teacher Education Guidelines: Basic & Advanced. 45p. 1991. pap. text ed. 6.00 (0-935989-36-6, NAEYC 211) Natl Assn Child Ed.

National Association for the Preservation & Perpetuation of Storytelling Staff, comp. Best-Loved Stories at the National Storytelling Festival. 224p. 1991. pap. 14.95 (1-879991-00-4, Natl Storytell) Natl Assn Preserv & Perpet Storytelling.

National Association for the Prevention of Addiction to Narcotics. Developments in the Field of Drug Abuse: Proceedings. Senay, Edward, ed. 1130p. 1975. 69.95 (0-87073-388-5) Transaction Pubs.

National Association for the Promotion of Social Science Trades' Societies Committee. Trades' Societies & Strikes: Report of the Committee on Trades' Societies Presented at the 4th Annual Meeting, Glasgow, Sept. 1860. LC 67-20514. (Reprints of Economic Classics Ser.). xxi, 651p. 1968. reprint ed. 57.50 (0-678-00347-5) Kelley.

National Association for Women Deans, Administrators & Counselors. Affirmative Action? 1976. pap. 6.00 (0-686-15381-2) Natl Assn Women.

National Association for Women Deans, Administrators & Counselors Staff. A Program for Optimizing Women's Leadership Skills (Owls) 1977. pap. 5.50 (0-686-23290-9) Natl Assn Women.

— A Symposium: Our Living History: Reminiscences of Black Participants in NAWDAC. 1980. pap. 3.00 (0-686-28001-6) Natl Assn Women.

National Association of Accountants, comp. Corporate Profitability & Logistics: Innovative Guidelines for Executives. 1987. 60.00 (0-318-33301-5) Coun Logistics Mgt.

National Association of Accountants Staff. NAA Statements on Management Accounting (1-18) Bound Volume of All Published Statements. 448p. 1990. 49.95 (0-13-611567-5) P-H.

— Statements on Management Accounting, No. 4K. 36p. 1990. pap. 9.95 (0-13-844465-X) P-H.

National Association of Accounting Staff. Management Accounting Terminology. 1991. pap. 9.95 (0-13-544602-3, Busn) P-H.

***National Association of Baptist Professors of Religion & Leschert, Dale F.** Hermeneutical Foundations of Hebrews: A Study in the Validity of the Epistle's Interpretation of Some Core Citations from the Psalms. (NABPR Dissertation Ser.: No. 10). 1995. write for info. (0-7734-2860-7) E Mellen.

National Association of Bond Lawyers Staff. Federal Taxation of Municipal Bonds: Statutes, Regulations, Rulings. Israel, Perry E. et al, eds. LC 93-35553. 6248p. 1993. disk 795.00 (0-13-300302-7) Aspen Law.

National Association of Broadcasters Staff. Advertising Revenues Per Television Household: A Market by Market Analysis. 51p. (Orig.). 1993. pap. 100.00 (0-89324-209-8) Natl Assn Broadcasters.

— Broadcasting Bibliography. rev. ed. Hill, Suan M., ed. 74p. 1989. 10.00 (0-89324-076-1) Natl Assn Broadcasters.

— Careers in Television. 32p. (Orig.). 1991. pap. 3.50 (0-89324-117-2) Natl Assn Broadcasters.

— Digital Audio Broadcasting: Status Report & Outlook. 69p. (Orig.). 1990. pap. 45.00 (0-89324-098-2) Natl Assn Broadcasters.

— The NAB Guide to AM & FM Radio Performance Measurements. 50p. (Orig.). 1990. pap. 60.00 (0-685-47799-1) Natl Assn Broadcasters.

— Radio Advertising's Missing Ingredient! The Optimum Effective Scheduling System. 2nd ed. 118p. (Orig.). 1993. pap. 50.00 (0-89324-206-3) Natl Assn Broadcasters.

— Radio Employee Compensation '90. 82p. (Orig.). 1990. pap. 100.00 (0-89324-093-1) Natl Assn Broadcasters.

— Radio Financial Report 1993. 225p. (Orig.). 1993. pap. 225.00 (0-89324-200-4) Natl Assn Broadcasters.

— Satellites & Broadcasting 1990: U. S. Domestic & International Market Directions & Issues. 42p. (Orig.). 1989. 60.00 (0-89324-075-3) Natl Assn Broadcasters.

— Trends in Radio Station Sales 1991-1993. 160p. (Orig.). 1993. pap. 225.00 (0-89324-201-2) Natl Assn Broadcasters.

— TV Financial Report 1993. 235p. (Orig.). 1993. pap. 225.00 (0-89324-148-2) Natl Assn Broadcasters.

— TV Market Analysis 1990. 135p. (Orig.). 1990. pap. 400.00 (0-89324-096-6) Natl Assn Broadcasters.

National Association of Church Personnel Administrators Staff. Working in the Catholic Church: An Attitudinal Survey. LC 93-19042. 184p. (Orig.). 1993. pap. 14.95 (1-55612-568-2) Sheed & Ward MO.

National Association of College & University Business Officers Staff. Administrative Procedures for Small Institutions. Welzenbach, Lanora, ed. 254p. 1985. 26.00 (0-915164-28-0) NACUBO.

— NACUBO Executive Briefing Series, 6 papers. McDonald, Deirdre & Reeder, Jefferson, eds. 1991. 37.50 (0-915164-63-9); 37.50 (0-915164-62-0); 37.50 (0-915164-65-5); 37.50 (0-915164-66-3); 37.50 (0-915164-67-1) NACUBO.

— National Symposium on Strategic Higher Education Finance & Management Issues: Proceedings. 246p. 1991. 65.00 (0-915164-68-X) NACUBO.

— Nineteen Ninety-Three NACUBO Endowment Study. 358p. 1994. 80.00 (0-685-59358-4); 28.00 (0-685-59359-2); 30.00 (0-685-59360-6) NACUBO.

— Nonpension Postretirement Benefits: Strategies for Colleges & Universities. Reeder, Jefferson, ed. 173p. 1992. 50.00 (0-915164-80-9) NACUBO.

National Association of College & University Business Officers & National Association of College & University Business Officers Staff. NACUBO Annual Membership Directory. 204p. 1994. 110.00 (0-685-48508-0) NACUBO.

National Association of College & University Business Officers Staff, jt. auth. see National Association of College.

National Association of Collegiate Director of Athletics Staff. National Directory of College Athletics, 1988-1989: Men's Edition. 1988. pap. 15.00 (0-318-41469-4) R Franks Ranch.

National Association of Collegiate Directors of Athletics Staff & National Association of Collegiate Director of Athletics Staff. The National Directory of College Athletics, 1988-1989: Women's Edition. 1988. pap. 11.00 (0-318-41470-8) R Franks Ranch.

National Association of Collegiate Director of Athletics Staff, jt. auth. see National Association of Collegiate Directors of Athletics Staff.

National Association of Credit Management Staff. Digest of Commercial Laws of the World, 11 bdrs. LC 65-22163. 1966. Approx. 4 releases per yr. write for info. (0-318-54751-1) Oceana.

— Digest of Commercial Laws of the World: Forms of Commercial Agreements, 2 vols., Set. 1984. ring bd. 200.00 (0-379-01045-3) Oceana.

— Digest of Intellectual Property Laws of the World, 3 vols. Nelson, Lester, ed. LC 65-22163. 1990. Approx. 4 releases per yr. write for info. (0-318-68974-X) Oceana.

National Association of Credit Management Staff & Nelson, Lester. Digest of Commercial Laws of the World, 11 bdrs. LC 65-22163. 1966. ring bd. 1,100.00 (0-379-01000-3) Oceana.

— Digest of Commercial Laws of the World: State Variations of Commercial Law, 2 vols. 1985. ring bd. 200.00 (0-379-01031-3); Approx. 4 releases per yr. write for info. (0-318-64270-0) Oceana.

— Digest of Intellectual Property Laws of the World, 3 vols., Set. LC 65-22163. 1990. ring bd. 495.00 (0-379-01015-1) Oceana.

National Association of Elementary School Principals Staff. Best Ideas from America's Blue Ribbon Schools: What Award-Winning Elementary & Middle School Principals Do. 120p. 1994. pap. 15.00 (0-8039-6177-4) Corwin Pr.

— Best Ideas from America's Blue Ribbon Schools Vol. 2: What Award-Winning Elementary & Middle School Principals Do. 128p. 1995. pap. 15.00 (0-8039-6272-X) Corwin Pr.

National Association of EMS Physicians Executive Staff. EMS Medical Directors' Handbook. 2nd ed. 544p. 1993. pap. 39.95 (0-8016-6580-9) Mosby Yr Bk.

National Association of EMS Physicians Staff. Quality Assurance in Prehospital Care. Swor, Robert A. et al, eds. LC 92-49237. 254p. 1993. pap. 32.95 (0-8016-6579-5) Mosby Yr Bk.

National Association of EMT's Pre-Hospital Life Support Committee, et al. Pre-Hospital Trauma Life Support. rev. ed. Butman, Alexander M. et al, eds. 358p. 1990. reprint ed. pap. text ed. 22.50 (0-940432-07-2) Educ Direction.

National Association of Home Builders NAHB Staff. Wood Frame House Construction. 280p. 1991. pap. text ed. 19.95 (0-8273-4739-1) Delmar.

National Association of Home Builders, Remodelors Council Staff. Quality Standards for the Professional Remodeler. rev. ed. LC 90-24100. 81p. 1991. reprint ed. 18.00 (0-86718-359-4) Home Builder.

National Association of Home Builders Research Foundation Staff. NAHB Thermal Performance Guidelines. 16p. 1983. pap. 8.00 (0-86718-192-3) Home Builder.

National Association of Home Builders Staff. Financing Land Acquisition & Development. LC 87-61069. 131p. 1987. pap. 32.00 (0-86718-281-4) Home Builder.

— The Future of Home Building: 1992-1994 & Beyond. 212p. 1992. pap. 35.00 (0-86718-468-X) Home Builder.

— Land Development. 7th ed. LC 87-60765. (Illus.). 344p. 1987. pap. 28.00 (0-86718-297-0) Home Builder.

— Profile of the New Home Buyer, 1991: Based on 1990 Home Buyers. 150p. 1991. pap. 65.00 (0-86718-467-1) Home Builder.

— Seniors Housing: A Development & Management Handbook. LC 87-62642. (Illus.). 121p. 1987. pap. 40.00 (0-86718-275-X) Home Builder.

— Understanding Building Codes & Standards in the United States. 35p. 1989. pap. 7.00 (0-86718-279-2) Home Builder.

***National Association of Home Builders Staff & Ratzlaff, Patricia.** The New Home Buyer's Workbook. Tuttle, John, ed. 32p. 1995. student ed 25.00 (0-86718-402-7) Home Builder.

National Association of Insurance Commissioners Staff. Nineteen Eighty-Five Proceedings of the National Association of Insurance Commissioners, Vol. II. Miller, Karen P., ed. 772p. 1985. 175.00 (0-89382-165-9) Nat Assn Insu Comm.

National Association of Insurance Commissioners Staff, ed. NAIC Model Laws, Regulations & Guidelines, 4 vols., Set. rev. ed. 1992. 250.00 (0-9601244-1-1) Nat Assn Insu Comm.

National Association of Investigating Specialists Staff. Investigator's Information Access Directory. Thomas, Ralph, ed. 350p. 1990. ring bd. 98.00 (0-317-99605-3) Thomas Pubns TX.

National Association of Investigative Specialists Staff. Investigator's International All-in-One Directory. Thomas, Ralph, ed. 95p. 1990. pap. text ed. 30.00 (0-317-99607-X) Thomas Pubns TX.

National Association of Investigative Specialists Staff & Thomas, Ralph D. American Directory of Private Investigative Specialists: 1988-1989. (Eighty-Five-Eighty-Six Ser.). 62p. 1985. pap. 14.95 (0-918487-14-5) Thomas Pubns TX.

— Investigator's International All-In-One Directory of the Investigative-Security Industry 1988-1989. 60p. 1985. pap. text ed. 30.00 (0-918487-15-3) Thomas Pubns TX.

National Association of Legal Assistants, Inc. Staff. NALA Manual for Legal Assistants. 2nd ed. Hannan, ed. 397p. (C). 1991. text ed. 55.75 (0-314-80780-2) West Pub.

National Association of Legal Assistants Staff. Manual for Legal Assistants. 529p. 1979. 18.95 (0-318-15095-6) Natl Assn Legal Secys.

National Association of Legal Assistants, Inc. Staff & Koerselman, Virginia. CLA Review Manual: A Practical Guide to CLA Exam Preparation. Hannan, ed. LC 93-8171. 700p. (C). 1993. pap. text ed. 67.00 (0-314-01349-0) West Pub.

National Association of Legal Secretaries (NALS) Staff. Manual for the Lawyer's Assistant. 2nd ed. 1118p. 1991. reprint ed. text ed. 32.95 (0-314-41162-3) West Pub.

National Association of Legal Secretaries Staff. Career Legal Secretary. 770p. 1993. reprint ed. text ed. 30.50 (0-314-32237-X) West Pub.

National Association of Legal Secretaries Staff, et al. NALS - Probate Handbook for the Lawyer's Assistant. 403p. (C). 1993. pap. text ed. write for info. (0-314-02351-8) West Pub.

National Association of Legal Secretary Staff & Aoki, Kaye. NALS - The Career Legal Secretary. 3rd ed. 864p. 1993. text ed. 31.50 (0-314-02353-4) West Pub.

National Association of Meat Purveyors Staff. The Meat Buyers Guide. U. S. Meat Export Federation Staff, tr. (Illus.). 218p. (Orig.). (JPN.). (C). 1991. pap. text ed. 39.00 (1-878154-01-X) Natl Assn Meat Purveyors.

— The Meat Buyers Guide. U. S. Meat Export Federation Staff, tr. (Illus.). 218p. (Orig.). (CHI.). 1991. pap. text ed. 39.00 (1-878154-02-8); pap. text ed. 39.00 (1-878154-03-6); pap. text ed. 39.00 (1-878154-05-2); pap. text ed. 39.00 (1-878154-06-0) Natl Assn Meat Purveyors.

— The Meat Buyers Guide. U. S. Meat Export Federation Staff, tr. (Illus.). 218p. (Orig.). (SPA.). (C). 1991. pap. text ed. 39.00 (1-878154-04-4) Natl Assn Meat Purveyors.

— The Meat Buyers Guide. (Illus.). 218p. (Orig.). (C). 1991. reprint ed. pap. text ed. 39.00 (1-878154-00-1) Natl Assn Meat Purveyors.

National Association of Professional Upholsterers Staff. The Art of Hand-Tying Coil Springs: A Set of How-to Diagrams. (Illus.). 22p. 1985. pap. text ed. 30.00 (0-9615307-0-7) Nat Assn Pro Upholsterers.

National Association of Rainbow Division Veterans. Forty-Second Rainbow Division History. LC 87-50364. 144p. 1987. 48.00 (0-938021-13-3) Turner Pub KY.

National Association of Real Estate Appraisers Staff. Residential Real Estate Appraisal. 196p. (C). 1989. text ed. 28.50 (0-935988-39-4, 372) Todd Pub.

National Association of Real Estate Appraisers Staff, comp. The Uniform Residential Appraisal Report Handbook. LC 88-50320. 142p. 1989. reprint ed. pap. text ed. 20.00 (0-935988-33-5, 341) Todd Pub.

National Association of Realtors, Economics & Research Division Staff. SIOR Industrial Real Estate Market Survey: 1986 Review-1987 Forecast. 240p. 1987. 20.00 (0-939623-06-4) Soc Industrial Realtors.

National Association of Realtors Staff. Real Estate Index, 2 vols., Set. 1987. 169.00 (0-938785-00-1) Natl Assoc Realtors.

— Real Estate Index, 2 vols., Vol. I. 1987. 99.00 (0-938785-01-X) Natl Assoc Realtors.

— Real Estate Index, 2 vols., Vol. II. 1987. 99.00 (0-938785-02-8) Natl Assoc Realtors.

— Real Estate Index - Supplement, Vol. 3. LC 86-23878. 1800p. 1988. 49.50 (0-938785-04-4) Natl Assoc Realtors.

— Real Estate Index, 1991. 1992. 15.00 (0-685-63292-X) Natl Assoc Realtors.

National Association of Realtors Staff, jt. auth. see Society of Industrial Realtors Staff.

National Association of Realtors Staff, jt. auth. see Society of Industrial.

National Association of Retired Federal Employees Staff. Open Season Guide: Federal Health Benefits & Premiums 1993. Brown, Gordon F., ed. 152p. (Orig.). 1992. pap. 9.95 (0-9631168-2-7) Natl Ret Fed Emps.

National Association of Review Appraisers & Mortgage Underwriters Staff. Establishing an Appraisal Quality Control Program. LC 89-50439. 97p. 1989. pap. text ed. 65.00 (0-935988-38-6, 357) Todd Pub.

National Association of Review Appraisers Staff & Arnold, Fayette F., III. Reviewing Condominium Projects. LC 80-53455. (Illus.). 156p. 1981. 21.50 (0-935988-21-1) Todd Pub.

National Association of Review Appraisers Staff & Everhart, Marion E. Land Classification for Land Uses, Management & Valuation. LC 82-74565. (Illus.). 220p. 1983. 19.50 (0-935988-23-8, 311) Todd Pub.

National Association of Safety & Health Professionals Staff. Handbook of Emergency Response & Toxic Chemical Releases. Cheremisinoff, Nicholas P., ed. (Illus.). 316p. 1992. 24.95 (0-925760-57-9) SciTech Pubs.

National Association of School Psychologists. Helping Children Grow Up in the 90's: A Resource Book for Parents & Teachers. 400p. 1992. pap. text ed. 35.00 (0-932955-07-X) Natl Assn Psych.

— Professional Conduct Manual. 2nd ed. pap. text ed. 12.00 (0-932955-12-6) Natl Assn Psych.

National Association of Secondary School Principals Staff. How Fares the Ninth Grade? A Day in the Life of a 9th Grader. Koerner, T., ed. (Orig.). 1985. pap. 12.00 (0-88210-167-6) Natl Assn Principals.

— Rank-in-Class & Other Factors in College Admissions. 60p. 1983. pap. text ed. 8.00 (0-88210-146-3) Natl Assn Principals.

— The School - College Connection: Relationships & Standards. 89p. reprint ed. pap. 25.40 (0-8357-4664-X, 2037604) Bks Demand.

— Student Learning Styles & Brain Behavior: Programs, Instrumentation, Research. LC 83-110391. (Illus.). 240p. reprint ed. pap. 68.40 (0-8357-5551-7, 2035170) Bks Demand.

An Asterisk (*) at the beginning of an entry indicates that the title is appearing in BIP for the first time.

— Workshops: Laboratories for Student Leaders. 1974. pap. 8.00 (*0-88210-057-2*) Natl Assn Principals.

National Association of Social Workers. Contemporary Developments in Social Work Research Methodology. 61p. reprint ed. pap. 25.00 (*0-7837-6546-0*, 2045683) Bks Demand.

— Impaired Social Worker Program: Resource Book. LC 87-24011. 43p. reprint ed. pap. 25.00 (*0-7837-6544-4*, 2045681) Bks Demand.

National Association of Social Workers Staff. Changing Services for Changing Clients. LC 69-18878. 139p. reprint ed. pap. 39.70 (*0-317-55467-0*, 2052205) Bks Demand.

— Social Group Work with Older People. Stein, Leon, ed. LC 79-8684. (Growing Old Ser.). 1980. reprint ed. lib. bdg. 18.95 (*0-405-12801-0*) Ayer.

***National Association of State Budget Officers Staff.** 1994 State Expenditure Report. (Illus.). 127p. (Orig.). Date not set. pap. text ed. 35.00 (*1-887253-01-7*) NASBD.

— Workforce Policies: State Activity & Innovations. 132p. (Orig.). 1995. pap. text ed. 25.00 (*1-887253-00-9*) NASBD.

National Association of State Budget Officers Staff, jt. auth. see National Governors' Association Staff.

National Association of State Development Agencies Staff. Directory of Incentives for Business Investment & Development in the United States: A State-by-State Guideline. 3rd ed. LC 86-157140. (Illus.). 790p. (C). 1991. lib. bdg. 163.00 (*0-87766-515-X*); pap. text ed. 75.00 (*0-87766-501-X*) Urban Inst.

National Association of State Textbook Administrators Staff, et al. Manufacturing Standards & Specifications for Textbooks. 1976. write for info. (*0-318-55921-8*) Textbk Specif.

National Association of Stove Manufacturers Staff, comp. Names of Stoves, Ranges, & Furnaces, 1876. 74p. 1992. pap. 12.50 (*0-9612204-1-4*) Autonomy Hse.

National Association of Towns & Townships Staff. Accidents Will Happen: A Small Town Guide to Planning for Hazardous Materials Response. (Illus.). 64p. (Orig.). 1990. pap. 10.00 (*0-925532-03-7*) Natl Assn Town & Twps.

— Getting Out from Under: Underground Storage Tank Alternatives for Small Towns. (Illus.). 80p. (Orig.). 1991. pap. text ed. 11.00 (*0-925532-07-X*) Natl Assn Town & Twps.

— Growing Our Own Jobs: A Small Town Guide to Creating Jobs Through Agricultural Diversification. (Illus.). 55p. (Orig.). 1988. pap. text ed. 10.00 (*0-925532-05-3*) Natl Assn Town & Twps.

— Harvesting Hometown Jobs: A Small Town Guide to Recycling. (Illus.). 35p. (Orig.). 1985. pap. text ed. 10.00 (*0-925532-04-5*) Natl Assn Town & Twps.

— Innovative Grassroots Financing: A Small Town Guide to Raising Funds & Cutting Costs. (Illus.). 64p. (Orig.). 1990. pap. text ed. 10.00 (*0-925532-06-1*) Natl Assn Town & Twps.

— Treat It Right: A Local Official's Guide to Small Town Wastewater Treatment. (Illus.). 64p. (Orig.). 1989. pap. 8.00 (*0-925532-02-9*) Natl Assn Town & Twps.

— Why Waste a Second Chance? A Small Town Guide to Recycling. (Illus.). 48p. (Orig.). 1989. pap. text ed. 10.00 (*0-925532-00-2*) Natl Assn Town & Twps.

National Association of Underwater Instructors. NAUI Standards & Procedures Manual. (Illus.). 1987. ring bd. 69.95 (*0-916974-35-9*, 200) NAUI.

National Association of Underwater Instructors Staff. NAUI Diving Log Book. 1973. 5.95 (*0-916974-05-7*, 382) NAUI.

— NAUI Training Record. 1973. 5.95 (*0-916974-06-5*, 385) NAUI.

National Association of Women Deans, Administrators & Counselors. Women Administrators in Education: A Review of Research, 1960-1975. 1979. pap. 5.00 (*0-686-23291-7*) Natl Assn Women.

National Association of Home Builders, Legal Department Staff. Contracts & Liability for Builders & Remodelers. (Illus.). 119p. 1993. pap. 25.00 (*0-86718-376-4*) Home Builder.

National Audubon Society Staff. Audubon's Birds of America. (Illus.). 435p. 1989. write for info. (*0-89659-425-4*) Abbeville Pr.

— Audubon's Birds of America. deluxe ed. (Illus.). 435p. 1989. ring bd. write for info. (*0-89659-427-0*) Abbeville Pr.

National Audubon Society Staff & Croxton Collaborative, Architects Staff. Audubon House: Building the Environmentally Responsible, Energy-Efficient Office. LC 93-46161. (Sustainable Design Ser.). 1994. text ed. 24.95 (*0-471-02496-1*) Wiley.

***National Audubon Society Staff & Kress, Stephen W.** The Audubon Society Bird Garden. LC 95-6748. 176p. 1995. 24.95 (*0-7894-0139-8*, 6-70475) Dorling Kindersley.

National Audubon Society Staff, jt. auth. see Conservation Foundation Staff.

National Bar Association, JCPS Office of Research-Judicial Council Staff. Elected & Appointed Black Judges in the United States. 85p. 1986. pap. 20.00 (*0-941410-75-7*) Jt Ctr Pol Studies.

National Board for Certified Counselors Staff, et al. A Work Behavior Analysis of Professional Counselors. LC 93-27915. 168p. 1993. 24.95 (*1-55959-053-X*) Accel Devel.

National Board of the Changing Relations Project Staff & Bach, Robert L. Changing Relations: Newcomers & Established Residents in U. S. Communities : A Report to the ford Foundation by the National Board of the Changing Relations Project. LC 92-46770. 1993. (*0-916584-48-8*) Ford Found.

National Bureau of Economic Research, Bureau of the Census: Conference on the Seasonal Analysis of Economic Time Series (1976: Washington DC). Seasonal Analysis of Economic Time Series. Zellner, Arnold, ed. LC 78-606108. (Economic Research Report Ser.: No. ER-1). 498p. reprint ed. pap. 142.00 (*0-317-55579-0*, 2056369) Bks Demand.

National Bureau of Economic Research Conference on the Economics of Physician & Patient Behavior (1978, Stanford, CA). The Economics of Physician & Patient Behavior. Fuchs, Victor R. & Newhouse, Joseph P., eds. (Journal of Human Resources Ser.: Vol. 13, Supplement). 262p. reprint ed. pap. 74.70 (*0-317-55574-X*, 2056367) Bks Demand.

National Bureau of Economic Research Staff. The Measurement & Behavior of Unemployment: A Conference of the Universities-National Bureau Committee for Economic Research. LC 57-5442. (National Bureau of Economic Research Ser.: Vol. 8). (Illus.). 615p. reprint ed. pap. 175.30 (*0-317-10942-1*, 2019641) Bks Demand.

— Measurement & Interpretation of Job Vacancies. (Other Conferences Ser.: No. 5). 603p. 1966. reprint ed. 156.80 (*0-87014-471-5*) Natl Bur Econ Res.

— NBER Macroeconomics Annual, 1986. Fischer, Stanley, ed. LC 87-642897. 417p. reprint ed. pap. 118.90 (*0-8357-7930-0*, 2052330) Bks Demand.

— Transportation Economics. (Universities-National Bureau Conference Ser.: No. 17). 482p. 1965. 124.80 (*0-87014-308-5*) Natl Bur Econ Res.

— Transportation Economics: A Conference of the Universities-National Bureau Committee for Economic Research. LC 65-11221. (National Bureau of Economic Research. Special Conference Ser.: No. 17). (Illus.). 480p. reprint ed. pap. 136.80 (*0-8357-7584-4*, 2056905) Bks Demand.

National Bureau of Standards. Low Temperature Mechanical Properties of Copper & Selected Copper Alloys. 165p. 1967. 24.75 (*0-317-34537-0*, 50) Intl Copper.

National Bureau of Standards, Cryogenics Division Staff. Grain Boundary Segregation in Copper & Copper Alloys. 59p. 1975. 8.85 (*0-317-34529-X*, 237) Intl Copper.

National Bureau of Standards Staff. Diffusion Rate Data & Mass Transport Phenomena for Cooper Systems. (INCRA Monograph). 322p. 1977. 20.00 (*0-317-42799-7*) Intl Copper.

National Bureau Special Staff, jt. auth. see Committee on Recent Economic Changes of the President's Conference on Unemployment.

***National Business Employment Weekly Staff.** National Business Employment Weekly Cover Letters. (National Business Employment Weekly Care Ser.). Date not set. text ed. 29.95 (*0-471-10671-2*) Wiley.

— National Business Employment Weekly Cover Letters. (National Business Employment Weekly Care Ser.). 1995. pap. text ed. 10.95 (*0-471-10672-0*) Wiley.

***National Business Forms Association Staff.** Partnering Tool Kit. 170p. 1991. pap. 198.00 (*0-614-02662-8*) Natl Assn Wholesale Dists.

National Cambridge Society Staff. Colors in Cambridge. (Illus.). 128p. 1991. 19.95 (*0-89145-270-2*) Collector Bks.

National Cancer Foundation, Inc. Staff, jt. auth. see Cancer Care, Inc. Staff.

***National Cargo Bureau, Inc. Staff.** General Information for Grain Loading. 2nd ed. Boyle, Edward, ed. (Illus.). 114p. 1994. pap. text ed. 7.50 (*0-9627009-1-6*) Natl Cargo Bureau.

National CASA Association Staff & National Council of Juvenile & Family Court Judges. Court Appointed Special Advocate (CASA) Manual. 239p. 1984. 20.00 (*0-318-21317-6*) Natl Juv & Family Ct Judges.

National Catholic Development Conference Staff. Bibliography of Fund Raising & Philanthropy. 2nd ed. LC 82-81523. 76p. 1982. 22.50 (*0-9603196-1-1*) Natl Cath Dev.

National Catholic Educational Association Staff. Directory of Catholic Boarding Schools. 1991. 5.30 (*1-55833-072-0*); pap. 4.00 (*0-685-48506-4*) Natl Cath Educ.

National Catholic Staff. Pope John Paul II. 1979. 17.50 (*0-8164-0109-8*) Harper SF.

National Catholic Vocation Council. Making Life Choices. 64p. 1987. pap. 4.95 (*0-89505-455-8*) Tabor Pub.

National Center fof State Courts Staff. Virginia Circuit Court Caseload Reporting System & Workload Analysis System: User's Guide. 86p. 1977. 5.16 (*0-685-15737-7*, MAB-136) Natl Ctr St Courts.

National Center for Children in Poverty Staff. Child Welfare Reform. 62p. (Orig.). 1991. pap. text ed. 8.00 (*0-926582-06-2*) NCCP.

***National Center for Education in Maternal & Child Health Staff.** Adolescent Health: Abstracts of Active Projects FY 1994. 350p. 1994. pap. text ed. write for info. (*1-57285-004-3*) Nat Ctr Educ.

— Emergency Medical Services for Children: Abstracts of Active Projects FY 1995. 170p. 1995. pap. text ed. write for info. (*1-57285-013-2*) Nat Ctr Educ.

***National Center for Education Statistics Staff, ed.** Digest of Educational Statistics 1994. 536p. 1994. pap. 33.00 (*0-89059-032-X*) Bernan Pr.

***National Center for Health Statistics Staff.** Advance Data from Vital & Health Statistics, Nos. 71-80. LC 94-1867. (Series Reports: Series 16, No. 8). 118p. Date not set. 8.00 (*0-614-02913-9*, 017-022-01239-1) Natl Ctr Health Stats.

— Advance Data from Vital & Health Statistics, Nos. 81-90. LC 94-1868. (Series Reports: Series 16, No. 9). 99p. Date not set. 7.50 (*0-614-02914-7*, 017-022-01240-5) Natl Ctr Health Stats.

— Advance Data from Vital & Health Statistics, Nos. 91-100. LC 94-1869. (Series Reports: Series 16, No. 10). 87p. Date not set. 6.00 (*0-614-02915-5*, 017-022-01245-6) Natl Ctr Health Stats.

— Advance Data from Vital & Health Statistics, Nos. 101-110. LC 94-1870. (Series Reports: Series 16, No. 11). 93p. Date not set. 6.00 (*0-614-02916-3*, 94PB-135928) Natl Ctr Health Stats.

— Advance Data from Vital & Health Statistics, Nos. 111-120. LC 94-1871. (Series Reports: Series 16, No. 12). 105p. Date not set. 7.50 (*0-614-02917-1*, PB94-142874) Natl Ctr Health Stats.

— Advance Data from Vital & Health Statistics, Nos. 121-130. LC 94-1872. (Series Reports: Series 16, No. 13). 98p. Date not set. 7.00 (*0-614-02918-X*, PB94-139748) Natl Ctr Health Stats.

— Advance Report of Final Natality Statistics, 1992 Vol. 43, No. 5. suppl. ed. (Monthly Vital Statistics Report Ser.). 88p. Date not set. write for info. (*0-614-02948-1*) Natl Ctr Health Stats.

— Advance Report of Maternal & Infant Health Data from the Birth Certificate, 1991 Vol. 42, No. 11. suppl. ed. (Monthly Vital Statistics Report Ser.). 32p. Date not set. write for info. (*0-614-02946-5*) Natl Ctr Health Stats.

— AIDS Knowledge & Attitudes for 1992. (Advance Data Ser.: No. 243). 16p. Date not set. write for info. (*0-614-02930-9*) Natl Ctr Health Stats.

— AIDS-Related Behavior among Women 15-44 Years of Age: United States, 1988 & 1990. (Advance Data Ser.: No. 239). 16p. Date not set. write for info. (*0-614-02926-0*) Natl Ctr Health Stats.

— Alcohol- & Drug-Related Visits to Hospital Emergency Departments: 1992 National Hospital Ambulatory Medical Care Survey. (Advance Data Ser.: No. 251). 16p. Date not set. write for info. (*0-614-02938-4*) Natl Ctr Health Stats.

— Annual Summary of Births, Marriages, Divorces, & Deaths Vol. 42, No. 13: United States, 1993. (Monthly Vital Statistics Report Ser.). 36p. Date not set. write for info. (*0-614-02947-3*) Natl Ctr Health Stats.

— Catalog of Electronic Data Products. 82p. Date not set. write for info. (*0-614-02955-4*) Natl Ctr Health Stats.

— Catalog of University Presentations 1994-95. 17p. Date not set. write for info. (*0-614-02956-2*) Natl Ctr Health Stats.

— Cause of Death Contributing to Changes in Life Expectancy: United States, 1984-89. LC 94-1851. (Series Reports: Series 20, No. 23). 35p. Date not set. 3.00 (*0-614-02920-1*, 017-022-01256-1) Natl Ctr Health Stats.

— Cesarean Delivery in the United States, 1990. LC 95-1929. (Series Reports: Series 21, No. 51). 24p. Date not set. 2.25 (*0-614-02923-6*, PB94-168234) Natl Ctr Health Stats.

— Characteristics of Elderly Home Health Patients: Premilinary Data from the 1992 National Home & Hospice Care Survey. (Advance Data Ser.: No. 247). 12p. Date not set. write for info. (*0-614-02934-1*) Natl Ctr Health Stats.

— Cognitive Aspects of Reporting Cancer Prevention Examinations & Tests. (Series Reports: Series 6, No. 7). 161p. Date not set. write for info. (*0-614-02905-8*) Natl Ctr Health Stats.

— Current Estimates from the National Health Interview Survey, 1992. LC 94-1517. (Series Reports: Series 10, No. 189). 269p. Date not set. 17.00 (*0-614-02907-4*, PB94 135811) Natl Ctr Health Stats.

— Detailed Diagnoses & Procedures, National Hospital Discharge Survey, 1991. LC 94-1776. (Series Reports: Series 13, No. 115). 290p. Date not set. 19.00 (*0-614-02908-2*, 017-022-01248-1) Natl Ctr Health Stats.

— Detailed Diagnoses & Procedures, National Hospital Discharge Survey, 1992. LC 94-1770. (Series Reports: Series 13, No. 118). 281p. Date not set. 18.00 (*0-614-02911-2*, 017-022-01261-8) Natl Ctr Health Stats.

— Development of the National Home & Hospice Care Survey. LC 94-1309. (Series Reports: Series 1, No. 33). 153p. Date not set. 11.00 (*0-614-02900-7*, 017-022-01265-1) Natl Ctr Health Stats.

— Dietary Intake of Vitamins, Minerals, & Fiber of Persons Ages 2 Months & over in the United States: Third National Health & Nutrition Examination Survey, Phase 1, 1988-91. (Advance Data Ser.: No. 258). 28p. Date not set. write for info. (*0-614-02945-7*) Natl Ctr Health Stats.

— Effect on Mortality Rates of the 1989 Change in Tabulating Race. LC 94-1853. (Series Reports: Series 20, No. 25). 28p. Date not set. 2.75 (*0-614-02922-8*, 017-022-01272-3) Natl Ctr Health Stats.

— Energy & Macronutrient Intake of Persons Ages 2 Months & over in the United States: Third National Health & Nutrition Examination Survey, Phase 1, 1988-91. (Advance Data Ser.: No. 255). 24p. Date not set. write for info. (*0-614-02942-2*) Natl Ctr Health Stats.

— Evaluation of National Health Interview Survey Diagnostic Reporting. LC 94-1394. (Series Reports: Series 2, No. 120). 116p. Date not set. 7.50 (*0-614-02903-1*, PB94-151214) Natl Ctr Health Stats.

— Firearm & Motor Vehicle Injury Mortality-Variations by State, Race, & Ethnicity: United States, 1990-91. (Advance Data Ser.: No. 242). 12p. Date not set. write for info. (*0-614-02929-5*) Natl Ctr Health Stats.

— Health Insurance & Cancer Screening among Women. (Advance Data Ser.: No. 254). 12p. Date not set. write for info. (*0-614-02941-4*) Natl Ctr Health Stats.

— Health Interview Survey, 1975. LC 82-80685. 1982. write for info. (*0-89138-926-1*, ICPSR 7672) ICPSR.

— Health of Foreign-Born Population: United States, 1989-90. (Advance Data Ser.: No. 241). 12p. Date not set. write for info. (*0-614-02928-7*) Natl Ctr Health Stats.

— Health, United States, 1993. LC 94-1232. 301p. Date not set. 19.00 (*0-614-02952-X*, 017-022-01252-9) Natl Ctr Health Stats.

— Health, United States, 1993 Chartbook. LC 94-12321. 92p. Date not set. write for info. (*0-614-02953-8*) Natl Ctr Health Stats.

— Healthy People 2000 Review, 1993. 171p. Date not set. write for info. (*0-614-02954-6*) Natl Ctr Health Stats.

— Hospices & Home Health Agencies: Data from the 1991 National Health Provider Inventory. (Advance Data Ser.: No. 257). 8p. Date not set. write for info. (*0-614-02944-9*) Natl Ctr Health Stats.

— Hospitalizations for Injury & Poisoning in the United States, 1991. (Advance Data Ser.: No. 252). 12p. Date not set. write for info. (*0-614-02939-2*) Natl Ctr Health Stats.

— Human Immunodeficiency Virus Antibody Testing in Women 15-44 Years of Age: United States, 1990. (Advance Data Ser.: No. 238). 16p. Date not set. write for info. (*0-614-02925-2*) Natl Ctr Health Stats.

— Infant Mortality by Birthweight & Other Characteristics: United States, 1985 Birth Cohort. LC 94-1852. (Series Reports: Series 20, No. 24). 36p. Date not set. 3.00 (*0-614-02921-X*, 017-022-01262-6) Natl Ctr Health Stats.

— Injury Prevention Measures in Households with Children in the United States, 1990. (Advance Data Ser.: No. 250). 16p. Date not set. write for info. (*0-614-02937-6*) Natl Ctr Health Stats.

— Investigation of Nonresponse Bias: Hispanic Health & Nutrition Examination Survey. LC 94-1393. (Series Reports: Series 2, No. 119). 75p. Date not set. 5.50 (*0-614-02902-3*, PB94-134996) Natl Ctr Health Stats.

— Mortality Surveillance System: Models from the Second Year. LC 94-1859. (Series Reports: Series 20, No. 22). 82p. Date not set. 5.50 (*0-614-02919-8*, 017-022-01273-1) Natl Ctr Health Stats.

— Mortality, 1989 Vol. II, Pt. A. LC 93-1101. (Vital Statistics of the United States Ser.). 730p. Date not set. 48.00 (*0-614-02950-3*, 017-022-01234-1) Natl Ctr Health Stats.

— Natality, 1989 Vol. I. LC 93-1100. (Vital Statistics of the United States Ser.). 508p. Date not set. 43.00 (*0-614-02949-X*, 017-022-01233-2) Natl Ctr Health Stats.

— National Ambulatory Medical Care Survey: 1992 Summary. (Advance Data Ser.: No. 253). 20p. Date not set. write for info. (*0-614-02940-6*) Natl Ctr Health Stats.

— The National Home & Hospice Care Survey: 1992 Summary. LC 94-1779. (Series Reports: Series 13, No. 117). 110p. Date not set. 7.00 (*0-614-02910-4*, 017-022-01271-5) Natl Ctr Health Stats.

— National Hospital Ambulatory Medical Care Survey: 1992 Emergency Department Summary. (Advance Data Ser.: No. 245). 12p. Date not set. write for info. (*0-614-02932-5*) Natl Ctr Health Stats.

— National Hospital Ambulatory Medical Care Survey: 1992 Outpatient Department Summary. (Advance Data Ser.: No. 248). 12p. Date not set. write for info. (*0-614-02935-X*) Natl Ctr Health Stats.

— National Hospital Discharge Survey: Annual Summary, 1992. LC 94-1779. (Series Reports: Series 13, No. 119). 63p. Date not set. 4.75 (*0-614-02912-0*, 017-022-01274-0) Natl Ctr Health Stats.

— National Medical Ambulatory Medical Care Survey: 1991 Summary. LC 94-1777. (Series Reports: Series 13, No. 116). 110p. Date not set. 6.50 (*0-614-02909-0*, 017-022-01288-3) Natl Ctr Health Stats.

— 1992 Summary: National Hospital Discharge Survey. (Advance Data Ser.: No. 249). 12p. Date not set. write for info. (*0-614-02936-8*) Natl Ctr Health Stats.

— Nursing Homes & Board & Care Homes. (Advance Data Ser.: No. 244). 8p. Date not set. write for info. (*0-614-02931-7*) Natl Ctr Health Stats.

— Office Visits to Dermatologists: National Ambulatory Medical Care Survey, United States, 1989-90. (Advance Data Ser.: No. 240). 12p. Date not set. write for info. (*0-614-02927-9*) Natl Ctr Health Stats.

— Office Visits to Psychiatrists: United States, 1989-90. (Advance Data Ser.: No. 237). 16p. Date not set. write for info. (*0-614-02924-4*) Natl Ctr Health Stats.

— An Overview of Home & Hospice Care Patients: Preliminary Data from the 1993 National Home & Hospice Care Survey. (Advance Data Ser.: No. 256). 12p. Date not set. write for info. (*0-614-02943-0*) Natl Ctr Health Stats.

— Plan & Operation of the National Hospital Ambulatory Medical Survey. LC 94-1310. (Series Reports: Series 1, No. 34). 78p. Date not set. 6.00 (*0-614-02901-5*, 017-022-01263-4) Natl Ctr Health Stats.

— Plan & Operation of the Third National Health & Nutrition Examination Survey, 1988-94. LC 94-1308. (Series Reports: Series 1, No. 32). 407p. Date not set. 25.00 (*0-614-02899-X*, 017-022-01260-0) Natl Ctr Health Stats.

— Prevalence & Characteristics of Persons with Hearing Trouble: United States, 1990-91. LC 94-1516. (Series Reports: Series 10, No. 188). 75p. Date not set. 5.50 (*0-614-02906-6*, PB94-156601) Natl Ctr Health Stats.

— Restricted Activity Days & Other Problems Associated with Use of Marijuana or Cocaine among Persons 18-24 Years of Age: United States, 1991. (Advance Data Ser.: No. 246). 12p. Date not set. write for info. (*0-614-02933-3*) Natl Ctr Health Stats.

N

— Statistical Issues in Analyzing the NHANES I Epidemiologic Followup Study. LC 94-1395. (Series Reports: Series 2, No. 121). 30p. Date not set. 2.75 (*0-614-02904-X*, 017-022-01258-8) Natl Ctr Health Stats.

— Vital Statistics of the United States, 1990 Life Tables Vol. II, Sect. 6. LC 94-1104. 20p. Date not set. 2.25 (*0-614-02951-1*, 017-022-01266-9) Natl Ctr Health Stats.

— Where to Write for Vital Records: Births, Death, Marriages, & Divorces. Cox, Klaudia, ed. 29p. pap. text ed. 1.75 (*0-8406-0375-4*) Natl Ctr Health Stats.

National Center for Health Statistics (U.S.) Staff, ed. see Clarke, Sally C. & Ventura, Stephanie J.

National Center for Law & Deafness Staff. Legal Rights: The Guide for Deaf & Hard of Hearing People. 4th rev. ed. LC 91-44372. (Illus.). 297p. 1992. pap. 19.95 (*1-56368-000-9*) Gallaudet Univ Pr.

National Center for Manufacturing Staff. Competing in World Class Manufacturing: American's Twenty-First Century Challenge. 410p. 1990. text ed. 45.00 (*1-55623-401-5*) Irwin Prof Pubng.

National Center for Research in Vocational Education. Math on the Job: Graphic Designer. (Orig.). 1987. pap. text ed. 14.95 (*0-923325-88-3*) Conover Co.

— Questions Frequently Asked about Vocational Education. 33p. 1987. 4.75 (*0-318-23416-5*, SN 57) Ctr Educ Trng Employ.

National Center for Research in Vocational Education Staff. Accept Responsibility Module, Connections: School & Work Transitions - Work Skills-Work Maturity Skills. 1987. write for info. (*0-318-67156-5*, SP100CB12) Ctr Educ Trng Employ.

— Adult Career Guidance, Options: Expanding Educational Services for Adults. 1987. 12.95 (*0-317-03853-2*, SP500FA) Ctr Educ Trng Employ.

— Aid Professional Growth Module, Competency-Based Career Guidance (CBCG) - Category D: Operating. 1985. 7.95 (*0-317-03854-0*, CG100D02) Ctr Educ Trng Employ.

— Apply for Jobs Module, Connections: School & Work Transitions - Work Skills-Job Search Skills. 1987. write for info. (*0-318-67157-3*, SP100CB04) Ctr Educ Trng Employ.

— Apprenticeship in Employment & Training Programs: An Action Planning Guidebook. 83p. 1983. 6.75 (*0-318-22035-0*, RD221) Ctr Educ Trng Employ.

— BASICS: Bridging Vocational & Academic Skills. 1987. 198.00 (*0-318-35278-8*, SP 300) Ctr Educ Trng Employ.

— The Bridger's Guide, Basics: Bridging Vocational & Academic Skills. 1987. 75.00 (*0-317-03855-9*, SP300A) Ctr Educ Trng Employ.

— Build a Guidance Program Planning Model Module, Competency-Based Career Guidance (CBCG) - Category A: Guidance Program Planning. 1985. 7.95 (*0-317-03856-7*, CG100A05) Ctr Educ Trng Employ.

— Career Passport Leader's Guide, Connections: School & Work Transitions - Career Passports. 1987. 9.50 (*0-317-03857-5*, SP100DA) Ctr Educ Trng Employ.

— Career Passport Student Workbook, Connections: School & Work Transitions - Career Passport. 1987. write for info. (*0-318-67158-1*, SP100DB) Ctr Educ Trng Employ.

— Career Portfolio, Connections: School & Work Transitions - Employment File. 1987. write for info. (*0-318-67159-X*, SP100EA02) Ctr Educ Trng Employ.

— Case Studies of Programs Serving Adults, Options: Expanding Educational Services for Adults. 1987. 39.95 (*0-317-03858-3*, SP500G) Ctr Educ Trng Employ.

— Certificates of Completion, PACE: A Program for Acquiring Competence in Entrepreneurship, 3 levels, Level 1. rev. ed. 1983. 5.00 (*0-317-06025-2*, RD240EA) Ctr Educ Trng Employ.

— Certificates of Completion, PACE: A Program for Acquiring Competence in Entrepreneurship, 3 levels, Level 2. rev. ed. 1983. 5.00 (*0-317-06026-0*, RD240EB) Ctr Educ Trng Employ.

— Certificates of Completion, PACE: A Program for Acquiring Competence in Entrepreneurship, 3 levels, Level 3. rev. ed. 1983. 5.00 (*0-317-06027-9*, RD240C) Ctr Educ Trng Employ.

— Certificates of Completion, PACE: A Program for Acquiring Competence in Entrepreneurship, 3 levels, Set. rev. ed. 1983. 20.00 (*0-317-03859-1*) Ctr Educ Trng Employ.

— Choosing the Type of Ownership Module, PACE: A Program for Acquiring Competence in Entrepreneurship, 3 levels. rev. ed. 1983. 2.50 (*0-317-06028-7*) Ctr Educ Trng Employ.

— Choosing the Type of Ownership Module, PACE: A Program for Acquiring Competence in Entrepreneurship, 3 levels, Level 1. rev. ed. 1983. 2.50 (*0-317-06029-5*, RD240AB5) Ctr Educ Trng Employ.

— Choosing the Type of Ownership Module, PACE: A Program for Acquiring Competence in Entrepreneurship, 3 levels, Level 2. rev. ed. 1983. 2.50 (*0-317-06030-9*, RD240BB5) Ctr Educ Trng Employ.

— Choosing the Type of Ownership Module, PACE: A Program for Acquiring Competence in Entrepreneurship, 3 levels, Level 3. rev. ed. 1983. 2.50 (*0-317-06031-7*, RD240CB5) Ctr Educ Trng Employ.

— Collaborate with the Community Module, Competency-Based Career Guidance (CBCG) - Category A: Guidance Program Planning. 1985. 7.95 (*0-317-03860-5*, CG100A03) Ctr Educ Trng Employ.

— Communicate & Use Evaluation-Based Decisions Module, Competency-Based Career Guidance (CBCG) - Category E: Evaluating. 1985. 6.95 (*0-317-03861-3*, CG100E02) Ctr Educ Trng Employ.

— Communicate Effectively Module, Connections: School & Work Transitions - Work Skills-Work Maturity Skills. 1987. write for info. (*0-318-67160-3*, SP100CB11) Ctr Educ Trng Employ.

— A Compendium of What Works for Vocational Educators in Dropout Prevention. 1988. 11.50 (*0-317-03862-1*, SP700DP03) Ctr Educ Trng Employ.

— Competency-Based Career Guidance (CBCG) Modules, 34 modules, Set. 1985. 245.00 (*0-317-03863-X*, CG100) Ctr Educ Trng Employ.

— Complying with Government Regulations Module, PACE: A Program for Acquiring Competence in Entrepreneurship, 3 levels. rev. ed. 1983. 2.50 (*0-317-06032-5*); Level 1. 2.50 (*0-317-06033-3*, RD240AB10); Level 2. 2.50 (*0-317-06034-1*, RD240BB10); Level 3. 2.50 (*0-317-06035-X*, RD240CB10) Ctr Educ Trng Employ.

— Conduct Computerized Guidance Module, Competency-Based Career Guidance (CBCG) - Category C: Implementing. 1985. 6.95 (*0-317-03864-8*, CG100C03) Ctr Educ Trng Employ.

— Conduct Placement & Referral Activities Module, Competency-Based Career Guidance (CBCG) - Category C: Implementing. 1985. 7.95 (*0-317-03866-4*, CG100C10) Ctr Educ Trng Employ.

— Conduct Staff Development Activities Module, Competency-Based Guidance (CBCG) - Category C: Implementing. 1985. 6.95 (*0-317-03865-6*, CG100B04) Ctr Educ Trng Employ.

— Connections: School & Work Transitions. 1987. 350.00 (*0-318-35279-6*, SP 100PR) Ctr Educ Trng Employ.

— The Connector's Guide, Connections: School & Work Transitions. 1987. 39.95 (*0-317-03867-2*, SP100AA) Ctr Educ Trng Employ.

— Cooperate with Others Module, Connections: School & Work Transitions - Work Skills-Work Maturity Skills. 1987. write for info. (*0-318-67161-1*, SP100CB13) Ctr Educ Trng Employ.

— Coordinate Career Resource Centers Module, Competency-Based Career Guidance (CBCG) - Category C: Implementing. 1985. 7.95 (*0-317-03868-0*, CG100C05) Ctr Educ Trng Employ.

— Counsel Individuals & Groups Module, Competency-Based Career Guidance (CBCG) - Category C: Implementing. 1985. 7.95 (*0-317-03869-9*, CG100C01) Ctr Educ Trng Employ.

— Create & Use an Individual Career Development Plan Module, Competency-Based Career Guidance (CBCG) - Category C: Implementing. 1985. 6.95 (*0-317-03870-2*, CG100C12) Ctr Educ Trng Employ.

— Credentials for Employment, Connections: School & Work Transitions - Employment File. 1987. write for info. (*0-318-67162-X*, SP100EA01) Ctr Educ Trng Employ.

— Dealing with Legal Issues Module, PACE: A Program for Acquiring Competence in Entrepreneurship, 3 levels. rev. ed. 1983. 2.50 (*0-317-06036-8*); Level 1. 2.50 (*0-317-06037-6*, RD240AB9); Level 2. 2.50 (*0-317-06038-4*, RD240BB9); Level 3. 2.50 (*0-318-67163-8*, RD240CB9) Ctr Educ Trng Employ.

— Determine Client & Environment Needs Module, Competency-Based Career Guidance (CBCG) - Category A: Guidance Program Planning. 1985. 7.95 (*0-317-03871-0*, CG100A06) Ctr Educ Trng Employ.

— Determining Your Potential As an Entrepreneur Module, PACE: A Program for Acquiring Competence in Entrepreneurship, 3 levels. rev. ed. 1983. Level 1. 2.50 (*0-318-67164-6*, RD240AB2); Level 2. 2.50 (*0-317-06041-4*, RD240BB2); Level 3. 2.50 (*0-317-06042-2*, RD240CB2); Level 1. write for info. (*0-318-67165-4*, RD240AB2) Ctr Educ Trng Employ.

— Develop a Work Experience Program Module, Competency-Based Career Guidance (CBCG) - Category C: Implementing. 1985. 6.95 (*0-317-03873-7*, CG100C07) Ctr Educ Trng Employ.

— Develop Ethical & Legal Standards Module, Competency-Based Career Guidance (CBCG) - Category C: Implementing. 1985. 6.95 (*0-317-04751-5*, CG100C19) Ctr Educ Trng Employ.

— Developing a Curriculum in Response to Change, Options: Expanding Educational Services for Adults. 1987. 39.95 (*0-317-03874-5*, SP500E) Ctr Educ Trng Employ.

— Developing the Business Plan Module, PACE: A Program for Acquiring Competence in Entrepreneurship, 3 levels. rev. ed. 1983. Level 1. 2.50 (*0-317-06043-0*, RD240AB3); Level 2. 2.50 (*0-317-06044-9*, RD240BB3); Level 3. 2.50 (*0-317-06045-7*, 2D240CB3) Ctr Educ Trng Employ.

— Dignity in the Workplace: A Labor Studies Curriculum Guide for Vocational Educators' Connections: School & Work Transitions - Coordinator's Resources. 1987. 18.50 (*0-317-03875-3*, SP100AC01) Ctr Educ Trng Employ.

— Dignity in the Workplace: A Student's Guide to Labor Unions, Connections: School & Work Transitions - Coordinator's Resources. 1987. 7.75 (*0-317-03876-1*, SP100AC02) Ctr Educ Trng Employ.

— Educator's Guide, Options: Expanding Educational Services for Adults. 1987. 5.25 (*0-317-03877-X*, SP500A) Ctr Educ Trng Employ.

— The Employer's Choice, Connections: School & Work Transitions, Set. 1987. 84.00 (*0-317-03879-6*, SP100BX) Ctr Educ Trng Employ.

— Employer's Choice Resource Manual, Connections: School & Work Transitions. 1987. 25.50 (*0-317-03880-X*, SP100BA01) Ctr Educ Trng Employ.

— Enhance Understanding of Individuals with Disabilities Module, Competency-Based Career Guidance (CBCG) - Category C: Implementing. 1985. 6.95 (*0-317-03881-8*, CG100C14) Ctr Educ Trng Employ.

— Ensure Program Operations Module, Competency-Based Career Guidance (CBCG) - Category D: Operating. 1985. 6.95 (*0-317-03882-6*, CG100D01) Ctr Educ Trng Employ.

— Es Tu Vida...Toma Control: It's Your Life...Take Charge Student Workbook, Dropout Prevention. (SPA.). 1988. write for info. (*0-318-67166-2*, SP700TC02) Ctr Educ Trng Employ.

— Establish a Career Development Theory Module, Competency-Based Career Guidance (CBCG) - Category A: Guidance Program Planning. 1985. 7.95 (*0-317-04752-3*, CG100A04) Ctr Educ Trng Employ.

— Evaluate Guidance Activities Module, Competency-Based Career Guidance (CBCG) - Category E: Evaluating. 1985. 7.95 (*0-317-04611-X*, CG100E01) Ctr Educ Trng Employ.

— Exhibit Positive Work Attitudes Module, Connections: School & Work Transitions - Work Skills-Work Maturity Skills. 1987. write for info. (*0-318-67167-0*, SP100CB08) Ctr Educ Trng Employ.

— Facilitate Follow-up & Follow-Through Module, Competency-Based Career Guidance (CBCG) - Category C: Implementing. 1985. 8.95 (*0-317-03885-0*, CG100C11) Ctr Educ Trng Employ.

— Financing the Business Module, PACE: A Program for Acquiring Competence in Entrepreneurship, 3 levels, Level 1. rev. ed. 1983. 2.50 (*0-318-67168-9*, RD240AB8) Ctr Educ Trng Employ.

— Financing the Business Module, PACE: A Program for Acquiring Competence in Entrepreneurship, 3 levels, Level 2. rev. ed. 1983. 2.50 (*0-318-67169-7*, RD240BB8) Ctr Educ Trng Employ.

— Financing the Business Module, PACE: A Program for Acquiring Competence in Entrepreneurship, 3 levels, Level 3. rev. ed. 1983. 2.50 (*0-318-67170-0*, RD240CB8) Ctr Educ Trng Employ.

— Handle Job Offers Module, Connections: School & Work - Work Skills-Job Search Skills. 1987. write for info. (*0-318-67171-9*, SP100CB06) Ctr Educ Trng Employ.

— Help Ethnic Minorities with Career Guidance Module, Competency-Based Career Guidance (CBCG) - Category C: Implementing. 1985. 7.95 (*0-317-04612-8*, CG100C15) Ctr Educ Trng Employ.

— Helping Process Overview Guidebook, Dropout Prevention. 1988. 6.50 (*0-317-03888-5*, SP700HP01) Ctr Educ Trng Employ.

— The Helping Process Professional Set, Dropout Prevention. 1988. 39.50 (*0-317-03887-7*, SP700HP) Ctr Educ Trng Employ.

— Identify & Plan for Guidance Program Change Module, Competency-Based Career Guidance (CBCG) - Category A: Guidance Program Planning. 1985. write for info. (*0-318-67172-7*) Ctr Educ Trng Employ.

— Implementation Guide; Basics: Bridging Vocational & Academic Skills - The Bridger's Guide. 1987. 10.95 (*0-317-03890-7*, SP300AA) Ctr Educ Trng Employ.

— Improve Public Relations & Community Involvement Module, Competency-Based Career Guidance (CBCG) - Category B: Supporting. 1985. 6.95 (*0-317-03891-5*, CB100B03) Ctr Educ Trng Employ.

— Influence Legislation Module, Competency-Based Career Guidance (CBCG) - Category B: Supporting. 1985. 19.95 (*0-317-03893-1*, CG100B01) Ctr Educ Trng Employ.

— Infuse Curriculum Plus Based Guidance Module, Competency-Based Career Guidance (CBCG) - Category C: Implementing. 1985. 7.95 (*0-317-03894-X*, CG100C04) Ctr Educ Trng Employ.

— Instructional Materials Development, Basics: Bridging Vocational & Academic Skills - Instructional Program Development. 1987. 13.95 (*0-317-04613-6*, SP300DA) Ctr Educ Trng Employ.

— Instructional Program Development, Basics: Bridging Vocational & Academic Skills. 1987. 50.00 (*0-317-03895-8*, SP300D) Ctr Educ Trng Employ.

— Instructor Guide, PACE: A Program for Acquiring Competence in Entrepreneurship, 3 levels, Level 1. rev. ed. 1983. 14.50 (*0-317-06049-X*, RD240AA) Ctr Educ Trng Employ.

— Instructor Guide, PACE: A Program for Acquiring Competence in Entrepreneurship, 3 levels, Level 2. rev. ed. 1983. 14.50 (*0-317-06050-3*, RD240BA) Ctr Educ Trng Employ.

— Instructor Guide, PACE: A Program for Acquiring Competence in Entrepreneurship, 3 levels, Level 3. rev. ed. 1983. 14.50 (*0-317-06051-1*, RD240CA) Ctr Educ Trng Employ.

— Interview for Jobs Module, Connections: School & Work Transitions - Work Skills-Job Search Skills. 1987. write for info. (*0-318-67173-5*, SP100CB05) Ctr Educ Trng Employ.

— Introduction to Connections, Connections: School & Work Transitions. 1987. 25.00 (*0-317-03897-4*, SP100AB) Ctr Educ Trng Employ.

— It's Your Life...Take Charge Professional Set, Dropout Prevention. 1988. 49.50 (*0-317-03898-2*, SP700TC) Ctr Educ Trng Employ.

— It's Your Life...Take Charge Student Workbook, Dropout Prevention. 1988. write for info. (*0-318-67174-3*, SP700C01) Ctr Educ Trng Employ.

— Job Placement in Employment & Training Programs: An Action Planning Guidebook. 121p. 1983. 9.00 (*0-318-22136-5*, RD218) Ctr Educ Trng Employ.

— Keeping the Business Records Module, PACE: A Program for Acquiring Competence in Entrepreneurship, 3 levels, Level 1. rev. ed. 1983. 2.50 (*0-317-06052-X*, RD240AB15) Ctr Educ Trng Employ.

— Keeping the Business Records Module, PACE: A Program for Acquiring Competence in Entrepreneurship, 3 levels, Level 2. rev. ed. 1983. 2.50 (*0-317-06053-8*, RD240BB15) Ctr Educ Trng Employ.

— Keeping the Business Records Module, PACE: A Program for Acquiring Competence in Entrepreneurship, 3 levels, Level 3. rev. ed. 1983. 2.50 (*0-317-06054-6*, RD240CB15) Ctr Educ Trng Employ.

— Linking with Employers, Options: Expanding Educational Services for Adults. 1987. 39.95 (*0-317-03900-8*, SP500D) Ctr Educ Trng Employ.

— Literacy Enhancement for Adults, Options: Expanding Educational Services for Adults. 1987. 9.50 (*0-317-03901-6*, SP500FB) Ctr Educ Trng Employ.

— Locating the Business Module, PACE: A Program for Acquiring Competence in Entrepreneurship, 3 levels, Level 1. rev. ed. 1983. 2.50 (*0-318-67175-1*, RD240AB7) Ctr Educ Trng Employ.

— Locating the Business Module, PACE: A Program for Acquiring Competence in Entrepreneurship, 3 levels, Level 1. rev. ed. 1983. Level 1. write for info. (*0-318-67176-X*, RD240AB7) Ctr Educ Trng Employ.

— Locating the Business Module, PACE: A Program for Acquiring Competence in Entrepreneurship, 3 levels, Level 2. rev. ed. 1983. 2.50 (*0-317-06056-2*, RD240BB7) Ctr Educ Trng Employ.

— Locating the Business Module, PACE: A Program for Acquiring Competence in Entrepreneurship, 3 levels, Level 3. rev. ed. 1983. 2.50 (*0-317-06057-0*, RD240CB7) Ctr Educ Trng Employ.

— Managing Customer Credit & Collections Module, PACE: A Program for Acquiring Competence in Entrepreneurship, Level 1. rev. ed. 1983. 2.50 (*0-317-06061-9*, RD240AB17) Ctr Educ Trng Employ.

— Managing Customer Credit & Collections Module, PACE: A Program for Acquiring Competence in Entrepreneurship, Level 2. rev. ed. 1983. 2.50 (*0-317-06062-7*, RD240BB17) Ctr Educ Trng Employ.

— Managing Customer Credit & Collections Module, PACE: A Program for Acquiring Competence in Entrepreneurship, Level 3. rev. ed. 1983. 2.50 (*0-318-67177-8*, RD240CB17) Ctr Educ Trng Employ.

— Managing Human Resources Module, PACE: A Program for Acquiring Competence in Entrepreneurship, 3 levels, Level 1. rev. ed. 1983. 2.50 (*0-317-06067-8*, RD240AB12) Ctr Educ Trng Employ.

— Managing Human Resources Module, PACE: A Program for Acquiring Competence in Entrepreneurship, 3 levels, Level 2. rev. ed. 1983. 2.50 (*0-317-06068-6*, RD240BB12) Ctr Educ Trng Employ.

— Managing Human Resources Module, PACE: A Program for Acquiring Competence in Entrepreneurship, 3 levels, Level 3. rev. ed. 1983. 2.50 (*0-317-06069-4*, RD240CB12) Ctr Educ Trng Employ.

— Managing Sales Efforts Module, PACE: A Program for Acquiring Competence in Entrepreneurship, 3 levels, Level 1. rev. ed. 1983. 2.50 (*0-318-67178-6*, RD240AB14) Ctr Educ Trng Employ.

— Managing Sales Efforts Module, PACE: A Program for Acquiring Competence in Entrepreneurship, 3 levels, Level 2. rev. ed. 1983. 2.50 (*0-317-06071-6*, RD240BB14) Ctr Educ Trng Employ.

— Managing Sales Efforts Module, PACE: A Program for Acquiring Competence in Entrepreneurship, 3 levels, Level 3. rev. ed. 1983. 2.50 (*0-317-06072-4*, RD240CB14) Ctr Educ Trng Employ.

— Managing the Business Module, PACE: A Program for Acquiring Competence in Entrepreneurship, 3 levels, Level 1. rev. ed. 1983. 2.50 (*0-317-06058-9*, RD240AB11) Ctr Educ Trng Employ.

— Managing the Business Module, PACE: A Program for Acquiring Competence in Entrepreneurship, 3 levels, Level 2. rev. ed. 1983. 2.50 (*0-317-06059-7*, RD240BB11) Ctr Educ Trng Employ.

— Managing the Business Module, PACE: A Program for Acquiring Competence in Entrepreneurship, 3 levels, Level 3. rev. ed. 1983. 2.50 (*0-317-06060-0*, RD240CB11) Ctr Educ Trng Employ.

— Managing the Finance Module, PACE: A Program for Acquiring Competence in Entrepreneurship, 3 levels, Level 1. rev. ed. 1983. 2.50 (*0-317-06064-3*, RD240AB16) Ctr Educ Trng Employ.

— Managing the Finance Module, PACE: A Program for Acquiring Competence in Entrepreneurship, 3 levels, Level 2. rev. ed. 1983. 2.50 (*0-317-06065-1*, RD240BB16) Ctr Educ Trng Employ.

— Managing the Finance Module, PACE: A Program for Acquiring Competence in Entrepreneurship, 3 levels, Level 3. rev. ed. 1983. 2.50 (*0-317-06066-X*, RD240CB16) Ctr Educ Trng Employ.

— Meet Initial Guidance Needs of Older Adults Module, Competency-Based Career Guidance (CBCG) - Category C: Implementing. 1985. 7.95 (*0-317-03902-4*, CG100C16) Ctr Educ Trng Employ.

— Obtaining Technical Assistance Module, PACE: A Program for Acquiring Competence in Entrepreneurship, 3 levels, Level 1. rev. ed. 1983. 2.50 (*0-317-06073-2*, RD240AB4) Ctr Educ Trng Employ.

— Obtaining Technical Assistance Module, PACE: A Program for Acquiring Competence in Entrepreneurship, 3 levels, Level 2. rev. ed. 1983. 2.50 (*0-317-06074-0*, RD240BB4) Ctr Educ Trng Employ.

— Obtaining Technical Assistance Module, PACE: A Program for Acquiring Competence in Entrepreneurship, 3 levels, Level 3. rev. ed. 1983. 2.50 (*0-317-06075-9*, RD240CB4) Ctr Educ Trng Employ.

— On the Job Student Book, Connections: School & Work Transitions - Employer's Choice. 1987. 7.25 (*0-317-04614-4*, SP100BB02) Ctr Educ Trng Employ.

— Options: Expanding Educational Services for Adults. 1987. 174.00 (*0-318-35280-X*, SP 500) Ctr Educ Trng Employ.

— Organize Guidance Program Development Team Module, Competency-Based Career Guidance (CBCG) - Category A: Guidance Program Planning. 1985. 7.95 (*0-317-04753-1*, CG100A02) Ctr Educ Trng Employ.

— Orientation to Options, Options: Expanding Educational Services for Adults. 1987. 25.00 (*0-317-03905-9*, SP500BVHS) Ctr Educ Trng Employ.

— Orientation to the World of Work Module, Connections: School & Work Transitions - Work Skills. 1987. write for info. (*0-318-67179-4*, SP100CB01) Ctr Educ Trng Employ.

— Planning the Marketing Strategy Module, PACE: A Program for Acquiring Competence in Entrepreneurship, 3 levels, Level 1. rev. ed. 1983. 2.50 (*0-317-06076-7*, RD240AB6) Ctr Educ Trng Employ.

— Planning the Marketing Strategy Module, PACE: A Program for Acquiring Competence in Entrepreneurship, 3 levels, Level 2. rev. ed. 1983. 2.50 (*0-317-06077-5*, RD240BB6) Ctr Educ Trng Employ.

— Planning the Marketing Strategy Module, PACE: A Program for Acquiring Competence in Entrepreneurship, 3 levels, Level 3. rev. ed. 1983. 2.50 (*0-318-67180-8*, RD240CB6) Ctr Educ Trng Employ.

— Practice Ethical Behavior Module, Connections: School & Work Transitions - Work Skills-Work Maturity Skills. 1987. write for info. (*0-318-67182-4*, SP100CB10) Ctr Educ Trng Employ.

— Practice Good Work Habits Module, Connections: School & Work Transitions - Work Skills-Work Maturity Skills. 1987. write for info. (*0-318-67181-6*, SP100CB09) Ctr Educ Trng Employ.

— Prepare for the Job Search Module, Connections: School & Work Transitions - Work Skills-Job Search Skills. 1987. write for info. (*0-318-67183-2*, SP100CB02) Ctr Educ Trng Employ.

— Present a Positive Image Module, Connections: School & Work Transitions - Work Skills-Work Maturity Skills. 1987. write for info. (*0-318-67184-0*, SP100CB07) Ctr Educ Trng Employ.

— Primer of Exemplary Strategies, Basics: Bridging Vocational & Academic Skills - The Bridger's Guide. 1987. 11.95 (*0-317-03906-7*, SP300AB) Ctr Educ Trng Employ.

— Priorities That Count Student Book, Connections: School & Work Transitions - Employer's Choice. 1987. 4.00 (*0-317-03907-5*, SP100BB01) Ctr Educ Trng Employ.

— Promote Equity & Client Advocacy Module, Competency-Based Career Guidance (CBCG) - Category C: Implementing. 1985. 6.95 (*0-317-03908-3*, CG100C17) Ctr Educ Trng Employ.

— Promoting the Business Module, PACE: A Program for Acquiring Competence in Entrepreneurship, 3 levels, Level 1. rev. ed. 1983. 2.50 (*0-318-67185-9*, RD240AB13); write for info. (*0-318-67186-7*, RD240AB13) Ctr Educ Trng Employ.

— Promoting the Business Module, PACE: A Program for Acquiring Competence in Entrepreneurship, 3 levels, Level 2. rev. ed. 1983. 2.50 (*0-317-06080-5*, RD240BB13) Ctr Educ Trng Employ.

— Promoting the Business Module, PACE: A Program for Acquiring Competence in Entrepreneurship, 3 levels, Level 3. rev. ed. 1983. 2.50 (*0-317-06081-3*, RD240CB13) Ctr Educ Trng Employ.

— Protecting the Business Module, PACE: A Program for Acquiring Competence in Entrepreneurship, 3 levels, Level 1. rev. ed. 1983. 2.50 (*0-317-06082-1*, RD240CB18) Ctr Educ Trng Employ.

— Protecting the Business Module, PACE: A Program for Acquiring Competence in Entrepreneurship, 3 levels, Level 2. rev. ed. 1983. 2.50 (*0-317-06083-X*, RD240BB18) Ctr Educ Trng Employ.

— Protecting the Business Module, PACE: A Program for Acquiring Competence in Entrepreneurship, 3 levels, Level 3. rev. ed. 1983. 2.50 (*0-317-06084-8*, RD240CB18) Ctr Educ Trng Employ.

— Provide Career Guidance to Girls & Women Module, Competency-Based Career Guidance (CBCG) - Category C: Implementing. 1985. 7.95 (*0-317-03910-5*, CG100C13) Ctr Educ Trng Employ.

— Provide for Employability Skill Development Module, Competency-Based Career Guidance (CBCG) - Category C: Implementing. 1985. 7.95 (*0-317-03911-3*, CG100C08) Ctr Educ Trng Employ.

— Provide for the Basic Skills Module, Competency-Based Career Guidance (CBCG) - Category C: Implementing. 1985. 7.95 (*0-317-03909-1*, CG100C09) Ctr Educ Trng Employ.

— Publicity Kit, Options: Expanding Educational Services for Adults. 1987. 29.95 (*0-317-03912-1*, SP500C) Ctr Educ Trng Employ.

— Resource Guide, PACE: A Program for Acquiring Competence in Entrepreneurship. rev. ed. 1983. 7.95 (*0-318-67187-5*, RD240D) Ctr Educ Trng Employ.

— Search for Available Jobs Module, Connections: School & Work Transitions - Work Skills-Job Search Skills. 1987. write for info. (*0-318-67188-3*, SP100CB03) Ctr Educ Trng Employ.

— Special Services for Adult Learners, Options: Expanding Educational Sources for Adults. 1987. 29.50 (*0-317-04616-0*, SP500F) Ctr Educ Trng Employ.

— Student's Choice Student Workbook, Dropout Prevention. 1988. write for info. (*0-318-67189-1*, SP700SC01) Ctr Educ Trng Employ.

— Supplemental Instructional Resources, Basics: Bridging Vocational & Academic Skill - Instructional Program Development. 1987. 7.95 (*0-317-03915-6*, SP300DB) Ctr Educ Trng Employ.

— Technique for Individualization: The Academic Development Plan, Basics: Bridging Vocational & Academic Skills - Targeting Teaching Techniques. 1987. 9.95 (*0-317-03918-0*, SP300EE) Ctr Educ Trng Employ.

— Technique for Management: Time for Learning, Basics: Bridging Vocational & Academic Skills - Targeted Teaching Techniques. 1987. 7.50 (*0-317-03919-9*, SP300EB) Ctr Educ Trng Employ.

— Technique for Remediation: Peer Tutoring with Audiocassette, Basics: Bridging Vocational & Academic Skills - Targeted Teaching Techniques. 1987. 13.95 (*0-317-03920-2*, SP300EC) Ctr Educ Trng Employ.

— Techniques of Joint Effort: The Vocational Academic Approach with Audiocassette, Basics: Bridging Vocational & Academic Skills - Targeted Teaching Techniques. 1987. 13.95 (*0-317-03916-4*, SP300EA) Ctr Educ Trng Employ.

— Tutor Clients Module, Competency-Based Career Guidance (CBCG) - Category C: Implementing. 1985. 7.95 (*0-317-03921-0*, CG100C02) Ctr Educ Trng Employ.

— Understanding the Nature of Small Business Module, PACE: A Program for Acquiring Competence in Entrepreneurship, 3 levels. rev. ed. 1983. Level 1. write for info. (*0-318-67190-5*, RD240AB1) Ctr Educ Trng Employ.

— Understanding the Nature of Small Business Module, PACE: A Program for Acquiring Competence in Entrepreneurship, 3 levels, Level 1. rev. ed. 1983. 6.50 (*0-317-06086-4*, RD240AB1) Ctr Educ Trng Employ.

— Understanding the Nature of Small Business Module, PACE: A Program for Acquiring Competence in Entrepreneurship, 3 levels, Level 2. rev. ed. 1983. 6.50 (*0-317-06087-2*, RD240BB1) Ctr Educ Trng Employ.

— Understanding the Nature of Small Business Module, PACE: A Program for Acquiring Competence in Entrepreneurship, 3 levels, Level 3. rev. ed. 1983. 6.50 (*0-318-67191-3*, RD240CB1) Ctr Educ Trng Employ.

— Use & Comply with Administrative Mechanisms Module, Competency-Based Career Guidance (CBCG) - Category B: Supporting. 1985. 7.95 (*0-317-03922-9*, CB100B05) Ctr Educ Trng Employ.

— Work Skills Instructor Guide, Connections: School & Work Transitions. 1987. 4.75 (*0-317-03924-5*, SP100CA02) Ctr Educ Trng Employ.

— Work Skills Modules, Connections: School & Work Transitions - Work Skills, 13 modules, Set. 1987. 39.00 (*0-317-03925-3*, SP100CA03) Ctr Educ Trng Employ.

— Work Skills Resource Manual, Connections: School & Work Transitions - Work Skills. 1987. 29.95 (*0-317-03926-1*, SP100CA01) Ctr Educ Trng Employ.

National Center for Small Communities Staff. The Americans with Disabilities Act: A Compliance Workbook for Small Communities. LC 92-17025. 1992. write for info. (*0-925532-08-8*) Natl Assn Town & Twps.

— Six Ways to Better Manage Your Town Government: What Every Small Town Government Official Needs to Know. LC 93-45605. 1994. 14.95 (*0-925532-10-X*) Natl Assn Town & Twps.

— Tapping Your Own Resources: A Decision-Maker's Guide for Small Town Drinking Water. 1993. write for info. (*0-925532-09-6*) Natl Assn Town & Twps.

National Center for State Courts. Alternatives to Incarceration: An Annotated Bibliography, 1978-80. 97p. 1981. 5.82 (*0-685-43728-0*, SRO-007) Natl Ctr St Courts.

— Backlog Reduction Program in the Supreme Court in New York City: First Interim Evaluation Report. 25p. 1982. 1.50 (*0-685-15459-9*, NERO-103) Natl Ctr St Courts.

— Case Filing & Disposition Reporting System for Circuit, Criminal, Chancery, & Law & Equity Courts of Tennessee, Vol. VI. 107p. 1976. 6.42 (*0-685-16628-7*, MAB-125) Natl Ctr St Courts.

— Citizen Settlement Program: Mediation of Small Claims. (Paul Reardon Ser.). 16p. 1982. 0.96 (*0-685-16810-7*, PRS-035) Natl Ctr St Courts.

— Civil Case Backlog Reduction: San Diego Superior Court. (Paul Reardon Ser.). 9p. 1982. 0.54 (*0-685-15472-6*, PRS-031) Natl Ctr St Courts.

— Data Collection & Analysis, with Recommendations, for the Tennessee Judicial Information System (TJIS), Vol. I. 160p. 1977. 9.60 (*0-685-16631-7*, MAB-122) Natl Ctr St Courts.

— Data Processing Options Assessment, Lehigh County (PA) Final Report. 17p. 1984. 1.02 (*0-685-16655-4*, NERO-141) Natl Ctr St Courts.

— Felony Backlog Elimination Program of the New York City Supreme Court: Paul Reardon Ser. 42p. 1982. 2.52 (*0-685-15531-5*, PRS-039) Natl Ctr St Courts.

— Information System for South Carolina Courts, No. 1. (Paul Reardon Ser.). 44p. 1981. 2.64 (*0-685-16659-7*, PRS-011) Natl Ctr St Courts.

— Master Plan for Tennessee Judicial Information System (TJIS) Program Development, Vol. III. 133p. 1976. 7.98 (*0-685-16676-7*, MAB-124) Natl Ctr St Courts.

— Pretrial Reimbursement Program. (Paul Reardon Ser.). 24p. 1982. 1.44 (*0-685-16769-0*, PRS-036) Natl Ctr St Courts.

— Public Affairs for the Judiciary: The Means By Which Public Confidence Can Be Fostered to Provide Effective & Efficient Judicial Service. (Paul Reardon Ser.). 13p. 1981. 0.78 (*0-685-15193-X*, PRS-019) Natl Ctr St Courts.

— Study of Caseflow Management. (Paul Reardon Ser.). 71p. 1981. 4.26 (*0-685-15702-4*, PRS-004) Natl Ctr St Courts.

— Volume & Delay in Appellate Courts: Preliminary Findings from a National Study. 185p. 1979. 11.10 (*0-685-16926-X*, NERO-091) Natl Ctr St Courts.

National Center for State Courts, Denver Staff. Policymakers' Views Regarding Issues in the Operation & Evaluation of Pretrial Release & Diversion Programs: Findings from a Questionnaire Survey. 152p. 1975. pap. write for info. (*0-89656-012-0*, R-016A) Natl Ctr St Courts.

— Research Priorities in Sentencing. 82p. 1975. pap. write for info. (*0-89656-013-9*, R-022) Natl Ctr St Courts.

National Center for State Courts Staff. Administration of Court Reporting in the State Courts. 48p. 1973. 2.88 (*0-685-15840-3*, MAB-001) Natl Ctr St Courts.

— Administration of the Massachusetts Courts. 62p. 1974. 3.72 (*0-685-15090-9*, MAB-002) Natl Ctr St Courts.

— Administrative Analysis of the King County (WA) District Courts. 179p. 1975. 10.74 (*0-685-15091-7*, MAB-003) Natl Ctr St Courts.

— Administrative Directives in the New York Unified Court System, 3 vols., Vol. I. 453p. 1981. write for info. (*0-318-61206-2*, NERO-098) Natl Ctr St Courts.

— Administrative Directives in the New York Unified Court System, 3 vols., Vol. II. 479p. 1981. 28.74 (*0-685-15092-5*, NERO-099) Natl Ctr St Courts.

— Administrative Directives in the New York Unified Court System, 3 vols., Vol. III. 282p. 1981. 16.92 (*0-685-15093-3*, NERO-100) Natl Ctr St Courts.

— Administrative Personnel Review: Eleventh Judicial Circuit, Dade County, Florida, Final Report. 66p. 1986. 4.00 (*0-685-15198-0*, SERO-017) Natl Ctr St Courts.

— Administrative Power in the Individual Massachusetts Courts. 125p. 1975. 7.50 (*0-685-15094-1*, NERO-005) Natl Ctr St Courts.

— Administrative Role of Chief Justices & Supreme Courts. 48p. 1979. pap. write for info. (*0-89656-038-4*, R-046) Natl Ctr St Courts.

— Administrative Staffing Implications of Court System Unification in North Dakota: Technical Assistance Report. 151p. 1981. 9.06 (*0-685-15200-6*, NCRO-016) Natl Ctr St Courts.

— Administrative Structure of the New York State Court System. 133p. 1980. 7.98 (*0-685-15095-X*, NERO-092) Natl Ctr St Courts.

— Administrative Unification of the Maine State Courts: Full Report. 204p. 1975. pap. write for info. (*0-89656-000-7*, R-020) Natl Ctr St Courts.

— Advisory Entities: Utilization by the Alabama Judicial System. 54p. 1975. 3.24 (*0-685-15096-8*, MAB-004) Natl Ctr St Courts.

— Alabama Judicial Article: Judicial Administration of Trial Courts, Rule-Making Power, Jury & Grand Jury, Entry & Withdrawal of Municipal Courts; Technical Assistance Report. 1974. 1.50 (*0-685-15015-1*, MAB-005) Natl Ctr St Courts.

— Alabama State Court System (Proposed) Personnel Rules. 1976. 2.28 (*0-685-15202-2*, MAB-006) Natl Ctr St Courts.

— Alabama Unified Judicial System Affirmative Action Evaluation: Technical Assistance Report. 42p. 1979. 2.52 (*0-685-15305-3*, NCRO, T/A-503) Natl Ctr St Courts.

— Alameda County Clerk Criminal-Corpus Division Workload Analysis. 101p. 1978. 6.06 (*0-685-15442-4*, WRO-020) Natl Ctr St Courts.

— Alaska Benchbook. 118p. 1978. 7.00 (*0-685-15064-X*, WRO-060) Natl Ctr St Courts.

— Alternate Court Reporting Techniques for Connecticut. 184p. 1979. 11.04 (*0-685-15843-8*, NERO-031) Natl Ctr St Courts.

— Alternative Sources of Financial & Technical Assistance for State Court Systems. 73p. 1979. 4.38 (*0-685-15170-0*, NERO-041) Natl Ctr St Courts.

— Alternatives to Incarceration: Resource Directory. 184p. 1981. 11.04 (*0-685-43729-9*, SRO-017) Natl Ctr St Courts.

— Analysis of Personnel Classification, Organizational Structure, & Financial Record Keeping Practices of the Circuit Court of Eau Claire County, Wisconsin. 52p. 1980. 3.12 (*0-685-15207-3*, DPO, T/A-504) Natl Ctr St Courts.

— Analysis of the Idaho Courts Information System. 56p. 1974. pap. 1.25 (*0-685-16640-6*, R-012) Natl Ctr St Courts.

— Analysis of the Jury System Serving Davidson County, Nashville, Tennessee. 11p. 1983. write for info. (*0-318-61288-7*, CJS-006) Natl Ctr St Courts.

— Analysis of the Puerto Rico Annual Report & Management & Statistical Information Systems. 179p. 1982. 10.74 (*0-685-16642-2*, MARO-010) Natl Ctr St Courts.

— Analysis of the Role for a Court Administrator in Lane County, Oregon. 39p. 1975. 2.34 (*0-685-15099-2*, MAB-008) Natl Ctr St Courts.

— Anchorage Law Library Analysis. 77p. 1977. 4.62 (*0-685-15347-9*, WRO-006) Natl Ctr St Courts.

— Anchorage Trial Courts Case Processing & Clerical Procedures Project: Analysis & Recommendations. 185p. 1978. 11.10 (*0-685-15448-3*, WRO-002) Natl Ctr St Courts.

— Anchorage Trial Courts Case Processing & Clerical Procedures Project: Appendix I: Desk Audits & Clerical Procedures. 217p. 1978. 13.02 (*0-685-15450-5*, WRO-001) Natl Ctr St Courts.

— Appellate Court Caseloads: Historical Trends With Caseload Statistics Appended. 59p. 1983. 3.54 (*0-685-16909-X*, NCSC-034) Natl Ctr St Courts.

— Appellate Court Delay: Structural Responses to the Problems of Volume & Delay. 184p. 1981. pap. write for info. (*0-89656-048-1*, R-056) Natl Ctr St Courts.

— Appellate Courts: Staff & Process in the Crisis of Volume. 276p. 1974. write for info. (*0-318-61304-2*, NCSC-005) Natl Ctr St Courts.

— Appellate Justice Improvement Project: Collected Papers. 269p. 1981. 16.14 (*0-685-16817-4*, NERO-076) Natl Ctr St Courts.

— Appellate Process & Staff Research Attorneys in the Appellate Division of the New Jersey Superior Court. 124p. 1974. pap. write for info. (*0-318-61305-0*, MAB-009) Natl Ctr St Courts.

— Appellate Process & Staff Research Attorneys in the Appellate Division of the New Jersey Superior Court. 34p. 1975. 2.04 (*0-685-16820-4*, MAB-010) Natl Ctr St Courts.

— Appellate Process & Staff Research Attorneys in the Illinois Appellate Court. 181p. 1974. pap. write for info. (*0-318-61306-9*, MAB-011) Natl Ctr St Courts.

— Appellate Process & Staff Research Attorneys in the Illinois Appellate Court. 18p. 1975. 1.08 (*0-685-16827-1*, MAB-012) Natl Ctr St Courts.

— Appellate Process & Staff Research Attorneys in the Supreme Court of Nebraska: 1972-73. 205p. 1974. pap. write for info. (*0-318-61307-7*, MAB-013) Natl Ctr St Courts.

— Appellate Process & Staff Research Attorneys in the Supreme Court of Nebraska: 1973-74. 92p. 1975. pap. write for info. (*0-318-61308-5*, MAB-014) Natl Ctr St Courts.

— Appellate Process & Staff Research Attorneys in the Supreme Court of Virginia. 71p. 1975. pap. write for info. (*0-318-61309-3*, MAB-016) Natl Ctr St Courts.

— Appellate Process in Rhode Island Supreme Court. 141p. 1977. 8.46 (*0-685-16836-0*, NERO-007) Natl Ctr St Courts.

— Appellate Settlement Conference: An Effective Procedural Reform? (Research Essay Ser.). 12p. 1978. 0.72 (*0-685-16773-9*, E-005) Natl Ctr St Courts.

— Appellate System in Kansas: Technical Assistance Report No. 2 in the Appellate Justice Improvement Project. 32p. 1980. 1.92 (*0-685-16838-7*, NERO, T/A-502) Natl Ctr St Courts.

— Appellate System in New Hampshire: Technical Assistance Report No. 4 in the Appellate Justice Improvement Project. 69p. 1980. 4.14 (*0-685-16840-9*, NERO, T/A-504) Natl Ctr St Courts.

— Appellate System in Oklahoma: Technical Assistance Report No. 1 in the Appellate Justice Improvement Project. 24p. 1980. 1.44 (*0-685-16846-8*, NERO, T/A-501) Natl Ctr St Courts.

— Appellate System in the North Carolina Court of Appeals: Technical Assistance Report No. 3 in the Appellate Justice Improvement Project. 131p. 1980. 7.86 (*0-685-16843-3*, NERO, T/A-503) Natl Ctr St Courts.

— Appellate System in Vermont: Technical Assistance Report No. 5 in the Appellate Justice Improvement Project. 49p. 1980. 2.94 (*0-685-16850-6*, NERO, T/A-505) Natl Ctr St Courts.

— Arizona Justice of the Peace Courts: Technical Assistance Project. 138p. 1984. 9.00 (*0-685-15016-X*, WRO, T/A-501) Natl Ctr St Courts.

— Arizona Superior Courts: Proposed Classification & Salary Plans. 456p. 1980. write for info. (*0-318-61224-0*, WRO-047) Natl Ctr St Courts.

— Arkansas Civil Benchbook. 283p. 1982. 17.00 (*0-685-15065-8*, SRO-013) Natl Ctr St Courts.

— Arkansas Fundamental Court Improvement Project. 1981. pap. write for info. (*0-318-61187-2*, SRO-006) Natl Ctr St Courts.

— Arkansas JPC Judicial Article Task Force: Judicial Personnel. 33p. write for info. (*0-318-61226-7*, SRO-019) Natl Ctr St Courts.

— Assessment of a Manual Case Monitoring System for the Third Judicial District Court, Salt Lake City, Utah. 41p. 1977. 2.46 (*0-685-15451-3*, MAB-017) Natl Ctr St Courts.

— Assessment of Audio Recording System for the North Dakota Supreme Court. 24p. 1975. 1.44 (*0-685-16272-9*, MAB-018) Natl Ctr St Courts.

— Assessment of Delaware County's Court of Common Pleas Courtroom Needs to Year 2000. 48p. 1979. 2.88 (*0-685-15156-5*, NERO-023) Natl Ctr St Courts.

— Assessment of Microfilm & Records Retention Programs in the Delaware County Court of Common Pleas, Media, Pennsylvania. 24p. 1978. 1.44 (*0-685-16557-4*, DPO, T/A-501) Natl Ctr St Courts.

— Assessment of the Adaptability of New PROMIS to a State Judicial Information System. 329p. 1979. 19.74 (*0-89656-034-1*, F-003) Natl Ctr St Courts.

— Assessment of the Juvenile Justice System in Philadelphia, 4 vols., Vol. I. 276p. 1984. 17.00 (*0-685-15037-2*, NERO-142) Natl Ctr St Courts.

— Assessment of the Juvenile Justice System in Philadelphia, 4 vols., Vol. II. 41p. 1984. 3.00 (*0-685-15038-0*, NERO-143) Natl Ctr St Courts.

— Assessment of the Juvenile Justice System in Philadelphia, 4 vols., Vol. III. 566p. 1984. 34.00 (*0-685-15039-9*, NERO-144) Natl Ctr St Courts.

— Atlantic County (NJ) Clerk's Office Criminal Case Operations: Final Report. 67p. 1980. 4.02 (*0-685-15455-6*, NERO-071) Natl Ctr St Courts.

— Audio-Recording in the Superior Court of District of Columbia. (Paul Reardon Ser.). 17p. 1982. 1.02 (*0-685-16276-1*, PRS-026) Natl Ctr St Courts.

National Center for State Courts Staff, et al. Audio-Video Technology & the Courts: Guide for Court Managers. LC 78-105951. (Courts' Equipment Analysis Project Ser.). (Illus.). 76p. 1977. pap. 0.70 (*0-89656-022-8*, R-034) Natl Ctr St Courts.

National Center for State Courts Staff. Automated Court Report Production: Increasing the Volume, Improving the Quality. (Paul Reardon Ser.). 44p. 1983. 2.64 (*0-685-16285-0*, PRS-040) Natl Ctr St Courts.

N

— Automated Options Assessment for the New York Supreme Court Appellate Division Second Department. 72p. 1983. 4.32 (*0-685-16643-0*, NERO-134) Natl Ctr St Courts.
— Automated Violations Bureau Citation Processing System. (Paul Reardon Ser.). 38p. 1982. 2.28 (*0-685-16645-7*, PRS-033) Natl Ctr St Courts.
— Automation Plan for the Kansas Appellate Courts. 57p. 1982. write for info. (*0-318-61280-1*, NCRO-072) Natl Ctr St Courts.
— Bailiff-Law Clerk Program. (Paul Reardon Ser.). 15p. 1981. 0.90 (*0-685-15335-5*, PRS-017) Natl Ctr St Courts.
— Bedford County (PA) Courthouse Facility Improvement Plan. 42p. 1982. 2.52 (*0-685-15348-7*, NERO-121) Natl Ctr St Courts.
— Bench Warrants: Their Insurance, Service, & Review. (Paul Reardon Ser.). 28p. 1981. 1.68 (*0-685-15151-4*, PRS-025) Natl Ctr St Courts.
— Bibliography: State Appellate Court Workload & Delay. 73p. 1979. 4.38 (*0-685-16910-3*, NERO-038) Natl Ctr St Courts.
— Bibliography: State Appellate Court Workload & Delay; 1979-82. 13p. 1983. 0.78 (*0-685-16911-1*, NCSC-030) Natl Ctr St Courts.
— Bibliography of Issues Relating to Women in the Judiciary. 59p. 1982. write for info. (*0-318-61325-5*, NCSC-029) Natl Ctr St Courts.
— Bibliography on State Bar Admission Practices & Procedures & Effects Upon Lawyer Competence & Delivery of Legal Services. 52p. 1980. 3.12 (*0-685-16748-8*, FR-004) Natl Ctr St Courts.
— Birmingham, Municipal Court Project Supporting Study. 250p. 1979. write for info. (*0-318-61194-5*, NRCO-074) Natl Ctr St Courts.
— Business Equipment & the Courts: Guide for Court Managers. (Illus.). 60p. 1977. pap. write for info. (*0-89656-018-X*, RG-030) Natl Ctr St Courts.
— Business Equipment & the Courts: Reference Manual. 363p. 1977. 22.00 (*0-89656-019-8*, RR-030) Natl Ctr St Courts.
— Calendar & Case File Management in the Marion County Circuit Court (Salem, Oregon) A Technical Assistance Report. 51p. 1985. 3.00 (*0-685-15761-X*, WRO, T/A-502) Natl Ctr St Courts.
— Calendar Management & Judge Rotation in North Carolina: Final Report. 184p. 1978. 11.04 (*0-685-15774-1*, SRO-002) Natl Ctr St Courts.
— Calendar Management in Magistrate Court Second Judicial Circuit, Siuox Falls, South Dakota: A Technical Assistance. 22p. 1985. 2.00 (*0-685-15779-2*, WRO, T/A-503) Natl Ctr St Courts.
— California Center for Judicial Education & Research: New Judge Education Services. (Paul Reardon Ser.). 31p. 1981. 1.86 (*0-685-15084-4*, PRS-012) Natl Ctr St Courts.
— California Consolidated Court Services Project. 65p. 1975. pap. write for info. (*0-318-61188-0*, MAB-019) Natl Ctr St Courts.
— California Continuing Judicial Studies Program. (Paul Reardon Ser.). 31p. 1981. 1.86 (*0-685-15085-2*, PRS-013) Natl Ctr St Courts.
— California Court of Appeals: Executive Summary. 40p. 1974. pap. write for info. (*0-318-61310-7*, R-013A) Natl Ctr St Courts.
— California Court of Appeals: Full Report. 344p. 1974. pap. write for info. (*0-318-61311-5*, R-013) Natl Ctr St Courts.
— California Jury Selection & Management Survey. 81p. 1976. pap. write for info. (*0-318-61289-5*, MAB-020) Natl Ctr St Courts.
— Case Counting in the Special Civil Part of the Essex County (NJ) Superior Court. 36p. 1985. 2.00 (*0-685-16627-9*, NERO-182) Natl Ctr St Courts.
— Case Processing in the First Judicial Circuit, Honolulu, Hawaii. 39p. 1982. 2.34 (*0-685-15461-0*, WRO-038) Natl Ctr St Courts.
— Case Processing in the York County (PA) Court of Common Pleas. 231p. 1979. 13.86 (*0-685-15463-7*, NERO-024) Natl Ctr St Courts.
— Case Tracking & Transcript Monitoring in Rhode Island: A Guide; Technical Assistance Report No. 6 in the Appellate Justice Improvement Project. 32p. 1980. 1.92 (*0-685-16296-6*, NERO, T/A-506) Natl Ctr St Courts.
— Caseflow Management Study for the Seventieth Judicial District Court, Saginaw, Michigan: Final Report. 108p. 1980. 7.00 (*0-685-15466-1*, NCRO-042) Natl Ctr St Courts.
— Caseload, Backlog, & Delay in the Fourth District Court of Appeals of Florida. 70p. 1973. pap. write for info. (*0-318-61322-0*, R-005) Natl Ctr St Courts.
— Catalog of Statistics Publications in the NCSC Library. 143p. 1984. 9.00 (*0-685-16629-5*, NCSC-045) Natl Ctr St Courts.
— Causal Analysis of the Relationship Between Learning Disabilities & Juvenile Delinquency. 103p. 1984. 6.18 (*0-685-16955-3*, LDJD-016) Natl Ctr St Courts.
— Change in Delinquent Behavior As a Function of Learning Disabilities: A Two-Year Longitudinal Study. 41p. 1981. 2.46 (*0-685-16958-8*, LDJD-009) Natl Ctr St Courts.
— Chief Judge's 1981 Plan to Reduce Trial Delay in New York City: A Progress Report. 37p. 1981. 2.22 (*0-685-15468-8*, NERO-097) Natl Ctr St Courts.
— Child Support Payment Procedures: Judicial Administration & Procedures Manual. 55p. 1976. 3.30 (*0-685-15100-X*, NCSC-027) Natl Ctr St Courts.
— Circuit & Family Court Management in the Second Judicial Circuit of Hawaii: A Technical Assistance Report. 42p. 1985. 3.00 (*0-685-15101-8*, WRO-057) Natl Ctr St Courts.
— Circuit Court Microfilming & Records Retention Project for the State of South Dakota. 213p. 1979. 12.78 (*0-685-16563-9*, NCRO-020) Natl Ctr St Courts.
— Citizens Handbook on Maine Courts. 77p. 1976. write for info. (*0-318-61219-4*, MAB-021) Natl Ctr St Courts.
— City of Phoenix Municipal Court Clerical Workflow Analysis. 118p. 1982. 7.08 (*0-685-15103-4*, WRO-040) Natl Ctr St Courts.
— City of Phoenix Municipal Court Clerical Workflow Analysis: Executive Summary. 42p. 1982. 2.52 (*0-685-15102-6*, WRO-041) Natl Ctr St Courts.
— Civil Case Scheduling in the Trumbull County (OH) Court of Common Pleas: Final Report. 52p. 1982. 3.12 (*0-685-15792-X*, NERO-122) Natl Ctr St Courts.
— Civil Case Scheduling in the Trumbull County (OH) Court of Common Pleas: Findings & Recommendations. 85p. 1982. 5.10 (*0-685-15785-7*, NERO-111) Natl Ctr St Courts.
— Civil Litigation in Alaska: Improvement Through Simplification. 64p. 1983. 3.84 (*0-685-15477-7*, WRO-051) Natl Ctr St Courts.
— Clark County (NV) Justice & District Courts Trial Delay. 72p. 1978. 4.32 (*0-685-15481-5*, WRO-034) Natl Ctr St Courts.
— Clark County (NV) Juvenile Court Affirmative Action Plan: Recommendations for Updating. 1980. write for info. (*0-318-61198-8*, WRO-010) Natl Ctr St Courts.
— Clemency: Legal Authority, Procedure & Structure. 120p. 1977. pap. write for info. (*0-89656-023-6*, R-035) Natl Ctr St Courts.
— Clerical Operations of the Office of the Clerk of Courts for the Supreme Court & Court of Appeals of Alaska. 72p. 1982. 4.32 (*0-685-15216-2*, NERO-119) Natl Ctr St Courts.
— Clerk of the District Court Manual, State of Idaho. 354p. 1978. 21.24 (*0-685-15219-7*, WRO-005) Natl Ctr St Courts.
— Clerks of Court in New Jersey: Final Report. 321p. 1981. 19.26 (*0-685-15220-0*, NERO-083) Natl Ctr St Courts.
— Collected Memoranda & Reports of the National Center for State Courts to the New York City Felony Backlog Reduction Program, October 1981-January 1982. 201p. 1983. 12.06 (*0-685-15483-1*, NERO-128) Natl Ctr St Courts.
— Collecting & Analyzing Court Statistics: Handbook Prepared for the New Hampshire Judicial Council. 68p. 1976. 4.08 (*0-685-16630-9*, MAB-022) Natl Ctr St Courts.
— Comments on Jury Management in Santa Barbara, California. 9p. 1986. 1.00 (*0-685-16705-4*, WRO-066) Natl Ctr St Courts.
— Community Work Service Program for Traffic Court. (Paul Reardon Ser.). 14p. 1981. 0.84 (*0-685-15057-7*, PRS-021) Natl Ctr St Courts.
— Comparative Analysis of Standardized Achievement Tests with Learning Disabled & Non-Learning Disabled Adolescent Boys. 20p. 1979. 1.20 (*0-685-16962-6*, LDJD-006) Natl Ctr St Courts.
— Comparative Records Management Systems & the Courts: Manual & Automated Alternatives. 51p. 1980. pap. write for info. (*0-89656-032-5*, R-044) Natl Ctr St Courts.
— Comparison of State Court Judicial Opinion Publishing Practices. 48p. 1976. 2.88 (*0-685-16859-X*, NERO-014) Natl Ctr St Courts.
— Compensation & Utilization of Court Reporters in Ventura County. 167p. 1974. 10.02 (*0-685-16306-7*, MAB-023) Natl Ctr St Courts.
— Computer-Aided Transcription in the Courts: Executive Summary. 67p. 1981. pap. write for info. (*0-89656-052-X*, R-058) Natl Ctr St Courts.
— Computer Analyses for Juror Utilization Operation Manual. 42p. 1984. 3.00 (*0-685-16706-2*, CJS-007) Natl Ctr St Courts.
— Computer Enters the Courtroom. (Paul Reardon Ser.). 169p. 1981. 10.14 (*0-685-16649-X*, PRS-010) Natl Ctr St Courts.
— Computerization, Records Management, & Caseflow Management in the Eleventh Judicial District of Nebraska (Grand Island) A Technical Assistance Report. 109p. 1984. 7.00 (*0-685-16567-1*, WRO-053) Natl Ctr St Courts.
— Computerized Case Processing, Records Management, & General Operation of Las Vegas Municipal Court. 29p. 1982. 1.74 (*0-685-15488-2*, WRO, T/A-500) Natl Ctr St Courts.
— Connecticut Court Reporting Services: Proposed Regulations. 90p. 1978. 5.40 (*0-685-16316-4*, NERO-032) Natl Ctr St Courts.
— Connecticut Forms Management Study. 26p. 1978. 1.56 (*0-685-16569-8*, NERO-078) Natl Ctr St Courts.
— Connecticut Office for Appeals Procedures Manual. 53p. 1986. 3.00 (*0-685-16861-1*, NERO-181) Natl Ctr St Courts.
— Connecticut Superior Court Clerks' Manual, Geographical Area. 276p. 1986. 17.00 (*0-685-15221-9*, NERO-179) Natl Ctr St Courts.
— Connecticut Superior Court Clerks' Manual, Judicial District. 286p. 1985. 17.00 (*0-685-15224-3*, NERO-168) Natl Ctr St Courts.
— Connecticut Trial Court Delay Reduction: Assistance to Judicial Department Staff Serving the Committee to Study the Rules of Civil Practice & Procedure. 207p. 1985. 13.00 (*0-685-15493-9*, NERO-178) Natl Ctr St Courts.
— Consideration in Selection of a Chief Justice: Comments & Materials. 59p. 1975. write for info. (*0-318-61203-8*, MAB-024) Natl Ctr St Courts.
— Consolidating Clerical Services in Ventura County. 45p. 1975. 2.70 (*0-685-15225-1*, MAB-025) Natl Ctr St Courts.
— Consolidation of Jury Management Services: California Court Services Project. 91p. 1975. 5.46 (*0-685-16708-9*, MAB-026) Natl Ctr St Courts.
— Consolidation of Professional Services & Witnesses: California Court Services Project. 54p. 1974. 3.24 (*0-685-16752-6*, MAB-027) Natl Ctr St Courts.
— Continuances in Civil Cases at the Franklin County Court of Common Pleas in Columbus, Ohio. 94p. 1981. 5.64 (*0-685-15497-1*, NERO-087) Natl Ctr St Courts.
— Continuing Judicial Education for Alabama Appellate Judges. 50p. 1975. 3.00 (*0-685-15086-0*, MAB-028) Natl Ctr St Courts.
— Controlling the Uncontrollable Elements in Court Budgets. (Paul Reardon Ser.). 6p. 1981. 0.36 (*0-685-15171-9*, PRS-007) Natl Ctr St Courts.
— Cost & Revenue of the Superior & Justice of the Peace Courts in Arizona. 105p. 1981. 6.30 (*0-685-15172-7*, WRO-031) Natl Ctr St Courts.
— Cost-Benefit Methodology for Evaluation of State Judicial Information Systems. 200p. 1979. 12.00 (*0-89656-033-3*, F-002) Natl Ctr St Courts.
— Cost Effective Electronic Recording System. (Paul Reardon Ser.). 9p. 1983. 0.54 (*0-685-16323-7*, PRS-042) Natl Ctr St Courts.
— Court Administration in New Mexico. 115p. 1975. pap. write for info. (*0-318-61207-0*, MAB-029) Natl Ctr St Courts.
— Court Automation Report: Ninth Judicial Circuit of Florida. 20p. 1984. write for info. (*0-318-61281-X*, NCSC-044) Natl Ctr St Courts.
— Court Facilities in Barnstable, Dukes, Nantucket, & Plymouth Counties, Massachusetts. 530p. 1975. 31.80 (*0-685-15350-9*, MAB-030) Natl Ctr St Courts.
— Court Facilities in Berkshire, Franklin, Hampden, & Hampshire Counties, Massachusetts. 510p. 1975. 30.60 (*0-685-15354-1*, MAB-031) Natl Ctr St Courts.
— Court Facilities in Bristol County (Massachusetts) Final Report. (On Loan Through NCSC Library). 212p. 1975. 12.72 (*0-685-15356-8*, MAB-032) Natl Ctr St Courts.
— Court Facilities in Essex County (Massachusetts) 375p. 1975. 22.50 (*0-685-15359-2*, MAB-033) Natl Ctr St Courts.
— Court Facilities in Middlesex County (Massachusetts) 524p. 1975. write for info. (*0-318-61245-3*, NERO-011) Natl Ctr St Courts.
— Court Facilities in Norfolk County (Massachusetts) 219p. 1975. 13.14 (*0-685-15365-7*, NERO-022) Natl Ctr St Courts.
— Court Facilities in Suffolk County (Massachusetts) 214p. 1975. 12.84 (*0-685-15368-1*, MAB-034) Natl Ctr St Courts.
— Court Facilities in Worcester County (Massachusetts) 469p. 1975. 28.14 (*0-685-15372-X*, MAB-035) Natl Ctr St Courts.
— Court Improvement Programs: A Guidebook for Planners. 308p. 1972. pap. write for info. (*0-318-61214-3*, R-002) Natl Ctr St Courts.
— Court Reform in Seven States. 171p. 1980. pap. write for info. (*0-89656-046-5*, R-054) Natl Ctr St Courts.
— Court-Related Data Processing in Montgomery County, Pennsylvania: A Technical Assistance Assessment Report. 24p. 1983. 2.00 (*0-685-16650-3*, NERO, T/A-523) Natl Ctr St Courts.
— Court Reporters Manual, State of Tennessee. 123p. 1975. 7.38 (*0-685-16328-8*, MAB-036) Natl Ctr St Courts.
— Court Reporting: Lessons from Alaska & Australia. 114p. 1974. write for info. (*0-318-61258-5*, R-010) Natl Ctr St Courts.
— Court Reporting Services in Maryland. 148p. 1976. 8.88 (*0-685-16338-5*, MARO-007) Natl Ctr St Courts.
— Court Reporting Services in New Jersey. 242p. 1978. 14.52 (*0-685-16346-6*, NERO-017) Natl Ctr St Courts.
— Court Reporting Services in South Dakota: Findings & Recommendations. 133p. 1977. 7.98 (*0-685-16350-4*, MAB-037) Natl Ctr St Courts.
— Court Reporting Services in the Lackawanna County (PA) Court of Common Pleas: Technical Assistance Report. 90p. 1982. 5.40 (*0-685-16356-3*, NERO, T/A-512) Natl Ctr St Courts.
— Court Selection: Student Litigation in State & Federal Courts. 220p. 1982. 13.20 (*0-685-16952-9*, NCSC-014) Natl Ctr St Courts.
— Court Services Package. 67p. 1973. pap. write for info. (*0-318-61220-8*, MAB-038) Natl Ctr St Courts.
— Court Space Needs for Cape May County, New Jersey. 168p. 1981. 10.08 (*0-685-15381-9*, NERO-086) Natl Ctr St Courts.
— Court Staffing Guidelines: A Survey with Recommendations. 59p. 1980. 3.54 (*0-685-15228-6*, NERO-049) Natl Ctr St Courts.
— Courtroom Needs Assessment & Court Space Review in Rockingham County, New Hampshire. 29p. 1981. 1.74 (*0-685-15375-4*, NERO-090) Natl Ctr St Courts.
— Courtroom Security: Closed Circuit Television & Microphone Including Supporting Materials. 113p. 1975. 6.78 (*0-685-15436-X*, MAB-040) Natl Ctr St Courts.
— Courts & the Community. 36p. 1978. pap. write for info. (*0-318-61221-6*, SC-002) Natl Ctr St Courts.
— Courts' Data Processing Action Plan for the Twenty-First & Twenty-Second Circuits of Missouri. 108p. 1972. 6.48 (*0-685-16652-X*, NCSC-001) Natl Ctr St Courts.
— Criminal Sentencing in Nebraska: The Feasibility of Empirically Based Guidelines. 352p. 1981. 21.12 (*0-685-16774-7*, NCRO-046) Natl Ctr St Courts.
— Cuyahoga County (OH) Court of Common Pleas Bureau of Support Operations Manual. 369p. 1985. 22.00 (*0-685-15337-1*, NERO-161) Natl Ctr St Courts.
— Cuyahoga County (OH) Court of Common Pleas Domestic Relations Operations Manual. 132p. 1985. 8.00 (*0-685-15339-8*, NERO-160) Natl Ctr St Courts.
— Data Processing & the Courts: Guide for Court Managers. (Illus.). 59p. 1977. pap. 1.50 (*0-89656-021-X*, RG-033) Natl Ctr St Courts.
— Data Processing & the Courts: Reference Manual. 539p. 1977. 32.34 (*0-685-16653-8*, RR-033) Natl Ctr St Courts.
— Defense Services in New Hampshire. 260p. 1976. Manuscript. 15.60 (*0-685-16944-8*, NERO-001) Natl Ctr St Courts.
— Definition & Prevalence of Learning Disabilities. 21p. 1978. Manuscript. 1.26 (*0-685-16963-4*, LDJD-013) Natl Ctr St Courts.
— Delay Reduction Plan: Kanawha County Circuit Court. 17p. 1985. 1.00 (*0-685-15503-X*, SERO-014) Natl Ctr St Courts.
— Deriving Measures of Delinquency from Self-Report Data. 50p. 1980. Manuscript. 3.00 (*0-685-16964-2*, LDJD-007) Natl Ctr St Courts.
— Description & an Analysis of a Selected Number of Judicial Councils, with Recommendations. 122p. 1975. Manuscript. 7.32 (*0-685-15152-2*, MAB-041) Natl Ctr St Courts.
— Description & Analysis of the Passaic County (NJ) Speedy Trial Demonstration Project: Interim Report. 12p. 1980. Manuscript. 0.72 (*0-685-15512-9*, NERO-063) Natl Ctr St Courts.
— Description of the Tax Certiorari. 45p. 1981. Manuscript. 2.70 (*0-685-15017-8*, NERO-093) Natl Ctr St Courts.
— Detroit Recorder's Court, Court Administrator-Clerk of Court Recruitment Project. 93p. 1978. 5.58 (*0-685-15230-8*, NCRO-002) Natl Ctr St Courts.
— Development & Implementation of an Accounting System for District Courts of Virginia. 18p. 1975. 1.08 (*0-685-15173-5*, MAB-042) Natl Ctr St Courts.
— District of Columbia Judicial System. 57p. 1974. 3.42 (*0-685-14999-4*, MAB-043) Natl Ctr St Courts.
— Early History of Sheriffs & County Clerks. 17p. 1975. 1.02 (*0-685-15236-7*, MAB-044) Natl Ctr St Courts.
— Economics & Politics of Crime, Courts, & Corrections... Strategies for the 80s: A Symposium. 106p. 1981. 6.36 (*0-685-15157-3*, SRO-014) Natl Ctr St Courts.
— El Paso Juvenile Court Conference Committees. (Paul Reardon Ser.). 10p. 1982. 0.60 (*0-685-15041-0*, PRS-030) Natl Ctr St Courts.
— Electronic & Photographic Media Coverage of Court Proceedings: An Annotated Bibliography. 39p. 1980. 2.34 (*0-685-16546-9*, FR-002) Natl Ctr St Courts.
— Equal Employment Opportunity-Assessment & Recommendations for the Clark County Juvenile Services; Sites Visits. 1980. write for info. (*0-318-61235-6*, WRO-007) Natl Ctr St Courts.
— Equal Employment Opportunity Program: Recommendations for the Court of Common Pleas, Cuyahoga County Juvenile Court. 18p. 1978. 1.08 (*0-685-15042-9*, NCRO-040) Natl Ctr St Courts.
— Equal Opportunity Program: Recommendations for the Superior Court of Los Angeles. 63p. 1978. 3.78 (*0-685-15317-7*, NCRO-041) Natl Ctr St Courts.
— Equal Opportunity Program: Recommendations for the Supreme Court of Florida. 40p. 1978. 2.40 (*0-685-15324-X*, NCRO-039) Natl Ctr St Courts.
— Establishing an Operational Definition of Juvenile Delinquency. 34p. 1978. 2.04 (*0-685-16966-9*, LDJD-010) Natl Ctr St Courts.
— Establishing the Reliability of Self-Reported Delinquency Data. 29p. 1978. 1.74 (*0-685-16968-5*, LDJD-008) Natl Ctr St Courts.
— Evaluating Pretrial Release Program. 63p. 1976. 3.78 (*0-685-16758-5*, MAB-045) Natl Ctr St Courts.
— Evaluation of a Proposed Electronic Transcription System for the Nineteenth Judicial District in Baton Rouge, Louisiana. 25p. 1974. 1.50 (*0-685-16414-4*, MAB-046) Natl Ctr St Courts.
— Evaluation of Audio Recording in the Masters & Chancery Courts, Maryland's Seventh Judicial Circuit. 22p. 1974. 1.32 (*0-685-16412-8*, MAB-047) Natl Ctr St Courts.
— Evaluation of Computerized Text-Processing & Photo-Composition Systems for the Connecticut Reporter of Judicial Decisions Office: Final Report. 36p. 1976. 2.16 (*0-685-16413-6*, NERO-013) Natl Ctr St Courts.
— Evaluation of Involuntary Civil Commitment in Milwaukee County: Final Report. 191p. 1983. 11.46 (*0-685-16971-5*, NCSC-033) Natl Ctr St Courts.
— Evaluation of Kentucky's & Innovative Approach to Making a Videotape Record of Trial Court Proceedings. 68p. 1985. 4.00 (*0-685-16532-9*, NERO-163) Natl Ctr St Courts.
— Evaluation of New Hampshire's Marital Masters Program. 36p. 1976. 2.16 (*0-685-15074-7*, NERO-009) Natl Ctr St Courts.
— Evaluation of Policy-Related Research on the Effectiveness of Pretrial Release Programs. 158p. 1974. pap. write for info. (*0-89656-002-3*, R-016) Natl Ctr St Courts.
— Evaluation of the Administrative Office of the Courts in Maine. 59p. 1977. 3.54 (*0-685-15104-2*, NERO-025) Natl Ctr St Courts.
— Evaluation of the Association for Children with Learning Disabilities Training Institute: Final Report. 116p. 1982. 6.96 (*0-685-16969-3*, NCSC-015) Natl Ctr St Courts.
— Evaluation of the District Court in Brockton's (MA) Computer Facility. 100p. 1979. 6.00 (*0-685-16656-2*, NERO-028) Natl Ctr St Courts.
— Evaluation of the Learning Disabilities-Juvenile Delinquency Remediation Program: Evaluation Design & Interim Results. 93p. 1979. 5.58 (*0-685-16972-3*, LDJD-005) Natl Ctr St Courts.
— Evaluation of the North Central Juvenile Care Center. 20p. 1981. 1.20 (*0-685-17026-8*, NCRO-030) Natl Ctr St Courts.

An Asterisk (*) at the beginning of an entry indicates that the title is appearing in BIP for the first time.

— Evaluation of the South Central (Iowa) Juvenile Care Center. 94p. 1979. 5.64 (*0-685-17028-4*, NCRO-022) Natl Ctr St Courts.
— Evaluation of the Superior Court of the District of Columbia Social Services Division's Management Information Systems Project. 30p. 1978. 1.80 (*0-685-16657-0*, MARO-008) Natl Ctr St Courts.
— Expediting Review of Felony Conviction after Trial: A Report of the Committee on Criminal Appeals of the Advisory Council on Appellate Justice. 28p. 1973. pap. write for info. (*0-318-61252-6*, MAB-048) Natl Ctr St Courts.
— Extension of Philadelphia's Victim-Witness Assistance Programs. 25p. 1984. 1.50 (*0-685-16754-2*, NERO-137) Natl Ctr St Courts.
— Facets of the Jury System: A Survey. Prescott, Elizabeth, ed. 124p. 1976. pap. write for info. (*0-89656-003-1*, R-028) Natl Ctr St Courts.
— Family Conciliation Unit of the Seventeenth Judicial Circuit of Florida. (Paul Reardon Ser.). 30p. 1981. 1.80 (*0-685-15053-4*, PRS-009) Natl Ctr St Courts.
— Federal Funding Assistance for State Courts. 76p. 1973. pap. write for info. (*0-318-61217-8*, MAB-049) Natl Ctr St Courts.
— Filing System & Records Management Review: United States Tax Court, Washington, D.C. 93p. 1985. 6.00 (*0-685-16578-7*, SERO-008) Natl Ctr St Courts.
— Final Project Report, Records Management in the Courts of Delaware: Accomplishments & Recommendations. 39p. 1985. 3.00 (*0-685-16575-2*, SERO-010) Natl Ctr St Courts.
— Finances & Operating Costs in Pennsylvania's Courts of Common Pleas. 186p. 1980. 11.16 (*0-685-15174-3*, NERO-070) Natl Ctr St Courts.
— Financial Aspects of Judicial Planning. 88p. 1977. 5.28 (*0-685-15175-1*, DC-006) Natl Ctr St Courts.
— Financial Impact of Adding a Judicial Position to the Orange County (CA) Superior Court. 33p. 1981. 1.98 (*0-685-15176-X*, WRO-032) Natl Ctr St Courts.
— Financial Integrity in the Courts: A Technical Assistance Report for Pennsylvania. 15p. 1985. 1.00 (*0-685-15177-8*, NERO, T/A-528) Natl Ctr St Courts.
— First National Symposium on Court Management. 1982. pap. write for info. (*0-89656-062-7*, R-068) Natl Ctr St Courts.
— Fiscal Administration in State-Funded Courts. 167p. 1981. pap. write for info. (*0-89656-053-8*, R-059) Natl Ctr St Courts.
— Forensic Mental Health Screening & Evaluation in Community & Regional Forensic Mental Health Centers. 222p. 1981. 13.32 (*0-685-16975-8*, OPS-004) Natl Ctr St Courts.
— Forensic Mental Health Screening & Evaluation in Community Corrections. 60p. 1981. 3.60 (*0-685-16979-0*, OPS-006) Natl Ctr St Courts.
— Forensic Mental Health Screening & Evaluation in Court Clinics. 164p. 1981. 9.84 (*0-685-16984-7*, OPS-002) Natl Ctr St Courts.
— Forensic Mental Health Screening & Evaluation in Jails. 95p. 1981. 5.70 (*0-685-16986-3*, OPS-003) Natl Ctr St Courts.
— Forensic Mental Health Screening & Evaluation of Client-Offenders: An Overview. 119p. 1981. 7.14 (*0-685-16989-8*, OPS-001) Natl Ctr St Courts.
— Fulton Alternative Community Enrichment Service Program. (Paul Reardon Ser.). 58p. 1982. 3.48 (*0-685-43730-2*, PRS-029) Natl Ctr St Courts.
— Further Observations on the Link Between Learning Disabilities & Juvenile Delinquency. 50p. 1979. 3.00 (*0-685-16991-X*, LDJD-014) Natl Ctr St Courts.
— General Juridiction Trial Judges Riding Circuit in State Court Systems: Technical Assistance Report. 17p. 1984. 1.02 (*0-685-15018-6*, NERO, T/A-517) Natl Ctr St Courts.
— Georgia Directory of Juvenile Justice Resources. 337p. 1983. 20.22 (*0-685-15043-7*, SERO-002) Natl Ctr St Courts.
— Guide to Computing Literature for Court Personnel. 26p. 1974. write for info. (*0-318-61239-9*, NERO-124) Natl Ctr St Courts.
— Guide to Juror Usage. 67p. 1974. 4.02 (*0-685-16710-0*, CJS-001) Natl Ctr St Courts.
— Guide to Jury System Management. 82p. 1975. 4.92 (*0-685-16713-5*, CJS-002) Natl Ctr St Courts.
— Guidebook of Projects for Prosecution & Defense Planning. 210p. 1973. write for info. (*0-318-61295-X*, MAB-050) Natl Ctr St Courts.
— Guidelines for Development of Computer Training Curricula for Court Personnel. 148p. 1974. pap. write for info. (*0-318-61240-2*, R-015) Natl Ctr St Courts.
— Guidelines for State Court Decision Making in the Life-Sustaining Medical Treatment. 2nd rev. ed. 250p. 1993. pap. text ed. write for info. (*0-314-02226-0*) West Pub.
— Guilty but Mentally Ill Verdict: An Empirical Study. 651p. 1985. 39.10 (*0-685-16995-2*, NCSC-046) Natl Ctr St Courts.
— Guilty but Mentally Ill Verdict: An Empirical Study; Executive Summary. 17p. 1985. 1.00 (*0-685-16999-5*, NCSC-047) Natl Ctr St Courts.
— Hawaii Benchbook. 96p. 1975. 5.76 (*0-685-15067-4*, WRO-019) Natl Ctr St Courts.
— Hawaii Guidebook for Videotaping. 79p. 1975. 4.74 (*0-685-16536-1*, WRO-004) Natl Ctr St Courts.
— Hawaii's Jury System, 2 vols., Set. 166p. 1976. 9.96 (*0-685-16714-3*, WRO-009) Natl Ctr St Courts.
— Hennepin County Courts Space Management Study: Final Report. 244p. 1979. 14.64 (*0-685-15385-1*, NCRO-008) Natl Ctr St Courts.
— Hennepin County Juvenile Justice Facilities, Space Program, & Site Studies: Final Report. 108p. 1978. 6.48 (*0-685-15387-8*, NCRO-011) Natl Ctr St Courts.
— Hennepin County Uniform Citation: Final Report. 200p. 1981. 12.00 (*0-685-16581-7*, NCRO-035) Natl Ctr St Courts.
— How Much Should We Charge for Justice? Fees & Statutory Costs Paid By Litigants in New York State. 55p. 1978. 3.30 (*0-685-15178-6*, NERO-020) Natl Ctr St Courts.
— Hudson County (NJ) CJP Evaluation. 53p. 1985. 3.00 (*0-685-16759-3*, NERO-169) Natl Ctr St Courts.
— Idea Whose Time Is Still to Come: The New Hampshire "Paperless Court" Project; Final Evaluation. 80p. 1983. 4.80 (*0-685-16658-9*, NERO-130) Natl Ctr St Courts.
— Illinois Appellate Automation Review: A Technical Assistance Report. 41p. 1986. 3.00 (*0-685-16863-8*, NERO, T/A-531) Natl Ctr St Courts.
— Impact of Domestic Relations Cases on the New Hampshire Superior Court: Analysis & Recommendations. 89p. 1974. 5.34 (*0-685-15054-2*, NERO-008) Natl Ctr St Courts.
— Implementation of Argersinger v. Hamlin: A Prescriptive Program Package. 86p. 1974. pap. write for info. (*0-318-61324-7*, R-009) Natl Ctr St Courts.
— Implementing the Model Annual Report. 1982. write for info. (*0-89656-061-9*, R-067) Natl Ctr St Courts.
— Improved Management & Organization of Court Support Services in New Jersey: Synthesis Volume, Final Report. 127p. 1981. 7.62 (*0-685-15238-3*, NERO-084) Natl Ctr St Courts.
— Improvements in Case Processing: Iowa Appellate Courts. 87p. 1982. 5.22 (*0-685-16914-6*, NCRO-060) Natl Ctr St Courts.
— Improving Academic Skill & Preventing Delinquency of Learning-Disabled Juvenile Delinquents: Evaluation of the ACLD Remediation Program. 378p. 1984. 22.68 (*0-685-17002-0*, LDJD-017) Natl Ctr St Courts.
— Indiana Records Management Project Report. 367p. 1982. 22.02 (*0-685-16584-1*, NCRO-058) Natl Ctr St Courts.
— Individual Calendar Program in the Criminal Division of the Allegheny County (Pittsburgh) Court of Common Pleas: Evaluation Report. 140p. 1983. 8.40 (*0-685-15798-9*, NERO-131) Natl Ctr St Courts.
— Initial Considerations in Organizing a Judicial Planning Effort: Scope & Structure. 51p. 1977. 3.06 (*0-685-15158-1*, DC-003) Natl Ctr St Courts.
— Internal Organization & Procedures of the Courts. 32p. 1978. pap. write for info. (*0-318-61208-9*, SC-004) Natl Ctr St Courts.
— Interpretation of Case Management Statistics in Connecticut Courts: Interim Technical Assistance Paper. 9p. 1979. 0.54 (*0-685-16632-5*, NERO-101) Natl Ctr St Courts.
— Involuntary Civil Commitment in Chicago. 228p. 1982. 13.68 (*0-685-17004-7*, NCSC-011) Natl Ctr St Courts.
— Involuntary Civil Commitment in Columbus, Ohio. 212p. 1982. 12.72 (*0-685-17005-5*, NCSC-010) Natl Ctr St Courts.
— Involuntary Civil Commitment in Los Angeles County. 114p. 1982. 6.84 (*0-685-17008-X*, NCSC-024) Natl Ctr St Courts.
— Involuntary Civil Commitment in the First Judicial Department, New York City. 142p. 1982. 8.52 (*0-685-17010-1*, NCSC-023) Natl Ctr St Courts.
— Involuntary Civil Commitment in Winston-Salem. 165p. 1982. 9.90 (*0-685-17009-8*, NCSC-013) Natl Ctr St Courts.
— Iowa Statewide Systems & Computer Inventory: Five-County Inventory with Survey Form for Statewide Inventory. 20p. 1984. 1.00 (*0-685-16660-0*, NERO-146) Natl Ctr St Courts.
— Issues in Automated Legal Research. 16p. 1977. 0.96 (*0-685-16663-5*, E-003) Natl Ctr St Courts.
— Jefferson Parish Juvenile Court Computerization Plan. 190p. 1984. 12.00 (*0-685-16664-3*, SERO-006) Natl Ctr St Courts.
— Jefferson Parish Juvenile Court Management Study. 75p. 1982. 4.50 (*0-685-15044-5*, SRO-016) Natl Ctr St Courts.
— Job Descriptions & a Compensation Schedule for Clerical Employees of the Massachusetts Supreme Judicial Court & Appeals Court. 108p. 1975. 6.48 (*0-685-15241-3*, MAB-051) Natl Ctr St Courts.
— Judicial Compensation Commissions. 51p. 1979. 3.00 (*0-89656-030-9*, R-042) Natl Ctr St Courts.
— Judicial Control Management. (Paul Reardon Ser.). 59p. 1981. 3.54 (*0-685-15105-0*, PRS-006) Natl Ctr St Courts.
— Judicial Council of Georgia, Administrative Office of the Courts: Technical Assistance Reports. 61p. 1978. 3.66 (*0-685-15159-X*, NCRO, T/A-504) Natl Ctr St Courts.
— Judicial Department of Connecticut: Equal Employment Opportunity Technical Assistance Report. 59p. 1979. 3.54 (*0-685-15329-0*, NCRO, T/A-502) Natl Ctr St Courts.
— Judicial Performance Evaluation: Issues & Options. 378p. 1983. 25.00 (*0-685-15083-6*, NCSC-032) Natl Ctr St Courts.
— Judicial Pilot Program of Santa Clara County, California: Evaluation Report. 48p. 1975. 2.88 (*0-685-15087-9*, MAB-052) Natl Ctr St Courts.
— Judicial Pilot Program of Santa Clara County, California: Evaluation Report II. 32p. 1976. 1.92 (*0-685-15088-7*, MAB-053) Natl Ctr St Courts.
— Judicial Retirement Plans: An Evaluation Model for Iowa. 39p. 1985. 3.00 (*0-685-15078-X*, NERO-173) Natl Ctr St Courts.
— Jurisdiction, Organization, & Size of Connecticut's New Intermediate Appellate Court. 124p. 1982. 7.44 (*0-685-16867-0*, NERO-140) Natl Ctr St Courts.
— Juror Phone-In System in the Ninth Judicial District of New York. (Paul Reardon Ser.). 55p. 1981. 3.30 (*0-685-16715-1*, PRS-014) Natl Ctr St Courts.
— Juror Utilization in the Cuyahoga County (OH) Court of Common Pleas. 50p. 1983. 3.00 (*0-685-16716-X*, NERO-129) Natl Ctr St Courts.
— Jury, Law Enforcement Witnesses, & Calendar Management in Marin County, California. 127p. 1983. 7.62 (*0-685-15812-8*, WRO-052) Natl Ctr St Courts.
— Jury Management in Imperial County. 59p. 1985. 4.00 (*0-685-16717-8*, WRO-059) Natl Ctr St Courts.
— Jury Management Study, Milwaukee County, Wisconsin. 64p. 1985. 4.00 (*0-685-16718-6*, NERO-177) Natl Ctr St Courts.
— Jury Management Study, Milwaukee County, Wisconsin: Analysis & Recommendations Report Task Two. 40p. 1984. 3.00 (*0-685-16719-4*, NERO-148) Natl Ctr St Courts.
— Jury System Management in Davidson County, Tennessee. 45p. 1986. 3.00 (*0-685-16721-6*, CJS-012) Natl Ctr St Courts.
— Jury Utilization & Management, Seventh Judicial Circuit, Rapid City, South Dakota. 255p. 1978. 15.30 (*0-685-16722-4*, NCRO-014) Natl Ctr St Courts.
— Justice Delayed: The Pace of Litigation in Urban Trial Courts: Executive Summary. 38p. 1978. write for info. (*0-318-61253-4*, RA-041) Natl Ctr St Courts.
— Justice in the States: Addresses & Papers of the National Conference on the Judiciary, Williamsburg, Virginia, 1971. 386p. 1971. pap. write for info. (*0-318-61209-7*, NCSC-004) Natl Ctr St Courts.
— Juvenile Court & Detention Facility, Minnehaha County, South Dakota. 29p. 1975. 1.74 (*0-685-15390-8*, MAB-055) Natl Ctr St Courts.
— Kalamazoo County District Court Consolidation Feasibility Study. 129p. 1980. 7.74 (*0-685-15000-3*, NCRO-029) Natl Ctr St Courts.
— Kansas Automation System. 50p. 1984. 3.00 (*0-685-16667-8*, NCSC-040) Natl Ctr St Courts.
— Kentucky Model Circuit Courts Project: A Conceptual Approach. 53p. 1974. 3.18 (*0-685-15001-1*, MAB-056) Natl Ctr St Courts.
— Laguna Pueblo Court: Court Improvement Plan & Management Audit. 480p. 1982. 28.80 (*0-685-15106-9*, NCRO-055) Natl Ctr St Courts.
— Lake County's (Illinois) Juvenile Justice Programs: A Community Approach to Treatment for Repeat Offenders & Court Liaison. (Paul Reardon Ser.). 22p. 1981. 1.32 (*0-685-43732-9*, PRS-016) Natl Ctr St Courts.
— Learning Disabilities & Juvenile Delinquency: A Handbook for Court Personnel, Judges, & Attorneys. 71p. 1979. 4.26 (*0-685-11620-4*, LDJD-001) Natl Ctr St Courts.
— Least Restrictive Alternatives in Involuntary Civil Commitment. 114p. 1983. 6.84 (*0-685-43733-7*, OPS-007) Natl Ctr St Courts.
— Libraries of the California Courts of Appeal: Survey with Recommendations. 43p. 1974. write for info. (*0-318-61249-6*, MAB-144) Natl Ctr St Courts.
— Link Between Learning Disabilities & Juvenile Delinquency: Interview Guide. 11p. 1979. 0.66 (*0-685-17012-8*, LDJD-004) Natl Ctr St Courts.
— Long-Range Plan for the State Judicial Information Systems Program. 115p. 1979. 6.90 (*0-89656-047-3*, F-006) Natl Ctr St Courts.
— Lorain County, Ohio, Child Support Enforcement Automation Planning Concepts: Final Report. 18p. 1985. 1.00 (*0-685-16668-6*, NERO-174) Natl Ctr St Courts.
— Los Angeles Municipal Court, Project Court: Final Report. 139p. 1979. 8.34 (*0-685-15019-4*, WRO-033) Natl Ctr St Courts.
— Los Angeles Municipal Court, Project Court: Phase II: Final Report. 113p. 1982. 6.78 (*0-685-15020-8*, WRO-039) Natl Ctr St Courts.
— Louisiana Clerks of Court Manual: Processing Criminal Cases in the District Court. 264p. 1975. 15.84 (*0-685-15245-6*, MAB-057) Natl Ctr St Courts.
— Louisiana Court of Appeals. 74p. 1981. 4.44 (*0-685-16874-3*, SRO-008) Natl Ctr St Courts.
— Louisiana Supreme Court: Personnel Policy Guide. 79p. 1980. 4.74 (*0-685-15248-0*, NCRO-033) Natl Ctr St Courts.
— Maine Juvenile Intake Service: York County Pilot Project. 56p. 1974. 3.36 (*0-685-15045-3*, NERO-043) Natl Ctr St Courts.
— Maine Superior Court Benchbook. 258p. 1976. 15.48 (*0-685-15068-2*, NERO-036) Natl Ctr St Courts.
— Maine Superior Court Clerks' Manual, 2 vols., Set. 399p. 1975. 23.94 (*0-685-15250-2*, MAB-058) Natl Ctr St Courts.
— Maine Traffic Court Study: Executive Summary. Steelman, David C., ed. 30p. 1975. pap. write for info. (*0-89656-004-X*, RA-018) Natl Ctr St Courts.
— Maine Traffic Court Study: Full Report. Steelman, David C., ed. (Illus.). 229p. 1975. write for info. (*0-89656-005-8*, R-018) Natl Ctr St Courts.
— Maine Trial Court Revision: Proposed Alternatives for Implementation. 80p. 1974. 4.80 (*0-685-15002-X*, MAB-059) Natl Ctr St Courts.
— Major Issues of Trial Court Financing in New Jersey: Final Report. 80p. 1981. 4.80 (*0-685-15179-4*, NERO-082) Natl Ctr St Courts.
— Management Analysis of the Broward County Clerk's Office: Seventeenth Judicial Circuit of Florida, Ft. Lauderdale. 34p. 1982. 2.04 (*0-685-15107-7*, SRO-012) Natl Ctr St Courts.
— Management Audit, Cuyahoga County Court of Common Pleas Domestic Relations Division & Bureau of Support. 50p. 1984. 3.00 (*0-685-15108-5*, NERO-150) Natl Ctr St Courts.
— Management Audit of the Ohio Supreme Court Clerk's Office, 3 vols., Vol. I. 60p. 1984. 4.00 (*0-685-15109-3*, NERO-154) Natl Ctr St Courts.
— Management Audit of the Ohio Supreme Court Clerk's Office, Vol. II. 35p. 1984. 2.00 (*0-685-15110-7*, NERO-155) Natl Ctr St Courts.
— Management Audit of the Ohio Supreme Court Clerk's Office, Vol. III. 62p. 1984. 4.00 (*0-685-15111-5*, NERO-156) Natl Ctr St Courts.
— Management Audit of the Orange County Superior Court. 152p. 1980. 9.12 (*0-685-15112-3*, WRO-029) Natl Ctr St Courts.
— Management of Tax Certiorari Cases in the New York State Unified Court System. 79p. 1982. 4.74 (*0-685-15021-6*, NERO-109) Natl Ctr St Courts.
— Management Review of the Maricopa County Office of the Clerk of the Superior Court. 215p. 1985. 13.00 (*0-685-15113-1*, WRO-067) Natl Ctr St Courts.
— Management Review of the Maricopa County Office of the Clerk of the Superior Court: Executive Summary. 118p. 1985. 7.00 (*0-685-15114-X*, WRO-068) Natl Ctr St Courts.
— Management Review of the West Virginia Court System. 472p. 1984. 28.32 (*0-685-15115-8*, SERO-003) Natl Ctr St Courts.
— Management Review of the Wichita Municipal Court. 104p. 1984. 6.00 (*0-685-15116-6*, SERO-005) Natl Ctr St Courts.
— Management Study of the Lafayette City Court, Lafayette, Louisiana. 1982. write for info. (*0-318-61210-0*, SRO-015) Natl Ctr St Courts.
— Managing Cases in the Fourth Judicial District (Boise), Idaho. 59p. 1985. 4.00 (*0-685-15549-8*, WRO-058) Natl Ctr St Courts.
— Managing the Hawaii Judiciary: An Era of Accomplishment, 1966-82. 149p. 1982. 8.94 (*0-685-15117-4*, WRO-049) Natl Ctr St Courts.
— Managing to Reduce Delay: An Abridged Version. 41p. 1982. 2.46 (*0-89656-064-3*, R-070) Natl Ctr St Courts.
— Manual for Clerks, Maine District Courts. 318p. 1975. 19.08 (*0-685-15252-9*, NERO-030) Natl Ctr St Courts.
— Manual for Processing Support Payments in the North Dakota District Courts. 33p. 1975. 1.98 (*0-685-15055-0*, MAB-060) Natl Ctr St Courts.
— Manual of Court Procedures, District Court of Vermont. 370p. 1977. 22.20 (*0-685-15118-2*, MAB-061) Natl Ctr St Courts.
— Manual of Court Procedures, Superior Court of Vermont. 195p. 1977. 11.70 (*0-685-15119-0*, MAB-062) Natl Ctr St Courts.
— Manual on Traffic Adjudication. 94p. 1977. 5.64 (*0-685-15058-5*, MAB-063) Natl Ctr St Courts.
— Marquette County (MI) Trial Court Management Audit. 260p. 1984. 15.60 (*0-685-15120-4*, NERO-139) Natl Ctr St Courts.
— Massachusetts Court Budget Book. 143p. 1976. 8.58 (*0-685-15180-8*, NERO-016) Natl Ctr St Courts.
— Massachusetts Courts: Summary & Recommendations. 210p. 1976. 12.60 (*0-685-15121-2*, MAB-064) Natl Ctr St Courts.
— Master Plan for Automation of the Kentucky Court of Justice. 35p. 1985. 2.00 (*0-685-16669-4*, NERO-175) Natl Ctr St Courts.
— Master Plan for Computerization of the Colorado Courts. 110p. 1985. 7.00 (*0-685-16671-6*, NCSC-042) Natl Ctr St Courts.
— Master Plan for Computerization of the New Jersey Courts. 180p. 1982. 10.80 (*0-685-16672-4*, R-074) Natl Ctr St Courts.
— Master Plan for Computerization of the New Jersey Courts: Management Summary. 21p. 1982. 1.26 (*0-685-16674-0*, R-073) Natl Ctr St Courts.
— Materials on Special Jury Techniques. 365p. 1984. 22.00 (*0-685-43707-8*, CJS-010) Natl Ctr St Courts.
— Materials Relating to the Maine Criminal Code. 306p. 1976. 18.36 (*0-685-15014-3*, MAB-065) Natl Ctr St Courts.
— Measuring the Performance for Different Types of Juvenile Courts. 183p. 1984. 10.98 (*0-685-15046-1*, NCSC-036) Natl Ctr St Courts.
— Medical Liability Review Panels in Arizona: An Evaluation. 147p. 1980. 8.82 (*0-685-15190-5*, WRO-030) Natl Ctr St Courts.
— Menominee Tribal Court Management Audit: Technical Assistance Report. 87p. 1982. 5.22 (*0-685-15034-8*, NCRO, T/A-509) Natl Ctr St Courts.
— Menominee Tribal Court Manual. 1982. write for info. (*0-318-61196-1*, NCRO-061) Natl Ctr St Courts.
— Mental Health Examinations in Criminal Justice Settings: Organization, Administration, & Program Evaluations. 658p. 1981. 39.48 (*0-685-17016-0*, NCSC-012) Natl Ctr St Courts.
— Mental Health Screening Unit. (Paul Reardon Ser.). 16p. 1982. 0.96 (*0-685-17018-7*, PRS-037) Natl Ctr St Courts.
— Methodology Manual for Jury Systems. 200p. 1981. 12.00 (*0-685-43708-6*, CJS-004) Natl Ctr St Courts.
— Methods of Speedy Case Processing. (Paul Reardon Ser.). 45p. 1981. 2.70 (*0-685-15560-9*, PRS-002) Natl Ctr St Courts.
— Michigan Court of Appeals Technology Assessment: A Technical Assistance Report. 13p. 1985. 1.00 (*0-685-16679-1*, NERO, T/A-525) Natl Ctr St Courts.
— Michigan Judicial Institute Court Administrative Personnel Development Program: Caseflow Management & Jury Utilization: Lansing, Michigan, February, 7-9, 1978, March 21-23, 1978. 52p. 1978. write for info. (*0-318-61229-1*, NCRO-070) Natl Ctr St Courts.

N

— Michigan Judicial Institute Court Administrative Personnel Development Program: Records Management, Final Report: Lansing, Michigan, May 1-3, 1978, May 16-18, 1978. 25p. 1978. write for info. (*0-318-61230-5*, NCRO-069) Natl Ctr St Courts.
— Michigan Uniform Vehicle Law Citation: Final Report. 162p. 1979. 9.72 (*0-685-15059-3*, NCRO-021) Natl Ctr St Courts.
— Microfilm & Records Disposition Options for the North Dakota Courts. 52p. 1976. 3.12 (*0-685-16586-8*, MAB-066) Natl Ctr St Courts.
— Microfilm & Records Management Recommendations for the Pennsylvania Supreme Court & the Supreme Court, Philadelphia, Pennsylvania. 33p. 1980. 1.98 (*0-685-16588-4*, NERO-062) Natl Ctr St Courts.
— Microfilm & the Courts: Reference Manual. 744p. 1976. 44.64 (*0-89656-008-2*, RR-026) Natl Ctr St Courts.
— Microfilming & Records Disposition for the Circuit Court of Jefferson County, Kentucky. 26p. 1976. 1.56 (*0-685-16596-5*, MAB-067) Natl Ctr St Courts.
— Microfilming Recommendations for the Charlotte County Circuit Court, Punta Gorda, Florida. 33p. 1977. 1.98 (*0-685-16590-6*, MAB-068) Natl Ctr St Courts.
— Microfilming Records of the Hawaii Judiciary. 36p. 1982. 2.16 (*0-685-16597-3*, WRO-037) Natl Ctr St Courts.
— Middlesex County, New Jersey: Reduction in Case Delay Through Defendant. (Paul Reardon Ser.). 19p. 1981. 1.14 (*0-685-15564-1*, PRS-008) Natl Ctr St Courts.
— Milwaukee County (WI) Circuit Court Technical Assistance Report. 16p. 1983. 1.00 (*0-685-16598-1*, NERO, T/A-524) Natl Ctr St Courts.
— Minnesota Citizens Conference on the Courts: Conference Report. 42p. 1981. 2.52 (*0-685-15191-3*, NCRO-037) Natl Ctr St Courts.
— Minnesota County Court Survey. 186p. 1974. pap. write for info. (*0-318-61222-4*, R-011) Natl Ctr St Courts.
— Minnesota District Court Survey. 166p. 1974. pap. write for info. (*0-318-61223-2*, R-014) Natl Ctr St Courts.
— Minnesota Financial Information Planning Study. 255p. 1979. 15.30 (*0-685-15181-6*, NCRO-019) Natl Ctr St Courts.
— Minnesota Personnel Standards & Information System Planning Study. 177p. 1979. 10.62 (*0-685-15263-4*, NCRO-013) Natl Ctr St Courts.
— Minnesota Supreme Court Automated Caseflow Management & Docketing Report: A Joint Publication of the National Center for State Courts & the Office of the Minnesota State Court Administrator. 131p. 1977. 7.86 (*0-685-15570-6*, NCRO-003) Natl Ctr St Courts.
— Model Court Development Project: Full Faith & Credit for Indian Court Judgements. 750p. 1982. 45.00 (*0-685-15035-6*, NCRO-050) Natl Ctr St Courts.
— Model for the Application of the Least Restrictive Alternative Doctrine in Involuntary Civil Commitment. 401p. 1984. 24.00 (*0-685-43735-3*, NCSC-041) Natl Ctr St Courts.
— Multi-Track Voice Writing: An Evaluation of a New Court Reporting Technique. 128p. 1973. 7.68 (*0-685-16415-2*, R-007) Natl Ctr St Courts.
— Multnomah County Attorney's Manual. 56p. 1981. 3.36 (*0-685-16746-1*, WRO-035) Natl Ctr St Courts.
— Multnomah County Circuit Court, 4 vols., Vol. I: Orientation. 108p. 1979. 6.48 (*0-685-15122-0*, WRO-015) Natl Ctr St Courts.
— Multnomah County Circuit Court, 4 vols., Vol. II: Civil Procedures. 163p. 1979. 9.78 (*0-685-15123-9*, WRO-016) Natl Ctr St Courts.
— Multnomah County Circuit Court, 4 vols., Vol. III: Domestic Relations. 149p. 1979. Vol. III:Domestic Relations, 149 pgs. 8.94 (*0-685-15124-7*, WRO-017) Natl Ctr St Courts.
— Multnomah County Circuit Court, 4 vols., Vol. IV: Criminal Procedures. 94p. 1979. 5.64 (*0-685-15125-5*, WRO-018) Natl Ctr St Courts.
— National Conference on Appellate Justice: Appellate Justice in the Federal Courts, Vol. IV. 213p. 1975. write for info. (*0-318-61315-8*, WRO-044) Natl Ctr St Courts.
— National Conference on Appellate Justice: Criminal Justice on Appeal, Vol. III. 1975. write for info. (*0-318-61314-X*, WRO-043) Natl Ctr St Courts.
— National Conference on Appellate Justice: Quantity & Quality in Appellate Justice, Vol. II. 191p. 1975. write for info. (*0-318-61313-1*, WRO-042) Natl Ctr St Courts.
— National Conference on Appellate Justice: Summary & Background, Vol. 1. 150p. 1975. write for info. (*0-318-61312-3*, WRO-023) Natl Ctr St Courts.
— National Conference on Appellate Justice: Supplement, Proceedings, & Conclusions, Vol. V. 140p. 1975. write for info. (*0-318-61316-6*, WRO-045) Natl Ctr St Courts.
— National Conference on Pretrial Release & Diversion, Chicago. 231p. 1975. 13.86 (*0-685-16760-7*, MAB-069) Natl Ctr St Courts.
— National Conference on Pretrial Release & Diversion, Chicago: Final Report. 113p. 1975. pap. write for info. (*0-318-61296-8*, MAB-070) Natl Ctr St Courts.
— National Conference on Pretrial Release & Diversion, San Francisco: Final Report. 85p. 1974. pap. write for info. (*0-318-61297-6*, MAB-072) Natl Ctr St Courts.
— National Conference on Pretrial Release & Diversion, San Francisco: Papers. 249p. 1974. 14.94 (*0-685-16761-5*, MAB-071) Natl Ctr St Courts.
— National Evaluation of the Jury Utilization & Management Demonstration Program: Final Report. 250p. 1979. 15.00 (*0-685-16729-1*, JUM-001) Natl Ctr St Courts.
— Nebraska County Court Information System Project: Final Report. 170p. 1980. write for info. (*0-318-61283-6*, NCSC-043) Natl Ctr St Courts.
— Nebraska Court Organization Project, 3 vols., I. 178p. 1977. 10.68 (*0-685-15003-8*, NCRO-024) Natl Ctr St Courts.
— Nebraska Court Organization Project, 3 vols., Vol. II. 125p. 1977. 7.50 (*0-685-15004-6*, NCRO-025) Natl Ctr St Courts.
— Nebraska Court Organization Project, 3 vols., Vol. III. 73p. 1977. Vol.III, 73 pgs. 4.38 (*0-685-15005-4*, NCRO-026) Natl Ctr St Courts.
— Nebraska Court Reporting Project: Final Report. 70p. 1975. pap. write for info. (*0-318-61259-3*, MAB-074) Natl Ctr St Courts.
— New Hampshire Court System Comprehensive Plan. 166p. 1978. 9.96 (*0-685-15160-3*, NERO-039) Natl Ctr St Courts.
— New Hampshire Court System Standards & Goals. 542p. 1975. 32.52 (*0-685-15161-1*, NERO-034) Natl Ctr St Courts.
— New Hampshire Juvenile Resources Manual. 119p. 1976. 7.14 (*0-685-17032-2*, MAB-075) Natl Ctr St Courts.
— New Hampshire Probate Court Manual, 2 vols., Vol. I. 357p. 1976. 21.42 (*0-685-15022-4*, NERO-002) Natl Ctr St Courts.
— New Hampshire Probate Court Manual, 2 vols., Vol. II. 329p. 1976. 19.74 (*0-685-15023-2*, NERO-003) Natl Ctr St Courts.
— New Jersey In-Court Management Personnel Survey. 80p. 1984. 5.00 (*0-685-15271-5*, NERO-157) Natl Ctr St Courts.
— New Jersey Municipal Court Procedures Manual. 243p. 1985. 15.00 (*0-685-15342-8*, NERO-162) Natl Ctr St Courts.
— New Jersey Probation Services: Final Report. 156p. 1981. 9.36 (*0-685-16807-7*, NERO-081) Natl Ctr St Courts.
— New Mexico Courts of Limited Jurisdiction. 232p. 1976. write for info. (*0-318-61195-3*, NCRO-071) Natl Ctr St Courts.
— New Mexico Management Study: Final Report. 190p. 1980. 11.40 (*0-685-15126-3*, WRO-028) Natl Ctr St Courts.
— New Orleans Municipal Court Management Audit: Final Report. 164p. 1982. 9.84 (*0-685-15127-1*, NCRO-056) Natl Ctr St Courts.
— New York Budget Review: A Study of the Judiciary's 1984-85 Budget Request. 45p. 1984. 2.70 (*0-685-15182-4*, NERO, T/A-515) Natl Ctr St Courts.
— New York City Felony Backlog Elimination Program of the New York State Unified Court System: Final Report. 24p. 1983. 1.44 (*0-685-15611-7*, NERO-133) Natl Ctr St Courts.
— New York Family Court Clerks Manual. 298p. 1983. write for info. (*0-318-61199-6*, NERO-132) Natl Ctr St Courts.
— New York Jury System Management Project for the Counties of New York, Queens, Nassau, & Delaware. 229p. 1983. 13.74 (*0-685-15128-X*, NERO-135) Natl Ctr St Courts.
— New York Practice & Procedure Rules Planning Project. 375p. 1983. 22.50 (*0-685-15153-0*, NERO-126) Natl Ctr St Courts.
— New York State Court Budget Review Manual. 60p. 1978. 3.60 (*0-685-15183-2*, NERO-018) Natl Ctr St Courts.
— New York Supreme & County Court Clerk's Manual. 550p. 1981. write for info. (*0-318-61211-9*, NERO-095) Natl Ctr St Courts.
— Newark (NJ) Municipal Court Violations Bureau Manual. 156p. 1986. 10.00 (*0-685-15269-3*, NERO-180) Natl Ctr St Courts.
— Nineteen Eighty-Four State Appellate Court Jurisdiction Guide for Statistical Reporting: Summary Tables. 117p. 1985. pap. write for info. (*0-318-61276-3*, R-096) Natl Ctr St Courts.
— Nineteen Eighty-Four State Trial Court Jurisdiction Guide for Statistical Reporting: Summary Tables. 110p. 1985. write for info. (*0-318-61279-8*, R-097) Natl Ctr St Courts.
— Nonjudicial Personnel Study of Oklahoma Court System, Vol. I. 146p. 1985. 9.00 (*0-685-15273-1*, SERO-012) Natl Ctr St Courts.
— Nonjudicial Personnel Study of Oklahoma Court System, Vol. II. 328p. 1985. 20.00 (*0-685-15274-X*, SERO-013) Natl Ctr St Courts.
— North Carolina Court of Appeals: Technical Assistance Diagnostic Report. 123p. 1980. 7.38 (*0-685-16884-0*, NERO-069) Natl Ctr St Courts.
— North Central Regional Conference: Conference Report, June 1-2, 1981. 106p. 1981. 6.36 (*0-685-15131-X*, NCRO-047) Natl Ctr St Courts.
— North Central Regional Conference: Conference Report: May 10-11, 1979. 109p. 1979. 6.54 (*0-685-15129-8*, NCRO-018) Natl Ctr St Courts.
— North Central Regional Conference: Conference Report, May 20-21, 1982. 114p. 1982. 6.84 (*0-685-15132-8*, NCRO-057) Natl Ctr St Courts.
— North Central Regional Conference: Conference Report, May 29-30, 1980. 245p. 1980. 14.70 (*0-685-15130-1*, NCRO-034) Natl Ctr St Courts.
— North Dakota Judicial Information System Project: Interim Report. 61p. 1975. 3.66 (*0-685-16682-1*, MAB-076) Natl Ctr St Courts.
— North Dakota Judicial Information System Project: State Judicial Management Information System Master Plan. 79p. 1976. 4.74 (*0-685-16683-X*, NCRO-004) Natl Ctr St Courts.
— Northeastern Regional Planning Conference, April 25-26, 1975: Summary of Comments. 40p. 1975. 2.40 (*0-685-15133-6*, NERO-006) Natl Ctr St Courts.
— Observations & Evaluation of the Small Claims Court, New Orleans, Louisiana. 30p. 1981. 1.80 (*0-685-15032-1*, DPO, T/A-503) Natl Ctr St Courts.
— Office Layout & Records Management Recommendations for the Licking County Municipal Court, Newark, Ohio. 303p. 1980. 18.18 (*0-685-15398-3*, NERO-061) Natl Ctr St Courts.
— Office of the Oregon State Court Administrator: An Analysis. 30p. 1976. 1.80 (*0-685-15134-4*, MAB-077) Natl Ctr St Courts.
— Oklahoma District Court Judges' Benchbook: Civil. 363p. 1981. write for info. (*0-318-61200-3*, SRO-009) Natl Ctr St Courts.
— Oklahoma District Court Judges' Benchbook: Criminal. 282p. 1980. write for info. (*0-318-61201-1*, SRO-011) Natl Ctr St Courts.
— Oklahoma Information Systems: Requirements Analysis & Conceptual Design. 161p. 1980. write for info. (*0-318-61284-4*, NCSC-026) Natl Ctr St Courts.
— One-Week-One-Trial Jury System: Jury Modification Plan for the Sixth Judicial Circuit Court, Oakland County, Michigan. (Paul Reardon Ser.). 10p. 1983. 0.60 (*0-685-16731-3*, PRS-043) Natl Ctr St Courts.
— Operation & Management of the Traffic Court, City of New Orleans. 237p. 1984. 14.00 (*0-685-15060-7*, SERO-007) Natl Ctr St Courts.
— Operation of the Appellate Process & Administration of the State Courts of Delaware. 115p. 1975. 6.90 (*0-685-16886-7*, MAB-078) Natl Ctr St Courts.
— Operations Review of the District Court of Dukes County (MA) 38p. 1975. 2.28 (*0-685-15135-2*, MAB-079) Natl Ctr St Courts.
— Oregon Court System Courtroom Clerks Training Program: Scripts. 29p. 1980. 1.74 (*0-685-15344-4*, WRO-026) Natl Ctr St Courts.
— Oregon Court System Courtroom Clerks Training Program: Workbook. 126p. 1980. 7.56 (*0-685-15345-2*, WRO-027) Natl Ctr St Courts.
— Oregon District Court Forms Project. 135p. 1977. 8.10 (*0-685-16601-5*, WRO-013) Natl Ctr St Courts.
— Organization & Management of the Erie County (PA) Court of Common Pleas: Final Report. 131p. 1985. 8.00 (*0-685-15136-0*, NERO-176) Natl Ctr St Courts.
— Organization & Management Study of the Administrative Office of the Courts, State of New Jersey. 277p. 1980. 16.62 (*0-685-15137-9*, NERO-051) Natl Ctr St Courts.
— Organization of the Administrative Structure of the Philadelphia Court of Common Pleas: Technical Assistance Report. 22p. 1984. 1.02 (*0-685-15006-2*, NERO, T/A-516) Natl Ctr St Courts.
— Overview of Judicial Immunity, Including Legal Representation. (Research Essay Ser.). 16p. 1978. 0.96 (*0-685-15089-5*, E-001) Natl Ctr St Courts.
— Passaic County (NJ) Speedy Trial Demonstration Project Evaluation: Interim Report 2. 20p. 1980. 1.20 (*0-685-15614-1*, NERO-073) Natl Ctr St Courts.
— Passaic County (NJ) Speedy Trial Demonstration Project Evalution: Final Evaluation Report. 98p. 1981. 5.88 (*0-685-15625-7*, NERO-085) Natl Ctr St Courts.
— Pennsylvania Court of Common Pleas Unit Cost Procedures Manual. 135p. 1982. 8.10 (*0-685-15184-0*, NERO-104) Natl Ctr St Courts.
— Pennsylvania Court of Common Pleas Unit Cost Procedures Manual: Executive Summary. 29p. 1982. 1.74 (*0-685-15185-9*, NERO-105) Natl Ctr St Courts.
— Pennsylvania Metropolitan Delay Project: A Report on Criminal Case Processing in Philadelphia & Allegheny County (Pittsburgh) Courts of Common Pleas, 3 vols., Vol. I. 229p. 1980. 13.74 (*0-685-15628-1*, NERO-065) Natl Ctr St Courts.
— Pennsylvania Metropolitan Delay Project: A Report on Criminal Case Processing in Philadelphia & Allegheny County (Pittsburgh) Courts of Common Pleas, 3 vols., Vol. II. 167p. 1980. 10.02 (*0-685-15629-X*, NERO-066) Natl Ctr St Courts.
— Pennsylvania Metropolitan Delay Project: A Report on Criminal Case Processing in Philadelphia & Allegheny County (Pittsburgh) Courts of Common Pleas, 3 vols., Vol. III. 67p. 1980. 4.02 (*0-685-15630-3*, NERO-067) Natl Ctr St Courts.
— Pennsylvania Superior Court Appellate Settlement Conference Design. 30p. 1979. 1.80 (*0-685-16916-2*, NERO-127) Natl Ctr St Courts.
— Pennsylvania Superior Court Automation: Technical Assistance Review. 37p. 1984. 2.00 (*0-685-16685-6*, NERO, T/A-522) Natl Ctr St Courts.
— Personnel & Operating Efficiency in the Butler County (OH) Court: A Technical Assistance Report. 41p. 1986. 3.00 (*0-685-15276-6*, NERO, T/A-532) Natl Ctr St Courts.
— Phase One Evaluation of Pretrial Delay Release Programs, 7 vols., Vol. I. 84p. 1976. 5.04 (*0-685-16762-3*, MAB-080) Natl Ctr St Courts.
— Phase One Evaluation of Pretrial Delay Release Programs, 7 vols., Vol. II. 33p. 1976. 19.98 (*0-685-16763-1*, MAB-081) Natl Ctr St Courts.
— Phase One Evaluation of Pretrial Delay Release Programs, 7 vols., Vol. III. 51p. 1976. 3.06 (*0-685-16764-X*, MAB-082) Natl Ctr St Courts.
— Phase One Evaluation of Pretrial Delay Release Programs, 7 vols., Vol. IV. 48p. 1976. 2.88 (*0-685-16765-8*, MAB-083) Natl Ctr St Courts.
— Phase One Evaluation of Pretrial Delay Release Programs, 7 vols., Vol. V. 35p. 1976. 2.10 (*0-685-16766-6*, MAB-084) Natl Ctr St Courts.
— Phase One Evaluation of Pretrial Delay Release Programs, 7 vols., Vol. VI. 33p. 1976. 1.98 (*0-685-16767-4*, MAB-085) Natl Ctr St Courts.
— Phase One Evaluation of Pretrial Delay Release Programs, 7 vols., Vol. VII. 54p. 1976. 3.24 (*0-685-16768-2*, MAB-086) Natl Ctr St Courts.
— Philadelphia Standards & Goals Exemplary Court Project: Final Evaluation. 137p. 1978. 8.22 (*0-685-15007-0*, NERO-027) Natl Ctr St Courts.
— Pike County (PA) Data Processing: A Technical Assistance Report. 9p. 1984. 0.54 (*0-685-16686-4*, NERO, T/A-521) Natl Ctr St Courts.
— Plan for Automating the York County (PA) Court of Common Pleas: Final Report. 103p. 1985. 6.00 (*0-685-16687-2*, NERO-170) Natl Ctr St Courts.
— Planning a Data Processing Initiative for the Pennsylvania Courts: A Technical Assistance Report. 17p. 1984. 1.02 (*0-685-16688-0*, NERO, T/A-518) Natl Ctr St Courts.
— Planning for Improved Records Management in the Clerk's Office of the Quincy Division, District Court Department of the Massachusetts Trial Court: Technical Assistance Report. 194p. 1981. 11.64 (*0-685-16602-3*, NERO, T/A-509) Natl Ctr St Courts.
— Polk County Courthouse Facilities Project, Des Moines, Iowa. 233p. 1979. 13.98 (*0-685-15402-5*, NCRO-010) Natl Ctr St Courts.
— Polk County Judicial Facilities Master Plan Project. 360p. 1979. 21.60 (*0-685-15162-X*, NCRO-027) Natl Ctr St Courts.
— Post-Adjudication Procedures in the Allegheny County (PA) Court of Common Pleas: Report of Findings, Vol. 5. 112p. 1982. 6.72 (*0-685-16775-5*, NERO-114) Natl Ctr St Courts.
— Post-Adjudication Procedures in the Dauphin County (PA) Court of Common Pleas: Report of Findings, Vol. 8. 81p. 1982. 4.86 (*0-685-16777-1*, NERO-110) Natl Ctr St Courts.
— Post-Adjudication Procedures in the Delaware County (PA) Court of Common Pleas: Report of Findings, Vol. 6. 81p. 1982. 4.86 (*0-685-43714-0*, NERO-116) Natl Ctr St Courts.
— Post-Adjudication Procedures in the Forest-Warren County (PA) Court of Common Pleas: Report of Findings, Vol. 10. 80p. 1982. 4.80 (*0-685-43715-9*, NERO-115) Natl Ctr St Courts.
— Post-Adjudication Procedures in the Lycoming County (PA) Court of Common Pleas: Report of Findings, Vol. 9. 75p. 1982. 4.50 (*0-685-43716-7*, NERO-106) Natl Ctr St Courts.
— Post-Adjudication Procedures in the Pennsylvania Court of Common Pleas: Report of Statewide Findings, Vol. 2. 152p. 1982. 9.12 (*0-685-43718-3*, NERO-113) Natl Ctr St Courts.
— Post-Adjudication Procedures in the Pennsylvania Courts of Common Pleas: Report of Findings, Vol. I. 172p. 1982. 10.32 (*0-685-43717-5*, NERO-117) Natl Ctr St Courts.
— Post-Adjudication Procedures in the Philadelphia (PA) Court of Common Pleas: Report of Findings, Vol. 4. 145p. 1982. 8.70 (*0-685-43719-1*, NERO-112) Natl Ctr St Courts.
— Post-Adjudication Procedures in the Susquehanna County (PA) Court of Common Pleas: Report of Findings, Vol. 11. 66p. 1982. 3.96 (*0-685-43720-5*, NERO-108) Natl Ctr St Courts.
— Post-Adjudication Procedures in the York County (PA) Court of Common Pleas: Report of Findings, Vol. 7. 84p. 1982. 5.04 (*0-685-16785-2*, NERO-107) Natl Ctr St Courts.
— Practical Observations on the Small Claims Court. 56p. 1979. pap. write for info. (*0-89656-039-2*, R-047) Natl Ctr St Courts.
— Preliminary Plan Design for the Franklin County Court of Common Pleas. 73p. 1978. 4.38 (*0-685-15163-8*, NERO-040) Natl Ctr St Courts.
— Preliminary Review of the Allegheny County Court of Common Pleas Criminal Division's Individual Calendar Program. 16p. 1982. 0.96 (*0-685-15817-9*, NERO, T/A-513) Natl Ctr St Courts.
— Pretrial Services Training & Clearinghouse Project: Final Report. 158p. 1975. 9.48 (*0-685-16770-4*, MAB-087) Natl Ctr St Courts.
— Price of Local Justice: A Cost of Operations of the Town & Village Courts in New York State. 45p. 1978. 2.70 (*0-685-15186-7*, NERO-019) Natl Ctr St Courts.
— Processing Juvenile Traffic Cases in Ventura County, California. 96p. 1975. 5.76 (*0-685-15047-X*, WRO-014) Natl Ctr St Courts.
— Producing a Judicial Plan. 144p. 1977. 8.64 (*0-685-15164-6*, DC-004) Natl Ctr St Courts.
— Programs for Improving the Image of the Judiciary. 94p. 1984. 6.00 (*0-685-15192-1*, ICM-001) Natl Ctr St Courts.
— Progress Report to the Advisory Committee on the Implementation of Amendment V to the Vermont Constitution Relating to the Organization of the Judicial System. 31p. 1974. write for info. (*0-318-61193-7*, NERO-125) Natl Ctr St Courts.
— Proposal & Analysis of a Unitary System for Review of Criminal Justice. 30p. 1974. write for info. (*0-318-61190-2*, MAB-088) Natl Ctr St Courts.
— Proposal for Limiting the Duty of the Trial Judge to Instruct the Jury Sua Sponte. 29p. 1974. 1.74 (*0-685-16732-1*, MAB-090) Natl Ctr St Courts.
— Proposal for the Design of a Caseflow Management System, Superior Court. 53p. 1975. 3.18 (*0-685-15642-7*, MAB-089) Natl Ctr St Courts.
— Proposed Judicial Article for the Constitution of the State of Washington. 107p. 1976. 6.42 (*0-685-15013-5*, MAB-091) Natl Ctr St Courts.
— Proposed One-Trial-One-Day Jury System for the Courts Serving Maricopa County, Arizona: Data Appendix. 71p. 1985. 5.00 (*0-685-43712-4*, CJS-009) Natl Ctr St Courts.
— Proposed One-Trial-One-Day Jury System for the Courts Serving Maricopa County, Arizona: Final Report. 77p. 1985. 5.00 (*0-685-16733-X*, CJS-008) Natl Ctr St Courts.

An Asterisk (*) at the beginning of an entry indicates that the title is appearing in BIP for the first time.

— Proposed Revision of Rules of Supreme Court & Appellate Session of Superior Court: To Implement Centralized Processing of Appeals in Connecticut. 80p. 1977. 4.80 (*0-685-16887-5*, NERO-037) Natl Ctr St Courts.
— Proposed Rules of Judicial Administration for Alabama Trial Courts. 68p. 1976. 4.08 (*0-685-15154-9*, MAB-092) Natl Ctr St Courts.
— Proposed Standards for Appellate Court Statistics: Report of the Appellate Statistics Committee, ABA Appellate Judges' Conference. 72p. 1973. write for info. (*0-318-61275-5*, MAB-093) Natl Ctr St Courts.
— Prosecution Alternative to Court Trial (PACT) Program: An Innovative Response to the Problem of DWI Adjudication in Phoenix, Arizona. (Paul Reardon Ser.). 21p. 1981. 1.26 (*0-685-16771-2*, PRS-023) Natl Ctr St Courts.
— Providing Legal Services to Indigents in Colorado. 126p. 1982. 7.56 (*0-685-16945-6*, WRO-050) Natl Ctr St Courts.
— Provisional Substantive & Procedural Guidelines for Involuntary Civil Commitment. 246p. 1982. 14.76 (*0-685-17020-9*, NCSC-022) Natl Ctr St Courts.
— Provisions for Disqualification & Substitution of Judges. (Research Essay Ser.). 6p. 1978. 0.36 (*0-685-15082-8*, E-009) Natl Ctr St Courts.
— Psychoeducational Diagnostic Services for Learning Disabled Youths: Research Procedures. 38p. 1977. 2.28 (*0-685-17022-5*, LDJD-011) Natl Ctr St Courts.
— Psychoeducational Diagnostic Services for Learning Disabled Youths: Validation Analysis. 80p. 1979. 4.80 (*0-685-17023-3*, LDJD-015) Natl Ctr St Courts.
— Public Image of Courts. 104p. 1978. 6.24 (*0-685-15194-8*, SC-001) Natl Ctr St Courts.
— Puerto Rico Court Reporting Study, Phase I. 132p. 1975. Phas I, 132 pgs. 7.92 (*0-685-16421-7*, WRO-024) Natl Ctr St Courts.
— Puerto Rico Court Reporting Study, Phase II. 30p. 1975. 1.80 (*0-685-16422-5*, WRO-025) Natl Ctr St Courts.
— Ramsey County Jury Study for the Second Judicial District: Final Report. 211p. 1979. 12.66 (*0-685-16735-6*, NCRO-017) Natl Ctr St Courts.
— Ramsey County Municipal Court Administrative Hearing Office. (Paul Reardon Ser.). 7p. 1982. 0.42 (*0-685-15024-0*, PRS-038) Natl Ctr St Courts.
— Recommendation for Developing an Integrated Municipal-Superior Court Automated Information System in Ventura County, California. 27p. 1976. 1.62 (*0-685-16689-9*, MAB-094) Natl Ctr St Courts.
— Recommendations for Improving the Use of Restitution As a Dispositional Alternative, As Administered by the Connecticut Adult Probation Division. 34p. 1975. 2.04 (*0-685-16753-4*, MAB-095) Natl Ctr St Courts.
— Recommendations Regarding Records Management & Space Utilization in the Clerk's Office of the New Salem District Court, Salem, Massachusetts. 57p. 1977. 3.42 (*0-685-15410-6*, MAB-096) Natl Ctr St Courts.
— Recommended Grievance & Appeal Procedures for the District of Columbia Courts. 30p. 1978. 1.80 (*0-685-15279-0*, MARO-009) Natl Ctr St Courts.
— Recommended Personnel Administration Standards for the Minnesota Judicial System: Executive Summary. 32p. 1978. 1.92 (*0-685-15280-4*, NCRO-009) Natl Ctr St Courts.
— Recommended Utlization of Legal Research Aides in the Supreme Court of Florida. 28p. 1973. write for info. (*0-318-61231-3*, MAB-097) Natl Ctr St Courts.
— Records Access & Subject Participation in Criminal Justice Research: A Preliminary Case Study. 34p. 1978. 2.04 (*0-685-16603-1*, LDJD-012) Natl Ctr St Courts.
— Records Management & Automation Needs Assessment Study for the Juvenile Court, Jefferson Parish, Louisiana. 132p. 1983. 7.92 (*0-685-16604-X*, SERO-001) Natl Ctr St Courts.
— Records Management in the Hawaii Judiciary: A New Direction. 133p. 1982. 7.98 (*0-685-16605-8*, WRO-046) Natl Ctr St Courts.
— Records Management Recommendations for Circuit Clerks of Franklin County, Goochland County, & Henry County Circuit Courts: State of Virginia. 80p. 1978. 4.80 (*0-685-16606-6*, DPO, T/A-502) Natl Ctr St Courts.
— Records Management Recommendations for the Idaho Supreme Court. 30p. 1976. 1.80 (*0-685-16607-4*, MAB-098) Natl Ctr St Courts.
— Records Management Review, Tenth Judicial Circuit Court, Saginaw, Michigan: A Technical Assistane Report. 21p. 1984. 1.26 (*0-685-15648-6*, NERO, T/A-519) Natl Ctr St Courts.
— Records Reorganization in a Court for the Idaho Supreme Court. (Paul Reardon Ser.). 16p. 1982. 0.96 (*0-685-16608-2*, PRS-034) Natl Ctr St Courts.
— Records Retention & Disposition Project, Fifth District, Minnesota: Final Project Report. 38p. 1981. 2.28 (*0-685-16611-2*, NCRO-045) Natl Ctr St Courts.
— Records Retention & Disposition Recommendations for the Circuit Court of Madison County. 14p. 1976. write for info. (*0-318-61272-0*, MAB-143) Natl Ctr St Courts.
— Red Lake Court of Indian Offenses: Management Audit. 52p. 1982. 3.12 (*0-685-15036-4*, NCRO, T/A-508) Natl Ctr St Courts.
— Red Lake Court of Tribal Offenses Court Manual. 450p. 1982. write for info. (*0-318-61197-X*, NCRO-067) Natl Ctr St Courts.
— Redistricting Arkansas Circuit & Chancery Courts. 87p. 1976. 5.22 (*0-685-15076-3*, MAB-099) Natl Ctr St Courts.
— Reduced Terms of Jury Service in the Federal Courts. 41p. 1986. 3.00 (*0-685-16737-2*, CJS-013) Natl Ctr St Courts.
— Reducing Court Recording Cost. (Paul Reardon Ser.). 25p. 1983. 1.50 (*0-685-16425-X*, PRS-044) Natl Ctr St Courts.
— Reducing the Paperwork Overload in Hudson County, New Jersey, Superior Court Law Division (Criminal) 29p. 1981. 1.74 (*0-685-16613-9*, NERO-089) Natl Ctr St Courts.
— Reducing the Time & Cost of the Appellate Process: Arizona Appellate Project Report. 40p. 1976. 2.40 (*0-685-16917-0*, MAB-100) Natl Ctr St Courts.
— Report of Technical Assistance Consultation to the State of Judicial Planning. 24p. 1976. 1.44 (*0-685-15165-4*, MAB-101) Natl Ctr St Courts.
— Report of the Alabama Trial Court Project. 148p. 1974. pap. write for info. (*0-318-61191-0*, MAB-102) Natl Ctr St Courts.
— Report of the Special Committee to Study the Nebraska Court System. 90p. 1978. 5.40 (*0-685-15008-9*, NCRO-036) Natl Ctr St Courts.
— Report on Judicial Redistricting for the Nebraska Supreme Court Legislature. 74p. 1982. write for info. (*0-318-61204-6*, NCSC-028) Natl Ctr St Courts.
— Report on Proposed Modification of the Judicial Retirement System of West Virginia. 157p. 1984. 10.00 (*0-685-15079-8*, SERO-004) Natl Ctr St Courts.
— Report on the Idaho Supreme Court Clerk's Office. 72p. 1974. 4.32 (*0-685-16890-5*, MAB-104) Natl Ctr St Courts.
— Report on the Montgomery County (AL) Office. 20p. 1977. 1.20 (*0-685-15417-3*, MAB-105) Natl Ctr St Courts.
— Report on Unpublished Opinions of the California Courts of Appeal. 23p. 1976. 1.38 (*0-685-16892-1*, MAB-106) Natl Ctr St Courts.
— Report to the California Judicial Council on Ways to Improve Trial Jury Selection & Management. 362p. 1978. pap. write for info. (*0-318-61291-7*, WRO-063) Natl Ctr St Courts.
— Report to the California Judicial Council on Ways to Improve Trial Jury Selection & Management: Executive Summary. 35p. 1978. pap. write for info. (*0-318-61292-5*, WRO-064) Natl Ctr St Courts.
— Report to the House of Delegates of the Nebraska State Bar Association from the Special Committee to Study the Nebraska Court System. 175p. 1978. write for info. (*0-318-61192-9*, NCRO-068) Natl Ctr St Courts.
— Report with Findings & Recommendations to the Conference of Chief Justices from Its Task Force on Lawyer Competence. 84p. 1982. 5.04 (*0-685-16751-8*, NCSC-021) Natl Ctr St Courts.
— Representation of Indigent Felony Defendants in the Cuyahoga County (OH) Court of Common Pleas. 144p. 1984. 8.64 (*0-685-16946-4*, NERO-138) Natl Ctr St Courts.
— Representation of Indigent Persons in the Courts of Lawrence County, Ohio. 62p. 1985. 4.00 (*0-685-16947-2*, NERO-166) Natl Ctr St Courts.
— Representation of Indigent Persons in the Courts of Scioto County, Ohio. 79p. 1985. 5.00 (*0-685-16948-0*, NERO-165) Natl Ctr St Courts.
— Requirements Analysis for Computerization of the New Jersey Courts, 2 vols., Vol. I. 498p. 1982. 29.88 (*0-685-16693-7*, R-075) Natl Ctr St Courts.
— Requirements Analysis for Computerization of the New Jersey Courts, 2 vols., Vol. II. 692p. 1982. 41.52 (*0-685-16694-5*, R-076) Natl Ctr St Courts.
— Requirements Definition Study of the San Mateo County Municipal Court. 290p. 1985. 18.00 (*0-685-15138-7*, WRO-065) Natl Ctr St Courts.
— Restitution: Background, Program, & Issues. 22p. 1977. 1.32 (*0-685-16757-7*, NERO-010) Natl Ctr St Courts.
— Restitution Program for Uninsured Offenders in Traffic Court. (Paul Reardon Ser.). 20p. 1981. 1.20 (*0-685-15061-5*, PRS-020) Natl Ctr St Courts.
— Review of Cobb County Jury System. 13p. 1983. write for info. (*0-318-61293-3*, CJS-005) Natl Ctr St Courts.
— Review of Pennsylvania Jury Monitoring, Technical Assistance: Final Report. 44p. 1985. 3.00 (*0-685-16740-2*, NERO, T/A-529) Natl Ctr St Courts.
— Review of Some Aspects of Court Reporting in San Joaquin County, California. 61p. 1986. 4.00 (*0-685-16429-2*, WRO-069) Natl Ctr St Courts.
— Review of the Administration & Operation of the Tucson City Court. 162p. 1985. 10.00 (*0-685-15139-5*, WRO-054) Natl Ctr St Courts.
— Review of the Automated Juror Selection Process in Santa Barbara County, California. 12p. 1985. 1.00 (*0-685-16738-0*, CJS-011) Natl Ctr St Courts.
— Review of the Calendar Management & Management Information Practices for the Eighteenth Judicial District (Araphoe County) of Colorado: A Technical Assistance Report. 106p. 1985. 7.00 (*0-685-15821-7*, WRO, T/A-504) Natl Ctr St Courts.
— Review of the Manual of Personnel Policies for the Judiciary of the State of Delaware: Comments & Suggestions. 18p. 1978. 1.08 (*0-685-15282-0*, NCRO-038) Natl Ctr St Courts.
— Revision of Forms for Use in Cases of Children in Need of Supervision (CHINS) in Massachusetts District Court. 50p. 1975. 3.00 (*0-685-16617-1*, MAB-107) Natl Ctr St Courts.
— Revolution in the Courts: Computers in the Housing Court of New York City. (Paul Reardon Ser.). 10p. 1983. 0.60 (*0-685-16696-1*, PRS-041) Natl Ctr St Courts.
— Rhode Island District Court Operations Manual. 365p. 1977. 21.90 (*0-685-15285-5*, NERO-047) Natl Ctr St Courts.
— Rhode Island Family Court Benchbook: Domestic Relations Matters, Vol.I. 237p. 1984. 14.00 (*0-685-15056-9*, NERO-151) Natl Ctr St Courts.
— Rhode Island Family Court Benchbook: Juvenile Matters, Vol. II. 206p. 1984. 13.00 (*0-685-15048-8*, NERO-152) Natl Ctr St Courts.
— Rhode Island Superior Court Operations Manual. 294p. 1978. 17.64 (*0-685-15287-1*, NERO-004) Natl Ctr St Courts.
— Role of Data in Judicial Planning. 101p. 1977. 6.06 (*0-685-15166-2*, DC-005) Natl Ctr St Courts.
— Rural Courts: The Effect of Space & Distance on the Administration of Justice. (Illus.). 136p. 1977. pap. write for info. (*0-89656-020-1*, R-032) Natl Ctr St Courts.
— Rural Courts: Trends & Implications. (Research Essay Ser.). 10p. 1977. 0.60 (*0-685-15025-9*, E-002) Natl Ctr St Courts.
— Rural Courts Workshop, Billings, Montana, 1976: Program & Materials. 161p. 1976. 9.66 (*0-685-15026-7*, MAB-108) Natl Ctr St Courts.
— Saginaw Circuit Court Management Study Report, 2 vols., Vol. I. 83p. 1982. 4.98 (*0-685-15140-9*, NCRO-064) Natl Ctr St Courts.
— Saginaw Circuit Court Management Study Report, 2 vols., Vol. II. 114p. 1982. 6.84 (*0-685-15141-7*, NCRO-065) Natl Ctr St Courts.
— Saginaw District Court Implementation Project: Final Report. 26p. 1981. 1.56 (*0-685-15009-7*, NCRO-059) Natl Ctr St Courts.
— Scott County Improvement Project. 19p. 1981. 1.14 (*0-685-15167-0*, PRS-003) Natl Ctr St Courts.
— Screening & Evaluation in Centralized Forensic Mental Health Facilities. 108p. 1981. 6.48 (*0-685-17025-X*, OPS-005) Natl Ctr St Courts.
— Screening & Summary Calendar Procedures at the District of Columbia Court of Appeals: An Evaluation. 42p. 1978. 2.52 (*0-685-15831-4*, MARO-005) Natl Ctr St Courts.
— Selected Salary Data: Massachusetts Judicial Department. 185p. 1978. 11.10 (*0-685-15080-1*, NERO-026) Natl Ctr St Courts.
— Selection of a Court Recording Method for the District Courts of Oregon. 29p. 1973. pap. write for info. (*0-318-61263-1*, R-003) Natl Ctr St Courts.
— Senior Citizen Participation in the Courts. (Paul Reardon Ser.). 11p. 1981. 0.66 (*0-685-15195-6*, PRS-024) Natl Ctr St Courts.
— Sentencing Felons in New Mexico: A Proposal for Guidelines Committee to the New Mexico Supreme Court. 81p. 1985. 5.00 (*0-685-43722-1*, WRO-062) Natl Ctr St Courts.
— Sentencing Procedures & Practices: An Annotated Bibliography. 31p. 1979. 1.86 (*0-685-16788-7*, FR-003) Natl Ctr St Courts.
— Separate but Subservient: Court Budgeting in the American States. 230p. 1975. pap. write for info. (*0-318-61218-6*, MAB-110) Natl Ctr St Courts.
— Seventh Judicial Circuit, South Dakota: A Caseflow Management System. 58p. 1976. 3.48 (*0-685-15682-6*, NCRO-005) Natl Ctr St Courts.
— Seventh Judicial District Requirements Analysis: State of Iowa. 317p. 1984. 19.00 (*0-685-15144-1*, NERO-167) Natl Ctr St Courts.
— Sheriffs in New Jersey: Final Report. 120p. 1981. 7.20 (*0-685-15291-X*, NERO-079) Natl Ctr St Courts.
— Short History of the Massachusetts Courts. 74p. 1975. 4.44 (*0-685-15010-0*, NERO-042) Natl Ctr St Courts.
— Simple Procedure to Speed Disposition of Appealed Civil Cases in Tennessee. (Paul Reardon Ser.). 3p. 1981. 0.18 (*0-685-16923-5*, PRS-005) Natl Ctr St Courts.
— Simplified Criminal Case Processing in the Massachusetts District Courts. (Paul Reardon Ser.). 19p. 1982. 1.14 (*0-685-15687-7*, PRS-027) Natl Ctr St Courts.
— Small Claims Courts: Operations & Prospects. (Research Essay Ser.). 11p. 1978. 0.66 (*0-685-15033-X*, E-006) Natl Ctr St Courts.
— South Central Juvenile Care Center: Evaluation Project. 55p. 1978. 3.30 (*0-685-17030-6*, NCRO-023) Natl Ctr St Courts.
— South Dakota State Court Administrator: Filing System Report & Manual. 18p. 1975. write for info. (*0-318-61274-7*, MAB-145) Natl Ctr St Courts.
— Space Needs for the Civil Courthouse in Atlantic City: Final Report. 95p. 1980. 5.70 (*0-685-15425-4*, NERO-072) Natl Ctr St Courts.
— Space Use Plan for the Berkshire County Court Complex (Pittsfield, MA) 37p. 1980. 2.22 (*0-685-15429-7*, NERO-068) Natl Ctr St Courts.
— St. Joseph Circuit Court: Final Report. 110p. 1981. 6.60 (*0-685-15142-5*, NCRO-048) Natl Ctr St Courts.
— St. Joseph County Circuit & Superior Court. 17p. 1982. 1.02 (*0-685-15143-3*, NCRO-054) Natl Ctr St Courts.
— Standards for Publication of Judicial Opinions: A Report of the Committee on Use of Appellate Court Energies of the Advisory Council for Appellate Justice. 46p. 1973. 2.76 (*0-685-16896-4*, MAB-111) Natl Ctr St Courts.
— State Appellate Growth Documentary Appendix. 290p. 1983. 17.40 (*0-685-16899-9*, NCSC-035) Natl Ctr St Courts.
— State Court Caseload Statistics: Annual Report 1977. 461p. 1982. pap. write for info. (*0-318-61277-1*, R-078) Natl Ctr St Courts.
— State Court Caseload Statistics: Annual Report 1978. 473p. 1983. pap. write for info. (*0-318-61278-X*, R-080) Natl Ctr St Courts.
— State Court Caseload Statistics: Annual Report 1979. 496p. 1983. pap. 3.00 (*0-685-16633-3*, R-090) Natl Ctr St Courts.
— State Court Caseload Statistics: Annual Report 1980. 494p. 1984. pap. write for info. (*0-89656-078-3*, R-092) Natl Ctr St Courts.
— State Court Caseload Statistics: Annual Report 1981. 1985. pap. write for info. (*0-89656-079-1*, R-093) Natl Ctr St Courts.
— State Court Information Systems: State of the Art, Vol. I. 1980. write for info. (*0-318-61285-2*) Natl Ctr St Courts.
— State Court Model Annual Report. 1980. write for info. (*0-89656-042-2*, R-050) Natl Ctr St Courts.
— State Court Perspective on Case Management in the U. S. Tax Court. 26p. 1985. 2.00 (*0-685-15694-X*, WRO-056) Natl Ctr St Courts.
— State Court Records Retention Study. 224p. 1985. 14.00 (*0-685-16620-1*, SERO-009) Natl Ctr St Courts.
— State Courts: A Blueprint for the Future. 360p. 1978. write for info. (*0-318-61215-1*, R-038) Natl Ctr St Courts.
— State Courts & the Death Penalty After Furman v. Georgia. 30p. 1973. pap. write for info. (*0-318-61299-2*, R-004) Natl Ctr St Courts.
— State Judicial Information Systems State of the Art, 1978. LC 79-16279. 344p. 1979. 20.64 (*0-89656-035-X*, F-004) Natl Ctr St Courts.
— State Judicial Training Profile. rev. ed. 84p. 1976. 5.04 (*0-89656-014-7*, R-024) Natl Ctr St Courts.
— State of Delaware Administrative Office of the Courts: Technical Assistance Report. 23p. 1978. 1.38 (*0-685-15145-X*, NCRO, T/A-506) Natl Ctr St Courts.
— State of Maryland Court Clerks' Association: Procedural Manual for Court Clerks. 328p. 1977. 19.68 (*0-685-15294-4*, MARO-003) Natl Ctr St Courts.
— State of Nebraska State Court Organization Profile. 166p. 1977. 9.96 (*0-685-15011-9*, MAB-113) Natl Ctr St Courts.
— State of North Dakota District Court Benchbook. 128p. 1982. 7.68 (*0-685-15071-2*, NCRO-051) Natl Ctr St Courts.
— Steps to Create an Appellate Settlement Conference: Follow-up Technical Assistance to the North Carolina Court of Appeal. 72p. 1981. 4.32 (*0-685-16924-3*, NERO, T/A-511) Natl Ctr St Courts.
— Student Litigation: A Compilation & Analysis of Civil Cases Involving Students, 1971-81. 208p. 1982. 12.48 (*0-685-16954-5*, NCSC-016) Natl Ctr St Courts.
— Study for the Birmingham (AL) Municipal Court. 228p. 1980. 13.68 (*0-685-15027-5*, SRO-003) Natl Ctr St Courts.
— Study of Court Filing Fees. 138p. 1975. 8.28 (*0-685-15187-5*, MAB-114) Natl Ctr St Courts.
— Study of Jury Management in Selected Pennsylvania Counties: Berks, Blair, Chester, McKean, Northumberland & Westmoreland. 160p. 1984. 10.00 (*0-685-16742-9*, NERO-147) Natl Ctr St Courts.
— Study of Massachusetts Court Facilities: Summary & Evaluation Volume With Recommendations. 183p. 1975. 10.98 (*0-685-15433-5*, NERO-021) Natl Ctr St Courts.
— Study of Plea Bargaining in Municipal Courts of the State of New Jersey. 106p. 1974. 6.36 (*0-685-16772-0*, NERO-050) Natl Ctr St Courts.
— Study of Structural Characteristics, Policies & Operational Procedures in Metropolitan Juvenile Center, 2 vols., Vol. I. 302p. 1982. 18.12 (*0-685-15050-X*, NCSC-018) Natl Ctr St Courts.
— Study of Structural Characteristics, Policies & Operational Procedures in Metropolitan Juvenile Center, 2 vols., Vol. II. 131p. 1982. 7.86 (*0-685-15051-8*, NCSC-019) Natl Ctr St Courts.
— Study of Structural Characteristics, Policies, & Operational Procedures in Metropolitan Juvenile Courts: Executive Summary. 177p. 1982. 10.62 (*0-685-15049-6*, NCSC-017) Natl Ctr St Courts.
— Study of the Appellate System in Minnesota. 58p. 1974. 3.48 (*0-685-16900-6*, MAB-116) Natl Ctr St Courts.
— Study of the Boston Housing Court. 91p. 1974. 5.46 (*0-685-15028-3*, MAB-117) Natl Ctr St Courts.
— Study of the New Jersey Appellate Division's Clerk's Office. 236p. 1979. 14.16 (*0-685-16901-4*, NERO-029) Natl Ctr St Courts.
— Successful Affirmative Action Tactics in a Large Urban Trial Court. (Paul Reardon Ser.). 26p. 1981. 1.56 (*0-685-15332-0*, PRS-001) Natl Ctr St Courts.
— Suggestions for Improved Case Processing & Case Assignment in the Portage County (OH) Municipal Court: Technical Assistance Report. 92p. 1981. 5.52 (*0-685-15714-8*, NERO, T/A-510) Natl Ctr St Courts.
— Suggestions for Improvement of Jury Management in Rhode Island. 25p. 1982. 1.50 (*0-685-16743-7*, NERO-102) Natl Ctr St Courts.
— Summary & Analysis of Statutory Provisions Relating to the Records of the Circuit Courts, District Courts, & Magistrates of Virginia. 91p. 1976. 5.46 (*0-685-16622-8*, MAB-119) Natl Ctr St Courts.
— Superior Court Clerk's Office at Providence (RI) Observations & Recommendations. 40p. 1978. 2.40 (*0-685-15146-8*, NERO-077) Natl Ctr St Courts.
— Superior Court of New Hampshire: Management Issues at the Hillsborough County Courthouse; Technical Assistance Report. 145p. 1980. 8.70 (*0-685-15147-6*, NERO-060) Natl Ctr St Courts.
— Supervisor's Addendum to the Personnel Policy Guide of the Louisiana Supreme Court. 145p. 1980. 8.70 (*0-685-15297-9*, NCRO-032) Natl Ctr St Courts.
— Supreme Court of Louisiana Personnel Management Study: Technical Assistance Report. 163p. 1980. 9.78 (*0-685-15300-2*, NCRO-031) Natl Ctr St Courts.
— Supreme Court of Ohio: Operations Review. 110p. 1985. 7.00 (*0-685-16902-2*, NERO-171) Natl Ctr St Courts.
— Supreme Court of Virginia: Technical Assistance Report. 145p. 1979. 8.70 (*0-685-15148-4*, NCRO, T/A-505) Natl Ctr St Courts.
— Surrogates in New Jersey: Final Report. 230p. 1981. 13. 80 (*0-685-15075-5*, NERO-080) Natl Ctr St Courts.
— Survey of Judicial Salaries in State Court System: Volumes I-III. 107p. 1974. 6.42 (*0-685-15081-X*, MAB-120) Natl Ctr St Courts.

N

— Survey of Jurors in Selected Pennsylvania Counties. 25p. 1983. 1.50 (*0-685-16745-3*, NERO-136) Natl Ctr St Courts.
— Survey of State Supreme Courts With Intermediate Appellate Courts: Technical Assistance Report. 114p. 1980. 6.84 (*0-685-16903-0*, NERO, T/A-508) Natl Ctr St Courts.
— Survey of the Status of Judicial Planning in State Courts: Paper Number Five. 147p. 1978. 8.82 (*0-685-15168-9*, DC-007) Natl Ctr St Courts.
— Technology & Management in Court Reporting Systems. 34p. 1973. write for info. (*0-318-61264-X*, MAB-121) Natl Ctr St Courts.
— Technology & the Courts: An Update. (Research Essay Ser.). 10p. 1978. 0.60 (*0-685-16437-3*, E-008) Natl Ctr St Courts.
— Tennessee Courthouse Facilities, Profile & Evaluation, Vol. II. 127p. 1977. write for info. (*0-318-61251-8*, SRO-001) Natl Ctr St Courts.
— Tension of Popular Participation. (Research Essay Ser.). 12p. 1977. 0.72 (*0-685-15196-4*, E-004) Natl Ctr St Courts.
— Texas Appellate Courts, 2 vols., Vol. I. 103p. 1980. 6.18 (*0-685-16905-7*, SRO-004) Natl Ctr St Courts.
— Texas Appellate Courts, 2 vols., Vol. II. 162p. 1980. 9.72 (*0-685-16906-5*, SRO-005) Natl Ctr St Courts.
— Texas Appellate Courts II Project: A Study for the Court of Appeals Fifth Supreme Judicial District, Dallas, Texas. 244p. 1981. write for info. (*0-318-61320-4*, SRO-010) Natl Ctr St Courts.
— Texas Appellate Courts III Project: A Continuation Study on the Implementation of S. J. R. 36. 167p. 1982. 10.02 (*0-685-16904-9*, SRO-018) Natl Ctr St Courts.
— Third Judicial Circuit Court of Michigan: Technical Assistance Report. 216p. 1979. 12.96 (*0-685-15149-2*, NCRO-012) Natl Ctr St Courts.
— Traffic Adjudication in Virginia: Report & Recommendations. 185p. 1977. 11.10 (*0-685-15062-3*, MAB-126) Natl Ctr St Courts.
— Transcript Preparation in New Hampshire: Technical Assistance Report. 46p. 1980. 2.76 (*0-685-16443-8*, NERO, T/A-507) Natl Ctr St Courts.
— Transcripts by Connecticut Court Reporters. 158p. 1978. 9.48 (*0-685-16447-0*, NERO-033) Natl Ctr St Courts.
— Trial Court Review of Verdicts: A National Survey, Vol. 3. (Post-Adjudication Ser.). 165p. 1982. 9.90 (*0-685-15155-7*, NERO-118) Natl Ctr St Courts.
— Unified Court System for Vermont: Full Report. 278p. 1974. write for info. (*0-89656-015-5*, R-017) Natl Ctr St Courts.
— Union County (New Jersey) District Court Pro Se Assistance Program. (Paul Reardon Ser.). 85p. 1981. 5.10 (*0-685-16949-9*, PRS-018) Natl Ctr St Courts.
— User Manual for Portotype Proportionality Review System. 746p. 1984. 44.76 (*0-685-16795-X*, NCSC-039) Natl Ctr St Courts.
— User's Introductory Handbook: NCSC Computerized Interactive Research System (CONRES) 30p. 1974. 1.80 (*0-685-15346-0*, MAB-127) Natl Ctr St Courts.
— Utah Appellate System: A Review. 82p. 1985. 5.00 (*0-685-16907-3*, WRO-061) Natl Ctr St Courts.
— Utah Courts of Limited Jurisdiction: Analysis & Recommendations. 146p. 1976. 8.76 (*0-685-15029-1*, WRO-003) Natl Ctr St Courts.
— Utah Supreme Court Project Report. 78p. 1977. 4.68 (*0-685-15012-7*, WRO-022) Natl Ctr St Courts.
— Victims, Witnesses, & Courts. 122p. 1986. 8.00 (*0-685-16755-0*, NCSC-050) Natl Ctr St Courts.
— Virginia Circuit Court Caseload Reporting Study: Detail Design Document. 190p. 1976. 11.40 (*0-685-16530-2*, MAB-132) Natl Ctr St Courts.
— Virginia Circuit Court Caseload Reporting Study: Final Report. 184p. 1977. 11.04 (*0-685-15721-0*, MAB-133) Natl Ctr St Courts.
— Virginia Circuit Court Caseload Reporting Study: Requirements Document. 86p. 1976. 5.16 (*0-685-15734-2*, MAB-135) Natl Ctr St Courts.
— Virginia Circuit Court Reporting: General Design Document. 148p. 1976. 8.88 (*0-685-16531-0*, MAB-134) Natl Ctr St Courts.
— Virginia Traffic Adjudication Study: Findings & Issues Document. 162p. 1976. 9.72 (*0-685-15063-1*, MAB-137) Natl Ctr St Courts.
— Virginia Uniform Docketing & Caseload Reporting System. 181p. 1976. 10.86 (*0-685-15741-5*, MAB-138) Natl Ctr St Courts.
— Volume & Delay in the Colorado Court of Appeals. 100p. 1980. 6.00 (*0-685-16928-6*, NERO-055) Natl Ctr St Courts.
— Volume & Delay in the Florida District Court of Appeals; First District. 98p. 1980. 5.88 (*0-685-16929-4*, NERO-054) Natl Ctr St Courts.
— Volume & Delay in the Illinois Appellate Court, First District. 107p. 1980. 6.42 (*0-685-16930-8*, NERO-058) Natl Ctr St Courts.
— Volume & Delay in the Indiana Court of Appeals. 107p. 1980. 6.42 (*0-685-16935-9*, NERO-074) Natl Ctr St Courts.
— Volume & Delay in the Montana Supreme Court. 98p. 1980. 5.88 (*0-685-16937-5*, NERO-053) Natl Ctr St Courts.
— Volume & Delay in the Nebraska Supreme Court. 97p. 1980. 5.82 (*0-685-16938-3*, NERO-057) Natl Ctr St Courts.
— Volume & Delay in the New Jersey Superior Court, Appellate Division. 97p. 1980. 5.82 (*0-685-16940-5*, NERO-056) Natl Ctr St Courts.
— Volume & Delay in the Ohio Court of Appeals, Eighth District. 103p. 1980. 6.18 (*0-685-16941-3*, NERO-059) Natl Ctr St Courts.
— Volume & Delay in the Oregon Court of Appeals. 92p. 1980. 5.52 (*0-685-18345-9*, NERO-052) Natl Ctr St Courts.
— Volume & Delay in the Virginia Supreme Court. 101p. 1980. 6.06 (*0-685-16942-1*, NERO-075) Natl Ctr St Courts.
— Volunteerism: An Initiative for Accountability in Our Justice System. (Paul Reardon Ser.). 25p. 1982. 1.50 (*0-685-15197-2*, PRS-028) Natl Ctr St Courts.
— Washington Appellate Courts Project: Final Report. 255p. 1975. 15.30 (*0-685-16908-1*, MAB-139) Natl Ctr St Courts.
— Washington Benchbook: Criminal. 334p. 1976. 20.04 (*0-685-15072-0*, MAB-140) Natl Ctr St Courts.
— Washington District Court Weighted Caseload Project. 55p. 1977. 3.30 (*0-685-15749-0*, WRO-011) Natl Ctr St Courts.
— Washington Pattern Forms. 448p. 1978. 26.88 (*0-685-16623-6*, WRO-021) Natl Ctr St Courts.
— Washington Superior Court Weighted Caseload Project. 74p. 1977. 4.44 (*0-685-15756-3*, WRO-012) Natl Ctr St Courts.
— Washington Trial Courts, Statistical Reporting System Report. 68p. 1978. 4.08 (*0-685-16638-4*, WRO-008) Natl Ctr St Courts.
— Wayne County Court Financing Study: Executive Summary. 15p. 1980. 0.90 (*0-685-15188-3*, NCRO-044) Natl Ctr St Courts.
— Wayne County Court Financing Study: Final Report. 204p. 1980. 12.24 (*0-685-15189-1*, NCRO-043) Natl Ctr St Courts.
— White Paper for the New Hampshire Judicial Council. 15p. 1982. 0.90 (*0-685-15169-7*, NERO-123) Natl Ctr St Courts.
— Will County Circuit Clerk's Study: Recordkeeping, Administration, Management, Vol. II. 120p. 1977. 7.20 (*0-685-15150-6*, MAB-141) Natl Ctr St Courts.
— Wisconsin Appellate Practice & Procedure Study: Final Report. 189p. 1975. pap. write for info. (*0-318-61321-2*, R-021) Natl Ctr St Courts.
— Wisconsin Appellate Process Study: Preliminary Report. Mueller, John E. et al, eds. 67p. 1975. pap. write for info. (*0-318-54513-6*, NCRO-066) Natl Ctr St Courts.
— Wisconsin Law Clerk Evaluation. 74p. 1978. 4.44 (*0-685-15302-9*, NCRO-006) Natl Ctr St Courts.
— Wisconsin Municipal Court Study: Executive Summary. 70p. 1982. write for info. (*0-318-61213-5*, NCRO-052) Natl Ctr St Courts.
— Wisconsin Municipal Court Study: Final Report. 76p. 1982. 4.56 (*0-685-15030-5*, NCRO-053) Natl Ctr St Courts.
— Wisconsin Rural Courts: A Technical Assistance Report. 55p. 1984. 3.30 (*0-685-15031-3*, NERO, T/A-520) Natl Ctr St Courts.
— Word Processing & Data Processing Needs of the Ninth District (Ohio) Court of Appeals. 21p. 1985. 2.00 (*0-685-16700-3*, NERO-164) Natl Ctr St Courts.
— Word Processing in the Courts. Bureau of Justice Statistics, ed. LC 84-14860. 60p. (Orig.). 1984. pap. write for info. (*0-89656-077-5*, R-091) Natl Ctr St Courts.
— Word Processing Needs in the Domestic Relations Division & Bureau of Support, Cuyahoga County (Ohio) Court of Common Pleas: A Technical Assistance Report. 8p. 1985. 1.00 (*0-685-16702-X*, NERO, T/A-527) Natl Ctr St Courts.
— Wyoming District Court Criminal Benchbook. 208p. 1976. 12.48 (*0-685-15073-9*, MAB-142) Natl Ctr St Courts.
— York County (ME) Juvenile Intake Service Evaluation. 74p. 1975. 4.44 (*0-685-15052-6*, NERO-044) Natl Ctr St Courts.

National Center for State Courts Staff & Conti, Samuel. Description & Analysis of the Passaic County (NJ) Speedy Trial Demonstration Project. 85p. 1980. 5.10 (*0-685-37387-8*, NERO-064) Natl Ctr St Courts.

National Center for State Courts Staff & Edelman, Daniel B. Equal Employment Opportunity in the Judicial Branch: An Outline of Policy & Law. 28p. (Orig.). 1981. pap. write for info. (*0-89656-054-6*, R-060) Natl Ctr St Courts.

National Center for State Courts Staff & National Court Statistics Project Staff. State Court Caseload Statistics: Annual Report 1976. 440p. 1980. pap. 3.00 (*0-89656-044-9*, R-052) Natl Ctr St Courts.

National Center for State Courts Staff, et al. Implementing Delay Reduction & Delay Prevention Programs in Urban Trial Courts: Preliminary Findings from Current Research. 35p. 1985. Manuscript. write for info. (*0-318-61244-5*, R-095) Natl Ctr St Courts.

National Center for State Courts, State Judicial Information Systems Project Staff. Automated Information Systems: Implementation Guidelines. 46p. 1983. pap. write for info. (*0-89656-067-8*, R-077) Natl Ctr St Courts.

National Center for State Courts, State Court Planning Capabilities Project Staff. Judicial Planning Bibliography. 64p. 1979. 3.84 (*0-685-43381-1*, DC-002) Natl Ctr St Courts.

National Center for State Courts Task Force on Principles for Assessing Judicial Resources Staff. Assessing the Need for Judicial Resources: Guidelines for a New Process; Preliminary Draft. Aikman, Alexander B. & Flango, Victor E., eds. 67p. 1983. pap. write for info. (*0-89656-069-4*, R-081) Natl Ctr St Courts.

National Center on Women & Family Law Staff. Battered Women: The Facts. 42p. (Orig.). 1990. pap. text ed. 20.00 (*0-929396-02-2*) Natl Ctr Women & Family Law Inc.
— Mediation - a Guide for Advocates & Attorneys Representing Battered Women. 106p. 1990. 40.00 (*0-929396-04-9*) Natl Ctr Women & Family Law Inc.
— Supplement to Interstate Child Custody Disputes, 1990: Practice, Policy & Law. 550p. (Orig.). 1990. pap. text ed. 50.00 (*0-929396-03-0*) Natl Ctr Women & Family Law Inc.

National Centre for Australian Studies Staff. Who's Who of Australian Children's Writers. 180p. 1992. pap. 35.00 (*0-909532-99-0*) D W Thorpe.

***National Centre for Australian Studies Staff, comp. Monash Biographical Dictionary of 20th Century Australia. 592p. 1994. 85.00 (*1-875589-19-8*) D W Thorpe.**
Over 2,000 men & women who have made their mark on modern-day Australia are described in a lively new dictionary co-produced by D. W. Thorpe & Monash University. Reflecting the private personalities of household names & headliners alike, capsule biographies range in length from 100 to 500 words & generally provide a brief bibliography for further research. From Dame Nellie Melba to Kylie Minogue, the selection covers all aspects of Australian endeavor & every level of society. Indeed, over one quarter of the entries are women & one third are still alive. Extensive cross-referencing links related figures. *Publisher Provided Annotation.*

— Who's Who of Australian Writers. 2nd ed. 700p. 1995. 80.00 (*1-875589-20-1*) D W Thorpe.

National Child Labor Committee. Proceedings of the National Child Labor Committee, 1905, Vol. 1. Bremner, Robert H., ed. LC 74-1699. (Children & Youth Ser.). 1974. 36.95 (*0-405-05976-0*) Ayer.

National Children's Bureau Staff & Pilling, Doria. Escape from Disadvantage. 250p. 1990. 60.00 (*1-85000-678-4*, Falmer Pr); pap. 29.00 (*1-85000-679-2*, Falmer Pr) Taylor & Francis.

National Civic League Staff. Handbook for Council Members. 5th ed. LC 76-9624. 40p. 1992. 10.00 (*0-916450-51-1*) Nat Civic League.
— Healthy Communities Directory. 1994. write for info. (*0-916450-50-3*) Nat Civic League.
— Healthy Communities Resource Guide. 1994. write for info. (*0-916450-49-X*) Nat Civic League.

National Clearinghouse for Professions in Special Education Staff. Introducing Students to Careers in Special Education & Related Services. (Professional Action Ser.). 25p. 1992. 5.00 (*0-86586-230-3*, R638) Coun Exc Child.
— Promoting Special Education Career Awareness. (Professional Action Ser.). 57p. 1992. 10.00 (*0-86586-229-X*, R639) Coun Exc Child.

National Clearinghouse for Professions in Special Education Staff, jt. auth. see Cook, Lynne.

National Clearinghouse on Licensure, Enforcement, & Regulation Staff & Council of State Governments Staff. Antitrust, Competition Policy & State Professional Regulation: A Manual for Regulators. Zeitlin, Kim, ed. LC 85-622991. 48p. 1985. 15.00 (*0-87292-059-3*, C-32) Coun State Govts.

National Cloak & Suit Co. Staff. Women's Fashions of the Early 1900s: An Unabridged Republication of "New York Fashions, 1909" unabridged ed. LC 92-21805. (Illus.). 128p. 1992. reprint ed. pap. text ed. 10.95 (*0-486-27276-1*) Dover.

National Coalition for Haitian Refugees, jt. auth. see Americas Watch Committee (U. S.).

National Coalition for Haitian Refugees, jt. auth. see Americas Watch Staff.

National Coalition for Music Education Staff, ed. Building Support for School Music: A Practical Guide. 64p. (Orig.). (C). 1991. 8.00 (*0-940796-97-X*, 1004) Music Ed Natl.

National Coalition for the Homeless Staff & Harris, Dana. Homelessness in America. Stickney, Arthur H., ed. (Illus.). 256p. 1996. 69.95 (*0-89774-869-7*, 2123) Oryx Pr.

National Coalition of Advocates for Students Staff. Criteria for Evaluating an AIDS Curriculum. rev. ed. 23p. 1992. reprint ed. pap. 4.00 (*1-880002-02-7*) Natl Coal Advocates.

National College of Chiropractic Staff. Manual of Chiropractic Diagnosis & Therapeutics. 500p. 1993. pap. 39.95 (*0-8016-6468-3*) Mosby Yr Bk.

National College of Juvenile and Family Law Staff. Glossary of Selected Legal Terms for Juvenile Justice Personnel. 10p. 1978. 3.00 (*0-318-36218-X*) Natl Juv & Family Ct Judges.

National Collegiate Athletic Association Staff. NCAA Basketball's Finest: All-Time Great Collegiate Players & Coaches. (Illus.). 200p. 1991. text ed. 13.95 (*0-685-48840-3*); pap. 7.95 (*0-9624436-9-7*) Triumph Bks.
— NCAA Final Four Record & Fact Book: 1994 Edition. (Illus.). 200p. 1993. pap. 8.95 (*1-880141-45-0*) Triumph Bks.
— NCAA Final Four Record & Fact Book - (1939-1991) (Illus.). 200p. 1991. text ed. 21.95 (*1-880141-02-7*); pap. 7.95 (*0-9624436-7-0*) Triumph Bks.
— 1994 Official NCAA Football Record & Fact Book. rev. ed. (Illus.). 1994. pap. 14.95 (*1-880141-75-2*) Triumph Bks.
— Official NCAA Basketball Record & Fact Book, 1994. (Illus.). 700p. 1993. pap. 13.95 (*1-880141-46-9*) Triumph Bks.
— Official NCAA Final Four Records Book 1996. rev. ed. (Illus.). 192p. 1995. pap. 13.95 (*1-57243-034-6*) Triumph Bks.
— Official NCAA Football Record & Fact Book, 1991. (Illus.). 500p. 1991. text ed. 29.95 (*1-880141-01-9*); pap. 10.95 (*0-9624436-6-2*) Triumph Bks.
— Official NCAA Football Record & Fact Book, 1993. (Illus.). 564p. 1993. pap. 13.95 (*1-880141-44-2*) Triumph Bks.
— Official NCAA Football Record Book 1995. rev. ed. (Illus.). 500p. 1995. pap. 16.95 (*1-57243-032-X*) Triumph Bks.
— Official Rules of Basketball 1996. (Official Rules Ser.). (Illus.). 181p. 1995. pap. 8.95 (*1-57243-049-4*) Triumph Bks.
— Official 1995 NCAA Basketball Record & Fact Book. rev. ed. (Illus.). 500p. 1994. pap. 14.95 (*1-880141-76-0*) Triumph Bks.
— Official 1995 NCAA Final Four Records Book. rev. ed. (Illus.). 200p. 1994. pap. 9.95 (*1-880141-77-9*) Triumph Bks.

***National Collegiate Athletics Association Staff.** Official NCAA Basketball Records Book 1996. (Illus.). 624p. 1995. pap. 16.95 (*1-57243-033-8*) Triumph Bks.

***National Comm. on Correctional Health Care Staff & Anno, B. Jay.** Prison Health Care: Guidelines for the Management of an Adequate Delivery System, 1992. 350p. 1991. 55.00 (*0-929561-04-X*) NCCHC.

National Commission of Family Foster Care Staff, comp. A Blueprint for Fostering Infants, Children, & Youth in the 1990s. 155p. 1991. pap. 14.95 (*0-87868-441-7*) Child Welfare.

National Commission on Allied Health Education Staff. The Future of Allied Health Education. LC 79-9666. (Jossey-Bass Series in Higher Education). 314p. reprint ed. pap. 89.50 (*0-8357-4955-X*, 2037887) Bks Demand.

National Commission on Community Health Services. Health Is a Community Affair: Report. LC 66-27415. 266p. 1966. pap. 12.95 (*0-674-38451-2*) HUP.

National Commission on Crime & Justice Staff. A Call to Action: An Analysis & Overview of the United States Criminal Justice System, with Recommendations. Thurston, Linda M., ed. LC 91-68516. 102p. (Orig.). 1993. pap. 8.00 (*0-88378-067-4*) Third World.

National Commission on Excellence in Education. Meeting the Challenge of a Nation at Risk. LC 84-50559. (Illus.). 128p. (Orig.). 1984. pap. 9.95 (*0-917191-04-8*) USA Res.
— A Nation at Risk: The Full Account. 2nd ed. USA Research, Inc. Staff, ed. (Illus.). 128p. (Orig.). (C). 1994. pap. 12.95 (*0-917191-02-1*) USA Res.

National Commission on Law Observance & Enforcement Staff. Report on the Police, No. 14, June 26, 1931. LC 77-154578. (Police in America Ser.). 1971. reprint ed. 13.95 (*0-405-03376-1*) Ayer.

National Commission on Resources for Youth. You're the Tutor. 66p. 1970. pap. 2.00 (*0-912041-03-X*) Natl Comm Res Youth.

National Commission on Secondary Vocational Education Staff. The Unfinished Agenda. 35p. 1985. 4.75 (*0-318-22226-4*, IN289) Ctr Educ Trng Employ.

National Commission on the Environment Staff. Choosing a Sustainable Future: The Report of the National Commission on the Environment. LC 92-35267. (Illus.). 190p. (C). 1992. 25.00 (*1-55963-231-3*); pap. 15.00 (*1-55963-232-1*) Island Pr.

National Commission on the Insanity Defense, (U. S.) & National Mental Health Association (U. S.) Staff. Myths & Realities: A Report of the National Commission on the Insanity Defense. LC 83-60609. (Illus.). 50p. 1983. 3.95 (*0-317-00680-0*, PE0902SH) Natl Mental Health.
— Myths & Realities: Hearing Transcript of the National Commission on the Insanity Defense. LC 83-60608. 214p. 1983. 9.95 (*0-317-00681-9*, PE0903SH) Natl Mental Health.

National Committee Against Discrimination in Housing. Fair Housing & Exclusionary Land Use: Historical Overview, A Summary of Litigation & a Comment with Research Bibliography. LC 74-13552. (Urban Land Institute Research Report Ser.: No. 23). 80p. reprint ed. pap. 25.00 (*0-317-26005-7*, 2023884) Bks Demand.

National Committee for Citizens in Education. Beyond the Bake Sale: An Educator's Guide to Working with Parents & Citizens. 160p. 1986. 10.95 (*0-934460-22-1*) NCCE.
— One School at a Time: School Based Management- A Process for Change. 96p. 1985. pap. 10.95 (*0-934460-23-X*) NCCE.

National Committee for Clinical Laboratory Standards. Activated Partial Thromboplastin Time Test (APTT) Proposed Guideline, Vol. 2. 1982. 40.00 (*1-56238-056-7*, H29-P) Natl Comm Clin Lab Stds.
— Additives to Blood Collection Devices - Herapin: Tentative Standard, Vol. 8. rev. ed. 1988. 40.00 (*1-56238-053-2*, H24-T) Natl Comm Clin Lab Stds.
— Antifungal Susceptibility Testing: Committee Report, Vol. 5. 1985. 40.00 (*1-56238-083-4*, M20-CR) Natl Comm Clin Lab Stds.
— Assessing the Quality of Radioimmunoassay Systems: Approved Guideline, Vol. 5. 1985. 40.00 (*1-56238-073-7*, LA1-A) Natl Comm Clin Lab Stds.
— Blood Collection on Filter Paper for Neonatal Screening Programs: Approved Standard, Vol. 9. 1988. 40.00 (*1-56238-074-5*, LA4-A) Natl Comm Clin Lab Stds.
— Blood Gas Preanalytical Considerations: Specimen Collection, Calibration, & Controls - Tentative Guideline, Vol. 9. 1989. 40.00 (*1-56238-015-X*, C27-T) Natl Comm Clin Lab Stds.

N

An Asterisk (*) at the beginning of an entry indicates that the title is appearing in BIP for the first time.

— Citrate Agar Electrophoresis for Confirming Identifications of Variant Hemoglobins: Tentative Guideline, Vol. 8. 1988. 40.00 (*1-56238-052-4*, H23-T) Natl Comm Clin Lab Stds.

— Clinical Laboratory Procedure Manuals: Approved Guideline, Vol. 4. 1984. 40.00 (*1-56238-023-0*, GP2-A) Natl Comm Clin Lab Stds.

— Collection & Transportation of Single-Collection Urine Specimens: Proposed Guideline, Vol. 5. 1985. 40.00 (*1-56238-027-3*, GP8-P) Natl Comm Clin Lab Stds.

— Development of Definitive Methods for the National Reference System for the Clinical Laboratory, Vol. 2. (Approved Guideline Ser.: Vol. 2). 1991. 40.00 (*1-56238-104-0*, NRSCL1-A) Natl Comm Clin Lab Stds.

— Development of Reference Methods for the National Reference System for the Clinical Laboratory, Vol. 4. (Approved Guideline Ser.: Vol. 4). 1984. 40.00 (*1-56238-105-9*, NRSCL2-A) Natl Comm Clin Lab Stds.

— Enzyme & Fluorescence Immunoassays: Tentative Guideline, Vol. 6. 1986. 40.00 (*1-56238-067-2*, D14-T) Natl Comm Clin Lab Stds.

— Evaluation & Performance Criteria for Multiple Component Test Products Intended for the Detection & Quantitation of Rubella Antibody, Vol. 5. 1985. 40.00 (*1-56238-069-9*, I/LA6-P) Natl Comm Clin Lab Stds.

— Glossary & Guidelines for Immunodiagnostic Procedures, Reagents, & Reference Materials: Approved Guideline, Vol. 6. 1986. 40.00 (*1-56238-064-8*, D11-A) Natl Comm Clin Lab Stds.

— Histochemical Method for Leukocyte Alkaline Phosphatase: Proposed Standard, Vol. 4. 1984. 40.00 (*1-56238-051-6*, H22-P) Natl Comm Clin Lab Stds.

— Immunoprecipitin Assays: Procedures for Evaluating the Performance of Materials, Vol. 6. (Approved Guideline Ser.: Vol. 6). 1986. 40.00 (*1-56238-065-6*, DI2-A) Natl Comm Clin Lab Stds.

— Inventory Control Systems for Laboratory Supplies: Proposed Guidelines, Vol. 3. 1983. 40.00 (*1-56238-026-5*, GP6-P) Natl Comm Clin Lab Stds.

— Leukocyte Differential Counting: Tentative Standard, Vol. 4. 1991. 40.00 (*1-56238-131-8*, H20-A) Natl Comm Clin Lab Stds.

— Method for Reticulocyte Counting: Proposed Standard, Vol. 5. 1985. 40.00 (*1-56238-046-X*, H16-P) Natl Comm Clin Lab Stds.

— Methods for Dilution Antimicrobial Susceptibility Tests for Bacteria That Grow Aerobically, Vol. 10: Approved Standard, Vol. 8. 2nd ed. 1990. 40.00 (*1-56238-080-X*, M7-A2) Natl Comm Clin Lab Stds.

— Nomenclature & Definitions for Use in the National Reference System for the Clinical Laboratory: Proposed Guideline, Vol. 5. 1985. 40.00 (*1-56238-093-1*, NRSCL8-P) Natl Comm Clin Lab Stds.

— One-Stage Prothrombin Time Test (PT) Proposed Guideline, Vol. 2. 1982. 40.00 (*1-56238-055-9*, H28-P) Natl Comm Clin Lab Stds.

— Percutaneous Collection of Arterial Blood for Laboratory Analysis: Approved Standard, Vol. 5. 1991. 40.00 (*1-56238-130-X*, H11-A2) Natl Comm Clin Lab Stds.

— Performance Characteristics for Devices Measuring PO2 & PCO2 in Blood Samples: Tentative Standard, Vol. 9. 1991. 40.00 (*1-56238-135-0*, C21-A) Natl Comm Clin Lab Stds.

— Performance Standards for Antimicrobial Disk Susceptibility Tests, Vol. 10: Approved Standard, Vol. 8. 4th ed. 1990. 40.00 (*1-56238-078-8*, M2-A4) Natl Comm Clin Lab Stds.

— Preparation of a Rubella IgM Antibody Reference Material: Proposed Guideline, Vol. 5. 1985. 40.00 (*1-56238-071-0*, I/LA8-P) Natl Comm Clin Lab Stds.

— Procedure for the Determination of Fibrinogen in Biological Samples: Proposed Guideline, Vol. 2. 1991. 40.00 (*1-56238-124-5*, H30-T) Natl Comm Clin Lab Stds.

— Procedures for the Handling & Processing of Blood Specimens: Tentative Standard, Vol. 4. 1984. 40.00 (*1-56238-110-5*, H18-A) Natl Comm Clin Lab Stds.

— Quantitative Measurement of Fetal Hemoglobin by the Alkali Denaturation Method, Vol. 10: Approved Guideline, Vol. 6. 1989. 40.00 (*1-56238-043-5*, H13-A) Natl Comm Clin Lab Stds.

— Reference Agar Dilution Procedure for Antimicrobic Susceptibility Testing of Anaerobic Bacteria: Tentative Standard, Vol. 9. 1990. 40.00 (*1-56238-099-0*, M11-A2) Natl Comm Clin Lab Stds.

— Reference Procedure for the Human Erythrocyte Sedimentation Rate (E.S.R.) Test: Approved Standard. 2nd ed. 1988. 40.00 (*1-56238-034-6*, H2-A2) Natl Comm Clin Lab Stds.

— Reference Procedure for the Quantitative Determination of Hemoglobin in Blood: Approved Standard, Vol. 4. 1984. 40.00 (*1-56238-045-1*, H15-A) Natl Comm Clin Lab Stds.

— Romanowsky Blood Stains: Proposed Standard, Vol. 6. 1986. 40.00 (*1-56238-059-1*, H32-P) Natl Comm Clin Lab Stds.

— Specimen Handling & Use of Rubella Serology Tests in the Clinical Laboratory: Proposed Guideline, Vol. 4. 1984. 40.00 (*1-56238-070-2*, I/LA7-P) Natl Comm Clin Lab Stds.

— Temperature Monitoring & Recording in Blood Bank: Tentative Guideline, Vol. 7. 1987. 40.00 (*1-56238-077-X*, I16-T) Natl Comm Clin Lab Stds.

— Use of Devices for Collection of Skin Puncture Blood Specimens: Approved Guideline, Vol. 5. 1985. 40.00 (*1-56238-109-1*, H14-A2) Natl Comm Clin Lab Stds.

— User Comparison of Quantitative Clinical Laboratory Methods Using Patient Samples: Proposed Guideline, Vol. 5. 1985. 40.00 (*1-56238-021-4*, EP9-P) Natl Comm Clin Lab Stds.

— User Evaluation of Precision Performance of Clinical Chemistry Devices: Tentative Guideline, Vol. 4. 1984. 40.00 (*1-56238-145-8*, EP5-T2) Natl Comm Clin Lab Stds.

National Committee for Clinical Laboratory Standards Staff. Agglutination Analyses: Characteristics of Antibody, Methodology, Limitations, & Clinical Validation, Vol. 6. (Tentative Guideline Ser.: Vol. 6). 1986. 40.00 (*1-56238-066-4*, DI3-T) Natl Comm Clin Lab Stds.

— Definitions of Quantities & Conventions Related to Blood pH & Gas Analysis. 2nd ed. (Tentative Standard Ser.: Vol. 2). 1991. 40.00 (*1-56238-138-5*, C12-T2) Natl Comm Clin Lab Stds.

— Development of Certified Reference Materials for the National Reference System for the Clinical Laboratory, Vol. 4. (Approved Guideline Ser.: Vol. 4). 1991. 40.00 (*1-56238-106-7*, NRSCL3-A) Natl Comm Clin Lab Stds.

— Evacuated Tubes for Blood Specimen Collection. 3rd ed. (Approved Standard Ser.). 1991. 40.00 (*1-56238-107-5*, H1-A2) Natl Comm Clin Lab Stds.

— Internal Quality Control Testing: Principles & Definitions, Vol. 7. (Approved Guideline Ser.: Vol. 7). 1991. 40.00 (*1-56238-112-1*, C24-A) Natl Comm Clin Lab Stds.

— Preparation & Testing of Reagent Water in the Clinical Laboratory. 3rd ed. (Tentative Guideline Ser.: Vol. 8). 1991. 40.00 (*1-56238-127-X*, C3-A2) Natl Comm Clin Lab Stds.

National Committee for Injury Prevention & Control Staff. Injury Prevention: Meeting the Challenge. (Illus.). 320p. 1989. 24.95 (*0-19-506248-5*) OUP.

National Committee for Mental Health. State Hospitals in the Depression. Grob, Gerald N., ed. LC 78-22579. (Historical Issues in Mental Health Ser.). 1980. reprint ed. lib. bdg. 17.95 (*0-405-11931-3*) Ayer.

National Committee of Japanese Historians Staff, ed. Historical Studies in Japan (Seven) 1983-1987. 358p. 1991. pap. 63.00 (*90-04-09292-7*) E J Brill.

National Committee on Pay Equity. The Wage Gap: Women Have Made Slow, Steady Progress in the Labor Market since 1979 but the Wage Gap Has Not Narrowed Significantly. (Briefing Papers: No. 1). 7p. 1989. pap. 4.00 (*0-685-29940-6*) Inst Womens Policy Rsch.

National Committee on Pay Equity & Institute for Women's Policy Research Staff. OPM Comparable Worth - Pay Equity Study Overstates Women's Progress in Federal Workforce. 10p. 1987. pap. 5.00 (*0-685-29950-3*) Inst Womens Policy Rsch.

National Committee on Uniform Traffic Laws & Ordinances Staff. Uniform Vehicle Code & Model Traffic Ordinance 1992. (Orig.). 1992. pap. 22.00 (*0-317-05952-1*) Natl Comm Traffic.

National Committee to Save America's Cultural Collections Staff. Caring for Your Collections: Preserving & Protecting Your Art & Other Collectibles. (Illus.). 208p. 1992. 39.95 (*0-8109-3174-5*) Abrams.

***National Communications Forum Staff.** Proceedings of the National Communications Forum, Vol. 44, 1990. fac. ed. LC 86-642827. (Illus.). 1058p. 1990. reprint ed. pap. 180.00 (*0-7837-7723-X*, 2029173) Bks Demand.

— Proceedings of the National Communications Forum, Vol. 45, 1991. fac. ed. LC 86-642827. (Illus.). 783p. 1991. reprint ed. pap. 180.00 (*0-7837-7724-8*, 2029173) Bks Demand.

— Proceedings of the National Communications Forum, Vol. 38: 1984. LC 45-8478. reprint ed. pap. 160.00 (*0-317-55371-2*, 2029173) Bks Demand.

National Community Education Association Staff. So You're on the Council. Boo, Mary R., ed. (Illus.). 20p. 1987. student ed. 2.50 (*0-932399-02-9*) Natl Comm Ed.

National Computer Dealers Association Editors, ed. Computer Blue Book, Spring 1986. rev. ed. 350p. 1986. pap. 12.95 (*0-933325-03-7*) NACD TX.

***National Computing Centre Staff.** Handbook of Data Communications. LC 95-6719. 1995. pap. write for info. (*1-85554-637-X*) Blackwell Pubs.

National Conference & Workshop Staff. Environmental Stress Screening of Electronic Hardware: Proceedings of the 1st National Conference & Workshop, March 1979. LC 62-38584. (Orig.). 1979. pap. text ed. 65.00 (*0-915414-59-7*) Inst Environ Sci.

National Conference of Catholic Bishops. The Challenge of Peace: God's Promise & Our Response. 152p. (Orig.). 1983. pap. 3.95 (*1-55586-863-0*) US Catholic.

— Economic Justice for All: Pastoral Letter in Catholic Social Teaching & U. S. Economy. 208p. 1986. pap. 3.95 (*1-55586-101-6*) US Catholic.

— Environment & Art in Catholic Worship: Study Edition. 38p. 1993. pap. 6.00 (*0-929650-65-4*, EADOC) Liturgy Tr Pubns.

— A Pastoral Statement for Catholics on Biblical Fundamentalism English & Spanish. Herrera, Marina, tr. 20p. (Orig.). (ENG & SPA.). 1987. pap. 1.95 (*1-55586-161-X*) US Catholic.

— Shorter Christian Prayer. 670p. 1988. 7.95 (*0-89942-408-2*, 408/10) Catholic Bk Pub.

— Statement on School-Based Clinics. (Orig.). 1987. pap. 0.95 (*1-55586-196-2*) US Catholic.

National Conference of Catholic Bishops, Ad Hoc Committee on Marriage & Family Life. A Family Perspective in Church & Society: A Manual for All Pastoral Leaders. 60p. (Orig.). 1988. pap. 7.95 (*1-55586-191-1*) US Catholic.

National Conference of Catholic Bishops Ad Hoc Committee Staff. Encounters with Faith: A Handbook for Observance of the Fifth Centenary of Evangelization in the Americas. 88p. (Orig.). (C). 1991. pap. 8.95 (*1-55586-416-3*) US Catholic.

National Conference of Catholic Bishops, Committee on Marriage & Family Staff. Families at the Center: A Handbook for Parish Ministry with a Family Perspective. 52p. (Orig.). 1990. pap. 3.95 (*1-55586-337-X*) US Catholic.

National Conference of Catholic Bishops, International Commission on English in the Liturgy & Bishops' Committee on the Liturgy Secretariat Staff. Liturgy Documentary Series 5: General Instruction of the Liturgy of the Hours. 78p. (Orig.). (C). 1983. pap. 4.50 (*1-55586-898-3*) US Catholic.

National Conference of Catholic Bishops Staff. Called & Gifted: The American Catholic Laity: Reflections of the American Bishops Commemorating the Fifteenth Anniversary of the Issuance of the "Decree on the Apostolate of the Laity" 4p. 1980. pap. 0.75 (*1-55586-727-8*) US Catholic.

— Complementary Norms. 56p. (Orig.). (C). 1991. pap. 3.95 (*1-55586-433-3*) US Catholic.

— Heritage & Hope: Evangelization in the United States. Herrera, Marina, tr. 108p. (Orig.). (ENG & SPA.). (C). 1990. pap. 5.95 (*1-55586-386-8*) US Catholic.

— Justicia Economica para Todos: Economic Justice for All. 208p. (Orig.). (SPA.). 1987. pap. 3.95 (*1-55586-146-6*) US Catholic.

— Norms for Priests & Their Third Age. 6p. (Orig.). 1988. pap. 0.50 (*1-55586-207-1*) US Catholic.

— Pastoral Letters of the United States Catholic Bishops, 1983-1988, Vol. V. 797p. 1989. 39.95 (*1-55586-200-4*) US Catholic.

— Rite of Christian Initiation of Adults. International Commission on English in the Liturgy Staff, ed. 404p. 1988. 17.95 (*0-89942-355-8*, 355-22); pap. 7.95 (*0-89942-358-2*, 358-04) Catholic Bk Pub.

— To the Ends of the Earth: A Pastoral Statement on World Mission 1987. 32p. (Orig.). 1987. pap. 3.95 (*1-55586-112-1*) US Catholic.

— Together, a New People: Pastoral Statement on Migrants & Refugees. 32p. (Orig.). 1987. pap. 3.95 (*1-55586-147-4*) US Catholic.

— Toward Peace in the Middle East: Perspectives, Principles, & Hope. 52p. (Orig.). 1989. pap. 2.95 (*1-55586-325-6*) US Catholic.

— United in Service: Reflections on the Presbyteral Council. 20p. (Orig.). (C). 1992. pap. 1.95 (*1-55586-482-1*) US Catholic.

National Conference of Catholic Bishops Staff & NCCB Ad Hoc Committee on the Moral Evaluation of Deterrence Staff. Building Peace: A Pastoral Reflection on the Response to the Challenge of Peace & a Report on The Challenge of Peace & Policy Developments, 1983-1988. 96p. (Orig.). 1988. pap. 3.95 (*1-55586-229-2*) US Catholic.

National Conference of Catholic Bishops Staff & United States Catholic Conference. Prayers for the Beginning of Life. 16p. (Orig.). 1989. pap. 1.95 (*1-55586-297-7*) US Catholic.

— Prayers of the Advent & Christmas Seasons. 45p. (Orig.). 1989. pap. 2.50 (*1-55586-300-0*) US Catholic.

— Prayers of the Lenten & Easter Seasons. 63p. (Orig.). 1989. pap. 2.75 (*1-55586-301-9*) US Catholic.

— A Treasury of Catholic Prayer. 80p. (Orig.). 1989. pap. 3.95 (*1-55586-296-9*) US Catholic.

National Conference of Catholic Bishops Staff & United States Catholic Conference Staff. Catholic Household Blessings & Prayers. 444p. (Orig.). 1989. pap. 8.95 (*1-55586-292-6*) US Catholic.

National Conference of Catholic Bishops Staff, jt. auth. see Bishops' Committee for Pastoral Research Staff.

National Conference of Catholic Bishops Staff, jt. auth. see Bishops' Committee on Priestly Life.

National Conference of Catholic Bishops Staff, ed. see Bishops' Committee on the Laity Staff.

National Conference of Catholic Bishops Staff, jt. auth. see Bishops' Committee on the Liturgy Staff.

National Conference of Catholic Bishops Staff, jt. auth. see Bishops' Committee on Vocations Staff.

National Conference of Catholic Bishops Staff, jt. auth. see Secretarist for Black Catholics Staff.

National Conference of Charities & Correction Staff. History of Child Saving in the United States. LC 70-108228. (Criminology, Law Enforcement, & Social Problems Ser.: No. 111). 1971. reprint ed. 28.00 (*0-87585-111-8*) Patterson Smith.

National Conference of CUSL Staff. National Conference of Commissioners on Uniform State Laws Handbooks, 10 vols., Set, 1980-1989. LC 06-25307. 1982. lib. bdg. 325.00 (*0-89941-317-X*, 302830) W S Hein.

National Conference of Social Work Staff. Social Work in the Current Scene, Nineteen Fifty: Selected Papers of the National Conference of Social Work, 77th. LC 72-3382. (Essay Index Reprint Ser.). 1977. reprint ed. 25.95 (*0-8369-2915-2*) Ayer.

***National Conference of State Legislatures Staff.** How Laws Are Made. Lang, Natalie & Martina, Krissie, eds. (Illus.). 160p. 1996. pap. 19.95 (*0-89774-944-8*, 2208) Oryx Pr.

— Issues Outlook, 1993: A Survey of State Legislative Priorities. 44p. 1992. pap. text ed. 30.00 (*1-55516-990-2*, 9350) Natl Conf State Legis.

National Conference of State Trial Judges. Standards Relating to Court Delay Reduction. LC 85-62250. 22p. 1985. pap. write for info. (*0-89707-181-6*, 484-0002-01) Amer Bar Assn.

National Conference of State Trial Judges Judical Benchbook Committee. Benchbook Planning Manual: With Civil & Criminal Law Model Outlines. LC 84-72182. 82p. 1985. pap. 10.00 (*0-89707-153-0*, 484-0003) Amer Bar Assn.

National Conference on Bail & Criminal Justice Staff. Proceedings & Interim Report of the National Conference on Bail & Criminal Justice, May 27-29, 1964 & May 1964-April 1965. Fogelson, Robert M., ed. LC 74-3839. (Criminal Justice in America Ser.). 1974. reprint ed. 33.95 (*0-405-06156-0*) Ayer.

National Conference on Motion Pictures Staff & Motion Picture Producers & Distributors of America Staff. The Community & the Motion Picture: Report of the National Conference on Motion Pictures, New York, 1929. LC 77-160242. (Moving Pictures Ser.). 96p. 1971. reprint ed. lib. bdg. 17.95 (*0-89198-043-1*) Ozer.

National Conference on Quality Beer & Brewing Staff, jt. auth. see American Homebrewers Association Staff.

National Conference on Rational Psychotherapy Staff. Twenty Years of Rational Therapy: Proceedings of the National Conference on Rational Psychotherapy, 1st. Wolfe, Janet & Brand, Eileen, eds. LC 76-57312. 1977. pap. 1.00 (*0-917476-08-5*) Inst Rational-Emotive.

National Conference on Social Welfare Staff. Social Work Practice: Proceedings. Incl. Ninety-Eighth Annual Meeting. LC 05-85377. 1971. text ed. 35.00 (*0-231-03588-8*); LC 05-85377. write for info. (*0-318-51415-X*) Col U Pr.

National Conference on Technology & Education Staff. Technology & Education: Policy, Implementation, Evaluation-Proceedings of the National Conference on Technology & Education, January 26-28, 1981. 340p. 1981. lib. bdg. 20.00 (*0-318-03015-2*) Inst Educ Lead.

National Conference on the Diabetic Foot Staff. The Foot in Diabetes: Proceedings of the First National Conference on the Diabetic Foot, Malvern, May 1986. Connor, H. et al, eds. LC 86-32514. (Wiley-Medical Publication Ser.). 182p. reprint ed. pap. 51.90 (*0-8357-6982-8*, 2052359) Bks Demand.

National Conference on the Future of Social Work Research Staff. Future of Social Work Research: Selected Papers - National Conference, October 15-18, 1978, San Antonio, TX. Fanshel, David, ed. LC 79-92733. 208p. reprint ed. pap. 59.30 (*0-7837-6534-7*, 2045670) Bks Demand.

National Conference on the Psychological Aspects of Disability Staff. Rehabilitation Psychology: Proceedings. Neff, Walter S., ed. LC 75-183150. 337p. reprint ed. pap. 96.10 (*0-7837-0492-5*, 2040816) Bks Demand.

National Conference on Thermal Spray, Second, Long Beach, CA Staff. Second National Conference on Thermal Spray: 31 October-2 November, 1984, Hyatt Regency Long Beach, Long Beach, California. LC 85-71832. (Illus.). 152p. pap. 43.40 (*0-7837-1864-0*, 2042065) Bks Demand.

National Congress on Pressure Vessels & Piping Staff. Dynamics of Fluid-Structure Systems in the Energy Industry: Presented at the Third National Congress on Pressure Vessel & Piping, San Francisco, California, June 25-29, 1979. Au-Yang, M. K. & Brown, S. J., eds. LC 79-51763. (PVP Ser.: No. 39). 234p. reprint ed. pap. 66.70 (*0-8357-6997-6*, 2039050) Bks Demand.

— Flow Induced Vibrations: Presented at the Third National Congress on Pressure Vessel & Piping Technology, San Francisco, CA, June 25-29, 1979. Chen, Shoei-Sheng & Bernstein, Martin D., eds. LC 79-50128. 158p. reprint ed. pap. 45.10 (*0-317-08572-7*, 2021116) Bks Demand.

— Lifeline Earthquake Engineering - Buried Pipelines, Seismic Risk, & Instrumentation: Presented at the Third National Congress on Pressure Vessels & Piping, San Francisco, California, June 25-29, 1979. Ariman, Teoman et al, eds. LC 79-50126. (PVP Ser.: No. 34). (Illus.). 291p. reprint ed. pap. 83.00 (*0-8357-2870-6*, 2039106) Bks Demand.

— Pressure Vessels & Piping: Verification & Qualification of Inelastic Analysis Computer Programs, Proceedings of the National Congress on Pressure Vessels & Piping, 2nd, San Francisco, 1975. Corum, J. M. & Wright, W. B., eds. LC 75-8090. (Illus.). 117p. reprint ed. pap. 33.40 (*0-317-08401-1*, 2016813) Bks Demand.

— Safety Relief Valves: Prepared at the Third National Congress on Pressure Vessels & Piping, San Francisco, CA, June 24-29, 1979. Haupt, R. W. & Meyer, R. A., eds. LC 79-50127. (PVP Ser.: No. 33). (Illus.). 200p. reprint ed. pap. 57.00 (*0-8357-3523-0*, 2056813) Bks Demand.

***National Consortium for Environmental Education & Training Staff.** EE Toolbox Slide Resource Kit. 20p. 1994. 49.95 (*0-614-00509-4*) Natl Consort EET.

— Getting Started: A Guide to Bringing Environmental Education into Your Classroom. 140p. 1994. 9.95 (*1-884782-00-0*) Natl Consort EET.

***National Consortium for Physical Education & Recreation for Individuals with Disabilities Staff.** Adapted Physical Education National Standards. Kelly, Luke E., ed. LC 95-3492. 224p. (Orig.). 1995. pap. text ed. write for info. (*0-87322-962-2*, BNCP0962) Human Kinetics.

National Consumer Law Center, Inc. Staff. Credit Discrimination. LC 93-86621. (Consumer Credit & Sales Legal Practice Ser.) 360p. 1993. pap. 60.00 (*1-881793-10-9*) Nat Consumer Law.

— Fair Credit Reporting Act. 3rd ed. LC 94-69832. (Consumer Credit & Sales Legal Practice Ser.). 594p. 1994. pap. 70.00 (*1-881793-26-5*) Nat Consumer Law.

— Odometer Law. 3rd ed. LC 92-64461. (Consumer Credit & Sales Legal Practice Ser.). 304p. 1992. pap. 60.00 (*1-881793-05-2*) Nat Consumer Law.

— The Regulation of Rural Electric Cooperatives. LC 93-84977. (Utility Law Practice Ser.). 208p. 1993. pap. 60.00 (*1-881793-08-7*) Nat Consumer Law.

— Repossessions. 2nd ed. LC 88-61108. (Consumer Credit & Sales Legal Practice Ser.). 334p. 1988. pap. 60.00 (*0-943116-58-9*) Nat Consumer Law.

N

— Tenants' Rights to Utility Service: 1993. LC 93-86927. (Utility Law Practice Ser.). 180p. 1994. pap. 60.00 (*1-881793-19-2*) Nat Consumer Law.

National Consumer Law Center, Inc. Staff, et al. Consumer Bankruptcy Law & Practice. 4th ed. LC 92-64462. (Consumer Credit & Sales Legal Practice Ser.). 837p. 1992. pap. 90.00 (*1-881793-06-0*) Nat Consumer Law.

National Consumer Law Center Staff. Consumer Law Training Manual & Repossession Materials. 262p. 1986. 18.50 (*0-685-23172-0*, 41,264) NCLS Inc.

— Sales of Goods & Services. 2nd ed. LC 89-63232. (Consumer Credit & Sales Legal Practice Ser.). 790p. (Orig.). 1989. pap. 70.00 (*0-943116-67-8*) Nat Consumer Law.

— Surviving Debt: Counseling Families in Financial Trouble. LC 92-81748. 272p. (Orig.). 1992. pap. 15.00 (*1-881793-07-9*) Nat Consumer Law.

— Truth in Lending. 2nd ed. LC 89-63233. (Consumer Credit & Sales Legal Practice Ser.). 798p. (Orig.). 1989. pap. 70.00 (*0-943116-66-X*) Nat Consumer Law.

— Truth in Lending Case Summaries. 3rd ed. 350p. (Orig.). 1983. pap. 15.00 (*0-941077-04-7*, 22,250) NCLS Inc.

National Contract Management Assn. Staff. Small Business Contracting. (National Contract Management Association Workshop Ser.). 50p. (Orig.). 1990. pap. 10.95 (*0-940343-58-4*) Natl Contract Mgmt.

National Contract Management Association Staff. Conducting Contract Closeout. 2nd ed. Rankin, Anne M., ed. (National Contract Management Association Workshop Ser.). 80p. 1993. pap. 10.95 (*0-940343-39-8*) Natl Contract Mgmt.

— Understanding Technical Data Rights. 2nd ed. Rankin, Anne M., ed. (National Contract Management Association Workshop Ser.). 54p. 1993. pap. 10.95 (*0-940343-38-X*) Natl Contract Mgmt.

National Council for the Social Studies Staff. An Annotated Bibliography of Historical Fiction for the Social Studies. 112p. 1992. pap. text ed. 14.95 (*0-8403-7516-6*) Kendall-Hunt.

— Curriculum Standards for Social Studies Expectations of Excellence. LC 94-68635. (NCSS Bulletin Ser.: No. 89). (Orig.). 1994. pap. 15.00 (*0-87986-065-0*) Nat Coun Soc Studies.

— Evaluation in Social Studies. Berg, Harry D., ed. LC 31-6192. (Yearbook Ser.: 35). 265p. reprint ed. pap. 75.60 (*0-317-20134-4*, 2023189) Bks Demand.

National Council for Vocational Qualifications Staff. British Qualifications. 744p. 1989. text ed. 74.95 (*0-8464-1406-6*); pap. text ed. 64.95 (*0-8464-1407-4*) Beekman Pubs.

National Council of American Soviet Friendship Staff. Science in Soviet Russia. LC 74-25151. (History, Philosophy & Sociology of Science Ser.). 1975. reprint ed. 18.95 (*0-405-06635-X*) Ayer.

National Council of Architectural Registration Boards Staff. National Council of Architectural Registration Boards Examination Handbook, 1988, 2 vols., Set. Houseman, William et al, eds. 1988. pap. 95.00 (*0-941575-06-3*) NCARB.

— NCARB 1983 Architect Registration Examination Handbook. (Illus.). 177p. 1983. pap. text ed. 36.00 (*0-9607310-1-6*) NCARB.

— NCARB 1984 Architect Registration Examination Handbook, 3 vols., Set. (Illus.). 1984. pap. text ed. 54.00 (*0-9607310-2-4*) NCARB.

National Council of Churches of Christ in the U. S. A., jt. auth. see Division of Education.

National Council of Churches of Christ in the U. S. A., Division of Education & Ministry, Inclusive Language Lectionary Committee. An Inclusive-Language Lectionary: Readings for Year A. enl. rev. ed. 292p. 1986. pap. 11.99 (*0-664-24051-8*, Westminster) Westminster John Knox.

National Council of Churches of Christ Staff. Inclusive Language Lectionary: Readings for Year A. rev. ed. LC 86-16930. 288p. 1986. pap. 12.95 (*0-8298-0746-2*) Pilgrim OH.

— An Inclusive Language Lectionary: Readings for Year B. rev. ed. LC 87-8164. 264p. 1984. pap. 12.95 (*0-8298-0782-9*) Pilgrim OH.

— An Inclusive-Language Lectionary: Readings for Year C. rev. ed. LC 88-13799. 272p. 1988. pap. 12.95 (*0-8298-0791-8*) Pilgrim OH.

— Inclusive-Language Psalms. LC 87-2244. 160p. (Orig.). 1987. pap. 10.95 (*0-8298-0747-0*) Pilgrim OH.

National Council of Instructors in Landscape Architecture Staff. Specialization in Landscape Architectural Education: Proceedings NCILA, 1975, Texas A & M, July 10-12. 98p. pap. 28.00 (*0-8357-3042-5*, 2039297) Bks Demand.

National Council of Jewish Women, Omaha Section Staff. The Kitchen Connection. Kutler, Sandy & Polikov, Sheila, eds. (Illus.). (Orig.). 1983. pap. 11.95 (*0-9612406-0-1*) Omaha Sec Nat.

National Council of Jewish Women Staff. Abortion: Challenges Ahead. (Illus.). 25p. (Orig.). 1985. pap. text ed. 5.00 (*0-941840-19-0*) NCJW.

— Adolescent Girls in the Juvenile Justice System. (Illus.). 89p. 1984. pap. text ed. 4.50 (*0-941840-18-2*) NCJW.

— Caring for Older Adults: A Handbook. 1993. 4.00 (*0-614-06653-0*) NCJW.

— Choosing Family Child Care: A Handbook for Parents. (Illus.). 21p. 1990. 3.00 (*0-685-62941-4*) NCJW.

— Como Elegir Una Casa Particular Donde Le Cuiden a Su Nino: Manual Para Padres. (Illus.). 21p. 1992. 3.00 (*0-685-62942-2*) NCJW.

— Domestic Violence Program Guide: "A Family Affair" 14p. (Orig.). 1983. pap. text ed. 3.00 (*0-941840-12-3*) NCJW.

— Employers & Family Day Care. (Illus.). 50p. 1991. 10.00 (*0-685-62940-6*) NCJW.

— An Employers Guide to Eldercare: Institute on Aging, Work, & Health. 1991. 4.00 (*0-614-06654-9*) NCJW.

— The Hard Questions in Family Day Care: National Issues & Exemplary Programs. 122p. 1991. 18.95 (*0-685-62943-0*) NCJW.

— Juvenile Waiver. (Illus.). (Orig.). 1985. pap. text ed. 3.50 (*0-941840-22-0*) NCJW.

— A Marketing Kit for Family Day Care Providers. 1990. 10.00 (*0-614-06656-5*) NCJW.

— Options for the 90's: Employer Support for Child Care. 22p. 1991. 10.00 (*0-685-62939-2*) NCJW.

— The Partnership Guide: Strategies for Supporting Family Day Care in Your Community. 49p. 1991. 15.00 (*0-685-62944-9*) NCJW.

— Self Help for Seniors. 30p. (Orig.). 1983. pap. text ed. 4.00 (*0-941840-14-X*) NCJW.

— Working with Employers & Other Community Partners. Date not set. 10.00 (*0-614-06655-7*) NCJW.

National Council of Jewish Women Staff & Leviton, Shirley I. Social Security Background Paper. 25p. (C). 1983. pap. text ed. 2.50 (*0-941840-11-5*) NCJW.

National Council of Juvenile & Family Court Judges. Judicial Review of Children in Placement Deskbook. 195p. 1981. 20.00 (*0-318-21318-4*) Natl Juv & Family Ct Judges.

National Council of Juvenile & Family Court Judges, jt. auth. see National CASA Association Staff.

National Council of Juvenile Court Judges Staff. Guides for Juvenile Court Judges. 145p. 1963. 1.50 (*0-318-15366-1*) Natl Coun Crime.

National Council of Negro Women Staff. The Black Family Reunion Cookbook: Recipes & Food Memories from the National Council of Negro Women, Inc. LC 92-41128. (Illus.). 224p. 1993. pap. 12.00 (*0-671-79629-1*, Fireside) S&S Trade.

— Celebrating Our Mothers' Kitchens: Words of Wisdom & Treasured Recipes. Wimmer, Glen, ed. (Illus.). 224p. 1994. 15.95 (*1-879958-23-6*) Tradery Hse.

National Council of Staff, Program & Organizational Development Staff. Community Colleges, the Future & SPOD (Staff, Program & Organizational Development) Brass, Richard J., ed. LC 84-61248. 162p. (Orig.). 1984. pap. 6.95 (*0-913507-01-6*) New Forums.

National Council of Teachers of English. English for Today, Bk. 5: Life in English Speaking Countries. 1967. 1.95 (*0-07-046108-2*) McGraw.

— English for Today, Book 5: Our Changing Culture. 2nd ed. (gr. 10-12). 1976. text ed. 12.72 (*0-07-045816-2*) McGraw.

National Council of Teachers of English, Comparative Literature Committee. Yearbook of Comparative & General Literature, No. 32, 1983. 160p. pap. 45.60 (*0-317-30475-5*, 2024821) Bks Demand.

— Yearbook of Comparative & General Literature, No. 31, 1982. 167p. reprint ed. pap. 47.60 (*0-317-29731-7*, 2022204) Bks Demand.

— Yearbook of Comparative & General Literature, No. 33, 1984. 128p. pap. 36.50 (*0-685-15956-6*, 2026243) Bks Demand.

National Council of Teachers of English Staff. English for Today. 2nd ed. Incl. Bk. 1. At Home & at School. 1973. text ed. 13.60 (*0-07-045802-2*); Bk. 2. World We Live In. 1973. text ed. 13.60 (*0-07-045806-5*); Bk. 3. Way We Live. 1973. text ed. 13.60 (*0-07-045810-3*); write for info. (*0-318-54193-9*) McGraw.

— Reading in an Age of Mass Communication: Report of the Committee on Reading at the Secondary School & College Levels. Gray, William S., ed. LC 70-167390. (Essay Index Reprint Ser.). 1977. reprint ed. 13.95 (*0-8369-2811-3*) Ayer.

National Council of Teachers of English Staff, jt. auth. see International Reading Association Staff.

***National Council of Teachers of Mathematics Staff.** Assessment Standards for School Mathematics. LC 95-17267. (Illus.). 102p. (Orig.). 1995. pap. write for info. (*0-87353-419-0*) NCTM.

— Cumulative Index: The Arithmetic Teacher, 1954-1973. LC 56-37587. 128p. 1974. pap. 12.00 (*0-87353-027-6*) NCTM.

— Cumulative Index: The Arithmetic Teacher, 1974-1983. 34p. (Orig.). 1984. pap. 11.50 (*0-87353-216-3*) NCTM.

— Cumulative Index: The Mathematics Teacher, 1966-1975. LC 42-24844. 96p. 1977. pap. 10.00 (*0-87353-029-2*) NCTM.

— Cumulative Index: The Mathematics Teacher, 1976-1985. 68p. (Orig.). 1988. pap. 11.50 (*0-87353-262-7*) NCTM.

— Enrichment Mathematics for High School. LC 63-14060. (National Council of Teachers of Mathematics Yearbook Ser.: 28th). 398p. reprint ed. pap. 113.50 (*0-685-15865-9*, 2027060) Bks Demand.

— Enrichment Mathematics for the Grades. LC 63-14059. (National Council of Teachers of Mathematics Yearbook Ser.: 27th). 378p. reprint ed. pap. 107.80 (*0-685-15828-4*, 2027056) Bks Demand.

— Evaluation in Mathematics. LC 61-11906. (National Council of Teachers of Mathematics Yearbook Ser.: 26th). 222p. reprint ed. pap. 63.30 (*0-685-15811-X*, 2027055) Bks Demand.

— The Growth of Mathematical Ideas, Grades K-12. LC 60-1738. (National Council of Teachers of Mathematics Yearbook Ser.: 24th). 517p. reprint ed. pap. 147.40 (*0-685-15790-3*, 2027053) Bks Demand.

— Historical Topics for the Mathematics Classroom. rev. ed. LC 89-12208. (Illus.). 542p. 1989. pap. 28.00 (*0-87353-281-3*) NCTM.

— Instruction in Arithmetic. LC 60-7488. (National Council of Teachers of Mathematics Yearbook Ser.: 25th). 372p. reprint ed. pap. 106.10 (*0-685-15802-0*, 2027054) Bks Demand.

— Instructional Aids in Mathematics. LC 76-189323. (National Council of Teachers of Mathematics Yearbook Ser.: 34th). 460p. reprint ed. pap. 131.10 (*0-685-15857-8*, 2027059) Bks Demand.

— The Learning of Mathematics: Its Theory & Practice. (National Council of Teachers of Mathematics Yearbook Ser.: 21st). 365p. reprint ed. pap. 104.10 (*0-685-15754-7*, 2027052) Bks Demand.

— Organizing Data & Dealing with Uncertainty. rev. ed. LC 79-9281. (Illus.). 135p. (J). (gr. 5-8). 1979. pap. 10.00 (*0-87353-141-8*) NCTM.

— The Teaching of Secondary School Mathematics. LC 27-7119. (National Council of Teachers of Mathematics Yearbook Ser.: 33rd). 441p. reprint ed. pap. 125.70 (*0-685-15850-0*, 2027058) Bks Demand.

National Council on Aging Staff. Myth & Reality of Aging, 1974. LC 79-84576. 1979. write for info. (*0-89138-971-7*) ICPSR.

National Council on Compensation Insurance Staff. National Council Workmen's Compensation Unit Statistical Plan Manual. (Illus.). 1983. write for info. (*0-318-58248-1*) Natl Comp Ins.

National Council on Crime & Delinquency Staff. Community Crime Prevention: An Annotated Bibliography. 1983. 4.50 (*0-318-02049-1*) Natl Coun Crime.

— Executive Summary of the National Evaluation of Delinquency Prevention: Final Report. 1980. 1.50 (*0-318-02056-4*) Natl Coun Crime.

National Council on Crime & Delinquency Staff & O'Leary, Vincent. Correctional Policy Inventory. 1970. ring bd. 4.10 (*0-318-02051-3*) Natl Coun Crime.

— Frames of Reference in Sentencing & Parole Inventory. 1977. ring bd. 4.10 (*0-318-02052-1*) Natl Coun Crime.

National Council on Governmental Accounting Staff. Governmental Accounting & Financial Reporting Principles. LC 79-87496. (NCGA Statement: No. 1). (Illus.). 49p. 1979. pap. 10.00 (*0-686-84258-8*) Municipal.

National Council on Public History. The Records of Government. LC 87-3384. 192p. 1987. reprint ed. lib. bdg. 22.50 (*0-89464-231-6*) Krieger.

National Council on Radiation Protection & Measurements Editors. Biological Effects & Exposure Criteria for Radiofrequency Electromagnetic Fields. LC 86-2451. (Report Ser.: No. 86). 400p. 1986. pap. text ed. 40.00 (*0-913392-80-4*) NCRP Pubns.

National Council on Radiation Protection & Measurements Staff. Carbon-14 in the Environment. LC 84-29586. (Report Ser.: No. 81). 65p. 1985. pap. text ed. 25.00 (*0-913392-73-1*) NCRP Pubns.

— Evaluation of Occupational & Environmental Exposures to Radon & Radon Daughters in the United States. LC 84-4756. (Report Ser.: No. 78). 204p. 1984. pap. text ed. 30.00 (*0-913392-68-5*) NCRP Pubns.

— Exposures from the Uranium Series with Emphasis on Radon & Its Daughters. LC 84-3420. (Report Ser.: No. 77). 131p. 1984. pap. text ed. 30.00 (*0-913392-67-7*) NCRP Pubns.

— General Concepts for the Dosimetry of Internally Deposited Radionuclides. LC 85-8965. (Report Ser.: No. 84). 109p. 1985. pap. text ed. 25.00 (*0-913392-77-4*) NCRP Pubns.

— Induction of Thyroid Cancer by Ionizing Radiation. LC 84-21441. (Report Ser.: No. 80). 70p. 1985. pap. text ed. 25.00 (*0-913392-72-3*) NCRP Pubns.

— Iodine-129: Evaluation of Releases from Nuclear Power Generation. LC 83-23145. (Report Ser.: No. 75). 74p. 1983. pap. text ed. 20.00 (*0-913392-65-0*) NCRP Pubns.

— Neutron Contamination from Medical Electron Accelerators. LC 84-19848. (Report Ser.: No. 79). 128p. 1984. pap. text ed. 25.00 (*0-913392-70-7*) NCRP Pubns.

— Operational Radiation Safety-Training. LC 82-62031. (Report Ser.: No. 71). 1983. 20.00 (*0-913392-60-X*) NCRP Pubns.

— Protection in Nuclear Medicine & Ultrasound Diagnostic Procedures in Children. LC 83-61834. (Report Ser.: No. 73). 81p. 1983. pap. text ed. 20.00 (*0-913392-63-4*) NCRP Pubns.

— Radiation Protection & Measurements for Low-Voltage Neutron Generators. LC 83-62802. (Report Ser.: No. 72). 80p. 1983. pap. text ed. 20.00 (*0-913392-61-8*) NCRP Pubns.

— Radiological Assessment: Predicting the Transport, Bioaccumulation, & Uptake by Man of Radionuclides Released to the Environment. LC 84-4773. (Report Ser.: No. 76). 300p. 1984. pap. text ed. 35.00 (*0-913392-66-9*) NCRP Pubns.

National Council on Radiation Protection Staff. A Handbook of Radioactivity Measurement Procedures. 2nd ed. LC 84-25423. (Report Ser.: No. 58). 600p. 1985. text ed. 50.00 (*0-913392-71-5*) NCRP Pubns.

— Mammography - A User's Guide. LC 85-32102. (Report Ser.: No. 85). 185p. (Orig.). 1986. pap. text ed. 30.00 (*0-913392-79-0*) NCRP Pubns.

National Council on the Aging, Inc. Staff. Respite Resource Guide. 40p. 1990. 8.00 (*0-910883-51-3*) Natl Coun Aging.

National Council on the Aging Staff, ed. see Alvarez, Ronald A. & Kline, Susan C.

National Council on the Aging Staff, ed. see Hettlinger, Richard F. & Worth, Grace.

National Council on the Handicapped. On the Threshold of Independence: Progress on Legislative Recommendations Toward Independence. 100p. (Orig.). 1988. write for info. (*0-936825-01-4*) Nat Coun Handicapped.

National Court Statistics Project Staff, jt. auth. see National Center for State Courts Staff.

National Crime Prevention Council Staff. Making a Difference: Young People in Community Crime Prevention. LC 85-61344. (Illus.). 150p. (Orig.). pap. 10.00 (*0-934513-00-7*) Natl Crime DC.

National Crime Prevention Institute. The Use of Locks in Physical Crime Prevention. (Illus.). 88p. 1987. pap. text ed. 21.95 (*0-409-90092-3*) Buttrwrth-Heinemann.

National Crime Prevention Institute Staff. Understanding Crime Prevention. (Illus.). 207p. (C). 1986. text ed. 30.95 (*0-409-90075-3*) Buttrwrth-Heinemann.

National Curriculum Editors. The English Book: A Perma-Bound Teach & Use Handbook for the Secondary Level. Snodgrass, Mary E., ed. (Illus.). 252p. (YA). (gr. 7 up). 1991. text ed. 14.65 (*0-7804-1950-2*, 089669) Perma-Bound.

National Curriculum Publishing Editors. Great American English Handbook. rev. ed. Snodgrass, Mary E., ed. (Illus.). 235p. (YA). (gr. 7 up). 1991. reprint ed. lib. bdg. 14.65 (*0-8000-2426-5*, 122550) Perma-Bound.

National Dairy Council Staff. Food Models: For Early Childhood Educators, Set. (Illus.). 1992. teacher ed write for info. (*1-55647-015-0*) Natl Dairy Coun.

— Food...Early Choices Program. rev. ed. (J). (ps-00). 1979. write for info. (*1-55647-491-1*) Natl Dairy Coun.

— Growth Record. (Illus.). 8p. (J). (gr. 3-4). 1988. pap. text ed. write for info. (*1-55647-003-7*) Natl Dairy Coun.

— Lifesteps: Nutrition & Your Busy Lifestyle. 1992. teacher ed write for info. (*1-55647-711-2*); student ed write for info. (*1-55647-715-5*) Natl Dairy Coun.

— Lifesteps: Weight Management. 2nd ed. 1990. teacher ed write for info. (*1-55647-882-8*); student ed write for info. (*1-55647-885-2*) Natl Dairy Coun.

— Newer Knowledge of Milk. 49p. 1988. pap. text ed. write for info. (*1-55647-300-1*) Natl Dairy Coun.

— Uncle Jim's Dairy Farm: A Summer Visit with Aunt Helen & Uncle Jim. (Illus.). 4p. (J). (gr. 3-6). 1980. Set incls. 12 user's guides & 1 tchr's. guide. write for info. (*1-55647-611-6*); vhs write for info. (*1-55647-634-5*) Natl Dairy Coun.

National Dairy Council Staff & Dairy Council of California Staff. Smart Moves. (Illus.). (YA). 1990. teacher ed write for info. (*1-55647-172-6*); student ed write for info. (*1-55647-173-4*); vhs write for info. (*1-55647-171-8*); write for info. (*1-55647-174-2*) Natl Dairy Coun.

***National Dance Association.** National Standards for Dance Education: What Every Young American Should Know & Be Able to Do in Dance. LC 94-46773. 1994. 15.00 (*0-87127-200-8*, Dance Horizons) Princeton Bk Co.

National Data & Research Staff. Investigating Medical Professionals. 98p. 1990. pap. text ed. 35.00 (*0-918487-38-2*) Thomas Pubns TX.

National Democratic Institute for International Affairs Staff. An Assessment of the elections in Cameroon October 11, 1992. 260p. (ENG & FRE.). 1993. pap. 9.95 (*1-880134-19-5*) Natl Demo Inst.

— An Assessment of the Senegalese Electoral Code. 140p. (ENG & FRE.). 1991. pap. 6.00 (*1-880134-07-1*) Natl Demo Inst.

— Coordinating Observers for Niger's 1993 Elections. 170p. (ENG & FRE.). 1993. pap. 10.95 (*1-880134-22-5*) Natl Demo Inst.

— Democracies in Regions of Crisis: Botswana, Costa Rica & Israel. LC 90-60684. 145p. 1990. pap. 7.95 (*1-880134-03-9*) Natl Demo Inst.

— An Evaluation of the Elections in Ethiopia, June 21, 1992. 160p. 1992. pap. 9.95 (*1-880134-18-7*) Natl Demo Inst.

— The June Nineteen Ninety Elections in Bulgaria. 117p. 1990. pap. 6.00 (*1-880134-00-4*) Natl Demo Inst.

— The May Nineteen Ninety Elections in Romania. 133p. 1991. pap. 6.00 (*1-880134-05-5*) Natl Demo Inst.

— The May Seventh, Nineteen Eighty-Nine Panamanian Elections. 126p. 1989. pap. 6.00 (*1-880134-01-2*) Natl Demo Inst.

— Nation Building: The U. N. & Namibia. 130p. 1990. pap. 6.95 (*1-880134-06-3*) Natl Demo Inst.

— The National Elections in Paraguay, 1993. 200p. Date not set. pap. 10.95 (*1-880134-24-1*) Natl Demo Inst.

— NDI Handbook on Election Monitoring. Date not set. pap. 9.95 (*1-880134-17-9*) Natl Demo Inst.

— The Nineteen Eighty-Nine Paraguayan Elections: A Foundation for Democratic Change. 68p. 1989. pap. 6.00 (*1-880134-02-0*) Natl Demo Inst.

— The Nineteen Ninety General Elections in Guatemala. 114p. 1991. pap. 10.95 (*1-880134-11-X*) Natl Demo Inst.

— The Nineteen Ninety General Elections in Haiti. 123p. (Orig.). 1991. pap. 10.95 (*1-880134-08-X*) Natl Demo Inst.

— The 1993 Elections in Senegal. 250p. (ENG & FRE.). Date not set. pap. 10.95 (*1-880134-21-7*) Natl Demo Inst.

— The October Nineteen Ninety Elections in Pakistan. 236p. 1991. pap. 10.00 (*1-880134-04-7*) Natl Demo Inst.

— Promoting Participation in Yemen's 1993 Elections. 150p. 1994. pap. 8.95 (*1-880134-23-3*) Natl Demo Inst.

— Reforming the Philippine Electoral Process: Developments 1986-88. 86p. 1991. pap. 8.95 (*1-880134-10-1*) Natl Demo Inst.

— Voting for Greater Pluralism: The May 26, 1991 Municipal Elections in Paraguay. 97p. 1992. pap. 8.95 (*1-880134-13-6*) Natl Demo Inst.

National Democratic Institute for International Affairs Staff & Carter Center of Emory University Staff. The October Thirty-First, Nineteen Ninety-One Presidential & Legislative Elections in Zambia. 167p. 1992. pap. 9.95 (*1-880134-14-4*) Natl Demo Inst.

National Democratic Institute for International Affairs Staff & International Republican Institute Staff. The Nineteen Ninety-Two Elections in Romania. 160p. Date not set. pap. 9.95 (*1-880134-20-9*) Natl Demo Inst.

An Asterisk (*) at the beginning of an entry indicates that the title is appearing in BIP for the first time.

— The October Thirteenth, Nineteen Ninety-One Legislative & Municipal Elections in Bulgaria. 136p. 1992. pap. 9.95 (*1-880134-12-8*) Natl Demo Inst.

National Dissemination Association (NDA) Staff. Educational Programs That Work (EPTW) The Catalogue of the National Diffusion Network (NDN) 20th ed. (EPTW Ser.). 260p. 1994. pap. text ed. 14.95 (*1-57035-004-3*, 6PB20) Sopris.

National Drug Abuse Conference Inc. Staff. Critical Concerns in the Field of Drug Abuse: Proceedings of the National Drug Abuse Conference, 3rd, New York, 1976. LC 78-12871. 1464p. reprint ed. pap. 180.00 (*0-685-16051-3*, 2027085) Bks Demand.

National Drug Abuse Conference, 2nd, 1975, New Orleans. Drug Abuse: Modern Trends, Issues, & Perspectives: Proceedings of the Second National Drug Abuse Conference, Inc., New Orleans, Louisiana, 1975. Schecter, Arnold et al, eds. LC 78-4091. 1254p. reprint ed. pap. 180.00 (*0-685-16089-0*, 2027089) Bks Demand.

National Editorial Board, New & Letters Staff. American Civilization on Trial: Black Masses As Vanguard. 4th ed. (Illus.). 48p. 1983. pap. 2.00 (*0-914441-03-5*) News & Letters.

National Education Association, Committee on Secondary School Studies. Report of the Committee on Secondary School Studies, Appointed at the Meeting of the National Education Association. LC 70-89222. (American Education: Its Men, Institutions & Ideas, Ser. 1). 1978. reprint ed. 21.95 (*0-405-01403-1*) Ayer.

National Education Association of the United States Staff. A Teacher Survey NEA Report: Computers in the Classroom. 98p. reprint ed. pap. 28.00 (*0-317-55509-X*, 2029543) Bks Demand.

National Education Association Staff. How Letters Make Words. 1983. pap. 1.95 (*0-380-82685-2*) Avon.

— Learning to Add. 1983. pap. 1.95 (*0-380-82719-0*) Avon.

— Learning to Subtract. 1983. pap. 1.95 (*0-380-82735-2*) Avon.

— Shapes & Patterns. 1983. pap. 1.95 (*0-380-82701-8*) Avon.

National Effective Transfer Consortium Staff. Enhancing Transfer Effectiveness: A Model for the 1990s. 1990. pap. 18.50 (*0-87117-250-X*) Am Assn Comm Coll.

National Election Studies, Center for Political Studies Staff & Miller, Warren E. American National Election Study, 1978, I. 2nd ed. LC 79-91223. 1979. write for info. (*0-89138-957-1*) ICPSR.

— American National Election Study, 1978, II. 2nd ed. LC 79-91223. 1979. write for info. (*0-89138-958-X*) ICPSR.

— American National Election Study, 1978, Set. 2nd ed. LC 79-91223. 1979. write for info. (*0-89138-963-6*) ICPSR.

— American National Election Study, 1980, 5 vols. LC 82-82378. 1982. Vol. I, Pre & Post Election Surveys. write for info. (*0-89138-921-0*); Vol. II, Major Panel File, Jan. & June. write for info. (*0-89138-922-9*); Vol. III, Major Panel File, Sept. & Nov. write for info. (*0-89138-916-4*); Vol. IV, Appendix A, Contextual Data. write for info. (*0-89138-923-7*); Vol. V, Appendix B, Notes & Questionares. write for info. (*0-89138-924-5*) ICPSR.

— American National Election Study, 1980, 5 vols., Set. LC 82-82378. 1982. write for info. (*0-89138-925-3*, ICPSR 7763) ICPSR.

— American National Election Study, 1984: Appendix: Notes & Questionnaire. 2nd ed. LC 86-80606. (American National Election Studies). 529p. 1986. write for info. (*0-89138-887-7*) ICPSR.

— American National Election Study, 1984: Pre & Post-Election Survey. 2nd ed. LC 86-80607. (American National Election Studies). 642p. 1986. write for info. (*0-89138-886-9*) ICPSR.

— American National Election Study, 1986: Appendices. 2nd ed. LC 87-83560. (American National Election Studies). 1988. write for info. (*0-89138-880-X*) ICPSR.

National Election Studies Center for Political Studies Staff & Miller, Warren E. American National Election Study, 1986: Post-Election Survey. 2nd ed. LC 87-83559. (American National Election Studies). 439p. 1988. write for info. (*0-89138-879-6*) ICPSR.

National Election Studies Staff & Miller, Warren E. American National Election Study, 1982, 2 vols. LC 85-117505. 1983. Vol. 1, Post Election Survey File. write for info. (*0-89138-902-4*); Vol. II, Appendix A: Notes & Questionnaire. write for info. (*0-89138-900-8*) ICPSR.

— American National Election Study, 1982, 2 vols., Set. LC 85-117505. 1983. write for info. (*0-89138-899-0*) ICPSR.

— American National Election Study, 1988: Pre- & Post-Election Survey & Appendix. 2nd ed. LC 89-82313. 724p. 1990. write for info. (*0-89138-872-9*); write for info. (*0-89138-871-0*) ICPSR.

National Election Studies Staff, et al. American National Election Study, 1990: Post-Election Survey. 2nd ed. LC 92-70528. (American National Election Studies). 772p. 1992. write for info. (*0-89138-865-6*) ICPSR.

National Electric Safety Code, ANSI C2 Staff. NESC Interpretations Second Interim Collection, 1991-1993. (Illus.). 68p. (Orig.). 1990. pap. 35.00 (*1-55937-025-4*) IEEE Standards.

National Electrical Manufacturers Association, Power Equipment Division Staff. Review of the Report, "Proposal for a Greater New Bedford, MA PCB Health Study" 15.00 (*0-317-05981-5*) Natl Elec Mfrs.

National Electronic Packaging & Production Conference Staff. National Electronic Packaging & Production Conference, 1985 East: Proceedings of the Technical Program, Boston, MA, June 19-21, 1985. 541p. 1985. reprint ed. pap. 154.20 (*0-685-16086-6*, 2027687) Bks Demand.

— National Electronic Packaging & Production Conference, 1985 West: Proceedings of the Technical Program, Anaheim CA, 1993. 973p. 1985. reprint ed. pap. 180.00 (*0-317-27240-3*, 2025090) Bks Demand.

— National Electronic Packaging & Production Conference, 1986 East: Proceedings of the Technical Program, Boston, MA, June 10-12, 1986. 452p. 1986. reprint ed. pap. 128.90 (*0-317-55765-3*, 2029366) Bks Demand.

— National Electronic Packaging & Production Conference, 1986 West: Proceedings of the Technical Program, Anaheim, CA, February 25-27, 1986, 2 vols., 1. 536p. 1986. reprint ed. pap. 152.80 (*0-685-16078-5*, 2027686) Bks Demand.

— National Electronic Packaging & Production Conference, 1986 West: Proceedings of the Technical Program, Anaheim, CA, February 25-27, 1986, 2 vols., 2. 486p. 1986. reprint ed. pap. 138.60 (*0-685-16079-3*, 2027686) Bks Demand.

— National Electronic Packaging & Production Conference, 1987 West: Proceedings of the Technical Program, February 24-26, 1987, 2 vols., 1. (Illus.). 596p. 1987. pap. 169.90 (*0-685-20418-9*, 2030237) Bks Demand.

— National Electronic Packaging & Production Conference, 1987 West: Proceedings of the Technical Program, February 24-26, 1987, 2 vols., 2. (Illus.). 487p. 1987. pap. 138.80 (*0-685-20419-7*, 2030237) Bks Demand.

— National Electronic Packaging & Production Conference, 1988 East: Proceedings of the Technical Program, June 13-16, 1988, Boston, MA. (Illus.). 515p. 1988. reprint ed. pap. 146.80 (*0-685-23807-5*, 2032914) Bks Demand.

— National Electronic Packaging & Production Conference, 1988 West: Proceedings of the Technical Program, February 24-26, 1987. 947p. 1988. reprint ed. pap. 180.00 (*0-685-23805-9*, 2032911) Bks Demand.

— National Electronic Packaging & Production Conference, 1989 West: Proceedings of the Technical Program; NEPCON West '89, Anaheim, CA, March 6-9, 1989, Vol. 1. (Illus.). 978p. 1989. reprint ed. pap. 180.00 (*0-8357-6738-8*, 2035394) Bks Demand.

— National Electronic Packaging & Production Conference, 1989 West: Proceedings of the Technical Program; NEPCON West '89, Anaheim, CA, March 6-9, 1989, Vol. 2. (Illus.). 1010p. 1989. reprint ed. pap. 180.00 (*0-8357-6739-6*, 2035394) Bks Demand.

— National Electronic Packaging & Production Conference, 1990 Vol. 1: Proceedings of the Technical Program, Anaheim, CA, February 25-27, 1986. 1990. Vol. 1, 984p. 180.00 (*0-7837-0145-4*, 2040435) Bks Demand.

— National Electronic Packaging & Production Conference, 1990 East: Proceedings of the Technical Program, Boston, MA, June 19-21, 1985. 1056p. 1990. pap. 180.00 (*0-7837-0148-9*, 2040437) Bks Demand.

— National Electronic Packaging & Production Conference, 1990 West Vol. 2: Proceedings of the Technical Program, Anaheim, CA, February 25-27, 1986. 984p. 1990. Vol. 2, 929p. 180.00 (*0-7837-0146-2*, 2040435) Bks Demand.

— National Electronic Packaging & Production Conference, 1991 West: Proceedings of the Technical Program, Anaheim CA, 1993, Vol. 1. 782p. 1991. pap. 180.00 (*0-7837-0149-7*, 2040438) Bks Demand.

— National Electronic Packaging & Production Conference, 1991 West: Proceedings of the Technical Program, Anaheim CA, 1993, Vol. 2. 705p. 1991. pap. 180.00 (*0-7837-0150-0*, 2040438) Bks Demand.

— National Electronic Packaging & Production Conference, 1991 West: Proceedings of the Technical Program, Anaheim CA, 1993, Vol. 3. 923p. 1991. pap. 180.00 (*0-7837-0151-9*, 2040438) Bks Demand.

— National Electronic Packaging & Production Conference, 1992 East: Proceedings of the Technical Program, Boston, MA, June 19-21, 1985. 467p. 1992. reprint ed. pap. 133.10 (*0-7837-2688-0*, 2043066) Bks Demand.

— National Electronic Packaging & Production Conference, 1992 West: Proceedings of the Technical Program, Anaheim CA, 1993, Vol. 1. (Illus.). 464p. 1992. reprint ed. pap. 132.30 (*0-7837-3073-X*, 2043065) Bks Demand.

— National Electronic Packaging & Production Conference, 1992 West: Proceedings of the Technical Program, Anaheim CA, 1993, Vol. 2. (Illus.). 663p. 1992. reprint ed. pap. 180.00 (*0-7837-3074-8*, 2043065) Bks Demand.

— National Electronic Packaging & Production Conference, 1993 West: Proceedings of the Technical Program, Anaheim CA, 1993, Vol. 1. (Illus.). 562p. 1993. reprint ed. pap. 160.20 (*0-7837-7036-7*, 2046851) Bks Demand.

— National Electronic Packaging & Production Conference, 1993 West: Proceedings of the Technical Program, Anaheim CA, 1993, Vol. 2. (Illus.). 579p. 1993. reprint ed. pap. 165.10 (*0-7837-7037-5*, 2046851) Bks Demand.

— National Electronic Packaging & Production Conference, 1993 West: Proceedings of the Technical Program, Anaheim CA, 1993, Vol. 3. 878p. reprint ed. pap. 180.00 (*0-7837-7041-3*, 2046852) Bks Demand.

— National Electronic Packaging & Production Conference, 1993 West: Proceedings of the Technical Program, Anaheim CA, 1993, Vol. 3. (Illus.). 805p. 1992. reprint ed. pap. 180.00 (*0-7837-3075-6*, 2043065) Bks Demand.

— National Electronic Packaging & Production Conference, 1993 West: Proceedings of the Technical Program, Anaheim CA, 1993, Vol. 3. (Illus.). 974p. 1993. reprint ed. pap. 180.00 (*0-7837-7038-3*, 2046851) Bks Demand.

— National Electronic Packaging & Production Conference, 1994 West: Proceedings of the Technical Program, Anaheim CA, 1993. 529p. 1984. reprint ed. pap. 150.80 (*0-317-19835-1*, 2023060) Bks Demand.

— National Electronic Packaging & Production Conference, 1994 West: Proceedings of the Technical Program, Anaheim CA, 1993, Vol. 1. (Illus.). 840p. 1994. reprint ed. pap. 180.00 (*0-7837-7039-1*, 2046852) Bks Demand.

— National Electronic Packaging & Production Conference, 1994 West: Proceedings of the Technical Program, Anaheim CA, 1993, Vol. 2. (Illus.). 852p. 1994. reprint ed. pap. 180.00 (*0-7837-7040-5*, 2046852) Bks Demand.

— National Electronic Packaging & Production, 1993 East: Proceedings of the Technical Program, Bayside Exposition Center, Boston, Massachusetts, June 14-17, 1993. (Illus.). 600p. 1993. reprint ed. pap. 171.00 (*0-7837-7035-9*, 2046850) Bks Demand.

National Electronics Conference Staff. National Electronics Conference: Proceedings: Regency Hyatt O'Hare, Chicago, Illinois, October 6-8, 1975, Vol. 30. Tranter, William H., ed. 369p. reprint ed. pap. 105.20 (*0-685-15937-X*, 2026806) Bks Demand.

— National Electronics Conference: Proceedings: The Conrad Hilton Hotel, Chicago, Illinois, December 8-10, 1969, Vol. 25. 972p. reprint ed. pap. 180.00 (*0-685-15924-8*, 2026805) Bks Demand.

National Elevator Industry, Inc. Safety Committee Staff, jt. auth. see Elevator World, Inc. Staff.

National Emergency Nurses' Association Staff. Standards for Emergency Nursing Practice. 101p. 1993. write for info. (*0-8016-8094-8*) Mosby Yr Bk.

National Employment Law Project Staff, jt. auth. see Hernandez, Theresa.

***National Employment Screening Services Staff.** The Guide to Background Investigations: A Comprehensive Source Directory for Employee Screening & Background Investigations. 6th ed. (Illus.). 1320p. 1994. pap. 129.50 (*0-425-05382-2*) Nat Employ Screen.

— The National Employment Screening Directory, 1987: A Guide to Background Investigations. (National Employment Screening Directory Ser.). (Illus.). 320p. 1987. pap. 95.00 (*0-941233-14-6*) Source Okla.

— Social Security Number Guide. 3rd ed. 16p. reprint ed. write for info. (*0-318-69321-6*) Source Okla.

National Endowment for Financial Education Academic Staff. The Financial Planner's Desk Reference: A Glossary of Terms. (Illus.). 238p. (Orig.). (C). 1994. pap. 29.95 (*1-884383-01-7*) Natl Endowment.

***National Engineering Consortium Staff.** Annual Review of Communications Vol. 46. fac. ed. LC 86-642827. 1132p. 1992. pap. 180.00 (*0-7837-8644-1*, 2047852) Bks Demand.

National Environmental Satellite, Data & Information Service Staff & Satellite Applications Lab Staff. Polar Orbiter Satellite Imagery Interpretation. (NWA Publication Ser.: No. 2-88). 42p. (C). 1988. sl. 84.00 (*1-883563-06-2*) Natl Weather.

— Satellite Imagery Indicators of Turbulence. (NWA Publication Ser.: No. 1-91). 17p. (C). 1991. sl. 84.00 (*1-883563-08-9*) Natl Weather.

— Winds of the World as Seen in Satellite Imagery. (NWA Publication Ser.: No. 1-90). 21p. 1990. sl. 84.00 (*1-883563-07-0*) Natl Weather.

National Environmental Training Staff, jt. auth. see National Safety Council Staff.

National Evaluation Systems Inc. Staff. Official TASP Test Study Guide. 1992. pap. 12.00 (*0-89056-007-2*) Natl Eval Systs.

— Official Tasp Test Study Guide. 1993. pap. 12.00 (*0-89056-010-2*) Natl Eval Systs.

National Executive Committee - Socialist Labor Party Staff, jt. auth. see De Leon, Daniel.

National Executive Committee of Mlp, Usa, ed. see Marxist-Leninist Party, USA Staff.

National Executive Committee of the MLP, U. S. A., ed. see Marxist-Leninist Party, U. S. A. Staff.

National Executive Committee of the MLP, USA, ed. see Marxist-Leninist Party, USA Staff.

National Financial Staff. Secrets of Classified Advertising. 1974. 1.00 (*0-918898-02-1*) Lincoln Pub.

National Fire Prevention Association Staff. Fire Prevention Code: NFPA 1. 1992. 26.50 (*0-317-46506-6*, 1-92) Natl Fire Prot.

***National Fire Protection Assn. Staff.** Life Safety Code. 316p. 1994. 39.50 (*0-614-03121-4*) Natl Fire Prot.

— Life Safety Code & Handbook 2 vols. 1994. 99.50 (*0-614-03122-2*, 101SET94) Natl Fire Prot.

— Life Safety Code Handbook: 1994 Edition. (Illus.). 1994. 77.50 (*0-614-03123-0*, 101HB94) Natl Fire Prot.

National Fire Protection Association Staff. Aircraft Fire & Explosion Investigators. 1991. 16.75 (*0-317-63438-0*, 422M-91) Natl Fire Prot.

— Aircraft Fueling Ramp Drainage. 1992. 16.75 (*0-317-63430-5*, 415-92) Natl Fire Prot.

— Aircraft Hangars. 31p. 1990. 20.25 (*0-317-63425-9*, 409-90) Natl Fire Prot.

— Aircraft Rescue & Fire Fighting Operational Procedures. 110p. 1991. 26.50 (*0-317-63421-6*, 402M-91) Natl Fire Prot.

— Airport - Community Emergency Planning. 68p. 1991. 22.25 (*0-317-63441-0*, 424M-91) Natl Fire Prot.

— Airport Fire Fighter Professional Qualifications. 1994. 16.75 (*0-317-63522-0*, 1003-94) Natl Fire Prot.

— Assembly Seating, Tents & Membrane Structures. 29p. 1994. 20.25 (*0-317-63308-2*, 102-94) Natl Fire Prot.

— Automotive & Marine Service Station Code. 1993. 16.75 (*0-317-63064-4*, 30A-93) Natl Fire Prot.

— Automotive Fire Apparatus. 74p. 1991. 22.25 (*0-317-63553-0*, 1901-91) Natl Fire Prot.

— Building Fire Service Training Centers. 17p. 1992. 16.75 (*0-317-63544-1*, 1402-92) Natl Fire Prot.

— Carbon Dioxide Extinguishing Systems. 46p. 1993. 2.25 (*0-317-63044-X*, 12-93) Natl Fire Prot.

— Care, Use, & Maintenance of Fire Hose Including Connections & Nozzles. 19p. 1993. 20.25 (*0-317-63566-2*, 1962-93) Natl Fire Prot.

— Cellulose Nitrate Motion Picture Film. 18p. 1988. 16.75 (*0-317-63072-5*, 40-94) Natl Fire Prot.

— Chimneys, Fireplaces, Vents, & Solid Fuel Burning Appliances. 39p. 1992. 18.75 (*0-317-63331-7*, 211-92) Natl Fire Prot.

— Classification of Class I Hazardous Locations for Electrical Installations in Chemical Plants. 40p. 1992. 20.25 (*0-317-63463-1*, 497A-92) Natl Fire Prot.

— Classification of Gases, Vapors & Dusts for Electrical Equipment in Hazardous (Classified) Locations. 1991. 16.75 (*0-317-63466-6*, 497M-91) Natl Fire Prot.

— Coal Preparation Plants. 1994. 16.75 (*0-317-63317-1*, 120-94) Natl Fire Prot.

— Code for Unmanned Rockets. 1994. 16.75 (*0-317-63530-1*, 1122-94) Natl Fire Prot.

— Compressed Natural Gas (CNG) Vehicular Fuel Systems. 25p. 1992. 20.25 (*0-685-18969-4*, 52-92) Natl Fire Prot.

— Construction & Fire Protection of Marine Terminals, Piers & Wharves. 28p. 1990. 20.25 (*0-317-63403-8*, 307-90) Natl Fire Prot.

— Construction & Protection of Aircraft Engine Test Facilities. 1994. 16.75 (*0-317-63439-9*, 423-94) Natl Fire Prot.

— Construction & Protection of Aircraft Loading Walkways. 1990. 15.50 (*0-317-63434-8*, 417-90) Natl Fire Prot.

— Construction & Protection of Airport Terminal Buildings. 1993. 16.75 (*0-317-63432-1*, 416-93) Natl Fire Prot.

— Cutting & Welding Processes. 1994. 16.75 (*0-317-63200-0*, 51B-94) Natl Fire Prot.

— Deluge Foam-Water Sprinkler & Spray Systems. 1994. 20.25 (*0-317-63053-9*, 16-94) Natl Fire Prot.

— Designing & Design Verification Tests for Fire Department Ground Ladders. 1994. 20.25 (*0-317-63563-8*, 1931-94) Natl Fire Prot.

— Dry Chemical Extinguishing Systems. 1994. 20.25 (*0-317-63055-5*, 17-94) Natl Fire Prot.

— Dry Cleaning Plants. 1990. 16.75 (*0-317-63066-0*, 32-90) Natl Fire Prot.

— Electrical Code for One- & Two-Family Dwellings. 180p. 1993. 26.50 (*0-317-63214-0*, 70A-93) Natl Fire Prot.

— Electrical Equipment Maintenance. 158p. 1994. 26.50 (*0-317-63215-9*, 70B-90) Natl Fire Prot.

— Emergency & Standby Power Systems. 29p. 1993. 20.25 (*0-317-63314-7*, 110-93) Natl Fire Prot.

— Explosion Venting. 60p. 1994. 22.25 (*0-685-18971-6*, 68-94) Natl Fire Prot.

— Explosives in Motor Vehicle Terminals. 1992. 16.75 (*0-317-63468-2*, 498-92) Natl Fire Prot.

— Facilities Handling Radioactive Materials. 1994. 20.25 (*0-317-63502-6*, 801-94) Natl Fire Prot.

— Fire Apparatus Driver-Operator Professional Qualifications. 18p. 1993. 16.75 (*0-317-63520-4*, 1002-93) Natl Fire Prot.

— Fire Department Operations in Properties Protected by Sprinkler & Standpipe Systems. 1994. 16.75 (*0-317-63050-4*, 13E-94) Natl Fire Prot.

— Fire Department Portable Pumping Units. 1993. 16.75 (*0-317-63558-1*, 1921-93) Natl Fire Prot.

— Fire Department Safety Officer. 1992. 16.75 (*0-317-63552-2*, 1521-92) Natl Fire Prot.

— Fire Doors & Windows. 77p. 1990. 22.25 (*0-317-63230-2*, 80-92) Natl Fire Prot.

— Fire Fighter Professional Qualifications. 20p. 1992. 20.25 (*0-317-63519-0*, 1001-92) Natl Fire Prot.

— Fire Flow Testing & Marking of Hydrants. 1988. 16.75 (*0-317-63396-1*, 291-88) Natl Fire Prot.

— Fire Hazard Properties of Flammable Liquids, Gases, & Volatile Solids. 94p. 1991. 22.25 (*0-317-63411-9*, 325M-91) Natl Fire Prot.

— Fire Hazards in Oxygen-Enriched Atmospheres. 43p. 1994. 22.25 (*0-614-03114-1*, 53-94) Natl Fire Prot.

— Fire Hose. 1992. 16.75 (*0-317-63565-4*, 1961-92) Natl Fire Prot.

— Fire Incident Data Coding Guide. 2nd ed. 38p. 1987. spiral bd. 12.50 (*0-317-63592-1*, SPP-42A) Natl Fire Prot.

— Fire Litigation Handbook & Supplement, Set. 113.50 (*0-317-46511-2*, 87-SET-86) Natl Fire Prot.

— Fire Officer Professional Qualifications. 15p. 1992. 16.75 (*0-317-63525-5*, 1021-92) Natl Fire Prot.

— Fire Protection for Archives & Records Centers. 1986. 20.25 (*0-317-63355-4*, 232AM-91) Natl Fire Prot.

— Fire Protection for Fossil Fueled Steam Electric Generation Plants. 48p. 1992. 20.25 (*0-317-63508-5*, 850-92) Natl Fire Prot.

— Fire Protection for Laboratories Using Chemicals. 46p. 1991. 20.25 (*0-317-63079-2*, 45-91) Natl Fire Prot.

— Fire Protection for Light Water Nuclear Power Plants. 30p. 1993. 20.25 (*0-317-63507-7*, 803-93) Natl Fire Prot.

— Fire Protection for Limited Access Highways, Tunnels, Bridges, Elevated Roadways, & Air Right Structures: 1987. 11p. 1992. 16.75 (*0-317-07394-X*, 502-92) Natl Fire Prot.

— Fire Protection for Mobile Surface Mining Equipment. 1990. 16.75 (*0-317-63318-X*, 121-90) Natl Fire Prot.

— Fire Protection in Planned Building Groups. 1990. 16.75 (*0-317-63535-2*, 1141-90) Natl Fire Prot.

— Fire Protection Standard for Marinas & Boatyards: 1990. 1990. 20.25 (*0-317-07389-3*, 303-90) Natl Fire Prot.

— Fire Protection Training Reports & Records. 21p. 1989. 20.25 (*0-317-63542-5*, 1401-89) Natl Fire Prot.

— Fire Reporting Field Incident Manual. 79p. 1990. 22.25 (*0-317-63511-5*, 902M-90) Natl Fire Prot.

— Fire Reporting Property Survey Manual. 79p. 1986. 22.25 (*0-317-63512-3*, 903-92) Natl Fire Prot.

— Fire-Retardant Impregnated Wood & Fire Retardant Coatings for Building Materials. 1992. 16.75 (*0-317-63500-X*, 703-92) Natl Fire Prot.

— Fire Service & the Law Book. 5.75 (*0-317-46513-9*, B7-FSP-3B) Natl Fire Prot.

— Fire Service Instructor Professional Qualifications. 1992. 16.75 (*0-685-19007-2*, 1041-92) Natl Fire Prot.

— Fire Service Life Safety Rope, Harnesses, & Hardware. 1990. 16.75 (*0-317-63576-X*, 1983-90) Natl Fire Prot.

N

An Asterisk (*) at the beginning of an entry indicates that the title is appearing in BIP for the first time.

— Fire Tests of Window Assemblies. 1990. 16.75 (*0-317-63372-4*, 257-90) Natl Fire Prot.

— Firesafety in Racetrack Stables. 1991. 16.75 (*0-317-63322-8*, 150-91) Natl Fire Prot.

— Fixed Guideway Transit Systems. 37p. 1993. 20.25 (*0-317-63321-X*, 130-93) Natl Fire Prot.

— Flammable & Combustible Liquids Code. 61p. 1990. 21.50 (*0-317-63063-6*, 30-90) Natl Fire Prot.

— Flammable & Combustible Liquids Code: 1993 Edition. 1993. 21.50 (*0-614-03116-8*, 30-93) Natl Fire Prot.

— Flammable & Combustible Liquids Code Handbook. 4th ed. 510p. 1993. 64.75 (*0-317-63618-9*, 30HB93) Natl Fire Prot.

— Gaseous Hydrogen Systems at Consumer Sites. 1994. 16.75 (*0-317-63083-0*, 50A-94) Natl Fire Prot.

— General Storage. 29p. 1990. 20.25 (*0-317-63339-2*, 231-90) Natl Fire Prot.

— Gloves for Structural Fire Fighters. 23p. 1993. 20.25 (*0-317-63571-9*, 1973-93) Natl Fire Prot.

— Guard Service in Fire Loss Prevention. 1992. 16.75 (*0-317-63488-7*, 601-92) Natl Fire Prot.

— Halon Thirteen-One Fire Extinguishing Systems. 65p. 1992. 22.25 (*0-317-63045-8*, 12A-92) Natl Fire Prot.

— Halon Twelve-Eleven Fire Extinguishing Systems. 44p. 1990. 20.25 (*0-317-63046-6*, 12B-90) Natl Fire Prot.

— Health Care Facilities. 229p. 1993. 32.25 (*0-317-63302-3*, 99-93) Natl Fire Prot.

— Health Care Facilities Standard & Handbook, 2 vols. rev. ed. Klein, Burton R., ed. 1993. 89.50 (*0-317-63277-9*, 99SET93) Natl Fire Prot.

— Hypobaric Facilities. 22p. 1993. 20.25 (*0-317-63303-1*, 99-B93) Natl Fire Prot.

— Identification of the Fire Hazards of Materials. 15p. 1990. 16.75 (*0-317-63501-8*, 704-90) Natl Fire Prot.

— Incident Follow-Up Report Manual. 1992. 20.25 (*0-317-63513-1*, 904-92) Natl Fire Prot.

— Incinerators, Waste & Linen Handling Systems & Equipment. 19p. 1990. 16.75 (*0-685-18974-0*, 82-90) Natl Fire Prot.

— Industrial Furnaces Using a Special Processing Atmosphere. 90p. 1991. 22.25 (*0-317-63286-8*, 86C-91) Natl Fire Prot.

— Industrial Furnaces Using Vacuum As an Atmosphere. 54p. 1990. 22.25 (*0-317-63287-6*, 86D-90) Natl Fire Prot.

— Installation & Operation of Pulverized Fuel Systems. 31p. 1992. 20.25 (*0-685-18979-1*, 8503-92) Natl Fire Prot.

— Installation, Maintenance, & Use of Central Station Signaling Systems. 269p. 1993. 32.25 (*0-614-03119-2*, 72-93) Natl Fire Prot.

— Installation, Maintenance, & Use of Public Fire Service Communication Systems. 38p. 1994. 20.25 (*0-317-63538-7*, 1221-94) Natl Fire Prot.

— Installation of Air Conditioning & Ventilation Systems. 21p. 1993. 20.25 (*0-317-63292-2*, 90A-93) Natl Fire Prot.

— Installation of Centrifugal Fire Pumps. 60p. 1993. 22.25 (*0-317-63058-X*, 20-93) Natl Fire Prot.

— Installation of Closed-Head Foam-Water Sprinkler Systems. 22p. 1994. 20.25 (*0-317-63054-7*, 16A-94) Natl Fire Prot.

— Installation of Private Fire Service Mains. 28p. 1992. 20.25 (*0-685-18943-0*, 24-92) Natl Fire Prot.

— Installation of Sprinkler Systems. 124p. 1994. 28.50 (*0-317-63047-4*, 13-94) Natl Fire Prot.

— Installation of Sprinkler Systems in One- & Two-Family Dwellings & Mobile Homes. 1994. 20.25 (*0-317-63049-0*, 13D-94) Natl Fire Prot.

— Installation of Warm Air Heating & Air Conditioning Systems. (Eighty-Ninety Ser.). 1993. 16.75 (*0-317-63294-9*, 90B-93) Natl Fire Prot.

— Investigation of Fires of Electrical Origin. 38p. 1988. 20.25 (*0-317-63515-8*, 907M-88) Natl Fire Prot.

— Life Safety Code. 327p. 1991. 39.50 (*0-317-63039-3*, 101-91) Natl Fire Prot.

— Life Safety Code & Handbook, 2 vols. 1991. 99.50 (*0-685-18984-8*, 101SET91) Natl Fire Prot.

— Life Safety Code Handbook. (Illus.). 1991. 77.50 (*0-317-63038-5*, 101HB91) Natl Fire Prot.

— Liquefied Hydrogen Systems at Consumer Sites. 1994. 16.75 (*0-317-63084-9*, 50B-94) Natl Fire Prot.

— Liquefied Petroleum Gases Standard & Handbook, 2 vols. Walls, Wilbur L., ed. 1992. 79.75 (*0-317-63074-1*, 58SET92) Natl Fire Prot.

— Low Expansion Foam & Combined Agent Systems. 51p. 1994. 22.25 (*0-317-63041-5*, 11-94) Natl Fire Prot.

— Manufacture of Aluminum & Magnesium Power. 1993. 16.75 (*0-317-63492-5*, 651-93) Natl Fire Prot.

— Manufacture of Organic Coatings. 1987. 20.25 (*0-317-63069-5*, 35-87) Natl Fire Prot.

— Manufacture, Transportation, & Storage of Fireworks. 1988. 20.25 (*0-317-63533-6*, 1124-88) Natl Fire Prot.

— Manufacture, Transportation, Storage, & Use of Explosive Materials. 36p. 1992. 20.25 (*0-317-63460-7*, 495-92) Natl Fire Prot.

— Marinas & Boatyards. 23p. 1990. 20.25 (*0-317-63401-1*, 303-90) Natl Fire Prot.

— Method of Test for Heat & Visible Smoke Release Rates for Materials & Products. 1994. 20.25 (*0-317-63394-5*, 263-94) Natl Fire Prot.

— Methods of Fire Tests of Roof Coverings. 1993. 16.75 (*0-317-63368-6*, 256-93) Natl Fire Prot.

— Mobile Foam Apparatus. 1990. 16.75 (*0-317-63043-1*, 11C-90) Natl Fire Prot.

— Motor Freight Terminals. 1990. 16.75 (*0-317-63484-4*, 513-90) Natl Fire Prot.

— National Electrical Code: 1987. 1987. pap. 32.50 (*0-317-63036-9*, 70-87); ring bd. 36.50 (*0-317-63035-0*, 70-87LL) Natl Fire Prot.

— National Electrical Code 1987 Handbook. (Illus.). 1000p. 1987. 65.00 (*0-317-63034-2*, 70-87HB) Natl Fire Prot.

— National Fire Codes, 1992, 12 vols. (Illus.). 1993. 700.00 (*0-317-63577-8*, NFC93ST) Natl Fire Prot.

— National Fuel Gas Code: 1988. 234p. 1992. 24.50 (*0-317-07374-5*, 54-92) Natl Fire Prot.

— Nuclear Research Reactors. 17p. 1993. 16.75 (*0-317-63506-9*, 802-93) Natl Fire Prot.

— Organization for Fire Services. 49p. 1994. 20.25 (*0-317-63536-0*, 1201-94) Natl Fire Prot.

— Ovens & Furnaces. 76p. 1990. 20.75 (*0-317-63285-X*, 86-90) Natl Fire Prot.

— Oxygen-Fuel Gas Systems for Welding, Cutting, & Allied Processes. 17p. 1992. 16.75 (*0-317-63085-7*, 51-92) Natl Fire Prot.

— Parking Structures. 1991. 16.75 (*0-685-18981-3*, 88A-91) Natl Fire Prot.

— Personal Alert Safety Systems (PASS) for Fire Fighters. 22p. 1993. 20.25 (*0-317-63575-1*, 1982-88) Natl Fire Prot.

— Pneumatic Conveying Systems for Handling Combustible Materials. 1990. 16.75 (*0-317-63491-7*, 650-90) Natl Fire Prot.

— Portable Fire Extinguishers. 52p. 1990. 22.75 (*0-317-63040-7*, 10-90) Natl Fire Prot.

— Portable Shipping Tanks for Flammable & Combustible Liquids. 1990. 16.75 (*0-317-63418-6*, 386-90) Natl Fire Prot.

— Prevention of Fire & Dust Explosions in Facilities Manufacturing & Handling Starch. 21p. 1989. 20.25 (*0-317-63207-8*, 61A-89) Natl Fire Prot.

— Prevention of Fire & Dust Explosions in Feed Mills. 20p. 1989. 20.25 (*0-685-18970-8*, 61C-89) Natl Fire Prot.

— Prevention of Fire & Dust Explosions in the Milling of Agricultural Commodities for Human Consumption. 20p. 1989. 20.75 (*0-317-63210-8*, 61D-89) Natl Fire Prot.

— Prevention of Fires & Explosions in Wood Processing & Woodworking Facilities. 1987. 15.50 (*0-317-63498-4*, 664-87) Natl Fire Prot.

— Prevention of Furnace Explosions in Fuel-Oil & Natural Gas-Fired Single Burner Boiler-Furnaces. 35p. 1992. 20.25 (*0-317-63236-1*, 8501-92) Natl Fire Prot.

— Processing & Finishing of Aluminum. 1987. 16.75 (*0-317-63212-4*, 65-87) Natl Fire Prot.

— Production, Processing, Handling, & Storage of Titanium. 1987. 16.75 (*0-317-63447-X*, 481-87) Natl Fire Prot.

— Production, Processing, Handling, & Storage of Zirconium. 1987. 16.75 (*0-317-63448-8*, 482-87) Natl Fire Prot.

— Professional Qualifications for Fire Inspector, Fire Investigator, & Fire Prevention Education Officer: NFPA 1031. 1993. 16.75 (*0-317-46518-X*, B7-NFPA-103-87) Natl Fire Prot.

— Protection from Exposure Fires. 1993. 16.75 (*0-317-63231-0*, 80A-93) Natl Fire Prot.

— Protection of Electronic Computer - Data Processing Equipment. 1992. 16.75 (*0-317-63226-4*, 75-92) Natl Fire Prot.

— Protection of Records. 1991. 16.75 (*0-317-63352-X*, 232-91) Natl Fire Prot.

— Protective Clothing for Structural Fire Fighting. 1991. 20.25 (*0-317-63569-7*, 1971-91) Natl Fire Prot.

— Public Firesafety Symbols. 1991. 20.25 (*0-317-63323-6*, 170-91) Natl Fire Prot.

— Purged & Pressurized Enclosures for Electrical Equipment. 21p. 1993. 20.25 (*0-317-63461-5*, 496-93) Natl Fire Prot.

— Rack Storage of Materials. 57p. 1991. 22.25 (*0-317-63340-6*, 231C-91) Natl Fire Prot.

— Removal of Smoke & Grease-Laden Vapors from Commercial Cooking Equipment. 1991. 20.25 (*0-317-63298-1*, 96-91) Natl Fire Prot.

— Roof Coverings & Roof Deck Constructions. 1992. 16.75 (*0-317-63329-5*, 203-92) Natl Fire Prot.

— Roof-Top Heliport Construction & Protection. 1990. 16.75 (*0-317-63436-4*, 418-90) Natl Fire Prot.

— RUniform Coding for Fire Protection. 113p. 1990. 26.50 (*0-317-63509-3*, 901-90) Natl Fire Prot.

— Safe Storage of Pyroxylin Plastics. (Forty Ser.). 1993. 15.50 (*0-317-63073-3*, 40E-93) Natl Fire Prot.

— Safeguarding Building Construction & Demolition Operations. 1989. 15.50 (*0-317-63358-9*, 241-89) Natl Fire Prot.

— Screw Threads & Gaskets for Fire Hose Connections. 1993. 20.25 (*0-317-63568-9*, 1963-85) Natl Fire Prot.

— Self-Contained Breathing Apparatus for Fire Fighters. 1992. 20.25 (*0-317-63573-5*, 1981-92) Natl Fire Prot.

— Smoke & Draft-Control Door Assemblies. 1993. 16.75 (*0-317-63312-0*, 105-89) Natl Fire Prot.

— Solvent Extraction Plants. 1993. 20.25 (*0-317-63070-9*, 36-93) Natl Fire Prot.

— Spray Application Using Flammable & Combustible Materials. 27p. 1989. 20.25 (*0-317-63067-9*, 33-89) Natl Fire Prot.

— Standard Glossary of Terms Relating to Chimneys, Vents, & Heat-Producing Appliances. 1992. 16.75 (*0-317-63300-7*, 97-92) Natl Fire Prot.

— Standard Method of Test for Critical Radiant Flux of Floor Covering Systems Using a Radiant Heat Energy Source. 1990. 16.75 (*0-317-63364-3*, 253-90) Natl Fire Prot.

— Standard Method of Test for Determining Resistance of Mock-Up Upholstered Furniture Material Assemblies to Ignition by Smoldering Cigarettes. 99p. 1994. 16.75 (*0-317-63383-X*, 261-89) Natl Fire Prot.

— Standard Method of Test for Fire & Smoke Characteristics of Wires & Cables. 1994. 16.75 (*0-685-18990-2*, 262-90) Natl Fire Prot.

— Standard Methods of Fire Tests for Flame-Resistant Textiles & Films. 1989. 15.50 (*0-317-63499-2*, 701-89) Natl Fire Prot.

— Standard Methods of Fire Tests of Door Assemblies. 1990. 16.75 (*0-317-63362-7*, 252-90) Natl Fire Prot.

— Standard Methods of Tests & Classification System for Cigarette Ignition Resistance of Components of Upholstered Furniture. 1994. 16.75 (*0-317-63378-3*, 260-89) Natl Fire Prot.

— Standard on Live Fire Training Evolutions in Structures. 1992. 16.75 (*0-317-63545-X*, 1403-92) Natl Fire Prot.

— Standard Research Test Method for Determining Smoke Generation of Solid Materials. 20p. 1989. 18.75 (*0-317-63373-2*, 258-89) Natl Fire Prot.

— Standard Test Method for Potential Heat of Building Materials. 1993. 16.75 (*0-317-63377-5*, 259-93) Natl Fire Prot.

— Standard Types of Building Construction. 1992. 16.75 (*0-317-07387-7*, 220-92) Natl Fire Prot.

— Standpipe & Hose Systems. 1993. 20.25 (*0-317-63051-2*, 14-93) Natl Fire Prot.

— Static Electricity. 30p. 1993. 20.25 (*0-317-63227-2*, 77-88) Natl Fire Prot.

— Station-Work Uniforms for Fire Fighters. 1990. 16.75 (*0-317-63572-7*, 1975-90) Natl Fire Prot.

— Stationary Combustion Engines & Gas Turbines. 1994. 16.75 (*0-317-63071-7*, 37-90) Natl Fire Prot.

— Storage & Handling of Liquefied Petroleum Gases. 100p. 26.50 (*0-317-63204-3*, 58-92) Natl Fire Prot.

— Storage, Handling, & Processing of Magnesium. 23p. 1993. 20.25 (*0-317-63445-3*, 480-87) Natl Fire Prot.

— Storage of Ammonium Nitrate. 1993. 16.75 (*0-317-63456-9*, 490-93) Natl Fire Prot.

— Storage of Baled Cotton. 1989. 16.75 (*0-317-63346-5*, 231E-89) Natl Fire Prot.

— Storage of Flammable & Combustible Liquids on Farms & Isolated Construction Projects. 1993. 16.75 (*0-317-63420-8*, 395-88) Natl Fire Prot.

— Storage of Flammable & Combustible Liquids Within Underground Metal & Non-Metal Mines (Other Than Coal) 1994. 20.25 (*0-317-63319-8*, 122-90) Natl Fire Prot.

— Storage of Forest Products. 1990. 16.75 (*0-317-63080-6*, 46-90) Natl Fire Prot.

— Storage of Pesticides in Portable Containers. 1994. 16.75 (*0-317-63078-4*, 43D-86) Natl Fire Prot.

— Storage of Roll Paper. 1987. 16.75 (*0-317-63351-1*, 231F-87) Natl Fire Prot.

— Storage of Rubber Tires. 1989. 16.75 (*0-317-63344-9*, 231D-89) Natl Fire Prot.

— Supervision of Valves Controlling Water Supplies for Fire Protection. 1988. 16.75 (*0-317-63062-8*, 26-88) Natl Fire Prot.

— Tank Vehicles for Flammable & Combustible Liquids. 1990. 16.75 (*0-317-63417-8*, 385-90) Natl Fire Prot.

— Training Standard on Initial Fire Attack. 1988. 16.75 (*0-317-63547-6*, 1410-88) Natl Fire Prot.

— Truck Fire Protection. 1994. 16.75 (*0-317-63483-6*, 513-90) Natl Fire Prot.

— Use, Maintenance, & Service Testing of Fire Department Ground Ladders. 1989. 16.75 (*0-317-63564-6*, 1932-89) Natl Fire Prot.

— Water-Cooling Towers. 1992. 20.25 (*0-317-63332-5*, 214-92) Natl Fire Prot.

— Water Spray Fixed Systems for Fire Protection. 43p. 1990. 20.25 (*0-317-63052-0*, 15-90) Natl Fire Prot.

— Water Supplies for Suburban & Rural Fire Fighting. 63p. 1993. 22.25 (*0-317-63539-5*, 1231-89) Natl Fire Prot.

— Water Tanks for Private Fire Protection. 63p. 1993. 20.75 (*0-317-63060-1*, 22-93) Natl Fire Prot.

— Wet Chemical Extinguishing Systems. 1990. 16.75 (*0-317-63056-3*, 17A-90) Natl Fire Prot.

— Wetting Agents. 1990. 16.75 (*0-317-63057-1*, 18-90) Natl Fire Prot.

National Fire Protection Association Staff & Richman, Harold. Engine Company Fireground Operations. 2nd ed. (Illus.). 205p. 1986. 38.00 (*0-317-63589-1*, FSP-75) Natl Fire Prot.

National Fire Safety Protection Association Staff. Firesafety Concepts Tree. 1994. 16.75 (*0-317-63485-2*, 550-94) Natl Fire Prot.

National Fire Service Incident Management System Consortium Model Procedures Committee Staff. Model Procedures Guide for Structural Firefighting. (Illus.). 72p. (Orig.). 1993. pap. text ed. 10.00 (*0-87939-108-1*) IFSTA.

National Flag Foundation Staff, jt. auth. see Allegheny Trails Council, Boy Scouts of America.

National Flag Foundation Staff, jt. auth. see Murfin, James.

National Fluid Power Association Staff. National Fluid Power Association Directory & Member Guide, 1993-94. 192p. 1993. 150.00 (*0-942220-30-7*) Natl Fluid Power.

National Fluid Power Association Staff, ed. IFPAC - Proceedings of the International Fluid Power Applications Conference: Empirical Design & Applications. 522p. 1992. 30.00 (*0-942220-27-7*) Natl Fluid Power.

— Proceedings of the Forty-Sixth National Conference on Fluid Power. 440p. 1994. 60.00 (*0-942220-31-5*) Natl Fluid Power.

— Your Guide to Cost Reduction Through Pneumatics Automation. (Illus.). 64p. (Orig.). (C). 1990. pap. 3.00 (*0-942220-23-4*) Natl Fluid Power.

— Your Guide to the Electronic Control of Fluid Power. (Illus.). 64p. (Orig.). 1992. pap. 5.00 (*0-942220-28-5*) Natl Fluid Power.

National Food Processors Association Staff. Food Labeling & Advertising: Finding Better Ways to Communicate About Nutrition. 52p. (C). 1985. pap. 15.00 (*0-937774-12-X*) Food Processors.

— Food Labeling & Advertising II: Giving Americans More Facts on Diet & Health: Proceedings. 61p. 1987. pap. text ed. 15.00 (*0-937774-16-2*) Food Processors.

— Packaging Alternatives for Food Processors: Proceedings. 101p. (Orig.). 1984. pap. text ed. 25.00 (*0-937774-11-1*) Food Processors.

National Football League Staff. Make the Right Call: The Official Playing Rules of the National Football League. (Illus.). 144p. 1993. 24.95 (*1-880141-54-X*); pap. 8.95 (*1-880141-53-1*) Triumph Bks.

— Make the Right Call: The Ultimate Guide to Every Game Situation. rev. ed. 220p. 1994. pap. 12.95 (*1-880141-88-4*) Triumph Bks.

— NFL's Make the Right Call: The NFL's Own Interpretations & Guidelines Plus Hundreds of Official Rulings on Game Situations. (Illus.). 220p. 1995. pap. 13.95 (*1-57243-046-X*) Triumph Bks.

— Official NFL Record & Fact Book, 1994. (Illus.). 1994. pap. 14.95 (*1-56305-674-7*) Workman Pub.

— Official Rules of the NFL. (Official Rules Ser.). (Illus.). Date not set. write for info. (*0-614-06492-9*) Triumph Bks.

National Football League Staff, comp. Official National Football League Record & Fact Book, 1993. 392p. (Orig.). 1993. pap. 14.95 (*1-56305-468-X*, 3468) Workman Pub.

National Football League Staff, ed. Official Rules of the NFL, 1994-95. 190p. 1994. pap. 8.95 (*1-880141-86-8*) Triumph Bks.

National Foreign Assessment Center Staff. Directory of Soviet Research Organization. LC 79-121624. 300p. reprint ed. pap. 85.50 (*0-8357-2914-1*, 2039153) Bks Demand.

National Forensic Center Staff. Forensic Services Directory, 1981. 800p. 1981. text ed. 52.50 (*0-685-05353-9*) West Pub.

National Forum for School Science Staff. The Science Curriculum: The Report of the 1986 National Forum for School Science. (This Year in School Science Ser.: No. 1986). 285p. reprint ed. pap. 81.30 (*0-8357-2823-4*, 2039059) Bks Demand.

— Science Teaching: The Report of the 1985 National Forum for School Science. Champagne, Audrey B. & Hornig, Leslie E., eds. (AAAS Publication Ser.: No. 86-6). 250p. reprint ed. pap. 71.30 (*0-7837-0060-1*, 2040307) Bks Demand.

— Students & Science Learning: Papers from the 1987 National Forum for School Science. Champagne, Audrey B. & Hornig, Leslie E., eds. (AAAS Publication Ser.: No. 87-29). 181p. reprint ed. pap. 51.60 (*0-8357-2824-2*, 2039060) Bks Demand.

***National Forum on the Future of Children & Family.** Effective Services for Young Children: Report of a Workshop. fac. ed. Schorr, Lisbeth B. et al, eds. LC 91-62826. 126p. 1994. pap. 36.00 (*0-7837-7560-1*, 2047313) Bks Demand.

***National Forum on Water Management Policy Staff.** Water Resouces Administration in the United States: Policy, Practice, & Emerging Issues: Selected Papers from the American Water Resources Association National Forum on Water Management Policy, June 28-July 1, 1992, Washington, DC. Reuss, Martin, ed. LC 93-7668. (Illus.). 326p. Date not set. reprint ed. pap. 93.00 (*0-7837-9226-3*, 2049977) Bks Demand.

National Foundation for Ileitis & Colitis Staff. The Crohn's Disease & Ulcerative Colitis Fact Book. Banks, Peter A. et al, eds. (Illus.). 208p. 1983. text ed. 18.95 (*0-684-17967-9*, Scribners) S&S Trade.

National Foundation for Long Term Care Staff. Enhancing Job Performance Through Staff Development. 214p. 9.95 (*0-318-17109-0*, 110004) Am Health Care Assn.

***National Foundation for U.C. & W.C. Staff.** Employer's Unemployment Compensation Cost Control Handbook. 52p. (Orig.). 1995. pap. text ed. 20.00 (*0-9646875-1-8*) NFUCWC.

National Fuel Efficiency Service Ltd. Staff. Boiler Operators Handbook. 2nd ed. (C). 1990. lib. bdg. 39.50 (*1-85333-285-2*) G & T Inc.

National Gallery Art Staff. The Age of Correggio & the Carraci: Painting in Emilia in the Sixteenth & Seventeenth Centuries. 602p. 1987. 90.00 (*0-521-34019-5*) Cambridge U Pr.

National Gallery in London Staff. Little Book of English Verse. 60p. 1994. 7.95 (*0-8118-0532-8*) Chronicle Bks.

National Gallery, London. Christmas Decorations. (Illus.). (J). (gr. 8 up). 1993. pap. 12.95 (*0-316-59890-9*) Little.

National Gallery of Art of London Staff. The ABCs of Art. (Illus.). 32p. (J). 1994. 7.95 (*0-87663-631-8*) Universe.

National Gallery of Art Staff. The ABCs of Art: Wall Frieze. (J). (ps-3). 1994. pap. 6.50 (*1-55550-912-6*) Universe.

— Conservation Research. 1992. 35.00 (*0-89468-178-8*) Natl Gallery Art.

— The Easter Story. LC 92-19505. (Illus.). 64p. 1993. 22.50 (*0-8212-1978-2*) Bulfinch Pr.

— Joy to the World: A Christmas Songbook, the Federal Style & Beyond. LC 92-753969. (Illus.). 128p. 1992. 19.95 (*0-8478-1588-9*) Rizzoli Intl.

— Noble Beasts: Animals in Art. LC 94-4651. (Illus.). 112p. 1994. 24.95 (*0-8212-2109-4*) Bulfinch Pr.

— Places to Remember Travel Log. (Illus.). 128p. 1994. 9.95 (*1-55550-911-8*) Universe.

— A Renaissance Christmas. (Illus.). 64p. (J). 1991. 19.95 (*0-8212-1875-1*) Bulfinch Pr.

National Gallery of Art (U. S.) Staff, jt. auth. see Walker, John.

***National Gallery of Arts Staff.** Milton Avery: Works on Paper. LC 94-30900. 1994. write for info. (*0-89468-207-5*) Natl Gallery Art.

National Gallery of Canada, Ottawa Staff. Catalogue of the Library of the National Gallery of Canada, First Supplement, 6 vols., Set. (Library Catalogs & Supplements). 1981. lib. bdg. 800.00 (*0-8161-0291-0*, Hall Library) G K Hall.

An Asterisk (*) at the beginning of an entry indicates that the title is appearing in BIP for the first time.

National Gallery of Canada Staff. Catalogue of the Library of the National Gallery of Canada, 8 vols., Set. 1973. Eight Vols. lib. bdg. 870.00 (0-8161-1043-3, Hall Library) G K Hall.

National Gallery of Ireland Staff. Little Book of Irish Verse. 60p. 1993. 7.95 (0-8118-0508-5) Chronicle Bks.

National Gardening Association Staff. Book of Cucumbers, Melons & Squash. 1987. pap. 4.95 (0-394-74988-X, Villard Bks) Random.

— Book of Eggplant, Okra & Peppers. 1987. pap. 4.95 (0-394-74990-1, Villard Bks) Random.

— Book of Lettuce & Greens. 1987. pap. 4.95 (0-394-74991-X, Villard Bks) Random.

— Book of Tomatoes. 1987. pap. 4.95 (0-394-75000-4, Villard Bks) Random.

— Cucumbers, Melons & Squash. LC 86-40341. 88p. 1987. pap. 4.95 (0-317-56629-6, Villard Bks) Random.

— Eggplant, Okra & Peppers. LC 86-40342. 1987. pap. 4.95 (0-317-56626-1, Villard Bks) Random.

— Gardening: The Complete Guide to Growing America's Favorite Fruits & Vegetables. (Illus.). 432p. 1986. write for info. (0-201-10866-6); pap. 19.18 (0-201-10855-0) Addison-Wesley.

— Lettuce & Greens. LC 86-40343. 1987. pap. 4.95 (0-317-56625-3, Villard Bks) Random.

— National Gardening Association Guide to Kids' Gardening. 148p. 1990. pap. text ed. 14.95 (0-471-52092-6) Wiley.

— Tomatoes. 1987. pap. 4.95 (0-317-56624-5, Villard Bks) Random.

National Gardening Association Staff & Buczacki, Stefan T. Gardeners' Questions Answered. LC 86-15759. 160p. 1987. 19.95 (0-317-56609-1, Villard Bks) Random.

National Geographic Editors. Exploring Our Living Planet. LC 88-22540. (Illus.). 1994. 35.00 (0-87044-760-2) Natl Geog.

— National Geographic: The Photographs. (Illus.). 1994. pap. write for info. (0-87044-987-7) Natl Geog.

— National Geographic Guide to the Civil War National Battlefield Parks. (Illus.). 1993. pap. 12.00 (0-87044-878-1) Natl Geog.

National Geographic Society Book Division. Wonders of the Ancient World: National Geographic Atlas of Archaeology. LC 94-16650. 1994. 34.95 (0-87044-982-6) Natl Geog.

— Wonders of the Ancient World: National Geographic Atlas of Archaeology. deluxe ed. LC 94-16650. 1994. pap. 46.95 (0-87044-983-4) Natl Geog.

National Geographic Society Book Division Staff. The Builders: Marvels of Engineering. Newhouse, Elizabeth L., ed. LC 92-30615. (Illus.). 288p. 1992. 41.95 (0-87044-837-4) Natl Geog.

— The Builders: Marvels of Engineering. Newhouse, Elizabeth L., ed. LC 92-30615. (Illus.). 288p. 1994. pap. 40.00 (0-87044-836-6) Natl Geog.

— Crossing America: National Geographic's Guide to the Interstates. LC 94-16464. 1994. pap. 21.95 (0-87044-985-0) Natl Geog.

— Exploring Canada's Spectacular National Parks. 200p. 1995. 16.00 (0-7922-2735-2) Natl Geog.

— National Geographic's Guide to Scenic Highways & Byways. LC 95-16166. (Illus.). 1995. write for info. (0-7922-2950-9) Natl Geog.

— National Geographic's Guide to Scenic Highways & Byways. deluxe ed. LC 95-16166. (Illus.). 1995. write for info. (0-7922-2951-7) Natl Geog.

— National Parks of North America. 1995. write for info. (0-7922-2954-1) Natl Geog.

— National Parks of North America. deluxe ed. 336p. 1995. write for info. (0-7922-2955-X) Natl Geog.

— Raging Forces: Earth in Upheaval. 200p. 1995. 16.00 (0-7922-2736-0) Natl Geog.

— Whales, Dolphins & Porpoises. 232p. 1995. write for info. (0-7922-2952-5) Natl Geog.

— Whales, Dolphins & Porpoises. deluxe ed. 232p. 1995. write for info. (0-7922-2953-3) Natl Geog.

— Wild Animals of North America. deluxe rev. ed. 406p. 1995. write for info. (0-7922-2960-6) Natl Geog.

— Wild Animals of North America. rev. ed. 406p. 1995. 54.00 (0-7922-2958-4) Natl Geog.

***National Geographic Society Editorial Staff.** The White House: An Historical Guide. 18th ed. 1995. 12.95 (0-912308-53-2); pap. 9.95 (0-912308-52-4) White House Hist.

National Geographic Society Staff. Adventures in Your National Parks. Crump, Donald J., ed. (Books for World Explorers Series 10: No. 2). (J). (gr. 3-8). 1994. pap. 12.50 (0-87044-707-6) Natl Geog.

— Animal Architects. Crump, Donald J., ed. LC 87-12198. (Books for World Explorers Series 8: No. 4). (Illus.). 104p. (J). (gr. 3-8). 1994. 12.50 (0-87044-612-6) Natl Geog.

— Animals at Play, Set. Crump, Donald J., ed. (Books for Young Explorers Ser.: Set 15, No. 2). (Illus.). (J). (gr. k-4). 1994. pap. 8.00 (0-87044-739-4) Natl Geog.

— Animals in Summer, Set. Crump, Donald J., ed. (Books for Young Explorers Ser.: Set 15, No. 1). (Illus.). (J). (gr. k-4). 1994. pap. 8.00 (0-87044-738-6) Natl Geog.

— Busy Beavers, Set. Crump, Donald J., ed. (Books for Young Explorers Ser.: Set 15, No. 3). (Illus.). (J). (gr. k-4). 1994. pap. 8.00 (0-87044-740-8) Natl Geog.

— The Emerald Realm: Earth's Precious Rain Forests. Crump, Donald J., ed. LC 90-6260. (Special Publications Series 25: No. 2). (Illus.). (YA). 1990. pap. 16.00 (0-87044-790-4) Natl Geog.

— Excursion to Enchantment. Crump, Donald J., ed. LC 88-19520. (Special Publications Series 23: No. 2). (Illus.). (YA). 1988. pap. 16.00 (0-87044-667-3) Natl Geog.

— Exploring Your Solar System. Crump, Donald J., ed. (Books for World Explorers Series 10: No. 3). (J). (gr. 3-8). 1993. pap. 12.50 (0-87044-703-3) Natl Geog.

— Historical Atlas of the United States. rev. ed. LC 93-32201. 1993. pap. 100.00 (0-87044-970-2) Natl Geog.

— The Incredible Machine. Poole, Robert M., ed. LC 85-29731. (Illus.). 384p. 1994. pap. 35.00 (0-87044-619-3) Natl Geog.

— Journey into China. 5th ed. LC 82-14132. (Illus.). 518p. 1984. lib. bdg. 23.95 (0-87044-461-1) Natl Geog.

— Lion Cubs. (Illus.). (J). Date not set. pap. 16.00 (0-87044-871-4) Natl Geog.

— National Geographic Animals Showing Off, Set. Crump, Donald J., ed. (Pop-Up Set Ser.: No. 3). (Illus.). (J). (ps-5). 1994. pap. 16.00 (0-87044-724-6) Natl Geog.

— National Geographic Atlas of the World. 6th deluxe rev. ed. LC 92-27845. (Special Publications Series 26). (Illus.). 1993. pap. 100.00 (0-87044-835-8) Natl Geog.

— National Geographic Picture Atlas of Our Fifty States. Sedeen, Margaret, ed. (Illus.). 1994. pap. 25.00 (0-87044-859-5) Natl Geog.

— National Geographic Picture Atlas of Our World. rev. ed. LC 93-4514. (Illus.). 256p. 1993. lib. bdg. write for info. (0-87044-964-8) Natl Geog.

— National Geographic Picture Atlas of Our World. rev. ed. LC 93-4514. (Illus.). 256p. 1994. pap. 25.00 (0-87044-960-5) Natl Geog.

— National Geographic Unlocking the Secrets of the Unknown. Newhouse, Elizabeth L., ed. (Illus.). 1993. pap. 16.00 (0-87044-908-7) Natl Geog.

— Our Inviting Eastern Parklands. LC 94-19638. 200p. 1994. 16.00 (0-87044-978-8) Natl Geog.

— Strange Animals of the Sea. (Books for World Explorers Ser.). (Illus.). Date not set. pap. 12.50 (0-87044-686-X) Natl Geog.

— You Won't Believe Your Eyes. Crump, Donald J., ed. LC 86-7637. (Books for World Explorers Series 8: No. 3). (Illus.). 104p. (J). (gr. 3-8). 1994. 12.50 (0-87044-611-8) Natl Geog.

National Geographic Society Staff, ed. Books for Young Explorers, 4 vols., Set. (J). (gr. k-4). 1988. 13.95 (0-87044-737-8) Natl Geog.

— Books for Young Explorers, 4 vols., Set 15. (J). (gr. k-4). 1988. lib. bdg. 16.95 (0-87044-742-4) Natl Geog.

— The Incredible Incas & Their Timeless Land. LC 74-28805. (Special Publications Series 10: No. 2). (Illus.). 200p. 1975. 12.95 (0-87044-177-9); lib. bdg. 12.95 (0-87044-182-5) Natl Geog.

— National Geographic Atlas of the World, Series 26. 6th rev. ed. (Special Publications). (Illus.). 1990. 65.00 (0-87044-834-X) Natl Geog.

— Primitive Worlds: People Lost in Time. LC 73-830. (Special Publications Series 8: No. 2). 1973. 8.95 (0-87044-127-2) Natl Geog.

National Geographic Society Staff, ed. see Aikman, Lonnelle.

National Geographic Society Staff, jt. auth. see Hirschland, Roger.

National Geographic Society Staff, jt. auth. see Kostyal, Karen.

National Geographic Society Staff, jt. auth. see McCauley, Jane.

National Geographic Society Staff, jt. auth. see McGrath, Susan.

National Geographic Society Staff, jt. auth. see McKelway, Margaret.

National Geographic Society Staff, jt. auth. see Stuart, Gene S.

***National Geographic Staff.** ABC in the Woods. (Little Learners' Library). (J). (ps). 1994. 4.50 (0-7922-1832-9) Natl Geog.

— At the Zoo. (J). (ps-3). 1993. 16.00 (0-87044-872-2) Natl Geog.

— Fun at the Fair. (J). (ps). 1993. 4.50 (0-7922-1919-8) Natl Geog.

— Houses Around Our World. (Little Learners' Library). (J). (ps). 1994. 4.50 (0-7922-1994-5) Natl Geog.

— My House. (J). (ps). 1993. 4.50 (0-7922-1835-3) Natl Geog.

— My Own Little World. (Little Learners' Library). (J). (ps). 1994. 4.50 (0-7922-1830-2) Natl Geog.

— National Geographic: The Photographs. (Illus.). 1994. pap. 50.00 (0-87044-986-9) Natl Geog.

— National Geographic Amazing Mammals '95. 1994. 9.95 (0-7922-2710-7) Random.

— National Geographic Amazing Otters. Date not set. pap. 8.00 (0-87044-770-X) Random.

— Opposites. (Little Learners' Library). (J). (ps). 1994. 4.50 (0-7922-1917-1) Natl Geog.

— Pile of Puppies. (J). (ps). 1993. 4.50 (0-7922-1834-5) Natl Geog.

— Why in the World. Crump, Donald J., ed. LC 85-18862. (Books for World Explorers Series 7: No. 1). (Illus.). 104p. 1994. 12.50 (0-87044-573-1) Natl Geog.

National Geographic Staff, jt. auth. see McGrath, Susan.

National Geographic Staff, jt. auth. see Rinard, Julie.

National Geographical Society Staff, ed. Books for Young Explorers, 4 vols., Set 1. Incl. Dinosaurs. LC 72-91418. 1972. (0-318-54543-8); Treasures in the Sea. 1972. (0-318-54544-6); Dogs Working for People. 1972. (0-318-54545-4); Lion Cubs. 1972. (0-318-54546-2); (J). (ps-3). 1972. Set lib. bdg. 16.95 (0-87044-300-3) Natl Geog.

National Glass Association Staff. Auto Glass Supervision. Date not set. pap. text ed. 49.95 (1-56393-007-2) National Glass Assn.

— Auto Glass Technician Manual: Instructor's Edition. 114p. 1993. pap. text ed. 69.95 (1-56393-006-4) National Glass Assn.

— Basic Guide to Glass & Glazing: Instructor's Manual. 116p. 1993. pap. text ed. 69.95 (1-56393-005-6) National Glass Assn.

— Basic Guide to Glass & Glazing: Level I. 1993. pap. text ed. 49.95 (1-56393-004-8) National Glass Assn.

— Master Auto Glass Technician Supervisory Manual. (Illus.). 70p. 1990. pap. 29.95 (1-56393-003-X) National Glass Assn.

— Senior Auto Glass Technician Manual. (Illus.). 120p. 1990. pap. 29.95 (1-56393-002-1) National Glass Assn.

National Governors' Assoc. Staff, ed. see Forcella, Domenic.

National Governors' Association Staff. Community Service: A Resource Guide for States. Glass, Karen, ed. 40p. (Orig.). 1989. pap. text ed. 10.00 (1-55877-053-4) Natl Governor.

— Directory of Governors of the American States, Commonwealths, & Territories, 1989. 68p. (Orig.). 1989. pap. text ed. 8.95 (1-55877-034-8) Natl Governor.

— Directory of Governors of the American States, Commonwealths, & Territories, 1990. Miller, Mark, ed. 76p. (Orig.). 1990. pap. text ed. 8.95 (1-55877-073-9) Natl Governor.

— Governors' Staff Directory, 1989. 75p. (Orig.). 1989. pap. text ed. 7.50 (1-55877-035-6) Natl Governor.

— Health Issues in Rural America. (New Alliances for Rural America Ser.). 120p. (Orig.). 1988. pap. text ed. 6.00 (1-55877-015-1) Natl Governor.

— Policy Positions, 1988-89. (Policy Positions Ser.). 280p. (Orig.). 1988. pap. text ed. 15.00 (1-55877-023-2) Natl Governor.

— Policy Positions, 1989-90. Miller, Mark, ed. 316p. (Orig.). 1989. pap. text ed. 15.00 (1-55877-064-X) Natl Governor.

— Results in Education: 1988. (Time for Results Ser.). (Orig.). 1988. pap. text ed. 12.50 (1-55877-013-5) Natl Governor.

National Governors' Association Staff & National Association of State Budget Officers Staff. Fiscal Survey of the States - October 1988. 50p. (Orig.). 1988. pap. text ed. 20.00 (1-55877-024-0) Natl Governor.

National Graves Association of Ireland Staff. The Last Post. MacCiarnain, Seamus & Conlon, Vincent, eds. (Illus.). 234p. 1986. 10.00 (0-9616291-0-X) Natl Graves Assn.

***National Grid Co. Staff.** A Practical Guide to Computer Virsuses. (Illus.). 248p. (Orig.). 1995. pap. write for info. (1-85554-218-8, Pub. by NCC Blackwell UK) Blackwell Pubs.

***National Hairdressing Federation Staff.** Setting up Your Own Salon. (Illus.). 144p. 1994. pap. 19.95 (0-632-03889-6, Pub. by Blckwell Sci Pubns UK) Blackwell Sci.

***National Health - Education Consortium Staff.** Florida's Youth, Florida's Future. 20p. 1993. 12.00 (0-937846-52-X) Inst Educ Lead.

— Texas' Youth, Texas' Future. 20p. 1993. 12.00 (0-937846-50-3) Inst Educ Lead.

***National Health & Education Consortium Staff.** Putting Children First: State-Level Collaboration Between Education & Health. 50p. 1995. 10.00 (0-937846-43-0) Inst Educ Lead.

— Starting Young: School-Based Health Centers at the Elementary Level. 50p. 1995. 10.00 (0-937846-42-2) Inst Educ Lead.

National Health Bureau of America Staff. Perfect Health, Vol. II: How to Be Young at 60 & Live to Be 100. 55p. 1976. reprint ed. spiral bd. 4.40 (0-7873-0633-9) Mokelumne.

National Health Law Program Staff, jt. auth. see Michigan Legal Services Staff.

National Health Lawyers Association Staff. Health Law Practice Guide, 3 vols. King, Marylou, ed. LC 93-17568. (Health Law Ser.). 1993. 450.00 (0-87632-912-1) Clark Boardman Callaghan.

National Heat Transfer Conference. Fouling in Heat Exchange Equipment: Presented At the 20th ASME-AICHE Heat Transfer Conference, Milwaukee, WI, August 2-5, 1981, (Sponsored by the Heat Transfer Equipment (K-10) Committee of the ASME Heat Transfer Division) Chenoweth, James M. & Impagliazzo, Mike, eds. LC 81-65617. (HTD Ser.: Vol. 17). 110p. reprint ed. pap. 31.40 (0-685-15213-8, 2056159) Bks Demand.

National Heat Transfer Conference Staff. Basic Aspects of Two Phase Flow & Heat Transfer: Presented at the 22nd National Heat Transfer Conference & Exhibition, Niagara Falls, New York, August 5-8, 1984. Dhir, V. K. & Schrock, V. E., eds. LC 84-71692. (HTD Ser.: Vol. 34). 189p. pap. 53.90 (0-7837-0205-1, 2040501) Bks Demand.

— Condensation Heat Transfer: Presented at the 18th National Heat Transfer Conference, San Diego, CA, August 6-8, 1979. Marto, P. J. & Kroeger, P. G., eds. LC 79-53410. 124p. reprint ed. pap. 35.40 (0-318-35019-X, 2030887) Bks Demand.

— Experimental & Analytical Modeling of LWR Safety Experiments: Presented at the 19th National Heat Transfer Conference, Orlando, Florida, July 27-30, 1980. Hochreiter, L. E. & Sozzi, G. L., eds. LC 80-66050. (HTD Ser.: Vol. 7). (Illus.). 144p. reprint ed. pap. 41.10 (0-8357-2836-6, 2039072) Bks Demand.

— Fundamentals of Natural Convection - Electronic Equipment Cooling: Presented at the 22nd National Heat Transfer Conference & Exhibition, Niagara Falls, New York, August 5-8, 1984. Witte, L. C. & Saxena, L. S., eds. LC 84-71690. (HTD Ser.: Vol. 32). 103p. pap. 29.40 (0-7837-0204-3, 2040500) Bks Demand.

— Natural Convection in Enclosures: Presented at the 19th National Heat Transfer Conference, Orlando, Florida, July 27-30, 1980. Torrance, K. E. & Catton, I., eds. LC 80-65786. (HTD Ser.: Vol. 8). (Illus.). 128p. reprint ed. pap. 36.50 (0-8357-2814-5, 2039053) Bks Demand.

— Nonequilibrium Interfacial Transport Processes: Presented at the 18th National Heat Transfer Conference, San Diego, California, August 6-8, 1979. Chen, J. C. & Bankoff, S. G., eds. LC 79-53412. (Illus.). 95p. reprint ed. pap. 27.10 (0-8357-2868-4, 2039104) Bks Demand.

— Thermal-Hydraulics in Nuclear Power Technology: Presented at the 20th National Heat Transfer Conference, Milwaukee, Wisconsin, August 2-5, 1981. Sun, K. H. et al, eds. LC 81-65616. (HTD Ser.: Vol. 15). (Illus.). 92p. reprint ed. pap. 26.30 (0-8357-2815-3, 2039054) Bks Demand.

National Herbart Society Staff. National Herbart Society Yearbooks One to Five 1895-1899, 5 Vols, Set. LC 70-89209. (American Education: Its Men, Institutions & Ideas, Ser. 1). 1978. reprint ed. 47.95 (0-405-01448-1) Ayer.

***National History Standards Task Force Staff.** National Standards for United States History: Exploring the American Experience. (National History STandards Project Ser.). (Illus.). 310p. (Orig.). (C). 1994. pap. text ed. 24.95 (0-9633218-1-1) Natl Ctr Hist.

— National Standards for World History: Exploring Paths to the Present. (National History STandards Project Ser.). (Illus.). 310p. (Orig.). (C). 1994. pap. text ed. 24.95 (0-9633218-2-X) Natl Ctr Hist.

National Hockey League Staff. Hockey Rules in Pictures. (Sports Rules in Pictures Ser.). (Illus.). 96p. 1992. pap. 8.95 (0-399-51772-3, Perigree Bks) Berkley Pub.

— National Hockey League Official Rule Book. (Illus.). 180p. 1993. 19.95 (1-880141-56-6); pap. 7.95 (1-880141-55-8) Triumph Bks.

— NHL Official Guide & Record Book 1995-96. rev. ed. (Illus.). 448p. 1995. pap. 18.95 (1-57243-035-4) Triumph Bks.

— 1994-95 National Hockey League Official Guide & Record Book. rev. ed. (Illus.). 448p. 1994. pap. 16.95 (1-880141-78-7) Triumph Bks.

— Official NHL Stanley Cup Fact Book. (Illus.). 224p. 1995. pap. 12.95 (1-57243-045-1) Triumph Bks.

— Official Rules of the NHL 1996. rev. ed. (Official Rules Ser.). (Illus.). 160p. 1995. pap. 8.95 (1-57243-036-2) Triumph Bks.

National Hockey League Staff, ed. National Hockey League Official Guide & Record Book 1992-93. (Illus.). 432p. (Orig.). 1992. lib. bdg. 39.95 (1-880141-18-3); pap. 16.95 (1-880141-17-5) Triumph Bks.

— National Hockey League Official Guide & Record Book, 1993-94. (Illus.). 432p. 1993. pap. 16.95 (1-880141-43-4) Triumph Bks.

***National Hospice Organization, 1991 Ethics Committee Staff.** Do-Not Resuscitate (DNR) Decisions in the Context of Hospice Care. 32p. 1992. 10.50 (0-931207-19-3) Natl Hospice.

***National Hospice Organization, Alternative Care Task Force Staff.** Alternative Care Programs in Hospice. 29p. 1991. 10.50 (0-931207-11-8) Natl Hospice.

***National Hospice Organization, Commercial Reimbursement Task Force Staff.** Commercial Reimbursement Insurance Monograph. 10p. Date not set. lp 7.35 (0-931207-25-8) Natl Hospice.

— Managed Care Monograph. 37p. 1993. 10.50 (0-931207-21-5) Natl Hospice.

***National Hospice Organization, Ethics Committee.** Discontinuation of Hospice Care: Ethical Issues. 15p. 1993. 15.75 (0-931207-22-3) Natl Hospice.

***National Hospice Organization Staff.** Hospice Bereavement Bibliography. 48p. Date not set. ring bd. 15.75 (0-931207-26-6) Natl Hospice.

— Hospice Bibliography. 185p. 1993. ring bd. 26.25 (0-931207-29-0) Natl Hospice.

— Hospice Legislation: 1977-1994. 252p. (C). 1995. ring bd. 60.00 (0-931207-34-7) Natl Hospice.

— Hospice Services Guidelines & Definitions. Brandt, Katherine, ed. 8p. (Orig.). 1995. pap. 7.35 (0-931207-31-2) Natl Hospice.

— 1993 Hospice Personnel Compensation Study. 21p. 1993. 105.00 (0-931207-13-4) Natl Hospice.

— Standards of a Hospice Program of Care. 40p. 1993. ring bd. 31.50 (0-931207-20-7) Natl Hospice.

— Volunteer Training Curriculum. Bates, Ira J. & Brandt, Katherine E., eds. 147p. 1990. ring bd. 45.00 (0-931207-06-1) Natl Hospice.

***National Hospice Organization, Standards & Accreditation Committee Staff.** Quality Assurance: A Primer for Hospice Programs. 38p. 1989. 10.50 (0-931207-17-7) Natl Hospice.

National Housing Law Project Staff. FMHA Housing Programs: Tenants' & Purchasers' Rights. 400p. (Orig.). 1982. pap. 60.00 (0-9606098-2-2) Natl Housing Law.

— HUD Housing Programs: Tenants' Rights. 475p. (Orig.). 1981. pap. 75.00 (0-9606098-0-6) Natl Housing Law.

— HUD Housing Programs: Tenants' Rights 1985 Supplement. 600p. (Orig.). 1985. pap. 45.00 (0-9606098-5-7) Natl Housing Law.

— Outline of New Developments Since the Writing of HUD Housing Programs: Tenants Rights, 1985 Supplement. 42p. 1987. pap. 4.50 (0-685-23181-X, 41,125) NCLS Inc.

— The Subsidized Housing Handbook: How to Provide, Preserve & Manage Housing for Lower-Income People. 500p. (Orig.). 1982. pap. 35.00 (0-9606098-3-0) Natl Housing Law.

National Housing Law Project Staff & Johnson, Sara E. Preserving HUD-Assisted Housing for Use by Low-Income Tenants: An Advocate's Guide. 484p. (Orig.). 1985. pap. 25.00 (0-941077-05-5, 38,900) NCLS Inc.

National Immigration Project of the National Lawyer's Guild Staff. Immigration Act of 1990 Handbook: The Complete Guide to the 1990 Ace, 1992. 1992. pap. 79.50 (0-87632-822-2) Clark Boardman Callaghan.

***National In-Line Hockey Association Staff.** Official Rules of In-Line Hockey. (Illus.). 144p. 1995. pap. 8.95 (1-57243-061-3) Triumph Bks.

N

An Asterisk (*) at the beginning of an entry indicates that the title is appearing in BIP for the first time.

National Incinerator Conference Staff. Resource Recovery Through Incineration: Proceedings; Papers Presented at 1974 National Incinerator Conference, Miami, Florida, May 12-15, 1974. LC 70-124402. 380p. reprint ed. pap. 108.30 (*0-317-29795-3*, 2016866) Bks Demand.

National Industrial Conference Board, Inc. Staff. Trade Associations: Their Economic Significance & Legal Status. 2nd rev. ed. LC 25-12032. xiv, 388p. 1982. reprint ed. lib. bdg. 47.50 (*0-89941-164-9*, 302310) W S Hein.

— The Work of the International Labor Organization. 1983. reprint ed. lib. bdg. 40.00 (*0-89941-211-4*, 303010) W S Hein.

National Industrial Conference Board Staff. The Banking Situation in the United States. Bruchey, Stuart, ed. LC 80-1188. (Rise of Commercial Banking Ser.). (Illus.). 1981. reprint ed. lib. bdg. 18.95 (*0-405-13671-4*) Ayer.

National Industrial Council Staff & Du Preez, B. G., eds. Consolidated Agreements of the Motor Industry. 1989. ring bd. write for info. (*0-7021-2263-7*, Pub. by Juta SA) W W Gaunt.

National Industrial Council Staff & Levy, David, eds. Consolidated Agreements of the National Industrial Council for the Iron, Steel, Engineering & Metallurgical Industry. 1987. ring bd. write for info. (*0-7021-1920-2*, Pub. by Juta SA) W W Gaunt.

National Industrial Fuel Efficiency Service Ltd. Staff. Boiler Operators Handbook. Graham & Trotman Ltd. Staff, ed. 155p. 1981. pap. text ed. 23.50 (*0-86010-251-3*) G & T Inc.

National Information Center for Educational Media Staff. Audiocassette Finder: A Subject Guide to Educational & Literary Materials on Audiocassettes. 2nd ed. Korney, Stephanie, ed. 925p. 1989. 95.00 (*0-937548-14-6*) Natl Info Ctr NM.

— Index to AV Producers & Distributors. 7th ed. LC 82-60346. 1989. pap. 75.00 (*0-937548-13-8*) Natl Info Ctr NM.

— Science & Computer Literacy Audiovisuals: A Teacher's Sourcebook. Johnstone, J. C., ed. 275p. (Orig.). 1986. pap. 49.95 (*0-89320-101-4*) Natl Info Ctr NM.

— Vocational & Technical Audiovisuals: A Teacher's Sourcebook. Johnstone, J. C., ed. 450p. (Orig.). 1986. pap. 49.95 (*0-89320-100-6*) Natl Info Ctr NM.

— Wellness Media: An Audiovisual Sourcebook for Health & Fitness. Johnstone, J. C., ed. 330p. (Orig.). 1986. pap. 49.95 (*0-89320-107-3*) Natl Info Ctr NM.

National Information Standards Organization. International Standard Serial Numbering. 16p. 1992. reprint ed. pap. 20.00 (*0-88738-992-9*, Z39.9) Transaction Pubs.

National Information Standards Organization Staff. American National Standard for Computerized Book Ordering: Abstract: Approved October 10, 1992 by the American National Standards Institute. LC 93-16162. (National Information Standards Ser.). 1993. pap. 40.00 (*0-88738-931-7*) Transaction Pubs.

— Codes for the Representation of Names of Countries: ANSI-NISO-ISO 3166. 76p. (C). 1993. pap. 50.00 (*0-88738-937-6*) Transaction Pubs.

— Common Command Language for On-Line Interactive Information Retrieval, Z39.58, 1992. 30p. 1993. 35.00 (*0-88738-940-6*) Transaction Pubs.

— Common Command Language for Online Interactive Information Retrieval, Z39.58-1992. LC 93-40322. (National Information Standards Ser.). 25p. 1994. 48.00 (*1-880124-03-3*) NISO.

— Computer Software Description, Z39.67-1993. LC 93-45764. (National Information Standards Ser.: No. 1041-5653). 16p. 1994. 45.00 (*1-880124-05-X*) NISO.

— GILS Report. (National Information Standards Ser.). 1994. write for info. (*1-880124-11-4*) NISO.

— Information Interchange Format, Z39.2-1994. LC 94-9641. (National Information Standards Ser.). 1994. 30.00 (*1-880124-08-4*) NISO.

— Information Interchange, 1992. 16p. (C). 1992. pap. 25.00 (*0-88738-938-4*, Z39.2) Transaction Pubs.

— Printed Information on Spines, Z39.41-1990. 20.00 (*0-88738-944-9*) Transaction Pubs.

— Serial Item & Contribution Identifier, 1991. 1992. 40.00 (*0-88738-943-0*, Z39.56) Transaction Pubs.

— Single-Tier Steel Bracket Library Shelving. LC 94-45135. (National Information Standards Ser.). 1995. write for info. (*1-880124-09-2*) NISO.

— Volume & File Structure of CD-ROM for Information Exchange: ANSI-NISO-ISO 9660. LC 93-3113. 64p. (C). 1993. pap. 48.00 (*0-88738-936-8*) Transaction Pubs.

— Z39.23 - 1990 Standard Technical Report Number (STRN) Format & Creation. (National Information Standards Ser.). 17p. 1995. write for info. (*1-880124-13-0*) NISO.

— Z39.43 - 1993 Standard Address Number for the Publishing Industry. (National Information Standards Ser.). 14p. 1995. write for info. (*1-880124-14-9*) NISO.

— Z39.53 - 1994 Codes for the Representation of Languages for Information Interchange. LC 94-36086. (National Information Standards Ser.). 1995. 35.00 (*1-880124-10-6*) NISO.

— Z39.56 - 1991 Serial Item & Contribution Identifier. (National Information Standards Ser.). 38p. 1995. write for info. (*1-880124-15-7*) NISO.

— Z39.57 - 1989 Holdings Statements for Non-Serial Items. (National Information Standards Ser.). 67p. 1995. write for info. (*1-880124-16-5*) NISO.

— Z39.63 - 1989 Interlibrary Loan Data Elements. (National Information Standards Ser.). 59p. 1995. write for info. (*1-880124-17-3*) NISO.

— Z39.66 - 1992 Durable Hardcover Binding for Books. (National Information Standards Ser.). 22p. 1995. write for info. (*1-880124-18-1*) NISO.

— Z39.9 - 1992 International Standard Serial Numbering (ISSN) (National Information Standard Ser.). 18p. 1995. write for info. (*1-880124-12-2*) NISO.

National Insecurity Council Staff. It's a Conspiracy! 252p. 1992. 9.95 (*1-879682-10-9*) Earth Works.

National Insecurity Council Staff & Litchfield, Michael. It's a Conspiracy! II: More of America's Favorite Conspiracy Theories! 1993. pap. 9.95 (*1-879682-34-6*) Earth Works.

National Inst. for Social Work Staff. The Swing Directory of Social Welfare Information Networks. (C). 1988. 35.00 (*0-685-31908-3*, Pub. by Natl Inst Soc Work) St Mut.

National Institue for Social Work Staff, ed. Personal Social Services Council: At Home in a Boarding House. 1981. 20.00 (*0-317-40623-X*, Pub. by Natl Inst Soc Work) St Mut.

National Institute for Burn Medicine Staff. International Bibliography on Burns: 1985 Supplement. Feller, Irving, ed. LC 71-94573. 120p. 1986. pap. 25.00 (*0-917478-16-9*) Natl Inst Burn.

— International Bibliography on Burns: 1986 Supplement. Feller, I., ed. LC 71-94573. 134p. 1986. pap. 25.00 (*0-917478-17-7*) Natl Inst Burn.

National Institute for Explication Staff. Children of Conflict: Nicaragua. Barker, Barry, ed. (Illus.). 1989. 17.00 (*0-317-93725-1*) W T Swengros.

National Institute for Exploration Members. Egypt Images of Adventure. Nichols, Tim et al, eds. (Illus.). 132p. 1988. 24.95 (*0-942529-01-4*) Viewfinder Pubns.

National Institute for Occupational Safety & Health Staff, jt. auth. see U. S. Environmental Protection Agency Staff.

National Institute for Social Work Staff. The Barclay Report: Social Workers, Their Role & Tasks. Report of an Independent Working Party. (C). 1982. 60.00 (*0-685-40349-1*, Pub. by Natl Inst Soc Work) St Mut.

— Helping People Work Together: A Guide to Participative Working Practices. (C). 1987. text ed. 40.00 (*0-902789-42-2*, Pub. by Natl Inst Soc Work) St Mut.

— Residential Care for Elderly People: Using Research to Improve Practice. (C). 1988. text ed. 45.00 (*0-902789-49-X*, Pub. by Natl Inst Soc Work) St Mut.

National Institute for Social Work Staff, ed. The Barclay Report: Papers from a Discussion Day. 1983. 40.00 (*0-317-40566-7*, Pub. by Natl Inst Soc Work) St Mut.

— Nineteen Twenty-Four to Nineteen Eighty-Three: Commentary by a Social Servant. 1984. 35.00 (*0-317-40568-3*, Pub. by Natl Inst Soc Work) St Mut.

— PSSC, the Case History of an Advisory Non-Governmental Organisation: 1973-1980. 1981. 15.00 (*0-317-42889-6*) St Mut.

National Institute for Social Work Staff, ed. see Epstein, Laura.

National Institute for Social Work Staff, ed. see Payne, Chris & Scott, Tony.

National Institute for the Control of Pharmaceutical & Biological Products Staff, ed. Colour Atlas of Chinese Traditional Drugs, Vol. 1. (Illus.). 300p. 1987. text ed. 110.00 (*0-945345-09-7*, Pub. by Sci Pr CH) Lubrecht & Cramer.

National Institute for Trial Advocacy, U. S. A., jt. auth. see Siemer, Deanne C.

National Institute for Urban Wildlife Staff. Wildlife Habitat Conservation Teacher's Pac Series: An Environmental Education Teaching Aid, 9 vols. 5.00 (*0-318-04278-9*) Natl Inst Urban Wildlife.

National Institute for Work & Learning. Getting a Job in the Computer Age. LC 86-776. 101p. (Orig.). 1986. pap. 3.95 (*0-87866-440-8*) Petersons Guides.

National Institute of Business Management Staff. Mastering the Business Interview. 1992. pap. 7.95 (*0-425-13188-2*) Berkley Pub.

— Three Hundred Sixty Most Guarded Secrets of Executive Success. 381p. 1990. write for info. (*1-880024-00-4*) Natl Inst Busn.

National Institute of Construction Law, Inc. Editorial Board Staff. Construction & Design Law, 5 vols., Set. suppl. ed. 1993. ring bd. 400.00x (*0-87215-849-7*) Michie Butterworth.

— Construction & Design Law Digest. Separate bound vols., 1984-1985. 100.00 (*0-87473-363-4*); Bound vol., 1985. 125.00 (*0-87215-979-5*); Bound vol., 1986. 110.00 (*0-87473-271-9*); Bound volume, 1988. 110.00 (*0-87473-491-6*); Bound vol., 1990. 110.00 (*0-87473-655-2*) Michie Butterworth.

— Construction & Design Law Digest. 1990. ring bd. 150.00 (*0-685-57944-1*) Michie Butterworth.

National Institute of Justice Staff & United States Department of Justice Staff. Quality of Prisoner Self-Reports: Arrest & Conviction Response Errors. Marquis, Kent H. & Ebener, Patricia A., eds. LC 81-168320. xvii, 176p. 1981. 15.00 (*0-8330-0300-3*, R-2637) Rand Corp.

National Institute of Mental Health Staff. Disasters & Mental Health: Contemporary Perspectives & Innovation in Services to Disaster Victims. Sowder, Barbara J. & Lystad, Mary, eds. LC 86-20616. (Illus.). 412p. 1986. reprint ed. pap. text ed. 18.50 (*0-88048-261-3*, 48-261-3) Am Psychiatric.

— How to Define & Research Stress. Eichler, Anita et al, eds. LC 86-20633. (Illus.). 160p. 1986. pap. text ed. 14.00 (*0-88048-268-0*, 48-268-0) Am Psychiatric.

— The Mental Health of the Child: Program Reports. Segal, Julius, ed. 1973. 19.95 (*0-405-03149-1*) Ayer.

National Institute of Mental Health (U. S.) Staff. The Neuroscience of Mental Health. LC 84-601129. 94p. reprint ed. pap. 26.80 (*0-8357-7855-X*, 2036232) Bks Demand.

National Institute of Public Health & Environmental Protection Staff, jt. auth. see Scenario Committee on Aging Staff.

National Institute of Senior Centers Staff. Senior Center Standards & Self-Assessment Workbook: Guidelines for Practice 1990 Edition. Ericson, Helen, ed. 200p. 1990. 25.00 (*0-910883-56-4*) Natl Coun Aging.

National Institute on Adult Daycare, a Constituent Unit of the National Council on the Aging, Inc. Staff. Standards & Guidelines for Adult Day Care. 2nd ed. LC 90-13518. 244p. 1990. pap. text ed. 25.00 (*0-910883-54-8*) Natl Coun Aging.

***National Institute on Drug Abuse, National Research Council Committee.** Development of Medications for the Treatment of Opiate & Cocaine Addictions: Issues for the Government & Private Sector. 272p. (Orig.). (C). 1995. pap. text ed. 37.00 (*0-309-05244-0*) Natl Acad Pr.

National Institutes of Health, Health & Human Services Dept. Staff. Bibliography of the History of Medicine, No. 25: 1985-1989. 1464p. 1990. text ed. 25.00 (*0-16-026803-6*) USGPO.

— Catalogue of Seventeenth Century Printed Books in the National Library of Medicine. 1329p. 1989. text ed. 45.00 (*0-16-002651-2*) USGPO.

National Issues Forum Institute Staff. The Boundaries of Free Speech: How Free Is Too Free? 32p. 1991. 2.95 (*0-8403-6924-7*) Kendall-Hunt.

— Criminal Violence: What Direction Now for the War on Crime? 32p. 1994. 2.95 (*0-8403-7435-6*) Kendall-Hunt.

— The Health Care Cost Explosion. abr. ed. 32p. 1993. 2.95 (*0-8403-8657-5*) Kendall-Hunt.

— The Poverty Puzzle: What Should Be Done to Help the Poor? 32p. 1993. 2.95 (*0-8403-8651-6*) Kendall-Hunt.

— The Poverty Puzzle: What Should Be Done to Help the Poor? abr. ed. 32p. 1993. 2.95 (*0-8403-8652-4*) Kendall-Hunt.

National Issues Forum Staff. America's Role in the World. 32p. 1991. 2.95 (*0-8403-6925-5*) Kendall-Hunt.

— Boundaries of Free Speech: Deciding How Free Is Too Free. abr. ed. 32p. 1991. 2.95 (*0-8403-6927-1*) Kendall-Hunt.

— Coping with AIDS. abr. ed. 48p. (C). 1988. 2.95 (*0-8403-4837-1*) Kendall-Hunt.

— The Day Care Dilemma: Who Should Be Responsible for the Children. 48p. 1989. 2.95 (*0-8403-5264-6*) Kendall-Hunt.

— The Day Care Dilemma: Who Should Be Responsible for the Children. 48p. 1989. teacher ed, per. 15.00 (*0-8403-5266-2*) Kendall-Hunt.

— The Drug Crisis: Public Strategies for Breaking the Habit. 80p. 1989. teacher ed 15.00 (*0-8403-5272-7*) Kendall-Hunt.

— Energy Options: Finding a Solution to the Power Predicament. 32p. 1991. 2.95 (*0-8403-6923-9*) Kendall-Hunt.

— Energy Options: Finding a Solution to the Power Predicament. abr. ed. 32p. 1991. 2.95 (*0-8403-6926-3*) Kendall-Hunt.

— The Environment at Risk: Responding to Growing Dangers. 48p. 1989. teacher ed 15.00 (*0-8403-5269-7*) Kendall-Hunt.

— The Environment at Risk: Responding to Growing Dangers. abr. ed. 32p. 1989. 2.95 (*0-8403-5268-9*) Kendall-Hunt.

— The Farm Crisis: Who's in Trouble, How to Respond. abr. ed. 36p. 1988. 2.95 (*0-8403-4782-0*) Kendall-Hunt.

— The Health Crisis: Containing Costs, Expanding Coverage. 32p. 1992. 2.95 (*0-8403-7432-1*) Kendall-Hunt.

— The Public Debt: Breaking the Habit of Deficit Spending. abr. ed. 32p. 1988. 2.95 (*0-8403-4794-4*) Kendall-Hunt.

— The Trade Gap: Regaining the Competitive Edge. abr. ed. 32p. 1988. 2.95 (*0-8403-4788-X*) Kendall-Hunt.

National Issues Forums Institute Staff. The Four Trillion Dollar Debt: Tough Choices about Soaring Federal Deficits. 36p. 1993. 2.95 (*0-8403-8653-2*) Kendall-Hunt.

— The Four Trillion Dollar Debt: Tough Choices about Soaring Federal Deficits. abr. ed. 32p. 1993. 2.95 (*0-8403-8654-0*) Kendall-Hunt.

— The Health Care Cost Explosion. 32p. 1993. 2.95 (*0-8403-8656-7*) Kendall-Hunt.

— The Health Care Crisis: Containing Costs, Expanding Coverage. abr. ed. 32p. 1992. 2.95 (*0-8403-7433-X*) Kendall-Hunt.

— Prescription for Prosperity: Four Paths to Economic Renewal. 32p. 1992. 2.95 (*0-8403-7438-0*) Kendall-Hunt.

National Issues Forums Staff. Growing up at Risk. 32p. (C). 1990. 2.95 (*0-8403-6028-2*) Kendall-Hunt.

— Growing up at Risk. abr. ed. 32p. (C). 1990. 2.95 (*0-8403-6029-0*) Kendall-Hunt.

— Regaining the Competitive Edge: Are We up to the Job? abr. ed. 32p. (C). 1990. 2.95 (*0-8403-5941-1*) Kendall-Hunt.

***National Issues Staff.** Admission Decisions. abr. ed. (Abridged Ser.). 76p. 1994. 49.50 (*0-7872-0501-X*) Kendall-Hunt.

— Contested Values. abr. ed. (Abridged Ser.). 76p. 1994. 49.50 (*0-7872-0502-8*); 2.95 (*0-8403-9891-3*) Kendall-Hunt.

— Course Implementation Guide. 112p. 1988. ring bd. 25.00 (*0-8403-4799-5*) Kendall-Hunt.

— Education: How Do We Get the Results We Want? 32p. 1992. disk 3.50 (*0-8403-8138-7*) Kendall-Hunt.

— Education (Issues in Brief Package) 12p. 1992. boxed 10.00 (*0-8403-8139-5*) Kendall-Hunt.

— Juvenile Violence. abr. ed. (Abridged Ser.). 76p. 1994. 49.50 (*0-7872-0500-1*) Kendall-Hunt.

— People & Politics: Who Should Govern? 48p. 1992. disk 2.95 (*0-8403-8091-7*) Kendall-Hunt.

— Politics in the Twenty-First Century. 48p. 1993. 4.00 (*0-8403-8393-2*) Kendall-Hunt.

National Issues Staff & Schwartzhoff, James P. Health Care for the Elderly: Moral Dilemmas, Mortal Choices. 48p. 1988. 2.95 (*0-8403-4796-0*) Kendall-Hunt.

National Japanese American Historical Society Staff. Japanese American Oral History Guide. 46p. 1992. pap. text ed. 6.50 (*1-881506-01-0*) Natl Japnse Am HS.

National Jewish Center for Learning & Leadership Staff. Sacred Times. (Illus.). 132p. 1992. write for info. (*0-9633329-0-2*) Natl Jew Ctr Lrn & Ldership.

National Jewish Welfare Board Staff. Bibliography of Jewish Instrumental Music. 60p. 1993. reprint ed. lib. bdg. 69.00 (*0-7812-9686-2*) Rprt Serv.

— Bibliography of Jewish Vocal Music. 66p. 1993. reprint ed. lib. bdg. 69.00 (*0-7812-9687-0*) Rprt Serv.

***National Judicial College Staff.** Americans with Disabilities Act - An Instructional Guide for Judges & Court Administrators. 448p. 1994. ring bd. 50.00 (*0-614-06248-9*) Natl Judicial Coll.

— Planning - Conducting a Course: "Managing Trials Effectively" 273p. 1994. ring bd. 35.00 (*0-614-06247-0*) Natl Judicial Coll.

***National Judicial College Staff & ABA-JAD National Conference of State Trial Judges Staff.** Capital Cases Benchbook. 383p. 1994. ring bd. 35.00 (*0-614-06244-6*) Natl Judicial Coll.

— The Judge's Book. 2nd ed. 437p. 1994. 39.95 (*0-614-06246-2*) Natl Judicial Coll.

National Jury Project Staff. Jurywork: Systematic Techniques, 2 vols., Set. 2nd ed. LC 82-22635. 1983. ring bd. 230.00 (*0-87632-322-0*) Clark Boardman Callaghan.

National Labor Relations Board Staff. Annual Reports of the National Labor Relations Board, 1936-1965. 10 Vols, Set. LC 79-136753. 1971. reprint ed. 18.95 (*0-405-01715-4*) Ayer.

National Lampoon Staff. That's Sick! A Collection of the Rudest & Crudest Cartoons from National Lampoon. 1994. pap. 8.95 (*0-8092-3695-8*) Contemp Bks.

— This Time You've Gone Too Far! A Sick & Twisted Cartoon Collection. (Illus.). 128p. 1995. pap. 8.95 (*0-8092-3567-6*) Contemp Bks.

National Lawyers Guild. National Immigration Project Staff, et al. Immigration Law & Crimes. LC 84-4281. 1984. ring bd. 140.00 (*0-87632-436-7*) Clark Boardman Callaghan.

National Lawyers Guild, San Francisco Bay Area Chapter, Anti-Sexism Committee, et al. Sexual Orientation & the Law. LC 84-24213. (Civil Rights Law Ser.). 1985. ring bd. 135.00 (*0-87632-454-5*) Clark Boardman Callaghan.

***National Lawyers Guild Staff.** Civil Rights Litigation & Attorney Fees Annual Handbook, Vol. 10. (Civil Rights Ser.). 1994. pap. 115.00 (*0-614-07303-0*) Clark Boardman Callaghan.

— Employee & Union Member Guide to Labor Law, 2 vols. LC 81-10090. 1992. ring bd. 235.00 (*0-87632-113-9*) Clark Boardman Callaghan.

National Lawyers Guild Staff & Klieman, Rikki. Representation of Witnesses Before Federal Grand Juries. 3rd ed. LC 83-15607. (Criminal Law Ser.). (C). 1984. ring bd. 145.00 (*0-87632-426-X*) Clark Boardman Callaghan.

National Leadership Commission on Health Care Staff. For the Health of a Nation: A Shared Responsibility. LC 89-11013. 206p. 1989. pap. 30.00 (*0-910701-51-2*, 0879) Health Admin Pr.

National League for Nursing Staff. Criteria & Guidelines for Evaluation of Associate Degree Programs in Nursing. rev. ed. 46p. 1991. pap. text ed. 5.95 (*0-88737-535-9*, 23-2439) Natl League Nurse.

— Criteria & Guidelines for Evaluation of Baccalaureate & Higher Degree Programs in Nursing. rev. ed. 74p. 1992. pap. text ed. 6.95 (*0-88737-552-9*, 15-2474) Natl League Nurse.

— Criteria & Guidelines for Evaluation of Diploma Programs in Nursing. rev. ed. 50p. 1992. pap. text ed. 5.95 (*0-88737-538-3*, 16-2444) Natl League Nurse.

— Criteria & Guidelines for Evaluation of Practical Nursing Programs. rev. ed. 64p. 1992. pap. text ed. 5.95 (*0-88737-539-1*, 38-2445) Natl League Nurse.

National League for Nursing Staff, ed. Gerontology in the Nursing Curriculum. (C). 1992. pap. text ed. 5.95 (*0-88737-570-7*, 14-2506) Natl League Nurse.

— Perspectives in Nursing 1991-1993. 224p. (C). 1992. pap. text ed. 25.95 (*0-88737-550-2*) Natl League Nurse.

— Scholarships & Loans for Nursing Education, 1992-1993. rev. ed. 112p. 1992. pap. text ed. 12.95 (*0-88737-560-X*) Natl League Nurse.

***National League for Nursing Staff, rev.** Scholarships & Loans for Nursing Education 1994-1995. rev. ed. 118p. 1994. 15.95 (*0-88737-614-2*) Natl League Nurse.

National League of Cities Staff. Building City Council Leadership Skills: A Casebook of Models & Methods. 158p. 1980. 20.00 (*0-317-35151-6*, 3504); 10.00 (*0-317-35152-4*) Natl League Cities.

National Legal Resource Center for Child Advocacy & Protection, jt. auth. see American Bar Association, Young Lawyers Division Staff.

National Legal Resources Center for Child Advocacy & Protection Staff. Protecting Children Through the Legal System. 972p. 1981. pap. 20.00 (*0-685-18987-2*, 549-0023-01) Amer Bar Assn.

— Representing Learning Disabled Children: A Manual for Attorneys. 152p. 1985. pap. 10.00 (*0-685-18991-0*, 549-0020-01) Amer Bar Assn.

National Lesbian & Gay Survey Staff. Proust, Cole Porter, Michelangelo, Marc Almond & Me: Writings by Gay Men on Their Lives & Lifestyles. LC 92-37658. 224p. 1993. pap. 15.95 (*0-415-08914-X*, A9971, Routledge NY) Routledge.

— What a Lesbian Looks Like: Writings by Lesbians on Their Lives & Lifestyles. 192p. 1992. pap. 14.95 (*0-415-08100-9*, A9591) Routledge.

N

An Asterisk (*) at the beginning of an entry indicates that the title is appearing in BIP for the first time.

National Library Canada Staff. Canadian ISBN Publishers' Directory. 473p. (Orig.). 1992. pap. 77.35 (*0-660-57481-0*, Pub. by Canada Commun Grp CN) Accents Pubns.
— Interlibrary Loan Services Manual: Interlibrary Loan Policies in Canada. 564p. (Orig.). 1993. pap. 64.95 (*0-660-14957-5*, Pub. by Canada Commun Grp CN) Accents Pubns.
National Library of Anthropology & History Staff, Mexico City. Catalogo de la Biblioteca Nacional de Antropologia y Historia - Catalogs of the National Library of Anthropology & History, 10 vols., Set. 1972. lib. bdg. 960.00 (*0-8161-0918-4*, Hall Library) G K Hall.
National Library of Ireland Staff. Manuscript Sources for the History of Irish Civilisation, 11 Vols, Set. 1970. lib. bdg. 1,200.00 (*0-8161-0662-2*, Hall Library) G K Hall.
— Manuscript Sources for the History of Irish Civilisation: First Supplement, 3 vols., Set. MacLochlainn, Alf, ed. 1979. lib. bdg. 430.00 (*0-8161-0248-1*, Hall Library) G K Hall.
— Sources for the History of Irish Civilization: Articles in Irish Periodicals, 9 vols., Set. 1970. lib. bdg. 1,090.00 (*0-8161-0858-7*, Hall Library) G K Hall.
National Library of Medicine Staff. Cumulated Index Medicus, Vol. 11: Nineteen Seventy. LC 74-8462. 1975. reprint ed. 48.95 (*0-405-18895-1*) Ayer.
— Cumulative Index Medicus, Vol. 13, 8 vols. LC 74-8462. 1975. 455.00 (*0-405-06650-3*) Ayer.
National Library of Peru Staff. Author Catalog of the Peruvian Collection of the National Library of Peru, 6 vols., Set. De Gaviria, Maria C., ed. 1979. lib. bdg. 755.00 (*0-8161-0250-3*, Hall Library) G K Hall.
***National Library Staff.** Canadian Marc Communication Format for Bibliographic Data. 1993. 123.50x (*0-660-15355-6*, Pub. by Canada Commun Grp CN) Accents Pubns.
National Live Stock & Meat Board Staff. Cooking Today's Beef. LC 88-700115. 1988. teacher ed, vhs 10.00 (*0-88700-008-8*) Natl Live Stock.
— Manufacturing Guidelines for Processed Pork Products. (Illus.). 60p. (Orig.). (C). 1985. pap. text ed. 10.00 (*0-88700-005-3*) Natl Live Stock.
National Live Stock & Meat Board Staff & Breidenstein, B. C. Manufacturing Guidelines for Processed Beef Products. (Illus.). 60p. 1983. 10.00 (*0-88700-001-0*) Natl Live Stock.
National Lubricating Grease Institute Staff. Glossary: Definition of Terms Relating to the Lubricating Grease Industry. 1984. teacher ed, pap. 4.00 (*0-9613935-4-8*) Natl Lubrica Grease.
— NLGI Lubricating Grease Guide. 2nd rev. ed. Ehrlich, Mel, ed. (Illus.). 148p. 1994. pap. 26.00 (*0-9613935-1-3*) Natl Lubrica Grease.
— NLGI Production Survey Report. 15p. 1994. pap. 40.00 (*0-614-04567-3*) Natl Lubrica Grease.
— NLGI Steady Flow Charts for Grease. (Illus.). 16p. 1982. student ed, pap. 6.00 (*0-9613935-3-X*) Natl Lubrica Grease.
National Machine Tool Builders Association Staff. Shop Math. LC 82-13534. (NMTBA Shop Practices Ser.). 140p. (C). 1982. pap. 13.95 (*0-471-07841-7*) P-H.
National Management Association Staff. The NMA Handbook for Managers. 416p. 1987. 39.95 (*0-13-622903-4*) P-H.
National Manpower Institute Staff & Wirtz, Willard. The Boundless Resource: A Prospectus for an Education-Work Policy. 205p. 1975. 10.00 (*0-915220-10-5*) Natl Inst Work.
National Maritime Museum Staff. Van de Velde Drawings: A Catalogue of Drawings in the National Maritime Museum Made by the Elder & the Younger William Van de Velde, Vol. 2: The Ingram Volume. LC 58-14763. 372p. reprint ed. pap. 106.10 (*0-317-27097-4*, 2024551) Bks Demand.
National Maritime Museum Staff, ed. Concise Catalogue of Oil Paintings in the National Maritime Museum. (Illus.). 600p. 1988. 99.50 (*1-85149-076-0*) Antique Collect.
National Master Ch'ing Liang. Flower Adornment Sutra Preface. Buddhist Text Translation Society, tr. (Illus.). 244p. (Orig.). (C). 1979. pap. 7.00 (*0-685-00938-6*) Buddhist Text.
— Flower Adornment Sutra Prologue: Vol. I, The First Door. Buddhist Text Translation Society, tr. (Illus.). 252p. (Orig.). (C). 1981. pap. 10.00 (*0-917512-66-9*) Buddhist Text.
— Flower Adornment Sutra Prologue, Vol. II: The Second Door, Pt. I. Buddhist Text Translation Society, tr. (Illus.). 280p. (Orig.). (C). 1981. pap. 10.00 (*0-685-57674-4*) Buddhist Text.
— Flower Adornment Sutra Prologue, Vol. III: The Second Door, Pt. II. Buddhist Text Translation Society Staff, tr. (Illus.). 220p. (Orig.). (C). 1983. pap. 10.00 (*0-917512-98-7*) Buddhist Text.
— Flower Adornment Sutra Prologue, Vol. III: The Second Door, Pt. II, Set. Buddhist Text Translation Society Staff, tr. (Illus.). 220p. (Orig.). (C). 1983. 38.00 (*0-685-57848-8*) Buddhist Text.
— Flower Adornment Sutra Prologue, Vol. IV: The Second Door, Part III. Buddhist Text Translation Society, tr. 170p. (Orig.). (C). 1983. pap. 8.00 (*0-88139-009-7*) Buddhist Text.
National Mastitis Council. Laboratory & Field Handbook on Bovine Mastitis. LC 87-81736. (Illus.). 212p. (Orig.). (C). 1987. 27.50 (*0-932147-03-8*) Hoard & Sons Co.
National Mental Health Association (U. S.) Staff, jt. auth. see National Commission on the Insanity Defense, (U. S.).
National Meteorological Service of China Staff. The Cloud Atlas of China. 336p. 1984. text ed. 211.00 (*0-677-31290-3*) Gordon & Breach.
National Methadone Maintenance Conference (2nd: 1969: New York) Staff. Methadone Maintenance: Papers. Einstein, Stanley, ed. LC 79-149717. (Illus.). 263p. reprint ed. pap. 75.00 (*0-685-23595-5*, 2027996) Bks Demand.
National Middle School Association Staff. This We Believe. 40p. 1992. 6.00 (*1-56090-019-9*) Natl Middle Schl.
National MS Society Staff. Creative Will: An Exhibition of Works by Thirty-One Artists with Multiple Sclerosis. LC 93-84778. (Illus.). 96p. (Orig.). 1993. pap. 19.95 (*1-56640-597-1*) Pomegranate Calif.
National Municipal League, Committee on Metropolitan Government. The Government of Metropolitan Areas in the United States. (Metropolitan America Ser.). 408p. 1974. reprint ed. 31.95 (*0-405-05405-X*) Ayer.
National Museum of African Art, Smithsonian Institution Libraries Staff. Catalog of the Library of the National Museum of African Art Branch of the Smithsonian Institution Libraries, 3 vols., Vol. 2. 1650p. 1991. Set. text ed. 595.00 (*0-8161-0521-9*) G K Hall.
***National Museum of American Art, Smithsonian Institution Staff.** National Museum of American Art. 280p. 1995. 40.00 (*0-8212-2216-3*) Bulfinch Pr.
***National Museum of American Art, Smithsonian Institution Staff & Stahl, Joan.** American Artists in Photographic Portraits: From the Peter A. Juley & Son Collection, National Museum of American Art, Smithsonian Institution. LC 95-3974. (Pictorial Archive Ser.). (Illus.). 96p. (Orig.). 1995. pap. text ed. 13.95 (*0-486-28659-2*) Dover.
***National Museum of American Art Staff.** American Art No. 4, Set. 1994. pap. 15.00 (*0-937311-19-7*) Natl Mus Amer Art.
National Museum of American Art Staff & Bermingham, Peter. American Art in the Barbizon Mood. LC 76-14950. 1977. fiche, lib. bdg. 22.50 (*0-226-69413-5*) U Ch Pr.
National Museum of American Art Staff, jt. auth. see Everett, Gwen.
National Museum of American History Staff, et al. Planispheric Astrolabes from the National Museum of American History. LC 83-600270. (Smithsonian Studies in History & Technology: 45). 239p. reprint ed. pap. 68.20 (*0-317-20136-0*, 2023165) Bks Demand.
National Museum of Natural History, Canada Staff. A Natural History Notebook of North American Animals. write for info. (*0-318-59594-X*) S&S Trade.
***National Museum of the American Indian (NMAI) Staff & Akwe:kon Press Staff.** Native American Expressive Culture. (Illus.). 174p. 1995. 17.95 (*1-55591-301-6*) Fulcrum Pub.
National Negro Conference Staff. Proceedings of the National Negro Conference, 1909. LC 69-18544. (American Negro: His History & Literature, Ser. No. 2). 1968. reprint ed. 18.95 (*0-405-01890-8*) Ayer.
National Neighbors Inc. Staff. Fair Housing Resource Directory. (Illus.). 234p. (Orig.). 1994. pap. text ed. 10.00 (*0-9640789-0-2*) Nat Neighbors.
National Network of Grantmakers Staff. Grant Seekers Guide. 3rd rev. ed. 832p. 1989. pap. 27.95 (*0-918825-84-9*) Moyer Bell.
National Network of Runaway & Youth Services Staff. Safe Choices Guide: AIDS & HIV Policies & Prevention Programs for High-Risk Youth. 252p. 1990. ring bd. 30.00 (*1-878848-01-1*) Natl Res Ctr.
National Notary Magazine Editors. Arizona Notary Law Primer. LC 93-85882. 1993. pap. 10.95 (*0-933134-29-0*) Natl Notary.
— The California Notary Law Primer. 14th ed. 112p. 1993. 10.95 (*0-933134-30-4*) Natl Notary.
— Connecticut Notary Law Primer. LC 87-62621. 1988. pap. 10.95 (*0-933134-24-X*) Natl Notary.
— Earning Extra Income As a Notary. LC 93-85330. 1993. pap. 10.95 (*0-933134-34-7*) Natl Notary.
— Florida Notary Law Primer. 3rd ed. 1992. pap. 10.95 (*0-933134-70-3*) Natl Notary.
— Missouri Notary Law Primer. 3rd ed. 1993. pap. 10.95 (*0-933134-31-2*) Natl Notary.
— New Jersey Notary Law Primer. 1994. pap. 10.95 (*0-933134-37-1*) Natl Notary.
— New York Notary Law Primer. 1987. 10.95 (*0-933134-22-3*) Natl Notary.
— North Carolina Notary Law Primer. LC 92-80094. 1992. pap. 10.95 (*0-933134-68-1*) Natl Notary.
— Notary Home Study Course. LC 84-63136. 1993. 36.95 (*0-933134-28-2*) Natl Notary.
— Oregon Notary Law Primer. LC 90-60968. 1990. pap. 10.95 (*0-933134-60-6*) Natl Notary.
— Sorry, No Can Do! 1994. pap. 15.95 (*0-685-72113-2*) Natl Notary.
— Texas Notary Law Primer. 4th ed. 1989. pap. 10.95 (*0-933134-56-8*) Natl Notary.
— Utah Notary Law Primer. 1988. pap. 10.95 (*0-933134-55-X*) Natl Notary.
— Washington Notary Law Primer. 2nd ed. LC 86-60899. 1993. pap. 10.95 (*0-933134-27-4*) Natl Notary.
— Why Fingerprint? 2nd ed. LC 92-83795. 1992. pap. 10.95 (*0-933134-74-6*) Natl Notary.
National Obscenity Law Center Staff. Obscenity Law Reporter, 2 vols., Set. 1986. ring bd. 300.00 (*0-9614159-1-6*) Natl Obscenity.
National Obscenity Law Center Staff, ed. see Weaver, George M.
National Oceanic & Atmospheric Administration Staff. Aeronautical Chart Users Guide. (Government Reprints Ser.). (Illus.). 104p. (C). 1994. pap. text ed. 13.95 (*1-56027-192-2*, ASA-CUG) Av Suppl & Acad.
National Oceanic & Atmospheric Administration Staff, jt. auth. see Federal Aviation Administration Staff.
National Oceanographic & Atmospheric Administration Staff. Current & Tide Tables for Puget Sound, Deception Pass, the San Juans, Gulf Islands & Strait of Juan de Fuca, 1990. abr. ed. Island Canoe, Inc. Staff, ed. 96p. 1989. pap. 5.95 (*0-918439-11-6*) Island Canoe.
— Current & Tide Tables, 1992: For Puget Sound, Deception Pass, the San Juans, Gulf Islands & Strait of Juan de Fuca. abr. ed. Island Canoe Staff, ed. 96p. 1991. pap. 5.95 (*0-918439-15-9*) Island Canoe.
— Current & Tide Tables (1994) for Puget Sound, Deception Pass, the San Juans, Gulf Islands & Strait of Juan De Fuca. Island Canoe Staff, ed. 1993. pap. 6.95 (*0-918439-17-5*) Island Canoe.
National Office Products Association Staff. Marketing Your Product to the Federal Government: An Introduction to GSA Schedule Contracts. (Illus.). 183p. write for info. (*0-318-62124-X*) Natl Office Products.
***National Oil & Gass Resource Assessment Team, ed.** Potential Additions to Technically Recoverable Resources of Oil & Gas: Onshore & State Waters of the United States. LC 94-45974. (Circular Ser.: No. 1118). 1995. write for info. (*0-615-00463-6*) US Geol Survey.
National Opinion Research Center Staff. General Social Survey, 1976. 1977. write for info. (*0-89138-158-9*) ICPSR.
National Organization of Social Security Claimants' Representatives. Social Security Practice Guide, 4 vols. 1984. Updates. ring bd. write for info. (*0-8205-1637-6*) Bender.
National Outdoor Leadership School Staff. The NOLS Cookery: Experience the Art of Outdoor Cooking. LC 88-60635. 112p. 1991. pap. 8.95 (*0-8117-3083-2*) Stackpole.
National P. R. Task Force on Educational Policy Staff. Toward a Language Policy for Puerto Ricans in the U. S. An Agenda for a Community in Movement. 21p. 1982. pap. 3.00 (*1-878483-16-1*) Hunter Coll CEP.
National Park & Conservation Association Staff. Our Endangered Parks. 320p. 1994. pap. 10.95 (*0-935701-84-2*) Foghorn Pr.
National Park Foundation. The Complete Guide to America's National Parks: The Official & Only Comprehensive Guide to 367 National Parks. LC 93-86476. 540p. 1994. pap. 14.95 (*0-679-02676-2*) Fodors Travel.
National Park Foundation Staff. Complete GD AM PK 1986. 1986. pap. 7.95 (*0-685-14507-7*) Viking Penguin.
— Mirror of America: Literary Encounters with the National Parks. Harmon, David, ed. 1989. 25.00 (*0-911797-50-5*); pap. 13.95 (*0-911797-51-3*) R Rinehart.
National Park Service Staff. Castillo de San Marcos: A Guide to Castillo de San Marcos National Monument. LC 92-40413. (Illus.). 64p. (Orig.). 1994. pap. 2.75 (*0-912627-59-X*) Natl Park Serv.
— Chesapeake & Ohio Canal. LC 88-25305. (Handbook Ser.: No. 142). (Illus.). (Orig.). 1991. pap. 4.50 (*0-912627-43-3*, 024-005-01076-9) Natl Park Serv.
— Congress Hall: Capitol of the U. S. 1790-1800. LC 90-13556. (Handbook Ser.: No. 147). (Illus.). 49p. (Orig.). 1991. pap. 1.50 (*0-912627-42-5*, 024-005-01074-2) Natl Park Serv.
— Craters of the Moon National Monument, Idaho. LC 89-13670. (Handbook Ser.: No. 139). (Illus.). 64p. 1991. pap. 2.75 (*0-912627-44-1*, 024-005-01077-7) Natl Park Serv.
— First Mothers: The Stories of the Women Whose Sons Became President of the United States. 58p. (Orig.). 1990. pap. 4.50 (*0-915992-49-3*) Eastern Acorn.
— National Parks for the Twenty-First Century: The Vail Agenda. LC 92-60471. (Illus.). 160p. (Orig.). 1994. pap. 14.95 (*0-9603410-7-2*) Natl Pk Found.
— National Register of Historic Places. 2nd ed. Savage, Beth L., ed. (Illus.). 923p. 1994. pap. 98.00 (*0-89133-254-5*) Preservation Pr.
— North Cascades. (Handbook Ser.: No. 131). (Illus.). 112p. (Orig.). 1986. pap. text ed. 4.50 (*0-912627-31-X*) Natl Park Serv.
— Sequoia & Kings Canyon: A Guide to Sequoia & Kings Canyon National Parks, California. LC 91-37844. (Handbook Ser.: No. 145). (Illus.). 128p. (Orig.). 1992. pap. 4.50 (*0-912627-47-6*, 024-005-01095-9) Natl Park Serv.
— Washington, D. C. LC 87-600287. (Handbook Ser.: No. 102). (Illus.). 176p. (Orig.). 1988. pap. 5.00 (*0-912627-36-0*) Natl Park Serv.
— Yosemite. LC 88-17932. (Handbook Ser.: No. 138). (Illus.). 144p. (Orig.). 1989. pap. 5.50 (*0-912627-37-9*) Natl Park Serv.
National Park Service Staff & Mobium Corporation Staff. Apostle Islands. LC 87-600289. (Handbook Ser.: No. 141). (Illus.). 64p. (Orig.). 1988. pap. 2.25 (*0-912627-35-2*) Natl Park Serv.
***National Park Service Staff & National Register of Historic Places Staff.** African American Historic Places. Savage, Beth L. et al, eds. LC 94-33218. (Illus.). 623p. (Orig.). 1994. pap. 25.95 (*0-89133-253-7*) Preservation Pr.
National Park Service Staff & Pigeon, Robert. Seventeen-Eighty-Seven: A Daily Journal of the Constitutional Convention. (Illus.). 192p. 1987. 9.98 (*0-914373-07-2*) Wieser & Wieser.
National Park Service Staff, ed. see Hayden, Elizabeth W.
National Park Service Staff, ed. see London, Mark.
National Park Service, U.S. Department of the Interior, Historic American Buildings Survey - Historic American Engineering Record Staff & Burns, John E. Recording Historic Structures. (Illus.). 270p. 1989. pap. 19.95 (*1-55835-021-7*) AIA Press.
***National Parks & Conservation Association Staff.** Everglades: Tiny Folios. LC 94-46988. (Tiny Folio Ser.). (Illus.). 320p. 1995. 11.95 (*1-55859-827-8*) Abbeville Pr.
— Investing in Park Futures - The National Park System Plan: A Blueprint for Tomorrow: Executive Summary. 44p. (C). 1988. pap. 9.95 (*0-940091-20-8*) Natl Parks & Cons.
— Investing in Park Futures - The National Park System Plan: A Blueprint for Tomorrow, Vol. I: To Preserve Unimpaired: The Challenge of Protecting Park Resources. (C). 1988. pap. 9.95 (*0-940091-21-6*) Natl Parks & Cons.
— Investing in Park Futures - The National Park System Plan: A Blueprint for Tomorrow, Vol. III: Parks & People: A Natural Relationship. (C). 1988. pap. 8.50 (*0-940091-23-2*) Natl Parks & Cons.
— Investing in Park Futures - The National Park System Plan: A Blueprint for Tomorrow, Vol. VI: Planning & Public Involvement: Constituency Building for the Parks. (C). 1988. pap. 4.50 (*0-940091-26-7*) Natl Parks & Cons.
— Investing in Park Futures - The National Park System Plan: A Blueprint for Tomorrow, Vol. VII: Land Acquisition: Completing the Parks. (C). 1988. pap. 4.95 (*0-940091-27-5*) Natl Parks & Cons.
— National Park Activist Guide: A Manual for Citizen Action. 1993. write for info. (*0-318-72303-4*) Natl Parks & Cons.
— Yellowstone. LC 94-18570. (Stylebooks Ser.). (Illus.). 320p. 1994. 11.95 (*1-55859-825-1*) Abbeville Pr.
National Parks & Conservation Staff. National Parks in Crisis. 17p. 1993. write for info. (*0-318-72304-2*) Natl Parks & Cons.
National Parks Service - Cordova Historical Society Staff. Cordova to Kennecott, Alaska. Spude, Robert et al, eds. (Illus.). 52p. (C). 1988. pap. 8.95 (*0-9623320-0-3*) Cordova Historical.
National Passive Solar Conference Staff. Passive Eighty-One: Proceedings of the National Passive Solar Conference, 6th, Portland, Oregon, 1981. Hayes, John & Kolar, William, eds. LC 81-12741. 1982. pap. text ed. 60.00 (*0-89553-032-5*) Am Solar Energy.
— Passive Solar State of the Art: Proceedings of the National Passive Solar Conference, 2nd, Philadelphia, 1978, 3 vols., Set. Prowler, Don, ed. LC 78-61242. 1978. pap. text ed. 50.00 (*0-89553-008-2*) Am Solar Energy.
— Proceedings of the National Passive Solar Conference, 3rd, San Jose, 1979. Miller, Harry et al, eds. 1979. pap. text ed. 80.00 (*0-89553-015-5*) Am Solar Energy.
— Proceedings of the National Passive Solar Conference, 5th, Amherst, 1980, 2 vols., Set. Hayes, John & Snyder, Rachel, eds. (Illus.). 1980. pap. text ed. 60.00 (*0-89553-025-2*) Am Solar Energy.
National Pastoral Life Center Staff, illus. Vatican Two: Act Two - Families: Participant's Guide. 64p. (Orig.). 1990. pap. 3.95 (*0-8146-1972-X*) Liturgical Pr.
— Vatican Two: Act Two - Living in God's World: Convener's Guide. 74p. (Orig.). 1990. pap. text ed. 6.95 (*0-8146-1971-1*) Liturgical Pr.
— Vatican Two: Act Two - Living in God's World: Participant's Guide. 61p. 1990. pap. 3.95 (*0-8146-1970-3*) Liturgical Pr.
National Perinatal Epidemiology Unit, Oxford Staff & World Health Organization Staff, eds. Classified Bibliography of Controlled Trials in Perinatal Medicine, 1940-1984. 1986. 49.95 (*0-19-261566-1*) OUP.
National Phonograph Company Staff. Edison Phonograph Monthly, 1903-1916. Moore, Wendell, ed. Incl. Vol. 1, 1903. 190p. 15.95 (*0-934281-50-5*); Vol. 2, 1904. 194p. 15.95 (*0-934281-51-3*); Vol. 3, 1905. 190p. 15.95 (*0-934281-52-1*); Vol. 4, 1906. 222p. 15.95 (*0-934281-53-X*); Vol. 5, 1907. 226p. 15.95 (*0-934281-54-8*); Vol. 6, 1908. 308p. 17.95 (*0-934281-55-6*); Vol. 7, 1909. 334p. 17.95 (*0-934281-56-4*); Vol. 8, 1910. 309p. 19.95 (*0-934281-57-2*); Vol.9. Edison Phonograph Monthly, 1903-1916. 309p. 1911. 25.00 (*0-934281-58-0*); (Illus.). reprint ed. write for info. (*0-318-59213-4*) W Moore Pub.
— Edison Phonograph Monthly, 1903-1916, Vol.9. Moore, Wendell, ed. (Edison Phonograph Monthly, 1903-1916). 309p. 1911. 25.00 (*0-934281-58-0*) W Moore Pub.
National Plan Service, Inc. Country Rustic Home Plans. (Illus.). 32p. (Orig.). reprint ed. pap. 3.95 (*0-934039-03-8*, A48) Natl Plan Serv.
National Plan Service Inc. Staff. One & One-Half & Two Story Home Plans. (Illus.). 32p. reprint ed. pap. 3.95 (*0-934039-05-4*, A55) Natl Plan Serv.
National Plan Service, Inc. Staff, ed. Affordable Ranch Homes. (Illus.). 32p. (Orig.). reprint ed. pap. 3.95 (*0-934039-04-6*, A42) Natl Plan Serv.
— America's Best Project Plans, No. A100. (Ucando Ser.). (Illus.). 64p. 1990. per., pap. 4.95 (*0-934039-30-5*) Natl Plan Serv.
— The Best Small Home Plans. (Illus.). 32p. (Orig.). reprint ed. pap. 3.95 (*0-934039-06-2*, A49) Natl Plan Serv.
— Better Living Home Plans. (Illus.). 32p. reprint ed. pap. 3.95 (*0-934039-19-4*, A36) Natl Plan Serv.
— Build Your Own Garage Manual. (Illus.). 88p. 1987. pap. 12.95 (*0-934039-26-7*, A270) Natl Plan Serv.
— Classic Designs. (Illus.). 32p. reprint ed. pap. 3.95 (*0-934039-24-0*, A35) Natl Plan Serv.
— Consumer Approved Home Designs, No. A132. (Illus.). 88p. 1990. per., pap. 5.95 (*0-934089-29-1*) Natl Plan Serv.
— Contemporary Home Plans. (Illus.). 32p. reprint ed. pap. 3.95 (*0-934039-21-6*, A47) Natl Plan Serv.
— Duplex-Townhouse Plans. rev. ed. (Illus.). 32p. (Orig.). reprint ed. pap. 3.95 (*0-934039-08-9*, A51) Natl Plan Serv.
— Early American Colonial Homes. rev. ed. (Illus.). 32p. reprint ed. pap. 3.95 (*0-934039-12-7*, A39) Natl Plan Serv.
— Energy Saving Home Plans. (Illus.). 32p. (Orig.). reprint ed. pap. 3.95 (*0-934039-07-0*, A56) Natl Plan Serv.

N

An Asterisk (*) at the beginning of an entry indicates that the title is appearing in BIP for the first time.

— Energy Saving New Home Plans, Bk. 2. (Illus.). 32p. reprint ed. pap. 4.95 (*0-934039-15-1*, A103) Natl Plan Serv.

— Garage Plans. rev. ed. (Illus.). 20p. reprint ed. pap. 3.95 (*0-934039-23-2*, A57) Natl Plan Serv.

— Home Designs for Narrow Lots, No. A-131. (Illus.). 88p. (Orig.). 1986. per. 5.95 (*0-934039-01-1*, A-131) Natl Plan Serv.

— Multi-Level...Hillside Home Plans. (Illus.). 32p. reprint ed. pap. 3.95 (*0-934039-16-X*, A41) Natl Plan Serv.

— A Portfolio of Best Selling House Plans. (Illus.). 32p. reprint ed. pap. 3.95 (*0-934039-22-4*, A34) Natl Plan Serv.

— Practical Contemporary Home Plans. (Illus.). 32p. (Orig.). reprint ed. pap. 3.95 (*0-934039-09-7*, A52) Natl Plan Serv.

— Selected Small Homes...Keyed to the Times. rev. ed. (Illus.). 32p. reprint ed. pap. 3.95 (*0-934039-11-9*, A37) Natl Plan Serv.

— Tudor Homes & Other Popular Designs. (Illus.). 32p. (Orig.). 1987. pap. 3.95 (*0-934039-02-X*, A70) Natl Plan Serv.

— Vacation Homes. (Illus.). 32p. reprint ed. pap. 3.95 (*0-934039-14-3*, A50) Natl Plan Serv.

National Plan Service Staff, ed. Quality Home Designs. (Illus.). 32p. reprint ed. 4.95 (*0-934039-34-8*, A103) Natl Plan Serv.

— Sunbelt Designs: Outdoor Living...Indoors. (Illus.). (Orig.). 1988. pap. 3.95 (*0-934039-27-5*, A72) Natl Plan Serv.

— Transitional Home Designs, No. A104. (Illus.). 32p. reprint ed. 4.95 (*0-934039-35-6*) Natl Plan Serv.

— Victorian & Country Home Designs, No. A102. (Illus.). 32p. reprint ed. 4.95 (*0-934039-33-X*) Natl Plan Serv.

National Plan Service Staff, ed. see Bynre, Randy.

National Plan Service Staff, ed. see Byrne, Randy.

National Planning Association, Center for Economic & Demographic Projections Staff. Basic Maps of the U. S. Economy, Nineteen Sixty-Seven to Nineteen Ninety. 304p. 1979. 25.00 (*0-686-28102-0*) Natl Planning.

National Planning Association Committee of New England Staff, ed. The Economic State of New England: Report of the Committee of New England of the National Planning Association. 738p. 1954. 100.00 (*0-317-27450-3*) Elliots Bks.

National Planning Association Staff. The Creole Petrolum Corporation in Venezuela. Bruchey, Stuart & Bruchey, Eleanor, eds. LC 76-5019. (American Business Abroad Ser.). 1976. reprint ed. lib. bdg. 19.95 (*0-405-09286-5*) Ayer.

— The Firestone Operations in Liberia. Bruchey, Stuart & Bruchey, Eleanor, eds. LC 76-5020. (American Business Abroad Ser.). (Illus.). 1976. reprint ed. 17.95 (*0-405-09287-3*) Ayer.

— The General Electric Company in Brazil. Bruchey, Stuart & Bruchey, Eleanor, eds. LC 76-5021. (American Business Abroad Ser.). (Illus.). 1976. reprint ed. 19.95 (*0-405-09288-1*) Ayer.

— Stanvac in Indonesia. Bruchey, Stuart & Bruchey, Eleanor, eds. LC 76-5022. (American Business Abroad Ser.). (Illus.). 1976. reprint ed. 19.95 (*0-405-09289-X*) Ayer.

— The United Fruit Company in Latin America. Bruchey, Stuart & Bruchey, Eleanor, eds. LC 76-5023. (American Business Abroad Ser.). (Illus.). 1976. reprint ed. 31.95 (*0-405-09290-3*) Ayer.

National Police Chiefs & Sheriffs Information Bureau Staff. National Directory of Law Enforcement Administrators, Vol. XXVII. 552p. 1991. 49.00 (*1-880245-01-9*) NPCS Info.

National Police Convention Staff. Official Proceedings of the National Police Convention. LC 70-154579. (Police in America Ser.). 1971. reprint ed. 13.95 (*0-405-03379-6*) Ayer.

National Portrait Gallery of the Smithsonian Institution Staff, jt. auth. see Denker, Eric.

National Portrait Gallery, Smithsonian Institution Staff, et al. Arnold Newman's Americans: National Portrait Gallery, Smithsonian Institution. (Illus.). 160p. 1992. pap. 35.00 (*0-8212-1901-4*) Bulfinch Pr.

National Powder Metallurgy Conference, Chicago IL Staff. National Powder Metallurgy Conference Proceedings, 1972. (Progress in Powder Metallurgy Ser.: No. 28). (Illus.). 322p. reprint ed. pap. 91.80 (*0-7837-1741-5*, 2057272) Bks Demand.

National Powder Metallurgy Conference Staff. National Powder Metallurgy Conference Proceedings: Proceedings of the 1977 National Powder Metallurgy Conference, Sponsored by the Metal Powder Industries Federation & the American Powder Metallurgy Institute, May 24-25, 1977, Detroit Plaza Hotel, Detroit, Michigan. Mocarski, Stanley & Pietrocini, Thomas W., eds. (Progress in Powder Metallurgy Ser.: No. 33). 283p. reprint ed. pap. 80.70 (*0-7837-3165-5*, 2042813) Bks Demand.

— National Powder Metallurgy Conference Proceedings: Proceedings of the 1978 National Powder Metallurgy Conference, April 24-26, 1978, Los Angeles, CA & the 1979 National Powder Metallurgy Conference, June 4-6, 1979, Cincinnati, OH. Hoffman, James et al, eds. (Progress in Powder Metallurgy Ser.: Vol. 34-35). (Illus.). 439p. reprint ed. pap. 125.20 (*0-7837-1556-0*, 2041849) Bks Demand.

— National Powder Metallurgy Conference Proceedings: Proceedings of the 1982 National Powder Metallurgy Conference, Sponsored by the Metal Powder Industries Federation & the American Powder Metallurgy Institute, May 24-27, 1982, Westin Bonaventure Hotel, Montreal, Quebec, Canada. Bewley, James G. & McGee, Sherwood W., eds. (Progress in Powder Metallurgy Ser.: No. 38). 283p. reprint ed. pap. 80.70 (*0-7837-3164-7*, 2042814) Bks Demand.

— National Powder Metallurgy Conference Proceedings, 1974. Smith, Gaylord D., ed. (Progress in Powder Metallurgy Ser.: No. 31). 312p. reprint ed. pap. 89.00 (*0-8357-6991-7*, 2057075) Bks Demand.

— National Powder Metallurgy Conference Proceedings, 1975. Halter, Richard F., ed. (Progress in Powder Metallurgy Ser.: No. 30). 213p. reprint ed. pap. 60.80 (*0-8357-6990-9*, 2057074) Bks Demand.

National Press Photographers Association, Region XI Staff. One Day in Washington. LC 84-21818. (Illus.). 192p. 1985. 24.95 (*0-88089-005-3*) Madrona Pubs.

National Press Photographers Association Staff & Universith of Missouri School of Journalism Staff, eds. The Best of Photojournalism, No. 18: Newspaper & Magazine Pictures of the Years. (Best of Photojournalism Ser.). (Illus.). 256p. (Orig.). 1993. pap. 21.95 (*1-56138-296-5*) Running Pr.

National Press Photographers Association Staff & University of Missouri School of Journalism Staff, eds. The Best of Photojournalism: Nineteen Newspaper & Magazine Pictures of the Year. (Illus.). 256p. (Orig.). 1994. pap. 21.95 (*1-56138-412-7*) Running Pr.

National Prison Association Staff. Proceedings of the Annual Congress of the National Prison Association of the United States. LC 77-154586. (Police in America Ser.). 1971. reprint ed. 16.95 (*0-405-03377-X*) Ayer.

National Quantum Electronics Conference Staff. Quantum Electronics & Electo-Optics: Proceedings of the Fifth National Quantum Electronics Conference, Hull University, Hull, September 1981. Knight, Peter, ed. LC 82-24778. (Illus.). 477p. reprint ed. pap. 136.00 (*0-8357-4315-2*, 2037114) Bks Demand.

National Quantum Electronics Conference (4th: 1979: Edinburgh) Staff. Laser Advances & Applications: Proceedings of the Fourth National Quantum Electronics Conference, Heriot-Watt University, Edinburgh, September, 1979. LC 80-40119. (Illus.). 300p. reprint ed. pap. 85.50 (*0-685-20659-9*, 2030445) Bks Demand.

National Quarantine & Sanitary Convention Staff. Proceedings of the National Quarantine & Sanitary Convention, 1st-4th: Original Anthology. Rosenkrantz, Barbara G., ed. LC 76-40668. (Public Health in America Ser.). 1977. reprint ed. lib. bdg. 89.95 (*0-405-09877-4*) Ayer.

***National Quotation Bureau Editorial Staff.** National Quotation Bureau Stock Summary. (Orig.). 1913. pap. text ed. 40.00 (*1-57447-000-0*) Nat Quot Bur.

***National Quotation Bureau Staff.** National Quotation Bureau Bond Summary. (Orig.). 1913. pap. text ed. 35.00 (*1-57447-001-9*) Nat Quot Bur.

National Recreation & Park Association Staff. Aging & Leisure. (Illus.). 136p. reprint ed. pap. 38.80 (*0-7837-1547-1*, 2041835) Bks Demand.

— Demand for Recreation in America. (Quest for Quality Ser.: No. 1). 39p. reprint ed. pap. 25.00 (*0-7837-1537-4*, 2041819) Bks Demand.

National Recreation & Park Association Staff & Weir, Lebert H. Europe at Play: A Study of Recreation & Leisure. 63.95 (*0-405-19033-6*) Ayer.

National Register of Historic Places Staff, jt. auth. see National Park Service Staff.

***National Register Press Editing Staff, ed. America's Corporate Finance Directory 1995. LC 67-22770. 1600p. 1995. 479.00 (*0-87217-940-0*) Natl Register. AMERICA'S CORPORATE FINANCE DIRECTORY 1995 profiles 5,000 of America's leading companies including their 18,000 subsidiaries & 31,000 outside service firms. Entries provide vital corporate statistics, such as sales earnings, assets, liabilities, stock exchange ticker symbol, even details about the company's pension plan, contact information, & a listing of wholly-owned U.S. subsidiaries. Each entry also lists up to 23 financial service firms, including insurance brokers, insurers, pension managers, investment bankers, auditors, legal counsel & registrars. Hardbound format makes it easy to use!** *Publisher Provided Annotation.*

— Co-op Source Directory Fall 1995: The Guide to Co-operative Advertising Programs. 1460p. 1995. pap. 375.00 (*0-87217-867-6*) Natl Register.

— Co-op Source Directory Spring 1995: The Guide to Co-operative Advertising Programs. 1460p. (Orig.). 1995. pap. 375.00 (*0-87217-866-8*) Natl Register.

— Corporate Finance Sourcebook 1995: The Guide to Major Capital Investment Sources & Related Financial Services. LC 86-642719. 2200p. (Orig.). 1995. pap. 479.00 (*0-87217-944-3*) Natl Register.

— Direct Marketing Market Place: The Networking Source of the Direct Marketing Industry. LC 79-649244. 1323p. 1995. pap. 189.00 (*0-87217-329-1*) Natl Register.

— Directory of Corporate Affiliations: Who Owns Whom, 5 vols. Incl. Directory of Corporate Affiliations: Master Index Volume I. LC 67-22770. 1812p. 1995. pap. (*0-87217-160-4*); Directory of Corporate Affiliations: Master Index Volume II. LC 67-22770. 2150p. 1995. pap. (*0-87217-161-2*); Directory of Corporate Affiliations: U. S. Public Companies. LC 67-22770. 2372p. 1995. pap. (*0-87217-163-9*); Directory of Corporate Affiliations: U. S. Private Companies. LC 67-22770. 1476p. 1995. pap. (*0-87217-164-7*); Directory of Corporate Affiliations: International Public & Private Companies. LC 67-22770. 1922p. 1995. pap. (*0-87217-162-0*); LC 67-22770. 950.00 (*0-87217-165-5*) Natl Register.

— Standard Directory of Advertisers: Business Classifications Edition. LC 15-21147. 2062p. 1995. pap. 479.00 (*0-87217-239-2*) Natl Register.

— Standard Directory of Advertisers: Geographic Edition. LC 15-21147. 2024p. 1995. pap. 479.00 (*0-87217-240-6*) Natl Register.

— Standard Directory of Advertisers: Indexes. LC 15-21147. 1056p. 1995. pap. write for info. (*0-87217-241-4*) Natl Register.

— Standard Directory of Advertising Agencies, January 1995: The Agency Red Book. LC 66-6149. 1500p. 1995. pap. 479.00 (*0-87217-032-2*) Natl Register.

— Standard Directory of Advertising Agencies, July 1995: Business Classifications Edition. LC 66-6149. 1500p. 1995. pap. 479.00 (*0-87217-033-0*) Natl Register.

— Standard Directory of International Advertisers & Agencies: The International Red Book. LC 15-21147. 1298p. 1995. pap. 379.00 (*0-87217-146-9*) Natl Register.

National Register Publishing Staff. America's Corporate Finance Directory 1994. 2300p. 1994. 525.00 (*0-87217-939-7*) Natl Register.

— Co-op Source Directory, March, 1994. 1252p. 1994. 399.00 (*0-87217-864-1*) Natl Register.

— Corporate Finance Sourcebook, 1994. LC 86-642719. 1878p. 1994. pap. 450.00 (*0-87217-943-5*) Natl Register.

— Direct Marketing Market Place, 1994: The Directory of the Direct Marketing Industry. LC 79-649244. 1179p. 1994. 179.99 (*0-87217-328-3*) Natl Register.

— Directory of Corporate Affiliations - International, 1994. LC 67-22770. 1784p. 1994. 685.00 (*0-87217-182-5*) Natl Register.

— Directory of Corporate Affiliations - U.S. Private, 1994. LC 87-659005. 1900p. 1994. 685.00 (*0-87217-202-3*) Natl Register.

— Directory of Corporate Affiliations - U.S. Public, 1994, 2 vols., Set. LC 67-22770. 2900p. 1994. 795.00 (*0-87217-154-X*) Natl Register.

— Standard Directory of International Advertisers & Agencies, 1994. LC 84-62414. 1430p. 1993. 375.00 (*0-87217-145-0*) Natl Register.

***National Register Publishing Staff, ed. Directory of Corporate Affiliations Library, 5 Vols. 1995. 950.00 (*0-87217-157-4*) Natl Register. The new 1995 edition of the DIRECTORY OF CORPORATE AFFILIATIONS LIBRARY, the definitive source of who owns whom, is now available exclusively as a completely updated, comprehensive 5-volume series. Only the most influential public & private companies in the U.S. & overseas are included - those with at least $10 million in revenue. Everything you & your patrons need to know about corporate linkage is at your fingertips. At-a-glance "family tree" listings make it easy to determine exactly who owns whom, & provide you with valuable insights into corporate hierarchy & the responsibilities of parent companies, subsidiaries, affiliates & divisions. For 1995, over 117,000 of the world's leading companies with 286,000 key executives have been selected for inclusion. Over 5,000 companies are all-new to this edition. The set features a 2-volume master Index, offering quick access to individual entries by company name, brand name, S.I.C. code, personnel, & geographic location. The three other volumes feature the latest information about new mergers, acquisitions, management changes, & more. Five volumes of essential business information at one low price! Your cost for the DIRECTORY OF CORPORATE AFFILIATIONS LIBRARY is only $950.00. You get the Directory of Corporate Affiliations/ U.S. Public, Directory of Corporate Affiliations/U.S. Private, & Directory of Corporate Affiliations/International, plus the 2- volume Master Index.** *Publisher Provided Annotation.*

— Standard Directory of Advertisers, 1994. LC 15-21147. 1809p. 1994. Geographic ed. with supplements. 575.00 (*0-87217-238-4*); Geographic ed. without supplements. 475.00 (*0-87217-235-X*); Business Classsifications ed. with supplements. 575.00 (*0-87217-237-6*); Business Classifications ed. without supplements. 475.00 (*0-87217-234-1*) Natl Register.

— Standard Directory of Advertising Agencies 1994. LC 66-6149. 1500p. 1994. 575.00 (*0-87217-045-4*) Natl Register.

— Standard Directory of Advertising Agencies 1995. 1500p. 1995. 579.00 (*0-87217-037-5*) K G Saur.

National Research Center of the Arts Staff, ed. Americans & the Arts, No. V: Highlights. 32p. (Orig.). 1988. pap. 2.00 (*0-915400-65-0*, ACA Bks) Am Council Arts.

National Research Conference on Smoking Behavior (2nd: 1966: University of Arizona) Staff. Studies & Issues in Smoking Behavior. Zagona, Salvatore V., ed. LC 67-28650. 277p. reprint ed. pap. 79.00 (*0-685-20953-9*, 2031489) Bks Demand.

National Research Council. Acid Deposition: Long-Term Trends. 520p. (Orig.). 1986. pap. 34.95 (*0-309-03647-X*) Natl Acad Pr.

— Active Tectonics: Impact on Society. 280p. 1986. text ed. 29.95 (*0-309-03638-0*) Natl Acad Pr.

— Antarctic Treaty System: An Assessment. 456p. (Orig.). 1986. text ed. 45.95 (*0-309-03640-2*) Natl Acad Pr.

— An Assessment of Research-Doctorate Programs in the U. S. Engineering. 193p. (C). 1982. pap. text ed. 19.95 (*0-309-03336-5*) Natl Acad Pr.

— An Assessment of Research-Doctorate Programs in the United States: Humanities. 244p. (C). 1982. pap. text ed. 14.95 (*0-309-03333-0*) Natl Acad Pr.

— Astronomy & Astrophysics. (Space Science in the Twenty-First Century Series: Imperatives for the Decades 1995 to 2015). 84p. 1988. pap. text ed. 14.95 (*0-309-03875-8*) Natl Acad Pr.

— Atomic, Molecular, & Optic Physics. (Physics Through the 1990's Ser.). 200p. 1986. pap. text ed. 24.50 (*0-309-03575-9*) Natl Acad Pr.

— Behavioral & Social Science: Fifty Years of Discovery. 312p. 1986. text ed. 29.50 (*0-309-03588-0*) Natl Acad Pr.

— The Behavioral & Social Sciences: Achievements & Opportunities. Gerstein, Dean R. et al, eds. 304p. 1988. 29.50 (*0-309-03749-2*) Natl Acad Pr.

— Bereavement: Reactions, Consequences, & Care. 312p. 1984. pap. 29.95 (*0-309-03438-8*) Natl Acad Pr.

— Comparable Worth: New Directions for Research. 192p. 1985. pap. text ed. 19.95 (*0-309-03534-1*) Natl Acad Pr.

— The Competitive Status of the U. S. Civil Aviation Manufacturing Industry. 168p. 1985. pap. 19.95 (*0-309-03399-3*) Natl Acad Pr.

— Complex Mixtures: Methods for In Vivo Toxicity Testing. 240p. 1988. text ed. 35.00 (*0-309-03778-6*) Natl Acad Pr.

— Computer Chips & Paper Clips: Technology & Women's Employment, Vol I. Hartman, Heidi I. et al, eds. 216p. 1986. pap. text ed. 19.95 (*0-309-03688-7*) Natl Acad Pr.

— Computer Chips & Paper Clips, Vol. 2: Technology & Women's Employment. Hartmann, Heidi I. et al, eds. (Case Studies & Policy Perspectives). 456p. 1987. pap. 34.95 (*0-309-03727-1*) Natl Acad Pr.

— Condensed-Matter Physics. (Physics Through the 1990's Ser.). 328p. 1986. pap. text ed. 31.50 (*0-309-03577-5*) Natl Acad Pr.

— Criminal Careers & "Career Criminals", Vol. I. Blumstein, Alfred et al, eds. 458p. 1986. text ed. 34.95 (*0-309-03684-4*) Natl Acad Pr.

— Criminal Careers & "Career Criminals", Vol II. Cohen, Jacqueline et al, eds. 404p. 1986. text ed. 49.95 (*0-309-03683-6*) Natl Acad Pr.

— Designing Foods: Animal Product Options in the Marketplace. 384p. 1988. 39.95 (*0-309-03798-0*); pap. text ed. 29.95 (*0-309-03795-6*) Natl Acad Pr.

— Diet, Nutrition, & Cancer. 496p. 1982. pap. 29.95 (*0-309-03280-6*) Natl Acad Pr.

— Dredging Coastal Ports: An Assessment of the Issues. 212p. 1985. pap. text ed. 21.50 (*0-309-03628-3*) Natl Acad Pr.

— Ecological Knowledge & Environmental Problem Solving: Concepts & Case Studies. 400p. 1986. pap. text ed. 29.95 (*0-309-03645-3*) Natl Acad Pr.

— The Effects on the Atmosphere of a Major Nuclear Exchange. 193p. 1985. pap. text ed. 24.95 (*0-309-03528-7*) Natl Acad Pr.

— Electricity in Economic Growth. 165p. (Orig.). 1986. pap. text ed. 19.95 (*0-309-03677-1*) Natl Acad Pr.

— Elementary-Particle Physics. (Physics Through the 1990's Ser.). 248p. 1986. pap. text ed. 24.50 (*0-309-03576-7*) Natl Acad Pr.

— Engineering Employment Characteristics. (Engineering Education & Practice in the United States Ser.). 94p. 1985. pap. text ed. 12.50 (*0-309-03586-4*) Natl Acad Pr.

— Engineering in Society. (Engineering Education & Practice in the United States Ser.). 132p. 1985. pap. text ed. 15.95 (*0-309-03592-9*) Natl Acad Pr.

— Engineering Infrastructure Diagramming & Modeling. (Engineering Education & Practice in the United States Ser.). 156p. (Orig.). 1986. pap. text ed. 15.95 (*0-309-03639-9*) Natl Acad Pr.

— Engineering Undergraduate Education. (Engineering Education & Practice in the United States Ser.). 104p. (Orig.). 1986. pap. text ed. 12.50 (*0-309-03642-9*) Natl Acad Pr.

— An Evaluation of the Role of Microbiological Criteria for Foods & Food Ingredients. 456p. 1985. text ed. 49.95 (*0-309-03497-3*) Natl Acad Pr.

— Frontiers in Chemical Engineering: Research Needs & Opportunities. 232p. 1988. pap. text ed. 29.95 (*0-309-03793-X*) Natl Acad Pr.

An Asterisk (*) at the beginning of an entry indicates that the title is appearing in BIP for the first time.

— Fundamental Physics & Chemistry. (Space Science in the Twenty-First Century Series: Imperatives for the Decades 1995 to 2015). 108p. 1988. pap. text ed. 14.95 (*0-309-03841-3*) Natl Acad Pr.

— Global Tropospheric Chemistry: A Plan for Action. 194p. 1984. pap. 24.95 (*0-309-03481-7*) Natl Acad Pr.

— Gravitation, Cosmology, & Cosmic-Ray Physics. (Physics Through the 1990's Ser.). 192p. 1986. pap. text ed. 24.50 (*0-309-03579-1*) Natl Acad Pr.

— Ground Water Quality Protection: State & Local Strategies. 309p. 1986. pap. text ed. 29.95 (*0-309-03685-2*) Natl Acad Pr.

— Hazardous Waste Site Management: Water Quality Issues. 224p. 1988. pap. text ed. 27.95 (*0-309-03790-5*) Natl Acad Pr.

— Health Risks of Radon & Other Internally Deposited Alpha-Emitters: BEIR IV. 624p. 1988. 54.95 (*0-309-03797-2*); pap. text ed. 44.95 (*0-309-03789-1*) Natl Acad Pr.

— Immigration Statistics: A Story of Neglect. 328p. 1985. pap. text ed. 29.95 (*0-309-03589-9*) Natl Acad Pr.

— Immunodeficient Rodents: A Guide to Their Immunobiology, Husbandry, & Use. 260p. 1989. text ed. 29.95 (*0-309-03796-4*) Natl Acad Pr.

— Improving Indicators of the Quality of Science & Mathematics Education in Grades 1-12. Murnane, Richard J. & Raizen, Senta A., eds. 232p. 1988. pap. text ed. 22.95 (*0-309-03740-9*) Natl Acad Pr.

— Issues in Marine & Intermodal Transportation. LC 93-5129. (Transportation Research Record Ser.: No. 1383). 94p. pap. text ed. 25.00 (*0-309-05453-2*) Transport Res Bd.

— Life Sciences Space Science in the Twenty-First Century Series. 160p. 1988. pap. text ed. 19.95 (*0-309-03880-4*) Natl Acad Pr.

— Managing Microcomputers in Large Organizations. 151p. 1985. pap. text ed. 19.95 (*0-309-03492-2*) Natl Acad Pr.

— The Mono Basin Ecosystem: Effects of Changing Lake Level. 288p. 1987. pap. text ed. 22.50 (*0-309-03777-8*) Natl Acad Pr.

— The New Engineering Research Centers: Purposes, Goals & Expectations. 224p. 1986. pap. text ed. 25.95 (*0-309-03598-8*) Natl Acad Pr.

— Nuclear Physics. (Physics Through the 1990's Ser.). 240p. 1986. pap. text ed. 24.50 (*0-309-03547-3*) Natl Acad Pr.

— Nutrient Adequacy: Assessment Using Food Consumption Surveys. 160p. 1986. pap. text ed. 19.95 (*0-309-03634-8*) Natl Acad Pr.

— Nutrient Requirements of Cats. rev. ed. 88p. 1986. pap. text ed. 19.95 (*0-309-03682-8*) Natl Acad Pr.

National, Research Council. Nutrient Requirements of Dairy Cattle. 6th rev. ed. 168p. 1989. pap. text ed. 19.95 (*0-309-03826-X*) Natl Acad Pr.

National Research Council. Nutrient Requirements of Dogs. rev. ed. 88p. 1985. pap. text ed. 19.95 (*0-309-03496-5*) Natl Acad Pr.

— Nutrient Requirements of Swine. 9th rev. ed. 104p. 1988. pap. text ed. 14.95 (*0-309-03779-4*) Natl Acad Pr.

— Nutritional Energetics of Domestic Animals & Glossary of Energy Terms. 54p. (Orig.). 1981. pap. text ed. 12.00 (*0-309-03127-3*) Natl Acad Pr.

— Office Workstations in the Home. LC 85-3022. 168p. 1985. pap. text ed. 19.95 (*0-309-03483-3*) Natl Acad Pr.

— Overview: Imperatives for the Decades 1995 to 2015. (Space Science in the Twenty-First Century Series: Imperatives for the Decades 1995 to 2015). 108p. 1988. pap. text ed. 14.95 (*0-309-03838-3*) Natl Acad Pr.

— Perspectives on Urban Infrastructure. 216p. 1984. pap. 19.95 (*0-309-03439-6*) Natl Acad Pr.

— Planetary & Lunar Exploration. (Space Science in the Twenty-First Century Ser.). 128p. 1988. pap. text ed. 14. 95 (*0-309-03885-5*) Natl Acad Pr.

— Plasmas & Fluids. (Physics Through the 1990's Ser.). 336p. 1986. pap. 31.50 (*0-309-03548-1*) Natl Acad Pr.

— Population Growth & Economic Development: Policy Questions. 120p. (Orig.). (C). 1986. pap. text ed. 24.95 (*0-309-03641-0*) Natl Acad Pr.

— Preservation of Historical Records. 108p. 1986. text ed. 17.95 (*0-309-03681-X*) Natl Acad Pr.

— Productive Agriculture & a Quality Environment. 335p. reprint ed. pap. 95.50 (*0-317-28677-3*, 2055290) Bks Demand.

— Prudent Practices for Handling Hazardous Chemicals in Laboratories. 291p. (C). 1981. 24.95 (*0-309-03128-1*) Natl Acad Pr.

— Reducing Hazardous Waste Generation: An Evaluation & a Call for Action. 76p. 1985. pap. text ed. 9.95 (*0-309-03498-1*) Natl Acad Pr.

— Regulating Pesticides. 288p. 1980. pap. text ed. 24.95 (*0-309-02946-5*) Natl Acad Pr.

— Responding to Changes in Sea Level: Engineering Implications. LC 87-21965. 160p. 1987. pap. text ed. 24. 95 (*0-309-03781-6*) Natl Acad Pr.

— Safety of Dams: Flood & Earthquake Criteria. 320p. 1985. pap. 29.95 (*0-309-03532-5*) Natl Acad Pr.

— Science & Creationism: A View from the National Academy of Sciences. 28p. (C). 1984. pap. 5.00 (*0-309-03440-X*) Natl Acad Pr.

— Science & Stewardship in the Antarctic. Commission on Geosciences, Environment, & Resources Staff, ed. 127p. (Orig.). (C). 1993. pap. text ed. 25.00 (*0-309-04947-4*) Natl Acad Pr.

— Selenium in Nutrition. rev. ed. 174p. (C). 1983. pap. text ed. 19.95 (*0-309-03375-6*) Natl Acad Pr.

— Social & Economic Aspects of Radioactive Waste Disposal: Considerations for Institutional Management. 175p. 1984. pap. 19.95 (*0-309-03444-2*) Natl Acad Pr.

— Soil Conservation, Vol. 1: An Assessment of the National Resources Inventory. 112p. 1986. pap. text ed. 14.95 (*0-309-03649-6*) Natl Acad Pr.

— Soil Conservation, Vol. 2: An Assessment of the National Resources Inventory. 314p. 1986. pap. text ed. 24.95 (*0-309-03675-5*) Natl Acad Pr.

— Solar & Space Physics. (Space Science in the Twenty-First Century Series: Imperatives for the Decades 1995 to 2015). 150p. 1988. pap. text ed. 17.95 (*0-309-03848-0*) Natl Acad Pr.

— Support Organizations for the Engineering Community. (Engineering Education & Practice in the United States Ser.). 80p. 1986. pap. text ed. 10.50 (*0-309-03629-1*) Natl Acad Pr.

— Tinnitus: Facts, Theories, & Treatments. 150p. (C). 1982. pap. text ed. 14.95 (*0-309-03328-4*) Natl Acad Pr.

— Toxicity Testing: Strategies to Determine Needs & Priorities. 382p. 1984. pap. 34.95 (*0-309-03433-7*) Natl Acad Pr.

— Urban Policy in a Changing Federal System. 278p. 1985. pap. text ed. 24.95 (*0-309-03591-0*) Natl Acad Pr.

— Video Displays, Work, & Vision. 273p. 1983. pap. 19.95 (*0-309-03388-8*) Natl Acad Pr.

— Water Chemicals Codex. 73p. (C). 1982. pap. text ed. 12. 95 (*0-309-03338-1*) Natl Acad Pr.

— Women's Work, Men's Work: Sex Segregation on the Job. 186p. (Orig.). (C). 1986. pap. text ed. 29.95 (*0-309-03429-9*) Natl Acad Pr.

National Research Council, ed. Improving Productivity in U. S. Marine Container Terminals. 205p. 1986. pap. text ed. 32.50 (*0-309-03694-1*) Natl Acad Pr.

National Research Council, jt. auth. see Institute of Medicine.

National Research Council, Academy Industry Program & Office of International Affairs Staff. Europe 1992: The Implication of Market Integration for R&D-Intensive Firms. 180p. 1991. pap. text ed. 18.00 (*0-309-04332-8*) Natl Acad Pr.

National Research Council, Agricultural Board Staff. Peat Control Strategies for the Future. reprint ed. pap. 95.80 (*0-317-28680-3*, 2055289) Bks Demand.

National Research Council, Agricultural Board. Pest Control Strategies for the Future. 383p. reprint ed. pap. 109.20 (*0-317-39635-8*, 2055289) Bks Demand.

National Research Council Assembly of Life Sciences-Food & Nutrition Board. Assessing Changing Food Consumption Patterns. 296p. (C). 1981. pap. text ed. 24. 95 (*0-309-03135-4*) Natl Acad Pr.

National Research Council, Astronomy & Astrophysics Survey Committee Staff. The Decade of Discovery in Astronomy & Astrophysics. 200p. (C). 1991. pap. text ed. 24.95 (*0-309-04381-6*) Natl Acad Pr.

— Working Papers: Astronomy & Astrophysics Panel Reports. 356p. (C). 1991. pap. text ed. 35.00 (*0-309-04383-2*) Natl Acad Pr.

National Research Council, Board on Acience & Technology for International Development Staff. Lost Crops of Africa: Grains. 425p. (Orig.). (C). 1995. pap. 34.95 (*0-309-04990-3*) Natl Acad Pr.

National Research Council, Board on Agriculture & Board on Science & Technology for International Development, Committee on Sustainable Agriculture & the Environment in the Humid Tropics Staff. Sustainable Agriculture & the Environment in the Humid Tropics. LC 92-36869. 720p. (C). 1993. text ed. 49.95 (*0-309-04749-8*) Natl Acad Pr.

National Research Council, Board on Agriculture Staff. Agriculture & the Undergraduate: Proceedings. 268p. (C). 1992. pap. text ed. 33.00 (*0-309-04682-3*) Natl Acad Pr.

— Investing in the National Research Initiative: An Update of the Competitive Grants Program in the U. S. Department of Agriculture (15) 80p. (Orig.). (C). 1994. pap. text ed. 20.00 (*0-309-05235-1*) Natl Acad Pr.

***National Research Council, Board on Atmospheric Sciences & Climate Staff.** Ozone Depletion, Greenhouse Gases, & Climate Change: Proceedings of a Joint Symposium. fac. ed. LC 88-31544. (Illus.). 136p. 1989. pap. 38.80 (*0-7837-7565-2*, 2036997) Bks Demand.

National Research Council, Board on Global Change Staff. Solar Influences on Global Change. 180p. (Orig.). (C). 1994. pap. text ed. 25.00 (*0-309-05148-7*) Natl Acad Pr.

National Research Council, Board on Marine Salvage Issues Staff. Purposeful Jettison of Petroleum Cargo. 216p. (Orig.). (C). 1994. pap. text ed. 33.00 (*0-309-05081-2*) Natl Acad Pr.

National Research Council Board on Ocean Science & Policy. Disposal of Industrial & Domestic Wastes: Land & Sea Alternatives. 210p. 1984. pap. 19.95 (*0-309-03484-1*) Natl Acad Pr.

National Research Council, Building Research Board Staff. Committing to the Cost of Ownership: Maintenance & Repair of Public Buildings. (Special Report Ser.: No. 60). 53p. (Orig.). 1990. pap. text ed. 30.00 (*0-917084-07-1*) Am Public Works.

***National Research Council, Climate Research Committee.** GOALS (Global Ocean-Atmosphere-Land System) for Predicting Seasonal-to-Interannual Climate: A Program of Observation, Modeling, & Analysis. 116p. (Orig.). (C). 1994. pap. text ed. 27.00 (*0-309-05180-0*) Natl Acad Pr.

National Research Council, Commission of Behavioral & Social Sciences & Education Staff. The Transition to Democracy: Proceedings of a Workshop. 104p. 1991. pap. text ed. 19.00 (*0-309-04441-3*) Natl Acad Pr.

National Research Council, Commission on Behavioral & Social Sciences & Education Staff. A Census That Mirrors America: Interim Report. 108p. (Orig.). (C). 1993. pap. text ed. 29.00 (*0-309-04979-2*) Natl Acad Pr.

National Research Council, Commission on Engineering & Technical Systems Staff. Aeronautical Technologies for the Twenty-First Century. (Illus.). 314p. (Orig.). (C). 1992. pap. text ed. 38.00 (*0-309-04732-3*) Natl Acad Pr.

— Commercialization of New Materials for a Global Economy. 80p. (C). 1993. pap. text ed. 25.00 (*0-309-04734-X*) Natl Acad Pr.

— Learning to Change: Opportunities to Improve the Performance of Smaller Manufacturers. 152p. (C). 1993. text ed. 26.00 (*0-309-04982-2*) Natl Acad Pr.

National Research Council, Commission on Geosciences, Environment, & Resources, Ocean Studies Board Staff. Oceanography in the Next Decade: Building New Partnerships. LC 92-34458. 216p. (C). 1992. pap. text ed. 39.95 (*0-309-04794-3*) Natl Acad Pr.

National Research Council, Commission on Geosciences, Environment, & Resources Staff. Application of Analytical Chemistry to Oceanic Carbon Studies. 96p. (Orig.). (C). 1993. pap. text ed. 26.00 (*0-309-04928-8*) Natl Acad Pr.

— Coastal Meteorology: A Review of the State of the Science. 112p. (C). 1992. pap. text ed. 24.00 (*0-309-04687-4*) Natl Acad Pr.

— Environmental Science in the Coastal Zone: Issues for Further Research. 184p. 1994. pap. text ed. 35.00 (*0-309-04980-6*) Natl Acad Pr.

— National Geomagnetic Initiative. 264p. (Orig.). (C). 1993. pap. text ed. 28.00 (*0-309-04977-6*) Natl Acad Pr.

— Radioactive Waste Repository Licensing: Synopsis of a Symposium. 112p. (C). 1992. pap. text ed. 19.00 (*0-309-04691-2*) Natl Acad Pr.

National Research Council, Commission on Life Sciences Staff. Assessment of the Possible Health Effects of the Ground Wave Emergency Network. 180p. (Orig.). (C). 1993. pap. text ed. 33.00 (*0-309-04777-3*) Natl Acad Pr.

— A Biological Survey for the Nation. 224p. (Orig.). (C). 1993. pap. text ed. 26.00 (*0-309-04984-9*) Natl Acad Pr.

— Plant Biology Research & Training for the 21st Century. 80p. (C). 1992. pap. text ed. 19.00 (*0-309-04679-3*) Natl Acad Pr.

***National Research Council Commission on Natural Resources.** Assigning Economic Value to Natural Resources. 196p. (Orig.). (C). 1994. pap. text ed. 29.00 (*0-309-05143-6*) Natl Acad Pr.

— Atmosphere-Biosphere Interactions: Toward a Better Understanding of the Ecological Consequences of Fossil Fuel Combustion. 280p. (C). 1981. pap. text ed. 24.95 (*0-309-03196-6*) Natl Acad Pr.

National Research Council, Commission on Natural Resources. Nutrient Requirements of Fish. 124p. (C). 1993. pap. text ed. 24.95 (*0-309-03187-7*) Natl Acad Pr.

National Research Council Commission on Natural Resources. Nutrient Requirements of Goats: Angora, Dairy, & Meat Goats in Temperate & Tropical Countries. 84p. (C). 1981. pap. text ed. 19.95 (*0-309-03185-0*) Natl Acad Pr.

National Research Council, Commission on Physical Science, Mathematics, & Applications Staff. Information Technology in the Service Society: A 21st Century Lever. 300p. (Orig.). (C). 1993. pap. text ed. 29. 00 (*0-309-04876-1*) Natl Acad Pr.

National Research Council, Commission on Physical Sciences, Mathematics, & Applications Staff. Atomic, Molecular, & Optical Science: An Investment in the Future. 224p. (Orig.). (C). 1994. pap. text ed. 30.00 (*0-309-05032-4*) Natl Acad Pr.

National Research Council, Commission on PHysical Sciences, Mathematics, & Applications Staff. Breaking the Mold: Forging a Common Defense Manufacturing Vision. 110p. (Orig.). (C). 1993. pap. text ed. 24.00 (*0-309-04789-7*) Natl Acad Pr.

— Currency Features for Visually Impaired People. 100p. (Orig.). (C). 1995. pap. text ed. 27.00 (*0-309-05194-0*) Natl Acad Pr.

— Demographic Effects of Economic Reversals in Sub-Saharan Africa. (Population Dynamics of Sub-Saharan Africa Ser.). 208p. (Orig.). (C). 1993. pap. text ed. 33.00 (*0-309-04898-2*) Natl Acad Pr.

— Drilling & Excavation Technologies for the Future. 176p. (Orig.). (C). 1994. pap. text ed. 27.00 (*0-309-05076-6*) Natl Acad Pr.

— Factors Affecting Contraceptive Use in Sub-Saharan Africa. (Population Dynamics of Sub-Saharan Africa Ser.). 272p. (Orig.). (C). 1993. pap. text ed. 35.00 (*0-309-04944-X*) Natl Acad Pr.

— Fourth Dimension in Building: Strategies for Minimizing Obsolescence. 114p. (Orig.). (C). 1993. pap. text ed. 28. 00 (*0-309-04842-7*) Natl Acad Pr.

— Health Effects of Ingested Fluoride. 206p. (Orig.). (C). 1993. pap. text ed. 35.00 (*0-309-04975-X*) Natl Acad Pr.

— Materials Research Agenda for the Automobile & Aircraft Industries. 83p. 1993. pap. text ed. 25.00 (*0-309-04985-7*) Natl Acad Pr.

— Mathematical Research in Materials Science: Opportunities & Perspectives. 144p. (Orig.). (C). 1993. pap. text ed. 23.00 (*0-309-04930-X*) Natl Acad Pr.

— A Reassessment of the Marine Salvage Posture of the United States. 144p. (Orig.). (C). 1994. pap. text ed. 33. 00 (*0-309-05149-5*) Natl Acad Pr.

— Toward a Coordinated Spatial Data Infrastructure for the Nation. 192p. (Orig.). (C). 1993. pap. text ed. 24.00 (*0-309-04899-0*) Natl Acad Pr.

— Workload Transition: Implications for Individual & Team Performance. Huey, Beverly M. & Wickens, Christopher D., eds. 304p. (Orig.). (C). 1993. pap. text ed. 36.00 (*0-309-04796-X*) Natl Acad Pr.

National Research Council, Commission on PHysical Sciences, Mathematics, & Applications Staff & Committee on Academic Careers for Experimental Computer Scientists Staff. Academic Careers of Experimental Computer Scientists. 152p. (Orig.). (C). 1993. pap. text ed. 27.00 (*0-309-04931-8*) Natl Acad Pr.

National Research Council, Commission on Behavioral & Social Sciences Staff & National Research Council Staff. Population & Land Use in Developing Countries: Report of a Workshop. 172p. (Orig.). (C). 1993. pap. text ed. 26.50 (*0-309-04838-9*) Natl Acad Pr.

National Research Council Commission on Physical Sciences, Mathematics, & Applications Staff, ed. see Pimentel, George C. & Coonrod, Janice A.

National Research Council, Committee for the Study of the Causes & Consequences of the Internationalization of U. S. Manufacturing Staff. The Internationalization of U. S. Manufacturing: Causes & Consequences. 180p. 1990. pap. text ed. 15.00 (*0-309-04331-X*) Natl Acad Pr.

National Research Council, Committee on Vision Staff. Advances in Photoreception: Proceedings of a Symposium on Frontiers of Visual Science. 160p. 1990. pap. text ed. 16.00 (*0-309-04240-2*) Natl Acad Pr.

National Research Council, Committee on Managing Global Genetic Resources Staff. Agricultural Crop Issues & Policies. (Managing Global Genetic Resources Ser.). 480p. (C). 1994. text ed. 49.95 (*0-309-04430-8*) Natl Acad Pr.

National Research Council, Committee on Ground Water Cleanup Alternatives Staff. Alternatives for Ground Water Cleanup. 336p. (C). 1994. text ed. 39.95 (*0-309-04994-6*) Natl Acad Pr.

National Research Council, Committee on Vision Staff. Clean Ships, Clean Ports, Clean Oceans: Controlling Garbage & Plastic Wastes at Sea. 300p. (C). 1994. text ed. 42.95 (*0-309-05137-1*) Natl Acad Pr.

National Research Council, Committee on Infectious Diseases of Mice & Rats Staff. Companion Guide to Infectious Disease of Mice & Rats. 108p. 1991. pap. text ed. 12.00 (*0-309-04283-6*) Natl Acad Pr.

National Research Council, Committee on Vision Staff. The Competitive Edge: Research Priorities for U. S. Manufacturing. 184p. 1991. text ed. 24.95 (*0-309-04784-6*) Natl Acad Pr.

National Research Council, Committee on Competitiveness of the U. S. Minerals & Metals Industry Staff. Competitiveness of the U. S. Minerals & Metals Industries. 160p. 1990. text ed. 22.95 (*0-309-04245-3*) Natl Acad Pr.

National Research Council, Committee on Disasters & the Mass Media Staff. Disasters & the Mass Media: Proceedings of the Committee on Disasters & the Mass Media Workshop, February 1979. LC 79-27615. (Illus.). 315p. reprint ed. pap. 89.80 (*0-8357-4270-9*, 2037066) Bks Demand.

National Research Council, Committee on Earthquake Engineering Staff. Earthquake Engineering for Concrete Dams: Design, Performance, & Research Needs. 158p. 1991. pap. text ed. 19.00 (*0-309-04336-0*) Natl Acad Pr.

National Research Council, Committee on Enabling Technologies for Unified Life-Cycle Engineering of Structural Components Staff. Enabling Technologies for Unified Life-Cycle Engineering of Structural Components. 112p. 1991. pap. text ed. 19.00 (*0-309-04492-8*) Natl Acad Pr.

National Research Council, Committee on Vision Staff. Fulfilling the Promise: Biology Education in the Nation's Schools. 168p. 1990. 19.95 (*0-309-05147-9*) Natl Acad Pr.

— Ground Water Recharge Using Waters of Impaired Quality. 304p. (Orig.). (C). 1994. pap. text ed. 39.00 (*0-309-05142-8*) Natl Acad Pr.

National Research Council, Committee on Haze in National Parks & Wilderness Areas Staff. Haze in the Grand Canyon: An Evaluation of the Winter Haze Intensive Tracer Experiment. 108p. 1990. pap. text ed. 17.00 (*0-309-04341-7*) Natl Acad Pr.

National Research Council, Committee on Vision Staff. Health Risks of Exposure to Radon: Time for Reassessment? 114p. (Orig.). (C). 1994. pap. text ed. 27. 00 (*0-309-05087-1*) Natl Acad Pr.

— Hierarchical Structures in Biology as a Guide for New Materials Technology. 144p. (Orig.). (C). 1994. pap. text ed. 38.00 (*0-309-04638-6*) Natl Acad Pr.

National Research Council, Committee on Advances in Assessing Human Exposure to Airborne Pollutants Staff. Human Exposure Assessment for Airborne Pollutants: Advances & Opportunities. 344p. 1991. pap. text ed. 35.00 (*0-309-04284-4*) Natl Acad Pr.

National Research Council, Committee on Natural Disaster Staff. Hurricane Hugo, Puerto Rico, the Virgin Islands, & Charleston, South Carolina, Sept. 17-22, 1989. (Natural Disaster Studies). 296p. 1994. pap. 39.00 (*0-309-04475-8*) Natl Acad Pr.

National Research Council, Committee on Hypersonic Technology for Military Application Staff. Hypersonic Technology for Military Application. 94p. 1990. pap. text ed. 15.00 (*0-309-04229-1*) Natl Acad Pr.

National Research Council, Committee on Engineering Design Theory & Methodology Staff. Improving Engineering Design: Designing for Competitive Advantage. 120p. 1991. pap. text ed. 19.00 (*0-309-04478-2*) Natl Acad Pr.

National Research Council, Committee on In Situ Bioremediation Staff. In Situ Bioremediation: When Does It Work? LC 93-5531. 215p. 1993. text ed. 29.95 (*0-309-04896-6*) Natl Acad Pr.

National Research Council, Committee on National Research Urban Policy Staff. Inner-City Poverty in the United States. 290p. 1990. text ed. 34.95 (*0-309-04279-8*) Natl Acad Pr.

National Research Council, Committee on Dogs Staff. Lab Animal Management: Dogs. LC 94-960. 152p. (Orig.). (C). 1994. pap. text ed. 24.95 (*0-309-04744-7*) Natl Acad Pr.

N

An Asterisk (*) at the beginning of an entry indicates that the title is appearing in BIP for the first time.

National Research Council, Committee on Vision Staff. Learning, Remembering, Believing: Enhancing Human Performance. Druckman, Daniel & Bjork, Robert A., eds. 416p. (C). 1994. 39.95 (*0-309-04993-8*) Natl Acad Pr.

National Research Council, Committee on Managing Global Genetic Resources: Agricultural Imperatives Staff. Livestock. (Managing Global Genetic Resources Ser.). 296p. (C). 1993. text ed. 34.95 (*0-309-04394-8*) Natl Acad Pr.

National Research Council, Committee on Wastewater Management for Coastal Urban Areas Staff. Managing Wastewater in Coastal Urban Areas. LC 93-1845. 496p. (Orig.). (C). 1993. text ed. 49.95 (*0-309-04826-5*) Natl Acad Pr.

National Research Council, Committee on Vision Staff. Meeting the Nation's Needs for Biomedical & Behavioral Scientists. 174p. (Orig.). (C). 1994. pap. text ed. 27.00 (*0-309-05086-3*) Natl Acad Pr.

— Microwave Processing of Materials. 164p. (Orig.). (C). 1994. pap. text ed. 35.00 (*0-309-05027-8*) Natl Acad Pr.

National Research Council, Committee on Advances in Navigation & Piloting Staff. Minding the Helm: Marine Navigation & Piloting. 528p. (C). 1994. text ed. 54.95 (*0-309-04829-X*) Natl Acad Pr.

National Research Council, Committee on Natural Disasters Staff. The New Year's Eve Flood on Oahu, Hawaii, December 31, 1987-January 1, 1988. (Natural Disaster Studies: Vol. 1). 88p. 1990. pap. 19.00 (*0-309-04433-2*) Natl Acad Pr.

National Research Council, Committee on Vision Staff. Nutrient Requirements of Laboratory Animals. 4th rev. ed. 350p. (Orig.). (C). 1995. pap. text ed. 34.95 (*0-309-05126-6*) Natl Acad Pr.

National Research Council, Committee on Setting Federal Standards to Control Building Life-Cycle Costs Staff. Pay Now or Pay Later: Controlling Cost of Ownership from Design Throughout the Service Life of Public Buildings. 72p. (C). 1991. pap. text ed. 19.00 (*0-309-04481-2*) Natl Acad Pr.

National Research Council, Committee on Haze in National Parks & Wilderness Areas Staff. Protecting Visibility in National Parks & Wilderness Areas. 316p. (Orig.). (C). 1993. pap. text ed. 38.00 (*0-309-04844-3*) Natl Acad Pr.

National Research Council, Committee on Bioprocess Engineering Staff. Putting Biotechnology to Work: Bioprocess Engineering. LC 92-61717. 132p. (Orig.). (C). 1992. pap. text ed. 24.00 (*0-309-04785-4*) Natl Acad Pr.

National Research Council, Committee on Vision Staff. Radiation-Dose Reconstruction for Epidemiology. 140p. (C). 1995. text ed. 29.95 (*0-309-05099-5*) Natl Acad Pr.

— Radiological Assessments for the Resettlement of Rongelap in the Republic of the Marshall Islands. 124p. (Orig.). (C). 1994. pap. text ed. 37.00 (*0-309-05049-9*) Natl Acad Pr.

— Ranking Hazardous-Waste Sites for Remedial Action. 312p. (Orig.). (C). 1994. pap. text ed. 30.00 (*0-309-05134-7*) Natl Acad Pr.

— Reactor-Related Options for the Disposition of Excess Weapons Plutonium. 200p. (Orig.). (C). 1995. pap. text ed. 27.00 (*0-309-05145-2*) Natl Acad Pr.

National Research Council, Committee on the Recognition & Alleviation of Pain & Distress in Laboratory Animals Staff. Recognition & Alleviation of Pain & Distress in Laboratory Animals. 160p. 1992. text ed. 29.95 (*0-309-04275-5*) Natl Acad Pr.

National Research Council, Committee on Global Change Staff. Research Strategies for the U. S. Global Change Research Program. 294p. 1990. pap. text ed. 28.00 (*0-309-04348-4*) Natl Acad Pr.

National Research Council, Committee on Fracture Characterization & Fluid Flow Staff. Rock Fractures & Fluid Flow: Contemporary Understanding & Application. (C). 1995. text ed. 72.95 (*0-309-04996-2*) Natl Acad Pr.

National Research Council, Committee on Rodents Staff. Rodents. (Laboratory Animal Management Ser.). 190p. (Orig.). (C). 1995. pap. text ed. 24.95 (*0-309-04936-9*) Natl Acad Pr.

National Research Council, Committee on Vision Staff. The Role of Public Agencies in Fostering New Technology & Innovation in Building. Lemer, Andrew C. & Dibner, David R., eds. LC 92-62883. 142p. (Orig.). 1993. pap. text ed. 28.00 (*0-309-04783-8*) Natl Res Coun.

National Research Council, Committee on Biology Teacher Inservice Programs Staff. The Role of Scientists in the Professional Development of Science Teachers. 176p. (C). 1995. text ed. 27.95 (*0-309-04999-7*) Natl Acad Pr.

National Research Council, Committee on Natural Disasters Staff. Saragosa, Texas, Tornado, May 22, 1987: An Evaluation of the Warning System. (Natural Disaster Studies: Vol. 2). 76p. 1991. pap. text ed. 19.00 (*0-309-04435-9*) Natl Acad Pr.

National Research Council, Committee on Women in Science & Engineering, Ad Hoc Panel on Interventions Staff. Science & Engineering Programs: On Target for Women? Matyas, Marsha L. & Dix, Linda S., eds. LC 92-61248. (Illus.). 240p. (Orig.). (C). 1992. pap. text ed. 29.00 (*0-309-04778-1*) Natl Acad Pr.

National Research Council, Committee on Vision Staff. Science & Judgment in RIsk Assessment. 672p. (Orig.). (C). 1994. text ed. 69.95 (*0-309-04894-X*) Natl Acad Pr.

National Research Council, Committee on Planetary Biology & Chemical Evolution Staff. The Search for Life's Origins: Progress & Future Directions in Planetary Biology & Chemical Evolution. 160p. 1990. pap. text ed. 16.00 (*0-309-04246-1*) Natl Acad Pr.

National Research Council, Committee on Haze in National Parks & Wilderness Areas Staff. Setting Priorities for Land Conservation. 150p. (Orig.). (C). 1993. pap. text ed. 39.95 (*0-309-04836-2*) Natl Acad Pr.

National Research Council, Committee on Long-Term Soil & Water Conservation Policy. Soil & Water Quality: An Agenda for Agriculture. 442p. (C). 1993. text ed. 54.95 (*0-309-04933-4*) Natl Acad Pr.

***National Research Council, Committee on Vision Staff.** Sources of Medical Technology: Universities & Industry, Vol. 5. Gelijns, Annetine C. & Rosenberg, Nathan, eds. (Medical Innovation at the Crossroads Ser.). 280p. (Orig.). (C). 1995. pap. text ed. 25.00 (*0-309-05189-4*) Natl Acad Pr.

National Research Council, Committee on Structural Adhesives for Aerospace Use. Structural Adhesives with Emphasis on Aerospace Applications: A Report of the Ad Hoc Committee on Structural Adhesives for Aerospace Use, National Materials Advisory Board, National Research Council. LC 75-17033. (Treatise on Adhesion & Adhesives Ser.: Vol. 4). 264p. reprint ed. pap. 75.30 (*0-685-16321-0*, 2027122) Bks Demand.

National Research Council, Committee on Tank Vessel Design Alternatives Staff. Tanker Spills: Prevention by Design. 384p. 1991. text ed. 39.95 (*0-309-04377-8*) Natl Acad Pr.

National Research Council, Committee on National Statistics Staff. Teacher Supply, Demand, & Quality: Policy Issues, Models, & Data Bases. Boe, Erling E. & Gifford, Dorothy M., eds. LC 92-50735. 344p. (C). 1992. pap. text ed. 44.00 (*0-309-04792-7*) Natl Acad Pr.

National Research Council, Committee on a Treatise on Marine Ecology & Paleoecology Staff. Treatise on Marine Ecology & Paleoecology. Hedgpeth, Joel W., ed. LC 57-4669. (Geological Society of America, Memoir Ser.: No. 67, Vol. 1). 1352p. pap. 180.00 (*0-318-34695-8*, 2031784) Bks Demand.

National Research Council, Committee on Nuclear Engineering Education Staff. U. S. Nuclear Engineering Education: Status & Prospects. 180p. (C). 1990. pap. text ed. 19.00 (*0-309-04280-1*) Natl Acad Pr.

National Research Council, Committee on Vision Staff. Virtual Reality: Scientific & Technological Challenges. Mavor, Anne S. & Durlach, N. I., eds. 542p. (C). 1994. text ed. 59.95 (*0-309-05135-5*) Natl Acad Pr.

National Research Council, Committee on Mathematical Sciences in the Year 2000 Staff & National Research Council, Committee on Vision Staff. Moving Beyond Myths: Revitalizing Undergraduate Mathematics. 80p. 1991. pap. text ed. 7.95 (*0-309-04489-8*) Natl Acad Pr.

National Research Council, Committee on Vision Staff, jt. auth. see National Research Council, Committee on Mathematical Sciences in the Year 2000 Staff.

National Research Council Committee on Environmental Research. Research to Protect, Restore, & Manage the Environment. 256p. (Orig.). (C). 1993. pap. text ed. 28.00 (*0-309-04929-6*) Natl Acad Pr.

National Research Council Committee on Low-Frequency Sound & Marine Mammals. Low-Frequency Sound & Marine Mammals: Current Knowledge & Research Needs. 92p. (Orig.). (C). 1994. pap. text ed. 25.00 (*0-309-05025-1*) Natl Acad Pr.

National Research Council Committee on Next-Generation Currency Design. Counterfeit Deterrent Features for the Next-Generation Currency Design. 144p. (Orig.). (C). 1994. pap. text ed. 29.00 (*0-309-05028-6*) Natl Acad Pr.

National Research Council Committee on Psychiatric Investigations. The Problem of Mental Disorder. Grob, Gerald N., ed. LC 78-22580. (Historical Issues in Mental Health Ser.). 1980. reprint ed. lib. bdg. 30.95 (*0-405-11932-1*) Ayer.

National Research Council Committee on Women in Science & Engineering. Women Scientists & Engineers Employed in Industry: Why So Few? 144p. (Orig.). (C). 1993. text ed. write for info. (*0-318-72775-7*); pap. text ed. 29.00 (*0-309-04991-1*) Natl Acad Pr.

***National Research Council, Committee to Review the Outer Continental Shelf Environmental Studies Program Staff.** An Assessment of Atlantic Bluefin Tuna. 168p. (Orig.). (C). 1994. pap. text ed. 29.00 (*0-309-05181-9*) Natl Acad Pr.

— Assessment of the U. S. Outer Continental Shelf Environmental Studies Program, No. 3: Social & Economic Studies. LC 89-63847. 164p. (Orig.). (C). 1993. pap. text ed. 30.00 (*0-309-04835-4*) Natl Acad Pr.

— Priorities for Coastal Ecosystem Science. 116p. (Orig.). (C). 1995. pap. text ed. 29.00 (*0-309-05096-0*) Natl Acad Pr.

National Research Council, Engineering Research Board Staff. Directions in Engineering Research: An Assessment of Opportunities & Needs. 364p. 1987. pap. text ed. 34.95 (*0-309-03747-6*) Natl Acad Pr.

National Research Council, Geophysics Study Committee Staff. Material Fluxes on the Surface of the Earth. LC 94-20773. (Studies in Geophysics). 192p. (C). 1994. text ed. 39.95 (*0-309-04745-5*) Natl Acad Pr.

National Research Council, Geotechnical Board Staff. Practical Lessons from the Loma Prieta Earthquake. 288p. (Orig.). (C). 1994. pap. text ed. 39.00 (*0-309-05030-8*) Natl Acad Pr.

National Research Council, Institute of Medicine, Committee on Drug Use in the Workplace Staff. Under the Influence: Drugs & the American Workforce. Normand, Jacques et al, eds. 336p. (C). 1993. text ed. 39.95 (*0-309-04885-0*) Natl Acad Pr.

National Research Council, Manufacturing Studies Board Staff. Toward a New Era in United States Manufacturing: The Need for a National Vision. LC 86-50832. (Illus.). 190p. reprint ed. pap. 54.20 (*0-8357-4222-9*, 2037007) Bks Demand.

***National Research Council, Mapping Science Committee.** Promoting the National Spatial Data Infrastructure Through Partnerships. 128p. (Orig.). (C). 1995. pap. text ed. 24.00 (*0-309-05141-X*) Natl Acad Pr.

National Research Council, Mathematical Sciences Education Board Staff. Everybody Counts: A Report to the Nation on the Future of Mathematics Education. 128p. 1989. pap. text ed. 7.95 (*0-309-03977-0*) Natl Acad Pr.

— Measuring Lead Exposure in Infants, Children, & Other Sensitive Populations. 356p. (Orig.). (C). 1993. pap. text ed. 39.00 (*0-309-04927-X*) Natl Acad Pr.

— Measuring What Counts: A Conceptual Guide for Mathematics Assessment. 236p. 1993. pap. text ed. 17.95 (*0-309-04981-4*) Natl Acad Pr.

— Measuring What Counts: A Policy Brief. 32p. 1993. pap. text ed. 3.95 (*0-309-04986-5*) Natl Acad Pr.

National Research Council, NRenaissance Committee Staff. Realizing the Information Future: The Internet & Beyond. 320p. (Orig.). (C). 1994. pap. 24.95 (*0-309-05044-8*) Natl Acad Pr.

National Research Council of Canada, Associate Committee on Geotechnical Research, Muskeg Subcommittee. Muskeg Engineering Handbook. MacFarlane, Ivan C., ed. LC 78-447167. (Canadian Building Ser.: No. 3). 320p. reprint ed. pap. 91.20 (*0-685-15867-5*, 2056114) Bks Demand.

National Research Council, Office of International Affairs Staff. Dual-Use Technologies & Export Administration in the Post-Cold War Era. 232p. (Orig.). (C). 1994. pap. text ed. 33.00 (*0-309-05031-6*) Natl Acad Pr.

— U. S. - Japan Technology Linkages in Biotechnology: Challenges for the 1990's. 106p. (C). 1992. pap. text ed. 19.00 (*0-309-04699-8*) Natl Acad Pr.

National Research Council, Office of the Home Secretary Staff. Biographical Memoirs, Vol. 61. 512p. (C). 1992. text ed. 59.00 (*0-309-04746-3*) Natl Acad Pr.

— Biographical Memoirs, Vol. 64. 500p. 1994. 59.00 (*0-309-04978-4*) Natl Acad Pr.

***National Research Council, Panel on Census Requirements in the Year 2000 & Beyond.** Modernizing the U. S. Census. Edmonston, Barry & Schultze, Charles, eds. 480p. (Orig.). (C). 1994. pap. text ed. 45.00 (*0-309-05182-7*) Natl Acad Pr.

National Research Council, Panel on Confidentiality & Data Access Staff. Private Lives & Public Policies: Confidentiality & Accessibility of Government Statistics. Jabine, Thomas B. & De Wolf, Virginia A., eds. LC 93-31312. 288p. (C). 1993. text ed. 34.95 (*0-309-04743-9*) Natl Acad Pr.

National Research Council, Panel on Dosimetric Assumptions Affecting the Application of Radon Risk Estimates Staff. Comparative Dosimetry of Radon in Homes & Mines. 256p. 1991. text ed. 29.95 (*0-309-04484-7*) Natl Acad Pr.

National Research Council, Panel on Effects of Past Global Change on Life Staff. Effects of Past Global Change on Life. (Studies in Geophysics). 200p. (C). 1994. text ed. 34.95 (*0-309-05127-4*) Natl Acad Pr.

National Research Council, Panel on Employer Policies & Working Families Staff. Work & Family: Policies for a Changing Workforce. Ferber, Marianne A. & O'Farrell, M. Brigid, eds. 268p. 1991. 29.95 (*0-309-04277-1*) Natl Acad Pr.

National Research Council, Panel on High Risk Youth Staff. Losing Generations: Adolescents in High-Risk Settings. Zeldin, Shepherd, ed. 288p. (Orig.). (C). 1993. pap. text ed. 29.95 (*0-309-04828-1*) Natl Acad Pr.

National Research Council, Panel on International Capital Transactions Staff. Following the Money: U. S. Finance in the World Economy. Kester, Anne Y., ed. 200p. 1994. text ed. 24.95 (*0-309-04883-4*) Natl Acad Pr.

National Research Council, Panel on Monitoring the Social Impact of the AIDS Epidemic Staff. The Social Impact of AIDS in the United States. 336p. 1993. 34.95 (*0-309-04628-9*) Natl Acad Pr.

National Research Council, Panel on Needle Exchange & Bleach Distribution Programs Staff & Institute of Medicine Staff. Proceedings-Workshop on Needle Exchange & Bleach Distribution Programs. 320p. (Orig.). (C). 1994. pap. text ed. 39.00 (*0-309-05084-7*) Natl Acad Pr.

National Research Council, Panel on Organizational Linkages. Organizational Linkages: Understanding the Productivity Paradox. Harris, Douglas H., ed. 320p. (Orig.). 1994. text ed. 44.95 (*0-309-04934-2*) Natl Acad Pr.

National Research Council, Panel on Poverty & Family Assistance Staff. Measuring Poverty: A New Approach. Citro, Constance F. et al, eds. 500p. (C). 1995. text ed. 44.95 (*0-309-05128-2*) Natl Acad Pr.

National Research Council, Panel on Research on Child Abuse & Neglect Staff. Understanding Child Abuse & Neglect. LC 93-29640. 408p. (C). 1993. text ed. 44.95 (*0-309-04889-3*) Natl Acad Pr.

National Research Council Panel on Sentencing Research & Blumstein, Alfred. Research on Sentencing: The Search for Reform, 2 vols., Vol. I. LC 83-4048. 315p. (C). 1983. 29.95 (*0-309-03347-0*) Natl Acad Pr.

— Research on Sentencing: The Search for Reform, 2 vols., Vol. II. LC 83-4048. 489p. (C). 1983. pap. text ed. 39.95 (*0-309-03383-7*) Natl Acad Pr.

National Research Council, Panel on Small Spacecraft Tech Staff, Nat Res Coun Staff. Technology for Small Spacecraft. 156p. (Orig.). (C). 1994. pap. text ed. 27.00 (*0-309-05075-8*) Natl Acad Pr.

National Research Council, Panel on the Understanding & Control of Violent Behavior Staff. Understanding & Preventing Violence, Vol. 2: Biobehavioral Influences. Reiss, Albert J., Jr. et al, eds. 560p. (Orig.). (C). 1994. pap. text ed. 45.00 (*0-309-04649-1*) Natl Acad Pr.

National Research Council, Panel on the Understanding & Control of Violet Behavior Staff. Understanding & Preventing Violence, Vol. 3: Social Influences. 592p. (Orig.). (C). 1994. pap. text ed. 45.00 (*0-309-05080-4*) Natl Acad Pr.

National Research Council, Panel on the Understanding & Control of violent Behavior Staff. Understanding & Preventing Violence, Vol. 4: Consequences & Control. Reiss, Albert J., Jr. et al, eds. 408p. (Orig.). (C). 1994. pap. text ed. 39.00 (*0-309-05079-0*) Natl Acad Pr.

National Research Council, Panel on the Understanding & Control of Violent Behavior Staff & Roth, Jeffrey A. Understanding & Preventing Violence. Reiss, Albrt J., Jr., ed. LC 92-32138. 480p. (C). 1992. text ed. 49.95 (*0-309-04594-0*) Natl Acad Pr.

National Research Council, Panel to Evaluate the Survey of Income & Program Participation, Committee on National Statistics Commission on Behavioral & Social Sciences & Education Staff. The Future of the Survey of Income & Program Participation. Citro, Constance F. & Kalton, Graham, eds. LC 92-62584. 298p. (Orig.). 1993. pap. text ed. 38.00 (*0-309-04795-1*) Natl Res Coun.

***National Research Council, Panel to Evaluate the Survey of Income & Program Participation, Committee on National Statistics Commission on Behavioral &.** Counting People in the Information Age: Final Report. Steffey, Duane L. & Bradburn, Norman M., eds. 240p. (Orig.). (C). 1994. pap. text ed. 29.00 (*0-309-05178-9*) Natl Acad Pr.

National Research Council, Physics Survey Committee Staff. Scientific Interfaces & Technological Applications. LC 85-32039. (Physics Through the 1990's Ser.). 284p. reprint ed. pap. 81.00 (*0-7837-3570-7*, 2043428) Bks Demand.

National Research Council Polymer Science & Engineering Committee Staff. Polymer Science & Engineering: The Shifting Research Frontiers. 192p. (C). 1994. text ed. 34.95 (*0-309-04998-9*) Natl Acad Pr.

***National Research Council, Population Committee.** Demography of Aging. Martin, Linda G. & Preston, Samuel H., eds. 424p. (Orig.). (C). 1994. pap. text ed. 39.00 (*0-614-03583-X*) Natl Acad Pr.

National Research Council, Safe Drinking Water Committee. Drinking Water & Health, Vol. 5. 157p. 1983. pap. text ed. 18.95 (*0-309-03381-0*) Natl Acad Pr.

— Drinking Water & Health, Vol. 6. 457p. 1986. pap. text ed. 39.95 (*0-309-03687-9*) Natl Acad Pr.

— Drinking Water & Health: Selected Issues in Risk Assessment, Vol. 9. 284p. 1989. pap. text ed. 29.95 (*0-309-03897-9*) Natl Acad Pr.

— Drinking Water & Health, Vol. 7: Disinfectants & Disinfectant By-Products. 212p. 1987. pap. text ed. 19.95 (*0-309-03741-7*) Natl Acad Pr.

— Drinking Water & Health, Vol. 8: Pharmacokinetics in Risk Assessment. 512p. 1987. pap. text ed. 43.50 (*0-309-03775-1*) Natl Acad Pr.

National Research Council, Safety of Marine Pipelines Committee. Improving the Safety of Marine Pipelines. 156p. (Orig.). (C). 1994. pap. text ed. 32.00 (*0-309-05047-2*) Natl Acad Pr.

National Research Council, Science & Technology for International Development Staff. Food Aid Projections for the Decade of the 1990s. 194p. 1989. pap. text ed. 20.00 (*0-309-04268-2*) Natl Acad Pr.

***National Research Council, Solar-Terrestrial Research Committee.** A Space Physics Paradox: Why Has Increased Funding Been Accompanied by Decreased Effectiveness in the Conduct of Space Physics Research? 112p. (Orig.). (C). 1994. pap. text ed. 29.00 (*0-309-05177-0*) Natl Acad Pr.

National Research Council Staff. Acid Deposition: Atmospheric Processes in Eastern North America. LC 83-61851. (Review of Current Scientific Understanding Ser.). 391p. reprint ed. pap. 111.50 (*0-7837-5038-2*, 2044714) Bks Demand.

— Agricultural Biotechnology: Strategies for National Competitiveness. LC 87-12181. 221p. reprint ed. pap. 63.00 (*0-7837-2776-3*, 2043167) Bks Demand.

— Airborne Geophysics & Precise Positioning: Scientific Issues & Future Directions. 200p. (Orig.). (C). 1994. pap. text ed. 30.00 (*0-309-05183-5*) Natl Acad Pr.

— The Airliner Cabin Environment: Air Quality & Safety. 318p. 1986. pap. text ed. 29.95 (*0-309-03690-9*) Natl Acad Pr.

— Assessing Evaluation Studies: The Case of Bilingual Education Strategies. 138p. (C). 1992. pap. text ed. 22.00 (*0-309-04728-5*) Natl Acad Pr.

— Assessment of the U. S. Outer Continental Shelf Environmental Studies Program, Vol. 1: Physical Oceanography. LC 89-63847. 153p. reprint ed. pap. 43.70 (*0-7837-5037-4*, 2044713) Bks Demand.

— Assessment of the U. S. Outer Continental Shelf Environmental Studies Program, Vol. 2: Ecology. 162p. 1992. pap. 21.00 (*0-309-04598-3*) Natl Acad Pr.

— Beam Technologies for Integrated Processing. 106p. 1992. pap. 19.00 (*0-309-04635-1*) Natl Acad Pr.

— Biologic Markers in Reproductive Toxicology. 420p. 1989. pap. 32.95 (*0-309-03979-7*) Natl Acad Pr.

— Biologic Markers in Urinary Toxicology. 210p. (Orig.). (C). 1995. pap. text ed. 27.00 (*0-309-05228-9*) Natl Acad Pr.

— Biologic Markers of Pulmonary Toxicology. 196p. 1989. 34.95 (*0-309-03992-4*); pap. 24.95 (*0-309-03990-8*) Natl Acad Pr.

— Catalysis Looks to the Future. 96p. 1991. pap. 19.00 (*0-309-04584-3*) Natl Acad Pr.

— Causes & Effects of Stratospheric Ozone Reduction: An Update. 339p. (C). 1982. pap. text ed. 29.95 (*0-309-03248-2*) Natl Acad Pr.

N

An Asterisk (*) at the beginning of an entry indicates that the title is appearing in BIP for the first time.

— Changing Economics of Medical Technology, Vol. 2. 224p. 1991. text ed. 24.95 (*0-309-04491-X*) Natl Acad Pr.

— The Changing Nature of Telecommunications & Information Infrastructure. 125p. (Orig.). (C). 1995. pap. text ed. 27.00 (*0-309-05091-X*) Natl Acad Pr.

— Climate, Climatic Change & Water Supply. (Studies in Geophysics). 132p. 1977. pap. 14.95 (*0-309-02625-3*) Natl Acad Pr.

— Coal: Energy for the Future. 320p. (Orig.). (C). 1995. text ed. 39.95 (*0-309-05232-7*) Natl Acad Pr.

— Contraceptive Use & Controlled Fertility: Health Issues for Women & Children. 172p. 1989. pap. text ed. 18.00 (*0-309-04096-5*) Natl Acad Pr.

— Democratization in Africa: African Views, African Voices. (Project on Democratization Ser.). 94p. (Orig.). (C). 1992. pap. text ed. 22.00 (*0-309-04797-8*) Natl Acad Pr.

— Diet & Health: Implications for Reducing Chronic Disease Risk. 768p. 1989. 54.95 (*0-309-03994-0*) Natl Acad Pr.

— Discovering the Brain. 194p. 1991. 22.95 (*0-309-04529-0*) Natl Acad Pr.

— The Earth's Electrical Environment. (Studies in Geophysics). 263p. 1986. text ed. 28.95 (*0-309-03680-1*) Natl Acad Pr.

— Education & Training in the Care & Use of Laboratory Animals: A Guide for Developing Institutional Programs. 152p. (C). 1991. pap. text ed. 11.95 (*0-309-04382-4*) Natl Acad Pr.

— The Effect of Genetic Variance on Nutritional Requirements of Animals: Proceedings of a Symposium, University of Maryland, College Park, Maryland, July 31, 1974. LC 75-10567. 129p. reprint ed. pap. 36.80 (*0-7837-1638-9*, 2041931) Bks Demand.

— The Effects on Human Health of Subtherapeutic Use of Antimicrobials in Animal Feeds. LC 80-81486. 376p. 1980. pap. text ed. 29.95 (*0-309-03044-7*) Natl Acad Pr.

— Engineering Education & Practice in the United States: Foundations of Our Techno-Economic Future. LC 85-60423. (Illus.). 150p. reprint ed. pap. 42.80 (*0-7837-5355-1*, 2045117) Bks Demand.

— Environmental Information for Outer Continental Shelf Oil & Gas Decisions in Alaska. 270p. (Orig.). (C). 1994. pap. text ed. 49.00 (*0-309-05036-7*) Natl Acad Pr.

— Environmental Tobacco Smoke: Measuring Exposures & Assessing Health Effects. LC 86-28622. 351p. reprint ed. pap. 100.10 (*0-7837-1299-5*, 2041440) Bks Demand.

— Estimating Probabilities of Extreme Floods: Methods & Recommended Research. LC 87-34839. 157p. reprint ed. pap. 44.80 (*0-8357-4268-7*, 2037064) Bks Demand.

— Expanding the Vision of Sensor Materials. 175p. (Orig.). (C). 1994. pap. text ed. 33.00 (*0-309-05175-4*) Natl Acad Pr.

— Fateful Choices: The Future of the U. S. Academic Research Enterprise. 72p. 1992. pap. 19.00 (*0-309-04643-2*) Natl Acad Pr.

— The Field of Solar Physics: Review & Recommendations for Ground-Based Solar Research. 72p. 1989. pap. text ed. 15.00 (*0-309-04082-5*) Natl Acad Pr.

— Field Testing Genetically Modified Organisms: Framework for Decisions. 184p. 1989. pap. text ed. 24.95 (*0-309-04076-0*) Natl Acad Pr.

— Film Badge Dosimetry in Atmospheric Nuclear Tests. 244p. 1989. pap. text ed. 22.00 (*0-309-04079-5*) Natl Acad Pr.

— Foreign Participation in U.S. Research & Development: Asset or Liability? (Prospering in a Global Economy Ser.). 150p. (Orig.). (C). 1995. text ed. 24.95 (*0-309-05095-2*) Natl Acad Pr.

— Fostering Flexibility in the Engineering Work Force. 180p. (C). 1990. pap. text ed. 17.00 (*0-309-04276-3*) Natl Acad Pr.

— The Funding of Young Investigators in the Biological & Biomedical Sciences. 128p. (Orig.). (C). 1994. pap. text ed. 24.00 (*0-309-05077-4*) Natl Acad Pr.

— Future National Research Policies Within the Industrialized Nations. 170p. 1992. pap. 19.00 (*0-309-04642-4*) Natl Acad Pr.

— The Future of Statistical Software: Proceedings of a Symposium. 100p. 1991. pap. 19.00 (*0-309-04599-1*) Natl Acad Pr.

— Genetic Engineering of Plants: Agricultural Research Opportunities & Policy Concerns. 96p. 1984. pap. text ed. 12.95 (*0-309-03434-5*) Natl Acad Pr.

— Geodesy in the Year 2000. 186p. 1990. pap. text ed. 20.00 (*0-309-04145-7*) Natl Acad Pr.

— Global Change & Our Common Future: Papers from a Forum. 244p. 1989. pap. text ed. 24.00 (*0-309-04089-2*) Natl Acad Pr.

— Global Dimensions of Intellectual Property Rights in Science & Technology. Wallerstein, Mitchel B. et al, eds. 450p. (C). 1993. text ed. 49.95 (*0-309-04833-8*) Natl Acad Pr.

— Grasslands & Grassland Sciences in Northern China. 230p. (C). 1992. pap. text ed. 31.00 (*0-309-04684-X*) Natl Acad Pr.

— Ground Water & Soil Contamination Remediation: Toward Compatible Science, Policy & Public Perception. 272p. 1990. pap. text ed. 24.00 (*0-309-04184-8*) Natl Acad Pr.

— Ground Water at Yucca Mountain: How High Can It Rise? 242p. (Orig.). (C). 1992. pap. text ed. 34.00 (*0-309-04748-X*) Natl Acad Pr.

— Ground Water Vulnerability Assessment: Predicting Relative Contamination Potential. 1993. 34.95 (*0-309-04799-4*) Natl Acad Sci.

— Headline News, Science Views, No. II. Jarmul, David, ed. 256p. 1993. pap. 19.95 (*0-309-04834-6*) Natl Acad Pr.

— Health Effects of Exposure to Low Levels of Ionizing Radiation: Beir V. 436p. 1990. pap. 39.95 (*0-309-03995-9*) Natl Acad Pr.

— High School Biology Today & Tomorrow. 364p. (C). 1989. text ed. 39.95 (*0-309-04028-0*) Natl Acad Pr.

— Human Factors Research Needs for an Aging Population. 110p. 1990. pap. text ed. 15.00 (*0-309-04178-3*) Natl Acad Pr.

— Human Factors Specialists' Education & Utilization: Results of a Survey. Van Cott, Harold P. & Huey, Beverly M., eds. 144p. 1992. 19.00 (*0-309-04693-9*) Natl Acad Pr.

— Hypersonic Technology for Military Application. LC 90-60076. (Illus.). 118p. reprint ed. pap. 33.70 (*0-8357-4265-2*, 2037061) Bks Demand.

— In the Mind's Eye: Enhancing Human Performance. 304p. 1992. 29.95 (*0-309-04398-0*) Natl Acad Pr.

— Infectious Diseases of Mice & Rats, Set. 415p. 1991. text ed. 60.00 (*0-309-03794-8*) Natl Acad Pr.

— Information Technology & Manufacturing: A Research Agenda. 240p. (Orig.). (C). 1994. pap. text ed. 33.00 (*0-309-05179-7*) Natl Acad Pr.

— Information Technology & the Conduct of Research: The User's View. 88p. 1989. pap. text ed. 12.95 (*0-309-03888-X*) Natl Acad Pr.

— Intellectual Property Issues in Software. 128p. 1991. text ed. 17.00 (*0-309-04344-1*) Natl Acad Pr.

— Irrigation-Induced Water Quality Problems. 120p. 1989. text ed. 24.95 (*0-309-04036-1*) Natl Acad Pr.

— Issues in Risk Assessment. LC 92-61838. 374p. (Orig.). (C). 1993. pap. text ed. 46.50 (*0-309-04786-2*) Natl Acad Pr.

— Keeping the U.S. Computer & Communications Industry Competitive: Convergence of Computing, Communications, & Entertainment. 90p. (Orig.). (C). 1995. pap. text ed. 25.00 (*0-309-05089-8*) Natl Acad Pr.

— Liquid Crystalline Polymers. (Illus.). 122p. (Orig.). (C). 1990. pap. text ed. 17.00 (*0-309-04231-3*) Natl Acad Pr.

— Losing Generations: Adolescents in High-Risk Settings. 288p. (Orig.). (C). 1995. pap. text ed. 19.95 (*0-309-05234-3*) Natl Acad Pr.

— Management of Technology: The Hidden Competitive Advantage. 51p. reprint ed. pap. 25.00 (*0-8357-6917-8*, 2037976) Bks Demand.

— Managing Water Resources in the West under Conditions of Climate Uncertainty: A Proceeding. 358p. (C). 1991. pap. text ed. 39.00 (*0-309-04677-7*) Natl Acad Pr.

— Materials for High-Density Electronic Packaging & Interconnection. 156p. (C). 1990. pap. text ed. 19.00 (*0-309-04233-X*) Natl Acad Pr.

— Medically Assisted Conception: An Agenda for Research. 370p. 1989. pap. text ed. 29.00 (*0-309-04128-7*) Natl Acad Pr.

— Monitoring Human Tissues for Toxic Substances. 224p. 1991. 27.00 (*0-309-04437-5*) Natl Acad Pr.

— Natural Disaster Studies, Vol. 5, The March 5, 1987 Ecuador Earthquake: Mass Wasting & Socioeconomic Effects. 184p. 1991. pap. 19.00 (*0-309-04444-8*) Natl Acad Pr.

— NEEM: A Tree for Solving Problems. 152p. (C). 1992. pap. text ed. 19.00 (*0-309-04686-6*) Natl Acad Pr.

— New Horizons in Electrochemical Science & Technology. 164p. 1987. pap. text ed. 17.95 (*0-309-03735-2*) Natl Acad Pr.

— North American Continent-Ocean Transects Program. 104p. (C). 1989. pap. text ed. 15.00 (*0-309-04177-5*) Natl Acad Pr.

— The Nuclear Weapons Complex: Management for Health, Safety & the Environment. 156p. 1989. pap. text ed. 19.00 (*0-309-04179-1*) Natl Acad Pr.

— Nutrient Requirements of Horses, Set. 5th rev. ed. 112p. 1989. disk, pap. 17.95 (*0-309-03989-4*) Natl Acad Pr.

— Nutrient Requirements of Laboratory Animals: Rat, Mouse, Gerbil, Guinea Pig, Hamster, Vole, Fish. 3rd rev. ed. LC 78-15118. (Nutrient Requirements of Domestic Animals Ser.: No. 10). (Illus.). 104p. reprint ed. pap. 29.70 (*0-7837-5983-5*, 2045790) Bks Demand.

— Nutrient Requirements of Mink & Foxes. 72p. 1982. pap. text ed. 12.95 (*0-309-03325-X*) Natl Acad Pr.

— Nutrient Requirements of Nonhuman Primates. LC 78-60949. (Nutrient Requirements of Domestic Animals Ser.: No. 14). 93p. reprint ed. pap. 26.60 (*0-7837-2778-X*, 2043169) Bks Demand.

— Nutrient Requirements of Poultry. 8th rev. ed. 71p. 1984. pap. text ed. 12.95 (*0-309-03486-8*) Natl Acad Pr.

— Nutrient Requirements of Sheep. 6th ed. (Nutrient Requirement Ser.). 112p. 1985. pap. text ed. 19.95 (*0-309-03596-1*) Natl Acad Pr.

— Nutrition Education in U. S. Medical Schools. 141p. 1985. pap. text ed. 19.50 (*0-309-03587-2*) Natl Acad Pr.

— Nutritional Energetics of Domestic Animals & Glossary of Energy Terms. 2nd rev. ed. LC 80-28912. 60p. reprint ed. pap. 25.00 (*0-8357-4998-3*, 2037931) Bks Demand.

— On the Shoulders of Giants: New Approaches to Numeracy. Steen, Lynn A., ed. 184p. 1990. 17.95 (*0-309-04234-8*) Natl Acad Pr.

— On Time to the Doctorate: A Study of the Lengthening Time to Completion for Doctorates in Science & Engineering. 163p. 1990. pap. text ed. 19.00 (*0-309-04085-X*) Natl Acad Pr.

— Opportunities in Biology. LC 89-13098. (Illus.). 468p. reprint ed. pap. 133.40 (*0-7837-5356-X*, 2045118) Bks Demand.

— Opportunities in Chemistry. 334p. (C). 1985. text ed. 34.95 (*0-309-03633-X*) Natl Acad Pr.

— Our Seabed Frontier: Challenges & Choices. 150p. 1989. pap. text ed. 17.00 (*0-309-04126-0*) Natl Acad Pr.

— Pesticides & Groundwater Quality: Issues & Problems in Four States. 136p. 1986. pap. text ed. 17.95 (*0-309-03676-3*) Natl Acad Pr.

— Pesticides in the Diets of Infants & Children. LC 93-14961. 408p. 1993. pap. 47.95 (*0-309-04875-3*) Natl Acad Pr.

— Precollege Science & Mathematics Teachers: Monitoring Supply, Demand, & Quality. 266p. 1990. pap. text ed. 25.00 (*0-309-04197-X*) Natl Acad Pr.

— Preparing for the Workplace: Charting a Course for Federal Postsecondary Training Policy. LC 93-37934. 224p. (C). 1993. text ed. 34.95 (*0-309-04935-0*) Natl Acad Pr.

— Preventing Drug Abuse: What Do We Know? 176p. 1993. 32.95 (*0-309-04627-0*) Natl Acad Pr.

— Probability & Algorithms. 188p. (Orig.). (C). 1992. pap. text ed. 26.00 (*0-309-04776-5*) Natl Acad Pr.

— The Proceedings: Fifth International Converence on Numerical Ship Hydrodynamics, No. 5. 744p. (C). 1990. text ed. 50.00 (*0-309-04241-0*) Natl Acad Pr.

— Prudent Practices for Disposal of Chemicals from Laboratories. 304p. 1983. 24.95 (*0-309-03390-X*) Natl Acad Pr.

— Prudent Practices for Safety in Laboratories. 380p. (Orig.). (C). 1995. text ed. 54.95 (*0-309-05229-7*) Natl Acad Pr.

— The Psychological Well-Being of Nonhuman Primates. 130p. (Orig.). (C). 1995. pap. text ed. 24.95 (*0-309-05233-5*) Natl Acad Pr.

— Recruitment, Retention, & Utiliation of Federal Scientists & Engineers. 192p. 1990. pap. 17.00 (*0-309-04330-1*) Natl Acad Pr.

— Rediscovering Geography: New Relevance for the New Century. 300p. (Orig.). (C). 1995. text ed. 29.95 (*0-309-05199-1*) Natl Acad Pr.

— Regulating Pesticides in Food: The Delaney Paradox. LC 87-61095. (Illus.). 288p. reprint ed. pap. 82.10 (*0-7837-5984-3*, 2045791) Bks Demand.

— Renewing U. S. Mathematics: A Plan for the 1990s. 148p. (C). 1990. pap. text ed. 15.00 (*0-309-04228-3*) Natl Acad Pr.

— Research Directions in Computational Mechanics: A Series. 144p. (C). 1991. pap. text ed. 19.00 (*0-309-04648-3*) Natl Acad Pr.

— Research-Doctorate Programs in the United States: Continuity & Change. 550p. (C). 1995. text ed. 54.95 (*0-614-03358-6*) Natl Acad Pr.

— Research Opportunities for Materials with Ultrafine Microstuctures. 130p. 1990. pap. text ed. 19.00 (*0-309-04183-X*) Natl Acad Pr.

— Restoring & Protecting Marine Habitat: The Role of Engineering & Technology. 212p. (Orig.). (C). 1994. pap. text ed. 27.00 (*0-309-04843-5*) Natl Acad Pr.

— A Review of the National Energy Modeling System (NEMS) LC 93-205713. 164p. 1992. pap. 19.00 (*0-309-04634-3*) Natl Acad Pr.

— A Review of the USGS National Water Assessment Pilot Program. 164p. 1990. pap. text ed. 15.00 (*0-309-04292-5*) Natl Acad Pr.

— A Safer Future: Reducing the Impacts of Natural Disasters. 76p. 1991. pap. 12.95 (*0-309-04546-0*) Natl Acad Pr.

— Safety of Tourist Submersibles. 162p. 1991. pap. text ed. 19.00 (*0-309-04232-1*) Natl Acad Pr.

— Scaling Up: A Research Agenda for Software Engineering. 100p. 1989. pap. text ed. 15.00 (*0-309-04131-7*) Natl Acad Pr.

— Sea-Level Change. (Studies in Geophysics). 256p. 1990. 29.95 (*0-309-04039-6*) Natl Acad Pr.

— Separations Technology & Transmutation Systems. 700p. (Orig.). (C). 1995. text ed. 79.95 (*0-309-05226-2*) Natl Acad Pr.

— Snow Avalanche Hazards & Mitigation in the United States. 96p. 1990. pap. text ed. 15.00 (*0-309-04335-2*) Natl Acad Pr.

— Soviet-American Dialogue in the Social Sciences: Research Workshops on Interdependence among Nations. 84p. (C). 1990. pap. text ed. 15.00 (*0-309-04289-5*) Natl Acad Pr.

— Spatial Statistics & Digital Image Analysis. 244p. 1991. pap. text ed. 25.00 (*0-309-04376-X*) Natl Acad Pr.

— Standards, Conformity Assessment, & Trade: Into the 21st Century. 220p. (Orig.). (C). 1995. text ed. 34.95 (*0-309-05236-X*) Natl Acad Pr.

— Star 21: Strategic Technologies for the Army in the Twenty-First Century. 334p. 1992. 34.95 (*0-309-04629-7*) Natl Acad Pr.

— Status & Applications of Diamond & Diamond-Like Materials: An Emerging Technology. 114p. 1990. pap. text ed. 15.00 (*0-309-04196-1*) Natl Acad Pr.

— A Strategy for the Detection & Study of Extrasolar Planetary Materials, 1990-2000. 96p. 1990. pap. text ed. 15.00 (*0-309-04193-7*) Natl Acad Pr.

— Toward a National Health Care Survey: A Data System for the 21st Century. Wonderlich, Gooloo S., ed. 204p. (C). 1992. pap. text ed. 27.00 (*0-309-04692-0*) Natl Acad Pr.

— Toward Sustainability: Soil & Water Research Priorities for Developing Countries. 76p. 1991. pap. 9.95 (*0-309-04641-6*) Natl Acad Pr.

— The U. S. Global Change Research Program: An Assessment in the FY 1991 Plans. 128p. 1990. pap. 15.00 (*0-309-04328-X*) Natl Acad Pr.

— The U. S. National Plant Germplasm System: The U. S. National Plant Germplasm System. 196p. 1990. 19.95 (*0-309-04390-5*) Natl Acad Pr.

— Underutilized Resources As Animal Feedstuffs. LC 83-13311. 273p. reprint ed. pap. 77.90 (*0-7837-2779-8*, 2043170) Bks Demand.

— Undiscovered Oil & Gas Resources: An Evaluation of the Department of the Interior's 1989 Assessment Procedures. 192p. 1991. pap. text ed. 23.00 (*0-309-04533-9*) Natl Acad Pr.

— The United States Antarctic Research Report to the Scientific Committee on Antarctic Research (SCAR), No. 32, 1990. 104p. 1991. pap. 19.00 (*0-309-04626-2*) Natl Acad Pr.

— Using Oil Spill Dispersants on the Sea. 352p. 1989. pap. text ed. 29.95 (*0-309-03882-0*) Natl Acad Pr.

— Valuing Health Risks, Costs, & Benefits for Environmental Decision Making: Report of a Conference. 244p. 1990. pap. text ed. 24.00 (*0-309-04195-3*) Natl Acad Pr.

— Vetiver Grass: A Thin Green Line Against Erosion. LC 92-50175. 188p. (Orig.). (C). 1993. pap. text ed. 12.00 (*0-309-04269-0*) Natl Acad Pr.

National Research Council Staff, ed. Fishing Vessel Safety. 308p. 1991. 34.95 (*0-309-04379-4*) Natl Acad Pr.

National Research Council Staff & Commission on Behavioral & Social Sciences & Education, National Research Council Staff. Myopia: Prevalence & Progression. 126p. 1989. pap. text ed. 15.00 (*0-309-04081-7*) Natl Acad Pr.

National Research Council Staff & National Academy of Sciences Staff. Supercomputers: Directions in Technology & Applications. 112p. 1989. pap. text ed. 17.00 (*0-309-04088-4*) Natl Acad Pr.

National Research Council Staff, jt. auth. see Board on Agriculture Staff.

National Research Council Staff, jt. auth. see Commission on Engineering.

National Research Council Staff, jt. auth. see Commission on Physical Sciences, Mathematics,.

National Research Council Staff, jt. auth. see Committee on Geosciences, Environment.

National Research Council Staff, jt. auth. see Institute of Medicine, Commission on Life Science Staff.

National Research Council Staff, jt. auth. see Low-Altitude Wind Shear.

National Research Council Staff, jt. auth. see National Research Council, Commission on Behavioral.

National Research Council Staff, jt. auth. see Panel on Foreign Trade Statistics Staff.

National Research Council Staff, et al. Science & the National Parks. LC 92-26303. (Illus.). 136p. (C). 1992. pap. text ed. 19.95 (*0-309-04781-1*) Natl Acad Pr.

National Research Council Staff (U. S.). Rethinking Urban Policy: Urban Development in An Advanced Economy. Hanson, Royce, ed. LC 83-19422. 231p. reprint ed. pap. 65.90 (*0-7837-3738-6*, 2043430) Bks Demand.

N

***National Research Council, Steering Committee on Rights & Responsibilities in Networked Communities.** Rights & Responsibilities of Participants in Networked Communities. Denning, Dorothy E. & Lin, Herbert S., eds. 172p. (Orig.). (C). 1994. pap. text ed. 25.00 (*0-309-05090-1*) Natl Acad Pr.

National Research Council, Subcommittee on Metabolic Modifiers Staff. Metabolic Modifiers: Effects on the Nutrient Requirements of Food-Producing Animals. 96p. (Orig.). (C). 1994. pap. text ed. 27.95 (*0-309-04997-0*) Natl Acad Pr.

— Recommended Dietary Allowances. 10th ed. 302p. 1989. 24.95 (*0-309-04041-8*); pap. 14.95 (*0-309-04633-5*) Natl Acad Pr.

National Research Council, System Security Study Committee Staff. Computers at Risk: Safe Computing in the Information Age. 320p. 1990. pap. 27.95 (*0-309-04388-3*) Natl Acad Pr.

***National Research Council, Technology & Telecommunications; Issues & Impact Committee.** Research Recommendations to Facilitate Distributed Work. 84p. (Orig.). (C). 1994. pap. text ed. 25.00 (*0-309-05185-1*) Natl Acad Pr.

National Research Council, Transportation Research Board Staff. Geometric Design of Interchanges. LC 92-45821. (Transportation Research Record Ser.: No. 1375). Date not set. write for info. (*0-309-05419-2*) Transport Res Bd.

— Safety Research: Heavy Vehicles, Information Systems, & Crash Studies & Methods. LC 92-45740. (Transportation Research Record Ser.: No. 1377). 1993. write for info. (*0-309-05417-6*) Transport Res Bd.

National Research Council (U. S.), Advisory Board on Military Personnel Supplies Staff. Hospital Patient Feeding Systems: Proceedings of a Symposium Held at Radisson South Hotel, Minneapolis, MN, October 19-21, 1981. LC 82-61132. (Illus.). 373p. reprint ed. pap. 106.40 (*0-8357-6811-2*, 2035494) Bks Demand.

National Research Council (U. S.), Astronomy Survey Committee Staff. Challenges to Astronomy & Astrophysics: Working Documents of the Astronomy Survey Committee. LC 83-60509. (Illus.). 296p. reprint ed. pap. 84.40 (*0-8357-6810-4*, 2035493) Bks Demand.

National Research Council (U. S.), Carbon Dioxide Assessment Committee Staff. Changing Climate. LC 83-62680. (Illus.). 520p. reprint ed. pap. 148.20 (*0-8357-6592-X*, 2035987) Bks Demand.

National Research Council (U. S.), Committee on Biologic Markers of Air-Pollution Damage in Trees Staff. Biologic Markers of Air-Pollution Stress & Damage in Forests. LC 89-62584. 377p. reprint ed. pap. 107.50 (*0-7837-0345-7*, 2040664) Bks Demand.

National Research Council (U. S.), Committee on Military Nutrition & Research. Cognitive Testing Methodology: Proceedings of a Workshop Held on June 11-12, 1984. 214p. reprint ed. pap. 61.00 (*0-8357-7688-3*, 2036039) Bks Demand.

National Research Council (U. S.), Committee on Atomic & Molecular Science Staff. Directory of Atomic, Molecular, & Optical Scientists. LC 86-62825. 191p. reprint ed. pap. 54.50 (*0-8357-6812-0*, 2035495) Bks Demand.

National Research Council (U. S.), Committee on Disposition of Offshore Platforms Staff. Disposal of Offshore Platforms. 99p. reprint ed. pap. 28.30 (*0-8357-7692-1*, 2036043) Bks Demand.

National Research Council (U. S.), Committee on Electromagnetic Pulse Environment Staff. Evaluation of Methodologies for Estimating Vulnerability to Electromagnetic Pulse Effects: A Report. 111p. reprint ed. pap. 31.70 (*0-8357-7705-7*, 2036060) Bks Demand.

National Research Council (U. S.), Committee on Vapor-Phase Organics Staff. Feasibility of Assessment of Health Risks from Vapor-Phase Organic Chemicals in Gasoline & Diesel Exhaust. 67p. reprint ed. pap. 25.00 (*0-8357-7707-3*, 2036063) Bks Demand.

National Research Council (U. S.), Committee on the Effective Implementation of Advanced Manufacturing Technology Staff. Human Resource Practices for Implementing Advanced Manufacturing Technology. 83p. reprint ed. pap. 25.00 (*0-8357-7696-4*, 2036048) Bks Demand.

National Research Council (U. S.), Committee on Biologic Markers of Air-Pollution Damage in Trees Staff. Improving Risk Communication. LC 89-9464. 58p. 1989. reprint ed. pap. 25.00 (*0-8357-7686-7*, 2036036) Bks Demand.

National Research Council (U. S.), Committee on Biologic Effects of Atmospheric Pollutants Staff. Lead: Airborne Lead in Perspective. LC 71-186214. (Its Biologic Effects of Atmospheric Pollutants Ser.). 344p. reprint ed. pap. 98.10 (*0-8357-7700-6*, 2036053) Bks Demand.

National Research Council (U. S.), Committee on Nutrition of the Mother & Preschool Child Staff. Nutrition Services in Perinatal Care. 82p. reprint ed. pap. 25.00 (*0-8357-7702-2*, 2036056) Bks Demand.

National Research Council (U. S.), Committee on Ocean Waste Transportation Staff. Ocean Disposal Systems for Sewage Sludge & Effluent. LC 84-61848. 136p. reprint ed. pap. 38.80 (*0-8357-2695-9*, 2040232) Bks Demand.

National Research Council (U. S.), Committee on Protection Against Mycotoxins Staff. Protection Against Trichothecene Mycotoxins. LC 83-62917. (Illus.). 239p. reprint ed. pap. 68.20 (*0-8357-6813-9*, 2035496) Bks Demand.

National Research Council (U. S.), Committee on Biologic Markers of Air-Pollution Damage in Trees Staff. The Role of Manufacturing Technology in Trade Adjustment Strategies. 64p. reprint ed. pap. 25.00 (*0-8357-7685-9*, 2036035) Bks Demand.

National Research Council, U. S. Geodynamics Committee Staff. Mount Rainier: Active Cascade Volcano. 128p. (Orig.). (C). 1994. pap. text ed. 29.00 (*0-309-05083-9*) Natl Acad Pr.

National Research Council (U. S.), Geophysics Study Committee Staff. Climate in Earth History. LC 82-18857. (Studies in Geophysics). 212p. reprint ed. pap. 60.50 (*0-7837-0349-X*, 2040668) Bks Demand.

National Research Council (U. S.), Marine Board Staff. Criteria for the Depths of Dredged Navigational Channels. 177p. reprint ed. pap. 50.50 (*0-8357-7710-3*, 2036066) Bks Demand.

National Research Council (U. S.), Marine Board, Committee on the National Salvage Posture Staff. Marine Salvage in the United States. 159p. reprint ed. pap. 45.40 (*0-8357-7706-5*, 2036061) Bks Demand.

National Research Council (U. S.), Marine Board, Committee on U. S. Shipbuilding Technology Staff. Toward More Productive Naval Shipbuilding. 214p. reprint ed. pap. 61.00 (*0-8357-7704-9*, 2036058) Bks Demand.

National Research Council, U. S. National Committee for the International Union of Psychological Science Staff. Behavioral Measures of Neurotoxicity. 452p. 1990. 42.50 (*0-309-04047-7*) Natl Acad Pr.

National Research Council (U. S.), Panel on Alternative Policies Affecting the Prevention of Alcohol Abuse & Alcoholism Staff. Alcohol & Public Policy: Beyond the Shadow of Prohibition. Moore, Mark H. & Gerstein, Dean R., eds. LC 81-11217. 477p. reprint ed. pap. 136.00 (*0-7837-0351-1*, 2040670) Bks Demand.

— Continuing Education of Engineers. LC 85-62019. (Engineering Education & Practice in the United States Ser.). 102p. 1985. pap. 29.10 (*0-7837-7451-6*, 2049173) Bks Demand.

National Research Council (U. S.), Panel to Review the Status of Basic Research on School-Age Children Staff. Development During Middle Childhood: The Years from Six to Twelve. Collins, W. Andrew, ed. LC 84-11457. 448p. reprint ed. pap. 127.70 (*0-7837-0350-3*, 2040669) Bks Demand.

National Research Council (U. S.), Panel on Engineering Graduate Education & Research Staff. Engineering Graduate Education & Research. LC 85-71643. 131p. reprint ed. pap. 37.40 (*0-7837-0348-1*, 2040667) Bks Demand.

National Research Council (U. S.) Panel on Earthquake Loss Estimation Methodology Staff. Estimating Losses From Future Earthquakes. 249p. reprint ed. pap. 71.00 (*0-8357-7697-2*, 2036049) Bks Demand.

National Research Council (U. S.), Panel on Energy Demand Analysis Staff. Improving Energy Demand Analysis. Stern, Paul C., ed. LC 84-60902. (Illus.). 134p. reprint ed. pap. 38.20 (*0-8357-6809-0*, 2035492) Bks Demand.

National Research Council (U. S.), Panel on Quality Criteria for Water Reuse Staff. Quality Criteria for Water Reuse. LC 82-61430. (Illus.). 153p. reprint ed. pap. 43.70 (*0-8357-6815-5*, 2035498) Bks Demand.

National Research Council (U. S.), Panel on Technology & Women's Employment Staff. Technology & Employment Effects: Interim Report. 160p. reprint ed. pap. 45.60 (*0-8357-7687-5*, 2036038) Bks Demand.

National Research Council (U. S.), Panel on Alternative Policies Affecting the Prevention of Alcohol Abuse & Alcoholism Staff. Toward the Prevention of Alcohol Problems: Government, Business, & Community Action. Gerstein, Dean R., ed. LC 84-16543. 188p. reprint ed. pap. 53.60 (*0-8357-6816-3*, 2035499) Bks Demand.

National Research Council U. S. Staff. Asbestiform Fibers: Nonoccupational Health Risks. LC 84-60249. 352p. reprint ed. pap. 100.40 (*0-7837-2041-6*, 2042308) Bks Demand.

National Research Council (U. S.) Staff. Causes & Effects of Stratospheric Ozone Reduction, an Update: A Report. LC 82-81229. 351p. reprint ed. pap. 100.10 (*0-8357-3446-3*, 2039706) Bks Demand.

National Research Council U. S. Staff. The Competitive Status of the U. S. Steel Industry: A Study of the Influences of Technology in Determining International Industrial Competitive Advantage. LC 84-63017. 172p. reprint ed. pap. 49.10 (*0-7837-2038-6*, 2042306) Bks Demand.

— Diet, Nutrition, & Cancer: Directions for Research. LC 83-61699. 86p. reprint ed. pap. 25.00 (*0-7837-2039-4*, 2042305) Bks Demand.

National Research Council (U. S.) Staff. Drinking Water & Health, Vol. 1. LC 77-89284. 948p. reprint ed. pap. 180.00 (*0-8357-2696-7*, 2040233) Bks Demand.

— Drinking Water & Health, Vol. 4. LC 77-89284. 311p. reprint ed. pap. 88.70 (*0-8357-3448-X*, 2039708) Bks Demand.

National Research Council U. S. Staff. Drinking Water & Health, 1980, Vol. 3. LC 77-89284. 427p. pap. 121.70 (*0-7837-1075-5*, 2041604) Bks Demand.

National Research Council (U. S.) Staff. Engineering Technology Education. LC 85-62838. 59p. reprint ed. pap. 25.00 (*0-8357-3447-1*, 2039707) Bks Demand.

— Laboratory Animal Housing: Proceedings of a Symposium Held at Hunt Valley, Maryland, September 22-23, 1976. LC 78-12545. 228p. reprint ed. pap. 65.00 (*0-8357-3450-1*, 2039711) Bks Demand.

— Models for Biomedical Research: A New Perspective. LC 85-60945. 192p. reprint ed. pap. 54.80 (*0-8357-3451-X*, 2039712) Bks Demand.

National Research Council U. S. Staff. New Directions for Biosciences Research in Agriculture: High-Reward Opportunities. LC 85-60580. 136p. reprint ed. pap. 38.80 (*0-7837-2037-8*, 2042304) Bks Demand.

— Poultry Inspection: The Basis for a Risk-Assessment Approach. LC 87-60910. 177p. reprint ed. pap. 50.50 (*0-7837-2042-4*, 2042309) Bks Demand.

National Research Council, U. S. Staff. Quantitative Modeling of Human Performance in Complex, Dynamic Systems. Baron, Sheldon et al, eds. LC 89-63540. 108p. reprint ed. pap. 30.80 (*0-7837-1298-7*, 2041439) Bks Demand.

National Research Council U. S. Staff. What Is America Eating? Proceedings of a Symposium. LC 85-62945. 183p. reprint ed. pap. 52.20 (*0-7837-2088-2*, 2042364) Bks Demand.

National Research Council (U. S.), Steering Committee for the Petroleum in the Marine Environment Update Staff. Oil in the Sea: Inputs, Fates, & Effects. LC 85-60541. 621p. reprint ed. pap. 177.00 (*0-7837-0347-3*, 2040666) Bks Demand.

***National Research Council (U. S.), Transportation Research Board Staff & Research & Technology Coordinating Committee (U. S.).** Highway Research: Current Programs & Future Directions. LC 94-42203. (Special Report, Transportation Research Board, National Research Council: Vol. 244). 1994. write for info. (*0-309-06054-0*) Transport Res Bd.

National Research Council (U. S.), Working Group on Simulation Staff. Human Factors Aspects of Simulation. Jones, Edward R. et al, eds. 165p. reprint ed. pap. 47.10 (*0-8357-7698-0*, 2036050) Bks Demand.

***National Research Council, Unit Manufacturing Committee.** Unit Manufacturing Processes: Issues & Opportunities in Research. 228p. (Orig.). (C). 1995. pap. text ed. 39.00 (*0-309-05192-4*) Natl Acad Pr.

***National Research Council (US) Panel of Plasma Processing of Materials Staff.** Plasma Processing of Materials: Scientific Opportunities & Technological Challenges. fac. ed. LC 91-66812. (Illus.). 87p. 1994. pap. 25.00 (*0-7837-7559-8*, 2047312) Bks Demand.

***National Research Council (US) Staff.** Fairness in Employment Testing: Validity Generalization, Minority Issues, & the General Aptitude Test Battery. fac. ed. Hartigan, John A. & Wigdor, Alexandra K., eds. LC 89-32841. (Illus.). 368p. 1994. pap. 104.90 (*0-7837-7569-5*, 2047322) Bks Demand.

— Frontiers in Chemical Engineering: Research Needs & Opportunities. fac. ed. LC 88-4120. (Illus.). 231p. 1994. pap. 65.90 (*0-7837-7561-X*, 2047314) Bks Demand.

— Improving Risk Communication. fac. ed. LC 89-9464. (Illus.). 352p. 1994. pap. 100.40 (*0-7837-7564-4*, 2047317) Bks Demand.

— Nutrient Requirements of Rabbits. 2nd fac. rev. ed. LC 77-6318. 36p. 1994. pap. 25.00 (*0-7837-7562-8*, 2047315) Bks Demand.

— Pesticide Resistance: Strategies & Tactics for Management. fac. ed. LC 84-25919. 482p. 1994. pap. 137.40 (*0-7837-7558-X*, 2047311) Bks Demand.

— Surface Coal Mining Effects on Ground Water Recharge. fac. ed. LC 90-60773. (Illus.). 169p. 1990. pap. 48.20 (*0-7837-7567-9*, 2047320) Bks Demand.

— Women in Science & Engineering: Increasing Their Numbers in the 1990s; a Statement on Policy & Strategy. fac. ed. LC 91-66811. (Illus.). 164p. 1991. pap. 46.80 (*0-7837-7563-6*, 2047316) Bks Demand.

National Research Council, Water Science & Technology Board Staff. Sustaining Our Water Resources. 128p. (Orig.). (C). 1993. pap. text ed. 25.00 (*0-309-04948-2*) Natl Acad Pr.

National Resources Committee. Our Cities: Their Role in the National Economy. LC 73-11923. (Metropolitan America Ser.). (Illus.). 108p. 1974. reprint ed. 18.95 (*0-405-05406-8*) Ayer.

National Resources Defense Council Staff, et al. Hazardous Waste Surface Impoundments: The Nation's Most Serious & Neglected Threat to Groundwater. 49p. 1983. 5.00 (*0-318-20476-2*) Natl Resources Defense Coun.

National Restaurant Assn. Educational Foundation Staff. Managing Foodservice Facilities & Equipment: Student Manual. 80p. (Orig.). 1990. pap. text ed. write for info. (*0-915452-50-2*) Educ Found.

National Restaurant Association, Educational Foundation Staff. Sirviendo Alimentos Sanos: Una Guia Para Empleados de la Industria Gastronomica. (ServSafe Ser.). (Illus.). 52p. (Orig.). (SPA.). (C). 1990. pap. text ed. 5.95 (*0-915452-55-3*) Educ Found.

***National Retail Federation Staff.** User Guide: NRF Color & Size Codes. 111p. 1995. pap. 100.00 (*0-9645599-0-0*) Nat Retail Fed.

***National Retail Hardware Association Staff.** Advanced Course Hardware Retail. 640p. 1995. 15.40 (*0-7872-0487-0*) Kendall-Hunt.

— Building Materials Prod. KNWLG. 420p. 1995. 69.99 (*0-7872-0492-7*) Kendall-Hunt.

— Custom Course in Hardware. 1000p. 1995. 99.99 (*0-7872-0512-5*) Kendall-Hunt.

— Home Depot Custom Course. 1000p. 1995. 49.00 (*0-7872-0508-7*) Kendall-Hunt.

National Retail Merchants Association Staff. Profitable Retail Television Advertising. 1977. pap. 15.00 (*0-87102-058-0*, 60-7661) Natl Ret Merch.

— Retail Accounting Manual. rev. ed. 45.00 (*0-87102-008-4*, 26-6132) Natl Ret Merch.

National Review Ser. Letters from Al. 1994. pap. 5.95 (*0-8362-1754-3*) Andrews & McMeel.

***National R&S Committee on High School Choirs Staff.** Guide for the Beginning Choral Director. (Monograph Ser.: No. 1). 41p. 1972. 5.00 (*0-614-05588-1*) Am Choral Dirs.

National Safe Workplace Institute Staff. Sacrificing of America's Youth: The Problem of Child Labor & What to Do about It. 208p. (Orig.). 1992. pap. 8.95 (*0-685-60856-5*) Natl Safe Workplace.

National Safe Workplace Institute Staff & Kinney, Joseph A. Faces: The Toll of Workplace Death on American Families. 230p. (Orig.). 1989. 22.95 (*0-9622842-0-3*); pap. text ed. 16.95 (*0-9622842-1-1*) Natl Safe Workplace.

National Safety Council. Guards Illustrated: Ideas for Mechanical Safety. 3rd ed. LC 69-21916. 125p. reprint ed. pap. 35.70 (*0-317-29136-X*, 2025014) Bks Demand.

— Guards Illustrated: Ideas for Mechanical Safety. 4th ed. LC 80-83322. 93p. reprint ed. pap. 26.60 (*0-685-15371-1*, 2026666) Bks Demand.

National Safety Council Industrial Division, Power Press & Forging Section Staff. Forging Safety Manual. LC 89-63767. (Illus.). 89p. (Orig.). (C). 1990. pap. 17.95 (*0-87912-148-3*, 12977-0000) Natl Safety Coun.

— Power Press Safety Manual. 4th ed. LC 89-60472. (Illus.). 64p. (Orig.). (C). 1989. pap. 22.95 (*0-87912-142-4*, 12974-0000) Natl Safety Coun.

National Safety Council, International Air Transport Section, Industrial Division Staff. Aviation Ground Operations Safety Handbook. 3rd ed. LC 87-63466. 162p. 1988. pap. 34.95 (*0-87912-138-6*, 12963-0000) Natl Safety Coun.

National Safety Council Public Employee Committee Staff. Public Employee Safety & Health Management. LC 89-63761. (Illus.). 386p. (C). 1990. 74.95 (*0-87912-143-2*, 12934-0000) Natl Safety Coun.

National Safety Council Staff. Accident Facts, 1984. 97p. pap. 27.70 (*0-8357-5037-X*, 2025010) Bks Demand.

— Accident Facts, 1985. 98p. pap. 28.00 (*0-8357-5036-1*, 2026711) Bks Demand.

— Accident Facts, 1987. (Illus.). 109p. reprint ed. pap. 31.10 (*0-8357-5038-8*, 2033113) Bks Demand.

— Accident Facts, 1988. (Illus.). 107p. reprint ed. pap. 30.50 (*0-8357-6875-9*, 2035573) Bks Demand.

— Accident Facts, 1989. (Illus.). 107p. reprint ed. pap. 30.50 (*0-7837-1098-4*, 2041630) Bks Demand.

— Accident Facts, 1990. 112p. reprint ed. pap. 32.00 (*0-7837-6436-7*, 2046436) Bks Demand.

— Accident Facts, 1991. LC 91-60648. 112p. reprint ed. pap. 32.00 (*0-7837-6437-5*, 2046437) Bks Demand.

— Accident Facts, 1992. LC 91-60648. (Illus.). 112p. Date not set. reprint ed. pap. 32.00 (*0-7837-9215-8*, 2049965) Bks Demand.

— Accident Prevention Manual for Industrial Operations, 2 vols. McElroy, Frank E., ed. LC 80-81376. pap. write for info. (*0-8357-5043-4*, 2032042) Bks Demand.

— Accident Prevention Manual for Industrial Operations. 7th ed. LC 74-79025. 1533p. reprint ed. pap. 180.00 (*0-8357-5039-6*, 2020315) Bks Demand.

— Accident Prevention Manual for Industrial Operations. 544p. reprint ed. pap. 155.10 (*0-8357-5040-X*, 2029208) Bks Demand.

— Accident Prevention Manual for Industrial Operations, Vol. 1, Administration & Programs. McElroy, Frank E., ed. LC 80-81376. 768p. pap. 180.00 (*0-8357-5044-2*) Bks Demand.

— Accident Prevention Manual for Industrial Operations, Vol. 2, Engineering & Technology. McElroy, Frank E., ed. LC 80-81376. pap. 160.00 (*0-685-73966-X*) Bks Demand.

— Accident Prevention Manual for Industrial Operations, Vols. 1 & 2. 9th ed. LC 86-63578. (Occupational Safety & Health Ser.). (Illus.). 541p. reprint ed. Vol. 1, Administration & Programs, 541p. pap. 154.20 (*0-7837-3071-3*, 2042632) Bks Demand.

— Accident Prevention Manual for Industrial Operations, Vols. 1 & 2. LC 86-63578. (Occupational Safety & Health Ser.). (Illus.). 512p. reprint ed. Vol. 2, Engineering & Technology, 512p. pap. 146.00 (*0-7837-3072-1*, 2042632) Bks Demand.

— Bloodborne Pathogens: Four Color Edition. LC 93-26138. 1993. pap. 13.75 (*0-86720-818-X*) Jones & Bartlett.

— Bloodborne Pathogens - Academic. LC 92-49476. 80p. 1992. teacher ed 15.00 (*0-86720-772-8*); teacher ed 395.00 (*0-86720-798-1*); pap. text ed. 12.50 (*0-86720-771-X*); vhs 195.00 (*0-86720-775-2*); sl. 195.00 (*0-86720-773-6*) Jones & Bartlett.

— Bloodborne Pathogens (Smithkline) 1993. pap. 12.50 (*0-86720-793-0*) Jones & Bartlett.

— CPR: 1992 Guidelines. 2nd ed. (Emergency Care Ser.). 120p. (C). 1993. teacher ed, pap. text ed. 15.00 (*0-86720-811-2*) Jones & Bartlett.

— CPR Manual: 1992 Guidelines. LC 92-40649. 128p. 1992. pap. text ed. 12.50 (*0-86720-784-1*); vhs 225.00 (*0-86720-794-9*) Jones & Bartlett.

— CPR Review Manual. LC 93-46698. (Emergency Care Ser.). (C). 1994. pap. text ed. 3.00 (*0-86720-849-X*) Jones & Bartlett.

— Essentials of First Aid & CPR. LC 94-10092. 1994. pap. 14.95 (*0-86720-979-8*) Jones & Bartlett.

— F&G NSC FirstAid - CPR Level One. 2nd ed. (Emergency Care Ser.). 96p. 1993. pap. 7.50 (*0-86720-792-2*) Jones & Bartlett.

— First Aid. (Emergency Care Ser.). 178p. (C). 1992. teacher ed 15.00 (*0-86720-781-7*); teacher ed 395.00 (*0-86720-780-9*); pap. 19.95 (*0-86720-755-8*) Jones & Bartlett.

— First Aid - CPR Infants & Children: Instructor's Manual. 2nd ed. (Emergency Care Ser.). 150p. (C). 1994. pap. text ed. 15.00 (*0-86720-838-4*) Jones & Bartlett.

— First Aid & CPR. 2nd ed. LC 92-42883. 1993. teacher ed 10.00 (*0-86720-791-4*); teacher ed 795.00 (*0-86720-802-3*); pap. text ed. 30.00 (*0-86720-785-X*); teacher ed, disk 50.00 (*0-86720-801-5*) Jones & Bartlett.

— First Aid & CPR, Level 1. 96p. 1991. teacher ed 11.00 (*0-86720-157-6*); teacher ed 650.00 (*0-86720-161-4*); pap. 7.50 (*0-86720-154-1*); 100.00 (*0-86720-230-0*); 30.00 (*0-86720-165-7*); 40.00 (*0-86720-166-5*) Jones & Bartlett.

— First Aid & CPR, Level 2. 192p. 1991. pap. 12.00 (*0-86720-155-X*); 100.00 (*0-86720-231-9*) Jones & Bartlett.

— First Aid & CPR, Level 3. 288p. 1991. pap. 21.00 (*0-86720-156-8*); 100.00 (*0-86720-232-7*) Jones & Bartlett.

— First Aid & CPR: Academic Version. 288p. 1991. teacher ed 10.00 (*0-86720-195-9*); teacher ed 795.00 (*0-86720-194-0*); pap. 30.00 (*0-86720-193-2*); teacher ed, disk 50.00 (*0-86720-164-9*); teacher ed, disk 195.00 (*0-86720-168-1*); teacher ed, Apple II 195.00 (*0-86720-169-X*) Jones & Bartlett.

— First Aid & CPR: Academic Version, Set. 288p. 1991. trans. 150.00 (*0-86720-163-0*); sl. 150.00 (*0-86720-162-2*); sl. 195.00 (*0-86720-086-3*) Jones & Bartlett.

— First Aid & CPR: Infants & Children. 2nd ed. LC 93-35537. 208p. 1994. pap. 22.50 (*0-86720-835-X*) Jones & Bartlett.

— First Aid & CPR: Level 2. 2nd ed. LC 93-21366. 186p. 1994. pap. 12.00 (*0-86720-825-2*) Jones & Bartlett.

— First Aid & CPR: Level 3. 2nd ed. LC 93-23167. 288p. 1994. pap. 21.00 (*0-86720-824-4*) Jones & Bartlett.

— First Aid & CPR for Infants & Children. (First Aid Ser.). 224p. (C). 1992. teacher ed 15.00 (*0-86720-759-0*); teacher ed 450.00 (*0-86720-800-7*); pap. text ed. 22.50 (*0-86720-249-1*); PAL First Aid. vhs 325.00 (*0-86720-273-4*); PAL CPR. vhs 225.00 (*0-86720-274-2*); vhs 225.00 (*0-86720-762-0*); vhs 195.00 (*0-86720-763-9*); sl. 150.00 (*0-86720-761-2*) Jones & Bartlett.

— First Aid Guide. (Illus.). 63p. (Orig.). 1991. pap. 200.00 (*0-86720-170-3*); vhs 295.00 (*0-86720-158-4*); 10.00 (*0-86720-234-3*) Jones & Bartlett.

— First Aid Guide. 2nd ed. 64p. 1993. pap. text ed. write for info. (*0-86720-803-1*) Jones & Bartlett.

— Fundamentals of Industrial Hygiene. 2nd ed. Olishifski, Julian B., ed. LC 78-58307. (N.S.C. Occupational Safety & Health Ser.). 1297p. reprint ed. pap. 180.00 (*0-685-20909-1*, 2032043) Bks Demand.

— Learn to Swim, Journey One. (J). 1993. pap. text ed. 50.00 (*0-86720-788-4*) Jones & Bartlett.

— Learn to Swim, Journey Three. 1993. pap. text ed. 50.00 (*0-86720-790-6*) Jones & Bartlett.

— Learn to Swim, Journey Two. 1993. pap. text ed. 50.00 (*0-86720-789-2*) Jones & Bartlett.

— Meat Industry Safety Guidelines. 2nd ed. LC 78-52082. (Illus.). 112p. reprint ed. pap. 32.00 (*0-7837-0579-4*, 2040923) Bks Demand.

— National Safety Council - First Aid - CPR I-III: Instructor's Manual. 2nd ed. 216p. 1993. pap. text ed. 15.00 (*0-86720-795-7*) Jones & Bartlett.

— National Safety Council Teaching Package: Bloodborne Pathogens. 1992. ring bd. 395.00 (*0-86720-774-4*) Jones & Bartlett.

— National Safety Council Teaching Package: Infants & Children. 1992. ring bd. 450.00 (*0-86720-760-4*) Jones & Bartlett.

— Power Press & Safety Manual. 2nd ed. 96p. reprint ed. pap. 27.40 (*0-317-29052-5*, 2025011) Bks Demand.

N

An Asterisk (*) at the beginning of an entry indicates that the title is appearing in BIP for the first time.

— Power Press Safety Manual. 3rd ed. LC 79-63712. (Illus.). 107p. reprint ed. pap. 30.50 (*0-8357-6425-7*, 2035793) Bks Demand.

— Primeros Auxilios y RCP. (Emergency Care Ser.). 100p. (C). 1994. pap. text ed. 12.50 (*0-86720-847-3*) Jones & Bartlett.

— Product Safety: Management Guidelines. LC 88-61858. (Illus.). 189p. (Orig.). 1989. 43.95 (*0-87912-140-8*, 17656-0000) Natl Safety Coun.

— Safeguarding Concepts Illustrated. 5th ed. LC 86-61185. (Illus.). 94p. reprint ed. pap. 26.80 (*0-7837-5569-4*, 2045346) Bks Demand.

— Scuba Diving First Aid. LC 94-48302. (Emergency Care Ser.). 65p. 1995. pap. 12.50 (*0-86720-944-5*) Jones & Bartlett.

— Stress Management. LC 94-16818. 1994. pap. 13.75 (*0-86720-980-1*) Jones & Bartlett.

National Safety Council Staff & Ellis & Associates Staff. National Safety Council Coordinated Manual, Learn to Swim. (Emergency Care Ser.). 150p. (C). 1993. pap. text ed. 40.00 (*0-86720-808-2*) Jones & Bartlett.

— National Safety Council, Learn to Swim: Instructor's Manual. (Emergency Care Ser.). 100p. (C). 1993. pap. text ed. 15.00 (*0-86720-809-0*) Jones & Bartlett.

***National Safety Council Staff & National Environmental Training Staff.** Hazardous Communication & Awareness. (Emergency Care Ser.). 50p. 1995. spiral bd., pap. 8.00 (*0-86720-940-2*) Jones & Bartlett.

National Safety Council Staff & Thygerson. CPR Manual. (First Aid Ser.). (C). 1992. pap. text ed. 12.50 (*0-86720-192-4*); vhs 195.00 (*0-86720-159-2*); 10.00 (*0-86720-233-5*) Jones & Bartlett.

***National Safety Council Staff & Thygerson, Alton.** First Aid Pocket Guide. LC 94-21045. (Emergency Care Ser.). 96p. 1995. pap. 7.95 (*0-86720-843-0*) Jones & Bartlett.

National Safety Council Staff, et al. Nursing Assessment - Bloodborne Valuepack. (Nursing-Health Science Ser.). (C). 1993. text ed. 50.00 (*0-86720-690-X*) Jones & Bartlett.

National SAMPE Symposium & Exhibition Staff. Advancing Technology in Materials & Processes: National SAMPE Symposium & Exhibition, 30th, Disneyland Hotel, Anaheim, California, March 19-21, 1985. (Science of Advanced Materials & Process Enginnering Ser.: No. 30). 1699p. reprint ed. pap. 180.00 (*0-7837-1283-9*, 2041424) Bks Demand.

— Material & Process Applications - Land, Sea, Air Space, 26th, National SAMPE Symposium & Exhibition. LC 81-183027. (Science of Advanced Materials & Process Enginnering Ser.: No. 26). 893p. reprint ed. pap. 180.00 (*0-7837-1279-0*, 2041420) Bks Demand.

— Materials & Processes - Continuing Innovations: National SAMPE Symposium & Exhibition, 28th, Disneyland Hotel, Anaheim, California, April 12-14, 1983. LC 83-177138. (Science of Advanced Materials & Process Enginnering Ser.: No. 28). 1571p. reprint ed. pap. 180.00 (*0-7837-1281-2*, 2041422) Bks Demand.

— Materials Overview for 1982: National SAMPE Symposium & Exhibition, 27th, Town & Country Hotel, San Diego, California, May 4-6, 1982. LC 82-179801. (Science of Advanced Materials & Process Enginnering Ser.: No. 27). 1080p. reprint ed. pap. 180.00 (*0-7837-1280-4*, 2041421) Bks Demand.

— The Nineteen-Eighties, Payoff Decade for Advanced Materials: 25th National SAMPE Symposium & Exhibition, Town & Country Hotel, San Diego, California, May 6-8, 1980. LC 80-133416. (Science of Advanced Materials & Process Enginnering Ser.: No. 25). 790p. reprint ed. pap. 180.00 (*0-7837-1278-2*, 2041419) Bks Demand.

— Selective Application of Materials for Products & Energy: 23rd National SAMPE Symposium & Exhibition, Disneyland Hotel, Anaheim, California, May 2-4, 1978. LC 78-105428. (Science of Advanced Materials & Process Enginnering Ser.: No. 23). 1260p. reprint ed. pap. 180.00 (*0-7837-1277-4*, 2041418) Bks Demand.

— Technology Vectors: National SAMPE Symposium & Exhibition, 29th, MGM Grand Hotel, Reno, Nevada, April 3-5, 1984. LC 84-215021. (Science of Advanced Materials & Process Enginnering Ser.: No. 29). 1638p. reprint ed. pap. 180.00 (*0-7837-1282-0*, 2041423) Bks Demand.

National SAMPE Technical Conference Staff. Bicentennial of Materials: National SAMPE Technical Conference, 8th, Sea-Tac Motor Inn, Seattle, Washington, October 12-14, 1976. LC 76-381464. (National SAMPE Technical Conference Ser.: No. 8). 518p. reprint ed. pap. 147.70 (*0-7837-1288-X*, 2041429) Bks Demand.

— Hi-Tech Review, 1984: National SAMPE Technical Conference, 16th, Clarion Four Seasons Motor Inn, Albuquerque, New Mexico, October 9-11, 1984. LC 84-251355. (National SAMPE Technical Conference Ser.: No. 16). 792p. reprint ed. pap. 180.00 (*0-7837-1292-8*, 2041433) Bks Demand.

— Material & Process Advances '82: National SAMPE Technical Conference, 14th, Sheraton Hotel, Atlanta, Georgia, October 12-14, 1982. LC 82-232953. (National SAMPE Technical Conference Ser.: No. 14). 584p. reprint ed. pap. 166.50 (*0-7837-1290-1*, 2041431) Bks Demand.

— Materials on the Move: The Sixth National SAMPE Technical Conference, Dayton, OH, October 8-10, 1974. LC 74-194771. (National SAMPE Technical Conference Ser.: No. 6). 477p. reprint ed. pap. 136.00 (*0-7837-1286-3*, 2041427) Bks Demand.

— Materials Review '75: National SAMPE Technical Conference, 7th, Hilton Inn, Albuquerque, New Mexico, October 14-16, 1975. LC 75-332485. (National SAMPE Technical Conference Ser.: No. 7). 548p. reprint ed. pap. 156.20 (*0-7837-1287-1*, 2041428) Bks Demand.

— Technology Transfer: National SAMPE Technical Conference, 13th, Mount Airy Lodge, Mount Pocono, Pennsylvania, October 13-15, 1981. LC 82-103085. (National SAMPE Technical Conference Ser.: No. 13). 711p. reprint ed. pap. 180.00 (*0-7837-1289-8*, 2041430) Bks Demand.

— Twenty-Twenty Vision in Materials for 2000: National SAMPE Technical Conference, 15th, Marriott Inn, Cincinnati, Ohio, October 4-6, 1983. LC 83-231242. (National SAMPE Technical Conference Ser.: No. 15). 795p. reprint ed. pap. 180.00 (*0-7837-1291-X*, 2041432) Bks Demand.

National School Boards Assoc. Staff, jt. auth. see American Assoc. of School Administrators Staff.

National School Boards Association, jt. auth. see American Association of School Administrators Staff.

National School Boards Association, jt. auth. see American Association of School Administrators.

National School Boards Association, jt. auth. see American Association of School Administrators Staff.

National School Boards Association, Office of General Counsel Staff. State Statutes on School District Collective Bargaining. rev. ed. 350p. 1993. ring bd. 100.00 (*0-88364-176-3*) Natl Sch Boards.

National School Boards Association Staff. School Law in Review, 1993. 130p. (Orig.). 1993. pap. 35.00 (*0-88364-148-8*) Natl Sch Boards.

— Violence in the Schools: How America's School Boards Are Safeguarding Our Children. (NSBA Best Practices Ser.). 115p. (Orig.). 1993. pap. 15.00 (*0-88364-180-1*) Natl Sch Boards.

National School Boards Association Staff, ed. Crisis Management in the Schools: The Legal Implications. 717p. 1992. ring bd. 200.00 (*0-88364-149-6*) Natl Sch Boards.

National School Boards Association Staff, jt. auth. see American Association of School Administrators Staff.

National School Public Relations Association Staff. Evaluating Your PR Investment. 1986. 17.95 (*0-87545-048-2*, 411-13364) Natl Sch PR.

— One Hundred One PR Ideas You Can Use Now... & More. 1986. ring bd. 45.00 (*0-317-57022-6*, 418-13985) Natl Sch PR.

— Rally School Support: Your Campaign to Build Commitment for Education in a Democratic Society. 1986. 42.00 (*0-317-57023-4*, 418-13982) Natl Sch PR.

— School PR: The Complete Book. 1986. 29.95 (*0-87545-051-2*, 411-13346) Natl Sch PR.

National School Services Staff. Assessing & Improving Student Achievement: Guidebook. (C). 1994. 25.00 (*0-932957-97-8*) Natl School.

— Assessing & Improving Student Achievement: Training Manual. (C). 1994. 95.00 (*0-932957-85-4*) Natl School.

— Coaching & Supervising Teachers. (C). 1991. teacher ed 85.00 (*0-932957-80-3*) Natl School.

— Coaching & Supervising Teachers: Guidebook. (C). Date not set. 25.00 (*0-932957-59-5*) Natl School.

— Curriculum Development & Alignment. (C). Date not set. teacher ed 95.00 (*0-932957-82-X*) Natl School.

— Curriculum Development & Alignment: Guidebook. (C). Date not set. 25.00 (*0-932957-95-1*) Natl School.

— Desarrollo y Alineacion del Curriculo: Guia. (SPA.). (C). Date not set. student ed 25.00 (*0-932957-71-4*); teacher ed 125.00 (*0-932957-83-8*) Natl School.

— Dirigiendo y Supervisando a los Maestros: Guia - Guidebook. (SPA.). (C). Date not set. student ed 25.00 (*0-932957-68-4*); teacher ed 125.00 (*0-932957-81-1*) Natl School.

— Estrategias Practicas para el Mejoramiento de la Escuela: Guia - Guidebook. (SPA.). (C). 1994. 25.00 (*0-932957-69-2*) Natl School.

— Estrategias Practicas para el Mejoramiento de la Escuela - Teacher Manual. (SPA.). (C). 1992. teacher ed 125.00 (*0-932957-57-9*) Natl School.

— Helen's Helpful Homework Hints: Training Guide. (Illus.). 1995. 10.95 (*0-932957-02-1*) Natl School.

— Management System for Teachers. 290p. (C). 1988. teacher ed 110.00 (*0-932957-87-0*); 95.00 (*0-932957-88-9*) Natl School.

— Management System for Teachers: Guidebook. (C). Date not set. 25.00 (*0-932957-78-1*) Natl School.

— Practical Strategies for School Improvement. (C). 1991. teacher ed 95.00 (*0-932957-56-0*) Natl School.

— Practical Strategies for School Improvement: Guidebook. (C). Date not set. 25.00 (*0-932957-58-7*) Natl School.

— Programa para el Mejoramiento del Aprovechamiento del Estudiante: Guia - Guidebook. (SPA.). (C). 1994. student ed 25.00 (*0-932957-67-6*) Natl School.

— Programa para el Mejoramiento del Aprovechamiento del Estudiante - Training Manual. (SPA.). (C). 1993. student ed 125.00 (*0-932957-74-9*) Natl School.

— Sistema de Manejo para Maestros: Guia - Guidebook. (SPA.). (C). 1994. student ed 25.00 (*0-932957-70-6*) Natl School.

— Sistema de Manejo para Maestros - Leaders Manual. (SPA.). (C). 1991. teacher ed 125.00 (*0-932957-79-X*) Natl School.

National School Supply & Equipment Association Staff. Guide to Effective Business Practices in Buying School Supplies, Industrial Materials, Equipment & Services, No. 9002. 20p. 1990. pap. 5.00 (*0-910170-53-3*) Assn Sch Busn.

National Science Foundation Staff. Human Evolution. Kornberg, Warren, ed. (Mosaic Reader Ser.). 64p. (Orig.). 1982. pap. text ed. 5.00 (*0-89529-174-6*) Avery Pub.

National Science Foundation Staff & Veziroglu, T. Nejat. Two Phase Flow & Heat Transfer Symposium Workshop: Proceedings of Condensed Paper, Ft. Lauderdale, Florida 10-76. 140.00 (*0-08-022135-1*, Pub. by Pergamon Repr UK) Franklin.

National Science Foundation Staff, et al. Geographic Information Systems & Their Application in Geotechnical Earthquake Engineering: Proceedings of a Workshop Sponsored by the National Science Foundation Through the Earthquake Hazard Mitigation Program & the Geomechanical, Geotechnical, & Geo-Environmental Systems Program. Frost, J. David & Chameau, Jean-Lou A., eds. LC 93-5432. 1993. write for info. (*0-87262-973-2*) Am Soc Civil Eng.

National Science Resources Center Staff, et al. Science for Children: Resources for Teachers. 192p. 1988. pap. 9.95 (*0-309-03934-7*) Natl Acad Pr.

National Security Archive Staff. Iran: The Making of U. S. Policy, 1977-1980, Guide & Index, 2 vols., Vols. 1 & 2. Hooglund, Eric et al, eds. (Making of U. S. Policy Ser.). (Illus.). (C). 1990. Set: Vol. 1, 609p.; Vol. 2, 990p. 900.00 (*0-89887-068-2*) Chadwyck-Healey.

National Security Archive Staff & Chadwyck-Healey Staff. Afghanistan: The Making of U. S. Policy, 1973-1990, Guide & Index, 2 vols., Set. Galster, Steve, ed. (Making of U. S. Policy Ser.). (Illus.). 1991. 900.00 (*0-89887-075-5*) Chadwyck-Healey.

— The Berlin Crisis, 1958-1962: Guide & Index, 2 vols., Set. Chang, Laurence, ed. (Making of U. S. Policy Ser.). (Illus.). 1992. 900.00 (*0-89887-096-8*) Chadwyck-Healey.

— Cuban Missile Crisis, 1962: The Making of U. S. Policy, 1962, Guide & Index, Set: Vol. 1, & 2. Chang, Laurence et al, eds. (Making of U. S. Policy Ser.). (Illus.). (C). 1990. Set: Vol. 1, 940p.; Vol. 2, 1220p. 900.00 (*0-89887-071-2*) Chadwyck-Healey.

— El Salvador: The Making of U. S. Policy, 1977-1984, 2 vols., Set, Vols. 1 & 2. Di Vinenzo, Janet et al, eds. (Making of U. S. Policy Ser.). (Illus.). (C). 1989. Set: Vol. 1, 760p.; Vol. 2, 760p. 900.00 (*0-89887-062-3*) Chadwyck-Healey.

— Military Uses of Space, 1945-1991: Guide & Index, Set. Richelson, Jeffrey, ed. (Making of U. S. Policy Ser.). (Illus.). 1992. 900.00 (*0-89887-092-5*) Chadwyck-Healey.

— Nicaragua: The Making of U. S. Policy, 1978-1990, Guide & Index, 2 vols., Set. Kornbluh, Deter, ed. (Making of U. S. Policy Ser.). (Illus.). 1991. 900.00 (*0-89887-088-7*) Chadwyck-Healey.

— Nuclear Non-Proliferation, 1945-1991: Guide & Index, 2 vols., Set. Foran, Virginia 230 1992, ed. (Making of U. S. Policy Ser.). (Illus.). 900.00 (*0-89887-094-1*) Chadwyck-Healey.

— The Philippines: U. S. Policy During the Marcos Years, 1965-1986, Guide & Index, 3 vols., Set. Nelson, Craig, ed. (Making of U. S. Policy Ser.). (Illus.). 1990. 900.00 (*0-89887-077-1*) Chadwyck-Healey.

— South Africa: The Making of U. S. Policy, 1962-1989, Guide & Index, 2 vols., Set. Mokoena, Kenneth, ed. (Making of U. S. Policy Ser.). (Illus.). 1992. 900.00 (*0-89887-073-9*) Chadwyck-Healey.

— The U. S. Intelligence Community: Organizations, Operations & Management, 1947-1989, Guide & Index. Richelson, Jeffrey T., ed. (Making of U. S. Policy Ser.). 1990. 900.00 (*0-89887-083-6*) Chadwyck-Healey.

National Semiconductor Staff. Series 32000, Programmer's Reference Manual. (Illus.). 323p. 1987. pap. 31.95 (*0-13-806936-0*) P-H.

National Seminars Staff. The Polished Professional. (Business Desk Reference Ser.). 128p. (Orig.). 1994. pap. 8.95 (*1-56414-146-2*) Career Pr Inc.

— Powerful Writing Skills. (Business Desk Reference Ser.). 128p. (Orig.). 1994. pap. 8.95 (*1-56414-145-4*) Career Pr Inc.

National Senior Citizen Law Center Staff. Representing Older Persons: An Advocates Manual. Chiplin, Alfred J., Jr., ed. 142p. 1990. reprint ed. 45.00 (*0-685-15260-X*, 38,950) NCLS Inc.

National Sex Forum Staff. The SAR Guide for a Better Sex Life. 128p. 1975. 5.95 (*0-317-34149-9*) Specific Pr.

National SIDS Council of Australia Staff, et al, eds. Proceedings of the Second Sudden Infant Death Syndrome International Conference. (Illus.). 1993. pap. 50.00 (*0-916859-52-5*) Perinatology.

National Social Science & Law Center Staff. Interpreting Evaluation Studies of Social Services Programs. (Illus.). 71p. (Orig.). 1984. pap. 8.00 (*0-941077-06-3*, 38,475) NCLS Inc.

National Society Daughters of the American Revolution Staff, jt. ed. see Colorado State Society Staff.

National Society for Performance & Instruction Staff. Introduction to Performance Technology. Smith, Martin, ed. LC 86-60742. (Illus.). 273p. 1986. per. 22.50 (*0-9616690-0-4*) Natl Soc Perform & Inst.

National Society of Colonial Dames of America in the Commonwealth of Virginia Staff. Register of Albemarle Parish, Surry & Sussex Counties, 1739-1788. Richards, Gertrude R., ed. (Illus.). 275p. 1984. reprint ed. 32.50 (*0-89308-545-6*) Southern Hist Pr.

National Society of Colonial Dames of America Staff. Church Music & Musical Life in Pennsylvania in the Eighteenth Century, 3 vols. in 4 pts. LC 79-38037. (Illus.). reprint ed. Vol. 3, Pt. 1. write for info. (*0-404-08093-6*); reprint ed. Vol. 3, Pt. 2. write for info. (*0-404-08094-4*) AMS Pr.

— Church Music & Musical Life in Pennsylvania in the Eighteenth Century, 3 vols. in 4 pts., 1. LC 79-38037. (Illus.). reprint ed. write for info. (*0-404-08091-X*) AMS Pr.

— Church Music & Musical Life in Pennsylvania in the Eighteenth Century, 3 vols. in 4 pts., 2. LC 79-38037. (Illus.). reprint ed. write for info. (*0-404-08092-8*) AMS Pr.

— Church Music & Musical Life in Pennsylvania in the Eighteenth Century, 3 vols. in 4 pts., Set. LC 79-38037. (Illus.). reprint ed. 195.00 (*0-404-08090-1*) AMS Pr.

National Society of Film Critics Members Staff. Produced & Abandoned: The Best Films You've Never Seen. Sragow, Michael, ed. LC 90-5853. (Illus.). 392p. (Orig.). 1990. pap. 9.95 (*0-916515-84-2*) Mercury Hse Inc.

***National Society of Film Critics Staff.** Flesh & Blood: The National Society of Film Critics on Sex, Violence, & Censorship. Keough, Peter, ed. LC 94-39759. 1995. pap. 14.95 (*1-56279-076-5*) Mercury Hse Inc.

— Foreign Affairs: The National Society of Film Critics' Video Guide to Foreign Films. Huffhines, Kathy S., ed. LC 91-9960. (Illus.). 592p. (Orig.). 1991. pap. 14.95 (*1-56279-016-1*) Mercury Hse Inc.

National Society of Professional Engineers Staff, jt. ed. see American Society of Civil Engineers Staff.

National Society of Public Accountants Staff. Portfolio of Accounting Systems for Small & Medium-Sized Businesses. rev. ed. (Illus.). 1977. text ed. 64.95 (*0-13-685305-6*, Busn) P-H.

National Society of Sales Training Executives Staff. The Sales Manager's Guide to Training & Developing Your Team. Higgens, Raymond A., ed. LC 92-11933. 216p. 1992. 25.00 (*1-55623-652-2*) Irwin Prof Pubng.

National Society of the Colonial Dames of America in the State of Virginia Staff. The Parish Register of Christ Church, Middlesex Co., Virginia, from 1625 to 1812. 360p. 1988. reprint ed. 37.50 (*0-89308-631-2*, VA 91) Southern Hist Pr.

— The Parish Register of St. Peter's, New Kent County, Virginia, 1680-1787. 206p. 1989. reprint ed. 17.50 (*0-685-60491-8*, 5100) Clearfield Co.

National Society of the Colonial Dames of America Staff. The Parish Register of Saint Peter's, New Kent County, Virginia, 1680-1787. iv, 206p. 1988. reprint ed. pap. text ed. 12.50 (*1-55613-119-4*) Heritage Bk.

National Soft Drink Association Staff. NSDA Legal Briefing Conference: Proceedings - September 23-25, 1985, Four Seasons Hotel, Washington, D.C. 287p. write for info. (*0-318-61971-7*) Natl Soft Drink.

***National Solid Waste Management Staff.** NSWMA Recycling Handbook. LC 95-14479. 288p. 1995. 55.00 (*1-56670-068-X*, L1068) Lewis Pubs.

National Standards Information Organization. Extended Latin Alphabet Coded Character Set for Bibliographic Use (ANSEL) 16p. 1992. 20.00 (*0-88738-959-7*, Z39.47) Transaction Pubs.

***National Storytelling Association Staff.** National Storytelling Directory: 1995 Edition. 1994. pap. 11.95 (*1-879991-18-7*) Natl Assn Preserv & Perpet Storytelling.

***National Storytelling Association Staff, comp.** Many Voices: Stories from American History. 1995. pap. 19.95 (*0-614-04561-4*) Natl Assn Preserv & Perpet Storytelling.

National Street Law Institute Staff, et al. Consumer Law, Competencies in Law & Citizenship. 107p. (C). 1982. pap. text ed. 24.50 (*0-314-65089-X*) West Pub.

National Strength & Conditioning Association Staff. Essentials of Strength Training & Conditioning. Baechle, Thomas R., ed. LC 94-3915. (Illus.). 560p. 1994. text ed. 45.00x (*0-87322-694-1*, BNSC0694) Human Kinetics.

National Structural Engineering Conference Staff. Methods of Structural Analysis: Proceedings of the National Structural Engineering Conference, August 22-25, 1976, Madison, Wisconsin, 2 vols., 1. Saul, William E. & Payrot, Alain H., eds. reprint ed. pap. 131.80 (*0-317-10736-4*, 2019541) Bks Demand.

— Methods of Structural Analysis: Proceedings of the National Structural Engineering Conference, August 22-25, 1976, Madison, Wisconsin, 2 vols., 2. Saul, William E. & Payrot, Alain H., eds. reprint ed. pap. 138.80 (*0-317-10737-2*) Bks Demand.

National Student Nurses' Association, Inc. Staff. Maternal-Newborn Nursing. LC 93-37630. (NSNA Review Ser.). 263p. 1994. pap. text ed. 18.95 (*0-8273-5674-9*) Delmar.

— Pediatric Nursing. Speer, Kathleen M., ed. LC 93-37960. (NSNA Review Ser.). 229p. 1994. pap. text ed. 19.95 (*0-8273-5670-6*) Delmar.

National Symposium on Building Family Strengths (2nd: 1979: University of Nebraska-Lincoln) Staff. Family Strengths Two: Positive Models for Family Life. Stinnett, Nick et al, eds. LC 80-50917. (Illus.). 528p. reprint ed. pap. 150.50 (*0-8357-3816-7*, 2036543) Bks Demand.

National Symposium on Building Family Strengths (3rd: 1980: University of Nebraska-Lincoln) Staff. Family Strengths Three: Roots of Well-Being. Stinnett, Nick et al, eds. LC 81-50712. (Illus.). 405p. reprint ed. pap. 115.50 (*0-8357-3817-5*, 2036544) Bks Demand.

National Symposium on Building Family Strengths (4th: 1982: University of Nebraska-Lincoln) Staff. Family Strengths Four: Positive Support Systems. Stinnett, Nick et al, eds. LC 82-51287. (Illus.). 611p. reprint ed. pap. 174.20 (*0-8357-3818-3*, 2036545) Bks Demand.

National Symposium on Deafness in Childhood Staff. Deafness in Childhood. McConnell, Freeman & Ward, Paul H., eds. LC 67-21653. 349p. reprint ed. pap. 99.50 (*0-8357-3260-6*, 2039481) Bks Demand.

National Symposium on Fracture Mechanics (5th, 1971, University of Illinois. Fracture Toughness Part 2: Proceedings. LC 72-78745. (ASTM Special Technical Publication Ser.: No. 514). 199p. reprint ed. pap. 56.80 (*0-685-15514-5*, 2026699) Bks Demand.

National Symposium on the Application of Psychology to the Teaching & Learning of Music (1978-1979, Ann Arbor, MI) Staff. Documentary Report of the Ann Arbor Symposium. LC 81-154469. (Illus.). 382p. reprint ed. pap. 108.90 (*0-8357-4572-4*, 2037457) Bks Demand.

N

National Symposium on the Applications of Psychology to the Teaching & Learning of Music Staff. Documentary Report of the Ann Arbor Symposium on the Applications of Psychology to the Teaching & Learning of Music, Session Three: Motivation & Creativity. LC 83-139075. (Illus.). 71p. pap. 25.00 (*0-8357-4558-9*, 2037458) Bks Demand.

National Symposium on the Future Availability of Ground Water Resources Staff. Proceedings of the National Symposium on the Future Availability of Ground Water Resources. Borden, Robert C. & Lyke, William L., eds. LC 92-70847. (AWRA Technical Publication Ser.: No. TPS-92-1). 485p. reprint ed. pap. 138.30 (*0-7837-6283-6*, 2045998) Bks Demand.

National Symposium on Wetlands (1978: Lake Buena Vista, FL). Wetland Functions & Values: The State of Our Understanding, Proceedings of the National Symposium of Wetlands Held in Disneyworld Village, Lake Buena Vista, Florida, November 7-10. LC 79-93316. (American Water Resources Association Technical Publication Ser.: TPS 79-2). 684p. reprint ed. pap. 180.00 (*0-685-15246-4*, 2027149) Bks Demand.

National TCA Book Committee Staff, et al. Lionel Trains: Standard of the World, 1900-1943. 2nd ed. (Illus.). 256p. (YA). 1989. reprint ed. 34.95 (*0-917896-02-5*) TCA PA.

National Technical Information Service Staff, ed. Corporate Author Authority List, 1987, 2 vols., Set. (Corporate Author Authority List Ser.). 2143p. 1987. 210.00 (*0-8103-2106-8*) Gale.

National Textbook Company Staff. Klett's Modern German & English Dictionary. 2nd ed. 1312p. 1993. 17.95 (*0-8442-2871-0*, Natl Textbk) NTC Pub Grp.

— National Textbook Company's Beginner's French & English Dictionary. 1992. pap. 7.95 (*0-8442-1476-0*, Natl Textbk) NTC Pub Grp.

— National Textbook Company's New College French & English Dictionary (Plain Edge) 1991. 17.95 (*0-8442-1481-7*, Natl Textbk) NTC Pub Grp.

— National Textbook Company's New College French & English Dictionary (Thumb Index) 1990. 19.95 (*0-8442-1480-9*, Natl Textbk) NTC Pub Grp.

— National Textbook Company's New College Greek & English Dictionary. 1990. 29.95 (*0-8442-8473-4*, Natl Textbk) NTC Pub Grp.

— NTC's Classical Dictionary. 1990. 29.95 (*0-8442-5473-8*, Natl Textbk) NTC Pub Grp.

— NTC's Compact Russian & English Dictionary. 1993. 17.95 (*0-8442-4283-7*); pap. 12.95 (*0-8442-4284-5*) NTC Pub Grp.

— NTC's Dictionary of Japan's Cultural Code Words. 1994. 17.95 (*0-8442-8391-6*) NTC Pub Grp.

— NTC's New Japanese & English Character Dictionary. 1994. 49.95 (*0-8442-8434-3*) NTC Pub Grp.

— Vox Compact Spanish & English Dictionary. 2nd ed. 1994. 12.95 (*0-8442-7985-4*); pap. 8.95 (*0-8442-7986-2*) NTC Pub Grp.

National Tooling & Machining Assn, ed. see Foster, Lowell.

National Tooling & Machining Association Staff. Advanced Diemaking: Instructor's Guide. xxxx, 21p. 1981. pap. 5.95 (*0-910399-35-2*, 5004) Natl Tool & Mach.

— Measuring & Gaging in the Machine Shop. 178p. (Orig.). 1981. pap. 18.25 (*0-910399-27-1*, 5023) Natl Tool & Mach.

National Toothpick Holder Coll. Staff. Toothpick Holders: Glass, China, & Metal. (Illus.). 152p. 1993. pap. 29.95 (*0-915410-88-5*) Antique Pubns.

National Toothpick Holder Collectors Society Staff. Toothpick Holders: China, Glass, & Metal. (Illus.). 152p. 1993. 37.95 (*0-915410-89-3*) Antique Pubns.

***National Tourist Board Staff.** Activity Holidays 95. (Illus.). 144p. (Orig.). 1995. pap. 8.95 (*0-7117-0805-3*, Pub. by Jarrold Pub UK) Seven Hills Bk.

National Transportation Act Review Commission Staff. Competition in Transportation: Policy & Legislation in Review. 474p. (Orig.). Date not set. pap. 55.25 (*0-660-14959-1*, Pub. by Canada Commun Grp CN) Accents Pubns.

National Trust for Historic Preservation in the United States Staff. Historic Preservation Tomorrow: Revised Report on Principles & Guidelines for Historic Preservation in the United States, Second Workshop, Williamsburg, Virginia. LC 69-10744. 68p. reprint ed. pap. 25.00 (*0-317-10190-0*, 2004590) Bks Demand.

National Trust for Historic Preservation Library of the University of Maryland Staff. Index to Historic Preservation Periodicals, 1987-90. suppl. ed. 400p. 1992. lib. bdg. 95.00 (*0-8161-0524-3*) G K Hall.

National Trust for Historic Preservation Staff. Curious Architecture: Views from America's Past. (National Trust for Historic Preservation, Past-Age Postcard Ser.). (Illus.). 20p. (Orig.). 1991. 7.95 (*0-89133-165-4*) Preservation Pr.

— Landmark Yellow Pages: Where to Find All the Names, Addresses, Facts & Figures You Need. 2nd ed. (Illus.). 395p. 1993. pap. 19.95 (*0-89133-169-7*) Preservation Pr.

— Menus for Special Occasions from Historic Hotels of America. LC 92-10274. (Illus.). 176p. 1992. 29.95 (*0-89133-173-5*) Preservation Pr.

— Recipes from Historic Hotels of America. (Illus.). 176p. 1991. 29.95 (*0-89133-163-8*) Preservation Pr.

— Reusing America's Schools: A Guide for Local Officials, Developers, Neighborhood Residents, Planners, & Preservationists. (Illus.). 96p. (Orig.). 1991. pap. 14.95 (*0-89133-184-0*) Preservation Pr.

National Trust for Historic Preservation Staff, et al. America's Forgotten Architecture. LC 76-9467. (Illus.). 312p. 1976. 20.00 (*0-394-49692-2*); pap. 14.95 (*0-394-73228-6*, NT C72) Pantheon.

National Trust Staff. Belton House. (Illus.). 96p. 1991. pap. 10.95 (*0-7078-0113-3*, Pub. by Natl Trust UK) Trafalgar.

— Beningbrough Hall. (Illus.). 96p. 1991. pap. 10.95 (*0-7078-0136-2*, Pub. by Natl Trust UK) Trafalgar.

— Bodiam Castle. (Illus.). 64p. 1991. pap. 9.95 (*0-7078-0137-0*, Pub. by Natl Trust UK) Trafalgar.

— Buckland Abbey. (Illus.). 64p. 1991. pap. 9.95 (*0-7078-0114-1*, Pub. by Natl Trust UK) Trafalgar.

— Cotehele House. (Illus.). 96p. 1991. pap. 10.95 (*0-7078-0117-6*, Pub. by Natl Trust UK) Trafalgar.

— Investigating Family History. (Illus.). 32p. 1994. pap. 6.95 (*0-7078-0133-8*, Pub. by Natl Trust UK) Trafalgar.

— Investigating Gardens. (Illus.). 32p. (J). (gr. 5-8). 1993. pap. 6.95 (*0-7078-0146-X*, Pub. by Natl Trust UK) Trafalgar.

— Investigating the Civil War. (Illus.). 32p. (J). (gr. 5-8). 1993. pap. 6.95 (*0-7078-0111-7*, Pub. by Natl Trust UK) Trafalgar.

— Investigating the Story of Farm Animals. (Illus.). 32p. 1994. pap. 6.95 (*0-7078-0134-6*, Pub. by Natl Trust UK) Trafalgar.

— Investigating the Tudors. (Illus.). 32p. 1994. pap. 6.95 (*0-7078-0168-0*, Pub. by Natl Trust UK) Trafalgar.

— Investigating the Victorians. (Illus.). 32p. (J). (gr. 3-6). 1994. pap. 6.95 (*0-7078-0167-2*, Pub. by Natl Trust UK) Trafalgar.

— Montacute House. (Illus.). 96p. 1991. pap. 11.95 (*0-7078-0138-9*, Pub. by Natl Trust UK) Trafalgar.

— Penrhyn Castle. (Illus.). 96p. 1991. pap. 9.95 (*0-7078-0115-X*, Pub. by Natl Trust UK) Trafalgar.

— Wimpole Hall. (Illus.). 96p. 1991. pap. 11.95 (*0-7078-0139-7*, Pub. by Natl Trust UK) Trafalgar.

National Trust Staff & Maddison, John. Blickling Hall. (Illus.). 96p. 1988. pap. 9.95 (*0-7078-0086-2*, Pub. by Natl Trust UK) Trafalgar.

National Underwriter Company, ed. see Hammond, J. D.

National Underwriter Staff. All about Medicare, 1993. 7th ed. 100p. 1993. pap. 8.95 (*0-87218-107-3*, N97) Natl Underwriter.

— Health Insurers - 1991. 1991. 37.00 (*0-87218-082-4*) Natl Underwriter.

— Life Insurers - 1991. 1991. 37.00 (*0-87218-081-6*) Natl Underwriter.

— Social Security Manual, 1992. 32th ed. 288p. 1992. pap. 12.50 (*0-87218-492-7*) Natl Underwriter.

— Social Security Manual, 1993. 33th ed. 288p. 1993. pap. 12.95 (*0-87218-106-5*, N96) Natl Underwriter.

— Tax Facts, Insurance & Employee Benefits Edition: 1992 Edition. 912p. (Orig.). 1992. pap. 24.95 (*0-87218-498-6*) Natl Underwriter.

— Tax Facts, Investments Edition: 1992 Edition. 600p. (Orig.). 1992. pap. 24.95 (*0-87218-499-4*) Natl Underwriter.

National Underwriter, Statistical Products Dept. Staff, ed. National Underwriter Profiles: Health Insurers. 304p. 1992. pap. 37.50 (*0-87218-088-3*) Natl Underwriter.

— National Underwriter Profiles: Life Insurers. 448p. 1992. pap. 37.50 (*0-87218-089-1*) Natl Underwriter.

— National Underwriter Profiles: Property - Casualty Insurers. 896p. 1992. pap. 37.50 (*0-87218-087-5*) Natl Underwriter.

National Underwriter, Statistical Products Dept. Staff, ed. see Ward Financial Group Staff.

National University Continuing Education Association Staff, jt. auth. see NUCEA Staff.

National Urban League Staff. Black Americans & Public Policy: Perspectives of the National Urban League. LC 88-61131. 98p. (Orig.). (C). 1988. pap. text ed. 14.95 (*0-685-33317-5*) Natl Urban.

— Children of the Sixties: The Power of the Ballot, a Handbook for Black Political Participation. 158p. (Orig.). (C). 1984. pap. text ed. 20.00 (*0-914758-12-8*) Natl Urban.

National Users Group. Multi-State Information System - Theoretical & Practical Issues: Proceedings of the Fourth Annual National Users Group Conference. King, James A., ed. 206p. 1980. pap. 10.00 (*0-936934-00-X*) N S Kline Inst.

***National Veterans Legal Services Program Ser.** The Veterans Self-Help Guide on VA Claims. 24p. (Orig.). 1995. pap. 5.00 (*1-878902-10-5*) Natl Vet Legal.

National Waste Processing Conference Staff. Energy Conservation Through Waste Utilization: Proceedings of 1978 National Waste Processing Conference - Including Discussions: Papers Presented at 1978 National Waste Processing Conference, Chicago, IL, May 7-10, 1978. LC 70-124402. 580p. reprint ed. pap. 165.30 (*0-8357-8711-7*, 2033648) Bks Demand.

— From Waste to Resource Through Processing: Proceedings of the 1976 National Waste Processing Conference: Papers Presented at 1976 National Waste Processing Conference, Boston, MA, May 23-26, 1976, Seventh Biennial Conference. LC 76-368694. 595p. reprint ed. pap. 169.60 (*0-8357-8721-4*, 2033646) Bks Demand.

— From Waste to Resource Through Processing. Supplement: Discussions: Papers Presented at 1976 National Waste Processing Conference, Boston, MA, May 23-26, 1976: Seventh Biennial Conference. LC 70-124402. 156p. reprint ed. pap. 44.50 (*0-8357-8722-2*, 2033647) Bks Demand.

— Meeting the Challenge: Proceedings of 1982 National Waste Processing Conference: Tenth Biennial Conference: Papers Presented at 1982 National Waste Processing Conference, New York, New York, May 2-5, 1982. LC 70-124402. (Illus.). 503p. reprint ed. pap. 143.40 (*0-8357-2862-5*, 2039098) Bks Demand.

— Resource Recovery Today & Tomorrow: Proceedings of 1980 National Waste Processing Conference, Ninth Biennial Conference: Papers Presented at 1980 National Waste Processing Conference, Washington, DC, May 11-14, 1980. LC 70-124402. 633p. reprint ed. pap. 180.00 (*0-8357-8759-1*, 2033649) Bks Demand.

— Resource Recovery Today & Tomorrow. Supplement: Discussions: Papers Presented at 1980 National Waste Processing Conference, Washington, DC, May 11-14, 1980: Ninth Biennial Conference. LC 70-124402. 215p. reprint ed. pap. 61.30 (*0-8357-8760-5*, 2033650) Bks Demand.

National Water Well Association, Committee on Waterwell Standards. Water Well Specifications: A Manual of Technical Standards & General Contractual Conditions for Construction of Water Wells. LC 80-80552. (Illus.). 156p. 1981. 13.00 (*0-912722-04-5*) Prem Press.

National Water Well Association Staff. Design & Construction of Water Wells. (Illus.). 256p. 1988. text ed. 54.95 (*0-442-26907-2*) Van Nos Reinhold.

National Water Well Association Staff, ed. Radon in Ground Water: Hydrogeologic Impact & Application to Indoor Airborne Contamination. (Illus.). 550p. 1987. 79.95 (*0-87371-117-3*, TD427) Lewis Pubs.

National Wetlands Policy Forum Staff. Issues in Wetlands Protection: Background Papers Prepared for the National Wetlands Policy Forum. Bingham, Gail et al, eds. LC 90-1631. 256p. (Orig.). 1990. pap. 17.50 (*0-89164-119-X*) World Wildlife Fund.

— Protecting America's Wetlands: An Action Agenda - the Final Report of the National Wetlands Policy Forum. 69p. (Orig.). 1988. pap. text ed. 10.00 (*0-89164-118-1*) World Wildlife Fund.

National Wildflower Research Center. Wildflower Handbook: The National Wildflower Research Center. (Illus.). 346p. 1992. reprint ed. pap. 12.95 (*0-89658-201-9*) Voyageur Pr.

National Wildflower Research Center Staff. Wildflowers of North America. (Postcard Collection Ser.). (Illus.). 30p. 1992. pap. 8.95 (*0-89658-202-7*) Voyageur Pr.

National Wildlife Federation Staff. Amazing Mammals I. (J). (gr. k-8). 1991. pap. 7.95 (*0-945051-29-8*, 75023) Natl Wildlife.

— Amazing Mammals II. (J). (gr. k-8). 1991. pap. 7.95 (*0-945051-30-1*, 75024) Natl Wildlife.

— Astronomy Adventures. (J). (gr. k-8). 1991. pap. 7.95 (*0-945051-31-X*, 75022) Natl Wildlife.

— Birds, Birds, Birds. (J). (gr. k-8). 1991. pap. 7.95 (*0-945051-32-8*, 75004) Natl Wildlife.

— Digging into Dinosaurs. (J). (gr. k-8). 1991. pap. 7.95 (*0-945051-33-6*, 75002) Natl Wildlife.

— Discovering Deserts. (J). (gr. k-8). 1991. pap. 7.95 (*0-945051-34-4*, 75005) Natl Wildlife.

— Diving into Oceans. (J). (gr. k-8). 1991. pap. 7.95 (*0-945051-36-0*, 75042) Natl Wildlife.

— Endangered Species. (J). (gr. k-8). 1991. pap. 7.95 (*0-945051-37-9*, 75033) Natl Wildlife.

— Geology: The Active Earth. (J). (gr. k-8). 1991. pap. 7.95 (*0-945051-38-7*, 75032) Natl Wildlife.

— Incredible Insects. (J). (gr. k-8). 1991. pap. 7.95 (*0-945051-39-5*, 75001) Natl Wildlife.

— Let's Hear It for Herps. (J). (gr. k-8). 1991. pap. 7.95 (*0-945051-42-5*, 75034) Natl Wildlife.

— Pollution: Problems & Solutions. (J). (gr. k-8). 1991. pap. 7.95 (*0-945051-40-9*, 75045) Natl Wildlife.

— Rain Forests: Tropical Treasures. (J). (gr. k-8). 1991. pap. 7.95 (*0-945051-41-7*, 75044) Natl Wildlife.

— Trees Are Terrific. (J). (gr. k-8). 1991. pap. 7.95 (*0-945051-43-3*, 75021) Natl Wildlife.

— Wading into Wetlands. (J). (gr. k-8). 1991. pap. 7.95 (*0-945051-44-1*, 75025) Natl Wildlife.

— Wild about Weather. (J). (gr. k-8). 1991. pap. 7.95 (*0-945051-45-X*, 75003) Natl Wildlife.

— Wild & Crafty. (J). (gr. k-8). 1991. pap. 7.95 (*0-945051-46-8*, 75043) Natl Wildlife.

National Women's Advisory Board on Sailing Staff. Women's Sailing Resource. 1994. pap. 3.00 (*0-914747-04-5*) Offshore Sail Schl.

National Women's Health Network Staff, ed. Abortion Then & Now: Creative Responses to Restricted Access. 110p. (Orig.). 1992. pap. 12.95 (*0-939522-00-4*) Nat Womens Hlth Netwk.

***National Writers Union Staff.** Byline: An Insider's Guide to Chicago-Area Print Media. 1994. pap. 14.95 (*0-9637796-0-5*) Nat Writ Union.

— National Writers Union Guide to Freelance Rates & Standard Practice. 216p. 1995. pap. 19.95 (*0-9644208-0-5*) Natl Writ Union.

***Nations Bible Society Staff, tr.** God's Word: Today's Bible Translation That Says What It Means. 1577p. 1995. 24.99 (*0-529-10312-5*) World Bible.

Nations, Bob, Jr. Ritual Crime Conduct Beyond the Law. 144p. 1991. student ed 19.95 (*0-914513-14-1*) Haughton.

Nations, Howard & Kilpatrick, John. Texas Workers' Compensation Law. 1990. write for info. (*0-8205-1735-6*, 735) Bender.

Nations, Opal L. The Marvels of Professor Pettingruel. (Illus.). 1978. 5.00 (*0-685-50395-X*) Black Stone.

***Natiuk, Robert.** Your Destiny: Your Life & Work Become One. rev. ed. 96p. 1994. pap. 8.00 (*1-884667-07-4*) Gage Res & Develop.

Nativ, Ronit. Hydrogeology & Hydrochemistry of the Ogallala Aquifer, Southern High Plains, Texas Panhandle & Eastern New Mexico. (Report of Investigations Ser.: RI 177). (Illus.). 64p. 1988. 3.00 (*0-317-03112-0*) Bur Econ Geology.

Native Womens Association Staff. Native Indian Wild Game, Fish & Wild Foods Cookbook. Hunt, David, ed. 304p. 1992. 24.95 (*1-56523-008-6*) Fox Chapel Pub.

Natividad, Irene, jt. ed. see Gall, Susan.

Natividad, Josephine C. My Oneness with God. Gabrawy, M., tr. LC 89-90122. (Illus.). 160p. (Orig.). (ARA.). 1989. pap. 4.95 (*0-685-25931-5*) J C Natividad.

Natividad, Oscar, tr. see Carlson, Daniel J.

Natke, H. G., ed. Application of System Identification in Engineering. (CISM International Centre for Mechanical Sciences Ser.: Vol. 296). (Illus.). 583p. 1988. pap. 70.00 (*0-387-82052-3*) Spr-Verlag.

Natke, Hans & Yao, James T. Structural Safety Evaluation Based on System Identification Approaches: Proceedings of the Workshop at Lambrecht-Pfalz. x, 502p. (C). 1988. pap. 94.00 (*3-528-06313-0*, Pub. by Vieweg & Sohn GW) Ballen Bkslr.

Natke, Hans G., et al. Safety Evaluation Based on Identification: Approaches Related to Time-Variant & Nonlinear Structures. x, 324p. 1993. pap. 70.00 (*3-528-06535-4*, Pub. by Vieweg & Sohn GW) Ballen Bkslr.

Natkiel, Richard, jt. auth. see Ferrel, Robert H.

Natkiel, Richard, jt. auth. see Ferrell, Robert.

Natkin, Robert. Subject Matter & Abstraction in Exile. (Illus.). 56p. 1993. pap. 9.95 (*1-870626-58-3*, Pub. by Claridge Pr UK) Paul & Co Pubs.

Natl. Inst. for Social Work Staff. The Barclay Report: Social Workers, Their Role & Tasks. (C). 1987. 65.00 (*0-685-28599-5*, Pub. by Natl Inst Soc Work) St Mut.

Natl. Inst. of Standards & Technology (NIST) Staff & Breitenberg, Maureen. Directory of European Regional Standards - Related Organizations. 184p. 1991. pap. 27.00 (*0-912702-58-3*) Global Eng Doc.

Natl Register Staff, ed. Working Press of the Nation, 1994, 1. 1993. 165.00 (*0-8352-3427-4*) Natl Register.

— Working Press of the Nation, 1994, 2. 1993. 165.00 (*0-8352-3428-2*) Natl Register.

— Working Press of the Nation, 1994, 3. 1993. 165.00 (*0-8352-3429-0*) Natl Register.

— Working Press of the Nation, 1994, 4. 1993. 165.00 (*0-8352-3430-4*) Natl Register.

— Working Press of the Nation, 1994, Set. 1993. 330.00 (*0-8352-3426-6*) Natl Register.

— Working Press of the Nation, 1994, Vols. 1 & 2. 1993. Vol. 1 & 2. 270.00 (*0-8352-3431-2*) Natl Register.

Natland, James, jt. ed. see Taylor, Brian.

Natland, Manley L., et al. A System of Stages for Correlation of Magallanes Basin Sediments. LC 74-75964. (Geological Society of America, Memoir Ser.: No. 139). 202p. reprint ed. pap. 57.60 (*0-317-28976-4*, 2023735) Bks Demand.

NATO Advanced Research Workshop on Mathematics Education & Technology. Learning from Computers - Mathematics Education & Technology: Proceedings of the NATO Advanced Research Workshop on Mathematics Education & Technology, Held in Villard-de-Lans, Grenoble, France, May 6-11, 1993. Keitel, Christine & Ruthven, Kenneth, eds. LC 93-34948. (NATO ASI Series F: Computer & Systems Sciences, Special Programme AET: Vol. 121). 1993. 88.00 (*0-387-57277-5*) Spr-Verlag.

NATO Advanced Research Workshop on Prediction of Interannual Climate Variations Staff. Prediction of Interannual Climate Variations. Shukla, J., ed. LC 93-18453. (ASI Series 1, Global Environmental Change: Vol. 6). 1993. 139.00 (*0-387-54591-3*) Spr-Verlag.

NATO Advanced Research Workshop on Recent Research Advances in the Fluid Mechanics of Turbulent Jets & Plumes. Recent Research Advances in the Fluid Mechanics of Turbulent Jets & Plumes. Do Castelo, Viana, ed. LC 94-684. (NATO Advanced Study Institutes Series E, Applied Sciences: Vol. 255). 1994. lib. bdg. 199.00 (*0-7923-2699-7*) Kluwer Ac.

NATO Advanced Research Workshop on Software for Parallel Computation. Software for Parallel Computation: Proceedings of the NATO Advanced Research Workshop on Software for Parallel Computation, Held at Cetraro, Cosenza, Italy, June 22-26, 1992. Kowalik, Janusz S. & Grandinetti, Lucio, eds. LC 93-16443. (NATO ASI Series F: Computer & Systems Sciences, Special Programme AET: Vol. 106). 1993. 98.00 (*0-387-56451-9*) Spr-Verlag.

***NATO Advanced Research Workshop on the Future of the Defence Firm Staff.** The Future of the Defence Firm - New Challenges, New Directions: Proceedings of the NATO Advanced Research Workshop on the Future of the Defence Firm, Hecla Island, Manitoba, Canada, 21-23 May 1992. Latham, Andrew & Hooper, Nicholas, eds. LC 94-23942. (NATO ASI, Series D, Behavioural Sciences: No. 79). 1995. write for info. (*0-7923-3268-7*) Spr-Verlag.

NATO Advanced Study Institute (1974: Newcastle upon Tyne) Staff. The Physics & Chemistry of Minerals & Rocks. Strens, R. G., ed. LC 75-6930. (Illus.). 715p. reprint ed. pap. 180.00 (*0-685-20682-3*, 2030471) Bks Demand.

NATO Advanced Study Institute (1975: University of Leicester). The Early History of the Earth: Based on the Proceedings of a NATO Advanced Study Institute Held at the University of Leicester, April 5-11, 1975. Windley, Brian F., ed. LC 75-26610. 629p. reprint ed. pap. 179.30 (*0-317-55705-X*, 2029266) Bks Demand.

NATO Advanced Study Institute in Information Science (1972: Champion, PA.). Information Science Search for Identity: Proceedings of the 1972 NATO Advanced Study Institute in Information Science Held at Seven Springs, Champion, Pennsylvania, August 12-20, 1972. Debons, Anthony, ed. LC 73-85383. (Books in Library & Information Science: Vol. 7). 511p. reprint ed. pap. 145.70 (*0-685-15742-3*, 2027809) Bks Demand.

An Asterisk (*) at the beginning of an entry indicates that the title is appearing in BIP for the first time.

NATO Advanced Study Institute on Mechanical Properties & Deformation Behavior of Materials Having Ultra-Fine Microstructures. Mechanical Properties & Deformation Behavior of Materials Having Ultra-Fine Microstructures: Proceedings of the NATO Advanced Study Institute, Porto Novo, Portugal, June 28 - July 10, 1992. Nastasi, Michael A. et al, eds. LC 93-12427. (NATO Advanced Study Institutes Series E, Applied Sciences: No. 233). 640p. (C). 1993. lib. bdg. 232.00 (*0-7923-2195-2*) Kluwer Ac.

***NATO Advanced Study Institute on Mobile Particulate Systems Staff.** Mobile Particulate Systems: Proceedings of the NATO Advanced Study Institute, Cargese, Corsica, France, July 4-15, 1994. Guazzelli, Elisabeth, ed. LC 95-9886. (NATO Advanced Science Institutes Series C: Vol. 287). 408p. (C). 1995. lib. bdg. 192.00 (*0-7923-3437-X*) Kluwer Ac.

***NATO Advanced Study Institute on Modern Aspects of Small-Angle Scattering Staff.** Modern Aspects of Small-Angle Scattering: Proceedings of the NATO Advanced Study Institute on Modern Aspects of Small-Angle Scattering, Como, Italy, May 12-22, 1993. Brumberger, H., ed. LC 94-40632. (NATO ASI, Series C). 480p. (C). 1994. lib. bdg. 215.00 (*0-7923-3251-2*) Kluwer Ac.

***NATO Advanced Study Institute on Solar Physics Staff.** Solar Physics: The Proceedings of NATO Advanced Study Institute on Solar Physics Held at Lagonissi, Athens, Greece, September 1965. fac. ed. Xanthakis, John N., ed. LC 67-29173. (Illus.). 551p. Date not set. pap. 157.10 (*0-7837-7365-X*, 2047174) Bks Demand.

***NATO Advanced Study Institute on the Gamma Ray Sky with COMPTON GRO & SIGMA Staff.** The Gamma Ray Sky with Compton GRO & SIGMA: Proceedings of the NATO ASI, Les Houches, France, January 25 - February 4, 1994. Signore, M. et al, eds. LC 95-9888. (NATO Advanced Science Institutes Series C: Vol. 401). 436p. (C). 1995. lib. bdg. 124.00 (*0-7923-3440-X*) Kluwer Ac.

NATO Advanced Study Institute on the Origin of the Solar System (1976: University of Newcastle upon Tyne) Staff. The Origin of the Solar System. Dermott, S. F., ed. LC 77-7547. (Illus.). 686p. reprint ed. pap. 180.00 (*0-685-20754-4*, 2030395) Bks Demand.

NATO Advanced Study Institute Staff. Atmospheric Effects on Radar Target Identification & Imaging: Proceedings of the NATO Advanced Study Institute, Goslar, 1975. Jeske, H., ed. (Mathematical & Physical Sciences Ser.: No. 27). 1976. lib. bdg. 112.50 (*90-277-0769-3*) Kluwer Ac.

— Charged & Reactive Polymers, No. 1, Polyelectrolytes: Proceedings of the NATO Advanced Study Institute, Forges-les-Eaux, June 18-28, 1972. Selegny, Eric et al, eds. LC 73-91435. 300p. 1974. lib. bdg. 172.50 (*90-277-0434-1*) Kluwer Ac.

— Chemical Spectroscopy & Photochemistry in the Vacuum: Proceedings of the NATO Advanced Study Institute, 1973. Sandorfy, Camille et al, eds. LC 73-91209. (NATO Advanced Studies Institute Ser.: No. C-8). 1974. lib. bdg. 149.50 (*90-277-0418-X*) Kluwer Ac.

— Combinatorial Programming: Methods & Application, Proceedings of the NATO Advanced Study Institute, Versailles, France, September 2-13, 1974. Roy, B., ed. (NATO Advanced Study Institutes Ser.: No. C19). 386p. 1975. pap. text ed. 42.50 (*90-277-0506-2*) Kluwer Ac.

— Computational Techniques in Quantum Chemistry & Molecular Physics: Proceedings of the NATO Advanced Study Institute, C15, Ramsau, Germany, 1974. Diercksen, G. H., ed. LC 75-9913. 568p. 1975. lib. bdg. 136.50 (*90-277-0588-7*) Kluwer Ac.

— Cytopharmacology of Secretion: Proceedings of the NATO Advanced Study Institute, Venice & Milan, June 16-23, 1973. fac. ed. Ceccarelli, B. et al, eds. LC 74-76090. (Advances in Cytopharmacology Ser.: No. 2). (Illus.). 398p. Date not set. pap. 113.50 (*0-7837-7287-4*, 2047019) Bks Demand.

— Earthquake Displacement Fields & the Rotation of the Earth: Proceedings of the NATO Advanced Study Institute Conference, Department of Geophysics, University of Western Ontario, London, Canada, June 22-28, 1969. Mansinha, L. et al, eds. LC 72-118130. (Astrophysics & Space Science Library: No. 20). 308p. 1970. lib. bdg. 84.00 (*90-277-0159-8*) Kluwer Ac.

— Electronic States of Inorganic Compounds - New Experimental Techniques: Proceedings of the NATO Advanced Study Institute, Inorganic Laboratory, St. John's College, Oxford, September 8-18, 1974. Day, P., ed. LC 75-17752. (NATO Advanced Study Institute Ser: No. C20). 541p. 1975. lib. bdg. 136.50 (*90-277-0627-1*) Kluwer Ac.

— Geodynamics of Iceland & the North Atlantic Area: Proceedings of the NATO Advanced Study Institute, University of Iceland, Reykjavik, Iceland, July 1-7, 1974. Kristjansson, L., ed. LC 74-27848. (NATO Advanced Study Institute Ser.: No. C11). 323p. 1974. lib. bdg. 84.00 (*90-277-0505-4*) Kluwer Ac.

— Interstellar Medium: Proceedings of the NATO Advanced Study Institute, Schliersee, Germany, April, 1973. Pinkau, K., ed. LC 73-91208. (NATO Advanced Study Institutes Ser.: No. C-6). 1974. lib. bdg. 80.00 (*90-277-0417-1*) Kluwer Ac.

— The Lives of the Neutron Stars: Proceedings of the NATO Advanced Study Institute, Kemer, Turkey August 29-September 12, 1993. Alpar, M. A. et al, eds. LC 94-40636. (NATO ASI, Series C). 592p. (C). 1994. lib. bdg. 269.00 (*0-7923-3246-6*) Kluwer Ac.

— Long-Time Predictions in Dynamics: Proceedings of the NATO Advanced Study Institute held in Cortina d'Ampezzo, Italy, August 3-16, 1975. Szebehely, Victor G. & Tapley, Byron D., eds. LC 76-7373. (NATO Advanced Study Institute Ser.: No. 26). 1975. lib. bdg. 89.00 (*90-277-0692-1*) Kluwer Ac.

— Modern Aspects of Mass Spectrometry: Proceedings of the NATO Advanced Study Institute on Mass Spectrometry, 2nd, 1966. Reed, Rowland I., ed. LC 68-16994. 401p. reprint ed. pap. 114.30 (*0-317-08735-5*, 2020703) Bks Demand.

— Modern Topics in Micro Wave Propagation & Air-Sea Interaction: Proceedings of the NATO Advanced Study Institute, Sorrento, Italy, June, 1973. Zancla, A., ed. LC 73-91210. (NATO ASI Series C: No. 5). 1973. lib. bdg. 89.00 (*90-277-0419-8*) Kluwer Ac.

— The Physics of Non-Thermal Radio Sources: Proceedings of the NATO Advanced Study Institute, Urbino, 1975. Setti, Giancarlo, ed. (Mathematical & Physical Sciences Ser.: No. 28). 1976. lib. bdg. 70.00 (*90-277-0753-7*) Kluwer Ac.

— Physics of the Solar Corona: Proceedings of the NATO Advanced Study Institute on Physics of the Solar Corona, Cavouri-Vouliagmeni, Athens, 1970. Macris, C. J., ed. LC 76-154741. (Astrophysics & Space Science Library: No. 27). 345p. 1971. lib. bdg. 103.00 (*90-277-0204-7*) Kluwer Ac.

— Reactions on Polymers: Proceedings of the NATO Advanced Study Institute, No. C-4, Troy, N. Y., July, 1973. Moore, James A., ed. LC 73-91207. 1973. lib. bdg. 112.50 (*90-277-0416-3*) Kluwer Ac.

— Recent Advances in Dynamical Astronomy: Proceedings of the NATO Advanced Study Institute in Dynamical Astronomy, Cortina D'ampezzo, August, 1972. Tapley, Byron D. & Szebehely, Victor G., eds. LC 73-83571. (Astrophysics & Space Science Library: No. 39). 490p. 1973. lib. bdg. 140.00 (*90-277-0348-5*) Kluwer Ac.

— Scattering Theory in Mathematical Physics: Proceedings of the NATO Advanced Study Institute, Denver, Colorado, June, 1973. LaVita, J. A. & Marchand, J. P., eds. LC 73-91205. 1974. lib. bdg. 99.00 (*90-277-0414-7*) Kluwer Ac.

— Semiclassical Methods in Molecular Scattering & Spectroscopy: Proceedings of the NATO Advanced Study Institute, Cambridge, England, September, 1979. Child, M. S., ed. (NATO Advanced Study Institutes Series C, Mathematical & Physical Sciences: No. 53). 344p. 1980. lib. bdg. 89.00 (*90-277-1082-1*) Kluwer Ac.

— Structure & Evolution of the Galaxy: Proceedings of the NATO Advanced Study Institute, Athens, Greece, September 8-19, 1969. Mavaridis, L. N., ed. LC 77-135107. (Astrophysics & Space Science Library: No. 22). 312p. 1971. lib. bdg. 89.00 (*90-277-0177-6*) Kluwer Ac.

— Studies in Mathematical Physics: Lectures in Mathematical Physics at the NATO Advanced Study Institute, Istanbul, Turkey, August, 1970, Vol. 1. Barut, Asim O., ed. LC 73-88587. (NATO Advanced Study Institutes Ser.: No. C-1). 1973. lib. bdg. 84.00 (*90-277-0405-8*) Kluwer Ac.

— The Theory & Application of Differential Games: Proceedings of the NATO Advanced Study Institute, University of Warwick, Coventry England, August 27 - September 6, 1974. Grote, J. D., ed. LC 74-34041. (NATO Advanced Study Institutes Ser.: No. C13). 310p. 1975. lib. bdg. 84.00 (*90-277-0581-X*) Kluwer Ac.

NATO Advanced Study Institute Staff & Holtet, Jan A. ELF-VLF Radio Wave Propagation: Proceedings of the NATO Advanced Study Institute, Spatind, Norway, April 17-27, 1974. LC 74-83870. 450p. 1974. lib. bdg. 112.50 (*90-277-0503-8*) Kluwer Ac.

NATO Advanced Study Institute Staff & Ribeiro, F. Ramoa. Zeolites: Proceedings: Science & Technology, NATO Advanced Study Institute on Zeolites, Portugal, 1983. 1984. lib. bdg. 191.50 (*90-247-2935-1*) Kluwer Ac.

NATO ASI & AMS Summer Seminar in Applied Mathematics Staff. Geometrical Methods for the Theory of Linear Systems: Proceedings of the NATO ASI & AMS Summer Seminar in Applied Mathematics held at Harvard University, Cambridge, MA, June 18-29, 1979. Byrnes, Christopher I. & Martin, Clyde F., eds. (NATO ASI Series C, Mathematical & Physical Sciences: No. 62). 313p. 1980. lib. bdg. 89.00 (*90-277-1154-2*) Kluwer Ac.

NATO Economic Directorate Staff, ed. CMEA: Energy Nineteen Eighty to Nineteen Ninety. (NATO Colloquia Ser.). 337p. 1982. 45.00 (*0-89250-341-6*) Orient Res Partners.

NATO Study Institute Staff & Thoft-Christensen, P. Continuum Mechanics Aspects of Geodynamics & Rock Fracture Mechanics: Proceedings of the NATO Study Institute, Reykjavik, Iceland, August 11-20, 1974. LC 74-34161. (NATO Advanced Study Institutes Ser.: No. C12). 273p. 1974. lib. bdg. 70.00 (*90-277-0504-6*) Kluwer Ac.

Natoli, Charles M. Nietzsche & Pascal on Christianity. LC 83-49020. (American University Studies: Philosophy: Ser. V, Vol. 3). 200p. (Orig.). (C). 1985. pap. text ed. 24.25 (*0-8204-0071-8*) P Lang Pubs.

Natoli, E. Cats of the World. 1988. 16.99 (*0-517-65496-2*) Random Hse Value.

Natoli, Joseph. Hauntings: Popular Film & American Culture 1990-1992. (SUNY Series in Postmodern Culture). 160p. (C). 1994. 44.50 (*0-7914-2153-8*); pap. 14.95 (*0-7914-2154-6*) State U NY Pr.

— Mots d'Ordre: Disorder in Literary Worlds. LC 91-26005. (SUNY Series, The Margins of Literature). 290p. (C). 1992. 57.50 (*0-7914-1111-7*); pap. 18.95 (*0-7914-1112-5*) State U NY Pr.

Natoli, Joseph, ed. Literary Theory's Future(s) LC 88-31742. 352p. 1989. 34.95 (*0-252-01599-1*); pap. 14.95 (*0-252-06049-0*) U of Ill Pr.

— Tracing Literary Theory. LC 86-24982. 400p. 1987. pap. 14.95 (*0-252-01384-0*) U of Ill Pr.

Natoli, Joseph & Hutcheon, Linda, eds. A Postmodern Reader. LC 92-39294. 584p. (C). 1993. 59.50 (*0-7914-1637-2*); pap. 19.95 (*0-7914-1638-0*) State U NY Pr.

Natoli, Joseph P. & Rusch, Frederik L., comps. Psychocriticism: An Annotated Bibliography. LC 84-4689. (Bibliographies & Indexes in World Literature Ser.: No. 1). xxiii, 268p. 1984. text ed. 55.00 (*0-313-23641-0*, NPL/, Greenwood Pr) Greenwood.

Natoli, Marie D. American Prince, American Pauper: The Contemporary Vice-Presidency in Perspective. LC 84-28965. (Contributions in Political Science Ser.: No. 134). xiv, 204p. 1985. text ed. 45.00 (*0-313-24750-1*, NAR/, Greenwood Pr) Greenwood.

Natoli, Salvatore, ed. see Georges, Daniel E.

Natoli, Salvatore, ed. see Lakshmanan, T. R. & Chatterjee, Lata.

Natoli, Salvatore J., ed. Careers in Geography. 6th rev. ed. LC 74-77075. (Illus.). 1994. 3.00 (*0-89291-184-0*) Assn Am Geographers.

— Strengthening Geography in the Social Studies. LC 88-61299. (Bulletin Ser.: No. 8). (Illus.). 127p. 1989. reprint ed. pap. 9.95 (*0-87986-056-1*, BU810088) Nat Coun Soc Studies.

Natoli, Salvatore J. & Bond, Andrew R. Geography in Internationalizing the Undergraduate Curriculum. (Resource Publications in Geography). 90p. (Orig.). 1985. pap. 10.00 (*0-89291-194-8*) Assn Am Geographers.

Natoli, Salvatore J., ed. see Baumann, Duane & Dworkin, Daniel.

Natoli, Salvatore J., ed. see Cook, Earl.

Natoli, Salvatore J., ed. see Greenberg, Michael, et al.

Natoli, Salvatore J., ed. see Lord, J. Dennis.

Natoli, Salvatore J., ed. see Roseman, Curtis C.

Natoli, Salvatore J., ed. see Salter, Christopher & Lloyd, William.

Natoli, Salvatore J., ed. see Smith, Christopher J.

Natoli, Salvatore J., ed. see Stutz, Frederick P.

Natoli, Salvatore J., ed. see Wiseman, Robert.

Natori, S., et al, eds. Mycotoxins & Phycotoxins Nineteen Eighty-Eight: A Collection of Invited Papers Presented at the 7th International IUPAC Symposium, Tokyo, Japan, 16-19 Aug., 1988. (Bioactive Molecules Ser.: No. 10). 496p. 1989. 164.00 (*0-444-88028-3*) Elsevier.

Natorp, Paul. Die Ethica des Demokritos. vi, 198p. 1970. reprint ed. write for info. (*0-318-70980-5*, Pub. by Georg Olms GW) Lubrecht & Cramer.

— Forschungen Zur Geschichte Des Erkenntnisproblems Im Altertum. Protagoras, Demokrit, Epikuruund die Skepsis. viii, 316p. 1990. reprint ed. write for info. (*3-487-01087-9*, Pub. by Georg Olms GW) Lubrecht & Cramer.

Natov, Roni. Leon Garfield. (Twayne's English Authors Ser.: No. 505). 176p. 1994. text ed. 22.95 (*0-8057-7042-9*, Twayne) Macmillan.

Natow. The Anti-Oxidant Counter. 1994. mass mkt. 5.99 (*0-671-78320-3*) PB.

Natow, Annette. Fast Food Nutrition Counter. 1994. mass mkt. 5.99 (*0-671-89475-7*) PB.

Natow, Annette B. & Heslin, Jo-Ann. The Diabetes Carbohydrate & Calorie Counter. Peters, Sally, ed. 288p. (Orig.). 1991. mass mkt. 5.99 (*0-671-69565-7*) PB.

— The Supermarket Nutrition Counter. Rubinstein, Julie, ed. 608p. (Orig.). 1995. mass mkt. 5.99 (*0-671-78328-9*) PB.

Natow, Annette B. & Heslin, JoAnn. The Fat Attack Plan. Zion, Claire, ed. 400p. 1991. reprint ed. pap. 6.50 (*0-671-73426-1*) PB.

Natow, Annette B. & Heslin, Joann. The Pregnancy Nutrition Counter. Peters, Sally, ed. 304p. (Orig.). 1992. mass mkt. 5.99 (*0-671-69563-0*, Pocket Star Bks) PB.

Natow, Annette B. & Hesun, Jo-Ann. The Cholesterol Counter. 3rd rev. ed. Peters, Sally, ed. 592p. 1993. mass mkt. 5.99 (*0-671-75173-5*) PB.

— The Sodium Counter. Peters, Sally, ed. 576p. (Orig.). 1993. mass mkt. 5.99 (*0-671-69566-5*) PB.

Natriello, Gary. Schooling Disadvantaged Children: Racing Against Catastrophe. 272p. (C). 1990. text ed. 40.95 (*0-8077-3015-7*); pap. text ed. 18.95 (*0-8077-3014-9*) Tchrs Coll.

Natriello, Gary, ed. School Dropouts: Patterns & Policies. enl. ed. 192p. 1986. reprint ed. pap. 16.95 (*0-8077-2835-7*) Tchrs Coll.

Natriuretic Hormone Symposium Staff. Regulation of Body Fluid Volumes by the Kidney: Proceedings of the Natriuretic Hormone Symposium, Czechoslovakia, June, 1969. Cort, J. H. & Lichardus, B., eds. (Illus.). 192p. 1970. 54.50 (*3-8055-0772-0*) S Karger.

Natsolim. Gniezniks, Polonian Pioneers. LC 83-60206. (Illus.). 304p. (Orig.). 1984. pap. text ed. 15.00 (*0-918020-06-9*) Masspac Pub.

Natsuki, Shizuko. Murder at Mount Fuji. 1987. reprint ed. pap. 2.95 (*0-345-33761-1*) Ballantine.

— Obituary Arrives at Two O'Clock. 1988. pap. 3.50 (*0-345-35237-8*) Ballantine.

— The Third Lady. 256p. (Orig.). 1987. pap. 2.95 (*0-345-33765-4*) Ballantine.

Natsume, Soseki. Botchan. Sasaki, Umeji, tr. LC 68-11794. 192p. 1968. reprint ed. pap. 8.95 (*0-8048-1620-4*) C E Tuttle.

— I Am a Cat. Ito, Aiko & Wilson, Graeme, trs. LC 78-182064. 220p. 1972. reprint ed. pap. 12.95 (*0-8048-1621-2*) C E Tuttle.

— I Am a Cat, Bk. II. Ito, Aiko & Wilson, Graeme, trs. LC 78-182064. 268p. 1979. pap. 12.95 (*0-8048-1280-2*) C E Tuttle.

— I Am a Cat, Vol. 3. Ito, Aiko & Wilson, Graeme, trs. 270p. 1993. pap. 12.95 (*0-8048-1860-6*) C E Tuttle.

Natsume Soseki. The Wayfarer. Beongcheon Yu, tr. & intro. by. LC 66-26974. 326p. reprint ed. pap. 93.00 (*0-7837-3625-8*, 2043491) Bks Demand.

Natta, G. & Danusso, F. Contributions of G. Natta & His School to Polymer Chemistry, 2 vols., Set. LC 63-10026. (Stereoregular Polymers & Stereospecific Polymerizations Ser.). 1967. 379.00 (*0-08-010156-9*, Pub. by Pergamon Repr UK) Franklin.

Natter, Elizabeth U., jt. auth. see Harker, Donald F.

Natter, Irving. Natter's New York City Education Bluebook, 1987-88. rev. ed. 50p. 1987. pap. 2.95 (*0-936143-02-9*) Natter Pub.

— Natter's New York City Education Bluebook, 1988-89. rev. ed. 50p. 1988. pap. 2.95 (*0-936143-03-7*) Natter Pub.

— Natter's New York City Education Bluebook, 1992-93. rev. ed. 54p. 1992. pap. 3.50 (*0-936143-07-X*) Natter Pub.

— Natter's New York City Education Bluebook, 1993-94. rev. ed. 54p. 1993. pap. 3.50 (*0-936143-08-8*) Natter Pub.

— Natter's New York City Education Bluebook, 1994-95. rev. ed. 54p. 1994. pap. 3.50 (*0-936143-09-6*) Natter Pub.

— Natter's 1986-87 New York City Education Bluebook. rev. ed. 50p. 1986. pap. 2.95 (*0-936143-01-0*) Natter Pub.

***Natter, Wolfgang, et al.** Objectivity & Its Other. 1995. lib. bdg. 40.00 (*0-89862-542-4*) Guilford Pr.

— Objectivity & Its Other. 1995. pap. text ed. 18.95 (*0-89862-545-9*) Guilford Pubns.

Natterer, F. The Mathematics of Computerized Tomography. LC 85-29591. 222p. 1986. text ed. 225.00 (*0-471-90959-9*) Wiley.

Natterson, Joseph. Beyond Countertransference: The Therapist's Subjectivity in the Therapeutic Process. LC 90-14542. 256p. 1991. 30.00 (*0-87668-558-0*) Aronson.

Natterson, Joseph M. The Dream in Clinical Practice. LC 80-65142. 520p. 1993. pap. 40.00 (*1-56821-091-4*) Aronson.

***Natterson, Joseph M. & Friedman, Raymond J.** A Primer of Clinical Intersubjectivity. LC 94-43799. 184p. 1995. pap. 25.00 (*1-56821-446-4*) Aronson.

Natterstad, J. H. Francis Stuart. (Irish Writers Ser.). 88p. 1975. 8.50 (*0-8387-7895-X*); pap. 1.95 (*0-8387-7979-4*) Bucknell U Pr.

Natterstad, Jerry, jt. auth. see Levenson, Leah.

Natterstad, Jerry H., jt. auth. see Levenson, Leah.

Natti, Susanna, jt. auth. see Abler, David A.

Nattier, Jan. Once upon a Future Time: Studies in a Buddhist Prophecy of Decline. LC 91-42549. (Nanzan Studies in Asian Religions: Vol. 1). 352p. (C). 1992. text ed. 60.00 (*0-89581-925-2*, Asian Human Pr); pap. text ed. 25.00 (*0-89581-926-0*, Asian Human Pr) Jain Pub Co.

Nattiez, Jean-Jacques. Music & Discourse: Toward a Semiology of Music. Abbate, Carolyn, tr. (Illus.). 254p. 1990. text ed. 49.50 (*0-691-09136-6*); pap. text ed. 17.95 (*0-691-02714-5*) Princeton U Pr.

— Proust As Musician. Puffett, Derrick, tr. (C). 1989. 49.95 (*0-521-36349-7*) Cambridge U Pr.

— Wagner Androgyne: A Study in Interpretation. Spencer, Stewart, tr. LC 92-23250. (Illus.). 401p. (C). 1993. text ed. 39.50 (*0-691-09141-2*) Princeton U Pr.

***Nattiez, Jean-Jacques, ed.** The Boulez-Cage Correspondence. 192p. 1995. pap. 14.95 (*0-521-48558-4*) Cambridge U Pr.

Nattiez, Jean-Jacques, ed. see Boulez, Pierre.

***Nattrass, Leonora.** William Cobbett: The Politics of Style. (Cambridge Studies in Romanticism: No. 11). 263p. (C). 1995. 54.95 (*0-521-46036-0*) Cambridge U Pr.

Nattrass, M. Malin's Clinical Diabetes. 2nd ed. 500p. 1993. 110.00 (*0-412-30860-6*) Chapman & Hall.

Nattrass, Nicoli & Ardington, Elisabeth, eds. The Political Economy of South Africa. 328p. 1990. pap. 19.95 (*0-19-570562-9*) OUP.

Natu, Bal. Conversations with the Awakener. 115p. 1991. pap. 10.00 (*1-880619-00-8*) Sheriar Found.

— Glimpses of the God-Man, Meher Baba, Vol. IV. LC 79-913293. (Illus.). 218p. (Orig.). 1984. pap. 10.00 (*0-913078-52-2*) Sheriar Pr.

— Glimpses of the God-Man Meher Baba, Vol. VI. 360p. (Orig.). 1994. pap. 12.00 (*1-880619-05-9*) Sheriar Found.

— Glimpses of the God-Man, Meher Baba: Vol. III, February 1952 - February 1953. LC 79-913293. (Illus.). 344p. (Orig.). 1982. pap. 10.00 (*0-913078-44-1*) Sheriar Pr.

— Glimpses of the God-Man, Meher Baba, Vol. 2: Jan. 1949-Jan. 1952. (Illus.). 406p. 1979. pap. 10.00 (*0-913078-38-7*) Sheriar Pr.

— More Conversations with the Awakener. 108p. (Orig.). 1993. pap. 10.00 (*1-880619-07-5*) Sheriar Found.

Natu, Bal, intro. Glimpses of the God-Man, Meher Baba, Vol. V. LC 79-913293. 326p. (Orig.). 1988. pap. 10.00 (*0-913078-60-3*) Sheriar Pr.

***Natural.** Asthma & Allergies: The Natural Way of Healing. 1995. mass mkt. 4.99 (*0-440-21662-1*) Dell.

— Chronic Pain: The Natural Way of Healing. 1995. mass mkt. 4.99 (*0-440-21658-3*) Dell.

— Stress, Anxiety, & Depression: The Natural Way of Healing. 1995. mass mkt. 4.99 (*0-440-21659-1*) Dell.

— Women's Health: The Natural Way of Healing. 1995. mass mkt. 4.99 (*0-440-21661-3*) Dell.

Natural Choices Company Staff. The Nontoxic Baby: Reducing Harmful Chemicals from Your Baby's Life. 88p. (Orig.). 1991. pap. 9.95 (*0-914955-09-8*) Lotus Pr WI.

N

Natural Environment Research Council Staff. Geology of the Kintail District. 74p. 1993. pap. 55.00 (0-11-884484-9, HM44849, Pub. by HMSO UK) UNIPUB.

Natural Fibers Information Center Staff. History of Cotton in Texas. 50p. (Orig.). 1989. pap. 5.00 (0-87755-317-3) Bureau Busn UT.

Natural Fibers Research & Information Center Staff. Natural Fibers Fact Book 1993. (Illus.). 50p. 1992. pap. 15.00 (0-87755-329-7) Bureau Busn UT.

***Natural Health Magazine Editors & Jacobi, Dana.** The Natural Health Cookbook: More than 150 Recipes to Sustain & Heal the Body. LC 95-8. 272p. 1995. 23.00 (0-684-80398-4) S&S Trade.

Natural Health Magazine Editors & Mayeell, Mark. The Natural Health First-Aid Guide: The Definitive Handbook of Natural Remedies for Treating Minor Emergencies. LC 93-11906. 1994. pap. 14.00 (0-671-79273-3) PB.

Natural Health Magazine Editors Staff, jt. auth. see Mayell, Mark.

Natural History Museum, London, England Staff, comp. Creepy Crawlies: Ladybugs, Lobsters, & Other Amazing Arthropods. LC 90-27531. (Illus.). 108p. (J). 1991. 14.95 (0-8069-8336-1) Sterling.

***Natural History Museum (London), General Library Staff.** A Catalogue of Manuscripts & Drawings in the General Library of the Natural History Museum. LC 95-6190. (Historical Studies in the Life & Earth Sciences: No. 4). 1995. write for info. (0-7201-2291-0, Mansell Pub) Cassell.

***Natural History Museum Staff.** Flora of Glamorgan. 448p. 1994. pap. 59.95 (0-11-310046-9, HM00469, Pub. by HMSO UK) UNIPUB.

— Rocks & Minerals. LC 87-26514. (Eyewitness Bks.). (Illus.). 64p. (J). (gr. 5 up). 1988. 17.00 (0-394-89621-1) Knopf Bks Yng Read.

— Rocks & Minerals. LC 87-26514. (Eyewitness Bks.). (Illus.). 64p. (J). (gr. 5 up). 1988. lib. bdg. 16.99 (0-394-99621-6) Knopf Bks Yng Read.

Natural History Museum Staff, comp. Creepy Crawlies: Ladybugs, Lobsters & Other Amazing Arthropods. LC 90-27531. (Illus.). 108p. (J). (gr. 4-10). 1992. pap. 9.95 (0-8069-8337-X) Sterling.

Natural Resources Defense Council Staff. Ebb Tide for Pollution: Actions for Cleaning up Coastal Waters. 1989. 7.00 (0-317-01843-4) Natl Resources Defense Coun.

— For Our Kids' Sake: How to Protect Your Child Against Pesticides in Foods. 90p. 1989. 7.95 (0-317-01840-X) Natl Resources Defense Coun.

Natural Resources Defense Council Staff & Edgerton, Lynne T. The Rising Tide: Global Warming & World Sea Levels. LC 90-5376. 136p. 1991. 29.95 (1-55963-068-X); pap. 17.95 (1-55963-067-1) Island Pr.

Natural Resources Defense Council Staff, jt. auth. see Garland, Ann W.

Natural Science Centers Conference Staff. Natural Science Centers Conference 1974, Nashville, Tennessee: Proceedings. Gardner, John F., ed. (Illus.). (Orig.). 1975. 5.00 (0-916544-04-4) Natural Sci Youth.

Natural Science for Youth Foundation Staff, ed. Changing Emphasis in Environmental Education: Proceedings of the Natural Science Centers Conference 1972-Jacksonville Florida. (Illus.). (Orig.). 1973. 5.00 (0-916544-02-8) Natural Sci Youth.

***Natural World Press Staff.** Waterproof Guide to the Middle Mckenzie River. (Illus.). 2p. 1994. 5.95 (0-939560-03-8) Natural World.

Naturalization, jt. auth. see President's Commission On Immigration.

Nature Conservancy Staff. Information Resources in Central America 1993: Belize: An Institutional Directory of Natural Resource & Environmental Information. Baker, Douglas S. & Chaves, Renan E., eds. 120p. (Orig.). (SPA.). 1993. pap. write for info. (0-9624590-0-3) Nature VA.

— Information Resources in Central America 1993: Costa Rica: An Institutional Directory of Natural Resource & Environmental Information. Baker, Douglas S. & Chaves, Renan E., eds. 450p. (Orig.) (SPA.). 1993. pap. write for info. (0-9624590-6-2) Nature VA.

— Information Resources in Central America 1993: El Salvador: An Institutional Directory of Natural Resource & Environmental Information. Baker, Douglas S. & Chaves, Renan E., eds. 150p. (Orig.). (SPA.). 1993. pap. write for info. (0-9624590-5-4) Nature VA.

— Information Resources in Central America 1993: Guatemala: An Institutional Directory of Natural Resource & Environmental Information. Baker, Douglas S. & Chaves, Renan E., eds. 200p. (Orig.). (SPA.). 1993. pap. write for info. (0-9624590-1-1) Nature VA.

— Information Resources in Central America 1993: Honduras: An Institutional Directory of Natural Resource & Environmental Information. Baker, Douglas S. & Chaves, Renan E., eds. 150p. (Orig.). (SPA.). 1993. pap. write for info. (0-9624590-3-8) Nature VA.

— Information Resources in Central America 1993: Nicaragua: An Institutional Directory of Natural Resource & Environmental Information. Baker, Douglas S. & Chaves, Renan E., eds. 120p. (Orig.). (SPA.). 1993. pap. write for info. (0-9624590-4-6) Nature VA.

— Information Resources in Central America 1993: Panama: An Institutional Directory of Natural Resource & Environmental Information. Baker, Douglas S. & Chaves, Renan E., eds. 200p. (Orig.). (SPA.). 1993. pap. write for info. (0-9624590-2-X) Nature VA.

Nature Conservancy of Washington Staff. Preserving Washington's Wild Lands: A Guide to the Nature Conservancy's Preserves in Washington. LC 92-85124. (Orig.). 1992. pap. 14.95 (0-89886-350-3) Mountaineers.

Naturman, Louis, ed. Polymer-Plastics Technology & Engineering, Vol. 2. LC 73-9411. (Illus.). 270p. reprint ed. pap. 77.00 (0-685-23625-0, 2029006) Bks Demand.

— Polymer-Plastics Technology & Engineering, Vol. 3. LC 73-94111. (Illus.). 268p. reprint ed. pap. 76.40 (0-685-23626-9, 2029007) Bks Demand.

Natvig, Jacob B., et al, eds. Amyloid & Amyloidosis 1991. (C). 1991. lib. bdg. 270.00 (0-7923-1089-6) Kluwer Ac.

Natzke, John R. & Volakis, John L. Diffraction by Parallel Resistive Half Plane Structures. (University of Michigan Report Ser.: No. 390968-2-T). 36p. reprint ed. pap. 25.00 (0-7837-4622-9, 2044345) Bks Demand.

Natzmer, Oldwig, jt. auth. see Rauss, Erhard.

Nau, Arlo. Peter in Matthew: Discipleship, Diplomacy, & Dispraise. (Good News Studies: No. 36). 200p. (Orig.). 1992. pap. text ed. 12.95 (0-8146-5700-1, M Glazier) Liturgical Pr.

Nau, B. S., ed. Fluid Sealing. 450p. 1989. 173.00 (0-387-51383-3) Spr-Verlag.

— Fluid Sealing: Proceedings of the 11th International Conference, Cannes, France, 8-10 April, 1987, Organized by BHRA, The Fluid Engineering Center, Cranfield, England. 795p. 1987. 169.25 (1-85166-100-X, Pub. by Elsevier Applied Sci UK) Elsevier.

Nau, Dana, jt. auth. see Kim, Steve M.

Nau, Douglas S. The New CRIS Case Studies. 57p. 1982. pap. 15.50 (1-881678-03-2) CRIS.

Nau, Erika, jt. auth. see Turner Publishing Co. Staff.

Nau, Erika S. Huna Self-Awareness: The Wisdom of the Ancient Hawaiians. rev. ed. (Illus.). 224p. (Orig.). 1992. pap. 10.95 (0-87728-743-0) Weiser.

— Self-Awareness Through Huna: Hawaii's Ancient Wisdom. Grunwald, Stefan, ed. LC 80-27842. 160p. (Orig.). 1981. pap. 5.95 (0-89865-099-2) Donning Co.

Nau, Henry R. The Myth of America's Decline: Leading the World Economy into the 1990s. (Illus.). 448p. 1990. 39.95 (0-19-506001-6) OUP.

— The Myth of America's Decline: Leading the World Economy into the 1990s. 440p. 1992. pap. 12.95 (0-19-507272-3) OUP.

Nau, Henry R., ed. Domestic Trade Politics & the Uruguay Round. 240p. 1988. pap. text ed. 16.00 (0-231-06823-9) Col U Pr.

— Domestic Trade Politics & the Uruguay Round. LC 88-25762. 234p. reprint ed. pap. 66.70 (0-7837-0424-0, 2040747) Bks Demand.

Nau, Henry R. & Quigley, Kevin F., eds. The Allies & East-West Economic Relations: Past Conflicts & Present Choices. 42p. 1989. pap. 4.00 (0-87641-306-8) Carnegie Ethics & Intl Affairs.

Nau, Jim. Ball Culture Guide: The Encyclopedia of Seed Germination. 2nd ed. LC 93-31746. (Illus.). 144p. (C). 1993. pap. text ed. 39.00 (1-883052-01-7) Ball Pub.

Naubert. Cezanne: Masterworks. 1992. 15.99 (0-517-06629-7) Random Hse Value.

Nauche, R., ed. Progress of Analytical Chemistry in the Iron & Steel Industry, EUR 14113. 616p. 1992. pap. 80.00 (92-826-3877-4, CD-NA-14113-EN-C, Pub. by Europ Com) UNIPUB.

Nauck, August. Tragicae Dictionis Index, Spectans ad Tragicorum Graecorum Fragmenta. xxxii, 738p. 1962. reprint ed. write for info. (0-318-70981-3, Pub. by Georg Olms GW); reprint ed. write for info. (0-318-72057-4, Pub. by Georg Olms GW) Lubrecht & Cramer.

— Tragicorum Graecorum Fragmenta. suppl. ed. 44p. 1983. reprint ed. Supplement, 44p. write for info. (0-318-70982-1, Pub. by Georg Olms GW) Lubrecht & Cramer.

— Tragicorum Graecorum Fragmenta. xxvi, 1048p. 1983. reprint ed. write for info. (3-487-00622-7, Pub. by Georg Olms GW) Lubrecht & Cramer.

Naudain, Barbara, ed. see Fourth Pacific Islands Conference of Leaders Staff.

Naudain, Barbara, jt. ed. see Halapua, Sitiveni.

Naudascher, E., ed. see IUTAM-IAHR Symposium Staff.

Naudascher, Eduard. Flow-Induced Vibrations: An Engineering Guide. (Hydraulic Structures Design Manual Ser.: Vol. 7). (Illus.). 450p. (C). 1994. text ed. 105.00 (90-5410-131-8, Pub. by A A Balkema NE) Ashgate Pub Co.

— Hydrodynamic Forces. (Hydraulic Structures Design Manual Ser.: No. 3). (Illus.). 307p. (C). 1990. text ed. 70.00 (90-6191-993-2, Pub. by A A Balkema NE) Ashgate Pub Co.

Naude, Alain, tr. see Hahnemann, Samuel.

Naude, Alain, ed. see Wright-Hubbard, Elizabeth.

Naude, Gabriel. Considerations Politiques Sur Les Coups d'Etat. 115p. (GER.). 1993. reprint ed. write for info. (3-487-09628-5, Pub. by Georg Olms GW) Lubrecht & Cramer.

— Considerations Politiques Sur les Coups d'Etat. 115p. reprint ed. write for info. (0-318-71380-2, Pub. by Georg Olms GW) Lubrecht & Cramer.

***Naude, Piet.** The Zionist Christian Church in South Africa: A Case-Study in Oral Theology. LC 94-39459. 164p. 1995. text ed. 79.95 (0-7734-9147-3) E Mellen.

Naude, Virginia N., ed. Sculptural Monuments in an Outdoor Environment. (Illus.). 116p. (Orig.). 1985. pap. write for info. (0-943836-04-2) Penn Acad Art.

Nauden, Jean B., jt. auth. see Sauliner, Jacqueline.

Naudet, Jean, jt. auth. see De Seynes, Claude.

Naudin, Jean-Bernard, et al. Renoir's Table: The Art of Living & Dining with One of the World's Greatest Impressionist Painters. LC 94-7792. 1994. 35.00 (0-671-89845-0) S&S Trade.

Nauen, Elinor, ed. Diamonds are a Girl's Best Friend: Women Writers on Baseball. 276p. 1994. 22.95 (0-571-19819-8) Faber & Faber.

Nauen, Lindsay B., ed. Guide to the Wisconsin Jewish Archives at the State Historical Society of Wisconsin. LC 74-16073. (Guides to Historical Resources Ser.). 28p. 1974. pap. 1.00 (0-87020-145-X) State Hist Soc Wis.

Nauert, Charles G., Jr. The Age of Renaissance & Reformation. LC 81-40034. 330p. 1982. reprint ed. pap. text ed. 23.50 (0-8191-1862-1) U Pr of Amer.

Nauert, Charles G. Agrippa & the Crisis of Renaissance Thought. LC 65-63002. (Illinois, University, Illinois Studies in the Social Sciences Ser.: Vol. 55). 382p. reprint ed. pap. 108.90 (0-8357-5273-9, 2019027) Bks Demand.

— Humanism & the Culture of Renaissance Europe. (New Approaches to European History Ser.: No. 7). (Illus.). 240p. (C). 1995. write for info. (0-521-40364-2); pap. write for info. (0-521-40724-9) Cambridge U Pr.

Nauert, Peter W., jt. auth. see Callaghan, Ed.

Naughton, Barry. Growing Out of the Plan: Chinese Economic Reform, 1978-1993. (Illus.). 375p. (C). 1995. 49.95 (0-521-47055-2) Cambridge U Pr.

Naughton, Bill. Spit Nolan. (Illustrated Short Stories Ser.). 1987. lib. bdg. 13.95 (0-88682-122-3) Creative Ed.

Naughton, Edmund. McCabe. 192p. 1991. reprint ed. pap. 3.50 (0-8439-3025-X) Dorchester Pub Co.

***Naughton, Gabriel.** Chardin. (Color Library). (Illus.). (C). 1995. pap. 14.95 (0-7148-3336-3, Pub. by Phaidon Press UK) Chronicle Bks.

— Chardin. (Color Library). (Illus.). 128p. (C). 1995. 19.95 (0-7148-3337-1, Pub. by Phaidon Press UK) Chronicle Bks.

Naughton, James. Colloquial Czech. (Colloquial Ser.). 320p. 1988. audio 29.95 (0-415-00076-9, A2567, RKP); pap. 16.95 (0-7102-0857-X, 08575, RKP); audio 15.95 (0-7102-1104-X, 1104X, RKP) Routledge.

Naughton, James, tr. see Hrabal, Bohumil.

Naughton, Jim. My Brother Stealing Second. LC 88-22035. (Trophy Keypoint Bk.). 288p. (YA). (gr. 7 up). 1991. pap. 3.95 (0-06-447017-2, Trophy) HarpC Child Bks.

— Taking to the Air: The Rise of Michael Jordan. (Illus.). 272p. 1992. 18.95 (0-446-51629-5) Warner Bks.

— Taking to the Air: The Rise of Michael Jordan. 288p. 1993. mass mkt. 4.99 (0-446-36401-0) Warner Bks.

Naughton, John. Exercise Testing: Physiological, Biomechanical & Clinical Principles. (Illus.). 240p. 1988. 35.00 (0-87993-245-7) Futura Pub.

Naughton, John, tr. see Bonnefoy, Yves.

Naughton, John, ed. see Bonnefoy, Yves.

Naughton, John T. The Poetics of Yves Bonnefoy. LC 87-5097. (Illus.). x, 60p. 1984. 20.00 (0-226-56947-0); pap. 6.95 (0-318-39964-4) U Ch Pr.

Naughton, Lee. Sand Through My Fingers. large type ed. 1990. 21.95 (0-7089-2129-9) Ulverscroft.

Naughton, Michael J. The Good Stewards: Practical Applications of the Papal Social Vision of Work. 163p. (Orig.). (C). 1992. lib. bdg. 38.50 (0-8191-8598-1); pap. text ed. 19.50 (0-8191-8599-X) U Pr of Amer.

Naughton, Renee. The Book Report & Library Talk Directory of Sources. 105p. 1991. spiral bd. 19.95 (0-938865-09-9) Linworth Pub.

Naughton, Renee, jt. ed. see Graef, Robert.

Naughton, Sean. Nine Hundred Words of Wisdom: The Real Truth about 900. DeMarco, Barbara, ed. (Orig.). 1993. student ed 99.00 (0-9638246-1-9); pap. 198.00 (0-9638246-0-0); audio 98.00 (0-9638246-2-7) Future Freedom.

Naughton, T. Raymond, jt. auth. see Goebel, Julius.

Naugle. Illustrated Network Book. 1994. pap. 42.95 (0-442-01826-6) Van Nos Reinhold.

Naugle, D., ed. Ordering Disorder: Prospect & Retrospect in Condensed Matter Physics. (AIP Conference Proceedings Ser.: No. 286). (Illus.). 352p. 1993. text ed. 125.00 (1-56396-255-1, AIP Pr) Am Inst Physics.

Naugle, Helen H., ed. see Johnson, Samuel.

Naugle, Matthew G. The Illustrated Network Book: A Graphic Guide to Understanding Computer Networks. (Illus.). 512p. 1994. pap. 42.95 (0-442-01790-1) Van Nos Reinhold.

— Local Area Networking. 288p. 1991. text ed. 38.00 (0-07-046455-3) McGraw.

— Network Protocol Handbook. LC 93-2013. (Computer Communications Ser.). 521p. 1993. text ed. 49.50 (0-07-046461-8) McGraw.

Naugle, Ronald, jt. auth. see Crews, Patricia C.

Naugol'nykh, K. A. & Ostrovsky, L. A. Nonlinear Acoustics. (Research Trends in Physics Ser.). (Illus.). 336p. 1994. boxed 85.00 (1-56396-338-8) Am Inst Physics.

Naugolnykh, K. A. & Ostrovsky, L. A. Nonlinear Wave Processes in Acoustics. (Texts in Applied Mathematics Ser.: No. 8). (Illus.). 290p. (C). 1995. write for info. (0-521-39080-X); pap. write for info. (0-521-39984-X) Cambridge U Pr.

Nauhaus, Gerd. The Marriage Diaries of Robert & Clara Schumann: From Their Wedding Day to the Russia Trip. Ostwald, Peter, tr. & pref. by. (Illus.). 256p. 1993. text ed. 35.00 (1-55553-171-7) NE U Pr.

Nauheim, Ferd. Letter Perfect: How to Write Business Letters That Work. 1982. text ed. 34.95 (0-442-88021-9) Van Nos Reinhold.

Nauheim, Stephen A. A Lawyer's Guide to International Business Transactions: United States Taxation of International Business Transactions, Pt. III, Folio 4. 2nd ed. 112p. 1982. pap. 5.00 (0-8318-0424-6, B424) Am Law Inst.

***Naui & Tophook Staff.** Adventures in Scuba Diving CD-ROM. 1995. cd-rom write for info. (0-916974-63-4, 296) NAUI.

NAUI Staff. Advanced Diving Technology & Techniques. 3rd ed. (Illus.). 298p. 1992. pap. 29.95 (0-916974-54-5, 097) NAUI.

— Libro Detext. (Illus.). 188p. 1994. pap. 22.95 (0-916974-56-1, 090SP) NAUI.

— Mastering Advanced Scuba Diving Interactive CD-ROM. 1995. cd-rom write for info. (0-916974-61-8, 297) NAUI.

— The NAUI Textbook One. 8th ed. (Illus.). 188p. 1992. pap. 22.95 (0-916974-53-7, 090) NAUI.

***Naujok, Michael.** This Is Boat Interior Construction. (Illus.). 138p. Date not set. 39.95 (0-7136-3612-2) Sheridan.

Naujoks, Bob, jt. auth. see Jacobson, Dick.

Nault, Andy. Staying Alive in Alaska's Wild. Loftin, Tee, ed. (Illus.). 224p. (Orig.). (J). (gr. 5 up). 1980. pap. 8.95 (0-934812-01-2) Tee Loftin.

Nault, Clifford A., Jr., jt. ed. see Ludwig, Richard M.

Nault, L. R. & Rodriguez, J. G., eds. The Leafhoppers & Planthoppers. LC 85-5383. 500p. 1985. text ed. 135.00 (0-471-80611-0, Wiley-Interscience) Wiley.

***Naum.** Zenobia. 1995. pap. text ed. (0-8101-1255-8) Northwestern U Pr.

Naum, Gellu. My Tired Father. 30p. 1987. pap. 4.00 (0-934301-07-7) Inkblot Pubns.

— Zenobia. Brook, James & Vlad, Sasha, trs. LC 95-10848. (Writings from an Unbound Europe Ser.). 1995. write for info. (0-8101-1254-X) Northwestern U Pr.

Nauman, Ann & Dearman, Marvene. Making Every Minute Count: Time Management for Librarians. (Illus.). 100p. (C). 1991. write for info. (0-931315-06-9) Lib Learn Res.

Nauman, Ann K. Biographical Handbook of Education: Five Hundred Contributions to the Field. 238p. 1985. pap. text ed. 16.95 (0-8290-0722-9) Irvington.

Nauman, Chuck, jt. auth. see Strain, Dave.

Nauman, E. B. Chemical Reactor Design. LC 91-45050. 456p. (C). 1992. reprint ed. lib. bdg. 67.95 (0-89464-707-5) Krieger.

— Introductory Systems Analysis for Process Engineers. (Chemical Engineering Ser.). 264p. 1990. text ed. 44.95 (0-409-90254-3) Buttrwrth-Heinemann.

Nauman, E. B. & Buffham, B. A. Mixing in Continuous Flow Systems. LC 82-24858. (Wiley-Interscience Publication Ser.). (Illus.). 297p. reprint ed. pap. 85.30 (0-7837-2369-5, 2057858) Bks Demand.

Nauman, Eileen. Medical Astrology. 3rd rev. ed. (Illus.). 298p. (Orig.). 1993. reprint ed. pap. 19.95 (0-9634662-2-4) Blue Turtle.

Nauman, Eileen & Gent, Ruth. Colored Stones & Their Meaning. 26p. 1988. pap. 4.95 (0-9634662-1-6) Blue Turtle.

Nauman, Elmo, Jr. Exorcism Through the Ages. (Illus.). 256p. 1974. pap. 3.95 (0-8065-0450-1, Citadel Pr) Carol Pub Group.

Nauman, Joel & Wagoner, J. Electronic Music Technique. 1984. text ed. write for info. (0-582-28281-0) Macmillan.

Nauman, St. Elmo, Jr. The New Dictionary of Existentialism. 1972. pap. 2.95 (0-8065-0281-9, Citadel Pr) Carol Pub Group.

Naumani, Shibli. Umar the Great, 2. 14.50 (0-933511-80-9) Kazi Pubns.

***Naumann.** Customer Satisfaction Measurement & Management: Using the Voice of the Customer. (SB-Marketing Education Ser.). 1995. text ed. 27.95 (0-538-84439-6) S-W Pub.

Naumann, Albert & Alexander, Grover, eds. Developing the Space Frontier. (Advances in the Astronautical Sciences Ser.: Vol. 52). (Illus.). 1983. fiche 45.00 (0-87703-185-1, Pub. by Am Astro Soc) Univelt Inc.

Naumann, Bernd, et al, eds. Language & Earth: Elective Affinities Between the Emerging Sciences of Linguistics & Geology. LC 91-35106. (Studies in the History of the Language Sciences: No. 66). xvi, 435p. 1992. 118.00x (1-55619-361-0) Benjamins North Am.

Naumann, C. M., et al. Verbreitungsatlas der Gattung Zygaena Fabricius, 1775: Lepidoptera, Zygaenidae. (Theses Zoologicae Ser.: Vol. 5). (Illus.). 144p. 1985. lib. bdg. 50.00 (3-7682-1405-2) Koeltz Sci Bks.

Naumann, Clas M., et al. Spezifitaet & Variabilitaet im Zygaena-Purpuralis- Komplex (Lepidoptera, Zygaenidae) (Theses Zoologicae Ser.: Vol. 2). (Illus.). 264p. 1983. reprint ed. 92.50 (3-7682-1339-0) Koeltz Sci Bks.

Naumann, Cynthia E., ed. see Cutburth, Ronald W.

Naumann, Earl. Creating Customer Value: The Path to Sustainable Competitive Advantage. LC 94-159. 1995. text ed. 24.95 (0-538-83847-7) S-W Pub.

Naumann, Francis, jt. auth. see Johns, Jasper.

Naumann, Francis M. The Mary & William Sisler Collection. LC 84-61714. 324p. 1984. 40.00 (0-87070-591-1, 0-8109-6072-9) Mus of Modern Art.

— New York Dada, 1915-23. LC 93-34280. 1994. write for info. (0-8109-3676-3) Abrams.

Naumann, Francis M., jt. ed. see Kuenzli, Rudolf E.

Naumann, G. O. & Apple, D. J. Pathology of the Eye. (Illus.). xxxv, 998p. 1986. 380.00 (0-387-96044-9) Spr-Verlag.

Naumann, Gottfried O., jt. auth. see Lang, Gerhard K.

***Naumann, H. H., et al, eds.** Head & Neck Surgery Vol. 1, Pt. II: Face, Nose & Facial Skull. LC 95-11552. 1995. write for info. (0-86577-590-7) Thieme Med Pubs.

Naumann, Hans H. Differential Diagnosis in Otorhinolaryngology: Symptoms, Syndromes, & Interdisciplinary Issues. LC 93-26903. 1993. 79.00 (0-86577-507-9) Thieme Med Pubs.

Naumann, K. Chemistry of Plant Protection, Vol. 4: Synthetic Pyrethroid Insecticides, Structures & Properties. Bowers, W. S. et al, eds. (Illus.). xvi, 241p. 1990. 169.00 (0-387-51313-2) Spr-Verlag.

— Chemistry of Plant Protection, Vol. 5: Synthetic Pyrethroid Insecticides, Chemistry & Patents. Bowers, W. S. et al, eds. (Illus.). 412p. 1990. 251.00 (0-387-51314-0) Spr-Verlag.

***Naumann, Nelly.** Die Einheimische Religion Japans. 264p. (GER.). 1994. 85.75 (90-04-10178-0) E J Brill.

N

An Asterisk (*) at the beginning of an entry indicates that the title is appearing in BIP for the first time.

Naumann, O. H., ed. see Lang, Gerhard K. & Gotfried.

Naumann, Otto, ed. Illustrated Bartsch, Vol. 6: Netherlandish Artists. 1980. 140.00 (*0-89835-006-9*) Abaris Bks.

— Illustrated Bartsch, Vol. 7: Netherlandish Artists. 1978. 140.00 (*0-89835-007-7*) Abaris Bks.

Naumburg, Margaret. Dynamically Oriented Art Therapy: Its Principles & Practice. (Illus.). 168p. (C). 1987. reprint ed. 32.95 (*0-9613309-1-0*) Magnolia St Pub.

— An Introduction to Art Therapy: Studies of the "Free" Art Expression of Behavior Problem Children & Adolescents As a Means of Diagnosis & Therapy. rev. ed. LC 73-78074. (Illus.). 240p. 1973. pap. text ed. 17.95 (*0-8077-2425-4*) Tchrs Coll.

Naumenko, Evgenii V. Central Regulation of the Pituitary-Adrenal Complex. LC 73-17250. (Studies in Soviet Science). 205p. reprint ed. pap. 58.50 (*0-317-28730-3*, 2020686) Bks Demand.

Naumenko, Maria. The Life of Saint Seraphim Wonderworker of Sarov. (Illus.). 22p. (Orig.). (J). (gr. 5-10). 1992. pap. 3.00 (*0-88465-049-9*) Holy Trinity.

— The Life of Saint Seraphim Wonderworker of Sarov: (Zhitie Prepodobnovo Serpahima, Sarovskovo Chudotvortsa) (Illus.). 22p. (Orig.). (RUS.). (J). (gr. 5-10). 1992. pap. 3.00 (*0-88465-052-9*) Holy Trinity.

Naumes, Margaret J., jt. auth. see Naumes, William.

Naumes, William & Naumes, Margaret J. Business. (Illus.). 704p. 1987. text ed. write for info. (*0-13-091307-3*) P-H.

Naumkin & Isaev. War & Peace in the Gulf: Domestic Politics & Regional Relations into the 1990's. 140p. 1991. 50.00 (*0-86372-134-6*, Pub. by Ithaca UK) Paul & Co Pubs.

Naumkin, Pavel I. & Shishmarev, Ilia A. Nonlinear Nonlocal Equations in the Theory of Waves. LC 93-8452. (Translations of Mathematical Monographs: Vol. 133). 312p. 1994. 149.00 (*0-8218-4573-X*) Am Math.

Naumkin, Vitaly. Island of the Phoenix. 352p. 1992. 79.00 (*0-86372-137-0*, Pub. by Ithaca UK) Paul & Co Pubs.

Naumkin, Vitaly, ed. State, Religion & Society in Central Asia: A Post-Soviet Critique. 306p. 1994. 65.00 (*0-86372-162-1*, Pub. by Ithaca UK) Paul & Co Pubs.

Naumkin, Vitaly, ed. see Rezvan, Efim.

Naumkin, Vitaly V. Central Asia & Transcaucasia: Ethnicity & Conflict. LC 93-31624. (Contributions in Political Science Ser.: No. 339). 256p. 1994. text ed. 59.95 (*0-313-29154-3*, Greenwood Pr) Greenwood.

Naumoff, Lawrence. From Portfolio of American Business. (Illus.). 36p. 1981. pap. 2.95 (*0-933974-03-5*) Bull City.

— Silk Hope, N. C. 1995. pap. 11.00 (*0-15-600207-8*) HarBrace.

— Silk Hope, N. C. A Novel. 1994. 21.95 (*0-15-188900-7*) HarBrace.

— Taller Women: A Cautionary Tale. LC 91-131. 1992. 21.95 (*0-15-187991-5*) HarBrace.

— Taller Women: A Cautionary Tale. (Harvest American Writing Ser.). 1994. pap. 10.95 (*0-15-688162-4*) HarBrace.

Naumoff, Olga. About the Splendid Macedonians: A Coloring Book & Much, Much More. (Illus.). 64p. (J). 1982. pap. 4.95 (*0-941983-00-5*) Splendid Assocs.

Naumov. Nonlinear Control Systems. 1990. 75.95 (*0-8493-7127-9*, QA402) CRC Pr.

Naumov, N. P. The Ecology of Animals. Levine, Norman D., ed. Plous, Frederick K., Jr., tr. LC 71-170965. (Illus.). 661p. (RUS.). reprint ed. 180.00 (*0-8357-9670-1*, 2014926) Bks Demand.

Naumov, Oleg V., jt. ed. see Lih, Laras T.

Naumova, T. N. Apomixis in Angiosperms: Nucellar & Integumentary Embryony. Mershchikova, I., tr. 1992. 130.95 (*0-8493-4570-7*, QK826) CRC Pr.

Naumovich, Epshtein M. Ottsovstvo. LC 92-17804. 160p. (Orig.). (RUS.). 1992. pap. 12.00 (*1-55779-045-0*) Hermitage.

Naunin, D. H., ed. see Bausiere, R., et al.

Naunin, D. H., ed. see Buxbaum, A. & Schierau, K.

Naunton, Robert. Fragmenta Regalia: Sixteen Thirty. Arber, Edward, ed. 272p. 1984. pap. 17.50 (*0-87556-577-8*) Saifer.

— Fragmenta Regalia, or, Observations on Queen Elizabeth, Her Times & Favorites. Cerovski, John S., ed. LC 82-49310. (Illus.). 120p. 1985. 26.50 (*0-918016-71-1*) Folger Bks.

Naunyn, Bernhard. Memories, Thoughts & Convictions. LC 94-2999. (Resources in Medical History Ser.). 1994. 30.00 (*0-88135-059-1*, Sci Hist) Watson Pub Intl.

Naur, Maja. Political Mobilization & Industry in Libya. (Illus.). 268p. (Orig.). 1986. pap. text ed. 52.50 (*0-317-65573-6*) Coronet Bks.

Naur, Peter. Computing: A Human Activity. (Illus.). 640p. (C). 1992. pap. text ed. 29.25 (*0-201-58069-1*) Addison-Wesley.

Nauratil, Marcia J. The Alienated Librarian. LC 88-34797. (New Directions in Information Management Ser.: No. 20). 139p. 1989. text ed. 45.00 (*0-313-25996-8*, NLL/, Greenwood Pr) Greenwood.

— Public Libraries & Nontraditional Clienteles: The Politics of Special Services. LC 84-19342. (New Directions in Librarianship Ser.: No. 8). xi, 180p. 1985. text ed. 45.00 (*0-313-23819-7*, NAP/, Greenwood Pr) Greenwood.

Nauroth, Holger. The Luftwaffe - from the North Cape to Tobruk 1939-1945: An Illustrated History. LC 91-61441. (Illus.). 236p. 1991. 29.95 (*0-88740-361-1*) Schiffer.

Nauroth, Holger & Held, Werner. German Fighters in World War Two: The Night Fighters. LC 91-61123. (Illus.). 232p. 1991. 29.95 (*0-88740-356-5*) Schiffer.

— The Messerchmitt Bf110-over All Fronts, 1939-1945. LC 90-62987. (Illus.). 248p. 1991. 29.95 (*0-88740-286-0*) Schiffer.

Nauroy, J. F., jt. ed. see Le Tirant, P.

Naus, Joseph I. Data Quality Control & Editing. LC 74-19804. (Statistics, Textbooks & Monographs: Vol. 10). 216p. reprint ed. pap. 61.60 (*0-685-16052-1*, 2027086) Bks Demand.

Naus, Joseph I., jt. auth. see Neff, Norman D.

Nauser, Markus, jt. ed. see Steiner, Dieter.

Nausner, Jacob, tr. The Talmud of Babylonia--An American Translation, No. XVII: Sotah. (Brown Judaic Studies). 1984. 31.95 (*0-89130-777-X*, 14 00 72); pap. 23.50 (*0-89130-778-8*, 14 00 72) Scholars Pr GA.

Nauss, W. John, Jr., jt. auth. see Seward, George C.

Nauta. Fundamental Neuroanatomy. LC 84-28675. (C). 1995. pap. text ed. write for info. (*0-7167-1723-9*) W H Freeman.

Nauta, Bram. Analog CMOS Filters for Very High Frequencies. LC 92-27778. (International Series in Engineering & Computer Science, VLSI, Computer Architecture, & Digital Screen Processing). (C). 1992. lib. bdg. 73.00 (*0-7923-9272-8*) Kluwer Ac.

Nauta, Doede. The Meaning of Information. LC 79-173382. (Approaches to Semiotics Ser.: No. 20). (Illus.). 314p. 1972. text ed. 57.35 (*90-279-1996-8*) Mouton.

Nauta, Paul, jt. ed. see Fang, Josephine Riss.

Nauta Staff. Diccionario de la Lengua Espanola: Dictionary of the Spanish Language, 2 vols., Set. 704p. (SPA.). 1978. 195.00 (*0-8288-4887-4*, S50030) Fr & Eur.

— Diccionario Enciclopedico Areas, 10 vols., Set. 4140p. (SPA.). 1990. 1,495.00 (*0-7859-5843-6*, 8427813597) Fr & Eur.

— Diccionario Enciclopedico Areas, Vol. 2. 424p. (SPA.). 1990. 150.00 (*0-7859-5844-4*, 8427813619) Fr & Eur.

— Diccionario Enciclopedico Areas, Vol. 3. 404p. (SPA.). 1990. 150.00 (*0-7859-5845-2*, 8427813627) Fr & Eur.

— Diccionario Enciclopedico Areas, Vol. 4. 424p. (SPA.). 1990. 150.00 (*0-7859-5846-0*, 8427813635) Fr & Eur.

— Diccionario Enciclopedico Areas, Vol. 5. 416p. (SPA.). 1990. 150.00 (*0-7859-5847-9*, 8427813643) Fr & Eur.

— Diccionario Enciclopedico Areas, Vol. 6. 416p. (SPA.). 1990. 150.00 (*0-7859-5848-7*, 8427813651) Fr & Eur.

— Diccionario Enciclopedico Areas, Vol. 7. 416p. 1990. 150.00 (*0-7859-6457-6*) Fr & Eur.

— Diccionario Enciclopedico Areas, Vol. 8. 408p. (SPA.). 1990. 150.00 (*0-7859-5849-5*, 8427813678) Fr & Eur.

— Diccionario Enciclopedico Areas, Vol. 9. 408p. (SPA.). 1990. 150.00 (*0-7859-5850-9*, 8427813686) Fr & Eur.

— Diccionario Enciclopedico Areas, Vol. 10. 404p. (SPA.). 1990. 150.00 (*0-7859-5851-7*, 8427813694) Fr & Eur.

— Enciclopedia de la Tecnica y de la Mecanica, 8 vols., Set. 5th ed. 2920p. (SPA.). 1975. 595.00 (*0-8288-5866-7*, S14237) Fr & Eur.

— Enciclopedia De los Animales. 400p. (SPA.). 1976. 75.00 (*0-8288-5661-3*, S50536) Fr & Eur.

— Enciclopedia General, 10 vols., Set. 4092p. (SPA.). 1978. 750.00 (*0-8288-5225-1*, S50465) Fr & Eur.

— Enciclopedia Medica Familiar, 2 vols., Set. 5th ed. 448p. (SPA.). 1979. pap. 75.00 (*0-8288-4742-8*, S50532) Fr & Eur.

— Enciclopedia Universal Nauta, 10 vols., Set. 10th ed. 2144p. (SPA.). 1978. 795.00 (*0-8288-5230-8*, S12303) Fr & Eur.

— Mi Primera Enciclopedia, 2 vols., Set. 7th ed. 420p. (SPA.). (J). 1978. 65.00 (*0-8288-5254-5*, S26910) Fr & Eur.

— Multidiccionario. 544p. (SPA.). 1979. 38.95 (*0-8288-4825-4*, S50514) Fr & Eur.

Nauta, Walle J. Neuroanatomy: Selected Papers of Walle J. H. Nauta. LC 93-10358. (Contemporary Neuroscientists Ser.). (Illus.). 614p. 1993. Acid-free paper. 99.50 (*0-8176-3539-4*) Birkhauser.

Nautilus Publishing, Inc. Staff. Fishing Vessels of the United States, 1993: A Complete Directory of All Vessels over 85 Feet. Udbye, Andreas & Angelsen, Jan E., eds. (Illus.). 360p. (Orig.). 1992. pap. 29.95 (*0-9634338-0-6*) Nautilus Pub.

— Fishing Vessels of the United States, 1994: 1,400 Vessels - 850 Photos, a Complete Directory of All Vessels over 79 Feet Registered Length. Udbye, Andreas, ed. (Illus.). 448p. (Orig.). 1994. pap. 29.95 (*0-9634338-1-4*) Nautilus Pub.

***Nautilus Publishing Staff. Fishing Vessels of the U. S. 1995-96 Edition. Udbye, Andreas, ed. (Illus.). 480p. (Orig.). 1995. pap. 29.95 (*0-9634338-3-0*) Nautilus Pub.**

A complete illustrated directory of all boats with a registered length of 79 feet & above. This is the third edition of this directory, further expanded & improved with more technical data & photographs. Contains technical & ownership information on USA's 1,400 largest commercial fishing boats. Approx. 1,000 photos. Vessels are listed alphabetically. Owners listed alphabetically in separate section, including addresses & many phone & FAX Nos. Statistical & introductory section with many graphs & tables, incl. rankings, averages & distributions. The directory contains some display advertising. This is a unique guidebook, & has become a popular & essential tool for boat owners, crew members, suppliers, governmental institutions, as well as job applicants & maritime historians. Provides the simplest way for reaching the nation's largest boat owners. Also available is a ring binder with technical & ownership information on 6,700 fishing vessels from 50 to 78 feet. ***Publisher Provided Annotation.***

Nautiyal, K. P. Proto-Historic India. (C). 1989. 76.00 (*0-8364-2481-6*, Pub. by Agam II) S Asia.

Nava, Julian. Mexican Americans: A Brief Look at Their History. (Illus.). 55p. pap. 1.50 (*0-686-74906-5*) ADL.

Nava, Marinella. The Book of Knitting. (Illus.). 160p. 1984. pap. 10.95 (*0-312-08942-2*) St Martin.

— A Day in the Park. (Wire-O-Board Bks.). (Illus.). 24p. (J). (gr. 2 up). 1994. 7.95 (*1-55550-992-4*) Universe.

Nava, Mica. Changing Cultures: Feminism, Youth & Consumerism. (Theory, Culture & Society Ser.). 256p. (C). 1992. text ed. 55.00 (*0-8039-8607-6*); pap. text ed. 21.95 (*0-8039-8608-4*) Sage.

***Nava, Mica & O'Shea, Alan, eds.** Modern Times: Reflections on a Century of English Modernity. LC 95-16372. 1995. write for info. (*0-415-06932-7*); pap. write for info. (*0-415-06933-5*) Routledge.

***Nava, Michael.** Created Equal: Why Gay Rights Matter to America. 1995. pap. 8.95 (*0-312-11764-7*, Stonewall Inn) St Martin.

— Goldenboy. 215p. 1991. reprint ed. pap. 8.95 (*1-55583-130-3*) Alyson Pubns.

— The Hidden Law. (Los Angeles Mysteries Ser.). 1994. mass mkt. 4.99 (*0-345-38406-7*) Ballantine.

— How Town. (Los Angeles Mysteries Ser.). mass mkt. 4.99 (*0-345-36987-4*) Ballantine.

— The Little Death. 165p. 1986. pap. 7.95 (*0-932870-96-1*) Alyson Pubns.

Nava, Michael, ed. Finale: Stories of Mystery & Suspense. LC 89-85942. 287p. (Orig.). 1989. pap. 8.95 (*1-55583-161-3*) Alyson Pubns.

Nava, Michael & Dawidoff, Robert. Created Equal: Why Gay Rights Matter to America. 144p. 1994. 17.95 (*0-312-10443-X*, Stonewall Inn) St Martin.

Navabi, Zainalabedin. VHDL: Analysis Modeling of Digital Systems. 1992. text ed. write for info. (*0-07-046472-3*) McGraw.

Navabpour, Reza. Iran. (World Bibliographical Ser.: No. 81). 308p. 1988. lib. bdg. 65.00 (*1-85109-036-3*) ABC-CLIO.

Navajas, Gonzalo. Mimesis Y Cultura en la Ficcion: Teoria de la Novella. (Serie A: Monagrafias, CXV). 214p. (SPA.). (C). 1985. 53.00 (*0-7293-0212-1*, Pub. by Tamesis Bks Ltd UK) Boydell & Brewer.

Navajata. A Divine Life in a Divine Body. 260p. 1991. pap. 11.95 (*0-685-54536-9*) Aurobindo Assn.

Navajo School of Indian Basketry Staff. Indian Basket Weaving. (Illus.). 1971. reprint ed. pap. 4.95 (*0-486-22616-6*) Dover.

Naval Historical Center Staff. The United States Naval Railway Batteries in France. rev. ed. (Illus.). 97p. (C). 1988. pap. 5.00 (*0-945274-00-9*) Naval Hist Ctr.

Naval Observatory Library Staff. Catalog of the Naval Observatory Library, Washington, D.C., 6 vols., Set. 1977. lib. bdg. 655.00 (*0-8161-0031-4*, Hall Library) G K Hall.

Naval Ocean Systems Center Staff. EREPS: Engineer's Refractive Effects Prediction System Software & User's Manual, Set. (Telecom Engineering Library). 200p. 1990. disk 250.00 (*0-89006-455-5*) Artech Hse.

Naval War College Staff. Sound Military Decision. Hatendorf, John B. & Hughes, Wayne P., Jr., eds. LC 91-45244. (Classics of Sea Power Ser.). (Illus.). 243p. 1992. 34.95 (*1-55750-752-X*) Naval Inst Pr.

Navantes, S. The Imitation of St. Therese of the Child Jesus. Grace, Mary, tr. LC 79-1132. 227p. reprint ed. pap. 64.70 (*0-317-28171-2*, 2022572) Bks Demand.

Navaretta, jt. ed. see Moore.

Navaretta, Cynthia. American Women Artists: Works on Paper & an American Album. LC 85-62160. (Illus.). 45p. 1985. pap. 7.00 (*0-9602476-5-3*) Midmarch Arts-WAN.

— Guide to Women's Art Organizations & Directory for the Arts. rev. ed. LC 82-80588. (Illus.). 1982. pap. text ed. 8.50 (*0-9602476-3-7*) Midmarch Arts-WAN.

— Whole Arts Directory. LC 87-62289. (Arts Guide Ser.). (Illus.). 172p. (Orig.). 1987. 12.95 (*0-9602476-7-X*) Midmarch Arts Pr.

***Navaretta, Cynthia & Marxer, Donna.** Artists Colonies Retreats & Study Centers. 32p. 1995. 6.00 (*1-877675-17-2*) Midmarch Arts-WAN.

***Navaretti, et al.** Beyond the Multifibre Arrangement: Third World Competition & Restructuring Europe's Textile Industry. 250p. (Orig.). 1995. pap. 32.00 (*92-64-14326-2*, Pub. by Econ & Coop Dev FR) OECD.

Navari, Cornelia, ed. The Condition of States. 256p. 1991. 90.00 (*0-335-09668-9*, Open Univ Pr); pap. 36.00 (*0-335-09667-0*, Open Univ Pr) Taylor & Francis.

Navaro, Anna, tr. see Swart, Susan.

Navarra, Anthony. Cobweb to a Star & Other Poems. (Illus.). 176p. (Orig.). 1988. pap. text ed. 8.95 (*0-9612678-2-8*) Abbott Pr.

— Whisperings on the Porch: A Collection of Haiku. (Illus.). 128p. (Orig.). 1992. pap. 6.95 (*0-9632041-3-0*) Japan Am Comm.

Navarra, Antonio, ed. see Commission of the European Communities Staff.

Navarra, Ferdinand. Yo He Tocado el Arca de Noe: Noah's Ark: I Touched It. (SPA.). 4.95 (*84-7228-406-9*, 220982, Pub. by Edit Clie SP) TSELF.

***Navarra, Ignazio, ed.** Atre e Storie a Sciacca, Celtabellotta, e Burgio del XV el XVII Secolo: Italian Stories & Art. xvi, 144p. 1986. pap. 15.00 (*0-89304-554-3*) Cross-Cultrl NY.

Navarra, Marcel M. Marcel M. Navarra: Cebuano Short Stories. Maceda, Teresita G., ed. & tr. by. 346p. 1986. pap. text ed. 8.00 (*0-8248-1098-8*, Pub. by U of Philippines Pr) UH Pr.

Navarra, Tova. The New Jersey Shore a Vanishing Splendor. LC 84-9337. (Illus.). 112p. 1985. pap. 9.95 (*0-8453-4793-4*, Cornwall Bks) Assoc Univ Prs.

— On My Own: Helping Kids Help Themselves. (Illus.). 128p. (J). (gr. 2-8). 1993. pap. 6.95 (*0-8120-1563-0*) Barron.

— Playing It Smart: What to Do When You're on Your Own. (Illus.). 128p. (J). (gr. 2-8). 1989. 12.95 (*0-8120-6131-4*) Barron.

Navarra, Tova & Lipkowitz, Myron. Allegeries A-Z. LC 93-33379. 352p. 1994. 40.00 (*0-8160-2824-9*) Facts on File.

Navarra, Tova, et al. Therapeutic Communication: A Guide to Effective Interpersonal Skills for Health Care Professionals. LC 88-43159. 158p. 1990. pap. 22.00 (*1-55642-075-7*) SLACK Inc.

Navarre, Monty, jt. ed. see Miller, Newton W.

Navarre, Yves. Cronus' Children. Girven, Howard, tr. 320p. 1990. pap. 14.95 (*0-7145-4014-5*) Riverrun NY.

— Our Share of Time. Di Bernardi, Dominic & Domke, Noelle, trs. LC 86-72136. Orig. Title: Le Temps Uoulu. 240p. 1988. reprint ed. pap. 9.95 (*0-916583-28-7*) Dalkey Arch.

— Sweet Tooth. Watson, Donald, tr. 1980. 14.95 (*0-7145-3522-2*) Riverrun NY.

— Swimming Pools at War. Watson, Donald, tr. (Publications Ser.: No. 1). 168p. (Orig.). 1983. pap. 8.95 (*0-913745-00-6*) Ubu Repertory.

Navarrete, Ignacio. Orphans of Petrarch: Poetry & Theory in the Spanish Renaissance. LC 93-4559. (Publications of the Center for Medieval & Renaissance Studies: Vol. 25). 1994. 40.00 (*0-520-08373-3*) U CA Pr.

***Navarrete, Pablo F.** Planning, Estimating & Control of Chemical Construction Projects. LC 95-124. (Chemical Industries Ser., Vol. 63: Cost Engineering Ser.: Vol. 22). 1995. write for info. (*0-8247-9359-5*) Dekker.

Navarrette, Francis G. American National Government & Politics in the Economy: A Primer of American Political Economy. 304p. (C). 1993. per., pap. text ed. 21.95 (*0-8403-8700-8*) Kendall-Hunt.

— Pragmatics of California Government & Politics. 192p. (C). 1992. pap. text ed. 15.95 (*0-8403-8022-4*) Kendall-Hunt.

— Pragmatics of Political Power in American National Government. 304p. (C). 1992. pap. text ed. 28.95 (*0-8403-7657-X*) Kendall-Hunt.

***Navarrette, Ruben.** Darker Shade of Crimson: Odyssey of a Harvard Chicano. 1994. pap. 11.95 (*0-553-37427-3*) Bantam.

Navarrette, Ruben, Jr. A Darker Shade of Crimson: Odyssey of a Harvard Chicano. LC 93-7985. 1993. 21.95 (*0-553-08998-6*) Bantam.

Navarria, F. L. & Pelfer, P. G. The Standard Model & Just Beyond. 520p. 1993. text ed. 121.00 (*981-02-1319-0*) World Scientific Pub.

Navarria, F. L., et al. Experimental Apparatus for High Energy Physics & Astrophysics. 564p. 1991. text ed. 151.00 (*981-02-0465-5*) World Scientific Pub.

Navarro. Mechanics & Physics of Aerating Grain. 1995. write for info. (*0-8493-4542-1*) CRC Pr.

— Species. 1995. mass mkt. (*0-553-57404-3*) Bantam.

Navarro-Almanza, Jose L., tr. see Chamberlin, Thomas W., et al.

Navarro, Armando. The Demographics of California's Latinos: Maps & Statistics. 19p. 1988. pap. 8.50 (*1-883638-09-7*) Rose Inst.

— Mexican American Youth Organization: Avant-Garde of the Chicano Movement in Texas. 1995. write for info. (*0-292-75556-2*); pap. write for info. (*0-292-75557-0*) U of Tex Pr.

Navarro, Aurelia, ed. see Appleton, Nancy.

Navarro, Aurelia, ed. see Hatengdi, M. U.

Navarro, C. F. Early Geometry. (Start Smart Ser.). (Illus.). 64p. (Orig.). (J). (gr. 2-3). 1990. pap. text ed. 6.50 (*1-878396-04-8*) Start Smart Bks.

— Prefixes & Suffixes. Navarro, Judith, ed. (Start Smart Ser.). 80p. 1990. student ed 7.50 (*0-685-35594-2*) Start Smart Bks.

— Thinking with Words. Navarro, Judith, ed. (Start Smart Ser.). 64p. 1990. student ed 6.50 (*1-878396-05-6*) Start Smart Bks.

Navarro, Carlos. Categories. (Start Smart Ser.). (J). (gr. k-2). 1990. student ed 4.50 (*1-878396-02-1*) Start Smart Bks.

— Early Reading Through Phonics, Vol. I. Kurfehs, Judith, ed. (Start Smart Ser.). (Illus.). 64p. 1989. student ed 4.50 (*0-685-30107-9*) Start Smart Bks.

— Early Reading Through Phonics, Vol. II. Kurfehs, Judith, ed. (Start Smart Ser.). (Illus.). 64p. 1989. student ed 3.50 (*0-685-30104-4*) Start Smart Bks.

— Verbal Correspondences. (Start Smart Ser.). (J). (gr. k-2). 1990. student ed 4.50 (*1-878396-00-5*) Start Smart Bks.

— Word Games to Learn By: Categories. Navarro, Judith, ed. (Start Smart Ser.). (Illus.). 32p. 1989. student ed 3.50 (*0-685-30103-6*) Start Smart Bks.

— Word Games to Learn By: Distinctions. Navarro, Judith, ed. (Start Smart Ser.). 32p. 1989. student ed 3.50 (*0-685-30105-2*) Start Smart Bks.

— Word Games to Learn By: Verbal Correspondences. Navarro, Judith, ed. (Start Smart Ser.). 32p. 1989. student ed 3.50 (*0-685-30106-0*) Start Smart Bks.

Navarro Dagnino, Juan. Vocabulario Maritimo Ingles-Espanol y Espanol-Ingles. 5th ed. 151p. (ENG & SPA.). 1976. pap. 19.95 (*0-8288-5766-0*, S12239) Fr & Eur.

Navarro, Eliseo, comp. Chicano Community: A Selected Bibliography for Use in Social Work Education. 1971. 3.30 (*0-318-35332-6*) Coun Soc Wk Ed.

Navarro, Gilbert, jt. auth. see Shea, Mary E.

Navarro, Gilbert, jt. auth. see Shea, Mary.

N

Navarro, J. & Schmitz, J., eds. Paediatric Gastroenterology. Barefoot, Brian, tr. (Illus.). 576p. 1992. 165.00 (0-19-261771-0) OUP.

Navarro, J. Nelson. Marine Diatoms Associated with Mangrove Prop Roots in the Indian River, Florida, U. S. A. (Bibliotheca Phycologica Ser.: Vol. 61). (Illus.). 151p. (Orig.). 1982. pap. text ed. 35.00 (3-7682-1337-4) Lubrecht & Cramer.

Navarro, Jose L. Blue Day on Main Street. LC 73-88742. 1973. pap. 4.00 (0-88412-063-5) TQS Pubns.

***Navarro, Juan C., ed.** Community Organizations in Latin America. 157p. (Orig.). 1994. 18.50x (0-940602-75-X) IADB.

Navarro, Judith, ed. see Navarro, C. F.

Navarro, Judith, ed. see Navarro, Carlos.

Navarro, Marysa, jt. auth. see Fraser, Nicholas.

Navarro, Peter. Bill Clinton's Agenda for America: Will It Make You Rich or Poor. write for info. (0-9635289-0-4) Williams OR.

— Job Opportunities under Clinton - Gore: Where Will the Big Paychecks Come From. write for info. (0-9635289-1-2) Williams OR.

— The Policy Game: How Special Interests & Ideologues Are Stealing America. 360p. (C). 1986. pap. 18.95 (0-669-14112-7) Free Pr.

Navarro, R. Lacasa & De Bustamante, I. Diaz. Spanish-English - English-Spanish Dictionary of Law, Economics & Politics. 4th ed. 761p. 1991. 149.00 (84-7130-306-X, Pub. by Edit De Derecho) IBD Ltd.

Navarro, Tomas. Studies in Spanish Phonology. Abraham, Richard D., tr. LC 68-31043. (Miami Linguistics Ser.: No. 4). 1968. 9.95 (0-87024-096-X) U of Miami Pr.

Navarro, Vicente. Class Struggle, the State & Medicine: An Historical & Contemporary Analysis of the Medical Sector in Great Britain. 1978. lib. bdg. 16.95 (0-88202-122-2) Watson Pub Intl.

— Crisis, Health & Medicine: A Social Critique. 300p. 1986. 32.50 (0-422-60580-8, 1006, Pub. by Tavistock UK); pap. 13.95 (0-422-60170-5, 9760, Pub. by Tavistock UK) Routledge Chapman & Hall.

— Dangerous to Your Health: The Crisis of Medical Care in the United States. (Cornerstone Bks.). 144p. (J). (ps-12). 1993. text ed. 22.00 (0-85345-864-2); pap. text ed. 10.00 (0-85345-865-0) Monthly Rev.

Navarro, Vicente, ed. Health & Medical Care in the U. S. A Critical Analysis. LC 77-70380. (Policy, Politics, Health & Medicine Ser.: Vol. 1). 162p. 1977. pap. 15.00x (0-89503-000-4) Baywood Pub.

— Imperialism, Health, & Medicine. LC 80-67832. (Policy, Politics, Health & Medicine Ser.: Vol. 3). 285p. (Orig.). (C). 1981. pap. text ed. 21.00x (0-89503-019-5) Baywood Pub.

— Why the United States Does Not Have a National Health Program. (Policy, Politics, Health & Medicine Ser.). 266p. 1992. pap. text ed. 24.00 (0-89503-105-1) Baywood Pub.

Navarro, Vicente & Berman, Daniel, eds. Health & Work under Capitalism: An International Perspective, Vol. 5. (Policy, Politics, Health & Medicine Ser.: Vol. 5). 311p. 1983. pap. text ed. 21.00x (0-89503-035-7) Baywood Pub.

Navarro, Vincente. The Politics of Health Policy: The U. S. Reforms, 1980-1993. 260p. 1994. 49.95 (1-55786-317-2); pap. 19.95 (1-55786-318-0) Blackwell Pubs.

Navarro, Yvonne. First Name Reverse Dictionary: Given Names Listed by Meaning. LC 92-50314. 217p. 1993. lib. bdg. 29.95 (0-89950-748-4) McFarland & Co.

Navas, Deborah. Things We Lost, Gave Away, Bought High & Sold Low. LC 92-53612. 152p. 1992. 16.95 (0-87074-336-8) SMU Press.

Navas, Gerardo. La Dialectica del Desarrollo Nacional: El Caso de Puerto Rico. LC 77-5824. (Planning Ser.: No. G-3). 1978. 6.40 (0-8477-2436-0) U of PR Pr.

Navas, Gerardo, ed. Crisis, Planificacion y el Desarrollo Social-Nacional. LC 77-22995. (Planning Ser.: No. S-3). 327p. 1978. pap. 6.00 (0-8477-2437-9) U of PR Pr.

— Geography & Planning, No. 1. 67p. 1977. pap. text ed. 2.80 (0-8477-2433-6) U of PR Pr.

Navas R, Jose J., tr. see McMullin, Rian E. & Casey, Bill.

Navas Ruiz, Ricardo, ed. see Hartzenbusch, Juan E.

Navascues Palacio, Pedro. Monasterios de Espana. 5th ed. (Illus.). 334p. 1988. 295.00x (84-239-5271-1) Elliots Bks.

Navasky, Bruno P., tr. & sel. Festival in My Heart: Poems by Japanese Children. LC 93-18251. (J). 1993. 29.95 (0-8109-3314-4) Abrams.

Navasky, Victor. Book about Journals: Public Opinion. 1986. write for info. (0-670-81342-7) Viking Penguin.

— Naming Names. 482p. 1981. pap. 8.95 (0-14-005942-3, Penguin Bks) Viking Penguin.

Navasky, Victor, jt. auth. see Cerf, Christopher.

Navatana, ed. see Jwala, pseud. & Smith, Roul.

Navathe, Shamkant B., jt. auth. see Elmasri, Ramez A.

Navazelskis, Ina. Alexander Dubcek. (World Leaders - Past & Present Ser.). (Illus.). 112p. (YA). (gr. 5 up). 1991. 17. 95 (1-55546-831-4) Chelsea Hse.

— Leonid Brezhnev. (World Leaders - Past & Present Ser.). (Illus.). 112p. (YA). (gr. 5 up). 1988. lib. bdg. 17.95 (0-87754-513-8) Chelsea Hse.

Navch, Z. & Lieberman, A. S. Landscape Ecology. (Environmental Management Ser.). (Illus.). xxviii, 356p. 1989. pap. 49.00 (0-387-97169-6) Spr-Verlag.

Nave, Brenda C., jt. auth. see Nave, Carl R.

Nave, Carl R. & Nave, Brenda C. Physics for the Health Sciences. 3rd ed. (Illus.). 432p. (C). 1985. pap. text ed. 39.50 (0-7216-1309-8) SCP.

Nave, Eric, jt. auth. see Rusbridger, James.

Nave, Jean R. How to Become a CEO Through Sales. 150p. 1985. pap. 8.95 (0-930115-01-5) Windemere Pr.

— The Quest for Success Rediscovering American Business Values. Orig. Title: Quest ...in Search of Values. 104p. 1987. pap. 9.95 (0-930115-08-2) Windemere Pr.

— Tool Kit for Going into Business. 125p. 1986. 295.00 (0-930115-06-6) Windemere Pr.

— Traveling a Road of Success. (Illus.). 30p. (Orig.). 1985. pap. 12.95 (0-930115-05-8) Windemere Pr.

— Women... The World's Greatest Salesmen! 96p. (Orig.). 1984. pap. 6.95 (0-930115-00-7) Windemere Pr.

Nave, Mark J. Power Line Filter Design for Switched-Mode Power Supplies. (Illus.). 224p. 1991. text ed. 54.95 (0-442-00453-2) Van Nos Reinhold.

Nave, Orville J. Nave's Topical Bible. 1616p. 1988. 24.95 (0-917006-02-X) Hendrickson MA.

— Nave's Topical Bible. Moody Press Staff, ed. (C). pap. 4.99 (0-8024-0030-2) Moody.

Nave, Orville J., ed. Nave's Topical Bible. (Reference Library Edition). 1616p. 1988. 24,99 (0-529-06591-6) World Bible.

Nave, Patricia S., ed. see Hackman, R., et al.

Nave, Yolanda. Breaking Up: From Heartache to Happiness in 48 Pages. LC 84-40680. (Illus.). 48p. (Orig.). 1984. pap. 3.95 (0-89480-839-7, 839) Workman Pub.

— Welcome to Our Company: Your Office Manual. LC 88-40251. 96p. 1988. pap. 5.95 (0-89480-608-4, 1608) Workman Pub.

Naveen, Ron. Antarctica. (Carolina Biology Readers Ser.). (Illus.). 16p. (Orig.). (YA). (gr. 10 up). 1992. pap. text ed. 2.75 (0-89278-124-6, 45-9624) Carolina Biological.

Naveen, Ron, et al. Wild Ice: Antarctic Journeys. (Illus.). 224p. 1990. 35.00 (0-87474-395-8) Smithsonian.

Naveh, Eyal J. Crown of Thorns: Political Martyrdom in American from Abraham Lincoln to Martin Luther King, Jr. 248p. (C). 1992. pap. text ed. 16.50 (0-8147-5776-6) NYU Pr.

***Naveh, J. & Shaked, S.** Magic Spells & Formulae: Aramaic Incantations of Late Antiquity. (Illus.). 296p. 1993. text ed. 28.00x (965-223-841-4, Pub. by Magnes Press IS) Eisenbrauns.

Naveh, Joseph. Early History of the Alphabet: An Introduction to West Semitic Epigraphy & Palaeography. 2nd ed. ix, 213p. (C). 1987. text ed. 25.00 (0-685-74242-3, Pub. by Magnes Press IS) Eisenbrauns.

Naveh, Joseph & Shaked, S. Amulets & Magic Bowls: Aramaic Incantations of Late Antiquity. 2nd ed. (Illus.). 340p. 1987. text ed. 28.00 (0-685-74254-7, Pub. by Magnes Press IS) Eisenbrauns.

Naveh, Z. & Lieberman, A. S. Landscape Ecology: Theory & Application. (Environmental Management Ser.). (Illus.). 335p. 1983. 59.50 (0-387-90849-8) Spr-Verlag.

— Landscape Ecology: Theory & Application. 2nd ed. (Illus.). 400p. 1993. pap. write for info. (3-540-94059-6) Spr-Verlag.

— Landscape Technology: Theory & Application. 2nd rev. ed. (Illus.). 472p. 1994. reprint ed. pap. 49.95 (0-387-94059-6) Spr-Verlag.

Naveh, Zev, jt. ed. see Bakshi, Trilochan S.

Naveira, A. M., ed. Differential Geometry. (Lecture Notes in Mathematics Ser.: Vol. 1045). viii, 194p. 1984. pap. 27.00 (0-387-12882-4) Spr-Verlag.

Naveira, A. M., et al, eds. Differential Geometry, Pensacola 1985. (Lecture Notes in Mathematics Ser.: Vol. 1209). 306p. 1986. pap. 39.30 (0-387-16801-X) Spr-Verlag.

Navel, Georges. Travaux. (FRE.). 1979. pap. 10.95 (0-7859-4127-4) Fr & Eur.

Naver, Judith E., ed. see Wise, Beth A. & Levin, Amy.

Naversen, Ken, photos. Beautiful America's San Diego. (Illus.). 80p. 1993. 17.95 (0-89802-629-6); pap. 12.95 (0-89802-632-6) Beautiful Am.

***Naversen, Kenneth.** Beautiful America's Orange County. (Illus.). 80p. 1995. 17.95 (0-89802-663-6); pap. 12.95 (0-89802-662-8) Beautiful Am.

— East Coast Victorians: Castles & Cottages. LC 90-860. (Illus.). 256p. 1990. 39.95 (0-89802-552-4); pap. 29.95 (0-89802-550-8) Beautiful Am.

Naves, Raymond, ed. see De Voltaire, Francois-Marie.

NAVI Staff. Beginning with Christ. rev. ed. 1980. pap. 10.00 (0-89109-159-9) NavPress.

Navi Staff. Prayer: Beholding Gods Glory. 1991. pap. 2.00 (0-89109-549-7) NavPress.

Navia, Luis E. The Presocratic Philosophers: An Annotated Bibliography. LC 93-16207. 752p. 1993. 110.00 (0-8240-9776-9, SS704) Garland.

— Socrates: The Man & His Philosphy. (Illus.). 376p. (Orig.). 1985. pap. text ed. 25.50 (0-8191-4855-5) U Pr of Amer.

— The Socratic Presence: A Study of the Sources. LC 93-13758. (Illus.). 416p. 1993. 61.00 (0-8153-1478-7, H1787) Garland.

— Socratic Testimonies. (Illus.). 380p. (Orig.). 1987. pap. text ed. 31.00 (0-8191-6115-2) U Pr of Amer.

Navia, Luis E. & Kelly, Eugene, eds. Ethics & the Search for Values. LC 80-82123. 530p. (C). 1980. pap. text ed. 23. 95x (0-87975-139-8) Prometheus Bks.

Navias, Martin S. Going Ballistic: The Build-up of Missiles in the Middle East. (Illus.). 270p. 1992. 45.00 (1-85753-020-9, Pub. by Brasseys UK) Brasseys Inc.

— Nuclear Weapons & British Strategic Planning, 1955-1958. (Nuclear History Program Ser.). 280p. 1991. 59.00 (0-19-827754-7, 12190) OUP.

Navickas. Consciousness & Reality. 1976. pap. text ed. 74.50 (90-247-1775-2) Kluwer Ac.

Navidi, Marjorie, jt. auth. see Radel, Stanley R.

Navigation Commission of ICAO Staff, jt. auth. see Dangerous Goods Panel of Air Staff.

Navigators Staff. Beginning a New Life. rev. ed. (Studies in Christian Living: Bk. 2). 32p. 1981. pap. 3.00 (0-89109-078-9) NavPress.

— The Character of the Christian. rev. ed. (Design for Discipleship Ser.: Bk. 4). 48p. 1980. pap. 3.00 (0-89109-039-8) NavPress.

— Design for Discipleship Series: Leader's Guide. 80p. (Orig.). 1980. pap. 4.00 (0-89109-043-6) NavPress.

— Developing Your Faith. rev. ed. (Studies in Christian Living: Bk. 5). 32p. 1981. pap. 3.00 (0-89109-081-9) NavPress.

— Foundations for Faith. rev. ed. (Design for Discipleship Ser.: Bk. 5). 48p. 1980. pap. 3.00 (0-89109-040-1) NavPress.

— Growing as a Christian. rev. ed. (Studies in Christian Living: Bk. 4). 32p. 1981. pap. 3.00 (0-89109-080-0) NavPress.

— Growing in Christ (Thirteen Chapters) 1957. pap. 5.00 (0-89109-157-2) NavPress.

— Growing in Discipleship. rev. ed. (Design for Discipleship Ser.: Bk. 6). (Illus.). 48p. 1980. pap. 3.00 (0-89109-041-X) NavPress.

— Knowing Jesus Christ. rev. ed. (Studies in Christian Living: Bk. 1). 32p. 1981. pap. 3.00 (0-89109-077-0) NavPress.

— Lessons on Assurance. (Growing in Christ Ser.). 32p. 1982. reprint ed. pap. text ed. 3.50 (0-934396-28-0) Churches Alive.

— Lessons on Assurance: Learn God's Promises for Salvation, Answered Prayer, Victory over Sin, Forgiveness & Guidance. rev. ed. (Growing in Christ Ser.). 32p. 1980. pap. 3.00 (0-89109-160-2) NavPress.

— Lessons on Christian Living. (Growing in Christ Ser.). 46p. 1982. pap. text ed. 3.50 (0-934396-29-9) Churches Alive.

— Lessons on Christian Living: Learn & Apply God's Principles for Maturing in the Christian Life. rev. ed. (Growing in Christ Ser.). 48p. 1980. pap. 3.00 (0-89109-162-9) NavPress.

— The Navigator Bible Studies Handbook. rev. ed. Lee-Thorp, Karen, ed. LC 79-87654. (Illus.). 120p. 1994. pap. 7.00 (0-89109-075-4, NavPr) NavPress.

— Our Hope in Christ. rev. ed. (Design for Discipleship Ser.: Bk. 7). 48p. 1980. pap. 3.00 (0-89109-042-8) NavPress.

— Serving Others. rev. ed. (Studies in Christian Living: Bk. 6). 32p. 1981. pap. 3.00 (0-89109-082-7) NavPress.

— The Spirit-Filled Christian. rev. ed. (Design for Discipleship Ser.: Bk. 2). (Illus.). 48p. 1980. pap. 3.00 (0-89109-037-1) NavPress.

— Talking with Christ. rev. ed. (Studies in Christian Living: Bk. 3). 32p. 1981. pap. 3.00 (0-89109-079-7) NavPress.

— Walking with Christ. rev. ed. (Design for Discipleship Ser.: Bk. 3). (Illus.). 48p. 1980. pap. 3.00 (0-89109-038-X) NavPress.

Navigators Staff, ed. New Testment Lessonmaker: Create Your Own Customized Bible Study on Any Passage in the New Testament in Minutes. LC 92-81117. 432p. (Orig.). 1992. pap. 19.00 (0-89109-688-4) NavPress.

Naviglio, Antonio, jt. auth. see Cumo, Maurizio.

Naviglio, Antonio, jt. ed. see Cumo, Maurizio.

Naville. Bibliographie des Ecrits d'Andre Gide Depuis 1891 Jusqu'a Sa Mort. (FRE.). 15.95 (0-8288-9780-8, F102790) Fr & Eur.

Naville, E. The Text of the Old Testament. (British Academy, London, Schweich Lectures on Biblical Archaeology Series, 1930). 1974. reprint ed. pap. 20.00 (0-8115-1257-6) Periodicals Srv.

Naville, Pierre, et al, eds. Revolution Surrealiste. No. One - Twelve. LC 68-28660. (Contemporary Art Ser.). (Illus.). (FRE.). 1968. reprint ed. 74.95 (0-405-00706-X) Ayer.

Navin, B. North Sea Passage Pilot. (Illus.). 1991. 59.95 (0-85288-157-6, Pub. by Imray Laurie Norie & Wilson UK) Bluewater Bks.

Navin, Brian. Cruising Guide to Germany & Denmark. (Illus.). 180p. 1994. 63.95 (0-85288-191-6, Pub. by Imray Laurie Norie & Wilson UK) Bluewater Bks.

— Cruising Guide to the Netherlands. (Illus.). 176p. (C). 1989. text ed. 42.95 (0-85288-131-2, Pub. by Imray Laurie Norie & Wilson UK) Bluewater Bks.

— North Sea Passage Pilot. 200p. 1987. 95.00 (0-85288-102-9, Pub. by Imray Laurie Norie & Wilson UK) St Mut.

Navin, Richard. Richard Navin: The Mycenae Circle. LC 80-1216. (Illus.). 20p. 1981. pap. 5.00 (0-89207-028-5) S R Guggenheim.

Navin, Sheryl & Cusack, Lynette. A Carer's Guide to Good Health. 61p. (Orig.). 1994. pap. 6.95 (0-85572-207-X, Pub. by Hill Content Pubng AT) Seven Hills Bk.

Navin, Thomas R. Copper Mining & Management. LC 78-2669. 450p. reprint ed. pap. 128.30 (0-317-28914-4, 2020438) Bks Demand.

Navinchandra, D. Exploration & Innovation in Design: Towards a Computational Model. Loveland, D. W. et al, eds. (Symbolic Computation - Artificial Intelligence Ser.). (Illus.). xi, 194p. 1990. 43.00 (0-387-97481-4) Spr-Verlag.

Navlakha, Suren. Elite & Social Change: A Study of Elite Formation in India. 180p. (C). 1989. text ed. 24.00 (0-8039-9627-6) Sage.

Navon, David H. Semiconductor Microdevices & Materials. 400p. (C). 1986. text ed. 69.25 (0-03-063983-2); Solutions manual. write for info. (0-03-063984-0) SCP.

Navon, I. M., jt. auth. see Le Dimet, F. X.

Navon, Robert. Autumn Songs: Poems on Love, Nature, Beauty, & Life. LC 82-73411. 96p. (Orig.). 1983. pap. 4.95 (0-9609866-1-8) Selene Bks.

— Cosmic Patterns, Vol. 1: An Explanation of the Underlying Intuitive Structure of the World in Its Mythical, Natural, Historical, & Cultural Manifestations. 303p. (Orig.). 1993. pap. 25.00 (0-933601-22-0) Selene Bks.

— The Harmony of the Spheres: Speculations on Western Man's Ever-Changing Views of the Cosmos, from Hesiod (700 B. C.) to Newton (1650 A. D.) LC 91-90481. 240p. 1991. 29.95 (0-933601-19-0) Selene Bks.

— Patterns of the Universe. xii, 116p. (Orig.). 1977. 18.00 (0-9609866-8-5); pap. 12.00 (0-9609866-2-6) Selene Bks.

Navon, Robert, ed. Fragments of the Lost Writings of Proclus. Taylor, Thomas, tr. LC 87-63418. (Great Works of Philosophy Ser.: Vol. 5). 128p. (C). 1995. reprint ed. pap. 15.00 (0-933601-12-3) Selene Bks.

— Fragments of the Lost Writings of Proclus, Vol. V. Taylor, Thomas, tr. LC 87-63418. (Great Works of Philosophy Ser.: Vol. 5). 128p. (C). 1995. reprint ed. text ed. 28.00 (0-933601-11-5) Selene Bks.

— The Platonic Theology, 2 vols. in 1. abr. rev. ed. Taylor, Thomas, tr. (Great Works of Philosophy: Vol. 1). xxvi, 222p. (C). 1995. reprint ed. pap. 25.00 (0-9609866-6-9) Selene Bks.

— The Sibylline Oracles. Terry, Milton, tr. (Great Works of Philosophy Ser.: Vol. 7). 267p. 1995. reprint ed. pap. 22. 50 (0-933601-08-5) Selene Bks.

Navon, Robert, ed. see Gautier, Theophile.

Navon, Robert, jt. ed. see Guthrie, Kenneth.

Navon, Robert, ed. see Pythagoras.

Navon, Yitzhak. The Six Days & the Seven Gates. 1980. 6.00 (0-930832-57-4); pap. 4.00 (0-686-70336-7) Herzl Pr.

Navon, Yoram, tr. see Leibowitz, Yeshayahu.

Navon, Ziva B., ed. The Glorious Sephardic Heritage. 120p. (Orig.). (YA). (gr. 6-12). 1992. pap. text ed. 10.00 (0-685-57455-5) Central Agency.

Navone, John. Communicating Christ. (C). 1988. 39.00 (0-85439-127-4, Pub. by St Paul Pubns UK) St Mut.

— Gospel of Love: A Narrative Theology. LC 84-81247. (Good News Studies: Vol. 12). 159p. 1984. pap. 8.95 (0-8146-5437-1) Liturgical Pr.

— Seeking God in Story. 250p. 1990. pap. text ed. 11.95 (0-8146-1919-3) Liturgical Pr.

— Self-Giving & Sharing: The Trinity & Human Fulfillment. 162p. (C). 1989. pap. 11.95 (0-8146-1774-3) Liturgical Pr.

— Towards a Theology of Story. (C). 1988. 39.00 (0-85439-136-3, Pub. by St Paul Pubns UK) St Mut.

Navone, John & Cooper, Thomas. Tellers of the Word. 1981. 23.00 (0-317-01341-6); pap. 14.00 (0-317-03298-4) Haymkt-Doyma.

— Tellers of the Word. 341p. 1981. 23.00 (0-929754-03-4); pap. 14.00 (0-929754-04-2) Jesuit Educ Ctr Human Dev.

NavPress Staff. Submitting: Letting God Use Others to Lead Me. (Love One Another Ser.). 64p. (Orig.). 1993. pap. 5.00 (0-89109-786-4, NavPr) NavPress.

— Your Life in Christ. rev. ed. (Design for Discipleship Ser.: Bk. 1). 31p. 1980. pap. 3.00 (0-89109-036-3) NavPress.

Navratil, Helen, ed. see Navratil, Sidney J., et al.

Navratil, James, jt. ed. see Schulz, Wallace W.

Navratil, James D. Nuclear Chemistry. 382p. 1993. boxed write for info. (0-13-626904-4) P-H.

Navratil, James D. & Schulz, W. W. Actinide Recovery from Waste & Low Grade Sources. (Radioactive Waste Management Ser.: Vol. 6). xiv, 386p. 1982. text ed. 190. 00 (3-7186-0105-2) Gordon & Breach.

Navratil, James D., jt. ed. see King, C. Judson.

Navratil, James D., jt. ed. see Li, Norman N.

Navratil, James D., jt. auth. see Macasek, Fedor.

Navratil, James D., jt. ed. see Schultz, Wallace W.

Navratil, James D., ed. see Tascher, Sylvia.

Navratil, James M. Medical Trivia. LC 86-82986. 200p. 1989. 12.50 (0-937557-06-4) Litarvan Lit.

Navratil, Sidney J., et al. Alcan Trail Blazers. Lloyd, John K. & Navratil, Helen, eds. (Illus.). 68p. (Orig.). 1992. pap. 14.00 (0-9633018-0-2) Six Hund Forty-Eight Mem.

***Navratilova, M. & Nickles.** The Total Zone. 1995. mass mkt. 6.99 (0-345-38867-4) Ballantine.

Navratilova, Martina & Nickles, Liz. The Total Zone. LC 94-10182. 1994. 21.00 (0-679-43390-2, Villard Bks) Random.

Navratilova, Martina & Vecsey, George. Martina. 1986. mass mkt. 5.99 (0-449-20982-2, Crest) Fawcett.

— Martina: Autobiography. LC 84-48894. (Illus.). 287p. 1985. 16.95 (0-394-53640-1) Knopf.

Navroth. The Ito School of Tsuba Makers. 1986. reprint ed. pap. 4.95 (0-910704-56-2) Hawley.

Navrotsky, A. & Weidner, D. J., eds. Perovskite: A Structure of Great Interest to Geophysics & Materials Sciences. (Geophysical Monograph Ser.: Vol. 45). 146p. 1989. 27.00 (0-87590-071-2) Am Geophysical.

Navrotsky, Alexandra. Physics & Chemistry of Earth Materials. LC 93-43135. (Cambridge Topics in Mineral Physics & Chemistry Ser.: No. 6). (Illus.). 250p. (C). 1994. 79.95 (0-521-35378-5); pap. 34.95 (0-521-35894-9) Cambridge U Pr.

Navrotsky, Alexandra, jt. ed. see O'Keeffe, Michael.

Navrozov, Lev. Prose from the Book That Was Not Published in 1968. 112p. (Orig.). 1984. pap. 14.00 (0-914265-00-8) New Eng Pub MA.

Navtikov, G. I., ed. Anatoly Kalashnikov Re(Hon) 576p. 1993. 45.00 (1-85183-062-6, Silent Bks) St Mut.

Navy Department Staff. Manual for Overhaul, Repair & Handling of Hamilton Ship Chronometer with Parts Catalog. (Illus.). 98p. 1988. pap. 14.95 (0-930163-33-8) Arlington Bk.

— Manual for Overhaul, Repair & Handling of Hamilton 35-Size Chronometer Watch with Parts Catalog. (Illus.). 63p. 1988. pap. 9.95 (0-930163-35-4) Arlington Bk.

— Manual for Overhaul, Repair & Handling of U. S. Navy Mechanical, Boat & Deck Clocks: Chelsea Type with Parts Catalog. (Illus.). 101p. 1988. pap. 14.95 (0-930163-20-6) Arlington Bk.

Navy Manufacturing Technology Program Staff, jt. auth. see U. S. Department of Commerce, National Bureau of Standards Staff.

Nawab, Ali. Some Moral & Religious Teachings of Al-Ghazzali. pap. 5.50 (0-933511-60-4) Kazi Pubns.

Nawab, Syed N. & Naqvi, Haider. Development Economics: A New Paradigm. LC 92-40700. 208p. (C). 1993. text ed. 28.95 (0-8039-9469-9) Sage.

Nawalany, Marek, jt. auth. see Zijl, Wouter.

N

An Asterisk (*) at the beginning of an entry indicates that the title is appearing in BIP for the first time.

Nawawi, Mahiudin A. Minhaj et Talibin: A Manual of Muhammadan Law According to the School of Shafii. 1992. reprint ed. 72.00 (*81-7013-097-2*, Pub. by Navrang) S Asia.

Nawaz, Tawfique, comp. The New International Economic Order: A Bibliography. LC 79-28077. 200p. 1980. text ed. 47.95 (*0-313-22111-1*, NAI/, Greenwood Pr) Greenwood.

Naworski, Priscilla, jt. auth. see Ikeda, Joanne.

Nawrath, Alfred. The Aegean World. LC 77-87872. (Illus.). 1977. 30.00 (*0-88331-097-X*) J J Binns.

Nawratzki, I., ed. see Jerusalem Conference on Impaired Vison in Childhood Staff.

Nawrocki, Dennis A. & Holleman, Thomas J. Art in Detroit Public Places. LC 80-10400. (Illus.). 160p. 1980. pap. 9.95 (*0-8143-1649-2*) Wayne St U Pr.

Nawrocki, Helene K. The Nurse's Book of Courage. 61p. 1993. pap. 14.95 (*0-9636792-0-1*); audio 14.95 (*0-9636792-1-X*) Ctr Nursing Excell.

Nawroth, Harry O. Lest We Forget. 97p. Date not set. pap. 4.95 (*1-883537-51-7*) Nawroth Pub.

— Thoughts about Jesus & Mary. 109p. Date not set. pap. 4.95 (*1-883537-50-9*) Nawroth Pub.

— We Do Have a Choice: Please Choose Jesus. 110p. Date not set. pap. 4.95 (*1-883537-52-5*) Nawroth Pub.

Nawy, Edward G. Prestressed Concrete: A Fundamental Approach. 832p. (J). 1988. text ed. 84.00 (*0-13-698375-8*) P-H.

— Prestressed Concrete: A Fundamental Approach. 2nd ed. LC 95-13788. 1995. text ed. 81.00 (*0-13-123480-3*) P-H.

— Reinforced Concrete: A Fundamental Approach. 3rd ed. LC 95-13792. 1995. write for info. (*0-13-123498-6*) P-H.

— Reinforced Concretes: A Fundamental Approach. 2nd ed. 758p. 1989. text ed. 87.00 (*0-13-771767-9*) P-H.

— Simplified Reinforced Concrete. (Illus.). 320p. (C). 1986. text ed. 29.95 (*0-317-29670-1*) P-H.

Nawyn, William E. American Protestantism's Response to Germany's Jews & Refugees, 1933-1941. LC 81-7552. (Studies in American History & Culture: No. 30). 342p. reprint ed. pap. 97.50 (*0-8357-1208-7*, 2070108) Bks Demand.

Naxerova, A. Technisches Woerterbuch, Vol. 1. (CZE & GER.). 1970. 89.95 (*0-8288-6554-X*, M-7649, Pub. by O Brandstetter Verlag GW) Fr & Eur.

— Technisches Woerterbuch, Vol. 2. (CZE & GER.). 1972. 89.95 (*0-8288-6422-5*, M-7650, Pub. by O Brandstetter Verlag GW) Fr & Eur.

Naxon, Jan L. & Rosenthal, Beth E. Dallas Entrees: A Restaurant Guide & Celebrity Cookbook (with a Primer to California Wines) 144p. (Orig.). 1982. pap. 5.95 (*0-910163-00-6*) Artichoke Pub.

Nay, Robert L., ed. Firearms Regulations in Various Foreign Countries. 203p. (Orig.). (C). 1992. pap. text ed. 40.00 (*1-56806-107-2*) Diane Pub.

Nay, Tim. Legal-Financial Planning Guide for Families. 2nd ed. 100p. 1990. pap. text ed. 15.00 (*1-877592-14-5*) GSH&MC.

Nay, Tim, jt. auth. see Byrlat, Katherine.

Naya, Seiji. Private Sector Development & Enterprise Reforms in Growing Asian Economies. 119p. 1990. pap. 9.95 (*1-55815-083-8*) ICS Pr.

Naya, Seiji & Takayama, Akira, eds. Economic Development in East & Southeast Asia: Essays in Honor of Professor Shinichi Ichimura. 340p. 1990. text ed. 44. 50 (*981-3035-64-1*, Pub. by Inst SE Asian Studies SI) Ashgate Pub Co.

Naya, Seiji, jt. ed. see Imada, Pearl.

Naya, Seiji, jt. ed. see Lee, Chung H.

Naya, Seiji, et al. ASEAN-U. S. Initiative: Assessment & Recommendations for Improved Eco Relations. 206p. 1989. pap. 26.50 (*981-3035-22-6*, Pub. by Inst SE Asian Studies SI) Ashgate Pub Co.

Naya, Seiji, et al, eds. Lessons in Development: A Comparative Study of Asia & Latin America. LC 89-19996. 361p. 1989. 34.95 (*1-55815-051-X*); pap. 14.95 (*1-55815-052-8*) ICS Pr.

Nayak, B. U. New Trends in Indian Art & Archeology: S. R. Rao's 70th Birthday Felicitation Volume, 2 vols., I. (C). 1992. write for info. (*81-85689-13-X*, Pub. by Aditya Prakashan II) S Asia.

— New Trends in Indian Art & Archeology: S. R. Rao's 70th Birthday Felicitation Volume, 2 vols., II. (C). 1992. write for info. (*81-85689-14-8*, Pub. by Aditya Prakashan II) S Asia.

— New Trends in Indian Art & Archeology: S. R. Rao's 70th Birthday Felicitation Volume, 2 vols., Set. (C). 1992. 165.00 (*81-85689-12-1*, Pub. by Aditya Prakashan II) S Asia.

Nayak, Debi P., ed. The Molecular Biology of Animal Viruses, 2 vols., 2. LC 76-29295. (Illus.). 579p. reprint ed. pap. 165.10 (*0-8357-6220-3*, 2034556) Bks Demand.

— The Molecular Biology of Animal Viruses, 2 vols., Vol. 1. LC 76-29295. (Illus.). 552p. reprint ed. pap. 157.40 (*0-8357-6219-X*, 2034556) Bks Demand.

Nayak, G. C. Philosophical Reflections. (C). 1987. 11.50 (*81-208-0421-X*, Pub. by Motilal Banarsidass II) S Asia.

Nayak, Nitin & Ray, Asok. Intelligent Seam Tracking for Robotic Welding. LC 93-3303. 1993. 69.00 (*0-387-19826-1*) Spr-Verlag.

Nayak, P. K. Blood, Women & Territory: An Analysis of Clan Feuds of Dongria Konds. (Sociological Publications in Honour of Dr. K. Ishwaran: No. 2). xviii, 238p. 1990. text ed. 32.50 (*81-85047-43-X*, Pub. by Reliance Pub Hse II) Apt Bks.

Nayak, P. K. & Mahajan, Anil, eds. Human Encounter with Drought. xxii, 151p. 1991. text ed. 30.00 (*81-85047-84-7*, Pub. by Reliance Pub Hse II) Apt Bks.

Nayak, P. Ranganath, jt. auth. see Deschamps, Jean-Philippe.

Nayak, P. Ranganath, jt. auth. see Ketteringham, John M.

Nayak, Panda U. Pakistan Society & Politics. 1985. 22.50 (*0-8364-1348-2*, Pub. by S Asia Pubs II) S Asia.

Nayak, Pandav. Pakistan: Political Economy of a Developing State. 1988. 48.50 (*81-7050-049-4*, Patriot) S Asia.

*__Nayak, Pradeep.__ Politics of the Ayodhya Dispute. (C). 1993. 22.50x (*81-7169-252-4*, Commonwealth) S Asia.

Nayak, Pulin, jt. ed. see Basu, Kaushik.

Nayak, Purshottam. Disguised Unemployment & Under-Employment in Agriculture. 174p. 1990. text ed. 27.50 (*0-685-33222-5*, Pub. by Radiant Pubs II) S Asia.

Nayak, R. K. & Siddiqui, H. Y. Social Work & Social Development. 1989. 23.50 (*81-85060-32-0*, Pub. by Gitanjali Prakashan) S Asia.

Nayak, Radhakant. Administrative Justice in India. 248p. 1989. text ed. 26.00 (*0-8039-9576-8*) Sage.

*__Nayapati.__ Using FTP. 1995. pap. (*0-7897-0238-X*) Que.

Nayar, Baldar R. American Geopolitics & India. 246p. 1976. 15.95 (*0-318-37228-2*) Asia Bk Corp.

Nayar, Baldev R. India's Mixed Economy. (C). 1989. 57.00 (*0-86132-217-7*) S Asia.

— The Political Economy of India's Public Sector: Policy & Performance. 1990. 48.50 (*0-86132-264-9*, Pub. by Popular Prakashan II) S Asia.

— State & International Aviation in India: Performance & Policy on the Eve of Aviation Globalization. (C). 1994. 34.00 (*81-7304-093-1*, Pub. by Manohar II) S Asia.

Nayar, Indira, tr. see Bronshtein, Z. S.

Nayar, Kuldip. In Jail. 152p. 1978. 9.95 (*0-7069-0647-0*) Asia Bk Corp.

— The Judgement: Inside Story of the Emergency in India. 228p. 1977. 14.95 (*0-7069-0557-1*) Asia Bk Corp.

— Report on Afghanistan. 1981. 12.00 (*0-8364-0690-7*, Pub. by Allied II) S Asia.

*__Nayar, Lali & Suxena, Rajul.__ Who's Afraid of Indian Cooking? Book of Menus. (C). 1994. 22.50 (*81-86112-64-2*, Pub. by UBS Pubs Dist II) S Asia.

Nayar, M. P. Meaning of India Flowering Plants Name. (C). 1988. text ed. 50.00 (*0-685-22103-2*, Scientific) St Mut.

Nayar, Sobhana. Bhatkhande's Contribution to Music: A Historical Perspective. (C). 1989. 32.00 (*0-86132-238-X*, Pub. by Popular Prakashan II) S Asia.

Nayar, Sushila, tr. see Gandhi, M. K.

Nayar, T. S. Pollen Flora of Maharashtra State. (International Bioscience Ser.: No. 14). (Illus.). 175p. 1990. 65.00 (*1-55528-221-0*, Messers Today & Tomorrow) Scholarly Pubns.

Nayar, Usha. Women Teachers in South Asia, Nudity & Discontinuity With Change. (C). 1988. 22.50 (*81-7001-048-9*, Pub. by Chanakya II) S Asia.

*__Nayatani, Yoshinobu, et al.__ The Seven New QC Tools: Practical Applications for Managers. Loftus, John H., tr. (Illus.). 180p. 1994. pap. text ed. 34.95 (*4-88319-004-8*, 190048, Pub. by Three A JA) Qual Resc.

Naydan, Michael, tr. see Tsvetaeva, Marina I.

Naydan, Theodore D. Secret Trout Flies: The Book of Unrevealed Patterns. (Illus.). 63p. 1989. pap. text ed. write for info. (*0-318-65818-6*) T D Naydan.

Nayden, Michael, tr. see Kostenko, Lina.

*__Nayder.__ Walkie Collins. Date not set. 22.95 (*0-8057-7059-3*, Twayne) Macmillan.

*__Naydler, Jeremy.__ The Temple of the Cosmos: The Ancient Egyptian Experience of the Sacred. 224p. 1995. pap. 16. 95 (*0-89281-555-8*) Inner Tradit.

Nayer, H. S., et al, eds. Progress in Powder Metallurgy, Vol. 39. (Illus.). 696p. 1983. pap. 20.00 (*0-918404-61-4*) Metal Powder.

Nayer, Judith E., ed. see Block, Arlene.

Nayer, Judith E., ed. see Evans, Karen.

Nayer, Judith E., ed. see Jonson, Liz & Silliman, Emery.

Nayer, Judith E., ed. see Silliman, Emery & Jonson, Liz.

Nayer, Judith E., ed. see Wise, Beth A.

Nayer, Judith E., ed. see Wise, Beth A. & Sokoloff, Myka-Lynne.

Nayer, Judith E., ed. see Wise, Beth A.

Nayer, Judith E., ed. see Wise, Beth A. & Block, Arlene.

*__Nayer, Judy.__ Birds. (At Your Fingertips Ser.). (Illus.). 10p. (J). (ps-2). 1995. bds. 6.95 (*1-56293-545-3*) McClanahan Bk.

— Dinosaurs. (At Your Fingertips Ser.). (Illus.). 12p. (J). (ps-2). 1993. bds. 6.95 (*1-56293-336-1*) McClanahan Bk.

— The Happy Little Dinosaur. (Storytime Bks.). (Illus.). 24p. (Orig.). (J). (gr. k-1). 1990. pap. 0.99 (*1-878624-34-2*) McClanahan Bk.

— The Happy Little Engine. (Storytime Bks.). 24p. (Orig.). (J). (gr. k-1). 1990. pap. 0.99 (*1-878624-43-1*) McClanahan Bk.

— The Human Body. (At Your Fingertips Ser.). (Illus.). 10p. (J). (ps-2). 1995. bds. 6.95 (*1-56293-546-1*) McClanahan Bk.

— Insects. (At Your Fingertips Ser.). (Illus.). 12p. (J). (ps-2). 1993. bds. 6.95 (*1-56293-335-3*) McClanahan Bk.

— Jungle Life. (At Your Fingertips Ser.). (Illus.). 10p. (J). (ps-2). 1992. bds. 6.95 (*1-56293-221-7*) McClanahan Bk.

— Little Bear's First Christmas. (Illus.). 24p. (J). (ps-2). 1994. 0.99 (*1-56293-498-8*) McClanahan Bk.

— Mammals. (At Your Fingertips Ser.). (Illus.). 12p. (J). (ps-2). 1993. bds. 6.95 (*1-56293-337-X*) McClanahan Bk.

— My First Numbers. (Learn Today for Tomorrow Ser.). (Illus.). 32p. (J). (ps). 1991. student ed 1.95 (*1-56293-166-0*) McClanahan Bk.

— My First Picture Dictionary. (Storytime Bks.). (Illus.). 24p. (J). (ps-2). 1992. pap. 0.99 (*1-56293-110-5*) McClanahan Bk.

— Night Animals. (At Your Fingertips Ser.). (Illus.). 10p. (J). (ps-2). 1992. bds. 6.95 (*1-56293-223-3*) McClanahan Bk.

— North American Indians. (At Your Fingertips Ser.). (Illus.). 10p. (J). (ps-2). 1995. bds. 6.95 (*1-56293-548-8*) McClanahan Bk.

— Reptiles. (At Your Fingertips Ser.). (Illus.). 10p. (J). (ps-2). 1992. bds. 6.95 (*1-56293-220-9*) McClanahan Bk.

— Rocks & Minerals. (At Your Fingertips Ser.). (Illus.). 10p. (J). (ps-2). 1995. bds. 6.95 (*1-56293-547-X*) McClanahan Bk.

— Sea Creatures. (At Your Fingertips Ser.). (Illus.). 10p. (J). (ps-2). 1992. bds. 6.95 (*1-56293-222-5*) McClanahan Bk.

— Space. (At Your Fingertips Ser.). (Illus.). 12p. (J). (ps-2). 1993. bds. 6.95 (*1-56293-338-8*) McClanahan Bk.

— Who Wears Shoes? (Interactive Photo Big Bks.). (Illus.). 16p. (J). (ps-2). 1994. pap. text ed. 14.95 (*1-56784-303-4*) Newbridge Comms.

Nayer, Judy, ed. Mother Goose. (Storytime Bks.). (Illus.). 24p. (J). (ps-2). 1992. pap. 0.99 (*1-56293-105-9*) McClanahan Bk.

— My First Book of Christmas Carols. (Storytime Christmas Bks.). (Illus.). 24p. (J). (ps-2). 1991. pap. 0.99 (*1-56293-117-2*) McClanahan Bk.

— Rhymes to Count On. (Storytime Bks.). (Illus.). 24p. (J). (ps-2). 1992. pap. 0.99 (*1-56293-104-0*) McClanahan Bk.

Nayer, Louise. The Houses Are Covered in Sound: Poems. LC 89-81826. 59p. (Orig.). 1990. pap. 10.00 (*0-9619744-2-7*) Blue Light Pr.

*__Nayfeh & Mook.__ Nonlinear Oscillations. (Classics Library). 1995. pap. text ed. 59.95 (*0-471-12142-8*) Wiley.

Nayfeh, Ali H. Introduction to Perturbation Techniques. LC 80-15233. 519p. 1981. text ed. 104.00 (*0-471-08033-0*, Wiley-Interscience) Wiley.

— Introduction to Perturbation Techniques. LC 80-15233. (Classics Library). 536p. 1993. pap. text ed. 54.95 (*0-471-31013-1*) Wiley.

— Methods of Normal Form. 232p. 1993. text ed. 54.95 (*0-471-59354-0*) Wiley.

— Perturbation Methods. LC 72-8068. (Pure & Applied Mathematics Ser.). 425p. 1973. text ed. 113.95 (*0-471-63059-4*) Wiley.

— Problems in Perturbation. LC 85-3173. 556p. 1985. text ed. 79.95 (*0-471-82292-2*) Wiley.

Nayfeh, Ali H. & Mook, Dean T. Nonlinear Oscillations. LC 78-27102. (Pure & Applied Mathematics Ser.). 704p. 1979. text ed. 144.00 (*0-471-03555-6*, Wiley-Interscience) Wiley.

Nayfeh, M. H. & Clark, C. W., eds. Atomic Excitation & Recombination in External Fields. LC 85-9780. 492p. 1985. text ed. 216.00 (*2-88124-043-7*) Gordon & Breach.

Nayler, G. H. Dictionary of Mechanical Engineering. 3rd ed. (Illus.). 400p. 1985. text ed. 84.95 (*0-408-01505-5*) Buttrwrth-Heinemann.

Nayler, J. Concise Encyclopaedic Dictionary of Astronautics. 1964. 20.50 (*0-444-99986-8*) Elsevier.

Nayler, W. G. Amlodipine. LC 93-23381. (Illus.). 325p. 1993. pap. 125.00 (*0-387-56698-8*) Spr-Verlag.

— The Endothelins. (Illus.). 208p. 1990. 77.00 (*0-387-52856-3*) Spr-Verlag.

— Second Generation of Calcium Antagonists. (Illus.). xiii, 226p. 1991. pap. 89.00 (*0-387-54215-9*) Spr-Verlag.

Nayler, Winifred. Calcium Antagonists. 347p. 1988. text ed. 73.00 (*0-12-514645-0*) Acad Pr.

Naylon, John. Western Europe: Economic & Social Studies: Spain. 192p. (C). 1988. pap. 60.00 (*0-317-93198-9*, Pub. by P Chapman Pub UK) St Mut.

*__Naylor.__ Construction Project Management & Scheduling. 96p. 1995. teacher ed 14.00 (*0-8273-5734-6*) Delmar.

— Simulation in Business Planning & Decision-Making. 130p. 1981. 36.00 (*0-685-66780-4*, SS09-1) Soc Computer Sim.

— Television Writer's Guide. 4th ed. 1995. pap. text ed. 47. 00 (*0-943728-75-4*) Lone Eagle Pub.

Naylor & Ralston. Large Animal Clinical Nutrition. (Illus.). 592p. 1991. 75.00 (*0-8016-2902-0*) Mosby Yr Bk.

Naylor, A. R., jt. auth. see Letchford, Frank.

Naylor, A. R., ed. see Letchford, Frank & Naylor, A. R.

Naylor, A. R., ed. see Spare, Austin O. & Wallace, William.

Naylor, A. R., ed. see Wallace, William.

Naylor, A. W. & Sell, George R. Linear Operator Theory in Engineering & Science. (Applied Mathematical Sciences Ser.: Vol. 40). (Illus.). 624p. 1994. 59.00 (*0-387-90748-3*) Spr-Verlag.

Naylor, Alice P., jt. auth. see Borders, Sarah G.

Naylor, Anthony, ed. see Crowley, Aleister.

Naylor, B., jt. auth. see Kim, K.

Naylor, B. Phyllis, ed. see Hodges, William N.

Naylor, C. David. Private Practice, Public Payment: Canadian Medicine & the Politics of Health Insurance, 1911-1966. 324p. (C). 1986. pap. text ed. 22.95 (*0-7735-0568-7*, Pub. by McGill CN) U of Toronto Pr.

Naylor, C. David, ed. Canadian Health Care & the State: A Century of Evolution. 288p. 1992. 49.95 (*0-7735-0934-8*, Pub. by McGill CN); pap. 22.95 (*0-7735-0949-6*, Pub. by McGill CN) U of Toronto Pr.

Naylor, C. W. God's Will & How to Know It. 1986. pap. 8.99 (*0-88019-200-3*) Schmul Pub Co.

— Heart Talks. 279p. 1982. reprint ed. pap. 3.00 (*0-686-36257-8*) Faith Pub Hse.

— The Redemption of Howard Gray. 72p. pap. 0.50 (*0-686-29162-X*) Faith Pub Hse.

Naylor, Charles, jt. auth. see Disch, Thomas M.

Naylor, Chris. The PC Compendium, Vol. 1. 340p. 1987. 25. 95 (*1-85058-087-1*, Pub. by Sigma Pr UK) Bk Clearing Hse.

Naylor, Chris, jt. auth. see Forsyth, Richard S.

Naylor, Colin, ed. Contemporary Artists. 3rd ed. 1989. 145. 00 (*0-912289-96-1*) St James Pr.

— Contemporary Designers. 2nd ed. (Illus.). 641p. 1990. lib. bdg. 145.00 (*0-912289-69-4*) St James Pr.

— Contemporary Masterworks. (Illus.). 933p. 1992. lib. bdg. 139.00 (*1-55862-083-4*, 200104) St James Pr.

— Contemporary Photographers. 2nd ed. 1988. 145.00 (*0-912289-79-1*) St James Pr.

Naylor, D. Geology of Offshore Ireland & West Britain. Shannon, P. M., ed. 174p. 1982. lib. bdg. 76.50 (*0-86010-340-4*); pap. text ed. 38.50 (*0-86010-430-3*) G & T Inc.

Naylor, D., jt. auth. see Duff, George F.

Naylor, D., jt. auth. see Shannon, P. M.

Naylor, David, et al. Coronary Artery Bypass Graft Surgery & Percutaneous Transluminal Coronary Angioplasty: Ratings of Appropriateness & Necessity by a Canadian Panel. LC 93-33095. 1993. write for info. (*0-8330-1452-8*, MR-128-CWF) Rand Corp.

Naylor, David T. & Diem, Richard A. Social Studies for the Twenty-First Century. 416p. (C). 1987. text ed. write for info. (*0-07-555483-6*) McGraw.

Naylor, E. & Hartnoll, E. G., eds. Cyclic Phenomena in Marine Plants & Animals. 1979. 203.00 (*0-08-023217-5*, Pub. by Pergamon Repr UK) Franklin.

Naylor, E. W. An Elizabethan Virginal Book. LC 70-87638. (Music Ser.). 1970. reprint ed. lib. bdg. 35.00 (*0-306-71792-1*) Da Capo.

Naylor, E. W., tr. see Bie, Oskar.

Naylor, Edward W. The Poets & Music. LC 80-16489. (Music Reprint Ser.). 1980. reprint ed. 29.50 (*0-306-76038-X*) Da Capo.

— The Poets & Music. LC 78-66913. (Encore Music Editions Ser.). (Illus.). 1979. reprint ed. 20.75 (*0-88355-753-3*) Hyperion Conn.

— Shakespeare & Music. 2nd ed. LC 65-16244. (Illus.). 1972. reprint ed. 17.95 (*0-405-08814-0*) Ayer.

— Shakespeare & Music. LC 06-1277. reprint ed. 20.00 (*0-404-04652-5*) AMS Pr.

— Shakespeare & Music. LC 65-16244. (Music Reprint Ser.). 1965. reprint ed. lib. bdg. 32.50 (*0-306-70908-2*) Da Capo.

Naylor, Edward W., ed. Shakespeare Music. LC 75-171080. 68p. 1973. reprint ed. lib. bdg. 19.50 (*0-306-70275-4*) Da Capo.

Naylor, Eric W., ed. The Text & Concordances of the Escorial Manuscript of the Arcipreste de Talavera of Alfonso Martinez de Toledo. (Spanish Ser.: No. 12). 6p. 1983. 10.00 (*0-942260-38-4*) Hispanic Seminary.

Naylor, Eric W., jt. auth. see Benson, Robert G.

Naylor, Eric W., ed. see De Avinon, Juan.

Naylor, Geoffrey, jt. auth. see McIver, Colin.

Naylor, Gloria. Bailey's Cafe. LC 91-42089. 1992. 19.95 (*0-15-110450-6*) HarBrace.

— Bailey's Cafe. LC 93-13117. (Vintage Contemporaries Ser.). 1993. pap. 11.00 (*0-679-74821-0*, Vin) Random.

— Bailey's Cafe. large type ed. LC 93-9846. 333p. 1993. pap. 16.95 (*0-8161-5720-0*) Hall.

— Mama Day. 1993. pap. 10.00 (*0-394-25625-5*, Vin) Random.

— Selected from The Women of Brewster Place. abr. ed. (Writers' Voices Ser.). 64p. (Orig.). 1991. pap. text ed. 3.50 (*0-929631-33-1*, Signal Hill) New Readers.

Naylor, Gloria R. Linden Hills. (Contemporary American Fiction Ser.). 320p. 1986. pap. 10.00 (*0-14-008829-6*, Penguin Bks) Viking Penguin.

— Mama Day. (Contemporaries Ser.). 1989. pap. 11.00 (*0-679-72181-9*, Vin) Random.

— The Women of Brewster Place. (Contemporary American Fiction Ser.). 208p. 1983. pap. 10.00 (*0-14-006690-X*, Penguin Bks) Viking Penguin.

— The Women of Brewster Place: A Novel in Seven Stories. 1988. pap. 4.50 (*0-318-37688-1*, Penguin Bks) Viking Penguin.

*__Naylor, Grant.__ Red Dwarf, 2 vols. in 1. 432p. 1993. 10.98 (*1-56865-049-3*, GuildAmerica) Dblday Bk Music.

— Red Dwarf: Better Than Life. 304p. (Orig.). 1993. pap. 4.99 (*0-451-45231-3*, ROC) NAL-Dutton.

— Red Dwarf: Infinity Welcomes Careful Drivers. 304p. 1992. pap. 4.99 (*0-451-45201-1*, ROC) NAL-Dutton.

Naylor, H. & Hagger, S. First Certificate Handbook: Key. (C). 1988. 35.00 (*0-85950-908-7*, Pub. by S Thornes Pubs UK) St Mut.

Naylor, Harriet H. The Role of the Volunteer Director in the Care of the Terminal Patient & the Family. 1981. 19. 95 (*0-405-13092-9*) Ayer.

— The Role of the Volunteer in the Care of the Terminal Patient & the Family. 1981. 17.95 (*0-405-13091-0*) Ayer.

*__Naylor, Henry F. W.__ Construction Project Management: Planning & Scheduling. 304p. 1995. 44.95 (*0-8273-5733-8*) Delmar.

Naylor, Honey. Insider's Guide to New Orleans. Rosenberg, Dan, ed. LC 93-41742. (Insider's Guide Ser.). (Illus.). 256p. (Orig.). 1994. pap. 9.95 (*1-55832-063-6*) Harvard Common Pr.

Naylor, J. Marketing. 1985. 60.00 (*0-85297-071-4*, Pub. by Inst Bankers UK) St Mut.

— Practical Theory of Tanning Leather: 1890-1987. (Illus.). 150p. 1991. pap. 20.00 (*0-87556-359-7*) Saifer.

Naylor, James. The New Democracy: Challenging the Social Order in Industrial Ontario, 1914-1925. 288p. 1992. text ed. 55.00 (*0-8020-5953-8*); pap. text ed. 18.95 (*0-8020-6886-3*) U of Toronto Pr.

Naylor, James B. Under Mad Anthony's Banner. 1993. reprint ed. lib. bdg. 89.00 (*0-7812-5393-4*) Rprt Serv.

Naylor, Jay H., jt. auth. see Jensen, Clayne R.

*__Naylor, John.__ Operations Management. 288p. 1995. pap. 37.50 (*0-7121-1054-2*, Pub. by Pitman Pub Ltd UK) Trans-Atl Phila.

Naylor, John & Senior, Barbara. Incompressible Unemployment: Cause, Consequences & Alternatives. 214p. 1988. text ed. 54.95 (*0-566-05530-9*, Pub. by Avebury Pub UK) Ashgate Pub Co.

Naylor, John, jt. auth. see Senoir, Barbara.

Naylor, John F. A Man & an Institution: Sir Maurice Hankey, the Cabinet Secretariat & the Custody of Cabinet Secrecy. LC 83-20930. 416p. 1984. 79.95 (*0-521-25583-X*) Cambridge U Pr.

N

An Asterisk (*) at the beginning of an entry indicates that the title is appearing in BIP for the first time.

Naylor, Keith, jt. auth. see St. Clair, Barry.

Naylor, Kim. Discovery Guide to Rajasthan with Delhi & Agra. 224p. (C). 1990. 90.00 (0-902743-49-X, Pub. by IMMEL Pubng UK) St Mut.
— Discovery Guide to Vietnam. 224p. (C). 1990. 79.00 (0-907151-71-X, Pub. by IMMEL Pubng UK) St Mut.
— Discovery Guide to West Africa: The Niger & Gambia River Route. 224p. (C). 1990. 79.00 (0-902743-67-8, Pub. by IMMEL Pubng UK) St Mut.
— Guide to Rajasthan. (Travel Guides Ser.). (Illus.). 160p. 1989. pap. 14.95 (0-87052-368-6) Hippocrene Bks.
— Mali. (Let's Visit Places & Peoples of the World Ser.). (Illus.). 96p. (J). (gr. 5 up). 1988. 14.95 (1-55546-181-6) Chelsea Hse.

Naylor, Lynne. Television Directors Guide. 2nd ed. 1994. 40.00 (0-943728-59-2) Lone Eagle Pub.
— Television Writers Guide. 3rd ed. 1993. pap. 45.00 (0-943728-56-8) Lone Eagle Pub.

Naylor, Maria, ed. Authentic Indian Designs. LC 74-17711. (Illus.). 256p. 1975. reprint ed. pap. 9.95 (0-486-23170-4) Dover.

Naylor, N., ed. Marketing. (C). 1989. 40.00 (0-85297-175-3, Pub. by Inst Bankers UK) St Mut.

Naylor, N., jt. ed. see McIver, M.

Naylor, Natalie A, ed. The Roots & Heritage of Hempstead Town. (Illus.). 256p. 1994. lib. bdg. 25.00 (1-55787-124-8, NY71063) Hrt of the Lakes.
— The Roots & Heritage of Hempstead Town. (Illus.). 256p. 1994. pap. 15.00 (1-55787-109-4, NY71064) Heart of the Lakes.

Naylor, Natalie A., jt. ed. see Krieg, Joann P.

Naylor, Natalie A., et al. Long Island's History & Cultural Heritage: An Integrative Curriculum Resource for Educators. LC 92-63132. (Illus.). 70p. 1992. pap. 7.00 (0-943526-23-X) Parrish Art.

Naylor, Natalie A., et al, eds. Theodore Roosevelt: Many-Sided American. (Long Island Studies). (Illus.). 678p. 1992. lib. bdg. 55.00 (1-55787-085-3, NY71048) Hrt of the Lakes.

Naylor, Patrick. Introduction to Metal Ceramic Technology. (Illus.). 1992. text ed. 68.00 (0-86715-237-0) Quint Pub Co.

Naylor, Peter. Discovering Dowsing & Divining. 1980. pap. 4.50 (0-913714-54-2) Legacy Books.
— Discovering Dowsing & Divining. 1989. pap. 25.00 (0-85263-516-8, Pub. by Shire UK) St Mut.

Naylor, Phillip C. & Heggoy, Alf A. The Historical Dictionary of Algeria. 2nd ed. LC 93-26302. (African Historical Dictionaries Ser.: No. 59). 1993. write for info. (0-8108-2748-4) Scarecrow.

Naylor, Phillip C., jt. ed. see Entelis, John P.

Naylor, Phyllis R. The Agony of Alice. LC 85-7957. 144p. (J). (gr. 4-9). 1985. text ed., lib. bdg. 13.95 (0-689-31143-5, Atheneum Bks Young) S&S Childrens.
— Alice in April. (J). (gr. 4-7). 1995. pap. 3.50 (0-440-40944-6) Dell.
— Alice in April. LC 92-17016. 176p. (J). (gr. 4-8). 1993. text ed. 14.95 (0-689-31805-7, Atheneum Bks Young) S&S Childrens.
— Alice In-Between. LC 93-8167. 160p. (J). (gr. 5-9). 1994. text ed. 14.95 (0-689-31890-1, Atheneum Bks Young) S&S Childrens.
— Alice in Rapture, Sort Of. (J). (gr. 4-7). 1991. pap. 3.50 (0-440-40462-2) Dell.
— Alice in Rapture, Sort Of. LC 88-8174. 176p. (J). (gr. 3-7). 1989. text ed. 13.95 (0-689-31466-3, Atheneum Bks Young) S&S Childrens.
— Alice the Brave. LC 94-32340. (J). 1995. write for info. (0-689-80095-9, Atheneum S&S) S&S Trade.
— All about Alice. (J). (gr. 4-7). 1994. pap. 3.50 (0-440-40918-7) Dell.
— All but Alice. LC 91-28722. 160p. (J). (gr. 4-8). 1992. text ed. 13.95 (0-689-31773-5, Atheneum Bks Young) S&S Childrens.
— An Amish Family. 18.95 (0-8488-0109-1, Amereon Hse) Amereon Ltd.
— Beetles, Lightly Toasted. LC 87-911. 144p. (J). (gr. 3-7). 1987. text ed. 13.95 (0-689-31355-1, Atheneum Bks Young) S&S Childrens.
— Being Danny's Dog. LC 95-5280. (J). 1995. write for info. (0-689-31756-5, Atheneum Bks Young) S&S Childrens.
— Bernie & the Bessledorf Ghost. 144p. (J). 1992. pap. 3.50 (0-380-71351-9, Camelot) Avon.
— Bernie & the Bessledorf Ghost. LC 88-29389. (Bessledorf Mysteries Ser.). 144p. (J). (gr. 3-7). 1990. text ed. 13.95 (0-689-31499-X, Atheneum Bks Young) S&S Childrens.
— The Bodies in the Bessledorf Hotel. 112p. 1988. pap. 2.99 (0-380-70485-4, Camelot) Avon.
— The Bodies in the Bessledorf Hotel. LC 86-3602. 144p. (J). (gr. 3-7). 1986. text ed. 13.95 (0-689-31304-7, Atheneum Bks Young) S&S Childrens.
— The Boy with the Helium Head. (J). (ps-3). 1992. 3.50 (0-440-40644-7, YB) Dell.
— Boys Against Girls. LC 93-37683. (Illus.). (J). 1994. 14.95 (0-385-32081-7) Delacorte.
— Boys Start the War. LC 92-249. (J). (gr. 4-7). 1993. 14.95 (0-385-30814-0) Doubleday.
— Boys Start the War - The Girls Get Even. (J). (gr. 4-7). 1994. mass mkt. 4.99 (0-440-40971-3) Dell.
— The Dark of the Tunnel. LC 84-20441. 216p. (YA). (gr. 8 up). 1985. lib. bdg. 14.95 (0-689-31098-6, Atheneum Bks Young) S&S Childrens.
— Ducks Disappearing. LC 95-10281. (Illus.). (J). 1996. write for info. (0-689-13902-0, Atheneum Bks Young) S&S Childrens.
— Eddie, Incorporated. LC 79-22589. (Illus.). 112p. (J). (gr. 4-6). 1980. text ed. 13.95 (0-689-30754-3, Atheneum Bks Young) S&S Childrens.
— The Face in the Bessledorf Funeral Parlor. LC 92-32613. 160p. (J). (gr. 3-7). 1993. text ed. 13.95 (0-689-31802-2, Atheneum Bks Young) S&S Childrens.
— The Fear Place. LC 93-38891. (J). 1994. text ed. 14.95 (0-689-31866-9, Atheneum Bks Young) S&S Childrens.
— The Girls Got Even. LC 92-43047. (J). 1993. 13.95 (0-385-31029-3) Delacorte.
— The Grand Escape. LC 91-40816. (Illus.). 160p. (J). (gr. 3-7). 1993. text ed. 14.00 (0-689-31722-0, Atheneum Bks Young) S&S Childrens.
— Grand Escape. 1994. mass mkt. 3.99 (0-440-40968-3) Dell.
— How I Came to Be a Writer. LC 86-32283. (Illus.). 144p. (J). (gr. 4). 1987. reprint ed. pap. 4.95 (0-689-71129-8, Aladdin Paperbacks) S&S Childrens.
— How Lazy Can You Get? (J). (gr. 4-7). 1992. pap. 3.50 (0-440-40608-0) Dell.
— How Lazy Can You Get? (J). (gr. k-6). 1993. 17.00 (0-8446-6691-2) Peter Smith.
— Ice. LC 95-5279. (J). 1995. write for info. (0-689-80005-3, Atheneum Bks Young) S&S Childrens.
— Josie's Troubles. (J). (gr. 4-7). 1994. pap. 3.50 (0-440-40862-8) Dell.
— Josie's Troubles. LC 90-47641. (Illus.). 112p. (J). (gr. 3-7). 1992. text ed. 13.95 (0-689-31659-3, Atheneum Bks Young) S&S Childrens.
— The Keeper. LC 85-20029. 228p. (YA). (gr. 5 up). 1986. text ed. 14.95 (0-689-31204-0, Atheneum Bks Young) S&S Childrens.
— Keeping a Christmas Secret. LC 88-29277. (Illus.). 32p. (J). (ps-2). 1989. text ed. 13.95 (0-689-31447-7, Atheneum Bks Young) S&S Childrens.
— Keeping a Christmas Secret. LC 93-12248. (Illus.). 32p. (J). (gr. k-2). 1993. reprint ed. pap. 4.95 (0-689-71760-1, Aladdin Paperbacks) S&S Childrens.
— King of the Playground. (Illus.). 32p. (J). (ps-3). 1991. text ed. 13.95 (0-689-31558-9, Atheneum Bks Young) S&S Childrens.
— King of the Playground. LC 93-25125. (Illus.). 32p. (J). (ps-3). 1994. reprint ed. pap. 4.95 (0-689-71802-0, Aladdin Paperbacks) S&S Childrens.
— The Mad Gasser of Bessledorf Street. 112p. (J). 1992. pap. 3.50 (0-380-71350-0, Camelot) Avon.
— Maudie in the Middle. (J). 1990. reprint ed. pap. 3.25 (0-440-40324-3, Yearling Classics) Dell.
— Night Cry. LC 83-15569. 168p. (J). (gr. 5-9). 1984. text ed. 14.95 (0-689-31017-X, Atheneum Bks Young) S&S Childrens.
— Old Sadie & the Christmas Bear. LC 84-2995. (Illus.). 32p. (J). (ps-2). 1984. text ed. 13.95 (0-689-31052-8, Atheneum Bks Young) S&S Childrens.
— One of the Third-Grade Thonkers. (J). (gr. 4-7). 1991. pap. 3.99 (0-440-40407-X) Dell.
— One of the Third-Grade Thonkers. LC 88-3130. (Illus.). 144p. (J). (gr. 3-7). 1988. text ed. 13.95 (0-689-31424-8, Atheneum Bks Young) S&S Childrens.
— Reluctantly Alice. 196p. (J). (gr. 5 up). 1992. pap. 3.50 (0-440-40685-4, YB) Dell.
— Reluctantly Alice. LC 90-37956. 192p. (J). (gr. 3-7). 1991. text ed. 13.95 (0-689-31681-X, Atheneum Bks Young) S&S Childrens.
— Send No Blessings. 240p. (J). (gr. 5 up). 1992. pap. 3.99 (0-14-034859-X) Puffin Bks.
— Send No Blessings. LC 89-28024. 240p. (YA). (gr. 7 up). 1990. text ed. 14.95 (0-689-31582-1, Atheneum Bks Young) S&S Childrens.
— Shiloh. 144p. (J). (gr. 3-7). 1992. mass mkt. 3.99 (0-440-40752-4, YB) Dell.
— Shiloh. LC 90-603. 144p. (J). (gr. 3-7). 1991. text ed. 13.95 (0-689-31614-3, Atheneum Bks Young) S&S Childrens.
— Shiloh. large type ed. 160p. (J). (gr. 4-8). 1995. lib. bdg. 16.95 (1-885885-10-5, Cornerstone FL) Pages Inc FL.
— To Walk the Skypath. (J). (gr. 4-7). 1992. 3.50 (0-440-40636-6, YB) Dell.
— The Witch Herself. 1992. 17.00 (0-8446-6543-6) Peter Smith.
— Witch Returns. (J). (gr. 4-7). 1993. pap. 3.50 (0-440-40815-6) Dell.
— Witch Weed. (Illus.). 192p. (J). (gr. 4-7). 1992. pap. 3.50 (0-440-40708-7, YB) Dell.
— Witch's Eye. (J). (gr. 4-7). 1991. pap. 3.50 (0-440-40514-9, YB) Dell.
— Witch's Sister. 1992. 18.75 (0-8446-6544-4) Peter Smith.
— The Year of the Gopher. LC 86-17317. 224p. (YA). (gr. 7 up). 1987. text ed. 14.95 (0-689-31333-0, Atheneum Bks Young) S&S Childrens.
— Year of the Gopher. 1993. pap. 3.50 (0-440-21591-9) Dell.

Naylor, Phyllis R. & Reynolds, Lura S. Maudie in the Middle. LC 87-3470. (Illus.). 176p. (J). (gr. 2-6). 1988. text ed. 14.95 (0-689-31395-0, Atheneum Bks Young) S&S Childrens.

Naylor, R. T. Hot Money: The Politics of Debt. 504p. (Orig.). 1990. pap. text ed. 12.95 (0-04-440188-4) Routledge Chapman & Hall.

Naylor-Reynolds, Phyllis. The Agony of Alice. (J). (gr. k-6). 1988. pap. 3.50 (0-440-40051-1, YB) Dell.
— The Witch Herself. (J). (gr. k-6). 1988. pap. 3.50 (0-440-40044-9) Dell.
— Witch Water. (J). (gr. k-6). 1988. pap. 3.50 (0-440-40038-4, YB) Dell.

Naylor, Robert A. La Influencia Britanica en el Comercio Centroamericano Durante las Primeras Decadas de la Independencia: 1821-1851. LC 87-72666. (Monograph Ser.: No. 3). 400p. (Orig.). (SPA.). 1987. pap. 16.50 (0-910443-04-1) CIRMA.
— Penny Ante Imperialism: The Mosquito Shore & the Bay of Honduras, 1600-1914. LC 87-45735. (Illus.). 320p. 1989. 42.50 (0-8386-3323-4) Fairleigh Dickinson.

Naylor, Robert E. The Baptist Deacon. 1955. 11.99 (0-8054-3501-8) Broadman.
— A Messenger's Memoirs: Sixty-One Southern Baptist Convention Meetings. (Illus.). 304p. (Orig.). 1995. pap. 16.95 (1-881576-46-9) Providence Hse.
— A Messenger's Memoirs: Sixty-One Southern Baptist Convention Meetings. deluxe ed. (Illus.). 304p. (Orig.). 1995. 29.95 (1-881576-48-5) Providence Hse.

Naylor, Sharon. One Thousand One Ways to Save Money... And Still Have a Dazzling Wedding. (Illus.). 288p. 1994. pap. 9.95 (0-8092-3657-5) Contemp Bks.

Naylor, T. H. & Thomas, C., eds. Optimization Models for Strategic Planning. (Studies in Management Science & Systems: Vol. 10). 1984. 87.00 (0-444-86831-3, I-542-83, North Holland) Elsevier.

***Naylor, Thomas, et al.** The Search for Meaning Workbook. 88p. (Orig.). 1994. pap. 8.95 (0-687-00440-3) Abingdon.

Naylor, Thomas H. The Cold War Legacy. 224p. 1991. text ed. 24.95 (0-669-24984-X) Free Pr.
— Corporate Planning Models. LC 77-93329. 1979. text ed. write for info. (0-201-05226-1) Addison-Wesley.
— The Gorbachev Strategy: Opening the Closed Society. LC 86-40219. 272p. 1987. text ed. 24.95 (0-669-13831-2) Free Pr.
— Simulation Models in Corporate Planning. LC 78-31258. (Praeger Special Studies). 312p. 1979. text ed. 55.00 (0-275-90398-2, C0398, Praeger Pubs) Greenwood.

Naylor, Thomas H. & Polzer, Charles W., eds. Pedro de Rivera & the Military Regulations for Northern New Spain, 1724-1729: A Documentary History of His Frontier Inspection & the Reglamento de 1729. LC 88-26098. 367p. 1988. 45.00 (0-8165-1070-9) U of Ariz Pr.
— The Presidio & Militia on the Northern Frontier of New Spain: A Documentary History - 1570-1700, Vol. I. LC 86-13283. 756p. 1986. 65.00 (0-8165-0903-4) U of Ariz Pr.

Naylor, Thomas H., ed. see Design of Computer Simulation Experiments Symposium Staff.

Naylor, Thomas H., et al. The Search for Meaning. LC 93-23618. 224p. 1994. 18.95 (0-687-02586-9) Abingdon.
— SIMPLAN: A Computer Based Planning System for Government. LC 74-75956. 189p. reprint ed. pap. 53.90 (0-317-20449-1, 2023426) Bks Demand.

Naylor, Tom L. The Trumpet & Trombone in Graphic Arts, Fifteen Hundred to Eighteen Hundred. Glover, Stephen L., ed. LC 79-10044. (Brass Research Ser.: No. 9). (Illus.). 1979. lib. bdg. 30.00 (0-914282-20-4) Brass Pr.

***Naylor, Trace.** Computer Troubles: Troubleshoot Them First. (Illus.). 86p. 1995. pap. 24.00 (1-886793-05-0) CompuTutor.

Naylor, W. Patrick. Beginner's Guide to Saving & Investing: Ten Steps to Financial Success. LC 94-6692. 262p. 1994. pap. 14.95 (1-883695-04-X) Edition Q.

Naylor, Wanda & Warda, Mark. How to Make a North Carolina Will. LC 94-66934. 95p. (Orig.). 1994. pap. 9.95 (0-913825-92-1) Sphinx Pub FL.
— How to Start a Business in North Carolina. LC 94-66931. 132p. (Orig.). 1994. pap. 16.95 (0-913825-93-X) Sphinx Pub FL.

***Nayman, Michele.** Jetlag. (Ninety's Title Ser.). 224p. (Orig.). 1995. pap. 11.99 (1-85242-361-7) Serpents Tail.

Naysmith, Kenneth J. Psychic Growth: Dangers & Ecstasies. 168p. 1977. pap. write for info. (0-89540-037-5, SB-037) Sun Pub.

Naythons, Matthew. The Face of Mercy: Medicine at War - A Photographic History. (Illus.). 1993. 40.00 (0-679-42744-9) Random.
— The Mission: Inside the Church of Jesus Christ of Latter-Day Saints. (Illus.). 1995. 49.95 (0-446-51889-1) Warner Bks.
— Sarajevo. 128p. 1994. 29.95 (0-446-51824-7) Warner Bks.

Nayyar, Deepak. India's Exports & Export Policies in the 1960s. LC 75-46206. (Cambridge South Asian Studies: Vol. 19). 410p. reprint ed. pap. 116.90 (0-685-16100-5, 2027248) Bks Demand.
— Industrial Growth & Stagnation: The Debate in India. 350p. 1994. 19.95 (0-19-563442-X) OUP.
— Migration, Remittances & Capital Flow: The Indian Experience. 144p. 1994. 13.95 (0-19-563345-8) OUP.

Nayyar, Kuldip. Report on Afghanistan. 212p. 1980. 15.95 (0-318-37264-9) Asia Bk Corp.

Nayyar, Mohinder L. Piping Handbook. 6th ed. 1992. text ed. 99.50 (0-07-046881-8) McGraw.

Nayyar, Sushila. Kasturba, Wife of Gandhi. (C). 1948. pap. 7.00 (0-87574-000-6) Pendle Hill.

Naz, R. Dictionnaire de Droit Canonique, 7 vols., Set. (FRE.). 1965. 1,195.00 (0-8288-6739-9, M-6423) Fr & Eur.

Naz, Rajesh K., ed. Immunology of Reproduction. 1992. 173.00 (0-8493-5191-X, QP252) CRC Pr.

Nazaikinskii, V. E., jt. auth. see Maslov, V. P.

Nazaikinskii, Vladimir E., et al. Contact Geometry & Linear Differential Equations. LC 92-24930. (Expositions in Mathematics Ser.: No. 6). vii, 216p. (C). 1992. lib. bdg. 82.95 (3-11-013381-4) De Gruyter.

Nazar, Krystyna, et al, eds. International Perspectives in Exercise Physiology. LC 89-37079. (Illus.). 248p. 1990. text ed. 38.00x (0-87322-283-0, BNAZ0283) Human Kinetics.

Nazarain, Soheil, et al. Development & Testing of a Siesmic Pavement Analyzer. 165p. (Orig.). (C). 1993. pap. text ed. 15.00 (0-309-05753-1, SHRP-H-375) SHRP.

Nazaraki, Muneshige & Frabetti, Guiliano. Ukiyo-E Masterpieces in European Collections, Vol. 5: Victoria & Albert Museum II. (Illus.). 272p. 1989. 300.00 (0-87011-876-5) Kodansha.

Nazarea-Sandoval, Virginia D. Local Knowledge & Rural Development in the Philippines. (Food Systems & Agrarian Change Ser.). (Illus.). 264p. 1995. 49.95 (0-8014-2801-7) Cornell U Pr.

Nazarenk, I. I. & Ermakov, A. N. Selenium & Tellurium. (Analytical Chemistry of the Elements Ser.). 249p. 1970. text ed. 62.50 (0-7065-1256-1, Pub. by Keter Pub IS) Coronet Bks.

Nazarenko, I. Kalinka: Russian National Folk Songs. 96p. (C). 1987. 60.00 (0-317-92397-8, Pub. by Collets UK) Pro-Am Music.

Nazarenko, O. K., jt. auth. see Paton, B. E.

Nazarenko, V. A. Germanium. (Analytical Chemistry of the Elements Ser.). 328p. 1970. text ed. 80.50 (0-7065-1435-1, Pub. by Keter Pub IS) Coronet Bks.

Nazareno, Rodolfo L., jt. auth. see Chua, Romulo L.

***Nazareth.** The General Is Up. Date not set. per. 10.95 (0-920661-19-X) InBook.

Nazareth, Brig J. Creative Thinking in Warfare. 1987. 34.00 (81-7062-035-X, Pub. by Lancer II) S Asia.

Nazareth, J. L. Computer Solution of Linear Programs. (Monographs on Numerical Analysis). (Illus.). 254p. 1988. 39.95 (0-19-504278-6) OUP.

Nazareth, John L. The Newton-Cauchy Framework: A Unified Approach to Unconstrained Nonlinear Minimization. LC 93-49417. (Lecture Notes in Computer Science Ser.: Vol. 769). xii, 101p. 1994. pap. 26.00 (0-387-57671-1) Spr-Verlag.

Nazareth, Ralph, ed. see Gomes, Antonio.

Nazareth, Ralph, jt. ed. see Sorensen, Lynda.

Nazarian, Bruce. Recording Production Techniques for Musicians. (Illus.). 96p. 1988. pap. 14.95 (0-8256-1177-6, AM69402) Music Sales.

Nazario. Anarcoma. Metz, Bernd, ed. Rosenthal, David, tr. (Illus.). 64p. 1984. 9.95 (0-87416-000-6) Catalan Communs.

Nazario, Manuel A. El Habla Campesina del Pais. LC 89-5385. 616p. (Orig.). (SPA.). 1990. pap. 28.00 (0-8477-3635-0) U of PR Pr.
— Origenes y Desarrollo del Espanol en Puerto Rico: Siglos XVI y XVII. LC 80-21477. 470p. 1982. 15.00 (0-8477-3197-9); pap. 12.00 (0-8477-3198-7) U of PR Pr.

Nazario, Thomas A. Street Law: A Course in Practical Law: California Supplement. 2nd ed. (Illus.). 480p. 1984. pap. text ed. 35.50 (0-314-84398-1) West Pub.

***Nazarko, Linda.** Nursing in Nursing Homes. LC 94-49058. 1995. write for info. (0-632-03987-6) Blackwell Sci.

Nazaroff, Pavel. Hunted Through Central Asia. Burr, Malcolm, tr. (Illus.). 352p. 1993. pap. 10.95 (0-19-285295-7) OUP.

Nazaroff, W. W., et al. Airborne Particles in Museums: Research in Conservation, No. 2. LC 92-35622. (Illus.). 144p. (Orig.). 1993. pap. 25.00 (0-89236-187-5) J P Getty Trust.

Nazaroff, William W. & Nero, Anthony V., eds. Radon & Its Decay Products in Indoor Air. LC 87-8915. (Environmental Science & Technology Ser.). 518p. 1988. text ed. 129.00 (0-471-62810-7) Wiley.

Nazarov, Bakhtiar, ed. Essays in Uzbek History, Culture, & Language. (Uralic & Altaic Ser.: Vol. 156). 128p. 1993. 25.00 (0-933070-29-2) Ind U Res Inst.

Nazarov, S. A. & PLamenevsky, Boris A. Elliptic Problems in Domains with Piecewise Smooth Boundaries. LC 94-7660. (Expositions in Mathematics Ser.). vii, 525p. 1994. 148.95 (3-11-013522-1) De Gruyter.

***Nazarov, V. M. & Frontasieva, M. V., eds.** Activation Analysis in Environmental Protection. (Illus.). 520p. (C). 1995. pap. text ed. 60.00 (0-911767-90-8) Hadronic Pr Inc.

Nazel, Joe. Black Cop. 1993. pap. 3.95 (0-87067-761-6) Holloway.
— Foxtrap. 1986. pap. 2.50 (0-87067-280-0, BH280) Holloway.
— Killer Cop. rev. ed. (Black Cop Ser.: No. 3). (Orig.). 1984. pap. 3.50 (0-87067-321-1) Holloway.
— Thurgood Marshall. 1993. pap. 3.95 (0-87067-584-2, Melrose Sq) Holloway.

Nazel, Joseph. B. B. King: Jazz Musician. (Black American Ser.). (Illus.). 208p. (YA). 1995. 4.95 (0-87067-792-6, Melrose Sq) Holloway.
— Black Fury. (Orig.). 1976. pap. 2.95 (0-87067-058-1, BH058) Holloway.
— Death for Hire. (Orig.). 1990. pap. 3.50 (0-87067-342-4) Holloway.
— Delta Crossing. (Orig.). 1984. pap. 2.75 (0-87067-712-8, BH712) Holloway.
— Finders Keepers, Losers Weepers. (Orig.). 1987. pap. 3.25 (0-87067-728-4) Holloway.
— Iceman, No. Five: Spinning Target. (Orig.). 1974. pap. 2.25 (0-87067-090-5, BH090) Holloway.
— Iceman, No. Four: Sunday Fix. (Orig.). 1974. pap. 2.25 (0-87067-089-1, BH089) Holloway.
— Iceman, No. One: Billion Dollar Death. (Orig.). pap. 2.25 (0-87067-086-7, BH086) Holloway.
— Iceman, No. Seven: The Shakedown. (Orig.). 1975. pap. 2.25 (0-87067-092-1, BH092) Holloway.
— Iceman, No. Six: Canadian Kill. (Orig.). 1974. pap. 2.25 (0-87067-091-3, BH091) Holloway.
— Iceman, No. Three: Slick Revenge. (Orig.). pap. 2.25 (0-87067-088-3, BH088) Holloway.
— Iceman, No. Two: The Golden Shaft. (Orig.). pap. 2.25 (0-87067-087-5, BH087) Holloway.
— Langston Hughes. (Black American Ser.). (Illus.). 192p. (Orig.). (YA). 1994. pap. 3.95 (0-87067-591-5, Melrose Sq) Holloway.
— Martin Luther King, Jr. 1991. pap. 3.95 (0-87067-573-7, Melrose Sq) Holloway.
— Richard Pryor. (Orig.). 1980. pap. 2.25 (0-87067-013-1, BH013) Holloway.
— Satan's Master. (Orig.). 1983. pap. 2.50 (0-87067-259-2, BH259) Holloway.
— Street Wars. (Orig.). 1987. pap. 2.50 (0-87067-284-3) Holloway.

An Asterisk (*) at the beginning of an entry indicates that the title is appearing in BIP for the first time.

— Uprising. (Orig.). 1976. pap. 2.50 (*0-87067-295-9*, BH295) Holloway.
— The Wolves of Summer. (Orig.). 1984. pap. 3.50 (*0-87067-339-4*, BH339) Holloway.
Nazem. Applied Time Series for Business & Economic Forecasting. (Statistics: Textbooks & Monographs: Vol. 93). 448p. 1988. 125.00 (*0-8247-7913-4*) Dekker.
Nazemetz, John, et al. Workbook to Introduction to Industrial & Systems Engineering. 3rd ed. 1993. pap. text ed. 15.40 (*0-13-489485-5*) P-H.
Nazey, Sonia, jt. ed. see Loughlin, John.
Nazigian, Arthur. Teach Them Diligently. 1986. pap. 2.99 (*0-8010-6747-2*) Baker Bk.
Nazim, M. Accountancy. 1987. 100.00 (*0-317-61963-2*) St Mut.
Nazim, M. A Coprehensive Foundation in Accountancy. 1985. 90.00 (*0-946796-04-1*) St Mut.
Nazir-Ali, Michael. Islam: A Christian Perspective. LC 84-3615. 186p. (Orig.). 1984. pap. 12.99 (*0-664-24527-7*, Westminster) Westminster John Knox.
Nazir, Pervaiz. Local Development in the Global Economy: The Case of Pakistan. 219p. 1991. text ed. 68.95 (*1-85628-106-X*, Pub. by Avebury Pub UK) Ashgate Pub Co.
***Nazmi, Nader.** Economic Policy & Stabilization in Latin America. (Illus.). 288p. 1995. 55.00 (*1-56324-583-3*); pap. 24.95 (*1-56324-584-1*) M E Sharpe.
***Nazri, F. A., et al, eds.** Solid State Ionics: 1994 MRS Fall Meeting, Boston, MA, Vol. IV. (MRS Symposium Proceedings Ser.). 1995. 77.00 (*1-55899-271-5*, 369K4) Materials Res.
Nazri, G., et al, eds. Solid State Ionics: Materials Research Society Symposium Proceedings, Vol. 135. 1989. text ed. 55.00 (*1-55899-008-9*) Materials Res.
Nazri, G. A., ed. see Armand, M.
Nazri, G. A., et al, eds. Solid State Ionics II: Materials Research Society Symposium Proceedings, Vol. 210. 722p. 1991. text ed. 58.00 (*1-55899-102-6*) Materials Res.
Nazri, Gholam-Abbas, jt. ed. see Julien, Christian.
Nazvi, Hamida K. Agricultural, Industrial & Urban Dynamism under the Sultans of Delhi, 1206-1555. 1986. 26.00 (*81-215-0002-8*, Pub. by Munshiram Manoharial II) S Asia.
Nazworth, Lenora H. The Pride of Dixie. 1993. 13.95 (*0-8034-9025-9*) Bouregy.
— River's Call. 1993. 13.95 (*0-8034-8994-3*) Bouregy.
Nazzari, Muriel. Disappearance of the Dowry: Women, Families, & Social Change in Sao Paulo, Brazil, 1600-1900. 272p. 1991. 37.50 (*0-8047-1928-4*) Stanford U Pr.
Nazzaro-Boston, Jean, ed. Exceptional Timetables: Historical Events Affecting the Handicapped & Gifted. 1977. pap. text ed. 5.00 (*0-86586-031-9*, P157) Coun Exc Child.
***NBA Conditioning Coaches Staff.** Condition the NBA Way: Pro Basketball Insiders' Strengthening Secrets. 208p. 1994. 19.95 (*1-56977-886-8*) Cadell & Davies.
NBA Properties Inc. National Basketball Encyclopedia. 1994. pap. 39.95 (*0-679-43293-0*) Random.
NBC News Division Staff & Pearce, Alan. NBC News Division & the Economics of Prime Time Access, Washington D. C., September 1973: Proceedings, 2 vols. in 1. Sterling, Christopher H., ed. LC 78-21730. (Dissertations in Broadcasting Ser.). 1980. lib. bdg. 31.95 (*0-405-11768-X*) Ayer.
NBPA Staff & Armstead. Sergeant's Assessment Center: A Training Manual for Law Enforcement Officers, Vol. I. 224p. 1993. per. 19.95 (*0-8403-8713-X*) Kendall-Hunt.
— Sergeant's Assessment Center: A Training Manual for Law Enforcement Officers, Vol. II. 176p. per. 19.95 (*0-8403-8714-8*) Kendall-Hunt.
NCA Staff. NCA Review for the Clinical Laboratory Sciences. 2nd ed. 1989. 32.95 (*0-316-59925-5*) Little.
NCAA Staff. NCAA Football's Finest All-Time Great Players & Coaches. 1991. 21.95 (*1-880141-03-5*); pap. 7.95 (*0-9624436-8-9*) Triumph Bks.
— Official Rules of Basketball, 1995. 190p. 1994. pap. 8.95 (*1-880141-89-2*) Triumph Bks.
NCARB. NCARB Architect Registration Examination Handbook, 1990, 2 vols., Set, Vols. I & II. FAIA Staff et al, eds. (A. R. E. Handbook Ser.). (Illus.). (Orig.). 1990. Set: Vol. I, 243p.; Vol. II, 166p. pap. 95.00 (*0-941575-12-8*) NCARB.
NCARB Staff. Architect Overseas Practice Standards: A Guide to Selected Countries. 115p. (Orig.). 1987. pap. text ed. 5.00 (*0-941575-02-0*) NCARB.
— NCARB Architect Registration Examination Handbook, 1989, 2 vols., Set, Vols. 1 & 2. FAIA Staff et al, eds. (A. R. E. Handbook Ser.). (Illus.). (Orig.). 1989. Set: Vol. 1, 218p.; Vol. 2, 192p. pap. 95.00 (*0-941575-09-8*) NCARB.
— NCARB 1987 Architect Registration Examination Handbook, 2 vols., Set. Houseman, William et al, eds. (Illus.). (Orig.). 1987. pap. text ed. 67.50 (*0-941575-03-9*) NCARB.
— NCARB 1987 Architect Registration Examination Handbook, 2 vols., Vol. 1. Houseman, William et al, eds. (Illus.). 171p. (Orig.). 1987. pap. text ed. 54.00 (*0-941575-04-7*) NCARB.
— NCARB 1987 Architect Registration Examination Handbook, 2 vols., Vol. 2. Houseman, William et al, eds. (Illus.). 120p. (Orig.). 1987. pap. text ed. 27.00 (*0-941575-05-5*) NCARB.
NCCB Ad Hoc Committee on the Moral Evaluation of Deterrence Staff, jt. auth. see National Conference of Catholic Bishops Staff.
NCCB, Bishops' Committee for Pastoral Research & Practices Staff. Faithful to Each Other Forever. (Marriage Is a Sacrament Ser.). 164p. 1989. 22.95 (*1-55586-252-7*) US Catholic.
NCCB, Bishops' Committee on the Liturgy Staff. Bishops' Committee on the Liturgy Newsletter, 1976-1980. 271p. 1981. 5.95 (*1-55586-803-7*) US Catholic.
NCCB, Bishops' Committee on the Liturgy Staff, jt. auth. see NCCB, International Commission on English in the Liturgy Staff.
NCCB Committee on Priestly Life & Ministry. A Shepherd's Care: Reflections on the Changing Role of Pastor. 84p. (Orig.). 1987. pap. 4.95 (*1-55586-166-0*) US Catholic.
NCCB Committee on the Liturgy Staff, jt. auth. see International Commission on English in the Liturgy Staff.
NCCB, International Commission on English in the Liturgy Staff & NCCB, Bishops' Committee on the Liturgy Staff. Rite of Christian Initiation of Adults: Study Edition. 396p. 1988. 7.95 (*1-55586-214-4*) US Catholic.
NCCB, Secretariat of the Bishops' Committee on the Liturgy Staff. The Liturgy of the Hours. (Study Text Ser.: No. 7). 57p. 1981. 3.95 (*1-55586-802-9*) US Catholic.
— Norms Governing Liturgical Calendars. (Liturgy Documentary Ser.: No. 6). 176p. 1984. 6.95 (*1-55586-928-9*) US Catholic.
NCCB Staff. The Church in Our Day. 78p. 1967. 1.25 (*1-55586-041-9*) US Catholic.
— He Aqui a Tu Madre: La Mujer de Fe. 65p. (SPA.). 1973. 2.95 (*1-55586-069-9*) US Catholic.
— Rito de la Iniciacion Cristiana de Adultos. 384p. (SPA.). Date not set. Study ed. student ed 12.95 (*1-55586-509-7*) US Catholic.
— Rito de la Iniciacion Cristiana de Adultos. 384p. (SPA.). 1981. Ritual ed. 34.95 (*1-55586-435-X*) US Catholic.
NCCB Staff, jt. auth. see Committee for Pro-Life Activities Staff.
NCCE Staff & Marburger, Carl L. Who Controls the Schools. 1978. pap. 3.50 (*0-934460-06-X*) NCCE.
NCCL. The Attack on Higher Education. 1978. 25.00 (*0-317-54632-5*, Pub. by NCCL UK) St Mut.
— Civil Disorder & Civil Liberties: Evidence to the Scarman Inquiry. 1981. 30.00 (*0-901108-96-0*, Pub. by NCCL UK) St Mut.
— Civil Liberties & the Miners' Dispute. 40p. (C). 1988. 30.00 (*0-946088-11-X*, Pub. by NCCL UK) St Mut.
— Civil Liberties 1984. Wallington, Peter, ed. 1984. 40.00 (*0-317-54657-0*, Pub. by NCCL UK) St Mut.
— Civil Liberty Briefings: Campaigning on the Public Order Bill, No. 2. 40p. 1984. 20.00 (*0-317-54648-1*, Pub. by NCCL UK) St Mut.
— Civil Liberty Briefings: Police Accountability, No. 3. 40p. 1984. 25.00 (*0-317-54652-X*, Pub. by NCCL UK) St Mut.
— Civil Liberty Briefings: Police & Criminal Evidence, No. 1. 40p. 1984. 40.00 (*0-685-17736-X*, Pub. by NCCL UK) St Mut.
— Civil Rights for Civil Servants. 95p. 1988. 35.00 (*0-946088-09-8*, Pub. by NCCL UK) St Mut.
— The Death of Blair Peach. (C). 1988. 21.00 (*0-901108-91-X*, Pub. by NCCL UK) St Mut.
— Southall: April Twenty-Third, 1979. (C). 1988. 21.00 (*0-901108-85-5*) St Mut.
NCCL Inquiry Staff. Stonehenge. (C). 1988. 21.00 (*0-946088-28-4*, Pub. by NCCL UK) St Mut.
NCCL Staff. Ethnic Minority Language Leaflets. (PAN.). (C). 1988. 21.00 (*0-685-33947-5*, Pub. by NCCL UK) St Mut.
— Hereford, 1984. 1984. 20.00 (*0-317-54887-5*, Pub. by NCCL UK) St Mut.
— Information Sheets on the Prevention of Terrorism Act. (C). 1988. 21.00 (*0-946088-14-4*, Pub. by NCCL UK) St Mut.
— Know Your Rights. 1986. 39.00 (*0-946088-22-5*) St Mut.
— Know Your Rights! (C). 1990. pap. text ed. 39.00 (*0-946088-38-1*, Pub. by NCCL UK) St Mut.
— Making a Complaint Against the Police. (URD.). (C). 1988. 30.00 (*0-685-45098-8*, Pub. by NCCL UK) St Mut.
— The National Council for Civil Liberties: The First Fifty Years. 1984. 20.00 (*0-317-54885-9*, Pub. by NCCL UK) St Mut.
— No Way in Wapping. 1988. 21.00 (*0-946088-27-6*, Pub. by NCCL UK) St Mut.
— A People's Charter: Liberty's Bill of Rights: A Consultation Document. 80p. (C). 1991. text ed. 39.00 (*0-946088-39-X*, Pub. by NCCL UK) St Mut.
— Public Order Campaign Badges: Protest: While You Still Can in Red & Black. 1988. 24.00 (*0-317-54913-8*, Pub. by NCCL UK) St Mut.
— The Purging of the Civil Service. 95p. 1988. 21.00 (*0-946088-17-9*, Pub. by NCCL UK) St Mut.
— Strip Searching: Women Remand Prisoners at Armagh Prison, 1982-85. (C). 1988. 40.00 (*0-946088-20-9*, Pub. by NCCL UK) St Mut.
— Submissions to the Royal Commission on Criminal Procedure. 1979. 20.00 (*0-317-54922-7*, Pub. by NCCL UK) St Mut.
NCCLS Staff. Antimicrobial Susceptibility Testing (SC2) 3rd ed. 200p. 1991. text ed. 160.00 (*1-56238-113-X*) Natl Comm Clin Lab Stds.
— Evaluation Protocols (SC1) 250p. 1991. text ed. 160.00 (*1-56238-000-1*) Natl Comm Clin Lab Stds.
— General Chemistry (SC8) 4th ed. 320p. 1991. text ed. 160.00 (*1-56238-116-4*) Natl Comm Clin Lab Stds.
— General Hematology (SC7) 4th ed. 370p. 1991. text ed. 160.00 (*1-56238-114-8*) Natl Comm Clin Lab Stds.
— Immunoassay (SC6) 4th ed. 300p. 1991. text ed. 190.00 (*1-56238-115-6*) Natl Comm Clin Lab Stds.
— PH & Blood Gas (SC5) 220p. 1989. text ed. 100.00 (*1-56238-149-0*) Natl Comm Clin Lab Stds.
— Physician's Office Laboratory Guidelines & Procedure Manual (POL1-2-T2) 200p. 1989. pap. text ed. 125.00 (*1-56238-159-8*) Natl Comm Clin Lab Stds.
— Specimen Collection (SC2) 400p. 1991. text ed. 265.00 (*1-56238-147-4*) Natl Comm Clin Lab Stds.
***NCEA (Minzey-LeTarte) Staff.** Reforming Public Schools Through Community Education. 256p. 1994. 24.95 (*0-8403-9568-X*) Kendall-Hunt.
***NCEO Staff.** The Employee Ownership Communications Sourcebook. (Illus.). 154p. (Orig.). Date not set. pap. 50.00 (*0-926902-28-8*) NCEO.
— Marketing Your Employee Ownership. (Illus.). 27p. Date not set. pap. 15.00 (*0-926902-27-X*) NCEO.
— NCEO Newsletters, 1989. 70p. (Orig.). (C). 1989. pap. text ed. 15.00 (*0-926902-12-1*) NCEO.
— NCEO Newsletters, 1990. 67p. (Orig.). (C). 1991. pap. text ed. 15.00 (*0-926902-19-9*) NCEO.
— NCEO Newsletters, 1991. 75p. (Orig.). (C). 1992. pap. text ed. 15.00 (*0-926902-22-9*) NCEO.
— NCEO Newsletters, 1992. 75p. (Orig.). 1993. pap. text ed. 15.00 (*0-685-66242-X*) NCEO.
N.C.E.S.R.D. Staff. A Conversation Between James Comer & Ronald Edmonds. 96p. 1989. pap. text ed. 12.00 (*0-8403-5281-6*) Kendall-Hunt.
NCMA Staff. Contract Challenge. 2nd ed. Barrientos, Mary, ed. (National Contract Management Association Workshop Ser.). 104p. 1994. pap. 13.50 (*0-940343-40-1*) Natl Contract Mgmt.
— Submitting Cost or Pricing Data. 2nd ed. (Workshop Ser.). 62p. 1993. pap. 10.95 (*0-940343-60-6*) Natl Contract Mgmt.
— Total Quality Management. (Workshop Ser.). 58p. 1989. pap. 10.95 (*0-940343-61-4*) Natl Contract Mgmt.
***NcNaught, John J.** Massachusetts Evidence: A Courtroom Evidence. LC 87-62743. 391p. 1988. ring bd. 95.00 (*0-944490-66-2*) Mass CLE.
NcNeir, Bob, jt. auth. see Clark, J. Michael.
NCR Corporation Staff. Guide to SCSI: Understanding the Small Computer System Interface. 1989. pap. 19.95 (*0-13-796855-8*) P-H.
— NCR Stakeholder Essay Competition National Winners, 1988: Creating Value for Stakeholders. (Illus.). 73p. (Orig.). 1988. pap. text ed. 11.95 (*0-925738-00-X*) NCR Law.
NCR Corporation Staff, et al. Transforming the Enterprise Through COOPERATION: An Object Oriented Solution. 160p. 1992. pap. text ed. 19.00 (*0-13-088451-0*) P-H.
***NCR Recognition Services Staff.** Designing Documents for Image-Based Recognition. 1993. pap. 36.00 (*0-89258-277-4*, R038) Assn Inform & Image Mgmt.
NCSL Children, Families & Social Services Committee Staff. Family Policy: Recommendations for State Action. Romig, Candace L., ed. (Illus.). 180p. (Orig.). 1989. pap. 25.00 (*1-55516-627-X*, 6115) Natl Conf State Legis.
***NCSL Children Families Program Staff.** 1994 Summary of Children Youth & Family Legislation. 200p. 1994. 20.00 (*1-55516-649-0*, 6131) Natl Conf State Legis.
NCSL Children, Youth & Families Program Staff. State Legislative Summary, 1993: Children, Youth, & Family Issues. 192p. 1993. pap. text ed. 20.00 (*1-55516-647-4*, 6130) Natl Conf State Legis.
NCSL Fiscal Affairs Staff. NCSL State Budget Update: February 1992. (State Legislative Reports: Vol. 17, No. 4). 22p. 1992. pap. text ed. 5.00 (*1-55516-276-2*, 7302-1704) Natl Conf State Legis.
NCSL Fiscal Staff. State Budget Update: April 1992. (State Legislative Reports: Vol. 17, No. 7). 13p. 1992. pap. text ed. 5.00 (*1-55516-279-7*, 7302-1707) Natl Conf State Legis.
***NCSL Health Program Staff.** Maternal & Child Health Legislation 1994. 75p. 1995. 15.00 (*1-55516-609-1*, 6650) Natl Conf State Legis.
NCSL Legislative Management Staff. Campaign Finance Legislation, 1993. 28p. (Orig.). 1994. 5.00 (*1-55516-745-4*, 9363) Natl Conf State Legis.
— State Legislators' Occupations, 1994: A Survey. 35p. 1994. 20.00 (*1-55516-746-2*, 7138) Natl Conf State Legis.
***NCSL Legislative Management Staff & Root, Monica.** Directory of Legislative Leaders 1995. 137p. 1994. 15.00 (*1-55516-744-6*, 7141) Natl Conf State Legis.
NCSL Staff. Directory of Legislative Leaders, 1993. 112p. 1993. pap. text ed. 15.00 (*1-55516-742-X*, 7135) Natl Conf State Legis.
— Election Results Directory, 1993. 282p. 1993. 35.00 (*1-55516-741-1*, 9351) Natl Conf State Legis.
— Election Results Directory, 1994. 300p. 1994. pap. 35.00 (*1-55516-743-8*, 9357) Natl Conf State Legis.
— Election Results Directory, 1995. 282p. 1995. 35.00 (*1-55516-748-9*, 9367) Natl Conf State Legis.
— The HIV-AIDS Fact Finder. 125p. 1993. pap. 25.00 (*1-55516-702-0*, 6640) Natl Conf State Legis.
— Issues Outlook, 1994. 45p. 1994. 30.00 (*1-55516-992-9*, 9355) Natl Conf State Legis.
— 1995 State Legislative Priorities: An Opinion Survey of Leading Lawmakers. 45p. 1995. 30.00 (*1-55516-925-2*, 9368) Natl Conf State Legis.
***NCSL State-Federal Relations Staff.** Summary of One Hundred Second Congress, Second Session, (1992) (State-Federal Issue Brief Ser.: Vol. 5, No. 5). 13p. 1992. 6.50 (*1-55516-899-X*, 8500-0505) Natl Conf State Legis.
NCSS Staff. Alan F. Griffin on Teaching. 92p. 1992. per. 14.95 (*0-8403-8147-6*) Kendall-Hunt.
— Children's Literature & Social Studies: Selecting & Using Notable Books in the Classroom. 96p. 1993. per. 13.95 (*0-8403-8951-5*) Kendall-Hunt.
— Voices of Teachers: Report of a Survey on Social Studies SD 173. 96p. 1991. per. 10.95 (*0-8403-6451-2*) Kendall-Hunt.
NCSU Acid Deposition Program Staff. International Directory of Acid Deposition Researchers, 1985-86 Edition. 2nd ed. 1986. 12.95 (*0-935577-08-4*) Acid Rain Found.
NCTM Commission on Teaching Standards for School Mathematics Staff. Professional Standards for Teaching Mathematics. LC 90-26154. (Illus.). 196p. (Orig.). 1991. pap. 25.00 (*0-87353-307-0*) NCTM.
***NCTM Staff.** Connecting Mathematics Across the Curriculum, 1995 Yearbook: 1995 Yearbook. House, Peggy A. & Coxford, Arthur F., eds. LC 94-48261. (Yearbook Ser.: 1995). (Illus.). 245p. (J). (gr. k-12). 1995. 20.00 (*0-87353-394-1*) NCTM.
— Cumulative Index: The Mathematics Teacher, 1908-1965. LC 42-24844. 207p. 1967. pap. 12.00 (*0-87353-028-4*) NCTM.
— Directory of NCTM Individual Members, 1994. 1012p. (Orig.). 1994. pap. 40.00 (*0-87353-382-8*) NCTM.
— Executive Summary: Curriculum & Evaluation Standards for School Mathematics. (Illus.). 15p. (Orig.). 1989. pap. 1.50 (*0-87353-331-3*) NCTM.
— Executive Summary: Professional Standards for Teaching Mathematics. 16p. (Orig.). 1991. pap. 1.50 (*0-87353-332-1*) NCTM.
— Guidelines for the Use of Calculators in Competitions. 24p. (Orig.). 1989. pap. 7.50 (*0-87353-286-4*) NCTM.
Ncube, Mthuli. Development Dynamics: Theories & Lessons from Zimbabwe. 242p. 1991. text ed. 55.95 (*1-85628-087-X*, Pub. by Avebury Pub UK) Ashgate Pub Co.
NCYM Peace Committee, ed. Faith into Action. 40p. (Orig.). 1985. pap. 2.00 (*0-942727-13-4*) NC Yrly Pubns Bd.
Ndachi, Teresa, ed. see True, Adiaha.
Ndagala, Daniel K. Territory, Pastoralists & Livestock: Resource Control among the Kisongo Maasai. (Uppsala Studies in Cultural Anthropology: No. 18). 192p. (Orig.). 1992. pap. 47.50x (*91-554-2877-0*, Pub. by Almqv & Wiksell SW) Coronet Bks.
Ndatshe, Vivienne, jt. auth. see Moodie, T. Dunbar.
Ndebe, Barnabas S., teller. Tales from Bandiland. (Liberian Studies Monograph Ser.: No. 4). (Illus.). 311p. 1974. 12.00 (*0-916712-07-9*) Arden Assocs.
Ndebele, Njabulo S. Fools & Other Stories. (Readers International Ser.). 280p. (C). 1986. reprint ed. pap. 11.95 (*0-930523-20-2*) Readers Intl.
— South African Literature & Culture: Rediscovery of the Ordinary. LC 93-47154. 1994. text ed. 59.95 (*0-7190-4051-5*, Pub. by Manchester Univ Pr UK); text ed. 19.95 (*0-7190-4052-3*, Pub. by Manchester Univ Pr UK) St Martin.
Ndego, Anne, ed. see Onuzo, Okey.
Ndeti, Kivuto & Gray, Kenneth R., eds. The Second Scramble for Africa: A Response & a Critical Analysis of the Challenges Facing Contemporary Sub-Saharan Africa. 417p. 1992. pap. text ed. 19.95 (*9966-835-73-3*) Prof World Peace.
Ndlovu, Duma, ed. Woza Afrika! A Collection of South African Plays. LC 86-20762. 272p. 1986. pap. 14.95 (*0-8076-1170-0*) Braziller.
Ndlovu, Lindani B. The System of Protection & Industrial Development in Zimbabwe. 246p. 1994. 59.95 (*1-85628-870-6*, Pub. by Avebury Pub UK) Ashgate Pub Co.
Ndongko, Wilfred A. & Vivekananda, Franklin. Bilateral & Multinational Economic Cooperation in West Africa. 350p. 1990. pap. 109.50x (*91-86702-09-2*, Pub. by Almqv & Wiksell SW) Coronet Bks.
— Critical Essays on African & Third World Economic Development, Vol. 1: Africa, the Awakening Giant. 218p. (Orig.). 1989. pap. 84.50x (*91-86702-05-X*, Pub. by Almqv & Wiksell SW) Coronet Bks.
— Economic Development of Cameroon. 230p. (Orig.). 1990. pap. 67.50 (*91-86702-07-6*, Pub. by Almqv & Wiksell SW) Coronet Bks.
Ndreca, Mikel. Albanian-Serbocroatian Dictionary: Fjalor Shallor Shqip-Serbokrpatisht-Shqip. 228p. (ALB & SER.). 1987. pap. 19.95 (*0-8288-1091-5*, F78710) Fr & Eur.
Ndu, Pol. Songs for Seers. LC 73-91413. 35p. 1974. pap. 2.95 (*0-88357-036-X*) NOK Pubs.
Ndubisi, Forster. Planning Implementation Tools & Techniques: A Resource Book for Local Governments. (Illus.). 224p. (Orig.). 1992. pap. text ed. 20.00 (*0-911847-04-9*) U GA Inst Community.
Ndulo, Muna, jt. ed. see Osei-Hwedie, Kwaku.
Ndyajunwoha, Gaston Z., jt. auth. see Nagel, Walter H.
N.E. Thing Enterprises. Magic Eye: A New way of Looking at the World. 1993. 12.95 (*0-8362-7006-1*) Andrews & McMeel.
— Magic Eye Gallery: A Showing of 88 Images. (Illus.). 32p. 1995. 12.95 (*0-8362-7044-4*) Andrews & McMeel.
— Magic Eye II: Now You See It... 1994. 12.95 (*0-8362-7009-6*) Andrews & McMeel.
***N.E. Thing Enterprises Staff.** Disney's Magic Eye: A Book of Postcards. (Illus.). 64p. 1995. pap. 8.95 (*0-8362-3207-0*) Hyperion.
***Ne-Zheng Sun.** Inverse Problems in Groundwater Modeling. LC 94-22252. (Theory & Applications of Transport in Porous Media Ser.: Vol. 6). 1994. lib. bdg. 132.00 (*0-7923-2987-2*) Kluwer Ac.
NEA, jt. auth. see OECD Staff.
NEA Staff, jt. auth. see Kaufman, Les.
NEA Staff, jt. auth. see OECD Staff.
***Neack, Laura, et al, eds.** Foreign Policy Analysis: Continuity & Change in Its Second Generation. 448p. 1995. pap. text ed. write for info. (*0-13-060575-1*) P-H.
Neacsu, L. Dictionary of Ecology: Dictionar de Ecologie. (RUM.). 1982. write for info. (*0-8288-1405-8*, M15838) Fr & Eur.
Nead, Linda, jt. ed. see Marcus, Laura.

N

Nead, Lynda. Myths of Sexuality: Representations of Women in Victorian Britain. (Illus.). 240p. 1990. pap. text ed. 21.95x (*0-631-17257-2*) Blackwell Pubs.

Neade, William. The Double Armed Man. limited ed. LC 68-59329. (Illus.). 51p. 1971. boxed 10.00 (*0-87387-022-0*) Shumway.

Neaderland, Louise. Artist at Work. 1982. 5.00 (*0-942561-08-2*) Bone Hollow.

— A Book of Short Stories. (Illus.). 1986. 25.00 (*0-942561-11-2*) Bone Hollow.

— The Disposable History of the World. (Illus.). (C). 1987. 15.00 (*0-942561-01-5*) Bone Hollow.

— Distress Signals. 58p. 1985. 3.00 (*0-942561-07-4*) Bone Hollow.

— A Mideast Kaleidoscope. (Illus.). 45p. 1983. 15.00 (*0-942561-05-8*) Bone Hollow.

— Missing Persons. 32p. 1988. 15.00 (*0-942561-10-4*) Bone Hollow.

— Nuclear Fan. (Illus.). 1984. 10.00 (*0-942561-02-3*) Bone Hollow.

— Open Roads-Empty Nests. (Illus.). 16p. 1988. 5.00 (*0-942561-12-0*) Bone Hollow.

— Our Glass. (Illus.). 1984. 25.00 (*0-317-91061-2*) Bone Hollow.

— Sadat's Journey. (Illus.). 1981. 5.00 (*0-942561-14-7*) Bone Hollow.

— Scenic Tunnels. (Illus.). 16p. (Orig.). 1983. pap. 12.00 (*0-942561-03-1*) Bone Hollow.

— La Strada. (Illus.). 1986. 12.00 (*0-942561-06-6*) Bone Hollow.

— Straitjacket. (Illus.). 1987. 5.00 (*0-942561-00-7*) Bone Hollow.

— Where Is Home? Basic Elements. (Illus.). 1986. 10.00 (*0-942561-09-0*) Bone Hollow.

Neaderland, Louise & Crist, Steve. Empress Bullett. (Illus.). 1982. 12.00 (*0-942561-13-9*) Bone Hollow.

Neaderland, Louise O. Desert Storm - Desert Sand. (Illus.). 1992. 12.00 (*0-942561-17-1*) Bone Hollow.

— Dialogues. (Illus.). 13p. (Orig.). 1990. 12.00 (*0-942561-15-5*) Bone Hollow.

— Farewells. (Illus.). 20p. 1990. spiral bd. write for info. (*0-942561-16-3*) Bone Hollow.

— Leningrad 8-9-91 - 8-24-91: St. Petersburg 1903. (Illus.). 65p. 1992. 35.00 (*0-942561-19-8*) Bone Hollow.

Neag, Michael, jt. ed. see Riga, Alan T.

Neagles, James C. Confederate Research Sources: A Guide to Archive Collections. LC 86-72004. (Illus.). 286p. (Orig.). 1986. pap. 14.95 (*0-916489-16-7*) Ancestry.

— Summer Soldiers: A Survey & Index of Revolutionary War Courts-Martial. LC 85-73273. (Illus.). 290p. 1986. 19.95 (*0-916489-05-1*) Ancestry.

— U. S. Military Records. LC 94-3848. (Illus.). 455p. 1994. 39.95 (*0-916489-55-8*) Ancestry.

Neagoe, Peter. Winning a Wife, & Other Stories. LC 78-152951. (Short Story Index Reprint Ser.). 1977. reprint ed. 20.95 (*0-8369-3866-6*) Ayer.

Neal. Emergency Interventional Radiology. 1989. 115.00 (*0-316-59927-1*) Little.

Neal & Clark. Hypnotism & Hypnotic Suggestion. 1987. pap. 8.95 (*0-917914-62-7*) Lindsay Pubns.

Neal & Schuman. Storytellers Sourcebook. 2nd ed. 1996. 99.00 (*0-8103-5485-3*) Gale.

Neal, tr. see Donner, Neal & Stevenson, Daniel B., eds.

Neal, et al. Nursing Diagnosis Care Plans for DRGs. 458p. 1990. 25.95 (*0-935236-58-9*) Genl Med Pub.

Neal & Associates Staff, ed. see Swift, Catherine G.

Neal, A. Life Contingencies. (C). 1977. 130.00 (*0-685-45045-7*, Pub. by Witherby & Co UK) St Mut.

Neal, A. W. Formation & Use of Industrial by-Products: A Guide. 1975. 25.00 (*0-8464-0420-6*) Beekman Pubs.

Neal, Adrian. The Path of Life. 64p. Date not set. pap. 5.00 (*1-878096-29-X*) Best E TX Pubs.

Neal, Alan C. & Wright, Frank B., eds. The European Communities' Health & Safety Legislation. 432p. 1993. pap. 99.95 (*0-412-46690-2*) Chapman & Hall.

Neal, Alfred C. Business Power & Public Policy. LC 81-7348. 176p. 1981. text ed. 45.00 (*0-275-90686-8*, C0686, Praeger Pubs) Greenwood.

Neal, Arminta. Exhibits for the Small Museum. LC 76-21812. (Illus.). 169p. 1976. pap. 14.95 (*0-910050-23-6*) AASLH.

— Help! For the Small Museum. 2nd ed. LC 86-30407. (Illus.). 176p. 1987. pap. 21.95 (*0-87108-720-0*) Pruett.

Neal, Bill. Bill Neal's Southern Cooking. enl. rev. ed. LC 88-37258. xv, 204p. 1989. 24.95 (*0-8078-1859-3*); pap. 13.95 (*0-8078-4255-9*) U of NC Pr.

— Biscuits, Spoonbread & Sweet Potato Pie. (Knopf Cooks America Ser.). (Illus.). 320p. 1990. 25.00 (*0-394-55941-X*) Knopf.

— Gardener's Latin: A Lexicon. 1992. 14.95 (*0-945575-94-7*) Algonquin Bks.

Neal, Bill & Perry, David. Good Old Grits Cookbook: Have Grits Your Way. LC 90-50946. (Illus.). 160p. (Orig.). 1991. pap. 6.95 (*0-89480-865-6*, 1865) Workman Pub.

Neal, Bill, ed. see Lawrence, Elizabeth.

Neal, Brook, tr. see Sakabe, Yoshio.

Neal, Carl B. Leonard Shoun & His Wife Barbara Slemp of Johnson County, Tennessee & Their Descendants. 283p. 1985. reprint ed. 28.95 (*0-932807-10-0*); reprint ed. pap. 21.95 (*0-932807-09-7*) Overmountain Pr.

Neal, Charles. Revelation: The Road to Overcoming. LC 89-51876. 214p. 1990. 8.95 (*0-87159-140-5*) Unity Bks.

— Sumac. 301p. (Orig.). 1994. pap. write for info. (*0-9638727-0-2*) Flame Grape.

***Neal, Charles D.** The Life & Times of a Fly Caught up in a Spider's Web: This Is the Way It Is. 1994. 18.95 (*0-533-11062-9*) Vantage.

Neal, Charles L. Parabolas del Evangelio. 144p. 1983. reprint ed. pap. 4.50 (*0-311-04338-0*) Casa Bautista.

Neal, Chellis, ed. see Hoefler, Patricia A.

Neal, Chellis E., ed. see Hoefler, Patricia A.

Neal, Christine C., ed. see Montgomery Museum of Fine Arts Staff.

***Neal, Connie.** Dancing in the Arms of God: Finding Intimacy & Fulfillment in Your Only True Love. 176p. 1995. pap. 14.99 (*0-310-20113-6*) Zondervan.

— Getting Your House (& Life) in Order. 1994. 8.98 (*0-88365-859-3*) Galahad Bks.

Neal, Daniel. The History of New-England... to the Year of Our Lord, 1700, 2 vols., Set. LC 75-31125. reprint ed. 64.00 (*0-404-13760-1*) AMS Pr.

Neal, David. The Rule of Law in a Penal Colony: Law & Politics in Early New South Wales. (Studies in Australian History). 224p. (C). 1992. 59.95 (*0-521-37264-X*) Cambridge U Pr.

Neal, David E., ed. Tumors in Urology: Biology & Clinical Management. LC 94-14579. 1994. write for info. (*0-387-19867-9*) Spr-Verlag.

Neal, Diane & Kremm, Thomas W. The Lion of the South: General Thomas C. Hindman. LC 93-9917. 306p. 1993. text ed. 24.95 (*0-86554-422-0*, MUP/H338) Mercer Univ Pr.

Neal, Donn C., ed. Consortia & Interinstitutional Cooperation. (ACE-Oryx Series on Higher Education). 224p. (C). 1988. 27.95 (*0-02-922510-8*, ACE-Oryx) Oryx Pr.

Neal, Dorothy. Telephone Techniques. 1989. pap. 8.70 (*0-07-046156-2*) McGraw.

Neal, Dorothy A., et al. Procedures for the Electronic Office. 464p. 1988. text ed. 22.56 (*0-07-046146-5*) McGraw.

Neal, Dorothy J., jt. auth. see Neal, James E., Jr.

Neal, Emily G. Celebration of Healing: An Emily Gardiner Neal Reader. Cassel, Anne, ed. LC 92-10866. 210p. 1992. pap. 12.95 (*1-56101-028-6*) Cowley Pubns.

Neal, Eric. Exercises with Your Dictionary. 88p. (C). 1989. 40.00 (*0-7175-0195-7*, Pub. by S Thornes Pubs UK) St Mut.

— A Sentence Dictionary. 432p. (C). 1988. 40.00 (*0-7175-0194-9*, Pub. by S Thornes Pubs UK) St Mut.

Neal, Ernest G. The Natural History of Badgers. LC 85-29248. (Illus.). 264p. reprint ed. pap. 75.30 (*0-7837-6690-4*, 2046307) Bks Demand.

Neal, Frank. Sectarian Violence: The Liverpool Experience, 1819-1914. LC 87-26030. 304p. 1988. text ed. 75.00 (*0-7190-1483-2*, Pub. by Manchester Univ Pr UK) St Martin.

— Sectarian Violence: The Liverpool Experience, 1819-1914: An Aspect of Anglo-Irish History. LC 87-26030. 284p. 1991. text ed. 24.95 (*0-7190-2348-3*, Pub. by Manchester Univ Pr UK) St Martin.

Neal, H. Roger. Streetwise Investing in Rental Properties: A Detailed Strategy for Financial Independence. LC 93-32874. 1994. 15.95 (*1-882877-03-9*) Panoply Pr.

Neal, Homer A. & Wilson, Jack M., eds. The Future of U.S. Doctoral Programs in Physics. (Illus.). 131p. (Orig.). (C). 1990. pap. 12.00 (*0-917853-39-3*, TC-5) Am Assn Physics.

Neal, James E., Jr. Effective Phrases for Performance Appraisals: A Guide to Successful Evaluations. 160p. (C). 1991. spiral bd. write for info. (*0-9609006-6-7*) Neal Pubns Inc.

— Effective Phrases for Performance Appraisals: A Guide to Successful Evaluations. 5th ed. LC 87-92043. 144p. 1988. pap. 6.95 (*0-9609006-5-9*) Neal Pubns Inc.

— Effective Phrases for Performance Appraisals: A Guide to Successful Evaluations. 7th ed. LC 93-85362. 176p. 1994. pap. 8.95 (*1-882423-07-0*) Neal Pubns Inc.

— Effective Resume Writing: A Guide to Successful Employment. LC 90-63084. 104p. (Orig.). (C). 1991. pap. 7.95 (*0-9609006-8-3*) Neal Pubns Inc.

— Effective Resume Writing: A Guide to Successful Employment. 2nd ed. 104p. (Orig.). (C). 1991. pap. write for info. (*0-318-68552-3*) Neal Pubns Inc.

— How to Make a Fortune in Self-Publishing. LC 93-92808. 106p. (Orig.). 1994. pap. text ed. 7.95 (*1-882423-29-1*) Neal Pubns Inc.

— Your Slice of the Melon: A Guide to Greater Job Success. 2nd ed. LC 87-92044. 144p. (C). 1989. pap. 4.95 (*0-9609006-1-6*) Neal Pubns Inc.

Neal, James E., Jr. & Neal, Dorothy J. Effective Letters for Business, Professional & Personal Use: A Guide to Successful Correspondence. 92p. 1989. pap. 5.95 (*0-9609006-9-1*) Neal Pubns Inc.

— Effective Letters for Business, Professional & Personal Use: A Guide to Successful Correspondence. 2nd ed. LC 93-92688. 132p. 1994. pap. text ed. 6.95 (*1-882423-00-3*) Neal Pubns Inc.

***Neal, James R.** Tempest. LC 93-93905. 112p. (Orig.). 1994. pap. 7.00 (*1-56002-344-9*) Aegina Pr.

Neal, John. The Down-Easters, 2 vols. LC 78-64083. reprint ed. 75.00 (*0-404-17310-1*) AMS Pr.

— Log of the Mahina. LC 76-150419. (Illus.). 284p. 1995. pap. 16.95 (*0-918074-02-9*) Pacific Intl.

— Logan, a Family History, 2 vols. LC 78-64085. reprint ed. 75.00 (*0-404-17330-6*) AMS Pr.

— Rachel Dyer. LC 64-10667. 1979. reprint ed. 50.00 (*0-8201-1263-1*) Schol Facsimiles.

— Rachel Dyer, a North American Story. 1988. reprint ed. lib. bdg. 49.00 (*0-7812-0003-2*) Rprt Serv.

Neal, John, jt. auth. see Marrett, Barbara.

Neal, John L., et al. Burning Douglas-Fir Slash: Physical, Chemical & Microbial Effects in the Soil. (Oregon State University, Forest Research Laboratory, Research Papers: No. 1). 35p. reprint ed. pap. 25.00 (*0-8357-7482-1*, 2026109) Bks Demand.

Neal, John R. Disunion & Restoration in Tennessee. LC 78-164390. (Black Heritage Library Collection). 1977. reprint ed. 15.95 (*0-8369-8849-3*) Ayer.

***Neal, John W.** Mother Was a Minister: Evangelizing the World - Beginning at Home. 64p. 1994. pap. 8.95 (*1-881576-32-9*) Providence Hse.

Neal, Joseph C., Jr. Getting Serious about Stewardship. LC 93-80741. 100p. (Orig.). 1993. pap. text ed. 6.00 (*1-883667-05-4*) Christian Meth.

Neal, Joseph C., jt. auth. see James, Douglas A.

Neal, Judith. Fun Projects for Kids: A Teacher's Guide to Classroom Art. LC 83-7657. (Reference Bks.). (Illus.). 136p. (J). (gr. k-6). 1983. lib. bdg. 16.05 (*0-516-00821-8*) Childrens.

Neal, Julia. The Kentucky Shakers. LC 82-1871. (Illus.). 120p. 1982. 13.00 (*0-8131-1458-6*) U Pr of Ky.

Neal, Kenneth L. Where Art Thou? Van Treese, James B., ed. (Illus.). 232p. 1992. pap. 8.95 (*1-880416-50-6*) NW Pub.

Neal, Larry. Archeological Survey of Clearcut Areas along Little River, McCurtain & Pushmataha Counties, Oklahoma. George, Preston, ed. (Archeological Resource Survey Report Ser.: No. 32). (Illus.). 201p. (C). 1988. pap. text ed. 6.00 (*1-881346-21-8*) Univ OK Archeol.

— Hoodoo Hollerin Bebop Ghosts. LC 73-88972. (Illus.). 87p. 1974. 12.95 (*0-88258-011-6*) Howard U Pr.

— The Rise of Financial Capitalism: International Capital Markets in the Age of Reason. (Studies in Monetary & Financial History). (Illus.). 288p. (C). 1991. 49.95 (*0-521-38205-X*) Cambridge U Pr.

— The Rise of Financial Capitalism: International Capital Markets in the Age of Reason. (Studies in Monetary & Financial History). (Illus.). 288p. (C). 1993. pap. 16.95 (*0-521-45738-6*) Cambridge U Pr.

— Visions of a Liberated Future: Black Arts Movement Writings. 224p. (Orig.). 1989. pap. 10.95 (*0-938410-77-6*) Thunders Mouth.

Neal, Larry, ed. War Finance. (International Library of Macroeconomic & Financial History: Vol. 12). 1880p. 1994. 499.95 (*1-85278-663-9*, Pub. by E Elgar Pub UK) Ashgate Pub Co.

Neal, Larry & Edginton, Christopher R., eds. EXETRA Perspectives: Concepts in Therapeutic Recreation. (Illus.). 232p. 1982. 10.00 (*0-943272-03-3*) Inst Recreation Res.

Neal, Larry L., ed. The Next Fifty Years: Health, Physical Education, Recreation, Dance. 179p. 1971. pap. 10.00 (*0-943272-08-4*) Inst Recreation Res.

Neal, Larry L., jt. ed. see Fairchild, Effie L.

***Neal, Lori S., comp.** Abstracts of Vital Records from Raleigh, NC Newspapers 1820-1829. 791p. 1995. 50.00 (*0-614-04973-3*) N C Genealogical.

Neal, M. Custom Draperies in Interior Design. 208p. 1982. 40.25 (*0-444-00640-0*) P-H.

Neal, M. C. Hawaiian Helicinidae. (BMB Ser.). 1969. reprint ed. 15.00 (*0-527-02231-4*) Periodicals Srv.

— Hawaiian Marine Algae. (BMB Ser.). 1969. reprint ed. 15.00 (*0-527-02173-3*) Periodicals Srv.

Neal, M. T., et al, eds. Bibliography on Postsecondary Accreditation. 107p. 1984. 9.50 (*0-318-17661-0*) Coun Postsecondary Accredit.

Neal, Margaret B., et al. Balancing Work & Caregiving: For Children, Adults & Elders. (Applications of Family Caregiving Ser.: Vol. 3). (Illus.). 292p. (C). 1993. text ed. 48.00 (*0-8039-4281-8*); pap. text ed. 24.00 (*0-8039-4282-6*) Sage.

Neal, Margaret T. And Set Aglow a Sacred Flame. (Illus.). 1983. 8.50 (*0-317-00833-1*) Puddingstone.

Neal, Margo C. Nursing Diagnosis Care Plans for Diagnosis-Related Groups. 496p. 1990. pap. 35.00 (*0-86720-418-4*) Jones & Bartlett.

Neal, Marie A. From Nuns to Sisters: An Expanding Vocation. LC 89-51579. 160p. (Orig.). 1990. pap. 9.95 (*0-89622-400-7*) Twenty-Third.

Neal, Marie C. In Gardens of Hawaii. rev. ed. (Special Publication Ser.: No. 50). (Illus.). 944p. 1965. 35.00 (*0-910240-33-7*) Bishop Mus.

Neal, Marshall. Seven Churches. (Illus.). 108p. (Orig.). 1977. pap. 3.95 (*0-89084-062-8*) Bob Jones Univ Pr.

Neal, Maynard, et al, intros. Hydraulic Institute Engineering Data Book. 2nd ed. (Hydraulic Institute Ser.). (Illus.). 205p. 1991. text ed. 79.00 (*1-880952-01-7*, S200) Hydraulic Inst.

Neal, Michael W., jt. auth. see Howard, Philip H.

Neal, Nancy. Lucinda-Linda, Where Are You? abr. ed. 117p. 1995. pap. 7.95 (*1-56901-486-8*) NW Pub.

Neal, Patricia A. Management Information Systems for the Fee-for-Service Prepaid Medical Group. (Going Prepaid Ser.). 154p. (Orig.). 1986. pap. 31.00 (*0-933948-76-X*, 9559) Ctr Res Ambulatory.

***Neal, Philip.** Endangered Species. (Conservation 2000 Ser.). 64p. (J). (gr. 6-9). 1995. 24.95 (*0-7134-7202-2*, Pub. by Batsford UK) Trafalgar.

— Energy, Power Sources & Electricity. (Considering Conservation Ser.). (Illus.). 48p. (YA). (gr. 6-9). 1989. 19.95 (*0-85219-776-4*, Pub. by Batsford UK) Trafalgar.

— The Greenhouse Effect. (Considering Conservation Ser.). (Illus.). 64p. (YA). (gr. 7-10). 1989. 19.95 (*0-85219-822-1*, Pub. by Batsford UK) Trafalgar.

— The Oceans. (Conservation 2000 Ser.). (Illus.). 64p. (YA). (gr. 6-9). 1993. 24.95 (*0-7134-6712-6*, Pub. by Batsford UK) Trafalgar.

— The Ozone Layer: Conservation 2000. (Illus.). 64p. (YA). (gr. 7-10). 1994. 24.95 (*0-7134-6713-4*, Pub. by Batsford UK) Trafalgar.

Neal, Philip, jt. auth. see Palmer, Joy.

Neal, Richard. School Based Management: A Detailed Guide for Successful Implementation. 211p. (Orig.). 1991. pap. 21.95 (*1-879639-15-7*) Natl Educ Serv.

Neal, Richard B., ed. The Stanford Two-Mile Accelerator. LC 68-24364. (Illus.). 1183p. reprint ed. pap. 180.00 (*0-8357-3820-5*, 2057030) Bks Demand.

Neal, Richard G. Time Wasters - Time Savers: Sixty-One Ways to Beat the Clock. 88p. 1994. pap. 16.00 (*0-910170-64-9*) Assn Sch Busn.

Neal, Robert D., jt. ed. see Lorentzen, Karen M.

***Neal, Roger.** The Story of Little Blue Hound: A Crystal Tale. 56p. (J). (gr. 1-5). 1995. pap. 7.95 (*1-55605-261-8*, Cloverdale) Wyndhall Pr.

Neal, Rosemary C. Elizabeth City County, Virginia, (now the City of Hampton) Deeds, Wills, Court Orders, etc. 1634, 1659, 1688-1702. 331p. (Orig.). 1986. pap. 18.50 (*1-55613-014-7*) Heritage Bk.

Neal, S. Lincoln the Politician. 1999. write for info. (*0-670-80883-0*) Viking Penguin.

Neal-Silva, Eduardo, et al. Motivos de conversacion Essentials of Spanish: Second year. 2nd ed. 416p. (C). 1988. student ed 16.50 (*0-394-36506-2*); pap. text ed. 27.95 (*0-394-36509-7*) Random.

Neal, Steve. Dark Horse: A Biography of Wendell Wilkie. LC 89-22614. (Illus.). xii, 371p. 1989. reprint ed. 35.00 (*0-7006-0454-5*); reprint ed. pap. 14.95 (*0-7006-0453-7*) U Pr of KS.

— The Eisenhowers. LC 84-40412. (Illus.). xii, 508p. 1984. reprint ed. pap. 14.95 (*0-7006-0260-7*) U Pr of KS.

— McNary of Oregon: A Political Biography. LC 85-13692. 1985. 17.95 (*0-87595-173-2*) Oregon Hist.

Neal, Steve, ed. They Never Go Back to Pocatello: The Selected Essays of Richard Neuberger. (Illus.). 416p. 1988. 22.50 (*0-87595-201-1*) Oregon Hist.

Neal, T. Lynn. Avatar of the Bowmaster. LC 92-74369. 304p. 1994. pap. 12.95 (*1-56002-214-0*) Aegina Pr.

Neal, Thomas A. Farewell My Book. (Los Angeles Miscellany Ser.: No. 14). (Illus.). 44p. 1983. 30.00 (*0-87093-314-0*) Dawsons.

Neal, Tommy, jt. auth. see Walker, Robert J.

***Neal, Valerie, et al.** Space Flight. 256p. 1995. text ed. 27.50 (*0-02-860007-X*); pap. 18.00 (*0-02-860040-1*) Macmillan.

Neal, Valerie, ed. Where Next, Columbus? The Future of Space Exploration. (Illus.). 256p. 1994. 35.00 (*0-19-509277-5*) OUP.

Neal, Valerie, ed. see Tipler, Paul A.

Neal, Viola P. Fragments of Experience: A Spiritual Journey. LC 78-822. 1978. 4.95 (*0-87516-280-0*) DeVorss.

Neal, Viola P. & Karagulla, Shafica. Through the Curtain. 2nd ed. LC 83-71171. 360p. 1993. reprint ed. pap. 13.95 (*0-87516-517-6*) DeVorss.

Neal, Viola P., jt. auth. see Chaplin, Annabel.

Neal, Virgil. Hypnotism & Hypnotic Suggestion. (Illus.). 93p. 1984. reprint ed. pap. text ed. 15.00 (*0-87556-379-1*) Saifer.

Neal, W. G., jt. auth. see Hall, Richard N.

***Neal, Wes.** The Handbook on Athletic Perfection. 248p. (Orig.). (YA). (gr. 6 up). 1993. pap. 8.95 (*1-887002-07-3*) Cross Trng.

— The Handbook on Coaching Perfection. 248p. (Orig.). (YA). (gr. 6 up). 1993. pap. 8.95 (*1-887002-08-1*) Cross Trng.

Neal, William A., jt. auth. see Moller, James H.

Neal, William D., ed. First Annual Advanced Research Techniques Forum. 408p. (Orig.). 1991. pap. 35.00 (*0-87757-218-6*) Am Mktg.

Neal, William J., et al. Living with the South Carolina Shore. LC 83-20515. (Living with the Shore Ser.). (Illus.). xiii, 218p. (C). 1984. 29.95 (*0-8223-0522-4*); pap. 14.95 (*0-8223-0524-0*) Duke.

Neal, William W., ed. see Kaplan, Norman M. & Lieberman, Ellin.

Nealand-Staley, Harriet C. Mariner Cheney: My Dad. (Illus.). 136p. 1992. 19.95 (*1-882266-00-5*) Newburyport.

Neale. None but the Sinners: Religious Categories in the Gospel of Luke. 200p. (C). 1991. 22.50 (*1-85075-314-8*, Pub. by Sheffield Acad UK) CUP Services.

Neale, Andrew. Narrow Gauge & Miniature Railways from Old Picture Postcards. 60p. (C). 1987. 35.00 (*0-9511108-0-2*, Pub. by Picton UK) St Mut.

***Neale, Bill & Holmes, David.** Post Completion Auditing: A Guide to Effective Re-Evaluation of Investment Projects. 224p. 1990. 113.00 (*0-273-03286-0*, Pub. by Pitman Pubng UK) St Mut.

Neale, Caroline. Writing "Independent" History: African Historiography, 1960-1980. LC 84-15756. (Contributions in Afro-American & African Studies: No. 85). ix, 208p. 1985. text ed. 49.95 (*0-313-24652-1*, NID/, Greenwood Pr) Greenwood.

Neale, Ernest R. & Williams, H., eds. Collected Papers on Geology of the Atlantic Region: Hugh Lilly Memorial Volume. LC 77-433692. (Geological Association of Canada. Special Paper Ser.: No. 4). 293p. reprint ed. pap. 83.60 (*0-685-17109-4*, 2027839) Bks Demand.

Neale, Frances. The Handbook of Performance Management. 172p. (C). 1992. pap. 90.00 (*0-85292-483-6*, Pub. by IPM Hse UK) St Mut.

Neale, Frances A. Law Enforcement Communicators Handbook. (Illus.). 180p. 1990. student ed 18.00 (*0-9626115-0-6*) PCS Pub.

Neale, J. & Flenley, J., eds. The Quaternary in Britain: Essays Reviews & Original Work on the Quarternary Published in Honour of Lewis Penny on His Retirement. (Illus.). 278p. 1981. 116.00 (*0-08-026254-6*, Pub. by Pergamon Repr UK) Franklin.

Neale, J. E. Queen Elizabeth the First. 435p. (C). 1992. reprint ed. pap. 13.95 (*0-89733-362-4*) Academy Chi Pubs.

Neale, J. M. Good King Wenceslas. LC 88-3633. (Illus.). 24p. (J). (ps up). 1988. 11.95 (*0-525-44420-3*, DCB) Dutton Child Bks.

— Good King Wenceslas. (Illus.). 24p. (J). 1993. pap. 4.99 (*0-14-054942-0*, Puff Unicorn) Puffin Bks.

Neale, J. M., jt. ed. see Carstensen, L. L.

Neale, J. W. The Taxonomy, Morphology & Ecology of Recent Ostracoda. 1969. 35.00 (*0-934454-77-9*) Lubrecht & Cramer.

Neale, John & Osborn, James M. Quene's Maiesties Passage Through the Citie of London to Westminster the day before her Coronation. 1960. 49.50 (0-685-26707-5) Elliots Bks.

Neale, John A. Neale: Charter & Records of Neales of Berkley, Yate & Corsham, England. 263p. 1993. reprint ed. lib. bdg. 51.00 (0-685-68822-4); reprint ed. pap. 41.00 (0-8328-3725-3) Higginson Bk Co.

Neale, John M. Essays on Liturgiology & Church History. LC 70-173070. reprint ed. 55.00 (0-404-04667-3) AMS Pr.

— A History of the Holy Eastern Church, 5 vols., Set. LC 74-144662. reprint ed. 325.00 (0-404-04670-3) AMS Pr.

— A History of the So-Called Jansenist Church of Holland. LC 71-133820. reprint ed. 49.50 (0-404-04656-8) AMS Pr.

— Hymns of the Eastern Church. LC 77-131029. reprint ed. 39.50 (0-404-04666-5) AMS Pr.

— Voices from the East: Documents of the Present State & Working of the Oriental Church. LC 75-173069. reprint ed. 20.00 (0-404-04659-2) AMS Pr.

Neale, John M., ed. A Commentary on the Psalms from Primitive & Mediaeval Writers, 4 vols. LC 78-130990. 1976. reprint ed. 275.00 (0-404-04680-0) AMS Pr.

Neale, John M. & Forbes, G. H. The Ancient Liturgies of the Gallican Church. LC 71-131030. reprint ed. 57.50 (0-404-04655-X) AMS Pr.

Neale, John M., jt. auth. see Davison, Gerald C.

Neale, John M., ed. see Durantis, Gulielmus.

Neale, Jonathan. Laughter of Heroes. 1993. pap. 11.99 (1-85242-279-3) Serpents Tail.

Neale, Kenneth J. Discovering Essex in London. 1993. pap. 17.00 (0-86025-406-2, Pub. by Ian Henry Pubns UK) Empire Pub Srvs.

Neale, M. J. Bearings. (Tribology Handbooks Ser.). (Illus.). 180p. 1993. pap. write for info. (0-7506-0979-6) Buttrwrth-Heinemann.

— Component Failure: A Tribology Handbook. (Authored (Royalty) Ser.). 1994. 39.00 (1-56091-451-3, R-137) Soc Auto Engineers.

— Drives & Seals: A Tribology Handbook. 180p. 1993. 39.00 (1-56091-452-1, R-138) Soc Auto Engineers.

— Lubrication. (Illus.). 160p. 1993. text ed. write for info. (0-7506-0882-X) Buttrwrth-Heinemann.

— Lubrication: A Tribology Handbook. 160p. 1993. 39.00 (1-56091-392-4, R-130) Soc Auto Engineers.

Neale, M. J., ed. Bearings. LC 93-10932. (Tribology Handbook). 180p. 1993. 39.00 (1-56091-393-2, R-131) Soc Auto Engineers.

— Tribology Handbook. (Illus.). 540p. 1973. text ed. 125.00 (0-408-00082-1) Buttrwrth-Heinemann.

Neale, Margaret A. & Bazerman, Max H. Cognition & Rationality in Negotiation. 240p. 1991. text ed. 42.95 (0-02-922515-9) Free Pr.

Neale, Margaret A., jt. auth. see Bazerman, Max H.

Neale, Margaret A., jt. auth. see Northcraft, Gregory B.

Neale, Michael C. Methodology for Genetic Studies of Twins & Families. 524p. (C). 1992. lib. bdg. 181.50 (0-7923-1874-9) Kluwer Ac.

Neale, Michael J. Component Failures, Maintenance & Repair. (Tribology Handbooks Ser.). (Illus.). 144p. 1995. pap. 4,795.00 (0-7506-0980-X) Buttrwrth-Heinemann.

— Drives & Seals. LC 93-20740. (Tribology Handbooks Ser.). (Illus.). 152p. 1994. write for info. (0-7506-0981-8) Buttrwrth-Heinemann.

Neale, R., jt. auth. see Miles, D.

Neale, R. S., ed. History & Class: Essential Readings in Theory & Interpretation. 256p. 1984. pap. 15.95 (0-631-13135-3) Blackwell Pubs.

Neale, Robert. The Common Writer: Theory & Practice for Writers & Teachers. 160p. 1993. pap. 16.95 (0-19-558221-7) OUP.

Neale, Robert, ed. Writers on Writing: An Anthology. 272p. 1993. pap. 19.95 (0-19-558256-X) OUP.

Neale, Robert & Hull, Thomas. Origami, Plain & Simple. (Illus.). 112p. (Orig.). 1994. pap. 10.95 (0-312-10516-9) St Martin.

Neale, Robert E. Loneliness, Solitude, & Companionship. LC 83-26065. 131p. (Orig.). reprint ed. pap. 37.40 (0-7837-2631-7, 2042981) Bks Demand.

— Tricks of the Imagination. (Illus.). 215p. 1991. 30.00 (0-945296-04-5) Hermetic Pr.

Neale, Roderick F., jt. ed. see Smith, S. Desmond.

Neale-Silva, E. Estudios Sobre Jose Eustasio Rivera I-the Arte Poetico: Tierra De Promision. (RHM Ser.: Vol. XIV). 84p. (SPA.). 1948. 2.00 (0-318-14263-5) Hispanic Inst.

Neale-Silva, Eduardo. Cesar Vallejo en Su Fase Trilcica. 664p. 1976. pap. 10.00x (0-299-06774-2) U of Wis Pr.

— Horizonte Humano: Vida de Jose Eustasio Rivera. 510p. (Orig.). (SPA.). 1960. 17.50 (0-299-02000-2) U of Wis Pr.

Neale-Silva, Eduardo & Lipski, John M. El Espanol en Sintesis. LC 80-25769. 393p. (C). 1981. text ed. 38.75 (0-03-058133-8) HB Coll Pubs.

Neale-Silva, Eduardo & Nicholas, Robert L. Adelante. (C). 1985. student ed, audio 220.00 (0-07-554511-X) McGraw.

— Adelante. 2nd ed. LC 80-21015. (C). 1981. text ed. 24.50 (0-394-33282-2) Random.

— Adelante. 3rd ed. (C). 1985. text ed. write for info. (0-07-554508-X) McGraw.

— Adelante. 3rd ed. (C). 1985. student ed, pap. text ed. 13.03 (0-07-554509-8) McGraw.

— En Camino. 3rd ed. (C). 1985. audio 233.16 (0-07-554507-1) McGraw.

Neale, Stephen. Descriptions. 200p. 1989. 40.00 (0-262-14045-4) MIT Pr.

— Descriptions. 304p. 1993. pap. 16.00 (0-262-64031-7, Bradford Bks) MIT Pr.

— Genre. 74p. 1987. reprint ed. pap. 7.95 (0-85170-094-2, Pub. by British Film Inst UK) Ind U Pr.

Neale, Steve & Krutnik, Frank. Popular Film & Television Comedy. 288p. 1990. 52.50 (0-415-04691-2, A4311); pap. 13.95 (0-415-04692-0, A4315) Routledge.

Neale, Tom. An Island to Oneself: Six Years on a Desert Island. LC 90-7546. (Illus.). 270p. 1990. reprint ed. 24.95 (0-918024-76-5) Ox Bow.

— Streets & Seasons. 16p. 1981. pap. 2.00 (0-941160-00-9) Ghost Pony Pr.

Neale, Walter. Life of Ambrose Bierce. LC 77-93773. reprint ed. 20.00 (0-404-04668-1) AMS Pr.

— Life of Ambrose Bierce. (BCL1-PS American Literature Ser.). 489p. 1992. reprint ed. lib. bdg. 99.00 (0-7812-6678-5) Rprt Serv.

Neale, Walter C. Developing Rural India: Policies, Politics, & Progress. LC 85-63424. (Perspectives on Asian & African Development Ser.: No. 3). 263p. 1990. 29.00 (0-913215-15-5) Riverdale Co.

— Monies in Societies. LC 76-519. (Cross-Cultural Themes Ser.). 128p. 1976. pap. text ed. 7.95 (0-88316-525-2) Chandler & Sharp.

Nealen, Mary K. The Poor in the Ecclesiology of Juan Luis Segundo. LC 91-3910. (American University Studies: Theology & Religion: Ser. VII, Vol. 113). 190p. (C). 1992. text ed. 35.95 (0-8204-1595-2) P Lang Pubs.

Nealey, Stanley M. Nuclear Power Development: Prospects in the 1990s. LC 89-38237. 1990. pap. text ed. 19.95 (0-935470-53-0) Battelle.

Neall, Lynne C., ed. see Burns, Jim, et al.

Neall, Ralph E. How Long, O Lord? Wheeler, Gerald, ed. 160p. 1988. 12.95 (0-8280-0399-8) Review & Herald.

Nealon, Jeffrey T. Double Reading: Postmodernism after Deconstruction. LC 93-636. 208p. 1993. 27.50 (0-8014-2853-X) Cornell U Pr.

Nealon, Thomas F. Management of the Patient with Cancer. 3rd ed. (Illus.). 784p. 1986. text ed. 145.00 (0-7216-1075-7) Saunders.

Nealon, Thomas F., Jr. & Nealon, William H. Fundamental Skills in Surgery. 4th ed. LC 93-32194. (Illus.). 480p. 1994. text ed. 42.00 (0-7216-6460-1) Saunders.

Nealon, Timothy, jt. auth. see Steldt, Paul.

Nealon, William H., jt. auth. see Nealon, Thomas F., Jr.

***Neals, Betty.** Dearest Mary Jane. large type ed. (Harlequin Romance Ser.). 1995. 18.95 (0-263-14076-8, Pub. by Mills & Boon UK) Thorndike Pr.

— The Quiet Professor. large type ed. (Harlequin Ser.). 17.95 (0-263-13358-3, Pub. by Mills & Boon UK) Thorndike Pr.

***Nealy, Eleanor.** Amazon Spirit: Daily Meditation for Lesbians in Recovery. 1995. pap. 10.00 (0-399-51940-8) Berkley Pub.

Nealy, Kenneth. Multiple Choice Questions in Preparation for the AP Chemistry Examination. 129p. 1992. student ed 12.95 (1-878621-20-3) D & S Mktg Syst.

— Multiple Choice Questions in Preparation for the AP Chemistry Examination. 2nd ed. 116p. 1992. student ed 15.95 (1-878621-19-X) D & S Mktg Syst.

Nealy, William. Kayak: The Animated Manual of Intermediate & Advanced Whitewater Technique. LC 86-8526. (Illus.). 190p. (Orig.). 1986. pap. 14.95 (0-89732-050-6) Menasha Ridge.

— Kayaks to Hell. LC 82-14247. (Illus.). 144p. 1982. pap. 5.95 (0-89732-010-7) Menasha Ridge.

— Mountain Bike! A Manual of Beginning to Advanced Technique. LC 91-40292. (Illus.). 172p. (Orig.). 1992. pap. 14.95 (0-89732-114-6) Menasha Ridge.

— A Mountain Bike Way of Knowledge. LC 89-27655. (Illus.). 128p. 1989. pap. 6.95 (0-89732-097-2) Menasha Ridge.

— Skiing Tales of Terror. 144p. 1990. pap. 6.95 (0-89732-106-5) Menasha Ridge.

— Whitewater Home Companion: Southeastern Rivers, Vol. II. LC 81-9854. (Illus.). 176p. (Orig.). 1984. pap. 12.95 (0-89732-025-5) Menasha Ridge.

— Whitewater Home Companion, Southeastern Rivers, Vol. 1. LC 81-9854. (Illus.). 176p. (Orig.). 1981. pap. 9.95 (0-89732-028-X) Menasha Ridge.

— Whitewater Tales of Terror. LC 83-22051. (Illus.). 120p. (Orig.). 1983. pap. 6.95 (0-89732-024-7) Menasha Ridge.

***Neaman, Evelyn.** Folk Rhymes from Around the World. (Illus.). 64p. (Orig.). (J). 1992. pap. 10.95 (0-88865-081-7, Pub. by Pacific Educ Pr CN) Orca Bk Pubs.

Neaman, Judith S. & Silver, Carole G. Kind Words: A Thesaurus of Euphemisms. rev. ed. 432p. 1989. 22.95 (0-8160-1896-0) Facts on File.

— Kind Words: A Thesaurus of Euphemisms. 432p. 1991. reprint ed. pap. 10.95 (0-380-71247-4) Avon.

Neaman, Linda. Foot Facts. 20p. (Orig.). 1980. pap. 3.00 (0-917061-05-5) Top Stories.

Neamat, C. Scenes de France. (C). 1982. 35.00 (0-7175-1005-0, Pub. by S Thornes Pubs UK) St Mut.

***Neamatalla, Georgeanne S. & Harper, Pamela B.** Family Planning Counseling & Voluntary Sterilization. rev. ed. 1994. pap. text ed. write for info. (1-885063-05-9) AVSC Int.

Neame, Alan, tr. The Prayers of Saint Francis. 3rd rev. ed. LC 94-10222. 112p. 1994. pap. 6.95 (1-56548-066-X) New City.

Neame, Alan, tr. see Camara, Dom H.

Neame, Alan, tr. see Cantalamessa, Raniero.

Neame, Alan, tr. see Carretto, Carlo.

Neamen, Donald A. Semiconductor Physics & Devices. 550p. (C). 1992. text ed. 72.50 (0-256-08405-X) Irwin.

Neamen, Mimi & Strong, Mary. Literature Circles: Cooperative Learning for Grades 3-8. (Illus.). 175p. (J). (gr. 3-8). 1992. pap. text ed. 18.00 (0-87287-987-9) Teacher Ideas Pr.

Neamen, Mimi, jt. auth. see Strong, Mary.

Neamtu, Celia. Woman's Ritual Headwear (Romania) Popescu-Judetz, Eugenia, tr. (Illus.). 110p. (Orig.). 1981. pap. 10.00 (0-936922-03-6) Tamburitza.

Neander, Johann A. General History of the Christian Religion & Church, 9 vols., Set. rev. ed. Torrey, Joseph, tr. reprint ed. lib. bdg. 495.00 (0-404-09590-9) AMS Pr.

Neapolitan, Richard E. Probabilistic Reasoning in Expert Systems: Theory & Algorithms. 433p. 1990. text ed. 65.00 (0-471-61840-3) Wiley.

Near, Anne. A Dubious Journey: From Class to Class. LC 92-76050. (Illus.). (Orig.). 1993. pap. 10.00 (0-9635674-0-3) Hereford Pub.

Near, Anne, et al. Downwardly Mobile for Conscience Sake: Ten Autobiographical Sketches: Each a Personal Search for Justice, Peace, & Eco-sanity. 206p. (Orig.). 1993. pap. 10.00 (0-931803-03-9) T Paine Inst.

Near, Doris, jt. auth. see Brendel, LeRoy A.

Near, Henry. The Kibbutz Movement: A History, 2 vols., Vol. 1: Origins & Growth, 1909-1939. (Littman Library of Jewish Civilization). (Illus.). 464p. 1992. lib. bdg. 80.00 (0-19-710069-4, Pub. by Littman Lib Jew UK) Bnai Brith Bk.

— The Kibbutz Movement: A History, 2 vols., Vol. 2: Crisis & Achievement, 1940-1990. (Littman Library of Jewish Civilization). (Illus.). 1992. lib. bdg. write for info. (0-19-710079-1, Pub. by Littman Lib Jew UK) Bnai Brith Bk.

Near, Holly. The Great Peace March. LC 92-25170. (Illus.). 32p. (J). (gr. 2-5). 1993. 15.95 (0-8050-1941-3, Bks Young Read) H Holt & Co.

— Singing for Our Lives. 1982. pap. 10.00 (0-9608774-2-8) Hereford Pub.

Near, Holly & Langley, Jeff. Words & Music. 136p. (Orig.). 1982. pap. text ed. 10.00 (0-9608774-1-X) Redwood Records.

Near, Janet P., jt. auth. see Miceli, Marcia P.

Near, Jean G. Open Sesame. LC 82-91113. (Illus.). 78p. 1983. pap. 4.95 (0-9609166-1-X) J Near.

Near, Jean H. G. A Genealogical Study of the Descendants of Joshua & Anna Gowan. LC 82-80136. (Illus.). 559p. 1983. 75.00 (0-9609166-0-1) J Near.

Near, Pinkney L. Three Masters of Landscape: Fragonard, Robert, & Boucher. LC 81-16180. (Illus.). 56p. 1981. pap. 1.50 (0-917046-11-0) Va Mus Arts.

Near, Pinkney L., jt. auth. see Rewald, John.

Nearing, Helen. The Good Life Album. 1974. pap. 10.00 (0-87690-144-5) Soc Sci Inst.

— Light on Aging & Dying: Wise Words Selected by Helen Nearing. 1995. 12.95 (0-88448-179-4) Tilbury Hse.

— Loving & Leaving the Good Life. 224p. 1992. reprint ed. pap. 14.95 (0-930031-63-6) Chelsea Green Pub.

— Simple Food for the Good Life. 309p. (Orig.). 1985. reprint ed. pap. 9.95 (0-913299-24-3) Stillpoint.

— Wise Words on the Good Life. 192p. 1980. 15.00 (0-686-73458-0) Soc Sci Inst.

Nearing, Helen & Nearing, Scott. The Good Life: Helen & Scott Nearing's 60 Years of Self-Sufficiency. LC 89-43162. (Illus.). 448p. 1989. pap. 14.00 (0-8052-0970-0) Schocken.

— Living the Good Life: How to Live Sanely & Simply in a Troubled World. LC 73-127820. (Illus.). 1987. reprint ed. 15.00 (0-8052-3363-6); reprint ed. pap. 7.95 (0-8052-0300-1) Schocken.

Nearing, Helen K., jt. auth. see Nearing, Scott.

Nearing, Patrick. Out Walking Free. Ingram, tr. 150p. 1995. pap. 7.95 (1-56901-366-7) NW Pub.

***Nearing, Richard & Hoff, David.** Arizona Military Installations: 1752-1992. (Illus.). 80p. (Orig.). 1995. pap. 20.00 (0-9635455-1-5) GEM Pub AZ.

Nearing, Ryam. Loving More: The Polyfidelity Primer. 3rd ed. LC 92-70873. (Illus.). 96p. (Orig.). 1992. pap. 12.00 (0-9622144-1-8) Paradise Educ.

Nearing, Scott. Anthracite: An Instance of Natural Resource Monopoly. LC 78-169772. (Select Bibliographies Reprint Ser.). 1977. reprint ed. 20.95 (0-8369-5992-2) Ayer.

— Black America. LC 69-17730. (Illus.). 275p. 1986. pap. 10.00 (0-685-16626-0) Schocken.

— Free Born: An Unpublishable Novel. LC 72-4737. (Black Heritage Library Collection). 1977. reprint ed. 25.95 (0-8369-9115-X) Ayer.

— The Making of a Radical: A Political Autobiography. 320p. 10.00 (0-685-83849-8); pap. 5.00 (0-685-83850-1) Soc Sci Inst.

— Man's Search for the Good Life. 160p. pap. 10.00 (0-685-83853-6) Soc Sci Inst.

— New Education: A Review of Progressive Education Movements of the Day. LC 75-89210. (American Education: Its Men, Institutions & Ideas, Ser. 1). 1974. reprint ed. 19.95 (0-405-01449-X) Ayer.

— A Scott Nearing Reader: The Good Life in Bad Times. Sherman, Steve, ed. LC 88-29528. (Illus.). 333p. 1989. 32.50 (0-8108-2144-3) Scarecrow.

— Whither China? An Economic Interpretation of Recent Events in the Far East. LC 75-39029. (China Studies). (Illus.). vi, 255p. 1977. reprint ed. 21.40 (0-88355-385-6) Hyperion Conn.

Nearing, Scott & Freeman, Joseph. Dollar Diplomacy: A Study in American Imperialism. LC 74-111703. (American Imperialism: Viewpoints of United States Foreign Policy, 1898-1941 Ser.). 1979. reprint ed. 25.95 (0-405-02040-6) Ayer.

Nearing, Scott & Nearing, Helen K. U. S. A. Today. LC 55-12158. 254p. 1955. 15.00 (0-685-83846-3); pap. 5.00 (0-685-83847-1) Soc Sci Inst.

Nearing, Scott & Russell, Bertrand. Bolshevism & the West: A Debate. 1973. 250.00 (0-87968-070-9) Gordon Pr.

Nearing, Scott, jt. auth. see Nearing, Helen.

Nearman, Hubert, tr. see Jiyu-Kennett, P. T., ed.

Nearman, Hubert, tr. see Jiyu-Kennett, P. T. & MacPhillamy, Daizui, eds.

Nearman, Hubert, tr. see Zenji, Keizan.

Neary, D., jt. auth. see Crossman, A. R.

Neary, Donal. The Calm Beneath the Storm: Reflections & Prayers for Young People. 80p. 1984. pap. 4.95 (0-8294-0470-8) Loyola Univ Pr.

— The Calm Beneath the Storm: Reflections & Prayers for Young People. 77p. 1989. pap. 22.00 (0-86217-096-6, Pub. by Veritas IE) St Mut.

— Forty Masses with Young People. 176p. (Orig.). 1994. pap. 19.95 (0-89622-630-1) Twenty-Third.

— Pilgrim in Advent. 80p. (Orig.). 1995. pap. 4.95 (1-85607-116-2, Pub. by Columba Pr IE) Twenty-Third.

— Pilgrim in Lent: Prayer for Every Day. 96p. (Orig.). 1992. pap. text ed. 4.95 (0-8146-2123-6) Liturgical Pr.

Neary, G. & Munson, R. Chronic Radiation Hazards: Experimental Study Fast Neutrons. LC 57-14862. 1957. 89.00 (0-08-009053-2, Pub. by Pergamon Repr UK) Franklin.

***Neary, Ian, ed.** Leaders & Leadership in Japan. 224p. (C). 1995. text ed. 70.00 (1-873410-41-7, Pub. by Curzon Pr UK) Humanities.

— War, Revolution & Japan. 128p. (C). 1993. pap. 25.00 (1-873410-08-5, Pub. by Japan Library) Humanities.

***Neary, Ian & Goodman, Roger, eds.** Case Studies on Human Rights in Japan. 192p. (C). 1995. text ed. 70.00 (1-873410-35-2, Pub. by Curzon Pr UK) Humanities.

Neary, J. Peter & Van Wijnbergen, Sweder, eds. Natural Resources & the Macroeconomy. 336p. 1986. 40.00 (0-262-14041-1) MIT Pr.

Neary, Jack. Jerry Finnegan's Sister. 1993. 4.95 (0-87129-300-5, J23) Dramatic Pub.

— To Forgive, Divine. 1990. pap. 4.75 (0-8222-1159-9) Dramatists Play.

Neary, John. Something & Nothingness: The Fiction of John Updike & John Fowles. LC 90-25137. 288p. (C). 1991. 24.95 (0-8093-1742-7) S Ill U Pr.

Neary, Kevin & Smith, Dave. The Ultimate Disney Trivia Book, Bk. 2. LC 94-2207. (Illus.). 208p. (J). 1994. pap. 9.95 (0-7868-8024-4) Hyperion.

Neary, Kevin, jt. auth. see Smith, Dave.

Neary, Michael. Our Hide & Seek God. 128p. (Orig.). 1992. pap. text ed. 8.95 (0-8146-2085-X) Liturgical Pr.

Neary, Paul, jt. auth. see Davis, Alan.

Neary, Peter. Newfoundland in the North Atlantic World, 1929-1949. (Illus.). 500p. (C). 1988. text ed. 44.95 (0-7735-0668-3, Pub. by McGill CN) U of Toronto Pr.

***Neary, Peter & Hiller, James, eds.** Twentieth Century Newfoundland: Explorations. 384p. 1995. pap. 19.95 (1-55081-072-3, Pub. by Breakwater Bks CN) Paul & Co Pubs.

Neary, Peter & O'Flaherty, Patrick, eds. By Great Waters: A Newfoundland & Labrador Anthology. LC 73-91561. (Social History of Canada Ser.). 1974. pap. 10.95 (0-8020-6233-4) U of Toronto Pr.

Neary, Peter, jt. ed. see Hiller, James.

Neary, R. Patrick, ed. see Moran, John P.

Neary, Robert D., jt. auth. see Herdman, Robert K.

Neas, Virginia L. Knife Rests. LC 86-90691. (Illus.). 87p. (Orig.). 1987. 16.95 (0-9617836-0-5); pap. 11.95 (0-9617836-1-3) Glassy Mount.

Neasi, Barbara. Just Like Me. LC 83-23154. (Rookie Reader Ser.). (Illus.). 32p. (J). (ps-2). 1984. lib. bdg. 10.35 (0-516-02047-1); pap. 2.95 (0-516-42047-X) Childrens.

— Just Like Me Big Book. (Rookie Readers Big Bks.). (Illus.). 32p. (J). (ps-2). 1988. lib. bdg. 22.95 (0-516-49506-2) Childrens.

— Listen to Me. LC 86-10664. (Rookie Reader Ser.). (Illus.). 32p. (J). (ps-2). 1986. lib. bdg. 10.35 (0-516-02072-2); pap. 2.95 (0-516-42072-0) Childrens.

— Listen To Me Big Book. (Rookie Readers Big Bks.). (Illus.). 32p. (J). (ps-2). 1988. lib. bdg. 22.95 (0-516-49507-0) Childrens.

— Sweet Dreams. LC 87-15083. (Rookie Reader Ser.). (Illus.). 32p. (J). (ps-2). 1987. lib. bdg. 10.35 (0-516-02084-6); pap. 2.95 (0-516-42084-4) Childrens.

Neasi, Barbara J. Dulces Suenos: Sweet Dreams. LC 87-15083. (Rookie Reader Ser.). (Illus.). 32p. (SPA.). (J). (ps-2). 1991. lib. bdg. 10.35 (0-516-32084-X); pap. 2.95 (0-516-52084-9) Childrens.

— Escuchame (Listen to Me) LC 86-10665. (Rookie Readers - Spanish Ser.). (Illus.). 32p. (SPA.). (J). (ps-2). 1988. lib. bdg. 10.35 (0-516-32072-6); lib. bdg. 22.95 (0-516-59507-5); pap. 2.95 (0-516-52072-5) Childrens.

— Igual Que Yo (Just Like Me) LC 83-23154. (Rookie Readers - Spanish Ser.). (Illus.). 32p. (SPA.). (J). (ps-2). 1988. lib. bdg. 10.35 (0-516-32047-5); lib. bdg. 22.95 (0-516-59506-7); pap. 2.95 (0-516-52047-4) Childrens.

Neason, Rebecca. Guises of the Mind. Ryan, Kevin, ed. (Star Trek: The Next Generation Ser.). 288p. (Orig.). 1993. mass mkt. 5.50 (0-671-79831-6) PB.

Neat, K. P., tr. see Shereshevsky, Mikhail I.

Neat, K. P., tr. see Vainstein, B. S.

Neat, Kenneth P., ed. & tr. The Games of Tigran Petrosian, Vol. 1: 1942-1965. (Russian Chess Ser.). 480p. 1991. 49.95 (0-08-037144-2, Pub. by CHES UK) Macmillan.

Neat, Kenneth P., ed. see Alekhine, A.

Neat, Kenneth P., tr. see Averbakh, Y.

Neat, Kenneth P., tr. see Averbakh, Y. & Checkover, V.

Neat, Kenneth P., tr. see Botvinnik, Mikhael M.

Neat, Kenneth P., tr. see Bronstein, David & Smolyan, Georgy.

Neat, Kenneth P., tr. see Estrin, Yakov B. & Glaskov, I. B.

Neat, Kenneth P., tr. see Karpov, Anatoly.

Neat, Kenneth P., tr. see Kasparov, Gary.

Neat, Kenneth P., tr. see Livshitz, August.

Neat, Kenneth P., tr. see Neishtadt, J.

Neat, Kenneth P., tr. see Polugayevsky, Lyev.

Neat, Kenneth P., ed. see Shekhtman, E. I.

Neat, Kenneth P., tr. see Shereshevsky, Mikhail I. & Slutsky, Leonid M.

Neat, Kenneth P., tr. see Suetin, A. S.

N

Neat, Kenneth P., tr. see Tal, M., et al.

Neatby, H. Blair. William Lyon Mackenzie King, 3 vols. Incl. Vol. 3. Prism of Unity, 1932-1939. (Illus.). 1976. 40.00 (*0-8020-5381-5*); write for info. (*0-318-56158-1*) U of Toronto Pr.

— William Lyon Mackenzie King: A Political Biography, Vol. 2: 1924-1932: The Lonely Heights. LC 59-347. (Illus.). 474p. reprint ed. pap. 135.10 (*0-8357-8375-8*, 2034057) Bks Demand.

— William Lyon Mackenzie King, Vol. II: The Lonely Heights, 1924-1932. 366p. 1963. text ed. 100.00 (*0-8020-1261-2*) U of Toronto Pr.

Neatby, H. Blair, et al. Imperial Relations in the Age of Laurier: Essays. LC 72-431730. (Canadian Historical Readings Ser.: No. 6). 92p. reprint ed. pap. 26.30 (*0-8357-3630-X*, 2036358) Bks Demand.

Neatby, Herbert B. William Lyon MacKenzie King: The Lonely Heights. LC 79-9143. (Scholarly Reprint Ser.: Vol. 2: 1924-1932). 464p. reprint ed. pap. 132.30 (*0-317-27005-2*, 2023656) Bks Demand.

Neatby, Hilda, et al. Queen's University, Vol. 1: Eighteen Forty-One to Nineteen Seventeen: Not to Yield, Vol. I. Gibson, Frederick W. & Graham, Roger, eds. (Illus.). 1978. 49.95 (*0-7735-0336-6*, Pub. by McGill CN) U of Toronto Pr.

Neate, Francis & McCormick, Roger. Bank Confidentiality. 1990. 140.00 (*0-406-17948-4*, U.K.) Butterworth Legal Pubs.

Neate, Francis W., ed. Using Set-Off As Security: A Comparative Survey for Practitioners. (C). 1990. lib. bdg. 150.00 (*1-85333-363-8*, Pub. by Graham & Trotman UK) Kluwer Ac.

Neate, Jill. High Asia: An Illustrated History of the World's 7000 Metre Peaks. (Illus.). 224p. (Orig.). 1990. 46.00 (*0-89886-238-8*) Mountaineers.

— Mountaineering Literature. 2nd enl. rev. ed. 296p. (Orig.). 1987. pap. 29.95 (*0-938567-04-7*, Mntn Bks) Cloudcap.

***Neate, Jill, ed.** Mountaineering in the Andes. (C). 1993. 45.00x (*0-907649-64-5*, Pub. by Expedit Advisory Centre UK) St Mut.

Neather, E. J. Mastering French. (Mastering Languages Ser.). (Illus.). 288p. (Orig.). 1991. pap. 11.95 (*0-87052-055-5*); audio 12.95 (*0-87052-060-1*) Hippocrene Bks.

Neathery, T. L., ed. Southeastern Section Field Guide. (DNAG Centennial Field Guides Ser.: No. 6). (Illus.). 477p. 1986. 40.50 (*0-8137-5406-2*) Geol Soc.

Neave, Airey. The Escape Room. 1982. pap. 2.50 (*0-89083-922-0*) Zebra.

Neave, Charles, jt. auth. see St. Laurent, Jonathan.

Neave, David & Waterson, Edward. Lost Houses of East Yorkshire. (C). 1989. text ed. 35.00 (*0-9513966-0-9*) St Mut.

Neave, Edwin. The Economic Organisation of a Financial System. 240p. (C). 1991. text ed. 74.00 (*0-415-05353-6*, A4886) Routledge.

Neave, G., ed. Research Perspectives on the Transition from School to Work. 144p. 1978. 13.75 (*90-265-0278-8*, Pub. by Swets Pub Serv NE) Taylor & Francis.

Neave, Guy. The Teaching Nation: Prospects for Teachers in the European Community. 180p. 1992. text ed. 77.00 (*0-08-041381-1*, Pergamon Pr) Elsevier.

Neave, Guy & Jenkinson, Sally. Research & Higher Education in Sweden. 112p. 1983. pap. text ed. 32.00x (*91-22-00624-9*, Pub. by Almqv & Wiksell SW) Coronet Bks.

Neave, Guy & Van Vught, Frans A., eds. The Winds of Change: Government & Higher Education Relationships over Three Continents: A Report to the World Bank. LC 93-23566. (Issues in Higher Education Ser.: Vol. 2). 1994. text ed. 83.00 (*0-08-042391-4*, Ed Skills Dallas) Elsevier.

Neave, Guy, jt. ed. see Clark, Burton R.

Neave, Guy, ed. see Van Vught, Frans.

Neave, Henry R. The Deming Dimension. 464p. (C). 1990. 40.00 (*0-945320-08-6*); pap. 20.00 (*0-945320-36-1*) SPC Pr.

— Elementary Statistics Tables. LC 92-22598. (Orig.). 1992. write for info. (*0-415-08458-X*, Routledge NY) Routledge.

Neave, Judy. Pressed Flower Crafting. (Illus.). 32p. (Orig.). 1994. pap. 8.95 (*1-884555-03-9*) P Depke Bks.

***Neave, M.** Sackville & Neave Property Law: Cases & Materials. 5th ed. 1072p. 1994. pap. 133.00 (*0-409-30529-4*, Austral) Butterworth Legal Pubs.

Neave, M., et al. Property Law: Cases & Materials. 4th ed. 1988. Australia. 100.00 (*0-409-49287-6*); Australia. pap. 94.00 (*0-409-49288-4*) Butterworth Legal Pubs.

Neave, M. A., jt. auth. see Bradbrook, A. J.

Neave, M. A., jt. auth. see Hardingham, I. J.

Neaverson, Peter, jt. auth. see Palmer, Marilyn.

Neaves, Pat. From Granny with Love Recipes from My Heart. (Illus.). 184p. 1991. spiral bd. 10.95 (*1-879806-00-2*) From My Heart.

— Little Black CookBook. (Illus.). 140p. 1992. spiral bd. 9.95 (*1-879806-01-0*) From My Heart.

Neba, Aaron S. Modern Geography of the Republic of Cameroon. 2nd ed. LC 87-70017. (Illus.). xii, 204p. 1987. 32.50 (*0-941815-01-3*); pap. 22.50 (*0-941815-00-5*) Neba Pubs.

***Nebabin, V.G.** Methods & Techniques of Radar Recognition. LC 94-29878. 1994. 79.00 (*0-89006-719-8*) Artech Hse.

***Nebalainen, David E & Callery, Marjana F.** Quality Systems in the Blood Bank & Laboratory Environment. (Illus.). (C). Date not set. pap. text ed. write for info. (*1-56395-038-3*) Am Assn Blood.

***Nebbe, Linda L.** Nature As a Guide: Using Nature in Counseling, Therapy, & Education. LC 95-60563. (Illus.). 256p. (C). 1995. pap. text ed. 14.95x (*0-932796-72-9*) Ed Media Corp.

Nebbia, Claudio, jt. auth. see Figa-Talamanca, Alessandro.

Nebe, G., jt. auth. see Plesken, W.

Nebebe, Fassil. Statistics with Minitab. 1990. 9.25 (*0-685-51813-2*) Ginn Pr.

Nebehay, Christian M. Gustav Klimt: From Drawing to Painting. LC 94-1415. 1994. write for info. (*0-8109-3510-4*) Abrams.

***Nebeker, Frederik.** Calculating the Weather: Meteorology in the Twentieth Century. (International Geophysics Ser.: Vol. 60). (Illus.). 336p. 1995. text ed. 59.95 (*0-12-515175-6*) Acad Pr.

Nebeker, Frederik, jt. auth. see Weber, Ernst.

Nebeker, R. Sparks of Genius: Portraits of Electrical Engineering Excellence. LC 93-15916. (Illus.). 280p. 1994. text ed. 34.95 (*0-7803-1033-0*, PC03822) Inst Electrical.

Nebel, B. Reasoning & Revision in Hybrid Representation Systems. Siekmann, Joerg H., ed. (Lecture Notes in Artificial Intelligence Ser.: Vol. 422). xii, 270p. 1990. pap. 32.70 (*0-387-52443-6*) Spr-Verlag.

Nebel, Bernard J. & Wright, Richard T. Environmental Science: The Way the World Works. 4th ed. 624p. (C). 1992. text ed. write for info. (*0-13-285446-5*) P-H.

— Environmental Science: The Way the World Works. 4th ed. LC 92-37954. 1993. write for info. (*0-13-285544-5*) P-H.

***Nebel, Bernhard & Dreschler-Fischer, Leonie, eds.** KI-94: Advances in Artificial Intelligence: Proceedings of the 18th German Annual Conference on Artificial Intelligence, Saarbrucken, Germany, September 18-23, 1994. LC 94-35132. (Lecture Notes in Computer Science, Vol. 861). 1994. 58.00 (*0-387-58467-6*) Spr-Verlag.

— KI-94: Advances in Artificial Intelligence: Proceedings of the 18th German Annual Conference on Artificial Intelligence, Saarbrucken, Germany, September 18-23, 1994. LC 94-35132. (Artificial Intelligence: 861). 1994. 58.00 (*3-540-58467-6*) Spr-Verlag.

Nebel, Bernhard, jt. ed. see Lakemeyer, Gerhard.

Nebel, Bernhard, et al, eds. Principles of Knowledge Representation & Reasoning: Proceedings of the Third International Conference (KR '92) LC 92-34433. (Representation & Reasoning Ser.). 1992. 49.95 (*1-55860-262-3*) Morgan Kaufmann.

Nebel, Cecile. The Dark Side of Creativity: Blocks, Unfinished Works & the Urge to Destroy. 175p. 1988. 18.50 (*0-87875-346-X*) Whitston Pub.

Nebel, Ed. Managing Hotels Effectively. (Illus.). 544p. 1991. text ed. 44.95 (*0-442-23814-2*) Van Nos Reinhold.

— Managing Hotels Effectively. 1993. pap. 20.95 (*0-442-01501-1*) Van Nos Reinhold.

Nebel, Frederick. The Adventures of Cardigan. LC 88-5233. (Dime Detective Bk.). 208p. 1988. pap. 9.95 (*0-89296-950-4*) Mysterious Pr.

— Six Deadly Dames. LC 80-12120. 189p. 1980. 18.95 (*0-8398-2654-0*) Boulevard.

Nebel, Martin. Vegetationskundliche Untersuchungen in Hoehenlohe. (Dissertationes Botanicae Ser.: Vol. 97). (Illus.). 262p. (GER.). 1986. pap. text ed. 71.50 (*3-443-64009-5*) Lubrecht & Cramer.

Nebelsick, Harold P. Renaissance & Reformation & the Rise of Science. 320p. 1992. pap. text ed. 33.95 (*0-567-09604-1*, Pub. by T & T Clark UK) Bks Intl VA.

Nebendahl, D., ed. Expert Systems, Pt. 2: Practical Applications. (Illus.). 328p. 1991. text ed. 63.00 (*3-8009-4104-X*) VCH Pubs.

Nebenhaus, Kathy, ed. see Elsden, Larry & Elsden, Judy.

Nebenhaus, Kathy, ed. see Muggleton, Pat, et al.

Nebenhaus, Kathy, ed. see Tucker, Michael.

Nebenzahl, Kenneth. Atlas of Columbus & the Great Discoveries. Fagan, Elizabeth & Leverenz, Jon, eds. (Illus.). 176p. (GER & SPA.). 1990. 75.00 (*0-528-83407-X*) Rand McNally.

Nebenzal, Harold. Cafe Berlin. 288p. 1994. pap. 10.00 (*0-380-72169-4*) Avon.

Nebert & Burrell. Marine Environmental Studies in Boca de Quadra & Smeaton Bay: Physical Oceanography, 1980. (IMS Report Ser.: No. R81-5). 59p. 5.25 (*0-914500-12-0*) U of AK Inst Marine.

Nebes, Norbert. Funktionsanalyse Von Kana Yaf Alu. (Studien Zur Sprachwissenschaft Ser.: Vol. 1). xiv, 222p. 1982. write for info. (*3-487-07300-5*, Pub. by Georg Olms GW) Lubrecht & Cramer.

Nebesky, Richard, jt. auth. see King, John.

***Nebesky, Richard, et al.** Russia, Ukraine & Belarus: Travel Survival Kit. (Illus.). 960p. 1996. pap. 24.95 (*0-86442-320-9*) Lonely Planet.

Nebesky-Wojkowitz, Rene De. Oracles & Demons of Tibet: The Cult & Iconography of the Tibetan Protective Deities. (C). 1993. 58.00 (*0-8364-2866-8*, Pub. by Book Faith II) S Asia.

— Tibetan Religious Dances. Von Furer-Haimendorf, Christoph, ed. (Religion & Society Ser.: No. 2). 1976. text ed. 60.00 (*90-279-7621-X*) Mouton.

Neblett, Genon H., jt. auth. see Wheeler, Mary B.

Neblett, Hester, jt. auth. see Hart, Martha A.

Neblett, William. Sherlock's Logic. (Orig.). 19.95 (*0-88029-723-9*) Dorset Pr.

Neblock, Nita, ed. Breaking Through Stone Walls: Where Do I Go From Here? (Illus.). 1989. pap. 5.00 (*0-913233-15-3*) AFRA.

— Genealogy Potpourri: Everything You Always Wanted to Know - But Didn't Know Who to Ask. (Illus.). 1988. pap. 5.00 (*0-913233-14-5*) AFRA.

— Migration of Church Groups to Midwest: Routes & Sources. (Illus.). 52p. 1987. pap. 5.00 (*0-913233-12-9*) AFRA.

— Roots in the Mid-West. (Illus.). 79p. 1991. pap. 5.00 (*0-913233-22-6*) AFRA.

— Threads in the Genealogical Tapestry. (Illus.). 38p. 1990. pap. 5.00 (*0-913233-18-8*) AFRA.

Neboiss, Arthur. Atlas of Trichoptera of the SW Pacific: Australian Region. (Entomologica Ser.). 1986. lib. bdg. 154.50 (*90-6193-575-X*) Kluwer Ac.

Nebor, Leos. Children of the World: Czechoslovakia. LC 87-42638. (Illus.). 64p. (J). (gr. 5-6). 1988. lib. bdg. 21.26 (*1-55532-216-6*) Gareth Stevens Inc.

Nebraska Curriculum Development Center Staff. A Curriculum for English, Units 82-84: Student Manual: The Hero. 197p. reprint ed. pap. 56.20 (*0-8357-3819-1*, 2052332) Bks Demand.

Nebraska Flying Boxcars Staff. The Fightn' 451st Bombardment Group. LC 89-51930. 240p. 1990. 48.00 (*0-938021-77-X*) Turner Pub KY.

Nebraska Library Commission Staff. Our Books, Our Wings: Books that Nebraskans Read & Treasure. 300p. (Orig.). (YA). (gr. 7). 1989. pap. 8.95 (*0-685-29054-9*) NE Library Commission.

Nebraska Sociological Feminist Collective. A Feminist Ethic for Social Science Research. LC 87-27377. (Women's Studies: Vol. 1). 250p. 1988. lib. bdg. 89.95 (*0-88946-120-1*) E Mellen.

Nebraska Symposium on Motivation Staff. Nebraska Symposium on Motivation, 1955. Jones, Marshall R., ed. LC 53-11655. (Current Theory & Research in Motivation Ser.: No. 3). 284p. reprint ed. pap. 81.00 (*0-7837-6597-5*, 2046163) Bks Demand.

— Nebraska Symposium on Motivation, 1956. Jones, Marshall R., ed. LC 53-11655. (Current Theory & Research in Motivation Ser.: No. 4). 319p. reprint ed. pap. 91.00 (*0-7837-6598-3*, 2046164) Bks Demand.

— Nebraska Symposium on Motivation, 1957. Jones, Marshall R., ed. LC 53-11655. (Current Theory & Research in Motivation Ser.: No. 5). 442p. reprint ed. pap. 126.00 (*0-7837-6599-1*, 2046165) Bks Demand.

— Nebraska Symposium on Motivation, 1958. Jones, Marshall R., ed. LC 53-11655. (Current Theory & Research in Motivation Ser.: No. 6). 288p. reprint ed. pap. 82.10 (*0-7837-6600-9*, 2046166) Bks Demand.

— Nebraska Symposium on Motivation, 1959. Jones, Marshall R., ed. LC 53-11655. (Current Theory & Research in Motivation Ser.: No. 7). 253p. reprint ed. pap. 72.20 (*0-7837-6601-7*, 2046167) Bks Demand.

— Nebraska Symposium on Motivation, 1960. Jones, Marshall R., ed. LC 53-11655. (Current Theory & Research in Motivation Ser.: No. 8). 280p. reprint ed. pap. 79.80 (*0-7837-6602-5*, 2046168) Bks Demand.

— Nebraska Symposium on Motivation, 1961. Jones, Marshall R., ed. LC 53-11655. (Current Theory & Research in Motivation Ser.: No. 9). 220p. reprint ed. pap. 62.70 (*0-7837-6603-3*, 2046169) Bks Demand.

— Nebraska Symposium on Motivation, 1962. Jones, Marshall R., ed. LC 53-11655. (Current Theory & Research in Motivation Ser.: No. 10). 344p. reprint ed. pap. 98.10 (*0-7837-6604-1*, 2046170) Bks Demand.

— Nebraska Symposium on Motivation, 1963. Jones, Marshall R., ed. LC 53-11655. (Current Theory & Research in Motivation Ser.: No. 11). 214p. reprint ed. pap. 61.00 (*0-7837-6605-X*, 2046171) Bks Demand.

— Nebraska Symposium on Motivation, 1964. Levine, David, ed. LC 53-11655. (Current Theory & Research in Motivation Ser.: No. 12). 294p. reprint ed. pap. 83.80 (*0-7837-6606-8*, 2046172) Bks Demand.

— Nebraska Symposium on Motivation, 1965. Levine, David, ed. LC 53-11655. (Current Theory & Research in Motivation Ser.: No. 13). 356p. reprint ed. pap. 101.50 (*0-7837-6607-6*, 2046173) Bks Demand.

— Nebraska Symposium on Motivation, 1966. Levine, David, ed. LC 53-11655. (Current Theory & Research in Motivation Ser.: No. 14). 219p. reprint ed. pap. 62.50 (*0-7837-6608-4*, 2046174) Bks Demand.

— Nebraska Symposium on Motivation, 1967. Levine, David, ed. LC 53-11655. (Current Theory & Research in Motivation Ser.: No. 15). 345p. reprint ed. pap. 98.40 (*0-7837-6609-2*, 2046175) Bks Demand.

— Nebraska Symposium on Motivation, 1968. Arnold, William J., ed. LC 53-11655. (Current Theory & Research in Motivation Ser.: No. 16). 347p. reprint ed. pap. 98.90 (*0-7837-6610-6*, 2046178) Bks Demand.

— Nebraska Symposium on Motivation, 1970. Arnold, William J. & Page, Monte M., eds. LC 53-11655. (Current Theory & Research in Motivation Ser.: No. 18). 302p. reprint ed. pap. 86.10 (*0-7837-6611-4*, 2046176) Bks Demand.

— Nebraska Symposium on Motivation, 1971. Cole, James K., ed. LC 53-11655. (Current Theory & Research in Motivation Ser.: No. 19). 316p. reprint ed. pap. 90.10 (*0-7837-6612-2*, 2046177) Bks Demand.

— Nebraska Symposium on Motivation, 1972. Cole, James K. & Jensen, Donald D., eds. LC 53-11655. (Current Theory & Research in Motivation Ser.: No. 20). 353p. reprint ed. pap. 100.70 (*0-7837-6613-0*, 2046179) Bks Demand.

— Nebraska Symposium on Motivation, 1973. Cole, James K. & Dienstbier, Richard, eds. LC 53-11655. (Current Theory & Research in Motivation Ser.: No. 21). 339p. reprint ed. pap. 96.70 (*0-7837-6614-9*, 2046180) Bks Demand.

— Nebraska Symposium on Motivation, 1974. Cole, James K. & Sonderegger, Theo B., eds. LC 53-11655. (Current Theory & Research in Motivation Ser.: No. 22). 328p. reprint ed. pap. 93.50 (*0-7837-6615-7*, 2046181) Bks Demand.

— Nebraska Symposium on Motivation, 1975: Conceptual Foundations of Psychology. Arnold, William J., ed. LC 53-11655. (Current Theory & Research in Motivation Ser.: No. 23). 614p. reprint ed. pap. 175.00 (*0-7837-6616-5*, 2046182) Bks Demand.

— Nebraska Symposium on Motivation, 1976: Personal Construct Psychology. Landfield, Alvin W., ed. LC 53-11655. (Current Theory & Research in Motivation Ser.: No. 24). 379p. reprint ed. pap. 108.10 (*0-7837-6617-3*, 2046183) Bks Demand.

— Nebraska Symposium on Motivation, 1977: Social Cognitive Development. Keasey, Charles B., ed. LC 53-11655. (Current Theory & Research in Motivation Ser.: No. 25). 373p. reprint ed. pap. 106.40 (*0-7837-6618-1*, 2046184) Bks Demand.

— Nebraska Symposium on Motivation, 1978: Human Emotion. Dienstbier, Richard A., ed. LC 53-11655. (Current Theory & Research in Motivation Ser.: No. 26). 347p. reprint ed. pap. 98.90 (*0-7837-6619-X*, 2046185) Bks Demand.

— Nebraska Symposium on Motivation, 1979: Beliefs, Attitudes, & Values. Page, Monte M., ed. LC 53-11655. (Current Theory & Research in Motivation Ser.: No. 27). 377p. reprint ed. pap. 107.50 (*0-7837-6620-3*, 2046186) Bks Demand.

— Nebraska Symposium on Motivation, 1980: Cognitive Processes. Flowers, John H., ed. LC 53-11655. (Current Theory & Research in Motivation Ser.: No. 28). 265p. reprint ed. pap. 75.60 (*0-7837-6621-1*, 2046187) Bks Demand.

— Nebraska Symposium on Motivation, 1981: Response Structure & Organization. Bernstein, Daniel J., ed. LC 53-11655. (Current Theory & Research in Motivation Ser.: No. 29). 279p. reprint ed. pap. 79.60 (*0-7837-6622-X*, 2046188) Bks Demand.

— Nebraska Symposium on Motivation, 1982: Personality - Current Theory & Research. Page, Monte M., ed. LC 53-11655. (Current Theory & Research in Motivation Ser.: No. 30). 292p. reprint ed. pap. 83.30 (*0-7837-6623-8*, 2046189) Bks Demand.

— Nebraska Symposium on Motivation, 1983: Theories of Schizophrenia & Psychosis. Spaulding, William D. & Cole, James K., eds. LC 53-11655. (Current Theory & Research in Motivation Ser.: No. 31). 391p. reprint ed. pap. 111.50 (*0-7837-6624-6*, 2046190) Bks Demand.

Nebreda, E. Bibliographia Augustiniana Seu Operum Collectio Quae, Divi Augustini Vitam et Doctrinam Quadantenus exponunt. (Classical Studies Ser.). (LAT.). reprint ed. lib. bdg. 39.50 (*0-697-00013-3*) Irvington.

Nebrera, Gregorio T., ed. see Quintero, Serafin Y.

Nebrija, A. Romance Vocabulary in Latin: Vocabulario de Romance en Latin. 200p. (LAT & SPA.). 1981. pap. 45.00 (*0-8288-1617-4*, S39785) Fr & Eur.

NEBSS Staff & NRMC Staff, eds. Writing Skills. (Open Learning for Supervisory Management Ser.: 302). (Illus.). 106p. 1986. 25.95 (*0-08-070072-1*, Pub. by PPL UK) Elsevier.

NEC-TAS Health Focus Group Staff & Fenichel, Emily. Promoting Health Through Part H: Promoting the Health of Infants & Toddlers with Disabilities Through Part H of the Individuals with Disabilities Evaluation Act. 49p. (Orig.). 1991. pap. 7.00 (*0-943657-17-2*) Zero To Three.

Necas, J. & Hlavacek, I. Mathematical Theory of Elastic & Elasto-Plastic Bodies: An Introduction. (Studies in Applied Mechanics: Vol. 3). 342p. 1991. 120.00 (*0-444-99754-7*) Elsevier.

Necas, J., jt. ed. see Galdi, G. P.

Necas, Jindric. Introduction to the Theory of Nonlinear Elliptic Equations. 163p. 1986. text ed. 115.00 (*0-471-90894-0*) Wiley.

Necas, Jindrich, jt. ed. see Galdi, Giovanni P.

Necatigil, Zaim M. The Cyprus Question & the Turkish Position in International Law. 2nd ed. LC 92-28431. 542p. 1993. 69.00 (*0-19-825846-1*) OUP.

Necchi, Orlando, Jr. Revision of the Genus Batrachospermum Roth (Rhodophyta, Batrachospermales) in Brazil. (Bibliotheca Phycologica Ser.: Vol. 84). (Illus.). 220p. 1990. pap. text ed. 76.50 (*3-443-60011-5*, Pub. by Gebruder Borntraeger GW) Lubrecht & Cramer.

Nechaeva, Nina T., ed. Improvement in Desert Ranges in Soviet Central Asia. (Advances in Desert & Arid Land Technology & Development Ser.). 342p. 1985. text ed. 295.00 (*3-7186-0222-9*) Gordon & Breach.

Nechama Tec. They Chose to Fight: Jewish Partisians in Belorussia During World War II. LC 92-33501. 1993. 30.00 (*0-19-507595-1*) OUP.

Nechas, Eileen. Unequal Treatment. 1994. 22.00 (*0-671-79186-9*) S&S Trade.

Nechas, Eileen & Foley, Denise. What Do I Do Now? LC 92-16458. 1992. pap. 12.00 (*0-671-76848-4*, Fireside) S&S Trade.

Necheles-Jansyn, Ruth F. The Mediator Revisited: Profile of a Profession, 1960s & 1985. LC 90-42215. (Institute of Management & Labor Relations Ser.: No. 3). 209p. 1990. 25.00 (*0-8108-2351-9*) Scarecrow.

Necheles, Ruth F. Abbe Gregoire, 1787-1831: The Odyssey of an Egalitarian. LC 75-105987. 333p. (C). 1971. text ed. 55.00 (*0-8371-3312-2*, NAG/&, Greenwood Pr) Greenwood.

Neches, William H., et al, eds. Pediatric Cardiac Catheterization. (Perspectives in Pediatric Cardiology Ser.: Vol. 3). (Illus.). 472p. 1991. 85.00 (*0-87993-500-6*) Futura Pub.

Nechiporenko, Oleg. Passport to Assassination: The Never Before Told Story of Lee Harvey Oswald by the KGB Colonel. 1993. 22.50 (*1-55972-210-X*, Birch Ln Pr) Carol Pub Group.

Nechis, Barbara. Watercolor from the Heart. (Illus.). 144p. (Orig.). 1993. 29.95 (*0-8230-1624-2*, Watsn-Guptill) Watsn-Guptill.

Nechodom, Kerry, illus. & adapt. The Rainbow Bridge: A Chumash Legend. 32p. (Orig.). (J). (gr. k-3). 1992. pap. 6.95 (*0-944627-36-6*) Sand River Pr.

An Asterisk (*) at the beginning of an entry indicates that the title is appearing in BIP for the first time.

*Nechols, James, ed. Biological Control in the Western United States. (Illus.). 376p. 1995. pap. 25.00 (1-879906-21-X, 3361) ANR Pubns CA.

Necholson, John. Chi-la-pe & the White Buffalo. (Indian Culture Ser.). 44p. (J). (gr. 2-10). 1981. pap. 5.95 (0-89992-064-0) Coun India Ed.

Nechvatal, A., jt. auth. see Tedder, J. M.

Nechvatal, A., jt. auth. see Tedder, John M.

Necipoglu, Gulcru. Architecture, Ceremonial & Power: The Topkapi Palace in the Fifteenth & Sixteenth Centuries. (Illus.). 384p. 1992. 55.00x (0-262-14050-0) MIT Pr.

*Necipoglu, Gulru. The Topkapi Scroll - Geometry & Ornament in Islamic Architecture. (Sketches & Albums Ser.). (Illus.). 384p. 1995. 160.00 (0-89236-335-5, Getty Ctr Hist Art & Human) J P Getty Trust.

Neck, Philip A. & Nelson, Robert E., eds. Small Enterprise Development: Policies & Programmes. 2nd rev. ed. (Management Development Ser.: No. 14). xiii, 282p. (Orig.). 1987. pap. 28.00 (92-2-105699-6) Intl Labour Office.

Neck, R. & Agilvsg, G. Field Guide - Butterflies of Texas. 224p. 1995. pap. write for info. (0-87719-243-X) Gulf Pub.

Neckar, Lance, jt. ed. see Condon, Patrick M.

Neckebrouck, Valeer, jt. ed. see Cornille, Catherine.

Necker, M. Burk. The Auschwitz Chimneys Smoke. rev. ed. (Illus.). 140p. 1993. pap. 12.50 (1-877582-19-0) Ardor Pub.

— Gold, Silver & Uranium from Seas & Oceans: The Emerging Technology. rev. ed. (Illus.). 330p. (C). 1991. 77.00 (1-877582-17-4); pap. 68.00 (1-877582-12-3) Ardor Pub.

Necker, Maksymilian B. The Essence & Meaning of Life. (Illus.). 160p. (Orig.). 1991. write for info. (1-877582-10-7); pap. 18.50 (1-877582-11-5) Ardor Pub.

— Folks in Cockeyed Pictures: Collection of Parodies, Japes, Jokes, Anectodes & Pastiches. (Illus.). 116p. (Orig.). 1989. pap. 9.95 (1-877582-09-3) Ardor Pub.

— Heart & Wit: Short Stories. (Illus.). 210p. (Orig.). 1991. pap. 16.50 (1-877582-16-6) Ardor Pub.

— The Holocaust Verses. rev. ed. (Illus.). 140p. (Orig.). 1990. pap. 12.50 (1-877582-13-1) Ardor Pub.

— The Human Menagerie: Collection of Satires & Parodies. rev. ed. (Illus.). 126p. (Orig.). 1990. pap. 14.50 (1-877582-14-X) Ardor Pub.

— Politicos, Dumbbells & Quacks. (Illus.). 170p. (Orig.). 1993. pap. 14.50 (1-877582-15-8) Ardor Pub.

— Sir Mistake & Mister Blunder: Collection of Satires & Parodies. 122p. (Orig.). 1989. pap. 13.50 (1-877582-07-7) Ardor Pub.

Necker, Wilhelm. The German Army of Today, Nineteen Forty-Three. (Illus.). 1976. reprint ed. 15.00 (0-85409-896-8) Charles River Bks.

Neckermann, Peter. The Unification of Germany: The Anatomy of a Peaceful Revolution. 160p. 1992. text ed. 22.50 (0-88033-230-1) Col U Pr.

Neckers, ed. New Directions in Photodynamic Therapy. 1987. 45.00 (0-89252-882-6, 847) SPIE.

Neckers, D. C., jt. auth. see Kumar, G. Sudesh.

Neckers, Douglas C., ed. Selected Papers on Photochemistry. LC 92-29753. (Milestone Ser.: Vol. MS 65). 1992. 109.00 (0-8194-1057-8); pap. 124.00 (0-8194-1056-X) SPIE.

*Neckers, Douglas C., et al. Advances in Photochemistry, Vol. 19. (Advances in Photochemistry). 325p. 1994. text ed. 125.00 (0-471-04912-3) Wiley.

Neckers, James W. The Building of a Department: Chemistry at Southern Illinois University, 1927-1967. LC 78-13384. (Illus.). 197p. 1979. 12.95 (0-8093-0901-7) S Ill U Pr.

Neckler. Safekeeping. 1984. pap. 3.50 (0-449-12704-4) Fawcett.

Necoechea, Miguel. In Defense of Mexico. 1976. lib. bdg. 59.95 (0-8490-2042-5) Gordon Pr.

Nectou, Jean-Michel, ed. Gabriel Faure: His Life Through His Letters. Underwood, J. A., tr. (Illus.). 320p. 1984. 40.00 (0-7145-2768-8) M Boyars Pubs.

Nectoux, Jean-Michel. Gabriel Faure: A Musical Life. (Illus.). 640p. (C). 1991. 89.95 (0-521-23524-3) Cambridge U Pr.

— New Grove Twentieth Century French. 1986. 25.00 (0-393-02284-6) Norton.

— New Grove Twentieth-Century French Masters: Faure, Debussy, Satie, Ravel, Poulenc, Messaien. 1986. pap. 14. 95 (0-393-30350-0) Norton.

Nedaud & Marcello. Zorro in Old California. (Illus.). 1990. 10.95 (0-913035-13-0); pap. 6.95 (0-913035-12-2) Eclipse Bks.

Nedbalek, Lani. Wahiawa: From Dream to Community. LC 84-51437. (Illus.). 128p. (Orig.). 1984. pap. 6.95 (0-930117-01-8) Wonder View Pr.

— Waipahu: A Brief History. (Illus.). 64p. (Orig.). 1984. pap. 3.95 (0-930117-00-X) Wonder View Pr.

Nedd, Kester J., ed. South Florida Rehab & Healthcare Directory, 1991. 490p. 1991. 39.00 (1-879657-00-7, Nedmar Graphics) HealthNet Pages.

Nedd, LaRue E. Black Laws: Nature of African Reality. 126p. 1990. pap. write for info. (1-883762-00-6, 029916637) HomeBased Comm.

— The Psych War: Interracial Battle for Mind Control. 23p. 1990. pap. 4.50 (1-883762-01-4, 038769464) HomeBased Comm.

— Why We Shouldn't Call Our Foreparents Slaves. 20p. Date not set. pap. 5.00 (1-883762-02-2) HomeBased Comm.

Nedderman, R. M. Statics & Kinematics of Granular Materials. (Illus.). 424p. (C). 1992. 99.95 (0-521-40435-5) Cambridge U Pr.

Nedderman, R. M., jt. auth. see Kay, John M.

Neddermeyer, Henning, ed. Scanning Tunneling Microscopy. LC 92-38479. (Perspectives in Condensed Matter Physics Ser.: Vol. 6). 272p. (C). 1993. lib. bdg. 122.00 (0-7923-2065-4) Kluwer Ac.

*Neddings, Nel. Philosophy of Education. LC 95-8820. 1995. write for info. (0-8133-8430-3) Westview.

Nedelkoff, D. Dan. One-Half of a Telephone Conversation. 1976. 1.00 (0-685-67938-1) Windless Orchard.

Nedell, Harold. The New Fox Terrier. LC 87-22649. (Illus.). 384p. 1987. 29.95 (0-87605-122-0) Howell Bk.

Nedelsky, Jennifer. Private Property & the Limits of American Constitutionalism: The Madisonian Framework & Its Legacy. 336p. 1990. 29.95 (0-226-56970-5) U Ch Pr.

— Private Property & the Limits of American Constitutionalism: The Madisonian Framework & Its Legacy. xiv, 343p. 1994. pap. text ed. 15.95 (0-226-56971-3) U Ch Pr.

Nederhood, Joel. Promises, Promises, Promises. LC 79-18889. (Voices Study Ser.). (Orig.). (YA). (gr. 10-12). 1979. teacher ed 8.50 (0-933140-78-9); pap. text ed. 6.25 (0-933140-09-6) CRC Pubns.

Nederlander, Caren. Changing Views - The Impressionist Photographs of Caren Nederlander, Ph.D. (Illus.). 30p. (Orig.). 1988. pap. 10.00 (0-9622466-0-3) C Nederlander.

Nederlander, Munin. Kitezh: The Russian Grail Legends. 304p. 1991. 29.95 (1-85538-037-4, Pub. by Aquarian Pr UK) Thorsons SF.

Nederman, Cary J. Community & Consent: The Secular Political Theory of Marsiglio of Padua's Defensor Pacis. LC 94-16779. 192p. reprint ed. lib. bdg. 57.50 (0-8476-7943-8); reprint ed. pap. 22.95 (0-8476-7944-6) Rowman.

Nederman, Cary J. & Forhan, Kate L., eds. Medieval Political Theory: A Reader: The Quest for the Body Politic, 1100-1400. LC 92-26387. 224p. 1993. 55.00 (0-415-06488-0, A9926, Routledge NY); pap. 15.95 (0-415-06489-9, A9930, Routledge NY) Routledge.

Nederman, Cary J., ed. see John of Salisbury.

Nederman, Cary J., ed. see Marsiglio of Padua.

*Nederpelt, R. P., et al. Selected Papers on Automath. LC 94-34022. (Studies in Logic & the Foundations of Mathematics: Vol. 133). 1994. write for info. (0-444-89822-0) Elsevier.

Nederveen, A., jt. auth. see Houtman, P.

Nedges, Charles S. Electrical Control of Fluid Power. 3rd ed. LC 77-156757. (Illus.). 256p. 1987. pap. 13.95 (0-9605644-9-7) Womack Educ Pubns.

Nedham, Marchamont, tr. see Selden, John.

Nedjalkov, Vladimir P. & Comrie, Bernard, eds. Typology of Resultative Constructions. LC 88-2598. (Typological Studies in Language: Vol. 12). xx, 573p. (C). 1988. reprint ed. 144.00x (0-915027-78-X); reprint ed. pap. 42. 95x (0-915027-79-8) Benjamins North Am.

Nedjati, Z. M. Human Rights under the European Convention. LC 78-23469. (European Studies in Law Ser.: Vol. 8). 298p. 1979. 89.75 (0-444-85218-2, North Holland) Elsevier.

*Nedo, M. Ludwig Wittgenstein-Wiener Ausgabe: Einfuhrung-Introduction. 148p. 1994. 24.50 (0-387-82498-7) Spr-Verlag.

— Philosophische Bemerkungen, 1. (Ludwig Wittgenstein, Wiener Ausgabe). 196p. 1994. 98.00 (0-387-82499-5) Spr-Verlag.

— Philosophische Betrachtungen, 2. (Ludwig Wittgenstein, Wiener Ausgabe). 333p. 1994. 125.00 (0-387-82502-9) Spr-Verlag.

Nedobeck, Don. Nedobeck's Alphabet Book. (Illus.). 16p. (J). (gr. 1-8). 1993. reprint ed. 9.95 (0-944314-00-7) New Wrinkle.

— Nedobeck's Numbers Book. 26p. (J). (gr. 1-8). 1988. 9.95 (0-944314-01-5) New Wrinkle.

Nedobeck, Don, illus. Nedobecks Twelve Days of Christmas. (J). (gr. 1-8). 1988. reprint ed. lib. bdg. 9.95 (0-944314-02-3) New Wrinkle.

Nedoluha, Gerald E., jt. ed. see Clegg, Andrew W.

Nedoncelle, Maurice. The Personalist Challenge: Intersubjectivity & Ontology. Gerard, Francois C. et al, trs. LC 83-26293. (Pittsburgh Theological Monographs: No. 27). 1994. pap. 10.00 (0-915138-29-8) Pickwick.

Nedreaas, Torborg. Music from a Blue Well. Lee, Bibbi, tr. LC 87-19026. (European Women Writers Ser.). vi, 238p. 1988. 21.00 (0-8032-3315-9) U of Nebr Pr.

— Nothing Grows by Moonlight. Lee, Bibbi, tr. LC 87-5000. (European Women Writers Ser.). vi, 198p. 1987. 15.95 (0-8032-3313-2) U of Nebr Pr.

Nedvetsky, Andrei G., intro. Khiva. (Great Photographic Archives Ser.). (Illus.). 128p. 1995. 35.00 (1-873938-27-6, Pub. by Garnet Pubng Ltd UK) Paul & Co Pubs.

Nedwell, D. B. & Brown, C. M., eds. Sediment Microbiology. (Society for General Microbiology Special Publications: No. 7). 1982. text ed. 95.00 (0-12-515380-5) Acad Pr.

*Nee, A. Y., et al, eds. Advanced Fixture Design for FMS. (Advanced Manufacturing Ser.). 1994. 89.00 (0-387-19908-X) Spr-Verlag.

*Nee, D. Y. Holistic Social Transformation: The New World Order. (C). 1996. pap. 20.00 (0-9639876-1-5) Inst For Systs.

— Radicalizinag the World Through Social Engineering: The New World Order. 272p. (Orig.). (C). 1993. pap. 38.00 (0-9639876-0-7) Inst For Systs.

Nee, Eric. The UniForum Guide to Graphical User Interfaces. Gold, Jordan, ed. (Illus.). 25p. (Orig.). pap. text ed. 9.95 (0-936593-16-4) UniForum.

Nee, John G. Engineering Graphics Problems. 226p. (C). 1985. pap. write for info. (0-02-386030-8) Macmillan.

— Jig & Fixture Design & Detailing. LC 78-71562. (Illus.). (C). 1979. pap. 17.95 (0-911168-41-9) Prakken.

— Mechanical Engineering Technology: Product Design & Drafting Problems. LC 83-60332. (Illus.). 163p. (C). 1983. pap. 11.95 (0-911168-52-4) Prakken.

*Nee, Patrick W. The Internationalist Business Guide to Africa: Guide for International Business & Investment. 200p. (Orig.). 1995. pap. 24.95 (0-9633905-6-2) Intlnatlist Pub Co.

— The Internationalist Business Guide to Eastern Europe & Russia: Guide for International Business & Investment. 200p. (Orig.). 1995. pap. 24.95 (0-9633905-4-6) Intlnatlist Pub Co.

— The Internationalist Business Guide to Mexico, Canada & Latin America: Guide for International Business & Investment. 200p. (Orig.). 1995. pap. 24.95 (0-9633905-1-1) Intlnatlist Pub Co.

— The Internationalist Business Guide to Middle East & Southern Asia: Guide for International Business & Investment. 200p. (Orig.). 1995. pap. 24.95 (0-9633905-5-4) Intlnatlist Pub Co.

— The Internationalist Business Guide to Pacific Rim & Southeast Asia: Guide for International Business & Investment. 200p. (Orig.). 1995. pap. 24.95 (0-9633905-2-X) Intlnatlist Pub Co.

— The Internationalist Business Guide to Western Europe: Guide for International Business & Investment. 200p. (Orig.). 1995. pap. 24.95 (0-9633905-3-8) Intlnatlist Pub Co.

— The Internationalist Business & Investment Guides Series: Guides for International Business & Investment, 6 bks., Set. (Orig.). 1995. pap. 99.95 (0-9633905-7-0) Intlnatlist Pub Co.

— The Lone Gunman. 195p. 1992. pap. 12.50 (0-9633905-0-3) Intlnatlist Pub Co.

Nee, T. S. Aguas Refrescantes. Orig. Title: Through the Year. 270p. (SPA.). 1992. pap. 5.25 (0-8254-1500-4) Kregel.

— La Cruz en la Vida Cristiana Normal. Orig. Title: The Cross in the Normal Christian Life. 144p. (SPA.). 1993. pap. 4.99 (0-8254-1501-2) Kregel.

— L' Homme Spirituel. 434p. (FRE.). 1991. pap. 15.95 (0-8297-1527-4) Life Pubs Intl.

— No Ameis al Mundo. Orig. Title: Love Not the World. 96p. (SPA.). 1992. pap. 3.99 (0-8254-1502-0) Kregel.

— El Obrero Cristiano Normal. Orig. Title: The Normal Christian Worker. 112p. (SPA.). 1992. pap. 3.99 (0-8254-1503-9) Kregel.

— Que Hare, Senor? Orig. Title: What Shall This Man Do?. 228p. (SPA.). 1992. pap. 5.99 (0-8254-1504-7) Kregel.

— Sentaos, Andad, Estad Firmes. Orig. Title: Sit, Walk, Stand. 80p. (SPA.). 1992. pap. 3.50 (0-8254-1505-5) Kregel.

— Transformados en Su Semejanza. Orig. Title: Transformed into His Image. 144p. (SPA.). 1992. pap. 4.99 (0-8254-1506-3) Kregel.

— La Vida Cristiana Normal. Orig. Title: Normal Christian Worker. 128p. (SPA.). 1992. pap. 3.99 (0-8254-1509-8) Kregel.

Nee, Tham S., jt. auth. see Leok, Goh C.

Nee, Victor. Community & Change in Revolutionary China. LC 91-3848. (Harvard Studies in Sociology). 168p. 1991. 16.00 (0-8240-9840-4) Garland.

— The Cultural Revolution at Peking University. LC 77-81790. 91p. reprint ed. pap. 26.00 (0-318-34967-1, 2030765) Bks Demand.

Nee, Victor & De Bary Nee, Brett. Longtime Californ' A Documentary Study of an American Chinatown. 438p. 1986. reprint ed. 45.00 (0-8047-1335-9); reprint ed. pap. 14.95 (0-8047-1336-7) Stanford U Pr.

Nee, Victor & Mozingo, David, eds. State & Society in Contemporary China. LC 82-46010. 269p. 1983. 39.95 (0-8014-1570-5); pap. 16.95 (0-8014-9253-X) Cornell U Pr.

Nee, Victor & Stark, David, eds. Remaking the Economic Institutions of Socialism: China & Eastern Europe. 424p. 1989. 49.50 (0-8047-1494-0); pap. 16.95 (0-8047-1495-9) Stanford U Pr.

Nee, Victor, jt. ed. see Lyons, Thomas.

Nee, Watchman. Aids to "Revelation" Kaung, Stephen, tr. 122p. 1983. pap. 4.00 (0-935008-60-8) Christian Fellow Pubs.

— Assembling Together. Kaung, Stephen, tr. (Basic Lesson Ser.: Vol. 3). 147p. 1973. 6.50 (0-935008-01-2); pap. 4.50 (0-935008-02-0) Christian Fellow Pubs.

— Back to the Cross. Fader, Herbert L., ed. Kaung, Stephen, tr. 171p. (Orig.). 1988. pap. 4.50 (0-935008-70-5) Christian Fellow Pubs.

— A Balanced Christian Life. Kaung, Stephen, tr. 174p. 1981. pap. 4.50 (0-935008-53-5) Christian Fellow Pubs.

— The Better Covenant. Kaung, Stephen, tr. 167p. 1982. 8.00 (0-935008-56-X); pap. 5.00 (0-935008-55-1) Christian Fellow Pubs.

— The Body of Christ: A Reality. Kaung, Stephen, tr. 90p. 1978. pap. 3.50 (0-935008-13-6) Christian Fellow Pubs.

— El Cantar De Los Cantares: Song of Songs-Commentary. (SPA.). 5.50 (84-7228-156-6, 220137, Pub. by Edit Clie SP) TSELF.

— Changed into His Likeness. 1992. pap. 4.95 (0-87508-410-9) Chr Lit.

— Changed into His Likeness. 1978. pap. 4.99 (0-8423-0228-X) Tyndale.

— The Character of God's Workman. Fader, Herbert L., ed. Kaung, Stephen, tr. 229p. (Orig.). 1988. pap. 5.50 (0-935008-69-1) Christian Fellow Pubs.

— Christ the Sum of All Spiritual Things. Kaung, Stephen, tr. 96p. 1973. pap. 3.50 (0-935008-14-4) Christian Fellow Pubs.

— The Church & the Work, 3 vols. Kaung, Stephen, tr. 550p. (CHI.). 1982. reprint ed. 30.00 (0-935008-57-8); reprint ed. pap. text ed. 17.00 (0-935008-58-6) Christian Fellow Pubs.

— Come, Lord Jesus. Kaung, Stephen, tr. 258p. 1976. 8.00 (0-935008-15-2); pap. 6.00 (0-935008-16-0) Christian Fellow Pubs.

— The Communion of the Holy Spirit. Fader, Herbert L., ed. Kaung, Stephen, tr. 1994. pap. 4.50 (0-935008-79-9) Christian Fellow Pubs.

— Conhecimento Espiritual. Orig. Title: Spiritual Knowledge. 144p. (POR.). 1986. 3.95 (0-8297-0781-6) Life Pubs Intl.

— Consejos Para una Vida Santa: Thoughts for a Holy Life. (SPA.). 4.95 (84-7645-234-9, 223259, Pub. by Edit Clie SP) TSELF.

— Consejos Sobre la Vida Cristiana: Thoughts on Christian Living. (SPA.). 5.95 (84-7645-233-0, 223260, Pub. by Edit Clie SP) TSELF.

— El Cuerpo De Cristo: La Realidad: The Body of Crist: A Reality. (SPA.). 3.25 (84-7645-269-1, 223303, Pub. by Edit Clie SP) TSELF.

— Do All to the Glory of God. Kaung, Stephen, tr. (Basic Lesson Ser.: Vol. 5). 214p. 1974. 7.00 (0-935008-03-9); pap. 5.50 (0-935008-04-7) Christian Fellow Pubs.

— Escudrinad las Escrituras: Search the Scriptures. (SPA.). 4.95 (84-7645-289-6, 223342, Pub. by Edit Clie SP) TSELF.

— The Finest of the Wheat, Vol. I. Kaung, Stephen & Fader, Herbert L., eds. 456p. 1992. 15.00 (0-935008-75-6); pap. 10.00 (0-935008-76-4) Christian Fellow Pubs.

— The Finest of the Wheat, Vol. II. Kaung, Stephen & Fader, Herbert L., eds. 527p. 1993. 15.00 (0-935008-77-2); pap. 10.00 (0-935008-78-0) Christian Fellow Pubs.

— From Faith to Faith. Fader, Herbert L., ed. 120p. 1984. pap. 4.50 (0-935008-62-4) Christian Fellow Pubs.

— From Glory to Glory. Fader, Herbert L., ed. Kaung, Stephen, tr. & intro. by. 142p. (Orig.). 1985. pap. 4.50 (0-935008-64-0) Christian Fellow Pubs.

— Full of Grace & Truth, Vol. I. Kaung, Stephen, tr. 205p. 1980. pap. 4.50 (0-935008-49-7) Christian Fellow Pubs.

— Full of Grace & Truth, Vol. II. Kaung, Stephen, tr. 147p. 1981. pap. 4.50 (0-935008-51-9) Christian Fellow Pubs.

— Gleanings in the Fields of Boaz. Fader, Herbert L., ed. Kaung, Stephen, tr. 136p. (Orig.). 1987. pap. 4.50 (0-935008-68-3) Christian Fellow Pubs.

— The Glory of His Life. Kaung, Stephen, tr. 117p. 1976. pap. 4.50 (0-935008-18-7) Christian Fellow Pubs.

— God's Plan & the Overcomers. Kaung, Stephen, tr. 83p. 1977. pap. 3.50 (0-935008-19-5) Christian Fellow Pubs.

— God's Work. Kaung, Stephen, tr. 64p. 1974. pap. 3.50 (0-935008-20-9) Christian Fellow Pubs.

— The Good Confession. Kaung, Stephen, tr. (Basic Lesson Ser.: Vol. 2). 114p. 1973. 6.00 (0-935008-05-5); pap. 4.00 (0-935008-06-3) Christian Fellow Pubs.

— Gospel Dialogue. Kaung, Stephen, tr. 197p. 1975. 8.00 (0-935008-21-7); pap. 5.00 (0-935008-22-5) Christian Fellow Pubs.

— Grace for Grace. Kaung, Stephen, tr. 114p. 1983. pap. text ed. 4.00 (0-935008-59-4) Christian Fellow Pubs.

— El Hombre Espiritual: The Spiritual Man, 3 bks., Tomo I. (SPA.). 5.95 (84-7645-206-3, 223252, Pub. by Edit Clie SP) TSELF.

— El Hombre Espiritual: The Spiritual Man, 3 bks., Tomo II. (SPA.). 6.75 (84-7645-207-1, 223253, Pub. by Edit Clie SP) TSELF.

— El Hombre Espiritual: The Spiritual Man, 3 bks., Tomo III. (SPA.). 6.95 (84-7645-208-X, 223254, Pub. by Edit Clie SP) TSELF.

— La Iglesia Gloriosa: The Glorious Church. (SPA.). 5.95 (84-7228-799-8, 220482, Pub. by Edit Clie SP) TSELF.

— La Iglesia Normal: The Normal Church. (SPA.). 5.50 (84-7228-798-X, 220484, Pub. by Edit Clie SP) TSELF.

— Interpreting Matthew. Fader, Herbert L., ed. Kaung, Stephen, tr. 288p. (Orig.). 1989. 12.00 (0-935008-71-3); pap. 6.50 (0-935008-72-1) Christian Fellow Pubs.

— Joyful Heart. 1979. pap. 5.95 (0-87508-417-6) Chr Lit.

— The Joyful Heart. Chen, Ruth T., tr. (CHI.). 1985. write for info. (0-941598-91-8); pap. write for info. (0-941598-24-1) Living Spring Pubns.

— The Joyful Heart. 1977. pap. 5.99 (0-8423-1975-1) Tyndale.

— The King & the Kingdom of Heaven. Kaung, Stephen, tr. 386p. 1978. 10.00 (0-935008-23-3); pap. 7.00 (0-935008-24-1) Christian Fellow Pubs.

— The Latent Power of the Soul. Kaung, Stephen, tr. 86p. 1972. pap. 3.50 (0-935008-25-X) Christian Fellow Pubs.

— Let Us Pray. Kaung, Stephen, tr. 87p. 1977. pap. 3.50 (0-935008-26-8) Christian Fellow Pubs.

— La Liberacion del Espiritu. 112p. 1968. 3.95 (0-88113-255-1) Edit Betania.

— The Life that Wins. Fader, Herbert L., ed. Kaung, Stephen, tr. & intro. by. 157p. (Orig.). 1986. 11.00 (0-935008-65-9); pap. 5.00 (0-935008-66-7) Christian Fellow Pubs.

— A Living Sacrifice. Kaung, Stephen, tr. (Basic Lesson Ser.: Vol. 1). 115p. 1972. 6.00 (0-935008-07-1); pap. 4.00 (0-935008-08-X) Christian Fellow Pubs.

— The Lord My Portion. Fader, Herbert L. & O'Dell, James P., eds. 246p. (Orig.). 1984. pap. 4.50 (0-935008-61-6) Christian Fellow Pubs.

— Love Not the World. 1970. pap. 4.95 (0-87508-412-5) Chr Lit.

— Love Not the World. 124p. 1993. pap. text ed. 5.70 (1-883137-05-5) Christ Stewards.

— Love Not the World. 125p. 1977. pap. 4.99 (0-8423-3850-0) Tyndale.

— Love One Another. Kaung, Stephen, tr. (Basic Lesson Ser.: Vol. 6). 235p. 1975. 7.00 (0-935008-09-8); pap. 5.50 (0-935008-10-1) Christian Fellow Pubs.

— The Messenger of the Cross. Kaung, Stephen, tr. 154p. (Orig.). 1980. pap. text ed. 4.50 (0-935008-50-0) Christian Fellow Pubs.

N

An Asterisk (*) at the beginning of an entry indicates that the title is appearing in BIP for the first time.

— The Ministry of God's Word. Kaung, Stephen, tr. 282p. 1971. 8.00 (*0-935008-27-6*); pap. 6.00 (*0-935008-28-4*) Christian Fellow Pubs.

— The Mystery of Creation. Kaung, Stephen, tr. 149p. 1981. pap. 4.50 (*0-935008-52-7*) Christian Fellow Pubs.

— Normal Christian Life. 1979. pap. 5.95 (*0-87508-414-1*) Chr Lit.

— The Normal Christian Life. 1977. pap. 5.99 (*0-8423-4710-0*) Tyndale.

— Not I, but Christ. Kaung, Stephen, tr. (Basic Lesson Ser.: Vol. 4). 143p. 1974. 6.50 (*0-935008-11-X*); pap. 4.50 (*0-935008-12-8*) Christian Fellow Pubs.

— Obra de Dios: Work of God. (SPA.). 2.95 (*84-7645-270-5*, 223355, Pub. by Edit Clie SP) TSELF.

— Practical Issues of This Life. Kaung, Stephen, tr. 163p. 1975. pap. 5.00 (*0-935008-29-2*) Christian Fellow Pubs.

— The Prayer Ministry of the Church. Kaung, Stephen, tr. 128p. 1973. pap. 4.50 (*0-935008-30-6*) Christian Fellow Pubs.

— Preguntas Vitales Sobre el Evangelio: Crucial Question on the Gospel. (SPA.). 4.95 (*84-7645-235-7*, 223258, Pub. by Edit Clie SP) TSELF.

— Salvacion del Alma: Salvation of the Soul. (SPA.). 3.95 (*84-7645-237-3*, 223276, Pub. by Edit Clie SP) TSELF.

— The Salvation of the Soul. Kaung, Stephen, tr. 115p. 1978. pap. 4.50 (*0-935008-31-4*) Christian Fellow Pubs.

— Sit, Walk, Stand. 1991. pap. 4.95 (*0-87508-419-2*) Chr Lit.

— Sit, Walk, Stand. 1977. pap. 4.99 (*0-8423-5893-5*) Tyndale.

— Song of Songs. 1992. pap. 4.95 (*0-87508-420-6*) Chr Lit.

— The Spirit of Judgment. Fader, Herbert L. et al, eds. Kaung, Stephen, tr. 158p. (Orig.). 1984. pap. 4.50 (*0-935008-63-2*) Christian Fellow Pubs.

— The Spirit of the Gospel. Fader, Herbert L., ed. 100p. (Orig.). 1986. pap. 4.50 (*0-935008-67-5*) Christian Fellow Pubs.

— The Spirit of Wisdom & Revelation. Kaung, Stephen, tr. 160p. 1980. pap. 4.50 (*0-935008-48-9*) Christian Fellow Pubs.

— Spiritual Authority. Kaung, Stephen, tr. 191p. 1972. pap. 5.00 (*0-935008-35-7*) Christian Fellow Pubs.

— Spiritual Knowledge. Kaung, Stephen, tr. 124p. 1973. 5.50 (*0-935008-36-5*); pap. 4.50 (*0-935008-37-3*) Christian Fellow Pubs.

— Spiritual Man. Kaung, Stephen, tr. 694p. 1968. pap. 10.00 (*0-935008-39-X*) Christian Fellow Pubs.

— Spiritual Reality or Obsession. Kaung, Stephen, tr. 64p. 1970. pap. 3.50 (*0-935008-41-1*) Christian Fellow Pubs.

— Table in the Wilderness. 1979. pap. 5.95 (*0-87508-422-2*) Chr Lit.

— Take Heed. Kaung, Stephen & Fader, Herbert L., eds. 204p. (Orig.). 1991. pap. 5.00 (*0-935008-74-8*) Christian Fellow Pubs.

— Testimony of God. Kaung, Stephen, tr. 123p. 1979. pap. 4.00 (*0-935008-44-6*) Christian Fellow Pubs.

— Ven Senor Jesus: Come Lord Jesus. (SPA.). 5.95 (*84-7228-844-7*, 222902, Pub. by Edit Clie SP) TSELF.

— Wayfarer in the Land. 1975. reprint ed. pap. 4.99 (*0-8423-7823-5*) Tyndale.

— What Shall This Man Do? 1979. pap. 5.95 (*0-87508-427-3*) Chr Lit.

— What Shall This Man Do? 1978. pap. 5.99 (*0-8423-7910-X*) Tyndale.

— Whom Shall I Send? Kaung, Stephen, tr. 89p. 1979. pap. 3.50 (*0-935008-45-4*) Christian Fellow Pubs.

— Worship God. Kaung, Stephen & Fader, Herbert L., eds. 107p. (Orig.). 1990. pap. 4.50 (*0-935008-73-X*) Christian Fellow Pubs.

— Ye Search the Scriptures. Kaung, Stephen, tr. 173p. 1974. 8.00 (*0-935008-46-2*); pap. 5.00 (*0-935008-47-0*) Christian Fellow Pubs.

Neeb, James & Harper, Shelly. Civil Action for Childhood Sexual Abuse. 392p. 1994. boxed 75.00 (*0-409-91493-2*, CN) Butterworth Legal Pubs.

Neeb, Karl-Hermann. Invariant Subsemigroups of Lie Groups. LC 93-17164. (Memoirs of the American Mathematical Society Ser.: No. 499). 193p. 1993. 36.00 (*0-8218-2562-3*) Am Math.

Neeb, Karl-Hermann, jt. auth. see Hilgert, J.

Neeb, Karl-Hermann, jt. auth. see Hilgert, Joachim.

Neebe. Primer on Linear Programming. 1991. 15.00 (*0-536-58006-5*) Ginn Pr.

Need, Richard. Basic Electricity. rev. ed. (Illus.). 32p. 1983. 3.00 (*0-8354-7686-3*) Intl Film.

Needell, Allan, ed. The First Twenty-Five Years in Space: A Symposium. LC 83-600210. 164p. (C). 1989. pap. 14.95 (*0-87474-713-9*) Smithsonian.

Needell, Claire. Not a Balancing Act. (Burning Deck Poetry Ser.). 64p. (Orig.). 1993. pap. 8.00 (*0-930901-89-4*) Burning Deck.

— Not a Balancing Act. deluxe ed. (Burning Deck Poetry Ser.). 64p. (Orig.). 1993. Signed ed. pap. 15.00 (*0-930901-90-8*) Burning Deck.

Needell, Jeffrey D. A Tropical Belle Epoque: Elite Culture & Society in Turn-of-the-Century Rio de Janeiro. (Cambridge Latin American Studies: No. 62). (Illus.). 300p. 1988. 69.95 (*0-521-33374-1*) Cambridge U Pr.

Needham, A. & Kerkut, G. A. Uniqueness of Biological Materials. LC 64-21694. (International Series Mono on Pure & Applied Mathematics: Vol. 25). 1965. 250.00 (*0-08-010748-6*, Pub. by Pergamon Repr UK) Franklin.

Needham, Barrie. Physical Planning & Environmental Policy in the Netherlands: A Guide to English-Language Publications. LC 92-5721. (CPL Bibliographies Ser.: No. 280). (Illus.). 1992. 20.00 (*0-86602-280-5*) Coun Plan Librarians.

Needham, Barrie & Koenders, Patrick. Urban Land & Property Markets in the Netherlands. 240p. 1993. 75.00 (*1-85728-051-2*, Pub. by UCL Pr UK) Taylor & Francis.

***Needham, Bobbe.** Beastly Abodes: Homes for Birds, Bats, Butterflies & Other Backyard Wildlife. LC 95-16330. (Illus.). 144p. 1995. 21.95 (*0-8069-3168-X*, Lark Bks) Sterling.

Needham, Brian, ed. Case Studies of Coastal Management: Experience from the United States. (Illus.). 117p. (Orig.). (C). 1993. pap. text ed. 30.00 (*1-56806-579-5*) Diane Pub.

Needham, Christina W. & Morales, Carmen A. Manual Para la Practica Docente: Programa a Base de Competencias. Objectivos Operacionales-Instrumentos de Evaluacion. 82p. (SPA.). 1980. pap. 5.00 (*0-8477-2744-0*) U of PR Pr.

Needham, Christopher D., ed. Reader in Social Science Documentation. LC 75-8049. 538p. 1983. text ed. 65.00 (*0-313-24047-7*, ZRO/, Greenwood Pr) Greenwood.

Needham, Christopher D. & Herman, Esther, eds. Study of Subject Bibliography with Special Reference to the Social Sciences. LC 75-630095. (Student Contribution Ser.: No. 3). 1970. pap. 5.00 (*0-911808-05-1*) U of Md Lib Serv.

Needham, Claude. The Original Handbook for the Recently Deceased. (Illus.). 144p. 1992. 100.00 (*0-89556-093-3*) Gateways Bks & Tapes.

— The Original Handbook for the Recently Deceased. (Illus.). 144p. 1993. pap. 12.50 (*0-89556-068-2*) Gateways Bks & Tapes.

Needham, D. Descubriendo la Oracion (Discovering Prayer) (SPA.). Date not set. 1.79 (*1-56063-359-X*, 498252) Editorial Unilit.

Needham, D. Barrie. How Cities Work: An Introduction. 1977. 86.00 (*0-08-020529-1*, Pub. by Pergamon Repr UK) Franklin.

Needham, David & Dransfield, Robert. Business Studies "A" Level Workbook. LC 92-43624. 1993. 10.99 (*0-07-707607-9*) McGraw.

Needham, David, jt. auth. see Dransfield, Robert.

Needham, David, et al. Teaching Business Studies. LC 92-20520. 1992. 15.99 (*0-07-707602-8*) McGraw.

***Needham, David C.** Birthright. 1995. pap. 10.99 (*0-88070-738-0*) Questar Pubs.

— Birthright: Christian, Do You Know Who You Are? LC 79-90682. (Critical Concern Ser.). 293p. 1979. pap. 9.99 (*0-930014-75-8*, Multnomah Bks) Questar Pubs.

— Close to His Majesty: An Invitation to Walk with God. Libby, Larry R., ed. LC 87-11298. 154p. 1987. pap. 8.99 (*0-88070-332-6*, Multnomah Bks) Questar Pubs.

Needham, Dorothy M., jt. auth. see Teich, Mikulas.

Needham, Francine L. Get Rid of Your Hang-Ups with the Key to Your Unconscious. LC 91-76665. (Illus.). 224p. (Orig.). 1993. pap. 9.95 (*0-9630889-4-7*) Gallandat.

Needham, G. I., ed. see Aelfric.

Needham, Helen C. & Menefee, Mark, eds. Superfund: A Legislative History, 3 Vols., Set. LC 84-10208. 1982. ring bd. 325.00 (*0-911937-08-0*) Environ Law Inst.

Needham, Henry B. Double Squeeze. LC 75-150557. (Short Story Index Reprint Ser.). (Illus.). 1977. reprint ed. 20.95 (*0-8369-3854-2*) Ayer.

Needham, J. Trans-Pacific Echoes & Resonance; Listening Once Again. 132p. 1991. pap. text ed. 7.00 (*0-9625118-8-9*) World Scientific Pub.

Needham, James G. Guide to the Study of Freshwater Biology. 5th ed. 1989. pap. 10.95 (*0-8162-6310-8*) Holden-Day.

Needham, James G. & Needham, Paul R. A Guide to the Study of Fresh-Water Biology: With Special Reference to Aquatic Insects & Other Invertebrate Animals. (Illus.). 88p. 1930. spiral bd. 31.95x (*0-398-04377-9*) C C Thomas.

— A Guide to the Study of Freshwater Biology. 5th ed. 1962. text ed. write for info. (*0-07-046137-6*) McGraw.

***Needham, Joan F.** Gerontological Nursing. LC 94-25559. 384p. 1994. pap. text ed. 28.95 (*0-8273-6226-9*) Delmar.

— Gerontological Nursing: A Restorative Approach. LC 92-10237. (Plans of Care for Specialty Practice Ser.). 384p. 1994. pap. text ed. 28.95 (*0-8273-5138-0*) Delmar.

Needham, Joan F., jt. auth. see Hegner, Barbara.

Needham, John. The Completest Mode. 210p. 1982. 22.50 (*0-85224-387-1*, Pub. by Edinburgh U Pr UK) Col U Pr.

Needham, Joseph. Chemistry of Life: Eight Lectures on the History of Biochemistry. LC 78-85733. (Illus.). 1970. 59.95 (*0-521-07379-0*) Cambridge U Pr.

— The Grand Titration: Science & Society in East & West. LC 76-483302. (Canadian University Paperbooks Ser.: No. 226). 350p. reprint ed. pap. 99.80 (*0-8357-4161-3*, 2036935) Bks Demand.

— Gunpowder as the Fourth Power, East & West. 76p. (C). 1985. pap. text ed. 36.00 (*962-209-072-9*, Pub. by Hong Kong U Pr HK) St Mut.

— A History of Embryology. 2nd ed. LC 74-26280. (History, Philosophy & Sociology of Science Ser.). 1979. reprint ed. 33.95 (*0-405-06607-4*) Ayer.

— Moulds of Understanding: A Pattern of Natural Philosophy. (Modern Revivals in Philosophy Ser.). 320p. 1993. 69.95 (*0-7512-0209-6*, Pub. by Gregg Revivals UK) Ashgate Pub Co.

— Order & Life. 1968. pap. 8.95 (*0-262-64001-5*) MIT Pr.

— Science & Civilisation in China, 6 vols. Incl. Vol. 1. Introductory Orientations. (Illus.). xxxiv, 318p. 1956. 94.95 (*0-521-05799-X*); Vol. 2. History of Scientific Thought. (Illus.). xxiv, 698p. 1991. 140.00 (*0-521-05800-7*); Vol. 3. Mathematics & the Sciences of the Heavens & the Earth. (Illus.). xlviii, 878p. 1959. 190.00 (*0-521-05801-5*); Vol. 4. Physics & Physical Technology: Part 1 Physics. (Illus.). xxxiv, 434p. 1962. 115.00 (*0-521-05802-3*); Vol. 4. Physics & Physical Technology: Part 2 Mechanical Engineering. (Illus.). lvi, 760p. 1991. 160.00 (*0-521-05803-1*); Vol. 4. Physics & Physical Technology: Part 3 Civil Engineering & Nautics. (Illus.). lviii, 932p. 1971. 190.00 (*0-521-07060-0*); Vol. 5. Chemistry & Chemical Technology: Part 1 Paper & Printing. (Illus.). 350p. 1985. 125.00 (*0-521-08690-6*); Vol. 5. Chemistry & Chemical Technology: Part 2 Spagyrical Discovery & Invention: Magisteries of Gold & Immortality. (Illus.). xlviii, 600p. 1974. 130.00 (*0-521-08571-3*); Vol. 5. Chemistry & Chemical Technology: Part 3 Spagyrical Discovery & Invention: Historical Survey from Cinnabar Elixirs to Synthetic Insulin. (Illus.). xxxv, 481p. 1976. 125.00 (*0-521-21028-3*); Vol. 4. Chemistry & Chemical Technology: Part 4 Spagyrical Discovery & Invention: Apparatus & Theory. (Illus.). xlviii, 756p. 1980. 160.00 (*0-521-08573-X*); Vol. 5. Chemical & Chemical Technology: Part 5 Spagyrical Discovery & Invention: Physiological Alchemy. (Illus.). 550p. 1983. 135.00 (*0-521-08574-8*); Vol. 5. Military Technology: The Gunpowder Epic: Part 7. (Illus.). 600p. 1987. 140.00 (*0-521-30358-3*); Vol. 6. Biology & Biological Technology Pt. 1: Botany. (Illus.). 756p. 1986. 140.00 (*0-521-08731-7*); Vol. 6. Biology & Biological Technology Pt. 2: Agriculture. (Illus.). 724p. 1984. 140.00 (*0-521-25076-5*); write for info. (*0-318-51294-7*) Cambridge U Pr.

— Science in Traditional China. (Illus.). 144p. (C). 1982. pap. text ed. 11.95 (*0-674-79439-7*) HUP.

— A Selection from the Writings of Joseph Needham. Davies, Mansel, ed. LC 93-31507. 487p. 1994. lib. bdg. 39.95 (*0-89950-903-7*) McFarland & Co.

— Time & Eastern Man. LC 65-29667. (Royal Anthropological Institute, Occasional Paper Ser.: No. 21). 62p. reprint ed. pap. 25.00 (*0-317-28751-6*, 2055492) Bks Demand.

— Time, the Refreshing River. 280p. 1986. reprint ed. 57.50 (*0-85124-429-7*, Pub. by Spokesman Bks UK); reprint ed. pap. 26.50 (*0-85124-439-4*, Pub. by Spokesman Bks UK) Coronet Bks.

— Within the Four Seas: The Dialogue of East & West. 1979. pap. 8.95 (*0-8020-6360-8*) U of Toronto Pr.

Needham, Joseph & Gwei-Djen. Trans-Pacific Echoes & Resonances: Listening Once Again. 106p. 1985. text ed. 30.00 (*9971-950-86-3*) World Scientific Pub.

Needham, Joseph & Pagel, Walter, eds. Background to Modern Science. LC 74-26281. (History, Philosophy & Sociology of Science Ser.). 1975. reprint ed. 21.95 (*0-405-06608-2*) Ayer.

Needham, Joseph & Yates, Robin D. Science & Civilization in China: Military Technology, Pt. 6, Missiles & Sieges; Vol. 5 Chemistry & Chemical Technology. (Science & Civilization in China Ser.). (Illus.). 552p. (C). 1994. 130.00 (*0-521-32727-X*) Cambridge U Pr.

Needham, Joseph, tr. see Sung Tz'u.

Needham, Joseph, et al. The Hall of Heavenly Records: Korean Astronomical Instruments & Clocks 1380-1780. (Illus.). 220p. 1986. 74.95 (*0-521-30368-0*) Cambridge U Pr.

— Heavenly Clockwork: The Great Astronomical Clocks of Medieval China. rev. ed. (Illus.). 312p. 1986. 84.95 (*0-521-32276-6*) Cambridge U Pr.

Needham, K. Essential French Dictionary. (Essential Guides Ser.). (Illus.). 64p. (J). (gr. 6 up). 1994. lib. bdg. 12.96 (*0-88110-709-3*, Usborne); pap. 5.95 (*0-7460-1004-4*, Usborne) EDC.

— Essential German Dictionary. (Essential Dictionaries Ser.). (Illus.). 64p. (YA). (gr. 6 up). 1995. lib. bdg. 12.96 (*0-88110-739-5*, Usborne); pap. 5.95 (*0-7460-1006-0*, Usborne) EDC.

***Needham, Kate.** The Dinosaurs. LC 95-14023. (Time Trekkers Visit the...Ser.). (Illus.). (J). 1995. lib. bdg. write for info. (*1-56294-942-X*, Copper Beech Bks) Millbrook Pr.

— Why Do People Eat? (Starting Point Science Ser.). (Illus.). 24p. (J). (gr. 1-5). 1993. lib. bdg. 11.96 (*0-88110-638-0*, Usborne); pap. 3.95 (*0-7460-1302-7*, Usborne) EDC.

***Needham, Kate & Gibson, Gay.** Collecting Things. (How to Make Ser.). (Illus.). 32p. (J). (gr. 2-6). 1995. lib. bdg. 12.96 (*0-88110-774-3*, Usborne); pap. 5.95 (*0-7460-2081-3*, Usborne) EDC.

Needham, Lawrence D., jt. ed. see Bialostosky, Don H.

Needham, Nicholas R. Thomas Erskine of Linlathen: His Life & Theology, 1788-1837. LC 92-7135. (Rutherford Studies in Historical Theology). 452p. 1992. reprint ed. lib. bdg. 109.95 (*0-7734-1645-5*) E Mellen.

Needham, Paul. The Printer & the Pardoner: An Unrecorded Indulgence, Printed by William Caxton for the Hospital of St. Mary Rounceval, Charing Cross. LC 85-18120. 101p. 1986. 35.00 (*0-8444-0508-6*) Lib Congress.

Needham, Paul & Oldelsted, Jan, eds. Changing Positions. (Philosophical Studies, University of Uppsala: No.38). x, 278p. (Orig.). 1986. pap. 45.00x (*0-317-65665-1*) Coronet Bks.

Needham, Paul, tr. see Lindahl, Lars.

Needham, Paul R., jt. auth. see Needham, James G.

Needham, Phil. Community in Mission: A Salvationist Ecclesiology. (Orig.). 1987. pap. 6.95 (*0-86544-043-3*) Salv Army Suppl South.

Needham, Randall W. When the Tempter Comes: Victory over Habits. 60p. (Orig.). 1993. pap. 3.95 (*0-9636067-0-0*) Grace TX.

Needham, Rodney. Circumstantial Deliveries. LC 81-1247. (Quantum Bks.: No. 21). (Illus.). 100p. 1981. 32.00 (*0-520-04389-8*) U CA Pr.

— Exemplars. LC 83-24326. (Illus.). 272p. 1985. 37.50 (*0-520-05200-5*) U CA Pr.

— Mamboru: History & Structure in a Domain of Northwestern Sumba. LC 86-18061. 202p. 1987. 49.95 (*0-19-823400-7*) OUP.

— Primordial Characters. LC 78-17230. 104p. reprint ed. pap. 29.70 (*0-7837-5314-4*, 2044712) Bks Demand.

— Reconnaissances. LC 81-160186. 132p. reprint ed. pap. 37.70 (*0-8357-8298-0*, 2034013) Bks Demand.

Needham, Rodney, ed. Right & Left: Essays on Dual Symbolic Classification. LC 73-82982. 1974. P759. pap. 7.50 (*0-226-56996-9*, P759) U Ch Pr.

— Right & Left: Essays on Dual Symbolic Classification. LC 73-82982. 488p. reprint ed. pap. 139.10 (*0-685-23833-4*, 2056614) Bks Demand.

— Structure & Sentiment: A Test Case in Social Anthropology. LC 62-9738. xii, 136p. 1984. pap. text ed. 11.95 (*0-226-56989-6*, Midway Reprint) U Ch Pr.

Needham, Rodney, tr. see Durkheim, Emile & Mauss, Marcel.

Needham, Rodney, ed. see Hocart, A. M.

Needham, Rodney, ed. see Levi-Strauss, Claude.

Needham, Rodney, ed. see Wake, Charles S.

Needham, Sara L. Heart of the Gods. Wells, Helen S., ed. (Illus.). 101p. (Orig.). (C). 1993. pap. 10.00 (*0-9639901-0-1*) Fascinatn.

***Needham, Stephen M., photos.** The International Garlic Cookbook. (Illus.). 1995. 12.95 (*0-00-225056-X*, Harp PBks) HarpC.

Needham, Stuart & Macklin, Mark G., eds. Alluvial Archaeology in Britain. (Oxbow Monographs in Archaeology: No. 27). (Illus.). 276p. 1992. pap. 61.00 (*0-946897-52-2*, Pub. by Oxbow Bks UK) David Brown.

Needham, Terence. Vascular Laboratory Quality Assurance Manual. 1995. write for info. (*0-941022-26-9*) Appleton Davies.

Needham, Walter. A Book of Country Things. LC 75-22098. (Illus.). 176p. 1992. reprint ed. pap. 11.95 (*0-911469-09-5*) A C Hood.

Needle, Ann V., ed. IBC - Donoghue Mutual Funds Almanac. 23th rev. ed. (Illus.). 264p. 1992. pap. 39.95 (*0-913755-14-1*) Donoghue Organ Inc.

Needle, Ann V., ed. see IBC - Donoghue Inc. Staff.

Needle, D. Business in Context. 384p. 1990. pap. 34.50 (*0-412-02661-9*, A4463, Chap & Hall NY) Chapman & Hall.

Needle, Jan. The Bully. large type ed. (Illus.). (J). (gr. 1-8). 1994. 16.95 (*0-7451-2223-X*, Galaxy Child Lrg Print) Chivers N Amer.

Needle, Stacy. Other Routes into College: Alternative Admission. 1991. 14.00 (*0-679-73140-7*) McKay.

Needleman, A., jt. ed. see Noor, A. K.

Needleman, Carla. The Work of Craft: An Inquiry into the Nature of Crafts & Craftsmanship. LC 92-16920. 160p. 1993. reprint ed. pap. 10.00 (*4-7700-1701-4*) Kodansha.

Needleman, Carolyn E., jt. auth. see Needleman, Martin L.

Needleman, Herbert L. Human Lead Exposure. 280p. 1991. 167.00 (*0-8493-6034-X*, RC347) CRC Pr.

Needleman, Herbert L. & Bellinger, David, eds. Prenatal Exposure to Toxicants: Developmental Consequences. LC 93-34394. (Series in Environmental Toxicology). 352p. 1994. 90.00 (*0-8018-4704-4*) Johns Hopkins.

Needleman, Herbert L. & Landrigan, Philip J. Raising Healthy Children: Protecting Your Child from Common Environmental Health Threats. LC 93-38108. 1994. 20.00 (*0-374-24643-2*); pap. 12.00 (*0-374-52392-4*) FS&G.

***Needleman, Jacob.** Gurdjieff: Meetings with a Remarkable Man, Vol. 1. Baker, George, ed. 380p. 1995. 34.50 (*0-8264-0800-1*) Continuum.

— The Heart of Philosophy. 1986. pap. 13.00 (*0-06-250645-5*, PL 4133) Harper SF.

— The Indestructible Question. Orig. Title: Consciousness & Tradition. 208p. 1994. reprint ed. 10.95 (*0-14-019364-2*, Arkana) Viking Penguin.

— Lost Christianity: A Journey of Rediscovery to the Center of Christian Experience. (Classic Edition Ser.). 240p. 1993. pap. 15.95 (*1-85230-132-5*) Element MA.

— Money & the Meaning of Life. 1994. pap. 15.00 (*0-385-26242-6*) Doubleday.

— Sin & Scientism. (Broadside Editions Ser.). 26p. (Orig.). (C). 1986. pap. 3.95 (*0-9609850-7-7*) Rob Briggs.

— Sorcerers. LC 86-8733. 235p. 1986. 16.95 (*0-916515-10-9*) Mercury Hse Inc.

Needleman, Jacob & Appelbaum, David, eds. Real Philosophy: An Anthology of the Universal Search for Meaning. 352p. 1991. pap. 11.00 (*0-14-019256-5*, Arkana) Viking Penguin.

Needleman, Jacob, et al. Religion for a New Generation. 2nd ed. Scott, Kenneth J., ed. 592p. (C). 1977. pap. write for info. (*0-02-385990-3*) Macmillan.

Needleman, Marilyn J. Werbel Multiple Choice Practice Questions for New York Addendum Property & Casualty Insurance. rev. ed. 112p. (C). 1994. pap. text ed. 11.95 (*1-884803-01-6*) Werbel Pub.

Needleman, Martin L. & Needleman, Carolyn E. Guerrillas in Bureaucracy: The Community Planning Experiment in the United States. LC 73-19806. (Wiley Series in Urban Research). 384p. reprint ed. pap. 109.50 (*0-317-09577-3*, 2015176) Bks Demand.

Needler, Martin. Latin American Politics in Perspective. 12.00 (*0-8446-2639-2*) Peter Smith.

Needler, Martin C. The Concepts of Comparative Politics. LC 90-43159. 176p. 1991. text ed. 45.00 (*0-275-93652-X*, C3652, Praeger Pubs); pap. text ed. 15.95 (*0-275-93653-8*, B3653, Praeger Pubs) Greenwood.

An Asterisk (*) at the beginning of an entry indicates that the title is appearing in BIP for the first time.

— An Introduction to Latin American Politics: The Structure of Conflict. 2nd ed. (Illus.). 256p. 1983. pap. text ed. 30.00 (*0-13-486035-7*) P-H.

— Mexican Politics: The Containment of Conflict. 2nd ed. LC 89-29672. 176p. 1990. text ed. 45.00 (*0-275-93428-4*, C3428, Praeger Pubs); pap. text ed. 17.95 (*0-275-93429-2*, B3429, Praeger Pubs) Greenwood.

— The Problem of Democracy in Latin America. (Illus.). 192p. 1987. text ed. 35.00 (*0-669-15333-8*) Free Pr.

***Needler, Toby & Goodman, Bonnie.** Exploring Global Art. 198p. 1991. ring bd. 25.00 (*0-614-02979-1*) Amer Forum.

Needles, Belverd E., Jr. Financial Accounting. 1982. Computer-assisted practice in financial acctg.; avail. Cook's Solar Energy Systems. 11.95 (*0-685-42657-2*); 3.50 (*0-685-42658-0*) HM.

— Financial Accounting. 3rd ed. LC 88-81351. 1988. Incl. test bank, instr's. handbook, working papers. student ed 17.56 (*0-318-36901-X*); write for info. (*0-318-63324-8*); trans. write for info. (*0-318-63325-6*) HM.

— Financial Accounting, Set I. (C). 1981. Computer-assisted practice set I. student ed. pap. 18.36 (*0-395-30480-6*) HM.

Needles, Belverd E., jt. ed. see Burns, Jane O.

Needles, Belverd E., Jr., et al. Financial & Managerial Accounting. 2nd ed. (C). 1991. write for info. (*0-395-43349-5*) HM Soft Schl Col Div.

— Principles of Accounting. 3rd ed. LC 86-80401. 1058p. (C). 1987. text ed. 47.16 (*0-685-18701-2*); 17.56 (*0-685-18702-0*) HM.

— Principles of Financial & Managerial Accounting. LC 87-80110. 950p. (C). 1988. Transparencies two sets. trans. 159.96 (*0-685-73860-4*); 15.96 (*0-685-73859-0*) HM.

Needles, Edward, comp. Historical Memoir of the Pennsylvania Society for Promoting the Abolition of Slavery for the Relief of Free Negroes Unlawfully Held in Bondage & for Improving the Condition of the African Race. LC 77-82207. (Anti-Slavery Crusade in America Ser.). 1980. reprint ed. 23.95 (*0-405-00645-4*) Ayer.

Needles, Howard L. Textile Fibers, Dyes, Finishes, & Processes: A Concise Guide. LC 86-5203. (Illus.). 227p. 1986. 36.00 (*0-8155-1076-4*) Noyes.

Needles, Howard L. & Zeronian, S. Haig, eds. Historic Textile & Paper Materials: Conservation & Characterization. LC 85-20094. (Advances in Chemistry Ser.: No. 212). (Illus.). xii, 464p. 1986. 76.95 (*0-8412-0900-6*) Am Chemical.

— Historic Textile & Paper Materials, No. 2: Conservation & Characterization. LC 89-38410. (Symposium Ser.: No. 410). (Illus.). 249p. 1989. 54.95 (*0-8412-1683-5*) Am Chemical.

Needles, Mark. Electronic Calculators in Business. LC 81-6599. 349p. reprint ed. pap. 99.50 (*0-7837-4051-4*, 2043881) Bks Demand.

***Needle's Prayse Staff & O'Steen, Darlene.** The Proper Stitch: A Guide for Counted Thread. Cockerham, Barbara, ed. (Illus.). 144p. 1994. 39.95 (*0-932437-03-6*) Symbol Exc Pubs.

Needman, J. R. Handbook of Microbiological Investigations for Laboratory Animal Health. 1979. text ed. 91.00 (*0-12-515950-1*) Acad Pr.

Neef, Joseph. Sketch of a Plan: Method of Education. LC 79-89211. (American Education: Its Men, Institutions & Ideas, Ser. 1). 1977. reprint ed. 18.95 (*0-405-01450-3*) Ayer.

Neef, Marian, jt. auth. see Nagel, Stuart S.

Neef, Marian, jt. auth. see Nagel, Stuart.

Neef, Marian, jt. ed. see Nagel, Stuart.

Neegele, N., ed. Air Pollution Damage to Vegetation. (C). 1991. text ed. 375.00 (*0-89771-612-4*, Pub. by Intl Bk Distr II) St Mut.

***Neel.** Death Among the Dons. (Illus.). (J). 1995. mass mkt. 5.50 (*0-671-89952-X*) PB.

Neel, Benjamin G. & Kumar, Ramesh, eds. The Molecular Basis of Human Cancer. (Illus.). 496p. 1993. 95.00 (*0-87993-554-5*) Futura Pub.

Neel, Boyd. The Story of an Orchestra. 1988. reprint ed. lib. bdg. 49.00 (*0-7812-0773-8*) Rprt Serv.

— The Story of an Orchestra. LC 71-181218. 133p. 1950. reprint ed. 19.00 (*0-403-01629-0*) Scholarly.

Neel, Carol, tr. see Dhuoda.

Neel, Charles D. & Sampson, Kenneth. Prehistoric Rock Art of the Cross Timbers Management Unit, East Central Oklahoma: An Introductory Study. (Archeological Resource Survey Report Ser.: No. 27). (Illus.). 130p. (C). 1986. pap. text ed. 8.50 (*1-881346-18-8*) Univ OK Archeol.

***Neel, David.** The Great Canoes. LC 95-10804. (Illus.). 136p. (C). 1995. pap. 27.95 (*0-295-97482-6*) U of Wash Pr.

— Our Chiefs & Elders: Words & Photographs of Native Leaders. LC 92-24652. (Illus.). 192p. 1992. 39.95 (*0-295-97217-3*) U of Wash Pr.

— Our Chiefs & Elders: Words & Photographs of Native Leaders. LC 92-24652. 160p. 1995. pap. 24.95 (*0-7748-0502-1*) U of Wash Pr.

Neel, James V. Physician to the Gene Pool: Genetic Lessons & Other Stories. LC 93-36614. 1994. text ed. 27.95 (*0-471-30844-7*) Wiley.

Neel, James V. & Schull, William J. Human Heredity. LC 54-12698. (College Library of Biolobical Sciences Ser.). 369p. reprint ed. pap. 105.20 (*0-317-20631-1*, 2024122) Bks Demand.

***Neel, James V. & Schull, William J., eds.** The Children of Atomic Bomb Survivors: A Genetic Study. fac. ed. LC 91-10042. (Illus.). 523p. 1994. pap. 149.10 (*0-7837-7566-0*, 2047319) Bks Demand.

Neel, Janet. Death among the Dons. 240p. 1993. 19.95 (*0-312-10450-2*) St Martin.

— Death among the Dons. large type ed. LC 94-14548. 369p. 1994. 20.95 (*0-8161-7439-3*) Hall.

— Death of a Partner. 1991. 16.95 (*0-312-05411-4*) St Martin.

— Death of a Partner. Chelius, Jane, ed. 256p. 1994. reprint ed. mass mkt. 4.99 (*0-671-74839-4*) PB.

— Death on Site. Chelius, Jane, ed. 288p. 1993. reprint ed. mass mkt. 4.99 (*0-671-73581-0*) PB.

— Death's Bright Angel. Chelius, Jane, ed. 288p. 1991. reprint ed. mass mkt. 4.99 (*0-671-73579-9*) PB.

Neel, Jasper. Aristotle's Voice: Rhetoric, Theory, & Writing in America. LC 94-9931. 264p. (C). 1994. 34.95 (*0-8093-1933-0*) S Ill U Pr.

— Plato, Derrida, & Writing. LC 87-28439. 268p. (C). 1988. text ed. 29.95 (*0-8093-1440-1*) S Ill U Pr.

Neel, Jasper P., ed. Options for the Teaching of English: Freshman Composition. LC 78-62655. (Options for Teaching Ser: No. 2). vii, 120p. (Orig.). 1978. pap. 19.75 (*0-87352-301-6*) Modern Lang.

Neel, Jasper P., ed. see Modern Language Association of America Staff.

Neel, John, ed. see Gentry, Roosevelt & Henderson, William T.

Neel, Peg. How to Pray According to God's Word. 72p. 1982. pap. 2.25 (*0-88144-004-3*, CPS-004) Christian Pub.

Neel, S. S. Treating Neck Pain Problems the Natural Way: Goodbye Pain in the Neck. (Illus.). 114p. (Orig.). 1991. pap. 14.95 (*0-9694691-0-1*) Gordon Soules Bk.

***Neel, Steven M.** The Wedding Ceremony & a Lot More! How to Plan for a Successful Wedding Day. Wray, Rhonda, ed. (Illus.). 1995. pap. 10.95 (*1-56608-012-6*, B122) Meriwether Pub.

Neel, William C. The Desk Top Risk Manager: An Employer's Guide to Reducing the Cost of Workers Compensation & Other Employee Benefits. 220p. 1991. 145.00 (*0-9628805-0-7*) ECMS.

***Neelakanta, Perambur S., ed.** Handbook of Electromagnetic Monolithic & Composite Materials. 800p. 1995. 129.95 (*0-8493-2500-5*, 2500) CRC Pr.

Neelakanta, Perambur S. & DeGroff, Dolores F. Neural Network Modeling: Statistical Mechanics & Cybernetic Perspectives. 256p. 1994. 69.95 (*0-8493-2488-2*, 2488) CRC Pr.

Neelamkavil, Francis. Computer Simulation & Modelling. 400p. 1987. text ed. 70.50 (*0-471-91129-1*) Wiley.

Neelands, Jonothan. Making Sense of Drama: A Guide to Classroom Practice. vi, 122p. (Orig.). (C). 1985. pap. text ed. 17.50 (*0-435-18658-2*) Heinemann.

— Structuring Drama Work: A Handbook of Available Forms in Theatre & Drama. Goode, Tony, ed. (Illus.). 87p. (C). 1990. pap. 19.50 (*0-521-37635-1*) Cambridge U Pr.

Neeld, Elizabeth H. Seven Choices. 1990. 19.95 (*0-517-57371-7*, C P Pubs) Crown Pub Group.

— Seven Choices: Taking the Steps to New Life after Losing Someone You Love. 1992. pap. 12.95 (*0-385-30672-5*, Delta) Dell.

Neeld, Elizabeth H., ed. see Harper, Tommie F.

Neeld, Elizabeth H., jt. auth. see Muller, Mary B.

Neeld, Judith. Naming the Island. 64p. (Orig.). 1988. pap. 5.95 (*0-939395-08-8*) Thorntree Pr.

— Scripts for a Life in Three Parts. (Stone Country Press Ser.: No. 6). 1978. pap. 4.95 (*0-930020-05-7*) Stone Country.

— Sea Fire. limited ed. 22p. (Orig.). 1987. pap. 5.00 (*0-938566-34-2*) Adastra Pr.

***Neeley, Bill.** The Last Comanche Chief: The Life & Times of Quanah Parker. 288p. 1995. text ed. 24.95 (*0-471-11722-6*) Wiley.

Neeley, Deta P. A Child's Story of the Book of Mormon. LC 87-19903. 382p. (J). (gr. 1-6). 1987. 13.95 (*0-87579-101-8*) Deseret Bk.

Neeley, G. Steven. The Constitutional Right to Suicide: A Legal & Philosophical Examination. LC 92-32235. (American University Studies, V, Philosophy: Vol. 146). 240p. (C). 1994. text ed. 41.95 (*0-8204-2032-8*) P Lang Pubs.

***Neeley, George.** Valparaiso: A Pictorial History. (Indiana Pictorial History Ser.). 1990. write for info. (*0-943963-11-7*) G Bradley.

Neeley, Gwen C. Miss Ima & the Hogg Family. (Illus.). 96p. (J). (gr. 4 up). 1992. lib. bdg. 12.95 (*0-937460-78-8*); pap. 8.95 (*0-937460-79-6*) Hendrick-Long.

Neeley, L. Paden. Accounting Principles & Practices. 5th ed. LC 94-19432. 1995. pap. 48.95 (*0-538-83194-4*) S-W Pub.

Neeley, L. Paden & Imke, Frank. Accounting Principles & Practices. 4th ed. 1072p. (C). 1990. text ed. write for info. (*0-318-68084-X*, AV63DA) S-W Pub.

Neeley, Mary A., jt. auth. see Muskat, Beth T.

Neels, Betty. At Odds with Love. (Romance Ser.). 1994. mass mkt. 2.99 (*0-373-03323-0*, 1-03323-2) Harlequin Bks.

— At Odds with Love. large type ed. 1994. 17.95 (*0-263-13653-1*, Pub. by Mills & Boon Ltd UK) Chivers N Amer.

— The Awakened Heart. (Romance Ser.). 1994. mass mkt. 2.99 (*0-373-03339-7*, 1-03339-8) Harlequin Bks.

— The Awakened Heart. large type ed. (Harlequin Romance Ser.). 1994. 18.95 (*0-263-13824-0*) Thorndike Pr.

— A Christmas Wish. 1995. pap. 2.99 (*0-373-03389-3*, 1-03389-3) Harlequin Bks.

— Dearest Love: (Sealed with a Kiss) (Romance Ser.). 1995. mass mkt. 2.99 (*0-373-03355-9*, 1-03355-4) Harlequin Bks.

— The Final Touch. large type ed. 1992. reprint ed. lib. bdg. 18.95 (*0-263-12902-0*) Thorndike Pr.

— A Girl in a Million. 1994. mass mkt. 2.99 (*0-373-03315-X*, 1-03315-8) Harlequin Bks.

— A Happy Meeting. (Romance Ser.). 1993. mass mkt. 2.99 (*0-373-03267-6*, 1-03267-1) Harlequin Bks.

— A Happy Meeting. large type ed. (Harlequin Ser.). 1993. reprint ed. lib. bdg. 18.95 (*0-263-13278-1*, Pub. by Mills & Boon UK) Thorndike Pr.

— The Hasty Marriage. 243p. 1994. 18.95 (*0-7505-0687-3*) Ulverscroft.

— Heaven is Gentle. large type ed. 267p. 1993. 21.95 (*0-7505-0561-3*) Ulverscroft.

— A Little Moonlight. large type ed. 285p. 1991. reprint ed. lib. bdg. 18.95 (*0-263-12696-X*, Pub. by Mills & Boon UK) Thorndike Pr.

— Magic in Vienna. large type ed. LC 94-3361. 253p. 1994. pap. 15.95 (*0-8161-7455-5*) Hall.

— The Most Marvellous Summer. (Romance Ser.: No. 185). 1992. pap. 2.89 (*0-373-03185-8*, 1-03185-5) Harlequin Bks.

— The Most Marvellous Summer. large type ed. 285p. 1992. reprint ed. lib. bdg. 18.95 (*0-263-12813-X*, Pub. by Mills & Boon UK) Thorndike Pr.

— The Quiet Professor. (Romance Ser.). 1993. mass mkt. 2.99 (*0-373-03279-X*, 1-03279-6) Harlequin Bks.

— Romantic Encounter. (Romance Ser.). 1993. pap. 2.89 (*0-373-03249-8*, 1-03249-9) Harlequin Bks.

— Romantic Encounter. large type ed. 1993. reprint ed. lib. bdg. 18.95 (*0-263-13184-X*, Pub. by Mills & Boon UK) Thorndike Pr.

— Secret Infatuation. (Romance Ser.). 1995. mass mkt. 2.99 (*0-373-03363-X*, 1-03363-8) Harlequin Bks.

— An Unlikely Romance. large type ed. 1992. reprint ed. lib. bdg. 18.95 (*0-263-12091-6*, Pub. by Mills & Boon UK) Thorndike Pr.

— A Valentine for Daisy. large type ed. (Harlequin Ser.). 1994. 18.95 (*0-263-13723-6*, Pub. by Mills & Boon UK) Thorndike Pr.

— A Valentine for Daisy: (Kids & Kisses) (Romance Ser.). 1995. pap. 2.99 (*0-373-03347-8*, 1-03347-1) Harlequin Bks.

— Wedding Bells for Beatrice. (Romance Ser.). 1995. mass mkt. 2.99 (*0-373-03371-0*, 1-03371-1) Harlequin Bks.

— Wedding Bells for Beatrice. large type ed. 1995. 18.95 (*0-263-13939-5*) Thorndike Pr.

Neels, Betty & James, Ellen. Two for the Heart. (Romance Ser.). 1994. mass mkt. 2.99 (*0-373-03299-4*, 1-03299-4) Harlequin Bks.

Neelsen, John P., ed. Gender, Caste & Power in South Asia: Social Status & Mobility in a Transitional Society. (C). 1991. 30.00 (*81-85425-44-2*, Pub. by Manohar II) S Asia.

— Social Inequality & Political Structures: Studies in Class Formation & Interest Articulation in an Indian Coalfield & Its Rural Hinterland. 1983. 27.50 (*0-8364-1071-8*, Pub. by Manohar II) S Asia.

Neely. Emergency Response to Chemical Spills. 425.00 (*0-87371-733-3*, TK) Lewis Pubs.

***Neely, Alan.** Christian Mission: A Case Study Approach. (American Society of Missiology Ser.: No. 21). 250p. (Orig.). 1995. pap. 19.95 (*1-57075-008-4*) Orbis Bks.

Neely, Alan, ed. see Bosch, David J.

Neely, Alan, tr. see Dussel, Enrique D.

Neely, Alan, ed. see Shenk, Wilbert R.

Neely, Alex. Applications Exercises Using VP-Planner, dBASE III-III Plus & Wordstar with VP-Planner, dBASE III-III Plus & Wordstar Student Software Disks. 150p. (C). 1987. pap. write for info. (*0-675-20844-0*, Merrill Pub Co) Macmillan.

— Applications Exercises Using VP-Planner with Student Software Disk. 100p. (C). 1987. pap. write for info. (*0-675-20921-8*, Merrill Pub Co) Macmillan.

Neely, Alex, et al. Applications Exercises Using Lotus 1-2-3, dBASE III-III Plus & Wordstar. 150p. (C). 1987. pap. write for info. (*0-675-20902-1*, Merrill Pub Co) Macmillan.

Neely, Alfred S., IV. Ethics-in-Government Laws: Are They Too "Ethical"? LC 84-3033. (AEI Studies: No. 402). 58p. 1984. pap. 10.75 (*0-8447-3550-7*) Am Enterprise.

Neely, Barbara. Blanche among the Talented Tenth. 240p. 1994. 19.95 (*0-312-11248-3*) St Martin.

— Blanche among the Talented Tenth. 240p. 1995. 5.95 (*0-14-025036-0*, Penguin Bks) Viking Penguin.

— Blanche on the Lam. 192p. 1993. mass mkt. 5.95 (*0-14-017439-7*, Penguin Bks) Viking Penguin.

Neely, Carol T. Broken Nuptials in Shakespeare's Plays. LC 84-29947. 272p. reprint ed. pap. 77.60 (*0-7837-3325-9*, 2057731) Bks Demand.

— Broken Nuptials in Shakespeare's Plays. LC 93-24730. 264p. 1993. reprint ed. pap. 14.95 (*0-252-06362-7*) U of Ill Pr.

Neely, Charles. Tales & Songs of Southern Illinois: Timeless Folklore in Story & Verse. 296p. 1989. reprint ed. 18.95 (*0-9623990-3-5*); reprint ed. pap. 12.95 (*0-9623990-2-7*) Crossfire Pr.

***Neely, Cynthia, et al.** Guide to Georgetown-Silver Plume Historic District. 3rd ed. LC 95-7719. 48p. 1995. pap. 6.95 (*1-55566-151-3*) Johnson Bks.

Neely, Cynthia H. & Lyerly, Elaine M. Mister Cookie Breakfast Cookbook. LC 86-2386. (Illus.). 32p. (J). (gr. k-4). 1986. pap. 3.25 (*0-88289-493-5*) Pelican.

Neely, Dan & Watson, Gary, eds. The Landscape Below Ground. 222p. (C). Date not set. pap. 25.00 (*1-881956-06-7*); pap. text ed. 35.00 (*0-685-75083-3*) Int Soc Arboricult.

Neely, Daniel K. Technicians Guide to Servicing Two-Way FM Radio. (Illus.). 1978. 14.95 (*0-13-898635-5*, Parker Publishing Co) P-H.

Neely, Esther J. Chateau Laurens. (Crime Court Mystery Ser.). 240p. (Orig.). 1986. pap. 2.95 (*0-8439-5005-6*) Dorchester Pub Co.

— South Wind. 320p. 1983. pap. 3.25 (*0-8439-2019-X*) Dorchester Pub Co.

Neely, Glenn. Mastering Elliott Wave: Presenting the Neely Method. 1990. 95.00 (*0-930233-44-1*) Windsor.

Neely, J. Practical Mettallurgy & Materials of Industry. 3rd ed. 1989. text ed. 62.00 (*0-13-683236-9*) P-H.

Neely, James W. & Isacoff, Eric G. Carbonaceous Adsorbents for the Treatment of Ground & Surface Waters. LC 82-8930. (Pollution Engineering & Technology Ser.: No. 21). (Illus.). 240p. reprint ed. pap. 68.40 (*0-7837-5373-X*, 2045137) Bks Demand.

Neely, John & Kibbe, Richard. Modern Materials & Manufacturing Processes. LC 86-15907. 480p. 1987. text ed. 45.50 (*0-471-81443-1*) P-H.

Neely, John E. Practical Metallurgy & Materials of Industry. 4th ed. LC 93-32364. 1993. text ed. 59.00 (*0-13-177270-8*) P-H.

***Neely, Joseph L.** Bumps in the Road: Overcoming Obstacles on the Journey to Success. 64p. 1995. 5.95 (*1-56245-192-8*) Great Quotations.

— Chosen Words, Favorite Sayings of Famous People. 1994. 5.95 (*1-56245-163-4*) Great Quotations.

Neely, Keith. Street Dancer. Forman, David B., ed. LC 90-91640. 265p. (Orig.). 1990. pap. 8.95 (*0-936174-06-4*) Jems Comm.

Neely, Margery & Haines, James. Parents Work Is Never Done: Helping Children from 16-30 Grow Toward Psychological Well-Being. 280p. 1989. 17.95 (*0-88282-027-3*); pap. 9.95 (*0-88282-057-5*) New Horizon NJ.

***Neely, Margery A.** Quality Interviews with Adult Students & Trainees: A Communication Course in Student Personnel & In-Service Training. (Illus.). 384p. 1992. pap. 38.95 (*0-398-06302-8*) C C Thomas.

— Quality Interviews with Adult Students & Trainees: A Communication Course in Student Personnel & In-Service Training. (Illus.). 384p. (C). 1992. text ed. 71.95x (*0-398-05813-X*) C C Thomas.

Neely, Mark E., Jr. The Abraham Lincoln Encyclopedia. (Quality Paperbacks Ser.). (Illus.). 368p. 1984. pap. 18.95 (*0-306-80209-0*) Da Capo.

— The Fate of Liberty: Abraham Lincoln & Civil Liberties. 304p. 1991. 24.95 (*0-19-506496-8*) OUP.

— The Fate of Liberty: Abraham Lincoln & Civil Liberties. 304p. 1992. reprint ed. pap. 11.95 (*0-19-508032-7*) OUP.

— The Last Best Hope of Earth: Abraham Lincoln & the Promise of America. LC 93-22863. 224p. 1993. text ed. 24.95 (*0-674-51125-5*) HUP.

— The Last Best Hope of Earth: Abraham Lincoln & the Promise of America. 224p. 1995. pap. 12.95 (*0-674-51126-3*, NEELAX) HUP.

Neely, Mark E., Jr. & McMurtry, R. Gerald. The Insanity File: The Case of Mary Todd Lincoln. LC 92-1743. 420p. (C). 1993. reprint ed. pap. 14.95 (*0-8093-1895-4*) S Ill U Pr.

Neely, Mark E., Jr., jt. auth. see Holzer, Harold.

Neely, Mark E., Jr., et al. The Confederate Image: Prints of the Lost Cause. LC 86-30797. (Illus.). xiv, 258p. 1987. 39.95 (*0-8078-1742-2*) U of NC Pr.

Neely, Martina. West Virginia Italian Heritage Festival Cookbook. (Illus.). 112p. (Orig.). 1980. pap. 5.00 (*0-686-37047-3*) Back Fork Bks.

Neely, Martina & Neely, William. The International Chili Society Official Chili Cookbook. (Illus.). 224p. 1982. pap. 9.95 (*0-312-41989-9*) St Martin.

Neely, Patricia A., jt. auth. see Chancey, Tina.

***Neely, Paula & Clinger, Dave M.** Insiders' Guide to Greater Richmond. 4th ed. 1995. 14.95 (*0-912367-75-X*) Insiders Guide.

— Insiders' Guide to Richmond, Virginia. 3rd ed. (Travel Book Ser.). 1994. 12.95 (*0-912367-59-8*) Insiders Guide.

Neely, Richard. How Courts Govern America. LC 81-1048. 256p. (C). 1983. pap. 14.00 (*0-300-02980-2*, Y-455) Yale U Pr.

— The Product Liability Mess: How Business Can Be Rescued from State Court Politics. 325p. 1988. text ed. 32.95 (*0-02-922680-5*) Free Pr.

— Shattered. LC 90-50635. Orig. Title: The Plastic Nightmare. 240p. 1991. pap. 9.00 (*0-679-73498-8*, Vin) Random.

— Take Back Your Neighborhood: A Case for Modern-Day "Vigilantism" 1990. 18.95 (*1-55611-182-7*) D I Fine.

— Tragedies of Our Own Making: How Private Choices Have Created Public Bankruptcy. 184p. 1994. 19.95 (*0-252-02038-3*) U of Ill Pr.

— The Walter Syndrome. 224p. 1993. pap. 3.95 (*0-88184-917-0*) Carroll & Graf.

Neely, Sharlotte. Snowbird Cherokees: People of Persistence. LC 90-11308. (Illus.). 192p. 1991. 30.00 (*0-8203-1327-0*) U of Ga Pr.

— Snowbird Cherokees: People of Persistence. (Brown Thrasher Bks.). (Illus.). 192p. 1993. pap. 14.95 (*0-8203-1575-3*) U of Ga Pr.

Neely, Sylvia. Lafayette & the Liberal Ideal, 1814-1824: Politics & Conspiracy in an Age of Reaction. LC 90-25649. (Illus.). 368p. (C). 1991. 39.95 (*0-8093-1733-8*) S Ill U Pr.

Neely, Sylvia, tr. see Fraysse, Olivier.

Neely, Tim. Hooping It Up: The Complete History of Notre Dame Basketball. LC 85-25324. (Illus.). 462p. 1985. pap. 12.95 (*0-912083-05-0*) Diamond Communications.

Neely, Virginia L. Alaska Calls. (Illus.). 208p. (Orig.). 1983. pap. 9.95 (*0-88839-970-7*) Hancock House.

***Neely, W. Brock.** Introduction to Chemical Exposure & Risk Assessment. 192p. 1994. 49.95 (*1-56670-094-9*, L1094) Lewis Pubs.

Neely, W. Brock & Blau, Gary E., eds. Environmental Exposure from Chemicals, Vol. I. 256p. 1985. 168.00 (*0-8493-6165-6*, TD196) CRC Pr.

— Environmental Exposure from Chemicals, Vol. II. 192p. 1985. 156.00 (*0-8493-6166-4*, TD196) CRC Pr.

Neely, Wayne C. Agricultural Fair. LC 73-181962. reprint ed. 17.50 (*0-404-04669-X*) AMS Pr.

Neely, Wesley B. Chemicals in the Environment: Distribution, Transport, Fate, Analysis. LC 80-23443. (Pollution Engineering & Technology Ser.: Vol. 13). (Illus.). 255p. reprint ed. pap. 72.70 (*0-685-24138-6*, 2033010) Bks Demand.

Neely, William. Alone in the Crowd: The Jim Gilmore Story. LC 88-70765. (Illus.). 192p. 1988. 18.50 (*0-89404-083-9*) Aztex.

— Stand on It: A Novel by Stroker Ace. LC 73-10414. 294p. 1990. reprint ed. 19.95 (*0-89404-082-0*); reprint ed. pap. 9.95 (*0-89404-081-2*) Aztex.

— Tire Wars: Racing with Goodyear. LC 93-72137. (Illus.). 192p. 1993. 29.95 (*0-89404-091-X*) Aztex.

Neely, William, jt. auth. see Neely, Martina.

Neely, William C. I Can't Be Addicted Because. 7p. (Orig.). 1986. pap. 1.50 (*0-89486-391-6*, 5308B) Hazelden.

Neely, William L. O.S.S., One Sad Sack: Private Neely Disciplines the Military. Shields, Allan, ed. LC 94-75402. (Illus.). 200p. (Orig.). 1994. pap. 8.95 (*1-882803-06-X*) Jerseydale Ranch.

— Wild Bill Neely & the Pagan Brothers' Golden Goat Winery. Shields, Allan, ed. LC 92-74907. 125p. 1992. pap. 7.95 (*1-882803-02-7*) Jerseydale Ranch.

— Wilderness Treks by Foot, Canoe, & Adobe Rocker, & Father's Far-Flung Fables. Shields, Allan, ed. LC 94-80241. (Illus.). xvi, 122p. (Orig.). 1995. pap. 7.95 (*1-882803-10-8*) Jerseydale Ranch.

— A Yosemite Naturalist's Odyssey. LC 94-77019. (Illus.). 300p. (Orig.). 1994. pap. 9.95 (*1-882803-08-6*) Jerseydale Ranch.

Neely, William T., jt. auth. see Esterly, Richard W.

Neeman, A. Ueda Theory: Theorems & Problems. LC 89-15176. (MEMO Ser.: Vol. 81/415). 123p. 1989. pap. 21.00 (*0-8218-2478-3*, MEMO 81/415) Am Math.

Ne'eman, Nira & Barthal, Lea. The Metaphoric Body: Guide to Expressive Therapy Through Images & Archetypes. 200p. 1993. pap. 27.00 (*1-85302-152-0*) Taylor & Francis.

Ne'eman, Y. & Eizenberg, E. Membranes & Other Extendons. 350p. (C). 1995. text ed. 68.00 (*981-02-0630-5*); pap. text ed. 36.00 (*981-02-0631-3*) World Scientific Pub.

Ne'eman, Y., jt. ed. see Sudarshan, E. C.

Neeman, Yaakov, ed. Conference on the Tax Consequences of American Investments in Israel: Proceedings. Nov. 12-14, 1972. x, 337p. (Orig.). 1974. 20.00 (*0-8377-0902-4*) Rothman.

***Neenan, Colin.** In Your Dreams. LC 94-31058. (J). 1995. write for info. (*0-15-200885-3*); pap. write for info. (*0-15-200884-5*) HarBrace.

Neenan, David, jt. auth. see Lynch, Dudley.

Neenan, Thomas & Hancock, Greg. Let's Blow thru Europe. rev. ed. LC 91-50886. (Illus.). 256p. 1992. pap. 10.95 (*0-914457-46-2*) Mustang Pub.

Neenan, William B., jt. ed. see Mathewson, Kent.

Neenan, William B., ed. see Social Security Conference Staff.

Neer. Shoulder Reconstruction. 624p. 1990. text ed. 164.00 (*0-7216-2832-X*) Saunders.

Neer, Frances. Dancing in the Dark: When Your Sight Begins to Change. LC 93-23291. 128p. 1994. 10.95 (*0-9637839-0-4*, Wildstar Pub) Rebecca Hse.

***Neerakuckrejasohoni.** Status of Girls in Development Strategies. (C). 1994. text ed. 28.00 (*81-241-0019-5*, Pub. by Har-Anand Pubns II) S Asia.

Neerdael, B., et al. Baccus Backfill Experiment at the Hades Underground Research Facility at Mol, EUR 14155. 67p. 1992. pap. 11.00 (*92-826-4397-2*, CD-NA-14155-EN-C, Pub. by Europ Com) UNIPUB.

— Geomechanical Behaviour of Boom Clay under Ambient & Temperature Conditions, No. 14154. 115p. 1992. pap. 17.00 (*92-826-4061-2*, CD-NA-14154-EN-C, Pub. by Europ Com) UNIPUB.

Neergaard, Ejler B., jt. auth. see Richardson, I. W.

Neerskov, Hans K. & Hunt, Dave. A Invasao Secreta. 212p. (POR.). 1991. pap. 8.95 (*0-8297-1640-8*) Life Pubs Intl.

— Je Brislerai les Verrous De Fe. 272p. (FRE.). 1990. pap. 5.95 (*0-8297-1427-8*) Life Pubs Intl.

Nees-Hatlen, Virginia, jt. ed. see Burnes, A. Patricia.

Nees, Lawrence. The Gundohinus Gospels. LC 80-82036. (Medieval Academy Bks.: No. 95). 1987. 40.00 (*0-910956-93-6*) Medieval Acad.

— A Tainted Mantle: Hercules & the Classical Tradition at the Carolingian Court. LC 90-48242. (Middle Ages Ser.). (Illus.). 392p. (C). 1991. text ed. 42.95 (*0-8122-8216-7*) U of Pa Pr.

Nees, Richard. Electronic Image Communications: A Guide to Networking Image Files. (Illus.). 100p. 1994. pap. text ed. 40.00 (*0-88736-922-7*) Learned Info.

Nees, Richard, jt. auth. see Cinnamon, Barry.

Neese, George. Three Years in the Confederate Horse Artillery. 1988. 40.00 (*0-89029-071-7*) Morningside Bkshop.

Neese, Harvey C. The Almanac of Rural Living. (Illus.). 1976. per. 6.95 (*0-686-16740-6*) N & N Resources.

— Home Gardening: Practical & Simple. 1978. write for info. (*0-686-23016-7*) N & N Resources.

Neese, L. H. Observers from Another Planet. LC 90-55251. 125p. (Orig.). 1991. pap. 7.95 (*1-56002-060-1*) Aegina Pr.

Neese, William A. Aircraft Hydraulic Systems. 3rd ed. 526p. (C). 1991. 48.95 (*0-89464-562-5*) Krieger.

Neeser, Robert W. Statistical & Chronological History of the United States Navy, 1775-1907, 2 vols., Set. (BCL1 - U. S. History Ser.). 1991. reprint ed. lib. bdg. 150.00 (*0-7812-6044-2*) Rprt Serv.

Neeson, Eoin. Civil War, 1922-23. 350p. 1988. pap. 19.95 (*1-85371-013-X*, Pub. by Poolbeg Pr IE) Dufour.

— First Book of Irish Myths & Legends. 126p. 1988. pap. 9.95 (*0-85342-858-1*, Pub. by Mercier Pr IE) Dufour.

— A History of Irish Forestry. (Illus.). 384p. 1991. 59.95 (*0-946640-70-X*, Pub. by Lilliput Pr Ltd IE); pap. 29.95 (*0-946640-71-8*, Pub. by Lilliput Pr Ltd IE) Irish Bks Media.

— Second Book of Irish Myths & Legends. 128p. 1988. pap. 10.95 (*0-85342-859-X*, Pub. by Mercier Pr IE) Dufour.

Neeson, Francis J., jt. auth. see McCalley, Stuart W.

Neeson, J. M. Commoners: Common Right, Enclosure & Social Change in England, 1700-1820. LC 92-28461. (Past & Present Publications). (Illus.). 400p. (C). 1993. 59.95 (*0-521-44054-8*) Cambridge U Pr.

Neesse, Gottfried. Heraklit Heute. viii, 148p. 1982. write for info. (*3-487-07157-6*, Pub. by Georg Olms GW) Lubrecht & Cramer.

Neetens, A., ed. Intraocular Lenses & Corneal Endothelium. (Journal: Ophthalmologica: Vol. 187, No. 2). (Illus.). x, 68p. 1983. pap. 41.75 (*3-8055-3758-1*) S Karger.

Neetens, A., jt. ed. see Daroff, R.

Neetens, A., et al, eds. The Visual System in Meyelin Disorders. (Monographs in Ophthalmology). 1984. lib. bdg. 191.50 (*90-6193-807-4*) Kluwer Ac.

Neethling, J., ed. & pref. The Journal of Contemporary Roman-Dutch Law. 1993. 97.00 (*0-685-71202-8*) Butterworth Legal Pubs.

Neethling, J., et al. Case Book on the Law of Delict - Vonnisbundel oor die Deliktereg. 759p. 1991. pap. write for info. (*0-7021-2593-8*, Pub. by Juta SA) W W Gaunt.

Neev, D., et al. Mediterranean Coasts of Israel & Sinai: Holocene Tectonism From Geology, Geophysics, & Archaeology. 144p. 1987. 32.00 (*0-8448-1495-4*, Crane Russak) Taylor & Francis.

Neev, David, jt. auth. see Emery, K. O.

Neev, Elan. Wholistic Healing: How to Harmonize Your Body, Mind & Spirit with Life, for Freedom, Joy, Health, Beauty, Love, Money & Psychic Powers. rev. ed. LC 77-71152. (Illus.). 1977. 49.95 (*0-685-00146-6*); pap. 6.95 (*0-686-96648-1*) Ageless Bks.

— Wholistic Healing: How to Harmonize Your Body, Mind & Spirit with Life, for Freedom, Joy, Health, Beauty, Love, Money & Psychic Powers. 4th limited ed. LC 77-71152. (Illus.). 1977. 10.95 (*0-918482-01-1*) Ageless Bks.

Neev, Elan Z. Cosmic Doodlings for Self-Realization & Self-Coloring. (Illus.). (Orig.). 1980. pap. 6.95 (*0-918482-03-8*) Ageless Bks.

— God the Generous Capitalist or How to Borrow All You Need from the Universal Bank of Infinite Abundance. (Illus.). (Orig.). Date not set. pap. text ed. 7.95 (*0-918482-05-4*) Ageless Bks.

— How to Be Selfishly Good. (Illus.). (Orig.). 6.95 (*0-918482-06-2*) Ageless Bks.

Neeves, D'Reen, illus. God Cares for Me. (Board Bks.). 12p. (J). (ps-2). 1991. bds. 6.99 (*0-7459-2059-4*) Lion USA.

— God Cares for the Earth. (Board Bks.). 12p. (J). (ps-2). 1991. bds. 6.99 (*0-7459-2060-8*) Lion USA.

Neeves, R., jt. auth. see Sweetgall, R.

Neeves, Robert, ed. see Sweetgall, Rob.

Neeves, Robert, jt. auth. see Sweetgall, Robert.

Nef. Princess Navina Visits Malvolia. (Illus.). 64p. (Orig.). 1990. pap. 8.95 (*0-915728-09-5*) Lytton Pub.

Nef, John U. Conquest of the Material World. LC 64-15804. 1964. lib. bdg. 25.00 (*0-226-57121-1*) U Ch Pr.

— The Rise of the British Coal Industry, 2 vols., Set. LC 71-37902. (Select Bibliographies Reprint Ser.). 1977. reprint ed. 89.95 (*0-8369-6740-2*) Ayer.

— Rise of the British Coal Industry, 2 vols., Set. (Illus.). 1966. reprint ed. 95.00 (*0-7146-1346-0*, BHA-01346, Pub. by F Cass Pubs UK) Intl Spec Bk.

— The United States & Civilization. 2nd rev. ed. LC 67-28465. 451p. reprint ed. pap. 128.60 (*0-317-09261-8*, 2020136) Bks Demand.

Nef, Karl. Outline of the History of Music. (Music Book Index Ser.). 400p. 1992. reprint ed. lib. bdg. 89.00 (*0-7812-9483-5*) Rprt Serv.

Nefedov, O. M., jt. auth. see Kolesnikov, S. P.

Nefedov, O. M., et al. Synthesis Structure & Properties of the First Examples of Germacyclopropenes (Germirenes) & 1,2-Digermacyclobutenes. (SSR Chemistry Reviews Ser.). 64p. 1988. 20.00 (*0-318-39941-5*) Gordon & Breach.

Nefedov, V. I. X-Ray Photoelectron Spectroscopy of Solid Surfaces. viii, 200p. 1987. lib. bdg. 130.00 (*90-6764-080-8*, Pub. by VSP NE) Coronet Bks.

Nefedova, I. Masterpieces of Latvian Painting. (Illus.). 352p. (C). 1988. text ed. 375.00 (*0-685-40272-X*, Pub. by Collets) St Mut.

***Neff.** Women & Their Emotions. 1995. pap. 8.99 (*0-8024-9531-1*) Moody.

Neff, jt. auth. see Day.

Neff, Bernice. Let's Dry It. (Illus.). 112p. (Orig.). 1984. pap. 7.95 (*0-88839-981-2*) Hancock House.

Neff, Bettye C., jt. auth. see Fox, Janet.

Neff, Blake, jt. auth. see Ratcliff, Donald.

Neff, Blake J. & Ratcliff, Donald, eds. Handbook of Family Religious Education. 290p. 1995. pap. 17.95 (*0-89135-095-0*) Religious Educ.

Neff, Carole C., jt. auth. see Nathan, Max, Jr.

***Neff, Donald.** Fallen Pillars: U. S. Policy Towards Palestine & Israel, 1947-1994. 200p. 1995. pap. 15.00 (*0-88728-259-8*) Inst Palestine.

— Warriors Against Israel. 600p. (Orig.). 1988. 19.95 (*0-915597-59-4*) Amana Bks.

— Warriors at Suez. 479p. 1987. pap. 9.95 (*0-915597-58-6*) Amana Bks.

— Warriors for Jerusalem. 430p. pap. 9.95 (*0-915597-57-8*) Amana Bks.

Neff, E. C. A Chronicle, Together with a Little Romance, Regarding Rudolf & Jacob Naf, of Frankford Pennsylvania, & Their Descendants, Including an Account of the Neffs in Switzerland & America. (Illus.). 352p. 1989. reprint ed. lib. bdg. 65.50 (*0-8328-0898-9*); reprint ed. pap. 55.50 (*0-8328-0899-7*) Higginson Bk Co.

***Neff, Eileen, ed. & intro.** Arcades of Philadelphia the Present: Manuscripts of the 1992-93 Pew Fellowships in the Arts Disciplinary Winners in Poetry. (Illus.). 36p. (Orig.). 1995. 10.00 (*0-939084-26-0*) R Mus & Lib.

Neff, Emery E. Carlyle & Mill; an Introduction to Victorian Thought. (BCL1-PR English Literature Ser.). 435p. 1992. reprint ed. lib. bdg. 99.00 (*0-7812-7492-3*) Rprt Serv.

— The Poetry of History: The Contribution of Literature & Literary Scholarship to the Writing of History Since Voltaire. LC 47-30933. 258p. (C). 1961. pap. text ed. 18.50 (*0-231-08525-7*) Col U Pr.

***Neff, Emily B. & Shackelford, George T.** American Painters in the Age of Impressionism. LC 94-40856. 1994. pap. 35.00 (*0-89090-064-7*) Mus Fine TX.

Neff, Fred. Basic Karate Handbook. LC 75-38471. (Fred Neff's Self-Defense Library). (Illus.). 56p. (J). (gr. 5 up). 1976. lib. bdg. 14.95 (*0-8225-1150-9*, Lerner Publctns) Lerner Group.

— Basic Self-Defense Manual. LC 75-38473. (Fred Neff's Self-Defense Library). (Illus.). 56p. (J). (gr. 5 up). 1976. lib. bdg. 14.95 (*0-8225-1152-5*, Lerner Publctns) Lerner Group.

— Hand-Fighting Manual for Self-Defense & Sport Karate. LC 75-38475. (Fred Neff's Self-Defense Library). (Illus.). 56p. (J). (gr. 5 up). 1977. lib. bdg. 11.95 (*0-8225-1154-1*, Lerner Publctns) Lerner Group.

— Karate Is for Me. LC 79-16900. (Sports for Me Bks.). (Illus.). 48p. (J). (gr. 2-5). 1980. lib. bdg. 13.50 (*0-8225-1090-1*, Lerner Publctns) Lerner Group.

— Lessons from the Art of Kempo: Subtle & Effective Self-Defense. (Fred Neff's Secrets of Self-Defense Ser.). (Illus.). 96p. (J). (gr. 5 up). 1987. lib. bdg. 14.95 (*0-8225-1160-6*, Lerner Publctns); pap. 4.95 (*0-8225-9532-X*, Lerner Publctns) Lerner Group.

— Lessons from the Samurai: Ancient Self-Defense Strategies & Techniques. (Fred Neff's Secrets of Self-Defense Ser.). (Illus.). 96p. (J). (gr. 5 up). 1987. lib. bdg. 14.95 (*0-8225-1161-4*, Lerner Publctns); pap. 4.95 (*0-8225-9531-1*, Lerner Publctns) Lerner Group.

— Lessons from the Western Warriors. (Fred Neff's Secrets of Self-Defense Ser.). (Illus.). 112p. (J). (gr. 5 up). 1994. lib. bdg. 14.95 (*0-8225-1166-5*, Lerner Publctns) Lerner Group.

— Lessons from the Western Warriors: Dynamic Self-Defense Techniques. (Fred Neff's Secrets of Self-Defense Ser.). (Illus.). 96p. (J). (gr. 5 up). 1987. lib. bdg. 14.95 (*0-8225-1159-2*, Lerner Publctns); pap. 4.95 (*0-8225-9533-8*, Lerner Publctns) Lerner Group.

Neff, Glenda, ed. The Writer's Essential Desk Reference. 352p. 1991. 19.95 (*0-89879-477-3*) Writers Digest.

Neff, Hector, ed. Chemical Characterization of Ceramic Pastes in Archaeology. LC 92-4933. (Monographs in World Archaeology: No. 7). 304p. (C). 1992. pap. text ed. 35.00 (*0-9629110-6-2*) Prehistory Pr.

Neff, Helen, jt. auth. see Westminster Presbyerian Church, Interpretive Arts Committee.

Neff, Herbert P., Jr. Basic Electromagnetic Fields. 2nd ed. 638p. (C). 1986. text ed. 66.50 (*0-06-044783-4*) Krieger.

— Continuous & Discrete Linear Systems. LC 90-48559. 530p. (C). 1991. reprint ed. lib. bdg. 59.50 (*0-89464-541-2*) Krieger.

Neff, J. A. Optical Enhancements to Computing Technology. 1992. 62.00 (*0-8194-0691-0*, 1563) SPIE.

Neff, Jack. The Designer's Guide to Making Money with Your Desktop Computer. (Illus.). 128p. 1992. pap. 19.95 (*0-89134-439-X*, 30423) North Light Bks.

— Make Your Woodworking Pay for Itself. (Illus.). 128p. 1992. 16.95 (*0-89879-536-2*) Writers Digest.

Neff, James. City Beat: Stories from the Heart of Cleveland. ix, 231p. 1983. 13.95 (*0-939738-55-4*) Zubal Inc.

— Unfinished Murder: The Capture of a Serial Rapist. Grose, William, ed. LC 94-34008. 352p. (Orig.). 1995. 22.00 (*0-671-73185-8*) PB.

Neff, Janet A. Trauma Nursing: The Art & Science. LC 92-16291. 808p. 1992. 49.95 (*0-8016-6655-4*) Mosby Yr Bk.

Neff, Jerry M. Polycyclic Aromatic Hydrocarbons in the Aquatic Environment: Sources, Fates & Biological Effects. (Illus.). 262p. 1979. 84.75 (*0-85334-832-4*, Pub. by Elsevier Applied Sci UK) Elsevier.

Neff, Joanna, ed. see Altman, Sandra.

Neff, John A., jt. auth. see Tate, Skip.

Neff, John H., jt. auth. see Castleman, Riva.

Neff, Kelly J. Everyday Life in Two Worlds: A Psychic's Experience. 192p. (Orig.). 1994. pap. 9.95 (*1-878901-95-8*) Hampton Roads Pub Co.

***Neff, Ken & Doering, David.** Troubleshooting NetWare 3.12. LC 94-42768. 1994. pap. text ed. 34.95 (*1-55851-432-5*) M&T Bks.

Neff, Larry M., ed. Selections from Arthur D. Graeff's Scholla. LC 79-166008. (Pennsylvania German Folklore Ser.: Vol. 5). 1971. 15.00 (*0-911122-27-3*) Penn German Soc.

Neff, Larry M. & Weiser, Frederick S., eds. The Account Book of Conrad Weiser: Berks County, Pennsylvania, 1746-1760. LC 81-84666. (Sources & Documents Ser.: No. 6). (Illus.). 1981. 15.00 (*0-911122-43-5*) Penn German Soc.

Neff, Lavonne. God's Gift Baby. (Arch Bks.). (J). (gr. k-4). 1977. pap. 1.89 (*0-570-06113-X*, 59-1230) Concordia.

Neff, LaVonne. One of a Kind: Making the Most of Your Child's Uniqueness. Heaney, Liz, ed. LC 93-40255. 197p. (Orig.). 1993. reprint ed. pap. 9.95 (*0-935652-20-5*) Ctr Applications Psych.

Neff, LaVonne, tr. see Ellul, Jacques.

Neff, Marsha J., jt. auth. see Dietl, L. Kay.

Neff, Miriam. Devotions for Women in the Workplace. 1991. pap. 7.99 (*0-8024-1727-2*) Moody.

— Helping Teens in Crisis. LC 92-42900. 1993. 8.99 (*0-8423-6823-X*) Tyndale.

— Women & Their Emotions. (Orig.). 1983. pap. 7.99 (*0-8024-5151-9*) Moody.

Neff, Norman D. & Naus, Joseph I. Vol. 6. (Selected Tables in Mathematical Statistics). 207p. 1980. 27.00 (*0-8218-1906-2*) Am Math.

Neff, Pauline. Tough Love: How Parents Can Deal with Drug Abuse. 160p. 1984. reprint ed. pap. 10.95 (*0-687-42407-0*) Abingdon.

Neff, Rena. Napkin Magic. Pemno, Karen, ed. 64p. (Orig.). 1990. pap. 3.49 (*0-942320-36-0*) Am Cooking.

Neff, Rena & Perrino, Karen. The Junior Chef. 64p. 1992. pap. 3.49 (*0-942320-41-7*) Am Cooking.

***Neff, Richard B. & Smallson, Fran.** NAFTA: Protecting & Enforcing Intellectual Property Rights in North America. LC 94-26390. 1994. write for info. (*0-07-172611-X*) Shepards-McGraw.

***Neff, Robert C.** Japan's Hidden Hot Springs. (Illus.). 196p. (Orig.). 1995. pap. 12.95 (*0-8048-1949-1*) C E Tuttle.

Neff, Ronald L., jt. auth. see Mey, Vander Brenda J.

Neff, Rose A. & Weimer, Maryellen, eds. Classroom Communication: Collected Readings for Effective Discussion & Questioning. 93p. (Orig.). (C). 1989. pap. text ed. 22.50 (*0-912150-08-4*) Magna Pubns.

Neff, Rose A., jt. auth. see Weimer, Maryellen.

Neff, Severine, tr. see Schoenberg, Arnold.

Neff, Severine, ed. see Schoenberg, Arnold.

Neff, Severine, tr. see Schoenberg, Arnold.

Neff, Stephen. Friends but No Allies: The Triumph of Capitalism & the Law of Nations. 1990. text ed. 37.50 (*0-231-07142-6*) Col U Pr.

Neff, Susan A., jt. auth. see Lunn, Terry.

Neff, Terry, ed. see Atkinson, D. Scott, et al.

Neff, Terry, ed. see Danoff, Michael, et al.

Neff, Terry, ed. see Dunlop, Ian & Warren, Lynne.

Neff, Terry, ed. see Jacob, Mary J. & McEvilley, Thomas.

Neff, Terry, ed. see Warren, Lynne.

Neff, Terry, ed. see Wright, Beryl J., et al.

Neff, Terry A., ed. Open Spain - Espana Abierta: Contemporary Documentary Photography in Spain. Fontanella, Lee, tr. (Illus.). 264p. (ENG & SPA.). 1992. write for info. (*0-932026-27-3*) Columbia College Chi.

— Within This Garden. (Illus.). (Orig.). (C). 1993. pap. 29.95 (*0-932026-30-3*) Columbia College Chi.

— Within This Garden: Photographs by Ruth Thorne-Thomsen. (Illus.). (Orig.). 1993. 45.00 (*0-89381-549-7*) Aperture.

Neff, Terry A., ed. see Curtis, Verna P. & Tilendis, Robert M.

Neff, Terry A., ed. see Hooks, Bell.

Neff, Walter S. Work & Human Behavior. 3rd ed. LC 85-1219. (Illus.). 360p. (C). 1985. pap. text ed. 25.95 (*0-202-30320-9*) Aldine de Gruyter.

Neff, Walter S., ed. see National Conference on the Psychological Aspects of Disability Staff.

Neff, Wanda F. Victorian Working Women. LC 77-181963. reprint ed. 29.50 (*0-404-04676-2*) AMS Pr.

Neff, William A. The Neff-Naf Family History. LC 91-66144. (Illus.). 480p. 1991. 42.50 (*0-9630457-0-9*) Neff & Assocs.

Neffgen, H. Grammar & Vocabulary of the Samoan Language. Stock, Arnold B., tr. LC 75-35206. reprint ed. 21.50 (*0-404-14229-X*) AMS Pr.

Nefsky, Marilyn F. Stone Houses & Iron Bridges: Tradition & the Place of Women in Contemporary Japan. LC 91-18444. (Toronto Studies in Religion: Vol. 12). 260p. (C). 1992. text ed. 47.95 (*0-8204-1568-5*) P Lang Pubs.

Neft, David S. Cincinnati Reds Trivia Book. 1993. pap. 9.99 (*0-312-08736-5*) St Martin.

— Sports Encyclopedia: Baseball 1995. 1995. pap. 19.99 (*0-312-11897-X*) St Martin.

— The Sports Encyclopedia of Baseball. 1989. 29.95 (*0-312-02033-3*) St Martin.

Neft, David S. & Cohen, Richard M. The Football Encyclopedia. 1024p. 1991. 49.95 (*0-312-05089-5*) St Martin.

— The Sports Encyclopedia: Baseball. 8th ed. LC 85-1833. 610p. 1988. 29.95 (*0-685-20014-0*) St Martin.

— The Sports Encyclopedia: Baseball, 1994. (Illus.). 688p. (Orig.). 1994. pap. 19.99 (*0-312-10551-7*) St Martin.

— The Sports Encyclopedia, Pro Football. 1989. pap. 18.95 (*0-318-42737-0*) St Martin.

Neft, David S., jt. auth. see Cohen, Richard M.

Neft, David S., et al. The Boston Red Sox Trivia Book. LC 92-44102. 1993. pap. 9.99 (*0-312-08712-8*, Pub. by Thomas Dunne Bks) St Martin.

— The Cincinnati Reds Trivia Book. LC 92-44101. 1993. write for info. (*0-312-98736-6*, Pub. by Thomas Dunne Bks) St Martin.

— The Dodgers Trivia Book. LC 92-43020. 1993. pap. 9.99 (*0-312-08839-6*) St Martin.

— The Football Encyclopedia: The Complete History of Professional Football from 1892 to the Present. 2nd ed. 1088p. 1994. 49.95 (*0-312-11435-4*) St Martin.

— The Sports Encyclopedia: Pro Football. 11th ed. 740p. 1993. pap. 19.99 (*0-312-09393-4*) St Martin.

— The Sports Encyclopedia of Pro Football. (Illus.). 768p. (Orig.). 1994. pap. 19.99 (*0-312-11073-1*) St Martin.

Neftci, Salih N., jt. auth. see Dunn, Robert M., Jr.

Nefzawi, Sheikh. The Perfumed Garden: A Pillow Book. Burton, Richard F., tr. LC 94-1609. (Illus.). 64p. 1994. 8.00 (*0-06-251082-7*) Harper SF.

***Nefzger, Carl.** Traits of a Winner: The Formula for Developing Thoroughbred Racehorses. (Illus.). 320p. 1994. 34.95 (*0-929346-33-5*) R Meerdink Co Ltd.

Negahban, Ezat. Excavations at Haft Tepe, Iran. (University Museum Monographs: No. 70). (Illus.). xx, 156p. 1990. 75.00 (*0-934718-89-X*) U PA Mus Pubns.

***Negahban, Ezat O.** Marlik: The Complete Excavation Report. LC 94-32410. (University Museum Monograph: Vol. 87). 1995. write for info. (*0-924171-32-4*) U PA Mus Pubns.

An Asterisk (*) at the beginning of an entry indicates that the title is appearing in BIP for the first time.

Negandhi, Anant R., ed. China's Trade with the Industrialized Countries: Socio-Economic & Political Perspectives. (Research in International Business & International Relations Ser.: Vol. 2). 1986. 73.25 (*0-89232-530-5*) Jai Pr.
— Interorganization Theory. LC 74-21887. 293p. reprint ed. pap. 83.60 (*0-7837-0503-4*, 2040827) Bks Demand.
— Research in International Business & International Relations, Vol. 3. 1988. 73.25 (*0-89232-649-2*) Jai Pr.
Negandhi, Anant R. & Savara, Arun M., eds. International Strategic Management. 288p. 1989. text ed. 52.95 (*0-669-20108-1*) Free Pr.
Negandhi, Anant R. & Schran, Peter, eds. Research in International Business & International Relations, Vol. 4: China & India: Foreign Investment & Economic Development. 1990. 73.25 (*1-55938-121-3*) Jai Pr.
Negandhi, Anant R. & Thomas, Howard, eds. Research in International Business & International Relations, Vol. 1: Multinational Corporations & State-Owned Enterprises: A New Challenge in International Business. 1986. 73.25 (*0-89232-529-1*) Jai Pr.
Negandhi, Arnant. Advances in International Comparative Management: Supplement 1. Beyond Theory Z: Global Rationalization Strategies of American, German & Japanese Multinational Comp. 73.25 (*0-89232-445-7*) Jai Pr.
Negas, T., ed. see Symposium on Materials & Processes for Wireless Communications Staff, et al.
Negash, Askale. Haile Selassie. (World Leaders - Past & Present Ser.). (Illus.). 112p. (YA). (gr. 5 up). 1989. 17.95 (*1-55546-850-0*) Chelsea Hse.
Negash, Tekeste. Italian Colonialism in Eritrea, 1882-1941: Policies, Praxis, & Impact. (Studia Historica Upsaliensia: No. 148). 217p. (Orig.). 1987. pap. 43.50x (*91-554-2111-3*, Pub. by Uppsala Univ Acta Univ Uppsaliensis SW) Coronet Bks.
***Negativland.** Fair Use: The Story of the Letter U & the Numeral 2. LC 94-69077. (Illus.). 288p. (Orig.). 1995. pap. 19.95 (*0-9643496-0-4*) Seeland.
Negbaur, Brad. How to Marry Money: The Rich Have to Marry Someone--Why Not You? LC 94-17640. 1994. 8.95 (*0-8065-1589-9*, Citadel Pr) Carol Pub Group.
Negedly, R. Elsevier's Dictionary of Fishery, Processing, Fish & Shellfish Names of the World. 624p. (ENG, FRE, GER, LAT & SPA.). 1990. 200.00 (*0-444-88039-9*) Elsevier.
— Elsevier's Dictionary of Fishery, Processing, Fish & Shellfish Names of the World. 624p. (ENG, FRE, GER, LAT & SPA.). 1990. 295.00 (*0-8288-9214-8*) Fr & Eur.
Negele, J. W. & Vogt, Erich, eds. Advances in Nuclear Physics, Vol. 12. LC 67-29001. 272p. 1981. 79.50 (*0-306-40708-6*, Plenum Pr) Plenum.
— Advances in Nuclear Physics, Vol. 13. LC 67-29001. 334p. 1984. 89.50 (*0-306-41313-2*, Plenum Pr) Plenum.
— Advances in Nuclear Physics, Vol. 14. LC 67-29001. 302p. 1984. 89.50 (*0-306-41524-0*, Plenum Pr) Plenum.
— Advances in Nuclear Physics, Vol. 15. LC 67-29001. 232p. 1985. 89.50 (*0-306-41864-9*, Plenum Pr) Plenum.
— Advances in Nuclear Physics, Vol. 16. LC 67-29001. 342p. 1985. 89.50 (*0-306-41997-1*, Plenum Pr) Plenum.
— Advances in Nuclear Physics, Vol. 17. LC 67-29001. 386p. 1986. 89.50 (*0-306-42333-2*, Plenum Pr) Plenum.
— Advances in Nuclear Physics, Vol. 18. LC 67-29001. 474p. 1988. 95.00 (*0-306-42700-1*, Plenum Pr) Plenum.
— Advances in Nuclear Physics, Vol. 19. (Illus.). 396p. 1989. 95.00 (*0-306-43046-0*, Plenum Pr) Plenum.
— Advances in Nuclear Physics, Vol. 20. (Illus.). 390p. 1991. 95.00 (*0-306-43861-5*, Plenum Pr) Plenum.
— Advances in Nuclear Physics, Vol. 21. 1994. 95.00 (*0-306-44548-4*, Plenum Pr) Plenum.
Negele, James R., jt. auth. see Fisk, Edward R.
Negele, John W. & Orland, Henri. Quantum Many-Particle Systems. (Frontiers in Physics Ser.). (Illus.). 500p. (C). 1988. 49.95 (*0-201-12593-5*, Adv Bk Prog) Addison-Wesley.
Negendank, Jorg F. & Zolitschka, B., eds. Paleolimnology of European Maar Lakes. (Lecture Notes in Earth Sciences Ser.: Vol. 49). (Illus.). x, 514p. 1993. pap. write for info. (*3-540-56570-1*) Spr-Verlag.
Negendank, Jorg F. & Zolitschka, Bernd, eds. Paleolimnology of European Maar Lakes. LC 93-4663. (Lecture Notes in Earth Sciences Ser.: Vol. 49). 1993. 109.00 (*0-387-56570-1*) Spr-Verlag.
Negev, Abraham, ed. Dictionnaire Archeologique de la Bible: Archeological Dictionary of the Bible. 350p. (FRE.). 1970. 75.00 (*0-8288-6510-8*, M-6117) Fr & Eur.
Negev, Avraham. Nabatean Archaeology Today. LC 86-5280. (Hagop Kevorkian Series on Near Eastern Art & Civilization). 160p. 1986. 55.00x (*0-8147-5760-X*) NYU Pr.
Negev, Avraham, ed. The Archaeological Encyclopedia of the Holy Land. 3rd ed. (Illus.). 400p. 1990. 29.95 (*0-13-044090-6*) P-H Gen Ref & Trav.
Neggers, Carla. Bewitching. (Temptation Ser.). 1993. mass mkt. 2.99 (*0-373-25552-7*, 1-25552-0) Harlequin Bks.
— Finders Keepers. (Men Made in America Ser.). 1994. pap. 3.99 (*0-373-45195-4*, 1-45195-4) Harlequin Bks.
— Minstrel's Fire. 1990. reprint ed. 18.95 (*0-7278-4040-1*) Severn Hse.
— Night Watch: Lovers & Legends. (Temptation Ser.). 1993. mass mkt. 2.99 (*0-373-25561-6*, 1-25561-1) Harlequin Bks.
— Tempting Fate. 352p. (Orig.). 1993. mass mkt. 4.99 (*0-425-13073-8*) Berkley Pub.
— Wisconsin Wedding. (Tyler Ser.: No. 503). 1992. mass mkt. 3.99 (*0-373-82503-X*, 1-82503-3) Harlequin Bks.
Neggers, Gladys. Vocabulario Culto. 2nd ed. 168p. (SPA.). 1977. pap. 17.95 (*0-8288-5535-8*, S50023) Fr & Eur.
Neggi, Dwijendra N. Sacred Tales of India. (C). 1991. reprint ed. 8.50 (*0-685-48886-1*, Pub. by Asian Educ Servs II) S Asia.
Negi, J. G. & Saraf, P. D. Anisotropy in Geoelectromagnetism. (Methods in Geochemistry & Geophysics Ser.: Vol. 28). 1989. 133.50 (*0-444-87495-X*) Elsevier.
***Negi, S. S.** Biodiversity & Its Conservation in India. (C). 1993. 31.00x (*81-85182-88-4*, Pub. by Indus Pub II) S Asia.
— A Dictionary of Forestry. (C). 1988. 62.50 (*81-7136-010-6*, Pub. by Periodical Expert India) St Mut.
— Elements of General Silviculture. 316p. 1988. 100.00 (*81-7089-092-6*, Pub. by Intl Bk Distr II) St Mut.
— Forest Types of India, Nepal & Bhutan. (C). 1989. 187.50 (*81-7136-012-2*, Pub. by Periodical Expert India) St Mut.
— Forestry in SAARC Countries. (C). 1992. 225.00 (*81-7136-035-1*, Pub. by Periodical Expert India) St Mut.
— Forests & Forestry in Nepal. (Illus.). 205p. (C). 1994. 20.00x (*81-7024-581-8*, Pub. by Ashish Pub Hse II) Nataraj Bks.
— Fundamentals of Forestry, Vol. 3: Introductory Soil Science. 101p. (C). 1983. 55.00 (*0-685-22308-6*, Scientific) St Mut.
— Fundamentals of Silviculture. (C). 1987. 95.00 (*0-685-21845-7*, Pub. by Intl Bk Distr II) St Mut.
— Geo-Botany of India. (C). 1986. 75.00 (*81-7136-005-X*, Pub. by Periodical Expert India) St Mut.
— Handbook of Forest. 690p. (C). 1986. 175.00 (*0-685-21846-5*, Pub. by Intl Bk Distr II) St Mut.
— Handbook of Forestry. 690p. 1986. 85.00 (*0-685-49625-2*, Pub. by Intl Bk Distr II) St Mut.
— Handbook of Forestry. 690p. (C). 1986. 275.00 (*0-685-61465-4*, Pub. by Intl Bk Distr II); text ed. 175.00 (*0-685-52013-7*, Pub. by Intl Bk Distr II) St Mut.
— Handbook of National Parks, Sanctuaries & Bisphere Reserves in India. (C). 1991. 25.00 (*81-85182-59-0*, Pub. by Indus Pub II) S Asia.
— Handbook of Social Forestry. 178p. 1986. 75.00 (*0-685-49624-4*, Pub. by Intl Bk Distr II) St Mut.
— Handbook of Social Forestry. 178p. (C). 1986. 120.00 (*81-7089-037-3*, Pub. by Intl Bk Distr II); 150.00 (*0-685-61464-6*, Pub. by Intl Bk Distr II); text ed. 110.00 (*0-685-52014-5*, Pub. by Intl Bk Distr II) St Mut.
— A Handbook of the Himalaya. (C). 1990. 58.50 (*81-85182-35-3*, Pub. by Indus Pub II) S Asia.
— Himachal Pradesh: The Land & People. (C). 1993. 24.00x (*81-85182-90-6*, Pub. by Indus Pub II) S Asia.
— Himalayan Forests & Forestry. (C). 1990. 48.00 (*81-85182-44-2*, Pub. by Indus Pub II) S Asia.
— Himalayan Rivers, Lakes & Glaciers. (C). 1991. 20.00 (*81-85182-61-2*, Pub. by Indus Pub II) S Asia.
— Himalayan Wildlife: Habitat & Conservation. (C). 1992. 24.00 (*81-85182-68-X*, Pub. by Indus Pub II) S Asia.
— Indian Forestry Through the Ages. (C). 1995. 28.00x (*81-7387-020-9*, Pub. by Indus Pub II) S Asia.
— India's Forests, Forestry & Wildlife. (C). 1994. text ed. 48.00 (*81-7387-010-1*, Pub. by Indus Pub II) S Asia.
— Managing the Himalayan Environment. (C). 1986. 75.00 (*81-7136-006-8*, Pub. by Periodical Expert India) St Mut.
— Manual of Wildlife in India. 1993. 175.00 (*81-7089-166-3*, Pub. by Intl Bk Distr II) St Mut.
— Minor Forest Products. (C). 1992. 125.00 (*81-7136-038-6*, Pub. by Periodical Expert India) St Mut.
— Operation Pushpak. (C). 1987. 22.50 (*81-7136-008-4*, Pub. by Periodical Expert India) St Mut.
— Principal of Land Management & Soil Conservation. (C). 1991. 170.00 (*81-7136-016-5*, Pub. by Periodical Expert India) St Mut.
— Tribal Development & Administration, 1986. 167p. (C). 1986. 125.00 (*81-7089-038-1*, Pub. by Intl Bk Distr II) St Mut.
— Tribal Welfare Development & Administration. 167p. (C). 1986. text ed. 125.00 (*0-685-52015-3*, Pub. by Intl Bk Distr II) St Mut.
Negin, Gary A. Teaching Thinking & Literacy. 148p. (Orig.). (C). 1992. lib. bdg. 35.50 (*0-8191-8478-0*); pap. text ed. 18.00 (*0-8191-8479-9*) U Pr of Amer.
Negishi, Ei-Ichi. Organometallics in Organic Synthesis: General Discussions & Organometallics of Main Group Metals in Organic Synthesis, Vol. 1. LC 79-16818. 548p. 1980. 49.00 (*0-471-03193-3*, Wiley-Interscience) Krieger.
Negishi, T. History of Economic Theory. (Advanced Textbooks in Economics Ser.: No. 26). 400p. 1989. 49.50 (*0-444-70437-X*, North Holland) Elsevier.
Negishi, Takashi. Economic Theories in a Non-Walrasian Tradition. (Historical Perspectives on Modern Economics Ser.). (Illus.). 208p. 1985. 64.95 (*0-521-25967-3*) Cambridge U Pr.
— Economic Theories in a Non-Walrasian Tradition. (Historical Perspectives on Modern Economics Ser.). (Illus.). 208p. (C). 1989. pap. 22.95 (*0-521-37860-5*) Cambridge U Pr.
— General Equilibrium Theory: The Collected Essays of Takashi Negishi, Vol. I. (Economists of the Twentieth Century Ser.). 416p. 1994. 74.95 (*1-85278-937-9*, Pub. by E Elgar Pub UK) Ashgate Pub Co.
— The History of Economics: The Collected Essays of Takashi Negishi, Vol. II. (Economists of the Twentieth Century Ser.). 364p. 1994. 69.95 (*1-85278-938-7*, Pub. by E Elgar Pub UK) Ashgate Pub Co.
Negishi, Takashi, jt. auth. see Itoh, Motoshige.
Negishi, Takashi, jt. ed. see Sato, Ryuzo.
Neglen, P. Surgical Treatment of Acute Venous Thrombosis. (Medical Intelligence Unit Ser.). 1995. write for info. (*1-57059-045-1*) R G Landes.
Negley, Glenn R. Political Authority & Moral Judgement. LC 65-13654. 173p. reprint ed. pap. 49.40 (*0-317-20448-3*, 2023427) Bks Demand.
Negley-Parker, Esther, jt. auth. see Araoz, Daniel L.
Neglia, Erminio & Ordaz, Luis. Repertorio Selecto del Teatro Hispanoamericano Contemporaneo. LC 79-15199. 111p. 1982. 1.00 (*0-87918-042-0*) ASU Lat Am St.
Negoesco, Stephen. Soccer. 144p. (C). 1993. pap. text ed. write for info. (*0-697-10059-6*) Brown & Benchmark.
Negoita, ed. Cybernetics & Applied Systems. 376p. 1992. 150.00 (*0-8247-8677-7*) Dekker.
Negoita, C. V. Fuzzy Systems, Vol. 2. (Cybernetics & Systems Ser., Abacus Bks.). (Illus.). 111p. 1981. text ed. 53.00 (*0-85626-164-5*) Gordon & Breach.
Negoita, Constantin PHD. The Cybernetic Conspiracy: Mind Over Matter. LC 88-80257. 1988. pap. 8.95 (*0-941404-69-2*) New Falcon Pubns.
Negovskii, Vladimir A. Acute Problems in Resuscitation & Hypothermia: Proceedings of a Symposium on the Application of Deep Hypothermia in Terminal States, Sept. 15-19, 1964. Haigh, Basil, tr. LC 65-20214. 98p. reprint ed. pap. 28.00 (*0-8357-5090-6*, 2020667) Bks Demand.
— Resuscitation & Artificial Hypothermia. Haigh, Basil, tr. LC 62-21589. 328p. reprint ed. pap. 93.50 (*0-317-07804-6*, 2020658) Bks Demand.
Negovsky, V. A., et al, eds. Postresuscitation Disease. 392p. 1984. 171.00 (*0-444-80488-9*) Elsevier.
Negre, Herve. Petit Larousse de la Medecine, Vol. 1. 975p. (FRE.). 1988. pap. 19.95 (*0-7859-4845-7*) Fr & Eur.
Negreiros, Almada, jt. illus. see Levine, David.
Negrepontis, S., jt. auth. see Comfort, W. W.
Negrey, Cynthia. Gender, Time, & Reduced Work. LC 92-11955. (SUNY Series in the Sociology of Work). (Illus.). 148p. 1993. 59.50 (*0-7914-1407-8*); pap. 19.95 (*0-7914-1408-6*) State U NY Pr.
Negri, Antonio. Marx Beyond Marx: Lessons on the Grundrisse. Orig. Title: Marx Oltre Marx. 248p. 1991. pap. 10.00 (*0-936756-25-X*) Autonomedia.
— The Politics of Subversion: A Manifesto for the Twenty-First Century. Newell, James, tr. 200p. 1989. text ed. 49.95 (*0-7456-0601-6*) Blackwell Pubs.
— The Savage Anomaly: The Power of Spinoza's Metaphysics & Politics. Hardt, Michael, tr. & frwd. by. 284p. 1990. text ed. 44.95 (*0-8166-1876-3*); pap. text ed. 18.95 (*0-8166-1877-1*) U of Minn Pr.
Negri, Antonio, jt. auth. see Hardt, Michael.
Negri, M., jt. ed. see Genazzani, A. R.
Negri, M., et al, eds. Clinical Perspectives of Endogenous Opioids Production. LC 92-14001. 437p. 1992. text ed. 174.95 (*0-471-93542-5*, Wiley-Liss) Wiley.
Negri, Paul, ed. Great Sonnets. LC 94-6460. 96p. (Orig.). 1994. pap. 1.00 (*0-486-28052-7*) Dover.
***Negri, Romana.** The Newborn in the Intensive Care Unit: A Neuropsychoanalytic Prevention Model. 285p. 1994. pap. text ed. 34.95 (*0-614-07215-8*, Pub. by Karnac Bks UK) Brunner-Mazel.
Negri, Sharon. The Other Side of Now. LC 88-26870. 72p. (Orig.). 1989. pap. 7.00 (*0-931846-35-8*) Wash Writers Pub.
Negri, Toni, jt. auth. see Guattari, Felix.
Negrin, Howard, jt. ed. see Lightman, Marjorie.
Negrin, S., ed. The Great Harmony: Teachings & Observations of the Way of the Universe. LC 77-77387. (Illus.). 128p. (Orig.). 1977. pap. 5.95 (*0-87810-033-4*) Times Change.
Negrin, Su. Begin at Start: Some Thoughts on Personal Liberation & World Change. LC 72-87031. (Illus.). 176p. (Orig.). 1972. 15.95 (*0-87810-520-4*); pap. 7.95 (*0-87810-020-2*) Times Change.
Negrine, Ralph M. Politics & the Mass Media in Britain. (Illus.). 284p. 1989. 45.00 (*0-415-01529-4*, A3282); pap. 17.95 (*0-415-01530-8*, A3286) Routledge.
— Politics & the Mass Media in Britain. 2nd ed. LC 93-18010. 1994. write for info. (*0-415-09468-2*) Routledge.
Negrine, Ralph M., ed. Satellite Broadcasting: The Politics & Implications of the New Media. 320p. 1988. lib. bdg. 65.00 (*0-415-00109-9*) Routledge.
Negrini, R., et al. Fault Tolerance Through Reconfiguration in VLSI & WSI Arrays. (Computer Systems Ser.). 320p. 1989. 47.50 (*0-262-14044-6*) MIT Pr.
***Negrino.** Using Microsoft Office for MacIntosh, Special Edition. 1994. pap. 34.99 (*0-7897-0017-4*) Que.
***Negrino, Tom.** Upgrading Your Mac Illustrated. (Illus.). 1994. pap. 24.99 (*1-56529-917-5*) Que.
Negro Pavon, Dalmacio, ed. see Mill, John Stuart.
Negro, Sergio P. Times & Seasons: Homilies for the Church Year. LC 94-76370. 200p. 1994. pap. 15.00 (*0-9641404-9-7*, WordWrks) Sixth St Pr.
Negro-Vilar, Andrea & Conn, P. Michael, eds. Peptide Hormones: Effects & Mechanisms of Action, Vol. I. 272p. 1988. 191.00 (*0-8493-6719-0*, QP572) CRC Pr.
— Peptide Hormones: Effects & Mechanisms of Action, Vol. II. 224p. 1988. 148.00 (*0-8493-6720-4*, CRC Reprint) Franklin.
— Peptide Hormones: Effects & Mechanisms of Action, Vol. III. 224p. 1988. 168.00 (*0-8493-6721-2*) CRC Pr.
Negro-Vilar, Andres, ed. Male Reproduction & Fertility. 406p. 1983. text ed. 173.50 (*0-89004-746-4*) Raven.
Negron De Montilla, Aida. Americanization in Puerto Rico & the Public School System, 1900-1930. 282p. 1975. 5.00 (*0-8477-2727-0*) U of PR Pr.
Negron-Portillo, Mariano & Mayo-Santana, Raul. La Esclavitud Urbana en San Juan de Puerto Rico. LC 92-72980. (Illus.). 137p. (Orig.). (SPA.). (C). 1992. pap. 6.95 (*0-929157-19-2*) Ediciones Huracan.
Negroni, Andrea L. & Platt, Larry. Residential Mortgage Lending: State Regulation Manual, 6 vols. 1990. Mid-Atlantic, Northeast, Southeast, North Central, South Central & West. 275.00 (*0-685-74210-5*) Clark Boardman Callaghan.
Negroni, Iraida. El Gran Dilema Humano: La Vida, Complicada e Incomprendida. (Illus.). 372p. (Orig.). (SPA.). (C). 1988. pap. 12.00 (*0-9620054-0-1*) I Negroni.
Negroni, Maria, tr. see Committee to Protect Journalists Staff.
Negroni, Maria, tr. see Ransome, Arthur.
Negroni, Maria, tr. see Shulevitz, Uri.
***Negroponte.** Being Digital. pap. 12.00 (*0-679-76290-6*) Random.
***Negroponte, Nicholas.** Being Digital. 1995. 23.00 (*0-679-43919-6*) Knopf.
***Negroponte, Nicholaus.** Being Digital, Compact Disc. Date not set. 15.00 (*0-679-44145-X*) Random.
Negrotti, M., ed. Understanding the Artificial: On the Future Shape of Artificial Intelligence. (Artificial Intelligence & Society Ser.). (Illus.). xi, 164p. 1991. pap. 69.00 (*0-387-19612-9*) Spr-Verlag.
Negru, John. Computer Typesetting. (Illus.). 208p. 1988. pap. 49.95 (*0-442-26696-0*) Van Nos Reinhold.
— Desktop Typographics. LC 90-49702. (Illus.). 192p. 1991. pap. 24.95 (*0-442-00179-7*) Van Nos Reinhold.
Negrutiu, I. & Gharti-Chhetri, G., eds. A Laboratory Guide to Cellular & Molecular Techniques for Higher Plants. (Biomethods Ser.: Vol. 4). 392p. 1991. 147.50 (*0-8176-2542-9*) Birkhauser.
Negrutiu, Radu. Elastic Analysis of Slab Structures. 1987. lib. bdg. 172.50 (*90-247-3367-7*) Kluwer Ac.
Negt, Oskar & Kluge, Alexander. Public Sphere & Experience: Analysis of the Bourgeois & Proletarian Public Sphere. Labanyi, Peter et al, trs. LC 93-610. (Theory & History of Literature Ser.: Vol. 85). 327p. (C). 1993. text ed. 44.95 (*0-8166-2031-8*) U of Minn Pr.
Negulescu, Ioan A., jt. auth. see Uglea, Constantin V.
Negulescu, M. Municipal Waste Waters Treatment. (Devlopments in Water Science Ser.: No. 23). 596p. 1986. 161.75 (*0-444-99561-7*) Elsevier.
***Negus.** Leg Ulcers. 1995. write for info. (*0-7506-1697-0*, Focal) Buttrwrth-Heinemann.
***Negus, et al.** Novell's Guide to UNIX System V & UnixWare 4.2. 1995. cd-rom 39.99 (*0-7821-1720-1*) Sybex.
***Negus, A.** The Ghosts of Dictatorship. 1994. 16.95 (*0-533-10994-9*) Vantage.
Negus, Brenda, ed. see Dechert Price & Rhoads Staff.
Negus, Brenda M. Donoghue's Money Fund Directory, 1990 Edition. 100p. (Orig.). 1990. pap. 19.00 (*0-685-33379-5*) Donoghue Organ Inc.
Negus, Brenda M., ed. Donoghue's Money Fund Directory, 1990-1991. (Illus.). 112p. 1990. pap. 19.00 (*0-913755-09-5*) Donoghue Organ Inc.
Negus, Chris & Schumer, Larry. Novell's Guide to UNIXWare 1.1. LC 93-85744. 817p. 1994. pap. 34.99 (*0-7821-1292-7*) Sybex.
Negus, D. Leg Ulcers: A Practical Approach to Management. (Illus.). 208p. 1991. 85.00 (*0-7506-1034-4*) Buttrwrth-Heinemann.
Negus, Joan. Astro-Alchemy: Making the Most of Your Transits. 156p. 1985. pap. 9.95 (*0-917086-82-1*) ACS Pubns.
— Basic Astrology: A Guide for Teachers & Students. 128p. 1978. pap. 8.95 (*0-917086-14-7*) ACS Pubns.
— Basic Astrology: A Workbook for Students. 64p. 1978. pap. 5.95 (*0-917086-15-5*) ACS Pubns.
— Cosmic Combinations: A Book of Astrological Exercises. 168p. (Orig.). 1982. pap. 8.95 (*0-917086-37-6*) ACS Pubns.
Negus, Keith. Producing Pop: Culture & Conflict in the Popular Music Industry. 192p. 1993. pap. 15.95 (*0-340-57512-3*, B0097, Pub. by E Arnold UK) Routledge Chapman & Hall.
Negus, Kenneth. Grimmelshausen. LC 73-17215. (Twayne's World Authors Ser.). 178p. (C). 1974. lib. bdg. 17.95 (*0-8057-2405-2*) Irvington.
Negus, Sue & Harris, Steve. Windows: Troubleshooting Guide. (Illus.). 400p. 1992. pap. 44.95 (*0-7506-0814-5*) Buttrwrth-Heinemann.
Negwer, Martin. Organic Chemical Drugs & their Synonyms, 3 vols., Set. 6th ed. LC 86-32496. 2470p. 1987. lib. bdg. 225.00 (*3-05-500156-7*, Pub. by Akademie GW) VCH Pubs.
***Nehamas, A. & Woodruff, P., trs.** Phaedrus. LC 94-46613. (Classics Ser.). 112p. (C). 1995. text ed. 27.95x (*0-87220-221-6*); pap. text ed. 5.95x (*0-87220-220-8*) Hackett Pub.
Nehamas, Alexander. Nietzsche: Life As Literature. LC 85-5589. 240p. 1985. 29.95 (*0-674-62435-1*) HUP.
— Nietzsche: Life As Literature. LC 85-5589. 240p. 1987. pap. 15.95 (*0-674-62426-2*) HUP.
Nehamas, Alexander, jt. ed. see Furley, David J.
Nehammer, C. F., jt. auth. see Stock, C. J.
Nehari, Zeev. Conformal Mapping. LC 74-27513. (Illus.). 416p. 1975. reprint ed. pap. text ed. 7.95 (*0-486-61137-X*) Dover.
Nehemias, Paulette. A Tree in Sprocket's Pocket: Stories about God's Green Earth. LC 92-26033. (God's Green Earth Ser.: Bk. 1). (Illus.). 128p. (Orig.). (J). (gr. 3-5). 1993. pap. 4.99 (*0-570-04730-7*) Concordia.
— Wiggler's Worms: Stories about God's Green Earth. LC 92-28486. (God's Green Earth Ser.). (Illus.). 128p. (Orig.). (J). (gr. 3-5). 1993. pap. 4.99 (*0-570-04731-5*) Concordia.
Nehemkis, Alexis M., jt. auth. see Gerber, Kenneth E.
Nehemkis, Peter, jt. auth. see Eells, Richard.
Neher, Andre. Jewish Thought & Scientific Revolution of the Sixteenth Century: David Gans (1541-1613) & His Times. Maisel, David, tr. LC 85-21797. (Littman Library of Jewish Civilization). (Illus.). 294p. 1986. 20.00 (*0-19-710057-0*, Pub. by Littman Lib Jew UK) Bnai Brith Bk.

— They Made Their Souls Anew: Ils Ont Refait Leur Ame. Maisel, David, tr. LC 89-38685. (SUNY Series in Modern Jewish Literature & Culture). 179p. 1990. 59.50 (*0-7914-0315-7*); pap. 19.95 (*0-7914-0316-5*) State U NY Pr.

Neher, Andrew. The Psychology of Transcendence. 384p. 1990. pap. 8.95 (*0-486-26167-0*) Dover.

Neher, Barbara L. From the Kitchen of the Royal Chef. (Illus.). 200p. (Orig.). 1985. ring bd. 14.95 (*0-685-10568-7*) Directed Media.

Neher, Clark & Mungkandi, Wiwat, eds. U. S. - Thailand Relations in a New International Era, No. 33. (Research Papers & Policy Studies). 350p. (Orig.). 1990. pap. 20.00 (*1-55729-018-0*) IEAS.

Neher, Clark D. Politics in Southeast Asia. rev. ed. 316p. 1987. 24.95 (*0-87047-010-8*); pap. 15.95 (*0-87047-011-6*) Schenkman Bks Inc.

— Southeast Asia in the New International Era. 2nd ed. (Politics in Asia & the Pacific Ser.). 242p. (C). 1994. text ed. 58.00 (*0-8133-1988-9*); pap. text ed. 19.95 (*0-8133-1989-7*) Westview.

Neher, E. Jordan Triple Systems by the Grid Approach. (Lecture Notes in Mathematics Ser.: Vol. 1280). xii, 193p. 1987. pap. 30.00 (*0-387-18362-0*) Spr-Verlag.

Neher, E. C., tr. see Lestienne, Remy.

Neher, Erwin, jt. ed. see Sakmann, Bert.

Neher, Evelyn. Four-Harness Huck. 40p. 1967. reprint ed. pap. text ed. 10.00 (*0-9600854-1-6*) E Neher.

— Inkle. (Illus.). 313p. 1974. 25.00 (*0-9600854-2-4*) E Neher.

Neher, James A. A Christian's Guide to Today's Catholic Charismatic Movement. vi, 134p. 1987. pap. 6.95 (*0-944788-99-8*) IBRI.

Neher, Philip A. Natural Resource Economics: Conservation & Exploitation. (Illus.). 432p. (C). 1990. pap. 32.95 (*0-521-31174-8*) Cambridge U Pr.

— Natural Resource Economics: Conservation & Exploitation. (Illus.). 432p. (C). 1990. 79.95 (*0-521-32358-4*) Cambridge U Pr.

Neher, Philip A., et al, eds. Rights Based Fishing. (C). 1989. lib. bdg. 172.00 (*0-7923-0246-X*) Kluwer Ac.

Neher, William W., et al. Public Speaking: A Rhetorical Approach. 3rd ed. 288p. (C). 1993. per. 28.95 (*0-8403-9197-8*) Kendall-Hunt.

N

***NEHGS Staff.** The New England Historical & Genealogical Register: 1866, XX. 398p. (Orig.). 1994. pap. 25.00 (*1-55613-977-2*) Heritage Bk.

— New England Historical & Genealogical Register Vol. 29: 1875. (Illus.). 513p. (Orig.). 1995. pap. text ed. 25.00 (*0-7884-0195-5*) Heritage Bk.

— The New England Historical & Genealogical Register Vol. XIX: 1865. 394p. (Orig.). 1994. pap. 25.00 (*1-55613-976-4*) Heritage Bk.

— New England Historical & Genealogical Register, 1851, Vol. 5. 486p. reprint ed. pap. 25.00 (*1-55613-708-7*) Heritage Bk.

— New England Historical & Genealogical Register, 1874, Vol. 28. (Illus.). 500p. 1995. reprint ed. pap. text ed. 25.00 (*0-7884-0194-7*) Heritage Bk.

— New England History & Genealogy Reg. Vol. 26: 1872. 464p. 1995. reprint ed. pap. text ed. 25.00 (*0-7884-0126-2*) Heritage Bk.

NEHGS Staff, ed. New England Historical & Genealogical Register, Vol. VI: 1852. 402p. reprint ed. pap. 25.00 (*1-55613-709-5*) Heritage Bk.

Nehls, Edward H., ed. D. H. Lawrence: A Composite Biography, 3 vols. 1959. write for info. (*0-318-56169-7*) U of Wis Pr.

— D. H. Lawrence: A Composite Biography, 3 vols, 1. 1959. 35.00 (*0-299-81501-3*) U of Wis Pr.

— D. H. Lawrence: A Composite Biography, 3 vols, 2. 1959. 35.00 (*0-299-81502-1*) U of Wis Pr.

Nehls, H. Michael. The Colors of Christmas. Sherer, Michael L., ed. (Orig.). 1986. pap. 4.15 (*0-89536-838-2*, 6862) CSS OH.

Nehls, Nadine, jt. auth. see Morgenbesser, Mel.

Nehlsen, Nancy & Stewart, Marjabelle Y. Princess Marjabelle Visits Lollygag Lake: Marjabelle Stewart's Introduction to Manners. (Princess Marjabelle Ser.). (Illus.). 32p. (J). (ps). 1994. 14.95 (*0-88331-214-X*) Luce.

Nehmer, J., ed. Experiences with Distributed Systems. (Lecture Notes in Computer Science Ser.: Vol. 309). 292p. 1988. pap. 36.00 (*0-387-19333-2*) Spr-Verlag.

Nehr, Ellen. Doubleday Crime Club Compendium, 1928-1991. 1992. lib. bdg. 75.00 (*0-9634420-0-7*) Offspring Pr.

Nehrbass, Arthur F. Dead Easy. 320p. 1993. pap. 4.99 (*0-451-17704-5*, Onyx) NAL-Dutton.

— Dead Heat. 336p. 1994. 19.95 (*0-525-93664-5*, Dutton) NAL-Dutton.

— Dead Heat. 384p. 1995. pap. 4.99 (*0-451-40570-6*, Onyx) NAL-Dutton.

Nehrbass, Richard. Dark of Night. 1994. mass mkt. 4.50 (*0-06-109163-4*, Harp PBks) HarpC.

— Perfect Death for Hollywood. 1993. mass mkt. 4.99 (*0-06-109042-5*, Harp PBks) HarpC.

Nehring, Donna, ed. see Rapp, Doris G.

Nehring, James. The Schools We Have, the Schools We Want: An American Teacher on the Front Line. LC 92-14016. (Education-Higher Education Ser.). 200p. 1992. 26.95 (*1-55542-457-0*) Jossey-Bass.

— Why Do We Gotta Do This Stuff, Mr. Nehring? Notes from a Teacher's Day in School. LC 89-1352. 192p. 1989. 15.95 (*0-87131-574-2*) M Evans.

Nehring, Neil. Flowers in the Dustbin: Culture, Anarchy, & Postwar England. LC 92-42085. 330p. 1993. text ed. 47.50 (*0-472-09526-9*); pap. text ed. 17.95 (*0-472-06526-2*) U of Mich Pr.

Nehring, Radine T. Dear Earth... A Love Letter from Spring Hollow. LC 94-28966. 176p. 1995. 17.95 (*0-9636620-2-3*) Brett Bks. The unforgettable chronicle of a couple who traded secure jobs & the rat race for a life of simplicity & quiet joy. "Read it & dream."--BOOKLIST "Radine reminds us that dreams are meant to be dreamed -- that woods are meant to be walked in -- & the Earth is meant to be cared for. She is a wonderfully warm, descriptive writer who will have you sitting on her bench in the woods -- watching & loving the things around you -- & loving her gentle company as well. You should give this book to everyone you love..."--MIKE FLYNN, Host, FOLK SAMPLER, National Public Radio. "Nehring's book is a must!"--DR. NEIL COMPTON, Conservationist & Pulitzer Prize nominee. National advertising & promotion. Brett Books, Inc., P.O. Box 290-637, Brooklyn, NY 11229-0011. Phone & FAX: 718-376-5470. Distributed by INDEPENDENT PUBLISHERS GROUP: 1-800-888-4741. *Publisher Provided Annotation.*

Nehrling, Arno & Nehrling, Irene. Gardening for Flower Arrangement. LC 75-20966. Orig. Title: Flower Growing for Flower Arrangement. 256p. 1976. reprint ed. pap. 5.95 (*0-486-23263-8*) Dover.

Nehrling, Irene, jt. auth. see Nehrling, Arno.

Nehrt, Lee C. International Marketing of Nuclear Power Plants. LC 65-24596. (Indiana University Social Science Ser.: No. 22). 419p. reprint ed. 119.50 (*0-8357-9220-X*, 2015462) Bks Demand.

Nehru, J. Selected Works of Jawaharlal Nehru, 7. Gopal, S., ed. LC 72-900197. 1975. 14.00 (*0-685-40473-0*) S Asia.

— Selected Works of Jawaharlal Nehru, Vols. 1-4. Gopal, S., ed. 1973. 12.75 (*0-318-55754-1*) S Asia.

— Selected Works of Jawaharlal Nehru, Vols. 5-6. Gopal, S., ed. 1973. 13.75 (*0-318-55755-X*) S Asia.

Nehru, J. & Gopal, S. Selected Works of Jawaharlal Nehru, 8. 1976. 15.00 (*0-88386-376-6*) S Asia.

— Selected Works of Jawaharlal Nehru, 9. 1977. 15.00 (*0-685-66727-8*) S Asia.

— Selected Works of Jawaharlal Nehru, 10. 1977. 15.00 (*0-8364-0344-4*) S Asia.

— Selected Works of Jawaharlal Nehru, 11. 1978. 16.00 (*0-8364-0345-2*) S Asia.

Nehru, Jawaharlal. An Autobiography: Centenary Edition. 640p. 1989. 19.95 (*0-19-562395-9*); pap. 9.95 (*0-19-562361-4*) OUP.

— Discovery of India. 1990. pap. 11.95 (*0-19-562359-2*) OUP.

— Glimpses of World History. 1032p. 1990. pap. 13.95 (*0-19-562360-6*) OUP.

— Glimpses of World History: Centenary Edition. 1032p. 1989. 22.50 (*0-19-562396-7*) OUP.

— Independence & After. LC 75-134120. (Essay Index Reprint Ser.). 1977. 29.95 (*0-8369-2003-1*) Ayer.

— India's Foreign Policy. 612p. 1985. reprint ed. 34.95 (*0-940500-94-9*, Pub. by Pubns Div II) Asia Bk Corp.

— Letters to Chief Ministers, 1947-1964, Vol. 1: 1947-1949. Parthasarathi, G., ed. (Illus.). 584p. 1988. 34.00 (*0-19-561881-5*) OUP.

— Letters to Chief Ministers, 1947-1964, Vol. 2: 1950-1952. (Illus.). 600p. 1987. 34.00 (*0-19-562012-7*) OUP.

— Letters to Chief Ministers, 1947-1964, Vol. 3: 1952-1954. (Illus.). 706p. 1988. 34.00 (*0-19-562180-8*) OUP.

— Letters to Chief Ministers, 1947-1964, Vol. 4: 1954-1957. (Illus.). 704p. 1990. 34.00 (*0-19-562338-X*) OUP.

— Letters to Chief Ministers, 1947-1964, Vol. 5: 1958-1964. (Illus.). 668p. 1990. 34.00 (*0-19-562512-9*) OUP.

— Selected Works of Jamaharlal Nehru, Vol. 16, Pt. II. Gopal, S., ed. (Illus.). 800p. 1995. 18.95 (*0-19-563681-3*) OUP.

— Selected Works of Jawaharlal Nehru, Vol. 13. Gopal, Sarvepalli, ed. (Illus.). 520p. 1993. 13.95 (*0-19-563086-6*) OUP.

— Selected Works of Jawaharlal Nehru, Vol. 14. Gopal, Sarvepalli, ed. (Illus.). 644p. 1993. 13.95 (*0-19-563096-3*) OUP.

— Selected Works of Jawaharlal Nehru, Vol. 15, Pt. I. 2nd ed. Gopal, S., ed. 593p. write for info. (*0-318-72311-5*) OUP.

— Selected Works of Jawaharlal Nehru: Second Series, Vol. 3. Gopal, Sarvepalli, ed. (Illus.). 554p. 1987. 34.50 (*0-19-561849-1*) OUP.

— Selected Works of Jawaharlal Nehru: Second Series, Vol. 5. Gopal, Sarvepalli, ed. (Illus.). 646p. 1988. 34.50 (*0-19-562011-9*) OUP.

— Selected Works of Jawaharlal Nehru: Second Series, Vol. 6. Gopal, Sarvepalli, ed. (Illus.). 582p. 1989. 29.95 (*0-19-562141-7*) OUP.

— Selected Works of Jawaharlal Nehru: Second Series, Vol. 7. Gopal, Sarvepalli, ed. (Illus.). 814p. 1989. 34.50 (*0-19-562337-1*) OUP.

— Selected Works of Jawaharlal Nehru: Second Series, Vol. 8. Gopal, Sarvepalli, ed. 514p. 1990. 29.95 (*0-19-562513-7*) OUP.

— Selected Works of Jawaharlal Nehru: Second Series, Vol. 9. Gopal, Sarvepalli, ed. (Illus.). 560p. 1992. 29.95 (*0-19-562654-0*) OUP.

— Selected Works of Jawaharlal Nehru: Second Series, Vol. 10. Gopal, Sarvepalli, ed. (Illus.). 588p. 1991. 18.95 (*0-19-562838-1*) OUP.

— Selected Works of Jawaharlal Nehru: Second Series, Vol. 12. Gopal, Sarvepalli, ed. (Illus.). 524p. 1992. 19.95 (*0-19-562964-7*) OUP.

— Selected Works of Jawaharlal Nehru: Second Series, Vol. 14, Pt. II. Gopal, S., ed. 530p. 1995. 12.95 (*0-19-563309-1*) OUP.

Nei, Masatoshi. Molecular Evolutionary Genetics. 448p. 1989. text ed. 86.00 (*0-231-06320-2*); pap. text ed. 31.50 (*0-231-06321-0*) Col U Pr.

Nei, Masatoshi, jt. auth. see Roychoudhury, Arun K.

Neibacher, Susan. Homeless People & Health Care: An Unrelenting Challenge. (Paper Ser.: No. 14). 32p. 1990. 5.00 (*0-934459-62-2*) United Hosp Fund.

Neibart, Wally & Charles, Mickey. Sportshots. (Illus.). 120p. 1982. pap. 4.95 (*0-943588-00-6*) Baron-Scott Enterp.

***Neibauer.** Home Improvement: Total Planning on Your Computer. 1995. pap. text ed. 24.95 (*1-56276-334-2*) Ziff-Davis.

— Your Health: Total Healthcare Planning on Your Computer. 1995. pap. text ed. 18.95 (*1-56276-302-4*) Ziff-Davis.

Neibauer, Alan. El ABC de MC Word. 373p. 1992. pap. text ed. 22.95 (*968-6346-21-X*, Pub. by Ventura Ediciones MX) Computer & Tech.

— El ABC del MS Word para Windows. 415p. 1992. pap. text ed. 24.95 (*968-6346-57-0*, Pub. by Ventura Ediciones MX) Computer & Tech.

— Word for Windows Version X Secrets & Solutions. LC 93-87708. 740p. 1994. pap. 24.99 (*0-7821-1392-3*) Sybex.

— Your First C-C Plus Plus Program. LC 93-87421. 367p. 1994. pap. 24.99 (*0-7821-1414-8*) Sybex.

Neibauer, Alan R. El ABC de WordPerfect 5.1. 306p. 1991. pap. text ed. 24.95 (*968-6346-24-4*, Pub. by Ventura Ediciones MX) Computer & Tech.

— El ABC de WordPerfect 5.1 para Windows. 312p. 1993. pap. text ed. 24.95 (*968-6346-51-1*, Pub. by Ventura Ediciones MX) Computer & Tech.

— El ABC Excel 4 para Windows. 292p. 1993. pap. text ed. 24.95 (*968-6346-58-9*, Pub. by Ventura Ediciones MX) Computer & Tech.

— The ABCs of Microsoft Word for Windows Version 2.0. 2nd ed. LC 91-67704. 417p. 1992. pap. 19.95 (*0-7821-1052-5*) Sybex.

— ABCs of Windows 3.1. LC 91-67907. 306p. (C). 1992. pap. 19.95 (*0-89588-839-4*) Sybex.

— The ABCs of Word 6 for Windows: Version X. LC 93-86869. 292p. 1993. 19.99 (*0-7821-1415-6*) Sybex.

— The ABCs of WordPerfect 5.1 for DOS. LC 89-63762. 352p. 1989. 19.95 (*0-89588-672-3*) Sybex.

— ABCs of WordPerfect 6 for DOS. LC 93-84822. 309p. 1993. pap. 19.95 (*0-7821-1177-7*) Sybex.

— The ABCs of WordPerfect 6 for Windows. LC 93-86064. 310p. 1993. 19.99 (*0-7821-1384-2*) Sybex.

— The Hand-Me-Down PC Handbook. LC 90-70872. 367p. 1990. pap. 19.95 (*0-89588-702-9*) Sybex.

— Mastering Q & A 4. 633p. 1991. pap. 27.95 (*0-89588-735-5*) Sybex.

— Moving Data Across Windows - An Easy Guide to Object Linking & Embedding. 1995. 19.99 (*0-7821-1562-4*) Sybex.

— Pushbutton Guide to Word 6.0 for Windows. LC 94-66141. 249p. 1994. pap. 16.99 (*0-7821-1527-6*) Sybex.

— WordPerfect Tips & Tricks. 4th ed. LC 89-52178. 685p. (Orig.). 1990. pap. 27.95 (*0-89588-681-2*) Sybex.

Neibauer Press Staff. Childrens Church Promotion. (Illus.). 48p. 1990. 7.95 (*1-878259-06-7*) Neibauer Pr.

— Church Year I. (Illus.). 48p. 1987. 5.95 (*0-685-28913-3*, 1451) Neibauer Pr.

— Clip Art for Afro American Churches. (Illus.). 48p. 1990. 7.95 (*1-878259-00-8*) Neibauer Pr.

— How to Organize a Mission Program. 166p. 1990. 25.95 (*1-878259-02-4*) Neibauer Pr.

Neibaur, James L. Movie Comedians: The Complete Guide. LC 84-43204. 255p. 1986. lib. bdg. 32.50 (*0-89950-163-X*) McFarland & Co.

— The RKO Features: A Complete Filmography of the Feature Films Released or Produced by RKO Radio Pictures, 1929-1960. LC 92-56669. (Illus.). 344p. 1994. lib. bdg. 45.00 (*0-89950-787-5*) McFarland & Co.

— Tough Guy: The American Movie Macho. LC 88-27309. (Illus.). 232p. 1989. lib. bdg. 27.50x (*0-89950-382-9*) McFarland & Co.

Neibaur, James L. & Okuda, Ted. The Jerry Lewis Films: An Analytical Filmography of the Enigmatic Comic Genius. LC 94-30905. 336p. 1994. lib. bdg. 37.50x (*0-89950-961-4*) McFarland & Co.

***Neibel, Benjamin W. & Gjesdahl, Maurice S.** Production Engineering. (Illus.). 148p. 1971. text ed. 14.75 (*92-833-1003-9*, 310039, Pub. by APO JA); pap. text ed. 11.00 (*92-833-1004-7*, 310047, Pub. by APO JA) Qual Resc.

Neible, Stephen & Waring, Michael, eds. Molecular Aspects of Anticancer Drug-DNA Interactions, Vol. II. (Topics in Molecular & Structural Biology Ser.). 336p. 1994. 97.00 (*0-8493-7773-0*, Z7773) CRC Pr.

Neibuhr, Reinhold. Children of the Light & Children of the Dark. 1985. pap. 13.50 (*0-684-15027-1*, Scribners) S&S Trade.

— Love & Justice: Selections from the Shorter Writings of Reinhold Niebuhr. Robertson, D. B., ed. (Library of Theological Ethics). 320p. 1992. pap. 13.99 (*0-664-25322-9*) Westminster John Knox.

Neiburger, E. J. & Neiburger, S. The Dentists' Handbook. LC 92-73278. (Illus.). 350p. (Orig.). 1993. pap. text ed. 37.50 (*0-914555-01-4*) Andent Inc.

Neiburger, Ellis J. Computers for Professional Practice. LC 83-72626. (Illus.). 281p. 1984. pap. 14.95 (*0-914555-00-6*) Andent Inc.

Neiburger, S., jt. auth. see Neiburger, E. J.

Neice, K. C. & Bartell, D. P. A Faunistic Survey of the Organisms Associated with Ants of Western Texas. (Graduate Studies: No. 25). (Illus.). 36p. (Orig.). 1982. pap. 6.00 (*0-89672-096-9*) Tex Tech Univ Pr.

Neich, Roger. Painted Histories: Early Maori Figurative Painting. (Auckland University Press Book Ser.). (Illus.). 392p. 1994. 75.00 (*1-86940-087-9*) OUP.

Neidecker, Elizabeth A. School Programs in Speech-Language: Organization & Management. (Illus.). 1980. text ed. write for info. (*0-13-794321-0*) P-H.

Neidecker, Elizabeth A. & Blosser, Jean L. School Programs in Speech-Language: Organization & Management. 3rd ed. 400p. 1992. text ed. write for info. (*0-13-792268-X*) P-H.

***Neidell, Norman S.** Stratigraphic Modeling & Interpretation: Geophysical Principles & Techniques. (Continuing Education Course Note Ser.: No. 13). (Illus.). 141p. 1979. pap. 15.00 (*0-89181-162-1*) AAPG.

Neider, Charles. The Authentic Death of Hendry Jones. LC 92-30094. (Western Literature Ser.). 224p. (C). 1993. reprint ed. pap. 13.00 (*0-87417-206-3*) U of Nev Pr.

— Mozart & the Archbooby. (Contemporary American Fiction Ser.). 96p. (Orig.). 1991. pap. 8.95 (*0-14-015402-7*, Penguin Bks) Viking Penguin.

— Overflight. 235p. 1986. 15.95 (*0-88282-026-5*) New Horizon NJ.

Neider, Charles, ed. The Autobiography of Mark Twain. LC 90-55053. (Illus.). 384p. 1990. reprint ed. pap. 13.00 (*0-06-092025-4*, PL) HarpC.

— Fabulous Insects. LC 68-16960. (Essay Index Reprint Ser.). 1977. 20.95 (*0-8369-0736-1*) Ayer.

— Great Short Stories. 560p. 1989. pap. 11.95 (*0-88184-457-8*) Carroll & Graf.

— Stature of Thomas Mann. LC 68-16961. (Essay Index Reprint Ser.). 1977. 29.95 (*0-8369-0737-X*) Ayer.

— Tolstoy: Tales of Courage & Conflict. 578p. 1985. pap. 11.95 (*0-88184-165-X*) Carroll & Graf.

Neider, Charles, intro. Great Shipwrecks & Castaways: Authentic Accounts of Disasters at Sea. 238p. 1990. 19.95 (*0-88029-464-7*) Marboro Bks.

— Short Novels of the Masters. 642p. (C). 1989. pap. 12.95 (*0-88184-487-X*) Carroll & Graf.

Neider, Linda, jt. auth. see Berkman, Harold.

Neiderbach, Shelley. Invisible Wounds: Crime Victims Speak. LC 86-22742. 281p. 1986. pap. 19.95 (*0-918393-30-2*) Harrington Pk.

— Invisible Wounds: Crime Victims Speak. LC 86-14831. 281p. 1986. 24.95 (*0-86656-525-6*); text ed. 44.95 (*0-86656-460-8*) Haworth Pr.

Neiderhaus, Lee B. Computer-Assisted Diagnosis & Medical Services: Subject Analysis with Bibliography. LC 83-45292. 168p. 1984. 39.50 (*0-88164-072-7*); pap. 34.50 (*0-88164-073-5*) ABBE Pubs Assn.

— Radon: Index of Modern Information. LC 88-47619. 150p. 1988. 44.50 (*0-88164-766-7*); pap. 39.50 (*0-88164-767-5*) ABBE Pubs Assn.

Neiderhiser, Richard. You Can Be Sanctified Wholly. (Christian Living Ser.). 40p. 1988. pap. 2.50 (*0-8341-1217-5*) Beacon Hill.

Neiderman, Andrew. After Life. 1993. mass mkt. 4.99 (*0-425-13974-3*) Berkley Pub.

— Angel of Mercy. LC 93-31259. 256p. 1994. 22.95 (*0-399-13926-5*, Putnam) Putnam Pub Group.

— Duplicates. 272p. (Orig.). 1994. pap. text ed. 4.99 (*0-425-14395-3*) Berkley Pub.

— Illusion. 288p. 1993. lib. bdg. 20.00 (*0-7278-4462-8*) Severn Hse.

— The Maddening. 320p. 1987. pap. text ed. 5.50 (*0-425-09898-2*) Berkley Pub.

— The Need. 288p. 1993. mass mkt. 4.99 (*0-425-13662-0*) Berkley Pub.

— Perfect Little Angels. (Orig.). 1991. 18.95 (*0-7278-4150-5*) Severn Hse.

— Reflection. 384p. (Orig.). 1986. mass mkt. 3.50 (*0-373-97027-7*, Wrldwide Lib) Harlequin Bks.

— Sight Unseen. 304p. 1987. pap. 3.95 (*0-8217-2038-4*) Zebra.

— Sister, Sister. 1992. mass mkt. 5.99 (*0-425-12846-6*) Berkley Pub.

— The Solomon Organization. 272p. 1994. mass mkt. 4.99 (*0-425-14281-7*) Berkley Pub.

— The Solomon Organization. LC 92-36566. 256p. 1993. 21.95 (*0-399-13806-4*, Putnam) Putnam Pub Group.

— Teacher's Pet. 336p. 1986. pap. 3.95 (*0-8217-1927-0*) Zebra.

***Neiderman, Derrick.** This Is Not Your Father's Stopicking Book. LC 95-2485. 1995. 35.00 (*0-8129-2216-6*) Random.

Neidermyer, Dan. Scripture Plays: Ten Plays from the Holy Bible. Zapel, Arthur, ed. LC 88-37687. (Illus.). 192p. (Orig.). 1989. pap. text ed. 9.95 (*0-916260-57-7*, B-150) Meriwether Pub.

Neides, Daniel m., jt. auth. see Weinstock, Michael B.

Neidhardt, E. Joseph, et al. No-Gimmick Guide to Managing Stress: Effective Options for Every Lifestyle. 2nd rev. ed. (Psychology Ser.). 136p. 1990. pap. 11.95 (*0-88908-886-1*) Self-Counsel Pr.

Neidhardt, Frederick C., et al. Physiology of the Bacterial Cell: A Molecular Approach. (Illus.). 508p. (C). 1990. text ed. 51.95 (*0-87893-608-4*) Sinauer Assocs.

Neidhardt, Frederick C., et al, eds. Escherichia Coli & Salmonella Typhimurium: Cellular & Molecular Biology. (Illus.). 1654p. 1987. pap. 79.00 (*0-914826-85-9*) Am Soc Microbio.

Neidhardt, H., jt. auth. see Exner, P.

An Asterisk (*) at the beginning of an entry indicates that the title is appearing in BIP for the first time.

Neidhardt, I. Technical Dictionary of TV Engineering: TV Electronics in Four Languages. LC 64-20643. (ENG, FRE, GER & RUS.). 1964. 139.00 (*0-08-010860-1*, Pub. by Pergamon Repr UK) Franklin.

Neidhardt, Jane E., ed. see Ketner, Joseph D., et al.

Neidhardt, P. Technical Dictionary of Electronics. LC 67-24527. 673.00 (*0-08-012434-8*, Pub. by Pergamon Repr UK) Franklin.

Neidhardt, Ralph, jt. auth. see Pellerin, Bill.

Neidhardt, W. Jim, jt. auth. see Loder, James E.

Neidhart, Joseph, jt. auth. see Krakow, Barry.

Neidig, D. F. & Hudson, H. S., eds. Solar Physics in the 1990s. (Advances in Space Research Ser.: Vol. 8). 1989. pap. 78.00 (*0-08-037371-2*, Pergamon Pr) Elsevier.

***Neidig,.** Enthalpy of Hydration. (Modular Laboratory Program in Chemistry Ser.). 12p. (C). 1989. pap. text ed. 1.25x (*0-87540-370-0*) Chem Educ Res.

***Neidig, H. A.** Enthalpy of Neutralization. (Modular Laboratory Program in Chemistry Ser.). 16p. (C). 1988. pap. text ed. 1.25x (*0-87540-346-8*) Chem Educ Res.

***Neidig, H. A., ed.** Classification & Properties of Matter. (Modular Laboratory Program in Chemistry Ser.). 11p. (C). 1988. pap. text ed. 1.25x (*0-87540-348-4*) Chem Educ Res.

— Preparing & Studying Oxygen & Some of Its Compounds. (Modular Laboratory Program in Chemistry Ser.). 11p. (C). 1992. pap. text ed. 1.25x (*0-87540-413-8*) Chem Educ Res.

***Neidig, H. A. & Spencer, J. N.** Charles's Law. (Modular Laboratory Program in Chemistry Ser.). 8p. (C). 1990. pap. text ed. 1.25x (*0-87540-384-0*) Chem Educ Res.

— Chemical Models: Ball-&-Stick Models of Organic Compounds. (Modular Laboratory Program in Chemistry Ser.). 10p. (C). 1994. pap. text ed. 1.25x (*0-87540-435-9*) Chem Educ Res.

— Density of Liquids & Solids. (Modular Series in Solid State Devices). 12p. (C). 1990. pap. text ed. 1.25x (*0-87540-383-2*) Chem Educ Res.

— Determining the Molar Concentration of a Sodium Hydroxide Solution. (Modular Laboratory Program in Chemistry Ser.). 12p. (C). 1992. pap. text ed. 1.25x (*0-87540-394-8*) Chem Educ Res.

— Diffusion of Gases. (Modular Laboratory Program in Chemistry Ser.). 7p. (C). 1990. pap. text ed. 1.25x (*0-87540-385-9*) Chem Educ Res.

— Double Replacement Reactions. (Modular Laboratory Program in Chemistry Ser.). 12p. (C). 1991. pap. text ed. 1.25x (*0-87540-390-5*) Chem Educ Res.

— The Empirical Formula of an Oxide. (Modular Laboratory Program in Chemistry Ser.). 12p. (C). 1990. pap. text ed. 1.25x (*0-87540-388-3*) Chem Educ Res.

— The Gas Burner & Glass Working. (Modular Laboratory Program in Chemistry Ser.). 12p. (C). 1990. pap. text ed. 1.25x (*0-87540-381-6*) Chem Educ Res.

— Heat of Neutralization. (Modular Laboratory Program in Chemistry Ser.). 12p. (C). 1989. pap. text ed. 1.25x (*0-87540-368-9*) Chem Educ Res.

— Introducing the Qualitative Analysis of a Group of Cations. (Modular Laboratory Program in Chemistry Ser.). 12p. (C). 1992. pap. text ed. 1.25x (*0-87540-396-4*) Chem Educ Res.

— Percent Water in a Hydrate. (Modular Laboratory Program in Chemistry Ser.). 7p. (C). 1990. pap. text ed. 1.25x (*0-87540-387-5*) Chem Educ Res.

***Neidig,.** pH, Acids, & Bases. (Modular Laboratory Program in Chemistry Ser.). 11p. 1992. pap. text ed. 1.25x (*0-87540-397-2*) Chem Educ Res.

***Neidig, H. A. & Spencer, J. N.** Safety Practices in the Chemistry Laboratory. (Modular Laboratory Program in Chemistry Ser.). 8p. (C). 1994. pap. text ed. 1.25x (*0-87540-380-8*) Chem Educ Res.

— Single Replacement Reactions & Relative Reactivity. (Modular Laboratory Program in Chemistry Ser.). 12p. (C). 1990. pap. text ed. 1.25x (*0-87540-389-1*) Chem Educ Res.

— Stoichiometry of the Reaction of Magnesium with Hydrochloric Acid. (Modular Laboratory Program in Chemistry Ser.). 12p. (C). 1989. pap. text ed. 1.25x (*0-87540-369-7*) Chem Educ Res.

— Titrating Vinegar. (Modular Laboratory Program in Chemistry Ser.). 11p. (C). 1992. pap. text ed. 1.25x (*0-87540-395-6*) Chem Educ Res.

***Neidig,.** Transfer & Measurement of Chemicals. (Modular Laboratory Program in Chemistry Ser.). 12p. (C). 1990. pap. text ed. 1.25x (*0-87540-382-4*) Chem Educ Res.

***Neidig, H. A. & Spencer, J. N.** Writing Lewis Symbols & Lewis Structures. (Modular Laboratory Program in Chemistry Ser.). 8p. (C). 1994. pap. text ed. 1.25x (*0-87540-434-0*) Chem Educ Res.

Neidig, H. A., ed. see Alcock, John W.

Neidig, H. A., ed. see Bailey, David N.

Neidig, H. A., ed. see Bedenbaugh, John H., et al.

Neidig, H. A., ed. see Bergo, Conrad H., et al.

Neidig, H. A., ed. see Billingham, E. J.

Neidig, H. A., ed. see Borst, Kenneth E. & Viens, Robert E.

Neidig, H. A., ed. see Boyles, James G., et al.

Neidig, H. A., ed. see Brown, William H.

Neidig, H. A., ed. see Carter, K. N.

Neidig, H. A., ed. see Clemens, Donald F. & McAllister, Warren A.

Neidig, H. A., ed. see Deckey, George.

Neidig, H. A., ed. see Deekey, George.

Neidig, H. A., ed. see Dingledy, David P.

Neidig, H. A., ed. see Douville, Judith A. & Douville, Phillip R.

Neidig, H. A., ed. see Everett, Grover W., Jr.

Neidig, H. A., ed. see Farrer, Leslie.

Neidig, H. A., ed. see Foster, Judith C.

Neidig, H. A., jt. auth. see Gillette,.

Neidig, H. A., ed. see Gillette,.

Neidig, H. A., jt. auth. see Gillette, M. L.

Neidig, H. A., ed. see Gillette, M. & Johnson, S. R.

Neidig, H. A., ed. see Glogovsky, Robert L.

Neidig, H. A., ed. see Good, William E., Jr. & Patterson, George S.

Neidig, H. A., ed. see Griswold, Norman E.

Neidig, H. A., ed. see Gunter, S. Kay & Birk, James P.

Neidig, H. A., ed. see Hudak, Norman J.

Neidig, H. A., ed. see Kieffer, William F.

Neidig, H. A., ed. see Markolo, Peter G.

Neidig, H. A., ed. see Markow, Peter G.

Neidig, H. A., ed. see Marks, R. L.

Neidig, H. A., ed. see McKone, Harold T.

Neidig, H. A., ed. see Melford, S. J. & Anysas, J. A.

Neidig, H. A., ed. see Metz, Clyde R.

Neidig, H. A., ed. see Metz, Clyde.

Neidig, H. A., ed. see Milio, Frank R. & Loffredo, William M.

Neidig, H. A., ed. see Mitchell, Richard S.

Neidig, H. A., ed. see Moews, Paul C., Jr., et al.

Neidig, H. A., ed. see Nicholson, Elva Mae & Ramsay, O. Bertrand.

Neidig, H. A., ed. see Patterson, George S.

Neidig, H. A., ed. see Pinnell, Robert P.

Neidig, H. A., ed. see Randy, Donald C. & Gillette, M. L.

Neidig, H. A., ed. see Reed, Roberta G. & Kotz, John C.

Neidig, H. A., ed. see Reichenbach, Wendy A.

Neidig, H. A., ed. see Rioux, Frank & Foster, Judith C.

Neidig, H. A., ed. see Schreck, James O. & Loffredo, William M.

Neidig, H. A., ed. see Spencer, J. N.

Neidig, H. A., ed. see Squattrito, Philip J.

Neidig, H. A., ed. see Stafford, Don.

Neidig, H. A., ed. see Suffredini, Constance.

Neidig, H. A., ed. see Suttles, Nancy L.

Neidig, H. A., ed. see Wolthuis, Enno.

Neidig, H. A., ed. see Yoke, John T.

Neidig, H. A., ed. see Zanella, Andrew W.

***Neidig, H. A., et al.** Preparation of Strontium Iodate Monohydrate. (Modular Laboratory Program in Chemistry Ser.). 12p. (C). 1988. pap. text ed. 1.25x (*0-87540-347-6*) Chem Educ Res.

— Synthesis of Strontium Iodate Monohydrate. (Modular Laboratory Program in Chemistry Ser.). 12p. (C). 1987. pap. text ed. 1.25x (*0-87540-341-7*) Chem Educ Res.

***Neidig, H. Anthony & Spencer, J. N.** Introducing Equilibrium. (Modular Laboratory Program in Chemistry Ser.). 12p. (C). 1991. pap. text ed. 1.25x (*0-87540-392-1*) Chem Educ Res.

— Solutions. (Modular Laboratory Program in Chemistry Ser.). 12p. (C). 1991. pap. text ed. 1.25x (*0-87540-391-3*) Chem Educ Res.

Neidig, H. Anthony & Stratton, Wilmer J., eds. Modern Experiments for Introductory College Chemistry. 2nd ed. 1989. 20.00 (*0-910362-27-0*) Chem Educ.

Neidig, H. Anthony, jt. auth. see Gillette,.

Neidig, H. Anthony, ed. see Gillette,.

Neidig, H. Anthony, jt. auth. see Gillette, M. L.

Neidig, H. Anthony, jt. auth. see Gillette, Marcia.

***Neidig, H. Anthony, et al.** Separating the Components of a Binary Mixture. (Modular Laboratory Program in Chemistry Ser.). 11p. (C). 1989. pap. text ed. 1.25x (*0-87540-374-3*) Chem Educ Res.

— Separating the Components of a Ternary Mixture. (Modular Laboratory Program in Chemistry Ser.). 12p. (C). 1989. pap. text ed. 1.25x (*0-87540-375-1*) Chem Educ Res.

Neidig, Peter H. & Friedman, Dale H. Spouse Abuse: A Treatment Program for Couples. LC 84-61187. 256p. (Orig.). 1984. pap. text ed. 17.95 (*0-87822-234-0*, 2340) Res Press.

***Neiditz, Minerva.** Business Writing at Its Best. 240p. (C). 1993. text ed. 22.95 (*0-256-14855-4*) Irwin.

Neiditz, Minerva H. Business Writing at Its Best. 288p. 1993. text ed. 20.00 (*0-7863-0137-6*) Irwin Prof Pubng.

— On the Way: Poems by Minerva Heller Neiditz. Leffler, Merrill, ed. LC 87-62924. 27p. (C). 1988. write for info. (*0-9618881-0-5*) Paper Moon Pr.

Neidjie, Bill. Story About Feeling. 180p. (C). 1990. 36.00 (*0-9588101-0-9*, Pub. by Pascoe Pub AT) St Mut.

Neidl, Raymond E., jt. auth. see Ott, James D.

Neidle & Yagiela. Pharmacology & Therapeutics for Dentistry. 3rd ed. (Illus.). 768p. 1989. text ed. 56.95 (*0-8016-3262-5*) Mosby Yr Bk.

Neidle, Amos, jt. ed. see Ehrenpreis, Seymour.

Neidle, C. & Nunez-Cedeno, R. A., eds. Studies in Romance Languages: Selected Proceedings of the 15th Linguistic Symposium on Romance Languages. (Publications in Language Sciences). xiv, 318p. 1987. pap. 67.90 (*90-6765-294-6*) Mouton.

Neidle, Carol. The Role of Case in Russian Syntax. (C). 1988. lib. bdg. 114.50 (*1-55608-042-5*) Kluwer Ac.

Neidle, Michael. Emergency & Security Lighting Handbook. 120p. 1988. text ed. 24.95 (*0-434-91436-3*) Buttrwrth-Heinemann.

Neidle, S., ed. Nucleic Acid Structure, Pt. 3. LC 87-6137. (Topics in Molecular & Structural Biology Ser.). 230p. 1987. lib. bdg. 130.00 (*0-89573-606-3*) VCH Pubs.

Neidle, Stephen. DNA Structure & Recognition: In Focus. (In Focus Ser.). (Illus.). 122p. (C). 1994. pap. text ed. 16.95 (*0-19-963419-X*, IRL Pr) OUP.

Neidle, Stephen & Waring, Michael, eds. Molecular Aspects of Anticancer Drug-DNA Interactions, Vol. 1. LC 93-8201. (Topics in Molecular & Structural Biology Ser.). 1993. 97.00 (*0-8493-7770-6*) CRC Pr.

Neidle, Stephen & Waring, Michael J. Molecular Aspects of Anti-Cancer Drug Action. (Topics in Molecular & Structural Biology Ser.: Vol. 3). 404p. 1983. lib. bdg. 155.00 (*0-89573-079-0*) VCH Pubs.

Neidle, Stephen, ed. see Atkins, E. D.

***Neidleman, Saul & Laskin, Allen L., eds.** Advances in Applied Microbiology, Vol. 40. (Illus.). 319p. 1995. text ed. 79.00 (*0-12-002640-6*) Acad Pr.

Neidleman, Saul L., ed. Advances in Applied Microbiology, Vol. 34. (Serial Publication Ser.). 315p. 1989. text ed. 92.00 (*0-12-002634-1*) Acad Pr.

Neidleman, Saul L. & Laskin, Allen I. Advances in Applied Microbiology, Vol. 35. (Serial Publication Ser.). 312p. 1990. text ed. 91.00 (*0-12-002635-X*) Acad Pr.

Neidleman, Saul L. & Laskin, Allen I., eds. Advances in Applied Microbiology, Vol. 36. (Illus.). 364p. 1991. text ed. 75.00 (*0-12-002636-8*) Acad Pr.

— Advances in Applied Microbiology, Vol. 37. (Illus.). 385p. 1992. text ed. 85.00 (*0-12-002637-6*) Acad Pr.

— Advances in Applied Microbiology, Vol. 38. (Illus.). 319p. 1993. text ed. 75.00 (*0-12-002638-4*) Acad Pr.

— Advances in Applied Microbiology, Vol. 39. (Illus.). 352p. 1993. text ed. 79.00 (*0-12-002639-2*) Acad Pr.

***Neidner, James Q.** Angel from Heaven. (Illus.). 120p. (Orig.). 1995. pap. 9.95 (*0-9642737-0-5*) J Q Neidner.

Neidorf, Charles. French Morocco, the 1943-44 Tour Hassan Issues. (Illus.). 1957. pap. 3.75 (*0-912574-03-8*) Collectors.

Neidorf, Mary. Operantics with Wolfgang Amadeus Mozart. LC 86-14435. 32p. (Orig.). (J). (gr. 3-6). 1987. pap. 4.95 (*0-86534-092-7*) Sunstone Pr.

Neie, Herbert. The Doctrine of the Atonement in the Theology of Wolfhart Pannenberg. (Theologische Bibliothek Toepelmann Ser.: Vol. 36). (C). 1978. 80.80 (*3-11-007506-7*) De Gruyter.

Neie, Winifred C. The Princess & Sorcerer: Recovering from Incest Through the Use of Fairy Tales & the Imagination. 175p. 1991. 38.50 (*1-879041-09-X*, Coventure Ltd); pap. 17.95 (*1-879041-08-1*, Coventure Ltd) Sigo Pr.

Neier, Areyeh, ed. see Helsinki Watch Staff.

Neier, Areyeh, ed. see Kushen, Robert.

Neier, Aryeh. Draining the Sea: An Americas Watch Report. LC 86-113890. 77p. 1985. 8.00 (*0-938579-03-7*, Am Watch) Hum Rts Watch.

Neier, Aryeh, ed. see Goldstein, Eric.

Neifeld, Morris R. Cooperative Consumer Credit. Bruchey, Stuart & Carosso, Vincent P., eds. LC 78-18972. (Small Business Enterprise in America Ser.). (Illus.). 1979. reprint ed. lib. bdg. 19.95 (*0-405-11475-3*) Ayer.

Neifert, Marianne E. Dr. Mom's Parenting Guide. 336p. 1993. reprint ed. pap. 5.99 (*0-451-17363-5*, Sig) NAL-Dutton.

Neifert, Marianne E., et al. Dr. Mom. 544p. 1987. pap. 5.99 (*0-451-16311-7*, Sig) NAL-Dutton.

Neifert, Marianne R., jt. ed. see Neville, Margaret C.

Neiger, Alexander. Atlas of Practical Proctology. 2nd enl. rev. ed. LC 89-71714. 170p. 1990. text ed. 98.00 (*0-920887-76-7*) Hogrefe & Huber Pubs.

Neiger, Elisabeth. Gastronomic Dictionary in Five Languages. 5th ed. 144p. (ENG, FRE, GER, ITA & SPA.). 1986. pap. 49.95 (*0-8288-0159-2*, M8448) Fr & Eur.

— Gastronomisches Woerterbuch: German, French, English, Italian, Spanish. 8th ed. 144p. (ENG, FRE & GER.). 1991. pap. 49.95 (*0-7859-7080-0*) Fr & Eur.

Neiger, L., jt. auth. see Beekman-Love, Gilian.

Neighbarger, Randy L. An Outward Show: Music for Shakespeare on the London Stage, 1660-1830. LC 92-5423. (Contributions to the Study of Music & Dance Ser.: No. 27). 340p. 1992. text ed. 55.00 (*0-313-27805-9*, NML, Greenwood Pr) Greenwood.

Neighbors, Charles, ed. see Carlson, Richard R.

***Neighbors, Chuck.** Power Plays: Drama for Worship Services & Other Gatherings. (Orig.). 1995. audio 9.99 (*0-8010-5236-X*); audio 9.99 (*0-8010-5239-4*) Baker Bk.

— Power Plays: Drama for Worship Services & Other Gatherings, Vol. 5. 64p. (Orig.). 1995. pap. 15.99 (*0-8010-5235-1*) Baker Bk.

— Power Plays: Drama for Worship Services & Other Gatherings, Vol. 6. 64p. (Orig.). 1995. pap. 15.99 (*0-8010-5238-6*) Baker Bk.

— Power Plays Vol. 3: Drama for Worship Services & Other Gatherings. 80p. (Orig.). 1995. pap. 15.99 (*0-8010-5045-6*); audio 9.99 (*0-8010-5047-2*) Baker Bk.

— Power Plays Vol. 4: Drama for Worship Services & Other Gatherings. 64p. (Orig.). 1995. pap. 15.99 (*0-8010-5046-4*); audio 9.99 (*0-8010-5048-0*) Baker Bk.

Neighbors, Chuck, ed. Power Plays, Vol. 1: Drama for Worship Services & Other Gatherings. LC 93-38799. 80p. (Orig.). 1994. pap. 15.99 (*0-8010-6793-6*); audio 9.99 (*0-8010-6795-2*) Baker Bk.

— Power Plays, Vol. 2: Drama for Worship Services & Other Gatherings. LC 93-38799. 80p. (Orig.). 1994. pap. 15.99 (*0-8010-6794-4*); audio 9.99 (*0-8010-6796-0*) Baker Bk.

Neighbors, Marianne, jt. auth. see Jackson, Janet E.

Neighbour, Oliver. The Music of William Byrd, Vol. III: Consort & Keyboard Music. 1979. 60.00 (*0-520-03486-4*) U CA Pr.

Neighbour, R. The Inner Apprentice: An Awareness-Centered Approach to Vocational Training. (C). 1992. lib. bdg. 39.50 (*0-7923-8983-2*) Kluwer Ac.

— The Inner Consultation: Developing an Effective & Intuitive Consulting Style. 336p. (C). 1987. lib. bdg. 61.00 (*0-7462-0040-4*) Kluwer Ac.

Neighbour, Ralph. Contacto en el Espiritu. Martinez, Jose L., ed. Kratzig, Guillermo, tr. 120p. (SPA.). 1983. pap. 4.25 (*0-311-09098-2*) Casa Bautista.

Neighbour, Ralph, Jr. Journey into Discipleship. 96p. 1.50 (*0-318-13660-0*) Brotherhd Comm.

Neighbour, Ralph W., Jr. La Iglesia del Futuro. Martinez, Jose L., tr. Orig. Title: Future Church. 256p. 1983. pap. 3.95 (*0-311-17024-2*) Casa Bautista.

— Sigueme. 128p. 1986. reprint ed. student ed 3.35 (*0-311-13836-5*); reprint ed. 3.50 (*0-311-13837-3*) Casa Bautista.

— Sigueme, Edicion para Ninos. Geiger, Mary J. & Ditmore, Shirley, trs. (Illus.). 64p. (Orig.). (SPA.). (J). 1989. pap. 2.65 (*0-311-13848-9*) Casa Bautista.

— Sigueme 2. Martinez, Mario, tr. (Illus.). 128p. (Orig.). (SPA.). 1989. pap. 3.75 (*0-311-13843-8*) Casa Bautista.

Neighbours, Kenneth F. Robert Simpson Neighbors & the Texas Frontier. 1975. 12.95 (*0-685-04884-5*) Texian.

Neihardt, Elizabeth R. & Allen, Jo A. Family Therapy with the Elderly. (Sourcebooks for the Human Services Ser.: Vol. 22). (Illus.). 225p. (C). 1992. 39.95 (*0-8039-4498-5*); pap. 18.95 (*0-8039-4499-3*) Sage.

***Neihardt, Hilda.** Black Elk & Flaming Rainbow: Personal Memories of the Lakota Holy Man & John Neihardt. LC 94-26350. 1995. 20.00 (*0-8032-3338-8*) U of Nebr Pr.

Neihardt, John. Black Elk Speaks. 1976. 4.95 (*0-87129-304-8*, B22) Dramatic Pub.

Neihardt, John G. All Is but a Beginning: Youth Remembered, 1881-1901. LC 85-28955. x, 173p. 1986. reprint ed. 16.95 (*0-8032-3311-6*); reprint ed. pap. 6.50 (*0-8032-8355-5*) U of Nebr Pr.

— The Ancient Memory & Other Stories. LC 91-2603. xiv, 230p. 1991. 19.95 (*0-8032-3327-2*) U of Nebr Pr.

— Black Elk Speaks. LC 88-14317. xx, 311p. 1979. 25.00 (*0-8032-3301-9*); pap. 9.95 (*0-8032-8359-8*) U of Nebr Pr.

— Black Elk Speaks: Being the Life Story of a Holy Man of the Ogalala Sioux. (Native American Voices Ser.). (Illus.). 280p. reprint ed. write for info. (*0-7835-1750-5*) Time-Life.

— A Cycle of the West: Golden Anniversary Edition. LC 91-38033. (Illus.). xiv, 524p. 1992. 100.00 (*0-8032-3323-X*) U of Nebr Pr.

— The Dawn Builder. LC 90-21279. (Landmark Edition Ser.). 335p. 1991. reprint ed. 35.00 (*0-8032-3330-2*) U of Nebr Pr.

— The Divine Enchantment: A Mystical Poem. 1974. 250.00 (*0-87968-168-3*) Gordon Pr.

— The Divine Enchantment: A Mystical Poem & Poetic Values: Their Reality & Our Need of Them. LC 88-38263. (Landmark Edition Ser.). iv, 144p. 1989. reprint ed. 32.50 (*0-8032-3319-1*) U of Nebr Pr.

— The End of the Dream & Other Stories. LC 90-43667. xxviii, 115p. 1991. 19.95 (*0-8032-3326-4*) U of Nebr Pr.

— The Giving Earth: A John G. Neihardt Reader. LC 90-28609. (Illus.). xviii, 301p. 1991. 25.00 (*0-8032-3325-6*) U of Nebr Pr.

— Indian Tales & Others. LC 88-14337. vi, 306p. 1988. reprint ed. pap. 10.95 (*0-8032-8358-X*) U of Nebr Pr.

— Life's Lure: Landmark Edition. 277p. 1991. 45.00 (*0-8032-3333-7*) U of Nebr Pr.

— Lyric & Dramatic Poems. LC 90-21713. (Landmark Edition Ser.). xiv, 239p. 1991. reprint ed. 30.00 (*0-8032-3329-9*) U of Nebr Pr.

— Man-Song. viii, 117p. 1991. 35.00 (*0-8032-3332-9*) U of Nebr Pr.

— The Mountain Men. LC 70-134770. (Illus.). xvi, 369p. 1971. reprint ed. pap. 11.95 (*0-8032-5733-3*, Bison Books) U of Nebr Pr.

— Patterns & Coincidences: A Sequel to "All Is But a Beginning" LC 77-24199. x, 123p. 1978. 15.00 (*0-8032-3312-4*) U of Nebr Pr.

— The River & I. LC 92-15792. (Illus.). x, 326p. 1992. reprint ed. 45.00 (*0-8032-3335-3*) U of Nebr Pr.

— The Sacred Hoop. Date not set. 3.00 (*0-87129-447-8*, SA8) Dramatic Pub.

— The Splendid Wayfaring: Jedediah Smith & the Ashley-Henry Men, 1822-1831. LC 71-116054. (Illus.). xii, 290p. 1970. reprint ed. pap. 9.95 (*0-8032-5723-6*, Bison Books) U of Nebr Pr.

— The Twilight of the Sioux. LC 74-134771. xiv, 292p. 1971. reprint ed. pap. 10.95 (*0-8032-5734-1*, Bison Books) U of Nebr Pr.

— When the Tree Flowered: The Story of Eagle Voice, a Sioux Indian. LC 90-19669. xxii, 248p. 1991. reprint ed. pap. 8.95 (*0-8032-8363-6*, Bison Books) U of Nebr Pr.

Neiheisel, Steven R. Corporate Strategy & the Politics of Goodwill Vol. 40: A Political Analysis of Corporate Philanthropy in America. LC 93-6959. (American University Studies: No. X). 202p. (C). 1994. text ed. 38.95 (*0-8204-2128-6*) P Lang Pubs.

Neiiendam, Maureen, tr. see Sorensen, Villy.

Neijssel, O. M., et al, eds. Proceedings of the Fourth European Congress on Biotechnology, 1987, 4 vols., Set. 2600p. 1988. 700.00 (*0-444-42831-3*) Elsevier.

Neil. Electromanipulation of Cells. 1994. write for info. (*0-8493-4476-X*) CRC Pr.

Neil & McIntyre. Lipids & Liproteins in Clinical Practice. 160p. 1991. 50.00 (*0-7234-0946-3*) Mosby Yr Bk.

Neil, Abbot. Hulkamania! Hulk Hogan America's Hero. 1985. pap. 3.50 (*0-317-19507-7*) PB.

Neil, Barbara. The Possession of Delia Sutherland. LC 93-34160. 1994. 22.00 (*0-385-47215-3*, N A Talese) Doubleday.

— The Possession of Delia Sutherland. large type ed. LC 94-25968. 453p. 1995. lib. bdg. 18.95 (*0-7862-0293-9*) Thorndike Pr.

Neil, C. Lang. The Modern Conjurer: And Drawing Room Entertainer. 389p. 1994. 30.00 (*1-885366-05-1*); pap. 14.95 (*1-885366-06-X*) Visionary CA.

Neil, Carey. Puffin Cove. (Illus.). 180p. 1984. pap. 11.95 (*0-88839-156-0*) Hancock House.

Neil, Cecily, et al, eds. Coping with Closures: An International Comparison of Mine Town Experiences. LC 91-12918. (Illus.). 416p. 1991. 99.50 (*0-415-06651-4*, A6471) Routledge.

Neil, David H., jt. auth. see Rutherford, Clarice.

N

An Asterisk (*) at the beginning of an entry indicates that the title is appearing in BIP for the first time.

Neil, Dorothy. By Canoe & Sailing Ship They Came. Brainard, Lee, ed. LC 89-63170. (Illus.). 296p. (Orig.). 1989. pap. 18.89 (*0-9624462-0-3*) Spindrift Pub.
Neil, E., jt. auth. see Dickens, F.
Neil, James M. Construction Cost Estimating for Project Control. (Illus.). 336p. 1982. text ed. 50.00 (*0-13-168757-3*) P-H.
***Neil, Joanna.** La Comedie de l'Innocence. (Horizon Ser.). (FRE.). 1994. pap. 3.50 (*0-373-39292-3*, 1-39292-7) Harlequin Bks.
— Flame of Love. large type ed. 1994. 17.95 (*0-263-13768-6*, Pub. by Mills & Boon Ltd UK) Chivers N Amer.
Neil, Marilyn. Stars, Wings, & Fun Things: Three Hundred Sixty-Five Activities for Children. (Illus.). 68p. (Orig.). (J). (gr. k-3). 1991. pap. text ed. 8.95 (*0-945301-05-7*) Druid Pr.
***Neil, Morag.** Suns & Moons. LC 94-68901. (Illus.). 80p. 1995. 12.95 (*0-8478-1858-6*) Rizzoli Intl.
Neil, R. & Watts, R., eds. Caring & Nursing: Explorations in Feminist Perspectives. 275p. 1990. pap. 29.95 (*0-88737-501-4*) Natl League Nurse.
Neil, Randy. The Official Pompom Girl's Handbook. LC 83-3184. (Illus.). 173p. 1983. pap. 6.95 (*0-312-58222-6*, Pub. by Marek) St Martin.
***Neil, Richard.** Stress: Taming the Tyrant. 118p. 1994. per. 8.95 (*1-57258-001-1*) Teach Servs.
Neil, Richard L. His Coming. Wheeler, Gerald, ed. 120p. (Orig.). 1988. pap. 7.50 (*0-8280-0413-7*) Review & Herald.
Neil, S., jt. auth. see Elwood, R.
Neil Snarr & Associates Staff. Sandinista Nicaragua, Pt. 2: Economy, Politics, & Foreign Policy: an Annotated Bibliography with Analytical Introductions. (Resources on Contemporary Issues Ser.: No. 5). 191p. 1990. pap. 40.00 (*0-87650-256-7*) Pierian.
Neil, William. Acts. (New Century Bible Ser.). 272p. 1973. 8.95 (*0-551-00336-7*) Attic Pr.
— The Acts of the Apostles. rev. ed. Black, Matthew, ed. (New Century Bible Commentary Ser.). 272p. 1981. pap. 14.99 (*0-8028-1904-4*) Eerdmans.
— Harper's Bible Commentary. 1975. pap. 12.00 (*0-06-066091-0*) Harper SF.
— The Pocket Bible Commentary. LC 63-7607. 544p. 1975. reprint ed. pap. 7.95 (*0-06-066090-2*, RD 92) Harper SF.
Neilan, Ruth E. American Military Movement Relating Sacred Dance. Adams, Doug, ed. & intro. by. (Orig.). 1985. pap. 3.00 (*0-941500-37-3*) Sharing Co.
Neilan, Sarah. The Braganza Pursuit. large type ed. 400p. 1984. 15.95 (*0-7089-1076-9*) Ulverscroft.
— Paradise. large type ed. 560p. 1984. 15.95 (*0-7089-1188-9*) Ulverscroft.
Neild, A. Bayne, Jr., ed. see Osbourne, Alan.
Neild, Eric. With Pegasus in India: The Story of 153rd Gurkha Parachute Battalion. (Airborne Ser.: No. 21). (Illus.). 110p. 1990. reprint ed. 27.50 (*0-89839-150-4*) Battery Pr.
Neild, Robert, jt. ed. see Boserup, Anders.
Neill. Modern Retail Risk Management. 1981. 39.95 (*0-409-49051-2*) Buttrwrth-Heinemann.
Neill & Hairn. Complete Denture Prosthetics. 3rd ed. 151p. 1991. pap. 75.00 (*0-7236-2063-6*, Pub. by John Wright UK) Buttrwrth-Heinemann.
Neill, A. S. Summerhill School: A New View of Childhood. rev. ed. Lamb, Albert, ed. LC 92-34957. 1993. 22.95 (*0-312-08860-4*) St Martin.
***Neill, Alex & Ridley, Aaron.** The Philosophy of Art: Readings Ancient & Modern. LC 94-37453. 1995. pap. text ed. write for info. (*0-07-046192-9*) McGraw.
Neill, Brian, ed. see Rampton, Richard & Sharp, Victoria.
Neill, C. R., ed. see Roads & Transportation Association of Canada, Project Committee on Bridge Hydraulics.
***Neill, Catherine A. & Clark, Edward B., eds.** The Developing Heart: A History of Pediatric Cardiology. LC 95-3082. (Developments in Cardiovascular Medicine Ser.: Vol. 162). 176p. (C). 1995. lib. bdg. 62.00 (*0-7923-3375-6*) Kluwer Ac.
Neill, Catherine A., et al. The Heart of a Child: What Families Need to Know about Heart Disorders in Children. 384p. 1993. 24.95 (*0-8018-4234-4*) Johns Hopkins.
Neill, Ed. Letters to Ted. 1992. pap. 5.00 (*1-55673-482-4*, 7932) CSS OH.
Neill, Edward D. Abraham Lincoln & His Mailbag: Two Documents. Blegen, Theodore C., ed. LC 64-23313. (Publications of the Minnesota Historical Society). 60p. reprint ed. pap. 25.00 (*0-8357-3316-5*, 2039540) Bks Demand.
— The History of Minnesota: From the Earliest French Explorations to the Present Time. LC 75-112. (Mid-American Frontier Ser.). 1975. reprint ed. 51.95 (*0-405-06879-4*) Ayer.
— History of Ramsey County & City of St. Paul, Minnesota. 650p. 1994. reprint ed. lib. bdg. 65.00 (*0-8328-3851-9*) Higginson Bk Co.
— History of Ramsey County & the City of St. Paul, MN. 650p. 1993. reprint ed. lib. bdg. 67.50 (*0-8328-3487-4*) Higginson Bk Co.
— History of the Minnesota Valley. 1016p. 1994. reprint ed. lib. bdg. 105.00 (*0-8328-3849-7*) Higginson Bk Co.
— History of the Upper Mississippi Valley. 717p. 1994. reprint ed. lib. bdg. 72.50 (*0-8328-3850-0*) Higginson Bk Co.
Neill, Edward D., ed. Glimpses of the Nation's Struggle: Third Series, Minnesota. (Military Order of the Loyal Legion of the United States Ser.: Vol. 28). 530p. 1992. reprint ed. 40.00 (*1-56837-183-7*) Broadfoot.
Neill, Edward D. & Bryant, Charles S. History of Rice County, Minnesota. 603p. 1994. reprint ed. lib. bdg. 62.50 (*0-8328-3856-X*) Higginson Bk Co.
— History of the Minnesota Valley. 1016p. 1994. reprint ed. lib. bdg. 105.00 (*0-8328-3838-1*) Higginson Bk Co.
Neill, Gene. I'm Gonna Bury You! 11th rev. ed. (Illus.). 210p. 1991. reprint ed. pap. 5.00 (*0-9608028-0-0*) Voice of Triumph.
Neill, George W., jt. auth. see Neill, Shirley B.
Neill, Humphrey B. Art of Contrary Thinking. 4th ed. LC 54-7837. 1963. pap. 7.95 (*0-87004-110-X*) Caxton.
— The Ruminator: A Collection of Thoughts & Suggestions on Contrary Thinking. LC 92-82739. 128p. (C). 1992. reprint ed. pap. 11.00 (*0-87034-105-7*) Fraser Pub Co.
— Tape Reading & Market Tactics. LC 73-115001. 1984. reprint ed. 16.00 (*0-87034-074-3*) Fraser Pub Co.
Neill, Isobel. An End of Darkness. large type ed. (Romance Ser.). 272p. 1994. pap. 14.95 (*0-7089-7546-1*, Trailtree Bookshop) Ulverscroft.
— The Law of Love. large type ed. (Romance Ser.). 1994. pap. 14.95 (*0-7089-7621-2*, Linford) Ulverscroft.
— Nothing to Lose. large type ed. (Romance Ser.). 1994. pap. 14.95 (*0-7089-7610-7*, Linford) Ulverscroft.
Neill, J., et al. A Need for Care? Elderly Applicants for Local Authority Homes. 255p. 1988. text ed. 59.95 (*0-566-05716-6*, Pub. by Avebury Pub UK) Ashgate Pub Co.
Neill, John. Records & Reminiscences of Bonhill Parish. 280p. (C). 1986. 49.00 (*0-9506620-0-3*) St Mut.
Neill, John R. Lucky Bucky in Oz. (Illus.). (J). (gr. 3 up). 1992. 24.95 (*0-929605-17-9*) Books Wonder.
— The Runaway in Oz. (Illus.). 244p. (YA). (gr. 3 up). 1995. 24.95 (*0-929605-39-X*) Books Wonder.
— The Scalawagons in Oz. (Illus.). 309p. (J). (gr. 3 up). 1991. 24.95 (*0-929605-12-8*) Books Wonder.
— The Wonder City of Oz. (Illus.). 318p. (J). (gr. 2 up). 1990. pap. 24.95 (*0-929605-07-1*) Books Wonder.
Neill, John R. & Kniskern, David P., eds. From Psyche to System: The Evolving Therapy of Carl Whitaker. LC 81-22933. (Guilford Family Therapy Ser.). 409p. 1982. lib. bdg. 45.00 (*0-89862-050-3*) Guilford Pr.
— From Psyche to System: The Evolving Therapy of Carl Whitaker. LC 81-22933. (Guilford Family Therapy Ser.). 409p. 1989. pap. 21.95 (*0-89862-519-X*) Guilford Pr.
Neill, June. Assessing Elderly People for Residential Care: A Practical Guide. (C). 1989. 59.00 (*0-685-28581-2*, Pub. by Natl Inst Soc Work); 30.00 (*0-685-40335-1*, Pub. by Natl Inst Soc Work); 35.00 (*0-902789-59-7*, Pub. by Natl Inst Soc Work); 40.00 (*0-7855-0087-1*, Pub. by Natl Inst Soc Work) St Mut.
Neill, Lou Anne, jt. auth. see Inglefield, Ruth K.
Neill-Mareci, Debra, jt. illus. see Hollinger, Candace.
Neill, Mary, jt. auth. see Chervin, Ronda.
Neill, Mary G. The Communion of Scholars: Chinese Art at Yale. (Illus.). 148p. 1988. reprint ed. pap. 14.95 (*0-295-96791-9*) U of Wash Pr.
Neill, Mary G., jt. auth. see Okada, Barbara T.
Neill, Nancy. More Than Bricks & Mortar: A History of the Atlanta Athletic Club. LC 87-51024. (Illus.). 141p. 1988. text ed. 25.00 (*0-9613474-2-2*) W H Wolfe.
Neill, Peter. Acoma. LC 77-92932. 1978. pap. 3.95 (*0-918172-03-9*) Leetes Isl.
— Maritime America: Art & Artifacts from America's Great Nautical Collections. (Illus.). 256p. 1988. 45.00 (*0-917439-11-2*) Balsam Pr.
Neill, Peter, ed. Maritime America: Art & Artifacts from America's Great Nautical Collections. 1988. 45.00 (*0-8109-1527-8*) Abrams.
Neill, Peter & Krohn, Barbara E. The Great Maritime Museums of the World. (Illus.). 304p. 1991. 60.00 (*0-917439-12-0*) Balsam Pr.
Neill, Peter, ed. see Cunningham, Louisa.
Neill, Richard & Gilbert, Lela. Taking on Donahue & TV Morality. 8.99 (*0-88070-690-2*) Questar Pubs.
Neill, Richard, jt. auth. see Sturges, Paul.
Neill, Robert H. Beware the Barking Bumblebees: And Forty-Three More Nature Talks. Rolfes, Ellen, ed. (Something to Talk about Ser.). 96p. (J). (gr. k-6). 1993. spiral bd. 5.95 (*1-879958-18-X*) Tradery Hse.
— Don't Fish under the Dingleberry Tree. 1991. 19.95 (*0-9617591-9-4*) MS River Pub.
— The Flaming Turkey. LC 86-62509. (Illus.). 208p. 1986. 17.95 (*0-9617591-0-0*) MS River Pub.
— The Flaming Turkey. (Illus.). 180p. 1990. 17.95 (*0-685-38754-2*) Robertson Pubns.
— Going Home. (Illus.). 200p. 1987. 17.95 (*0-9617591-2-7*) MS River Pub.
— The Jakes. 1989. 17.95 (*0-9617591-4-3*) MS River Pub.
— Magnolia Club. 1990. 25.00 (*0-9617591-7-8*) MS River Pub.
— Voice of Jupiter Pluvius. 1990. 17.95 (*0-9617591-8-6*) MS River Pub.
Neill, Robert H. & Baugh, Jim R. How to Lose Your Farm in Ten Easy Lessons & Cope with It. 150p. 1987. 6.95 (*0-9617591-1-9*) MS River Pub.
Neill, Robert H., ed. see Southeast Out Press Writers Assoc. Staff.
Neill, Robin. A History of Canadian Economic Thought. (History of Economic Thought Ser.). 320p. 1991. 49.95 (*0-415-05412-5*, A6247) Routledge.
— A New Theory of Value: The Canadian Economics of H. A. Innis. LC 77-185867. (Canadian University Paperbooks Ser.: No. 120). 167p. reprint ed. pap. 47.60 (*0-8357-4162-1*, 2036936) Bks Demand.
Neill, S. D. Clarifying McLuhan: An Assessment of Process & Product. LC 92-36609. (Contributions to the Study of Mass Media & Communications Ser.: No. 37). 168p. 1993. text ed. 47.95 (*0-313-28444-X*, NCM, Greenwood Pr) Greenwood.
— Dilemmas in the Study of Information: Exploring the Boundaries of Information Science. LC 91-24835. (Contributions in Librarianship & Information Science Ser.: No. 70). 208p. 1992. text ed. 49.95 (*0-313-27734-6*, NDN, Greenwood Pr) Greenwood.
Neill, S. E. Lexikon Zur Weltmission. (GER.). 95.00 (*3-7974-0054-3*, M-7190); 95.00 (*0-8288-7912-5*, M7190) Fr & Eur.
Neill, S. R., jt. auth. see Campbell, Jim.
Neill, Sean. Classroom Nonverbal Communication. (International Library of Psychology). (Illus.). 228p. (C). 1991. text ed. 65.00 (*0-415-02663-6*, A5247) Routledge.
Neill, Sean & Caswell, Chris. Body Language for Competent Teachers. LC 92-24744. 1993. pap. 17.95 (*0-415-06660-3*, A9892, Routledge NY) Routledge.
Neill, Shirley B. The Competency Movement: Problems & Solutions. (Critical Issues Report Ser.: No. 2). (Illus.). 1978. pap. 8.95 (*0-87652-020-4*, 021-00510) Am Assn Sch Admin.
— School Energy Crisis: Problems & Solutions. (Critical Issues Report Ser.: No. 1). (Illus.). 1977. pap. 8.95 (*0-87652-045-X*, 02100380) Am Assn Sch Admin.
— Staff Dismissal. (Critical Issues Report Ser.: No. 3). 1978. pap. 8.95 (*0-686-02455-9*, 02100512) Am Assn Sch Admin.
Neill, Shirley B. & Neill, George W. Only the Best: Annual Guide to Highest-Rated Education Software-Multimedia for Preschool-Grade 12. 144p. 1991. 27.95 (*0-936423-04-8*) Ed News Serv.
— Only the Best, 1985-1989: The Cumulative Guide to Highest-Rated Educational Software, Preschool - Grade 12. 313p. 1989. 49.95 (*0-8352-2851-7*) Bowker.
— Only the Best, 1991: The Annual Guide to the Highest-Rated Educational Software, Preschool-Grade 12. 144p. 1990. pap. 29.95 (*0-8352-2952-1*) Bowker.
Neill, Shirley B., ed. see American Association of School Administrators Staff.
Neill, Shirley B., ed. see Pine, Patricia.
Neill, Stephen. Anglicanism. 4th ed. 1978. pap. 23.00 (*0-19-520033-0*) OUP.
— Christian Faith & Other Faiths. LC 84-19123. 304p. 1984. pap. 15.99 (*0-87784-337-6*, 337) InterVarsity.
— History of Christian Missions. (History of the Church Ser.: Vol. 6). (Orig.). 1964. mass mkt. 5.95 (*0-14-020628-0*, Penguin Bks) Viking Penguin.
— A History of Christianity in India 1707-1858. (Illus.). 592p. 1985. 130.00 (*0-521-30376-1*) Cambridge U Pr.
— Jesus Through Many Eyes: Introduction to the Theology of the New Testament. LC 75-36455. 228p. 1976. pap. 12.00 (*0-8006-1220-5*, 1-1220, Fortress Pr) Augsburg Fortress.
— The Pelican History of the Church: A History of the Christian Missions, Vol. 6. 512p. 1987. pap. 7.95 (*0-14-022736-9*, Penguin Bks) Viking Penguin.
Neill, Stephen & Wright, N. T. The Interpretation of the New Testament, 1861-1986. 2nd ed. 480p. 1988. pap. text ed. 15.95 (*0-19-283057-0*) OUP.
Neill, Stephen, et al. When Will Ye Be Wise? Kilmister, C. A., ed. 208p. (Orig.). 1984. reprint ed. pap. 6.95 (*0-685-09580-0*) St Thomas.
Neill, Thomas. Incidents in the Early History of Pullman & the State College of Washington. 1977. pap. 7.50 (*0-87770-175-X*) Ye Galleon.
Neill, W., jt. ed. see Elder, T.
Neill, Wilfred T. Archaeology & a Science of Man. 1978. text ed. 50.00 (*0-231-03661-2*) Col U Pr.
— Twentieth-Century Indonesia. LC 72-11718. (Illus.). 413p. 1973. text ed. 57.00 (*0-231-03547-0*); pap. text ed. 20.50 (*0-231-08316-5*) Col U Pr.
Neill, Wilfred T. & Allen, E. Ross. Florida's Seminole Indians. rev. ed. LC 65-3660. (Illus.). 1965. reprint ed. pap. 4.95 (*0-8200-1018-9*) Great Outdoors.
Neill, William. Making Tracks: Poems in Scots, English & Gaelic with Translation. 96p. (C). 1989. 39.00 (*0-903065-65-7*, Pub. by G Wright Pub Ltd) St Mut.
— Straight Lines. 98p. (Orig.). 1992. pap. 12.95 (*0-85640-475-6*, Pub. by Blackstaff Pr IE) Dufour.
— Wild Places. 200p. 1989. pap. 35.00 (*0-946487-11-1*, Pub. by Luath Pr UK) St Mut.
Neill, William, photos. Grand Canyon National Park Postbox Collection. (Illus.). 1993. boxed 10.95 (*0-8118-0295-7*) Chronicle Bks.
— Yosemite National Park Postbox Collection. 1993. boxed 10.95 (*0-8118-0277-9*) Chronicle Bks.
***Neill, William J., et al.** Reimaging the Pariah City: Urban Development in Belfast & Detroit. 251p. 1995. boxed, pap. 59.95 (*1-85628-480-8*, Pub. by Avebury Pub UK) Ashgate Pub Co.
Neilland, Sean K., II. Award Winners. 15p. Date not set. pap. 5.00 (*0-9619612-0-1*) S Neilland.
***Neillands, Robin.** The Conquest of the Reich: D-Day to VE Day-A Soldiers' History. (Illus.). 304p. 1995. 24.95 (*0-8147-5781-2*) NYU Pr.
— The Hundred Years War. 422p. 1990. 29.95 (*0-415-00148-X*, A4939) Routledge.
— The Hundred Years War. (Illus.). 370p. 1991. pap. 16.95 (*0-415-07149-6*, A6681) Routledge.
— The Wars of the Roses. (Illus.). 256p. 1993. 29.95 (*0-304-34080-4*, Pub. by Cassell UK) Sterling.
Neillands, Robin, jt. auth. see Bartelski, Konrad.
Neils, Elaine M. Reservation to City: Indian Migration & Federal Relocation. LC 78-144044. (Research Papers Ser.: No. 131). 198p. 1971. pap. 12.00 (*0-89065-038-1*) U Chicago Comm Geo.
Neils, Jenifer. Goddess & Polis: The Panathenaic Festival in Ancient Athens. (Illus.). 200p. 1992. pap. text ed. 25.00 (*0-691-00223-1*) Princeton U Pr.
Neils, Jenifer, ed. see Cleveland Museum of Art Staff.
Neils, Patricia. China Images in the Life & Times of Henry Luce. 384p. 1990. lib. bdg. 50.50 (*0-8476-7634-X*) Rowman.
Neils, Patricia, ed. United States Attitudes Toward China: The Impact of American Missionaries. LC 89-78510. (Studies on Modern China). 304p. 1990. 46.95 (*0-87332-632-6*) M E Sharpe.
Neils, Selma M. The Klickitat Indians. LC 85-72818. (Illus.). 240p. (Orig.). 1985. pap. 12.95 (*0-8323-0446-8*) Binford Mort.
***Neilsen, Allan R.** Critical Thinking & Reading: Empowering Learners to Think & Act. (Monographs on Teaching Critical Thinking). (Illus.). 54p. (C). 1989. pap. 8.95 (*0-927516-02-0*) ERIC-REC.
Neilsen, Lorri. Literacy & Living: The Literate Lives of Three Adults. LC 88-35973. 150p. (Orig.). (C). 1989. pap. 14.95 (*0-435-08493-3*) Heinemann.
Neilsen, Mark. Eight Key Issues in Modern Society: A Catholic Perspective. LC 89-63787. 80p. (Orig.). 1990. pap. 2.95 (*0-89243-311-6*) Liguori Pubns.
Neilsen, Mark, ed. I Am with You Always: A Living Faith Prayer Companion. (Illus.). 169p. (Orig.). 1991. pap. 7.95 (*0-9629585-0-6*) Crtve Commns MO.
Neilsen, Nicki J. The Red Dragon & St. George's. (Illus.). 66p. 1983. pap. 7.50 (*0-9607358-2-8*) Fathom Pub.
Neilsen, Philip, ed. The Sting in the Wattle. 270p. Date not set. pap. 16.95 (*0-7022-2565-7*, Pub. by Univ Queensland Pr AT) Intl Spec Bk.
Neilsen, Shelly. I Love Animals. Berg, Julie, ed. LC 93-18955. (Target Earth Ser.). (J). 1993. 14.96 (*1-56239-191-7*) Abdo & Dghtrs.
— I Love Animals. Berg, Julie, ed. LC 93-18955. (Target Earth Ser.). (J). 1993. pap. 7.49 (*1-56239-406-1*) Abdo & Dghtrs.
Neilson, Alasdair. Fate of Organic Chemicals in the Aquatic Environment. 1994. write for info. (*0-87371-597-7*) Lewis Pubs.
Neilson, Andrew. Monza Protest. 1987. pap. 2.95 (*0-449-13048-7*) Fawcett.
Neilson, Bruce J. & Cronin, L. Eugene, eds. Estuaries & Nutrients. LC 81-83901. (Contemporary Issues in Science & Society Ser.). (Illus.). 656p. 1981. 99.50 (*0-89603-035-0*) Humana.
***Neilson, D. & Das, M. P., eds.** Computational Approaches to Novel Condensed Matter Systems: Applications to Classical & Quantum Systems. LC 95-13989. 280p. 1995. 89.50 (*0-306-44986-2*, Plenum Pr) Plenum.
Neilson, D., jt. ed. see Das, M. P.
Neilson, D. G. Principles & Practice of Farm Management Accounting. Mallyon. 3rd ed. x, 293p. 1986. pap. 46.00 (*0-455-20645-7*, Pub. by Law Bk Co) W W Gaunt.
Neilson, Eric, ed. see Alderman, Michael H. & Mitch, William E.
Neilson, Francis. Churchill & Yalta. (Revisionist Historiography Ser.). 1979. lib. bdg. 250.00 (*0-685-96613-5*) Revisionist Pr.
— The Churchill Legend: Winston Churchill As Fraud, Fakir & War-Monger. 1983. lib. bdg. 79.95 (*0-87700-001-8*) Revisionist Pr.
— Churchill's War Memoirs. (Revisionist Historiography Ser.). 1979. lib. bdg. 250.00 (*0-87700-275-4*) Revisionist Pr.
— The Copyright Tyranny. 1979. lib. bdg. 39.95 (*0-685-96615-1*) Revisionist Pr.
— Cultural Tradition & Other Essays. LC 69-18935. (Essay Index Reprint Ser.). 1977. 20.95 (*0-8369-1046-X*) Ayer.
— Cultural Tradition & Other Essays. 228p. 1957. 2.00 (*0-911312-82-X*) Schalkenbach.
— The Devil & All: A Churchill Satire. 1971. 250.00 (*0-87700-019-0*) Revisionist Pr.
— Escort of Lies: War Propaganda. (Revisionist Historiography Ser.). 1979. lib. bdg. 39.00 (*0-685-96621-6*) Revisionist Pr.
— The Freudians & the Oedipus Complex. 1971. 250.00 (*0-87700-013-1*) Revisionist Pr.
— From Ur to Nazareth: An Economic Inquiry into the Religious & Political History of Israel. 1971. 250.00 (*0-87700-010-7*) Revisionist Pr.
— The Garden of Doctor Persuasion. 1971. 250.00 (*0-87700-018-2*) Revisionist Pr.
— Hate, the Enemy of Peace. (Studies in Pacifism). 1991. lib. bdg. 75.00 (*0-8490-4405-7*) Gordon Pr.
— A History of Trade. 1979. lib. bdg. 250.00 (*0-685-96624-0*) Revisionist Pr.
— History Versus Patriotism: Diplomacy up a Blind Alley. (Revisionist Historiography Ser.). 1979. lib. bdg. 44.50 (*0-685-96625-9*) Revisionist Pr.
— How Diplomats Make War. 1986. lib. bdg. 250.00 (*0-8490-3847-2*) Gordon Pr.
— How Diplomats Make War. 382p. 1984. pap. 5.00 (*0-930439-06-6*) Schalkenbach.
— In Quest of Justice. 135p. 1944. 1.00 (*0-911312-31-5*) Schalkenbach.
— A Key to Culture: The Great Books. 1971. 250.00 (*0-87700-064-6*) Revisionist Pr.
— The Last Mile. 1971. 250.00 (*0-685-26316-9*) Revisionist Pr.
— The Makers of War. 1971. 250.00 (*0-87700-002-6*) Revisionist Pr.
— My Life in Two Worlds, 2 vols., Set. 1971. 300.00 (*0-87700-004-2*) Revisionist Pr.
— The Nietzsche-Wagner Rift. 1979. lib. bdg. 150.00 (*0-685-96632-1*) Revisionist Pr.
— Our Garden: Reflections on Nature. 1971. 250.00 (*0-87700-015-8*) Revisionist Pr.
— Philanthropy & Peace. 1979. lib. bdg. 39.95 (*0-685-96634-8*) Revisionist Pr.
— A Poem. 1971. 59.95 (*0-87700-066-2*) Revisionist Pr.
— Poems. 1971. 250.00 (*0-87700-006-9*) Revisionist Pr.
— Portents: Scares Old & New. 1979. lib. bdg. 39.00 (*0-685-96635-6*) Revisionist Pr.
— Recent Books on World War Two. (Revisionist Historiography Ser.). 1979. lib. bdg. 39.95 (*0-685-96636-4*) Revisionist Pr.
— Shakespeare & the Tempest. LC 74-30004. 181p. 1970. reprint ed. text ed. 65.00 (*0-8371-7385-X*, NEST, Greenwood Pr) Greenwood.

An Asterisk (*) at the beginning of an entry indicates that the title is appearing in BIP for the first time.

— The Story of the Freeman. 1971. 250.00 (*0-87700-011-5*) Revisionist Pr.

— A Study of Macbeth for the Stage. 1981. lib. bdg. 250.00 (*0-686-72851-3*) Revisionist Pr.

— A Task for Diogenes: A Satire. 1971. 250.00 (*0-87700-017-4*) Revisionist Pr.

— Taxes Are Devilish Things. 1979. lib. bdg. 39.95 (*0-685-96638-0*) Revisionist Pr.

— Teilhard de Chardin's Vision of the Future. 1979. lib. bdg. 250.00 (*0-685-96640-2*) Revisionist Pr.

— The Threat of International Chaos. 1979. lib. bdg. 39.95 (*0-685-96641-0*) Revisionist Pr.

— Tolstoy's Message for Our Times. 1979. lib. bdg. 39.00 (*0-685-96643-7*) Revisionist Pr.

— Toynbee's Study of History. 1979. lib. bdg. 49.95 (*0-685-96644-5*) Revisionist Pr.

— The Tragedy of Europe. 1971. 275.00 (*0-87700-003-4*) Revisionist Pr.

— Unrest in the Middle East. 1979. lib. bdg. 39.95 (*0-685-96646-1*) Revisionist Pr.

Neilson, G. W. & Enderby, J. E., eds. Water & Aqueous Solutions. (Illus.). 362p. 1986. 118.00 (*0-85274-576-1*) IOP Pub.

Neilson, G. W., jt. auth. see Bellisent-Funel, M. C.

Neilson, Gena. Favorite Rhymes. (Illus.). (J). (ps-1). 1986. pap. 9.95 (*0-937763-02-0*) Lauri Inc.

Neilson, Gena, illus. Dinosaurs. (J). (ps-1). 1986. spiral bd. 9.95 (*0-937763-00-4*) Lauri Inc.

— It's Your Birthday. (J). (ps-1). 1986. spiral bd. 9.95 (*0-937763-03-9*) Lauri Inc.

— Noah's Ark. (J). (ps-1). 1986. spiral bd. 9.95 (*0-937763-01-2*) Lauri Inc.

Neilson, George. John Barbour: Poet & Translator. (BCL1-PR English Literature Ser.). 57p. 1992. reprint ed. lib. bdg. 59.00 (*0-7812-7167-3*) Rprt Serv.

***Neilson, Gregory G.** Karl the Kodiak & the Scratching Bear Contest. (Illus.). 18p. (J). 1994. text ed. 12.50 (*0-930329-84-8*) KABEL Pubs.

Neilson, Helen P. What the Cow Said to the Calf: Native American Historical Biography. LC 93-84752. 200p. (Orig.). (C). 1993. pap. text ed. 17.95 (*1-880222-15-9*) Red-Apple Pub.

Neilson, J. Reports of the European Communities, 1952-1977: An Index to Authors & Chairmen. 576p. 1981. text ed. 110.00 (*0-7201-1592-2*, Mansell Pub) Cassell.

Neilson, James P. & Chambers, S. E., eds. Obstetric Ultrasound Vol. 1. (Illus.). 320p. 1993. 75.00 (*0-19-262224-2*) OUP.

— Obstetric Ultrasound Vol. 2. (Illus.). 250p. 1995. text ed. 79.00 (*0-19-262373-7*) OUP.

Neilson, James P., jt. auth. see Willocks, James.

Neilson, Joseph. Memories of Rufus Choate: With Some Consideration of His Studies, Methods, & Opinions, & of His Style As a Speaker & Writer. xx, 460p. 1985. reprint ed. lib. bdg. 37.50 (*0-8377-0909-1*) Rothman.

Neilson, Keith. Strategy & Supply: The Anglo-Russian Alliance, 1914-17. 240p. 1984. text ed. 55.00 (*0-04-940072-X*) Routledge Chapman & Hall.

***Neilson, Keith & Errington, Elizabeth J., eds.** Navies & Global Defense: Theories & Strategy. LC 95-2239. 232p. 1995. text ed. 55.00 (*0-275-94898-6*, Praeger Pubs) Greenwood.

Neilson, Keith & Haycock, Ronald G., eds. The Cold War & Defense. LC 90-30926. 224p. 1990. text ed. 49.95 (*0-275-93556-6*, C3556, Praeger Pubs) Greenwood.

Neilson, Keith & McKercher, B. J., eds. Go Spy the Land: Military Intelligence in History. LC 92-234. 222p. 1992. text ed. 47.95 (*0-275-93708-9*, C3708, Praeger Pubs) Greenwood.

Neilson, Keith, jt. ed. see Haycock, Ronald G.

Neilson, Keith, jt. ed. see Ion, A. Hamish.

Neilson, Melanie. Civil Noir. LC 91-67073. 96p. (Orig.). 1992. pap. 8.95 (*0-937804-45-2*) Segue NYC.

Neilson, Melanie, jt. auth. see Anderson, Michael.

Neilson, Melany. Even Mississippi. 216p. 1989. 26.95 (*0-8173-0440-1*) U of Ala Pr.

Neilson, N., ed. The Cartulary & Terrier of the Priory of Bilsongton, Kent. (British Academy, London, Records of the Social & Economic History of England & Wales Ser.: Vol. 7). 1972. reprint ed. pap. 40.00 (*0-8115-1247-9*) Periodicals Srv.

— A Terrier of Fleete, Lincolnshire. Bd. with Eleventh Century Inquisition of St. Augustine's Canterbury. (British Academy, London, Record of the Social & Economic History of Wngland & Wales. Series: Vol. 4). 1974. reprint ed. Set pap. 40.00 (*0-8115-1244-4*) Periodicals Srv.

Neilson, Peter, ed. Life-Adventures of Zamba, an African Negro King. LC 70-133162. (Black Heritage Library Collection). 1977. 27.95 (*0-8369-8717-9*) Ayer.

Neilson, Philip. Imagined Lives: A Study of David Malouf. 1990. pap. 29.95 (*0-7022-2274-7*, Pub. by Univ Queensland Pr AT) Intl Spec Bk.

— Imago. (Orig.). 1993. pap. 10.95 (*0-7022-2566-5*, Pub. by Univ Queensland Pr AT) Intl Spec Bk.

Neilson, Stefan. Characteristics of Excellence. 81p. 1986. student ed, audio 69.95 (*0-9606110-1-0*) AEON-Hierophant.

Neilson, Stefan & Theolke, Shay. Winning Colors for Elementary Students. (Personality Language & Winning Colors Ser.). (Illus.). 89p. 1990. teacher ed 30.00 (*1-880830-12-4*); student ed 20.00 (*1-880830-13-2*); teacher ed, pap. 30.00 (*1-880830-22-1*) AEON-Hierophant.

Neilson, Stefan & Thoelke, Shay. Color Me Changing - Succeeding: Personality Language Development. (Personality Language Ser.). (Illus.). 55p. (Orig.). 1988. pap. write for info. (*1-880830-23-X*); spiral bd. 15.00 (*1-880830-00-0*) AEON-Hierophant.

— Color Me Winning. (Personality Language Ser.). (Illus.). 50p. (J). (gr. 4-6). 1989. spiral bd. 20.00 (*1-880830-02-7*) AEON-Hierophant.

— Communicate. (Personality Language Ser.). (Illus.). 112p. 1988. text ed., spiral bd. 40.00 (*1-880830-03-5*); pap. 42.00 (*1-880830-24-8*) AEON-Hierophant.

— Communication Power Tools: Getting to Winning Colors. LC 90-84510. (Personality Language & Winning Colors Ser.). (Illus.). 59p. 1990. student ed, spiral bd. 30.00 (*1-880830-04-3*) AEON-Hierophant.

— Here's Looking at You Kid! Color Me Winning. LC 90-84509. (Personality Language Ser.). (Illus.). 118p. 1992. teacher ed 35.00 (*1-880830-06-X*); teacher ed, pap. 35.00 (*1-880830-21-3*); spiral bd. 20.00 (*1-880830-07-8*) AEON-Hierophant.

— Personality Language: Youth's Road to Excellence. (Illus.). 121p. 1988. student ed 20.00 (*1-880830-09-4*) AEON-Hierophant.

— Personality Language: Youth's Road to Excellence. rev. ed. (Illus.). 121p. 1988. pap. write for info. (*1-880830-25-6*); spiral bd. 40.00 (*0-9606110-6-1*) AEON-Hierophant.

— Winning Colors Power Pack: Adult. (Illus.). 101p. (C). 1988. teacher ed 30.00 (*1-880830-15-9*) AEON-Hierophant.

— Winning Colors Power Pack: Adult. rev. ed. (Illus.). 72p. (C). 1988. spiral bd. 20.00 (*1-880830-14-0*) AEON-Hierophant.

— Winning Colors Power Pack: Student. (Personality Language Ser.). (Illus.). 102p. 1988. teacher ed 30.00 (*1-880830-17-5*); student ed, spiral bd. 20.00 (*1-880830-16-7*) AEON-Hierophant.

— Winning Colors Series. rev. ed. Salisbury, George, ed. (Illus.). (C). 1995. pap. text ed. 19.50 (*1-880830-26-4*) AEON-Hierophant.

Neilson, Stefan F. & Thoelke, Shay. Personality Language. LC 81-66718. (Illus.). 168p. (Orig.). 1981. spiral bd. 9.95 (*0-9606110-0-2*) AEON-Hierophant.

Neilson, Suzanne, ed. see Wilson, James F., et al.

Neilson, William A. & Thorndike, Ashley H. The Facts About Shakespeare. reprint ed. 69.00 (*0-403-03058-7*) Somerset Pub.

Neiman, jt. auth. see Wolf.

Neiman, Barbara L. Come Behind the Veil. Dean, Athena, ed. (Illus.). 112p. (Orig.). Date not set. pap. write for info. (*0-9622413-4-2*) Wine Pr Pub.

***Neiman, Carol.** Miracles: The Extraordinary, the Impossible, & the Divine. (Illus.). 224p. 1995. 22.95 (*0-670-85582-0*, Viking Studio) Studio Bks.

Neiman, Catrina, et al, eds. David Rabinowitch: Tyndale Constructions in Five Planes with West Fenestration, Sculpture for Max Imdahl. LC 89-51859. (Illus.). 160p. 1990. 60.00 (*0-9624258-0-X*); pap. 40.00 (*0-9624258-1-8*) Flynn Gallery.

Neiman, Harvey L. & Yao, James S., eds. Angiography of Vascular Disease. LC 84-17564. (Illus.). 624p. reprint ed. pap. 177.90 (*0-7837-6239-9*, 2045953) Bks Demand.

Neiman, Irving G. Murder Once Removed. 1972. pap. 4.75 (*0-8222-0793-1*) Dramatists Play.

Neiman, LeRoy. An American in Paris. LC 94-263. 1994. write for info. (*0-8109-1950-8*) Abrams.

— Big-Time Golf. (Illus.). 176p. 1992. 45.00 (*0-8109-3666-6*) Abrams.

— Carnaval. (Illus.). 1981. 100.00 (*0-937608-01-7*) Knoedler.

***Neiman, M. B. & Gal, D.** The Kinetic Isotope Method & Its Application. 310p. (C). 1971. 48.00x (*963-05-9999-6*, Pub. by Akad Kiado HU) St Mut.

Neiman, Marcus L., ed. Life in the Music Classroom. 64p. (C). 1992. teacher ed 8.00 (*1-56545-010-8*) Music Ed Natl.

Neiman Marcus Staff. Pure & Simple: An Incircle Cookbook. 1991. 19.95 (*0-9629473-0-X*) Neiman-InCircle.

Neiman, Max, jt. ed. see Kempton, Willett.

Neiman, Morris. A Century of Modern Hebrew Literary Criticism, 1784-1884. 1983. 25.00 (*0-88125-011-2*) Ktav.

Neiman, Richard S., et al, eds. Hodgkin's Disease II: Pathological Considerations. LC 73-23030. (Hodgkin's Disease Ser.: Vol. 2). 141p. 1974. text ed. 21.00 (*0-8422-7194-5*) Irvington.

Neiman, Susan. Slow Fire: Jewish Notes from Berlin. LC 91-52699. 320p. 1992. 22.50 (*0-8052-4112-4*) Schocken.

— The Unity of Reason: Rereading Kant. 288p. 1994. 37.00 (*0-19-506768-1*) OUP.

Neimark, A. V. Percolation & Fractals in Colloid & Interface Science. 400p. (C). 1995. text ed. 48.00 (*981-02-0734-4*) World Scientific Pub.

Neimark, Anne E. A Deaf Child Listened: Thomas Gallaudet, Pioneer in American Education. LC 82-23942. 160p. (J). (gr. 7-p). 1983. 14.00 (*0-688-01719-3*) Morrow Jr Bks.

— Diego Rivera, Artist of the People. LC 91-25209. (Illus.). 128p. (J). (gr. 3-7). 1992. lib. bdg. 16.89 (*0-06-021784-7*) HarpC Child Bks.

Neimark, Edith. Adventures in Thinking. 360p. (C). 1987. pap. text ed. 20.00 (*0-15-501895-7*) HB Coll Pubs.

Neimark, Edith D., et al, eds. Moderators of Competence. (Jean Piaget Symposium Ser.). 240p. (C). 1985. text ed. 49.95 (*0-89859-531-2*) L Erlbaum Assocs.

Neimark, Jill. Bloodsong. LC 94-15060. 288p. 1994. pap. 9.95 (*0-452-27296-3*, Plume) NAL-Dutton.

— Bloodsong. LC 93-261. 1993. 20.00 (*0-679-42005-3*) Random.

— Ice Cream. LC 84-10915. (Illus.). (J). (gr. 2-6). 1986. pap. 11.95 (*0-8038-9290-X*) Hastings.

Neimark, Jill, jt. auth. see Weiner, Marcella B.

Neimark, Marilyn, ed. Advances in Public Interest Accounting, Vol. 1. 1986. 73.25 (*0-89232-516-X*) Jai Pr.

Neimark, Marilyn, et al, eds. Advances in Public Interest Accounting, Vol. 2. 1987. 73.25 (*0-89232-698-0*) Jai Pr.

— Advances in Public Interest Accounting, Vol. 3. 275p. 1990. 73.25 (*0-89232-784-7*) Jai Pr.

Neimark, Marilyn K. The Hidden Dimensions of Annual Reports: Sixty Years of Social Conflict at General Motors. (Critical Accounting Research Ser.). 269p. (C). 1995. text ed. 39.95x (*1-55876-054-7*) Wiener Pubs Inc.

— The Hidden Dimensions of Annual Reports: Sixty Years of Social Conflict at General Motors. (Critical Accounting Research Ser.). 269p. (C). 1995. pap. text ed. 24.95x (*1-55876-100-4*) Wiener Pubs Inc.

Neimark, Paul & Berkowitz, Gerald. A Doctor Discusses Care of the Back. 1990. pap. 6.00 (*0-910304-04-1*) Budlong.

Neimark, Paul & Matlin, Samuel. Doctor Discusses Female Surgery. (Illus.). 1992. pap. 6.00 (*0-686-65550-8*) Budlong.

Neimark, Paul, jt. auth. see Owens, Jesse.

Neimark, Paul, jt. auth. see Scheimann, Eugene.

Neimark, Paul, et al. A Doctor Discusses Your Life After the Baby Is Born. (Illus.). 1993. pap. 6.00 (*0-685-46338-9*) Budlong.

Neimark, Philip J. The Way of the Orisa. LC 92-53903. 240p. 1993. pap. 12.00 (*0-06-250557-2*) Harper SF.

Neimark, Yu. I. & Landa, P. S. Stochastic & Chaotic Oscillations. (C). 1992. lib. bdg. 200.00 (*0-7923-1530-8*) Kluwer Ac.

Neimat, Marie-Anne K. Search Mechanisms for Large Files. LC 81-13036. (Computer Science: Distributed Database Systems Ser.: No. 11). 130p. reprint ed. pap. 37.10 (*0-685-20839-7*, 2070064) Bks Demand.

Neimeijer, Rudo, jt. auth. see Hoorweg, Jan.

***Neimeyer, Charles P.** America Goes to War: A Social History of the Continental Army. (American Social Experience Ser.). (Illus.). 240p. 1995. 35.00 (*0-8147-5780-4*) NYU Pr.

Neimeyer, Greg, jt. ed. see Neimeyer, Robert.

Neimeyer, Greg J. Constructivist Assessment: A Casebook. (Counseling Psychologist Casebook Ser.: Vol. 2). (Illus.). 248p. (C). 1992. 39.95 (*0-8039-4830-1*); pap. 18.95 (*0-8039-4831-X*) Sage.

Neimeyer, Greg J. & Neimeyer, Robert A., eds. Advances in Personal Construct Psychology, Vol. 1. 287p. 1989. 73.25 (*1-55938-081-0*) Jai Pr.

***Neimeyer, Juanita.** Hobby Ceramist's Guide to Finishing Products: How to Correctly Use Ceramic Decorating & Repairing Media. Bayer, Gregory W., ed. 56p. (Orig.). 1994. pap. 7.99 (*1-879825-14-7*) Jones Publish.

Neimeyer, Robert & Neimeyer, Greg, eds. A Personal Construct Therapy Casebook. LC 87-4601. 336p. 1987. 33.95 (*0-8261-5530-8*) Springer Pub.

Neimeyer, Robert A. The Development of Personal Construct Psychology. LC 84-17367. 186p. reprint ed. pap. 53.10 (*0-7837-6806-0*, 2046638) Bks Demand.

Neimeyer, Robert A., ed. Death Anxiety Handbook. (Series in Death Education, Aging, & Health Care). 312p. 1994. 54.50 (*1-56032-282-9*, Pub. by Paul Chapman UK) Taylor & Francis.

***Neimeyer, Robert A. & Mahoney, Michael J., eds.** Constructivism in Psychotherapy. 480p. 1995. text ed. 49.95 (*1-55798-279-1*) Am Psychol.

Neimeyer, Robert A., jt. ed. see Epting, Franz R.

Neimeyer, Robert A., jt. auth. see Liles, Larry E.

Neimeyer, Robert A., jt. ed. see Neimeyer, Greg J.

Neimeyer, Robert A., jt. ed. see Wass, Hannelore.

Neimi, Helena R. Porcelain Dollmaking in Detail. (Illus.). 60p. (Orig.). 1980. pap. text ed. 15.00 (*0-9607800-0-9*) H R Niemi.

Neinast, Helen & Ettinger, Tom. With Heart & Mind & Soul. 250p. 1994. pap. 14.95 (*0-8358-0695-2*) Upper Room Bks.

Neinast, Helen R. Albert Schweitzer. 1989. pap. 2.95 (*0-687-60015-4*) Abingdon.

Neinast, Helen R., comp. Contemporary Spiritual Classics: Albert Schweitzer. LC 89-50644. 60p. (Orig.). 1989. pap. 2.95 (*0-8358-0605-7*) Upper Room Bks.

Neinast, Helen R. & Ettinger, Thomas C. What about God Now That You're off to College: A Prayerguide for First-Year Students. LC 91-67171. 240p. 1992. text ed. 19.95 (*0-8358-0655-3*) Upper Room Bks.

Neinhuys, J. W., tr. see Temam, Roger.

Neinken, Mortimer L. The U. S. Ten Cent Stamps of 1855-59. (Illus.). 252p. 1960. 30.00 (*0-912574-07-0*) Collectors.

Neinstein, Lawrence S. Adolescent Health Care: A Practical Guide. rev. ed. (Illus.). 1112p. 1991. pap. 59.00 (*0-683-06373-1*) Williams & Wilkins.

— Adolescent Health Care: A Practical Guide. 2nd rev. ed. (Illus.). 1112p. 1991. 59.00 (*0-683-06374-X*) Williams & Wilkins.

— Issues in Reproductive Management. LC 93-33909. 1993. 45.00 (*0-86577-505-2*) Thieme Med Pubs.

Neinstein, Lawrence S. & Katz, Barbara. Contraception & Chronic Illness: A Clinician's Sourcebook. LC 86-70099. 98p. 1986. pap. 24.95 (*0-9603332-5-8*) Am Health Consults.

Neirynck, J., jt. auth. see Boite, R.

Neirynck, Jacques, jt. auth. see Hasler, Martin.

Neis, Klaus J. & Brandner, Percy. Hysteroscopy: Textbook & Atlas. LC 94-17573. (Illus.). 1994. write for info. (*3-13-799701-1*) Thieme Med Pubs.

Neis, Klaus J. & Hepp, Hermann. Hysteroscopy. (Illus.). 128p. 1994. text ed. 79.00 (*0-86577-489-7*) Thieme Med Pubs.

Neis, Marlys E. & Kingdon, Ruth T. Leadership in Transition: A Practical Guide to Shared Governance. LC 90-91945. 113p. 1990. 24.95 (*0-9627557-0-2*) Nova I.

Neis, Marlys E., jt. auth. see Kingdon, Ruth T.

***Neis, Sandra L.** Growing Readers: Their Care & Feeding. LC 93-80702. (Illus.). 136p. (Orig.). 1994. pap. 14.95 (*0-9639769-8-2*) Learning Tree.

Neisen, Joseph H. Reclaiming Pride: Daily Reflections on Contemporary Gay & Lesbian Life. 380p. (Orig.). 1994. pap. 8.95 (*1-55874-312-X*, 312X) Health Comm.

Neisendorfer, Joseph. Primary Homotopy Theory. LC 80-12109. (Memoirs of the American Mathematical Society Ser.: No. 25/232). 67p. 1983. reprint ed. pap. 16.00 (*0-8218-2232-2*, MEMO 25/232) Am Math.

Neises, Charles P. The Beatles Reader: A Selection of Contemporary Views, News & Reviews of the Beatles in Their Heyday. LC 84-60267. (Rock & Roll Remembrances Ser.: No. 6). 232p. 1991. reprint ed. 28.50 (*1-56075-024-3*) Popular Culture.

Neises, M., et al, eds. Der Geriatrische Tumorpatient. (Beitraege zur Onkologie, Contributions to Oncology Ser.: Vol. 45). (Illus.). viii, 234p. 1994. 92.00 (*3-8055-5808-2*) S Karger.

Neish, W. J. Xanthines & Cancer: An Experimental Study of Tumour Inhibition. 192p. (C). 1988. pap. 35.00 (*0-08-036399-7*, Pub. by Aberdeen U Pr) Macmillan.

Neishstadt. Test Your Tactical Ability. 1992. pap. 24.95 (*0-7134-4013-9*, Pub. by Batsford UK) Trafalgar.

Neishtadt, I. Paul Keres Chess Master Class. 182p. 1983. 29.90 (*0-08-023122-5*, Pergamon Pr); 17.90 (*0-08-029719-6*, Pergamon Pr) Elsevier.

Neishtadt, Iakov. Queen Sacrifice. LC 90-40805. (Russian Chess Ser.). 266p. 1990. pap. 17.95 (*0-08-037158-2*, Pub. by CHES UK); pap. 14.95 (*0-685-47231-0*, Pub. by CHES UK) Macmillan.

Neishtadt, J. Play the Catalan: Closed Variation & Catalan Opening after 1 d4 d5 2 c4. LC 87-2262. (Illus.). 190p. 1988. 33.90 (*0-08-032063-5*, Pergamon Pr); pap. 19.90 (*0-08-032062-7*, Pergamon Pr) Elsevier.

— Play the Catalan, Vol. 1: Open Variation. Neat, Kenneth P., tr. LC 87-2262. (Chess Ser.). (Illus.). 258p. 1987. 37.90 (*0-08-029741-2*, Pergamon Pr); pap. 23.90 (*0-08-029740-4*, Pergamon Pr) Elsevier.

Neishtadt, Yakov. Attacking the King. (Chess Library). 160p. 1992. pap. 16.95 (*0-02-029438-7*, Collier S&S) S&S Trade.

Neissa, Peter A. The Drug Lord. 210p. 1990. 23.00 (*0-685-38358-X*) Floricanto Pr.

Neisser, Arden. The Other Side of Silence. LC 89-71507. 301p. 1990. pap. 13.95 (*0-930323-64-5*) Gallaudet Univ Pr.

Neisser, Eric. Recapturing the Spirit: Essays on the Bill of Rights at 200. 291p. 1991. 19.95 (*0-945612-22-2*); pap. text ed. 12.95 (*0-945612-23-0*) Madison Hse.

Neisser, Ulric, ed. Memory Observed: Remembering in Natural Contexts. LC 81-15197. (Illus.). (C). 1995. pap. text ed. 23.95 (*0-7167-1372-1*) W H Freeman.

— The Perceived Self: Ecological & Interpersonal Sources of Self Knowledge. (Emory Symposia in Cognition Ser.: No. 5). (Illus.). 384p. (C). 1994. 49.95 (*0-521-41509-8*) Cambridge U Pr.

— The School Achievement of Minority Children: New Perspectives. 208p. (C). 1986. text ed. 39.95 (*0-89859-685-8*) L Erlbaum Assocs.

Neisser, Ulric & Fivush, Robyn, eds. The Remembering Self: Construction & Accuracy in the Self-Narrative. LC 93-40556. (Emory Symposia in Cognition Ser.: Vol. 6). 240p. (C). 1994. 49.95 (*0-521-43194-8*) Cambridge U Pr.

Neisser, Ulric & Winograd, Eugene. Remembering Reconsidered: Ecological & Traditional Approaches to the Study of Memory. (Emory Symposia in Cognition Ser.: No. 2). (Illus.). 420p. 1988. 59.95 (*0-521-33031-9*) Cambridge U Pr.

***Neisser, Ulric & Winograd, Eugene, eds.** Remembering Reconsidered: Ecological & Traditional Approaches to the Study of Memory. (Emory Symposia in Cognition Ser.: No. 2). (Illus.). 399p. (C). 1995. pap. 24.95 (*0-521-48500-2*) Cambridge U Pr.

Neisser, Ulric, jt. ed. see Winograd, Eugene.

Neistadt, Maureen E. & Freda, Maureen. Choices: A Guide to Sex Counseling with Physically Disabled Adults. LC 86-2888. 132p. 1987. text ed. 14.50 (*0-89874-903-4*); pap. 9.95 (*0-89464-201-4*) Krieger.

Neisworth, John, jt. auth. see Bagnato, Stephen J.

Neisworth, John T., jt. auth. see Smith, Robert M.

Neite, Heinz. Untersuchungen ueber Veraenderungen in den Buchenschuerzen der Kalk-Buchenwaelder des Teutoburger Waldes. (Dissertationes Botanicae Ser.: Vol. 108). (Illus.). 104p. 1987. pap. text ed. 38.50 (*3-443-64020-6*) Lubrecht & Cramer.

Neito, Eva M., et al, eds. Notable Hispanic American Women. 465p. 1993. 65.00 (*0-8103-7578-8*, 003318) Gale.

Neito, M. M., jt. ed. see Goldman, T.

Neittaanmaki, P., ed. Numerical Methods for Free Boundary Problems. (International Series of Numerical Mathematics: Vol. 99). xv, 439p. 1991. 116.00 (*0-8176-2641-7*) Birkhauser.

Neittaanmaki, P. & Tiba, D. Optimal Control of Nonlinear Parabolic Systems: Theory, Algorithms & Applications. LC 93-45312. (Pure & Applied Mathematics Ser.). 424p. 1994. 150.00 (*0-8247-9081-2*) Dekker.

Neittaanmaki, P., jt. auth. see Haslinger, J.

Neittaanmaki, P., jt. auth. see Makela, M. M.

Neittaanmaki, P., jt. auth. see Marinov, C. A.

***Neittaarmaki, P., et al.** Inverse Problems & Optimal Design in Electricity & Magnetism. (Monographs in Electrical & Electronic Engineering: No. 35). (Illus.). 384p. 1995. 80.00 (*0-19-859383-X*) OUP.

Neitz, Mary J. Charisma & Community: A Study of Religion in American Culture. 275p. 1987. 39.95x (*0-88738-130-8*) Transaction Pubs.

***Neitzel.** Dress I'll Wear to the Party. 1995. pap. (*0-688-14261-3*, Mulberry) Morrow.

— Environmental Compliance Handbook Set. 2nd ed. Date not set. pap. text ed. 195.00 (*0-471-12437-0*) Wiley.

N

*Neitzel, Charlotte L. The RCRA Compliance Handbook. rev. ed. (Environmental Compliance Handbook Ser.). 1994. pap. text ed. 54.95 (0-471-11266-6) Wiley.
— RCRA Compliance Handbook. 2nd ed. (Environmental Compliance Handbook Ser.: Vol. 3). 1992. pap. 49.95 (0-7816-0071-5) Exec Ent Pubns.
Neitzel, Duane A., jt. ed. see Becker, C. Dale.
Neitzel, Jill E. The Regional Organization of the Hohokam in the American Southwest: A Stylistic Analysis of Red-on-Buff Pottery. LC 90-28291. (Evolution of North American Indians Ser.). 215p. 1991. reprint ed. 20.00 (0-8240-2509-1) Garland.
Neitzel, Jill E., jt. ed. see Carr, Christopher.
Neitzel, Robert S. The Grand Village of the Natchez Indians Revisited. Galloway, Patricia K., ed. LC 83-620022. (Mississippi Department of Archives & History Archaeological Reports). 215p. 1983. pap. 15.00 (0-938896-35-0) Mississippi Archives.
Neitzel, Shirley. The Bag I'm Taking to Grandma's. LC 94-4115. (Illus.). 32p. (J). 1995. lib. bdg. 14.93 (0-688-12961-7) Greenwillow.
— The Bag I'm Taking to Grandma's. LC 94-4115. (Illus.). 32p. (J). (ps up). 1995. 15.00 (0-688-12960-9) Greenwillow.
— The Dress I'll Wear to the Party. LC 91-30906. (Illus.). 32p. (J). (ps-4). 1992. 14.00 (0-688-09959-9); lib. bdg. 13.93 (0-688-09960-2) Greenwillow.
— Jacket I Wear in the Snow. LC 88-18767. (Illus.). 32p. (J). (ps up). 1989. 15.00 (0-688-08028-6); lib. bdg. 13.93 (0-688-08030-8) Greenwillow.
— The Jacket I Wear in the Snow. Cohr, Amy, ed. LC 92-43789. (Illus.). 32p. (J). (ps up). 1994. reprint ed. pap. 4.95 (0-688-04587-1, Mulberry) Morrow.
Neitzke, Frederic W. A Software Law Primer. LC 83-23508. 176p. 1984. text ed. 37.95 (0-442-26866-1) Van Nos Reinhold.
Neitzke, John J., jt. auth. see Crabill, Delmar C.
*Neizmann, Claus W. Calcium Regulation by Calcium Binding Proteins in Neurodegenerative Disorders. Braun, K., ed. (Neuroscience Intelligence Unit Ser.). 141p. 1995. write for info. (1-57059-260-8) R G Landes.
Nejad, Aaron, jt. auth. see Bradley, Keith R.
*Nejar, Carlos. Carlos Nejar. Picciotto, tr. (QRL Poetry Book Ser.: Vol. XXII). 20.00 (0-614-06392-2); pap. 10.00 (0-614-06393-0) Quarterly Rev.
Nekam, Alexander. The Personality Conception of the Legal Entity. LC 38-37803. (Harvard Studies in the Conflict of Laws: Vol. 3). 131p. 1978. reprint ed. lib. bdg. 40.00 (0-89941-128-2, 301060) W S Hein.
Nekliudova, M. Ivanov, Alexander. (C). 1985. 50.00 (0-685-34440-1, Pub. by Collets) St Mut.
Neklyudova, M. Alexander Ivanov. (Illus.). (C). 1988. 50.00 (0-569-51981-0, Pub. by Collets UK) Pro-Am Music.
*Nekola, Charlotte. Dream House. 175p. 1993. pap. 12.00 (1-55597-225-X) Graywolf.
— Dream House: A Memoir. 192p. 1993. 18.95 (0-393-03433-X) Norton.
Nekola, Charlotte & Rabinowitz, Paula, eds. Writing Red: An Anthology of American Women Writers, 1930-1940. LC 89-25023. 368p. 1987. pap. text ed. 15.95 (0-935312-76-5) Feminist Pr.
Nekrasov, George M. North of Gallipoli, No. 343: The Black Sea Fleet at War, 1914-1917. 200p. 1992. text ed. 28.00 (0-88033-240-9) Col U Pr.
Nekrasov, Nikolai A. Poems. Soskice, Juliet, tr. LC 76-23889. (Classics of Russian Literature Ser.). 1977. reprint ed. 15.00 (0-88355-503-4); reprint ed. pap. 10.00 (0-88355-504-2) Hyperion Conn.
— Who Can Be Happy & Free in Russia. LC 72-120571. reprint ed. 39.50 (0-404-04677-0) AMS Pr.
— Who Can Be Happy & Free in Russia ? Soskice, Juliet, tr. LC 76-23891. (Classics of Russian Literature Ser.). 1977. reprint ed. pap. 10.00 (0-88355-505-0) Hyperion Conn.
Nekrasov, Victor. Po Obe Storony Steny. LC 84-81387. (Povesti i Rasskazy Ser.). 216p. (RUS.). 1985. 12.50 (0-911971-12-2) Effect Pub.
Nekrasova, Maria. Lacquer Miniatures from Palekh. (Illus.). 1984. 50.00 (0-317-57266-0, Pub. by Collets UK) St Mut.
Nekrich, Aleksandr. Forsake Fear: Memoirs of an Historian. 336p. (RUS.). (C). 1990. text ed. 39.95 (0-04-445682-4) Routledge Chapman & Hall.
Nekrich, Aleksandr & Heller, Mikhail. Utopia in Power: The History of the Soviet Union from 1917 to the Present. 880p. 1988. reprint ed. pap. 16.00 (0-671-64535-8) Summit Bks.
Nel, Christo, jt. auth. see McLagan, Patricia.
Nel, H., jt. auth. see Jones, R. J.
Nel, Philip J. The Structure & Ethos of the Wisdom Admonitions in Proverbs. (Beiheft zur Zeitschrift fuer die Alttestamentliche Wissenschaft Ser.: Vol. 158). xii, 142p. 1982. 66.95 (3-11-008750-2) De Gruyter.
Nelan, Joseph. College Math: A Space Odyssey. 180p. (Orig.). (C). 1994. pap. text ed. 25.00 (1-878045-24-5) Whittier Pubns.
Nelder, J. A. & Kime, R. D. Computers in Biology. (Wykeham Science Ser.: No. 32). 168p. (C). 1974. 14.00 (0-8448-1159-9, Crane Russak) Taylor & Francis.
Nelder, J. A., jt. auth. see Baker, R. J.
Nelder, J. A., jt. auth. see McCullagh, Peter.
Nelesen, J. H. Mr. Washington's Trolley Music. 32p. (J). (ps-4). 1987. 7.99 (0-570-04151-1, 56-1611) Concordia.
Nelesen, James H. The Most Important Christmas. 32p. (J). (gr. 5-9). 1985. 7.99 (0-570-04110-4, 56-1521) Concordia.
Nelessen, Anton C. Visions for a New American Dream: Process, Principles, & an Ordinance to Plan & Design Small Communities. 2nd ed. LC 94-71145. (Illus.). 374p. 1994. reprint ed. lib. bdg. 65.00 (1-884829-01-5); reprint ed. pap. 50.00 (1-884829-00-7) Planners Pr.
Neligh, Robert D., ed. The Brownsea Trail: A Brave, Clean, & Reverent Path. LC 92-81312. (Illus.). 300p. 1993. 21.95 (0-9631648-5-6); pap. 12.95 (0-9631648-6-4) Ambush Pub.
Nelipa, N. F. Photoproduction & Scattering of Pi-Mesons. (Russian Tracts on the Physical Sciences Ser.). (Illus.). 108p. 1961. text ed. 105.00 (0-677-20430-2) Gordon & Breach.
Nelipa, N. F., jt. auth. see Chaichian, M.
Nelis, G. F., et al. Peptic Ulcer Diseases: Basic & Clinical Aspects. (Developments in Gastroenterology Ser.). 1985. lib. bdg. 157.50 (0-89838-759-0) Kluwer Ac.
Nelischer, Maurice, ed. Handbook of Landscape Architectural Construction, Vol. 1. 2nd ed. 385p. 1985. 45.00 (0-941236-09-9, Landscape Architecture) Am Landscape Arch.
— Handbook of Landscape Architectural Construction, Vol. II: Site Works. LC 85-80042. 1988. 45.00 (0-318-37707-1, Landscape Architecture) Am Landscape Arch.
Nelken, Andrea, ed. see Van Hook, Beverly.
Nelken, D., ed. The Limits of the Legal Process: A Study of Landlords, Law & Crime. 1983. text ed. 88.00 (0-12-515280-9) Acad Pr.
*Nelken, David. The Futures of Criminology. 256p. 1994. 69.95 (0-8039-8714-5) Sage.
— The Futures of Criminology. 1994. pap. 21.95 (0-8039-8715-3) Sage.
Nelken, David, ed. White Collar Crime. (International Library of Criminology & Criminal Justice). 656p. 1994. 168.95 (1-85521-376-1, Pub. by Dartmth Pub UK) Ashgate Pub Co.
Nelken, Halina. Images of a Lost World: Jewish Motifs in Polish Painting. 1991. text ed. 49.50 (1-85043-354-2, Pub. by I B Tauris UK) St Martin.
Nelkin, Dorothy. Jetport: The Boston Airport Controversy. LC 74-78793. (Social Policy Ser.). 200p. 1974. 29.95x (0-87855-111-5); pap. 16.95x (0-87855-591-9) Transaction Pubs.
— On the Season: Aspects of the Migrant Labor System. LC 76-632774. (ILR Paperback Ser.: No. 8). 98p. 1970. pap. 3.50 (0-87546-041-0) ILR Pr.
— Science As Intellectual Property: Who Controls Research? LC 83-3805. (AAAS Series on Issues in Science & Technology). 142p. reprint ed. pap. 40.50 (0-7837-6741-2, 2046369) Bks Demand.
— Science As Intellectual Property: Who Controls Scientific Research. (AAAS Issues in Science & Technology Ser.). 130p. 1983. text ed. 15.95 (0-685-08670-4); pap. text ed. 7.95 (0-685-08671-2) Free Pr.
— Science As Intellectual Property: Who Controls Scientific Research. 130p. 1983. text ed. write for info. (0-318-57876-X); pap. text ed. 15.95 (0-02-949090-1) Macmillan.
— Selling Science: How the Press Covers Science & Technology. 2nd ed. 1995. pap. text ed. write for info. (0-7167-2595-9) W H Freeman.
Nelkin, Dorothy, ed. Controversy: Politics of Technical Decisions. 3rd ed. (Focus Editions Ser.: Vol. 8). (Illus.). 320p. 1992. 49.95 (0-8039-4466-7); pap. 24.95 (0-8039-4467-5) Sage.
— The Language of Risk: Conflicting Perspectives on Occupational Health. LC 85-2211. (Sage Focus Edition Ser.: No. 71). 200p. reprint ed. pap. 57.00 (0-7837-4565-6, 2044094) Bks Demand.
Nelkin, Dorothy & Brown, Michael S. Workers at Risk: Voices from the Workplace. LC 83-9319. (Illus.). xviii, 220p. 1984. lib. bdg. 22.50 (0-226-57127-0) U Ch Pr.
— Workers at Risk: Voices from the Workplace. LC 83-9319. (Illus.). xviii, 220p. 1986. pap. text ed. 9.95 (0-226-57128-9) U Ch Pr.
*Nelkin, Dorothy & Lindee, M. Susan. The DNA Mystique: The Gene as a Cultural Icon. LC 94-48711. 1995. text ed. write for info. (0-7167-2709-9) W H Freeman.
Nelkin, Dorothy & Pollak, Michael. The Atom Besieged: Extraparliamentary Dissent in France & Germany. (Illus.). 256p. 1981. pap. 9.95x (0-262-64021-X) MIT Pr.
Nelkin, Dorothy & Tancredi, Laurence. Dangerous Diagnostics: The Social Power of Biological Information. LC 93-32571. 1994. pap. text ed. 12.95 (0-226-57129-7) U Ch Pr.
Nelkin, Dorothy, jt. auth. see Jasper, James M.
Nelkin, Dorothy, et al, eds. A Disease of Society: Cultural & Institutional Responses to AIDS. 240p. (C). 1991. 54.95 (0-521-40411-8); pap. 17.95 (0-521-40743-5) Cambridge U Pr.
Nelkowski, H., ed. Einstein Symposium Berlin, on Occasion of the One Hundredth Anniversary of His Birthday. (Lecture Notes in Physics Ser.: Vol. 100). 550p. 1980. pap. 34.00 (0-387-09718-X) Spr-Verlag.
Nell, Edward. Prosperity & Public Spending: Transformation Growth & the Role of Government. (Studies in International Political Economy). 224p. 1988. text ed. 37.95 (0-04-339044-7); pap. text ed. 17.95 (0-04-339045-5) Routledge Chapman & Hall.
Nell, Edward J. Transformational Growth & Effective Demand: Economics after the Capital Critique. 675p. 1991. text ed. 100.00 (0-8147-5769-3) NYU Pr.
Nell, Edward J., ed. Growth, Profits, & Property: Essays in the Revival of Political Economy. LC 76-47192. (Illus.). 320p. 1984. pap. 32.95 (0-521-31918-8) Cambridge U Pr.
Nell, Edward J. & Semmler, Willi, eds. Nicholas Kaldor & Mainstream Economics: Confrontation or Convergence? LC 90-8893. 400p. 1991. text ed. 69.95 (0-312-05356-8) St Martin.
Nell, Edward J., jt. auth. see Deleplace, Ghislain.
Nell, Lynda, et al. Hog Heaven: Recipes from the Durning House. Date not set. 19.95 (0-9639218-0-0) Hog Heaven.
Nell, Onora. Acting on Principle: An Essay on Kantian Ethics. LC 74-20647. 167p. reprint ed. pap. 47.60 (0-8357-5083-3, 2022725) Bks Demand.
Nell, Terril A. Flowering Potted Plants: Prolonging Shelf Performance: Postproduction Care & Handling. LC 92-45173. (Postproduction Ser.). (Illus.). 96p. (Orig.). (C). 1993. pap. 42.00 (0-9626796-8-2) Ball Pub.
Nell, Varney R., ed. Entitled! Free Papers in Appalachia Concerning Antebellum Freeborn Negroes & Emancipated Blacks of Montgomery County, Virginia. LC 81-80481. 102p. lib. bdg. 18.50 (0-915156-47-4) Natl Genealogical.
Nell, Victor. Lost in a Book: The Psychology of Reading for Pleasure. LC 87-14283. 1988. 42.00 (0-300-04115-2) Yale U Pr.
— Lost in a Book: The Psychology of Reading for Pleasure. 350p. (C). 1990. reprint ed. pap. 17.00 (0-300-04906-4) Yale U Pr.
Nell, W. C. The Colored Patriots of the American Revolution. 1973. 59.95 (0-87968-907-2) Gordon Pr.
Nell, William C. Colored Patriots of the American Revolution. LC 68-29013. (American Negro: His History & Literature, Ser. No. 1). 1978. reprint ed. 31.95 (0-405-01832-0) Ayer.
— Services of Colored Americans in the Wars of 1776 & 1812. LC 78-144663. reprint ed. 27.50 (0-404-00202-1) AMS Pr.
Nellas & Panayiotis. Deification in Christ: The Nature of the Human Person. LC 86-31479. (Contemporary Greek Theologians Ser.: No. 5). 254p. (Orig.). 1991. pap. 13.95 (0-88141-030-6) St Vladimirs.
Nelle, Susan, jt. auth. see Allen, Mark.
Nelle, Susan, jt. auth. see Gonzalez, Jean.
Nellen, Henk J. M. & Rabbie, Edwin, eds. Hugo Grotius, Theologian: Essays in Honor of G.H.M Posthumus Meyjes. LC 93-46252. (Studies in the History of Christian Thought: Vol. 55). 1994. text ed. 77.25 (90-04-10000-8) E J Brill.
Nelles, H. V., jt. auth. see Armstrong, Christopher.
Nelles, Verlag, comp. Paris. rev. ed. (Nelles Guides Ser.). (Illus.). 258p. 1992. pap. 14.95 (3-88618-382-3, Pub. by Nelles Verlag GW) Seven Hills Bk.
Nelles Verlag Staff, comp. China. (Nelles Guides Ser.). (Illus.). 256p. 1993. pap. 14.95 (3-88618-393-9, Pub. by Nelles Verlag GW) Seven Hills Bk.
Nellhaus, Arlynn. The Heart of Jerusalem. (Illus.). 336p. 1988. pap. 12.95 (0-912528-79-6) John Muir.
Nelli, Bert. The Winning Tradition: A History of Kentucky Wildcat Basketball. LC 84-7306. (Illus.). 176p. 1984. 20.00 (0-8131-1519-1) U Pr of Ky.
Nelli, Humbert O., ed. Index & Guide to Walford's Insurance Cyclopaedia. LC 75-38801. (Research Monograph: No. 67). 633p. 1976. spiral bd. 60.00 (0-88406-099-3) GA St U Busn Pr.
Nelli, Humbert O. & Ewedemi, Soga. A Bibliography of Insurance History. 2nd ed. LC 76-6938. (Research Monograph: No. 70). 120p. 1976. spiral bd. 19.95 (0-88406-106-X) GA St U Busn Pr.
Nelli, Humbert S. The Business of Crime: Italians & Syndicate Crime in the United States. LC 80-27196. xiv, 314p. (C). 1981. reprint ed. pap. text ed. 15.95 (0-226-57132-7) U Ch Pr.
Nelli, Rene. Dictionnaire des Heresies Meridionales. 384p. (FRE.). 18.50 (0-8288-9194-X) Fr & Eur.
— Spiritualite de l'Heresie: le Catharisme. LC 78-63189. (Heresies of the Early Christian & Medieval Era Ser.: Second Ser.). reprint ed. 39.50 (0-404-16226-6) AMS Pr.
*Nelligan, Emile. Selected Poems. Widdows, P. F., tr. (Essential Poets Ser.: No. 73). 96p. 1995. 10.00 (1-55071-034-6) Guernica Editions.
Nelligan, Emily, illus. Heart of the Flower: Poems for the Sensuous Gardener. LC 90-24639. 128p. (Orig.). 1991. pap. 13.95 (0-9619111-2-3) Chicory Blue.
*Nelligan, Murray H. Old Arlington: The Story of the Lee Mansion National Memorial. (Illus.). 480p. 1995. write for info. (1-57420-052-6); pap. write for info. (1-57420-051-8) Chatelaine.
Nelligan, Tom. Commuter Trains to Central Terminal. 1986. pap. 7.95 (0-915276-45-3) Quadrant Pr.
Nellis, David W. Seashore Plants of South Florida & the Caribbean. LC 93-40713. (Illus.). 160p. 1994. 27.95 (1-56164-026-3); pap. 19.95 (1-56164-056-5) Pineapple Pr.
Nellis, David W., jt. auth. see Dammann, Arthur E.
Nellis, Elwyn A. A SCORE That Counts: The Story of the Service Corps of Retired Executives. (Illus.). 188p. 1989. 7.50 (0-9623466-0-8) SCOREA.
Nellis, John. Contract Plans & Public Enterprise Performance: Les Contrats de Plan et Leur Role Dans l'Amelioration de la Performance des Enterprises Publiques. (Discussion Paper Ser.: No. 48). 100p. 1989. English, 100 pp. 7.95 (0-8213-1188-3, 20048) World Bank.
— Improving the Performance of Soviet Enterprises. (Discussion Paper Ser.: No. 118). 24p. 1991. pap. 6.95 (0-8213-1777-6, 11777) World Bank.
— Public Enterprises in Sub-Saharan Africa. 72p. 1986. 7.95 (0-8213-0845-9, 20001) World Bank.
Nellis, John, jt. auth. see Lee, Barbara.
Nellis, John, jt. auth. see Nunberg, Barbara.
Nellis, John, jt. auth. see Shirley, Mary.
Nellis, John R. Les Enterprises Publiques dans l'Afrique au Sud du Sahara. 48p. (FRE.). 1988. 7.95 (0-8213-1157-3, BK1157) World Bank.
Nellis, Joseph G. Essence of Business Statistics. 1992. 53.33 (0-13-284688-8) P-H.
Nellis, Joseph G. & Parker, David. The Essence of Business Economics. LC 92-12062. (Essence of Management Ser.). 1992. pap. write for info. (0-13-284761-2) P-H.
Nellis, Joseph G., jt. auth. see Fleming, Michael C.
Nellis, W. J., et al, eds. Shock Waves in Condensed Matter: 1981 (Menlo Park) LC 82-70014. (AIP Conference Proceedings Ser.: No. 78). 715p. 1982. lib. bdg. 43.00 (0-88318-177-0) Am Inst Physics.
Nellist, Cassandra L. Child's First Book about Hawaii. (Illus.). 24p. (J). (ps). 1987. 8.95 (0-916630-58-7) Pr Pacifica.
Nellist, J. & Nicholl, B., eds. ASE Science Teacher's Handbook. (C). 1989. 140.00 (0-09-156340-2, Pub. by S Thornes Pubs UK) St Mut.
Nellist, John. Understanding Telecommunications & Lightwave Systems: An Entry-Level Guide. LC 92-8099. (Illus.). 200p. (C). 1992. pap. 24.95 (0-7803-0418-7, PP0314-5) Inst Electrical.
*Nellist, John G. Understanding Telecommunications & Lightwave Systems. 2nd ed. LC 95-11535. 1995. pap. write for info. (0-7803-1113-2) Inst Electrical.
Nello, Arthur. Heriot. 1992. pap. 13.95 (0-87949-335-6) Ashley Bks.
Nello, Susan S. The New Europe: Changing Economic Relations Between East & West. 320p. (C). 1992. text ed. 57.50 (0-472-10373-3) U of Mich Pr.
NelloZuech, ed. Handbook of Intelligent Sensors for Industrial Automation. 544p. 1992. 54.95 (0-201-55022-9) Addison-Wesley.
Nells, Robert. Walk a Straight Line to Freedom. 1991. 7.95 (0-533-08956-5) Vantage.
Nelms & Pym. Cardigan Welsh Corgis. (KW Ser.). (Illus.). 192p. 1990. lib. bdg. 11.95 (0-86622-573-0, KW-203) TFH Pubns.
Nelms, Brenda. The Third Republic & the Centennial of 1789. McNeill, William H. & Pinkney, David H., eds. (Modern European History Ser.). 312p. 1987. lib. bdg. 15.00 (0-8240-8039-4) Garland.
Nelms, Henning. Magic & Showmanship: A Handbook for Conjurers. LC 68-58047. (Orig.). 1969. pap. 6.95 (0-486-22337-X) Dover.
— Only an Orphan Girl. 1944. pap. 4.75 (0-8222-0855-5) Dramatists Play.
— A Primer of Stagecraft. 1941. pap. 5.95 (0-8222-0914-4) Dramatists Play.
— Scene Design: A Guide to the Stage. LC 74-25249. (Illus.). 96p. 1975. reprint ed. pap. 5.95 (0-486-23153-4) Dover.
— Thinking with a Pencil. (Illus.). 368p. 1986. pap. 14.95 (0-89815-052-3) Ten Speed Pr.
Nelms, I., ed. Fashion & Clothing Technology. (C). 1976. 65.00 (0-7175-0682-7, Pub. by S Thornes Pubs UK) St Mut.
Nelms, R. M., ed. see De Doncker, R. W., et al.
Nelsen, Brent F. The State Offshore: Petroleum, Politics, & State Intervention on the British & Norwegian Continental Shelves. LC 90-21037. 272p. 1991. text ed. 59.95 (0-275-93835-2, C3835, Praeger Pubs) Greenwood.
Nelsen, Brent F., ed. Norway & the European Community: The Political Economy of Integration. LC 92-45109. 264p. 1993. text ed. 57.95 (0-275-94211-2, C4211, Praeger Pubs) Greenwood.
Nelsen, Jan L., jt. auth. see Nelsen, Marjorie R.
Nelsen, Jane. Positive Discipline. 1987. pap. 10.00 (0-345-34856-7, Ballantine Trade) Ballantine.
— Positive Discipline. 2nd ed. LC 87-91180. 242p. 1987. pap. 7.95 (0-9606896-1-3) Sunrise Pr.
— Positive Discipline for Preschoolers: A Practical Guide to Raising Preschoolers. 1994. pap. 12.95 (1-55958-497-1) Prima Pub.
— Understanding: Eliminating Stress & Finding Serenity in Life & Relationships. LC 85-63353. 141p. 1986. pap. 8.95 (0-9606896-2-1) Sunrise Pr.
Nelsen, Jane & Glenn, H. Stephen. Time Out: A Guide for Parents & Teachers Using Popular Discipline Methods to Empower & Encourage Children. 2nd ed. Erwin, Cheryl, ed. 111p. 1992. pap. 6.95 (0-9606896-8-0, B105) Sunrise Pr.
Nelsen, Jane & Lott, Lynn. I'm on Your Side: Resolving Conflict with Your Teenage Son or Daughter. 304p. 1991. pap. 9.95 (1-55958-059-3) Prima Pub.
Nelsen, Jane, jt. auth. see Glenn, H. Stephen.
Nelsen, Jane, et al. Clean & Sober Parenting: A Guide to Help Recovering Parents Rebuild Trust, Create Structure & Routine from Chaos, Improve Communication & Share Feelings, Learn Parenting Skills, & Give up Guilt & Shame. 275p. (Orig.). 1992. pap. 10.95 (1-55958-165-4) Prima Pub.
— Positive Discipline A-Z. 350p. (Orig.). 1993. pap. 14.95 (1-55958-312-6) Prima Pub.
— Positive Discipline for Single Parents: A Practical Guide to Raising Children Who Are Responsible, Respectful, & Resourceful. LC 93-17738. 1993. pap. 10.95 (1-55958-355-X) Prima Pub.
— Positive Discipline in the Classroom: How to Effectively Use Class Meetings & Other Positive Discipline Strategies. 175p. (Orig.). 1993. pap. 14.95 (1-55958-311-8) Prima Pub.
Nelsen, Jane T., ed. A Prairie Populist: The Memoirs of Luna Kellie. LC 91-41361. (Singular Lives: The Iowa Series in North American Autobiography). (Illus.). 209p. 1992. text ed. 25.95x (0-87745-368-3); pap. 11.95 (0-87745-369-1) U of Iowa Pr.
Nelsen, John & Law, Scott. Alco RSD Seven & Fifteen. Hundman, Robert L. & Lee, Cathy H., eds. (Dataseries Ser.). (Illus.). 100p. 1988. 14.50 (0-945434-09-X) Hundman Pub.
Nelsen, Judith C. Communication Theory & Social Work Practice. LC 79-20361. 1980. lib. bdg. 12.50 (0-226-57151-3) U Ch Pr.
Nelsen, Karen. Books by Kids! Helping Young Children Create Their Own Books. (J). (gr. k-3). 1993. pap. 9.99 (0-86653-930-1) Fearon Teach Aids.

N

An Asterisk (*) at the beginning of an entry indicates that the title is appearing in BIP for the first time.

Nelsen, Marjorie R. & Nelsen, Jan L. Peak with Books: An Early Childhood Resource Guide. 2nd rev. ed. (Illus.). 228p. 1991. 19.95 (*0-9630495-1-8*) Partners in Learn.

Nelsen, Philip T., jt. ed. see Hampton, Robert G.

Nelsen, Rodney, ed. see Westheimer, Mary.

Nelsen, Roger B. Proofs Without Words: Exercises in Visual Thinking. LC 93-86338. (Classroom Resource Materials Ser.). 160p. (Orig.). 1993. pap. 29.50 (*0-88385-700-6*) Math Assn.

Nelsen, William C. Renewal of the Teacher-Scholar: Faculty Development in the Liberal Arts College. LC 82-135931. 116p. (Orig.). reprint ed. pap. 33.10 (*0-7837-1649-4*, 2041946) Bks Demand.

Nelsen, William C. & Siegel, Michael E., eds. Effective Approaches to Faculty Development. LC 79-93173. 159p. (Orig.). reprint ed. pap. 45.40 (*0-7837-1647-8*, 2041941) Bks Demand.

Nelson. Advanced Run Book. (Runner's World Ser.). 1983. 10.95 (*0-02-499480-4*) Macmillan.

— Current Therapy in Neonatal-Peri. 3rd ed. 544p. Date not set. 83.00 (*1-55664-382-9*) Mosby Yr Bk.

— Current Therapy in Neonatal-Perinatal Medicine. 2nd ed. 506p. 1990. 83.00 (*1-55664-070-6*) Mosby Yr Bk.

— Current Therapy in Pediatric Infectious Disease. 2nd ed. 386p. (C). 1988. 52.00 (*1-55664-038-2*) Mosby Yr Bk.

— Current Therapy in Pediatric Infectious Diseases. 3rd ed. 448p. 1993. 79.00 (*1-55664-349-7*) Mosby Yr Bk.

— Environmental Emergencies. 1985. pap. text ed. 30.95 (*0-7216-1163-X*) Saunders.

— Gas Mixtures: Preparation & Control. 1992. 75.00 (*0-87371-298-6*, T) Lewis Pubs.

— Mechanical Trades Pocket Manual. (Orig.). 1986. 10.95 (*0-02-588660-6*) Macmillan.

— NDE Near Death Experiences. 177p. 1995. 14.95 (*1-55517-160-5*) CFI Dist.

— Principles & Practice of Neuropathology. 528p. 1993. 119.00 (*0-8016-6456-X*) Mosby Yr Bk.

— Pulmonary Development: Transition from Intrauterine to Extrauterine Life. (Lung Biology in Health & Disease Ser.: Vol. 27). 536p. 1985. 170.00 (*0-8247-7316-0*) Dekker.

— Understanding Cardiology. 1991. write for info. (*0-8151-6347-9*, Yr Bk Med Pubs) Mosby Yr Bk.

Nelson & Beckel. Nursing Care Plans for the Pediatric Patient. 400p. 1987. pap. text ed. 29.95 (*0-8016-3909-3*) Mosby Yr Bk.

Nelson & Catalano, Robert A. Atlas of Ocular Motility. 256p. 1989. text ed. 121.00 (*0-7216-2628-9*) Saunders.

Nelson, jt. auth. see Blauvelt.

Nelson, et al. Pediatric Ophthalmology. 3rd ed. (Illus.). 544p. 1991. text ed. 138.00 (*0-7216-2599-1*) Saunders.

— Proceedings of the Winter Simulation Conference, 1991. 1262p. 1991. 150.00 (*0-685-66846-0*, WSC-91) Soc Computer Sim.

— Transport Theory, Invariant Imbedding, & Integral Equations: Proceedings in Honor of G. M. Wing's 65th Birthday. (Lecture Notes in Pure & Applied Mathematics Ser.: Vol. 115). 480p. 1989. 160.00 (*0-8247-8158-9*) Dekker.

***Nelson, et al, eds.** Delaware 1782 Tax Assessment & Census List. 270p. 1994. text ed. 31.00 (*1-887061-04-5*) DE Geneal Soc.

Nelson, A. A Long Hard Day on the Ranch. (Illus.). 24p. (J). (ps-8). 1989. pap. 4.95 (*0-88753-184-9*, Pub. by Black Moss Pr CN) Firefly Bks Ltd.

Nelson, A. M., jt. auth. see Parker, W. S.

Nelson, A. Thomas & Miller, Paul B. Modern Management Accounting. 2nd ed. LC 80-23023. 589p. reprint ed. pap. 167.90 (*0-7837-6549-5*, 2045686) Bks Demand.

Nelson, A. Tom & Miller, Paul W. Modern Management Accounting. 2nd ed. (C). 1981. text ed. 35.50 (*0-673-16115-3*) HarpCollege.

***Nelson, Adie & Robinson, Barrie W.** Gigolos & Madames Bountiful: Illusions of Gender, Power & Intimacy. 344p. 1994. 24.95 (*0-8020-0613-2*) U of Toronto Pr.

Nelson, Al P., jt. auth. see Keating, Lawrence A.

Nelson, Alan. Five-Minute Ministry: Ten Simple Principles for You to Make a Difference. LC 93-15177. 144p. (Orig.). 1994. pap. 8.99 (*0-8010-6790-1*) Baker Bk.

Nelson, Alan, ed. Cambridge. (Records of Early English Drama Ser.). 1100p. 1989. 175.00 (*0-8020-5751-9*) U of Toronto Pr.

Nelson, Alan H. Early Cambridge Theatres: College, University, & Town Stages, 1464-1720. LC 93-31690. (Illus.). 185p. (C). 1994. 59.95 (*0-521-43177-8*) Cambridge U Pr.

Nelson, Alan H., ed. see Medwall, Henry.

Nelson, Albert J. Emerging Influentials in State Legislatures: Women, Blacks, & Hispanics. LC 91-8604. 168p. 1991. text ed. 45.00 (*0-275-93829-8*, C3829, Praeger Pubs) Greenwood.

Nelson, Alfred L., et al, eds. The Adelphi Calendar Project, 1806-1850: Sans Pareil Theatre 1806-1819 - Adelphi Theatre 1819-1850. LC 89-11968. (London Stage 1800-1900 Ser.: No. 1). 248p. 1990. 195.00 (*0-313-25882-1*, DUG/, Greenwood Pr) Greenwood.

— The Adelphi Theatre Calendar: The Adelphi Calendar Project 1806-1900 - the Adelphi Theatre 1850-1900, Pt. II. LC 89-11968. (London Stage, 1800-1900 - a Documentary Record & Calendar of Performances Ser.). 296p. 1993. 225.00 (*0-313-28882-8*, GR8882) Greenwood.

Nelson, Alice B. Four Ducks on a Pond. vi, 92p. 1983. reprint ed. 11.95 (*0-911570-19-5*) Vermont Bks.

Nelson, Alice J. Virginia Lineages, Letters & Memories. (Illus.). x, 302p. 21.50 (*0-9614497-0-5*) A J Nelson.

Nelson, Alice R. The Goodness of St. Rocque & Other Stories. LC 73-18594. reprint ed. 32.50 (*0-404-11405-9*) AMS Pr.

Nelson, Alvar. Responses to Crime: An Introduction to Swedish Criminal Law & Administration. Getz, Jerome L., tr. (New York University Criminal Law Education & Research Center Monograph: No. 6). vi, 90p. 1972. pap. text ed. 8.50 (*0-8377-0900-8*) Rothman.

Nelson, Alvin F. Inquiry & Reality: A Discourse in Pragmatic Synthesis. LC 75-46077. 192p. reprint ed. pap. 54.80 (*0-317-09210-3*, 2021573) Bks Demand.

Nelson, Andrew. Modern Reader's Japanese-English Character Dictionary. 2nd rev. ed. LC 61-11973. 1110p. (ENG & JPN.). 1962. 49.95 (*0-8048-0408-7*) C E Tuttle.

Nelson, Andrew, jt. auth. see Solomon, Brian.

Nelson, Anita, illus. Loon & Deer Were Traveling: A Story of the Upper Skagit. LC 92-5450. (Adventures in Storytelling Ser.). 24p. (J). (ps-3). 1992. lib. bdg. 13.95 (*0-516-05140-7*); pap. 5.95 (*0-516-45140-5*) Childrens.

Nelson, Anita, jt. illus. see Schoonover, pat.

Nelson, Anita, jt. illus. see Schoonover, Pat.

Nelson, Anita, jt. illus. see Thiewes, Sam.

Nelson, Anna K., ed. see Kennan, George F.

Nelson, Annabel, jt. auth. see Behrens, Laurence.

Nelson, Annabelle. How to Focus the Distractible Child. LC 85-61724. 110p. (Orig.). 1986. pap. text ed. 8.95 (*0-88247-747-1*) R & E Pubs.

— The Learning Wheel: Ideas & Activities for Multicultural & Holistic Lesson Planning. LC 93-27890. 1994. 30.00 (*0-913705-91-8*) Zephyr Pr AZ.

— Living the Wheel: Working with Emotion, Terror & Bliss Through Imagery. (Illus.). 208p. (Orig.). 1993. pap. 10. 95 (*0-87728-782-1*) Weiser.

Nelson, Annie G. After the Storm. LC 76-14493. 131p. 1976. reprint ed. 10.00 (*0-87152-243-8*) Reprint.

— The Dawn Appears. LC 76-18799. 135p. 1976. reprint ed. 10.00 (*0-87152-244-6*) Reprint.

— Don't Walk on My Dreams. LC 76-18308. (Illus.). 121p. 1976. reprint ed. 10.00 (*0-87152-245-4*) Reprint.

Nelson, Annika M., illus. Folk Wisdom of Mexico - Proverbios y Dichos Mexicanos. LC 93-30338. 80p. (ENG & SPA.). 1994. 9.95 (*0-8118-0513-1*) Chronicle Bks.

Nelson, Anson & Nelson, Fanny. Memorials of Sarah Childress Polk: Wife of the Eleventh President of the United States. LC 73-22435. (Illus.). 322p. 1974. reprint ed. 20.00 (*0-87152-163-6*) Reprint.

— Sarah Childress Polk: Wife of the 11th President of the United States. LC 93-74429. (Signature Ser.). (Illus.). 284p. 1994. reprint ed. 30.00 (*0-945707-07-X*) Amer Political.

Nelson, Antonya. The Expendables. 208p. 1992. pap. 8.00 (*0-380-71452-3*) Avon.

— The Expendables. LC 89-31444. (Flannery O'Connor Award for Short Fiction Ser.). 208p. 1990. 19.95 (*0-8203-1156-1*) U of Ga Pr.

— Family Terrorists: Seven Stories & a Novella. LC 93-45826. 1994. 19.95 (*0-395-68679-2*) HM.

— In the Land of Men. 240p. 1993. reprint ed. pap. 8.00 (*0-380-71488-4*) Avon.

— In the Land of Men: Stories. braille ed. 430p. 1994. text ed. 34.40 (*1-56956-505-8*, BR9446) W A T Braille.

Nelson, Ardel E., jt. auth. see Gilbert, G. Ronald.

Nelson, Ardis. Cabrera Infante in the Menippean Tradition. Lathrop, Thomas et al, eds. 123p. Date not set. 15.75 (*0-936388-20-X*); pap. 10.75 (*0-936388-15-3*) Juan de la Cuesta.

Nelson, Arlene J. Accounts, Designs & Roses. (Teachings of the Master, Sinat Schirah "Suggestions for Learning" Ser.). 240p. (Orig.). 1988. pap. 12.95 (*0-685-26083-6*, TXU 307-298) Loveline Prodns.

— Placements. (Teachings of the Master, Sinat Schirah, "Suggestions for Learning" Ser.). 200p. (Orig.). 1988. pap. 9.95 (*0-685-26084-4*, TXU 309-553) Loveline Prodns.

Nelson, Arlene J., ed. Teachings of the Master Sinat Schirah: "Suggestions for Learning" 240p. (Orig.). 1988. pap. 12.95 (*0-685-45297-2*) Loveline Prodns.

***Nelson, Arthur C.** System Development Charges for Water, Wastewater, & Stormwater Facilities. LC 94-23520. 176p. 1995. 59.95 (*1-56670-037-X*, L1037) Lewis Pubs.

Nelson, Arthur C., ed. Development Impact Fees. LC 88-70565. (Illus.). 389p. 1988. pap. 34.95 (*0-685-19734-4*) Planners Pr.

Nelson, Arthur C., jt. auth. see Knaap, Gerrit.

Nelson, Arthur C., et al. Growth Management Principles & Practices. LC 94-70284. (Illus.). 250p. (Orig.). 1995. lib. bdg. 49.00 (*0-918286-93-X*); pap. 39.95 (*0-918286-92-1*) Planners Pr.

Nelson, Arty. Technicolor Pulp. 224p. 1995. 18.95 (*0-446-51819-0*) Warner Bks.

Nelson, B. A. Coming Triumph of Mexican Irredentism. 24p. 1984. pap. 2.00 (*0-936247-01-0*) Amer Immigration.

***Nelson, Barbara.** Igniting the Flame: Clinical Pastoral Education for Nurses. xvii, 164p. (C). 1995. pap. 14.95 (*1-55605-258-8*) Wyndhall Pr.

— Summer of Rescue. LC 93-80393. 270p. 1994. 18.95 (*1-878448-58-7*) MacMurray & Beck.

— Summer of Rescue: A Novel. LC 95-1262. 1995. 11.00 (*0-684-80114-0*, Scribners) S&S Trade.

Nelson, Barbara, jt. auth. see Timpson, William.

Nelson, Barbara J. Making an Issue of Child Abuse: Political Agenda Setting for Social Problems. LC 83-18044. xiv, 170p. 1986. pap. text ed. 10.95 (*0-226-57201-3*) U Ch Pr.

Nelson, Barbara J. & Chowdhury, Najma, eds. Women & Politics Worldwide. LC 93-28668. 832p. (C). 1994. 55. 00 (*0-300-05407-6*); pap. 25.00 (*0-300-05408-4*) Yale U Pr.

Nelson, Barbara J., jt. auth. see Evans, Sara M.

Nelson, Barbara N., jt. auth. see Evans, Sara M.

Nelson, Barbara W. The Share Rental Survival Guide: Open Your Door to Fun & Profit. (Orig.). 1989. write for info. (*0-318-63724-3*) Mediawrite.

Nelson, Barry. Country-Western Dancing. (Illus.). 72p. (Orig.). 1993. pap. 6.95 (*0-911007-29-6*) Prairie Hse.

***Nelson, Barry L.** Stochastic Modeling: Analysis & Simulation. (Industrial Engineering & Management Science Ser.). 1995. text ed. 46.00 (*0-07-046213-5*) McGraw.

Nelson, Becky, ed. see Allen, Loyd.

Nelson, Becky, ed. see Bates, Beverly.

Nelson, Becky, ed. see Bolton, Joy.

Nelson, Becky, ed. see Brown, Pam.

Nelson, Becky, ed. see Browning, James.

Nelson, Becky, ed. see Butler, Cathy.

Nelson, Becky, ed. see Clendinning, Monte M.

Nelson, Becky, ed. see Climer, Ron.

Nelson, Becky, ed. see Crim, Lottie & McAlister, Katsy.

Nelson, Becky, ed. see Dean, Jennifer K.

Nelson, Becky, ed. see Dickson, Charles.

Nelson, Becky, ed. see Dixon, Michael C.

Nelson, Becky, ed. see Dockrey, Karen.

Nelson, Becky, ed. see Edwards, Judy.

Nelson, Becky, ed. see Harris, Doris.

Nelson, Becky, ed. see Howard, David.

Nelson, Becky, ed. see Marler, Malcolm.

Nelson, Becky, ed. see Parham, Robert.

Nelson, Becky, ed. see Serratt, Mary L.

Nelson, Becky, ed. see Smith, Melanie.

Nelson, Becky, ed. see Sutton, Jan, et al.

Nelson, Becky, ed. see Taylor, Larry & O'Brien, Dellanna.

Nelson, Becky, ed. see Taylor, Laurie.

Nelson, Becky, ed. see Wood, Randy.

Nelson, Ben A., jt. ed. see Wait, Walter K.

Nelson, Benjamin. Monarch Notes on Tennessee Williams' Major Plays. (Orig.). (C). pap. 3.95 (*0-671-00650-9*, Arco Test) P-H Gen Ref & Trav.

— On the Roads to Modernity - Conscience, Science, & Civilizations: Selected Writings. Huff, Toby E., ed. LC 79-21321. 340p. 1981. 41.00 (*0-8476-6209-8*) Rowman.

— Tennessee Williams. 1961. 20.00 (*0-8392-1111-2*) Astor-Honor.

Nelson, Benjamin, ed. Freud & the Twentieth Century. 11. 25 (*0-8446-2097-1*) Peter Smith.

Nelson, Bernie. Mind Control Wars: They Promise Immortality Using New Human-Alien Technologies That Could Trigger the Apocalypse. LC 94-77607. 240p. (Orig.). 1995. pap. 12.95 (*0-9641923-0-6*) Lightword Pubng.

Nelson, Beth. George Crabbe & the Progress of Eighteenth-Century Narrative Verse. LC 75-5147. 189p. 1976. 18.00 (*0-8387-1736-5*) Bucknell U Pr.

Nelson, Betty P. Private Knowledge. 256p. 1993. pap. 11.95 (*0-312-09897-9*) St Martin.

— Pursuit of Bliss. 288p. 1992. 18.95 (*0-312-08169-3*) St Martin.

— Pursuit of Bliss. 360p. 1994. pap. 10.95 (*0-312-11049-9*) St Martin.

— Uncertain April. LC 94-2666. 1994. 20.95 (*0-312-11086-3*) St Martin.

— Uncertain April. 336p. 1994. 20.95 (*0-312-11084-7*) St Martin.

— The Weight of Light. 320p. 1993. pap. 12.95 (*0-312-09936-3*) St Martin.

Nelson, Bill. Implementing Standards of Good Behavior. LC 79-11414. 53p. 1979. pap. 3.75 (*0-934332-15-0*) LEpervier Pr.

— Tex Watson: The Man the Madness the Manipulation. 256p. (Orig.). 1991. pap. 10.95 (*0-9629084-0-1*) Pen Power.

Nelson, Blake. Girl. 1994. pap. 11.00 (*0-671-89707-1*, Touchstone Bks) S&S Trade.

Nelson, Bob. One Thousand One Ways to Reward Employees. (Illus.). 192p. (Orig.). 1993. pap. 7.95 (*1-56305-339-X*, 3339) Workman Pub.

***Nelson, Bob, ed.** Sagas of the Central Coast: History from the Pages of Central Coast Magazine. (Illus.). 128p. (Orig.). 1995. pap. 14.95 (*0-9646930-0-3*) R J Nelson.

— Santa Maria Style Barbecue Cookbook: Favorite Recipes from California's Central Coast. (Illus.). 120p. (Orig.). Date not set. pap. 14.95 (*0-9646930-1-1*) R J Nelson.

Nelson, Bonnie E. Science & Computer Activities for Children 3 to 9 Years Old. 2nd rev. ed. (Illus.). 146p. (J). (gr. k-3). 1988. 28.00 (*0-931642-21-3*) Lintel.

***Nelson, Bonnie F.** Mabel's Cats. (J). 1995. 7.95 (*0-533-11261-3*) Vantage.

Nelson, Bonnie R. A Guide to Published Library Catalogs. LC 81-16558. 358p. 1982. 27.50 (*0-8108-1477-3*) Scarecrow.

Nelson, Brent A. America Balkanized: Immigration's Challenge to Government. LC 94-4306. 1994. 10.00 (*0-936247-14-2*) Amer Immigration.

— Assimilation: The Ideal & the Reality. 27p. 1987. pap. 3.00 (*0-936247-07-X*) Amer Immigration.

Nelson, Brent F. & Stubb, Alexander C-G., eds. The European Union: Readings on the Theory & Practice of European Integration. LC 94-19158. 312p. (C). 1994. lib. bdg. 49.50 (*1-55587-505-X*); pap. text ed. 19.95 (*1-55587-506-8*) Lynne Rienner.

Nelson, Brian. Western Political Thought: From Theory & Ideology. 352p. (C). 1982. text ed. write for info. (*0-13-951640-9*) P-H.

Nelson, Brian, ed. Naturalism in the European Novel: Critical Essays. LC 91-19724. (European Studies Ser.). 288p. 1992. 54.95 (*0-85496-627-7*) Berg Pubs.

Nelson, Brian, jt. auth. see Giono, Jean.

Nelson, Brian, ed. see Llobera, Josep R.

Nelson, Brian, tr. see Zola, Emile.

Nelson, Brian, et al, eds. The European Community in the Nineteen Nineties: Economics, Politics, Defence. (International Issues - Questions Internationales Ser.). 246p. 1992. 46.75 (*0-85496-758-3*) Berg Pubs.

— The Idea of Europe: Problems of National & Transnational Identity. (European Studies Ser.). 192p. 1992. 39.95 (*0-85496-757-5*) Berg Pubs.

***Nelson, Brian R.** Western Political Thought: From Socrates to the Age of Ideology. 2nd ed. LC 94-48427. 1995. text ed. write for info. (*0-13-191172-4*) P-H.

Nelson, Brian W., jt. auth. see Zucker, William V.

Nelson, Bruce. Workers on the Waterfront: Seamen, Longshoremen, & Unionism in the 1930s. LC 87-28749. 384p. 1990. pap. 11.95 (*0-252-06144-6*) U of Ill Pr.

Nelson, Bruce, ed. Portland: A Collection of 19th Century Engravings. (Illus.). 1976. pap. 6.95 (*0-9600612-6-6*) Greater Portland.

Nelson, Bruce & Nelson, Dwight. And What Do You Do? Biblical Perspectives on Vocation & Work. 1984. pap. 1.95 (*0-910452-54-7*) Covenant.

Nelson, Bruce, jt. auth. see Zimmerman, David.

Nelson, Bruce C. Beyond the Martyrs: A Social History of Chicago's Anarchists, 1870-1900. (Class & Culture Ser.). 352p. (C). 1988. text ed. 40.00 (*0-8135-1344-8*); pap. text ed. 15.00 (*0-8135-1345-6*) Rutgers U Pr.

***Nelson, Bruce L.** Hunting Big Whitetails: Tactics Guaranteed to Make You a More Successful Whitetail Hunter. (Illus.). 272p. (Orig.). 1995. pap. 17.95 (*0-9645972-8-4*) Buck Pubng.

Nelson, Bruce W., ed. Environmental Framework of Coastal Plain Estuaries. LC 71-187849. (Geological Society of America, Memoir Ser.: No. 133). 640p. reprint ed. pap. 180.00 (*0-317-29121-1*, 2025027) Bks Demand.

Nelson, Bryan. The Gannet. LC 78-57690. (Illus.). 1978. 30. 00 (*0-931130-01-8*) Harrell Bks.

— The Gannet. 1989. pap. 25.00 (*0-7478-0018-9*, Pub. by Shire UK) St Mut.

— Living with Seabirds. (Island Biology Ser.: Vol. 2). (Illus.). 240p. 1987. 25.00 (*0-85224-523-8*, Pub. by Edinburgh U Pr UK) Col U Pr.

Nelson, Bryce E. Good Schools: The Seattle Public School System, 1901-1930. LC 88-6916. (Illus.). 192p. 1988. 20. 00 (*0-295-96668-8*) U of Wash Pr.

Nelson, Buck. My Trip to Mars, the Moon & Venus. 33p. 1988. reprint ed. spiral bd. 5.50 (*0-7873-1199-5*) Mokelumne.

Nelson, Burrell E. Vascular Plants of the Medicine Bow Mountains, Wyoming. rev. ed. 393p. 1984. pap. text ed. 12.00 (*0-936204-19-2*) Jelm Mtn.

***Nelson, Byron.** Byron Nelson: The Little Black Book: Anecdotes, Memories & Lessons on the 50th Anniversary of One Man's Greatest Year in Golf. LC 95-15760. 1995. write for info. (*1-56530-180-3*) Summit TX.

— Byron Nelson's Winning Golf. limited ed. 192p. 1992. reprint ed. 50.00 (*0-87833-021-6*) Taylor Pub.

— Byron Nelson's Winning Golf. 192p. 1992. reprint ed. 18. 95 (*0-87833-800-4*); reprint ed. pap. 9.95 (*0-87833-801-2*) Taylor Pub.

— How I Played the Game. 1994. mass mkt. 9.95 (*0-440-50637-9*) Dell.

— How I Played the Game. LC 92-37339. 304p. 1993. 19.95 (*0-87833-819-5*) Taylor Pub.

— Our Home Forever: The Hupa Indians of Northern California. LC 88-1213. (Illus.). 224p. 1988. reprint ed. pap. 9.95 (*0-935704-47-7*) Howe Brothers.

Nelson, Byron & Dennis, Larry. Shape Your Swing the Modern Way. rev. ed. (Classics of Golf Ser.). (Illus.). 126p. 1985. 28.00 (*0-940889-06-4*) Classics Golf.

Nelson, C., jt. ed. see Gunnar, M. R.

Nelson, C. Donald. Practical Procedures for Children with Language Disorders: Preschool-Adolescence. LC 90-32276. 94p. 1991. pap. text ed. 14.00 (*0-89079-235-6*, 3503) Buttrwrth-Heinemann.

Nelson, C. Ellis. Congregations: Their Power to Form & Transform. LC 87-35252. 264p. 1988. pap. 14.99 (*0-8042-1601-0*, John Knox) Westminster John Knox.

— Helping Teenagers Grow Morally: A Guide for Adults. 128p. (Orig.). 1992. pap. 11.99 (*0-664-25305-9*) Westminster John Knox.

— How Faith Matures. 252p. 1989. pap. 14.99 (*0-8042-0750-X*) Westminster John Knox.

— Where Faith Begins. 1984. pap. 9.99 (*0-8042-1471-9*, John Knox) Westminster John Knox.

Nelson, C. Hans & Nilsen, Tor H. Modern & Ancient Deep Sea Fan Sedimentation. (Short Course Notes Ser.: No. 14). 404p. 1984. pap. 38.00 (*0-918985-41-2*) SEPM.

Nelson, C. J., jt. ed. see McDonald, M. B., Jr.

Nelson, C. Michael & Pearson, Cheryll A. Integrating Services for Children & Youth With Emotional & Behavioral Disorders, No. 1. (Current Issues in Special Education Ser.). 206p. (Orig.). (C). 1991. pap. text ed. 25.00 (*0-86586-218-4*, P364) Coun Exc Child.

Nelson, C. Michael, jt. auth. see Kerr, Mary M.

Nelson, C. Michael, et al. Special Education in the Criminal Justice System. 352p. (C). 1987. pap. write for info. (*0-675-20477-1*, Merrill Pub Co) Macmillan.

Nelson, C. R., ed. Chemistry of Coal Weathering. (Coal Science & Technology Ser.: Vol. 14). 1989. 141.00 (*0-444-88088-7*, CST 14) Elsevier.

Nelson, C. Robert, jt. auth. see Ewen, Dale.

Nelson, Candice J., jt. auth. see Magleby, David B.

Nelson, Candice J., jt. ed. see Thurber, James A.

Nelson, Carl. Devotions for the Alcoholic Christian. Sherer, Michael, ed. (Orig.). 1988. pap. 5.00 (*1-55673-033-0*, 8817) CSS OH.

— Orchestral Studies, Vol. 1. Date not set. pap. 8.95 (*0-685-69110-1*, Pub. by Wilhelm Hansen DK) Music Sales.

N

An Asterisk (*) at the beginning of an entry indicates that the title is appearing in BIP for the first time.

— Protecting the Past from Natural Disasters. (Illus.). 192p. (Orig.). 1991. pap. 14.95 (*0-89133-178-6*) Preservation Pr.

Nelson, Carl A. Global Success: International Business Tactics for the 1990's. 1990. 27.95 (*0-8306-3506-8*) TAB Bks.

— Import - Export: How to Get Started in International Trade. 1989. pap. text ed. 14.95 (*0-07-156008-4*) McGraw.

— Import-Export: How to Profit in International Trade. 228p. 1989. pap. 14.95 (*0-8306-4052-5*, Liberty Hse) TAB Bks.

— Import/Export: How to Get Started in International Trade. 2nd ed. LC 95-16132. 1995. pap. write for info. (*0-07-046276-3*) McGraw.

— Managing Globally: A Complete Guide to Competing Worldwide. 320p. 1993. 65.00 (*0-7863-0121-X*) Irwin Prof Pubng.

— Mechanical Trades Pocket Manual. 3rd ed. 364p. (Orig.). 1990. pap. 14.95 (*0-02-588665-7*) Macmillan.

— Millwrights & Mechanics Guide. 4th ed. 1040p. 1989. text ed. 31.00 (*0-02-588591-X*) Macmillan.

***Nelson, Carletta L.** Marriages of Alleghany County, Virginia, 1822 - 1872. 508p. (Orig.). 1994. pap. text ed. 35.00 (*0-7884-0038-X*) Heritage Bk.

Nelson, Carlos I., jt. auth. see Mulvaney, Rebekah M.

Nelson, Carol. How to Market Women. 1994. pap. 19.95 (*0-8103-9484-7*) Gale.

— Integrated Advertising: How to Make Image Advertising & Direct Response Work Together for Bigger Profits. 213p. 1992. 34.95 (*0-85013-218-5*) Dartnell Corp.

Nelson, Carol, ed. Women's Market Handbook. 400p. 1993. 64.95 (*0-8103-9139-2*, 101791) Gale.

Nelson, Carol, jt. auth. see Musser, Charles.

Nelson, Carol F., jt. auth. see Nelson, Horace G.

Nelson, Carolyn. Basic Skills Nursery Rhymes Workbook. (Basic Skills Workbooks). 32p. (gr. k-1). 1983. 1.98 (*0-8209-0565-8*, EEW-6) ESP.

Nelson, Carolyn & Seccombe, Matthew, eds. British Newspapers & Periodicals, 1641-1700: A Short-Title Catalogue of Serials Printed in England, Scotland, Ireland & British America. LC 86-33171. xx, 724p. 1988. 300.00 (*0-87352-174-9*) Modern Lang.

Nelson, Cary. Our Last First Poets: Vision & History in Contemporary American Poetry. LC 81-5082. 239p. reprint ed. pap. 68.20 (*0-317-28191-7*, 2022783) Bks Demand.

— Our Last First Poets: Vision & History in Contemporary American Poetry. LC 81-5082. 240p. 1984. reprint ed. pap. 11.95 (*0-252-01140-6*) U of Ill Pr.

— Repression & Recovery: Modern American Poetry & the Politics of Cultural Memory, 1910-1945. LC 89-40264. (Wisconsin Project on American Writers Ser.). (Illus.). 256p. 1989. text ed. 24.95 (*0-299-12340-5*) U of Wis Pr.

— Repression & Recovery: Modern American Poetry & the Politics of Cultural Memory, 1910-1945. LC 89-40264. (Wisconsin Project on American Writers Ser.). (Illus.). 352p. (C). 1992. reprint ed. pap. 15.95 (*0-299-12344-8*) U of Wis Pr.

Nelson, Cary, ed. Theory in the Classroom. LC 85-16531. 288p. 1986. pap. 13.95 (*0-252-01471-5*) U of Ill Pr.

Nelson, Cary & Folsom, Ed, eds. W. S. Merwin: Essays on the Poetry. LC 85-24531. (Illus.). 424p. 1987. 27.50 (*0-252-01277-1*) U of Ill Pr.

Nelson, Cary & Grossberg, Lawrence, eds. Marxism & the Interpretation of Culture. LC 87-5981. 752p. 1988. 39.95 (*0-252-01108-2*); pap. 18.95 (*0-252-01401-4*) U of Ill Pr.

Nelson, Cary & Hendricks, Jefferson. Edwin Rolfe: A Biographical Essay & Guide to the Rolfe Archive at the University of Illinois at Urbana-Champaign. (Illus.). 124p. 1990. 24.95 (*0-252-01794-3*); pap. 11.95 (*0-252-06179-9*) U of Ill Pr.

Nelson, Cary, jt. ed. see Berube, Michael.

Nelson, Cary, ed. see Merwin, W. S.

Nelson, Cary, ed. see Rolfe, Edwin.

Nelson, Catherine C. Mary's Invisible Friend. LC 94-60717. (Illus.). 44p. (J). (gr. k-4). 1995. 6.95 (*1-55523-710-X*) Winston-Derek.

Nelson, Cathy. Being Grown up Is Not What I Thought! (Coralville Capers Ser.). (Illus.). 28p. (Orig.). (J). (gr. 1-3). 1994. pap. 6.00 (*0-9637845-0-1*) Thumbprnt Pub.

Nelson-Cave, Wendy. Broadway Theatre Posters. (Illus.). 112p. 1993. 14.98 (*0-8317-5166-5*) Smithmark.

Nelson, Charles. The Boy Who Picked the Bullets Up. (Meadowland Ser.). 1988. pap. 7.95 (*0-317-68068-4*) Carol Pub Group.

— Boy Who Picked the Bullets Up. 1988. pap. 9.95 (*0-8216-2002-9*, Univ Books) Carol Pub Group.

— Panthers in the Skins of Men. 1989. pap. 9.95 (*0-8216-2006-1*, Univ Books) Carol Pub Group.

— The Trees of Ireland. (Illus.). 240p. 1993. 75.00 (*1-874675-24-4*, Pub. by Lilliput Pr Ltd IE); pap. 36.95 (*1-874675-25-2*, Pub. by Lilliput Pr Ltd IE) Irish Bks Media.

Nelson, Charles, ed. see Nelson, Mexico Mike.

Nelson, Charles, jt. illus. see Walsh, Wendy.

***Nelson, Charles A., ed.** Basic & Applied Perspectives on Learning, Cognition, & Development: The Minnesota Symposia on Child Psychology, Vol. 28. (Minnesota Symposia on Child Psychology Ser.). 250p. 1995. text ed. 40.00 (*0-8058-1833-2*) L Erlbaum Assocs.

— Memory & Affect in Development: The Minnesota Symposia on Child Psychology. (Minnesota Symposium on Child Psychology Ser.: Vol. 26). 288p. 1993. text ed. 49.95 (*0-8058-1261-X*) L Erlbaum Assocs.

— Threats to Optimal Development: Integrating Biological, Psychological, & Social Risk Factors: The Minnesota Symposia on Child Psychology, Vol. 29. (Minnesota Symposium on Child Psychology Ser.). 360p. 1994. text ed. 59.95 (*0-8058-1510-4*) L Erlbaum Assocs.

Nelson, Charles A. & Cavey, Robert D. Ethics, Leadership & the Bottom Line: An Executive Reader. 1991. pap. 22.50 (*0-88427-081-5*) North River.

Nelson, Charles G. Systems Programming with Modula-3. 288p. 1991. pap. text ed. 34.67 (*0-13-590464-1*, 260501) P-H.

***Nelson, Charles L.** The Book of the Knight Zifar: A Translation of El Libro del Cavallero Zifar. LC 82-21940. (Studies in Romance Languages: No. 27). reprint ed. pap. 93.50 (*0-7837-9585-8*, 2060334) Bks Demand.

Nelson, Charles R. Applied Time Series Analysis for Managerial Forecasting. LC 72-88942. 350p. 1973. text ed. 42.95 (*0-8162-6366-3*) Holden-Day.

— The Investor's Guide to Economic Indicators. 193p. 1989. pap. text ed. 14.95 (*0-471-51329-6*) Wiley.

Nelson, Charles W., jt. auth. see Keedy, Mervin L.

***Nelson, Christena.** Sharing the Articles of Faith: Child-Centered Learning Activities. (Illus.). (Orig.). 1994. pap. 6.95 (*0-87579-943-4*) Deseret Bk.

Nelson, Christena C. Gospel of Jesus Christ Can Bring Me Peace. (Illus.). 1993. pap. 6.95 (*0-87579-816-0*) Deseret Bk.

— Sharing Time for Special Occassions. (Illus.). 51p. 1993. pap. 6.95 (*0-87579-815-2*) Deseret Bk.

Nelson, Christina. Interior Decorating. Horn, Jan, ed. LC 92-70586. (Illus.). 112p. (Orig.). 1992. pap. 9.95 (*0-89721-245-2*, UPC 05971) Ortho Info.

Nelson, Christina H. Directly from China: Export Goods for the American Market, 1784-1930. (Orig.). 1985. pap. 15.00 (*0-87577-152-1*, Peabody Museum) Peabody Essex Mus.

Nelson, Christine A., jt. auth. see Pescar, Susan C.

Nelson, Christopher. Mapping the Civil War: Featuring Rare Maps from the Library of Congress. LC 92-17799. (Illus.). 1992. 39.95 (*1-56373-001-4*) Fulcrum Pub.

Nelson, Christopher, jt. auth. see Nelson, Roberta.

Nelson, Claudia. Boys Will Be Girls: The Feminine Ethic & British Children's Fiction, 1857-1917. LC 90-20004. (Illus.). 216p. (C). 1991. text ed. 35.00 (*0-8135-1681-1*) Rutgers U Pr.

— Invisible Men: Fatherhood in Victorian Periodicals, 1850-1910. LC 94-18033. 344p. 1995. 45.00 (*0-8203-1699-7*) U of Ga Pr.

Nelson, Claudia & Vallone, Lynne, eds. The Girl's Own: Cultural Histories of the Anglo-American Girl, 1830-1915. LC 93-29651. (Illus.). 304p. (C). 1994. 45.00 (*0-8203-1615-6*) U of Ga Pr.

Nelson, Clifford, ed. Pioneer Churchman: The Narrative & Journal of J. W. C. Dietrichson, 1844-1850. Kaasa, Harris & Rosholt, Malcolm, trs. 265p. 1973. 12.00 (*0-87732-053-5*) Norwegian-Am Hist Assn.

Nelson, Clifford A., tr. see Giertz, Bo.

Nelson, Cordner. Careers in Pro Sports. rev. ed. Rosen, Ruth, ed. LC 89-37641. (Careers in Depth Ser.). (Illus.). 143p. (YA). (gr. 7-12). 1992. lib. bdg. 14.95 (*0-8239-1456-9*) Rosen Group.

— Runners' World Advanced Running Book. 200p. (Orig.). 1983. pap. 10.95 (*0-89037-273-X*) Anderson World.

Nelson, Craig. Bad TV: The Very Best of the Very Worst. LC 94-14967. 1995. 9.95 (*0-385-31359-4*, Delta) Dell.

Nelson, Craig, ed. see National Security Archive Staff & Chadwyck-Healey Staff.

Nelson, Cyndi, jt. auth. see Miller, Millie.

Nelson, Cyril I. The Quilt Engagement Calendar 1995. (Illus.). 116p. 1994. 10.95 (*0-525-93595-9*, Viking Studio) Studio Bks.

Nelson, D. F., ed. Low Frequency Properties of Dielectric Crystals: Piezoelectric, Pyroelectric & Related Constants, Vol. 29. (Landolt-Boernstein Ser.). 450p. 1993. 1,275.00 (*0-387-55065-8*) Spr-Verlag.

Nelson, D. F., ed. see Every, A. G. & McCurdy, A. K.

Nelson, D. W., et al, eds. Chemical Mobility & Reactivity in Soil Systems. (Special Publication Ser.). 262p. 1983. pap. 12.00 (*0-89118-771-5*) Soil Sci Soc Am.

Nelson, Dalmas H. Administrative Agencies of the U. S. A. Their Decisions & Authority. LC 63-13433. (Wayne State University Studies: No. 15: Political Science). 352p. reprint ed. pap. 100.40 (*0-8357-5108-2*, 2027652) Bks Demand.

Nelson, Dan, jt. auth. see Judd, Ron.

Nelson, Dana. Gonzalo de Berceo y el "Alixandre" Vindicacion de un Estilo. (Spanish Ser.: No. 63). xi, 505p. (SPA.). 1991. 30.00 (*0-940639-57-2*) Hispanic Seminary.

— The Word in Black & White: Writing "Race" in American Literature, 1638-1867. 208p. 1992. 45.00 (*0-19-506592-1*) OUP.

Nelson, Dana, ed. see Rush, Rebecca.

Nelson, Dana D. The Word in Black & White: Reading "Race" in American Literature 1638-1867. 189p. 1994. reprint ed. pap. 13.95 (*0-19-508927-8*) OUP.

***Nelson, Danette L.** Genetic Connections: A Guide to Documenting Your Individual & Family Health History. LC 94-67892. (Illus.). 1995. text ed. 39.95 (*0-9639154-2-8*); pap. 34.95 (*0-9639154-3-6*) Sonters Pubng.

***Nelson, Danette L. & Waters, Cynthia V.** Genetic Connections: A Guide to Documenting Your Individual & Family Health History. Roerden, Chris et al, eds. LC 94-67892. (Illus.). 335p. 1995. 44.95 (*0-9639154-1-X*) Sonters Pubng.

Nelson, Daniel. American Rubber Workers & Organized Labor, 1900-1941. (Illus.). 520p. 1988. text ed. 49.50 (*0-691-04752-9*) Princeton U Pr.

— Farm & Factory in the Heartland: Work & Workers in the American Midwest, 1880 to 1990. LC 94-45185. (Midwestern History & Culture Ser.). 1995. write for info. (*0-253-32883-7*) Ind U Pr.

— Frederick W. Taylor & the Rise of Scientific Management. LC 79-5411. 288p. 1980. 29.50 (*0-299-08160-5*) U of Wis Pr.

— Managers & Workers: Origins of the New Factory System in the United States, 1880-1920. 246p. 1975. 32.50 (*0-299-06900-1*) U of Wis Pr.

— Managers & Workers: Origins of the New Factory System in the United States, 1880-1920. 246p. 1979. pap. 13.95 (*0-299-06904-4*) U of Wis Pr.

— Managers & Workers: Origins of the Twentieth-Century Factory System in the United States, 1880-1920. rev. ed. LC 95-6356. 1995. write for info. (*0-299-14880-7*); pap. write for info. (*0-299-14884-X*) U of Wis Pr.

— Unemployment Insurance: The American Experience, 1915-1935. (Illus.). 320p. 1969. 27.50 (*0-299-05200-1*) U of Wis Pr.

— Unemployment Insurance: The American Experience, 1915-1935. LC 69-16114. (Illus.). 323p. reprint ed. pap. 92.10 (*0-7837-1660-5*, 2041957) Bks Demand.

Nelson, Daniel, ed. A Mental Revolution: Scientific Management since Taylor. (Historical Perspectives on Business Enterprise Ser.). 248p. 1992. lib. bdg. 49.50 (*0-8142-0567-4*) Ohio St U Pr.

Nelson, Daniel M. The Priority of Prudence: Virtue & Natural Law in Thomas Aquinas & the Implications for Modern Ethics. 224p. 1992. text ed. 28.50 (*0-271-00778-8*) Pa St U Pr.

Nelson, Daniel N. Balkan Imbroglio: Politics & Security in Southeastern Europe. (C). 1991. pap. text ed. 33.50 (*0-8133-7956-3*) Westview.

— Democratic Centralism in Romania: A Study of Local Communist Politics. (East European Monographs: No. 69). 186p. 1980. text ed. 45.00 (*0-914710-63-X*) East Eur Quarterly.

— Elite-Mass Relations in Communist Systems. 240p. 1988. text ed. 45.00 (*0-312-00741-8*) St Martin.

— Romanian Politics in the Ceausescu Era. 236p. 1988. text ed. 86.00 (*2-88124-261-8*) Gordon & Breach.

***Nelson, Daniel N., ed.** After Authoritarianism: Democracy or Disorder? LC 95-5267. (Contributions in Political Science Ser.: Vol. 360). 200p. 1995. text ed. 59.95 (*0-313-29393-7*, Greenwood Pr) Greenwood.

— After Authoritarianism: Democracy or Disorder? 200p. 1995. pap. text ed. 18.95 (*0-275-95330-0*, Greenwood Pr) Greenwood.

— Local Politics in Communist Countries. LC 78-58121. 240p. 1980. 21.00 (*0-8131-1398-9*) U Pr of Ky.

— Romania after Tyranny. LC 91-26080. 311p. (C). 1992. pap. text ed. 42.50 (*0-8133-1348-1*) Westview.

Nelson, Daniel N. & Anderson, Roger B., eds. Soviet-American Relations: Understanding Differences, Avoiding Conflicts. LC 88-19726. 211p. (C). 1988. 40.00 (*0-8420-2300-3*); pap. text ed. 15.95 (*0-8420-2326-7*) Scholarly Res Inc.

Nelson, Daniel N. & Welsh, William A. The Politics & Government of Eastern Europe. (C). 1929. text ed. 30.00 (*0-86531-740-2*); pap. text ed. 14.95 (*0-86531-741-0*) Westview.

Nelson, Daniel N., jt. ed. see Lampe, John R.

Nelson, Daniel N., jt. auth. see Menon, Rajan.

Nelson, Dave. I Never Pay Taxes - I Always Get a Refund: or Myths, Mysteries, Fallacies, Fables & Facts about the IRS & Taxes. 32p. 1992. pap. 7.95 (*0-9635607-0-0*) D S Nelson.

***Nelson, David.** Menu: San Diego County - The Best 200 Restaurants. 1994. pap. 12.95 (*0-9628274-7-9*) D Thomas Pub.

— Natural Immunity. 844p. 1990. text ed. 104.00 (*0-12-514555-1*) Acad Pr.

— San Diego Cooks! Delicious Recipes from San Diego's 40 Best Restaurants. 208p. (Orig.). 1991. reprint ed. lib. bdg. 29.00x (*0-8095-5859-9*) Borgo Pr.

Nelson, David, tr. see Bhattacarya, Jagadishvara.

Nelson, David, jt. auth. see Coody, Betty.

Nelson, David, et al. Multicultural Mathematics. LC 92-17031. (Illus.). 1993. 13.95 (*0-19-282241-1*) OUP.

Nelson, David, et al, eds. Statistical Mechanics of Membranes & Surfaces: 5th Jerusalem Winter School for Theoretical Physics. 272p. (C). 1989. text ed. 53.00 (*9971-5-0722-6*); pap. text ed. 36.00 (*9971-5-0734-X*) World Scientific Pub.

Nelson, David C. A New World for Jon. 188p. 1992. 8.95 (*1-55523-514-X*) Winston-Derek.

Nelson, David J., Jr. Cracking the Pavement. (Minority Poet Ser.). (Illus.). 57p. 1989. pap. 4.00 (*1-880046-01-6*) Baculite Pub.

Nelson, David K., ed. see Nelson, Gail & Foard, Pamela.

Nelson, David L. & Brownstein, Bernard H., eds. YAC Libraries: A User's Guide. LC 93-13780. (University of Wisconsin Biotechnology Center Biotechnical Resource Ser.). (Illus.). 240p. 1993. pap. text ed. 39.95 (*0-7167-7014-8*) OUP.

Nelson, David L. & George, Thomas F., eds. Chemistry of High-Temperature Superconductors, No. 2. LC 88-19314. (ACS Symposium Ser.: No. 377). (Illus.). ix, 340p. 1988. 64.95 (*0-8412-1541-3*) Am Chemical.

Nelson, David L., et al, eds. Chemistry of High-Temperature Supconductors. LC 87-19314. (ACS Symposium Ser.: No. 351). (Illus.). xi, 349p. 1987. 69.95 (*0-8412-1431-X*) Am Chemical.

Nelson, David M. The Anatomy of a Game: Football, the Rules, & the Men Who Made the Game. LC 91-51009. 1994. Alk. paper. 25.00 (*0-87413-455-2*) U Delaware Pr.

Nelson, David N. Bibliography of South Asia. LC 94-613. (Area Bibliographies Ser.: No. 4). 484p. 1994. text ed. 52.50 (*0-8108-2854-5*) Scarecrow.

— Bridles & Bits of Cowboy Poetry. (Illus.). 60p. (Orig.). 1994. pap. text ed. 8.00 (*1-886615-00-4*) D N Nelson.

— Reflections. (Illus.). 45p. (Orig.). 1994. pap. text ed. 10.00 (*1-886615-03-9*) D N Nelson.

— Stress Management: Does Anyone in Chicago Know about It? LC 92-93554. 96p. (Orig.). 1992. pap. 12.95 (*0-88100-078-7*) Natl Writ Pr.

***Nelson, David T., ed.** The Diary of Elisabeth Koren 1853-1855. LC 94-66634. 381p. 1994. pap. 12.95 (*1-57216-008-X*) Penfield.

Nelson, David T., tr. see Koren, Elizabeth.

Nelson, Dawn. Compassionate Touch: Hands-on Caregiving for the Elderly, the Ill & the Dying. 1993. pap. 13.95 (*0-88268-149-4*) Station Hill Pr.

Nelson, Dean. New Father's Survival Guide: Devotions for the First Year of Parenthood. LC 93-49451. 1994. 9.99 (*0-8066-2591-0*) Augsburg Fortress.

***Nelson, Deborah L. & Howicz, Jennifer L.** Uniform Commercial Code Legal Forms, 2 vols. 3rd ed. LC 94-37285. 1994. 200.00 (*0-615-00337-0*) Clark Boardman Callaghan.

— Williston on Sales, 3 vols. 5th ed. LC 94-46505. 1994. 265.00 (*0-615-00522-5*) Clark Boardman Callaghan.

Nelson, Debra L. & Quick, James C. Organizational Behavior: Foundations, Realities, & Challenges. Leyh, ed. LC 93-27987. 650p. (C). 1994. text ed. 65.25 (*0-314-02640-1*) West Pub.

— Organizational Behavior: Foundations, Realities, & Challenges. alternate ed. LC 94-37592. 650p. 1994. pap. text ed. 53.25 (*0-314-04709-3*) West Pub.

Nelson, Dee W., ed. The Crisp Pine: A Collection of Winning Poems, 1980-1989. (Illus.). 120p. (Orig.). (C). 1990. pap. 10.00 (*0-9626793-0-5*) AAUW Pr.

Nelson, Dennis. Advanced Random Vibration & Shock. (Illus.). 250p. (C). 1990. student ed 100.00 (*0-918247-10-1*) Tustin Tech.

— Food Combining Simplified: Twenty-Eight Recipes Included. rev. ed. (Illus.). 64p. 1988. pap. 2.50 (*0-9612188-2-7*) Nelsons Bks.

— Maximizing Your Nutrition. 128p. (Orig.). 1988. pap. 3.50 (*0-9612188-3-5*) Nelsons Bks.

Nelson, Dennis R., jt. ed. see Stanley-Samuelson, David W.

Nelson, Derek. The Ads That Won the War. (Illus.). 160p. 1992. 34.95 (*0-87938-591-X*) Motorbooks Intl.

— Moonshiners, Bootleggers & Rumrunners. (Illus.). 192p. 1995. pap. 24.95 (*0-7603-1000-9*) Motorbooks Intl.

— Moonshiners, Bootleggers, & Rumrunners. LC 95-5913. 1995. pap. write for info. (*0-87938-956-7*) Motorbooks Intl.

— The Posters that Won the War. (Illus.). 160p. 1991. 34.95 (*0-87938-515-4*) Motorbooks Intl.

Nelson, Derek, jt. auth. see Parsons, Dave.

Nelson, Derek, jt. auth. see Parsons, David L.

Nelson, Derk, jt. auth. see Parsons, Dave.

Nelson, Dianne. A Brief History of Male Nudes in America: Stories by Dianne Nelson. LC 93-809. (Flannery O'Connor Award for Short Fiction Ser.). 136p. (C). 1993. 19.95 (*0-8203-1571-0*) U of Ga Pr.

Nelson, Donald, ed. see CODASYL COBOL Committee Staff.

Nelson, Donald E., jt. auth. see Humphrey, Sherry H.

Nelson, Donald F. COBOL 85 for Programmers. 250p. 1988. pap. 26.75 (*0-444-01232-X*) Elsevier.

Nelson, Donald M. Arsenal of Democracy: The Story of American War Production. LC 72-2378. (FDR & the Era of the New Deal Ser.). 439p. 1973. reprint ed. lib. bdg. 45.00 (*0-685-01352-9*) Da Capo.

Nelson, Donald T. & Schneiter, Paul H. Gifts-in-Kind: The Fund Raiser's Guide to Acquiring, Managing, & Selling Charitable Contributions Other than Cash & Securities. 178p. 1991. 29.95 (*0-930807-23-5*, 600318) Fund Raising.

Nelson, Dorothy. Glengary at Final Anchor. 146p. 1984. 12.00 (*0-87770-320-5*) Ye Galleon.

***Nelson, Doug.** Hotcakes to High Stakes: The Chuckwagon Story. (Illus.). 192p. 1993. 39.95 (*1-55059-056-1*) Temeron Bks.

Nelson, Douglas, jt. auth. see Nelson, Ray.

Nelson, Douglas, jt. auth. see Parker, Thomas.

Nelson, Doyal & Worth, Joan. How to Choose & Create Good Problems for Primary Children. LC 83-6218. (Illus.). 40p. 1983. pap. 8.50 (*0-87353-205-8*) NCTM.

Nelson, Drew. Wild Voices. (Illus.). 96p. (J). (gr. 3 up). 1991. 15.95 (*0-399-21798-3*, Philomel Bks) Putnam Pub Group.

Nelson, Dwight, jt. auth. see Nelson, Bruce.

***Nelson, Dwight K.** The Claim: Nine Radical Claims of Jesus That Can Revolutionize Your Life. LC 94-26480. 1994. pap. 1.95 (*0-8163-1236-2*) Pacific Pr Pub Assn.

Nelson, E. A., tr. see Speyr, Adrienne von.

Nelson, E. A., tr. see Von Balthasar, Hans U.

Nelson, E. B., ed. Well Cementing. (Developments in Petroleum Science Ser.: No. 28). 496p. 1990. 138.50 (*0-444-88751-2*) Elsevier.

Nelson, E. Clifford. The Rise of World Lutheranism: An American Perspective. LC 80-2376. 445p. reprint ed. pap. 126.90 (*0-317-55549-9*, 2029618) Bks Demand.

Nelson, E. Clifford, ed. Lutherans in North America. rev. ed. LC 74-26337. (Illus.). 576p. 1980. pap. 29.00 (*0-8006-1409-7*, 1-1409) Augsburg Fortress.

Nelson, E. W., jt. auth. see McLean, William G.

Nelson, Eastin, jt. auth. see Conference on Economic Development Staff.

Nelson, Edna C. Magnificent Percheron. (Illus.). (Orig.). 1963. pap. 5.95 (*0-87505-115-4*) Borden.

Nelson, Edward. Dynamical Theories of Brownian Motion. LC 72-38239. (Mathematical Notes Ser.). 146p. reprint ed. pap. 41.70 (*0-685-15536-6*, 2052178) Bks Demand.

— Predicative Arithmetic. (Mathematical Notes Ser.: No. 32). (Illus.). 199p. 1987. text ed. 24.95 (*0-691-08455-6*) Princeton U Pr.

— Quantum Fluctuations. LC 84-26449. (Physics Ser.). 155p. 1985. pap. 19.95 (*0-691-08379-7*) Princeton U Pr.

— Radically Elementary Probability Theory. (Annals of Mathematics Studies: No. 117). (Illus.). 86p. 1987. text ed. 45.00 (*0-691-08473-4*); pap. text ed. 16.95 (*0-691-08474-2*) Princeton U Pr.

An Asterisk (*) at the beginning of an entry indicates that the title is appearing in BIP for the first time.

Nelson, Edward W. The Eskimo about Bering Strait. LC 83-600094. (Classics of Smithsonian Anthropology Ser.: No. 4). (Illus.). 520p. 1983. pap. text ed. 29.95 (*0-87474-671-X*, NEEBP) Smithsonian.
— Lower California & Its Natural Resources. LC 66-24189. (Illus.). 1966. 49.50x (*0-910950-00-8*) Ransom Dist Co.
— Music & Worship. 176p. 1985. spiral bd. 13.25 (*0-311-72642-9*) Casa Bautista.
— Que Mi Pueblo Adore. Mussiett, Salomon C., tr. 184p. (SPA.). 1986. pap. 5.50 (*0-311-17029-3*) Casa Bautista.
Nelson, Edwin L., jt. auth. see Fuda, George E.
Nelson, Elden. I Hate WordPerfect: A Friendly Guide to WordPerfect. 1993. pap. 16.95 (*1-56529-212-X*) Que.
— I Hate WordPerfect 6. 1993. pap. 16.95 (*1-56529-361-4*) Que.
***Nelson, Eldon.** WordPerfect for Windows Quickstart. 2nd ed. 1994. disk, pap. 29.99 (*1-56529-786-5*) Que.
Nelson, Eleanor R., ed. see Kanter, Arnold B.
Nelson, Elizabeth. The British Counter-Culture, 1966-1973: A Study of the Underground Press. 256p. 1989. text ed. 45.00 (*0-312-02766-4*) St Martin.
— Coping with Drugs & Sports. (Coping Ser.). (YA). (gr. 7-12). 1992. lib. bdg. 15.95 (*0-8239-1342-2*) Rosen Group.
— How to Write a Lesson Plan for Adult Classes. 7p. 1994. student ed 5.00 (*0-918328-17-9*) Carma.
— Orange County Children's Directory 1992. 1991. pap. 4.95 (*1-877609-05-6*) Riviera Pubns.
— Professional Teaching Techniques: A Handbook for Teaching Adults Any Subject. 87p. 1994. student ed 10.95 (*0-918328-16-0*); pap. 7.95 (*0-918328-15-2*) Carma.
— San Diego Children's Directory 1992. 1991. pap. 3.95 (*1-877609-04-8*) Riviera Pubns.
— San Diego Children's Directory 1993. 1992. pap. 4.95 (*1-877609-06-4*) Riviera Pubns.
Nelson, Elizabeth, jt. ed. see Hollandsworth, Cynthia.
Nelson, Elizabeth, ed. see Riviera Publications Staff.
Nelson, Elizabeth A., ed. Orange County Children's Directory. 110p. 1989. pap. 4.95 (*1-877609-00-5*) Riviera Pubns.
Nelson, Elizabeth A., ed. see Riviera Publications Staff.
Nelson, Elizabeth R. Monarch Notes on Hardy's Far from the Madding Crowd. (Orig.). (C). pap. 3.95 (*0-671-00890-0*, Arco Test) P-H Gen Ref & Trav.
Nelson, Elva L., ed. see Ranganathananda, Swami.
Nelson, Emmanuel S. AIDS: The Literary Response. 360p. 1992. text ed. 23.95 (*0-8057-9029-2*, Twayne); pap. 14.95 (*0-8057-9032-2*, Twayne) Macmillan.
— Bharati Mukherjee: Critical Perspectives, Vol. 1663. LC 93-18145. 256p. 1993. 38.00 (*0-8153-1173-7*, H1663) Garland.
Nelson, Emmanuel S., ed. Contemporary Gay American Novelists: A Bio-Bibliographical Critical Sourcebook. LC 92-25762. 456p. 1993. text ed. 69.50 (*0-313-28019-3*, NCY, Greenwood Pr) Greenwood.
— Reworlding: The Literature of the Indian Diaspora. LC 91-40939. (Contributions to the Study of World Literature Ser.: No. 42). 208p. 1992. text ed. 49.95 (*0-313-27794-X*, NLI, Greenwood Pr) Greenwood.
— Writers of the Indian Diaspora: A Bio-Bibliographical Critical Sourcebook. LC 92-27898. 504p. 1993. text ed. 89.50 (*0-313-27904-7*, NWI/, Greenwood Pr) Greenwood.
Nelson, Emmanuel S., intro. Critical Essays: Gay & Lesbian Writers of Color. LC 93-30614. (Journal of Homosexuality: Vol. 26, Nos. 2-3). 250p. 1993. lib. bdg. 39.95 (*1-56024-482-8*) Haworth Pr.
— Critical Essays: Gay & Lesbian Writers of Color. LC 93-30614. (Journal of Homosexuality: Vol. 26, Nos. 2-3). 250p. 1994. pap. 14.95 (*1-56023-048-7*) Haworth Pr.
Nelson Engineering & Research, Inc. NEAR Conference on Missile Aerodynamics, Monterey, CA, Oct. 31-Nov. 2, 1988: Proceedings. 1989. 65.00 (*0-9620629-1-X*) Nielsen Engineering & Res Inc.
Nelson, Eric. The Interpretation of Waking Life. 81p. 1991. 16.95 (*1-55728-197-1*); pap. 9.95 (*1-55728-198-X*) U of Ark Pr.
— The Light Bringers. LC 83-50966. (Series Eight). 52p. 1983. pap. 7.00 (*0-931846-23-4*) Wash Writers Pub.
— On Call. (Moonsquilt Chadbook Ser.). 28p. (Orig.). 1983. pap. 3.50 (*0-943216-04-4*) MoonsQuilt Pr.
Nelson, Eric & McMillen, Lauretta. The Crimson & Blue Handbook: Stories, Stats & Stuff about KU Basketball. (Illus.). 160p. (Orig.). 1993. pap. 9.95 (*1-880652-31-5*) Wichita Eagle.
Nelson, Eric G., et al. Telecommunications Trade Issues: An Overview of the Regulatory Framework & Analyses of Current Events. (Illus.). 45p. (Orig.). 1989. pap. 53.00 (*0-940919-16-8*) NA Telecomm Assn.
Nelson-Erichsen, Jean. Copito: The Christmas Chihuahua. LC 82-72080. (Copito Stories). (Illus.). 80p. (J). (gr. k-5). 1982. pap. 3.50 (*0-943864-07-0*) Davenport.
Nelson-Erichsen, Jean & Erichsen, Heino R. Butterflies in the Wind: Spanish - Indian Children with White Parents. Gantley, Juleen & Cramer, Lorraine, eds. (Illus.). 355p. (Orig.). (C). 1992. pap. 18.00 (*0-935366-19-9*) Los Ninos.
— How to Adopt from Asia, Europe & the South Pacific. (Illus.). 230p. 1991. pap. 16.95 (*0-685-56353-7*) Los Ninos.
— How to Adopt from Latin America. (How to Adopt Ser.: No. 1). (Illus.). 150p. (Orig.). (C). 1985. pap. 16.95 (*0-935366-25-3*) Los Ninos.
— How to Adopt Internationally: A Guide for Agency-Directed & Independent Adoption. Gantley, Juleen, ed. (Illus.). 200p. (Orig.). (C). 1993. pap. 25.00 (*0-935366-18-0*) Los Ninos.
Nelson, Erland, jt. ed. see Price, Thomas R.
Nelson, Ersie L. Black American History Word Search Puzzles: The Black Contribution to the World of America, Vol. 1. 64p. 1993. write for info. (*0-9635801-0-8*) Ersie Nelson.
Nelson, Esther. Cotton Patch Cooking. (Black Folktales & Recipes Ser.: No. 1). (Illus.). 80p. 1981. pap. 3.00 (*0-686-32790-X*) Folks Pubns.
Nelson, Esther M. An Analysis of Content of Student-Teaching Courses. LC 70-177100. (Columbia University. Teachers College. Contributions to Education Ser.: No. 723). reprint ed. 37.50 (*0-404-55723-6*) AMS Pr.
Nelson, Ethel R., ed. Three Hundred Seventy-Five Meatless Recipes: Century 21 Cookbook. LC 94-61582. 164p. (Orig.). 1993. spiral bd. 7.95 (*0-945383-41-X*) Teach Servs.
Nelson, Ethel R. & Broadberry, Richard E. Genesis & the Mystery Confucius Couldn't Solve. LC 93-50090. (Illus.). 176p. (Orig.). 1994. pap. 9.99 (*0-570-04635-1*) Concordia.
Nelson, Eugene. Break Their Haughty Power: Joe Murphy in the Heyday of the Wobblies. LC 93-16106. (Illus.). 367p. (Orig.). 1993. pap. 12.00 (*0-910383-31-6*) Ism Pr.
Nelson, Eugene, intro. Crystal Gazing in the Amber Fluid & Other Wobbly Poems. 64p. (Orig.). 1992. pap. 10.00 (*0-88286-206-5*) C H Kerr.
Nelson, Eve, jt. ed. see DeMirjian, Arto, Jr.
Nelson, Evelyn G. & Nelson, Frederick J. The Island of Guam: Description & History from a 1934 Perspective. LC 92-85517. (Illus.). 250p. 1992. 15.00 (*0-9618941-2-1*) Ana Pubns.
Nelson, Fanny, jt. auth. see Nelson, Anson.
***Nelson, Fern K.** This Was Jackson's Hole: Incidents & Profiles from the Settlement of Jackson Hole. LC 94-25082. (Illus.). 384p. 1994. pap. 15.95 (*0-931271-25-8*) Hi Plains Pr.
Nelson, Florence. The Astrological Let Me Be Book. (Illus.). 1977. pap. 2.50 (*0-918328-01-2*) Carma.
— How to Teach a Demonstration-Type Subject. 10p. 1981. 3.50 (*0-918328-03-9*); pap. 3.50 (*0-686-96688-0*) Carma.
— How to Teach a Lecture-Type Subject. 12p. 1980. pap. 3.50 (*0-918328-06-3*) Carma.
— How to Use the Basic Seven Professional Teaching Techniques. 8p. 1978. 3.00 (*0-918328-09-8*) Carma.
— How to Write a Lesson Plan for Adult Classes. rev. ed. 6p. 1978. 5.00 (*0-918328-10-1*) Carma.
— Teaching for Craft Retailers. 8p. 1984. 3.50 (*0-918328-12-8*) Carma.
— Yes You Can Teach. LC 77-73639. (Illus.). 56p. 1977. spiral bd. 5.00 (*0-918328-00-4*) Carma.
Nelson, Florence, jt. auth. see Dlugosch, Sharon.
Nelson, Florence E., jt. auth. see Dlugosch, Sharon E.
***Nelson, Florencia B.** The School of the South - La Escuela del Sur: El Taller Torres-Garcia & Its Legacy. LC 91-73445. (Illus.). 22p. (J). 1991. pap. 5.00 (*0-614-02733-0*) A M Huntington Art.
Nelson, Florencia B., ed. see Barnitz, Jacqueline.
Nelson, Forrest D., jt. auth. see Aldrich, John H.
Nelson, Frances, ed. Jones Journeys. 1986. lib. bdg. write for info. (*0-318-60844-8*) Borgo Pr.
— Jones Journeys, 1-4. LC 84-646414. 1986. write for info. (*0-8095-6935-3*) Borgo Pr.
— Jones Journeys, 5. LC 84-646414. 1986. lib. bdg. 22.00x (*0-8095-6936-1*) Borgo Pr.
— Jones Journeys, 6. LC 84-646414. 1986. lib. bdg. 22.00x (*0-8095-6937-X*) Borgo Pr.
— Jones Journeys, 7. LC 84-646414. 1986. lib. bdg. 22.00x (*0-8095-6938-8*) Borgo Pr.
— Jones Journeys, 8. LC 84-646414. 1986. lib. bdg. 22.00x (*0-8095-6939-6*) Borgo Pr.
— Jones Journeys, 9. LC 84-646414. 1986. lib. bdg. 22.00x (*0-8095-6940-X*) Borgo Pr.
— Jones Journeys, 10. LC 84-646414. 1986. lib. bdg. 22.00x (*0-8095-6941-8*) Borgo Pr.
— Jones Journeys, 11. LC 84-646414. 1986. lib. bdg. 22.00x (*0-8095-6942-6*) Borgo Pr.
— Jones Journeys, 12. 1986. lib. bdg. 22.00x (*0-8095-6943-4*) Borgo Pr.
— Jones Journeys, 13. 1986. lib. bdg. 22.00x (*0-8095-6944-2*) Borgo Pr.
— Jones Journeys, 14. 1986. lib. bdg. 22.00x (*0-8095-6954-X*) Borgo Pr.
— Jones Journeys, 15. 1986. lib. bdg. 22.00x (*0-8095-6955-8*) Borgo Pr.
— Miller Monitor, 6 vols., 1. 1986. lib. bdg. 22.00x (*0-8095-6907-8*) Borgo Pr.
— Miller Monitor, 6 vols., 2. 1986. lib. bdg. 22.00x (*0-8095-6908-6*) Borgo Pr.
— Miller Monitor, 6 vols., 3. 1986. lib. bdg. 22.00x (*0-8095-6909-4*) Borgo Pr.
— Miller Monitor, 6 vols., 4. 1986. lib. bdg. 22.00x (*0-8095-6910-8*) Borgo Pr.
— Miller Monitor, 6 vols., 5. 1986. lib. bdg. 22.00x (*0-8095-6911-6*) Borgo Pr.
— Miller Monitor, 6 vols., 6. 1986. lib. bdg. 22.00x (*0-8095-6912-4*) Borgo Pr.
— Russell Register, 8 vols. 1986. write for info. (*0-318-60850-2*) Borgo Pr.
— Russell Register, 8 vols., 1. LC 83-10269. 1986. lib. bdg. 22.00x (*0-8095-6928-0*) Borgo Pr.
— Russell Register, 8 vols., 2. LC 83-10269. 1986. lib. bdg. 22.00x (*0-8095-6929-9*) Borgo Pr.
— Russell Register, 8 vols., 3. LC 83-10269. 1986. lib. bdg. 22.00x (*0-8095-6930-2*) Borgo Pr.
— Russell Register, 8 vols., 4. LC 83-10269. 1986. lib. bdg. 22.00x (*0-8095-6931-0*) Borgo Pr.
— Russell Register, 8 vols., 5. LC 83-10269. 1986. lib. bdg. 22.00x (*0-8095-6932-9*) Borgo Pr.
— Russell Register, 8 vols., 6. LC 83-10269. 1986. lib. bdg. 22.00x (*0-8095-6933-7*) Borgo Pr.
— Russell Register, 8 vols., 7. LC 83-10269. 1986. lib. bdg. 22.00x (*0-8095-6934-5*) Borgo Pr.
— Russell Register, 8 vols., 8. LC 83-10269. 1986. lib. bdg. 22.00x (*0-8095-6945-0*) Borgo Pr.
— Russell Register, 9. 1986. lib. bdg. 22.00 (*0-685-73971-6*) Borgo Pr.
— Russell Register, 10. 1986. lib. bdg. 22.00x (*0-8095-6957-4*) Borgo Pr.
— Russell Register, Vol. 9. 1987. lib. bdg. 22.00x (*0-8095-6956-6*) Borgo Pr.
— Vanderpool Newsletter. 1986. write for info. (*0-318-60888-X*); write for info. (*0-318-60889-8*) Borgo Pr.
— Vanderpool Newsletter, 1. 1986. lib. bdg. 22.00x (*0-8095-6916-7*) Borgo Pr.
— Vanderpool Newsletter, 2. 1986. lib. bdg. 22.00x (*0-8095-6917-5*) Borgo Pr.
— Vanderpool Newsletter, 3. 1986. lib. bdg. 22.00x (*0-8095-6918-3*) Borgo Pr.
— Vanderpool Newsletter, 4. 1986. lib. bdg. 22.00x (*0-8095-6919-1*) Borgo Pr.
— Vanderpool Newsletter, 5. 1986. lib. bdg. 22.00x (*0-8095-6920-5*) Borgo Pr.
— Vanderpool Newsletter, 6. 1986. lib. bdg. 22.00x (*0-8095-6921-3*) Borgo Pr.
— Vanderpool Newsletter, 7. 1986. lib. bdg. 22.00x (*0-8095-6922-1*) Borgo Pr.
— Vanderpool Newsletter, 8. 1986. lib. bdg. 22.00x (*0-8095-6923-X*) Borgo Pr.
— Vanderpool Newsletter, 9. 1986. lib. bdg. 22.00x (*0-8095-6924-8*) Borgo Pr.
— Vanderpool Newsletter, 10. 1986. lib. bdg. 22.00x (*0-8095-6925-6*) Borgo Pr.
— Vanderpool Newsletter, 11. 1986. lib. bdg. 22.00x (*0-8095-6926-4*) Borgo Pr.
— Vanderpool Newsletter, 12. 1986. lib. bdg. 22.00x (*0-8095-6927-2*) Borgo Pr.
— Vanderpool Newsletter, 13. 1986. lib. bdg. 22.00x (*0-8095-6958-2*) Borgo Pr.
— Vanderpool Newsletter, 14. 1986. lib. bdg. 22.00x (*0-8095-6959-0*) Borgo Pr.
Nelson, Frances & Hardy, Sheila, eds. Campbell Contacts in America, 1979-1985, 7 vols. 1986. lib. bdg. write for info. (*0-318-60841-3*) Borgo Pr.
— Campbell Contacts in America, 1979-1985, Vol. 1. LC 85-642854. 1986. lib. bdg. 22.00x (*0-8095-6900-0*) Borgo Pr.
— Campbell Contacts in America, 1979-1985, Vol. 2. LC 85-642854. 1986. lib. bdg. 22.00x (*0-8095-6901-9*) Borgo Pr.
— Campbell Contacts in America, 1979-1985, Vol. 3. LC 85-642854. 1986. lib. bdg. 22.00x (*0-8095-6902-7*) Borgo Pr.
— Campbell Contacts in America, 1979-1985, Vol. 4. LC 85-642854. 1986. lib. bdg. 22.00x (*0-8095-6903-5*) Borgo Pr.
— Campbell Contacts in America, 1979-1985, Vol. 5. LC 85-642854. 1986. lib. bdg. 22.00x (*0-8095-6904-3*) Borgo Pr.
— Campbell Contacts in America, 1979-1985, Vol. 6. LC 85-642854. 1986. lib. bdg. 22.00x (*0-8095-6905-1*) Borgo Pr.
— Campbell Contacts in America, 1979-1985, Vol. 7. LC 85-642854. 1986. lib. bdg. 22.00x (*0-8095-6906-X*) Borgo Pr.
— Campbell Contacts in America, 1979-1987, Vol. 8. 1986. lib. bdg. 22.00 (*0-685-73969-4*) Borgo Pr.
— Campbell Contacts in America, 1979-1987, Vol. 8. 1987. Vol. 9, 1987. lib. bdg. 22.00x (*0-8095-6946-9*) Borgo Pr.
— Campbell Contacts in America, 1979-1987, Vol. 9. 1986. lib. bdg. 22.00x (*0-8095-6947-7*) Borgo Pr.
— Nelson Notes, 5 vols. 1986. write for info. (*0-318-60849-9*) Borgo Pr.
— Nelson Notes, 5 vols., 1. 1986. lib. bdg. 22.00x (*0-8095-6913-2*) Borgo Pr.
— Nelson Notes, 5 vols., 2. 1986. lib. bdg. 22.00x (*0-8095-6914-0*) Borgo Pr.
— Nelson Notes, 5 vols., 4. 1986. lib. bdg. 22.00x (*0-8095-6948-5*) Borgo Pr.
— Nelson Notes, 5 vols., 5. 1986. lib. bdg. 22.00x (*0-8095-6949-3*) Borgo Pr.
Nelson, Frances S., ed. see Stakel, Charles J.
Nelson, Frederick C., tr. see Lalanne, Michel, et al.
Nelson, Frederick J., jt. auth. see Nelson, Evelyn G.
Nelson, G. K. To Be a Farmer's Boy. (J). (gr. 5-12). 1991. 30.00 (*0-86299-872-7*); pap. 18.00 (*0-7509-0182-9*) A Sutton Pub.
Nelson, G. Kenneth & Cramer, Joe J., Jr. Budgeting Problems. LC 68-28845. (Illus.). 182p. reprint ed. 51.90 (*0-8357-9849-6*, 2012524) Bks Demand.
Nelson, G. L., et al. Light Agricultural & Industrial Structures. (Illus.). 650p. 1988. text ed. 79.95 (*0-442-26777-0*) Chapman & Hall.
Nelson, G. Lynn. Writing & Being: Taking Back Our Lives Through the Power of Language. Geiger, Lura I., ed. 160p. (Orig.). 1994. pap. 14.95 (*1-880913-11-9*) LuraMedia.
Nelson, G. S., et al. Evaluation of the STD II Programme (1987-1991) (EUR Ser.: No. 14945). 146p. 1993. pap. 25.00 (*92-826-5783-3*, CG-NA-14945-ENC, Pub. by Europ Com) UNIPUB.
***Nelson, Gail & Foard, Pamela.** In Concert: The Freelance Musician's Keys to Financial Success. Nelson, David K., ed. LC 94-92250. (Illus.). 96p. (Orig.). 1994. pap. 16.95 (*0-9633888-2-7*, KFS1) Preludes Nouveaux.
— Wedding Music Essentials. rev. ed. LC 93-85452. 90p. 1993. pap. 19.95 (*0-9633888-1-9*, PNWM02) Preludes Nouveaux.
Nelson, Gail, jt. auth. see Foard, Pamela.
Nelson, Gail A., jt. auth. see Hauser, Paula.
Nelson, Gail L., jt. auth. see Nelson, Lynn T.
Nelson, Gale. Stare Decisis. (Burning Deck Poetry Ser.). 144p. (Orig.). 1991. pap. 9.00 (*0-930901-72-X*) Burning Deck.
— Stare Decisis. deluxe ed. (Burning Deck Poetry Ser.). 144p. (Orig.). 1991. Signed. pap. 15.00 (*0-930901-73-8*) Burning Deck.
Nelson, Gareth & Platnick, Norman. Biogeography. Head, John J., ed. LC 83-70604. (Carolina Biology Readers Ser.: No. 119). (Illus.). 16p. (C). (gr. 10 up). 1986. pap. 2.75 (*0-89278-319-2*, 45-9719) Carolina Biological.
Nelson, Gareth & Platnick, Norman I. Systematics & Biogeography: Cladistics & Vicariance. LC 80-20828. (Illus.). 592p. 1981. text ed. 86.00 (*0-231-04574-3*) Col U Pr.
Nelson, Gareth & Rosen, Donn E., eds. Vicariance Biogeography: A Critique. LC 80-15351. (Illus.). 616p. 1981. text ed. 88.50 (*0-231-04808-4*) Col U Pr.
Nelson, Garrett M. & Braun, Eddie. Earthquake Preparedness Guide: California Edition. (Orig.). 1989. pap. 2.95 (*0-685-30794-8*) MXM Imaging.
— Official Earthquake Preparedness Guide: National Edition. (Orig.). 1989. pap. 2.95 (*0-9625260-1-0*) MXM Imaging.
— Official Earthquake Preparedness Guides: California Edition. (Orig.). 1989. pap. 2.95 (*0-9625260-0-2*) MXM Imaging.
Nelson, Gary J., ed. Health Effects of Dietary Fatty Acids. 284p. (C). 1991. 95.00 (*0-935315-31-4*) AOCS Pr.
— Health Effects of Dietary Fatty Acids. 284p. 1992. pap. 40.00 (*0-935315-44-6*) AOCS Pr.
***Nelson, Gary M., et al.** The Field of Adult Services: Social Work Practice & Administration. 400p. (C). 1995. lib. bdg. 34.95 (*0-87101-250-2*, 2502) Natl Assn Soc Wkrs.
Nelson, Gene E. Beating the Bureaucrats: How to Get All You Earned from Social Security, Vol. 2. 1990. pap. 14.95 (*0-9623810-3-9*) White Plume Pr.
— Is Love Really Worth It? (Where Do You Go When Love Dies? Ser.: Vol. 2). (Illus.). 64p. (Orig.). 1992. pap. 7.95 (*0-9623810-7-1*) White Plume Pr.
— The Last Rose of Love. (Where Do You Go When Love Dies? Ser.: Vol. 3). (Illus.). 64p. (Orig.). 1992. pap. 7.95 (*0-9623810-8-X*) White Plume Pr.
— Little Flower & Other Love Poems. (Illus.). 1991. pap. 7.95 (*0-9623810-4-7*) White Plume Pr.
— Seven-O-Nine Bus down Broadway. (Illus.). 64p. (Orig.). 1992. pap. 7.95 (*0-9623810-9-8*) White Plume Pr.
— Social Security for Business Owners: How to Get Your Retirement Benefits. LC 89-90331. (Beating the Bureaucrats Ser.). 88p. (Orig.). (C). 1989. pap. 9.95 (*0-9623810-0-4*) White Plume Pr.
— Social Security for Business Owners: How to Get Your Retirement Benefits. (Beating the Bureaucrats Ser.). (Orig.). 1990. pap. text ed. 9.95 (*0-9623810-1-2*) White Plume Pr.
— Where Do You Go When Love Dies? (Illus.). (Orig.). 1991. pap. 7.95 (*0-9623810-5-5*) White Plume Pr.
Nelson, Geoffrey K. Seen & Not Heard: Memories of Childhood in the Early 20th Century. LC 93-33708. 1994. 30.00 (*0-7509-0460-7*) A Sutton Pub.
***Nelson, George.** Outside In. 63p. (Orig.). (YA). (gr. 5-12). 1994. pap. 4.00 (*1-57514-119-1*, 1075) Encore Perform Pub.
Nelson, George, intro. Chairs. (Twentieth Century: Landmarks in Design Ser.: Vol. 3). (Illus.). 188p. 1994. reprint ed. 55.00 (*0-926494-02-3*) Acanthus Pr.
Nelson, George, ed. see Herman Miller Staff.
Nelson, George E. The Introductory Biological Sciences in the Traditional Liberal Arts College. LC 74-177101. (Columbia University. Teachers College. Contributions to Education Ser.: No. 501). (C). reprint ed. 37.50 (*0-404-55501-2*) AMS Pr.
Nelson, George R., ed. Freedom & Welfare: Social Patterns in the Northern Countries of Europe. LC 72-98784. 539p. 1970. reprint ed. text ed. 79.50 (*0-8371-2903-6*, NEFR, Greenwood Pr) Greenwood.
Nelson, Gerald D. & Krause, John L. Clinical Photography in Plastic Surgery. (Illus.). 176p. 1987. 79.95 (*0-316-60315-5*, Little Med Div) Little.
Nelson, Gerry. Armageddon: The Diary of Vladimir Brezynski. 198p. 1983. 12.95 (*0-914701-00-2*) New Comet.
Nelson, Gersham. Legacy of Fourteen Ninety-Two. (Illus.). 232p. (Orig.). (C). 1994. pap. text ed. 17.00 (*1-878045-35-0*) Whittier Pubns.
Nelson, Gertrud. Clip Art for Celebration & Service. 188p. 1992. pap. 15.00 (*0-8146-6083-5*, Pueblo Bks) Liturgical Pr.
— Clip Art for Feasts & Seasons. 216p. 1992. pap. 15.95 (*0-8146-6041-X*, Pueblo Bks) Liturgical Pr.
Nelson, Gertrud M. Here All Dwell Free: Stories to Heal the Wounded Feminine. 384p. 1993. pap. 12.00 (*0-449-90789-9*, ExPress) Fawcett.
— Pocket Prayers. 1995. pap. (*0-385-47847-X*) Doubleday.
— To Dance with God: Family Ritual & Community Celebration. 176p. 1986. pap. 12.95 (*0-8091-2812-8*) Paulist Pr.
Nelson, Gideon. Biological Principles with Human Applications. 3rd ed. 435p. 1989. Net. pap. text ed. write for info. (*0-471-61775-X*); Net. student ed 22.95 (*0-471-61867-5*) Wiley.
***Nelson, Gil.** Exploring Wild North Florida. (Illus.). 224p. 1995. pap. 14.95 (*1-56164-091-3*) Pineapple Pr.
— Exploring Wild Northwest Florida. (Illus.). 224p. 1995. pap. 14.95 (*1-56164-086-7*) Pineapple Pr.
— Trees of Florida. LC 93-41607. (Illus.). 352p. 1994. 29.95 (*1-56164-053-0*); pap. 19.95 (*1-56164-055-7*) Pineapple Pr.
Nelson, Gillian. Highland Bridges. (Illus.). 1990. pap. 17.75 (*0-08-037744-0*, Pub. by Aberdeen U Pr) Macmillan.
— Walking in the Garden. 1994. lib. bdg. 19.00 (*0-7278-4619-1*) Severn Hse.
Nelson, Ginger K. Pirate's Revenge. Kratoville, Betty L., ed. (Meridian Bks.). (Illus.). 64p. (J). (gr. 3-9). 1989. lib. bdg. 4.95 (*0-87879-654-1*) High Noon Bks.
Nelson, Gladys T. War Drums at Eden Prairie. (Illus.). (J). (gr. 5-9). 1977. 5.95 (*0-87839-023-5*) North Star.

Nelson, Glenn C. Ceramics: A Potter's Handbook. LC 83-12633. (Illus.). (C). 1984. pap. text ed. 34.75 (0-03-063227-7) HB Coll Pubs.

— Ceramics: A Potter's Handbook. 5th ed. LC 83-12633. (Illus.). (C). 1984. 34.50 (0-03-064163-2) HB Coll Pubs.

Nelson, Gordon. Hibrow Cow: More Alaskan Stories & Recipes. LC 89-15018. (Illus.). 215p. 1989. pap. 9.95 (0-88240-354-0) Alaska Northwest.

Nelson, Gordon L., ed. Fire & Polymers: Hazards Identification & Prevention. LC 90-34195. (ACS Symposium Ser.: No. 425). (Illus.). 610p. 1990. 99.95 (0-8412-1779-3) Am Chemical.

Nelson, Gordon L., jt. auth. see Alper, Joseph.

Nelson, Gordon R. Lowbush Moose & Other Alaskan Recipes. LC 78-16515. (Illus.). 1978. pap. 9.95 (0-88240-112-2) Alaska Northwest.

Nelson, Grant S. Real Estate Transfer, Finance & Development: Cases & Materials On. Whitman, Dale A., ed. (American Casebook Ser.). 1333p. 1993. reprint ed. text ed. 50.00 (0-314-00568-4) West Pub.

Nelson, Grant S. & Whitman, Dale A. Land Transactions & Finance. 2nd ed. (Black Letter Ser.). 466p. (C). 1992. reprint ed. pap. text ed. 20.00 (0-314-68969-9) West Pub.

— Real Estate Finance Law. LC 85-13660. (Hornbook Ser.). 1052p. 1991. student ed, text ed. 36.50 (0-314-91412-9) West Pub.

— Real Estate Finance Law. 3rd ed. LC 93-43024. (Hornbook Ser.). 1002p. 1994. text ed. 37.50 (0-314-03453-6) West Pub.

— Real Estate Finance Law, 2 vols., Vol. 1. 3rd ed. (Practitioner's Treatise Ser.). 842p. 1993. text ed. 62.50 (0-314-02296-1) West Pub.

— Real Estate Finance Law, 2 vols., Vol. 2. (Practitioner's Treatise Ser.). 825p. 1993. text ed. 62.50 (0-314-02434-4) West Pub.

Nelson, Grant S. & Whitman, Dean D. Real Estate Finance Law: Nineteen Eighty-Eight Pocket Part. 2nd ed. (Hornbook Ser.). 137p. 1990. reprint ed. pap. text ed. 11.00 (0-314-50082-0) West Pub.

Nelson, H. F., ed. Thermal Design of Aeroassisted Orbital Transfer Vehicles. LC 85-3853. (PAAS Ser.: Vol. 96). (Illus.). 566p. 1985. 81.95 (0-915928-94-9) AIAA.

Nelson, H. Roice, Jr. New Technologies in Exploration Geophysics. LC 82-21120. 282p. 1983. 19.00 (0-87201-321-9) Gulf Pub.

Nelson, Hank & McCormack, Gavan. The Burma-Thailand Railway. 192p. 1994. pap. 17.95 (1-86373-577-1, Pub. by Allen Unwin AT) Paul & Co Pubs.

Nelson, Hanna. The Z-Mail Handbook: Three Interfaces for E-Mail. (Nutshell Handbook Ser.). 462p. (Orig.). 1991. pap. 29.95 (0-937175-76-5) OReilly & Assocs.

Nelson, Harland S. Charles Dickens. (English Authors Ser.: No. 314). 264p. (C). 1981. text ed. 21.95 (0-8057-6805-X, Twayne) Macmillan.

Nelson, Harold B., intro. Sounding the Depths: One Hundred Fifty Years of American Seascape. (Illus.). 112p. (C). 1989. pap. 18.95 (0-87701-598-8) Am Fed Arts.

Nelson, Harold D. Sudan: A Country Study. 3rd ed. LC 83-2718. (Area Handbook Ser.: DA Pam 550-27). (Illus.). 393p. 1983. 10.00 (0-16-001596-0, S/N 008-020-00440-5) USGPO.

Nelson, Harold D., ed. Algeria: A Country Study. 4th ed. LC 86-3583. (DA Pam Area Handbook Ser.: No. 550-44). (Illus.). 440p. 1983. text ed. 17.00 (0-16-001650-9, S/N 008-020-01091-0) USGPO.

— Costa Rica: A Country Study. 2nd ed. LC 84-16888. (Area Handbook Ser.: DA Pam 550-90). 367p. 1984. 14.00 (0-16-001610-X, S/N 008-020-01009-0) USGPO.

— Morocco: A Country Study. LC 85-600265. (DA Pam Area Handbook Ser.: No. 550-49). (Illus.). 476p. (YA). (gr. 9-12). 1986. 15.00 (0-16-001640-1, S/N 008-020-01072-3) USGPO.

— Mozambique: A Country Study. LC 85-6027. (DA Pam Area Handbook Ser.: No. 550-61). (Illus.). 375p. 1985. text ed. 12.00 (0-16-001622-3, S/N 008-020-01033-2) USGPO.

— Tunisia: A Country Study. 3rd ed. LC 86-3351. (DA Pam Area Handbook Ser.: No. 550-89). Orig. Title: Area Handbook for the Republic of Tunisia. (Illus.). 407p. 1988. 17.00 (0-16-001651-7, S/N 008-020-01092-8) USGPO.

— Zimbabwe: A Country Study. 2nd ed. LC 83-11946. (Area Handbook Ser.: DA Pam 550-171). 393p. 1983. 8.00 (0-16-001598-7, S/N 008-020-00964-4) USGPO.

Nelson, Harold E., et al. Quantitative Methods for Life Safety Analysis: Proceedings of the 1986 Symposium. 1988. 35.30 (0-318-24020-3) Society Fire Protect.

Nelson, Harold H. The Great Hypostyle Hall at Karnak: Vol. 1--The Wall Reliefs. Murnane, William J., ed. LC 81-80596. (Oriental Institute Publications: No. 106). (Illus.). 1981. lib. bdg. 90.00 (0-918986-30-3) Orientl Inst Pr IT.

— Key Plans Showing Locations of Theban Temple Decorations. LC 42-21551. (Oriental Institute Publications: No. 56). (Illus.). 1941. lib. bdg. 30.00 (0-226-62154-5, OIP56) U Ch Pr.

Nelson, Harold H. & Holscher, Uvo. Medinet Habu, Nineteen Twenty Four-Twenty Eight. LC 29-13423. (Illus.). 1929. pap. text ed. 5.00 (0-226-62320-3, OIC5) U Ch Pr.

Nelson, Harold N., ed. Freedom of the Press from Hamilton to the Warren Court. LC 66-22578. (Orig.). (C). 1967. write for info. (0-672-51005-7, Bobbs); pap. 8.40 (0-672-60120-6, AHS74, Bobbs) Macmillan.

Nelson, Harold W. Leon Trotsky & the Art of Insurrection, 1905-1917. 250p. 1986. 37.50 (0-7146-3272-4, Pub. by F Cass Pubs UK); pap. text ed. 19.50 (0-7146-4065-4, Pub. by F Cass Pubs UK) Intl Spec Bk.

Nelson, Harold W., jt. ed. see Luvaas, Jay.

*Nelson, Harry. Knowing What the Problem Is & Getting It Solved: State Reform in Long-Term Care. 19p. (Orig.). 1994. pap. text ed. write for info. (0-9629870-3-4) Milbank Memorial.

— The Resistance of the Air to Stone-dropping Meteors. LC 53-12359. (Augustana College Library Publication Ser.: No. 24). 37p. 1953. pap. 3.00 (0-910182-19-1) Augustana Coll.

Nelson, Harry & Jurmain, Robert. Introduction to Physical Anthropology. 5th ed. Simon & Perlee, Clyde, eds. 640p. (C). 1991. pap. text ed. 41.75 (0-314-80906-6) West Pub.

Nelson, Harry, jt. auth. see Jurmain, Robert.

Nelson, Harry, et al. Essentials of Physical Anthropology. Perlee, Clyde & Simon, eds. 352p. (C). 1992. pap. text ed. 38.25 (0-314-93440-5) West Pub.

Nelson, Havelock & Gonzales, Michael. Bring the Noise: A Guide to Rap Music & Hip-Hop Culture. (Illus.). 224p. 1991. 12.00 (0-517-58305-4, Harmony) Crown Pub Group.

Nelson-Heern, Laurie, jt. ed. see Harris, Diana.

Nelson, Helge. The Swedes & the Swedish Settlements in North America, 2 vols. in one. Scott, Franklyn D., ed. LC 78-15197. (Scandinavians in America Ser.). (Illus.). 1979. reprint ed. lib. bdg. 50.95 (0-405-11654-3) Ayer.

*Nelson, Henry S. Doctor with Big Shoes. (Illus.). 288p. (Orig.). 1995. pap. 17.95 (1-881576-45-0) Providence Hse.

Nelson-Herber, Joan, jt. auth. see Herber, Harold L.

Nelson, Herbert B. English Essentials: With Self-Scoring Exercises. (Quality Paperback Ser.: No. 52). 206p. (Orig.). 1977. reprint ed. pap. 14.00 (0-8226-0052-8) Littlefield.

Nelson, Hilda. Francois Baucher: The Man & His Method. 192p. 1990. 110.00 (0-85131-534-8, Pub. by J A Allen & Co UK) St Mut.

Nelson, Hilda, tr. see De Pluvinel, Antoine.

*Nelson, Hilde L. & Nelson, James L. The Patient in the Family: An Ethics of Medicine & Families. LC 94-33652. 224p. 1995. 59.95x (0-415-91128-1, B4910, Routledge NY); pap. 16.95 (0-415-91129-X, B4914, Routledge NY) Routledge.

Nelson, Horace G. & Nelson, Carol F. The College Journal. 320p. 1994. 28.95 (0-9638311-0-0) Primary Publns.

Nelson, Horatio. Nelson's Last Diary: A Facsimile. Warner, Oliver, ed. LC 70-165752. 80p. reprint ed. pap. 25.00 (0-317-30444-5, 2024924) Bks Demand.

Nelson, Howard. Creatures. 47p. (Orig.). 1983. pap. 4.50 (0-914946-40-4) Cleveland St Univ Poetry Ctr.

— Robert Bly: An Introduction to the Poetry. Unterecker, John, ed. LC 83-14481. (Columbia Introductions to Twentieth-Century American Poetry Ser.). 1984. text ed. 31.50 (0-231-05310-X) Col U Pr.

Nelson, Howard, ed. On the Poetry of Galway Kinnell: The Wages of Dying. 1988. 39.50 (0-472-09376-2); pap. 13.95 (0-472-06376-6) U of Mich Pr.

Nelson, Humphrey. The Little Man & the Little Oyster. LC 89-12198. (Illus.). 88p. 1990. 9.95 (0-935693-11-4) Mason Cty Hist.

Nelson, Ireene, intro. Atlas of Youth Camps in America-Alabama. LC 77-85081. (Illus.). 1978. pap. text ed. 2.00 (0-9601464-1-5) I J Nelson.

Nelson, Ivar, jt. auth. see Hart, Patricia.

*Nelson, J. Black Beauty: Poems about Our People. 1995. 7.95 (0-614-05145-2) House Nia.

Nelson, J., jt. auth. see Michaelis, John U.

Nelson, J. C., tr. see Aumiaux, M.

Nelson, J. C., tr. see Jagoda, A. & De Villepin, M.

*Nelson, J. C. C. Operational Amplifier Circuits: Analysis & Design. LC 94-32724. 175p. 1994. pap. 22.95 (0-7506-9468-8) Buttrwrth-Heinemann.

Nelson, J. H., comp. The Madura Country: A Manual. (Illus.). (C). 1989. reprint ed. 62.50 (81-206-0424-5, Pub. by Asian Educ Servs II) S Asia.

*Nelson, J. R. Bonnie: The Development of the Triumph Bonneville. (Illus.). 184p. 1995. pap. 24.95 (0-85429-957-2) Motorbooks Intl.

Nelson, J. Robert. On the New Frontiers of Genetics & Religion. 192p. (Orig.). (C). 1994. pap. 12.99 (0-8028-0741-0) Eerdmans.

— Science & Our Troubled Conscience. LC 80-8045. 187p. (Orig.). reprint ed. pap. 53.30 (0-317-55550-2, 2029619) Bks Demand.

Nelson, J. Robert, ed. Life As Liberty, Life As Trust. 104p. (Orig.). 1992. pap. 9.99 (0-8028-0637-6) Eerdmans.

— Life As Liberty, Life As Trust. fac. ed. LC 92-6287. 104p. 1992. reprint ed. pap. 29.70 (0-7837-7968-2, 2047724) Bks Demand.

Nelson, J. Russell, ed. see Conference on Understanding Profits (1964: Macalester College & University of Minnesota) Staff.

Nelson, J. S., jt. auth. see Winfield, I. J.

Nelson, Jack. Terror in the Night: The Klan's Campaign Against the Jews. LC 92-29539. (Illus.). 304p. 1993. 22.00 (0-671-69223-2) S&S Trade.

Nelson, Jack & Roberts, Gene, Jr. The Censors & the Schools. LC 77-23390. 208p. 1977. reprint ed. text ed. 55.00 (0-8371-9687-6, NECE, Greenwood Pr) Greenwood.

Nelson, Jack, jt. auth. see Bass, Jack.

Nelson, Jack A., ed. The Disabled, the Media, & the Information Age. LC 93-7700. (Contributions to the Study of Mass Media & Communications Ser.: No. 42). 264p. 1994. text ed. 55.00 (0-313-28472-5, NDM/, Greenwood Pr) Greenwood.

Nelson, Jack E. Christian Missionizing & Social Transformation: A History of Conflict & Change in Eastern Zaire. LC 91-46755. 224p. 1992. text ed. 49.95 (0-275-94246-5, C4246, Praeger Pubs) Greenwood.

Nelson, Jack K., jt. auth. see Thomas, Jerry R.

Nelson, Jack L. & Green, Vera M., eds. International Human Rights: Contemporary Issues. 300p. 1980. text ed. 25.00 (0-930576-37-3) E M Coleman Ent.

Nelson, Jack L., et al. Critical Issues in Education: A Dialectic Approach. 2nd ed. LC 92-19341. 1992. pap. text ed. write for info. (0-07-046211-9) McGraw.

Nelson, Jackie & Halpern-Segal, Janice. My Trip. (Illus.). 24p. (Orig.). (J). (ps-3). 1989. pap. 6.95 (0-685-29177-4) Take Along Pubns.

Nelson, Jacquelyn S. Indiana Quakers Confront the Civil War. LC 91-8983. 324p. (C). 1991. 19.95 (0-87195-064-2) Ind Hist Soc.

Nelson, James, ed. Alaska Review. (Illus.). 84p. (Orig.). 1989. pap. 11.95 (0-9623681-0-5, Moosehorn Pubns) AK ReView Inc.

Nelson, James & Davis, Terry. Protect Your Business. LC 93-27225. (Small Business Sourcebooks Ser.). 1993. 17.95 (0-942061-69-1) Sourcebks.

— Protect Your Business: Top Cops Help You Safeguard Against Shoplifting, Employee Theft, & More. (Small Business Sourcebooks Ser.). 170p. 1993. pap. 8.95 (0-942061-66-7) Sourcebks.

Nelson, James A. How to Enjoy Living. LC 82-70774. 160p. (Orig.). 1982. pap. 4.95 (0-89636-087-3) Accent CO.

Nelson, James B. Between Two Gardens: Reflections on Sexuality & Religious Experience. LC 83-11119. 208p. (Orig.). 1983. pap. 12.95 (0-8298-0681-4) Pilgrim OH.

— Body Theology. 176p. (Orig.). 1992. pap. 12.99 (0-664-25379-2) Westminster John Knox.

— Embodiment: An Approach to Sexuality & Christian Theology. LC 78-55589. 304p. 1979. pap. 16.99 (0-8066-1701-2, 10-2071, Augsburg) Augsburg Fortress.

— The Intimate Connection: Male Sexuality, Masculine Spirituality. LC 87-29487. 144p. (Orig.). 1988. pap. 12.99 (0-664-24065-8, Westminster) Westminster John Knox.

Nelson, James B. & Longfellow, Sandra P., eds. Sexuality & The Sacred: Sources For Theological Reflection. LC 93-39390. 432p. (Orig.). 1994. pap. 24.99 (0-664-25529-9) Westminster John Knox.

Nelson, James B. & Rohricht, Jo Anne. Human Medicine: Ethical Perspective on Today's Medical Issues. rev. ed. LC 84-12411. 240p. (Orig.). 1984. pap. 15.99 (0-8066-2086-2, 10-3187, Augsburg) Augsburg Fortress.

Nelson, James D. Awakening. 1989. pap. 9.95 (0-8306-9000-X) TAB Bks.

Nelson, James G. The Early Nineties: A View from the Bodley Head. LC 70-139718. 401p. reprint ed. pap. 114.30 (0-7837-2303-2, 2057391) Bks Demand.

— Elkin Mathews: Publisher to Yeats, Joyce, Pound. LC 89-40265. 304p. (Orig.). (C). 1990. text ed. 37.50 (0-299-12240-9); pap. text ed. 16.75 (0-299-12244-1) U of Wis Pr.

— The Last Refuge. LC 72-87214. 230p. reprint ed. pap. 65.60 (0-317-28423-1, 2022314) Bks Demand.

— Sir William Watson. LC 66-28912. (Twayne's English Authors Ser.). 1966. lib. bdg. 17.95 (0-89197-938-7); pap. text ed. 6.95 (0-8290-2025-X) Irvington.

— The Sublime Puritan: Milton & the Victorians. LC 74-8794. (Illus.). 209p. 1974. reprint ed. text ed. 38.50 (0-8371-7586-0, NESP, Greenwood Pr) Greenwood.

Nelson, James H., Jr. Manual of Basic Pelvic Surgery. 170p. 1994. pap. 37.00 (0-07-105400-6) Hlth Prof Div.

Nelson, James H., jt. auth. see Taymor, Melvin L.

Nelson, James K., Jr., ed. Computer Utilization in Structural Engineering. LC 89-6774. 574p. 1989. pap. text ed. 53.00 (0-87262-698-9, 698) Am Soc Civil Eng.

— Electronic Computation. LC 59-65010. (Conference Proceedings Ser.). 794p. 1983. pap. 60.00 (0-87262-351-3) Am Soc Civil Eng.

Nelson, James L., jt. auth. see Nelson, Hilde L.

Nelson, James M. Health & Welfare Benefit Plans: A Legal Guide to Planning & Management. 440p. 1994. ring bd. 95.00 (0-88063-371-9) Michie Butterworth.

— Health & Welfare Benefit Plans: A Legal Guide to Planning & Management. suppl. ed. 360p. 1993. 39.00 (0-685-74395-0) Butterworth Legal Pubs.

Nelson, James S. & McKeever, Paul E. Clinical Neuropathology. (C). 1994. disk 600.00 (1-56815-020-2) Image Premast.

Nelson, Jan, ed. see De Troyes, Chretien.

Nelson, Jan A., ed. The Old French Crusade Cycle, Vol. II: Le Chevalier au Cygne & La Fin d'Elias. LC 85-8443. (Illus.). xivii, 550p. 1985. 60.00 (0-8173-0272-7) U of Ala Pr.

Nelson, Jan A. & Mickel, Emanuel J., eds. La Naissance Du Chevalier Au Cygne. LC 76-30489. (Old French Crusade Cycle Ser.: Vol. 1). 496p. 1977. 34.50 (0-8173-8501-0) U of Ala Pr.

Nelson, Jane. Understanding: Eliminating Stress & Finding Serenity in Life & Relationships. rev. ed. Bookman Productions Staff, ed. 192p. 1988. pap. 9.95 (0-914629-72-7) Prima Pub.

Nelson, Jane & Lott, Lynn. Positive Discipline for Teenagers: Resolving Conflict with Your Teenage Son or Daughter. LC 93-36383. 1994. pap. 10.95 (1-55958-441-6) Prima Pub.

Nelson, Jane A. Form & Image in the Fiction of Henry Miller. LC 69-10515. 230p. reprint ed. pap. 65.60 (0-685-15760-1, 2027673) Bks Demand.

Nelson, Jane V. Mabel Dodge Luhan. (Western Writers Ser.: No. 55). (Illus.). 50p. (Orig.). 1982. pap. 3.95 (0-88430-029-3) Boise St U W Writ Ser.

Nelson, Janet. Charles the Bold. (Medieval World Ser.). 344p. (C). 1992. pap. text ed. 17.95 (0-582-05584-9) Longman.

Nelson, Janet L. Politics & Ritual in Early Medieval Europe. 440p. 1986. text ed. 60.00 (0-907628-59-1) Hambledon Press.

Nelson, Janet L., ed. The Annals of St-Bertin: Ninth-Century Histories, Vol. 1. LC 91-4030. 256p. 1992. text ed. 69.95 (0-7190-3425-6, Pub. by Manchester Univ Pr UK); text ed. 24.95 (0-7190-3426-4, Pub. by Manchester Univ Pr UK) St Martin.

Nelson, Janet L., jt. ed. see Gibson, Margaret T.

Nelson, Jeanne D., jt. auth. see Gibbons, Andy.

Nelson, Jefferson E., jt. auth. see Good, William V.

Nelson, Jeffrey. The Dinosaur Hunt Activity Book. (Orig.). (J). 1994. pap. 2.99 (0-8125-9439-8) Tor Bks.

— Dinosaur Jokes & Riddles Book. (Illus.). 24p. (J). (gr. 3 up). 1988. pap. 1.95 (1-56288-341-0) Checkerboard.

— Monster Jokes & Riddles. (Illus.). 24p. (J). (gr. 3 up). 1988. pap. 1.95 (1-56288-342-9) Checkerboard.

— Outerspace Jokes & Riddles Book. (Jokes & Riddles Bks.). (Illus.). 24p. (J). (gr. 3 up). 1988. pap. 1.95 (1-56288-343-7) Checkerboard.

— Spooky Jokes & Riddles Books. (Illus.). 24p. (J). (gr. 3 up). 1988. pap. 1.95 (1-56288-344-5) Checkerboard.

Nelson, Jeffrey A., jt. auth. see McNichol, Andrea.

Nelson, Jeffrey N., ed. The Poetry of Robert Tofte, 1597-1620: A Critical Old-Spelling Edition. LC 94-9802. (Renaissance Imagination Ser.). 360p. 1994. 82.00 (0-8153-1091-9) Garland.

Nelson, Jeffrey S. Animal Jokes & Riddles. LC 90-27676. (Illus.). 24p. (J). (gr. 3 up). 1991. pap. 1.95 (1-56288-016-0) Checkerboard.

— Family Jokes & Riddles. (Illus.). 24p. (J). (gr. 3 up). 1991. pap. 1.95 (1-56288-015-2) Checkerboard.

— Jungle Jokes & Riddles. (Illus.). 24p. (J). (gr. 3 up). 1991. pap. 1.95 (1-56288-017-9) Checkerboard.

— Spooky Jokes & Riddles. LC 89-123851. (J). 1988. pap. 1.95 (0-02-689070-4, Mac Bks Young Read) S&S Childrens.

— Yucky Jokes & Riddles. (Illus.). 24p. (J). (gr. 3 up). 1991. pap. 1.95 (1-56288-014-4) Checkerboard.

Nelson, Jennifer K., et al. Mayo Clinic Diet Manual: A Handbook of Nutrition Practices. 7th ed. LC 93-43747. 1994. write for info. (0-8151-6348-7) Mosby Yr Bk.

Nelson, Jenny. Archibald & the Crunch Machine. (Illus.). 40p. (J). (gr. 2-4). 1990. pap. 5.95 (1-55037-114-2, Pub. by Annick CN) Firefly Bks Ltd.

Nelson, Jerome L. Libel: A Basic Program for Beginning Journalists. LC 73-13006. 121p. reprint ed. pap. 34.50 (0-685-15327-4, 2026659) Bks Demand.

Nelson, Jill. Volunteer Slavery: My Authentic Negro Experience. LC 92-51078. 243p. 1993. 21.95 (1-879360-24-1) Noble Pr.

— Volunteer Slavery: My Authentic Negro Experience. 256p. 1994. 9.95 (0-14-023716-X, Penguin Bks) Viking Penguin.

*Nelson, Jim. Careers in Law Enforcement: Interviewing for Results. 1995. pap. 27.50 (0-614-06593-3) Graduate Group.

Nelson, Jim, jt. auth. see Ellrod, Gary.

Nelson, Jim, jt. auth. see Potterfield, Peter.

Nelson, Jo, jt. auth. see Munson, Shirley.

Nelson, Joan. Abortion. LC 91-15566. (Overview Ser.). (Illus.). 112p. (J). (gr. 5-8). 1992. lib. bdg. 16.95 (1-56006-128-6) Lucent Bks.

*Nelson, Joan, ed. Precarious Balance Vol. I: Democratic Consolidation & Economic Reform in Eastern Europe & Latin America. 1994. pap. 14.95 (0-614-05562-8) ICS Pr.

— Precarious Balance Vol. II: Democratic Consolidation & Economic Reform in Eastern Europe & Latin America. 1994. pap. 14.95 (1-55815-323-3) ICS Pr.

Nelson, Joan E. Kids Who Kill Kids. LC 93-85136. 284p. (Orig.). (YA). (gr. 8-12). 1994. pap. 12.95 (0-9637293-1-4) Storm Pub.

— Mommy, Where Are You? (Orig.). 1994. reprint ed. pap. 10.95 (0-9637293-7-3) Storm Pub.

Nelson, Joan M. Migrants, Urban Poverty, & Instability in Developing Nations. LC 74-9752. (Harvard University. Center for International Affairs. Occasional Papers in International Affairs: No. 22). reprint ed. 11.50 (0-404-54622-6) AMS Pr.

— Teaching Self-Defense: Steps to Success. LC 93-31620. (Illus.). 160p. 1994. pap. 19.95x (0-87322-620-8, PNEL0620) Human Kinetics.

Nelson, Joan M., ed. Economic Crisis & Policy Choice: The Politics of Adjustment in the Third World. (Illus.). 406p. (Orig.). 1990. text ed. 52.50 (0-691-07821-1); pap. text ed. 15.95 (0-691-02310-7) Princeton U Pr.

— Intricate Links: Democratization & Market Reforms in Latin America & Eastern Europe. (U. S. - Third World Policy Perspectives Ser.: No. 20). 256p. (C). 1994. 32.95 (1-56000-177-1) Transaction Pubs.

— Intricate Links: Democratization & Market Reforms in Latin America & Eastern Europe. (U. S. - Third World Policy Perspectives Ser.: No. 20). 256p. (C). 1994. pap. 17.95 (1-56000-759-1) Transaction Pubs.

Nelson, Joan M. & Eglinton, Stephanie J. Encouraging Democracy: What Role for Conditioned Aid? LC 92-14033. (Policy Essay Ser.: No. 4). 80p. (Orig.). 1992. pap. text ed. 9.95 (1-56517-004-0) Overseas Dev Council.

— Global Goals, Contentious Means: Issues of Multiple Aid Conditionality. LC 93-23293. (Policy Essay Ser.: No. 10). 136p. (C). 1993. pap. text ed. 9.95 (1-56517-012-1) Overseas Dev Council.

Nelson, Joan M., jt. auth. see Huntington, Samuel P.

Nelson, Joan M., et al, eds. The Politics of Economic Adjustment: Fragile Coalitions. 224p. 1990. 32.95 (0-88738-283-5); pap. 17.95 (0-88738-787-X) Transaction Pubs.

Nelson, JoAnne. Count by Twos. (Explore & Learn Ser.). (Illus.). 16p. (Orig.). (J). (gr. k-2). 1990. pap. 3.95 (1-878624-10-5) McClanahan Bk.

An Asterisk (*) at the beginning of an entry indicates that the title is appearing in BIP for the first time.

— Feeling Fit, That's It! LC 92-37719. (Primarily Health Ser.). (Illus.). (J). (gr. k-2). 1994. pap. 5.95 (*0-935529-58-6*) Comprehen Health Educ.
— Friends All Around. LC 92-4657. (Primarily Health Ser.). (Illus.). 24p. (Orig.). (J). (gr. k-2). 1993. pap. 5.95 (*0-935529-17-9*) Comprehen Health Educ.
— Good Grief! Good Grief! LC 92-6685. (Primarily Health Ser.). (Illus.). 24p. (Orig.). (J). (gr. k-2). 1993. pap. 5.95 (*0-935529-18-7*) Comprehen Health Educ.
— How Do You Feel? LC 91-36336. (Primarily Health Ser.). (Illus.). 24p. (Orig.). (J). (gr. k-2). 1993. pap. write for info. (*0-935529-15-2*) Comprehen Health Educ.
— It's up to Me! LC 93-9349. (Primarily Health Ser.). (Illus.). (J). (gr. k-2). 1995. 5.95 (*0-935529-63-2*) Comprehen Health Educ.
— Nose to Toes. LC 91-34706. (Primarily Health Ser.). (Illus.). 24p. (Orig.). (J). (gr. k-2). 1993. pap. 5.95 (*0-935529-16-0*) Comprehen Health Educ.
— Our Friend, the Earth. LC 92-37716. (Primarily Health Ser.). (Illus.). (J). (gr. k-2). 1995. pap. 5.95 (*0-935529-59-4*) Comprehen Health Educ.
— Play It Safe. LC 93-12173. (Primarily Health Ser.). (Illus.). (J). (gr. k-2). 1995. 5.95 (*0-935529-62-4*) Comprehen Health Educ.
— We Are Family. LC 93-12176. (Primarily Health Ser.). (Illus.). (J). (gr. k-2). 1995. 5.95 (*0-935529-60-8*) Comprehen Health Educ.
— What Next? LC 91-35731. (Primarily Health Ser.). (Illus.). 24p. (Orig.). (J). (gr. k-2). 1993. pap. 5.95 (*0-935529-19-5*) Comprehen Health Educ.
— When I'm Sick. LC 93-9348. (Primarily Health Ser.). (Illus.). (J). (gr. k-2). 1995. 5.95 (*0-935529-61-6*) Comprehen Health Educ.
— Where's Mittens? LC 91-9373. (Primarily Health Ser.). (Illus.). 24p. (Orig.). (J). (gr. k-2). 1993. pap. 5.95 (*0-935529-14-4*) Comprehen Health Educ.

Nelson, Joel. Economic Inequality: Conflict Without Change. LC 82-4164. 1982. text ed. 53.00 (*0-231-05416-5*); pap. text ed. 19.50 (*0-231-05417-3*) Col U Pr.

***Nelson, Joel I.** Post-Industrial Capitalism. 206p. (C). 1995. 45.00 (*0-8039-7332-2*); pap. 21.95 (*0-8039-7333-0*) Sage.

Nelson, John. Bonnie: The Development History of the Triumph Bonneville. 165p. pap. 17.95 (*0-85429-257-8*, F257, Pub. by G T Foulis Ltd) Haynes Pubns.
— Colonial Classics You Can Build Today: Plans & Drawings for 80 Authentic Projects, All Exact Replicas of Early American Antiques. LC 85-26171. (Illus.). 256p. (Orig.). 1986. pap. 19.95 (*0-8117-2025-X*) Stackpole.
— Drafting for Trades & Industry. LC 77-91450. (Drafting Ser.). teacher ed 15.00 (*0-8273-1641-0*) Delmar.
— Drafting for Trades & Industry - Architectural. LC 77-91450. (Drafting Ser.). 138p. (C). 1979. pap. text ed. 24.95 (*0-8273-1839-1*) Delmar.
— Drafting for Trades & Industry - Basic Skills. LC 77-91450. (Drafting Ser.). 464p. (C). 1979. pap. text ed. 32.95 (*0-8273-1841-3*) Delmar.
— Drafting for Trades & Industry - Civil. LC 77-91450. (Drafting Ser.). 942p. (C). 1979. pap. text ed. 24.95 (*0-8273-1844-8*) Delmar.
— Drafting for Trades & Industry - Mechanical & Electronic. LC 77-91450. (Drafting Ser.). 328p. (C). 1979. pap. text ed. 24.95 (*0-8273-1846-4*) Delmar.
— Early American Classics: Thirty-Three Projects for Woodworkers with Complete Plans & Instructions. LC 91-47001. (John Nelson Woodworking Ser.). (Illus.). 192p. 1992. pap. 16.95 (*0-8117-2535-9*) Stackpole.
— Matrix of the Gods. 288p. (Orig.). 1994. pap. 10.95 (*1-878901-97-4*) Hampton Roads Pub Co.
— Starborn. 1993. 8.95 (*1-878901-59-1*) Hampton Roads Pub Co.
— Starborn: A Mystical Tale. rev. ed. Friedman, Robert S., ed. LC 78-22108. 124p. 1987. pap. 5.95 (*0-915442-68-X*) Donning Co.
— Transformations. 272p. 1988. pap. 8.95 (*0-89865-549-8*) Hampton Roads Pub Co.
— Wintering on the Cortez. Ingram, tr. 230p. 1995. pap. 8.95 (*0-7610-0446-7*) NW Pub.

Nelson, John, jt. auth. see Nelson, Joyce.

Nelson, John, et al. The Rhetoric of the Human Sciences: Language & Argument in Scholarship & Public Affairs. LC 86-34030. (Rhetoric of the Human Sciences Ser.). (Illus.). 408p. (C). 1987. text ed. 35.00 (*0-299-11020-6*) U of Wis Pr.
— Rhetoric of the Human Sciences: Language & Argument in Scholarship & Public Affairs. LC 86-34030. (Illus.). 408p. 1991. pap. 16.95 (*0-299-11024-9*) U of Wis Pr.

Nelson, John, et al, prefs. Management of Uranium Mill Tailings, Low Level Waste & Hazardous Waste: Proceedings of the Seventh Symposium, 2 vols. (Orig.). 1985. pap. text ed. 38.00 (*0-910069-08-5*) Geotech Engineer Prog.

Nelson, John A. Basic Blueprint Reading. 1990. text ed. 28.95 (*0-07-157469-7*) McGraw.
— Basic Blueprint Reading. (Illus.). 256p. 1989. 28.95 (*0-8306-4273-0*); pap. 19.95 (*0-8306-3273-5*) TAB Bks.
— Build Your Own Grandfather Clock & Save. (Illus.). 144p. 1988. 19.95 (*0-8306-9053-0*, 3053); pap. 12.95 (*0-8306-9353-X*, 3053) TAB Bks.
— Clockmaking: Eighteen Antique Designs for the Woodworker. (Illus.). 240p. (Orig.). 1994. pap. 16.95 (*0-8117-2526-X*) Stackpole.
— Clockmaking: Eighteen Antique Designs for the Woodworker. (Illus.). 176p. (Orig.). 1989. 25.95 (*0-8306-9164-2*); pap. 18.95 (*0-8306-3164-X*) TAB Bks.
— Clocks: Full-Size Designs, Ready to Cut. (Scroll Saw Pattern Book Ser.). (Illus.). 96p. 1995. pap. 14.95 (*0-8117-3073-5*) Stackpole.
— Country Classics: Authentic Projects You Can Build in One Weekend. Atwater, Sally, ed. LC 88-20027. (Illus.). 224p. (Orig.). 1989. pap. 16.95 (*0-8117-2277-5*) Stackpole.
— Early American Classics. 1993. 25.50 (*0-8446-6720-X*) Peter Smith.
— Easy-to-Make Antique Furniture Reproductions: 15 Small Projects. (Illus.). 128p. 1988. reprint ed. pap. 5.95 (*0-486-25671-5*) Dover.
— Fancy Fretwork: 39 Full-Size Designs, Ready to Cut. LC 94-33616. (Scroll Saw Pattern Book Ser.). (Illus.). 96p. 1995. pap. 14.95 (*0-8117-3024-7*) Stackpole.
— Fifty-Two Country Projects for the Weekend Woodworker. LC 92-8580. (Illus.). 160p. 1992. pap. 12.95 (*0-8069-8625-5*) Sterling.
— Fifty-Two Decorative Weekend Woodworking Projects. LC 93-15288. (Illus.). 160p. 1993. pap. 12.95 (*0-8069-0392-9*) Sterling.
— Fifty-Two Holiday Wood Projects. LC 94-42100. (Illus.). 164p. 1995. pap. 14.95 (*0-8069-0652-9*) Sterling.
— 52 Toys & Puzzles for the Weekend Woodworker. LC 94-2372. (Illus.). 160p. 1994. pap. 12.95 (*0-8069-0644-8*) Sterling.
— Fifty Two Weekend Woodworking Projects. LC 91-9954. (Illus.). 160p. 1991. pap. 12.95 (*0-8069-8300-0*) Sterling.
— Folk Art Weather Vanes: Authentic American Patterns for Wood & Metal. LC 89-26368. (Illus.). 160p. (Orig.). 1990. pap. 16.95 (*0-8117-2406-9*) Stackpole.
— Handbook of Architectural & Civil Drafting. 296p. 1983. pap. 33.95 (*0-442-26864-5*) Chapman & Hall.
— One Hundred and Ten Easy to Make Woodworking. 1993. 9.99 (*0-517-09300-6*) Random Hse Value.
— Plain & Simple Fun: 59 Full-Size Designs, Ready to Cut. (Scroll Saw Pattern Book Ser.). (Illus.). 96p. 1995. pap. 14.95 (*0-8117-3025-5*) Stackpole.
— Trains, Planes, & Automobiles: Full-Size Designs, Ready to Cut. (Scroll Saw Pattern Book Ser.). (Illus.). 96p. 1995. pap. 14.95 (*0-8117-3072-7*) Stackpole.
— Weekend Woodworker. LC 89-70250. (Illus.). 304p. 1990. 23.95 (*0-87857-894-3*, 14-997-0); pap. 14.95 (*0-87857-904-4*, 14-997-1) Rodale Pr Inc.
— Woodworker's Jackpot. 1991. 24.95 (*0-8306-5316-3*) TAB Bks.
— Woodworker's Jackpot: Forty-Nine Step-by-Step Projects. (Illus.). 240p. (Orig.). 1989. 22.95 (*0-8306-9154-5*); pap. 16.95 (*0-8306-3154-2*) TAB Bks.

Nelson, John A. & Nelson, Joyce C. Patterns & Projects for the Scroll Saw. LC 90-44284. 224p. (Orig.). 1991. pap. 14.95 (*0-8117-3040-9*) Stackpole.

Nelson, John A., jt. auth. see Goetsch, David L.

Nelson, John C. Renaissance Theory of Love: The Context of Giordano Bruno's Eroici Furori. LC 58-7170. 288p. reprint ed. pap. 82.10 (*0-317-09244-8*, 2005782) Bks Demand.

Nelson, John C., tr. see Boisseau, M., et al.

Nelson, John C., tr. see Halley, Pierre.

Nelson, John C., tr. see Pelloso, Pierre.

***Nelson, John D.** Nineteen Ninety Five Pocket Book of Pediatric Antimicrobial Therapy. 11th ed. 106p. 1994. pap. text ed. 13.95 (*0-683-06406-1*) Williams & Wilkins.
— Pocketbook of Pediatric Antimicrobial Therapy 1993-94. 10th ed. 112p. 1993. pap. 12.00 (*0-683-06405-3*) Williams & Wilkins.

Nelson, John D. & Miller, Debora J. Expansive Soils: Problems & Practice in Foundation & Pavement Engineering. 288p. 1992. text ed. 69.95 (*0-471-51186-2*) Wiley.

Nelson, John D., jt. ed. see McCracken, George H.

Nelson, John E. Healing the Split: Integrating Spirit into Our Understanding of the Mentally Ill. rev. ed. (SUNY Series in the Philosophy of Psychology). 442p. (C). 1994. 49.50 (*0-7914-1985-1*); pap. 16.95 (*0-7914-1986-X*) State U NY Pr.

Nelson, John F., jt. auth. see Coleman, Gary C.

Nelson, John G. Wheelchair Vagabond. 1975. 14.95 (*0-933261-10-1*) Twin Peaks Pr.

Nelson, John H. Cosmic Patterns. 80p. 1974. 6.00 (*0-86690-133-7*, N1355-014) Am Fed Astrologers.
— Negro Character in American Literature. LC 73-128982. reprint ed. 29.50 (*0-404-00203-X*) AMS Pr.
— The Negro Character in American Literature. (BCL1-PS American Literature Ser.). 146p. 1992. reprint ed. lib. bdg. 69.00 (*0-7812-6616-5*) Rprt Serv.

Nelson, John H. & Kemp, Kenneth C. Laboratory Experiments: Chemistry--the Central Science. 4th ed. Brown & LeMay, H. Eugene, Jr., eds. (Illus.). 464p. (C). 1988. pap. text ed. write for info. (*0-13-129800-3*) P-H.

Nelson, John L. The Beginners Guide to Flight Instruction. 2nd ed. (Practical Flying Ser.). (Illus.). 208p. 1989. pap. 15.95 (*0-8306-2443-0*) TAB Bks.

Nelson, John M. & Ross, Sandi B. Medical Practice Handbook. (Practice & Financial Management Ser.). 144p. 1990. text ed. 47.50 (*0-87489-582-0*) Med Economics.

Nelson, John O. Opportunities in Religious Service Careers. (Illus.). 160p. 1988. 13.95 (*0-8442-6484-9*, VGM Career Bks); pap. 10.95 (*0-8442-6485-7*, VGM Career Bks) NTC Pub Grp.

Nelson, John O., jt. auth. see Machan, Tibor R.

Nelson, John R. Auditing in a Microcomputer Environment: Student's Workbook. Holman, Richard, ed. (Media-Assisted Training Ser.). 44p. 1986. pap. text ed. 15.00 (*0-89413-152-4*) Inst Inter Aud.
— Auditing in a Microcomputer Environment: Videotape & Instructor's Guide. Holman, Richard, ed. (Media-Assisted Training Ser.). 44p. 1986. pap. text ed. 400.00 (*0-89413-153-2*) Inst Inter Aud.

Nelson, John R., Jr. Liberty & Property: Political Economy & Policymaking in the New Nation, 1789-1812. LC 86-21373. (Johns Hopkins University Studies in Historical & Political Science: No. 2). 256p. 1987. text ed. 32.50 (*0-8018-3440-6*) Johns Hopkins.

Nelson, John S., ed. Tradition, Interpretation, & Science: Political Theory in the American Academy. LC 86-7098. (SUNY Series in Political Theory: Contemporary Issues). 372p. (C). 1986. 59.50 (*0-88706-371-3*); pap. 19.95 (*0-88706-373-X*) State U NY Pr.
— What Should Political Theory Be Now? LC 82-19167. (SUNY Series in Political Theory: Contemporary Issues). 607p. (C). 1984. 59.50 (*0-87395-694-X*); pap. 19.95 (*0-87395-695-8*) State U NY Pr.

***Nelson, Johnnie R.** Kwanzaa Love. (Illus.). 40p. (Orig.). 1994. pap. 6.00 (*0-9623205-3-6*) House Nia.

Nelson, Johnnierenee. Positive Passage: Everyday Kwanzaa Poems. (Illus.). 48p. (Orig.). (J). (gr. 1 up). 1991. pap. 7.00 (*0-9623205-1-X*) House Nia.
— A Quest for Kwanzaa: Poems by Johnnierenee Nelson. (Illus.). 40p. (Orig.). 1988. pap. 6.00 (*0-9623205-0-1*) House Nia.
— Values of the African American Family: The Kwanzaa Canons. (Illus.). 48p. (Orig.). 1993. pap. 9.00 (*0-9623205-2-8*) House Nia.

Nelson, Johnny. Texas Land Grab. 1979. reprint ed. pap. 1.25 (*0-8439-0671-5*) Dorchester Pub Co.

Nelson-Jones, John & Nuttall, Graeme. Employee Ownership: Legal & Tax Aspects. 170p. 1987. 120.00 (*1-85190-033-0*, Pub. by Fourmat Pub UK) St Mut.

Nelson-Jones, John & Stewart, Peter. A Practical Guide to Package Holiday Law & Contracts. 1987. 120.00 (*1-85190-041-1*, Pub. by Fourmat Pub UK) St Mut.
— A Practical Guide to Package Holiday Law & Contracts. 300p. 1993. 90.00 (*0-85459-810-3*, Pub. by Tolley Pubng UK) St Mut.

Nelson-Jones, Richard. Group Leadership: A Training Approach. LC 91-25842. 336p. (C). 1992. pap. 32.95 (*0-534-17010-2*) Brooks-Cole.
— Lifeskills Helping: Helping Others Through a Systematic People Approach. 352p. (C). 1993. pap. 25.95 (*0-534-19674-8*) Brooks-Cole.
— Personal Responsibility & Therapy: An Integrative Approach. 214p. 1987. 42.00 (*0-89116-777-3*) Hemisp Pub.

Nelson-Jones, Rodney & Burton, Frank. Medical Negligence Case Law. 432p. (C). 1990. text ed. 150.00 (*1-85190-087-X*, Pub. by Tolley Pubng UK) St Mut.
— Personal Injury Limitation Law. 362p. 1994. pap. text ed. 75.00 (*0-406-02447-2*, UK) Butterworth Legal Pubs.

Nelson-Jones, Rodney & Nuttall, Graeme. Tax & Interest Tables, 1988-89. (Illus.). 80p. (C). 1988. 100.00 (*1-85190-047-0*, Pub. by Fourmat Pub UK) St Mut.

Nelson-Jones, Rodney & Stewart, P. Product Liability: The New Law under the Consumer Protection Act, 1987. 208p. (C). 1988. 90.00 (*1-85190-049-7*, Pub. by Fourmat Pub UK) St Mut.

Nelson-Jones, Rodney & Stewart, Peter. Product Liability: The New Law under the Consumer Protection Act 1987. 208p. 1987. 128.00 (*1-85190-034-9*, Pub. by Fourmat Pub UK) St Mut.

Nelson, Joseph F. So You Want to Build a Live Steam Locomotive. LC 74-75879. (Illus.). 164p. 1978. reprint ed. 20.95 (*0-914104-01-2*) Wildwood Pubns MI.

Nelson, Joseph S. Fishes of the World. 2nd ed. LC 83-19684. 523p. 1984. text ed. 79.95 (*0-471-86475-7*) Wiley.
— Fishes of the World. 3rd ed. LC 93-37462. 688p. 1994. text ed. 79.95 (*0-471-54713-1*) Wiley.

Nelson, Josephus & Farley, Judith. Full Circle: Ninety Years of Service in the Main Reading Room. LC 91-14571. 64p. 1991. 6.00 (*0-8444-0726-7*) Lib Congress.

Nelson, Joy, jt. auth. see Irwin, Phyllis.

Nelson, Joyce. The Perfect Machine: Television & the Bomb. (Illus.). 192p. (Orig.). 1991. lib. bdg. 39.95 (*0-86571-234-4*); pap. 12.95 (*0-86571-235-2*) New Soc Pubs.
— Sultans of Sleaze: Public Relations & the Media. 160p. (Orig.). 1993. 29.95 (*1-56751-003-5*); pap. 12.95 (*1-56751-002-7*) Common Courage.

Nelson, Joyce & Nelson, John. Holiday Woodworking Projects: 90 Patterns for Festive Decorations. LC 93-17075. (Illus.). 160p. 1993. pap. 12.95 (*0-8117-2547-2*) Stackpole.

Nelson, Joyce C., jt. auth. see Nelson, John A.

Nelson, Joyce I. A Matter of Life & Death: Recent Death Rates among the South Dakotan Elderly. (Studies in Historical Demography). 225p. 1990. reprint ed. 50.00 (*0-8240-3361-2*) Garland.

***Nelson, Judd O., et al, eds.** Immunmoanalysis of Agrochemicals: Emerging Technologies. LC 95-5968. (ACS Symposium Ser.: No. 586). 1995. write for info. (*0-8412-3149-4*) Am Chemical.

***Nelson, Judith.** Beau Guest. braille ed. 377p. 1991. text ed., vinyl bd. 30.16 (*1-56956-404-3*, BR8402) W A T Braille.
— Two Hearts Trump. 208p. (Orig.). 1993. pap. 3.99 (*0-515-11253-4*) Jove Pubns.

Nelson, Judith G. Six Keys to Recruiting, Orienting & Involving Nonprofit Board Members: A Guide to Building Your Board. (Nonprofit Governance Ser.: No. 42). 58p. (Orig.). (C). 1992. reprint ed. pap. text ed. 20.00 (*0-925299-11-1*) Natl Ctr Nonprofit.

Nelson, Judy, jt. auth. see Faulkner, Sandra.

Nelson, Julianne, jt. ed. see Sato, Ryuzo.

Nelson, Julie A., jt. ed. see Ferber, Marianne A.

Nelson, June K. Harry Bertoia, Printmaker: Monotypes & Other Monographics. LC 87-32780. (Great Lakes Bks.). (Illus.). 235p. 1987. 39.95 (*0-8143-1964-5*); pap. 19.95 (*0-8143-2063-5*) Wayne St U Pr.

Nelson, K., ed. Internationales Zuchtbuch, 1988. (Illus.). (GER.). 1988. write for info. (*0-913934-13-5*) Chicago Zoo.
— Picosecond & Femtosecond Spectroscopy from Laboratory to Real World. 1990. 42.00 (*0-8194-0250-8*, VOL. 1209) SPIE.

Nelson, K., jt. auth. see French, L. A.

Nelson, K. D. Design & Construction of Small Earth Dams. (Illus.). 128p. 1985. pap. 27.95 (*0-909605-34-3*, Pub. by Inkata Pr AT) Intl Spec Bk.
— Design & Construction of Small Earth Dams. (C). 1991. text ed. 125.00 (*81-7233-003-0*, Pub. by Scientific Pubs II) St Mut.
— Design & Construction of Small Earth Dams. 128p. (C). 1988. reprint ed. 160.00 (*0-685-54224-6*, Scientific) St Mut.

Nelson, K. E., jt. ed. see Speidel, G.

Nelson, K. Ray, jt. auth. see Smith, J. David.

***Nelson, Kai.** Moral Concerns. 240p. 1995. 16.95 (*1-55111-013-X*) Broadview Pr.

***Nelson, Karin B. & Ellenberg, Jonas H., eds.** Febrile Seizures. fac. ed. LC 80-5898. (Illus.). 378p. Date not set. pap. 107.80 (*0-7837-7526-1*, 2046979) Bks Demand.

Nelson, Karl & Stanton, Barry. Life on the Line: The Karl Nelson Story. LC 93-27769. (Illus.). 192p. 1993. 19.95 (*1-56796-051-0*) WRS Group.

Nelson, Katherine. Making Sense: The Acquisition of Shared Meaning. (Developmental Psychology Ser.). 1985. text ed. 59.00 (*0-12-515420-8*) Acad Pr.

Nelson, Katherine, ed. Event Knowledge: Structure & Function in Development. 288p. (C). 1986. text ed. 49.95 (*0-89859-657-2*) L Erlbaum Assocs.
— Narratives from the Crib. LC 88-28455. (Illus.). 368p. 1989. 36.00 (*0-674-60118-1*) HUP.

Nelson, Katherine A., jt. auth. see Trevino, Linda K.

Nelson, Kathryn E., et al. Voices from the Field: Lessons from the Family Academy. LC 94-18656. 1994. write for info. (*0-934842-30-2*) CSPA.

Nelson, Kathryn P. Gentrification & Distressed Cities: An Assessment of Trends in Intrametropolitan Migration. LC 87-40370. (Social Demography Ser.). 224p. (C). 1988. pap. text ed. 16.25 (*0-299-11164-4*) U of Wis Pr.

Nelson, Kay. Friendly Windows 3.1. 1993. pap. 6.99 (*0-679-79183-3*) Random.
— Friendly WordPerfect for Windows. Date not set. write for info. (*0-679-75332-X*) Random.
— Friendly WordPerfect 5.1. 1993. pap. 5.99 (*0-679-79185-X*) Random.
— Writing Your Life Story: A Legacy to Your Family. (Illus.). 79p. (Orig.). 1989. pap. 8.95 (*0-9623302-0-5*) Wstwnds Pubns.

Nelson, Kay H. & Huse, Nancy, eds. The Critical Response to Tillie Olsen. LC 93-41228. (Critical Responses in Arts & Letters Ser.: No. 10). 304p. 1994. text ed. 59.95 (*0-313-28714-7*, Greenwood Pr) Greenwood.

Nelson, Kay S. A Bonnie Scottish Cookbook. LC 89-7778. 144p. (Orig.). 1989. pap. 10.95 (*0-939009-25-0*) EPM Pubns.
— One-Dish Meals from Around the World. 1993. pap. 14.95 (*0-8128-8551-1*, Scrbrough Hse) Madison Bks UPA.
— Soups from Around the World. 1993. pap. 14.95 (*0-8128-8552-X*, Scrbrough Hse) Madison Bks UPA.
— Stews & Ragouts: Simple & Hearty One-Dish Meals. 1978. reprint ed. pap. 5.95 (*0-486-23662-5*) Dover.

Nelson, Kay Y. Friendly Macintosh. 1993. pap. 6.99 (*0-679-79191-4*) Random.
— The Little DOS 5 Book. (Illus.). 160p. 1991. pap. 12.95 (*0-938151-43-6*) Peachpit Pr.
— The Little DOS 6 Book. (Illus.). 232p. 1993. pap. 13.00 (*1-56609-056-3*) Peachpit Pr.
— The Little OS-2 Book: 2.1 Edition. (Illus.). 176p. (Orig.). 1993. pap. 13.00 (*1-56609-047-4*) Peachpit Pr.
— Little System 7.1-7.5 Book. 180p. 1994. pap. 13.95 (*1-56609-151-9*) Peachpit Pr.
— The Little Windows Book, 3.1 Edition. (Illus.). 144p. 1992. pap. 12.95 (*0-938151-81-9*) Peachpit Pr.
— The Little Windows 95 Book. 375p. 1995. pap. 17.95 (*1-56609-181-0*) Peachpit Pr.
— One-Two-Three for Windows Answers: Certified Tech Support. 1994. pap. text ed. 16.95 (*0-07-882068-5*) McGraw.
— Voodoo DOS: Tips & Tricks with an Attitude Through Version 6.0. 2nd ed. pap. 21.95 (*1-56604-046-9*) Ventana Pr.
— Voodoo Mac. (Illus.). 307p. pap. 21.95 (*1-56604-028-0*) Ventana Pr.
— Voodoo Mac: Mastery Tips & Masterful Tricks. 2nd ed. (Illus.). 350p. 1994. disk, pap. 24.95 (*1-56604-177-5*) Ventana Pr.
— Voodoo Windows: Tips & Tricks with an Attitude. (Illus.). 282p. (C). 1992. pap. 19.95 (*1-56604-005-1*) Ventana Pr.
— Voodoo Windows 95: Mastery Tips & Masterful Tricks. 2nd ed. (Illus.). 375p. 1995. disk 24.94 (*1-56604-145-7*) Ventana Pr.

Nelson, Kay Y., jt. auth. see Harvey, Greg.

Nelson, Kay Yarborough. Word for Windows 6.0 Slick Tricks. 1994. pap. 16.00 (*0-679-79175-2*) Random.

Nelson, Keith & Van Kleeck, Anne E., eds. Children's Language, Vol. 6. 366p. 1987. text ed. 89.95 (*0-89859-760-9*) L Erlbaum Assocs.

Nelson, Keith, ed. see Grattan, C. H.

Nelson, Keith E., ed. Children's Language, Vol. 3. 522p. (C). 1982. text ed. 89.95 (*0-89859-264-X*) L Erlbaum Assocs.
— Children's Language, Vol. 4. 496p. 1983. text ed. 89.95 (*0-89859-272-0*) L Erlbaum Assocs.
— Children's Language, Vol. 5. 472p. (C). 1985. text ed. 89.95 (*0-89859-346-8*) L Erlbaum Assocs.

Nelson, Keith E. & Reger, Zita, eds. Children's Language, Vol. 8. 304p. 1994. text ed. 59.95 (*0-8058-1367-5*) L Erlbaum Assocs.

*Nelson, Keith L. The Making of Detente: Soviet-American Relations in the Shadow of Vietnam. LC 94-34423. 248p. 1994. text ed. 35.00x (0-8018-4883-0) Johns Hopkins.
— Victors Divided: America & the Allies in Germany, 1918-1923. LC 72-87203. 463p. reprint ed. pap. 132.00 (0-318-34901-9, 2031308) Bks Demand.
Nelson, Keith L. & Olin, Spencer C. Why War? Ideology, Theory, & History. LC 78-51746. 1980. pap. 13.00 (0-520-04279-4) U CA Pr.
Nelson, Kelly, jt. ed. see Atkinson, Robert.
Nelson, Ken & Dyville, Jack. A Country Christmas Carol. (Illus.). 36p. (Orig.). 1985. pap. 3.50 (0-88680-235-0); 12.50 (0-88680-247-4) I E Clark.
Nelson, Kennard. Flower & Plant Production in the Greenhouse. 4th ed. (Illus.). 220p. 1991. 26.60 (0-8134-2843-2); teacher ed 6.95 (0-8134-2850-5); text ed. 19.95 (0-685-38376-8) Interstate.
Nelson, Kennard S. Greenhouse Management for Flower & Plant Production. 2nd ed. 252p. 1980. 29.25 (0-8134-2070-9, 2070); teacher ed 4.95 (0-8134-2324-4); text ed. 21.95 (0-685-02544-6) Interstate.
Nelson, Kenneth A. Electrical Engineering Quick Reference Cards. (Engineering Reference Manual Ser.). 70p. 1991. spiral bd. 18.95 (0-912045-21-3) Prof Pubns CA.
Nelson, Kenneth C. Understanding Station Carrier. LC 73-85629. (Basic Ser.). (Illus.). 68p. (Orig.). (C). 1983. pap. 13.95 (1-56016-005-5) ABC TeleTraining.
Nelson, Kent. The Straight Man. LC 77-88656. 144p. 1978. pap. 3.50 (0-916870-11-1, Blk Lizard) Creat Arts Bk.
Nelson, Kerry, ed. see Douglas County Historical Society Staff.
Nelson, Kevin. Baseball's Even Greater Insults: More of the Game's Most Outrageous & Irreverent Remarks. LC 92-32597. (Illus.). 240p. (Orig.). 1993. pap. 9.00 (0-671-76066-1, Fireside) S&S Trade.
— The Greatest Golf Shot Ever Made: And Other Lively & Entertaining Tales from the Lore & History of Golf. (Illus.). 256p. (Orig.). 1992. 21.00 (0-671-75002-X, Fireside) S&S Trade.
— Pickle, Pepper, & Tip-In-Too. 1994. pap. 15.00 (0-671-87956-1, Fireside) S&S Trade.
— Talkin' Trash: Basketball's Greatest Insults. LC 93-4342. 1993. pap. 10.00 (0-671-76067-X) S&S Trade.
Nelson, Kim L. Bioprocess Engineering: Systems, Equipment & Facilities. Lyderson, Bjorn K. et al, eds. LC 93-44639. 1994. text ed. 89.95 (0-471-03544-0, Wiley-Interscience) Wiley.
Nelson, Kirk. North of the Red River. Van Treese, James B., ed. 178p. 1994. pap. 7.95 (1-56901-199-0) NW Pub.
— The Second Coming. (Orig.). 1986. pap. 8.95 (0-9617119-0-6) Wright Pub VA.
Nelson, Klayton E. Harvesting & Handling California Table Grapes for Market. LC 79-51948. (Illus.). 76p. 1979. pap. 10.00 (0-931876-33-8, 1913) ANR Pubns CA.
Nelson, Kou K., jt. auth. see Frost, Dan R.
Nelson, Kristine, jt. ed. see Adams, Paul.
*Nelson, Kristine E. & Landsman, Miriam J. Alternative Models of Family Preservation: Family-Based Services in Context. 266p. 1992. pap. 30.95 (0-398-06303-6) C C Thomas.
— Alternative Models of Family Preservation: Family-Based Services in Context. 266p. (C). 1992. text ed. 51.95x (0-398-05810-5) C C Thomas.
Nelson, L. N., jt. ed. see Nelson, P. N.
Nelson-L'Aloge, Virginia, ed. see L'Aloge, Bob.
*Nelson, Larry E. Bullets, Ballots & Rhetoric: Confederate Policy for the U. S. Presidential Contest of 1864. LC 79-27869. 249p. 1980. pap. 71.00 (0-7837-8396-5, 2059207) Bks Demand.
Nelson, Larry R., jt. auth. see Clancy, Gary.
Nelson, Laura L., ed. see Milam, June M.
*Nelson, Lee. Beyond the Veil. 142p. 1994. pap. 10.95 (1-55517-166-4) CFI Dist.
— Beyond the Veil, No. II. 163p. 1995. pap. 10.95 (1-55517-172-9) CFI Dist.
— Beyond the Veil, No. III. 151p. 1994. pap. 10.95 (1-55517-165-6) CFI Dist.
Nelson, Lee, ed. Storm Testament: Porter Rockwell, Walkara, Butch Cassidy, Storm Testament, 4 bks., Set. 1992. boxed 39.95 (1-56684-009-0, Council Pr) Pubs Dist Ctr Inc.
Nelson, Lee & Nelson, Miriam G. Concordance to Epistle to the Son of the Wolf. 282p. (Orig.). 1985. 11.95 (0-933770-45-6) Kalimat.
Nelson, Lee H. The Colossus of 1812: An American Engineering Superlative. 64p. 1989. pap. text ed. 25.00 (0-87262-737-3) Am Soc Civil Eng.
Nelson, Leon. The Bonding Book. 1985. 49.95 (0-87814-267-3, D4238) PennWell Bks.
Nelson, Leonard B. Pediatric Ophthalmology. (Major Problems in Clinical Pediatrics Ser.: Vol. 25). (Illus.). 288p. 1984. text ed. 69.95 (0-7216-1191-5) Saunders.
Nelson, Leonard B., jt. auth. see Catalano, Robert A.
Nelson, Leonard T., jt. auth. see Bennett, Albert B., Jr.
Nelson, Leslie W., jt. auth. see Lorbeer, George C.
Nelson, Lester, jt. auth. see National Association of Credit Management Staff.
Nelson, Lester, ed. see National Association of Credit Management Staff.
Nelson, Lewis B. History of the U. S. Fertilizer Industry. Parker, J. Harold, ed. LC 91-205883. (Illus.). 522p. 1990. text ed. 45.00 (0-87077-004-7) TVA.
Nelson, Lin, et al. Turning Things Around: A Women's Occupational & Environmental Health Resource Guide. (Illus.). 162p. (Orig.). 1990. pap. 12.95 (0-939522-01-2) Nat Womens Hlth Netwk.
Nelson, Linda, jt. ed. see Little, Judith W.
Nelson, Linda, ed. see McKinley, Robert K.
*Nelson, Linda A. & Lewis, Rob. In Digging Through Grandma's Attic: Walnut, Iowa. (Illus.). 20p. (Orig.). 1994. pap. 7.95 (0-9640662-1-1) R Lewis Pub.
Nelson, Linda L., jt. ed. see Spence, Richard B.
Nelson, Lisa. Ice Age Mammals of the Colorado Plateau. (Northern Arizona University Colorado Plateau Research Ser.). 24p. 1990. pap. 9.00 (0-9624990-0-5) Ctr Study First Am.
Nelson, Lisa, ed. see Charlip, Remy.
Nelson, Lisa M. Bright Smiles & Blue Skies: Positive Music for Today's Kids. (Illus.). 16p. (Orig.). (J). (gr. k-6). 1990. audio, pap. 9.95 (0-9627863-0-6) Brght Ideas CA.
— Freddy Bear's Wakeful Winter. (Illus.). 32p. (Orig.). (J). (ps-4). 1994. pap. text ed. 6.95 (1-883212-02-2, BIP401) Brght Ideas CA.
Nelson, Louella. Days of Fire. (American Romance Ser.). 1993. mass mkt. 3.39 (0-373-16479-3, 1-16479-7) Harlequin Bks.
— Emerald Fortune. (American Romance Ser.: No. 379). 1991. pap. 2.95 (0-373-16379-7) Harlequin Bks.
Nelson, Lowry. Cuba: The Measure of a Revolution. LC 77-187163. 258p. reprint ed. pap. 73.60 (0-8357-8855-5, 2033275) Bks Demand.
— The Minnesota Community: Country & Town in Transition. LC 60-10191. 185p. reprint ed. pap. 52.80 (0-317-29451-2, 2055893) Bks Demand.
— The Mormon Village: A Study in Social Origins. 1972. 59.95 (0-8490-0673-2) Gordon Pr.
Nelson, Lowry, Jr. Poetic Configurations: Essays in Literary History & Criticism. 352p. 1992. text ed. 35.00 (0-271-00800-8) Pa St U Pr.
Nelson, Lowry, Jr., jt. ed. see Jackson, Robert L.
Nelson, Lowry, Jr., ed. see Pulsiano, Phillip & Skaptason, Jon.
Nelson, Lowry, Jr., ed. see Weingartner, Russel.
Nelson, Lycette, tr. see Blanchot, Maurice.
Nelson, Lyle M., jt. ed. see Lerner, Daniel.
Nelson, Lynda B., jt. auth. see Madsen, Donna L.
*Nelson, Lynda M. The Little Red Buckets. Florence, Giles et al, eds. (Illus.). 91p. (Orig.). (J). 1995. pap. 4.95x (0-9645810-9-4) Galleon Pubns.
*Nelson, Lynn. Creating Commands on the AS-400. (FastStart Ser.). (Illus.). 82p. (Orig.). 1994. pap. 59.00 (1-884322-32-8) Comp Applicatns.
Nelson, Lynn A. Learning to Print Animal Alphabet Book. (J). 1990. 9.95 (0-88047-221-9, D9007) DOK Pubs.
Nelson, Lynn D. & Kuzes, Irina Y. Radical Reform in Yeltsin's Russia: Successes & Failures. (Illus.). 256p. 1995. 60.00 (1-56324-479-9); pap. text ed. 22.95 (1-56324-480-2) M E Sharpe.
Nelson, Lynn D., et al. Property to the People: The Struggle for Radical Economic Reform in Russia. LC 93-5692. 320p. 1993. pap. text ed. 19.95 (1-56324-274-5) M E Sharpe.
— Property to the People: The Struggle for Radical Economic Reform in Russia. LC 93-5692. 280p. 1994. text ed. 59.95 (1-56324-273-7) M E Sharpe.
Nelson, Lynn H. The Chronicle of San Juan de la Pena: A Fourteenth-Century Official History of the Crown of Aragon. LC 91-8495. (Middle Ages Ser.). 160p. (C). 1991. text ed. 27.95x (0-8122-3068-X); pap. text ed. 12.95 (0-8122-1352-1) U of Pa Pr.
— Global Perspectives, Vol. II, Since 1600: Source Readings from World Civilizations. 492p. (C). 1989. pap. text ed. 18.00 (0-15-529617-5) HB Coll Pubs.
— Who Knows: From Quine to a Feminist Empiricism. 336p. (C). 1990. 34.95 (0-87722-647-4) Temple U Pr.
— Who Knows: From Quine to a Feminist Empiricism. 336p. 1992. pap. 18.95 (1-56639-007-9) Temple U Pr.
Nelson, Lynn H., ed. Global Perspectives, Vol. I, 3000 B.C. to 1600 A.D. Source Readings from World Civilizations. 430p. (C). 1988. pap. text ed. 18.00 (0-15-529616-7) HB Coll Pubs.
— The Human Perspective: Reading in World Civilization, 2 vols., Vol. I: The Ancient World to the Early Modern Era. 328p. (C). 1987. Vol. I: The Ancient World to the Early Modern Era, 328pgs. pap. text ed. 17.50 (0-15-540392-3) HB Coll Pubs.
— The Human Perspective: Reading in World Civilization, Vol. II: The Modern World Through 20th Century. 384p. (C). 1987. Vol. II: The Modern World Through the Twentieth Century, 384pgs. pap. text ed. 17.50 (0-15-540393-1) HB Coll Pubs.
Nelson, Lynn H. & Peebles, Patrick. Classics of Eastern Thought. 608p. (C). 1991. pap. text ed. 20.00 (0-15-507655-8) HB Coll Pubs.
Nelson, Lynn H. & Shirk, Melanie. Liutprand of Cremona, Mission to Constantinople 968 A.D. 62p. 1972. pap. 5.00 (0-87291-039-3) Coronado Pr.
Nelson, Lynn H., jt. auth. see Drummond, Steven K.
Nelson, Lynn T. & Nelson, Gail L. Encyclopedia of Reflexology: A Working Professional's Text. 2nd ed. (Illus.). 430p. 1988. 79.95 (0-9623429-0-4) Digits Intl.
— The Encyclopedia of Reflexology: A Working Professional's Text. 3rd ed. (Illus.). 435p. (C). 1990. pap. 79.95 (0-9623429-2-0) Digits Intl.
— Introduction to Hand & Foot Reflexology. (Illus.). (C). 1990. write for info. (0-318-65302-8) Digits Intl.
— Introduction to Reflexology. (Illus.). 56p. (Orig.). (C). 1990. pap. 19.95 (0-9623429-9-8) Digits Intl.
Nelson, M. A., jt. ed. see Hukins, D. W.
Nelson, M. E., ed. Pets-R-Permitted Hotel, Motel, Kennel & Petsitter Directory. 320p. 1995. pap. 10.95 (1-56471-795-X) Annenberg.
— Pets-R-Permitted Hotel, Motel, Kennel & Petsitter Directory: Petcare Options When You Travel. 288p. (Orig.). 1993. pap. 9.95 (1-56471-779-8) Annenberg.
Nelson, M. E., ed. see Annenberg Communications Staff.
Nelson, M. J., et al. Denny Reading Test. 1973. text ed. 22.72 (0-395-17986-6) HM.
Nelson, M. W. Los Testigos de Jehova. 130p. 1984. reprint ed. pap. 3.95 (0-311-06352-7) Casa Bautista.
Nelson, Malcolm A., jt. auth. see George, Diana Hume.
Nelson, Margaret, et al. Ladder Ranch Research Project: A Report of the First Season. (Maxwell Museum Papers: No. 1). (Illus.). 105p. 1984. pap. 10.00 (0-912535-02-4) Max Mus.
*Nelson, Margaret C., et al, eds. Equity Issue for Women in Archeology. LC 94-33016. (Archeological Papers: No. 5). 1994. write for info. (0-913167-67-3) Am Anthro Assn.
Nelson, Margaret K. Negotiated Care: The Experience of Family Day Care Providers. 400p. 1991. 34.95 (0-87722-728-4) Temple U Pr.
Nelson, Margaret K., jt. ed. see Abel, Emily K.
Nelson, Margaret V. Study of Judicial Review in Virginia, 1789-1928. LC 47-31482. (Columbia University. Studies in the Social Sciences: No. 532). reprint ed. 20.00 (0-404-51532-0) AMS Pr.
Nelson, Marguerite. Desert Nurse. large type ed. (Linford Romance Library). 240p. 1992. pap. 14.95 (0-7089-7211-X, Trailtree Bookshop) Ulverscroft.
Nelson, Marguerite H. Teacher Stories: Teaching Archetypes Revealed by Analysis. 122p. (Orig.). 1993. pap. text ed. 10.40 (0-911168-86-9) Prakken.
*Nelson, Mariah B. The Stronger Women Get, the More Men Love Football. 320p. 1995. reprint ed. pap. 11.00 (0-380-72527-4) Avon.
— The Stronger Women Get, the More Men Love Football: Sex & Sports in America. LC 93-44358. 1994. 22.95 (0-15-181393-0) HarBrace.
*Nelson, Marian. Guide to Worldwide Postal-Code & Address Formats, 1994. 3rd ed. 150p. 1995. spiral bd. 129.50 (0-9630677-3-7) Nelson Assocs.
Nelson, Marie. Judith, Juliana, & Elene: Three Fighting Saints. LC 91-17515. (American University Studies: English Language & Literature: Ser. IV, Vol. 135). 210p. 1992. 37.95 (0-8204-1576-6) P Lang Pubs.
Nelson, Marie C. Bitter Bread: The Famine in Norrbotten, 1867-1868. (Studia Historica Upsaliensia: No. 153). 192p. (Orig.). 1988. pap. 43.50x (91-554-2264-0, Pub. by Uppsala Univ Acta Univ Uppsaliensis SW) Coronet Bks.
Nelson, Marie C., ed. The Narcissistic Condition: A Fact of Our Lives & Times. LC 76-20724. (Self-in-Process Ser.: Vol. 1). 300p. 1977. 43.95 (0-87705-250-6) Human Sci Pr.
Nelson, Marie C. & Eigen, Michael, eds. Evil: Self & Culture. (Self-in-Process Ser.: Vol. 4). 352p. 1984. 42.95 (0-89885-143-2) Human Sci Pr.
Nelson, Marie C. & Ikenberry, Jean, eds. Psychosexual Imperatives: Their Role in Identity Formation. LC 78-17739. (Self-in-Process Ser.: Vol. 2). 397p. 1979. 45.95 (0-87705-302-2) Human Sci Pr.
Nelson, Marie W. At the Point of Need: Teaching Basic & ESL Writers. 269p. (C). 1990. pap. text ed. 23.00 (0-86709-265-3, 0265) Boynton Cook Pubs.
Nelson, Marilyn M. Practical Guide to Neutral Networks with Disks. 1991. 36.95 (0-201-52376-0) Addison-Wesley.
*Nelson, Marion, et al. Material Culture & People's Art among the Norwegians in America. (Special Publications). 228p. 1994. 30.00 (0-87732-082-9) Norwegian-Am Hist Assn.
Nelson, Marion J. Art Pottery of the Midwest. Brown, Susan, ed. LC 88-51176. (Illus.). 120p. (Orig.). 1988. pap. text ed. 25.00 (0-938713-03-5) Univ MN Art Mus.
Nelson, Marjorie. Pawns & Symbols. (Star Trek Ser.: No. 26). 288p. (Orig.). 1988. mass mkt. 5.50 (0-671-66497-2, Pocket Star Bks) PB.
*Nelson, Mark. C++ Program Guide to Standard Template Library. 1995. pap. 39.99 (1-56884-314-3) IDG Bks.
— Data Compression: A C Plus Plus Developers. 1995. pap. 39.99 (1-56884-323-2) IDG Bks.
— The Data Compression Book. 527p. (Orig.). 1991. pap. 29.95 (1-55851-214-4); disk, pap. 39.95 (1-55851-216-0) M&T Bks.
— The Data Compression Book. 2nd ed. 600p. 1995. disk, pap. 39.95 (1-55851-434-1) M&T Bks.
— Serial Communications Programming in C & C Plus Plus: An Object-Oriented Approach. 400p. (Orig.). 1992. pap. 32.95 (1-55851-281-0) M&T Bks.
Nelson, Mark & Alling, Abigail. Life under Glass: The Inside Story of Biosphere 2. 312p. 1993. pap. 16.95 (1-882428-07-2) Biosphere Pr.
Nelson, Mark, jt. auth. see Allen, John.
Nelson, Mark A., jt. auth. see Verheiden, Mark.
Nelson, Mark E. An Econometric Study of Residential Electricity Demand: A Conditional Demand Analysis of End-Use Equipment Consumption. Sweeney, T. J. & Loeffler, L., eds. (Illus.). 155p. 1994. 795.00 (1-56471-005-X) Annenberg.
Nelson, Mark L. Bibliography of Old Time Saddlemakers. 98p. (Orig.). 1992. pap. 20.00 (0-9632094-1-8) Nelson Pub.
Nelson, Marlin L., ed. Readings in Third World Missions: A Collection of Essential Documents. LC 76-45803. 294p. 1976. pap. 7.95 (0-87808-319-7) William Carey Lib.
Nelson, Martha. On Being a Deacon's Wife. LC 72-96150. 96p. 1973. 11.99 (0-8054-3505-0) Broadman.
— On Being a Deacon's Wife: Study Guide. LC 72-96150. 1991. 2.99 (0-8054-3507-7) Broadman.
Nelson, Martia. Coming Home: The Return to True Self. 240p. 1993. pap. 12.95 (1-882591-11-9) Nataraj Pub.
— Coming Home: The Return to True Self. rev. ed. 256p. 1995. pap. 12.95 (1-882591-23-2) Nataraj Pub.
Nelson, Mary, ed. Family Life Educator: Selected Articles, Vols. 1-3. 108p. 1985. pap. text ed. 14.95 (0-941816-18-4) ETR Assocs.
— Family Life Educator: Teaching Tools, Vols. 1-3. 72p. 1985. pap. text ed. 14.95 (0-941816-19-2) ETR Assocs.
Nelson, Mary & Clark, Kay, eds. The Educator's Guide to Preventing Child Sexual Abuse. 250p. 1986. pap. text ed. 19.95 (0-941816-17-6) ETR Assocs.
Nelson, Mary, ed. see Abbey, Nancy & Wagman, Ellen.
Nelson, Mary, ed. see Bignell, Steven.
Nelson, Mary, jt. auth. see Keet, Robert B.
Nelson, Mary, ed. see Quackenbush, Marcia & Villarreal, Sylvia.
Nelson, Mary, ed. see Stronck, David.
Nelson, Mary, ed. see Strong, Bryan & DeVault, Christine.
Nelson, Mary A., jt. auth. see Reams, Bernard D., Jr.
Nelson, Mary A., jt. ed. see Reams, Bernard D., Jr.
Nelson, Mary Ann, jt. auth. see Reams, Bernard D., Jr.
Nelson, Mary B. Let's Talk Turkey. Van Treese, James B., ed. 158p. 1995. pap. 7.95 (1-56901-012-9) NW Pub.
Nelson, Mary C. Artists of the Spirit: New Prophets in Art & Mysticism. Mackenzie, Anne, ed. LC 94-10117. (Illus.). 264p. (Orig.). 1994. pap. 25.00 (0-916955-14-1) Arcus Pub.
*Nelson, Mary S. Fruit That Bends the Bough. 100p. 1995. 16.00 (1-886029-05-9) Zeppelin Pr.
Nelson, Maxine F. Collectible Vernon Kilns. 1994. pap. 18.95 (0-89145-584-1) Collector Bks.
Nelson, Meryl. All American Cooking: Savory Recipes from Savvy Creative Cooks Across America. LC 91-6652. 125p. 1992. pap. 7.95 (0-88247-902-4, 902-4) R & E Pubs.
— Meryl Nelson's When You're Out of... Cookbook. rev. ed. Sing, Shirley, ed. LC 83-51044. (Illus.). 104p. 1983. pap. 4.95 (0-941900-06-1) This N That.
— This for That: A Treasury of Savy Substitutions for the Creative Cook. 3rd ed. Sing, Shirley & Thoman, Frances, eds. LC 90-62126. (Illus.). 112p. 1991. pap. 6.95 (0-88247-847-8) R & E Pubs.
Nelson, Meryl & Thoman, Frances. Meryl Nelson's Cooking Coast to Coast. Sing, Shirley, ed. LC 83-51697. (Illus.). 120p. (Orig.). 1984. pap. 3.95 (0-941900-08-8) This N That.
Nelson-Metlay, Valerie, tr. see Graham, Bill.

Nelson, Mexico Mike. Mexico's Colonial Heart: Including Mexico City. Nelson, Charles, ed. LC 94-90360. (Sanborn's Travelog - Mexico by Land Ser.). (Illus.). 240p. (Orig.). 1995. pap. 15.95 (1-878166-17-4) Wanderlust Pubns. This is the only book of its kind--a guide for people who drive in Mexico. Readers who fly & rent cars will benefit just as much as those who drive from the border. More than a guidebook, this volume has detailed directions that take the reader by the hand & direct him, mile by mile, through the heartland of Mexico. Coupled with unique maps of every major town he'll encounter & photographs to excite his interest, the reader can use this to plan his trip before he leaves. Armchair travelers will buy it for the collection of humorous & poignant anecdotes by the author that give the reader a true feel for what it's like to travel "real" Mexico. The author's expertise has been recognized by: WALL STREET JOURNAL, NY TIMES, WASHINGTON POST, AP, US NEWS & WORLD REPORT, TEXAS MONTHLY & more. He's the media spokesperson for Mexico's surface tourism program & has lived in or traveled Mexico for more than 20 years. He has done extensive radio, TV & print interviews & in-store signings to promote his other book, MEXICO FROM THE DRIVER'S SEAT & has an aggressive plan to do the same for this one. To order, contact: Sunbelt Publications, 1-800-626-6579 or directly to: Wanderlust Publications, 210-686-3601. ***Publisher Provided Annotation.***

Nelson, Michael. The Development of Tropical Lands: Policy Issues in Latin America. LC 72-12363. (Resources for the Future Ser.). 323p. 1973. 27.00 (0-8018-1488-X) Johns Hopkins.
— The Development of Tropical Lands: Policy Issues in Latin America. LC 72-12363. (Illus.). 326p. reprint ed. pap. 93.00 (0-685-20405-7, 2030212) Bks Demand.
— Historical Documents on Presidential Elections, 1787-1988. 902p. 1991. 93.00 (0-87187-607-8) Congr Quarterly.
Nelson, Michael, ed. The Elections of Nineteen Ninety-Two. 192p. 1993. 30.95 (0-87187-937-9); pap. 19.95 (0-87187-657-4) Congr Quarterly.
— A Heartbeat Away: Report of the Task Force on the Vice-Presidency. 120p. 1988. text ed. 18.95 (0-318-35969-3); pap. text ed. 9.95 (0-318-35970-7) Routledge Chapman & Hall.
— The Presidency A to Z: A Ready Reference Encyclopedia. rev. ed. LC 94-17668. (Encyclopedia of American Government Ser.: Vol. 2). 1994. 125.00 (1-56802-056-2); pap. 59.95 (1-56802-006-6) Congr Quarterly.
Nelson, Michael, jt. auth. see CQ Inc. Staff.
Nelson, Michael, jt. auth. see Hargrove, Erwin C.

An Asterisk (*) at the beginning of an entry indicates that the title is appearing in BIP for the first time.

Nelson, Michael, jt. ed. see Heard, Alexander.
Nelson, Michael, jt. auth. see Milkis, Sidney M.
Nelson, Michael E., jt. auth. see Watts, Mark T.
Nelson, Michael G., jt. ed. see Bandopadhyay, Sukumar.
Nelson, Michael J. Managing Health Professionals. 216p. 1990. pap. 25.50 (0-412-33350-3, A4446) Chapman & Hall.
Nelson, Mico. The Cutting Edge of Audio Production & Post Production: Theory, Equipment & Techniques. 265p. 1994. 39.95 (0-86729-304-7) Knowledge Indus.
Nelson, Mike. Baja Driver's Travelog. (Mexico by Land Ser.). 52p. (Orig.). 1993. pap. 14.95 (1-878166-07-7) Wanderlust Pubns.
— Mexico from the Driver's Seat: Tales of the Road from Baja to the Yucatan. (Sanborn's Mexico Bks.). 129p. (Orig.). 1991. pap. 8.95 (1-878166-04-2) Wanderlust Pubns.
— Mexico's Gulf Driver's Travelog North to South: Border to Acayucan. (Mexico by Land Ser.). 90p. (Orig.). 1993. pap. 14.95 (1-878166-09-3) Wanderlust Pubns.
— Mexico's Gulf Driver's Travelog South to North: Acayucan to Border. (Mexico by Land Ser.). 90p. (Orig.). 1993. pap. 14.95 (1-878166-12-3) Wanderlust Pubns.
— Mexico's West Coast Driver's Travelog. (Mexico by Land Ser.). 80p. (Orig.). 1993. pap. 19.95 (1-878166-10-7) Wanderlust Pubns.
— Mexico's West Coast Driver's Travelog South to North: Mazatlan Nogales. (Mexico by Land Ser.). (Illus.). 80p. (Orig.). 1993. pap. 19.95 (1-878166-15-8) Wanderlust Pubns.
— Monterrey-Saltillo Driver's Travelog: South Texas Gateways. 2nd ed. (Mexico by Land Ser.). (Illus.). 60p. 1994. pap. 14.95 (1-878166-14-X) Wanderlust Pubns.
— Oaxaca & Chiapas Driver's Travelog. (Mexico by Land Ser.). 60p. (Orig.). 1993. pap. 9.95 (1-878166-11-5) Wanderlust Pubns.
— Ruta Maya Driver's Travelog. (Mexico by Land Ser.). 150p. (Orig.). 1993. pap. 19.95 (1-878166-08-5) Wanderlust Pubns.
— Sanborn's R. V. Guide to Mexico: For Campers Too! 2nd ed. Yelland, Christopher, ed. (Illus.). 53p. 1993. pap. 6.95 (1-878166-06-9) Wanderlust Pubns.
Nelson, Mike, ed. see Shroeder, Rick & Riser, Mel.
Nelson, Mike D. The World's Worst Cookbook. 104p. (Orig.). 1994. pap. 8.95 (1-56790-137-9) Cool Hand Comms.
Nelson, Milward D. The Syriac Version of the Wisdom of Ben Sira Compared to the Greek & Hebrew Materials. LC 87-28674. (Society of Biblical Literature Dissertation Ser.). 140p. 1989. 18.95 (1-55540-193-7, 06 21 07); pap. 12.95 (1-55540-194-5, 06 21 07) Scholars Pr GA.
Nelson, Miriam G., jt. auth. see Nelson, Lee.
***Nelson-Morrill, Creston, ed.** Florida Caregivers Handbook. 2nd rev. ed. 276p. pap. 14.95 (0-9638162-0-9) HlthTrac Res.
— Florida Caregivers Handbook: An Essential Resource Guide for Caregivers & Their Older Loved Ones. LC 91-71913. 248p. (Orig.). 1991. pap. 14.95 (1-879919-99-0) HealthTrac.
Nelson-Morrill, Creston, ed. see Polangin, Richard F. & Feigenbaum, Ernest.
Nelson, Murry. Children & Social Studies. 2nd ed. 400p. (C). 1992. text ed. 45.75 (0-15-507266-8) HB Coll Pubs.
Nelson, Murry R. Children & Social Studies: Creative Teaching in the Elementary Classroom. 374p. (C). 1987. text ed. 37.25 (0-15-507265-X, NELSON) HB Coll Pubs.
Nelson, Murry R., ed. The Future of the Social Studies. 90p. (Orig.). 1994. pap. 14.95 (0-89994-378-0) Soc Sci Ed.
Nelson, N. S. The Compleat Slug. LC 85-61964. (Illus.). 76p. (Orig.). 1986. pap. 6.50 (0-935195-12-2) Plaid Pony Pubns.
Nelson, Nancy. Any Time, Any Place, Any River: The Nevills of Mexican Hat. LC 91-67399. (Illus.). 85p. (Orig.). 1991. pap. 9.95 (0-9611678-8-2) Red Lake Bks.
— Evenings with Cary Grant. large type ed. 748p. 1992. reprint ed. lib. bdg. 22.95 (1-56054-342-6) Thorndike Pr.
— Evenings with Cary Grant. large type ed. 748p. 1992. pap. 14.95 (1-56054-937-8) Thorndike Pr.
— Evenings with Cary Grant: Recollections in His Own Words & by Those Who Knew Him Best. 448p. 1993. mass mkt. 5.99 (0-446-36398-7) Warner Bks.
— Evenings with Cary Grant: Recollections in His Own Words & by Those Who Knew Him Best. (Illus.). 384p. 1991. 23.00 (0-688-10610-2) Morrow.
***Nelson, Nancy O., ed.** Private Voices, Public Lives: Women Speak on the Literary Life. 384p. (Orig.). 1995. pap. 16.95 (0-929398-88-2) UNTX Pr.
Nelson, Nancy O., ed. see Manfred, Frederick.
Nelson, Nathan, ed. Organellar Proton-ATPases. (Medical Intelligence Unit Ser.). 220p. 1995. 89.00 (1-57059-115-6) R G Landes.
Nelson, Nici. Why Has Development Neglected Rural Women? A Review of the South Asian Literature. LC 79-40235. (Women in Development Ser.: Vol. 1). (Illus.). 1979. 55.00 (0-08-023377-5, Pub. by Pergamon Repr UK) Franklin.
Nelson, Nici, ed. African Women in the Development Process. 144p. 1981. 35.00 (0-7146-3175-2, Pub. by F Cass Pubs UK) Intl Spec Bk.
Nelson, Nici, jt. ed. see Wright, Susan.
Nelson, Nickola W. Childhood Language Disorder in Context: Infancy Through Adolescence. (Illus.). 640p. (C). 1993. text ed. write for info. (0-675-21203-0) Macmillan.
Nelson, Nigel. Body Talk. LC 93-27780. (Nonverbal Communications Ser.). (Illus.). 32p. (J). (gr. k-2). 1993. 12.95 (1-56847-099-1) Thomson Lrning.
— Codes. LC 93-40962. (Nonverbal Communications Ser.). (Illus.). 32p. (J). (gr. k-2). 1994. 12.95 (1-56847-157-2) Thomson Lrning.
— Signs & Symbols. LC 93-27779. (Nonverbal Communications Ser.). (Illus.). 32p. (J). (gr. k-2). 1993. 12.95 (1-56847-100-9) Thomson Lrning.
— Space. LC 93-7257. 32p. (J). (gr. k-2). 1993. 14.95 (1-56847-109-2) Thomson Lrning.
— Writing & Numbers. LC 93-40963. (Nonverbal Communications Ser.). (Illus.). 32p. (J). (gr. k-2). 1994. 12.95 (1-56847-158-0) Thomson Lrning.
Nelson, Noelle. A Winning Case: How to Use Persuasive Communication Techniques for Successful Trial Work. 384p. 1991. 49.95 (0-13-932278-7, 720303) P-H.
Nelson, Norm, ed. see Strain, Dave & Nauman, Chuck.
Nelson, O., ed. Plant Transposable Elements: Alaskan Aviation History. LC 88-21917. (Basic Life Sciences Ser.: Vol. 47). (Illus.). 416p. 1990. 105.00 (0-306-43001-0, Plenum Pr); Vol. 1, 1897-1928, 550 p. write for info. (0-318-63137-7, Plenum Pr); Vol. 2, 1929-1930, 550 p. write for info. (0-318-63138-5, Plenum Pr) Plenum.
Nelson, O. Edward. The Product Life Cycle of Titanium. 20p. (Orig.). 1990. pap. 20.00 (0-935297-11-1) Titanium.
Nelson, O. N. History of the Scandinavians & Successful Scandinavians in the U. S, 2 vols., Set. LC 68-31266. (American History & Americana Ser.: No. 47). 1969. reprint ed. lib. bdg. 150.00 (0-8383-0198-3) M S G Haskell Hse.
Nelson, O. T. The Girl Who Owned a City. 192p. (YA). (gr. 6 up). 1977. mass mkt. 3.99 (0-440-92893-1, LFL) Dell.
— The Girl Who Owned a City. 204p. (YA). (gr. 5 up). 1995. pap. 3.95 (0-8225-9670-9, Runestone Pr) Lerner Group.
— The Girl Who Owned a City. LC 94-29210. 204p. (YA). (gr. 5 up). 1995. 18.95 (0-8225-3152-6, Runestone Pr) Lerner Group.
Nelson, Oliver. The Cowman's Southwest. Debo, Angie, ed. LC 86-11231. (Illus.). 343p. 1986. reprint ed. pap. 8.95 (0-8032-8356-3, Bison Books) U of Nebr Pr.
Nelson, Opal W. What You Should Know Before Going into the Hospital. pap. 2.95 (0-8217-1361-2) Zebra.
Nelson, Otto, jt. ed. see Goebel, Ulrich.
Nelson, P. A. & Elliott, S. J. Active Control of Sound. 436p. 1993. pap. text ed. 49.95 (0-12-515426-7) Acad Pr.
Nelson, P. C. Bible Doctrines. LC 81-82738. 128p. (YA). (gr. 9-12). 1981. pap. 2.95 (0-88243-479-9, 02-0479) Gospel Pub.
Nelson, P. N. & Nelson, L. N., eds. Oregon Gold! 104p. 1983. pap. 5.95 (0-942652-00-2) Wind River Scri.
***Nelson, P. P. & Laubach, S. E., eds.** Rock Mechanics: Models & Measurements, Challenges from the Industry: Proceedings of the First North American Rock Mechanics Symposium, Austin, Texas, June 1994. (Illus.). 1200p. (C). 1994. text ed. 85.00 (90-5410-386-8) Ashgate Pub Co.
Nelson-Pallmeyer, Jack. Brave New World Order: Can We Pledge Allegiance? LC 91-37238. 1992. pap. 9.95 (0-88344-785-1) Orbis Bks.
— Politics of Compassion: A Biblical Perspective on World Hunger, the Arms Race & U. S. Policy in Central America. LC 85-25809. 128p. (Orig.). 1986. pap. 11.95 (0-88344-356-2) Orbis Bks.
— War Against the Poor: Low Intensity Conflict & Christian Faith. LC 88-38165. 125p. 1989. pap. 10.95 (0-88344-589-1, 589-1) Orbis Bks.
***Nelson, Pamela, tr.** Landscapes. LC 94-49714. (First Discovery Art Bk.). (Illus.). (ENG & FRE.). (J). 1995. 11.95 (0-590-50216-6, Cartwheel) Scholastic Inc.
***Nelson, Pamela B.** Ethnic Images in Toys & Games. LC 90-81444. (Illus.). 51p. 1990. 5.00 (0-937437-07-7) Balch IES Pr.
Nelson, Pamela B., ed. Armenian Rugs: Fabric of a Culture. LC 87-71500. (Illus.). 40p. 1988. 10.00 (0-937437-04-2) Balch Inst Ethnic Studies.
Nelson, Pat. Magic Minutes: Quick Read-Alouds for Every Day. LC 92-35887. (Illus.). 1993. 18.50 (0-87287-996-8) Teacher Ideas Pr.
Nelson, Patty. Teacher's Bag of Tricks. (Illus.). 80p. (J). (gr. 2-6). 1986. pap. text ed. 7.95 (0-86530-132-8) Incentive Pubns.
Nelson, Paul. Average Nights. LC 77-75758. 62p. 1977. per. 3.75 (0-934332-04-5) LEpervier Pr.
— Days Off. LC 82-20294. (Virginia Commonwealth University Series for Contemporary Poetry). 70p. 1982. 10.95 (0-8139-0965-1) U Pr of Va.
— The Hard Shapes of Paradise. LC 87-19221. (Alabama Poetry Ser.). 96p. (Orig.). 1988. 15.95 (0-8173-0391-X); pap. 9.95 (0-8173-0392-8) U of Ala Pr.
— Narrative & Morality: A Theological Inquiry. LC 86-43034. 192p. 1987. 27.50 (0-271-00485-1) Pa St U Pr.
— The World Bank & Non-Governmental Organizations: The Limits of Apolitical Development. LC 95-7825. (International Political Economy Ser.). 1995. write for info. (0-312-12620-4) St Martin.
***Nelson, Paul, ed.** The Creationist Writings of Byron C. Nelson. LC 95-1065. (Creationism in Twentieth-Century America: Vol. 5). 536p. 1995. 100.00 (0-8153-1806-5) Garland.
Nelson, Paul, jt. auth. see Nestmann, Mark.
Nelson, Paul A., ed. see Poulsen, Peter.
Nelson, Paul D. Anthony Wayne: Soldier of the Early Republic. LC 84-48543. (Illus.). 380p. 1985. 29.95 (0-253-30751-1) Ind U Pr.
— General James Grant: Scottish Soldier & Royal Governor of East Florida. LC 92-28134. 216p. 1993. 29.95 (0-8130-1175-2) U Press Fla.
— William Alexander, Lord Stirling. LC 85-16473. (Illus.). 256p. 1987. 32.95 (0-8173-0283-2) U of Ala Pr.
— William Tryon & the Course of Empire: A Life in British Imperial Service. LC 90-11998. (Illus.). xiii, 250p. (C). 1990. 27.50 (0-8078-1917-4) U of NC Pr.
***Nelson, Paul E. & Pearson, Judy.** Confidence in Public Speaking. 304p. (C). 1995. pap. write for info. (0-697-24635-3) Brown & Benchmark.
— Confidence in Public Speaking. 5th ed. 368p. (C). 1993. pap. text ed. write for info. (0-697-12934-9) Brown & Benchmark.
Nelson, Paul E., jt. auth. see Pearson, Judy.
Nelson, Paul E., et al. Fusarium Species: An Illustrated Manual for Identification. LC 82-62197. (Illus.). 226p. 1983. teacher ed 45.00 (0-271-00349-9) Pa St U Pr.
Nelson, Paul M., ed. Transportation Noise Reference Book. LC 86-29944. (Illus.). 540p. 1987. text ed. 129.00 (0-408-01446-6) Buttrwrth-Heinemann.
Nelson, Paul V. Greenhouse Operation & Management. 4th ed. 512p. 1991. text ed. 71.00 (0-13-365198-3) P-H.
— Greenhouse Operations & Management. 3rd ed. LC 84-22256. (C). 1985. teacher ed write for info. (0-8359-2584-6, Reston) P-H.
Nelson, Paula. The Joy of Money: The Guide to Women's Financial Freedom. 224p. 1986. reprint ed. 18.95 (0-9616661-0-2) Joy Money Pub.
Nelson, Paula M. After the West Was Won: Homesteaders & Town-Builders in Western South Dakota, 1900-1917. LC 86-11405. (Illus.). 238p. (C). 1986. reprint ed. pap. 13.95 (0-87745-250-4) U of Iowa Pr.
— The Prairie Winnows Out Its Own: The West River Country of South Dakota in the Years of Depression & Dust. (Illus.). 240p. 1995. text ed. 27.95x (0-87745-525-2) U of Iowa Pr.
Nelson, Pauline, jt. auth. see Daubert, Todd.
Nelson, Pauline, jt. auth. see Saikali, Diana.
Nelson, Pearl A. The First Year: Retirement Journal. Kirchhofer, M. V., ed. (Illus.). 163p. (Orig.). 1982. pap. 5.95 (0-932910-41-6) Potentials Development.
Nelson, Pearl A., jt. auth. see Lazow, Alfred.
Nelson, Peggy. How to Create Powerful Newsletters: Easy Ways to Avoid the Pitfalls that 80 Percent of All Newsletters Face. 260p. 1992. 30.00 (0-929387-86-4) Bonus Books.
Nelson, Peter. Dangerous Waters. Ashby, Ruth, ed. (Sylvia Smith-Smith Novel Ser.). 224p. (Orig.). (J). 1992. pap. 3.50 (0-671-74891-2, Archway) PB.
— Deadly Games. (Sylvia Smith-Smith Novel Ser.). 240p. (YA). 1992. pap. 2.99 (0-671-74890-4, Archway) PB.
— Death Threat. (YA). (gr. 9-12). 1993. mass mkt. 3.50 (0-06-106104-2, Harp PBks) HarpC.
— Double Dose. (Mollie Fox Mystery Ser.: No. 2). (YA). 1992. mass mkt. 3.50 (0-06-106101-8, Harp PBks) HarpC.
— First to Die. (Mollie for Mysteries Ser.: No. 1). (YA). 1994. pap. 1.99 (0-06-106223-5, Pub. by Haags Gemeentemuseum) HarpC.
— Fourth-Quarter Fix. (Mollie Fox Mystery Ser.: No. 4). (YA). 1992. mass mkt. 3.50 (0-06-106103-4, Harp PBks) HarpC.
— Scarface. MacDonald, Patricia, ed. (Sylvia Smith-Smith Novel Ser.). 224p. (Orig.). (J). 1991. pap. 2.99 (0-671-70585-7, Archway) PB.
— Six Deadly Lies. (YA). 1993. mass mkt. 3.50 (0-06-106110-7, Harp PBks) HarpC.
— Sylvia Smith-Smith. Ashby, Ruth, ed. (J). 1993. reprint ed. pap. 2.99 (0-671-70586-5, Archway) PB.
— Ten Practical Tips for Environmental Reporting. 57p. Date not set. pap. text ed. 6.75 (0-9626584-6-4) Ctr Foreign Journalists.
— Third Degree. (Mollie Fox Mystery Ser.: No. 3). (YA). 1992. mass mkt. 3.50 (0-06-106102-6, Harp PBks) HarpC.
— Treehouses. LC 93-32568. 1994. pap. 19.95 (0-395-62949-7) HM.
Nelson, Peter, tr. see Antoine, Charles.
***Nelson, Peter K.** Leadership & Discipleship: A Study of Luke 22: 24-30. LC 94-26261. (SBL Dissertation Ser.: No. 138). 350p. 1994. 32.95 (1-55540-900-8, 062138); pap. 21.95 (1-55540-901-6) Scholars Pr GA.
Nelson, Peter R., et al, eds. The Frontiers of Statistical Computation, Simulation, & Modeling, Vol. 1: Proceedings of the ICOSCO-I Conference (First International Conference on Statistical Computing, Cesme, Izmir, Turkey, March-April 1987) LC 90-85328. (Series in Mathematical & Management Sciences: Vol. 25). 450p. 1991. 110.00 (0-935950-27-3) Am Sciences Pr.
Nelson, Philip, illus. Coinage of William Wood. 1978. reprint ed. pap. 8.00 (0-915262-21-5) S J Durst.
Nelson, Philip B. Corporations in Crisis: Behavioral Observations for Bankruptcy Policy. LC 81-1415. 222p. 1981. text ed. 49.95 (0-275-90687-6, C0687, Praeger Pubs) Greenwood.
Nelson, Philip B., jt. auth. see Hilke, John C.
Nelson, Philip B., et al. In Search of Mediocrity. (Illus.). 112p. (Orig.). 1986. pap. 4.95 (0-9615870-0-8) Woodside Pr.
Nelson, Philip E., et al. Principles of Aseptic Processing & Packaging. 2nd ed. LC 79-57624. 257p. (Orig.). 1993. pap. 60.00 (0-937774-03-0) Food Processors.
Nelson, Phillip G. & Lieberman, Melvyn, eds. Excitable Cells in Tissue Culture. LC 80-8106. 440p. 1981. 95.00 (0-306-40516-4, Plenum Pr) Plenum.
Nelson, Polly. Defending the Devil: The Story of Ted Bundy's Last Lawyer. LC 93-23411. 1994. write for info. (0-688-10823-7) Morrow.
Nelson, Portia. There's a Hole in My Sidewalk. 128p. 1989. reprint ed. pap. 6.95 (0-9621159-0-8) Stonebarn.
— There's a Hole in My Sidewalk: The Romance of Self-Discovery. 1993. pap. 7.95 (0-941831-87-6) Beyond Words Pub.
Nelson, Priscilla P., et al, eds. Design & Performance for Deep Foundations: Piles & Piers in Soil & Soft Rock: Proceedings of a Session Sponsored by the Committees on Deep Foundations & Rock Mechanics of the Geotechnical Engineering Division of the American Society of Civil Engineers in Conjunction with the ASCE Convention in Dallas, Texas, October 24-28, 1993. LC 93-31658. (Geotechnical Special Publication Ser.: No. 36). 1993. write for info. (0-87262-987-2) Am Soc Civil Eng.
Nelson, R., jt. ed. see Balassa, Bela A.
Nelson, R. A. Geologic Analysis of Naturally Fractured Reservoirs. LC 85-17183. (Contributions in Petroleum Geology & Engineering Ser.: Vol. 1). (Illus.). 320p. 1985. 47.00 (0-87201-575-0) Gulf Pub.
Nelson, R. D., Jr. Dispersing Powders in Liquids. (Handbook of Powder Technology Ser.: No. 7). 244p. 1988. 82.00 (0-444-43004-0) Elsevier.
Nelson, R. D., jt. auth. see Daintith, J.
Nelson, R. J. The Logic of Mind. 1982. lib. bdg. 136.50 (90-277-1399-5) Kluwer Ac.
— The Logic of Mind. enl. rev. ed. (C). 1989. pap. text ed. 45.50 (90-277-2822-4) Kluwer Ac.
— The Logic of Mind. 2nd enl. rev. ed. (C). 1989. lib. bdg. 137.00 (90-277-2819-4) Kluwer Ac.
— Naming & Reference. LC 91-45969. (Problems of Philosophy: Their Past & Present Ser.). 304p. 1992. 45.00 (0-415-00939-1, A1619) Routledge.
— Play Within a Play. LC 72-87356. (Theatre, Film & the Performing Arts Ser.). 182p. 1971. reprint ed. lib. bdg. 29.50 (0-306-71580-5) Da Capo.
Nelson, R. R. Understanding Technical Change: An Evolutionary Process. (Lectures in Economics Ser.: Vol. 8). 80p. 1987. pap. 37.50 (0-444-70207-5, North Holland) Elsevier.
Nelson, R. Ryan. End User Computing: Concepts, Issues & Applications. 383p. 1989. Net. pap. text ed. write for info. (0-471-61359-2) Wiley.
Nelson, Rachel W., jt. auth. see Webb, Sheyann.
Nelson, Ralph, jt. auth. see Preston, Paul.
Nelson, Ralph C., tr. see Allard, Jean-Louis.
Nelson, Ralph L. Economic Factors in the Growth of Corporation Giving. LC 70-104182. 116p. 1970. 19.95 (0-87154-615-9) Russell Sage.
— Economic Factors in the Growth of Corporation Giving. (Occasional Papers: No. 111). 136p. 1970. reprint ed. 35.40 (0-685-61351-8) Natl Bur Econ Res.
— The Investment Policies of Foundations. LC 66-30032. 204p. 1967. 24.95 (0-87154-614-0) Russell Sage.
— Merger Movements in American Industry, 1895-1956. LC 59-11082. (National Bureau of Economic Research. General Ser.: No. 66). 198p. reprint ed. pap. 56.50 (0-317-09557-9, 2051756) Bks Demand.
— Merger Movements in American Industry, 1895-1956. (General Ser.: No. 66). 198p. 1959. reprint ed. 49.50 (0-87014-065-5) Natl Bur Econ Res.
Nelson, Ramon W. & Woodward, John B. Island Life, Island Toil: The House of David on High Island. (Illus.). 192p. 1991. 29.00 (0-931781-07-8) Jennings Pr.
***Nelson, Randolph.** Probability, Stochastic Processes & Queueing Theory: The Mathematics of Computer Performance Modelling. LC 95-4041. 1995. write for info. (0-387-94452-4) Spr-Verlag.
Nelson, Randy, ed. The Overlook Martial Arts Reader. 356p. 1989. 19.95 (0-87951-347-0) Overlook Pr.
Nelson, Randy F. The Martial Arts Index: An Annotated Bibliography. LC 88-11243. 456p. 1988. 71.00 (0-8240-4435-5, SS451) Garland.
Nelson, Randy F., ed. The Overlook Martial Arts Reader: Classic Writings on Philosophy & Technique. 356p. 1992. reprint ed. pap. 14.95 (0-87951-459-0) Overlook Pr.
Nelson, Randy J. An Introduction to Behavioral Endocrinology. LC 94-34729. (Illus.). 500p. (C). 1994. text ed. 47.95 (0-87893-615-7) Sinauer Assocs.
***Nelson, Ray, et al.** A Dinosaur Ate My Homework. (Illus.). 48p. (J). (gr. k-6). 1994. 14.95 (1-56977-400-5) Flying Rhino.
Nelson, Ray. I Never Met One Stranger. 450p. (Orig.). (J). (gr. 12). 1989. pap. write for info. (0-318-65128-9) Raynel.
— Sleeper. (Illus.). 105p. (YA). 1995. pap. 9.95 (0-9623068-1-9) Raynel.
Nelson, Ray, Jr. & Kelly, Doug. The Seven Seas of Billy's Bathtub. (Illus.). 48p. (J). (gr. 1-5). 1993. 12.95 (1-883772-00-1) Flying Rhino.
Nelson, Ray & Kelly, Douglas. Connie & Bonnie's Birthday Blastoff. (Illus.). 48p. (J). (gr. 1-5). 1994. 12.95 (1-883772-02-8) Flying Rhino.
— Connie & Bonnie's Birthday Blastoff. (Illus.). 48p. (J). (gr. k-6). 1994. 14.95 (1-56977-403-X) Flying Rhino.
— The Seven Seas of Billy's Bathtub. (Illus.). 48p. (J). (gr. k-6). 1994. 14.95 (1-56977-406-4) Flying Rhino.
— Shrews Can't Hoop!? (Illus.). 48p. (J). (gr. k-6). 1994. 14.95 (1-56977-418-8) Flying Rhino.
— Wooden Teeth & Jelly Beans: The Tupperman Files. (Illus.). 48p. (J). (gr. k-6). 1995. 12.95 (0-614-05022-7) Flying Rhino.
***Nelson, Ray & Nelson, Douglas.** Greetings from America: Postcards from Donovan Willoughby. 2nd ed. Tronslin, Andrea, ed. LC 92-14819. (Illus.). 48p. (J). (gr. k-5). Date not set. 14.95 (1-56977-409-9) Flying Rhino.
Nelson, Ray F. Dogheaded Death. (Centurion Books). 184p. (Orig.). 1989. pap. 9.95 (0-89407-079-7) Strawberry Hill.
Nelson, Ray R. I Never Met One Stranger: A Personal Journey. 435p. (Orig.). (YA). (gr. 12). 1989. pap. 10.45 (0-9623068-0-0) Raynel.
Nelson, Raymond. Kenneth Patchen & American Mysticism. LC 83-27384. xxiii, 187p. 1984. 27.50 (0-8078-1610-8) U of NC Pr.

N

Nelson, Raymond A. Computerizing Warehouse Operations. 250p. 1985. text ed. 39.95 (0-13-163924-2, Busn) P-H.
Nelson, Raymond S. And the Kansas Wind Blows: Poems about the People, the Land. (Illus.). 96p. (Orig.). 1991. pap. 7.95 (0-9627947-1-6) Hearth KS.
— Hemingway: Expressionist Artist. LC 79-4640. 113p. reprint ed. pap. 32.30 (0-317-30474-7, 2024822) Bks Demand.
— Prairie Sketches. LC 92-73894. (Illus.). 96p. (Orig.). 1992. pap. 8.95 (0-9627947-8-3) Hearth KS.
— Thy Love Is Better Than Wine. LC 93-81210. (Illus.). 96p. (Orig.). 1994. pap. 9.95 (1-882420-11-X, 1-882420-11-X) Hearth KS.
Nelson, Raymond S., ed. see Shaw, George Bernard.
Nelson, Rebecca, ed. see Johnston, Sammie.
Nelson, Rebecca, ed. see Serratt, Mary L.
Nelson, Rebecca S. Games & Activities with Base Ten Blocks, Bk. 1. (Illus.). 64p. (J). (gr. 1-4). 1987. pap. text ed. 8.95 (0-914040-57-X) Cuisenaire.
— Games & Activities with Base Ten Blocks, Bk. 2. 64p. (J). (gr. 1-4). 1987. pap. text ed. 8.95 (0-914040-58-8) Cuisenaire.
Nelson-Rees, W. A. Paintings by Selden Connor Gile, 1877-1947, Vol. II. (Illus.). 36p. 1983. 10.00 (0-938842-03-X) WIM Oakland.
Nelson-Rees, W. A. & Coran, James L. Kirby Waite. (Illus.). 36p. 1983. 5.00 (0-938842-04-8) WIM Oakland.
Nelson-Rees, Walter A. Albert Thomas DeRome, 1885-1959: Being a Story of His Life & a Picture Diary of His Oils & Watercolors. LC 87-51379. (Illus.). 164p. 1988. 60.00 (0-938842-06-4) WIM Oakland.
— John O'Shea, Eighteen Seventy-Six to Nineteen Fifty-Six: The Artist's Life As I Know It. LC 85-50075. (Illus.). 179p. 1985. 45.00 (0-938842-05-6) WIM Oakland.
— Lillie May Nicholson: 1884-1964 an Artist Rediscovered. LC 80-53867. (Illus.). 88p. 1981. 25.00 (0-938842-00-5) WIM Oakland.
Nelson-Rees, Walter A., jt. auth. see Coran, James L.
Nelson, Rex. The Hillary Factor: The Story of America's First Lady. 256p. 1993. 21.95 (0-9636477-0-9); pap. 10.95 (0-9636477-1-7) Gallen Pub Fnd.
Nelson, Rex, jt. auth. see Hudson, Alvin.
Nelson, Richard. Aesthetic Frontiers: The Machiavellian Tradition & the Southern Imagination. LC 90-32055. 336p. 1990. 39.50 (0-87805-439-1) U Pr of Miss.
— An American Comedy & Other Plays. 1984. pap. 12.95 (0-933826-70-2) PAJ Pubns.
— Columbus & the Discovery of Japan. 144p. (Orig.). 1992. pap. 8.95 (0-571-16857-4) Faber & Faber.
— First & Second Kings. LC 87-9883. (Interpretation: A Bible Commentary for Teaching & Preaching Ser.). 252p. 1987. 22.00 (0-8042-3109-5, John Knox) Westminster John Knox.
— The Island Within. LC 90-55685. 304p. 1991. 11.00 (0-679-73239-X, Vin) Random.
— Life Sentences. 96p. (Orig.). 1993. pap. 8.95 (0-571-19831-7) Faber & Faber.
— New England. 92p. (Orig.). 1995. pap. 10.95 (0-571-17510-4) Faber & Faber.
— Principia Scriptoriae with Between East & West. 144p. 1991. pap. 12.95 (0-571-12905-6) Faber & Faber.
— Sensibility & Sense. 96p. 1989. pap. 7.95 (0-571-15329-1) Faber & Faber.
— Some Americans Abroad. 99p. 1990. pap. 7.95 (0-571-14158-7) Faber & Faber.
— Two Shakespearean Actors. 103p. (Orig.). 1990. pap. 8.95 (0-571-16103-0) Faber & Faber.
Nelson, Richard, ed. Strictly Dishonorable & Other Lost American Plays. LC 86-5782. (Illus.). 260p. (Orig.). (C). 1986. pap. 10.95 (0-930452-55-0) Theatre Comm.
Nelson, Richard, intro. Travels in Alaska. (Illus.). 336p. 1993. pap. 12.00 (0-14-017021-9, Penguin Bks) Viking Penguin.
Nelson, Richard & Gelman, Alexander. Misha's Party. 96p. (Orig.). 1994. pap. 9.95 (0-571-17117-6) Faber & Faber.
***Nelson, Richard & Jones, David.** Making Plays: The Writer-Director Relationship in the Theater Today. Chambers, Colin, ed. 165p. (Orig.). 1995. pap. 11.95 (0-571-16354-8) Faber & Faber.
Nelson, Richard, jt. auth. see Feldman, Edward C.
***Nelson, Richard A.** A Chronology & Glossary of Propaganda in the United States. LC 94-47427. 1995. text ed. write for info. (0-313-29261-2, Greenwood Pr) Greenwood.
Nelson, Richard A., jt. auth. see Heath, Robert L.
Nelson, Richard B., jt. ed. see Hart, Gary C.
Nelson, Richard C. Choice Awareness: Systematic, Eclectic Counseling Theory. LC 90-81967. 352p. (Orig.). (C). 1990. pap. text ed. 17.95 (0-932796-30-3) Ed Media Corp.
— Choosing: A Better Way to Live. LC 78-67188. (Illus.). 1978. pap. 5.95 (0-932570-00-3) Guidelines Pr.
— On the CREST: Growing Through Effective Choices. LC 92-70821. (Illus.). 192p. (Orig.). (C). 1992. pap. text ed. 9.95 (0-932796-39-7) Ed Media Corp.
— Success Is a Choice. (Orig.). 1979. pap. write for info. (0-932570-01-1) Guidelines Pr.
Nelson, Richard C., jt. auth. see Miller, Doris I.
Nelson, Richard C., et al. Working with Adolescents: Building Effective Communication & Choice-Making Skills. LC 94-70340. 144p. (Orig.). (C). 1994. pap. text ed. 16.95 (0-932796-61-3) Ed Media Corp.
Nelson, Richard D. Raising up a Faithful Priest: Community & Priesthood in Biblical Theology. LC 93-10361. 1993. pap. 19.99 (0-664-25437-3) Westminster John Knox.
Nelson, Richard E. & Galas, Judith. The Power to Prevent Suicide: A Guide for Teens Helping Teens. Espeland, Pamela, ed. LC 94-5594. (Illus.). 136p. (Orig.). (YA). (gr. 6 up). 1994. pap. 11.95 (0-915793-70-9) Free Spirit Pub.
Nelson, Richard K. Hunters of the Northern Forest: Designs for Survival among the Alaskan Kutchin. 2nd ed. LC 86-7085. (Illus.). 320p. (C). 1986. pap. text ed. 12.95 (0-226-57181-5) U Ch Pr.
— Hunters of the Northern Ice. LC 78-75136. (Illus.). 1972. pap. text ed. 12.95 (0-226-57176-9) U Ch Pr.
— Make Prayers to the Raven: A Koyukon View of the Northern Forest. LC 82-8441. xvi, 292p. 1986. pap. 13.95 (0-226-57163-7) U Ch Pr.
— Shadow of the Hunter: Stories of Eskimo Life. LC 80-11091. (Illus.). xiv, 282p. 1983. pap. 12.95 (0-226-57180-7) U Ch Pr.
— Shadow of the Hunter: Stories of Eskimo Life. LC 80-11091. 296p. reprint ed. pap. 84.40 (0-685-23649-8, 2026494) Bks Demand.
Nelson, Richard R., ed. National Innovation Systems. (Illus.). 560p. 1993. 52.00 (0-19-507616-8); pap. 29.95 (0-19-507617-6) OUP.
Nelson, Richard R. & Winter, Sidney G. An Evolutionary Theory of Economic Change. 400p. 1985. pap. 19.95 (0-674-27228-5) HUP.
Nelson, Richard R., ed. see Conference on Families & the Economy Staff.
Nelson, Richard R., jt. auth. see Ostry, Sylvia.
Nelson, Richard R., et al. Structural Change in a Developing Economy: Colombia's Problems & Prospects. LC 72-146645. (Rand Corporation Research Study Ser.). (Illus.). 336p. reprint ed. pap. 95.80 (0-685-44421-X, 2032642) Bks Demand.
Nelson, Richard W. & Couto. Essentials of Small Animal Internal Medicine. 1042p. 1992. 93.95 (0-8016-3334-6) Mosby Yr Bk.
Nelson, Richard W., jt. auth. see Rubin, Seymour J.
Nelson-Richards, Melsome. Beyond the Sociology of Agrarian Transformation: Economy & Society in Zambia, Nepal & Zanzibar. Ishwaran, K., ed. LC 87-20931. (Monographs & Theoretical Studies in Sociology & Anthropology in Honour of Nels Anderson: Vol. 20). (Illus.). v, 141p. (Orig.). 1988. pap. 34.50 (90-04-08282-4) E J Brill.
***Nelson, Rick.** Babymaker: Fertility, Fraud & the Fall of Doctor Cecil Jacobson. 1994. mass mkt. 5.99 (0-553-56162-6) Bantam.
Nelson, Rick & Nelson, Sheila. Black Sea Cruising Guide. (Illus.). 200p. 1995. pap. 57.95 (0-85288-173-8, Pub. by Imray Laurie Norie & Wilson UK) Bluewater Bks.
***Nelson, Ridley.** Dryland Management: The "Desertification" Problem. (Technical Paper Ser.: No. 116). 48p. 1990. 6.95 (0-614-02770-5, 11444) World Bank.
Nelson, Riki K. Borders-Grenzen. 128p. (ENG & GER.). 1991. 9.50 (0-9614462-4-2) Ariadne CA.
Nelson, Rob & Cowan, Jon. Revolution X: A Survival Guide for Our Generation. 208p. 1994. 9.95 (0-14-023532-9, Penguin Bks) Viking Penguin.
Nelson, Robert. The Job Hunt. LC 85-27921. 64p. (Orig.). 1986. pap. 2.95 (0-89815-160-0) Ten Speed Pr.
Nelson, Robert & Christensen, Carl J. Foundations of Music: A Computer-Assisted Introduction (Apple II) 2nd ed. LC 92-12695. 236p. (C). 1993. pap. 37.95 (0-534-18829-X) Intl Thomson.
— Foundations of Music: A Computer-Assisted Introduction (Macintosh) 2nd ed. 236p. (C). 1993. pap. 37.95 (0-534-18828-1) Intl Thomson.
Nelson, Robert, tr. see Sanchez, Victor.
***Nelson, Robert A.** The Great Book of Hemp: The Complete Guide to the Commerical, Medicinal & Psychotropic Uses of the World's Most Extraordinary Plant. (Illus.). 256p. 1995. pap. 19.95 (0-89281-541-8, Park St Pr) Inner Tradit.
— SI: The International System of Units. 2nd ed. (Illus.). 132p. 1983. 10.00 (0-318-41552-6, OP45) Am Assn Physics.
Nelson, Robert B. Decision Point. 224p. 1992. pap. 14.95 (0-89815-485-5) Ten Speed Pr.
Nelson, Robert B. Empowering Employees Through Delegation. 175p. 1993. 17.00 (1-55623-847-9) Irwin Prof Pubng.
Nelson, Robert B. Louder & Funnier. LC 85-2575. 196p. (Orig.). 1985. pap. 5.95 (0-89815-142-2) Ten Speed Pr.
Nelson, Robert B. & Economy, Peter J. Better Business Meetings. LC 94-9330. (Briefcase Books Ser.). 175p. 1994. text ed. 17.00 (0-7863-0188-0) Irwin Prof Pubng.
— Better Business Meetings International Editon. LC 94-9330. (Briefcase Books Ser.). 192p. 1994. pap. 13.95 (0-7863-0205-4) Irwin Prof Pubng.
Nelson, Robert B. & Wallick, Jenifer. The Presentation Primer: Getting Your Point Across. 168p. 1993. text ed. 17.00 (1-55623-846-0) Irwin Prof Pubng.
Nelson, Robert B., jt. ed. see Briggs, James I.
***Nelson, Robert C.** Elementary Technical Mathematics. 6th ed. LC 94-26683. 640p. 1995. pap. 51.95 (0-534-94554-6) PWS Pubs.
— Flight Stability & Automatic Control. 320p. 1989. text ed. write for info. (0-07-046218-6) McGraw.
Nelson, Robert E., Jr. W. I. N. N. Against Suicide. Parker, Diane, ed. 80p. (Orig.). 1993. pap. 6.95 (1-56875-049-8) R & E Pubs.
Nelson, Robert E., jt. ed. see Neck, Philip A.
Nelson, Robert F. Summer Shoes. Van Treese, James B., ed. 260p. 1993. pap. 8.95 (1-56901-045-5) NW Pub.
Nelson, Robert H. The Making of Federal Coal Policy. LC 83-7155. (Duke Press Policy Studies). (Illus.). xi, 261p. (C). 1983. 41.95 (0-8223-0497-X) Duke.
— Public Lands & Private Rights: The Failure of Scientific Management. 312p. (C). 1995. lib. bdg. 61.50 (0-8476-8008-8); pap. 24.95 (0-8476-8009-6) Rowman.
— Reaching for Heaven on Earth: The Theological Meaning of Economics. 1993. pap. 16.95 (0-8226-3024-9) Littlefield.
— Reaching for Heaven on Earth: The Theological Meaning of Economics. 320p. (C). 1991. text ed. 24.95 (0-685-38894-8) Rowman.
Nelson, Robert J. Pascal: Adversary & Advocate. LC 81-6330. 296p. 1982. 37.00 (0-674-65615-6) HUP.
— Willa Cather & France: In Search of the Lost Language. LC 87-24484. 192p. (C). 1988. 24.95 (0-252-01502-9) U of Ill Pr.
Nelson, Robert J. & Oxenhandler, Neal, eds. Aspects of French Literature. LC 61-5992. (FRE.). 1961. 49.50 (0-89197-037-1); pap. text ed. 29.95 (0-89197-038-X) Irvington.
***Nelson, Robert J. & Weales, Gerald, eds.** Enclosure: A Collection of Plays. LC 74-23084. 282p. 1975. 16.95 (0-679-50531-8) Boulevard.
Nelson, Robert J., jt. ed. see Weales, Gerald.
Nelson, Robert L. & Trubek, David M., eds. Lawyers' Ideals - Lawyers' Practices: Transformations in the American Legal System. LC 91-55533. 320p. 1992. 42.50 (0-8014-2461-5); pap. 16.95 (0-8014-9710-8) Cornell U Pr.
Nelson, Robert S. The Iconography of Preface & Miniature in the Byzantine Gospel Book. LC 80-15335. (College Art Association Monograph Ser.: Vol. 36). (Illus.). 180p. 1985. reprint ed. 35.00 (0-271-00404-5) Pa St U Pr.
Nelson, Robert V. Understanding Basic Energy Terms. LC 81-2888. 1981. lib. bdg. 10.00 (0-86663-806-7); pap. text ed. 8.00 (0-86663-807-5) Ide Hse.
Nelson, Robert V., et al. E Equals MC Squared: Energy - Management, Conservation & Communication, 17 vols. Ide, Arthur F., ed. (Illus.). (Orig.). 1981. write for info. (0-86663-800-8); pap. write for info. (0-86663-801-6) Ide Hse.
Nelson, Roberta & Nelson, Christopher. Parents As Resident Theologians. 2nd ed. 36p. 1990. pap. 10.00 (1-55896-194-1) Unitarian Univ.
— Parents As Social Justice Educators. 48p. 1993. 15.00 (1-55896-314-6) Unitarian Univ.
Nelson, Rodney. The Boots Brevik Saga. LC 78-11771. 1978. pap. 6.95 (0-914974-19-X) Holmgangers.
— Oregon Scroll. 1976. pap. 3.00 (0-914974-11-4) Holmgangers.
— Thor's Home. (Kestrel Ser.: No. 8). 28p. 1983. pap. 3.00 (0-914974-40-8) Holmgangers.
— Villy Sadness: A Novella. 114p. 1987. pap. 7.95 (0-89823-093-4) New Rivers Pr.
Nelson, Rodney, ed. see Finnerty, Margaret.
Nelson, Rodney, ed. see Phillips, Amy.
Nelson, Rodney, ed. see Sanford, Charles W., Jr.
Nelson, Rodney B., III. Beaumont: America's First Physiologist. LC 89-82643. (Illus.). 400p. 1990. 42.00 (0-9625624-0-8) Grant Hse Pr.
— The Franklin Institute Illinois' First Medical School. (Illus.). v, 94p. (Orig.). 1991. pap. 9.95 (0-9625624-2-4) Grant Hse Pr.
Nelson, Roger L., jt. auth. see Seippel, Robert G.
Nelson, Roger M. & Currier, Dean P. Clinical Electrotherapy. 2nd ed. (Illus.). 422p. (C). 1991. boxed 42.95 (0-8385-1334-4, A1334-0) Appleton & Lange.
Nelson, Roger M., jt. auth. see Currier, Dean P.
Nelson, Roland H., jt. auth. see Edinger, Lois V.
Nelson, Ronald E. Human Geography: People, Cultures & Landscapes. (C). 1993. pap. 32.00 (0-03-025414-0) HB Coll Pubs.
Nelson, Ronald E., ed. Illinois: Land & Life in the Prairie State. (Regional Geography Ser.). (Illus.). 368p. 1978. per. 19.95 (0-8403-1831-6) Kendall-Hunt.
Nelson, Ronald R. & Schweizer, Peter. The Soviet Concepts of Peace, Peaceful Coexistence & Detente. LC 87-34520. 198p. (Orig.). (C). 1988. lib. bdg. 47.00 (0-8191-6832-7, Natl Forum Found); pap. text ed. 22.00 (0-8191-6833-5, Natl Forum Found) U Pr of Amer.
Nelson, Rosemary O. & Hayes, Steven C., eds. Conceptual Foundations of Behavioral Assessment. LC 85-27363. (Guilford Behavioral Assessment Ser.). 544p. 1986. lib. bdg. 65.00 (0-89862-142-9) Guilford Pr.
Nelson, Ross. Running Visual Basic for Windows. 2nd ed. LC 93-13651. 328p. 1993. pap. 22.95 (1-55615-564-6) Microsoft.
Nelson, Roy, ed. Vingtieme Siecle: La Problematique du Discours. LC 81-50963. (Michigan Romance Studies: vol. 6). 127p. (Orig.). 1986. pap. 9.00 (0-939730-05-7) Mich Romance.
Nelson, Roy & Wilson, Robin J., eds. Graph Colourings. (Pitman Research Notes in Mathematics Ser.). 1990. pap. text ed. 57.95 (0-470-21509-7) Halsted Pr.
***Nelson, Roy C.** Industrialization & Political Affinity: Industrial Policy in Brazil. LC 95-3434. (Thunderbird/Routledge Series in International Management). 1995. write for info. (0-415-12528-6) Routledge.
***Nelson, Roy J.** Causality & Narrative in French Fiction from Zola to Robbe-Grillet. 245p. 1990. 49.50 (0-8142-0504-6) Ohio St U Pr.
Nelson, Roy P. The Cartoonist. LC 93-94236. (Illus.). 179p. (Orig.). 1994. pap. 9.95 (0-9639729-0-1) Seven Gab Pr.
— Design of Advertising. 7th ed. (Illus.). 432p. 1994. boxed write for info. (0-697-12933-0) Brown & Benchmark.
— Publication Design. 5th ed. 336p. (C). 1991. pap. write for info. (0-697-08620-8) Brown & Benchmark.
Nelson, Roy P., jt. auth. see Copperud, Roy H.
Nelson, Ruby. Door of Everything. 1963. pap. 8.95 (0-87516-069-7) DeVorss.
Nelson, Rudolph. The Making & Unmaking of an Evangelical Mind: The Case of Edward Carnell. 320p. 1988. 64.95 (0-521-34263-5) Cambridge U Pr.
***Nelson, Russell M.** The Gateway We Call Death. 1995. 10.95 (0-87579-953-1) Deseret Bk.
— The Power Within Us. LC 88-20299. ix, 160p. 1988. 13.95 (0-87579-154-9) Deseret Bk.
Nelson, Russell S., jt. ed. see Wrone, David R.
Nelson, Ruth & Williams, Roger. Handbook of Rocky Mountain Plants. 4th ed. (Illus.). 400p. 1992. pap. 19.95 (0-911797-96-3) R Rinehart.
Nelson, Ruth A. Plants of Zion National Park: Wildflowers, Trees, Shrubs & Ferns. LC 74-28958. (Illus.). 344p. 1976. pap. text ed. 9.95 (0-915630-01-X) Zion.
***Nelson, Ruth E.** The House on the Hill. 200p. (Orig.). Date not set. 9.95 (0-9643648-2-4) R E Nelson.
— Tall Trees Fall. 194p. (Orig.). 1993. write for info. (0-9643648-0-8) R E Nelson.
— Yesterday Is Today. 160p. (Orig.). 1994. 8.00 (0-9643648-1-6) R E Nelson.
Nelson, S. A. The ABC of Stock Speculation. LC 63-22761. 1964. reprint ed. 16.00 (0-87034-054-9) Fraser Pub Co.
Nelson, S. H., jt. auth. see Grogono, Peter.
Nelson, Sally, jt. auth. see Spiegelberg, Emma J.
Nelson, Samuel A. The A B C of Stock Speculation. LC 89-60256. 232p. 1989. reprint ed. 45.00 (1-55888-805-5) Omnigraphics Inc.
Nelson, Samuel H. Colonialism in the Congo Basin, 1880-1940. LC 94-18278. (Monographs in International Studies, Africa Ser.: No. 64). 248p. (Orig.). (C). 1994. pap. text ed. 23.00x (0-89680-180-2) Ohio U Pr.
Nelson, Samuel J. Mississippian Faunas of Western Canada. (Geological Association of Canada. Special Paper Ser.: No. 2). 100p. reprint ed. pap. 28.50 (0-685-17118-3, 2027837) Bks Demand.
Nelson, Sara, tr. see Vierci, Pablo.
Nelson, Sarah. The Archaeology of Korea. (World Archaeology Ser.). (Illus.). 288p. (C). 1993. 69.95 (0-521-40443-6); pap. 27.95 (0-521-40783-4) Cambridge U Pr.
— Ulster's Uncertain Defenders: Protestant Political, Paramilitary, & Community Groups & the Northern Ireland Conflict. (Irish Studies). 206p. 1987. pap. text ed. 14.95 (0-8156-2418-2) Syracuse U Pr.
Nelson, Sarah M., ed. The Archaeology of Northeast China: Beyond the Great Wall. LC 94-9966. 1995. 65.00x (0-415-11755-0, B4521, Routledge NY) Routledge.
Nelson, Sarah M. & Kehoe, Alice B., eds. Powers of Observation: Alternative Views in Archeology. 1990. write for info. (0-913167-42-8) Am Anthro Assn.
Nelson, Scott. No Experience Necessary. LC 90-60085. 1990. 12.95 (0-916990-25-7) META Pubns.
Nelson, Scott A. The Discourses of Algernon Sidney, Vol. 24, No. 45. LC 91-58939. 176p. 1993. 33.50 (0-8386-3438-9) Fairleigh Dickinson.
Nelson, Sharlene, jt. auth. see Nelson, Ted.
Nelson, Sharlene P. & Nelson, Ted W. Umbrella Guide to Washington Lighthouses. (Illus.). 160p. 1990. pap. 10.95 (0-914143-24-7, Umbrella Bks) Epicenter Pr.
Nelson, Sharon R., jt. auth. see Reed, Kathlyn L.
Nelson, Sheila, jt. auth. see Nelson, Rick.
Nelson, Sherry & Shaw, Jackie. You Can Paint Anything in Oils or Acrylics. (Illus.). 32p. (Orig.). 1987. pap. 7.95 (0-941284-38-7) J Shaw Studio.
Nelson, Shirley. Fair Clear & Terrible: The Story of Shiloh, a Strange Fragment of American History. Mirabelli, Margaret & Dumbleton, Susanne, eds. (Illus.). 448p. 1989. 21.95 (0-945167-17-2) British Amer Pub.
— The Last Year of the War. (Northcote Bks.). 1989. reprint ed. pap. 11.99 (0-87788-484-6) Shaw Pubs.
Nelson-Stafford, Barbara. From Kitchen to Consumer: An Entrepreneur's Guide to Commercial Food Production. (Illus.). 343p. 1991. pap. text ed. 33.00 (0-12-662770-3) Acad Pr.
Nelson, Stanley. The Brooklyn Book of the Dead. 108p. pap. 6.00 (0-912292-22-9) The Smith.
— The Brooklyn Book of the Dead. deluxe limited ed. 108p. 50.00 (1-882986-01-6) The Smith.
— Driftin on a Nightriff. (Illus.). 24p. (Orig.). 1988. pap. 3.50 (0-945085-04-4) Sub Rosa.
— Immigrant, Bk. I. 84p. 1990. pap. 9.95 (0-913559-14-8) Birch Brook Pr.
— Immigrant, Bk. II. 112p. 1993. pap. 11.95 (0-913559-21-0) Birch Brook Pr.
— Nightriffer. (Illus.). 108p. 1988. pap. 5.95 (0-685-67672-2) Birch Brook Pr.
— Nightriffer. deluxe limited ed. (Illus.). 108p. 1988. pap. 25.00 (0-913559-02-4) Birch Brook Pr.
— One Hundred One Fragments of a Prayer. Gauthier, Guy, ed. (Midnight Sun Ser.). (Illus.). 1979. 2.00 (0-935292-00-4) Midnight Sun.
— The Travels of Ben Sira. LC 77-82687. (Illus.). 70p. (Orig.). 1978. pap. 6.00 (0-912292-44-X) The Smith.
— The Unknowable Light of the Alien. LC 80-53431. 180p. (Orig.). 1981. pap. 7.50 (0-912292-65-2) The Smith.
Nelson, Stanley, ed. The Scene - Four. LC 77-70415. (Scene Award Ser.). (Illus.). 272p. 1977. pap. 8.00 (0-912292-42-3) The Smith.
— Scene - One. LC 72-89382. (Scene Award Ser.). 212p. 1972. pap. 8.00 (0-912292-27-X) The Smith.
— The Scene - Three. LC 72-89382. (Scene Award Ser.). 196p. 1975. pap. 8.00 (0-912292-38-5) The Smith.
— Scene - Two. LC 70-94633. (Scene Award Ser.). 192p. 1974. pap. 8.00 (0-912292-34-2) The Smith.
Nelson, Stephen. Only a Paper Moon: The Theatre of Billy Rose. Brockett, Oscar, ed. LC 87-5001. (Theater & Dramatic Studies: No. 42). 184p. reprint ed. 52.20 (0-8357-1796-8, 2070746) Bks Demand.
— Quattro Pro for Windows at Work. 1992. pap. 24.95 (0-201-58139-6) Addison-Wesley.
Nelson, Stephen D., et al, eds. AAAS Science & Technology Policy Yearbook, 1992. 400p. 1993. pap. 19.95 (0-87168-503-5, 92-24S) AAAS.
Nelson, Stephen L. Excel 4 pour Windows Memopoche. 250p. 1993. pap. 32.95 (0-7859-5642-5, 2736110080) Fr & Eur.
— Field Guide to Microsoft Access for WIndows 95. 1995. 9.95 (1-55615-875-0) Microsoft.

N

An Asterisk (*) at the beginning of an entry indicates that the title is appearing in BIP for the first time.

— Field Guide to Microsoft PowerPoint for Windows 95. 1995. 9.95 (1-55615-841-6) Microsoft.
— Field Guide to Microsoft Word for Windows 95. 1995. 9.95 (1-55615-832-7) Microsoft.
— Field Guide to PCs. 1995. 9.95 (1-55615-842-4) Microsoft.
— Field Guide to PowerPoint 4 for Windows. LC 94-3489. 1994. 9.95 (1-55615-693-6) Microsoft.
— Mastering Quicken 3 for Windows. LC 93-86306. 519p. 1993. 19.99 (0-7821-1371-0) Sybex.
— Mastering Quicken 4 for Windows. LC 94-68475. 547p. 1994. pap. 19.99 (0-7821-1580-2) Sybex.
— Microsoft Money. 2nd ed. 1992. pap. 19.95 (1-55615-510-7) Microsoft.
— The Power of Improv 2.1 for Windows. 2nd ed. LC 93-86062. 715p. 1993. 34.99 (0-7821-1440-7) Sybex.

Nelson, Steve. Excel Power Presentations: High-Impact Graphics That Make You Look Good. LC 92-36799. 1992. disk 34.95 (0-201-63294-2) Addison-Wesley.
— Field Guide to Microsoft Access. 1994. pap. 9.95 (1-55615-581-6) Microsoft.
— Field Guide to Windows. 2nd ed. 1994. pap. 9.95 (1-55615-675-8) Microsoft.
— Field Guide to Windows 3.1. 1994. pap. 9.95 (1-55615-640-5) Microsoft.
— Quicken for DOS for Dummies. (Illus.). 360p. 1993. pap. 16.95 (1-56884-006-3) IDG Bks.
— Quicken 3 for Windows for Dummies. (Illus.). 384p. 1993. pap. 16.95 (1-56884-005-5) IDG Bks.

Nelson, Steve & Rollins, Jack. Frosty the Snowman: Book & Cookie Cutter Set. (Illus.). 17p. (J). (ps-2). 1993. Incl. 2 cookie cutters. pap. 3.95 (0-590-69016-7, Cartwheel) Scholastic Inc.

Nelson, Steve, et al. Steve Nelson, American Radical. LC 80-26528. 475p. 1981. 49.95 (0-8229-3441-8) U of Pittsburgh Pr.
— Steve Nelson, American Radical. LC 80-26528. (Series in Social & Labor History). (Illus.). 448p. 1992. pap. 19.95 (0-8229-5471-0) U of Pittsburgh Pr.

***Nelson, Steve L.** QR-Quicken 4 for Windows for Dummies. 1994. pap. 9.95 (1-56884-950-8) IDG Bks.
— Quickbooks 3 for Dummies. 1994. pap. 19.99 (1-56884-227-9) IDG Bks.
— Quicken 4 for Windows for Dummies. 2nd ed. 1994. pap. 19.95 (1-56884-209-0) IDG Bks.
— Quicken 5 for MACs for Dummies. 1994. pap. 19.95 (1-56884-211-2) IDG Bks.
— Quicken 8 for DOS for Dummies. 1994. pap. 19.95 (1-56884-210-4) IDG Bks.

Nelson, Steven. Guinea Pigs As a New Pet. (Illus.). 64p. (Orig.). 1990. pap. 5.95 (0-86622-613-3, TU-006) TFH Pubns.

Nelson, Susan, ed. Underground Space Ninety-One - Ninety-Two, First Annual Edition. 100p. (Orig.). (C). 1991. pap. text ed. 50.00 (0-9612412-7-6) Lineal Pub Co.

Nelson, Susan, tr. see Mihura, Miguel.

Nelson, Susan C., jt. auth. see Breneman, David.

Nelson, Susan R., ed. Groundworks: North American Underground Projects, 1980-1989. (Illus.). (Orig.). 1989. pap. 45.00 (0-9622383-0-9) AUSA.

Nelson, Suzann J., jt. auth. see Martin, Janet L.

Nelson, Suzanne, ed. see Townswick, Jane.

***Nelson, T. G.** Children, Parents, & the Rise of the Novel. LC 94-47663. 1995. write for info. (0-87413-558-3) U Delaware Pr.

Nelson, T. J. & Wullert, J. R., II. Electronic Information Display Technologies. 250p. 1995. text ed. 53.00 (981-02-1301-8) World Scientific Pub.

Nelson, Ted & Nelson, Sharlene. Umbrella Guide to California Lighthouses. Olson, B. G., ed. (Umbrella Guides Ser.). (Illus.). 160p. (Orig.). 1993. pap. 12.95 (0-945397-21-6, Umbrella Bks) Epicenter Pr.
— Umbrella Guide to Oregon Lighthouses. Ummel, Christine, ed. (Illus.). 128p. 1994. pap. 10.95 (0-945397-27-5, Umbrella Bks) Epicenter Pr.

Nelson, Ted, et al, eds. Legal & Regulatory Affairs Manual. 1982. pap. 15.00 (0-686-37426-6) Coun NY Law.

Nelson, Ted W., jt. auth. see Nelson, Sharlene P.

Nelson, Teresa. Special Occasions. (Illus.). 28p. 1985. pap. 5.95 (0-933491-02-6) Hot off Pr.

Nelson, Thelma R. Hughes of North Carolina Ancestral Journal of the Hughes Families & Their Interlinks. (Illus.). 380p. 1994. reprint ed. lib. bdg. 67.00 (0-8328-4080-7); reprint ed. pap. 57.00 (0-8328-4081-5) Higginson Bk Co.

Nelson, Theodor. Computer Lib-Dream Machines. LC 87-19706. (Illus.). 336p. (Orig.). 1987. pap. 18.95 (0-914845-49-7, Tempus Bks) Microsoft.

***Nelson, Theodor H.** Literary Machines 93.1. rev. ed. (Illus.). 286p. 1992. pap. 25.00 (0-89347-062-7) Mindful Pr.

Nelson, Theresa. And One for All. (J). (gr. 4-7). 1991. pap. 3.50 (0-440-40456-8) Dell.
— And One for All. LC 88-22490. 192p. (J). (gr. 6-8). 1989. 15.95 (0-531-05804-2); lib. bdg. 15.99 (0-531-08404-3) Orchard Bks Watts.
— The Beggars' Ride. LC 90-52515. 256p. (YA). (gr. 6 up). 1992. 15.95 (0-531-05896-4); lib. bdg. 15.99 (0-531-08496-5) Orchard Bks Watts.
— Beggar's Ride. (YA). 1994. mass mkt. 3.99 (0-440-21887-X) Dell.
— Devil Storm. LC 87-5493. 224p. (J). (gr. 5-7). 1987. 15.95 (0-531-05711-9); lib. bdg. 15.99 (0-531-08311-X) Orchard Bks Watts.
— Earthshine: A Novel. LC 94-8793. 192p. (J). (gr. 6-9). 1994. 15.95 (0-531-06867-6); lib. bdg. 15.99 (0-531-08717-4) Orchard Bks Watts.
— The Twenty-Five Cent Miracle. LC 85-17061. 224p. (YA). (gr. 7 up). 1986. lib. bdg. 14.95 (0-02-724370-2, Bradbury S&S) S&S Childrens.
— The Twenty-Five Cent Miracle. LC 89-6822. 224p. (J). (gr. 4-7). 1989. reprint ed. pap. 3.95 (0-689-71326-6, Aladdin Paperbacks) S&S Childrens.

Nelson, Theresa M. For the Love of Casey. Mattingly, Jennie, ed. LC 87-50991. 230p. (Orig.). (J). (gr. 7 up). 1987. pap. 8.95 (1-55523-083-0) Winston-Derek.

Nelson, Theron R. The Management Science System. 150p. (C). 1988. pap. text ed. 25.95 (0-256-05655-2) Irwin.

Nelson, Theron R. & Potter, Thomas A. Real Estate Law: Concepts & Applications. Burvikovs, ed. LC 93-36562. 600p. (C). 1994. text ed. 52.00 (0-314-02824-2) West Pub.

Nelson, Thomas A. Kubrick: Inside a Film Artist's Maze. LC 80-8845. (Illus.). 288p. 1982. 39.95 (0-253-14648-8); pap. 12.95 (0-253-20283-3, MB-283) Ind U Pr.
— Shakespeare's Comic Theory: A Study of Art & Artifice in the Last Plays. (De Proprietatibus Litterarum, Ser. Practica: No. 57). 95p. (Orig.). 1972. text ed. 13.85 (3-10-800281-3) Mouton.

Nelson, Thomas A., jt. auth. see Cirrincione, J. A.

Nelson, Thomas A., jt. auth. see Cirrincione, Joseph A.

Nelson, Thomas A., jt. auth. see Schouppe, F. X.

Nelson, Thomas B. & Lockhoven, Hans B. The World's Submachine Guns: Developments from 1915 to 1963, Vol. I. rev. ed. 1985. 29.95 (0-686-15931-4) TBN Ent.

Nelson, Thomas B. & Musgrave, Daniel D. The World's Machine Pistols & Submachine Guns: Developments from 1963-1980, Vol. 2A. 1980. 29.95 (0-686-15933-0) TBN Ent.

Nelson, Thorana S. & Trepper, Terry S., eds. 101 Interventions in Family Therapy. LC 91-22252. 452p. 1992. lib. bdg. 49.95 (0-86656-902-2) Haworth Pr.

Nelson, Timothy, ed. see Young, Natalie B.

Nelson, Tina & Lanza, Janet. An Illustrated Guide to Northeastern Forest Trees. (Marginal Media Bioguide Ser.: No. 4). (Illus.). 50p. (J). 1983. pap. 3.00 (0-942788-11-7) Iris Visual.

Nelson, Tom. The Adventures of Bishop Delgazo. LC 90-72008. (Illus.). 96p. (Orig.). 1992. pap. 8.00 (1-56002-089-X, Univ Edtns) Aegina Pr.
— Math in Geography. (Math Is Everywhere Ser.). (Illus.). 48p. 1994. teacher ed. pap. text ed. 6.45 (1-55799-331-9, EMC 115) Evan-Moor Corp.

Nelson, Truman. God in Love: The Sexual Revolution of John Humphrey Noyes. write for info. (0-393-01636-6) Norton.

Nelson, V. & Carroll, B. Fault-Tolerant Computing. LC 86-46205. 419p. 1987. 9.95 (0-8186-8677-4, 677) IEEE Comp Soc.

Nelson, Vaunda M. Mayfield Crossing. 96p. (J). 1994. pap. 3.99 (0-380-72179-1, Camelot) Avon.
— Mayfield Crossing. LC 92-10564. (Illus.). 96p. (J). (gr. 3-7). 1993. 14.95 (0-399-22331-2, Putnam) Putnam Pub Group.
— Possibles. LC 94-44386. (J). 1995. write for info. (0-399-22823-3, Putnam) Putnam Pub Group.

Nelson, Vera J. Scent of Water. (Western Americana Bks.). 104p. (Orig.). 1973. pap. 5.00 (0-913626-19-8) S S S Pub Co.

***Nelson, Victor P.** Digital Logic Circuit Analysis & Design. 2nd ed. LC 94-35122. 1995. text ed. 69.00 (0-13-463894-8) P-H.

Nelson, Victoria. On Writer's Block: Removing the Barriers to Creativity. LC 92-38147. 192p. 1993. pap. 9.95 (0-395-64727-4) HM.

***Nelson, Vincent.** Entertainment Law Vol. 1. 1994. 112.00 (0-421-50150-2, Pub. by Sweet & Maxwll) W W Gaunt.

Nelson, Vincent E. The Structural Geology of the Cache Creek Area, Gros Ventre Mountains, Wyoming. LC 43-15519. (Augustana College Library Publication Ser.: No. 18). 46p. 1942. pap. 3.00 (0-910182-13-2) Augustana Coll.

Nelson, Virginia. Learning to Listen in English, Set. 144p. 1990. student ed, audio 39.95 (0-8442-0689-X, Natl Textbk) NTC Pub Grp.
— Listening to Communicate in English, Set. 144p. 1990. student ed, audio 39.95 (0-8442-0692-X, Natl Textbk) NTC Pub Grp.
— The Marriage Contract. (Orig.). 1980. pap. 1.95 (0-449-14355-4, GM) Fawcett.

***Nelson, Virginia J. & Clements, Colin.** Bluff Your Way in Hollywood. (Bluffers Ser.). 75p. (Orig.). 1993. pap. 3.95 (1-57143-032-6) RDR Bks.

Nelson, Vita & Korn, Donald J. Create & Manage Your Own Mutual Fund: Buy Stocks Directly from America's Blue Chip Companies. 220p. 1994. 15.95 (0-8119-0773-2) LIFETIME.

Nelson, Vivian, jt. auth. see Roller, William.

Nelson, W. Checklist of the Issues of the Press of New Jersey, 1723-1800. 1969. 5.00 (0-87556-223-X) Saifer.
— High Temperature Aspects of Hypersonic Flow: Proceedings of the Agard-NATO Special Meeting, Rhode-Saint-Genese, April, 1962. LC 63-17827. 1964. 322.00 (0-08-010288-3, Pub. by Pergamon Repr UK) Franklin.

***Nelson, W. Dale.** The President Is at Camp David. LC 94-37083. (Illus.). 260p. 1995. 24.95 (0-8156-0318-5) Syracuse U Pr.

Nelson, W. Ed, jt. auth. see Dufour, John W.

Nelson, W. M., jt. auth. see Lee, Edward G.

Nelson, W. N. Illustrated Dictionary of the Bible: Diccionario Ilustrado de la Biblia. 10th ed. (Illus.). 735p. (SPA.). 1982. 59.95 (0-8288-1204-7, S34921) Fr & Eur.

Nelson, Waldo E., ed. see Behrman, Richard E., et al.

***Nelson, Walter & Lindsey, George, eds.** Nelson's America's Best Money Managers 1995. 200p. 1995. per., pap. 135.00 (0-922460-68-X) Nelson Pubns.
— Nelson's Directory of Institutional Real Estate 1993. 2000p. 1993. per. 275.00 (0-922460-33-7) Nelson Pubns.
— Nelson's Directory of Institutional Real Estate 1995. 2200p. 1995. per., pap. 295.00 (0-922460-55-8) Nelson Pubns.
— Nelson's Directory of Investment Managers 1993, 2 vols., I. 4500p. 1993. write for info. (0-922460-27-2) Nelson Pubns.
— Nelson's Directory of Investment Managers 1993, 2 vols., II. 4500p. 1993. write for info. (0-922460-31-0) Nelson Pubns.
— Nelson's Directory of Investment Managers 1993, 2 vols., Set. 4500p. 1993. per. 435.00 (0-922460-32-9) Nelson Pubns.
— Nelson's Directory of Investment Managers 1995, 2 vols., Set. 4600p. 1995. per., pap. 495.00 (0-922460-65-5) Nelson Pubns.
— Nelson's Directory of Investment Managers 1995, Vol. I. 1995. per., pap. write for info. (0-922460-63-9) Nelson Pubns.
— Nelson's Directory of Investment Managers 1995, Vol. II. 1995. per., pap. write for info. (0-922460-64-7) Nelson Pubns.
— Nelson's Directory of Investment Research 1993, 2 vols. 1993. Vol. I: U.S., 1300p. write for info. (0-922460-24-8); Vol. II: International, 1000p. write for info. (0-922460-25-6); write for info. (0-318-69661-4) Nelson Pubns.
— Nelson's Directory of Investment Research 1993, 2 vols., Set. 1993. per. 495.00 (0-922460-26-4) Nelson Pubns.
— Nelson's Directory of Investment Research 1995, 2 vols., Set. 3700p. 1995. per., pap. 535.00 (0-922460-58-2) Nelson Pubns.
— Nelson's Directory of Investment Research 1995, Vol. I. 1995. per., pap. write for info. (0-922460-56-6) Nelson Pubns.
— Nelson's Directory of Investment Research 1995, Vol. II. 1995. per., pap. write for info. (0-922460-57-4) Nelson Pubns.
— Nelson's Directory of Neglected Stock Opportunities 1993. 750p. 1993. per. 225.00 (0-922460-35-3); Incl. electronic diskette database. per. 375.00 (0-685-61605-3) Nelson Pubns.
— Nelson's Directory of Plan Sponsors & Tax-Exempt Funds 1993, 3 vols., I. 4100p. 1992. write for info. (0-922460-28-0) Nelson Pubns.
— Nelson's Directory of Plan Sponsors & Tax-Exempt Funds 1993, 3 vols., II. 4100p. 1992. write for info. (0-922460-29-9) Nelson Pubns.
— Nelson's Directory of Plan Sponsors & Tax-Exempt Funds 1993, 3 vols., III. 4100p. 1992. write for info. (0-922460-39-6) Nelson Pubns.
— Nelson's Directory of Plan Sponsors & Tax-Exempt Funds 1993, 3 vols., Set. 4100p. 1992. per. 475.00 (0-922460-30-2) Nelson Pubns.
— Nelson's Directory of Plan Sponsors 1995, 3 vols., Set. 5700p. 1995. per., pap. 495.00 (0-922460-62-0) Nelson Pubns.
— Nelson's Directory of Plan Sponsors 1995, Vol. I. 1995. per., pap. write for info. (0-922460-59-0) Nelson Pubns.
— Nelson's Directory of Plan Sponsors 1995, Vol. II. 1995. per., pap. write for info. (0-922460-60-4) Nelson Pubns.
— Nelson's Directory of Plan Sponsors 1995, Vol. III. 1995. per., pap. write for info. (0-922460-61-2) Nelson Pubns.
— Nelson's Guide to Pension Fund Consultants 1993. 700p. 1993. per. 295.00 (0-922460-34-5) Nelson Pubns.
— Nelson's Guide to Pension Fund Consultants 1995. 700p. 1995. per., pap. 345.00 (0-922460-66-3) Nelson Pubns.
— Nelson's-NIMA Directory of Minority & Woman-Owned Investment Managers 1993. 400p. 1993. per. 125.00 (0-922460-36-1) Nelson Pubns.
— Nelson's TechReSource 1993. 1000p. 1993. write for info. (0-318-69662-2) Nelson Pubns.
— Nelson's TechResources 1995. 700p. 1995. per., pap. 95.00 (0-922460-67-1) Nelson Pubns.
— Nelson's 401(k) Marketplace Directory 1993. 2000p. 1992. per. 495.00 (0-922460-37-X); Incl. electronic diskette database. per. 1,495.00 (0-685-61606-1) Nelson Pubns.

Nelson, Walter, et al, eds. Nelson's Directory of Investment Research, 1990. 15th rev. ed. 1600p. 1990. 350.00 (0-922460-03-5) Nelson Pubns.
— Nelson's Directory of Investment Research, 1991. 16th ed. 2400p. 1992. Vol. 1: U.S., 1500p. write for info. (0-922460-14-0); Vol. 2: International, 900p. write for info. (0-318-68056-4) Nelson Pubns.
— Nelson's Directory of Investment Research, 1991, Set. 16th ed. 2400p. 1992. 450.00 (0-922460-13-2) Nelson Pubns.
— Nelson's Directory of Plan Sponsors & Tax-Exempt Funds, 1992. 2100p. 1992. 275.00 (0-685-50170-1) Nelson Pubns.

Nelson, Walter R. History of Goshen. (Illus.). 471p. 1992. reprint ed. lib. bdg. 47.00 (0-685-54708-6) Higginson Bk Co.

Nelson, Walter R., et al, eds. Nelson's Directory of Investment Managers, 1989. 2nd rev. ed. 900p. 1989. write for info. (0-922460-02-7) Nelson Pubns.

***Nelson, Warren.** T. C. Hammond. 178p. 1994. pap. 9.95 (0-85151-672-6) Banner of Truth.

Nelson, Warren L., et al. Always Bet on the Butcher: Warren Nelson & Casino Gaming, 1930s-1980s. LC 94-21183. (Illus.). 242p. 1994. 21.95 (1-56475-368-9) U NV Oral Hist.

Nelson, Wayne. Accelerated Testing: Statistical Models, Test Plans & Data Analysis. (Series in Probability & Mathematics). 601p. 1990. text ed. 110.00 (0-471-52277-5) Wiley.
— Applied Life Data Analysis. LC 81-14779. (Probability & Mathematical Statistics: Applied Probability & Statistics Section Ser.). 634p. 1982. text ed. 112.00 (0-471-09458-7, Wiley-Interscience) Wiley.

Nelson, Wayne E. & Glass, Henry. International Playtime. 1992. pap. 22.99 (0-86653-990-5) Fearon Teach Aids.

Nelson, Wayne F. The Best Kept Secret on Wall Street: How to Invest in Convertible Securities Like the Pros. LC 93-21502. 193p. 1993. 24.95 (0-7931-0720-2, 560887) Dearborn Finan.

***Nelson, Wendell.** Of Stones, Steam & the Earth: The Pleasures & Meanings of a Sauna. (Illus.). 88p. (Orig.). 1993. pap. 9.95 (0-9632975-3-8) Finnish Amer.
— Of Stones, Steam & the Earth: The Pleasures & Meanings of a Sauna. (Illus.). 88p. (Orig.). 1994. pap. 9.95 (0-9632975-7-0) Finnish Amer.

Nelson, Wesley. The Art of Bridge Building. 1989. pap. 3.95 (0-910452-69-5) Covenant.

Nelson, Wesley W. God's Friends: Called to Believe & Belong. 1985. 15.95 (0-910452-59-8); 19.95 (0-00-669930-8) Covenant.

Nelson, Wilfred H. Instrumental Methods for Rapid Microbiological Analysis. LC 85-15726. 219p. 1985. lib. bdg. 60.00 (0-89573-137-1) VCH Pubs.
— Physical Methods for Microorganisms Detection. 176p. 1991. 133.00 (0-8493-4140-X, QR69) CRC Pr.

Nelson, Wilfred H., ed. Modern Techniques for Rapid Microbiological Analysis. 263p. 1991. text ed. 69.50 (1-56081-001-7) VCH Pubs.

***Nelson, William.** Documents Relating to the Colonial History of the State of New Jersey, Vol. XXIII Vol. XXIII: Calendar of New Jersey Wills, 1670-1730, Vol. 1. (Illus.). 662p. 1994. reprint ed. pap. text ed. 42.00 (1-55613-988-8) Heritage Bk.
— Fact or Fiction: The Dilemma of the Renaissance Storyteller. LC 73-77990. 121p. reprint ed. pap. 34.50 (0-7837-4096-4, 2057919) Bks Demand.
— Interference Handbook. Orr, William I., ed. (Illus.). 252p. 1991. pap. 11.95 (0-8230-8709-3, RAC Bks) Watsn-Guptill.
— New Jersey Biographical & Genealogical Notes. 222p. 1992. reprint ed. pap. 21.50 (0-685-60395-4, 4005) Clearfield Co.

***Nelson, William & Van Doren Honeyman, A.** Documents Relating to the Colonial History of the State of New Jersey: Calendar of N. J. Wills, Administrations, Etc., 1730 - 1750, 2 vols., No. 2. 708p. (Orig.). 1994. pap. text ed. 42.00 (0-7884-0041-X) Heritage Bk.

Nelson, William, jt. ed. see Clayton, W. Woodford.

Nelson, William, jt. ed. see Ferguson, John.

N

Nelson, William A. Vermont Criminal Practice & Procedure. 1993. ring bd. 170.00 (0-88063-788-9) Butterworth Legal Pubs.
— Vermont Criminal Practice & Procedure. 830p. 1993. ring bd. 170.00 (1-56257-360-8) Michie Butterworth.

Nelson, William E. The Americanization of the Common Law: The Impact of Legal Change of Massachusetts Society, 1760-1830. LC 74-21231. (Studies in Legal History). 288p. (C). 1975. pap. 13.95 (0-674-02972-0) HUP.
— Americanization of the Common Law: The Impact of Legal Change on Massachusetts Society, 1760-1830. LC 74-21231. 288p. 1994. reprint ed. pap. 18.00 (0-8203-1587-7) U of Ga Pr.
— Dispute & Conflict Resolution in Plymouth County, Massachusetts, 1725-1825. LC 80-17403. (Studies in Legal History). 224p. reprint ed. pap. 63.90 (0-8357-3900-7, 2036632) Bks Demand.
— The Fourteenth Amendment: From Political Principle to Judicial Doctrine. LC 87-35226. 288p. (Orig.). 1990. text ed. 32.00 (0-674-31625-8) HUP.
— The Fourteenth Amendment: From Political Principle to Judicial Doctrine. 272p. (Orig.). (C). 1995. pap. text ed. 14.95 (0-674-31626-6) HUP.

Nelson, William E. & Reid, John P. The Literature of American Legal History. LC 85-61965. (New York University School of Law, Linden Studies in Legal History). 356p. 1985. Annual Survey of American Law Suppl. lib. bdg. 47.50 (0-379-20819-9) Oceana.

Nelson, William F., jt. auth. see Davis, Harold T.

Nelson, William H. The American Tory. 224p. 1992. reprint ed. pap. text ed. 12.95 (1-55553-148-2) NE U Pr.

Nelson, William J. Almost a Territory: America's Attempt to Annex the Dominican Republic. LC 89-40204. (Illus.). 152p. 1990. 32.50 (0-87413-380-7) U Delaware Pr.
— The Real Truth about Health: The Book That Takes the Work Out of Being Healthy. Musey, Charles W., ed. LC 85-82587. (Illus.). 287p. (Orig.). 1987. lib. bdg. 13.95 (0-936987-01-4) Kaptur Pr.

Nelson, William R. Interference Handbook. 2nd ed. LC 81-51709. (Illus.). 247p. 1981. 11.95 (0-933616-01-5) Radio Pubns.
— Planting Design: A Manual of Theory & Practice. (Illus.). 1985. text ed. 23.80 (0-87563-268-8) Stipes.

Nelson, William S., ed. Christian Way in Race Relations. LC 79-134121. (Essay Index Reprint Ser.). 1977. 21.95 (0-8369-2004-X) Ayer.

Nelson, Willie. Willie. 1988. 18.95 (0-318-35175-7) S&S Trade.
— Willie: Autobiography. 1989. mass mkt. 4.95 (0-671-68075-7) PB.
— Willie Nelson Lyrics, 1957-1994. 1995. 16.95 (0-312-11917-8) St Martin.

Nelson, Wilson E. The Roots of American Bureaucracy, 1830-1900. 224p. 1982. 34.50 (0-674-77945-2) HUP.

Nelson, Wilton M. Protestantism in Central America. LC 84-13727. 96p. reprint ed. pap. 27.40 (0-685-20790-0, 2030069) Bks Demand.

Nelson, Wilton M., ed. Diccionario Ilustrado de la Biblia. (Illus.). 735p. (SPA.). 1974. 20.95 (0-89922-033-9); pap. 17.95 (0-89922-099-1) Edit Caribe.

An Asterisk (*) at the beginning of an entry indicates that the title is appearing in BIP for the first time.

Nelson, Yvette. Celebrating the Eucharist. (Discovering Program Ser.). (Illus.). 73p. (Orig.). (YA). (gr. 7-8). 1992. teacher ed 6.00 (0-88489-270-0); pap. text ed. 2.80 (0-88489-269-7) St Marys.

— Exploring the Story of Israel: Discovering Program. (Illus.). 32p. (Orig.). 1992. student ed 3.30 (0-88489-267-0); teacher ed 6.00 (0-88489-268-9) St Marys.

— Gathering to Celebrate. Zanzig, Tom, ed. (Discovering Program Ser.). (Illus.). 80p. (J). (gr. 6-8). 1994. teacher ed 6.00 (0-88489-301-4); pap. text ed. 2.80 (0-88489-300-6) St Marys.

— We'll Come When It Rains. LC 82-61649. (Minnesota Voices Project Ser.: No. 11). (Illus.). 70p. 1982. pap. 3.00 (0-89823-043-8) New Rivers Pr.

Nelson, Yvette, jt. auth. see Bitney, James.

Neltz, Mary A. Dysfunctional Family Cooking. 32p. 1993. pap. 4.95 (1-883849-02-0) Nine Hund Forty Six Pr.

***Nema.** Maat Magick: A Guide to Self-Initiation. (Illus.). 288p. 1995. reprint ed. pap. 14.95 (0-87728-827-5) Weiser.

Nema, Faraja. Book of the Imperials. LC 87-71067. (Illus.). 88p. (C). 1987. 12.95 (0-318-23420-3); text ed. 11.00 (0-943799-03-1); lib. bdg. 10.97 (0-317-89465-X); pap. 7.95 (0-318-23422-X); pap. text ed. 6.00 (0-318-23423-8) Maan Found Grp.

Nema, N. Phytomedicine, a Treatise on Plant Diseases. (C). 1988. 197.50 (81-7136-009-2, Pub. by Periodical Expert India) St Mut.

***Neman, Beth S.** Teaching Students to Write. 2nd ed. 480p. (C). 1995. pap. text ed. 19.95 (0-19-506428-3) OUP.

— Writing Effectively. 2nd ed. 560p. (C). 1990. text ed. 34.50 (0-06-044807-5) HarpCollege.

Neman, Beth S. & Smythe. Writing Effectively in Business. (C). 1991. text ed. 40.50 (0-06-044809-1) HarpCollege.

Nemaneic, Allison, et al. Diabetes Care Made Easy: A Simple Step-by-Step Guide for Controlling Your Diabetes. LC 92-11193. (J). 1992. 9.95 (1-56561-013-X) Chronimed.

Nemanich, R. J., et al, eds. Chemical Surface Preparation, Passivation & Cleaning for Semiconductor Growth & Processing. (Materials Research Society Symposium Proceedings Ser.: Vol. 259). 1992. text ed. 57.00 (1-55899-154-9) Materials Res.

— Thin Films--Interfaces & Phenomena: Symposium Proceedings, Vol. 54. (Materials Research Society Symposium Proceedings Ser.). 1986. text ed. 55.00 (0-931837-19-7) Materials Res.

***Nemaniec, Allison.** Diabetes Care Made Easy, for Kids: A Simple Step by Step Guide for Controlling Your Diabetes. 1993. pap. 9.95 (1-56561-014-8) Chronimed.

***Nemapare, Prisca & Neumann, Richard.** Fundamentals of Meal Management. LC 95-3064. (Illus.). 242p. (C). 1995. text ed. 52.95x (0-398-05991-8); pap. text ed. 31.95x (0-398-05992-6) C C Thomas.

Nemat-Nasser, S. Mechanics Today. LC 72-10430. (Pergamon Mechanics Today Ser.: No. 6). 1981. 98.00 (0-08-024749-0, Pub. by Pergamon Repr UK) Franklin.

— Variational Methods in the Mechanics of Solids: Proceedings of the IUTAM Symposium, Sept. 11-13, 1978. LC 80-41529. (Illus.). 426p. 1980. 171.00 (0-08-024728-8, Pub. by Pergamon Repr UK) Franklin.

Nemat-Nasser, S., ed. Hydraulic Fracturing & Geothermal Energy. 1983. lib. bdg. 169.00 (90-247-2855-X) Kluwer Ac.

— Mechanics Today, Set. Incl. Vol. 1. 1974. 166.00 (0-08-017246-6); Vol. 2. 1975. 145.00 (0-08-018113-9); Vol. 3. 1976. 135.00 (0-08-019882-1); Vol. 4. 1978. 180.00 (0-08-021792-3); Vol. 5. 1980. 240.00 (0-08-024249-9); Vol. 6. 1981. pap. text ed. 40.00 (0-08-027318-1); 1978. 121.00 (0-08-022682-5, Pub. by Pergamon Repr UK) Franklin.

Nemat-Nasser, S. & Hori, Motoo. Micromechanics: Overall Properties of Heterogeneous Materials. LC 93-11093. (Applied Mathematics & Mechanics Ser.). 687p. 1993. 120.00 (0-444-89881-6, North Holland) Elsevier.

Nemat-Nasser, S., ed. see American Society of Mechanical Engineers Staff.

Nemazee, Susan, jt. auth. see Lowry, Glenn D.

Nembach, Paul A., jt. auth. see Douglas, James A.

Nemcova, B. Fairy Tales from Czechoslovakia, Vol. I. Velinsky, L., tr. (Illus.). 305p. (Orig.). (CZE.). (J). (gr. 4 up). 1987. pap. 39.50 (0-685-19314-4) KABEL Pubs.

Nemcova, Bozena. Granny: Scenes from Country Life. Pargeter, Edith, tr. LC 76-48902. 349p. 1977. reprint ed. text ed. 35.00 (0-8371-9355-9, NEGR, Greenwood Pr) Greenwood.

Nemcova, Jeanne, tr. see Lustig, Arnost.

Nemcova, Jeanne, tr. see Skvorecky, Josef.

Nemcsics, Antal. Colour Dynamics: Environmental Colour Design. 448p. 1993. text ed. 71.00 (0-13-138199-7) P-H.

Nemec, David. The Baseball Challenger Quiz Book. 192p. (Orig.). 1991. pap. 3.99 (0-451-16943-3, Sig) NAL-Dutton.

— The Beer & Whiskey League. 256p. 1994. 27.95 (1-55821-285-X) Lyons & Burford.

— The Great American Baseball Team Book. 432p. (Orig.). 1993. pap. 4.99 (0-451-17567-0, Sig) NAL-Dutton.

— The Great American Baseball Team Book: 1995 Updated Edition. 432p. (Orig.). 1995. pap. 4.99 (0-451-18336-3, Sig) NAL-Dutton.

— Great Baseball Feats, Facts, & Firsts. rev. ed. 432p. 1989. pap. 4.99 (0-451-16124-6, Sig) NAL-Dutton.

— Great Baseball Feats, Facts, & Firsts: 1995 Updated Edition. 432p. (Orig.). 1995. pap. 4.99 (0-451-18342-8, Sig) NAL-Dutton.

— The Most Extraordinary Baseball Quiz Book Ever. rev. ed. 192p. 1990. pap. 3.99 (0-451-16450-4, Sig) NAL-Dutton.

— One Thousand & One Fascinating Baseball Facts. rev. ed. 1994. 12.98 (0-681-00449-5) Longmeadow Pr.

— The Rules of Baseball. (Illus.). 192p. 1994. 24.95 (1-55821-279-5); pap. 16.95 (1-55821-280-9) Lyons & Burford.

Nemec, Dulci. White Fury. 150p. (Orig.). 1989. pap. 3.49 (0-9618998-4-0) Nemec Pub.

Nemec, E. P. Manager's Handbook. LC 87-71781. (Illus.). 158p. (Orig.). 1987. pap. 4.45 (0-9618998-0-8) Nemec Pub.

Nemec, Frantisek & Moudry, Vladimir. The Soviet Seizure of Subcarpathian Ruthenia. LC 79-2916. 375p. 1980. reprint ed. 30.00 (0-8305-0085-5) Hyperion Conn.

Nemec, Gale B. Living with Cats. LC 92-25706. 1993. 8.00 (0-688-10022-8, Quill) Morrow.

Nemec, I., jt. auth. see Kolar, V.

Nemec, J. & Drexler, J. Endurance of Mechanical Structures: Physical & Statistical Approaches. (Developments in Civil Engineering Ser.: No. 29). 468p. 1990. 148.75 (0-444-98807-6) Elsevier.

Nemec, Jack. Universe of Cartoons. LC 87-91984. (Illus.). 120p. (Orig.). 1987. pap. 3.95 (0-9618998-3-2) Nemec Pub.

Nemec, James M. & Matthews, Jaymie M., eds. New Perspectives on Stellar Pulsation & Pulsating Variable Stars. (Illus.). 454p. (C). 1993. 59.95 (0-521-44382-2) Cambridge U Pr.

Nemec, Jaromir, et al, eds. Prediction & Perception of Natural Hazards: Proceedings Symposium, 22-26 October 1990, Perugia, Italy. LC 93-4585. (Advances in Natural & Technological Hazards Research Ser.: Vol. 2). 216p. (C). 1993. lib. bdg. 69.00 (0-7923-2355-6) Kluwer Ac.

Nemec, John. Article Writing Guidelines. 14p. 1987. 1.75 (0-9618998-2-4) Nemec Pub.

— Naked in the Night. 160p. (Orig.). 1991. pap. 3.49 (0-9618998-8-3) Nemec Pub.

— Present Your Sale. LC 87-90713. 50p. (Orig.). 1987. 2.95 (0-9618998-1-6) Nemec Pub.

— Raging Passion. 160p. (Orig.). 1991. pap. 3.49 (0-9618998-7-5) Nemec Pub.

— Vacationer's Choice. (Illus.). 163p. (Orig.). 1989. pap. 4.45 (0-9618998-5-9) Nemec Pub.

— Wild for Kicks. 160p. (Orig.). 1991. pap. 3.49 (0-9618998-6-7) Nemec Pub.

Nemec, Ludvik. Infant Jesus of Prague. 1978. 2.25 (0-89942-129-6, 129/04) Catholic Bk Pub.

***Nemecek, Larry.** Star Trek: The Next Generation Companion. 1995. pap. 14.00 (0-671-88340-2) PB.

Nemeck, Francis K. & Coombs, Marie T. Contemplation. (Way of the Christian Mystics Ser.). 151p. 1982. pap. 9.95 (0-8146-5283-2) Liturgical Pr.

— Spiritual Journey. LC 85-45664. 230p. (Orig.). 1986. pap. 10.95 (0-8146-5546-7) Liturgical Pr.

— The Way of Spiritual Direction. LC 84-81254. 220p. 1985. pap. 10.95 (0-8146-5447-9) Liturgical Pr.

Nemeck, Francis K., jt. auth. see Coombs, Maria T.

Nemeck, Francis K., jt. auth. see Hermit, Marie T.

Nemecz, E. Clay Minerals. 548p. 1981. 227.00 (0-569-08686-8) St Mut.

***Nemeczek, Alfred.** Van Gogh in Arles. (Illus.). 128p. 1995. 25.00 (3-7913-1484-X) Pegasus.

Nemenyi, R. Controlled Atmospheres for Heat Treatment. (Illus.). 225p. 1984. 108.00 (0-08-019883-X, Pub. by Pergamon Repr UK) Franklin.

Nemeroff. Neuroendocrinology. 1992. 93.95 (0-8493-8844-9, QP356) CRC Pr.

Nemeroff, C. B. & Dunn, A. J., eds. Peptides, Hormones & Behavior. (Illus.). 944p. 1984. text ed. 150.00 (0-88331-174-7) Luce.

Nemeroff, Charles, ed. Neuropeptides & Psychiatric Disorders. LC 90-924. (Progress in Psychiatry Ser.: No. 29). 224p. 1991. text ed. 30.00 (0-88048-185-4) Am Psychiatric.

Nemeroff, Charles B., ed. Neuropeptides in Psychiatric & Neurological Disorders. LC 87-45487. (Series in Contemporary Medicine & Public Health). 368p. 1987. text ed. 65.00 (0-8018-3514-3) Johns Hopkins.

Nemeroff, Charles B. & Loosen, Peter T., eds. Handbook of Clinical Psychoneuroendocrinology. LC 86-31837. 502p. 1987. lib. bdg. 75.00 (0-89862-698-6) Guilford Pr.

Nemeroff, Charles B., jt. ed. see De Souza, Errol B.

Nemeroff, Charles B., jt. ed. see Kitabgi, Patrick.

Nemeroff, Charles B., jt. ed. see Schatzberg, Alan F.

***Nemerov, Alexander.** Frederic Remington & Turn-of-the-Century America. LC 95-1223. (Publications in the History of Art). 1995. write for info. (0-300-05566-8) Yale U Pr.

Nemerov, Harold. War Stories: Poems about Long Ago & Now. LC 87-5097. (Illus.). x, 60p. 1989. pap. 7.95 (0-226-57243-9) U Ch Pr.

Nemerov, Howard. The Collected Poems of Howard Nemerov. LC 77-544. 536p. 1981. pap. 16.95 (0-226-57259-5) U Ch Pr.

— The Homecoming Game: A Novel. LC 92-15687. 264p. (Orig.). 1992. reprint ed. pap. 12.95 (0-8262-0870-3) U of Mo Pr.

— A Howard Nemerov Reader. 552p. 1991. 24.95 (0-8262-0776-6) U of Mo Pr.

— A Howard Nemerov Reader. 552p. 1993. pap. 16.95 (0-8262-0936-X) U of Mo Pr.

— Inside the Onion. LC 83-9312. 72p. (C). 1985. pap. 6.95 (0-226-57245-5) U Ch Pr.

— Journal of the Fictive Life. LC 81-10449. (C). 1981. pap. 5.95 (0-226-57261-7) U Ch Pr.

— The Melodramatists. LC 91-40801. 352p. (C). 1992. reprint ed. pap. 14.95 (0-8262-0846-0) U of Mo Pr.

— New & Selected Poems. LC 60-14236. 1963. pap. 9.95 (0-226-57247-1, PP6) U Ch Pr.

— Oak in the Acorn: On Remembrance of Things Past & On Teaching Proust, Who Will Never Learn. LC 86-21087. 168p. 1987. text ed. 27.50 (0-8071-1385-9) La State U Pr.

— Sentences. LC 80-17702. 86p. 1983. pap. 8.95 (0-226-57262-5) U Ch Pr.

— Tall Story. adapted ed. Lindsey, Howard, ed. 1959. pap. 4.75 (0-8222-1109-2) Dramatists Play.

— Trying Conclusions: New & Selected Poems, 1961-1991. 152p. 1991. 18.95 (0-226-57263-3) U Ch Pr.

— War Stories: Poems about Long Ago & Now. LC 87-5097. 72p. (C). 1987. 10.95 (0-226-57242-0) U Ch Pr.

Nemerov, Howard, et al. Ethics of Change: Humanistic Values vs. Technological Imperatives. LC 88-83425. (Proceedings of the February Forums Ser.: Vol. II). (Illus.). 222p. (Orig.). 1989. pap. text ed. 15.00 (1-882070-03-8) Atlantic Ctr Arts.

Nemerow, Nelson L. Stream, Lake, Estuary & Ocean Pollution. 2nd rev. ed. (Environmental Engineering Ser.). (Illus.). 464p. 1991. text ed. 69.95 (0-442-00767-1) Van Nos Reinhold.

— Zero Population for Industry: Waste Minimalization through Industrial Complexes. LC 95-10072. 1995. text ed. 54.95 (0-471-12164-9) Wiley.

Nemerow, Nelson L. & Dasgupta, Avijit. Industrial & Hazardous Waste Treatment. LC 90-49704. (Illus.). 752p. 1991. text ed. 95.00 (0-442-31934-7) Van Nos Reinhold.

Nemerowicz, Gloria M. Children's Perceptions of Gender & Work Roles. LC 79-11783. 201p. 1979. text ed. 49.95 (0-275-90399-0, C0399, Praeger Pubs) Greenwood.

Nemerowitz Morris, Gloria, jt. auth. see Gora, Jo Ann.

Nemes, Claire. A Picture Book of Dinosaurs. LC 89-37331. (Picture Book of...Ser.). (Illus.). 24p. (J). (gr. 1-4). 1990. lib. bdg. 9.59 (0-8167-1900-4); pap. text ed. 2.50 (0-8167-1901-2) Troll Assocs.

***Nemes, Claire, ed.** Young Tom Edison: Great Inventor. LC 95-8107. (First-Start Biography Ser.). (Illus.). 32p. (J). (gr. k-2). 1995. lib. bdg. 11.59 (0-8167-3776-2); pap. text ed. 3.50 (0-8167-3777-0) Troll Assocs.

Nemes, L. Information Control Problems in Manufacturing Automation, Vol. 5. 500p. 1993. text ed. 69.00 (9971-5-0100-7) World Scientific Pub.

Nemes, L., jt. ed. see Puente, E. A.

Nemes, Laszlo, tr. see Mika, Jozsef & Torok, Tibor.

Nemes, Sylvester. Learn How to Fly Fish in One Day: Quickest Way to Start Tying Flies, Casting Flies, & Catching Fish. LC 85-20802. (Illus.). 128p. (Orig.). 1986. pap. 10.95 (0-8117-2185-X) Stackpole.

— The Soft-Hackled Fly: A Trout Fisherman's Guide. LC 93-12705. (Illus.). 130p. 1993. reprint ed. 19.95 (0-8117-1670-8) Stackpole.

— The Soft-Hackled Fly Addict. LC 93-12707. (Illus.). 144p. 1993. reprint ed. 19.95 (0-8117-1671-6) Stackpole.

Nemes, T. Cybernetic Machines. 260p. 1970. text ed. 200.00 (0-677-60570-6) Gordon & Breach.

Nemeshegyi, Peter. The Meaning of Christianity. 128p. 1982. pap. 3.95 (0-8091-2464-5) Paulist Pr.

***Nemeskurty, I.** Nous, les Hongrois. 384p. (FRE.). 1994. 62.00 (963-05-6688-5, Pub. by A K HU) Intl Spec Bk.

Nemeskurty, Istvan. A History of Hungarian Literature. 572p. 1982. 75.00 (0-569-08791-0, Pub. by Collets UK) Pro-Am Music.

Nemeskurty, Istvan & Szanto, Tibor. A Pictorial Guide to the Hungarian Cinema (1901-1984) 210p. 1985. 60.00 (0-317-61348-0, Pub. by Collets UK) Pro-Am Music.

Nemessuri, M., jt. auth. see Szende, O.

Nemessuri, Mihaly, jt. auth. see Szende, Otto.

Nemet-Nejat, Murat, tr. see Veli, Orhan.

Nemet, Roslyn. Cook to Your Heart's Content. 1981. pap. 1.75 (0-8439-0870-X) Dorchester Pub Co.

— Cooking Cues from A to Z. (Orig.). 1981. pap. 1.95 (0-8439-8013-3) Dorchester Pub Co.

— Investment Tips for Today's Woman. (Orig.). 1981. pap. 2.25 (0-8439-8038-9) Dorchester Pub Co.

Nemeth, Charles P. Anderson's Directory of Criminal Justice Education, 1990-91. LC 87-654284. 800p. (C). 1990. pap. text ed. 59.95 (0-87084-195-5) Anderson Pub Co.

— Business Forms for Paralegals. LC 94-41808. (Paralegals Law Library). 1995. text ed. 98.00 (0-471-01998-4) Wiley.

— The Case of Archbishop Lefebure: Trial by Canon Law. 173p. 1994. pap. text ed. 9.95 (0-935952-50-0) Angelus Pr.

— Delaware Corporate Practice for the Paralegal: With Forms. LC 94-70885. 400p. 1995. ring bd. 49.50 (0-614-05668-3) Bisel Co.

— Estate Planning & Administration for Paralegals. (Paralegal Law Library). 576p. 1993. text ed. 98.00 (0-471-58745-1) Wiley.

— Evidence Handbook for Paralegals. (Paralegal Law Library). 280p. 1993. text ed. 98.00 (0-471-58746-X) Wiley.

— Florida Corporate Practice for the Paralegal: With Forms. 403p. 1995. 49.50 (0-614-05669-1) Bisel Co.

— Legal Research & Writing Exercises for Paralegals. (Illus.). 171p. (Orig.). (C). 1992. student ed, pap. 8.95 (0-916951-00-6) Adams & Ambrose.

— Legal Research & Writing Exercises for Paralegals: Teacher's Answer Key. 41p. (Orig.). (C). 1992. student ed, pap. 7.50 (0-916951-01-4) Adams & Ambrose.

— Litigation, Pleadings & Arbitration. 508p. 1991. 49.00 (0-87084-616-7) Anderson Pub Co.

— New Jersey Corporate Practice for the Paralegal: With Forms. LC 94-72418. 399p. 1995. 49.50 (0-614-05670-5) Bisel Co.

— Paralegal Internships Manual. 1995. per. write for info. (0-929563-21-2) Pearson Pubns.

— The Paralegal Resource Manual. 1476p. 1989. 79.00 (0-87084-606-X) Anderson Pub Co.

— Paralegal Workbook, No. 1. 363p. 1989. pap. 24.95 (0-87084-610-8) Anderson Pub Co.

— Paralegal Workbook, No. 2. 286p. 1989. pap. 24.95 (0-87084-611-6) Anderson Pub Co.

— Pennsylvania Corporate Practice for the Paralegal: With Forms. LC 94-70887. 494p. 1994. ring bd. 49.50 (0-614-05667-5) Bisel Co.

— Private Security & the Investigative Process. LC 90-84734. (Illus.). 359p. (C). 1992. pap. text ed. 34.95 (0-87084-626-4) Anderson Pub Co.

— Private Security & the Law. (Illus.). 250p. (C). 1989. pap. text ed. 25.95 (0-87084-625-6) Anderson Pub Co.

— A Status Report on Contemporary Criminal Justice Education: A Definition of the Discipline & an Assessment of Its Curricula, Faculty & Program Characteristics. LC 88-7998. (Mellen Studies in Education: Vol. 3). 250p. 1989. lib. bdg. 89.95 (0-88946-938-5) E Mellen.

Nemeth, Charles P. & VanHorn, Grayson P. Real Estate Foreclosure: Paralegal Practice & Procedure. LC 94-11917. 1994. text ed. 98.00 (0-471-30722-X, Pub. by Wiley Law Pubns) Wiley.

Nemeth, David J. The Architecture of Ideology: Neo-Confucian Imprinting on Cheju Island, Korea. (UC Publications in Geography: Vol. 26). (Orig.). 1988. pap. 50.00 (0-520-09713-0) U CA Pr.

Nemeth, Doris I., et al, eds. The Poet, Nineteen Eighty-One. (Autumn Ser.). (Illus.). 400p. 1981. pap. 11.00 (0-932192-03-3) Fine Arts Soc.

— The Poet, Nineteen Eighty-Three. (Autumn Ser.: 1983). (Illus.). 400p. 1983. pap. 11.50 (0-932192-05-X) Fine Arts Soc.

***Nemeth, Evi.** Unix System Administration Handbook. 2nd ed. 816p. 1995. pap. 52.00 (0-13-151051-7) P-H.

Nemeth, G., ed. Mathematical Approximations of Special Functions. 128p. (C). 1992. pap. text ed. 85.00 (1-56072-052-2) Nova Sci Pubs.

Nemeth, G. & Kuttig, H. Isodose Atlas for Use in Radiotherapy. 272p. 1981. lib. bdg. 117.00 (90-247-2476-7) Kluwer Ac.

Nemeth, G. & Zentai, P. Seventy-Two Hours in Budapest: A Guidebook. 116p. (C). 1989. pap. 40.00 (0-685-37547-1, Pub. by Collets) St Mut.

***Nemeth, I. & Vizkelety, A., eds.** Ex Libris & Manuscriptis Quellen, Editionen, Untersuchungen zur Osterreichischen & Ungarischen Geistesgeschichte. (Schriftenreihe des Komitees Osterreich-Ungarn: Band 3). 276p. (GER.). 1994. pap. 42.00 (963-05-6680-X, Pub. by A K HU) Intl Spec Bk.

Nemeth, J. Turkish Grammar. (Publications in Near & Middle East Studies: Ser. B, No. 1). 1962. 22.00 (90-279-0100-7) Mouton.

Nemeth, K. Application of Electro-Ultrafiltration (EUF) in Agricultural Production. 1982. pap. text ed. 47.00 (90-247-2641-7) Kluwer Ac.

Nemeth, Laszlo. Guilt. Gulyas, Gyula, tr. LC 66-76589. 1966. 22.50 (0-7206-3845-3) Dufour.

***Nemeth, Maria.** You & Money: A Guide to Personal Integrity & Financial Abundance. 256p. 1995. pap. 14.95 (0-929999-05-3) Tzedakah Pubns.

***Nemeth, Sally.** Sally's Shorts. 1995. pap. 4.75 (0-8222-1454-7) Dramatists Play.

***Nemett, Barry.** Images, Objects & Ideas. 324p. (C). 1992. pap. text ed. write for info. (0-697-27459-4) Brown & Benchmark.

— Images, Objects, & Ideas: Viewing the Visual Arts. 352p. (C). 1992. pap. text ed. 42.75 (0-03-021782-2) HB Coll Pubs.

Nemetz, Jennifer, ed. Directory of Women's & Childrens Wear Specialty Stores, 1993. 1100p. 1992. pap. 180.00 (0-86730-569-X, CSG Info Servs) Lebhar Friedman.

Nemetz, Jennifer, ed. see Prueher, Terry.

Nemetz, Peter N. & Hankey, Marilyn. Economic Incentives for Energy Conservation. LC 83-17064. 352p. 1984. 45.95 (0-471-88768-4, Wiley-Interscience) Krieger.

Nemetz, Rowena. Bo's Search for Love & Understanding. LC 86-10379. (Illus.). 48p. (Orig.). (J). (gr. 1-6). 1986. pap. 5.95 (0-941992-09-8) Los Arboles Pub.

Nemhauser, G. L., et al, eds. Optizmation: Handbooks in Operations Research & Management Science, Vol. 1. 700p. 1989. 115.00 (0-444-87284-1, North Holland) Elsevier.

Nemhauser, George L. Introduction to Dynamic Programming. LC 66-21046. (Series in Decision & Control). 270p. reprint ed. pap. 77.00 (0-317-08720-7, 2013053) Bks Demand.

Nemhauser, George L. & Wolsey, Laurence A. Integer & Combinatorial Optimization. LC 87-34067. (Discrete Mathematics Ser.). 763p. 1988. text ed. 125.00 (0-471-82819-X) Wiley.

Nemiah, John C. Foundations of Psychopathology. 1966. pap. 18.95 (0-19-501137-6) OUP.

Nemiah, John C., jt. ed. see Gold, Judith H.

Nemilov. Vitreous State: Thermodynamic & Kinetic Aspects. 1994. write for info. (0-8493-3782-8) CRC Pr.

Nemilova, I. S. French Painting of the Eighteenth Century in the State Hermitage. 268p. 1985. 175.00 (0-317-61270-0) St Mut.

Nemiro, Beverly A. & Hamilton, Donna M. High Altitude Cookbook. LC 67-12738. 1980. 25.00 (0-394-51308-8) Random.

Nemiroff, Diana. Canadian Biennial of Contemporary Art. (Illus.). 188p. 1990. pap. 24.95 (0-88884-595-2) U Ch Pr.

— Jana Sterbak: States of Being - Corps a Corps. (Illus.). 96p. 1991. pap. 24.95 (0-88884-616-9) U Ch Pr.

Nemiroff, Diana, ed. Land, Spirit, Power: First Nations at the National Gallery of Canada. (Illus.). 275p. 1992. pap. 39.95 (0-88884-650-9) U Ch Pr.

***Nemiroff, Diana & Kuspit, Donald.** Roland Poulin: Sculpture. 43p. 1995. pap. 29.95 (0-88884-634-7) U Ch Pr.

N

Nemiroff, Greta H. Reconstructing Education: Towards a Pedagogy of Critical Humanism. LC 91-33944. 224p. 1992. text ed. 52.95 (*0-89789-266-6*, H266, Bergin & Garvey); pap. text ed. 16.95 (*0-89789-267-4*, G267, Bergin & Garvey) Greenwood.

Nemiroff, Marc A. & Annunziata, Jane. A Child's First Book about Play Therapy. LC 90-49954. (Illus.). 60p. (Orig.). (J). 1990. 19.95 (*1-55798-112-4*); pap. text ed. write for info. (*1-55798-088-6*) Am Psychol.

Nemiroff, Robert, ed. see Hansberry, Lorraine.

Nemiroff, Robert A. & Colarusso, Calvin A. New Dimensions in Adult Development. LC 89-43165. 576p. 1990. text ed. 40.00 (*0-465-05010-7*) Basic.

Nemiroff, Robert A. & Colarusso, Calvin A., eds. The Race Against Time: Psychotherapy & Psychoanalysis in the Second Half of Life. LC 84-17683. (Critical Issues in Psychiatry Ser.). 350p. 1985. 47.50 (*0-306-41753-7*, Plenum Pr) Plenum.

Nemiroff, Robert A., jt. auth. see Colarusso, Calvin A.

Nemiroff, Robert A., et al, eds. On Loving, Hating, & Living Well: The Public Psychoanalytic Lectures of Ralph R. Greenson, M.D. LC 92-1438. (Monograph Series of the Ralph R. Greenson Memorial Library of the San Diego Psychoanalytic Institute & Society). 382p. 1992. text ed. 50.00 (*0-8236-3790-5*) Intl Univs Pr.

Nemirovitch-Dantchenko, Vladimir. My Life in the Russian Theatre. LC 67-18053. (Illus.). 1968. pap. 3.45 (*0-87830-520-3*, Theatre Arts Bks) Routledge Chapman & Hall.

Nemirovskaias, M. A. Watercolours & Drawings of the Eighteenth & First Half of the Nineteenth Century in the Tretyakov Gallery. (Illus.). 162p. (ENG & RUS.). 1982. 173.00 (*0-317-57485-X*, Pub. by Collets UK) St Mut.

Nemirovski, Arkadii, jt. auth. see Nesterov, Yurii.

Nemirovskii, E. D. Adrei Chokhov. 108p. (RUS.). 1982. 35. 00 (*0-317-40836-4*, Pub. by Collets UK) Pro-Am Music.

Nemirovsky, A. S. & Yudin, D. B. Problem Complexity & Method Efficiency in Optimization. LC 82-11065. 388p. 1983. text ed. 220.00 (*0-471-10345-4*) Wiley.

Nemirovsky, Irene. Life of Chekhov. LC 74-7101. (Studies in Russian Literature & Life: No. 100). 1974. lib. bdg. 59.95 (*0-8383-1865-7*) M S G Haskell Hse.

Nemirow, Steven, et al. Coyote's Journal. LC 82-70807. (Illus.). 176p. (Orig.). 1982. pap. 8.95 (*0-914728-38-5*) Wingbow Pr.

Nemko, Barbara, jt. auth. see Nemko, Marty.

Nemko, Martin. How to Get an Ivy League Education at a State University. 784p. 1988. pap. 10.95 (*0-380-75375-8*) Avon.

Nemko, Martin, jt. ed. see Hatfield, Susan R.

Nemko, Marty & Nemko, Barbara. How to Get Your Child a "Private School" Education in a Public School. 228p. 1988. 12.95 (*0-89815-279-8*); pap. 8.95 (*0-89815-277-1*) Ten Speed Pr.

Nemmers, Erwin E. Hobson & Underconsumption. LC 73-186784. (Reprints of Economic Classics Ser.). xi, 152p. 1972. reprint ed. 27.50 (*0-678-00672-5*) Kelley.

— Twenty Centuries of Catholic Church Music. LC 78-17248. 213p. 1978. reprint ed. text ed. 35.00 (*0-313-20542-6*, NETW, Greenwood Pr) Greenwood.

Nemnick, Mary B., jt. auth. see Jandt, Fred E.

Nemo, John, ed. see Kavanagh, Patrick & O'Connor, P. J.

Nemodruk, A. A. & Karalova, Z. K. Analytical Chemistry of Boron. 248p. 1971. text ed. 68.00 (*0-7065-0750-9*, Pub. by Keter Pub IS) Coronet Bks.

Nemoianu, Anca M. The Boat's Gonna Leave: A Study of Children Learning a Second Language from Conversations with Other Children. (Pragmatics & Beyond Ser.: Vol. 1, No. 1). vi, 116p. 1980. pap. 29.00x (*90-272-2507-9*) Benjamins North Am.

Nemoianu, Virgil. The Taming of Romanticism: European Literature & the Age of the Biedermeier. (Studies in Comparative Literature: No. 37). 320p. 1984. 37.00 (*0-674-86802-1*) HUP.

— A Theory of the Secondary: Literature, Progress, & Reaction. LC 88-83620. (Parallax: Re-Visions of Culture & Society Ser.). 272p. 1989. text ed. 38.00x (*0-8018-3731-6*) Johns Hopkins.

Nemoianu, Virgil & Royal, Robert, eds. The Hospitable Canon: Essays on Literary Play, Scholarly Choice & Popular Pressures. LC 91-8337. (Cultura Ludens Ser.: Vol. 4). vii, 270p. 1991. 74.00x (*1-55619-152-9*) Benjamins North Am.

— Play, Literature, Religion: Essays in Cultural Intertextuality. LC 91-4056. 221p. 1992. 49.50 (*0-7914-0935-X*); pap. 16.95 (*0-7914-0936-8*) State U NY Pr.

Nemore, Arnold L. & Mangum, Garth L. Reorienting the Federal - State Employment Service. (Policy Papers in Human Resources & Industrial Relations Ser.: No. 8). (Orig.). 1968. pap. 5.00 (*0-87736-108-8*) U of Mich Inst Labor.

Nemoto, Makoto, jt. auth. see Ikeda, Daisaku.

Nemoto, Maseo. Total Quality Control for Management: Strategies & Techniques from Toyota & Toyoda Gosei. 270p. 1987. 24.95 (*0-13-925637-7*) P-H.

Nemoto, T., jt. auth. see Mauchline, J.

Nemoy, Elizabeth M. Speech Correction Through Story-Telling Units. 1973. text ed. 6.00 (*0-686-09399-2*) Expression.

Nemoy, Leon. Arabic Manuscripts in the Yale University Library. (Connecticut Academy of Arts & Sciences Ser., Trans.: Vol. 40). 1956. pap. 100.00 (*0-685-22894-0*) Elliots Bks.

Nemoy, Leon & Moreen, Vera B., eds. Tarih: A Volume of Occasional Papers in Near Eastern Studies, Vol. 1. 129p. 1990. pap. text ed. 17.50 (*0-685-57085-1*, Ctr Judaic Studies) Eisenbrauns.

Nemoy, Leon, jt. ed. see Katsh, Abraham I.

Nemoy, Sheldon & Aiken, C. J. Looking Good with CorelDRAW! Hundreds of Tips, Techniques & Ideas for Creating Great Art on Your Computer. 2nd ed. (Illus.). 328p. 1993. pap. 27.95 (*1-56604-061-2*) Ventana Pr.

— Looking Good with CorelDRAW! Hundreds of Tips, Techniques & Ideas for Creating Great Art on Your Computer. 3rd ed. (Illus.). 350p. 1994. pap. 27.95 (*1-56604-162-7*) Ventana Pr.

Nemschak, F., ed. World Economy & East-West Trade, Vol. 1. 1977. pap. 39.00 (*0-387-81390-X*) Spr-Verlag.

Nemser, C. Ben Cunningham: A Life with Color. 92p. 1989. text ed. 38.00 (*0-9622235-0-6*) Gordon & Breach.

Nemser, Cindy. Ben Cunningham - A Life with Color. (Illus.). 92p. 1989. write for info. (*0-318-64797-4*) JPL Art Pubs.

Nemser, W., jt. auth. see Dezso, L.

Nemser, William. Experimental Study of Phonological Interference in the English of Hungarians. LC 68-66741. (Uralic & Altaic Ser.: Vol. 105). 191p. (Orig.). 1971. pap. text ed. 12.00 (*0-87750-043-6*) Res Inst Inner Asian Studies.

Nemy, Enid. Judith Leiber: The Art of the Handbag. LC 94-17787. (Illus.). 1994. write for info. (*0-8109-3571-6*); pap. write for info. (*0-8109-2609-1*) Abrams.

***Nemzow, Martin.** The Ethernet Management Guide. 3rd ed. LC 95-5552. 1995. text ed. 50.00 (*0-07-046380-8*) McGraw.

— Implementing Wireless Networks. LC 94-43753. 1995. text ed. 50.00 (*0-07-046377-8*) McGraw.

Nemzow, Martin A. Computer Performance Optimization. LC 93-42960. 1994. pap. text ed. 39.95 (*0-07-911689-2*) McGraw.

— Ethernet Management Guide: Keeping the Link. 2nd ed. 1992. text ed. 48.00 (*0-07-046320-4*) McGraw.

— FDDI Networking: Planning, Installation, & Management. (Computer Communications Ser.). 450p. 1993. text ed. 45.00i (*0-07-046322-0*) McGraw.

— Keeping the Link: Ethernet Installation & Management. 384p. 1988. text ed. 43.00 (*0-07-046302-6*) McGraw.

— The Token-Ring Management Guide. (Computer Communications Ser.). 450p. 1993. text ed. 48.00i (*0-07-046321-2*) McGraw.

Nenarkomova, I. Sizov. Art Treasures from the Museums of the Moscow Kremlin. 111p. 1980. 75.00 (*0-569-08692-2*, Pub. by Collets UK) St Mut.

Nenarokov, A. Illustrated History of the Great October Socialist Revolution. (Illus.). 400p. (C). 1987. 100.00 (*0-685-31510-X*, Pub. by Collets UK) Pro-Am Music.

***Nenaskev, Mikhail.** An Ideal Betrayed: Testimonies of a Prominent & Loyal Member of the Soviet Establishment. 176p. 1995. pap. 14.95 (*1-871871-25-5*) Paul & Co Pubs.

Nencel, Lorraine & Pels, Peter, eds. Constructing Knowledge: Authority & Critique in Social Science. (Inquiries in Social Construction Ser.). 256p. (C). 1991. text ed. 55.00 (*0-8039-8401-4*); pap. text ed. 22.50 (*0-8039-8402-2*) Sage.

Nenci, I., jt. auth. see Castagnetta, L.

Nene, Y. L. & Thapliyal, P. N. Fungicides in Plant Disease Control. 3rd ed. 670p. (C). 1993. text ed. 60.00 (*1-881570-22-3*) Intl Sci Pub.

Nene, Y. L., et al, eds. The Pigeonpea. 490p. 1991. text ed. 99.00 (*0-85198-657-9*) CAB Intl.

Nenida, Pablo. Pablo Nenida: Selected Poems. 512p. 1990. pap. 13.95 (*0-395-54418-1*) HM.

Nenneman, Richard A. The New Birth of Christianity: Why Religion Persists in a Scientific Age. LC 91-50501. 208p. 1992. 19.00 (*0-06-250615-3*) Harper SF.

***Nenner, Howard.** The Right to Be King: The Succession to the Crown of England, 1603-1714. LC 95-14389. (Studies in Legal History). 1995. write for info. (*0-8078-2247-7*) U of NC Pr.

***Nenner, Irene, et al, eds.** Molecules & Grains in Space. (AIP Conference Proceedings Ser.: No. 312). 832p. 1994. text ed. 145.00x (*1-56396-355-8*) Am Inst Physics.

Nennessy, John. Second Manassas Battlefield Map Study. (Virginia Civil War Battles & Leaders Ser.). (Illus.). 504p. 1991. 39.95 (*1-56190-009-5*) H E Howard.

Nenninger, Timothy K. The Leavenworth Schools & the Old Army: Education, Professionalism, & the Officer Corps of the United States Army, 1881-1918. LC 77-91105. (Contributions in Military History Ser.: No. 15). 173p. 1978. text ed. 49.95 (*0-313-20047-5*, NFL/) Greenwood.

Nenninger, Timothy K., jt. ed. see Ryan, Garry D.

Nennius. History of the Britons. Giles, J. A., tr. pap. 3.95 (*0-89979-019-4*) British Am Bks.

— Nennius's "History of the Brittons" Wade-Evans, A. W., tr. Bd. with Annals of Britons of Court Pedigree of Hywel the Good. (Church Historical Society, London, N. S. Ser.: No. 34). 1974. reprint ed. Set pap. (*0-317-15134-7*) Periodicals Srv.

Nennius Abbot of Bangor. The Irish Nennius from Leabhar Na H-Uidre & Homilies & Legends from Leabhar Breac. Hogan, Edmund, ed. LC 78-72685. (Royal Irish Academy. Todd Lecture Ser.: Vol. 6). reprint ed. 16.50 (*0-404-60566-4*) AMS Pr.

Nenno, Mary K. & Brophy, Paul C. Housing & Local Government. LC 82-9174. (Municipal Management Ser.). (Illus.). 260p. (Orig.). (C). 1982. text ed. 28.00 (*0-87326-025-2*); pap. text ed. 21.00 (*0-87326-026-0*) Intl City-Cnty Mgt.

Nenno, Robert B., jt. auth. see Gallo, Michael A.

Nenno, Robert B., jt. auth. see Gilligan, Lawrence G.

Nenon, T., ed. see Husserl, Edmund.

Nenon, Thomas J., Jr., tr. see Marx, Werner.

Nenot, J. C. & Stather, J. W. The Toxicity of Plutonium, Americium & Curium. (Commission of the European Communities Ser.: EUR 6157). (Illus.). 1979. pap. 96.00 (*0-08-023440-2*, Pub. by Pergamon Repr UK) Franklin.

Nentl, Jerolyn. Beaver. LC 83-5323. (Wildlife Habits & Habitats Ser.). (Illus.). 48p. (J). (gr. 5). 1983. text ed. 12. 95 (*0-89686-219-4*, Crstwood Hse) Silver Burdett Pr.

— The Caribou. LC 83-26254. (Wildlife Habits & Habitats Ser.). (Illus.). 48p. (J). (gr. 5). 1984. text ed. 12.95 (*0-89686-244-5*, Crstwood Hse) Silver Burdett Pr.

— The Grizzly. LC 83-22354. (Wildlife Habits & Habitats Ser.). (Illus.). 48p. (J). (gr. 5). 1984. text ed. 12.95 (*0-89686-245-3*, Crstwood Hse) Silver Burdett Pr.

— The Mallard. LC 83-2087. (Wildlife Habits & Habitats Ser.). (Illus.). 48p. (J). (gr. 5). 1983. text ed. 12.95 (*0-89686-221-6*, Crstwood Hse) Silver Burdett Pr.

— Raccoon. LC 83-21072. (Wildlife Habits & Habitats Ser.). (Illus.). 48p. (J). (gr. 5). 1984. text ed. 12.95 (*0-89686-246-1*, Crstwood Hse) Silver Burdett Pr.

Nentvig, Juan. Rudo Ensayo: A Description of Sonora & Arizona in 1764. Pradeau, Alberto F. & Rasmussen, Robert R., trs. LC 79-20420. 160p. 1980. 19.95 (*0-8165-0696-5*) U of Ariz Pr.

Nentwich, Phyllis F. Handbook of IV Medications, 1991. 544p. 1991. pap. 25.00 (*0-86720-441-9*) Jones & Bartlett.

— Intravenous Therapy. 512p. 1990. boxed 50.00 (*0-86720-419-2*) Jones & Bartlett.

***Nentwig, Joachim.** Parat Lexikon Folientechnik. 550p. (GER.). 1991. 165.00 (*0-7859-8417-8*, 3527281819) Fr & Eur.

Nentwig, Joachim, et al. Chemistry Made Easy, 2 vols., Set, Pts. I & II. 750p. (C). 1992. Set. pap. text ed. 59.95 (*1-56081-549-3*) VCH Pubs.

— General & Inorganic Chemistry Made Easy. 744p. (C). 1992. pap. text ed. 34.95 (*1-56081-502-7*) VCH Pubs.

— Organic Chemistry Made Easy. 558p. (C). 1992. pap. text ed. 59.95 (*1-56081-548-5*) VCH Pubs.

Nentwig, K. Elsevier's Dictionary of Opto-Electronics & Electro-Optics in English, German, French & Spanish. 296p. (ENG, FRE, GER & SPA.). 1986. 295.00 (*0-8288-9242-3*, F92345) Fr & Eur.

— Elsevier's Dictionary of Optoelectronics & Electro-Optics: In English, French, German & Spanish. 296p. 1986. 151. 50 (*0-444-42617-5*) Elsevier.

— Elsevier's Dictionary of Solar Technology. 214p. (ENG, FRE, GER, ITA & SPA.). 1985. 250.00 (*0-8288-9255-5*, M15475) Fr & Eur.

— Elsevier's Dictionary of Solar Technology: In English, German, French, Spanish & Italian. 214p. 1985. 123.00 (*0-444-42459-8*) Elsevier.

Nentwig, W. Spiders of Panama. (Flora & Fauna Handbook Ser.: No. 12). (Illus.). 274p. (Orig.). 1993. pap. 49.95 (*1-877743-18-6*) Sandhill Crane.

Nentwig, W., ed. Ecophysiology of Spiders. (Illus.). 465p. 1987. 231.00 (*0-387-17034-0*) Spr-Verlag.

Neocleus, C. International Typewriting (Home) (C). 1983. pap. 65.00 (*0-85950-143-4*, Pub. by S Thornes Pubs UK) St Mut.

— International Typewriting (Horizontal) 7th ed. 268p. (C). 1991. pap. 40.00x (*0-7478-1183-0*, Pub. by S Thornes Pubs UK) St Mut.

Neog, Maheswar. Srihastamuktavali: A Text of Ancient Indian Aescetics. (C). 1991. 30.00 (*81-208-0829-0*, Pub. by Motilal Banarsidass II) S Asia.

Neogy, Prithwish, jt. auth. see Haar, Francis.

Neophyton, Andrea. Fresh Flower Arranger's Companion. 1994. 10.98 (*0-7858-0099-9*) Bk Sales Inc.

Neou, Vivian. Internet: Domain Administration. (C). 1993. pap. text ed. 24.00 (*0-13-511180-3*) P-H.

— Internet: Mailing Lists. rev. ed. Hardie, Edward T., ed. LC 93-30775. 1993. pap. 29.00 (*0-13-289661-3*) P-H.

— Internet Mailing Lists Manager for Windows Users. 1995. disk, pap. 39.95 (*0-13-193988-2*) P-H.

Nepal National Commission for UNESCO Staff. Records of the Second General Assembly. (UNESCO Reports). 136p. 1966. 12.50 (*0-318-17087-6*, 68) Am-Nepal Ed.

***Nepaulsingh, Colbert.** Apples of Gold in Filigrees of Silver: Jewish Writing in the Eye of the Inquisition. (New Perspectives: Jewish Life & Thought Ser.). 200p. (C). 1995. 40.00 (*0-8419-1358-7*); pap. 18.00 (*0-8419-1361-7*) Holmes & Meier.

Nepaulsingh, Colbert I. Towards a History of Literary Composition in Medieval Spain. (Romance Ser.). 302p. 1986. text ed. 45.00 (*0-8020-2570-6*) U of Toronto Pr.

***Neperud, Ron, ed.** Toward a Post-Postmodern Art Education. 272p. (C). 1995. pap. text ed. 21.95x (*0-8077-3444-6*) Tchrs Coll.

— Toward a Post-Postmodern Art Education. 272p. (C). 1995. text ed. 45.00x (*0-8077-3445-4*) Tchrs Coll.

Neperud, Ronald W., jt. ed. see Farley, Frank H.

Nephew, John. Creature Catalog. (Dungeons & Dragons Ser.). (Illus.). 1993. pap. 15.00 (*1-56076-593-3*) TSR Inc.

— The Dymrak Dread. (Dungeons & Dragons Ser.). 1991. DDA4. pap. 6.95 (*1-56076-073-7*, DDA4) TSR Inc.

— Mystara Monstrous Compendium. (Advanced Dungeons & Dragons 2nd Ed. Accessory Ser.: MC19). 1994. pap. 18.00 (*1-56076-875-4*) TSR Inc.

— Night Howlers. 1992. 10.95 (*1-56076-392-2*) TSR Inc.

Nephew, Sara. Building Block Quilts. LC 89-82476. (Illus.). 64p. (Orig.). 1990. pap. 14.95 (*0-9621172-1-8*) Clearview Triangle.

— Building Block Quilts 2. (Illus.). 64p. 1991. pap. 14.95 (*0-9621172-2-6*) Clearview Triangle.

— Easy & Elegant Quilts. (Illus.). 64p. (Orig.). 1994. pap. 15.95 (*0-9621172-3-4*) Clearview Triangle.

— Equilateral Triangle Patchwork: Complete Instructions for 11 Quilts. (Illus.). 56p. 1992. reprint ed. pap. 5.95 (*0-486-27048-3*) Dover.

— Mock Applique. LC 95-67105. (Illus.). 72p. (Orig.). 1995. pap. 15.95 (*0-9621172-4-2*) Clearview Triangle.

— My Mother's Quilts: Designs from the Thirties. (Orig.). 1993. pap. 6.95 (*0-486-27417-9*) Dover.

— Quilt Designs from the Thirties. LC 93-41394. (Illus.). 1994. reprint ed. pap. 7.95 (*0-486-28156-6*) Dover.

Nephew, Sara A. Stars & Flowers: Three-Sided Patchwork. LC 88-72380. (Illus.). 56p. (Orig.). 1989. pap. 12.95 (*0-9621172-0-X*) Clearview Triangle.

Nephrology Symposium Staff. Glomerulonephritis: Proceedings of the Nephrology Symposium, 3rd, Hannover, June 1975. Sterzel, R. B., ed. (Contributions to Nephrology Ser.: Vol. 2). (Illus.). 200p. 1976. 41.00 (*3-8055-2318-1*) S Karger.

— Interstitial Nephropathies: Proceedings of the Nephrology Symposium, 6th, Hannover, May 1978. Kuhn, K., ed. (Contributions to Nephrology Ser.: Vol. 16). (Illus.). 1979. pap. 64.00 (*3-8055-2979-1*) S Karger.

***Nepo, Mark.** Acre of Light: Living with Cancer. 1994. pap. 9.95 (*0-87886-138-6*) Greenfld Rev Lit.

— Fire Without Witness: Michelangelo in the Sistine Chapel. (Illus.). 407p. 1988. 19.95 (*0-945167-06-7*) British Amer Pub.

Nepomnyashchy, A. A., jt. auth. see Simanovskii, I. B.

***Nepomnyashchy, Catharine T.** Abram Tertz & the Poetics of Crime. LC 94-40946. (Studies of the Harriman Institute). 1995. write for info. (*0-300-06210-9*) Yale U Pr.

Nepomnyashchy, Catharine T., tr. see Tertz, Abram, pseud.

Neporent, Liz, jt. auth. see Hart, Leisa.

Neppe, Joseph. The Choices of Daniel Trigo. 199p. 1992. 13.95 (*0-944070-87-6*); pap. 10.95 (*0-685-65662-4*) Targum Pr.

Neppe, Vernon M. Innovative Psychopharmacotherapy. 238p. 1989. 52.50 (*0-88167-490-7*) Raven.

Neprash, Ivan V., et al. Glory Filled the Land. 205p. 1989. lib. bdg. 17.95 (*0-926474-00-6*) Intl Awakening Pr.

Neprash, Jerry A. Brookhart Campaigns in Iowa, 1920-1926. LC 68-58612. (Columbia University. Studies in the Social Sciences: No. 366). reprint ed. 20.00 (*0-404-51366-2*) AMS Pr.

Nepstad, Daniel & Schwartzman, Stephen, eds. Non-Timber Products from Tropical Forests: Evaluation of a Conservation & Development Strategy. LC 92-14911. (Advances in Economic Botany Ser.: Vol. 9). 176p. 1992. pap. text ed. 18.95 (*0-89327-376-7*) NY Botanical.

Nepstad, Ellsworth P. Experiences of a Farm Boy. 1993. 7.95 (*0-8062-4772-X*) Carlton.

Nepstad, Verna. Prayer Adventure for Boys & Girls. (Illus.). 48p. (Orig.). 1993. teacher ed, pap. 8.95 (*0-88243-348-2*, 02-0348) Gospel Pub.

— Prayer Adventure for Boys & Girls: A Prayer Soldier's Manual. (Illus.). 80p. (J). (gr. 3-5). 1993. student ed 6.95 (*0-88243-338-5*, 02-0338) Gospel Pub.

Nequam, Alexander. Speculum Speculationum. Thomson, Rodney M., ed. (Auctores Britannici Medii Aevi Ser.: No. XI). (Illus.). 532p. 1988. 125.00 (*0-19-726067-5*) OUP.

Nequatewa, Edmund. Truth of a Hopi: Stories Relating to the Origins, Myths, & Clan Histories of the Hopi. 2nd ed. LC 73-78419. (Illus.). 128p. 1993. reprint ed. pap. 12.95 (*0-87358-386-8*) Northland AZ.

Ner, Sonia, ed. see O'Boyle, Lily G. & Alejandro, Reynaldo.

Ner, Yehuda. Patterns of Heartbreak: How to Stop Finding Mr. Wrong. 1992. pap. 5.50 (*1-56171-141-1*, S P I Bks) Sure Sellers.

Neracher, Mark, see Training Mark, pseud..

Nerad, T. A., ed. American Type Culture Collection Catalogue of Protists. 18th ed. 100p. 1993. pap. text ed. write for info. (*0-930009-50-9*) ATCC.

Neraudau, Jean-Pierre. Dictionnaire d'Histoire de l'Art. 544p. (FRE.). 1985. 125.00 (*0-8288-1417-1*, F26160) Fr & Eur.

***Nerbern, Kent.** West Coast Reverie. 192p. (Orig.). 1996. pap. 12.95 (*1-880032-81-3*) New Wrld Lib.

Nerbonne, John, et al. German in Head-Driven Phrase Structure Grammar. LC 93-40350. (CSLI Lecture Notes Ser.: No. 46). 1993. 49.95 (*1-881526-30-5*); pap. 21.95 (*1-881526-29-1*) Ctr Study Language.

Nerbonne, Michael A., jt. ed. see Schow, Ronald L.

Nerbun, Ann. Our Power to Love. LC 91-73633. (Illus.). 10p. 1990. pap. 6.00 (*0-89870-382-4*) Ignatius Pr.

Nerburn, Kent. Letters to My Son: A Father's Wisdom on Manhood, Women, Life, & Love. LC 94-18879. 240p. 1994. pap. 10.95 (*1-880032-49-X*) New Wrld Lib.

— Neither Wolf nor Dog: On Forgotten Roads with an Indian Elder. LC 94-21558. 224p. 1994. pap. 11.95 (*1-880032-37-6*) New Wrld Lib.

Nerburn, Kent, ed. The Soul of an Indian: And Other Writings from Ohiyesa (Charles Alexander Eastman) LC 93-24678. (Classic Wisdom Collection). 96p. 1993. 12.95 (*1-880032-23-6*) New Wrld Lib.

Nerburn, Kent, ed. & intro. The Wisdom of the Great Chiefs. LC 93-47415. (Classic Wisdom Collection). 96p. 1994. 12.95 (*1-880032-40-6*) New Wrld Lib.

***Nercessian, Y. T.** Armenian Coins & Their Values. LC 94-94430. (Illus.). 304p. 1995. boxed 36.50 (*0-9606842-8-X*) ANS.

— Armenian Numismatic Bibliography & Literature. LC 83-73256. 729p. 1984. boxed 50.00 (*0-9606842-2-0*) ANS.

— Attribution & Dating of Armenian Bilingual Trams. (Illus.). 48p. (Orig.). 1983. 6.75 (*0-9606842-1-2*) ANS.

— Bank Notes of Armenia. LC 86-70860. 416p. 1988. boxed 30.00 (*0-9606842-5-5*) ANS.

Nercessian, Y. T., ed. Studies in Honor of Dr. Paul Z. Bedoukian, Armenian Numismatic Journal, 1989, Vol. 15: Essays Dedicated in Honor of Dr. Paul Z. Bedoukian on the Fortieth Year of His Contributions. (Illus.). 192p. (ARM & ENG.). 1989. 30.00 (*0-9606842-6-3*) ANS.

Nerdinger, Winfried. Walter Gropius. (Illus.). 312p. (Orig.). (ENG & GER.). 1986. pap. 24.95 (*3-7861-1448-X*) Harvard Art Mus.

— The Walter Gropius Archive, Vol. II: (1930-1936) LC 90-3058. 500p. 1990. reprint ed. 295.00 (*0-8240-3341-8*) Garland.

— The Walter Gropius Archive, Vol. III: (1936-1957) LC 90-3058. (Illus.). 500p. 1990. reprint ed. 325.00 (*0-8240-3342-6*) Garland.

N

Nerdinger, Winifred, ed. Walter Gropius, 1911-1930: Collection of the Busch-Reisinger Museum. LC 90-3058. (Walter Gropius Archive Ser.: Vol. I of 4). (Illus.). 500p. 1990. reprint ed. 290.00 (0-8240-3340-X) Garland.

Nerenberg, Arnie. Love & Estrangement in the Baha'i Community. (Orig.). 1986. 14.95 (0-933770-47-2) Kalimat.

***Nerenberg, Arnold.** Hi Mom & Dad, I'm Here. (Orig.). 1994. pap. text ed. 9.95 (1-878113-06-2) Bell Pubns.

— Path of the Wrong Way. (C). 1987. pap. write for info. (1-878113-00-3) Bell Pubns.

Nerenz, jt. auth. see Ariew.

Nerenz, Anne, jt. auth. see Ariew, Robert.

***Nereson, Sally.** Outside the Lines but on the Page: Perspectives on Writing in an Individualized, Writing-Intensive Baccalaureate Degree Program. Bridwell-Bowles, Lillian & Olson, Mark, eds. (Technical Report Ser.: No. 8). 38p. (Orig.). (C). 1994. pap. 3.50 (1-881221-14-8) U Minn Ctr Interdis.

Neressian, Nancy J. Faraday to Einstein: Constructing Meaning in Scientific Theories. 1984. lib. bdg. 85.50 (90-247-2997-1) Kluwer Ac.

Nergaard, Bea, ed. see Nightingale, Florence.

Nergaard, R. Arnfinn. The Smedvig Production Unit. 1989. 150.00 (90-6314-520-9, Pub. by Lorne & MacLean Marine) St Mut.

Nerhood, Harry W., jt. ed. see Tupper, Harmon.

Nerhot, Patrick. Law, Writing, Meaning: An Essay in Legal Hermeneutics. (Law & Society Ser.). 224p. (C). 1993. text ed. 65.00 (0-7486-0391-3, Pub. by Edinburgh U Pr UK) Col U Pr.

Nerhot, Patrick, ed. Legal Knowledge & Analogy: Fragments of Legal Epistemology, Hermeneutics & Linguistics. (C). 1991. lib. bdg. 89.00 (0-7923-1065-9) Kluwer Ac.

Neri, Filippo. Introduction to Electronic Defense Systems. (Radar Library). 480p. 1991. text ed. 85.00 (0-89006-553-5) Artech Hse.

Neri, Helene M., tr. see Schaefer, Udo.

Neri, Joseph. So I Said to the Little Old Man. Edwards, Kristen, ed. (Illus.). 96p. (Orig.). (J). (gr. k-6). 1994. lib. bdg. 14.99 (0-9639428-1-6); pap. 12.95 (0-9639428-3-2) Tympanon Prods.

Neri, L., jt. auth. see Anderson, R. T.

Neri, Louise & Crugier, Bice, eds. Collaboration Sigmar Polke. (Parkett Art Magazine Ser.: No. 30). (Illus.). 220p. 1991. pap. 19.50 (3-907509-80-3, Pub. by Parkett Pubs SZ) Dist Art Pubs.

Neri, Penelope. Beloved Scoundrel. 1983. pap. 3.75 (0-8217-1259-4) Zebra.

— Bold Breathless Nights. 1989. mass mkt. 4.50 (0-8217-2780-X) Zebra.

— Cherish the Night. 1992. mass mkt. 5.99 (0-8217-3654-X) Zebra.

— Crimson Angel. 1986. pap. 3.95 (0-317-39257-3) Zebra.

— Desert Captive. 512p. 1988. pap. 3.95 (0-8217-2447-9) Zebra.

— Enchanted. 608p. 1993. mass mkt. 4.99 (0-8217-4318-X) Zebra.

— Forever & Beyond. 1990. mass mkt. 4.95 (0-8217-3115-7) Zebra.

— Forever in His Arms. 560p. 1991. mass mkt. 4.95 (0-8217-3385-0) Zebra.

— Hearts Enchanted. 1984. pap. 3.75 (0-8217-1432-5) Zebra.

— Jasmine Paradise. 1983. pap. 3.75 (0-8217-1170-9) Zebra.

— Loving Lies. (Romance Ser.). 528p. 1987. pap. 3.95 (0-8217-2034-1) Zebra.

— Midnight Captive. 1989. pap. 3.95 (0-8217-2593-9) Zebra.

— No Sweeter Paradise. 480p. 1993. mass mkt. 5.99 (0-8217-4024-5) Zebra.

— Passion's Betrayal. 1985. pap. 3.95 (0-8217-1568-2) Zebra.

— Passion's Rapture. (Orig.). 1982. pap. 3.50 (0-89083-912-3) Zebra.

— Sea Jewel. 496p. 1986. pap. 3.95 (0-8217-1888-6) Zebra.

— Silver Rose. 576p. 1988. pap. 3.95 (0-8217-2275-1) Zebra.

— This Stolen Moment. 432p. 1994. mass mkt. 5.99 (0-8217-4584-0) Zebra.

Neri, Renee. Our Family Grows. 40p. 1985. pap. 3.95 (0-89529-299-8) Avery Pub.

Neri, Rita, ed. U. S. & Japan Foreign Trade: An Annotated Bibliography of Socioeconomic Perspectives. (Reference Library of Social Science). 332p. 1988. lib. bdg. 48.00 (0-8240-8471-3) Garland.

Neri, Rodolpho. The Blue Planet. 1989. 10.95 (0-533-08166-1) Vantage.

Neri Serneri, G. G., jt. ed. see Born, G. V.

Nerin, William. You Can't Grow up Till You Go Back Home: A Safe Journey to See Your Parents As Human. 192p. 1993. 22.95 (0-8245-1225-1) Crossroad NY.

Nerin, William F. Family Reconstruction: Long Day's Journey into Light. (Professional Bks.). (Illus.). 1986. 22.95 (0-393-70017-8) Norton.

— You Can't Grow up Till You Go Back Home: A Safe Journey to See Your Parents As Human. LC 92-42915. (Illus.). 194p. 1995. reprint ed. 22.95 (0-9646789-0-X) Magic Mtn.

Nering, Evar D. Linear Algebra & Matrix Theory. 2nd ed. LC 76-91646. 352p. (C). 1970. Net. text ed. write for info. (0-471-63178-7) Wiley.

Nering, Evar D. & Tucker, Albert W. Linear Programs & Related Problems. (Computer Science & Scientific Computing Ser.). 584p. 1992. text ed. 49.95 (0-12-515440-2) Acad Pr.

Nerlich, Brigitte. Change in Language: Whitney, Breal & Wegener. 224p. 1990. 47.50 (0-415-00991-X, A4081) Routledge.

— Semantic Theories in Europe, 1830-1930: From Etymology to Contextuality. LC 91-42523. (Studies in the History of the Language Sciences: No. 59). xii, 346p. 1992. 74.00x (1-55619-354-8) Benjamins North Am.

Nerlich, Brigitte, tr. see Keller, Rudi.

Nerlich, Graham. Values & Valuing: Speculations on the Ethical Life of Persons. 232p. 1990. 55.00 (0-19-824847-4) OUP.

— What Spacetime Explains: Metaphysical Essays on Space & Time. LC 93-27336. 272p. (C). 1994. 49.95 (0-521-45261-9) Cambridge U Pr.

Nerlich, Grahm. The Shape of Space. 2nd ed. LC 93-28935. 320p. (C). 1994. pap. 22.95 (0-521-45645-2) Cambridge U Pr.

— The Shape of Space. 2nd ed. LC 93-28935. 320p. (C). 1994. 74.95 (0-521-45014-4) Cambridge U Pr.

Nerlich, Michael. Ideology of Adventure: Studies in Modern Consciousness, 1100-1750, 2 vols., 1. LC 86-19354. (Theory & History of Literature Ser.: Vols. 42 & 43). 1988. pap. text ed. 14.95 (0-8166-1538-1) U of Minn Pr.

— Ideology of Adventure: Studies in Modern Consciousness, 1100-1750, 2 vols., 2. LC 86-19354. (Theory & History of Literature Ser.: Vols. 42 & 43). 1988. pap. text ed. 14.95 (0-8166-1541-1) U of Minn Pr.

— Ideology of Adventure: Studies in Modern Consciousness, 1100-1750, 2 vols., Vol. 1. LC 86-19354. (Theory & History of Literature Ser.: Vols. 42 & 43). 272p. 1988. text ed. 39.95 (0-8166-1537-3) U of Minn Pr.

— Ideology of Adventure: Studies in Modern Consciousness, 1100-1750, 2 vols., Vol. 2. LC 86-19354. (Theory & History of Literature Ser.: Vols. 42 & 43). 194p. 1988. text ed. 39.95 (0-8166-1540-3) U of Minn Pr.

Nerlich, Michael, ed. Cervantes's Exemplary Novels & the Adventure of Writing. (Hispanic Issues Ser.: Vol. 6). 1990. pap. text ed. 14.95 (0-8166-2014-8) U of Minn Pr.

Nerlich, Michael & Spadaccini, Nicholas, eds. Cervantes's Exemplary Novels & the Adventure of Writing. (Hispanic Issues Ser.). 365p. (Orig.). (C). 1990. pap. 14.95 (0-910235-35-X) Prisma Bks.

Nerlich, Michael, jt. auth. see Talens, Jenaro.

Nerlove, Marc, et al. Analysis of Economic Time Series: A Synthesis. LC 78-26059. (Economic Theory, Econometrics & Mathematical Economics Ser.). 1979. text ed. 75.00 (0-12-515750-9) Acad Pr.

Nerlove, Marc. Issues in Contemporary Economics, Vol. II: Aspects of Macroeconomics & Econometrics. (International Economic Association Book Ser.). 300p. 1991. text ed. 100.00x (0-8147-5767-7) NYU Pr.

— Modernizing Traditional Agriculture. 20p. 1988. pap. 6.95 (1-55815-033-1) ICS Pr.

***Nerlove, Marc, et al.** Analysis of Economic Time Series: A Synthesis. rev. ed. (Economic Theory, Econometrics, & Mathematical Economics Ser.). (Illus.). 486p. 1995. boxed write for info. (0-12-515751-7) Acad Pr.

Nerlove, Miriam. Christmas. Tucker, Kathy, ed. LC 89-70737. (Illus.). 24p. (J). (ps-1). 1990. 11.95 (0-8075-1148-X) A Whitman.

— Christmas: An Albert Whitman Prairie Book. (J). (ps-3). 1993. pap. 4.95 (0-8075-1147-1) A Whitman.

— Easter. Mathews, Judith, ed. LC 89-35394. (Illus.). 24p. (J). (ps-1). 1989. 11.95 (0-8075-1871-9); pap. 4.95 (0-8075-1872-7) A Whitman.

— Flowers on the Wall. LC 94-31289. (Illus.). 1995. write for info. (0-689-50614-7, McElderry) S&S Childrens.

— Halloween. Levine, Abby, ed. LC 88-36858. (Illus.). 24p. (J). (ps-1). 1989. lib. bdg. 11.95 (0-8075-3131-6); pap. 4.95 (0-8075-3130-8) A Whitman.

— Hanukkah. Levine, Abby, ed. LC 88-36648. (Illus.). 24p. (J). (ps-1). 1989. lib. bdg. 11.95 (0-8075-3143-X); pap. 4.95 (0-8075-3142-1) A Whitman.

— I Made a Mistake. LC 85-6018. (Illus.). 32p. (J). (ps-2). 1985. text ed. 13.95 (0-689-50327-X, McElderry) S&S Childrens.

— I Meant to Clean My Room Today. LC 87-16968. (Illus.). 32p. (J). (ps-3). 1988. text ed. 13.95 (0-689-50438-1, McElderry) S&S Childrens.

— If All the World Were Paper. Tucker, Kathy, ed. LC 90-39217. (Illus.). 32p. (J). (gr. k-3). 1991. 13.95 (0-8075-3535-4) A Whitman.

— Just One Tooth. LC 88-19488. (Illus.). 32p. (J). (ps-3). 1989. text ed. 13.95 (0-689-50465-9, McElderry) S&S Childrens.

— Passover. Levine, Abby, ed. LC 89-35393. (Illus.). 24p. (J). (ps-1). 1989. 11.95 (0-8075-6360-9); pap. 4.95 (0-8075-6361-7) A Whitman.

— Purim. Levine, Abby, ed. LC 91-19516. (Illus.). 24p. (J). (ps-1). 1992. lib. bdg. 11.95 (0-8075-6682-9) A Whitman.

— Purim. LC 91-19516. (Albert Whitman Prairie Bks.). (Illus.). 24p. (J). (ps-1). 1994. pap. 4.95 (0-8075-6683-7) A Whitman.

— Thanksgiving. Mathews, Judith, ed. LC 89-49363. (Illus.). 24p. (J). (ps-1). 1990. lib. bdg. 11.95 (0-8075-7818-5) A Whitman.

— Thanksgiving: An Albert Whitman Prairie Book. (J). (ps-3). 1993. pap. 4.95 (0-8075-7817-7) A Whitman.

— Valentine's Day. Mathews, Judith, ed. LC 91-19289. (Illus.). 24p. (J). (ps-1). 1992. lib. bdg. 11.95 (0-8075-8454-1) A Whitman.

— Valentine's Day. LC 91-19289. (Albert Whitman Prairie Bks.). (Illus.). 24p. (J). (ps-1). 1994. pap. 4.95 (0-8075-8455-X) A Whitman.

Nerman, Birger. Poetic Edda in the Light of Archaeology. LC 76-43954. (Viking Society for Northern Research: Extra Ser.: Vol. 4). (Illus.). reprint ed. 39.50 (0-404-60024-7) AMS Pr.

***Nerman, Maud.** The Cermony of Innocence. 240p. Date not set. pap. 8.95 (0-7610-0298-7) NW Pub.

Nermut, M. V. & Steven, A. C., eds. Animal Virus Structure. (Perspectives in Virus Structure Ser.: Vol. 3). 466p. 1987. 177.00 (0-444-80879-5) Elsevier.

Nerney, Catherine. Called to Be Faithful: Reflections on Cycle B Readings for the Sundays of Lent. 1985. 2.50 (0-8091-9339-6) Paulist Pr.

— Mark's Gospel Enrollment in the School of Discipleship. 1987. 2.50 (0-8091-9331-0) Paulist Pr.

— Promise of Glory. 1985. pap. 1.25 (0-8091-9334-5) Paulist Pr.

Nero, Ann B. Essential Skills in Geography. Radner, Barbara, ed. (Illus.). 94p. (Orig.). (J). (gr. 4-9). 1987. teacher ed 7.92 (0-528-17919-5); pap. text ed. 3.96 (0-528-17918-7) Rand McNally.

Nero, Anthony V. A Guidebook to Nuclear Reactors. LC 77-76183. (Illus.). 304p. reprint ed. pap. 86.70 (0-7837-4676-8, 2044422) Bks Demand.

Nero, Anthony V., jt. ed. see Nazaroff, William W.

Nero, Jacqueline E. Pressing Toward the Mark: A Guide to Healing for Victims of Sexual Abuse: Incest, Child Molestation, Rape & Sexual Harassment. 80p. (Orig.). 1992. pap. write for info. (0-9632213-0-2) J E Nero.

Nerode, A. & Matiyasevich, Y. V., eds. Logical Foundations of Computer Science: Proceedings of the Third International Symposoium, LFCS '94, St. Petersburg, Russia, July 11-14, 1994. LC 94-19257. 1994. 58.00 (0-387-58140-5) Spr-Verlag.

Nerode, A. & Shore, R., eds. Recursion Theory. LC 84-18525. (Proceedings of Symposia in Pure Mathematics Ser., Humboldt State University, Arcata, CA, July 29-August 16, 1974: Vol. 42). 528p. 1985. text ed. 82.00 (0-8218-1447-8, PSPUM-42) Am Math.

Nerode, Anil & Marek, Wiktor, eds. Logic Programming & Non-Monotonic Reasoning: Proceedings of the First International Workshop, June 22-24, 1991, Washington, DC. (Illus.). 352p. 1992. 32.50 (0-262-64027-9) MIT Pr.

Nerode, Anil & Shore, Richard. Logic for Applications. LC 93-27846. (Texts & Monographs in Computer Science). 1993. 39.95 (0-387-94129-0) Spr-Verlag.

Nerode, Anil, jt. auth. see Crossley, J. N.

Nerode, Anil, jt. auth. see Pereira, Luis M.

Nerode, Anil, et al, eds. Logical Foundations of Computer Science - Tver '92: Second International Symposium, Tver, Russia, July 20-24, 1992, Proceedings. LC 92-18642. (Lecture Notes in Computer Science Ser.: Vol. 620). ix, 514p. 1992. pap. 74.00 (0-387-55707-5) Spr-Verlag.

Nerone, Joh. The Culture of the Press in the Early Republic: Cincinnati, 1793-1848. (Nineteenth Century American Political & Social History Ser.). 310p. 1989. reprint ed. 20.00 (0-8240-4070-8) Garland.

Nerone, John. Violence Against the Press in U. S. History. (Communication & Society Ser.). 320p. (C). 1994. 39.95 (0-19-507166-2); pap. text ed. 16.95 (0-19-508698-8) OUP.

Nerone, John C., ed. see Berry, William E.

Neroni, Rosalind. The Porcupine's Princess. 29p. 1978. pap. 2.50 (0-914946-12-9) Cleveland St Univ Poetry Ctr.

Nerou, Jean-Pierre, jt. auth. see Bergeron, Marcel.

Nerovich, Peter. Reupholstering at Home. LC 91-67017. (Illus.). 176p. 1992. pap. 14.95 (0-88740-376-X) Schiffer.

Neroznak, V. P., jt. auth. see Diakonov, I. M.

Nerozzi, D., jt. auth. see Meltzer, H. Y.

Nerozzi, Dina, et al, eds. Hypothalamic Dysfunction in Neuropsychiatric Disorders. (Advances in Biochemical Psychopharmacology Ser.: Vol. 43). (Illus.). 382p. 1987. text ed. 69.00 (0-88167-304-8) Raven.

Nerpin, S. V. & Chudnovskii, A. F. Heat & Mass Transfer in the Plant-Soil-Air System. Sivaramakrishnan, M. M., tr. 367p. (C). 1985. text ed. 95.00 (90-6191-446-9, Pub. by A A Balkema NE) Ashgate Pub Co.

— Physics of the Soil. 480p. 1970. text ed. 110.00 (0-7065-0610-3, Pub. by Keter Pub IS) Coronet Bks.

Ners, Krzysztof, et al. Beyond Assistance: Report of the IEWS Task Force on Western Assistance to Transition in the Czech & Slovak Federal Republic, Hungary, & Poland. LC 92-18010. 1992. 12.85 (0-913449-32-6) Inst EW Stud.

Nersesian, Arthur. Tompkins Square & Other Illfated Riots. (Illus.). 48p. 1990. pap. 2.95 (0-685-56991-8) SPD-Small Pr Dist.

Nersesian, Roy L. Computer Simulation in Business Decision Making: A Guide for Managers, Planners, & MIS Professionals. LC 88-32390. 268p. 1989. text ed. 65.00 (0-89930-408-7, NCR/, Quorum Bks) Greenwood.

— Computer Simulation in Financial Risk Management: A Guide for Business Planners & Strategists. LC 90-45146. 240p. 1991. text ed. 59.95 (0-89930-578-4, NCD, Quorum Bks) Greenwood.

— Corporate Planning, Human Behavior, & Computer Simulation: Forecasting Business Cycles. LC 89-37650. 249p. 1990. text ed. 59.95 (0-89930-458-3, NCB/, Greenwood Pr) Greenwood.

Nersesian, Roy L., jt. auth. see Heely, James A.

Nersessian. Armenia. (World Bibliographical Ser.). 1993. lib. bdg. 92.00 (1-85109-144-0) ABC-CLIO.

***Nersessian, Edward & Kopff, Richard G., eds.** Textbook of Psychoanalysis. 859p. 1995. boxed 110.00 (0-88048-507-8, 8507) Am Psychiatric.

Nersessian, Nancy J. Faraday to Einstein: Constructing Meaning in Scientific Theories. (Science & Philosophy Ser.). 216p. 1990. pap. text ed. 34.50 (0-7923-0950-2) Kluwer Ac.

Nersessian, Nancy J., ed. The Process of Science: Contemporary Philosophical Approaches to Understanding Scientific Practice. (Science & Philosophy Ser.: No. 3). 234p. 1987. lib. bdg. 99.50 (90-247-3425-8) Kluwer Ac.

Nersessian, Vrej. The Tondrakian Movement: Religious Movements in the Armenian Church from the Fourth to the Tenth Centuries. LC 88-4066. (Princeton Theological Monograph Ser.: No. 15). 156p. 1988. reprint ed. pap. 10.00 (0-915138-99-9) Pickwick.

Nerson, Jean M., jt. auth. see Walden, Kim.

Nerson, Jean-Marc, jt. ed. see Meyer, Bertrand.

Nersoyan, H. J. Andre Gide: The Theism of an Atheist. LC 69-17717. 1969. 39.95x (0-8156-2135-3) Syracuse U Pr.

Nersoyan, Tiran, jt. ed. see Fries, Paul R.

Neruda, Jan. Tales of the Little Quarter. Pargeter, Edith, tr. LC 76-49935. 296p. 1977. reprint ed. text ed. 45.00 (0-8371-9344-3, NELQ, Greenwood Pr) Greenwood.

Neruda, Pablo. Antologia Essencial. (SPA.). 1971. 14.95 (0-8288-2542-4, S20078) Fr & Eur.

— Antologia Poetica. 509p. (SPA.). 1982. 9.95 (0-685-60725-9, S39023) Fr & Eur.

— Antologia Poetica 1. 43th ed. 304p. 1990. pap. 12.95 (0-7859-5197-0) Fr & Eur.

— Antologia Poetica 2. 3rd ed. 256p. 1988. pap. write for info. (0-7859-5198-9) Fr & Eur.

— Art of Birds. Schmitt, Jack, tr. LC 84-7585. (Texas Pan American Ser.). (Illus.). 87p. 1985. reprint ed. 19.95 (0-292-70371-6) U of Tex Pr.

— The Book of Questions. O'Daly, William, tr. LC 91-72064. 96p. (Orig.). 1991. 19.00 (1-55659-040-7); pap. 11.00 (1-55659-041-5) Copper Canyon.

— Canto General. (SPA.). 1968. 12.50 (0-8288-2532-7) Fr & Eur.

— Canto General. Schmitt, Jack, tr. LC 90-39070. (Latin American Literature & Culture Ser.: No. 7). 418p. 1991. 38.00 (0-520-05433-4) U CA Pr.

— Canto General. 1993. pap. 15.00 (0-520-08279-6) U CA Pr.

— Canto General. 2nd ed. 496p. 1988. pap. 13.95 (0-7859-5186-5) Fr & Eur.

— The Captain's Verses. Walsh, Donald D., tr. & intro. by. LC 72-80977. 160p. (ENG & SPA.). 1972. pap. 8.95 (0-8112-0457-X, NDP345) New Directions.

— Confieso Que He Vivido. 464p. (SPA.). 1984. pap. 10.95 (0-7859-5004-4) Fr & Eur.

— Crepusculario. 3rd ed. 104p. 1987. pap. 12.95 (0-7859-5199-7) Fr & Eur.

— Espana en el Corazon. Spain in the Heart. Schaaf, Richard, tr. 180p. (ENG & SPA.). 1992. 29.95 (0-685-47548-4) Floricanto Pr.

— Extravagaria. Reid, Alastair, tr. LC 92-37189. (Texas Pan American Ser.). 303p. (C). 1993. reprint ed. pap. 14.95 (0-292-72083-1) U of Tex Pr.

— Five Decades: Poems 1925-1970. Belitt, Ben, ed. & tr. by. 464p. 1987. pap. 14.50 (0-8021-3035-6) Grove-Atltic.

— Geografia Infructuosa. (SPA.). 1973. write for info. (0-8288-2537-8) Fr & Eur.

— The Heights of Macchu Picchu: Bilingual Edition. Tarn, Nathaniel, tr. 71p. 1967. pap. 10.00 (0-374-50648-5) FS&G.

— Incitement to Nixonicide. Kowit, Steve, tr. 1076p. 27.50 (0-9600306-3-8) Fr & Eur.

— Incitement to Nixonicide. Kowit, Steve, tr. 1979. pap. 5.00 (0-685-04198-0) Quixote.

— Incitement to Nixonicide & Praise for the Chilean Revolution. 2nd ed. Kowit, Steve, tr. (Illus.). 82p. 1980. pap. 6.00 (0-686-68219-X) Quixote.

— Jardin de Invierno. 3rd ed. 104p. (SPA.). 1983. pap. 12.95 (0-685-74087-0) Fr & Eur.

— Late & Posthumous Poems, 1968-1974: (Bilingual Edition) Belitt, Ben, ed. & tr. by. 288p. 1989. pap. 11.95 (0-8021-3145-X) Grove-Atltic.

— Let the Railsplitter Awake & Other Poems. Waldeen, tr. LC 88-6150. (Illus.). 96p. (Orig.). 1989. pap. 4.95 (0-7178-0668-5) Intl Pubs Co.

— Love: Ten Poems by Pablo Neruda. 48p. 1995. pap. 6.95 (0-7868-8148-8) Hyperion.

— El Mary y las Campanas. 80p. (SPA.). 1976. pap. 19.95 (0-7859-5003-6) Fr & Eur.

— Memoirs. St. Martin, Hardie, tr. 1978. pap. 7.95 (0-14-004661-5, Penguin Bks) Viking Penguin.

— Memoirs. 1992. pap. 9.95 (0-14-018628-X, Penguin Bks) Viking Penguin.

— Memorial De Isla Negra. 2nd ed. 312p. (SPA.). 1982. pap. 12.95 (0-7859-5000-1) Fr & Eur.

— Neruda's Garden: An Anthology of Odes. Miller, Yvette E., ed. Jacketti, Maria, tr. LC 94-25088. (Discoveries Ser.). 250p. 1994. pap. 17.95 (0-935480-68-4) Lat Am Lit Rev Pr.

— Nuevas Odas Elementales. (SPA.). 1964. 9.95 (0-8288-2535-1, S20092) Fr & Eur.

— Odas Elementales. 3rd ed. 276p. (SPA.). 1988. pap. 12.95 (0-7859-4999-2) Fr & Eur.

— Odes to Common Things. Krabbenhoft, Ken, tr. LC 93-39665. (Illus.). 152p. (ENG & SPA.). 1994. 22.50 (0-8212-2080-2) Bulfinch Pr.

— Odes to Opposites. Krabbenhoft, Ken, tr. (Illus.). 152p. 1995. 22.50 (0-8212-2227-9) Bulfinch Pr.

— One Hundred Love Sonnets: Cien Sonetos de Amor. Tapscott, Stephen, tr. (Texas Pan American Ser.). 232p. 1986. 22.50 (0-292-76029-9); pap. 10.95 (0-292-76028-0) U of Tex Pr.

— Residence on Earth & Other Poems. Walsh, Donald D., tr. & intro. by. LC 72-93972. Orig. Title: Residencia en la Tierra. 1973. pap. 12.95 (0-8112-0467-7, NDP340) New Directions.

— Residence on Earth & Other Poems: Bilingual Edition. Flores, Angel, tr. LC 76-75462. 205p. 1976. 40.00 (0-87752-205-7) Gordian.

— Residencia en la Tierra. 5th ed. 160p. (SPA.). 1989. pap. 16.95 (0-7859-4996-8) Fr & Eur.

— La Rosa Separada. 4th ed. 112p. (SPA.). 1990. pap. 16.95 (0-7859-5001-X) Fr & Eur.

— The Sea & the Bells. O'Daly, William, tr. LC 88-70585. 136p. (Orig.). 1988. pap. 10.00 (1-55659-019-9) Copper Canyon.

— Seaquake - Maremoto. Maloney, Dennis & Giacchetti, Maria, trs. 80p. 1993. pap. 9.00 (1-877727-32-6) White Pine.

An Asterisk (*) at the beginning of an entry indicates that the title is appearing in BIP for the first time.

— Selected Odes of Pablo Neruda. Peden, Margaret S., tr. LC 90-10707. 388p. 1990. 40.00 (*0-520-05944-1*); pap. 13.00 (*0-520-07172-7*) U CA Pr.

— Selected Poems. Belitt, Ben, ed. & tr. by. 320p. (ENG & SPA.). 1989. Bilingual ed. pap. 10.95 (*0-8021-5102-7*) Grove-Atltic.

— A Separate Rose. O'Daly, William, tr. LC 84-73338. 80p. (Orig.). 1985. pap. 9.00 (*0-914742-88-4*) Copper Canyon.

— Spain in the Heart: Hymn to the Glories of the People at War. Schaaf, Richard, tr. LC 92-71332. 150p. (Orig.). 1993. pap. 12.95 (*0-9632363-1-8*) Azul Edits.

— Still Another Day. O'Daly, William, tr. LC 84-70299. 80p. (ENG & SPA.). 1984. pap. 9.00 (*0-914742-77-9*) Copper Canyon.

— The Stones of Chile. Maloney, Dennis, tr. 1987. 10.00 (*0-934834-01-6*) White Pine.

— Stones of the Sky. Nolan, James, tr. LC 87-71140. 80p. (Orig.). 1987. 15.00 (*1-55659-006-7*); pap. 10.00 (*1-55659-007-5*) Copper Canyon.

— Tercera Residencia. 4th ed. 112p. (SPA.). 1990. pap. 14.95 (*0-7859-4997-6*) Fr & Eur.

— Twenty Love Poems & a Song of Despair. (Illus.). 80p. 1993. 12.95 (*0-8118-0320-1*) Chronicle Bks.

— Twenty Love Poems & a Song of Despair. LC 70-481699. (Cape Editions Ser.). 1976. mass mkt. 4.95 (*0-14-042205-6*, Penguin Bks) Viking Penguin.

— Twenty Love Poems & a Song of Despair. Merwin, W. S., tr. 88p. 1993. 8.95 (*0-14-018648-4*, Penguin Classics) Viking Penguin.

— Two Thousand. Schaaf, Richard, tr. LC 92-70941. 88p. (Orig.). 1992. pap. 10.95 (*0-9632363-0-X*) Azul Edits.

— Veinte Poemas De Amor y una Cancion Desesperada. 3rd ed. 129p. (SPA.). 1991. pap. 10.95 (*0-7859-4995-X*) Fr & Eur.

— Los Versos Del Capitan. 2nd ed. 126p. (SPA.). 1977. pap. 19.95 (*0-7859-4998-4*) Fr & Eur.

— Windows That Open Inward: Images of Chile. Reid et al, trs. (Illus.). 1984. 25.00 (*0-934834-51-2*) White Pine.

— Winter Garden. O'Daly, William, tr. LC 86-71837. 80p. (Orig.). 1986. 15.00 (*0-914742-99-X*); pap. 9.00 (*0-914742-93-0*) Copper Canyon.

— The Yellow Heart. O'Daly, William, tr. LC 89-81834. 112p. (Orig.). 1990. 17.00 (*1-55659-028-8*); pap. 10.00 (*1-55659-029-6*) Copper Canyon.

Neruda, Pablo & Reid, Alastair. Fully Empowered. Reid, Alastair, tr. LC 94-7998. 144p. 1994. reprint ed. pap. 10.95 (*0-8112-1281-5*, NDP 792) New Directions.

Neruda, Pablo, et al. Three Spanish American Poets: Pellicer, Neruda, Andrade. Mallan, Lloyd, ed. Wicker, Mary, tr. 1977. lib. bdg. 59.95 (*0-8490-2747-0*) Gordon Pr.

***Neruzow, Martin.** Enterprise Network Performance Optimization. LC 94-3427. 1995. text ed. 50.00 (*0-07-911889-5*) McGraw.

Nerval, Gerard. Oeuvres, 2 vols., Vol. 1. deluxe ed. Beguin & Richer, eds. (Pleiade Ser.). (FRE.). 99.95 (*2-07-011067-2*) Schoenhof.

— Oeuvres, 2 vols., Vol. 2. Beguin & Richer, eds. (Pleiade Ser.). (FRE.). 88.95 (*2-07-011029-X*) Schoenhof.

Nerval, Gerard de. Les Chimeres. 94p. (FRE.). 1966. pap. 11.95 (*0-7859-5388-4*) Fr & Eur.

— Les Confidences de Nicolas. 236p. 1945. 50.00 (*0-686-54813-2*) Fr & Eur.

— Le Nouveau Genre ou le Cafe d'un Theatre: Scenes I a X. 112p. 1969. 6.95 (*0-686-54816-7*) Fr & Eur.

— Petits Chateaux de Boheme: Prose et Poesie. 96p. 1973. reprint ed. 32.00 (*0-686-54808-6*) Fr & Eur.

— Sylvie: Recollections of Valois. LC 77-10266. (Illus.). 168p. reprint ed. 24.00 (*0-404-16318-1*) AMS Pr.

— The Women of Cairo: Scenes of Life on the Orient, 2 Vols., Set. LC 77-87652. 720p. reprint ed. 115.00 (*0-404-16420-X*) AMS Pr.

Nervi, Pier L. Aesthetics & Technology in Building. Einaudi, R., tr. LC 65-16686. (Charles Eliot Norton Lectures: 1961-1962). (Illus.). 210p. 1965. 22.00 (*0-674-00701-8*) HUP.

Nervig, Robert M., ed. Advances in Carriers & Adjuvants for Veterinary Biologics. LC 85-23969. 202p. 1986. text ed. 25.95 (*0-8138-0273-3*) Iowa St U Pr.

Nervo, A. Amada Inmovil. 143p. (SPA.). 1972. 9.95 (*0-8288-7128-0*, S8371) Fr & Eur.

— Perlas Misticas. 147p. (SPA.). 1973. 9.95 (*0-8288-7122-1*) Fr & Eur.

Nery, R. Cancer: An Enigma in Biology & Society. LC 85-72852. 436p. 1986. text ed. 34.95 (*0-914783-09-2*) Charles.

Nerys, Dee. Fortune-Telling by Playing Cards: A New Guide to the Ancient Art of Cartomancy. (Illus.). 160p. (Orig.). 1988. pap. 8.95 (*0-85030-266-8*) Sterling.

Nes, David W. & Parish, Edward J., eds. Analysis of Sterols & Other Biologically Significant Steroids. 341p. 1989. text ed. 109.00 (*0-12-515445-3*) Acad Pr.

Nes, W. David. Isopentenoids & Other Natural Products: Evolution & Function. LC 94-25742. (ACS Symposium Ser.: No. 562). (Illus.). 257p. 1994. 69.95 (*0-8412-2934-1*) Am Chemical.

Nes, W. David, jt. ed. see Fuller, Glenn.

Nes, W. David, jt. ed. see Patterson, Glenn W.

Nes, W. David, et al, eds. Isopentenoids in Plants: Biochemistry & Function. LC 83-23167. (Illus.). 614p. reprint ed. pap. 175.00 (*0-7837-4307-6*, 2043998) Bks Demand.

— Regulation of Isopentenoid Metabolism. LC 92-17807. (ACS Symposium Ser.: Vol. 497). (Illus.). 270p. 1992. 66.95 (*0-8412-2457-9*) Am Chemical.

***Nesaule, Agate.** A Woman in Amber. 285p. 1995. 24.00 (*1-56947-046-4*) Soho Press.

Nesbett, Peter, jt. auth. see Hills, Patricia.

Nesbit. Railway Children. (J). 1994. 14.95 (*0-8050-3129-4*) H Holt & Co.

Nesbit, Debra L., ed. see Hoskin, Theresa.

Nesbit, Dorothy D. Videostyle in Senate Campaigns. LC 88-2166. 192p. 1988. text ed. 26.00x (*0-87049-582-8*) U of Tenn Pr.

Nesbit, E. The Enchanted Castle. LC 91-46267. (Books of Wonder). (Illus.). 304p. (YA). 1992. 20.00 (*0-688-05435-8*) Morrow Jr Bks.

— Five Children & It. Kemp, Sandra, ed. (World's Classics Ser.). (Illus.). 224p. (J). 1994. pap. 7.95 (*0-19-283163-1*) OUP.

— The Railway Children. (Classics Ser.). 240p. (J). (gr. 5 up). 1994. pap. 3.50 (*0-14-036671-7*) Puffin Bks.

— The Railway Children. (Classics for Young Readers Ser.). 64p. (J). 1994. 5.98 (*0-86112-983-0*) Brimax Bks.

— Whereyouwanttogoto & Other Unlikely Tales. Cott, Jonathan, ed. LC 93-18685. (Little Barefoot Books). (Illus.). 220p. 1993. 6.00 (*1-56957-909-1*) Barefoot Bks.

Nesbit, Edith. Caesars Dialogue. LC 73-38215. (English Experience Ser.: No. 480). 154p. 1972. reprint ed. 14.00 (*90-221-0480-X*) Walter J Johnson.

— The Deliverers of Their Country. LC 85-9389. (Illus.). 32p. (J). (gr. 3-5). 1991. pap. 15.95 (*0-88708-005-7*, Picture Book Studio) S&S Childrens.

— Enchanted Castle. 231p. (J). 1981. reprint ed. lib. bdg. 10.95 (*0-89966-361-3*) Buccaneer Bks.

— Enchanted Castle. 179p. (J). 1981. reprint ed. lib. bdg. 16.95 (*0-89967-035-0*) Harmony Raine.

— Five Children & It. (Illus.). 224p. (J). (gr. 4-6). 1985. pap. 3.50 (*0-14-035061-6*, Puffin) Puffin Bks.

— Five Children & It. 208p. (J). (gr. 4-7). 1988. pap. 3.25 (*0-590-42146-8*, Apple Classics) Scholastic Inc.

— Five Children & It. 188p. (J). 1981. reprint ed. lib. bdg. 21.95 (*0-89966-362-1*) Buccaneer Bks.

— Five Children & It. 182p. (J). 1981. reprint ed. lib. bdg. 21.95 (*0-89967-036-9*) Harmony Raine.

— Railway Children. (J). (gr. 4 up). 1993. pap. 3.25 (*0-553-21415-2*, Bantam Classics) Bantam.

— Railway Children. (J). (gr. 4-7). 1992. pap. 3.50 (*0-440-40602-1*) Dell.

— The Railway Children. (J). 1993. 12.95 (*0-679-42534-9*, Everymans Lib) Knopf.

— The Railway Children. 256p. 1992. 2.95 (*0-451-52561-2*, Sig Classics) NAL-Dutton.

— The Railway Children. (World's Classics Ser.). 224p. (J). 1991. pap. 4.95 (*0-19-282659-X*, 11912) OUP.

— The Railway Children. (J). (gr. 5-8). 1988. 16.00 (*0-8446-6345-X*) Peter Smith.

— The Railway Children. (Classics Ser.). 240p. (J). (gr. 3-7). 1983. pap. 2.95 (*0-14-035005-5*, Puffin) Puffin Bks.

— Story of the Amulet. (J). 1986. pap. 3.50 (*0-14-035063-2*, Puffin) Puffin Bks.

— Story of the Treasure Seekers. (Classics Ser.). (J). (gr. 3 up). 1987. pap. 2.99 (*0-14-035058-6*, Puffin) Puffin Bks.

— Story of the Treasure Seekers. (Classics Ser.). (J). (gr. 4-6). 1987. pap. 2.25 (*0-685-03990-0*, Puffin) Puffin Bks.

— Whereyouwantogoto: And Other Unlikely Tales. LC 93-18685. (Little Barefoot Bks.). (Illus.). 224p. (J). 1993. 6.00 (*1-56957-904-0*) Shambhala Pubns.

— The Wouldbegoods. (J). (gr. 5-8). 1988. 17.25 (*0-8446-6347-6*) Peter Smith.

— The Wouldbegoods. (Classics Ser.). 283p. (J). (gr. 5 up). 1986. pap. 3.99 (*0-14-035059-4*, Puffin) Puffin Bks.

Nesbit, Evelyn. Railway Children. (Illus.). 192p. (YA). 1992. 9.99 (*0-517-07011-1*, Derrydale Bks) Random Hse Value.

Nesbit Group Staff & Brown, Diane E. CorelDRAW! for Windows at a Glance: The Fastest & Easiest Way to Learn CorelDRAW! 4.0 for Windows. LC 93-49610. 128p. (Orig.). 1994. pap. 15.95 (*1-55622-409-5*) Wordware Pub.

Nesbit, Jeffrey A. Absolutely Perfect Summer. 211p. (Orig.). (YA). (gr. 9-12). 1990. pap. 6.99 (*0-87788-005-0*) Shaw Pubs.

— All the King's Horses. 192p. (Orig.). (YA). (gr. 9-12). 1990. pap. 6.99 (*0-87788-040-9*) Shaw Pubs.

— The Great Nothing Strikes Back. 256p. (Orig.). (YA). (gr. 9-12). 1991. pap. 6.99 (*0-87788-323-8*) Shaw Pubs.

— The Puzzled Prodigy. (Capital Crew Ser.). (Orig.). (J). (gr. 3-6). 1992. pap. 1.00 (*0-89693-075-0*, Victor Books) SP Pubns.

— The Sioux Society. LC 92-20199. (Young Adult Fiction Ser.). 1992. 6.99 (*0-87788-748-9*) Shaw Pubs.

***Nesbit, Lois.** Richard Meier Sculpture. (Illus.). 56p. 1995. pap. 25.00 (*0-8478-1848-9*) Rizzoli Intl.

Nesbit, Martha G. Savannah: Crown of the Colonial Coast. (Urban Tapestry Ser.). (Illus.). 208p. 1992. 39.50 (*0-9628128-7-0*) Towery Pub.

— Savannah Collection: Favorite Recipes from Savannah Cooks. (Illus.). 250p. 1986. bds. 10.95 (*0-9617126-0-0*) M Nesbit.

Nesbit, Molly. Atget's Seven Albums. (Illus.). 440p. (C). 1994. text ed. 60.00 (*0-300-03580-2*) Yale U Pr.

— Atget's Seven Albums. (Illus.). 440p. (C). 1994. pap. 30.00 (*0-300-05916-7*) Yale U Pr.

Nesbit, Paul W. Garden of God's. 5th rev. ed. LC 88-90928. (Illus.). 1988. pap. 5.00 (*0-911746-08-0*) Nesbit.

— New Techniques for Efficient Teaching. (Illus.). 1947. 1.75 (*0-911746-03-X*); pap. 1.00 (*0-911746-05-6*) Nesbit.

— Nez-Bits. (Illus.). 1946. pap. 0.75 (*0-911746-04-8*) Nesbit.

Nesbit, Robert & Miller, Arthur. Making Sales Manager: All You Need to Know to Lead & Succeed. 225p. 1992. 24.95 (*1-55738-400-2*) Probus Pub Co.

Nesbit, Robert C. The History of Wisconsin, Vol. III: Urbanization & Industrialization, 1873-1893. (Illus.). 720p. 1985. 30.00 (*0-87020-243-X*) State Hist Soc Wis.

— Wisconsin: A History. 2nd rev. ed. (Illus.). 600p. (C). 1990. 25.00 (*0-299-10800-7*) U of Wis Pr.

Nesbit, Roy C. Illustrated History of the RAF. 1991. 29.99 (*0-517-03379-8*) Random Hse Value.

Nesbit, William, ed. World Energy: Will There Be Enough in 2020? (Decisionmakers Bookshelf Ser.: Vol. 6). (Illus.). 88p. (Orig.). 1979. pap. 2.50 (*0-931032-06-7*) Edison Electric.

Nesbit, William & Williams, Samuel W. Two Black Views of Liberia: Four Months in Liberia, or African Colonization Exposed Four Years in Liberia, a Sketch of the Life of Rev. Samuel Williams. LC 70-92234. (American Negro: His History & Literature, Ser. No. 3). 1970. reprint ed. 16.95 (*0-405-01936-X*) Ayer.

Nesbit, William M. Sumerian Records from Drehem. LC 15-2779. (Columbia University. Oriental Studies: No. 8). (Illus.). reprint ed. 12.50 (*0-404-50498-1*) AMS Pr.

Nesbitt, Alexander. Decorative Alphabets & Initials. (Illus.). 21.50 (*0-8446-0820-3*) Peter Smith.

— Decorative Initials & Alphabets. (Illus.). 1959. pap. 6.95 (*0-486-20544-4*) Dover.

— The History & Technique of Lettering. Orig. Title: Lettering: The History & Technique of Lettering As Design. 1950. pap. 6.95 (*0-486-20427-8*) Dover.

— Two Hundred Decorative Title Pages. (Illus.). (Orig.). 1964. pap. 8.95 (*0-486-21264-5*) Dover.

***Nesbitt, Caroline.** The Pony Breeder's Companion: A Guide for Owners & Breeders. LC 95-15647. (Illus.). 288p. 1995. 29.95 (*0-87605-996-5*) Howell Bk.

Nesbitt, Cecil J., jt. auth. see Butcher, Marjorie V.

Nesbitt, David. FoxPro 2.5 at a Glance. 1994. pap. 15.95 (*1-55622-342-0*) Wordware Pub.

— Learn PowerBuilder 5.0 for Windows in a Day. 1995. disk, pap. 15.95 (*1-55622-471-0*) Wordware Pub.

— Paradox for Windows at a Glance: The Fastest & Easiest Way to Learn Borland Paradox for Windows. LC 93-17702. 1993. 15.95 (*1-55622-345-5*) Wordware Pub.

Nesbitt, David, jt. auth. see Jones, Edward C.

Nesbitt, David D., jt. auth. see Nesbitt Group Staff.

Nesbitt, Gemma. Garden Graphics: How to Map & Plan Your Garden. (Illus.). 192p. 1993. 35.00 (*0-913643-11-4*) Capabilitys.

Nesbitt, Gene H. & Ackerman, Lowell J. Dermatology for the Small Animal Practitioner Exotics - Feline - Canine. 1991. pap. 55.00 (*1-884254-02-0*) Vet Lrn Syst.

Nesbitt Group & Teglovic, Eugene W. Quattro Pro 4.0 at a Glance: The Fastest & Easiest Way to Learn Quattro Pro 4.0. LC 93-20072. (At a Glance Ser.). 128p. 1993. 15.95 (*1-55622-355-2*) Wordware Pub.

Nesbitt Group Staff & Craig, John. Paradox 4.5 at a Glance. LC 94-7375. 128p. 1994. pap. 15.95 (*1-55622-411-7*) Wordware Pub.

Nesbitt Group Staff & Nesbitt, David D. FoxPro 2.5 for Windows at a Glance: The Fastest & Easiest Way to Learn FoxPro for Windows. LC 93-47373. 136p. 1994. pap. 15.95 (*1-55622-343-9*) Wordware Pub.

— Microsoft Windows at a Glance: The Fastest & Easiest Way to Learn Windows 3.1. LC 93-29892. (At a Glance Ser.). 111p. (Orig.). 1993. pap. 15.95 (*1-55622-341-2*) Wordware Pub.

Nesbitt Hawes, R. & Lindley, B. Training of Youth in Industry, Vol. 4: Engineering. 5th ed. LC 66-19079. 1966. 98.00 (*0-08-011726-0*, Pub. by Pergamon Repr UK) Franklin.

***Nesbitt, Henrietta.** White House Diary. (American Autobiography Ser.). 314p. 1995. reprint ed. lib. bdg. 89.00 (*0-7812-8600-X*) Rprt Serv.

***Nesbitt, John, ed.** Wyoming Journeys. (Illus.). 32p. (Orig.). 1995. pap. 5.00 (*0-917557-04-2*) Wyo Writers.

***Nesbitt, John & Oikonomides, Nicolas, eds.** Catalogue of Byzantine Seals at Dumbarton Oaks & in the Fogg Museum of Art Vol. 2: South of the Balkans, the Islands, South of Asia Minor. LC 91-12861. (Illus.). 248p. 1994. 35.00x (*0-88402-226-9*, BYS2, Dumbarton Rsch Lib) Dumbarton Oaks.

— Catalogue of Byzantine Seals at Dumbarton Oaks & in the Fogg Museum of Art, Vol. 1: Italy, North of the Balkans, North of the Black Sea. LC 91-12861. (Illus.). 276p. 1991. 30.00 (*0-88402-194-7*, BYS1, Dumbarton Oaks) Dumbarton Oaks.

Nesbitt, John, jt. ed. see Miller, Timothy S.

Nesbitt, John A., et al, eds. Recreation & Leisure Service for the Disadvantaged. LC 76-115026. (Illus.). 612p. reprint ed. 174.50 (*0-8357-9419-9*, 2014568) Bks Demand.

Nesbitt, John D. One-Eyed Cowboy Wild. LC 93-32741. 180p. 1994. 19.95 (*0-8027-4135-5*) Walker & Co.

— One-Eyed Cowboy Wild. large type ed. LC 94-26349. 1994. pap. 17.95 (*0-8161-7477-6*) Hall.

— Twin Rivers. 1995. 19.95 (*0-8027-4152-5*) Walker & Co.

***Nesbitt, Kate, ed.** Theorizing a New Agenda for Architecture: An Anthology of Architectural Theory 1965-1995. (Illus.). 384p. 1995. 50.00 (*1-56898-053-1*); pap. 34.95 (*1-56898-054-X*) Princeton Arch.

Nesbitt, Kate D. Gwinnett County, Georgia: Eighteen-Fifty Census with Mortality Schedule. 242p. 1986. 10.00 (*0-317-56128-6*) Gwinnett Hist.

Nesbitt, Lee T., Jr., jt. ed. see Sanders, Charles V.

Nesbitt, Lewis M. Gold Fever, Vol. 11. LC 74-355. 214p. 1974. reprint ed. 20.95 (*0-405-05916-7*) Ayer.

— Hell Hole of Creation: The Exploration of Abyssinian Danakil. LC 74-15072. (Illus.). reprint ed. 26.00 (*0-404-12116-0*) AMS Pr.

Nesbitt, Lois. Richard Meier Collages. 1991. 24.95 (*0-312-05672-9*) St Martin.

Nesbitt, Lois, tr. see Virivid, Paul, et al.

Nesbitt, Lois, jt. ed. see Wong, Tony.

Nesbitt, Mark. If the South Won Gettysburg. LC 80-52561. (Illus.). 107p. (Orig.). 1980. pap. 6.95 (*0-937740-01-2*) Reliance Pub.

— If the South Won Gettysburg. (Illus.). 124p. (Orig.). (C). 1993. reprint ed. pap. text ed. 6.95 (*0-939631-69-5*) Thomas Publications.

— Rebel Rivers: A Guide to the Civil War Sites on the Potomac, Rappahannock, York, & James. LC 93-20180. (Illus.). 166p. 1993. pap. 12.95 (*0-8117-2538-3*) Stackpole.

— Saber & Scapegoat: J. E. B. Stuart & the Gettysburg Controversy. (Illus.). 272p. 1994. 19.95 (*0-8117-0915-9*) Stackpole.

— 35 Days to Gettysburg: The Campaign Diaries of Two American Enemies. LC 92-13397. (Illus.). 208p. 1992. 16.95 (*0-8117-1757-7*) Stackpole.

— Through Blood & Fire: Selected Civil War Papers of Major General Joshua Chamberlain. (Illus.). 192p. 1996. 19.95 (*0-8117-1750-X*) Stackpole.

Nesbitt, Mark V. Ghosts of Gettysburg: Spirits, Apparitions & Haunted Places of the Battlefield. (Illus.). 84p. (C). 1991. pap. text ed. 4.95 (*0-939631-41-5*) Thomas Publications.

— More Ghosts of Gettysburg: Spirits, Apparitions & Haunted Places of the Battlefield. (Illus.). 100p. (C). 1992. pap. text ed. 4.95 (*0-939631-51-2*) Thomas Publications.

Nesbitt, Murray B. Labor Relations in the Federal Government Service. LC 75-44255. 559p. reprint ed. pap. 159.40 (*0-317-29421-0*, 2024306) Bks Demand.

Nesbitt, Perry L., ed. see Phillips, Patricia C.

Nesbitt, Prexy. Apartheid in Our Living Rooms: U. S. Foreign Policy & South Africa. (Midwest Research Monograph Ser.: No. 3). 58p. 1986. pap. 5.50 (*0-915987-02-3*) Political Rsch Assocs.

***Nesbitt, Steven M.** British Pensions Policy Making in the 1980's: The Rise & Fall of a Policy Community. 176p. 1995. 54.95 (*1-85628-498-0*, Pub. by Avebury Pub UK) Ashgate Pub Co.

Nesbitt, Susan & Krasner, Melvin I. The Financial Condition of New York City Voluntary Hospitals: The First Year of NYPHRM. (Paper Ser.: No. 2). 24p. 1985. 5.00 (*0-934459-10-X*) United Hosp Fund.

Nesbitt, W. H., ed. Boone & Crockett Club's 18th Big Game Awards. (Illus.). 306p. 1984. 24.95 (*0-940864-05-3*) Boone & Crockett.

Nesbitt, W. H. & Reneau, Jack, eds. Boone & Crockett Club's Twentieth Big Game Awards. (Illus.). 480p. 1990. 34.95 (*0-940864-16-9*) Boone & Crockett.

— Records of North American Big Game. 9th ed. (Illus.). 512p. 1988. 49.95 (*0-940864-13-4*) Boone & Crockett.

— Records of North American Elk & Mule Deer. 1991. LC 91-73121. (Illus.). viii, 264p. (Orig.). 1991. pap. 16.95 (*0-940864-18-5*) Boone & Crockett.

— Records of North American Whitetail Deer. (Illus.). 246p. 1987. pap. 14.95 (*0-940864-12-6*) Boone & Crockett.

— Records of North American Whitetail Deer. 1991. 2nd ed. LC 91-973120. (Illus.). viii, 312p. (Orig.). 1991. pap. 16.95 (*0-940864-17-7*) Boone & Crockett.

Nesbitt, W. H. & Wright, Philip L., eds. Records of North American Big Game. 8th deluxe limited ed. (Records of North American Big Game Ser.). (Illus.). xii, 412p. 1981. 199.00 (*0-940864-01-0*) Boone & Crockett.

— Records of North American Big Game. 8th ed. (Records of North American Big Game Ser.). (Illus.). xii, 412p. 1981. 29.95 (*0-940864-00-2*) Boone & Crockett.

Nesbitt, William A. & Abramowitz, Norman. Teaching Youth about Conflict & War. Bloomstein, Charles, ed. LC 73-75291. (Teaching Social Studies in an Age of Crisis: No. 5). 112p. reprint ed. pap. 32.00 (*0-317-08320-1*, 2005099) Bks Demand.

Nesbitt, William H. Boone & Crockett Clubs Twenty-First Big Game Award, 1989-1991. 1992. 39.95 (*1-879356-19-8*) Wolfe Pub Co.

Nesci, Catherine. La Femme mode d'emploi: Balzac, de la Physiologie du mariage a La Comedie humaine. LC 92-71331. (French Forum Monographs: No. 81). 247p. (Orig.). (FRE.). 1992. pap. 17.95 (*0-917058-86-0*) French Forum.

Nesdoly, Samuel J. Among the Soviet Evangelicals. (Orig.). 1986. pap. 8.95 (*0-85151-489-8*) Banner of Truth.

Neseman, Dale & Thebo, Jack. So That's How They're Spending Our Money! Your Federal Taxes at Work. (Illus.). 144p. (Orig.). 1991. pap. 6.95 (*0-9629343-0-5*) Neseman Enter.

Nesenoff, Norman, ed. see CES Industries, Inc. Staff.

Nesenoff, Norman, jt. auth. see CES Industries, Inc. Staff.

Nesetril, J., ed. Topological, Algebraical, & Combinatorial Structures: Frolik's Memorial Volume. LC 93-275. (Topics in Discrete Mathematics Ser.: No. 8). 1993. write for info. (*0-444-89236-2*, North Holland) Elsevier.

Nesetril, J. & Fiedler, M., eds. Fourth Czechoslovakian Symposium on Combinatorics, Graphs & Complexity. LC 92-14160. (Annals of Discrete Mathematics Ser.: Vol. 51). 1992. write for info. (*0-444-89543-4*, North Holland) Elsevier.

Nesetril, J., et al, eds. Mathematics of Ramsey Theory. (Algorithms & Combinatorics Ser.: Vol. 5). (Illus.). 281p. 1990. 72.00 (*0-387-18191-1*) Spr-Verlag.

Nesfield-Cookson, Bernard. William Blake: Prophet of Universal Brotherhood. 480p. (Orig.). (C). 1989. 33.00x (*0-8095-7102-1*) Borgo Pr.

Neshati, Amin, tr. see Daneshvar, Simin.

Neshati, Amin, tr. see Taj of Saltana.

Nesheim, Eric, ed. see Rude, Steve.

Nesheim, John L. High Tech Start Up: The Complete How-to-Handbook for Creating Successful New High Tech Companies. Brett, Elaine, ed. LC 91-29695. 303p. 1992. reprint ed. 49.50 (*0-914405-71-3*) Electronic Trend.

Nesheim, Malden C., jt. auth. see Austic, Richard E.

***Nesheim, Paul & Noble, Weston.** Building Beautiful Voices. Foss, Scott, ed. 180p. (Orig.). (C). 1995. pap. text ed. 25.00 (*0-89328-138-7*, 30-1054R) Lorenz Corp.

An Asterisk (*) at the beginning of an entry indicates that the title is appearing in BIP for the first time.

Nesher, Pearla & Kilpatrick, Jeremy. Mathematics & Cognition: A Research Synthesis by the International Group for the Psychology of Mathematics Education. (International Commission on Mathematical Instruction Study Ser.). 180p. (C). 1990. pap. 21.95 (*0-521-36787-5*) Cambridge U Pr.

Neshyba, S., et al, eds. Poleward Flows along Eastern Ocean Boundaries. (Coastal & Estuarine Studies: Vol. 34). ix, 374p. 1989. 65.00 (*0-387-97175-0*) Spr-Verlag.

Nesi, jt. auth. see Smith.

Nesi, Frank A., jt. ed. see Spoor, Thomas C.

Nesi, Thomas J., jt. auth. see Wolfe, M. Michael.

Nesin, Ali, jt. auth. see Borovik, Alexandre.

Nesin, Aziz. Istanbul Boy, Part III: The Climb. Jacobson, Joseph S., tr. 232p. (Orig.). 1991. pap. 9.95 (*0-292-73864-1*, Pub. by Ctr Mid East Stud) U of Tex Pr.

— Turkish Stories from Four Decades. Mitler, Louis, tr. & intro. by. 160p. (Orig.). 1991. text ed. 25.00 (*0-89410-687-2*); pap. 13.00 (*0-89410-688-0*) Three Continents.

Nesis, Gennady. Exchanging to Win in the Endgame. 160p. 1991. pap. 14.95 (*0-02-008671-7*) Macmillan.

— Tactical Chess Exchanges. (Chess Library). 128p. 1992. pap. 16.95 (*0-02-029437-9*, Pub. by Gebrueder Borntraeger GW) Macmillan.

— Tactics in the French. 1994. pap. 19.95 (*0-8050-3279-7*) H Holt & Co.

— Tactics in the Grunfeld. (Batsford Chess Library). 176p. 1993. pap. 19.95 (*0-8050-2638-X*, Owl) H Holt & Co.

— Tactics in the Sicilian. (Batsford Chess Library). 192p. 1993. pap. 19.95 (*0-8050-2934-6*) H Holt & Co.

Neslehova, Mahulena. Bohumil Kubista. 328p. 1984. 158.00 (*0-317-61238-7*, Pub. by Collets UK) Pro-Am Music.

Neslen, Barbara. Crock-It. (Illus.). 176p. 1991. pap. 12.95 (*0-9629290-9-3*) Star Feather.

Nesler, T. P. & Bergersen, E. P. Mysids in Fisheries. LC 91-71560. (Symposium Ser.: No. 9). 204p. 1991. pap. 33.50 (*0-913235-71-7*) Am Fisheries Soc.

Nesman, Edgar G. Peasant Mobilization & Rural Development. 148p. 1981. pap. text ed. 11.95 (*0-87073-718-X*) Schenkman Bks Inc.

***Nesme-Ribes, Elizabeth.** The Solar Engine & Its Influence of Terrestrial Atmosphere & Climate. LC 94-34430. 1994. 214.00 (*3-540-58417-X*) Spr-Verlag.

Nesmelov, Arsenij. Bez Rossii. (Illus.). 480p. (Orig.). 1990. 35.00 (*1-878445-57-X*) Antiquary CT.

Nesmeyanov, A., jt. auth. see Yoffe, S.

Nesmeyanov, A. N. Selected Works in Organic Chemistry. 1963. 481.00 (*0-08-010158-5*, Pub. by Pergamon Repr UK) Franklin.

Nesmeyanov, A. N. & Baranov, V. Handbook of Radiochemical Exercises. LC 62-9182. 1965. 192.00 (*0-08-010157-7*, Pub. by Pergamon Repr UK) Franklin.

Nesmith, Alisa A., ed. see Peppers, Jerome G.

Nesmith, Anna M., ed. see Kissinger, Charles C.

Nesmith, Bruce. Battlesystem Arena. (Advanced Dungeons & Dragons Ser.). 1991. pap. 15.00 (*1-56076-141-5*) TSR Inc.

— From the Shadows. (Advanced Dungeons & Dragons, Second Edition; Al-Qadim Ser.). (Illus.). 1992. pap. 9.95 (*1-56076-356-6*, RQ3) TSR Inc.

— The New Republican Coalition: The Reagan Campaigns & White Evangelicals. LC 92-40964. (American University Studies, X, Political Science: Vol. 41). 192p. (C). 1994. text ed. 39.95 (*0-8204-2138-3*) P Lang Pubs.

— Touch of Death. (Advanced Dungeons & Dragons Ser.). 1991. pap. 6.95 (*1-56076-144-X*) TSR Inc.

— Unsung Heroes. (Advanced Dungeons & Dragons, Second Edition; Al-Qadim Ser.). (Illus.). 1993. pap. 9.95 (*1-56076-423-6*) TSR Inc.

***Nesmith, Eleanor L.** Instant Architecture. (Illus.). 240p. 1995. pap. 10.00 (*0-449-90699-X*) Fawcett.

Nesmith, James W. Two Addresses. 56p. 1978. pap. 5.95 (*0-87770-202-0*) Ye Galleon.

Nesmith, Lynn. Health Care Architecture: Designs for the Future. 1994. 39.99 (*1-56496-136-2*) Rockport Pubs.

***Nesmith, Lynn, ed.** Health Care Architecture. (Illus.). 192p. 1995. 39.95 (*1-55835-135-3*) AIA Press.

Nesmith, Mary E. An Objective Determination of Stories & Poems for the Primary Grades. LC 78-117102. (Columbia University. Teachers College. Contributions to Education Ser.: No. 255). reprint ed. 37.50 (*0-404-55255-2*) AMS Pr.

Nesmith, Samuel P., jt. auth. see Martinello, Marian L.

Nesmith, Timothy E., jt. auth. see Batchelor, Andrew J., Jr.

Nesmith, Tom, ed. Canadian Archival Studies & the Rediscovery of Provenance. (Society of American Archivists & Association of Canadian Archivists Ser.). (Illus.). 526p. 1993. 59.50 (*0-8108-2660-7*) Scarecrow.

Neso, E. Fake It. LC 90-71973. 204p. (Orig.). 1992. pap. 8.95 (*1-56002-033-4*) Aegina Pr.

Nesovich, Peter. Reupholstering at Home: A Do-It Yourself Manual for Turning Old Furniture into New Showpieces. (Illus.). 1988. pap. 9.95 (*0-517-53819-9*, Crown) Crown Pub Group.

Nespeca, Sue M., ed. see Association of Library Service to Children Staff.

***Nespeca, Sue McCleaf.** Library Programming for Families with Young Children. LC 94-37894. (A How-to-do-it Manual Ser.: 45). 1994. write for info. (*1-55570-181-7*) Neal-Schuman.

Nesper, Kathy, jt. auth. see Wessel, Helen.

***Nespor, Jan.** Knowledge in Motion: Space, Time & Curriculum in Undergraduate Physics & Management. LC 94-31140. 172p. 1994. 69.00x (*0-7507-0270-2*) Taylor & Francis.

— Knowledge in Motion: Space, Time & Curriculum in Undergraduate Physics & Management. LC 94-31140. (Knowledge, Identity & School Life Ser.: Vol. 2). 166p. 1994. pap. 24.95x (*0-7507-0271-0*, Falmer Pr) Taylor & Francis.

Nespor, M. & Vogel, G. Prosodic Phonology. (Studies in Generative Grammar). xiv, 328p. 1986. pap. 75.00 (*90-6765-242-3*) Mouton.

Nespor, Marina, jt. ed. see Mascaro, Joan.

Nespoulous, J. L. & Villiard, P., eds. Morphology, Phonology & Aphasia. (Neuropsychology Ser.). (Illus.). 304p. 1990. 60.00 (*0-387-97183-1*) Spr-Verlag.

Nespoulous, J. L., et al. The Biological Foundations of Gestures: Motor & Semiotic Aspects. 336p. (C). 1986. text ed. 69.95 (*0-89859-645-9*) L Erlbaum Assocs.

Ness, Arlin E., jt. auth. see Brendtro, Larry K.

Ness, Arthur J. & Ward, John M. The Konigsberg Manuscript. LC 89-80415. (Illus.). 196p. 1989. 89.00 (*0-936186-31-3*) Edit Orphee.

Ness, Beatrice. Creativite et Mystification Dans l'Oeuvre Romanesque de Marguerite Yourcenar: Cinq Lectures Genetiques. LC 93-85869. (North Carolina Studies in the Romance Languages & Literatures). 210p. (C). 1994. pap. text ed. 25.00 (*0-8078-9251-3*) U of NC Pr.

***Ness, Brian, ed.** Actor's Training Guide. 80p. 1994. pap. 5.00 (*1-56850-043-2*) Chicago Plays.

***Ness, Caroline.** Let's Be Friends. (Illus.). 22p. (J). 1995. 5.95 (*0-694-00725-0*, Festival) HarpC Child Bks.

— Let's Get a Puppy. (Illus.). 22p. (J). 1995. 5.95 (*0-694-00724-2*, Festival) HarpC Child Bks.

— Star Signs: A Child's Guide to Astrology. (J). (ps-3). 1994. 12.95 (*1-57036-011-1*) Turner Pub GA.

Ness, David. Keys to Planning for Long-Term Custodial Care. (Retirement Keys Ser.). 160p. 1991. pap. 5.95 (*0-8120-4593-9*) Barron.

Ness, E. Sam, Bangs, & Moonshine. (J). (gr. 4 up). 1971. pap. 3.95 (*0-03-080111-7*) H Holt & Co.

Ness, Eliot & Fraley, Oscar. The Untouchables. 224p. 1987. mass mkt. 4.99 (*0-671-64449-1*) PB.

Ness, Eliot, jt. auth. see Fraley, Oscar.

Ness, Erik, ed. see Johnson, Denny.

Ness, Evaline. Sam, Bangs & Moonshine. LC 66-10113. (Illus.). 48p. (J). (ps-2). 1966. 14.95 (*0-8050-0314-2*, Bks Young Read) H Holt & Co.

— Sam, Bangs & Moonshine. LC 66-10113. (Illus.). 48p. (J). (ps-2). 1971. pap. 5.95 (*0-8050-0315-0*, Bks Young Read) H Holt & Co.

— Sam, Bangs y Hechizo de Luna. Alonso, Liwayway, tr. (Illus.). 48p. (SPA.). (J). Date not set. 14.95 (*1-880507-12-9*) Lectorum Pubns.

Ness, Frederic W. An Uncertain Glory: Letters of Cautious but Sound Advice. LC 74-152812. (Jossey-Bass Higher Education Ser.). 168p. reprint ed. 47.90 (*0-8357-9353-2*, 2013820) Bks Demand.

Ness, Frederic W., jt. ed. see Jellema, William W.

Ness, Gayl D. & Ando, Hirofumi. The Land Is Shrinking: Population Planning in Asia. LC 83-48048. 256p. 1984. 38.00 (*0-8018-2982-8*) Johns Hopkins.

Ness, Gayl D., et al, eds. Population - Environment Dynamics: Ideas & Observations. 350p. (C). 1992. text ed. 47.50 (*0-472-10395-4*) U of Mich Pr.

Ness, George T., Jr. Under the Eagle's Wings: The Army on the Eve of Civil War, 2 vols., 1. 650p. 1983. write for info. (*0-89126-112-5*) MA-AH Pub.

— Under the Eagle's Wings: The Army on the Eve of Civil War, 2 vols., 2. 650p. 1983. write for info. (*0-89126-113-3*) MA-AH Pub.

— Under the Eagle's Wings: The Army on the Eve of Civil War, 2 vols., Set. Vols. 1 & 2. 650p. 1983. Set. 69.00 (*0-685-06169-8*) MA-AH Pub.

Ness, Indoe. Tax Planning for Disposition of Business Interest. 2nd ed. 704p. Supplemented semi-annually. 155.00 (*0-7913-0627-5*) Warren Gorham & Lamont.

— Tax Planning for Disposition of Business Interest. 2nd suppl. ed. 704p. 48.00 (*0-7913-0932-0*); 50.75 (*0-685-51110-3*) Warren Gorham & Lamont.

Ness, Jean, jt. auth. see Aune, Elizabeth.

Ness, Pamela M. Assisi Embroidery. (Illus.). 1978. pap. 3.50 (*0-486-23743-5*) Dover.

— Norwegian Smyrna Cross Stich: Technique & Thirty-Nine Charted Designs. (Illus.). 48p. 1982. pap. 2.95 (*0-486-24274-9*) Dover.

Ness, Paul, jt. ed. see Anderson, Kenneth C.

***Ness, Paul Van.** Understanding Business Statistics. 176p. (C). 1991. student ed, text ed. 17.50 (*0-256-09340-7*) Irwin.

Ness, S. Chemical Sampling Methods Handbook. 1994. text ed. write for info. (*0-442-01463-5*) Van Nos Reinhold.

Ness, Sally A. Body, Movement, & Culture: Kinesthetic & Visual Symbolism in a Philippine Community. LC 92-15310. (Contemporary Ethnography Ser.). (Illus.). 312p. (Orig.). (C). 1992. text ed. 41.95 (*0-8122-3110-4*); pap. text ed. 17.95 (*0-8122-1383-1*) U of Pa Pr.

Ness, Shirley A. Air Monitoring for Toxic Exposures. LC 90-38159. (Illus.). 624p. 1991. text ed. 85.00 (*0-442-20639-9*) Van Nos Reinhold.

— Surface & Dermal Sampling for Toxic Exposures. 1994. text ed. 69.95 (*0-442-01465-1*) Van Nos Reinhold.

Ness, Theodore & Vogel, Eugene L. Taxation of the Closely-Held Corporation. 4th ed. 1991. Cumulative supplements, semi-annual. 135.00 (*0-685-45578-5*, TCHC) Warren Gorham & Lamont.

— Taxation of the Closely Held Corporation. 5th ed. 1991. text ed. 155.00 (*0-685-69545-X*, TCHC) Warren Gorham & Lamont.

Ness, Thomas E. Marketing in Action: A Decision Game Student's Manual. 5th ed. Day, Ralph L., tr. (C). 1984. text ed. 29.95 (*0-256-02650-5*) Irwin.

Ness, Tor, jt. auth. see Andenaes, Olav.

Nessan, Craig. Orthopraxis or Heresy. (American Academy of Religion Academy Ser.). 1989. pap. 22.95 (*1-55540-299-2*) Scholars Pr GA.

***Nesse, Randolph M. & Williams, George C.** Why We Get Sick: The New Science of Darwinian Medicine. LC 94-27651. 1994. 24.00 (*0-8129-2224-7*, Times Bks) Random.

Nesse, William D. Introduction to Optical Mineralogy. 2nd ed. (Illus.). 352p. (C). 1991. text ed. 45.00 (*0-19-506024-5*) OUP.

Nessel, Denise, jt. auth. see Dixon, Carol N.

Nessel, Denise D. & Jones, Margaret B. Language-Experience Approach to Reading: A Handbook for Teachers of Reading. LC 80-27822. (Orig.). 1981. pap. 15.95 (*0-8077-2596-X*) Tchrs Coll.

Nessel, Denise D., et al. Thinking Through the Language Arts. 857p. (C). 1989. text ed. write for info. (*0-02-386601-2*) Macmillan.

Nesselrath, Heinz-Gunther. Die Atticshe Mittlere Komodie: Ihre Stellung in der Antiken Literatur & Literaturgeschichte. (Untersuchungen zur Antiken Literatur und Geschichte Ser.: No. 36). x, 395p. (GER.). (C). 1990. lib. bdg. 166.15 (*3-11-012196-4*) De Gruyter.

— Lukians Parasitendialog: Untersuchungen und Kommentar. (Untersuchungen aur Antiken Literatur und Geschichte Ser.: Vol. 22). xi, 559p. (GER.). 1985. 234.65 (*3-11-010277-3*) De Gruyter.

Nesselrath, Heinz-Gunther, ed. see Kassel, Rudolf.

Nesselroade, J. B. & Cattell, Raymond B., eds. Handbook of Multivariate Experimental Psychology. 2nd ed. LC 88-9806. (Perspectives on Individual Differences Ser.). (Illus.). 996p. 1988. 125.00 (*0-306-42526-2*, Plenum Pr) Plenum.

Nesselroade, John R. & Baltes, Paul B., eds. Longitudinal Methodology in the Study of Behavior & Development. LC 79-23265. 1979. text ed. 63.00 (*0-12-515660-X*) Acad Pr.

Nesselroade, John R. & Von Eye, Alexander, eds. Individual Development & Social Change: Explanatory Analysis. 1985. text ed. 68.00 (*0-12-515620-0*) Acad Pr.

Nesselroth. Lautreamont's Imagery: A Stylistic Approach. 14.95 (*0-685-34929-2*) Fr & Eur.

Nesselson, Lisa, jt. auth. see Fitch, Brian T.

Nessen, Robert L. Real Estate Finance & Taxation: Structuring Complex Transactions. (Real Estate Practice Library). 294p. 1990. text ed. 120.00 (*0-471-62161-7*) Wiley.

Nessen, Ron & Neuman, Johanna. Knight & Day. 256p. 1995. 21.95 (*0-312-85588-5*) Forge NYC.

Nesset, Kirk. The Stories of Raymond Carver: A Critical Study. 150p. (C). 1994. text ed. 34.95 (*0-8214-1099-7*); pap. text ed. 14.95 (*0-8214-1100-4*) Ohio U Pr.

Nessim, Susan. Cancervive: The Challenge of Life after Cancer. large type ed. 1993. 21.95 (*1-56895-007-1*) Wheeler Pub.

Nessim, Susan & Ellis, Judith. Cancervive: The Challenge of Life after Cancer. 256p. 1992. pap. 10.95 (*0-395-62432-0*) HM.

Nessmith, William C., jt. auth. see Sloshberg, Willard.

Nessmuk, pseud. Woodcraft & Camping. (Illus.). 105p. 1963. pap. 3.95 (*0-486-21145-2*) Dover.

Nesson, Charles R. Evidence, 1988. 1988. 25.00 (*1-55917-164-2*, 7306); audio 135.00 (*1-55917-162-6*); vhs 495.00 (*1-55917-163-4*) Natl Prac Inst.

Nesson, Fern L. Great Waters: A History of Boston's Water Supply. LC 82-40342. (Illus.). 134p. reprint ed. pap. 38.20 (*0-8357-6521-0*, 2035892) Bks Demand.

Nestel, B. L. Development of Animal Production Systems. (World Animal Science Ser.: Vol. 2A). 350p. 1984. 146.25 (*0-444-42050-9*, I-474-83) Elsevier.

Nestel, Barry, jt. auth. see Daniels, Doug.

Nestel, P. J., jt. ed. see Fidge, N. H.

Nestell, Merlynd, tr. see Akhiezer, N. I. & Glazman, I. M.

***Nester, Dean.** A Second Chance. 283p. 1995. pap. 7.99 (*0-9647710-0-4*) Sable Pub.

Nester, Emery, jt. auth. see Baker, Don.

Nester, Eugene W. & Verma, Desh P., eds. Advances in Molecular Genetics of Plant-Microbe Interactions, Vol. 2. LC 92-35081. (Current Plant Science & Biotechnology in Agriculture Ser.). 640p. (C). 1992. lib. bdg. 137.50 (*0-7923-2045-X*) Kluwer Ac.

Nester, Eugene W., et al. Microbiology: A Human Perspective. 832p. (C). 1994. text ed. write for info. (*0-697-12760-5*) Wm C Brown Pubs.

— Microbiology: A Human Perspective. 832p. (C). 1994. student ed write for info. (*0-697-14788-6*) Wm C Brown Pubs.

Nester, Mary A. Pre-Employment Testing & the ADA. (ADA Practice Ser.). 16p. 1994. pap. 9.00 (*0-685-72821-8*) LRP Pubns.

Nester-Niederman, Julie. Participation in Development: An Evaluation of Animation Rurale in Senegal. (Graduate Student Term Paper Ser.). 19p. 1984. pap. text ed. 2.00 (*0-941934-48-9*) Indiana Africa.

***Nester, William.** Ends of the Earth. 560p. 1995. pap. 12.95 (*1-56901-904-5*) NW Pub.

— International Relations: Geopolitical & Geoeconomic Conflict & Cooperation. LC 94-32955. 608p. (C). 1995. pap. 27.75 (*0-673-99305-1*) HarpCollege.

Nester, William R. European Power & the Japanese Challenge. LC 93-17512. 304p. 1993. text ed. 55.00 (*0-8147-5777-4*) NYU Pr.

— The Foundation of Japanese Power. LC 90-34055. 418p. 1990. 62.95 (*0-87332-755-1*) M E Sharpe.

— Japan & the Third World: Patterns, Power, & Prospects. LC 91-32530. 260p. 1992. text ed. 45.00 (*0-312-07251-1*) St Martin.

— Japanese Industrial Targeting: The Neomercantilist Path to Economic Superpower. LC 90-20560. 312p. 1991. text ed. 55.00 (*0-312-05782-2*) St Martin.

— Japan's Growing Power over East Asia & the World Economy: Ends & Means. LC 89-35713. 300p. 1990. text ed. 55.00 (*0-312-03530-6*) St Martin.

Nesterenko, I. F., jt. auth. see Brekhman, I. I.

Nesterenko, V. V., jt. auth. see Barbashov, B. M.

Nesterov, Yurii & Nemirovski, Arkadii. Interior Point Polynomial Methods in Convex Programming. (Miscellaneous Bks.: No. 13). ix, 405p. 1993. 68.50 (*0-89871-319-6*) Soc Indus-Appl Math.

Nestingen, Jan, ed. see Brandt, Betty.

Nestingen, Signe L. & Lewis, Laurel. Growing Beyond Abuse: A Workbook for Survivors of Sexual Exploitation or Childhood Sexual Abuse. 192p. 1991. 15.95 (*0-9628703-0-7*) Omni Recovery.

Nestle, Joan. A Restricted Country. LC 87-26671. 192p. (Orig.). 1987. lib. bdg. 20.95 (*0-932379-38-9*); pap. 9.95 (*0-932379-37-0*) Firebrand Bks.

Nestle, Joan, ed. The Persistent Desire: A Femme-Butch Reader. LC 92-6166. 503p. (Orig.). 1992. pap. 14.95 (*1-55583-190-7*) Alyson Pubns.

Nestle, Joan & Holoch, Naomi, eds. Women on Women: An Anthology of American Lesbian Short Fiction. 1990. pap. 11.95 (*0-452-26388-3*, Plume) NAL-Dutton.

Nestle, Joan & Preston, John. Sister & Brother: Lesbians & Gay Men Write about Their Lives Together. LC 94-9158. 356p. 1994. 22.00 (*0-06-251055-X*) Harper SF.

Nestle, Joan, jt. ed. see Holoch, Naomi.

Nestle, Marion. Nutrition in Clinical Practice. LC 85-60806. 330p. (Orig.). 1985. pap. 16.95 (*0-930010-11-6*) Jones Med.

Nestle, Walter. Die Struktur Des Eingangs in Der Attiscshen Tragodie. No. 10. viii, 133p. 1967. reprint ed. write for info. (*0-318-70984-8*, Pub. by Georg Olms GW) Lubrecht & Cramer.

Nestle, Wilhelm. Vom Mythos Zum Logos: Die Selbstentfaltung Des Griechischen Denkens Von Homer Bis Auf Die Sophistik und Sokrates. Bolle, Kees W., ed. LC 77-79147. (Mythology Ser.). (GER.). 1978. reprint ed. lib. bdg. 50.95 (*0-405-10556-8*) Ayer.

Nestlebaum, Chana. The Mookster's Mitzvah Mishaps. LC 91-75362. (Illus.). 32p. (J). (gr. k-4). 1991. 11.95 (*0-910818-26-6*); pap. 8.95 (*0-910818-27-4*) Judaica Pr.

Nestler, ed. Automated Testing of Electro-Optical Systems. 1988. 38.00 (*0-89252-976-8*, 941) SPIE.

Nestler, Eric J., jt. auth. see Hyman, Steven E.

Nestler, Harold. A Bibliography of New York State Communities. 3rd ed. 312p. 1990. pap. 20.00 (*1-55613-330-8*) Heritage Bk.

Nestmann, Frank & Hurrelman, Klaus, eds. Social Networks & Social Support in Childhood & Adolescence. LC 94-544. (Prevention & Intervention in Childhood & Adolescence Ser.: Vol. 16). xii, 441p. (C). 1994. lib. bdg. 84.95 (*3-11-014360-7*) De Gruyter.

Nestmann, Mark. How to Achieve Personal & Financial Privacy in a Public Age. 4th ed. 260p. reprint ed. pap. 68.00 (*0-9627953-1-3*) LPP.

—Privacy 1995. 208p. 1995. 100.00 (*3-9520851-0-3*, Pub. by W Beck Verlag SZ) Tattered Cover.
PRIVACY 1995, the first edition of the annually updated PRIVACY SERIES, documents GLOBAL SURVEILLANCE INFRASTRUCTURE that tracks assets & information across international borders & permits world governments to seize property & invade privacy. The PRIVACY SERIES exists because this infrastructure is complex, evolving, & demands rigorous & continuing research. ANYONE wishing to protect privacy & wealth must deal with global surveillance. Most privacy literature & "experts" in the LUCRATIVE asset protection industry pretend surveillance doesn't exist or claim that dealing with it requires full government disclosure. As a result, most asset protection plans are designed to protect wealth only from civil litigation--NOT world governments. The PRIVACY SERIES reveals alternatives that are LESS COMPLEX, LESS EXPENSIVE, require LITTLE OR NO DISCLOSURE & can be MUCH MORE EFFECTIVE. To purchase PRIVACY 1995 & ensure prompt automatic delivery of updates place a standing order with The Tattered Cover Bookstore (Business Section), 800-833-9327, ext. 250; FAX 303-399-2279. Wholesale orders by case only: 16 books, $960. Contact W. Beck Verlag, Bahnhofstrasse 52, CH-8001 Zurich; +41-1-214-6562; Facsimile: +41-1-214-6519, attention J. Bossert or M. Noser.
Publisher Provided Annotation.

Nestmann, Mark & Nelson, Paul. Corporate Espionage: How to Stop Thieves, Saboteurs & Spies from Bankrupting Your Business. (Orig.). 1991. pap. write for info. (*0-9627953-0-5*) LPP.

An Asterisk (*) at the beginning of an entry indicates that the title is appearing in BIP for the first time.

Nestor, Helen. Family Portraits in Changing Times. (Illus.). 144p. 1992. 39.95 (*0-939165-16-3*); pap. 22.95 (*0-939165-15-5*) NewSage Press.

Nestor-Iskander. Nestor-Iskander: The Tale of Constantinople (of Its Origin & Capture in the Year 1453) Hanak, Walter & Philippides, Marios, eds. Philippides, Marios, tr. (Late Byzantine & Ottoman Studies: No. 5). 192p. (ENG & SLA.). 1993. text ed. 60.00 (*0-89241-503-7*) Caratzas.

Nestor, J. J., Jr., jt. ed. see Vickery, B. H.

Nestor, Joanne P. & Glotzer, Judith A. Teaching Nutrition. 302p. 1981. pap. text ed. 20.00 (*0-89011-559-1*) Abt Bks.

Nestor, Joanne P. & Glotzer, Judith A., eds. Teaching Nutrition: A Review of Programs & Research. 302p. 1984. reprint ed. pap. text ed. 27.00 (*0-8191-4115-1*) U Pr of Amer.

Nestor, Larry, jt. auth. see Peterson, Gary.

Nestor, Lisa. Atoms & Molecules. (C). 1993. 7.75 (*1-56870-076-8*) RonJon Pub.

Nestor, Pauline. Charlotte Bronte's "Jane Eyre" LC 92-17623. (Critical Studies of Key Texts). 1992. text ed. 35.00 (*0-312-08423-4*); pap. 12.95 (*0-312-08601-6*) St Martin.

Nestor, Pauline, ed. Villette: Charlotte Bronte. LC 91-41407. (New Casebooks Ser.). 184p. 1992. text ed. 45.00 (*0-312-07909-5*) St Martin.

Nestorian Church Staff. Liturgy & Ritual: The Liturgy of the Holy Apostles Adai & Mari. LC 79-131032. reprint ed. 29.50 (*0-404-03997-9*) AMS Pr.

Nestorius Patriarch Of Constantinople. The Bazaar of Heracleides. Driver, G. R., tr. LC 77-84705. reprint ed. 42.00 (*0-404-16112-X*) AMS Pr.

Nestorova, Tatyana. American Missionaries among the Bulgarians: 1858-1912. 160p. 1987. text ed. 36.00 (*0-88033-114-3*, 218) East Eur Quarterly.

— Rise & Fall Soviet Union. 176p. 1993. per. 29.95 (*0-8403-8467-X*) Kendall-Hunt.

Nestrick, William V. Constructional Activities of Adult Males. LC 76-177115. (Columbia University. Teachers College. Contributions to Education Ser.: No. 780). reprint ed. 37.50 (*0-404-55780-5*) AMS Pr.

Nestroy, Johann. Der Talisman: Posse mit Gesang in drei Akten. Herles, Helmut, ed. 135p. (C). 1971. 15.25 (*3-11-001869-1*) De Gruyter.

Nestroy, Johann N. Johann Nestroy's Saemtliche Werke, 15 Vols, Set. Von Brukner, Fritz & Rommell, Otto, eds. LC 77-173072. reprint ed. 1,147.50 (*0-404-04690-8*) AMS Pr.

Nestyev, Israel V. Prokofiev. Jonas, Florence, tr. LC 60-11631. 111p. reprint ed. pap. 30.00 (*0-7837-1224-3*, 2041755) Bks Demand.

Netanyahu, B. The Origins of the Inquisition in Fifteenth Century Spain. LC 92-53643. 1995. 50.00 (*0-679-41065-1*) Random.

***Netanyahu, Benjamin.** Fighting Terrorism: How Democracies Can Defeat Domestic & International Terrorism. 150p. Date not set. 15.00 (*0-374-15492-9*) FS&G.

— A Place Among the Nations: Israel & the World. LC 92-43310. 1993. 24.95 (*0-553-08974-9*) Bantam.

Netanyahu, Benjamin, ed. International Terrorism: Challenge & Response. 383p. 1982. pap. 19.95 (*0-87855-894-2*) Transaction Pubs.

— Terrorism: How the West Can Win. 272p. 1987. mass mkt. 4.50 (*0-380-70321-1*) Avon.

Neter, E., ed. see International Convocation on Immunology Staff.

Neter, John, et al. Applied Linear Regression Models. 2nd ed. 688p. (C). 1988. text ed. 69.95 (*0-256-07068-7*) Irwin.

— Applied Linear Statistical Models. 3rd ed. 1184p. (C). 1990. text ed. 72.95 (*0-256-08338-X*) Irwin.

— Applied Statistics. 3rd ed. 1006p. (C). 1988. student ed 19.00 (*0-685-18748-9*, H03312); Instr's. manual. teacher ed write for info. (*0-205-10331-6*, H03296); boxed 56.00 (*0-205-10328-6*, H03288); write for info. (*0-318-62190-8*, H03304) Allyn.

— Applied Statistics. 4th ed. 1040p. (C). 1992. text ed. 61.00 (*0-205-13478-5*) Allyn.

Neterowicz, Eva M., jt. auth. see Bowers, Stephen R.

Neth, Mary C. Preserving the Family Farm: Women, Community, & the Foundations of Agribusiness in the Midwest, 1900-1940. (Revisiting Rural America Ser.). 272p. 1995. text ed. 39.95x (*0-8018-4898-9*) Johns Hopkins.

Neth, Michael, ed. The Hellas Notebook, Vol. XVI, No. E.7. LC 94-3196. (Bodleian Shelley Manuscripts). 322p. 1994. 165.00 (*0-8240-5874-7*) Garland.

Neth, Rolf, et al, eds. Modern Trends in Human Leukemia, No. VIII. (Haematology & Blood Transfusion Ser.: Vol. 32). (Illus.). 592p. 1990. pap. 181.00 (*0-387-50967-4*) Spr-Verlag.

— Modern Trends in Human Leukemia IX: New Results in Clinical & Biological Research Including Pediatric Oncology; Organized on Behalf of the Deutsche Gesellschaft fur Hamatologie und Onkologie, Wilsede, June 17-21, 1990. LC 92-2334. (Haematology & Blood Transfusion - Haematologie und Bluttransfusion Ser.: Vol. 35). (Illus.). 480p. 1992. 198.00 (*0-387-54360-0*); pap. 198.00 (*3-540-54360-0*) Spr-Verlag.

— Modern Trends in Human Leukemia Three. (Illus.). 1979. 85.20 (*0-387-08999-3*) Spr-Verlag.

Nethercot, Arthur H. First Five Lives of Annie Besant. LC 59-11624. (Illus.). 431p. reprint ed. pap. 122.90 (*0-8357-9645-0*, 2013621) Bks Demand.

— The Last Four Lives of Annie Beasant. LC 63-25862. 499p. reprint ed. pap. 142.30 (*0-317-28137-2*, 2024102) Bks Demand.

— Men & Supermen: The Shavian Portrait Gallery. 2nd ed. LC 65-16245. 1972. 23.95 (*0-405-08815-9*) Ayer.

Nethercot, D. A. Limit States Design of Structural Steelwork. 2nd ed. 296p. 1991. pap. write for info. (*0-412-39700-5*) Chapman & Hall.

Nethercott, Arthur H. Reputation of Abraham Cowley: Sixteen Sixty - Eighteen Hundred. (English Literature Ser.: No. 33). 1970. reprint ed. pap. 22.95 (*0-8383-0057-X*) M S G Haskell Hse.

— Reputation of the Metaphysical Poets During the Age of Johnson & the Romantic Revival. LC 72-98993. (English Literature Ser.: No. 33). 1970. reprint ed. pap. 22.95 (*0-8383-0058-8*) M S G Haskell Hse.

Netherland, et al. Perspectives in Introductory Biology. 7th ed. 160p. 1992. teacher ed, spiral bd. 17.95 (*0-88725-174-9*) Hunter Textbks.

Netherland, Eric, jt. auth. see Trampe, Greg.

Netherlands Institute for Law of the Sea Staff, ed. International Organizations & the Law of the Sea: Documentary Yearbook 1989. 800p. (C). 1991. lib. bdg. 254.50 (*0-7923-1201-5*) Kluwer Ac.

Netherlands Institute for the Law of the Sea (NILOS) Staff, ed. International Organizations & the Law of the Sea: Documentary Yearbook, 1987. (C). 1990. lib. bdg. 205.00 (*1-85333-162-7*) Kluwer Ac.

Netherlands Institute for the Law of the Sea Staff. International Organizations & the Law of the Sea: Documentary Yearbook 1992. 944p. (C). 1994. lib. bdg. 322.00 (*0-7923-2614-8*) Kluwer Ac.

Netherlands Institute for the Law of the Sea Staff, ed. International Organizations & the Law of the Sea: Documentary Yearbook 1985. 650p. 1987. lib. bdg. 202.50 (*90-247-3488-6*) Kluwer Ac.

— International Organizations & the Law of the Sea: Documentary Yearbook 1986. (C). 1988. lib. bdg. 215.00 (*1-85333-104-X*) Kluwer Ac.

— International Organizations & the Law of the Sea: Documentary Yearbook 1988. 680p. 1990. lib. bdg. 215.00 (*1-85333-455-3*, Pub. by Graham & Trotman UK) Kluwer Ac.

— International Organizations & the Law of the Sea: Documentary Yearbook, 1990. 752p. (C). 1992. lib. bdg. 247.00 (*0-7923-1600-2*) Kluwer Ac.

Netherlands, Ministry of Agriculture & Fisheries Staff & Nijdam, J., eds. Elsevier's Dictionary of Horticulture. 561p. (DAN, DUT, ENG, FRE, GER, ITA, LAT, SPA & SWE.). 1970. 161.75 (*0-444-40812-6*) Elsevier.

Netherly, Patricia J., jt. ed. see Henderson, John S.

Nethersole-Thompson, Desmond. The Oystercatcher. 1989. pap. 25.00 (*0-85263-949-X*, Pub. by Shire UK) St Mut.

Nethersole-Thompson, Desmond & Nethersole-Thompson, Maimie. Greenshanks. LC 78-67031. (Illus.). 1979. 27.50 (*0-931130-02-6*) Harrell Bks.

— Waders: Their Breeding Haunts & Watchers. (Illus.). 424p. 1991. text ed. 34.95 (*0-85661-042-9*, 784642, Pub. by Poyser UK) Acad Pr.

— Waders: Their Breeding Haunts & Watchers. (Illus.). 424p. 1991. 42.00 (*0-685-50063-2*, 784642) Acad Pr.

Nethersole-Thompson, Desmond & Watson, Adam. The Cairngorms. 324p. (C). 1986. 40.00 (*0-906664-12-8*, Pub. by Mercat Pr Bks UK) St Mut.

Nethersole-Thompson, Maimie, jt. auth. see Nethersole-Thompson, Desmond.

Netherton, Cliff. History of the Sport of Casting: Golden Years. LC 83-72846. (Illus.). 388p. 1983. lib. bdg. 24.95 (*0-9605960-2-X*); pap. 14.95 (*0-9605960-3-8*) Am Casting.

— History of the Sport of Casting: People, Events, Records, Tackle & Literature - Early Times. LC 81-65632. (Illus.). 404p. 1981. lib. bdg. 24.95 (*0-9605960-0-3*); pap. 14.95 (*0-9605960-1-1*) Am Casting.

Netherton, H. Eugene. Boy Meets Girl. 112p. (Orig.). 1975. pap. 2.00 (*0-686-31977-X*) Netherton.

— Will Drafting Explained. 84p. 1987. 9.95 (*0-318-21767-8*) Netherton.

Netherton, John. At the Water's Edge: Wading Birds of North America. LC 93-21365. 1994. 29.95 (*0-89658-233-7*) Voyageur Pr.

— Florida - A Guide to Nature & Photography. Badger, David, ed. LC 90-81715. (Illus.). 96p. 1990. 29.95 (*0-9620582-2-X*); pap. 19.95 (*0-9620582-1-1*) Cumberland Val Pr.

— Of Breath & Earth: A Book of Days. (Illus.). 120p. 1994. 14.95 (*0-87358-589-5*) Northland AZ.

— Tennessee: A Bicentennial Celebration. (Illus.). 128p. 1995. 39.95 (*1-56579-126-6*) Westcliffe Pubs Inc.

Netherton, John, photos. Radnor Lake: Nashville's Walden. LC 84-51576. (Illus.). 72p. 1985. reprint ed. 18.95 (*0-934395-17-9*) Rutledge Hill Pr.

Netherton, John & Duhl, David. A Guide to Photography & the Smoky Mountains. Badger, David, ed. LC 88-70895. (Illus.). 96p. (Orig.). 1988. pap. 17.95 (*0-9620582-0-3*) Cumberland Val Pr.

Netherton, John, jt. photos see Baker, Howard.

Netherton, Nan. Books & Beyond: Fairfax County Public Library's First Fifty Years. (Illus.). (Orig.). 1990. pap. 9.95 (*0-9623689-0-3*) Fairfax Cnty Pub Lib.

Netherton, Nan & Rose, Ruth P. Memories of Beautiful Burke, Virginia. LC 88-71085. (Illus.). 1988. 19.95 (*0-9620619-0-5*) Burke Hist Soc.

Netherton, Nan, et al. Fairfax County, Virginia: A History. LC 77-95356. (Illus.). 1978. 15.00 (*0-686-24339-0*) Fairfax County.

Netherton, Ross D. Fairfax County in Virginia: Pictorial History. 1989. 22.50 (*0-89865-319-3*) Donning Co.

Nethery, Mary. Hannah & Jack. LC 93-4651. (Illus.). (J). 1995. text ed. 15.95 (*0-02-768125-4*, Bradbury S&S) S&S Childrens.

Nethery, Susan, jt. auth. see McIlhaney, Joe S.

***Nethus, Marie, ed.** Video Forum: A Videography for Libraries: Latino Issue. 60p. Date not set. write for info. (*1-884188-02-8*) Nat Video.

Netifnet, Dadisi M. Poetry for Today's Young Black Revolutionary Minds. LC 91-66856. 102p. 1992. pap. 6.95 (*1-55523-479-8*) Winston-Derek.

Netland, Harold A. Dissonant Voices: Religious Pluralism & the Question of Truth. xii, 324p. (Orig.). 1991. pap. 14.99 (*0-8028-0602-3*) Eerdmans.

Neto, A. Lins, jt. auth. see Camacho, Cesar.

Neto-Advogados, Pinhiero, ed. Doing Business in Brazil. 1982. ring bd. 360.00 (*1-56425-008-3*) Transnatl Juris Pubns.

Neto, J. V. Dictionary of Telecommunications: Dicionario de Telecommunicacoes. 689p. (ENG & POR.). 1981. 75.00 (*0-8288-0184-3*, F45000) Fr & Eur.

***Neto, Jose R.** The Christianization of Pyrrhonism: Scepticism & Faith in Pascal, Kierkegaard & Shestov. LC 95-1251. (International Archives of the History of Ideas Ser.: Vol. 144). 1995. lib. bdg. write for info. (*0-7923-3381-0*) Kluwer Ac.

Neto, Jose R. & Maia Neto, Jose R. Macho de Assis, the Brazilian Pyrrhonian. LC 94-3008. (Studies in Romance Literatures: Vol. 5). 240p. 1994. 35.95 (*1-55753-051-3*) Purdue U Pr.

Neto, Teixeira A. Pomba-Gira: Enchantments to Invoke the Formidable Powers of the Female Messenger of the Gods. Dow, Carol L., tr. & intro. by. (Illus.). 63p. 1992. pap. 11.95 (*1-878738-04-6*) Tech Sacred.

Netravali, A. N., ed. Visual Communications Systems. LC 88-34726. (Illus.). 552p. 1989. text ed. 69.95 (*0-87942-250-5*, PC02410) Inst Electrical.

Netravali, A. N. & Haskell, B. G. Digital Pictures: Representation & Compression. LC 87-32722. (Applications of Communications Theory Ser.). 602p. 1988. 105.00 (*0-306-42791-5*, Plenum Pr) Plenum.

***Netravali, Arun N. & Haskell, Barry G.** Digital Pictures: Representation, Compression & Standards. 2nd ed. LC 94-42988. (Applications of Communications Theory Ser.). 686p. 1995. 95.00 (*0-306-44917-X*, Plenum Pr) Plenum.

Netsch, Dawn Clark, jt. auth. see Mandelker, Daniel R.

Netschert, Bruce C. The Mineral Foreign Trade of the United States in the Twentieth Century: A Study in Mineral Economics. Bruchey, Stuart, ed. LC 76-39836. (Nineteen Seventy-Seven Dissertations Ser.). (Illus.). 1977. lib. bdg. 47.95 (*0-405-09916-9*) Ayer.

Netschert, Bruce C. & Landsberg, Hans H. The Future Supply of the Major Metals: A Reconnaissance Survey. LC 61-18125. 71p. reprint ed. pap. 25.00 (*0-7837-3047-0*, 2042871) Bks Demand.

— The Future Supply of the Major Metals: A Reconnaissance Survey. LC 76-58923. (Resources for the Future Ser.). (Illus.). 65p. 1978. reprint ed. text ed. 49.75 (*0-8371-9472-5*, NEMM, Greenwood Pr) Greenwood.

Netschert, Bruce C. & Schurr, S. H. Atomic Energy Applications with Reference to Underdeveloped Countries: A Preliminary Survey. LC 57-1745. 143p. reprint ed. pap. 40.80 (*0-7837-3046-2*, 2042872) Bks Demand.

Netsell, Ronald. A Neurobiologic View of Speech Production & the Dysarthrias. (Illus.). 164p. (C). 1991. reprint ed. pap. text ed. 34.95 (*1-879105-25-X*, 0080) Singular Publishing.

Netsky, Ron. The Graphic Art of Harold Faye. LC 87-3223. (Illus.). 32p. (Orig.). 1987. pap. 3.50 (*0-943651-00-X*) Hudson Riv.

Nett, Louise M., jt. auth. see Petty, Thomas L.

Nettancourt, D. Incompatibility in Angiosperms. (Monographs on Theoretical & Applied Genetics: Vol. 3). 1977. 50.00 (*0-387-08112-7*) Spr-Verlag.

Nettel, Reginald. The Orchestra in England: A Social History. 1988. reprint ed. lib. bdg. 49.00 (*0-7812-0774-6*) Rprt Serv.

Nettel, S. Wave Physics: Oscillations Solitions & Chaos. 1992. 39.00 (*0-387-55715-6*) Spr-Verlag.

— Wave Physics: Oscillations, Solitons, Chaos. 272p. 1995. 39.00 (*3-540-58504-4*) Spr-Verlag.

— Wave Physics: Up to Solitons & Chaos. (Illus.). 260p. (C). 1992. text ed. 33.00 (*0-387-53295-1*) Spr-Verlag.

***Nettel, Stephen.** Wave Physics: Oscillations, Solitons, Chaos. 2nd enl. ed. 1994. write for info. (*0-387-58504-4*) Spr-Verlag.

Nettelbeck, Colin. Forever French: Exile in the United States, 1939-1945. 211p. 1992. 49.95 (*0-85496-632-3*) Berg Pubs.

Nettelbeck, Colin W., ed. War & Identity in France. 176p. 1987. pap. 15.50 (*0-423-51700-7*) Routledge Chapman & Hall.

Nettelbeck, F. A. Americruiser. 64p. (Orig.). 1984. pap. 8.95 (*0-317-11782-3*) Illuminati.

— Americruiser. deluxe limited ed. 64p. (Orig.). 1984. 20.00 (*0-317-13028-5*) Illuminati.

— Hands on a Mirror. 32p. (Orig.). 1987. 5.00 (*0-934301-09-3*) Inkblot Pubns.

Nettelbeck, T., jt. auth. see Bollard, J.

Nettelbeck, T., jt. ed. see Luszcz, M.

Nettels, Curtis P. Emergence of a National Economy, 1775-1815. LC 89-10649. (Economic History of the United States Ser.). 451p. 1977. reprint ed. pap. text ed. 20.95 (*0-87332-096-4*) M E Sharpe.

— The Money Supply of the American Colonies. 1972. 59.95 (*0-8490-0663-5*) Gordon Pr.

— Money Supply of the American Colonies Before 1720. LC 64-22242. (Library of Money & Banking History). 300p. 1964. reprint ed. 39.50 (*0-678-00061-1*) Kelley.

— Roots of American Civilization: A History of American Colonial Life. 2nd ed. LC 63-8707. (Illus.). reprint ed. write for info. (*0-89197-386-9*); reprint ed. pap. text ed. write for info. (*0-89197-925-5*) Irvington.

Nettels, Elsa. Language, Race & Social Class in Howells's America. LC 87-18895. 248p. 1988. text ed. 27.00 (*0-8131-1629-5*) U Pr of Ky.

Netten, Ann. A Positive Environment: Physical & Social Influences on People with Senile Dementia in Residential Care. LC 92-44396. 110p. 1993. 49.95 (*1-85742-107-8*, Pub. by Ashgate UK); pap. 23.95 (*1-85742-112-4*, Pub. by Ashgate UK) Ashgate Pub Co.

Netten, Ann & Beecham, Jeni. Costing Community Care: Theory & Practice. LC 93-16351. 180p. 1993. 58.95 (*1-85742-098-5*, Pub. by Ashgate UK); pap. 27.95 (*1-85742-102-7*, Pub. by Ashgate UK) Ashgate Pub Co.

Netter, Edith M., ed. Land Use Law: Issues for the Eighties, Pt. II. LC 81-83016. 341p. (Orig.). 1984. pap. 8.00 (*0-918286-36-0*) Planners Pr.

Netter, Frank H. Atlas of Human Anatomy. Colacino, Sharon, ed. LC 89-60477. (Illus.). 592p. 1989. 120.00 (*0-914168-18-5*); pap. text ed. 49.95 (*0-914168-19-3*) CIBA Med.

Netter, Frank H., illus. The C I B A Collection of Medical Illustrations, 12 bks., Set. Incl. Vol. 1, Pt. 1. Nervous System: Anatomy & Physiology. LC 53-2151. (Illus.). 1983. 50.00 (*0-914168-10-X*); Vol. 1, Pt. 2. Nervous System: Neurologic & Neuromuscular Disorders. LC 53-2151. 1986. 52.00 (*0-914168-11-8*); Vol. 2. Reproductive System. LC 53-2151. 1974. 47.50 (*0-914168-02-9*); Vol. 3, Pt. 1. Digestive System: Upper Digestive Tract. LC 53-2151. 1974. 39.00 (*0-914168-03-7*); Vol. 3, Pt. 2. Digestive System: Lower Digestive Tract. LC 53-2151. 1974. 41.00 (*0-914168-04-5*); Vol. 3, Pt. 3. Digestive System: Liver, Biliary Tract & Pancreas. LC 53-2151. 1974. 38.00 (*0-914168-05-3*); Vol. 4. Endocrine System & Selected Metabolic Diseases. LC 53-2151. 1974. 47.50 (*0-914168-06-1*); Vol. 5. Heart. LC 53-2151. 1974. 55.00 (*0-914168-07-X*); Vol. 6. Kidneys, Ureters & Urinary Bladder. LC 53-2151. 1974. 55.00 (*0-914168-08-8*); Vol. 7. Respiratory System. LC 53-2151. 1974. 55.00 (*0-914168-09-6*); Vol. 8, Pt. 1. Musculoskeletal System: Anatomy, Physiology & Metabolic Disorders. LC 53-2151. 1974. 55.00 (*0-914168-14-2*); Musculoskeletal System - Developmental Disorders, Tumors, Rheumatic Diseases & Joint Replacement. LC 53-2151. 1974. 58.50 (*0-914168-15-0*); Musculoskeletal System - Developmental Disorders, Tumors, Rheumatic Diseases & Joint Replacement. LC 53-2151. 1974. 58.50 (*0-914168-15-0*); LC 53-2151. (Illus.). 1974. Complete set. 475.00 (*0-914168-00-2*) CIBA Med.

Netter, Klaus, jt. ed. see Hiader, Hubert.

Netter, P., ed. Psychobiology: Psychophysiological & Psychohumoral Processes Combined. (Journal: Neuropsychobiology: Vol. 28, No. 1-2, 1993). (Illus.). 112p. 1993. pap. 108.00 (*3-8055-5853-8*) S Karger.

Netter, Thomas. Fasciculi Zizaniorium Magistri Johannis Wyclif Cum Tritico. Shirley, Walter W., ed. (Rolls Ser.: No. 5). 1972. reprint ed. 45.00 (*0-8115-1006-9*) Periodicals Srv.

Nettesheim, P., et al, eds. Morphology of Experimental Respiratory Carcinogenesis: Proceedings. LC 73-609398. (AEC Symposium Ser.). 500p. 1970. pap. 20.50 (*0-87079-277-6*, CONF-700501); fiche 9.00 (*0-87079-278-4*, CONF-700501) DOE.

Nettesheim, Paul, jt. auth. see Thomassen, David G.

Nettesheim, Paul, jt. auth. see Witschi, Hanspeter.

Nettheim, G., jt. auth. see Chisholm, R.

Netting, Ellen, et al. Social Work Macro-Practice. LC 92-18943. 279p. (C). 1993. text ed. 41.95 (*0-8013-0464-4*, 78281) Longman.

Netting, Robert M. Balancing on an Alp: Ecological Change & Continuity in a Swiss Mountain Community. LC 81-358. (Illus.). 436p. 1981. 64.95 (*0-521-23743-2*) Cambridge U Pr.

— Cultural Ecology. 2nd ed. (Illus.). 131p. (Orig.). 1986. pap. text ed. 9.50 (*0-88133-204-6*) Waveland Pr.

— Hill Farmers of Nigeria. LC 84-45539. (American Ethnological Society Monographs: No. 46). 1988. reprint ed. 37.50 (*0-404-62944-X*) AMS Pr.

— Smallholders, Householders: Farm Families & the Ecology of Intensive, Sustainable Agriculture. (Illus.). 416p. (C). 1993. 49.50 (*0-8047-2061-4*); pap. 16.95 (*0-8047-2102-5*) Stanford U Pr.

Nettl, Bruno. Blackfoot Musical Thought: Comparative Perspectives. LC 88-28450. (World Music Ser.). 210p. 1989. 21.00 (*0-87338-370-2*) Kent St U Pr.

— Cheremis Musical Styles. LC 60-64259. (Indiana University Folklore Institute Monograph Ser.: Vol. 14). 126p. reprint ed. pap. 36.00 (*0-317-09424-6*, 2050045) Bks Demand.

— Heartland Excursions: Ethnomusicological Reflections on Schools of Music. 168p. 1995. pap. text ed. 12.95 (*0-252-06468-2*) U of Ill Pr.

— Heartland Excursions: Ethnomusicological Reflections on Schools of Music. (Music in American Life Ser.). 1995. write for info. (*0-252-02135-5*) U of Ill Pr.

— Music in Primitive Culture. LC 56-8551. 220p. reprint ed. 62.70 (*0-8357-9167-X*, 2016730) Bks Demand.

— The Study of Ethnomusicology: Twenty-Nine Issues & Concepts. LC 82-7065. 424p. 1983. pap. 14.95 (*0-252-01039-6*) U of Ill Pr.

— The Study of Ethnomusicology: Twenty-Nine Issues & Concepts. LC 82-7065. 422p. reprint ed. pap. 120.30 (*0-8357-3554-0*, 2034454) Bks Demand.

— The Western Impact on World Music Change, Adaption, & Survival. 232p. 1985. write for info. (*0-317-46649-6*) Macmillan.

Nettl, Bruno, ed. Eight Urban Musical Cultures: Tradition & Change. LC 77-25041. (Illus.). 336p. 1978. 29.95 (*0-252-00208-3*) U of Ill Pr.

Nettl, Bruno & Bohlman, Philip V. Comparative Musicology & Anthropology of Music: Essays in the History of Ethnomusicology. (Chicago Studies in Ethnomusicology). (Illus.). 400p. 1991. pap. text ed. 18.95 (*0-226-57409-1*) U Ch Pr.

Nettl, Bruno & Foltin, Bela. Daramad of Chahargah: A Study in the Performance Practice of Persian Music. LC 74-175174. (Detroit Monographs in Musicology: No. 2). 84p. 1972. pap. 6.00 (0-911772-51-0) Info Coord.

Nettl, Bruno & Myers, Helen. Folk Music in the United States: An Introduction. exp. rev. ed. LC 76-84. 190p. 1976. pap. 13.95 (0-8143-1557-7) Wayne St U Pr.

Nettl, Bruno, jt. auth. see Blacking, John.

Nettl, Bruno, et al. Excursions in World Music. 304p. (C). 1991. pap. text ed. write for info. (0-13-299025-3) P-H.

— Folk & Traditional Music of the Western Continents. 3rd ed. 304p. 1989. pap. text ed. 33.33 (0-13-323247-6) P-H.

Nettl, P. Story of Dance Music. (Ballroom Dance Ser.). 1986. lib. bdg. 79.95 (0-8490-3253-9) Gordon Pr.

— Story of Dance Music. (Ballroom Dance Ser.). 1985. lib. bdg. 79.95 (0-87700-692-X) Revisionist Pr.

Nettl, Paul. The Beethoven Encyclopedia: His Life & Art from A to Z. LC 94-17636. 1994. 12.95 (0-8065-1539-2, Citadel Pr) Carol Pub Group.

— Beethoven Handbook. LC 75-33885. 335p. 1975. reprint ed. text ed. 38.50 (0-8371-8540-8, NEBH, Greenwood Pr) Greenwood.

— Book of Musical Documents. LC 73-88991. 381p. 1969. text ed. 65.00 (0-8371-2116-7, NEMD, Greenwood Pr) Greenwood.

— Mozart & Masonry. 1987. 16.95 (0-88029-159-1) Dorset Pr.

— Mozart & Masonry. LC 78-114564. (Music Ser.). 1970. reprint ed. lib. bdg. 25.00 (0-306-71922-3) Da Capo.

— The Other Casanova: A Contribution to Eighteenth-Century Music & Manners. LC 73-107872. (Music Ser.). (Illus.). 1970. reprint ed. lib. bdg. 39.50 (0-306-71896-0) Da Capo.

— Story of Dance Music. LC 77-88992. 370p. 1970. reprint ed. text ed. 35.00 (0-8371-2114-0, NEDM, Greenwood Pr) Greenwood.

Nettlau, M. La Premiere Internationale en Espagne. (Illus.). 683p. (FRE.). 1969. lib. bdg. 196.00 (90-277-0103-2) Kluwer Ac.

Nettlau, Max. Anarchism in England One Hundred Years Ago. 1971. 59.95 (0-8490-1422-0) Gordon Pr.

— Anarchy Through the Times. Johnson, Scott, tr. 1978. lib. bdg. 300.00 (0-8490-1397-6) Gordon Pr.

— History of Anarchism, 3 vols., Set. (Men & Movements in the History & Philosophy of Anarchism Ser.). 1978. lib. bdg. 900.00 (0-685-57774-0) Revisionist Pr.

— The Unfolding of Anarchism: Its Origins & Historical Development to the Year 1864. (Men & Movements in the History & Philosophy of Anarchism Ser.). 1978. lib. bdg. 49.95 (0-685-06650-9) Revisionist Pr.

Nettleford, Rex. Caribbean Cultural Identity: The Case of Jamaica. (Afro-American Culture & Society Monograph Ser.: Vol. 1). (Illus.). 239p. 1978. 15.95 (0-934934-00-2) UCLA CAAS.

Nettleford, Rex, ed. Jamaica in Independence: Essays on the Early Years. 364p. (C). 1991. pap. text ed. 19.95 (976-605-094-5, 00685, Pub. by Heinemann Pubs JM) Heinemann.

Nettleford, Rex, jt. ed. see Hyatt, Vera L.

Nettler. Criminal Careers, 3 vols. Incl. Vol. 1. Explaining Criminals. 220p. 1982. 16.95 (0-87084-600-0); Vol. 3. Lying, Cheating, Stealing. 143p. 1982. pap. 15.95 (0-87084-602-7); Vol. 4. Responding to Crime. 191p. 1982. 16.95 (0-87084-603-5); 1982. write for info. (0-685-10468-0) Anderson Pub Co.

Nettler, Gwynn. Criminology Lessons: Arguments about Crime, Punishment, & the Interpretation of Conduct, with Advice for Individuals & Prescriptions for Public Policy. LC 88-71498. (Illus.). 342p. (Orig.). (C). 1988. pap. text ed. 26.95 (0-87084-604-3) Anderson Pub Co.

Nettler, Gwynne. The Relationship Between Attitude & Information Concerning the Japanese in America. Zuckerman, Harriet & Merton, Robert K., eds. LC 79-9016. (Dissertations on Sociology Ser.). 1980. lib. bdg. 21.95 (0-405-12984-X) Ayer.

— Responding to Crime. (Criminal Careers Ser.: Vol. 4). 200p. 1982. pap. 16.95 (0-685-49833-6) Anderson Pub Co.

Nettler, Ronald L. Past Trials & Present Tribulations: A Muslim Fundamentalist's View of the Jews. LC 87-9313. (SIAS Ser.). 100p. 1987. 28.00 (0-08-034791-6, Pergamon Pr) Elsevier.

Nettles, Bea. Breaking the Rules: A Photo Media Cookbook. 3rd ed. LC 77-12930. (Illus.). 64p. (C). 1992. pap. text ed. 12.50 (0-930810-08-2) Inky Pr.

— Flamingo in the Dark: Images. (Orig.). 1979. 35.00 (0-930810-01-5) Inky Pr.

— Knights of Assisi: A Journey Through the Tarot. (Illus.). 24p. (Orig.). 1990. pap. 10.00 (0-930810-06-6) Inky Pr.

— Life's Lessons: A Mother's Journal. (Illus.). 72p. (Orig.). 1990. pap. 15.00 (0-930810-05-8) Inky Pr.

— Skirted Garden: Nineteen Seventy to Nineteen Ninety. (Illus.). 80p. (Orig.). 1990. pap. 5.00 (0-930810-04-X) Inky Pr.

Nettles, Bea, photos & text. Complexities. (Illus.). 48p. (Orig.). 1992. pap. 15.00 (0-930810-07-4) Inky Pr.

— Grace's Daughter. (Illus.). 48p. (Orig.). 1994. pap. 8.00 (0-930810-09-0) Inky Pr.

— Turning Fifty. (Illus.). 64p. (Orig.). 1995. pap. 10.00 (0-930810-11-2) Inky Pr.

Nettles, Bea, jt. auth. see Nettles, Grace.

Nettles, Gala, jt. auth. see Freeman, Bill.

Nettles, Grace & Nettles, Bea. Corners. (Illus.). 104p. 1989. pap. 14.95 (0-930810-03-1) Inky Pr.

Nettles, Jack, jt. auth. see McNellis, Jerry.

Nettles, John. Bergerac's Jersey. (Illus.). 156p. 1992. pap. 17.95 (0-563-36178-6, BBC-Parkwest) Parkwest Pubns.

— John Nettles Jersey: A Personal History of the People & Places. (Illus.). 240p. 1993. 29.95 (0-563-36318-5, BBC-Parkwest) Parkwest Pubns.

Nettles, Joseph E. So Beloved Cousins: The Life & Times of Solon B. Cousins, Jr. LC 82-23986. x, 178p. 1983. 12.95 (0-86554-070-5, H53) Mercer Univ Pr.

Nettles, Michael T., ed. The Effect of Assessment on Minority Student Participation. LC 85-645339. (New Directions for Institutional Research Ser.: No. IR 65). 1990. 16.95 (1-55542-828-2) Jossey-Bass.

— Equity & Excellence in Educational Testing & Assessment. (Evaluation in Education & Human Services Ser.). 400p. (C). 1994. lib. bdg. 69.95 (0-7923-9531-X) Kluwer Ac.

— Toward Black Undergraduate Student Equality in American Higher Education. LC 87-24956. (Contributions to the Study of Education Ser.: No. 25). 240p. 1988. text ed. 55.00 (0-313-25616-0, NBK/, Greenwood Pr) Greenwood.

***Nettles, Sarah A.** Growing up with E. Z. Mezure: E. Z. Makes Measuring Easy! (Illus.). (Orig.). (J). (gr. 3-5). Date not set. pap. text ed. 8.50 (1-882293-06-1) Activity Resources.

Nettles, Thomas J. By His Grace & for His Glory: A Historical, Theological, & Practical Study of the Doctrines of Grace in Baptist Life. LC 85-71180. 442p. 1991. pap. text ed. 14.99 (0-8010-6742-1) Baker Bk.

Nettleship, David N. & Birkhead, Tim R., eds. The Atlantic Alcidae: The Evolution, Distribution & Biology of the Auks Inhabiting the Atlantic Ocean & Adjacent Water Areas. 1986. text ed. 108.00 (0-12-515670-7); pap. text ed. 39.95 (0-12-515671-5) Acad Pr.

Nettleship, E. N., et al, eds. Seabirds on Islands: Threats, Case Studies & Action Plans. (Birdlife Conservation Ser.). (Illus.). 350p. 1994. pap. 32.00 (1-56098-526-7) Smithsonian.

Nettleship, H., ed. see Persius Flaccus, Aulus.

Nettleship, Henry. Lectures & Essays, Second Series. Haverfield, F., ed. LC 72-336. (Essay Index Reprint Ser.). 1977. reprint ed. 23.95 (0-8369-2812-1) Ayer.

Nettleship, Henry, ed. see Vergilius.

Nettleship, Martin, jt. ed. see Givens, R. Dale.

Nettleship, Martin A., et al, eds. War, Its Causes & Correlates. (World Anthropology Ser.). (Illus.). xviii, 814p. 1975. 82.35 (90-279-7659-7) Mouton.

Nettleship, R. L., ed. see Green, Thomas H.

Nettleship, Richard L. Theory of Education in the Republic of Plato. LC 68-54676. (Classics in Education Ser.). 1968. pap. text ed. 6.00 (0-8077-1849-1) Tchrs Coll.

***Nettleton, Asahel.** Asahel Nettleton: Sermons from the Second Great Awakening. 500p. 1995. 35.95 (0-9641803-3-2) Internat Outreach.

Nettleton, D. H., jt. ed. see Fox, N. P.

Nettleton, David. Chosen to Salvation: Select Thoughts on the Doctrine of Election. LC 83-11062. 180p. 1984. pap. 5.95 (0-87227-094-7) Reg Baptist.

Nettleton, George H. Yale in the World War, 2 vols. 1925. 300.00 (0-685-40002-6) Elliots Bks.

Nettleton, George H., ed. Specimens of the Short Story. LC 75-94740. (Short Story Index Reprint Ser.). 1977. 19.95 (0-8369-3120-3) Ayer.

Nettleton, George H. & Case, Arthur E., eds. British Dramatists from Dryden to Sheridan. 2nd ed. LC 75-2443. 975p. (C). 1975. pap. 30.00 (0-8093-0743-X) S Ill U Pr.

Nettleton, Joyce A. Omega-3 Fatty Acids & Health. LC 94-20759. 1994. write for info. (0-412-98861-5, Chap & Hall NY) Chapman & Hall.

Nettleton, L. L. Gravity & Magnetics for Geologists & Seismologists. (Geophysical Monograph Ser.: No. 1). 121p. 1971. pap. 6.00 (0-931830-10-9, 481) Soc Expl Geophys.

Nettleton, Lewis L. Gravity & Magnetics in Oil Prospecting. LC 75-17899. (McGraw-Hill International Series in the Earth & Planetary Sciences). 480p. reprint ed. pap. 136.80 (0-317-10446-2, 2051921) Bks Demand.

Nettleton, M. A. Gaseous Detonations: Their Nature, Causes & Control. 250p. 1987. 77.50 (0-412-27040-4, 1150) Chapman & Hall.

Nettleton, Myrtle. History of the Kauffman & Harrison Families. 141p. 1983. 9.95 (0-87770-294-2) Ye Galleon.

Nettleton, Sarah. Power, Pain & Dentistry. 192p. 1992. 90.00 (0-335-09723-5, Open Univ Pr); pap. 32.00 (0-335-09722-7, Open Univ Pr) Taylor & Francis.

— The Sociology of Health & Illness. 280p. (C). 1995. 54.95 (0-7456-0893-0); pap. 22.95 (0-7456-0894-9) Blackwell Pubs.

Netto, C. & Wagener, G. Japanischer Humor. (Asian Folklore & Social Life Monographs: No. 34). (GER.). 1901. 18.00 (0-89986-034-6) Oriental Bk Store.

***Netton.** Popular Dictionary of Islam. LC 92-13600. 1992. pap. 18.50 (0-7007-0233-4, Pub. by Curzon Pr UK) Humanities.

Netton, Ian R. Al-Farabi & His School. LC 91-42233. (Arabic Thought & Culture Ser.). 208p. 1992. 62.50 (0-415-03594-5, A7566); pap. 16.95 (0-415-03595-3, A7570) Routledge.

— Allah Transcendant: Studies in the Structure & Semiotics of Islamic Philosophy, Theology & Cosmology. 448p. (C). 1994. pap. 29.95 (0-7007-0287-3, Pub. by Curzon Pr UK) Humanities.

— Muslim Neoplatonism. 1991. pap. text ed. 25.00 (0-7486-0251-8, Pub. by Edinburgh U Pr UK) Col U Pr.

— A Popular Dictionary of Islam. LC 92-13600. 244p. 1992. pap. 18.50 (0-391-03756-0) Humanities.

— Seek Knowledge: Thought & Travel in the House of Islam. 150p. (C). 1996. text ed. 49.95 (0-7007-0339-X, Pub. by Curzon Pr UK); pap. 17.50 (0-7007-0340-3, Pub. by Curzon Pr UK) Humanities.

— Text & Trauma: An East-West Primer. 268p. (C). 1995. text ed. 59.95 (0-7007-0325-X, Pub. by Curzon Pr UK); pap. 19.95 (0-7007-0326-8, Pub. by Curzon Pr UK) Humanities.

Netton, Ian R., ed. Golden Roads: Migration, Pilgrimage & Travel in Medieval & Modern Islam. 288p. (C). 1993. pap. 29.95 (0-7007-0243-1, Pub. by Curzon Pr UK) Humanities.

— Middle East Materials in United Kingdom & Irish Libraries: A Directory: a MELCOM Guide to Libraries & Other Institutions in Britain & Ireland with Islamic & Middle Eastern Books & Materials. LC 82-23574. 136p. reprint ed. pap. 38.80 (0-7837-5318-7, 2045057) Bks Demand.

Network Development & MARC Standards Office. USMARC Format for Community Information: Including Guidelines for Content Designation. LC 92-45199. 1993. write for info. (0-8444-0779-8) Lib Congress.

Network Development & MARC Standards Office Staff. USMARC Format for Authority Data: Including Guidelines for Content Designation. LC 93-26502. 1993. write for info. (0-8444-0802-6) Lib Congress.

Network Development & MARC Standards Office Staff, ed. USMARC Code List for Geographic Areas. LC 94-9550. 1994. write for info. (0-8444-0812-3) Lib Congress.

Network Development Staff & MARC Standards Office Staff. USMARC Code List for Relators, Sources, Description Conventions. LC 93-30404. 1993. write for info. (0-8444-0806-9) Lib Congress.

***Network Development Staff & MARC Standards Office Staff, eds.** Format Integration & Its Effect on the USMARC Bibliographic Format. LC 94-49541. 1995. pap. write for info. (0-8444-0873-5) Lib Congress.

Network Management Forum. Discovering Omnipoint: A Common Approach to the Integrated Management of Networked Information. LC 92-82680. 224p. (C). 1993. pap. text ed. 32.00 (0-13-106121-6) P-H.

Network of Egyptian Professional Women Staff. Egyptian Women in Social Development: A Resource Guide. 550p. 1988. pap. 35.00 (977-424-184-3, Pub. by Am Univ Cairo Pr UA) Col U Pr.

Netzel, Sally. Alice in Wonderland - the Musical. (Stage Magic Play Ser.). (Illus.). 56p. (Orig.). 1991. pap. 4.00 (0-88680-342-X); 15.00 (0-88680-343-8) I E Clark.

— Cinderella. (Illus.). 32p. (J). (ps up). 1981. pap. 3.00 (0-88680-028-5) I E Clark.

— The Dark Castle. (Illus.). 27p. (Orig.). 1993. pap. 4.00 (0-88680-379-9); 40.00 (0-685-66606-9) I E Clark.

— Puss in Boots. (Illus.). 32p. (J). (gr. k up). 1979. pap. 3.50 (0-88680-157-5) I E Clark.

Netzer, A. Ambrose. How to Parent Carefully: A Handbook on Parenting & Self Care. LC 85-70262. (Illus.). 146p. (Orig.). 1985. pap. 9.95 (0-9614588-0-1) Center Creative Life.

***Netzer, Carol.** Cutoffs: How Family Members Who Sever Relationships Can Reconnect. 256p. 1995. pap. 13.95 (0-88282-138-5) New Horizon NJ.

Netzer, Corinne T. Brand Name Calorie Counter. 1991. mass mkt. 4.99 (0-440-21109-3) Dell.

— Cholesterol Content of Food. rev. ed. 1992. mass mkt. 4.50 (0-440-20739-8) Dell.

— Complete Book of Food Counts. 1991. mass mkt. 6.99 (0-440-21271-5) Dell.

— Corinne T. Netzer Carbohydrate Gram Counter. 1994. mass mkt. 4.99 (0-440-21665-6) Dell.

— Corinne T. Netzer Dieter's Diary. 1992. mass mkt. 6.95 (0-440-50410-4) Dell.

— Corinne T. Netzer Encyclopedia of Food Values. 1992. pap. 25.00 (0-440-50367-1) Dell.

— Corinne T. Netzer Fat Gram Counter. 1992. mass mkt. 4.99 (0-440-20740-1) Dell.

— Corinne T. Netzer Low-Fat Diary. 1995. pap. 6.95 (0-440-50695-6) Dell.

— Corinne T. Netzer 1995 Calorie Counter. 1995. pap. 4.99 (0-440-21760-1) Dell.

— Corinne T. Netzer's, 3 vols. 1990. boxed 12.85 (0-440-36012-9) Dell.

— Dieter's Calorie Counter. 3rd ed. 1992. mass mkt. 8.99 (0-440-50321-3, Dell Trade Pbks) Dell.

— Fiber Counter. 1994. mass mkt. 4.50 (0-440-21483-1) Dell.

— One Hundred & One Low Calorie Recipes. 1993. mass mkt. 8.99 (0-440-50416-3) Dell.

— One Hundred & One Low Cholesterol Recipes. 1993. mass mkt. 8.99 (0-440-50417-1) Dell.

— One Hundred & One Low Sodium Recipes. 1993. mass mkt. 8.99 (0-440-50419-8) Dell.

— One Hundred & One Vegetarian Recipes. LC 93-46366. (Corinne T. Netzer Good Eating Ser.). 1994. text ed. 8.99 (0-440-50597-6) Dell.

— One Hundred One High Fiber Recipes. 1993. mass mkt. 8.99 (0-440-50420-1) Dell.

— One Hundred One High Fiber Recipes. large type ed. (Good Eating Ser.). 1993. 20.95 (1-56895-026-8) Wheeler Pub.

— One Hundred One Low Fat Recipes. 1993. mass mkt. 9.99 (0-440-50418-X) Dell.

Netzer, David W., jt. ed. see Jensen, Gordon E.

Netzer, Dick. Economics of the Property Tax. LC 65-28602. (Studies of Government Finance). 344p. reprint ed. pap. 98.10 (0-685-16229-X, 2056253) Bks Demand.

Netzer, Dick, jt. ed. see Bellush, Jewel.

Netzer, Nancy. Cultural Interplay in the Eighth Century: The Trier Gospels & the Makings of a Scriptorium at Echternach. LC 93-17800. (Studies in Palaeography & Codicology: No. 3). (Illus.). 282p. (C). 1994. 64.95 (0-521-41255-2) Cambridge U Pr.

— Medieval Objects in the Museum of Fine Arts, Boston: Metalwork. (Illus.). 200p. 1991. pap. 24.95 (0-87846-327-5) Mus Fine Arts Boston.

Netzer, Nancy & Swarzenski, Hanns. Medieval Objects in the Museum of Fine Arts, Boston: Medieval Enamels & Glass. Spear, Judy, ed. LC 85-63531. (Illus.). 171p. 1986. 40.00 (0-87846-263-5); pap. 17.50 (0-87846-274-0) Mus Fine Arts Boston.

Netzer, Roland L. Echoes from the Hills, Vol. I: A Defined Guide to Country Sayings. LC 90-80819. 350p. 1990. write for info. (0-9625768-0-8) Echo Pub MO.

Netzhammer, Beverly S., jt. auth. see Lerner, B. Rosie.

Netzley, Patricia D. The Assassination of President John F. Kennedy. LC 93-20818. (American Events Ser.). (Illus.). 96p. (J). (gr. 6 up). 1994. text ed. 14.95 (0-02-768127-0, New Dscvry Bks) Silver Burdett Pr.

Netzorg, Morton J. Backward, Turn Backward: A Study of Books for Children in the Philippines, 1866-1945. (Illus.). xx, 246p. 1985. 22.50 (971-08-2402-3, Pub. by Natl Bk Store PH); pap. 15.00 (0-318-18464-8, Pub. by Natl Bk Store PH) Cellar.

Neu, jt. auth. see Ellner.

***Neu, et al.** New Macrolides, Azalides & Streptogramin in Clinical Practice. (Infectious Disease & Therapy Ser.). 656p. 1995. write for info. (0-8247-9311-0) Dekker.

— The New Macrolides, Azalides, & Streptogramins: Pharmacology & Clinical Applications. (Infectious Disease & Therapy Ser.: Vol. 8). 248p. 1993. 125.00 (0-8247-9038-3) Dekker.

Neu, C. R., jt. auth. see Steiner, Andrea.

Neu, Charles E. The Troubled Encounter: The United States & Japan. LC 79-4541. 272p. 1979. reprint ed. pap. 17.00 (0-88275-951-5) Krieger.

— An Uncertain Friendship: Theodore Roosevelt & Japan, 1906-1909. LC 67-27091. 357p. reprint ed. pap. 101.80 (0-7837-4172-3, 2059021) Bks Demand.

Neu, Charles E., jt. ed. see Cooper, John M., Jr.

Neu, Clyde W., jt. auth. see Redinbaugh, Larry D.

Neu, Elisabeth, tr. see Van Dulmen, Richard.

Neu, H. & Bain, D., eds. National Energy Planning & Management in Developing Countries. 1983. lib. bdg. 131.50 (90-277-1589-0) Kluwer Ac.

Neu, H. C., ed. Fosfomycin Trometamol Single Dose: Significance & Management of Lower UTI's - Journal: Chemotherapy, Vol. 36, Suppl. 1, 1990. (Illus.). iv, 56p. 1990. pap. 17.00 (3-8055-5325-0) S Karger.

Neu, H. C. & Reeves, D. S., eds. Ciprofloxacin: Microbiology-Pharmacokinetics-Clinical Experience. (Current Topics in Infectious Diseases & Clinical Microbiology Ser.: Vol. 1). viii, 132p. (C). 1986. pap. 26.00 (3-528-07938-X, Pub. by Vieweg & Sohn GW) Ballen Bkslr.

Neu, H. C. & Sabath, L. D., eds. Ein Praktischer Leitfaden fuer die Therapeutische Anwendung von Cefotiam. (Pharmanual Ser.: Vol. 3). (Illus.). vi, 182p. 1983. pap. 45.00 (3-8055-3694-1) S Karger.

Neu, H. C. & Williams, J. D., eds. New Trends in Urinary Tract Infections. (Illus.). x, 358p. 1988. 197.00 (3-8055-4637-8) S Karger.

Neu, H. C., ed. see International Ciprofloxacin Workshop Staff.

Neu, Harold C., ed. New Antibacterial Strategies. (Illus.). 340p. (Orig.). 1991. pap. text ed. 66.00 (0-443-04448-1) Churchill.

Neu, Harold C., jt. ed. see Welton, Andrew.

Neu, Irene D. Erastus Corning, Merchant & Financier: 1794-1872. LC 77-22015. (Illus.). 212p. 1977. reprint ed. text ed. 38.50 (0-8371-9791-0, NEEC, Greenwood Pr) Greenwood.

Neu, Irene D., jt. auth. see Taylor, George.

Neu, Jerome, ed. The Cambridge Companion to Freud. (Companions to Philosophy Ser.). 350p. (C). 1991. pap. 18.95 (0-521-37779-X) Cambridge U Pr.

Neu, John, ed. ISIS Cumulative Bibliography, 1966-1975, Vol. 1: Personalities & Institutions. 514p. 1980. text ed. 200.00 (0-7201-1515-9, Mansell Pub) Cassell.

— ISIS Cumulative Bibliography, 1966-1975, Vol. 2: Subjects, Periods & Civilizations. 720p. 1985. text ed. 200.00 (0-7201-1516-7, Mansell Pub) Cassell.

Neu, John, jt. auth. see Lindsay, Robert O.

Neu, John, jt. ed. see Lindsay, Robert O.

Neu, John, et al, eds. Chemical, Medical, & Pharmaceutical Books Printed Before 1800: In the Collections of the University of Wisconsin Libraries. 288p. 1965. 27.50 (0-299-03680-4) U of Wis Pr.

Neu, Lynn. Seeking Justice. (Discovering Program Ser.). (Illus.). 75p. (Orig.). 1990. text ed. 2.80 (0-88489-208-5); teacher ed 6.00 (0-88489-209-3) St Marys.

Neubacher, G. Little Red Riding Hood. (Traditional Fairy Tales Ser.). (Illus.). 32p. (J). (gr. 1-4). 1989. lib. bdg. 6.95 (0-88625-214-8) Durkin Hayes Pub.

Neubacher, Gerda. Tales from the Beechy Woods: Fluff's Birthday. (Illus.). 32p. (J). (ps-00). 1983. 10.95 (0-88625-044-7) Durkin Hayes Pub.

Neubart, Jack. Industrial Photography. (Illus.). 144p. 1989. pap. 22.50 (0-8174-4017-8, Amphoto) Watsn-Guptill.

— The Photographer's Guide to Exposure. (Illus.). 144p. 1988. pap. 18.95 (0-8174-5424-1, Amphoto) Watsn-Guptill.

Neubauer, A. D. Catalogue of the Hebrew Manuscripts in the Bodleian Library & in the College Libraries of Oxford, Vol. I. 624p. 1995. 130.00 (0-19-951357-0) OUP.

Neubauer, Adolphe. La Geographie Du Talmud. xl, 468p. 1967. reprint ed. write for info. (0-318-71381-0, Pub. by Georg Olms GW) Lubrecht & Cramer.

Neubauer, Alexander. Conversations on Writing Fiction: Interviews with 13 Distinguished Teachers of Fiction Writing in America. LC 93-25533. (Illus.). 256p. (Orig.). 1994. pap. 12.00 (0-06-273223-4, Harper Ref) HarpC.

***Neubauer, David W.** America's Court & the Criminal Justice System. 5th ed. LC 95-2518. 1996. text ed. 44.95 (0-534-23952-8) Intl Thomson.

An Asterisk (*) at the beginning of an entry indicates that the title is appearing in BIP for the first time.

— America's Courts & the Criminal Justice System. 4th ed. LC 91-32391. 489p. (C). 1992. text ed. 44.95 (*0-534-15432-8*) Intl Thomson.

— Judicial Process: Law, Courts, & Politics in the United States. LC 90-49598. 452p. (C). 1991. text ed. 33.95 (*0-534-15384-4*) Intl Thomson.

Neubauer, F., jt. ed. see Von Raumer, J. F.

Neubauer, F. F. Portfolio Management: The Concept of Profit Potentials; Its Application. 3rd ed. 110p. 1990. 52.00 (*90-6544-500-5*) Kluwer Law Tax Pubs.

Neubauer, Franz-Freidrich, jt. auth. see Demb, Ada.

Neubauer, Fred, jt. auth. see Lessem, Ronnie.

Neubauer, Glennon H. Real Estate's Ambiguous Language: You Ought'a Understand. LC 92-74245. 112p. 1993. pap. 14.95 (*1-882399-19-6*) Ethos Grp Pub.

Neubauer, Joan R. From Memories to Manuscript: The Five Step Method of Writing Your Life Story. LC 93-43942. 32p. 1994. 7.95 (*0-916489-56-6*) Ancestry.

Neubauer, John A. The Emancipation of Music. LC 85-14355. 264p. 1986. 32.00 (*0-300-03577-2*) Yale U Pr.

Neubauer, Karl W. European Library Networks. LC 89-37179. 448p. (C). 1990. text ed. 75.00 (*0-89391-157-7*) Ablex Pub.

Neubauer, Patricia. Beneath Bare Cherry Trees: Haiku for Winter. LC 87-90531. (Illus.). 56p. (Orig.). 1987. 45.00 (*0-9617265-2-0*); pap. 15.00 (*0-9617265-3-9*) Neubauer Pr.

— Beneath Bare Cherry Trees: Haiku for Winter. limited ed. LC 87-90531. (Illus.). 56p. (Orig.). 1987. write for info. (*0-9617265-4-7*) Neubauer Pr.

— Leaves & Wind Chimes: Haiku for Autumn. LC 86-90529. (Illus.). 50p. (Orig.). 1986. write for info. (*0-9617265-0-4*); pap. 15.00 (*0-9617265-1-2*) Neubauer Pr.

Neubauer, Peter, jt. ed. see Solnit, Albert J.

Neubauer, Peter B. Nature's Thumbprint: The Role of Genetics in Human Development. 1990. 17.26 (*0-201-09254-9*) Addison-Wesley.

Neubauer, Peter B., jt. auth. see Eissler, Ruth S.

Neubauer, Peter B., jt. auth. see Flapan, Dorothy.

***Neubauer, Raymond L.** The Visionary Universe: A Prophecy. (Illus.). 273p. (Orig.). 1995. pap. 8.95 (*0-914220-00-4*, A441941) Bay Rainbows Pr.

Neubauer, Richard E. The Intelligent Building Sourcebook. LC 85-45877. 350p. 1987. text ed. 68.00 (*0-88173-019-X*) Fairmont Pr.

Neubauer, Russell H. Naturally Occuring Biological Immunosuppressive Factors & Their Relationship to Disease. 304p. 1979. 113.95 (*0-8493-5243-6*, RC268, CRC Reprint) Franklin.

Neubauer, William. Nurse March. large type ed. 1991. 18.95 (*0-7927-0741-9*, CH021, Curley Lrg Print); pap. 16.95 (*0-7927-0742-7*, CS0127, Curley Lrg Print) Chivers N Amer.

Neubeck, Deborah K. Guide to the Microfilm Edition of The Frank B. Kellogg Papers. LC 78-63612. 56p. 1978. pap. 2.00 (*0-87351-126-3*) Minn Hist.

***Neubeck, Ken.** A-10 "Mini" in Action. (Mini in Action Ser.). (Illus.). 50p. 1995. pap. 5.95 (*0-89747-335-3*) Squad Sig Pubns.

***Neubeck, Kenneth J. & Glasberg, Davita S.** Sociology: A Critical Approach. LC 95-2208. 1995. write for info. (*0-07-046315-8*) McGraw.

***Neubecker, Otfried.** Grosses Wappen-Bilder-Lexikon. 2nd ed. 1147p. (GER.). 1992. 150.00 (*0-7859-8544-1*, 3894410302) Fr & Eur.

Neubecker, Ottfried. German & French for Heraldry: Deutsch und Franzoesisch Fuer Heraldiker. 108p. (FRE & GER.). 1983. 59.95 (*0-8288-1480-5*, M15253) Fr & Eur.

— Wappen-Bilder-Lexikon: German, French & English. 418p. (ENG, FRE & GER.). 1974. 49.95 (*0-7859-8519-0*, 3870450223) Fr & Eur.

Neubecker, William, ed. Antique Auto Body Metal Work for the Restorer. LC 82-62579. (Vintage Craft Ser.: No. 1). (Illus.). 1969. pap. 6.95 (*0-911160-01-9*) Post Group.

Neuber, Keith A., et al. Needs Assessment: A Model for Community Planning. (Human Services Guides Ser.: Vol. 14). 107p. 1980. pap. 17.95 (*0-8039-1396-6*) Sage.

***Neuberg.** Triumph of Pan, Vol. 1. 1995. 45.00 (*1-871438-55-1*) Atrium Pubs.

Neuberg, Leland G. Conceptual Anomalies in Economics & Statistics: Lessons from the Social Experiment. (Illus.). 475p. 1989. 79.95 (*0-521-30444-X*) Cambridge U Pr.

***Neuberg, Roger.** Obstetrics: A Practical Manual. (Illus.). 256p. 1995. pap. 35.00 (*0-19-263007-5*) OUP.

Neuberger, A. & Brocklehurst, K., eds. Hydrolytic Enzymes. (New Comprehensive Biochemistry Ser.: Vol. 16). 436p. 1988. 123.00 (*0-444-80886-8*) Elsevier.

Neuberger, A. & Van Deenen, L. L. Comprehensive Biochemistry, Section 6: History of Biochemistry, Vols. 30-32. Incl. Vol. 30. Pt. 1: Proto-Biochemistry; Part 2: From Proto-Biochemistry to Biochemistry. 1972. 137.00 (*0-444-41024-4*); Vol. 32. Pt. 4: Early Studies on Biosynthesis. 1977. 112.00 (*0-444-41544-0*); 1977. write for info. (*0-318-51831-7*, North Holland) Elsevier.

Neuberger, A. & Van Deenen, L. L., eds. Modern Physical Methods in Biochemistry, Part B. (New Comprehensive Biochemistry Ser.: No. 11B). 320p. 1988. 97.50 (*0-444-80968-6*) Elsevier.

— Modern Physical Methods in Biochemistry, Pt. A. (New Comprehensive Biochemistry Ser.: Vol. 11). 428p. 1986. 110.25 (*0-444-80649-0*) Elsevier.

Neuberger, A., jt. ed. see Florkin, M.

Neuberger, Anne E. The Girl-Son. LC 94-6725. (Adventures in Time Ser.). 132p. (J). (gr. 3-6). 1994. 19.95 (*0-87614-846-1*, Carolrhoda) Lerner Group.

Neuberger, Benjamin. Involvement, Invasion & Withdrawal: Qadhdhafi's Libya & Chad 1969-1981. 80p. (Orig.). 1982. pap. text ed. 6.95 (*0-8156-7049-4*) Syracuse U Pr.

Neuberger, Egon & Lara, Juan. The Foreign Trade Practices of Centrally Planned Economies & Their Effects on U. S. International Competitiveness. LC 77-90040. 56p. 1977. 3.00 (*0-89068-043-4*) Natl Planning.

Neuberger, Egon, ed. see Conference on International Trade & Central Planning (1966-1967: University of Southern California) Staff.

Neuberger, I., ed. Arne Beurling: Collected Works, 2 vols., Set. (Contemporary Mathematicians Ser.). 900p. 1990. 95.00 (*0-8176-3412-6*) Birkhauser.

— Arne Beurling: Collected Works, 2 vols., Vol. I. (Contemporary Mathematicians Ser.). 512p. 1989. 52.00 (*0-8176-3415-0*) Birkhauser.

— Arne Beurling: Collected Works, 2 vols., Vol. II. (Contemporary Mathematicians Ser.). 384p. 1989. 52.00 (*0-8176-3416-9*) Birkhauser.

Neuberger, James & Lucey, Michael, eds. Liver Transplantation: Practice & Management. 250p. 1994. pap. text ed. 54.00 (*0-685-72221-X*, BMJ Pubng Grp) Amer Coll Phys.

Neuberger, Joan. Hooliganism: Crime, Culture, & Power in St. Petersburg, 1900-1914. LC 92-34003. (Studies on the History of Society & Culture: Vol. 19). 1993. 42.00 (*0-520-08011-4*) U CA Pr.

***Neuberger, Julia.** Things That Matter: An Anthology of Women's Spiritual Poetry. LC 94-46616. 1995. 21.00 (*0-312-11899-6*, Pub. by Thomas Dunne Bks) St Martin.

— Whatever's Happening to Women? 218p. 1992. pap. 19.95 (*1-85626-046-1*) Trafalgar.

Neuberger, M. S., jt. ed. see Calabi, F.

Neuberger, Marc ., jt. auth. see Dorfman, Len.

Neuberger, Marc J., jt. auth. see Dorfman, Len.

Neuberger, Max. The Historical Development of Experimental Brain & Spinal Cord Physiology Before Flourens. Clarke, Edwin, ed. & tr. by. LC 81-47604. 424p. 1982. text ed. 70.00 (*0-8018-2380-3*) Johns Hopkins.

Neuberger, Phyllis J. Suppose You Were a Kitten. LC 82-91105. (Illus.). (J). (gr. 1-3). 1982. pap. 2.95 (*0-9610050-0-9*) P J Neuberger.

Neuberger, Richard L. Our Promised Land. LC 88-34684. 398p. (C). 1989. reprint ed. pap. 12.95 (*0-89301-129-0*) U of Idaho Pr.

Neuberger, Richard L. & Loe, Kelley. An Army of the Aged. LC 72-2379. (FDR & the Era of the New Deal Ser.). 332p. 1973. reprint ed. lib. bdg. 39.50 (*0-306-70518-4*) Da Capo.

Neuberger, Ruth, ed. see Longinus.

***Neuberger, Sarah.** David & the Dummy & Other Stories for Children. 1995. 7.95 (*0-533-11425-X*) Vantage.

Neuberger, Thomas. Foundation: Building Sentence Skills. 3rd ed. 432p. 1988. teacher ed write for info. (*0-318-63326-4*) HM.

— Foundation: Building Sentence Skills, 3 Vols. 3rd ed. LC 88-81352. 432p. (C). 1988. pap. 32.36 (*0-395-35028-X*) HM.

Neubert. Paul Wonner. 1989. pap. 15.00 (*0-932499-36-8*) Lapis Pr.

Neubert, Albrecht & Shreve, Gregory. Translation As Text. LC 92-7731. (Translation Studies Ser.: No. 1). 184p. (C). 1992. 27.00 (*0-87338-469-5*) Kent St U Pr.

***Neubert, Christopher & Withiam, Jack, Jr.** How to Handle Your Own Contracts. 256p. 1994. lib. bdg. 37.00x (*0-8095-7623-6*) Borgo Pr.

— How to Handle Your Own Contracts. exp. rev. ed. LC 90-23740. (Illus.). 256p. 1991. pap. 14.95 (*0-8069-8256-X*) Sterling.

Neubert, Diether, et al. Risk Assessment of Prenatally-Induced Adverse Health Effects. LC 92-26482. 1992. 125.00 (*0-387-55890-X*) Spr-Verlag.

Neubert, Emil. My Ideal-Jesus, Son of Mary. LC 88-50578. 111p. 1988. reprint ed. pap. 3.50 (*0-89555-338-4*) TAN Bks Pubs.

Neubert, G. Dictionary of Hydraulics & Pneumatics: English-German-Russian-Spanish & French. 226p. (ENG, FRE, GER, RUS & SPA.). 1973. 95.00 (*0-7859-0814-5*, M-8178) Fr & Eur.

Neubert, George W., text. Paul Wonner: Abstract Realist. LC 81-67616. (Illus.). 72p. (Orig.). 1981. pap. 15.00 (*0-911291-07-5*) Fellows Cont Art.

Neubert, George W., jt. auth. see Garver, Thomas H.

Neubert, Gloria A. Improving Teaching Through Coaching. LC 88-61695. (Fastback Ser.: No. 277). 50p. (Orig.). (C). 1988. pap. 1.25 (*0-87367-277-1*) Phi Delta Kappa.

Neubert, Gloria A. & Binko, James B. Inductive Reasoning in the Secondary Classroom. 128p. 1992. 11.95 (*0-8106-3010-9*) NEA.

Neubert, Gloria A., jt. auth. see McAllister, Elizabeth A.

Neubert, Gunter. Dictionary of Hydraulics & Pneumatics. 226p. 1980. 60.00 (*0-569-08523-3*, Pub. by Collets UK) St Mut.

— Parat Dictionary of Fluidics: English-German, German-English. 259p. (ENG & GER.). 1993. 150.00 (*0-7859-6959-4*) Fr & Eur.

Neubert, Gunter, ed. Technical Dictionary of Hydraulics & Pneumatics. (C). 1973. 110.00 (*0-08-016958-9*, Pub. by Pergamon Repr UK) Franklin.

Neubert, K., jt. auth. see Buehrens, Carol.

Neubert, Kevin, jt. auth. see Buehrens, Carol.

Neuborne, Burt, jt. auth. see Friedman, Leon.

Neuburg, Abtei. Hedera Sorten. 2nd ed. (Illus.). 135p. (GER.). 1987. 25.00 (*0-937233-32-3*) Am Ivy Soc.

Neuburger, jt. auth. see Koneman, Elmer W.

Neuburger, Henry & Fraser, Neil. Economic Policy Analysis: A Rights-Based Approach. 208p. 1993. 59.95 (*1-85628-505-7*, Pub. by Avebury Pub UK) Ashgate Pub Co.

Neuburger, Hugh. German Banks & German Economic Growth from Unification to World War I. Bruchey, Stuart, ed. LC 77-77182. (Dissertations in European Economic History Ser.). 1978. lib. bdg. 23.95 (*0-405-10795-1*) Ayer.

Neuchterlein, Anne M. Improving Your Multiple Staff Ministry: How to Work Together More Effectively. LC 89-30879. 160p. (Orig.). 1989. pap. 13.99 (*0-8066-2422-1*, 9-2422) Augsburg Fortress.

Neuchterlein, Anne M. & Hahn, Celia A. The Male-Female Church Staff: Celebrating the Gifts - Confronting the Challenges. LC 90-83134. 80p. (Orig.). 1990. pap. 9.95 (*1-56699-038-6*, AL119) Alban Inst.

Neudeck, Gerold W. The Bipolar Junction Transistor. LC 81-14977. (Modular Series on Solid State Devices: No. 3). (Illus.). 85p. 1983. pap. write for info. (*0-201-05322-5*) Addison-Wesley.

— The Bipolar Junction Transistor. 2nd ed. (Modular Series on Solid State Devices: Vol. III). (Illus.). 128p. (C). 1989. pap. text ed. 20.50 (*0-201-12297-9*) Addison-Wesley.

— The PN Junction Diode. LC 81-14979. (Modular Series on Solid State Devices: No. 2). (Illus.). 120p. 1983. pap. write for info. (*0-201-05321-7*) Addison-Wesley.

— The PN Junction Diode. 2nd ed. (Modular Series on Solid State Devices). (Illus.). 160p. (C). 1989. pap. text ed. 20.50 (*0-201-12296-0*) Addison-Wesley.

Neudeck, Gerold W., jt. auth. see Pierret, Robert F.

Neudecker, Heinz, jt. auth. see Magnus, Jan R.

***Neudecker, Joan & Politano, Colleen.** Adrift! Boating Safety for Children. LC 94-31922. (Child Survival Ser.). (Illus.). 64p. (J). 1994. 6.99 (*0-934802-98-X*) ICS Bks.

Neuder, Gustav F. & Ullrich, Heinz M. Dictionary of Radiological Engineering. (ENG, FRE & GER.). (C). 1979. pap. text ed. 53.10 (*3-11-007807-4*) De Gruyter.

Neudorfer, Paul O. & Hassul, Michael. Introduction to Circuit Analysis. 600p. 1989. text ed. write for info. (*0-205-11373-7*, H13733) P-H.

— Introduction to Circuit Analysis. 600p. 1990. teacher ed write for info. (*0-318-63886-X*, H13741) P-H.

Neue, Friedrich. Formenlehre der Lateinischen Sprache, 4 vols. in 3, Set. 3151p. 1985. reprint ed. write for info. (*3-487-07703-5*, Pub. by Georg Olms GW) Lubrecht & Cramer.

— Formenlehre der Lateinischen Sprache, 4 vols. in 3, Vol. I: Das Substantivum. 3151p. 1985. reprint ed. write for info. (*0-318-71183-4*, Pub. by Georg Olms GW) Lubrecht & Cramer.

— Formenlehre der Lateinischen Sprache, 4 vols. in 3, Vol. II: Adjektiva, Numeralia etc. 3151p. 1985. reprint ed. write for info. (*0-318-71184-2*, Pub. by Georg Olms GW) Lubrecht & Cramer.

— Formenlehre der Lateinischen Sprache, 4 vols. in 3, Vol. III: Das Verbum. 3151p. 1985. reprint ed. write for info. (*0-318-71185-0*, Pub. by Georg Olms GW) Lubrecht & Cramer.

— Formenlehre der Lateinischen Sprache, 4 vols. in 3, Vol. IV: Register Mit Zusatzen und Verbesserungen. 3151p. 1985. reprint ed. write for info. (*0-318-71186-9*, Pub. by Georg Olms GW) Lubrecht & Cramer.

Neue Slowenische Kunst Staff, ed. NSK: New Slovenian Art, Neue Slowenische Kunst. (Illus.). 288p. (C). 1992. 60.00 (*1-878923-05-6*) Amok Bks.

Neueder, R., jt. auth. see Barthel, J.

Neuefeind, Wilhelm & Riezman, Raymond G., eds. Economic Theory & International Trade: Essays in Memoriam J. Trout Radar. LC 92-26243. (Illus.). x, 306p. 1992. 109.00 (*0-387-55737-7*) Spr-Verlag.

Neuendorf, Wayne. An Engineer's Notebook: A Collection of Original Articles, Practical Ideas & Other Stuff about Recording. LC 89-92332. (Illus.). 155p. (Orig.). 1990. pap. 12.95 (*0-9624890-6-9*) Spiral Pr.

Neuenschwander, Brody. Letterwork: Creative Letterforms in Graphic Design. (Illus.). 160p. (C). 1993. pap. 29.95 (*0-7148-2909-9*, Pub. by Phaidon Press UK) Chronicle Bks.

Neuenschwander, Evonne, et al, eds. Tapestry of Praise. 1986. 7.95 (*0-685-68291-9*, MB-566) Lillenas.

Neuenschwander, Jan, jt. auth. see Otensmann, John R.

Neuenschwander, Jan, jt. auth. see Ottensmann, John R.

Neuenschwander, John N. Oral History & the Law. LC 85-13686. (Oral History Association Pamphlet Ser.: No. 1). 4.00 (*0-317-01097-2*) Oral Hist.

Neuenschwander, Leon F. & Peters, William J. Slash & Burn: Farming in the Third World Forest. LC 88-1155. (Illus.). 156p. 1988. 14.95 (*0-89301-123-1*) U of Idaho Pr.

Neuenswander, Helen L. & Arnold, Dean E. Cognitive Studies of Southern Mesoamerica. LC 77-80015. (Museum of Anthropology Publications: No. 3). 283p. 1977. 10.95 (*0-88312-152-2*) Summer Instit Ling.

— Cognitive Studies of Southern Mesoamerica, 4 fiche, Set. LC 77-80015. (Museum of Anthropology Publications: No. 3). 283p. 1977. fiche 16.00x (*0-88312-250-2*) Summer Instit Ling.

Neuerburg, Norman. California Missions to Cut Out, Vol. I. (J). (gr. 4-9). 1993. pap. 4.95 (*0-88388-177-2*) Bellerophon Bks.

— California Missions to Cut Out, Vol. 2. (J). (gr. 4-9). 1993. pap. 4.95 (*0-88388-185-3*) Bellerophon Bks.

— The Decoration of the California Missions. (Illus.). 80p. (Orig.). 1987. pap. 6.95 (*0-88388-131-4*) Bellerophon Bks.

— Saints of the California Missions. (Illus.). 48p. (Orig.). 1989. pap. 8.95 (*0-88388-139-X*) Bellerophon Bks.

Neufang, Otger. Electronics Lexicon: Lexikon der Elektronik. 815p. (ENG & GER.). 1983. 185.00 (*0-8288-0292-0*, M8754) Fr & Eur.

Neufang, Otger & Ruhl, Horst. German & English Electronics Dictionary: Elektronik-Worterbuch. 421p. (ENG & GER.). 1986. pap. 185.00 (*0-8288-1376-0*, M426) Fr & Eur.

Neufeld, jt. auth. see Dobell.

Neufeld, Arthur H., jt. ed. see Drance, Stephen M.

Neufeld, Dietmar. Reconceiving Texts as Speech Acts: An Analysis of 1 John. LC 94-1367. (Biblical Interpretation Ser.: Vol. 7). 1994. 54.50 (*90-04-09853-4*) E J Brill.

Neufeld, E. P. The Financial System of Canada. LC 70-178200. 635p. 1972. text ed. 45.00 (*0-312-28980-4*) St Martin.

Neufeld, Edward P. A Global Corporation: A History of the International Development of Massey-Ferguson Limited. LC 76-403976. (Illus.). 474p. reprint ed. pap. 135.10 (*0-8357-4740-9*, 2037660) Bks Demand.

Neufeld, Elsie K. Dancing in the Dark: A Sister Grieves. LC 90-83830. 200p. (Orig.). 1990. pap. 8.95 (*0-8361-3537-7*) Herald Pr.

Neufeld, Evelyn. Homework! 64p. (J). (gr. k-2). 1987. pap. text ed. 8.95 (*0-914040-56-1*) Cuisenaire.

Neufeld, Gerald & Plattner, Bernhard, eds. Upper Layer Protocols: Proceedings of the IFIP International Conference on Upper Layer Protocols, Architectures & Applications, Vancouver, B.C., Canada, 27-29 May, 1992. LC 92-37889. (IFIP Transactions C: Communication Systems Ser.: Vol. 6). 1992. write for info. (*0-444-89766-6*, North Holland) Elsevier.

Neufeld, Gerald, jt. auth. see Immers, Richard C.

Neufeld, Gerald G. The Fifteen Forty-One User's Guide. 1986. 19.95 (*0-89303-738-9*) S&S Trade.

Neufeld, Henry N. & Schneeweiss, Adam. Coronary Artery Disease in Infants & Children. LC 83-766. (Illus.). 189p. reprint ed. pap. 53.90 (*0-7837-1491-2*, 2057187) Bks Demand.

Neufeld, Herman A. Mary Neufeld & the Repphun Story: From the Molotschna to Manitoba. LC 88-70276. (Illus.). 240p. 1988. 16.75 (*0-945608-07-1*) C Joyce Gall.

— The Repphun Family: Circas: 1840-50s to 1988. LC 88-192584. 57p. 1988. 15.00 (*0-945608-10-1*) C Joyce Gall.

Neufeld, Herman A., comp. Flashback: Neufeld Family Newsletters, March 1977 to Dec. 1989, Vol. II. (Illus.). 360p. 1990. 49.50 (*0-945608-08-X*) C Joyce Gall.

— Flashback: Neufeld Family Newsletters, Oct. 1959 - Dec. 1976, Vol. I. (Illus.). 342p. 1988. pap. write for info. (*0-945608-06-3*) C Joyce Gall.

Neufeld, Jacob. Development of Ballistic Missiles in the United Air Force, 1945-1960. LC 89-71109. (Illus.). 425p. 1990. pap. 23.00 (*0-16-021154-9*, S/N 008-070-00641-3) USGPO.

Neufeld, Jacqueline K. A Handbook for Technical Communication. (Illus.). 224p. (C). 1987. pap. text ed. 14.75 (*0-13-382292-3*) P-H.

***Neufeld, John.** Almost a Hero. LC 94-12785. (J). 1995. 15.00 (*0-689-31971-1*, Atheneum S&S) S&S Trade.

— Edgar Allan. 1969. pap. 2.95 (*0-451-15870-9*, Sig) NAL-Dutton.

— Edgar Allan. LC 68-31175. (Illus.). (J). (gr. 5-8). 1968. 22.95 (*0-87599-149-1*) S G Phillips.

— Lisa, Bright & Dark. 1970. pap. 2.95 (*0-451-16093-2*, AE1983, Sig) NAL-Dutton.

— Lisa, Bright & Dark. (J). (gr. 7 up). 1969. 22.95 (*0-87599-153-X*) S G Phillips.

— Sharelle. 240p. 1984. pap. 2.50 (*0-451-12783-8*, Sig Vista) NAL-Dutton.

— Small Civil War. 1983. pap. 2.25 (*0-449-70082-8*) Fawcett.

Neufeld, John J., tr. Daut Niehe Tastament. 483p. (GER.). 1988. 15.95 (*0-919797-76-8*) Kindred Prods.

Neufeld, Jonathan, jt. auth. see Grimmett, Peter.

Neufeld, Jonathan, tr. see Huberman, Michael, et al.

Neufeld, Judith B., ed. LILRC Handbook of Programs & Services. 1994. ring bd. 25.00 (*0-938435-34-5*) LI Lib Resources.

Neufeld, Judith B., intro. Long Island Union List of Periodicals, 5 vols. 1994. pap. 275.00 (*0-938435-35-3*) LI Lib Resources.

Neufeld, M. Lynne, et al, eds. Abstracting & Indexing Services in Perspective: Miles Conrad Memorial Lectures 1969-1983. LC 82-84484. viii, 305p. 1983. text ed. 27.50 (*0-87815-043-9*) Info Resources.

Neufeld, Maurice F. Poor Countries & Authoritarian Rule. LC 65-63408. (International Report: No. 6). 256p. 1965. 5.00 (*0-87546-010-0*) ILR Pr.

— A Representative Bibliography of American Labor History. LC 64-63608. (ILR Bibliography Ser.: No. 6). 160p. 1964. 4.50 (*0-87546-021-6*) ILR Pr.

Neufeld, Michael J. The Skilled Metalworkers of Nuremberg: Craft & Class in the Industrial Revolution. LC 88-23875. (Class & Culture Ser.). 240p. (C). 1989. text ed. 45.00 (*0-8135-1394-4*) Rutgers U Pr.

Neufeld, P. Elementary Aspects of Corrosion. (C). 1988. 170.00 (*0-901994-56-1*, Pub. by Fuel Metallurgical Jrnl UK) St Mut.

Neufeld, Richard W. Advances in Investigation of Psychological Stress. (Health Psychology-Behavioral Medicine Ser.). 453p. 1989. text ed. 75.00 (*0-471-81598-5*) Wiley.

Neufeld, Ronald D., ed. Energy - Environmental Opportunities for Civil Engineers. 154p. 1988. 17.00 (*0-87262-655-5*) Am Soc Civil Eng.

Neufeld, Ronald D. & Casson, Leonard W., eds. Hazardous & Industrial Waste: Proceedings of the Mid-Atlantic Industrial Waste Conference, 23rd. 400p. 1991. 75.00 (*0-87762-862-9*) Technomic.

Neufeld, Ronald D. & Goodwin, Richard W., eds. Emerging Energy - Environmental Trends & the Engineer. 59p. 1983. pap. 14.00 (*0-87262-380-7*) Am Soc Civil Eng.

N

Neufeld, Rose. Exploring Nontraditional Jobs for Women. rev. ed. Rosen, Ruth, ed. (Careers in Depth Ser.). (YA). (gr. 7-12). 1989. lib. bdg. 14.95 (*0-8239-0971-9*) Rosen Group.

Neufeld, Victor R. & Norman, Geoffrey R., eds. Assessing Clinical Competence. LC 84-10555. (Medical Education Ser.: Vol. 7). 384p. 1984. 39.95 (*0-8261-3330-4*) Springer Pub.

Neufeld, W. P. The Liver Causes Heart Attacks. 159p. (Orig.). 1991. pap. 11.95 (*0-88925-816-3*) Gordon Soules Bk.

Neufeld, William. From Faith to Faith: The History of the Manitoba Mennonite Brethren Church. (Illus.). 260p. (Orig.). 1989. pap. 15.95 (*0-919797-92-X*) Kindred Prods.

Neufelder, Ann M. Ensuring Software Reliability. LC 92-25561. (Quality & Reliability Ser.: Vol. 38). 264p. 1992. 79.75 (*0-8247-8762-5*) Dekker.

Neufelder, Jerome N. & Coelho, Mary C., eds. Writings on Spiritual Direction by Great Christian Masters. 224p. (Orig.). 1982. pap. 11.95 (*0-8164-2420-9*) Harper SF.

Neufeldt. The Poems of Patrick Branwell Bronte: A New Text & Commentary. LC 90-38464. 590p. 1990. 62.00 (*0-8240-4590-4*, H1050) Garland.

Neufeldt-Fast, Arnold, tr. see Jungel, Eberhard.

Neufeldt, Harvey G. & McGee, Leo, eds. Education of the African American Adult: An Historical Overview. LC 89-25925. (Contributions in Afro-American & African Studies: No. 134). 288p. 1990. text ed. 55.00 (*0-313-25972-0*, MGK/, Greenwood Pr) Greenwood.

Neufeldt, Harvey G., jt. comp. see McGee, Leo.

Neufeldt, Leonard. The House of Emerson. LC 81-16208. 272p. reprint ed. pap. 77.60 (*0-7837-6174-0*, 2045896) Bks Demand.

Neufeldt, Leonard N. The Economist: Henry Thoreau & Enterprise. 232p. 1989. 45.00 (*0-19-505789-9*) OUP.

Neufeldt, Leonard N. & Simmons, Nancy C., eds. The Writings of Henry D. Thoreau Journal, Vol. 4: 1851-1852. (Illus.). 450p. 1992. text ed. 45.00 (*0-691-06535-7*) Princeton U Pr.

Neufeldt, Ronald. F. Max Muller & the Rg-Veda. 1980. 16.00 (*0-8364-0040-2*) S Asia.

Neufeldt, Ronald W., ed. Karma & Rebirth: Post Classical Developments. LC 84-16304. 357p. 1986. 64.50 (*0-87395-990-6*); pap. 21.95 (*0-87395-989-2*) State U NY Pr.

***Neufeldt, Susan.** Structured Supervision for First Practicum. 1995. write for info. (*1-55620-146-X*) Am Coun Assn.

Neufeldt, Victor A., ed. A Bibliography of the Manuscripts of Patrick Branwell Bronte. LC 93-8646. 184p. 1993. 52.00 (*0-8153-1563-5*) Garland.

Neufeldt, Victoria, ed. Webster's New World Dictionary. rev. ed. 704p. 1990. Trade pbk. pap. 10.99 (*0-446-39164-6*); mass mkt. 4.50 (*0-446-36026-0*) Warner Bks.

Neufeldt, Victoria, ed. see Webster's New World Dictionaries Staff.

Neuffer, Claude & Neuffer, Irene. Correct Mispronunciations of Some South Carolina Names. LC 83-5947. 191p. 1983. 15.95 (*0-87249-424-1*); pap. 9.95 (*0-87249-556-6*) U of SC Pr.

— The Name Game: From Oyster Point to Keowee. LC 72-76383. (Illus.). 1979. 6.00 (*0-87844-009-7*) C H Neuffer.

Neuffer, Claude H. Names in South Carolina, Vols. XXV-XXX: 1978-1983. 296p. 1984. reprint ed. pap. 20.00 (*0-87152-404-X*) Reprint.

— Names in South Carolina, 1954-65: Vols. I-XII. LC 76-29026. 1976. reprint ed. 25.00 (*0-87152-248-9*) C H Neuffer.

— Names in South Carolina, 1966-83: Vols. XIII-XXX. 1983. 5.00 (*0-686-18734-2*) C H Neuffer.

Neuffer, Irene, jt. auth. see Neuffer, Claude.

***Neuffer, M. G., et al.** Mutants of Maize. (Illus.). 450p. (C). 1995. 300.00 (*0-87969-443-2*); pap. 150.00 (*0-87969-444-0*) Cold Spring Harbor.

Neuffer, Mark, jt. auth. see Amigo, Eleanor.

Neufield, Michael J. Rocket & the Reich. 1994. 24.95 (*0-02-922895-6*) Free Pr.

Neugaard, Edward. A Motif-Index of Medieval Catalan Folktales. LC 92-16905. (Medieval & Renaissance Texts & Studies: Vol. 96). 128p. 1992. 18.00 (*0-86698-110-1*) MRTS.

Neugaard, Edward J., ed. & tr. Anthology of Catalan Folktales. LC 94-16323. (Catalan Studies: Vol. 16). 1994. write for info. (*0-8204-2530-3*) P Lang Pubs.

Neugart, R., et al, eds. Nuclei Far from Stability & Atomic Masses & Fundamental Constants, 1992: The Proceedings of the 6th International Conference on Nuclei Far from Stability & the 9th International Conference on Atomic Masses & Fundamental Constants Held in Mainz, Germany, 19-24 July 1992. (Institute of Physics Conference Ser.: No. 132). 1040p. 1993. 290.00 (*0-7503-0262-3*) IOP Pub.

Neugarten, Bernice L., ed. Middle Age & Aging: A Reader in Social Psychology. LC 68-55150. 1968. pap. text ed. 20.00 (*0-226-57382-6*) U Ch Pr.

Neugarten, Bernice L., jt. auth. see Coleman, Richard P.

Neugarten, Bernice L., et al. Personality in Middle Life & Late Life: Empirical Studies. Stein, Leon, ed. LC 79-8677. (Growing Old Ser.). (Illus.). 1980. reprint ed. lib. bdg. 25.95 (*0-405-12794-4*) Ayer.

Neugebauer. Handbook of Mediators in Septic Shock. 1993. 189.95 (*0-8493-3548-5*, RC182) CRC Pr.

Neugebauer, Bonnie, ed. Alike & Different: Exploring Our Humanity with Young Children. rev. ed. LC 92-61315. (Illus.). 186p. 1992. reprint ed. pap. 8.00 (*0-935989-52-8*, 240) Natl Assn Child Ed.

— The Anti-Ordinary Thinkbook: A Stimulating Tool for Staff Training & Team-Building in Early Childhood Programs. (Illus.). 24p. (Orig.). (C). 1991. pap. 10.00 (*0-942702-08-5*) Child Care.

— The Wonder of It: Exploring How the World Works. (Beginnings Bks.). (Illus.). 88p. (Orig.). (C). 1989. pap. 16.00 (*0-942702-05-0*) Child Care.

Neugebauer, C. A., ed. see International Conference on Structure & Properties of Thin Films Staff.

Neugebauer, C. A., et al. The Packaging of Power Semiconductor Devices. (Electrocomponent Science Monographs: Vol. 7). 98p. 1986. text ed. 46.00 (*2-88124-135-2*) Gordon & Breach.

Neugebauer, Gerry, jt. auth. see Goodstein, David.

Neugebauer, Hermann & Windischbaur, Gerhard, eds. Surface Topography & Body Deformity: Proceedings of 5th International Symposium on Surface Topography & Body Deformity, September 19-October 1, 1989, Vienna, Austria. 240p. (Orig.). 1990. pap. 65.00 (*1-56081-303-2*) G F Verlag.

Neugebauer, Janet M., ed. All That Matters: The Texas Plains in Photographs & Poems. LC 92-16575. 144p. 1992. 22.50 (*0-89672-291-0*) Tex Tech Univ Pr.

Neugebauer, O. Astronomy & History: Selected Essays. (Illus.). 538p. 1983. pap. 48.00 (*0-387-90844-7*) Spr-Verlag.

Neugebauer, O. & Parker, R. A. Egyptian Astronomical Texts: Decans, Planets, Constellations & Zodiacs, Vol. 3. LC 60-15723. (Brown Egyptological Studies: No. 6). (Illus.). reprint ed. 28.20 (*0-8357-9045-2*, 2012292); reprint ed. 53.00 (*0-685-07740-3*) Bks Demand.

Neugebauer, O. & Sachs, A. Mathematical Cuneiform Texts. (American Oriental Ser.: Vol. 29). 1945. 26.00 (*0-940490-29-3*) Am Orient Soc.

Neugebauer, O., jt. auth. see Swerdlow, N. M.

Neugebauer, Otto. The Exact Sciences in Antiquity. 2nd ed. LC 69-20421. (Illus.). 1969. reprint ed. pap. 6.95 (*0-486-22332-9*) Dover.

Neugebauer, Richard. Certuv Kamen. (Illus.). 110p. (CZE.). 1983. reprint ed. 16.95 (*0-86516-024-4*); reprint ed. pap. 8.95 (*0-685-06791-2*) Bolchazy-Carducci.

***Neugebauer, Roger, ed.** Developing Staff Skills. (Best of Exchange Ser.). (Illus.). 48p. (Orig.). (C). 1990. pap. 10.00 (*0-942702-07-7*) Child Care.

— Fostering Improved Staff Performance. (Best of Exchange Ser.). 48p. (Orig.). (C). 1991. pap. 10.00 (*0-942702-10-7*) Child Care.

— On Being a Leader. (Best of Exchange Ser.). (Illus.). 48p. (Orig.). (C). 1990. pap. 10.00 (*0-942702-06-9*) Child Care.

— Parent Relations: Building an Active Partnership. (Best of Exchange Ser.). 48p. (Orig.). (C). 1994. pap. 10.00 (*0-942702-13-1*) Child Care.

— Taking Stock: Tools for Teacher, Director, & Center Evaluation. (Best of Exchange Ser.). (Illus.). 48p. (Orig.). (C). 1994. pap. 10.00 (*0-942702-12-3*) Child Care.

Neugebauer, Wolfgang, ed. Schule & Absolutismus in Preussen: Akten zum Preussischen Elementarschulwesen Bis 1806. (Veroeffentlichungen der Historischen Kommission zu Berlin, Band 67, Beitraege zu Inflation und Wiederaufbau in Deutschland und Europa 1914-1924: Vol. 33). vii, 814p. (C). 1992. lib. bdg. 195.40 (*3-11-012304-5*) De Gruyter.

Neugeboren, Jay. Poli - a Mexican Boy in Early Texas. LC 88-64094. (Multicultural Texas Ser.). (Illus.). 120p. (J). (gr. 7 up). 1992. pap. 7.95 (*0-931722-74-8*) Corona Pub.

Neugent, William, et al. Technology Assessment: Methods for Measuring the Level of Computer Security. LC 85-600600. (Computer Science & Technology Ser.). (Illus.). 216p. (Orig.). 1985. pap. 8.00 (*0-16-000210-9*, S/N 003-003-02686-7) USGPO.

Neugroschal, Joachim, tr. see Bataille, Georges.

Neugroschel, Joachim, ed. & tr. The Shtetl: A Creative Anthology of Jewish Life in Eastern Europe. 584p. 1990. 25.00 (*0-87951-356-X*); pap. 15.95 (*0-87951-380-2*) Overlook Pr.

Neugroschel, Joachim, intro. Great Tales of Jewish Occult & Fantasy: The Dybbuk & 30 Other Classic Stories. 720p. 1991. reprint ed. 12.99 (*0-517-06005-1*) Random Hse Value.

Neugroschel, Joachim, tr. & comp. Great Works of Jewish Fantasy. LC 85-900. (Illus.). 710p. 1987. 27.95 (*0-87951-229-6*); pap. 15.95 (*0-87951-242-3*) Overlook Pr.

Neugroschel, Joachim, tr. see Arp, J. Hans.

Neugroschel, Joachim, tr. see Barbieri, Renzo.

Neugroschel, Joachim, tr. see Bruckner, Pascal.

Neugroschel, Joachim, tr. see Canetti, Elias.

Neugroschel, Joachim, tr. see Cirillo, Stefano & DiBlasio, Paola.

Neugroschel, Joachim, tr. see Ehrenburg, Ilya.

Neugroschel, Joachim, tr. see Hartling, Peter.

Neugroschel, Joachim, tr. see Hervier, Julien.

Neugroschel, Joachim, tr. see Hildesheimer, Wolfgang.

Neugroschel, Joachim, tr. see Junger, Ernst.

Neugroschel, Joachim, tr. see Kafka, Franz.

Neugroschel, Joachim, tr. see Kolbowski, Silvia, et al.

Neugroschel, Joachim, tr. see Landolfi, Tommaso.

Neugroschel, Joachim, tr. see Lernet-Holenia, Alexander.

Neugroschel, Joachim, tr. see Nossack, Hans E.

Neugroschel, Joachim, tr. see Roth, Joseph.

Neugroschel, Joachim, tr. see Schweitzer, Albert.

Neugroschel, Joachim, tr. see Sergeant, Philippe.

Neugroschel, Joachim, tr. see Sperber, Manes.

Neugroschel, Joachim, tr. see Vogt, Paul, et al.

Neugroschez, Joachim, tr. see Jelinek, Elfriede.

Neuhart, John, et al. Eames Design: The Work of the Office of Charles & Ray Eames 1941-1978. (Illus.). 464p. 1989. 95.00 (*0-8109-0879-4*) Abrams.

Neuharth, Al. Confessions of an S. O. B. 432p. 1992. pap. 5.99 (*0-451-17272-8*, Sig) NAL-Dutton.

Neuharth, Allen H. Buscapade: Plain Talk Across the U. S. A. 1987. 16.95 (*0-944347-00-2*) USA Today Bks.

— Window on the World: Faces, Places & Plain Talk from 32 Countries. (Illus.). 256p. 1988. write for info. (*0-944347-16-9*) USA Today Bks.

Neuharth, Allen H., et al. Profiles of Power: How the Governors Run Our 50 States. (Illus.). 1988. 9.95 (*0-944347-14-2*) USA Today Bks.

Neuhaus, A., jt. auth. see Gebhardt, M.

Neuhaus, Bo & Neuhaus, Lindy. It's Okay, God, We Can Take It. Seidl, Tony, ed. 160p. 1989. 14.95 (*0-89015-733-2*) Sunbelt Media.

***Neuhaus, David, illus.** The Drug-Alert Series, 9 vols., Set. 64p. (J). (gr. 2-4). 1991. lib. bdg. 134.82 (*0-8050-3448-X*) TFC Bks NY.

Neuhaus, David & Williamson, Michael. The Nuclear Overhauser Effect in Stereochemical & Conformational Analysis. LC 88-33963. 522p. 1989. lib. bdg. 105.00 (*1-56081-616-3*) VCH Pubs.

— Nuclear Overhauser Effect in Stereochemical & Conformational Analysis. LC 88-33963. 522p. 1992. pap. 60.00 (*0-685-62697-0*) VCH Pubs.

Neuhaus, Edmund C. & Astwood, William. Practicing Psychotherapy: Basic Techniques & Practical Issues. LC 79-25464. 208p. 1980. 35.95 (*0-87705-467-3*); pap. 22.95 (*0-89885-230-7*) Human Sci Pr.

Neuhaus, Eugen. Drawn from Memory: A Self-Portrait. LC 64-23486. (Illus.). 1964. 17.95 (*0-87015-129-0*) Pacific Bks.

— The History & Ideals of American Art. LC 31-15072. 462p. reprint ed. pap. 131.70 (*0-317-10174-9*, 2050859) Bks Demand.

Neuhaus, Eugen, tr. see Doerner, Max.

Neuhaus, Heike. Plastidaere Mosaikgene: Struktur und Funktion des Chloroplasten-Gens fuer die Trnalys aus Sinapsis Alba L. (Dissertationes Botanicae Ser.: Vol. 115). (Illus.). 110p. (GER.). 1988. pap. 43.00 (*3-443-64027-3*) Lubrecht & Cramer.

Neuhaus, Heinrich. The Art of Piano Playing. Leibovitch, K. A., tr. LC 89-2585. 240p. 1989. 32.00 (*0-89341-556-1*, Longwood Academic) Hollowbrook.

— The Art of Piano Playing. Leibovitch, K. A., tr. LC 89-2585. 240p. 1995. pap. 22.50 (*0-89341-756-4*, Longwood Academic) Hollowbrook.

Neuhaus, Joseph E., jt. auth. see Holtzmann, Howard M.

Neuhaus, Karsta. Cassell Business Companion: Spain. 1993. 19.95 (*0-304-34761-2*, Pub. by Cassell UK) Sterling.

Neuhaus, Lindy, jt. auth. see Neuhaus, Bo.

Neuhaus, Richard, jt. auth. see Berger, Peter L.

Neuhaus, Richard J. America Against Itself: Moral Vision & the Public Order. LC 91-51112. (C). 1992. text ed. 19.95 (*0-268-00633-4*) U of Notre Dame Pr.

— Democracy & the Renewal of Public Education, Vol. 4. (Encounter Ser.). 184p. (Orig.). 1987. pap. 11.99 (*0-8028-0204-4*) Eerdmans.

— Dispensations: The Future of South Africa as South Africans See It. LC 86-2150. 333p. reprint ed. pap. 95.00 (*0-8357-8562-9*, 2034922) Bks Demand.

— Freedom for Ministry: A Guide for the Perplexed Who Are Called to Serve. rev. ed. xiv, 258p. 1992. pap. 14.99 (*0-8028-0622-8*) Eerdmans.

— The Naked Public Square: Religion & Democracy in America. 280p. 1986. reprint ed. pap. 19.99 (*0-8028-0080-7*) Eerdmans.

Neuhaus, Richard J., ed. Augustine Today. (Encounter Ser.). 168p. (Orig.). (C). 1993. pap. text ed. 12.99 (*0-8028-0216-8*) Eerdmans.

— The Bible, Politics, & Democracy. (Encounter Ser.: Vol. 5). 224p. 1987. pap. 12.99 (*0-8028-0205-2*) Eerdmans.

— Biblical Interpretation in Crisis: The Ratzinger Conference on Bible & Church, Vol. 9. (Encounter Ser.). 1989. pap. 10.99 (*0-8028-0209-5*) Eerdmans.

— Confession, Conflict, & Community. (Encounter Ser.: Vol. 3). 128p. (Orig.). 1986. pap. 7.99 (*0-8028-0203-6*) Eerdmans.

— Different Gospels: The Meaning of Apostasy, Vol. 10. (Encounter Ser.). 1989. pap. 9.99 (*0-8028-0210-9*) Eerdmans.

— Guaranteeing the Good Life: Medicine & the Return of Eugenics. 368p. (Orig.). (C). 1990. pap. 17.99 (*0-8028-0213-3*) Eerdmans.

— Jews in Unsecular America. (Encounter Ser.: Vol. 6). 160p. (Orig.). 1987. pap. 10.99 (*0-8028-0206-0*) Eerdmans.

— Law & the Ordering of Our Life Together. (Encounter Ser.: Vol. 11). 196p. (Orig.). (C). 1989. pap. 14.99 (*0-8028-0211-7*) Eerdmans.

— Reinhold Niebuhr Today. (Encounter Ser.: Vol. 12). 144p. (Orig.). (C). 1989. pap. 11.99 (*0-8028-0212-5*) Eerdmans.

— Theological Education & Moral Formation. (Encounter Ser.: No. 15). x, 236p. 1992. pap. 18.99 (*0-8028-0215-X*) Eerdmans.

Neuhaus, Richard J. & Cromartie, Michael, eds. Piety & Politics: Evangelicals & Fundamentalists Confront the World. LC 87-19942. 434p. (Orig.). (C). 1988. pap. text ed. 12.95 (*0-89633-108-3*) Ethics & Public Policy.

Neuhaus, Richard J. & Weigel, George, eds. Being Christian Today: An American Conversation. 310p. (C). 1992. 24.95 (*0-89633-164-4*) Ethics & Public Policy.

Neuhaus, Richard J., ed. see Berger, Peter, et al.

Neuhaus, Richard J., ed. see Billington, James, et al.

Neuhaus, Richard J., ed. see Johnson, Paul, et al.

Neuhaus, Richard J., jt. auth. see Klenicki, Leon.

Neuhaus, Ruby, jt. auth. see Atchinson, William E.

Neuhaus, Ruby H. Long Term Care Administration: Teamwork & Effective Management. 200p. (Orig.). (C). 1990. lib. bdg. 45.00 (*0-8191-7860-8*); pap. text ed. 23.50 (*0-8191-7861-6*) U Pr of Amer.

Neuhaus, W., tr. see Gerber, H. U.

Neuhausel, Patricia A., jt. auth. see Mansmann, Patricia A.

Neuhauser, Charles. Third World Politics: China & the Afro-Asian People's Solidarity Organization, 1957-1967. LC 76-2492. (East Asian Monographs: No. 27). 107p. 1968. pap. 11.00 (*0-674-88455-8*) HUP.

Neuhauser, Duncan. Coming of Age. 2nd ed. LC 93-81268. 375p. 1994. 25.00 (*1-56793-009-3*, 0519) Health Admin Pr.

Neuhauser, Duncan, jt. ed. see Crichton, Anne.

Neuhauser, Duncan, jt. ed. see Kovner, Anthony R.

Neuhauser, E. F., jt. ed. see Edwards, C. A.

Neuhauser, Peg C. Corporate Legends & Lore: The Power of Storytelling as a Management Tool. LC 93-14759. 240p. 1993. text ed. 22.95 (*0-07-046326-3*) McGraw.

— Tribal Warfare in Organizations. 1990. pap. 17.00 (*0-88730-444-3*) Harper Busn.

Neuhausl, R., jt. ed. see Bohn, U.

Neuhausl, R., et al, eds. Chorological Phenomena in Plant Communities. (Advances in Vegetation Science Ser.). 1985. lib. bdg. 182.00 (*90-6193-515-6*) Kluwer Ac.

Neuhausler, Johann. Dachau. (Holocaust Ser.). 1991. lib. bdg. 62.95 (*0-8490-4465-0*) Gordon Pr.

Neuhoff, V. & Friend, J., eds. Cell to Cell Signals in Plants & Animals Progress Report. (NATO ASI Series H: Cell Biology: Vol. 51). (Illus.). 386p. 1991. 139.00 (*0-387-53739-2*) Spr-Verlag.

Neuhoff, Volker. Scientists in Conference: The Congress Organizer's Handbook, The Congress Visitor's Companion. Schoenfeld, R., tr. LC 88-20974. 223p. 1987. lib. bdg. 55.00 (*0-89573-591-1*) VCH Pubs.

Neuhoff, Walther. Die Pilze Mitteleuropas, Vol. 2B: Die Milchlinge (Lactarii) Walther Neuhoff. (Illus.). 1956. 120.00 (*3-7682-0520-7*) Lubrecht & Cramer.

Neuhold, jt. auth. see Ott.

Neuhold, Erich J., ed. Formal Description of Programming Concepts: Proceedings of the Working Conference, St. Andrews N.B. Canada, August, 1977. 648p. 1978. 77.00 (*0-444-85107-0*, North Holland) Elsevier.

Neuhold, Erich J. & Chroust, G., eds. Formal Models in Programming: Proceedings of the IFIP TC2 Working Conference on the Role of Abstract Models in Information Processing, Vienna, Austria, 30 January-1 February, 1985. 426p. 1986. 79.50 (*0-444-87888-2*, North Holland) Elsevier.

Neuhold, Erich J. & Paul, M., eds. Formal Description of Programming Concepts. (IFIP State-of-the-Art Reports). (Illus.). ix, 507p. 1991. 69.00 (*0-387-53961-1*) Spr-Verlag.

Neuhold, Erich J., jt. auth. see Furtado, A. L.

Neuhold, Hanspeter, ed. The European Neutrals in the 1990s: New Challenges & Opportunities. 279p. (C). 1991. pap. text ed. 48.00 (*0-8133-8315-3*) Westview.

***Neuhold, Hanspeter, et al, eds.** Political & Economic Transformation in East-Central Europe. (Austrian Institute for International Affairs Ser.). (C). 1994. pap. text ed. 54.95 (*0-8133-8892-9*) Westview.

Neuhold, N. P., ed. Environmental Protection & International Law. (International Environmental Law & Policy Ser.). (C). 1992. lib. bdg. 92.50 (*1-85333-611-4*, Pub. by Graham & Trotman UK) Kluwer Ac.

Neuhouser, Frederick. Fichte's Theory of Subjectivity. 180p. (C). 1990. pap. 16.95 (*0-521-39938-6*) Cambridge U Pr.

Neuhuber, W. L., jt. ed. see Zenker, W.

***Neuitt, Jennifer, et al.** How to Excel in Leasing Apartments. (Illus.). 325p. (Orig.). 1995. pap. 29.95 (*0-9645538-0-5*) NCMHI.

Neukirch, J. Class Field Theory. LC 85-14846. (Grundlehren der Mathematischen Wissenschaften Ser.: Vol. 280). 155p. 1986. 75.00 (*0-387-15251-2*) Spr-Verlag.

Neukomm, P. A., ed. see Biotelemetry International Symposium Staff.

Neukrantz, Klaus. Barricades in Berlin. LC 78-68131. 1978. pap. 2.95 (*0-916650-07-3*) Banner Pr.

Neukrug, Ed. Theory, Practice, & Trends in Human Services: An Overview of an Emerging Profession. LC 93-20941. 1994. text ed. 45.95 (*0-534-22278-1*) Brooks-Cole.

Neuleib, Janice, jt. auth. see Scharton, Maurice.

Neulen, Leon N. Problem Solving in Arithmetic. LC 70-177116. (Columbia University. Teachers College. Contributions to Education Ser.: No. 483). (C). reprint ed. 37.50 (*0-404-55483-0*) AMS Pr.

Neulen, Lester N. State Aid for Educational Projects in the Public Schools. LC 73-177117. (Columbia University. Teachers College. Contributions to Education Ser.: No. 308). reprint ed. 37.50 (*0-404-55308-7*) AMS Pr.

***Neuliep, James W.** Human Communication Theory: Applications & Case Studies. 1994. pap. 36.25 (*0-13-142226-X*) P-H.

Neuliep, James W., ed. Replication Research in the Social Sciences. 530p. 1991. 55.00 (*0-8039-4091-2*); pap. 25.95 (*0-8039-4092-0*) Sage.

Neuls-Bates, Carol, jt. ed. see Block, Adrienne F.

Neumaier, A. Interval Methods for Systems of Equations. (Encyclopedia of Mathematics & Its Applications Ser.: No. 37). (Illus.). 226p. (C). 1991. 74.95 (*0-521-33196-X*) Cambridge U Pr.

— Introduction to Numerical Analysis. (Illus.). 300p. (C). 1995. write for info. (*0-521-33323-7*) Cambridge U Pr.

Neumaier-Dargyay, E. K. The Sovereign All-Creating Mind-the Motherly Buddha: A Translation of the Kun Byed Rgyal Po'i Mdo. LC 91-2500. (SUNY Series in Buddhist Studies). 246p. 1992. 59.50 (*0-7914-0895-7*); pap. 19.95 (*0-7914-0896-5*) State U NY Pr.

Neumaier-Dargyay, Eva K., jt. ed. see Joy, Morny.

***Neumaier, Diane, ed.** Reframings: New American Feminist Photography. LC 94-46914. (Illus.). 1995. write for info. (*1-56639-331-0*) Temple U Pr.

— Reframings: New American Feminist Photography. LC 94-46914. (Illus.). 304p. (C). 1995. pap. write for info. (*1-56639-332-9*) Temple U Pr.

An Asterisk (*) at the beginning of an entry indicates that the title is appearing in BIP for the first time.

Neumaier, Diane, jt. ed. see Kahn, Douglas.
Neumaier, J. J., ed. see Durrenmatt, Friedrich.
Neuman, Abraham A. Landmarks & Goals: Historical Studies & Addresses. xv, 370p. 1953. 16.95 (*0-685-70563-3*, Ctr Judaic Studies) Eisenbrauns.
Neuman, Alma. Always Straight Ahead: A Memoir. LC 92-20844. viii, 176p. (C). 1993. 24.95 (*0-8071-1792-7*) La State U Pr.
Neuman, Arlene C. Hearing Aids: Recent Developments. Levitt, Harry, ed. (Mini Monographs in Communication Sciences Ser.). 39p. 1993. pap. 10.00 (*0-912752-34-3*) York Pr.
***Neuman, Betty M., ed.** The Neuman Systems Model. 3rd ed. LC 94-30479. 1994. pap. text ed. 38.95 (*0-8385-6701-0*) Appleton & Lange.
Neuman, Brunon. Polish-French Medical Dictionary: Dictionnaire Medical Polonais-Francais. 2nd ed. 1984. 50.00 (*0-8288-1854-1*, M15407) Fr & Eur.
Neuman, Colleen. Riverview, Tape 23. 1993. 2.50 (*0-87129-286-6*, R53) Dramatic Pub.
Neuman, Dagmar. The Origin of Arithmetic Skills: A Phenomenographic Approach. (Goteborg Studies in Educational Sciences: No. 62). 352p. 1987. pap. 59.50x (*91-7346-194-6*, Pub. by Acta U Gothenburg SW) Coronet Bks.
Neuman, Daniel M. The Life of Music in North India: The Organization of an Artistic Tradition. (Illus.). 279p. 1990. reprint ed. pap. text ed. 16.95 (*0-226-57516-0*) U Ch Pr.
Neuman de Veguar, C., jt. auth. see Farrell, R. T.
Neuman, Donald B. Experiences in Science for Young Children. LC 76-53185. (C). 1978. teacher ed 10.00 (*0-8273-1643-7*); pap. text ed. 17.95 (*0-8273-1642-9*) Delmar.
— Experiences in Science for Young Children. LC 76-53185. (Illus.). 176p. (C). 1992. reprint ed. pap. text ed. 13.50x (*0-88133-682-3*) Waveland Pr.
— Experiencing Elementary Science. 434p. (C). 1993. text ed. 44.95 (*0-534-18822-2*) Intl Thomson.
Neuman, Frantisek. Global Properties of Linear Ordinary Differential Equations. (C). 1992. lib. bdg. 131.50 (*0-7923-1269-4*) Kluwer Ac.
Neuman, Fred G. Irvin S. Cobb. (American Newspapermen 1790-1933 Ser.). (Illus.). 274p. 1975. reprint ed. 27.00 (*0-8464-0011-1*) Beekman Pubs.
Neuman, Gerard G. Origins of Human Aggression: Dynamics & Etiology. LC 86-15370. 200p. 1987. 35.95 (*0-89885-324-9*) Human Sci Pr.
Neuman, Johanna, jt. auth. see Nessen, Ron.
Neuman, M. Useful & Harmful Interactions of Antibiotics. LC 84-1607. 1985. 154.00 (*0-8493-6061-7*, CRC Reprint) Franklin.
Neuman, Margaret W., jt. auth. see Neuman, William F.
Neuman, Mark & Payne, Michael, eds. Perspective: Art, Literature, Participation. LC 85-24330. (Review Ser.: Vol. 30, No. 1). (Illus.). 160p. 1986. 22.00 (*0-8387-5104-0*) Bucknell U Pr.
Neuman, Maurice. Dictionnaire des Medicaments: Dictionary of Medications. 432p. (FRE.). 1971. pap. 35.00 (*0-8288-6446-2*, M-6424) Fr & Eur.
Neuman, Michael R., et al, eds. Physical Sensors for Biomedical Applications. 168p. 1980. 98.95 (*0-8493-5975-9*, R857, CRC Reprint) Franklin.
Neuman, Nancy, jt. auth. see Greenberg, Michael R.
Neuman, Patricia O. Moving: The What, When, Where, & How of It. (Illus.). 132p. 1981. pap. 5.95 (*0-89651-450-1*) M & O Pub.
***Neuman, Pearl.** The Egypt Game. Friedland, J. & Kessler, R., eds. (Novel-Ties Ser.). (J). (gr. 5-7). 1994. student ed, pap. text ed. 15.95 (*1-56982-067-8*) Lrn Links.
— The Stories Julian Tells. Friedland, J. & Kessler, R., eds. (Novel-Ties Ser.). (J). (gr. 1-3). 1994. pap. text ed. 15.95 (*1-56982-054-6*) Lrn Links.
— When Winter Comes. (Real Readers Ser.: Level Blue). (Illus.). 32p. (J). (gr. 1-4). 1989. lib. bdg. 19.97 (*0-8172-3519-1*); pap. 4.95 (*0-8114-6723-6*) Raintree Steck-V.
Neuman, Phyllis. Conveyancing of Freehold Property. 1980. 45.00 (*0-686-97093-4*, Pub. by Fourmat Pub UK) St Mut.
Neuman, R. Emil. The Complete Handbook of Health Tips. rev. ed. 256p. 1986. pap. 12.95 (*0-9614924-1-4*) United Res CA.
— Complete Handbook of U. S. Government Benefits. rev. ed. (Illus.). 326p. 1993. pap. 15.95 (*0-685-65181-9*) Kesend Pub Ltd.
— How to Collect Big Dollars from Uncle Sam. rev. ed. 325p. 1986. pap. 12.95 (*0-9614924-2-2*) United Res CA.
— How You Can Achieve Financial Independence in Mail Order Working Out of Your Home. (Illus.). 168p. (Orig.). 1986. pap. 9.95 (*0-9614924-3-0*) United Res CA.
— Paradise Found: How to Live in North America's Best Climate for under 500 Dollars a Month. rev. ed. (Illus.). 148p. (C). 1987. pap. 9.95 (*0-9614924-0-6*) United Res CA.
— Write Perfect Letters for Any Occasion. (Illus.). 240p. (Orig.). 1990. pap. 12.95 (*0-9614924-5-7*) United Res CA.
Neuman, Regina, jt. auth. see Brinton, Donna.
Neuman, Robert. Robert de Cotte & the Perfection of Architecture in Eighteenth-Century France. LC 93-30046. 1994. 55.00 (*0-226-57437-7*) U Ch Pr.
Neuman, Robert W. An Introduction to Louisiana Archaeology. LC 83-19973. (Illus.). xvi, 368p. 1990. pap. 14.95 (*0-8071-1651-3*) La State U Pr.
— The Sonota Complex & Associated Sites on the Northern Great Plains. (Publications in Anthropology: No. 6). 216p. 1975. pap. 6.00 (*0-686-20022-5*) Nebraska Hist.
Neuman, Robert W., ed. Historical Archaeology of the Eastern United States: Papers from the R. J. Russell Symposium. LC 82-84033. (Geoscience & Man Ser.: Vol. 23). 69p. 1983. pap. 10.00 (*0-938909-31-2*) Geosci Pubns LSU.
Neuman, Robert W., jt. ed. see West, Frederick H.
Neuman, Salley. MS-DOS Quick Reference. 1993. pap. 9.95 (*1-56539-137-3*) Color Cnty.
Neuman, Sally. Easy Upgrading & Troubleshooting. (Illus.). 256p. (Orig.). 1993. pap. 19.95 (*1-56529-152-2*) Que.
— MS-DOS 6 Quick Reference. (Illus.). 192p. 1993. pap. 9.95 (*1-56529-137-9*) Que.
— MS DOS 6.2 Quick Reference. 1993. pap. 9.99 (*1-56529-645-1*) Que.
Neuman, Scott. Anonymous Dinner Guest. 1988. 3.00 (*0-685-25016-4*) Windless Orchard.
Neuman, Seev. Strategic Information Systems: Competition Through Information Technologies. LC 93-17343. (Illus.). 320p. (C). 1994. text ed. write for info. (*0-02-386690-X*) Macmillan.
Neuman, Shirley. Some One Myth: Yeat's Autobiographical Prose. (Illus.). 160p. 1982. pap. 19.95 (*0-318-40003-0*, Pub. by Colin Smythe Ltd UK) Dufour.
— Some One Myth: Yeats' Autobiographies. (New Yeats' Papers: No. XIX). (Illus.). 112p. 1982. pap. 23.00 (*0-85105-369-6*, Pub. by Dolmen Pr IE) Dufour.
Neuman, Shirley, ed. Autobiography & Questions of Gender. 1992. text ed. 29.50 (*0-7146-3422-0*, Pub. by F Cass Pubs UK) Intl Spec Bk.
Neuman, Shirley & Nadel, Ira B., eds. Gertrude Stein & the Making of Literature. 236p. 1988. 35.00 (*1-55553-025-7*) NE U Pr.
Neuman, Shirley & Stephenson, Glennis, eds. Reimagining Women: Representations of Women in Culture. 352p. 1993. 60.00 (*0-8020-2777-6*); pap. 24.95 (*0-8020-6825-1*) U of Toronto Pr.
Neuman, Stefanie G. Military Assistance in Recent Wars: The Dominance of the Superpowers. LC 86-16911. (Washington Papers: No. 122). 199p. 1987. text ed. 45.00 (*0-275-92219-7*, C2219, Praeger Pubs) Greenwood.
Neuman, Stephanie G. & Harkavy, Robert E. The Lessons of Recent Wars in the Third World Comparative Dimensions, Vol. II. LC 83-47912. 288p. 1987. text ed. 45.00 (*0-669-09852-3*) Free Pr.
Neuman, Susan & Panoff, Renee. Exploring Feelings. LC 82-81894. (Illus.). 230p. (Orig.). 1983. lib. bdg. 26.95 (*0-89334-205-X*, 205-X) Humanics Ltd.
Neuman, Susan B. Literacy in the Television Age. Dervin, Brenda, ed. (Communication & Information Science Ser.). 256p. (C). 1991. text ed. 39.50 (*0-89391-485-1*) Ablex Pub.
***Neuman, Susan B. & McCormick, Sandra, eds.** Single-Subject Experimental Research: Applications for Literacy. 256p. 1995. pap. 16.00 (*0-87207-128-6*) Intl Reading.
Neuman, Susan B. & Panoff, Renee. Exploring Feelings. LC 82-81894. 224p. (Orig.). (ps-2). 1983. pap. 16.95 (*0-89334-037-5*) Humanics Ltd.
Neuman, Susan B. & Roskos, Kathleen A. Language & Literacy Learning in the Early Years: An Integrated Approach. (Illus.). 320p. (C). 1993. pap. text ed. 28.75 (*0-03-076846-2*) HB Coll Pubs.
Neuman, W. Lawrence. Social Research Methods: Qualitative & Quantitative Approaches. 2nd ed. LC 93-11234. 538p. 1993. text ed. 46.00 (*0-205-14548-5*) Allyn.
Neuman, W. Russell. The Future of the Mass Audience. (Illus.). 208p. (C). 1991. pap. 14.95 (*0-521-42404-6*) Cambridge U Pr.
— The Future of the Mass Audience. (Illus.). 208p. (C). 1992. 54.95 (*0-521-41347-8*) Cambridge U Pr.
— The Paradox of Mass Politics. LC 86-288. (Illus.). 264p. 1986. pap. 16.50 (*0-674-65460-9*) HUP.
Neuman, W. Russell, et al. Common Knowledge: News & the Construction of Political Meaning. LC 92-5992. (American Politics & Political Economy Ser.). (Illus.). 168p. (C). 1992. pap. text ed. 11.95 (*0-226-57440-7*) U Ch Pr.
Neuman, William F. & Neuman, Margaret W. The Chemical Dynamics of Bone Mineral. LC 58-5491. 221p. reprint ed. pap. 63.00 (*0-317-28183-6*, 2020202) Bks Demand.
Neuman, William I., tr. see Ignacio Talbo, Paco, II.
Neuman, William I., tr. see Taibo, Paco I., II.
Neumann. Legal Reasoning & Legal Writing. 1990. 22.00 (*0-316-60379-1*) Little.
Neumann, et al. Financial Management: Concepts & Applications for Health Care Providers. 2nd ed. 656p. (C). 1992. pap. text ed. 45.95 (*0-8403-8365-7*) Kendall-Hunt.
Neumann, A. L. & Lusby, Keith S. Beef Cattle. 8th ed. LC 86-16. 326p. 1986. Net. text ed. write for info. (*0-471-82535-2*) Wiley.
Neumann, Alfred. King Haber, & Other Stories. LC 71-128743. (Short Story Index Reprint Ser.). 1977. 19.95 (*0-8369-3634-5*) Ayer.
Neumann, Angelo. Personal Recollections of Wagner. LC 76-16506. (Music Reprint Ser.). 329p. 1976. reprint ed. 45.00 (*0-306-70843-4*) Da Capo.
Neumann, Anna, jt. auth. see Bensimon, Estela M.
Neumann, Arthur H. Elephant Hunting in East Equatorial Africa. Resnick, Mike, ed. (Library of African Adventure Ser.: Vol. 3). 496p. 1994. 24.95 (*0-312-10458-8*) St Martin.
Neumann, B. H., jt. auth. see Kim, A. C.
Neumann, B. H., jt. ed. see Kim, A. C.
Neumann, B. H., et al, eds. The International Conference on the Theory of Groups: Proceedings. 418p. 1967. text ed. 200.00 (*0-677-10780-3*) Gordon & Breach.
Neumann, Balthasar, ed. Neresheim Abbey Church: Balthasar Neumann. (Opus Ser.). (Illus.). 60p. 1993. 39.95 (*3-8030-2706-3*, Pub. by Ernst Wasmuth GW) Dist Art Pubs.
Neumann, Bernd & Horn, Werner, eds. ECAI Ninety-Two: Tenth European Conference on Artificial Intelligence, August 3-7, 1992, Vienna, Austria: Proceedings. LC 92-22694. 876p. 1992. pap. text ed. 139.00 (*0-471-93608-1*) Wiley.
***Neumann, Bruce R., et al.** Financial Management: Concepts. 656p. (C). 1994. per., pap. text ed. 46.95 (*0-7872-0405-6*) Kendall-Hunt.
Neumann, D. & Jenner, H. A., eds. The Zebra Mussel Dreissena Polymorphia: Ecology, Biological Monitoring & First Applications in the Water Quality Management. (Limnologie Aktuell Ser.: Vol. 4). (Illus.). 263p. 1992. pap. text ed. 89.60 (*0-685-65636-5*, Pub. by G Fischer Verlag GW) Lubrecht & Cramer.
***Neumann, D. A., et al, eds.** Neutron Scattering in Materials Science: 1994 MRS Fall Meeting, Boston, MA, Vol. 376. (MRS Symposium Proceedings Ser.). 1995. 77.00 (*1-55899-278-2*, 376K4) Materials Res.
Neumann, Daniele, jt. auth. see Limousin, Odile.
***Neumann, Dietrich, ed.** Film Architecture: Set Designs from "Metropolis" to "Blade Runner" (Illus.). 224p. 1995. pap. 60.00 (*3-7913-1605-2*) Pegasus.
Neumann, Don A. Holy Week in the Parish. (American Essays in Liturgy Ser.). 56p. (Orig.). 1991. pap. text ed. 3.95 (*0-8146-1949-5*) Liturgical Pr.
Neumann-Duscha. Beverages: Three-Language Technical Dictionary. 424p. (ENG, FRE & GER.). 1986. 225.00 (*0-8288-7915-X*) Fr & Eur.
Neumann, E., et al, eds. Electroporation & Electrofusion in Cell Biology. (Illus.). 454p. 1989. 105.00 (*0-306-43043-6*, Plenum Pr) Plenum.
Neumann, E. G. Single-Mode Fibers. (Optical Sciences Ser.: Vol. 57). (Illus.). 560p. 1988. 109.00 (*0-387-18745-6*) Spr-Verlag.
Neumann, Eckhard. Bauhaus & Bauhaus People: Personal Opinions & Recollections of Former Bauhaus Members & Their Contemporaries. rev. ed. Richter, Eva & Lorman, Alba, trs. LC 92-19324. 1993. text ed. 34.95 (*0-442-01279-9*) Van Nos Reinhold.
Neumann, Eduardo G. Benefactors & Notable Men of Puerto Rico, 2 vols., Set. (Puerto Rico Ser.). 1979. lib. bdg. 250.00 (*0-8490-2871-X*) Gordon Pr.
Neumann, Edward S. & Bondada, Murthy V., eds. Automated People Movers: Engineering & Management in Major Activity Centers. 846p. 1985. 61.00 (*0-87262-488-9*) Am Soc Civil Eng.
Neumann, Else-Ragnhild & Ramberg, Ivar B., eds. Petrology & Geochemistry of Continental Rifts. (NATO Advanced Study Institutes Series C: No. 36). 1978. lib. bdg. 89.00 (*90-277-0866-5*) Kluwer Ac.
Neumann, Else-Ragnhild, jt. ed. see Ramberg, Ivar B.
Neumann, Emanuel. In the Arena. 1976. 10.00 (*0-685-82596-5*) Herzl Pr.
Neumann, Erich. Amor & the Psyche: The Psychic Development of the Feminine: A Commentary on the Tale by Apoleius. Manheim, Ralph, tr. (Bollingen Ser.: Vol. 54). (C). 1990. pap. text ed. 9.95 (*0-691-01772-7*) Princeton U Pr.
— Archetypal World of Henry Moore. Hull, R. F., tr. (Bollingen Ser.: Vol. LXVIII). (Illus.). 216p. 1984. text ed. 35.00 (*0-691-09702-X*) Princeton U Pr.
— Art & the Creative Unconscious. Manheim, Ralph, tr. (Bollingen Ser.: Vol. 61). (Illus.). 1959. pap. 12.95x (*0-691-01773-5*) Princeton U Pr.
— Creative Man: Five Essays. Rolfe, Eugene, tr. LC 79-16711. (Bollinger Ser.: 61; 2). (Illus.). 1979. pap. 12.95 (*0-691-01848-0*) Princeton U Pr.
— Fear of the Feminine & Other Essays on Feminine Psychology: Five Essays. Matthews, Boris et al, trs. LC 93-32444. (Essays of Erich Neumann Ser.: Vol. 4). 1994. 39.95 (*0-691-03474-5*); pap. 12.95 (*0-691-03473-7*) Princeton U Pr.
— The Great Mother: An Analysis of the Archetype. Manheim, Ralph, tr. (Bollingen Ser.: Vol. 47). 628p. 1964. pap. 16.95 (*0-691-01780-8*) Princeton U Pr.
— Origins & History of Consciousness. Hull, R. F., tr. (Bollingen Ser.: Vol. 42). (Illus.). 1954. pap. 16.95 (*0-691-01761-1*) Princeton U Pr.
Neumann, Erich P., jt. ed. see Noelle-Neumann, Elisabeth.
Neumann, Ernst-Georg, jt. auth. see Meyer, Erwin.
Neumann, Ewald. GRE Vocabulary Builder. 2nd rev. ed. (Vocabulary Builder Ser.). 64p. (C). 1994. pap. text ed. 24.95 (*0-9625001-1-9*) Spargo Comns.
— SAT Vocabulary Builder. (Vocabulary Builder Ser.). 64p. (C). 1992. audio 24.95 (*0-9625001-2-7*) Spargo Comns.
— TOEFL Vocabulary Builder. rev. ed. (Vocabulary Builder Ser.). 80p. (C). 1994. pap. text ed. 24.95 (*0-9625001-4-3*) Spargo Comns.
***Neumann, F.** Questions & Problems in Auditing. 466p. 1995. spiral bd. 29.80x (*0-87563-540-7*) Stipes.
Neumann, F., jt. auth. see Habenicht, U. F.
Neumann, Franz. Gesammelte Werke, 3 vols., Set. 1990. reprint ed. 225.00 (*3-262-01422-2*) Periodicals Srv.
Neumann, Franz L., et al. The Cultural Migration: The European Scholar in America. Metzger, Walter P., ed. LC 76-55140. (Academic Profession Ser.). 1977. reprint ed. lib. bdg. 17.95 (*0-405-10041-8*) Ayer.
Neumann, Frederick. New Essays on Performance Practice. LC 89-34600. (Illus.). 262p. (C). 1992. reprint ed. text ed. 55.00 (*1-878822-12-8*); reprint ed. pap. text ed. 19.95 (*1-878822-13-6*) Univ Rochester Pr.
— Ornamentation & Improvisation in Mozart. LC 85-42694. (Illus.). 244p. (C). 1989. 75.00 (*0-691-09130-7*); pap. text ed. 29.95 (*0-691-02711-0*) Princeton U Pr.
— Ornamentation in Baroque & Post-Baroque Music. LC 77-72130. (Illus.). 630p. 1978. 99.50 (*0-691-09123-4*); pap. 32.50x (*0-691-02707-2*) Princeton U Pr.
— Performance Practices of the Seventeenth & Eighteenth Centuries. 616p. 1993. 50.00 (*0-02-873300-2*) Schirmer Bks.
— Violin Left Hand Technique. 9.00 (*0-318-18118-5*) Am String Tchrs.
Neumann, G. Surface Self-Diffusion of Metals. 1972. 36.00 (*0-87849-501-0*, Pub. by Trans Tech GW) LPS Dist Ctr.
Neumann, George B. A Study of International Attitudes of High School Students with Special Reference to Those Nearing Completion of Their High School Courses. LC 77-177118. (Columbia University. Teachers College. Contributions to Education Ser.: No. 239). reprint ed. 37.50 (*0-404-55239-0*) AMS Pr.
Neumann, George C. & Kravic, Frank J. Collector's Illustrated Encyclopedia of the American Revolution. (Illus.). 286p. 1990. reprint ed. 32.95 (*0-9605666-7-8*); reprint ed. pap. 21.95 (*0-9605666-8-6*) Scurlock Pub.
— Swords & Blades of the American Revolution. (Illus.). 288p. 1991. reprint ed. 35.95 (*0-9605666-9-4*); reprint ed. pap. 23.95 (*1-880655-00-4*) Scurlock Pub.
Neumann, George R., jt. auth. see Kiefer, Nicholas M.
Neumann, H. Varieties of Groups. (Ergebnisse der Mathematik und Ihrer Grenzgebiete Ser.: Vol. 37). 1967. 65.00 (*0-387-03779-9*) Spr-Verlag.
Neumann, H. D. Introduction to Manual Medicine. (Illus.). 130p. 1989. pap. 31.00 (*0-387-50612-8*) Spr-Verlag.
Neumann, H. G., jt. ed. see Dekant, Wolfgang.
Neumann, Hans H. Foreign Travel & Immunization Guide Series. 12th ed. 96p. (Orig.). 1987. pap. 24.95 (*0-87489-466-2*) Med Economics.
Neumann, Hans H., jt. auth. see Dardick, Kenneth R.
Neumann, Harry. Liberalism. LC 91-70429. 359p. 1991. 29.95 (*0-89089-455-8*) Carolina Acad Pr.
Neumann, Holm W. The Paleopathology of the Archaic Modoc Rock Shelter Inhabitants. (Reports of Investigations Ser.: No. 11). (Illus.). 68p. 1967. pap. 2.50 (*0-89792-034-1*) Ill St Museum.
Neumann, I. Biotaxonomische Untersuchungen an Einigen Hefen der Gattung Saccharomyces. 1972. 24.00 (*3-7682-5440-2*) Lubrecht & Cramer.
Neumann, Inge S. European War Crimes Trials: A Bibliography. Rosebaum, Robert A., ed. LC 77-18934. 113p. 1978. reprint ed. text ed. 38.50 (*0-313-20210-9*, NEEW) Greenwood.
Neumann, Irmgard, tr. see Boltzius, John M. & Gronau, Christian I.
Neumann, J. Multilingual Dictionary of Technical Terms in Cartography. 500p. (ENG, FRE & SPA.). 1992. 450.00 (*0-8288-7914-1*, 3598107641) Fr & Eur.
Neumann, J. J. The Polyporaceae of Wisconsin. 1971. reprint ed. 36.00 (*3-7682-0704-8*) Lubrecht & Cramer.
Neumann, James W. Listening to Your Own Body: A Guide to the Neurological Problems That Afflict Us As We Grow Older. LC 86-7985. 127p. 1987. 14.95 (*0-917561-22-8*); pap. 6.95 (*0-917561-26-0*) Adler & Adler.
***Neumann, Jeff & Ruth, Romy.** The Naturalist Collector: The Best Book on Card Collecting. Robinson, Rita & Frank, Alan, eds. LC 94-69480. (Illus.). 128p. (YA). (gr. 9 up). 1994. pap. 14.95 (*0-9643339-0-2*) Rockefel Pub.
Neumann, Jens, jt. auth. see Hufner, Klaus.
Neumann, K. Stochastic Project Networks: Temporal Analysis, Scheduling & Cost Minimization. (Lecture Notes in Economics & Mathematical Systems Ser.: Vol. 344). (Illus.). xii, 237p. 1990. pap. 34.00 (*0-387-52664-1*) Spr-Verlag.
Neumann, K. & Pallaschke, D., eds. Contributions to Operations Research. (Lecture Notes in Economics & Mathematical Systems Ser.: Vol. 240). v, 190p. 1985. pap. 36.00 (*0-387-15205-9*) Spr-Verlag.
Neumann, K. & Steinhardt, U. GERT Networks & the Time-Oriented Evaluation of Projects. (Lecture Notes in Economics & Mathematical Systems Ser.: Vol. 172). (Illus.). 1979. 32.00 (*0-387-09705-8*) Spr-Verlag.
Neumann, K. H., jt. ed. see Elixmann, D.
Neumann, K. H., et al, eds. Primary & Secondary Metabolism of Plant Cell Cultures. LC 85-17257. (Proceedings in Life Sciences Ser.). (Illus.). 400p. 1985. 139.00 (*0-387-15797-2*) Spr-Verlag.
Neumann, Karl & Rosenbaum, Maury, eds. The Business Traveler's Guide to Good Health on the Road: The Nation's Leading Health, Travel, & Business Experts Tell How to Maximize Your Health While Traveling. 212p. 1994. pap. 12.95 (*1-56561-036-9*, 004233) Chronimed.
Neumann, Ken. The Authenticity of the Pauline Epistles in the Light of Stylostatistical Analysis. (Society of Biblical Literature Dissertation Ser.). 403p. 1990. 25.95 (*1-55540-428-6*, 06 21 20); pap. 16.95 (*1-55540-429-4*) Scholars Pr GA.
Neumann, Klaus. Not the Way It Really Was: Constructing the Tolai Past. LC 91-28884. (Pacific Islands Monograph Ser.: No. 10). (Illus.). 328p. (C). 1992. text ed. 34.00 (*0-8248-1333-2*) UH Pr.
Neumann, Linda, jt. auth. see Anderson, Rita.
Neumann, Linda C., jt. auth. see Anderson, Rita.
Neumann, Manfred & Roskamp, Karl W., eds. Public Finance & Performance of Enterprises: Proceedings of the 43rd Congress of the International Institute of Public Finance, Paris, 1987. LC 89-5521. 512p. (C). 1989. 49.95 (*0-8143-2269-7*) Wayne St U Pr.
Neumann, Manfred J., ed. Monetary Policy & Uncertainty: Collected Papers from the 1982-1984 Konstanz Seminars. 262p. 1986. pap. 46.00 (*3-7890-1257-2*, Pub. by Nomos Verlags GW) Intl Bk Import.
Neumann, Michael. What's Left? Radical Politics & the Radical Psyche. 240p. 1988. pap. 7.95 (*0-921149-22-0*) Broadview Pr.
Neumann-Neurode, D. & Kaiser, W. Baby Gymnastics. LC 67-26321. 1967. 23.00 (*0-08-012305-8*, Pub. by Pergamon Repr UK) Franklin.

N

Neumann, Peter G. Computer-Related Risks. 320p. (C). 1995. text ed. 24.75 (*0-201-55805-X*) Addison-Wesley.

Neumann, Peter J. Playing a Virginia Moon. LC 93-25563. (YA). 1994. 14.95 (*0-395-66562-0*) HM.

Neumann, Peter M., ed. Plant Growth & Leaf-Applied Chemicals. 192p. 1988. 174.00 (*0-8493-5414-5*, SB128) CRC Pr.

Neumann, Peter M., et al. Groups & Geometry. LC 93-270. (Illus.). 264p. (C). 1994. pap. 29.95 (*0-19-853451-5*) OUP.

Neumann, Phyllis L. Marin County Bike Trails. (Illus.). 128p. (Orig.). 1989. pap. 11.95 (*0-9621694-0-4*) Penngrove Pubns.

Neumann, Pierre-Louis, jt. auth. see Birjandi, Abbas.

Neumann, Randall D., jt. ed. see Brown, David E.

Neumann, Richard, jt. auth. see Nemapare, Prisca.

***Neumann, Robert L.** Crystals of Light. 56p. 1995. pap. 8.00 (*0-8059-3776-5*) Dorrance.

Neumann, Ruth, jt. auth. see Lindsay, Alan.

Neumann, Sarah, ed. see Ouellette, Deborah.

Neumann, Udo, jt. auth. see Goddard, Dale.

Neumann, Victor. The Temptation of Homo Europaeus. LC 93-73007. (East European Monographs: No. CCCLXXXIV). 269p. 1994. 39.00 (*0-88033-281-6*) East Eur Quarterly.

Neumann, Walter D., jt. auth. see Eisenbud, David.

Neumann, William. The Genesis of Pearl Harbor. 1979. lib. bdg. 42.50 (*0-685-96396-9*) Revisionist Pr.

Neumann, William L. America Encounters Japan: From Perry to MacArthur. (Goucher College Ser.). 366p. 1963. reprint ed. 52.00 (*0-8018-0485-X*) Johns Hopkins.

Neumark, David. Geschichte der Judischen Philosophie des Mittelalters, 3 vols., 1. Katz, Steven, ed. LC 79-7149. (Jewish Philosophy, Mysticism & History of Ideas Ser.). 1980. reprint ed. lib. bdg. 44.95 (*0-405-12280-2*) Ayer.

— Geschichte der Judischen Philosophie des Mittelalters, 3 vols., Set. Katz, Steven, ed. LC 79-7149. (Jewish Philosophy, Mysticism & History of Ideas Ser.). 1980. reprint ed. lib. bdg. 132.95 (*0-405-12279-9*) Ayer.

— Geschichte der Judischen Philosophie des Mittelalters, 3 vols., Vol. 2, Pt. 1. Katz, Steven, ed. LC 79-7149. (Jewish Philosophy, Mysticism & History of Ideas Ser.). 1980. reprint ed. lib. bdg. 44.95 (*0-405-12281-0*) Ayer.

— Geschichte der Judischen Philosophie des Mittelalters, 3 vols., Vol. 2, Pt. 2. Katz, Steven, ed. LC 79-7149. (Jewish Philosophy, Mysticism & History of Ideas Ser.). 1980. reprint ed. lib. bdg. 44.95 (*0-405-12282-9*) Ayer.

— Journal of Jewish Lore & Philosophy, Vol. 1. 1919. 25.00 (*0-87068-092-7*) Ktav.

***Neumayer, Bob.** Drinking Helps You Drive Straight. 248p. 1995. pap. 12.95 (*1-56796-085-5*) WRS Group.

Neumayer, Erwin. Lines on Stone: The Prehistoric Rock Art of India. (C). 1993. 54.00x (*81-7304-046-X*, Pub. by Manohar II) S Asia.

Neumayer, Lisa, ed. see Costello, Jeanne & Witty, Doreen.

***Neumayr, Anton.** Dictators in the Mirror of Medicine: Napoleon, Hitler, Stalin. rev. ed. Parent, David J., tr. (Illus.). 450p. 1995. text ed. 34.95 (*0-936741-09-0*) Medi-Ed Pr.

— Hummel, Weber, Mendelssohn, Schumann, Brahams, Bruckner: Notes on Their Lives, Works, & Medical Histories. Clarke, Bruce C., tr. (Music & Medicine Ser.: Vol. 2). (Illus.). 1995. write for info. (*0-936741-07-4*) Medi-Ed Pr.

— Music & Medicine: Haydn, Mozart, Beethoven, Schubert, Notes on Their Lives, Works & Medical Histories. Clarke, Bruce C., tr. LC 94-21413. (Music & Medicine Ser.: Vol. 1). (Illus.). 416p. 1994. 32.95 (*0-936741-05-8*) Medi-Ed Pr.

Neumayr, Sharon. American Literature Activities Kit: Ready-to-Use Worksheets for Secondary Students. 256p. 1992. pap. 24.95 (*0-87628-110-2*) Ctr Appl Res.

— World Literature Activities Kit: Ready-to-Use Worksheets. 288p. 1994. pap. 27.95 (*0-87628-948-0*) Ctr Appl Res.

Neumeier, G. Occupational Exposure Limits. (EUR Ser.: No. 14491). 132p. 1993. pap. 19.00 (*92-826-4820-6*, CE-NA-14491-EN-C, Pub. by Europ Com) UNIPUB.

Neumeier, Marty & Glaser, Byron. Action Alphabet. LC 84-25322. (Illus.). 56p. (J). (ps-1). 1985. 14.00 (*0-688-05703-9*); lib. bdg. 13.93 (*0-688-05704-7*) Greenwillow.

Neumeier, Rolf, jt. auth. see Zamir, Jan R.

***Neumeister, Michel & Weiss, Maud B., photos.** The Challenge of Piety: Satmar Hasidim in New York. (Illus.). 144p. 1995. 45.00 (*3-929078-22-8*) Dist Art Pubs.

Neumeister, Susan M., jt. ed. see Hartman, Donald K.

Neumeyer, David & Tepping, Susan. A Guide to Schenkerian Analysis. 160p. (C). 1991. pap. text ed. write for info. (*0-13-497215-5*) P-H.

Neumeyer, David, tr. see Von Cube, Felix-Eberhard.

Neumeyer, Kathleen, jt. auth. see Giler, Janet Z.

Neumeyer, Ken. Sailing the Farm: Independence on Thirty Feet - A Survival Guide to Homesteading the Ocean. LC 81-51896. 256p. (Orig.). 1981. pap. 9.95 (*0-89815-051-5*) Ten Speed Pr.

Neumeyer, Peter F., ed. Twentieth Century Interpretations of The Castle. 1969. pap. 1.25 (*0-13-120378-9*, Spectrum Bks) P-H.

Neumeyer, Peter F., tr. see Buchholz, Quinn.

Neumeyer, Susan L. Minnesota Wills & Estate Planning. 400p. 1993. ring bd. 105.00 (*1-56257-262-8*) Michie Butterworth.

Neumyer, Marsha M. & Auer, Arthur I., eds. The Noninvasive Vascular Laboratory: Current Issues & Clinical Developments. 1995. text ed. write for info. (*0-941022-28-5*) Appleton Davies.

***Neumyer, Marsha M. & Thiele, Brian L.** Techniques of Abdominal Vascular Sonography. Date not set. vhs write for info. (*0-941022-32-3*) Appleton Davies.

— Techniques of Abdominal Vascular Sonography. 1995. text ed. write for info. (*0-941022-27-7*) Appleton Davies.

Neumyer, Marsha M., et al. Vascular Laboratory Physician's Manual: Indications, Interpretation, & Clinical Decision Making. 1995. write for info. (*0-941022-29-3*) Appleton Davies.

Neuneck, Gotz, jt. auth. see Muller, Erwin.

Neuner, A. Pilze: Alle wichtigen Pilze nach Farbfotos bestimmen. (Illus.). 143p. 1983. pap. text ed. 10.00 (*3-405-12048-9*) Lubrecht & Cramer.

Neuner, Gerd, et al. Lehrerhandbuch, Pt. 2. write for info. (*3-468-49927-2*) Langenscheidt.

Neuner, Gerd & Desmarets, Peter. Deutsch Konkret, Level 1. Incl. Set. Textbook, 3 vols. 256p. 1983. 15.50 (*0-88729-754-4*); Lehrbuch. 96p. 1983. pap. text ed. 12.00 (*3-468-49850-0*); English Workbook. 128p. 1984. 9.95 (*3-468-96746-2*); Arbeitsbuch. 79p. 1983. 9.50 (*3-468-49851-9*); Glossar English. 17p. 1984. 4.95 (*3-468-49853-5*); Glossar French. 17p. 1984. 4.95 (*3-468-49854-3*); Teacher's Manual. 56p. 1984. 13.25 (*3-468-96747-0*); Lehrerhandreichungen. 112p. 1984. 11.95 (*3-468-49852-7*); Cassette 1A. 1984. 20.00 (*3-468-84430-1*); Cassette 1B. 1984. 29.95 (*3-468-84431-X*); Begleitheft zu Cassette 1B. 5.50 (*3-468-49859-4*); Folien, 30 transparencies. 1984. 109.95 (*3-468-84434-4*); Tests. 42.50 (*3-468-96743-8*); Resource Pkg. 49.95 (*3-468-49882-9*); write for info. (*0-318-68076-9*) Langenscheidt.

Neuner, Gerd & Vahle, Fredrik. Paule Puhmanns Paddelboot Liederbuch mit Hinweisen fuer den Unterricht. 71p. 15.95 (*3-468-49845-4*); audio 20.00 (*3-468-84516-2*) Langenscheidt.

Neuner, Gerd, et al. Uebungstypologie zum Kommunikativen Deutschunterricht. 184p. pap. 26.50 (*3-468-49430-0*) Langenscheidt.

Neuner, J. & Dupuis, J., eds. The Christian Faith. rev. ed. LC 82-22700. 740p. 1990. pap. 16.95 (*0-8189-0453-4*) Alba.

***Neuner, Josef.** Walking with Him: A Biblical Guide Through Thirty Days of Spiritual Exercises. 290p. (C). 1985. 7.95 (*0-8294-0533-X*, Campion Bks) Loyola Univ Pr.

Neunzert, Helmut, ed. Mathematics in Industry, Second European Symposium: Proceedings. (C). 1988. lib. bdg. 129.50 (*90-277-2732-5*) Kluwer Ac.

— Proceedings of the Second Workshop on Road-Vehicle-Systems & Related Mathematics June 20-25, 1987, ISI Torino. (C). 1989. lib. bdg. 112.50 (*0-7923-0243-5*) Kluwer Ac.

Neunzig, H. H. Moths of America North of Mexico: Fascicle 15.2 Pyraloidea, Pyralidae: Phycitinae: Acrobasis & Allies. Hodges, Ronald W. et al, eds. LC 85-51913. (Illus.). xii, 113p. (Orig.). 1986. pap. text ed. 45.00 (*0-933003-01-3*) Wedge Entomological.

— The Moths of America North of Mexico, Fascicle 15.3: Pyraloidea, Pyralidae Phycitinae (Part) Hodges, Ronald W. et al, eds. LC 90-70020. (Illus.). 165p. (C). 1990. pap. text ed. 55.00 (*0-933003-05-6*) Wedge Entomological.

Neupaver, Albert J., jt. comp. see Lall, Chaman.

***Neupert, Ricardo & Goldstein, Sidney.** Urbanization & Population Redistribution in Mongolia. LC 94-39475. (East-West Center Occasional Papers: No. 122). 1994. pap. text ed. write for info. (*0-86638-166-X*) EW Ctr HI.

***Neupert, Richard.** The End: Narration & Closure in the Cinema. (Contemporary Film & Television Ser.). (Illus.). 208p. (Orig.). 1995. pap. text ed. 19.95x (*0-8143-2525-4*) Wayne St U Pr.

Neupert, Richard, tr. see Aumont, Jacques, et al.

Neupert, Walter & Lill, Roland, eds. Membrane Biogenesis & Protein Targeting. LC 92-24428. (New Comprehensive Biochemistry Ser.: Vol. 22). 1992. write for info. (*0-444-89638-4*) Elsevier.

Neural Network Laboratory Staff. The Brain Simulator: Tutorial Software for Neural Circuit Design. (Illus.). 91p. (C). 1988. pap. 99.00 (*0-944365-05-1*) Abbot Foster.

Neurath, A. R., jt. ed. see Van Regenmortel, M. H.

Neurath, A. R., jt. ed. see Van Regenmortel, Marc H.

Neurath, Hans. Perspectives in Biochemistry, Vol. 1. LC 89-409. (Illus.). 251p. 1989. pap. 14.95 (*0-8412-1621-5*) Am Chemical.

Neurath, Maria & Cohen, R. S., eds. Empiricism & Sociology: The Life & Work of Otto Neurath. Foulkes, Paul, tr. LC 72-95889. (Vienna Circle Collection Ser.: No. 1). 1973. lib. bdg. 140.00 (*90-277-0258-6*); pap. text ed. 64.00 (*90-277-0259-4*) Kluwer Ac.

Neurath, Maria, ed. see Neurath, Otto.

Neurath, Otto. Philosophical Papers Nineteen Thirteen to Nineteen Forty-Six. Cohen, Robert S. & Neurath, Maria, eds. 1983. lib. bdg. 140.00 (*90-277-1483-5*) Kluwer Ac.

Neurath, Otto, et al, eds. Foundations of the Unity of Science: Toward an International Encyclopedia of Unified Science, 2. LC 56-553. (Foundations of the Unity of Science Ser.: Vols. 1 & 2). 1971. lib. bdg. 25.00 (*0-226-57588-8*) U Ch Pr.

Neurath, Paul. From Malthus to the Club of Rome & Back: Problems of Limits to Growth, Population Control, & Migrations. (Columbia University Seminars Ser.). 244p. 1994. text ed. 60.00 (*1-56324-407-1*); pap. text ed. 24.95 (*1-56324-408-X*) M E Sharpe.

Neureiter, Paul R. Love in an Age of Paranoia. LC 91-67927. 244p. 1992. 12.00 (*1-56002-192-6*, Univ Edtns) Aegina Pr.

Neuringer, Charles & Lettieri, Dan J. Suicidal Women: Their Thinking & Feeling Patterns. LC 81-6294. 250p. 1982. text ed. 26.95 (*0-89876-023-2*) Gardner Pr.

Neuringer, Sheldon. The Carter Administration, Human Rights & the Agony of Cambodia. LC 93-23577. 108p. 1993. 59.95 (*0-7734-9367-0*) E Mellen.

Neuringer, Sheldon M. American Jewry & United States Immigration Policy, 1881-1953. Cordasco, Francesco, ed. LC 80-883. (American Ethnic Groups Ser.). 1981. lib. bdg. 54.95 (*0-405-13444-4*) Ayer.

Neurobiological & Equilibriometric Society. Vertigo, Nausea, Tinnitus & Hearing Loss in Cardiovascular Diseases: Proceedings of the Scientific Meeting of the Neurobiological & Equilibriometric Society, 13th, Bad Kissingen, 21-23 March, 1986. Claussen, C. F. & Kirtane, M. V., eds. (International Congress Ser.: No. 708). 540p. 1987. 169.25 (*0-444-80825-6*, Excerpta Medica) Elsevier.

Neusch, Donna R. & Siebenaler, Alan F. The High Performance Enterprise: Reinventing the People Side of Your Business. LC 92-60670. 360p. 1993. 35.00 (*0-939246-29-5*) Oliver Wight.

— The High Performance Enterprise: Reinventing the People Side of Your Business. 2nd ed. 400p. 1995. 35.00 (*0-939246-83-X*) Oliver Wight.

Neuschatz, Michael. The Golden Sword: The Coming of Capitalism to the Colorado Mining Frontier. LC 85-27026. (Contributions in American Studies: No. 84). 313p. 1986. text ed. 55.00 (*0-313-25104-5*, NGS/, Greenwood Pr) Greenwood.

Neuschotz, Nilson. Welcome to Multi.Mac. 1995. pap. 27.95 (*1-55828-339-0*) H Holt & Co.

Neuse, Erna. Der Erzahler in der Deutschen Kurzgeschichte. (Studies in German Literature, Linguistics & Culture: Vol. 60). 230p. (GER.). 1991. 55.00 (*0-938100-92-0*) Camden Hse.

Neuse, Erna K., ed. Neue Deutsche Prosa. LC 68-30796. (Illus.). (Orig.). (GER.). (C). 1968. pap. text ed. 9.95 (*0-8290-2383-6*) Irvington.

Neuse, Richard. Chaucer's Dante: Allegory & Epic Theater in "The Canterbury Tales" 332p. 1991. 45.00 (*0-520-07241-3*) U CA Pr.

Neuse, Werner. Geschichte der Erlebten Rede und des Inneren Monologs in der Deutschen Prosa. LC 89-77256. (American University Studies: Germanic Languages & Literature: Ser. I, Vol. 88). 599p. (GER.). (C). 1990. text ed. 102.95 (*0-8204-1153-1*) P Lang Pubs.

Neuser, Jacob. Sifre to Numbers, Part I. (Brown Judaic Studies). (C). 1986. pap. 23.95 (*1-55540-009-4*) Scholars Pr GA.

— Sifre to Numbers, Part II. (Brown Judaic Studies). (C). 1986. pap. 20.95 (*1-55540-011-6*) Scholars Pr GA.

Neuser, Wilhelm H., ed. Calvinus Sacrae Scripturae Professor (Calvin As Confessor of Holy Spirit) LC 93-41123. 296p. 1994. pap. 24.99 (*0-8028-0716-X*) Eerdmans.

Neushel, Kristen B. Word of Honor: Interpreting Noble Culture in Sixteenth-Century France. LC 88-47916. 256p. 1989. 29.95 (*0-8014-2181-0*) Cornell U Pr.

Neusius, Phillip D. Archaeological Excavations at the Kruse Bluffbase No. 3 Site, Monroe County, Illinois. LC 85-71910. (Center for Archaeological Investigations Research Paper Ser.: No. 51). (Illus.). x, 95p. 1985. pap. 6.50 (*0-88104-057-6*) Center Archaeo.

***Neusner.** The Price of Excellence: Universities in Conflict During the Cold War Era. 224p. 1995. 22.95 (*0-8264-0853-2*) Continuum.

Neusner, Jacob. Abo Addresses & Other Recent Essays on Judaism in Time & Eternity. LC 93-39349. (USF Studies in the History of Judaism). 232p. 1994. 77.95 (*1-55540-933-4*, 240022) Scholars Pr GA.

— The Academic Study of Judaism: Essays & Reflections. LC 82-204699. (Libraries Bibliography: No. 15). 25.00 (*0-87068-431-0*) Ktav.

— The Academic Study of Judaism: Essays & Reflections. LC 75-5782. (Brown Judaic Studies). (C). 1982. reprint ed. pap. 17.50 (*0-89130-218-2*, 14-00-35) Scholars Pr GA.

— The Academic Study of Judaism: Essays & Reflections I. (Library of Sephardic History & Thought: No. 3). 25.00 (*0-87068-712-3*) Ktav.

— American Judaism: Adventure in Modernity. reprint ed. pap. 9.95 (*0-87068-681-X*) Ktav.

— Ancient Israel after Catastrophe: The Religious World View of the Mishnah. LC 82-15972. (Richard Lectures). 94p. reprint ed. pap. 26.80 (*0-7837-1771-7*, 2041968) Bks Demand.

— Ancient Judaism: Debates & Disputes. (Studies in History of Judaism). 244p. 1990. 54.95 (*1-55540-479-0*, 24 00 05) Scholars Pr GA.

— Ancient Judaism & Modern Category Formation: "Judaism," "Midrash," "Messianism," & Canon in the Past Quarter-Century. LC 85-30416. (Studies in Judaism). 138p. (Orig.). (C). 1986. lib. bdg. 42.00 (*0-8191-5395-8*, Studies in Judaism) U Pr of Amer.

— Ancient Judaism Debates & Disputes, Third Series: Essays on the Formation of Judaism, Dating Sayings, Methods in the History Of... LC 93-15667. (USF Studies in the History of Judaism: No. 3). 328p. 1993. 89.95 (*1-55540-872-9*, 240083) Scholars Pr GA.

— Androgynous Judaism: Masculine & Feminine in the Dual Torah. LC 93-32291. 216p. 1993. 30.00 (*0-86554-428-X*, MUP/H342) Mercer Univ Pr.

— Approaches to Ancient Judaism. (New Ser.: Vol. 2). 215p. 1990. 59.95 (*1-55540-545-2*, 24 00 17) Scholars Pr GA.

— Approaches to Ancient Judaism, New Series, Vol. 3. (USF Studies in the History of Judaism). 249p. 1993. 64.95 (*1-55540-830-3*, 240056) Scholars Pr GA.

— Approaches to Ancient Judaism, New Series, Vol. 4: Religious & Theological Studies. (South Florida Studies in the History of Judaism). 198p. 1993. 17.00 (*1-55540-868-0*, 240081) Scholars Pr GA.

— Are There Really Tannaitic Parallels to the Gospels? A Refutation of Morton Smith. (USF Studies in the History of Judaism). 186p. 1993. 59.95 (*1-55540-867-2*, 240080) Scholars Pr GA.

— The Bavli: An Introduction. (USF Studies in the History of Judaism). 230p. (C). 1992. 59.95 (*1-55540-697-1*, 240042) Scholars Pr GA.

— The Bavli & Its Sources: The Question of Tradition in the Case of Tractate Sukkah. LC 87-4665. (Brown Judaic Studies). 226p. 1987. 29.95 (*1-55540-117-1*, 14-00-85) Scholars Pr GA.

— The Bavli That Might Have Been: The Tosefta's Theory of Mishnah Commentary Compared with the Bavli's. 215p. 1991. 59.95 (*1-55540-575-4*, 24 00 18) Scholars Pr GA.

— The Bavli's Intellectual Character: The Generative Problematic in Bavli Baba Qamma Chapter One & Bavli Shabbat Chapter One. LC 92-33003. (USF Studies in the History of Judaism: Vol. 62). 235p. 1992. 59.95 (*1-55540-773-0*, 24 00 62) Scholars Pr GA.

— The Bavli's Massive Miscellanies. (USF Studies in the History of Judaism). 298p. (C). 1992. 64.95 (*1-55540-698-X*, 240043) Scholars Pr GA.

— The Bavli's One Statement: The Metapropositional Program of Babylonian Talmud Tractate Zebahim, Chapters 1 & 5. 284p. 1991. 69.95 (*1-55540-637-8*, 24 00 30) Scholars Pr GA.

— The Bavli's One Voice. (USF Studies in the History of Judaism). 554p. 1991. 89.95 (*1-55540-604-1*, 240024) Scholars Pr GA.

— The Bavli's Primary Discourse: Mishnah Commentary. (USF Studies in the History of Judaism). 190p. (C). 1992. 59.95 (*1-55540-689-0*, 240038) Scholars Pr GA.

— The Bavli's Unique Voice, Vol. 3. (USF Studies in the History of Judaism). 311p. 1993. 74.95 (*1-55540-841-9*, 240073) Scholars Pr GA.

— The Bavli's Unique Voice, Vol. 4. (USF Studies in the History of Judaism). 342p. 1993. 74.95 (*1-55540-863-X*, 240076) Scholars Pr GA.

— The Bavli's Unique Voice, Vol. 5. (USF Studies in the History of Judaism). 226p. 1993. 64.95 (*1-55540-864-8*, 240077) Scholars Pr GA.

— The Bavli's Unique Voice, Vol. 6. (USF Studies in the History of Judaism). 276p. 1993. 74.95 (*1-55540-865-6*, 240078) Scholars Pr GA.

— The Bavli's Unique Voice, Vol. 7. (USF Studies in the History of Judaism). 315p. 1993. 74.95 (*1-55540-866-4*, 240079) Scholars Pr GA.

— The Bavli's Unique Voice: A Systematic Comparison of the Talmud of Babylonia & the Talmud of the Land of Israel, 2 vols., Vol. 1. LC 93-20017. (USF Studies in the History of Judaism: Vols. 71 & 72). 367p. 1993. 79.95 (*1-55540-834-6*, 24 00 71) Scholars Pr GA.

— The Bavli's Unique Voice: A Systematic Comparison of the Talmud of Babylonia & the Talmud of the Land of Israel, 2 vols., Vol. 2. LC 93-20017. (USF Studies in the History of Judaism: Vols. 71 & 72). 185p. 1993. 59.95 (*1-55540-835-4*, 24 00 72) Scholars Pr GA.

— Between Time & Eternity: The Essentials of Judaism. 196p. (C). 1975. pap. 21.95 (*0-8221-0160-2*) Intl Thomson.

— Canon & Connection: Intertextuality in Judaism. LC 86-26798. (Studies in Judaism). 316p. (Orig.). (C). 1987. pap. text ed. 26.00 (*0-8191-5797-X*, Studies in Judaism) U Pr of Amer.

— The Canonical History of Ideas: The Place of the So-called Tannaite Midrashim: Mekhilta Attributed to R. Ishmael, Sifra, Sifre to Numbers, & Sifre to Deuteronomy. (Studies in History of Judaism). 240p. 1990. 54.95 (*1-55540-436-7*, 24 00 04) Scholars Pr GA.

— Children of the Flesh, Children of the Promise: A Rabbi Talks with Paul. 168p. (Orig.). 1995. pap. 14.95 (*0-8298-1026-9*) Pilgrim OH.

— Christian Faith & the Bible of Judaism: The Judaic Encounter with Scripture. (Brown Judaic Studies). 232p. 1991. 59.95 (*1-55540-498-7*, 140208) Scholars Pr GA.

— Christian Faith & the Bible of Judaism: The Judaic Encounter with Scripture. LC 87-20177. 221p. reprint ed. pap. 63.00 (*0-8357-4366-7*, 2037195) Bks Demand.

— The City of God in Judaism: And Other Comparative & Methodological Studies. 367p. 1991. 74.95 (*1-55540-586-X*, 24 00 23) Scholars Pr GA.

— The Classics of Judaism: A Textbook & Reader. LC 94-12970. 512p. (Orig.). (C). 1995. pap. 29.99 (*0-664-25455-1*) Westminster John Knox.

— Comparative Midrash: The Plan & Program of Genesis Rabbah & Leviticus Rabbah. (Brown Judaic Studies). (C). 1986. 29.95 (*0-89130-958-6*, 14-01-11); pap. 23.95 (*0-89130-959-4*) Scholars Pr GA.

— Confronting Creation: How Judaism Reads Genesis. 397p. 1991. text ed. 39.95 (*0-87249-732-1*) U of SC Pr.

— Conservative, American & Jewish-I Wouldn't Have It Any Other Way. LC 93-78463. 240p. 1993. pap. 9.99 (*1-56384-048-0*) Huntington Hse.

— Death & Birth of Judaism: The Impact of Christianity, Secularism, & the Holocaust on Jewish Faith. LC 92-41013. (USF Studies in the History of Judaism: No. 66). 380p. 1993. reprint ed. pap. 54.95 (*1-55540-811-7*, 24 00 66) Scholars Pr GA.

— Decoding the Talmud's Exegetical Program: From Detail to Principle in the Bavli's Quest for Generalization: Babylonian Talmud Tractate Shabbat. LC 92-39001. (USF Studies in the History of Judaism). 276p. 1992. 64.95 (*1-55540-804-4*, 240067) Scholars Pr GA.

— The Discourse of the Bavli: Language, Literature, & Symbolism. (USF Studies in the History of Judaism). 248p. (C). 1991. 59.95 (*1-55540-650-5*, 240034) Scholars Pr GA.

An Asterisk (*) at the beginning of an entry indicates that the title is appearing in BIP for the first time.

— The Documentary Foundation of Rabbinic Culture: Mopping Up After Debates with Gerald L. Bruns, S. J. D. Cohen, Arnold Maria Goldberg, Susan Handelman, Christine Hayes, James Kugel, Peter Schaefer, Eliezer Segal, E. P. Sanders & Lawrence H. Schiffman. LC 95-1939. (South Florida Studies in the History of Judaism: No. 113). 1995. write for info. (*0-7885-0092-9*) Scholars Pr GA.

— The Economics of the Mishnah: Chicago Studies in the History of Judaism. 200p. 1990. lib. bdg. 45.00 (*0-226-57655-8*); pap. text ed. 14.95 (*0-226-57656-6*) U Ch Pr.

— The Enchantments of Judaism: Rites of Transformation from Birth Through Death. (USF Studies in the History of Judaism). 242p. 1991. 24.95 (*1-55540-589-4*, 240021) Scholars Pr GA.

— Esther Rabbah I: An Analytical Tradition. LC 89-36888. (Brown Judaic Studies). 193p. 1989. 51.95 (*1-55540-382-4*, 14-01-82) Scholars Pr GA.

— First-Century Judaism in Crisis: Yohanan ben Zakkai & the Renaissance of Torah. 1982. 14.95 (*0-87068-728-X*) Ktav.

— First Principles of Systemic Analysis: The Case of Judaism Within the History of Religion. LC 87-25235. (Studies in Judaism). 172p. (C). 1988. lib. bdg. 34.00 (*0-8191-6598-0*, Studies in Judaism) U Pr of Amer.

— Form-Analytical Comparison in Rabbinic Judaism. (USF Studies in the History of Judaism). 147p. (C). 1992. 59.95 (*1-55540-700-5*, 240045) Scholars Pr GA.

— The Formation of Judaism: In Retrospect & Prospect. 276p. 1991. 59.95 (*1-55540-573-8*) Scholars Pr GA.

— The Formation of the Jewish Intellect: Making Connections & Drawing Conclusions in the Traditional System of Judaism. LC 88-18374. (Brown Judaic Studies). 192p. 1988. 48.95 (*1-55540-255-0*, 14 01 51) Scholars Pr GA.

— Formative Judaism. LC 82-16746. (Brown Judaic Studies). 182p. (C). 1982. pap. 14.50 (*0-89130-594-7*, 14 00 37) Scholars Pr GA.

— Formative Judaism: Religious, Historical, & Literary Studies. (Brown Judaic Studies). (C). 1985. 31.95 (*0-89130-850-4*, 14-00-91); pap. 22.95 (*0-89130-851-2*) Scholars Pr GA.

— Formative Judaism: Religious, Historical & Literary Studies-Third Series. LC 83-8662. (Brown Judaic Studies). 212p. (C). 1983. pap. 16.00 (*0-89130-633-1*, 14 00 46) Scholars Pr GA.

— Formative Judaism - Religious Historical & Literary Studies: Fourth Series - Problems of Classification & Composition. (Brown Judaic Studies: No. 76). 222p. (C). 1984. 25.95 (*0-89130-782-6*, 14 00 76); pap. 17.95 (*0-89130-783-4*) Scholars Pr GA.

— Formative Judaism II. LC 82-25072. (Brown Judiac Studies). 198p. 1983. pap. 14.50 (*0-89130-614-5*, 14 00 41) Scholars Pr GA.

— Formative Judaism, Seventh Series: Religious, Historical, & Literary Studies. LC 93-40719. (USF Studies in the History of Judaism). 222p. 1994. 69.95 (*1-55540-928-8*, 240094) Scholars Pr GA.

— The Fortress Introduction to American Judaism: What the Books Say, What the People Do. LC 93-14856. 160p. 1994. pap. 11.00 (*0-8006-2670-2*, 1-2670, Fortress Pr) Augsburg Fortress.

— Foundations of Judaism. (USF Studies in the History of Judaism). 126p. 1993. 49.95 (*1-55540-887-7*, 240086) Scholars Pr GA.

— The Foundations of the Theology of Judaism, Torah, Pt. 2: An Anthology. (USF Studies in the History of Judaism). 160p. (C). 1992. 59.95 (*1-55540-699-8*, 240044) Scholars Pr GA.

— From Description to Conviction: Essays on the History & Theology of Judaism. LC 87-25274. (Brown Judaic Studies). 162p. 1987. 31.95 (*1-55540-118-X*, 14-00-86) Scholars Pr GA.

— From Mishnah to Scripture: The Problem of the Unattributed Saying. LC 84-10527. (Brown Judaic Studies). 135p. (C). 1984. 21.95 (*0-89130-759-1*, 14 00 67); pap. 14.95 (*0-89130-749-4*) Scholars Pr GA.

— From Politics to Piety: The Emergence of Pharisaic Judaism. pap. 9.95 (*0-87068-677-1*) Ktav.

— From Text to Historical Context In Rabbinic Judaism: Historical Facts in Systemic Documents, One; The Mishanah, Tosefta, Abot, Sifra, Sifra to Numbers & Sifre. LC 93-38730. 325p. 1994. 89.95 (*1-55540-927-X*, 240093) Scholars Pr GA.

— From Text to Historical Context in Rabbinic Judaism, Vol. 2: Historical Facts in Systemic Documents. (USF Studies in the History of Judaism). 260p. 1994. 74.95 (*1-55540-955-5*, 240103) Scholars Pr GA.

— From Text to Historical Context in Rabbinic Judaism, Vol. 3: Historical Facts in Systemic Documents. (USF Studies in the History of Judaism). 286p. 1994. 74.95 (*1-55540-956-3*, 240104) Scholars Pr GA.

— From Tradition to Imitation: The Plan & Program of Pesiqta Rabbati & Pesiqta deRab Kahana. LC 87-4664. (Brown Judaic Studies). 249p. 1987. 25.95 (*1-55540-113-9*, 14-00-80) Scholars Pr GA.

— Genesis & Judaism: The Perspective of Genesis Rabbah, an Analytical Anthology. (C). 1985. 30.95 (*0-89130-940-3*, 14-01-08); pap. 23.95 (*0-89130-941-1*) Scholars Pr GA.

— Genesis Rabbah: The Judaic Commentary to the Book of Genesis, Vol. I. (C). 1985. pap. 28.75 (*0-89130-932-2*) Scholars Pr GA.

— Genesis Rabbah: The Judaic Commentary to the Book of Genesis, Vol. II. (C). 1985. pap. 31.55 (*0-89130-934-9*) Scholars Pr GA.

— Genesis Rabbah: The Judaic Commentary to the Book of Genesis, Vol. III. (C). 1985. 33.95 (*0-89130-935-7*, 14-01-06); pap. 30.55 (*0-89130-936-5*) Scholars Pr GA.

— A History of the Jews in Babylonia I: The Parthian Period. LC 84-5363. (Brown Judaic Studies). 292p. (C). 1984. pap. 22.00 (*0-89130-738-9*, 14 00 62) Scholars Pr GA.

— How the Talmud Shaped Rabbinic Discourse. (USF Studies in the History of Judaism). 180p. (C). 1991. 54.95 (*1-55540-649-1*, 240033) Scholars Pr GA.

— How to Study the Bavli. (USF Studies in the History of Judaism). 248p. (C). 1992. 59.95 (*1-55540-688-2*, 240037) Scholars Pr GA.

— In Search of Talmudic Biography: The Problem of the Attributed Saying. LC 84-10526. (Brown Judaic Studies). 148p. 1984. 20.95 (*0-89130-752-4*, 14 00 70); pap. 15.95 (*0-89130-758-3*) Scholars Pr GA.

— In the Margins of the Yerushalmi: Glosses on the English Translation. LC 83-20113. (Brown Judaic Studies). 160p. (C). 1983. pap. 15.00 (*0-89130-663-3*, 14 00 55) Scholars Pr GA.

— The Incarnation of God: The Character of Divinity in Formative Judaism. LC 92-33002. (USF Studies in the History of Judaism: No. 63). 239p. 1992. 59.95 (*1-55540-778-1*, 24 00 63) Scholars Pr GA.

— The Integrity of Leviticus Rabbah: The Problem of the Autonomy of a Rabbinic Document. (Brown Judaic Studies). 1985. 27.95 (*0-89130-852-0*, 14-00-93); pap. 22.50 (*0-89130-853-9*) Scholars Pr GA.

— An Introduction to Judaism: A Textbook & Reader. 448p. (Orig.). 1992. pap. 24.99 (*0-664-25348-2*) Westminster John Knox.

— Introduction to Rabbinic Literature. LC 93-28109. (Anchor Bible Reference Library). 1994. 40.00 (*0-385-47093-2*) Doubleday.

— Invitation to the Talmud: A Teaching Book. LC 83-48422. 400p. 1989. pap. 15.00 (*0-06-066112-7*) Harper SF.

— Israel after Calamity: The Book of Lamentations. 1995. pap. 13.00 (*1-56338-105-2*) TPI PA.

— Israel & Iran in Talmudic Times: A Political History. (Illus.). 266p. (Orig.). (C). 1987. lib. bdg. 49.50 (*0-8191-5729-5*, Studies in Judaism) U Pr of Amer.

— Israel in America: A Too-Comfortable Exile? (Studies in Judaism). 216p. (C). 1994. reprint ed. pap. text ed. 22.00 (*0-8191-7533-1*) U Pr of Amer.

— Israel's Love Affair with God: Song of Songs. LC 93-18503. pap. 14.95 (*1-56338-052-8*) TPI PA.

— Israel's Politics in Sasanian Iran: Jewish Self-Government in Talmudic Times. (Studies in Judaism). (Illus.). 202p. (Orig.). (C). 1987. pap. text ed. 22.50 (*0-8191-5726-0*, Studies in Judaism) U Pr of Amer.

— Jesus: A Jewish Dissent. LC 92-16395. 1993. 21.00 (*0-385-42466-3*) Doubleday.

— The Jewish War Against the Jews: Reflections on Golah, Shoah, & Torah. LC 84-9657. 157p. 1984. 12.95 (*0-88125-050-3*) Ktav.

— Jews & Christians: The Myth of a Common Tradition. LC 90-44866. 176p. (Orig.). (C). 1991. pap. 14.95 (*0-334-02465-X*) TPI PA.

— Judaic Law from Jesus to the Mishnah: A Systematic Reply to Professor E. P. Sanders. LC 93-15668. (USF Studies in the History of Judaism: No. 84). 329p. 1993. 74.95 (*1-55540-873-7*, 240084) Scholars Pr GA.

— The Judaic Law of Baptism: Tractate Miqvaot in the Mishnah & the Tosefta: A Form-Analytical Translation & Commentary & a Legal & Religious History. LC 95-1936. (South Florida Studies in the History of Judaism: No. 112). 1995. write for info. (*0-7885-0091-0*) Scholars Pr GA.

— Judaism: The Classical Statement, the Evidence of the Bavli. LC 85-28875. (Chicago Studies in the History of Judaism). 288p. 1986. 37.00 (*0-226-57620-5*) U Ch Pr.

— Judaism: The Evidence of the Mishnah. LC 87-24328. (Brown Judaic Studies). 527p. 1988. 62.95 (*1-55540-181-3*, 14-01-29) Scholars Pr GA.

— Judaism after the Death of "The Death of God" LC 94-35373. (South Florida Studies in the History of Judaism). Date not set. write for info. (*0-7885-0048-1*) Scholars Pr GA.

— Judaism & Christianity in the Age of Constantine: History, Messiah, Israel, & the Initial Confrontation. LC 87-5952. (Chicago Studies in the History of Judaism). xvi, 248p. 1987. 27.50 (*0-226-57652-3*) U Ch Pr.

— Judaism & Its Social Metaphors: Israel in the History of Jewish Thought. 251p. (C). 1989. 59.95 (*0-521-35471-4*) Cambridge U Pr.

— Judaism & Scripture: The Evidence of Leviticus Rabbah. LC 85-20497. (Chicago Studies in the History of Judaism). 664p. 1986. 50.00 (*0-226-57614-0*) U Ch Pr.

— Judaism & Story: The Evidence of the Fathers According to Rabbi Nathan. LC 91-37130. (Chicago Studies in the History of Judaism). 320p. 1992. 49.00 (*0-226-57630-2*) U Ch Pr.

— Judaism & Zoroastrianism at the Dusk of Late Antiquity: How Two Ancient Faiths Wrote down Their Great Traditions. (USF Studies in the History of Judaism). 202p. 1993. 59.95 (*1-55540-889-3*, 240087) Scholars Pr GA.

— Judaism As Philosophy: The Method & Message of the Mishnah. 317p. 1991. text ed. 39.95 (*0-87249-736-4*) U of SC Pr.

— The Judaism Behind the Texts: The Generative Premises of Rabbinic Literature; The Mishnah, the Division of Appointed Times, Women, Vol. IA. LC 93-35682. (USF Studies in the History of Judaism: No. 89-90). 242p. 1994. 74.95 (*1-55540-915-6*, 240089) Scholars Pr GA.

— The Judaism Behind the Texts: The Generative Premises of Rabbinic Literature; The Mishnah, the Division of Appointed Times, Women, Vol. IB. LC 93-35682. (USF Studies in the History of Judaism: No. 89-90). 264p. 1994. 74.95 (*1-55540-916-4*, 240090) Scholars Pr GA.

— Judaism Behind the Texts IC. (USF Studies in the History of Judaism). 236p. 1994. 74.95 (*1-55540-934-2*, 240097) Scholars Pr GA.

— The Judaism Behind the Texts II: The Generative Premises of Rabbinic Literature. LC 93-39348. (USF Studies in the History of Judaism: No. 98). 269p. 1994. 74.95 (*1-55540-935-0*, 240098) Scholars Pr GA.

— The Judaism Behind the Texts III: The Later Midrash Compilations; Genesis Rabbah, Leviticus Rabbah, & Pesiqta DeRab Kahana. LC 93-48298. (USF Studies in the History of Judaism: Vol. 99). 270p. 1994. 74.95 (*1-55540-947-4*, 240099) Scholars Pr GA.

— The Judaism Behind the Texts IV: The Latest Midrash Compilations; Song of Songs Rabbah, Ruth Rabbah, Esther Rabbah I, & Lamentations Rabbati. LC 93-48299. (USF Studies in the History of Judaism: Vol. 100). 223p. 1994. 74.95 (*1-55540-948-2*, 240100) Scholars Pr GA.

— The Judaism Behind the Texts V: The Generative Premises of Rabbinic Literature; The Talmuds of the Land of Israel & of Babylonia. LC 93-48300. (USF Studies in the History of Judaism: Vol. 101). 325p. 1994. 74.95 (*1-55540-949-0*, 240101) Scholars Pr GA.

— Judaism, Christianity, & Zoroastrianism in Talmudic Babylonia. (Brown Judaic Studies). 248p. 1990. 49.95 (*1-55540-474-X*) Scholars Pr GA.

— Judaism in Modern Times: An Introduction & Reader. LC 94-29537. 256p. 1995. 49.95 (*1-55786-683-X*) Blackwell Pubs.

— Judaism in Modern Times: An Introduction & Reader. LC 94-29537. 256p. (C). 1995. pap. 19.95 (*1-55786-684-8*) Blackwell Pubs.

— Judaism in Society: The Evidence of the Yerushalmi: Toward the Natural His. (USF Studies in the History of Judaism). 318p. 1991. 69.95 (*1-55540-574-6*, 240020) Scholars Pr GA.

— Judaism in the American Humanities. LC 81-1798. (Brown Judaic Studies). (C). 1981. pap. text ed. 21.00 (*0-89130-480-0*, 14-00-28) Scholars Pr GA.

— Judaism in the American Humanities: Second Series: Jewish Learning & the New Humanities. (Brown Judaic Studies). 136p. (C). 1983. pap. 14.50 (*0-89130-618-8*, 14 00 42) Scholars Pr GA.

— Judaism in the Beginning of Christianity. LC 83-48000. 112p. (C). 1984. pap. 10.00 (*0-8006-1750-9*, 1-1750) Augsburg Fortress.

— Judaism in the Matrix of Christianity. 2nd ed. 148p. 1991. 64.95 (*1-55540-607-6*, 24 00 08) Scholars Pr GA.

— Judaism States Its Theology: The Talmudic Re-Presentation. (USF Studies in the History of Judaism). 202p. 1993. 74.95 (*1-55540-890-7*, 240088) Scholars Pr GA.

— The Judaism the Rabbis Take for Granted. LC 93-49771. (USF Studies in the History of Judaism: No. 102). 270p. 1994. 74.95 (*1-55540-954-7*, 240102) Scholars Pr GA.

— Judaism Without Christianity: An Introduction to the System of the Mishnah. 1990. pap. 19.95 (*0-88125-333-2*) Ktav.

— Judaism's Theological Voice: The Melody of the Talmud. LC 94-33405. (Chicago Studies in the History of Judaism). 1995. pap. text ed. 14.95 (*0-226-57649-3*) U Ch Pr.

— Judaism's Theological Voice: The Melody of the Talmud. LC 94-33405. (Chicago Studies in the History of Judaism). 1995. lib. bdg. 39.95 (*0-226-57648-5*) U Ch Pr.

— Language as Taxonomy: The Rules for Using Hebrew & Aramaic in the Babylonian Talmud. 256p. 1991. 59.95 (*1-55540-538-X*) Scholars Pr GA.

— The Law Behind the Laws: The Bavli's Essential Discourse. (USF Studies in the History of Judaism). 212p. (C). 1992. 59.95 (*1-55540-674-2*, 240035) Scholars Pr GA.

— Learn Mishnah. LC 78-5482. (Illus.). (J). (gr. 5-6). 1978. pap. 5.95 (*0-87441-310-9*) Behrman.

— Learn Talmud. (Illus.). (gr. 9). 1979. pap. 5.95 (*0-87441-292-7*) Behrman.

— Lectures on Judaism in the Academy & in the Humanities. (Studies in History of Judaism). 291p. 1990. 59.95 (*1-55540-413-8*) Scholars Pr GA.

— Lectures on Judaism in the History of Religions. (Studies in History of Judaism). 400p. 1990. 72.95 (*1-55540-480-4*) Scholars Pr GA.

— Major Trends in Formative Judaism: First Series. LC 83-20176. (Brown Judaic Studies). 126p. (C). 1983. pap. 15.25 (*0-89130-668-4*, 14 00 60) Scholars Pr GA.

— Major Trends in Formative Judaism: Second Series: Texts, Contents, & Contexts. LC 83-20176. (Brown Judaic Studies). 160p. 1984. pap. text ed. 16.00 (*0-89130-727-3*, 14 00 61) Scholars Pr GA.

— Major Trends in Formative Judaism: Third Series: The Three Stages in the Formation of Judaism. (Brown Judaic Studies). (C). 1985. 23.95 (*0-89130-898-9*, 14-00-99); pap. 19.25 (*0-89130-899-7*) Scholars Pr GA.

— The Making of the Mind of Judaism: The Formative Age. LC 87-28528. (Brown Judaic Studies). 184p. 1987. 23.95 (*1-55540-197-X*, 14-01-33) Scholars Pr GA.

— Making the Classics in Judaism: The Three Stages of Literary Formation. LC 89-35719. (Brown Judaic Studies). 282p. 1989. 53.95 (*1-55540-377-8*, 14 01 80) Scholars Pr GA.

— Medium & Message in Judaism: First Series. LC 89-35718. (Brown Judaic Studies). 169p. 1989. 49.95 (*1-55540-378-6*, 14 01 79) Scholars Pr GA.

— Meet Our Sages. LC 80-12771. (Illus.). 128p. (J). (gr. 5-8). 1980. pap. text ed. 5.95 (*0-87441-327-3*) Behrman.

— Mekhilta According to Rabbi Ishmael: An Introduction to Judaisms First Scriptural Encyclopaedia. LC 88-30829. (Brown Judaic Studies). 280p. 1989. 42.95 (*1-55540-262-3*, 14-01-52) Scholars Pr GA.

— Mekhilta According to Rabbi Ishmael - An Analytical Translation: Pisha, Beshallah, Shirata & Vayassa, Vol. 1. LC 88-11442. (Brown Judaic Studies). 288p. 1989. 46.95 (*1-55540-237-2*, 14-01-48) Scholars Pr GA.

— Mekhilta According to Rabbi Ishmael, Vol. 2: An Analytical Translation. LC 88-11442. (Brown Judaic Studies). 282p. 1989. 43.95 (*1-55540-269-0*, 14 01 54) Scholars Pr GA.

— The Memorized Torah: The Mnemonic System of the Mishnah. (Brown Judaic Studies). (C). 1985. 22.95 (*0-89130-866-0*, 14-00-96); pap. 18.95 (*0-89130-867-9*) Scholars Pr GA.

— Messiah in Context: Israel's History & Destiny in Formative Judaism. (Studies in Judaism). 288p. (C). reprint ed. lib. bdg. 45.00 (*0-8191-6904-8*, Studies in Judaism) U Pr of Amer.

— Method & Meaning in Ancient Judaism. LC 79-9881. (Brown Judaic Studies: No. 10). 219p. reprint ed. pap. 62.50 (*0-7837-5398-5*, 2045162) Bks Demand.

— Method & Meaning in Ancient Judaism: Fourth Series. LC 88-27015. (Brown Judaic Studies). 287p. 1989. 51.95 (*1-55540-323-9*, 14 01 68) Scholars Pr GA.

— Method & Meaning in Ancient Judaism II. LC 80-21781. (Brown Judaic Studies). (C). 1981. pap. 29.50 (*0-89130-416-9*, 140015) Scholars Pr GA.

— Method & Meaning in Ancient Judaism, Third Series. LC 80-19449. (Brown Judaic Studies: No. 16). 255p. reprint ed. pap. 72.70 (*0-7837-5425-6*, 2045189) Bks Demand.

— The Midrash: An Introduction. LC 89-18274. 256p. 1994. reprint ed. pap. text ed. 20.00 (*1-56821-357-3*) Aronson.

— Midrash in Context: Exegesis in Formative Judaism. 1988. 37.95 (*1-55540-218-6*, 14 01 41) Scholars Pr GA.

— The Mishnah: A New Translation. LC 87-21531. (C). 1988. text ed. 75.00 (*0-300-03065-7*) Yale U Pr.

— The Mishnah: A New Translation. 1162p. (C). 1991. reprint ed. pap. text ed. 35.00 (*0-300-05022-4*) Yale U Pr.

— The Mishnah: An Introduction. LC 88-38460. 256p. 1994. reprint ed. pap. text ed. 20.00 (*1-56821-358-1*) Aronson.

— The Mishnah: Introduction & Reader. LC 91-38147. 256p. (Orig.). (C). 1992. pap. 16.95 (*1-56338-021-8*) TPI PA.

— Mitzvah. (J). (gr. 6-8). pap. 6.95 (*0-317-70156-8*) Behrman.

— Mitzvah: Basic Jewish Ideas. (Ser.). (Orig.). (gr. 6-8). 1981. pap. 4.95 (*0-940646-25-0*) Rossel Bks.

— Mother of the Messiah in Judaism: The Book of Ruth. LC 93-31398. 1993. pap. 12.00 (*1-56338-061-7*) TPI PA.

— The Oral Torah: The Sacred Books of Judaism: An Introduction. (USF Studies in the History of Judaism). 258p. (C). 1991. 64.95 (*1-55540-638-6*, 240031) Scholars Pr GA.

— Oral Tradition in Judaism: The Case of the Mishnah. LC 87-12056. (Albert Bates Lord Studies in Oral Tradition: Vol. 1). 176p. 1987. 31.00 (*0-8240-7849-7*, H764) Garland.

— Paradigms in Passage: Patterns of Change in the Contemporary Study of Judaism. (Studies in Judaism). 218p. (C). 1988. lib. bdg. 35.00 (*0-8191-6899-8*, Studies in Judaism) U Pr of Amer.

— The Peripatetic Saying: The Problem of the Thrice-Told Tale in the Canon of Talmudic Literature. (Brown Judaic Studies: No. 89). 208p. (C). 1985. 19.95 (*0-89130-830-X*, 14 00 89); pap. 16.95 (*0-89130-831-8*) Scholars Pr GA.

— The Pharisees: Rabbinic Perspectives. LC 85-5783. (Studies in Ancient Judaism). 300p. (Orig.). 1985. pap. text ed. 19.95 (*0-88125-067-8*) Ktav.

— The Philosophical Mishnah: The Initial Probe. LC 88-33716. (Brown Judaic Studies). 254p. 1989. 51.95 (*1-55540-310-7*, 14 01 63) Scholars Pr GA.

— The Philosophical Mishnah, Vol. 2: The Tractate's Agenda: From Abodah Zarah Through Moed Qatan. LC 88-33716. (Brown Judaic Studies). 303p. 1989. 65.95 (*1-55540-326-3*, 14 01 64) Scholars Pr GA.

— The Principal Parts of the Bavli's Discourse: A Preliminary Taxonomy. LC 92-25795. (USF Studies in the History of Judaism: No. 53). 237p. 1992. 64.95 (*1-55540-750-1*, 240053) Scholars Pr GA.

— Purity in Rabbinic Judaism: A Systematic Account. LC 93-40720. (USF Studies in the History of Judaism: No. 95). 217p. 1994. 69.95 (*1-55540-929-6*, 240095) Scholars Pr GA.

— Rabbi Talks with Jesus: An Intermillennial, Interfaith Exchange. LC 93-36807. 1994. mass mkt. 9.00 (*0-385-47306-0*, Image Bks) Doubleday.

— Rabbinic Judaism: Debates & Disputes. LC 94-27844. (USF Studies in the History of Judaism: No. 107). 310p. 1994. 79.95 (*0-7885-0006-6*, 240107) Scholars Pr GA.

— Rabbinic Judaism: The Documentary History of Its Formative Age 70-600 C. E. 413p. (C). 1994. 42.00 (*1-883053-06-4*) CDL Pr.

— Rabbinic Literature & the New Testament: What We Cannot Show, We Do Not Know. 176p. (Orig.). (C). 1994. pap. 17.00 (*1-56338-074-9*) TPI PA.

— Rabbinic Political Theory: Religion & Politics in the Mishnah. (Chicago Studies in the History of Judaism). 288p. 1991. lib. bdg. 49.95 (*0-226-57650-7*); pap. text ed. 22.50 (*0-226-57651-5*) U Ch Pr.

— Reading & Believing. LC 86-30399. (Brown Judaic Studies). 138p. (C). 1986. 27.50 (*0-89130-976-4*, 14-01-13); pap. 20.50 (*0-89130-977-2*) Scholars Pr GA.

— Religion & the Social Order: What Kinds of Lessons Does History Teach? LC 94-33696. (South Florida-Rochester-Saint Louis Studies on Religion & the Social Order: Vol. 11). 1994. write for info. (*0-7885-0054-6*) Scholars Pr GA.

— A Religion of Pots & Pans? Modes of Philosophical & Theological Discourse in Ancient Judaism. LC 88-30828. (Brown Judaic Studies). 228p. 1989. 41.95 (*1-55540-283-6*, 140156) Scholars Pr GA.
— Religious Study of Judaism: Context, Text, Circumstance, Vol. 3. (Studies in Judaism). 234p. (Orig.). 1987. lib. bdg. 50.00 (*0-8191-6047-4*, Studies in Judaism); pap. 22.50 (*0-8191-6048-2*, Studies in Judaism) U Pr of Amer.
— The Religious Study of Judaism: Description, Analysis & Interpretation. LC 85-30411. (Studies in Judaism: Vol. 1). 188p. (Orig.). (C). 1986. pap. text ed. 20.50 (*0-8191-5394-X*, Studies in Judaism) U Pr of Amer.
— The Religious Study of Judaism: Description, Analysis, Interpretation-The Centrality of Context. LC 85-30411. (Studies in Judaism: Vol. 2). 230p. (Orig.). (C). 1986. lib. bdg. 50.00 (*0-8191-5450-4*, Studies in Judaism); pap. text ed. 23.00 (*0-8191-5451-2*, Studies in Judaism) U Pr of Amer.
— The Religious Study of Judaism: Description, Analysis, Interpretation, Vol. IV: Ideas of History Ethics, Ontology, & Religion in Formative Judaism. LC 85-30411. (Studies in Judaism). 210p. (C). 1988. lib. bdg. 34.00 (*0-8191-7142-5*) U Pr of Amer.
— The Rules of Composition of the Talmud of Babylonia. 280p. 1991. 59.95 (*1-55540-539-8*) Scholars Pr GA.
— School, Court, Public Administration. LC 87-4632. (Brown Judaic Studies). 306p. 1987. 36.95 (*1-55540-115-5*, 14-00-83) Scholars Pr GA.
— Self-Fulfilling Prophecy: Exile & Return in the History of Judaism. (Studies in History of Judaism). 260p. 1990. 64.95 (*1-55540-494-4*) Scholars Pr GA.
— A Short History of Judaism: Three Meals, Three Epochs. LC 92-7929. 244p. (Orig.). 1992. pap. 15.00 (*0-8006-2552-8*, 1-2552, Fortress Pr) Augsburg Fortress.
— Sifra in Perspective: The Documentary Comparison of the Midrashim of Ancient Judaism. LC 88-10073. (Brown Judaic Studies). 277p. 1988. 41.95 (*1-55540-232-1*, 14-01-46) Scholars Pr GA.
— Sifre to Deuteronomy: An Analytical Transtation, Vol. I: Pisqaot One Through One Hundred Forty-Three. LC 87-9779. (Brown Judaic Studies: Vol. 1). 366p. 1987. 31.95 (*1-55540-145-7*, 14-00-98) Scholars Pr GA.
— Sifre to Deuteronomy: An Introduction. LC 87-16687. (Brown Judaic Studies). 210p. 1987. 25.95 (*1-55540-168-6*, 14-01-24) Scholars Pr GA.
— The Social Study of Judaism, Vol. 1: Essays & Reflections. LC 88-33664. (Brown Judaic Studies). 270p. 1989. 46.95 (*1-55540-306-9*, 14 01 60) Scholars Pr GA.
— Sources & Traditions: Types of Compositions in the Talmud of Babylonia. (USF Studies in the History of Judaism). 212p. (C). 1992. 59.95 (*1-55540-675-0*, 240036) Scholars Pr GA.
— Sources of the Transformation of Judaism: From Philosophy to Religion in the Classics of Judaism: A Reader. LC 92-42836. (USF Studies in the History of Judaism: Vol. 68). 307p. 1993. 74.95 (*1-55540-813-3*, 240068) Scholars Pr GA.
— Struggle for the Jewish Mind: Debates & Disputes on Judaism Then & Now. (Studies in Judaism). 200p. (Orig.). (C). 1988. lib. bdg. 32.00 (*0-8191-6689-8*) U Pr of Amer.
— Studying Classical Judaism: A Primer. 192p. (Orig.). 1991. pap. 15.99 (*0-664-25136-6*) Westminster John Knox.
— Systemic Analysis of Judaism. LC 87-32401. (Brown Judaic Studies). 144p. 1988. 30.95 (*1-55540-204-6*, 14-01-37) Scholars Pr GA.
— The Talmud: A Close Encounter. LC 91-17994. 224p. (Orig.). 1991. pap. 15.00 (*0-8006-2498-X*, 1-2498, Fortress Pr) Augsburg Fortress.
— The Talmud in Babylonia Vol. XII: Hagigah: An Academic Commentary. (USF Academic Commentary Ser.). 175p. 1994. 59.95 (*1-55540-984-9*, 243007) Scholars Pr GA.
— The Talmud in Babylonia Vol. XXVI: Bavli Tractate Honayot: An Academic Commentary. (USF Academic Commentary Ser.). 155p. 1994. 59.95 (*1-55540-985-7*, 243008) Scholars Pr GA.
— The Talmud in Babylonia Vol. XXVII: Bavli Tractate Shebuot: An Academic Commentary. (USF Academic Commentary Ser.). 321p. 1994. 74.95 (*1-55540-986-5*, 243009) Scholars Pr GA.
— The Talmud in Babylonia, Vol. XXXIII Temurah: An Academic Commentary. (USF Academic Commentary Ser.). 261p. 1994. 74.95 (*1-55540-987-3*, 243010) Scholars Pr GA.
— The Talmud in Babylonia, Vol. XXXV Meilah & Tamid: An Academic Commentary. (USF Academic Commentary Ser.). 170p. 1994. 59.95 (*1-55540-988-1*, 243011) Scholars Pr GA.
— The Talmud of Babylonia: A Complete Outline. LC 94-36299. (USF Academic Commentary Ser.: No. 27). Date not set. write for info. (*0-7885-0053-8*) Scholars Pr GA.
— The Talmud of Babylonia: An American Translation: Shabbat II.A. LC 92-37135. (Brown Judaic Studies: No. 270). 192p. 1992. 59.95 (*1-55540-797-8*, 14 02 70) Scholars Pr GA.
— The Talmud of Babylonia: An American Translation: XI: Tractate Moed Qatan. LC 92-13780. (Brown Judaic Studies: No. 252). 232p. 1992. 59.95 (*1-55540-725-0*, 140252) Scholars Pr GA.
— The Talmud of Babylonia: An American Translation: XIII.A: Tractate Yebamot. LC 92-13781. (Brown Judaic Studies: No. 250-251). 230p. 1992. 69.95 (*1-55540-722-6*, 140250) Scholars Pr GA.
— The Talmud of Babylonia: An American Translation: XIII.B: Tractate Yebamot. (Brown Judaic Studies). 204p. 1992. 59.95 (*1-55540-723-4*, 140251) Scholars Pr GA.
— The Talmud of Babylonia: An American Translation: XIII.C: Tractate Yebamot. (Brown Judaic Studies). 223p. 1992. 69.95 (*1-55540-733-1*, 140256) Scholars Pr GA.
— The Talmud of Babylonia: An American Translation: XIII.D: Tractate Yebamot. (Brown Judaic Studies). 206p. 1992. 59.95 (*1-55540-745-5*, 140261) Scholars Pr GA.
— The Talmud of Babylonia: An American Translation: XIV.A: Tractate Ketubot. LC 92-16852. (Brown Judaic Studies). 202p. 1992. 59.95 (*1-55540-734-X*, 140257) Scholars Pr GA.
— The Talmud of Babylonia: An American Translation: XIV.B: Tractate Ketubot. (Brown Judaic Studies). 202p. 1992. 59.95 (*1-55540-735-8*, 140258) Scholars Pr GA.
— The Talmud of Babylonia: An American Translation: XIV.C: Tractate Ketubot. (Brown Judaic Studies). 213p. 1992. 59.95 (*1-55540-744-7*, 140260) Scholars Pr GA.
— The Talmud of Babylonia: An American Translation: XV.A: Tractate Nedarim. (American Academy of Religion Academy Ser.). 187p. 1992. 59.95 (*1-55540-751-X*, 140262) Scholars Pr GA.
— The Talmud of Babylonia: An American Translation: XX.A: Tractate Baba Qamma. (Brown Judaic Studies). 221p. 1992. 59.95 (*1-55540-702-1*, 140247) Scholars Pr GA.
— The Talmud of Babylonia: An American Translation: XX.B: Tractate Baba Qamma. (Brown Judaic Studies). 248p. 1992. 64.95 (*1-55540-703-X*, 140248) Scholars Pr GA.
— The Talmud of Babylonia: An American Translation: XX.C: Tractate Baba Qamma. (Brown Judaic Studies). 238p. 1992. 59.95 (*1-55540-704-8*, 140249) Scholars Pr GA.
— The Talmud of Babylonia: An American Translation: XXII.A: Tractate Baba Batra. (Brown Judaic Studies). 245p. 1992. 59.95 (*1-55540-667-X*, 140239) Scholars Pr GA.
— The Talmud of Babylonia: An American Translation: XXII.B: Tractate Baba Batra. (Brown Judaic Studies). 198p. 1992. 59.95 (*1-55540-668-8*, 140240) Scholars Pr GA.
— The Talmud of Babylonia: An American Translation: XXII.C: Tractate Baba Batra. (Brown Judaic Studies). 199p. 1992. 59.95 (*1-55540-673-4*, 140241) Scholars Pr GA.
— The Talmud of Babylonia: An American Translation: XXVII.A: Tractate Shebuot. (Brown Judaic Studies). 192p. 1992. 59.95 (*1-55540-685-8*, 140242) Scholars Pr GA.
— The Talmud of Babylonia: An American Translation: XXVII.B: Tractate Shebuot. (Brown Judaic Studies). 246p. 1992. 59.95 (*1-55540-686-6*, 140243) Scholars Pr GA.
— The Talmud of Babylonia: Pesahim IV. A: An American Translation: Tractate Pesahim IV. A Chapter One. (Brown Judaic Studies). 221p. 1993. 59.95 (*1-55540-826-5*, 140281) Scholars Pr GA.
— The Talmud of Babylonia: Pesahim IV D: An American Translation: Tractate Pesahim IV Chapters 7 & 8. (Brown Judaic Studies). 228p. 1992. 59.95 (*1-55540-842-7*, 140284) Scholars Pr GA.
— The Talmud of Babylonia Vol. VI: Sukkah: An Academic Commentary. (USF Academic Commentary Ser.: Series No. 6). 315p. 1994. 59.95 (*1-55540-983-0*, 243006) Scholars Pr GA.
— The Talmud of Babylonia, an Academic Commentary, Vol. XI, Moed Qatan. LC 94-8120. (USF Academic Commentary Ser.: Vol. 1). 218p. 1994. 69.95 (*1-55540-973-3*, 243001) Scholars Pr GA.
— The Talmud of Babylonia, an Academic Commentary, Vol. XXXIV, Keritot. LC 94-8120. (USF Academic Commentary Ser.: Vol. 1). 270p. 1994. 74.95 (*1-55540-972-5*, 243002) Scholars Pr GA.
— The Talmud of Babylonia, an Academic Commentary Vol. XVII. LC 94-8120. (USF Studies in the History of Judaism). 286p. 1994. 79.95 (*1-55540-978-4*, 243003) Scholars Pr GA.
— The Talmud of Babylonia, an Academic Commentary Vol. V: Yoma. (USF Academic Commentary Ser.: Series No. 13). 434p. 1994. 99.95 (*0-7885-0002-3*, 243013) Scholars Pr GA.
— The Talmud of Babylonia, an Academic Commentary Vol. VIII: Bavli Tractate Rosh Hashanah, No. VIII. (USF Academic Commentary Ser.: Series No. 12). 162p. 1994. 74.95 (*0-7885-0012-0*, 243012) Scholars Pr GA.
— The Talmud of Babylonia, an Academic Commentary Vol. XX: Bavli Tractate Baba Qamma, No. XX. (USF Academic Commentary Ser.: No. 15). 666p. 1994. 139.95 (*0-7885-0004-X*, 243015) Scholars Pr GA.
— The Talmud of Babylonia, an Academic Commentary Vol. XXIV: Makkot, No. XXIV. LC 94-8120. (USF Academic Commentary Ser.: Series No. 4). 162p. 1994. 59.95 (*1-55540-979-2*, 243004) Scholars Pr GA.
— The Talmud of Babylonia, an Academic Commentary Vol. XXX: Bavli Tractate Hullin, No. XXX. (USF Academic Commentary Ser.: Series No. 17). 803p. 1994. 149.95 (*0-7885-0016-3*, 243017) Scholars Pr GA.
— The Talmud of Babylonia, an Academic Commentary Vol. XXXI: Bavli Tractate Bekhorot, No. XXI. (USF Academic Commentary Ser.: Series No. 16). 359p. 1994. 89.95 (*0-7885-0005-8*, 243016) Scholars Pr GA.
— The Talmud of Babylonia, an Academic Commentary Vol. XXXVI: Bavli Tractate Niddah, No. XXXVI. (USF Academic Commentary Ser.). 434p. 1994. 99.95 (*0-7885-0003-1*, 243014) Scholars Pr GA.
— The Talmud of Babylonia, an American Translation: Baba Batra, Pt. D. LC 91-14855. (Brown Judaic Studies). 256p. 1994. 64.95 (*0-7885-0021-X*, 140297) Scholars Pr GA.
— The Talmud of Babylonia, an American Translation: Baba Batra, Pt. E. LC 91-14855. (Brown Judaic Studies). 256p. 1994. 64.95 (*0-7885-0022-8*, 140298) Scholars Pr GA.
— The Talmud of Babylonia, an American Translation Vol. A: Yoma. LC 94-28396. (Brown Judaic Studies). 232p. 1994. 59.95 (*0-7885-0007-4*, 140294) Scholars Pr GA.
— The Talmud of Babylonia, an American Translation Vol. B: Yoma. LC 94-28396. (Brown Judaic Studies). 238p. 1994. 59.95 (*0-7885-0008-2*, 140295) Scholars Pr GA.
— The Talmud of Babylonia: An American Translation, Vol. XXIX: Tractate Menahot Chapters 1-3. (Brown Judaic Studies). 219p. 1991. 59.95 (*1-55540-646-7*, 140235) Scholars Pr GA.
— The Talmud of Babylonia: An American Translation, Vol. XXIX C: Tractate Menahot. (Brown Judaic Studies). 211p. 1991. 59.95 (*1-55540-662-9*, 140237) Scholars Pr GA.
— The Talmud of Babylonia: An American Translation, Vol. XXV.A: Tractate Abod. (Brown Judaic Studies). 228p. 1991. 59.95 (*1-55540-594-0*, 140227) Scholars Pr GA.
— The Talmud of Babylonia: An American Translation, Vol. XXV.B: Tractate Abod. (Brown Judaic Studies). 238p. 1991. 59.95 (*1-55540-595-9*, 140228) Scholars Pr GA.
— The Talmud of Babylonia: An American Translation, Vol. XXVIII.B: Tractate Zebahim. 230p. 1991. 59.95 (*1-55540-635-1*, 140233) Scholars Pr GA.
— The Talmud of Babylonia: An American Translation, Vol. XXXIV: Keritot. (Brown Judaic Studies). 226p. 1991. 59.95 (*1-55540-546-0*, 140223) Scholars Pr GA.
— The Talmud of Babylonia: Erubin III. D: An American Translation: Tractate Eurbin III. D Chapters 7-10. (Brown Judaic Studies). 213p. 1993. 59.95 (*1-55540-822-2*, 140279) Scholars Pr GA.
— The Talmud of Babylonia: Eurbin III. A: An American Translation: Tractate Eurbin III. A-B Chapters 1 & 2. (Brown Judaic Studies). 229p. 1993. 59.95 (*1-55540-814-1*, 140276); Pt. A, 213 p. write for info. (*0-318-70138-3*); Pt. B, 206p. write for info. (*0-318-70139-1*) Scholars Pr GA.
— The Talmud of Babylonia: Eurbin III. B: An American Translation: Tractate Eurbin III. B Chapters 3 & 4. (Brown Judaic Studies). 206p. 1993. 59.95 (*1-55540-815-X*, 140277) Scholars Pr GA.
— The Talmud of Babylonia: Eurbin III. C: An American Translation: Tractate Eurbin III. C Chapters 5 & 6. (Brown Judaic Studies). 223p. 1993. 59.95 (*1-55540-821-4*, 140278) Scholars Pr GA.
— The Talmud of Babylonia: Pesahim IV. B: An American Translation: Tractate Pesahim IV. B Chapters 2 & 3. (Brown Judaic Studies). 231p. 1993. 64.95 (*1-55540-827-3*, 140282) Scholars Pr GA.
— The Talmud of Babylonia: Pesahim IV. E: An American Translation: Tractate Pesahim IV. E, Chaps. 9 & 10. (Brown Judaic Studies). 228p. 1993. 64.95 (*1-55540-843-5*) Scholars Pr GA.
— The Talmud of Babylonia: Shabbat II. C: An American Translation: Tractate Shabbat II. C Chapters 7-10. (Brown Judaic Studies). 215p. 1993. 59.95 (*1-55540-808-7*, 140273) Scholars Pr GA.
— The Talmud of Babylonia: Shabbat II. D: An American Translation: Tractate Shabbat II. D Chapters 11-17. (Brown Judaic Studies). 230p. 1993. 59.95 (*1-55540-809-5*, 140274) Scholars Pr GA.
— The Talmud of Babylonia: Shabbat II. E: An American Translation: Tractate Shabbat II. E Chapters 18-24. (Brown Judaic Studies). 221p. 1993. 59.95 (*1-55540-812-5*, 140275) Scholars Pr GA.
— The Talmud of the Land of Israel: A Preliminary Translation & Explanation, Rosh Hashanah, Vol. 16. Goldman, Edward A., tr. (Chicago Studies in the History of Judaism). 136p. 1988. lib. bdg. 26.00 (*0-226-57675-2*) U Ch Pr.
— The Talmud of the Land of Israel: A Preliminary Translation & Explanation, Sukkah, Vol. 17. (Chicago Studies in the History of Judaism). 160p. 1988. lib. bdg. 26.00 (*0-226-57676-0*) U Ch Pr.
— Talmudic Thinking: Language, Logic, Law. LC 91-48456. 212p. 1992. text ed. 34.95 (*0-87249-825-5*) U of SC Pr.
— Telling Tales: Making Sense of Christian & Judiac Nonsense: The Urgency & Basis for Judaeo-Christian Dialogue. LC 92-29802. 176p. (Orig.). 1993. pap. 10.99 (*0-664-25371-7*) Westminster John Knox.
— There We Sat Down: Talmudic Judaism in the Making. pap. 9.95 (*0-87068-676-3*) Ktav.
— Torah: From Scroll to Symbol in Formative Judaism. (Brown Judaic Studies). 1988. 34.95 (*1-55540-219-4*, 14 01 36) Scholars Pr GA.
— Torah from Our Sages: Pirke Avot. 214p. 1986. pap. 9.95 (*0-685-43435-4*) Rossel Bks.
— The Torah in the Talmud: A Taxonomy of the Uses of Scripture in the Talmud: Tractate Qiddushin in the Talmud of Babylonia & the Talmud of the Land of Israel, 2 vols., Vol. 1. LC 92-46278. (USF Studies in the History of Judaism: Nos. 69 & 70). 197p. 1993. 59.95 (*1-55540-828-1*, 24 00 69) Scholars Pr GA.
— The Torah in the Talmud: A Taxonomy of the Uses of Scripture in the Talmud: Tractate Qiddushin in the Talmud of Babylonia & the Talmud of the Land of Israel, 2 vols., Vol. 2. LC 92-46278. (USF Studies in the History of Judaism: Nos. 69 & 70). 194p. 1993. 59.95 (*1-55540-829-X*, 24 00 70) Scholars Pr GA.
— Torah Through the Ages: A Short History of Judaism. LC 89-20646. 192p. (C). 1990. text ed. 21.95 (*0-334-02456-0*) TPI PA.
— The Tosefta: An Introduction. LC 92-10435. (USF Studies in the History of Judaism: No. 47). 422p. 1992. 89.95 (*1-55540-713-7*, 240047) Scholars Pr GA.
— Tosefta: Structure & Sources. LC 86-15638. (Brown Judaic Studies). (C). 1986. 41.95 (*1-55540-049-3*, 14-01-12) Scholars Pr GA.
— The Tosefta: Translated from the Hebrew Sixth Division Tororot, the Order of Purities. 1991. 74.95 (*1-55540-477-4*) Scholars Pr GA.
— The Tosefta, Translated from the Hebrew: Pt. II. Moed. The Order of Appointed Times. 59.50 (*0-87068-691-7*) Ktav.
— The Tosefta, Translated from the Hebrew: Pt. III Nashim. The Order of Women. 59.50 (*0-87068-684-4*) Ktav.
— The Tosefta Translated from the Hebrew: The Order of Purities, Pt. 6. 59.50 (*0-87068-430-2*) Ktav.
— The Tosefta Translated from the Hebrew I. Zeraim: The Order of Seeds. 1986. 59.50 (*0-87068-693-3*) Ktav.
— The Tosefta Translated from the Hebrew IV. Neziqin: The Order of Damages. 1981. 59.50 (*0-87068-692-5*) Ktav.
— The Tosefta Translated from the Hebrew V. Qodoshim: The Order of Holy Things. 1980. 59.50 (*0-87068-340-3*) Ktav.
— Tradition as Selectivity. 246p. 1990. 59.95 (*1-55540-478-2*, 240009) Scholars Pr GA.
— The Transformation of Judaism from Philosophy to Religion. 368p. 1992. 34.95 (*0-252-01805-2*) U of Ill Pr.
— Translating the Classics of Judaism: In Theory & in Practice. LC 89-6281. (Brown Judaic Studies). 158p. 1989. 46.95 (*1-55540-353-0*, 14 01 76) Scholars Pr GA.
— The Twentieth Century Construction of "Judaism" Essays on the Religion of Torah in the History of Religion. (USF Studies in the History of Judaism). 392p. (C). 1991. 74.95 (*1-55540-645-9*, 240032) Scholars Pr GA.
— Tzedakah: Can Jewish Philanthropy Buy Jewish Survival? (Brown Judaic Studies). 126p. 1990. 44.95 (*1-55540-475-8*) Scholars Pr GA.
— Understanding American Judaism: Toward the Description of a Modern Religion, 2 vols. Incl. Vol. 1. Synagogue & the Rabbi. pap. 14.95 (*0-87068-280-6*); Vol. 2. Reform, Orthodoxy, Conservatism, & Reconstructionism. pap. 14.95 (*0-87068-279-2*); Set pap. write for info. (*0-318-54061-4*) Ktav.
— Understanding Jewish Theology. 1973. pap. 16.95 (*0-87068-215-6*) Ktav.
— Understanding Rabbinic Judaism: From Talmudic to Modern Times. 1974. pap. 14.95 (*0-87068-238-5*) Ktav.
— Understanding Seeking Faith: Essays on the Case of Judaism Vol. 1: Debates on Method Reports of Results. LC 86-20316. (Brown Judaic Studies). 158p. (C). 1986. 29.95 (*1-55540-053-1*, 14-01-16) Scholars Pr GA.
— Understanding Seeking Faith: Essays on the Case of Judaism Vol. 3: Society, History, & the Political & Philosophical Uses of Judaism. LC 86-20316. (Brown Judaic Studies). 334p. 1989. 46.95 (*1-55540-270-4*, 14-01-53) Scholars Pr GA.
— Understanding Seeking Faith: Essays on the Case of Judaism Vol. 2: Literature, Religion & the Social Study of Judaism. LC 86-20316. (Brown Judaic Studies). 250p. 1987. 31.95 (*1-55540-114-7*, 14-00-73) Scholars Pr GA.
— Uniting the Dual Torah: Sifra & the Problem of the Mishnah. 272p. (C). 1990. 74.95 (*0-521-38125-8*) Cambridge U Pr.
— Vanquished Nation, Broken Spirit: The Virtues of the Heart in Formative Judaism. 208p. 1987. 44.95 (*0-521-32832-2*) Cambridge U Pr.
— The Way of Torah: An Introduction to Judaism. 5th ed. LC 92-12408. 212p. (C). 1993. pap. 19.95 (*0-534-16938-4*) Intl Thomson.
— Who, Where & What Is "Israel"? Zionist Perspectives on Israeli & American Judaism. LC 88-33976. (Studies in Judaism). 176p. (C). 1989. lib. bdg. 35.00 (*0-8191-7360-6*, Studies in Judaism) U Pr of Amer.
— Why No Gospels in Talmudic Judaism? (Brown Judaic Studies). 100p. 1987. 31.95 (*1-55540-198-8*, 14-01-35); pap. 12.95 (*1-55540-199-6*) Scholars Pr GA.
— Why There Never Was a "Talmud of Caesarea" Saul Lieberman's Mistake. LC 94-35372. (South Florida Studies in the History of Judaism: No. 108). 193p. 1994. 69.95 (*0-7885-0047-3*, 240108) Scholars Pr GA.
— The Wonder-Working Lawyers of Talmudic Bablonia: The Theory & Practice of Judaism in Its Formative Age. LC 87-6161. (Studies in Judaism). (Illus.). 372p. (Orig.). (C). 1987. lib. bdg. 50.50 (*0-8191-6287-6*, Studies in Judaism); pap. text ed. 29.00 (*0-8191-6288-4*, Studies in Judaism) U Pr of Amer.
— Writing with Scripture: The Authority & Uses of the Hebrew Bible in the Torah of Formative Judaism. (USF Studies in the History of Judaism). 188p. (Orig.). 1993. 49.95 (*1-55540-886-9*, 240085) Scholars Pr GA.
— Wrong Ways & Right Ways in the Study of Formative Judaism: Critical Methid & Literature, History & the History of Religion. LC 88-4546. (Brown Judaic Studies). 275p. 1988. 39.95 (*1-55540-228-3*, 14-01-45) Scholars Pr GA.
— Yerushalmi-the Talmud of the Land of Israel: An Introduction. LC 91-19713. 208p. 1993. 30.00 (*0-87668-812-1*) Aronson.

Neusner, Jacob, ed. The Academy & Traditions of Jewish Learning. LC 92-36348. (Judaism in Cold War America, 1945-1990 Ser.: Vol. 9). 344p. 1993. 56.00 (*0-8153-0081-6*) Garland.
— The Alteration of Orthodoxy. LC 92-37155. (Judaism in Cold War America, 1945-1990 Ser.: Vol. 8). 264p. 1993. 46.00 (*0-8153-0077-8*) Garland.
— Ancient Judaism: Debates & Disputes. LC 84-5532. (Brown Judaic Studies). 292p. (C). 1985. 33.50 (*0-89130-755-9*); pap. 21.95 (*0-89130-746-X*, 14 00 64) Scholars Pr GA.
— The Challenge of America: Can Judaism Survive in Freedom? LC 92-33631. (Judaism in Cold War America, 1945-1990 Ser.: Vol. 1). 320p. 1993. 53.00 (*0-8153-0074-3*) Garland.
— The Christian & Judaic Invention of History. 256p. 1991. 44.95 (*1-55540-320-4*, 01 00 55); pap. 29.95 (*1-55540-321-2*) Scholars Pr GA.

An Asterisk (*) at the beginning of an entry indicates that the title is appearing in BIP for the first time.

— Conserving Conservative Judaism: Reconstructionist Judaism. LC 92-35453. (Judaism in Cold War America, 1945-1990 Ser.: Vol. 7). 376p. 1993. 59.00 (*0-8153-0078-6*) Garland.
— Contemporary Judaic Fellowship in Theory & Practice. 1972. 20.00 (*0-87068-187-7*) Ktav.
— Dictionary of Biblical Judaism, 2 vols., 1. 1994. lib. bdg. 62.50 (*0-685-71134-X*) Macmillan.
— Dictionary of Biblical Judaism, 2 vols., 2. 1994. lib. bdg. 62.50 (*0-02-897289-9*) Macmillan.
— Dictionary of Biblical Judaism, 2 vols., Set. 1994. text ed. 125.00 (*0-685-59239-1*) Macmillan.
— In the Aftermath of the Holocaust. LC 92-35029. (Judaism in Cold War America, 1945-1990 Ser.: Vol. 2). 280p. 1993. 44.00 (*0-8153-0079-4*) Garland.
— Israel & Zion in American Judaism: The Zionist Fulfillment. LC 92-34800. (Judaism in Cold War America, 1945-1990 Ser.: Vol. 3). 240p. 1993. 40.00 (*0-8153-0073-5*) Garland.
— Judaism & Christianity: The New Relationship. LC 92-36226. (Judaism in Cold War America, 1945-1990 Ser.: Vol. 4). 224p. 1993. 38.00 (*0-8153-0075-1*) Garland.
— Judaism in Late Antiquity Vol. 1: The Literary & Archaeological Sources. (Nahe und der Mittlere Osten: No. 16). 268p. 1994. 80.00 (*90-04-10129-2*) E J Brill.
— Judaism in Late Antiquity Vol. 2: Historical Syntheses. LC 94-30825. (Handbuch der Orientalistik Ser.: Vol. 17). 340p. 1994. 114.50 (*90-04-10130-6*) E J Brill.
— Judaism Transcends Catastrophe: God, Torah, & Israel Beyond the Holocaust. 1994. 30.00 (*0-86554-460-3*) Mercer Univ Pr.
— The Literature of Formative Judaism: Controversies on the Literature of Formative Judaism. LC 92-13897. (Origins of Judaism Ser.: Vol. 13). 400p. 1991. 65.00 (*0-8240-8184-6*) Garland.
— The Literature of Formative Judaism: The Talmuds. LC 90-13900. (Origins of Judaism Ser.: Vol. 10). 496p. 1991. 75.00 (*0-8240-8181-1*) Garland.
— New Humanities & Academic Disciplines. LC 83-16893. 224p. 1984. pap. text ed. 27.50 (*0-299-09750-1*) U of Wis Pr.
— Our Sages, God & Israel: An Anthology of the Jerusalem Talmud. LC 84-23793. 179p. (C). 1985. 19.95 (*0-940646-18-8*) Rossel Bks.
— The Pharisees & Other Sects. LC 90-13893. (Origins of Judaism Ser.: Vol. 2). 1126p. 1991. 150.00 (*0-8240-8173-0*) Garland.
— The Rabbinate in America: Reshaping an Ancient Calling. LC 92-37068. (Judaism in Cold War America, 1945-1990 Ser.: Vol. 10). 256p. 1993. 42.00 (*0-8153-0082-4*) Garland.
— The Reformation of Reform Judaism. LC 92-33290. (Judaism in Cold War America, 1945-1990 Ser.: Vol. 6). 272p. 1993. 47.00 (*0-8153-0076-X*) Garland.
— The Religious Renewal of Jewry. LC 92-34799. (Judaism in Cold War America, 1945-1990 Ser.: Vol. 5). 344p. 1993. 56.00 (*0-8153-0080-8*) Garland.
— The Study of Ancient Judaism, Vol. 1: Mishnah, Midrash, Siddur. LC 92-19867. 194p. 1992. 69.95 (*1-55540-741-2*) Scholars Pr GA.
— Take Judaism, for Example: Studies Toward the Comparison of Religions. LC 92-17940. 244p. 1992. 69.95 (*1-55540-743-9*, 24 00 51) Scholars Pr GA.
— The Talmud of the Land of Israel: A Preliminary Translation & Explanation. Avery-Peck, Alan J. & Jaffee, Martin S., trs. xii, 570p. 1987. write for info. (*0-318-62141-X*) U Ch Pr.
— The Talmud of the Land of Israel: A Preliminary Translation & Explanation, Vol. 6: Terumot. Avery-Peck, Alan J. & Jaffee, Martin S., trs. (Chicago Studies in the History of Judaism). 504p. 1987. lib. bdg. 75.00 (*0-226-57663-9*) U Ch Pr.
— The Talmud of the Land of Israel: A Preliminary Translation & Explanation- Vol. 25, Gittin. (Chicago Studies in the History of Judaism). 270p. 1985. lib. bdg. 33.00 (*0-226-57684-1*); lib. bdg. 33.00 (*0-226-57683-3*) U Ch Pr.
— The Talmud of the Land of Israel: A Preliminary Translation & Explanation: Vol. 19, Megillah. LC 86-25284. (Chicago Studies in the History of Judaism). x, 188p. (C). 1987. lib. bdg. 29.00 (*0-226-57678-7*); lib. bdg. 37.50 (*0-226-57677-9*) U Ch Pr.
— Talmud of the Land of Israel: A Preliminary Translation & Explanation, Vol. 2. Brooks, Roger, tr. LC 89-5136. (Chicago Studies in the History of Judaism). 364p. 1990. lib. bdg. 54.95 (*0-226-57659-0*) U Ch Pr.
— The Talmud of the Land of Israel: A Preliminary Translation & Explanation, Vol. 22: Ketubot. (Chicago Studies in the History of Judaism). 384p. 1985. lib. bdg. 49.00 (*0-226-57681-7*) U Ch Pr.
— The Talmud of the Land of Israel: A Preliminary Translation & Explanation, Vol. 22: Ketubot. Zahavy, Tzvee, tr. (Chicago Studies in the History of Judaism). 312p. 1989. lib. bdg. 48.00 (*0-226-57658-2*) U Ch Pr.

Neusner, Jacob, ed. & tr. The Talmud of the Land of Israel: A Preliminary Translation & Explanation : Hagigah & Moed Qatan, Vol. 20. LC 85-29037. (Chicago Studies in the History of Judaism). 242p. 1986. lib. bdg. 35.00 (*0-226-57679-5*) U Ch Pr.
— The Talmud of the Land of Israel: A Preliminary Translation & Explanation- Vol. 25, Gittin. (Chicago Studies in the History of Judaism). 248p. 1985. lib. bdg. 31.00 (*0-226-57682-5*) U Ch Pr.
— The Talmud of the Land of Israel: A Preliminary Translation & Explanation, Sheqalim, (Chicago Studies in the History of Judaism: Vol. 15). 190p. 1990. lib. bdg. 35.00 (*0-226-57674-4*) U Ch Pr.
— The Talmud of the Land of Israel: A Preliminary Translation & Explanation-Vol. 26, Qiddushin. 1984. lib. bdg. 25.00 (*0-226-57688-4*); lib. bdg. 25.00 (*0-226-57689-2*) U Ch Pr.
— The Talmud of the Land of Israel: A Preliminary Translation & Explanation-Vol. 26, Qiddushin. 1984. lib. bdg. 25.00 (*0-226-57687-6*) U Ch Pr.
— The Talmud of the Land of Israel: A Preliminary Translation & Explanation-Vol. 26, Qiddushin. 1984. lib. bdg. 25.00 (*0-226-57686-8*) U Ch Pr.
— The Talmud of the Land of Israel: A Preliminary Translation & Explanation-Vol. 30, Baba Batra. 1982. lib. bdg. 27.00 (*0-226-57693-0*); lib. bdg. 29.00 (*0-226-57694-9*) U Ch Pr.
— The Talmud of the Land of Israel: A Preliminary Translation & Explanation-Vol. 30, Baba Batra. 1983. lib. bdg. 31.00 (*0-226-57692-2*) U Ch Pr.
— The Talmud of the Land of Israel: A Preliminary Translation & Explanation-Vol. 30, Baba Batra. 1984. lib. bdg. 19.00 (*0-226-57695-7*) U Ch Pr.
— The Talmud of the Land of Israel: A Preliminary Translation & Explanation-Vol. 30, Baba Batra. 1984. lib. bdg. 25.00 (*0-226-57690-6*) U Ch Pr.
— The Talmud of the Land of Israel: A Preliminary Translation & Explanation-Vol. 30, Baba Batra. 1984. lib. bdg. 45.00 (*0-226-57691-4*) U Ch Pr.
— The Talmud of the Land of Israel: Yebamot. LC 86-11406. (Chicago Studies in the History of Judaism). x, 514p. (C). 1987. lib. bdg. 58.00 (*0-226-57680-9*) U Ch Pr.

Neusner, Jacob, ed. The Talmud of the Land of Israel: A Preliminary Translation & Explanation, Vol. 5: Shebiit. Avery-Peck, Alan J., tr. (Chicago Studies in the History of Judaism). 400p. 1991. lib. bdg. 65.00 (*0-226-57662-0*) U Ch Pr.
— The Talmud of the Land of Israel: A Preliminary Translation & Explanation, Vol. 9: Hallah. (Chicago Studies in the History of Judaism). 200p. 1991. lib. bdg. 35.00 (*0-226-57666-3*) U Ch Pr.

Neusner, Jacob, ed. & tr. The Talmud of the Land of Israel, a Preliminary Translation & Explanation, Vol. 11: Shabbat. (Chicago Studies in the History of Judaism). 464p. 1991. lib. bdg. 75.00 (*0-226-57670-1*) U Ch Pr.
— The Talmud of the Land of Israel, a Preliminary Translation & Explanation, Vol. 12: Erubin. LC 90-10963. (Chicago Studies in the History of Judaism). 296p. 1990. lib. bdg. 50.00 (*0-226-57669-8*) U Ch Pr.
— The Talmud of the Land of Israel, Vol. 10: A Preliminary Translation & Explanation, Orlah & Bikkurim. LC 90-20468. (Chicago Studies in the History of Judaism). 184p. 1991. lib. bdg. 39.95 (*0-226-57667-1*) U Ch Pr.

Neusner, Jacob, ed. The Talmud of the Land of Israel, Vol. 3: Demai. Sarason, Richard S., tr. LC 93-18738. (Chicago Studies in the History of Judaism). 376p. (C). 1993. lib. bdg. 65.00 (*0-226-57660-4*) U Ch Pr.
— The Talmud of the Land of Israel, Vol. 8: Maaser Sheni. Brooks, Roger, tr. LC 92-25277. (Chicago Studies in the History of Judaism). 216p. (HEB.). (C). 1993. lib. bdg. 42.00 (*0-226-57665-5*) U Ch Pr.
— Understanding American Judaism: Toward the Description of Modern Religion, 2 vols. Incl. Vol.1. Synagogue & the Rabbi. (*0-318-56726-1*); Vol.II. Reform, Orthodoxy, Conservatism, & Reconstruction. (*0-318-56727-X*); Set pap. 9.95 (*0-686-95149-2*) ADL.
— World Religions in America: An Introduction. LC 93-32886. 320p. (Orig.). 1994. text ed. 22.00 (*0-664-22053-3*); pap. 12.99 (*0-664-25300-8*) Westminster John Knox.

Neusner, Jacob, tr. The Fathers According to Rabbi Nathan. LC 86-17656. (Brown Judaic Studies). 274p. 1986. 43.95 (*1-55540-051-5*, 14-01-14) Scholars Pr GA.
— Pesiqta deRab Kahana: An Analytical Translation, 2 pts. 245p. 1987. write for info. (*0-318-61736-6*) Scholars Pr GA.
— Pesiqta deRab Kahana: An Analytical Translation, 2 pts., Pt. 1. LC 86-26042. (Brown Judaic Studies). 245p. 1987. 36.95 (*1-55540-072-8*, 14-01-22) Scholars Pr GA.
— Pesiqta deRab Kahana: An Analytical Translation, 2 pts., Pt. 2. LC 86-26042. (Brown Judaic Studies). 245p. 1987. 36.95 (*1-55540-073-6*, 14-01-23) Scholars Pr GA.
— Scriptures of the Oral Torah: Sanctification & Salvation in the Sacred Books of Judaism. (Brown Judaic Studies). 1990. 74.95 (*1-55540-499-5*) Scholars Pr GA.
— The Talmud of Babylonia: An American Translation. 248p. 1991. 59.95 (*1-55540-606-8*); 64.95 (*1-55540-636-X*) Scholars Pr GA.
— The Talmud of Babylonia: An American Translation: XXI Tractate Bava Mesia, 4 vols., 8. (Brown Judaic Studies Ser.). 1990. 59.59 (*1-55540-505-3*) Scholars Pr GA.
— The Talmud of Babylonia: An American Translation: XXI Tractate Bava Mesia, 4 vols., A. 1990. write for info. (*0-318-68028-9*) Scholars Pr GA.
— The Talmud of Babylonia: An American Translation: XXI Tractate Bava Mesia, 4 vols., A. (Brown Judaic Studies Ser.). 1990. 59.59 (*1-55540-504-5*) Scholars Pr GA.
— The Talmud of Babylonia: An American Translation: XXI Tractate Bava Mesia, 4 vols., C. (Brown Judaic Studies Ser.). 1990. 59.59 (*1-55540-506-1*) Scholars Pr GA.
— The Talmud of Babylonia: An American Translation: XXI Tractate Bava Mesia, 4 vols., D. (Brown Judaic Studies Ser.). 1990. 59.59 (*1-55540-507-X*) Scholars Pr GA.
— The Talmud of Babylonia: Tractate Pesahim IV.C-E, Set, Chaps. 4-6. LC 93-319. (Brown Judaic Studies: Nos. 283-285). 246p. 1993. Set. 59.95 (*1-55540-833-8*, 14 02 83) Scholars Pr GA.
— The Talmud of Babylonia: Tractate Qiddushin XIX.A-B, A. LC 92-30644. (Brown Judaic Studies: Nos. 267 & 268). 1992. 59.95 (*1-55540-776-5*, 14 02 67) Scholars Pr GA.
— The Talmud of Babylonia: Tractate Qiddushin XIX.A-B, B. LC 92-30644. (Brown Judaic Studies: Nos. 267 & 268). 1992. 59.95 (*1-55540-777-3*, 14 02 68) Scholars Pr GA.
— The Talmud of Babylonia--An American Translation, No. I: Berakhot. (Brown Judaic Studies). 1984. 36.95 (*0-89130-808-3*, 14 00 78); pap. 31.95 (*0-89130-809-1*, 14 00 78) Scholars Pr GA.
— The Talmud of Babylonia--An American Translation, No. VI: Tractate Sukkah. (Brown Judaic Studies). 1984. 35.75 (*0-89130-786-9*, 14 00 74); pap. 23.50 (*0-89130-788-5*, 14 00 74) Scholars Pr GA.
— The Talmud of Babylonia--An American Translation, No. XXIIIA: Sanhedrin, Ch. 1-3. (Brown Judaic Studies). 1984. 25.95 (*0-89130-799-0*, 14 00 81); pap. 19.50 (*0-89130-800-8*) Scholars Pr GA.
— The Talmud of Babylonia--An American Translation, No. XXXII: Arakhin. (Brown Judaic Studies). 1984. 27.95 (*0-89130-739-7*, 14 00 63); pap. 18.25 (*0-89130-754-0*, 14 00 63) Scholars Pr GA.
— The Talmud of Babylonia: An American Translation: Gittin XVIII.A & Gittin XVIII.B, Vol. A. LC 92-30643. (Brown Judaic Studies: Nos. 265 & 266). 199p. 1992. 59.95 (*1-55540-774-9*, 14 02 65) Scholars Pr GA.
— The Talmud of Babylonia: An American Translation: Gittin XVIII.A & Gittin XVIII.B, Vol. B. LC 92-30643. (Brown Judaic Studies: Nos. 265 & 266). 185p. 1992. 59.95 (*1-55540-775-7*, 14 02 66) Scholars Pr GA.
— The Talmud of Babylonia: An American Translation: IX: Tractate Nidarim. LC 92-25792. (Brown Judaic Studies: No. 262-263). 199p. 1992. 59.95 (*0-685-74478-7*, 14 02 62); 59.95 (*1-55540-752-8*, 14 02 63) Scholars Pr GA.
— The Talmud of Babylonia: Hagigah XII: An American Translation: Tractate Hagigah XII. LC 92-247132. (Brown Judaic Studies: Vol. 280). 203p. 1993. 59.95 (*1-55540-823-0*, 14 02 80) Scholars Pr GA.
— The Talmud of the Land of Israel: A Preliminary Translation & Explanation, Yoma, Vol. 14. (Chicago Studies in the History of Judaism). 224p. 1991. lib. bdg. 40.00 (*0-226-57673-6*) U Ch Pr.

Neusner, Jacob & Brooks, Roger, trs. Sifra: The Rabbinic Commentary on Leviticus. (Brown Judaic Studies). (C). 1985. pap. 19.25 (*0-89130-914-4*) Scholars Pr GA.

***Neusner, Jacob & Chilton, Bruce D.** Revelation: The Torah & the Bible. 176p. (Orig.). 1995. pap. 17.00 (*1-56338-124-9*) TPI PA.

Neusner, Jacob & Frerichs, Ernest S., eds. Goodenough on the History of Religion & on Judaism. LC 86-20320. (Brown Judaic Studies). 168p. 1987. pap. 31.95 (*1-55540-062-0*, 14-01-21) Scholars Pr GA.
— New Perspectives on Ancient Judaism: Judaic & Christian Interpretation of Texts: Contents & Contexts, Vol. 3. 226p. (C). 1987. pap. text ed. 24.00 (*0-8191-6563-8*, Studies in Judaism) U Pr of Amer.
— To See Ourselves As Others See Us: Christians, Jews, "Others" in Late Antiquity. (Studies in Humanities). (Orig.). 1985. pap. 29.95 (*0-89130-820-2*, 00 01 09) Scholars Pr GA.

Neusner, Jacob & Jaffee, Martin S., eds. The Talmud of the Land of Israel: A Preliminary Translation & Explanation - Maaserot, Vol. 7. LC 87-5852. (Chicago Studies in the History of Judaism). xii, 284p. (C). 1987. lib. bdg. 25.00 (*0-226-57664-7*) U Ch Pr.

Neusner, Jacob & Neusner, Noam, eds. To Grow in Wisdom: An Anthology of Abraham Joshua Heschel. 234p. 1990. 19.95 (*0-8191-7464-5*) Madison Bks UPA.

Neusner, Jacob, jt. auth. see Chilton, Bruce.

Neusner, Jacob, jt. auth. see Greeley, Andrew M.

Neusner, Jacob, ed. see Jaffee, Martin.

Neusner, Jacob, ed. see Mandelbaum, Irving J.

Neusner, Jacob, ed. see Novak, David.

Neusner, Jacob, jt. auth. see Silverman, Morris.

Neusner, Jacob, tr. see Stemberger, Gunter.

Neusner, Jacob, et al. From Ancient Israel to Modern Judaism: Intellect in Quest of Understanding, 1. 1989. 77.95 (*1-55540-335-2*, 14 01 59) Scholars Pr GA.
— From Ancient Israel to Modern Judaism: Intellect in Quest of Understanding, 2. 1989. write for info. (*1-55540-341-7*, 14 01 73) Scholars Pr GA.
— From Ancient Israel to Modern Judaism: Intellect in Quest of Understanding, 3. 1989. write for info. (*1-55540-342-5*, 14 01 74) Scholars Pr GA.
— From Ancient Israel to Modern Judaism: Intellect in Quest of Understanding, 4. 1989. write for info. (*1-55540-343-3*, 14 01 75__001) Scholars Pr GA.
— Religious Writings & Religious Systems. (Studies in Religion: Vol. 1). 1989. 53.95 (*1-55540-296-8*, 14 70 01) Scholars Pr GA.

Neusner, Jacob, et al, eds. Judaisms & Their Messiahs at the Turn of the Christian Era. 375p. 1988. 64.95 (*0-521-34146-9*); pap. 19.95 (*0-521-34940-0*) Cambridge U Pr.
— New Perspectives on Ancient Judaism: Religion, Literature, & Society in Ancient Israel, Formative Christianity & Judaism, Vol. II. LC 87-23027. 184p. (C). 1988. lib. bdg. 44.00 (*0-8191-6597-2*) U Pr of Amer.
— New Perspectives on Ancient Judaism, Vol. 1: Religion Literature, & Society in Ancient Israel, Formative Christianity & Judaism. (Brown Judaic Studies). 1990. 54.95 (*1-55540-497-9*) Scholars Pr GA.
— Religion, Literature, & Society in Ancient Israel, Formative Christianity & Judaism: Formative Judaism. (New Perspectives on Ancient Judaism Ser.: Vol. I). 170p. (Orig.). (C). 1987. pap. text ed. 19.00 (*0-8191-6514-X*, Studies in Judaism) U Pr of Amer.
— Religion, Science, & Magic: In Concert & in Conflict. 288p. 1992. reprint ed. pap. 18.95 (*0-19-507911-6*) OUP.

Neusner, Noam, jt. ed. see Neusner, Jacob.

Neuss, Paula. Fifteenth-Century English Drama. (Illus.). 160p. 1970. 71.00 (*0-85991-091-1*) Boydell & Brewer.

Neuss, Paula, ed. see Skelton, John.

Neustadt, Egon. The Lamps of Tiffany. LC 78-142102. (Illus.). 224p. 1970. 195.00 (*0-913158-01-1*) Neustadt.

Neustadt, Gail K., jt. auth. see Glickstein, Joan K.

Neustadt, Kathy. Clambake: A History & Celebration of an American Tradition. LC 91-45599. (Illus.). 240p. 1992. lib. bdg. 40.00 (*0-87023-782-9*); pap. text ed. 16.95x (*0-87023-799-3*) U of Mass Pr.

Neustadt, L. W. Optimization: A Theory of Necessary Conditions. 1976. 65.00x (*0-691-08141-7*) Princeton U Pr.

Neustadt, L. W., ed. Proceedings of the First International Congress on Programming & Control. (Proceedings in Applied Mathematics Ser.: No. 1). iv, 261p. 1966. 32.50 (*0-89871-155-X*) Soc Indus-Appl Math.

***Neustadt, Lucien W.** Optimization: A Theory of Necessary Conditions. LC 76-3010. Date not set. reprint ed. pap. 125.20 (*0-7837-9401-0*, 2060146) Bks Demand.

Neustadt, Richard, ed. see Kennedy, Robert F.

Neustadt, Richard E. Presidency & Legislation: The Growth of Central Clearance. (Reprint Series in Social Sciences). (C). 1993. reprint ed. pap. text ed. 1.00 (*0-8290-3230-4*, PS-216) Irvington.
— Presidential Power: The Politics of Leadership from FDR to Carter. LC 79-19474. 286p. (C). 1980. pap. write for info. (*0-02-386670-5*) Macmillan.
— Presidential Power & the Modern Presidents: The Politics of Leadership from Roosevelt to Reagan. 1989. 22.95 (*0-02-922975-8*) Free Pr.

Neustadt, Richard E. & May, Ernest R. Thinking in Time: The Uses of History for Decision Makers. 350p. (Orig.). 1988. 27.95 (*0-02-922790-9*); pap. 12.95 (*0-02-922791-7*) Free Pr.

Neustadt, Richard M. The Birth of Electronic Publishing: Legal & Economic Issues in Telephone, Cable & Over-the-Air Teletext & Videotext. LC 82-6614. (Professional Librarian Ser.). 146p. 1982. text ed. 35.95 (*0-86729-030-7*, Hall Reference) Macmillan.

Neustaedter, Randall. Homeopathic Pediatrics: Assessment & Case Management. 337p. 1991. 39.95 (*1-55643-120-1*) North Atlantic.
— The Immunization Decision: A Guide for Parents. (Family Health Ser.). 120p. (Orig.). 1990. pap. 8.95 (*1-55643-071-X*) North Atlantic.

Neustupny, Evzen. Archaeological Method. LC 92-1711. (Illus.). 192p. (C). 1993. 44.95 (*0-521-38076-6*) Cambridge U Pr.

Neustupny, J. V., ed. Post-Structural Approaches to Language: Language Theory in a Japanese Context. 307p. 1978. pap. 17.50 (*0-86008-194-X*, Pub. by U of Tokyo JA) Col U Pr.

Neususs, Floris M., et al. Experimental Vision: The Evolution of the Photogram since 1919. LC 93-61702. (Illus.). 88p. (Orig.). 1994. pap. 22.95 (*1-879373-73-4*) R Rinehart.

Neutens, James J. Healthy Sexual Development, Course I. (Discover Ser.). (Illus.). 144p. (J). (gr. 6-8). 1993. 18.95 (*0-7854-0053-2*, 15162); text ed. 7.95 (*0-7854-0052-4*, 15161) Am Guidance.
— Healthy Sexual Development, Course II. (Discover Ser.). (Illus.). 144p. (YA). (gr. 9-12). 1993. 18.95 (*0-7854-0055-9*); text ed. 7.95 (*0-7854-0054-0*, 15163) Am Guidance.

Neutens, James J., jt. auth. see Rubinson, Laurna.

Neutra, Dione, tr. & comp. Richard Neutra: Promise & Fulfillment, 1919-1932: Selections from the Letters & Diaries of Richard & Dione Neutra. LC 85-2245. 264p. 1986. 24.95 (*0-8093-1228-X*) S Ill U Pr.

Neutra, Richard J. Wie Baut Amerika? Baubucher, Vol. 1. (Bauhaus Ser.). 1990. reprint ed. 37.00 (*3-601-00289-2*); reprint ed. pap. 28.00 (*0-685-44711-1*) Periodicals Srv.

Neutrelle, Dale. Wild Things to Cook. 1974. pap. 5.00 (*0-916552-00-4*) Acoma Bks.

Neuts. Structured Stochastic Matrices of M-G-1 Type & Their Applications. (Probability Ser.: Vol. 5). 512p. 1989. 150.00 (*0-8247-8283-6*) Dekker.

***Neuts, Marcel F.** Algorithmic Probability: A Collection of Problems. 1995. write for info. (*0-412-99691-X*) Chapman & Hall.
— Matrix-Geometric Solutions in Stochastic Models: An Algorithmic Approach. unabridged ed. 332p. 1995. pap. text ed. 8.95 (*0-486-68342-7*) Dover.
— Matrix-Geometric Solutions in Stochastic Models: An Algorithmic Approach. LC 80-8872. (Johns Hopkins Series in the Mathematical Sciences: No. 2). 348p. reprint ed. pap. 99.20 (*0-7837-5378-0*, 2045142) Bks Demand.

Neutze, Grahame M. Economic Policy & the Size of Cities. LC 67-89992. (Illus.). xi, 136p. 1965. 27.50 (*0-678-05190-9*) Kelley.

Neuville, H. Richmond, Jr. Monarch Notes on Dostoyevsky's the Brothers Karamazov. (Orig.). (C). pap. 3.95 (*0-671-00556-1*, Arco Test) P-H Gen Ref & Trav.

Neuville, Maureen B. Sometimes I Get All Scribbly. (Illus.). 120p. (Orig.). 1991. pap. 10.00 (*0-941187-64-0*) M Abel Assocs.
— Sometimes I Get All Scribbly: Living with Attention-Deficit/Hyperactivity Disorder. 2nd ed. LC 94-41588. 100p. (C). 1995. pap. text ed. 14.00 (*0-89079-667-X*, 6976) PRO-ED.

Neuville, Pierre. Pequeno Diccionario Medico Practico: Small Practical Medical Dictionary. 8th ed. 240p. (SPA.). 1987. pap. 10.95 (*0-7859-4945-3*) Fr & Eur.

Neuvonen, E. K. Finnish-Spanish-Finnish Dictionary. 452p. (FIN & SPA.). 1980. pap. 59.95 (*0-8288-4698-7*, S37816) Fr & Eur.

Neuweiler, Phillip F. Big Game Trails in the Far North. Lapasta, Douglas, ed. (Illus.). 320p. 1990. 35.00 (*0-937708-20-8*) Great Northwest.

Neuwelt, E. A., ed. Implications of the Blood - Brain Barrier & Its Manipulation, Vol. 1: Basic Science Aspects. (Illus.). 434p. 1989. 89.50 (*0-306-42628-5*, Plenum Med Bk) Plenum.

N

An Asterisk (*) at the beginning of an entry indicates that the title is appearing in BIP for the first time.

— Implications of the Blood - Brain Barrier & Its Manipulation, Vol. 1: Basic Science Aspects, Set with Vol. 2. (Illus.). 434p. 1989. 165.00 (*0-318-32869-0*, Plenum Med Bk) Plenum.

— Implications of the Blood - Brain Barrier & Its Manipulation, Vol. 1: Clinical Aspects. (Illus.). 668p. 1989. 115.00 (*0-306-42637-4*, Plenum Med Bk) Plenum.

— Implications of the Blood - Brain Barrier & Its Manipulation, Vol. 1: Clinical Aspects, Set with Vol. 1. (Illus.). 668p. 1989. 165.00 (*0-318-32870-4*, Plenum Med Bk) Plenum.

Neuwirt, J. & Ponka, P. Regulation of Hemoglobin Synthesis. 1977. lib. bdg. 56.50 (*90-247-1999-2*) Kluwer Ac.

Neuwirth, Gertrud, ed. see Weber, Max M.

Neuwirth, L. P., ed. Knots, Groups, & 3-Manifolds: Papers Dedicated to the Memory of R. H. Fox. LC 75-5619. (Annals of Mathematics Studies: No. 84). 345p. 1975. 55.00 (*0-691-08170-0*) Princeton U Pr.

Neuzil, E. F., jt. auth. see Miller, John A.

Neva, Franklin A. Basic Clinical Parasitology. 6th ed. (Illus.). 400p. 1994. text ed. 36.95 (*0-8385-0624-0*, A0624-5) Appleton & Lange.

Nevada Wildlife Record Book Committee Staff. Nevada Wildlife Record Book. 2nd ed. (Illus.). 346p. 1990. 29.00 (*0-9622467-0-0*) NV WRBC.

— Nevada Wildlife Record Book, 1990. 2nd ed. (Illus.). 250p. 1990. write for info. (*0-318-64890-3*) NV WRBC.

Nevadomski, Stacie, ed. Environmental & Urban Issues. write for info. (*0-318-63044-3*) Fla Atlantic.

***Nevaer, Louis E.** Strategies for Business in Mexico: Free Trade & the Emergence of North America, Inc. LC 95-6921. 1995. text ed. write for info. (*0-89930-882-1*, Quorum Bks) Greenwood.

Nevaer, Louis E. & Deck, Steven A. Corporate Financial Planning & Management in a Deficit Economy. LC 86-25582. 190p. 1987. text ed. 59.95 (*0-89930-202-5*, NCF/, Quorum Bks) Greenwood.

— The Management of Corporate Business Units: Portfolio Strategies for Turbulent Times. LC 87-32586. 246p. 1988. text ed. 55.00 (*0-89930-284-X*, NVP/, Quorum Bks) Greenwood.

— The Protectionist Threat to Corporate America: The U. S. Trade Deficit & Management Responses. LC 88-39910. 239p. 1989. text ed. 55.00 (*0-89930-363-3*, NEW, Quorum Bks) Greenwood.

— Strategic Corporate Alliances: A Study of the Present, a Model for the Future. LC 90-30010. 240p. 1990. text ed. 55.00 (*0-89930-361-7*, Quorum Bks) Greenwood.

Nevai, Lucia. Star Game. LC 87-16159. (Iowa Short Fiction Award Ser.). 161p. 1987. 19.95 (*0-87745-174-5*) U of Iowa Pr.

Nevai, Paul, ed. Orthogonal Polynomials: Theory & Practice: Proceedings of the NATO Advanced Study Institute on "Orthogonal Polynomials & Their Applications" Held in Columbus, Ohio, U. S. A. May 22 - June 3, 1989. (C). 1989. lib. bdg. 169.00 (*0-7923-0569-8*) Kluwer Ac.

Nevai, Paul & Pinkus, Alan, eds. Progress in Approximation Theory. (Illus.). 916p. 1991. text ed. 225.00 (*0-12-516750-4*) Acad Pr.

Nevai, Paul G. Orthogonal Polynomials. LC 78-32112. (Memoirs of the American Mathematical Society Ser.: No. 213). 185p. 1991. reprint ed. pap. 18.00 (*0-8218-2213-6*, MEMO-213) Am Math.

Nevala, Steve, jt. auth. see Linsenman, Bob.

Nevalinna, Olavi. Convergence of Iterations for Linear Equations. LC 93-3187. (Lectures in Mathematics ETH Zurich). vii, 177p. 1993. Alk. paper. 29.00 (*0-8176-2865-7*); Alk. paper. pap. write for info. (*0-318-70050-6*) Birkhauser.

Nevanlinna, F. & Nevanlinna, R. Absolute Analysis. Emig, P., tr. LC 73-75652. (Grundlehren der Mathematischen Wissenschaften Ser.: Vol. 102). (Illus.). 280p. 1973. 72.00 (*0-387-05917-2*) Spr-Verlag.

Nevanlinna, R., jt. auth. see Nevanlinna, F.

Nevanlinna, Saara & Taavitsainen, Irma, eds. St. Katherine of Alexandria: The Late Middle English Prose Legend in Southwell Minster, No. MS7. LC 93-36296. (Illus.). 160p. (C). 1993. text ed. 53.00 (*0-85991-391-0*, DS Brewer) Boydell & Brewer.

Nevares, Dora, et al. Delinquency in Puerto Rico: The 1970 Birth Cohort Study. LC 90-32108. (Contributions in Criminology & Penology Ser.: No. 31). 248p. 1990. text ed. 55.00 (*0-313-27456-8*, NVD/, Greenwood Pr) Greenwood.

Nevares-Muniz, Dora. Derecho Penal Puertorriqueno: Parte General. 352p. 1983. pap. text ed. 20.00 (*0-914939-00-9*) Instituto Desarrollo.

— Sumario de Derecho Procesal Penal Puertorriqueno. 2nd ed. 296p. (SPA.). 1986. pap. text ed. 20.00 (*0-317-38881-9*) Instituto Desarrollo.

— Sumario de Derecho Procesal Penal Puertorriqueno. 2nd suppl. ed. 296p. (SPA.). 1986. 10.00 (*0-685-11823-1*) Instituto Desarrollo.

Nevaskar, Balwant S. Capitalists Without Capitalism: The Jains of India & the Quakers of the West. LC 72-98709. (Contributions in Sociology Ser.: No. 6). 252p. 1971. text ed. 59.95 (*0-8371-3297-5*, NCA/, Greenwood Pr) Greenwood.

Neve, Brian. Film & Politics in America: A Social Tradition. LC 92-5196. (Studies in Film, Television & the Media). 192p. 1992. 69.95 (*0-415-02619-9*, A7920, Routledge NY); pap. 16.95 (*0-415-02620-2*, A7924, Routledge NY) Routledge.

Neve, Brian, jt. ed. see Davies, Philip J.

Neve, Christopher. Unquiet Landscape: Places & Ideas in Twentieth-Century English Painting. (Illus.). 166p. 1991. 45.00 (*0-571-15291-0*) Faber & Faber.

***Neve, Ernest F.** Things Seen in Kashmir. (C). 1993. 18.00 (*81-7041-821-6*, Pub. by Anmol II) S Asia.

Neve, Herbert, ed. Homeward Journey: Readings in African Studies. LC 93-28433. 340p. (J). 1994. 45.95 (*0-86543-407-7*); pap. 14.95 (*0-86543-408-5*) Africa World.

Neve, J. Concordance to the Poetical Works of William Cowper. LC 68-26363. (Studies in Poetry: No. 38). 1969. reprint ed. lib. bdg. 69.95 (*0-8383-0289-0*) M S G Haskell Hse.

Neve, Jean & Favier, Alain, eds. Selenium in Medicine & Biology: Proceedings of the Second International Congress on Trace Elements in Medicine & Biology. xx, 428p. (C). 1989. lib. bdg. 193.35 (*0-89925-503-5*) De Gruyter.

— Selenium in Medicine & Biology: Proceedings of the Second International Congress on Trace ELements in Medicine & Biology. xx, 428p. (C). 1989. lib. bdg. 234.65 (*3-11-011770-3*) De Gruyter.

Neve, John. A Concordance to the Poetical Works of William Cowper. (BCL1-PR English Literature Ser.). 504p. 1992. reprint ed. lib. bdg. 99.00 (*0-7812-7340-4*) Rprt Serv.

Neve, Michael, ed. see Darwin, Charles.

Neve, P. L. & Van Kappen, O. Moorman, eds. Conservare Jura. 224p. 1988. pap. 27.00 (*90-6544-370-3*) Kluwer Law Tax Pubs.

Neve, Richard. The Complete Builder's Guide: A 1726 Dictionary of Builders Terms & Usage. 45.00 (*0-89979-004-6*) British Am Bks.

Nevel, Bonnie & Harnik, Peter. Railroads Recycled: How Local Initiative & Federal Support Launched the Rails-to-Trails Movement, 1965-1990. 104p. (Orig.). 1990. 12.95 (*0-925794-03-1*) Rails Trails.

Neveling, Ulrich. Terminologie de la Documentation. Wersig, Gernot, ed. 274p. (ENG, FRE, GER, RUS & SPA.). 1976. pap. 85.00 (*0-8288-5756-3*, M6529) Fr & Eur.

Nevelow, Mark, ed. see Baker, Kyle.

Nevelow, Mark, ed. see Hempel, Marc.

Nevelow, Mark, ed. see Messner-Loebs, William.

Nevels, Lourene A. & Coche, Judith M. Powerful Wisdom: Voices of Distinguished Women Psychotherapists. LC 93-3621. (Social & Behavioral Science Ser.). 190p. 1993. 26.95 (*1-55542-570-4*) Jossey-Bass.

Nevel'son, M. B. & Has'minskii, R. Z. Stochastic Approximation & Recursive Estimation. LC 76-48298. (Translations of Mathematical Monographs: Vol. 47). 244p. 1976. 75.00 (*0-8218-1597-0*, MMONO47) Am Math.

Neven, Damien, et al. Merger in Daylight: The Economics & Politics of European Merger Control. 296p. (C). 1994. pap. 29.95 (*1-898128-01-4*) Brookings.

Neverdon-Morton, Cynthia. Afro-American Women of the South & the Advancement of the Race, 1895-1925. LC 88-17481. (Illus.). 288p. 1989. text ed. 41.00x (*0-87049-583-6*); pap. 18.95 (*0-87049-684-0*) U of Tenn Pr.

Neverov, Alexander, pseud. City of Bread. LC 72-90302. (Soviet Literature in English Translation Ser.). (Illus.). 242p. 1973. reprint ed. 20.25 (*0-88355-013-X*) Hyperion Conn.

Neverow-Turk, Vara & Hussey, Mark, eds. Virginia Woolf: Selected Papers from the Second Annual Conference on Virginia Woolf. LC 92-46424. 280p. (Orig.). (C). 1993. lib. bdg. 57.00 (*0-944473-12-1*); pap. text ed. 24.00 (*0-944473-13-X*) Pace Univ Pr.

Neverow-Turk, Vara, jt. ed. see Hussey, Mark.

Neverow, Vara, jt. ed. see Hussey, Mark.

Neves, A. C., jt. ed. see Nowak, A.

Neves, Claudio, jt. ed. see Magoon, Orville T.

Neves, Gorcalo. Kompreni: Rakontoj. 56p. 1993. pap. text ed. 3.95 (*1-882251-07-5*) Eldonejo Bero.

***Neves, Jose C.** The Palace & Gardens of Fronteira: Seventeenth & Eighteenth Century Portuguese Style. (Illus.). 148p. 1995. 50.00 (*0-935748-98-9*) Scala Books.

Neves, Margaret, tr. see Torres, Antonio.

Neves, Margaret A., tr. see Amado, Jorge.

Neves, Margaret A., tr. see Ribeiro, Edgard T.

Nevett, T. R., jt. auth. see Miracle, Gordon E.

Nevett, Terence, ed. Cases in Advertising Management. 320p. 1992. pap. 24.95 (*0-8442-3368-4*, NTC Busn Bks) NTC Pub Grp.

Nevett, Terence & Fullerton, Ronald A., eds. Historical Perpectives in Marketing: Essays in Honor of Stanley C. Hollander. LC 87-45770. 272p. 1988. text ed. 45.00 (*0-669-16968-4*) Free Pr.

Neveu, Jacques. Theorie des Semi-Groupes de Markov. LC 58-9788. (California University Publications in Statistics: Vol. 2 No. 14). 80p. reprint ed. pap. 25.00 (*0-317-08330-9*, 2021185) Bks Demand.

Neviaser, Robert J., ed. Controversies in Hand Surgery. (Illus.). 232p. 1990. text ed. 64.00 (*0-443-08433-5*) Churchill.

Neviaser, Robert J., et al. Emergency Orthopaedic Radiology. LC 84-23679. (Illus.). 295p. reprint ed. pap. 84.10 (*0-7837-6241-0*, 2045955) Bks Demand.

Nevid, Jeffrey, jt. auth. see Rathus, Spencer A.

***Nevid, Jeffrey S.** Choices: Sex in the Age of Standards. 1995. pap. 15.95 (*0-205-16941-4*) Allyn.

Nevid, Jeffrey S., jt. auth. see Rathus, Spencer A.

***Nevid, Jeffrey S., et al.** Human Sexuality in a World of Diversity. 2nd ed. LC 94-33693. 1994. text ed. write for info. (*0-205-16407-2*) Allyn.

***Nevidjon, Brenda.** Building a Legacy: Voices Oncology Nurses. LC 95-4063. (Nursing Ser.). 500p. 1995. 49.95 (*0-86720-727-2*) Jones & Bartlett.

Nevile, Liddy & Noss, Richard. Proceedings of Logo Mathematics Education Conference. (C). 1992. 90.00 (*0-86431-132-X*, Pub. by Aust Council Educ Res AT) St Mut.

Nevile, Pran. Lahore: A Sentimental Journey. (C). 1993. 16.00 (*81-7023-253-8*, Pub. by Allied II) S Asia.

Nevill, A. M. Properties of Concrete. 3rd ed. 438p. 1986. pap. text ed. 67.95 (*0-470-20552-0*) Halsted Pr.

Nevill, A. M. & Chatterton, M., eds. New Concrete Technologies & Building Design. 134p. reprint ed. pap. 38.20 (*0-317-08590-5*, 2020983) Bks Demand.

Nevill, Antonia, tr. see Agulhon, Maurice.

Nevill, Antonia, tr. see Furet, Francois.

Nevill, Antonia, tr. see Lancel, Serge.

Nevill, Antonia, tr. see Le Glay, Marcel, et al.

Nevill, Antonia, tr. see Richard, Yann.

Nevill, W. The Castell of Pleasure. (EETS, OS Ser.: No. 179). 1972. reprint ed. 26.00 (*0-527-00176-7*) Periodicals Srv.

Neville. Awakened Imagination: Including "The Search" 94p. 1993. reprint ed. pap. 8.95 (*0-87516-656-3*) DeVorss.

— The Law & the Promise. 156p. 1984. reprint ed. pap. 7.95 (*0-87516-532-X*) DeVorss.

— The Power of Awareness. 124p. 1993. reprint ed. pap. 8.95 (*0-87516-655-5*) DeVorss.

— Resurrection. 1966. 9.95 (*0-87516-076-X*) DeVorss.

— Seedtime & Harvest. 160p. 1985. reprint ed. pap. 7.95 (*0-87516-557-5*) DeVorss.

— Your Faith Is Your Fortune. 1941. pap. 8.95 (*0-87516-078-6*) DeVorss.

Neville, A. & Kirkwood, A. Hospital Handbook on Multiculturalism & Religion. 1994. pap. 3.95 (*0-85574-921-0*, Pub. by E J Dwyer AT) Morehouse Pub.

Neville, A. C. Biology of Fibrous Composites: Development Beyond the Cell Membrane. (Illus.). 275p. (C). 1993. 64.95 (*0-521-41051-7*) Cambridge U Pr.

— Symposia of the Royal Entomological Society of London: Insect Ultrastructure. 190p. 1984. 35.00 (*0-317-07180-7*) St Mut.

Neville, A. G. & Ashe, A. W. Equity Proceedings with Precedents New South Wales. 1981. Australia. 102.00 (*0-409-49039-3*) Butterworth Legal Pubs.

Neville, A. M., ed. Biochemical & Immunologic Diagnosis of Cancer. (Journal: Tumor Biology: Vol. 8, No. 2-3, 1987). (Illus.). 124p. 1987. pap. 65.75 (*3-8055-4665-3*) S Karger.

Neville, A. W. Backward Glances I. Steely, Skipper, ed. (Illus.). 320p. 1983. 20.00 (*0-915263-25-4*) Wright Pr.

— Backward Glances II. Steely, Skipper, ed. & intro. by. (Illus.). 321p. 1985. 20.00 (*0-915263-26-2*) Wright Pr.

— Backward Glances, Three. Steely, Skipper, ed. (Illus.). 303p. 1985. 20.00 (*0-915263-27-0*) Wright Pr.

Neville, Adam, et al. Concrete Technology. 438p. 1987. pap. text ed. 67.95 (*0-470-20716-7*) Wiley.

Neville, Adam M. & Wainwright, P. High Alumina Cement Concrete. LC 76-354854. 201p. reprint ed. pap. 57.30 (*0-317-08024-5*, 2016302) Bks Demand.

Neville, Amelia. The Fantastic City San Francisco. 1992. reprint ed. lib. bdg. 75.00 (*0-7812-5069-2*) Rprt Serv.

Neville, Amelia R. The Fantastic City: Memoirs of the Social & Romantic Life of Old San Francisco. LC 75-1863. (Leisure Class in America Ser.). (Illus.). 1975. reprint ed. 29.95 (*0-405-06929-4*) Ayer.

Neville, Brad W., et al. Color Atlas of Clinical Oral Pathology. LC 89-13980. (Illus.). 385p. 1991. text ed. 99.50 (*0-8121-1311-X*) Williams & Wilkins.

— Oral & Maxillofacial Pathology. LC 94-20442. (Illus.). 688p. 1995. text ed. 55.00 (*0-7216-6695-7*) Saunders.

Neville, Charles W. Invariant Subspaces of Hardy Classes on Infinitely Connected Open Surfaces. (Memoirs Ser.: No. 2/160). 151p. 1975. pap. 19.00 (*0-8218-1860-0*, MEMO 2/160) Am Math.

***Neville, David, et al.** Promoting Positive Parenting. 164p. 1995. pap. 25.95 (*1-85742-266-X*, Pub. by Arena UK) Ashgate Pub Co.

Neville, David J. Arguments from Order in Synoptic Source Criticism: A History & Critique. (New Gospel Studies: No. 7). 386p. 1993. text ed. 25.00 (*0-86554-399-2*, MUP/H325) Mercer Univ Pr.

Neville, Deborah, jt. auth. see Coleman, Bob.

Neville, E. W. Planets in Synastry: Astrological Patterns of Relationships. 276p. 1989. pap. 14.95 (*0-924608-01-3*, Whitford Pr) Schiffer.

— Tarot for Lovers. Lockhart, Julie, ed. LC 87-62096. (Illus.). 252p. (Orig.). 1987. pap. 14.95 (*0-914918-75-3*, Whitford Pr) Schiffer.

Neville, Emily C. Berries Goodman. LC 65-19485. (Trophy Bk.). (J). (gr. 5-9). 1975. pap. 3.95 (*0-06-440072-7*, Trophy) HarpC Child Bks.

— Berries Goodman. (J). (gr. 5-9). 1992. 18.50 (*0-8446-6584-3*) Peter Smith.

— The China Year. LC 90-39899. 256p. (J). (gr. 5-9). 1991. lib. bdg. 15.89 (*0-06-024384-8*) HarpC Child Bks.

— It's Like This, Cat. LC 62-21292. (Illus.). 192p. (J). (gr. 5-9). 1963. 15.00 (*0-06-024390-2*) HarpC Child Bks.

— It's Like This, Cat. (Illus.). 192p. (J). (gr. 5-9). 1964. 15.00 (*0-614-03780-8*) HarpC Child Bks.

— It's Like This, Cat. LC 62-21292. (Illus.). 192p. (YA). (gr. 5-9). 1964. lib. bdg. 14.89 (*0-06-024391-0*) HarpC Child Bks.

— It's Like This, Cat. LC 62-21292. (Trophy Bk.). (Illus.). 192p. (J). (gr. 5-9). 1975. pap. 3.95 (*0-06-440073-5*, Trophy) HarpC Child Bks.

— Newbery Award Library I: It's Like This Cat - Julie of the Wolves - Onion John - Sounder, 4 bks., Set. (J). (gr. 4-6). 1985. Boxed set. pap. 15.80 (*0-06-440162-6*) HarpC Child Bks.

Neville, Georgina & Neville, Robert. Family Walks in Oxfordshire. 64p. 1987. 30.00 (*0-905392-21-3*) St Mut.

Neville, Graham, ed. The Diaries of Edward Lee Hicks: Bishop of Lincoln 1910-1919. (Publications of the Lincoln Record Society: Vol. 82). 256p. 1993. 35.00 (*0-901503-55-X*) Boydell & Brewer.

Neville, Gwen K. Kinship & Pilgrimage: Rituals of Reunion in American Protestant Culture. 178p. 1987. 35.00 (*0-19-504338-3*) OUP.

— The Mother Town: Civic Ritual, Symbols, & Experience in the Borders of Scotland. (Illus.). 176p. 1994. 35.00 (*0-19-508837-9*); pap. 16.95 (*0-19-509032-2*) OUP.

Neville, Helen, et al. No-Fault Parenting. (Illus.). 400p. 1984. 24.95 (*0-87196-671-9*) Facts on File.

Neville, Jim. Swimming the Channel. 192p. 1994. 18.95 (*0-312-11337-4*, Pub. by Thomas Dunne Bks) St Martin.

Neville, John D., comp. Bacon's Rebellion: Abstracts of Materials in the Colonial Records Project. LC 76-24548. xv, 427p. 1976. pap. text ed. 7.95 (*0-917394-00-3*) VA State Lib.

***Neville, John F.** The Press, the Rosenbergs & the Cold War. LC 94-22655. 208p. 1995. text ed. 55.00 (*0-275-94995-8*, Praeger Pubs) Greenwood.

Neville, Jonathan. Questions & Answers: Contracts. 2nd rev. ed. (Winning in Law School Ser.). 175p. (Orig.). 1992. pap. text ed. 12.95 (*0-915667-21-5*) Spectra Pub Co.

Neville, Joyce. How to Share Your Faith Without Being Offensive. LC 89-33291. 148p. (Orig.). 1989. reprint ed. pap. 7.95 (*0-8192-1479-5*) Morehouse Pub.

Neville, Katherine. A Calculated Risk. LC 92-52663. 1992. 19.50 (*0-345-35136-3*, Ballantine Trade) Ballantine.

— A Calculated Risk. 1994. mass mkt. 5.99 (*0-345-38682-5*) Ballantine.

— The Eight. 608p. 1990. mass mkt. 6.99 (*0-345-36623-9*) Ballantine.

— The Eight. 1994. mass mkt. 5.99 (*0-345-90133-9*) Ballantine.

Neville, Kathleen. Yellowbuddy: The Runaway School Bus. (J). (gr. 4-7). 1993. pap. 8.95 (*0-933905-22-X*) Claycomb Pr.

Neville, Kris. The Science Fiction of Kris Neville. Malzberg, Barry N. & Greenberg, Martin H., eds. LC 83-10514. (Alternatives Ser.). 254p. (C). 1984. 19.95 (*0-8093-1112-7*) S Ill U Pr.

Neville, Kris, jt. auth. see Lee, Henry.

Neville, Kris, jt. auth. see Rejda, L. J.

Neville, Margaret C. & Daniel, C. W., eds. The Mammary Gland: Development, Regulation, & Function. LC 87-18606. (Illus.). 648p. 1987. 120.00 (*0-306-42641-2*, Plenum Pr) Plenum.

Neville, Margaret C. & Neifert, Marianne R., eds. Lactation: Physiology, Nutrition & Breast Feeding. LC 83-17652. 482p. 1983. 95.00 (*0-306-41311-6*, Plenum Pr) Plenum.

Neville, Margaret C., jt. ed. see Jensen, Robert C.

Neville, Margot. My Bad Boy. large type ed. (Linford Mystery Library). 400p. 1992. pap. 14.95 (*0-7089-7234-9*, Linford) Ulverscroft.

Neville, Mark. Died: Not Yet. (Graphic Works Ser.). 36p. 1992. pap. text ed. 2.00 (*0-943123-22-4*) Arjuna Lib Pr.

— The Time Dog. Mycue, Edward, ed. (Took Modern Poetry in English Ser.: No. 16). (Illus.). 32p. (Orig.). 1991. pap. 4.00 (*1-879457-15-6*) Norton Coker Pr.

Neville, Mary. The Christmas Tree Ride. LC 91-28853. (Illus.). 32p. (J). (ps-3). 1992. lib. bdg. 14.95 (*0-8234-0956-2*) Holiday.

Neville, Mary, ed. If a Poem Bothers You. (Illus.). 64p. (Orig.). (J). (gr. 2-6). 1991. pap. 7.00 (*0-913678-14-7*) New Day Pr.

Neville, P. Feral Cats in Tunisia. 1984. 25.00 (*0-317-43897-2*) St Mut.

— Humane Control of an Urban Cat Colony. 1983. 30.00 (*0-317-43898-0*) St Mut.

Neville, P. & Remfry, J. Effect of Neutering on Two Groups of Feral Cats. 1984. 16.00 (*0-685-12473-8*) St Mut.

Neville, Peter. Do Dogs Need Shrinks? What to Do When Man's Best Friend Misbehaves. 288p. 1992. pap. 12.95 (*0-8065-1332-2*, Citadel Pr) Carol Pub Group.

— A Traveller's History of Ireland. LC 92-5756. (Traveller's History Ser.). (Illus.). 288p. (Orig.). 1993. pap. 13.95 (*1-56656-110-8*) Interlink Pub.

— Traveller's History of Russia & the U. S. S. R. rev. ed. LC 90-34708. (Traveller's History Ser.). (Illus.). 336p. (Orig.). 1994. pap. 13.95 (*1-56656-143-4*) Interlink Pub.

Neville, Peter, jt. auth. see Kagan, Sharon L.

Neville, Peter, jt. auth. see O'Farrell, Valerie.

Neville, R. C. Solar Energy Conversion: The Solar Cell. (Studies in Electrical & Electronic Engineering: Vol. 13). 298p. 1978. 107.75 (*0-444-41712-5*) Elsevier.

***Neville, Rhonda.** Guilty by Association. 264p. 1995. pap. 8.95 (*1-56901-539-2*) NW Pub.

***Neville, Richard C.** Solar Energy Conversion: The Solar Cell. 2nd ed. LC 94-39734. 1995. write for info. (*0-444-89818-2*) Elsevier.

Neville, Robert. Deathday. 400p. (Orig.). 1986. pap. 3.95 (*0-8439-2805-0*) Dorchester Pub Co.

Neville, Robert, ed. see Benson, John.

Neville, Robert, jt. auth. see Neville, Georgina.

Neville, Robert C. Behind the Masks of God: An Essay Toward Comparative Theology. LC 90-36353. 200p. (C). 1991. 49.50 (*0-7914-0578-8*); pap. 16.95 (*0-7914-0579-6*) State U NY Pr.

— The Cosmology of Freedom. 385p. (C). 1994. text ed. 59.50x (*0-7914-2757-9*); pap. text ed. 19.95x (*0-7914-2758-7*) State U NY Pr.

— Creativity & God: A Challenge to Process Theology. 163p. (C). 1995. text ed. 49.50x (*0-7914-2821-4*); pap. text ed. 16.95x (*0-7914-2822-2*) State U NY Pr.

— Eternity & Time's Flow. LC 92-27081. (SUNY Series in Philosophy & SUNY Series in Religious Studies). 268p. (C). 1993. 49.50 (*0-7914-1599-6*); pap. 16.95 (*0-7914-1600-3*) State U NY Pr.

— God the Creator: On the Transcendence & Presence of God. LC 90-27103. (Illus.). 320p. (C). 1992. reprint ed. 49.50 (*0-7914-0843-4*); reprint ed. pap. 16.95 (*0-7914-0844-2*) State U NY Pr.

An Asterisk (*) at the beginning of an entry indicates that the title is appearing in BIP for the first time.

— The Highroad Around Modernism. LC 91-47542. (SUNY Series in Philosophy). 339p. (C). 1992. 59.50 (*0-7914-1151-6*); pap. 19.95 (*0-7914-1152-4*) State U NY Pr.

— Normative Cultures. 288p. (C). 1995. text ed. 49.50x (*0-7914-2577-0*); pap. text ed. 16.95x (*0-7914-2578-9*) State U NY Pr.

— The Puritan Smile: A Look Toward Moral Reflection. LC 86-30162. 248p. 1987. 59.50 (*0-88706-542-2*); pap. 19.95 (*0-88706-543-0*) State U NY Pr.

— Reconstruction of Thinking. LC 81-5347. 350p. 1981. 59.50 (*0-87395-494-7*); pap. 19.95 (*0-87395-495-5*) State U NY Pr.

— Recovery of the Measure: Interpretation & Nature. LC 89-11444. 369p. 1989. 59.50 (*0-7914-0098-0*); pap. 19.95 (*0-7914-0099-9*) State U NY Pr.

— Soldier, Sage, Saint. LC 77-75798. 141p. 1989. reprint ed. pap. 15.00 (*0-8232-1036-7*) Fordham.

— The Tao & the Daimon. LC 82-5888. 281p. 1983. 59.50 (*0-87395-661-3*); pap. 19.95 (*0-87395-662-1*) State U NY Pr.

— A Theology Primer. LC 90-19636. 221p. (C). 1991. 39.50 (*0-7914-0849-3*); pap. 12.95 (*0-7914-0850-7*) State U NY Pr.

— The Truth of Broken Symbols. LC 95-2363. (Religious Studies Ser.). 256p. (C). 1994. text ed. 59.50x (*0-7914-2741-2*); pap. text ed. 19.95x (*0-7914-2742-0*) State U NY Pr.

Neville, Robert C., ed. New Essays in Metaphysics. LC 86-30011. (SUNY Series in Systematic Philosophy). 321p. (C). 1986. 57.50 (*0-88706-357-8*); pap. 18.95 (*0-88706-471-X*) State U NY Pr.

Neville, Robert G., jt. ed. see Benson, John.

Neville, Susan. Indiana Winter. LC 93-40692. 1994. pap. 12.95 (*0-253-20879-3*) Ind U Pr.

— Indiana Winter. LC 93-40692. 1994. 27.95 (*0-253-34004-7*) Ind U Pr.

— The Invention of Flight. LC 83-24142. (Flannery O'Connor Award for Short Fiction Ser.). 144p. 1984. 15.95 (*0-8203-0706-8*) U of Ga Pr.

Neville, William. Serve It Up: Volleyball for Life. LC 93-36096. (Illus.). 190p. (Orig.). (C). 1993. pap. text ed. 13.95x (*1-55934-110-6*) Mayfield Pub.

Neville, William J., jt. auth. see United States Volleyball Association Staff.

***Neville, Williams.** Chronology of the Expanding World, 1492 to 1762. LC 94-30476. 1994. 75.00 (*0-13-326406-8*) S&S Trade.

Nevin, Ann, jt. auth. see Leff, Herb.

Nevin, Bruce E. Astrology Inside Out. (Illus.). 320p. (Orig.). 1982. pap. 18.95 (*0-914918-19-2*, Whitford Pr) Schiffer.

Nevin, David & Savell, Isabelle K. John Charles Fremont-the Pathfinder. (Illus.). 12p. 1989. pap. 2.50 (*0-911183-38-8*) Rockland County Hist.

Nevin, J. A., jt. ed. see Commons, Michael L.

***Nevin, John D.** Nevin Genealogica (Some Desc. of Daniel Nevin, Cumberland Valley, Pa., 1770), 2 vols. in 1. 435p. 1995. reprint ed. lib. bdg. 75.00 (*0-8328-4452-7*); reprint ed. pap. 65.00 (*0-8328-4453-5*) Higginson Bk Co.

Nevin, John W. The Anxious Bench: Chambersburg, PA 1844. Kuklick, Bruce, ed. Bd. with Mystical Presence (Philadelphia, PA 1846) 56p. (American Religious Thought of the 18th & 19th Centuries Ser.). 312p. 1987. Set lib. bdg. 45.00 (*0-8240-6970-6*) Garland.

Nevin, Mark. Born to Succeed. (Illus.). 145p. (Orig.). 1983. pap. 7.95 (*0-553-13843-X*) M Nevin.

Nevin, Pat. Ireland, Where Our Roots Go Deep. LC 87-82207. 320p. 1987. 30.00 (*0-86140-255-3*, Pub. by Colin Smythe Ltd UK); pap. 12.95 (*0-86140-259-6*, Pub. by Colin Smythe Ltd UK) Dufour.

Nevin, Paul F. The Survival Economy: Micro-Enterprises in Latin America. 94p. (Orig.). 1985. pap. 4.95 (*0-89192-385-3*) Interbk Inc.

Nevin, Thomas R. Irving Babbitt: An Intellectual Study. LC 83-27407. xi, 194p. 1984. 29.95 (*0-8078-1595-0*) U of NC Pr.

— Simone Weil: Portrait of a Self-Exiled Jew. LC 91-9784. xvi, 488p. (C). 1991. 34.95 (*0-8078-1999-9*) U of NC Pr.

***Nevins.** Child with Cochlear Impairment. 1995. 45.00 (*1-56593-160-2*, 1140) Singular Publishing.

— Diary of Battle: The Personal Journals of Colonel Charles S. Wainwright, 1861-1865. 1993. 35.00 (*1-879664-15-1*) Stan Clark Military.

Nevins, A., ed. see Laugel, Auguste.

Nevins, Albert J. American Martyrs: From 1542. LC 86-64002. 180p. (Orig.). 1987. pap. 6.95 (*0-87973-488-4*, 488) Our Sunday Visitor.

— Answering a Fundamentalist. LC 90-60644. 144p. (Orig.). 1990. pap. 6.95 (*0-87973-433-7*, 433) Our Sunday Visitor.

— Builders of Catholic America. LC 85-72363. 250p. (Orig.). 1985. pap. 7.95 (*0-87973-582-1*, 582) Our Sunday Visitor.

— Called to Serve: A Guidebook for Altar Servers. LC 81-82546. 48p. (J). (gr. 4 up). 1981. pap. 14.95 (*0-87973-663-1*, 663) Our Sunday Visitor.

— Catholicism: The Faith of Our Fathers. LC 94-68930. 192p. (Orig.). 1995. pap. 14.95 (*0-87973-650-X*, 650) Our Sunday Visitor.

— Life after Death. LC 83-61888. 136p. (Orig.). 1983. pap. 6.95 (*0-87973-612-7*, 612) Our Sunday Visitor.

— The Life of Jesus Christ. 248p. (Orig.). 1987. pap. 12.95 (*0-87973-500-7*, 500) Our Sunday Visitor.

— My Baptismal Book. 20p. (J). (ps). 1971. pap. 4.95 (*0-87973-360-8*, 360) Our Sunday Visitor.

— A Saint for Your Name: Saints for Boys. LC 79-92504. (Illus.). 120p. (YA). (gr. 7 up). 1980. pap. 5.95 (*0-87973-320-9*, 320) Our Sunday Visitor.

— A Saint for Your Name: Saints for Girls. LC 79-92502. (Illus.). 104p. (YA). (gr. 7 up). 1980. pap. 5.95 (*0-87973-321-7*, 321) Our Sunday Visitor.

— Strangers at Your Door: How to Respond to Jehovah's Witnesses, the Mormons, Televangelists, Cults, & More. LC 88-61111. 160p. (Orig.). 1988. pap. 6.95 (*0-87973-496-5*, 496) Our Sunday Visitor.

Nevins, Albert J., ed. Father Smith Instructs Jackson. rev. ed. LC 75-628. 278p. 1975. pap. 7.95 (*0-87973-864-2*) Our Sunday Visitor.

Nevins, Allan. The American States During & After the Revolution, 1775-1789. (BCL1 - U. S. History Ser.). 728p. 1991. reprint ed. lib. bdg. 109.00 (*0-7812-6134-1*) Rprt Serv.

— American States During & After the Revolution, 1775-1798. LC 68-56552. xviii, 728p. 1969. reprint ed. 49.50 (*0-678-00510-9*) Kelley.

— A Century of Political Cartoons: Caricature in the United States from 1800 to 1900. (BCL1 - U. S. History Ser.). 190p. 1991. reprint ed. lib. bdg. 69.00 (*0-7812-6038-8*) Rprt Serv.

— Emergence of Modern America, 1865-1878. LC 77-145207. (Illus.). 1971. reprint ed. 95.00 (*0-403-01127-2*) Scholarly.

— The Emergence of Modern America, 1865-1878. (History - United States Ser.). 446p. 1993. reprint ed. lib. bdg. 99.00 (*0-7812-4906-6*) Rprt Serv.

— Fremont: Pathmarker of the West. LC 91-40734. (Illus.). xiv, 704p. 1992. reprint ed. pap. 19.95 (*0-8032-8364-4*, Bison Books) U of Nebr Pr.

— Fremont, the World's Greatest Adventurer. 1992. reprint ed. lib. bdg. 75.00 (*0-7812-5070-6*) Rprt Serv.

— History of the Bank of New York & Trust Company, 1784-1934. LC 75-41774. (Companies & Men: Business Enterprises in America Ser.). (Illus.). 1978. reprint ed. 26.95 (*0-405-08088-3*) Ayer.

— James Truslow Adams: Historian of the American Dream. LC 68-16627. (Illus.). 329p. reprint ed. pap. 93.80 (*0-8357-6168-1*, 2034455) Bks Demand.

— Ordeal of the Union, Vol. 1. 1072p. 1992. pap. 25.00 (*0-02-035441-X*, Collier S&S) S&S Trade.

— Ordeal of the Union, Vol. 2. 1072p. 1992. pap. 25.00 (*0-02-035442-8*, Collier S&S) S&S Trade.

— Ordeal of the Union, Vol. 3. 1072p. 1992. pap. 25.00 (*0-02-035443-6*, Collier S&S) S&S Trade.

— Ordeal of the Union, Vol. 4. 1072p. 1992. pap. 25.00 (*0-02-035445-2*, Collier S&S) S&S Trade.

— Pocket History of the U. S. Sacco, Maryanne, ed. 1992. pap. 7.50 (*0-671-79023-4*) PB.

— The State Universities & Democracy. LC 77-9308. 171p. 1977. reprint ed. text ed. 38.50 (*0-8371-9705-8*, NESU, Greenwood Pr) Greenwood.

Nevins, Allan, ed. Diary of Philip Hone 1828-1851, 2 Vols. in 1. LC 77-112559. (Rise of Urban America Ser.). (Illus.). 1970. reprint ed. 57.95 (*0-405-02468-1*) Ayer.

— Letters of Grover Cleveland, 1850-1908. LC 70-123752. (American Public Figures Ser.). 1970. reprint ed. lib. bdg. 75.00 (*0-306-71982-7*) Da Capo.

Nevins, Allan & Commager, Henry S. A Pocket History of the United States. (gr. 10 up). 1991. mass mkt. 4.95 (*0-671-62992-1*) PB.

Nevins, Allan & Hill, Frank E. Ford, 3 vols. Incl. Vol. 1. Times, the Man, the Company. LC 75-41775. 1976. (*0-318-50821-4*); Vol. 2. Expansion & Challenge, 1915-1933. LC 75-41775. 1976. (*0-318-50822-2*); Vol. 3. Decline & Rebirth: 1933-1962. LC 75-41775. 1976. (*0-318-50823-0*); LC 75-41775. (Companies & Men: Business Enterprises in America Ser.). (Illus.). 1976. reprint ed. 154.95 (*0-405-08089-1*) Ayer.

Nevins, Allan & Krout, John A., eds. The Greater City: New York, 1898 to 1948. LC 81-4173. (Illus.). vii, 260p. 1981. reprint ed. text ed. 59.75 (*0-313-23072-2*, NEGC, Greenwood Pr) Greenwood.

Nevins, Allan, ed. see Strong, George T.

Nevins, Allan, ed. see Wainwright, Charles S.

Nevins, Allen. American Press Opinion, Washington to Coolidge: A Documentary Record of Editorial Leadership & Criticism, 1785-1927. (BCL1 - U. S. History Ser.). 598p. 1991. reprint ed. lib. bdg. 99.00 (*0-7812-6023-X*) Rprt Serv.

Nevins, Christopher B., jt. auth. see Warren, Winthrop D.

Nevins, Dan. Brainpuzzlers: Amazing Math Games & Puzzles. (J). (gr. 4-7). 1994. pap. 2.95 (*0-8167-3193-4*) Troll Assocs.

— Three-Dee Mouse Mazes. (Illus.). 48p. (Orig.). (J). (gr. 8-11). 1987. pap. 2.95 (*0-8431-1883-0*) Price Stern.

Nevins, Deborah, ed. Grand Central Terminal: City Within the City. LC 82-81177. (Illus.). 148p. (Orig.). 1982. 25.00 (*0-9606892-2-2*) Municipal Art Soc.

Nevins, Deborah, jt. auth. see Bogart, Michele.

Nevins, Deborah, et al. Architects' Drawings from the Collection of Barbara Pine. (Illus.). 48p. (Orig.). 1987. pap. 15.00 (*0-941680-05-3*) M&L Block.

Nevins, Edward. Forces of the British Empire - 1914. LC 92-15109. (Illus.). 288p. 1992. 65.00 (*0-918339-18-9*) Vandamere.

***Nevins, Elizabeth.** Date Tripping with Friends & Lovers: The Fun, Whimsical, Inexpensive, Outrageous, Extravagant, Sensual, Romantic, & Simple Book of Things to Do on a Date. LC 94-92458. (Illus.). 384p. (Orig.). 1995. pap. 9.95 (*0-9643977-0-6*) Sun Tea Bks.

Nevins, Ellen. Real Bosses Don't Say Thank You. (Illus.). 138p. (Orig.). 1983. pap. 4.95 (*0-914359-00-2*) Nevins Pub Co.

Nevins, Frances M. The One Hundred Twenty Hour Clock. 216p. 1986. 15.95 (*0-8027-5657-3*) Walker & Co.

Nevins, Francis M., Jr. Bar-Twenty: The Life of Clarence E. Mulford, Creator of Hopalong Cassidy, with Seven Original Stories Reprinted. LC 92-56670. (Illus.). 264p. 1993. lib. bdg. 32.50 (*0-89950-870-7*) McFarland & Co.

— Cornell Woolrich-Morkrets Poet. LC 86-2266. 46p. 1986. reprint ed. lib. bdg. 27.00x (*0-89370-538-1*) Borgo Pr.

— The Films of Hopalong Cassidy. LC 88-40500. (Illus.). 328p. 1988. pap. 19.95 (*0-936505-09-5*) World Yesterday.

— The Ninety Million Dollar Mouse. 1987. 16.95 (*0-8027-5683-2*) Walker & Co.

Nevins, Francis M., Jr. & Greenberg, Martin H., eds. The Adventures of Henry Turnbuckle: Detective Comedies by Jack Ritchie. LC 86-31372. (Mystery Makers Ser.). 386p. 1987. 29.95 (*0-8093-1397-9*) S Ill U Pr.

— Buffet for Unwelcome Guests: The Best Short Mysteries of Christianna Brand. LC 83-526. (Mystery Makers Ser.). 316p. 1983. 17.95 (*0-8093-1140-2*) S Ill U Pr.

— Exeunt Murderers: The Best Mystery Stories of Anthony Boucher. LC 83-19513. (Mystery Makers Ser.). 320p. 1983. 19.95 (*0-8093-1099-6*) S Ill U Pr.

— Leopold's Way: Detective Stories by Edward D. Hoch. LC 84-27554. (Mystery Makers Ser.). 359p. 1985. 24.50 (*0-8093-1233-6*) S Ill U Pr.

Nevins, Francis M., Jr. & Stanich, Ray. The Sound of Detection: Ellery Queen's Adventures in Radio. LC 85-25462. viii, 109p. 1985. reprint ed. lib. bdg. 25.00x (*0-89370-556-X*, Brownstone Bks); reprint ed. pap. 15.00x (*0-941028-01-1*, Brownstone Bks) Borgo Pr.

Nevins, Francis M., Jr., jt. auth. see Greenberg, Martin H.

Nevins, Francis M., Jr., ed. see Hoch, Edward D.

Nevins, Francis M., Jr., ed. see Slesar, Henry.

Nevins, Iris. Fabric Marbling. 1988. pap. text ed. 12.50 (*0-9620400-1-0*) Iris Nevins.

— One Hundred Five Helpful Marbling Hints. 1991. pap. text ed. 12.50 (*0-9620400-2-9*) Iris Nevins.

— Traditional Marbling. rev. ed. (C). 1988. pap. 15.00 (*0-9620400-0-2*) Iris Nevins.

Nevins, Jane, ed. see Gordon, Barry.

Nevins, Kathy. Dot-to-Dot Dinos. (Illus.). 48p. (Orig.). (J). (gr. 2 up). 1989. bds. 2.95 (*0-8431-2338-9*) Price Stern.

***Nevins, Michael.** The Jewish Doctor: A Narrative History. 1996. write for info. (*1-56821-533-9*) Aronson.

Nevins, Randi J., jt. auth. see Gorden, William I.

Nevins, Randi J., jt. auth. see Rubin, Rebecca B.

Nevins, William. Thoughts on Popery. Grob, Gerald, ed. LC 76-46093. (Anti-Movements in America Ser.). 1977. reprint ed. lib. bdg. 19.95 (*0-405-09966-5*) Ayer.

Nevinson, Henry W. Between Two Wars. 1972. 69.95 (*0-87968-725-8*) Gordon Pr.

— Books & Personalities. LC 68-16962. (Essay Index Reprint Ser.). 1977. reprint ed. 20.95 (*0-8369-0738-8*) Ayer.

— Changes & Chances. 1972. 69.95 (*0-87968-834-3*) Gordon Pr.

— Dawn in Russia or Scenes in the Russian Revolution. LC 77-115569. (Russia Observed Ser.). (Illus.). 1971. reprint ed. 25.95 (*0-405-03088-6*) Ayer.

— Essays in Freedom & Rebellion. LC 67-28761. (Essay Index Reprint Ser.). 1977. 19.95 (*0-8369-0739-6*) Ayer.

— Essays, Poems & Tales of Henry Nevinson. Brailsford, Henry, ed. 1977. lib. bdg. 59.95 (*0-8490-1788-2*) Gordon Pr.

— Farewell to America. 1973. 250.00 (*0-87968-103-9*) Gordon Pr.

— Films of Time. 1973. 69.95 (*0-8490-0166-8*) Gordon Pr.

— Fire of Life. 1972. 69.95 (*0-8490-0169-2*) Gordon Pr.

— Goethe: Man & Poet. 1974. 69.95 (*0-8490-0244-3*) Gordon Pr.

— Goethe: Man & Poet. LC 77-164619. (Select Bibliographies Reprint Ser.). 1977. reprint ed. 20.95 (*0-8369-5902-7*) Ayer.

— In the Dark Backward. LC 72-111854. (Essay Index Reprint Ser.). 1977. 20.95 (*0-8369-1621-2*) Ayer.

— Last Changes, Last Chances. 1972. 69.95 (*0-8490-0487-X*) Gordon Pr.

— More Changes, More Chances. 1973. 69.95 (*0-8490-0671-6*) Gordon Pr.

— Running Accompaniments. 1972. 69.95 (*0-8490-0980-4*) Gordon Pr.

— Thomas Hardy. LC 72-2084. (Studies in Thomas Hardy: No. 14). 1972. reprint ed. lib. bdg. 39.95 (*0-8383-1466-X*) M S G Haskell Hse.

— Visions & Memories. 1972. 69.95 (*0-8490-1262-7*) Gordon Pr.

Nevis, Joel A. FUSAC '88 ACEFO: Proceedings of the Sixth Annual Meeting of the Finno-Ugric Studies Association of Canada. LC 89-34253. 158p. (C). 1989. lib. bdg. 44.50 (*0-8191-7492-0*, Pub. by Finno-Ugric Studies CN) U Pr of Amer.

***Nevis, Joel A., et al, eds.** Clitics: A Comprehensive Bibliography 1892-1991. LC 94-27029. (Library & Information Sources in Linguistics). xxvii, 233p. 1994. lib. bdg. 69.00 (*1-55619-252-5*) Benjamins North Am.

Nevis, St. Kitts & Jagdeo, Tirbani P. Caribbean Contraceptive Prevalence Surveys. 1985. write for info. (*0-916683-16-8*) Intl Plan Parent.

Nevison, Christopher H., et al. Laboratories for Parallel Programming. LC 93-46893. (Computer Science: Artificial Intelligence Ser.). 325p. (C). 1994. spiral bd. 40.00 (*0-86720-470-2*) Jones & Bartlett.

Nevison, John M. Spreadsheet Design for 1-2-3. 1989. pap. 21.95 (*0-13-838160-7*) P-H.

***Nevitt, Lee R.** Memories & More: A Bit of Sharing. 140p. (Orig.). 1995. pap. write for info. (*1-885591-48-9*) Morris Pubng.

Nevitt, Peter K., et al. Equipment Leasing for Commercial Bankers. LC 87-5532. (Illus.). 136p. (Orig.). 1987. pap. text ed. 43.00 (*0-936742-37-2*) Robt Morris Assocs.

Nevitte, Neil. The Decline of Deference. 320p. 1995. pap. 19.95 (*1-55111-031-8*) Broadview Pr.

Nevitte, Neil & Gibbins, Roger. New Elites in Old States: The Ideologies of Equality in the Anglo-American Democracies. 224p. 1991. 27.50 (*0-19-540803-9*) OUP.

***Nevitte, Neil & Kornberg, Allan, eds.** Minorities & the Canadian State. 320p. 1995. pap. 37.00 (*0-8095-4930-1*) Borgo Pr.

Nevitte, Neil, jt. ed. see Feldman, Elliot J.

Nevius, Blake. American Novel: Sinclair Lewis to the Present. LC 76-103094. (Goldentree Bibliographies Series in Language & Literature). (C). 1970. pap. text ed. write for info. (*0-88295-524-1*) Harlan Davidson.

— Ivy Compton-Burnett. LC 74-110600. (Columbia Essays on Modern Writers Ser.: No. 47). (Orig.). 1970. pap. text ed. 7.50 (*0-231-02988-8*) Col U Pr.

Nevius, Blake, ed. see Cooper, James Fenimore.

Nevkapil, Jiri, jt. ed. see Chloupek, Jan.

Nevo, B. & Jager, R. S., eds. Educational & Psychological Testing: The Test Taker's Outlook. (Illus.). 321p. 1993. pap. 29.50 (*0-88937-057-5*) Hogrefe & Huber Pubs.

Nevo, Baruch, ed. Scientific Aspects of Graphology: A Handbook. (Illus.). 362p. (C). 1987. 56.95x (*0-398-05245-X*) C C Thomas.

— Scientific Aspects of Graphology: A Handbook. (Illus.). 362p. 1987. pap. 34.95 (*0-398-06304-4*) C C Thomas.

Nevo, D., jt. auth. see Smilansky, M.

***Nevo, David.** School-Based Evaluation: A Dialogue for School Improvement. LC 94-46676. 1995. text ed. 67.00 (*0-08-041942-9*, Pergamon Pr) Elsevier.

Nevo, David, jt. auth. see Glasman, Naftaly.

Nevo, David, jt. auth. see Lewy, Arieh.

Nevo, Eviatar & Reig, Osvaldo A., eds. Evolution of Subterranean Mammals at the Organismal & Molecular Levels. (Progress in Clinical & Biological Research Ser.). 434p. 1990. text ed. 155.95 (*0-471-56711-6*) Wiley.

Nevo, Eviatar, jt. auth. see Karlin, Samuel.

Nevo, Joseph & Pappe, Ilan, eds. Jordan in the Middle East: The Making of A Pivotal State. LC 94-4617. 1994. 28.50 (*0-7146-3454-9*, Pub. by F Cass Pubs UK) Intl Spec Bk.

Nevo, Ruth. Comic Transformations in Shakespeare. 1981. pap. 13.95 (*0-416-73890-7*, NO.6351) Routledge Chapman & Hall.

— Shakespeare's Other Language. 160p. 1987. text ed. 39.50 (*0-416-06402-7*) Routledge Chapman & Hall.

Nevo, Ruth, tr. see Amichai, Yehuda.

Nevsky, Y. G. & Gorovoy, A. V. Russian-English Dictionary of Sports Terms & Phrases. 224p. 1983. 30.00 (*0-317-39527-0*, Pub. by Collets) St Mut.

Nevzorov, B. A. Corrosion of Structural Materials in Sodium. 112p. 1970. text ed. 31.00 (*0-7065-0710-X*, Pub. by Keter Pub IS) Coronet Bks.

New, jt. auth. see Petersen.

New Age Journal Editors & Miller, Ronald S. As Above, So Below: Paths to Spiritual Renewal in Daily Life. 346p. (Orig.). 1992. pap. 14.95 (*0-87477-659-7*) J P Tarcher.

New American Foundation Staff. Unity in Diversity: An Index to the Publications of Conservative & Libertarian Institutions. Birch, Carol L., ed. LC 82-20552. 284p. 1983. 25.00 (*0-8108-1599-0*) Scarecrow.

New American Roget's College Thesaurus Editors. The New American Roget's College Thesaurus. 1986. pap. 3.50 (*0-317-47644-0*) NAL-Dutton.

New, Anne L. Raise More Money for Your Nonprofit Organization: A Guide to Evaluating & Improving Your Fundraising. (Orig.). 1991. pap. text ed. 14.95 (*0-87954-388-4*) Foundation Ctr.

***New Atlantean Press Staff.** Vaccine Exemptions: A State-by-State Summary of Legal Exemptions to "Mandatory" Vaccine Laws. 16p. (Orig.). 1995. pap. 10.00 (*1-881217-07-8*) New Atlantean.

New, Bill D., jt. auth. see Wright, D. Franklin.

New Careers Center, Inc. Staff & Frey, Judith. College Degrees You Can Earn from Home: How to Earn a First-Class Degree Without Attending Class. 181p. 1995. pap. 14.95 (*0-911781-12-9*) Live Oak Pubns.

New Careers Center, Inc. Staff & Glenn, Reed. The Ten Best Opportunities for Starting a Home Business Today. 200p. (Orig.). 1993. pap. 14.95 (*0-911781-10-2*) Live Oak Pubns.

New, Carl R., jt. auth. see Wolf, Charles, Jr.

New, Charles. Life, Wanderings & Labours in Eastern Africa. (Illus.). 529p. 1971. reprint ed. 45.00 (*0-7146-1876-4*, BHA-01876, Pub. by F Cass Pubs UK) Intl Spec Bk.

New City Press Editorial Staff, ed. see Lubich, Chiara.

New City Press Editorial Staff, tr. see Lubich, Chiara.

New Combined Bible Dictionary & Concordance Staff. New Combined Bible Dictionary & Concordance. (Direction Bks.). 456p. 1965. pap. 7.99 (*0-8010-6680-8*) Baker Bk.

***New, David.** Daring to Dream Again: Breaking Through Barriers That Hold Us Back, Small Group Leader's Guide. (1994 50-Day Spiritual Adventure Ser.). (Illus.). 52p. (Orig.). 1993. student ed, pap. text ed. 9.99 (*1-879050-18-8*) Chapel of Air.

New, David S. Old Testament Quotations in the Synoptic Gospels, & the Two-Document Hypothesis. LC 93-36734. (Septuagint & Cognate Studies: No. 37). 147p. 1993. 23.95 (*1-55540-920-2*); pap. 15.95 (*1-55540-921-0*) Scholars Pr GA.

New Dimensions Foundation Staff, ed. Worlds Beyond: The Everlasting Frontier. LC 78-54345. 320p. 1978. pap. 6.95 (*0-915904-36-5*) And-Or Pr.

New, Dorothy. Bedtime Friends. (J). 1994. 8.95 (*0-8062-4873-4*) Carlton.

New, Elisa. The Regenerate Lyric: Theology & Innovation in American Poetry. LC 92-23412. (Cambridge Studies in American Literature & Culture: No. 64). (Illus.). 288p. (C). 1993. 59.95 (*0-521-43021-6*) Cambridge U Pr.

New Engalnd Historic Genealogical Society Staff. The New England Historical & Genealogical Register, 1861, Vol. 15. (Illus.). 375p. 1993. reprint ed. pap. text ed. 25.00 (*1-55613-840-7*) Heritage Bk.

New England Aquarium Staff & Kaufman, Les. Do Fishes Get Thirsty? Questions Answered by the New England Aquarium. (Illus.). 40p. (YA). (gr. 5 up). 1991. lib. bdg. 15.82 (*0-531-10992-5*) Watts.

N

New England Association for Women in Psychology Staff, ed. Current Feminist Issues in Psychotherapy. LC 82-15721. (Women & Therapy Ser.: Vol. 1, No. 3). 115p. 1983. text ed. 29.95 (*0-86656-206-0*) Haworth Pr.

New England Banking Institute Staff. Bank Operations. 184p. 1991. pap. 30.00 (*0-536-57797-8*) Ginn Pr.

— Branch Management. 328p. 1991. pap. 27.00 (*0-536-58058-8*) Ginn Pr.

— Fundamentals of Banking. 2nd ed. 316p. 1991. 34.00 (*0-536-57950-4*) Ginn Pr.

New England Deaconess Hospital & Harvard Medical School Mind-Body Medical Institute Associates Staff, et al. The Wellness Book: The Comprehensive Guide to Maintaining Health & Treating Stress-Related Illness. LC 92-39899. (Illus.). 1993. pap. 14.00 (*0-671-79750-6*) S&S Trade.

New England Historic & Genealogical Society Staff. The New England Historical & Genealogical Register, 1857, Vol. XI. xii, 380p. 1993. reprint ed. pap. text ed. 25.00 (*1-55613-777-X*) Heritage Bk.

— The New England Historical & Genealogical Register, 1863, Vol. XVII. (Illus.). 387p. (Orig.). 1994. reprint ed. pap. text ed. 25.00 (*1-55613-937-3*) Heritage Bk.

— New England Historical & Genealogical Register, 1864, Vol. XVIII. (Illus.). 409p. (Orig.). 1994. reprint ed. pap. text ed. 25.00 (*1-55613-938-1*) Heritage Bk.

New England Historic, Genealogical Society Staff. The New England Historical & Genealogical Register, 1847. (Register Ser.). (Illus.). 400p. 1992. reprint ed. pap. text ed. 25.00 (*1-55613-606-4*) Heritage Bk.

New England Historic Genealogical Society Staff. The New England Historical & Genealogical Register, Vol. XVI, 1862. (Illus.). 397p. 1993. reprint ed. pap. text ed. 25.00 (*1-55613-841-5*) Heritage Bk.

***New England Historic-Genealogical Society Staff.** The New England Historical & Genealogical Register, Vol. 24. 451p. (Orig.). 1994. pap. text ed. 25.00 (*0-7884-0071-1*) Heritage Bk.

New England Historic Genealogical Society Staff. The New England Historical & Genealogical Register, Vol. IX: 1855. 388p. (Orig.). 1993. reprint ed. pap. text ed. 25.00 (*1-55613-744-3*) Heritage Bk.

— The New England Historical & Genealogical Register, Vol. 10: 1856. 379p. (Orig.). 1993. reprint ed. pap. text ed. 25.00 (*1-55613-745-1*) Heritage Bk.

— The New England Historical & Genealogical Register, Vol. 13: 1859. iv, 387p. (Orig.). 1993. pap. 22.00 (*1-55613-813-X*) Heritage Bk.

— New England Historical & Genealogical Register, 1860, Vol. 14. v, 390p. (Orig.). 1993. reprint ed. pap. text ed. 25.00 (*1-55613-814-8*) Heritage Bk.

— The New England Historical & Genealogical Register, 1867 Vol. 21, 1867. 399p. (Orig.). 1994. pap. text ed. 25.00 (*0-7884-0012-6*) Heritage Bk.

— The New England Historical & Genealogical Registry, 1868 Vol. 22,1868, Vol. 22. 500p. (Orig.). 1994. pap. text ed. 25.00 (*0-7884-0013-4*) Heritage Bk.

— Vital Records of Tisbury, Massachusetts, to the Year Eighteen Fifty. ii, 244p. reprint ed. pap. 19.00 (*1-55613-555-6*) Heritage Bk.

New England Historic Genealogical Society Staff & Mayhew, Catherine M. Vital Records of Chilmark, Massachusetts to the Year 1850 with an Addenda by Catherine Merwin Mayhew. 153p. 1992. reprint ed. pap. 16.50 (*1-55613-543-2*) Heritage Bk.

New England Historical & Genealogical Society Staff. New England Historical & Genealogical Register, Vol. VII, 1853. 388p. 1992. reprint ed. pap. text ed. 25.00 (*1-55613-687-0*) Heritage Bk.

— New England Historical & Genealogical Register, Vol. VIII, 1854. 388p. 1992. reprint ed. pap. text ed. 25.00 (*1-55613-688-9*) Heritage Bk.

— The New England Historical & Genealogical Register, 1849, Vol. III. 418p. 1992. reprint ed. pap. 25.00 (*1-55613-641-2*) Heritage Bk.

— The New England Historical & Genealogical Register, 1858, Vol. XII. vi, 379p. 1993. reprint ed. pap. text ed. 25.00 (*1-55613-778-8*) Heritage Bk.

— The New England Historical & Genealogical Register, 1873, Vol. 27. 464p. (Orig.). 1995. pap. text ed. 25.00 (*0-7884-0183-1*) Heritage Bk.

New England Historical Genealogical Society Staff. The Greenlaw Index of the New England Historic Genealogical Society. 1979. lib. bdg. 225.50 (*0-8161-0312-7*, Hall Library) G K Hall.

New England Marine Advisory Service. Seafood Sourcebook: A Consumer's Guide to Information on Food from Our Oceans & Lakes. 46p. 1978. 1.00 (*0-686-36979-3*, P762) Sea Grant Pubns.

New England Press Editors. Vermont Bed & Breakfasts. LC 91-61244. 74p. (Orig.). 1991. pap. 8.95 (*0-933050-92-5*) New Eng Pr VT.

— Vermont Inns & Bed & Breakfast Inns. LC 93-83757. 128p. (Orig.). 1993. pap. 8.95 (*1-881535-04-5*) New Eng Pr VT.

***New England Press Staff, ed.** Vermont Inns & Bed & Breakfast Inns. LC 95-68733. (Illus.). 136p. (Orig.). 1995. pap. text ed. 9.95 (*1-881535-19-3*) New Eng Pr VT.

New England Publishing Associates, Inc. Staff, ed. see Ryan, Bernard, Jr.

New England Publishing Associates Staff, ed. see Hand, Larry E.

New England Regional Commission. The New England Regional Plan: An Economic Development Strategy. LC 81-50584. 158p. reprint ed. 45.10 (*0-685-15819-5*, 2027533) Bks Demand.

New England Regional Office of the American Friends Service Committee Staff. The Deadly Connection: Nuclear War & U. S. Intervention. Gerson, Joseph, ed. (Illus.). 266p. 1986. lib. bdg. 39.95 (*0-86571-068-6*); pap. 12.95 (*0-86571-067-8*) New Soc Pubs.

New England Science Fiction Association Staff. NESFA Index: Science Fiction Magazines & Original Anthologies 1975. 36p. 1976. pap. 5.00 (*0-915368-04-8*) New Eng SF Assoc.

— The NESFA Index: Science Fiction Magazines & Original Anthologies 1976. 38p. 1977. pap. 5.00 (*0-915368-05-6*) New Eng SF Assoc.

New England Society of Jungian Analysts Staff, ed. The Analytic Life: Personal & Professional Aspects of Being a Jungian Analyst. 78p. 1988. pap. 11.95 (*0-938434-28-4*) Sigo Pr.

New England Water Works Association Staff. Taking the Bull by the Horns: Adopting a Proactive Approach to Public Relations. 149p. 1991. student ed 30.00 (*1-881198-00-6*) New Eng Water Wks.

— Treatment Practices of New England Surface Water Supplies. 80p. 1994. 22.50 (*1-881198-01-4*) New Eng Water Wks.

New Farm Staff, et al. What Really Happens When You Cut Chemicals? Shirley, Christopher & Bowman, Greg, eds. LC 92-41471. 1993. write for info. (*0-913107-16-6*) Rodale Inst.

New Fourth World Movement Staff, tr. see Wresinski, Joseph.

New Hampshire Bicentennial Conference on the History of Geology (1976: University of New Hampshire) Staff. Two Hundred Years of Geology in America: Proceedings of the New Hampshire Bicentennial Conference on the History of Geology. Schneer, Cecil J., ed. LC 78-63149. (Illus.). 399p. reprint ed. pap. 113.80 (*0-8357-7522-4*, 2036029) Bks Demand.

New Hampshire Staff. Forest Laws of New Hampshire. xxviii, 217p. write for info. (*0-318-60196-6*) Equity Pubng NH.

New Hampshire State Legislature Staff. Provincial & State Papers, 18 vols., Set. Bouton, Nathaniel & Hammond, I. W., eds. LC 70-173073. reprint ed. 1,690.00 (*0-404-07450-2*) AMS Pr.

New Holland Publ. Ltd. Staff. Patchwork. (C). 1989. 35.00 (*1-85368-076-1*, Pub. by New Holland Pubs UK) St Mut.

— Table Decorating. (C). 1989. 50.00 (*0-685-32436-2*, Pub. by New Holland Pubs UK) St Mut.

New Hope Church Family & Friends Staff. In the Spirit of Christmas: Thanksgiving-Advent-Epiphany: Selections for Daily Use. Daily, Lois, ed. LC 87-26059. (Illus.). 136p. (Orig.). 1987. pap. 8.95 (*0-944741-00-2*) Legacy Hse CA.

New Individualist Review Journal Staff. New Individualist Review. LC 65-35281. 1024p. 1992. pap. 8.50 (*0-86597-065-3*) Liberty Fund.

New Initiatives for Full Employment Staff. Jobs for All: A Plan for the Economic & Social Revitalization of America. 112p. (Orig.). 1994. pap. 9.50 (*0-945257-55-4*) Apex Pr.

New International Bartender's Guide Staff. The New International Bartender's Guide. LC 84-8375. 320p. 1989. 6.95 (*0-394-54038-7*) Random.

New International Version of Bible Staff. The Lost Boy. (Stories from the Great Book Ser.). (Illus.). (Orig.). (J). 1986. pap. 4.95 (*0-918789-07-9*) FreeMan Prods.

— The Stowaway. (Stories from the Great Book Ser.). (Illus.). (Orig.). (J). 1986. pap. 4.95 (*0-918789-09-5*) FreeMan Prods.

New International Version of the Bible Staff. Daniel & the Lions. (Stories from the Great Book Ser.). (Orig.). (J). 1986. pap. 4.95 (*0-918789-08-7*) FreeMan Prods.

— The Giant & the Boy. (Stories from the Great Book Ser.). (Illus.). (Orig.). (J). 1986. pap. 4.95 (*0-918789-06-0*) FreeMan Prods.

New Internationalist Publication Staff, comp. Women: A World Report. LC 85-13573. (Illus.). 376p. 1987. pap. 8.95 (*0-19-505064-9*) OUP.

New Int'l Version Staff, tr. Life Application Bible Study Guide: Daniel. 96p. 1990. 4.99 (*0-8423-2731-2*, 022731-2) Tyndale.

— Life Application Bible Study Guide: I, II Timothy & Titus. 96p. 1990. 4.99 (*0-8423-2734-7*, 022734-7) Tyndale.

— NIV Life Application Bible Study Guide: Philippians & Colossians. 96p. 1990. 4.99 (*0-8423-2733-9*, 022733-9) Tyndale.

New Jersey Adjutant-General Office Staff. Records of Officers & Men of New Jersey in Wars 1791-1815. 410p. 1993. reprint ed. pap. 42.50 (*0-685-69932-3*, 4035) Clearfield Co.

New Jersey Appellate Practice Study Committee. New Jersey Appellate Practice Handbook. 3rd ed. 92p. 1993. ring bd. 65.00 (*0-685-65972-0*) NJ Inst CLE.

New Jersey Association of Legal Secretaries Staff. New Jersey Legal Secretary's Handbook. rev. ed. 570p. 1984. ring bd. 50.00x (*0-87215-721-0*) Michie Butterworth.

— New Jersey Legal Secretary's Handbook. suppl. ed. 574p. 1991. ring bd. 40.00 (*0-87473-859-8*) Michie Butterworth.

New Jersey Conference of Social Work Staff. Negro in New Jersey. LC 74-78772. (Illus.). 116p. 1969. reprint ed. text ed. 49.75 (*0-8371-1411-X*, NNJ&, Negro U Pr) Greenwood.

New Jersey Historical Society Staff. Records of the Town of Newark, New Jersey: From Its Settlement in 1666 to Its Incorporation As a City in 1836. 302p. 1990. reprint ed. pap. 20.00 (*1-55613-292-1*) Heritage Bk.

New Jersey Institute for Continuing Legal Education Staff. Criminal Trial Practice (Seminar Materials) 403p. 1988. pap. 55.00 (*0-685-14626-X*) NJ Inst CLE.

— Workers' Compensation Practice: Seminar Materials. 93p. 1992. 35.00 (*0-317-57862-6*) NJ Inst CLE.

New Jersey Institute for Continuing Legal Education Staff & Lunin, Joseph. Forms for Practice under the New Jersey Nonprofit Corporation Act (1991) (Illus.). 80p. 95.00 (*0-685-08690-9*) NJ Inst CLE.

New Jersey Self-Help Clearinghouse Staff. The Self-Help Group Directory. 10th ed. DeGirolamo, Gail & White, Barbara, eds. 480p. 1992. 20.00 (*0-9634322-1-4*) St C-R Med Ctr.

New Jersey State Museum Staff, et al. The Hollywood Indian: Stereotypes of Native Americans in Films. (Illus.). 80p. (Orig.). 1981. 5.95 (*0-938766-00-7*) NJ State Mus.

New Jersey Supreme Court Committee on Model Jury Charges - Civil Staff. Model Jury Charges - Civil. 4th ed. 813p. 1992. ring bd. 75.00 (*0-685-65971-2*) NJ Inst CLE.

New Jersey Supreme Court Committee on Model Jury Charges - Criminal Staff. Model Jury Charges - Criminal. 3rd ed. 658p. 1990. ring bd. 75.00 (*0-939457-03-2*) NJ Inst CLE.

— Model Jury Charges - Criminal. 3rd suppl. ed. 658p. 1991. 39.00 (*0-685-58685-5*) NJ Inst CLE.

— Model Jury Charges - Criminal. 3rd suppl. ed. 658p. 1992. 39.00 (*0-685-58686-3*) NJ Inst CLE.

New Jersey Supreme Court Staff. In the Matter of Karen Quinlan Vol. 1: The Complete Legal Briefs, Court Proceedings, & Decision in the Superior Court of New Jersey. LC 75-42525. 575p. 1975. text ed. 55.00 (*0-313-26920-3*, U6920, Greenwood Pr) Greenwood.

New Jersey Supreme Court Staff, et al. In the Matter of Karen Quinlan Vol. 2: The Complete Briefs, Oral Arguments, & Opinion in the New Jersey Supreme Court, Vol. 2. LC 76-14598. 344p. 1976. text ed. 50.00 (*0-313-26921-1*, U6921, Greenwood Pr) Greenwood.

New Jewish Agency Staff. New Shalom Seders. 1985. pap. 12.95 (*0-915361-22-1*) Modan-Adama Bks.

New Jewish Agenda Staff, comp. The Shalom Seders: Three Passover Haggadahs. LC 83-25857. (Illus.). 104p. 1984. pap. 12.95 (*0-915361-03-5*, 09747-1) Modan-Adama Bks.

New, Joan, ed. see Sterne, Laurence.

New, Joan C. Knocking down Pears. Zarucchi, Roy & Page, Carolyn, eds. (Chapbook Ser.). (Illus.). 24p. (Orig.). 1990. pap. 5.00 (*0-9623862-7-8*) Nightshade Pr.

— The River Bend. LC 92-82885. (Orig.). 1993. pap. 8.50 (*0-933598-44-0*) NC Wesleyan Pr.

— The River Bend. deluxe limited ed. LC 92-82885. (Orig.). 1993. pap. 17.00 (*0-933598-45-9*) NC Wesleyan Pr.

New, John F. Anglican & Puritan: The Basis of Their Opposition, 1558-1640. 140p. 1964. 22.50 (*0-8047-0066-4*) Stanford U Pr.

— The Renaissance & Reformation: A Short History. 2nd ed. 201p. (C). 1977. pap. text ed. write for info. (*0-07-554681-7*) McGraw.

New, John F., ed. Oliver Cromwell: Pretender, Puritan, Statesman, Paradox? LC 76-23190. (European Problem Studies). 128p. 1977. reprint ed. pap. text ed. 9.50 (*0-03-085178-5*) Krieger.

New Left Review Staff, ed. Western Marxism - A Critical Reader. 354p. 1977. pap. text ed. 16.95 (*0-902308-29-7*, A1021, Pub. by Verso NLB UK) Routledge Chapman & Hall.

New Life Inc. Staff, jt. auth. see Prince, Matthew S.

New Life Ministries International Staff, tr. see Clendennen, B. H.

New Line Cinema Staff, ed. see Barstow, Jack.

New Line Cinema Staff, ed. see Chaskin, David.

New Line Cinema Staff, ed. see Craven, Wes & Wagner, Bruce.

New Line Cinema Staff, ed. see Kotzwinkle, William & Helgeland, Brian.

New Line Cinema Staff, ed. see Talalay, Rachel.

New, Lloyd K., intro. The Institute of American Indian Arts, Alumni Exhibition. LC 73-92099. (Illus.). 72p. 1974. pap. 3.25 (*0-88360-003-X*) Amon Carter.

New, Maria I., ed. Congenital Adrenal Hyperplasia. (Annals Ser.: Vol. 458). 290p. 1985. text ed. 66.00 (*0-89766-311-X*); pap. text ed. 66.00 (*0-89766-312-8*) NY Acad Sci.

New, Maria I. & Levine, Leonore S., eds. Adrenal Diseases in Childhood. (Pediatric & Adolescent Endocrinology Ser.: Vol. 13). (Illus.). viii, 236p. 1984. 132.00 (*3-8055-3777-8*) S Karger.

New, Melvyn. Laurence Sterne As Satirist: A Reading of Tristram Shandy. LC 70-79524. 1969. 18.95 (*0-8130-0278-8*) U Press Fla.

— Telling New Lies: Seven Essays in Fiction, Past & Present. 256p. (C). 1992. lib. bdg. 27.95 (*0-8130-1120-5*) U Press Fla.

— Tristram Shandy: A Book for Free Spirits. (Twayne's Masterworks Ser.: No. 132). 125p. 1994. text ed. 22.95 (*0-8057-8358-X*, Pub. by Royal Botanic Garden UK); pap. 12.95 (*0-8057-4450-9*, Pub. by Royal Botanic Garden UK) Macmillan.

New, Melvyn, ed. Approaches to Teaching Sterne's Tristram Shandy. LC 88-28977. (Approaches to Teaching World Literature Ser.: No. 20). x, 174p. (Orig.). 1989. text ed. 37.50 (*0-87352-515-9*, AP20C); pap. 18.00x (*0-87352-516-7*, AP20P) Modern Lang.

— The Complete Novels & Selected Writings of Amy Levy, 1861-1889. LC 92-41443. 576p. 1993. lib. bdg. 49.95 (*0-8130-1199-X*); pap. 24.95 (*0-8130-1200-7*) U Press Fla.

— Tristram Shandy. LC 91-35819. (New Casebooks Ser.). 200p. 1992. text ed. 45.00 (*0-312-07566-9*) St Martin.

New, Melvyn, ed. see Sterne, Laurence.

New Mexico Legal Press Staff & Sirotkin, Eric. Labor & Employment in New Mexico. 400p. 1994. ring bd. write for info. (*0-409-25715-X*) Butterworth Legal Pubs.

New Mexico Native Plant Protection Advisory Committee Staff. A Handbook of Rare & Endemic Plants of New Mexico. LC 83-16865. 309p. reprint ed. pap. 88.10 (*0-7837-5863-4*, 2045582) Bks Demand.

New Mexico People & Energy Collective Staff, et al. Red Ribbons for Emma. limited ed. LC 80-83883. (Illus.). 48p. (Orig.). (J). (gr. 3 up). 1981. pap. 12.00 (*0-938678-07-8*) New Seed.

New Mexico State University Staff, jt. auth. see IUPAC Staff.

New Orleans Academy of Ophthalmology Staff. Pediatric Ophthalmology & Strabismus. (Transactions of the New Orleans Academy of Ophthalmology Ser.). (Illus.). 560p. 1986. text ed. 129.00 (*0-88167-164-9*) Raven.

New Orleans Times Staff. Picayunes Creole Cookbook. 1989. 24.95 (*0-394-57652-7*) Random.

New, Peter J. Fiction & Purpose in "Utopia," "Rasselas," "The Mill on the Floss," & "Women in Love" LC 84-18390. 256p. 1985. text ed. 29.95 (*0-312-28810-7*) St Martin.

New, R. R., ed. Liposomes: A Practical Approach. (Practical Approach Ser.). (Illus.). 320p. 1990. pap. 44.00 (*0-19-963077-1*, IRL Pr) OUP.

New, Rebecca, jt. auth. see Mallory, Bruce.

***New Riders Development Group Staff.** CNE Short Course. (Illus.). 800p. (Orig.). 1995. pap. text ed. 60.00 (*1-56205-446-5*) New Riders Pub.

— Digital Productions on the Mbone & the Internet. (Illus.). 300p. (Orig.). 1995. pap. 32.00 (*1-56205-397-3*) New Riders Pub.

— Implementing Internet Security. (Illus.). 300p. (Orig.). 1995. pap. 35.00 (*1-56205-471-6*) New Riders Pub.

— Inside Adobe Illustrator for Windows, New Version. (Illus.). 850p. (Orig.). 1995. pap. text ed. 39.99 (*1-56205-370-1*) New Riders Pub.

— Inside TCP-IP. (Illus.). (Orig.). 1994. pap. 39.99 (*1-56205-354-X*) New Riders Pub.

— Inside the World Wide Web. (Illus.). 800p. (Orig.). 1995. pap. text ed. 39.99 (*1-56205-412-0*) New Riders Pub.

— Internet Agents: Robots, Spiders, Fish, & Worms. (Illus.). 350p. (Orig.). 1995. pap. 32.00 (*1-56205-463-5*) New Riders Pub.

— Internet Firewalls & Network Security. (Illus.). 400p. (Orig.). 1995. pap. text ed. 35.00 (*1-56205-437-6*) New Riders Pub.

— Internet Professional Reference. (Illus.). 1200p. (Orig.). 1995. pap. text ed. 55.00 (*1-56205-473-2*) New Riders Pub.

— Internet Professional Reference. (Illus.). 1200p. (Orig.). 1995. pap. 39.99 (*1-56205-411-2*) New Riders Pub.

— Kai's Power Tools Filters & Effects. (Illus.). 320p. (Orig.). 1995. pap. text ed. 45.00 (*1-56205-480-5*) New Riders Pub.

— LAN Server Engineer Certification Handbook. (Illus.). 1300p. (Orig.). 1995. pap. 89.99 (*1-56205-406-6*) New Riders Pub.

— The More Than Complet ObjectPAL Command Reference. (Illus.). 700p. (Orig.). 1994. pap. 35.00 (*1-56205-346-9*) New Riders Pub.

— NetWare Training Guide: CNA Study Guide. LC 94-34769. (Illus.). 800p. (Orig.). 1994. pap. 50.00 (*1-56205-365-5*) New Riders Pub.

— Photoshop 3 Filters & Effects. (Illus.). 336p. (Orig.). 1995. pap. text ed. 45.00 (*1-56205-448-1*) New Riders Pub.

— Photoshop 3.0 for Beginners. (Illus.). 600p. (Orig.). 1995. pap. text ed. 29.99 (*1-56205-422-8*) New Riders Pub.

— The 3D Studio Plug-in Reference. (Illus.). 312p. (Orig.). 1995. pap. text ed. 55.00 (*1-56205-431-7*) New Riders Pub.

New Riders Development Group Staff, et al. The More Than Complete NetWare Command Reference. (Illus.). 800p. (Orig.). 1995. pap. 35.00 (*1-56205-317-5*) New Riders Pub.

***New Riders Development Staff, et al.** Inside Unix. 1994. disk, pap. 39.99 (*1-56205-401-5*) New Riders Pub.

***New Riders Development Staff.** NetWare Training Guide Netware TCP IP & Netware NFS. 800p. 1994. disk, pap. 50.00 (*1-56205-409-0*) New Riders Pub.

— Network Security with Windows NT Server. 300p. 1995. disk, pap. 35.00 (*1-56205-371-X*) New Riders Pub.

***New Riders Development Staff & Tidrow, Robert.** NLW Riders Official Compuserve Yellow Pages. 636p. 1994. pap. 29.99 (*1-56205-396-5*) New Riders Pub.

New Riders Editors. Riding the Internet Highway. 1993. pap. 16.95 (*1-56205-192-X*) New Riders Pub.

New Riders Publishing Staff. Adobe Photoshop Now! 300p. 1994. pap. 35.00 (*1-56205-200-4*) New Riders Pub.

— AutoCAD 3D Design & Presentation. (Illus.). 448p. (Orig.). 1991. 29.95 (*0-934035-81-4*) New Riders Pub.

— CorelDRAW! Now! 310p. 1993. 21.95 (*1-56205-131-8*) New Riders Pub.

— Don't Panic! It's Only Netware. 300p. 1993. pap. 18.95 (*1-56205-203-9*) New Riders Pub.

— Inside AutoCAD, Release 13.0 for Windows & NT. 1500p. 1995. Incl. diskette. disk 40.00 (*1-56205-319-1*) New Riders Pub.

— Inside Corelventura 5. 630p. 1995. cd-rom, pap. 40.00 (*1-56205-341-8*) New Riders Pub.

— Killer AutoCAD Utilities. 800p. 1993. pap. 45.00 (*1-56205-204-7*) New Riders Pub.

— New Riders Reference Guide to AutoCAD, Release 12. (Illus.). 577p. (Orig.). 1992. pap. 19.95 (*1-56205-058-3*) New Riders Pub.

— OS - 2 Certification Handbook. 1300p. 1995. pap. 89.99 (*1-56205-407-4*) New Riders Pub.

New Riders Staff. Inside Excel 5 for Windows. 1994. pap. 39.95 (*1-56205-218-7*) New Riders Pub.

— Inside Word for Windows 6. 1993. pap. 39.95 (*1-56205-209-8*) New Riders Pub.

An Asterisk (*) at the beginning of an entry indicates that the title is appearing in BIP for the first time.

New River Valley Bicycle Club Staff. Cycling the New River Valley. 68p. (Orig.). 1993. pap. 5.75 (*0-936015-42-X*) Pocahontas Pr.

New, Robert C. Your Employees Are Stealing You Blind. 172p. 1994. pap. 12.95 (*0-87425-966-5*) Human Res Dev Pr.

New Salem Journal Printing Staff, tr. see Diede, Pauline N.

New Seed Press Collective Staff. A Book about Us. (Illus.). (J). (ps-5). 1977. pap. 4.95 (*0-938678-04-3*) New Seed.

New, Silva, jt. ed. see Lake, Kirsopp.

New Statesman Staff. New Statesmanship. Hyams, E., ed. LC 72-128281. (Essay Index Reprint Ser.). 1977. 23.95 (*0-8369-1891-6*) Ayer.

New Student Programs Staff. General Education Program. 2nd ed. 16p. 1993. 0.43 (*0-8403-8647-8*) Kendall-Hunt.

— Settling In: A Guide to the University of Rhode island. 2nd ed. 96p. 1993. per. 10.45 (*0-8403-8510-2*) Kendall-Hunt.

New, T. R. Associations Between Insects & Plants. 113p. 1990. pap. 19.95 (*0-86840-099-8*, Pub. by New South Wales Univ Pr AT) Intl Spec Bk.

— Butterfly Conservation. (Illus.). 230p. 1992. pap. 29.95 (*0-19-553228-7*) OUP.

— Insect Conservation. (Entomologica Ser.). 1984. lib. bdg. 94.00 (*90-6193-507-5*) Kluwer Ac.

— An Introduction to Invertebrate Conservation Biology. (Illus.). 200p. 1995. 55.00 (*0-19-854052-3*); pap. 27.95 (*0-19-854051-5*) OUP.

— Psocoptera of the Oriental Region: A Review. (Oriental Insects Supplements Ser.: No. 6). 1977. 30.00 (*1-877711-16-0*) Assoc Pubs FL.

New, T. R. & Collins, N. M. Swallowtail Butterflies: An Action Plan for Their Conservation. (Illus.). 40p. 1991. pap. 16.00 (*2-8317-0061-2*, Pub. by IUCN SZ) Island Pr.

New, Tim. Insects as Predators. 1991. pap. 19.95 (*0-86840-276-1*, Pub. by New South Wales Univ Pr AT) Intl Spec Bk.

New, Timothy & Theischinger, Gunther, eds. Handbuch der Zoologie - Handbook of Zoology: A Natural History of the Phyla of the Animal Kingdom, Band IV - Vol. IV. v, 101p. (ENG & GER.). (C). 1993. lib. bdg. 200.00 (*3-11-013566-3*) De Gruyter.

***New Tokyo Photographers Staff, contrib.** Deja-vu 18. 130p. 1995. pap. 25.00 (*4-309-90338-X*) Dist Art Pubs.

New Troubadours Staff. The New Troubadours Songbook. Crabtree, Philip et al, eds. (Illus.). 92p. (Orig.). 1981. pap. 10.00 (*0-936878-02-9*) Lorian Pr.

New Valaam Monks Staff, ed. Father Gerasim of New Valaam. LC 89-64024. (Acquisition of the Holy Spirit in Russia Ser.). (Illus.). 112p. 1990. pap. 5.00 (*0-938635-29-8*) St Herman AK.

New, W. H. Canadian Writers, Nineteen Twenty to Nineteen Fifty-Nine, Vol. 68. (Dictionary of Literary Biography Ser.: Vol. 68). 1988. 128.00 (*0-8103-1746-X*) Gale.

— Dreams of Speech & Violence: The Art of the Short Story in Canada & New Zealand. 302p. 1987. text ed. 35.00 (*0-8020-5663-6*) U of Toronto Pr.

— A History of Canadian Literature. 1993. pap. 19.95 (*1-56131-040-9*) New Amsterdam Bks.

New, W. H., ed. Canadian Writers since 1960, 2nd Series, Vol. 60. (Dictionary of Literary Biography Ser.). 416p. 1987. 128.00 (*0-8103-1738-9*) Gale.

— Dictionary of Literary Biography, Vol. 92: Canadian Writers, 1890-1920, Vol. 92. LC 89-48355. (Illus.). 487p. 1990. text ed. 128.00 (*0-8103-4572-2*) Gale.

— Literary History of Canada, Vol. 4: Canadian Literature in English. 492p. 1990. text ed. 60.00 (*0-8020-5685-7*); pap. text ed. 24.95 (*0-8020-6610-0*) U of Toronto Pr.

New Ways to Work Staff, ed. New Policies for Part-Time & Contingent Workers. 67p. 1992. 5.00 (*0-685-66556-9*, G-006) New Ways Work.

New Ways to Work Staff & Batz, Julie. Work Sharing: An Alternative to Layoffs. rev. ed. 24p. (Orig.). 1991. pap. text ed. 12.00 (*0-940173-25-5*) New Ways Work.

New, William H., ed. Inside the Poem: Essays in Honour of Donald Stephens. 320p. 1993. pap. 22.00 (*0-19-540925-6*) OUP.

— Native Writers & Canadian Writing. 352p. 1991. pap. 21.95 (*0-7748-0371-1*) U of Wash Pr.

New Woman Magazine Editors. Sounds Like a New Woman: A Decade of New Women, Old Ladies, & Thumps on the Head. (Illus.). 96p. (Orig.). 1993. pap. 8.95 (*0-14-017636-5*, Penguin Bks) Viking Penguin.

New World Dictionary Editors. Misspeller's Dictionary. 1983. 5.00 (*0-671-46864-2*) S&S Trade.

New World Foundation Staff. How to Get to Heaven. 100p. (Orig.). 1991. pap. 7.77 (*1-879964-01-5*) New World TX.

New World Foundation Staff, ed. The Bible II: How to Get to Heaven. 630p. (Orig.). (C). 1991. pap. 14.95 (*1-879964-00-7*) New World TX.

New World Library Group Staff. The Gift of Sobriety: One Hundred Twelve Reasons Not to Drink Today. 64p. 1993. pap. 4.95 (*1-880032-24-4*) New Wrld Lib.

New World Press Staff, ed. see China Sports Editorial Board Staff.

New York Academy of Medicine Editors. New York Academy of Medicine, Illustration Catalog. 3rd enl. ed. 1976. lib. bdg. 40.00 (*0-8161-0038-1*, Hall Library) G K Hall.

New York Academy of Medicine Staff. Author Catalog of the Library of the New York Academy of Medicine, 43 Vols, Set. 1970. lib. bdg. 4,290.00 (*0-8161-0829-3*, Hall Library) G K Hall.

— Author Catalog of the Library of the New York Academy of Medicine, 1st Suppl, 4 vols, Set. 1974. lib. bdg. 545.00 (*0-8161-0851-X*, Hall Library) G K Hall.

— The End of Life: Guidelines for Health Professionals Concerning Death Certificates, Autopsies & Organ & Tissue Donations. rev. ed. Hirsch, Charles & Messite, Jacqueline, eds. (Illus.). 1994. pap. text ed. 10.00 (*0-924143-03-7*) NY Acad Med.

— Freud & Contemporary Culture. Galdston, Iago, ed. LC 77-142674. (Essay Index Reprint Ser.). 1977. 13.95 (*0-8369-2112-7*) Ayer.

— Freud & Contemporary Culture. Galdston, Iago, ed. LC 57-10551. 111p. reprint ed. pap. 31.70 (*0-317-10589-2*, 2050990) Bks Demand.

— Frontiers in Medicine. LC 70-142675. (Essay Index Reprint Ser.). 1977. 19.95 (*0-8369-2113-5*) Ayer.

— Future in Medicine: The March of Medicine, 1949, Laity Lectures, No. 14. LC 74-167391. (Essay Index Reprint Ser.). 1977. reprint ed. 19.95 (*0-8369-2465-7*) Ayer.

— Landmarks in Medicine. LC 74-142676. (Essay Index Reprint Ser.). 1977. 23.95 (*0-8369-2114-3*) Ayer.

— March of Medicine: Lectures to the Laity, 1943. LC 78-142677. (Essay Index Reprint Ser.). 1977. reprint ed. 19.95 (*0-8369-2466-5*) Ayer.

— March of Medicine: Lectures to the Laity, 1944. LC 78-142677. (Essay Index Reprint Ser.). 1977. reprint ed. 17.95 (*0-8369-2467-3*) Ayer.

— March of Medicine Laity Lectures, No. 4. LC 78-142677. (Essay Index Reprint Ser.). 1977. reprint ed. 19.95 (*0-8369-2212-3*) Ayer.

— March of Medicine, Laity Lectures No. 5. LC 78-142677. (Essay Index Reprint Ser.). 1977. 19.95 (*0-8369-2115-1*) Ayer.

— March of Medicine, Laity Lectures No. 6. LC 78-142677. (Essay Index Reprint Ser.). 1977. 19.95 (*0-8369-2116-X*) Ayer.

— March of Medicine, Laity Lectures No. 7. LC 78-142677. (Essay Index Reprint Ser.). 1977. 20.95 (*0-8369-2117-8*) Ayer.

— Medicine & Anthropology. Galdston, Iago, ed. LC 71-142678. (Essay Index Reprint Ser.). 1977. 19.95 (*0-8369-2118-6*) Ayer.

— Medicine & Science. Galdston, Iago, ed. LC 75-142679. (Essay Index Reprint Ser.). 1977. 18.95 (*0-8369-2122-4*) Ayer.

— Medicine in a Changing Society. Galdston, Iago, ed. LC 70-142680. (Essay Index Reprint Ser.). 1977. 19.95 (*0-8369-2123-2*) Ayer.

— Medicine in the Postwar World: The March of Medicine, 1947, Laity Lectures, No. 12. LC 78-167392. (Essay Index Reprint Ser.). 1977. reprint ed. 17.95 (*0-8369-2468-1*) Ayer.

— Medicine Today: The March of Medicine, 1946 (Laity Lectures, No. 11) LC 71-167393. (Essay Index Reprint Ser.). 1977. reprint ed. 19.95 (*0-8369-2469-X*) Ayer.

— Milestones in Medicine. LC 73-142681. (Essay Index Reprint Ser.). 1977. 21.95 (*0-8369-2119-4*) Ayer.

— Ministry & Medicine in Human Relations. Galdston, Iago, ed. LC 77-142682. (Essay Index Reprint Ser.). 1977. 19.95 (*0-8369-2120-8*) Ayer.

— Modern Attitudes in Psychiatry. LC 70-142683. (Essay Index Reprint Ser.). 1977. 19.95 (*0-8369-2121-6*) Ayer.

— Perspectives in Medicine. LC 75-152204. (Essay Index Reprint Ser.). 1977. 19.95 (*0-8369-2813-X*) Ayer.

— Portrait Catalog, 5 vols. suppl. ed. 1971. First Suppl. 1959-65. lib. bdg. 120.00 (*0-8161-0733-5*, Hall Library); Second Suppl. 1965-71. lib. bdg. 120.00 (*0-8161-0900-1*, Hall Library) G K Hall.

— Portrait Catalog, 5 vols, Set. 1971. lib. bdg. 360.00 (*0-8161-0233-3*, Hall Library) G K Hall.

— Portrait Catalog: Third Supplement, 1971-1975. 1976. lib. bdg. 120.00 (*0-8161-0034-9*, Hall Library) G K Hall.

— Society & Medicine. Galdston, Iago, ed. LC 74-142684. (Essay Index Reprint Ser.). 1977. 17.95 (*0-8369-2124-0*) Ayer.

— Subject Catalog of the Library of the New York Academy of Medicine, 34 Vols, Set. 1970. lib. bdg. 3,550.00 (*0-8161-0826-9*, Hall Library) G K Hall.

— Subject Catalog of the Library of the New York Academy of Medicine, 1st Supplement, 4 vols., Set. 1974. lib. bdg. 545.00 (*0-8161-0184-1*, Hall Library) G K Hall.

New York Academy of Sciences Staff. Airborne Contagion: Proceedings of the New York Academy of Sciences, Nov. 7-9, 1979, Vol. 353. Kundsin, Ruth B., ed. LC 80-27061. (Annals Ser.). 341p. 1980. 69.00 (*0-89766-095-1*); pap. 69.00 (*0-89766-096-X*) NY Acad Sci.

— Genetic Variation of Viruses: Proceedings of the New York Academy of Sciences, Nov. 28-30, 1979, Vol. 354. Palese, Peter & Roizman, Bernard, eds. LC 80-25770. (Annals Ser.). 507p. 1980. 99.00 (*0-89766-097-8*); pap. 99.00 (*0-89766-098-6*) NY Acad Sci.

— Immunological Tolerance to Self & Non-Self: Proceedings of the New York Academy of Sciences, Annals of October 19-21, 1987, Vol. 392. Battisto, Jack R. & Claman, Henry N., eds. 436p. 1982. 80.00 (*0-89766-174-5*); pap. write for info. (*0-89766-175-3*) NY Acad Sci.

— International Conference on Carriers & Channels in Biological Systems, Second: Proceedings of the New York Academy of Sciences, Feb. 4-6, 1980, Vol. 358. (Annals Ser.). 387p. 1980. 77.00 (*0-89766-105-2*); pap. 77.00 (*0-89766-106-0*) NY Acad Sci.

— Micronutrient Interactions: Proceedings of the New York Academy of Sciences, Feb. 20-22, 1980, Vol. 355. Levander, Orville A. & Cheng, Lorraine, eds. LC 80-25622. 372p. 1980. pap. 74.00 (*0-89766-100-1*) NY Acad Sci.

— Modulation of Cellular Interactions by Vitamin A & Derivatives: Proceedings of the New York Academy of Sciences on Retinoids, March 10-12, 1980, Vol. 359. De Luca, Luigi M. & Shapiro, Stanley S., eds. 431p. 1981. pap. 85.00 (*0-89766-108-7*) NY Acad Sci.

— Nonlinear Dynamics: Proceedings of the New York Academy of Sciences, Dec. 17-21, 1979. Helleman, Robert H., ed. LC 80-72072. (Annals Ser.: Vol. 357). 507p. 1980. 100.00 (*0-89766-103-6*) NY Acad Sci.

— Vitamin E: Biochemical, Hematological, Clinical Aspects, Annals Nov. 11-13, 1981, Vol. 393. Lubin, Bertram & Machlin, Lawrence J., eds. 506p. 1982. 95.00 (*0-89766-176-1*); pap. write for info. (*0-89766-177-X*) NY Acad Sci.

New York Architectural League Staff. Resorts of the Catskills. LC 79-65868. (Illus.). 113p. 1979. 15.00 (*0-685-72096-9*) Gal Assn NY.

New York Association for Improving the Condition of the Poor Staff. AICP First Annual Reports Investigating Poverty, Nos. 1-10. LC 77-137179. (Poverty U. S. A. Historical Record Ser.). 1978. reprint ed. 35.95 (*0-405-03117-3*) Ayer.

New York Association of Realtors Staff & Harwood, Bruce M. New York Real Estate. (C). 1981. text ed. 34.00 (*0-8359-4894-3*, Reston) P-H.

***New York Bar Association Criminal Litigation Committee of the Environmental Law Section Staff.** Environmental Crimes. Elder, Michael S., ed. 334p. 1995. 60.00 (*0-942954-73-4*) NYS Bar.

***New York Bar Association Staff.** Public Sector Labor & Employment Law - 1995 Supplement. Townley, Rosemary A., ed. 440p. 1995. pap. text ed. 45.00 (*0-942954-77-7*) NYS Bar.

New York Book Fair Staff. In Search of Song, Vol. 5. Fisher, Barbara & Spiegel, Richard, eds. (Illus.). 40p. (Orig.). (J). (gr. k-9). 1983. pap. 2.00 (*0-934830-30-4*) Ten Penny.

New York Botanical Garden Institute of Urban Horticulture, ed. see Rose, Graham.

New York Botanical Garden Library Staff, comp. Biographical Notes Upon Botanists, 3 Vols, Set. 1974. lib. bdg. 370.00 (*0-8161-0695-9*, Hall Library) G K Hall.

New York Botanical Garden Staff. American Garden Guides: Perennial Gardening. 224p. 1994. 25.00 (*0-679-41431-2*) Pantheon.

— Index to Economic Botany: Volumes 1-20, 1947-1966. (Economic Botany Ser.). 1967. pap. 7.50 (*0-89327-213-2*) NY Botanical.

— Mycologia Index: Volumes 1-58, 1909-1966. LC 57-51730. (Mycologia Ser.). 1968. 20.00 (*0-89327-215-9*) NY Botanical.

New York Botanical Garden Staff, ed. see Bush-Brown, James & Bush-Brown, Louise.

New York Chamber of Commerce & Industry Staff. New York: A City of Neighborhoods. (Illus.). (Orig.). 1984. 17.95 (*0-9613808-0-2*); pap. 14.95 (*0-317-20537-4*) NY Chamber.

New York City Board of Alderman, Committee on General Welfare. Preliminary Report of the Committee on General Welfare in the Matter of a Request of the Conference of Organized Labor Relative to Educational Facilities. Meeting of June 26, 1917. LC 73-11924. (Metropolitan America Ser.). 350p. 1974. reprint ed. 28.95 (*0-405-05407-6*) Ayer.

New York City Commission. Report of a Preliminary Scheme of Improvements: Staten Island. LC 73-2910. (Metropolitan America Ser.). 118p. 1974. reprint ed. 11.95 (*0-405-05408-4*) Ayer.

New York City Common Council Staff. Report of the Special Committee of the New York City Board of Aldermen on the New York City Police Department: New York City Common Council Document, No. 53. LC 72-154582. (Police in America Ser.). 1971. reprint ed. 26.95 (*0-405-03378-8*) Ayer.

New York City Landmarks Preservation Committee, jt. auth. see Dolkart, Andrew S.

New York City Museum of Modern Art Max Weber, Retrospective Exhibition, 1907-1930, 1969 Staff, et al. Three American Modernist Painters: Max Weber, with an Introduction by Alfred H. Barr, Jr.; Maurice Sterne by H. M. Kallen, with a Note by the Artist; Stuart Davis by James Johnson Sweeney. 1969. reprint ed. 20.95 (*0-405-01528-3*, 15554) Ayer.

New York City Museum of Modern Art Staff. Twenty Centuries of Mexican Art: Viento Siglos de Arte Mexicano. LC 79-169322. (Museum of Modern Art Publications in Reprint). (Illus.). 200p. 1972. reprint ed. 25.95 (*0-405-01580-1*) Ayer.

New York City Museum of Modern Art Staff, et al. Three American Romantic Painters: Burchfield, Stettheimer, Watkins. 1969. 18.95 (*0-405-01538-0*, 15564) Ayer.

New York Colony. New York Marriages Previous to 1784. LC 67-30757. 618p. 1984. reprint ed. 30.00 (*0-8063-0259-3*) Genealog Pub.

New York Committee of Fifteen, et al. Prostitution in America: Three Investigations, 1975. Syracuse Moral Survey Committee, ed. Massachusetts Commission for Investigation of White Slave Traffic, tr. (Social Problems & Social Policy Ser.). 1976. 41.95 (*0-405-07511-1*) Ayer.

New York Committee of Merchants for the Relief of Colored People Suffering from the Late Riots. Anti-Negro Riots in the North, Eighteen Sixty-Three. LC 69-18537. (American Negro: His History & Literature, Ser. No. 2). 1969. reprint ed. 19.95 (*0-405-01848-7*) Ayer.

New York Constitutional Convention Staff. Reports of the Proceedings & Debates of the New York Constitutional Convention, 1821. LC 72-133168. (Law, Politics & History Ser.). 1970. reprint ed. lib. bdg. 85.00 (*0-306-70069-7*) Da Capo.

New York Genealogical & Biographical Society Staff. Minisink Valley Reformed Dutch Church Records, 1716-1830. (Illus.). 395p. 1992. reprint ed. pap. 26.00 (*1-55613-556-4*) Heritage Bk.

New York Gold Staff. Conceptual People Photography 6: Portrait, Lifestyle, Fashion & Beauty. (Illus.). 128p. 1994. 22.95 (*0-8230-6317-8*, Watsn-Guptill) Watsn-Guptill.

— Conceptual Still Life Photography Six: General Still Life, Food & Interiors. (Illus.). 128p. 1994. 22.95 (*0-8230-6318-6*) Watsn-Guptill.

— Direct Stock 3. (Illus.). 142p. 1994. pap. 24.95 (*0-8230-6316-X*, Watsn-Guptill) Watsn-Guptill.

— Gold Book's Eye: On Still Life Photography & on People Photography, 2 vols. in 1. 112p. 1994. pap. 22.95 (*0-8230-6380-1*) Watsn-Guptill.

New York Historical Society Staff. American Landscape & Genre Paintings in the New York Historical Society: A Catalog of the Collection Including Historical, Narrative & Marine Art, 3 vols., Set. (Illus.). 1982. lib. bdg. 400.00 (*0-8161-0364-X*, Hall Library) G K Hall.

— Collections of the New York Historical Society, First Series, 5 vols. in 4, 1. reprint ed. 72.00 (*0-404-11071-1*) AMS Pr.

— Collections of the New York Historical Society, First Series, 5 vols. in 4, 2. reprint ed. 72.00 (*0-404-11072-X*) AMS Pr.

— Collections of the New York Historical Society, First Series, 5 vols. in 4, 3. reprint ed. 72.00 (*0-404-11073-8*) AMS Pr.

— Collections of the New York Historical Society, First Series, 5 vols. in 4, Set. reprint ed. 375.00 (*0-404-11070-3*) AMS Pr.

— Collections of the New York Historical Society, First Series, 5 vols. in 4, Vols. 4 & 5. reprint ed. 90.00 (*0-404-11074-6*) AMS Pr.

— Colonel Stephen Kemble's Journals & British Army Orders, 1775-1778. Billias, George, ed. LC 72-8999. (American Revolutionary Ser.). reprint ed. lib. bdg. 35.00 (*0-8398-1355-4*) Irvington.

New York Institute of Finance. How the Bond Market Works. 1988. pap. 15.95 (*0-13-423310-7*) NY Inst Finance.

— The Successful Sales Assistant's Handbook. (Illus.). 288p. student ed 25.00 (*0-13-860305-7*) NY Inst Finance.

New York Institute of Finance Staff. After the Trade Is Made - An Operation Training Manual: Study Guide. (Illus.). 224p. 1987. 24.95 (*0-13-858721-3*) NY Inst Finance.

— Asset Plays: Profiting from Undervalued Stock. 1988. 29.95 (*0-317-03938-5*) NY Inst Finance.

— Asset Plays: Profiting from Undervalued Stocks. 1988. 24.95 (*0-13-049819-X*) P-H.

— Fixed Income Investments: A Personal Seminar. 1990. pap. 21.95 (*0-13-322207-1*) NY Inst Finance.

— Fixed Income Investments: A Personal Seminar. LC 92-23622. 1992. 79.95 (*0-13-159252-1*) P-H.

— Futures: A Personal Seminar. (Illus.). 260p. 1988. pap. 21.95 (*0-13-658196-X*) NY Inst Finance.

— Introduction to Brokerage Operation Department Procedures. (Illus.). 175p. 1979. 11.95 (*0-13-478982-2*) NY Inst Finance.

— Introduction to Brokerage Operations Department Procedures. 2nd ed. 1988. pap. 12.95 (*0-13-478975-X*) P-H.

— Investor's Rights Manual. 1988. pap. 17.95 (*0-13-799099-5*) NY Inst Finance.

— New York Institute of Finance Guide to Investing. LC 87-11323. (Illus.). 288p. 1987. pap. 15.00 (*0-13-620436-8*) NY Inst Finance.

— New York Institute of Finance Guide to Investing. 2nd ed. 1992. pap. 17.95 (*0-13-617598-8*) P-H.

— Real Estate Investment Trusts. 320p. 1988. 17.95 (*0-13-763228-2*) NY Inst Finance.

— Securities Analysis: A Personal Seminar. 240p. 1989. pap. 21.95 (*0-13-658204-4*) NY Inst Finance.

— Securities Industry Glossary. 2nd ed. 1988. pap. 12.95 (*0-13-798778-1*) P-H.

— Stocks, Bonds, Options, Futures: Investments & Their Markets. 1991. pap. 18.95 (*0-13-847369-2*, Busn) P-H.

— Technical Analysis: A Personal Seminar. 1989. pap. 21.95 (*0-13-898370-4*) NY Inst Finance.

— Trading Stocks on the Over-the-Counter Market. 1988. 21.50 (*0-13-926007-2*) NY Inst Finance.

New York, Kings Country, Grand Jury Staff. A Presentment Concerning the Enforcement of the City of New York of the Laws Against Gambling by the Grand Jury for the Additional Extraordinary Special & Trial Term. LC 73-3844. (Criminal Justice in America Ser.). 1974. reprint ed. 19.95 (*0-405-06148-X*) Ayer.

New York Knicks Staff. Knicks Media Guide, 1993-1994. 1993. pap. 8.00 (*0-671-89023-9*) S&S Trade.

New York Landmarks Conservancy Staff. Repairing Old & Historic Windows. (Illus.). 208p. (Orig.). 1992. pap. 24.95 (*0-89133-185-9*) Preservation Pr.

New York Metropolitan Museum of Art Staff. Tiffany Address Book. (Illus.). 128p. 1991. 16.95 (*0-8212-1878-6*) Bulfinch Pr.

New York-New Jersey Trail Conference Staff. Guide to the Long Path. 2nd ed. 58p. 1987. pap. 5.95 (*0-9603966-4-0*) NY-NJ Trail Confer.

— Guide to the Long Path. 3rd ed. LC 92-19099. 1992. write for info. (*1-880775-00-X*) NY-NJ Trail Confer.

***New York Newsday Staff.** Fiscal Fitness. (Illus.). 208p. 1995. pap. 9.95 (*0-8362-7046-0*) Andrews & McMeel.

New York Organ Co. Vocalian Organ. (Illus.). 25p. 1981. pap. 6.00 (*0-913746-16-9*) Organ Lit.

New York Public Library & Library of Congress MARC Tapes Staff. Bibliographic Guide to Technology: 1990, 2 vols., Set. (Bibliographic Guides Ser.). 1020p. 1991. lib. bdg. 350.00 (*0-8161-7150-5*) G K Hall.

New York Public Library, Art & Architecture Div. Staff. Bibliographic Guide to Art & Architecture, 1990, 2 vols. large type ed. 1335p. 1991. 320.00 (*0-8161-7131-9*, Biblio Guides) G K Hall.

An Asterisk (*) at the beginning of an entry indicates that the title is appearing in BIP for the first time.

New York Public Library Art & Architecture Division Staff & Library of Congress Staff. Bibliographic Guide to Art & Architecture, 1991, 2 vols., Vol. 2. (Bibliographic Guides Ser.). 960p. 1992. text ed. 335.00 (*0-8161-7152-1*) G K Hall.

New York Public Library for the Performing Arts Staff, jt. auth. see Dance Collection Staff.

New York Public Library Map Division & the Geography & Map Division of the Library of Congress Staff. Bibliographic Guide to Maps & Atlases, 1990. (Bibliographic Guides Ser.). 770p. 1991. lib. bdg. 300.00 (*0-8161-7143-2*) G K Hall.

New York Public Library, Music Div. Staff. Bibliographic Guide to Music, 1990. large type ed. 792p. 1991. 210.00 (*0-8161-7146-7*, Hall Reference) Macmillan.

New York Public Library OCLC Tapes Staff, jt. auth. see Columbia University Teachers College OCLC Tapes Staff.

New York Public Library, Research Libraries, Rare Division Staff. The Imprint Catalog in the Rare Book Division, 21 vols., Set. 1979. lib. bdg. 2,120.00 (*0-8161-0092-6*, Hall Library) G K Hall.

New York Public Library, Research Libraries Staff. Bibliographic Guide to Theatre Arts: 1990. large type ed. 244p. 1991. 185.00 (*0-8161-7149-1*, Hall Reference) Macmillan.

— Catalog of Government Publications, Economics Division, 40 vols., Set. 1972. lib. bdg. 4,350.00 (*0-8161-0781-5*, Hall Library) G K Hall.

— Catalog of Government Publications, Supplement 1974, 2 vols., Set. 1976. lib. bdg. 240.00 (*0-8161-0060-8*, Hall Library) G K Hall.

— Catalog of the Theatre & Drama Collections, 2 pts. Incl. Set. Drama Collection: Listing by Cultural Origin, 6 vols. 1970. 640.00 (*0-685-01808-3*); Set. Drama Collection: Author Listing, 6 vols. 1970. lib. bdg. 985.00 (*0-8161-0106-X*); Set. Theatre Collection: Books on the Theatre, 9 vols. 1970. lib. bdg. 790.00 (*0-8161-0107-8*); 1970. write for info. (*0-318-52340-X*, Hall Library) G K Hall.

— Catalog of the Theatre & Drama Collections, Pt. 3. 30 Vols. Non-book Collection. 1976. lib. bdg. 3,990.00 (*0-8161-1195-2*, Hall Library) G K Hall.

— Catalog of the Theatre & Drama Collections: First Supplement to Pt. 1, Drama Collection. 1973. lib. bdg. 120.00 (*0-8161-0745-9*, Hall Library) G K Hall.

— Catalog of the Theatre & Drama Collections: First Supplement to Pt. 2, Theatre Collection, 2 vols, Set. 1973. lib. bdg. 310.00 (*0-8161-0747-5*, Hall Library) G K Hall.

— Catalog of the Theatre & Drama Collections, Supplement 1974. 1976. lib. bdg. 120.00 (*0-8161-0058-6*, Hall Library) G K Hall.

— Dictionary Catalog & Shelf List of the Spencer Collection of Illustrated Books & Manuscripts & Fine Bindings, 2 vols., Set. 1970. lib. bdg. 220.00 (*0-8161-0862-5*, Hall Library) G K Hall.

— Dictionary Catalog of Jewish Collection, 14 Vols, Set. 1970. lib. bdg. 1,365.00 (*0-8161-0409-3*, Hall Library) G K Hall.

— Dictionary Catalog of Materials on New York City. 1977. lib. bdg. 330.00 (*0-8161-0079-9*, Hall Library) G K Hall.

— Dictionary Catalog of the Albert A. & Henry W. Berg Collection of English & American Literature, First Supplement. 1975. lib. bdg. 120.00 (*0-8161-0014-4*, Hall Library) G K Hall.

— Dictionary Catalog of the Art & Architecture Division, Supplement 1974. 1976. lib. bdg. 95.00 (*0-8161-0061-6*, Hall Library) G K Hall.

— Dictionary Catalog of the Art & Architecture Division, The Research Libraries of The New York Public Library, 30 vols., Set. 1975. lib. bdg. 3,380.00 (*0-8161-1157-X*, Hall Library) G K Hall.

— Dictionary Catalog of the Dance Collection, Performing Arts Research Center, 10 vols., Set. 1974. lib. bdg. 940.00 (*0-8161-1124-3*, Hall Library) G K Hall.

— Dictionary Catalog of the Henry W. & Albert A. Berg Collection of English & American Literature, 5 Vols, Set. 1970. lib. bdg. 535.00 (*0-8161-0870-6*, Hall Library) G K Hall.

— Dictionary Catalog of the History of the Americas Collection, 28 Vols, Set. 1970. lib. bdg. 2,520.00 (*0-8161-0540-5*, Hall Library) G K Hall.

— Dictionary Catalog of the History of the Americas Collection, First Supplement, 9 vols., Set. 1974. lib. bdg. 1,085.00 (*0-8161-0771-8*, Hall Library) G K Hall.

— Dictionary Catalog of the Jewish Collection, First Supplement, 8 vols., Set. 5424p. 1975. lib. bdg. 960.00 (*0-8161-0773-4*, Hall Library) G K Hall.

— Dictionary Catalog of the Local History & Genealogy Division, 20 vols., Set. 1974. lib. bdg. 1,760.00 (*0-8161-0784-X*, Hall Library) G K Hall.

— Dictionary Catalog of the Manuscript Division, 2 Vols, Set. 1970. lib. bdg. 170.00 (*0-8161-0750-5*, Hall Library) G K Hall.

— Dictionary Catalog of the Map Division, 10 vols., Set. 1971. lib. bdg. 1,090.00 (*0-8161-0783-1*, Hall Library) G K Hall.

— Dictionary Catalog of the Music Collection. 2nd ed. 1983. lib. bdg. 6,865.00 (*0-8161-0374-7*, Hall Library) G K Hall.

— Dictionary Catalog of the Music Collection, 33 Vols, Set. 1974. lib. bdg. 2,750.00 (*0-8161-0709-2*, Hall Library) G K Hall.

— Dictionary Catalog of the Music Collection, Supplement II, 10 vols., Set. 1978. lib. bdg. 1,490.00 (*0-8161-0760-2*, Hall Library) G K Hall.

— Dictionary Catalog of the Music Collection, Supplement 1974. 1976. lib. bdg. 95.00 (*0-8161-0059-4*, Hall Library) G K Hall.

— Dictionary Catalog of the Oriental Collection, 16 Vols, Set. 1970. lib. bdg. 1,320.00 (*0-8161-0410-7*, Hall Library) G K Hall.

— Dictionary Catalog of the Oriental Collection: First Supplement, 8 vols., Set. 1976. lib. bdg. 1,100.00 (*0-8161-0775-0*, Hall Library) G K Hall.

— The Dictionary Catalog of the Prints Division, 5 vols., Set. 1975. lib. bdg. 545.00 (*0-8161-1148-0*, Hall Library) G K Hall.

— Dictionary Catalog of the Rare Book Division, 21 vols, Set. 1971. lib. bdg. 2,280.00 (*0-8161-0782-3*, Hall Library) G K Hall.

— Dictionary Catalog of the Rare Book Division: First Supplement. 1973. lib. bdg. 125.00 (*0-8161-1089-1*, Hall Library) G K Hall.

— Dictionary Catalog of the Schomburg Collection of Negro Literature & History, 9 vols. LC 66-1573. 1973. Supp. 1, 2 vols. lib. bdg. 130.00 (*0-8161-0735-1*, Hall Library); Supp. 2, 4 vols. lib. bdg. 485.00 (*0-8161-0820-X*, Hall Library) G K Hall.

— Dictionary Catalog of the Schomburg Collection of Negro Literature & History, 9 vols., Set. LC 66-1573. 1973. lib. bdg. 915.00 (*0-8161-0632-0*, Hall Library) G K Hall.

— Dictionary Catalog of the Slavonic Collection, 44 vols., Set. 2nd rev. ed. 1974. lib. bdg. 4,355.00 (*0-8161-0777-7*, Hall Library) G K Hall.

— Music Subject Headings, Vol. 1. 2nd enl. ed. 1970. lib. bdg. 80.00 (*0-8161-0739-4*, Hall Library) G K Hall.

— Subject Catalog of the World War One Collection, 4 Vols, Set. 1970. lib. bdg. 310.00 (*0-8161-0559-6*, Hall Library) G K Hall.

— Subject Headings, 5 Vols, Set. 1970. lib. bdg. 375.00 (*0-8161-0368-2*, Hall Library) G K Hall.

— Theatre Subject Headings, Vol. 1. 2nd enl. ed. 1970. lib. bdg. 75.00 (*0-8161-0740-8*, Hall Library) G K Hall.

— United States Local History Catalog, 2 vols., Set. 1115p. 1975. lib. bdg. 180.00 (*0-8161-1147-2*, Hall Library) G K Hall.

New York Public Library, Schomburg Center for Research in Black Culture Staff, ed. Index to the Schomburg Clipping File. 1986. 80.00 (*0-89887-035-6*) Chadwyck-Healey.

New York Public Library Schomburg Collection of Negro Literature & History Staff. Bibliographic Guide to Black Studies: 1991. (Bibliographic Guides Ser.). 545p. 1992. text ed. 160.00 (*0-8161-7153-X*) G K Hall.

***New York Public Library Staff.** Bibliograhpic Guide to Psychology 1994. 1995. 205.00 (*0-7838-2195-6*) G K Hall.

— Bibliographic Guide to Art & Architecture, 1987. 1384p. 1988. lib. bdg. 300.00 (*0-8161-7087-8*, Biblio Guides) G K Hall.

— Bibliographic Guide to Art & Architecture, 1988. 1175p. 1989. lib. bdg. 300.00 (*0-8161-7097-5*, Biblio Guides) G K Hall.

— Bibliographic Guide to Art & Architecture, 1989, 2 vols. (C). 1990. lib. bdg. 320.00 (*0-8161-7116-5*, Biblio Guides) G K Hall.

— Bibliographic Guide to Art & Architecture, 1993, 2 vols. Incl. Vol. 2. Bibliographic Guide to Art & Architecture, 1993. 592p. 1994. 175.00 (*0-7838-2067-4*, Biblio Guides); 350.00 (*0-7838-2065-8*) G K Hall.

— Bibliographic Guide to Art & Architecture, 1994 Vol. 1. 1995. 190.00 (*0-7838-2162-X*) G K Hall.

— Bibliographic Guide to Art & Architecture, 1994 Vol. 2. 1995. 190.00 (*0-7838-2163-8*) G K Hall.

— Bibliographic Guide to Black Studies: 1989. 400p. (C). 1989. Catalog. lib. bdg. 150.00 (*0-8161-7110-6*, Hall Reference) Macmillan.

— Bibliographic Guide to Black Studies: 1993. 399p. 1994. 170.00 (*0-7838-2068-2*, Biblio Guides) G K Hall.

— Bibliographic Guide to Business & Economics, 3 Vols. 1816p. 1994. 575.00 (*0-7838-2069-0*, Biblio Guides) G K Hall.

— Bibliographic Guide to Business & Economics, 1987. 2256p. 1988. lib. bdg. 520.00 (*0-8161-7086-X*, Hall Reference) Macmillan.

— Bibliographic Guide to Business & Economics, 1989, 3 vols., Set. (C). 1990. lib. bdg. 540.00 (*0-8161-7117-3*, Hall Reference) Macmillan.

— Bibliographic Guide to Business & Economics, 1994 Vol. 1. (Reference Library). 1995. 210.00 (*0-7838-2166-2*) G K Hall.

— Bibliographic Guide to Business & Economics, 1994 Vol. 2. (Reference Library). 1995. 210.00 (*0-7838-2167-0*) G K Hall.

— Bibliographic Guide to Conference Publications, 1993, 2 Vols. Incl. Vol. 1. Bibliographic Guide to Conference Publications, 1993. 640p. 1994. 170.00 (*0-7838-2074-7*, Biblio Guides); 340.00 (*0-7838-2073-9*, Biblio Guides) G K Hall.

— Bibliographic Guide to Conference Publications, 1994, 2 vols. Incl. Bibliographic Guide to Conference Publications, 1994 Vol. 1. 1995. 185.00 (*0-7838-2170-0*); Bibliographic Guide to Conference Publications, 1994 Vol. 2. 1995. 185.00 (*0-7838-2171-9*); 365.00 (*0-7838-2169-7*) G K Hall.

— Bibliographic Guide to Conference Publications, 1987. 1392p. 1988. lib. bdg. 300.00 (*0-8161-7096-7*, Hall Reference) Macmillan.

— Bibliographic Guide to Conference Publications, 1988. (Bibliographic Guides Ser.). 1235p. 1989. lib. bdg. 300.00 (*0-8161-7073-8*, Hall Reference) Macmillan.

— Bibliographic Guide to Conference Publications, 1989. 1200p. (C). 1989. lib. bdg. 310.00 (*0-8161-7111-4*, Hall Reference) Macmillan.

— Bibliographic Guide to Dance, 1990. (Bibliographic Guides Ser.). 1150p. 1991. lib. bdg. 360.00 (*0-8161-7136-X*) G K Hall.

— Bibliographic Guide to Dance, 1993, 3 Vols. Incl. Bibliographic Guide to Dance, 1993, Vol. 1. 686p. 1994. 160.00 (*0-7838-2077-1*, Biblio Guides); 480.00 (*0-7838-2076-3*, Biblio Guides) G K Hall.

— Bibliographic Guide to Dance, 1994, 3 vols. Incl. Bibliographic Guide to Dance, 1994 Vol. 1. 1995. 170.00 (*0-7838-2173-5*); Bibliographic Guide to Dance, 1994 Vol. 2. 1995. 170.00 (*0-7838-2174-3*); Bibliographic Guide to Dance, 1994 Vol. 3. 1995. 170.00 (*0-7838-2175-1*); 510.00 (*0-7838-2172-7*) G K Hall.

— Bibliographic Guide to East Asian Studies, 1989. (Monograph Ser.). 350p. (C). 1990. lib. bdg. 160.00 (*0-8161-7126-2*) G K Hall.

— Bibliographic Guide to East Asian Studies, 1993. 432p. 1994. 185.00 (*0-7838-2080-1*, Biblio Guides) G K Hall.

— Bibliographic Guide to East Asian Studies, 1994. 1995. 200.00 (*0-7838-2176-X*) G K Hall.

— Bibliographic Guide to Education, 1993. 432p. 1994. 315.00 (*0-7838-2081-X*, Biblio Guides) G K Hall.

— Bibliographic Guide to Education 1994. 1995. 335.00 (*0-7838-2177-8*) G K Hall.

— Bibliographic Guide to Goverment Publications, 1993 - U.S., 2 Vols. 944p. 1994. 520.00 (*0-7838-2086-0*, Biblio Guides) G K Hall.

— Bibliographic Guide to Government Publications - U. S. 1987. 1448p. 1988. lib. bdg. 435.00 (*0-8161-7089-4*, Hall Reference) Macmillan.

— Bibliographic Guide to Government Publications - U. S. 1988. 1175p. 1989. lib. bdg. 455.00 (*0-8161-7102-5*, Hall Reference) Macmillan.

— Bibliographic Guide to Government Publications - Foreign: 1983, 2 vols., Set. 1195p. 1984. lib. bdg. 350.00 (*0-8161-6995-0*, Hall Reference) Macmillan.

— Bibliographic Guide to Government Publications - Foreign: 1988. 1720p. 1989. lib. bdg. 505.00 (*0-8161-7103-3*, Hall Reference) Macmillan.

— Bibliographic Guide to Government Publications-Foreign: 1987. 1808p. 1988. lib. bdg. 495.00 (*0-8161-7090-8*, Hall Reference) Macmillan.

— Bibliographic Guide to Government Publications, 1993 - Foriegn, 2 Vols. 1664p. 1994. 575.00 (*0-7838-2083-6*, Biblio Guides) G K Hall.

— Bibliographic Guide to Government Publications 1994 Vol. 1: Foreign. 1995. 300.00 (*0-7838-2180-8*) G K Hall.

— Bibliographic Guide to Government Publications, 1994 Vol. 1: U. S. 1995. 275.00 (*0-7838-2183-2*) G K Hall.

— Bibliographic Guide to Government Publications 1994 Vol. 2: Foreign. 1995. 300.00 (*0-7838-2181-6*) G K Hall.

— Bibliographic Guide to Government Publications, 1994 Vol. 2: U. S. 1995. 275.00 (*0-7838-2184-0*) G K Hall.

— Bibliographic Guide to Latin American Studies, 2 Vols. 1668p. 1994. 550.00 (*0-7838-2089-5*, Biblio Guides) G K Hall.

— Bibliographic Guide to Latin American Studies, 1994 Vol. 1. 1995. 290.00 (*0-7838-2186-7*) G K Hall.

— Bibliographic Guide to Latin American Studies, 1994 Vol. 2. 1995. 290.00 (*0-7838-2187-5*) G K Hall.

— Bibliographic Guide to Law: 1987. 1544p. 1988. lib. bdg. 315.00 (*0-8161-7095-9*, Hall Reference) Macmillan.

— Bibliographic Guide to Law 1994 Vol. 1. 1995. 190.00 (*0-7838-2189-1*) G K Hall.

— Bibliographic Guide to Law 1994 Vol. 2. 1995. 190.00 (*0-7838-2190-5*) G K Hall.

— Bibliographic Guide to Maps & Atlases, 1987. 880p. 1988. lib. bdg. 300.00 (*0-8161-7085-1*, Hall Reference) Macmillan.

— Bibliographic Guide to Maps & Atlases, 1993. 535p. 1994. 325.00 (*0-7838-2095-X*, Biblio Guides) G K Hall.

— Bibliographic Guide to Microform Publications. (Bibliographic Guides Ser.). 600p. (C). 1990. lib. bdg. 250.00 (*0-8161-7129-7*) G K Hall.

— Bibliographic Guide to Microform Publications. (Bibliographic Guides Ser.). 600p. 1989. lib. bdg. 250.00 (*0-8161-7106-8*, Hall Reference) Macmillan.

— Bibliographic Guide to Microform Publications, 1993. 535p. 1994. 275.00 (*0-7838-2096-8*, Biblio Guides) G K Hall.

— Bibliographic Guide to Middle Eastern Studies, 1993. 497p. 1994. 195.00 (*0-7838-2097-6*, Biblio Guides) G K Hall.

— Bibliographic Guide to Middle Eastern Studies 1994. 1995. 205.00 (*0-7838-2192-1*) G K Hall.

— Bibliographic Guide to Middle Eastern Studies, 1990 Edition. (Bibliographic Guides Ser.). 800p. 1991. text ed. 195.00 (*0-8161-7151-3*) G K Hall.

— Bibliographic Guide to Music, 1987. 752p. 1988. lib. bdg. 205.00 (*0-8161-7093-2*, Hall Reference) Macmillan.

— Bibliographic Guide to Music, 1988. (Bibliographic Guides Ser.). 690p. 1989. lib. bdg. 205.00 (*0-8161-7075-4*, Hall Reference) Macmillan.

— Bibliographic Guide to Music, 1993. 767p. 1994. 235.00 (*0-7838-2098-4*, Biblio Guides) G K Hall.

— Bibliographic Guide to North American History: 1987. 768p. 1988. lib. bdg. 275.00 (*0-8161-7092-4*, Hall Reference) Macmillan.

— Bibliographic Guide to North American History: 1989. (C). 1990. lib. bdg. 290.00 (*0-8161-7118-1*, Hall Reference) Macmillan.

— Bibliographic Guide to North American History: 1993. 808p. 1994. 315.00 (*0-7838-2099-2*, Biblio Guides) G K Hall.

— Bibliographic Guide to Psychology: 1987. 152p. 1988. lib. bdg. 175.00 (*0-8161-7094-0*, Hall Reference) Macmillan.

— Bibliographic Guide to Psychology: 1989. 150p. 1989. lib. bdg. 190.00 (*0-8161-7114-9*) G K Hall.

— Bibliographic Guide to Psychology: 1993. 224p. 1994. 195.00 (*0-7838-2100-X*, Biblio Guides) G K Hall.

— Bibliographic Guide to Soviet & East European Studies: 1987. 2360p. 1988. lib. bdg. 545.00 (*0-8161-7091-6*, Hall Reference) Macmillan.

— Bibliographic Guide to Soviet & East European Studies 1994 Vol. 1. 1995. 220.00 (*0-7838-2197-2*) G K Hall.

— Bibliographic Guide to Soviet & East European Studies 1994 Vol. 2. 1995. 220.00 (*0-7838-2198-0*) G K Hall.

— Bibliographic Guide to Soviet & East European Studies 1994 Vol. 3. 1995. 220.00 (*0-7838-2199-9*) G K Hall.

— Bibliographic Guide to Technology: 1987. 1080p. 1988. lib. bdg. 360.00 (*0-8161-7088-6*, Hall Reference) Macmillan.

— Bibliographic Guide to Technology 1994 Vol. 1. 1995. 180.00 (*0-7838-2201-4*) G K Hall.

— Bibliographic Guide to Technology 1994 Vol. 2. 1995. 180.00 (*0-7838-2202-2*) G K Hall.

— Bibliographic Guide to the Environment 1994. 1995. 185.00 (*0-7838-2178-6*) G K Hall.

— Bibliographic Guide to Theater Arts: 1989. (Bibliographic Guides Ser.). 200p. (C). 1989. lib. bdg. 200.00 (*0-8161-7115-7*, Hall Reference) Macmillan.

— Bibliographic Guide to Theatre Arts: 1987. 264p. 1988. lib. bdg. 190.00 (*0-8161-7084-3*, Hall Reference) Macmillan.

— Bibliographic Guide to Theatre Arts 1994. 1995. 205.00 (*0-7838-2203-0*) G K Hall.

— Dictionary Catalog of the Schomburg Collection of Negro Literature & History, Supplement 1974. 1976. lib. bdg. 120.00 (*0-8161-0062-4*, Hall Library) G K Hall.

— Index to Dance Periodicals: 1990: Dance Collection of the Performing Arts Research Center at the New York Public Library. annuals 400p. 1991. text ed. 125.00 (*0-8161-0523-5*) G K Hall.

— Index to Dance Periodicals 1992. 1993. text ed. 150.00 (*0-8161-0605-3*) G K Hall.

— phic Guide to the Environment, 1993. 392p. 1994. 175.00 (*0-7838-2082-8*, Biblio Guides) G K Hall.

New York Public Library Staff, comp. Bibliographic Guide to Dance, 1991, 3 vols., Set. (Bibliographic Guides Ser.). 1800p. 1992. text ed. 450.00 (*0-8161-7157-2*) G K Hall.

New York Public Library Staff, ed. Bibliographic Guide to Black Studies: 1985, Vol. 1. 1985. lib. bdg. 115.00 (*0-8161-7019-3*, Biblio Guides) G K Hall.

— Bibliographic Guide to Maps & Atlases, 1985. 1986. lib. bdg. 225.00 (*0-8161-7027-4*, Hall Reference) Macmillan.

New York Public Library Staff & Library of Congress Staff. Bibliographic Guide to Business & Economics, 1991, 3 vols., Vol. 3. (Bibliographic Guides Ser.). 1560p. 1992. text ed. 550.00 (*0-8161-7154-8*) G K Hall.

— Bibliographic Guide to Maps & Atlases, 1988. 675p. 1989. lib. bdg. 300.00 (*0-8161-7105-X*, Hall Reference) Macmillan.

— Guide to Festschriften. (Festschriften Collection of the New York Public Library). 1977. lib. bdg. 170.00 (*0-8161-0069-1*, Hall Library) G K Hall.

New York Public Library Staff & Library of Congress Staff, comps. Bibliographic Guide to East Asian Studies, 1991. (Bibliographic Guides Ser.). 600p. 1992. text ed. 175.00 (*0-8161-7158-0*) G K Hall.

— Bibliographic Guide to Middle Eastern Studies, 1991. (Bibliographic Guides Ser.). 500p. 1992. text ed. 195.00 (*0-8161-7172-6*) G K Hall.

— Bibliographic Guide to the Environment, 1991. (Bibliographic Guides Ser.). 250p. 1992. text ed. 165.00 (*0-8161-7222-6*) G K Hall.

New York Public Library Staff & University of Texas Austin Staff. Bibliographic Guide to Latin American Studies: 1987. 2048p. 1988. lib. bdg. 520.00 (*0-8161-7083-5*, Hall Reference) Macmillan.

New York Public Library Staff, jt. auth. see LC Marc Tapes Staff.

New York Public Library Theatre & Drama Collections Staff & Library of Congress Staff. Bibliographic Guide to Theatre Arts: 1991. (Bibliographic Guides Ser.). 203p. 1992. text ed. 195.00 (*0-8161-7170-X*) G K Hall.

***New York Rangers Staff.** Official 1994-95 New York Rangers Media Guide. rev. ed. 320p. 1995. pap. 9.95 (*1-57243-054-0*) Triumph Bks.

New York Society for General Semantics Staff, ed. see Daly, T. P.

New York Spanish Institute Staff, tr. see Pace, Edgardo, ed.

***New York State Bar Association.** Environmental Law Index. Gerrard, Michael B. et al, eds. LC 94-65586. 313p. 1994. 50.00 (*0-942954-68-8*) NYS Bar.

New York State Bar Association Committee on Federal Courts. Individual Judges Rules, Procedures & Forms in United States District Courts of the Southern, Eastern, Northern & Western Districts of New York. LC 86-62411. 363p. 1986. 60.00 (*0-942954-13-0*) NYS Bar.

***New York State Bar Association Staff.** Antitrust Law in New York State. Hubbard, Robert, ed. 400p. (Orig.). 1994. pap. text ed. 50.00 (*0-614-07027-9*) NYS Bar.

— Collections & the Enforcement of Money Judgements. Getman, Jack et al, eds. LC 84-60393. 467p. 1985. text ed. 60.00 (*0-942954-05-X*) NYS Bar.

— Corporate Practice Handbook. Merritt, Raymond W. & Ennico, Clifford R., eds. LC 92-61676. 995p. (Orig.). 1992. text ed. 95.00 (*0-942954-55-6*) NYS Bar.

— Federal Civil Practice. LC 89-61058. 1038p. 1990. 90.00 (*0-942954-23-8*) NYS Bar.

— Federal Rules of Civil Procedure: 1993 Amendments. Arenson, Gregory K. & Wise, Robert F., Jr., eds. LC 94-65587. 204p. 1994. pap. text ed. (*0-942954-67-X*) NYS Bar.

— The Grand Jury in New York. Gray, Lawrence N., ed. LC 94-65728. 240p. 1994. pap. 44.00 (*0-942954-69-6*) NYS Bar.

— Handling the Basic Workers' Compensation Case in New York. Magro, Michael V., ed. LC 84-60392. 266p. 1985. 50.00 (*0-942954-06-8*) NYS Bar.

— Law Firm Mergers. Sambal, Nancy G., ed. LC 86-62410. 124p. 1986. 25.00 (*0-942954-12-2*) NYS Bar.

An Asterisk (*) at the beginning of an entry indicates that the title is appearing in BIP for the first time.

— Medical Malpractice: Strategic & Practical Principles. Devine, Robert, ed. LC 85-61222. 261p. 1985. text ed. 50.00 (0-942954-08-4) NYS Bar.
— Medical Malpractice in New York. Devine, Robert, ed. & pref. by. LC 92-63000. 570p. 1993. 90.00 (0-942954-54-8) NYS Bar.
— New York Criminal Practice Handbook-1994 Supplement. Gray, Lawrence N., ed. 229p. 1994. pap. text ed. 40.00 (0-942954-72-6) NYS Bar.
— New York Lawyer's Deskbook. LC 89-64413. 900p. 1990. ring bd. 80.00 (0-942954-33-5) NYS Bar.
— New York Lawyer's Formbook. LC 90-50851. 800p. 1991. ring bd. 80.00 (0-942954-35-1) NYS Bar.
— The Partnership Handbook. Merritt, Raymond W. & Helpern, Martin, eds. LC 85-62739. 917p. 1985. 70.00 (0-942954-09-2) NYS Bar.
— Pitfalls of Practice. White, Joanne M., ed. LC 93-86813. 348p. (Orig.). 1993. pap. text ed. 45.00 (0-942954-65-3) NYS Bar.
— ProForms NYSBA Electronic Legal Forms. 55p. 1994. pap. text ed. 140.00 (0-942954-71-8) NYS Bar.
— Real Estate Titles. Pedowitz, James M., ed. LC 83-60951. (Illus.). 877p. 1984. 70.00 (0-942954-04-1) NYS Bar.
— Real Estate Titles. 2nd ed. Pedowitz, James M., ed. & pref. by. LC 93-86812. (Illus.). 1216p. 1994. text ed. 95.00 (0-942954-66-1) NYS Bar.
— Real Estate Titles Update, 1988. Pedowitz, James M., ed. 50p. 1989. pap. 20.00 (0-942954-15-7) NYS Bar.
— The Treatise on New York Environmental Law. Robinson, Nicholas A. & Hopkins, James D., eds. LC 92-53528. 1000p. 1992. 95.00 (0-685-56517-3) NYS Bar.
New York State Board for Chiropractic. Chiropractic Staff. iii, 35p. write for info. (0-318-61630-0) NYS Ed Dept.
New York State Chamber of Commerce Staff. Papers & Proceedings of the Committee on the Police Problem, City of New York. LC 79-154581. (Police in America Ser.). 1971. reprint ed. 51.95 (0-405-03364-8) Ayer.
New York State Commission on Relief for Widowed Mothers. Report of the New York State Commission on Relief for Widowed Mothers. LC 74-1696. (Children & Youth Ser.: Vol. 18). 602p. 1974. reprint ed. 48.95 (0-405-05973-6) Ayer.
New York State Commission to Investigate Provision for the Mentally Deficient. Report of the State Commission to Investigate Provision for the Mentally Deficient. LC 75-17234. (Social Problems & Social Policy Ser.). (Illus.). 1976. reprint ed. 96.95 (0-405-07503-0) Ayer.
New York State Committee on State Prisons. Investigation of the New York State Prisons. LC 74-3828. (Criminal Justice in America Ser.). 1974. reprint ed. 87.95 (0-405-06159-5) Ayer.
New York State Crime Commission. Crime & the Community. LC 74-3820. (Criminal Justice in America Ser.). 1974. reprint ed. 25.95 (0-405-06158-7) Ayer.
— Report of the Crime Commission, 1925: Legislative Document Number 23. LC 74-3840. (Mass Violence in America Ser.). 1974. reprint ed. 53.95 (0-405-06157-9) Ayer.
New York State Department of Transportation Staff, jt. auth. see Coon, William F.
New York State Division of Library Development Staff, jt. auth. see New York State Library Staff.
New York State Education Department, Bureau of Adult Occupational Education Staff. Handbook for Teachers of Adult Occupational Education. 96p. 1977. 4.95 (0-318-15481-1, SN20) Ctr Educ Trng Employ.
New York State Humane Association Staff. Overpopulation of Cats & Dogs: Causes, Effects, & Prevention. Anchel, Marjorie, ed. LC 90-82350. 260p. 1990. 25.00 (0-8232-1296-3) Fordham.
New York State Legislature, Joint Committee Investigating Seditious Activities. Revolutionary Radicalism, 4 vols. in 5, Set. LC 78-12114. (Civil Liberties in American History Ser.). 1971. reprint ed. lib. bdg. 295.00 (0-306-71974-6) Da Capo.
New York State Legislature, Joint Committee Investigating Seditious Activities, ed. Revolutionary Radicalism: Its History, Purpose & Tactics, 6 vols., Set. 1980. lib. bdg. 1,200.00 (0-8490-3152-4) Gordon Pr.
New York State Legislature Staff. Family Law, N.Y.S. 425p. 1994. Updated annually. ring bd. 18.95 (0-930137-44-2) Looseleaf Law.
— Town Law, New York State. annuals 350p. 1994. Updated annually. ring bd. 14.95 (0-930137-41-8) Looseleaf Law.
— Village Law, New York State. annuals 200p. 1994. Updated annually. ring bd. 12.95 (0-930137-42-6) Looseleaf Law.
New York State Library Staff. African American Bibliography: The Arts. 21p. 1990. 2.00 (0-317-05244-6) NYS Library.
— Annotated Lists & Indexes of the NYS Assembly & Senate Document Series, 1831-1918, 3 vols., Set. 1992. 50.00 (0-317-05247-0) NYS Library.
New York State Library Staff & New York State Division of Library Development Staff. Directory of Library Systems in New York State. 191p. 1992. 8.00 (0-317-05248-9) NYS Library.
New York State Motor Truck Association Staff. Heavy Advanced Brake Systems. LC 94-10791. 237p. 1994. pap. 29.95 (0-8273-6894-1) Delmar.
***New York State Off. of Business Permits & Reg. Assist. Staff.** The Official Directory of New York State Business Permits. 1993. 25.00 (0-942954-60-2) NYS Bar.
***New York State Office of Business Permits & Reg. Assist. Staff.** The Official Directory of New York State Business Permits. 1792p. 1992. pap. 35.00 (0-942954-51-3) NYS Bar.
New York State Organized Crime Task Force Staff. Corruption & Racketeering in the New York City Construction Industry: Interim Report. LC 87-37928. (ILR Paperback Ser.: No. 19). 160p. 1988. pap. 10.95 (0-87546-136-0) ILR Pr.
New York State Preservation League Staff. Preservation Directory: A Guide to Programs, Organizations, & Agencies in New York State. rev. ed. (Illus.). 232p. 1989. pap. 15.00 (0-942000-06-4) Pres League NYS.
New York State Supreme Court, Appellate Division Staff. The Investigation of the Magistrated Courts in the First Judicial Department & the Magistrates Thereof, & of Attorneys-at-Law Practicing in Said Courts: Final Report of Samuel Seabury, Referee. LC 74-3842. (Criminal Justice in America Ser.). 1974. reprint ed. 25.95 (0-405-06160-9) Ayer.
New York Stock Exchange, Office of the Hearing Board. Hearing Board Decisions: Index Outline of Procedures. write for info. (0-318-61975-X) NYSE Inc.
New York Times Company Women's Magazines Staff & Sheehan, Carol S. The Hunter Douglas Guide to Window Decorating: The Complete Reference for Designing Beautiful Window Treatments. Date not set. 14.95 (0-9636751-0-9) G&J USA Pubs.
New York Times Editors. Give Us This Day... A Report on the World Food Crisis. LC 75-1038. 1975. 15.95 (0-405-06644-9) Ayer.
— Introduction to a Good Reading Habit. 36p. 1981. pap. text ed. write for info. (0-912853-03-4) NY Times.
— New York Times Atlas of the World. 4th rev. ed. 1994. 75.00 (0-8129-2420-7, Times Bks) Random.
— New York Times Crossword Puzzles of the 1960s, Vol. 4. 1994. pap. 7.95 (0-8129-6367-9, Times Bks) Random.
— New York Times Crossword Puzzles of the 1970s, Vol. 4. 1994. pap. 7.95 (0-8129-6368-7, Times Bks) Random.
— New York Times Crossword Puzzles of the 1980s, Vol. 4. 1994. pap. 7.95 (0-8129-6369-5, Times Bks) Random.
— New York Times Skillbuilder Crosswords: Three-Star Strategist Level Puzzles, Vol. 2. 1994. pap. 8.00 (0-8129-2307-3, Times Bks) Random.
— New York Times Skillbuilder Crosswords: Two-Star Apprentice Level Puzzles. (Vol. 2). 1994. pap. 8.00 (0-8129-2306-5, Times Bks) Random.
— New York Times Sports Hall of Fame. 1980. 14.95 (0-405-13942-X) Ayer.
— New York Times Traveler's Pocket Atlas. 1994. pap. 10.00 (0-8129-2421-5, Times Bks) Random.
— New York Times Update 1979, Set 1. (Great Contemporary Issues Ser.). 1979. 38.95 (0-405-18421-2, 1772) Ayer.
— New York Times Update 1979, Set 2. (Great Contemporary Issues Ser.). 38.95 (0-405-18422-0, 1773) Ayer.
— The Newspaper, Its Making & Its Meaning. LC 80-2891. (BCL Ser.: Vols. I & II). reprint ed. 26.00 (0-404-18069-8) AMS Pr.
— Update, Set One, 1981. (Great Contemporary Issues Ser.). 55.95 (0-405-13941-1) Ayer.
— Update, Set Two, 1980. (Great Contemporary Issues Ser.). 1980. 38.95 (0-405-13781-8) Ayer.
New York Times Staff. New York Times Book of Sports Legends. 1991. 25.00 (0-8129-1798-7) Random.
— New York Times Crossword Puzzles of the 1960's, Vol. 3. 1994. pap. 7.95 (0-8129-2335-9, Times Bks) Random.
— New York Times Crossword Puzzles of the 1970's, Vol. 3. 1994. pap. 7.95 (0-8129-2334-0, Times Bks) Random.
— New York Times Crossword Puzzles of the 1980's, Vol. 3. 1994. pap. 7.95 (0-8129-2333-2, Times Bks) Random.
— New York Times Crosswords of the 1960s Vol. 6. 1995. pap. 7.95 (0-8129-2548-3, Times Bks) Random.
— New York Times Crosswords of the 1970s Vol. 6. 1995. pap. 7.95 (0-8129-2549-1, Times Bks) Random.
— New York Times Crosswords of the 1980s Vol. 6. 1995. pap. 7.95 (0-8129-2550-5, Times Bks) Random.
— The New York Times Handy Crossword Book, No. 3. 1994. mass mkt. 3.99 (0-8041-1318-1) Ivy Books.
— The New York Times Handy Crossword Book, No. 3. 1994. mass mkt. 3.99 (0-8041-1317-3) Ivy Books.
— The New York Times Handy Crossword Book, No. 4. 1994. mass mkt. 3.99 (0-8041-1319-X) Ivy Books.
— The New York Times Handy Crossword Book, No. 5. 1995. mass mkt. 3.99 (0-8041-1320-3) Ivy Books.
— The New York Times Handy Crossword Book, No. 6. 1995. mass mkt. 4.99 (0-8041-1321-1) Ivy Books.
— The New York Times Handy Crossword Book, No. 7. 1995. mass mkt. 4.99 (0-8041-1337-8) Ivy Books.
— New York Times Handy Crossword Book, No. 8. 1995. mass mkt. 4.99 (0-8041-1348-3) Ivy Books.
— The New York Times Handy Crossword Book No. 9. 1995. mass mkt. 4.99 (0-8041-1389-0) Ivy Books.
— New York Times Skillbuilder Crossword: One-Star Beginner Puzzles. 1994. pap. 8.00 (0-8129-2302-2, Times Bks) Random.
— New York Times Skillbuilder Crossword One-Star Beginner Puzzles Vol. 4. 1995. pap. 8.50 (0-8129-2555-6, Times Bks) Random.
— New York Times Skillbuilder Crossword Three-Star Strategist Puzzles Vol. 4. 1995. pap. 8.50 (0-8129-2557-2, Times Bks) Random.
— New York Times Skillbuilder Crossword Two-Star Apprentice Puzzles Vol. 4. 1995. pap. 8.50 (0-8129-2556-4, Times Bks) Random.
— New York Times Skillbuilder Crosswords: One-Star Beginner Level Puzzles, Vol. 2. 1994. pap. 8.00 (0-8129-2305-7, Times Bks) Random.
— New York Times Skillbuilder Crosswords: Three-Star Strategist Puzzles. 1994. pap. 8.00 (0-8129-2304-9, Times Bks) Random.
— New York Times Skillbuilder Crosswords: Two-Star Apprentice Puzzles. 1994. pap. 8.00 (0-8129-2303-0, Times Bks) Random.
— Page One. 1992. 17.98 (0-88365-809-7) Galahad Bks.
— Page One: 1994 Edition Major Events 1920-1994 As Presented in the New York Times. 1994. 19.98 (0-88365-884-4) Galahad Bks.
— The Times Atlas of the World. 8th ed. (Illus.). 1990. 159.95 (0-8129-1874-6, Times Bks) Random.
New York Transit Museum Staff. I've Been Working on the Subway: The Folklore & Oral History of Transit. (Illus.). 54p. (Orig.). (J). (gr. 5-10). 1991. teacher ed, pap. 5.00 (0-9637492-9-3) NY Transit Mus.
New York University, Burma Research Project Staff, et al. Japanese & Chinese Language Sources on Burma: An Annotated Bibliography. Trager, Frank N., ed. LC 57-13287. (Behavior Science Bibliographies Ser.). 151p. reprint ed. pap. 43.10 (0-317-10647-3, 2010453) Bks Demand.
New York University, Division of General Education. Proceedings of the New York University Conference on Practice & Procedure Under the Immigration & Nationality Act (McCarran-Walter Act) Held on June 13,1953: Proceedings. Sellin, Henry, ed. LC 54-7877. xii, 145p. reprint ed. lib. bdg. 22.50 (0-8371-7684-0, NYUP) Greenwood.
New York University Libraries Staff. Fales Library Checklist, 2 Vols. Grieder, Theodore, ed. 1970. write for info. (0-318-50581-9) AMS Pr.
— Fales Library Checklist, 2 Vols, 1. Grieder, Theodore, ed. LC 71-122494. 1970. 97.50 (0-404-07947-4) AMS Pr.
— Fales Library Checklist, 2 Vols, 2. Grieder, Theodore, ed. LC 71-122494. 1970. 97.50 (0-404-07948-2) AMS Pr.
— Fales Library Checklist, 2 Vols, Set. Grieder, Theodore, ed. LC 71-122494. 1970. 195.00 (0-404-07946-6) AMS Pr.
— Fales Library Checklist: First Supplement. LC 71-122494. 1973. 95.00 (0-404-11203-X) AMS Pr.
— Fales Library Checklist: Second Supplement. Grieder, Theodore, ed. LC 77-21906. 1977. 95.00 (0-404-16025-5) AMS Pr.
New York University School of Law Staff, ed. Annual Survey of American Law, 1942-1991, 56 vols., Set. LC 46-30523. 1942. lib. bdg. 2,057.50 (0-379-12200-6) Oceana.
— Annual Survey of American Law, 1980-1991, 22 vols., Set. 807.50 (0-614-02966-X) Oceana.
New York University Society Staff. Modern Music & Musicians. 616p. 1991. reprint ed. lib. bdg. 119.00 (0-7812-9345-6) Rprt Serv.
— The World's Best Music, 6 vols., Set. 1991. reprint ed. lib. bdg. 540.00 (0-7812-9365-0) Rprt Serv.
New York Vietnam Veterans Memorial Commission. Dear America: Letters Home from Vietnam. Edelman, Bernard, ed. 276p. 1985. 13.95 (0-393-01998-5) Norton.
New York Women's Handbook Group Staff, jt. auth. see ACT-UP - New York Women.
New York World Staff. The Conning Tower Book. 1972. 59.95 (0-87968-931-5) Gordon Pr.
New York Writer's Program Staff. A Maritime History of New York. LC 72-2083. (American History & Americana Ser.: No. 47). 1972. reprint ed. lib. bdg. 75.00 (0-8383-1460-0) M S G Haskell Hse.
New Yorker Magazine Editors. The Complete Book of Covers from the New Yorker 1925-1989. LC 89-45280. (Illus.). 400p. 1989. 75.00 (0-394-57841-4) Knopf.
— The New Yorker Book of Doctor Cartoons & Psychiatrist Cartoons. (Illus.). 1993. 18.00 (0-679-43069-5) Knopf.
— The New Yorker Book of Lawyer Cartoons. (Illus.). 1993. 18.00 (0-679-43068-7) Knopf.
— The New Yorker Book of Poems. LC 74-13031. 1974. reprint ed. pap. 18.45 (0-688-07877-X, Quill) Morrow.
— New Yorker Book of War Pieces. LC 75-167394. (Essay Index Reprint Ser.). 1977. reprint ed. 31.95 (0-8369-2470-3) Ayer.
New Yorker Magazine Staff. New Yorker Book of Cat Cartoons. (Illus.). 1990. 19.00 (0-394-58795-2) Knopf.
New Yorker Staff. Fifty Five Short Stories from the New Yorker. (BCL1-PS American Literature Ser.). 480p. 1993. reprint ed. lib. bdg. 99.00 (0-7812-6935-0) Rprt Serv.
— The New Yorker Book of Cat Cartoons. LC 90-53070. (Illus.). 112p. 1992. pap. 9.00 (0-679-74276-X) Knopf.
Newacheck, Paul W. Estimating Medicaid Eligible Pregnant Women & Children Living Below 185 Percent of Poverty: Strategies for Improving State Perinatal Programs. Feinstein, Gerry R., ed. 32p. (Orig.). 1988. pap. text ed. 15.00 (1-55877-010-0) Natl Governor.
Newall, Christopher. The Art of Lord Leighton. (Illus.). 144p. (C). 1993. reprint ed. pap. 24.95 (0-7148-2957-9, Pub. by Phaidon Press UK) Chronicle Bks.
— Victorian Watercolors. (Illus.). 140p. (C). 1993. reprint ed. pap. 24.95 (0-7148-2811-4, Pub. by Phaidon Press UK) Chronicle Bks.
Newall, Christopher, jt. auth. see Wilcox, Scott.
Newall, Venetia. An Egg at Easter: A Folklore Study. LC 72-146724. (Illus.). 448p. 1989. 27.50 (0-253-31942-0) Ind U Pr.
Newark Beth Israel Medical Center, Dietary Department Staff. Diet Manual. LC 80-82889. 92p. (Orig.). 1980. pap. 10.00 (0-937714-00-3) Newark Beth.
Newark Museum Junior Museum Staff. Explore Tibet. 32p. 1992. pap. 9.95 (1-55939-017-4) Snow Lion Pubns.
Newark Museum Quarterly, jt. auth. see Dietz, Ulysses G.
Newark, Tim. The Barbarians: Warriors & Wars of the Dark Ages. (Illus.). 160p. 1988. pap. 16.95 (0-7137-2042-5, Pub. by Blandford Pr UK) Sterling.
— Celtic Warriors 400 B. C. to A. D. 1600. (Illus.). 160p. 1994. pap. 16.95 (0-7137-2043-3, Pub. by Blandford Pr UK) Sterling.
— Medieval Warlords. (Illus.). 160p. (Orig.). 1990. pap. 16.95 (0-7137-2234-7, Pub. by Blandford Pr UK) Sterling.
Neway. Fermentation Process Development of Industrial Organisms. (Bioprocess Technology Ser.: Vol. 4). 344p. 1989. 125.00 (0-8247-7917-7) Dekker.
Neway, Julie M. Information Specialist As Team Player in the Research Process. LC 85-5488. (New Directions in Librarianship Ser.: No. 9). xiv, 194p. 1985. text ed. 45.00 (0-313-24508-8, NEI/, Greenwood Pr) Greenwood.
Newaz, G. M. Advances in Thermoplastic Matrix Composite Materials. LC 89-17634. (Special Technical Publication Ser.: No. STP 1044). (Illus.). 315p. 1989. text ed. 64.00 (0-8031-1272-6, 04-010440-33) ASTM.
Newaz, Golam, ed. Proceedings of the American Society for Composites: Eighth Technical Conference: Composite Materials, Mechanics & Processing. LC 93-61006. 1150p. 1993. text ed. 225.00 (1-56676-103-4) Technomic.
Newaz, Golam M., ed. Delamination in Advanced Composites. LC 90-71549. 475p. 1991. 65.00 (0-87762-753-3) Technomic.
Newball, Harold H., ed. Immunopharmacology of the Lung. LC 83-1799. (Lung Biology in Health & Disease Ser.: No. 19). 540p. reprint ed. pap. 153.90 (0-7837-3346-1, 2043304) Bks Demand.
Newbattle Abbey Staff. Registrum S. Marie De Neubotle. Innes, Cosmo, ed. LC 74-173074. (Bannatyne Club, Edinburgh. Publications: No. 89). reprint ed. 42.50 (0-404-52819-8) AMS Pr.
Newbegin, Wade. R. M. Wade & Co. & Family: Four Generations. Bledsoe, Helen W., ed. 112p. (Orig.). 1991. write for info. (0-9630153-0-3) R M Wade.
Newberg, Herbert B. Attorney Fee Awards. suppl. ed. 1986. Supplemented semiannually. text ed. 95.00 (0-07-046344-1) Shepards-McGraw.
— Newberg on Class Actions, 6 vols. 3rd ed. LC 92-38102. (Trial Practice Ser.). 3000p. 1992. text ed. 510.00 (0-07-172314-5) Shepards-McGraw.
— Newberg on Class Actions: A Manual for Group Litigation at Federal & State Levels, 5 vols., Set. LC 76-46479. 1985. text ed. 475.00 (0-07-046354-9) Shepards-McGraw.
***Newberg, Paula R.** Judging the State: Courts & Constitutional Politics in Pakistan. (South Asian Studies: No. 59). 304p. (C). 1995. 54.95 (0-521-45289-9) Cambridge U Pr.
Newberg, Paula R., ed. New Directions in Telecommunications Policy, 2 vols., Vol. 1. LC 89-1446. (Duke Press Policy Studies). 1989. pap. text ed. 29.50 (0-8223-0941-6) Duke.
— New Directions in Telecommunications Policy, 2 vols., Vol. 1: Regulatory Policy: Telephone & Mass Media. LC 89-1446. (Duke Press Policy Studies). 414p. 1989. mass mkt. 70.50 (0-8223-0916-5) Duke.
— New Directions in Telecommunications Policy, 2 vols., Vol. 2. LC 89-1446. (Duke Press Policy Studies). 1989. pap. text ed. 26.95 (0-8223-0948-3) Duke.
— New Directions in Telecommunications Policy, 2 vols., Vol. 2: Information Policy & Economic Policy. LC 89-1446. (Duke Press Policy Studies). 346p. 1989. lib. bdg. 68.00 (0-8223-0923-8) Duke.
— The Politics of Human Rights. LC 79-1998. (UNA-USA Book Ser.). 1981. 50.00x (0-8147-5754-5); pap. 16.50x (0-8147-5755-3) NYU Pr.
Newberger, D., jt. auth. see Black, S.
Newberger, Devra. Full House Family Scrapbook. (J). (gr. 4-7). 1992. pap. 3.95 (0-590-45706-3) Scholastic Inc.
— Scary Stories to Drive You Batty. LC 94-21667. (Illus.). 32p. (J). (gr. 2-6). 1994. pap. text ed. 2.95 (0-8167-3534-4) Troll Assocs.
Newberger, E. Unhappy Families: Clinical & Research Perspectives on Family Violence. 192p. 1989. pap. 35.00 (0-88416-504-3, Yr Bk Med Pubs) Mosby Yr Bk.
Newberger, Eli H. Child Abuse. (Clinical Pediatrics Ser.). 1982. 52.95 (0-316-60410-0) Little.
Newberger, Joe & Hendricks, Elrod. The Ultimate Baseball Players Yearbook. (Illus.). 96p. (J). (gr. 3-9). 1991. student ed 12.95 (0-9629307-0-9) Batboy Pr.
Newberger-Speregen, Devra. Hip Hop Till You Drop. (Full House Ser.: No. 4). (YA). 1994. mass mkt. 3.99 (0-671-88291-0, Minstrel Bks) PB.
— Stephanie: Phone Call from a Flamingo. (Full House Ser.). 128p. (Orig.). (J). (gr. 5 up). 1993. mass mkt. 3.99 (0-671-88004-7, Minstrel Bks) PB.
Newberne, P. M. Trace Substances & Health: A Handbook, Pt. 2. 192p. 1982. 99.75 (0-8247-1850-X) Dekker.
Newberne, Paul M., ed. Trace Substances & Health, Pt. 1, 1976: A Handbook. LC 75-25167. (Illus.). 412p. reprint ed. pap. 117.50 (0-7837-0705-3, 2041037) Bks Demand.
Newberry, Arthur S. Caught on the Fly. (Illus.). 306p. 1989. reprint ed. 30.00 (0-9620609-1-7) Meadow Run Pr.
Newberry, Benjamin H., et al. A Holistic Conceptualization of Stress & Disease. LC 86-82021. (Stress in Modern Society Ser.: No. 7). 1991. 32.50 (0-404-63258-0) AMS Pr.
Newberry, Clare T. April's Kittens. LC 40-32442. (Illus.). 32p. (J). (gr. k-3). 1940. 17.00 (0-06-024400-3); lib. bdg. 16.89 (0-06-024401-1) HarpC Child Bks.
— Kittens ABC. (J). Date not set. 14.95 (0-06-024450-X); lib. bdg. 14.89 (0-06-024451-8) HarpC Child Bks.
— Marshmallow. LC 89-20052. (Illus.). 32p. (J). (ps-3). 1990. 17.00 (0-06-024460-7) HarpC Child Bks.
Newberry, Conrad F., comp. Perspectives in Aerospace Design. 1026p. 1991. 79.95 (0-685-59651-6) AIAA.
Newberry, David M. & Stiglitz, Joseph E. The Theory of Commodity Price Stabilization: A Study in the Economics of Risk. (Illus.). 1981. pap. 32.50 (0-19-828438-1) OUP.
Newberry, David M., jt. ed. see Szekely, Istvan P.
Newberry, Julia R. Julia Newberry's Diary. (American Biography Ser.). 176p. 1991. reprint ed. lib. bdg. 59.00 (0-7812-8295-0) Rprt Serv.

N

Newberry, Kevin. Shell's Golf Guide to Greater Houston. 2nd ed. (Illus.). 484p. 1993. pap. 14.95 (1-883369-02-9) Twnty-Frst Media.

Newberry Library, Chicago Staff. Bibliographical Inventory to the Early Music in the Newberry Library, Chicago, Illinois. Krummel, Donald W., ed. 1978. lib. bdg. 85.00 (0-8161-0042-X, Hall Library) G K Hall.

— Catalogue of the Greenlee Collection, 2 vols, Set. 1970. lib. bdg. 220.00 (0-8161-0903-6, Hall Library) G K Hall.

— Dictionary Catalog of the Edward E. Ayer Collection of Americana & American Indians, 16 Vols, Set. 1970. lib. bdg. 1,280.00 (0-8161-0586-3, Hall Library) G K Hall.

— Dictionary Catalog of the Edward E. Ayer Collection of Americana & American Indians, First Supplement, 3 vol., Set. 1970. lib. bdg. 365.00 (0-8161-0810-2, Hall Library) G K Hall.

— Dictionary Catalogue of the History of Printing from the John M. Wing Foundation, 6 Vols, Set. 1970. lib. bdg. 655.00 (0-8161-0587-1, Hall Library) G K Hall.

— Dictionary Catalogue of the History of Printing from the John M. Wing Foundation, First Supplement, 3 vols., Set. 1970. lib. bdg. 365.00 (0-8161-0809-9, Hall Library) G K Hall.

— Genealogical Index of the Newberry Library, Chicago, 4 vols., Set. 1970. lib. bdg. 380.00 (0-8161-0498-0, Hall Library) G K Hall.

Newberry Library Staff. Narratives of Captivity among the Indians of North America, with Supplement I. 1974. reprint ed. 35.00 (1-55888-193-X) Omnigraphics Inc.

Newberry, Lida, et al. Daytrips from New York. (Earl Steinbicker Guide Ser.). (Illus.). 350p. (Orig.). 1994. pap. 14.95 (0-8038-9332-9) Hastings.

Newberry, Lynn & Fisher, M. Frances. The Food Book. LC 80-19009. (Illus.). 368p. 1986. text ed. 28.60 (0-87006-565-3) Goodheart.

***Newberry, Mark A.** Textbook of Hemodialysis for Patient Care Personnel. (Illus.). 606p. 1989. pap. 49.95 (0-398-06305-2) C C Thomas.

— Textbook of Hemodialysis for Patient Care Personnel. (Illus.). 606p. (C). 1989. text ed. 99.95x (0-398-05516-5) C C Thomas.

Newberry, P. E. Ancient Egyptian Scarabs. 278p. pap. 25.00 (0-89005-092-9) Ares.

Newberry, P. F. The Design of an Extendible Graph Editor. (Lecture Notes in Computer Science Ser.: Vol. 704). xv, 184p. 1993. pap. 35.00 (0-387-57090-X) Spr-Verlag.

Newberry, P. G., jt. auth. see Wright, A.

***Newberry, Sandra.** Seclusion Room. 1995. 13.95 (0-8062-5275-8) Carlton.

Newberry, Sara, ed. see Maguire, Majorie R. & Maguire, Daniel.

Newberry, Thomas. The Newberry Reference Bible. LC 73-189203. 1064p. 1992. lib. bdg. 49.99 (0-8254-3315-0); lib. bdg. 54.99 (0-8254-3318-5) Kregel.

— The Newberry Reference Bible. deluxe ed. LC 73-189203. 1064p. 1992. 79.99 (0-8254-3299-5); 84.99 (0-8254-3298-7) Kregel.

Newberry, Tina T. Kelli Tyler Extraordinaire. 120p. (Orig.). (J). (gr. 4-6). 1990. pap. text ed. 3.50 (0-936625-91-0, New Hope AL) Womans Mission Union.

Newbert, Chris. Within a Rainbowed Sea. 1987. 75.00 (0-941831-09-4); 95.00 (0-685-19505-8); pap. 34.95 (0-941831-52-3) Beyond Words Pub.

— Within a Rainbowed Sea. deluxe ed. 1987. 2,250.00 (0-941831-04-3) Beyond Words Pub.

Newbert, Christopher. Within a Rainbowed Sea: Ten Year Anniversary Edition. 2nd ed. Berry, Paul, ed. LC 94-21962. (Illus.). 220p. 1994. 75.00 (0-941831-99-X); pap. text ed. 39.95 (1-885223-00-5) Beyond Words Pub.

***Newbert, Christopher & Wilms, Birgitte.** In a Sea of Dreams. (Illus.). 204p. 1995. 75.00 (0-9642736-5-9) Fourth Day Pub.

***Newbery, David & Stern, Nicholas, eds.** Theory of Taxation for Developing Countries. 712p. 1987. 32.95 (0-614-02857-4, 60541) World Bank.

Newbery, J. G. Classic Convertibles. (Illus.). 112p. 1995. 14.98 (0-8317-1165-5) Smithmark.

— Muscle Cars. LC 94-19959. 1994. 19.98 (1-57145-007-6) Thunder Bay CA.

Newbery, J. G. & Horton, Chris. Sportscars Album. 256p. 1993. 19.98 (0-681-41868-0) Longmeadow Pr.

Newbery, P. G., jt. auth. see Wright, A.

Newbery, Timothy J., et al. Italian Renaissance Frames. (Illus.). 112p. 1990. pap. 16.95 (0-87099-589-8, Abrams) Metro Mus Art.

Newbigging, Thomas. Fables & Fabulists: Ancient & Modern. LC 76-37799. (Essay Index Reprint Ser.). 1977. reprint ed. 19.95 (0-8369-2615-3) Ayer.

Newbigin, Leslie. Mission in Christ's Way: Bible Studies. (Mission Ser.: No. 8). 48p. (Orig.). 1987. pap. 2.90 (2-8254-0900-6) Wrld Coun Churches.

Newbigin, Lesslie. Foolishness to the Greeks. 160p. (Orig.). 1986. pap. 12.99 (0-8028-0176-5) Eerdmans.

— Gospel in a Pluralist Society. 1990. pap. 14.99 (0-8028-0426-8) Eerdmans.

— Mission Agenda 2000. Jackson, Eleanor, ed. 208p. (Orig.). (C). 1994. pap. 14.99 (0-8028-0730-5) Eerdmans.

— Mission in Christ's Way: A Gift, a Command, an Assurance. 48p. 1988. pap. 2.95 (0-377-00190-2) Friendship Pr.

— The Open Secret. 192p. 1995. pap. 12.99 (0-8028-0829-8) Eerdmans.

— Proper Confidence: Faith, Doubt, & Certainty in Christian Discipleship. 112p. (Orig.). 1995. pap. 7.99 (0-8028-0856-5) Eerdmans.

— Truth to Tell: The Gospel As Public Truth. xvi, 74p. (Orig.). 1991. pap. 6.99 (0-8028-0607-4) Eerdmans.

— Unfinished Agenda. 352p. 1993. pap. 60.00 (0-7152-0687-7, Pub. by St Andrew UK) St Mut.

Newble, D. I. & Cannon, Robert. Handbook for Clinical Teachers. 148p. 1983. lib. bdg. 0.01 (0-85200-728-0) Kluwer Ac.

— A Handbook for Medical Teachers. 2nd ed. 160p. (C). 1987. lib. bdg. 28.50 (0-85200-673-X) Kluwer Ac.

***Newble, David.** A Handbook for Medical Teachers. 3rd ed. LC 94-22258. (Illus.). 185p. (C). 1994. lib. bdg. 32.00 (0-7923-8850-X) Kluwer Ac.

***Newble, David & Cannon, Robert.** Handbook for Teachers in Universities & Colleges. 176p. 1995. pap. 27.95x (0-7494-1669-6, Pub. by Kogan Page Educ UK) Taylor & Francis.

— A Handbook for Teachers in Universities & Colleges: A Guide to Improving Teaching Methods. LC 89-6044. 144p. 1989. pap. 15.95 (0-312-03196-3) St Martin.

— A Handbook for Teachers in Universities & Colleges: A Guide to Improving Teaching Methods. rev. ed. 162p. 1991. pap. 29.95 (0-7494-0512-0, Pub. by Kogan Page Educ UK) Taylor & Francis.

Newble, David, et al. The Certification & Recertification of Doctors: Issues in the Assessment of Clinical Competence. LC 92-48562. (Illus.). 220p. (C). 1994. 69.95 (0-521-43187-5) Cambridge U Pr.

Newble-De Graaf, Jane. Duchesse Lace: An Introduction. (Illus.). 120p. 1989. 39.95 (0-7134-5629-9, Pub. by Batsford UK) Trafalgar.

Newbold. Dr. Newbold's Revolutionary New. 1977. 1.25 (0-89256-014-2, Rawson Assocs) Macmillan.

Newbold & Bos, Theodore. Introductory Business & Economic Forecasting. 2nd ed. (C). 1994. text ed. 60.95 (0-538-82874-9, HG60BA) S-W Pub.

Newbold, Charles E., Jr., jt. auth. see O'Neil, Mike S.

***Newbold, Chris A.** 30 "Secrets" to Saving Money on Your Auto Insurance. (Illus.). (Orig.). 1995. pap. text ed. 9.95 (0-9646190-0-8) Newbold Ins.

Newbold, Greg. Punishment & Politics: The Maximum Security Prison in New Zealand. 304p. 1989. 39.95 (0-19-558179-2) OUP.

Newbold, H. L. Dr. Cox's Couch. 1979. 10.00 (0-8184-0282-2) Carol Pub Group.

— Dr. Newbold's Diet to Cure Incurable Diseases. Orig. Title: Dr. Newbold's Nutrition for Your Nerves. 385p. 1994. reprint ed. 29.98x (0-941683-30-3) Instant Improve.

— Dr. Newbold's Nutrition for Your Nerves. 368p. (Orig.). 1993. pap. 14.95 (0-87983-606-7) Keats.

— The Psychiatric Programming of People: Neo-Behavioral Orthomolecular Psychiatry. 170p. 1972. 56.00 (0-08-016791-8, Pub. by Pergamon Repr UK) Franklin.

Newbold, Henry. Long John. 1979. 10.00 (0-8184-0276-8) Carol Pub Group.

Newbold, Pat, jt. auth. see Diebel, Anne.

Newbold, Patt & Diebel, Anne. Paper Hat Tricks I: A Big Book of Hat Patterns Holidays, Careers, Characters, & Animals. (Illus.). 36p. (Orig.). 1988. pap. text ed. 13.95 (1-56422-999-8, Paper Hat) Start Reading.

— Paper Hat Tricks II: A Big Book of Hat Patterns Farm, Ocean, & Insect Hats. (Illus.). 36p. (Orig.). 1990. pap. text ed. 13.95 (1-56422-998-X, Paper Hat) Start Reading.

— Paper Hat Tricks, Vol. 4: A Big Book of Hat Patterns, Folklore, Fairytales, Foreign Lands & Long Ago Hats. 39p. (J). (ps-5). 1992. pap. text ed. 13.95 (1-56422-996-3, Paper Hat) Start Reading.

— Paper Hat Tricks, Vol. 5: A Big Book of Hat Patterns, Circus, Sports, Fun Foods, & Safety First Hats. 39p. (J). (ps-5). 1992. pap. text ed. 13.95 (1-56422-995-5, Paper Hat) Start Reading.

Newbold, Patt, jt. auth. see Diebel, Anne.

Newbold, Paul. Statistics for Business & Economics. (Illus.). 864p. (C). 1984. text ed. write for info. (0-13-845140-0) P-H.

— Statistics for Business & Economics. 4th ed. LC 94-33610. 1994. text ed. write for info. (0-13-181595-4) P-H.

Newbold, Paul & Bos, Theodore. Stochastic Parameter Regression Models. (Quantitative Applications in the Social Sciences Ser.: Vol. 51). 1985. 9.95 (0-8039-2425-9) Sage.

***Newbold, Peter & Wilson, Martin.** Practical Capital Allowances. 220p. 1994. boxed 88.00 (0-406-03484-2, UK) Butterworth Legal Pubs.

Newbold, Philip A., jt. auth. see Mack, Ken E.

***Newbolt, Henry.** The Island Race. LC 94-24513. (Decadents, Symbolists, Anti-Decadents Ser.). 1995. 48.00 (1-85477-152-3, Pub. by Woodstock Bks UK) Cassell.

Newbolt, Henry J. Studies, Green & Gray. LC 68-8485. (Essay Index Reprint Ser.). 1977. reprint ed. 20.95 (0-8369-0740-X) Ayer.

Newbolt, Henry J., comp. An English Anthology of Prose-Poetry: Showing the Main Stream of English Literature Through Six Centuries (14th Century-19th Century) LC 75-168785. (Granger Index Reprint Ser.). 1977. reprint ed. 50.95 (0-8369-6305-9) Ayer.

***Newbolt, Peter.** G. A. Henty, 1832-1902: A Bibliographical Study of His British Editions with Short Accounts of His Publishers, Illustrators, & Designers, & Notes on Production Methods Used for His Books. (Illus.). 650p. 1996. 85.95 (1-85928-208-3, Pub. by Scolar Pr UK) Ashgate Pub Co.

Newborn, Monty, jt. auth. see Levy, David N.

Newborn, Sasha, ed. First Person Intense, a Prose Anthology. LC 77-642342. 192p. (C). 1978. pap. 5.00 (0-930012-14-3) Bandanna Bks.

Newborn, Sasha, tr. see Sappho.

Newborn, Tony. Secrets of International Identity Change: New I. D. in Canada, England, Australia & New Zealand. (Illus.). 120p. 1985. pap. 17.95 (0-87364-532-4) Paladin Pr.

Newborne, M. J. A Guide to Freight Consolidation for Shippers. LC 76-10119. 1977. pap. 8.00 (0-87408-004-5) Intl Thom Trans Pr.

Newbould, Brian, contrib. Franz Schubert: Symphony No. 7 in E, D729: Realization by Brian Newbould. (Illus.). 220p. 1992. 45.00 (0-85958-471-2, Pub. by Hull Univ Pr UK) Paul & Co Pubs.

Newbould, Christopher & Beresford, Christine. The Glosters: An Illustrated History of a County Regiment. LC 92-34324. 1992. 20.00 (0-7509-0041-5) A Sutton Pub.

Newbould, Christopher, jt. auth. see Beresford, Christine.

Newbould, Gerald D. & Luffman, George A. Successful Business Policies. LC 78-70561. 235p. 1979. text ed. 55.00 (0-275-90400-8, C0400, Praeger Pubs) Greenwood.

Newbould, Ian. Whiggery & Reform, 1830-41: The Politics of Government. LC 89-62180. 410p. 1991. 47.50 (0-8047-1759-1) Stanford U Pr.

Newbound, Betty. Blue Ridge Dinnerware. 3rd ed. 1989. pap. 14.95 (0-89145-391-1) Collector Bks.

— Collector's Encyclopedia of Milk Glass. 1994. pap. 24.95 (0-89145-626-0) Collector Bks.

— Collector's Guide to Blue Ridge Dinnerware. 1994. pap. 18.95 (0-89145-583-3) Collector Bks.

Newbro, Frank. Life Against Itself. LC 92-90941. 238p. (Orig.). 1992. pap. 4.75 (0-9633736-0-9) F Newbro.

Newbrough, Jennie & Greenwood, Carol. Support Group Leaders Guide. 150p. 1993. pap. 12.95 (1-56616-005-7, 572047) Aglow Communs.

Newbrun. Cariology. 3rd ed. (Illus.). 392p. 1989. text ed. 58.00 (0-86715-205-2) Quint Pub Co.

Newburn, R. L., Jr., et al, eds. Comets in the Post-Halley Era, 2 vols., Set. (C). 1991. lib. bdg. 196.00 (0-7923-1164-7); pap. text ed. 61.50 (0-7923-1165-5) Kluwer Ac.

Newburn, Tim. Disaster & After: Social Work in the Aftermath of Disaster. 160p. 1993. pap. 37.50 (1-85302-170-9, Pub. by J Kingsley Pubs UK) Taylor & Francis.

— Making a Difference? Social Work after Hillsborough. 1993. pap. 35.00 (0-902789-81-3, Pub. by Natl Inst Soc Work) St Mut.

Newburn, Tim & Stanko, Elizabeth, eds. Just Boys Doing the Business: Men, Masculinities & Crime. 256p. 1994. 69.95 (0-415-09321-X, B3742) Routledge.

***Newburn, Tim & Stanko, Elizabeth A., eds.** Just Boys Doing Business? Men, Masculinities & Crime. 304p. 1995. pap. 18.95 (0-415-09320-1, C0402) Routledge.

Newbury. CoBuild English Learner's Dictionary. (C). 1990. pap. text ed. 23.50 (0-06-632697-4) HarpCollege.

Newbury, Anthony. All You Can Eat Diet. (Orig.). 1986. pap. 14.95 (0-9601978-4-2) Health Res Las Vegas.

Newbury, Catharine. The Cohesion of Oppression: Clientship & Ethnicity in Ruanda, 1860-1960. (Illus.). 336p. (C). 1993. text ed. 47.00 (0-231-06256-7); pap. 18.50 (0-231-06257-5) Col U Pr.

Newbury, Colin. British Policy Towards West Africa: Selected Documents, 2 vols., Set. (Modern Revivals in African Studies). 1992. 125.95 (0-7512-0084-0, Pub. by Gregg Pub UK) Ashgate Pub Co.

— British Policy Towards West Africa Vol. 1: Selected Documents. 1992. Vol. 1, 1786-1874. 62.95 (0-7512-0082-4, Pub. by Gregg Pub UK) Ashgate Pub Co.

— British Policy Towards West Africa Vol. 2: Selected Documents. 1992. Vol. 2, 1875-1914. write for info. (0-7512-0083-2, Pub. by Gregg Pub UK) Ashgate Pub Co.

Newbury, Colin W. The Diamond Ring: Business, Politics, & Precious Stones in South Africa, 1867-1945. (Illus.). 448p. 1990. 89.00 (0-19-821775-7) OUP.

— The Western Slave Coast & Its Rulers: European Trade & Administration among the Yoruba & Adja-Speaking Peoples of Southwestern Nigeria, Southern Dahomey & Togo. LC 83-12619. ix, 234p. 1983. reprint ed. text ed. 55.00 (0-313-23967-3, NEWE) Greenwood.

Newbury, Dale E., ed. see Heinrich, K. F.

Newbury, Dale E., et al. Advanced Scanning Electron Microscopy & X-Ray Microanalysis. LC 85-28261. 466p. 1986. 49.50 (0-306-42140-2, Plenum Pr) Plenum.

Newbury, David. Kings & Clans: Ijwi Island & the Lake Kivu Rift, 1780-1840. LC 91-28932. (Illus.). 384p. (Orig.). (C). 1992. lib. bdg. 50.00 (0-299-12890-3); pap. 19.95 (0-299-12894-6) U of Wis Pr.

Newbury, Donald. Survivor after the Pole Shift. abr. ed. 270p. 1995. pap. 8.95 (1-56901-476-0) NW Pub.

Newbury, Kenneth. Life Skills Handbook. (Illus.). 48p. (YA). (gr. 9-12). 1993. 9.95 (0-7854-0057-5, 15168); text ed. 6.95 (0-7854-0056-7, 15167) Am Guidance.

Newbury, L. E. I Now Start My Life Story. (C). 1989. 22.00 (0-7223-2216-X, Pub. by A H S Ltd UK) St Mut.

Newbury, Nathan, et al. Princeton Problems in Physics with Solutions. 336p. 1991. pap. text ed. 19.95 (0-691-02449-9) Princeton U Pr.

Newbury, Paul A. A Geography of Agriculture. LC 86-18154. 334p. reprint ed. pap. 95.20 (0-7837-4031-X, 2043860) Bks Demand.

Newbury, Robert L. Secret Doors & Treasure. LC 90-71968. 64p. (J). 1993. pap. 6.95 (1-56002-029-6, Univ Edtns) Aegina Pr.

Newbury, Susan L., jt. auth. see Delgado-Gomez, Angel.

Newbury, Susan L., jt. auth. see Fiering, Norman.

Newbury, Susan L., jt. auth. see Johnson, Julie G.

***Newbury, Tim.** The Ultimate Garden Designer. (Illus.). 256p. 1995. 35.00 (0-7063-7335-9, Pub. by Ward Lock UK) Sterling.

Newby & Niemeier, eds. Formability of Metallic Materials, 2,000 A.D. - STP 753. 331p. 1981. 39.50 (0-8031-0742-0, 04-753000-23) ASTM.

Newby, Bruce & Clayton, George B. Operational Amplifiers. 3rd ed. (Illus.). 559p. 1993. pap. 34.95 (0-7506-0640-1) Buttrwrth-Heinemann.

Newby, Bruce W. G. Electronic Signal Conditioning. LC 93-51084. 1994. 18.50 (0-7506-1844-2) Buttrwrth-Heinemann.

Newby, Elizabeth L. Bracera Con Esperanza. 144p. 1992. pap. 8.95 (0-944350-23-2) Friends United.

— Migrant with Hope. 144p. 1992. pap. 7.95 (0-8054-7218-5) Friends United.

Newby, Eric. Round Ireland in Low Gear. 308p. 1989. pap. 11.00 (0-14-009588-8, Penguin Bks) Viking Penguin.

Newby, Eric, comp. A Book of Travellers' Tales. 576p. 1987. pap. 10.95 (0-14-009567-5, Penguin Bks) Viking Penguin.

Newby, F. How to Find Out about Patents. LC 66-30632. 1967. 83.00 (0-08-012333-3, Pub. by Pergamon Repr UK) Franklin.

***Newby-Fraser, Paula & Mora, John.** Paula Newby-Fraser's Peak Fitness for Women. LC 94-40070. (Illus.). 216p. (Orig.). 1995. pap. write for info. (0-87322-672-0, PNEW0672) Human Kinetics.

Newby, Gordon D. A History of the Jews of Arabia: From Ancient Times to Their Eclipse under Islam. Denny, Frederick M., ed. (Studies in Comparative Religion). 189p. (C). 1988. text ed. 34.95 (0-87249-558-2) U of SC Pr.

— The Making of the Last Prophet: A Reconstruction of the Earliest Biography of Muhammad. 276p. (Orig.). 1989. pap. 18.95 (0-87249-623-6) U of SC Pr.

Newby, Grace, jt. auth. see Albritton, Clarice.

***Newby, Greg B., ed.** Web Site Yellow Pages. 400p. 1995. pap. 29.95 (0-88736-996-0) Mecklermedia.

Newby, Gregory B. Directory of Directories on the Internet. (Supplement to Small Computers in Libraries Ser.: No. 33). 175p. 1993. pap. text ed. 29.50 (0-88736-768-2) Mecklermedia.

Newby, Gregory B., jt. auth. see Peek, Robin P.

Newby, Hayes A. & Popelka, Gerald R. Audiology. 6th ed. 512p. (C). 1992. text ed. write for info. (0-13-051921-9) P-H.

Newby, Howard, ed. International Perspectives in Rural Sociology. LC 77-21274. 230p. reprint ed. pap. 65.60 (0-317-07765-1, 2022403) Bks Demand.

Newby, Howard, jt. ed. see Bell, Colin.

Newby, Howard, jt. ed. see Buttel, Frederick H.

Newby, Howard, jt. auth. see Lee, David.

Newby, Howard, et al. Property, Paternalism, & Power: Class & Control in Rural England. LC 78-20301. 432p. reprint ed. pap. 123.20 (0-8357-6797-3, 2035473) Bks Demand.

Newby, I. A. Plain Folk in the New South: Social Change & Cultural Persistence, 1880-1915. LC 88-17439. 588p. 1989. text ed. 42.50 (0-8071-1456-1) La State U Pr.

Newby, I. A., ed. Civil War & Reconstruction, 1850-1877. (Literature of History Ser.). (Orig.). (C). 1971. pap. text ed. 14.95 (0-89197-081-9) Irvington.

Newby, Idus A. Jim Crow's Defense: Anti-Negro Thought in America, Nineteen Hundred to Nineteen Thirty. LC 80-11253. xv, 230p. 1980. reprint ed. text ed. 35.00 (0-313-22353-X, NEJC, Greenwood Pr) Greenwood.

— Jim Crow's Defense: Anti-Negro Thought in America, 1900-1930. LC 65-20297. 246p. reprint ed. pap. 70.20 (0-317-28771-0, 2051684) Bks Demand.

Newby, James R. Reflections from the Light of Christ: 5 Quaker Classics. LC 80-7477. 126p. 1980. 7.95 (0-913408-55-7) Friends United.

Newby, John R., ed. Source Book on Forming of Steel Sheet: A Discriminative Selection of Outstanding Articles from the Periodical & Reference Literature. LC 76-28176. (American Society for Metals. Engineering Bookshelf Ser.). (Illus.). 399p. reprint ed. pap. 113.80 (0-317-11148-5, 2019498) Bks Demand.

Newby, Leroy W. Into the Guns of Ploesti. (Illus.). 250p. 1991. pap. 12.95 (0-87938-494-8) Motorbooks Intl.

— Target Ploesti. 384p. 1986. pap. 3.50 (0-8217-1902-5) Zebra.

Newby, Leroy W., jt. auth. see Armstrong, Robert H.

Newby, Lorraine D. Waukegan Schools: A History in Sketches, 1840's-1990's. Schornick, Lynn, ed. LC 89-52037. (Illus.). 48p. (Orig.). 1989. pap. 10.00 (0-9625103-0-0) Waukegan Pk Dist.

Newby, M. & Poole, E. Investigating Food - Pupils Book. (C). 1990. 60.00 (0-685-47487-9, Pub. by S Thornes Pubs UK) St Mut.

Newby, P. H. Saladin in His Time. 1992. 19.95 (0-88029-775-1) Marboro Bks.

***Newby, Peter, ed.** The Mammoth Book of Astounding Word Games. 512p. 1995. pap. 9.95 (0-7867-0213-3) Carroll & Graf.

Newby, Richard. The Structure of English: A Handbook of English Grammar. 112p. 1987. pap. 8.95 (0-521-34996-6) Cambridge U Pr.

Newby, Rick. Great Escapes: Montana State Parks. (Illus.). 80p. 1988. pap. 5.95 (0-937959-42-1) Falcon Pr MT.

— Old Friends Walking in the Mountains. (Illus.). 104p. (Orig.). 1994. pap. 11.95 (1-56044-312-X) Falcon Pr MT.

Newby, Rick, jt. auth. see Grosskopf, Linda A.

Newby, Rick, jt. auth. see Grosskopf, Linda.

Newby, Robert. King Midas. (Books about Awareness & Caring Ser.). (Illus.). 64p. (J). (gr. 1-6). 1990. lib. bdg. 15.95 (1-878363-25-5) Forest Hse.

— King Midas: With Selected Sentences in American Sign Language. LC 90-4908. (Illus.). 72p. (J). (gr. 1-5). 1990. 14.95 (0-930323-75-0); vhs 38.20 (0-930323-77-7); vhs 29.00 (0-930323-71-8) Gallaudet Univ Pr.

— Sleeping Beauty. (Awareness & Caring - Sign Language Storybook Ser.). (Illus.). 64p. (J). (gr. k-3). 1992. lib. bdg. 15.95 (1-56674-035-5) Forest Hse.

— Sleeping Beauty: With Selected Sentences in American Sign Language. LC 91-29729. (Illus.). 64p. (J). (gr. 1-7). 1992. vhs 38.20 (*1-56368-009-2*, Pub. by K Green Pubns) Gallaudet Univ Pr.

— Sleeping Beauty: With Selected Sentences in American Sign Language. LC 91-29729. (Illus.). 64p. (J). (gr. 1-7). 1992. 14.95 (*0-930323-97-1*); vhs 29.00 (*0-930323-98-X*) Gallaudet Univ Pr.

Newby, T. J. & Stokes, C. R., eds. Local Immune Responses of the GUT. LC 83-26321. 264p. 1984. 129.00 (*0-8493-5534-6*, QR186, CRC Reprint) Franklin.

***Newby, Tony.** Validating Your Training. 136p. (C). 1992. pap. 45.00x (*0-7494-0551-1*, Pub. by IPM Hse UK) St Mut.

Newcity, Michael. Tax Reform in Russia: Statutes, Regulations & Treaties. 1994. ring bd. 185.00 (*1-56425-001-6*) Transnatl Juris Pubns.

Newcity, Michael A. Taxation in the Soviet Union. LC 85-19359. 406p. 1986. text ed. 59.95 (*0-275-92005-4*, C2005, Praeger Pubs) Greenwood.

***Newcomb.** Arrow Keeper's Song. 1995. mass mkt. (*0-553-56955-4*) Bantam.

Newcomb, jt. auth. see Connable.

Newcomb, Anthony. The Madrigal at Ferrara, Fifteen Seventy-Nine to Fifteen Ninety-Seven, 2 vols., Vol. 1. LC 78-573. (Princeton Studies in Music: No. 7). 318p. reprint ed. pap. 82.70 (*0-8357-4646-1*, 2037577) Bks Demand.

— The Madrigal at Ferrara, Fifteen Seventy-Nine to Fifteen Ninety-Seven, 2 vols., Vol. 2. LC 78-573. (Princeton Studies in Music: No. 7). 230p. reprint ed. pap. 65.60 (*0-8357-4647-X*) Bks Demand.

Newcomb, Benjamin H. Franklin & Galloway: A Political Partnership. LC 72-75205. 344p. reprint ed. pap. 98.10 (*0-8357-8136-4*, 2033842) Bks Demand.

— Political Partisanship in the American Middle Colonies, 1700-1776. 328p. (C). 1995. text ed. 37.50 (*0-8071-1875-3*) La State U Pr.

Newcomb, Charles K. The Journals of Charles King Newcomb. Johnson, Judith K., ed. LC 46-3324. (Brown University Studies: 10). 310p. reprint ed. 88.40 (*0-685-15762-8*, 2027520) Bks Demand.

Newcomb, Donald L. & Rimler, George W. The Reduction in Force Testament. LC 89-92738. 84p. (Orig.). 1989. pap. text ed. 24.95 (*0-9625257-0-7*) LACY Pub VA.

Newcomb, Duane. Small Space, Big Harvest: Turn Your Small Garden into a Vegetable Factory - Naturally. LC 92-39921. 264p. (Orig.). 1993. pap. 14.95 (*1-55958-289-8*) Prima Pub.

Newcomb, Duane & Newcomb, Karen. California Vegetable Patch: The Organic Gardener's Complete Reference Almanac. LC 94-17780. 1995. pap. 20.00 (*0-06-258554-1*) HarpC West.

Newcomb, Everett W., Jr. The Creatures Nobody Loves. LC 91-66375. (Illus.). 48p. (J). (gr. 4-6). 1991. pap. 3.95 (*0-9627974-3-X*) Tabby Hse Bks.

Newcomb, Franc J. Hosteen Klah: Navaho Medicine Man & Sand Painter. LC 64-20759. (Civilization of the American Indian Ser.: No. 73). (Illus.). 227p. 1972. reprint ed. pap. 15.95 (*0-8061-1008-2*) U of Okla Pr.

— Navaho Folktales. LC 90-39570. (Illus.). 228p. 1990. reprint ed. pap. 11.95 (*0-8263-1231-4*) U of NM Pr.

Newcomb, Geneva R. Please Hold My Hand. (Illus.). 78p. (Orig.). 1989. 9.95 (*0-9622762-1-9*); pap. 4.95 (*0-9622762-0-0*) Non-Fictitious.

Newcomb, H. R. United States Copper Cents (1816-1857) (Illus.). 1988. reprint ed. lib. bdg. 45.00 (*0-942666-51-8*) S J Durst.

Newcomb, H. T. The Work of the Interstate Commerce Commission. Bruchey, Stuart, ed. LC 80-1334. (Railroads Ser.). (Illus.). 1981. reprint ed. lib. bdg. 15.95 (*0-405-13808-3*) Ayer.

Newcomb, Horace, ed. Television: The Critical View. 5th ed. 512p. (C). 1994. pap. text ed. 19.95 (*0-19-508528-0*) OUP.

Newcomb, Howard R. United States Copper Cents Eighteen Sixteen to Eighteen Fifty-Seven. LC 81-50923. (Illus.). 288p. 1981. reprint ed. lib. bdg. 50.00 (*0-88000-127-5*) Quarterman.

Newcomb, J. B. Genealogical Memoir of the Newcomb Family Containing Records of Nearly Every Person of the Name in America from 1635-1874. (Illus.). 600p. 1989. reprint ed. lib. bdg. 86.00 (*0-8328-0902-0*); reprint ed. pap. 76.00 (*0-8328-0903-9*) Higginson Bk Co.

Newcomb, Joan I. John F. Kennedy: An Annotated Bibliography. LC 77-7568. 143p. 1977. 20.00 (*0-8108-1042-5*) Scarecrow.

Newcomb, John. The Book of Graphic Problem Solving: How to Get Visual Ideas When You Need Them. 256p. 1984. pap. 39.95 (*0-8352-1895-3*) Bowker.

Newcomb, John T. Wallace Stevens & Literary Canons. LC 91-31930. 1992. 35.00 (*0-87805-525-8*) U Pr of Miss.

Newcomb, Karen, jt. auth. see Newcomb, Duane.

Newcomb, Kerry. Scorpion. 1994. mass mkt. 4.99 (*0-553-29447-4*) Bantam.

Newcomb, Kerry & Schaefer, Frank. Pandora Man. 1980. pap. 1.95 (*0-449-24205-6*, Crest) Fawcett.

Newcomb, L. H., et al. Methods of Teaching Agriculture. 2nd ed. 362p. 1993. 29.95 (*0-8134-2952-8*) Interstate.

Newcomb, Lawrence. Newcomb's Wildflower Guide: An Ingenious New Key System for Quick, Positive Field Identification of Wildflowers, Flowering Shrubs & Vines. (Illus.). 520p. 1977. 24.95 (*0-316-60441-0*) Little.

— Newcomb's Wildflower Guide: An Ingenious New Key System for Quick, Positive Field Identification of Wildflowers, Flowering Shrubs & Vines. (Illus.). 520p. 1989. pap. 17.95 (*0-316-60442-9*) Little.

Newcomb, Michael D. Drug Use in the Workplace. LC 87-34921. 180p. 1988. text ed. 55.00 (*0-86569-182-7*, Auburn Hse) Greenwood.

Newcomb, Mildred. The Imagined World of Charles Dickens. 256p. 1989. text ed. 47.50 (*0-8142-0482-1*) Ohio St U Pr.

Newcomb, Norma. Boss Lady. large type ed. (Dales Ser.). 192p. 1994. pap. 16.95 (*1-85389-435-4*, Dales) Ulverscroft.

— Brownstone Angel. large type ed. 1992. 19.95 (*0-7927-0911-X*, Curley Lrg Print); pap. 17.95 (*0-7927-0912-8*, Curley Lrg Print) Chivers N Amer.

Newcomb, Peggy C. Popular Annuals of Eastern North America, 1865-1914. LC 84-1674. (Illus.). 208p. (Orig.). 1985. pap. 15.00 (*0-88402-138-6*) Dumbarton Oaks.

Newcomb, Rexford. Spanish-Colonial Architecture in the United States. 1990. pap. 12.95 (*0-486-26263-4*) Dover.

Newcomb, Richard. Future Resources: Their Geostatistical Appraisal. 179p. 1982. 20.00 (*0-937058-13-0*) West Va U Pr.

Newcomb, Richard F. Iwo Jima. 320p. 1988. pap. 3.95 (*0-553-27547-X*) Bantam.

Newcomb, Robert D. & Marshall, Edwin C. Public Health & Community Optometry. 2nd ed. (Illus.). 424p. 1990. text ed. 59.95 (*0-409-90107-5*) Buttrwrth-Heinemann.

Newcomb, Robert T. Janissa. 1943. 8.00 (*0-685-08807-3*) Destiny.

Newcomb, Robinson. Mobile Home Parks: An Analysis of Characteristics, Pt. 1. LC 76-167878. (Urban Land Institute, Technical Bulletin Ser.: No. 66). 80p. reprint ed. pap. 25.00 (*0-317-29759-7*, 2017357) Bks Demand.

Newcomb, S. B. & Bennett, M. J., eds. Microscopy of Oxidation 2: Proceedings of the 2nd International Conference Held in Selwyn College, University of Cambridge, March 1993. (Illus.). 600p. 1993. 170.00 (*0-901716-50-2*, Pub. by Inst Materials UK) Ashgate Pub Co.

Newcomb, Sarah, jt. auth. see Ajemian, Shari.

Newcomb, Simon. His Wisdom, the Defender. LC 74-16513. (Science Fiction Ser.). (Illus.). 338p. 1975. reprint ed. 28.95 (*0-405-06308-3*) Ayer.

— Plain Man's Talk on the Labor Question. LC 77-89756. (American Labor, from Conspiracy to Collective Bargaining Ser., No. 1). 195p. 1978. reprint ed. 17.95 (*0-405-02143-7*) Ayer.

— Principles of Political Economy. LC 65-26372. (Reprints of Economic Classics Ser.). xvi, 548p. 1966. reprint ed. 49.50 (*0-678-00156-1*) Kelley.

Newcomb, T. P. & Spurr, R. T. A Technical History of the Motorcar. (Illus.). 430p. 1989. 91.00 (*0-85274-074-3*) IOP Pub.

Newcomb, Theodore M. & Wilson, Everett K., eds. College Peer Groups: Problems & Prospects for Research. LC 65-29033. (Monographs in Social Research: No. 8). 1966. 10.95 (*0-202-09002-7*) NORC.

Newcomb, Theodore M., jt. auth. see Feldman, Kenneth A.

Newcomb, Tim, jt. auth. see Keiter, Robert S.

Newcomb, V. N. Practical Accounting for Business Studies. LC 82-11103. 380p. reprint ed. pap. 108.30 (*0-317-41955-2*, 2025984) Bks Demand.

— Practical Calculations for Business Studies: Problems & Applications for Students in Africa. LC 80-42019. 164p. reprint ed. pap. 46.80 (*0-318-34688-5*, 2031760) Bks Demand.

Newcomb, William W., Jr. German Artist on the Texas Frontier: Friedrich Richard Petri. LC 77-28620. (Illus.). 258p. 1978. 35.00 (*0-292-72717-8*) U of Tex Pr.

— The Indians of Texas: From Prehistoric to Modern Times. LC 60-14312. (Texas History Paperbacks Ser.: No. 4). (Illus.). 422p. (C). 1961. 29.95 (*0-292-73271-6*); pap. 12.95 (*0-292-78425-2*) U of Tex Pr.

Newcomb, William W., jt. ed. see Davis, Edward M.

Newcombe, Barry. Tennis: Tactics of Success. (Illus.). 80p. (YA). (gr. 10-12). 1992. pap. 8.95 (*0-7063-7098-8*, Pub. by Ward Lock UK) Sterling.

***Newcombe, D. G.** Henry VIII & the English Reformation. LC 94-39263. (Lancaster Pamphlets Ser.). 1995. write for info. (*0-415-10728-8*) Routledge.

Newcombe, David S. Inherited Biochemical Disorders & Uric Acid Metabolism. 298p. reprint ed. pap. 85.00 (*0-317-26192-4*, 2052074) Bks Demand.

Newcombe, David S., et al, eds. Clinical Immunotoxicology. 464p. 1992. 100.00 (*0-88167-830-9*) Raven.

Newcombe, Ellen. Mentoring Programs for New Teachers. 24p. 1988. pap. 5.95 (*1-56602-021-2*) Research Better.

— Perspectives on Teacher Induction: A Review of the Literature & Promising Program Models. 98p. 1990. pap. 16.95 (*1-56602-033-6*) Research Better.

Newcombe, Howard B. Handbook of Record Linkage: Methods for Health & Statistical Studies, Administration, & Business. (Illus.). 224p. 1988. 55.00 (*0-19-261732-X*) OUP.

Newcombe, P. Judson. Voice & Diction. 2nd ed. (Illus.). 317p. (C). 1991. pap. text ed. 32.95 (*0-89892-063-9*) Contemp Pub Co of Raleigh.

***Newcombe, Tod.** The Local Government Guide to Imaging Systems: Planning & Implementation. (Special Report Ser.). (Illus.). 120p. 1995. pap. 70.00 (*0-87326-097-X*) Intl City-Cnty Mgt.

Newcombe, Tod, ed. Solutions for Technology-Sharing Networks, 1988-89. 484p. (Orig.). 1988. pap. 25.00 (*1-55657-007-4*) Pub Tech Inc.

Newcome, Robert & Newcome, Zita. Little Lion. (Illus.). 32p. (J). (ps-1). 1993. 17.95 (*1-85681-181-6*, Pub. by J MacRae UK) Trafalgar.

Newcome, Zita. Rosie Goes Exploring. (Illus.). 32p. (J). (ps-00). 1992. 11.95 (*1-85681-170-0*, Pub. by J MacRae UK) Trafalgar.

Newcome, Zita, jt. auth. see Newcome, Robert.

Newcomer, C. Armour. Cole's Cavalry: Or, Three Years in the Saddle in the Shenandoah Valley. LC 76-126245. (Select Bibliographies Reprint Ser.). 1977. 16.95 (*0-8369-5472-6*) Ayer.

Newcomer, James. Lady Morgan the Novelist. LC 89-43054. 104p. 1990. 26.50 (*0-8387-5177-6*) Bucknell U Pr.

— Maria Edgeworth. LC 77-125886. (Irish Writers Ser.). 94p. 1975. pap. 1.95 (*0-8387-7732-5*) Bucknell U Pr.

— The Resonance of Grace. pap. 5.00 (*0-318-04288-6*) Latitudes Pr.

Newcomer, Larry R. SELECT...SQL: The Relational Database Language. 446p. (C). 1991. pap. write for info. (*0-02-386693-4*) McGraw.

Newcomer, Lawrence. Schaum's Outline of Structured COBOL Programming. 2nd ed. (Schaum's Outline Ser.). 1994. pap. text ed. 13.95 (*0-07-038019-8*) McGraw.

Newcomer, Lawrence R. Schaum's Outline of Theory & Problems of Programming with Advanced Structured COBOL: With File Structured Systems Development & Interactive Considerations. (Illus.). 350p. (C). 1986. pap. text ed. 11.95 (*0-07-037999-8*) McGraw.

— Schaum's Outline of Theory & Problems of Programming with Structured COBOL. (Illus.). 375p. (C). 1984. pap. text ed. 12.95 (*0-07-037998-X*) McGraw.

Newcomer, Mabel. A Century of Higher Education for American Women. LC 75-40214. 1976. reprint ed. 19.95 (*0-89201-002-9*) Zenger Pub.

— Separation of State & Local Revenues in the United States. LC 68-56675. (Columbia University. Studies in the Social Sciences: No. 180). reprint ed. 17.50 (*0-404-51180-5*) AMS Pr.

Newcomer, Phyllis L. Readings in Emotional Disturbance. LC 93-5040. 245p. 1993. pap. text ed. 19.00 (*0-89079-588-6*, 6666) PRO-ED.

— Understanding & Teaching Emotionally Disturbed Children & Adolescents. 2nd rev. ed. LC 92-33990. (C). 1993. text ed. 39.00 (*0-89079-575-4*, 6575) PRO-ED.

Newcomer, Ruth, jt. ed. see Woolfolk, Doug.

Newcomer, Victor D. & Young, Edward M., Jr. Geriatric Dermatology: Clinical Diagnosis & Practical Therapy. LC 88-9192. (Illus.). 720p. 1989. 159.50 (*0-89640-149-9*) Igaku-Shoin.

***Newdick.** Scented Gifts. 1995. 9.99 (*0-517-12154-9*) Random Hse Value.

***Newdick, Christopher.** Who Should We Treat? Law, Patients, & Resources in the NHS. 320p. 1995. 49.95 (*0-19-825924-7*); pap. 21.00 (*0-19-825925-5*) OUP.

Newdick, Jane. At Home with Herbs. LC 94-20669. (Illus.). 224p. 1994. 29.95 (*0-88266-886-2*, Storey Pub) Storey Comm Inc.

— The Birthday Book. (Illus.). 160p. 1995. 9.98 (*0-8317-0689-9*) Smithmark.

— Country Flower Style: Creating the Natural Look. (Illus.). 120p. 1995. 24.95 (*0-7892-0013-9*) Abbeville Pr.

— Five Minute Centerpiece. 1991. 18.00 (*0-517-58226-0*, Crown) Crown Pub Group.

— Five Minute Flower Arranger. 1989. 18.00 (*0-517-57342-3*, Crown) Crown Pub Group.

— Flower Arranger's Handbook. 1994. 12.99 (*0-517-12052-6*) Random Hse Value.

— Flower Arranging. 1989. 29.99 (*0-517-68027-0*) Random Hse Value.

— Period Flowers: Designs for Today Inspired by Centuries of Floral Art. (Illus.). 160p. 1991. 30.00 (*0-517-58428-X*, Crown) Crown Pub Group.

— Victorian Flowercrafts. (Illus.). 128p. 1994. 17.95 (*0-87596-603-9*) Rodale Pr Inc.

Newdick, Robert S., jt. auth. see Sutton, William A.

***Newell.** Using Nursing Case Management to Improve Health Outcomes: Recasting Theory, Tools & Care Delivery. 350p. 1994. 59.00 (*0-8342-0623-4*) Aspen Pub.

Newell & Lee. Applied Process Control: A Case Study. 1989. text ed. 26.80 (*0-13-040940-5*) P-H.

Newell, jt. auth. see Spitz, Margaret R.

Newell, A. C., ed. see Benjamin, T. B. & Benney, D. J.

Newell, Abraham. Hillside View of Industrial History: A Study of Industrial Evolution in the Pennine Highlands. LC 73-119540. (Reprints of Economic Classics Ser.). (Illus.). vii, 281p. 1971. reprint ed. 39.50 (*0-678-00695-4*) Kelley.

Newell, Alan C. Solitons in Mathematics & Physics. LC 84-71051. (CBMS-NSF Regional Conference Ser.: No. 48). xvi, 244p. (Orig.). 1985. text ed. 38.25 (*0-89871-196-7*) Soc Indus-Appl Math.

Newell, Alan C., jt. auth. see Moloney, Jerome V.

Newell, Alex. The Soliloquies in Hamlet: The Structural Design. LC 89-46410. (Illus.). 192p. 1991. 36.50 (*0-8386-3404-4*) Fairleigh Dickinson.

Newell, Allen. Unified Theories of Cognition. (Illus.). 549p. 1990. 47.00 (*0-674-92099-6*) HUP.

— Unified Theories of Cognition. 549p. 1994. pap. 21.00 (*0-674-92101-1*) HUP.

Newell, Allen & Simon, Herbert A. Human Problem Solving. LC 79-152528. (Illus.). 1972. text ed. 52.00 (*0-13-445403-0*) P-H.

Newell, Ann. Moon Puddles. (Illus.). 30p. (Orig.). 1983. pap. text ed. 4.50 (*0-912549-02-5*) Bread & Butter.

Newell, Arlo. Blessed Assurance as Revealed in Scripture. 1989. pap. 3.95 (*0-685-51751-9*, D1550) Warner Pr.

— The Church of God As Revealed in Scripture. 1983. pap. 1.95 (*0-87162-269-6*, D4775) Warner Pr.

Newell, Arlo F. Receive the Holy Spirit. 1984. pap. 3.95 (*0-87162-409-5*, D6431) Warner Pr.

Newell, Arlo F., ed. see Byrum, Russell R.

Newell, Arthur. A Knight of the Toilers. LC 74-22799. reprint ed. 39.50 (*0-404-58455-1*) AMS Pr.

***Newell, Bruce, et al.** Pocket Guide to Basic Canoeing. (Illus.). 28p. 1994. spiral bd. 12.95 (*1-886127-00-X*) Greycliff Pub.

Newell, C. F. Application of Queueing Theory. 2nd ed. (Monographs on Statistics & Applied Probability). 220p. 1982. 42.50 (*0-412-24500-0*, 6620) Chapman & Hall.

Newell, Cam, ed. see Restany, Pierre.

Newell, Charldean, ed. Effective Local Government Manager. 2nd ed. LC 93-17353. (Municipal Management Ser.). 1993. 39.95 (*0-87326-090-2*); pap. 32.00 (*0-87326-091-0*) Intl City-Cnty Mgt.

Newell, Charldean, jt. auth. see Ammons, David N.

Newell, Charldean, jt. auth. see Kraemer, Richard H.

Newell, Chester. History of the Revolution in Texas. LC 72-9462. (Far Western Frontier Ser.). (Illus.). 230p. 1978. reprint ed. 24.95 (*0-405-04990-0*) Ayer.

***Newell, Christopher.** The Grosvenor Gallery Exhibitions: Change & Continuity in the Victorian Art World. (Art, Patrons & Public Ser.). (Illus.). 230p. (C). 1994. 79.95 (*0-521-46493-5*) Cambridge U Pr.

Newell, Claire, jt. auth. see Mcdowell, Ian.

Newell, Clarence A. Class Size & Adaptability, Including Observations on Invention: A Study of Selected Elementary School Classes in New Jersey. LC 70-177119. (Columbia University. Teachers College. Contributions to Education Ser.: No. 894). reprint ed. 37.50 (*0-404-55894-1*) AMS Pr.

— Human Behavior in Educational Administration: A Behavioral Science Interpretation. (Illus.). 1978. text ed. write for info. (*0-13-444638-0*) P-H.

— Old Glass Paperweights of Southern New Jersey: An American Folk Art. LC 87-62586. (Illus.). 96p. 1989. pap. 15.00 (*0-9619547-0-1*) Papier Presse.

Newell, Clayton. The Framework of Operational Warfare. (Operational Level of War Ser.). 256p. 1991. 30.00 (*0-415-05045-6*, A6243) Routledge.

Newell, Clayton R. & Krause, Michael D., eds. On Operational Art. 1994. write for info. (*0-318-72957-1*) USGPO.

Newell, Coke. Dying Words: Colombian Journalists & the Cocaine Warlords. Maxwell, Marilyn C., ed. 192p. (Orig.). 1991. pap. 23.00 (*0-9630149-0-0*) Red Mesa.

Newell, Colin. Methods & Models in Demography. LC 88-45079. 217p. 1988. reprint ed. pap. 18.95 (*0-89862-451-7*) Guilford Pr.

Newell, D. G., ed. Campylobacter: Progress in Research. (Illus.). 400p. 1982. lib. bdg. 121.00 (*0-85200-455-9*) Kluwer Ac.

Newell, David. Aspects of Employment Law. 217p. (C). 1990. 78.00 (*1-85190-105-1*, Pub. by Tolley Pubng UK) St Mut.

— The Law of Journalism. 1995. boxed write for info. (*0-406-02602-5*, UK) Butterworth Legal Pubs.

Newell, David M. If Nothin' Don't Happen. LC 74-7745. (Illus.). 256p. 1975. 19.95 (*0-394-49312-5*, 49312) Knopf.

Newell, David W. & Aaslid, Rune. Transcranial Doppler. 288p. 1992. 173.50 (*0-88167-836-8*) Raven.

Newell, Diane, ed. The Development of the Pacific Salmon-Canning Industry: A Grown Man's Game. (Illus.). 336p. (C). 1989. text ed. 49.95 (*0-7735-0717-5*, Pub. by McGill CN) U of Toronto Pr.

Newell, Dianne. Tangled Webs: Indians & the Law in Canada's Pacific Coast Fisheries. (Illus.). 288p. 1993. 40.00 (*0-8020-0547-0*); pap. 18.95 (*0-8020-7746-3*) U of Toronto Pr.

Newell, E. T. The Coinages of Demetrius Poliorcetes. (Illus.). 1978. 70.00 (*0-916710-36-X*) Obol Intl.

— The Seleucid Mint of Antioch. (Illus.). 1978. 50.00 (*0-916710-38-6*) Obol Intl.

— Some Cypriote "Alexanders" (Illus.). iii, 29p. 1974. pap. 5.00 (*0-916710-14-9*) Obol Intl.

Newell, Edward T. The Coinage of the Eastern Seleucid Mints, from Seleucus I to Antiochus III. (Numismatic Studies: No. 1). (Illus.). 363p. 1978. reprint ed. 40.00 (*0-89722-174-5*) Am Numismatic.

— Coinage of the Western Seleucid Mints, from Seleucus I to Antiochus III. (Numismatic Studies: No. 4). (Illus.). 552p. 1977. reprint ed. 50.00 (*0-89722-183-4*) Am Numismatic.

— The Dated Alexander Coinage of Sidon & Ake. LC 78-63544. (Yale Oriental Series: Researches: No. 2). reprint ed. 24.50 (*0-404-60272-X*) AMS Pr.

— The Pre-Imperial Coinage of Roman Antioch. 45p. 1980. reprint ed. pap. 5.00 (*0-916710-66-1*) Obol Intl.

— Royal Greek Portrait Coins. LC 88-73216. (Illus.). 110p. 1990. pap. 12.00 (*0-942666-60-7*) S J Durst.

— Standard Ptolemaic Silver. suppl. ed. (Illus.). 1981. reprint ed. (*0-318-55575-1*) S J Durst.

— Standard Ptolemaic Silver. LC 80-70056. (Illus.). 1981. reprint ed. pap. 6.00 (*0-915262-49-5*) S J Durst.

Newell, Elaine. When Your Long-Term Marriage Ends: A Workbook for Divorced Women. LC 94-405. 144p. 1994. pap. 14.95 (*0-89390-291-8*) Resource Pubns.

Newell, Frank W. Ophthalmology: Principles & Concepts. 7th ed. 587p. 1991. 54.95 (*0-8016-3633-7*) Mosby Yr Bk.

Newell, Frederick H. Water Resources: Present & Future Uses. LC 72-2859. (Use & Abuse of America's Natural Resources Ser.). (Illus.). 350p. 1972. reprint ed. 23.95 (*0-405-04523-9*) Ayer.

Newell, G. F. The M-M Service System with Ranked Servers in Heavy Traffic. (Lecture Notes in Economics & Mathematical Systems Ser.: Vol. 231). xi, 126p. 1984. 28.00 (*0-387-13377-1*) Spr-Verlag.

Newell, Gale E. & Newell, Sydney B. Introduction to Microcomputing. 2nd ed. 808p. 1989. Net. text ed. write for info. (*0-471-60764-9*) Wiley.

Newell, George E. & Durst, Russel K., eds. Exploring Texts: The Role of Discussion & Writing in the Teaching & Learning of Literature. 352p. (YA). (gr. 8-12). 1993. text ed. 42.95 (*0-926842-24-2*) CG Pubs Inc.

Newell, Gordon, ed. see McCurdy, James G.

Newell, Gordon R. Ships of the Inland Sea: The Story of the Puget Sound Steamboats. 2nd ed. (Illus.). 257p. 1960. 14.95 (*0-8323-0039-X*) Binford Mort.

N

***Newell, Guy R., ed.** Cancer Prevention in Clinical Medicine. fac. ed. LC 83-22994. (Illus.). 271p. Date not set. pap. 77.30 (*0-7837-7220-3*, 2047078) Bks Demand.

Newell, Guy R. & Hong, Waun K., eds. The Biology & Prevention of Aerodigestive Tract Cancers. LC 92-21811. (Advances in Experimental Medicine & Biology Ser.: Vol. 320). 1992. 65.00 (*0-306-44244-2*, Plenum Pr) Plenum.

Newell, Henry H., jt. auth. see Schwerin, Horace S.

Newell, Herbert M. & Newell, Jeanie P. History of Fayette County Baptist Association. 1968. 15.00 (*0-317-13829-4*) Banner Pr AL.

Newell, J. D. & Gabrielson, Ira W., eds. Medicine Looks at the Humanities. LC 87-17925. 206p. (Orig.). (C). 1987. lib. bdg. 44.00 (*0-8191-6607-3*) U Pr of Amer.

Newell, James, ed. St. James Encyclopedia of Mortgage & Real Estate Finance. 400p. 1991. lib. bdg. 55.00 (*1-55862-154-7*) St James Pr.

Newell, James, tr. see Negri, Antonio.

Newell, James, tr. see Villari, Rosario.

Newell, Jeanie P., jt. auth. see Newell, Herbert M.

Newell, John, jt. auth. see Calder, Nigel.

Newell, John D. & Kelsey, Charles A., eds. Digital Imaging in Diagnostic Radiology. (Illus.). 163p. 1990. text ed. 64.00 (*0-443-08634-6*) Churchill.

***Newell, John D., Jr. & Kelsey, Charles A., eds.** Digital Imaging in Diagnostic Radiology. fac. ed. LC 90-2231. (Illus.). 173p. 1990. reprint ed. pap. 49.40 (*0-7837-7876-7*, 2047633) Bks Demand.

Newell, John D., Jr. & Tarver, Robert D., eds. Thoracic Radiology. LC 92-49207. 192p. 1993. 100.00 (*0-88167-983-6*) Raven.

Newell, K. W., ed. Health by the People. 1975. 14.40 (*0-686-16783-X*) World Health.

Newell, Karl M. & Corcos, Daniel M. Variability & Motor Control. LC 92-33077. (Illus.). 520p. 1993. text ed. 65.00x (*0-87322-424-8*, BNEW0424) Human Kinetics.

Newell, Karl M., ed. see North American Society for the Psychology of Sport & Physical Activity Staff.

***Newell, Lavone.** Skagit Valley Fare: A Cookbook Celebrating Bounty & Beauty in the Pacific Northwest. (Illus.). 240p. (Orig.). 1995. pap. 19.95 (*0-9615580-5-9*) Island Pubs WA.

Newell, Leonard A., jt. ed. see Conrad, C. Eugene.

Newell, Leonard E., jt. auth. see Lamb, Sydney M.

Newell, Leslie, jt. auth. see Schambach, Frank.

Newell, Linda K. & Avery, Valeen T. Mormon Enigma: Emma Hale Smith. 2nd ed. LC 93-32626. (Illus.). 432p. 1994. pap. 16.95 (*0-252-06291-4*) U of Ill Pr.

Newell, Liz. Why Sarah Ran Away with the Veterinarian. LC 93-27524. 171p. 1994. 22.00 (*1-877946-45-1*) Permanent Pr.

***Newell, Lloyd.** May Peace Be with You: Messages from "The Spoken Word" LC 94-22202. xi, 263p. 1994. 13.95 (*0-87579-866-7*) Deseret Bk.

Newell, Lloyd D. The Divine Connection: Understanding Your Inherent Worth. LC 92-33191. xii, 275p. 1992. 7.99 (*0-87579-645-1*) Deseret Bk.

Newell, Margaret, jt. auth. see Efurd, Martha.

Newell, Marie-Louise, jt. ed. see Mok, Jacqueline.

Newell, Mike. Aestiuation. (Illus.). 56p. (Orig.). 1992. pap. 5.00 (*1-880977-02-8*) Watusi.

Newell, Mindy. The Catwoman: Her Sister's Keeper. O'Neil, Dennis, ed. (Illus.). 104p. 1991. pap. 9.95 (*0-930289-97-8*) DC Comics.

Newell, Mindy, et al. Catwoman: Her Sister's Keeper. (Illus.). 1992. reprint ed. pap. 9.99 (*0-446-39366-5*) Warner Bks.

Newell, Norman D. Creation & Evolution: Myth or Reality. Anshen, Ruth N., ed. LC 84-17858. (Convergence Ser.). 266p. 1984. pap. text ed. 12.95 (*0-275-91792-4*, B1792, Praeger Pubs) Greenwood.

— Late Paleozoic Pelecypods: Pectinacea & Mytilacea, State Geological Survey of Kansas, Vol. 10, Pts. 1 & 2. Gould, Stephen J., ed. LC 79-8337. (History of Paleontology Ser.). (Illus.). 1980. reprint ed. lib. bdg. 26.95 (*0-405-12722-7*) Ayer.

Newell, P. & Stevenson, J. Fighting the Revolution: Makhno, Durruti & Zapata. 1984. lib. bdg. 79.95 (*0-87700-645-8*) Revisionist Pr.

Newell, Patricia J., jt. auth. see Lavrack, Kevin R.

***Newell, Pete.** Basketball Post Play. (Illus.). (Orig.). 1995. pap. 14.95 (*1-57028-030-4*) Masters Pr IN.

Newell, Peter. Hole Book. 1976. 18.95 (*0-8488-1440-1*) Amereon Ltd.

— The Hole Book. (Illus.). 52p. 1988. reprint ed. lib. bdg. 19.95 (*0-89966-597-7*) Buccaneer Bks.

— The Hole Book. LC 84-52396. (Illus.). 50p. (J). (gr. k-4). 1985. reprint ed. 14.95 (*0-8048-1498-8*) C E Tuttle.

— Rocket Book. LC 91-3120. (J). (gr. 4-7). 1992. pap. 3.95 (*0-486-26961-2*) Dover.

— The Rocket Book. LC 69-12080. (Illus.). 52p. (J). (gr. k-4). 1969. reprint ed. 14.95 (*0-8048-0505-9*) C E Tuttle.

— The Rocket Book. (Illus.). 48p. (J). (gr. 4-7). 1992. reprint ed. pap. 3.95 (*0-685-52838-3*) Dover.

— The Slant Book. LC 67-12304. (Illus.). 50p. (J). (gr. k-4). 1967. reprint ed. 16.95 (*0-8048-0532-6*) C E Tuttle.

Newell, Peter, jt. auth. see Berkman, Alexander.

Newell, Peter E. Zapata of Mexico. (Orig.). 1980. pap. 5.50 (*0-932366-08-2*) Black Thorn Bks.

Newell, Peter S. Topsys & Turvys. LC 87-51208. 72p. (J). (gr. k-4). 1988. 12.95 (*0-8048-1551-8*) C E Tuttle.

— Topsys & Turvys. (Illus.). 76p. (J). (gr. 3-7). pap. 3.50 (*0-486-21231-9*) Dover.

— Topsys & Turvys, No. 2. LC 87-51208. 72p. (J). (gr. k-4). 1988. 12.95 (*0-8048-1552-6*) C E Tuttle.

Newell, R. A., ed. see British Computer Society Staff.

Newell, R. C. Biology of Intertidal Animals. 781p. 1979. 175.00 (*0-9506920-0-X*) St Mut.

Newell, R. R., et al. An Inquiry into the Ethnic Resolution of Mesolithic Regional Groups: The Study of Their Decorative Ornaments in Time & Space. LC 90-2418. (Illus.). xxxii, 488p. 1990. 125.75 (*90-04-09097-5*) E J Brill.

Newell, R. W. Objectivity, Empiricism & Truth. (Studies in Philosophical Psychology). 126p. 27.50 (*0-7102-0897-9*, 08979, RKP) Routledge.

***Newell, Ray.** The Morris Minor. 1989. pap. text ed. 25.00 (*0-7478-0149-5*, Pub. by Shire UK) St Mut.

— Original Morris Minor. (Illus.). 128p. 1993. 34.95 (*1-870979-43-5*, Pub. by Bay View Bks UK) Motorbooks Intl.

Newell, Richard S. Politics of Afghanistan. Park, Richard L., ed. LC 78-176487. (Illus.). 254p. 1972. 38.50 (*0-8014-0688-9*) Cornell U Pr.

Newell, Robert. Interviewing Skills for Nurses & Other Health Care Professionals: A Structured Approach. LC 93-10048. 1994. write for info. (*0-415-07793-1*); pap. write for info. (*0-415-07794-X*) Routledge.

***Newell, Robert, ed.** Developing Your Career in Nursing. LC 95-11758. 1996. write for info. (*0-304-33226-7*); pap. write for info. (*0-304-33228-3*) Cassell.

Newell, Robert B., intro. Conference on Control Engineering, Fourth, 1990: Control Technology for Australian Industry. (Illus.). 238p. (Orig.). 1990. pap. 72.00 (*0-85825-502-2*) Accents Pubns.

Newell, Robert H. The Orpheus C. Kerr Papers. (BCL1-PS American Literature Ser.). 1992. reprint ed. lib. bdg. 79.00 (*0-7812-6805-2*) Rprt Serv.

— Orpheus C. Kerr Papers, 3 Vols, Set. LC 78-169922. reprint ed. 115.00 (*0-404-03670-8*) AMS Pr.

— Smoked Glass. LC 70-171060. reprint ed. 32.50 (*0-404-03663-5*) AMS Pr.

— Walking Doll: Or, the Asters & Disasters of Society. LC 74-171061. reprint ed. 41.50 (*0-404-03664-3*) AMS Pr.

***Newell, Steve.** Golf Rules: A Player's Guide. (Illus.). 80p. 1995. pap. 9.95 (*0-7137-2487-0*, Pub. by Blandford Pr UK) Sterling.

— How to Play Golf. (Illus.). 160p. 1995. 14.98 (*0-8317-4498-7*) Smithmark.

***Newell, Susan.** The Healthy Organization: Fairness, Ethics, & Effective Management. LC 94-43132. (Essential Business Psychology Ser.). 208p. 1995. 49.95 (*0-415-12677-0*, C0546); pap. 15.95 (*0-415-10327-4*, C0547) Routledge.

Newell, Sydney B., jt. auth. see Newell, Gale E.

Newell, Theron A. Coco: A Story for Dog Lovers. (Illus.). 16p. (Orig.). 1986. pap. 2.00 (*0-9610080-1-6*) Dentan Pr.

— My Friend God: This Amazing Universe! Who Made It? LC 82-73698. (Illus.). 92p. 1983. 9.95 (*0-9610080-0-8*) Dentan Pr.

Newell, Tom, jt. auth. see Ellis, Dale.

Newell, Tom, jt. auth. see Johnson, Kevin.

Newell, Tom, jt. auth. see Young, Steve.

Newell, W. Casting of Steel. 1955. 252.00 (*0-08-009016-8*, Pub. by Pergamon Repr UK) Franklin.

— Vocabulary of Foundry Practice in Six Languages. LC 62-15654. (CZE, ENG, FRE, GER, POL & RUS.). 1963. 126.00 (*0-08-009740-5*, Pub. by Pergamon Repr UK) Franklin.

Newell, Waller R., jt. auth. see Emberley, Peter C.

Newell, William. Basic Sign Communication: Student Materials. pap. 19.95 (*0-913072-56-7*, SL074) Natl Assn Deaf.

— Basic Sign Communication: Vocabulary. (Basic Sign Communication Ser.). (Illus.). 162p. (Orig.). (C). 1983. pap. text ed. 12.95 (*0-913072-55-9*) Natl Assn Deaf.

Newell, William H. Interdisciplinary Undergraduate Programs: A Directory. LC 85-62972. 1986. 34.95 (*0-9615764-0-5*) Assoc Integ.

— Population Change & Agricultural Development in 19th Century France. Bruchey, Stuart, ed. LC 77-77783. (Dissertations in European Economic History Ser.). (Illus.). 1978. lib. bdg. 29.95 (*0-405-10796-X*) Ayer.

Newell, William H., ed. Ancestors. (World Anthropology Ser.). xvi, 404p. 1976. 56.15 (*3-10-800162-0*) Mouton.

***Newell, William L.** The Secular Magi: Marx, Freud, & Nietzsche on Religion. 240p. (C). 1994. pap. text ed. 24.95 (*0-8191-9588-X*) U Pr of Amer.

— Truth Is Our Mask: An Essay on Theological Method. LC 89-39428. 148p. (Orig.). (C). 1990. pap. text ed. 17.00 (*0-8191-7621-4*) U Pr of Amer.

Newell, William R. The Book of the Revelation. 408p. 1994. pap. 14.99 (*0-8254-3325-8*) Kregel.

— Hebrews: Verse by Verse. LC 94-37701. 504p. 1995. pap. 16.99 (*0-8254-3327-4*, 95-017) Kregel.

— Romanos: Versiculo por Versiculo. Orig. Title: Romans: Verse by Verse. 464p. (SPA.). 1984. pap. 11.99 (*0-8254-1507-1*) Kregel.

— Romans, Verse-by-Verse. 576p. 1995. pap. 16.99 (*0-8254-3326-6*) Kregel.

Newell, William W. Games & Songs of American Children. 2nd ed. 1903. pap. 6.50 (*0-486-20354-9*) Dover.

— Games & Songs of American Children. 254p. 1992. reprint ed. pap. 19.95 (*0-685-70004-6*, 7700) Clearfield Co.

— Games & Songs of Children. 1973. 59.95 (*0-8490-0209-5*) Gordon Pr.

— King Arthur & the Table Round: Tales Chiefly after the Old French of Chretien of Troveso with an Account of Arthurian Romance, 2 vols. 1976. lib. bdg. 250.00 (*0-8490-2115-4*) Gordon Pr.

Newels, Margarete. Los Generos Dramaticos en las Poeticas del Siglo de Oro. (Serie A: Monagrafias, XXXV). (Illus.). 223p. (Orig.). (SPA.). (C). 1973. pap. 36.00 (*0-900411-78-3*, Pub. by Tamesis Bks Ltd UK) Boydell & Brewer.

Newendorp, Paul D. Decision Analysis for Petroleum Exploration. LC 75-10936. 680p. 1976. 89.95 (*0-87814-064-6*, P4032) PennWell Bks.

Newenhuyse, Elizabeth. Sometimes I Feel Like Running Away. 208p. (Orig.). 1993. pap. 7.99 (*1-55661-317-2*) Bethany Hse.

Newenhuyse, Elizabeth C. Am I the Only Crazy Mom on the Planet? 1994. pap. 9.99 (*0-310-38631-4*) Zondervan.

— Great Expectations of a Hopeless Romantic. 208p. (Orig.). 1993. pap. 1.80 (*1-56476-096-0*, Victor Books) SP Pubns.

Newenhuyse, Elizabeth C., ed. Encouragement for Couples: Lifelong Love & Partnership. (Pocketpac Bks.). 80p. (Orig.). 1993. pap. 2.99 (*0-87788-213-4*) Shaw Pubs.

— Strength from the Psalms: Verses to Comfort, Uplift, & Challenge. (Pocketpac Bks.). 80p. (Orig.). 1993. pap. 2.99 (*0-87788-799-3*) Shaw Pubs.

Newey, Charles & Weaver, Graham. Materials in Action: Principles & Practice. (Illus.). 405p. 1990. pap. text ed. 39.95 (*0-7506-0390-9*) Buttrwrth-Heinemann.

Newey, Deni. Months of the Year Quiet Book. (Illus.). 45p. 1990. pap. 9.98 (*0-88290-363-2*) Horizon Utah.

Newey, Eric. Something Wholesale: My Life & Times in the Rag Trade. large type ed. 256p. 1991. 9.97 (*1-85089-281-4*, Pub. by ISIS UK) Transaction Pubs.

Newey, Judge. Newey: The Official Referees' Courts - Practice & Procedure. 1988. U.K. pap. 38.00 (*0-406-11340-8*) Butterworth Legal Pubs.

Newey, Vincent. Cowper's Poetry: A Critical Study & Reassessment. LC 82-6843. (English Texts & Studies: No. 20). 378p. (C). 1982. text ed. 45.00 (*0-389-20079-4*, N6851) B&N Imports.

***Newey, Vincent, ed.** Centering the Self: Subjectivity, Society & Reading from Thomas Gray to Thomas Hardy. 300p. 1995. 59.95 (*1-85928-151-6*, Pub. by Scolar Pr UK) Ashgate Pub Co.

Newey, Vincent & Thompson, Ann, eds. Literature & Nationalism. 288p. (C). 1991. text ed. 64.00 (*0-389-20954-6*) B&N Imports.

Newey, Vincent, jt. ed. see Beatty, Bernard.

Newfarmer, Richard. Transnational Conglomerates & the Economics of Dependent Development. Altman, Edward I. & Walter, Ingo, eds. LC 78-13842. (Contemporary Studies in Economic & Financial Analysis: Vol. 23). 420p. 1980. lib. bdg. 73.25 (*0-89232-110-5*) Jai Pr.

***Newfield, Christopher.** The Emerson Effect: Individualism & Submission in America. 280p. 1996. 45.00x (*0-226-57698-1*); pap. 16.95x (*0-226-57700-7*) U Ch Pr.

***Newfield, Christopher & Strickland, Ronald, eds.** After Political Correctness: The Humanities & Society in the 1990s. LC 94-33692. (Cultural Studies - Politics & Culture Subs). 1995. text ed. 79.95 (*0-8133-2336-3*) Westview.

— After Political Correctness: The Humanities & Society in the 1990s. LC 94-33692. (Cultural Studies - Politics & Culture Subs). (C). 1995. pap. text ed. 24.95 (*0-8133-2337-1*) Westview.

Newfield, Dalton. Young Winston: 1874-1898: A Biography Using Stamps. (Educational Ser.: No. 2). (Illus.). 16p. 1990. pap. 5.00 (*0-943879-04-3*) Intl Churchill Soc.

Newfield, Jack. Robert Kennedy: A Memoir. LC 87-30685. 324p. 1988. pap. 11.00 (*0-452-26064-7*, Plume) NAL-Dutton.

Newfield, Jane, jt. auth. see Krueger, David W.

Newfield, Marcia. The Life of Louis Pasteur. (Pioneers in Health & Medicine Ser.). (Illus.). 80p. (J). (gr. 4-7). 1991. lib. bdg. 13.98 (*0-941477-67-3*) TFC Bks NY.

— Where Did You Put Your Sleep? LC 83-2785. (Illus.). 32p. (J). (gr. k-4). 1983. text ed. 13.95 (*0-689-50286-9*, McElderry) S&S Childrens.

Newfield, Phillippa. Neuroanesthesia. 2nd ed. 1991. 65.00 (*0-316-60471-2*) Little.

Newfield, Phillippa & Cottrell, James E. Handbook of Neuroanesthesia: Clinical & Physiologic Essentials. 437p. 1983. 29.50 (*0-316-60470-4*) Little.

Newgarden, Albert, ed. The Field Sales Manager: A Manual of Practice. LC 60-12757. (American Management Association, Management Report Ser.: No. 48). 380p. reprint ed. pap. 108.30 (*0-317-28269-7*, 2022614) Bks Demand.

Newhall, Arthur. Calligraphy. (How to Draw & Paint Ser.). (Illus.). 32p. (Orig.). 1990. pap. 5.95 (*1-56010-064-8*, HT-227) W Foster Pub.

— Calligraphy & Lettering Design. (Artist's Library). (Illus.). 64p. (Orig.). 1990. pap. 6.95 (*1-56010-031-1*, AL15) W Foster Pub.

Newhall, Barker. The Barker Family of Plymouth Colony & County. (Illus.). 102p. 1988. reprint ed. lib. bdg. 29.00 (*0-8328-0188-7*); reprint ed. pap. 19.00 (*0-8328-0189-5*) Higginson Bk Co.

Newhall, Beaumont. The Daguerreotype in America. (Illus.). 176p. 1976. reprint ed. pap. 14.95 (*0-486-23322-7*) Dover.

— Dorothea Lange Looks at the American Country Woman. LC 67-18363. (Illus.). 72p. 1967. reprint ed. 12.95 (*0-88360-027-7*); reprint ed. pap. 9.95 (*0-88360-026-9*) Amon Carter.

— The History of Photography: From 1839 to the Present Day. 5th rev. ed. (Illus.). 1982. pap. 29.95 (*0-87070-381-1*) Mus of Modern Art.

— Photography & the Book. 1983. pap. 10.00 (*0-89073-066-0*) Boston Public Lib.

— Supreme Instants: The Photography of Edward Weston. 191p. 1986. 50.00 (*0-317-53697-4*) Little.

Newhall, Beaumont, ed. Eliot Porter: The Grand Canyon. (Illus.). 152p. 1992. 29.95 (*3-7913-1233-2*, Pub. by Prestel) TeNeues.

— Photography: Essays & Images; Illustrated Readings in the History of Photography. (Illus.). 328p. 1981. 32.50 (*0-87070-387-0*, 0-8109-6108-3) Mus of Modern Art.

Newhall, Beaumont, intro. Todd Webb Photographs: Early Western Trails & Some Ghost Towns. rev. ed. LC 79-10354. (Illus.). 37p. 1979. pap. 7.95 (*0-88360-032-3*) Amon Carter.

Newhall, Beaumont & Calderone, Mary. Edward Steichen: The Early Years 1900-1927, a Portfolio of 12 Prints. limited ed. (Illus.). 1981. 1,800.00 (*0-89381-074-6*) Aperture.

Newhall, Beaumont, ed. see Davidson, Kathryn & Glassman, Elizabeth.

Newhall, Beaumont, et al. Brett Weston: Master Photographer. Christopher, Carol W. & Featherstone, David, eds. (Illus.). 180p. 1989. 95.00 (*0-9616515-3-9*) Photog West Graphics.

Newhall, Charles L. The Adventures of Jack: Or Life on A Wave. 93p. 1981. 10.95 (*0-87770-263-2*) Ye Galleon.

Newhall, David S. Clemenceau: A Life at War. LC 90-20994. (Illus.). 724p. 1991. lib. bdg. 139.95 (*0-88946-785-4*) E Mellen.

Newhall, Fales H. & Terry, Milton S. Whedon's Commentary on the Old Testament, Vol. 1: Genesis-Exodus. 1987. 21.99 (*0-88019-216-X*) Schmul Pub Co.

Newhall, George N. Sunspots, Dust & Rainfall. (Illus.). 208p. (Orig.). (C). 1990. text ed. 20.00 (*0-9619881-0-X*); per. 16.00 (*0-9619881-1-8*) S & G Pub.

Newhall, Guy. Settlement of Estates & Fiduciary Law in Massachusetts, 3 vols. 4th suppl. ed. 1992. Suppl. 1992. 50.00 (*0-317-03269-0*) Lawyers Cooperative.

— Settlement of Estates & Fiduciary Law in Massachusetts, 3 vols., Set. 4th ed. 315.00 (*0-318-11944-7*) Lawyers Cooperative.

Newhall, James, jt. auth. see Lewis, Alonzo.

Newhall, James R., jt. auth. see Lewis, Alonzo.

Newhall, Nancy. From Adams to Stieglitz: Early Pioneers of Twentieth-Century Photography. (Writers & Artists on Photography Ser.). (Illus.). 310p. 1989. 39.95 (*0-89381-372-9*); pap. 16.95 (*0-89381-373-7*) Aperture.

Newhall, Nancy & Metcalf, Paul, eds. Time in New England. limited ed. (Illus.). 256p. 1980. 350.00 (*0-89381-061-4*) Aperture.

Newhall, Nancy, jt. auth. see Adams, Ansel.

Newhall, Richard. The Crusades. rev. ed. (Illus.). 64p. (C). 1991. pap. text ed. 2.25 (*1-877891-03-7*) Paperbook Pr Inc.

***Newham, Lucy.** Beef Cattle: Breeding, Feeding, & Showing. 164p. Date not set. 39.95 (*0-7506-7902-6*, Pub. by Inkata Pr AT) Intl Spec Bk.

Newham, Paul. The Outlandish Adventures of Orpheus in the Underworld. LC 93-24490. (Illus.). 32p. 1994. 15.00 (*1-56957-908-3*) Barefoot Bks.

— The Singing Cure: An Introduction to Voice Movement Therapy. LC 93-34739. 1994. pap. 15.00 (*0-87773-997-8*) Shambhala Pubns.

Newhauser, Richard & Alford, John A., eds. Literature & Religion in the Later Middle Ages: Philological Stuies in Honor of Siegfrid Wenzel. (Medieval & Renaissance Texts & Studies: Vol. 118). 400p. 1994. 25.00 (*0-86698-172-1*) MRTS.

Newhnam, Rex E. Away with Arthritis. 1994. 12.50 (*0-533-10814-4*) Vantage.

Newhold, Paul, jt. auth. see Granger, C. W.

Newhouse. Understanding MRI. 1991. 53.95 (*0-316-60474-7*) Little.

Newhouse, Dora. The Encyclopedia of Homonyms-Sound Alikes: Condensed & Abridged Edition. LC 76-50944. (Illus.). (J). (gr. 6-12). 1978. pap. 6.95 (*0-918050-00-6*) Newhouse Pr.

— How to Become an American Citizen: Amnesty - Legalization - Voter Registration. 8th ed. LC 88-90865. (Illus.). (ENG & SPA.). 1989. pap. 8.95 (*0-918050-61-8*) Newhouse Pr.

— How to Work or Communicate in a Hotel, Motel or Inn: Como Trabajar O Comunicar en un Hotel, Motel O Posada. LC 77-80666. (Illus.). (ENG & SPA.). 1977. pap. 3.95 (*0-918050-05-7*) Newhouse Pr.

— How to Work or Communicate in a Private Home: Como Trabajar O Communicar en un Casa Privada. LC 77-80665. (Illus.). (ENG & SPA.). 1977. pap. 3.95 (*0-918050-03-0*) Newhouse Pr.

— How to Work or Communicate in a Restaurant or Bar: Como Trabajar O Comunicar en un Restaurante O Bar. LC 77-80667. (Illus.). (ENG & SPA.). 1977. pap. 3.95 (*0-918050-06-5*) Newhouse Pr.

— Illustrated Homonyms 'Sound-Alikes' - Homonimos 'Sonidos Identicos' (Illus.). (ENG & SPA.). 1979. 9.95 (*0-918050-09-X*); pap. 6.95 (*0-918050-27-8*) Newhouse Pr.

Newhouse, Dora, illus. Homonyms Plus. (J). (gr. 6-12). 1979. teacher ed 6.95 (*0-918050-41-3*); student ed 6.95 (*0-918050-42-1*); 4.95 (*0-918050-44-8*) Newhouse Pr.

Newhouse, Edward. This Is Your Day. LC 74-2800. (Labor Movement in Fiction & Non-Fiction Ser.). reprint ed. 45.00 (*0-404-58456-X*) AMS Pr.

Newhouse, Elizabeth L., ed. Inventors & Discoverers: Changing Our World. (Illus.). 320p. 1988. 36.95 (*0-87044-752-1*); pap. 24.95 (*0-87044-751-3*) Natl Geog.

— National Geographic's Guide to the National Parks of the United States. 432p. 1989. Bk. only. 18.95 (*0-685-44964-5*) Natl Geog.

— National Geographic's Guide to the National Parks of the United States. rev. ed. LC 92-5851. (Illus.). 432p. 1992. pap. 26.50 (*0-87044-885-4*) Natl Geog.

Newhouse, Elizabeth L., ed. see McDowell, Bart.

Newhouse, Elizabeth L., ed. see National Geographic Society Book Division Staff.

Newhouse, Elizabeth L., ed. see National Geographic Society Staff.

Newhouse, Elizabeth L., ed. see Scott, John A.

Newhouse, Flower A. The Christward Way. 396p. 1984. pap. 14.00 (*0-910378-19-3*) Christward.

An Asterisk (*) at the beginning of an entry indicates that the title is appearing in BIP for the first time.

— Disciplines of the Holy Quest. 5th ed. LC 59-15553. (Illus.). 1959. 14.00 (0-910378-05-3) Christward.

— Drama of Incarnation. 4th ed. 1948. 10.00 (0-910378-04-5) Christward.

— Gateways into Light. 3rd ed. LC 74-75517. 160p. 1974. pap. 10.00 (0-910378-09-6) Christward.

— Here Are Your Answers, Vol. I. 3rd ed. LC 49-16192. 247p. 1948. 12.00 (0-910378-01-0) Christward.

— Here Are Your Answers, Vol. II. 2nd ed. LC 76-103410. 227p. 1969. 12.00 (0-910378-06-1) Christward.

— Here Are Your Answers, Vol. III. Boult, Pamela, ed. LC 82-73083. 222p. 1982. 12.00 (0-910378-18-5) Christward.

— The Journey Upward. Bengtson, Athene, ed. LC 78-74955. 191p. (Orig.). 1978. pap. 10.00 (0-910378-15-0) Christward.

— Kingdom of the Shining Ones. 8th ed. 195p. 1955. 14.00 (0-910378-03-7) Christward.

— The Meaning & Value of the Sacraments. 2nd ed. LC 77-186123. 123p. 1971. 11.00 (0-910378-07-X) Christward.

— A Measure of Days. LC 85-72907. 64p. (Orig.). 1985. pap. 7.00 (0-910378-20-7) Christward.

— Prayers of a Mystic. LC 86-71083. 100p. (Orig.). 1986. pap. 7.00 (0-910378-21-5) Christward.

— Rediscovering the Angels & Natives of Eternity. 8th ed. (Illus.). 156p. 1966. 14.00 (0-910378-02-9) Christward.

— The Sacred Heart of Christmas. 2nd ed. Bengtson, Athene, ed. LC 78-74956. (Illus.). 93p. 1978. pap. 8.00 (0-910378-14-2) Christward.

— Songs of Deliverance. LC 72-94582. 250p. 1972. 12.00 (0-910378-08-8) Christward.

— These, Too, Shall Be Loved. 2nd ed. LC 76-49246. 104p. 1976. pap. 7.00 (0-910378-11-8) Christward.

— Through Lent to Resurrection. Bengtson, Melodie N., ed. LC 77-77088. (Illus.). 72p. 1977. pap. 7.00 (0-910378-13-4) Christward.

— Travel with Inner Perceptiveness. (Illus.). 112p. (Orig.). 1979. pap. text ed. 7.00 (0-910378-16-9) Christward.

Newhouse, Flower A., et al. Insights into Reality. 2nd ed. LC 75-36869. 191p. 1975. pap. 10.00 (0-910378-10-X) Christward.

Newhouse, George, jt. auth. see Ezell, Elaine.

***Newhouse, Janette K.** Rural & Urban Patterns: An Exploration of How Older Adults Use In-Home Care. Bruchey, Stuart, ed. LC 94-22166. (Studies on the Elderly in America). (Illus.). 1995. 66.00 (0-8153-1631-3) Garland.

Newhouse, John. The Sporty Game. LC 81-48123. 1982. 22.95 (0-394-51447-5) Knopf.

Newhouse, Joseph P. & Insurance Experiment Group Staff. Free for All? Lessons from the Rand Health Insurance Experiment. LC 93-1356. 501p. (C). 1994. 49.95 (0-674-31846-3) HUP.

Newhouse, Joseph P., jt. ed. see Fuchs, Victor R.

Newhouse, Joseph P., ed. see National Bureau of Economic Research Conference on the Economics of Physician & Patient Behavior (1978, Stanford, CA).

Newhouse, M., jt. auth. see Morgenroth, Konrad.

***Newhouse, Margaret.** Outside the Ivory Tower: A Guide for Academics Considering Alternative Careers. 164p. (Orig.). 1993. pap. 13.00 (0-943747-08-2) Harvard OCS.

***Newhouse, Miriam & Messaline, Peter.** The Actor's Survival Kit. rev. ed. 202p. 1993. pap. text ed. 17.00 (0-88924-216-X, Pub. by Simon & Pierre Pub CN) Empire Pub Srvs.

Newhouse, Sue. Creative Hand Embroidery. (Illus.). 64p. (Orig.). (YA). 1993. pap. 14.95 (0-85532-727-8, Pub. by Search Pr UK) A Schwartz & Co.

Newhouse, Susan M., jt. auth. see Mabee, Carleton.

***Newhouse, Tom & Routh, David.** Ejaculation Control Manual: Extended Lovemaking. 74p. (Orig.). 1992. pap. write for info. (0-9625096-1-2) Starside Pub.

Newick, Glenn. The Ultimate in Rifle Accuracy. (Illus.). 210p. (Orig.). 1990. pap. 11.95 (0-88317-159-7) Stoeger Pub Co.

Newiger, Hans-Joachim. Untersuchungen zu Gorgias' Schrift Ueber das Nichtseiende. (C). 1973. 89.25 (3-11-003432-8) De Gruyter.

Newing, Edward G., jt. ed. see Conrad, Edgar W.

Newing, Francis. First Impressions: Printing the Church Magazine & Other Literature. (C). 1989. 20.00 (0-9510086-8-4, Pub. by Jay Bks UK) St Mut.

***Newington, Irene.** Presents. (Fun to Do Ser.). (Illus.). 32p. (J). 1995. lib. bdg. write for info. (1-887238-05-0) Fitzgerald.

Newitt, Malyn. A History of Mozambique. LC 93-7477. (Illus.). 400p. 1995. text ed. 57.50 (0-253-34006-3); pap. 24.95 (0-253-34007-1) Ind U Pr.

Newitt, Paul M. Nineteen Sixty-Eight & One Half Ford Mustang GT-California Special Recognition Guide & Owner's Manual. (Illus.). 68p. (Orig.). (C). 1989. pap. 12.95 (0-9624730-0-6) P M Newitt.

Newitt, Simon. Four Wheel Driving. (Illus.). 128p. 1991. pap. 24.95 (1-85532-144-0, Pub. by Osprey Pubng Ltd UK) Motorbooks Intl.

Newkirk, jt. auth. see Sullivan.

Newkirk, Dennis. Almanac of Soviet Manned Space Flight. (Illus.). 378p. 1990. 29.95 (0-87201-848-2) Gulf Pub.

Newkirk, G., ed. see International Astronomical Union Staff.

Newkirk, G. F., jt. auth. see Quayle, D. B.

Newkirk, Ingrid. Free the Animals! The Inside Story of the Animal Liberation Front & Its Founder, "Valerie" LC 91-51222. (Illus.). 372p. (Orig.). 1992. pap. 13.95 (1-879360-11-X) Noble Pr.

— Save the Animals! One Hundred One Easy Things You Can Do. 1990. mass mkt. 4.95 (0-446-39234-0) Warner Bks.

Newkirk, Ingrid, jt. auth. see People for the Ethical Treatment of Animals Staff.

Newkirk, J. B. & Wernick, J. H., eds. Direct Observation of Imperfections in Crystals: Proceedings. LC 61-16633. 629p. reprint ed. pap. 179.30 (0-317-08753-3, 2000684) Bks Demand.

Newkirk, J. B., ed. see International Conference on Structure & Properties of Thin Films Staff.

Newkirk, Jay. Hey Batter! LC 86-82532. 260p. (Orig.). 1987. pap. 7.95 (0-9617711-0-0) HR Press.

Newkirk, Lois, ed. Hudson: A Survey of Historic Buildings in an Ohio Town. LC 88-8442. (Illus.). 319p. reprint ed. pap. 91.00 (0-7837-5126-5, 2044854) Bks Demand.

Newkirk, R. A. The Eriophyid Mites of Alfred Nalepa. (Thomas Say Foundation Ser.: Vol. 9). 138p. 1984. 25.00 (0-938522-22-1) Entomol Soc.

Newkirk, Robert, Jr., jt. ed. see Anderson, Douglas T.

Newkirk, Sally L. Some Tastes of Home. (Illus.). 480p. 1989. 14.95 (0-9620596-0-9) S L Newkirk.

Newkirk, Sandra L., tr. see Schusdziarra, Heinrich & Schusdziarra, Volker.

Newkirk, Sandra L., tr. see Tellington-Jones, Linda & Bruns, Ursula.

***Newkirk, Terrye.** The Martyrs of Compiegne: The Mantle of Elijah As Prophets of the Modern Age. LC 94-29671. 48p. 1995. 3.95 (0-935216-51-0) ICS Pubns.

***Newkirk, Thomas.** Critical Thinking & Writing: Reclaiming the Essay. Harste, Jerome, ed. & intro. by. LC 89-23515. (Monographs on Teaching Critical Thinking). 56p. (C). 1989. pap. 8.95 (0-927516-04-7) ERIC-REC.

— More Than Stories: The Range of Children's Writing. LC 88-26067. (Illus.). 228p. (Orig.). (C). 1989. pap. 18.00 (0-435-08490-9, 08490) Heinemann.

— To Compose: Teaching Writing in High School & College. 2nd ed. LC 89-31484. 312p. 1989. pap. text ed. 19.50 (0-435-08496-8) Heinemann.

— Workshop 4: The Teacher as Researcher. (Workshop for & by Teachers Ser.: Vol. 4). 187p. 1992. pap. text ed. 16.00 (0-435-08728-2, Pub. by Heinemann Educ Bks UK) Heinemann.

Newkirk, Thomas, ed. Nuts & Bolts: A Practical Guide to Teaching College Composition. LC 92-42069. 216p. (C). 1993. pap. text ed. 18.50 (0-86709-321-8, 0321) Boynton Cook Pubs.

— Workshop 5 - by & for Teachers: The Writing Process Revisited. 188p. (C). 1993. pap. text ed. 16.00 (0-435-08798-3, 08798) Heinemann.

Newkirk, Thomas & Atwell, Nancie, eds. Understanding Writing: Ways of Observing, Learning & Teaching. 2nd ed. LC 87-11872. 178p. (Orig.). 1987. reprint ed. pap. text ed. 20.00 (0-435-08441-0) Heinemann.

Newkirk, Thomas & McLure, Patricia. Listening In: Children Talk about Books (& Other Things) 176p. 1993. pap. 14.95 (0-435-08713-4, 08713) Heinemann.

Newkirk, Tom, jt. auth. see Tobin, Lad.

Newkirk, William & Linden, Richard. Managing Emergency Medical Services: Principles & Practices. 272p. 1984. 27.95 (0-317-58947-4) P-H.

Newkirk, William & Linden, William. Managing in the Emergency Medical Services: Principles & Practice. (C). 1984. text ed. 41.00 (0-8359-4198-1, Reston) P-H.

Newkirk, William L., ed. Occupational Health Services: Practical Strategies for Improving Quality & Controlling Costs. LC 93-26520. 332p. 1993. pap. 56.95 (1-55648-108-X, 155400) AHPI.

Newkome, George R. & Paudler, William W. Contemporary Hetercyclic Chemistry: Syntheses, Reactions & Applications. LC 82-4795. 422p. 1982. text ed. 99.95 (0-471-06279-0, Wiley-Interscience) Wiley.

Newkome, George R., et al, eds. Pyridine & Its Derivatives, Vol. 14. LC 59-103038. (Chemistry of Heterocyclic Compounds Ser.: Vol. 14, Pt. 5). 714p. 1984. text ed. 430.00 (0-471-05072-5, 1-079) Wiley.

Newkumet, Vynola B. & Meredith, Howard L. Hasinai: A Traditional History of the Caddo Confederacy. (Illus.). 160p. 1988. 16.95 (0-89096-342-8) Tex A&M Univ Pr.

***Newland.** Pathology: Examination & Board Review. (C). 1995. pap. text ed. 26.95 (0-8385-7719-9) Appleton & Lange.

Newland, Adrian C., et al, eds. Cambridge Medical Reviews: Haematological Oncology, Vol. 1. (Illus.). 260p. (C). 1991. 89.95 (0-521-40193-3) Cambridge U Pr.

Newland, Amy R. & Uhlenbeck, Chris. Ukiyo-E. 112p. 1994. 14.98 (0-8317-6116-4) Smithmark.

Newland, Chester A. Professional Public Executives. LC 80-81209. (PAR Classics Ser.: No. 1). 222p. reprint ed. pap. 63.30 (0-8357-4219-9, 2037004) Bks Demand.

Newland, D. E. Introduction to Random Vibrations & Spectral Analysis. 2nd ed. LC 74-75025. (Illus.). 352p. 1986. pap. text ed. 64.95 (0-470-20553-9) Halsted Pr.

— An Introduction to Random Vibrations, Spectral & Wavelet Analysis. 3rd ed. 477p. 1994. pap. text ed. 64.95 (0-470-22153-4) Halsted Pr.

— Mechanical Vibration Analysis & Computation. LC 08-822017. 1989. text ed. 86.95 (0-470-21388-4) Halsted Pr.

Newland, David H. Mineral Resources of the State of New York. 315p. 1993. reprint ed. lib. bdg. 89.00 (0-7812-5150-8) Rprt Serv.

Newland, Ernest T. BLAT Manual. 1971. pap. 7.50 (0-252-00886-3) U of Ill Pr.

— Blind Learning Aptitude Test. 1971. 50.00 (0-252-00881-2) U of Ill Pr.

Newland, Guy. The Two Truths in the Madhyamika Philosophy of the Ge-luk-ba Order of Tibetan Buddhism. 1992. 35.00 (0-937938-80-7); pap. 19.95 (0-937938-79-3) Snow Lion Pubns.

Newland, Guy, tr. Compassion, a Tibetan Analysis: A Buddhist Monastic Textbook. (Advanced Book - Blue Ser.). 168p. (Orig.). 1984. pap. 12.95 (0-86171-024-X) Wisdom MA.

Newland, James. Carpenter's Assistant. 1990. 19.99 (0-517-03303-8) Random Hse Value.

Newland, James R., ed. see Ishikawa, G.

Newland, John. Primal Instinct. 432p. 1994. mass mkt. 4.50 (0-8217-4651-0) Zebra.

Newland, Joseph N., jt. auth. see Davis, Barbara.

Newland, Kathleen. City Limits: Emerging Constraints on Urban Growth. 1980. pap. write for info. (0-916468-37-2) Worldwatch Inst.

— Global Employment & Economic Justice: The Policy Challenge. LC 79-63577. (Worldwatch Papers). 1979. pap. 5.00 (0-916468-27-5) Worldwatch Inst.

— Infant Mortality & the Health of Societies. 1981. pap. write for info. (0-916468-46-1) Worldwatch Inst.

— International Migration: The Search for Work. LC 79-56318. (Worldwatch Papers). 1979. pap. 5.00 (0-916468-32-1) Worldwatch Inst.

— Productivity: The New Economic Context. LC 82-50699. (Worldwatch Papers). 1982. pap. 5.00 (0-916468-48-8) Worldwatch Inst.

— Refugees: The New International Politics of Displacement. LC 81-50523. (Worldwatch Papers). 1981. pap. 5.00 (0-916468-42-9) Worldwatch Inst.

— Women & Population Growth: Choice Beyond Childbearing. LC 77-91827. (Worldwatch Papers). 1977. pap. 5.00 (0-916468-15-1) Worldwatch Inst.

— Women in Politics: A Global Review. 1975. pap. write for info. (0-916468-02-X) Worldwatch Inst.

Newland, Kathleen, ed. The International Relations of Japan. LC 90-42912. 248p. 1990. text ed. 24.95 (0-312-05357-6) St Martin.

Newland, Kathleen & Soedjatmoko, Kamala C., eds. Transforming Humanity: The Visionary Writings of Soedjatmoko. LC 93-5181. (Library of Management for Development). 224p. 1994. 42.00 (1-56549-025-8); pap. 18.95 (1-56549-026-6) Kumarian Pr.

Newland, Kathleen, jt. auth. see Eckholm, Erik.

Newland, Kathleen, jt. ed. see Grant, Rebecca.

***Newland, Loren E.** Hotel Protection Management: Guest Protection & Reasonable Care. 250p. (Orig.). (C). 1995. write for info. (1-886081-00-X) TNZ Pubs.

Newland, Mary R. The Hebrew Scriptures: The Biblical Story of God's Promise to Israel & Us. Nagel, Stephan, ed. (Illus.). 261p. (Orig.). (YA). (gr. 10-11). 1990. pap. text ed. 12.40 (0-88489-231-X); teacher ed, spiral bd. 18.95 (0-88489-232-8) St Marys.

— The Year & Our Children: Planning the Family Activities for Christian Feasts & Seasons. 2nd ed. 192p. 1995. pap. 11.95 (1-885553-37-4) Firefly Press.

Newland, Patricia. A Tapestry of Daily Prayer. (Illus.). 190p. 1993. reprint ed. pap. 7.99 (0-89283-771-3, Charis) Servant.

Newland, Samuel J. Cossacks in the German Army, 1941-1945. 1991. 39.50 (0-7146-3351-8, Pub. by F Cass Pubs UK) Intl Spec Bk.

***Newlands, Anne.** The Group of Seven: And Tom Thomson An Introduction. (Illus.). 64p. (YA). 1995. text ed. 17.95 (1-895565-53-7); pap. 9.95 (1-895565-54-5) Firefly Bks Ltd.

Newlands, Carole, tr. Peter Ramus's Attack on Cicero: Text & Translation of Ramus's Brutinae Quaestiones. 282p. (C). 1992. text ed. 24.50 (1-880393-00-X); pap. text ed. 13.95 (1-880393-01-8) Hermagoras Pr.

***Newlands, Carole E.** Playing with Time: Ovid & the "Fasti" LC 95-2919. (Studies in Classical Philology: Vol. 55). 256p. 1995. 42.50 (0-8014-3080-1) Cornell U Pr.

***Newlands, George.** God in Christian Perspective. 1994. text ed. 49.95 (0-567-09657-2, Pub. by T & T Clark UK); pap. text ed. 29.95 (0-567-29259-2, Pub. by T & T Clark UK) Bks Intl VA.

Newlin, Algie. Charity Cook. LC 81-66294. 120p. (Orig.). 1981. pap. 8.95 (0-913408-66-2) Friends United.

***Newlin, Algie I.** Friends "at the Spring" A History of Spring Monthly Meeting. 1984. pap. 7.50 (0-614-04682-3) NC Frnds Hist Soc.

Newlin, Claude M. Life & Writings of Hugh Henry Brackenridge. 1971. 12.00 (0-911858-20-2) Appel.

— Philosophy & Religion in Colonial America. LC 68-23317. 212p. 1968. reprint ed. text ed. 55.00 (0-8371-0184-0, NEPR, Greenwood Pr) Greenwood.

Newlin, Deborah L. The Tonkawa People: A Tribal History From Earliest Times to 1893. Richardson, Gale, ed. (Museum Journal Ser.). (Illus.). 119p. 1982. pap. 5.00 (0-911618-07-4) West Tex Mus.

Newlin, Dika. Bruckner-Mahler, Schoenberg: Music Book Index. 293p. 1993. reprint ed. lib. bdg. 79.00 (0-7812-9582-3) Rprt Serv.

— Schoenberg Remembered: Diaries & Recollections 1938-1976. LC 79-19128. (Illus.). 1980. 36.00 (0-918728-14-2) Pendragon NY.

Newlin, Dika, tr. see Leibowitz, Rene.

Newlin, Dika, tr. see Werner, Eric.

***Newlin, Gary.** Simple Kaleidoscopes: Sixteen Spectacular Scopes to Make. LC 95-4591. (Illus.). 112p. 1995. 19.95 (0-8069-3154-X, Lark Bks) Sterling.

***Newlin, George.** Everyone in Dickens. 2506p. 1995. text ed. 275.00 (0-313-29580-8, Greenwood Pr) Greenwood.

— Everyone in Dickens Vol. II: Plots, People & Publishing Particulars in the Complete, Vol. 2. LC 95-2453. 1995. text ed. 125.00 (0-313-29582-4, Greenwood Pr) Greenwood.

***Newlin, George, ed.** Everyone in Dickens Vol. I: Plots, People & Publishing Particulars in the Complete. LC 95-2453. 1995. text ed. 125.00 (0-313-29581-6, Greenwood Pr) Greenwood.

— Everyone in Dickens Vol. III: Characteristics & Commentaries, Tables & Tabulations: A Taxonomy, Vol. 3. 1995. text ed. 95.00 (0-313-29583-2, Greenwood Pr) Greenwood.

Newlin, J. Shipley, Jr., jt. auth. see Frick, Elizabeth.

Newlin, Jeanne T., intro. Our Town on Stage: The Original Promptbook in Fascimile. (Barry & Mary Bingham Series in the Harvard Theatre Collection: No. 1). (Illus.). 96p. 1990. 29.95 (0-674-64760-2) HUP.

Newlin, John. The World Is Your Market. LC 93-33154. 1994. 24.95 (1-55958-439-4) Prima Pub.

Newlin, Jon, jt. auth. see Bookhardt, D. Eric.

Newlin, Keith. Hardboiled Burlesque: Raymond Chandler's Comic Style. LC 85-25473. (Brownstone Mystery Guides Ser.: Vol. 1). 50p. 1984. reprint ed. lib. bdg. 20.00x (0-89370-555-1, Brownstone Bks); reprint ed. pap. 10.00x (0-941028-03-8, Brownstone Bks) Borgo Pr.

Newlin, Keith, ed. see Thomas, et al.

Newlin, Lana S. Surviving Sixth Grade. Morey, Cathy, ed. (Illus.). 90p. (J). (gr. 5-7). 1990. 16.95 (0-9625413-0-3); pap. 9.95 (0-9625413-1-1) Christmans.

Newlin, Nancy L. The Gem of Edenvale: The Historic Hayes Mansion of San Jose, California. (Illus.). (Orig.). 1994. pap. 24.95 (0-9641102-0-2) Renasci.

***Newlin, Nicholas P.** Adelhelm Abbey. 1995. 19.95 (0-533-11426-8) Vantage.

Newlin, Richard, ed. & intro. Richard Diebenkorn: Works on Paper. LC 86-82665. 293p. 1987. 65.00 (0-940619-00-8) Houston Fine Art Pr.

Newlin, Richard, jt. auth. see Adams, Ben Q.

Newlin, Virginia S., jt. auth. see Sherman, Pecki.

Newlin, William V. The Down East Guide to the Lakes & Ponds of Mt. Desert. LC 89-50792. (Illus.). 208p. (Orig.). 1989. pap. 12.95 (0-89272-270-3) Down East.

***Newling, D. W., ed.** Prostate Cancer: Hormonal Treatment & Treatment of Advanced Disease. (Journal: European Urology: Vol. 26, Suppl. 1, 1994). (Illus.). iv, 34p. 1994. pap. 20.00 (3-8055-6111-3) S Karger.

Newling, Donald W., jt. ed. see Kurth, K. H.

Newlon, Howard, Jr., ed. A Selection of Historic American Papers on Concrete, 1876-1926. LC 76-47294. (American Concrete Institute Publication Ser.: SP-52). 342p. reprint ed. pap. 97.50 (0-317-27231-4, 2025081) Bks Demand.

Newlove, Donald. First Paragraphs: Inspired Openings for Writers & Readers. 176p. 1993. pap. 9.95 (0-8050-2597-9) H Holt & Co.

— Invented Voices. 1994. 16.95 (0-8050-2979-6); pap. 9.95 (0-8050-2592-8) H Holt & Co.

— Painted Paragraph. 1995. pap. 9.95 (0-8050-2591-X) H Holt & Co.

— Painted Paragraphs: Inspired Description for Writers & Readers. 192p. 1993. 14.95 (0-8050-2978-8) H Holt & Co.

Newlove, George H. Consolidated Balance Sheets. LC 82-48380. (Accountancy in Transition Ser.). 309p. 1982. lib. bdg. 15.00 (0-8240-5325-7) Garland.

Newlove, Jean. Laban for Actors & Dancers: Putting Laban's Movement Theory into Practice: A Step-by-Step Guide. LC 93-40376. 1993. pap. write for info. (0-87830-044-9, Theatre Arts Bks) Routledge Chapman & Hall.

Newlove, John. The Night the Dog Smiled. 80p. (C). 1986. 18.00 (0-920763-33-2, Pub. by ECW Press CN); pap. 9.00 (0-920763-31-6, Pub. by ECW Press CN) Genl Dist Srvs.

Newlun, Chester O. Teaching Children to Summarize in Fifth Grade History. LC 75-177120. (Columbia University. Teachers College. Contributions to Education Ser.: No. 404). (C). reprint ed. 37.50 (0-404-55404-0) AMS Pr.

Newlyn, Dennis, jt. auth. see Watson, Edward R.

Newlyn, Lucy. Paradise Lost & the Romantic Reader. LC 92-463. 340p. (C). 1993. 59.00 (0-19-811277-7, Clarendon Pr) OUP.

Newman. Development Through Life: A Psychosocial Approach. 5th ed. LC 90-25467. 708p. (C). 1991. text ed. 49.95 (0-534-15396-8) Brooks-Cole.

— Linear Mathematics. 1991. 28.00 (0-536-57952-0) Ginn Pr.

— Quantitative Methods in Aquatic Ecotoxicology. 1995. write for info. (0-87371-622-1) Lewis Pubs.

— Vademecum of Antibiotics: Vadecum de los Antibioticos. (SPA.). 1981. pap. 19.95 (0-8288-4681-2, S34979) Fr & Eur.

Newman & Eisenschiml. CWL: American Iliad. 700p. 1995. 14.98 (0-8317-1337-2) Smithmark.

Newman & Madey, eds. Free Electron Lasers: Critical Reviews. 1987. 48.00 (0-89252-773-0, 738) SPIE.

Newman & Scott. Pediatric Nursing. (Clinical Rotation Guide Ser.). 293p. 1989. 14.95 (0-87434-206-6) Springhouse Pub.

Newman & Smith. Geriatric Care Plans. 334p. 1991. 29.95 (0-87434-263-5) Springhouse Pub.

***Newman & Szterenfeld.** Guide to Doing Business in Mexico. 1995. pap. text ed. 14.95 (0-07-046378-6) McGraw.

Newman, jt. auth. see Biuso.

Newman, A. Monoclonal Antibodies: Molecular Structure & Characteristics. 270p. 1988. 129.00 (0-685-20123-6) Elsevier.

Newman, A. C., ed. Chemistry of Clays & Clay Minerals. 480p. 1987. text ed. 156.95 (0-471-01141-X) Wiley.

Newman, Al. Fibber E. Frog. LC 93-77685. (Illus.). 32p. (J). (ps-3). 1993. reprint ed. text ed. 8.95 (0-89334-213-0); reprint ed. pap. 3.95 (0-89334-217-3) Humanics Ltd.

— Fraid E. Cat. LC 93-77687. (Illus.). 32p. (J). (ps-3). 1993. reprint ed. 8.95 (0-89334-215-7); reprint ed. pap. 3.95 (0-89334-219-X) Humanics Ltd.

— Giggle E. Goose. LC 93-77684. (Illus.). 32p. (J). (ps-3). 1993. reprint ed. 8.95 (0-89334-212-2); reprint ed. pap. 3.95 (0-89334-216-5) Humanics Ltd.

— Grub E. Dog. LC 93-77686. (Illus.). 32p. (J). (ps-3). 1993. reprint ed. 8.95 (0-89334-214-9); reprint ed. pap. 3.95 (0-89334-218-1) Humanics Ltd.

N

— It's a Dog's Life Pet Diary. (Other Dog Bks.). (Illus.). 1990. 9.95 (*0-87714-152-5*) Denlingers.

Newman, Albert H. History of Anti-Pedobaptism: From the Rise of Pedobaptism to A.D. 1609. LC 71-144664. reprint ed. 52.00 (*0-404-04686-X*) AMS Pr.

— A Manual of Church History, 2 vols., Set. 1977. lib. bdg. 250.00 (*0-8490-2205-3*) Gordon Pr.

***Newman, Alexander.** Non-Compliance in Winnicott's Words: A Companion to the Writings & Work of D. W. Winnicott. 500p. 1995. 75.00 (*0-8147-5786-3*); pap. 25.00 (*0-8147-5785-5*) NYU Pr.

***Newman, Amy.** Order, or Disorder. (CSU Poetry Ser.: No. XLVIII). 75p. (Orig.). 1995. pap. 10.00 (*1-880834-42-1*) Cleveland St Univ Poetry Ctr.

— Order, or Disorder. (CSU Poetry Ser.: No. XLVIII). 75p. (Orig.). 1995. 15.00 (*1-880834-43-X*) Cleveland St Univ Poetry Ctr.

Newman, Amy, ed. Defining Modern Art: Selected Writings of Alfred H. Barr. (Illus.). 302p. 1986. 39.95 (*0-8109-0715-1*) Abrams.

Newman, Amy, ed. see Phelan, Ellen.

Newman, Anabel P. & Beverstock, Caroline. Adult Literacy: Contexts & Challenges. LC 90-38481. 230p. reprint ed. pap. 65.60 (*0-7837-4588-5*, 2044307) Bks Demand.

Newman, Andrew. The Physical Basis of Predication. (Studies in Philosophy). 325p. (C). 1992. 54.95 (*0-521-41131-9*) Cambridge U Pr.

Newman, Andy. The Uncle's Handbook (& Aunt's Too) One Hundred One Things to Do with Kids. 160p. (Orig.). 1993. pap. 8.00 (*0-380-77192-6*) Avon.

Newman, Anne & Suk, Julie, eds. Bear Crossings: An Anthology of North American Poets. 124p. 1983. pap. 6.95 (*0-917990-08-0*) New South Co.

Newman, Anny. Die Chronik des Popen von Duklja Kroatische Fassung: Untersuchung zu Schrift und Sprache. (Illus.). 231p. (Orig.). (GER.). (C). 1988. pap. text ed. 17.95 (*0-317-92494-X*) Intercult Commns.

***Newman, Anthony.** Bach & the Baroque: European Source Materials from the Baroque & Early Classical Periods with Special Emphasis on the Music of J. S. Bach. 2nd ed. LC 94-5326. 1995. lib. bdg. 48.00 (*0-945193-64-5*); pap. 32.00 (*0-945193-76-9*) Pendragon NY.

Newman, Arnold. Tropical Rainforest. (Illus.). 256p. 1990. 45.00 (*0-8160-1944-4*) Facts on File.

Newman, Art. The Illustrated Treasury of Medical Curiosa. (Illus.). 304p. 1988. text ed. 39.95 (*0-07-046301-8*) Hlth Prof Div.

Newman, Arthur J., ed. In Defense of the American Public School. LC 78-19570. 1979. 30.50 (*0-8211-1307-0*); text ed. write for info. (*0-685-03224-8*) McCutchan.

— In Defense of the American Public School. LC 78-15699. 192p. 1978. pap. text ed. 18.95 (*0-87073-999-9*) Transaction Pubs.

— In Defense of the American Public School. LC 78-15699. 288p. reprint ed. pap. 82.10 (*0-8357-8917-9*, 2033582) Bks Demand.

Newman, Barbara. Biology Research Activities. Kutscher, Eugene, ed. (Illus.). 1988. teacher ed write for info. (*0-318-64016-3*); student ed write for info. (*0-318-64017-1*) Alpha Pub MD.

— From Virile Woman to WomanChrist: Studies in Medieval Religion & Literature. LC 94-37704. (Middle Ages Ser.). (Illus.). 424p. 1995. text ed. 39.95 (*0-8122-3273-9*); pap. text ed. 18.95 (*0-8122-1545-1*) U of Pa Pr.

— Sister of Wisdom: St. Hildegard's Theology of the Feminine. LC 86-16094. 288p. (C). 1987. pap. 12.00 (*0-520-06615-4*) U CA Pr.

— Striking a Balance: Dancers Talk about Dancing. rev. ed. LC 91-44442. (Illus.). 402p. 1992. reprint ed. pap. 17.95 (*0-87910-154-7*) Limelight Edns.

Newman, Barbara & Newman, Philip. When Kids Go to College: A Parent's Guide to Changing Relationships. 208p. 1992. 40.00 (*0-8142-0561-5*); pap. 19.95 (*0-8142-0562-3*) Ohio St U Pr.

Newman, Barbara & Spatt, Leslie E. Sadler's Wells Royal Ballet "Swan Lake" (Illus.). 143p. 1983. 29.95 (*0-903102-72-2*, Pub. by Dance Bks UK) Princeton Bk Co.

Newman, Barbara, ed. see Hildegard of Bingen, St.

***Newman, Barbara M. & Newman, Philip R.** Development Through Life: A Psychosocial Approach. 6th ed. 763p. 1995. text ed. 49.95 (*0-534-23334-1*) Brooks-Cole.

Newman, Barclay M. & Nida, Eugene A. A Handbook on Paul's Letter to the Romans. LC 93-39491. (UBS Handbook Ser.). Orig. Title: Translators Handbook on Paul's Letter to the Romans. vii, 325p. 1994. reprint ed. 14.00 (*0-8267-0160-4*, 102680) Untd Bible Soc.

— A Handbook on the Acts of the Apostles. LC 92-40063. (UBS Handbook Ser.). Orig. Title: Translator's Handbook on the Acts of the Apostles. vii, 542p. 1993. reprint ed. 16.00 (*0-8267-0159-0*, 102677) Untd Bible Soc.

— A Handbook on the Gospel of John. LC 92-40060. (UBS Handbook Ser.). Orig. Title: Translator's Handbook on the Gospel of John. viii, 681p. 1993. reprint ed. 18.00 (*0-8267-0158-2*, 102726) Untd Bible Soc.

Newman, Barclay M. & Stine, Philip C. A Handbook on the Gospel of Matthew. LC 92-25802. (UBS Handbook Ser.). Orig. Title: Translator's Handbook on the Gospel of Matthew. x, 911p. 1993. reprint ed. 18.00 (*0-8267-0155-8*, 102725) Untd Bible Soc.

Newman, Barclay M., jt. auth. see Bratcher, Robert G.

***Newman, Barry.** The Bear's World: Remedy for the Blues. (Illus.). (Orig.). 1994. pap. 9.95 (*0-9642844-4-8*) Chubby Bear.

Newman, Benjamin. Searching for the Figure in the Carpet in the Tales of Henry James: Reflections of an Ordinary Reader. (American University Studies: English Language & Literature: Ser. IV, Vol. 49). 194p. (C). 1987. text ed. 39.00 (*0-8204-0442-X*) P Lang Pubs.

Newman, Bernard. The New Europe. LC 72-4581. (Essay Index Reprint Ser.). 1977. reprint ed. 31.95 (*0-8369-2963-2*) Ayer.

Newman, Bernard, jt. auth. see Wilson, Ken.

Newman, Bernard H. & Oliverio, Mary E. Business Communications: A Managerial Approach. LC 76-21593. 1976. pap. 4.95 (*0-686-17616-2*) Monong Pub.

Newman, Bertram. Edmund Burke. LC 71-102251. (Select Bibliographies Reprint Ser.). 1977. 30.95 (*0-8369-5136-0*) Ayer.

Newman, Beryl. When Descanso Was Young: Early Settlers & Ranchers Descanso, 1845-1947. (Illus.). 204p. (Orig.). Date not set. pap. 12.00 (*0-938711-25-3*) Tecolote Pubns.

Newman, Beryl E. Simply Benjamin. LC 94-60119. (Illus.). 320p. 1994. pap. 9.95 (*1-55523-684-7*) Winston-Derek.

Newman, Betsy & Mara, Joseph. Reading, Writing & TV: A Video Handbook for Teachers. 190p. 1995. pap. 25.00 (*0-917846-33-8*, 95583) Highsmith Pr.

***Newman, Bob.** Commonsense Outdoor Survival: How to Survive in the Wilderness for Five Days. (Nuts-n-Bolts Ser.). (Illus.). 32p. 1994. pap. 4.95 (*0-89732-166-9*) Menasha Ridge.

— The Complete Guide to Fly Fishing Maine: Where, When, & How to Take Maine's Best Fighting Fish. LC 94-14256. 144p. 1994. pap. 13.50 (*0-89272-348-3*) Down East.

— Inshore Fishing the Carolina Coasts: A Complete Guide to Fishing All Coastal Waters of the Carolinas. Bledsoe, Jerry, ed. LC 94-70668. (Illus.). 165p. (Orig.). 1994. pap. 13.95 (*1-878086-27-8*) Down Home NC.

— Land navigation. (Nuts-N-Bolts Guides Ser.). 1995. 4.95 (*0-89732-178-2*) Menasha Ridge.

— Nuts-'n-Bolts, Weather Forecasting for Outdoor Enthusiasts. (Nuts-N-Bolts Guides Ser.). (Illus.). 32p. 1995. pap. 4.95 (*0-89732-179-0*) Menasha Ridge.

— Wilderness Wayfinding: How to Survive in the Wilderness As You Travel. (Illus.). 160p. 1994. pap. 15.00 (*0-87364-760-2*) Paladin Pr.

Newman, Bobby. The Reluctant Alliance: Behaviorism & Humanism. 130p. (C). 1992. 21.95 (*0-87975-727-2*) Prometheus Bks.

Newman, Bruce I. The Marketing of the President: Political Marketing As Campaign Strategy. LC 93-32450. (C). 1993. text ed. 46.00 (*0-8039-5137-X*); pap. text ed. 22.95 (*0-8039-5138-8*) Sage.

Newman, Bruce I. & Sheth, Jagdish N. A Theory of Political Choice Behavior. LC 86-15152. (Praeger Series in Public & Nonprofit Sector Marketing). 199p. 1987. text ed. 49.95 (*0-275-92187-5*, C2187, Praeger Pubs) Greenwood.

Newman, Bruce I. & Sheth, Jagdish N., eds. Political Marketing: Readings & Annotated Bibliography. LC 85-26866. (Reading Ser.). 259p. (Orig.). 1986. pap. text ed. 29.00 (*0-87757-180-5*) Am Mktg.

— Political Marketing: Readings & Annotated Bibliography. LC 85-26866. 269p. (Orig.). reprint ed. pap. 76.70 (*0-7837-2494-2*, 2042659) Bks Demand.

Newman, C. E., et al, eds. Ovarian Cancer: Proceedings of the International Symposium on Ovarian Cancer, 24-25 September 1979, Birmingham. LC 80-40166. (Illus.). 260p. 1980. 50.00 (*0-08-025532-9*, Pergamon Pr) Elsevier.

Newman, C. J., jt. ed. see Smith, T. J.

Newman, C. T. The Newman Report: Interim Report, Eighth Coast Guard District Offshore Operations Liason Staff, 1 June 1973. 109p. (Orig.). 1985. pap. text ed. 50.85 (*0-934114-67-6*) Marine Educ.

Newman, Cade Newman & Horn, Bill. Nutrition & Aids. 450p. 1993. 54.00 (*0-8342-0308-1*, 20308) Aspen Pub.

Newman, Carey C. Paul's Glory-Christology: Tradition & Rhetoric. (Novum Testamentum, Supplements Ser.: Vol. 69). xvi, 305p. 1991. 91.50 (*90-04-09463-6*) E J Brill.

Newman, Carol, ed. see Hildebrand, Verna.

Newman, Carol, ed. see Morton, Ruth.

Newman, Carole, jt. auth. see Newman, Isadore.

Newman, Charles. A Child's History of America: Some Ribs & Riffs for the Sixties. LC 82-73500. 307p. 1973. 13.95 (*0-89366-245-3*) Ultramarine Pub.

— The Post-Modern Aura: The Act of Fiction in an Age of Inflation. 203p. 1985. reprint ed. 29.95 (*0-8101-0668-X*); reprint ed. pap. 14.95 (*0-8101-0669-8*) Northwestern U Pr.

— The Promisekeeper: A Tephramancy. LC 76-139651. 1971. 25.00 (*0-671-20822-5*) Ultramarine Pub.

— There Must Be More to Love Than Death: Three Short Novels. LC 76-17743. 217p. 1976. 12.95 (*0-89366-257-7*) Ultramarine Pub.

— White Jazz. LC 86-46072. 213p. (Orig.). 1984. pap. 7.95 (*0-385-18863-3*) Ultramarine Pub.

Newman, Charles L. & Amos, William E., eds. Parole: Legal Issues, Decision-Making, Research. 430p. 1975. 15.00 (*0-87945-034-7*); pap. 8.95 (*0-685-01623-4*) Fed Legal Pubn.

***Newman, Chris.** Essential American Government. 112p. (C). 1995. pap. text ed. 18.95 (*0-7872-1066-8*) Kendall-Hunt.

— Phillip's Dream World: A Coloring Book. (Illus.). 52p. (Orig.). (J). 1992. pap. 5.95 (*0-9635004-3-0*) Flying Heart.

Newman, Christopher. Backfire. 320p. 1990. mass mkt. 5.99 (*0-449-13295-1*, GM) Fawcett.

— Dead End Game. 320p. (Orig.). 1995. pap. text ed. 5.99 (*0-425-14564-6*) Berkley Pub.

— Dead End Game. 256p. (Orig.). 1994. 21.95 (*0-399-13952-4*, Putnam) Putnam Pub Group.

— Killer. LC 94-32236. 1995. write for info. (*0-399-14044-1*, Putnam) Putnam Pub Group.

— Knock-Off. 1989. mass mkt. 5.99 (*0-449-13294-3*) Fawcett.

— Mid-Town North. 1991. mass mkt. 5.95 (*0-449-14689-8*, GM) Fawcett.

— Midtown South. (Orig.). 1986. mass mkt. 5.99 (*0-449-13064-9*, GM) Fawcett.

— Nineteenth Precinct. (Orig.). 1992. mass mkt. 5.99 (*0-449-14732-0*, GM) Fawcett.

— Precinct Command. 1993. mass mkt. 4.99 (*0-449-14795-9*, GM) Fawcett.

— Sixth Precinct. 320p. (Orig.). 1987. mass mkt. 4.95 (*0-449-13174-2*, GM) Fawcett.

Newman, Claire M. & Turkel, Susan. Chance It! Probability Simulation. (C). 1984. pap. 4.00 (*0-89824-056-5*); teacher ed. pap. 5.00 (*0-89824-057-3*); Apple II 15.00 (*0-685-42710-2*); 4.00 (*0-89824-068-9*) Trillium Pr.

Newman, Claire M., jt. auth. see Artzt, Alice F.

Newman, D. & Wilson, K. Models in Plant Physiology & Biochemistry, Vol. 1. LC 87-9363. 1987. reprint ed. 90.00 (*0-8493-4343-7*, CRC Reprint) Franklin.

— Models in Plant Physiology & Biochemistry, Vol. 2. LC 87-9363. 1987. reprint ed. 95.00 (*0-8493-4344-5*, CRC Reprint) Franklin.

— Models in Plant Physiology & Biochemistry, Vol. 3. LC 87-9363. 1987. reprint ed. 86.00 (*0-8493-4345-3*, CRC Reprint) Franklin.

Newman, D., jt. auth. see Price, C.

Newman, D. J. Approximation with Rational Functions. LC 79-14971. (CBMS Regional Conference Series in Mathematics: No. 41). 52p. 1981. reprint ed. pap. 19.00 (*0-8218-1691-8*, CBMS-41) Am Math.

— A Problem Seminar. (Problem Books in Mathematics). 113p. 1982. 34.50 (*0-387-90765-3*) Spr-Verlag.

Newman, D. J., jt. auth. see Bak, J.

Newman, D. J., jt. auth. see MacKeown, P. K.

Newman, D. L., jt. auth. see Van Der Tuin, J. D.

Newman, D. M., jt. ed. see Lingeman, James E.

Newman, Daisy. The Autumn's Brightness. 251p. 1991. pap. 10.95 (*0-944350-18-6*) Friends United.

— Diligence in Love. 252p. 1992. pap. 11.95 (*0-944350-22-4*) Friends United.

— I Take Thee, Serenity. large type ed. LC 94-5392. 470p. 1994. 21.95 (*0-8161-7492-X*) Hall.

— I Take Thee Serenity. LC 89-11798. 310p. 1989. reprint ed. pap. 10.95 (*0-944350-09-7*) Friends United.

— Indian Summer of the Heart. LC 82-6226. 376p. 1990. pap. 11.95 (*0-944350-15-1*) Friends United.

— A Procession of Friends. (C). 1988. 100.00 (*0-913408-59-X*, Pub. by W Sessions UK) St Mut.

Newman, Danny. Subscribe Now: Building Arts Audiences Through Dynamic Subscription Promotion. 3rd ed. LC 77-81452. (Illus.). 300p. (C). 1977. pap. 13.95 (*0-930452-01-1*) Theatre Comm.

Newman, David. David Newman's Movie Quiz Book. Spradlin, Kelly A. & Spradlin, Michael P., eds. 208p. (Orig.). 1993. pap. 12.50 (*1-881892-01-8*) Spradlin & Assocs.

— Population, Settlement, & Conflict: Israel & the West Bank. (Update Ser.). (Illus.). 64p. (C). 1991. pap. 13.95 (*0-521-40804-0*) Cambridge U Pr.

Newman, David, ed. The Impact of Gush Emunim: Politics & Settlement in the West Bank. LC 84-40370. 256p. 1985. text ed. 39.95 (*0-312-40972-9*) St Martin.

Newman, David B. Taxation of Financially Distressed Businesses, 1 vol. LC 93-9101. (Tax Ser.). 1993. 120.00 (*0-685-67256-5*) Clark Boardman Callaghan.

Newman, David H., jt. auth. see Hyde, William F.

***Newman, David M.** Sociology, Exploring the Architecture of Everyday Life. LC 94-38140. 1995. pap. write for info. (*0-8039-9004-9*) Pine Forge.

***Newman, David M., ed.** Sociology, Exploring the Architecture of Everyday Life: Readings. LC 94-28139. 1995. pap. write for info. (*0-8039-9054-5*) Pine Forge.

Newman, David R. Worship As Praise & Empowerment. LC 88-2506. 168p. 1988. pap. 10.95 (*0-8298-0774-8*) Pilgrim OH.

Newman, Debra L., comp. Black History: A Guide to Civilian Records in the National Archives. LC 84-16597. (Illus.). 379p. 1984. pap. 15.00 (*0-911333-31-2*, 200030); boxed 25.00 (*0-911333-21-5*, 100030) National Archives & Recs.

Newman, Denis, et al. The Construction Zone: Working for Cognitive Change in School. (Learning in Doing: Social, Cognitive & Computational Perspectives Ser.). (Illus.). 160p. (C). 1989. pap. 16.95 (*0-521-38942-9*) Cambridge U Pr.

Newman, Denise. The Blood Flower. 8p. 1993. 15.00 (*0-9632085-3-5*) Em Pr.

Newman, Donald G. & Larock, Bruce E. Engineer-in-Training: Examination Review. 3rd ed. 600p. 1991. text ed. 49.95 (*0-471-50827-6*) Wiley.

Newman, Donald J. Introduction to Criminal Justice. 3rd ed. 564p. (C). 1986. 8.95 (*0-685-08613-5*) McGraw.

***Newman, Donald J., ed.** James Boswell, Psychological Interpretations. LC 94-43702. 1995. text ed. 39.95 (*0-312-12142-3*) St Martin.

Newman, Donald J. & Anderson, Patrick. Introduction to Criminal Justice. 4th ed. (Illus.). 576p. (C). 1989. text ed. 33.95 (*0-394-38269-2*); write for info. (*0-394-38687-6*) Random.

Newman, Donald J., jt. auth. see Anderson, Patrick R.

Newman, E. Colonial Coins of Virginia. 2nd ed. 1990. pap. 15.00 (*0-942666-50-X*) S J Durst.

— Continental Currency of 1776 & Fugio Cent Varieties. (Illus.). 1982. reprint ed. pap. 6.00 (*0-915262-90-8*) S J Durst.

Newman, E. M. Seeing London. 1972. 59.95 (*0-8490-1017-9*) Gordon Pr.

— Seeing Paris. 1972. 59.95 (*0-8490-1018-7*) Gordon Pr.

Newman, Ed. Hot Air & Gas: The Basics of Balloons. LC 92-70713. (Illus.). 52p. (Orig.). (J). (gr. 4-12). 1992. pap. 6.95 (*0-9632038-0-0*) Greenway Pub.

Newman, Edgar L., ed. Historical Dictionary of France from the 1815 Restoration to the Second Empire. LC 85-17728. 1915p. 1987. text ed. 195.00 (*0-313-22751-9*, NDH/) Greenwood.

— Historical Dictionary of France from the 1815 Restoration to the Second Empire, 1. LC 85-17728. 1915p. 1987. text ed. 125.00 (*0-313-26045-1*, NDH/01) Greenwood.

— Historical Dictionary of France from the 1815 Restoration to the Second Empire, Vol. 2. LC 85-17728. 1915p. 1987. text ed. 125.00 (*0-313-26046-X*, NDH/02) Greenwood.

Newman, Edwin. A Civil Tongue. LC 76-11607. 1976. 9.95 (*0-672-52267-5*, Bobbs) Macmillan.

— Edwin Newman, on Language. 1992. 9.98 (*0-88365-795-3*) Galahad Bks.

— I Must Say. 312p. 1989. pap. 9.95 (*0-446-39099-2*) Warner Bks.

— Strictly Speaking: Will America Be the Death of English? LC 74-6525. 224p. 1974. 9.95 (*0-672-51990-9*, Bobbs) Macmillan.

Newman, Edwin S. & Wypyski, Eugene M. U. S. International Trade Reports, 7 binders. LC 81-11181. (First Ser.). 1981. New Series, incl. U. S. Court of International Trade-Rules. 1986 On. ring bd. 760.00 (*0-379-20798-2*); Approx. 2 releases per yr. write for info. (*0-318-54765-1*) Oceana.

Newman, Eric. The Early Paper Money of America. 3rd ed. LC 76-8365. (Illus.). 480p. 1990. 49.95 (*0-87341-120-X*) Krause Pubns.

Newman, Eric P. Coins of Colonial Virginia. 2nd ed. (Illus.). 1990. pap. 20.00 (*0-915262-67-3*) S J Durst.

Newman, Eric P., ed. Studies on Money in Early America. LC 76-6790. (Illus.). 222p. reprint ed. pap. 63.30 (*0-7837-6359-X*, 2046071) Bks Demand.

Newman, Eric P., jt. auth. see Madous, H. Michael.

Newman, Ernest. Elgar. 3rd ed. LC 74-24163. reprint ed. 34.50 (*0-404-13058-5*) AMS Pr.

— Essays from the World of Music. LC 77-17326. (Music Reprint Ser.). (Illus.). 1978. reprint ed. lib. bdg. 29.50 (*0-306-77519-0*) Da Capo.

— Essays from the World of Music, Vol. 1. 1986. 14.95 (*0-7145-3548-6*) Riverrun NY.

— Gluck & the Opera: A Study in Musical History. LC 76-43929. (Music & Theatre in France in the 17th & 18th Centuries Ser.). reprint ed. 35.00 (*0-404-60176-6*) AMS Pr.

— Gluck & the Opera: A Study in Musical History. LC 76-7579. 300p. 1976. reprint ed. text ed. 59.75 (*0-8371-8849-0*, NEGO, Greenwood Pr) Greenwood.

— Gluck & the Opera: A Study in Musical History. 300p. 1990. reprint ed. lib. bdg. 69.00 (*0-7812-9064-3*) Rprt Serv.

— Hugo Wolf. 279p. 1990. reprint ed. lib. bdg. 69.00 (*0-7812-9100-3*) Rprt Serv.

— The Life of Richard Wagner, Vol. 1. LC 76-22682. reprint ed. pap. 148.00 (*0-318-34828-4*, 2031699) Bks Demand.

— The Man Liszt. (Music Book Index Ser.). 313p. 1992. reprint ed. lib. bdg. 89.00 (*0-7812-9484-3*) Rprt Serv.

— More Essays from the World of Music. 1986. 14.95 (*0-7145-3549-4*) Riverrun NY.

— More Essays from the World of Music. LC 77-17332. (Music Reprint Ser.: 1978). (Illus.). 1978. reprint ed. lib. bdg. 35.00 (*0-306-77520-4*) Da Capo.

— A Musical Critic's Holiday. 330p. 1990. reprint ed. lib. bdg. 79.00 (*0-7812-9129-1*) Rprt Serv.

— A Musical Motley. LC 76-10332. (Music Reprint Ser.). 1976. lib. bdg. 35.00 (*0-306-70784-5*) Da Capo.

— A Musical Motley. 291p. 1990. reprint ed. lib. bdg. 69.00 (*0-7812-9001-5*) Rprt Serv.

— Musical Studies. LC 68-25297. (Studies in Music: No. 42). 1969. reprint ed. lib. bdg. 75.00 (*0-8383-0309-9*) M S G Haskell Hse.

— Musical Studies: Music Book Index. 319p. 1993. reprint ed. lib. bdg. 89.00 (*0-7812-9706-0*) Rprt Serv.

— Richard Strauss. LC 79-94279. (Select Bibliographies Reprint Ser.). 1977. 21.95 (*0-8369-5053-4*) Ayer.

— Richard Strauss. 144p. 1990. reprint ed. lib. bdg. 59.00 (*0-7812-9092-9*) Rprt Serv.

— Stories of the Great Operas & Their Composers, 3 vols. 1990. reprint ed. lib. bdg. 148.00 (*0-7812-9158-5*) Rprt Serv.

— Stories of the Great Operas & Their Composers, 3 vols., Set. 1988. reprint ed. lib. bdg. 249.00 (*0-7812-0408-9*) Rprt Serv.

— Stories of the Great Operas & Their Composers, 3 vols., Set. reprint ed. 195.00 (*0-403-01632-0*) Scholarly.

— Unconscious Beethoven: An Essay in Musical Psychology. 154p. 1990. reprint ed. lib. bdg. 59.00 (*0-7812-9045-7*) Rprt Serv.

— Wagner: As Man & Artist. LC 85-18155. (Illus.). 432p. 1985. reprint ed. pap. 15.95 (*0-87910-052-4*) Limelight Edns.

— Wagner As Man & Artist. 1963. 12.75 (*0-8446-2653-8*) Peter Smith.

— The Wagner Operas. 729p. 1991. pap. text ed. 19.95 (*0-691-02716-1*) Princeton U Pr.

Newman, Ernest, ed. see Day, John A.

Newman, Ernest, tr. see Schweitzer, Albert.

Newman, Evelyn S., jt. auth. see Sherman, Susan R.

Newman, F. X., ed. The Meaning of Courtly Love: Papers from the First CEMERS Conference. LC 68-25571. 102p. (C). 1968. 57.50 (*0-87395-038-0*); pap. 18.95 (*0-87395-222-7*) State U NY Pr.

Newman, Felice, tr. see Galgoczi, Erzsebet.

Newman, Frances. Dead Lovers are Faithful Lovers: A Novel by Frances Newman. LC 93-39195. (Brown Thrasher Bks.). 312p. 1994. reprint ed. pap. 17.95 (*0-8203-1588-5*) U of Ga Pr.

An Asterisk (*) at the beginning of an entry indicates that the title is appearing in BIP for the first time.

— Frances Newman's Letters. (American Biography Ser.). 372p. 1991. reprint ed. lib. bdg. 79.00 (*0-7812-8296-9*) Rprt Serv.

— The Hard-Boiled Virgin. Hardwick, Elizabeth, ed. LC 76-51674. (Rediscovered Fiction by American Women Ser.). 1977. lib. bdg. 29.95 (*0-405-10052-3*) Ayer.

— The Hard-Boiled Virgin: A Novel by Frances Newman. LC 80-16376. (Brown Thrasher Bks.). 306p. 1994. reprint ed. 17.95 (*0-8203-0526-X*) U of Ga Pr.

Newman, Frances, ed. see Laforgue, Jules.

Newman, Francis W. Regal Rome, an Intro to Roman History. 1852. 20.00 (*0-8196-1556-0*) Biblo.

Newman, Francis X., ed. Social Unrest in the Late Middle Ages: Papers of the Fifteenth Annual Conference of the Center for Medieval & Early Renaissance Studies. LC 85-28420. (Medieval & Renaissance Texts & Studies: Vol. 39). (Illus.). 160p. 1986. 16.00 (*0-86698-071-7*) MRTS.

Newman, Frank. Higher Education & the American Resurgence. LC 85-21357. 268p. 1985. pap. text ed. 8.00 (*0-931050-28-6*) Carnegie Fnd Advan Teach.

Newman, Frank & Weissbrodt, David. International Human Rights: Law, Policy & Process, Problems & Materials. 812p. 1990. 54.00 (*0-87084-368-0*) Anderson Pub Co.

Newman, Frank C., jt. auth. see Lillich, Richard B.

Newman, Fred. The Myth of Psychology. LC 91-76608. 229p. 1991. pap. 12.95 (*0-9628621-2-6*) Castillo Intl.

Newman, Fred & Holzman, Lois. Lev Vygotsky: Revolutionary Scientist. LC 92-28810. (Critical Psychology Ser.). 192p. 1993. 49.95 (*0-415-06441-4*, A5802, Routledge NY); pap. 16.95 (*0-415-06442-2*, B0216, Routledge NY) Routledge.

*__Newman, Fred, et al.__ Let's Develop! A Guide to Continuous Personal Growth. LC 94-68612. 272p. 1994. pap. 11.95 (*0-9628621-6-9*) Castillo Intl.

Newman, Frederick L. & Sorenson, James E. Integrated Clinical & Fiscal Management in Mental Health. Caddy, Glenn R., ed. LC 85-6219. (Developments in Clinical Psychology Ser.). 408p. 1986. text ed. 52.50 (*0-89391-233-6*) Ablex Pub.

Newman, Frederick R. Mouthsounds. LC 80-51513. (Illus.). 128p. 1980. pap. 6.95 (*0-89480-128-7*, 427) Workman Pub.

Newman, G. C., jt. auth. see Person, R. J.

Newman, G. F. Operation Bad Apple: (Royal Court Writers Ser.). 43p. 1988. pap. 6.95 (*0-413-50270-8*, A0198) Heinemann.

Newman, G. R. & Hobot, J. A. Resin Microscopy & On-Section Immunocytochemistry. LC 93-14253. (Laboratory Ser.). 221p. 1993. 49.00 (*0-387-56429-2*) Spr-Verlag.

Newman, Gene & Tada, Joni E. All God's Children: Ministry with Disabled Persons. rev. ed. LC 92-28627. 128p. 1993. pap. 10.99 (*0-310-59381-6*) Zondervan.

Newman, Gene, jt. auth. see Newman, Marsha.

Newman, George. Interpreters of Nature: Essays. LC 68-20325. (Essay Index Reprint Ser.). 1977. 20.95 (*0-8369-0741-8*) Ayer.

— One Hundred & One Ways to Be a Long-Distance Super-Dad. LC 81-66803. (Illus.). 112p. (Orig.). 1981. pap. 7.95 (*0-88247-800-1*) R & E Pubs.

Newman, Gerald. Happy Birthday, Little League. LC 88-38158. (First Bks.). 64p. (J). (gr. 3-6). 1989. lib. bdg. 13. 23 (*0-531-10687-X*) Watts.

Newman, Gerald & Layfield, Eleanor N. Allergies. LC 91-33862. (Venture Bks.). (Illus.). 112p. (YA). (gr. 7-12). 1992. lib. bdg. 14.28 (*0-531-12516-5*) Watts.

Newman Gordon, Pauline. Dictionnaire des Idees dans l'Oeuvre de Marcel Proust. (FRE.). 1968. 59.95 (*0-8288-6634-1*, M-6624) Fr & Eur.

Newman, Graeme & Newman, Tamsin. Australia: Hippocrene Companion Guide. 252p. 1992. pap. 16.95 (*0-7818-0041-2*) Hippocrene Bks.

— Companion Guide to Australia. (Companion Guides Ser.). 252p. (Orig.). 1991. pap. 16.95 (*0-87052-034-2*) Hippocrene Bks.

Newman, Graeme, jt. auth. see Marongiu, Pietro.

Newman, Graeme R., ed. Crime & Deviance: A Comparative Perspective. LC 80-11629. (Sage Annual Reviews of Studies in Deviance: No. 4). 335p. reprint ed. pap. 95.50 (*0-8357-8501-7*, 2034777) Bks Demand.

Newman, Grant. Teaching Children Music: Fundamentals of Music & Method. 3rd ed. 400p. (C). 1989. student ed write for info. (*0-697-03652-9*); spiral bd. write for info. (*0-697-03644-8*) Brown & Benchmark.

— Teaching Children Music: Fundamentals of Music & Method. 4th ed. 400p. (C). 1995. spiral bd. write for info. (*0-697-12540-8*) Brown & Benchmark.

— Teaching Children Music: Fundamentals of Music & Method. 4th ed. 80p. (C). 1995. student ed, pap. text ed. write for info. (*0-697-12541-6*) Brown & Benchmark.

Newman, Gray. Business Internationals Guide to Doing Business in Mexico. 1992. text ed. 34.95 (*0-07-009339-3*) McGraw.

Newman, Gwen, illus. Perennials: A Southern Celebration of Foods & Flavors. LC 83-81825. vi, 426p. 1984. 14.95 (*0-9612234-0-5*) Perennial Pubns.

Newman, H. Michael. Direct Digital Control of Building Systems: Theory & Practice. (Series of Practical Construction Guides). 264p. 1994. text ed. 54.95 (*0-471-51696-1*) Wiley.

Newman, H. Morton, jt. auth. see Blake, Fay M.

Newman, Harold. Effective Language Arts Practices in the Elementary School: Selected Readings. LC 75-38951. 894p. reprint ed. pap. 180.00 (*0-317-07902-6*, 2011880) Bks Demand.

— Extending Reading Horizons. 95p. (Orig.). (C). 1994. pap. text ed. 20.00 (*0-9613577-4-6*) Prestige Educ.

— Extending Reading Horizons: A College Reader. LC 93-40696. 1994. write for info. (*0-9613577-5-4*) Prestige Educ.

— An Illustrated Dictionary of Jewelry. LC 86-51260. (Illus.). 336p. 1994. reprint ed. pap. 24.95 (*0-500-27452-5*) Thames Hudson.

— An Illustrated Dictionary of Silverware. LC 86-51576. (Illus.). 384p. 1987. 39.95 (*0-500-23456-6*) Thames Hudson.

— Parents & Teachers Ask about Reading. 115p. 1986. pap. text ed. 15.00 (*0-9613577-1-1*) Prestige Educ.

— Reading - Learning - Enjoying: A College Reader. LC 88-19495. 94p. (C). 1988. pap. text ed. 15.00 (*0-9613577-2-X*) Prestige Educ.

— Reading for Understanding & Stimulation: A College Reader. (Orig.). (C). 1990. pap. text ed. write for info. (*0-9613577-3-8*) Prestige Educ.

— Upgrading Your College Reading: Study Skills. 108p. (Orig.). (C). 1984. pap. 15.00 (*0-9613577-0-3*) Prestige Educ.

— Veilleuses: A Collector's Guide. (Illus.). 176p. 1988. 45.00 (*0-8453-4755-1*, Cornwall Bks) Assoc Univ Prs.

Newman, Harold & Savage, George. An Illustrated Dictionary of Ceramics. LC 85-51073. (Illus.). 1985. pap. 24.95 (*0-500-27380-4*) Thames Hudson.

Newman, Harry & Davis, Clinton T., eds. Beyond Tradition: Transcripts of the First National Symposium on Non-Traditional Casting. (Illus.). 122p. (Orig.). 1988. pap. 15. 00 (*0-927340-00-3*) Non-Traditional.

*__Newman, Harry W.__ Anne Arundel Gentry: A Genealogical History of Twenty-Two Pioneers of Anne Arundel County & Their Descendants. 668p. 1995. reprint ed. lib. bdg. 69.50 (*0-8328-4692-9*) Higginson Bk Co.

— Charles County Gentry. (Illus.). 321p. 1990. reprint ed. 25.00 (*0-685-60386-5*, 4095) Clearfield Co.

— The Flowering of the Maryland Palatinate: An Intimate & Objective HIstory of the Province of Maryland to the Overthrow of Proprietory Rule in 1654. LC 83-82451. (Illus.). 359p. 1985. reprint ed. 25.00 (*0-8063-1051-0*) Genealog Pub.

— Maryland Revolutionary Records: Data Obtained from 3,050 Pension Claims & Bounty Land Applications, Including 1,000 Marriages of Maryland Soldiers & a List of 1,200 Proved Services of Soldiers & Patriots of Other States. LC 67-28367. 155p. 1993. reprint ed. 17.50 (*0-8063-0257-7*) Genealog Pub.

— To Maryland from Overseas. LC 84-82536. 190p. 1991. reprint ed. 20.00 (*0-8063-1109-6*) Genealog Pub.

Newman, Harvey & Scherer, Judith. Planned Placement of Community Care Facilities: Balancing the Rights & Needs of Clients & the Community. 85p. 1978. pap. 5.00 (*0-88156-076-6*) Comm Serv Soc NY.

Newman, Harvey, et al. Self-Evaluation for Planning in Human Services Organizations. 180p. 1986. ring bd. write for info. (*0-318-61139-2*) AMACOM.

— Self-Evaluation for Planning in Human Services Organizations. LC 86-48283. 180p. 1987. ring bd. 65.00 (*0-8144-1145-2*) AMACOM.

Newman, Henry. Hymns. 1983. pap. 9.95 (*0-87193-199-0*) Dimension Bks.

Newman, Henry W. Acute Alcoholic Intoxication: A Critical Review. x, 207p. 1941. 29.50 (*0-8047-0995-5*) Stanford U Pr.

— Acute Alcoholic Intoxication: A Critical Review. fac. ed. LC 41-28278. 111p. 1941. reprint ed. pap. 30.00 (*0-7837-7919-4*, 2047675) Bks Demand.

Newman, Herta. Virginia Woolf & the Problem of Character. (Origins of Modernism Ser.: Vol. 3). 250p. Date not set. 34.00 (*0-8240-5172-6*, H1328) Garland.

Newman, Horatio H., ed. Evolution, Genetics & Eugenics. LC 32-26475. (Illus.). 620p. 1970. reprint ed. text ed. 89. 50 (*0-8371-1880-8*, NEEV, Greenwood Pr) Greenwood.

Newman, I. A., jt. ed. see Hopper, K.

Newman, Isadore. Basic Procedures in Conducting Survey Research. 4th ed. 39p. 1976. pap. text ed. 1.00 (*0-917180-04-6*) I Newman.

Newman, Isadore, ed. Computer-Assisted Instructions. Four Selected Articles & a Cross Referenced, Annotated Bibliography. 141p. 1975. pap. text ed. 4.00 (*0-917180-03-8*) I Newman.

Newman, Isadore & Benz, Carolyn. Multiple Linear Regression: A Workbook, Syllabus, Readings; Problems & Exams. 1979. pap. text ed. 7.25 (*0-917180-07-0*) I Newman.

Newman, Isadore & Newman, Carole. Conceptual Statistics for Beginners. 2nd ed. 298p. (C). 1994. pap. text ed. 28. 50 (*0-8191-9420-4*) U Pr of Amer.

— Thirty-Eight, Twenty-Two, Thirty-Six Conceptual Statistics for Beginners. 4th ed. 207p. 1977. pap. text ed. 5.50 (*0-917180-06-2*) I Newman.

Newman, Isadore, et al. An Introduction to the Basic Concepts & Techniques of Measurement & Evaluation. 4th ed. 210p. 1976. reprint ed. pap. text ed. 5.00 (*0-917180-05-4*) I Newman.

Newman, Isidora. Fairy Flowers. 1976. 20.95 (*0-8488-0596-8*) Amereon Ltd.

Newman, J., jt. auth. see Knight, David C.

Newman, J. C., Jr. & Elber, Wolf, eds. Mechanics of Fatigue Crack Closure, STP 982. LC 88-6303. (Special Technical Publication (STP) Ser.). (Illus.). 650p. 1988. text ed. 105.00 (*0-8031-0996-2*, 04-982000-30) ASTM.

Newman, J. C., Jr. & Loss, F. J., eds. Elastic-Plastic Fracture Mechanics Technology, STP 896. LC 85-22965. (Illus.). 185p. 1986. text ed. 30.00 (*0-8031-0449-9*, 04-896000-30) ASTM.

Newman, J. D., ed. The Physiological Control of Mammalian Vocalization. (Illus.). 438p. 1988. 105.00 (*0-306-43003-7*, Plenum Pr) Plenum.

Newman, J. G., et al. Static SIMS Handbook of Polymer Analysis. LC 90-62564. (Illus.). 200p. (Orig.). 1991. write for info. (*0-9627026-0-9*); pap. write for info. (*0-9627026-1-7*) Perkin-Elmer.

Newman, J. Robert, jt. auth. see Edwards, Ward.

Newman, J. Wilson. The Private Sector. (Credibility of Institutions, Policies & Leadership Ser.: Vol. 6). 140p. (Orig.). 1985. lib. bdg. 39.00 (*0-8191-4765-6*, Pub. by White Miller Center); pap. 15.00 (*0-8191-4766-4*) U Pr of Amer.

Newman, Jacqueline M. Melting Pot: An Annotated Bibliography & Guide to Food & Nutrition Information for Ethnic Groups in America. 2nd ed. LC 92-46351. 256p. 1993. 38.00 (*0-8240-7756-3*, SS708) Garland.

*__Newman, James A.__ Making a Living. (Illus.). 120p. (Orig.). (J). (gr. 2-8). 1991. pap. 7.95 (*0-9642980-0-7*) J A Newman.

Newman, James C., Jr., ed. see Reuter, Walter G.

*__Newman, James L.__ The Peopling of Africa: A Geographic Interpretation. LC 94-28259. 1995. write for info. (*0-300-06003-3*) Yale U Pr.

Newman, James L., jt. ed. see Griffith, Daniel A.

Newman, James R., ed. The World of Mathematics, 4 vols., Set. LC 88-20040. 2784p. 1988. boxed 99.95 (*1-55615-149-7*, Tempus Bks); boxed 50.00 (*1-55615-148-9*, Tempus Bks) Microsoft.

Newman, James R., ed. see Clifford, William K.

Newman, James R., jt. auth. see Kasner, Edward.

Newman, James R., jt. auth. see Nagel, Ernest.

Newman, James W. Release Your Brakes! 304p. 1993. reprint ed. pap. 14.95 (*0-9638918-0-4*) Pace Orgztn.

Newman, Jane O. Pastoral Conventions: Poetry, Language, & Thought in Seventeenth-Century Nuremburg. LC 89-49002. 320p. 1990. text ed. 48.50 (*0-8018-3996-3*) Johns Hopkins.

Newman, Janet, jt. auth. see Itzen, Catherine.

Newman, Jason, et al. Street Law: A Course in the Law of Corrections. 79p. 1976. teacher ed 5.75 (*0-8299-1014-X*); pap. text ed. 7.50 (*0-8299-1013-1*) West Pub.

Newman, Jay. Competition in Religious Life. (Editions SR Ser.: Vol. 11). 264p. (C). 1989. pap. 28.50 (*0-88920-989-8*, Pub. by Wilfrid Laurier CN) Humanities.

— Fanatics & Hypocrites. LC 86-9436. 151p. 1986. 29.95x (*0-87975-348-X*) Prometheus Bks.

— Foundations of Religious Tolerance. 192p. 1982. 30.00 (*0-8020-5591-5*); pap. 11.95 (*0-8020-6507-4*) U of Toronto Pr.

— The Journalist in Plato's Cave. LC 88-48022. 208p. 1990. 36.50 (*0-8386-3349-8*) Fairleigh Dickinson.

— The Mental Philosophy of John Henry Newman. 224p. (C). 1986. text ed. 28.50 (*0-88920-186-2*, Pub. by Wilfrid Laurier CN) Humanities.

— On Religious Freedom. 256p. 1991. pap. 25.00 (*0-7766-0308-6*, Pub. by Univ Ottawa Pr CN) Paul & Co Pubs.

Newman, Jean C. Pedro Salinas & His Circumstance. LC 83-10778. (Illus.). 274p. (C). 1984. pap. 11.95 (*0-913480-56-8*) Inter Am U Pr.

Newman, Jeanne. The Tenant's Leasing Handbook. 208p. 1991. pap. 19.95 (*0-7931-0317-7*, 4105-11) Dearborn Finan.

Newman, Jennifer. Exquisite Embroidery. (Illus.). 144p. 1993. 27.95 (*1-86351-079-6*, Pub. by S Milner AT) Sterling.

— Exquisite Embroidery. (Milner Craft Ser.). (Illus.). 160p. 1995. pap. 19.95 (*1-86351-154-7*, Pub. by S Milner AT) Sterling.

Newman, Jennifer L. The Dead Hours. (Illus.). 18p. (Orig.). 1991. pap. text ed. 5.95 (*1-56315-020-4*) Sterling Hse.

Newman, Jenny, ed. Faber Book of Seductions. 366p. 1991. pap. 12.95 (*0-571-13751-2*) Faber & Faber.

Newman, Jeremiah. The Postmodern Church. 157p. 1990. 10.00 (*1-85182-064-7*) Lumen Christi.

Newman, Jerry. Green Earrings & a Felt Hat. LC 92-29056. (Illus.). 48p. (J). (gr. 1-3). 1993. 14.95 (*0-8050-2392-5*, Bks Young Read) H Holt & Co.

Newman, Jerry M., jt. auth. see Milkovich, George T.

Newman, Jim. Control Systems: A "How to" Guide for Control Installations in R-C Model Aircraft. (Illus.). 23p. 1985. pap. 6.95 (*0-911295-01-1*) Air Age.

— Four Hundred Great R-C Modeling Tips. 76p. 1987. 12. 95 (*0-911295-05-4*) Air Age.

— Four Hundred Great R-C Modeling Tips, Vol. II. 66p. 1991. 12.95 (*0-911295-17-8*) Air Age.

— Four Hundred One R-C Tech Tips. 74p. 1991. 12.95 (*0-911295-11-9*) Air Age.

— 402 Radio Control Car Tech Tips. Jeffcoat, Karen, ed. (Illus.). 74p. (Orig.). 1994. pap. 12.95 (*0-911295-27-5*) Air Age.

— Two Hundred Fifty Great R-C Marine Tips. (Illus.). 48p. (Orig.). 1991. pap. 9.95 (*0-911295-16-X*) Air Age.

Newman, Jim & Raymond, Kathleen Z. Workshop Wisdom Dollhouse Crafting Tips from Nutshell News. Kraszewski, Andrea L., ed. (Illus.). 64p. 1992. pap. text ed. 9.95 (*0-89024-150-3*, 10-7745) Greenberg Bks.

Newman, Jim & Yarrish, Gerry, illus. R-C Car Troubleshooting: Two Hundred Tech Tricks, Vol. 1. 74p. (Orig.). 1992. pap. 12.95 (*0-911295-22-4*) Air Age.

Newman, Joan, ed. see Kulvinskas, Viktoras.

*__Newman, Joan T.__ Pediatric Nursing. 2nd ed. LC 94-33613. (Clinical Rotation Guides Ser.). 1994. pap. 15.95 (*0-87434-737-8*) Springhouse Pub.

Newman, John. Old High German Reader. 158p. (Orig.). (C). 1981. pap. text ed. 8.65 (*0-89894-012-5*) Advocate Pub Group.

— Oswald & the CIA. 627p. 1995. 28.00 (*0-7867-0131-5*) Carroll & Graf.

Newman, John & Hilfinger, Ann. Vietnam War Literature: An Annotated Bibliography of Imaginative Works about Americans Fighting in Vietnam. 2nd ed. LC 88-15747. 299p. 1988. 27.50 (*0-8108-2155-9*) Scarecrow.

Newman, John, et al. Workers' Benefits from Bolivia's Emergency Social Fund. (Living Standards Measurement Study Working Paper Ser.: No. 77). 52p. 1991. 6.95 (*0-8213-1765-2*, 11765) World Bank.

Newman, John E. How to Stay Cool, Calm, & Collected When the Pressure's On: A Stress-Control Plan for Businesspeople. 176p. 1993. pap. 15.95 (*0-8144-7765-8*) AMACOM.

Newman, John E. & Hinrichs, John R. Performance Evaluation for Professional Personnel. (Studies in Productivity: Highlights of the Literature Ser.: Vol. 14). 48p. 1980. pap. 55.00 (*0-89361-021-6*) Work in Amer.

— Performance Evaluation for Professional Personnel, Vol. 14. LC 80-20739. (Studies in Productivity, Highlights of the Literature). 1982. pap. 35.00 (*0-685-05451-9*, Pergamon Pr) Elsevier.

Newman, John H. Apologia Pro Vita Sua. 432p. 1993. pap. 8.50 (*0-460-87232-X*, Everyman's Classic Lib) C E Tuttle.

— Apologia Pro Vita Sua. 1989. mass mkt. 9.95 (*0-385-12646-8*, Image Bks) Doubleday.

— Apologia Pro Vita Sua. Culler, Arthur D., ed. (C). 1956. pap. 9.96 (*0-395-05109-6*) Norton.

— Apologia Pro Vita Sua. (C). 1968. pap. text ed. 12.95 (*0-393-09766-8*) Norton.

— Apologia pro Vita Sua. Ker, Ian, ed. & intro. by. 608p. 1995. 12.95 (*0-14-043374-0*, Penguin Classics) Viking Penguin.

— Apologia Pro Vita Sua: Being a History of His Religious Opinions. Svaglic, Martin J., ed. & intro. by. (Oxford English Texts Ser.). 664p. 1991. 140.00 (*0-19-811840-6*) OUP.

— Blessed Art Thou among Women. 1985. pap. 5.95 (*0-87193-076-5*) Dimension Bks.

— Conscience Consensus. 1992. pap. 15.00 (*0-385-42280-6*) Doubleday.

— An Essay in Aid of a Grammar of Assent. LC 78-51523. 1979. reprint ed. pap. text ed. 13.95 (*0-268-01000-5*) U of Notre Dame Pr.

— An Essay on the Development of Christian Doctrine. LC 89-40021. (Series in the Great Books: No. 4). 480p. (C). 1989. pap. text ed. 14.95 (*0-268-00921-X*) U of Notre Dame Pr.

— The Idea of a University: Defined & Illustrated. O'Connell, Daniel M., ed. 498p. (C). Date not set. reprint ed. 9.95 (*0-8294-0585-2*, Campion Bks) Loyola Univ Pr.

— The Idea of University. Svaglic, Martin J., ed. LC 82-7019. (Series in the Great Books). 428p. 1982. reprint ed. pap. text ed. 12.95 (*0-268-01150-8*) U of Notre Dame Pr.

— The Kingdom Within: Discourses to Mixed Congregations. 1984. pap. 14.95 (*0-87193-216-4*) Dimension Bks.

— Lead Kindly Light. Helms, Hal M., ed. LC 87-60611. (Living Library). 210p. (Orig.). 1987. pap. text ed. 8.95 (*0-941478-78-5*) Paraclete MA.

— The Letters & Diaries of John Henry Cardinal Newman, Vol. 6: The Via Media & Froude's Remains, January 1837 to December 1838. Tracey, Gerard, ed. 1984. 59. 00 (*0-19-920141-2*) OUP.

— The Letters & Diaries of John Henry Newman. Dessain, Charles S. & Gornall, Thomas, eds. Incl. Vol. 23. Defeat at Oxford-Defence at Rome, January to December 1867. 1973. 38.50 (*0-19-920040-8*); 1973. write for info. (*0-318-54853-4*) OUP.

— Loss & Gain. Hill, Alan G., ed. & intro. by. (World's Classics Ser.). 352p. 1986. pap. 6.95 (*0-19-281687-X*) OUP.

— Mary the Second Eve. 40p. 1982. reprint ed. pap. 2.50 (*0-89555-181-0*) TAN Bks Pubs.

— A Newman Anthology. Lilly, W. S., ed. 1977. lib. bdg. 59.95 (*0-8490-2341-6*) Gordon Pr.

— On Consulting the Faithful in Matters of Doctrine. Coulson, John, ed. LC 62-9877. 128p. 1985. reprint ed. pap. 7.95 (*0-934134-51-0*) Sheed & Ward MO.

— The Philosophical Notebook, 2 vols., Set. Sillem, E., ed. Incl. Vol. 1. General Introduction. 257p. 1970. text ed. (*0-318-54065-7*); Vol. 2. Text. v, 218p. 1970. text ed. (*0-318-54066-5*); 1970. 95.00 (*0-912116-13-7*) Learned Pubns.

— Prayers, Poems, & Meditations. 208p. 1990. 12.95 (*0-8245-1004-6*) Crossroad NY.

— Prayers, Verses & Devotions. LC 88-81571. 766p. 1989. 31.95 (*0-89870-217-8*) Ignatius Pr.

— Reason for Faith: Nine Sermons. 2nd ed. 145p. 1990. reprint ed. pap. 6.95 (*0-940147-08-4*) Source Bks CA.

— A Reason for the Hope Within: Sermons on the Theory of Religious Belief. 368p. 1985. pap. 14.95 (*0-87193-219-9*) Dimension Bks.

— Sermons 1824-1843, Vol. I: Sermons on the Liturgy & Sacraments & on Christ the Mediator. Murray, Placid, ed. 408p. 1992. 89.00 (*0-19-920088-2*) OUP.

— Sermons 1824-1843, Vol. II: Sermons on Biblical History, Sin & Justification, the Christian Way of Life, & Biblical Theology. Blehl, Vincent F., ed. 496p. 1994. 90.00 (*0-19-920401-2*) OUP.

— Taking on the Heart of Christ: Meditations & Devotions. 1990. pap. 5.95 (*0-87193-276-8*) Dimension Bks.

— The Uses of Knowledge: Selections from the Idea of a University. Ward, Leo L., ed. (Crofts Classics Ser.). 128p. 1948. pap. text ed. write for info. (*0-88295-063-0*) Harlan Davidson.

— Verses on Various Occasions. 1992. 18.95 (*0-87193-282-2*) Dimension Bks.

— The Via Media of the Anglican Church. 496p. 1990. 98. 00 (*0-19-826693-6*) OUP.

— Who Is a Christian? 1985. pap. 16.95 (*0-87193-188-5*) Dimension Bks.

Newman, John H., tr. see Athanasius.

N

Newman, John H., et al, eds. Tracts for the Times, 6 Vols, 1. 1841. write for info. (*0-404-04711-4*) AMS Pr.
— Tracts for the Times, 6 Vols, 2. 1841. write for info. (*0-404-04712-2*) AMS Pr.
— Tracts for the Times, 6 Vols, 3. 1841. write for info. (*0-404-04713-0*) AMS Pr.
— Tracts for the Times, 6 Vols, 4. 1841. write for info. (*0-404-04714-9*) AMS Pr.
— Tracts for the Times, 6 Vols, 5. 1841. write for info. (*0-404-04715-7*) AMS Pr.
— Tracts for the Times, 6 Vols, 6. 1841. write for info. (*0-404-04716-5*) AMS Pr.
— Tracts for the Times, 6 Vols, Set. 1841. lib. bdg. 450.00 (*0-404-04710-6*) AMS Pr.
Newman, John K. The Classical Epic Tradition. LC 85-40766. (Studies in Classics). 576p. 1986. text ed. 30.00 (*0-299-10510-5*) U of Wis Pr.
Newman, John L. & Gertler, Paul J. Family Productivity, Labor Supply, & Welfare in a Low-Income Country. LC 92-27891. (Living Standards Measurement Study Working Paper Ser.: No. 87). 65p. 1992. 6.95 (*0-8213-2253-2*, 12253) World Bank.
Newman, John M. JFK & Vietnam: Deception, Intrigue, & the Struggle for Power. 528p. 1992. 22.95 (*0-446-51678-3*) Warner Bks.
Newman, John N. Marine Hydrodynamics. 1977. 55.00 (*0-262-14026-8*) MIT Pr.
Newman, John Q. Be Your Own Dick: Private Investigating Made Easy. LC 92-70018. 113p. (Orig.). 1992. pap. 12.00 (*1-55950-083-2*, 55090) Loompanics.
— Heavy Duty New Identity. LC 90-64229. 72p. 1991. pap. 10.95 (*1-55950-062-X*, 61116) Loompanics.
Newman, John S. Electrochemical Systems. 2nd ed. 576p. 1991. text ed. 79.00 (*0-13-248758-6*, 310103) P-H.
Newman, John W. & Birkel, Michael, eds. The Lamb's War: Essays in Honor of Hugh Barbour. 286p. (Orig.). 1991. pap. write for info. (*0-318-68396-2*) Earlham College Pr.
Newman, John W., jt. ed. see Birkel, Michael L.
Newman, Josef. Family Values. 1992. disk 14.95 (*1-882833-00-7*) Scribe Agency.
Newman, Joseph W. America's Teachers: An Introduction to Education. 2nd ed. LC 93-16924. 355p. (Orig.). (C). 1994. teacher ed write for info. (*0-8013-1424-0*, 76491); pap. text ed. 31.95 (*0-8013-0843-7*, 78910) Longman.
— The Energy Machine of Joseph Newman: An Invention Whose Time Has Come. 4th ed. Soule, Evan R., Jr., ed. (Illus.). 333p. 1986. 38.45 (*0-9613835-4-2*) J Newman Pub.
— Energy Machine of Joseph Newman: An Invention Whose Time Has Come. 5th ed. Soule, Evan R., ed. (Illus.). 355p. 1987. 38.45 (*0-9613835-5-0*) J Newman Pub.
— The Energy Machine of Joseph Newman: An Invention Whose Time Has Come. 7th ed. Soule, Evan R., Jr., ed. & illus. by. LC 84-90652. 488p. 1995. text ed. 59.95 (*0-9613835-7-7*) J Newman Pub.
Newman, Joyce. Jean-Baptiste de Lully & His Tragedies Lyriques. Buelow, George J., ed. LC 79-12289. (Studies in Musicology: No. 1). 280p. 1991. pap. 19.00 (*0-8357-1915-4*) Univ Rochester Pr.
***Newman, Judie.** The Ballistic Bard: Postcolonial Fictions. LC 95-16018. 1995. write for info. (*0-340-53914-3*, Pub. by E Arnold UK); pap. write for info. (*0-340-53915-1*, Pub. by E Arnold UK) Routledge Chapman & Hall.
— Nadine Gordimer. (Contemporary Writers Ser.). 96p. 1988. pap. text ed. 9.95 (*0-415-00660-0*) Routledge.
— Saul Bellow & History. LC 83-8708. 192p. 1984. text ed. 35.00 (*0-312-69981-6*) St Martin.
Newman, Judith. The Craft of Children's Writing. LC 85-5830. 72p. (Orig.). (C). 1985. pap. 7.95 (*0-435-08233-7*) Heinemann.
— Parents from Hell: Unexpurgated Tales of Good Intentions. LC 94-43447. 1995. write for info. (*0-452-27234-3*, Plume) NAL-Dutton.
Newman, Judith M., ed. Finding Our Own Way: Teachers Exploring Their Assumptions. LC 89-15442. 168p. (Orig.). 1989. pap. 17.95 (*0-435-08501-8*) Heinemann.
— Whole Language: Theory in Use. LC 85-17636. x, 204p. (Orig.). 1985. pap. text ed. 20.00 (*0-435-08244-2*) Heinemann.
Newman, Judy. Beautiful Boxes to Create, Cover & Decorate. (Illus.). 1992. 19.95 (*1-86351-008-7*, Pub. by S Milner AT) Sterling.
— Paper Tole: Three Dimensional Decoupage. (Illus.). 72p. 1994. pap. 12.95 (*1-86351-144-X*, Pub. by S Milner AT) Sterling.
Newman, K. O., tr. see Von Economo, Constantin.
Newman, Karen. Fashioning Femininity & English Renaissance Drama. LC 90-23374. (Women in Culture & Society Ser.). (Illus.). 208p. 1991. pap. text ed. 11.95 (*0-226-57709-0*) U Ch Pr.
— Shakespeare's Rhetoric of Comic Character: Dramatic Convention in Classical & Renaissance Comedy. 128p. 1985. 18.95 (*0-416-37990-7*, 9116) Routledge Chapman & Hall.
Newman, Katharine D. Never Without a Song: The Years & Songs of Jennie Devlin, 1865-1952. LC 93-6387. (Music in American Life Ser.). (Illus.). 272p. 1994. 39.95 (*0-252-02081-2*); pap. 16.95 (*0-252-06371-6*) U of Ill Pr.
Newman, Katherine. Law & Economic Organization: A Comparative Study of Preindustrial Societies. LC 83-7169. 264p. 1983. pap. 18.95 (*0-521-28966-1*) Cambridge U Pr.
Newman, Katherine, ed. see Newman, Preston.
Newman, Katherine, ed. see Runnells, Robert R.
Newman, Katherine S. Declining Fortunes: The Withering of the American Dream. 288p. 1994. reprint ed. pap. 12.00 (*0-465-01594-8*) Basic.
— Falling From Grace. 1989. pap. 12.00 (*0-679-72397-8*, Vin) Random.
— Falling from Grace: The Experience of Downward Mobility in the American Middle Class. 304p. 1988. text ed. 29.95 (*0-02-923121-3*) Free Pr.
***Newman, Kathleen, ed.** Latin American Cinema. (Special Issue of Iris Ser.: No. 13). 1995. pap. 12.95 (*0-253-30014-2*) Ind U Pr.
Newman, Kenneth, jt. auth. see Bacal, Howard A.
Newman, Kim. Anno-Dracula. 400p. 1993. 21.00 (*0-88184-967-7*) Carroll & Graf.
— Anno Dracula. 416p. 1994. mass mkt. 5.99 (*0-380-72345-X*) Avon.
— Bad Dreams. 280p. 1995. mass mkt. 4.95 (*0-7867-0227-3*) Carroll & Graf.
— The Bloody Red Baron. 320p. 1995. 21.00 (*0-7867-0252-4*) Carroll & Graf.
— Jago. 536p. 1993. 22.00 (*0-88184-868-9*) Carroll & Graf.
— The Night Mayor. 202p. 1992. pap. 3.95 (*0-88184-768-2*) Carroll & Graf.
— The Quorum. 310p. 1994. 21.00 (*0-7867-0132-3*) Carroll & Graf.
Newman, Kim, jt. ed. see Jones, Stephen.
Newman, Kim, jt. ed. see McAuley, Paul J.
Newman, Laura. Make Your Juicer Your Drug Store. LC 66-125414. (Illus.). 192p. 1978. pap. 4.95 (*0-87904-001-7*) Lust.
Newman, Lawrence, et al. Comparative Probate Law Studies. LC 76-76208. xii, 837p. 1976. pap. 45.00 (*0-685-42779-X*, B192) Am Law Inst.
Newman, Lawrence & Kalter, Albert. Postmortem Estate Planning. LC 76-4993. xiii, 154p. 1976. Incl. 1976 Suppl. 7.00 (*0-685-09574-6*, B195/B196) Am Law Inst.
Newman, Lawrence, jt. auth. see Kalter, Albert.
Newman, Lawrence G. Texas Corporation Law. 850p. 1994. ring bd. 115.00 (*1-55943-158-X*) Michie Butterworth.
— Texas Corporation Law, No. 1. suppl. ed. 850p. 1988. Suppl. 1, 10/88. 40.00 (*0-685-66113-X*) Butterworth Legal Pubs.
— Texas Corporation Law, No. 2. suppl. ed. 850p. 1990. Suppl. 2, 11/90. 32.50 (*0-685-66114-8*) Butterworth Legal Pubs.
— Texas Corporation Law, No. 3. suppl. ed. 850p. 1992. Suppl. 3, 8/92. 35.00 (*0-685-70055-0*) Butterworth Legal Pubs.
Newman, Lawrence W. International Litigation in the United States. Date not set. 95.00 (*1-56425-020-2*) Transnatl Juris Pubns.
Newman, Lawrence W. & Burrows, Michael. The Practice of International Litigation. 1993. 95.00 (*1-56425-005-9*) Transnatl Juris Pubns.
Newman, Lea B. A Reader's Guide to the Short Stories of Herman Melville. (Reference Bks.). 344p. 1986. text ed. 45.00 (*0-8161-8653-7*, Hall Reference) Macmillan.
Newman, Leonard, ed. Measurement Challenges in Atmospheric Chemistry. LC 92-38528. (Advances in Chemistry Ser.: No. 232). 350p. 1992. 94.95 (*0-8412-2470-6*) Am Chemical.
Newman, Leslea. Belinda's Bouquet. (Illus.). 24p. (J). (gr. k-3). 1991. 6.95 (*1-55583-154-0*) Alyson Pubns.
— Every Woman's Dream. LC 94-15390. 200p. (Orig.). 1994. pap. 9.95 (*0-934678-62-6*) New Victoria Pubs.
— Fat Chance. LC 94-7692. 224p. (J). (gr. 3-7). 1994. 14.95 (*0-399-22760-1*, Putnam) Putnam Pub Group.
— Gloria Goes to Gay Pride. (Illus.). 48p. (Orig.). (J). (ps-2). 1991. pap. 7.95 (*1-55583-185-0*) Alyson Pubns.
— Good Enough to Eat. LC 86-16228. 272p. (Orig.). 1986. lib. bdg. 18.95 (*0-932379-22-2*); pap. 8.95 (*0-932379-21-4*) Firebrand Bks.
— Heather Has Two Mommies. (Illus.). 38p. (J). (ps-3). 1991. reprint ed. pap. 7.95 (*1-55583-180-X*) Alyson Pubns.
— In Every Laugh a Tear. LC 92-27744. 256p. (Orig.). 1992. pap. 9.95 (*0-934678-46-4*) New Victoria Pubs.
— Lesbian Love Poems. Date not set. write for info. (*0-345-39483-6*) Ballantine.
— A Letter to Harvey Milk. LC 88-3923. 176p. (Orig.). 1988. lib. bdg. 18.95 (*0-932379-44-3*); pap. 8.95 (*0-932379-43-5*) Firebrand Bks.
— Love Me Like You Mean It. 98p. (Orig.). 1993. reprint ed. pap. 8.95 (*1-878533-14-2*) Clothespin Fever Pr.
— Remember That. LC 94-27874. (Illus.). (J). 1995. write for info. (*0-395-66589-2*, Clarion Bks) HM.
— Saturday Is Pattyday. (Illus.). 24p. (J). (ps-5). 1993. lib. bdg. 14.95 (*0-934678-52-9*); pap. 6.95 (*0-934678-51-0*) New Victoria Pubs.
— Secrets. LC 90-31303. 206p. (Orig.). 1990. pap. 8.95 (*0-934678-24-3*) New Victoria Pubs.
— SomeBody to Love: A Guide to Loving the Body You Have. LC 91-34617. 208p. (Orig.). 1991. pap. 10.95 (*1-879427-03-6*) Third Side Pr.
— Sweet Dark Places: Poetry by Leslea Newman. 109p. 1991. pap. 8.95 (*0-939821-01-X*) HerBooks.
— Too Far Away to Touch, Close Enough to See. LC 93-30327. (Illus.). (J). 1995. 14.95 (*0-395-68968-6*, Clarion Bks) HM.
— Writing from the Heart: Inspirations & Exercises for Women Who Want to Write. 160p. 1993. pap. 12.95 (*0-89594-641-6*) Crossing Pr.
Newman, Leslea, ed. Eating Our Hearts Out: Women & Food. LC 92-33669. 1993. pap. 12.95 (*0-89594-569-X*) Crossing Pr.
— The Femme Mystique. (Illus.). 319p. (Orig.). 1995. pap. 11.95 (*1-55583-255-5*) Alyson Pubns.
— A Loving Testimony: Remembering Loved Ones Lost to Aids. 448p. 1995. pap. 14.95 (*0-89594-752-8*) Crossing Pr.
Newman, Leslea, intro. Bubbe Meisehs by Shayneh Maidelehs: Poetry by Jewish Granddaughters about Our Grandmothers. 112p. (Orig.). 1989. pap. text ed. 8.00 (*0-939821-00-1*) HerBooks.
***Newman, Linda A.** Maintaining Function in Older Adults. LC 95-13936. 1995. write for info. (*0-7506-9568-4*) Buttrwrth-Heinemann.
Newman, Linda P., jt. auth. see Ansari, Mary B.
Newman, Lindsay, ed. see Hervouet, Yves.
Newman, Louis. Genesis: The Student's Guide, Pt. 2. pap. 4.95 (*0-8381-0404-5*) United Syn Bk.
— Pebbles & Sand. LC 77-99935. (Illus.). 96p. pap. 6.00 (*0-912292-12-1*) The Smith.
— Teacher's Supplement to Genesis the Student's Guide Pt. 1. pap. 2.95 (*0-8381-0403-7*) United Syn Bk.
Newman, Louis, ed. see Newman, Shirley.
Newman, Louis E. The Sanctity of the Seventh Year: A Study of Mishnah Tractate Shebiit. LC 83-8683. (Brown Judaic Studies). 276p. (C). 1983. pap. 13.00 (*0-89130-630-7*, 14 00 44) Scholars Pr GA.
Newman, Louis E., jt. ed. see Dorff, Elliot N.
Newman, Louis I. Jewish Influence on Christian Reform Movements. LC 26-883. (Columbia University. Oriental Studies: No. 23). reprint ed. 45.00 (*0-404-50513-9*) AMS Pr.
Newman, Louis I., ed. The Talmudic Anthology. LC 45-9682. 1978. pap. text ed. 19.95 (*0-87441-303-6*) Behrman.
Newman, Louis I., tr. & comp. The Hasidic Anthology. LC 87-70172. 740p. 1987. 40.00 (*0-87668-968-3*) Aronson.
***Newman, Louise M.** Men's Ideas, Women's Realities: Popular Science, 1870-1915. LC 84-1072. (Athene Ser.). 367p. 1985. pap. 104.60 (*0-7837-8952-1*, 2049664) Bks Demand.
Newman, Louise M., ed. Men's Ideas - Women's Realities: Popular Science, 1870-1915. (Athene Ser.). 368p. (C). pap. text ed. 19.95 (*0-685-53793-5*) Tchrs Coll.
— Men's Ideas, Women's Realities: "Popular Science", Eighteen Seventy to Nineteen Fifteen. (Athene Ser.). 384p. 1984. text ed. 55.00 (*0-08-031930-0*, Pergamon Pr); pap. text ed. 19.95 (*0-08-031929-7*, Pergamon Pr) Elsevier.
Newman, Lowell S., jt. auth. see Rohrbach, Peter T.
***Newman, Lucile.** Hunger in History: Food Shortage, Poverty & Deparivation. 1989. pap. text ed. 21.95 (*1-55786-628-7*) Blackwell Pubs.
Newman, Lucile, ed. Hunger in History: Food Shortage, Poverty & Deparivation. 1989. text ed. 54.95 (*1-55786-044-0*) Blackwell Pubs.
***Newman, Lucile F.** Women's Medicine: A Cross-Cultural Study of Indigenous Fertility Regulation. 203p. (Orig.). (C). 1995. pap. text ed. 16.00 (*0-8135-2257-9*) Rutgers U Pr.
Newman, Lucile F., ed. Women's Medicine: A Cross Cultural Study of Indigenous Fertility Regulation. (Douglass Ser.). 226p. (C). 1985. text ed. 35.00 (*0-8135-1067-8*) Rutgers U Pr.
Newman, M., jt. auth. see James, I.
Newman, M. E., jt. auth. see Lee, J. S.
Newman, M. H. Elements of the Topology of Plane Sets of Points. (Illus.). vii, 214p. 1992. reprint ed. pap. 6.95 (*0-486-67037-6*) Dover.
Newman, M. T. Indian Skeletal Material from the Central Coast of Peru. (Harvard University Peabody Museum of Archaeology & Ethnology Papers). 1969. reprint ed. pap. 15.00 (*0-527-01270-X*) Periodicals Srv.
Newman, Marc T. A Rhetorical Analysis of Popular American Film. 400p. (C). 1993. pap. text ed. 34.95 (*0-8403-9003-3*) Kendall-Hunt.
Newman, Margaret. Step Family Realities: How to Overcome Difficulties & Have a Happy Family. 254p. (Orig.). 1994. 24.95 (*1-879237-70-9*); pap. 11.95 (*1-879237-69-5*) New Harbinger.
***Newman, Margaret A.** A Developing Discipline: Selected Works of Margaret Newman. LC 94-23657. 1995. pap. 29.95 (*0-88737-638-X*) Natl League Nurse.
— Health as Expanding Consciousness. 2nd ed. 150p. 1994. 35.95 (*0-88737-620-7*, 14-2626) Natl League Nurse.
Newman, Marjorie. Bible People: Old & New Testaments. 1992. 3.98 (*0-8317-0830-1*) Smithmark.
Newman, Marjorie, ed. My Book of Favorite Prayers. LC 89-82555. (Illus.). 28p. (J). (ps-2). 1990. pap. 9.99 (*0-8066-2469-8*, 9-2469) Augsburg Fortress.
Newman, Mark. Entrepreneurs of Profits & Pride: From Black-Appeal to Radio Soul. LC 88-5887. 202p. 1988. text ed. 55.00 (*0-275-92888-8*, C2888, Praeger Pubs) Greenwood.
— Sea Gnomes: An Under-Sea Odyssey. abr. ed. 600p. 1995. pap. 12.95 (*1-56901-456-6*) NW Pub.
Newman, Mark, jt. photos see Domico, Terry.
Newman, Mark J., jt. ed. see Powell, Michael F.
Newman, Marsha. Fire & Glory: The Millennial Story I. 229p. 1989. 12.95 (*0-9608658-5-3*) Wellspring Utah.
— Fire & Glory: The Millennial Story II. 226p. 1989. 12.95 (*0-9608658-4-5*) Wellspring Utah.
— The Lightning & the Storm. 229p. 1986. 9.95 (*0-9608658-2-9*) Wellspring Utah.
— A Love Beyond Time. 329p. 1987. 14.95 (*0-9608658-3-7*) Wellspring Utah.
— Reflections of Eve & Her Daughters. (Illus.). 1981. 6.95 (*0-9608658-0-2*) Wellspring Utah.
Newman, Marsha & Miller, Barbara. The Jewels of Vicarey Harbor. 208p. (Orig.). (YA). (gr. 11-12). 1993. pap. 5.95 (*0-9608658-8-8*) Wellspring Utah.
Newman, Marsha & Newman, Gene. She Shall Be Called Woman. 1981. pap. write for info. (*0-318-56398-3*) Wellspring Utah.
***Newman, Martha G.** The Boundaries of Charity: Cistercian Culture & Ecclesiastical Reform, 1098-1180. LC 95-14016. (Figurae: Reading Medieval Culture Ser.). (Illus.). 466p. 1996. 55.00x (*0-8047-2512-8*) Stanford U Pr.
Newman, Martin. Industrial Electronics & Controls. LC 85-17828. (Electronic Technology Ser.). 450p. 1986. text ed. 42.50 (*0-471-05274-4*) P-H.
Newman, Mary A., tr. see De Ventos, Xavier R.
Newman, Mary J. CPR Bluebook. 148p. 1984. 11.95 (*0-317-47412-X*) Jems Comm.
Newman, Matt & Lemay, Nita K. Human Reproductive Systems. (Illus.). (J). (gr. 5-8). 1980. pap. text ed. 165.00 (*0-89290-101-2*, A794-SATC) Soc for Visual.
Newman, Matt, et al. Developing Self-Esteem. LC 80-730732. (Illus.). 1980. pap. text ed. 165.00 (*0-89290-152-7*, A602-SATC) Soc for Visual.
Newman, Matthew. Dwight Gooden. LC 86-16527. (Sports Close-Ups 2 Ser.). (Illus.). 48p. (J). (gr. 5-6). 1986. text ed. 11.95 (*0-89686-317-4*, Crstwood Hse) Silver Burdett Pr.
— Larry Bird. LC 86-16524. (Sports Close-Ups 2 Ser.). (Illus.). 48p. (J). (gr. 5-6). 1986. text ed. 11.95 (*0-89686-314-X*, Crstwood Hse) Silver Burdett Pr.
— Lynette Woodard. LC 86-19737. (Sports Close-Ups 2 Ser.). (Illus.). 48p. (J). (gr. 5-6). 1986. text ed. 11.95 (*0-89686-316-6*, Crstwood Hse) Silver Burdett Pr.
— Mary Decker Slaney. LC 86-16525. (Sports Close-Ups 2 Ser.). (Illus.). 48p. (J). (gr. 5-6). 1986. text ed. 11.95 (*0-89686-319-0*, Crstwood Hse) Silver Burdett Pr.
— Patrick Ewing. LC 86-16522. (Sports Close-Ups 2 Ser.). (Illus.). 48p. (J). (gr. 5-6). 1986. text ed. 11.95 (*0-89686-315-8*, Crstwood Hse) Silver Burdett Pr.
— Watch-Guard Dogs. LC 85-19542. (Working Dogs Ser.). (Illus.). 48p. (J). (gr. 5-6). 1985. text ed. 11.95 (*0-89686-287-9*, Crstwood Hse) Silver Burdett Pr.
Newman, Maxwell H. Elements of the Topology Plane Sets of Points. LC 85-12548. viii, 214p. 1985. reprint ed. text ed. 59.75 (*0-313-24956-3*, NETO, Greenwood Pr) Greenwood.
Newman, Michael. The Complete Guide to Everything Romantic: Unique & Creative Ideas. LC 94-20220. 1995. 15.95 (*0-8065-1547-3*, Citadel Pr) Carol Pub Group.
Newman, Michael, jt. auth. see Kalinovska, Milena.
Newman, Michael, jt. ed. see Mazey, Sonia.
Newman, Michael C. & McIntosh, A. Metal Ecotoxicology: Concepts & Applications. (Advances in Trace Substances Research Ser.). 1991. 79.95 (*0-87371-411-3*, QH545) Lewis Pubs.
***Newman, Michael E.** Computer Applications in Agriculture & Agribusiness. 172p. 1994. pap. text ed. 14.95 (*0-8134-2976-5*) Interstate.
Newman, Michael G. & Kornman, Kenneth G. Antibiotic - Antimicrobial Use in Dental Practice. (Illus.). 1990. pap. text ed. 30.00 (*0-86715-172-2*) Quint Pub Co.
Newman, Michael G., jt. ed. see Nisengard, Russell J.
***Newman, Michael W.** Harrison Town: Stories of Grace. LC 95-7715. 1995. write for info. (*0-570-04825-7*) Concordia.
Newman, Mike. Secret Buddies. 250p. (Orig.). 1992. pap. 11.95 (*1-879194-09-0*) GLB Pubs.
Newman, Mike & Rhyne, Tom, eds. Electronic Design Automation Frameworks: When Will the Promise Be Realized? Proceedings of the Third IFIP WG 10.2 - WG 10.5 Workshop on Electronic Design Automation Frameworks in Cooperation with GI - ITG FG 3.5.6 - 5.2.6, Bad Lippspringe, Germany, 23-25 March, 1992. LC 92-29454. (IFIP Transactions A: Computer Science & Technology Ser.). 1992. write for info. (*0-444-89820-4*, North Holland) Elsevier.
Newman, Milda, tr. see Greimas, Algirdas J.
Newman, Mildred & Berkowitz, Bernard. How to Be Your Own Best Friend. 1986. mass mkt. 4.95 (*0-345-34239-9*) Ballantine.
Newman, Mildred & Berkowitz, Bernard, eds. How to Be Awake & Alive. 128p. 1983. pap. 3.95 (*0-345-31683-5*) Ballantine.
Newman, Molly. Shooting Stars. 1988. pap. 4.75 (*0-8222-1023-1*) Dramatists Play.
Newman, Molly & Damashek, Barbara. Quilters. 1986. pap. 4.75 (*0-8222-0928-4*) Dramatists Play.
Newman, Mona. Night of a Thousand Stars. large type ed. 320p. 1987. 16.95 (*0-7089-1628-7*) Ulverscroft.
Newman, Morris. Integral Matrices. (Pure & Applied Mathematics Ser.: Vol. 45). 1972. text ed. 91.00 (*0-12-517850-6*) Acad Pr.
Newman, Morton. Design & Construction of Wood Framed Buildings. 1994. text ed. 49.00 (*0-07-046363-8*) McGraw.
— Standard Handbook of Structural Details for Building Contruction. 2nd ed. 1993. text ed. 93.50 (*0-07-046352-2*) McGraw.
— Standard Structural Details for Building Construction. 1967. text ed. 70.00 (*0-07-046345-X*) McGraw.
— Structural Details for Concrete Construction. 1988. pap. text ed. 30.95 (*0-07-046360-3*) McGraw.
— Structural Details for Masonry Construction. 1988. pap. text ed. 30.95 (*0-07-046361-1*) McGraw.
— Structural Details for Wood Construction. 1988. pap. 30.95 (*0-07-046358-1*) McGraw.
— Structure Details for Steel Construction. 1988. pap. text ed. 30.95 (*0-07-046359-X*) McGraw.
Newman, Moshe, jt. auth. see Becher, Mordechai.
Newman, N., ed. Computer Systems - Software & Architecture. (C). 1989. 110.00 (*0-09-159451-0*, Pub. by S Thornes Pubs UK) St Mut.
Newman, N. A., ed. Early Christian-Muslim Dialogue. LC 93-61140. xvii, 776p. 1994. 59.95x (*0-944788-91-2*) IBRI.
Newman, N. A., ed. see Noldeke, Theodor.
Newman, Nancy. Competence in Cloze: Level D, Science. 56p. 1990. student ed 4.25 (*0-910307-87-3*) Comp Pr.
— Competence in Cloze: Level F, Social Studies. 54p. 1990. student ed 4.25 (*0-910307-96-2*) Comp Pr.
Newman, Nancy K., ed. see Davis, Charles.
Newman, Nancy M. Neuro-Ophthalmology: A Practical Text. (Illus.). 480p. (C). 1992. boxed 95.00 (*0-8385-6698-7*, A6698-3) Appleton & Lange.
Newman, Nanette. Spider the Horrible Cat. LC 92-17242. (Illus.). (J). 1993. 13.95 (*0-15-277972-8*) HarBrace.

N

An Asterisk (*) at the beginning of an entry indicates that the title is appearing in BIP for the first time.

— There's a Bear in the Bath! LC 93-12877. (J). 1994. 13.95 (*0-15-285512-2*) HarBrace.

Newman, Nicholas. Newmanship: The Sailing Scene Observed. (Illus.). 112p. (Orig.). 1985. pap. 6.95 (*0-229-11753-8*, Adlard Coles) Sheridan.

Newman, Oksana & Foster, Allan, eds. Environmental Statistics Handbook: Europe. 800p. 1993. 90.00 (*1-873477-60-0*, 055563, Gale Res Intl) Gale.

— European Market Share Reporter, No. 1. 368p. 1993. 160.00 (*1-873477-35-X*, Gale Res Intl) Gale.

Newman, P., et al. River Water Quality - Ecological Assessment & Control, EUR 14606. 754p. 1992. 95.00 (*92-826-2929-5*, CR-NA-14606-EN, Pub. by Europ Com) UNIPUB.

Newman, P. B. House on the Saco. 1977. pap. 6.95 (*0-87233-038-9*) Bauhan.

— Paula: A Narrative Poem. limited ed. LC 74-25862. (Living Poets' Library Ser.). 1975. pap. 2.50 (*0-686-10402-1*) Dragons Teeth.

Newman, P. J. & Agg, A. R., eds. Environmental Protection of the North Sea. 1988. 185.00 (*0-434-91370-7*) Buttrwrth-Heinemann.

Newman, P. P. Neurophysiology. (Illus.). 455p. 1980. text ed. 35.00 (*0-88331-165-8*) Luce.

Newman, P. R. Atlas of the English Civil War. (Illus.). 144p. 1985. text ed. 35.00 (*0-02-906540-2*) Macmillan.

— The Old Service: Royalist Regimental Colonels & the Civil War, 1642-46. LC 93-14678. (C). 1993. text ed. 69.95 (*0-7190-3752-2*, Pub. by Manchester Univ Pr UK) St Martin.

Newman, Pamela & Lynch, Alfred F. Behind Closed Doors: A Guide to Successful Meetings. (Illus.). 192p. 1983. 18.50 (*0-13-072025-9*) P-H.

Newman, Pamela, et al. Egyptian Peaks. (Illus.). 60p. (Orig.). (J). (gr. 4-12). 1988. pap. 24.95 (*0-943804-66-3*) U of Denver Teach.

Newman, Paul. Nominal & Verbal Plurality in Chadic. (Publications in African Languages & Linguistics: No. 12). 164p. 1990. pap. 60.00 (*90-6765-499-X*) Mouton.

— Optical Resolution Procedures for Chemical Compounds: Alcohols, Phenols, Thiols, Aldehydes & Ketones, Vol. 3. 738p. 1984. lib. bdg. 57.50 (*0-9601918-4-4*) Optical Resolution.

— Optical Resolution Procedures for Chemical Compounds, Vol. 1: Amines & Related Compounds. 1978. 52.50 (*0-9601918-0-1*) Optical Resolution.

— Optical Resolution Procedures for Chemical Compounds, Vol. 2: Acids, 2 pts. LC 78-61452. 1981. Pt. I, 566p. write for info. (*0-9601918-1-X*); Pt. II, 580p. write for info. (*0-9601918-2-8*) Optical Resolution.

— Optical Resolution Procedures for Chemical Compounds, Vol. 2: Acids, 2 pts., Set. LC 78-61452. 1981. 79.00 (*0-9601918-3-6*) Optical Resolution.

Newman, Paul & Botre, Robert D. Current Approaches to African Linguistics, Vol. 5. (Publications in African Languages & Linguistics: No. 8). viii, 266p. 1989. pap. 83.10 (*90-6765-324-1*) Mouton.

Newman, Paul & Newman, Roxana M., eds. Modern Hausa-English Dictionary. 168p. 1988. pap. 11.95 (*0-19-575303-8*) OUP.

Newman, Paul, jt. auth. see Moorhouse, John.

Newman, Paul B. The Ladder of Love. LC 74-94634. 80p. 1970. pap. 6.00 (*0-912292-15-6*) The Smith.

Newman, Paul B., ed. see Kratt, Mary N.

Newman, Paul W. A Spirit Christology: Recovering the Biblical Paradigm of Christian Faith. LC 87-10390. 258p. (Orig.). (C). 1987. lib. bdg. 49.00 (*0-8191-6375-9*); pap. text ed. 24.00 (*0-8191-6376-7*) U Pr of Amer.

Newman, Peter, ed. see Eatwell, John.

Newman, Peter, et al. The New Palgrave Dictionary of Money & Finance, 3 Vols., Set. 2580p. 1992. 595.00 (*1-56159-041-X*, Stockton Pr) Groves Dictionaries.

Newman, Peter C. Caesars of the Wilderness: The Story of the Hudson's Bay Company. 480p. 1988. pap. 10.95 (*0-14-011456-4*, Penguin Bks) Viking Penguin.

— Company of Adventurers: The Story of the Hudson's Bay Company. 448p. 1987. pap. 9.95 (*0-14-010139-X*, Penguin Bks) Viking Penguin.

Newman, Peter R. Companion to Irish History. 256p. 1991. lib. bdg. 27.95 (*0-8160-2572-X*) Facts on File.

— Companion to the English Civil Wars. (Illus.). 256p. 1991. 29.95 (*0-8160-2237-2*) Facts on File.

Newman, Peter W. & Kenworthy, Jeffrey R. Cities & Automobile Dependence: A Sourcebook. (Illus.). xviii, 388p. 1989. text ed. 79.95 (*1-85742-103-5*, Pub. by Ashgate UK) Ashgate Pub Co.

Newman, Philip, jt. auth. see Newman, Barbara.

Newman, Philip, jt. auth. see Sizer, Richard.

Newman, Philip R., jt. auth. see Newman, Barbara M.

Newman, Phyllis. Just in Time: Notes from My Life. LC 89-49726. 224p. 1990. reprint ed. pap. 12.95 (*0-87910-138-5*) Limelight Edns.

Newman, Phyllis E. & Craven, Sue. Newman's Conveyancing Practice & Procedure. 214p. (C). 1991. 110.00 (*1-85190-108-6*, Pub. by Tolley Pubng UK) St Mut.

Newman, Phyllis E., jt. auth. see Gittins, Vera D.

Newman, Preston. The Land Stacks Up. LC 85-90788. 95p. (Orig.). 1985. pap. 4.95 (*0-9619636-0-3*) K Newman.

— The Land Stacks Up. 2nd ed. Newman, Katherine, ed. LC 85-90788. (Illus.). 128p. (Orig.). 1993. pap. 5.95 (*0-936015-33-0*) Pocahontas Pr.

Newman, R. C., jt. ed. see Frankel, G. S.

Newman, R. S. Grassroots Education in India: A Challenge for Policy-Makers. 192p. 1989. text ed. 27.50 (*81-207-0951-9*, Pub. by Sterling Pubs II) Apt Bks.

Newman, Ralph A. Law of Labor Relations. LC 53-10762. viii, 310p. 1953. lib. bdg. 36.00 (*0-89941-615-2*, 501940) W S Hein.

Newman, Rayce A. The Hollywood Connection: The Drug Supplier to the Stars Tells All. 1994. pap. 5.99 (*1-56171-326-0*, S P I Bks) Sure Sellers.

Newman, Raymond J. Orthogeriatrics: Comprehensive Orthopedic Care for the Elderly Patient. (Illus.). 224p. 1992. 135.00 (*0-7506-1371-8*) Buttrwrth-Heinemann.

Newman, Rebecca. Belly Dancer in the Barrel of Oil. LC 84-90336. 1984. 10.00 (*0-87212-177-1*) Libra.

Newman, Renee. The Diamond Ring Buying Guide: How to Spot Value & Avoid Ripoffs. 4th ed. LC 93-9741. (Illus.). 151p. (C). 1993. pap. 12.95 (*0-929975-20-0*) Intl Jewelry Pubns.

— Diamonds: Fascinating Facts. (Gemstones Ser.). (Illus.). 16p. (C). 1990. 3.95 (*0-929975-01-4*) Intl Jewelry Pubns.

— Emerald & Tanzanite Buying Guide. (Illus.). 156p. (Orig.). (C). 1995. pap. 19.95 (*0-929975-23-5*) Intl Jewelry Pubns.

— The Gold Jewelry Buying Guide. LC 93-17583. (Illus.). 170p. (Orig.). (C). 1993. pap. 19.95 (*0-929975-19-7*) Intl Jewelry Pubns.

— The Pearl Buying Guide. 2nd ed. LC 93-43758. (Illus.). 188p. (Orig.). (C). 1994. pap. 19.95 (*0-929975-22-7*) Intl Jewelry Pubns.

— The Ruby & Sapphire Buying Guide: How to Spot Value & Ripoffs. 2nd ed. LC 93-9054. (Illus.). 204p. (C). 1994. pap. 19.95 (*0-929975-21-9*) Intl Jewelry Pubns.

Newman, Richard. Afro-American Education, 1907-1932: A Bibliographic Index. LC 83-24869. 198p. 1995. 45.00 (*0-931186-05-6*) Lambeth Pr.

— The Complete Guide to College Success: What Every Student Needs to Know. (Illus.). 320p. 1996. 50.00 (*0-8147-5783-9*); pap. 15.95 (*0-8147-5784-7*) NYU Pr.

— Lemuel Haynes: A Bio-Bibliography. LC 83-24877. 160p. 1995. 40.00 (*0-03-118604-1*) Carlson Pub.

— Lemuel Haynes: A Bio-Bibliography. LC 83-24877. 138p. 1984. 40.00 (*0-931186-04-8*) Lambeth Pr.

— Words Like Freedom: Afro-American Books & Manuscripts in the Henry W. & Albert A. Berg Collection of English & American Literature. (Illus.). vii, 33p. (Orig.). 1989. pap. 10.00 (*0-87104-413-7*) NY Pub Lib.

— Workers & Unions in Bombay, Nineteen Eighteen to Nineteen Twenty-Nine: A Study of Organisation in the Cotton Mills. 1982. pap. 22.00 (*0-686-91580-1*) S Asia.

Newman, Richard, comp. Black Access: A Bibliography of Afro-American Bibliographies. LC 83-8537. xxviii, 249p. 1984. text ed. 49.95 (*0-313-23282-2*, NEB/, Greenwood Pr) Greenwood.

Newman, Richard, ed. Black Preacher to White America: The Collected Writings of Lemuel Haynes, 1774-1833. LC 89-48246. 291p. 1989. 75.00 (*0-926019-24-4*) Carlson Pub.

— Nine Decades of Scholarship. 83p. 1986. pap. 3.00 (*0-87104-288-6*) NY Pub Lib.

— Treasures from The New York Public Library. (Illus.). 134p. (Orig.). 1985. pap. 19.95 (*0-87104-286-X*) NY Pub Lib.

Newman, Richard, intro. The Negro Churchman, 2 vols., Set. 1990. reprint ed. 160.00 (*0-527-66370-0*) Periodicals Srv.

Newman, Richard, jt. auth. see Tomasek, Jaroslav.

Newman, Richard G. Supplier Price Analysis: A Guide for Purchasing, Accounting, & Financial Analysts. LC 91-33084. 200p. 1992. text ed. 55.00 (*0-89930-545-8*, NSR/, Quorum Bks) Greenwood.

***Newman, Richard L.** Heads-Up Displays: Designing the Way Ahead. 350p. 1994. 76.95 (*0-291-39811-1*, Pub. by Avebury Pub UK) Ashgate Pub Co.

— On Wings of Evil. 368p. (Orig.). 1988. pap. 3.95 (*0-8439-2658-9*) Dorchester Pub Co.

— Siege of Orbitor. 1980. pap. 2.25 (*0-8439-0814-9*) Dorchester Pub Co.

Newman, Robert. The Case of the Baker Street Irregular. 1994. 18.25 (*0-8446-6762-5*) Peter Smith.

— The Case of the Baker Street Irregular. LC 77-15463. 232p. (J). (gr. 3-7). 1984. pap. 4.95 (*0-689-70766-5*, Aladdin Paperbacks) S&S Childrens.

— The Case of the Vanishing Corpse. 1994. 18.25 (*0-8446-6765-X*) Peter Smith.

— The Case of the Vanishing Corpse. LC 79-22078. 228p. (J). (gr. 4-6). 1985. pap. 4.95 (*0-689-71037-2*, Aladdin Paperbacks) S&S Childrens.

— Merlin's Mistake. (Illus.). (J). (gr. 5-9). 15.75 (*0-8446-6187-2*) Peter Smith.

— The Testing of Tertius. (Illus.). (J). (gr. 5-9). 19.75 (*0-8446-6188-0*) Peter Smith.

Newman, Robert, jt. auth. see Magee, Doug.

Newman, Robert C. Baptists & the American Tradition. LC 76-7166. 76p. 1976. pap. 1.95 (*0-87227-008-4*) Reg Baptist.

Newman, Robert C., ed. The Evidence of Prophecy: Fulfilled Prediction As a Testimony to the Truth of Christianity. LC 88-82536. 150p. 1988. pap. 6.95 (*0-944788-98-X*) IBRI.

Newman, Robert C. & Eckelmann, Herman J., Jr. Genesis One & the Origin of the Earth. LC 77-72526. 158p. 1989. pap. 6.95 (*0-944788-97-1*, N4) IBRI.

Newman, Robert C., jt. auth. see Fawcett, Cheryl.

Newman, Robert D. Transgressions of Reading: Narrative Engagement As Exile & Return. LC 92-13546. (Post-Contemporary Interventions Ser.). (Illus.). 192p. 1992. lib. bdg. 39.95 (*0-8223-1280-8*); pap. text ed. 15.95 (*0-8223-1296-4*) Duke.

— Understanding Thomas Pynchon. (Understanding Contemporary American Literature Ser.). 1986. 34.95 (*0-87249-485-3*); pap. 14.95 (*0-87249-486-1*) U of SC Pr.

Newman, Robert D. & Thorton, Weldon, eds. Joyce's Ulysses: The Larger Perspective. LC 86-40399. (Illus.). 312p. 1987. 40.00 (*0-87413-316-5*) U Delaware Pr.

Newman, Robert P. The Cold War Romance of Lillian Hellman & John Melby. LC 88-22659. (Illus.). xvi, 376p. (C). 1989. 29.95 (*0-8078-1815-1*) U of NC Pr.

— Owen Lattimore & the "Loss" of China. 685p. 1992. 35.00 (*0-520-07388-6*) U CA Pr.

— Truman & the Hiroshima Cult. 260p. 1995. 34.95 (*0-87013-403-5*) Mich St U Pr.

***Newman, Robin G.** How to Meet a Mensch in New York: A Decent, Responsible Person Even Your Mother Would Love. LC 94-21404. (Illus.). 1994. 9.95 (*1-885492-04-9*) City & Co.

Newman, Rochelle & Fowler, Donna M. Space, Structure, & Form. (Illus.). 320p. 1995. pap. 39.95 (*0-9614504-5-2*) Pythagorean Pr.

Newman, Rochelle, jt. auth. see Boles, Martha.

Newman, Roger C. Murtagh & the Vikings. (Hawthorn Series in Irish History). (Illus.). 96p. (Orig.). (J). (gr. 5-8). 1986. 9.95 (*0-947962-05-0*, Pub. by Childrens Pr IE); pap. 5.95 (*0-947962-06-9*, Pub. by Childrens Pr IE) Irish Bks Media.

Newman, Roger K. Hugo Black: A Biography. LC 94-10233. 944p. 1994. 30.00 (*0-679-43180-2*) Pantheon.

Newman, Roger K., jt. auth. see De Grazia, Edward.

Newman, Ron. The HBJ Workbook for Freshman Composition. 448p. (C). 1992. pap. text ed. 14.75 (*0-03-079567-2*) HB Coll Pubs.

Newman, Roxana M. An English-Hausa Dictionary. LC 89-51452. 344p. (C). 1990. text ed. 35.00 (*0-300-04702-9*) Yale U Pr.

Newman, Roxana M., jt. ed. see Newman, Paul.

Newman, Roy R. & Brooks, Pat. The Budding Fig Tree. LC 87-62894. 1988. pap. text ed. 2.50 (*0-932050-39-5*) New Puritan.

Newman, Ruth, jt. ed. see Cliver, Dean O.

***Newman, Ruth G. & Ketchum, Bradford W., Jr., eds.** How to Really Recruit, Motivate & Lead Your Team: Managing People. 1994. pap. 15.95 (*0-614-03641-0*) Inc Pub MA.

Newman, Ruth G., et al. Communicating in Business Today. LC 86-81357. 626p. (C). 1987. text ed. 30.50 (*0-669-06344-4*); Instr.'s guide. teacher ed 2.00 (*0-669-06343-6*) Heath.

Newman, S., jt. auth. see Mallick, P. K.

Newman, S. L. Salaries & Attitudes: A Profile of the Internal Auditing Profession. Holman, Richard, ed. 80p. 1984. pap. text ed. 27.00 (*0-89413-126-5*, 411) Inst Inter Aud.

Newman, Sally, jt. auth. see Kramer, Cynthia.

Newman, Sally, ed. see Smith, Thomas B., et al.

Newman, Samuel P. Elements of Political Economy. LC 68-30535. (Reprints of Economic Classics Ser.). xi, 324p. 1973. reprint ed. 39.50 (*0-678-00691-1*) Kelley.

Newman, Sandra & Reschovsky, James. Federal Policy & the Mobility of Older Homeowners: The Effects of the One-Time Capital Gains Exclusion. LC 84-29745. (ISR Research Report Ser.). 104p. (Orig.). 1985. pap. text ed. 10.00 (*0-87944-302-2*) Inst Soc Res.

Newman, Sandra C. Indian Basket Weaving: How to Weave Pomo, Yurok, Pima & Navajo Baskets. LC 73-79779. (Illus.). 108p. 1974. reprint ed. pap. 12.95 (*0-87358-112-1*) Northland AZ.

Newman, Sandra J. Federal Policy & the Mobility of Older Homeowners: The Effects of the One-Time Capital Gains Exclusion. LC 84-29745. (Institute for Social Research, Research Report Ser.). 98p. (Orig.). reprint ed. pap. 28.00 (*0-7837-5265-2*, 2045003) Bks Demand.

Newman, Sandra J., ed. Worlds Apart? Long-Term Care in Australia & the United States. LC 87-29770. (Home Health Care Services Quarterly Ser.: Vol. 8, No. 3). (Illus.). 113p. 1988. text ed. 32.95 (*0-86656-703-8*) Haworth Pr.

Newman, Sandra J. & Owen, Michael S. Residential Displacement in the United States, 1970-1977. LC 82-12101. (Institute for Social Research, Research Report Ser.). 106p. reprint ed. pap. 30.30 (*0-685-17866-8*, 2029469) Bks Demand.

Newman, Sandra J. & Schnare, Ann B. Beyond Bricks & Mortar: Reexamining the Purpose & Effects of Housing Assistance. LC 92-23289. (Urban Institute Report Ser.: No. 92-3). 152p. (Orig.). (C). 1992. lib. bdg. 46.50 (*0-87766-584-2*); pap. text ed. 18.50 (*0-87766-585-0*) Urban Inst.

— Subsidizing Shelter: The Relationship Between Welfare Reform & Housing Assistance. LC 87-34026. (Urban Institute Report Ser.: No. 88-1). (Illus.). 206p. (Orig.). (C). 1988. pap. text ed. 23.00 (*0-87766-414-5*) Urban Inst.

Newman, Sara W., jt. auth. see Gilman, Sid.

Newman, Sasha M., et al. Felix Vallotton. (Illus.). 328p. 1991. 65.00 (*1-55859-312-8*) Abbeville Pr.

— Felix Vallotton. LC 91-66233. 328p. (C). 1991. pap. 35.95 (*0-89467-057-3*) Yale Art Gallery.

Newman, Sasha N., ed. see Weber, Nicholas F.

Newman, Seymour, jt. ed. see Paul, D. R.

***Newman, Sharan.** Death Comes As Epiphany. 320p. 1995. mass mkt. 4.99 (*0-8125-2293-1*) Forge NYC.

— Death Comes As Epiphany. 320p. 1993. 19.95 (*0-312-85419-6*) Tor Bks.

— The Devil's Door. 384p. 1994. 21.95 (*0-312-85420-X*) Forge NYC.

— The Devil's Door. 416p. 1995. mass mkt. 4.99 (*0-8125-2295-8*) Forge NYC.

— The Wandering Arm of St. Anne. 1995. 20.95 (*0-312-85829-9*) Forge NYC.

Newman, Sharon. Guinevere. 296p. 1984. pap. 5.95 (*0-312-35321-9*) St Martin.

— Guinevere Evermore. 288p. 1986. pap. 6.95 (*0-312-35324-3*) St Martin.

— Treasures from Yesteryear Vol. I. White, Janet, ed. LC 94-38618. (Illus.). 88p. (Orig.). 1995. pap. 19.95 (*1-56477-039-7*, B169) That Patchwork.

— Treasures from Yesteryear Vol. II. White, Janet, ed. (Illus.). 88p. (Orig.). 1995. pap. 19.95 (*1-56477-063-X*, B212) That Patchwork.

Newman, Sharon, jt. auth. see Petillon, Mary.

Newman, Shirlee P. The Incas. Rosoff, Iris, ed. LC 91-31378. (First Bks.). (Illus.). 64p. (J). (gr. 3-5). 1992. lib. bdg. 12.90 (*0-531-20004-3*) Watts.

— The Incas. (First Bks.). (Illus.). 64p. (J). (gr. 5-8). 1992. pap. 5.95 (*0-531-15637-0*) Watts.

— The Inuits. LC 93-18370. (First Bks.). (Illus.). 64p. (J). (gr. 4-6). 1993. lib. bdg. 13.93 (*0-531-20073-6*) Watts.

— The Inuits. (First Bks.). (Illus.). 64p. (J). (gr. 5-8). 1994. pap. 5.95 (*0-531-15702-4*) Watts.

— Inuits. (First Bks.). (J). (gr. 4-7). 1994. pap. 5.95 (*0-531-15701-6*) Watts.

Newman, Shirley. A Child's Introduction to the Early Prophets. LC 75-14052. (Illus.). 128p. (J). (gr. 3-4). 1975. pap. 7.50x (*0-87441-244-7*); teacher ed, pap. 14.95x (*0-87441-227-7*) Behrman.

— A Child's Introduction to the Early Prophets, No. 2. LC 75-14052. (Illus.). 128p. (J). (gr. 3-4). 1975. student ed, pap. 2.95x (*0-87441-269-2*) Behrman.

— A Child's Introduction to Torah. Newman, Louis, ed. (Illus.). 128p. (Orig.). (J). (gr. 2-3). 1972. pap. text ed. 7.50 (*0-87441-067-3*) Behrman.

— Introduction to Kings, Later Prophets & Writings, Vol. 3. Rossel, Seymour, ed. (Child's Introduction to Bible Ser.). (Illus.). 160p. (Orig.). (J). (gr. 4-5). 1981. student ed, pap. 4.50 (*0-685-00733-2*); pap. text ed. 7.95x (*0-87441-336-2*) Behrman.

Newman, Shirley, jt. auth. see Rosenberg, Amye.

Newman, Stanley. E As in Erudite: The Expert's Guide to Crossword Puzzles. 1993. pap. 8.00 (*0-06-096987-3*, PL) HarpC.

— F as in Fulgent: The Expert's Book of Crossword Puzzles. 1993. pap. 8.00 (*0-06-096985-7*, PL) HarpC.

— Random House Cryptic Crossword Book Vol. 2. 1995. pap. 10.00 (*0-8129-2562-9*, Times Bks) Random.

— Random House Cryptic Crosswords, Vol. 1. 1994. pap. 10.00 (*0-8129-6371-7*, Times Bks) Random.

— Random House Sunday Crossword Puzzles Vol. 1. 1995. pap. 8.00 (*0-8129-2554-8*, Times Bks) Random.

— Random House Ultrahard Crosswords, Vol. 1. 1994. pap. 8.00 (*0-8129-6372-5*, Times Bks) Random.

— Ultimate Crossword Puzzle Book. 1994. pap. 5.99 (*0-517-10160-2*) Random Hse Value.

— Zuni Law: A Field of Values, with an Appendix. Incl. Practical Zuni Orthography. 1954. (*0-318-54046-0*); (HU PMP Ser.). 1954. 32.00 (*0-527-01312-9*) Periodicals Srv.

Newman, Stanley, ed. B As in Bravura. (Expert's Book of Crosswords Ser.). 64p. (Orig.). 1991. pap. 8.00 (*0-06-096555-X*, PL) HarpC.

— C As in Cognoscenti. (Expert's Guide of Crosswords Ser.). 64p. (Orig.). 1991. pap. 8.00 (*0-06-096570-3*, PL) HarpC.

— Expert's Book of Crosswords. (Illus.). 64p. (Orig.). 1994. pap. 8.00 (*0-06-096986-5*, PL) HarpC.

— H As in Habile. (Illus.). 64p. (Orig.). 1994. pap. 8.00 (*0-06-096988-1*, PL) HarpC.

— The Random House Handy Crossword Book, No. 1. 1995. mass mkt. 4.99 (*0-8041-1322-X*) Ivy Books.

— The Random House Handy Crossword Book, No. 2. 1995. mass mkt. 4.99 (*0-8041-1339-4*) Ivy Books.

— The Random House Handy Crossword Book No. 3. 1995. pap. 4.99 (*0-8041-1340-8*) Ivy Books.

Newman, Stanton, jt. auth. see Geber, Beryl.

***Newman, Stanton, et al.** Understanding Rheumatoid Arthritis. LC 95-16023. 1996. write for info. (*0-415-10540-4*); pap. write for info. (*0-415-10541-2*) Routledge.

Newman, Stephen A., ed. Acid & Sour Gas Treating Processes. LC 84-25339. 820p. 1985. 47.00 (*0-87201-839-3*) Gulf Pub.

— Thermodynamics of Aqueous Systems with Industrial Applications. LC 80-16044. (ACS Symposium Ser.: No. 133). 1980. 86.95 (*0-8412-0569-8*) Am Chemical.

— Thermodynamics of Aqueous Systems with Industrial Applications. suppl. ed. LC 80-16044. (ACS Symposium Ser.: No. 133). 1980. 14.95 (*0-8412-0590-6*) Am Chemical.

Newman, Stephen L. Liberalism at Wit's End: The Libertarian Revolt Against the Modern State. LC 84-7108. 192p. 1984. 32.50 (*0-8014-1747-3*) Cornell U Pr.

Newman, Steve & Marsh, Ed. Last Action Hero: The Making of the Arnold Schwarzenegger Film - The Official Moviebook. (Illus.). 128p. (Orig.). 1993. pap. 9.95 (*1-55704-174-1*) Newmarket.

Newman, Steven A., jt. ed. see Tusa, Ronald J.

Newman, Steven M. Worldwalk. 560p. 1990. mass mkt. 5.95 (*0-380-71150-8*) Avon.

Newman, Steven M., jt. auth. see Sholly, Dan R.

Newman, Steven T., jt. ed. see Case, Keith.

Newman, Stewart A. A Free Church Perspective: A Study in Ecclesiology. 113p. (Orig.). 1986. pap. 8.95 (*0-913029-12-2*) Stevens Bk Pr.

Newman, Stuart, jt. auth. see Souter, Nick.

Newman, Stuart A., jt. auth. see Hall, Brian K.

Newman, Susan. Dont Be S. A. D. A Teenage Guide to Handling Stress, Anxiety & Depression. (J). 1991. lib. bdg. 12.98 (*0-671-72610-2*, Julian Messner); lib. bdg. 7.95 (*0-671-72611-0*, Julian Messner) Silver Burdett Pr.

— Let's Always: Promises to Make Love Last. LC 94-16788. 144p. (Orig.). 1995. pap. 8.00 (*0-399-51901-7*, Perigree Bks) Berkley Pub.

— Little Things Long Remembered: Making Your Children Feel Special Every Day. LC 92-42897. 1993. 12.50 (*0-517-59302-5*, Crown) Crown Pub Group.

— Parenting an Only Child. 1990. pap. 12.95 (*0-385-24964-0*) Doubleday.

N

***Newman, Susan B.** Literacy in the Television Age. (Illus.). 248p. 1995. pap. write for info. (*1-56750-162-1*) Ablex Pub.

— Literacy in the Television Age. 2nd ed. (Illus.). 248p. 1995. write for info. (*1-56750-161-3*) Ablex Pub.

***Newman, Susan D.** With Heart & Hand: The Black Church Working to Save Black Children. LC 94-39334. 1995. pap. 8.00 (*0-8170-1223-0*) Judson.

Newman-Swaney, Laura J. Eighty Years A-Growing. Laube, Gary, ed. (Illus.). 48p. 1994. pap. 8.95 (*0-8059-3530-4*) Dorrance.

Newman, T. C. & Odell, P. L. The Generation of Random Variates. 1971. 17.95 (*0-85264-194-X*) Lubrecht & Cramer.

Newman, Tamsin, jt. auth. see Newman, Graeme.

Newman, Teresa & Watkinson, Ray. Ford Maddox Brown: And the Pre-Raphaelite Circle. (Illus.). 226p. 1992. 100. 00 (*0-7011-3186-1*, Pub. by Chatto & Windus UK) Trafalgar.

Newman, Thelma R. & Merrill, Virginia H. The Complete Book of Making Miniatures. (Arts & Crafts Ser.). (Illus.). 328p. 1975. pap. 16.95 (*0-517-52460-0*, Crown) Crown Pub Group.

Newman, Thomas, jt. auth. see Ostrager, Barry R.

***Newman, Thomas E.** Electricity & Electronics. LC 94-37494. 1994. 39.95 (*0-02-801253-4*) Glencoe.

Newman, Thomas R. New York Appellate Practice, 2 vols. 1985. Updates. ring bd. write for info. (*0-8205-1519-1*) Bender.

Newman, Thomas R., jt. auth. see Ostrager, Barry R.

Newman, Vicky, jt. auth. see Cumming, Candy.

***Newman, Victor.** Problem Solving for Results. 200p. 1995. 48.95 (*0-566-07566-0*, Pub. by Gower UK) Ashgate Pub Co.

Newman, W. A. C., jt. auth. see Rose, T. K.

Newman, W. S. & Stipcich, S. Nuclear Winter & the New Defense Systems: Problems & Perspectives, the 4th International Seminar on Nuclear War. (Science & Culture Ser.). 532p. 1992. text ed. 123.00 (*981-02-1187-2*) World Scientific Pub.

— SDI, Computer Simulations, New Proposals to Stop the Arms Race: Fifth International Seminar on Nuclear War. (Science & Culture Ser.). 396p. 1992. text ed. 121.00 (*981-02-1188-0*) World Scientific Pub.

— The Technical Basis for Peace: Third International Seminar on Nuclear War. (Science & Culture Ser.). 400p. 1992. text ed. 121.00 (*981-02-1186-4*) World Scientific Pub.

Newman, Walter H., jt. ed. see Abel, Francis L.

Newman, Walter S. & Salwen, Bert S., eds. AmerInds & Their Paleoenvironments in Northeastern North America, Vol. 288. 1977. 37.00 (*0-89072-034-7*) NY Acad Sci.

Newman, Wilda B., jt. auth. see Mount, Ellis.

***Newman, William.** Gehennical Fire: The Lives of George Starkey, an American Alchemist in the Scientific Revolution. (Illus.). 364p. 1994. text ed. 49.95 (*0-674-34171-6*, NEWGEH) HUP.

— Interactive System Design. (C). 1995. text ed. 43.25 (*0-201-63162-8*) Addison-Wesley.

Newman, William A. & Ross, Arnold, eds. Antarctic Cirripedia. LC 74-129339. (Antarctic Research Ser.: Vol. 14). (Illus.). 257p. 1971. 32.00 (*0-87590-114-X*) Am Geophysical.

Newman, William A., jt. auth. see Grupe, Fritz H.

Newman, William H. Administrative Action: The Techniques of Organization & Management. 2nd ed. 1963. text ed. 48.00 (*0-13-007195-1*) P-H.

— Birth of a Successful Joint Venture. LC 92-10759. 1992. 15.50 (*0-8191-8724-0*); 40.50 (*0-8191-8723-2*) U Pr of Amer.

Newman, William H., jt. auth. see Yavitz, Boris.

Newman, William I., et al, eds. Nonlinear Dynamics & Predictability of Geophysical Phenomena, IUGG, 1994, Vol. 18. LC 94-20388. (Geophysical Monograph Ser.: Vol. 83). 107p. 1994. 28.00 (*0-87590-469-6*) Am Geophysical.

Newman, William M. Charters of St-Fursy of Peronne. LC 75-36479. (Medieval Academy Bks.: No. 85). 1977. 25. 00 (*0-910956-59-6*) Medieval Acad.

— Le Domaine Royal Sous les Premiers Capetiens (987-1180) LC 80-2014. reprint ed. 41.50 (*0-404-18581-9*) AMS Pr.

— Interactive Systems Design. Date not set. text ed. write for info. (*0-07-046343-3*) McGraw.

— The Kings, the Court & Royal Power in France in the Eleventh Century. LC 80-2030. reprint ed. 28.00 (*0-404-18582-7*) AMS Pr.

Newman, William M. & Halvorson, Peter L. Patterns in Pluralism: A Portrait of American Religion, 1952-1971. LC 79-55177. 1980. pap. 5.00 (*0-914422-10-3*) Glenmary Res Ctr.

Newman, William M., jt. auth. see Boudreau, Frances A.

Newman, William M., jt. auth. see Halvorson, Peter L.

Newman, William R. The Summa Perfectionis of Pseudo-Geber: A Critical Edition, Translation & Study. LC 91-25350. (CTAI Ser.: No. 35). iv, 785p. 1991. 214.50 (*90-04-09464-4*) E J Brill.

Newman, William S. Beethoven on Beethoven: Playing His Piano Music His Way. 1991. pap. 14.95 (*0-393-30719-0*) Norton.

— The Pianist's Problems. 4th ed. LC 83-19020. (Music Reprint Ser.). (Illus.). 208p. 1984. reprint ed. lib. bdg. 25.00 (*0-306-76213-7*) Da Capo.

— The Pianist's Problems. (Quality Paperbacks Ser.). (Illus.). x, 208p. 1986. reprint ed. pap. 10.95 (*0-306-80269-4*) Da Capo.

— Six Keyboard Sonatas from the Classical Era Score. 67p. reprint ed. pap. 25.00 (*0-317-09725-3*, 2004336) Bks Demand.

— The Sonata in the Baroque Era. 4th ed. (C). 1983. text ed. 18.95 (*0-393-95275-4*) Norton.

— The Sonata in the Classic Era. 3rd ed. (C). 1983. text ed. 22.50 (*0-393-95286-X*) Norton.

— The Sonata since Beethoven: The Third & Final Volume of a History of the Sonata Idea. LC 76-80924. 880p. reprint ed. pap. 180.00 (*0-8357-3860-4*, 2036593) Bks Demand.

Newman, William S., ed. Diabelli Variations: Sixteen Contemporaries of Beethoven on a Waltz Tune. 31p. reprint ed. pap. 25.00 (*0-317-09716-4*, 2004337) Bks Demand.

Newmann, Anna, jt. auth. see Bensimon, Estela M.

Newmann, Dana. The Compleat Teacher's Almanack: A Practical Guide to Every Day of the Year. 384p. 1991. 24.95 (*0-87628-243-5*) P-H.

— The Early Childhood Teacher's Almanac: Activities for Every Month of the Year. (Illus.). 192p. (Orig.). 1984. pap. 24.95 (*0-87628-287-7*) Ctr Appl Res.

— New Early Childhood Teacher's Almanac: Fun Activities for Every Month of the Year. rev. ed. LC 92-14012. (Illus.). 1992. pap. 27.95 (*0-87628-606-6*) Ctr Appl Res.

— The New Teacher's Almanac: Practical Ideas for Every Day of the School Year. 1980. 24.95 (*0-87628-604-X*) Ctr Appl Res.

Newmann, Frances. Dead Lovers Are Faithful Lovers. LC 76-51673. (Rediscovered Fiction by American Women Ser.). 1977. lib. bdg. 33.95 (*0-405-10051-5*) Ayer.

Newmann, Fred M., ed. Student Engagement & Achievement in American Secondary Schools. LC 92-15727. 240p. (C). 1992. 38.00 (*0-8077-3183-8*); pap. 17. 95 (*0-8077-3182-X*) Tchrs Coll.

Newmann, Fred M., jt. auth. see Archbald, Doug A.

Newmann-Solow, Sharon. Sign Language Interpreting: A Basic Resource Book. (Illus.). 107p. (C). 1981. text ed. 11.95 (*0-913072-45-1*); pap. text ed. 9.95 (*0-913072-44-3*) Natl Assn Deaf.

Newmarch, Jan. Logic Programming: Prolog & Stream Parallel Languages. 288p. 1991. boxed 35.00 (*0-13-539842-8*) P-H.

— The X Window System & Motif: A Fast Tract Approach. LC 92-25196. (C). 1992. pap. text ed. 34.50 (*0-201-53931-4*) Addison-Wesley.

Newmarch, Rosa. The Concert-Goer's Library of Descriptive Notes, 2 vols. in 1. LC 70-160984. (Select Bibliographies Reprint Ser.). 1977. reprint ed. 21.95 (*0-8369-5852-7*) Ayer.

— The Music of Czechoslovakia. LC 77-26269. (Music Reprint Ser.: 1978). 1978. reprint ed. lib. bdg. 32.50 (*0-306-77563-8*) Da Capo.

— Tchaikovsky: His Life & Works, with Extracts from His Writings, & the Diary of His Tour Abroad in 1888. LC 68-25298. (Studies in Music: No. 42). 1968. reprint ed. lib. bdg. 75.00 (*0-8383-0310-2*) M S G Haskell Hse.

Newmarch, Rosa H. The Concert Goer's Library of Descriptive Notes. 1990. reprint ed. lib. bdg. 79.00 (*0-7812-9165-8*) Rprt Serv.

— The Music of Czechoslovakia. (Music Book Index Ser.). 244p. 1992. reprint ed. lib. bdg. 79.00 (*0-7812-9510-6*) Rprt Serv.

— The Russian Opera. LC 72-109807. (Illus.). 403p. 1972. reprint ed. text ed. 79.50 (*0-8371-4298-9*, NERO, Greenwood Pr) Greenwood.

— Tchaikovsky: His Life & Works with Extracts from His Writings and the Diary of His Tour Abroad in 1888. LC 69-14011. 232p. 1969. reprint ed. text ed. 55.00 (*0-8371-1116-1*, NETC, Greenwood Pr) Greenwood.

— Tchaikovsky: His Life & Works, with Extracts from His Writings, & the Diary of His Tour Abroad in 1888. 232p. 1990. reprint ed. lib. bdg. 69.00 (*0-7812-0775-4*, 10093) Rprt Serv.

Newmark, Ann. Chemistry. LC 92-54480. (Eyewitness Science Ser.). (Illus.). 64p. (J). (gr. 7 up). 1993. 15.95 (*1-56458-231-0*) Dorling Kindersley.

Newmark, Charles S. Major Psychological Assessment Instruments, Vol. I. 1985. text ed. 66.00 (*0-205-08457-5*, H84577, Longwood Div) Allyn.

— Major Psychological Assessment Instruments, Vol. II. 416p. 1989. text ed. 69.00 (*0-205-11923-9*, H19235) Allyn.

Newmark, Charles S., ed. MMPI: Clinical & Research Trends. LC 79-17777. (Praeger Special Studies). 464p. 1979. 49.95 (*0-03-048926-1*, Praeger Pubs) Greenwood.

Newmark, Deborah, jt. auth. see King, Trisha.

Newmark, Eileen. Women's Roles: A Cross-Cultural Perspective. 128p. 1981. pap. 10.25 (*0-08-026073-X*, Pergamon Pr) Elsevier.

Newmark, Harris. Sixty Years in Southern California, 1853-1913. Newmark, Maurice H. & Newmark, Marco R., eds. 744p. 1984. 25.00 (*0-87093-186-5*) Dawsons.

— Sixty Years in Southern California, 1853-1913. 1992. reprint ed. lib. bdg. 75.00 (*0-7812-5071-4*) Rprt Serv.

Newmark, Irving S., jt. auth. see Newmark, Jerry.

Newmark, Jerry & Newmark, Irving S. Happiness Through Superficiality: The War Against Meaningful Relationships. (Illus.). 176p. (Orig.). 1991. pap. 11.95 (*0-932767-02-8*, NMI Pubs) Newmark Mgmt Inst.

Newmark, Joseph. Mathematics As a Second Language. 4th ed. LC 85-30646. (Mathematics Ser.). (C). 1987. text ed. write for info. (*0-201-05885-5*) Addison-Wesley.

— Mathematics for Elementary School Teachers. (Illus.). 750p. (C). 1991. text ed. 52.75 (*0-201-19123-7*) Addison-Wesley.

— Statistics & Probability in Modern Life. 5th ed. 736p. (C). 1992. text ed. 56.00 (*0-03-072867-3*) SCP.

Newmark, Kevin. Beyond Symbolism: Textual History & the Future of Reading. LC 91-55056. 256p. 1991. 34.95 (*0-8014-2577-8*) Cornell U Pr.

Newmark, Leonard, jt. auth. see Bloomfield, Morton W.

Newmark, Leonard, et al. Spoken Albanian. LC 79-56549. 348p. 1980. pap. 10.00 (*0-87950-005-0*); audio 70.00 (*0-87950-007-7*); audio 80.00 (*0-87950-008-5*) Spoken Lang Serv.

Newmark, Leonard D., et al. Standard Albanian: A Reference Grammar for Students. LC 81-52125. 368p. 1982. 49.50 (*0-8047-1129-1*) Stanford U Pr.

Newmark, Marco R., ed. see Newmark, Harris.

Newmark, Maurice H., ed. see Newmark, Harris.

Newmark, Maxim. Dictionary of Foreign Words & Phrases. LC 70-88915. 245p. 1969. reprint ed. text ed. 35.00 (*0-8371-2103-5*, NEFW, Greenwood Pr) Greenwood.

— Dictionary of Spanish Literature. LC 72-141263. 314p. 1972. reprint ed. text ed. 35.00 (*0-8371-5859-1*, NESL, Greenwood Pr) Greenwood.

Newmark, Maxim, jt. ed. see Kendris, Christopher.

Newmark, Michael E. & Penry, J. Kiffin. Genetics of Epilepsy: A Review. 132p. 1980. 45.00 (*0-89004-394-9*) Raven.

Newmark, Nathan M. Selected Papers by Nathan M. Newmark. LC 76-25684. (Civil Engineering Classics Ser.). (Illus.). 897p. reprint ed. pap. 180.00 (*0-317-08325-2*, 2019537) Bks Demand.

Newmark, Nathan M. & Hall, William J. Earthquake Spectra & Design. 103p. 1982. 25.00 (*0-943198-22-4*) Earthquake Eng.

Newmark, Peter. About Translation. (Multilingual Matters Ser.: No. 74). 208p. 1991. 89.00 (*1-85359-118-1*, Pub. by Multilingual Matters UK); pap. 32.00 (*1-85359-117-3*, Pub. by Multilingual Matters UK) Taylor & Francis.

— Paragraphs on Translation. LC 92-42551. 1993. 59.00 (*1-85359-192-0*, Pub. by Multilingual Matters UK); pap. 19.50 (*1-85359-191-2*, Pub. by Multilingual Matters UK) Taylor & Francis.

Newmeyer, F. J., ed. Linguistics: The Cambridge Survey, Vol. 1: Linguistic Theory: Foundations. 512p. (C). 1989. pap. 29.95 (*0-521-37580-0*) Cambridge U Pr.

— Linguistics: The Cambridge Survey, Vol. 2: Linguistic Theory: Extensions & Implications. 328p. (C). 1989. pap. 22.95 (*0-521-37581-9*) Cambridge U Pr.

— Linguistics: The Cambridge Survey, Vol. 3: Language: Psychological & Biological Aspects. 368p. (C). 1989. pap. 22.95 (*0-521-37582-7*) Cambridge U Pr.

— Linguistics: The Cambridge Survey, Vol. 4: Language: The Socio-Cultural Context. 304p. (C). 1989. pap. 22.95 (*0-521-37583-5*) Cambridge U Pr.

Newmeyer, Frederick J. English Aspectual Verbs. LC 74-77826. (Janua Linguarum, Series Practica: No. 203). (Illus.). 95p. (Orig.). 1975. pap. text ed. 37.70 (*90-279-3392-8*) Mouton.

— Generative Linguistics. LC 94-32379. (History of Linguistic Thought Ser.). 1995. 45.00 (*0-415-11553-1*) Routledge.

— Grammatical Theory: Its Limits & Its Possibilities. LC 83-3549. 208p. 1983. pap. text ed. 12.95 (*0-226-57719-8*) U Ch Pr.

— Linguistic Theory of America. 2nd ed. (C). 1986. text ed. 75.00 (*0-12-517151-X*); pap. text ed. 40.00 (*0-12-517152-8*) Acad Pr.

— The Politics of Linguistics. viii, 172p. 1988. pap. text ed. 9.95 (*0-226-57722-8*) U Ch Pr.

Newmeyer, Frederick J., ed. Linguistics: The Cambridge Survey, Vol. 3: Psychological & Biological Aspects. 1988. 64.95 (*0-521-30835-6*) Cambridge U Pr.

— Linguistics: The Cambridge Survey, Vol. 4: The Socio-Cultural Context. 1988. 69.95 (*0-521-30834-8*) Cambridge U Pr.

Newmeyer, John. August Thirty-Two, Two Thousand: And Other Essays for a New Millennium. LC 94-71771. (Illus.). 172p. 1994. 12.95 (*0-9641233-0-4*) Bright Moon.

Newmeyer, William L. Primary Care of Hand Injuries. LC 78-31444. 310p. reprint ed. pap. 88.40 (*0-8357-3248-7*, 2057144) Bks Demand.

Newmyer & Newmyer, Joseph, Jr. Intermediate Algebra. 3rd ed. 448p. (C). 1982. pap. write for info. (*0-675-09912-9*, Merrill Pub Co) Macmillan.

NewMyer, David A., jt. auth. see Wolfe, Harry P.

Newmyer, Frank, jt. auth. see Schroeder, Roger.

Newmyer, Joseph, Jr., jt. auth. see Klentos, Gus.

Newmyer, Joseph, Jr., jt. auth. see Newmyer.

Newmyer, Marina, ed. Washington Black Book: The Directory to the Washington Press Corps. LC 88-5181. 500p. (Orig.). 1988. pap. 103.50 (*0-8191-6878-5*) Madison Bks UPA.

Newmyer, R. Kent. Supreme Court Justice Joseph Story: Statesman of the Old Republic. LC 84-11886. (Studies in Legal History). (Illus.). 508p. reprint ed. pap. 144.80 (*0-7837-6854-0*, 2046683) Bks Demand.

— Supreme Court Under Marshall & Taney. Franklin, John H. & Wakelyn, Jon L., eds. LC 68-29540. (American History Ser.). 192p. (C). 1969. pap. text ed. write for info. (*0-88295-746-5*) Harlan Davidson.

Newmyer, Stephen. Statius Silvae (Selections) (Latin Commentaries Ser.). 117p. (Orig.). (C). 1987. pap. text ed. 7.00 (*0-929524-52-7*) Bryn Mawr Commentaries.

Newmyer, Stephen T. Herodotus, Bk. 3. (Greek Commentaries Ser.). 174p. (Orig.). (C). 1986. pap. text ed. 8.00 (*0-929524-14-4*) Bryn Mawr Commentaries.

Newnam, Thomas A., jt. auth. see Brown, Waln K.

Newnan, C. Dean, jt. auth. see Newnan, Donald G.

Newnan, Donald G. Civil Engineering License Problems & Solutions: Problems & Solutions. 12th ed. (Illus.). 350p. 1995. 29.50 (*0-910554-91-9*, 919) Engineering.

— Civil Engineering License Review: Text. 12th ed. (Illus.). 736p. 1995. 49.50 (*0-910554-90-0*, 900) Engineering.

— Compound Interest Tables. 30p. (Orig.). 1991. pap. text ed. 2.50x (*0-910554-08-0*, 08-0) Engineering.

— Engineer-in-Training License Review. 12th ed. LC 94-2763. (Illus.). 976p. 1995. 58.50 (*0-910554-88-9*, 88-9) Engineering.

— Engineering Economic Analysis, 2 vols., Set. 4th ed. LC 90-40779. (Illus.). 578p. (C). 1991. text ed. 59.50x (*0-910554-83-8*) Engineering.

— Engineering Economics Review. 2nd ed. 78p. 1989. pap. 9.95 (*0-910554-72-2*) Engineering.

Newnan, Donald G., ed. Engineering Economic Analysis Exam File. LC 90-3901. (Exam File Ser.). (Illus.). 298p. (Orig.). (C). 1991. pap. text ed. 17.50x (*0-910554-81-1*) Engineering.

Newnan, Donald G. & Lindskog, Robert E. Civil Engineering License Exam File. 11th ed. LC 90-22318. (Exam File Ser.). (Illus.). 380p. 1991. pap. 39.50 (*0-910554-84-6*) Engineering.

Newnan, Donald G. & Newnan, C. Dean. Engineer-in-Training Exam File. 11th ed. LC 89-23413. (Exam File Ser.). 346p. (Orig.). 1990. pap. 17.50 (*0-910554-78-1*) Engineering.

Newnan, Donald G., et al. Engineering Economic Analysis, 2 vols. 5th ed. LC 94-24798. 908p. (C). 1995. text ed. 59.50x (*0-910554-93-5*, 935) Engineering.

Newnan, Edna S. Michigan Nature Association - In Retrospect: Celebrating 28 Years of Preserving Michigan's Wild & Rare Natural Lands, 1960-1988. Daubendiek, Bertha A., ed. LC 88-62060. (Illus.). 99p. 1989. 29.75 (*0-318-37923-6*) MI Nature Assn.

Newnan Junior Service League Staff. A Taste of Georgia Two: In the Southern Manor. (Illus.). 298p. 1991. spiral bd. 12.95 (*0-9611002-1-4*) Newnan JSL.

Newnes, Craig, ed. Death, Dying & Society: A Special Issue of Psychology & Psychotherapy. 180p. 1990. text ed. 29. 95 (*0-86377-177-7*) L Erlbaum Assocs.

Newnham, Jeffrey, jt. ed. see Evans, Graham.

Newnham, Rex. Here's Health. 1994. 17.00 (*0-533-10823-3*) Vantage.

Newnham, Richard, ed. German Short Stories. (Orig.). (gr. 9 up). 1965. pap. 9.00 (*0-14-002040-3*, Penguin Bks) Viking Penguin.

Newnham, Robert E., ed. Applied Crystal Chemistry & Physics. (Transactions of the American Crystallographic Association Ser.: Vol. 11). 117p. 1975. pap. 25.00 (*0-686-47114-8*) Polycrystal Bk Serv.

Newport & Meier, eds. The Acquisition of American Sign Language. (Crosslinguistic Study of Language Acquisition Ser.). 80p. 1990. pap. 14.95 (*0-89859-849-4*) L Erlbaum Assocs.

Newport, Cris. Sparks Might Fly. LC 94-15387. 192p. (Orig.). 1994. pap. 9.95 (*0-934678-61-8*) New Victoria Pubs.

— The White Bones of Truth. 210p. (Orig.). 1995. pap. 10. 95 (*1-886383-15-4*) Pride OH.

Newport, Dan & Schultz, Joe. Planning a Running Event: A Manual on the Administration of a Successful Running Race. (Quest for Quality Ser.: No. 2). 50p. reprint ed. pap. 25.00 (*0-7837-1551-X*, 2041844) Bks Demand.

Newport, Frank, jt. auth. see Rothenberg, Stuart.

Newport Harbor Art Museum Staff. Just Before the War: Urban America from 1935 to 1941. (Illus.). 1968. 5.95 (*0-8079-0147-4*); pap. 2.95 (*0-8079-0148-2*) October.

Newport, John P. Demonios, Demonios, Demonios. Canclini, Arnoldo, tr. 110p. (Orig.). (SPA.). 1987. pap. 5.50 (*0-311-05765-9*) Casa Bautista.

— El Leon y el Cordero. Zorzoli, Ruben O., tr. 352p. (Orig.). (SPA.). 1989. pap. 8.50 (*0-311-04359-3*) Casa Bautista.

— The Lion & the Lamb. LC 85-29887. 1986. 14.99 (*0-8054-1324-3*) Broadman.

Newport, John R. Avionic System Design. LC 94-11904. 1994. write for info. (*0-8493-2465-3*) CRC Pr.

— Fuzzy Rule Based Computer Design. 256p. 1995. 69.95 (*0-8493-7834-6*, 7834) CRC Pr.

***Newquist, H. P.** Virtual Reality. LC 95-9900. (J). 1995. write for info. (*0-590-48408-7*) Scholastic Inc.

Newquist, H. P., jt. auth. see Prown, Pete.

Newquist, Harvey. Music & Technology. (Illus.). 208p. 1989. pap. 16.95 (*0-8230-7578-8*, Billboard Bks) Watsn-Guptill.

Newquist, Jerreld L., ed. see Cannon, George Q.

Newquist, Roy. Conversations with Joan Crawford. (Illus.). 1980. 10.00 (*0-8065-0720-9*, Citadel Pr) Carol Pub Group.

***Newquist, Trini.** Phoenix Baby Resource Guide, 93-94. (Illus.). 304p. (Orig.). (C). 1993. pap. text ed. 9.95 (*0-9637868-0-6*) AZ Baby Res.

***Newsam, Barbara & Newsam, David.** Making Money Teaching Music. (Illus.). 240p. (Orig.). 1995. pap. 18.99 (*0-89879-657-1*) Writers Digest.

Newsam, Barbara S. Complete Student Assistance Program Handbook: Techniques & Materials for Alcohol-Drug Prevention & Intervention in Grades 7-12. LC 92-22749. (Illus.). 302p. 1992. spiral bd. 34.95 (*0-87628-878-6*) Ctr Appl Res.

Newsam, David, jt. auth. see Newsam, Barbara.

***Newsday Staff.** Long Island User's Guide: How to Make Sense of Schools, Government, Health & Education. Heisler, Robert, ed. (Illus.). 448p. (Orig.). 1994. pap. 11. 95 (*1-885134-03-7*) Newsday.

— Rush to Burn: Solving America's Garbage Crisis? LC 89-1939. (Illus.). 269p. (Orig.). 1989. 25.00 (*1-55963-001-9*); pap. 15.95 (*1-55963-000-0*) Island Pr.

***Newsday Staff & Carter, Sylvia.** Eats NYC. 192p. 1995. pap. 8.95 (*0-8362-0809-9*) Andrews & McMeel.

***Newsday Staff & Reel, Bill.** Get Reel: The Brooklyn Boy & Other Stories of Faith in the City. 192p. 1995. pap. 8.95 (*0-8362-0810-2*) Andrews & McMeel.

Newsham, Bradley. All the Right Places: Traveling Light Through China, Japan, & Russia. 1989. 16.95 (*0-394-57410-9*, Villard Bks) Random.

***Newsham, Ian, illus.** A Treasury of Irish Stories. LC 95-3009. 1995. pap. 5.95 (*1-85697-595-9*, Kingfisher LKC) LKC.

An Asterisk (*) at the beginning of an entry indicates that the title is appearing in BIP for the first time.

Newsham, N. GCSE Biology Practical Assessment - Evaluation Pack. (C). 1989. text ed. 110.00 (*0-09-176100-X*, Pub. by S Thornes Pubs UK) St Mut.
— GCSE Biology Practical Assessment - Workpack & Teacher's Guide. (C). 1989. text ed. 300.00 (*0-09-173147-X*, Pub. by S Thornes Pubs UK) St Mut.
— GCSE Biology Practical Assessment Additional Teacher's Guide. (C). 1989. 40.00 (*0-09-173142-9*, Pub. by S Thornes Pubs UK) St Mut.
Newsholme, Arthur. The Elements of Vital Statistics. 3rd rev. ed. LC 75-38139. (Demography Ser.). (Illus.). 1976. reprint ed. 31.95 (*0-405-07992-3*) Ayer.
— Evolution of Preventive Medicine. LC 75-23748. reprint ed. 37.50 (*0-404-13354-1*) AMS Pr.
— Public Health & Insurance. LC 78-19270. 1979. 28.95 (*0-405-10617-3*) Ayer.
Newsholme, Christopher. Willows, the Genus Salix. (Illus.). 224p. 1992. 34.95 (*0-88192-261-7*) Timber.
Newsholme, E. A. & Start, C. Regulation in Metabolism. LC 72-5721. (Illus.). 363p. reprint ed. pap. 103.50 (*0-7837-5205-9*, 2044933) Bks Demand.
Newsholme, Eric, et al. Keep on Running: The Science of Training & Performance. LC 93-49630. 1994. 45.00 (*0-471-94313-4*) Wiley.
— Keep on Running: The Science of Training & Performance. LC 93-49630. 1994. pap. text ed. 17.95 (*0-471-94314-2*) Wiley.
Newsholme, Eric A. & Leech, Anthony R. Biochemistry for the Medical Sciences. 952p. 1984. pap. text ed. 89.95 (*0-471-90058-3*) Wiley.
***Newsinger, John.** The Fenians. LC 94-32946. (Socialist History of Britain Ser.). (C). 1994. text ed. 34.95 (*0-7453-0900-3*, Pub. by Pluto Pr UK) Westview.
***Newsom, Brad.** The Athletics of Voice: A Handbook for Teachers & Students of Singing. Windward, Shirley, ed. (Illus.). 108p. (C). 1995. pap. text ed. 15.00 (*0-9644358-0-2*) NewWind.
Newsom, Carol. The Songs of the Sabbath Sacrifice: Edition, Translation, & Commentary. (Harvard Semitic Museum Monographs). (C). 1985. 39.95 (*0-89130-918-7*, 04-04-27) Scholars Pr GA.
Newsom, Carol A. & Ringe, Sharon H., eds. The Women's Bible Commentary. 384p. 1992. text ed. 23.00 (*0-664-21922-5*) Westminster John Knox.
— The Women's Bible Commentary. 416p. 1995. reprint ed. pap. 19.00 (*0-664-25586-8*) Westminster John Knox.
Newsom, D. Earl. The Birth of Oklahoma. (Illus.). 178p. (J). (gr. 5-12). 1983. 14.95 (*0-934188-08-4*) Evans Pubns.
— Drumright II (& Shamrock, Pemeta, Oilton & Olive) A Thousand Memories. (Illus.). 288p. 1987. 19.95 (*0-934188-25-4*) Evans Pubns.
Newsom, David. David Newsom: The Western Observer, 1805-1882. LC 72-92062. (Illus.). 330p. 1972. pap. 7.95 (*0-87595-040-X*) Oregon Hist.
Newsom, David D. Can Negotiation Be Taught? (Pew Case Studies in International Affairs). 50p. (C). 1992. pap. text ed. 2.50 (*1-56927-448-7*) Geo U Inst Dplmcy.
— Diplomacy & the American Democracy. LC 87-45438. 240p. 1988. 25.00 (*0-253-31816-5*); pap. 9.95 (*0-253-20470-4*, MB-470) Ind U Pr.
Newsom, David D., ed. Diplomacy under a Foreign Flag: When Nations Break Relations. LC 89-19983. 144p. (Orig.). 1990. pap. text ed. 9.95 (*0-934742-46-4*) Geo U Inst Dplmcy.
— Diplomacy under a Foreign Flag: When Nations Break Relations. LC 89-19983. 144p. (Orig.). 1990. text ed. 39.95 (*0-312-04051-2*) St Martin.
— Diplomatic Record, 1989-1990. (Illus.). 250p. 1990. text ed. 73.00 (*0-8133-1142-X*) Westview.
— The Diplomatic Record, 1989-1990. (Diplomatic Record Ser.). (Illus.). 256p. (Orig.). 1991. pap. text ed. 12.50 (*0-934742-65-0*) Geo U Inst Dplmcy.
— The Diplomatic Record, 1990-1991. (Diplomatic Record Ser.). (Illus.). 337p. 1992. pap. text ed. 12.50 (*0-934742-66-9*) Geo U Inst Dplmcy.
— The Diplomatic Record, 1990-1991. (Illus.). 331p. 1992. text ed. 61.00 (*0-8133-1386-4*) Westview.
— Private Diplomacy with the Soviet Union. LC 86-28926. 166p. (Orig.). (C). 1987. pap. text ed. 14.50 (*0-8191-5821-6*, Inst Study Diplomacy) U Pr of Amer.
Newsom, David D., ed. & frwd. Private Diplomacy with the Soviet Union. LC 86-28926. 156p. (Orig.). 1987. pap. text ed. 14.50 (*0-934742-40-5*) Geo U Inst Dplmcy.
Newsom-Davis, J. M. & Weatherall, David, eds. Health Policy & Technological Innovation. LC 93-21164. 1993. write for info. (*0-412-54250-1*, Chap & Hall NY) Chapman & Hall.
Newsom, Doug & Carrell, Bob. Public Relations Writing: Form & Style. 3rd ed. 458p. (C). 1991. pap. 26.95 (*0-534-14388-1*) Intl Thomson.
Newsom, Doug & Wollert, James A. Media Writing: Preparing Information for the Mass Media. 2nd ed. 444p. (C). 1988. pap. 28.95 (*0-534-08712-4*) Intl Thomson.
Newsom, Doug, et al. This Is PR: The Realities of Public Relations. 5th ed. LC 92-10718. 615p. (C). 1993. text ed. 54.95 (*0-534-17262-8*) Intl Thomson.
***Newsom, Doug A. & Carrell, Bob J., eds.** Silent Voices. (Illus.). 256p. (Orig.). (C). 1995. lib. bdg. 47.00 (*0-8191-9854-4*) U Pr of Amer.
— Silent Voices. 256p. (Orig.). (C). 1995. pap. text ed. 29.50 (*0-8191-9855-2*) U Pr of Amer.
***Newsom, Douglas & Carrell, Bob.** Public Relations Writing: Form & Style. 4th ed. LC 94-33763. 504p. 1995. pap. 27.95 (*0-534-25500-0*) Intl Thomson.
Newsom, Earl D. The Cherokee Strip: Its History & Grand Opening. (Oklahoma Legacies Ser.). (Illus.). (Orig.). 1992. pap. 10.95 (*0-913507-27-X*) New Forums.
Newsom, Ed. Blood Bullets. (Brannigan Ser.: No. 3). (Orig.). 1982. pap. 2.25 (*0-89083-920-4*) Zebra.
— Brannigan. 208p. (Orig.). 1981. pap. 1.95 (*0-89083-713-9*) Zebra.
— Brannigan, No. 4: The Peacekeeper. 1983. pap. 2.25 (*0-8217-1163-6*) Zebra.
— Comanchero Chase. (Brannigan Ser.: No 2). (Orig.). 1981. pap. 2.25 (*0-89083-858-5*) Zebra.
Newsom, Horton E. & Jones, John H., eds. Origin of the Earth. (Illus.). 384p. (C). 1990. 50.00 (*0-19-506619-7*) OUP.
Newsom, Iris, ed. Performing Arts at the Library of Congress. 167p. 1992. 26.00 (*0-16-036054-4*, 030-001-00136-9) Lib Congress.
Newsom, Jon, ed. Perspectives on John Philip Sousa. LC 83-600076. (Illus.). 152p. 1983. 17.00 (*0-16-004018-3*, S/N 030-001-00103-2) USGPO.
Newsom, Joseph C., jt. auth. see Newsom, Samuel.
Newsom, Lila. Recollections of Ninety-One Years. 1989. pap. 7.95 (*0-89137-116-8*) Quality Pubns.
Newsom, Mary M., jt. ed. see Burke, Edmund R.
Newsom, Peggy, jt. auth. see Raders, Sheri.
Newsom, Robert. Dickens on the Romantic Side of Familiar Things: Bleak House & the Novel Tradition. LC 88-70307. xvi, 173p. (C). 1988. reprint ed. pap. 12.70 (*0-9620150-0-8*) UCSC Dickens Project.
— A Likely Story: Probability & Play in Fiction. 258p. (Orig.). (C). 1988. text ed. 35.00 (*0-8135-1320-0*); pap. text ed. 15.00 (*0-8135-1357-X*) Rutgers U Pr.
Newsom, Robert S., jt. auth. see Glick, Rush G.
Newsom, Ron, jt. ed. see Dressler, Dennis W.
Newsom, Samuel. Japanese Garden Construction. 556p. reprint ed. 60.00 (*0-938290-10-X*) Apollo.
Newsom, Samuel & Newsom, Joseph C. Picturesque California Homes. LC 78-4248. (Illus.). 1978. reprint ed. pap. 18.95 (*0-912158-82-4*) Hennessey.
Newsome, A. R. Records of Emigrants from England & Scotland to North Carolina, 1774-1775. 30p. 1989. pap. 3.00 (*0-86526-134-2*) NC Archives.
Newsome, Albert R., jt. auth. see Lefler, Hugh T.
Newsome, Arden. Cork & Wood Crafts. LC 72-112370. (Illus.). 64p. (J). (gr. k-3). 1971. lib. bdg. 12.95 (*0-87460-229-7*) Lion Bks.
Newsome, D. H., ed. Weather Radar Networking: COST 73 Project: Final Report. LC 92-26375. 272p. (C). 1992. lib. bdg. 94.00 (*0-7923-1939-7*) Kluwer Ac.
Newsome, D. H. & Edwards, A. M., eds. Third River Basin Management Conference: Proceedings of a Conference Held in York, 4-8 July 1983 & Incorporating the Workshop on Advances in the Application of Mathematical Modelling to Water Quality Management Held in London, July 11-12 1983. (Illus.). 670p. 1984. pap. 130.00 (*0-08-031505-4*, Pergamon Pr) Elsevier.
Newsome, David. Bishop Westcott & the Platonic Tradition. LC 78-409427. (Bishop Westcott Memorial Lecture Ser.: Vol. 1968). 39p. reprint ed. pap. 25.00 (*0-8357-7279-9*, 2051381) Bks Demand.
— The Convert Cardinals: Newman & Manning. (Illus.). 384p. 1995. 55.00 (*0-7195-4635-4*, Pub. by John Murray UK) Trafalgar.
— On the Edge of Paradise: A. C. Benson; the Diarist. LC 80-12747. (Illus.). 416p. 1980. 25.00 (*0-226-57742-2*) U Ch Pr.
— The Parting of Friends: The Wilberforces & Henry Manning. LC 93-6749. (Illus.). 502p. 1993. 29.99 (*0-8028-3714-X*) Eerdmans.
Newsome, David A., ed. Retinal Dystrophies & Degenerations. (Illus.). 400p. 1988. text ed. 151.00 (*0-88167-186-X*) Raven.
Newsome, David H. Wilberforces & Henry Manning: The Parting of Friends. LC 67-2. (Illus.). 498p. 1966. 42.50 (*0-674-95280-4*) Belknap Pr.
Newsome, James D. By the Waters of Babylon: Palaces, Patriarchs & Prophecy. 176p. (Orig.). 1986. pap. 19.95 (*0-567-29103-0*, Pub. by T & T Clark UK) Bks Intl VA.
— Greeks, Romans, Jews: Currents of Culture & Belief in the New Testament World. LC 92-26308. (Illus.). 496p. 1992. pap. 29.95 (*1-56338-037-4*) TPI PA.
Newsome, James D., Jr. The Hebrew Prophets. LC 84-7601. 252p. (Orig.). 1986. pap. 13.99 (*0-8042-0113-7*, John Knox) Westminster John Knox.
— A Synoptic Harmony of Samuel, Kings, & Chronicles: With Related Passages from Psalms, Isaiah, Jeremiah & Ezra. LC 86-70160. 286p. 1990. pap. 12.99 (*0-8010-6783-9*) Baker Bk.
Newsome, Karen L. User Initiated Document Delivery. LC 91-75414. (Studies in Library & Information Science: No. 3). 1992. 32.50 (*0-404-64003-6*) AMS Pr.
Newsome, Lisa. Thinker Task Cards. (Illus.). 128p. 1992. student ed 11.95 (*0-86653-681-7*, 1415) Good Apple.
Newsome, Muriel. Watchful Eyes. 192p. (Orig.). 1993. pap. 3.99 (*1-55773-859-9*) Diamond.
Newsome, S. L., et al, eds. Design Theory Eighty-Eight. (Illus.). xi, 355p. 1989. 54.00 (*0-387-96976-4*) Spr-Verlag.
Newson, Adele S. Zora Neale Hurston: A Reference Guide. (Reference Guides to Literature Ser.). 110p. 1987. text ed. 30.00 (*0-8161-8902-1*, Hall Reference) Macmillan.
Newson, D. Earl. Drumright, the Glory Days of a Boom Town. LC 85-70033. (Illus.). 200p. 1985. 19.95 (*0-934188-17-3*) Evans Pubns.
Newson, David D. The Soviet Brigade in Cuba: A Study in Political Diplomacy. LC 86-45943. 142p. 1987. 25.00 (*0-253-35404-8*); pap. 7.95 (*0-253-20429-1*, MB-429) Ind U Pr.
Newson, E. F., jt. auth. see Bell, P. C.
Newson, E. F., jt. auth. see Bell, Peter C.
Newson, Elizabeth & Hipgrave, Tony. Getting Through to Your Handicapped Child: A Handbook for Parents, Foster-Parents, Teachers & Anyone Caring for Handicapped Children. LC 82-4310. 144p. 1983. pap. 12.25 (*0-521-27056-1*) Cambridge U Pr.
Newson, Herbert H. Medical & Health Practices & Defensive Medicine: New Research Bible of Current Trends. 160p. 1994. 51.50 (*0-7883-0200-0*); pap. 45.50 (*0-7883-0201-9*) ABBE Pubs Assn.
Newson, Linda A. Indian Survival in Colonial Nicaragua. LC 86-40078. (Civilization of the American Indian Ser.: Vol. 175). (Illus.). 496p. 1987. 42.50 (*0-8061-2008-8*) U of Okla Pr.
— Life & Death in Early Colonial Equador. LC 94-41571. (Civilization of the American Indian Ser.: Vol. 214). (Illus.). 505p. 1995. 45.00 (*0-8061-2697-3*) U of Okla Pr.
Newson, M. Managing the Human Impact on the Natural Environment Patterns & Processes. 282p. 1993. 335.00 (*81-7089-152-3*, Pub. by Intl Bk Distr II) St Mut.
Newson, Malcolm. Hydrology & the River Environment. (Illus.). 256p. (C). 1994. 49.95 (*0-19-874156-1*); pap. text ed. 22.95 (*0-19-874157-X*) OUP.
— Land, Water & Development: River Basin Systems & Their Sustainable Management. LC 91-39206. (Natural Environment: Problems & Management Ser.). (Illus.). 384p. 1992. 74.50 (*0-415-05711-6*, A7502); pap. 29.95 (*0-415-08031-2*, A7506) Routledge.
Newson, T. Housing Policy: An International Bibliography. 416p. 1986. text ed. 120.00 (*0-7201-1785-2*, Mansell Pub) Cassell.
Newson, T. & Potter, P. Housing Policy in Britain: An Information Sourcebook. 236p. 1985. text ed. 80.00 (*0-7201-1750-X*, Mansell Pub) Cassell.
Newson, T. M. Cen Pictures of St. Paul, Minnesota & Biographical Sketches of Old Settlers, Vol. I. 746p. 1993. reprint ed. lib. bdg. 75.00 (*0-8328-3473-4*) Higginson Bk Co.
— Pen Pictures of St. Paul, Minnesota & Biographical Sketches of Old Settlers, Vol. 1. 746p. 1994. reprint ed. lib. bdg. 75.00 (*0-8328-3839-X*) Higginson Bk Co.
— Thrilling Scenes among the Indians. LC 94-11835. 1994. 7.98 (*0-681-00759-1*) Longmeadow Pr.
Newspaper Enterprise Association Staff. The World Almanac Guide to Metrics. 1981. pap. 2.50 (*0-449-13828-3*, GM) Fawcett.
Newspaper Features Council Staff, jt. auth. see Nordling, Lee.
Newspaper Marketing Associates Staff. Headcheese Recipes: From Your Favorite Local Restaurants. (Illus.). 160p. 1989. pap. text ed. 12.95 (*0-9629776-0-8*) News Mktg Assocs.
Newstead, Stephen E., et al, eds. Human Assessment: Cognition & Motivation. (C). 1986. lib. bdg. 173.00 (*90-247-3331-6*) Kluwer Ac.
Newstrom, Harvey. Nutrients Catalog: Vitamins, Minerals, Amino Acids, Macronutrients - Beneficial Use, Helpers, Inhibitors, Food Sources, Intake Recommendations, & Symptoms of over or under Use. LC 92-56671. 558p. 1993. lib. bdg. 55.00 (*0-89950-784-0*) McFarland & Co.
Newstrom, John & Broad, Mary. Managing Transfer Training. (Illus.). 269p. 1992. 24.95 (*0-201-19274-8*) Addison-Wesley.
Newstrom, John W. & Davis, Keith. Organizational Behavior: Human Behavior at Work. 9th ed. LC 92-22097. (Series in Management). 1992. text ed. write for info. (*0-07-015603-4*) McGraw.
— Organizational Behavior: Human Behavior at Work. 9th ed. 1993. pap. text ed. write for info. (*0-07-015632-8*) McGraw.
— Organizational Behavior: Readings & Exercises. 8th rev. ed. 624p. (C). 1989. pap. text ed. write for info. (*0-07-015519-4*) McGraw.
Newstrom, John W. & Scannell, Edward. Games Trainers Play: Experimental Learning Exercises. (Illus.). 336p. 11.00 (*0-318-13272-9*); pap. 12.95 (*0-318-13271-0*, N E G T) Am Soc Train & Devel.
Newstrom, John W. & Scannell, Edward E. Game Trainers Play. 1980. text ed. 21.95 (*0-07-046408-1*) McGraw.
— Still More Games Trainers Play. 320p. 1991. pap. text ed. 21.95 (*0-07-046427-8*) McGraw.
Newstrom, John W., jt. auth. see Bittel, Lester R.
Newstrom, John W., jt. auth. see Bittle, Lester R.
Newstrom, John W., jt. auth. see Davis, Keith.
Newstrom, John W., jt. auth. see Pierce, Jan L.
Newstrom, John W., jt. auth. see Pierce, Jon L.
Newstrom, John W., jt. auth. see Scannell, Edward E.
Newsum, Gillian. Milton. (Illus.). 96p. 1991. 28.95 (*1-872082-20-3*, Pub. by Kenilworth Pr UK) Half Halt Pr.
Newsum, Gillian, jt. auth. see Eilberg, Ferdi.
Newsum, H. E. Class Language & Education: Class Struggle & Sociolinguistics in an African Situation. LC 89-81017. 97p. (C). 1989. 24.95 (*0-86543-139-6*); pap. 7.95 (*0-86543-140-X*) Africa World.
Newsum, H. E. & Abegunrin, Olayiwola. United States Foreign Policy Towards South Africa: Andrew Young & Beyond. LC 84-45784. 256p. 1987. text ed. 39.95 (*0-312-83324-5*) St Martin.
Newsweek, Education Department Staff & Foreign Policy Association Staff. Issues Today for Teachers. 96p. 1990. 14.95 (*0-685-50772-6*) Foreign Policy.
Newth, D. R. & Balls, M., eds. Maternal Effects in Development. LC 78-73812. (British Society for Developmental Biology Symposium Ser.: No. 4). (Illus.). 1980. 125.00 (*0-521-22685-6*) Cambridge U Pr.
Newth, John T. Tolley's Interest & Penalty Provisions. 350p. 1993. 105.00 (*0-85459-580-5*, Pub. by Tolley Pubng UK) St Mut.
Newth, Mette. The Abduction. Nunnally, Tiina & Murray, Steve, trs. (YA). (gr. 7 up). 1989. 14.95 (*0-374-30008-9*) FS&G.
— Abduction. (YA). 1993. pap. 3.95 (*0-374-40009-1*) FS&G.
Newth, Michael, tr. Chanson d'Asprmont. LC 88-31024. (Library of Medieval Literature). 292p. 1989. 20.00 (*0-8240-5618-3*) Garland.
Newth, Michael A. The Songs of Aliscans. LC 91-43662. (Library of Medieval Literature: Vol. 85B). 288p. 1992. 43.00 (*0-8153-0488-9*, GLML 85B) Garland.
Newth, Rebecca. Finding the Lamb. LC 82-7929. 80p. 1983. pap. 4.95 (*0-940170-05-1*) Open Bk Pubns.
— Great North Woods. 1994. pap. 12.00 (*0-9630310-1-5*) Will Hall.
— A Journey Whose Bones Are Mine. 64p. 1990. pap. 3.00 (*0-916562-16-6*) Truck Pr.
— The Oseberg Skiff. (Illus.). 64p. (Orig.). 1991. pap. 6.95 (*0-9630310-0-7*) Will Hall.
***Newton.** Amazing Grace. 1991. 15.95 (*1-56282-998-X*) Hyperion.
— Cat & Mouse. (Illus.). (J). 1995. mass mkt. 5.99 (*0-671-89738-1*) PB.
— Disaster Creek. large type ed. LC 93-37420. 331p. 1994. pap. 15.95 (*0-8161-5857-6*, Large Print Bks) Hall.
Newton, jt. auth. see Coleman.
Newton, jt. auth. see Winsor.
Newton, A. & Ford, J. E. The Production & Properties of Non-Woven Fabrics. 93p. 1973. 70.00 (*0-686-63785-2*) St Mut.
— Production & Properties of Non-Woven Fabrics, Vol. 5, No. 3. (C). 1973. pap. text ed. 90.00 (*0-685-54102-9*, Pub. by Textile Institue UK) St Mut.
Newton, A., jt. auth. see Burnip, M. S.
Newton, A. Edward. A Tribute to A. Edward Newton. 1972. 59.95 (*0-8490-1231-7*) Gordon Pr.
Newton, A. P., ed. Select Documents Relating to the Unification of South Africa. 574p. 1968. reprint ed. 65.00 (*0-7146-1777-6*, Pub. by F Cass Pubs UK) Intl Spec Bk.
Newton, A. R. Logic Synthesis for Integrated Circuit Design, Selected Papers On. 144p. 1987. pap. 24.95 (*0-87942-236-X*, PP02261) Inst Electrical.
Newton, A. Richard, jt. auth. see Saleh, Resve A.
***Newton, Adam Z.** Narrative Ethics. LC 94-19710. 1995. text ed. 42.50 (*0-674-60087-8*, NEWNAR) HUP.
Newton, Alan. Fabric Manufacture: A Handbook. (Illus.). 48p. (Orig.). 1993. pap. 13.50 (*1-85339-133-6*, Pub. by Intermed Tech UK) Women Ink.
Newton, Albert S. Biblical Interleaves in Prose & Verse. 56p. 1987. pap. 1.95 (*0-88028-070-0*, 901) Forward Movement.
***Newton, Alex.** Best Places to Stay in South America. (Illus.). 288p. (Orig.). 1995. pap. 14.95 (*1-55650-696-1*) Hunter NJ.
— Central Africa: A Travel Survival Kit. 2nd ed. (Illus.). 576p. (Orig.). 1994. pap. 16.95 (*0-86442-138-9*) Lonely Planet.
— West Africa: A Travel Survival Kit. 2nd ed. (Illus.). 752p. (Orig.). 1992. pap. 19.95 (*0-86442-137-0*) Lonely Planet.
***Newton, Alex & Else, David.** West Africa: Travel Survival Kit. 3rd ed. (Illus.). 900p. 1995. pap. 19.95 (*0-86442-294-6*) Lonely Planet.
Newton, Alexander H. Out of the Briars. LC 72-89385. (Black Heritage Library Collection). 1977. 17.95 (*0-8369-8637-7*) Ayer.
Newton, Alfred E. Derby Day & Other Adventures. LC 75-93368. (Essay Index Reprint Ser.). 1977. 28.95 (*0-8369-1365-5*) Ayer.
— End Papers. LC 70-90669. (Essay Index Reprint Ser.). 1977. 21.95 (*0-8369-1231-4*) Ayer.
— Magnificent Farce & Other Diversions of a Book-Collector. LC 73-121492. (Essay Index Reprint Ser.). 1977. 30.95 (*0-8369-1767-7*) Ayer.
— Thomas Hardy: Novelist or Poet. LC 70-160428. (Studies in Thomas Hardy: No. 14). 1971. reprint ed. lib. bdg. 32.95 (*0-8383-1298-5*) M S G Haskell Hse.
***Newton, Alice S.** The Sun Says When. 80p. 1994. 12.95 (*0-8233-0493-0*) Golden Quill.
Newton, Arthur P. Travel & Travellers of the Middle Ages. 1972. 59.95 (*0-8490-1228-7*) Gordon Pr.
Newton, Arthur P., ed. Great Age of Discovery. LC 79-99713. (Essay Index Reprint Ser.). 1977. 30.95 (*0-8369-1366-3*) Ayer.
— Sea Commonwealth, & Other Papers. Imperial Studies. LC 68-22114. (Essay Index Reprint Ser.). 1977. 12.95 (*0-8369-0742-6*) Ayer.
— Travel & Travellers of the Middle Ages. LC 67-23252. (History of Civilization Ser.). 1977. 17.95 (*0-8369-0743-4*) Ayer.
Newton, B. A., jt. ed. see Crompton, D. W.
Newton, Barry. A. C. Roessler Photo Cachet Catalogue. Mellone, Michael, ed. (Illus.). 1977. pap. 15.00 (*0-89794-002-4*) FDC Pub.
Newton, Bernard. Economics of Francis Amasa Walker, 1840-1897: American Economics in Transition. LC 66-22633. x, 208p. 1968. 29.50 (*0-678-00357-2*) Kelley.
Newton, Bradley R. Improvisation: Serious Fun for the Classroom. (Illus.). 80p. 1994. pap. 12.00 (*0-910707-21-9*) Ohio Psych Pr.
Newton, C. R. General Principles of Law. (C). 1983. 130.00 (*0-685-32810-4*, Pub. by Witherby & Co UK) St Mut.
Newton, C. R. & Graham, A. PCR. (Introduction to Biotechniques Ser.). 176p. (Orig.). 1994. pap. 47.50 (*1-872748-82-1*, Pub. by Bios Scientific UK) Coronet Bks.
Newton, Candelas. Lorca, Una Escritura en Trance: Libro de Poemas y Divan del Tamarit. LC 92-12286. (Purdue University Monographs in Romance Languages: Vol. 40). viii, 249p. (SPA.). 1992. 80.00 (*1-55619-308-4*); pap. 27.95 (*1-55619-309-2*) Benjamins North Am.
— Understanding Federico Garcia Lorca. (Understanding Modern European & Latin American Literature Ser.). 1995. write for info. (*1-57003-020-0*) U of SC Pr.

N

***Newton, Caroline G.** Newton. Rev. Roger Newton, Deceased 1683, & One Line of His Descendants, & Abner Newton, 1764-1852, His Ancestors & Descendants. (Illus.). 280p. 1995. reprint ed. lib. bdg. 54.00 (0-8328-4559-0); reprint ed. pap. 44.00 (0-8328-4560-4) Higginson Bk Co.

Newton, Cathryn & Laporte, Leo F. Ancient Environments. 3rd ed. 208p. (C). 1989. pap. text ed. write for info. (0-13-036476-2) P-H.

***Newton, Charles, et al.** Voyages & Visions: Nineteenth-Century European Images of the Middle East from the Victoria & Albert Museum. (Illus.). 128p. (C). 1995. 40.00 (0-295-97490-7) U of Wash Pr.

Newton, Charles H. Place Names in Arizona. rev. ed. Fessler, Diane M., ed. 64p. 1991. pap. 3.95 (0-935810-51-X) Primer Pubs.

Newton, Charly T. A History of Discoveries at Halicarnassus, Cnidus & Branchidae, 2 vols. in 3, Set. (Illus.). 1302p. Date not set. write for info. (0-318-70985-6, Pub. by Georg Olms GW) Lubrecht & Cramer.

— Travels & Discoveries in the Levant, 2 vols. in 1. (Illus.). xxvi, 635p. 1990. reprint ed. 102.70 (3-487-09149-6, Pub. by Georg Olms GW) Lubrecht & Cramer.

Newton, Chester & Holopainen, Eoro O., eds. Extratropical Cyclones: The Erik H. Palmen Memorial. (Illus.). 164p. 1990. 65.00 (1-878220-02-0) Am Meteorological.

Newton, Chester W., ed. Meteorology in the Southern Hemisphere. (Meteorological Monograph Ser.: Vol. 13, No. 35). (Illus.). 263p. 1972. 30.00 (0-933876-38-6) Am Meteorological.

Newton, Clyde. Dynamic Sumo. Pockell et al, eds. (Illus.). 112p. 1994. 30.00 (4-7700-1802-9) Kodansha.

Newton, Colin & Tarrant, Tony. Managing Change in Schools. (Educational Management Ser.). 208p. 1992. 69.95 (0-685-59499-8, A7522) Routledge.

Newton College of the Sacred Heart Staff. Physical Science Two. (C). 1972. text ed. 21.32 (0-13-671354-8); pap. text ed. 11.00 (0-13-671339-4); 46.00 (0-13-671156-1) P-H.

Newton, Connie. Quiche Quiche Quiche. 36p. (Orig.). 1983. pap. 2.75 (0-940844-15-X) Wellspring.

— Quick & Easy. 36p. (Orig.). 1989. pap. 2.75 (0-940844-32-X) Wellspring.

Newton, Crystal H., ed. Manual on the Building of Materials Databases. LC 93-36460. (ASTM Manual Ser.: No. MNL 19). (Illus.). 105p. 1993. text ed. 45.00 (0-8031-2052-4, 28-019093-63) ASTM.

Newton, D., ed. see RFPR Staff.

Newton, D. B. Ambush Reckoning - Hellbent for a Hangrope - Lurking Gun. 416p. 1993. pap. 5.99 (0-8439-3536-7) Dorchester Pub Co.

— Colt Wages. large type ed. LC 94-19825. 1994. 18.95 (0-7927-2132-2, Curley Lrg Print); pap. 17.95 (0-7927-2131-4, Curley Lrg Print) Chivers N Amer.

— Outcast of Ute Bend. large type ed. LC 94-14541. 1994. 18.95 (0-7927-2097-0, Curley Lrg Print); pap. 17.95 (0-7927-2096-2, Curley Lrg Print) Chivers N Amer.

— The Paxman Feud. large type ed. LC 93-49367. 1994. 18.95 (0-7927-1985-9, Curley Lrg Print); pap. 17.95 (0-7927-1984-0, Curley Lrg Print) Chivers N Amer.

— Sheriff of Sentinel. large type ed. LC 93-38348. 1994. 18.95 (0-7927-1905-0, Curley Lrg Print); pap. 16.95 (0-7927-1904-2, Curley Lrg Print) Chivers N Amer.

Newton, Dale, jt. auth. see Gaspord, John.

Newton, David. Global Warming. (Contemporary World Issues Ser.). 183p. 1993. lib. bdg. 39.50 (0-87436-711-5) ABC-CLIO.

— James Watson & Francis Crick. (Makers of Modern Science Ser.). (Illus.). 128p. (YA). (gr. 7-12). 1992. lib. bdg. 16.95 (0-8160-2558-4) Facts on File.

— 1920-1929. (Yearbooks in Science Ser.). (Illus.). 80p. (J). (gr. 5-8). 1995. lib. bdg. 16.98 (0-8050-3432-3) TFC Bks NY.

Newton, David E. AIDS Issues: A Handbook. LC 92-10071. (Issues in Focus Ser.). 144p. (J). (gr. 6 up). 1992. lib. bdg. 18.95 (0-89490-338-1) Enslow Pubs.

— Chemical Elements. LC 93-30044. (Venture Bks.). (Illus.). 128p. (YA). (gr. 9-12). 1994. lib. bdg. 14.28 (0-531-12501-7) Watts.

— Consumer Chemistry Projects for Young Scientists. LC 90-48499. (Illus.). 128p. (YA). (gr. 9-12). 1991. lib. bdg. 14.77 (0-531-11011-7) Watts.

— Earthquakes. (First Bks.). (Illus.). 64p. (J). (gr. 5-8). 1993. pap. 5.95 (0-531-15664-8) Watts.

— Earthquakes. LC 92-23291. (First Bks.). (J). 1993. lib. bdg. 13.93 (0-531-20054-X) Watts.

— Encyclopedia of Cryptology. 1996. lib. bdg. 60.00 (0-87436-772-7) ABC-CLIO.

— Gay Rights: Contemporary World Issues Ser. 225p. 1994. lib. bdg. 39.50 (0-87436-745-X) ABC-CLIO.

— Gun Control: An Issue for the Nineties. LC 91-23352. (Issues in Focus Ser.). (Illus.). 128p. (J). (gr. 6 up). 1992. lib. bdg. 17.95 (0-89490-296-2) Enslow Pubs.

— Hunting. (Impact Bks.). (Illus.). 144p. (YA). (gr. 9-12). 1992. lib. bdg. 14.42 (0-531-13022-3) Watts.

— Land Use A-Z. LC 89-78119. (Environment Reference Ser.). 128p. (J). (gr. 6 up). 1991. lib. bdg. 17.95 (0-89490-260-1) Enslow Pubs.

— Linus Pauling: Scientist & Advocate. LC 93-31719. (Makers of Modern Science Ser.). (Illus.). 128p. (J). 1994. 16.95 (0-8160-2959-8) Facts on File.

— Making & Using Scientific Equipment. LC 92-38039. (Experimental Science Book Ser.). (Illus.). 128p. (YA). (gr. 9-12). 1993. lib. bdg. 14.49 (0-531-11176-8); pap. 6.95 (0-531-15663-X) Watts.

— Particle Accelerations: From the Cyclotron to the Superconducting Super Collider. LC 88-31375. (Venture Bks.). (Illus.). 128p. (YA). (gr. 10-12). 1990. lib. bdg. 14.28 (0-531-10671-3) Watts.

— Science - Technology - Society Projects for Young Scientists. LC 91-17825. (Projects for Young Scientists Ser.). (Illus.). 144p. (YA). (gr. 9-12). 1991. lib. bdg. 14.77 (0-531-11047-8) Watts.

— Teen Violence: Out of Control. (Issues in Focus Ser.). (Illus.). 128p. (J). 1995. lib. bdg. 17.95 (0-89490-999-1) Enslow Pubs.

— Teen Violence: Out of Control. LC 95-6943. (Issues in Focus Ser.). (YA). (gr. 6 up). 1995. lib. bdg. 17.95 (0-89490-506-6) Enslow Pubs.

Newton, David E., jt. auth. see Siegel, Dorothy S.

Newton, Deborah. Designing Knitwear. Timmons, Christine, ed. 272p. 1992. 39.95 (0-942391-06-3) Taunton.

Newton, Dennis. Severe Weather Flying. 2nd ed. ASA Staff, ed. LC 91-71566. (Illus.). 190p. 1991. pap. 16.95 (1-56027-072-1, ASA-SWF) Av Suppl & Acad.

Newton, Derek, jt. auth. see Smith, David.

Newton, Derek A. Feed Your Eagles: Inspiring & Coaching Your Sales Team to the Top. rev. ed. 1993. 22.95 (1-55738-531-9) Probus Pub Co.

— Feed Your Eagles! Building & Managing a Top-Flight Sales Force. 1991. boxed 21.95 (0-13-310467-2) P-H.

Newton, Donna J. Scottie Showcase: A Pictorial Introduction to Scottie Dog Collectibles. (Illus.). 144p. 1988. pap. 15.00 (0-9620064-0-8) Country Scottie.

Newton, Douglas. Crocodile & Cassowary. 1994. pap. 9.95 (0-8109-6455-4) Abrams.

— Crocodile & Cassowary. (Illus.). 112p. 1971. pap. 9.95 (0-912294-42-6) Metro Mus Art.

— Primitive Sculpture from the Barbier Mueller Collection. LC 95-12486. (Illus.). 1995. write for info. (0-86565-962-1) Vendome.

— Teaching with Texts: Preparaing & Choosing Textual Materials. 130p. (Orig.). 1990. pap. text ed. 32.95 (0-8464-1451-1) Beekman Pubs.

Newton, Douglas & Barbier, Jean P., eds. Islands & Ancestors: Indigenous Styles of Southeast Asia. (Illus.). 364p. 1988. 80.00 (3-7913-0899-8, Pub. by Prestel) TeNeues.

Newton, Douglas, ed. see Bessieres, Albert.

Newton, Dwight B. Lone Gun. 1994. lib. bdg. 15.95 (0-7451-4612-0, Gunsmoke) Chivers N Amer.

***Newton, Earle & Knight, Doug, eds.** Understanding Change in Education: Rural & Remote Regions of Canada. 310p. (Orig.). (C). 1993. pap. text ed. 22.95x (1-55059-059-6) Temeron Bks.

***Newton, Earle & Newton, Patti.** Voices, Vision & Vitality: Redesigning Small Schools. 143p. (Orig.). (C). 1992. pap. text ed. 18.95x (1-55059-047-2) Temeron Bks.

Newton, Earle W., comp. Index to the Proceedings of the Vermont Historical Society, New Series, Volumes 1-10: Nineteen Thirty to Nineteen Forty-Two. 84p. 1946. ring bd. 3.75 (0-934720-09-6) VT Hist Soc.

Newton, Edward R., jt. auth. see Newton, Michael.

Newton, Eric. Tintoretto. LC 70-110275. (Illus.). 250p. 1972. reprint ed. text ed. 35.00 (0-8371-4501-5, NETI, Greenwood Pr) Greenwood.

Newton, Esther. Cherry Grove, Fire Island: Sixty Years in America's First Gay & Lesbian Town. LC 92-43092. (Illus.). 384p. 1993. 24.00 (0-8070-7926-X) Beacon Pr.

— Cherry Grove, Fire Island: Sixty Years in America's First Gay & Lesbian Town. 416p. 1995. pap. 14.00 (0-8070-7927-8) Beacon Pr.

— Mother Camp: Female Impersonators in America. LC 76-37634. 1979. pap. 9.95 (0-226-57760-0, P807) U Ch Pr.

Newton, Francis J. The Jazz Scene. LC 75-4748. (Roots of Jazz Ser.). 303p. 1975. reprint ed. lib. bdg. 35.00 (0-306-70685-7) Da Capo.

Newton, Frank, et al. Hispanic Mental Health Research: A Reference Guide. 696p. 1982. pap. 25.00 (0-520-04791-5) U CA Pr.

Newton, Fred P. Ole Man River & Me. write for info. (0-318-54680-9) Newton.

Newton, G. W., jt. auth. see Chandratillake, M. R.

Newton General Hospital Auxiliary Staff. The Best of the South. 254p. 1993. 14.95 (0-9638446-0-1) Newton Genrl Hosp.

Newton, Grant W. Bankruptcy & Insolvency Accounting, Vol. 1: Practice & Procedure. 5th ed. LC 93-36890. 1994. text ed. 130.00 (0-471-59834-8) Wiley.

— Bankruptcy & Insolvency Accounting, Vol. 2. 5th ed. LC 93-36890. 1994. Set. text ed. 240.00 (0-471-59833-X) Wiley.

— Bankruptcy & Insolvency Accounting: Practice & Procedure. 4th ed. 1989. text ed. 200.00 (0-471-51503-5); text ed. 105.00 (0-471-50525-0); 95.00 (0-471-50863-2) Wiley.

— Bankruptcy & Insolvency Accounting: Practice & Procedure. 4th suppl. ed. 400p. 1993. 65.00 (0-685-58445-3) Wiley.

— Economics & Business Finance. (Certificate in Management Accounting Review Ser.). (Illus.). 227p. 1984. 18.95 (0-918937-00-0); audio 100.00 (0-918937-07-8) Malibu Pub.

— Internal Reporting & Analysis. 2nd ed. (Certificate in Management Accounting Review Ser.). 304p. 1984. 19.95 (0-918937-03-5); audio 110.00 (0-918937-10-8) Malibu Pub.

— Public Reporting Standards & Auditing. 2nd ed. (Certificate in Management Accounting Review Ser.). 287p. 1983. 19.95 (0-918937-02-7); audio 120.00 (0-918937-09-4) Malibu Pub.

— Taxes, Current Pronouncements, & Updated CMA Questions: 1987-1988. (Illus.). 238p. 1987. 19.95 (0-918937-15-9) Malibu Pub.

Newton, Grant W. & Bailey, Andrew D. Decision Analysis, Including Modeling & Information Systems. (Certificate in Management Accounting Review Ser.). (Illus.). 300p. 1984. 19.95 (0-918937-04-3); audio 110.00 (0-918937-11-6) Malibu Pub.

Newton, Grant W. & Bloom, Gilbert D. Bankruptcy & Insolvency Taxation. 576p. 1991. text ed. 110.00 (0-471-50780-6) Wiley.

— Bankruptcy & Insolvency Taxation. 2nd ed. 720p. 1993. text ed. 135.00 (0-471-59837-2) Wiley.

Newton, H. Joseph. Timeslab: A Time Series Analysis Laboratory. LC 87-38202. 625p. (C). 1988. text ed. 68.95 (0-534-09198-9) Intl Thomson.

Newton, H. William, III. International Income Tax & Estate Planning. 2nd ed. LC 93-23251. (Tax & Estate Planning Ser.). 1993. write for info. (0-07-172502-4) Shepards-McGraw.

Newton, Harry. Newton's Telecom Dictionary. 1993. pap. 24.95 (0-936648-42-2) Telecom Lib.

Newton, Harry, jt. auth. see Teleconnect Magazine Research Group Staff.

Newton, Henry. In Far New Guinea. LC 75-35145. (Illus.). reprint ed. 27.00 (0-404-14161-7) AMS Pr.

Newton, Huey P. The Genius of Huey P. Newton. 34p. (Orig.). 1993. pap. 6.95 (1-56411-067-2) Untd Bros & Sis.

— Revolutionary Suicide. 1995. pap. 13.95 (0-86316-326-2) Writers & Readers.

— To Die for the People. Morrison, Toni, ed. 1995. pap. 12.95 (0-86316-327-0) Writers & Readers.

Newton, Huey P., jt. auth. see Erikson, Erik H.

***Newton-Hurt, Diana.** Elephantastic. (J). 1995. pap. 2.95 (1-85697-569-X, Kingfisher LKC) LKC.

Newton, Ian. Population Ecology of Raptors. LC 79-50279. (Illus.). 1979. 35.00 (0-931130-03-4) Harrell Bks.

— The Sparrowhawk. (Illus.). 420p. 1991. text ed. 39.95 (0-85661-041-0, 784641, Pub. by Poyser UK) Acad Pr.

Newton, Ian, ed. Lifetime Reproduction in Birds. 479p. 1990. text ed. 109.00 (0-12-517370-9) Acad Pr.

— Lifetime Reproduction in Birds. (Illus.). 496p. 1992. pap. text ed. 39.95 (0-12-517371-7) Acad Pr.

Newton, Ian & Olsen, Penny, eds. Birds of Prey. (Illus.). 240p. 1990. 40.00 (0-8160-2182-1) Facts on File.

Newton, Isaac. Correspondence, 4 vols. Turnbull, H. W. & Scott, J. F., eds. 1967. 74.50 (0-685-42030-2) Cambridge U Pr.

— Correspondence, 4 vols., 4. Turnbull, H. W. & Scott, J. F., eds. 1967. 79.95 (0-521-05815-5) Cambridge U Pr.

— The Correspondence of Isaac Newton, Vol. 3, 1688-1694. Turnbull, H. W., ed. LC 59-65134. 465p. reprint ed. pap. 132.60 (0-317-26385-4, 2024527) Bks Demand.

— Correspondence, 1709-1713, Vol. 5. Hall, A. R. & Tilling, Laura, eds. 1975. 120.00 (0-521-08721-X) Cambridge U Pr.

— Correspondence, 1713-1718, 6. Hall, A. R. & Tilling, Laura, eds. (Illus.). 500p. 1976. 120.00 (0-521-08722-8) Cambridge U Pr.

— Correspondence, 1713-1718, 7. Hall, A. R. & Tilling, Laura, eds. (Illus.). 500p. 1976. 120.00 (0-318-51278-5) Cambridge U Pr.

— Isaac Newton's Papers & Letters on Natural Philosophy & Related Documents. 2nd ed. Cohen, I. Bernard et al, eds. LC 77-72764. 558p. reprint ed. pap. 159.10 (0-7837-2236-2, 2057326) Bks Demand.

— Isaac Newton's Philosophiae Naturalis Principia Mathematica, 2 Vols, Set. Koyre, Alexander et al, eds. LC 75-78515. (Illus.). 964p. 1990. 120.00 (0-674-66475-2) HUP.

— Mathematical Papers, Vol. 4. Whiteside, D. T. & Hoskin, M. A., eds. 1971. 225.00 (0-521-07740-0) Cambridge U Pr.

— Mathematical Papers, Vol. 5: 1683-1684. Whiteside, D. T. et al, eds. LC 65-11203. (Illus.). 600p. 1972. 225.00 (0-521-08262-5) Cambridge U Pr.

— Mathematical Papers, Vol. 6: 1684-1691. Whiteside, D. T. & Hoskin, M. A., eds. LC 73-86046. (Illus.). 6000p. 1975. 225.00 (0-521-08719-8) Cambridge U Pr.

— Mathematical Papers, Vol. 7: 1691-1695. Whiteside, D. T. & Hoskin, M. A., eds. LC 65-11203. 1977. 250.00 (0-521-08720-1) Cambridge U Pr.

— Mathematical Papers, Vol. 8: 1697-1722. Whiteside, D. T., ed. LC 65-11203. (Illus.). 750p. 1981. 275.00 (0-521-20103-9) Cambridge U Pr.

— Mathematical Principles of Natural Philosophy & His System of the World (Principia) Motte, Andrew, tr. Incl. Vol. I. Motions of Bodies. 1901. pap. 15.00 (0-520-00928-2); Vol. II. System of the World. 1962. 65.00 (0-520-00927-4); Vol. II. System of the World. 1962. pap. 16.00 (0-520-00929-0); 1962. write for info. (0-318-56010-0) U CA Pr.

— Newton's Philosophy of Nature: Selected Writings. 1970. pap. 14.95 (0-02-849700-7) Free Pr.

— Newton's Philosophy of Nature: Selections of His Writings. Thayer, Horace S., ed. (Hafner Library of Classics). 208p. 1974. pap. 12.95 (0-685-43029-4) Free Pr.

— Observations upon the Prophecies of Daniel, & the Apocalypse of St. John. LC 91-74116. 323p. 1991. reprint ed. 19.95 (0-942487-02-8) Oregon Inst Sci Med.

— The Optical Papers of Isaac Newton: Vol. 1: The Optical Lectures, 1670-1672. Shapiro, Alan E., ed. LC 82-14751. (Illus.). 704p. 1984. 190.00 (0-521-25248-2) Cambridge U Pr.

— Opticks. 1952. pap. text ed. 9.95 (0-486-60205-2) Dover.

— The Preliminary Manuscripts for Isaac Newton's 1687 Principia: 1684-1686. (Cambridge University Library Newton Manuscripts Ser.). (Illus.). 300p. 1989. 130.00 (0-521-33499-3) Cambridge U Pr.

— The Principia, 2 vols. in 1, Set. Motte, Andrew, tr. LC 95-6733. (Great Minds Ser.). 472p. 1995. pap. 14.95 (0-87975-980-1) Prometheus Bks.

Newton, J. Extractive Metallurgy. LC 59-14124. 540p. reprint ed. pap. 153.90 (0-8357-9889-5, 2055265) Bks Demand.

Newton, J. Frank & Graham, Charles G. From Plan to Profit: A Management Handbook for Home Builders. LC 90-43916. 110p. (Orig.). 1990. pap. 20.00 (0-86718-327-6) Home Builder.

Newton, J. H., et al. History of the Pan-Handle: Being Historical Collections of the Counties of Ohio, Brooke, Marshall & Hancock, West Virginia. (Illus.). 540p. 1991. reprint ed. pap. 50.00 (1-55613-413-4) Heritage Bk.

Newton, J. M., jt. auth. see Hickey, A. E.

Newton, J. R. & Op Ten Berg, M., eds. Optimizing the Estrogen Dose in Oral Contraceptives. (Illus.). 79p. (C). 1992. text ed. 35.00 (1-85070-445-7) Prthnon Pub.

Newton, Jack & Teece, Philip. The Guide to Amateur Astronomy. (Illus.). 288p. 1989. 29.95 (0-521-34028-4) Cambridge U Pr.

— The Guide to Amateur Astronomy. 2nd ed. LC 93-40354. (Illus.). 368p. (C). 1995. 34.95 (0-521-44492-6) Cambridge U Pr.

Newton, James. The Deserted Village: Diary of Rev. James Newton of Nuneham Courtenay, 1736-86. Hannah, Gavin, ed. (Illus.). 192p. (C). 1992. text ed. 30.00 (0-7509-0205-1) A Sutton Pub.

— Uncommon Friends. 1989. pap. 10.95 (0-15-692620-2) HarBrace.

Newton, Jane. Good Morning Dogs! (Illus.). 20p. (Orig.). (J). (ps). 1991. pap. text ed. 4.95 (0-931571-08-1) Lifetime Pr.

***Newton, Janice.** The Feminist Challenge to the Canadian Left, 1900-1918. (Illus.). 272p. 1995. 44.95 (0-7735-1262-4); pap. 17.95 (0-7735-1291-8) U of Toronto Pr.

Newton, Janice, ed. Course Outlines on Women & Politics. 293p. (C). 1993. pap. 25.00 (0-88920-236-2, Pub. by Wilfrid Laurier CN) Humanities.

Newton, Jennifer. Preventing Mental Illness. 272p. 1988. text ed. 65.00 (0-7102-0930-4, RKP) Routledge.

— Preventing Mental Illness. 272p. 1992. pap. 22.00 (0-415-03902-9, B0249) Routledge.

— Preventing Mental Illness in Practice. 272p. 1992. 79.95 (0-415-04893-1, A6688) Routledge.

— Preventing Mental Illness in Practice. 240p. 1995. pap. 17.95 (0-415-11993-6, C0607) Routledge.

Newton, Jerry. Complete Book of Forms for the School Health Professional: Ready-to-Use Forms for the School Health Professional. 480p. 1987. text ed. 34.95 (0-13-156498-6) P-H.

— The New School Health Handbook: A Ready Reference for School Nurses & Educators. 352p. 1989. text ed. 29.95 (0-13-615923-0) P-H.

— School Health Handbook: A Ready Reference for School Nurses & Educators. LC 84-8382. 300p. 1984. 27.95 (0-13-793639-7, Busn) P-H.

Newton, Jill. Cat-Fish. LC 91-42858. (Illus.). 32p. (J). (ps up). 1992. 14.00 (0-688-11423-7); lib. bdg. 13.93 (0-688-11424-5) Lothrop.

— Don't Sit There! LC 93-23538. (Illus.). (J). 1994. write for info. (0-688-13309-6) Lothrop.

— Polar Bear Scare. (Illus.). (J). (ps-3). 1992. 15.00 (0-688-11232-3) Lothrop.

— Polar Bear Scare. LC 91-5304. (Illus.). (J). (ps-3). 1992. lib. bdg. 14.93 (0-688-11233-1) Lothrop.

Newton, Joe, jt. auth. see Durkin, John F.

Newton, Joe, jt. auth. see Newton, Willis.

Newton, John. Computers in Translation: A Practical Appraisal. 224p. 1992. write for info. (0-415-05432-X, A6955) Routledge.

— Letters of John Newton. 1976. pap. 5.95 (0-85151-120-1) Banner of Truth.

— Out of the Depths. LC 80-85340. (Illus.). 160p. 1991. pap. 8.99 (0-8254-3317-7) Kregel.

— Works of John Newton, 6 vols, Set. 1985. reprint ed. 159.95 (0-85151-460-X) Banner of Truth.

Newton, John & Bohrer, Dick. John Newton. (Golden Oldies Ser.). 128p. (Orig.). 1983. pap. 4.99 (0-8024-0251-8) Moody.

Newton, John H. Latacumba Assignment. 165p. (C). 1989. 45.00 (0-7223-2300-X, Pub. by A H S Ltd UK) St Mut.

Newton, John K., tr. see Ahmad, Jalal A.

Newton-John, Olivia, frwd. Vanishing Eden: The Plight of the Tropical Rain Forest. (Illus.). 304p. 1991. 49.95 (0-8120-6246-9) Barron.

Newton-John, Olivia & Hurst, Brian S. A Pig Tale. LC 92-44116. (Illus.). (J). 1993. pap. 12.00 (0-671-78778-0, S&S Bks Young Read) S&S Childrens.

Newton, John R., jt. ed. see Clayton, Stanley G.

Newton, Joseph, et al. California Real Estate. 576p. 1988. text ed. 53.00 (0-13-112442-0) P-H.

Newton, Joseph F. The Builders: A Story & Study of Freemasonry. 9th ed. (Illus.). 345p. 1985. reprint ed. 16.95 (0-88053-045-6, M 301) Macoy Pub.

— Builders: A Story & Study of Freemasonry. 10th ed. (Illus.). xxx, 315p. 1989. reprint ed. 16.95 (0-318-42073-2, M301) Macoy Pub.

— The Great Light in Masonry. 92p. 1992. reprint ed. pap. 12.95 (1-56459-046-1) Kessinger Pub.

— The Men's House: Masonic Papers & Addresses. xx, 241p. 1990. text ed. 12.95 (0-88053-037-5, M-86) Macoy Pub.

— Modern Masonry: A Brief Sketch of the Craft Since 1717. 92p. 1992. reprint ed. pap. 12.95 (1-56459-043-7) Kessinger Pub.

— Short Talks on Masonry. x, 243p. 1988. reprint ed. pap. 8.95 (0-88053-036-7, M-85) Macoy Pub.

— Some Living Masters of the Pulpit: Studies in Religious Personality. LC 71-152203. (Essay Index Reprint Ser.). 1977. reprint ed. 20.95 (0-8369-2287-5) Ayer.

— The Three Degrees & Great Symbols of Masonry. 112p. 1992. reprint ed. pap. 12.95 (1-56459-045-3) Kessinger Pub.

An Asterisk (*) at the beginning of an entry indicates that the title is appearing in BIP for the first time.

Newton, Joy. La Chauve-Souris et le Papillon Correspondance Montesquiou-Whistler. 264p. 1993. 60.00 (*0-85261-277-X*, Pub. by Univ of Glasgow UK) St Mut.

Newton, Judith. Starting Over: Feminism & the Politics of Cultural Critique. LC 94-10225. (Critical Perspectives on Women & Gender Ser.). 1994. text ed. 39.50 (*0-472-09482-3*); pap. text ed. 14.95 (*0-472-06482-7*) U of Mich Pr.

Newton, Judith J. & Spielman, Frankie E., eds. Data Administration: Management & Practice. (Proceedings of the Annual DAMA Symposium Ser.: No. 1). (Illus.). 130p. (Orig.). (C). 1992. pap. text ed. 29.95 (*1-56806-068-8*) Diane Pub.

— Data Administration: Standards & Techniques. (Proceedings of the Annual DAMA Symposium Ser.: No. 2). (Illus.). 164p. (Orig.). (C). 1992. pap. text ed. 29.95 (*1-56806-069-6*) Diane Pub.

Newton, Judith J., et al, eds. Managing Data: From Vision to Reality. (Proceedings of the Annual DAMA Symposium Ser.: No. 4). (Illus.). 158p. (Orig.). (C). 1992. pap. text ed. 29.95 (*1-56806-070-X*) Diane Pub.

Newton, Judith L. Women, Power & Subversion: Social Strategies in British Fiction, 1778-1860. 224p. 1985. pap. text ed. 12.95 (*0-416-41200-9*, 9761) Routledge Chapman & Hall.

Newton, Judith L. & Rosenfelt, D., eds. Feminist Literary Criticism & Social Change. 250p. (Orig.). 1986. 35.00 (*0-416-38700-4*, 9678); pap. 13.95 (*0-416-38710-1*, 9679) Routledge Chapman & Hall.

Newton, Judith M. & Tabuchi, Mayumi. Haiku, Origami & More: Worship & Study Resources from Japan. (Orig.). 1991. pap. 5.95 (*0-377-00217-8*) Friendship Pr.

Newton, Judith V. & Weiss, Carol. A Grand Tradition: The Hoosier Salon Art & Artists, 1925-1990. (Illus.). 500p. 1993. 75.00 (*0-9638360-0-5*) Hoosier Salon.

Newton, Judy A., jt. auth. see Newton, Michael.

Newton, Judy Ann, jt. ed. see Newton, Micheal.

Newton, K. & Steeds, W. Motor Vehicle. 11th ed. 1989. text ed. 74.95 (*0-7506-0407-7*) Buttrwrth-Heinemann.

Newton, K., et al. Motor Vehicle. 9th ed. 1972. 26.50 (*0-592-00070-2*) Transatl Arts.

Newton, K. C., jt. auth. see Edwards, A. C.

Newton, K. M., ed. George Eliot. 356p. (Orig.). (C). 1991. pap. text ed. 23.95 (*0-582-04064-7*, 78834) Longman.

Newton, Ken M. In Defense of Literary Interpretation: Theory & Practice. LC 86-3937. 192p. 1986. text ed. 29.95 (*0-312-41080-8*) St Martin.

— Interpreting the Text: A Critical Introduction to the Theory & Practice of Literary Interpretation. LC 90-8190. 224p. 1990. text ed. 45.00 (*0-312-04757-6*); pap. 16.95 (*0-312-04758-4*) St Martin.

Newton, Ken M., ed. Theory into Practice: A Reader in Modern Literary Criticism. LC 92-4348. 256p. 1992. text ed. 45.00 (*0-312-07996-6*) St Martin.

— Theory into Practice: A Reader in Modern Literary Criticism. LC 92-4348. 256p. 1992. pap. text ed. 16.95 (*0-312-07997-4*) St Martin.

— Twentieth-Century Literary Theory: A Reader. 277p. 1988. pap. 15.95 (*0-312-02025-2*) St Martin.

Newton, Kenneth, jt. ed. see Kaase, Max.

Newton, L. E. & Hausler, R. H., eds. CO2 Corrosion in Oil & Gas Production: Selected Papers, Abstracts, & References. 6th ed. LC 82-60734. 687p. 1984. 75.00 (*0-915567-06-7*) NACE Intl.

Newton, L. E., Jr. & Hausler, R. H., eds. CO2 Corrosion in Oil & Gas Production: Selected Papers, Abstracts, & References. LC 82-60734. 687p. 1984. 137.00 (*0-915567-01-6*) NACE Intl.

Newton, Lady. Legh Family of England: The House of Lyme, from Its Foundation to the End of the 18th Century. 423p. 1994. reprint ed. lib. bdg. 74.00 (*0-8328-4141-2*); reprint ed. pap. 64.00 (*0-8328-4142-0*) Higginson Bk Co.

Newton, Laura. Me & My Aunts. Fay, Ann, ed. LC 86-15950. (Albert Whitman Concept Bks.). (Illus.). 32p. (J). (gr. 2-5). 1986. lib. bdg. 13.95 (*0-8075-5029-9*) A Whitman.

Newton, Laura P. William the Vehicle King. LC 86-33412. (Illus.). 32p. (J). (ps-2). 1987. text ed. 13.95 (*0-02-768230-7*, Bradbury S&S) S&S Childrens.

Newton, Leon. Psycho-Politics in Government, Vol. 2: Theatre Version. rev. ed. 52p. 1993. pap. 15.95 (*0-915885-03-4*) Playwright MI.

Newton, Leon T. Psycho-Politics in Government, Vol. 1: A Dramatic Dialogue. LC 93-85663. 52p. (Orig.). 1993. pap. 9.95 (*0-915885-02-6*) Playwright MI.

Newton, Lewis. Social & Political History of Texas. 1993. reprint ed. lib. bdg. 75.00 (*0-7812-5946-0*) Rprt Serv.

Newton, Lewis W. The Americanization of French Louisiana: A Study of the Process of Adjustment Between French & Anglo-American Population of Louisiana. Cordasco, Francesco, ed. LC 80-884. (American Ethnic Groups Ser.). 1981. lib. bdg. 30.95 (*0-405-13445-2*) Ayer.

Newton, Lionel. Getting Right with God. LC 93-26920. 272p. 1994. 19.95 (*0-525-93754-4*, Dutton) NAL-Dutton.

— Getting Right with God. 288p. 1995. pap. 9.95 (*0-452-27147-9*, Plume) NAL-Dutton.

— Things To Be Lost. LC 94-32463. 256p. 1995. 19.95 (*0-525-93755-2*, Dutton) NAL-Dutton.

Newton, Lisa. Ethics in America Source Reader. 208p. 1988. pap. text ed. 26.67 (*0-13-290180-3*) P-H.

— Ethics in America Study Guide. 416p. 1988. pap. text ed. 26.67 (*0-13-290206-0*) P-H.

Newton, Lisa H. & Dillingham, Catherine K. Watersheds: Classic Cases in Environmental Ethics. 249p. 1994. pap. 17.95 (*0-534-21180-1*) Intl Thomson.

Newton, Lisa H. & Ford, Maureen M., eds. Taking Sides: Clashing Views on Controversial Issues in Business Ethics & Society. 3rd rev. ed. LC 93-50063. (Illus.). 384p. 1994. pap. text ed. 13.95 (*1-56134-247-5*) Dushkin Pub.

Newton, Lucilda A. Big Peanuts. (J). (ps-3). 1976. pap. 2.50 (*0-915374-17-X*, 17-X) Rapids Christian.

— Big Peanuts in Trouble. (J). (ps-3). 1976. pap. 2.50 (*0-915374-18-8*, 18-8) Rapids Christian.

Newton, Lynn D., ed. Primary Science: The Challenge of the Nineteen Nineties. LC 92-31457. 144p. 1992. 29.95 (*1-85359-176-9*, Pub. by Multilingual Matters UK) Taylor & Francis.

Newton, M. B., Jr., jt. ed. see Walker, H. J.

Newton, M. D. The Origins of Beowulf & the Pre-Viking Kingdom of East Anglia. 192p. (C). 1992. text ed. 63.00 (*0-85991-361-9*) Boydell & Brewer.

Newton, Marceline A. New Life Cookbook: Based on the Health & Nutritional Philosophy of the Edgar Cayce Readings. LC 76-15963. 1976. pap. 7.95 (*0-915442-13-2*) Donning Co.

Newton, Marjorie. Southern Cross Saints: The Mormons in Australia. LC 91-8229. (Mormons in the Pacific Ser.). (Illus.). 312p. (Orig.). 1991. pap. 12.95 (*0-939154-49-8*) Inst Polynesian.

Newton, Mark G., ed. Rivers to Skyscrapers: Ethics in Modern American Literature. LC 91-60154. 146p. 1991. pap. 12.95 (*0-945759-02-9*) St Leo Col Pr.

Newton, Melanie, jt. ed. see Tolz, Vera.

Newton, Merlin O. Armed with the Constitution: Jehovah's Witnesses in Alabama & the U. S. Supreme Court, 1939-1946. LC 94-3993. 1995. 29.95 (*0-8173-0736-2*) U of Ala Pr.

Newton, Michael. Armed & Dangerous: A Writer's Guide to Weapons. (Howdunit Ser.). 186p. 1990. pap. 15.99 (*0-89879-370-X*) Writers Digest.

— Bad Girls Do It! An Encyclopedia. LC 93-79481. 205p. (Orig.). (C). 1993. pap. 14.95 (*1-55950-104-9*, 34070) Loompanics.

— Bitter Grain: Huey Newton & the Black Panther Party. (Orig.). 1991. pap. 3.95 (*0-87067-751-9*) Holloway.

— Handbook of Weed & Insect Control Chemicals for Forest Resource Managers. LC 81-1629. 160p. 1981. pap. 17.95 (*0-917304-25-X*) Timber.

— Hunting Humans, Vol. I. 416p. 1992. mass mkt. 5.99 (*0-380-76396-6*) Avon.

— Hunting Humans, Vol. 2. 360p. 1993. mass mkt. 5.99 (*0-380-76509-8*) Avon.

— Hunting Humans: An Encyclopedia of Modern Serial Killers. LC 89-63826. 353p. 1990. text ed. 34.95 (*1-55950-026-3*) Loompanics.

— Journey of Souls: Case Studies of Life Between Lives. LC 94-15730. 288p. 1994. pap. 12.95 (*1-56718-485-5*) Llewellyn Pubns.

— The King Conspiracy. (Orig.). (J). (ps-12). 1987. pap. 3.25 (*0-87067-729-2*) Holloway.

— Raising Hell: An Encyclopedia of Devil Worship & Satanic Crime. 432p. (Orig.). 1993. mass mkt. 5.99 (*0-380-76837-2*) Avon.

— Serial Slaughter: What's Behind America's Murder Epidemic. LC 91-76992. 173p. (Orig.). 1992. pap. 19.95 (*1-55950-078-6*, 34061) Loompanics.

— Silent Rage: The Thirty-Year Odyssey of a Serial Killer. 1994. mass mkt. 4.99 (*0-440-21313-4*) Dell.

Newton, Michael & Newton, Edward R. Complications of Gynecologic & Obstetric Management. (Illus.). 544p. 1988. text ed. 79.50 (*0-7216-6764-4*) Saunders.

Newton, Michael & Newton, Judy A. The Ku Klux Klan: An Encyclopedia. LC 90-140008. 645p. 1990. 80.00 (*0-8240-2038-3*, SS499) Garland.

— Racial & Religious Violence in America: A Chronology. LC 90-22038. (Illus.). 742p. 1991. 90.00 (*0-8240-4848-2*, SS501) Garland.

— Terrorism in the United States & Europe, 1800-1959: An Annotated Bibliography. 522p. 1988. lib. bdg. 80.00 (*0-8240-5747-3*) Garland.

Newton, Michael & Newton, Judy Ann, eds. The FBI Most Wanted: An Encyclopedia. LC 89-11820. 356p. 1989. 50.00 (*0-8240-4779-6*, SS937) Garland.

***Newton, Miller.** Adolescence: Guiding Youth Through the Perilous Ordeal. 224p. (C). 1995. 27.00 (*0-393-70194-8*) Norton.

Newton, Miller, jt. auth. see Polson, Beth.

Newton, Milton B. Atlas of Louisiana: A Guide for Students. LC 79-186216. (Miscellaneous Publication Ser.: No. 72-1). 200p. 1972. pap. 12.00 (*0-938909-25-8*) Geosci Pubns LSU.

Newton, Milton B., Jr., ed. The Journal of John Landreth, Surveyor: An Expedition to the Gulf Coast November 15, 1818-May 19, 1819. LC 84-73203. 204p. 1985. 30.00 (*0-685-58831-9*); pap. 20.00 (*0-938909-33-9*) Geosci Pubns LSU.

Newton, Miranda H. London Architects' Houses. (Illus.). 160p. 1993. 75.00 (*0-7506-1270-3*, Butterwrth Archit) Buttrwrth-Heinemann.

***Newton, Norman.** Islay. (Pevensey Island Guides Ser.). (Illus.). 112p. 1995. pap. 14.95 (*0-907115-90-X*, Pub. by D & C Pub UK) Sterling.

— Shetland. (Pevensey Island Guides Ser.). (Illus.). 112p. 1995. pap. 14.95 (*0-907115-88-8*, Pub. by D & C Pub UK) Sterling.

— Skye. (Pevensey Island Guides Ser.). (Illus.). 112p. 1995. pap. 14.95 (*0-907115-89-6*, Pub. by D & C Pub UK) Sterling.

Newton, Norman T. Design on the Land: The Development of Landscape Architecture. LC 70-134955. (Illus.). 740p. 1971. 50.00 (*0-674-19870-0*) Belknap Pr.

Newton, P. Additional Book-Keeping Exercises. (C). 1989. 40.00 (*0-85950-841-2*, Pub. by S Thornes Pubs UK) St Mut.

***Newton, P. W., et al, eds.** Networking Spatial Information Systems. 1994. text ed. 79.95 (*0-471-94734-2*) Wiley.

Newton, Pam, illus. & ret. The Stonecutter: An Indian Folktale. 32p. (J). (ps-3). 1990. 14.95 (*0-399-22187-5*, Whitebird Bks) Putnam Pub Group.

Newton, Patti, jt. auth. see Newton, Earle.

Newton, Peter, et al, eds. Desktop Planning: Microcomputer Applications for Infrastructure & Services Planning & Management. (Illus.). 416p. 1990. 69.95 (*0-340-51945-2*, A4221, Pub. by E Arnold UK) Routledge Chapman & Hall.

Newton, Peter M. Sigmund Freud's Odyssey: From Youthful Dream to Mid-Life Crisis. 297p. 1994. lib. bdg. 21.95 (*0-89862-293-X*, 2293) Guilford Pr.

Newton, R. E. Wave Physics. (Illus.). 320p. (C). 1988. pap. text ed. 24.95 (*0-7131-2656-6*, Pub. by E Arnold UK) Routledge Chapman & Hall.

Newton, R. G. Inverse Schrodinger Scattering in Three Dimensions. (Texts & Monographs in Physics). 185p. 1989. 49.00 (*0-387-50563-6*) Spr-Verlag.

— Scattering Theory of Waves & Particles. 2nd ed. (Texts & Monographs in Physics). 800p. 1982. 99.00 (*0-387-10950-1*) Spr-Verlag.

Newton, Rae R., jt. auth. see Rudestam, Kjell E.

Newton, Randall. Inside Generic CADD 6. 2nd ed. 1992. pap. 29.95 (*1-56205-067-2*) New Riders Pub.

Newton, Raymann. Political "ISMS" & the Democratic Mind: A Treatise on the Origin, Nature & Outcome of the Modern Conflict over Political Sovereignty. De Roin, Gene, ed. LC 88-92701. 160p. (Orig.). (C). 1989. pap. text ed. 7.95 (*0-9622647-0-9*) Baron-Roth Pub.

Newton, Rebecca, ed. see LaMorte, Kathy & Lewis, Sharen.

Newton, Rena. Reviving Your First Love. LC 88-13760. 144p. (Orig.). 1989. pap. 6.99 (*0-8007-9139-8*) Chosen Bks.

***Newton, Richard.** How To Restore & Modify Your Corvette 1968-82. LC 95-13977. 1995. pap. write for info. (*0-7603-0052-6*) Motorbooks Intl.

— Illustrated Austin-Healey Buyers Guide. (MBI Buyers Guide Ser.). (Illus.). 144p. 1994. pap. 16.95 (*0-87938-935-4*) Motorbooks Intl.

— Illustrated Triumph Buyer's Guide. 2nd ed. (Illus.). 176p. 1994. pap. 16.95 (*0-87938-917-6*) Motorbooks Intl.

***Newton, Richard W., ed.** Color Atlas of Pediatric Neurology. LC 94-42132. (Illus.). 1994. 72.00 (*0-7234-1879-9*) Mosby Yr Bk.

Newton, Robert. Moon's Acceleration & Its Physical Origins, Vol. 1: As Deduced from Solar Eclipses. LC 78-2059. 1979. 65.00 (*0-8018-2216-5*) Johns Hopkins.

— Tokyo. LC 92-2498. (Cities at War Ser.). (Illus.). 96p. (YA). (gr. 6 up). 1992. lib. bdg. 14.95 (*0-02-768235-8*, Mac Bks Young Read) S&S Childrens.

Newton, Robert & Penman, Susanna. A Manual for Small-Scale Rabbit Production. 1991. pap. 16.00 (*81-204-0555-2*, Pub. by Oxford IBH II) S Asia.

Newton, Robert, jt. auth. see Marcell, Rita.

Newton, Robert R. Ancient Astronomical Observations & the Accelerations of the Earth & Moon. LC 70-122011. (Illus.). 329p. reprint ed. pap. 93.80 (*0-8357-9264-1*, 2013730) Bks Demand.

— Ancient Planetary Observations & the Validity of Ephemeris Time. LC 75-44392. 768p. 1976. 65.00 (*0-8018-1842-7*) Johns Hopkins.

— The Crime of Claudius Ptolemy. LC 77-4211. 1977. text ed. 50.00 (*0-8018-1990-3*) Johns Hopkins.

— Medieval Chronicles & the Rotation of the Earth. LC 78-39780. 848p. reprint ed. pap. 180.00 (*0-317-07955-7*, 2012291) Bks Demand.

— The Moon's Acceleration & Its Physical Origins, Vol. 2: As Deduced from General Lunar Observations. LC 78-20529. (C). 1984. text ed. 45.00 (*0-8018-2639-X*) Johns Hopkins.

— The Origins of Ptolemy's Astronomical Parameters. (Technical Publications of the Center for Archaeoastronomy: No. 4). (Illus.). 228p. (Orig.). 1982. pap. 12.00 (*0-912025-02-6*) JHU Applied Physics.

— The Origins of Ptolemy's Astronomical Tables. (Technical Publications of the Center for Archaeoastronomy: No. 5). (Illus.). 264p. (Orig.). 1985. pap. 12.00 (*0-912025-03-4*) JHU Applied Physics.

Newton, Roger G. What Makes Nature Tick? LC 93-9507. 269p. 1993. text ed. 27.95 (*0-674-95085-2*) HUP.

— What Makes Nature Tick? (Illus.). 269p. 1994. pap. text ed. 14.95 (*0-674-95082-8*, NEWWHX) HUP.

Newton, Roger G., jt. auth. see Gilbert, Robert P.

Newton, Ronald C. German Buenos Aires, 1900-1933: Social Change & Cultural Crisis. LC 77-7206. (Texas Pan-American Ser.). 243p. reprint ed. pap. 69.30 (*0-8357-7752-9*, 2036110) Bks Demand.

— The Nazi Menace in Argentina, 1931-1947. LC 91-20368. (Illus.). 540p. 1992. 49.50 (*0-8047-1929-2*) Stanford U Pr.

Newton, Roy, illus. A History of the Town of Grand Isle As Told by the People of the Town. 222p. (Orig.). 1991. pap. 16.00 (*0-9624658-1-X*) Landside Pr.

Newton, Roy G. & Davison, Sandra. The Conservation of Glass. (Illus.). 322p. 1989. text ed. 94.95 (*0-408-10623-9*) Buttrwrth-Heinemann.

Newton, Roy M. Seven South: The Adventures & Times of a Small Vermont Restaurant, 1972-1982. (Illus.). 250p. 1985. 14.95 (*0-930721-00-4*) Newton Pub.

Newton, Ruth & Lebowitz, Naomi. Dickens, Manzoni, Zola, & James: The Impossible Romance. 256p. 1990. text ed. 26.00 (*0-8262-0738-3*) U of Mo Pr.

***Newton, S.** Where Are You When I Need You? Date not set. pap. 4.99 (*0-517-12653-2*) Random.

Newton, Sarah E. Learning to Behave: A Guide to American Conduct Books Before 1900. LC 94-2849. 248p. 1994. text ed. 59.95 (*0-313-26752-9*, Greenwood Pr) Greenwood.

Newton, Saul, jt. auth. see Pearce, Jane.

Newton, Scott & Porter, Dilwyn. Joseph Chamberlain, 1836-1914: A Bibliography. LC 93-50544. (Bibliographies & Indexes in World History Ser.: No. 32). 152p. 1994. text ed. 55.00 (*0-313-28290-0*, Greenwood Pr) Greenwood.

***Newton, Shane.** Protecting a Will. 154p. 1994. 49.00 (*1-86287-142-6*, Pub. by Federation Pr AU) W W Gaunt.

Newton, Shirley, jt. auth. see Jones, Ursula.

Newton-Smith, W. H. The Rationality of Science. (International Library of Philosophy). 300p. 1981. pap. 14.95 (*0-7100-0913-5*, RKP) Routledge.

— The Structure of Time. 274p. 1984. pap. 14.95 (*0-7102-0389-6*, RKP) Routledge.

Newton-Smith, W. H., et al. Popper in China. 176p. 1992. 59.50 (*0-415-03717-4*, A6652) Routledge.

Newton, Stanley. MacKinac Island & Sault St. Marie. LC 76-4405. 1990. reprint ed. pap. 10.50 (*0-912382-19-8*) Black Letter.

Newton, Stanley D. Paul Bunyan of the Great Lakes. 4th ed. LC 85-70346. 1985. pap. 11.95 (*0-932212-42-5*) Avery Color.

Newton, Stella M. The Dress of the Venetians. 180p. 1988. text ed. 76.95 (*0-85967-735-4*, Pub. by Scolar Pr UK) Ashgate Pub Co.

***Newton, Steven.** German Battle Tactics on the Russian Front, 1941-1945. (Illus.). 320p. 1994. 24.95 (*0-88740-582-7*) Schiffer.

Newton, Steven H. The Battle of Seven Pines, May 31 - June 1, 1862. (Virginia Civil War Battles & Leaders Ser.). (Illus.). 147p. 1993. 19.95 (*1-56190-048-6*) H E Howard.

Newton, Suzanne. I Will Call It Georgie's Blues. (J). 1990. pap. 4.99 (*0-14-034536-1*, Puffin) Puffin Bks.

— Where Are You When I Need You? LC 92-31360. 208p. (YA). (gr. 7 up). 1993. pap. 3.99 (*0-14-034454-3*) Puffin Bks.

Newton, T. W. Kinetics of the Oxidation-Reduction Reactions of Uranium, Neptunium, Plutonium, & Americium Ions in Aqueous Solutions. LC 75-22030. (ERDA Critical Review Ser.). 142p. 1975. pap. 11.50 (*0-685-01477-0*, TID-26506); fiche 9.00 (*0-87079-252-0*, TID-26506) DOE.

Newton, Tanist. How to ....Salvage Your Marriage or Survive Your Divorce. LC 86-61005. (Metamorphosis Trilogy Ser.: Vol. 1). 212p. (Orig.). 1988. pap. 12.95 (*0-9616881-0-6*) New Vistas Pub.

Newton, Thomas, ed. see Curio, Augustine.

Newton, Thomas, tr. see Grataroius, Gulielmus.

Newton, Thomas, ed. see Seneca, Lucius Annaeus.

Newton, Thomas H. & Bilaniuk, Larissa T. Radiology of the Eye & Orbit. (Modern Neuroradiology Ser.: Vol. 4). 320p. 1990. 127.50 (*0-88167-662-4*, 2129) Raven.

Newton, Thomas H. & Potts, D. Gordon. Advanced Imaging Techniques. (Modern Neuroradiology Ser.: Vol. 2). 348p. 1983. 83.50 (*0-685-38980-4*, CL0002) Raven.

Newton, Thomas H., et al, eds. Computed Tomography of the Head & Neck. (Modern Neuroradiology Ser.: Vol. 3). (Illus.). 480p. 1988. text ed. 160.50 (*0-88167-392-7*) Raven.

***Newton, Tim.** Managing Stress: Subjectivity & Power in the Workplace. 176p. 1995. text ed. 65.00 (*0-8039-8643-2*); pap. text ed. 21.95 (*0-8039-8644-0*) Sage.

Newton, Velma. Commonwealth Caribbean Legal Systems: A Study of Small Jurisdictions. LC 89-46052. xxv, 325p. 1989. reprint ed. 73.00 (*0-912004-76-2*) W W Gaunt.

Newton, Verne W. Cambridge Spies: The American Cover-up of the Philby, Burgess, MacLean Scandal. 550p. 1991. 24.95 (*0-8191-8059-9*) Madison Bks UPA.

— The Cambridge Spies: The Untold Story of Maclean, Philby, & Burgess in America. LC 91-7889. 462p. 1993. pap. 14.95 (*1-56833-006-5*) Madison Bks UPA.

***Newton, Verne W., ed.** F. D. R. & the Holocaust. LC 95-8304. 1995. text ed. write for info. (*0-312-12226-8*) St Martin.

Newton, Vernon. Homage to a Cat: As It Were: Logscapes of the Lost Ages. LC 91-66800. (Orig.). 1991. pap. 9.95 (*0-9621570-5-8*) North Lights.

Newton, Violette, jt. auth. see Appelbee, Evelyn C.

Newton, Violette, jt. auth. see Ottenstein, Claire.

Newton, W. E., jt. ed. see Gibson, A. H.

Newton, Walter H., jt. auth. see Myers, William S.

Newton, Wayne & Maurice, Dick. Once Before I Go. 320p. 1991. mass mkt. 4.95 (*0-380-71405-1*) Avon.

Newton, Wesley P. The Perilous Sky: Evolution of United States Aviation Diplomacy Toward Latin America, 1919-1931. LC 77-84781. (Illus.). 1978. text ed. 15.00 (*0-87024-298-9*) U of Miami Pr.

Newton, Wesley P. & Rea, Robert R., eds. Wings of Gold: An Account of Naval Aviation Training in World War II. LC 86-7013. 352p. 1987. 35.95 (*0-8173-0319-7*) U of Ala Pr.

Newton, Wesley P., jt. auth. see McFarland, Stephen L.

Newton, William. Death Is for Losers. large type ed. 1991. pap. 13.95 (*0-7089-7003-6*) Ulverscroft.

— Don't Hold Your Breath. large type ed. (Linford Mystery Library). 288p. 1992. pap. 14.95 (*0-7089-7272-1*, Trailtree Bookshop) Ulverscroft.

— If the Price Is Right. large type ed. 1991. pap. 13.95 (*0-7089-7023-0*) Ulverscroft.

— It Never Comes Easy. large type ed. (Linford Mystery Library). 304p. 1993. pap. 14.95 (*0-7089-7347-7*, Trailtree Bookshop) Ulverscroft.

— The Night We Get Rich. large type ed. 1990. pap. 12.95 (*0-7089-7000-1*, Linford) Ulverscroft.

— Nothing Is for Free. large type ed. (Linford Mystery Library). 1991. pap. 13.95 (*0-7089-7132-6*) Ulverscroft.

— The Rio Contract. large type ed. 1991. pap. 13.95 (*0-7089-7027-3*) Ulverscroft.

— The Set-Up. large type ed. 1990. pap. 12.95 (*0-7089-6954-2*, Trailtree Bookshop) Ulverscroft.

N

— A Slice of the Cake. large type ed. (Linford Mystery Library). 1991. pap. 13.95 (0-7089-7087-7) Ulverscroft.
— The Smell of Money. large type ed. 1990. pap. 12.95 (0-7089-6996-8, Trailtree Bookshop) Ulverscroft.
— Someone Has to Take the Fall. large type ed. (Linford Mystery Library). 1991. pap. 13.95 (0-7089-7083-4) Ulverscroft.
— The Way to Get Dead. large type ed. (Linford Mystery Library). 1991. pap. 13.95 (0-7089-7071-0) Ulverscroft.
— You Can Deal Me In. large type ed. (Linford Mystery Library). 1991. pap. 13.95 (0-7089-7079-6) Ulverscroft.
— You Can Go Feet First. large type ed. (Linford Mystery Library). 1991. pap. 13.95 (0-7089-7067-2) Ulverscroft.
Newton, William E. & Nyman, C. J., eds. Nitrogen Fixation, Vol. 1: Proceedings of the First International Symposium, 1974, Pullman, WA. (Illus.). 319p. reprint ed. pap. 91.00 (0-685-24153-X, 2033027) Bks Demand.
Newton, William H., jt. auth. see Shepard's Citation, Inc. Staff.
Newton, Willis & Newton, Joe. The Newton Boys: Portrait of an Outlaw Gang. Middleton, David, ed. LC 93-43267. (Illus.). 332p. 1994. 24.95 (1-880510-15-4); pap. 16.95 (1-880510-16-2) State House Pr.
— The Newton Boys: Portrait of an Outlaw Gang. limited ed. Middleton, David, ed. LC 93-43267. (Illus.). 332p. 1994. 60.00 (1-880510-17-0) State House Pr.
Newtown Psych. Staff. Not Too High, Not Too Low: Stress Management Strategies for Professional Baseball Players & Their Fans. 224p. 1990. 17.95 (0-8403-6407-5) Kendall-Hunt.
Newville, Jack. New Engineering Concepts in Community Development. LC 67-28256. (Urban Land Institute, Technical Bulletin Ser.: 59). 58p. reprint ed. pap. 25.00 (0-317-09991-4, 2005776) Bks Demand.
Newville, Leslie J., tr. see Callinicos, Constantine.
Nex, Anthony, jt. auth. see Cook, Scott.
***Nexia International Staff.** International Handbook of Corporate & Personal Taxes. 2nd ed. 1994. 59.50 (0-412-54540-3, Blackie & Son-Chapman NY) Routledge Chapman & Hall.
— Tolley's Vat in Europe. 200p. (C). 1994. 105.00 (0-614-00331-8) St Mut.
***Nexia International Staff, ed.** Tolley's Vat in Europe. 200p. (C). 1994. 190.00x (0-85459-849-9) St Mut.
Nexo, John B. Camels. (Zoobooks Ser.). 24p. (J). (gr. 3). 1989. lib. bdg. 14.95 (0-88682-222-X) Creative Ed.
Nexo, Martin A. Pelle the Conqueror, Vol. 3: The Great Struggle. Murray, Steven T., tr. (Modern Classics Ser.: No. 6). 256p. (Orig.). Date not set. write for info. (0-940242-64-8); pap. write for info. (0-940242-63-X) Fjord Pr.
Next Computer Inc. Staff. Next Development Tools. 1991. pap. 26.95 (0-201-58132-9) Addison-Wesley.
— Next Operating System Software. 1991. pap. 24.95 (0-201-58131-0) Addison-Wesley.
NeXT Computer, Inc. Staff. NeXTstep Database Kit Concepts. LC 93-46024. (Nextstep Developer's Library). 1994. pap. 24.95 (0-201-40741-8) Addison-Wesley.
Next Computer Inc. Staff. NeXTstep Development Tools: Release 3. 1992. pap. 30.95 (0-201-63249-7) Addison-Wesley.
— NeXtstep General Reference: Release 3. 1992. pap. 49.95 (0-201-63248-9) Addison-Wesley.
— NeXTstep General Reference, Release 3, Vol. 1. 1992. pap. 44.95 (0-201-62220-3) Addison-Wesley.
— NeXTstep Network & System Administration: Release 3. 1992. pap. 34.95 (0-201-63254-3) Addison-Wesley.
— NeXTstep Object-Oriented Programming & the Objective-C Language: Release 3. 1993. pap. 24.95 (0-201-63251-9) Addison-Wesley.
— NeXTstep Operating System Software: Release 3. 1992. pap. 28.95 (0-201-63252-7) Addison-Wesley.
— NeXTstep Programming Interface Summary: Release 3. 1992. pap. 30.95 (0-201-63253-5) Addison-Wesley.
— NeXTstep User Interface Guidelines: Release 3. 1992. pap. 24.95 (0-201-63250-0) Addison-Wesley.
— Sound, Music, & Signal Processing on a Next Computer Concepts. 1991. pap. 19.95 (0-201-58137-X) Addison-Wesley.
Ney, jt. auth. see Joffe.
Ney, Denise M., jt. auth. see Zeman, Frances J.
Ney, George & Fadem, Susan S. Cat Condominiums & Other Feline Furniture. (Illus.). 128p. 1989. 16.95 (0-525-24709-2, Dutton) NAL-Dutton.
Ney, James W. Transformational Grammar: Essays for the Left Hand. (Edward Sapir Monograph Ser. in Language, Culture & Cognition: No. 16). vi, 169p. (Orig.). 1988. pap. 2.00 (0-933104-26-X) Jupiter Pr.
Ney, Jessica, ed. McBride's Characters of Middle Earth. (Middle Earth Ser.). (Illus.). 64p. (Orig.). (C). 1990. pap. 14.95 (1-55806-134-7, 8007) Iron Crown Ent Inc.
— The Necromancer's Lieutenant. (Middle Earth Ser.). (Illus.). 32p. (Orig.). (YA). (gr. 12). 1990. pap. 7.00 (1-55806-113-4, 8113) Iron Crown Ent Inc.
Ney, Jessica, ed. see Baur, Wolfgang.
Ney, Jessica, ed. see Birkner, Malthias & Birkner, Karen.
Ney, Jessica, ed. see Cooke, Tim.
Ney, Jessica, ed. see Crowdis, John.
Ney, Jessica, ed. see Crutchfield, Charles.
Ney, Jessica, ed. see Feild, William B., Jr. & Stassun, Peter G.
Ney, Jessica, ed. see Ferrone, John M.
Ney, Jessica, ed. see McKeage, Jeffrey.
Ney, Jessica, ed. see Rabuck, Mark.
Ney, Jessica, ed. see Staplehurst, Graham & Kubasch, Heike.
Ney, Jessica, ed. see Willner, Carl.
Ney, Jessica M., ed. see Wilson, William E.
Ney, John. Miami Today - the U. S. Tomorrow. 36p. 1988. pap. 3.00 (0-936247-11-8) Amer Immigration.
Ney, Marian W. Indian America: A Geography of North America Indians. (Illus.). 56p. 1977. 4.95 (0-935741-06-2) Cherokee Pubns.
Ney, P. E., jt. auth. see Athreya, K. B.
Ney, Peter, ed. Advances in Probability & Related Topics, Vol. 2. LC 75-79066. 262p. reprint ed. pap. 74.70 (0-8357-5178-3, 2027071) Bks Demand.
Ney, Peter & Port, Sidney, eds. Advances in Probability & Related Topics, 2 vols., 3. LC 75-79066. 422p. pap. 120.30 (0-8357-8391-X, 2027071) Bks Demand.
— Advances in Probability & Related Topics, 2 vols., Vol. 1. LC 75-79066. 229p. pap. 65.30 (0-8357-8390-1, 2027071) Bks Demand.
Ney, Philip G. & Peters, Anna. Ending the Cycle of Abuse: The Stories of Women Abused As Children & the Group Therapy Techniques That Helped Them Heal. LC 94-28150. 272p. 1995. 23.95 (0-87630-752-7) Brunner-Mazel.
Ney, Tara, ed. True & False Allegations of Child Sexual Abuse: Assessment & Case Management. LC 94-47941. 400p. 1995. 45.95 (0-87630-758-6) Brunner-Mazel.
Ney, Tara & Gale, Anthony, eds. Smoking & Human Behavior. LC 88-33844. 395p. reprint ed. pap. 112.60 (0-7837-5874-X, 2045594) Bks Demand.
— Smoking & Human Behaviour. 384p. 1989. text ed. 121.00 (0-471-92138-6) Wiley.
Ney, Tom. The Health-Lover's Guide to Super Seafood: 250 Delicious Ways to Enjoy the Ultimate in Natural Nutrition. LC 88-7878. 288p. 1991. pap. 13.95 (0-87857-950-8, 07-812-5) Rodale Pr Inc.
Ney, W. Roger, ed. Particle Counting in Radioactivity Measurements. (ICRU Report Ser.: No. 52). 84p. 1994. pap. text ed. 50.00 (0-913394-51-3) Intl Comm Rad Meas.
— Prescribing, Recording & Reporting Photon Beam Therapy. LC 93-3633. (ICRU Report Ser.: No. 50). 720p. (Orig.). 1993. pap. text ed. 50.00 (0-913394-48-3) Intl Comm Rad Meas.
— Stopping Powers & Ranges for Protons & Alpha Particles. (ICRU Report Ser.: No. 49). 260p. (Orig.). 1993. pap. text ed. 55.00 (0-913394-47-5) Intl Comm Rad Meas.
Ney, W. ROger, ed. see Fry, R. J.
Ney, W. Roger, ed. see ICRU Staff.
Neyen, Auguste. Biographie Luxembourgeoise, 3 vols., Set. lii, 1463p. 1973. reprint ed. write for info. (3-487-04295-9, Pub. by Georg Olms GW) Lubrecht & Cramer.
Neyer, B. T., ed. High Bandwidth Analog Applications of Phototonics II, Vol. 987. 1988. 45.00 (0-8194-0022-X) SPIE.
Neyfakh, A. A. & Timofeeva, M. Ya. Molecular Biology of Development: Molecular Events & Problems of Regulation. Kolchinsky, A. M., ed. 792p. 1985. 145.00 (0-306-41333-7, Plenum Pr) Plenum.
Neyhart, Charles A., Jr. & Kemp, Patrick S. Financial Accounting. 4th ed. 1992. pap. text ed. write for info. (0-07-021057-8) McGraw.
Neyland, Charlotte S. Southwest Traveler: A Travelers Guide to: Southwest Indian Arts & Crafts. (American Traveler Ser.). (Illus.). 48p. (Orig.). 1992. pap. 4.95 (1-55838-129-5) R H Pub.
Neyland, James. Booker T. Washington, Educator. Locke, Raymond F., ed. (Black American Ser.). (Illus.). 192p. (YA). 1993. pap. 3.95 (0-87067-599-0, Melrose Sq) Holloway.
— Crispus Attucks. 208p. 1995. 4.95 (0-87067-791-8) Holloway.
— The Dark Lady. 320p. (Orig.). 1994. pap. 3.95 (0-87067-744-6) Holloway.
— The Fever. 288p. (Orig.). 1994. pap. 3.95 (0-87067-743-8) Holloway.
— A Philip Randolph. 1994. pap. 3.95 (0-87067-777-2, Melrose Sq) Holloway.
— W. E. B. DuBois, Scholar & Activist. Locke, Raymond F., ed. (Black American Ser.). (Illus.). 192p. (YA). 1993. pap. 3.95 (0-87067-588-5, Melrose Sq) Holloway.
Neyland, James, told to. Politics, Fat-Cats & Honey-Money Boys: The Mem-Wars of Jerry Sadler. LC 83-63199. 336p. 1984. 15.95 (0-915677-01-6) Roundtable Pub.
Neyland, James E. George Washington Carver. (Orig.). 1992. pap. 3.95 (0-87067-583-4, Melrose Sq) Holloway.
Neyland, Leedell W. Unquenchable Black Fires. 204p. 1994. write for info. (0-9641539-0-4); pap. write for info. (0-9641539-1-2) Leney Educ.
Neylon, M. Wit & Wisdom. 1993. 56.00 (1-85594-050-7, Pub. by Attic Pr IE) St Mut.
Neylon, Margaret. Pathways: A Sourcebook of Live Options. (Illus.). 160p. (C). 1991. pap. 15.99 (1-85594-026-4, Pub. by Attic IE) InBook.
— The Wit & Wisdom of Women: A Thought Book. 160p. (C). 1990. pap. text ed. 24.00 (1-85594-010-8, Pub. by Attic Pr IE) St Mut.
Neyman, E., jt. auth. see Brainina, Z.
Neyman, J. & Pearson, E. K. Joint Statistical Papers. 299p. 1967. lib. bdg. 35.00 (0-85264-706-9) Lubrecht & Cramer.
Neyman, J., jt. ed. see Le Cam, Lucien M.
Neyman, Jerzy, ed. The Heritage of Copernicus: Theories: "Pleasing to the Mind" 1974. pap. 14.95 (0-262-64016-3) MIT Pr.
Neyman, Jerzy & Pearson, E. S. The Selected Papers of Jerzy Neyman & E. S. Pearson. Incl. Vol. 2. Joint Statistical Papers. 1967. 48.00 (0-520-00991-6); Vol. 3. Selection of Early Statistical Papers of J. Neyman. 80p. 1967. 48.00 (0-520-00992-4); write for info. (0-318-56013-5) U CA Pr.
Neymeyr, Ulrich. Die Christlichen Lehrer im Zweiten Jahrhundert: Ihre Lehrtatigkeit, ihr Selbstverstandnis und ihre Geschichte. LC 88-29247. (Supplements to Vigiliae Christianae Ser.: Vol. IV). 279p. (GER.). (C). 1989. text ed. 74.50 (90-04-08773-7) E J Brill.
Neyra, Carlos A. Biochemical Basis Plant Breeding: Carbon Metabolism, Vol. 1. 176p. 1985. 144.00 (0-8493-5741-1, SB123, CRC Reprint) Franklin.
Neyra, Carlos A., ed. Biochemical Basis of Plant Breeding, Vol. II. 192p. 1986. 144.00 (0-8493-5742-X, SB123, CRC Reprint) Franklin.
Neyrey, Jerome H. Christ Is Community: The Christologies of the New Testament. LC 85-47753. (Good News Studies: Vol. 13). 229p. 1985. pap. 12.95 (0-8146-5465-7) Liturgical Pr.
— First & Second Timothy, Titus, James, First Peter, Second Peter, Jude. Karris, Robert J., ed. (Collegeville Bible Commentary - New Testament Ser.: No. 9). 112p. (C). 1983. pap. 3.95 (0-8146-1309-8) Liturgical Pr.
— Paul, in Other Words: A Cultural Readings of His Letters. 252p. (Orig.). 1990. text ed. 20.00 (0-664-21925-X) Westminster John Knox.
— Resurrection Stories. (Zacchaeus Studies). 109p. (Orig.). 1988. pap. 7.95 (0-8146-5664-1) Liturgical Pr.
— Second Peter, Jude: A New Translation with Introduction & Commentary. LC 92-21142. (Anchor Bible Ser.: Vol. 37C). 1993. 28.00 (0-385-41362-9, Anchor NY) Doubleday.
Neyrey, Jerome H., ed. The Social World of Luke-Acts: Models for Interpretation. LC 91-3333. 432p. 1991. 19.95 (0-943575-48-6) Hendrickson MA.
Neyrey, Jerome H., jt. auth. see Malina, Bruce J.
Neyrohr, Deborah, jt. auth. see Brothers, Barbara.
Nez, Martha M. & Haburay, J. Keitz. Laboratory Manual for General Zoology. 176p. (C). 1993. spiral bd. 17.95 (0-8403-8541-2) Kendall-Hunt.
***Nez, Redwing T.** The Forbidden Talent. Murphy, Erin, ed. (Illus.). 32p. (J). (ps up). 1995. 14.95 (0-87358-605-0) Northland AZ.
Nezadal, Werner. Unkrautgesellschaften der Getreide- und Fruehjahrshackfruchtkulturen (Stellarietae Mediae) im Mediterranen Iberien. (Illus.). 206p. (GER.). 1990. pap. text ed. 89.50 (3-443-64052-4, Pub. by Gebruder Borntraeger GW) Lubrecht & Cramer.
Nezhat, Camran, et al. Modern Surgical Management of Endometriosis. LC 94-19130. 1995. 95.00 (0-387-94243-2) Spr-Verlag.
— Operative Gynecologic Laparascopy: Principles & Techniques. 352p. 1995. text ed. 115.00 (0-07-105422-7) Hlth Prof Div.
Nezhinskaya, Larissa. Doing Business in Russia: Basic Facts for the Pioneering Entrepreneur. 1995. pap. 19.95 (1-55571-168-5) Oasis Pr OR.
***Neziroglu.** Over & Over Again: Understanding Obsessive Compulsive Disorder. 1995. pap. 12.00 (0-02-874013-0) Free Pr.
Nezlin, M. V. Physics of Intense Beams in Plasmas. (Plasma Physics Ser.). (Illus.). 344p. 1993. 140.00 (0-7503-0186-4) IOP Pub.
Nezlin, M. V. & Snezhkin, E. N. Rossby Vortices, Spiral Structures, Solitons: Astrophysics & Plasma Physics in Shallow Water Experiments. Dobrolavsky, A. & Pletnev, A., trs. LC 93-28898. (Nonlinear Dynamics Ser.). (Illus.). 240p. 1993. 89.00 (0-387-50115-0) Spr-Verlag.
Neznanskii, Fridrich. Zapiski Sledovatelia (Notes of An Investigator) LC 89-61028. 342p. (Orig.). (RUS.). (C). 1990. pap. 16.00 (0-911971-44-0) Effect Pub.
Neznansky, Fridrikh. The Prosecution of Economic Crimes in the U. S. S. R., 1954-1984. Michta, Andrew, ed. (Orig.). 1985. pap. text ed. 75.00 (1-55831-031-2) Delphic Associates.
Neznek, Mary, jt. ed. see Janger, Michael.
Nezu, Arthur M. & Nezu, Christine M. Clinical Decision Making in Behavior Therapy: A Problem-Solving Perspective. LC 89-61522. 438p. (Orig.). 1989. pap. text ed. 21.95 (0-87822-317-7, 3183) Res Press.
Nezu, Arthur M., et al. Problem Solving Therapy for Depression: Theory Research & Clinical Guidelines. (Personality Processes Ser.). 274p. 1989. text ed. 45.00 (0-471-62885-9) Wiley.
Nezu, Christine M., jt. auth. see Nezu, Arthur M.
Nezu, Christine M., et al. Psychopathology in Persons with Mental Retardation: Clinical Guidelines for Assessment & Treatment. LC 92-61116. 342p. (Orig.). (C). 1992. pap. text ed. 21.95 (0-87822-328-2, 4625) Res Press.
Nezu, Masuo, tr. see Niwano, Nikkyo.
Nezunan. French-Polish Medical Dictionary. (FRE & POL.). 1990. 150.00 (0-8288-7273-2) Fr & Eur.
Nezworski, Teresa, jt. ed. see Belsky, Jay.
NFAIS Staff. Information Industry Human Resources - a 1990 Survey. Schipper, Wendy & Cunningham, Ann M., eds. (Report Series, 1991: No. 3). 250p. (Orig.). 1991. pap. text ed. 240.00 (0-942308-32-8) NFAIS.
***NFCYM Staff.** The Challenge of Catholic Youth: Called to Be Witnesses & Storytellers. 28p. 1993. 8.50 (0-89944-273-0) Don Bosco Multimedia.
***NFL Properties Staff, ed. & photos.** Good Days, Bad Days. (Illus.). 128p. (J). (gr. 3-9). 1995. 4.99 (0-14-036341-6) Puffin Bks.
NFLC Staff. Language Assessment for Feedback: Testing & Other Strategies. 160p. 1992. 29.95 (0-8403-7932-3) Kendall-Hunt.
***Ng & Hung.** Safety, Reliability & Applications of Emerging Intelligent Control. 1995. pap. text ed. write for info. (0-08-042374-4, Pergamon Pr) Elsevier.
***Ng, Alice N., ed.** The Quest for Excellence: A History of the Chinese University of Hong Kong, 1963-1993. 400p. 1994. 42.50x (962-201-606-5, Pub. by Chinese Univ HK) Coronet Bks.
Ng, Anthony & Wei, William. A Handbook of Practical Medical Terms. 172p. (C). 1989. pap. text ed. 35.00 (962-209-225-X, Pub. by Hong Kong U Pr HK) St Mut.
Ng, C., ed. Optical Methods for Time- & State-Resolved Chemistry. 1992. 70.00 (0-8194-0784-4, 1638) SPIE.
Ng, C. S., ed. Frontiers in Reproductive Endocrinology & Infertility. (C). 1988. lib. bdg. 63.00 (0-7462-0092-7) Kluwer Ac.
Ng, C. Y., ed. see Franzen, H. F.
Ng Chee Yuen & Wagner, Norbert, eds. Marketization in ASEAN. 156p. 1991. pap. text ed. 14.50 (981-3035-72-2, Pub. by Inst SE Asian Studies SI) Ashgate Pub Co.
Ng, Cheuk-Yiu, ed. Cluster Ions. LC 93-10286. (Current Topics in Ion Chemistry & Physics Ser.: Vol. 1). 400p. 1993. text ed. 144.00 (0-471-93830-0) Wiley.
— Vacuum Ultraviolet Photoionization & Photodissociation of Molecules & Clusters. 580p. (C). 1991. text ed. 150.00 (981-02-0430-2); pap. 48.00 (981-02-0431-0) World Scientific Pub.
Ng, Cheuk-Yiu & Baer, Michael, eds. State-Selected & State-to-State Ion-Molecule Reaction Dynamics: Experiment, Vol. 82. (Advances in Chemical Physics Ser.: Vol. 82, Pt. 1). 704p. 1992. text ed. 185.00 (0-471-53258-4) Wiley.
Ng, Cheuk-Yiu, jt. ed. see Baer, Michael.
Ng, Cheuk-Yiu, et al, eds. Unimolecular & Biomolecular Ion-Molecule Reaction Dynamics. LC 93-46718. (Ion Chemistry & Physics Ser.). 1994. text ed. 125.00 (0-471-93831-9) Wiley.
Ng, David. Developing Leaders for Youth Ministry. 64p. 1984. pap. 6.00 (0-8170-1032-7) Judson.
— La Juventud: (Spanish Translation of Youth in the Ministry of Disciples) Vazquez, Victor, ed. 128p. (Orig.). (SPA.). 1989. pap. 9.00 (0-8170-1153-6) Judson.
Ng, David & Thomas, Virginia. Children in the Worshipping Community. LC 80-84655. (Illus.). 128p. (Orig.). (C). 1981. pap. 9.99 (0-8042-1688-6, John Knox) Westminster John Knox.
Ng, Donna, ed. see Buck, Pearl S.
Ng, Donna, ed. see Cather, Willa.
Ng, Donna, ed. see Ellis, Trey.
Ng, Donna, ed. see Hawthorne, Nathaniel.
Ng, Donna, ed. see Lame Deer & Erodes.
Ng, Donna, ed. see Martin, Valerie.
Ng, Donna, ed. see Pelletier, Cathie.
Ng, Fae M. Bone. 208p. 1994. reprint ed. pap. 11.00 (0-06-097592-X, PL) HarpC.
— Bone: A Novel. 208p. 1993. 19.95 (1-56282-944-0) Hyperion.
Ng, Franklin. Chinese Amerian Struggle for Equality. LC 92-7472. (Discrimination Ser.). (YA). 1992. 22.60 (0-86593-181-X); lib. bdg. 16.95 (0-685-59290-1) Rourke Corp.
***Ng, Franklin, ed.** The Asian American Encyclopedia, 6 Vols. LC 94-33003. (Illus.). 1900p. (YA). 1994. lib. bdg. 449.95 (1-85435-677-1) Marshall Cavendish.
Ng, Franklin, et al, eds. New Visions in Asian American Studies: Diversity, Community, Power. LC 93-36427. (Association for Asian American Studies Ser.). 256p. (C). 1994. pap. text ed. 30.00 (0-87422-102-1) Wash St U Pr.
Ng, K. C. Electrical Network Theory. (Illus.). 1977. pap. text ed. 30.00 (0-8464-0362-5) Beekman Pubs.
Ng, K. C., tr. see Yuen Liao Fan.
Ng, K. W., et al. Algorithms & Computation: Proceedings, Fourth International Symposium, ISAAC '93, Hong Kong, December 1993. LC 93-44957. (Lecture Notes in Computer Science Ser.: Vol. 762). 1994. 78.00 (0-387-57568-5) Spr-Verlag.
***Ng, Kwok K.** Complete Guide to Semiconductor Devices. 1994. pap. 62.50 (0-07-035860-5) McGraw.
Ng Lam Sim Yuk, jt. ed. see Chik Hon Man.
Ng, N. H., tr. see Hua, Lo-Keng.
Ng, Nelson, jt. auth. see Pechar, Gary.
***Ng, Nelson K.** Metcalc Software: Metabolic Calculations in Exercise & Fitness. LC 95-10269. 80p. (Orig.). 1995. disk, pap. text ed. write for info. (0-87322-527-9, BNGN 0527) Human Kinetics.
Ng, Nelson K., jt. auth. see Pechar, Gary S.
Ng, Paul. Understanding Aerodynamic Characteristics of Windsurfing. 1992. pap. 12.95 (0-533-10271-5) Vantage.
Ng, Peter A. Modern Software Engineering: Foundation & Current Perspectives. 1990. text ed. 79.95 (0-442-26695-2) Van Nos Reinhold.
Ng, Peter Y., ed. New Peace County: A Chinese Gazetteer of the Hong Kong Region. 162p. (C). 1983. text ed. 36.00 (962-209-043-5, Pub. by Hong Kong U Pr HK) St Mut.
***Ng, Roxana, et al, eds.** Anti-Racism, Feminism, & Critical Approaches to Education. LC 95-5160. (Critical Studies in Education & Culture). 192p. 1995. text ed. 55.00 (0-89789-327-1, Bergin & Garvey); pap. text ed. 16.95 (0-89789-328-X, Bergin & Garvey) Greenwood.
Ng Sek Hong, jt. auth. see Lethbridge, David G.
Ng Shui Meng, ed. Socio-Economic Correlates of Mortality in Japan & ASEAN. 317p. 1987. pap. text ed. 16.75 (9971-988-21-6, Pub. by Inst SE Asian Studies SI) Ashgate Pub Co.
Ng Shui Meng, jt. ed. see Wong, Aline K.
Ng Sik Hung & Bradac, James J. Power in Language: Verbal Communication & Social Influence. LC 93-18762. (Language & Language Behaviors Ser.: Vol. 3). (Illus.). 227p. (C). 1993. text ed. 48.00 (0-8039-4422-5); pap. text ed. 21.95 (0-8039-4423-3) Sage.
Ng, Vivien W. Madness in Late Imperial China: From Illness to Deviance. LC 90-50237. 208p. 1990. 30.00 (0-8061-2297-8) U of Okla Pr.
Ng, W. Y. Interactive Multi-Objective Programming As a Framework for Computer-Aided Control System Design. (Lecture Notes in Control & Information Sciences Ser.: Vol. 132). (Illus.). xv, 182p. 1989. pap. 35.00 (0-387-51504-6) Spr-Verlag.

An Asterisk (*) at the beginning of an entry indicates that the title is appearing in BIP for the first time.

***Ng, Wendy L., et al, eds.** ReViewing Asian America: Locating Diversity. (Association for Asian American Studies Ser.: No. 6). 150p. (Orig.). 1995. pap. text ed. 29.00x (*0-87422-118-8*) Wash St U Pr.
Ng, Yew-Kwang, jt. auth. see Yang, Xiaokai.
Ng Yu-Kwan. T'ien-T'ai Buddhism & Early Madhyamika. LC 93-23160. 1993. text ed. 37.00 (*0-8248-1560-2*); pap. text ed. 22.00 (*0-8248-1561-0*) UH Pr.
Nga, B. H. & Lee, Y. K., eds. Microbiology Applications in Food Biotechnology: Proceedings of the Second Congress of the Singapore Society for Microbiology, Singapore, 31 Oct.-3 Nov. 1989. (Illus.). 232p. 1990. 55. 75 (*1-85166-530-7*) Elsevier.
Ngafua, Zizwe. Nommo (the Word) (Illus.). 56p. (Orig.). 1978. pap. 4.00 (*0-917886-04-6*) Shamal Bks.
Ngah, Nor bin. Kitab Jawi: Islamic Thought of the Malay Muslim Scholars. 64p. (Orig.). 1982. pap. text ed. 10.00 (*9971-902-48-6*, Pub. by Inst SE Asian Studies SI) Ashgate Pub Co.
Ngai-ha, Ng L. Interactions of East & West: Development of Public Education in Early Hong Kong. (Illus.). x, 186p. 1984. text ed. 32.50x (*962-201-291-4*) Coronet Bks.
Ngantcha, Frances. The Right of Innocent Passage & the Evolution of the International Law of the Sea: The Current Regime of "Free" Navigation in Coastal Waters of Third States. 256p. 1990. text ed. 49.00 (*0-86187-851-5*, Pub. by Pinter Pubs UK) St Martin.
Ngara, Emmanuel. Ideology & Form in African Poetry. LC 90-30115. (Studies in African Literature). 208p. (Orig.). 1990. pap. 19.50 (*0-435-08045-8*) Heinemann.
***Ngarjuna.** The Fundamental Wisdom of the Middle Way: Nagarjuna's Mulamadhyamakakarika. Garfield, Jay L., tr. & comment by. 336p. 1995. 39.95 (*0-19-510317-3*); pap. 12.95 (*0-19-509336-4*) OUP.
Ngata, Apirana N. Complete Manual of Maori Grammar & Conversation, with Vocabulary. 5th enl. rev. ed. LC 75-35261. (MAO.). reprint ed. 19.00 (*0-404-14433-0*) AMS Pr.
Ngate, Jonathan. Francophone African Fiction: Reading a Literary Tradition. Arnold, Stephen H. & Lang, George, eds. LC 88-70588. (Comparative Studies in African-Caribbean Literature Ser.). 250p. (C). 1988. 32.00 (*0-86543-087-X*); pap. 9.95 (*0-86543-088-8*) Africa World.
Ngate, Jonathan & Zimra, Clarisse, eds. Criss Crossing Boundaries in African Literatures 1986. (Annual Selected Papers of the African Literature Association). 197p. (Orig.). 1991. text ed. 24.00 (*0-89410-718-6*); pap. 15.00x (*0-89410-719-4*) Three Continents.
Ngcobo, A. B., jt. ed. see Rycroft, D. K.
Ngcobo, Lauretta. And They Didn't Die. 246p. 1991. 17.50 (*0-8076-1263-4*) Braziller.
Ngeyi, Stanley-Pierre. I See War, War, Real War Everywhere: America Stands Tall, Israel Survives by a Whisker, & Apartheid Dies. Lyonga, Lynne N., ed. (Illus.). 224p. (Orig.). 1993. pap. 10.40 (*0-9636079-0-1*) Mt Zion Pub.
Nghi, Nguyen Thanh, jt. auth. see Fistual, V. I.
Nghiem, Alex. NextStep Programming Primer: Writing Nextstep Applications. (Illus.). 656p. (C). 1993. pap. text ed. 42.00 (*0-13-605916-3*) P-H.
Nghieu Minh. Trang Mat. 140p. 1992. 15.00 (*0-9635574-2-4*) Alpha Bks VA.
Ngien, Dennis. The Suffering of God According to Martin Luther's Theologia Crucis. LC 94-11414. (American University Studies: Ser. VII, Vol. 181). 304p. (C). 1995. text ed. 46.95 (*0-8204-2582-6*) P Lang Pubs.
Ngo, Alita M. Open Heart. LC 93-61421. 44p. 1994. 7.95 (*1-55523-667-7*) Winston-Derek.
Ngo, Bach & Zimmerman, Gloria. The Classic Cuisine of Vietnam. 1986. pap. 11.00 (*0-452-25833-2*) NAL-Dutton.
Ngo Quang Truong. The Easter Offensive of 1972. 183p. 1989. reprint ed. pap. 20.00x (*0-923135-09-X*) Dalley Bk Service.
Ngo, T. T., ed. Electrochemical Sensors in Immunological Analysis. LC 87-1416. (Illus.). 372p. 1987. 85.00 (*0-306-42580-7*, Plenum Pr) Plenum.
— Molecular Interactions in Bioseparations. (Illus.). 495p. (C). 1994. 95.00 (*0-306-44435-6*, Plenum Pr) Plenum.
— Nonisotopic Immunoassay. LC 87-36105. (Illus.). 512p. 1988. 110.00 (*0-306-42811-3*, Plenum Pr) Plenum.
Ngo, T. T. & Lenhoff, Howard M., eds. Enzyme-Mediated Immunoassay. LC 85-16988. 498p. 1985. 110.00 (*0-306-42085-6*, Plenum Pr) Plenum.
Ngo Vinh Long. Before the Revolution. 320p. 1991. pap. text ed. 14.50 (*0-231-07679-7*) Col U Pr.
Ngoc Phuong, Cao. Learning True Love: How I Learned & Practiced Social Change in Vietnam. LC 93-31442. 258p. 1993. pap. 16.00 (*0-938077-50-3*) Parallax Pr.
Ngok, Lee. China's Defense Modernisation & Military Leadership. (Illus.). 400p. 1990. 47.00 (*0-08-033046-0*, Pergamon Pr) Elsevier.
Ng'ombe, James L. The King's Pillow & Other Plays. (Evans Africa Plays Ser.). 71p. 1991. pap. 4.95 (*0-237-50916-4*, Pub. by Evans Bros Ltd UK) Trafalgar.
Ngubane, Jordan K. An African Explains Apartheid. LC 75-35338. (Illus.). 243p. 1977. reprint ed. text ed. 59.75 (*0-8371-8565-3*, NGAE, Greenwood Pr) Greenwood.
Ngugi. The River Between. (African Writers Ser.). 152p. (C). 1965. pap. 9.95 (*0-435-90548-1*) Heinemann.
Ngugi Wa Mirii, jt. auth. see Ngugi Wa Thiong'o.
Ngugi, Wa T. Secret Lives. 144p. (C). 1992. pap. 8.95 (*0-435-90150-8*, 90150) Heinemann.
Ngugi Wa Thiongo. The Black Hermit. (African Writers Ser.). (C). 1968. pap. 9.95 (*0-435-90051-X*) Heinemann.
Ngugi Wa Thiong'o. Decolonising the Mind: The Politics of Language in African Literature. LC 86-4683. xiv, 114p. (Orig.). 1986. pap. 15.00 (*0-435-08016-4*, 08016) Heinemann.
— Detained: A Writer's Prison Diary. (African Writers Ser.). 232p. (Orig.). (C). 1981. pap. 11.95 (*0-435-90240-7*) Heinemann.
— Devil on the Cross. 256p. (C). 1987. pap. 10.95 (*0-435-90844-8*) Heinemann.
— A Grain of Wheat. (African Writers Ser.). 247p. 1987. pap. 8.95 (*0-435-90836-7*) Heinemann.
Ngugi wa Thiong'O. Matigari. Wangui wa Goro, tr. (African Writers Ser.). 175p. (Orig.). 1989. 17.95 (*0-435-90654-2*, 90654) Heinemann.
Ngugi Wa Thiong'o. Matigari. Wangui wa Goro, tr. (African Writers Ser.). 175p. (Orig.). (C). 1989. pap. 9.95 (*0-435-90546-5*, 90546) Heinemann.
Ngugi wa Thiong'o. Njamba Nene & the Flying Bus. Wangui wa Goro, tr. LC 88-70433. (Young Reader's Ser.). (Illus.). 34p. (J). (gr. 2-7). 1995. 12.95 (*0-86543-079-9*); pap. 5.95 (*0-86543-080-2*) Africa World.
— Njamba Nene's Pistol. Wangui wa Goro, tr. LC 88-70432. (Young Reader's Ser.). (Illus.). 32p. (J). (gr. 2-7). 1995. 12.95 (*0-86543-081-0*); pap. 5.95 (*0-86543-082-9*) Africa World.
Ngugi Wa Thiong'o. Weep Not Child. (African Writers Ser.). 136p. 1988. pap. 9.95 (*0-435-90830-8*) Heinemann.
Ngugi Wa Thiong'o & Ngugi Wa Mirii. I Will Marry When I Want. (African Writers Ser.). 122p. (Orig.). 1982. pap. 9.95 (*0-435-90246-6*) Heinemann.
Ngugi Wa Thiong'o, et al. The Trial of Dedan Kimathi. (African Writers Ser.). 1977. pap. 9.95 (*0-435-90191-5*) Heinemann.
Ngumy, James. The Boy Who Rode a Lion. (Junior African Writers Ser.). (Illus.). (J). (gr. 4-5). 1992. pap. 2.95 (*0-7910-2907-7*) Chelsea Hse.
Nguyen, Alina, ed. see Allen, James & Powell, Tag.
Nguyen, Alina, ed. see Davis, Samantha A.
Nguyen, Alina, ed. see Kelly, Dorothy V.
Nguyen, Alina, ed. see Ollivier, John J.
Nguyen, Anh, tr. see Lucas, Alice.
Nguyen Anh Tuan. South Vietnam: Trial & Experience. LC 86-23532. (Monographs in International Studies, Southeast Asia Ser.: No. 80). 186p. 1986. pap. text ed. 18.00 (*0-89680-141-1*, Ohio U Ctr Intl) Ohio U Pr.
Nguyen, Chi. Cooking the Vietnamese Way. (YA). (gr. 5 up). 1993. pap. 5.95 (*0-8225-9647-4*, Lerner Publctns) Lerner Group.
Nguyen, Chi & Monroe, Judy M. Cooking the Vietnamese Way. (Easy Menu Ethnic Cookbooks Ser.). (Illus.). 48p. (J). (gr. 5 up). 1985. lib. bdg. 14.95 (*0-8225-0914-8*, Lerner Publctns) Lerner Group.
Nguyen Chi Thien. Flowers from Hell. Huynh Sanh Thong, tr. LC 86-72981. (Lac-Viet Ser.: No. 1). 136p. 1984. pap. 10.00 (*0-938692-21-6*) Yale U SE Asia.
Nguyen, Christian. The Geography of War. 40p. (Orig.). 1995. pap. 8.00 (*0-939121-04-2*) Cooper Hse.
Nguyen, D. T., jt. auth. see MacBean, Alasdair I.
Nguyen, Dang. Vietnamese Pronunciation. LC 70-128082. (Pali Language Texts : Southeast Asia). 281p. reprint ed. pap. 80.10 (*0-685-17125-6*, 2027029) Bks Demand.
Nguyen Dihn-Hoa. Vietnamese-English Dictionary. LC 66-17773. 584p. 1991. pap. 19.95 (*0-8048-1712-X*) C E Tuttle.
Nguyen, Dinh H. Two Hundred One Vietnamese Verbs Fully Conjugated in All the Tenses. LC 79-14200. (J). (gr. 10-12). 1979. pap. text ed. 9.95 (*0-8120-2019-7*) Barron.
Nguyen, Dinh-Hoa. Essential English-Vietnamese Dictionary. 316p. 1983. 95.00 (*0-317-59313-7*, Pub. by Collets UK) Pro-Am Music.
Nguyen Dinh Tham. Studies on Vietnamese Language & Literature: A Preliminary Bibliography. (Southeast Asia Program Ser.: No. 10). 227p. (Orig.). 1992. pap. text ed. 15.00 (*0-87727-127-5*) Cornell SE Asia.
Nguyen Duy Hinh. Lam Son 719. 179p. 1989. reprint ed. pap. 18.50x (*0-923135-12-X*) Dalley Bk Service.
Nguyen Duy Hinh & Tran Dinh Tho. The South Vietnamese Society. 175p. 1989. reprint ed. pap. 18.50x (*0-923135-14-6*) Dalley Bk Service.
Nguyen, Elizabeth T., jt. auth. see Nash, Jesse W.
Nguyen, Elizabeth T., jt. ed. see Nash, Jesse W.
Nguyen, Gia K. & Kline, Tilde S. Essentials of Cytology: An Atlas - Text. LC 93-20139. (Illus.). 264p. 1993. pap. 98. 50 (*0-89640-231-2*) Igaku-Shoin.
Nguyen, Gia-Khanh. Essentials of Aspiration Biopsy Cytology. LC 90-5005. (Illus.). 200p. 1990. pap. 39.50 (*0-89640-188-X*) Igaku-Shoin.
Nguyen, H. T. & Rogers, G. S. Fundamentals of Mathematical Statistics. (Texts in Statistics Ser.). (Illus.). x, 432p. 1989. 39.80 (*0-387-97014-2*) Spr-Verlag.
— Fundamentals of Mathematical Statistics, Vol. II. (Texts in Statistics Ser.). xi, 422p. 1989. 39.80 (*0-387-97020-7*) Spr-Verlag.
Nguyen, H. T., jt. ed. see Goodman, I. R.
Nguyen Hien Duc. Rain Melody: Poems by Nguyen Hien Duc. Goforth, Ronald, ed. (Illus.). 111p. (Orig.). 1988. pap. 25.00 (*0-9622682-0-8*) H D Nguyen.
Nguyen-Hong-Nhiem, Lucy & Halpern, Joel M., eds. The Far East Comes Near: Autobiographical Accounts of Southeast Asian Students in America. LC 88-32687. (Illus.). 232p. 1989. 30.00 (*0-87023-671-7*); pap. 15.95x (*0-87023-672-5*) U of Mass Pr.
Nguyen, Hung P. Submarine Detection from Space: A Study of Russian Capabilities. LC 93-4992. 79p. 1993. pap. 25. 95 (*1-55750-639-6*) Naval Inst Pr.
Nguyen, Hung T., et al, eds. Theoretical Aspects of Fuzzy Control. LC 94-20860. 1995. text ed. 59.95 (*0-471-02079-6*) Wiley.
Nguyen-Khac, U. & Lutz, A. M., eds. Neutral Currents Twenty Years Later: Proceedings of the International Conference. 500p. 1994. text ed. 109.00 (*981-02-1752-8*) World Scientific Pub.
Nguyen, Kim-Anh. Vietnamese Word Book. LC 93-73560. (Illus.). 144p. (ENG & VIE.). (J). (gr. k-6). 1994. 15.95 (*1-880188-70-8*); pap. 11.95 (*1-880188-51-1*) Bess Pr.
Nguyen, L. T. & Pecht, M. G., eds. Electronic Packaging Reliability. LC 93-93270. 131p. Date not set. pap. 45.00 (*0-7918-1035-6*) ASME.
Nguyen, Luu T., ed. see Pecht, Michael G.
Nguyen, Luu T., jt. auth. see Tong, Ho-Ming.
Nguyen, Mai, ed. see Luong Si Hang.
Nguyen Ngoc Huy, jt. auth. see Young, Stephen B.
Nguyen Ngoc Huy, et al, trs. Le Code: Law in Traditional Vietnam, 3 vols., Set. LC 86-8371. 1735p. 1987. text ed. 175.00 (*0-8214-0630-2*) Ohio U Pr.
Nguyen, P. Essential English-Vietnamese Dictionary. 316p. (ENG & VIE.). 1983. 24.95 (*0-8288-1702-2*, M13014) Fr & Eur.
Nguyen, Phong & Campbell, Patricia S. From Rice Paddies & Temple Yards: Traditional Music of Vietnam. LC 89-52161. (Illus.). 88p. (Orig.). 1990. pap. 10.95 (*0-937203-32-7*); audio 8.95 (*0-937203-33-5*) World Music Pr.
— From Rice Paddies & Temple Yards: Traditional Music of Vietnam, Set. LC 89-52161. (Illus.). 88p. (Orig.). 1990. audio 14.95 (*0-937203-34-3*) World Music Pr.
Nguyen, Q. S., ed. Bifurcation & Stability of Dissipative Systems. (CISM International Centre for Mechanical Sciences Ser.: Vol. 327). (Illus.). v, 291p. 1993. pap. 65. 00 (*0-387-82437-5*) Spr-Verlag.
Nguyen, Q. S., jt. ed. see Bui, H. D.
Nguyen, Qui Duc. Where the Ashes Are: The Odyssey of a Vietnamese Family. LC 93-25869. 1994. 21.95 (*0-201-63202-0*) Addison-Wesley.
Nguyen, Quoc Khanh. Norsk - Vietnamesisk Ordbok. 501p. (NOR & VIE.). lib. bdg. 225.00 (*0-7859-3668-8*, 8200067572) Fr & Eur.
***Nguyen, T. D., et al, eds.** Structure & Properties of Multilayered Thin Films. (Symposium Proceedings Ser.: Vol. 382). 1995. text ed. 85.00 (*1-55899-285-5*) Materials Res.
***Nguyen, Than C.** Yellow Leaves: Children of the Rolling Thunder. 76p. (Orig.). 1994. 10.00 (*0-9631569-2-6*) Backyard Pr.
Nguyen, Thanh T., tr. see Weigl, Bruce, ed.
Nguyen The, H., jt. ed. see Pescia, G.
Nguyen Thi Thu-Lam. Fallen Leaves: Memoirs of a Vietnamese Woman from 1940-1975. LC 89-60488. (Lac-Viet Ser.: No. 11). vii, 224p. 1989. pap. 15.00 (*0-938692-39-9*) Yale U SE Asia.
Nguyen, Thu T. Dinh Duong Tri Lieu: Nutrition Therapy. LC 92-62316. (Illus.). 928p. 1993. 89.00 (*0-9635459-0-6*) T T Nguyen.
Nguyen, Thuyen. Advanced Programmer's Guide to Presentation Manager. 1990. pap. 29.95 (*0-13-004383-4*) P-H.
Nguyen, Tim & Little, Joseph R. Applied Excel: Creating Spreadsheets Systems for Others. 420p. 1989. pap. 22.95 (*0-13-039652-4*) P-H.
Nguyen, Tri Q. Third-World Development: Aspects of Political Legitimacy & Viability. LC 87-45959. (Illus.). 224p. 1989. 35.00 (*0-8386-3327-7*) Fairleigh Dickinson.
Nguyen Trieu Dan. A Vietnamese Family Chronicle: Twelve Generations on the Banks of the Hat River. LC 90-53513. (Illus.). 400p. 1991. lib. bdg. 32.50x (*0-89950-592-9*) McFarland & Co.
Nguyen, Truong, jt. auth. see Strang, Gilbert.
***Nguyen, Tuyet-Nga.** Fragrance of Flowers from the Old Garden. 1995. pap. 8.95 (*0-533-11362-8*) Vantage.
Nguyen, Van C. Vietnam under Communism, 1975-1982. LC 83-10754. (Illus.). xvi, 312p. 1983. pap. 9.95 (*0-8179-7852-6*) Hoover Inst Pr.
Nguyen Van Chuc. Viet Nam Chinh Su. 630p. 1992. 20.00 (*0-9635574-0-8*) Alpha Bks VA.
Nguyen Van Duong. Medicinal Plants of Vietnam, Cambodia & Laos. LC 93-92625. 528p. (Orig.). (C). 1993. pap. 49. 00 (*0-9637303-1-2*) N Van Duong.
***Nguyen-Van-Huy, Pierre.** Le Devenir et la Conscience Cosmique Chez Saint-Exupery. LC 94-38773. 188p. (FRE.). 1995. text ed. 79.95 (*0-7734-2912-3*) E Mellen.
Nguyen, Van-Khan. Viet-Anh, Anh-Viet Tu-Din Thong-Dun. 1723p. 1986. 125.00 (*0-317-59304-8*, Pub. by Collets UK) Pro-Am Music.
Nguyen Van Nghi. Acupuncture Energetics: Classification & Treatment of Disease in Traditional Chinese Medicine. Seem, Mark D., tr. (Illus.). 1000p. (Orig.). 1983. 75.00 (*0-910263-00-0*) Raiko.
Nguyen, Van T. Geothermal Energy: Resource & Utilization. 52p. 1984. pap. 10.00 (*0-318-41414-7*, IO-5) Am Assn Physics.
Nguyen, Van T., jt. ed. see Ehrlich, Daniel J.
Nguyen-vo, Thu-huong. Khmer-Viet Relations & the Third Indochina Conflict. LC 91-47179. 238p. 1992. lib. bdg. 32.50x (*0-89950-717-4*) McFarland & Co.
Nguyen, Xuan-Mai, tr. see Luong Si Hang.
***Nguyen Xuan Thu.** Vietnamese Phrasebook. 2nd ed. (Illus.). 160p. 1995. pap. 5.95 (*0-86442-347-0*) Lonely Planet.
***Ngwainmbi, Emmanuel K.** Communication Efficiency & Rural Development in Africa: The Case of Cameroon. (Illus.). 196p. (Orig.). (C). 1994. lib. bdg. 46.50 (*0-8191-9734-3*); pap. text ed. 27.50 (*0-8191-9735-1*) U Pr of Amer.
Ng'Weno, Fleur. Kenya. (Focus On Ser.). (Illus.). 32p. (YA). (gr. 7-10). 1992. 17.95 (*0-237-60194-X*, Pub. by Evans Bros Ltd UK) Trafalgar.
Nha, I. S., jt. ed. see Leung, K. C.
Nhan, Phan-Thein & Kim, Sangtae. Microstructures in Elastic Media: Principles & Computational Methods. (Illus.). 272p. 1994. 65.00 (*0-19-509086-1*) OUP.
Nhat Hanh, Thich. Being Peace. LC 87-2340. (Illus.). 115p. (Orig.). 1987. pap. 10.00 (*0-938077-00-7*) Parallax Pr.
— Breathe! You Are Alive: Sutra on the Full Awareness of Breathing. 2nd ed. Laity, Annabel, tr. LC 90-48425. 68p. 1990. pap. 6.00 (*0-938077-38-4*) Parallax Pr.
— The Heart of Understanding: Commentaries on the Prajnaparamita Heart Sutra. Levitt, Peter, ed. & intro. by. LC 88-15184. 54p. (Orig.). 1988. pap. 7.00 (*0-938077-11-2*) Parallax Pr.
— The Miracle of Mindfulness: A Manual on Meditation. Ho, Mobi, tr. LC 87-42852. (Illus.). 160p. (C). 1992. pap. 10.00 (*0-8070-1201-7*, BP 776) Beacon Pr.
— Old Path White Clouds: Walking in the Footsteps of the Buddha. LC 90-21483. (Illus.). 598p. 1990. 40.00 (*0-938077-40-6*); per., pap. 25.00 (*0-938077-26-0*) Parallax Pr.
— A Rose for Your Pocket. Sand, Elin, tr. 14p. (Orig.). 1987. pap. 3.50 (*0-938077-08-2*) Parallax Pr.
— The Sun My Heart: From Mindfulness to Insight Contemplation. Sand, Elin et al, trs. LC 88-17908. 139p. (Orig.). 1988. pap. 10.00 (*0-938077-12-0*) Parallax Pr.
— The Sutra on the Eight Realizations of the Great Beings. Truong, Diem T. & Melkonian, Carole, trs. 22p. 1987. pap. 3.00 (*0-938077-07-4*) Parallax Pr.
— Transformation & Healing: Sutra on the Four Establishments of Mindfulness. LC 90-49512. 180p. 1990. per. 12.00 (*0-938077-34-1*) Parallax Pr.
NHC Staff & Rhinehart. Studies in the History of a People, Vol. I. 304p. (C). 1993. per. 19.95 (*0-8403-8637-0*) Kendall-Hunt.
— Studies in the History of a People, Vol. II. 256p. (C). 1993. per. 19.95 (*0-8403-8638-9*) Kendall-Hunt.
NHK Overseas Broadcasting Department Staff & Mizutani, Nobuko. NHK's Let's Learn Japanese, Bk. II: A Practical Conversation Guide. Maeda, ed. (Illus.). 176p. 1993. pap. 15.00 (*4-7700-1784-7*); audio 40.00 (*4-7700-1785-5*) Kodansha.
— NHK's Let's Learn Japanese, Bk. III: A Practical Conversation Guide. Maeda, ed. (Illus.). 176p. 1993. pap. 15.00 (*4-7700-1786-3*); audio 40.00 (*4-7700-1787-1*) Kodansha.
— NHK's Let's Learn Japanese, Bk. IV: A Practical Conversation Guide. Maeda, ed. (Illus.). 176p. 1994. pap. 15.00 (*4-7700-1788-X*); audio 40.00 (*4-7700-1789-8*) Kodansha.
NHK Science & Technical Research Laboratories Staff. High Definition Television: Hi-Vision Technology. LC 92-17071. 1993. text ed. 64.95 (*0-442-00798-1*) Van Nos Reinhold.
Nhuong. Land I Lost. (J). 1982. 12.95 (*0-06-024592-1*); lib. bdg. 12.89 (*0-06-024593-X*) HarpC Child Bks.
Nhuong, Nuynh Quang. The Land I Lost: Adventures of a Boy in Vietnam. LC 80-8437. (Illus.). 128p. (J). (gr. 4-7). 1990. lib. bdg. 14.89 (*0-397-32448-0*, Lipp Jr Bks) HarpC Child Bks.
Ni Chuilleanain, Eilean, ed. see Edgeworth, Maria.
Ni, Daoshing. Crane-Style Chi Gong & Its Therapeutic Effects. (Illus.). 68p. (Orig.). 1984. pap. 10.95 (*0-937064-10-6*) SevenStar Comm.
Ni Dhinbhne, Eilis. Eating Women Is Not Recommended. 192p. (Orig.). (C). 1991. pap. 13.99 (*1-85594-029-9*, Pub. by Attic IE) InBook.
Ni Dhomhnaill, Nuala. Selected Poems - Rogha Danta. Hartnett, Michael, tr. & intro. by. LC 88-51546. 159p. (Orig.). (ENG & IRI.). 1988. pap. 14.95 (*1-85186-027-4*) Dufour.
***Ni Dhuibhne, Eilis.** The Bray House. 256p. (Orig.). 1990. pap. 11.95 (*0-614-05161-4*, Pub. by Attic IE) InBook.
— The Bray House. (Orig.). (C). 1989. 39.00 (*0-946211-96-5*, Pub. by Attic Pr IE) St Mut.
Ni Eidhin, Deirdre, tr. see Godon, B. & Boudreau, Armand, eds.
Ni, Hu-Ching. Gate to Infinity: Realizing Your Ultimate Potential. LC 93-13692. 1994. Alk. paper. 13.95 (*0-937064-68-8*) SevenStar Comm.
Ni, Hua-Ching. Ageless Counsel for Modern Life: Profound Commentaries on the I Ching by an Achieved Taoist Master. LC 91-53212. 256p. (Orig.). 1992. pap. 15.95 (*0-937064-50-5*) SevenStar Comm.
— Ascend the Spiritual Mountain. LC 92-37044. (Spiritual Expedition Ser.: Bk. 2). Orig. Title: Uncharted Voyage. 1994. pap. write for info. (*0-937064-58-0*) SevenStar Comm.
— Attaining Unlimited Life: Teachings of Chuang Tzu. LC 88-63990. 467p. (Orig.). 1989. 25.00 (*0-937064-23-8*); pap. 18.00 (*0-937064-18-1*) SevenStar Comm.
— Attune Your Body with Dao-In. LC 90-62781. (Master's Series of Taoist Internal Arts). 1992. pap. 14.95 (*0-937064-40-8*) SevenStar Comm.
— Awaken to the Great Path. (Spiritual Expedition Ser.: Bk. 1). 1994. pap. write for info. (*0-937064-57-2*) SevenStar Comm.
— Book of Changes & the Unchanging Truth. rev. ed. LC 89-64438. (Illus.). 696p. 1990. reprint ed. 35.00 (*0-937064-29-7*) SevenStar Comm.
— Book of Changes & the Unchanging Truth. rev. ed. LC 95-149. (Illus.). 704p. 1995. reprint ed. 35.00 (*0-937064-81-5*) SevenStar Comm.
— The Complete Works of Lao Tzu: Tao Teh Ching & Hua Hu Ching. LC 79-88745. 212p. 1979. reprint ed. pap. 12. 95 (*0-937064-00-9*) SevenStar Comm.
— Cosmic Tour Ba Gua. (Master's Series of Taoist Internal Arts). 1994. pap. write for info. (*0-937064-43-2*) SevenStar Comm.
Ni Hua Ching. Eight Thousand Years of Wisdom: Conversations with Taoist Master Ni, Hua Ching, Bk. 1. LC 83-51082. 248p. (Orig.). (C). 1983. pap. text ed. 12. 50 (*0-937064-07-6*) SevenStar Comm.
— Eight Thousand Years of Wisdom: Conversations with Taoist Master Ni, Hua Ching, Bk. 2. LC 83-51082. 248p. (Orig.). 1983. pap. text ed. 12.50 (*0-937064-08-4*) SevenStar Comm.

N

An Asterisk (*) at the beginning of an entry indicates that the title is appearing in BIP for the first time.

Ni, Hua-Ching. Enlightenment: Mother of Spiritual Independence: Teachings of Hui Neng. LC 88-63988. 264p. (Orig.). 1989. 22.00 (*0-937064-22-X*); pap. 12.50 (*0-937064-19-X*) SevenStar Comm.

— The Esoteric Tao Teh Ching. 192p. (Orig.). 1993. pap. 12.95 (*0-937064-49-1*) SevenStar Comm.

— Essence of Universal Spirituality. LC 90-60962. 282p. (Orig.). 1990. pap. 19.95 (*0-937064-35-1*) SevenStar Comm.

— Eternal Light. LC 90-62782. (Esoteric Teachings of the Tradition of Tao Ser.: Bk. 3). 208p. (Orig.). 1991. pap. 14.95 (*0-937064-38-6*) SevenStar Comm.

— The Gentle Path of Spiritual Progress. rev. ed. LC 90-61066. 288p. 1990. pap. 12.95 (*0-937064-33-5*) SevenStar Comm.

— Gentle Path T'ai Chi Chuan. (Master's Series of Taoist Internal Arts). 1994. pap. write for info. (*0-937064-28-9*) SevenStar Comm.

Ni Hua Ching. Guide to Inner Light. LC 90-60825. 168p. 1990. pap. text ed. 12.95 (*0-937064-30-0*) SevenStar Comm.

***Ni, Hua-Ching.** Guide to Your Total Well-Being. (Self Development Ser.). (Orig.). 1994. pap. 4.00 (*0-937064-78-5*) SevenStar Comm.

— Immortal Wisdom. LC 92-50542. (Orig.). 1994. pap. write for info. (*0-937064-53-X*) SevenStar Comm.

— Infinite Expansion T'ai Chi Chuan. (Master's Series of Taoist Internal Arts). 1994. pap. write for info. (*0-937064-42-4*) SevenStar Comm.

— Integal Nutrition. (Healthy Living Ser.). 32p. (Orig.). 1995. pap. 3.00 (*0-937064-84-X*) SevenStar Comm.

— Internal Growth Through Tao. LC 90-60824. 208p. (Orig.). 1991. pap. 13.95 (*0-937064-27-0*) SevenStar Comm.

— The Key to Good Fortune: Refining Your Spirit. 144p. (Orig.). 1991. pap. 12.95 (*0-937064-39-4*) SevenStar Comm.

— Less Stress, More Happiness. (Healthy Living Ser.). 32p. (Orig.). 1994. pap. 3.00 (*0-937064-55-6*) SevenStar Comm.

— The Light of All Stars Illuminates the Way. (Self-Development Ser.). 56p. (Orig.). 1994. pap. 4.00 (*0-937064-80-7*) SevenStar Comm.

— The Majestic Domain of the Heart. LC 93-2539. 1993. write for info. (*0-937064-69-6*) SevenStar Comm.

— The Mystical Universal Mother: The Teachings of Mother of Yellow Altar. LC 90-60709. 210p. (Orig.). 1992. pap. 14.95 (*0-937064-45-9*) SevenStar Comm.

— Nurture Your Spirits. LC 90-60827. 176p. 1991. pap. 12.95 (*0-937064-32-7*) SevenStar Comm.

— The Power of Natural Healing. LC 90-60823. 232p. (Orig.). 1991. pap. 14.95 (*0-937064-31-9*) SevenStar Comm.

— Progress along the Way: Life, Service & Realization. (Self Development Ser.). (Orig.). 1994. pap. 4.00 (*0-937064-79-3*) SevenStar Comm.

— Quest of Soul. LC 89-64093. (Esoteric Teachings of the Tradition of Tao Ser.: Bk. 2). 152p. (Orig.). 1991. pap. 11.95 (*0-937064-26-2*) SevenStar Comm.

— Self-Reliance & Constructive Change. LC 95-10463. (Course for Total Health Ser.). 64p. (Orig.). 1995. pap. 7.00 (*0-614-07230-1*) SevenStar Comm.

— Self-Reliance & Constructive Change: The Declaration of Spiritual Independence. LC 95-10463. 1995. pap. write for info. (*0-937064-85-8*) SevenStar Comm.

— Sky Journey T'ai Chi Chuan. (Master's Series of Taoist Internal Arts). 1994. pap. write for info. (*0-937064-41-6*) SevenStar Comm.

— Spiritual Messages of a Buffalo Rider, a Man of Tao. rev. ed. LC 90-60963. 240p. 1990. pap. 12.95 (*0-937064-34-3*) SevenStar Comm.

— Stepping Stones for Spiritual Success. LC 89-64020. 160p. (Orig.). 1990. pap. 12.95 (*0-937064-25-4*) SevenStar Comm.

— The Story of Two Kingdoms. LC 88-93051. (Esoteric Teachings of the Tradition of Tao Ser.: Bk. 1). 122p. 1989. 14.00 (*0-937064-24-6*) SevenStar Comm.

— Strength from Movement: Mastering Chi. LC 93-40503. (Illus.). 256p. (Orig.). 1994. pap. 16.95 (*0-937064-73-4*) SevenStar Comm.

— Tao: The Subtle Universal Law & the Integral Way of Life. LC 79-91720. (Illus.). 166p. (Orig.). 1979. pap. text ed. 7.50 (*0-937064-01-7*) SevenStar Comm.

— Tao Teh Ching. Sanchez-Piltz, Mark & Barrero, Olga V., trs. 112p. (Orig.). (SPA.). 1995. pap. 8.95 (*0-937064-92-0*) SevenStar Comm.

— The Taoist Inner View of the Universe & the Immortal Realm. LC 79-92389. (Illus.). 218p. (Orig.). 1979. pap. text ed. 14.95 (*0-937064-02-5*) SevenStar Comm.

— The Time Is Now for a Better Life & a Better World. LC 92-50854. 136p. (Orig.). 1993. pap. 10.95 (*0-937064-63-7*, Shrine Eternal) SevenStar Comm.

Ni, Hua Ching. The Uncharted Voyage Toward the Subtle Light. 423p. 1985. pap. text ed. 14.50 (*0-937064-09-2*) SevenStar Comm.

Ni, Hua-Ching. The Way of Integral Life. LC 88-63991. 408p. (Orig.). 1989. 20.00 (*0-937064-21-1*); pap. 14.00 (*0-937064-20-3*) SevenStar Comm.

— The Way, the Truth, & the Light. LC 92-50543. 232p. (Orig.). 1994. pap. 14.95 (*0-937064-56-4*) SevenStar Comm.

— Workbook for Spiritual Development of All People. rev. ed. LC 92-13036. 240p. 1992. pap. 14.95 (*0-937064-54-8*) SevenStar Comm.

***Ni, Hua-Ching, tr.** Hua Hu Ching: The Later Teachings of Lao Tzu. LC 94-36153. 1995. pap. 10.00 (*1-57062-079-2*) Shambhala Pubns.

Ni, Hua-Chung. Heavenly Way. LC 81-50158. (Illus.). 41p. (Orig.). 1981. pap. text ed. 2.50 (*0-937064-03-3*) SevenStar Comm.

***Ni, Lionel M., ed.** Parallel & Distributed Systems: Proceedings of the International Conference, Taiwan, Republic of China, 1994. LC 94-77037. 800p. 1994. pap. text ed. 160.00 (*0-8186-6555-6*, PR06555) IEEE Comp Soc.

***Ni, Maohing.** The Eight Treasures. LC 94-30068. 1994. 14.95 (*0-937064-74-2*) SevenStar Comm.

Ni, Maoshing. Applied Chinese Nutritional Analysis. (Orig.). 1994. write for info. (*0-937064-17-3*) SevenStar Comm.

— The Yellow Emperor's Classic of Medicine: A New Translation of the Neijing Suwen with Commentary. (Orig.). 1995. pap. 16.00 (*1-57062-080-6*) Shambhala Pubns.

Ni, Maoshing & McNease, Cathy. The Tao of Nutrition. rev. ed. LC 93-7783. 264p. 1993. pap. 14.95 (*0-937064-66-1*) SevenStar Comm.

Ni Suilleabhain, Eibhlis. Letters from the Great Blasket. 87p. 1988. pap. 8.95 (*0-85342-848-4*, Pub. by Mercier Pr IE) Dufour.

Ni, W. M., et al, eds. Nonlinear Diffusion Equations & Their Equilibrium States One. (Mathematical Sciences Research Institute Publications: Vol. 12). (Illus.). 350p. 1988. 43.00 (*0-387-96771-0*) Spr-Verlag.

— Nonlinear Diffusion Equations & Their Equilibrium States Two. (Mathematical Sciences Research Institute Publications: Vol. 13). (Illus.). 350p. 1988. 43.00 (*0-387-96772-9*) Spr-Verlag.

Ni, Wei-ming, et al, eds. Degenerate Diffusions: Proceedings of the IMA Workshop "Degenerate Diffusions" Held at the University of Minnesota from May 13-18, 1991. LC 93-10431. (IMA Volumes in Mathematics & Its Applications Ser.: Vol. 47). 1993. Acid-free paper. 49.00 (*0-387-94068-5*) Spr-Verlag.

Ni, Wei-Tou. Precision Measurement & Gravity Experiment: Proceedings & Symposium of the International School. 1988. 109.00 (*0-317-03850-8*) World Scientific Pub.

NIAE Staff. Architectural Education & the Built Future: Faculty Essay Competition, 1992. 80p. 1992. pap. text ed. 12.00 (*0-8403-8169-7*) Kendall-Hunt.

Niaki, Shahzad & Broscious, John A. Underground Tank Leak Detection Methods. LC 86-31159. (Pollution Technology Review Ser.: No. 139). (Illus.). 123p. 1987. 36.00 (*0-8155-1117-5*) Noyes.

— Underground Tank Leak Detection Methods: A State-of-the-Art Review. 136p. 1988. 47.00 (*0-89116-098-1*) Hemisp Pub.

***Niall, Brenda.** Georgiana: A Biography of Georgiana McCrae, Painter, Diarist, Pioneer. 368p. Date not set. 39.95 (*0-522-84513-4*) Intl Spec Bk.

— Martin Boyd: A Life. 1988. 39.95 (*0-522-84268-2*) Intl Spec Bk.

— Martin Boyd, a Life. (Illus.). 268p. 1990. reprint ed. pap. 19.95 (*0-522-84400-6*) Intl Spec Bk.

Niall, Ian. English Country Traditions. 75p. 1991. 30.00 (*0-87923-870-4*) Godine.

Niall, Michael. Bad Day at Black Rock. 16.95 (*0-8488-0107-5*, Amereon Hse) Amereon Ltd.

Nials, Fred, et al. Chacoan Roads in the Southern Periphery: Results of Phase II of the BLM Chaco Roads Project. No. 1. (Illus.). 214p. (Orig.). 1987. pap. write for info. (*0-318-68062-9*) Bureau of Land Mgmt NM.

Nials, Fred L., jt. auth. see Livingston, Stephanie D.

Nias, A. H. Clinical Radiobiology. 2nd ed. (Illus.). 304p. 1989. text ed. 59.00 (*0-443-03340-4*) Churchill.

Nias, A. H. & Dimbleby, Richard. An Introduction to Radiobiology. 360p. 1990. text ed. 52.95 (*0-471-92756-2*) Wiley.

Nias, Jennifer. Primary Teachers Talking: A Study of Teaching As Work. 208p. 1989. pap. 18.95 (*0-415-01115-9*, A3678) Routledge.

— Seeing a New: Teachers Theories of Action. (C). 1987. 41.00 (*0-7300-0448-1*, Pub. by Deakin Univ AT) St Mut.

Nias, Jennifer, ed. The Human Nature of Learning: Selections from the Work of M. L. J. Abercrombie. LC 93-13277. 160p. 1993. 79.00 (*0-335-09334-5*, Open Univ Pr); pap. 29.50 (*0-335-09333-7*, Open Univ Pr) Taylor & Francis.

— Teacher Socialisation: The Individual in the System. 151p. (C). 1986. 51.00 (*0-7300-0399-X*, Pub. by Deakin Univ AT) St Mut.

Nias, Jennifer & Groundwater-Smith, Susan, eds. The Enquiring Teacher. 200p. 1988. 65.00 (*1-85000-295-9*, Falmer Pr); pap. 33.00 (*1-85000-296-7*, Falmer Pr) Taylor & Francis.

Nias, Jennifer & Southworth, Geoff. Whole School Curriculum: Development in the Primary School. 270p. 1992. 80.00 (*0-7507-0064-5*, Falmer Pr); pap. 29.00 (*0-7507-0065-3*, Falmer Pr) Taylor & Francis.

Nias, Jennifer, jt. ed. see Biott, Colin.

Niatum, Duane. Drawings of the Song Animals. 1991. pap. 10.95 (*0-930100-44-1*) Holy Cow.

— Pieces. (Illus.). 20p. (Orig.). 1981. pap. 2.50 (*0-936574-07-0*) Strawberry Pr NY.

Niatum, Duane, ed. Harper's Anthology of Twentieth Century Native American Poetry. LC 86-45023. 352p. (Orig.). 1988. pap. 18.00 (*0-06-250666-8*) Harper SF.

Niazi, Kausar. Iqbal & the Third World. 40p. (Orig.). 1988. pap. 3.00 (*1-56744-298-6*) Kazi Pubns.

— Zulfiqar Ali Bhutto of Pakistan: The Last Days. (Illus.). 244p. (C). 1992. text ed. 27.50 (*0-685-56704-4*, Pub. by Vikas II) S Asia.

Niazi, Zamir. Press in Chains. 252p. 1987. 27.50 (*81-202-0182-5*, Pub. by Ajanta II) S Asia.

— The Web of Censorship. 250p. 1995. text ed. 24.00 (*0-19-577543-0*) OUP.

***Nibb, Stephen R.** War, Diplomacy, & Development: The United States & Mexico 1938-1954. Beezley, William H. & Ewell, Judith, eds. (Latin American Silhouettes Ser.). (Illus.). 320p. 1995. 50.00 (*0-8420-2550-2*) Scholarly Res Inc.

Nibbe, H., ed. see Sharpham, Edward.

Nibbi, Alessandra. Ancient Egypt & Some Eastern Neighbours. LC 81-16863. (Illus.). 221p. 1982. 24.00 (*0-8155-5062-6*, NP) Noyes.

Nibbrig, Chris H., ed. see Chinchilla, Madame, pseud.

Nibeck, Cecilia. Alaskan Halibut Recipes. (Illus.). 200p. 1989. write for info. (*0-9622117-0-2*) AK Anchorage.

— Moose & Caribou from Alaska. 1992. pap. 10.95 (*0-9622117-3-7*) AK Anchorage.

— Salmon Recipes from Alaska. (Illus.). 190p. 1987. pap. text ed. 10.95 (*0-9622117-1-0*) AK Anchorage.

Nibeck, Richard G., intro. Learning with Microcomputers, Readings from Instructional Innovator-5. 80p. 1983. pap. 10.95 (*0-89240-042-0*) Assn Ed Comm Tech.

Niblack, W., jt. ed. see Jamberdino, A. A.

Niblett, William R. Education, the Lost Dimension. LC 73-108845. 150p. 1970. reprint ed. text ed. 49.75 (*0-8371-3735-7*, NIED, Greenwood Pr) Greenwood.

Niblett, William R., ed. Higher Education: Demand & Response. LC 71-110637. (Jossey-Bass Higher Education Ser.). 286p. reprint ed. pap. 81.60 (*0-317-08582-4*, 2013821) Bks Demand.

Nibley, Hugh. The Ancient State: The Rulers & the Ruled. LC 91-8004. (Collected Works of Hugh Nibley: Vol. 10). 515p. 1991. 21.95 (*0-87579-375-4*) Deseret Bk.

— An Approach to the Book of Mormon. 3rd ed. LC 88-3585. (Collected Works of Hugh Nibley: Vol. 6). xvii, 541p. 1988. 19.95 (*0-87579-138-7*) Deseret Bk.

— Approaching Zion. LC 89-38824. (Collected Works of Hugh Nibley: Vol. 9). 631p. 1989. 19.95 (*0-87579-252-9*) Deseret Bk.

— Brother Brigham Challenges the Saints. Norton, Don E. & Ricks, Shirley S., eds. LC 93-38393. (Collected Works of Hugh Nibley: Vol. 13). xv, 541p. 1994. 23.95 (*0-87579-818-7*) Deseret Bk.

— Enoch the Prophet. LC 86-11437. (Collected Works of Hugh Nibley: Vol. 2). viii, 309p. 1986. 15.95 (*0-87579-047-X*) Deseret Bk.

— Lehi in the Desert. Bd. with World of the Jaredites. LC 87-32941. LC 87-32941. (Collected Works of Hugh Nibley: Vol. 5). xviii, 464p. 1988. reprint ed. 16.95 (*0-87579-132-8*) Deseret Bk.

— Lehi in the Desert & the World of the Jaredites. 9.95 (*0-88494-022-5*) Bookcraft Inc.

— Mormonism & Early Christianity. LC 87-25291. (Collected Works of Hugh Nibley: Vol. 4). 446p. 1987. 23.95 (*0-87579-127-1*) Deseret Bk.

— Of All Things: Classic Quotations from Hugh Nibley. LC 93-6508. xii, 292p. 1993. pap. 12.95 (*0-87579-678-8*) Deseret Bk.

— Old Testament & Related Studies. LC 85-27544. (Collected Works of Hugh Nibley: Vol. 1). xiv, 290p. 1986. 19.95 (*0-87579-032-1*) Deseret Bk.

— The Prophetic Book of Mormon. LC 88-30986. (Collected Works of Hugh Nibley: Vol. 8). xi, 595p. 1989. 19.95 (*0-87579-179-4*) Deseret Bk.

— Since Cumorah: The Book of Mormon. LC 88-3862. (Collected Works of Hugh Nibley: Vol. 7). xv, 512p. 1988. 16.95 (*0-87579-139-5*) Deseret Bk.

— Temple & Cosmos. LC 91-33320. (Collected Works of Hugh Nibley: Vol. 12). 597p. 1992. 24.95 (*0-87579-523-4*) Deseret Bk.

— Tinkling Cymbals & Sounding Brass: The Art of Telling Tales about Joseph Smith & Brigham Young. LC 91-11539. (Collected Works of Hugh Nibley: Vol. 11). xxii, 741p. 1991. 22.95 (*0-87579-516-1*) Deseret Bk.

— The World & the Prophets: Mormonism & Early Christianity. LC 87-620. (Collected Works of Hugh Nibley: Vol. 3). xii, 333p. 1987. 17.95 (*0-87579-078-X*) Deseret Bk.

Nibley, Hugh W. Nibley on the Timely & the Timeless. (Monograph Ser.: Vol. 1). 9.95 (*0-88494-338-0*) Bookcraft Inc.

Nibley, Preston. History of Joseph Smith by His Mother, Lucy Mack Smith. 9.95 (*0-88494-033-0*) Bookcraft Inc.

Nibley, Preston, comp. Three Mormon Classics. 9.95 (*0-88494-049-7*) Bookcraft Inc.

Niblo, Graham & Roller, Martin, eds. Geometric Group Theory, Vol. 1. (London Mathematical Society Lecture Note Ser.: No. 181). (Illus.). 350p. (C). 1993. pap. 34.95 (*0-521-43529-3*) Cambridge U Pr.

— Geometric Group Theory, Vol. 2. (London Mathematical Society Lecture Note Ser.: No. 182). (Illus.). 350p. (C). 1993. pap. 34.95 (*0-521-44680-5*) Cambridge U Pr.

Niblock, Tim. Class & Power in Sudan: The Dynamics of Sudanese Politics, 1898-1985. LC 86-23059. 370p. 1987. 64.50 (*0-88706-480-9*); pap. 21.95 (*0-88706-481-7*) State U NY Pr.

Niblock, Timothy C. Arab Politics: Class, Power & International Involvement. 256p. 1990. write for info. (*0-312-01972-6*); pap. write for info. (*0-312-01973-4*) St Martin.

Niblock, Timothy C. & Murphy, Emma, eds. Economic Liberalization in the Middle East. 288p. (C). 1993. text ed. 65.00 (*1-85043-600-2*, Pub. by I B Tauris UK) St Martin.

Nic Leodhas, Sorche. Always Room for One More. LC 65-12881. (Illus.). 32p. (J). (ps-2). 1972. pap. 5.95 (*0-8050-0330-4*, Bks Young Read) H Holt & Co.

Nica, A. A Mechanics of Aerospace Materials. (Materials Science Monographs: Vol. 9). 346p. 1981. 100.00 (*0-444-99729-6*) Elsevier.

Nica, Traian, tr. see Smarandache, Florentin.

Nicaise, Auguste. A Year in the Desert. 125p. 1980. 16.95 (*0-87770-237-3*) Ye Galleon.

Nicaise, Keith. IBM System 370: Assembler Language Program. (Illus.). 400p. 1990. 36.95 (*0-8306-7380-6*, Windcrest); pap. 24.95 (*0-8306-3380-4*, Windcrest) TAB Bks.

Nicaise, Keith H. IBM System 370 Assembly Language Programming. 1990. pap. 24.95 (*0-07-156234-6*) McGraw.

Nicander. The Poems & Poetical Fragments. Connor, W. R., ed. LC 78-18579. (Greek Texts & Commentaries Ser.). (Illus.). 1979. reprint ed. lib. bdg. 23.95 (*0-405-11422-2*) Ayer.

Nicandri, David. The Italians of Washington State. LC 77-81592. (Illus.). 71p. 1978. pap. 6.00 (*0-917048-08-3*) Wash St Hist Soc.

Nicandrus. Nicandri Colophonii Carminum. Bernabe, A., ed. Bd. XCI. Date not set. write for info. (*0-318-70986-4*, Pub. by Georg Olms GW) Lubrecht & Cramer.

NiCarthy, Ginny. Getting Free: You Can End Abuse & Take Back Your Life. 2nd enl. ed. LC 86-3774. (New Leaf Ser.). 352p. (Orig.). 1986. pap. 12.95 (*0-931188-37-7*) Seal Pr Feminist.

— The Ones Who Got Away: Women Who Left Abusive Partners. LC 87-20470. (New Leaf Ser.). 329p. (Orig.). 1987. pap. 12.95 (*0-931188-49-0*) Seal Pr Feminist.

NiCarthy, Ginny & Davidson, Sue. You Can Be Free: An Easy-to-Read Handbook for Abused Women. LC 88-36245. (New Leaf Ser.). 120p. (Orig.). 1989. pap. 8.95 (*0-931188-68-7*) Seal Pr Feminist.

NiCarthy, Ginny, et al. Talking It Out: A Guide to Groups for Abused Women. LC 84-23494. (New Leaf Ser.). 165p. (Orig.). 1984. pap. 12.95 (*0-931188-24-5*) Seal Pr Feminist.

— You Don't Have to Take It! A Woman's Guide to Confronting Emotional Abuse at Work. LC 93-12873. (New Leaf Ser.). 397p. (Orig.). 1993. pap. 14.95 (*1-878067-35-4*) Seal Pr Feminist.

Nicas, A. & Shadwick, W. F., eds. Differential Geometry, Global Analysis, & Topology. LC 92-5152. (Conference Proceedings, Canadian Mathematical Society Ser.: Vol. 12). 185p. 1992. 50.00 (*0-8218-6017-8*, CMSAMS/12C) Am Math.

Nicas, Andrew J. Induction Theorems for Groups of Homotopy Manifold Structures. LC 82-11546. (Memoirs of the American Mathematical Society Ser.: No. 39/267). 108p. 1982. pap. 16.00 (*0-8218-2267-5*, MEMO 39/267) Am Math.

***Nicassio, Perry M. & Smith, Timothy W., eds.** Managing Chronic Illness: A Biopsychosocial Perspective. (Application & Practice in Health Psychology Ser.). 440p. 1995. text ed. 49.95 (*1-55798-300-3*) Am Psychol.

Nicastro, Anthony J. Laboratory Astronomy: Experiments & Exercises. 208p. (C). 1989. spiral bd. write for info. (*0-697-08475-2*) Wm C Brown Pubs.

Niccolai, Giulia. Substitution: Bilingual Edition. Vangelisti, Paul, tr. 1975. per. 2.50 (*0-88031-020-0*) Invisible-Red Hill.

Niccolai, Guilia, tr. see Spatola, Adriano.

Niccoli, Gabriel. Cupid, Satyr & the Golden Age: Pastoral Dramatic Scences of the Late Renaissance. 249p. (C). 1989. text ed. 36.95 (*0-8204-0783-6*) P Lang Pubs.

Niccoli, Ottavia. Prophecy & People in Renaissance Italy. Cochrane, Lydia G., tr. (Illus.). 214p. (C). 1990. text ed. 55.00 (*0-691-05568-8*); pap. text ed. 14.95 (*0-691-00835-3*) Princeton U Pr.

Niccoli, Ria. Pembroke Welsch Corgis. 1989. 11.95 (*0-86622-513-7*, KW176) TFH Pubns.

Niccols, Richard. Beggars Ape. LC 37-5555. 1980. reprint ed. 50.00 (*0-8201-1178-3*) Schol Facsimiles.

— Expicedium. a Funeral Oration, Upon the Late Deceased Princesse, Elizabeth, Queen of England. LC 71-26332. (English Experience Ser.: No. 172). 24p. 1969. reprint ed. 25.00 (*90-221-0172-X*) Walter J Johnson.

— Sir Thomas Overbury's Vision (1616) & Other English Sources of Nathaniel Hawthorne's "The Scarlet Letter." LC 57-6417. 1979. 50.00 (*0-8201-1239-9*) Schol Facsimiles.

Nice, Claudia. Barnyards & Billygoats. 44p. 1982. pap. 6.50 (*1-56770-134-5*) S Scheewe Pubns.

— Creating Textures in Pen & Ink with Watercolor. LC 95-12916. (Illus.). 144p. 1995. 27.99 (*0-89134-595-7*) North Light Bks.

— Creative Quill. 44p. 1981. pap. 6.50 (*1-56770-133-7*) S Scheewe Pubns.

— Journey of Memories. 44p. 1986. pap. 6.50 (*1-56770-166-3*) S Scheewe Pubns.

— Pen & Brush Animals. 44p. 1986. pap. 6.50 (*1-56770-137-X*) S Scheewe Pubns.

— Scenes from Seasons Past. 96p. 1988. pap. 7.50 (*1-56770-183-3*) S Scheewe Pubns.

— Sketching Your Favorite Subjects in Pen & Ink. (Illus.). 144p. 1993. 22.95 (*0-89134-472-1*, 30473) North Light Bks.

— A Taste of Summer. 96p. 1990. pap. 7.50 (*1-56770-223-6*) S Scheewe Pubns.

— Wings & Wildflowers. 44p. 1983. pap. 6.50 (*1-56770-135-3*) S Scheewe Pubns.

Nice, David. Richard Strauss. (Illustrated Lives of the Great Composers Ser.). (Illus.). 144p. pap. 14.95 (*0-7119-1685-3*, OP45020) Omnibus NY.

— Tchaikovsky. LC 95-3359. (Compact Companions Ser.). 1995. 17.50 (*0-684-81357-2*) S&S Trade.

Nice, David C. Federalism: The Politics of Intergovernmental Relations. LC 86-60643. 256p. (C). 1986. pap. text ed. 14.00 (*0-312-28549-3*) St Martin.

— Policy Innovation in State Government. LC 93-24017. 200p. (C). 1994. text ed. 29.95 (*0-8138-0658-5*) Iowa St U Pr.

Nice, David C. & Fredericksen, Patricia. The Politics of Intergovernmental Relations. LC 94-15923. 1995. pap. text ed. 21.95 (*0-8304-1357-X*) Nelson-Hall.

Nice, David C., et al, eds. Government & Politics in the Evergreen State. LC 92-8476. (Illus.). 215p. (C). 1992. 18.95 (*0-87422-085-8*) Wash St U Pr.

An Asterisk (*) at the beginning of an entry indicates that the title is appearing in BIP for the first time.

Nice, James W. Putman's Digital Electronics: Lac Manual. (Illus.). 144p. 1986. pap. text ed. 25.00 (*0-13-212549-8*) P-H.
Nice, M. M. The Watcher at the Nest. (Illus.). 11.25 (*0-8446-2656-2*) Peter Smith.
Nice, Richard, tr. see Biardeau, Madeleine.
Nice, Richard, tr. see Bourdieu, Pierre.
Nice, Stephen D., jt. auth. see Hunter, Edna J.
Nice, Vivien E. Mothers & Daughters: A Distortion of a Relationship. 1996. 35.00 (*0-333-52528-0*, Pub. by Macm UK) St Martin.
— Mothers & Daughters: The Distortion of a Relationship. 1992. text ed. 39.95 (*0-312-06764-X*) St Martin.
Niceforo, Alfredo. Kultur und Fortschritt im Spiegel der Zahlen: Culture & Progress in the Mirror of Figures. Schumann, Eva, tr. LC 74-25772. 227p. 1975. reprint ed. 20.95 (*0-405-06526-4*) Ayer.
Nicely, Robert F., Jr., jt. ed. see Blume, Glendon W.
Nicely, Tom. Adam & His Work: A Bibliography of Sources by & about Paul Goodman (Nineteen Eleven to Nineteen Seventy-Two) LC 79-11662. (Author Bibliographies Ser.: No. 42). 362p. 1979. 32.50 (*0-8108-1219-3*) Scarecrow.
Nicephorus. Nicephori Archiepiscopi Constantinopolitani Opuscula Historica. De Boor, Carl G., ed. LC 75-7311. (Roman History Ser.). (GRE.). 1975. reprint ed. 28.95 (*0-405-07193-0*) Ayer.
***Nicetas.** Niceta of Remesiana: Sulpicius Severus, Vincent of Lerins, Prosper of Aquitaine: Grace & Free Will. Walsh, Gerald G. et al, trs. LC 50-5703. (Fathers of the Church Ser.: Vol. 7). 449p. Date not set. reprint ed. pap. 128.00 (*0-7837-9204-2*, 2049954) Bks Demand.
Nicewander, Dan L. Consumer Credit Regulations. 2nd ed. (Business Practice Library). 380p. 1991. 135.00 (*0-471-55305-0*) Wiley.
— Consumer Credit Regulations. 2nd suppl. ed. (Business Practice Library). 168p. 1992. 55.00 (*0-471-57729-4*) Wiley.
— Consumer Credit Regulations: 1991 Supplement. 2nd ed. 80p. 1991. ring bd. 45.00 (*0-471-55806-0*) Wiley.
Nicewander, Dan L., ed. see State Bar of Texas Legal Forms Committee.
***Nicewander, Merritt.** Clean Air Act Permitting: A Guidance Manual. LC 95-3028. 1995. write for info. (*0-87814-441-2*) PennWell Bks.
Nicgorski, Walter & Weber, Ronald, eds. An Almost Chosen People: The Moral Aspirations of Americans. LC 76-41343. 170p. reprint ed. pap. 48.50 (*0-8357-5325-5*, 2022062) Bks Demand.
Nicgorski, Walter, jt. ed. see Deutsch, Kenneth L.
Nichelason, Margery G. Homeless or Helpless? LC 92-19675. (Pro - Con Ser.). (Illus.). 112p. (YA). (gr. 6 up). 1993. lib. bdg. 17.50 (*0-8225-2606-9*, Lerner Publctns) Lerner Group.
Nichelatti, M. Topics on Diffusion in Emulsions. 152p. 1995. text ed. 48.00 (*981-02-1789-7*) World Scientific Pub.
Nichels, J. Two for the Road. 1988. 39.00 (*0-317-43671-6*, Pub. by Regency Press) St Mut.
Nichelsburg, George W. Jewish Literature Between the Bible & Mishnah. LC 80-16176. 332p. (Orig.). 1981. pap. 20.00 (*0-8006-1980-3*, 1-1980, Fortress Pr) Augsburg Fortress.
Nichelson, Oliver. Tesla's Fuelless Generator & Wireless Method. v, 48p. (Orig.). 1993. pap. 9.00 (*0-9636012-0-2*) Twty Frst Cent.
***NICHHD Workshop on the Testis Staff.** Testicular Development, Structure, & Function. fac. ed. Steinberger, Anna & Steinberger, Emil, eds. LC 78-68530. (Illus.). 556p. Date not set. pap. 158.50 (*0-7837-7249-1*, 2047056) Bks Demand.
Nichil, P. Lexique Francais-Anglais et Anglais-Francais des Termes d'usage Courant En Hydraulique et Pneumatique. 42p. (ENG & FRE.). 1974. pap. 8.95 (*0-686-56790-0*, M-6426) Fr & Eur.
Nichils, James L. General Fitzhugh Lee: A Biography. (Virginia Civil War Battles & Leaders Ser.). (Illus.). 244p. 1989. 19.95 (*0-930919-78-5*) H E Howard.
Nichiporovich, A. A., ed. Photosynthesis of Protective Systems. 192p. 1967. text ed. 51.50 (*0-7065-0589-1*, Pub. by Keter Pub IS) Coronet Bks.
Nichiren. The Awakening to the Truth. Ehara, N. R. et al, trs. LC 83-45457. Orig. Title: Kaimokusho. 1983. reprint ed. 28.50 (*0-404-20189-X*) AMS Pr.
Nichlaus, Jack & Bowden, Ken. Jack Nicklaus' Playing Lessons. 143p. 1983. 9.95 (*0-671-49557-7*) S&S Trade.
Nichol, Andrew, jt. auth. see Dummett, Ann.
Nichol, B. P. Art Facts: A Book of Contexts. LC 89-667. 168p. (Orig.). (C). 1990. pap. 15.00 (*0-925904-00-7*) Chax Pr.
— Once: A Lullaby. LC 85-9942. (Illus.). 24p. (J). (ps-1). 1986. 11.95 (*0-688-04284-8*); lib. bdg. 11.88 (*0-688-04285-6*) Greenwillow.
— Once: A Lullaby. LC 85-9942. (Illus.). 24p. (J). (ps up). 1992. pap. 4.95 (*0-688-04286-4*, Mulberry) Morrow.
— Translating Translating Apollinaire. 1979. pap. 10.00 (*0-87924-031-8*) Membrane Pr.
Nichol, B. P., jt. auth. see McCaffery, Steve.
Nichol, B. P., et al. Six Fillious. 1978. pap. 10.00 (*0-87924-032-6*) Membrane Pr.
Nichol, Barbara. Beethoven Lives Upstairs. LC 93-5774. (Illus.). 48p. (J). (gr. k-3). 1994. 15.95 (*0-531-06828-5*) Orchard Bks Watts.
Nichol, C. R. God's Woman. 1984. pap. 7.95 (*0-915547-52-X*) Abilene Christ U.
— Lord's Supper, Prayers, Thanksgiving. 1957. pap. 8.95 (*0-915547-62-7*) Abilene Christ U.
— Nichol Pocket Bible Encyclopedia. 1984. pap. 2.50 (*0-915547-55-4*) Abilene Christ U.
— Sound Doctrine, Vol. 1. 1984. pap. 6.95 (*0-915547-57-0*) Abilene Christ U.
— Sound Doctrine, Vol. 2. 1984. pap. 6.95 (*0-915547-58-9*) Abilene Christ U.
— Sound Doctrine, Vol. 3. 1984. pap. 6.95 (*0-915547-59-7*) Abilene Christ U.
— Sound Doctrine, Vol. 4. 1984. pap. 6.95 (*0-915547-60-0*) Abilene Christ U.
— Sound Doctrine, Vol. 5. 1984. pap. 6.95 (*0-915547-61-9*) Abilene Christ U.
Nichol, Catherine, jt. auth. see Museley, David.
Nichol, Claudia, et al. Scattered: Like Chaff in the Wind. (Illus.). 340p. (Orig.). 1989. pap. 13.95 (*0-9623121-0-X*) CompuWords.
Nichol, D. M. Greece & Byzantium. 19p. 1983. pap. 2.00 (*0-916586-94-4*) Holy Cross Orthodox.
Nichol, Don. Trees: Guardians of the Earth. (Illus.). 28p. (C). 1988. reprint ed. pap. text ed. 4.95 (*0-929660-03-X*) Morningtown.
Nichol, Francis D. The Midnight Cry: A Defense of William Miller & the Millerites. LC 72-8249. reprint ed. 52.00 (*0-404-11003-7*) AMS Pr.
Nichol, Gene R., jt. auth. see Redish, Martin H.
Nichol, Gene R., jt. auth. see Redishl, Martin H.
Nichol, Gloria. Christmas Companion. 96p. 1994. 10.98 (*0-8317-1223-6*) Smithmark.
***Nichol, James P.** Diplomacy in the Former Soviet Republics. LC 95-3353. 256p. 1995. text ed. 55.00 (*0-275-95192-8*, Praeger Pubs) Greenwood.
Nichol, John. American Literature: An Historical Sketch. 1972. 59.95 (*0-87968-607-3*) Gordon Pr.
— American Literature: An Historical Sketch, 1620-1880. LC 77-39071. (Essay Index Reprint Ser.). 1977. reprint ed. 26.95 (*0-8369-2706-0*) Ayer.
— Bites & Stings: The World of Venomous Animals. 160p. 1989. 19.95 (*0-8160-2233-X*) Facts on File.
— Byron. Morley, John, ed. LC 68-58390. (English Men of Letters Ser.). reprint ed. lib. bdg. 27.50 (*0-404-51722-6*) AMS Pr.
— The Mighty Rainforest. (Illus.). 200p. (Orig.). 1994. pap. 17.95 (*0-7153-0218-3*, Pub. by D & C Pub UK) Sterling.
— Thomas Carlyle. Morley, John, ed. LC 68-58391. (English Men of Letters Ser.). reprint ed. lib. bdg. 27.50 (*0-404-51723-4*) AMS Pr.
Nichol, Jon. Battle of Agincourt. (Resource Units: Middle Ages, 1066-1485 Ser.). (Illus.). 1974. reprint ed. pap. text ed. 12.95 (*0-582-39385-X*) Longman.
— The Castle. (Resource Units: Middle Ages, 1066-1485 Ser.). (Illus.). 24p. 1974. teacher ed, pap. text ed. 12.95 (*0-582-39379-5*) Longman.
— Edward I Campaigns in Wales & Scotland. (Resource Units: Middle Ages, 1066-1485 Ser.). (Illus.). 24p. 1974. teacher ed, pap. text ed. 12.95 (*0-582-39381-7*) Longman.
— The First & Third Crusades, 10 bks., Set. (Resource Units: Middle Ages, 1066-1485 Ser.). (Illus.). 24p. 1974. teacher ed, pap. text ed. 12.95 (*0-582-39377-9*) Longman.
— Joan of Arc. (Resource Units: Middle Ages, 1066-1485 Ser.). (Illus.). 24p. 1974. teacher ed, pap. text ed. 12.95 (*0-582-39386-8*) Longman.
— King John. (Resource Units: Middle Ages, 1066-1485 Ser.). (Illus.). 24p. 1974. teacher ed, pap. text ed. 12.95 (*0-582-39378-7*) Longman.
— Richard Third. (Resource Units: Middle Ages, 1066-1485 Ser.). (Illus.). 24p. 1974. teacher ed, pap. text ed. 12.95 (*0-582-39391-4*) Longman.
— Ships & Voyages. (Resource Units, Middle Ages, 1066-1485, Ser.). (Illus.). 24p. 1974. teacher ed, pap. text ed. 12.95 (*0-582-39388-4*) Longman.
— The Wars of the Roses. (Resource Units MIddle Ages, 1066-1485 Ser.). (Illus.). 24p. 1974. reprint ed. pap. 13.25 (*0-582-39390-6*) Longman.
Nichol, Norman. Robert Owen at New Lanark. (C). 1989. 50.00 (*1-85098-361-5*, Pub. by Jordanhill College UK) St Mut.
Nichol, R. T., tr. see Durer, Albrecht.
Nichol, Richard. Muscle Cars. 1987. 8.98 (*0-671-07525-X*) S&S Trade.
Nichol, Todd W., ed. see Preus, Herman A.
Nicholas. Letters of the Tsar to the Tsaritsa, 1914-1917. Vulliamy, C. E., ed. Hynes, A. L., tr. LC 75-37207. (Russian Studies: Perspectives on the Revolution). 324p. 1987. reprint ed. 28.00 (*0-88355-447-X*) Hyperion Conn.
Nicholas, II. Letters of the Tsar to the Tsaritsa, 1914-1917. Vulliamy, C. E., ed. Hynes, A. L., tr. 1976. lib. bdg. 59.95 (*0-8490-2155-3*) Gordon Pr.
***Nicholas.** Rottweilers. 1994. 11.95 (*0-7938-1073-6*) TFH Pubns.
— The Upper Extremity in Sports Medicine. (Illus.). 968p. 1989. 129.00 (*0-8016-3943-3*) Mosby Yr Bk.
Nicholas, jt. auth. see Scott, Sharon.
Nicholas, Alan, et al. Transforming Families & Communities: Christian Hope in a World of Change. 86p. 1987. pap. 5.00 (*0-88028-072-7*, 922) Forward Movement.
Nicholas, Anna. American Staffordshire Terrier. 1991. 9.95 (*0-86622-073-9*) TFH Pubns.
Nicholas, Anna K. American Staffordshire Terriers. (Illus.). 160p. 1990. lib. bdg. 9.95 (*0-86622-889-6*, KW158) TFH Pubns.
— Black & Tan Coonhounds. 1990. 11.95 (*0-86622-774-1*, KW-190) TFH Pubns.
— The Book of the English Springer Spaniel. (Illus.). 414p. 1983. 34.95 (*0-87666-744-2*, H 1060) TFH Pubns.
— Book of the German Shepherd Dog. (Illus.). 480p. 1983. 34.95 (*0-87666-562-8*, H-1062) TFH Pubns.
— Book of the Golden Retriever. (Illus.). 480p. 1983. 34.95 (*0-87666-738-8*, H-1058) TFH Pubns.
— The Book of the Labrador Retriever. (Illus.) 480p. 1983. 24.95 (*0-87666-748-5*, H 1059) TFH Pubns.
— The Book of the Miniature Schnauzer. (Illus.). 368p. 1986. 29.95 (*0-86622-151-4*, H-1080) TFH Pubns.
— The Book of the Poodle. (Illus.). 528p. 29.95 (*0-87666-736-1*, H-1033) TFH Pubns.
— The Book of the Rottweiler. (Illus.). 544p. 1981. 24.95 (*0-87666-735-3*, H-1035) TFH Pubns.
— The Book of the Shetland Sheepdog. (Illus.). 544p. 1984. 34.95 (*0-86622-036-4*, H-1064) TFH Pubns.
— Book of the West Highland White Terrier. (Illus.). 224p. 1993. 29.95 (*0-86622-663-X*, TS187) TFH Pubns.
— The Chow Chow. (Illus.). 256p. 1989. 19.95 (*0-86622-029-1*, PS-812) TFH Pubns.
— The Collie. (Illus.). 320p. 1986. 19.95 (*0-86622-723-7*, PS-825) TFH Pubns.
— A Complete Introduction to Cocker Spaniels. (Complete Introduction to...Ser.). (Illus.). 128p. (Orig.). 1987. pap. 5.95 (*0-86622-381-9*, CO-036S) TFH Pubns.
— Complete Introduction to Doberman Pinschers. (Complete Introduction to...Ser.). (Illus.). 128p. (Orig.). 1987. pap. 5.95 (*0-86622-376-2*, CO-033S) TFH Pubns.
— The Dalmatian. (Illus.). 320p. 1986. 19.95 (*0-86622-157-3*, PS-823) TFH Pubns.
— Finnish Spitz. (KW Ser.). (Illus.). 192p. 1989. lib. bdg. 9.95 (*0-86622-783-0*, KW-194) TFH Pubns.
— French Bulldogs. 1990. 11.95 (*0-86622-767-9*, KW-186) TFH Pubns.
— The Great Dane. (Illus.). 319p. (YA). (gr. 7 up). 1988. 19.95 (*0-86622-122-0*, PS-826) TFH Pubns.
— Jack Russell Terriers. (Illus.). 160p. 1989. 11.95 (*0-86622-597-8*, KW-164) TFH Pubns.
— The Maltese. (Illus.). 288p. 1984. 19.95 (*0-87666-569-5*, PS-803) TFH Pubns.
— Norwegian Elkhounds. (Illus.). 128p. 1988. 11.95 (*0-86622-437-8*, KW-110) TFH Pubns.
— Norwich Terriers. (Illus.). 192p. 1993. 11.95 (*0-86622-580-3*, KW209) TFH Pubns.
— The Poodle. (Illus.). 288p. 1984. text ed. 19.95 (*0-86622-033-X*, PS-814) TFH Pubns.
— The Professional's Book of Rottweilers. (TS Ser.). (Illus.). 446p. 1991. lib. bdg. 79.95 (*0-86622-625-7*, TS-147) TFH Pubns.
— The Samoyed. (Illus.). 320p. 1990. 19.95 (*0-86622-934-5*, PS-855) TFH Pubns.
— Staffordshire Bull Terriers. (Illus.). 1989. lib. bdg. 11.95 (*0-86622-594-3*, KW157) TFH Pubns.
— The Staffordshire Terriers: American Staffordshire Terrier & Staffordshire Bull Terrier. (TS Ser.). (Illus.). 256p. 1991. text ed. 39.95 (*0-86622-637-0*, TS-143) TFH Pubns.
— The World of Doberman Pinschers. (Illus.). 640p. 1986. 49.95 (*0-86622-123-9*, H-1082) TFH Pubns.
— The World of Rottweilers. (Illus.). 336p. 1986. 39.95 (*0-86622-124-7*, H-1083) TFH Pubns.
— World of the Chinese Shar-pei. 1992. 79.95 (*0-86622-199-9*) TFH Pubns.
Nicholas, Anna K. & Brearley, Joan McD. The Book of the Pekingese. (Illus.). 352p. 1975. 29.95 (*0-87666-348-X*, H-953) TFH Pubns.
Nicholas, Anna K. & Foy, Marcia. The Beagle. (Illus.). 320p. 1982. text ed. 19.95 (*0-86622-042-9*, PS-811) TFH Pubns.
— The Dachshund. (Breed Ser.). (Illus.). 320p. 1987. 19.95 (*0-86622-158-1*, PS-822) TFH Pubns.
Nicholas, Anna K. & Foy, Marcia A. The Fox Terrier. (Illus.). 320p. 1990. 19.95 (*0-86622-931-0*, PS-858) TFH Pubns.
Nicholas, Anna K., jt. auth. see Brearley, Joan McD.
Nicholas, Anna K., jt. auth. see Foy, Marcia A.
***Nicholas, Anne.** The Art of the New Zealand Tattoo. (Illus.). 132p. 1995. pap. 19.95 (*0-8065-1603-8*, Citadel Pr) Carol Pub Group.
Nicholas, Anne K. A Complete Introduction to Poodles. (Complete Introduction to...Ser.). (Illus.). 128p. (Orig.). 1987. pap. 5.95 (*0-86622-380-0*, CO-032S) TFH Pubns.
Nicholas, Barbara. Portable Pet. LC 83-22689. (Other Dog Bks.). 80p. 1983. pap. 5.95 (*0-87714-117-7*) Denlingers.
— The Portable Pet: How to Travel Anywhere with Your Dog or Cat. LC 83-22689. 96p. 1984. 12.95 (*0-916782-50-6*); pap. 5.95 (*0-916782-49-2*) Harvard Common Pr.
Nicholas, Barry. The French Law of Contract. 2nd ed. 296p. 1992. 59.00 (*0-19-876255-0*) OUP.
— Introduction to Roman Law. (Clarendon Law Ser.). 1976. 24.95 (*0-19-876063-9*) OUP.
Nicholas, Barry, jt. auth. see Jolowicz, Herbert F.
Nicholas, Bill, jt. auth. see McManus, Ed.
Nicholas, Charles, illus. Banner in the Sky. (Contemporary Motivators Ser.). (J). (gr. 4-12). 1978. pap. text ed. 2.25 (*0-88301-301-0*) Pendulum Pr.
— God Is My Co-Pilot. LC 78-50959. (Contemporary Motivators Ser.). (J). (gr. 4-12). 1978. pap. text ed. 2.25 (*0-88301-302-9*) Pendulum Pr.
— Hiroshima. LC 78-50861. (Contemporary Motivators Ser.). (J). (gr. 4-12). 1978. pap. text ed. 2.25 (*0-88301-304-5*) Pendulum Pr.
— Hot Rod. LC 78-50957. (Contemporary Motivators Ser.). (J). (gr. 4-12). 1978. pap. text ed. 2.25 (*0-88301-305-3*) Pendulum Pr.
— Just Dial a Number. LC 78-50860. (Contemporary Motivators Ser.). (J). (gr. 4-12). 1978. pap. text ed. 2.25 (*0-88301-306-1*) Pendulum Pr.
— Lost Horizon. (Contemporary Motivators Ser.). 32p. (Orig.). (YA). (gr. 3-5). 1979. pap. text ed. 2.25 (*0-88301-309-6*) Pendulum Pr.
Nicholas, D. Commodities Futures Trading: A Guide to Information Sources & Computerized Services. 154p. 1985. pap. text ed. 70.00 (*0-7201-1703-8*, Mansell Pub) Cassell.
Nicholas, D., comp. Peter Matthiessen: A Bibliography, Nineteen Fifty-One to Nineteen Seventy-Nine. LC 80-109000. (Illus.). 63p. 1980. 15.00 (*0-938364-00-6*) Orirana Pr.
Nicholas, D. & Erbach, G. Online Information Sources for Business & Current Affairs: An Evaluation. 320p. 1989. text ed. 110.00 (*0-7201-1878-6*, Mansell Pub) Cassell.
Nicholas, D., jt. auth. see Nicholas, R.
Nicholas, D., jt. ed. see Thijsen, J. M.
Nicholas, D., et al. End-Users of Online Information Systems: An Analysis. 168p. 1988. text ed. 80.00 (*0-7201-1995-2*, Mansell Pub) Cassell.
— Online Searching: Its Impact on Information Users. 168p. 1987. text ed. 75.00 (*0-7201-1887-5*, Mansell Pub) Cassell.
Nicholas, David. The Domestic Life of a Medieval City: Women, Children, & the Family in Fourteenth Century Ghent. LC 84-22011. (Illus.). x, 261p. 1985. 30.00 (*0-8032-3310-8*) U of Nebr Pr.
— The Evolution of the Medieval World: Society, Government & Thought in Europe, 312-1500. 560p. (C). 1992. text ed. 54.50 (*0-582-09256-6*, 79266) Longman.
— The Evolution of the Medieval World: Society, Government & Thought in Europe, 312-1500. 560p. (C). 1993. pap. text ed. 17.95 (*0-582-09257-4*, 79267) Longman.

— Medieval Flanders. 480p. (C). 1992. pap. text ed. 31.50 (*0-582-01678-9*, 79365) Longman.
— The Metamorphosis of a Medieval City: Ghent in the Age of the Arteveldes, 1302-1390. LC 86-27276. 381p. reprint ed. pap. 102.90 (*0-7837-6887-7*, 2046717); reprint ed. pap. 108.60 (*0-7837-6491-X*, 2046581) Bks Demand.
— The Middle East: Its Oil, Economies, & Investment Policies: A Guide to Sources of Financial Information. LC 80-28555. xxiv, 201p. 1981. text ed. 49.95 (*0-313-22986-4*, NME/, Greenwood Pr) Greenwood.
— The van Arteveldes of Ghent: The Varieties of Vendetta & the Hero in History. LC 88-3858. (Illus.). 232p. 1988. 29.95 (*0-8014-2149-7*) Cornell U Pr.
Nicholas, David, jt. ed. see Bachrach, Bernard S.
Nicholas, David R. Foundations of Biblical Inerrancy. pap. 2.99 (*0-88469-104-7*) BMH Bks.
— What's a Woman to Do in Church? 148p. 1979. 7.99 (*0-88469-123-3*) BMH Bks.
Nicholas, Edward. The Chaplain's Lady: Life & Love At Fort Mackinac. (Illus.). 82p. (Orig.). 1987. pap. 7.00 (*0-911872-56-6*) Mackinac Island.
Nicholas, F. W. Veterinary Genetics. (Illus.). 500p. 1987. 65.00 (*0-19-857569-6*) OUP.
Nicholas, Flamel, jt. auth. see Urbigerus, Baro.
Nicholas, Francis S., comp. Index to Schoolcraft's "Indian Tribes of the United States" reprint ed. 49.00 (*0-403-03611-9*) Scholarly.
***Nicholas, Frank W.** Introduction to Veterinary Genetics. (Illus.). 240p. 1996. 67.00 (*0-19-854293-3*); pap. 29.95 (*0-19-854292-5*) OUP.
Nicholas, G. P., ed. Holocene Human Ecology in Northeastern North America. LC 88-11113. (Interdisciplinary Contributions to Archaeology Ser.). (Illus.). 340p. 1988. 42.50 (*0-306-42869-5*, Plenum Pr) Plenum.
Nicholas, Geoff & Duncan, Andy. What Drum. 2nd ed. (Illus.). 113p. 1990. pap. 12.95 (*0-933224-52-4*, Pub. by Track Record UK) Bold Strummer Ltd.
Nicholas, H. G. British General Election of 1950. (Illus.). 353p. 1968. reprint ed. 35.00 (*0-7146-1568-4*, Pub. by F Cass Pubs UK) Intl Spec Bk.
— The Nature of American Politics. 2nd ed. 160p. 1986. 28.00 (*0-19-827483-1*) OUP.
— The United Nations As a Political Institution. 5th ed. 1975. pap. 15.95 (*0-19-519826-3*) OUP.

N

An Asterisk (*) at the beginning of an entry indicates that the title is appearing in BIP for the first time.

— The United States & Britain. Iriye, Akira, ed. LC 74-16681. (United States in the World, Foreign Perspectives Ser.). viii, 196p. 1975. lib. bdg. 13.00 (0-226-58002-4) U Ch Pr.

Nicholas, H. G., ed. Washington Despatches, 1941 to 1945: Weekly Political Reports from the British Embassy. LC 80-6208. xviii, 700p. (C). 1985. pap. text ed. 19.95 (0-226-58005-9) U Ch Pr.

Nicholas, Herbert G. Britain & the U. S. A. LC 63-10195. (Albert Shaw Lectures on Diplomatic History: 1961). 192p. reprint ed. pap. 54.80 (0-8357-7410-4, 2020728) Bks Demand.

Nicholas, Ilene M. The Proto-Elamite Settlement at TUV. Sumner, William M., ed. (University Museum Monographs: Malyan Excavation Reports: No. 69). 250p. 1989. text ed. 55.00 (0-934718-86-5) U PA Mus Pubns.

Nicholas, J. F. An Atlas of Models of Crystal Surfaces. 238p. 1965. text ed. 255.00 (0-677-00580-6) Gordon & Breach.

Nicholas, J. Karl & Nicholl, James R. Effective Argument: A Writer's Guide with Readings. 600p. 1991. pap. text ed. 22.00 (0-205-13063-1, H30638) Allyn.

Nicholas, J. Karl & Nicholl, James R., eds. Models for Effective Writing. LC 93-11808. 1994. write for info. (0-205-40017-5) Allyn.

Nicholas, J. Karl, jt. ed. see Farwell, Harold.

Nicholas, J. V. Traceable Temperatures: An Introduction of Temperatures, Measurement & Calibration. 1994. text ed. 89.95 (0-471-93803-3) Wiley.

***Nicholas, James A., ed.** The Lower Extremity & Spine in Sports Medicine. 2nd ed. LC 94-26126. 1994. write for info. (0-8151-6391-6) Mosby Yr Bk.

***Nicholas, James A., et al, eds.** The Upper Extremity in Sports Medicine. 2nd ed. LC 95-6355. 1995. write for info. (0-8151-6392-4) Mosby Yr Bk.

Nicholas, James C. State Regulation: Housing Prices. 140p. 1982. pap. text ed. 3.00 (0-88285-075-X) Transaction Pubs.

Nicholas, James C., ed. The Changing Structure of Infrastructure Finance. 98p. 1985. 15.00 (0-317-01542-7) Fla Atlantic.

— The Changing Structure of Infrastructure Finance. (Monograph: No. 85-5). (Illus.). 98p. 1985. pap. text ed. 5.25 (1-55844-092-5) Lincoln Inst Land.

Nicholas, James C., et al. A Practitioner's Guide to Development Impact Fees. LC 90-80606. (Illus.). 300p. (Orig.). 1991. lib. bdg. 54.95 (0-918286-70-0) Planners Pr.

Nicholas, James H., Jr., tr. see Kojeve, Alexandre.

Nicholas, Jeff. Death Valley: A Visual Interpretation. Leach, Nicky, ed. (Wish You Were Here Ser.). 64p. (Orig.). 1994. pap. 9.95 (0-939365-37-5) Sierra Pr CA.

— Islands in the Sky: Scenes from the Colorado Plateau. 1991. pap. 14.95 (0-939365-16-2) Sierra Pr CA.

— Islands in the Sky: Scenes of the Colorado Plateau. 1992. 24.95 (0-939365-19-7) Sierra Pr CA.

***Nicholas, Jeff, ed.** Arches National Park. (Wish You Were Here Postcard Bks.). (Illus.). 32p. (Orig.). 1995. pap. 4.95 (0-939365-48-0) Sierra Pr CA.

— Art on the Rocks. (Wish You Were Here Postcard Bks.). (Illus.). 32p. 1993. pap. 4.95 (0-939365-24-3) Sierra Pr CA.

— Bryce Canyon. (Wish You Were Here Postcard Bks.). (Illus.). 32p. 1992. pap. 4.95 (0-939365-06-5) Sierra Pr CA.

— Cactus Flowers. (Wish You Were Here Postcard Bks.). 32p. (Orig.). 1994. pap. 4.95 (0-939365-39-1) Sierra Pr CA.

— Carlsbad Caverns. (Wish You Were Here Postcard Bks.). (Illus.). 32p. (Orig.). 1995. pap. 4.95 (0-939365-46-4) Sierra Pr CA.

— Death Valley. (Wish You Were Here Postcard Bks.). 32p. (Orig.). 1994. pap. text ed. 4.95 (0-939365-40-5) Sierra Pr CA.

— Desert Dunes. (Wish You Were Here Postcard Bks.). 32p. (Orig.). 1994. pap. 4.95 (0-939365-41-3) Sierra Pr CA.

— Glen Canyon. (Wish You Were Here Postcard Bks.). (Illus.). 32p. 1993. pap. 4.95 (0-939365-28-6) Sierra Pr CA.

— Grand Canyon. (Wish You Were Here Postcard Bks.). (Illus.). 32p. 1990. pap. 4.95 (0-939365-11-1) Sierra Pr CA.

— Grand Teton. (Wish You Were Here Postcard Bks.). (Illus.). 32p. 1990. pap. 4.95 (0-939365-12-X) Sierra Pr CA.

— Monument Valley. (Wish You Were Here Postcard Bks.). (Illus.). 32p. 1993. pap. 4.95 (0-939365-27-8) Sierra Pr CA.

— Petrified Forest. (Wish You Were Here Postcard Bks.). (Illus.). 32p. (Orig.). 1995. pap. 4.95 (0-939365-47-2) Sierra Pr CA.

— Rocky Mountain National Park. (Wish You Were Here Postcard Bks.). (Illus.). 32p. (Orig.). 1995. pap. 4.95 (0-939365-45-6) Sierra Pr CA.

— Ruins of the Southwest. (Wish You Were Here Postcard Bks.). (Illus.). 32p. 1993. pap. 4.95 (0-939365-23-5) Sierra Pr CA.

— Sequoia & Kings Canyon. (Wish You Were Here Postcard Bks.). (Illus.). 32p. 1993. pap. 4.95 (0-939365-25-1) Sierra Pr CA.

— Wildlife of the Rockies. (Wish You Were Here Postcard Bks.). 32p. 1994. pap. 4.95 (0-939365-35-9) Sierra Pr CA.

— Yellowstone. (Wish You Were Here Postcard Bks.). (Illus.). 32p. 1992. pap. 4.95 (0-939365-05-7) Sierra Pr CA.

— Yellowstone Wildlife. (Wish You Were Here Postcard Bks.). (Illus.). 32p. 1994. pap. 4.95 (0-939365-34-0) Sierra Pr CA.

— Yosemite. 3rd ed. (Wish You Were Here Postcard Bks.). (Illus.). 32p. 1992. pap. 4.95 (0-939365-10-3) Sierra Pr CA.

— Zion. rev. ed. (Wish You Were Here Postcard Bks.). 32p. 1994. pap. 4.95 (0-939365-33-2) Sierra Pr CA.

Nicholas, Jeff, ed. see Gilmore, Jackie.

Nicholas, Jeff, ed. see Leach, Nicky.

Nicholas, Jeff, ed. see Wuerthner, George.

Nicholas, Jesse C. The J. C. Nichols Chronicle: The Authorized Story of the Man & His Company. LC 94-12824. 1994. 25.00x (0-7006-0685-8) U Pr of KS.

Nicholas, Joe. Language Diversity Surveys As Agents of Change. LC 93-50651. (Multilingual Matters Ser.: No. 102). 176p. 1994. 69.95 (1-85359-233-1, Pub. by Multilingual Matters UK); pap. 29.95 (1-85359-232-3, Pub. by Multilingual Matters UK) Taylor & Francis.

Nicholas, John M., ed. Images, Perception & Knowledge. (Western Ontario Ser.: No. 8). 1977. lib. bdg. 103.00 (90-277-0782-0) Kluwer Ac.

Nicholas, John R. Oh, What a Lovely War. LC 91-75916. 400p. 1991. pap. 12.95 (0-9630445-0-8) Harper Hse.

Nicholas, John S. Goethe, the Layman in Science. (Connecticut Academy of Arts & Sciences Ser., Trans.: Vol. 32). 1933. pap. 39.50 (0-685-22921-1) Elliots Bks.

Nicholas, Jonathan. On the Oregon Trail. (Illus.). 156p. 1992. 45.00 (1-55868-101-9) Gr Arts Ctr Pub.

***Nicholas, Jonathan & Forster, C. Bruce.** Portland. rev. ed. 111p. 1994. 39.95 (1-55868-164-7) Gr Arts Ctr Pub.

Nicholas, Kate. The Social Effects of Unemployment on Teesside, 1919-39. 254p. 1988. text ed. 79.95 (0-7190-1772-6, Pub. by Manchester Univ Pr UK) St Martin.

***Nicholas, Kristin.** Knitting the New Classics: 60 Exquisite Sweaters from Elite. LC 95-6205. (Illus.). 160p. 1995. 27.95 (0-8069-3172-8, Lark Bks) Sterling.

Nicholas, Lynn H. The Rape of Europa: The Fate of Europe's Treasures in the Third Reich & the Second World War. LC 93-11317. 1994. 27.50 (0-679-40069-9) Knopf.

— Rape of Europa: The Fate of Europe's Treasures in the Third Reich & the Second World War. 1995. pap. 15.00 (0-679-75686-8, Vin) Random.

Nicholas, Marta R., et al. Bangladesh: Birth of a Nation. Morehouse, Ward, ed. 160p. 1971. pap. 3.50 (0-88253-201-4) Ind-US Inc.

Nicholas, Mary. Mystery of Goodness & the Positive Moral Consequences of Psychotherapy. 288p. (C). 1994. 30.00 (0-393-70166-2) Norton.

Nicholas, Mary W. Change in the Context of Group Therapy. LC 84-1718. 272p. 1984. 39.95 (0-87630-358-0) Brunner-Mazel.

Nicholas, Michele, jt. auth. see Baron, Nick.

Nicholas, Nancy. Tales of an Inn. (Illus.). 56p. (Orig.). 1989. pap. 9.95 (0-9625274-0-8) Sevynmor Pr.

Nicholas, Nancy, ed. see Piercy, Marge.

Nicholas, Patty. Fiddlin for Fun Functionally - Piano Accompaniment. 72p. 1994. pap. text ed. 10.95 (0-87487-679-6) Summy-Birchard.

— Fiddlin for Fun Functionally - Student Book. 44p. 1994. pap. text ed. 6.95 (0-87487-678-8) Summy-Birchard.

— Fiddlin for Fun Functionally - Teacher Book. 56p. 1994. pap. text ed. 7.95 (0-87487-680-X) Summy-Birchard.

Nicholas, Paul. The Game of Insurance: How Insurance Is Conducted in California. LC 90-92961. (Illus.). 304p. (Orig.). 1990. pap. 17.95 (0-9626901-0-4) Jade Pub Co.

Nicholas, Phoebe O., ed. see American Psychological Association Staff.

Nicholas Prince of Greece. Political Memoirs, 1914-17. LC 72-1274. (Select Bibliographies Reprint Ser.). 1977. reprint ed. 34.95 (0-8369-6833-6) Ayer.

Nicholas, R. & Nicholas, D. Virology: An Information Profile. 244p. 1983. text ed. 75.00 (0-7201-1673-2, Mansell Pub) Cassell.

Nicholas, R., ed. see Haber, Paul.

***Nicholas, Robert.** Mundo Unido Vol. 1: Lectura y Escritura. Date not set. pap. text ed. write for info. (0-471-58484-3) Wiley.

Nicholas, Robert J. Fifty Creative Exercises, 2 bks., Bk. I. (YA). (gr. 7 up). 1991. pap. 12.95 (1-879777-00-2) Leonardos Work.

— Fifty Creative Exercises, 2 bks., Bk. II. (YA). (gr. 7 up). 1991. pap. 12.95 (1-879777-01-0) Leonardos Work.

— Fifty Creative Exercises, 2 bks., Set. (YA). (gr. 7 up). 1991. pap. 24.00 (1-879777-02-9) Leonardos Work.

Nicholas, Robert L., jt. auth. see Neale-Silva, Eduardo.

Nicholas, Robert L., et al. En Camino! A Cultural Approach to Beginning Spanish. 1990. teacher ed 15.95 (0-07-540859-7); student ed, teacher ed 150.00 (0-07-540861-9) McGraw.

— En Camino! A Cultural Approach to Beginning Spanish. 4th ed. 1990. text ed. write for info. (0-07-046189-9) McGraw.

— En Camino! A Cultural Approach to Beginning Spanish. 4th ed. 1990. write for info. (0-07-909501-1); student ed, pap. text ed. 14.90 (0-07-540856-2); student ed, teacher ed 15.95 (0-07-540862-7); write for info. (0-07-540860-0); write for info. (0-07-540863-5) McGraw.

— Motivos de Conversacion: Essentials of Spanish. 2nd ed. 1988. pap. text ed. write for info. (0-07-554175-0) McGraw.

— Motivos de Conversacion: Essentials of Spanish. 3rd ed. 1992. text ed. write for info. (0-07-046708-0) McGraw.

— Motivos de Conversacion: Essentials of Spanish. 3rd ed. 1992. Wkbk. - lab man. student ed, pap. text ed. write for info. (0-07-046714-5); Tapescript. pap. text ed. write for info. (0-07-046718-8) McGraw.

Nicholas, Robin. The Cowboy & His Lady. 1994. pap. 2.75 (0-373-91017-7, 5-91017-9); pap. 2.75 (0-373-19017-4, 5-19017-8) Harlequin Bks.

Nicholas, Ron. Small Group Leaders' Handbook. LC 82-68. 194p. (Orig.). 1982. pap. 9.99 (0-87784-372-4, 372) InterVarsity.

Nicholas, Ron, et al. Good Things Come in Small Groups. LC 85-778. 188p. 1985. pap. 9.99 (0-87784-917-X, 917) InterVarsity.

Nicholas, Stephen, ed. Convict Workers: Reinterpreting Australia's Past. (Studies in Australian History). (Illus.). 300p. (C). 1989. 59.95 (0-521-36126-5) Cambridge U Pr.

Nicholas, Susan C., et al. Rights & Wrongs: Women's Struggle for Legal Equality. 2nd ed. LC 86-2461. (Women's Lives - Women's Work Ser.). 112p. (Orig.). 1986. pap. 9.95 (0-935312-42-0) Feminist Pr.

Nicholas, T., jt. ed. see Liaw, P. K.

Nicholas, T., ed. see Metallurgical Society of AIME Staff.

Nicholas, Tawa. Three Centuries of American Music: A Collection of Sacred & Secular Music, Vol. I: Solo Song to 1865. (Library Catalogs Ser.). 400p. (C). 1989. lib. bdg. 80.00 (0-8161-0542-1) G K Hall.

Nicholas, Ted. The Complete Book of Corporate Forms. LC 80-67502. 256p. 1990. 69.95 (0-913864-54-4, 5615-06, Enter-Dearbrn) Dearborn Finan.

— Complete Book of Corporate Forms. rev. ed. LC 92-19051. 245p. 1992. pap. 19.95 (0-7931-0488-2, 561554) Dearborn Finan.

— Complete Guide to Business Agreements. rev. ed. 333p. 1992. pap. 19.95 (0-7931-0489-0, 561553) Dearborn Finan.

— The Complete Guide to Nonprofit Corporations. rev. ed. 248p. 1993. pap. 19.95 (0-7931-0615-X, 5615-66) Dearborn Finan.

— Complete Guide to "S" Corporations. 175p. 1993. pap. 19.95 (0-7931-0613-3, 561565) Dearborn Finan.

— Complete Non-Profit Corporation Handbook. Facenda, Ann, ed. 1986. ring bd. 69.95 (0-913864-95-1, 5615-41, Enter-Dearbrn) Dearborn Finan.

— The Corporate Forms Kit. 1995. pap. 19.95 (0-936894-91-1) Upstart Pub.

— The Executive's Business Letter Book: Ready-to-Use Business Letters for Business Owners & Executives. rev. ed. LC 92-19246. 386p. 1992. pap. 19.95 (0-7931-0491-2, 561552) Dearborn Finan.

— Forty-Three Ways to Raise Capital. 197p. (Orig.). 1991. pap. 29.95 (0-942103-19-X, 5615-16, Enter-Dearbrn) Dearborn Finan.

— The Golden Mailbox: How to Get Rich Direct Marketing Your Product. 212p. 1993. pap. 39.95 (0-7931-0486-6, 5615-17, Enter-Dearbrn) Dearborn Finan.

— How to Form Your Own Corporation Without a Lawyer for under 75 Dollars: 1992 Edition. 150p. 1992. pap. 19.95 (0-7931-0419-X, 5615-01, Enter-Dearbrn) Dearborn Finan.

— How to Form Your Own "S" Corporation & Avoid Double Taxation. 208p. 1995. pap. 21.95 (0-936894-94-6, 5614-3901, Upstart) Dearborn Finan.

— How to Gain Financial Freedom As an Independent Contractor: The Income Plan. 1991. pap. 19.95 (0-913864-55-2, 5615-05, Enter-Dearbrn) Dearborn Finan.

— How to Get Your Own Trademark. rev. ed. 185p. 1993. pap. 24.95 (0-7931-0487-4, 5615-0202) Dearborn Finan.

— How to Publish a Book & Sell a Million Copies. 256p. 1993. pap. 19.95 (0-7931-0620-6, 561567, Enter-Dearbrn) Dearborn Finan.

— Management for Entrepreneurs: How to Manage a Great Small Business. 142p. 1990. 29.95 (0-942103-10-6, 5615-29, Enter-Dearbrn) Dearborn Finan.

— The "S" Corporation Handbook. 1993. ring bd. 69.95 (0-7931-0614-1, 5615-42, Enter-Dearbrn) Dearborn Finan.

— Secrets of Entrepreneurial Leadership: Building Top Performance Through Trust & Teamwork. Orig. Title: Management for Entrepreneurs. 192p. 1992. 19.95 (0-7931-0493-9, 5615-61) Dearborn Finan.

— The Ted Nicholas Small Business Course. 352p. (Orig.). 1993. pap. 29.95 (0-7931-0725-3, 5615-69, Enter-Dearbrn) Dearborn Finan.

— Your Handbook to a Successful Home-Based Business: Your Guide to Wealth While Working in Your Own Home-Based Business. 123p. (Orig.). 1991. pap. 19.95 (0-942103-15-7, 5615-32, Enter-Dearbrn) Dearborn Finan.

Nicholas, Ted, jt. auth. see Shenson, Howard.

Nicholas, Thomas. Annals & Antiquities of the Counties & County Families of Wales, 2 vols., I. (Illus.). 964p. 1991. write for info. (0-8063-1316-1, 4103) Genealog Pub.

— Annals & Antiquities of the Counties & County Families of Wales, 2 vols., II. (Illus.). 964p. 1991. write for info. (0-8063-1315-3, 4103) Genealog Pub.

Nicholas, Toula. CPT - HCPCS Basic Coding Handbook. 85p. 1993. 35.00 (0-317-05425-2) Am Hlth Info.

Nicholas, Toula & Ertl, Linda. Basic ICD-9-CM Coding Handbook. 315p. 1992. 42.00 (0-317-05423-6) Am Hlth Info.

Nicholas, Warwick L. The Biology of Free-Living Nematodes. 2nd ed. (Illus.). 1984. 69.00 (0-19-857587-4) OUP.

***Nicholass, Ted.** The Business Agreements Kit. 1995. pap. 19.95 (0-936894-90-3) Upstart Pub.

Nicholaus, Bret, jt. auth. see Lowrie, Paul.

Nicholaus, J. Air Defence Weapons. (Army Library). (Illus.). 48p. (J). (gr. 3-8). 1989. lib. bdg. 18.60 (0-86592-423-6); lib. bdg. 13.95 (0-685-58578-6) Rourke Corp.

— Army Air Support. (Army Library). (Illus.). 48p. (J). (gr. 3-8). 1989. lib. bdg. 18.60 (0-86592-421-X) Rourke Corp.

— Artillery. (Army Library). (Illus.). 48p. (J). (gr. 3-8). 1989. lib. bdg. 18.60 (0-86592-419-8) Rourke Corp.

— Main Battle Tanks. (Army Library). (Illus.). 48p. (J). (gr. 3-8). 1989. 13.95 (0-685-58576-X); lib. bdg. 18.60 (0-86592-420-1) Rourke Corp.

— Rockets & Missiles. (Army Library). (Illus.). 48p. (J). (gr. 3-8). 1989. lib. bdg. 18.60 (0-86592-418-X); lib. bdg. 13.95 (0-685-58577-8) Rourke Corp.

— Tracked Vehicles. (Army Library). (Illus.). 48p. (J). (gr. 3-8). 1989. lib. bdg. 18.60 (0-86592-422-8); lib. bdg. 13.95 (0-685-58579-4) Rourke Corp.

Nicholaus, John. The Army Library, 6 bks., Set. (Illus.). 288p. (J). (gr. 3-8). 1989. lib. bdg. 111.60 (0-86592-417-1) Rourke Corp.

Nichole. Friends. 64p. (Orig.). 1993. pap. 8.95 (0-9637962-0-8) Joli Pubng.

Nicholes, Mike. Parts Department-Inventory Management. 6th ed. (Illus.). 505p. (Orig.). student ed 150.00 (0-685-10193-2) Mike Nicholes.

Nicholi, Armand M. New Harvard Guide to Psychiatry. LC 87-24115. (Illus.). 864p. 1988. 58.00 (0-674-61540-9) Belknap Pr.

Nicholl, B., jt. ed. see Nellist, J.

Nicholl, Boyd, jt. auth. see Bush, Neil L.

Nicholl, Charles. The Fruit Palace. LC 94-17942. 1994. pap. 12.00 (0-679-74364-2, Vin) Random.

— The Fruit Palace. 1987. pap. 3.95 (0-312-90725-7) St Martin.

— The Reckoning. LC 93-23694. 1994. 24.95 (0-15-175981-2) HarBrace.

— The Reckoning: The Murder of Christopher Marlowe. LC 95-3004. 1995. pap. 14.95 (0-226-58024-5) U Ch Pr.

Nicholl, Christopher. Bishop's University, 1843-1970. (Illus.). 360p. 1994. 39.95 (0-7735-1176-8, Pub. by McGill CN) U of Toronto Pr.

Nicholl, D., tr. see Dante Alighieri.

Nicholl, Desmond S. An Introduction to Genetic Engineering. (Studies in Biology). (Illus.). 150p. (C). 1994. 39.95 (0-521-43054-2); pap. 16.95 (0-521-43634-6) Cambridge U Pr.

Nicholl, Donald, tr. see Bochenski, Innocentius.

Nicholl, James R., jt. auth. see Nicholas, J. Karl.

Nicholl, James R., jt. ed. see Nicholas, J. Karl.

Nicholl, Malcolm J. Loser-Friendly Diet. LC 92-32952. 256p. 1993. 19.95 (0-87131-712-5) M Evans.

Nicholls, A. J. Freedom with Responsibility: The Social Market Economy in Germany, 1918-1963. LC 93-32122. 420p. 1994. 45.00 (0-19-820425-6, Old Oregon Bk Store) OUP.

— Weimar & the Rise of Hitler. 3rd ed. LC 90-48823. (Making of the Twentieth Century Ser.). (C). 1991. pap. text ed. 14.50 (0-312-05713-X) St Martin.

— Weimar & the Rise of Hitler. 3rd ed. LC 90-48823. (Making of the Twentieth Century Ser.). 192p. 1991. text ed. 45.00 (0-312-05795-4) St Martin.

Nicholls, Andy, jt. auth. see Allison, Charles.

Nicholls, Ann, jt. auth. see Hudson, Kenneth.

***Nicholls, Bruce J., ed.** The Unique Christ in Our Pluralistic World. LC 94-36248. (World Evangelical Fellowship Ser.). 285p. 1995. pap. 14.99 (0-8010-2013-1) Baker Bk.

Nicholls, C. S., ed. The Dictionary of National Biography: Missing Persons. 790p. 1993. 115.00 (0-19-865211-9) OUP.

Nicholls, C. S., jt. ed. see Blake, Lord.

Nicholls, Christine S., ed. see Smith, George.

Nicholls, D. Inorganic Chemistry in Liquid Ammonia. (Topics in Inorganic & General Chemistry: Vol. 17). 238p. 1979. 97.50 (0-444-41774-5) Elsevier.

— Proteins, Transmitters & Synapses. (Illus.). 288p. 1994. pap. 49.95 (0-632-03661-3, Pub. by Blckwell Sci Pubns UK) Blackwell Sci.

Nicholls, David. American Experimental Music 1890-1940. (Illus.). (C). 1990. 64.95 (0-521-34578-2) Cambridge U Pr.

— American Experimental Music, 1890-1940. (Illus.). 300p. (C). 1991. pap. 21.95 (0-521-42464-X) Cambridge U Pr.

— Deity & Domination: Images of God & the State in the Nineteenth & Twentieth Centuries. 336p. 1989. 29.95 (0-415-01171-X, A3381) Routledge.

— Francois Truffaut. (Illus.). 176p. 1994. pap. 24.95 (0-7134-6694-4, Pub. by Batsford UK) Trafalgar.

— From Dessalines to Duvalier: Race, Colour & National Independence in Haiti. LC 95-8893. (C). 1995. pap. text ed. 18.95 (0-8135-2240-4) Rutgers U Pr.

— From Dessalines to Duvalier: Race, Colour & National Independence in Haiti. rev. ed. LC 95-8893. 400p. (C). 1995. reprint ed. text ed. 50.00 (0-8135-2239-0) Rutgers U Pr.

— God & Government in an "Age of Reason" LC 95-14321. 1995. write for info. (0-415-01173-6) Routledge.

— The Lost Prime Minister: A Life of Sir Charles Dilke. LC 95-6072. 1995. 40.00 (1-85285-125-2) Hambledon Press.

— The Pluralist State: The Political Ideas of J. N. Figgis & His Contemporaries. LC 94-1157. 1994. write for info. (0-312-12163-6) St Martin.

Nicholls, David & Kerr, Fergus, eds. John Henry Newman: Reason, Rhetoric, & Romanticism. 224p. (C). 1992. 29.95 (0-8093-1758-3) S Ill U Pr.

Nicholls, David & Marsh, Peter, eds. Biographical Dictionary of Modern European Radicals & Socialists: 1780-1815, Vol. I. LC 87-36961. 360p. 1988. text ed. 55.00 (0-312-01968-8) St Martin.

Nicholls, David G. & Ferguson, Stuart J. Bioenergetics. 2nd ed. 255p. 1992. pap. text ed. 37.50 (0-12-518124-8) Acad Pr.

Nicholls, Delia, jt. auth. see Hatherly, Janelle.

Nicholls, Dorothy D., ed. Gleanings from a Cornish Notebook. (C). 1989. 30.00 (1-85022-025-5, Pub. by Dyllansow Truran UK) St Mut.

Nicholls, Elgiva. Tatting. (Knitting, Crocheting, Tatting Ser.). 144p. 1984. reprint ed. pap. 4.95 (0-486-24612-4) Dover.

***Nicholls, Florence Z.** Button Hand Book. 288p. 1994. pap. 29.95 (0-9629046-1-9) New Leaf Pubs.

An Asterisk (*) at the beginning of an entry indicates that the title is appearing in BIP for the first time.

Nicholls, G. Measure for Measure. (Text & Performance Ser.). (Illus.). 96p. (C). 1986. pap. 10.95 (*0-333-34982-2*, Pub. by Macmillan UK) Humanities.

Nicholls, George. History of the English Poor Law, 3 vols., 1. rev. ed. LC 66-19700. 1967. reprint ed. write for info. (*0-678-04040-0*) Kelley.

— History of the English Poor Law, 3 vols., 2. rev. ed. LC 66-19700. 1967. reprint ed. write for info. (*0-678-04041-9*) Kelley.

— History of the English Poor Law, 3 vols., 3. rev. ed. LC 66-19700. 1967. reprint ed. write for info. (*0-678-04042-7*) Kelley.

— History of the Irish Poor Law. LC 67-28454. (Reprints of Economic Classics Ser.). x, 424p. 1967. reprint ed. 49.50 (*0-678-00325-4*) Kelley.

— History of the Scotch Poor Law. LC 67-28455. (Reprints of Economic Classics Ser.). x, 288p. 1967. reprint ed. 45.00 (*0-678-00326-2*) Kelley.

Nicholls, George, jt. auth. see Mackay, Thomas.

Nicholls, H. R. Advanced Tactile Sensing for Robotics. (Series in Robotics & Automated Systems: No. 5). 250p. 1992. text ed. 81.00 (*981-02-0870-7*) World Scientific Pub.

Nicholls, Harry R. Study of Damage to a Residential Structure from Blast Vibrations. 71p. 1974. pap. 6.00 (*0-87262-074-3*) Am Soc Civil Eng.

Nicholls, Ian. Fifty Activities for Developing Supervisory Skills. 350p. 1994. ring bd. 139.95 (*0-87425-244-X*) Human Res Dev Pr.

Nicholls, J. Design Assignments GCSE & Standard Grade. (C). 1988. 230.00 (*0-09-173229-8*, Pub. by S Thornes Pubs UK) St Mut.

— Leadership of Customer-Driven TQM. (C). 1994. 150.00x (*0-946655-57-X*, Pub. by S Thornes Pubs UK) St Mut.

— Selling Professional Services: A Handbook for Professionals. (C). 1994. 150.00x (*0-946655-56-1*, Pub. by S Thornes Pubs UK) St Mut.

Nicholls, J. & Glass, R. Coloproctology. (Illus.). 244p. 1985. pap. 51.00 (*0-387-15140-0*) Spr-Verlag.

Nicholls, J., et al, eds. Modern Methods of Igneous Petrology: Understanding Magmatic Processes. (Reviews in Mineralogy Ser.: Vol. 24). 1990. per. 22.00 (*0-939950-29-4*) Mineralogical Soc.

Nicholls, J. E. Z User Workshop, York 1991: Proceedings of the Sixth Annual Z User Meeting York, 16-17 December 1991. Van Rijsbergen, C. J., ed. (Workshops in Computing Ser.). (Illus.). viii, 403p. 1992. pap. 69.00 (*0-387-19780-X*) Spr-Verlag.

Nicholls, J. E. & Van Rijsbergen, C. J., eds. Z User Workshop: Proceedings of the Fourth Annual Z User Meeting, 15 December 1989, Oxford, U. K. (Workshops in Computing Ser.). (Illus.). 288p. 1990. pap. 59.00 (*0-387-19627-7*) Spr-Verlag.

— Z User Workshop Oxford 1990: Proceedings of the Annual Meeting, 5th, December 17-18, 1990, U. K. (Workshops in Computing Ser.). ix, 387p. 1991. pap. 59.00 (*0-387-19672-2*) Spr-Verlag.

Nicholls, J. G. Repair & Regeneration of the Nervous System: Berlin, 1981 Proceedings. (Dahlem Workshop Reports: Vol. 24). 411p. 1982. 39.00 (*0-387-11649-4*) Spr-Verlag.

Nicholls, J. G., et al. From Neuron to Brain: A Cellular & Molecular Approach to the Function of the Nervous System. 3rd ed. LC 92-15974. (Illus.). 680p. (C). 1992. text ed. 51.95x (*0-87893-580-0*) Sinauer Assocs.

Nicholls, J. R., et al. Modelling of Erosion Corrosion Processes in Energy Conversion Systems, No. 14051. 314p. 1992. pap. 45.00 (*92-826-3978-9*, CD-NA-14051-EN-C, Pub. by Europ Com) UNIPUB.

Nicholls, J. W. The Matter of Courtesy: Medieval Courtesy Books & the Gawain-Poet. LC 84-24599. 241p. 1985. 79.00 (*0-85991-185-3*) Boydell & Brewer.

***Nicholls, John & Thorkildsen, Theresa, eds.** Reasons for Learning: Expanding the Conversation on Student-Teacher Collaboration. 192p. (C). 1995. pap. text ed. 16.95x (*0-8077-3397-0*) Tchrs Coll.

— Reasons for Learning: Expanding the Conversation on Student-Teacher Collaboration. 192p. (C). 1995. text ed. 34.00x (*0-8077-3398-9*) Tchrs Coll.

Nicholls, John, jt. auth. see Martin, Peter.

Nicholls, John, jt. ed. see Wells, Gordon.

Nicholls, John, et al. Beginning Writing. (English, Language & Education Ser.). 128p. 1990. pap. 27.00 (*0-335-09224-1*, Open Univ Pr) Taylor & Francis.

Nicholls, John E. Structure & Design of Programming Languages. LC 74-12801. (IBM Systems Programming Ser.). (Illus.). 592p. (C). 1975. text ed. write for info. (*0-201-14454-9*) Addison-Wesley.

Nicholls, John G. The Competitive Ethos & Democratic Education. LC 88-16303. (Illus.). 280p. 1989. 42.50 (*0-674-15417-7*) HUP.

— The Search for Connections: Studies of Regeneration in the Nervous System of the Leech. LC 86-22061. (Magnes Memorial Lectures Ser.: Vol. 2). (Illus.). 86p. (Orig.). 1987. pap. text ed. 21.95 (*0-87893-577-0*) Sinauer Assocs.

Nicholls, John G. & Hazzard, Susan P. Education As Adventure: Lessons from the Second Grade. LC 92-36030. 240p. (C). 1993. text ed. 37.00 (*0-8077-3240-0*); pap. text ed. 17.95 (*0-8077-3239-7*) Tchrs Coll.

Nicholls, Josephine H. Bayou Triste: A Story of Louisiana. LC 72-1516. (Black Heritage Library Collection). 1977. reprint ed. 26.95 (*0-8369-9040-4*) Ayer.

Nicholls, Judith, ed. Sing Freedom! Children's Poetry. (Illus.). 132p. (J). (gr. 3 up). 1992. 16.95 (*0-571-16513-3*); pap. 9.95 (*0-571-16514-1*) Faber & Faber.

— What on Earth? Poems with a Conservation Theme. (Illus.). 132p. (J). (gr. 2 up). 1989. pap. 8.95 (*0-571-15262-7*) Faber & Faber.

***Nicholls, Keith.** Volleyball. (Skills of the Game Ser.). (Illus.). 120p. 1995. pap. 16.95 (*1-85223-831-3*, Pub. by Crowood UK) Trafalgar.

***Nicholls, Lisa S.** Visual FoxPro 3.0 Power Toolkit: Cutting-Edge Tools & Techniques for Programmers. 800p. 1995. cd-rom, pap. text ed. 49.95 (*1-56604-241-0*) Ventana Pr.

Nicholls, M. G., et al. Legal Studies for South Australia: Years 11 & 12. 1989. Australia. pap. 31.00 (*0-409-49471-2*) Butterworth Legal Pubs.

Nicholls, Mark. Investigating the Gunpowder Plot. LC 90-20286. 251p. 1991. text ed. 39.95 (*0-7190-3225-3*, Pub. by Manchester Univ Pr UK) St Martin.

Nicholls, Martin. After Dinner Speeches. (Work Matters Ser.). 96p. 1991. pap. 4.95 (*0-7063-6816-9*, Pub. by Ward Lock UK) Sterling.

***Nicholls, Maureen.** Gold Pan Mining Company & Shops Breckenridge, Colorado. Gilliland, Mary E., ed. LC 94-66385. (Illus.). 64p. (Orig.). 1994. pap. text ed. 13.95 (*0-9641029-0-0*) Quandary Pubng.

Nicholls, P., et al, eds. Membrane Proteins. LC 77-30604. (Federation of European Biochemical Societies Ser.). 330p. 1978. 143.00 (*0-08-022626-4*, Pub. by Pergamon Repr UK) Franklin.

Nicholls, Paul. Tolley's Discrimination Law Handbook. 304p. 1991. 66.00 (*0-85459-425-6*, Pub. by Tolley Pubng UK) St Mut.

Nicholls, Paul & Ensor, Pat, eds. CD-ROM for Library Users: A Guide to Managing & Maintaining User Access. 200p. 1994. pap. 37.50 (*0-88736-940-5*) Learned Info.

Nicholls, Paul T. CD-ROM Buyer's Guide & Handbook: The Definitive Reference for CD-ROM Users, Third Edition of CD-ROM Collection. rev. ed. (Builder's Toolkit Ser.). 736p. 1993. pap. 44.95 (*0-910965-08-0*) Online.

— CD-ROM Collection Builder's Toolkit, 1992: The Definitive Reference for CD-ROM Buyers. 2nd ed. (Illus.). 470p. 1991. 39.95 (*0-910965-02-1*) Online.

Nicholls, Peter. The Biology of Oxygen. Head, J. J., ed. LC 81-67981. (Carolina Biology Readers Ser.: No. 100). (Illus.). 16p. (gr. 10 up). 1982. pap. 2.75 (*0-89278-300-1*, 45-9700) Carolina Biological.

— Cytochromes & Cell Respiration. 2nd ed. Head, J. J., ed. LC 78-55322. (Carolina Biology Readers Ser.: No. 66). (Illus.). 16p. (C). (gr. 10 up). 1984. pap. 2.75 (*0-89278-266-8*, 45-9666) Carolina Biological.

— Modernisms: A Literary Guide. 1995. 50.00 (*0-520-20102-7*); pap. 16.00 (*0-520-20103-5*) U CA Pr.

Nicholls, Peter, jt. ed. see Clute, John.

Nicholls, Peter J., jt. auth. see Sons, Linda R.

Nicholls, R. W., jt. auth. see Armstrong, B. H.

Nicholls, Rex & Vaughan, Patrick. The Gospel of Mark Illuminated. (Illus.). 128p. 1990. 49.95 (*0-7459-1440-3*) Lion USA.

Nicholls, Richard. Corpus Speculorum Etruscorum: Great Britain 2 Cambridge. Swaddling, Judith & Rasmussen, Tom, eds. LC 92-35756. (Illus.). 144p. (C). 1994. 95.00 (*0-521-43380-0*) Cambridge U Pr.

Nicholls, Richard, ed. see London, Jack.

Nicholls, Richard E. Beginning Hydroponics. rev. ed. LC 89-43022. (Illus.). 128p. 1990. pap. 8.95 (*0-89471-741-3*) Running Pr.

Nicholls, Robert P., jt. ed. see Ray, Mary H.

Nicholls, Roger A. Nietzsche in the Early Work of Thomas Mann. LC 55-9553. (University of California Publications in Social Welfare: Vol. 45). 128p. reprint ed. pap. 36.50 (*0-317-29559-4*, 2021252) Bks Demand.

Nicholls, Sandra & Hoadley-Maidment, Elizabeth. Current Issues in Teaching English As a Second Language to Adults. 160p. 1988. pap. text ed. 14.95 (*0-7131-8450-7*, Pub. by E Arnold UK) Routledge Chapman & Hall.

***Nicholls, William.** Christian Antisemitism: A History of Hate. LC 92-35713. 532p. 1995. pap. 30.00 (*1-56821-519-3*) Aronson.

Nicholls, William, ed. Modernity & Religion. (SR Supplements Ser.: No. 19). 250p. (C). 1987. pap. 19.95 (*0-88920-154-4*, Pub. by Wilfrid Laurier CN) Humanities.

Nicholls, William, jt. auth. see Kent, Ian.

Nicholls, Willis J. English Law for Business Studies. 3rd ed. LC 74-81551. 437p. reprint ed. pap. 124.60 (*0-317-30074-1*, 2020985) Bks Demand.

***Nicholoff, Jac A., ed. & intro.** Electroporation Protocaols for Microorganisms. (Methods in Molecular Biology Ser.: No. 47). (Illus.). 416p. 1995. spiral bd. 69.50 (*0-89603-310-4*) Humana.

Nicholoson, Daniel. Remembering His Benefit. 48p. 1988. pap. text ed. 2.95 (*0-88144-074-4*) Christian Pub.

Nicholoson, Michael. Mahatma Gandhi: Champion of Human Rights. LC 89-77589. (People Who Made a Difference Ser.). (Illus.). 64p. (J). (gr. 3-4). 1990. lib. bdg. 21.26 (*0-8368-0390-6*) Gareth Stevens Inc.

Nicholoson, Peter, jt. ed. see Horton, John.

Nichols. Ambulatory Gynecology. 2nd ed. 528p. 1995. 52.50 (*0-397-51325-9*) Lippincott.

— Bird Hunter. large type ed. 1991. 17.95 (*0-7451-8044-2*, AH092, Atlantic Lrg Print); pap. 15.95 (*0-7927-0508-4*, AS0128, Atlantic Lrg Print) Chivers N Amer.

— Birds of Algonquin Legend. 1995. (*0-472-10611-2*) U of Mich Pr.

— Gynecologic & Obstetric Surgery. 1232p. 1992. 115.00 (*0-8016-6245-1*) Mosby Yr Bk.

— The Johns Hopkins Hospital Golden Hour. (SPA.). 1992. 31.65 (*0-8016-6710-0*) Mosby Yr Bk.

— Medical-Surgical Nursing: A Study Guide. (Illus.). 320p. 1989. pap. text ed. 15.95 (*0-8016-5494-7*) Mosby Yr Bk.

— Moving & Learning: Text & Lessons Plan Manual. 3rd ed. 1993. 44.95 (*0-8016-7867-6*) Mosby Yr Bk.

— Moving & Learning: The Elementary School PE Experience. 2nd ed. (Illus.). 640p. 1990. 46.95 (*0-8016-5801-2*) Mosby Yr Bk.

— Moving & Learning: The Elementary School Physical Education Experience. (C). 1986. 28.00 (*0-8016-3851-8*) Mosby Yr Bk.

— Moving & Learning: The Elementary School Physical Education Experience. 3rd ed. 704p. 1994. 44.95 (*0-8016-7770-X*) Mosby Yr Bk.

— Moving & Learning Lesson Plan Manual. 2nd ed. 392p. 1990. pap. 18.95 (*0-8016-5802-0*) Mosby Yr Bk.

— Moving & Learning, Lessons Plan Manual. 3rd ed. 1993. 18.95 (*0-8016-7777-7*) Mosby Yr Bk.

— Moving & Learning Two Text & Lesson Plan Manual. 1990. 46.95 (*0-8016-3687-6*) Mosby Yr Bk.

— Nichols: Plays One. (Metuchen World Dramatists Ser.). 376p. 1991. pap. 17.95 (*0-413-64870-2*) Heinemann.

— Psychological Care in Physical Illness. 2nd ed. 248p. 1993. pap. 41.50 (*1-56593-134-3*, 0446) Singular Publishing.

— Re-Operative Gynecologic Surgery. 384p. 1990. 89.00 (*0-8151-6383-5*, Yr Bk Med Pubs) Mosby Yr Bk.

Nichols & Cameron. Textbook of Pediatric Cardiac Intensive Care. 1000p. 1994. 149.00 (*0-8016-6929-4*) Mosby Yr Bk.

Nichols & Evans. Lab Manual for Anatomy & Physiology. 240p. (C). 1992. pap. text ed. 16.95 (*0-8403-7968-4*) Kendall-Hunt.

Nichols & Ionson, eds. Sensing, Discrimination, & Signal Processing & Superconducting Materials & Instrumentation. 1988. 45.00 (*0-89252-914-8*, 879) SPIE.

Nichols & Pachard. Maine One Hundred Years Ago. (Historical Ser.). (Illus.). 1977. pap. 3.50 (*0-89540-049-9*, SB-049) Sun Pub.

Nichols & Woolson. Old Florida. (Historical Ser.). (Illus.). 1977. pap. 3.50 (*0-89540-054-5*, SB-054) Sun Pub.

Nichols, jt. auth. see Scala, Bea.

Nichols, et al. Golden Hour: The Handbook of Advanced Pediatric Life Support. 480p. 1990. pap. 30.95 (*0-8151-6395-9*, Yr Bk Med Pubs) Mosby Yr Bk.

***Nichols, Aidan.** Byzantine Gospel: Maximus the Confessor in Modern Scholarship. 280p. 1993. text ed. 39.95 (*0-567-09651-3*, Pub. by T & T Clark UK) Bks Intl VA.

— A Grammar of Consent: The Existence of God in Christian Tradition. LC 90-50978. (Library of Religious Philosophy: Vol. 6). (C). 1991. text ed. 31.95 (*0-268-01026-9*) U of Notre Dame Pr.

— The Holy Eucharist. 200p. 1991. pap. 15.95 (*0-685-51641-5*, Pub. by Veritas Publns IE) Ignatius Pr.

— Holy Eucharist. 200p. 1989. pap. 27.00 (*1-85390-182-2*, Pub. by Veritas IE) St Mut.

— Holy Order: The Apostolic Ministry from the New Testament to Vatican Two. 200p. (Orig.). 1991. pap. 16.95 (*1-85390-175-X*, Pub. by Veritas Publns IE) Ignatius Pr.

— The Panther & the Hind: A Theological History of Angelicanism. 208p. 1993. pap. text ed. 19.95 (*0-567-29232-0*, Pub. by T & T Clark UK) Bks Intl VA.

— Rome & the Eastern Churches: A Study in Schism. 240p. (Orig.). 1992. pap. text ed. 19.95 (*0-8146-5019-8*, M Glazier) Liturgical Pr.

— The Shape of Catholic Theology: An Introduction to Its Sources, Principles, & History. 250p. (Orig.). 1991. pap. text ed. 16.95 (*0-8146-1909-6*) Liturgical Pr.

— Theology in the Russian Diaspora: Church, Fathers, Eucharist in Nikolai Afanas'ev (1893-1966) 280p. (C). 1990. 74.95 (*0-521-36543-0*) Cambridge U Pr.

Nichols, Aidan, ed. see Ratzinger, Joseph C.

Nichols, Aidan, tr. see Von Balthasar, Hans U.

Nichols, Alan, Sr. Letters Home from the Lafayette Flying Corps. Nichols, Nancy A., ed. LC 92-28089. (Illus.). 320p. 1993. 24.95 (*0-9630274-0-9*); pap. 14.95 (*0-9630274-7-6*) J D Huff.

Nichols, Alan H. Higher Ground: A Sacred Mountain Primer. (Illus.). 224p. 1994. pap. 19.95 (*0-9630274-1-7*) J D Huff.

— Journey: A Bicycle Odyssey Through Central Asia. Nichols, Nancy A., ed. (Illus.). 221p. 1991. 22.95 (*0-9630274-4-1*) J D Huff.

Nichols, Alan H. & Nichols, Nancy A. Sacred Mountains of California. (Illus.). 224p. 1994. 35.00 (*0-9630274-3-3*) J D Huff.

Nichols, Albert L. Targeting Economic Incentives for Environmental Protection. (Regulation of Economic Activity Ser.). (Illus.). 248p. 1984. 30.00 (*0-262-14036-5*) MIT Pr.

Nichols, Ann E. Seeable Signs: The Iconography of the Seven Sacraments, 1350-1544. (Illus.). 384p. (C). 1993. text ed. 89.00 (*0-85115-342-9*) Boydell & Brewer.

Nichols, Ann E., jt. ed. see Davidson, Clifford.

Nichols, Anne. Abie's Irish Rose. LC 74-29510. (Modern Jewish Experience Ser.). 1975. reprint ed. 30.95 (*0-405-06736-4*) Ayer.

Nichols, Annie. Step by Step: Quick & Healthy Vegetarian. (Illus.). 96p. 1995. 9.98 (*0-8317-7847-4*) Smithmark.

Nichols, Ashton. The Poetics of Epiphany: Nineteenth Century Origins of the Modern Literary Moment. LC 86-16042. 272p. 1987. 31.50 (*0-8173-0327-8*) U of Ala Pr.

Nichols, Barry, illus. Opposite Song Big Book. (J). (ps-2). 1988. pap. text ed. 14.00 (*0-922053-06-5*) N Edge Res.

Nichols, Belia, jt. auth. see Nichols, Peter.

Nichols, Beverley. Down the Garden Path. 290p. 1986. reprint ed. pap. 19.95 (*1-85149-007-8*) Antique Collect.

Nichols, Bill. Blurred Boundaries. LC 94-2205. 1994. 29.95 (*0-253-34064-0*); pap. 12.95 (*0-253-20900-5*) Ind U Pr.

— Ideology & the Image: Social Representation in the Cinema & Other Media. LC 80-7684. (Illus.). 384p. 1981. 29.95 (*0-253-18287-5*); pap. 14.95 (*0-253-20256-6*, MB-256) Ind U Pr.

— Newsreel: Documentary Filmaking on the American Left. Jowett, Garth S., ed. LC 79-6681. (Dissertations on Film Ser.). 313p. 1980. 23.95 (*0-405-12914-9*) Ayer.

— Representing Reality: Issues & Concepts in Documentary. LC 91-2637. (Illus.). 336p. 1992. 39.95 (*0-253-34060-8*); pap. 17.50 (*0-253-20681-2*, MB-681) Ind U Pr.

Nichols, Bill, ed. Movies & Methods, Vol. I. LC 74-22968. 1977. pap. 18.00 (*0-520-03151-2*) U CA Pr.

— Movies & Methods, Vol. II. LC 74-22969. 1985. 55.00 (*0-520-05408-3*); pap. 18.00 (*0-520-05409-1*) U CA Pr.

***Nichols, Bradford.** POSIX Threads. 350p. 1995. 29.95 (*1-56592-115-1*) OReilly & Assocs.

Nichols, Breck. Big Book of Science Charts: My Body. (Illus.). 26p. (Orig.). 1992. student ed 14.95 (*1-55734-570-8*) Tchr Create Mat.

Nichols Brown, Ann L. Hillsborough Co, NH, Census, 1850, Pt. 3. (Illus.). 406p. (Orig.). 1993. pap. text ed. 33.00 (*1-55613-913-6*) Heritage Bk.

Nichols, Bruce & Loescher, Gil, eds. The Moral Nation: Humanitarianism & U. S. Foreign Policy Today. LC 88-40323. (C). 1990. text ed. 29.95 (*0-268-01372-1*); pap. text ed. 15.95 (*0-268-01398-5*) U of Notre Dame Pr.

Nichols, Buffy, jt. auth. see Nichols, Mark.

Nichols, Buford, jt. ed. see Lifschitz, Carlos H.

Nichols, Buford L., ed. Nutrition During Infancy. LC 88-80716. (Illus.). 440p. 1988. text ed. 41.00 (*0-932883-09-5*) Hanley & Belfus.

Nichols, C. D. Learning, Measurement & Discipline. 60p. (C). 1993. student ed 13.22 (*1-56870-057-1*) RonJon Pub.

Nichols, C. M., jt. auth. see Nichols, James.

Nichols, Carol S. Structure & Bonding in Condensed Matter. (Illus.). 312p. (C). 1994. 59.95 (*0-521-46283-5*) Cambridge U Pr.

— Structure & Bonding in Condensed Matter. (Illus.). 312p. (C). 1995. pap. 24.95 (*0-521-46822-1*) Cambridge U Pr.

Nichols, Carole. Votes & More for Women: Suffrage & After in Connecticut. LC 83-8405. (Women & History Ser.: No. 5). 92p. 1983. text ed. 29.95 (*0-86656-192-7*) Haworth Pr.

Nichols, Cecil B. Human Growth & Development Study Guide. 256p. 1993. per. 18.95 (*0-8403-8688-5*) Kendall-Hunt.

Nichols, Charle W. De Lyon. The Ultra-Fashionable Peerage of America. LC 75-1864. (Leisure Class in America Ser.). 1975. reprint ed. 16.95 (*0-405-06930-8*) Ayer.

Nichols, Charlene & Wright, Darlene. Loan Administration in the 90's: Looking Ahead, 10 vols., Set. 1994. text ed. write for info. (*1-880999-30-7*) Loan Admin.

— Loan Administration in the 90's: Looking Ahead, Vol. 1. 1994. text ed. 150.00 (*1-880999-21-8*) Loan Admin.

— Loan Administration in the 90's: Looking Ahead, Vol. 2. 1994. text ed. 150.00 (*1-880999-22-6*) Loan Admin.

— Loan Administration in the 90's: Looking Ahead, Vol. 3. 1994. text ed. 150.00 (*1-880999-23-4*) Loan Admin.

— Loan Administration in the 90's: Looking Ahead, Vol. 4. 1994. text ed. 150.00 (*1-880999-24-2*) Loan Admin.

— Loan Administration in the 90's: Looking Ahead, Vol. 5. 1994. text ed. 150.00 (*1-880999-25-0*) Loan Admin.

— Loan Administration in the 90's: Looking Ahead, Vol. 6. 1994. text ed. 150.00 (*1-880999-26-9*) Loan Admin.

— Loan Administration in the 90's: Looking Ahead, Vol. 7. 1994. text ed. 150.00 (*1-880999-27-7*) Loan Admin.

— Loan Administration in the 90's: Looking Ahead, Vol. 8. 1994. text ed. 150.00 (*1-880999-28-5*) Loan Admin.

— Loan Administration in the 90's: Looking Ahead, Vol. 9. 1994. text ed. 150.00 (*1-880999-29-3*) Loan Admin.

— Loan Administration in the 90's: Looking Ahead, Vol. 10. 1994. text ed. 150.00 (*1-880999-20-X*) Loan Admin.

Nichols, Charles S., Jr. & Shaw, Henry I., Jr. Okinawa: Victory in the Pacific. (Elite Unit Ser.: No. 19). (Illus.). 368p. 1989. reprint ed. 35.00 (*0-318-41699-9*) Battery Pr.

Nichols, Christopher. Dracula: Death of Nosferatu. 40p. 1991. pap. 2.50 (*0-87129-091-X*, D54) Dramatic Pub.

***Nichols, Christopher P. & Bentley, Earl.** Lamia. 1994. 5.00 (*0-87129-404-4*, L80) Dramatic Pub.

Nichols, Claude A. Moral Education among the North American Indians. LC 75-177112. (Columbia University. Teachers College. Contributions to Education Ser.: No. 427). reprint ed. 37.50 (*0-404-55427-X*) AMS Pr.

***Nichols, Clive.** Photographing Plants & Gardens. (Illus.). 160p. 1995. 34.95 (*0-7153-0135-7*, Pub. by D & C Pub UK) Sterling.

Nichols, Daniel E. Distance off Tables. LC 43-15657. 253p. reprint ed. pap. 72.20 (*0-7837-4377-7*, 2044117) Bks Demand.

***Nichols, David.** The Administration of Public Safety in Higher Education. (Illus.). 264p. 1987. pap. 33.95 (*0-398-06306-0*) C C Thomas.

— The Administration of Public Safety in Higher Education. (Illus.). 264p. 1987. 55.95x (*0-398-05330-8*) C C Thomas.

— University-Community Relations: Living Together Effectively. 142p. 1990. pap. 18.95 (*0-398-06307-9*) C C Thomas.

— University-Community Relations: Living Together Effectively. 142p. (C). 1990. text ed. 32.95x (*0-398-05680-3*) C C Thomas.

Nichols, David, ed. Ernie's America: The Best of Ernie Pyle's 1930s Travel Dispatches. LC 90-50173. 480p. 1990. pap. 14.95 (*0-679-73177-6*, Vin) Random.

— Ernie's War: The Best of Ernie Pyle's World War II Dispatches. LC 85-18390. (Illus.). 480p. 1986. 19.95 (*0-394-54923-6*) Random.

— Monitoring the Marine Environment. LC 78-71806. 220p. 1979. text ed. 65.00 (*0-275-90401-6*, C0401, Praeger Pubs) Greenwood.

Nichols, David & Terkel, Studs, eds. Ernie's War: The Best of Ernie Pyle's World War II Dispatches. (Illus.). 448p. 1987. pap. 12.00 (*0-671-64452-1*, Touchstone Bks) S&S Trade.

N

An Asterisk (*) at the beginning of an entry indicates that the title is appearing in BIP for the first time.

*Nichols, David, et al. Butterworth Scottish Family Law Service. 1994. ring bd. 275.00 (*0-406-01356-X*, UK) Butterworth Legal Pubs.
— The Law of Succession in Scotland. Date not set. pap. text ed. write for info. (*0-406-42500-0*, UK) Butterworth Legal Pubs.
Nichols, David H. & Anderson, George W. Clinical Problems, Injuries & Complications of Gynecologic Surgery. 2nd ed. 360p. 1988. 75.00 (*0-683-06496-7*) Williams & Wilkins.
***Nichols, David H. & Delancey, John O. L., eds.** Clinical Problems, Injuries & Complications of Gynecologic & Obstetric Surgery. rev. ed. LC 94-44911. 453p. 1995. 85.00 (*0-683-06497-5*) Williams & Wilkins.
Nichols, David H. & Randall, Clyde L. Vaginal Surgery. 3rd ed. (Illus.). 480p. 1989. 85.00 (*0-683-06494-0*) Williams & Wilkins.
Nichols, David K. The Myth of the Modern Presidency. 192p. (C). 1994. 32.50 (*0-271-01316-8*); pap. 13.95 (*0-271-01317-6*) Pa St U Pr.
Nichols, Dean. Copper Sands & The N. P. M. W. A. R. A. LC 93-71480. (Illus.). 1994. pap. 14.95 (*0-8323-0503-0*) Binford Mort.
— Islands of Experience. 80p. 1972. 12.50 (*0-682-47549-1*) Binford Mort.
— Kid on the River. LC 88-72057. (Illus.). 128p. (Orig.). 1988. pap. 9.95 (*0-8323-0463-8*) Binford Mort.
— A Poet's Sketch of His Biography. 96p. 1979. 12.50 (*0-682-49420-8*) Binford Mort.
— Two Cats for Puerto Rico & A Sailor's Yarns & Observations. LC 93-71481. (Illus.). 1993. pap. 14.95 (*0-8323-0502-2*) Binford Mort.
Nichols, Deborah L. & Smiley, F. E., eds. Excavations on Black Mesa, 1982: A Descriptive Report. LC 82-72189. (Center for Archaeological Investigations Research Paper Ser.: No. 39). (Illus.). xxxviii, 856p. (Orig.). 1984. fiche, pap. 30.00 (*0-88104-016-9*) Center Archaeo.
Nichols, Donald D. The Delirious Decade, Nineteen Sixty-Five to Nineteen Seventy-Five: A Social History of a Community College. (Illus.). 271p. (Orig.). (C). 1990. pap. text ed. 14.95 (*0-685-35415-6*) Tri-Nic Pr.
— The Delirious Decade, 1965-1975: A Social History of a Community College. (Illus.). 272p. (Orig.). (C). 1991. pap. text ed. 14.95 (*0-9626770-0-0*) Tri-Nic Pr.
Nichols, Donald H. Drinking - Driving Litigation: Criminal & Civil - Trial Notebook. LC 85-29890. (Criminal Law Ser.). 1987. ring bd. 115.00 (*0-685-59800-4*) Clark Boardman Callaghan.
— Drinking-Driving Litigation: Criminal & Civil, 5 vols. (Criminal Law Ser.). 1989. ring bd. 520.00 (*0-685-14562-X*) Clark Boardman Callaghan.
***Nichols, Donald H., ed.** The Drinking Driver in Minnesota, 1989. suppl. ed. 1994. 35.00 (*0-250-40744-2*) Butterworth Legal Pubs.
— The Drinking Driver in Minnesota, 1989. 2nd ed. 400p. 1994. ring bd. 115.00 (*0-86678-009-2*) Michie Butterworth.
Nichols, Donald R. The Income Investor: Choosing Investments That Pay Cash Today & Tomorrow. 212p. 1990. 19.95 (*0-88462-738-1*, 5608-08); pap. 12.95 (*0-7931-0025-9*, 5608-31) Dearborn Finan.
— The Personal Investor's Complete Book of Bonds. 240p. 1989. 23.95 (*0-88462-627-X*, 5608-14) Dearborn Finan.
— Personal Investor's Complete Book of Bonds. 240p. 1990. pap. 12.95 (*0-7931-0089-5*, 5608-43) Dearborn Finan.
— Starting Small, Investing Smart: What to Do with Five to Five Thousand Dollars. 2nd rev. ed. 200p. 1987. text ed. 26.00 (*1-55623-041-9*) Irwin Prof Pubng.
— Treasury Securities; Making Money with Uncle Sam. 224p. 1990. 24.95 (*0-7931-0016-X*, 5608-06) Dearborn Finan.
Nichols, Donald R., ed. The Handbook of Investor Relations. 400p. 1988. text ed. 57.00 (*0-87094-966-7*) Irwin Prof Pubng.
Nichols, Dwight O. Discover Truth & Be Free. 68p. (Orig.). 1994. pap. 4.95 (*0-9624064-1-4*) New Era Trng.
— Listening to Ourselves: The Key to Everything That Matters. 326p. 1993. 21.95 (*0-9624064-0-6*) New Era Trng.
Nichols, E. J. Issues in Education: A Comparative Analysis. 264p. (C). 1983. pap. 39.00 (*0-317-93194-6*, Pub. by P Chapman Pub UK) St Mut.
Nichols, E. Ray. No Escape from Love. LC 89-285. 1991. 14.95 (*0-87949-312-7*) Ashley Bks.
Nichols, Edward J. Towards Gettysburg: A Biography of General John F. Reynolds. 276p. 1988. reprint ed. 30.00 (*0-942211-64-2*) Olde Soldier Bks.
Nichols, Edward L. & Howes, H. L. Cathodo-luminescence & the Luminescence of Incandescent Solids. LC 28-21004. (Carnegie Institution of Washington Publication Ser.: No. 384). 358p. reprint ed. pap. 102.10 (*0-317-08547-6*, 2007882) Bks Demand.
Nichols, Edwin J., et al. Teaching Mathematics, Vol. 1: Culture, Motivation, History & Classroom Management. Ratteray, Oswald M., ed. (Illus.). 48p. (Orig.). 1986. pap. 3.50 (*0-941001-00-8*) Inst Indep Educ.
Nichols, Elisabeth. Young Chidren: Growing & Learning Together. (Orig.). 1990. pap. text ed. 3.95 (*0-935493-37-9*) Programs Educ.
Nichols, Elizabeth. Tune into Limericks. 1979. 7.50 (*0-913650-05-6*) CPP Belwin.

Nichols, Elizabeth L. Christian Holiday Verses. (Illus.). 24p. (Orig.). 1993. pap. text ed. 3.95 (*1-880473-05-4*) Fam Hist Educ.
Inspirational Christian verses--ideal for devotionals, family sharing, or personal inspiration. Twelve simple-language poems about Jesus Christ as Savior & Redeemer--with emphasis on his birth, resurrection & love; & Christmas, & Easter. Ideal gift. Cardstock cover; four-color reproductions of two Harry Anderson paintings--"The Prophet Isaiah Foretells Christ's Birth" & "Second Coming;" worth its price just for these paintings. Reader Responses: "A MOST INSPIRING BOOKLET OF POETRY ON THE BIRTH & MISSION OF THE SAVIOR." "THE AUTHOR HAS BEEN GIVEN THE GIFT OF INSIGHT & THE POWER TO SHARE THAT INSIGHT IN VERSE." "THE FEELINGS IT EVOKES PREPARES ME FOR THE GLORIOUS CELEBRATION OF THE SAVIOR'S PRICELESS GIFT TO US." "WE JUST READ CHRISTIAN HOLIDAY VERSES FOR FAMILY HOME EVENING AN EVENING WHERE THE WHOLE FAMILY SHARES TOGETHER<, & ENJOYED EVERY WORD OF IT." A few selected verses: "A child is born to Mary,/A baby dear & sweet;/An infant to be cared for/By loving hands petite"-(page 3). "It's true! 'tis true!/How can we know?/Kneel & pray, & ask for your heart/To know from within..."--(page 23). Order from: Family History Educators, Box 510606, Salt Lake City, UT 84151-0606. Phone & FAX: 801-359-7391. *Publisher Provided Annotation.*

—Genealogy in the Computer Age: Understanding FamilySearch (Ancestral File, International Genealogical Index, Social Security Death Index) rev. ed. (Illus.). 56p. 1994. pap. text ed. 9.95 (*1-880473-07-0*) Fam Hist Educ.
Describes & illustrates computer genealogy programs & files published by The Church of Jesus Christ of Latter-Day Saints (Mormons) available at thousands of locations. Simple-language text; glossary; 65 illustrations, prepares for a visiting library where FamilySearch (r) available. On compact disc, FamilySearch is used on personal computers with compact disc drives. Main files: Ancestral File--a pedigree-linked file for sharing genealogies, focusing on persons now deceased. Anyone can use or contribute to it (20 million names, 1994 edition); International Genealogical Index (tm)--240 million names, 1993-94 editions, from 90 countries; pre-1900s); Social Security Death Index--47 million records, deaths reported to U. S. Social Security, 1962-1993. Released by U. S. Government. Records can be copied from these files for use in personal computer genealogy software without rekeying the data. ALA recommended. "A must if you want to gain the most from the millions of names & records provided by FamilySearch."--review. "... has answered more questions for me & the many people who are asking me questions."--Librarian, Hawaii. Author: internationally recognized specialist; accredited genealogist. Order from: Family History Educators, Box 510606, Salt Lake City, UT 84151-0606. Phone & FAX 801-359-7391. *Publisher Provided Annotation.*

—The Genesis of Your Genealogy: Step-by-Step Instruction for the Beginner in Family History. 3rd enl. ed. (Illus.). 74p. (Orig.). 1992. pap. text ed. 8.95 (*1-880473-04-6*) Fam Hist Educ.
State-of-the-art, expert step-by-step instruction includes computers & genealogy; basic how-to of sources, resources, terminology; simple language; 42 illustrations. Three sections: basic information followed by steps guiding students through actions; "By the time students complete it, they will not only have learned about the subject, but will have the beginning of their family history recorded on pedigree charts & family group sheet (blank forms included); ...part 2 (provides) basic understanding of how computers are used in the field of family history...at home, in libraries & family history facilities. Part 3 is a glossary that not only defines but explains."--(review). Used as community college & university text. "Without doubt ... the most superb how- to book ever published for use by a beginner in genealogy."-- (letter). "so interesting it'll keep you going."--(review). "Author uses learning objectives, outline, question & answer, & action assignments to stimulate learning. Index supplemented by list of questions with page numbers."--(review). Author: internationally recognized specialist; accredited genealogist (A.G.). Order from: Family History Educators, Box 510606, Salt Lake City, Utah 84151- 0606. Phone & FAX:801-359-7391. *Publisher Provided Annotation.*

Nichols, Elizabeth L., illus. Finding Your Relationship to a Known Relative. enl. rev. ed. 6p. (Orig.). 1993. pap. 1.95 (*1-880473-06-2*) Fam Hist Educ.
Nichols, Ellen, ed. Northwest Originals: Oregon Women & Their Art. (Illus.). 112p. (Orig.). 1989. pap. 19.95 (*0-9624305-0-1*) MatriMedia.
Nichols, Eugene D. & Schwartz, Sharon L. Mathematics Dictionary & Handbook. 464p. (YA). (gr. 5-10). 1993. text ed. 28.95 (*1-882269-00-4*) N Schwartz Pub.
Nichols, Eve K. Mobilizing Against AIDS. enl. rev. ed. LC 88-30100. (Illus.). 387p. 1989. 34.50 (*0-674-57763-9*); pap. text ed. 12.95 (*0-674-57762-0*) HUP.
Nichols, Eve K. & Institute of Medicine - National Academy of Sciences Staff. Human Gene Therapy. LC 88-574. 264p. 1988. pap. text ed. 12.95 (*0-674-41480-2*) HUP.
Nichols, Forbes, jt. auth. see Shelton, Vaughan.
***Nichols, Frances S., ed.** Index to Schoolcraft's "Indian Tribes of the United States" (Bureau of American Ethnology Bulletins Ser.). 257p. 1995. lib. bdg. 89.00 (*0-7812-4152-9*) Rprt Serv.
Nichols, Frances S., ed. see Schoolcraft, Henry R.
Nichols, Francine H. & Humenick, Sharron S. Childbirth Education: Practice, Research & Theory. (Illus.). 544p. 1988. text ed. 52.50 (*0-7216-2052-3*) Saunders.
Nichols, Francis M. Britton: The French Text Carefully Revised with an English Translation, Introduction & Notes, Vol. I. LC 83-80259. 419p. 1983. reprint ed. lib. bdg. 158.00 (*0-912004-49-5*) W W Gaunt.
— Britton: The French Text Carefully Revised with an English Translation, Introduction & Notes, Vol. II. 398p. 1983. reprint ed. write for info. (*0-318-57311-3*) W W Gaunt.
Nichols, Francis M., tr. The Marvels of Rome. rev. ed. LC 86-45750. (Historical Travel Ser.). Orig. Title: Mirabilia Urbis Romae. (Illus.). 164p. 1986. pap. 8.95 (*0-934977-02-X*) Italica Pr.
Nichols, Frank. Curves. (J). 1989. pap. 3.95 (*0-85953-049-3*) Childs Play.
— Stencils. (J). 1989. pap. 3.95 (*0-85953-048-5*) Childs Play.
— Tangrams. (J). 1989. pap. 3.95 (*0-85953-050-7*) Childs Play.
Nichols, Frank, illus. Circles. (Shape Play Ser.). (Orig.). (J). (ps-2). 1976. pap. 3.95 (*0-85953-047-7*) Childs Play.
***Nichols, Frank R.** Tobe. LC 94-68961. 160p. 1994. lib. bdg. 22.95 (*0-923687-33-5*) Celo Valley Bks.
Nichols, Fred J., ed. An Anthology of Neo-Latin Poetry. LC 78-9944. 746p. reprint ed. pap. 180.00 (*0-8357-8027-9*, 2033843) Bks Demand.
Nichols, Frederick D. & Bear, James A., Jr. Monticello. LC 67-5861. 86p. reprint ed. pap. 25.00 (*0-7837-2022-X*, 2042297) Bks Demand.
Nichols, Frederick D. & Griswold, Ralph E. Thomas Jefferson, Landscape Architect. LC 77-10601. (Illus.). ix, 196p. 1981. pap. 8.95 (*0-8139-0899-X*) U Pr of Va.
Nichols, Gary. Healthcare Resource Directory: National Edition. Reed, Mark L., ed. 224p. (Orig.). 1993. pap. 25.00 (*0-933745-13-3*) Med Prod.
— Houston Medical Directory, 1993. 10th ed. Schellhous, Shirley & Reed, Mark L., eds. 850p. 1993. 54.95 (*0-933745-11-7*) Med Prod.
— Houston Medical Directory 1994. 11th ed. Schellhous, Shirley, ed. 750p. 1994. pap. 59.95 (*0-933745-14-1*) Med Prod.
— Houston Referral Directory, 1993. 3rd ed. Schellhous, Shirley & Reed, Mark L., eds. 136p. 1993. 14.95 (*0-933745-12-5*) Med Prod.
— Houston Referral Directory 1994. 4th ed. Schellhous, Shirley, ed. 150p. 1994. pap. 19.95 (*0-933745-15-X*) Med Prod.
Nichols, Gary C. River Runners' Guide to Utah & Adjacent Areas. LC 86-1688. (Bonneville Bks.). (Illus.). 130p. (Orig.). 1986. pap. 14.95 (*0-87480-254-7*) U of Utah Pr.
Nichols, Gary D. On-Line Process Analyzers. LC 87-30538. 300p. 1988. text ed. 107.00 (*0-471-86608-3*) Wiley.
Nichols, George. George Nichols, Salem Shipmaster & Merchant. LC 74-124245. (Select Bibliographies Reprint Ser.). 1977. reprint ed. 15.95 (*0-8369-5433-5*) Ayer.
— George Nichols, Salem Shipmaster & Merchant: An Autobiography. (American Biography Ser.). 89p. 1991. reprint ed. lib. bdg. 59.00 (*0-7812-8297-7*) Rprt Serv.
Nichols, George E. The Vegetation of Northern Cape Breton Island, Nova Scotia. (Connecticut Academy of Arts & Sciences Ser., Trans.: Vol. 22). 1918. pap. 100.00 (*0-685-22837-1*) Elliots Bks.
Nichols, George N. Focus: Pregnancy & Childbirth Problems in the Workplace. write for info. (*0-318-60956-8*) P-H.
Nichols, George W. The Story of the Great March. 394p. 1972. reprint ed. 24.00 (*0-87928-031-X*) Corner Hse.
Nichols, Geraldine C., intro. Escribir, Espacio Propio: Laforet, Matute, Moix, Tusquets, Riera y Roig por Sis Mismas. (Literature & Human Rights Ser.: Vol. 7). 244p. (Orig.). (SPA.). 1989. pap. 10.00 (*1-877660-04-3*) IFTSOIL.
Nichols, Geri. A Walking Tour of Historic Roscoe Village. (Illus.). 34p. (Orig.). 1989. pap. 3.50 (*1-880443-03-1*) Roscoe Village.
Nichols, Grace, jt. auth. see Agard, John.
Nichols, Grace, jt. ed. see Agard, John.
Nichols, H., jt. auth. see Clark, B.
Nichols, H. K. & Simpson, D. ESEC '87. (Lecture Notes in Computer Science Ser.: Vol. 289). xii, 404p. 1987. pap. 45.00 (*0-387-18712-X*) Spr-Verlag.
Nichols, Harold. McCoy Cookie Jars. 1988. 15.95 (*0-9617912-1-7*) Nichols Wrestling.
— McCoy Cookie Jars from the First to the Last. 2nd ed. LC 91-68550. (Illus.). 198p. (Orig.). 1992. pap. 18.95 (*0-9617912-2-5*) Nichols Wrestling.
— The Work of the Deacon & Deaconess. (Orig.). 1964. pap. 9.00 (*0-8170-0328-2*) Judson.
Nichols, Harold, ed. McCoy Pottery Co. Cookie Jars from the First to the Latest. (Illus.). 200p. (Orig.). 1987. write for info. (*0-318-62248-3*) Nichols Wrestling.
Nichols, Helen. Healing Love. Weinberger, Jane, ed. (Illus.). 200p. (Orig.). 1994. pap. 9.95 (*0-932433-38-3*) Windswept Hse.
Nichols, Herbert L., Jr. Moving the Earth: The Workbook of Excavation. 3rd ed. 1760p. 1988. text ed. 89.95 (*0-07-046483-9*) McGraw.
Nichols, Hugh, ed. Passages West: Nineteen Stories of Youth & Identity. LC 89-82162. 1990. pap. 12.95 (*0-917652-76-2*) Confluence Pr.
Nichols, Hugh, ed. see Maclean, Norman.
Nichols, I. A. History of Iowa Falls, Iowa. (Illus.). 365p. 1993. reprint ed. lib. bdg. 39.50 (*0-8328-2842-4*) Higginson Bk Co.
Nichols, J. Snowflake. LC 89-90662. 64p. (Orig.). (C). 1989. pap. 7.95 (*0-9622423-0-6*) Snowflake Pr.
Nichols, J. Alden. The Year of the Three Kaisers: Bismarck & the German Succession, 1887-1888. LC 86-7028. 432p. 1987. 39.95 (*0-252-01307-7*) U of Ill Pr.
Nichols, J. Bruce. The Uneasy Alliance: Religion, Refugee Work, & U. S. Foreign Policy. 332p. 1988. 30.00 (*0-19-504274-3*) OUP.
Nichols, J. L. & Crogman, William H. Progress of a Race. LC 69-18552. (American Negro: His History & Literature, Ser. No. 2). 1969. reprint ed. 21.95 (*0-405-01883-5*) Ayer.
Nichols, J. Randall. Ending Marriage, Keeping Faith: A New Guide Through the Spiritual Journey of Divorce. 240p. 1993. pap. 11.95 (*0-8245-1209-X*) Crossroad NY.
— Ending Marriage, Keeping Faith: A New Guide Through the Spiritual Journey of Divorce. 224p. 1991. 17.95 (*0-8245-1089-5*) Crossroad NY.
Nichols, James & Nichols, C. M. Bird Hunter. 192p. 1984. pap. 2.25 (*0-8439-2081-5*) Dorchester Pub Co.
Nichols, James, ed. see Annesley, Samuel, et al.
Nichols, James, ed. see Annesley, Samuel.
Nichols, James D. Bullwhacker. 192p. (Orig.). 1984. pap. 2.25 (*0-8439-2182-X*) Dorchester Pub Co.
Nichols, James H. & Wright, Colin. From Political Economy to Economics - & Back? 250p. (C). 1991. 24.95 (*1-55815-113-3*) ICS Pr.
Nichols, James O. The Departmental Guide to Implementation of Student Outcomes Assessment & Institutional Effectiveness. (Illus.). 72p. 1991. pap. 6.00 (*0-87586-096-6*) Agathon.
Nichols, James O., et al. A Practitioner's Handbook for Institutional Effectiveness & Student Outcomes Assessment. 2nd rev. ed. (Illus.). 300p. 1991. 30.00 (*0-87586-095-8*) Agathon.
Nichols, James R. Afterwords. 52p. 1986. pap. 4.95 (*0-89697-272-0*) Intl Univ Pr.
— Chemistry of the Farm & the Sea. LC 73-125755. (American Environmental Studies). 1974. reprint ed. 15.95 (*0-405-02681-1*) Ayer.
Nichols, Jane. Cut, Color, & Paste: Constructions for Special Times, K-2. (Illus.). 120p. (Orig.). 1988. pap. 9.95 (*0-673-38086-6*) GdYrBks.
Nichols, Janet. American Music Makers. (Illus.). 232p. (YA). (gr. 7 up). 1990. 19.95 (*0-8027-6957-8*); lib. bdg. 19.85 (*0-8027-6958-6*) Walker & Co.
— Casey Wooster's Pet Care Service. LC 93-7041. 128p. (J). (gr. 4-7). 1993. text ed. 12.95 (*0-689-31879-0*, Atheneum Bks Young) S&S Childrens.
— Women Music Makers. 224p. (YA). (gr. 7 up). 1992. 18.95 (*0-8027-8168-3*); lib. bdg. 19.85 (*0-8027-8169-1*) Walker & Co.
Nichols, Jeanne M. Leaning over the Edge: Poems. 64p. (Orig.). 1993. pap. 8.50 (*1-56474-058-7*) Fithian Pr.
Nichols, Jeff, jt. auth. see Simons, Jack.
Nichols, Jeffrey A. Getting Started in Metals. 1999. pap. text ed. 16.95 (*0-471-55557-6*) Wiley.
— How to Profit from the Coming Boom in Gold. 1992. text ed. 19.95 (*0-07-046488-X*) McGraw.
Nichols, Joan K. A Matter of Conscience: The Trial of Anne Hutchinson. LC 92-18087. (Stories of America Ser.). (Illus.). 101p. (J). (gr. 2-5). 1992. lib. bdg. 22.13 (*0-8114-7233-7*) Raintree Steck-V.
— New Orleans. LC 88-35915. (Downtown America Bks.). (Illus.). 60p. (J). (gr. 3 up). 1989. text ed. 13.95 (*0-87518-403-0*, Dillon Silver Burdett) Silver Burdett Pr.

An Asterisk (*) at the beginning of an entry indicates that the title is appearing in BIP for the first time.

— No Room for a Dog. 96p. (Orig.). (J). (gr. 4). 1995. pap. 3.50 (*0-380-77973-0*, Camelot Young) Avon.

Nichols, Johanna. Linguistic Diversity in Space & Time. LC 91-43682. (Illus.). 288p. 1992. 39.95 (*0-226-58056-3*) U Ch Pr.

— Predicate Nominals: A Partial Surface Syntax of Russian. LC 80-16745. (University of California Publications in Social Welfare: No. 97). 415p. reprint ed. pap. 118.30 (*0-685-23811-3*, 2032918) Bks Demand.

Nichols, Johanna & Woodbury, Anthony C., eds. Grammar Inside & Outside the Clause: Some Approaches to Theory from the Field. 419p. 1985. 79.95 (*0-521-26617-3*) Cambridge U Pr.

Nichols, John. Collection of All the Wills, Now Known To Be Extant, Of The Kings & Queens Of E. LC 04-25875. reprint ed. 55.00 (*0-404-04759-9*) AMS Pr.

— Conjugal Bliss: A Comedy of Marital Arts. LC 93-1245. 320p. 1994. 22.50 (*0-8050-2803-X*) H Holt & Co.

— Conjugal Bliss: A Comedy of the Marital Arts. 1995. pap. 5.99 (*0-345-38790-2*) Ballantine.

— An Elegy for September. 1993. mass mkt. 5.99 (*0-345-37994-2*) Ballantine.

— A Fragile Beauty: John Nichols' Milagro Country. (Illus.). 160p. 1995. 39.95 (*0-941270-85-8*) Ancient City Pr.

— A Ghost in the Music. 1987. pap. 7.95 (*0-393-30471-X*) Norton.

— Illustrations of the Manners & Expenses of Ancient Times in England in the 15th, 16th & 17th Centuries. LC 79-173078. reprint ed. 36.00 (*0-404-04688-6*) AMS Pr.

— Keep It Simple: A Defense of the Earth. (Illus.). 168p. 1993. 25.00 (*0-393-03386-4*); pap. 15.95 (*0-393-30901-0*) Norton.

— Literary Anecdotes of the Eighteenth Century, 9 Vols. LC 11-32672. reprint ed. 300.00 (*0-404-04720-3*) AMS Pr.

— The Milagro Beanfield War: Facsimile Anniversary Edition. (Illus.). 484p. 1993. 27.50 (*0-8050-2805-6*) H Holt & Co.

— Minor Lives: A Collection of Biographies. Annotated & with an Introduction on John Nichols & the Antiquarian & Anecdotal Movements of the Late Eighteenth Century. Hart, Edward L., ed. LC 73-131470. 402p. reprint ed. pap. 114.60 (*0-7837-4473-0*, 2044181) Bks Demand.

— On the Mesa. deluxe ed. (Illus.). 208p. 1995. 24.95 (*0-941270-86-6*) Ancient City Pr.

— Progresses & Public Processions of Queen Elizabeth, 3 Vols. LC 03-17051. reprint ed. 435.00 (*0-404-04770-X*) AMS Pr.

— Progresses, Processions & Magnificent Festivities of King James First, His Royal Consort, Family & Court, 4 vols., Set. LC 03-29463. reprint ed. 310.00 (*0-404-04780-7*) AMS Pr.

— Progresses, Processions & Magnificent Festivities of King James First, His Royal Consort, Family & Court, 4 Vols, Set. LC 03-29463. (Illus.). 1968. reprint ed. 120.00 (*0-527-67170-3*) Periodicals Srv.

— Sky's the Limit. 1990. pap. 14.95 (*0-393-30717-4*) Norton.

— Sky's the Limit: A Defense of the Earth. 1990. 25.00 (*0-393-02865-8*) Norton.

— Some Account of the Alien Priories, & of Such Lands As They Are Known to Have Possessed in England & Wales, 2 Vols. in 1. LC 72-173079. reprint ed. 47.50 (*0-404-04689-4*) AMS Pr.

— The Sterile Cuckoo. (Shoreline Bks.). 1987. pap. 7.95 (*0-393-30472-8*) Norton.

— Wizard of Loneliness. 320p. 1994. pap. 8.95 (*0-393-31073-6*) Norton.

Nichols, John, ed. Select Collection of Poems, with Notes Biographical & Historical, 8 vols. LC 11-29585. reprint ed. 380.00 (*0-404-04750-5*) AMS Pr.

— Select Collection of Poems, with Notes Biographical & Historical, 8 vols., Set. 1974. reprint ed. 400.00 (*0-527-67180-0*) Periodicals Srv.

***Nichols, John, photos & text.** On the Mesa. LC 95-15130. (Illus.). 1995. write for info. (*0-941270-87-4*) Ancient City Pr.

Nichols, John & Gough, Richard. Biblioteca Topographica Britannica, 10 Vols. LC 70-138264. reprint ed. 1,750.00 (*0-404-04740-8*) AMS Pr.

Nichols, John & Nichols, John B. Illustrations of the Literary History of the 18th Century, 8 Vols. LC 11-32673. reprint ed. 300.00 (*0-404-04730-0*) AMS Pr.

Nichols, John A. & Shank, M. Thomas, eds. Hidden Springs (Medieval Religious Women), Vol. III. (Cistercian Studies). 300p. 1992. write for info. (*0-87907-613-5*); pap. write for info. (*0-87907-913-4*) Cistercian Pubns.

— Medieval Religious Women I: Distant Echoes. (Cistercian Studies: No. 71). (C). 1984. 29.95 (*0-87907-871-5*); pap. 11.95 (*0-87907-971-1*) Cistercian Pubns.

Nichols, John B. Numerical Proportions of the Sexes at Birth. LC 07-23967. (American Anthropological Association Memoirs Ser.: No. 4). 1906. 15.00 (*0-527-00503-7*) Periodicals Srv.

Nichols, John B., jt. auth. see Nichols, John.

Nichols, John B., jt. auth. see Tillman, Barrett.

***Nichols, John D. & Nyholm, Earl.** A Concise Dictionary of Minnesota Ojibwe. expanded rev. ed. LC 94-35219. Orig. Title: Ojebwewi-Ikodowinan. (ENG & OJI.). 1995. 19.95 (*0-8166-2427-5*); pap. 9.95 (*0-8166-2428-3*) U of Minn Pr.

Nichols, John D., ed. see Kegg, Maude.

Nichols, John E. Guide to Hospital Security. 176p. 1983. text ed. 50.95 (*0-566-02359-8*) Ashgate Pub Co.

Nichols, John G., ed. Chronicle of Queen Jane & of Two Years of Queen Mary & Especially of the Rebellion of Sir Thomas Wyat. (Camden Society, London. Publications, First Ser.: No. 48). reprint ed. 24.00 (*0-404-50148-6*) AMS Pr.

— Chronicle of the Grey Friars of London. (Camden Society, London. Publications, First Ser.: No. 53). reprint ed. 32.50 (*0-404-50153-2*) AMS Pr.

— Descriptive Catalogue of the Works of the Camden Society. (Camden Society, London. Publications, First Ser.: No. 80B). reprint ed. 25.00 (*0-404-50208-3*) AMS Pr.

— Narrative of the Days of the Reformation. (Camden Society, London. Publications, First Ser.: No. 77). reprint ed. 85.00 (*0-404-50177-X*) AMS Pr.

Nichols, John G. & Bruce, John, eds. Wills from Doctors' Commons. (Camden Society, London. Publications, First Ser.: No. 83). reprint ed. 42.50 (*0-404-50183-4*) AMS Pr.

Nichols, John G., ed. see Machin, Henry.

Nichols, John G., ed. see Turpyn, Richard.

Nichols, John H. A Biblical Humanist. (Orig.). 1989. pap. 30.00 (*0-685-29796-9*) Unitarian Soc WH.

— A Biblical Humanist Companion. 157p. (Orig.). 1989. pap. 30.00 (*0-9624948-0-1*) Unitarian Soc WH.

Nichols, John S., jt. auth. see Soley, Lawrence C.

Nichols, John T. The Magic Journey. 1983. mass mkt. 5.99 (*0-345-31049-7*) Ballantine.

— The Milagro Beanfield War. 1987. mass mkt. 5.95 (*0-345-34446-4*) Ballantine.

— The Nirvana Blues. 608p. 1983. mass mkt. 5.95 (*0-345-30465-9*) Ballantine.

Nichols, Joseph, et al. UNIX Survival Guide. 352p. (C). 1987. pap. text ed. 28.00 (*0-03-000773-9*) HB Coll Pubs.

***Nichols, Judith.** Growing from Good to Great. 240p. 1995. text ed. 40.00 (*1-56625-035-8*) Bonus Books.

— Pinpointing Affluence. 300p. 1994. 40.00 (*0-944496-40-7*) Bonus Books.

Nichols, Judith E. Building Sales with Demographics & Psychographics: The Road to Your Most Profitable Markets. 289p. 1992. 29.95 (*0-85013-217-7*) Dartnell Corp.

— Changing Demographics - Fund Raising in the 1990s. LC 89-64110. 267p. 1990. 40.00 (*0-944496-11-3*) Precept Pr.

— Targeted Fund Raising: Defining & Refining Your Development Strategy. LC 91-77217. 210p. 1991. 40.00 (*0-944496-29-6*) Precept Pr.

***Nichols, Judy.** Changing Demographics. Date not set. 40.00 (*0-614-05017-0*, CD) Capitol Publns.

— Pinpointing Affluence. Date not set. 40.00 (*0-614-05015-4*, PA) Capitol Publns.

— Targeted Fund Raising. Date not set. 40.00 (*0-614-05016-2*, TFR) Capitol Publns.

Nichols, Julia, ed. see Broadfoot, Tom.

Nichols, K. Temor (Fear) El Enfermedad De-Decada (Sickness of Our Decade) (SPA.). Date not set. 2.49 (*1-56063-035-3*, 498061) Editorial Unilit.

Nichols, K. M. & Silberling, N. J. Upper Devonian to Upper Mississippian Strata of the Antler Foreland in the Leppy Hills, Easternmost Northern Nevada. 1994. write for info. (*0-318-70186-3*) US Interior.

Nichols, Karen, et al. Michael Graves: Buildings & Projects, 1982-1990. LC 89-10615. (Illus.). 351p. (Orig.). 1990. 49.95 (*0-910413-13-4*); pap. 34.95 (*0-910413-17-7*) Princeton Arch.

Nichols, Kate E. Leominster of To-Day. (Illus.). 361p. 1993. reprint ed. lib. bdg. 37.50 (*0-8328-3168-9*) Higginson Bk Co.

Nichols, Kathie. Sarah: A Story of Love & Adoption. (Illus.). 32p. (Orig.). (J). (gr. 2-4). 1992. pap. 6.95 (*0-943861-21-7*) Lone Tree.

— Sarah: A Story of Love & Adoption. LC 92-28414. (Illus.). (Orig.). 1992. 12.95 (*0-943861-22-5*) Lone Tree.

Nichols, Kathryn M. Smell It Like It Is: Tales from the Garlic Capital of the World. LC 91-36046. (Illus.). 112p. (Orig.). 1992. pap. 8.95 (*1-56474-008-0*) Fithian Pr.

Nichols, Kathryn M. & Silberling, N. J. Stratigraphy & Depositional History of the Star Peak Group (Triassic), Northwestern Nevada. LC 77-89753. (Geological Society of America, Special Paper Ser.: No. 178). (Illus.). 79p. reprint ed. pap. 25.00 (*0-8357-3146-4*, 2039409) Bks Demand.

Nichols, Keith A. Psychological Care in Physical Illness. LC 84-71617. 204p. 1984. pap. 13.95 (*0-914783-06-8*) Charles.

— Psychological Care in Physical Illness. 2nd ed. LC 92-49595. 1993. write for info. (*0-412-43560-8*) Chapman & Hall.

Nichols, Keith A. & Jenkinson, John. Groups & Group Work. 140p. 1990. pap. 23.00 (*0-412-34340-1*, A4404) Chapman & Hall.

Nichols, Ken. Traprock: Connecticut Rock Climbs. LC 81-71989. (Illus.). 479p. 1990. 20.00 (*0-930410-14-9*) Amer Alpine Club.

Nichols, Kenneth G. Physical Electronics: A Guide to the Study of Paper 344 of the CEI Examinations. (PPL Study Guide Ser.: No. 4). 52p. reprint ed. pap. 25.00 (*0-317-08575-1*, 2011488) Bks Demand.

Nichols, Kevin. Cornerstone. (C). 1988. 39.00 (*0-85439-157-6*, Pub. by St Paul Pubns UK) St Mut.

— Pastoral Catechetics in Action. (C). 1988. 30.00 (*0-85439-144-4*, Pub. by St Paul Pubns UK) St Mut.

— Voice of the Hidden Waterfall. (C). 1988. 39.00 (*0-85439-178-9*, Pub. by St Paul Pubns UK) St Mut.

Nichols, Kevin & Cummins, John. Into His Fullness. (C). 1988. 39.00 (*0-85439-171-1*, Pub. by St Paul Pubns UK) St Mut.

Nichols, Kim, jt. auth. see Nichols, Wendy.

Nichols, Larry. Law Enforcement Patrol Operations: Police Systems & Practices. LC 90-62594. (Illus.). 540p. 1990. teacher ed 39.00 (*0-8211-1309-7*) McCutchan.

Nichols, Larry, jt. auth. see Robbins, Ray.

Nichols, Larry A., jt. auth. see Mather, George A.

Nichols, Larry D., jt. auth. see Grantham, Charles E.

Nichols, Lawrence T., jt. auth. see Buono, Anthony F.

Nichols, Lee. African Writers at the Microphone. LC 83-50539. (Illus.). 281p. 1984. 25.00 (*0-89410-164-1*); pap. 12.00 (*0-89410-165-X*) Three Continents.

— Breakthrough on the Color Front. rev. ed. LC 93-24153. 1993. 24.00 (*0-89410-771-2*); pap. 15.00 (*0-89410-772-0*) Three Continents.

Nichols, Leigh, pseud. Shadowfires. 448p. 1987. pap. 3.95 (*0-380-75216-6*) Avon.

Nichols, Lonnie J. God, the Universe & Self. LC 82-74521. 96p. 1983. pap. 4.50 (*0-87516-515-X*) DeVorss.

Nichols, M. Q. White Roots: A Nichols Genealogy. (Illus.). 377p. 1983. 25.00 (*0-9612516-0-3*) M Q Nichols.

Nichols, Madaline W. Gaucho: Cattle Hunter, Cavalryman, Ideal of Romance. LC 68-58423. 161p. (C). 1968. reprint ed. 50.00 (*0-87752-077-1*) Gordian.

Nichols, Margaret H. Perfect Patchwork: The Sew-Easy Way. LC 93-2321. (Illus.). 168p. 1993. pap. 14.95 (*0-8069-0358-9*) Sterling.

Nichols, Margaret I. Guide to Reference Books for School Library Media Centers. 4th ed. 463p. 1992. lib. bdg. 38.50 (*0-87287-833-3*) Libs Unl.

— Reference Services & Sources in Small Public Libraries & School Media Centers. 125p. 1995. pap. text ed. 23.50 (*1-56308-289-6*) Libs Unl.

***Nichols, Marie H.** Rhetoric & Criticism. LC 63-7958. 161p. 1963. pap. 45.90 (*0-7837-8514-3*, 2049323) Bks Demand.

Nichols, Marilyn. The Journey Symbol. (Teilhard Studies). 1988. 3.50 (*0-89012-054-4*) Anima Pubns.

Nichols, Marion. Encyclopedia of Embroidery Stitches, Including Crewel. LC 72-97816. (Illus.). 224p. (Orig.). 1974. pap. 7.95 (*0-486-22929-7*) Dover.

Nichols, Marion, ed. see Briggs Company, Ltd. Staff.

Nichols, Mark & Nichols, Buffy. A Grassroots Survival Company Cookbook of Recipes, Remedies & Memories from the Great Depression. (Illus.). (Orig.). 1980. pap. 14.95 (*0-685-60296-6*) Grassrts Survival.

Nichols, Mary. The Danbury Scandals. large type ed. 1993. 18.95 (*0-263-13551-9*, Pub. by Mills & Boon Ltd UK) Chivers N Amer.

— Devil-May-Care. large type ed. 1994. 18.95 (*0-263-14007-5*, Pub. by Mills & Boon Ltd UK) Chivers N Amer.

— Reminiscences of Edgar Allan Poe. LC 74-4041. (Studies in Poe: No. 23). 1974. lib. bdg. 22.95 (*0-8383-2068-6*) M S G Haskell Hse.

— The Stubble Field. 432p. 1993. 25.95 (*1-85797-177-9*) Trafalgar.

Nichols, Mary & Young, Stanley. The Amazing L. A. Environment: A Handbook for Change. (Illus.). 160p. (Orig.). 1991. pap. 6.95 (*1-879326-11-6*) Living Planet Pr.

Nichols, Mary P. Citizens & Statesmen: A Study of Aristotle's Politics. 288p. 1991. pap. text ed. 22.00 (*0-8476-7703-6*) Rowman.

— Citizens & Statesmen: A Study of Aristotle's Politics. 288p. (C). 1991. text ed. 54.50 (*0-8476-7702-8*) Rowman.

— Socrates & the Political Community: An Ancient Debate. LC 86-14421. (SUNY Series in Political Theory: Contemporary Issues). 237p. 1987. 74.50 (*0-88706-395-0*); pap. 24.95 (*0-88706-396-9*) State U NY Pr.

***Nichols, Max.** John & Eleanor: A Sense of Community. 208p. 1995. 24.95 (*1-57178-014-9*) Coun Oak Bks.

Nichols, Maynard. Circulation, Water Quality, & Environmental Resources of Perseverance Bay, St. Thomas. (Illus.). 102p. 1977. 15.00 (*0-318-14612-6*) Isl Resources.

— Virgin Islands Bays: Modeling of Water Quality & Pollution Susceptibility. (Illus.). 92p. 1979. 12.50 (*0-318-14619-3*) Isl Resources.

— Water Sediments & Ecology of the Mangrove Lagoon & Benner Bay, St. Thomas. (Illus.). 159p. 1977. 20.00 (*0-318-14622-3*) Isl Resources.

Nichols, Michael. The Power of Family Therapy. rev. ed. 464p. (C). 1993. reprint ed. pap. text ed. 29.95 (*0-89876-204-9*, RC488.5.N5345) Gardner Pr.

Nichols, Michael, photos. Gorilla: The Struggle for Survival in the Virungas. (Illus.). 1992. 39.95 (*0-89381-310-9*); pap. 24.95 (*0-89381-349-4*) Aperture.

— The Great Apes: Between Two Worlds. LC 93-2261. 1993. 34.95 (*0-87044-947-8*) Natl Geog.

— The Great Apes: Between Two Worlds. deluxe ed. LC 93-2261. 1993. 49.95 (*0-87044-948-6*) Natl Geog.

— Keepers of the Kingdom: The New American Zoo. (Illus.). 132p. 1995. 34.95 (*1-56566-089-7*) Thomasson-Grant.

— Keepers of the Kingdom: The New American Zoo. (Illus.). 132p. 1995. pap. 19.95 (*1-56566-090-0*) Thomasson-Grant.

***Nichols, Michael P.** The Lost Art of Listening. (Guilford Family Therapy Ser.). 251p. 1995. lib. bdg. 19.95 (*0-89862-267-0*) Guilford Pr.

— The Self in the System: Expanding the Limits of Family Therapy. LC 87-13773. 328p. 1987. 31.95 (*0-87630-472-2*) Brunner-Mazel.

***Nichols, Michael P. & Paolino, Thomas J., Jr., eds.** Basic Techniques of Psychodynamic Psychotherapy. 360p. 1995. pap. 30.00 (*1-56821-618-1*) Aronson.

Nichols, Michael P. & Schwartz, Richard C. Family Therapy: Concepts & Methods. 3rd ed. LC 94-14096. 1994. text ed. write for info. (*0-205-16395-5*) Allyn.

Nichols, Michael P., jt. auth. see Minuchin, Salvador.

Nichols, Mike. Life, & Other Ways to Kill Time. 288p. 1988. 15.95 (*0-8184-0462-0*) Carol Pub Group.

— Real Men Belch Downwind: Modern Etiquette for the Primitive Man. Towle, Mike, ed. (Illus.). 142p. 1993. pap. 6.95 (*1-56530-054-8*) Summit TX.

Nichols, N. K. & Owens, D. H., eds. The Mathematics of Control Theory: Based on the Proceedings of a Conference on Control Theory, Organized by the Institute of Mathematics & Its Applications, & Held at the University of Strathclyde in September 1988. LC 92-23022. (Institute of Mathematics & Its Applications Conference Series, New Ser.: New Series 37). 1992. 110.00 (*0-19-853640-2*, Clarendon Pr) OUP.

Nichols, N. R. Round - Rounds Genealogy: Descendants of John Round of Swansen MA. (Illus.). 259p. reprint ed. lib. bdg. 49.00 (*0-8328-1670-1*); reprint ed. pap. 39.00 (*0-8328-1671-X*) Higginson Bk Co.

Nichols, Nancy. Reach for the Top: Women & the Changing Facts of Work Life. 1994. text ed. 24.95 (*0-07-103580-X*) McGraw.

Nichols, Nancy A. San Quentin Prison - Inside the Walls. Delahunty, James T., ed. (Illus.). 68p. (Orig.). 1991. pap. 9.95 (*0-9630115-2-9*) San Quentin Mus.

Nichols, Nancy A., intro. Reach for the Top: Women & the Changing Facts of Work Life. LC 93-34718. (Harvard Business Review Book Ser.). 208p. 1994. 24.95 (*0-87584-507-X*) Harvard Busn.

Nichols, Nancy A., ed. see Nichols, Alan H.

Nichols, Nancy A., jt. auth. see Nichols, Alan H.

Nichols, Nancy A., ed. see Nichols, Alan, Sr.

Nichols, Naomi M. Food Drying at Home. 1978. pap. 5.95 (*0-442-26029-6*) Van Nos Reinhold.

***Nichols, Nichelle.** Beyond Uhura: Star Trek & Other Memories. 336p. Date not set. pap. text ed. 5.99 (*1-57297-011-1*) Blvd Books.

— Beyond Uhura: Star Trek & Other Memories. 320p. 1995. 22.95 (*0-399-13993-1*) Putnam Pub Group.

Nichols, Nick. The Comfort Fairy Story. 24p. (J). (gr. k-4). 1990. 19.95 (*0-9632531-0-7*) N Squared Ent.

***Nichols, Nina D.** Ariadne's Lives. LC 94-31366. 1995. write for info. (*0-8386-3582-2*) Fairleigh Dickinson.

***Nichols, Nina D. & Bazzoni, Jana O.** Pirandello & Film. LC 94-32071. 1995. text ed. 45.00 (*0-8032-3336-1*) U of Nebr Pr.

Nichols, Patsie, ed. see Bureau of Deep Mine Safety, Mining & Reclamation Staff.

Nichols, Patsie, ed. see Bureau of Deep Mine Safety & Mining & Reclamation Staff.

Nichols, Patsie, ed. see Pennsylvania Bureau of Mining & Reclamation Staff & Bureau of Deep Mine Safety Staff.

N

Nichols, Paul. Social Survey Methods: A Guide for Development Workers. 132p. (C). 1991. text ed. 80.00 (*0-85598-125-3*, Pub. by Oxfam Pubns UK); pap. text ed. 32.00 (*0-85598-126-1*, Pub. by Oxfam Pubns UK) St Mut.

— Tough Tackle. (Blitz Ser.: No. 2). (J). 1988. pap. 2.95 (*0-345-35109-6*) Ballantine.

—Where in the World Did You Come From? (Illus.). 26p. (J). (ps-4). 1993. 17.95 (*1-884507-00-X*) Boyer-Caswell. Written & illustrated by public school teachers, this highly visual children's book gives young readers a first look at our global geography & wildlife; yet holds interest for older children. Beautiful primary color illustrations with a thoughtful text to entertain & teach. Unique die cuts discs (featuring metal grommets) picture twelve animals native to each continent. Children learn to identify by name animals from each continent as they turn the discs. Total of 84 animals on discs. This book promotes ecological awareness. Encourages children to think & draw conclusions. Reinforces learning by providing continent/animal index. Spill-proof film laminated cover; premium grade paper, Smythe-sewn & hardbound. Recommended for pre-K to 4th grade. RAVE REVIEWS FROM PARENTS, GRANDPARENTS - & CHILDREN - AS WELL AS TEACHERS! To order contact: Boyer-Caswell Publishing Co., 823 E. Main St., 14th Fl., Richmond, VA 23219. 804-648-6624, FAX: 804-648-9221. ***Publisher Provided Annotation.***

Nichols, Paul D., et al, eds. Cognitively Diagnostic Assessment. 480p. 1995. 89.95 (*0-8058-1588-0*); pap. 39.95 (*0-8058-1589-9*) L Erlbaum Assocs.

Nichols, Paul L. & Chen, Ta-Chuan. Minimal Brain Dysfunction: A Prospective Study. LC 80-18739. 352p. 1981. text ed. 69.95 (*0-89859-074-4*) L Erlbaum Assocs.

Nichols, Peter. Joe Egg. LC 68-21264. 87p. (Orig.). 1968. pap. 9.95 (*0-8021-5115-9*) Grove-Atltic.

— Nichols: Plays One. (Methuen World Dramatists Ser.). 376p. (C). 1991. pap. 17.95 (*0-685-63015-3*, A0560) Heinemann.

— Nichols: Plays Two. (Methuen World Dramatists Ser.). (C). 1992. pap. 13.95 (*0-413-65070-7*, A0561) Heinemann.

— Passion Play. (Methuen Modern Plays Ser.). 106p. 1981. pap. 9.95 (*0-413-47800-9*, A0361, Pub. by Methuen UK) Heinemann.

— A Piece of My Mind. (Methuen Modern Plays Ser.). 80p. 1988. pap. 9.95 (*0-413-17360-7*, A0210, Pub. by Methuen UK) Heinemann.

Nichols, Peter & Nichols, Belia. Mastodon Hunters to Mound Builders: North American Archaeology. (Illus.). 112p. (J). (gr. 4-7). 1992. 12.95 (0-89015-748-0) Sunbelt Media.

Nichols, Phillip. Homeopathy & the Medical Profession. 250p. 1988. lib. bdg. 57.50 (0-7099-1836-4, Pub. by Croom Helm UK) Routledge Chapman & Hall.

Nichols, Phillip D., ed. see Dare, Benjamin.

Nichols, Preston & Moon, Peter. Montauk Revisited: Adventures in Synchronicity. (Illus.). 224p. 1994. pap. 19.95 (0-9631889-1-7) Sky Bks NY.

***Nichols, Preston B. & Moon, Peter.** Encounter in the Pleiades: An Inside Look at UFO Phenomena. (Illus.). 225p. Date not set. pap. 19.95 (0-614-07051-1) Sky Bks NY.

— The Montauk Project: Experiments in Time. LC 91-91514. (Illus.). 160p. (Orig.). 1992. pap. 15.95 (0-9631889-0-9) Sky Bks NY.

— Pyramids of Montauk, No. 3: Explorations in Consciousness. (Illus.). 266p. 1995. pap. 19.95 (0-9631889-2-5) Sky Bks NY.

Nichols, R. Great Zodiac of Glastonbury. (Orig.). 1993. pap. 5.95 (1-55818-240-3) Holmes Pub.

— Spanish & Portuguese Gardens. 1976. 59.95 (0-8490-2646-6) Gordon Pr.

Nichols, R. W., ed. Acoustic Emission. (Illus.). 121p. 1976. 63.00 (0-85334-681-X, Pub. by Elsevier Applied Sci UK) Elsevier.

— Advances in Non-Destructive Examination for Structural Integrity: Proceedings of the International Seminar on Non-Destructive Examination in Relation to Structural Integrity, 2nd, Paris, Aug. 24-25, 1981. (Illus.). 447p. 1983. 142.25 (0-85334-158-3, I-459-82, Pub. by Elsevier Applied Sci UK) Elsevier.

— Developments in Pressure Vessel Technology, Vols. 1-3. 1980. Vol. 1: Flaw Analysis. 79.25 (0-85334-802-2, Pub. by Elsevier Applied Sci UK); Vol. 2: Inspecton & Testing. 79.25 (0-85334-806-5, Pub. by Elsevier Applied Sci UK); Vol. 3: Materials & Fabrication. 97.25 (0-85334-922-3, Pub. by Elsevier Applied Sci UK) Elsevier.

— Developments in Pressure Vessel Technology: Design for Specific Applications, Vol. 4. (Illus.). 311p. 1983. 106.25 (0-85334-223-7, I-339-83, Pub. by Elsevier Applied Sci UK) Elsevier.

— Developments in Stress Analysis for Pressurized Components, Vol. 1. (Illus.). 210p. 1977. 79.25 (0-85334-724-7, Pub. by Elsevier Applied Sci UK) Elsevier.

— Non-Destructive Examination in Relation to Structural Integrity. (Illus.). 290p. 1980. 88.25 (0-85334-908-8, Pub. by Elsevier Applied Sci UK) Elsevier.

— Pressure Vessel Codes & Standards. 312p. 1987. 101.00 (1-85166-048-8, Pub. by Elsevier Applied Sci UK) Elsevier.

— Trends in Reactor Pressure Vessel & Circuit Development. (Illus.). 380p. 1980. 106.25 (0-85334-872-3, Pub. by Elsevier Applied Sci UK) Elsevier.

Nichols, R. W. & Crutzen, S., eds. Ultrasonic Inspection of Heavy Section Steel Components: The PISC II Final Report. 698p. 1988. 192.75 (1-85166-155-7) Elsevier.

Nichols, R. W. & Dau, G. J., eds. Non-Destructive Examination for Pressurized Components: Proceedings of the International Seminar on Non-Destructive Examination in Relation to Structural Integrity, 3rd, 29-30 August 1983, Monterey, CA. (Illus.). 384p. 1985. 144.00 (0-85334-307-1, Pub. by Elsevier Applied Sci UK) Elsevier.

Nichols, R. W., jt. ed. see Farley, J. M.

Nichols, R. W., jt. ed. see Liu, Cengdian.

Nichols, R. W., et al, eds. Effective Non-Destructive Examination for Structural Integrity. 362p. 1987. 158.50 (1-85166-050-X, Pub. by Elsevier Applied Sci UK) Elsevier.

— Non-Destructive Examination in Relation to Structural Integrity: Proceedings of the 5th International Seminar Held in Davos, Switzerland, 26-27 Aug., 1987. 1989. 117.00 (1-85166-283-9) Elsevier.

Nichols, Ray. Treason, Tradition & the Intellectual: Julien Benda & Political Discourse. LC 78-7785. x, 270p. 1979. 29.95 (0-7006-0175-9) U Pr of KS.

Nichols, Renee E., ed. see White, Darryl R.

Nichols, Richard. Classic American Cars. 1992. pap. 19.95 (0-671-08193-4) S&S Trade.

Nichols, Robbie, jt. auth. see Molander, Roger C.

Nichols, Robert. Adventures in the High Wind: Poetic Observations & Other Lore. 144p. (Orig.). (C). 1990. pap. 7.95 (0-9627615-0-8) Mntn Muse Pub.

— Anthology of War Poetry, 1914-1918. 1973. 200.00 (0-87968-646-4) Gordon Pr.

— Arrival. LC 77-1362. (Daily Lives in Nghsi-Altai Ser.: Bk. 1). 1977. pap. 1.95 (0-8112-0653-X, NDP437) New Directions.

— Exile. LC 79-15330. (Daily Lives in Nghsi-Altai Ser.: Bk. 4). 1979. pap. 3.95 (0-8112-0732-3, NDP485) New Directions.

— From the Steam Room: A Comic Fiction. LC 93-13505. 240p. 1993. 18.95 (0-88448-129-8) Tilbury Hse.

— The Harditts in Sawna. LC 78-10765. (Daily Lives in Nghsi-Altai Ser.: Bk. 3). 1979. pap. 3.95 (0-8112-0684-X, NDP470) New Directions.

— In the Air. LC 90-26164. (Poetry & Fiction Ser.). 192p. 1991. text ed. 30.00 (0-8018-4195-X); pap. 10.95 (0-8018-4196-8) Johns Hopkins.

Nichols, Robert, jt. auth. see Larsh, Ed.

Nichols, Robert, jt. auth. see Larsh, Edward.

Nichols, Robert C., jt. auth. see Loehlin, John C.

Nichols, Robert L. & Stavrou, Theofanis G., eds. Russian Orthodoxy under the Old Regime. LC 78-3196. 230p. 1978. pap. text ed. 12.95 (0-8166-0847-4) U of Minn Pr.

Nichols, Robert M. Fantastica: Being the Smile of the Sphinx, & Other Tales of Imagination. LC 75-128744. (Short Story Index Reprint Ser.). 1977. 23.95 (0-8369-3635-3) Ayer.

***Nichols, Rod.** Successful Network Marketing for the Twenty-First Century. Wait, Erin, ed. (Successful Business Library Ser.). 225p. (Orig.). 1995. pap. 14.95 (1-55571-350-5) Oasis Pr OR.

Nichols, Roger. Black Hawk & the Warrior's Path. Kraut, Alan M. & Wakelyn, Jon L., eds. (American Biographical History Ser.). 190p. 1992. pap. text ed. write for info. (0-88295-884-4) Harlan Davidson.

— Debussy Remembered. (Illus.). 282p. 1992. 24.95 (0-931340-41-1, Amadeus Pr); pap. 12.95 (0-931340-42-X, Amadeus Pr) Timber.

Nichols, Roger & Halley, Patrick L. Stephen Long & America Frontier Expedition. LC 78-68878. (Illus.). 280p. 1980. 38.50 (0-87413-149-9) U Delaware Pr.

Nichols, Roger & McLeish, Kenneth, eds. Through Greek Eyes. 2nd ed. (Illus.). 144p. (C). 1991. pap. 12.95 (0-521-37756-0) Cambridge U Pr.

Nichols, Roger & Nichols, Sarah. Greek Everyday Life. McLeish, Kenneth & McLeish, Valerie, eds. (Aspects of Greek Life Ser.). (Illus.). 48p. (YA). (gr. 7-12). 1978. reprint ed. pap. text ed. 9.00 (0-582-20672-3, 70819) Longman.

Nichols, Roger & Smith, Richard L., eds. Claude Debussy: "Pelleas et Melisande" (Cambridge Opera Handbooks Ser.). (Illus.). 192p. (C). 1989. pap. 19.95 (0-521-31446-1) Cambridge U Pr.

Nichols, Roger, ed. see Debussy, Claude.

Nichols, Roger, tr. see Debussy, Claude.

Nichols, Roger, tr. see Livy.

Nichols, Roger L. The American Indian: Past & Present. 4th ed. 1992. pap. text ed. write for info. (0-07-046499-5) McGraw.

Nichols, Roger L., ed. American Frontier & Western Issues: A Historiographical Review. LC 85-30181. (Contributions in American History Ser.: No. 118). 312p. 1986. text ed. 49.95 (0-313-24356-5, NAF/, Greenwood Pr) Greenwood.

***Nichols, Roger L. & Halley, Patrick L.** Stephen Long & American Frontier Exploration. LC 94-36696. (Illus.). 280p. 1995. pap. 14.95 (0-8061-2724-4) U of Okla Pr.

Nichols, Ronald L., et al. Decision Making in Surgical Sepsis. 408p. (C). 1990. 62.00 (1-55664-053-6) Mosby Yr Bk.

Nichols, Ross. The Book of Druidry: History, Sites, & Wisdom. (Illus.). 1992. reprint ed. pap. 16.00 (1-85538-167-2, Pub. by Aquarian Pr UK) Thorsons SF.

Nichols, Roy C. Doing the Gospel: Local Congregations in Ministry. LC 90-33916. 1990. pap. 9.95 (0-687-11030-0) Abingdon.

Nichols, Roy F. Democratic Machine, 1850-1854. LC 68-1159. (Columbia University. Studies in the Social Sciences: No. 248). reprint ed. 20.00 (0-404-51248-8) AMS Pr.

— The Disruption of American Democracy. LC 83-45826. 1983. reprint ed. 48.50 (0-404-20190-3) AMS Pr.

— The Disruption of American Democracy. LC 48-6344. 630p. reprint ed. pap. 179.60 (0-317-42219-7, 2052043) Bks Demand.

— Franklin Pierce: Young Hickory of the Granite Hills. LC 93-70974. (Signature Ser.). (Illus.). 625p. 1993. reprint ed. 35.00 (0-945707-06-1) Amer Political.

Nichols, Sallie. Jung & Tarot: An Archetypal Journey. LC 80-53118. (Illus.). 416p. 1984. pap. 14.95 (0-87728-515-2) Weiser.

Nichols, Sarah, jt. auth. see Bieler, Henry G.

Nichols, Sarah, jt. auth. see Nichols, Roger.

Nichols, Spencer V. The Significance of Anthony Trollope. 1977. lib. bdg. 59.95 (0-8490-2604-0) Gordon Pr.

Nichols, Stephen G., jt. ed. see Bloch, R. Howard.

Nichols, Stephen G., Jr., ed. see De Lorris, Guillaume.

Nichols, Stephen G., Jr., jt. ed. see Lyons, John D.

Nichols, Stephen G., Jr., jt. ed. see Robinson, Franklin W.

Nichols, Steven, jt. auth. see Seiter, Charles.

Nichols, Stuart E. & Ostrow, David G., eds. Psychiatric Implications of Acquired Immune Deficiency Syndrome. LC 84-6187. (Clinical Insights Ser.). 151p. reprint ed. pap. 43.10 (0-8357-7822-3, 2036195) Bks Demand.

Nichols, Sue. Words on Target: For Better Christian Communication. LC 63-16410. (Illus.). (Orig.). 1963. pap. 6.99 (0-8042-1476-X, John Knox) Westminster John Knox.

Nichols, Susan K., pref. Patterns in Practice: Selections from the Journal of Museum Education. LC 91-66484. 391p. (Orig.). 1992. pap. 35.00 (1-880437-00-7) Mus Ed Round.

Nichols, Tawa. Three Centuries of American Music, Vol. 2: Solo Song, 1866-1910. (Collection of American Sacred & Secular Music). 400p. (C). 1989. Catalog. lib. bdg. 80.00 (0-8161-0543-X) G K Hall.

Nichols, Teresa. Student Teaching Handbook. 80p. (C). 1993. 6.95 (0-8403-8508-0) Kendall-Hunt.

Nichols, Terri V. Francis: The Knight of Assisi. (Illus.). 61p. (Orig.). (J). (ps-6). 1990. 21.95 (1-56814-002-9); pap. text ed. 4.95 (0-685-62404-8) CCC of America.

Nichols, Therese M. Basics of Workers Compensation Law for Legal Assistants. 3rd ed. 125p. 1991. pap. text ed. 24.95 (1-879563-06-1) Lexicon CA.

Nichols, Thomas L. A Biography of the Brothers Davenport. LC 75-36912. (Occult Ser.). 1976. reprint ed. 29.95 (0-405-07969-9) Ayer.

— Esoteric Anthropology: The Mysteries of Man. LC 75-180585. (Medicine & Society in America Ser.). (Illus.). 350p. 1972. reprint ed. 24.95 (0-405-03962-X) Ayer.

— Forty Years of American Life: 1812-1861, 2 vols., Set. (American Biography Ser.). 1991. reprint ed. lib. bdg. 148.00 (0-7812-8298-5) Rprt Serv.

— Journal in Jail. LC 71-125709. (American Journalists Ser.). 1978. reprint ed. 24.95 (0-405-01690-5) Ayer.

— Marriage: Its History, Character, & Results. LC 78-22161. (Free Love in America Ser.). reprint ed. 36.50 (0-404-60955-4) AMS Pr.

— Woman in All Ages & All Nations. 1972. 250.00 (0-8490-1314-3) Gordon Pr.

Nichols, Thomas M. The Sacred Cause: Civil-Military Conflict over Soviet National Security, 1917-1992. LC 92-34543. (Cornell Studies in Security Affairs). 280p. 1993. 33.50 (0-8014-2774-6) Cornell U Pr.

Nichols, Tim, ed. see National Institute for Exploration Members.

Nichols, Tom, jt. auth. see Ostroff, Harriet.

Nichols, V. Cars & Trucks Sticker Pad. (Illus.). 32p. (J). (gr. k-6). 1993. reprint ed. pap. 2.95 (1-879424-16-9) Nickel Pr.

— Dinosaur Coloring Book. (Illus.). 32p. (Orig.). (J). (gr. k-6). 1993. pap. 2.95 (1-879424-50-9) Nickel Pr.

— Flags of the World Sticker Atlas. (Illus.). 32p. (Orig.). (J). (gr. k-6). 1992. pap. 3.95 (1-879424-22-3) Nickel Pr.

— Funny Faces Sticker Pad. (Illus.). 32p. (J). (gr. k-6). 1993. reprint ed. pap. 2.95 (1-879424-31-2) Nickel Pr.

— Hunt for Humphrey. (Illus.). 32p. (J). (gr. k-6). 1992. pap. 1.95 (1-879424-15-0) Nickel Pr.

— Hunt for Humphrey. Turkow, E., tr. (Illus.). 32p. (ENG & SPA.). (J). (gr. k-6). 1992. pap. 1.95 (1-879424-23-1) Nickel Pr.

— The Incredible Dionsaur Activity Book. (Illus.). 128p. (J). (gr. k-6). Date not set. pap. 2.95 (1-879424-64-9) Nickel Pr.

— Large Print Puzzle Assortment. 384p. (Orig.). 1993. pap. 3.95 (1-879424-60-6) Nickel Pr.

— Notebook U. S. Atlas. (Illus.). 16p. 1993. pap. 1.95 (1-879424-44-4) Nickel Pr.

— Notebook World Atlas. (Illus.). 16p. (YA). (gr. 5-12). 1993. reprint ed. pap. 1.95 (1-879424-25-8) Nickel Pr.

— Student Planner & Assignment Book. 2nd ed. (Illus.). 120p. (YA). (gr. 5-12). 1993. reprint ed. pap. 3.95 (1-879424-20-7) Nickel Pr.

— U. S. Map & Sticker Book. (Illus.). 32p. (J). (gr. k-6). 1993. reprint ed. pap. 3.95 (1-879424-10-X) Nickel Pr.

— Webster's Dictionary. Kauffman, L., ed. (Illus.). 448p. 1993. reprint ed. pap. 2.99 (1-879424-00-2); reprint ed. pap. 1.99 (1-879424-12-6) Nickel Pr.

— Webster's Dictionary & Thesaurus. rev. ed. Kaufmann, L., ed. (C). 1991. reprint ed. pap. 7.95 (1-879424-14-2) Nickel Pr.

— Webster's English-French Rack Size. 288p. (Orig.). (ENG & FRE.). 1993. pap. 1.99 (1-879424-57-6) Nickel Pr.

— Webster's English Spanish Dictionary. 336p. (Orig.). (ENG & SPA.). 1992. pap. 1.99 (1-879424-11-8) Nickel Pr.

— Webster's English Spanish Rack Dictionary. 288p. (Orig.). (ENG & SPA.). 1993. pap. 1.99 (1-879424-58-4) Nickel Pr.

— Webster's English Spanish Vest Pocket. 192p. (Orig.). (ENG & SPA.). 1992. pap. 1.95 (1-879424-24-X) Nickel Pr.

— Webster's Giant Print Dictionary. Kauffman, L., ed. (Illus.). 288p. 1993. pap. 2.99 (1-879424-53-3) Nickel Pr.

— Webster's Thesaurus. Kauffman, L., ed. 288p. 1993. reprint ed. pap. 1.99 (1-879424-01-0) Nickel Pr.

— Webster's Two in One Dictionary & Thesaurus. Kauffman, L., ed. (Illus.). 352p. Date not set. pap. 1.99 (1-879424-42-8) Nickel Pr.

Nichols, V. & Kauffman, L. Webster's Speller. 288p. Date not set. pap. 1.99 (1-879424-02-9) Nickel Pr.

— Webster's Three Piece Box Set. 1024p. (Orig.). 1991. pap. 9.95 (1-879424-03-7) Nickel Pr.

— Webster's Vest Pocket Dictionary. 192p. 1992. reprint ed. pap. 1.95 (1-879424-33-9) Nickel Pr.

— Webster's Vest Pocket Thesaurus. 192p. 1993. reprint ed. pap. 1.95 (1-879424-34-7) Nickel Pr.

Nichols, Victoria & Thompson, Susan. Silk Stalkings: A Survey of Series Characters Created by Women Authors in Crime & Mystery Fiction. LC 88-10491. 448p. (Orig.). 1988. pap. 16.95 (0-88739-096-X, Blk Lizard) Creat Arts Bk.

Nichols, Vida. Growth Poles: An Investigation of Their Potential As a Tool for Regional Economic Development. (Discussion Paper Ser.: No. 30). 1969. pap. 10.00 (1-55869-051-4) Regional Sci Res Inst.

Nichols, Virginia. How to Show Your Own Dog. 1970. 14.95 (0-86622-698-2, PS-607) TFH Pubns.

Nichols, Virginia, ed. see Beal, Walter S., et al.

Nichols, Virginia, tr. see Bowser, Milton.

Nichols, Virginia A., jt. auth. see Crumbley, D. Larry.

Nichols, Virginia A., jt. ed. see Crumbley, D. Larry.

Nichols, W. Gary & Boykin, Milton L., eds. Arms Control & Nuclear Weapons: U. S. Policies & the National Interest. LC 86-29429. (Contributions in Military Studies: No. 59). 147p. 1987. text ed. 45.00 (0-313-25389-7, NAC/, Greenwood Pr) Greenwood.

Nichols, W. W. & O'Rourke, Michael F. McDonald's Blood Flow in Arteries: Theoretical, Experimental & Clinical Principles. 3rd ed. (Illus.). 456p. 1991. text ed. 110.00 (0-8121-1323-3) Williams & Wilkins.

Nichols, Wendy & Nichols, Kim. Wonderscience: A Developmentally Appropriate Guide to Hands-on Science for Young Children. LC 90-60081. 60p. (Orig.). (J). (ps-3). 1990. pap. 14.95 (0-9625907-0-3) Learning Expo.

Nichols, William C. Marital Therapy: An Integrative Approach. LC 88-11179. (Guilford Family Therapy Ser.). 282p. 1988. lib. bdg. 32.00 (0-89862-102-X) Guilford Pr.

— The Narrow Way: Examining Both Heaven & Hell & the Message of Salvation in Jesus Christ. 115p. 1993. pap. 6.50 (0-9641803-1-6) Internat Outreach.

— Treating Adult Survivors of Childhood Sexual Abuse. LC 91-50913. (Practitioner's Resource Ser.). 80p. 1992. pap. 14.70 (0-943158-68-0, TASBP, Prof Resc Pr) Pro Resource.

Nichols, William C., ed. Power & Family Therapy: A Special Issue of Contemporary Family Therapy. 75p. 1988. pap. 14.95 (0-89885-430-X) Human Sci Pr.

Nichols, William C. & Everett, Craig A. Systemic Family Therapy: An Integrative Approach. LC 85-17235. (Guilford Family Therapy Ser.). 442p. 1986. lib. bdg. 39.95 (0-89862-066-X) Guilford Pr.

***Nichols, Yuriko.** Bookshelf Collection Fifth-Eighth Graders. (Reading Skills Discovery Ser.). 144p. (J). 1994. 14.00 (1-880892-56-1) Fam Lrng Ctr.

— Common Sense Math for Kindergartners. 11p. 1993. Kit. pap. 12.00 (1-880892-68-5) Fam Lrng Ctr.

Nicholsen, Loren, ed. see Erwin, Richard E.

Nicholsen, Margaret. People in Books. LC 69-15811. 792p. 1977. 37.00 (0-8242-0587-1) Wilson.

Nicholsen, Shierry W., ed. see Adorno, Theodor W.

Nicholsen, Shierry W., tr. see Adorno, Theodor W.

Nicholsen, Shierry W., tr. see Habermas, Jurgen.

Nicholsen, Shierry W., ed. see Habermas, Jurgen.

Nicholsen, Shierry W., tr. see Habermas, Jurgen.

***Nicholson.** In the Dreamy Afternoon. Date not set. per. 8.99 (0-85449-119-8, Pub. by Gay Mens Pr UK) InBook.

— Translations of Eastern Poetry: Literature from the Arabic & Persian. (C). 1987. pap. 15.00 (0-7007-0196-6, Pub. by Curzon Pr UK) Humanities.

Nicholson, ed. Mathnawi of Jalaluddin Rumi, 3 vols., Set, Bks. II, IV, VI. (Gibb Collection Ser.). 1982. Set. 99.00 (0-906094-27-5, Pub. by Aris & Phillips UK) David Brown.

— Mathnawi of Jalaluddin Rumi, Vol. 2, Bks. I-II. (Gibb Collection Ser.). 1926. 35.00 (0-906094-08-9, Pub. by Aris & Phillips UK) David Brown.

— Mathnawi of Jalaluddin Rumi, Vol. 4, Bks. III-IV. (Gibb Collection Ser.). 1981. 35.00 (0-906094-09-7, Pub. by Aris & Phillips UK) David Brown.

— Mathnawi of Jalaluddin Rumi, Vol. 6, Bks. V-VI. (Gibb Collection Ser.). 1981. 35.00 (0-906094-10-0, Pub. by Aris & Phillips UK) David Brown.

Nicholson, A. S. & Ridd, J. E. Health, Safety & Ergonomics. (Illus.). 175p. 1988. text ed. 39.95 (0-408-02386-4) Buttrwrth-Heinemann.

Nicholson, Alasdair. The Cold War. Yapp, Malcolm et al, eds. (World History Ser.). (Illus.). 32p. (YA). (gr. 6-11). 1980. reprint ed. pap. text ed. 4.35 (0-89908-211-4) Greenhaven.

Nicholson, Andrew, ed. Don Juan, Cantos III-IV Manuscript: A Facsimile of the Fair Copy Manuscripts in the University of London Library. LC 92-19692. (Manuscripts of the Younger Romantics Ser.). 174p. 1992. 105.00 (0-8153-1145-1) Garland.

Nicholson, Andrew, tr. & intro. Don Juan, Cantos Ten, Eleven, Twelve, & Seventeen Manuscript: A Facsimile of the Original Draft Manuscripts in the University of London Library. LC 92-35185. (Manuscripts of the Younger Romantics, Lord Byron Ser.: No. 9). 1993. 122.00 (0-8153-1146-X) Garland.

Nicholson, Andrew, ed. see Byron.

Nicholson, Andrew, ed. see Gordon, George & Byron.

Nicholson, Andrew, ed. see Nicholson, Winifred.

Nicholson, Anne & Chorpenning, Charlotte B. The Magic Horn of Charlemagne. 69p. 1954. reprint ed. pap. 3.45 (0-87129-051-0, M75) Dramatic Pub.

Nicholson, Bertha M. Meditations on a D Major Scale. LC 87-63035. 1987. pap. 3.00 (0-87574-276-9) Pendle Hill.

Nicholson, Brinsley, ed. see Shakespeare, William.

Nicholson-Brown, Barbara, ed. Human Resource Management in Religiously Affiliated Institutions. 125p. 1991. 20.00 (0-910402-96-5) Coll & U Personnel.

Nicholson, Bruce K. Hi, Ho, Come to the Fair: Tales of the New York World's Fair, 1964-1965. LC 89-92227. 224p. (Orig.). 1989. pap. 13.95 (0-9624426-0-7) Pelagian Pr.

Nicholson, C. David, ed. Anti-Dementia Agents: Research & Prospects for Therapy. (Neuroscience Perspectives Ser.). (Illus.). 316p. 1994. boxed 69.95 (0-12-518055-1) Acad Pr.

Nicholson, Carol A., et al, eds. Law Library Systems Directory. LC 93-2893. (American Association of Law Libraries Publications Ser.: No. 44). xix, 332p. 1993. 45.00 (0-8377-0146-5) Rothman.

Nicholson, Charles. A Field Guide to Southern Speech. LC 89-14872. 86p. 1989. pap. 6.95 (0-87483-098-2) August Hse.

— WAIS-R Companion. 1989. 30.00 (0-88047-151-4, 9002) DOK Pubs.

Nicholson, Charles L. & Alcorn, Charles L. Educational Applications of the WISC-III: A Handbook of Interpretive Strategies & Remedial Recommendations. 100p. 1994. spiral bd. 42.50 (0-87424-294-0, W-294A) Western Psych.

Nicholson, Christina. The Savage Sands. 1978. pap. 2.25 (0-449-23762-1, Crest) Fawcett.

Nicholson, Clara & Nicholson, Judith, eds. Personalized Care Model for the Elderly. 540p. 1983. pap. text ed. 21.30 (0-317-00780-7) Elder.

Nicholson, Colin. Alexander Pope: Essays for the Tercentenary. (Illus.). 280p. 1988. text ed. 30.00 (0-08-036394-6, Pub. by Aberdeen U Pr) Macmillan.

— Writing & the Rise of Finance: Capital Satires of the Early Eighteenth Century. (Cambridge Studies in Eighteenth-Century English Literature & Thought: No. 21). 236p. (C). 1994. 54.95 (0-521-45323-2) Cambridge U Pr.

Nicholson, Colin, ed. Iain Crichton Smith: Critical Essays. 224p. 1992. 29.50 (0-7486-0340-9, Pub. by Edinburgh U Pr UK) Col U Pr.

An Asterisk (*) at the beginning of an entry indicates that the title is appearing in BIP for the first time.

— Under Cover: An Anthology of Contemporary Scottish Writing. 224p. 1994. pap. 15.95 (1-85158-548-6, Pub. by Mnstream UK) Trafalgar.

Nicholson, Colin & Orr, John, eds. Cinema & Fiction: New Modes of Adapting, 1950-1990. 240p. 1992. 55.00 (0-7486-0356-5, Pub. by Edinburgh U Pr UK) Col U Pr.

Nicholson, Colin, jt. ed. see Carnell, Geoffrey.

Nicholson, Cyn, jt. auth. see Pace, Denny F.

Nicholson, D. & Parsonage, N. G. Computer Simulation & the Statistical Mechanics of Adsorption. 1983. text ed. 156.00 (0-12-518060-8) Acad Pr.

Nicholson, D. H. The Mysticism of St. Francis of Assissi. 1977. lib. bdg. 250.00 (0-8490-2319-X) Gordon Pr.

Nicholson, Dale, jt. ed. see Friend, Diane.

Nicholson, Dan. From Hippie to Happy. (Orig.). 1984. pap. write for info. (0-88144-026-4, CPS026) Christian Pub.

Nicholson, Darrell. Wild Boars. (Nature Watch Bks.). (Illus.). 48p. (J). (gr. 2-5). 1987. lib. bdg. 19.95 (0-87614-308-7, Carolrhoda) Lerner Group.

Nicholson, David, ed. see Papgapitos, Karen.

Nicholson, David L. Spread Spectrum Signal Design: LPE & AJ Systems. Kahl, Sandy, ed. LC 87-38218. (Electrical Engineering, Telecommunications, & Signal Processing Ser.). 291p. (C). 1995. text ed. write for info. (0-7167-8150-6) W H Freeman.

Nicholson, Dorinda M. Pearl Harbor Child: A Child's View of Pearl Harbor-From Attack to Peace. (Illus.). 60p. (J). 1993. pap. write for info. (0-9631388-6-3) AZ Mem Mus.

Nicholson, Dorothy H. The Henry Family from the British Isles to America & Allied Families. LC 90-62578. (Illus.). 1990. lib. bdg. 65.00 (0-9627521-1-8) D H Nicholson.

Nicholson, Dwight R. Introduction to Plasma Theory. LC 91-36314. 304p. (C). 1992. reprint ed. lib. bdg. 61.95 (0-89464-677-X) Krieger.

Nicholson, E. W., jt. ed. see Baker, J.

***Nicholson, Elva Mae & Ramsay, O. Bertrand.** Estimating the Optimum pH & Temperature for Digestive Enzyme Activity. Neidig, H. A., ed. (Modular Laboratory Program in Chemistry Ser.). 12p. (C). 1994. pap. text ed. 1.25x (0-87540-444-8) Chem Educ Res.

Nicholson, Eric, tr. see Delumeau, Jean.

Nicholson, Frances, ed. Political & Economic Encyclopedia of Western Europe. 380p. 1990. lib. bdg. 85.00 (1-55862-072-9) St James Pr.

Nicholson, Frank C. Old German Love Songs. 1973. 59.95 (0-8490-0759-3) Gordon Pr.

Nicholson, G., jt. auth. see Poste, George.

Nicholson, G., jt. ed. see Poste, George.

Nicholson, Geoff. Day Trips to the Desert: A Sort of Travel Book. (Illus.). 190p. 1993. 34.95 (0-340-55371-5, Pub. by H & S UK) Trafalgar.

— Everything & More. 256p. 1995. 21.95 (0-312-13069-4) St Martin.

— The Food Chain. 184p. 1994. 21.95 (0-87951-508-2, Penguin Bks); pap. 10.95 (0-87951-544-9, Penguin Bks) Overlook Pr.

— Hunters & Gatherers. 215p. 1994. 21.95 (0-87951-559-7) Overlook Pr.

— Hunters & Gatherers. 215p. 1995. pap. 10.95 (0-87951-601-1) Overlook Pr.

— Still Life with Volkswagens. 233p. 1995. pap. 21.95 (0-87951-616-X) Overlook Pr.

Nicholson, George A. English Words with Native Roots & with Greek, Latin, or Romance Suffixes. LC 70-173081. (Chicago. University. Linguistic Studies in Germanic: No. 3). reprint ed. 27.50 (0-404-50283-0) AMS Pr.

Nicholson, Gilbert W. Studies on Tumor Formation. LC 51-3965. (Illus.). 649p. reprint ed. pap. 180.00 (0-317-41707-X, 2025720) Bks Demand.

Nicholson, Godfrey C. Death As Departure: The Johannine Descent-Ascent Schema. LC 81-18336. (Society of Biblical Literature Dissertation Ser.). 250p. (C). 1982. pap. 15.95 (0-89130-555-6, 060163) Scholars Pr GA.

Nicholson, Graeme. Illustrations of Being: Drawing upon Heidegger & upon Metaphysics. LC 91-35247. (Contemporary Studies in Philosophy & the Human Sciences). 312p. (C). 1992. text ed. 55.00 (0-391-03738-2) Humanities.

— Seeing & Reading. LC 83-12854. 292p. (C). 1989. pap. 18.50 (0-391-03618-1) Humanities.

Nicholson, Graeme, jt. ed. see Greenspan, Louis.

Nicholson, Graeme, jt. ed. see Misgeld, Dieter.

Nicholson, Gregoe D. Some Early Emigrants to America: And Early Emigrants to America from Liverpool. 110p. 1989. reprint ed. 12.95 (0-685-60504-3, 4110) Clearfield Co.

Nicholson, H. Structure of Interconnected Systems. (Control Engineering Ser.: No. 5). (Illus.). 258p. 1978. boxed 61.00 (0-901223-69-7, CE005) Inst Elect Eng.

Nicholson, H. B. & Berger, Rainer. Two Aztec Wood Idols: Iconographic & Chronologic Analysis. LC 68-58701. (Studies in Pre-Columbian Art & Archaeology: No. 5). (Illus.). 28p. 1968. pap. 6.00 (0-88402-026-6) Dumbarton Oaks.

Nicholson, H. B., jt. auth. see Cordy-Collins, Alana.

Nicholson, Heather J. & Nicholson, Ralph L. Distant Hunger: Agriculture, Food, & Human Values. LC 78-60761. (Science & Society: Series in Science, Technology, & Human Values: Vol. 3). (Illus.). 240p. 1979. pap. 6.95 (0-931682-00-2) Purdue U Pubns.

***Nicholson, Helen.** Templars, Hospitallers & Teutonic Knights: The Image of the Military Orders, 1128-1291. 224p. 1995. pap. 24.95 (0-7185-2277-X, Pub. by Leicester Univ Pr) St Martin.

Nicholson, Henry A. The Ancient Life-History of the Earth. 1980. 37.95 (0-405-12723-5) Ayer.

— The Ancient Life-History of the Earth: A Comprehensive Outline of the Principles & Leading Facts of Paleontological Science. Gould, Stephen J., ed. LC 79-83338. (History of Paleontology Ser.). (Illus.). 1980. reprint ed. lib. bdg. 30.00 (0-405-12724-3) Ayer.

***Nicholson, Ian.** Boat Data Book. 3rd ed. LC 94-35443. (Illus.). 192p. 1995. 30.00 (0-924486-78-3) Sheridan.

Nicholson, Irene. A Guide to Mexican Poetry. (Illus.). 96p. 1968. pap. 4.00 (0-912434-13-9) Ocelot Pr.

Nicholson, Irene, tr. see Castellanos, Rosario.

Nicholson, J. Boyd. The Watered Garden. (Illus.). 96p. 1994. 18.95 (1-882701-03-8) Gospel Folio.

Nicholson, J. Shield. The Effects of Machinery on Wages. LC 72-38263. (Evolution of Capitalism Ser.). 160p. 1972. reprint ed. 18.95 (0-405-04129-2) Ayer.

Nicholson, J. V. Forest Flora from Within Bihar & Orissa. 70p. (C). 1981. text ed. 60.00 (0-89771-615-9, Pub. by Intl Bk Distr II) St Mut.

Nicholson, James H. Calculator Enhancement for Single-Variable Calculus. 99p. (C). 1990. pap. text ed. 8.00 (0-15-505676-X) HB Coll Pubs.

Nicholson, James H. & Kenelly, John. Calculator Enhancement for Single Variable Calculus. (Clemson Calculator Enhancement Ser.). 196p. (C). 1992. pap. text ed. 12.00 (0-03-092728-5) SCP.

Nicholson, James W. Stories by Dixie. 1966. pap. 6.00 (0-87511-153-X) Claitors.

***Nicholson, Jeff.** Nicholson's Small Press Tirade. (Illus.). 104p. (Orig.). 1994. pap. 7.95 (1-885047-01-0) Bad Habit.

— Through the Habitrails. (Illus.). 144p. (Orig.). 1994. pap. 9.95 (1-885047-00-2) Bad Habit.

Nicholson, Jerome L. Cost Accounting: Theory & Practice. Brief, Richard P., ed. LC 77-87283. (Development of Contemporary Accounting Thought Ser.). 1978. reprint ed. lib. bdg. 31.95 (0-405-10911-3) Ayer.

Nicholson, Jill. Mother & Baby Homes: A Survey of Homes for Unmarried Mothers. 1968. 45.00 (0-317-05814-2, Pub. by Natl Inst Soc Work) St Mut.

***Nicholson, JoAnna.** How to Be Sexy Without Looking Sleazy. 150p. (Orig.). 1994. pap. 6.95 (1-57023-013-7) Impact VA.

— One Hundred Mistakes Working Women Make & How to Avoid Them: Dressing Smart in the 90's. 117p. 1994. pap. 9.95 (1-57023-009-9) Impact VA.

— One Hundred Ten Mistakes Working Women Make & How to Avoid Them: Dressing Smart in the '90s. LC 94-31928. 1994. 9.95 (1-57023-014-5) Impact VA.

Nicholson, Joanne, ed. see International Childbirth Education Association, Community Outreach Committee.

Nicholson, John. Cicero's Return from Exile: The Orations Post Reditum. LC 92-12191. (Classical Studies: Vol. 4). 174p. (C). 1992. text ed. 39.95 (0-8204-1945-1) P Lang Pubs.

— Homemade Houses. (J). (gr. 4-7). 1994. 14.95 (1-86373-489-9); pap. 6.95 (1-86373-516-X) IPG Chicago.

— Men & Women: How Different Are They? (Illus.). 240p. 1984. pap. 9.95 (0-19-286034-8) OUP.

— Men & Women: How Different Are They? 2nd ed. LC 92-30066. (Illus.). 240p. 1993. 14.95 (0-19-286157-3) OUP.

Nicholson, John B., Jr. Reading & the Art of Librarianship: Selected Essays of John B. Nicholson, Jr. LC 86-18442. (Collection Management Ser.: Vol. 8, Nos. 3/4). 281p. 1986. 49.95 (0-86656-585-X) Haworth Pr.

Nicholson, John G. Russian Normative Stress Notation. 176p. 1968. 29.95 (0-7735-0020-0, Pub. by McGill CN) U of Toronto Pr.

— Russian Normative Stress Notation. LC 67-31404. 187p. reprint ed. pap. 53.30 (0-7837-6929-6, 2046758) Bks Demand.

Nicholson, John R. Understanding & Using PageMaker 4.0. Leyh, ed. LC 92-28569. (Microcomputing Ser.). 416p. (C). 1993. pap. text ed. 26.75 (0-314-01269-9) West Pub.

— Understanding & Using Pagemaker 5.0. LC 94-11725. (Microcomputing Ser.). 1994. spiral bd. 26.75 (0-314-03972-4) West Pub.

Nicholson, John W., jt. auth. see Wilson, Alan D.

Nicholson, Jon & Williams, John. Detour's London. Caswell, Augustus, ed. LC 93-90988. (Detour Ser.). 304p. 1993. 13.95 (0-9635983-1-7) Detour Pubns.

Nicholson, Joseph S. Strikes & Social Problems. LC 72-4517. (Essay Index Reprint Ser.). 1977. reprint ed. 20.95 (0-8369-2964-0) Ayer.

Nicholson, Joseph W., jt. auth. see Mays, Benjamin E.

Nicholson, Judith, jt. ed. see Nicholson, Clara.

Nicholson, Kathleen. Turner's Classical Landscapes: Myth & Meaning. (Illus.). 360p. 1990. text ed. 55.00 (0-691-04080-X) Princeton U Pr.

Nicholson, Keith. Geothermal Fluids: Chemistry & Exploration Techniques. LC 93-29590. 1993. 89.00 (0-387-56017-3) Spr-Verlag.

Nicholson, Kenneth E., jt. auth. see Becnel, Irwin J., Jr.

Nicholson, Kenyon & Robinson, Charles K. The Flying Gerardos. 1949. pap. 4.75 (0-8222-0414-2) Dramatists Play.

***Nicholson, Laurel L., ed.** 401 (k) Plans. LC 94-47143. 1995. write for info. (0-87179-878-6) BNA.

Nicholson, Lewis & Frese, Dolores. Anglo-Saxon Poetry: Essays in Appreciation. LC 74-27893. 400p. 1977. pap. 14.95 (0-268-00576-1) U of Notre Dame Pr.

Nicholson, Lewis E. The Vercelli Book Homilies: Translations from the Anglo-Saxon. 184p. (C). 1991. lib. bdg. 38.00 (0-8191-8116-1) U Pr of Amer.

Nicholson, Lewis E., ed. Anthology of Beowulf Criticism. 1963. pap. 14.95 (0-268-00006-9) U of Notre Dame Pr.

***Nicholson, Linda & Seidman, Steven, eds.** Social Postmodernism: Beyond Identity Politics. (Cultural & Social Studies). 416p. (C). 1995. write for info. (0-521-47516-3); pap. write for info. (0-521-47571-6) Cambridge U Pr.

Nicholson, Linda J. Gender & History: The Limits of Social Theory in the Age of the Family. LC 85-21281. 256p. 1988. text ed. 40.50 (0-231-06220-6); pap. text ed. 15.00 (0-231-06221-4) Col U Pr.

Nicholson, Linda J., intro. Feminism - Postmodernism. 352p. 1989. 45.00 (0-415-90058-1, Routledge NY); pap. 14.95 (0-415-90059-X, Routledge NY) Routledge.

Nicholson, Linda J., ed. see Butler, Judith P.

***Nicholson, Lois.** Babe Ruth: Sultan of Swat. (Illus.). 170p. (YA). (gr. 7-12). 1995. 17.95 (0-9625427-1-7) Goodwood Pr.

— Cal Ripken, Jr. Quiet Hero. LC 93-22741. (Illus.). 112p. (J). (gr. 4-8). 1993. bds. 12.95 (0-87033-445-X, Tidewtr Pubs) Cornell Maritime.

— The Importance of Georgia O'Keefe. (Importance of... Ser.). (Illus.). 128p. (J). (gr. 5-9). 1995. lib. bdg. 16.95 (1-56006-055-7, 0557) Lucent Bks.

— Michael Jackson: Entertainer. (Black Americans of Achievement Ser.). (Illus.). 1994. 18.95 (0-7910-1929-2, Am Art Analog) Chelsea Hse.

— Oprah Winfrey: Entertainer. (Black Americans of Achievement Ser.). (Illus.). 1994. 18.95 (0-7910-1886-5, Am Art Analog) Chelsea Hse.

***Nicholson, Lois P.** Helen Keller: The Humantarian Who Became Deaf & Blind at Nineteen Months. LC 94-37512. (Great Achievers Ser.). (Illus.). 128p. (YA). (gr. 5 up). 1995. 18.95 (0-7910-2086-X) Chelsea Hse.

— Mike Schmidt. LC 94-23612. (Baseball Legends Ser.). (Illus.). 64p. (J). (gr. 3 up). 1995. lib. bdg. 14.95 (0-7910-2173-4) Chelsea Hse.

— Nolan Ryan. LC 95-3099. (Baseball Legends Ser.). (Illus.). 64p. (YA). (gr. 3 up). 1995. lib. bdg. 14.95 (0-7910-2174-2) Chelsea Hse.

Nicholson, Loren. Old Picture Postcards: A Historic Journey along California's Central Coast. (California Heritage Ser.: No. 1). (Illus.). 144p. (Orig.). (YA). (gr. 9-12). 1989. pap. 12.95 (0-9623233-1-4) CA HPA.

— Rails across the Ranchos: Centennial Edition of the Southern Pacific Coastal Line Railroad Centennial Years. 2nd ed. (California Heritage Ser.). (Illus.). 208p. (Orig.). reprint ed. pap. 18.95 (0-9623233-6-5) CA HPA.

— Romualdo Pacheco's California! The Mexican-American Who Won. (California Heritage Ser.: No. 2). (Illus.). 112p. (Orig.). (YA). (gr. 10-12). 1991. pap. text ed. 12.95 (0-9623233-2-2) CA HPA.

Nicholson, Louis P. George Washington Carver: Botanist & Ecologist. (Junior Black Americans of Achievement Ser.). (Illus.). 80p. (J). (gr. 3-6). 1993. lib. bdg. 14.95 (0-7910-1763-X, Am Art Analog) Chelsea Hse.

— George Washington Carver: Botanist & Ecologist. LC 93-38515. (Junior Black Americans of Achievement Ser.). (Illus.). 80p. (J). (gr. 3-6). 1994. write for info. (0-7910-2108-4); pap. 4.95 (0-7910-2114-9) Chelsea Hse.

Nicholson, Louise. Delhi, Agra, & Jaipur. (Asian Guides Ser.). 208p. 1988. pap. 12.95 (0-8442-9917-0, Passport Bks) NTC Pub Grp.

— The Festive Food of India & Pakistan. (Illus.). 60p. 1994. 8.95 (1-85626-051-8) Trafalgar.

— Fodor's London Companion: The Complete Guide for the Independent Traveler. 3rd ed. 1993. pap. 17.00 (0-679-02457-3) Fodors Travel.

— London. 1989. 16.95 (0-370-31032-2) Random.

Nicholson, M., jt. auth. see Sivertsen, J.

Nicholson, M. Jean, jt. auth. see Hein, Eleanor C.

Nicholson, M. P., ed. Architectural Management. 418p. 1992. 109.95 (0-442-31598-8) Chapman & Hall.

Nicholson, Marjorie H. Newton Demands the Muse: Newton's "Opticks" & the Eighteenth Century Poets. LC 78-13146. 178p. 1979. reprint ed. text ed. 35.00 (0-313-21044-6, NIND, Greenwood Pr) Greenwood.

***Nicholson, Mary E. & St. Pierre, Richard.** Instructor's Manual for "Sexuality: A Health Education Perspective" rev. ed. (Illus.). 75p. (C). 1991. teacher ed write for info. (0-910251-28-2) Venture Pub PA.

Nicholson, Mary J. Moments in Time with Mary John. LC 81-90608. (Illus.). 40p. 1982. pap. text ed. 5.50 (0-9607574-0-6) M J Nicholson.

Nicholson, Mary K. Separation & Divorce in North Carolina: Answers to the Most Commonly Asked Questions about Your Legal Rights. Bledsoe, Jerry, ed. LC 92-72659. 68p. (Orig.). 1992. pap. 7.95 (1-878086-16-2) Down Home NC.

Nicholson, Mavis. Martha Jane & Me. large type ed. 1993. 39.95 (0-7066-1014-8, Pub. by Remploy Pr CN) St Mut.

Nicholson, Meredith. A Hoosier Chronicle. 1975. lib. bdg. 23.40 (0-89966-144-0) Buccaneer Bks.

— The House of a Thousand Candles. 1975. lib. bdg. 16.70 (0-89966-142-4) Buccaneer Bks.

— The House of a Thousand Candles. LC 85-45892. (Library of Indiana Classics). (Illus.). 392p. 1986. 20.00 (0-253-32852-7); pap. 7.95 (0-253-20381-3, MB-381) Ind U Pr.

— The Port of Missing Men. 1975. lib. bdg. 17.25 (0-89966-143-2) Buccaneer Bks.

— Provincial American & Other Papers. LC 79-152205. (Essay Index Reprint Ser.). 1977. 20.95 (0-8369-2211-5) Ayer.

***Nicholson, Michael.** Causes & Consequences in International Relations: A Conceptual Analysis. 256p. 1995. text ed. 59.95 (1-85567-242-1, Pub. by Pinter Pubs UK) St Martin.

— Formal Theories in International Relations. (Studies in International Relations: No. 3). (Illus.). 272p. (C). 1990. pap. 19.95 (0-521-39967-X) Cambridge U Pr.

— Rationality & the Analysis of International Conflict. (Studies in International Relations). (Illus.). 288p. (C). 1992. pap. 19.95 (0-521-39810-X) Cambridge U Pr.

— The Structure of International Society: A Conceptual Analysis. 256p. 1995. (1-85567-243-X, Pub. by Pinter Pubs UK) St Martin.

Nicholson, Michael & Winner, David. Raoul Wallenberg. LC 88-2078. (People Who Have Helped the World Ser.). (Illus.). 68p. (J). (gr. 5-6). 1990. pap. 7.95 (0-8192-1525-2) Morehouse Pub.

— Raoul Wallenberg: The Swedish Diplomat Who Saved 100,000 Jews from the Nazi Holocaust Before Mysteriously Disappearing. Sherwood, Rhoda, ed. LC 88-2078. (People Who Have Helped the World Ser.). (Illus.). 68p. (J). (gr. 5-6). 1989. lib. bdg. 21.26 (1-55532-820-2) Gareth Stevens Inc.

Nicholson, N. & Clemie, C. The Good Interview Guide. (C). 1989. text ed. 35.00 (0-948032-39-1, Pub. by Rosters Ltd) St Mut.

— The Right Job for You. (C). 1989. text ed. 29.95 (0-948032-63-4, Pub. by Rosters Ltd) St Mut.

***Nicholson, Nigel, ed.** The Blackwell Encyclopedic Dictionary of Organizational Behavior. (Encyclopedia of Management Ser.). 550p. 1995. write for info. (0-631-18781-2) Blackwell Pubs.

Nicholson, Nigel & West, Michael. Managerial Job Change: Men & Women in Transition. (Management & Industrial Relations Ser.: No. 12). (Illus.). 300p. 1988. pap. 19.95 (0-521-35744-6) Cambridge U Pr.

Nicholson, Nigel, et al. The Dynamics of White Collar Unionism: A Study of Local Union Participation. LC 81-66682. (Organizational & Occupational Psychology Ser.). 1981. text ed. 104.00 (0-12-518020-9) Acad Pr.

Nicholson, Norman K. Panchayat Raj, Rural Development & the Political Economy of Village India. (Occasional Paper Ser.: No. 1). 61p. (Orig.). (C). 1973. pap. text ed. 4.95 (0-86731-014-6) Cornell CIS RDC.

Nicholson, Norman K. & Khan, Dilawar A. Basic Democracies & Rural Development in Pakistan. (Special Series on Rural Local Government: No. 10). 99p. (Orig.). (C). 1974. pap. text ed. 3.50 (0-86731-096-0) Cornell CIS RDC.

Nicholson, Norman K., jt. ed. see Russell, Clifford S.

Nicholson, Patrick J. Mr. Jim, The Biography of James Smither Abercrombie. LC 83-12608. 416p. 1983. 18.00 (0-87201-404-5) Gulf Pub.

— William Ward Watkin & the Rice Institute. 364p. 1991. 24.95 (0-88415-012-7) Gulf Pub.

Nicholson, Paul T. Egyptian Faience & Glass. 1989. pap. 25.00 (0-7478-0195-9, Pub. by Shire UK) St Mut.

Nicholson, Paul W. Nuclear Electronics. LC 73-8196. 402p. reprint ed. 114.60 (0-317-52891-2, 2026677) Bks Demand.

Nicholson, Peggy. Pure & Simple. (Romance Ser.). 1993. pap. 2.89 (0-373-03250-1, 1-03250-7) Harlequin Bks.

— Pure & Simple. large type ed. LC 93-13219. 1993. 13.95 (1-56054-758-8) Thorndike Pr.

— The Truth about George. (Romance Ser.). 1994. mass mkt. 2.99 (0-373-03322-2, 1-03322-4) Harlequin Bks.

Nicholson, Peggy & Warner, John F. The Case of the Furtive Firebug. (Kerry Hill Casecrackers Ser.: No. 1). 120p. (J). (gr. 4-7). 1994. 14.95 (0-8225-0709-9, Lerner Publctns) Lerner Group.

— The Case of the Lighthouse Ghost. (Kerry Hill Casecrackers Ser.: No. 2). 120p. (J). (gr. 4-7). 1994. 14.95 (0-8225-0710-2, Lerner Publctns) Lerner Group.

— The Case of the Mysterious Codes. (Kerry Hill Casecrackers Ser.: No. 4). 120p. (J). (gr. 4-7). 1994. 14.95 (0-8225-0712-9, Lerner Publctns) Lerner Group.

— The Case of the Squeaky Thief. (Kerry Hill Casecrackers Ser.: No. 3). 120p. (J). (gr. 4-7). 1994. 14.95 (0-8225-0711-0, Lerner Publctns) Lerner Group.

Nicholson, Peter. An Annotated Index to the Commentary on John Gower's "Confessio Amantis" (Medieval & Renaissance Texts & Studies: Vol. 62). 608p. 1989. 36.00 (0-86698-046-6) MRTS.

— The Barry Album. (Illus.). 48p. (C). 1987. pap. 13.00 (0-317-90464-7, Pub. by Picton UK) St Mut.

— Diesel Locomotives in Preservation, Vol. 2: Former BR LMSR Loco's. 28p. (C). 1987. pap. 35.00 (0-317-90465-5, Pub. by Picton UK) St Mut.

— New Carpenter's Guide of Eighteen Eighteen. (Illus.). 100p. 1993. reprint ed. pap. 40.00 (0-87556-826-2) Saifer.

Nicholson, Peter, ed. Gower's Confessio Amantis: A Critical Anthology. (Publications of the John Gower Society: No. III). 224p. (C). 1991. text ed. 70.00 (0-85991-318-X) Boydell & Brewer.

Nicholson, Peter & Parker, Janet. The Complete Rhodesian Ridgeback. (Illus.). 160p. 1991. 25.95 (0-87605-295-2) Howell Bk.

Nicholson, Peter P. The Political Philosophy of the British Idealists. (C). 1990. 84.95 (0-521-37102-3) Cambridge U Pr.

Nicholson, R. A. The Essence of Sufism. 1984. reprint ed. pap. 3.95 (0-916411-49-4, Near Eastern) Holmes Pub.

— Idea of Personality in Sufism. 12.50 (1-56744-051-7) Kazi Pubns.

— The Sufi Doctrine of the Perfect Man. 1984. reprint ed. pap. 3.95 (0-916411-48-6, Near Eastern) Holmes Pub.

Nicholson, R. A., ed. & tr. Selected Poems from the Divani Shamsi Tabriz. 432p. (C). 1994. text ed. 80.00 (0-7007-0277-6, Pub. by Curzon Pr UK) Humanities.

Nicholson, R. H. Inside the MCC: A Technical Guide to the Mission Control Center at the Johnson Space Center. (Illus.). 96p. (Orig.). 1991. pap. 9.95 (1-882123-30-1) Universal Radio Rsch.

Nicholson, Ralph L., jt. auth. see Nicholson, Heather J.

Nicholson, Ranald. The Edinburgh History of Scotland, Vol. 2: The Later Middle Ages. 695p. (C). 1986. pap. 75.00 (0-901824-84-4, Pub. by Mercat Pr Bks UK) St Mut.

N

An Asterisk (*) at the beginning of an entry indicates that the title is appearing in BIP for the first time.

*****Nicholson, Reynold.** Rumi: Poet & Mystic. 1995. pap. 10. 95 (*1-85168-096-9*) Onewrld Pubns.
— Tales of Mystic Meaning. 1995. pap. 11.95 (*1-85168-097-7*) Onewrld Pubns.
*****Nicholson, Reynold A.** Ecstasy in Islam. Date not set. pap. 3.95 (*1-55818-298-5*, Near Eastern) Holmes Pub.
— A Literary History of the Arabs. 536p. (C). 1930. text ed. 70.00 (*0-7007-0261-X*, Pub. by Curzon Pr UK) Humanities.
— A Literary History of the Arabs. 536p. (C). 1995. pap. 35. 00 (*0-7007-0336-5*, Pub. by Curzon Pr UK) Humanities.
— A Literary History of the Arabs. LC 74-401710. 538p. reprint ed. pap. 153.40 (*0-317-27312-4*, 2024502) Bks Demand.
— The Mystics of Islam. 192p. 1990. pap. 9.95 (*0-14-019168-2*, Penguin Bks) Viking Penguin.
— Studies in Islamic Mysticism. 288p. (C). 1994. pap. 19.95 (*0-7007-0278-4*, Pub. by Curzon Pr UK) Humanities.
Nicholson, Reynold A., tr. see Al-Hujwiri.
*****Nicholson, Robert.** Ancient China. (Journey into Civilization Ser.). (Illus.). 32p. (J). (gr. 3-7). 1994. lib. bdg. 14.95 (*0-7910-2702-3*) Chelsea Hse.
— Ancient China. (Journey into Civilization Ser.). (Illus.). 32p. (J). (gr. 3-7). 1994. pap. 7.95 (*0-7910-2726-0*) Chelsea Hse.
— Ancient Egypt. (Illus.). 32p. (J). (gr. 3-7). 1994. lib. bdg. 14.95 (*0-7910-2704-X*) Chelsea Hse.
— Ancient Egypt. (Illus.). 32p. (J). (gr. 3-7). 1994. pap. 7.95 (*0-7910-2728-7*) Chelsea Hse.
— Ancient Greece. LC 93-29442. (Journey into Civilization Ser.). (Illus.). 32p. (J). (gr. 3-7). 1994. 7.95 (*0-7910-2727-9*); lib. bdg. 14.95 (*0-7910-2703-1*) Chelsea Hse.
— The Aztecs. LC 93-29445. (Journey into Civilization Ser.). (Illus.). 32p. (J). (gr. 3-7). 1994. lib. bdg. 14.95 (*0-7910-2701-5*); pap. 7.95 (*0-7910-2725-2*) Chelsea Hse.
— Great Mysteries. Clayton, Caroline & Kelleher, Damian, eds. (Info Adventure Ser.). (Illus.). 32p. (J). (gr. 4-6). 1995. pap. 5.95 (*1-56847-315-X*) Thomson Lrning.
— Great Mysteries. Clayton, Caroline & Kelleher, Damian, eds. (Info Adventure Ser.). (Illus.). 32p. (J). (gr. 4-6). 1995. 12.95 (*1-56847-408-3*) Thomson Lrning.
— The Maya. (Journey into Civilization Ser.). (Illus.). 32p. (J). (gr. 3-7). 1994. lib. bdg. 14.95 (*0-7910-2705-8*) Chelsea Hse.
— The Maya. (Journey into Civilization Ser.). (Illus.). 32p. (J). (gr. 3-7). 1994. pap. 7.95 (*0-7910-2729-5*) Chelsea Hse.
— The Mongols. (Journey into Civilization Ser.). (Illus.). 32p. (J). (gr. 3-7). 1994. lib. bdg. 14.95 (*0-7910-2706-6*) Chelsea Hse.
— The Mongols. (Journey into Civilization Ser.). (Illus.). 32p. (J). (gr. 3-7). 1994. pap. 7.95 (*0-7910-2730-9*) Chelsea Hse.
— The Sioux. (Journey into Civilization Ser.). (Illus.). 32p. (J). (gr. 3-7). 1994. lib. bdg. 14.95 (*0-7910-2708-2*) Chelsea Hse.
— The Sioux. (Journey into Civilization Ser.). (Illus.). 32p. (J). (gr. 3-7). 1994. pap. 7.95 (*0-7910-2732-5*) Chelsea Hse.
— Los Siux. Araluce, Jose R., tr. (Raices Ser.). (Illus.). 32p. (SPA.). (J). 1993. 16.95 (*1-56492-092-5*) Laredo.
— The Ulysses Guide: Tours Through Joyce's Dublin. 150p. 1989. pap. 9.95 (*0-415-90144-8*, A3315, Routledge NY) Routledge.
— The Vikings. (Journey into Civilization Ser.). (Illus.). 32p. (J). (gr. 3-7). 1994. lib. bdg. 14.95 (*0-7910-2709-0*) Chelsea Hse.
— The Vikings. (Journey into Civilization Ser.). (Illus.). 32p. (J). (gr. 3-7). 1994. pap. 7.95 (*0-7910-2733-3*) Chelsea Hse.
— The Zulus. (Journey into Civilization Ser.). (Illus.). 32p. (J). (gr. 3-7). 1994. lib. bdg. 14.95 (*0-7910-2710-4*) Chelsea Hse.
— The Zulus. (Journey into Civilization Ser.). (Illus.). 32p. (J). (gr. 3-7). 1994. pap. 7.95 (*0-7910-2734-1*) Chelsea Hse.
Nicholson, Robert & Watts, Claire. La Antigua China: Hechos, Historias, Actividades. Araluce, Jose R., tr. (Raices Ser.). (Illus.). 32p. (SPA.). (YA). (gr. 6-10). 1993. 14.95 (*1-56492-093-3*) Laredo.
— El Antiguo Egipto: Hechos - Histoias - Actividades. Araluce, Jose R., tr. (Raices Ser.). (Illus.). 32p. (SPA.). (J). (gr. 6-10). 1993. 14.95 (*1-56492-094-1*) Laredo.
— Los Aztecas. Araluce, Jose R., tr. (Raices Ser.). (Illus.). 24p. (SPA.). (J). 1993. 14.95 (*1-56492-091-7*) Laredo.
Nicholson, Robert, jt. auth. see Watts, Claire.
Nicholson, Robert L. Joscelyn I, Prince of Edessa. LC 78-63352. (Crusades & Military Orders Ser.: Second Series). 120p. reprint ed. 31.50 (*0-404-17025-0*) AMS Pr.
— Tancred: A Study of His Career & Work. LC 79-29847. reprint ed. 29.50 (*0-404-15425-5*) AMS Pr.
Nicholson, Ronald. A Black Future? Jesus & Salvation in South Africa. LC 89-28280. 288p. (Orig.). (C). 1990. pap. text ed. 18.95 (*0-334-00120-X*) TPI PA.
Nicholson, Ronald A. Practical Footcare for Nurse Practitioners: A Training Manual & Clinical Handbook. LC 94-66314. (Illus.). 192p. (Orig.). (C). 1994. pap. text ed. 69.95 (*1-885421-01-X*) Practical Footcare.
— Practical Footcare for Physician Assistants: A Training Manual & Clinical Handbook. LC 94-66313. (Illus.). 192p. (Orig.). (C). 1994. pap. text ed. 69.95 (*1-885421-00-1*) Practical Footcare.
— Practical Footcare for Primary Care Physicians: A Training Manual & Clinical Handbook. LC 94-66215. (Illus.). 192p. (Orig.). (C). 1994. pap. text ed. 69.95 (*1-885421-02-8*) Practical Footcare.
Nicholson, Roy S. True Holiness: The Wesleyan-Arminian Emphasis. 1985. pap. 8.99 (*0-88019-195-3*) Schmul Pub Co.
Nicholson, S. Francis. Quaker Money. 290p. (Orig.). 1990. pap. 3.00 (*0-87574-290-4*) Pendle Hill.
Nicholson, Sheila A., ed. see Humble, Tracy W.
Nicholson, Shierry W., tr. see Adorno, Theodor W.
Nicholson, Shierry W., tr. see Habermas, Jurgen.
Nicholson, Shirley. Ancient Wisdom: Modern Insight. LC 84-40513. (Illus.). 198p. (Orig.). 1985. pap. text ed. 6.75 (*0-8356-0595-7*, Quest) Theos Pub Hse.
— Nyman's: The Story of a Sussex Garden. (Illus.). 192p. 1994. pap. 20.00 (*0-7509-0615-4*) A Sutton Pub.
— A Victorian Household. (Illus.). 224p. 1994. pap. 20.00 (*0-7509-0637-5*) A Sutton Pub.
Nicholson, Shirley, comp. Shamanism. LC 86-40405. 402p. (Orig.). 1987. pap. 11.95 (*0-8356-0617-1*, Quest) Theos Pub Hse.
Nicholson, Shirley, ed. The Goddess Re-Awakening: The Feminine Principle Today. LC 88-40488. 314p. (Orig.). 1989. pap. 10.95 (*0-8356-0642-2*, Quest) Theos Pub Hse.
Nicholson, Shirley & Rosen, Brenda, eds. Gaia's Hidden Life: The Unseen Intelligence of Nature. LC 92-50143. (Illus.). 290p. 1992. pap. 14.00 (*0-8356-0685-6*, Quest) Theos Pub Hse.
Nicholson, Shirley, ed. see Besant, Annie.
Nicholson, Shirley, ed. see Powell, Robert.
Nicholson-Smith, Donald, tr. see Debord, Guy.
Nicholson-Smith, Donald, tr. see Lefebvre, Henri.
Nicholson-Smith, Donald, tr. see Vaneigem, Raoul.
*****Nicholson, Stuart.** Billie Holiday. LC 95-16155. 1995. write for info. (*1-55553-248-9*) NE U Pr.
— Ella Fitzgerald: A Biography. LC 93-34359. 320p. 1994. text ed. 23.00 (*0-684-19699-9*, Scribners) S&S Trade.
— Ella Fitzgerald: A Biography of the First Lady of Jazz. (Illus.). 368p. 1995. reprint ed. pap. 14.95 (*0-306-80642-8*) Da Capo.
— Jazz, the Nineteen Eighties Resurgence: The 1980s Resurgence. 2nd ed. (Illus.). 352p. 1995. pap. 14.95 (*0-306-80612-6*) Da Capo.
Nicholson, Susan B. Encyclopedia of Antique Postcards. LC 94-14084. 1994. 19.95 (*0-87069-730-7*, Wallace-Hmestead) Chilton.
Nicholson, Susan B., jt. auth. see Banneck, Janet A.
Nicholson, Susan T., jt. auth. see Andrews, Charlotte J.
Nicholson, T. J., jt. ed. see Evans, D. D.
Nicholson, Vincent D. Cooperation & Coercion as Methods of Social Change. (C). 1934. pap. 3.00 (*0-87574-001-4*) Pendle Hill.
Nicholson, W. Keith. Elementary Linear Algebra with Applications. 2nd ed. 576p. (C). 1990. text ed. 57.95 (*0-534-92189-2*) PWS Pubs.
— Introduction to Abstract Algebra. 640p. 1993. text ed. 63. 95 (*0-534-93189-8*) PWS Pubs.
— Linear Algebra with Applications. 3rd ed. LC 93-28879. 1994. text ed. 64.95 (*0-534-93666-0*) PWS Pubs.
Nicholson, Walter. Intermediate Microeconomics & Its Application. 6th ed. LC 93-70170. 722p. (C). 1994. text ed. 66.50 (*0-03-074809-7*) Dryden Pr.
— Intermediate Microeconomics & Its Application. 6th ed. LC 93-70170. (C). 1994. disk 21.00 (*0-03-006462-7*) Dryden Pr.
— Intermediate Microeconomics & Its Applications. 5th ed. 768p. (C). 1990. text ed. 57.25 (*0-03-031392-9*) Dryden Pr.
— Intermediate Microeconomics & Its Applications: Instructor's Manual to Accompany. 6th ed. 146p. (C). 1994. pap. text ed. 28.00 (*0-03-074812-7*) Dryden Pr.
— Intermediate Microeconomics & Its Applications: Instructor's Manual to Accompany. 6th ed. 146p. (C). 1994. disk 21.00 (*0-03-006458-9*) Dryden Pr.
— Microeconomic Theory. 5th ed. 864p. (C). 1992. text ed. 57.75 (*0-03-055043-2*) Dryden Pr.
— Test Bank to Accompany Intermediate Microeconomics & Its Application. 6th ed. 97p. (C). 1994. pap. text ed. 28.00 (*0-03-006457-0*) Dryden Pr.
Nicholson, Watson. Historical Sources of DeFoe's Journal of the Plague Years. LC 68-54174. (British History Ser.: No. 30). (C). 1969. reprint ed. lib. bdg. 75.00 (*0-8383-0600-4*) M S G Haskell Hse.
— Struggle for a Free Stage in London. LC 65-27915. 1972. reprint ed. 24.95 (*0-405-08816-7*, Pub. by Blom Pubns UK) Ayer.
Nicholson, William. An Alphabet. LC 75-14747. (Illus.). 1975. reprint ed. 30.00 (*0-915346-02-8*) A Wofsy Fine Arts.
— Exposition of the Catechism. LC 72-173190. (Library of Anglo-Catholic Theology: No. 14). reprint ed. 12.50 (*0-404-52106-1*) AMS Pr.
— Shadowlands. 96p. 1991. pap. 7.95 (*0-452-26732-3*, Plume) NAL-Dutton.
Nicholson, William J., ed. Management of Assessed Risk for Carcinogens, Vol. 363. 290p. 1981. 58.00 (*0-89766-119-2*); pap. 58.00 (*0-89766-120-6*) NY Acad Sci.
Nicholson, William J. & Moore, John A., eds. Health Effects of Halogenated Aromatic Hydrocarbons. LC 79-12253. (Annals Ser.: Vol. 320). 730p. 1979. 117.00 (*0-89766-008-0*) NY Acad Sci.
Nicholson, William R. Colossians: Oneness with Christ. LC 73-81742. 284p. 1973. pap. 8.99 (*0-8254-3300-2*) Kregel.
Nicholson, Winifred. Unknown Colour: Paintings, Letters & Writings. Nicholson, Andrew, ed. (Illus.). 256p. 1987. 47.50 (*0-571-14950-2*) Faber & Faber.
Nichomachus the Pythagorean. The Manual of Harmonics. Levin, Flora, tr. (Illus.). 200p. (Orig.). 1993. 35.00 (*0-933999-42-9*); pap. 18.00 (*0-933999-43-7*) Phanes Pr.
Nichter, Mark. Essays on Anthropology & International Health. (C). 1989. lib. bdg. 130.00 (*0-7923-0005-X*); pap. text ed. 45.50 (*0-7923-0158-7*) Kluwer Ac.
Nichter, Mark, ed. Anthropological Approaches to the Study of Ethnomedicine. LC 92-20369. 1992. text ed. 58.00 (*2-88124-530-7*); pap. text ed. 24.00 (*2-88124-529-3*) Gordon & Breach.
Nichter, Rhoda. How to Stop Smoking Once & for All. Hammond, Debbie, ed. LC 79-12134. 1980. 22.95 (*0-87949-173-6*) Ashley Bks.
— Yes, I Do Mind If You Smoke. LC 77-83110. 1978. 22.95 (*0-87949-114-0*) Ashley Bks.
*****Nicieza, Fabian.** X-Men: Fatal Attractions. (X-Men Ser.). 256p. 1994. pap. 17.95 (*0-7851-0065-2*) Marvel Entmnt.
Nicieza, Fabian, et al. Adventures of Captain America, No. 4. 48p. 1991. 4.95 (*0-87135-814-X*) Marvel Entmnt.
— Adventures of Captain America, No. 1. 48p. 1991. 4.95 (*0-87135-811-5*) Marvel Entmnt.
— Adventures of Captain America, No. 2. 48p. 1991. 4.95 (*0-87135-812-3*) Marvel Entmnt.
— Adventures of Captain America, No. 3. 48p. 1991. 4.95 (*0-87135-813-1*) Marvel Entmnt.
— X-Men - Avengers: Bloodties. (Illus.). 128p. 1995. pap. 15.95 (*0-7851-0103-9*) Marvel Entmnt.
Nicita, Michael & Petrusha, Ronald. The Reader's Guide to Microcomputer Books. LC 84-15451. (Professional Librarian Ser.). 500p. 1984. text ed. 32.95 (*0-86729-122-2*, Hall Reference) Macmillan.
Nicjoll, Donald. Holiness. 1989. pap. 11.95 (*0-8091-3113-7*) Paulist Pr.
Nick, Dagmar. Summons & Sign. Barnes, Jim, tr. LC 80-18367. Orig. Title: Zeugnis & Zeichen. (Illus.). 124p. (Orig.). 1980. pap. 20.00 (*0-933428-02-2*) Chariton Review.
Nick, Jean M. A. & Bradley, Fern M., eds. Growing Fruits & Vegetables Organically: The Complete Guide to a Great-Tasting, More Bountiful, Problem-Free Harvest. (Illus.). 532p. 1994. 27.95 (*0-87596-586-5*) Rodale Pr Inc.
Nickalls, John L. & Penn, William, prefs. The Journal of George Fox. rev. ed. LC 85-80620. 789p. 1985. reprint ed. pap. 14.75 (*0-941308-05-7*) Phila Yrly Mtg RSOF.
*****Nickalls, R. W. & Ramasubramanian, R.** Interfacing the IBM-PC to Medical Equipment: The Art of Serial Communication. (Illus.). 421p. (C). 1995. 59.95 (*0-521-46280-0*) Cambridge U Pr.
Nickas, Paul. How to Make Money with Puts & Calls: The Smart Way to Unlimited Profits with the Least Amount of Risk. 1993. 39.95 (*0-9634155-3-0*) Sigma Pub Assocs.
Nickau, Klaus. Untersuchungen zur Textkritischen Methode des Zenodotos von Ephesos. (Untersuchungen zur Antiken Literatur und Geschichte Ser.: Vol. 16). (C). 1977. 103.10 (*3-11-001827-6*) De Gruyter.
*****Nickel, Amy, ed.** Roll Forming: Collected Articles & Technical Papers. (Illus.). 132p. (Orig.). (C). 1994. pap. 34.95 (*1-881113-07-8*) Croydon Grp.
— Sheet Metal Cutting: Collected Articles & Technical Papers. (Illus.). 144p. (Orig.). (C). 1994. pap. 29.95 (*1-881113-05-1*) Croydon Grp.
Nickel, Amy J., ed. see Conner, Gary B.
Nickel, Catherine, jt. ed. see Gonzalez-del-Valle, Luis T.
Nickel, David J. Acupressure for Athletes. 2nd rev. ed. LC 86-12097. (Illus.). 176p. 1987. pap. 10.95 (*0-8050-0128-X*, Owl) H Holt & Co.
Nickel, E., et al. Stability of Heavy Minerals. Fuechtbauer, H., ed. (Contributions to Sedimentology Monograph: No. 1). (Illus.). 125p. 1973. pap. text ed. 34.00 (*3-510-57001-4*) Lubrecht & Cramer.
Nickel, Ernest H. Mineral Reference Manual. 1990. pap. 16. 95 (*0-442-00344-7*) Chapman & Hall.
*****Nickel, Friedhelm.** Woerterbuch der Umwelttechnik. 290p. (GER.). 1990. 95.00 (*0-7859-8483-6*, 3802304217) Fr & Eur.
Nickel, Gerhard, ed. see International Congress of Applied Linguistics (2nd : 1969 : Cambridge).
Nickel, Gudrun. How to File for Adoption in Florida. LC 92-60730. 146p. (Orig.). 1993. pap. 19.95 (*0-913825-54-9*) Sphinx Pub FL.
— How to File for Guardianship in Florida. LC 92-60729. 122p. (Orig.). 1993. pap. 19.95 (*0-913825-53-0*) Sphinx Pub FL.
— How to Probate an Estate in Florida. 2nd ed. 130p. (Orig.). 1995. pap. 19.95 (*1-57248-003-3*) Sphinx Pub FL.
Nickel, Gudrun M. Debtors' Rights: Self-Help Legal Guide. LC 91-66962. 158p. 1992. pap. 12.95 (*0-913825-43-3*) Sphinx Pub FL.
Nickel, Heinrich L. Medieval Architecture of Eastern Europe. LC 82-6254. (Illus.). 210p. 1983. 65.00 (*0-8419-0811-7*) Holmes & Meier.
Nickel, Helmut, et al. Studies in European Arms & Armor: The C. Otto Von Kienbusch Collection in the Philadelphia Museum of Art. LC 91-47037. (Illus.). 208p. (C). 1991. pap. 49.95 (*0-8122-7963-8*, PA Mus Art) U of Pa Pr.
Nickel, James W. Making Sense of Human Rights. 1987. pap. 13.00 (*0-520-05994-8*) U CA Pr.
*****Nickel, Karl & Wohlfahrt, Michael.** Tailless Aircraft in Theory & Practice. LC 94-28604. (Education Ser.). Orig. Title: Schwanzlose Flugzeuge. (Illus.). 498p. 1994. 29.95 (*1-56347-094-2*, 94-2(890)) AIAA.
Nickel, Klaus G., ed. Corrosion of Advanced Ceramics Measurement & Modelling: Proceedings of the NATO Advanced Research Workshop, Tubingen, Germany, August 30-September 3, 1993. LC 94-13365. (NATO ASI Series E. Applied Sciences: Vol. 267). 1994. lib. bdg. 205.00 (*0-7923-2838-8*) Kluwer Ac.
Nickel-Pepin-Donat, B., jt. ed. see Charvosset, H.
Nickel, R., et al. Anatomy of the Domestic Birds. 1977. 71. 00 (*0-387-91134-0*) Spr-Verlag.
Nickel, R., et al, eds. The Locomotor System of the Domestic Mammals. (Anatomy of the Domestic Animals Ser.: Vol. 1). (Illus.). 520p. 1985. 88.00 (*0-387-91259-2*) Spr-Verlag.
Nickel, Steven. Torso. 264p. 1990. mass mkt. 4.95 (*0-380-70987-2*) Avon.
— Torso: The True Story of Eliot Ness & the Search for a Psychopathic Killer. LC 89-792. (Illus.). 232p. 1989. 18. 95 (*0-89587-072-X*) Blair.
Nickel, Sue S. Missed Blessings. 1993. 9.95 (*0-9637015-0-9*) Crossover OK.
Nickel, Tricia. Color & Personality. 68p. 1989. spiral bd. 9.95 (*0-941522-08-3*) Ken Kra Pubs.
Nickel, Vernon L. & Botte, Michael J., eds. Orthopaedic Rehabilitation. 2nd ed. (Illus.). 939p. 1992. text ed. 134. 95 (*0-443-08726-1*) Churchill.
Nickell. Forecasting on Your Microcomputer. 1991. 24.95 (*0-8306-6648-6*) TAB Bks.
Nickell, Eugenie, jt. auth. see Witherspoon, Del.
Nickell, Eugenie, jt. ed. see Witherspoon, Del.
Nickell, Joe. Ambrose Bierce Is Missing: And Other Historical Mysteries. LC 91-3049. (Illus.). 192p. 1991. 22.00 (*0-8131-1766-6*) U Pr of Ky.
— Camera Clues: A Handbook for Photographic Investigation. LC 94-15623. (Illus.). 240p. 1994. 26.95 (*0-8131-1894-8*) U Pr of Ky.
— Entities: Angels, Spirits, Demons, & Other Alien Beings. LC 94-44761. (Illus.). 300p. 1995. 24.95 (*0-87975-961-5*) Prometheus Bks.
— Inquest on the Shroud of Turin. 2nd rev. ed. LC 87-61608. (Illus.). 186p. 1988. pap. 19.95 (*0-87975-396-X*) Prometheus Bks.
— Looking for a Miracle: Weeping Icons, Relics, Stigmata, Visions & Healing Cures. (Illus.). 252p. 1993. 23.95 (*0-87975-840-6*) Prometheus Bks.
— The Magic Detectives: Join Them in Solving Strange Mysteries. (Young Readers Ser.). (Illus.). 115p. (J). (gr. 4-9). 1989. 9.95 (*0-87975-547-4*) Prometheus Bks.
— Pen, Ink & Evidence: A Study of Writing & Writing Materials for the Penman, Collector, & Document Detective. LC 90-38544. (Illus.). 240p. 1990. 75.00 (*0-8131-1719-4*) U Pr of Ky.
— Wonder-Workers! How They Perform the Impossible. (Young Readers Ser.). (Illus.). 80p. (Orig.). (YA). 1991. pap. 12.95 (*0-87975-688-8*) Prometheus Bks.
Nickell, Joe, ed. Psychic Sleuths: ESP & Sensational Cases. (Illus.). 251p. (C). 1994. 24.95 (*0-87975-880-5*) Prometheus Bks.
Nickell, Joe & Fischer, John F. Secrets of the Supernatural: Investigating the World's Occult Mysteries. (Illus.). 199p. 1991. 23.95 (*0-87975-461-3*); pap. 17.95 (*0-87975-685-3*) Prometheus Bks.
Nickell, Joe & Fischer, John F., eds. Mysterious Realms: Probing Paranormal, Historical, & Forensic Enigmas. 221p. 1992. 23.95 (*0-87975-765-5*) Prometheus Bks.
Nickell, Joe, jt. auth. see Baker, Robert A.
*****Nickell, Judy.** Enchanted Gardening. (Illus.). 227p. 1992. spiral bd. 25.00 (*0-9632261-3-4*) Canaima Pr.
— A Gardener's Guide to Cataloging Flower & Garden Slides: And Prints, Too. (Illus.). 36p. 1994. pap. 7.00 (*0-9632261-2-6*) Canaima Pr.
*****Nickell, Lawrence.** Red Devil. Owensby, Craig, ed. 128p. (Orig.). 1995. pap. 12.95 (*1-886371-14-8*) Eggman Pub.
Nickell, Louis G. Plant Growth Regulators: Agricultural Uses. (Illus.). 173p. 1981. 70.00 (*0-387-10973-0*) Spr-Verlag.
Nickell, Louis G., ed. Plant Growth Regulating Chemicals, 2 Vols., Vol. I. 288p. 1983. 168.00 (*0-8493-5002-6*, QK745) CRC Pr.
— Plant Growth Regulating Chemicals, 2 Vols., Vol. II. 264p. 1983. 168.00 (*0-8493-5003-4*, QK745) CRC Pr.
Nickell, Molli. Guerrillas of Goodness Handbook: One Hundred Seven Little Ways You Can Make a Big Difference in the World. 1994. pap. 59.40 (*1-56305-669-0*) Workman Pub.
— Guerrillas of Goodness Handbook: 108 Little Ways You Can Make a Big Difference in the World. LC 94-6241. 1994. pap. 4.95 (*1-56305-561-9*) Workman Pub.
— Healing the Whole Person, the Whole Planet. 225p. 1988. pap. 12.95 (*0-941831-14-0*) Beyond Words Pub.
— Life Before, During & After. 1989. pap. 12.95 (*0-941831-24-8*) Beyond Words Pub.
Nickell, Molli, ed. AIDS: Spirits Share Understanding & Comfort from the "Other" Side. 110p. 1986. 9.95 (*0-938283-99-5*) Spirit Speaks.
— Relationships: Yours-Mine-Ours. (Celebration of Discovery Ser.: Vol. III). (Illus.). 192p. 1989. pap. 12.95 (*0-938283-02-2*) Spirit Speaks.
Nickell, Samila S., ed. see Cook, Harvey A. & Pederson, Duane E.
*****Nickell, Stephen.** The Performance of Companies: The Relationship Between the External Environment, Management Strategies & Corporate Performance. (Mitsui Lectures in Economics). 128p. (C). 1995. 39.95x (*0-631-19731-1*) Blackwell Pubs.
Nickelodeon Staff. Postcards over the Edge. (Nickelodeon: The Ren & Stimpy Show Ser.). (J). 1992. pap. 5.95 (*0-448-40502-4*, G&D) Putnam Pub Group.
— Rugrats at the Movies. (Nickelodeon Rugrats Ser.). (J). 1992. pap. 2.25 (*0-448-40500-8*, G&D) Putnam Pub Group.
— Rugrats Monster in the Garage. (Nickelodeon Rugrats Ser.). (J). 1992. pap. 2.25 (*0-448-40501-6*, G&D) Putnam Pub Group.
Nickels, Cameron C. New England Humor: From the Revolutionary War to the Civil War. LC 93-320. (Illus.). 304p. (C). 1993. text ed. 36.00x (*0-87049-804-5*) U of Tenn Pr.
Nickels, Cameron C., ed. see Smith, Seba.
Nickels, George. The Gypsy Season. LC 80-12821. 1982. 22. 95 (*0-87949-187-6*) Ashley Bks.
Nickels, Hamilton. Codemaster: Secrets of Making & Breaking Codes. 144p. 1990. pap. 16.00 (*0-87364-564-2*) Paladin Pr.
— Secrets of Making & Breaking Codes. LC 94-18198. 1994. 6.95 (*0-8065-1563-5*, Citadel Pr) Carol Pub Group.

An Asterisk (*) at the beginning of an entry indicates that the title is appearing in BIP for the first time.

Nickels, Meryl. Love's Lying Eyes. 1990. mass mkt. 4.25 (0-8217-2883-0) Zebra.
Nickels, Sue, jt. auth. see Holly, Pat.
*Nickels, Thom. The Boy on the Bicycle. LC 92-82592. 384p. (Orig.). 1993. pap. 13.95 (1-877978-59-0, STARbks Pr) Woldt.
— The Cliffs of Aries. LC 88-71119. 192p. (Orig.). 1989. pap. 10.00 (0-916383-68-7) Aegina Pr.
— Two Novellas: Walking Water & After All This. 160p. (Orig.). 1989. pap. 8.95 (0-934411-22-0, Banned Bks) Edward-William Austin.
*Nickels, William, et al. Understanding Business, 1990. 2nd ed. 542p. (C). 1989. student ed, text ed. 16.95 (0-256-08058-5) Irwin.
— Understanding Canadian Business: Canadian. 704p. (C). 1994. text ed. 44.25 (0-256-10800-5) Irwin.
— Understanding Canadian Business: Canadian. (C). 1994. student ed, text ed. 15.00 (0-256-10801-3) Irwin.
Nickels, William G., et al. Understanding Business. 3rd ed. LC 92-17456. 984p. (C). 1992. text ed. 53.95 (0-256-09548-5) Irwin.
— Understanding Business, 1990. 2nd ed. 884p. (C). 1989. text ed. 53.95 (0-256-07623-5) Irwin.
Nickelsburg, George W., Jr., ed. Studies on the Testament of Abraham. LC 76-44205. (Society of Biblical Literature. Septuagint & Cognate Studies: No. 6). 350p. reprint ed. pap. 99.80 (0-7837-5436-1, 2045201) Bks Demand.
Nickelsburg, George W. & Stone, Michael E. Faith & Piety in Early Judaism: Texts & Documents. LC 82-71830. 256p. reprint ed. pap. 73.00 (0-318-34891-8, 2031257) Bks Demand.
— Faith & Piety in Early Judaism: Texts & Documents. LC 91-12033. 256p. (C). 1991. reprint ed. pap. 14.95 (1-56338-012-9) TPI PA.
Nickelsburg, Janet. Field Trips: Ecology for Youth Leaders. LC 66-14520. 126p. (C). reprint ed. 36.00 (0-8357-9048-7, 2013330) Bks Demand.
— Nature Activities for Early Childhood. 1976. pap. text ed. 16.50 (0-201-05097-8) Addison-Wesley.
Nickelson, Harry. Vietnam. LC 89-13100. (Overview Ser.). (Illus.). 80p. (J). (gr. 5-8). 1989. lib. bdg. 16.95 (1-56006-110-3) Lucent Bks.
Nickens. Boure (Boo-Ray) A Louisiana Card Game. 1972. 4.95 (0-685-37721-0) Claitors.
Nickens, Bessie. Walking the Log: Memories of a Southern Childhood. LC 94-10803. (Illus.). 32p. (J). (gr. 2 up). 1994. 14.95 (0-8478-1794-6) Rizzoli Intl.
Nickens, C., jt. auth. see Leigh, Janet.
Nickerson, Betty. Old & Smart: Women & Aging. 352p. 1991. pap. 16.95 (0-919970-08-7) All About Us.
Nickerson, Betty, ed. All about Us - Nous Autres: Creative Writing & Painting by & for Young People. (Illus.). 36p. (ENG & FRE.). (J). 1992. pap. 4.95 (0-685-61052-7) All About Us.
— Girls Will Be Women: Femmes de Demain. (Illus.). 75p. (ENG & FRE.). 1992. pap. 5.95 (0-919970-00-1) All About Us.
— Of You & Me: A Contemporary View of Human Rights by Young Canadians - Nous Autres: Vue Contemporaine Des Droits de la Personne par des Jeunes Canadiens. (Illus.). 96p. 1992. pap. 7.95 (0-919970-02-8) All About Us.
*Nickerson, Dan. Introduction to Co-Counseling. 1994. pap. 1.00 (0-913937-93-2) Rational Isl.
Nickerson, Dorothy. Witch of Sawtooth Mountain. LC 94-60453. 315p. 1995. pap. 7.95 (1-55523-690-1) Winston-Derek.
Nickerson, Edward A., ed. see Sheridan, Thomas.
Nickerson, Eileen T. The Dissertation Handbook: A Guide to Successful Dissertations. 2nd ed. 152p. (C). 1994. per. 22.95 (0-8403-8300-2) Kendall-Hunt.
Nickerson, Elinor. Golf: A Women's History. LC 85-43583. 167p. 1987. lib. bdg. 28.50x (0-89950-211-3) McFarland & Co.
— Racquet Sports: An Illustrated Guide. LC 82-17180. (Illus.). 192p. 1982. lib. bdg. 32.50x (0-89950-051-X) McFarland & Co.
Nickerson, Eve, jt. auth. see Thomsett, Kay.
Nickerson, Gifford S. Native North Americans in Doctoral Dissertations, 1971-1975: A Classified & Indexed Research Bibliography, No. 1232. 1977. 7.50 (0-686-19688-0) CPL Biblios.
Nickerson, Jane. Jane Nickerson's Florida Cookbook. LC 73-17413. (Illus.). 204p. 1973. 18.95 (0-8130-0443-8); spiral bd. 12.95 (0-8130-0816-6) U Press Fla.
Nickerson, Jane S. Short History of North Africa. LC 68-54233. 1961. 30.00 (0-8196-0219-1) Biblo.
Nickerson, Joshua. Days to Remember. 304p. 1988. 14.95 (0-9615051-1-7) Parnassus Imprints.
Nickerson, Joshua A. Days to Remember. 1988. pap. 14.95 (0-317-67586-9) Chatham His Soc.
Nickerson, Lloyd C., ed. see Barlow, Raymond E. & Kaiser, Joan E.
Nickerson, Lloyd C., ed. see Barlow, Raymond E. & Kaiser, Joan B.
Nickerson, Marie-Louise. The Modern Writer's Workbook. 2nd ed. (Illus.). 432p. (C). 1993. pap. write for info. (0-02-387480-5) Macmillan.
Nickerson, Marie-Louise, jt. auth. see Fergenson, Laraine.
Nickerson, Marjorie C. Burma Interlude. Nickerson, Thomas, ed. (Illus.). 128p. 1981. 3.00 (0-914916-55-6) Ku Paa.
Nickerson, Mike. Bakavi: Change the World I Want to Stay On. (Illus.). 119p. 1992. pap. 12.95 (0-919970-03-6) All About Us.
Nickerson, Patricia. Nickerson's Four-Star Management Workshop. 1989. 39.95 (0-13-622341-9) P-H.
— Nickerson's Four Star Management Workshop. 384p. 1988. 39.95 (0-685-37794-6) P-H.
Nickerson, Ray, et al. The Teaching of Thinking. 400p. (C). 1985. text ed. 49.95 (0-89859-539-8) L Erlbaum Assocs.
Nickerson, Raymond & Zodhiates, Philip. Technology in Education: Looking Toward 2020. 352p. (C). text ed. 69.95 (0-8058-0214-2); pap. 29.95 (0-8058-0297-5) L Erlbaum Assocs.
Nickerson, Raymond S. Looking Ahead: Human Factors in a Changing World. 456p. 1992. text ed. 89.95 (0-8058-1150-8); pap. 29.95 (0-8058-1151-6) L Erlbaum Assocs.
— Reflections on Reasoning. 160p. (C). 1986. 29.95 (0-89859-762-5); teacher ed write for info. (0-89859-764-1); pap. 16.50 (0-89859-763-3) L Erlbaum Assocs.
— Using Computers: Human Factors in Information Systems. 22.50 (0-317-42856-X) McGraw.
— Using Computers: Human Factors in Information Systems. 456p. 1986. reprint ed. pap. 14.50 (0-262-64022-8, Bradford Bks) MIT Pr.
Nickerson, Raymond S., ed. Attention & Performance VIII. LC 80-23850. (Attention & Performance Ser.). 864p. 1980. 150.00 (0-89859-038-8) L Erlbaum Assocs.
Nickerson, Richard P. Genetics: A Guide to Basic Concepts & Problem Solving. (C). 1990. pap. text ed. 26.50 (0-673-39684-3) HarpCollege.
Nickerson, Robert C. Computer Hardware: Module 2. LC 92-37221. (C). 1992. write for info. (0-06-501698-X, HarpT) HarpC.
— Computers: Concepts & Application. 2nd ed. (C). 1993. 51.00 (0-673-46790-2) HarpCollege.
— Computers: Concepts & Applications for Users. (C). 1989. pap. text ed. 31.75 (0-673-39828-5) HarpCollege.
— Computers: Concepts & Applications for Users. 2nd ed. (C). 1992. text ed. 47.00 (0-673-46554-3) HarpCollege.
— Computers: Concepts & Applications for Users with BASIC. (C). 1990. pap. text ed. 32.75 (0-673-46016-9) HarpCollege.
— Computers: Concepts & Applications with BASIC. 2nd ed. (C). 1992. write for info. (0-673-46690-6); text ed. 51.50 (0-673-46553-5) HarpCollege.
— Computers & Society: Module 5. LC 92-37224. (C). 1993. write for info. (0-06-501699-8) HarpCollege.
— Computers: Concepts & Applications: Study Guide. (C). 1990. pap. text ed. 13.50 (0-673-39866-8) HarpCollege.
— Fundamentals of FORTRAN 77 Programming: A Structured Approach. 3rd ed. (C). 1988. pap. text ed. 56.50 (0-673-39039-X) HarpCollege.
— Fundamentals of Programming in BASIC. 2nd ed. (C). 1987. pap. text ed. 42.50 (0-673-39040-3) HarpCollege.
— Fundamentals of QBasic Programming: Problem Solving & Application Development. 401p. (C). 1995. text ed. 37.00 (0-673-99378-7) HarpCollege.
— Fundamentals of Structured COBOL. (C). 1991. 15.50 (0-673-52137-0) HarpCollege.
— Fundamentals of Structured COBOL. (C). 1987. teacher ed write for info. (0-318-61087-6) Little.
— Fundamentals of Structured COBOL. 2nd ed. (C). 1987. pap. text ed. 35.50 (0-673-39044-6) HarpCollege.
— Fundamentals of Structured COBOL. 2nd ed. (C). 1987. student ed write for info. (0-318-61088-4); trans. write for info. (0-318-61089-2); disk write for info. (0-318-61090-6); disk write for info. (0-318-61091-4) Little.
— Fundamentals of Structured COBOL. 3rd ed. (C). 1991. pap. text ed. 60.00 (0-673-52113-3) HarpCollege.
— Fundamentals of Structured COBOL. 3rd ed. (C). 1991. 10.00 (0-673-52209-1) HarpCollege.
— QBasic Programming: Structured Applications. (C). 1993. text ed. 9.50 (0-06-501345-X) HarpCollege.
Nickerson, Robert C., jt. auth. see Russell.
Nickerson, Robert L., jt. auth. see Whalen, Harold B.
Nickerson, Roy. Hawaii, the Volcano State. (Illus.). 1978. 1.95 (0-930492-01-3) Hawaiian Serv.
— Lahaina: Royal Capital of Hawaii. Wirtz, Richard, ed. LC 77-94277. (Illus.). 1978. pap. 5.95 (0-930492-03-X) Hawaiian Serv.
— Sea Otters: A Natural History & Guide. rev. ed. (Illus.). (Orig.). (C). 1989. pap. 12.95 (0-87701-567-8) Chronicle Bks.
*Nickerson, S. Harold. Conversations of Silence. LC 94-45897. 226p. (Orig.). 1995. pap. 18.95 (0-86534-231-8) Sunstone Pr.
Nickerson, Sara. Martin the Cavebine. LC 88-71369. (Illus.). 28p. (Orig.). (J). (gr. 2-4). 1988. pap. 9.00 (0-935529-06-3) Comprehen Health Educ.
— Peter Parrot, Private Eye. LC 88-63800. (Illus.). 43p. (Orig.). (J). (gr. 3-5). 1988. pap. 9.00 (0-935529-07-1) Comprehen Health Educ.
Nickerson, Sheila. Feast of the Animals: An Alaska Bestiary. 68p. (Orig.). 1987. pap. 12.95 (0-9615529-4-8) Old Harbor Pr.
— Feast of the Animals, Vol. II: An Alaska Bestiary. LC 86-62524. (Illus.). 56p. (Orig.). 1991. 55.00 (0-9615529-9-9); pap. 12.95 (0-9615529-8-0) Old Harbor Pr.
— In the Compass of Unrest. 34p. (Orig.). 1988. pap. 4.00 (0-916155-04-8) Trout Creek.
— On Why the Quiltmaker Became a Dragon: A Visionary Poem. (Illus.). 59p. 1985. pap. 7.95 (0-318-18390-0) Vanessapress.
Nickerson, Sheila B. In Rooms of Falling Rain. LC 76-28466. (Orig.). 1976. lib. bdg. 8.00 (0-914476-56-4); pap. 4.00 (0-914476-59-9) Thorp Springs.
— Writers in the Public Library. LC 83-14859. xii, 276p. 1984. 36.00 (0-208-01872-7, Lib Prof Pubns) Shoe String.
Nickerson, Thomas, ed. see Nickerson, Marjorie C.
Nickerson, William. How I Turned One Thousand Dollars into Three Million in Real Estate-in My Spare Time. rev. ed. 1980. 25.00 (0-671-25368-9) S&S Trade.
*Nickl. Story of the Kind Wolf. 1994. mass mkt. 5.95 (0-200-72929-2) Criterion Bks.
Nickl, Peter. Crocodile, Crocodile. Cutler, Ebbitt, tr. Orig. Title: Krokodil, Krokodil. (Illus.). 32p. (J). 1989. 11.95 (0-940793-33-4, Crocodile Bks); pap. 7.95 (0-940793-32-6, Crocodile Bks) Interlink Pub.
— The Story of the Kind Wolf. LC 87-42923. (Illus.). 32p. (J). (gr. k-3). 1988. 14.95 (1-55858-066-2) North-South Bks NYC.
— The Story of the Kind Wolf. LC 87-42923. (Illus.). 32p. (J). (gr. k-3). 1994. pap. 5.95 (1-55858-058-1) North-South Bks NYC.
*Nickla, Harry. Student Handbook for Concepts of Genetics. 4th ed. (Illus.). 283p. (C). 1994. write for info. (0-02-386722-1, Merrill Pub Co) Macmillan.
— Student Handbook to Essentials of Genetics. (Illus.). 208p. (Orig.). (C). 1993. pap. write for info. (0-02-387483-X) Macmillan.
*Nicklas, John D. Am I Worthy? LC 94-92223. 100p. (Orig.). 1995. pap. 9.00 (0-9641766-0-2) Beauty Within.
Nicklas, Steven D. A General Survey of Coinage in the Roman Empire A. D. 294-408 & Its Relationship to Roman Military Deployment. LC 94-18059. 380p. 1994. text ed. 99.95 (0-7734-9104-X) E Mellen.
Nicklaus, Carol. Come Dance with Me. (Sports Ser.). (Illus.). 32p. (J). (ps-1). 1991. lib. bdg. 5.95 (0-671-73503-9); pap. 2.95 (0-671-73507-1) Silver Pr.
— The Go Club. (Sports Ser.). (Illus.). 32p. (J). (ps-1). 1991. lib. bdg. 5.95 (0-671-73500-4); pap. 2.95 (0-671-73505-5) Silver Pr.
— Silver Sports Series, 4 vols., Set. (Illus.). (J). (ps-1). 1991. lib. bdg. 23.80 (0-671-31271-5); pap. 11.80 (0-671-31272-3) Silver Pr.
Nicklaus, Carol, illus. I See You. (Sesame Street Babies Bks.). 5p. (J). (ps). 1994. 4.99 (0-679-86389-3) Random Bks Yng Read.
— Shake & Rattle. (Sesame Street Babies Bks.). 5p. (J). (ps). 1994. 6.99 (0-679-86387-7) Random Bks Yng Read.
— Squeaky Clean. (Sesame Street Babies Bks.). 5p. (J). (ps). 1994. 5.99 (0-679-86388-5) Random Bks Yng Read.
Nicklaus, Jack. Golf My Way. 1976. pap. 12.00 (0-671-22278-3, Fireside) S&S Trade.
— My Fifty-Five Ways to Lower Your Golf Score. (Illus.). 1985. pap. 9.00 (0-671-55395-X) S&S Trade.
— Play Better Golf. 1989. mass mkt. 5.50 (0-671-68492-2) PB.
— Play Better Golf: The Short Game & Scoring, Vol. II. 1986. mass mkt. 5.50 (0-671-52257-4) PB.
Nicklaus, Jack & Bowden, Ken. Jack Nicklaus' Lesson Tee: Fifteenth Anniversary Edition. (Illus.). 160p. 1992. pap. 13.00 (0-671-78007-7, Fireside) S&S Trade.
— Jack Nicklaus' Playing Lessons. LC 80-84953. (Illus.). 144p. 1981. pap. 15.00 (0-671-72313-8) Golf Digest.
— My Most Memorable Shots in the Majors: And What You Can Learn from Them. (Illus.). 128p. 1988. 14.95 (0-8129-1750-2, Times Bks) Random.
— Play Better Golf: Problems & Answers, Vol. 3. (Orig.). 1990. mass mkt. 4.99 (0-671-72765-6) PB.
Nickle, Keith F. The Synoptic Gospels: An Introduction. LC 79-92069. (Orig.). 1980. pap. 11.99 (0-8042-0422-5, John Knox) Westminster John Knox.
Nickle, Keith F. & Lull, Timothy F., eds. A Common Calling: The Witness of Our Reformation Churches in North America Today, the Report of the Lutheran-Reformed Committee for Theological Conversations, 1988-1992. LC 92-43096. 64p. 1993. 4.99 (0-8066-2665-8, 9-2665) Augsburg Fortress.
Nickle, William R., ed. Manual of Agricultural Nematology. 1064p. 1991. 250.00 (0-8247-8397-2) Dekker.
— Plant & Insect Nematodes. fac. ed. LC 84-4937. (Illus.). 943p. 1984. pap. 180.00 (0-7837-7715-9, 2047477) Bks Demand.
Nickles, jt. auth. see Navratilova, M.
*Nickles, Alfred E. The AS-400 Client-Server Series Bk. 1: Introduction. 130p. 1994. 99.00 (1-887519-01-7) C-S Technol.
— The AS-400 Client-Server Series Bk. 2: Getting Started. 182p. 1995. 99.00 (1-887519-02-5) C-S Technol.
— The Client-Server Marketing & Technology Report. 344p. 1993. 99.00 (1-887519-00-9) C-S Technol.
Nickles, Herbert L. Microsoft Works on the IBM PC: A Tool for Productivity. 269p. (C). 1992. pap. 27.95 (0-534-13340-1); 3.5 hd, pap. 30.95 (0-534-13348-7); 5.25 hd, pap. 30.95 (0-534-13349-5) Boyd & Fraser.
— Microsoft Works on the Macintosh: A Tool for Productivity. 327p. (C). 1991. pap. 30.95 (0-534-13338-X) Boyd & Fraser.
Nickles, Liz & Asseyev, Tamara. Always Kiss with Your Whiskers: Love Advice from My Cat. (Illus.). 64p. 1991. pap. 6.00 (0-671-74983-8) PB.
Nickles, Liz, jt. auth. see Navratilova, Martina.
Nickles, N. Beverly, jt. ed. see Spann, Milton G., Jr.
Nickles, Sara, ed. Drinking, Smoking, & Screwing: Great Writers on Good Times. LC 94-9336. 1994. 11.95 (0-8118-0784-3) Chronicle Bks.
Nickles, Steve. Lender Liability in Secured Financing: Major Causes & Effective Cures. 4th ed. 456p. 1989. pap. 45.00 (0-943380-04-9) PEG MN.
Nickles, Steve H. Negotiable Instruments. 2nd ed. LC 92-47440. (Black Letter Ser.). 565p. 1993. pap. text ed. 22.00 (0-314-01979-0) West Pub.
Nickles, Steve H. & Epstein, David G. Creditors' Rights & Bankruptcy. (Black Letter Ser.). 576p. 1990. reprint ed. pap. text ed. 20.00 (0-314-48841-3) West Pub.
Nickles, Steve H., jt. auth. see Epstein, David G.
Nickles, Steve H., jt. auth. see Speidel, Richard E.
Nickles, Steve H., et al. Teacher's Manual to Accompany Course Materials on Commercial Paper & Modern Payment Systems. (American Casebook Ser.). 146p. 1993. pap. text ed. write for info. (0-314-03587-7) West Pub.
Nickles, Steve M., et al. Modern Commercial Paper: The New Law of Negotiable Instruments (& Related Commercial Paper) (American Casebook Ser.). 650p. 1993. text ed. 45.50 (0-314-03240-1) West Pub.
Nickles, Thomas, ed. Scientific Discovery: Case Studies. (Boston Studies in the Philosophy of Science: No. 60). 386p. 1980. lib. bdg. 74.50 (90-277-1092-9); pap. text ed. 36.50 (90-277-1093-7) Kluwer Ac.
— Scientific Discovery, Logic & Rationality. (Boston Studies in the Philosophy of Science: No. 56). 400p. 1980. lib. bdg. 74.50 (90-277-1069-4) Kluwer Ac.
Nickles, Thomas, jt. ed. see Asquith, Peter D.
Nickless, Steve. Anatomy & Development of Formula Ford Race Cars. 1993. pap. 29.95 (0-87938-807-2) Motorbooks Intl.
Nicklin, D. J., jt. ed. see Potter, O. E.
Nicklin, Flip. With the Whale. (Illus.). 160p. 1990. 39.95 (1-55971-039-X, 0187); pap. 19.95 (0-685-74179-6) NorthWord.
— With the Whales. (Illus.). 160p. 1994. pap. 19.95 (1-55971-180-9) NorthWord.
Nicklin, Flip, photos. The Wonder of Whales. LC 92-16946. (Animal Wonders Ser.). (Illus.). (J). 1992. lib. bdg. 18.60 (0-8368-0857-6) Gareth Stevens Inc.
Nicklin, J. Bernard. Testimony in Stone. 1961. 6.00 (0-685-08818-9) Destiny.
*Nicklin, Joan. Four Outstanding Black Women Historians in Africa & the U. S. A. LC 95-67257. (African Women Ser.: No. 2). 50p. (Orig.). (C). 1995. pap. text ed. 5.00 (0-943324-60-2) Omenana.
— Patterns of Indigeneous Capitalist Formations in Pre-Colonial Africa & North America. LC 95-67260. (African Women Ser.: No. 1). 50p. (Orig.). (C). 1995. pap. text ed. 5.00 (0-943324-56-4) Omenana.
Nicklin, Stephen, jt. ed. see Miller, Klara.
*Nicklin, Walter. The Rappahannock River. (Virginia Heritage Publications). 48p. 1994. pap. 5.95 (1-885937-00-8) Casco Commns.
Nickman, Steven L. The Adoption Experiences. LC 85-8957. (Teen Survival Library). 192p. (J). (gr. 7 up). 1985. lib. bdg. 14.98 (0-671-50817-2, Julian Messner) Silver Burdett Pr.
— When Mom & Dad Divorce. (Illus.). 80p. (J). (gr. 3-6). 1986. lib. bdg. 10.98 (0-671-60153-9, Julian Messner) Silver Burdett Pr.
Nickolae, Barbara. Finders, Keepers. large type ed. 1991. 21.95 (0-7089-2375-5) Ulverscroft.
— Kiss Mommy Goodnight. 288p. (Orig.). 1994. pap. text ed. 4.99 (0-425-14043-1) Berkley Pub.
— Ties That Bind. 272p. (Orig.). 1993. mass mkt. 4.99 (0-425-13573-X) Berkley Pub.
— Ties That Bind. large type ed. LC 93-29304. (Orig.). 1993. 18.95 (0-8161-5885-1, Large Print Bks) Hall.
Nickolaisen, Robert H. Machine Drafting & Design. (Illus.). 560p. (C). 1986. text ed. 36.33 (0-317-46150-8, Reston) P-H.
Nickolaus, Martin, tr. see Marx, Karl.
*Nickolls, Brian. Making Character Dolls' Houses in 1-12 Scale. (Illus.). 192p. 1995. 29.95 (0-7153-0200-0, Pub. by D & C Pub UK) Sterling.
— Making Dolls Houses in One-Twelfth Scale. (Illus.). 192p. 1991. 29.95 (0-7153-9848-2, Pub. by D & C Pub UK) Sterling.
Nickoloff. Dermal Immune System. 1992. 161.00 (0-8493-5941-4, RL97) CRC Pr.
Nickols, Kevin, ed. see Stoutt, Glenn R. & Womack, Marvyn.
Nickon, A. & Silversmith, E. F. Organic Chemistry - The Name Game: Modern Coined Terms & Their Orgins. LC 86-30450. (Illus.). 360p. 1987. 170.00 (0-08-034481-X, Pergamon Pr); pap. 62.00 (0-08-035157-3, Pergamon Pr) Elsevier.
*Nicks, J. E. Cooking with Chef Dinosaur. Nicks, Mary, ed. (Illus.). 200p. 1995. pap. 11.95 (0-9642743-6-1) Jensen Pubng.
— Cost Estimating for Metal Stampers & Fabricators. Boeselager, Amy, ed. (Illus.). 160p. (Orig.). (C). 1993. pap. 29.95 (1-881113-04-3) Croydon Grp.
Nicks, Jensen E. BASIC Programming Solutions for Manufacturing. LC 82-137513. (Illus.). 297p. reprint ed. pap. 84.70 (0-8357-6496-6, 2035867) Bks Demand.
Nicks, Mary, ed. see Nicks, J. E.
Nicks, Mel J., jt. auth. see Ortwerth, John.
Nicks, Oran W. Far Travelers: The Exploring Machines. LC 85-1794. (NASA SP Ser.: No. 480). (Illus.). 267p. 1985. pap. 17.00 (0-16-004189-9, S/N 033-000-00957-7) USGPO.
Nicks, Oran W., ed. This Island Earth. LC 78-608969. (NASA EP Ser.: No. 250). (Illus.). 192p. 1987. 12.00 (0-16-004124-4, S/N 033-000-00321-8) USGPO.
Nicks, Walter. Jazz Dance Collection. 18p. (Orig.). (C). 1965. pap. text ed. 10.00 (0-932582-27-3) Dance Notation.
Nickse, Ruth S., jt. auth. see Quezada, Shelley.
*Nickson, Chris. Mariah Carey: Her Story. LC 95-9883. 1995. pap. 8.95 (0-312-13121-6) St Martin.
Nickson, Hilda. Now with His Love. large type ed. (Linford Romance Library). 317p. 1984. pap. 11.95 (0-7089-6027-8, Linford) Ulverscroft.
Nickson, Jeanne. Shadow of the Condor. 400p. (Orig.). 1994. mass mkt., pap. text ed. 4.99 (0-505-51975-5) Dorchester Pub Co.
— Tears of the Moon. 464p. 1992. pap. 4.50 (0-8439-3328-3) Dorchester Pub Co.
Nickson, Noel J., jt. ed. see Picken, Laurence.
Nickson, R. Andrew. Historical Dictionary of Paraguay. 2nd ed. (Latin American Historical Dictionaries Ser.: No. 24). (Illus.). 710p. 1992. 69.50 (0-8108-2643-7) Scarecrow.

— Local Government in Latin America. LC 94-43541. 250p. 1995. pap. text ed. 49.95 (*1-55587-366-9*) Lynne Rienner.

Nickul, Karl. The Skolt Lapp Community Suenjelsijd During the Year 1938. LC 77-87728. (Acta Lapponica Ser.: 5). (Illus.). 160p. 1983. reprint ed. 57.50 (*0-404-16504-4*) AMS Pr.

***Nickum, James E.** Dam Lies & Other Statistics: Taking the Measure of Irrigation in China, 1931-1991. LC 94-44338. (East-West Center Occasional Papers: Environment Ser.: Vol. 18). 1995. write for info. (*0-86638-168-6*) EW Ctr HI.

— Water Management Organizations in the People's Republic of China. LC 80-5458. (China Book Project Ser.). (Illus.). 285p. reprint ed. pap. 81.30 (*0-685-23742-7*, 2032783) Bks Demand.

Nickum, James E., ed. Metropolitan Water Use Conflicts in Asia & the Pacific. (Studies in Water Policy & Management). 219p. (C). 1994. pap. text ed. 55.00 (*0-8133-8779-5*) Westview.

Nickum, James E., ed. see Fourth Pacific Environmental Conference Staff.

NicLeodhas, Sorche. Always Room for One More. LC 65-12881. (Illus.). 32p. (J). (ps-2). 1965. 14.95 (*0-8050-0331-2*, Bks Young Read) H Holt & Co.

Nicleza, Fabian. X-Cutioner's Song: Starring the X-Men, X-Factor, & X-Force. 1994. pap. 24.95 (*0-7851-0025-3*) Marvel Entmnt.

Nicod, J., et al. Geomorphology & Geoecology - Karst. (Annals of Geomorphology Ser.: Suppl. 85). (Illus.). 144p. 1992. pap. text ed. 56.70 (*3-443-21085-6*, Pub. by Gebrueder Borntraeger GW) Lubrecht & Cramer.

Nicod, Pascal, jt. ed. see Peterson, Kirk L.

Nicodemi, F., ed. Scientific Highlights in Memory of Leon Van Hove, Napoli, Italy, October 25-26, 1991. LC 93-17108. (Twentieth Century Physics Ser.: Vol. 2). 180p. 1993. text ed. 67.00 (*981-02-1399-9*) World Scientific Pub.

Nicodemi, Olympia. Discrete Mathematics: A Bridge to Computer Science & Advanced Mathematics. LC 86-24616. (Illus.). 491p. (C). 1987. text ed. 57.50 (*0-314-28503-2*) West Pub.

Nicogossian, Arnauld E., et al. Space Physiology & Medicine. 3rd ed. (Illus.). 400p. 1993. text ed. 89.50 (*0-8121-1595-3*) Williams & Wilkins.

***Nicol.** Standard Catalog of German Coins, 1601 - Present. 1995. pap. text ed. 59.00 (*0-87341-272-9*) Krause Pubns.

***Nicol & Stretch.** Preschool Children in Troubled Families: Approaches to Intervention & Support. Date not set. pap. text ed. 29.95 (*0-471-95584-1*) Wiley.

Nicol, A. R., ed. Longitudinal Studies in Child Psychology & Psychiatry: Practical Lessons from Research Experience. LC 84-11802. (Studies in Child Psychiatry Ser.). 411p. 1985. text ed. 102.00 (*0-471-10441-8*) Wiley.

Nicol, Andrew & Rogers, Heather. Changing Contempt of Court. (C). 1988. 21.00 (*0-901108-92-8*, Pub. by NCCL UK) St Mut.

Nicol, Arthur R., ed. Longitudinal Studies in Child Psychology & Psychiatry: Practical Lessons from Research Experience. LC 84-11802. (Wiley Series on Studies in Child Psychiatry). 423p. reprint ed. pap. 120.60 (*0-8357-4945-2*, 2037876) Bks Demand.

Nicol, Bruce. Wind of Chance. 178p. (C). 1989. text ed. 40.00 (*0-946270-98-8*, Pub. by Pentland Pr UK) St Mut.

Nicol, C. W. Moving Zen: Karate As a Way to Gentleness. LC 74-11439. (Illus.). 1982. pap. 7.95 (*0-688-01181-0*, Quill) Morrow.

Nicol, Charles & Barabtarlo, Gennady, eds. A Small Alpine Form: Studies in Nabokov's Short Fiction. LC 92-22715. (Reference Library of the Humanities: Vol. 1580). 264p. 1992. 38.00 (*0-8153-0857-4*, H1580) Garland.

Nicol, Charles, jt. ed. see Rivers, J. E.

Nicol, D. M. The End of the Byzantine Empire. LC 80-19902. 109p. 1980. pap. 14.95 (*0-8419-5826-2*) Holmes & Meier.

Nicol, David. Structured Program Design: A Designer's Handbook. (Illus.). 256p. 1994. pap. 29.95 (*0-7506-1759-4*) Buttrwrth-Heinemann.

Nicol, David & Fujimoto, Richard, eds. Distributed Simulation, 1990. (Simulation Ser.: Vol. 22, No. 1). 230p. 1990. 50.00 (*0-911801-62-6*, SS22-1) Soc Computer Sim.

Nicol, Davidson, et al, eds. Regionalism & the New International Economic Order: Studies Presented to the UNITAR-CEESTEM Club of Rome Conference at the United Nations. LC 80-23706. (Policy Studies on International Development). 448p. 1981. pap. text ed. 46.00 (*0-08-026331-3*, Pergamon Pr) Elsevier.

Nicol, Donald M. A Biographical Dictionary of the Byzantine Empire. (Illus.). 156p. 39.95 (*1-85264-048-0*, Pub. by Seaby UK) Trafalgar.

— The Byzantine Lady: Ten Portraits, 1250-1500. LC 93-35728. (Illus.). 168p. (C). 1994. 39.95 (*0-521-45531-6*) Cambridge U Pr.

— Byzantium & Venice. (Illus.). 480p. (C). 1992. pap. 27.95 (*0-521-42894-7*) Cambridge U Pr.

— The Immortal Emperor: The Life & Legend of Constantine Palaiologos, Last Emperor of the Romans. (Illus.). 250p. (C). 1992. 39.95 (*0-521-41456-3*) Cambridge U Pr.

— The Immortal Emperor: The Life & Legend of Constantine Palaiologos, Last Emperor of the Romans. (Canto Book Ser.). (Illus.). 162p. (C). 1994. pap. 9.95 (*0-521-46717-9*) Cambridge U Pr.

— The Last Centuries of Byzantium, 1261-1453. 2nd ed. LC 92-46203. (Illus.). 528p. (C). 1993. 89.95 (*0-521-43384-3*); pap. 27.95 (*0-521-43991-4*) Cambridge U Pr.

— Studies in Late Byzantine History & Prosopography. (Collected Studies: No. CS242). (Illus.). 330p. (C). 1986. reprint ed. lib. bdg. 89.95 (*0-86078-190-9*, Pub. by Variorum UK) Ashgate Pub Co.

Nicol, G. T. Flex Manual. (Illus.). 120p. 1993. 15.00 (*1-882114-21-3*) Free Software.

***Nicol, Gloria.** The New Candle Book. (Illus.). 160p. 1995. 27.50 (*1-85967-066-0*, Lorenz Bks) Stewart Tabori & Chang.

Nicol, Iain G., ed. Schleiermacher & Feminism: Sources, Evaluations, & Responses. LC 92-26504. (Schleiermacher Studies & Translations: Vol. 12). 140p. 1992. text ed. 69.95 (*0-7734-9587-8*) E Mellen.

Nicol, J. A. The Eyes of Fishes. (Illus.). 328p. 1989. 90.00 (*0-19-857195-X*) OUP.

Nicol, Jim. Golf Resort Guide - East. 2nd ed. (Illus.). 350p. (Orig.). 1993. pap. 13.95 (*1-55650-568-X*) Hunter NJ.

— Golf Resort Guide - West. 2nd ed. (Illus.). 350p. (Orig.). 1993. pap. 13.95 (*1-55650-569-8*) Hunter NJ.

Nicol, Mary M. & Roth, Pamela K., eds. Ready, Set...Sing! (Songs for Sunday & Everyday) 96p. (Orig.). (J). 1989. pap. 9.00 (*0-8170-1155-2*) Judson.

***Nicol, Mike.** Horseman. LC 95-5841. 1995. 22.00 (*0-679-43766-5*) Knopf.

Nicol, N. D., et al. Catalog of the Islamic Coins, Glass Weights, Dies & Medals in the Egyptian National Library, Cairo. (American Research Center in Egypt, Catalogs Ser.: Vol. 3). (Illus.). xxviii, 314p. (ARA & ENG.). 1982. text ed. 52.50 (*0-89003-115-0*, Pub. by Amer Res Ctr Egypt UA) Eisenbrauns.

Nicol, Nancy M. & Walker, Stanley, eds. Basic Management for Staff Nurses: A Companion to Practice. 176p. (C). 1991. pap. text ed. 28.00 (*0-412-35520-5*, A5239) Chapman & Hall.

Nicol, Rory, et al. Preschool Children in Troubled Families: Approaches to Intervention & Support. LC 92-37834. (Series on Studies in Child Psychiatry). 250p. 1993. text ed. 63.95 (*0-471-93868-8*) Wiley.

***Nicol, Rosemary.** Irritable Bowel Syndrome: A Natural Approach. 296p. (Orig.). 1995. pap. 9.95 (*1-56975-030-0*) Ulysses Pr.

Nicol, Stewart H. A Book of Saints. 142p. 1993. pap. 30.00 (*0-7152-0693-1*) St Mut.

Nicola, Jill, jt. auth. see Coad, Peter.

Nicola-McLaughlin, Andree, jt. ed. see Braxton, Joanne.

Nicola, Michel. Arabic Key Reader: 1001 Nights. (ARA & ENG.). 1985. 6.95x (*0-86685-349-9*) Intl Bk Ctr.

— A Thousand & One Nights, Bk. 1. 56p. (ARA & ENG.). 1986. pap. 5.95 (*0-86685-371-5*) Intl Bk Ctr.

***Nicola, Nicos A., ed.** Guidebook to Cytokines & Their Receptors. (Illus.). 280p. 1995. pap. 39.50 (*0-19-859946-3*) OUP.

— Guidebook to Cytokines & Their Receptors. (Illus.). 280p. 1995. bds. 75.00 (*0-19-859947-1*) OUP.

Nicola, Nicos A., jt. auth. see Metcalf, Donald.

Nicola, Pier C. Imperfect General Equilibrium: The Economy As an Evolutionary Process, Individualistic, Discrete, Deterministic. (Lecture Notes in Economics & Mathematical Systems). 1994. 43.00 (*0-387-58102-2*) Spr-Verlag.

Nicolacopoulos, Pantelis, ed. Greek Studies in the Philosophy & History of Science. (C). 1990. lib. bdg. 144.00 (*0-7923-0717-8*) Kluwer Ac.

Nicolae, Petre. CMEA in Theory & Practice. Jones, Steven, ed. 90p. (Orig.). 1984. pap. text ed. 75.00 (*1-55831-032-0*) Delphic Associates.

Nicolaeff, A., tr. Selected Plays of Aleksei Arbuzov. LC 82-364. (Illus.). 336p. 1982. text ed. 38.00 (*0-08-024548-X*, Pub. by Pergamon Repr UK) Franklin.

Nicolaeff, Ariadne, tr. see Arbuzov, Aleksei.

Nicolaeff, Ariadne, tr. see Turgenev, Ivan.

Nicolaenko, B., et al, eds. Nonlinear Systems of Partial Differential Equations in Applied Mathematics, 2 pts., Pt. I. LC 85-15107. (Lectures in Applied Mathematics: Vol. 23). 470p. 1986. text ed. 61.00 (*0-8218-1125-8*, LAM 23.1) Am Math.

— Nonlinear Systems of Partial Differential Equations in Applied Mathematics, 2 pts., Pt. II. LC 85-15107. (Lectures in Applied Mathematics: Vol. 23). 387p. 1986. text ed. 61.00 (*0-8218-1126-6*, LAM 23.2) Am Math.

— Nonlinear Systems of Partial Differential Equations in Applied Mathematics, 2 pts., Set. LC 85-15107. (Lectures in Applied Mathematics: Vol. 23). 858p. 1986. text ed. 101.00 (*0-8218-1123-1*, LAM 23) Am Math.

Nicolai, Christoph F., et al, eds. Bibliothek der Schonen Wissenschaften und der Freyen Kunste, 12 vols. in 6, Set. 1979. reprint ed. write for info. (*3-487-06659-9*, Pub. by Georg Olms GW) Lubrecht & Cramer.

Nicolai, D. Miles. The Summer the Flowers Had No Scent. (Illus.). (J). 1978. pap. 2.75 (*0-933992-00-9*) Coffee Break.

— The Summer the Flowers Had No Scent. 3rd ed. (Color-A-Story Ser.). (Illus.). 28p. (J). (gr. 3-5). 1977. pap. 2.75 (*0-933992-19-X*) Coffee Break.

Nicolai, Friedrich, ed. Allgemeine Deutsche Bibliothek, 118 vols. reprint ed. write for info. (*0-318-71727-1*, Pub. by Georg Olms GW) Lubrecht & Cramer.

Nicolai, Jurgen. A Complete Introduction to Finches. (Complete Introduction to... Ser.). (Illus.). 128p. (Orig.). 1987. pap. 5.95 (*0-86622-293-6*, CO-006S) TFH Pubns.

Nicolai, Otto. Il Templario: And Excerpts from Other Operas. (Italian Opera 1810-40 Ser.: Vol. 26). 280p. 1991. 124.00 (*0-8240-6575-1*) Garland.

Nicolaides, A. N., jt. ed. see Salmasi, Abdul-Majeed.

Nicolaides, Andrew N. & Yao, James S., eds. Investigation of Vascular Disorders. LC 81-6194. (Illus.). 649p. reprint ed. pap. 180.00 (*0-7837-2589-2*, 2042751) Bks Demand.

Nicolaides, Andrew N., jt. ed. see Salmasi, Abdul-Majeed.

***Nicolaides, Anthony.** Algebra, No. 111. (C). 1990. pap. 39.95x (*1-872684-13-0*, Pub. by P A S S Pubns UK) St Mut.

— Analytical Mathematics, No. 11. (C). 1990. pap. 39.95x (*1-872684-14-9*, Pub. by P A S S Pubns UK) St Mut.

— Calculus, No. 111. (C). 1990. pap. 39.95x (*1-872684-12-2*, Pub. by P A S S Pubns UK) St Mut.

— Coordinate Geometry. 240p. 1994. 45.00 (*1-872684-04-1*, Pub. by P A S S Pubns UK) St Mut.

— Electrical & Electronic Principles, No. 11. (C). 1990. pap. 39.95x (*1-872684-10-6*, Pub. by P A S S Pubns UK) St Mut.

— Integral Calculus & Applications. 432p. 1994. 59.00 (*1-872684-09-2*, Pub. by P A S S Pubns UK) St Mut.

— Mathematics, No. 11. (C). 1990. pap. 39.95 (*1-872684-11-4*, Pub. by P A S S Pubns UK) St Mut.

— Pure Mathematics: Algebra. (C). 1990. pap. 39.95x (*1-872684-01-7*, Pub. by P A S S Pubns UK) St Mut.

— Pure Mathematics: Cartesianand Polar Curve Sketching. (C). 1990. pap. 39.95x (*1-872684-06-8*, Pub. by P A S S Pubns UK) St Mut.

— Pure Mathematics: Complex Numbers. (C). 1990. pap. 39.95x (*1-872684-00-9*, Pub. by P A S S Pubns UK) St Mut.

— Pure Mathematics: Differential Calculus & Applications. (C). 1990. pap. 39.95x (*1-872684-08-4*, Pub. by P A S S Pubns UK) St Mut.

— Pure Mathematics: Trigonometry. (C). 1990. pap. 39.95x (*1-872684-02-5*, Pub. by P A S S Pubns UK) St Mut.

— Vectors. 224p. (C). 1994. pap. 45.00x (*1-872684-03-3*, Pub. by P A S S Pubns UK) St Mut.

Nicolaides-Bouman, Ans, jt. ed. see Wald, Nicholas J.

Nicolaides, C. A., et al, eds. Atoms in Strong Fields. LC 89-48928. (NATO ASI Series B, Physics: Vol. 212). (Illus.). 550p. 1990. 135.00 (*0-306-43414-8*, Plenum Pr) Plenum.

Nicolaides, Cleanthes A. & Beck, Donald R., eds. Excited States in Quantum Chemistry. (NATO Advanced Study Institutes Series C, Mathematical & Physical Sciences: No. 46). 1978. lib. bdg. 121.50 (*90-277-0961-0*) Kluwer Ac.

Nicolaides, Cleanthes A., jt. ed. see Bitsakis, Eftichios.

Nicolaides, K. H., jt. ed. see Snijders, R. J.

Nicolaides, K. H., jt. ed. see Thorpe Beeston, J. G.

Nicolaides, Kimon. Natural Way to Draw: A Working Plan for Art Study. 1990. pap. 10.95 (*0-395-53007-5*) HM.

Nicolaides, Lou. Cafe U. S. A.: Where to Go for the Best Cup of Joe! Your Ultimate Annual Guide to Massachusetts. 1994. pap. 12.95 (*0-9637060-1-2*) Ludwig CA.

— Cafe U. S. A.: Where to Go for the Best Cup of Joe! Your Ultimate Annual Guide to the Coffee State. 1994. pap. 11.95 (*0-9637060-2-0*) Ludwig CA.

Nicolaides, Louis. Caffe' L.A. The Coffeehouse Directory for L.A. County. 1993. pap. 9.95 (*0-9637060-0-4*) Ludwig CA.

— Caffe U. S. A. Ventura, Santa Barbara & Central Coast Edition; Your Ultimate Guide to the Coffee. 1994. pap. 12.95 (*0-9637060-3-9*) Ludwig CA.

Nicolaides, Phedon. Liberalizing Trade in Services: Strategies for Success. LC 89-32087. (Chatham House Papers). 128p. (Orig.). 1989. pap. 14.95 (*0-87609-064-1*) Coun Foreign.

Nicolaides, Phedon, ed. Industrial Policy in the European Community: A Necessary Response to Economic Integration? LC 92-41377. 148p. (C). 1993. lib. bdg. 79.00 (*0-7923-2084-0*) Kluwer Ac.

Nicolaides, Roy A., jt. ed. see Gunzburger, Max D.

Nicolaidis, Stylianos, ed. Serotoninergic System, Feeding & Body Weight Regulation. 170p. 1988. pap. text ed. 40.00 (*0-12-518175-2*) Acad Pr.

Nicolaisen, Jay. Italian Opera in Transition, 1871-1893. LC 80-22512. (Studies in Musicology: No. 31). 324p. reprint ed. pap. 92.40 (*0-8357-1121-8*, 2070224) Bks Demand.

Nicolaisen, W. F. H., ed. Oral Tradition in the Middle Ages: Selected Papers from the 1988 CEMERS Conference. LC 93-14340. (Medieval & Renaissance Texts & Studies: Vol. 112). 1994. 24.00 (*0-86698-165-9*) MRTS.

Nicolaison, Nancy. The Visual Guide to Visual C Plus Plus: The Illustrated Plain-English Companion. (Illus.). 850p. 1994. pap. 29.95 (*1-56604-079-5*) Ventana Pr.

***Nicolaou.** Investor's Guide to Valuing Tradeable Instruments: Proven Valuation Techniques. 1995. 50.00 (*0-273-61243-3*, Pub. by Pitman Publishing UK) Krieger.

Nicolaou, M. & Hadjivassilis, I., eds. Design & Operation of Sewage Treatment Plants in Coastal Tourist Areas: Proceedings of the IAWPRC Conference Held in Limassol, Cyprus, November 3-4, 1987. (Water Science & Technology Ser.: No. 21). 158p. 1990. pap. 57.50 (*0-08-037374-7*, Pergamon Pr) Elsevier.

Nicolaou-Smokoviti, Litsa & Bruyn, Severyn T. International Issues in Social Economy: Studies in the United States & Greece. LC 88-3525. 375p. 1989. text ed. 79.50 (*0-275-92518-8*, C2518, Praeger Pubs) Greenwood.

Nicolas, jt. auth. see Will.

***Nicolas, A.** The Mid-Oceanic Ridges: Mountains Below Sea Level. (Geology, Tectonics, Structural Geology, Oceanographic Science Geochemistry, Volcanology). 192p. 1995. pap. 36.00 (*0-387-57380-1*) Spr-Verlag.

Nicolas, Adolphe. Principles of Rock Deformation. 1987. pap. text ed. 51.50 (*90-277-2369-9*) Kluwer Ac.

— Structures of Ophiolites & Dynamics of Oceanic Lithosphere. (C). 1989. lib. bdg. 137.00 (*0-7923-0255-9*) Kluwer Ac.

Nicolas, Adolphe & Poirier, J. P. Crystalline Plasticity & Solid State Flow in Metamorphic Rocks. LC 75-15981. (Selected Topics in Geological Sciences Ser.). (Illus.). 490p. reprint ed. pap. 139.70 (*0-685-20673-4*, 2030461) Bks Demand.

***Nicolas, Anna K.** Weimaraner. 1994. 11.95 (*0-86622-509-9*) TFH Pubns.

Nicolas, D. French-English - English-French Vocabulary of Genetic Engineering & Molelcular Biology. 100p. (ENG & FRE.). 1990. pap. 20.50 (*2-85608-035-9*) IBD Ltd.

Nicolas, Harris, ed. see Chaucer, Geoffrey.

Nicolas, John F. Complete Cookbook of American Fish & Shellfish. 1990. text ed. 44.95 (*0-442-23504-6*) Van Nos Reinhold.

Nicolas, John F., jt. auth. see Sonnenschmidt, Frederic.

Nicolas, Richard, jt. auth. see Guerin-Fermigier, Franette.

Nicolau, Alexander, et al, eds. Advances in Languages & Compilers for Parallel Processing. (Pitman Ser.). (Illus.). 480p. 1991. pap. 40.00 (*0-262-64028-7*) MIT Pr.

Nicolau, C. Experimental Methods in Biophysical Chemistry. LC 72-5720. 703p. reprint ed. 180.00 (*0-8357-9888-7*, 2016155) Bks Demand.

Nicolau, C., ed. Oxygen Transport in Red Blood Cells: Proceedings of the Twelfth Aharon Katzir-Katchalsky Conference, Tours, France, 4-7 April 1984. 200p. 1986. 90.00 (*0-08-030800-7*, Pub. by PPL UK) Elsevier.

Nicolau, C. & Paraf, A., eds. Liposomes, Drugs & Immunocompetent Cell Functions. LC 81-66683. 1981. text ed. 93.00 (*0-12-518660-6*) Acad Pr.

Nicolau D'Olwer, Luis. Fray Bernardino de Sahagun: A Biography, 1499-1590. Mixco, Mauricio, tr. LC 87-5842. 229p. (SPA.). 1987. text ed. 25.00 (*0-87480-269-5*) U of Utah Pr.

Nicolau, E. & Zaharia, D. Adaptive Arrays. (Studies in Electrical & Electronic Engineering: No. 35). 298p. 1989. 110.25 (*0-444-98889-0*) Elsevier.

Nicolaus-Cusanus, Cardinal. Of Learned Ignorance. Heron, Germain, tr. LC 78-14132. (Illus.). 1991. reprint ed. 23.00 (*0-88355-806-8*) Hyperion Conn.

Nicolaus, M. J. Horsehide Devotions. LC 92-85553. (Illus.). 368p. (Orig.). 1992. pap. 12.50 (*0-939644-91-6*) Media Pub.

Nicolaus of Cusa. The Catholic Concordance. Sigmund, Paul E., ed. (Texts in the History of Political Thought Ser.). 376p. 1992. 19.95 (*0-521-40207-7*) Cambridge U Pr.

Nicolay, Carol & Barrette, Judith. Assembling Course Materials: A Trainer's Action Guide. 128p. (C). 1992. pap. 39.95 (*0-89397-415-3*) Nichols Pub.

Nicolay, D., jt. ed. see Ouden, Den C.

Nicolay, Helen. Lincoln's Secretary: A Biography of John G. Nicolay. LC 70-138169. (Illus.). 363p. 1971. reprint ed. text ed. 59.75 (*0-8371-5626-2*, NILS, Greenwood Pr) Greenwood.

***Nicolay, John G.** The Outbreak of the Rebellion. (Illus.). 246p. 1995. pap. 12.95 (*0-306-80657-6*) Da Capo.

— The Outbreak of the Rebellion. (Illus.). 226p. 1989. reprint ed. 25.00 (*0-916107-36-1*) Broadfoot.

Nicole, Christopher. Bloody Sunrise. 384p. 1994. 22.00 (*0-7278-4556-X*) Severn Hse.

— Bloody Sunset. 1994. lib. bdg. 22.00 (*0-7278-4614-0*) Severn Hse.

— Days of Wine & Roses? 1991. 21.95 (*0-7278-4187-4*) Severn Hse.

— Iron Ships, Iron Men. 1987. 18.95 (*0-7278-1444-3*) Severn Hse.

— The Last Battle. 352p. 1993. lib. bdg. 20.00 (*0-7278-4454-7*) Severn Hse.

— The Passion & the Glory. 1991. 18.95 (*0-7278-1696-9*) Severn Hse.

— Raging Sea, Searing Sky. 1988. 18.95 (*0-7278-1613-6*) Severn Hse.

— The Regiment. large type ed. 1990. 21.95 (*0-7089-2226-0*) Ulverscroft.

— Resumption. 352p. 1993. lib. bdg. 20.00 (*0-7278-4398-2*) Severn Hse.

— The Seeds of Power. 1995. lib. bdg. 22.00 (*0-7278-4691-4*) Severn Hse.

— The Titans. 352p. 1992. 20.00 (*0-7278-4319-2*) Severn Hse.

— Wind of Destiny. 1988. 18.95 (*0-7278-1529-6*) Severn Hse.

Nicole, David. The Crusades. (Paper Soldiers of the Middle Ages Ser.: Bk. 1). (J). (gr. 1-9). 1992. pap. 3.95 (*0-88388-096-2*) Bellerophon Bks.

— The Hundred Years' War. (Paper Soldiers of the Middle Ages Ser.: Bk. 2). (J). (gr. 1-9). 1992. pap. 3.95 (*0-88388-142-X*) Bellerophon Bks.

Nicole, Eugene, jt. ed. see Caws, Mary A.

Nicole, Jules. Les Scolies Genevoises de l'Iliade, 2 vols. in 1. lxxxiii, 574p. 1966. reprint ed. write for info. (*0-318-70987-2*, Pub. by Georg Olms GW); reprint ed. write for info. (*0-318-71382-9*, Pub. by Georg Olms GW) Lubrecht & Cramer.

Nicole, Pierre. Oeuvres Philosophiques et Morales. xxiii, 475p. 1970. reprint ed. write for info. (*0-318-71383-7*, Pub. by Georg Olms GW) Lubrecht & Cramer.

Nicole, Pierre, jt. auth. see Arnauld, Antoine.

Nicoleau, Guitele, jt. ed. see Geismar, Kathryn.

***Nicolello, I.** Complete Pastrywork Techniques. 1993. pap. text ed. 32.95 (*0-470-23348-6*) Halsted Pr.

— Complete Pastrywork Techniques. 1993. pap. text ed. 12.95 (*0-470-23353-2*) Wiley.

Nicolello, L. G. & Dinsdale, J. Basic Pastrywork Techniques. 2nd ed. 239p. 1993. pap. text ed. 29.95 (*0-470-23349-4*) Halsted Pr.

Nicoles, William, tr. see Arminius, James.

Nicolescu, Basarab. Science, Meaning, & Evolution: The Cosmology of Jacob Boehme. Baker, Rob, tr. (Illus.). 256p. 1991. reprint ed. 17.95 (*0-930407-20-2*) Parabola Bks.

***Nicolet, Andre & Belmans, R., eds.** Electric & Magnetic Fields: From Numerical Models to Industrial Applications. LC 95-13990. 380p. 1995. 105.00 (*0-306-44991-9*, Plenum Pr) Plenum.

Nicolet, Art, ed. see Hubbard, Edward L.

Nicolet, Claude. Space, Geography, & Politics in the Early Roman Empire. (Illus.). 276p. 1990. text ed. 37.50 (*0-472-10096-3*) U of Mich Pr.

— The World of the Citizen in Republican Rome. LC 77-80474. 1980. pap. 15.00 (*0-520-06342-2*) U CA Pr.

An Asterisk (*) at the beginning of an entry indicates that the title is appearing in BIP for the first time.

Nicolet, M. A. & Picraux, S. T. Ion Mixing & Surface Layer Alloying: Recent Advances. LC 84-14773. (Illus.). 162p. 1985. 32.00 (*0-8155-1006-3*) Noyes.

Nicolet, M. A., et al, eds. Materials Characterization. (MRS Symposium Proceedings Ser.: Vol. 69). 1986. text ed. 44.00 (*0-931837-35-9*) Materials Res.

***Nicoletta, Julie.** The Architecture of the Shakers. LC 94-23258. (Illus.). 176p. 1995. 40.00 (*0-88150-310-X*) Countryman.

Nicoletti, B., et al, eds. Human Achondroplasia: A Multidisciplinary Approach. LC 88-25288. (Basic Life Sciences Ser.: Vol. 48). (Illus.). 514p. 1988. 120.00 (*0-306-43006-1*, Plenum Pr) Plenum.

Nicoletti, Giuseppe. Diccionario de Bacteriologia Humana. 320p. 1989. pap. write for info. (*0-7859-6034-1*, 8440435959) Fr & Eur.

***Nicolic, Predrag.** French: Advance Variation. 2nd ed. (Electronic Chessbooks Ser.). 80p. 1995. disk, pap. 25.00 (*0-614-07029-5*) Chess Combi.

***Nicolin.** Umberto Riva. 1994. pap. text ed. 28.95 (*84-252-1597-8*, Pub. by Gustavo Gili SP) Rizzoli Intl.

Nicolini, C. Structure & Dynamics of Biopolymers. (C). 1987. lib. bdg. 110.00 (*90-247-3527-0*) Kluwer Ac.

Nicolini, C., ed. Bioscience at the Physical Science Frontier. 270p. 1988. 115.00 (*0-89603-131-4*) Humana.

— Modeling & Analysis in Biomedicine: Proceedings of the 4th Course of the International School of Pure & Applied Biostructure, Erice, Italy, Oct. 18-27,1982. 552p. 1984. 108.00 (*9971-950-81-2*) World Scientific Pub.

Nicolini, Claudio. Biophysics & Cancer. LC 86-4926. 480p. 1986. 125.00 (*0-306-42122-4*, Plenum Pr) Plenum.

***Nicolini, Claudio, ed.** From Neural Networks & Biomolecular Engineering to Bioelectronics: Proceedings of the 1993 International Workshop on Electronics & Biotechnology Advances Held on the Isle of Elba, Italy, July 13-16, 1993. LC 95-11436. (Electronics & Biotechnology Advanced (EL.B.A.) Forum Ser.: Vol. 1). 251p. 1995. 85.00 (*0-306-44907-2*) Plenum.

— Molecular Basis of Human Cancer. (NATO ASI Series A, Life Sciences: Vol. 209). (Illus.). 210p. 1991. 79.50 (*0-306-44018-0*, Plenum Pr) Plenum.

Nicolini, Claudio, jt. ed. see Bradbury, E. Morton.

Nicolini, M. & Zatta, R. F., eds. Glycobiology & the Brain. LC 93-21168. (Studies in Neuroscience). 1994. 134.00 (*0-08-042283-7*, Pergamon Pr) Elsevier.

Nicolini, M., jt. auth. see Zatta, P.

Nicolini, M., et al, eds. Alzheimer's Disease & Related Disorders. (Advances in the Biosciences Ser.: Vol. 87). 474p. 1993. 180.00 (*0-08-042330-2*, Pergamon Pr) Elsevier.

Nicolini, Marino, ed. Platinum & Other Metal Coordination Compounds in Cancer Chemotherapy. (Developments in Oncology Ser.). (C). 1988. lib. bdg. 220.50 (*0-89838-358-7*) Kluwer Ac.

Nicolis, C. & Nicolis, G., eds. Irreversible Phenomena & Dynamical Systems Analysis in Geosciences. 1986. lib. bdg. 177.00 (*90-277-2363-X*) Kluwer Ac.

Nicolis, C., jt. auth. see Berger, A. L.

***Nicolis, G.** Introduction to Nonlinear Science. (Illus.). 260p. (C). 1995. write for info. (*0-521-46228-2*); pap. write for info. (*0-521-46782-9*) Cambridge U Pr.

Nicolis, G. & Baras, F., eds. Chemical Instabilities: Applications in Chemistry, Engineering, Geology, & Materials Science. 1983. lib. bdg. 145.50 (*90-277-1705-2*) Kluwer Ac.

Nicolis, G. & Prigogine, Ilya. Self-Organization in Non-Equilibrium Systems: From Dissipative Structures to Order Through Fluctuations. LC 76-49019. 491p. 1977. text ed. 150.00 (*0-471-02401-5*, Wiley-Interscience) Wiley.

Nicolis, G., jt. ed. see Nicolis, C.

Nicolis, G., et al. Order & Fluctuations in Equilibrium & Nonequilibrium Statistical Mechanics. LC 80-13215. 396p. 1981. 90.00 (*0-471-05927-7*) Krieger.

Nicolis, J. S. Chaos & Information Processing. 304p. 1991. text ed. 48.00 (*981-02-0076-5*) World Scientific Pub.

— Dynamics of Hierarchical Systems. (Synergetics Ser.: Vol. 25). (Illus.). 415p. 1986. 105.00 (*0-387-13323-2*) Spr-Verlag.

Nicoll, A. & Pusey, E. B. Bibliothecae Bodleianae Codicum Manuscriptorum Catalogi Partis Secundae Volumen Secundum, Arabicos Complectens, 2 vols in 1. (Illus.). viii, 535p. reprint ed. write for info. (*0-318-71539-2*, Pub. by Georg Olms GW) Lubrecht & Cramer.

Nicoll, Allardyce. Dryden As an Adapter of Shakespeare. LC 78-173083. reprint ed. 20.00 (*0-404-07848-6*) AMS Pr.

— English Theatre: A Short History. LC 75-98861. 252p. 1971. reprint ed. text ed. 35.00 (*0-8371-3133-2*, NIET, Greenwood Pr) Greenwood.

— Film & Theatre. LC 77-169335. (Literature of Cinema, Ser. 2). 272p. 1975. reprint ed. 19.95 (*0-405-03902-6*) Ayer.

— Stuart Masques & the Renaissance Stage. LC 63-23186. (Illus.). 1972. 30.95 (*0-405-08817-5*, Pub. by Blom Pubns UK) Ayer.

— Studies in Shakespeare. (BCL1-PR English Literature Ser.). 164p. 1992. reprint ed. lib. bdg. 69.00 (*0-7812-7300-5*) Rprt Serv.

— The Theatre & Dramatic Theory. LC 78-5609. 221p. 1978. reprint ed. text ed. 55.00 (*0-313-20433-0*, NITD, Greenwood Pr) Greenwood.

— Theory of Drama. LC 66-29422. 1972. reprint ed. 23.95 (*0-405-08818-3*, Pub. by Blom Pubns UK) Ayer.

— The World of Harlequin: A Critical Study of the Commedia Dell'arte. LC 76-18411. 259p. reprint ed. pap. 73.90 (*0-317-27311-6*, 2024501) Bks Demand.

Nicoll, Allardyce, ed. Shakespeare Survey: An Annual Survey of Shakespearian Study & Production, Vol. II. LC 49-1639. 139p. reprint ed. pap. 39.70 (*0-317-30413-5*, 2024944) Bks Demand.

Nicoll, Angus & Rudd, Peter, eds. British Paediatric Association Manual on Infections & Immunizations in Children. (Illus.). 376p. 1989. pap. 19.95 (*0-19-261785-0*) OUP.

Nicoll, Angus, jt. ed. see Rudd, Peter.

Nicoll, Graham. Corporate Crocodiles & Other Tales. 1993. pap. 11.95 (*1-875680-05-5*, Pub. by Busn & Prof Pubng AT) Pubs Dist MI.

Nicoll, Helen & Pienkowski, Jan. Meg on the Moon. (Illus.). 32p. (J). (ps). 1980. 15.95 (*0-434-95424-1*, Pub. by W Heinemann Ltd) Trafalgar.

— Mog's Box. (Illus.). 32p. (J). (ps-00). 1987. 15.95 (*0-434-95658-9*, Pub. by W Heinemann Ltd) Trafalgar.

— Mog's Mumps. (Meg & Mog Ser.). (Illus.). 32p. (J). (ps-1). 1983. 15.95 (*0-434-95640-6*, Pub. by W Heinemann Ltd) Trafalgar.

— Owl at School. (Illus.). 32p. (J). (ps). 1984. 15.95 (*0-434-95434-9*, Pub. by W Heinemann Ltd) Trafalgar.

— Owl at School. (Illus.). 32p. (J). (ps). 1984. 15.95 (*0-434-95431-4*, Pub. by W Heinemann Ltd) Trafalgar.

Nicoll, Henry J. Landmarks of English Literature. LC 72-3282. (English Literature Ser.: No. 33). (Illus.). 1972. reprint ed. lib. bdg. 52.95 (*0-8383-1500-3*) M S G Haskell Hse.

Nicoll, John. Diary of Public Transactions & Other Occurrences, Chiefly in Scotland. LC 71-173084. (Bannatyne Club, Edinburgh. Publications: No. 52). reprint ed. 37.50 (*0-404-52762-0*) AMS Pr.

Nicoll, Josephine, tr. see Von Boehn, Max.

Nicoll, Leslie H. Perspectives on Nursing Theory. (C). 1986. text ed. 20.25 (*0-673-39397-6*) HarpCollege.

— Perspectives on Nursing Theory. 2nd ed. (Illus.). 736p. 1992. 41.95 (*0-397-54911-3*); pap. 32.50 (*0-397-54910-5*) Lippincott.

Nicoll, Martin E. & Rathbun, Galen. African Insectivora & Elephant-Shrews: An Action Plan for Their Conservation. (Illus.). 58p. (Orig.). 1991. pap. 18.00 (*2-8317-0020-5*, Pub. by IUCN SZ) Island Pr.

Nicoll, Maurice. The New Man: An Interpretation of Some Parables & Miracles of Christ. LC 83-20279. 153p. (Orig.). 1984. pap. 14.00 (*0-394-72390-2*) Shambhala Pubns.

Nicoll, Mildred R., tr. see Steiner, Rudolf.

Nicoll, W. R. & Wise, Thomas J. Literary Anecdotes of the Nineteenth Century, 2 Vols. reprint ed. write for info. (*0-318-50641-6*) AMS Pr.

— Literary Anecdotes of the Nineteenth Century, 2 Vols, 1. LC 11-21329. reprint ed. 57.50 (*0-404-04718-1*) AMS Pr.

— Literary Anecdotes of the Nineteenth Century, 2 Vols, 2. LC 11-21329. reprint ed. 57.50 (*0-404-04719-X*) AMS Pr.

— Literary Anecdotes of the Nineteenth Century, 2 Vols, Set. LC 11-21329. reprint ed. 115.00 (*0-404-04717-3*) AMS Pr.

Nicoll, W. Robertson. The Problem of 'Edwin Drood' LC 72-1330. (Studies in Dickens: No. 52). 1972. reprint ed. lib. bdg. 49.95 (*0-8383-1442-2*) M S G Haskell Hse.

Nicoll, W. Robertson, ed. The Sermon Outline Bible, 12 vols., Set. 1987. reprint ed. text ed. 249.95 (*0-8010-6749-9*) Baker Bk.

Nicoll, William & Salmon, Trevor. Understanding the European Communities. (Illus.). 260p. (C). 1990. lib. bdg. 64.50 (*0-389-20912-0*); pap. 25.50 (*0-86003-709-6*) B&N Imports.

Nicolle, D. Romano-Byzantine Armies Fourth-Ninth Century. (Men-at-Arms Ser.: No. 247). (Illus.). 48p. pap. 11.95 (*1-85532-224-2*, 9218, Pub. by Osprey UK) Stackpole.

Nicolle, David. The Age of Charlemagne. (Men-at-Arms Ser.: No. 150). (Illus.). 48p. pap. 11.95 (*0-85045-042-X*, 9082, Pub. by Osprey UK) Stackpole.

— The Age of Tamerlane. (Men-at-Arms Ser.: No. 222). (Illus.). 48p. pap. 11.95 (*0-85045-949-4*, 9180, Pub. by Osprey UK) Stackpole.

— The Armies of Islam Seventh to Eleventh Centuries. (Men-at-Arms Ser.: No. 125). (Illus.). 48p. pap. 11.95 (*0-85045-448-4*, 9057, Pub. by Osprey UK) Stackpole.

— Armies of the Muslim Conquest. (Men-at-Arms Ser.: No. 255). (Illus.). 48p. pap. 11.95 (*1-85532-279-X*, 9226, Pub. by Osprey UK) Stackpole.

— Armies of the Ottoman Turks 1300-1774. (Men-at-Arms Ser.: No. 140). (Illus.). 48p. pap. 11.95 (*0-85045-511-1*, 9072, Pub. by Osprey UK) Stackpole.

— Arthur & the Anglo-Saxon Wars. (Men-at-Arms Ser.: No. 154). (Illus.). 48p. pap. 11.95 (*0-85045-548-0*, 9086, Pub. by Osprey UK) Stackpole.

— Attila & the Nomad Hordes. (Elite Ser.: No. 30). (Illus.). 64p. pap. 12.95 (*0-85045-996-6*, 9430, Pub. by Osprey UK) Stackpole.

— The Crusades. (Elite Ser.: No. 19). (Illus.). 64p. pap. 12.95 (*0-85045-854-4*, 9419, Pub. by Osprey UK) Stackpole.

— El Cid & the Reconquista, 1000-1492. (Men-at-Arms Ser.: No. 200). (Illus.). 48p. pap. 11.95 (*0-85045-840-4*, 9133, Pub. by Osprey UK) Stackpole.

— First Time Crew: Everything You Ever Wanted to Know but Never Dared Ask the Skipper. (Illus.). 112p. 1990. pap. 14.95 (*0-229-11845-3*, Adlard Coles) Sheridan.

— French Medieval Armies 1000-1300. (Men-at-Arms Ser.: No. 231). (Illus.). 48p. pap. 11.95 (*1-85532-127-0*, 9189, Pub. by Osprey UK) Stackpole.

— Gravelotte-St. Privat 1871. (Campaign Ser.: No. 21). (Illus.). 96p. pap. 14.95 (*1-85532-286-2*, 9520, Pub. by Osprey UK) Stackpole.

— Hattin 1187. (Campaign Ser.: No. 19). (Illus.). 96p. pap. 14.95 (*1-85532-284-6*, 9518, Pub. by Osprey UK) Stackpole.

— Hungary & the Fall of Eastern Europe 1000-1568. (Men-at-Arms Ser.: No. 195). (Illus.). 48p. pap. 11.95 (*0-85045-833-1*, 9128, Pub. by Osprey UK) Stackpole.

— Italian Medieval Armies 1300-1500. (Men-at-Arms Ser.: No. 136). (Illus.). 48p. pap. 11.95 (*0-85045-477-8*, 9068, Pub. by Osprey UK) Stackpole.

— The Janissary. (Elite Ser.). (Illus.). 64p. 1995. pap. 12.95 (*1-85532-413-X*, Pub. by Osprey UK) Stackpole.

— Lawrence & the Arab Revolts 1914-18. (Men-at-Arms Ser.: No. 208). (Illus.). 48p. pap. 11.95 (*0-85045-888-9*, 9141, Pub. by Osprey UK) Stackpole.

— The Mamluks 1250-1517. (Men-at-Arms Ser.). (Illus.). 48p. 1993. pap. 11.95 (*1-85532-314-1*, 9230, Pub. by Osprey UK) Stackpole.

— Moghul India 1523-1805. (Men-at-Arms Ser.). (Illus.). 48p. 1993. pap. 11.95 (*1-85532-344-3*, 9234, Pub. by Osprey UK) Stackpole.

— The Mongol Warlords: Ghengis Khan, Kublai Khan, Hulegu, & Tamerlane. (Illus.). 208p. 1990. 24.95 (*1-85314-104-6*, Pub. by Firebird Bks UK) Sterling.

— The Normans. (Elite Ser.: No. 9). (Illus.). 64p. pap. 12.95 (*0-85045-729-7*, 9408, Pub. by Osprey Pubng Ltd UK) Stackpole.

— The Ottoman Army 1914-18. (Men-at-Arms Ser.). (Illus.). 48p. 1994. pap. 11.95 (*1-85532-412-1*, 9240, Pub. by Osprey UK) Stackpole.

— Rome's Enemies, Vol. 5: The Desert Frontier. (Men-at-Arms Ser.: No. 243). (Illus.). 48p. pap. 11.95 (*1-85532-166-1*, 9203, Pub. by Osprey UK) Stackpole.

— Saladin & the Saracens Armies of the Middle East 1100-1300. (Men-at-Arms Ser.: No. 171). (Illus.). 48p. pap. 11.95 (*0-85045-682-7*, 9103, Pub. by Osprey UK) Stackpole.

— Saracen Faris 1100-1250 A. D. (Warrior Ser.). (Illus.). 64p. 1994. pap. 12.95 (*1-85532-453-9*, 9609, Pub. by Osprey UK) Stackpole.

— The Venetian Empire 1200-1700. (Men-at-Arms Ser.: No. 210). (Illus.). 48p. pap. 11.95 (*0-85045-899-4*, 9143, Pub. by Osprey UK) Stackpole.

— Yarmuk 636 AD. (Campaign Ser.). (Illus.). 96p. 1994. pap. 14.95 (*1-85532-414-8*, 9530, Pub. by Osprey UK) Stackpole.

***Nicollelo, Ildo & Foote, Rowland.** Complete Confectionery Techniques. LC 94-45597. 1995. pap. text ed. 29.95 (*0-470-23493-8*) Wiley.

Nicollian, Edward H. & Brews, John R. MOS (Metal Oxide Semiconductor) Physics & Technology. LC 81-7607. 906p. 1982. text ed. 181.95 (*0-471-08500-6*) Wiley.

***Nicollier, Alain.** Dictionnaire des Mots Suisses de la Langue Francaise. 171p. (FRE.). 1990. pap. 49.95 (*0-7859-8200-0*, 2881150055) Fr & Eur.

— Dictionnaire Encyclopedique Suisse. 1988. write for info. (*0-7859-8199-3*, 2-88115-001-2) Fr & Eur.

Nicollier, Alain, ed. European Universities, Nineteen Seventy-Five to Eighty-Five: Proceedings of the 5th General Assembly of the Standing Conference of Rectors & Vice-Chancellors of the European Universities, Bologna, 1974. LC 75-4331. 1975. pap. 106.00 (*0-08-019710-8*, Pub. by Pergamon Repr UK); French Ed. pap. 104.00 (*0-08-019711-6*, Pub. by Pergamon Repr UK) Franklin.

***Nicolls, M.** Festive Food of America. 1994. pap. 5.99 (*0-517-12872-1*) Random.

***Nicolo, F.** Robot Control 1994 (SYROCO '94) A Postscript Volume from the IFAC Symposium, Capri, Italy, 19-21 September 1994. Sciavicco, L. & Bonivento, C., eds. LC 95-5963. 1995. pap. 117.00 (*0-08-042227-6*, Pergamon Pr) Elsevier.

Nicoloff, Philip L. Emerson on Race & History: An Examination of English Traits. LC 80-2540. 1981. reprint ed. 33.50 (*0-404-19266-1*) AMS Pr.

Nicolosi, Alfredo, ed. HIV Epidemiology: Models & Methods. LC 93-30218. 384p. 1994. 85.00 (*0-7817-0118-X*) Raven.

Nicolosi, Joseph. Healing Homosexuality: Case Stories of Reparative Therapy. LC 92-16501. 240p. 1993. 30.00 (*0-87668-340-5*) Aronson.

— Reparative Therapy of Male Homosexuality: A New Clinical Approach. LC 91-4534. 376p. 1991. 40.00 (*0-87668-545-9*) Aronson.

Nicolosi, Lucille. Terminology of Communication Disorders: Speech - Language - Hearing. 3rd ed. 375p. 1989. pap. text ed. 28.95 (*0-683-06500-9*) Williams & Wilkins.

Nicols, Virginia S., jt. auth. see Gaudio, Peter E.

Nicolsky, R. & Escudero, R., eds. High Temperature Superconductivity: Proceedings of the Latin American Conference, Rio de Janeiro, Brazil, May 5-6, 1988. (Progress in High Temperature Superconductivity: Vol. 9). 504p. 1988. pap. 60.00 (*9971-5-0646-7*) World Scientific Pub.

Nicolson, Colin, jt. auth. see Boatswain, Timothy.

Nicolson, D. H., et al. An Interpretation of Van Rheede's Hortus Malabaricus. (Regnum Vegetabile Ser.: Vol. 119). 378p. 1988. lib. bdg. 118.00 (*3-87429-281-9*) Koeltz Sci Bks.

Nicolson, Dan H., et al. Flora of Dominica, Pt. 2: Dicotyledoneae. LC 90-10415. (Smithsonian Contributions to Botany Ser.: No. 77). 278p. reprint ed. pap. 79.30 (*0-8357-2611-8*, 2039931) Bks Demand.

***Nicolson, Doula & Ayers, Harry.** Individual Counselling Theory & Practice: A Reference Guide. (Resource Materials for Teachers Ser.). 96p. 1995. pap. 21.95x (*1-85346-373-6*, Pub. by D Fulton UK) Taylor & Francis.

Nicolson, G., jt. ed. see Poste, George.

Nicolson, Garth L., jt. ed. see Moloy, Peter.

Nicolson, Harold. The Congress of Vienna: A Study of Allied Unity 1812-1822. LC 46-7614. 312p. 1970. reprint ed. pap. 10.95 (*0-15-622061-X*, Harvest Bks) HarBrace.

— Diplomacy. 3rd ed. LC 88-31994. 168p. (C). 1989. reprint ed. pap. text ed. 12.00 (*0-934742-52-9*) Geo U Inst Dplmcy.

— Good Behavior: Being a Study of Certain Types of Civility. 11.75 (*0-8446-0822-X*) Peter Smith.

— Tennyson. LC 72-2100. (English Literature Ser.: No. 33). 1972. reprint ed. lib. bdg. 75.00 (*0-8383-1458-9*) M S G Haskell Hse.

Nicolson, Harold G. Byron, the Last Journey, April 1823-April 1824. (BCL1-PR English Literature Ser.). 288p. 1992. reprint ed. lib. bdg. 79.00 (*0-7812-7481-8*) Rprt Serv.

— Dwight Morrow. LC 75-2657. (Wall Street & the Security Market Ser.). (Illus.). 1975. reprint ed. 39.95 (*0-405-06982-0*) Ayer.

— Dwight Morrow. (History - United States Ser.). 409p. 1993. reprint ed. lib. bdg. 99.00 (*0-7812-4922-8*) Rprt Serv.

— The Evolution of Diplomatic Method: The Chichele Lectures Delivered at Oxford, November, 1953. LC 76-56181. 93p. 1977. reprint ed. text ed. 59.75 (*0-8371-9428-8*, NIDM, Greenwood Pr) Greenwood.

— Paul Verlaine. LC 77-10281. reprint ed. 49.50 (*0-404-16332-7*) AMS Pr.

— Sainte-Beuve. LC 77-20072. (Illus.). 274p. 1978. reprint ed. text ed. 59.75 (*0-313-20013-0*, NISB, Greenwood Pr) Greenwood.

— Small Talk. LC 72-152206. (Essay Index Reprint Ser.). 1977. reprint ed. 19.95 (*0-8369-2420-7*) Ayer.

— Swinburne. (BCL1-PR English Literature Ser.). 207p. 1992. reprint ed. lib. bdg. 79.00 (*0-7812-7706-X*) Rprt Serv.

— Swinburne. LC 70-145208. 1971. reprint ed. 39.00 (*0-403-00807-7*) Scholarly.

— Tennyson: Aspects of His Life. LC 74-145209. 308p. 1925. reprint ed. 15.00 (*0-403-00806-9*) Scholarly.

— Tennyson: Aspects of His Life, Character & Poetry. LC 72-12. (Select Bibliographies Reprint Ser.). 1977. reprint ed. 19.95 (*0-8369-9967-3*) Ayer.

— Tennyson, Aspects of His Life, Character & Poetry. (BCL1-PR English Literature Ser.). 308p. 1992. reprint ed. lib. bdg. 89.00 (*0-7812-7697-7*) Rprt Serv.

Nicolson, I. F. The Mystery of Crichel Down. (Illus.). 308p. 1987. 65.00 (*0-19-827492-0*) OUP.

Nicolson, Iain. Explore the World of Space & the Universe. (Illus.). 48p. (J). (gr. 3-7). 1992. write for info. (*0-307-15608-7*, 15608, Golden Pr) Western Pub.

— Illustrated World of Space. (J). (gr. 4-7). 1991. pap. 12.95 (*0-671-74127-6*, S&S Bks Young Read) S&S Childrens.

Nicolson, Ian. Cold-Moulded & Strip-Planked Wood Boatbuilding. (Illus.). 187p. 1991. 34.95 (*0-924486-14-7*) Sheridan.

— Small Steel Craft. (Illus.). 208p. 1971. 34.95 (*0-8464-1296-9*) Beekman Pubs.

— Surveying Small Craft. 3rd ed. (Illus.). 224p. 1994. 29.95 (*0-924486-58-9*) Sheridan.

Nicolson, Laian, jt. ed. see Moore, Patrick.

Nicolson, Louise. Best Baby Name Book. 1990. pap. 8.95 (*0-7225-2124-3*) Thorsons SF.

Nicolson, M. H., ed. see Conway, Anne.

Nicolson, Marjorie H. Pepys' Diary & the New Science. LC 65-26012. (Illus.). 217p. reprint ed. pap. 61.90 (*0-8357-3139-1*, 2039402) Bks Demand.

Nicolson, Marjorie H., ed. The Conway Letters: The Correspondence of Anne, Viscountess Conway, Henry More & Their Friends: 1642-1684. rev. ed. (Illus.). 544p. 1992. 98.00 (*0-19-824876-8*) OUP.

Nicolson, Marjorie H., ed. see Shadwell, Thomas.

Nicolson, Nigel. Portrait of a Marriage. LC 79-25497. 288p. (C). 1980. pap. 12.95 (*0-689-70597-2*, 257, Atheneum S&S) S&S Trade.

— The World of Jane Austen. (Illus.). 192p. 1995. pap. 17.95 (*0-297-83495-9*, Pub. by Orion) Trafalgar.

Nicolson, Nigel & Trautmann, Joanne, eds. The Letters of Virginia Woolf, Vol. I: 1888-1912. LC 76-40422. 531p. 1977. pap. 12.95 (*0-15-650881-8*, Harvest Bks) HarBrace.

— The Letters of Virginia Woolf, Vol. II: 1911-1922. LC 76-40422. (Illus.). 627p. 1978. pap. 5.95 (*0-15-650882-6*, Harvest Bks) HarBrace.

— The Letters of Virginia Woolf, Vol. III: 1923-1928. LC 76-40422. (Illus.). 600p. 1980. pap. 5.95 (*0-15-650883-4*, Harvest Bks) HarBrace.

— The Letters of Virginia Woolf, Vol. IV: 1929-1931. LC 76-40422. 472p. 1981. pap. 10.95 (*0-15-650884-2*, Harvest Bks) HarBrace.

— The Letters of Virginia Woolf, Vol. VI: 1936-1941. LC 75-25538. 576p. 1982. pap. 9.95 (*0-15-650887-7*, Harvest Bks) HarBrace.

Nicolson, Paula, jt. ed. see Ussher, Jane M.

Nicolson, Rod, jt. auth. see Scott, Peter.

Nicolson, Sheryl A. & Shipstead, Susan G. Through the Looking Glass: Observations in the Early Childhood Classroom. 448p. (C). 1994. pap. write for info. (*0-02-387491-0*, Merrill Pub Co) Macmillan.

Nicosia, Francis R. The Third Reich & the Palestine Question. 335p. 1986. text ed. 35.00 (*0-292-72731-3*) U of Tex Pr.

Nicosia, Francis R., ed. Central Zionist Archives, 1933-1945: Jerusalem. LC 89-16915. (Archives of the Holocaust Ser.: Vol. 3). 450p. 1990. 115.00 (*0-8240-5485-7*) Garland.

— Central Zionist Archives 1939-1945, Jerusalem. LC 89-16915. (Archives of the Holocaust Ser.: Vol. 4). 470p. 1990. reprint ed. 125.00 (*0-8240-5486-5*) Garland.

N

Nicosia, Francis R. & Stokes, Lawrence D., eds. Germans Against Nazism: Nonconformity, Opposition & Resistance in the Third Reich. (Illus.). 450p. 1991. 74.00 (0-85496-688-9) Berg Pubs.

Nicosia, Gerald. Lovers, Lunatics, Poets, Vets & Bargirls: Poems by Gerald Nicosia. (Illus.). 65p. (Orig.). (C). 1991. 50.00 (0-924047-06-2) Host Pubns.

— Lunatics, Lovers, Poets, Jet & Bargirls: Poems by Gerald Nicosia. (Illus.). 80p. (Orig.). 1991. pap. text ed. 9.50 (0-924047-05-4) Host Pubns.

— Memory Babe: A Critical Biography of Jack Kerouac. LC 93-33457. 1994. 18.00 (0-520-08569-8) U CA Pr.

— Memory Babe: A Critical Biography of Jack Kerouac. 768p. 1988. pap. 9.95 (0-14-058016-6, Penguin Bks) Viking Penguin.

***Nicosia, Joan E. & Petro, Jame A.** Manual of Burn Care. fac. ed. LC 82-25499. (Illus.). 166p. Date not set. pap. 47.40 (0-7837-7288-2, 2047018) Bks Demand.

Nicosia, Sal, jt. auth. see Pfaffle, A. E.

Nicoson, Michael. The Basic Essentials of Bicycle Touring. LC 92-47123. (Basic Essentials Ser.). (Illus.). 72p. (Orig.). 1993. pap. 5.99 (0-934802-73-4) ICS Bks.

Nicotera, Anne M. Interpersonal Communication in Friend & Mate Relationships. LC 92-3099. (SUNY Series, Human Communication Processes). 256p. 1993. 59.50 (0-7914-1351-9); pap. 19.95 (0-7914-1352-7) State U NY Pr.

***Nicotera, Anne M., ed.** Conflict in Organizations: Communicative Processes. (SUNY Series, Human Communication Processes). 288p. (C). 1995. 59.50x (0-7914-2665-3) State U NY Pr.

— Conflict in Organizations: Communicative Processes. (SUNY Series, Human Communication Processes). 288p. (C). 1995. pap. 19.95x (0-7914-2666-1) State U NY Pr.

Nicoud, J. D. Microprocessor Interface Design: Digital Circuits & Concepts. 1991. pap. 49.95 (0-442-31513-9) Chapman & Hall.

— Microprocessor Interface Design: Digital Circuits & Concepts. 288p. 1991. pap. write for info. (0-412-45140-9, E & FN Spon) Routledge Chapman & Hall.

Nicoud, J. D. & Wagner, F. Major Microprocessors: A Unified Approach Using CALM. 340p. 1987. 97.50 (0-444-70116-8, North Holland) Elsevier.

Nicoud, J. D., et al, eds. Microcomputer Architectures: Proceedings of the Third EUROMICRO Symposium on Microprocessing Microprogramming, October 1977, Amsterdam. 284p. 1978. 89.75 (0-444-85097-X, North Holland) Elsevier.

Nicoulin, M. The French Verb. (C). 1983. 35.00 (0-7175-1158-8, Pub. by S Thornes Pubs UK) St Mut.

Nicovich, Draunta L. God's Garden: A Vegetarian Cookbook. (Illus.). 168p. (Orig.). 1989. pap. 11.95 (0-9623040-7-7) Country Day.

Nicozisin, George. What Every Orthodox Christian Should Know. 1992. pap. 3.95 (0-937032-85-9) Light&Life Pub Co MN.

Nicshal, Ken K., jt. auth. see Kanski, Jack J.

Niculescu, Mihai, jt. auth. see Eliade, Mircea.

Niczow, Aleksandar. Black Book of Polish Censorship. LC 82-72611. 170p. (Orig.). 1982. pap. 7.95 (0-89708-095-5) And Bks.

Nida, Eugene, jt. auth. see Louw, J. P.

Nida, Eugene A. Language Structure & Translation: Essays by Eugene A. Nida. Dil, Anwar S., ed. LC 75-183. (Language Science & National Development Ser.). 300p. 1975. 39.50 (0-8047-0885-1) Stanford U Pr.

— Message & Missions: The Communication of the Christian Faith. rev. ed. LC 60-11785. (Illus.). 315p. 1990. pap. text ed. 10.95 (0-87808-756-7, WCL756-7) William Carey Lib.

— Synopsis of English Syntax. (Janua Linguarum, Series Practica: No. 19). (Orig.). 1966. pap. text ed. 40.00 (90-279-2430-9) Mouton.

— Towards a Science of Translating. (Illus.). 1964. 72.95 (90-04-02605-3) Adlers Foreign Bks.

Nida, Eugene A., jt. auth. see Arichea, Daniel C.

Nida, Eugene A., jt. auth. see Bratcher, Robert G.

Nida, Eugene A., jt. auth. see De Waard, Jan.

Nida, Eugene A., jt. auth. see Ellingworth, Paul.

Nida, Eugene A., jt. auth. see Newman, Barclay M.

Nida, Patricia C. & Heller, Wendy M. The Teenager's Survival Guide to Moving. LC 87-1134. 148p. (YA). 1987. reprint ed. pap. 2.95 (0-02-044510-5, Collier Bks Young) S&S Childrens.

Nida-Ruemelin, Julian, ed. Praktische Rationalitaet: Grundlagenprobleme und Ethische Anwendungen Des Rational Choice-Paradigmas. (Perspektiven der Analytischen Philosophie Ser.: No. 2). viii, 458p. (GER.). 1993. lib. bdg. 167.70 (3-11-013656-2) De Gruyter.

Nidditch, Peter H., ed. An Essay Concerning Human Understanding. (Clarendon Edition of the Works of John Locke Ser.). (Illus.). 924p. (C). 1979. reprint ed. pap. text ed. 21.00 (0-19-824595-5) OUP.

Nidditch, Peter H., ed. see Hume, David.

Nidditch, Peter H., ed. see Locke, John.

Nideffer, Robert M. An Athletes' Guide to Mental Training. LC 85-4305. 164p. (C). 1985. pap. text ed. 14.95 (0-931250-96-X, BNID0096) Human Kinetics.

— The Ethics & Practice of Applied Sport Psychology. 1981. pap. text ed. 14.95 (0-685-42270-4) Mouvement Pubns.

— Psyched to Win. LC 91-38529. 152p. 1992. pap. 11.95 (0-88011-463-0, PNID0463) Human Kinetics.

Nidetch, Jean T. Weight Watchers Quick Start Plus Program Cookbook. 1986. pap. 12.00 (0-452-26477-4, Plume) NAL-Dutton.

— Weight Watchers Quick Start Program Cookbook: Including the Full Exchange Plan. (Illus.). 416p. 1984. 18.50 (0-453-01010-5) NAL-Dutton.

— Weight Watchers Quick Success Program Cookbook. (Illus.). 448p. 1990. pap. 10.95 (0-452-26428-6, Plume) NAL-Dutton.

Nidhipraba, Bhanupong, jt. auth. see Warr, Peter G.

NiDhuibhne, Eilis. Blood & Water. 148p. (C). 1991. pap. 9.95 (0-946211-54-X, Pub. by Attic IE) InBook.

Nidich, Randi J., jt. auth. see Nidich, Sanford I.

Nidich, Sanford I. & Nidich, Randi J. Growing up Enlightened: How Maharishi School of the Age of Enlightenment Is Awakening the Creative Genius of Students & Creating Heaven on Earth. LC 90-61520. (Illus.). 233p. (Orig.). 1989. pap. 12.95 (0-923569-03-0) Maharishi Intl U Pr.

Nidiffer, Jana, jt. auth. see Levine, Arthur.

Niditch, B. Z. Exile. Schuler, Ruth W., ed. 16p. (Orig.). 1986. pap. text ed. 3.00 (0-317-46598-8) Heritage Trails.

Niditch, Susan. Chaos to Cosmos: Studies in Biblical Patterns of Creation. (Studies in Humanities: No. 6). (C). 1985. pap. 14.95 (0-89130-763-X, 00 01 06) Scholars Pr GA.

— Folklore & the Hebrew Bible. LC 93-17830. 1993. Alk. paper. 10.00 (0-8006-2590-0, Fortress Pr) Augsburg Fortress.

— The Symbolic Vision in Biblical Tradition. LC 83-8643. (Harvard Semitic Monographs). 270p. (C). 1983. 17.00 (0-89130-627-7, 04 00 30) Scholars Pr GA.

— War in the Hebrew Bible: A Study in the Ethics of Violence. LC 92-5787. 192p. (C). 1993. 32.00 (0-19-507638-9) OUP.

— War in the Hebrew Bible: A Study in the Ethics of Violence. 192p. 1995. pap. 10.95 (0-19-509840-4) OUP.

Niditch, Susan, ed. Text & Tradition: The Hebrew Bible & Folklore. (Society of Biblical Literature Semeia Studies). 1990. 29.95 (1-55540-440-5); pap. 19.95 (1-55540-441-3) Scholars Pr GA.

Nidl. Can Someone Please Tell Me Whe. 1984. pap. 17.95 (0-684-18230-0, Scribners) S&S Trade.

Nidle, Sheldon, jt. auth. see Essene, Virginia.

***Nie, Junhong & Linkens, Derek A.** Fuzzy-Neural Control: Principles, Algorithms & Applications. LC 94-47246. 1995. pap. text ed. 49.00 (0-13-337916-7) P-H.

Nie, Norman, jt. auth. see Verba, Sidney.

Nie, Norman H., jt. auth. see Verba, Sidney.

Nie, Norman H., et al. The Changing American Voter. LC 75-42429. 450p. 1980. 37.50 (0-674-10830-2); pap. 16.95 (0-674-10835-3) HUP.

— Social Structure & Political Participation: Development Relationships, Pt. I. (Reprint Series in Political Science). (C). 1993. reprint ed. pap. text ed. 1.00 (0-8290-2748-3, PS-519) Irvington.

Nie Zeng Jifen. Testimony of a Confucian Woman: The Autobiography of Mrs. Nie Zeng Jifen, 1852-1942. Kennedy, Micki & Kennedy, Thomas L., eds. LC 92-22989. (Illus.). 240p. 1993. 35.00 (0-8203-1509-5) U of Ga Pr.

Nieback. Conscience, War & the Selective Objector. 62p. 1968. 1.75 (0-318-15969-4) NISBCO.

Nieback, Paul L., ed. The Rent Control Debate. LC 85-1181. (Urban & Regional Policy & Development Studies). 160p. reprint ed. pap. 45.60 (0-7837-2468-3, 2042621) Bks Demand.

Niebauer, Abby. Sun Rose. 60p. 1985. pap. 14.00 (0-930513-01-0) Blackwells Pr.

— Three Windows. (Illus.). 60p. (Orig.). 1980. 140.00 (0-940592-05-3) Heyeck Pr.

Niebel. Engineering Maintenance Management. 2nd expanded rev. ed. (Industrial Engineering: Vol. 18). 384p. 1994. 125.00 (0-8247-9247-5) Dekker.

Niebel, Benjamin W. Motion & Time Study. 9th ed. LC 92-15051. 880p. (C). 1992. text ed. 70.95 (0-256-09248-6) Irwin.

Niebel, Benjamin W. & Baldwin, Edward N. Designing for Production. rev. ed. LC 63-14230. (Irwin Series in Management). 696p. reprint ed. pap. 180.00 (0-317-10722-4, 2001036) Bks Demand.

Niebel, Benjamin W., et al. Modern Wrestling: A Primer for Wrestlers, Parents, & Fans. LC 82-7478. (Illus.). 128p. (Orig.). (C). 1982. lib. bdg. 25.00 (0-271-00323-5); pap. text ed. 12.50 (0-271-00328-6) Pa St U Pr.

***Niebergall, Jane.** The Alaska Report. (Alaska Teaching Units Ser.). 123p. (Orig.). (C). 1994. teacher ed, pap. text ed. 9.95 (1-878051-16-4) Circumpolar Pr.

— Bears to Barely Bears: A Theme Unit about Alaskan Bears. (Alaskan Teaching Unit Ser.). (Illus.). 71p. (Orig.). (C). 1990. teacher ed, pap. 9.95 (1-870511-21-2) Circumpolar Pr.

***Nieberl, Helen R.** On the Trail: The Adventures of a Middle-Aged Tenderfoot. (Illus.). 104p. (Orig.). 1994. pap. 11.95 (0-9636921-1-9) Pack & Paddle.

Nieberle, jt. auth. see Cohrs, P.

Niebes, Joylyn. Children's Pages: A Parent Source Book for North Central Texas. 320p. (Orig.). 1986. pap. 8.95 (0-933547-02-1) Lauren Pubns.

— The Children's Pages: A Parent Source Book for the Dallas Area. 128p. (Orig.). 1985. pap. 8.95 (0-933547-00-5) Lauren Pubns.

Niebla, Gilberto G., et al. Paulo Freire on Higher Education: A Dialogue at the National University of Mexico. (Teacher Empowerment & School Reform Ser.). 201p. (C). 1994. text ed. 49.50x (0-7914-1873-1); pap. text ed. 16.95x (0-7914-1874-X) State U NY Pr.

Nieboehr, E., et al. Rare Earths. LC 67-11280. (Structure & Bonding Ser.: Vol. 22). iv, 1p. 1975. 51.00 (0-387-07268-3) Spr-Verlag.

Nieboer, Evert & Nriagu, Jerome O., eds. Nickel & Human Health: Current Perspectives. (Advances in Environmental Science & Technology Ser.). 704p. 1992. text ed. 159.00 (0-471-50076-3) Wiley.

Nieboer, Evert, jt. ed. see Nriagu, Jerome O.

Nieboer, Laura. My Child's Care. 50p. 1992. 25.00 (1-881782-00-X) State Art.

Niebuhr, Bruce R., jt. auth. see Rahr, Richard R.

Niebuhr, Carsten. Travels Through Arabia & Other Countries in the East, Vol. 1. (Folios Archive Library). (Illus.). 464p. 1994. 65.00 (1-873938-43-8, Pub. by Garnet Pubng Ltd UK) Paul & Co Pubs.

— Travels Through Arabia & Other Countries in the East, Vol. 2. (Folios Archive Library). (Illus.). 456p. 1994. 65.00 (1-873938-54-3, Pub. by Garnet Pubng Ltd UK) Paul & Co Pubs.

Niebuhr, Gary W. A Reader's Guide to the Private Eye Novel. LC 93-22212. (Reader's Guides to Mystery Novels Ser.). 323p. 1993. text ed. 45.00 (0-8161-1802-7) G K Hall.

Niebuhr, H. Richard. Christ & Culture. 1956. pap. text ed. 13.00 (0-06-130003-9, TB3, Torch) HarpC.

— Faith on Earth. 1989. 22.00 (0-300-04315-5) Yale U Pr.

— Faith on Earth: An Inquiry into the Structure of Human Faith. Niebuhr, Richard R., ed. 136p. (C). 1991. reprint ed. pap. text ed. 11.00 (0-300-05122-0) Yale U Pr.

— The Kingdom of God in America. 247p. 1988. pap. 15.95x (0-8195-6222-X, Wesleyan Univ Pr) U Pr of New Eng.

— Meaning of Revelation. 160p. 1967. pap. 7.00 (0-02-087750-1, Collier S&S) S&S Trade.

— Radical Monotheism & Western Culture: With Supplemental Essays. (Library of Theological Ethics). 112p. 1993. pap. 9.99 (0-664-25326-1) Westminster John Knox.

— The Responsible Self. LC 63-15955. 1978. pap. text ed. 11.00 (0-06-066211-5, RD 266) Harper SF.

Niebuhr, Reinhold. Beyond Tragedy: Essays on the Christian Interpretation of History. 1979. pap. text ed. write for info. (0-684-16410-8, SL38, Scribners) S&S Trade.

— Beyond Tragedy: Essays on the Christian Interpretation of History. LC 76-167397. (Essay Index Reprint Ser.). 1977. reprint ed. 26.95 (0-8369-2437-1) Ayer.

— The Children of Light & the Children of Darkness. 190p. (C). 1977. pap. write for info. (0-02-387530-5, Scribners) S&S Trade.

— Christian Realism & Political Problems. LC 75-128062. 203p. 1977. reprint ed. 25.00 (0-678-02757-9) Kelley.

— The Contribution of Religion to Social Work. LC 74-172444. reprint ed. 20.00 (0-404-04708-4) AMS Pr.

— Faith & History: A Comparison of Christian & Modern Views of History. 272p. 1977. text ed. 35.00 (0-684-15318-1, Scribners) S&S Trade.

— An Interpretation of Christian Ethics. 1986. reprint ed. pap. text ed. 12.00 (0-8164-2206-0) Harper SF.

— Irony of American History. 192p. 1982. text ed. 30.00 (0-684-17602-5, Scribners) S&S Trade.

— Leaves from the Notebook of a Tamed Cynic. LC 79-2992. (Harper's Ministers Paperback Library). 224p. 1980. pap. 7.95 (0-06-066231-X, RD 311) Harper SF.

— Leaves from the Notebook of a Tamed Cynic. LC 76-27833. (Prelude to Depression Ser.). 1976. reprint ed. lib. bdg. 25.00 (0-306-70852-3) Da Capo.

— Leaves from the Notebook of a Tamed Cynic. (American Biography Ser.). 198p. 1991. reprint ed. lib. bdg. 59.00 (0-7812-8299-3) Rprt Serv.

— Leaves from the Notebook of a Tamed Cynic. 152p. 1990. reprint ed. pap. 10.99 (0-664-25164-1) Westminster John Knox.

— Man's Nature & His Communities: Essays on the Dynamics & Enigmas of Man's Personal & Social Existence. 96p. (C). 1988. pap. 14.50 (0-8191-6743-6) U Pr of Amer.

— Moral Man & Immoral Society. 22.75 (0-8446-6221-6) Peter Smith.

— Moral Man & Immoral Society: A Study in Ethics & Politics. 320p. 1930. pap. 11.95 (0-684-71857-X, Scribners) S&S Trade.

— Pious & Secular America. LC 79-128063. 150p. 1977. reprint ed. 25.00 (0-678-02756-0) Kelley.

— Reinhold Niebuhr & the Issues of Our Time. Harries, Richard, ed. LC 86-180530. 215p. reprint ed. pap. 61.30 (0-7837-3188-4, 2042792) Bks Demand.

— Structure of Nations & Empires: A Study of the Recurring Patterns & Problems of the Political Order in Relation to the Unique Problems of the Nuclear Age. LC 72-128064. xi, 306p. 1977. reprint ed. 37.50 (0-678-02755-2) Kelley.

— The World Crisis & American Responsibility. Lefever, Ernest W., ed. LC 74-10643. 128p. 1974. reprint ed. text ed. 35.00 (0-8371-7649-2, NIWC, Greenwood Pr) Greenwood.

Niebuhr, Reinhold & Heimert, Alan. A Nation So Conceived: Reflections on the History of America from Its Early Visions to Its Present Power. LC 83-10708. 155p. 1983. reprint ed. text ed. 39.75 (0-313-23866-9, NINA, Greenwood Pr) Greenwood.

Niebuhr, Reinhold & Niebuhr, Ursula M. Justice & Mercy. 160p. 1991. pap. 7.99 (0-664-25170-6) Westminster John Knox.

Niebuhr, Richard H. The Social Sources of Denominationalism. 1984. 22.50 (0-8446-6150-3) Peter Smith.

Niebuhr, Richard R., ed. see Niebuhr, H. Richard.

Niebuhr, Ursula M., jt. auth. see Niebuhr, Reinhold.

Niebur, Jay E. & Fell, James E., Jr. Arthur Redman Wilfley: Miner, Inventor, & Entrepreneur. (Illus.). xii, 245p. 1981. pap. 8.95 (0-942576-25-X) CO Hist Soc.

Nieburgs, Herbert E., ed. see International Symposium on Detection & Prevention of Cancer Staff.

Niebyl, Jennifer R., jt. auth. see Russell, Keith P.

Niebyl, Karl H. Studies in the Classical Theories of Money. LC 70-173795. reprint ed. 18.75 (0-404-04709-2) AMS Pr.

Niebylski, Dianna C. The Poem on the Edge of the Word: The Limits of Language & the Uses of Silence in the Poetry of Mallarme, Rilke & Vallejo. LC 93-9536. (Studies in Modern Poetry: Vol. 1). 180p. 1993. 41.95 (0-8204-2107-3) P Lang Pubs.

Niechoda, Irene. A Sourcery for Books One & Two of B. P. Nichol's The Martyrology. 214p. (C). 1992. pap. text ed. 25.00 (1-55022-102-7, Pub. by ECW Press CN) Genl Dist Srvs.

Niecks, Frederick. Programme Music in the Last Four Centuries. LC 68-25299. (Studies in Music: No. 42). 1969. reprint ed. lib. bdg. 75.00 (0-8383-0311-0) M S G Haskell Hse.

— Programme Music in the Last Four Centuries: A Contribution to the History of Musical Expression. 548p. 1990. reprint ed. lib. bdg. 99.00 (0-7812-9122-4) Rprt Serv.

— Robert Schumann. LC 74-24167. (Dent's International Library of Books on Music). reprint ed. 39.50 (0-404-13065-8) AMS Pr.

Niedbala, W. Phthiracaroidea (Acari, Oribatida) Systematic Studies. 620p. 1991. 257.00 (0-444-98705-3) Elsevier.

Niedecker, Lorine. From This Condensery: The Complete Poems of Lorine Niedecker. Bertholf, Robert, ed. LC 85-80301. 336p. 1985. 30.00 (0-912330-57-0) Jargon Soc.

— From This Condensery: The Complete Poems of Lorine Niedecker. limited ed. Bertholf, Robert, ed. LC 85-80301. 336p. 1985. 100.00 (0-912330-58-9) Jargon Soc.

— The Granite Pail. LC 85-60860. 128p. 1985. pap. 11.95 (0-86547-215-7, North Pt Pr) FS&G.

Niedenthal, Paula M. & Kitayama, Shinobu, eds. The Heart's Eye: Emotional Influences in Perception & Attention. (Illus.). 289p. 1994. text ed. 55.00 (0-12-410560-2) Acad Pr.

Nieder, John & Thompson, Thomas. Forgive & Love Again. 1991. pap. 7.99 (0-89081-934-3) Harvest Hse.

Nieder, Philip C. The Cochlea As an Opto-Acoustic Device: A Unified Theory for the Function of the End Organ of Hearing in Mammals. LC 74-29191. (Illus.). 1974. 2.00 (0-915176-05-X) Woods Hole Pr.

Niederehe, Hans J., jt. auth. see Quilis, Antonio.

***Niederehe, Hans-Josef.** Bibliografia Cronologica de la Linguistica, la Gramatica y la Lexicografia del Espanol Desde los Principos Hasta el Ano 1600 (BICRES) Scholarly Edition. LC 94-36633. (Studies in the History of the Language Sciences: No. 76). (SPA.). 1994. lib. bdg. 100.00x (1-55619-612-1) Benjamins North Am.

Niederehe, Hans Josef & Haarmann, Harald, eds. In Memoriam Friedrich Diez: Proceedings of the Colloquium for the History of Romance Studies, Trier Oct. 2-4, 1975. (Studies in the History of Linguistics: No. 9). viii, 508p. 1976. 87.00x (90-272-0900-6) Benjamins North Am.

Niederehe, Hans-Josef & Koerner, E. F., eds. History & Historiography of Linguistics: Proceedings of the Fourth International Conference on the History of the Language Sciences, Trier, 24-28 August 1987, 2 vols., Set. LC 90-42546. (Studies in the History of the Language Sciences: Vol. 51). 1990. 236.00x (90-272-4534-7) Benjamins North Am.

— History & Historiography of Linguistics: Proceedings of the Fourth International Conference on the History of the Language Sciences, Trier, 24-28 August 1987, 2 vols., Vol. 1. LC 90-42546. (Studies in the History of the Language Sciences: Vol. 51). xii, 394p. 1990. write for info. (90-272-4541-X) Benjamins North Am.

— History & Historiography of Linguistics: Proceedings of the Fourth International Conference on the History of the Language Sciences, Trier, 24-28 August 1987, 2 vols., Vol. 2. LC 90-42546. (Studies in the History of the Language Sciences: Vol. 51). x, 452p. 1990. write for info. (90-272-4542-8) Benjamins North Am.

Niederer, Frances J. Hollins College: An Illustrated History. 2nd ed. LC 85-1785. (Illus.). 225p. 1986. 19.50x (0-8139-1083-8) U Pr of Va.

Niederhauser, Emil. The Rise of Nationality in Eastern Europe. 340p. 1982. 45.00 (0-317-54550-7, Pub. by Collets UK) Pro-Am Music.

Niederhauser, Hans R. & Frohlich, Margaret. Form Drawing. (Illus.). 57p. (Orig.). (J). 1974. pap. 10.00 (0-318-41110-5) Merc Pr NY.

Niederhauser, Warren D. & Meyer, E. Gerald, eds. Legal Rights of Chemists & Engineers. LC 77-9364. (Advances in Chemistry Ser.: No. 161). 1977. 24.95 (0-8412-0357-1); pap. 14.95 (0-8412-0537-X) Am Chemical.

Niederhellamnn, Annette. Arzt und Heilkunde in den fruhmittelalterlichen Leges: Eine Wort- und Sachkundliche Untersuchung, Vol. 12. 3053p. 1983. 142.35 (3-11-009607-2) De Gruyter.

Niederhoffer, Arthur, jt. auth. see Bloch, Herbert A.

Niederhoffer, Elaine, jt. auth. see Blumberg, Abraham S.

Niederhuber, John E., ed. Current Therapy in Oncology. LC 92-49914. (Current Therapy Ser.). 663p. 1992. 99.00 (1-55664-229-6) Mosby Yr Bk.

Niederland, William G. The Schreber Case: Psychoanalytic Profile of a Paranoid Personality. (Illus.). 196p. 1984. reprint ed. 29.95 (0-88163-025-X) Analytic Pr.

Niederland, William G. & Sholevar, Bahman. The Creative Process: A Psychoanalytic Discussion. LC 82-73946. (Criticism, Literary & Psychoanalytic Ser.). (Illus.). 90p. (Orig.). 1982. pap. 5.95 (0-911323-03-1) Concourse Pr.

Niederlander, Carol, et al. Practical Writing. 416p. (C). 1986. pap. text ed. 26.00 (0-03-071111-8) HB Coll Pubs.

Niederlehner, B. R., jt. auth. see Cairns, John, Jr.

Niederlinski, A., et al. EFPI - Expert for Process Identification: Software & User's Manual. 1994. text ed. 78.00 (981-02-1272-0) World Scientific Pub.

Niederman, Michael S., ed. Respiratory Infections in the Elderly. 400p. 1991. 68.50 (0-88167-817-1) Raven.

Niederman, Michael S., et al. Respiratory Infections: A Scientific Basis for Management. LC 93-35615. (Illus.). 688p. 1994. text ed. 129.00 (*0-7216-4347-7*) Saunders.

Niederman, Sharon. Hellish Relish: Sizzling Salsas & Devilish Dips from the Kitchens of New Mexico. LC 93-41280. 96p. 1994. 16.00 (*0-06-258539-8*) Harper SF.

— A Quilt of Words: Women's Diaries, Letters, & Original Accounts of Life in the Southwest, 1860-1960. LC 88-81621. 240p. 1988. pap. 10.95 (*1-55566-047-9*) Johnson Bks.

Niederman, Sharon, ed. Shaking Eve's Tree: Short Stories of Jewish Women. 290p. 1990. text ed. 27.50 (*0-8276-0356-8*); pap. 14.95 (*0-8276-0369-X*) JPS Phila.

Niederman, Sharon & Sagan, Miriam, eds. New Mexico Poetry Renaissance. (Illus.). 216p. 1994. pap. 14.95 (*1-878610-41-4*) Red Crane Bks.

***Niedermayer, Oskar & Sinnott, Richard, eds.** Public Opinion & International Governance. (Beliefs in Government Ser.: No. 2). (Illus.). 328p. 1995. 59.00 (*0-19-827958-2*) OUP.

Niedermayer, Walter. Into the Deep Misty Woods of the Ardennes. (Illus.). 170p. (Orig.). (YA). 1990. pap. text ed. 13.50 (*0-935648-30-5*) Halldin Pub.

— Remagen & Other Rhine Crossings. (Illus.). 67p. 1993. 9.95 (*0-935648-45-3*) Halldin Pub.

Niedermeier, Lynn, jt. auth. see Vest, Herb D.

Niedermeyer, E., ed. Epilepsy: Recent View on Its Theory, Diagnosis & Therapy of Epilepsy. (Modern Problems of Pharmacopsychiatry Ser.: Vol. 4). 1970. 83.25 (*3-8055-0529-9*) S Karger.

Niedermeyer, Ernst. The Epilepsies: Diagnosis & Management. (Illus.). 416p. 1990. 75.00 (*0-683-06513-0*) Williams & Wilkins.

Niedermeyer, Ernst & Da Silva, Fernando L., eds. Electroencephalography: Basic Principles, Clinical Applications, & Related Fields. 3rd rev. ed. LC 93-3005. (Illus.). 1189p. 1993. 155.00 (*0-683-06511-4*) Williams & Wilkins.

Niedermiller-Chaffins. Network Training Guide: Managing Netware Systems. 3rd ed. 856p. 1994. Incl. diskette. disk 70.00 (*1-56205-366-3*) New Riders Pub.

***Niedermiller-Chaffins, Debra.** Network Training Guide: Networking Technologies. 3rd ed. LC 94-33319. 600p. 1994. disk, pap. 70.00 (*1-56205-363-9*) New Riders Pub.

***Niedernostheide, F. J., ed.** Nonlinear Dynamics & Pattern Formation in Semiconductors & Devices. (Proceedings in Physics Ser.: Vol. 79). 272p. 1995. 89.00 (*0-387-58833-7*) Spr-Verlag.

— Nonlinear Dynamics & Pattern Formation in Semiconductors & Devices: Proceedings of the International Conference, Noorwijkerhout, the Netherlands, July 4-7, 1994. LC 95-2680. 1995. 89.00 (*3-540-58833-7*) Spr-Verlag.

Niederreiter, H., jt. auth. see Kuipers, Lauwerens.

Niederreiter, Harald, jt. auth. see Lidl, Rudolf.

Niederrieter, Harald. Random Number Generation & Quasi-Monte Carlo Methods. LC 92-12567. (CBMS-NSF Regional Conference Ser.: No. 63). vi, 241p. 1992. pap. 36.50 (*0-89871-295-5*) Soc Indus-Appl Math.

Niednagel, Jonathan P. Your Best Sport: How to Choose & Play It. LC 92-60519. (Illus.). 392p. (Orig.). 1992. pap. 19.95 (*0-916309-01-0*) Laguna Pr.

Niedner, Marie & Von Reden, Gussi. Knitted Lace. Kliot, Kaethe, ed. & tr. by. Orig. Title: Kunst-Stricken. (Illus.). 80p. 1993. pap. 12.00 (*0-916896-53-6*) Lacis Pubns.

Niedt, Friederich E. The Musical Guide, Pts. I-III: 1700-1721. Taylor, Irmgard C., ed. Poulin, Pamela L. & Taylor, Irmgard C., trs. (Early Music Ser.). (Illus.). 312p. 1989. 85.00 (*0-19-315251-7*) OUP.

Niedzialkowski, Stephan & Winslow, Jonathan. Beyond the Word: The World of Mime. LC 93-3164. 116p. 1993. pap. 12.95 (*1-879094-23-1*) Momentum Bks.

Niedzielski, Henri, jt. auth. see Mueller, Theodore.

Niedzwecki, John M., jt. ed. see Lutes, Loren D.

Nieft, Jerry W. Studies in Ephesians. (Bible Study Ser.). 36p. 1991. pap. 4.50 (*0-8309-0590-1*) Herald Hse.

— Studies in Galatians. (Bible Study Ser.). (Illus.). 36p. 1990. pap. 4.50 (*0-8309-0570-7*) Herald Hse.

Nieh Hua Ling. People, Twentieth Century. 288p. 1990. pap. text ed. 9.00 (*0-9625118-5-4*) World Scientific Pub.

Nieh, Hua-ling, ed. Literature of the Hundred Flowers: Criticism & Polemics, Vol. 1. LC 80-36748. (Modern Asian Literature Ser.). 338p. reprint ed. pap. 96.40 (*0-8357-4274-1*, 2037072) Bks Demand.

Nieh, Hualing, ed. Literature of the Hundred Flowers, 2 vols., Set. LC 80-36748. (Modern Asian Literature Ser.). 1981. text ed. 135.00 (*0-231-05264-2*) Col U Pr.

— Literature of the Hundred Flowers, 2 vols., Vol. II: Poetry & Fiction. LC 80-36748. (Modern Asian Literature Ser.). 618p. 1981. Vol. II, Poetry & Fiction, 618pp. text ed. 82.50 (*0-231-05076-3*) Col U Pr.

Niehans, Jurg. A History of Economic Theory: Classic Contributions, 1720-1980. LC 89-45489. (Illus.). 592p. 1989. text ed. 70.00x (*0-8018-3834-7*) Johns Hopkins.

— A History of Economic Theory: Classic Contributions, 1720-1980. 592p. 1994. reprint ed. pap. text ed. 25.95x (*0-8018-4976-4*) Johns Hopkins.

— International Monetary Economics. LC 83-14960. 352p. (C). 1984. text ed. 49.50 (*0-8018-3021-4*) Johns Hopkins.

— International Monetary Economics. LC 83-124960. 360p. 1986. reprint ed. pap. text ed. 17.95x (*0-8018-3408-2*) Johns Hopkins.

— The Theory of Money. LC 77-17247. (Illus.). 1980. text ed. 47.50x (*0-8018-2055-3*); pap. text ed. 16.95x (*0-8018-2372-2*) Johns Hopkins.

Niehaus, Earl F. Irish in New Orleans, Eighteen Hundred to Eighteen Sixty. LC 76-6359. (Irish Americans Ser.). 1976. reprint ed. 28.95 (*0-405-09352-7*) Ayer.

Niehaus, J. A. Fukatsu. LC 86-51459. 144p. (Orig.). 1987. pap. 8.00 (*0-916383-16-4*, Univ Edtns) Aegina Pr.

***Niehaus, Jeffrey J.** Covenant & Theophany in the Bible & Ancient Near East. 360p. 1995. pap. 18.99 (*0-310-49471-0*) Zondervan.

Niehaus, Joseph. The Sixth Sense: Practical Tips for Everyday Safety. (Illus.). (Orig.). 1990. pap. 11.95 (*0-933025-19-X*) Blue Bird Pub.

***Niehaus, Joseph & Sakora, Mary.** Hypnosis Unveiled. 82p. (YA). (gr. 7-12). 1994. pap. write for info. (*1-57515-056-5*) PPI Pubng.

Niehaus, R. J. & Price, K. F., eds. Bottom Line Results from Strategic Human Resource Planning. (Illus.). 313p. (C). 1991. 85.00 (*0-306-44187-X*, Plenum Pr) Plenum.

— Creating the Competitive Edge Through Human Resource Applications. LC 87-38076. (Illus.). 280p. 1988. 75.00 (*0-306-42827-X*, Plenum Pr) Plenum.

— Human Resource Strategies for Organizations in Transition. LC 90-6759. (Illus.). 344p. 1990. 85.00 (*0-306-43506-3*, Plenum Pr) Plenum.

Niehaus, Richard J. Strategic Human Resource Planning Applications. 248p. 1987. 75.00 (*0-306-42561-0*, Plenum Pr) Plenum.

Niehaus, Richard J., ed. Human Resource Policy Analysis: Organizational Application. LC 85-6577. 256p. 1985. text ed. 49.95 (*0-275-90218-8*, C0218, Praeger Pubs) Greenwood.

Niehaus, Theodore F. A Biosystematic Study of the Genus Brodiaea (Amaryllidaceae) LC 77-170326. (University of California Publications in Social Welfare: No. 60). (Illus.). 73p. reprint ed. pap. 25.00 (*0-8357-7259-4*, 2030678) Bks Demand.

— A Field Guide to Pacific States Wildflowers. (Peterson Field Guide Ser.). (Illus.). 432p. 1976. 24.95 (*0-395-21624-9*) HM.

— A Field Guide to Pacific States Wildflowers. (Peterson Field Guide Ser.). (Illus.). 432p. 1981. pap. 15.95 (*0-395-31662-6*) HM.

Niehaus, Theodore F. & Ripper, Charles L. Pacific State Wildflowers. (Peterson Field Guide Ser.: No. 22). (Illus.). 432p. 17.95 (*0-317-60659-X*); pap. 12.95 (*0-317-60660-3*) HM.

Niehaus, Theodore F., et al. A Field Guide to Southwestern & Texas Wildflowers. (Peterson Field Guide Ser.). 1984. 20.95 (*0-395-32876-4*); pap. 16.95 (*0-395-36640-2*) HM.

Niehaus, Thomas, et al. Resources for Latin American Jewish Studies: Essays on Using Jewish Reference Sources for the Study of Latin American Jewry; U. S. Library Collections on L. A. Jews; & U. S. Archival Resources for the Study of Jews in L. A. Elkin, Judith L., ed. LC 84-80219. (LAJSA Publication Ser.: No. 1). 59p. (Orig.). 1984. pap. text ed. 10.00 (*0-916921-00-X*) Lat Am Jewish Studies.

***Niehoff, Arthur.** On Becoming Human: A Journey of 5,000, 000 Years. LC 94-92303. (Illus.). 417p. (Orig.). (C). 1995. pap. 12.95 (*0-9643072-1-9*) Hominid Pr.

Niehoff, Arthur H. Another Side of History. LC 89-63072. 1990. 18.95 (*0-87212-233-6*) Libra.

Niehoff, Arthur H., jt. auth. see Arensberg, Conrad M.

Niehoff, M. The Figure of Joseph in Post-Biblical Jewish Literature. LC 91-35676. (Arbeiten zur Geschichte des Antiken Judentums & des Urchristentums Ser.: Vol. 16). 178p. 1992. 51.50 (*90-04-09556-X*) E J Brill.

Niehoff, Richard O. Floyd W. Reeves: Innovative Educator & Distinguished Practitioner of the Art of Public Administration. (Illus.). 348p. (C). 1991. lib. bdg. 47.00 (*0-8191-7921-3*) U Pr of Amer.

Niehr, Herbert. Der Hochste Gott: Alttestamentlicher JHWH-Glaube im Kontext Syrisch-Kanaanaischer Religion des 1.Jahrtausends v. Chr. (Beiheft zur Zeitschrift fuer die Alttestamentliche Wissenschaft Ser.: Band 190). x, 268p. (C). 1990. lib. bdg. 75.40 (*3-11-012342-8*) De Gruyter.

Niehuss, Merith. Arbeiterschaft in Krieg und Inflation: Soziale Schichtung und Lage der Arbeiter in Augsburg und Linz 1910-1925. (Veroeffentlichungen der Historischen Kommission zu Berlin, Band 67, Beitraege zu Inflation und Wiederaufbau in Deutschland und Europa 1914-1924: Band 3). xiv, 308p. (GER.). 1985. 89.25 (*3-11-009660-9*) De Gruyter.

Niejolt, G. Thomas-Lycklama. On the Road for Work: Migratory Workers on the East Coast of the United States. (Ser. on the Development of Societies: Vol. VII). 224p. 1980. lib. bdg. 40.50 (*0-89838-043-X*) Kluwer Ac.

Nieke, M. R., jt. ed. see Driscoll, S. T.

Niekisch, E. A., ed. see Burkel, E.

Niekro, Phil & Bird, Tom. Knuckleballs. LC 86-9902. 232p. 1986. 16.95 (*0-88191-042-2*) Freundlich.

Niel, A. The Man in Revolt. 109p. 1973. 4.95 (*0-318-37033-6*) Asia Bk Corp.

Niel, Jean-Francois M. Diccionario de Mitologia Universal, 2 vols. 1266p. 1991. pap. 95.00 (*0-7859-6254-9*, 8476723571) Fr & Eur.

— Diccionario De Mitologia Universal, Vol. 1. 1266p. 1991. pap. 95.00 (*0-7859-6489-4*) Fr & Eur.

— Diccionario de Mitologia Universal, Vol. 2. 1266p. 1991. pap. 95.00 (*0-7859-6255-7*, 8476723598) Fr & Eur.

Niel, Raymonde. French 2201 Workbook Preliminary Edition. 72p. 1992. spiral bd. 9.50 (*0-8403-7304-X*) Kendall-Hunt.

***Nieland, Ruth A. & Thuronyi, George F.** Answering the Call: The Telephone Pioneers Talking-Book Machine-Repair Program. LC 94-31658. 1994. pap. text ed. write for info. (*0-8444-0839-5*) Lib Congress.

Nield, D. A. & Bejan, Adrian. Convection in Porous Media. (Illus.). 424p. 1991. 69.00 (*0-387-97651-5*) Spr-Verlag.

Nield, Dorothea. Adventures in Patchwork. 84p. 1976. 8.95 (*0-263-05591-4*) Transatl Arts.

Nield, J. A Guide to the Best Historical Novels & Tales. 1972. 59.95 (*0-8490-0270-2*) Gordon Pr.

Nield, Jill S. & Houseman, Ginger. Fundamentals of Dental Hygiene Instrumentation. 2nd ed. LC 87-25975. (Illus.). 521p. 1988. pap. text ed. 35.95 (*0-8121-1130-3*) Williams & Wilkins.

Nield, R. Open-End Spinning. 56p. 1975. 40.00 (*0-686-63778-X*) St Mut.

Nield, Sarah. The Hong Kong Conveyancing & Property Ordinance. 414p. 1988. 119.00 (*0-409-99540-1*) Butterworth Legal Pubs.

Nieli, Russell. Wittgenstein: From Mysticism to Ordinary Language: A Study of Viennese Positivism & the Thought of Ludwig Wittgenstein. LC 86-23144. (SUNY Series in Philosophy). 261p. 1987. 59.50 (*0-88706-397-7*); pap. 19.95 (*0-88706-398-5*) State U NY Pr.

Nieli, Russell, ed. Racial Preference & Racial Justice: The New Affirmative Action Controversy. 544p. (C). 1991. 25.95 (*0-89633-147-4*) Ethics & Public Policy.

Niello, J. F., et al. Nuclear Physics: Proceedings of the 15th Workshop. 400p. 1993. text ed. 114.00 (*981-02-1374-3*) World Scientific Pub.

***Niels Bohr Library Staff.** Guide to the Archival Collections in the Niels Bohr Library at the American Institute of Physics. LC 94-28569. (International Catalog of Sources for History of Physics & Allied Science Ser.: Rept. 7). 1995. 140.00 (*1-56396-379-5*) Am Inst Physics.

Nielsen. Album of Nine Songs. Date not set. pap. 19.95 (*0-685-69294-9*, Pub. by Wilhelm Hansen DK) Music Sales.

— Direct Integral Theory. (Lecture Notes in Pure & Applied Mathematics Ser.: Vol. 61). 184p. 1980. 99.75 (*0-8247-6971-6*) Dekker.

— Illustrated Dictionary of Ground-Water Science. 1995. write for info. (*0-87371-446-6*) Lewis Pubs.

— Jeremy's Muffler. 1995. 16.00 (*0-689-80319-2*) Macmillan.

— Polymer Rheology. 216p. 1977. 110.00 (*0-8247-7550-3*) Dekker.

Nielsen, A. & Belcher, R. Kinetics of Precipitation. LC 64-15738. (International Series Mono on Analytical Chemistry: Vol. 18). 1964. 72.00 (*0-08-010735-4*, Pub. by Pergamon Repr UK) Franklin.

Nielsen, Alan. The Great Victorian Sacrilege: Preachers, Politics & "The Passion," 1879-1884. LC 90-53514. (Illus.). 304p. 1991. lib. bdg. 35.00x (*0-89950-586-4*) McFarland & Co.

Nielsen, Aldon L. Reading Race: White American Poets & Racial Discourse in the Twentieth Century. LC 88-3942. (South Atlantic Modern Language Association Award Study). 192p. 1990. pap. 12.00 (*0-8203-1273-8*) U of Ga Pr.

— Writing Between the Lines: Race & Intertextuality. LC 93-23000. 312p. 1994. 45.00 (*0-8203-1603-2*) U of Ga Pr.

Nielsen, Alfred C. Life in American Denmark. Scott, Franklyn D., ed. LC 78-15843. (Scandinavians in America Ser.). (Illus.). 1979. reprint ed. lib. bdg. 17.95 (*0-405-11655-1*) Ayer.

Nielsen, Anders, ed. see Aika, K.

Nielsen, Andreas. The German Air Force General Staff. Kennedy, Edward P., ed. (USAF Historical Studies: No. 173). 301p. 1959. reprint ed. pap. text ed. 32.95 (*0-89126-135-4*) MA-AH Pub.

— German Air Force General Staff. LC 68-22551. (German Air Force in World War 2 Ser.). 1968. reprint ed. 19.95 (*0-405-00043-X*) Ayer.

Nielsen, Andreas L. The Collection & Evaluation of Intelligence for the German Air Force High Command: Karlsruhe Study. (USAF Historical Studies: No. 171). 224p. 1955. reprint ed. pap. text ed. 27.00 (*0-89126-143-5*) MA-AH Pub.

***Nielsen, Arnold T.** Nitrocarbons. LC 94-41183. (Organic Nitro Chemistry Ser.). 1995. 115.00 (*1-56081-681-3*) VCH Pubs.

Nielsen, Arnold T., jt. ed. see Feuer, Henry.

***Nielsen, Arya.** Gua Sha: Traditional Technique for Modern Practice. LC 95-7286. 1995. write for info. (*0-443-05181-X*) Churchill.

Nielsen, Ashleea. Dolphin Tribe: Remembering the Human-Dolphin Connection. Patton, Sara, ed. 136p. (Orig.). 1993. pap. 12.95 (*0-9637429-3-0*) Dancing Dolphin.

***Nielsen, B. K.** English-Danish Comprehensive Dictionary. 1203p. (DAN & ENG.). 1994. write for info. (*0-7859-8756-8*) Fr & Eur.

— English-Danish Dictionary: Engelsk-Dansk Ordbog. (DAN & ENG.). 1981. 195.00 (*0-8288-4651-0*, M1270) Fr & Eur.

***Nielsen, Birgit.** Living Language German All the Way 2: Conversation, Grammar, Culture, Reading, Writing, Business. Schier, Helga & Suffrendini, Ana, eds. LC 95-5241. (Living Language Ser.). 1995. 15.00 (*0-517-88291-4*, Crown) Crown Pub Group.

Nielsen, Carl. For Young & Old, Bk. 1. Date not set. pap. 9.95 (*0-685-69060-1*, Pub. by Wilhelm Hansen DK) Music Sales.

— For Young & Old, Bk. 2. Date not set. pap. 9.95 (*0-685-69061-X*, Pub. by Wilhelm Hansen DK) Music Sales.

— Orchestral Studies, Vol. 2. Date not set. pap. 8.95 (*0-685-69111-X*, Pub. by Wilhelm Hansen DK) Music Sales.

— Orchestral Studies, Vol. 3. Date not set. pap. 8.95 (*0-685-69112-8*, Pub. by Wilhelm Hansen DK) Music Sales.

Nielsen, Cindy. In Pictures Glacier: The Continuing Story. LC 93-77022. (Illus.). 48p. 1993. pap. 6.95 (*0-88714-067-X*) KC Pubns.

***Nielsen, Claus.** Animal Evolution: Interrelationships of the Living Phyla. (Illus.). 528p. 1995. 85.00 (*0-19-854868-0*); pap. 40.00 (*0-19-854867-2*) OUP.

— Entoprocts. LC 88-29791. (Synopses of the British Fauna Ser.: No. 41). (Illus.). 131p. 1989. pap. text ed. 44.75 (*90-04-08886-5*) E J Brill.

Nielsen, Cynthia, jt. auth. see Hayden, Elizabeth W.

Nielsen, D. & Aller, L. Methods for Determining the Mechanical Integrity of Class II Injection Wells. 261p. 1984. 25.00 (*1-56034-032-0*, T164) Natl Water Well.

Nielsen, D. R., jt. auth. see Stewart, B. A.

Nielsen, David M., ed. Practical Handbook of Ground Water Monitoring. (Illus.). 920p. 1991. 89.95 (*0-87371-124-6*, TD426) Lewis Pubs.

Nielsen, David M. & Johnson, Ivan A., eds. Ground Water & Vadose Zone Monitoring, STP-1053. LC 89-17992. (Illus.). 312p. 1990. text ed. 49.00 (*0-8031-1275-0*, 04-010530-38) ASTM.

Nielsen, Donald W., jt. auth. see Yost, William A.

Nielsen, Dorothy & Evans, Claudia. My Child, My Friend. pap. 4.95 (*1-55503-273-7*, 0111813) Covenant Comms.

Nielsen, Duke. Partnering with Employees: A Practical System for Building Empowered Relationships. LC 93-3775. (Management Ser.). 130p. 1993. 27.95 (*1-55542-565-8*) Jossey-Bass.

Nielsen, Dulcimer, jt. auth. see James, Ed.

Nielsen, E. H. English-Danish. 3rd ed. 275p. 1987. reprint ed. pap. 33.00 (*87-01-95151-3*) IBD Ltd.

Nielsen, E. Hoegh. Dansk-Engelsk Ordbog: Danish & English. 4th ed. 336p. (DAN & ENG.). 1983. 49.95 (*0-8288-0528-8*, M1272) Fr & Eur.

Nielsen, E. Schmidt, jt. auth. see Traugott-Olsen, E.

Nielsen, Ebbe S. & Kristensen, Niels P. Primitive Ghost Moths. (Monographs on Australian Lepidoptera: Vol. 1). (Illus.). 230p. (C). 1989. text ed. 70.00 (*0-643-04999-1*, Pub. by CSIRO AT) Intl Spec Bk.

Nielsen, Ebbe S., jt. auth. see Robinson, Gaden S.

Nielsen, Elaine. Ogallala: A Century on the Trail, Vol. 1. (Illus.). 102p. 1984. 12.95 (*0-9614379-0-1*) Keith County Hist.

***Nielsen, Elaine A.** Waiting for the Harvest. LC 94-73475. 123p. (Orig.). (YA). (gr. 9-12). 1994. pap. 12.00 (*0-9625040-7-6*) Legendary Pub.

Nielsen, Erik & Nielsen, Hans F. Irregularities in Modern English: NOWELE Suppl. No. 2. 359p. (Orig.). 1986. pap. 30.00 (*87-7492-566-0*, Pub. by Odense Universitets Forlag DK) Coronet Bks.

Nielsen, Gary, intro. Borderline & Acting-Out Adolescents: A Developmental Approach. LC 81-20223. (Illus.). 256p. 1983. 35.95 (*0-89885-109-2*) Human Sci Pr.

Nielsen, George R. In Search of a Home: Nineteenth-Century Wendish Immigration. LC 89-31217. (Illus.). 232p. 1989. 19.95 (*0-89096-400-9*) Tex A&M Univ Pr.

Nielsen, Greg. Beyond Pendulum Power: Entering the Energy World. LC 88-70068. (Illus.). 153p. (Orig.). 1988. pap. 9.95 (*0-9619917-0-4*) Conscious Bks.

— MetaBusiness: Creating a New Global Culture. LC 90-86068. (Illus.). 136p. 1991. pap. 9.95 (*0-9619917-2-0*) Conscious Bks.

— Tuning to the Spiritual Frequencies. LC 89-91602. (Illus.). 224p. (Orig.). 1990. pap. 12.95 (*0-9619917-1-2*) Conscious Bks.

***Nielsen, Greg & Panza-Ella, Tracy.** Mother Earth Speaks: The Official Earth Day Book. 128p. 1995. pap. 14.95 (*0-9619917-3-9*) Conscious Bks.

Nielsen, Greg & Polansky, Joseph. Pendulum Power. 128p. (Orig.). 1987. pap. 8.95 (*0-89281-157-9*) Inner Tradit.

Nielsen, H. A. Where the Passion Is: A Reading of Kierkegaard's Philosophical Fragments. LC 83-6923. 209p. 1983. 27.95 (*0-8130-0742-9*) U Press Fla.

Nielsen, H. Dean, jt. ed. see Gopinathan, S.

Nielsen, H. O., ed. Environment & Pollution Measurement Sensors & Systems. 1990. 53.00 (*0-8194-0316-4*, VOL. 1269) SPIE.

Nielsen-Hamilton, Marit & Monroy, Alberto, eds. Current Topics in Developmental Biology, Vol. 24: Growth Factors & Development. 347p. 1990. text ed. 83.00 (*0-12-153124-4*) Acad Pr.

Nielsen, Hans F. The Germanic Languages: Origins & Early Dialectual Interrelations. rev. ed. LC 88-20795. 192p. (C). 1989. pap. 16.50 (*0-8173-0423-1*) U of Ala Pr.

Nielsen, Hans F., jt. ed. see Juul, Arne.

Nielsen, Hans F., jt. auth. see Nielsen, Erik.

Nielsen, Harald. Ancient Ophthamological Agents. (Acta Historica Scientarium Ser.: No. 31). 117p. (Orig.). 1974. pap. 24.00 (*87-7492-108-8*, Pub. by Odense Universitets Forlag DK) Coronet Bks.

Nielsen Hayden, Patrick, ed. see Nielsen Hayden, Teresa.

Nielsen Hayden, Teresa. Making Book. Nielsen Hayden, Patrick, ed. LC 93-87492. (Boskone Bks.). 160p. 1994. pap. 9.95 (*0-915368-55-2*) New Eng SF Assoc.

Nielsen, Helen. Detour. LC 87-70476. 192p. 1988. reprint ed. pap. 4.95 (*0-88739-080-3*, Blk Lizard) Creat Arts Bk.

— Sing Me a Murder. LC 87-70477. 176p. 1988. reprint ed. pap. 4.95 (*0-88739-079-X*, Blk Lizard) Creat Arts Bk.

Nielsen, Helle, ed. see Kurtzman, Harvey & Downs, Sarah.

Nielsen, Inge. Thermae Et Balnea: The Architecture & Cultural History of Roman Public Baths, 2 vols., Set. (Illus.). 400p. 1991. 125.00 (*87-7288-212-3*, Pub. by Aarhus Univ Pr DK) Coronet Bks.

Nielsen, J. Designing User Interfaces for International Use. (Advances in Human Factors-Ergonomics Ser.: No. 13). 230p. 1990. 107.75 (*0-444-88428-9*) Elsevier.

Nielsen, J. & Villadsen, J. Bioreaction Engineering Principles. (Illus.). 440p. 1994. 79.50 (*0-306-44688-X*, Plenum Pr) Plenum.

Nielsen, J., jt. auth. see Schmid, W.

Nielsen, J. Rud, ed. see Bohr, Niels.

Nielsen, Jack N. Missile Aerodynamics. 468p. (C). 1988. reprint ed. text ed. 40.00 (*0-9620629-0-1*) Nielsen Engineering & Res Inc.

***Nielsen, Jakob.** Multimedia & Hypertext: The Internet & Beyond. (Illus.). 480p. 1995. pap. text ed. 29.95 (*0-12-518408-5*, AP Prof) Acad Pr.

N

An Asterisk (*) at the beginning of an entry indicates that the title is appearing in BIP for the first time.

— Usability Engineering. (Illus.). 358p. 1993. 39.95 (*0-12-518405-0*, AP Prof) Acad Pr.
— Usability Engineering. (Illus.). 362p. 1994. pap. text ed. 29.95 (*0-12-518406-9*, AP Prof) Acad Pr.
Nielsen, Jakob, ed. Coordinating User Interfaces for Consistency. 144p. 1989. text ed. 43.00 (*0-12-518400-X*) Acad Pr.
Nielsen, Jakob & Mack, Robert L. Usability Inspection Methods. LC 93-48412. 1994. text ed. 44.95 (*0-471-01877-5*) Wiley.
Nielsen, James. Handbook of Federal Drug Law. 2nd ed. LC 91-37918. (Illus.). 225p. 1992. text ed. 33.00 (*0-8121-1439-6*) Williams & Wilkins.
Nielsen, James F., ed. see American Bankers Association Staff.
Nielsen, Jens E. How to Create Your Own Real-Estate Fortune Using Tax Shelters to Protect Your Profits. 4th ed. 126p. 1990. pap. 17.50 (*0-934311-84-6*) Intl Wealth.
— How to Create Your Own Real-Estate Fortune Using Tax Shelters to Protect Your Profits. 5th ed. 126p. 1992. pap. 17.50 (*1-56150-035-6*) Intl Wealth.
— How to Create Your Own Real-Estate Fortune Using Tax Shelters to Protect Your Profits. 6th ed. 126p. 1993. pap. 17.50 (*1-56150-085-2*) Intl Wealth.
— How to Create Your Own Real-Estate Fortune Using Tax Shelters to Protect Your Profits. 7th ed. 126p. 1994. pap. 17.50 (*1-56150-132-8*) Intl Wealth.
Nielsen, Jorgen. Muslims in Western Europe. (Islamic Surveys Ser.). (Illus.). 192p. 1992. 42.50 (*0-7486-0309-3*, Pub. by Edinburgh U Pr UK) Col U Pr.
— Muslims in Western Europe. (Islamic Surveys Ser.). 192p. 1992. pap. 27.50 (*0-685-61122-1*, Pub. by Edinburgh U Pr UK) Col U Pr.
— Muslims in Western Europe. 2nd ed. 192p. 1995. pap. 25.00 (*0-7486-0617-3*, Pub. by Edinburgh U Pr UK) Col U Pr.
Nielsen, Jorgen S., ed. International Documents on Palestine, 1972. 416p. 1975. 34.95 (*0-88728-015-3*) Inst Palestine.
— International Documents on Palestine, 1973. 592p. 1976. 34.95 (*0-88728-016-1*) Inst Palestine.
— International Documents on Palestine, 1974. 605p. 1977. 34.95 (*0-88728-017-X*) Inst Palestine.
Nielsen, Joseph P., jt. auth. see Fontaine, Richard A.
Nielsen, Joyce J. One-Two-Three Release 2.4 Quick Reference. (Quick Reference Ser.). (Illus.). (Orig.). 1992. pap. 9.95 (*0-88022-987-X*) Que.
— One-Two-Three Release 3.4 Quick Reference. 1992. pap. 9.95 (*1-56529-010-0*) Que.
Nielsen, Joyce M. Sex & Gender in Society: Perspectives on Stratification. 2nd ed. 293p. (Orig.). (C). 1990. pap. text ed. 13.95 (*0-88133-456-1*) Waveland Pr.
Nielsen, Joyce M., ed. Feminist Research Methods: Exemplary Readings in the Social Sciences. 262p. (C). 1990. pap. text ed. 21.50 (*0-8133-0577-2*) Westview.
Nielsen, Jurgen S., jt. ed. see Samir, Samir K.
Nielsen, K., jt. ed. see Hanen, M.
Nielsen, Kai. After the Demise of the Tradition: Rorty, Critical Theory, & the Fate of Philosophy. (C). 1991. text ed. 49.50 (*0-8133-8044-8*) Westview.
— Equality & Liberty: A Defense of Radical Egalitarianism. 336p. 1986. 61.50 (*0-8476-6758-8*); pap. 25.00 (*0-8476-7516-5*) Rowman.
— Ethics Without God. rev. ed. 207p. (C). 1989. reprint ed. pap. 18.95x (*0-87975-552-0*) Prometheus Bks.
— God & the Grounding of Morality. (Philosophica Ser.: No. 41). 230p. 1991. pap. 25.00 (*0-7766-0328-0*, Pub. by Univ Ottawa Pr CN) Paul & Co Pubs.
— God, Scepticism & Modernity. (Philosophica Ser.: No. 40). 250p. 1989. pap. 25.00 (*0-7766-0241-1*, Pub. by Univ Ottawa Pr CN) Paul & Co Pubs.
— Introduction to Metaphilosophy. 120p. (C). 1995. text ed. 59.00 (*0-8133-0666-3*) Westview.
— An Introduction to the Philosophy of Religion. LC 82-16843. 200p. 1983. text ed. 29.95 (*0-312-43310-7*) St Martin.
— Philosophy & Atheism. LC 84-63084. (Skeptic's Bookshelf Ser.). 231p. 1985. 29.95x (*0-87975-289-0*) Prometheus Bks.
— Why Be Moral? 300p. 1989. pap. text ed. 19.95 (*0-87975-519-9*) Prometheus Bks.
Nielsen, Kai & Hart, Hendrik. Search for Community in a Withering Tradition. 254p. (C). 1991. lib. bdg. 44.00 (*0-8191-7989-2*); pap. text ed. 25.00 (*0-8191-7990-6*) U Pr of Amer.
Nielsen, Kai & Patten, Stephen C., eds. Marx & Morality. 379p. 1993. pap. 15.00 (*0-919491-01-4*, Pub. by Univ Calgary CN) Paul & Co Pubs.
Nielsen, Kai, jt. auth. see Moreland, J. P.
Nielsen, Kai, jt. ed. see Ware, Robert.
Nielsen, Kjell. Software Development with C Plus Plus: Maximizing Reuse with Object Technology. (Illus.). 450p. 1994. pap. 39.95 (*0-12-518420-4*, AP Prof) Acad Pr.
Nielsen, Klas, jt. ed. see Mendell, Marguerite.
Nielsen, Klaus & Duncan, J. Robert, eds. Animal Brucellosis. 464p. 1990. 240.00 (*0-8493-5878-7*, SF809) CRC Pr.
Nielsen, L. A. Methods of Marking Fish & Shellfish. LC 92-74200. (Special Publication Ser.: No. 23). 208p. 1992. text ed. 39.50 (*0-913235-80-6*) Am Fisheries Soc.
Nielsen, L. A. & Johnson, D. L., eds. Fisheries Techniques. LC 83-71866. 468p. (C). 1983. text ed. 43.50 (*0-913235-00-8*) Am Fisheries Soc.
Nielsen, Laura F. Jeremy's Muffler. (Illus.). (J). 1995. text ed. 15.95 (*0-02-768135-1*, Bradbury S&S) S&S Childrens.
Nielsen, Lawrence E. Predicting the Properties of Mixtures: Mixture Rules in Science & Engineering. LC 77-16705. 108p. reprint ed. pap. 30.80 (*0-8357-3501-X*, 2034557) Bks Demand.
Nielsen, Leon & Brown, Robert D. Translocation of Wild Animals. (Illus.). 353p. 1988. pap. text ed. 19.50 (*0-685-24084-3*) IR Pubns.
Nielsen, Leslie. Leslie Nielsen: The Naked Truth. 1994. pap. 10.00 (*0-671-79578-3*) PB.
— Leslie Nielsen's Stupid Little Golf Book. 1995. 17.50 (*0-385-47598-5*) Doubleday.
Nielsen, Linda. Adolescence: A Contemporary View. 2nd ed. (Illus.). 760p. (C). 1991. text ed. 42.75 (*0-03-032853-5*) HB Coll Pubs.
Nielsen, Lisa C., tr. see Amir, Tami.
Nielsen, Lisa C., tr. see Assaf, Yael.
Nielsen, Lisa C., tr. see Bar, Amos.
Nielsen, Lisa C., tr. see Baram, Bella.
Nielsen, Lisa C., tr. see Blatchford, Claire.
Nielsen, Lisa C., tr. see Burla, Oded.
Nielsen, Lisa C., jt. auth. see Dean, David H.
Nielsen, Lisa C., tr. see Eitan, Ora.
Nielsen, Lisa C., tr. see Fleisher, Gila M.
Nielsen, Lisa C., tr. see Gelbart, Ofra.
Nielsen, Lisa C., tr. see Gelbert, Ofra.
Nielsen, Lisa C., tr. see Griffin, Gail M.
Nielsen, Lisa C., tr. see Harel, Nira.
Nielsen, Lisa C., tr. see Ofek, Uriel.
Nielsen, Lisa C., tr. see Sherrow, Victoria.
Nielsen, Lisa C., tr. see Shinhav, Chaya.
Nielsen, Lynn E., ed. see Osen, Mary E.
Nielsen, M. P. Limit Analysis & Concrete Plasticity. (Illus.). (C). 1984. text ed. 74.00 (*0-13-536623-2*) P-H.
Nielsen, Margaret, ed. see MacHaffie, Ingeborg S.
Nielsen, Margaret A., ed. see MacHaffie, Ingeborg S.
Nielsen Marketing Research Staff. Category Management: Positioning Your Organization to Win. 1993. 27.95 (*0-8442-3489-3*) NTC Pub Grp.
Nielsen, Mary, ed. see Penner, Mil & Schmidt, Carol.
Nielsen, Matt, ed. see Sumeria Staff.
Nielsen-McLellan, Karen L. Ginger Bear's Christmas Cookie Mystery. (Illus.). 32p. (J). (ps-1). 1992. 12.95 (*0-9634851-0-5*) Scand Descent.
Nielsen, Nancy. Black Widow Spider. LC 89-28271. (Wildlife Ser.). (Illus.). 48p. (J). (gr. 5). 1990. text ed. 12.95 (*0-89686-513-4*, Crstwood Hse) Silver Burdett Pr.
— Teen Alcoholism. LC 90-66. (Overview Ser.). (Illus.). 96p. (J). (gr. 5-8). 1990. lib. bdg. 16.95 (*1-56006-121-9*) Lucent Bks.
Nielsen, Nancy, ed. see Fisher, Gary & Cummings, Rhoda.
Nielsen, Nancy, ed. see Keiffer, Ann.
Nielsen, Nancy J. Bicycle Racing. LC 87-30489. (Super-Charged Ser.). (Illus.). 48p. (J). (gr. 5-6). 1988. text ed. 11.95 (*0-89686-361-1*, Crstwood Hse) Silver Burdett Pr.
— Carnivorous Plants. LC 91-34422. (First Bks.). (Illus.). 64p. (J). (gr. 3-6). 1992. lib. bdg. 13.93 (*0-531-20056-6*) Watts.
— Carnivorous Plants. (First Bks.). (Illus.). 64p. (J). (gr. 5-8). 1992. pap. 5.95 (*0-531-15644-3*) Watts.
— Helicopter Pilots. LC 88-12007. (At Risk Ser.). (Illus.). 48p. (J). (gr. 5-6). 1988. text ed. 11.95 (*0-89686-399-9*, Crstwood Hse) Silver Burdett Pr.
— Killer Whales: Orcas of the Pacific Ocean. (Animals & the Environment Ser.). 48p. (J). (gr. 3-4). 1994. lib. bdg. 13.35 (*1-56065-236-5*) Capstone Pr.
Nielsen, Nancy L. Blackberries & Dust. 20p. (Orig.). 1984. pap. 4.00 (*0-914473-01-8*) Stone Man Pr.
— East of the Light. 50p. (Orig.). 1984. pap. 6.95 (*0-914473-02-6*) Stone Man Pr.
Nielsen, Nancy L., jt. auth. see Brooks, Alan.
Nielsen, Nicki J. The Iditarod: Women on the Trail. LC 85-52335. (Illus.). 80p. 1986. pap. 12.00 (*0-9616191-0-4*) Wolfdog Pubns.
Nielsen, Niels. Die Gammafunktion, 2 vols. in 1. Incl. Integrallogarithmus. LC 64-13785. 1965. (*0-318-51338-2*); LC 64-13785. (GER.). 1965. 29.50 (*0-8284-0188-8*) Chelsea Pub.
***Nielsen, Niels C., Jr.** Christianity after Communism: Social, Political & Cultural Struggle in Russia. LC 94-29700. (C). 1994. text ed. 49.95 (*0-8133-2365-7*) Westview.
— Fundamentalism, Mythos, & World Religions. LC 92-37601. 186p. (C). 1993. 59.50 (*0-7914-1653-4*); pap. 19.95 (*0-7914-1654-2*) State U NY Pr.
Nielsen, Norman. Maverick of the Cloth. Van Treese, James B., ed. 384p. 1993. pap. 9.95 (*1-880416-94-8*) NW Pub.
Nielsen, Norman D. The Magic Castle Walls of Fame. (Illus.). 557p. (Orig.). 1987. pap. 24.50 (*0-9618175-0-X*) Nielsen Magic.
Nielsen, Norman R., jt. auth. see Walters, John R.
Nielsen, O. B. Chaos & Networks: Statistical & Probabilistic Aspects. LC 93-3333. 1993. write for info. (*0-412-46530-2*) Chapman & Hall.
Nielsen, P. Coastal Bottom Boundary Layers & Sediment Transport. 250p. 1992. text ed. 64.00 (*981-02-0472-8*); pap. text ed. 32.00 (*981-02-0473-6*) World Scientific Pub.
Nielsen, Patti. Living with It Daily: Meditations for People with Chronic Pain. LC 93-46867. 1994. 9.95 (*0-440-50555-0*) Dell.
Nielsen, Peter. Black Man's Place in South Africa. LC 70-109347. 149p. 1970. reprint ed. text ed. 45.00 (*0-8371-3619-9*, NIB&, Negro U Pr) Greenwood.
— Will of Iron: A Champion's Journey; a Strategy for Fitness. LC 92-27532. (Illus.). 227p. (Orig.). 1992. pap. 14.95 (*1-879094-19-3*) Momentum Bks.
Nielsen, Peter E., ed. Photochemical Probes in Biochemistry. (C). 1989. lib. bdg. 112.50 (*0-7923-0171-4*) Kluwer Ac.
Nielsen, Richard O. Sonar Signal Processing. (Artech House Acoustics Library). 445p. 1991. text ed. 95.00 (*0-89006-453-9*) Artech Hse.
Nielsen, Rick, jt. auth. see Rich, Bill.
***Nielsen, Robert R.** I Am! A New Discovery of Self. LC 95-69596. 64p. (Orig.). 1995. 19.95 (*1-886391-02-5*); pap. text ed. 12.95 (*1-886391-03-3*) Narwhal Pr.
Nielsen, Ruth & Jorgensen, Kurt, eds. Advances in Industrial Ergonomics & Safety 5. 800p. 1993. 210.00 (*0-7484-0061-3*, Pub. by Tay Francis Ltd UK) Taylor & Francis.
Nielsen, Ruth & Szyszczak, Erika. The Social Dimension of the European Community. 238p. (Orig.). 1991. pap. 87.50x (*87-17-03598-8*, Pub. by Almqv & Wiksell SW) Coronet Bks.
Nielsen, Scott. Mallards. (Illus.). 1994. pap. 24.95 (*0-89658-238-8*) Voyageur Pr.
Nielsen, Shelly. Caring. Wallner, Rosemary, ed. LC 91-73044. (Values Matter Ser.). (J). 1992. lib. bdg. 13.99 (*1-56239-064-3*) Abdo & Dghtrs.
— Christmas. Wallner, Rosemary, ed. LC 91-73034. (Holiday Celebrations Ser.). (J). 1992. lib. bdg. 13.99 (*1-56239-067-8*) Abdo & Dghtrs.
— Easter. Wallner, Rosemary, ed. LC 91-73032. (Holiday Celebrations Ser.). (J). 1992. lib. bdg. 13.99 (*1-56239-069-4*) Abdo & Dghtrs.
— Fun with A - a. LC 92-16038. (J). 1992. lib. bdg. 13.99 (*1-56239-134-8*) Abdo & Dghtrs.
— Fun with E - e. LC 92-16041. (J). 1992. lib. bdg. 13.99 (*1-56239-135-6*) Abdo & Dghtrs.
— Fun with I - i. LC 92-16040. (J). 1992. lib. bdg. 13.99 (*1-56239-136-4*) Abdo & Dghtrs.
— Fun with O - o. LC 92-16039. (J). 1992. lib. bdg. 13.99 (*1-56239-137-2*) Abdo & Dghtrs.
— Fun with U - u. LC 92-16042. (J). 1992. lib. bdg. 13.99 (*1-56239-138-0*) Abdo & Dghtrs.
— Gloria Estefan: International Pop Star. LC 93-26000. (Reaching for the Stars Ser.). 1993. lib. bdg. 12.94 (*1-56239-226-3*) Abdo & Dghtrs.
— Halloween. Wallner, Rosemary, ed. LC 91-73031. (Holiday Celebrations Ser.). (J). 1992. lib. bdg. 13.99 (*1-56239-070-8*) Abdo & Dghtrs.
— Hanukkah. Wallner, Rosemary, ed. LC 91-73029. (Holiday Celebrations Ser.). (J). 1992. lib. bdg. 13.99 (*1-56239-072-4*) Abdo & Dghtrs.
— I Love Air. LC 93-7597. (Target Earth Ser.). (J). 1993. lib. bdg. 14.96 (*1-56239-189-5*) Abdo & Dghtrs.
— I Love Air. LC 93-7597. (Target Earth Ser.). (J). 1993. pap. 7.49 (*1-56239-404-5*) Abdo & Dghtrs.
— I Love Dirt. Berg, Julie, ed. LC 93-18956. (Target Earth Ser.). (J). (gr. 3 up). 1993. lib. bdg. 14.96 (*1-56239-188-7*) Abdo & Dghtrs.
— I Love Dirt. Berg, Julie, ed. LC 93-18956. (Target Earth Ser.). (J). (gr. 3 up). 1993. pap. 7.49 (*1-56239-407-X*) Abdo & Dghtrs.
— Independence Day. Wallner, Rosemary, ed. LC 91-73030. (Holiday Celebrations Ser.). (J). 1992. lib. bdg. 13.99 (*1-56239-071-6*) Abdo & Dghtrs.
— Just Victoria. LC 86-2294. (Victoria Ser.). 130p. (J). (gr. 3-7). 1986. pap. 4.99 (*0-89191-609-1*, Chariot Bks) Chariot Family.
— Manners. Wallner, Rosemary, ed. LC 91-73042. (Values Matter Ser.). (J). 1992. lib. bdg. 13.99 (*1-56239-066-X*) Abdo & Dghtrs.
— More Victoria. LC 86-2280. (Victoria Ser.). 130p. (J). (gr. 3-7). 1986. pap. 4.99 (*0-89191-453-6*, Chariot Bks) Chariot Family.
— Only Kidding, Victoria. LC 86-8817. (Victoria Ser.). 130p. (J). (gr. 3-7). 1986. pap. 4.99 (*0-89191-474-9*, Chariot Bks) Chariot Family.
— Playing Fair. Wallner, Rosemary, ed. LC 92-73043. (Values Matter Ser.). (J). 1992. lib. bdg. 13.99 (*1-56239-065-1*) Abdo & Dghtrs.
— Self-Esteem. Wallner, Rosemary, ed. LC 91-73047. (Values Matter Ser.). (J). 1992. lib. bdg. 13.99 (*1-56239-061-9*) Abdo & Dghtrs.
— Sharing. Wallner, Rosemary, ed. LC 91-73045. (Values Matter Ser.). (J). 1992. lib. bdg. 13.99 (*1-56239-063-5*) Abdo & Dghtrs.
— Take a Bow, Victoria. LC 86-8818. (Victoria Ser.). 130p. (J). (gr. 3-7). 1986. pap. 4.99 (*0-89191-470-6*, Chariot Bks) Chariot Family.
— Telling the Truth. Wallner, Rosemary, ed. LC 91-73046. (Values Matter Ser.). (J). 1992. lib. bdg. 13.99 (*1-56239-062-7*) Abdo & Dghtrs.
— Thanksgiving. Wallner, Rosemary, ed. LC 91-73033. (Holiday Celebrations Ser.). (J). 1992. lib. bdg. 13.99 (*1-56239-068-6*) Abdo & Dghtrs.
— Trash! Trash! Trash! Berg, Julie, ed. LC 93-18952. (Target Earth Ser.). (J). 1993. lib. bdg. 14.96 (*1-56239-192-5*) Abdo & Dghtrs.
— Trash! Trash! Trash! Berg, Julie, ed. LC 93-18952. (Target Earth Ser.). (J). 1993. pap. 7.49 (*1-56239-408-8*) Abdo & Dghtrs.
Nielsen, Shelly & Berg, Julie. I Love Water. LC 93-18957. (Target Earth Ser.). (J). 1993. lib. bdg. 14.96 (*1-56239-190-9*) Abdo & Dghtrs.
— I Love Water. LC 93-18957. (Target Earth Ser.). (J). 1993. pap. 7.49 (*1-56239-405-3*) Abdo & Dghtrs.
— Love Earth: The Beauty Makeover. LC 93-18954. (Target Earth Ser.). (J). 1993. lib. bdg. 14.96 (*1-56239-198-4*) Abdo & Dghtrs.
— Love Earth: The Beauty Makeover. LC 93-18954. (Target Earth Ser.). (J). 1993. pap. 7.49 (*1-56239-409-6*) Abdo & Dghtrs.
***Nielsen, Susin.** Melanie. (Degrassi Book Ser.). (YA). 1995. bds. 16.95 (*1-55028-254-9*) Formac Dist Ltd.
— Melanie. (Degrassi Book Ser.). (YA). 1995. pap. 4.95 (*1-55028-256-5*) Formac Dist Ltd.
— Shane. (Degrassi Book Ser.). (YA). 1995. pap. 4.95 (*1-55028-235-2*) Formac Dist Ltd.
— Shane. (Degrassi Book Ser.). (YA). 1995. bds. 16.95 (*1-55028-237-9*) Formac Dist Ltd.
— Snake. (Degrassi Book Ser.). (YA). 1995. pap. 4.95 (*1-55028-368-5*) Formac Dist Ltd.
— Snake. (Degrassi Book Ser.). (YA). 1995. bds. 16.95 (*1-55028-370-7*) Formac Dist Ltd.
— Wheels. (Degrassi Book Ser.). (YA). 1995. pap. 4.95 (*1-55028-360-X*) Formac Dist Ltd.
— Wheels. (Degrassi Book Ser.). (YA). 1995. bds. 16.95 (*1-55028-362-6*) Formac Dist Ltd.
Nielsen, Suzanne & Hui, Y. H. Introduction to the Chemical Analysis of Foods. LC 93-44871. (Health Science Ser.). 700p. (C). 1994. boxed 57.50 (*0-86720-826-0*) Jones & Bartlett.
Nielsen, T. T. Bose Algebras: Complex & Real Wave Representations. (Lecture Notes in Mathematics Ser.: Vol. 1472). v, 132p. 1991. pap. 24.00 (*0-387-54041-5*) Spr-Verlag.
Nielsen, V. C., et al. Odour & Ammonia Emissions from Livestock Farming. 1991. 76.50 (*1-85166-717-2*) Elsevier.
Nielsen, V. C., et al, eds. Odour Preventing & Control of Organic Sludge & Livestock Farming: Proceedings of a Round-Table Seminar, Silso, U. K., 15 April 1985. 404p. 1986. 90.00 (*1-85166-010-0*) Elsevier.
Nielsen, Veneta L. Familiar As a Sparrow. LC 78-55118. 1978. 4.95 (*0-8425-1072-9*) BYU Scholarly.
— Looking for the Blue Rose: A Collection of Poems & Ponderings. 134p. 1990. 14.95 (*0-87421-149-2*) Utah St U Pr.
Nielsen, Virginia. A Faraway Love. 256p. 1982. pap. 2.75 (*0-449-14477-1*, GM) Fawcett.
— Secrets of Bellefleur. (Orig.). 1995. mass mkt. 5.99 (*0-345-38114-9*) Ballantine.
— To Love a Pirate. (Historical Ser.). 1993. mass mkt. 3.99 (*0-373-28761-5*, 1-28761-4) Harlequin Bks.
Nielsen, Waldemar. The Big Foundations. LC 72-3676. (Twentieth Century Fund Study). 475p. 1973. reprint ed. text ed. 54.00 (*0-231-03665-5*); reprint ed. pap. text ed. 20.50 (*0-231-03666-3*) Col U Pr.
Nielsen, Waldemar A. The Endangered Sector. LC 79-15772. 279p. 1979. text ed. 42.00 (*0-231-04688-X*) Col U Pr.
— The Great Powers & Africa. LC 77-83342. 447p. reprint ed. pap. 127.40 (*0-317-11017-9*, 2002947) Bks Demand.
Nielsen, Waldemar A., jt. auth. see Strassberg, Richard E.
Nielsen, Yvonne V. Verbal Elixirs: Thoughts to Peace of Mind; How to Have Heaven on Earth. 96p. 1991. pap. 16.95 (*0-9630324-0-2*) YV Prods.
Nielson, Aleene B., jt. auth. see Maker, C. June.
Nielson, Bill. Beacon Small-Group Bible Studies, I & II Thessalonians: The Distinguishing Marks of a Christian. 56p. 1981. pap. 3.95 (*0-8341-0738-4*) Beacon Hill.
Nielson, David G. Black Ethos: Northern Urban Negro Life & Thought, 1890-1930. LC 76-47169. (Contributions in Afro-American & African Studies: No. 29). 248p. 1977. text ed. 29.95 (*0-8371-9402-4*, NBE/, Greenwood Pr) Greenwood.
Nielson, David M. & Sapa, Martin N., eds. Current Practices in Ground Water & Vabose Zone Investigations. (Special Technical Publication Ser.: STP 1118). (Illus.). 435p. 1992. text ed. 49.00 (*0-8031-1462-1*, 04-011180-38) ASTM.
Nielson, Denis P., jt. auth. see Chatfield, Michael.
Nielson, Flemming & Nielson, Hanne R. Two-Level Functional Languages. (Tracts in Theoretical Computer Science Ser.: No. 34). (Illus.). 300p. (C). 1992. 44.95 (*0-521-40384-7*) Cambridge U Pr.
Nielson, Flemming, jt. auth. see Nielson, Hanne R.
Nielson, Greg, jt. auth. see Toth, Max.
Nielson, Gregory M. & Shriver, Bruce. Visualization in Scientific Computing. (Illus.). 304p. 1990. 85.00 (*0-8186-8979-X*, 1979) IEEE Comp Soc.
Nielson, Hanne R. & Nielson, Flemming. Semantics with Applications: A Formal Introduction. 240p. 1992. pap. text ed. 39.95 (*0-471-92980-8*) Wiley.
Nielson, Hanne R., jt. auth. see Nielson, Flemming.
***Nielson, Ingvar.** Wooden Toys: Step-by-Step Plans for over Fifty Colourful Toys. 1994. 18.95 (*1-870586-05-0*, Pub. by D Porteous Edits UK) Seven Hills Bk.
Nielson, Jakob. Jakob Nielsen: Collected Mathematical Papers, 2 Vols., Set. Hansen, Vagn L. & Topsoe, Fleming, eds. (Contemporary Mathematicians Ser.). 1986. lib. bdg. 160.00 (*0-8176-3152-6*) Birkhauser.
— Jakob Nielsen: Collected Mathematical Papers, 2 Vols., Vol. 1. Hansen, Vagn L. & Topsoe, Fleming, eds. (Contemporary Mathematicians Ser.). 472p. 1986. lib. bdg. 100.00 (*0-8176-3140-2*) Birkhauser.
— Jakob Nielsen: Collected Mathematical Papers, 2 Vols., Vol. 2. Hansen, Vagn L. & Topsoe, Fleming, eds. (Contemporary Mathematicians Ser.). 432p. 1986. lib. bdg. 100.00 (*0-8176-3151-8*) Birkhauser.
Nielson, James. Unread Herrings: Thomas Nashe & the Prosaics of the Real. LC 93-31708. (Renaissance & Baroque Studies & Texts: Vol. 11). 224p. 1994. 43.95 (*0-8204-2254-1*) P Lang Pubs.
Nielson, James, tr. see Serres, Michel.
Nielson, Jane E. & Nakata, John K. Mantle Origin & Flow Sorting of Megacryst-Xenolith Inclusions in Mafic Dikes of Blake Canyon, Arizona. No. 1541. 1993. write for info. (*0-318-71675-5*) US Geol Survey.
Nielson, John B. Beacon Small Group Bible Studies, Zehariah-Malachi: Prisoners of Hope. 80p. (Orig.). 1986. pap. 3.95 (*0-8341-1100-4*) Beacon Hill.
— The Towel & the Cross. 118p. (Orig.). 1983. pap. 4.95 (*0-8341-0847-X*) Beacon Hill.
Nielson, John M. Beacon Small-Group Bible Studies, Romans: More than Conquerors. Wolf, Earl C., ed. 88p. (Orig.). 1985. pap. 3.95 (*0-8341-0944-1*) Beacon Hill.
Nielson, John M. & Skillings, Otis. Bible Walk. (J). 1980. 5.25 (*0-685-68193-9*, MB-492); audio 10.98 (*0-685-68194-7*, TA-9016C); 6.00 (*0-685-68195-5*, L-9016C) Lillenas.
Nielson, Jon, ed. see Cole, Terrence.

An Asterisk (*) at the beginning of an entry indicates that the title is appearing in BIP for the first time.

***Nielson, Jonathan.** American Historians in War & Peace: Patriotism, Diplomacy & the Paris Peace Conference 1919 Value Pak. (C). 1994. write for info. (0-8403-9585-X); 43.00 (0-8403-9587-6); student ed, pap. text ed. write for info. (0-8403-9586-8) Kendall-Hunt.

Nielson, Jonathan M. Armed Forces on a Northern Frontier: The Military in Alaska's History, 1867-1987. LC 87-31781. (Contributions in Military Studies: No. 74). 301p. 1988. text ed. 49.95 (0-313-26030-3, NAE/, Greenwood Pr) Greenwood.

Nielson, Joyce. One-Two-Three Release 4 for Windows Quick Start. 544p. (Orig.). 1993. pap. 9.95 (0-685-70408-4) Que.

Nielson, K. Textiles for Today's Interiors. 1991. text ed. write for info. (0-442-01202-0) Van Nos Reinhold.

Nielson, Karla J. Window Treatments. (Illus.). 368p. 1990. text ed. 59.95 (0-442-26809-2) Van Nos Reinhold.

Nielson, Karla J. & Taylor, David A. Interiors: An Introduction. 2nd ed. (Illus.). 464p. 1994. pap. write for info. (0-697-12543-2) Brown & Benchmark.

Nielson, Kathleen B. Resting Secure: Poems by David, Solomon, Isaiah, & Habakkuk. (Challenge Bible Study Guides Ser.). 112p. (Orig.). 1993. pap. 4.99 (0-8010-6789-8) Baker Bk.

— This God We Worship: Poems by Moses, Hannah, David, & Hosea. (Challenge Bible Study Guides Ser.). 112p. (Orig.). 1993. pap. 4.99 (0-8010-6787-1) Baker Bk.

Nielson, Kathleen V. No One Prepared Me for This. 130p. (Orig.). 1989. pap. 7.95 (0-317-93837-1) IHC Home Health.

— No One Prepared Me for This. (Orig.). 1991. pap. 9.95 (0-9622967-0-8) IHC Home Health.

Nielson, L. & Landel, eds. Mechanical Properties of Polymers & Composites. 2nd expanded rev. ed. (Mechanical Engineering Ser.: Vol. 90). 544p. 1994. 150.00 (0-8247-8964-4) Dekker.

Nielson, Larry. How Would You Like to See the Slides of My Mission? A Tasteful Collection of Missionary Humor. LC 80-82708. (Illus.). 158p. (Orig.). 1980. pap. 8.98 (0-88290-153-2, 2040) Horizon Utah.

Nielson, Lavrans, illus. Sacred Art of Lavrans Nielson. 32p. (Orig.). 1992. pap. 24.95 (1-55612-461-9) Sheed & Ward MO.

Nielson, Linda. Adolescence: A Contemporary View. 700p. (C). 1986. text ed. 42.75 (0-03-070493-6) HB Coll Pubs.

Nielson, Nancy, jt. auth. see Robinson, James.

Nielson, Niels C., Jr., et al. Religions of the World. 3rd ed. LC 92-50025. (Illus.). 576p. (C). 1993. pap. text ed. 36.00 (0-312-05023-2) St Martin.

***Nielson, Norm.** Guns along the Comstock. Turner, Phyllis, ed. 207p. 1994. pap. 6.95 (0-9625020-4-9) Tales Nevada.

— Tales of Nevada!, Vol. 1. Lonse, Kris, ed. (Illus.). 230p. 1989. pap. 12.95 (0-685-29880-9) Tales Nevada.

— Tales of Nevada, Vol. 1. Lonse, Kris, ed. (Illus.). 230p. 1989. pap. 12.95 (0-9625020-0-6) Tales Nevada.

— Tales of Nevada!, Vol. 2. Wright, Karen, ed. (Illus.). 300p. 1990. pap. 12.95 (0-9625020-1-4) Tales Nevada.

— The West: The Way It Really Was! Nevada. Turner, Phyllis B., ed. 218p. (Orig.). 1994. pap. 12.95 (0-9625020-3-0) Tales Nevada.

Nielson, Norma L., et al. Financial Planning As an Employee Benefit. Brzezinski, Mary Jo, ed. LC 91-76439. 74p. (Orig.). 1991. pap. 37.00 (0-89154-431-3) Intl Found Employ.

Nielson, Norman, jt. auth. see Walters, John R.

Nielson, Palle. The Enchanted City. Morch, Dea T. & Doyle, Judith A., eds. Taylor, Alexander, tr. LC 87-71734. (Printworks Ser.). 72p. (Orig.). 1987. pap. 9.95 (0-915306-75-1) Curbstone.

Nielson, Paul. Inside the Norton Anti Virus: The Official Guide. (Illus.). (Orig.). 1992. pap. 26.95 (0-13-473463-7) Brady Compu Bks.

Nielson, Scott. Season with Eagles. (Illus.). 1994. pap. 16.95 (0-89658-247-7) Voyageur Pr.

Nielson, Stefan, jt. auth. see Thoelke, Shay.

Nielson, Thomas P. T'ang Poet-Monk Chiao-Jan. 64p. 1972. pap. 6.00 (0-939252-01-5) ASU Ctr Asian.

Nielson, Waldo. Right-of-Way: A Guide to Abandoned Railroads in the United States. rev. ed. (Illus.). 220p. 1992. pap. 19.95 (0-89288-001-5) Maverick.

Nielsson. Manual of Fertilizer Processing. (Fertilizer Science & Technology Ser.: Vol. 5). 544p. 1987. 199.00 (0-8247-7522-8) Dekker.

Nielsson, Gunnar P. Mediation under Crisis Management Conditions: The U. N. Secretary General & the Falkland - Malvinas Islands Crisis. (Pew Case Studies in International Affairs). 50p. (C). 1994. pap. text ed. 2.50 (1-56927-127-5) Geo U Inst Dplmcy.

Nielzen, S. & Olsson, O., eds. Structure & Perception of Electroacoustic Sound & Music: Proceedings of the Marcus Wallenberg Symposium, Lund, Sweden, 21-28 August, 1988. (International Congress Ser.: No. 846). 216p. 1989. 92.50 (0-444-81105-2, Excerpta Medica) Elsevier.

Niem, Freddie. Sons of the Moon. (Illus.). 121p. 1992. 45.00 (0-9624276-1-6) Orchid Hse.

Nieman, Charles. Gods Plan for the Family. 58p. (Orig.). 1985. 4.95 (0-914307-48-7) R Tilton Ministries.

— God's Plan for Your Financial Success. 230p. (Orig.). 1985. pap. text ed. 6.95 (0-914307-34-7) R Tilton Ministries.

— The Life of Excellence. 32p. (Orig.). 1985. student ed 4.95 (0-914307-37-1) R Tilton Ministries.

— Living Smart. 95p. 1988. 6.95 (0-89274-477-4) Harrison Hse.

— Prayer: An Invitation from God. 140p. (Orig.). (C). 1983. pap. text ed. 4.95 (0-914307-03-7, Harrison Hse) R Tilton Ministries.

— Thinking Big in Small Places. 43p. (Orig.). 1986. student ed 4.95 (0-914307-53-3) R Tilton Ministries.

— Wisdom & Guidance. 206p. (Orig.). 1984. pap. text ed. 6.95 (0-914307-19-3, Harrison Hse) R Tilton Ministries.

***Nieman, David C.** Fitness & Sports Medicine: A Health-Related Approach. 3rd ed. LC 94-23736. 1995. 48.95 (0-923521-30-5) Bull Pub.

— Fitness & Your Health. LC 92-22225. 1993. 29.95 (0-923521-23-2) Bull Pub.

Nieman, Donald G. Promises to Keep: African Americans & the Constitutional Order, 1776 to Present. (Bicentennial Essays on the Bill of Rights Ser.). (Illus.). 304p. (C). 1991. pap. text ed. 14.95 (0-19-505561-6) OUP.

Nieman, Donald G., ed. African Americans & Education in the South, 1865-1900. LC 93-38436. (African American Life in the Post-Emancipation South Ser.: Vol. 10). (Illus.). 464p. 1994. reprint ed. 70.00 (0-8153-1447-7) Garland.

— Church & Community among Black Southerners, 1856-1900. LC 93-37341. (African American Life in the Post-Emancipation South Ser.: No. 9). 424p. 1994. 73.00 (0-8153-1446-9) Garland.

— The Constitution, Law, & American Life: Critical Aspects of the Nineteenth-Century Experience. LC 91-21385. 232p. 1992. 35.00 (0-8203-1403-X) U of Ga Pr.

Nieman, Donald G., intro. The African-American Family in the South, 1861-1900. LC 93-37087. (African American Life in the Post-Emancipation South Ser.: Vol. 8). (Illus.). 368p. 1994. 64.00 (0-8153-1445-0) Garland.

— African-Americans & Non-Agricultural Labor in the South, 1865-1900. LC 93-37339. (African American Life in the Post-Emancipation South Ser.: Vol. 4). 400p. 1994. 64.00 (0-8153-1441-8) Garland.

— African-Americans & Southern Politics from Redemption to Disfranchisement. LC 93-36874. (African American Life in the Post-Emancipation South Ser.: Vol. 6). 360p. 1994. 58.00 (0-8153-1443-4) Garland.

— African-Americans & the Emergence of Segregation, 1865-1900. LC 93-29264. (African American Life in the Post-Emancipation South Ser.: Vol. 11). (Illus.). 464p. 1994. 65.00 (0-8153-1448-5) Garland.

— Black Freedom - White Violence, 1865-1900. LC 93-29265. (African American Life in the Post-Emancipation South Ser.: Vol. 7). 1994. 68.00 (0-8153-1444-2) Garland.

— Black Southerners & the Law, 1865-1900. LC 93-29263. (African American Life in the Post-Emancipation South Ser.: Vol. 12). 488p. 1994. 73.00 (0-8153-1449-3) Garland.

— The Day of the Jubilee: The Civil War Experience of Black Southerners. LC 93-33613. (African American Life in the Post-Emancipation South Ser.: No. 1). (Illus.). 408p. 1994. 63.00 (0-8153-1438-8) Garland.

— The Freedman's Bureau & Black Freedom. LC 93-36877. 424p. 1994. 66.00 (0-8153-1439-6) Garland.

— From Slavery to Sharecropping: White Land & Black Labor in the Rural South, 1865-1900. LC 93-36876. (African American Life in the Post-Emancipation South Ser.: Vol. 3). (Illus.). 434p. 1994. 69.00 (0-8153-1440-X) Garland.

— The Politics of Freedom: African Americans & the Political Process During Reconstruction. LC 93-36875. (Illus.). 432p. 1994. 66.00 (0-8153-1442-6) Garland.

Nieman, H. Pattern Analysis. (Information Sciences Ser.: Vol. 4). (Illus.). 305p. 1981. 47.00 (0-387-10792-4) Spr-Verlag.

Nieman, Jean. A World of Travel Tips. (Illus.). 270p. (Orig.). 1982. write for info. (0-9609388-0-X) Travel Inter.

Nieman, Nancy D., tr. see Rossetti, Ana & Suntree, Susan.

Niemand, Jasper, ed. see Judge, William Q.

Niemann, jt. auth. see Parnham, Michael J.

Niemann, Bernard J., Jr., jt. ed. see McLaughlin, John D.

Niemann, H. Pattern Analysis & Understanding. 2nd ed. (Information Sciences Ser.: Vol. 4). (Illus.). 360p. 1990. pap. 54.50 (0-387-51378-7) Spr-Verlag.

Niemann, H., et al, eds. Recent Advances in Speech Understanding & Dialog Systems. (NATO Asi Series F: Vol. 46). (Illus.). x, 521p. 1988. 110.00 (0-387-19245-X) Spr-Verlag.

Niemann, Henry. Rectification: Known-Unknown Birthtimes. 1990. pap. 20.95 (0-86690-373-9, 3043-014) Am Fed Astrologers.

Niemann, Henry, jt. auth. see Teles, Rubens.

Niemann, Linda. Boomer: Railroad Memoirs. 252p. (C). 1992. reprint ed. pap. 12.95 (0-939416-55-7) Cleis Pr.

Niemann, Walter. Brahms. 492p. 1990. reprint ed. lib. bdg. 89.00 (0-7812-9054-6) Rprt Serv.

Niemantsverdriet, J. W. Spectroscopy in Catalysis: An Introduction. LC 93-15537. 1993. 95.00 (1-56081-792-5) VCH Pubs.

Niemark, Ju. I. & Fufaev, N. A. Dynamics of Nonholonomic Systems. LC 72-3274. (Translations of Mathematical Monographs: No. 33). 518p. 1972. 123.00 (0-8218-1583-0, MMONO-33) Am Math.

Niemcewicz, Julian U. & Budka, Metchie J., eds. Under Their Vine & Fig Tree: Travels Through America in 1797-1799, 1805 with Some Further Account of Life in New Jersey, Vol. 14. (Illus.). 398p. 20.00 (0-686-81808-3) NJ Hist Soc.

Niemcryk, Steve J., jt. ed. see Bolek, Catherine S.

Niemeier, jt. ed. see Newby.

Niemeier, Jim. From the Inside Out: A Parole Planning Manual. 144p. (Orig.). 1991. pap. 14.95 (0-8134-2920-X) Interstate.

Niemeijer, J. W. & De Groot, Irene. Sailing Ships in Dutch Prints. Walker, Janet, ed. LC 82-80141. (Illus.). 32p. (Orig.). 1982. pap. 7.75 (0-88397-040-6) Art Srvc Intl.

Niemeijer, J. W. & Te Rijdt, R. J. Eighteenth-Century Watercolors from the Rijksmuseum Printroom, Amsterdam. Hoyle, Michael, tr. LC 93-492. 1993. write for info. (0-88397-107-0) Art Srvc Intl.

Niemela, Pirkko, jt. ed. see Bjorkqvist, Kaj.

Niemer, William T., jt. auth. see Snider, Ray S.

Niemeyer, Carl, ed. see Carlyle, Thomas.

Niemeyer, Eberhardt V. Revolution at Queretaro: The Mexican Constitutional Convention of 1916-1917. (Latin American Monographs: No. 33). 319p. reprint ed. pap. 91.00 (0-8357-7714-6, 2036071) Bks Demand.

Niemeyer, G. & Huber, Charles. Techniques in Clinical Electrophysiology of Vision. 1982. lib. bdg. 219.00 (90-6193-727-2) Kluwer Ac.

Niemeyer, Gerhart. Aftersight & Foresight: Selected Essays. LC 87-33418. 374p. (Orig.). (C). 1988. lib. bdg. 48.00 (0-8191-6840-8); pap. text ed. 32.00 (0-8191-6841-6) U Pr of Amer.

Niemeyer, Gerhart, ed. see Voegelin, Eric.

Niemeyer, Lucian, photos. Long-Legged Wading Birds of the North American Wetlands. LC 92-28154. (Illus.). 224p. 1993. 49.95 (0-8117-1889-1) Stackpole.

— Old Order Amish: Their Enduring Way of Life. (Illus.). 208p. 1993. 39.95 (0-8018-4426-6) Johns Hopkins.

— Shenandoah: Daughter of the Stars. LC 94-18981. (Illus.). 224p. 1994. 39.95 (0-8071-1966-0) La State U Pr.

Niemeyer, Lucian & Meyer, Eugene L. Chesapeake Country. (Illus.). 224p. 1990. 35.00 (1-55859-063-3) Abbeville Pr.

Niemeyer, Paul V. & Richards, Linda M. Maryland Rules Commentary with 1988 Supplement. 480p. 1984. 55.00x (0-87215-813-6) Michie Butterworth.

— Maryland Rules Commentary with 1988 Supplement. suppl. ed. 480p. 1988. 20.00 (0-87473-396-0) Michie Butterworth.

***Niemeyer, Paul V. & Schuette, Linda M.** Maryland Rules Commentary. 610p. 1993. 85.00 (0-614-06185-7) Michie Butterworth.

Niemeyer, Ralph W., tr. see De Broglie, Louis.

Niemeyer, Suzanne, ed. Money for Film & Video Artists: A Comprehensive Arts Resource Guide. LC 91-20784. 240p. (Orig.). 1991. pap. 14.95 (0-915400-93-6, ACA Bks) Am Council Arts.

— Money for Performing Artists: A Comprehensive Arts Resource Guide. LC 91-29393. 288p. (Orig.). 1991. pap. 14.95 (0-915400-96-0, ACA Bks) Am Council Arts.

— Money for Visual Artists: A Comprehensive Arts Resource Guide. LC 91-13168. 240p. (Orig.). 1991. pap. 12.95 (0-915400-91-X, ACA Bks) Am Council Arts.

— Research Guide to American Historical Biography, Vol. 4: Women & Minorities. LC 88-19316. 572p. 1990. lib. bdg. 63.00 (0-933833-21-0) Beacham Pub.

Niemeyer, Suzanne, ed. see Aspen Reference Group Staff.

Niemeyer, Suzanne, jt. ed. see Beetz, Kirk.

Niemeyer, Suzanne, jt. ed. see Di Lima, Sara N.

***Niemi.** Russell Banks. 1995. text ed. 22.95 (0-8057-4018-X) Macmillan.

Niemi, Albert W., Jr. State & Regional Patterns in American Manufacturing, 1860-1900. LC 73-13289. (Contributions in Economics & Economic History Ser.: No. 10). 209p. 1974. text ed. 69.50 (0-8371-7148-2, NAM, Greenwood Pr) Greenwood.

— U. S. Economic History. 2nd ed. LC 87-10730. (Illus.). 492p. 1987. reprint ed. pap. text ed. 32.00 (0-8191-6335-X) U Pr of Amer.

Niemi, Beth T., jt. auth. see Lloyd, Cynthia B.

Niemi, E. & Makelainen, P., eds. Tubular Structures: Papers & Discussion Presented at the Third International Symposium, Lappeenranta, Finland, 1-2 September, 1989. 468p. 1990. 101.00 (1-85166-474-2) Elsevier.

Niemi, H., et al, eds. Proceedings of the Third Finnish-Soviet Conference on Probability Theory & Mathematical Statistics. (Frontiers in Pure & Applied Probability Ser.: Vol. 1). 306p. 1994. 187.50 (90-6764-156-1) Coronet Bks.

Niemi, Helena R. Porcelain Dollmaking in Detail: Advanced Study Book, No. 2. (Orig.). 1985. pap. write for info. (0-9607800-2-5) H R Niemi.

— Porcelain Dollmaking in Detail: Porcelain Doll Business, No. 3. (Orig.). 1985. pap. write for info. (0-9607800-3-3) H R Niemi.

Niemi, John A., ed. Mass Media & Adult Education. LC 73-168491. 128p. 1971. pap. 14.95 (0-87778-025-0) Educ Tech Pubns.

Niemi, Judith. The Basic Essentials of Women in the Outdoors. LC 90-31389. (Basic Essentials Ser.). (Illus.). 72p. (Orig.). 1990. pap. 5.99 (0-934802-56-4) ICS Bks.

Niemi, Judith & Wieser, Barbara, eds. Rivers Running Free: Canoeing Stories by Adventurous Women. LC 92-23108. (Illus.). 289p. 1992. reprint ed. pap. 14.95 (1-878067-22-2) Seal Pr Feminist.

— Rivers Running Free: Stories of Adventurous Women. LC 87-71552. (Illus.). 300p. (Orig.). 1987. pap. 12.95 (0-943127-00-9) Bergamot Bks.

Niemi, Matt, jt. auth. see Sharp, Mary.

Niemi, Richard G. How Family Members Perceive Each Other: Political & Social Attitudes in Two Generations. LC 73-86913. (Illus.). 228p. 1974. 32.00 (0-300-01698-0) Yale U Pr.

Niemi, Richard G. & Weisberg, Herbert F., eds. Classics in Voting Behavior. LC 92-23085. 1992. 42.95 (0-87187-705-8); pap. 29.95 (0-87187-651-5) Congr Quarterly.

— Controversies in Voting Behavior. 2nd ed. LC 84-9605. (Illus.). 651p. reprint ed. pap. 180.00 (0-8357-8537-8, 2034840) Bks Demand.

Niemi, Richard G. & Wiesberg, Herbert F., eds. Controversies in Voting Behavior. 3rd ed. LC 92-22878. 433p. 1992. pap. text ed. 29.95 (0-87187-706-6) Congr Quarterly.

Niemi, Richard G., jt. auth. see Jennings, M. Kent.

Niemi, Richard G., jt. auth. see Stanley, Harold W.

Niemi, Richard G., et al. Trends in Public Opinion: A Compendium of Survey Data. LC 89-2213. (Documentary Reference Collections). 344p. 1989. text ed. 79.50 (0-313-25426-5, NTP/, Greenwood Pr) Greenwood.

***Niemi, Steven M. & Wilson, John E., eds.** Refinement & Reduction in Animal Testing. LC 93-84516. 138p. 1993. pap. 25.00 (0-614-06559-3) Scientists Ctr.

***Niemi, Steven M., et al, eds.** Rodents & Rabbits: Current Research Issues. LC 94-65718. 81p. 1994. pap. 30.00 (0-614-06558-5) Scientists Ctr.

***Niemiec, Richard P. & Walberg, Herbert J., eds.** Evaluating Chicago School Reform. LC 85-644749. (New Directions for Program Evaluation Ser.: No. 59). 110p. (Orig.). 1993. pap. 17.95 (1-55542-678-6) Jossey-Bass.

Niemiee, Dennis, jt. auth. see Langlos, Ruth.

Niemier, B. A., et al, eds. Formability Topics: Metallic Materials - STP 647. 279p. 1978. 27.75 (0-8031-0358-1, 04-647000-23) ASTM.

Nieminen, R. M., et al, eds. Many-Atom Interactions in Solids: Proceedings of the International Workshop, Pajulahti, Finland, June 5-9, 1989. (Proceedings in Physics Ser.: Vol. 48). (Illus.). viii, 319p. 1990. 68.00 (0-387-52657-9) Spr-Verlag.

Nieminen, Raija. Voyage to the Island. LC 90-19178. 265p. 1990. 17.95 (0-930323-62-9) Gallaudet Univ Pr.

Nieminski, John. John Nieminski: Somewhere a Roscoe. Liebow, Ely & Scott, Art, eds. LC 87-38833. (Brownstone Mystery Guides Ser.: No. 3). 61p. (C). 1987. reprint ed. lib. bdg. 20.00x (0-8095-6402-5, Brownstone Bks); reprint ed. pap. 10.00x (0-941028-06-2, Brownstone Bks) Borgo Pr.

Niemira, Michael P. & Kahan, Samuel D. Forecasting Economic Cycles. 432p. 1994. text ed. 55.00 (0-471-84544-2) Wiley.

Niemira, Michael P. & Zukowski, Gerald F. Trading the Fundamentals: The Trader's Complete Guide to Interpreting Economic Indicators & Monetary Policy. 300p. 1993. 37.50 (1-55738-450-9) Probus Pub Co.

Niemoeller, A. F., tr. see D'Hancarville.

***Niemoeller, Michael.** Stone Made Flesh. Wolverton, Terry, ed. 100p. (Orig.). 1995. pap. 9.95 (0-9629528-2-6) Silverton Bks.

Niemoller, Martin. Exile in the Fatherland: Martin Niemoller's Letters from Moabit Prison. Locke, Hubert G., ed. Kaemke, Ernst et al, trs. LC 86-491. 182p. (Orig.). reprint ed. pap. 51.90 (0-685-23459-2, 2032739) Bks Demand.

Niemtschek, Franz X. Life of Mozart. Mautner, Helen, tr. LC 78-66914. (Encore Music Editions Ser.). 1985. reprint ed. 16.00 (0-88355-754-1) Hyperion Conn.

— Life of Mozart. 1988. reprint ed. lib. bdg. 49.00 (0-7812-0253-1) Rprt Serv.

— Life of Mozart. LC 74-181224. 87p. 1956. reprint ed. 49.00 (0-403-01751-3) Scholarly.

Niemtzow, Richard C., ed. Transmembrane Potentials & Characteristics of Immune & Tumor Cells. 176p. 1985. 115.00 (0-8493-5688-1, RC267, CRC Reprint) Franklin.

***Niemuth, Neal D.** Owls for Kids. (Wildlife for Kids Ser.). (Illus.). 48p. (Orig.). (J). (gr. 3-7). 1995. pap. write for info. (1-55971-475-1) NorthWord.

Nienaber, Jeanne, jt. auth. see Mazmanian, Daniel A.

Niendorf, Robert M., jt. auth. see Ward, David J.

Niendorff, John S., ed. see Holmes, Ernest.

Niendorff, John S., ed. see Moseley, Naomi & Moseley, Douglas.

Nienhauser, W. H. Liu Tsung-Yuan. (Twayne's World Authors Ser.). (C). 1971. lib. bdg. 17.95 (0-8057-2538-5) Irvington.

Nienhauser, W. H., Jr., et al, eds. Critical Essays on Chinese Literature. x, 207p. 1976. text ed. 33.50 (962-201-019-9, Pub. by Chinese Univ HK) Coronet Bks.

Nienhauser, William H., Jr., ed. see Chien, Ssu-ma.

Nienhauser, William H., Jr., et al, eds. The Indiana Companion to Traditional Chinese Literature. LC 83-49511. 1052p. 1985. 75.00 (0-253-32983-3) Ind U Pr.

Nienhueser, Helen & Wolfe, John, Jr. Fifty-Five Ways to the Wilderness in Southcentral Alaska. 4th ed. (Illus.). 176p. 1994. pap. 12.95 (0-89886-389-9) Mountaineers.

Nienhuis, Arthur W., jt. ed. see Stamatoyannopoulos, George.

Nienhuis, H., jt. auth. see Meyer, C.

Nienhuis, P. H. & Smaal, A. C., eds. The Oosterschelde Estuary: A Case Study of a Changing Ecosystem. LC 94-14882. (Developments in Hydrobiology Ser.: Vol. 97). 624p. (C). 1994. lib. bdg. 280.00 (0-7923-2817-5) Kluwer Ac.

Nienhuys, J. W., tr. see Chaillou, Jacques.

Nienkamp, Jean, ed. see Tenney, Tabitha G.

Nienkirchen, Charles W. Albert Benjamin Simpson & the Pentecostal Movement: A Study in Continuity, Crisis & Change. 176p. 1992. pap. 9.95 (0-913573-99-X) Hendrickson MA.

Nienstedt, Vermadel P. & Smith, Lynn. Laugh to Keep from Crying. LC 83-91465. (Illus.). 90p. pap. 5.95 (0-9613010-0-7) Nienstedt VP & L Smith.

Nienstedt, W., jt. auth. see Hervonen, A.

Nieoczym, Adam, tr. see Krasucki, Florian, et al.

Niepold, G. The Battle for White Russia: The Destruction of Army Group Center, June 1944. Simpkin, Richard E., tr. 287p. 1987. 67.00 (0-08-033606-X, Pub. by Brasseys UK) Brasseys Inc.

Nier, M., jt. ed. see Courtot, M. E.

Nier, Susan, jt. auth. see Monastery of Arkashea Staff.

Nierenbe. Art of Negotiating. 1981. pap. 7.95 (0-671-62999-9) S&S Trade.

Nierenberg & Smith. Clinical Problems in Basic Pharmacology. (Illus.). 336p. 1988. pap. text ed. 19.95 (0-8016-3860-7) Mosby Yr Bk.

Nierenberg, Claudia, jt. auth. see McGurk, Russell.

Nierenberg, Gerald. The Complete Negotiator. 64p. 1989. student ed, audio 59.95 (0-13-162033-9) P-H.

Nierenberg, Gerard. The Complete Negotiator. 1991. pap. 8.95 (0-425-12779-6) Berkley Pub.

N

— How to Give & Receive Advice. 1975. 4.95 (0-318-20081-3) Nierenberg-Zeif.
— Negotiating the Big Sale. 208p. 1993. pap. 8.95 (0-425-13805-4) Berkley Pub.
Nierenberg, Gerard I. Art of Negotiating. 1989. mass mkt. 5.99 (0-671-70499-0) PB.
— The Art of Negotiating. 1990. student ed, audio 69.95 (0-924967-00-5) Intl Ctr Creat Think.
— Between the Word, Hidden Meanings in What People Say. 1985. 9.95 (0-671-60662-X) S&S Trade.
— Meta-Talk. 1981. pap. 4.95 (0-685-03973-0) PB.
— Negotiating the Big Sale. 250p. 1991. 27.00 (1-55623-621-2) Irwin Prof Pubng.
***Nierenberg, J.** Backcountry Companion for Denali National Park. (Illus.). 96p. 1995. pap. 8.95 (0-930931-03-3) Alaska Natural.
Nierenberg, Judith & Janovic, Florence. The Hospital Experience: A Complete Guide to Understanding & Participating in Your Own Care. LC 78-55658. (Illus.). 1978. 12.95 (0-672-52372-8, Bobbs); pap. 9.95 (0-672-52373-6, Bobbs) Macmillan.
Nierenberg, Nicolas. SQL Applications Programming. (Illus.). 304p. (Orig.). 1989. pap. 21.95 (0-8306-3214-X, Windcrest) TAB Bks.
Nierenberg, Ted, photos. The Beckoning Path: Lessons of a Lifelong Garden. (Illus.). 108p. 1993. 35.00 (0-89381-544-6) Aperture.
Nierenberg, William A., ed. Encyclopedia of Earth System Science, 4 vols., Set. (Illus.). 2629p. 1991. 950.00 (0-685-53442-1) Acad Pr.
— Encyclopedia of Earth Systems Science, 1. (Illus.). 3264p. 1991. text ed. 262.00 (0-12-226722-2) Acad Pr.
— Encyclopedia of Earth Systems Science, 2. (Illus.). 3264p. 1991. text ed. 262.00 (0-12-226723-0) Acad Pr.
— Encyclopedia of Earth Systems Science, 3. (Illus.). 3264p. 1991. text ed. 262.00 (0-12-226724-9) Acad Pr.
— Encyclopedia of Earth Systems Science, 4. (Illus.). 3264p. 1991. text ed. 262.00 (0-12-226725-7) Acad Pr.
— Encyclopedia of Earth Systems Science, Set, Vols. 1-4. (Illus.). 3264p. 1991. Set. 950.00 (0-685-47646-4) Acad Pr.
— Encyclopedia of Environmental Biology, 3 Vols. (Illus.). 1160p. 1995. boxed 475.00 (0-12-226730-3) Acad Pr.
— Encyclopedia of Environmental Biology Vol. 1, 3 vols., set. LC 94-24917. 1160p. 1995. write for info. (0-12-226731-1) Acad Pr.
— Encyclopedia of Environmental Biology Vol. 2. LC 94-24917. 1995. write for info. (0-12-226732-X) Acad Pr.
***Nierengarten, Ruth.** New Borns, 3 bks., Set. (Illus.). 96p. 1994. boxed 12.95 (0-87839-092-8) North Star.
Nierhaus, K. H., et al, eds. The Translational Apparatus. 1994. 149.50 (0-306-44538-7, Plenum Pr) Plenum.
Niering, William A. Wetlands. Elliott, Charles, ed. LC 84-48672. (Audubon Society Nature Guides Ser.). (Illus.). 638p. 1985. pap. 19.00 (0-394-73147-6) Knopf.
— Wetlands of North America. LC 91-9. (Illus.). 160p. 1991. pap. 12.98 (0-934738-93-9) Thomasson-Grant.
Niering, William A. & Spellenberg, Richard. Familiar Flowers of North America, Eastern Region. (Audubon Society Pocket Guides Ser.). 1987. pap. 4.95 (0-317-56707-1) Knopf.
— Familiar Flowers of North America, Western Region. (Audubon Society Pocket Guides Ser.). 1987. pap. 4.95 (0-317-56709-8) Knopf.
— Familiar Wildflowers of North America, 6 vols. (Illus.). 192p. 1988. write for info. (0-318-63230-6) Knopf.
— Familiar Wildflowers of North America, 6 vols., Set. (Illus.). 192p. 1988. 95.70 (0-318-36011-X) Knopf.
Nierman, J. Harris. Preparing Your Research Paper. (Illus.). 23p. (Orig.). (gr. 10 up). 1979. pap. 1.95 (0-935770-00-3) Creative Res & Educ.
Nierman, Judith. Floyd Dell: An Annotated Bibliography of Secondary Sources, 1910-1981. LC 84-13852. (Author Bibliographies Ser.: No. 69). 208p. 1984. 22.50 (0-8108-1718-7) Scarecrow.
Nierman, Lewis G. Lefty's Place. (Illus.). 32p. (J). (gr. 1-4). 1994. 18.95 (0-9636820-0-8) Kindness Pubns.
Nierman, W. C. & Maglott, D. R., eds. American Type Culture Collection - NIH Repository Catalogue of Human & Mouse DNA Probes & Libraries. 8th ed. 200p. 1995. pap. text ed. write for info. (0-930009-52-5) ATCC.
Nierman, W. C., jt. ed. see Maglott, D. R.
Niermann, Eleanor, ed. Papers of John L. Lewis: Guide to a Microfilm Edition. (Guides to Historical Resources Ser.). 12p. 1970. pap. 1.00 (0-87020-182-4) State Hist Soc Wis.
Niermann, Eleanor M., ed. Papers of the University Settlement Society of New York City: Guide to a Microfilm Edition. (Guides to Historical Resources Ser.). 1972. pap. 1.00 (0-87020-183-2) State Hist Soc Wis.
— The Papers of the University Settlement Society of New York City, 1886-1945: Guide to a Microfilm Edition. 15p. 1972. pap. 55.00 (0-685-48796-2) Chadwyck-Healey.
Niermann, Johannes. Woerterbuch der DDR Paedagogik. (GER.). 1974. pap. 24.95 (0-7859-0839-0, M-7032) Fr & Eur.
Niermeyer, J. F. Mediae Latinitatis Lexicon Minus. LC 92-42558. xvi, 1138p. (ENG, FRE & LAT.). 1993. reprint ed. 170.50 (90-04-07108-3) E J Brill.
***Nierop, Tom.** Systems & Regions in Global Politics: An Empirical Study of Diplomacy, International Organization & Trade. Date not set. text ed. 59.95 (0-470-22040-6) Wiley.
— Systems & Regions in Global Politics: An Empirical Study of Diplomacy, International Organization, & Trade, 1950-1991. LC 93-46291. (Belhaven Studies in Political Geography). 1995. text ed. 49.95 (0-471-94942-6) Wiley.
Nierstrasz, O. M., ed. ECOOP '93 - Object-Oriented Programming: Proceedings of the Seventh European Conference Held in Kaiserslautern, Germany, July 26-30, 1993. (Lecture Notes in Computer Science Ser.: Vol. 707). xi, 531p. 1993. pap. 72.00 (0-387-57120-5) Spr-Verlag.
Nierstrasz, O. M., ed. see Seventh European Conference on Object-Oriented Programming Staff.
***Nierstrasz, Oscar & Tsichritzis, Dennis, eds.** Object-Oriented Software Composition. LC 95-7616. (Object-Oriented Ser.). 1995. write for info. (0-13-220674-9) P-H Intl.
Nies, H., jt. auth. see Singer, C.
Nies, J. I. & LaBrecque, S. V. Creating Change. 1980. 3.50 (0-911365-16-8, A261-08448) Home Econ Educ.
Nies, James B. Historical, Religious & Economic Texts & Antiquities. LC 78-63522. (Babylonian Inscriptions in the Collection of James B. Nies Ser.: No. 2). reprint ed. 37.50 (0-404-60132-4) AMS Pr.
Nies, Judith. Seven Women: Portraits from the American Radical Tradition. 1978. pap. 10.95 (0-14-004792-1, Penguin Bks) Viking Penguin.
Nies, Kevin A. From Sorceress to Scientist: Biographies of Women Physical Scientists. (Lives of Women Scientists Ser.: Vol. I). (Illus.). 95p. (Orig.). (YA). (gr. 8 up). 1991. 30.00 (1-880211-00-9); pap. 14.99 (1-880211-01-7) Calif Video.
***Niesar, Gerald V., et al.** California Limited Liability Company Forms & Practice Manual. 584p. 1994. ring bd. 149.95 (0-9637468-8-X) Data Trace Legal.
Nieschlag, E., ed. Hormone Assays in Reproductive Medicine. (Journal: Hormone Research: Vol. 9, No. 6). (Illus.). 1978. pap. 25.00 (3-8055-2975-9) S Karger.
Nieschlag, E. & Behre, H. M., eds. Testosterone - Action, Deficiency, Substitution. (Illus.). 352p. 1990. 70.00 (0-387-52763-X) Spr-Verlag.
Nieschlag, E., et al, eds. Spermatogenesis - Fertilization Contraception: Molecular, Cellular, & Endocrine Events in Male Reproduction. LC 92-2300. (Schering Foundation Workshop Ser.: Vol. 4). (Illus.). 528p. 1992. 59.00 (0-387-55436-X); write for info. (3-540-55436-X) Spr-Verlag.
Niesen de Abruno, Laura E. The Refining Fire: Herakles & Other Heroes in T. S. Eliot's Works. (American University Studies: English Language & Literature: Ser. IV, Vol. 62). 188p. (C). 1988. text ed. 35.95 (0-8204-0550-7) P Lang Pubs.
Niesen, Karen L. & Onaga, Christine Y. Wisconsin Directory of International Institutions. 261p. 1993. pap. 25.00 (0-299-97079-5) U of Wis Pr.
***Niesen, Karen L., et al.** Burundi. LC 95-15771. (OIES Country Guide Ser.). 1995. write for info. (0-929851-44-7) Am Assn Coll Registrars.
Niesen, Thomas M. Beachcomber's Guide to California Marine Life. LC 93-29207. (Illus.). 180p. 1994. pap. 16.95 (0-88415-075-5) Gulf Pub.
— The Marine Biology Coloring Book. (Illus.). 224p. (Orig.). 1982. pap. 15.00 (0-06-460303-2, CO 303, Harper Ref) HarpC.
Niesewand, Nonie. Contemporary Details: A Visual Sourcebook of Architectural Features, Fittings, & Decorative Finishes for 20th-Century Homes. (Illus.). 192p. 1993. 35.00 (0-671-74958-7) S&S Trade.
— Designing with Flowers. (Illus.). 192p. 1986. 27.50 (0-517-55942-0, Crown) Crown Pub Group.
Nieshtadt, Yakov, ed. Catastrophe in the Opening. (Chess Ser.). (Illus.). 271p. 1980. 25.95 (0-08-023121-7, Pergamon Pr); pap. 14.95 (0-08-024097-6, Pergamon Pr) Elsevier.
Niesiecki, K. Herbarz Polski, 10 vols., Set. (Illus.). reprint ed. 800.00 (0-318-23353-3) Szwede Slavic.
Niesluchowski, Warren, tr. see Cooke, Lynne, et al.
Niess, Frank. A Hemisphere to Itself: A History of U. S.-Latin-American Relations. LC 89-18272. (C). 1990. text ed. 55.00 (0-86232-866-7, Pub. by Zed Books UK); pap. 17.50 (0-86232-867-5, Pub. by Zed Books UK) Humanities.
Niessen & Van Der Greef, eds. Liquid Chromatography - Mass Spectometry. (Chromatographic Science Ser.: Vol. 58). 524p. 1992. 175.00 (0-8247-8635-1) Dekker.
Niessen, M. & Peschar, J., eds. Comparative Research on Education: Overview, Strategy & Applications in Eastern & Western Europe. (Vienna Centre Ser.). 281p. 1982. 123.00 (0-08-027934-1, Pub. by Pergamon Repr UK) Franklin.
— International Comparative Research: Problems of Theory, Methodology & Organisation in Eastern & Western Europe. (Vienna Centre Ser.: No. 10). (Illus.). 184p. 1982. 47.00 (0-317-66833-1, Pergamon Pr) Elsevier.
Niessen, M., et al. International Comparative Research: Social Structure & Public Institutions in Eastern & Western Europe. LC 82-16519. (Vienna Centre Ser.). 184p. 1984. 76.00 (0-08-031334-5, Pub. by Pergamon Repr UK) Franklin.
Niessen, Sandra A. Batak Cloth & Clothing: A Dynamic Indonesian Tradition. (Asia Collection). (Illus.). 148p. 1994. 45.00 (967-65-3040-9) OUP.
Niessen, Walter R. Combustion & Incineration Processes: Applications in Environmental Engineering. 2nd expanded rev. ed. LC 94-29112. (Environmental Science & Pollution Ser.: Vol. 13). 680p. 1995. 175.00 (0-8247-9267-X) Dekker.
Nieswanger, Elithe, ed. see Jinarajadasa, C.
Nieswiadomy, Rose. Foundations of Nursing Research. 2nd ed. (Illus.). 360p. (C). 1992. pap. text ed. 31.95 (0-8385-2694-2, A2694-6) Appleton & Lange.
Niesz, Anita. Anita Niesz: Photographs. (Illus.). 152p. 1989. pap. 35.00 (3-7165-0672-9, Pub. by Benteli Verlag SZ) Dist Art Pubs.
Nietenhoefer, Ken. Fifty Ways to Enrich Your Life, Bk. 1. LC 94-96026. 152p. 1991. pap. 5.00 (0-9631681-0-X) Ken Co.
— Fifty Ways to Enrich Your Life, Bk. 2. LC 91-91567. 136p. 1994. pap. 6.00 (0-9631681-1-8) Ken Co.
Niethammer, Carolyn. American Indian Food & Lore. LC 73-7681. (Illus.). 191p. 1974. pap. 16.95 (0-02-010000-0, Collier S&S) S&S Trade.
— Daughters of the Earth. 304p. 1977. pap. 16.00 (0-02-096150-2, Collier S&S) S&S Trade.
— The Tumbleweed Gourmet: Cooking with Wild Southwestern Plants. LC 87-5948. 229p. 1987. 9.95 (0-8165-1021-0) U of Ariz Pr.
Niethammer, Lutz. Posthistoire: Has History Ended? Camiller, Patrick, tr. 200p. 1992. 29.95 (0-86091-395-3, A9730, Pub. by Verso UK) Routledge Chapman & Hall.
Nietmann, William F. The Unmaking of God. LC 93-49437. 240p. (Orig.). (C). Date not set. lib. bdg. 49.50 (0-8191-9435-2); pap. text ed. 28.50 (0-8191-9436-0) U Pr of Amer.
Nieto, jt. auth. see Szklo.
Nieto, Amparo Y. Esmorgantes. (Nueva Austral Ser.: Vol. 153). (SPA.). 1991. pap. text ed. 24.95x (84-239-1953-6) Elliots Bks.
Nieto, Angel. Mosquito! LC 94-55. (Illus.). (J). 1994. write for info. (0-590-29274-9) Scholastic Inc.
Nieto, Jose, ed. Valdes's Two Catechisms: The Dialogue on Christian Doctrine & the Christian Instruction for Children. Jones, William B. & Jones, Carol D., trs. (Illus.). 200p. (C). 1981. 16.50 (0-87291-151-9) Coronado Pr.
Nieto, M. The Titius-Bode Law of Planetary Distance. 173p. (C). 1972. 76.00 (0-08-016784-5, Pub. by Pergamon Repr UK) Franklin.
Nieto-Manjon, Luis. Diccionario Illustrado de Terminos Taurinos. 3rd ed. 438p. 1991. pap. 65.00 (0-7859-5751-0) Fr & Eur.
Nieto, Michael M., et al, eds. Science Underground. LC 83-70377. (AIP Conference Proceedings Ser.: No. 96). 446p. 1983. lib. bdg. 38.75 (0-88318-195-9) Am Inst Physics.
Nieto, Sonia. Affirming Diversity: The Sociopolitical Context of Multicultural Education. 335p. (Orig.). (C). 1992. pap. text ed. 35.95 (0-8013-0529-2, 78406) Longman.
— Affirming Diversity: The Sociopolitical Context of Multicultural Education. 2nd ed. LC 95-7931. (C). 1996. pap. text ed. 33.95 (0-8013-1420-8) Longman.
Nieto, Sonia, jt. ed. see Rivera, Ralph.
Nieto-Vesperinas, M. Scattering & Diffraction in Physical Optics. (Series In Pure & Applied Optics). 416p. 1991. text ed. 105.00 (0-471-61529-3) Wiley.
Nieto-Vesperinas, M., jt. ed. see Fiddy, M. A.
Nietschmann, Bernard. The Unknown War: The Miskito Nation, Nicaragua, & the United States. LC 89-7831. (Focus on Issues Ser.: No. 8). (Illus.). 120p. (Orig.). (C). 1989. lib. bdg. 37.00 (0-932088-41-4); pap. text ed. 16.50 (0-932088-42-2) Freedom Hse.
Nietz, Mary J., jt. auth. see Hall, John R.
Nietzel. Psychological Consultation. (C). 1986. pap. 19.95 (0-205-14426-8, H4426) Allyn.
Nietzel, G. P. & Smith, M. K., eds. Surface-Tension-Driven Flows. LC 93-73260. 88p. Date not set. pap. 35.00 (0-7918-1024-0) ASME.
Nietzel, M. & Winett, R. Behavioral Approaches to Community Psychology. LC 77-30566. 1977. 192.00 (0-08-020376-0, Pub. by Pergamon Repr UK) Franklin.
Nietzel, Michael. Crime & Its Modification: A Social Learning Perspective. LC 78-23984. (General Psychology Ser.: Vol. 77). (Illus.). 1979. pap. 24.00 (0-08-023877-7, Pergamon Pr) Elsevier.
Nietzel, Michael T., ed. Behavioral Community Psychology: A Special Issue of Behavioral Counseling & Community Interventions. 112p. 1984. pap. 16.95 (0-89885-179-3) Human Sci Pr.
Nietzel, Michael T., et al. Introduction to Clinical Psychology. 4th ed. LC 93-33601. 592p. 1993. text ed. write for info. (0-13-098518-X) P-H.
Nietzel, Mike, jt. auth. see Baker, Robert.
Nietzel, Shirley. Jacket I Wear in the Snow. (Big Book Ser.). (J). (ps-3). 1992. pap. 19.95 (0-590-72613-7) Scholastic Inc.
Nietzke, Ann. Natalie On the Street. 1994. pap. 14.95 (0-934971-41-2) Calyx Bks.
— Natalie On the Street. 1994. 24.95 (0-934971-42-0) Calyx Bks.
Nietzsche. Der Streit um "Nietzsches Geburt der Tragodie" (Olms Paperbacks Ser.: Bd. 40). 136p. 1989. pap. write for info. (3-487-02599-X, Pub. by Georg Olms GW) Lubrecht & Cramer.
Nietzsche, Frederich. My Sister & I. Levy, Oscar, tr. (Illus.). 340p. (C). 1990. reprint ed. pap. 9.95 (1-878923-01-3) Amok Bks.
***Nietzsche, Friederich W.** Thus Spoke Zarathustra. Kaufmann, Walter, tr. & pref. by. LC 95-15383. 1995. 14.50 (0-679-60175-9, Modern Lib) Random.
Nietzsche, Friedrich. The Anti-Christ. 190p. 1988. reprint ed. 9.00 (0-939482-10-X) Noontide.
— The Antichrist. LC 70-161338. (Atheist Viewpoint Ser.). 60p. 1972. reprint ed. 9.95 (0-405-03799-6) Ayer.
— The Antichrist & Twilight of the Gods. 1974. 300.00 (0-87968-210-8) Gordon Pr.
— Basic Writings of Nietzsche. Kaufmann, Walter, ed. & tr. by. LC 68-29392. 1977. 20.00 (0-394-60406-7, Modern Lib) Random.
— Beyond Good & Evil. 1974. lib. bdg. 300.00 (0-87968-207-8) Gordon Pr.
— Beyond Good & Evil. 1966. pap. 5.95 (0-394-70337-5) Random.
— Beyond Good & Evil. Zimmern, Helen, tr. (Great Books in Philosophy). 268p. 1989. reprint ed. pap. text ed. 8.95 (0-87975-558-X) Prometheus Bks.
— Beyond Good & Evil. Hollingdale, R. J., tr. 256p. 1990. reprint ed. mass mkt. 8.95 (0-14-044513-7, Penguin Classics) Viking Penguin.
— Beyond Good & Evil: Prelude to a Philosophy of the Future. Kaufmann, Walter, tr. 1989. pap. 10.00 (0-679-72465-6, Vin) Random.
— The Birth of Tragedy. 1974. 300.00 (0-87968-172-1) Gordon Pr.
— The Birth of Tragedy. Whiteside, Shaun, tr. 160p. 1994. pap. 8.95 (0-14-043339-2, Penguin Classics) Viking Penguin.
— The Birth of Tragedy. Kaufmann, Walter, tr. Bd. with Case of Wagner. 1967. Set pap. 9.00 (0-394-70369-3, Vin) Random.
— The Birth of Tragedy. unabridged ed. (Thrift Editions Ser.). 96p. 1995. pap. text ed. 1.00 (0-486-28515-4) Dover.
— The Birth of Tragedy & the Genealogy of Morals. Golffing, Francis, tr. Incl. Genealogy of Morals. LC 56-7535. 1956. (0-318-51722-1); LC 56-7535. 1956. Set mass mkt. 8.95 (0-385-09210-5, A81, Anchor NY) Doubleday.
— Briefwechsel: Kritische Gesamtausgabe, Section 1, Vol. 1. Colli, Giorgio & Montinari, Mazzino, eds. xiv, 452p. (C). 1975. 156.95x (3-11-005911-8) De Gruyter.
— Briefwechsel: Kritische Gesamtausgabe, Section 1, Vols. 2 & 3. Incl. Vol. 2. September 1864 - April 1869. 1975. 56.00 (3-11-006514-2); Vol. 3. October 1864 - March 1869. 1975. 52.00 (3-11-006558-4); (C). 1975. write for info. (0-318-51616-0) De Gruyter.
— Le Cas Wagner: Nietzsche Contre Wagner. (FRE.). 1991. pap. 9.95 (0-7859-3982-2) Fr & Eur.
— The Case of Wagner. 1974. lib. bdg. 300.00 (0-87968-203-5) Gordon Pr.
— Complete Works, 18 vols. 1974. 300.00 (0-87968-173-X) Gordon Pr.
— The Dawn of Day. 1974. 300.00 (0-87968-204-3) Gordon Pr.
— Daybreak: Thoughts on the Prejudices of Morality. Hollingdale, R. J., tr. LC 81-18017. (Texts in German Philosophy Ser.). 220p. 1982. pap. 16.95 (0-521-28662-X) Cambridge U Pr.
— Dithyrambs of Dionysus. Hollingdale, R. J., ed. & tr. by. (Austrian-German Culture Ser.). 96p. 1984. 25.00 (0-933806-15-9) Black Swan CT.
— Early Greek Philosophy & Other Essays. 1974. lib. bdg. 300.00 (0-87968-174-8) Gordon Pr.
— Ecce Homo. Hollingdale, R. J., tr. 144p. 1992. 7.95 (0-14-044515-3, Penguin Classics) Viking Penguin.
— Ecce Homo (Nietzsche's Autobiography) 1974. 300.00 (0-87968-211-6) Gordon Pr.
— The Gay Science. Kauffmann, Walter, tr. 1974. pap. 9.00 (0-394-71985-9, Vin) Random.
— Genealogy of Morals & Peoples & Countries. 1974. lib. bdg. 300.00 (0-87968-208-6) Gordon Pr.
— Human, All-Too-Human, 2 vols. 1974. lib. bdg. 600.00 (0-87968-201-9) Gordon Pr.
— Human, All Too Human: A Book for Free Spirits. Faber, Marion & Lehmann, Stephen, trs. LC 83-25955. xxviii, 274p. 1984. pap. 12.00 (0-8032-8353-9) U of Nebr Pr.
— Human, All-Too Human: Including Assorted Opinions & Maxims & the Wanderer & His Shadow. Hillingdale, R. J., tr. (Texts in German Philosophy Ser.). 500p. 1986. 69.95 (0-521-26543-6); pap. 17.95 (0-521-31945-5) Cambridge U Pr.
— Index to Nietzsche. Guppy, Robert, ed. Cohn, Paul V., tr. 1974. lib. bdg. 300.00 (0-87968-212-4) Gordon Pr.
— The Joyful Wisdom. 1974. lib. bdg. 300.00 (0-87968-205-1) Gordon Pr.
— Nietzsche: A Self-Portrait from His Letters. Fuss, Peter & Shapiro, Henry, eds. LC 73-134953. 208p. reprint ed. pap. 59.30 (0-8357-9170-X, 2014655) Bks Demand.
— A Nietzsche Reader. Hollingdale, R. J., tr. (Classics Ser.). (Orig.). 1978. pap. 9.95 (0-14-044329-0, Penguin Classics) Viking Penguin.
— Nietzsche-Studien, Vol. 4. Montinari, M., ed. (Internationales Jahrbuch fuer die Nietzsche-Forschung Ser.). (GER.). 1975. 142.35 (3-11-005844-8) De Gruyter.
— Nietzsche-Studien, Vol. 6. (Internationales Jahrbuch fuer die Nietzsche-Forschung Ser.). (C). 1977. 113.85 (3-11-007166-5) De Gruyter.
— Nietzsche-Studien, Vol. 7. (Internationales Jahrbuch fuer die Nietzsche-Forschung Ser.). (GER.). 1978. 126.95 (3-11-007338-2) De Gruyter.
— Nietzsche-Studien, Vol. 8. (Internationales Jahrbuch fuer die Nietzsche-Forschung Ser.). (GER.). 1979. 150.00 (3-11-007861-9) De Gruyter.
— Nietzsche-Studien, Vol. 9. Behler, Ernst et al, eds. (Internationales Jahrbuch fuer die Nietzsche-Forschung Ser.). (GER.). 1980. 157.70 (3-11-008241-1) De Gruyter.
— Nietzsche-Studien, Vol. 10-11. (Internationales Jahrbuch fuer die Nietzsche-Forschung Ser.). (GER.). 1982. 215.40 (3-11-008638-7) De Gruyter.
— Nietzsche-Studien, Vol. 12. (Internationales Jahrbuch fuer die Nietzsche-Forschung Ser.). (GER.). 1982. 176.95 (3-11-009507-6) De Gruyter.
— Nietzsche-Studien, Vol. 13. (Internationales Jahrbuch fuer die Nietzsche-Forschung Ser.). (GER.). 1984. 234.65 (3-11-009648-X) De Gruyter.
— Nietzsche-Studien, Vol. 14. (Internationales Jahrbuch fuer die Nietzsche-Forschung Ser.). (GER.). 1985. 153.85 (3-11-010207-2) De Gruyter.
— Nietzsche-Studien, Vol. 15. (Internationales Jahrbuch fuer die Nietzsche-Forschung Ser.). (GER.). 1986. 176.95 (3-11-010540-3) De Gruyter.

— Nietzsche-Studien, Vol.5. (Internationales Jahrbuch fuer die Nietzsche-Forschung Ser.). (C). 1976. 134.65 (*3-11-006656-4*) De Gruyter.

— Nietzsche-Studien: Internationales Jahrbuch fuer Die Nietzsche - Forschung, Vol. 2. Montinari, Mazzino et al, eds. vi, 368p. (C). 1973. 112.35 (*3-11-004332-7*) De Gruyter.

— Nietzsche-Studien: Internationales Jahrbuch fuer die Nietzsche-Forschung, Vol. 1. Montinari, Mazzino et al, eds. 470p. (C). 1972. 142.35 (*3-11-002224-9*) De Gruyter.

— Nietzsche-Studien: Internationales Jahrbuch fuer Die Nietzsche-Forschung, Vol. 3. Montinari, Mazzino et al, eds. (GER.). (C). 1974. 73.10 (*3-11-004726-8*) De Gruyter.

— Nietzsche Werke: Kritische Gesamtausgabe Sect. 8, Vol. 3: Nachgelassene Fragmente Anfang 1888-Anfang Januar 1889. Colli, Giorgio & Montinari, Mazzino, eds. LC 68-84293. 484p. (C). 1972. 104.65x (*3-11-004192-8*) De Gruyter.

— Nietzsche Werke. Kritische Gesamtausgabe: Sect. 3, Vol. 2: Nachgelassene Schriften 1870-1873. Colli, Giorgio & Montinari, Mazzino, eds. 400p. (C). 1973. 86.15 (*3-11-004312-2*) De Gruyter.

— Nietzsche Werke, Kritische Gesamtausgabe, Sect. 3, Vol. 1: Die Geburt der Tragoedie. Unzeitgemaesse Betrachtungen I-III (1872-1874) Colli, Giorgio & Montinari, Mazzino, eds. iv, 427p. (C). 1972. 92.35 (*3-11-004294-0*) De Gruyter.

— Nietzsche Werke, Kritische Gesamtausgabe, Sect. 5, Vol. 1: Morgenroethe, Nachgelassene Fragmente Anfang 1880 bis Fruehjahr 1881. (C). 1971. 150.80 (*3-11-001828-4*) De Gruyter.

— Nietzsche Werke: Kritische Gesamtausgabe, Sect. 5, Vol. 2: Idyllen aus Messina. Die Froehliche Wissenschaft. Nachgelassene Fragmente Fruehjahr 1881 bis Sommer 1882. viii, 587p. (GER.). (C). 1973. 127.70 (*3-11-004476-5*) De Gruyter.

— Nietzsche Werke: Kritische Gesamtausgabe, Sect. 7, Vol. 2: Nachgelassene Fragmente Fruehjahr bis Herbst 1884. iv, 324p. (C). 1973. 69.25 (*3-11-004797-7*) De Gruyter.

— Nietzsche, Werke, Kritische Gesamtausgabe, Sect. 8, Vol. 1: Nachgelassene Fragmente, Herbst 1885 bis Herbst 1887. Colli, Giorgio & Montinari, Mazzino, eds. viii, 360p. (GER.). (C). 1974. 73.85x (*3-11-004741-1*) De Gruyter.

— Nietzsche Werke: Kritische Gesamtausgabe, Section 7, Vol. 3: Nachgelassene Fragmente Herbst 1884 bis Herbst 1885. iv, 476p. (C). 1974. 101.55 (*3-11-004983-X*) De Gruyter.

— On the Advantage & Disadvantage of History for Life. Preuss, Peter, tr. LC 80-16686. (HPC Classics Ser.). 70p. (C). 1980. lib. bdg. 15.00 (*0-915144-95-6*); pap. text ed. 3.95 (*0-915144-94-8*) Hackett Pub.

— On the Future of Our Educational Institutions & Homer & Classical Philology. 1974. lib. bdg. 300.00 (*0-87968-200-0*) Gordon Pr.

— On the Genealogy of Morality & Other Writings. Ansell-Pearson, Keith & Diethe, Carol, eds. LC 93-41334. (Texts in the History of Political Thought Ser.). 288p. (C). 1994. 39.95 (*0-521-40459-2*); pap. 11.95 (*0-521-40610-2*) Cambridge U Pr.

— On the Genealogy of Morals. Kaufmann, Walter, tr. 1989. pap. 11.00 (*0-679-72462-1*, Vin) Random.

— On the Genealogy of Morals. Kaufman, Walter, tr. Bd. with Ecce Homo. 1967. Set pap. 5.95 (*0-394-70401-0*, Vin) Random.

— Philosophical Writings. (German Library: Vol. 48). 324p. 1995. 29.50 (*0-8264-0278-X*); pap. text ed. 14.95 (*0-8264-0279-8*) Continuum.

— Philosophy & Truth: Selections from Nietzsche's Notebooks of the Early 1870s. Breazeale, Daniel, ed. & tr. by. LC 76-53746. (Humanities Paperback Library). 192p. (C). 1990. pap. 15.95 (*0-391-03671-8*) Humanities.

— Philosophy in the Tragic Age of the Greeks. Cowan, Marianne, tr. 117p. 1962. pap. 7.95 (*0-89526-944-9*) Regnery Pub.

— Portable Nietzsche. Kaufmann, Walter, ed. (Portable Library: No. 62). 1977. pap. 13.95 (*0-14-015062-5*, Penguin Bks) Viking Penguin.

— Saemtliche Briefe: Kritische Studienausgabe in 8 Baenden. Colli, Giorgio & Montinari, Mazzino, eds. 3630p. 1986. pap. 121.55 (*3-11-010963-8*) De Gruyter.

— Saemtliche Werke: Kritische Studierausgabe, 15 vols. 8800p. (GER.). 1980. 199.95 (*3-11-008117-2*) De Gruyter.

— Thoughts Out of Season, 2 vols. 1974. lib. bdg. 600.00 (*0-87968-202-7*) Gordon Pr.

— Thus Spake Zarathustra. 1974. lib. bdg. 300.00 (*0-87968-206-X*) Gordon Pr.

— Thus Spake Zarathustra. (Great Books in Philosophy). (Illus.). 341p. 1993. pap. 9.95 (*0-87975-861-9*) Prometheus Bks.

— Thus Spake Zarathustra. Common, Thomas, tr. LC 83-42947. 1982. 14.50 (*0-394-60808-9*, Modern Lib) Random.

— Thus Spoke Zarathustra. Kaufmann, Walter, tr. 1961. mass mkt. 9.95 (*0-14-044118-2*, Penguin Classics) Viking Penguin.

— Thus Spoke Zarathustra. Kaufmann, Walter, tr. 1978. pap. 10.95 (*0-14-004748-4*, Penguin Classics) Viking Penguin.

— Twilight of the Idols & the Anti-Christ. Hollingdale, R. J., tr. (Classics Ser.). (Orig.). 1990. mass mkt. 9.95 (*0-14-044514-5*, Penguin Classics) Viking Penguin.

— Unmodern Observations. Arrowsmith, William, ed. 424p. (C). 1990. text ed. 45.00 (*0-300-04311-2*) Yale U Pr.

— Untimely Meditations. Hollingdale, R. J., tr. LC 83-6604. (Texts in German Philosophy Ser.). 250p. 1984. pap. 16.95 (*0-521-28927-0*) Cambridge U Pr.

— Will to Power. 1976. 70.95 (*0-8488-1112-7*) Amereon Ltd.

— Will to Power. Kaufmann, Walter, tr. 1968. pap. 15.00 (*0-394-70437-1*, Vin) Random.

— The Will to Power, 2 vols., Set. 1974. lib. bdg. 600.00 (*0-87968-209-4*) Gordon Pr.

Nietzsche, Friedrich Wilhelm. Unfashionable Observations. Gray, Richard T., tr. LC 94-6177. (Complete Works of Friedrich Nietzsche: Vol. 2). 1995. 29.95 (*0-8047-2382-6*) Stanford U Pr.

***Nieuwbeerta, Paul.** The Democratic Class Struggle in Twenty Countries 1945-1990. 247p. 1995. pap. 28.00 (*90-5170-336-8*, Pub. by Thesis Pubs NE) IBD Ltd.

Nieuweboer, Adele, jt. auth. see Berkvens-Stevelinck, Christiane.

***Nieuwenhiuzen, Agnes, ed.** The Written World: Youth & Literature. 349p. 1994. pap. 30.00 (*1-875589-30-9*) D W Thorpe.

Nieuwenhuijzen, H., jt. ed. see De Jager, C.

***Nieuwenhuis.** Teamwork in Neuro. 1993. 46.95 (*1-56593-121-1*, 0433) Singular Publishing.

Nieuwenhuis, B., ed. Biotechnology R & D in the European Communities, EUR 14089. 96p. 1992. pap. 9.00 (*92-826-3743-3*, CD-NA-14089-EN-C, Pub. by Europ Com) UNIPUB.

Nieuwenhuis, Paul & Wells, Peter. Motor Vehicles in the Environment: Principles & Practice. LC 94-2542. 1994. text ed. 54.95 (*0-471-94943-4*) Wiley.

Nieuwenhuis, Tom. Politics & Society in Early Modern Iraq. 1982. lib. bdg. 70.00 (*90-247-2576-3*) Kluwer Ac.

Nieuwenhuys, Olga. Children's Lifeworlds: Gender, Welfare & Labour in the Developing World. LC 93-17607. 1994. 69.95 (*0-415-09750-9*); pap. 19.95 (*0-415-09751-7*) Routledge.

Nieuwenhuys, R. Chemoarchitechture of the Brain. (Illus.). 256p. 1985. pap. 104.00 (*0-387-15349-7*) Spr-Verlag.

Nieuwenhuys, R., et al. The Human Central Nervous System. (Illus.). 440p. 1993. pap. 69.00 (*0-387-13441-7*) Spr-Verlag.

Nieuwenhuys, Rob. Mirror of the Indies: A History of Dutch Colonial Literature. Beekman, E. M., ed. Van Rosevelt, Frans, tr. LC 82-4755. (Library of the Indies). 368p. 1982. text ed. 37.50x (*0-87023-368-8*) U of Mass Pr.

***Nieuwkerk, Karin van.** A Trade Like Any Other: Female Singers & Dancers in Egypt. LC 94-26452. 1995. 35.00 (*0-292-78720-0*) U of Tex Pr.

Nieuwkoop, P. D. & Faber, J., eds. Normal Table of Xenopus Laevis (Daudin) A Systematical & Chronological Survey of the Development from the Fertilized Egg till the End of Metamorphosis. LC 94-11518. (Illus.). 252p. 1994. pap. 55.00 (*0-8153-1896-0*) Garland.

Nieuwkoop, P. D., et al. The Epigenetic Nature of Early Chordate Development. (Developmental & Cell Biology Ser.: No. 16). 368p. 1985. 89.95 (*0-521-25107-9*) Cambridge U Pr.

Nieuwkoop, Pieter D. & Sutasurya, Lien A. Primordial Germ Cells in the Chordates: Embryogenesis & Phylogenesis. LC 78-18101. (Developmental & Cell Biology Ser.: No. 7). 199p. reprint ed. pap. 56.80 (*0-318-34829-2*, 2031700) Bks Demand.

Nieuwolt, S. Tropical Climatology: An Introduction to the Climates of the Low Latitudes. LC 76-13454. 217p. reprint ed. pap. 61.90 (*0-318-34859-4*, 2031024) Bks Demand.

Nieuwstadt, F. T., ed. Flow Visualization & Image Analysis. LC 92-32223. (Fluid Mechanics & Its Applications Ser.: Vol. 14). 1993. lib. bdg. 133.00 (*0-7923-1994-X*) Kluwer Ac.

***Nieuwstadt, F. T. & Steketee, J. A., eds.** Selected Papers of J. M. Burgers. LC 94-39288. 1994. lib. bdg. 317.00 (*0-7923-3265-2*) Kluwer Ac.

Nieuwstadt, F. T & Van Dop, Han, eds. Atmospheric Turbulence & Air Pollution Modelling. rev. ed. 1984. lib. bdg. 49.00 (*0-318-01663-X*) Kluwer Ac.

Nieuwstadt, F. T., jt. ed. see Dijksman, J. F.

Nieuwwolt, Simone, jt. auth. see Seguenny, Andre.

Nieva, Veronica & Gutek, Barbara. Women & Work: A Psychological Perspective. LC 81-2713. 190p. 1981. text ed. 47.50 (*0-275-90688-4*, C0688, Praeger Pubs) Greenwood.

Nievergelt, J., jt. auth. see Lemperle, G.

Nievergelt, J., et al, eds. Documents, Preparation Systems: A Collection of Survey Articles. 280p. 1983. 59.00 (*0-444-86493-8*, 1-498-82, North Holland) Elsevier.

Nievergelt, Jurg, et al. Small Programs for Small Machines: Computers & Education. LC 84-28338. 240p. 1985. pap. write for info. (*0-201-11129-2*) Addison-Wesley.

Nievergelt, Jurg & Hinrichs, Klaus H. Algorithms & Data Structures: With Applications to Graphics & Geometry. 336p. 1992. text ed. 62.00 (*0-13-489428-6*) P-H.

***Nievergelt, Jurg & International Workshop on Advanced Research in Geographic Information Systems Staff, eds.** IGIS 94--Geographic Information Systems: Proceedings of International Workshop on Advanced Research in Geographic Information Systems, Monte Verita, Ascona, Switzerland, February, March, 1994. LC 94-42163. (Lecture Notes in Computer Science: Vol. 884). 292p. 1994. pap. 40.00 (*0-387-58795-0*) Spr-Verlag.

Nievergelt, Yves. Fractals on Hewlett-Packard's HP 28 & 48. (Illus.). 74p. 1991. spiral bd. write for info. (*0-318-68932-4*) EduCALC Pubns.

— Mathematics in Business Administration. 528p. (C). 1989. text ed. 57.95 (*0-256-06914-X*) Irwin.

Nieves-Aponte, Miguel. Fundamentos Sociales de la Educacion. enl. ed. LC 77-23509. 329p. 1978. pap. 5.00 (*0-8477-2734-3*) U of PR Pr.

Nieves, Ernesto R., illus. Juan Bobo: Four Folktales from Puerto Rico. LC 93-12936. (I Can Read Bk.). 64p. (J). (gr. k-3). 1994. 14.00 (*0-06-023389-3*) HarpC.

— Juan Bobo: Four Folktales from Puerto Rico. LC 93-12936. (I Can Read Bk.). 64p. (J). (gr. k-3). 1994. lib. bdg. 13.89 (*0-06-023390-7*) HarpC.

Nieves, Luis. El Exito Universitario a Traves de la Aplicacion de los Meodos de Autayuda: Un Manual de Asesoramiento y Planificacion para Estudiantes. 5.25 (*0-317-67874-4*) Educ Testing Serv.

Nieves, Luis R. Coping in College: Successful Strategies. 134p. 1986. mass mkt. 6.95 (*0-446-38483-6*) Warner Bks.

— El Exito Universitario a Traves de la Aplicacion de los Metodos de Autoayuda: Un Manual de Asesoramiento y Planificacion para Estudiantes. 1986. mass mkt. 5.25 (*0-446-38491-7*) Warner Bks.

Nieves, Myrna. Cuentos. 100p. (Orig.). (SPA.). 1991. pap. 8.00 (*0-685-26448-3*) Atabex Collection.

Nieves Sanchez, Maria, ed. Sumario de la Medicina, Francisco Lopez de Villalobos, I-1169: Biblioteca Nacional de Madrid. (Medieval Spanish Medical Texts Ser.: No. 13). 8p. (SPA.). 1987. 10.00 (*0-940639-09-2*) Hispanic Seminary.

— Tratado de la Phisonomia, I-51: Biblioteca Nacional, Madrid. (Medieval Spanish Medical Texts Ser.: No. 14). 8p. (SPA.). 1987. 10.00 (*0-940639-10-6*) Hispanic Seminary.

Nieves, Walter L., ed. see Maigne, Robert.

Nievo, Ippolito. Castle of Fratta. Edwards, Lovett F., tr. LC 74-10017. 589p. 1974. reprint ed. text ed. 38.50 (*0-8371-7660-3*, NICA, Greenwood Pr) Greenwood.

Niewahner, James, jt. auth. see Hicks, Vernon.

Niewahner, James H., jt. auth. see Hawkins, Charles E.

Niewerth, Hans. Lexikon der Planun und Organisation. (GER.). 1968. 65.00 (*0-8288-6651-1*, M-7235) Fr & Eur.

Niewiadoma, M. English-Polish Dictionary of Accounting with Polish Index. 280p. 1993. 98.00x (*83-85385-15-0*, Pub. by Centrum Kreowania PL) IBD Ltd.

— English-Polish Dictionary of Accounting with Polish Index. 280p. (ENG & POL.). 1993. write for info. (*0-7859-8771-1*) Fr & Eur.

Niewiadomski. Filter Handbook. 1989. 30.95 (*0-8493-7131-7*, TK) CRC Pr.

Niewiadomski, H. Rapeseed: Chemistry & Technology. (Developments in Food Science Ser.: No. 23). 448p. 1990. 118.00 (*0-444-98799-1*) Elsevier.

Niewiadomski, Henryk & Szczepanska, Hanna. By-Products & Waste Materials in Fat Technology. 352p. 1995. text ed. 69.95 (*0-13-109547-1*) P-H.

***Niewyk, Donald L.** Socialist, Anti-Semite, & Jew: German Social Democracy Confronts the Problem of Anti-Semitism, 1918-1933. LC 79-137123. 264p. 1971. pap. 75.30 (*0-7837-8519-4*, 2049328) Bks Demand.

Niewyk, Donald L., ed. The Holocaust: Problems & Perspectives of Interpretation. (Problems in European Civilization Ser.). 267p. (C). 1992. pap. text ed. write for info. (*0-669-27291-4*) Heath.

Niewyk, Donald L., tr. see Stoldt, Hans-Herbert.

Niezgodka, Marek, jr. see Meirmanov, Anvarbek M.

Niezing, Johan. Sociology, War & Disarmament: Studies in Peace Research. 131p. 1973. pap. text ed. 18.95 (*90-237-6223-1*) Transaction Pubs.

— Strategy & Structure: Studies in Peace Research II. 68p. 1978. pap. text ed. 17.95 (*90-265-0274-5*) Transaction Pubs.

NIF Staff. Admission Decisions: Should Immigration Be Restricted? 32p. 1994. 2.95 (*0-8403-9446-2*) Kendall-Hunt.

***Niffenegger, Bill.** Kai's Power Tools Finesse: The Official Book/CD-ROM. Date not set. cd-rom 45.00 (*0-679-76045-8*) Random.

— Photoshop Filters Toolkit with Disk: Amazing Special Effects with PhotoShop Painter & More. 1994. pap. 45.00 (*0-679-75324-9*) Random.

Nigal, Gedalyah. Magic, Mysticism, & Hasidism: The Supernatural in Jewish Thought. Levin, Edward, tr. LC 93-34030. 304p. 1994. 30.00 (*1-56821-033-7*) Aronson.

Nigam, J. K., jt. ed. see Prasad, Paras N.

***Nigam, N. C.** Applications of Random Vibrations. 557p. 1994. 114.00 (*0-387-19861-X*) Spr-Verlag.

Nigam, Santosh, et al, eds. Eicosanoids & Other Bioactive Lipids in Cancer, Inflammation, & Radiation Injury: Proceedings of the 2nd International Conference, September 17-21, 1991, Berlin, FRG. LC 92-23659. (Developments in Oncology Ser.: Vol. 71). 848p. (C). 1992. lib. bdg. 182.00 (*0-7923-1870-6*) Kluwer Ac.

Niger, Shmuel. Bilingualism in the History of Jewish Literature. Fogel, Joshua A., tr. LC 89-24789. 140p. (C). 1990. lib. bdg. 33.00 (*0-8191-7382-7*) U Pr of Amer.

Nigerian Resource Centre for Indigenous Knowledge Staff, tr. see Atte, O. David.

Nigg, B. M. & Herzog, W. Biomechanics of the Musculo-Skeletal System. LC 94-1827. 1994. text ed. 59.95 (*0-471-94444-0*) Wiley.

Nigg, Benno M., ed. Biomechanics of Running Shoes. LC 85-2460. 192p. 1986. text ed. 40.00x (*0-87322-002-1*, BNIG0002) Human Kinetics.

Nigg, Herbert N. & Seigler, David S., eds. Phytochemical Resources for Medicine & Agriculture. LC 92-20152. 1992. 95.00 (*0-306-44245-0*, Plenum Pr) Plenum.

Nigg, Joe. The Great Balloon Festival: A Season of Hot Air Balloon Meets Across North America. (Illus.). 208p. 1989. 39.95 (*0-9621741-0-6*) Free Flght Pr.

— Winegold: Short Stories. LC 85-51697. 71p. 1985. 15.00 (*0-933573-04-9*); pap. 7.00 (*0-933573-05-7*) Wayland Pr.

— Wonder Beasts: Tales & Lore of the Phoenix, the Griffin, the Unicorn, & the Dragon. LC 94-46797. (Illus.). 180p. 1995. lib. bdg. 24.50 (*1-56308-242-X*) Libs Unl.

Nigg, Walter. Heretics: Heresy Through the Ages. Winston, Clara, ed. Winston, Richard & Winston, Clara, trs. (Reprints Ser.). 412p. 1990. 19.95 (*0-88029-455-8*) Dorset Pr.

Niggli, Josephina. Mexican Folk Plays. Koch, Frederick H., ed. LC 76-1260. (Chicano Heritage Ser.). (Illus.). 1977. reprint ed. 23.95 (*0-405-09517-1*) Ayer.

— Mexican Village. LC 93-14886. 526p. (C). 1994. reprint ed. pap. 17.95 (*0-8263-1338-8*) U of NM Pr.

Niggli, Paul. Rocks & Mineral Deposits, Vol. 1. Parker, Robert L., tr. LC 53-8082. (Geology Texts Ser.). 573p. reprint ed. pap. 163.40 (*0-317-29240-4*, 2055547) Bks Demand.

Nigh, Douglas, jt. ed. see Toyne, Brian.

Nighbert, Esther. Learning Through Creative Dramatics. 1987. 8.50 (*0-88047-117-4*, 8619) DOK Pubs.

Nighswander, Ada. The Little Martins Learn to Love. (J). (ps-4). 1982. 6.95 (*0-686-30775-5*) Rod & Staff.

Nighswander, James K. On Becoming a Cosmetology Teacher. 1991. pap. text ed. 26.00 (*1-56253-086-0*) Milady Pub.

— School Discipline-A Planning & Resource Guide. 500p. 1987. teacher ed 2.50 (*0-932957-92-7*); teacher ed 200.00 (*0-932957-93-5*) Natl School.

***Nightbert, David F.** Shutout. 1995. 21.95 (*0-312-11890-2*) St Martin.

Nightengale, J. E. Contributions Towards the History of Early English Porcelain from Contemporary Sources. 1976. reprint ed. 12.50 (*0-85409-839-9*) Charles River Bks.

***Nightengale, Robert.** Little Big Horn. (Illus.). 364p. (Orig.). 1995. pap. 24.95 (*1-886768-00-5*) Blue Bk Pubns.

Nighthawk, MC, pseud. Rovers of the Night Sky. 214p. pap. 19.95 (*0-947898-01-8*, 5579) Stackpole.

Nightingale-Bamford School Staff. The Cooks' Book. Wolfson, Rita, ed. (Illus.). 224p. (Orig.). 1987. pap. text ed. 12.00 (*0-9618051-0-2*) Nightingale-Bamford Schl.

***Nightingale-Bamford School Staff, ed.** Poems for Life: Famous People Select Their Favorite Poem & Say Why It Inspires Them. LC 94-39896. (Illus.). 128p. 1995. 16.95 (*1-55970-286-9*) Arcade Pub Inc.

***Nightingale, Carl H.** On the Edge: A History of Poor Black Children & Their American Dreams. 272p. 1994. pap. 14.00 (*0-465-05219-3*) Basic.

Nightingale, Demetra S. & Haveman, Robert H., eds. The Work Alternative: Welfare Reform & the Realities of the Job Market. 230p. (C). 1995. 24.95 (*0-87766-623-7*) Urban Inst.

Nightingale, Demetra S., et al. Evaluation of the Massachusetts Employment & Training (ET) Choices Program. LC 90-19842. (Report Ser.: No. 91-1). (Illus.). 250p. (Orig.). (C). 1991. lib. bdg. 49.00 (*0-87766-499-4*); pap. text ed. 21.50 (*0-87766-500-1*) Urban Inst.

Nightingale, Derek. Local Management of Schools: At Work in the Primary School. (School Development & the Management of Change Ser.). 224p. 1990. 55.00 (*1-85000-648-2*, Falmer Pr); pap. 29.00 (*1-85000-649-0*, Falmer Pr) Taylor & Francis.

Nightingale, Donald V. Workplace Democracy: An Inquiry into Employee Participation in Canadian Work Organizations. 336p. 1982. pap. 18.95 (*0-8020-6470-1*) U of Toronto Pr.

Nightingale, Earl. Earl Nightingale's Greatest Discovery. 182p. 1987. 16.95 (*0-396-08928-3*) WC Stone PMA.

Nightingale, Elena O. & Goodman, Melissa. Before Birth: Prenatal Testing for Genetic Disease. (Illus.). 128p. 1990. 27.00 (*0-674-06390-2*); pap. text ed. 9.95 (*0-674-06391-0*) HUP.

Nightingale, Elena O. & Meister, Susan B., eds. Prenatal Screening, Policies, & Values: The Example of Neural Tube Defects. (Illus.). 160p. 1987. pap. 10.95 (*0-674-70075-9*) HUP.

Nightingale, Florence. Cassandra. LC 79-15175. 64p. (Orig.). 1980. pap. 5.95 (*0-912670-55-X*) Feminist Pr.

— Cassandra & Suggestions for Thought. Poovey, Mary, ed. (Women's Classics Ser.). 250p. 1992. text ed. 55.00x (*0-8147-5773-1*); pap. 18.95 (*0-8147-5775-8*) NYU Pr.

— Ever Yours, Florence Nightingale: Selected Letters. Vicinus, Martha & Nergaard, Bea, eds. (Illus.). 480p. 1990. text ed. 32.00 (*0-674-27020-7*) HUP.

— Letters from Egypt: A Journey on the Nile, 1849-1850. 1992. 24.95 (*0-8021-1532-2*) Grove-Atltic.

— Notes on Hospitals. 1976. lib. bdg. 150.00 (*0-8490-2357-2*) Gordon Pr.

— Notes on Nursing: What It Is, & What It Is Not. LC 79-79233. 1969. pap. 3.95 (*0-486-22340-X*) Dover.

— Notes on Nursing: What It Is, & What It Is Not. 140p. 1987. reprint ed. lib. bdg. 21.95 (*0-89966-604-3*) Buccaneer Bks.

— Notes on Nursing, Replica Edition: What it is, What it is Not. 79p. 1946. text ed. 14.95 (*0-397-54000-0*, 64-01046, Lippincott Nursing) Lippincott.

Nightingale, Florence & Barnum, Barbara S. Notes on Nursing: What It Is, & What It Is Not. LC 92-15476. 1992. 24.95 (*0-397-55007-3*) Lippincott.

Nightingale, Jean. Without a Gate. 363p. (Orig.). 1990. pap. 6.95 (*9971-972-92-1*) OMF Bks.

Nightingale, Jennifer L., jt. auth. see Nightingale, Nancy R.

***Nightingale, Kate, et al.** Learning to Care in the Operating Department. 2nd ed. 112p. 1994. pap. text ed. 18.95 (*1-56593-394-X*, 0816) Singular Publishing.

Nightingale, Ken. One Way Through the Jungle. 1975. pap. 2.50 (*0-85363-107-7*) OMF Bks.

Nightingale, Michael. Acupuncture. (Alternataive Health Ser.). (Illus.). 128p. (Orig.). 1994. pap. 12.95 (*0-8048-3004-5*) C E Tuttle.

***Nightingale, Nancy R. & Nightingale, Jennifer L.** Step-by-Step Meals: For People with Cognitive Challenges. 248p. 1993. pap. text ed., ring bd. 66.00 (*0-88450-639-8*, 4287) Commun Skill.

Nightingale, Neil. New Guinea: An Island Apart. (Illus.). 146p. 1993. 29.95 (*0-563-36161-1*, BBC-Parkwest) Parkwest Pubns.

***Nightingale, Pamela.** A Medieval Mercantile Community: The Grocers' Company & the Politics & Trade of London. LC 95-12262. 1995. write for info. (*0-300-06325-3*) Yale U Pr.

N

An Asterisk (*) at the beginning of an entry indicates that the title is appearing in BIP for the first time.

Nightingale, Peggy. Journey Through Darkness: The Writing of V. S. Naipaul. LC 86-13231. 255p. (Orig.). 1987. pap. text ed. 29.95 (*0-7022-2016-7*, Pub. by Univ Queensland Pr AT) Intl Spec Bk.

Nightingale, Peggy, ed. A Sense of Place in the New Literatures in English. 252p. 1986. text ed. 29.95 (*0-7022-1849-9*, Pub. by Univ Queensland Pr AT) Intl Spec Bk.

Nightingale, Peggy, jt. ed. see O'Neil, Mike.

Nightingale, Sandy. Cat's Knees & Bee's Whiskers. LC 92-39811. (Illus.). (J). 1993. 14.95 (*0-15-215364-0*) HarBrace.

— A Giraffe on the Moon. (J). (ps-1). 1992. 13.95 (*0-15-230950-0*, HB Juv Bks) HarBrace.

— I'm a Little Monster: Words & Pictures. LC 94-18345. (Illus.). 1995. 15.00 (*0-15-200309-6*) HarBrace.

— Pink Pigs A-Plenty. (J). (ps-3). 1992. 14.95 (*0-15-261882-1*, HB Juv Bks) HarBrace.

Nightingale, Susan & I.C.E., Inc. Staff. Electric Bread. rev. ed. LC 91-72650. (Illus.). 160p. 1993. reprint ed. 29.95 (*0-9629831-0-1*) Innov Cook Enter.

Nightingale, Susan, jt. auth. see I. C. E. Inc. Staff.

Nightingale, Tom & Hill, Mike. Birds of Bahrain. 288p. (C). 1990. 150.00 (*0-907151-79-5*, Pub. by IMMEL Pubng UK) St Mut.

Nigl, Alfred J. Biofeedback & Behavioral Strategies in Pain Treatment. LC 84-14083. 368p. 1984. text ed. 42.50 (*0-89335-203-9*) PMA Pub Corp.

Nigmatulin, R. I. Dynamics of Multiphase Media: Revised & Augmented Edition, 2 vols., Set. rev. ed. Friedly, John C., ed. Piterman, Mark A., tr. 1990. 199.00 (*1-56032-207-1*) Hemisp Pub.

— Dynamics of Multiphase Media: Revised & Augmented Edition, 2 vols., Vol. 1. rev. ed. Friedly, John C., ed. Piterman, Mark A., tr. 536p. 1990. 133.00 (*0-89116-316-6*) Hemisp Pub.

— Dynamics of Multiphase Media: Revised & Augmented Edition, 2 vols., Vol. 2. rev. ed. Friedly, John C., ed. Piterman, Mark A., tr. 384p. 1990. 105.00 (*0-89116-328-X*) Hemisp Pub.

Nigosian, S. A. World Faiths. 2nd ed. 234p. (Orig.). 1994. text ed. 35.00 (*0-312-10274-7*) St Martin.

— World Faiths. 2nd ed. 560p. 1993. pap. text ed. 20.00 (*0-312-08414-5*) St Martin.

— The Zoroastrian Faith: Tradition & Modern Research. 168p. 1993. 39.95 (*0-7735-1133-4*, Pub. by McGill CN); pap. 17.95 (*0-7735-1144-X*, Pub. by McGill CN) U of Toronto Pr.

Nigosian, Soloman A. World Faiths. LC 88-63092. 512p. (Orig.). 1990. text ed. 45.00 (*0-312-04019-9*) St Martin.

Nigosian, Solomon. Islam: The Way of Submission. 216p. (C). 1989. reprint ed. lib. bdg. 33.00x (*0-8095-7085-8*) Borgo Pr.

Nigrin, Albert. Neural Networks for Pattern Recognition. LC 93-10027. (Illus.). 404p. 1993. 50.00 (*0-262-14054-3*, Bradford Bks) MIT Pr.

Nigro. Decision Making in the Public Sector. (Public Administration & Public Policy Ser.: Vol. 25). 336p. 1984. 59.75 (*0-8247-7155-9*) Dekker.

Nigro, August J. The Diagonal Line. LC 83-50945. 192p. 1984. 32.50 (*0-941664-02-3*) Susquehanna U Pr.

*__Nigro, Debbie.__ The Working Mom on the Run Manual or What the Heck Happened to My Life? A.K.A. What the Heck Happened to My Life? 220p. 1995. pap. 9.95 (*1-57101-011-4*) MasterMedia Ltd.

Nigro, Felix A. & Nigro, Lloyd G. Modern Public Administration. 7th ed. 448p. (C). 1990. text ed. 29.50 (*0-06-044829-6*) HarpCollege.

Nigro, Felix A., jt. auth. see Nigro, Lloyd G.

Nigro, Kirsten F. Palabras Mas Que Comunes: Ensayos Sobre el Teatro de Jose Triana. 168p. 1993. pap. 32.00 (*0-89295-073-0*) Society Sp & Sp-Am.

Nigro, Lloyd G. & Nigro, Felix A. The New Public Personnel Administration. 4th ed. LC 92-61962. 348p. (C). 1994. boxed 44.00 (*0-87581-374-7*) Peacock Pubs.

Nigro, Lloyd G., jt. auth. see Nigro, Felix A.

Nigro, Salvatore S. Pontormo: Paintings. LC 93-31283. 1994. 75.00 (*0-8109-3727-1*) Abrams.

Nigro, Salvatore S., intro. Pontormo: Drawings. (Illus.). 160p. 1992. 75.00 (*0-8109-3717-4*) Abrams.

Nigro, Susan L. Laffs from the Bottom of the Pit: The Musicians Joke Book ... for Conductors Too! Parker, Diane, ed. Quinn, Kaye, tr. LC 92-54176. (Adult Edition Ser.). (Illus.). 80p. 1992. spiral bd. 5.95 (*0-88247-930-X*) R & E Pubs.

— Laffs from the Bottom of the Pit: The Musicians Joke Book...for Conductors Too! Parker, Diane, ed. LC 92-53718. (Illus.). 75p. (Orig.). 1992. spiral bd. 5.95 (*0-88247-921-0*) R & E Pubs.

— More Laffs from the Bottom of the Pit. LC 93-43756. 1994. 6.95 (*1-56875-082-X*) R & E Pubs.

Nigrosh, Leon. Sculpting Clay. (Illus.). 192p. 1992. 25.95 (*0-87192-236-3*) Davis Mass.

Nigrosh, Leon I. Claywork: Form & Idea in Ceramics Design. 3rd ed. LC 93-74643. (Illus.). 296p. 1995. text ed. 33.71 (*0-87192-285-1*) Davis Mass.

— Low Fire: Other Ways to Work in Clay. LC 79-56377. (Illus.). 112p. 1980. 19.95 (*0-87192-120-0*) Davis Mass.

Nigst, H., et al. Hand Surgery, Vol. 1. McGregor, Alan D., tr. (Illus.). 652p. 1988. text ed. 245.00 (*0-86577-233-9*) Thieme Med Pubs.

*__Niguidula, David.__ Introduction to Programming: A Graphical Approach. (Illus.). 750p. 1994. write for info. (*0-615-00245-5*) Addison-Wesley.

Niguidula, David & Van Dam, Andries. Pascal on the Macintosh. LC 86-20668. (C). 1987. pap. text ed. 36.75 (*0-201-16588-0*) Addison-Wesley.

*__Niguidula, David, et al.__ Object-Oriented Turbo Pascal: A Graphical Approach. 752p. (C). 1996. pap. text ed. 40.95x (*0-201-62883-X*) Addison-Wesley.

Nihan, James F. The Marxist Empire: Communist Dream - World Nightmare. 313p. 1990. pap. 26.80 (*0-89412-171-5*) Aegean Park Pr.

Nihei, Yasumitsu, jt. auth. see Stewart, Charles T., Jr.

Nihelena Ormazebel, Michel. Diccionaire Basque Pour Tous: Francais-Basque. 660p. 1975. pap. 6.95 (*0-7859-6033-3*, 8440082304) Fr & Eur.

Nihin Vogue Staff. Fine Crochet Lace. 2nd ed. (Illus.). 90p. 1982. pap. 13.95 (*0-87040-503-9*) Japan Pubns USA.

Nihon Vogue Staff. Basic Embroidery. (Illus.). 1986. pap. 7.95 (*0-87040-650-7*) Japan Pubns USA.

— Basic Lace. (Illus.). 1986. pap. 10.95 (*0-87040-651-5*) Japan Pubns USA.

— Beautiful Lace. LC 81-84803. (Illus.). 82p. 1982. pap. 11.95 (*0-87040-504-7*) Japan Pubns USA.

— The Best Collections of Cross Stitch Design & Handywork. LC 82-81054. (Illus.). 84p. 1982. pap. 12.95 (*0-87040-522-5*) Japan Pubns USA.

— Golden Lace. (Illus.). 90p. (Orig.). 1983. pap. 13.95 (*0-87040-562-4*) Japan Pubns USA.

— Hook Knitting: New Concepts in Crochet. (Illus.). 76p. (Orig.). 1986. pap. 15.95 (*0-87040-710-4*) Japan Pubns USA.

— Lace for Beginners. (Illus.). 82p. 1984. pap. 13.95 (*0-87040-567-5*) Japan Pubns USA.

— Lovely Cross Stitch Designs. (Illus.). 84p. (Orig.). 1983. pap. 11.95 (*0-87040-529-2*) Japan Pubns USA.

— Mohair Knitting. (Illus.). 80p. (Orig.). 1985. pap. 15.95 (*0-87040-610-8*) Japan Pubns USA.

— Sashiko: Traditional Japanese Quilt Designs. LC 88-80146. (Illus.). 42p. (Orig.). 1989. pap. 11.95 (*0-87040-769-4*) Japan Pubns USA.

— Simple Pineapple Crochet. (Illus.). 74p. 1995. pap. text ed. 15.00 (*0-87040-951-4*) Japan Pubns USA.

— White Sweaters. (Illus.). 61p. (Orig.). 1987. pap. 14.95 (*0-87040-652-3*) Japan Pubns USA.

Nihoul, J. C., ed. Coupled Ocean-Atmosphere Models: Proceedings of the Sixteenth International Liege Colloquium on Ocean Hydrodynamics Liege, Belgium, May 7-11, 1984. (Oceanography Ser.: 40). 768p. 1985. 146.25 (*0-444-42486-5*) Elsevier.

— Hydrodynamics of Semi-Enclosed Seas. (Oceanography Ser.: Vol. 34). 556p. 1982. 113.00 (*0-444-42077-0*, I-172-82) Elsevier.

— Marine Forecasting: Predictability & Modelling in Ocean Hydrodynamics. (Oceanography Ser.: Vol. 25). 1979. 113.00 (*0-444-41797-4*) Elsevier.

— Marine Interfaces Ecohydrodynamics: Proceedings of the 17th International Liege Colloquium on Ocean Hydrodynmics. (Oceanography Ser.: Vol. 42). 670p. 1986. 118.00 (*0-444-42626-4*) Elsevier.

— Marine Turbulence: Proceedings of the 11th International Colloquium. (Oceanography Ser.: Vol. 28). 378p. 1980. 95.00 (*0-444-41881-4*) Elsevier.

— Modelling of Marine Systems. LC 74-77585. (Oceanography Ser.: Vol. 10). 272p. 1975. 100.00 (*0-444-41232-8*) Elsevier.

— Remote Sensing of Shelf Sea Hydrodynamics: Proceedings of the International Liege Colloquium on Ocean Hydrodynamics, 15th, May 2-6, 1983. (Oceanography Ser.: No. 38). 354p. 1984. 105.25 (*0-444-42314-1*) Elsevier.

Nihoul, J. C. & Jamart, B. M., eds. Mesoscale-Synoptic Coherent Structures in Geophysical Turbulence: Proceedings of the 20th International Liege Colloquium on Ocean Hydrodynamics. (Oceanography Ser.). 842p. 1989. 148.75 (*0-444-87470-4*) Elsevier.

— Small-Scale Turbulence & Mixing in the Ocean: Proceeding of the 19th Liege Colloquium on Ocean Hydrodynamics, Liege, Belgium, 4-9 May, 1987. (Oceanography Ser.: 46). 542p. 1988. 123.00 (*0-444-42987-5*) Elsevier.

— Three-Dimensional Models of Marine & Estuarine Dyanmics. 360p. 1987. 146.25 (*0-444-42794-5*) Elsevier.

Nihoul, J. C., jt. auth. see Brasseur, P.

Nii, Koichi P., tr. see Nakahara, Yasuo.

Nii-owoo, Ife. A Is for Africa: Looking at Africa Through the Alphabet. LC 90-81575. (Young Reader's Ser.). (Illus.). 32p. (J). (ps-00). 1992. 12.95 (*0-86543-182-5*); pap. 5.95 (*0-86543-183-3*) Africa World.

*__Niihara, Koichi, et al, eds.__ Materials Processing & Design: Grain-Boundary-Controlled Properties of Fine Ceramics II. (Transactions Ser.: Vol. 44). 1994. 83.00 (*0-944904-78-5*, 1EBK01M) Am Ceramic.

*__Niimi.__ Progress in Microcirculation Research. LC 94-26568. 521p. 1994. 165.00 (*0-08-042503-8*, Pergamon Pr) Elsevier.

Niinikoski, J., jt. ed. see Aro, H.

Niiniluoto, I. & Tuomela, Raimo. Theoretical Concepts & Hypothetico-Inductive Inference. LC 73-83567. (Synthese Library: No. 53). 1973. lib. bdg. 84.00 (*90-277-0343-4*) Kluwer Ac.

Niiniluoto, Ilkka. Is Science Progressive? 1984. lib. bdg. 39.50 (*0-318-03669-X*) Kluwer Ac.

Niiro, Katsuyuki, jt. ed. see Boenau, A. Bruce.

Niitsuma, N., jt. auth. see Matsuda, T.

Nijboer, J. F., et al, eds. Forensic Expertise & the Law of Evidence: Proceedings of the Colloquium, Amsterdam, the Netherlands, August 1992. 204p. 1993. pap. 42.75 (*0-444-85777-X*, North Holland) Elsevier.

Nijdam, J., jt. ed. see Netherlands, Ministry of Agriculture.

Nijenhuis, Albert & Will, Herbert S. Combinatorial Algorithms: For Computers & Hard Calculators. 2nd ed. (Computer Science & Applied Mathematics Ser.). 1978. text ed. 66.00 (*0-12-519260-6*) Acad Pr.

Nijenhuis, Willem. Ecclesia Reformata. (Studies on the Reformation: Vol. II). 320p. 1994. 77.25 (*90-04-09465-2*, NLG135) E J Brill.

Nijhawan, B. R., ed. Production of Iron, Steel & High Quality Product Mix: Latest Technological Innovations & Processes. 316p. 1993. 108.00 (*0-87170-457-9*, 6258NR) ASM.

Nijholt, A. Context-Free Grammars: Covers, Normal Forms, & Parsing. (Lecture Notes in Computer Science Ser.: Vol. 93). 253p. 1980. pap. 28.00 (*0-387-10245-0*) Spr-Verlag.

Nijholt, A., ed. Computers & Languages: Theory & Practice - Studies in Computer Science & Artificial Intelligence. 482p. 1988. 87.25 (*0-444-70463-9*, North Holland) Elsevier.

Nijhout, H. Frederick. Insect Hormones. LC 93-42301. 1994. 35.00 (*0-691-03466-4*) Princeton U Pr.

Nijhout, H. Frederik. The Development & Evolution of Butterfly Wing Patterns. LC 90-24312. (Series in Comparative Evolutionary Biology). (Illus.). 336p. (C). 1991. 45.00 (*0-87474-921-2*); pap. text ed. 25.00 (*0-87474-917-4*) Smithsonian.

Nijhuis, Jan G., ed. Fetal Behaviour: Developmental & Perinatal Aspects. LC 92-12913. (Illus.). 312p. 1992. 78.00 (*0-19-262089-4*) OUP.

Nijhuis, Miep. Fuchsias: The Complete Handbook. (Illus.). 272p. 1994. 22.95 (*0-304-34387-0*, Pub. by Cassell UK) Sterling.

— One Thousand Fuchsias. (Illus.). 176p. 1994. 34.95 (*0-7134-7587-0*, Pub. by Batsford UK) Trafalgar.

Nijim, Basheer K., ed. American Church Politics & the Middle East. (Monograph Ser.: No. 15). 156p. (Orig.). 1982. pap. 6.95 (*0-937694-53-3*) Assn Arab-Amer U Grads.

Nijinska, Bronislava. Bronislava Nijinska: Early Memoirs. Nijinska, Irina & Rawlinson, Jean, eds. Rawlinson, Jean, tr. LC 92-13666. (Illus.). 576p. 1992. pap. 18.95 (*0-8223-1295-6*) Duke.

Nijinska, Irina, ed. see Nijinska, Bronislava.

Nijinsky, Romola, ed. The Diary of Vaslav Nijinsky. (Illus.). 1968. pap. 11.95 (*0-520-00945-2*) U CA Pr.

Nijinsky, Tamara. The Nijinsky Legacy. Sarda, Michel F. & Ray, Donnalee, eds. (Illus.). 144p. (Orig.). 1990. write for info. (*0-318-64825-3*) Bridgewood Pr.

Nijinsky, Vaslav. L' Apres-Midi D'Un Faune: Vaslav Nijinsky 1912. 140p. 1995. reprint ed. 49.95 (*0-87127-136-2*, Dance Horizons) Princeton Bk Co.

Nijkamp, E. P., et al, eds. Mediators in Airway Hyperreactivity. (Agents & Actions Supplements Ser.: Vol. 31). 296p. 1990. 67.00 (*0-8176-2513-5*) Birkhauser.

Nijkamp, H. J., et al, eds. Progress in Plant Cellular & Molecular Biology. (Current Plant Science & Biotechnology Ser.). (C). 1990. lib. bdg. 205.00 (*0-7923-0873-5*) Kluwer Ac.

Nijkamp, P. & Reichman, S. Transportation Planning in a Changing World. 320p. 1987. text ed. 59.95 (*0-566-05250-4*, Pub. by Avebury Pub UK) Ashgate Pub Co.

Nijkamp, P., jt. ed. see Coccossis, H.

Nijkamp, Peter. Environmental Policy Analysis: Operational Methods & Models. LC 79-41778. (Illus.). 299p. reprint ed. pap. 85.30 (*0-685-20599-1*, 2030533) Bks Demand.

— Impact Assessment & Evaluation in Transportation Planning. (Transportation, Research, Economics & Policy Ser.). 284p. (C). 1994. lib. bdg. 94.50 (*0-7923-2648-2*) Kluwer Ac.

— Sustainability of Urban Systems: A Cross-National Evolutionary Analysis of Urban Innovation. 323p. 1990. text ed. 68.95 (*1-85628-094-2*, Pub. by Avebury Pub UK) Ashgate Pub Co.

Nijkamp, Peter, ed. Environmental Economics, Vol. 2. 1976. pap. text ed. 39.00 (*90-207-0645-4*) Kluwer Ac.

— Europe on the Move. 362p. 1993. 68.95 (*1-85628-547-2*, Pub. by Avebury Pub UK) Ashgate Pub Co.

— New Borders & Old Barriers in Spatial Development. LC 94-7287. 1994. 63.95 (*1-85628-906-0*, Pub. by Avebury Pub UK) Ashgate Pub Co.

Nijkamp, Peter & Giaoutzi, Maria. Decision Support Models for Regional Sustainable Development: An Application of Geographic Information Systems & Evaluation Models to the Greek Sporades Islands. 314p. 1993. 59.95 (*1-85628-496-4*, Pub. by Avebury Pub UK) Ashgate Pub Co.

Nijkamp, Peter & Leitner, Helga, eds. Measuring the Unmeasurable: Analysis of Qualitative Spatial Data. Wrigley, Neil, tr. 1985. lib. bdg. 202.50 (*90-247-3124-0*) Kluwer Ac.

Nijkamp, Peter & Mills, E. S. Handbook of Regional & Urban Economics: Volumes One & Two. 1987. 150.00 (*0-444-87971-4*) Elsevier.

*__Nijkamp, Peter & Perrels, Adriaan.__ Sustaining Cities in Europe. 1994. 49.95 (*1-85383-229-4*, Pub. by Erthscan Pubns UK); pap. 24.95 (*1-85383-203-0*, Pub. by Erthscan Pubns UK) Island Pr.

Nijkamp, Peter & Reggiani, Aura. Interaction, Evolution, & Chaos in Space. LC 92-13515. (Illus.). xii, 276p. 1992. 98.00 (*3-540-55458-0*); 98.00 (*0-387-55458-0*) Spr-Verlag.

Nijkamp, Peter & Reggiani, Aura, eds. Nonlinear Evolution of Spatial Economic Systems. LC 93-34002. (Illus.). x, 285p. 1993. 98.00 (*0-387-57162-0*) Spr-Verlag.

Nijkamp, Peter & Rietveld, P. Information Systems for Integrated Regional Planning. (Contributions to Economic Analysis Ser.: Vol. 149). 1984. 82.00 (*0-444-86828-3*, 1-464-83) Elsevier.

Nijkamp, Peter & Rietveld, Piet. Cities in Transition: Problems & Policies. (NATO Advanced Study, Behavioral & Social Sciences Ser.: No. 4). 432p. 1981. lib. bdg. 89.00 (*90-286-2641-7*) Kluwer Ac.

Nijkamp, Peter, ed. see Batty, Michael, et al.

Nijkamp, Peter, jt. auth. see Chatterjee, Lata.

Nijkamp, Peter, jt. auth. see Fischer, M. M.

Nijkamp, Peter, jt. ed. see Fischer, Manfred M.

Nijkamp, Peter, jt. auth. see Giaoutzi, Maria.

Nijkamp, Peter, jt. ed. see Lakshmanan, T. R.

Nijkamp, Peter, jt. ed. see Mills, E. S.

Nijkamp, Peter, jt. auth. see Van Delft, A.

Nijkamp, Peter, jt. auth. see Van Lierop, F. J.

Nijkamp, Peter, et al. Euromobile: Transport, Communication & Mobility in Europe: A Cross-National Comparative Overview. 420p. 1990. text ed. 75.00 (*0-566-07150-9*, Pub. by Avebury Pub UK) Ashgate Pub Co.

— Missing Transport Networks in Europe. 215p. 1994. 59.95 (*1-85628-674-6*, Pub. by Avebury Pub UK) Ashgate Pub Co.

— Multicriteria Evaluation in Physical Planning. (Contributions to Economic Analysis Ser.: No. 185). 220p. 1990. 65.00 (*0-444-88851-9*, North Holland) Elsevier.

— Multicriteria Evaluation in Physical Planning. (Contributions to Economic Analysis Ser.: Vol. 185). 1990. 65.00 (*0-444-88124-7*) Elsevier.

— Multidimensional Spatial Data & Decision Analysis. LC 79-40518. (Illus.). 334p. reprint ed. pap. 95.20 (*0-685-20672-6*, 2030460) Bks Demand.

Nijman, Jan. The Geopolitics of Power & Conflict: Superpowers in the International System 1945-1992. 160p. 1993. text ed. 64.95 (*0-471-94735-0*) Chichester Pub.

— The Geopolitics of Power & Conflict: Superpowers in the International System 1945-1992. Date not set. text ed. 54.95 (*0-470-22011-2*) Halsted Pr.

Nijmeijer, H. & Schumacher, J. M., eds. Three Decades of Mathematical System Theory. (Lecture Notes in Control & Information Sciences Ser.: Vol. 135). (Illus.). vi, 562p. 1989. pap. 90.00 (*0-387-51605-0*) Spr-Verlag.

Nijmeijer, H. & Van der Schaft, A. Nonlinear Dynamical Control Systems. (Illus.). xiii, 467p. (C). 1991. 49.95 (*0-387-97234-X*) Spr-Verlag.

Nijmeijer, Peter, tr. see Barkan, Stanley H., ed.

Nijs, E. Breton de. Faded Portraits. Beekman, E M., ed. Sturtevant, Donald & Sturtevant, Elsje, trs. LC 81-19653. (Library of the Indies). Orig. Title: Vergeelde Portretten Uit Een Indisch Familie-Album. 192p. 1982. lib. bdg. 25.00 (*0-87023-363-7*) U of Mass Pr.

Nijs, Johan F., ed. Advanced Silicon & Semiconducting Silicon Alloy-Based Materials & Devices. (Illus.). 488p. 1994. 160.00 (*0-7503-0299-2*) IOP Pub.

Nijssen, Han, jt. auth. see Kullander, Sven O.

Nijura, Miguel. Maribel y la Extrana Familia. (Nueva Austral Ser.: Vol. 123). (SPA.). 1991. pap. text ed. 24.95x (*84-239-1923-4*) Elliots Bks.

Nik-Safiah, N. I., jt. auth. see Pathmanathan, I.

Nik-Uhernik. War Dogs, No. 2: M-16 Jury. 272p. 1985. pap. 2.75 (*0-8217-1539-9*) Zebra.

Nikaido, Hukukane. Convex Structures & Economic Theory. (Mathematics in Science & Engineering Ser.: Vol. 51). 1969. text ed. 136.00 (*0-12-519450-1*) Acad Pr.

— Monopolistic Competition & Effective Demand. LC 74-25623. (Princeton Studies in Mathematical Economics: No. 6). 158p. reprint ed. pap. 45.10 (*0-8357-6225-4*, 2034648) Bks Demand.

— Prices, Cycles, & Growth. (Studies in Dynamical Economic Science). (Illus.). 288p. (C). 1995. 39.95x (*0-262-14059-4*) MIT Pr.

Nikam, N. A. Some Concepts of Indian Culture. 212p. 1980. 15.95 (*0-318-36979-6*) Asia Bk Corp.

Nikam, N. A. & McKeon, Richard, eds. The Edicts of Asoka. LC 59-5748. (Midway Reprint Ser.). 1978. pap. text ed. 9.95 (*0-226-58611-1*) U Ch Pr.

Nikanne, Urpo, jt. ed. see Homberg, Anders.

Nikazy, Eddie M. Abstracts of Death Records for Johnson County, Tennessee, 1908 to 1941. 482p. (Orig.). 1992. pap. 33.00 (*1-55613-665-X*) Heritage Bk.

— Abstracts of Tennessee Death Records for Carter County, 1908-1925. 485p. 1993. pap. text ed. 32.50 (*1-55613-738-9*) Heritage Bk.

— Carter County, Tennessee Death Record Abstracts, 1926-1934. 335p. (Orig.). 1994. pap. text ed. 26.00 (*1-55613-953-5*) Heritage Bk.

— Carter County, Tennessee, Marriages, 1871-1920. ix, 322p. (Orig.). 1993. pap. 24.50 (*1-55613-765-6*) Heritage Bk.

— Sullivan Co., Tennessee Death Records, 1908-1918. 311p. (Orig.). 1994. pap. text ed. 22.00 (*0-7884-0099-1*) Heritage Bk.

— Washington Co., TN: Death Record Abstracts 1908-1916. 316p. (Orig.). 1994. pap. text ed. 23.00 (*0-7884-0100-9*) Heritage Bk.

Nikbakht, Ebsan, jt. auth. see Groppelli, A. A.

Nikbakht, Ehsan. Foreign Loans & Economic Performance: The Experience of the Less Developed Countries. LC 84-8296. 146p. 1984. text ed. 55.00 (*0-275-91235-3*, C1235, Praeger Pubs) Greenwood.

*__Nikbakht, Ehsan & Groppelli, A. A.__ Finance. 3rd ed. LC 94-28891. (Business Review Ser.). 1995. write for info. (*0-8120-1916-4*) Barron.

Nike Sport Research Laboratory Staff & Fixx, James F. Maximum Sports Performance: How to Achieve Your Full Potential in Speed, Endurance, Strength & Coordination. LC 84-17963. 1985. 17.95 (*0-394-53682-7*) Random.

Nikel, Casimir M., jt. auth. see Pfeiffer, Guy O.

Nikelly, John C., jt. ed. see Horvath, Csaba.

Nikephoros. Zeitschrift Fur Sport und Kultur Im Altertum, Bd. 1. Decker, Wolfgang et al, eds. 320p. 1988. write for info. (*3-615-00038-2*, Pub. by Georg Olms GW) Lubrecht & Cramer.

— Zeitschrift Fur Sport und Kultur Im Altertum, Bd. 2. Decker, Wolfgang et al, eds. 330p. 1989. write for info. (*3-615-00058-7*, Pub. by Georg Olms GW) Lubrecht & Cramer.

An Asterisk (*) at the beginning of an entry indicates that the title is appearing in BIP for the first time.

— Zeitschrift Fur Sport und Kultur Im Altertum, Bd. 3. Decker, Wolfgang et al, eds. 338p. 1990. write for info. (3-615-00067-6, Pub. by Georg Olms GW) Lubrecht & Cramer.

— Zeitscshrift fur Sport und Kultur Im Altertum, Band 4. Decker, Joachim et al, eds. 334p. (GER.). 1991. write for info. (3-615-00077-3, Pub. by Georg Olms GW) Lubrecht & Cramer.

Nikhilananda, Swami. Hinduism: Its Meaning for the Liberation of the Spirit. LC 58-6155. 220p. 1992. pap. 10.95 (0-911206-26-4) Ramakrishna.

— Holy Mother: Being the Life of Sri Sarada Devi, Wife of Sri Ramakrishna & Helpmate in His Mission. LC 62-13423. (Illus.). 384p. 1962. reprint ed. pap. 12.50 (0-911206-20-5) Ramakrishna.

— Man in Search of Immortality: Testimonials from the Hindu Scriptures. LC 68-101793. 112p. 1992. pap. 8.95 (0-911206-27-2) Ramakrishna.

— Vivekananda: A Biography. LC 53-7851. 256p. (C). 1989. pap. 12.50 (0-911206-25-6) Ramakrishna.

Nikhilananda, Swami, tr. The Bhagavad Gita. LC 44-33674. 404p. 1944. 14.50 (0-911206-09-4) Ramakrishna.

— The Bhagavad Gita (Pocket Edition) LC 44-33674. 256p. 1944. 10.50 (0-911206-10-8) Ramakrishna.

— Drg-Drsya-Viveka. 69p. Bilingual ed. pap. 1.95 (0-87481-402-2, Pub. by Advaita Ashrama II) Vedanta Pr.

— Gospel of Sri Ramakrishna. LC 58-8948. (Illus.). 1106p. (C). 1942. 29.50 (0-911206-01-9) Ramakrishna.

— Gospel of Sri Ramakrishna. abr. ed. LC 58-8948. 640p. 14.50 (0-911206-02-7) Ramakrishna.

— Mandukya Upanisad. Bilingual ed. 5.95 (0-87481-400-6, Pub. by Advaita Ashrama II) Vedanta Pr.

— Self-Knowledge: Sankara's "Atmabodha" LC 50-36440. 248p. (C). 1946. 12.95 (0-911206-11-6) Ramakrishna.

— Upanishads, 4 Vols, Set. LC 49-9558. 60.00 (0-911206-14-0) Ramakrishna.

— Upanishads, 4 Vols, Vol. I. LC 49-9558. 333p. 1949. 15.00 (0-911206-15-9) Ramakrishna.

— Upanishads, 4 Vols, Vol. II. LC 49-9558. 400p. 1952. 15.00 (0-911206-16-7) Ramakrishna.

— Upanishads, 4 Vols, Vol. III. LC 49-9558. 408p. 1956. 15.00 (0-911206-17-5) Ramakrishna.

— Upanishads, 4 Vols, Vol. IV. LC 49-9558. 424p. 1959. 15.00 (0-911206-18-3) Ramakrishna.

Niki, Hiromi & Becker, K. H., eds. The Tropospheric Chemistry of Ozone in the Polar Regions. LC 93-19454. (NATO ASI Series I: Global Environmental Change: Vol. 7). 1993. 185.00 (0-387-56683-X) Spr-Verlag.

Niki, K., jt. ed. see Dryhurst, G.

Nikias, Chrysostomos L. & Petropulu, Athina P. Higher Order Spectral Analysis: A Non-Linear Signal Processing Framework. LC 93-28. (Signal Processing Ser.). 430p. 1993. text ed. 71.00 (0-13-678210-8) P-H.

*Nikias, Chrysostomos L. & Shao, Min. Signal Processing with Alpha-Stable Distributions & Applications. LC 95-1482. (Adaptive & Learning Systems for Signal Processing, Communications & Control Ser.). 1995. write for info. (0-471-10647-X) Wiley-Interscience.

Nikiel, J. Topologies on Pseudo-Trees & Applications. LC 89-17764. (MEMO Ser.: Vol. 82/416). 116p. 1989. pap. 21.00 (0-8218-2479-1, MEMO 82/416) Am Math.

Nikiel, J., et al. Continuous Images of Arcs & Inverse Limit Methods. LC 93-17171. (Memoirs of the American Mathematical Society Ser.: No. 498). 80p. 1993. pap. 28.00 (0-8218-2561-5) Am Math.

Nikiforoff-Volgin, V. Dorozhnij Posokh. 188p. 1971. reprint ed. pap. 6.00 (0-317-30421-6) Holy Trinity.

— Zemlja Imjeninnitsa. 182p. 1960. reprint ed. pap. 6.00 (0-317-30418-6) Holy Trinity.

Nikiforov, A. & Uvarov, V. Special Functions of Mathematical Physics. 500p. 1988. 148.50 (0-8176-3183-6) Birkhauser.

Nikiforov, A. F., et al. Classical Orthogonal Polynomials of a Discrete Variable. Glowinski, R. et al, eds. (Computational Physics Ser.). (Illus.). 368p. 1992. text ed. 89.00 (0-387-51123-7) Spr-Verlag.

Nikiforov, G. A., jt. auth. see Ershov, V. V.

*Nikiforowa, Anna. Woerterbuch Wirtschatsrussisch: German-Russian. 496p. (GER & RUS.). 1993. 105.00 (0-7859-8380-5, 3464494063) Fr & Eur.

— Woerterbuch Wirtschatsrussisch: Russian-German. 496p. (GER & RUS.). 1994. 105.00 (0-7859-8381-3, 3464494071) Fr & Eur.

Nikiforuk, Andrew. The Fourth Horseman: A Short History of Epidemics, Plagues, Famine & Other Scourges. LC 93-2686. 192p. 1993. 18.95 (0-87131-721-4) M Evans.

Nikiforuk, G., ed. Prevention: Basic & Clinical Aspects. (Understanding Dental Caries (Ltd. Vol.) Ser.: Vol. 2). (Illus.). xiv, 290p. 1985. 46.50 (3-8055-3905-3) S Karger.

— Understanding Dental Caries, Vol. 1: Etiology & Mechanisms. (Illus.). xiv, 306p. 1985. 46.50 (3-8055-3864-2) S Karger.

— Understanding Dental Caries, Vols. 1 & 2, 2 vols., Set. (Illus.). xxviii, 596p. 1985. 93.00 (3-8055-3906-1) S Karger.

Nikinmaa, M. Vertebrate Red Blood Cells. (Zoophysiology Ser.: Vol. 28). (Illus.). 300p. 1990. 149.00 (0-387-51590-9) Spr-Verlag.

Nikirov, jt. auth. see Basseville.

Nikishin, et al. Rational Approximations & Orthogonality. LC 91-18793. (MMONO-92 Ser.). 221p. 1991. 90.00 (0-8218-4545-4, MMONO-92) Am Math.

*Nikitas, Matthew. Grand Finishes for Walls & Floors: Interior House Painting, Wallpapering, & Wood Floor Refinishing. LC 94-31857. (Illus.). 160p. 1994. pap. 16.95 (1-56440-487-0) Globe Pequot.

Nikitin, A., jt. auth. see Kortunov, A.

Nikitin, A. A., jt. auth. see Levinson, I. B.

Nikitin, A. G., jt. auth. see Fushchich, W. I.

Nikitin, E. E. & Umanskii, S. Y. Theory of Slow Atomic Collisions. (Chemical Physics Ser.: Vol. 30). (Illus.). 440p. 1984. 94.00 (0-387-12414-4) Spr-Verlag.

Nikitin, E. E., jt. auth. see Kondratiev, V. N.

Nikitin, Evengii. Theory of Thermally Induced Gas Phase Reactions. Schlag, E. W., tr. LC 66-12733. 167p. reprint ed. pap. 47.60 (0-317-09605-2, 2050961) Bks Demand.

Nikitin, N. I. The Chemistry of Cellulose & Wood. 704p. 1966. text ed. 149.50 (0-7065-0583-2, Pub. by Keter Pub IS) Coronet Bks.

Nikitin, P. D., jt. ed. see Al'benskii, A. V.

Nikitin, P. L. The Fundamentals of Political Economy. 430p. 1983. 35.00 (0-317-53756-3, Pub. by Collets) St Mut.

Nikitin, S. Global Controllability & Stabilization of Nonlinear Systems. (Series on Advances in Mathematics). 284p. 1994. text ed. 61.00 (981-02-1779-X) World Scientific Pub.

Nikitin, Valentin. Sumerki Smertnago Dnya - Twilight of a Mortal Day. (Orig.). (RUS.). 1990. pap. 8.00 (2-85065-189-3) Gnosis Pr.

Nikitin, Yakov. Asymptotic Efficiency of Nonparametric Tests. 250p. (C). 1995. 49.95 (0-521-47029-3) Cambridge U Pr.

Nikitin, Yu. P. & Rosental, I. L. Theory of Multiparticle Production Processes. (Studies in High Energy Physics: Vol. 6). 344p. 1988. 275.00 (3-7186-4809-1) Gordon & Breach.

Nikitin, Yu. P. & Rozental, I. L. High Energy Physics with Nuclei. 292p. 1986. text ed. 255.00 (3-7186-0172-9) Gordon & Breach.

Nikitina, T. S., et al, eds. Effect of Ionizing Radiation on High Polymers. (Russian Tracts on the Physical Sciences Ser.). (Illus.). 96p. 1963. text ed. 105.00 (0-677-20480-9) Gordon & Breach.

Nikitine, Basile V. The Fatal Years: Fresh Revelations on a Chapter of Underground History. LC 75-39058. (Russian Studies: Perspectives on the Revolution). 312p. 1977. reprint ed. 27.50 (0-88355-438-0) Hyperion Conn.

Nikkei Business Publications. Biotechnology Guide: Japan 1990-1991: Company Directory & Comprehensive Analysis Translated from the Section on Japanese Companies in Sekai no Baio Kigyo 800sha. 608p. 1993. reprint ed. pap. text ed. 250.00 (0-7167-7000-8) OUP.

Nikkila, E., jt. auth. see Mustajoki, A.

Niklas, Gerals R. & Stefanics, Charlotte. Ministry to the Sick. LC 82-4083. 143p. (Orig.). 1982. pap. 7.95 (0-8189-0429-1) Alba.

Niklas, Karl J. Plant Allometry: The Scaling of Form & Process. LC 94-2418. 1994. lib. bdg. 62.50 (0-226-58080-6); pap. text ed. 24.95 (0-226-58081-4) U Ch Pr.

— Plant Biomechanics: An Engineering Approach to Plant Form & Function. (Illus.). 640p. 1992. lib. bdg. 75.00 (0-226-58630-8); pap. text ed. 29.95 (0-226-58631-6) U Ch Pr.

Niklas, Karl J., ed. Paleobotany, Paleoecology, & Evolution, 2 vols., Set. LC 81-1838. 1981. text ed. 95.00 (0-275-90691-4, C06910, Praeger Pubs) Greenwood.

— Paleobotany, Paleoecology, & Evolution, 2 vols., Vol. 1. LC 81-1838. 1981. text ed. 69.50 (0-275-90690-6, C06901, Praeger Pubs) Greenwood.

— Paleobotany, Paleoecology, & Evolution, 2 vols., Vol. 2. LC 81-1838. 1981. text ed. 125.00 (0-275-90689-2, C06892, Praeger Pubs) Greenwood.

*Niklasson & Hoden. Connectionism in a Broad Perspective. (Illus.). 250p. (C). 1994. text ed. 70.00 (0-13-176751-8) P-H.

*Niklasson, Lars & Boden, Mikael B., eds. Current Trends in Connectionism. 392p. 1995. text ed. 69.95 (0-8058-1997-5) L Erlbaum Assocs.

Niklasson, Lars & Hoden, Mikael. Connectionism in a Broad Perspective. 1994. text ed. 46.50 (0-685-70922-1) P-H.

Niklaus, Robert L. To All Peoples: Missions World Book of the Christian & Missionary Alliance. LC 90-81150. (Illus.). 412p. 1990. 29.99 (0-87509-432-5) Chr Pubns.

Nikles, D. C., jt. auth. see Burley, J.

Nikles, D. G., et al. Progress & Problems of Genetic Improvement of Tropical Forest Trees, 2 Vols. 1978. 165.00 (0-85074-020-7) St Mut.

Nikles, G., jt. auth. see Burley, J.

*NIKO, Nicholas J. Koushiafes. Gods of the Universe. LC 95-94055. (Illus.). 400p. 1995. 20.00 (0-9607228-6-6) Gods Universe.

Nikola-Lisa, W. Bein' with You This Way. LC 93-5164. (Illus.). 32p. (J). (gr. k-3). 1994. 14.95 (1-880000-05-9) Lee & Low Bks.

— Bein' with You This Way. LC 93-5164. (Illus.). 32p. (J). (ps up). 1995. pap. 5.95 (1-880000-26-1) Lee & Low Bks.

— Night Is Coming. LC 90-3806. (Illus.). 32p. (J). (ps-2). 1991. 14.99 (0-525-44687-7, DCB) Dutton Child Bks.

— No Babies Asleep. LC 93-20589. (Illus.). 32p. (J). (ps-1). 1994. lib. bdg. 15.95 (0-689-31841-3, Atheneum S&S) S&S Trade.

— One, Two, Three Thanksgiving! Levine, Abby, ed. LC 90-28638. (Illus.). 32p. (J). (ps-1). 1991. 13.95 (0-8075-6109-6) A Whitman.

— Shake d'em Halloween Bones. LC 94-49738. (Illus.). (J). 1995. write for info. (0-395-73095-3) Ticknor & Flds Bks Yng Read.

— Storm. LC 92-22775. (Illus.). 32p. (J). (ps-2). 1993. text ed. 14.95 (0-689-31704-2, Atheneum Bks Young) S&S Childrens.

— Wheels Go Round. LC 93-38595. (Illus.). (J). 1994. 12.95 (0-385-32069-8) Doubleday.

Nikola, Tesla. Complete Patents. 500p. 35.00 (0-913022-44-6) Angriff Pr.

Nikola Tesla Museum Staff, ed. Nikola Tesla, 1856-1943: Lectures, Patents, Articles, 2 vols., Set. 1956. reprint ed. spiral bd. 71.50 (0-7873-0634-7) Mokelumne.

Nikolaev, A. V. Seismics of Heterogeneous & Turbid Media. 184p. reprint ed. text ed. 45.00 (0-7065-1535-8) Coronet Bks.

Nikolaev, E. S., jt. auth. see Samarskii, A.

Nikolaev, Mikhail. Detdom. Schweitzer, Victoria, ed. LC 84-51670. 150p. (Orig.). (RUS.). 1985. pap. 10.00 (0-89830-091-6) Russica Pubs.

Nikolaeva, I. A. Eighteen Twelve Borodino Panorama. (Illus.). (RUS.). 1982. 100.00 (0-685-18073-5, Pub. by Collets UK) St Mut.

Nikolaeva, P., jt. auth. see Kozhenikov, V.

Nikolaevskii, Boris I. Istoriia Odnogo Predatelia. LC 80-53079. 374p. (RUS.). 1980. reprint ed. pap. 12.00 (0-89830-026-6) Russica Pubs.

Nikolaevskij, V. N. Mechanics of Porous & Fractured Media. (Series in Theor-App. Mech: Vol. 8). 492p. 1990. text ed. 108.00 (9971-5-0383-2) World Scientific Pub.

Nikolai & Bazley. Intermediate Accounting. 6th ed. (C). 1994. text ed. 72.95 (0-538-82531-6, AC65FA) S-W Pub.

Nikolai, Robert J. Bioengineering Analysis of Orthodontic Mechanics. LC 84-5712. 493p. reprint ed. pap. 140.60 (0-7837-2848-4, 2057624) Bks Demand.

Nikolaidis, Efstratios & Perakis, Anastassios N. Partially Saturated Ocean Detection: Second Order Process Statistics, PARSAT Computer Program Manual. (University of Michigan, Dept. of Naval Architecture & Marine Engineering, Report Ser.: No. 291). 73p. reprint ed. pap. 25.00 (0-317-27121-0, 2024687) Bks Demand.

Nikolajeva, Maria. The Magic Code: The Use of Magical Patterns in Fantasy for Children. 163p. (Orig.). 1988. pap. 46.00x (91-22-01200-1, Pub. by Almqv & Wiksell SW) Coronet Bks.

*Nikolajeva, Maria, ed. Aspects & Issues in the History of Children's Literature. LC 94-43041. (Contributions to the Study of World Literature: Vol. 60). 224p. 1995. text ed. 55.00 (0-313-29614-6, Greenwood Pr) Greenwood.

Nikolajewsky, Boris I. Aseff the Spy. (Russian Ser.: Vol. 11). 1969. 25.00 (0-87569-011-4) Academic Intl.

Nikolay, Peter. All Colour Wok Cookbook. (Illus.). 128p. 1995. 9.95 (0-572-01767-7, Pub. by Foulsham UK) Atrium Pubs.

Nikolayev, A., jt. auth. see Nalin, Y.

Nikolayev, Aleksandr A. John Field. Doscher, David, ed. & intro. by. LC 73-79275. 1973. pap. 15.00 (0-913000-99-X) Maestro Scope.

Nikolenko, Lada. Francesco Ubertini Called Il Bacchiacca. LC 66-2377. 7.00 (0-685-71755-0) J J Augustin.

Nikolic, Jovan P., intro. Doba Iskusenja. LC 83-137480. 63p. (SER.). 1983. pap. 2.00 (0-931931-13-4) Ravnogorski.

Nikolic, M. Methods in Subnuclear Physics, Vol. 1. 516p. 1968. 190.00 (0-677-11950-X) Gordon & Breach.

— Methods in Subnuclear Physics, Vol. 5. viii, 364p. 1977. text ed. 275.00 (0-677-15920-X) Gordon & Breach.

— Methods in Subnuclear Physics, Vol. 5, 2 pts., Vol. 5. 1977. Set. text ed. 502.00 (0-677-15960-9) Gordon & Breach.

Nikolic, M., ed. Analysis of Scattering & Decay. 344p. (Orig.). 1968. text ed. 216.00 (0-677-12810-X) Gordon & Breach.

— Kinematics & Multi-Particle Systems. (Documents on Modern Physics Ser.). 324p. (Orig.). 1968. text ed. 216.00 (0-677-01800-2) Gordon & Breach.

Nikolic, M., ed. see International School of Elementary Particle Physics Staff.

Nikolic, Pedrag, ed. French: Advance Variation. (Electronic Chessbook Ser.). 64p. 1994. disk 25.00 (0-917237-05-6, Interchess) Chess Combi.

Nikolic-Zugic, Janko, ed. Intrathymic Development of T Cells. LC 93-41387. (Molecular Biology Intelligence Unit Ser.). 110p. 1994. 89.95 (1-57059-014-1, LN9014) R G Landes.

Nikoljukin, A. Russian Discovery of America. 508p. (C). 1986. 60.00 (0-685-31574-6, Pub. by Collets UK) Pro-Am Music.

Nikolov, Lyubomir. Pagan. Flint, Roland & Tcholakova, Viara, trs. (Poetry Ser.). 48p. (Orig.). 1992. pap. 9.95 (0-88748-146-9) Carnegie-Mellon.

Nikolov, N., jt. auth. see Varbanova, A.

Nikolowa, J., et al. Bulgarisch-Deutsches Phraseologisches Worterbuch: Bulgarian-German Phraseology Dictionary. 1088p. (BUL & GER.). 1977. 95.00 (0-8288-5295-2, M9833) Fr & Eur.

Nikolowski, W., et al. Kohabitations-und Fertilitaets-Stoerungen: Ein Leitfaden fuer die aerztliche Praxis. (Illus.). 1977. 16.00 (3-8055-2682-2) S Karger.

Nikolskaia, Tatiana, ed. see Tufanov, Aleksandr V.

Nikolski, N. K., jt. ed. see Havin, V. P.

Nikol'skii, G. V. Special Ichthyology: Israel Program for Scientific Translation. Lengy, J. I. & Krauthamer, Z., trs. (Illus.). 538p. (RUS.). 1989. reprint ed. 55.00 (1-55528-162-1, Pub. by Today & Tomorrows P & P II) Scholarly Pubns.

Nikolskii, G. V. Theory of Fish Population Dynamics As the Biological Background for Rational Exploitation & Management of Fishery Resources. Jones, R., ed. Bradley, J. E., tr. (Illus.). 323p. 1980. reprint ed. lib. bdg. 115.50 (3-87429-171-5) Koeltz Sci Bks.

Nikolskii, N. K. Topics on Toeplitz Operators & Spectral Function Theory. (Operator Theory Ser.: No. 42). 300p. 1989. 132.00 (0-8176-2344-2) Birkhauser.

Nikol'skii, N. K. Treatise on the Shift Operator. Peetre, J., tr. LC 84-26869. (Grundlehren der Mathematischen Wissenschaften Ser.: Vol. 273). (Illus.). 504p. 1986. 98.00 (0-387-15021-8) Spr-Verlag.

Nikol'skii, N. K., ed. Spectral Theory of Functions & Operators. LC 80-1102. (Proceedings of the Steklov Institute of Mathematics Ser.: No. 130). 233p. 1980. 70.00 (0-8218-3030-9, STEKLO-130) Am Math.

— Spectral Theory of Functions & Operators, II: 1983. LC 80-11102. (Proceedings of the Steklov Institute of Mathematics Ser.: Vol. 155). 176p. 1983. pap. text ed. 75.00 (0-8218-3072-4, STEKLOV 155) Am Math.

Nikol'skii, N. K., ed. see Steklov Institute of Mathematics, Academy of Sciences, U. S. S. R. Staff.

Nikol'skii, S. M. Approximation of Functions of Several Variables & Embedding Theorems. Danskin, J. M., tr. LC 74-4652. (Grundlehren der Mathematischen Wissenschaften Ser.: Vol. 205). 450p. 1975. 89.00 (0-387-06442-7) Spr-Verlag.

— Theory & Applications of Differentiable Functions of Several Variables, No. XII. LC 68-1677. 293p. 1990. pap. 154.00 (0-8218-3131-3, STEKLO-181) Am Math.

Nikolskii, S. M., ed. Differential Equations & Function Spaces: Dedicated to the Memory of Academician Sergei Lvovich Sobolev: Collection of Papers. LC 92-30907. 256p. 1992. 163.00 (0-8218-3146-1, STEKLO-192) Am Math.

— International Conference on Analytic Methods in Number Theory & Analysis. LC 86-47529. (Steklov Institute of Mathematics Ser.: Vol. 163). 319p. 1986. pap. text ed. 137.00 (0-8218-3090-2, STEKLO-163) Am Math.

Nikol'skii, S. M., ed. Theory & Applications of Differentiable Functions of Several Variables, No. VIII. LC 68-1677. (Proceedings of the Steklov Institute of Mathematics Ser.: Vol. 156). 284p. 1983. 115.00 (0-8218-3017-1, STEKLO-117) Am Math.

— Theory & Applications of Differentiable Functions of Several Variables, No. IX. LC 84-24501. (Proceedings of the Steklov Institute of Mathematics Ser.: Vol. 161). 253p. 1986. reprint ed. text ed. 80.00 (0-8218-3083-X, STEKLO-161) Am Math.

— Theory & Applications of Differentiable Functions of Several Variables, VII. LC 68-1677. (Proceedings of the Steklov Institute of Mathematics Ser.: Vol. 150). 336p. 1982. reprint ed. 137.00 (0-8218-3047-3, STEKLO/150C) Am Math.

— Theory & Applications of Differentiable Functions of Several Variables, 6, No. VI. (Proceedings of the Steklov Institute of Mathematics Ser.: No. 140). 312p. 1979. 113.00 (0-8218-3039-2, STEKLO-140) Am Math.

Nikol'skii, S. M., ed. see Steklov Institute of Mathematics, Academy of Sciences, U. S. S. R. Staff.

Nikol'skij, L. B., jt. auth. see Svejcer, Aleksandr D.

Nikol'skij, N. K., ed. see Ashurov, R. R., et al.

Nikol'skij, N. K., jt. auth. see Khavin, V. P.

Nikol'skij, N. K., ed. see Lyubich, Y. I.

Nikol'skij, S. M. & Gamkrelidze, R. V., eds. Analysis Three: Spaces of Differentiable Functions. Peetre, J., tr. (Encyclopaedia of Mathematical Sciences Ser.: Vol. 26). (Illus.). 232p. (RUS.). 1990. 65.00 (0-387-51866-5) Spr-Verlag.

Nikol'skij, S. M., jt. auth. see Maz'ya, V. G.

Nikolsky, S. M. A Course of Mathematical Analysis, 2 Vols. 460p. 1985. 110.00 (0-317-46603-8, Pub. by Collets UK) Pro-Am Music.

Nikonowa, O. N. & Zwilling, M. J. Russian-German Dictionary: Russisch-Deutsches Woerterbuch. 8th ed. 798p. (GER & RUS.). 1982. 75.00 (0-8288-1239-X, F60170) Fr & Eur.

Nikos, Cheryl, ed. Concerns of Small Business. 33p. 1992. pap. text ed. 10.00 (0-89834-125-6, 0323) Chamber Comm US.

— U. S. Chamber Watch on Small Business Legislation & Regulation (newsletter) 65.00 (0-685-62965-1) Natl Chamber Foun.

Nikos, Cheryl, ed. see U. S. Chamber of Commerce Staff & Fasman, Zachary D.

Nikovskis, Armins, tr. see Yoshikawa, Itsuji.

Niks, Mikhail. Type Without Tension. Ingram, tr. (Illus.). 1992. pap. 6.95 (1-880416-07-7) NW Pub.

Niku-Lari, A., ed. Advances in Surface Treatments: Proceedings of the AST World Conference, December 3-4, 1986, Paris. (AST Ser.: No. 5). (Illus.). 446p. 1987. 221.00 (0-08-034923-4) Franklin.

— Advances in Surface Treatments: Residual Stresses. (Advances in Surface Treatments Ser.: Vol. 4). 400p. 1987. 239.00 (0-08-034062-8, Pub. by PPL UK) Franklin.

— Advances in Surface Treatments: Technology, Applications, Effects, Vol. 1. (Illus.). 240p. 1984. 124.00 (0-08-031126-1, Pub. by Pergamon Repr UK) Franklin.

— Advances in Surface Treatments III: Technology, Applications, Effects, III. (Advances in Surface Treatments Ser.: Vol. 3). 270p. 1986. 116.00 (0-08-033464-4) Franklin.

— Structural Analysis System 4: CAD-CAM & Structural Analysis in Industry. (Structural Analysis Systems Ser.). (Illus.). 284p. 1986. 121.00 (0-08-034918-8, Pub. by Pergamon Repr UK) Franklin.

— Structural Analysis Systems: Finite, Boundary Element & Expert Systems in Structural Analysis. (Structural Analysis Systems Ser.: Vol. 6). (Illus.). 210p. 1987. 97.00 (0-08-034934-X, Pub. by Pergamon Repr UK) Franklin.

— Structural Analysis Systems: Software, Hardware, Capability, Compatibility, Applications, Vol. 2. LC 85-9419. (Illus.). 250p. 1986. 101.00 (0-08-032578-5, Pub. by Pergamon Repr UK) Franklin.

— Structural Analysis Systems I: Software, Hardware, Capability, Compatibility, Applications. (Structural Analysis Systems Ser.: Vol. 1). (Illus.). 250p. 1986. 132.00 (0-08-032577-7, Pub. by PPL UK) Franklin.

N

— Structural Analysis Systems III: Software, Hardware, Capability, Compatibility, Applications. (Structural Analysis Systems Ser.: Vol. 3). (Illus.). 250p. 1986. 118.00 (0-08-032582-3, Pub. by PPL UK) Franklin.

— Structural Analysis Systems, Vol. 5: Expert Systems in Structural Analysis. (Illus.). 218p. 1986. 94.00 (0-08-034919-6) Franklin.

Niku-Lari, A. & Al-Hassani, S. T., eds. Shot Peening: Proceedings of the 1st International Conference, Paris, 14-17 September 1981. 528p. 1982. 314.00 (0-08-027599-0, Pub. by Pergamon Repr UK) Franklin.

Niku-Lari, A. & Ghosh, S. K., eds. CAD-CAM & FEM in Metal Working. LC 88-19669. (Technology Transfer Handbook Ser.). (Illus.). 300p. 1988. 116.00 (0-08-035917-5, Pub. by Pergamon Repr UK) Franklin.

Nikulin, M. S., jt. auth. see Voinov, Vasilii G.

Nikulin, N. & Asvarishch, B. German & Austrian Painting in the Hermitage. (Illus.). 424p. (C). 1986. text ed. 450.00 (0-685-40301-7, Pub. by Collets) St Mut.

Nikulin, Nikolai. Anton Raphael Mengs. (Masters of World Painting Ser.). 1984. pap. 55.00 (0-317-57255-5, Pub. by Collets UK) St Mut.

— The Golden Age of Netherlandish Painting (Fifteenth Century) (Illus.). 398p. (ENG & RUS.). 1981. 174.00 (0-317-14235-6, Pub. by Collets UK) St Mut.

Nikulin, V. V. & Shafarevich, I. R. Geometries & Groups. (Soviet Mathematics Ser.). (Illus.). 265p. 1994. pap. 49.00 (0-387-15281-4) Spr-Verlag.

Nikuradse, Tamara & Matthews, Scott. To the Man I Love, Thank You for Being Mine. 160p. (Orig.). 1994. mass mkt. 5.99 (0-449-90914-X, Columbine) Fawcett.

Nikuradse, Tamara, jt. auth. see Matthews, Scott.

Nilamni, Madhu, ed. Aluminum Cast House Technology. (Illus.). 532p. 1993. 60.00 (0-87339-198-5) Minerals Metals.

Nilan, Robert A., ed. see International Barley Genetics Symposium Staff.

Nilan, Roxanne, jt. auth. see Davis, Margo.

Niland, D'Arcy. The Shiralee. 250p. 1992. reprint ed. lib. bdg. 25.95 (0-89966-941-7) Buccaneer Bks.

Niland, John & Clarke, Oliver, eds. Agenda for Change: An International Analysis of Industrial Relations in Transition. 224p. 1991. pap. 24.95 (0-04-442270-9, Pub. by Allen & Unwin Aust Pty AT) Paul & Co Pubs.

Niland, John, et al, eds. The Future of Industrial Relations: Global Change & Challenges. LC 93-48901. 384p. (C). 1994. text ed. 48.00 (0-8039-5547-2) Sage.

Niland, Kilmeny. A Bellbird in a Flame Tree: The Twelve Days of Christmas. LC 90-25869. 32p. (J). (ps-3). 1991. 12.95 (0-688-10797-4, Tambourine Bks); lib. bdg. 12.88 (0-688-10798-2, Tambourine Bks) Morrow.

***Niland, Kurt R. & Armstrong, Scott.** The Spirit of the Place Vol. 1: The Emerald-Coast Celebrates Its Finest Restaurants, Chefs, & Cuisine. (Illus.). 154p. 1995. pap. 18.95 (0-9645334-0-5) Oracle Pub.

Nila's, M. S. Law of Suspension. 3rd rev. ed. (C). 1994. 62.50 (81-7012-523-5, Pub. by Eastern Book II) St Mut.

Nilausen, Jesper. APPN Networks. LC 93-50760. 1994. pap. text ed. 42.95 (0-471-94447-5) Wiley.

— Token Ring Networks. LC 92-30182. 330p. 1992. pap. text ed. 37.00 (0-13-923376-8) P-H.

Nile, tr. see Celine, Louis-Ferdinand D.

Nile, Lauren N. Developing Diversity Training for the Workplace: A Guide for Trainers. 220p. 1994. ring bd. 129.95 (1-885077-40-8) NMCI Pubns.

Nile, Richard. Australian Aborigines. LC 92-17044. (Threatened Cultures Ser.). (Illus.). 48p. (J). (gr. 5-6). 1992. lib. bdg. 22.80 (0-8114-2303-4) Raintree Steck-V.

***Nile, Richard, ed.** Australian Civilisation. 288p. 1995. pap. 26.00 (0-19-553504-9) OUP.

Niles, ed. Saturday Mourning Fly in My Eye. (Illus.). 1990. pap. 9.95 (1-56060-022-5) Eclipse Bks.

Niles, Ann, ed. CD-ROM Book Index: An International Guide to Fulltext Books on CD-ROM. (Supplement to Computers in Libraries Ser.: No. 73). 300p. 1994. pap. 75.00 (0-88736-889-1) Learned Info.

Niles, B. Colombia. 1976. lib. bdg. 59.95 (0-8490-1642-8) Gordon Pr.

Niles-Beattie, Anita. The Trail to Tomorrow. LC 92-91104. (Illus.). 72p. 1993. pap. 9.00 (1-56002-278-7, Univ Edtns) Aegina Pr.

Niles, Blair. Strange Brother. LC 75-12341. (Homosexuality Ser.). 1975. reprint ed. 17.95 (0-405-07390-9) Ayer.

Niles, Bo. The Country Living Book of Country Kitchens. LC 85-60098. (Illus.). 1985. 29.95 (0-688-04267-8) Hearst Bks.

— Country Living Country Bears. (Illus.). 96p. 1991. 13.95 (0-688-10016-3, Hearst Marine Bks) Morrow.

— Country Living Country Decorating: Achieving the Country Look, Room by Room. Bramson, Ann, ed. LC 88-4112. (Illus.). 256p. 1988. 29.95 (0-688-08073-1) Hearst Bks.

— Living with Lace. LC 90-34556. (Illus.). 176p. 1990. 35.00 (1-55670-156-X) Stewart Tabori & Chang.

— Make Yourself at Home. 192p. (Orig.). 1995. pap. text ed. 4.99 (0-425-14536-0) Berkley Pub.

— White by Design. LC 84-228. (Illus.). 200p. 1984. 40.00 (0-941434-54-0); pap. 24.95 (1-55670-277-9) Stewart Tabori & Chang.

— A Window on Provence: One Summer's Sojourn into the Simple Life. LC 89-40699. (Illus.). 224p. 1990. 18.95 (0-670-82722-3, Viking) Viking Penguin.

***Niles, Bo & McNiff, Veronica.** The New York Book of Coffee & Cake. 1995. 15.00 (1-885492-20-0) City & Co.

— The New York Book of Tea: Where to Take Tea, Buy Tea & Teaware. 1995. 15.00 (1-885492-06-5) City & Co.

Niles, Cornelia D., ed. see Smithsonian Institution, Washington, D. C. Staff.

Niles, Douglas. Advanced Dungeons & Dragons: Complete Thief Manual. 2nd ed. 1990. pap. 10.95 (0-88038-780-7) TSR Inc.

— Advanced Dungeons & Dragons: Lankhmar, City of Adventure. 1985. pap. 12.00 (0-88038-247-3) TSR Inc.

— The Black Wizards. LC 87-51258. (Forgotten Realms Moonshae Trilogy Ser.: Bk. 2). 352p. (Orig.). 1988. pap. 4.95 (0-88038-563-4) TSR Inc.

— A Breach in the Watershed. 448p. (Orig.). 1995. pap. 13.00 (0-441-00208-0) Ace Bks.

— The Complete Book of Gnomes & Halflings. (Advanced Dungeons & Dragons, Second Edition; Al-Qadim Ser.). (Illus.). 1993. pap. 15.00 (1-56076-573-9) TSR Inc.

— The Coral Kingdom. (Druidhome Trilogy Ser.: Bk. 2). 320p. (Orig.). 1992. pap. 4.95 (1-56076-332-9) TSR Inc.

— Darkwalker on Moonshae. LC 86-51270. (Forgotten Realms Moonshae Trilogy Ser.: Bk. 1). 352p. (Orig.). 1987. pap. 4.95 (0-88038-451-4) TSR Inc.

— Darkwell. LC 88-50057. (Forgotten Realms Moonshae Trilogy Ser.: Bk. 3). 1989. pap. 4.95 (0-88038-717-3) TSR Inc.

— The Druid Queen. (Druidhome Trilogy Ser.: Bk. 3). 320p. (Orig.). 1993. pap. 4.95 (1-56076-568-2) TSR Inc.

— Emperor of Ansalon. (Villians Ser.: No. 3). 320p. (Orig.). 1993. 4.95 (1-56076-680-8) TSR Inc.

— Feathered Dragon: Forgotten Realms. LC 90-71498. (Forgotten Realms Maztica Trilogy Bks.: Bk. 3). 320p. (Orig.). 1991. 4.95 (1-56076-045-1) TSR Inc.

— Ironhelm. LC 89-51884. (Forgotten Realms Maztica Trilogy Bks.: Bk. 1). (Illus.). 320p. (Orig.). 1990. pap. 4.95 (0-88038-903-6) TSR Inc.

— The Kagonesti. (Lost Histories Ser.: No. 1). 320p. (Orig.). 1995. pap. 4.95 (0-7869-0091-1) TSR Inc.

— Kinslayer Wars. LC 90-71492. (Dragonlance Elven Nations Trilogy: Vol. 2). (Illus.). 320p. (Orig.). 1991. pap. 4.95 (1-56076-113-X) TSR Inc.

— Pawns Prevail. (First Quest Ser.). (Illus.). 288p. (Orig.). 1995. pap. 3.95 (1-56076-854-1) TSR Inc.

— Prophet of Moonshae: Forgotten Realms, Bk. 1. (Druidhome Trilogy Ser.). 320p. (Orig.). 1992. 4.95 (1-56076-319-1) TSR Inc.

— Suitors Duel. (First Quest Ser.). (Illus.). 288p. (Orig.). (YA). 1995. pap. 3.95 (1-56076-922-X) TSR Inc.

— Viperhand. LC 89-51885. (Forgotten Realms Maztica Trilogy Bks.: Bk. 2). 320p. (Orig.). 1990. pap. 4.95 (0-88038-907-9) TSR Inc.

Niles, Douglas, jt. auth. see Kirchoff, Mary.

Niles, Edward I. Federal Civil Procedure. 2nd ed. 700p. 1994. ring bd. 95.00 (1-55943-148-2) Michie Butterworth.

— Federal Civil Procedure. 2nd suppl. ed. 700p. 1993. 39.50 (0-685-70048-8) Butterworth Legal Pubs.

Niles, Edward I., jt. auth. see Faber, Stuart J.

Niles, Gayle L. & Snider, Douglas H. Woman's Counsel: A Legal Guide for Women. LC 84-11161. 240p. (Orig.). 1984. pap. 8.50 (0-912869-04-6) Arden Pr.

Niles, Grace G. Hoosac Valley: Its Legend & Its History. 584p. 1993. reprint ed. lib. bdg. 99.00 (0-7812-5191-5) Rprt Serv.

Niles, J. J., intro. Appalachian Photographs of Doris Ulmann. LC 70-137213. 1971. pap. 12.50 (0-912330-00-7, Inland Bk) Jargon Soc.

***Niles, John.** School-to-Work Toolkit: Building a State-Wide System. 1994. 150.00 (1-887410-50-3) Jobs for Future.

Niles, John D. Beowulf: The Poem & Its Tradition. LC 83-4308. 316p. reprint ed. pap. 91.20 (0-7837-2304-0, 2057392) Bks Demand.

Niles, John D. & Amodio, Mark, eds. Anglo-Scandinavian England: Norse-English Relations in the Period Before Conquest. LC 88-31728. (Old English Colloquium Ser.: No. 4). 94p. (Orig.). (C). 1989. lib. bdg. 29.00 (0-8191-7267-7, Old English Colloquium); pap. text ed. 17.00 (0-8191-7268-5, Old English Colloquium) U Pr of Amer.

Niles, John D., tr. see Luthi, Max.

Niles, John J. & Merton, Thomas. The Niles-Merton Songs: Opus 171 & 172. (Illus.). 95p. 1981. spiral bd. 15.95 (0-916656-16-0, MF755) Mark Foster Mus.

Niles, John J., jt. auth. see Hall, Bert.

Niles, John M., jt. auth. see Pease, John C.

Niles, Kathryn B. Food Preparation Recipes. LC 55-5964. 372p. reprint ed. pap. 106.10 (0-8357-9892-5, 2055187) Bks Demand.

Niles, Nathan O. & Haborak, George E. Calculus with Analytic Geometry. 2nd ed. (Illus.). 640p. 1982. text ed. write for info. (0-13-112011-5) P-H.

Niles, Nathaniel. The American Hero: A Sapphick Ode. 1975. 3.00 (0-89073-039-3) Boston Public Lib.

Niles, Phillip, ed. see Pelizza, John J.

Niles, Steve. Anxiety Times. 1991. pap. 12.95 (1-56060-118-3) Eclipse Bks.

— Fly in My Eye Exposed. 1991. pap. 12.95 (1-56060-122-1) Eclipse Bks.

— Words Without Pictures. 1990. 29.95 (1-56060-031-4); pap. 8.95 (1-56060-032-2) Eclipse Bks.

Niles, Steve, ed. Daughter of Fly in My Eye. (Illus.). 1990. 9.95 (1-56060-073-X) Eclipse Bks.

Niles, Steve, jt. auth. see Barker, Clive.

Niles, Susan A. Callachaca: Style & Status in an Inca Community. LC 87-16782. (Illus.). 264p. 1987. text ed. 32.95 (0-87745-177-X) U of Iowa Pr.

Niles, W. E. Taxonomic Investigations in the Genera Perityle & Laphamia (Compositae) (Memoirs Ser.: Vol. 21 (1)). (Illus.). 82p. 1970. 10.00 (0-89327-070-9) NY Botanical.

Nilges, Richard G. Cycles. LC 80-12889. 1983. pap. 14.95 (0-87949-182-5) Ashley Bks.

***Nilius, R. & Paquet, K. J., eds.** Praevention, Progressionshemmung & Rehabilitation Von Lebererkrankungen. (Illus.). x, 318p. 1995. 143.50 (3-8055-6171-7) S Karger.

Nilkanth, H. G., tr. see Desai, Mahadev.

Nill, Annegreth, jt. auth. see Caldwell, John.

Nill, Kimball R., jt. auth. see Fleschar, Manfred H.

Nilles. Making Telecommuting Happen: A Guide for Telemanagers & Telecommuters. 1994. pap. 24.95 (0-442-01857-6) Van Nos Reinhold.

Nilles, Burgandy & Thiewes, Sam, illus. Beauty & the Beast. (Favorite Fairy Tales Ser.). 24p. (J). 1993. lib. bdg. 10.95 (1-56674-061-4, HTS Bks) Forest Hse.

— Goldilocks & the Three Bears. (Favorite Fairy Tales Ser.). 24p. (J). (gr. k-4). 1993. lib. bdg. 10.95 (1-56674-063-0, HTS Bks) Forest Hse.

Nilles, Camilla J., intro. Rabelais et Montaigne: Chapitres Choisis. LC 91-29802. 596p. 1991. lib. bdg. 119.95 (0-7734-9704-8) E Mellen.

Nilles, Jack M. Exploring the World of the Personal Computer. (Illus.). 256p. 1982. 17.95 (0-13-297572-6); text ed. 19.39 (0-685-03857-2) P-H.

Nilles, Mary E. In a Large Circle of Relatives: A Genealogical Guide to the Early Community of Rollingstone, Minnesota. (Illus.). 525p. 1989. pap. 30.00 (0-9616845-1-8) M E Nilles.

— A Legacy from Luxembourg: A Historical Guide to the Early Settlement of Rollingstone, Minnesota. 154p. (Orig.). 1986. pap. 9.95 (0-9616845-0-X) M E Nilles.

Nilles, Myrah J. Fix My Hair Pretty: Hair Designs for Young Girls. (Illus.). 64p. (Orig.). 1985. pap. 6.95 (0-9613683-0-6) Nilles Pub.

***Nillsen, Rodney Victor.** Difference Spaces & Invariant Linear Forms. (Lecture Notes in Mathematics: Vol. 1586). 1994. write for info. (3-540-58323-8) Spr-Verlag.

— Difference Spaces & Invariant Linear Forms. (Lecture Notes in Mathematics: Vol. 1586). 1994. 30.00 (0-387-58323-8) Spr-Verlag.

Nilon, Charles H. Bibliography of Bibliographies in American Literature. LC 73-103542. 495p. reprint ed. pap. 141.10 (0-8357-7178-4, 2013299) Bks Demand.

Nilsen. Conference on Tools for the Simulationist, 1990. 36p. 1990. 10.00 (0-685-66845-2, MC90-1) Soc Computer Sim.

Nilsen, Alleen P. Presenting M. E. Kerr. (Twayne's Young Adult Authors Ser.: No. 527). 136p. 1986. text ed. 19.95 (0-8057-8202-8, Twayne) Macmillan.

Nilsen, Alleen P. & Donelson, Kenneth L. Literature for Today's Young Adults. 3rd ed. (C). 1989. text ed. 33.25 (0-673-38400-4) HarpCollege.

Nilsen, Alleen P., jt. auth. see Donelson, Kenneth L.

Nilsen, Angela, jt. auth. see Maxwell, Sarah.

***Nilsen, Dave & Chadwick, Frank.** Striker II: Miniature Warfare in the Far Future. (Travellers the New Era Ser.). (Illus.). 196p. (Orig.). 1994. pap. 20.00 (1-55878-173-0) Game Designers.

Nilsen, David. Ranger. (Twenty-Three Hundred AD Ser.). (Illus.). 64p. (Orig.). (YA). 1989. pap. 8.00 (1-55878-016-5) Game Designers.

Nilsen, Don L. English Adverbials. (Janua Linguarum, Ser. Practica: No. 125). 1972. pap. text ed. 42.35 (90-279-2146-6) Mouton.

— Humor in American Literature: A Selected Annotated Bibliography. LC 91-42821. 584p. 1992. 78.00 (0-8240-8395-4, H#1049) Garland.

— Humor Scholarship: A Research Bibliography. LC 92-38989. (Bibliographies & Indexes in Popular Culture Ser.). 416p. 1993. text ed. 65.00 (0-313-28441-5, NHS/) Greenwood.

— The Instrumental Case in English: Syntactic & Semantic Considerations. LC 72-94490. (Janua Linguarum, Ser. Minor: No. 156). (Illus.). 187p. 1973. pap. text ed. 43.10 (90-279-2387-6) Mouton.

— Toward a Semantic Specification of Deep Case. (Janua Linguarum, Ser. Minor: No. 152). 52p. (Orig.). 1972. text ed. 34.65 (90-279-2318-3) Mouton.

Nilsen, Frances S. & Salter, James L. Amerigo: The Amerigo Vespucci Story. LC 92-93878. (Illus.). 253p. (YA). (gr. 10-12). 1992. 14.95 (0-9633937-6-6) Shamrock TN.

Nilsen-Hamilton, Marit, ed. Growth Factors & Signal Transduction in Development. LC 94-6541. (Modern Cell Biology Ser.: Vol. 14). 1994. text ed. 99.95 (0-471-30539-1) Wiley.

Nilsen, Marit-Jentoft & Trendall, A. D. Corpus Vasorum Antiquorum, United States of America, Fascicule 3. (Illus.). 50p. 1990. 85.00 (0-89236-172-7) J P Getty Trust.

Nilsen, Mary Y. Real Living: A Small-Group Life Experience with the Gospel of Luke, Pt. 1. (Illus.). 1979. pap. text ed. 5.65 (0-03-021856-X) Harper SF.

— Real Living: A Small Group Life Experience with the Gospel of Luke, Pt. 2. (Illus.). 1980. pap. text ed. 5.65 (0-03-022141-2) Harper SF.

— A Time for Peace: Daily Meditations for Twelve-Step Living. Friedman, R. Cheryl, ed. LC 90-90177. (Illus.). 416p. (Orig.). 1990. pap. 8.95 (0-9627147-0-4) Zion Pub.

Nilsen, Per. Prince: A Documentary. (Illus.). 160p. pap. 25.95 (0-7119-1816-3, OP45376); pap. 16.95 (0-7119-3179-8) Omnibus NY.

Nilsen, Ragnar, ed. Tools for the Simulation Profession, 1989. 76p. 1989. pap. 20.00 (0-911801-53-7, EMC89-1) Soc Computer Sim.

Nilsen, Richard, ed. Helping Nature Heal: A Whole Earth Catalog. (Illus.). 176p. (Orig.). 1991. pap. 14.95 (0-89815-425-1) Ten Speed Pr.

Nilsen, Thomas R. Ethics of Speech Communication. 2nd ed. LC 72-86834. 1974. pap. 3.50 (0-672-61300-X, SC10, Bobbs) Macmillan.

Nilsen, Tor H., jt. ed. see Ingersoll, Raymond V.

Nilsen, Tor H., jt. auth. see Nelson, C. Hans.

***Nilsestuen, Rolf M.** The Kensington Runestone Vindicated. (Illus.). 222p. (C). 1995. lib. bdg. 36.50 (0-8191-9749-1) U Pr of Amer.

Nilson, Arthur H. Design of Concrete Structures. 11th ed. 1991. text ed. write for info. (0-07-046567-3) McGraw.

— Design of Prestressed Concrete. 2nd ed. 592p. 1987. Net. text ed. write for info. (0-471-83072-0) Wiley.

***Nilson, Carolyn.** Games That Drive Change. LC 95-17015. 1995. pap. write for info. (0-07-046589-4) McGraw.

— How to Manage Training: A Guide to Administration, Design, & Delivery. 275p. 1991. ring bd. 69.95 (0-8144-1150-9, 040530) AMACOM.

— How to Start a Training Program in Your Growing Business. 176p. 1992. 27.95 (0-8144-5032-6) AMACOM.

— Peer Training: Improved Performance One by One. LC 94-165. 1994. write for info. (0-13-104639-X) P-H.

— Team Games for Trainers. LC 93-3369. 304p. 1993. pap. text ed. 21.95 (0-07-046588-6) McGraw.

— Trainer's Complete Guide to Management & Supervisory Development. LC 92-15854. 1992. write for info. (0-13-410663-6) P-H.

— Training for Non-Trainers: A Do-It-Yourself Guide for Managers. 240p. 1991. pap. 16.95 (0-8144-7775-5) AMACOM.

— Training Program Workbook & Kit. 384p. 1989. text ed. 69.95 (0-13-926247-4) P-H.

Nilson, Donald E. & Kroenke, David M. Managing Information with Microcomputers: Featuring R BASE Series, Database Management Systems. Craig, Dorothy P., ed. LC 84-6651. (Illus.). (Orig.). 1984. 19.95 (0-916937-00-3) Microrim.

Nilson, Jeena, jt. auth. see Aslett, Don.

***Nilson, Jon.** Nothing Beyond the Necessary: Roman Catholicism & the Ecumenical Future. LC 95-11964. 120p. (Orig.). 1995. pap. 7.95 (0-8091-3576-0) Paulist Pr.

Nilson, Linda, ed. Natural Disasters & Public Policy. 200p. (Orig.). 1985. pap. 12.00 (0-918592-75-5) Pol Studies.

Nilson, Shirley, jt. auth. see Warnick, Kathleen.

***Nilson, Sue & Morgan, Andy.** Starting a Single Adult Ministry: Includes Ideas for the Small Church. Date not set. 16.95 (0-7814-5061-6, 87866) Cook.

***Nilson, Torsten H.** Chaos Marketing: How to Win in a Turbulent World. LC 95-1442. (Marketing for Professionals Ser.). 1995. pap. 19.95 (0-07-707991-4) McGraw.

— Value-Added Marketing: Marketing Management for Superior Results. 1992. text ed. 22.95 (0-07-707655-9) McGraw.

Nilsson. The Pleistocene. 1983. lib. bdg. 249.00 (90-277-1466-5) Kluwer Ac.

— Rocky Mountain National Park. 1978. pap. 5.95 (0-02-499400-6) Macmillan.

Nilsson, A., jt. ed. see Onvural, R. O.

Nilsson, Anders, jt. auth. see Abrahamsson, Hans.

Nilsson, Ann-Sofie. Political Uses of International Law. 194p. (Orig.). 1987. pap. 43.50 (91-7504-083-2, Pub. by Dialogos SW) Coronet Bks.

Nilsson, Annika. Greenhouse Earth. (Scientific Committee on Problems of the Environment Ser.). 219p. 1992. pap. text ed. 39.95 (0-471-93628-6) Wiley.

Nilsson, Arne, jt. ed. see Onvural, Raif O.

Nilsson, Birgit. Birgit Nilsson: My Memoirs in Pictures. Teal, Thomas, tr. (Quality Paperbacks Ser.). (Illus.). 127p. 1982. reprint ed. pap. 14.95 (0-306-80180-9) Da Capo.

Nilsson, Erik. Rocky Mountain National Park Trail Guide. LC 78-362. (Illus.). 187p. 1978. pap. 4.95 (0-89037-098-2) Anderson World.

Nilsson, Eriksson, jt. auth. see Nilsson, Ulf.

Nilsson, G oran E., jt. auth. see Lutz, Peter L.

Nilsson, Goran. Effects of Bisulphite & the Stability of Adrenaline. (Uppsala Dissertations from the Faculty of Science Ser.: No. 2). (Illus.). vii, 98p. (Orig.). 1986. pap. text ed. 23.50x (91-554-1888-0, Pub. by Uppsala Univ Acta Univ Upps aliensis SW) Coronet Bks.

Nilsson, Goran, jt. auth. see Lutz, Peter L.

Nilsson, James W. Electric Circuits. 2nd ed. LC 85-1380. (Electrical Engineering Ser.). 820p. (C). 1985. text ed. write for info. (0-201-12695-8); teacher ed write for info. (0-201-12696-6) Addison-Wesley.

— Electric Circuits. 3rd ed. (Electrical Engineering Ser.). (Illus.). 832p. (C). 1990. text ed. 61.25 (0-201-17288-7) Addison-Wesley.

— Electric Circuits. 5th ed. LC 94-17612. (C). 1996. text ed. 51.16 (0-201-55707-X) Addison-Wesley.

Nilsson, Jerker & Host, Viggo. Reseller Assortment Decision Criteria. 181p. (Orig.). 1987. pap. 33.50 (87-7288-079-1) Coronet Bks.

Nilsson, John A. Dealing Effectively with Counsel Abroad. (International Business Portfolios Ser.). 1988. write for info. (0-8205-1955-3) Bender.

Nilsson, K., jt. auth. see Brodersen, K.

Nilsson, Kare & Nilsson, Paasche. Norsk - Spansk Ordbok. 392p. (NOR & SPA.). lib. bdg. 150.00 (0-7859-3673-4, 8200075869) Fr & Eur.

Nilsson, Karen. A Wild Flower by Any Other Name: Sketches of Pioneer Naturalists Who Named Our Western Plants. LC 93-44015. 1994. 12.95 (0-935382-74-7) Tioga Pub Co.

Nilsson, Karen B. Wild Flower by Any Other Name: Sketches of Pioneer Naturalists Who Named Our Western Plants. LC 93-44015. (Illus.). 1994. pap. 14.95 (0-939666-76-6) Yosemite Assn.

Nilsson, L. G., ed. Perspectives on Memory Research. 416p. 1979. text ed. 79.95 (0-89859-483-9) L Erlbaum Assocs.

Nilsson, L. G. & Archer, Trevor, eds. Perspectives on Learning & Memory. (Comparative Cognition & Neuroscience Ser.). 352p. (C). 1985. 69.95 (0-89859-628-9) L Erlbaum Assocs.

Nilsson, L. G., jt. ed. see Archer, T.

Nilsson, L. G., jt. ed. see Hjelmquist, E.

Nilsson, Lennart. Behold Man. LC 73-14087. (Illus.). 1978. 29.95 (0-316-60751-7) Little.

— A Child Is Born: The Completely New Edition. (Illus.). 1990. 27.50 (0-385-30237-1, Sey Lawr) Delacorte.

An Asterisk (*) at the beginning of an entry indicates that the title is appearing in BIP for the first time.

Nilsson, Lennart & Swanberg, Lena K. How Was I Born? James, Clare, tr. LC 94-11908. (Illus.). (J). 1994. 18.95 (*0-385-31357-8*) Delacorte.

Nilsson, Magnus, jt. auth. see Lorentzi, Jakob.

Nilsson, Martin P. The Dionysiac Mysteries of the Hellenistic & Roman Age. LC 75-10643. (Ancient Religion & Mythology Ser.). (Illus.). 1980. reprint ed. 18.95 (*0-405-07261-9*) Ayer.

— A History of Greek Religion. Fielden, F. J., tr. LC 80-13430. 316p. 1980. reprint ed. text ed. 65.00 (*0-313-22466-8*, NIHG, Greenwood Pr) Greenwood.

— Imperial Rome. (Illus.). 376p. 1974. pap. 25.00 (*0-89005-546-7*) Ares.

— The Minoan-Mycenaean Religion. LC 70-162300. 1950. 20.00 (*0-8196-0273-6*) Biblo.

— The Mycenaean Origins of Greek Mythology. 21.00 (*0-8446-6208-9*) Peter Smith.

— The Mycenaean Origins of Greek Mythology. (Sather Classical Lectures: No. 8). 278p. (C). 1973. reprint ed. pap. 13.00 (*0-520-05073-8*) U CA Pr.

Nilsson, N. R., jt. ed. see Lundqvist, S. O.

Nilsson, Nancy M. Very Truly Yours, M. L. A Visit with Mary Lincoln. (Illus.). 36p. (Orig.). 1992. pap. 6.95 (*0-9629170-3-6*) Twinbrook Comms.

Nilsson, Nils, jt. auth. see Genesereth, Michael.

Nilsson, Nils A., ed. Boris Pasternak: Essays. 215p. 1977. pap. text ed. 30.00x (*91-22-00086-0*, Pub. by Almqv & Wiksell SW) Coronet Bks.

— Slavic Literatures & Modernism. (Nobel Symposium Ser.: No. 62). 318p. 1986. pap. text ed. 48.50x (*91-7402-180-X*, Pub. by Almqv & Wiksell SW) Coronet Bks.

— Velimir Chlebnikov. (Studies in Russian Literature: No. 20). 150p. (Orig.). 1985. pap. text ed. 25.00x (*91-22-00765-2*, Pub. by Almqv & Wiksell SW) Coronet Bks.

Nilsson, Nils-Ake, ed. Czeslaw Milosz: A Stockholm Conference, 1991. 112p. (Orig.). 1992. pap. 29.00x (*91-7402-231-8*, Pub. by Almqv & Wiksell SW) Coronet Bks.

Nilsson, Nils J. Principles of Artificial Intelligence. LC 86-2815. (Illus.). 476p. 1986. reprint ed. text ed. 54.95 (*0-934613-10-9*) Morgan Kaufmann.

Nilsson, Nils J., jt. ed. see Webber, Bonnie L.

Nilsson, Nils J., et al. Mathematical Foundations of Learning Machines. 1990. 25.95 (*1-55860-123-6*) Morgan Kaufmann.

Nilsson, Paasche, jt. auth. see Nilsson, Kare.

Nilsson, S., jt. auth. see Ekspong, Gosta.

Nilsson, Shirley. Stitching Free: Easy Machine Pictures. Townsend, Louise, ed. LC 93-21483. (Illus.). 80p. 1993. pap. 16.95 (*0-914881-68-X*) C & T Pub.

Nilsson, Stefan & Holmgreen, Susanne. Comparative Physiology & Evolution of the Autonomic Nervous System. LC 93-25356. (Autonomic Nervous System Ser.: Vol. 4). 1994. text ed. 104.00 (*3-7186-5137-8*) Gordon & Breach.

Nilsson, Sten & Pitt, David. Protecting the Atmosphere: The Climate Change Convention & Its Context. 160p. (Orig.). 1993. 22.50 (*1-85383-161-1*, Pub. by Erthscan Pubns UK) Island Pr.

Nilsson, Sten, jt. auth. see Virtanen, Yrjo.

Nilsson, Sten, et al. The Forest Resources of the Former European U. S. S. R. 500p. (C). 1992. text ed. 85.00 (*1-85070-425-2*) Prthnon Pub.

— Future Forest Resources of Western & Eastern Europe. 500p. (C). 1992. 85.00 (*1-85070-424-4*) Prthnon Pub.

Nilsson, Sven G., jt. auth. see Ragnarsson, Ingemar.

Nilsson, T. K., et al. Clinical Aspects of Fibrinolysis. (Illus.). 187p. 1991. 143.50x (*91-22-01436-5*, Pub. by Almqv & Wiksell SW) Coronet Bks.

Nilsson, Ulf. If You Didn't Have Me. Blecher, Lone T. & Blecher, George, trs. LC 86-21327. (Illus.). 128p. (J). (gr. 2-5). 1987. text ed. 13.95 (*0-689-50406-3*, McElderry) S&S Childrens.

Nilsson, Ulf & Maluszynski, Jan. Logic, Programming & Prolog. 289p. 1990. pap. text ed. 44.95 (*0-471-92625-6*) Wiley.

Nilsson, Ulf & Nilsson, Eriksson. Little Bunny & Friends. (J). 1993. pap. 2.99 (*0-517-11071-7*) Random Hse Value.

— Little Bunny Gets Lost. (J). 1993. pap. 2.99 (*0-517-11075-X*) Random Hse Value.

Nilsson, W. Achieving Strategic Goals Through Executive Development. LC 86-32201. 1987. 25.95 (*0-201-12751-2*) Addison-Wesley.

Nilus. Protocols of the Learned Elders of Zion. Marsden, Victor E., ed. & tr. by. 1977. lib. bdg. 250.00 (*0-8490-1388-7*) Gordon Pr.

Nilus of Sinai. Selected Texts on Prayer. pap. 0.25 (*0-89981-090-X*) Eastern Orthodox.

Nilus, Schema-Hieromonk. Prayers to the Most Holy Theotokos (The Virgin Mary) 1992. pap. 1.00 (*0-89981-134-5*) Eastern Orthodox.

Nim, A., ed. see Cajori, Florian.

Nim, Ahn Sang, ed. see Soon, Cho Wha.

Ni'Mat, Allah. History of the Afghans, 2 vols. in 1. Dorn, B., tr. LC 65-8824. 1965. reprint ed. 45.00 (*0-678-07265-5*) Kelley.

Nimbark, Ashakant, ed. Honeycomb. 1976. pap. 1.95 (*0-917428-01-3*) Dowling.

Nimbark, Jai. The Lotus Leaves. 12.00 (*0-89253-628-4*); 4.80 (*0-89253-629-2*) Ind-US Inc.

***Nimbersheim, Jack.** Windows 95 Revealed. 1994. 19.00 (*0-679-76177-2*) Knopf.

Nimble, Jack B. The Construction & Operation of Clandestine Drug Laboratories. 2nd rev. ed. LC 93-80258. (Illus.). 132p. (C). 1994. pap. 14.95 (*1-55950-108-1*, 85178) Loompanics.

Nimer, Kamal K. The Role of Women's Organizations in Eradicating Illiteracy in Jordan. LC 85-48189. 150p. 1986. 34.50 (*0-88164-512-5*); pap. 26.50 (*0-88164-513-3*) ABBE Pubs Assn.

Nimersheim, Jack. Best Book of DESQview. 1990. pap. 24.95 (*0-672-22727-4*, Bobbs) Macmillan.

— DOS: Includes DOS 6.0. LC 93-60387. (In Plain English Ser.). (Illus.). 144p. (Orig.). 1993. pap. 9.95 (*1-56664-029-6*) WorldComm.

— DOS Handbook. 1993. pap. 27.95 (*0-679-79151-5*) Random.

— First Book of Microsoft Windows, No. 3. 1990. pap. 16.95 (*0-672-27334-9*, Bobbs) Michie Butterworth.

— First Book of MS-DOS. 1990. pap. 16.95 (*0-672-27312-8*, Bobbs) Macmillan.

— First Book of MS-DOS. 2nd ed. 1991. pap. 16.95 (*0-672-27341-1*, Bobbs) Macmillan.

— First Book of Procomm Plus. 1990. pap. 16.95 (*0-672-27309-8*, Bobbs) Macmillan.

— First Book of Windows 3.1: Best Seller Edition. 1992. pap. 38.95 (*0-672-27419-1*) Alpha Bks IN.

— Friendly Excel 4.0 for Windows. 1993. pap. 5.99 (*0-679-79187-6*) Random.

— Friendly Word for Windows 2.0. 1993. pap. 5.99 (*0-679-79184-1*) Random.

— Friendly Word for Windows 6.0. 1994. pap. 6.99 (*0-679-79192-2*) Random.

— In Plain English: Microsoft Word for Windows. Hall, Kathryn, ed. (Illus.). 144p. Date not set. pap. text ed. 9.95 (*1-56664-078-4*) WorldComm.

— In Plain English: Windows 95. Hall, Kathryn, ed. (Illus.). 144p. Date not set. pap. text ed. 9.95 (*1-56664-074-1*) WorldComm.

— Norton PcANYWHERE(TM) The Complete Communications Guide. 320p. 1992. 29.95 (*0-8306-4021-5*, 4175, Windcrest); pap. 19.95 (*0-8306-4022-3*, 4175, Windcrest) TAB Bks.

— PCAnywhere: The Complete Communications Guide. 1992. pap. 19.95 (*0-07-046526-6*) McGraw.

— Windows X.0 Slick Tricks. (Slick Tricks Ser.). 1994. pap. 16.00 (*0-679-79178-7*) Random.

— Windows 3.1. LC 93-60164. (In Plain English Ser.). (Illus.). (Orig.). 1993. pap. 9.95 (*1-56664-007-5*) WorldComm.

Nimershein, Jack. DOS 6.2 Slick Tricks. 1994. pap. 16.00 (*0-679-79177-9*) Random.

Nimersheum, Jack. Friendly Excel 5.0 for Windows. Date not set. 6.99 (*0-679-75331-1*) Random.

Nimeth, Albert. Grow Old Gracefully. 1989. reprint ed. pap. 1.95 (*0-8199-0509-7*, Frncscn Herld) Franciscan Pr.

Nimeth, Albert J. I Like You, Just Because. LC 79-139971. (Illus.). (J). (gr. 5 up). 1971. 5.00 (*0-8199-0422-8*, Frncscn Herld) Franciscan Pr.

— In Your Time of Sorrow. 1976. pap. 0.75 (*0-8199-0566-6*, Frncscn Herld) Franciscan Pr.

— Joy. 1975. pap. 0.75 (*0-8199-0602-6*, Frncscn Herld) Franciscan Pr.

— Of Course I Love You. 1973. pap. 5.00 (*0-8199-0466-X*, Frncscn Herld) Franciscan Pr.

— Of Course I Love You. 1973. pap. 5.00 (*0-8199-0951-3*, Frncscn Herld) Franciscan Pr.

— Tenderly I Care. 1977. 5.00 (*0-8199-0952-1*, Frncscn Herld) Franciscan Pr.

— To Listen Is to Heal. 1984. 5.00 (*0-8199-0874-6*, Frncscn Herld) Franciscan Pr.

— To Listen Is to Heal. 1984. 5.00 (*0-8199-0950-5*, Frncscn Herld) Franciscan Pr.

Nimetz, Michael. Humor in Galdos: A Study of the Novelas Contemporaneas. LC 68-13921. (Yale Romanic Studies, Second Ser.: No. 18). 237p. reprint ed. pap. 67.60 (*0-317-29285-4*, 2022024) Bks Demand.

Nimetz, Michael, tr. see Alas, Leopoldo.

Nimick, Ellen H., et al. Juvenile Court Statistics, 1982. 45p. 1984. 10.00 (*0-318-36228-7*) Natl Juv & Family Ct Judges.

Nimick, Ellen H., jt. auth. see Hotzler, John L.

***Nimier, Marie.** The Giraffe. Feeney, Mary, tr. 200p. 1995. 17.95 (*1-56858-026-6*) FWEW.

Nimier, Roger. Les Enfants Tristes. (FRE.). 1983. pap. 12.95 (*0-7859-4184-3*) Fr & Eur.

— L' Etrangere. (FRE.). 1980. pap. 10.95 (*0-7859-4137-1*) Fr & Eur.

— Le Grand d'Espagne. (FRE.). 1975. pap. 10.95 (*0-7859-4036-7*) Fr & Eur.

— Le Hussard Bleu. 434p. (FRE.). 1977. pap. 11.95 (*0-7859-4088-X*, 2070369862) Fr & Eur.

Nimis, P. L. & Crovello, T. J., eds. Quantitative Approaches to Phytogeography. (Tasks for Vegetation Science Ser.). (C). 1990. lib. bdg. 188.50 (*0-7923-0795-X*) Kluwer Ac.

Nimis, Stephen A. Narrative Semiotics in the Epic Tradition: The Simile. LC 87-45323. 211p. reprint ed. pap. 60.20 (*0-7837-3722-X*, 2057900) Bks Demand.

Nimitz, Jon. An Explosion of Chemistry Jokes. LC 90-70457. (Illus.). 193p. (Orig.). 1992. pap. 9.95 (*1-56002-114-4*) Aegina Pr.

Nimitz, Jonathan S. Experiments in Organic Chemistry. 450p. 1989. boxed 39.00 (*0-685-27167-6*) P-H.

— Experiments in Organic Chemistry: From Microscale to Macroscale. 512p. 1990. text ed. 72.00 (*0-13-295718-3*) P-H.

Nimke, R. W. The Rutland Betterments - Statistics. LC 89-81530. (Rutland Ser.). (Illus.). 192p. (Orig.). 1989. 35.00 (*0-914960-90-3*); pap. 25.00 (*0-914960-77-6*) Academy Bks.

Nimley, Anthony J. Government & Politics in Liberia, Vol. I. LC 90-85696. (Illus.). 1813p. (C). 1991. pap. text ed. 75.00 (*0-9628498-0-4*) A J Nimley.

— Government & Politics in Liberia, Vol. II. LC 90-85696. 1554p. (C). 1991. pap. text ed. 75.00 (*0-9628498-1-2*) A J Nimley.

Nimmer. Treatise on the Theory of the First Amendment. 1984. Student Edition. student ed write for info. (*0-8205-0286-3*, 516) Bender.

Nimmer, David. The Journey Goes On. 109p. 1992. pap. 9.95 (*0-931714-49-4*) Nodin Pr.

Nimmer, Melville B. Nimmer on Copyright, 5 vols. 1978. Updates. ring bd. write for info. (*0-8205-1465-9*) Bender.

— Nimmer on Freedom of Speech. 1984. Updates. ring bd. write for info. (*0-8205-1516-7*) Bender.

Nimmer, Melville B., et al. Entertainment Litigation Including Unfair Competition, Defamation, Privacy, Illustrated, Cases & Materials On Copy & Other Aspects Of: Copy & Other Aspects Of. 4th ed. (American Casebook Ser.). 1177p. 1991. text ed. 54.00 (*0-314-83541-5*) West Pub.

Nimmer, Raymond. Commercial Asset-Based Financing: 1988-1990, 4 vols. annuals suppl. ed. 500.00 (*0-685-24490-3*) Clark Boardman Callaghan.

Nimmer, Raymond T. The Law of Computer Technology. 2nd ed. 688p. 1992. 125.00 (*0-7913-1270-4*) Warren Gorham & Lamont.

— The Law of Computer Technology. 2nd suppl. ed. 688p. 1992. Supplemented semi-annually; write for info. 50.00 (*0-685-55750-2*) Warren Gorham & Lamont.

Nimmer, Raymond T., jt. auth. see White, James J.

Nimmer, Raymond T., et al. Commercial Transactions: Secured Financing. 2nd ed. (Contemporary Legal Education Ser.). 685p. 1992. 37.00 (*0-87215-963-9*); 37.00 (*0-685-62351-3*) Michie Butterworth.

Nimmer, Ron, jt. auth. see Trantina, Gerry.

***Nimmo, Claude.** Collins-Robert Gem French Dictionary. 3rd ed. 630p. (ENG & FRE.). 1993. write for info. (*0-7859-7412-1*, 0004589777) Fr & Eur.

Nimmo, Dan, ed. Communication Yearbook,, No. 3. 704p. 1979. 49.95 (*0-87855-341-X*) Transaction Pubs.

— Communication Yearbook, No. 4. 752p. 1980. 49.95 (*0-87855-385-1*) Transaction Pubs.

Nimmo, Dan & Combs, James E. Mediated Political Realities. 2nd ed. 256p. (C). 1990. pap. text ed. 27.50 (*0-8013-0220-X*, 75878) Longman.

— Nightly Horrors: Crisis Coverage in Television Network News. LC 84-10464. 232p. 1985. 36.00x (*0-87049-443-0*); pap. 16.95 (*0-87049-625-5*) U of Tenn Pr.

— The Political Pundits. LC 91-34491. (Praeger Series in Political Communication). 208p. 1992. text ed. 55.00 (*0-275-93541-8*, C3541, Praeger Pubs); pap. text ed. 15.95 (*0-275-93545-0*, B3545, Praeger Pubs) Greenwood.

Nimmo, Dan & Mansfield, Michael W., eds. Government & the News Media: Comparative Dimensions. LC 82-73859. 306p. 1982. 18.95 (*0-918954-36-3*); pap. 13.50 (*0-918954-42-8*) Baylor Univ Pr.

Nimmo, Dan, jt. auth. see Combs, James.

Nimmo, Dan, jt. auth. see Savage, Robert L.

Nimmo, Dan, jt. auth. see Smith, Larry D.

Nimmo, Dan, jt. ed. see Swanson, David L.

Nimmo, Derek. Memorable Dinners: Portentous, Outrageous, & Exuberant, Recollected by the Rich & Rare. 1992. 29.95 (*1-870948-48-3*, Pub. by Quiller Pr UK) St Mut.

— Up Mount Everest Without a Paddle. large type ed. 168p. 1989. reprint ed. lib. bdg. 9.97 (*1-85089-325-X*, Pub. by ISIS UK) Transaction Pubs.

Nimmo, Dorothy. James Nayler Poems. 1993. pap. 20.00 (*1-85072-129-7*, Pub. by W Sessions UK) St Mut.

Nimmo, H. A., jt. ed. see Kaeppler, A. L.

Nimmo, H. Arlo. The Songs of Salanda: And Other Stories of Sulu. LC 93-42674. 248p. 1994. 22.50 (*0-295-97334-X*); pap. write for info. (*0-295-97335-8*) U of Wash Pr.

Nimmo, Ian, ed. Edinburgh: The New Town. 200p. (C). 1989. text ed. 50.00 (*0-85976-323-4*, Pub. by J Donald) St Mut.

Nimmo, J. C., jt. auth. see Bullen, A. H.

Nimmo, Jenny. Orchard of the Crescent Moon. 170p. (J). (gr. 5-9). 1990. pap. 2.95 (*0-8167-2265-X*) Troll Assocs.

— Rainbow & Mr. Zed. 144p. (J). 1994. 14.99 (*0-525-45150-1*) Dutton Child Bks.

— The Snow Spider. LC 87-5429. 144p. (J). (gr. 5 up). 1987. 11.95 (*0-525-44306-1*, DCB) Dutton Child Bks.

— The Snow Spider. 136p. (J). (gr. 5-9). 1990. pap. 2.95 (*0-8167-2264-1*) Troll Assocs.

— Ultramarine. large type ed. 296p. (J). 1992. 16.95 (*0-7451-1554-3*, Galaxy Child Lrg Print) Chivers N Amer.

Nimmo, John, jt. auth. see Jones, Elizabeth.

Nimmo, Joseph, Jr. Report in Regard to the Range & Ranch Cattle Business of the United States. LC 72-2860. (Use & Abuse of America's Natural Resources Ser.). 214p. 1972. reprint ed. 19.95 (*0-405-04524-7*) Ayer.

Nimmo, W., et al. Anaesthesia. 2nd ed. (Illus.). 2144p. 1994. write for info. (*0-632-03244-8*) Blackwell Sci.

***Nimmo, Walter S. & Tucker, Geoffrey T., eds.** Clincial Measurement in Drug Evaluation. LC 94-40650. 1994. text ed. 79.95 (*0-471-94391-6*) Wiley.

Nimmo, William F. Behind a Curtain of Silence: Japanese in Soviet Custody, 1945-1956. LC 88-5623. (Contributions in Military Studies: No. 78). (Illus.). 159p. 1988. text ed. 45.00 (*0-313-25762-0*, NCS/, Greenwood Pr) Greenwood.

— Japan & Russia: A Re-Evaluation in the Post-Soviet Era. LC 93-11847. (Contributions in Asian Studies: No. 3). 240p. 1994. text ed. 55.00 (*0-313-28440-7*, Greenwood Pr) Greenwood.

Nimmo, William F., ed. The Occupation of Japan: Grass Roots Level. (C). 1992. lib. bdg. 19.25 (*0-9606418-7-4*) Genl D MacArthur Fnd.

— The Occupation of Japan: The Impact of the Korean War. 189p. (C). 1986. lib. bdg. 19.25 (*0-9606418-6-6*) Genl D MacArthur Fnd.

Nimmons, Carol A. The Child-Care Worker Manual. Wren, Jim & Bowman, Suzanne, eds. (Illus.). 24p. 1989. teacher ed 3.00 (*0-89606-320-8*, 805TK); pap. 9.00 (*0-89606-267-8*, 805) Am Assn Voc Materials.

Nimmons, David, jt. auth. see Dubler, Nancy N.

Nimni, Ephraim. Marxism & Nationalism: The Theoretical Origins of the Political Crisis. 242p. (C). 1991. text ed. 70.00 (*0-7453-0358-7*, Pub. by Pluto Pr UK) Westview.

— Marxism & Nationalism: The Theoretical Origins of the Political Crisis. 242p. (C). 1994. pap. text ed. 21.00 (*0-7453-0730-2*, Pub. by Pluto Pr UK) Westview.

Nimni, Marcel E., ed. Collagen: Biochemistry, Biomechanics, Biotechnology, Vol. I. 384p. 1988. 175.00 (*0-8493-4601-0*, QP552, CRC Reprint) Franklin.

— Collagen: Biochemistry, Biomechanics, Biotechnology, Vol. II. 336p. 1988. 239.00 (*0-8493-4602-9*, QP552) CRC Pr.

— Collagen: Biochemistry, Biomechanics, Biotechnology, Vol. III. 368p. 1988. 176.00 (*0-8493-4603-7*, QP552, CRC Reprint) Franklin.

Nimni, Marcel E. & Kang, Andrew H. Collagen Vol. V: Pathobiochemistry. 288p. 1991. 205.00 (*0-8493-4605-3*, QP552) CRC Pr.

Nimni, Marcel E. & Olsen, Bjorn R., eds. Collagen Vol. IV: Molecular Biology. 208p. 1989. 179.00 (*0-8493-4604-5*, QP552) CRC Pr.

Nimnicht, Nona. In the Museum Naked. LC 78-1145. 1978. pap. 5.00 (*0-915016-19-2*) Second Coming.

Nimnicht, Nona, jt. ed. see Askew, Judith.

Nimocks, Walter. Milner's Young Men: The Kindergarten in Edwardian Imperial Affairs. LC 68-8588. 248p. reprint ed. pap. 70.70 (*0-317-20447-5*, 2023429) Bks Demand.

***Nimoy, Leonard.** I Am Spock. (Illus.). 320p. 1995. 24.95 (*0-7868-6182-7*) Hyperion.

— Vincent. 1985. 4.95 (*0-87129-386-2*, V17) Dramatic Pub.

— Warmed by Love. 150p. 1983. text ed. 16.95 (*0-88396-200-4*) Blue Mtn Pr CO.

Nimrod, Carl & Griener, Glenn, eds. Biomedical Ethics & Fetal Therapy. (Calgary Institute for the Humanities Ser.). 100p. (C). 1988. pap. 17.50 (*0-88920-962-6*, Pub. by Wilfrid Laurier CN) Humanities.

Nimrod, Naomi, jt. auth. see Broner, E. M.

Nims, Bonnie L. Just Beyond Reach. (Illus.). 48p. (J). 1992. 13.95 (*0-590-44077-2*, Scholastic Hardcover) Scholastic Inc.

— Where Is the Bear? Fay, Ann, ed. LC 87-25321. (Illus.). 24p. (J). (ps-2). 1988. lib. bdg. 11.95 (*0-8075-8933-0*) A Whitman.

— Where Is the Bear at School? Tucker, Kathy, ed. LC 89-37903. (Illus.). 24p. (J). (ps-1). 1989. 11.95 (*0-8075-8935-7*) A Whitman.

— Where Is the Bear in the City? Mathews, Judith, ed. LC 92-3390. (Illus.). 24p. (J). (ps-1). 1992. 11.95 (*0-8075-8937-3*) A Whitman.

Nims, Jack. The Wind As Messenger. LC 88-71117. 163p. (Orig.). 1989. pap. 8.00 (*0-916383-71-7*) Aegina Pr.

Nims, John F. The Harper Anthology of Poetry. (Illus.). 842p. (C). 1990. text ed. 28.50 (*0-06-044847-4*) HarpCollege.

— A Local Habitation: Essays on Poetry. (Poets on Poetry Ser.). 1985. pap. 13.95 (*0-472-06356-1*) U of Mich Pr.

— Selected Poems. LC 81-19820. (Phoenix Ser.). xii, 148p. 1982. pap. 6.95 (*0-226-58118-7*) U Ch Pr.

— The Six-Cornered Snowflake & Other Poems. LC 90-33222. 64p. 1990. 18.95 (*0-8112-1143-6*); pap. 9.95 (*0-8112-1144-4*, NDP700) New Directions.

— Zany in Denim. 91p. 1990. 14.95 (*1-55728-154-8*); pap. 6.95 (*1-55728-155-6*) U of Ark Pr.

Nims, John F., ed. Western Wind: An Introduction to Poetry. 3rd ed. 1992. text ed. write for info. (*0-07-046574-6*) McGraw.

Nims, John F., tr. Sappho to Valery: Poems in Translation. LC 89-38953. 435p. 1990. pap. 19.95 (*1-55728-141-6*) U of Ark Pr.

Nims, John F., tr. see St. John of the Cross.

Nims, Marion R., ed. see U. S. Council of National Defense Staff.

Nimsch, Hubertus. A Reference Guide to the Gymnosperms of the World. 92p. 1995. pap. 25.00 (*1-878762-52-4*) Koeltz Sci Bks.

Nimse, Gordon. Take What You Want. large type ed. (Dales Mystery Ser.). 422p. 1993. pap. 16.95 (*1-85389-372-2*, Medcom-Trainex) Ulverscroft.

Nimtz, August H. Islam & Politics in East Africa: The Sufi Order in Tanzania. LC 80-429. 250p. reprint ed. pap. 71.30 (*0-7837-2933-2*, 2057521) Bks Demand.

Nimtz, Sharon & Cousineau, Ruth. Tomato Imperative! Fried Green Tomatoes to Summer's Ripe Bounty, More Than 130 Recipes for Tomatoes, Fresh & Preserved. LC 93-35618. 1994. 14.95 (*0-316-60794-0*) Little.

Nimuendaju, Curt. The Serente. Lowie, Robert H., tr. LC 76-44769. reprint ed. 37.50 (*0-404-15873-0*) AMS Pr.

— The Serente. Lowie, Robert H., ed. & tr. by. (Frederick Webb Hodge Publications: No. 4). (Illus.). xii, 106p. 1967. reprint ed. pap. 5.00 (*0-916561-58-5*) Southwest Mus.

Nimz, Horst H., ed. Holzforschung: Supplement Issue in Honor of Guenther Stegmann. 158p. (GER.). (C). 1994. pap. text ed. 242.35 (*3-11-014247-3*, 10-94) De Gruyter.

Nimzovich, Aron. Chess Praxis. Orig. Title: Praxis of My System. (Illus.). 1936. pap. 6.95 (*0-486-20296-8*) Dover.

Nimzowitsch, Aron. Blockade. rev. ed. Platz, Joseph, tr. (Illus.). 65p. (Orig.). 1983. pap. 5.00 (*0-931462-07-X*) Chess Ent Inc.

— Chess Praxis: Twenty First Century Edition. Artz, Ken, ed. Du Mont, J., tr. 296p. 1993. pap. 17.95 (*1-880673-91-6*) Hays Pub.

— My System. rev. ed. 1979. 13.00 (*0-679-14025-5*) McKay.

— My System: Twenty-First Century Edition. Hays, Lou, ed. 260p. 1992. pap. 17.50 (*1-880673-85-1*) Hays Pub.

N

Nin, Anais. Children of the Albatross. LC 66-6826. 111p. 1959. pap. 6.95 (0-8040-0039-5) Swallow.
— Collages. LC 64-25338. (Illus.). 122p. 1964. 6.95 (0-8040-0045-X) Swallow.
— D. H. Lawrence: An Unprofessional Study. LC 64-16109. 110p. (Orig.). 1964. pap. 8.95 (0-8040-0067-0) Swallow.
— The Diary of Anais Nin, Vol. 5: 1947-1955. Stuhlmann, Gunther, ed. LC 77-2085. 275p. 1975. reprint ed. pap. 10.95 (0-15-626030-1, Harvest Bks) HarBrace.
— The Diary of Anais Nin, Vol. 6: 1955-1966. Stuhlmann, Gunther, ed. & pref. by. LC 77-3599. 414p. 1977. pap. 12.00 (0-15-626032-8, Harvest Bks) HarBrace.
— The Diary of Anais Nin, Vol. 7: 1966-1974. Stuhlmann, Gunther, ed. LC 66-12917. (Illus.). 368p. 1981. pap. 12.00 (0-15-626035-2, Harvest Bks) HarBrace.
— The Early Diary of Anais Nin: Vol. II, 1920-1923. LC 77-20314. 476p. 1983. reprint ed. pap. 12.95 (0-15-627248-2, Harvest Bks) HarBrace.
— The Early Diary of Anais Nin: Vol. III, 1923-1927. (Illus.). 316p. 1985. pap. 12.95 (0-15-627250-4, Harvest Bks) HarBrace.
— The Early Diary of Anais Nin: Volume 4, 1918-1927. 1986. pap. 14.95 (0-15-627251-2) HarBrace.
— The Early Diary of Anais Nin: 1914-1920, Vol. I. Sherman, Jean, tr. LC 79-18962. (Illus.). 1980. pap. 12.95 (0-15-652386-8, Harvest Bks) HarBrace.
— Fire: From "A Journal of Love" 400p. 1995. 25.00 (0-15-100088-3) HarBrace.
— Four-Chambered Heart. LC 66-6825. 187p. 1959. pap. 8.95 (0-8040-0121-9) Swallow.
— Henry & June. 1990. pap. 8.95 (0-15-640057-X) HarBrace.
— House of Incest. LC 61-65487. 72p. 1958. pap. 5.95 (0-8040-0148-0) Swallow.
— In Favor of the Sensitive Man & Other Essays. LC 75-38583. 176p. (Orig.). 1976. pap. 7.95 (0-15-644445-3, Harvest Bks) HarBrace.
— Incest. 1993. pap. 12.95 (0-15-644300-7) HarBrace.
— Ladders to Fire. rev. ed. LC 61-66834. (Cities of the Interior Ser.: Vol.). 192p. 1995. reprint ed. pap. 9.95 (0-8040-0181-2) Ohio U Pr.
— Literate Passion. 1989. pap. 12.95 (0-15-652791-X) HarBrace.
— Little Birds. 176p. 1990. mass mkt. 5.50 (0-671-68011-0) PB.
— La Maison de l'Inceste. (POR.). Cassette & Text. audio 24.95 (0-318-36212-0) Fr & Eur.
— The Mystic of Sex: Uncollected Writings, 1930-1974. 160p. (Orig.). 1995. lib. bdg. 29.00 (0-8095-4132-7) Borgo Pr.
— The Mystic of Sex: Uncollected Writings, 1930-1974. 160p. (Orig.). Date not set. pap. 10.95 (0-88496-391-8) Capra Pr.
— The Novel of the Future. LC 86-1895. 212p. 1986. reprint ed. pap. text ed. 10.95 (0-8040-0879-5) Swallow.
— A Photographic Supplement to the Diary of Anais Nin. LC 77-2085. 80p. (Orig.). 1974. pap. 7.95 (0-15-626024-7, Harvest Bks) HarBrace.
— Seduction of the Minotaur. LC 61-66834. 146p. (Orig.). 1961. pap. 7.95 (0-8040-0268-1) Swallow.
— Spy in the House of Love. LC 66-6833. 140p. 1959. pap. 7.95 (0-8040-0280-0) Swallow.
— A Spy in the House of Love. Rubenstein, Julie, ed. 176p. 1994. reprint ed. mass mkt. 5.50 (0-671-87139-0) PB.
— Under a Glass Bell. LC 94-32163. 101p. (Orig.). 1995. pap. 8.95 (0-8040-0302-5) Swallow.
— Waste of Timelessness: And Other Early Stories. LC 74-28648. viii, 110p. 1994. reprint ed. pap. 9.95 (0-8040-0981-3) Swallow.
— Winter of Artifice. LC 61-17530. 175p. (Orig.). 1961. pap. 7.95 (0-8040-0322-X) Swallow.
Ninan, K. N. Edible Oilseeds: Growth, Area Responses & Prospects. (C). 1989. 24.00 (81-204-0397-5, Pub. by Oxford IBH II) S Asia.
Ninan, Philip T., jt. ed. see Lery, Stephen T.
Nincic, Miroslav. Anatomy of Hostility: The U. S.-Soviet Rivalry in Perspective. 292p. (C). 1989. pap. text ed. 16.00 (0-15-502712-3) HB Coll Pubs.
— The Arms Race: The Political Economy of Military Growth. LC 81-13808. 224p. 1982. text ed. 49.95 (0-275-90869-0, C0869, Praeger Pubs) Greenwood.
— Democracy & Foreign Policy. 1992. text ed. 37.50 (0-231-07668-1) Col U Pr.
— Democracy & Foreign Policy: The Fall of Political Realism. 200p. 1994. pap. 16.50 (0-231-07669-X) Col U Pr.
— Democracy & Foreign Policy: The Fallacy of Political Realism. 224p. 1992. text ed. 37.50 (0-685-53218-6) Col U Pr.
— United States Foreign Policy. 407p. 1988. pap. 27.95 (0-87187-449-0) Congr Quarterly.
Nincic, Miroslav, jt. auth. see Stockholm International Peace Research Institute Staff.
Nind, Melanie & Hewett, David. Access to Communication: Developing the Basics of Communication with People with Severe Learning Difficulties Through Intensive Interaction. 244p. 1994. pap. 34.00 (1-85346-206-3, Pub. by D Fulton UK) Taylor & Francis.
Nind, T. E. Hydrocarbon Reservoir & Well Performance. 347p. 1989. 146.95 (0-412-34030-5) Chapman & Hall.
Ninde, Edward S. The Story of the American Hymn. LC 72-1708. (Illus.). reprint ed. 29.75 (0-404-09914-9) AMS Pr.
Nine, Jerry. Cattle Buyers & Cattle Poop by the Pound or by the Scoop. (Illus.). 64p. 1989. pap. write for info. (0-318-65802-X) Rocking Nine.
Nine, William G. & Wilson, Ronald G. The Appomattox Paroles April 9-15, 1865. (Virginia Civil War Battles & Leaders Ser.). (Illus.). 236p. 1989. 19.95 (0-930919-69-6) H E Howard.
Ninebrenner, Jan, jt. auth. see Davidson, James.
Nineham, Dennis, ed. see Evans, C. F.
Nineham, Dennis, ed. see Houlden, J. L.
Nineham, Dennis, ed. see Sweet, John.
Nineham, Dennis, ed. see Ziesler, John.
Nineham, Dennis E. The Gospel of St. Mark: Commentaries. (Orig.). 1964. pap. 7.95 (0-14-020489-X, Penguin Bks) Viking Penguin.
Ninemeier, Jack D. Management of Food & Beverage Operations. 2nd ed. Purvis, Jim, ed. LC 90-36083. (Illus.). 370p. 1990. text ed. 59.95 (0-86612-057-2) Educ Inst Am Hotel.
— Planning & Control for Food & Beverage Operations. 3rd ed. Davis, Daniel T., ed. LC 91-483. (Illus.). 399p. 1991. text ed. 59.95 (0-86612-055-6) Educ Inst Am Hotel.
Ninemeier, Jack D., jt. auth. see Kavanaugh, Raphael R.
Ninestein, Eleanor H. Introduction to Computer Mathematics. (C). 1986. text ed. 30.50 (0-673-18205-3) HarpCollege.
— Technical Math with Calculus. (C). 1991. text ed. 60.00 (0-673-18748-9) HarpCollege.
— Technical Math with Calculus. (C). 1991. 18.50 (0-673-46458-X) HarpCollege.
— Technical Mathematics. (C). 1991. text ed. 56.50 (0-673-18747-0); student ed write for info. (0-318-68849-2) HarpCollege.
***Nineteen Ninety-Four United Nations Convention Staff, The.** The 1994 United Nations Convention on the Law of the Sea: Basic Documents. LC 94-39925. (Nijhoff Law Specials: Vol. 8). 1995. pap. text ed. 56.00 (0-7923-3271-7, Pub. by M Nijhoff) Kluwer Ac.
Nineth European Symposium on Medieval Logic & Semantics Staff. Sophisms in Medieval Logic & Grammar: Acts of the Ninth European Symposium on Medieval Logic & Semantics, Held at St, Andrews, June 1990. Read, Stephen, ed. LC 93-16500. (Nijhoff International Philosophy Ser.: Vol. 48). 460p. (C). 1993. Alk. paper. lib. bdg. 157.50 (0-7923-2196-0) Kluwer Ac.
Ninety Niner Home Computer Magazine Editors. The Best of Ninety-Niner, Vol. I. (Illus.). 360p. (Orig.). 1984. pap. 19.95 (0-933094-11-6) Emerald Pub.
***Ninety-Second St. Y Parenting Center Staff, et al.** Wonderplay: More Than 200 Games, Crafts, & Creative Activities for Infants, Toddlers, & Preschoolers. (Illus.). 128p. 1995. pap. 12.95 (1-56138-575-1) Running Pr.
Ninfo, Vito & Chung, E. B., eds. Tumors & Tumor-Like Lesions of Soft Tissues. (Contemporary Issues in Surgical Pathology Ser.: Vol. 18). (Illus.). 295p. 1991. text ed. 95.00 (0-443-08672-9) Churchill.
Ning H. Chen. Process Reactor Design. 512p. (C). 1983. teacher ed write for info. (0-318-57278-8, H79049) P-H.
Ningshang Xu, jt. auth. see Latham, Rodney V.
***Ninh, Bao.** The Sorrow of War: A Novel. Palmos, Frank, ed. Thanhh, Vo B., tr. LC 94-22390. 1995. 21.00 (0-679-43961-7) Pantheon.
Ninham, B. W., jt. auth. see Barber, M. N.
Ninham, B. W., jt. auth. see Hughes, B. D.
Ninian, Stephen. Sir Owen Dixon: A Celebration. 41p. 1986. pap. 9.95 (0-522-84330-1) Intl Spec Bk.
Nininger, H. H. Arizona's Meteorite Crater. (Illus.). 1965. reprint ed. pap. 9.95 (0-910096-02-3) Am Meteorite.
— A Comet Strikes the Earth. rev. ed. (Illus.). 1969. pap. 3.00 (0-910096-04-X) Am Meteorite.
— Meteorites: A Photographic Study of Surface Features: Part 2: Orientation. Danielsen, T. L., ed. (Illus.). 75p. (Orig.). (C). 1993. pap. text ed. 25.00 (0-7881-0144-7) Diane Pub.
Ninio, Jacques. Molecular Approaches to Evolution. Lang, Robert, tr. LC 83-4253. (Illus.). 144p. 1983. 42.50 (0-691-08313-4); pap. 16.95 (0-691-08314-2) Princeton U Pr.
Niniowskyi, W. Ukrainian - English English - Ukrainian Dictionary. 1991. lib. bdg. 29.95 (0-8288-2634-X) Fr & Eur.
Niniows'kyi, W. Ukrainian-English - English-Ukrainian. 2nd rev. ed. 679p. 1990. pap. 30.00 (0-88431-319-0) IBD Ltd.
Niniowskyi, W. Ukrainian-English & English-Ukrainian Dictionary. 680p. 1992. pap. 21.00 (0-317-05517-8) Szwede Slavic.
Ninkovic, Tom. Reunion Handbook for School & Military Reunions. 222p. 1991. reprint ed. lib. bdg. 53.00x (0-8095-4650-7) Borgo Pr.
Ninkovic, Tom & Brown, Barbara. Family Reunion Handbook. 260p. 1992. reprint ed. lib. bdg. 35.00x (0-8095-4652-3) Borgo Pr.
Ninkovic, Tom & Masciangelo, Bill. Military Reunion Handbook. 214p. 1991. reprint ed. lib. bdg. 31.00x (0-8095-4651-5) Borgo Pr.
Ninkovich, F. A. The Diplomacy of Ideas: U. S. Foreign Policy & Cultural Relations, 1938-1950. 256p. 1981. 49.95 (0-521-23241-4) Cambridge U Pr.
***Ninkovich, Frank.** Germany & the United States. rev. ed. (International History Ser.: No. 2). (Illus.). 224p. 1994. text ed. 26.95x (0-8057-7928-0, Twayne); pap. 14.95 (0-8057-9223-6, Twayne) Macmillan.
— Germany & the United States: The Transformation of the German Question since 1945. (International History Ser.: No. 2). 256p. 1988. text ed. 26.95 (0-8057-7903-5, Twayne); pap. 12.95 (0-8057-9202-3, Twayne) Macmillan.
— Modernity & Power: A History of the Domino Theory in the Twentieth Century. LC 94-5733. 1994. lib. bdg. 49.95 (0-226-58650-2); pap. text ed. 19.95 (0-226-58651-0) U Ch Pr.
Ninkovich, Thomas, jt. auth. see Brown, Barbara E.
Ninman, Stefani B. The Malibu Million Dollar Rock. LC 79-53369. (Illus.). 36p. 1979. pap. 4.00 (0-930422-21-X) Dennis-Landman.
Ninness, H. A. & Glenn, Sigrid S. Applied Behavior Analysis & School Psychology: A Research Guide to Principles & Procedures. LC 87-29544. 304p. 1988. text ed. 65.00 (0-313-24267-4, NBA/, Greenwood Pr) Greenwood.
Ninness, H. A., et al. Assessment & Treatment of Emotional or Behavioral Disorders. LC 93-20502. 192p. 1993. text ed. 55.00 (0-275-94098-5, C4098, Praeger Pubs) Greenwood.
Nino, Carlos, ed. Rights. (International Library of Essays in Law & Legal Theory). 550p. 1992. text ed. 150.00 (0-8147-5771-5) NYU Pr.
Nino, Carlos S. The Ethics of Human Rights. 336p. 1994. reprint ed. pap. 24.00 (0-19-825869-0) OUP.
Nino, Raul. Breathing Light. (Illus.). 48p. (Orig.). 1991. pap. 6.00 (1-877636-10-X) March Abrazo.
Ninomiya. Flow Analysis Using a PC. 1991. 89.95 (0-8493-7733-1, Q) CRC Pr.
Ninomiya, H. & Onishi, K. Flow Analysis Using a PC. 212p. 1991. 74.00 (1-56252-077-6) Computational Mech MA.
Ninomiya, I. Synthesis of the Benzo(C) Phenanthridine Alkaloids. The Chemistry the Vancomycin Group of Antibiotics. 210p. 1984. 96.00 (0-569-08788-0, Pub. by Collets UK) Pro-Am Music.
Ninomiya, I. & Naito, T. Photochemical Synthesis. (Best Synthetic Methods Ser.). 350p. 1989. text ed. 113.00 (0-12-519490-0) Acad Pr.
— Recent Developments in the Chemistry of Natural Carbon Compounds, Vol. 10. 210p. (C). 1984. 150.00 (0-685-46655-8, Pub. by Collets) St Mut.
Ninomiya, Kazuji, tr. see Mori, Ogai.
Ninomiya, M. & Kikkawa, K. Quantum Gravity: Proceedings of the 7th Nishinomiya-Yukawa Memorial Symposium Nishinomuya City, 19-20 November 92. 216p. 1993. text ed. 67.00 (981-02-1460-X) World Scientific Pub.
Ninomiya, Sontoku. Sage Ninomiya's Evening Talks. Yamagata, Isoh, tr. LC 70-98786. 139p. 1970. reprint ed. text ed. 38.50 (0-8371-3134-0, NIEV, Greenwood Pr) Greenwood.
Ninomiya, T., jt. ed. see Yonezawa, F.
Ninomiya, Takamichi & Enright, D. J., eds. The Poetry of Living Japan. LC 78-11863. 104p. 1979. reprint ed. text ed. 45.00 (0-313-21210-4, NIPL, Greenwood Pr) Greenwood.
Ninommiya, T., jt. ed. see Kuo, K. H.
Ninotschka, Rose, jt. auth. see Robertson, Joe E.
Nintendo Staff. Super Mario Bros. Adventures. (Nintendo Comic Book & Cassette Ser.). (Illus.). 32p. (Orig.). (J). (gr. 1-7). 1991. pap. 6.95 (0-679-81822-7) Random Bks Yng Read.
Ninth International Conference Staff. Fundamentals of Computation Theory: Proceedings of the 9th International Conference, FCT '93, Szeged, Hungary, August 23-27, 1993. Esik, Zoltan, ed. (Lecture Notes in Computer Science Ser.: Vol. 710). ix, 471p. 1993. pap. write for info. (3-540-57163-9) Spr-Verlag.
Ninyerola, Alfonso. Jose Maria Sicilia: New Paintings. Bell, Suzanne, ed. Vidal, Africa, tr. (Illus.). 36p. 1990. pap. 0.20 (0-685-32872-4) Blum Helman.
Niobet, George. Larousse Dictionnaire Analogique. (FRE.). 1992. pap. 59.95 (0-8288-7857-9) Fr & Eur.
Niobey. Nouveau Larousse Dictionnaire Analogique. 856p. (FRE.). 1980. pap. 31.95 (0-8288-1942-4, M14296) Fr & Eur.
Niocaill, Gearoid M., jt. ed. see Monahan, Edward C.
Nioche, Brigitte. What Turns Men On? 224p. (Orig.). 1989. pap. 4.99 (0-451-16054-1, Sig) NAL-Dutton.
Niordson, F. I. Shell Theory. (Applied Mathematics & Mechanics Ser.: Vol. 29). 402p. 1985. 57.50 (0-444-87640-5, North Holland) Elsevier.
Niordson, F. I., ed. see International Union of Theoretical & Applied Mechanics Staff.
Niordson, F. I., ed. see Symposium of International Union of Theoretical & Applied Mechanics, Lyngby, Denmark, Aug. 1974.
Niosi, Jorge, ed. New Technology Policy & Social Innovations in the Firm. LC 94-15090. 1995. 60.00 (1-85567-259-6, Pub. by Pinter Pubs UK) St Martin.
— Technology & National Competitiveness: Oligopoly, Technological Innovation, & International Competition. 304p. (C). 1991. pap. text ed. 24.95 (0-7735-0859-7, Pub. by McGill CN) U of Toronto Pr.
Niphuis-Nell, M., ed. Demographic Aspects of the Changing Status of Women in Europe. (Publications of the Netherlands Inter-University Demographic Institute & the Population & Family Study Centre Ser.: Vol. 7). 1978. pap. text ed. 27.50 (90-207-0714-0) Kluwer Ac.
Nipkow, Tobias, jt. ed. see Barendregt, Hank.
Nipon, Pearl. Dining In - Philadelphia. (Dining in Ser.). 200p. (Orig.). 1982. pap. 8.95 (0-89716-039-8) P B Pubng.
Nipp, G. L. Quaternary Quadratic Forms: Computer Generated Tables. vii, 155p. 1991. pap. 59.00 (0-387-97601-9) Spr-Verlag.
Nipp, Luitgard. Kapitalausstattung im Landlichen Kleingewerbe in der 2. Halfte Des 19. Jahrunderts. Bruchey, Stuart, ed. LC 80-2818. (Dissertations in European Economic History Ser.). (Illus.). 1981. lib. bdg. 26.95 (0-405-14002-9) Ayer.
Nipp, S. H., jt. auth. see Beall, P. C.
Nipp, Susan H., jt. auth. see Beall, Pamela C.
***Nippel, Wilfried.** Public Order in Ancient Rome. (Key Themes in Ancient History Ser.). 176p. (C). 1995. write for info. (0-521-38327-7); pap. write for info. (0-521-38749-3) Cambridge U Pr.
Nippell, Janet, jt. auth. see Yandell, Ben.
Nipper, Jo-Ann. Journey into Forever. 1994. pap. 13.95 (0-533-10848-9) Vantage.
Nipperdey, Karl & Andresen, Georg, eds. Tacitus, Annalen, 2 vols., Bd. I: Ab Excessu Divi Augusti I-IV. 466p. (GER.). 1978. write for info. (3-296-15751-4, Pub. by Georg Olms GW) Lubrecht & Cramer.
— Tacitus, Annalen, 2 vols., Bd. II: Ab Excessu Divi Augusti XI-XVI. 347p. (GER.). 1978. write for info. (3-296-15752-2, Pub. by Georg Olms GW) Lubrecht & Cramer.
Nipperdey, Karl & Witte, Kurt, eds. Nepos, Cornelius. iii, 300p. 1967. write for info. (3-296-12000-9, Pub. by Georg Olms GW) Lubrecht & Cramer.
Nippold, Marilyn A., ed. Later Language Development: Ages Nine Through Nineteen. LC 90-52764. 271p. (Orig.). 1988. pap. text ed. 28.00 (0-89079-304-2, 1756) PRO-ED.
Nippon Bonsai Association Staff. Classic Bonsai of Japan. Bester, John, tr. (Illus.). 176p. 1989. 100.00 (0-87011-933-8) Kodansha.
Nippon Dental University Staff. Osseointegrated Implant Manual. (Illus.). 153p. 1994. pap. 150.00 (1-56386-014-7) Ishiyaku Euro.
Nippon Shuppan Hanbai Inc Staff, tr. see Kuwayama, Yasaburo, ed.
Nipps, Karen. Naturally Fond of Pictures: American Illustration of the 1840s & 1850s. (Illus.). 30p. 1989. pap. 6.00 (0-685-59303-7) Lib Co Phila.
Nips, Nick L. Driver Training. 1976. 2.00 (0-686-75954-0) Luna Bisonte.
Nique, Thomas A. & Tu, Harold K., eds. Anesthesia for Facial Plastic Surgery. LC 93-11651. 114p. 1993. 55.00 (0-86577-445-5); write for info. (3-13-783701-4) Thieme Med Pubs.
Niquette, Alan & Niquette, Beth. Building Your Christian Defense System. (Building...Ser.). (Orig.). (YA). (gr. 9-12). 1988. teacher ed 7.99 (1-55661-016-5); pap. text ed. 6.99 (1-55661-015-7) Bethany Hse.
Niquette, Beth, jt. auth. see Niquette, Alan.
Nir, Dov. The New Comprehensive Guide to Israel. 7.95 (0-87677-143-6) Hartmore.
— Region As a Socio-Environmental System: An Introduction to a Systemic Regional Geography. (C). 1990. lib. bdg. 92.00 (0-7923-0516-7) Kluwer Ac.
Nir, Yehuda, jt. auth. see Maslin, Bonnie.
Niramayananda. Call of the Spirit: Conversion with Swami Akhandananda. 170p. 1987. pap. 2.95 (0-87481-538-X, Pub. by Ramakrishna Math II) Vedanta Pr.
Niranjan, Shiva. Raja Rao, Novelist As Sadhaka. 154p. 1986. 13.50 (0-8364-1664-3, Pub. by Popular Prakashan II) S Asia.
Niranjana, Tejaswini. Siting Translation: History, Post-Structuralism, & the Colonial Context. LC 91-21487. 216p. 1992. 38.00 (0-520-07450-5) U CA Pr.
— Siting Translation: History, Post-Structuralism, & the Colonial Context. LC 91-21487. 216p. 1992. pap. 14.00 (0-520-07451-3) U CA Pr.
Niranjana, Tejaswini, ed. Interrogating Modernity: Culture & Colonialism in India. (C). 1993. 34.00 (81-7046-109-X, Pub. by Seagull Bks II) S Asia.
Nirash, K. L. & Iqbal, S. M., eds. The Culture of Kashmir. 244p. 1978. 16.95 (0-318-36980-X) Asia Bk Corp.
Nirav, Shunyam. Hawaiian Organic Growing Guide: Hawaii's "How-to-Grow-It" Gardening Encyclopedia for the Tropics & Subtropics. 3rd ed. LC 92-60821. (Illus.). 232p. 1992. pap. 14.95 (0-9633187-0-5) New Dawn Environ.
Nirdlinger, Charles F. Four Short Plays. LC 79-50027. (One-Act Plays in Reprint Ser.). 1980. reprint ed. 17.50 (0-8486-2052-6) Roth Pub Inc.
Nirenberg, Charles. Call Me Charlie: The Convenience Store Baron. 259p. 1992. 19.95 (0-9635419-0-0) Convenient.
Nirenberg, David Z., jt. auth. see Peaslee, James M.
Nirenberg, Jesse S. Getting Through to People. 224p. 1988. pap. text ed. 9.95 (0-13-355041-9) P-H.
— Getting Through to People. LC 63-15341. 1986. reprint ed. 10.95 (0-13-354860-0, Reward) P-H.
Nirenberg, John. The Living Organization: Transforming Teams into Workplace Communities. LC 92-37515. 300p. 1993. text ed. 30.00 (1-55623-943-2) Irwin Prof Pubng.
— Management Insight, 1989: Annual Planner & Sourcebook. 200p. (Orig.). 1988. pap. 19.95 (0-945693-00-1) Mgmt Insight.
— Management Insight, 1990: Annual Planner. 176p. 1989. pap. 14.95 (0-945693-02-8) Mgmt Insight.
Nirenberg, Louis. Lectures on Linear Partial Differential Equations. LC 73-4400. (CBMS Regional Conference Series in Mathematics: No. 17). 58p. 1992. reprint ed. pap. 16.00 (0-8218-1667-5, CBMS-17) Am Math.
Nirenberg, Sue, jt. auth. see Ruedy, Elisabeth.
Nirenberg, Ted D. & Maisto, Stephen. Developments in the Assessment & Treatment of Addictive Behaviors. Caddy, Glenn R., ed. LC 87-11446. (Developments in Clinical Psychology Ser.: Vol. 5). 400p. 1987. text ed. 59.50 (0-89391-170-4) Ablex Pub.
Nirenberg, Ted D., jt. ed. see Gomberg, Edith S.
Nirenberg, Ted D., jt. ed. see Miller, Peter M.
Nirenburg, S., ed. Progress in Machine Translation. LC 92-3503. 334p. 1992. 70.00 (90-5199-074-X, Pub. by IOS Pr NE) IOS Press.
Nirenburg, Sergei, jt. ed. see Goodman, Kenneth.
Nirenburg, Sergei, et al. Knowledge-Based Machine Translation. Goodman, Kenneth, ed. 250p. 1991. 44.95 (1-55860-128-7) Morgan Kaufmann.
Nirgiotis, Nicholas. Erie Canal: Gateway to the West. LC 92-24547. (First Bks.). (Illus.). 64p. (J). (gr. 5-8). 1993. lib. bdg. 13.93 (0-531-20146-5) Watts.
— Thomas Edison. LC 93-37028. (Cornerstones of Freedom Ser.). (Illus.). 32p. (J). (gr. 3-6). 1994. lib. bdg. 12.30 (0-516-06676-5) Childrens.
— Thomas Edison. (J). (gr. 3-6). 1994. pap. 3.95 (0-516-46676-3) Childrens.

An Asterisk (*) at the beginning of an entry indicates that the title is appearing in BIP for the first time.

Nirgun, Ma A., ed. see Osho.

Nirmal, Barry. CICS Application & System Programming: Tools & Techniques. 1993. pap. text ed. 39.95 (*0-471-58477-0*, GD3934) Wiley.

Nirmal, Barry K. CICS Application & System Programming: Tools & Techniques. 1991. 39.95 (*0-89435-393-4*) Wiley.

— MVS - TSO: Mastering CLISTs. 1993. pap. text ed. 39.95 (*0-471-58441-X*, GC3195) Wiley.

— MVS-TSO: Mastering Clists. LC 89-24367. 296p. 1990. pap. 34.95 (*0-89435-319-5*) Wiley.

— Programming Standards & Guidelines: COBOL Edition. (Illus.). 208p. (C). 1987. text ed. 35.00 (*0-13-729823-4*) P-H.

— REXX Tools & Techniques. 1993. pap. text ed. 44.95 (*0-471-58559-9*, GD4175) Wiley.

— REXX Tools & Techniques. 2nd ed. 1993. pap. 39.95 (*0-89435-417-5*) Wiley.

Niro. Yes to Life, A Healing Discovery. rev. ed. 260p. 1994. reprint ed. pap. 12.00 (*1-884886-01-9*) Starr Pubng.

Nirschel, Martin, ed. see DiMona, Joseph.

Nirvesha, Deva, ed. see Rajneesh, Osho.

Nisan, Mordechai. Minorities in the Middle East: A History of Struggle & Self-Expression. LC 91-52512. 312p. 1991. lib. bdg. 35.00x (*0-89950-564-3*) McFarland & Co.

— Towards a New Israel: The Jewish State & the Arab Question. LC 91-11936. (Studies in Modern Society: No. 24). 1992. 42.50 (*0-404-61631-3*) AMS Pr.

Nisan, Noam. Using Hard Problems to Create Pseudorandom Generators. (ACM Distinguished Dissertation, 1990 Ser.). 76p. 1991. 20.00 (*0-262-14051-9*) MIT Pr.

Nisanyan, Sevan, jt. auth. see Beazley, Mitchell.

Nisber, Jay N. The Random House Handbook of Business Terms. 352p. 1988. 14.95 (*0-394-53047-0*) Random.

Nisberg. Random House Dictionary of Business Terms. 1992. 6.00 (*0-679-41369-3*, Random Ref) Random.

Nisbert, Robert G., ed. see Cicero, Marcus T.

Nisbet-Brown, Eric, jt. auth. see Cooper, Edwin L.

Nisbet, E. G. Leaving Eden: To Protect & Manage the Earth. (Illus.). 465p. (C). 1991. pap. 16.95 (*0-521-42579-4*) Cambridge U Pr.

— Living Earth: A Short History of Life & Its Home. (Illus.). 238p. (C). 1992. text ed. 89.95 (*0-04-445855-X*, A8182); pap. text ed. 25.00 (*0-04-445856-8*, A8183) Routledge Chapman & Hall.

Nisbet, E. G., jt. ed. see Arndt, N. T.

Nisbet, E. G., jt. ed. see Bickle, M. J.

Nisbet, Euan G. The Young Earth: An Introduction to Archean Geology. 400p. 1987. text ed. 90.00 (*0-04-550045-2*); pap. text ed. 49.95 (*0-04-550049-5*) Routledge Chapman & Hall.

Nisbet, H. B., tr. see Hegel, Georg W.

Nisbet, H. B., ed. see Hegel, Georg W.

Nisbet, H. B., tr. see Kant, Immanuel.

Nisbet, Jack. Sky People. LC 84-61542. (Illus.). 128p. (Orig.). 1984. 12.95 (*0-931849-00-4*); pap. 5.95 (*0-931849-01-2*) Quartzite Bks.

— Sources of the River: Tracking David Thompson Across Western North America. LC 94-6478. 288p. 1994. 22.95 (*1-57061-020-7*) Sasquatch Bks.

— Sources of the River: Tracking David Thompson Across Western North America. LC 94-6478. 288p. 1995. pap. 14.95 (*1-57061-006-1*) Sasquatch Bks.

Nisbet, James C. Four Years on the Firing Line. (Illus.). 267p. 1992. reprint ed. 30.00 (*0-916107-24-8*) Broadfoot.

***Nisbet, James D.** Weathering Stock Market Storms: Learning about Risk Control Timing. (Illus.). 208p. (C). Date not set. 29.95 (*0-9640139-0-8*) Capital Bks.

Nisbet, Jan, ed. Natural Supports in School, at Work, & in the Community for People with Severe Disabilities. LC 92-9855. 368p. 1992. pap. text ed. 30.00 (*1-55766-101-4*) P H Brookes.

Nisbet, Jim. The Damned Don't Die. LC 85-73607. Orig. Title: The Gourmet. 144p. 1986. reprint ed. pap. 3.95 (*0-88739-004-8*, Blk Lizard) Creat Arts Bk.

— Death Puppet. LC 88-7905. 192p. 1989. 16.95 (*0-88739-136-2*, Blk Lizard) Creat Arts Bk.

— Lethal Injection. LC 87-70925. 160p. 1987. 15.95 (*0-88739-081-1*, Blk Lizard) Creat Arts Bk.

— Small Apt. (Thumbscrew Press Ser.). (Illus.). 68p. (Orig.). 1992. pap. 8.95 (*0-926664-12-3*) Bay Area Ctr Art & Tech.

Nisbet, John. The Impact of Research on Policy & Practice in Education. 96p. 1980. text ed. 17.50 (*0-08-025723-2*, Pergamon Pr) Elsevier.

Nisbet, John & Shucksmith, Janet. Learning Strategies. (Education Bks.). 144p. (C). 1986. text ed. 37.50 (*0-7102-0569-4*, RKP) Routledge.

— Learning Strategies. 112p. 1989. pap. 13.95 (*0-415-03111-7*) Routledge.

Nisbet, John, et al. Towards Community Education: An Evaluation of Community Schools. 144p. 1980. 20.00 (*0-08-025735-6*, Pergamon Pr) Elsevier.

Nisbet, Lee, ed. The Gun Control Debate: You Decide. 341p. (Orig.). (C). 1990. pap. 18.95 (*0-87975-618-7*) Prometheus Bks.

Nisbet, Louis J. & Winstanley, D. J., eds. Bioactive Microbial Products II: Development & Production. (Special Publications of the Society for General Microbiology). 1984. text ed. 55.00 (*0-12-519550-8*) Acad Pr.

Nisbet, Peter, ed. The Sketchbooks of George Grosz. LC 93-32084. (Illus.). 191p. 1995. pap. 24.95 (*0-916724-83-2*, 4882) Harvard Art Mus.

***Nisbet, Peter & Norris, Emilie.** The Busch-Reisinger Museum: History & Holdings. (Illus.). 125p. 1995. pap. 9.95 (*0-916724-79-4*, 4794) Harvard Art Mus.

Nisbet, Peter, tr. see Koschatzky, Walter.

Nisbet, Peter, et al. Twelve Artists From the German Democratic Republic. (Illus.). 171p. 1995. pap. 29.00 (*0-916724-71-9*, 4719) Harvard Art Mus.

***Nisbet, R. G.** Collected Papers on Latin Literature. 456p. 1995. 80.00 (*0-19-814948-4*) OUP.

Nisbet, R. M. & Gurney, W. S. Modelling Fluctuating Populations. LC 81-14668. 393p. reprint ed. pap. 112.10 (*0-685-20671-8*, 2030459) Bks Demand.

Nisbet, R. M. & Wood, S. N. Estimation of Mortality Rates in Stage Structured Populations. (Lecture Notes in Biomathematics Ser.). viii, 101p. 1991. pap. 24.00 (*0-387-53979-4*) Spr-Verlag.

Nisbet, Richard. Capacity of Negroes for Religious & Moral Improvement Considered. LC 73-100295. 207p. 1970. reprint ed. text ed. 45.00 (*0-8371-2940-0*, NIC&, Negro U Pr) Greenwood.

Nisbet, Robert. Conservatism: Dream & Reality. LC 86-1375. (Concepts in Social Thought Ser.). 128p. (Orig.). 1986. pap. text ed. 12.95 (*0-8166-1526-8*) U of Minn Pr.

— History of the Idea of Progress. 380p. (C). 1993. pap. text ed. 21.95 (*1-56000-713-3*) Transaction Pubs.

— Pieces of Eight. 145p. (C). 1982. pap. 30.00 (*0-85088-555-8*, Pub. by Gomer Pr UK) St Mut.

— Prejudices: A Philosophical Dictionary. 328p. 1983. pap. text ed. 9.95 (*0-674-70066-X*) HUP.

Nisbet, Robert & Perrin, Robert G. The Social Bond. 2nd ed. 1978. pap. text ed. write for info. (*0-07-553673-0*) McGraw.

Nisbet, Robert A. Emile Durkheim. LC 75-36358. 179p. 1976. reprint ed. text ed. 55.00 (*0-8371-8626-9*, NIEDU, Greenwood Pr) Greenwood.

— The Quest for Community: A Study in the Ethics of Order & Freedom. LC 90-32568. 300p. 1990. reprint ed. pap. 10.95 (*1-55815-058-7*) ICS Pr.

— The Social Group in French Thought. Zuckerman, Harriet & Merton, Robert K., eds. LC 79-9017. (Dissertations on Sociology Ser.). 1980. lib. bdg. 23.95 (*0-405-12985-8*) Ayer.

— The Sociological Tradition. rev. ed. LC 92-35189. 365p. (C). 1993. pap. text ed. 21.95 (*1-56000-667-6*) Transaction Pubs.

— Teachers & Scholars: A Memoir of Berkeley in Depression & War. 224p. (C). 1992. 34.95 (*1-56000-034-1*) Transaction Pubs.

Nisbet, Robert A. & Perrin, Robert G. The Social Bond: An Introduction to the Study of Society. 2nd ed. 1977. pap. text ed. 14.50 (*0-394-31215-5*, KnopfC) Knopf.

Nisbet, Robert A., jt. ed. see Merton, Robert K.

Nisbet, Robin G., ed. Cicero: In L. Calpurnium Pisonem Oratio. 240p. 1987. pap. 21.00 (*0-19-872131-5*) OUP.

Nisbet, Ulric. Onlie Begetter. LC 70-121234. (Studies in Shakespeare: No. 24). 1970. reprint ed. lib. bdg. 49.95 (*0-8383-1095-8*) M S G Haskell Hse.

Nisbett, Alec. The Sound Studio. 5th ed. (Illus.). 480p. 1993. pap. 39.95 (*0-240-51292-8*, Focal) Buttrwrth-Heinemann.

— The Sound Studio. 6th ed. LC 94-24609. 480p. 1995. pap. 49.95 (*0-240-51395-9*, Focal) Buttrwrth-Heinemann.

— Use of Microphones. 3rd ed. 184p. 1989. pap. 19.95 (*0-240-51291-X*, Focal) Buttrwrth-Heinemann.

Nisbett, E. G. & Melilli, Albert S., eds. Steel Forgings: STP 903. LC 86-14066. (Illus.). 610p. 1986. text ed. 59.00 (*0-8031-0465-0*, 04-903000-02) ASTM.

Nisbett, Edward G., jt. ed. see Melilli, Albert S.

Nisbett, Jean. The Complete Dolls' House Book. (Illus.). 208p. 1993. pap. 19.95 (*0-946819-44-0*, Pub. by Guild Mstr Craftsman UK) Sterling.

— The Secrets of the Dolls' House Makers. (Illus.). 200p. 1995. pap. 21.95 (*0-946819-54-8*) Sterling.

Nisbett, Richard E., ed. Rules for Reasoning. LC 92-39042. 454p. 1992. text ed. 89.95 (*0-8058-1256-3*); pap. 32.50 (*0-8058-1257-1*) L Erlbaum Assocs.

Nisbett, Richard E. & Ross, Lee. Human Inference: Strategies & Shortcomings of Social Judgement. 318p. 1985. pap. text ed. 35.80 (*0-13-445073-6*) P-H.

Nisbett, Richard E., jt. auth. see Ross, Lee.

Nischan, Bodo. Prince, People, & Confession: The Second Reformation in Brandenburg. LC 93-49639. (Illus.). 384p. (C). 1994. text ed. 48.95 (*0-8122-3242-9*) U of Pa Pr.

Nise. Control Systems. Elliott, Sally, ed. 844p. (C). 1992. text ed. 69.95 (*0-8053-5420-4*) Benjamin-Cummings.

Nise, Norman. Control Systems Engineering. 2nd ed. 800p. (C). 1995. text ed. 70.95 (*0-8053-5424-7*) Benjamin-Cummings.

Nisen, William G., et al. Marketing Your Software: Strategies for Success. (Illus.). 224p. 1984. pap. 16.95 (*0-201-00105-5*) Addison-Wesley.

Nisenfeld, A. E. Artificial Intelligence Handbook, 2 vols., Set. Davis, J. R., ed. 1989. text ed. 98.00 (*1-55617-135-8*, A135-8) Instru Soc.

— Artificial Intelligence Handbook, 2 vols., Vol. 1: Principles. Davis, J. R., ed. 250p. 1989. Vol. 1, Principles, 250p. text ed. 45.00 (*1-55617-133-1*, A133-1) Instru Soc.

— Artificial Intelligence Handbook, 2 vols., Vol. 2: Applications. Davis, J. R., ed. 350p. 1989. Vol. 2, Applications, 350p. text ed. 65.00 (*1-55617-134-X*, A134X) Instru Soc.

Nisenfeld, A. Eli. Centrifugal Compressors: Principles of Operation & Control. LC 82-80223. (Instrument Society of America: Monograph: No. 3). 253p. reprint ed. pap. 72.20 (*0-7837-5132-X*, 2044860) Bks Demand.

Nisenfeld, A. Eli & Seemann, Richard C. Distillation Columns. LC 80-85271. (Instrument Society of America: Monograph: No. 2). (Illus.). 256p. reprint ed. pap. 73.00 (*0-7837-5155-9*, 2044884) Bks Demand.

Nisenfeld, Eli. Industrial Evaporators: Principles of Operation & Control. 227p. 1985. 40.00 (*0-87664-693-3*, I693-3) Instru Soc.

Nisengard, Russell J. & Newman, Michael G., eds. Oral Microbiology & Immunology. 2nd ed. (Illus.). 512p. 1993. pap. text ed. 47.50 (*0-7216-6753-8*) Saunders.

Nisenoff, M., jt. ed. see Weinstock, H.

Nisenoff, M., et al. Progress in High-Temperature Superconducting Transistors & Other Devices. 1992. 53.00 (*0-8194-0728-3*, 1597) SPIE.

Nisenson, Eric. Ascension: John Coltrane & His Quest. (Illus.). 336p. 1993. 22.95 (*0-312-09838-3*) St Martin.

— Ascension: John Coltrane & His Quest. 298p. 1995. reprint ed. pap. 13.95 (*0-306-80644-4*) Da Capo.

Nisetich, Frank. Pindar & Homer. LC 88-46123. (American Journal of Philology Monographs: No. 4). 128p. 1989. text ed. 24.00 (*0-8018-3820-7*) Johns Hopkins.

Nisetich, Frank, tr. see Euripides.

Nisetich, Frank J. Pindar's Victory Songs. LC 79-3739. 384p. 1980. text ed. 45.00 (*0-8018-2350-1*); pap. text ed. 25.95 (*0-8018-2356-0*) Johns Hopkins.

Nisevich, N. I., jt. ed. see Marchuk, Guril I.

Nish, Dale L. Artistic Woodturning. LC 80-21302. (Illus.). 288p. 1980. 19.95 (*0-8425-1842-8*); pap. 15.95 (*0-8425-1826-6*) BYU Scholarly.

— Creative Woodturning. LC 75-6952. (Illus.). 280p. 1975. text ed. 15.95 (*0-8425-0469-9*); pap. text ed. 12.95 (*0-8425-1557-7*) BYU Scholarly.

Nish, Ian, ed. Britain & Japan: Biographical Portraits. 264p. (C). 1994. text ed. 70.00 (*1-873410-27-1*, Pub. by Japan Library) Humanities.

Nish, Ian H. The Anglo-Japanese Alliance: The Diplomacy of Two Island Empires 1894-1907. 2nd ed. LC 84-18600. 420p. (C). 1985. text ed. 50.00 (*0-485-13139-0*, Pub. by Athlone Pr UK) Humanities.

— Japan's Struggle with Internationalism: Japan, China & the League of Nations, 1931-1933. (Illus.). 280p. 1993. 59.95 (*0-7103-0437-4*, A7316, Pub. by Kegan Paul Intl UK) Routledge Chapman & Hall.

— The Origins of the Russo-Japanese War. (Origins of Modern Wars Ser.). 274p. (C). 1985. pap. text ed. 21.95 (*0-582-49114-2*, 73483) Longman.

Nish, Ian H., ed. Anglo-Japanese Alienation 1919-1952: Papers of the Anglo-Japanese Conference on the History of the Second World War. LC 81-18111. (Cambridge International Studies). 320p. 1982. 69.95 (*0-521-24061-1*) Cambridge U Pr.

— Contemporary European Writing on Japan: Scholarly Views from Eastern & Western Europe. 288p. (C). 1988. pap. 25.00 (*0-904404-60-9*, Pub. by Paul Norbury Pubns UK) Humanities.

Nish, Ian H., jt. ed. see Dunn, Charles.

Nishi, Kazuo. What Is Japanese Architecture: A Survey of Traditional Japanese Architecture with a List of Sites & a Map. Horton, Mack H., tr. LC 84-48695. (Illus.). 144p. (C). 1985. 25.00 (*0-87011-711-4*) Kodansha.

Nishi, M., et al, eds. Gastric Cancer. LC 93-31369. 1994. 260.00 (*0-387-70127-3*) Spr-Verlag.

Nishi, Masao, ed. see Campbell, John H.

Nishi, Toshio, tr. see Ito, Kiichi, et al.

Nishida, A., ed. Magnetospheric Plasma Physics. 364p. 1982. lib. bdg. 126.50 (*90-277-1345-6*) Kluwer Ac.

Nishida, Gordon M. & Tenorio, JoAnn M. What Bit Me? Identifying Hawaii's Stinging & Biting Insects & Their Kin. LC 92-33673. (Illus.). 80p. (Orig.). 1993. pap. 11.95 (*0-8248-1492-4*) UH Pr.

Nishida, Gordon M., jt. auth. see Renorio, JoAnn M.

Nishida, Hiroko. Japanese Porcelains from Burghley House. LC 86-80691. (Illus.). 284p. 1986. 50.00 (*0-913304-24-7*) Japan Soc.

Nishida, Hiroshi, jt. ed. see Grooters, Ronald K.

Nishida, Kitaro. Art & Morality. Dilworth, David A. & Viglielmo, Valdo H., trs. LC 72-92067. 228p. reprint ed. pap. 65.00 (*0-8357-6026-X*, 2034642) Bks Demand.

— An Inquiry into the Good. Abe, Masao & Ives, Christopher, trs. 218p. (C). 1992. reprint ed. pap. text ed. 13.00 (*0-300-05233-2*) Yale U Pr.

— Intelligibility & the Philosophy of Nothingness. Schinzinger, Robert, tr. LC 72-12319. (Illus.). 251p. 1973. reprint ed. text ed. 35.00 (*0-8371-6689-6*, NIIP, Greenwood Pr) Greenwood.

— Intuition & Reflection in Self-Consciousness. Viglielmo, Valdo H. et al, trs. LC 86-14538. (SUNY Series in Philosophy). 204p. (C). 1987. 74.50 (*0-88706-368-3*); pap. 24.95 (*0-88706-370-5*) State U NY Pr.

— Last Writings: Nothingness & the Religious Worldview. Dilworth, David A., tr. LC 86-30931. 176p. 1987. pap. text ed. 12.00 (*0-8248-1554-8*) UH Pr.

— A Study of God, 10 vols., Set. Viglielmo, V. H., tr. (Documentary Reference Collections). 1988. 395.00 (*0-318-35982-0*, CMJ/, Greenwood Pr) Greenwood.

— A Study of God, 10 vols., Vol. 2. Viglielmo, V. H., tr. (Documentary Reference Collections). 217p. 1988. lib. bdg. 45.00 (*0-313-26560-7*, CMJ02, Greenwood Pr) Greenwood.

Nishida, Koji, jt. auth. see Goto, Shiro.

Nishida, Shin-Ichi. Failure Analysis in Engineering Applications. 228p. 1992. 125.00 (*0-7506-1065-4*) Buttrwrth-Heinemann.

Nishida, T., jt. ed. see Mimura, M.

Nishida, T., et al, eds. Patterns & Waves: Qualitative Analysis of Nonlinear Differential Equations. (Studies in Mathematics & Its Applications: No. 18). 692p. 1987. 202.75 (*0-444-70144-3*, North Holland) Elsevier.

Nishida, Tina Y., jt. ed. see Nakanishi, Don T.

Nishida, Tina Y., jt. ed. see Nakanishi, Donald T.

Nishida, Toshisada, ed. The Chimpanzees of the Mahale Mountains: Sexual & Life History Strategies. (Illus.). 336p. 1990. 69.50 (*0-86008-462-0*, Pub. by U of Tokyo JA) Col U Pr.

Nishigauchi, Taisuke. Quantification in the Theory of Grammar. (C). 1990. lib. bdg. 82.00 (*0-7923-0643-0*) Kluwer Ac.

Nishiguchi, Toshihiro. Strategic Industrial Sourcing: The Japanese Advantage. LC 92-13254. (Illus.). 384p. 1994. 39.95 (*0-19-507109-3*) OUP.

Nishihara, Hiroshi, et al. Optical Integrated Circuits. 400p. 1989. text ed. 50.00 (*0-07-046092-2*) McGraw.

Nishihara, M., jt. ed. see Inoue, H.

Nishihara, M., jt. auth. see Koizumi, M.

Nishihara, Masashi. East Asian Security & the Trilateral Countries. 116p. 1986. 40.00x (*0-8147-5758-8*) NYU Pr.

— East Asian Security & the Trilateral Countries. (Triangle Papers). 1985. 6.00 (*0-8147-5759-6*) Trilateral Comm.

— Japanese & Sukarno's Indonesia: Tokyo-Jakarta Relations, 1951-1966. LC 75-35765. (Center for Southeast Asian Studies, Kyoto University). (Illus.). 262p. 1976. pap. text ed. 10.00 (*0-8248-0379-5*, Eastwest Ctr Pr) UH Pr.

Nishijima, K. Fields & Particles: Field Theory & Dispersion Relations. 4th ed. 465p. (C). 1969. pap. text ed. 33.56 (*0-685-53851-6*, Adv Bk Prog) Addison-Wesley.

Nishikawa, K. Plasma Physics - Basic Theory with Fusion Applications. Ecker, G. et al, eds. (Atoms & Plasmas Ser.: Vol. 8). (Illus.). 320p. 1990. 69.00 (*0-387-52481-9*) Spr-Verlag.

Nishikawa, K. & Wakatani, M. Plasma Physics: Basic Theory with Fusion Applications. 2nd rev. ed. LC 93-36463. 340p. 1994. pap. 59.00 (*0-387-56854-9*) Spr-Verlag.

Nishikawa, Kyotaro & Sano, Emily J. The Great Age of Japanese Buddhist Sculpture AD 600-1300. LC 82-82805. (Illus.). 160p. 1983. pap. 29.95 (*0-295-96010-8*) U of Wash Pr.

Nishikawa, Kyotaro, et al. The Great Age of Japanese Buddhist Sculpture, AD 600-1300. LC 82-82805. (Illus.). 152p. (Orig.). 1982. pap. 24.95 (*0-912804-08-4*) Kimbell Art.

Nishikawa, Machiko. Elegant Needlework. (Illus.). 120p. 1988. pap. 13.95 (*0-87040-750-3*) Japan Pubns USA.

Nishikawa, Shunsaku, ed. The Labor Market in Japan: Selected Readings. Mouer, Ross E., tr. 277p. 1980. 29.50 (*0-86008-262-8*, Pub. by U of Tokyo JA) Col U Pr.

Nishikawa, T., et al, eds. Tricontinental Symposium on Autoimmune Skin Diseases, Proceedings, Kyodai Kaikan, Kyoto - Japan, November 1, 1993. (Journal: Dermatology Ser.: Vol. 189, Suppl. 1, 1994). (Illus.). xii, 138p. 1994. pap. 119.25 (*3-8055-5993-3*) S Karger.

Nishikawa, Y. & Kaya, Y., eds. Energy Systems, Management & Economics: Selected Papers from the IFAC-IFORS-IAEE Symposium, Tokyo, Japan, 25-27 October 1989. (IFAC Symposia Ser.: No. 9014). 1990. 215.00 (*0-08-037021-7*, Pergamon Pr) Elsevier.

Nishimo, Akiyo, ed. Two Hundred Fifty Essential Kanji for Everyday Use. (Illus.). 232p. 1993. pap. 17.95 (*0-8048-1911-4*) C E Tuttle.

Nishimoto, A., jt. auth. see Tabuchi, K.

Nishimoto, Katsuyuki. Fractional Calculus: Integrations & Differentiations of Arbitrary Order, Vol. 1. xiii, 195p. (C). 1984. write for info. (*0-936285-06-0*, JPY8200, Pub. by Descartes JA) U New Haven Pr.

— Fractional Calculus: Integrations & Differentiations of Arbitrary Order, Vol. 2. xiv, 189p. (C). 1987. write for info. (*0-936285-07-9*, JPY9200, Pub. by Descartes JA) U New Haven Pr.

— Fractional Calculus: Integrations & Differentiations of Arbitrary Order, Vol. 3. (C). 1989. write for info. (*0-318-64057-0*, Pub. by Descartes JA) U New Haven Pr.

Nishimoto, Miyoko. The Now & Zen Epicure: Gourmet Cuisine for the Enlightened Palate. LC 91-13503. (Illus.). 240p. 1991. pap. 17.95 (*0-913990-78-7*) Book Pub Co.

Nishimoto, Taeg, tr. see Benjamin, Bernard, et al.

Nishimura, Eshin, jt. auth. see Sato, Giei.

Nishimura, H. How to Conquer Air Pollution: A Japanese Experience. (Studies in Environmental Science: Vol. 38). 1990. 100.00 (*0-444-88537-4*, SES 38) Elsevier.

Nishimura, Kimiko, tr. see Hidenobu Jinnai.

Nishimura, Kiyohiko G. Imperfect Competition, Differential Information, & Microfoundations of Macroeconomics. (Illus.). 248p. 1992. 39.95 (*0-19-828617-1*) OUP.

— Imperfect Competition, Differential Information, & Microfoundations of Macroeconomics. (Illus.). 248p. 1995. pap. 24.95 (*0-19-829039-X*) OUP.

Nishimura, Kyotaro. The Mystery Train Disappears. LC 90-3302. 1990. 16.95 (*0-942637-30-5*, Dembner NY) Barricade Bks.

Nishimura, Mari. The Twentieth-Century Composer Speaks: An Index of Interviews. LC 93-29548. (Reference Books in Music: No. 28). xxxii, 189p. 1993. 39.50 (*0-914913-29-8*) Fallen Leaf.

Nishimura, Masao, tr. see Pearson, Richard J., et al, eds.

Nishimura, N., jt. ed. see Kobayashi, Shoshichi.

Nishimura, Shoji. Developmental Diagnosis in Treatment of Handicapped Individuals. (Illus.). 240p. 1988. 27.50 (*0-87562-097-3*) Spec Child.

Nishimura, T., ed. Automatic Control in Aerospace: Selected Papers from the IFAC Symposium, Tsukuba, Japan, 17-21 July 1989. LC 90-31776. (IFAC Proceedings Ser.: No. 9006). (Illus.). 248p. 1990. 170.00 (*0-08-037027-6*, Pergamon Pr) Elsevier.

Nishimura, Tsutomu. The Words Book, Roman, Nepali English-Japanese & Japanese-English Nepali. (ENG, JPN & NEP.). 1991. 20.00 (*0-7855-0292-0*, Pub. by Ratna Pustak Bhandar) St Mut.

Nishimura, Tsutomu, ed. The Words Book (Roman) Nepali-English Japanese & Japanese-English Nepali. (C). 1984. 65.00 (*0-89771-086-X*, Pub. by Ratna Pustak Bhandar) St Mut.

Nishimura, Yoshifumi, jt. ed. see Kyogoku, Yoshimasa.

Nishimura, Yoshihisa. Bakudan Sensei. (Illus.). 100p. 1982. pap. 2.95 (*0-933704-43-7*) Dawn Pr.

Nishinari, Katsuyoshi & Doi, Etsushiro, eds. Food Hydrocolloids: Structure, Properties, & Functions. LC 93-44786. 510p. 1994. 125.00 (*0-306-44594-8*, Plenum Pr) Plenum.

An Asterisk (*) at the beginning of an entry indicates that the title is appearing in BIP for the first time.

Nishinuma, Y. & Espesser, R. UNIX - First Contact. Mariani, J. A., ed. Stewart, M. J., tr. (Computer Science Ser.). (Illus.). 258p. (C). 1988. pap. text ed. 30.00 (*0-333-43624-5*, Pub. by Macmill Press UK) Scholium Intl.

Nishio, Shojiro & Yonezawa, Akinori, eds. Object Technologies for Advanced Software: First JSSST International Symposium, Kanazawa, Japan, November 4-6, 1993: Proceedings. LC 93-32466. (Lecture Notes in Computer Science Ser.: Vol. 742). 1993. 78.00 (*0-387-57342-9*) Spr-Verlag.

Nishio, T., jt. auth. see Osaki, S.

Nishio, Yvonne. Longman ESL Literacy. 256p. 1991. teacher ed 29.95 (*0-8013-0579-9*, 78505); pap. text ed. 13.95 (*0-8013-0578-0*, 78504) Longman.

Nishioka. Tuftsin: Biochemistry, Immunology & Clinical Prospects. 1995. write for info. (*0-8493-6701-8*) CRC Pr.

Nishioka-Evans, Vicki, et al. Functional Living Skills for Adolescents & Adults with Mild & Moderate Disabilities: Budgeting Skills. 80p. 1988. pap. text ed. 13.00 (*0-944232-03-5*) Teaching Res.

Nishioka, H., jt. ed. see Seligman, T. H.

Nishioka, Hayward & West, James R. The Judo Textbook. LC 78-65737. (Japanese Arts Ser.). (Illus.). 1979. pap. 14.95 (*0-89750-063-6*, 210) Ohara Pubns.

Nishioka, Judy R., ed. see Fourth Pacific Environmental Conference Staff.

***Nishioka, K., et al.** Viral Hepatitis & Liver Disease. 824p. 1994. 260.00 (*0-387-70132-X*) Spr-Verlag.

Nishioka, Kusuya, et al. Hepatitis Viruses & Hepatocellular Carcinoma. 1986. text ed. 70.00 (*0-12-519930-9*) Acad Pr.

Nishioka, M., et al, eds. Autoimmune Hepatitis. 360p. 1994. 177.25 (*0-444-88196-4*) Elsevier.

Nishisato, Shizuhiko. Analysis of Categorical Data: Dual Scaling & Its Applications. LC 81-116307. (Mathematical Expositions Ser.: No. 24). 290p. reprint ed. pap. 82.70 (*0-8357-8023-6*, 2034012) Bks Demand.
— Elements of Dual Scaling: An Introduction to Practical Data Analysis. 400p. 1993. text ed. 79.95 (*0-8058-1209-1*) L Erlbaum Assocs.

Nishitani, Keiji. Religion & Nothingness. Van Bragt, Jan, tr. LC 81-4084. (Nanzan Studies in Religion & Culture: No. 1). 366p. 1982. pap. 14.00 (*0-520-04946-2*) U CA Pr.

Nishitani, T., jt. auth. see Kajitani, K.

Nishiura, E. Schaum's Outline of Mathematics for Nurses. 208p. 1986. pap. text ed. 11.95 (*0-07-046100-7*) McGraw.

Nishiura, Elizabeth, ed. American Battle Monuments: A Guide to Battlefields & Cemeteries of the United States Armed Forces. (Illus.). 450p. 1989. 74.00 (*1-55888-812-8*) Omnigraphics Inc.

Nishiura, T., jt. auth. see Aarts, J. M.

Nishiwaki Junzaburo. Gen'ei: Selected Poems of Nishiwaki Junzaburo, 1894-1982. Claremont, Yasuko, tr. (University of Sydney East Asian Ser.: No. 4). 120p. (C). 1991. pap. text ed. 15.00 (*0-9590735-8-2*, Pub. by Wild Peony Pty AT) UH Pr.

Nishiya, I., et al, eds. Flow Cytometry & Image Analysis for Clinical Applications: Proc. of the Internat. Symp., Morioka & Hanamaki, Iwate, Japan, July 1-3, 1990. (International Congress Ser.: No. 933). 380p. 1991. 158.75 (*0-444-81379-9*, Excerpta Medica) Elsevier.

Nishiyama, Chiaki & Leube, Kurt R., eds. The Essence of Hayek. (Publication Ser.: No. 301). lxviii, 419p. (C). 1984. lib. bdg. 27.50 (*0-8179-8011-3*); pap. text ed. 22.95 (*0-8179-8012-1*) Hoover Inst Pr.

Nishiyama, H. & Brown. Karate. 18.95 (*0-685-22002-8*) Wehman.

Nishiyama, Hidetaka & Brown, Richard C. Karate: Art of Empty-Hand Fighting. (Illus.). 246p. (YA). (gr. 9 up). 1991. pap. 19.95 (*0-8048-1668-9*) C E Tuttle.

Nishiyama, Kazuo. Hotel Japanese: Practical Japanese for the Hotel Industry. (Illus.). 144p. 1993. pap. 12.95 (*0-8048-1917-3*) C E Tuttle.

Nishiyama, T., et al, eds. Proceedings of the Twenty-Ninth International Geological Congress Pt. A: Metamorphic Reactions; Sandstone Petrology; Evaporite & Desert Environment. (Illus.). 316p. 1994. 147.50x (*90-6764-173-1*, Pub. by VSP NE) Coronet Bks.

Nishizawa, J., ed. Semiconductor Technologies. (Japan Annual Reviews in Electronics, Computers & Telecommunications Ser.: No. 19). 345p. 1987. 136.00 (*0-444-87934-X*, North Holland) Elsevier.
— Semiconductor Technologies: Japan Annual Reviews in Electronics, Computers & Telecommunications. (Jarect Ser.: Vol. 13). 1985. 95.00 (*0-685-09956-3*) Elsevier.

Nishizawa, Junichi, jt. auth. see Suto, Len.

Nishizawa, Tetsuo, tr. see Moran, Patrick R., ed.

Nishizeki, T. & Chiba, N. Planar Graphs: Theory & Algorithms. (Mathematics Studies, Vol.140: Annals of Discrete Mathematics, Vol. 32). 410p. 1988. 97.50 (*0-444-70212-1*, North Holland) Elsevier.

Nishizeki, T., jt. ed. see Saito, N.

Nishizuka, Yasutomi, et al. The Biology & Medicine of Signal Transduction. (Advances in Second Messenger & Phosphoprotein Research Ser.: Vol. 24). 784p. 1990. 109.50 (*0-88167-670-5*) Raven.

Nishizuka, Yasutomo, jt. ed. see Ito, Masao.

Nisitani, H., ed. Computational & Experimental Fracture Mechanics: Developments in Japan. LC 93-74382. (Topics in Engineering Ser.: Vol. 16). 436p. 1994. 147.00 (*1-56252-202-7*) Computational Mech MA.

***Niska, Algot.** Over Green Borders: The Memoirs of Algot Niska. Danielsson, J. Jerry, tr. Date not set. 16.95 (*0-533-11226-5*) Vantage.

Niska, Melvin. Toward Corporate Tomorrow. abr. ed. 260p. 1995. pap. 8.95 (*1-56901-381-0*) NW Pub.

Niskanen, Anthony S., ed. see RRN Inc. Staff.

Niskanen, William A. Bureaucracy & Public Economics. (John Locke Ser.). (Illus.). 320p. 1994. 67.95 (*1-85898-019-4*, Pub. by E Elgar Pub UK); pap. 23.95 (*1-85898-041-0*, Pub. by E Elgar Pub UK) Ashgate Pub Co.
— Reaganomics: An Insider's Account. (Illus.). 384p. 1988. 30.00 (*0-19-505394-X*) OUP.

Niskanen, William A., jt. ed. see Dorn, James A.

Nisker, Scoop. Crazy Wisdom. 240p. 1990. pap. 12.95 (*0-89815-350-6*) Ten Speed Pr.

Nisker, Wes S. If You Don't Like the News, Go Out & Make Some of Your Own. 1994. pap. 14.95 (*0-89815-626-2*) Ten Speed Pr.

Nisley, Rebecca G., jt. auth. see Landis, Thomas D.

Nisly, Paul W. Sweeping up the Heart: A Father's Lament for His Daughter. LC 92-4565. 108p. 1992. pap. 8.95 (*1-56148-069-X*) Good Bks PA.

Niso. American National Standard for Standard Address Number for the Publishing Industry. LC 93-149. (National Information Standards Ser.). 18p. (C). 1993. pap. 20.00 (*0-88738-933-3*) Transaction Pubs.
— Permanence of Paper, Z39.48-1992: Permanence of Paper for Publications & Documents in Libraries & Archives. 20p. (C). 1993. pap. 20.00 (*0-88738-932-5*) Transaction Pubs.

NISO Staff. Computerized Book Ordering, No. Z39.49, 1992. 50p. 1993. pap. 50.00 (*0-88738-942-2*) Transaction Pubs.
— Electronic Manuscript Preparation & Markup. (National Information Standards Ser.: No. Z39.59-1988). 96p. (C). 1991. pap. 75.00 (*0-88738-945-7*) Transaction Pubs.

Nisolle, M., jt. auth. see Donnez, J.

Nison, Steve. Beyond Candlesticks: More Japanese Charting Techniques. LC 94-4290. 1994. text ed. 65.00 (*0-471-00720-X*) Wiley.
— Japanese Candlestick: Charting Techniques. 1991. 65.00 (*0-13-931650-7*) P-H.

Nisonger, Thomas E. Collection Evaluation in Academic Libraries: A Literature Guide & Annotated Bibliography. LC 92-11037. 271p. 1992. lib. bdg. 37.00 (*0-87287-925-9*) Libs Unl.

Nisonoff, Alfred, jt. ed. see Greene, Mark I.

Niss, Bob. Faces of Maine. (Illus.). (Orig.). 1982. pap. 8.95 (*0-930096-20-7*) G Gannett.

Niss, M., et al. Teaching of Mathematical Modeling & Applications. (Mathematics & Its Applications Ser.). 426p. 1991. 89.00 (*0-13-892068-0*, 540301) P-H.

Niss, Mogens, ed. Cases of Assessment in Mathematics Education: An ICMI Study. LC 92-41538. (Diverse Ser.). 226p. (C). 1993. lib. bdg. 97.50 (*0-7923-2089-1*) Kluwer Ac.
— Investigations into Assessment in Mathematics Education. LC 92-41132. (ICMI Study Ser.). 1993. lib. bdg. 97.50 (*0-7923-2095-6*) Kluwer Ac.

Nissan, Alfred H. Lectures of Fiber Science in Paper. (Pulp & Paper Technology Ser.: No. 4). (Illus.). 163p. reprint ed. pap. 46.50 (*0-8357-8206-9*, 2033954) Bks Demand.

Nissan, Ephraim, ed. Advances in Computing & the Humanities, Vol. 1. 1988. 73.25 (*0-89232-683-2*) Jai Pr.

Nissan, Ephraim & Schmidt, Klaus. From Information to Knowledge. 420p. (Orig.). 1994. pap. text ed. 37.95 (*1-871516-50-1*, Pub. by Intellect Bks UK) Cromland.

Nissan Motor Company Staff. Business Japanese: A Guide to Communicating in Japanese. 300p. (ENG & JPN.). 1988. pap. 39.95 (*0-8288-0992-5*, M 900) Fr & Eur.

Nissani, Moti. Lives in the Balance: The Cold War & American Politics, 1945-1991. LC 90-27114. 323p. (Orig.). 1992. 20.00 (*1-882154-19-3*, UA10.N57); text ed. 22.00 (*1-882154-20-7*); pap. 12.00 (*1-882154-21-5*) Dowser Pub Grp.

Nissanka, H. S. Buddhist Psychotherapy: An Eastern Therapeutical Approach to Mental Problems. 1993. 27.50 (*0-7069-6883-2*, Pub. by Vikas II) S Asia.
— Buddist Psychotherapy: An Eastern Approach to Mental Problems. (C). 1995. 24.00x (*0-7069-9003-X*, Pub. by Vikas II) S Asia.

***Nissanka, H. S., ed.** Maha Bodhi Tree in Anuradhapura, Sri Lanka: The Oldest Historical Tree in the World. (C). 1994. 32.00 (*0-7069-7063-2*, Pub. by Vikas II) S Asia.

Nissanke, Machiko & Hewitt, Adrian, eds. Overcoming Economic Crisis in Developing Countries: Policies for Recovery & Development. 288p. 1994. 59.00 (*1-85567-152-2*, Pub. by Pinter Pubs UK) St Martin.

***Nissen, Bruce.** Fighting for Jobs: Case Studies of Labor-Community Coalitions Confronting Plant Closings. LC 94-34608. 224p. 1995. text ed. 49.50x (*0-7914-2567-3*); pap. 16.95x (*0-7914-2568-1*) State U NY Pr.

Nissen, Bruce, jt. ed. see Craypo, Charles.

Nissen, Bruce, jt. ed. see Larson, Simeon.

Nissen, Christopher. Ethics of Retribution in the Decameron & the Late Medieval Italian Novella: Beyond the Circle. LC 93-20916. 156p. 1993. text ed. 69.95 (*0-7734-9835-4*, Mellen Univ Pr) E Mellen.

Nissen, Georg N. Biographie W. A. Mozarts. (Olms Paperbacks Ser.: Vol. 37). 1991. write for info. (*3-487-06076-0*, Pub. by Georg Olms GW); pap. write for info. (*3-487-04548-6*, Pub. by Georg Olms GW) Lubrecht & Cramer.

Nissen, H., et al. Information Systems Research: Contemporary Approaches & Emergent Trends. 1991. 148.75 (*0-444-89029-7*) Elsevier.

Nissen, Hans J. The Early History of the Ancient Near East, 9000-2000 B.C. Lutzeier, Elizabeth & Northcott, Kenneth J., trs. (Illus.). 224p. 1988. 34.95 (*0-226-58656-1*) U Ch Pr.
— The Early History of the Ancient Near East, 9000-2000 B.C. Lutzeier, Elizabeth & Northcott, Kenneth J., trs. LC 87-25530. (Illus.). xiv, 216p. 1990. pap. text ed. 17.95 (*0-226-58658-8*) U Ch Pr.

Nissen, Hans J., et al. Archaic Bookkeeping: Early Writing & Techniques of the Economic Administration of the Ancient Near East. Larsen, Paul, tr. LC 93-909. (Illus.). 224p. 1993. 34.95 (*0-226-58659-6*) U Ch Pr.

Nissen, Heinrich. Italische Landeskunde, 2 vols. in 3, Set. Finley, Moses, ed. LC 79-4997. (Ancient Economic History Ser.). (GER.). 1979. reprint ed. lib. bdg. 143.95 (*0-405-12383-3*) Ayer.
— Italische Landeskunde, 2 vols. in 3, Vol. 2, Pt. 2. Finley, Moses, ed. LC 79-4997. (Ancient Economic History Ser.). (GER.). 1979. reprint ed. 47.95 (*0-405-12488-0*) Ayer.
— Italische Landeskunde, Vol. 1. 1979. 47.95 (*0-405-12385-X*) Ayer.
— Italische Landeskunde, Vol. 2, Pt. 1. 1979. 47.95 (*0-405-12386-8*) Ayer.
— Kritische untersuchungen uber die Quellen der Vierten und Funften Dekade des Livius. LC 75-7332. (Roman History Ser.). (GER.). 1975. reprint ed. 29.95 (*0-405-07109-4*) Ayer.

Nissen, Henrik S., ed. Scandinavia During the Second World War. Munch-Petersen, Thomas, tr. LC 82-2779. (Nordic Ser.: No. 9). 417p. reprint ed. pap. 118.90 (*0-7837-2932-4*, 2057522) Bks Demand.

Nissen, Mrs. Carl, ed. Index to the New Jersey Genesis, 1953-1971. 172p. 1973. 16.00 (*0-913478-03-2*) Hermosa.

Nissen, Richard, ed. The Most Romantic Hotels & Inns in Britain. (Illus.). 192p. 1985. pap. 9.95 (*0-312-54919-9*) St Martin.

Nissen, Steven, ed. Modern Methods in Protein Nutrition & Metabolism. (Illus.). 345p. 1991. text ed. 76.00 (*0-12-519570-2*) Acad Pr.

Nissenbaum, A., ed. Hypersaline Brines & Evaporitic Environments. (Developments in Sedimentology Ser.: Vol. 28). 270p. 1980. 84.25 (*0-444-41238-7*) Elsevier.

Nissenbaum, Helen. Emotion & Focus. (Center for the Study of Language & Information-Lecture Notes Ser.: No. 2). 156p. (C). 1985. pap. text ed. 8.95 (*0-937073-20-2*, 12211-5) Ctr Study Language.

Nissenbaum, Helen, jt. ed. see Johnson, Deborah G.

Nissenbaum, Stephen. Battle for Christmas. 1992. write for info. (*0-679-74038-4*); pap. write for info. (*0-679-41223-9*) McKay.
— Sex, Diet & Debility in Jacksonian America: Sylvester Graham & Health Reform. LC 79-8280. (Contributions in Medical History Ser.: No. 4). xvii, 198p. 1980. text ed. 49.95 (*0-313-21415-8*, NSY/, Greenwood Pr) Greenwood.
— Sex, Diet, & Debility in Jacksonian America: Sylvester Graham & Health Reform. 198p. (C). 1989. reprint ed. pap. 19.95 (*0-534-10915-2*) Intl Thomson.

Nissenbaum, Stephen, jt. auth. see Boyer, Paul.

Nissenbaum, Stephen, jt. ed. see Boyer, Paul.

Nissenbaum, Stephen, ed. see Hawthorne, Nathaniel.

***Nissenberg, David.** The Law of Commercial Trucking: Damages to Persons & Property. 1000p. 1994. 105.00 (*1-55834-165-X*) Michie Butterworth.

Nissenberg, Sandra K. Healthy Start Kids' Cookbook: Fun & Healthful Recipes That Kids Can Make Themselves. 192p. 1995. pap. 11.95 (*1-56561-054-7*) Chronimed.
— How Should I Feed My Child: From Pregnancy to Preschool. 1993. pap. 12.95 (*1-56561-035-0*) Chronimed.

***Nissenberg, Sandra K., et al.** Quick Meals for Healthly Kids & Busy Parents: Wholesome Family Recipes in 30 Minutes or Less. 300p. 1995. 12.95 (*1-56561-064-4*) Chronimed.

Nissenboim, Sylvia & Vroman, Christine. Interactions by Design: The Positive Interactions Program for Persons with Alzheimer's Disease & Related Disorders. rev. ed. LC 89-85538. (Series in Nonprofit Management). 100p. 1989. pap. 27.95 (*0-9621846-1-6*) Geri-Active.

***Nissenson.** Clinical Dialysis. 3rd ed. (C). 1995. text ed. 175.00 (*0-8385-1379-4*) Appleton & Lange.
— Macoy's Star Songs. 48p. reprint ed. pap. 1.00 (*0-88053-311-0*, S301) Macoy Pub.

Nissenson, Allen R. & Fine, Richard N., eds. Dialysis Therapy. 2nd ed. 417p. (Orig.). 1992. pap. text ed. 53.00 (*1-56053-058-8*) Hanley & Belfus.

Nissenson, Allen R., et al. Clinical Dialysis. 2nd ed. (Illus.). 768p. 1990. boxed 175.00 (*0-8385-1223-2*, A1223-5) Appleton & Lange.

***Nissenson, Marilyn & Jonas, Susan.** Snake Charm. LC 94-42669. 1995. write for info. (*0-8109-4456-1*) Abrams.
— The Ubiquitous Pig. (Illus.). 136p. 1992. 29.95 (*0-8109-3916-9*) Abrams.

Nissenson, Marilyn, jt. auth. see Jonas, Susan.

Nissenson, R. A., jt. ed. see Draper, M. W.

Nissenson, Robert A., jt. auth. see Halloran, Bernard P.

Nissenson, S. G. Patroon's Domain. 416p. 1993. reprint ed. lib. bdg. 99.00 (*0-7812-5192-3*) Rprt Serv.

Nissi Wang, jt. ed. see Jirui Chen.

Nissim-Momigliano, Luciana. Continuity & Change in Psychoanalysis: Letters from Milan. 184p. 1992. pap. 29.95 (*1-85575-009-0*, Pub. by Karnac Bks UK) Brunner-Mazel.

Nissim-Momigliano, Luciana & Robutti, Andreina. Shared Experience: The Psychoanalytic Dialogue. 278p. 1992. pap. 35.95 (*1-85575-034-1*, Pub. by Karnac Bks UK) Brunner-Mazel.

Nissim, Perahyah B. Perush Rabbenu Perahyah Ben Nissim Al Masskheth Shabbath. Hirschfeld, Boruch, ed. 339p. (HEB.). (C). 1988. 14.00 (*1-881255-04-2*) OFEQ Inst.

Nissim, Yves I. & Katz, Avishay, eds. Single Chamber Processing: Proceedings of the Joint Session on Single Chamber Processing of the 1992 E-MRS Spring Meeting Conference, Strasbourg, France, June 2-5, 1992. LC 92-42556. (European Materials Research Society Symposia Proceedings Ser.: Vol. 37). 1993. write for info. (*0-444-89915-4*, North Holland) Elsevier.

Nissim, Yves I. & Rosencher, Emmanuel, eds. Heterostructures on Silicon: One Step Further with Silicon. (C). 1989. lib. bdg. 155.00 (*0-7923-0124-2*) Kluwer Ac.

***Nissim, Yves I., et al, eds.** Integrated Processing for Micro & Optoelectronics: Proceedings of Symposium D on Integrated Processing for Micro & Optoelectronics of the 1993 E-MRS Spring Conference, Strasbourg, France, May 4-7, 1993. LC 94-22909. (European Materials Research Society Symposia Proceedings Ser.: Vol. 42). 1994. 200.00 (*0-444-81983-5*, North Holland) Elsevier.

Nissiotis, N. Interpreting Orthodoxy. 1980. pap. 2.95 (*0-937032-23-9*) Light&Life Pub Co MN.

***Nissley, Julia.** How To Probate an Estate: California. 8th ed. Warner, Ralph & Randolph, Mary, eds. LC 94-35334. 1994. pap. 34.95 (*0-87337-280-8*) Nolo Pr.

Nissman, David & Hagen, Ed. Law of Confessions. 2nd ed. LC 94-67910. 1994. 120.00 (*0-685-59837-3*) Clark Boardman Callaghan.

Nist, John. Style in English. LC 72-77824. 1969. pap. 1.75 (*0-672-60904-5*, CR18, Bobbs) Macmillan.

***Nist, Sherrie L. & Diehl, William.** Developing Textbook Thinking: Strategies for Success in College. 3rd ed. 393p. (C). 1994. pap. text ed. write for info. (*0-669-29779-8*) Heath.

Nist, Sherrie L. & Diehl, William A. Developing Textbook Thinking: Strategies for Success in College. 2nd ed. 399p. (C). 1990. pap. text ed. 17.50 (*0-669-20468-4*); Instr.'s guide. teacher ed 2.00 (*0-669-24428-7*) Heath.

Nist, Sherrie L. & Mohr, Carole. Improving Vocabulary Skills. 180p. 1990. pap. text ed. 7.30 (*0-944210-81-3*) Townsend NJ.

Nist, Sherrie L. & Simpson, Michele L. Developing Vocabulary Concepts for College Thinking. 416p. (C). 1993. pap. text ed. write for info. (*0-669-27914-5*); Instr.'s guide. teacher ed write for info. (*0-669-27916-1*) Heath.

Nista, Leila, jt. auth. see Anderson, Maxwell L.

Nista, Leila, jt. ed. see Anderson, Maxwell L.

Nister, Ernest. Animal Playmates. (Illus.). 10p. (J). 1990. 5.95 (*0-399-21957-9*, Philomel Bks) Putnam Pub Group.
— Christmas Toys. (Tiny Nisters Ser.). (Illus.). 10p. (J). (ps up). 1992. 4.95 (*0-399-21995-1*, Philomel Bks) Putnam Pub Group.
— Darling Babies. (Tiny Pull-the-Tab Bks.). (Illus.). 10p. (YA). 1994. 4.95 (*0-399-22722-9*, Philomel Bks) Putnam Pub Group.
— A Day in the Country. (Illus.). 10p. (J). 1990. 5.95 (*0-399-21959-5*, Philomel Bks) Putnam Pub Group.
— Ernest Nister's Book of Christmas. (Illus.). 12p. (J). 1991. 12.95 (*0-399-21799-1*, Philomel Bks) Putnam Pub Group.
— Farmyard Friends. (Four Tiny Nisters Ser.). (Illus.). 10p. (J). (ps up). 1991. 4.95 (*0-399-22110-7*, Philomel Bks) Putnam Pub Group.
— Favorite Animals. (Miniature Pop-Up & Pull-the-Tab Bks.). (Illus.). 10p. (J). 1989. 5.95 (*0-399-21728-2*, Philomel Bks) Putnam Pub Group.
— Good Friends. (Miniature Pop-ups & Pull-the-Tab Bks.). (Illus.). (J). 1989. 5.95 (*0-399-21729-0*, Philomel Bks) Putnam Pub Group.
— Hide-&-Seek. (Illus.). 20p. (J). (ps-8). 1992. 14.95 (*0-399-21810-6*, Philomel Bks) Putnam Pub Group.
— Keepsake Carousel. (J). 1993. 7.95 (*1-56397-081-3*) Boyds Mills Pr.
— Land of Sweet Surprises: An Antique Revolving Picture Books. (Illus.). (J). (gr. k up). 1983. 12.95 (*0-399-20993-X*, Philomel Bks) Putnam Pub Group.
— Little Dolls. (Four Tiny Nisters Ser.). (Illus.). 10p. (J). (ps up). 1991. 4.95 (*0-399-22107-7*, Philomel Bks) Putnam Pub Group.
— Magic Windows: An Antique Revolving Picture Book. (Illus.). 14p. (J). (ps up). 1981. 12.95 (*0-399-20773-2*, Philomel Bks) Putnam Pub Group.
— Merry Magic-Go-Round. (Illus.). (J). (gr. k up). 1983. lib. bdg. 12.95 (*0-399-20946-8*, Philomel Bks) Putnam Pub Group.
— Mother & Me. (Illus.). 10p. (J). 1990. 5.95 (*0-399-21958-7*, Philomel Bks) Putnam Pub Group.
— My Best Friend. (Illus.). 10p. (J). 1990. 5.95 (*0-399-21960-9*, Philomel Bks) Putnam Pub Group.
— My Little Pets. (Four Tiny Nisters Ser.). (Illus.). 10p. (J). (ps up). 1991. 4.95 (*0-399-22109-3*, Philomel Bks) Putnam Pub Group.
— Our Baby. (Illus.). 32p. (J). 1991. 15.95 (*0-399-21856-4*, Philomel Bks) Putnam Pub Group.
— Our Farmyard: A Pop-up Book with Punch-out Play Figures. (Illus.). 12p. (J). (ps-3). 1991. 13.95 (*0-525-44689-3*, DCB) Dutton Child Bks.
— Playtime Delights. (Illus.). 26p. (J). (ps up). 1993. 15.95 (*0-399-21898-X*, Philomel Bks) Putnam Pub Group.
— Pop up Mother Goose Favorites. (Illus.). 18p. (J). (ps up). 1989. 14.99 (*0-525-44504-8*, DCB) Dutton Child Bks.
— Rainbow Round-a-Bout. 10p. (J). 1993. 7.95 (*1-56397-088-0*) Boyds Mills Pr.
— Santa's Surprises. (Tiny Nisters Ser.). (Illus.). 10p. (J). (ps up). 1992. 4.95 (*0-399-21996-X*, Philomel Bks) Putnam Pub Group.
— Snowy Days. (Tiny Nisters Ser.). (Illus.). 10p. (J). (ps up). 1992. 4.95 (*0-399-21997-8*, Philomel Bks) Putnam Pub Group.
— Special Days. (Illus.). (J). (gr. k up). 1989. 5.95 (*0-399-21694-4*, Philomel Bks) Putnam Pub Group.
— Spring Gardens. (Tiny Pull-the-Tab Bks.). (Illus.). 10p. (YA). 1994. 4.95 (*0-399-22723-7*, Philomel Bks) Putnam Pub Group.
— Sunny Days. (Tiny Pull-the-Tab Bks.). (Illus.). 10p. (YA). 1994. 4.95 (*0-399-22721-0*, Philomel Bks) Putnam Pub Group.

An Asterisk (*) at the beginning of an entry indicates that the title is appearing in BIP for the first time.

— Tiny Tots. (Four Tiny Nisters Ser.). (Illus.). 10p. (J). (ps up). 1991. 4.95 (*0-399-22108-5*, Philomel Bks) Putnam Pub Group.

— Token of Love. (Tiny Pull-the-Tab Bks.). (Illus.). 10p. (YA). 1994. 4.95 (*0-399-22720-2*, Philomel Bks) Putnam Pub Group.

— Visiting Grandma. (Illus.). (J). (gr. k up). 1989. 5.95 (*0-399-21695-2*, Philomel Bks) Putnam Pub Group.

— Yuletide Delights. (Tiny Nisters Ser.). (Illus.). 10p. (J). (ps up). 1992. 4.95 (*0-399-21998-6*, Philomel Bks) Putnam Pub Group.

Nister, Ernest, illus. Baby's Memory Book: A Baby Record Book. 30p. 1986. 15.95 (*0-399-21292-2*, G&D) Putnam Pub Group.

— Moving Pictures: An Antique Picture Book. 12p. (J). (ps up). 1985. 11.95 (*0-399-21272-8*, Philomel Bks) Putnam Pub Group.

— Playtime Delights. 26p. (J). 1993. 15.95 (*0-685-66598-4*, Philomel Bks) Putnam Pub Group.

Nister, Ernest & Bingham, Clifton. Revolving Pictures. LC 79-12438. (Illus.). (J). (ps-4). 1981. 12.95 (*0-399-20802-X*, Philomel Bks) Putnam Pub Group.

Nistico, Giuseppe & Bolis, Liana, eds. Progress in Nonmammalian Brain Research, 3 Vols., Ill. 1983. 132.00 (*0-8493-6352-7*, CRC Reprint) Franklin.

— Progress in Nonmammalian Brain Research, 3 Vols., Vol. I. 208p. 1983. 115.00 (*0-8493-6350-0*, QP376, CRC Reprint) Franklin.

— Progress in Nonmammalian Brain Research, 3 Vols., Vol. II. 240p. 1983. 115.00 (*0-8493-6351-9*, CRC Reprint) Franklin.

Nistico, Giuseppe, jt. auth. see Muller, Engenio E.

Nistico, Giuseppe, et al, eds. Neurotransmitters, Seizures, & Epilepsy III. (Illus.). 528p. 1986. text ed. 108.50 (*0-88167-229-7*) Raven.

Nistral-Moret, Benjamin, ed. Esclavos Profugos Y Cimarrones Puerto Rico 1770-1870. LC 84-20885. (Illus.). 287p. (SPA.). 1984. text ed. 10.50 (*0-8477-0885-3*) U of PR Pr.

NISW Info. Service Staff. Social Work Update. (C). 1988. 90.00 (*0-685-28594-4*, Pub. by Natl Inst Soc Work) St Mut.

***NISW Information Service Staff.** A Guide to the Wagner Report. 1988. pap. 35.00 (*0-614-00736-4*, Pub. by Natl Inst Soc Work) St Mut.

— A Guide to the Wagner Report. (C). 1988. 23.00 (*0-7855-0094-4*, Pub. by Natl Inst Soc Work) St Mut.

***NISW Staff.** Assessment & Care Co-Ordination. 1993. 105.00 (*1-873153-13-9*, Pub. by Natl Inst Soc Work) St Mut.

— Community Care in Context. 1992. 90.00 (*0-614-07447-9*, Pub. by Natl Inst Soc Work) St Mut.

— The Wagner Report: Report of the Independent Review of Residential Care, 1988, Vol. 1: A Positive Choice (Report & Recommendations) (C). 1988. 59.00 (*0-685-28583-9*, Pub. by Natl Inst Soc Work) St Mut.

NISW Staff, ed. The Wagner Report: Report of the Independent Review of Residential Care, Vol. 11: The Research Reviewed (Background Information) (C). 1988. 75.00 (*0-685-28582-0*, Pub. by Natl Inst Soc Work) St Mut.

Niswander, Adam. The Charm: A Southwestern Supernatural Thriller. LC 93-26241. 288p. 1993. lib. bdg. 21.95 (*0-9626148-1-5*) Integra Pr.

— The Serpent Slayers: A Southwestern Supernatural Thriller. LC 94-1284. (Shaman Cycle Ser.: Bk. 2). 320p. 1994. lib. bdg. 21.95 (*0-9626148-2-3*) Integra Pr.

Niswander, Kenneth R. Manual of Obstetrics. 4th ed. 1991. 31.95 (*0-316-61173-5*) Little.

— Manual of Obstetrics: Diagnosis & Therapy. 3rd ed. (Brown Spiral Manual Ser.). 1987. spiral bd. 22.50 (*0-316-61139-5*) Little.

— Manual of Obstetrics Asia, No. 3. 1987. 10.95 (*0-316-61135-2*) Little.

— Manual of Obstetrics Asia, No. 4. 1991. 10.95 (*0-316-61171-9*) Little.

— Manual of Obstetrics ISE, No. 3. 1987. 15.95 (*0-316-61136-0*) Little.

— Obstetrics: Essentials of Clinical Practice. 2nd ed. 379p. 1981. 34.95 (*0-316-61147-6*) Little.

Niswender, G. D., et al, eds. Reproduction in Domestic Ruminants. (Journal of Reproduction & Fertility, Supplement Ser.: No. 34). 270p. 1987. 67.00 (*0-906545-12-9*) Portland NC.

Niswonger, Richard L. Arkansas Democratic Politics, 1896-1920. LC 89-5195. 344p. 1990. 29.95 (*1-55728-116-5*) U of Ark Pr.

— New Testament History. (History - New Testament Studies). 368p. 1992. 15.99 (*0-310-31201-9*) Zondervan.

Nitchie, Edward B. Lip Reading Made Easy. LC 84-52486. (Illus.). 130p. (Orig.). 1985. pap. 7.95 (*0-915179-22-9*) Loompanics.

Nitchie, Elizabeth. Mary Shelley, Author of Frankenstein. LC 72-100233. 255p. 1970. reprint ed. text ed. 55.00 (*0-8371-3689-X*, NIMS, Greenwood Pr) Greenwood.

— Reverend Colonel Finch. LC 40-33650. reprint ed. 20.00 (*0-404-04777-7*) AMS Pr.

— Vergil & the English Poets. LC 19-9760. reprint ed. 20.00 (*0-404-04778-5*) AMS Pr.

Nitchie, George W. Human Values in the Poetry of Robert Frost: A Study of a Poet's Convictions. LC 60-10813. 256p. reprint ed. pap. 73.00 (*0-317-20444-0*, 2023430) Bks Demand.

— Human Values in the Poetry of Robert Frost: A Study of a Poet's Convictions. LC 78-4612. 242p. 1978. reprint ed. 45.00 (*0-87752-199-9*) Gordian.

— Marianne Moore: An Introduction to the Poetry. LC 79-96998. (Introduction to Twentieth Century American Poetry Ser.). 205p. 1972. pap. text ed. 17.50 (*0-231-08312-2*) Col U Pr.

***Nitchman, Karoleigh K.** Karoleigh's Finger-Lickin' Lip Smacking' Quick-Fixin' Snackin' Book. Date not set. 15.95 (*1-883962-02-1*) Kristalex Pr.

— Whistlin' Dixie: A Tale of the South. (Orig.). Date not set. pap. 12.95 (*1-883962-01-3*) Kristalex Pr.

Nite, Norm N. Rock on Almanac: The First Four Decades of Rock 'n' Roll: A Chronology. 2nd ed. LC 92-52544. (Illus.). 576p. 1992. pap. 20.00 (*0-06-273157-2*, Harper Ref) HarpC.

Nitecki, jt. auth. see Misiurewicz.

***Nitecki, Alicia.** Recovered Land. LC 94-41650. (Illus.). 144p. 1995. 19.95 (*0-87023-976-7*) U of Mass Pr.

Nitecki, Andre, jt. ed. see Arnold, Stephen.

Nitecki, D. V., jt. ed. see Nitecki, M. H.

Nitecki, D. V., jt. ed. see Nitecki, M. N.

Nitecki, Danuta A., ed. Energies for Transition: Proceedings of the Fourth National Conference of the Association of College & Research Libraries. 248p. 1986. pap. text ed. 32.95 (*0-8389-6976-3*); pap. text ed. 23.95 (*0-685-67508-4*) Assn Coll & Res Libs.

Nitecki, Doris V., jt. ed. see Nitecki, Matthew H.

Nitecki, M. H. & Nitecki, D. V., eds. Origins of Anatomically Modern Human. (Interdisciplinary Contributions to Archaeology Ser.). (Illus.). 320p. (C). 1994. 49.50 (*0-306-44675-8*, Plenum Pr) Plenum.

Nitecki, M. N. & Nitecki, D. V., eds. The Evolution of Human Hunting. LC 87-34302. (Illus.). 472p. 1988. 95.00 (*0-306-42821-0*, Plenum Pr) Plenum.

Nitecki, Matthew H. Evolutionary Innovations. LC 90-10990. (Illus.). 330p. 1990. lib. bdg. 44.95 (*0-226-58694-4*) U Ch Pr.

— Evolutionary Innovations. LC 90-10990. (Illus.). 330p. 1990. pap. text ed. 17.95 (*0-226-58695-2*) U Ch Pr.

Nitecki, Matthew H., ed. Evolutionary Progress. LC 88-20835. (Illus.). 368p. 1989. lib. bdg. 42.50 (*0-226-58692-8*); pap. text ed. 16.95 (*0-226-58693-6*) U Ch Pr.

— Mazon Creek Fossils. LC 79-10104. 1979. text ed. 77.00 (*0-12-519650-4*) Acad Pr.

Nitecki, Matthew H. & Kitchell, Jennifer A. Evolution of Animal Behavior: Paleontological & Field Approaches. (Illus.). 224p. 1986. 39.95 (*0-19-504006-0*) OUP.

Nitecki, Matthew H. & Nitecki, Doris V., eds. Evolutionary Ethics. LC 92-47270. (SUNY Series in Philosophy & Biology). 368p. (C). 1993. 59.50 (*0-7914-1499-X*); pap. 19.95 (*0-7914-1500-7*) State U NY Pr.

— History & Evolution. LC 92-724. (SUNY Series in Philosophy & Biology). 269p. 1992. 59.50 (*0-7914-1211-3*); pap. 19.95 (*0-7914-1212-1*) State U NY Pr.

Nitecki, Matthew H., jt. ed. see Hoffman, Antoni.

Nitecki, Zbigniew H. & Guterman, Martin M. Differential Equations with Linear Algebra. 640p. (C). 1986. text ed. 55.00 (*0-03-002719-5*) SCP.

Nitecki, Zbigniew H., jt. auth. see Guterman, Martin M.

Nitka, Arthur & Kulbach, Joanna E. The Recorder Guide. (Illus.). 128p. pap. 14.95 (*0-8256-0020-0*, Oak) Music Sales.

Nitka, David, II. Allergic Reactions. 91p. 1994. pap. 7.00 (*0-9641196-0-9*) Champion Bks.

Nitkin, Karen, ed. see Rodengen, Jeffrey L.

Nitkina, N. V. & Mikheeva, G. V. Guide to Russian Periodicals & Serial Publications, 1728-1985. 550p. (C). 1993. text ed. 195.00 (*1-56072-059-X*) Nova Sci Pubs.

Nitkina, N. V. & Mikheeva, G. V., eds. Guide to Bibliographies of Russian Periodicals & Serials Publications, 1728-1985. 550p. (C). 1992. text ed. 195.00 (*1-56072-057-3*) Nova Sci Pubs.

Nitko, Anthony J. Educational Tests & Measurements. 2nd ed. 672p. (C). 1996. text ed. write for info. (*0-02-387651-4*) Macmillan.

Nitko, Anthony J., jt. auth. see Mulgrave, Norman.

Nitobe, Inazo. Bushido: The Soul of Japan. 228p. 1994. pap. 8.95 (*0-8048-1961-0*) C E Tuttle.

— Bushido, The Warrior's Code. Lucas, Charles, ed. LC 75-21718. (History & Philosophy Ser.). (Illus.). 1975. pap. text ed. 9.95 (*0-89750-031-8*, 303, Wehman) Ohara Pubns.

Nitobe, Inazo, pseud. The Intercourse Between the U. S. & Japan: An Historical Sketch. LC 72-82102. (Japan Library Ser.). 1973. reprint ed. lib. bdg. 24.00 (*0-8420-1397-0*) Scholarly Res Inc.

Nitobe, Inazo O. The Intercourse Between the United States & Japan: An Historical Sketch. LC 78-64252. (Johns Hopkins University. Studies in the Social Sciences. Thirtieth Ser. 1912: 8). reprint ed. 11.50 (*0-404-61356-X*) AMS Pr.

Nitopi, Bill. Cherokee Mist: The Lost Writings of Jimi Hendrix. 1994. pap. 10.00 (*0-06-092562-0*, PL) HarpC.

Nitsch, Bert, ed. see Nitsch, Susan L.

Nitsch, J., jt. ed. see Winter, C. J.

Nitsch, Roger M., et al, eds. Alzheimer's Disease: Amyloid Precursor Proteins, Signal Transduction, & Neuronal Transplantation. LC 93-26927. (Annals Ser.: Vol. 695). 1993. write for info. (*0-89766-853-7*); pap. 100.00 (*0-89766-854-5*) NY Acad Sci.

Nitsch, Sherry. The Euclidean Woman. LC 88-28753. 54p. 1988. pap. text ed. 3.00 (*0-943123-10-0*) Arjuna Lib Pr.

Nitsch, Susan L. How to Become a Freelance Secretary. Pasich, William, ed. (Illus.). 53p. 1983. pap. 3.95 (*0-943544-01-7*) Secretarial Pubns.

— How to Start & Operate a Secretarial Service. Davis, William & Nitsch, Bert, eds. (Illus.). 85p. (Orig.). 1982. pap. text ed. 7.95 (*0-943544-00-9*) Secretarial Pubns.

Nitsch, Thomas O., ed. On the Condition of Labor & the Social Question One Hundred Years Later: Commemorating the One Hundredth Anniversary of Rerum Novarum, & the Fiftieth Anniversary of the Association for Social Economics. LC 94-17918. (Toronto Studies in Theology: Vol. 69). 626p. 1994. text ed. 129.95 (*0-7734-9069-8*) E Mellen.

Nitsch, Twylah, jt. auth. see Sams, Jamie.

Nitsch, Twylah H. Creature Totems: Nature Teacher Medicine. Rinebold, Albert F., ed. (Illus.). 130p. (Orig.). 1991. pap. 16.00 (*0-9626135-1-7*) Aware Tribe.

***Nitsche, J.** Aluminium Production: Glossary of Technical Terms English-French-German-Spanish. 361p. (ENG, FRE & GER.). 1992. pap. 120.00x (*3-87017-182-0*) IBD Ltd.

Nitsche, J., jt. auth. see Lang, G.

Nitsche, J. C., jt. ed. see Davis, H. T.

Nitsche, Johannes C. Introduction to Minimal Surfaces, Vol. 1. (Illus.). 450p. 1989. 165.00 (*0-521-24427-7*) Cambridge U Pr.

Nitsche, M. Polygraph Dictionary of the Graphic Arts. 327p. (ENG & GER.). 1987. 125.00 (*0-8288-7916-8*) Fr & Eur.

Nitsche, M., jt. auth. see Trondt, Leonhard.

Nitsche, Michael. Polygraph Dictionary of the Graphic Arts & Communications Technology: English - German - Italian - French. 642p. (C). 128.00 (*3-87641-245-5*, 1-245) Perfect Graphic.

Nitsche, Michael & Trondt, Leonhard. Polygraph Dictionary of the Graphic Arts: German-English, English-German. 4th rev. ed. 339p. 1993. 55.00 (*0-685-52270-9*, 1-158) Perfect Graphic.

Nitschke, Diana L., et al, eds. The Seventh National Space Symposium Proceedings Report. (Illus.). 224p. 1991. pap. 50.00 (*0-9616962-5-7*) US Space Found.

Nitschke, Diane L., et al, eds. The Sixth National Space Symposium Proceedings Report. (Illus.). 198p. 1990. pap. 50.00 (*0-9616962-4-9*) US Space Found.

Nitschke, Martha. How to Fight Sexual Harassment & Win: A Woman's Guide to Survival in a Man's World. 160p. (Orig.). 1993. pap. 24.95 (*0-9630077-1-8*) Entrepress.

— How to Start Your Own One Hundred Thousand Dollar Nursing Agency: With As Little As One Week's Salary. (Illus.). 128p. 1991. pap. 35.00 (*0-9630077-0-X*) Entrepress.

Nitske, Robert. Mercedes Benz Production Model Forty-Six to Ninety. 1986. 39.95 (*0-87938-486-7*) Motorbooks Intl.

Nitta, Jiro. Death March on Mount Hakkoda. Westerhoven, James, tr. LC 91-24157. (Rock Spring Collection). 204p. (Orig.). 1991. pap. 10.95 (*0-9628137-2-9*, Rock Spring Collect) Stone Bridge Pr.

Nitter-Hauge, S., et al, eds. Cardiac Imaging: X-Ray, MR & Ultrasound: Proceedings of the Nycomed Scientific Symposium, 1990, Held in Bergen, 8-9 Oct., 1990. (International Congress Ser.: No. 922). 236p. 1991. 111.50 (*0-444-81441-8*, Excerpta Medica) Elsevier.

Nitterhouse, Denise, jt. auth. see Herzlinger, Regina E.

Nitti, Francesco. Catholic Socialism. 1976. lib. bdg. 69.95 (*0-8490-1586-3*) Gordon Pr.

Nitti, Francesco S. Population & the Social System. LC 75-38140. (Demography Ser.). (Illus.). 1976. reprint ed. 19.95 (*0-405-07993-1*) Ayer.

Nitti, J. J. Two Hundred & One Portuguese Verbs. 1977. pap. 9.95 (*0-8120-0330-6*) Barron.

Nitti, John J., ed. Juan Fernandez de Heredia's Aragonese Version of the Libro de Marco Polo. (Dialect Ser.: No. 1). (Illus.). xxxvi, 122p. 1980. 12.00 (*0-942260-13-9*) Hispanic Seminary.

Nittrouer, C. A. & Demaster, D. J., eds. Sedimentary Processes on the Amazon Continental Shelf. (Illus.). 336p. 1987. 39.50 (*0-08-033928-X*, Pergamon Pr) Elsevier.

Nityaswarupananda, Swami, tr. see Astavakra.

Nityo, P., ed. see Osho.

Nityo, Prabodh, ed. see Osho.

Nitz, Dwight V., jt. auth. see Brown, Herbert O.

Nitz, Hans-Jurgen, ed. The Early Modern World-System in Geographical Perspective. (Illus.). 415p. (Orig.). 1993. pap. 87.50 (*3-515-06094-4*) Coronet Bks.

Nitz, Irmela, tr. see Polyani, M.

Nitz, Lawrence H. Business Analysis & Graphics with Lotus 1-2-3. (Illus.). 176p. 1985. pap. 32.95 (*0-13-091604-8*) P-H.

— Business Analysis & Graphics with Lotus 1-2-3. write for info. (*0-318-59621-0*) S&S Trade.

***Nitz, Tim, ed.** Sapatq'ayn: Twentieth Century Nez Perce Artists. LC 91-62472. 60p. 1991. 20.00 (*0-917652-95-9*) Confluence Pr.

Nitzan, Menachem, ed. The Influence of Maternal Hormones on the Fetus & Newborn. (Pediatric & Adolescent Endocrinology Ser.: Vol. 5). (Illus.). 1979. pap. 79.25 (*3-8055-2902-3*) S Karger.

Nitzan, Shmuel & Paroush, Jacob. Collective Decision Making: An Economic Outlook. (Illus.). 120p. 1986. 49.95 (*0-521-30326-5*) Cambridge U Pr.

Nitzberg, Esther M. Hippocrates' Handmaidens: Women Married to Physicians. LC 90-41946. (Women Ser.: Vol. 4). 238p. 1990. pap. 19.95 (*0-918393-81-7*) Harrington Pk.

— Hippocrates' Handmaidens: Women Married to Physicians. LC 90-41947. (Women Ser.: Vol. 4). 238p. 1990. text ed. 59.95 (*0-86656-880-8*) Haworth Pr.

Nitzberg, M. & Mumford, D. Filtering, Segmentation & Depth. Goos, G. & Hartmanis, J., eds. (Lecture Notes in Computer Science Ser.: Vol. 662). 151p. 1993. pap. 35.00 (*0-387-56484-5*) Spr-Verlag.

Nitzberg, M., et al. Filtering, Segmentation, & Depth. LC 93-2797. (Lecture Notes in Computer Science Ser.: Vol. 662). 1993. write for info. (*3-540-56484-5*) Spr-Verlag.

Nitzberg, Ramon. Adaptive Signal Processing for Radar. (Radar Library). 424p. 1992. text ed. 88.00 (*0-89006-586-1*) Artech Hse.

Nitze, A. & Jenkins, T. A., eds. Perlevaus: Perceval - Le Haut Du Graal, 2 Vols. LC 71-159117. (Illus.). 926p. 1972. reprint ed. 250.00 (*0-87753-054-8*) Phaeton.

Nitze, Paul H. Recovery of Ethics. (Ethics & Foreign Policy Ser.). 1960. pap. 0.50 (*0-87641-104-9*) Carnegie Ethics & Intl Affairs.

— Tension Between Opposites: Reflections on the Practice & Theory of Politics. LC 93-12874. (Illus.). 384p. 1993. text ed. 22.00 (*0-684-19628-X*, Scribners) S&S Trade.

Nitze, Paul H. & Sullivan, Leonard. Securing the Seas: The Soviet Naval Challenge & Western Alliance Options. 464p. 1979. 22.50 (*0-317-33696-7*); 12.50 (*0-317-33697-5*) Atl Coun US.

Nitze, W. A. & Cross, T. P. Lancelot & Guinevere. 1973. 59.95 (*0-8490-0482-9*) Gordon Pr.

Nitze, William A. Arthurian Romance & Modern Poetry & Music. LC 76-122995. (Arthurian Legend & Literature Ser.: No. 1). (C). 1970. reprint ed. lib. bdg. 37.95 (*0-8383-1128-8*) M S G Haskell Hse.

Nitze, William N., jt. auth. see Cross, Tom P.

Nitzsch, Karl W. Die Romische Annalistik. xii, 355p. 1974. reprint ed. write for info. (*3-487-05190-7*, Pub. by Georg Olms GW) Lubrecht & Cramer.

Nitzsch, Paul F. Worterbuch der Alten Geographie. Hopfner, J. G., ed. xxviii, 648p. (GER.). 1983. reprint ed. write for info. (*3-487-06958-X*, Pub. by Georg Olms GW) Lubrecht & Cramer.

Nitzsche, Jane C. The Genius Figure in Antiquity & the Middle Ages. LC 74-17206. 201p. 1975. text ed. 40.00 (*0-231-03852-6*) Col U Pr.

Niu, Alan K., jt. ed. see Yu-Chong Lin.

***Niu-Niu.** No Tears for Mao. Amman, Enne & Amman, Peter, trs. 280p. 1995. 22.95 (*0-89733-410-8*) Academy Chi Pubs.

Niu, Xiaodong. Education East & West: The Influence of Mao Zedong & John Dewey. 200p. 1994. 64.95 (*1-883255-57-0*); pap. 44.95 (*1-883255-56-2*) Intl Scholars.

— Policy Education & Inequalities in Communist China since 1949. 122p. (C). 1992. lib. bdg. 32.50 (*0-8191-8335-0*) U Pr of Amer.

Niv. NIV Life Application Bible: Matthew. 160p. 1992. pap. 4.99 (*0-8423-2883-1*) Tyndale.

***Niv, M. D.** Reason in Madness: An Existential Approach to Psychiatric Disorders. 480p. (C). 1995. pap. 19.95 (*0-9634433-0-5*) EVER Pub.

Niva, George D., jt. auth. see Baughman, W. Henry.

Nivardus, Magister. Ysengrimus. Sypher, F. J. & Sypher, Eleanor, trs. (Illus.). 280p. 1980. 95.00 (*0-317-00052-7*) F Sypher.

Nivat, M., et al. Algebraic Methodology Software Technology (AMAST'91) Proceedings of the Third International Conference on Algebraic Methodology & Software Technology. LC 93-38672. (Workshops in Computing Ser.). 1994. 76.00 (*0-387-19852-0*) Spr-Verlag.

Nivat, Maurice & Perrin, D., eds. Automata on Infinite Words. (Lecture Notes in Computer Science Ser.: Vol. 192). iii, 216p. (ENG & FRE.). 1985. pap. 30.00 (*0-387-15641-0*) Spr-Verlag.

Nivat, Maurice & Podelski, Andreas, eds. Tree Automata & Languages. LC 92-17937. (Studies in Computer Science & Artificial Intelligence: Vol. 10). 1992. write for info. (*0-444-89026-2*, North Holland) Elsevier.

Nivat, Maurice, jt. ed. see Ait-Kaci, Hassan.

Nivat, Maurice, jt. ed. see Dauchet, M.

Nivat, Maurice, jt. ed. see Fuchi, K.

Nivat, Maurice, et al. Parallel Image Processing. (Series on Machine Perception). 268p. 1992. text ed. 45.00 (*981-02-1120-1*) World Scientific Pub.

Nivat, Maurice, et al, eds. Algebraic Methodology & Software Technology (AMAST '91) Proceedings of the Second International Conference on Algebraic Methodology & Software Technology, Iowa City, U. S. A. 22-25 May 1991. LC 92-33753. (Workshops in Computing Ser.). 1993. 89.00 (*0-387-19797-4*) Spr-Verlag.

Nivedita. Complete Works of Sister Nivedita, 5 vols., Set. Noble, Margaret, ed. Incl. Vol. 1. Our Master & His Message, the Master As I Saw Him, Kali the Mother, Lectures & Articles. 1967. 8.95 (*0-87481-112-0*); Vol. 2. Web of Indian Life, an Indian Study on Love & Death, Studies from an Eastern Home, Lectures & Articles. 1967. 8.95 (*0-87481-113-9*); Vol. 3. Indian Art, Cradle Tales of Hinduism, Religion & Dharma. 1967. 8.95 (*0-87481-114-7*); Vol. 4. Footfalls of Indian History, Bodh-Gaya, Civic Ideal & Indian Nationality, Hints on National Education in India. 1967. 8.95 (*0-87481-115-5*); Vol. 5. Lectures & Writings. 1967. 8.95 (*0-87481-226-7*); 1967. 65.00 (*0-87481-216-X*) Vedanta Pr.

— Cradle Tales of Hinduism. (Illus.). 329p. (J). (gr. 3-12). 1972. pap. 5.95 (*0-87481-170-8*, Pub. by Advaita Ashrama II); pap. 5.95 (*0-87481-131-7*, Pub. by Advaita Ashrama II) Vedanta Pr.

— Letters of Sister Nivedita. 1982. 25.00 (*0-87481-228-3*, Pub. by Advaita Ashrama II) Vedanta Pr.

— Master As I Saw Him. 5.95 (*0-87481-088-4*, Pub. by Advaita Ashrama II) Vedanta Pr.

— Notes of Some Wanderings. 3.00 (*0-87481-185-6*) Vedanta Pr.

— Siva & Buddha. pap. 1.00 (*0-87481-116-3*, Pub. by Advaita Ashrama II) Vedanta Pr.

Nivedita, Sr., jt. auth. see Coomaraswamy, Ananda K.

Nivelle, Armand. Fruehromantische Dichtungstheorie. (C). 1970. 76.15 (*3-11-002703-8*) De Gruyter.

***Niven & Barnes.** California Voodoo Game. 1994. pap. 5.99 (*0-517-12814-4*) Random.

Niven, Alexander C. From Moscow to Vladivostok: A Historical, Geographical, & Economic Guide for Travellers on the Trans-Siberian Railroad. (Illus.). 1985. pap. 8.00 (*0-940604-07-8*) Intl Inst Adv Stud.

— We Live in the Calm of Despotism: Notes & Observations of James Buchanan During His Ambassadorship in Russia, 1831-1833. 1983. pap. 3.00 (*0-940604-04-3*) Intl Inst Adv Stud.

Niven, B. M. Special Men, Special War: Portraits of the SAS & Dhofar. (Illus.). 76p. 1992. 21.95 (*0-911977-10-4*, Imago Prod) Seven Hills Bk.

Niven, Bruce M. The Mountain Kingdom: Portraits of Nepal & the Gurkhas. (Illus.). 96p. (Orig.). 1991. pap. 18.95 (*0-911977-07-4*, Imago Prod) Seven Hills Bk.

Niven, Catherine A. Psychological Care for Families: Before, During & after Birth. (Illus.). 192p. 1992. pap. 35.00 (*0-7506-0060-8*) Buttrwrth-Heinemann.

Niven, Catherine A. & Carroll, Douglas, eds. The Health Psychology of Women. LC 92-49332. 1993. text ed. 38.00 (*3-7186-5335-4*); pap. text ed. 20.00 (*3-7186-5336-2*) Gordon & Breach.

Niven, David, jt. auth. see Hilbert, Robert.

Niven, Ivan. Irrational Numbers. (Carus Monograph: No. 11). 164p. 1956. 28.00 (*0-88385-011-7*) Math Assn.

— The Mathematics of Choice. LC 65-17470. (New Mathematical Library: No. 15). 202p. 1975. pap. 16.00 (*0-88385-615-8*) Math Assn.

— Maxima & Minima Without Calculus. LC 80-81045. (Dolciani Mathematical Expositions Ser.: Vol. 6). 323p. (C). 1982. 20.00 (*0-88385-306-X*) Math Assn.

— Numbers: Rational & Irrational. LC 61-6226. (New Mathematical Library: No. 1). 140p. 1961. pap. 18.00 (*0-88385-601-8*) Math Assn.

Niven, Ivan, et al. An Introduction to the Theory of Numbers. 5th ed. 529p. 1991. Net. text ed. write for info. (*0-471-62546-9*) Wiley.

Niven, John. Coming of the Civil War, 1837-1861. Franklin, John H. & Eisenstadt, A. S., eds. (American History Ser.). 192p. (C). 1990. pap. text ed. write for info. (*0-88295-861-5*) Harlan Davidson.

— Gideon Welles: Lincoln's Secretary of Navy. LC 73-82671. (Illus.). 696p. 1994. pap. 17.95 (*0-8071-1912-1*) La State U Pr.

— John C. Calhoun & the Price of Union: A Biography. LC 88-11775. (Southern Biography Ser.). (C). 1993. pap. 12.95 (*0-8071-1858-3*) La State U Pr.

— Martin Van Buren: The Romantic Age of American Politics. (Illus.). 1983. 45.00 (*0-19-503238-1*) OUP.

— Niven: The Family of Niven, with Biographical Sketches & the Voyages, Letters & Diaries of Capt. John Niven. 252p. 1992. reprint ed. lib. bdg. 47.00 (*0-8328-2394-5*); reprint ed. pap. 37.00 (*0-8328-2395-3*) Higginson Bk Co.

— Salmon P. Chase: A Study in Paradox. (Illus.). 544p. 1995. 35.00 (*0-19-504653-6*) OUP.

Niven, John, et al, eds. The Salmon P. Chase Papers Vol. 1: Journals, 1829-1872. LC 93-16217. (Illus.). 880p. 1993. lib. bdg. 35.00 (*0-87338-472-5*) Kent St U Pr.

— The Salmon P. Chase Papers Vol. 2: Correspondence, 1823-1857. LC 94-16217. (Illus.). 520p. 1995. text ed. 35.00x (*0-87338-508-X*) Kent St U Pr.

Niven, Larry. Crashlander. 1994. mass mkt. 4.99 (*0-345-38168-8*, Del Rey) Ballantine.

— Flatlander: The Collected Tales of Gil "The Arm" Hamilton. 1995. mass mkt. 5.99 (*0-345-39480-1*, Del Rey) Ballantine.

— A Gift from Earth. 256p. 1987. pap. 3.95 (*0-345-35051-0*, Del Rey) Ballantine.

— The Gripping Hand. 1994. mass mkt. 5.99 (*0-671-79574-0*) PB.

— The Integral Trees. 1985. mass mkt. 4.95 (*0-345-32065-4*, Del Rey) Ballantine.

— Limits. 256p. 1985. mass mkt. 4.95 (*0-345-32142-1*, Del Rey) Ballantine.

— Long Arm of Gil Hamilton. 1986. pap. 3.95 (*0-345-34238-0*, Del Rey) Ballantine.

— The Magic Goes Away. 224p. 1985. mass mkt. 4.99 (*0-441-51554-1*) Ace Bks.

— Man Kzin Wars IV. 320p. 1991. mass mkt. 4.95 (*0-671-72079-1*) Baen Bks.

— Man-Kzin Wars V. 336p. 1992. mass mkt. 5.99 (*0-671-72137-2*) Baen Bks.

— N-Space. 704p. 1991. mass mkt. 5.99 (*0-8125-1001-1*) Tor Bks.

— Neutron Star. 1986. mass mkt. 4.95 (*0-345-33694-1*, Del Rey) Ballantine.

— Niven's Laws. 108p. 1984. 12.00 (*0-913896-24-1*) Owlswick Pr.

— Playgrounds of the Mind. 704p. 1992. mass mkt. 5.99 (*0-8125-1695-8*) Tor Bks.

— Protector. 224p. (Orig.). 1987. mass mkt. 4.95 (*0-345-35312-9*, Del Rey) Ballantine.

— Ringworld. 352p. (Orig.). 1985. mass mkt. 5.95 (*0-345-33392-6*, Del Rey) Ballantine.

— The Ringworld Engineers. 368p. 1985. mass mkt. 4.95 (*0-345-33430-2*, Del Rey) Ballantine.

— The Smoke Ring. 336p. 1988. mass mkt. 4.95 (*0-345-30257-5*, Del Rey) Ballantine.

— Tales of Known Space: The Universe of Larry Niven. 256p. (Orig.). 1985. mass mkt. 4.95 (*0-345-33469-8*, Del Rey) Ballantine.

— The Time of the Warlock. LC 84-51291. (Illus.). 1984. 20.00 (*0-916595-01-3*) SteelDragon Pr.

— World of Ptavvs. 192p. 1986. mass mkt. 4.99 (*0-345-34508-8*, Del Rey) Ballantine.

— A World Out of Time. 1986. mass mkt. 4.95 (*0-345-33696-8*, Del Rey) Ballantine.

Niven, Larry, creator. Man-Kzin Wars VI. 416p. (Orig.). 1994. mass mkt. 5.99 (*0-671-87607-4*) Baen Bks.

— Man-Kzin Wars VII. 352p. 1995. mass mkt. 5.99 (*0-671-87670-8*) Baen Bks.

Niven, Larry, ed. The Magic May Return. 256p. 1983. mass mkt. 4.99 (*0-441-51549-5*) Ace Bks.

Niven, Larry & Barnes, Steve. Dream Park II: The Barsoom Project. 1989. mass mkt. 4.99 (*0-441-16712-8*) Ace Bks.

Niven, Larry & Barnes, Steven. Achilles' Choice. 1992. mass mkt. 4.99 (*0-8125-1083-6*) Tor Bks.

— The California Voodoo Game. 1992. mass mkt. 5.99 (*0-345-38148-3*, Del Rey) Ballantine.

— The Descent of Anansi. 1991. pap. 3.95 (*0-8125-1292-8*) Tor Bks.

— Dream Park. 448p. 1982. mass mkt. 5.50 (*0-441-16730-6*) Ace Bks.

Niven, Larry & Byrne, John. Green Lantern: Ganthet's Tale. O'Neil, Dennis, ed. 64p. 1992. pap. 5.95 (*1-56389-026-7*) DC Comics.

Niven, Larry & Pournelle, Jerry. Footfall. 1986. mass mkt. 5.95 (*0-345-32344-0*, Del Rey) Ballantine.

— Inferno. Stern, Dave, ed. 240p. 1988. mass mkt. 5.99 (*0-671-67055-7*) PB.

— The Legacy of Heorot. Stern, Dave, ed. 400p. 1989. mass mkt. 5.99 (*0-671-69532-0*) PB.

— Lucifer's Hammer. 1985. mass mkt. 5.95 (*0-449-20813-3*, Crest) Fawcett.

— The Mote in God's Eye. Stern, Dave, ed. 576p. 1991. mass mkt. 5.99 (*0-671-74192-6*) PB.

— Oath of Fealty. Stern, Dave, ed. 1984. mass mkt. 5.99 (*0-671-53227-8*) PB.

***Niven, Larry & Pournelle, Larry.** The Mote in God's Eye. 480p. 1993. 9.98 (*1-56865-054-X*, GuildAmerica) Dblday Bk Music.

Niven, Larry, jt. auth. see Gerrold, David.

***Niven, Larry, et al.** Beowulf's Children. 1995. 23.95 (*0-312-85522-2*) Tor Bks.

— Fallen Angels. 384p. (Orig.). 1991. mass mkt. 5.95 (*0-671-72052-X*) Baen Bks.

— The Man-Kzin Wars. 304p. 1991. reprint ed. mass mkt. 5.99 (*0-671-72076-7*) Baen Bks.

— Man-Kzin Wars II. 320p. 1990. mass mkt. 5.99 (*0-671-72036-8*) Baen Bks.

— Man-Kzin Wars III. 320p. 1990. mass mkt. 5.99 (*0-671-72008-2*) Baen Bks.

Niven, Marian. The Altar & the Crown. LC 73-175112. (Seekers Ser.: Pt. I). 413p. 1971. 10.00 (*0-8164-0099-7*) Univ South Pr.

— A Doctor of Souls. LC 77-80171. (Seekers Ser.: Pt. III). 356p. 1977. 10.00 (*0-8164-0098-9*) Univ South Pr.

— The Inheritors. LC 77-80170. (Seekers Ser.: Pt. II). 252p. 1977. 10.00 (*0-8164-0097-0*) Univ South Pr.

— Melody Unheard. 296p. 1980. 10.00 (*0-8164-9217-4*) Univ South Pr.

Niven, Mary. Flanders Lace. (Illus.). 1988. 29.95 (*0-85219-691-1*) Branford.

Niven, Mary M. Personnel Management, Nineteen Thirteen to Nineteen Sixty-Three: The Growth of Personnel Management & the Development of the Institute. 174p. (C). 1978. 50.00 (*0-85292-199-3*) St Mut.

Niven, Neil. Health Psychology. 396p. 1989. pap. text ed. 26.00 (*0-443-03665-9*) Churchill.

— Health Psychology: An Introduction for Nurses & Other Health Care Professionals. LC 94-8465. 1994. write for info. (*0-443-04810-X*) Churchill.

Niven, Penelope. Carl Sandburg: A Biography. (Illus.). 864p. 1994. 19.95 (*0-252-02115-0*) U of Ill Pr.

Niven, Penelope, jt. auth. see Jones, James E.

Nivens, Beatryce. How to Choose a Career. (No Nonsense Career Guide Ser.). (Orig.). 1991. pap. 4.95 (*0-681-41045-0*) Longmeadow Pr.

— How to Re-enter the Work Force. (No Nonsense Career Guide Ser.). (Orig.). 1991. pap. 4.95 (*0-681-41046-9*) Longmeadow Pr.

— HT Reenter the Work Force. 1993. pap. 4.95 (*0-681-41389-1*) Longmeadow Pr.

Niver, Anthony. Gillnets & Gillnet Fishing. Wendes, ed. (Illus.). 144p. 1986. lib. bdg. write for info. (*0-318-60954-1*) Comtech Pubns.

***Niver, Kemp.** The First Twenty Years, a Segment of Film History. rev. ed. (Illus.). 176p. Date not set. 10.00 (*0-614-07425-8*) Historical Films.

***Niver, Kemp R.** D. W. Griffith: His Biograph Films in Perspective. (Illus.). 190p. Date not set. 15.00 (*0-614-07427-4*) Historical Films.

— D. W. Griffith: His Biograph Films in Perspective. LC 74-81838. (Illus.). 190p. 1974. 15.00 (*0-913986-06-2*) Renovare Co.

— D. W. Griffith's "The Battle at Elderbush Gulch" LC 72-85599. (Illus.). 1972. 7.50 (*0-913986-04-6*) Renovare Co.

— D. W. Griffith's the Battle at Elderbush Gulch. Date not set. 7.50 (*0-614-07428-2*) Historical Films.

— The Early Motion Pictures: The Paper Print Collection in the Library of Congress. Bergsten, Bebe, ed. LC 84-600185. 509p. 1985. 24.00 (*0-8444-0463-2*, 030-001-00110-5) Lib Congress.

— The First Twenty Years: A Segment of Film History. 2nd rev. ed. LC 68-58700. (Illus.). 176p. 1979. 10.00 (*0-913986-01-1*) Renovare Co.

— Klaw & Erlanger: Famous Plays in Pictures. (Illus.). 177p. Date not set. 15.00 (*0-614-07429-0*) Historical Films.

— Klaw & Erlanger: Famous Plays in Pictures. LC 75-44556. (Illus.). 177p. 1976. 15.00 (*0-913986-07-0*) Renovare Co.

— Mary Pickford: Comedienne. LC 72-103050. (Illus.). 156p. 1969. 10.00 (*0-913986-02-X*) Renovare Co.

— Mary Pickford, Comedienne. (Illus.). 156p. Date not set. 10.00 (*0-614-07430-4*) Historical Films.

Nivison, David S. The Life & Thought of Chang Hseuh-ch'eng (1738-1801) ix, 336p. 1966. 45.00 (*0-8047-0230-6*) Stanford U Pr.

Nivison, David S. & Wright, Arthur F., eds. Confucianism in Action. LC 59-7433. xiv, 390p. 1959. 47.50 (*0-8047-0554-2*) Stanford U Pr.

Nivola, Pietro S. The Politics of Energy Conservation. LC 85-48265. 294p. 1986. 32.95 (*0-8157-6088-4*); pap. 12.95 (*0-8157-6087-6*) Brookings.

— Regulating Unfair Trade. 284p. (C). 1993. 31.95 (*0-8157-6090-6*); pap. 12.95 (*0-8157-6089-2*) Brookings.

***Nivola, Pietro S. & Crandall, Robert W.** The Extra Mile: Rethinking Energy Policy for Automotive Transportation. 200p. (C). 1995. 31.95x (*0-8157-6092-2*); pap. 12.95x (*0-8157-6091-4*) Brookings.

Nivola, Pietro S. & Rosenbloom, David H., eds. Classic Readings in American Politics. 2nd ed. LC 88-63045. 523p. (C). 1989. pap. text ed. 19.00 (*0-312-02014-7*); pap. text ed. 0.59 (*0-312-02527-0*) St Martin.

Nivre, Joakim. Situations, Meaning & Communication: A Situation Theoretic Approach to Meaning in Language & Communication. (Gothenburg Monographs in Linguistics: No. 11). 238p. (Orig.). 1992. pap. 58.50x (*0-685-65633-0*, Pub. by Almqv & Wiksell SW) Coronet Bks.

Niwa, Fumio. Buddha Tree. LC 74-15259. 380p. 1971. pap. 12.95 (*0-8048-0995-X*) C E Tuttle.

— Buddha Tree. Strong, Kenneth, tr. 1966. 25.00 (*0-7206-1125-3*) Dufour.

Niwa, Kiyoshi. Knowledge Based Risk Management in Engineering: Case Study in Human Computer Cooperative Systems. (Engineering Management Ser.). 132p. 1989. text ed. 49.95 (*0-471-62893-X*) Wiley.

Niwa, S., et al, eds. Biomechanics in Orthopedics. LC 92-49957. 1993. write for info. (*4-431-70108-7*); write for info. (*3-540-70108-7*); 165.00 (*0-387-70108-7*) Spr-Verlag.

Niwano, Nichiko. The Inward Path. 168p. (Orig.). 1990. pap. 5.95 (*4-333-01422-0*, Pub. by Kosei Pub Co JA) C E Tuttle.

— Modern Meditations: A Buddhist Sampler. 152p. 1992. pap. 5.95 (*4-333-01477-8*, Pub. by Kosei Pub Co JA) C E Tuttle.

— My Father My Teacher: A Spiritual Journey. Gage, Richard L., tr. 144p. (Orig.). 1982. pap. 5.95 (*4-333-01095-0*, Pub. by Kosei Pub Co JA) C E Tuttle.

Niwano, Nikkyo. A Buddhist Approach to Peace. Nezu, Masuo, tr. (Illus.). 162p. 1977. 10.95 (*4-333-00308-3*, Pub. by Kosei Pub Co JA) C E Tuttle.

— A Guide to the Threefold Lotus Sutra. Langston, Eugene, tr. Orig. Title: Hokke-Sambu-Kyo-Nyumon. 168p. 1981. pap. 5.95 (*4-333-01025-X*, Pub. by Kosei Pub Co JA) C E Tuttle.

— Lifetime Beginner: An Autobiography. Gage, Richard L., tr. LC 79-374242. Orig. Title: Shoshin Issho & Niwano Nikkyo Jiden. (Illus.). 300p. 1990. 19.95 (*4-333-00336-9*, Pub. by Kosei Pub Co JA) C E Tuttle.

— The Meaningful Life. Gage, Richard L., tr. Orig. Title: Ningen No Ikigai. 126p. 1982. pap. 4.95 (*4-333-01027-6*, Pub. by Kosei Pub Co JA) C E Tuttle.

— The Richer Life. Gage, Richard L., tr. Orig. Title: Ningen Rashiku Ikiru. 138p. 1979. pap. 4.95 (*4-333-00351-2*, Pub. by Kosei Pub Co JA) C E Tuttle.

— Shakyamuni Buddha: A Narrative Biography. rev. ed. Miyasaka, Kojiro, tr. LC 80-154779. Orig. Title: Bukkyo No Inochi Hokekyo. (Illus.). 128p. 1980. pap. 4.95 (*4-333-01001-2*, Pub. by Kosei Pub Co JA) C E Tuttle.

— The Wholesome Family Life. Alexander, Joy, tr. Orig. Title: Ningen o Sodateru Kokoro. 182p. 1982. pap. 5.95 (*4-333-01026-8*, Pub. by Kosei Pub Co JA) C E Tuttle.

Nix. Urban Storm Modeling & Stimulation. 1994. 69.95 (*0-87371-527-6*) Lewis Pubs.

Nix, Don & Spiro, Rand, eds. Cognition, Education, & Multimedia: Exploring Ideas in High Technology. 232p. 1990. 49.95 (*0-8058-0036-0*) L Erlbaum Assocs.

Nix, Eileen, jt. auth. see Anderson, Alan H.

Nix, Evett D. Oklahombres, Particularly the Wilder Ones: Particularly the Wilder Ones. LC 92-37966. xxxiv, 316p. 1993. pap. 12.95 (*0-8032-8366-0*, Bison Books) U of Nebr Pr.

Nix, Garth. The Ragwitch. 320p. (J). 1995. pap. 3.99 (*0-8125-3506-5*) Tor Bks.

Nix, Gary W., ed. The Rights of the Hearing-Impaired Child. LC 77-85240. 1977. 2.95 (*0-88200-112-4*, P5543) Alexander Graham.

Nix, H. A. & Elliott, M. A., eds. Managing Aquatic Ecosystems. 174p. (C). 1975. text ed. 100.00 (*0-909436-01-0*, Pub. by Surrey Beatty & Sons AT) St Mut.

***Nix, Jacob.** The Sioux Uprising in Minnesota, 1862: Jacob Nix's Eyewitness History. Tolzmann, Don H., ed. & tr. by. Steinhauser, Gretchen & Reichmann, Eberhard, trs. (Illus.). xxii, 165p. (ENG & GER.). 1994. reprint ed. pap. text ed. 12.80 (*1-880788-02-0*) MKGAC & IGHS.

Nix, Jan. The Book of Regional American Cooking: Southwest. 120p. 1993. pap. 11.95 (*1-55788-074-3*, HP Books) Berkley Pub.

— Filo! Appetizers, Entrees, & Desserts. (Illus.). 142p. (Orig.). 1991. 20.95 (*0-89594-515-0*); pap. 8.95 (*0-89594-516-9*) Crossing Pr.

***Nix, Janeth J. & Smith, Margaret A.** Zinfandel Cookbook: Food to Go with California's Heritage Wine. Braasch, Barbara J., ed. (Illus.). 112p. (Orig.). 1994. pap. text ed. 14.95 (*0-9642901-0-3*) Toyon Hill Pr.

Nix, John, et al. Land & Estate Management. 225p. (C). 1981. text ed. 190.00 (*1-85341-038-1*, Pub. by Surrey Beatty & Sons AT) St Mut.

Nix, Neeleke, ed. see Parker-Fairbanks, Dixie, et al.

Nix, Nelleke. Nineteen Forty-Nineteen Forty-Five Remembered: 1940-1945 Translated from My Diary & Retold. (Illus.). 40p. 1992. 300.00 (*1-881067-01-7*); teacher ed 60.00 (*1-881067-04-1*); lib. bdg. 200.00 (*1-881067-03-3*); pap. 200.00 (*1-881067-00-9*); 280.00 (*1-881067-02-5*) N Nelleke Studio.

Nix, Rebekah, jt. auth. see Parker, Sue.

Nix, Shann. Wildcatting. 1994. mass mkt. 5.99 (*0-345-38754-6*) Ballantine.

— Wildcatting. LC 92-19020. 1993. 21.95 (*0-385-42411-6*) Doubleday.

Nix, Stephan J., ed. see Symposium on Monitoring, Modeling, & Mediating Water Quality Staff.

Nix, Susan W., jt. auth. see Nix, William E.

Nix, Verolga & Cleveland, Jefferson, eds. Songs of Zion. LC 81-8039. 352p. (Orig.). 1981. pap. 11.95 (*0-687-39121-0*); pap. 8.95 (*0-687-39120-2*) Abingdon.

Nix, W. D., et al, eds. Thin Films: Stresses & Mechanical Properties III. (Symposium Proceedings Ser.: Vol. 239). 1992. text ed. 66.00 (*1-55899-133-6*) Materials Res.

Nix, William E. & Nix, Susan W. The Irwin Guide to Stock Index Futures & Options. LC 83-73716. 275p. 1984. 50.00 (*0-87094-482-7*) Irwin Prof Pubng.

Nix, William E., jt. auth. see Geisler, Norman L.

Nixey, C. & Grey, T. C., eds. Recent Advances in Turkey Science. (Illus.). 373p. 1989. text ed. 99.95 (*0-408-00971-3*) Buttrwrth-Heinemann.

Nixon. Edgar Winners Collection. (J). Date not set. 14.00 (*0-06-023650-7*); lib. bdg. 13.89 (*0-06-023651-5*) HarpC Child Bks.

— Essentials of Pediatric Surgery. 1992. 75.00 (*0-7506-0013-6*) Buttrwrth-Heinemann.

— If You Were a Writer. (J). 1995. pap. 4.95 (*0-689-71900-0*, Aladdin Paperbacks) S&S Childrens.

— Organizational Structures of Companies, No. 1. 300p. 1992. 135.00 (*0-8103-8497-3*, 101446) Gale.

— Transputer & Occam Developments. LC 95-75772. (Transputer & Occam Engineering Ser.). Date not set. 69.50 (*90-5199-222-X*) IOS Press.

Nixon, jt. auth. see Weigel, Al.

Nixon, et al. New York Environmental Law Handbook. 3rd ed. (State Environmental Law Ser.). 368p. 1993. pap. text ed. 79.00 (*0-86587-332-1*) Gov Insts.

***Nixon, Alan J.** Equine Fracture Repair. LC 94-32748. (Illus.). 352p. 1995. text ed. write for info. (*0-7216-6754-6*) Saunders.

Nixon, Anthony. The Three English Brothers: Sir T. Sheley His Travels, Sir A. Sherley His Ambassage to the Christian Princes, Master R. Sheley His Wars Against the Turkes. LC 72-26473. (English Experience Ser.: No. 270). 80p. 1970. reprint ed. 30.00 (*90-221-0270-X*) Walter J Johnson.

***Nixon, Barbara B.** Behind the Question: Listen for Success in Job Interviews. 1995. 18.95 (*0-614-05150-9*); 18.95 (*0-614-05418-4*) SPECTRA Inc.

***Nixon, Bess S.** Triangle. 100p. Date not set. pap. 7.95 (*0-7610-0432-7*) NW Pub.

Nixon, Bruce, ed. New Approaches to Management Development. 130p. 1981. text ed. 49.95 (*0-566-02290-7*) Ashgate Pub Co.

Nixon, C. E., tr. & intro. Pacatus: Panegyric to the Emperor Theodosius. (Translated Texts for Historians Ser.). 128p. (Orig.). 1987. reprint ed. pap. text ed. 14.95 (*0-85323-076-5*, Pub. by Liverpool Univ Pr UK) U of Pa Pr.

Nixon, C. E. & Rodgers, Barbara S. In Praise of Later Roman Emperors: The Panegyrici Latini: Introduction, Translation, & Historical Commentary with the Latin Text of R.A.B. Mynors. LC 93-27872. (Transformation of the Classical Heritage: Vol. 21). (ENG.). 1994. 70.00 (*0-520-08326-1*) U CA Pr.

Nixon, D., ed. Unsteady Transonic Aerodynamics. (PAAS Ser.: Vol. 120). 385p. 1989. 69.95 (*0-930403-52-5*) AIAA.

Nixon, Daniel W. Cancer Recovery Eating Plan: The Right Foods to Help Fuel Your Recovery. 1994. pap. 25.00 (*0-8129-1983-1*, Times Bks) Random.

— Chemoprevention of Cancer. 144p. 1994. 99.95 (*0-8493-6850-2*, 6850) CRC Pr.

Nixon, David. The Year of the Locust. 138p. (Orig.). 1980. pap. 6.95 (*0-8341-0675-2*) Beacon Hill.

Nixon, David, ed. Transonic Aerodynamics. LC 82-4027. (PAAS Ser.: Vol. 81). (Illus.). 669p. 1982. 79.95 (*0-915928-65-5*) AIAA.

Nixon, Debra A., see Debra Ann, pseud..

Nixon, Dennis W. Marine & Coastal Law: Cases & Materials. LC 93-30986. 392p. 1994. text ed. 65.00 (*0-275-93763-1*, Praeger Pubs) Greenwood.

Nixon, Don W., jt. auth. see Gaddy, C. Welton.

Nixon, E. Anna. A Century of Planting: A History of the American Friends Mission in India. LC 85-72070. (Illus.). 493p. (Orig.). 1985. 16.95 (*0-913342-55-6*); pap. 11.95 (*0-913342-54-8*) Barclay Pr.

— On the Cutting Edge. LC 87-72972. (Illus.). 325p. 1987. pap. 11.95 (*0-913342-61-0*) Barclay Pr.

Nixon, Edgar B., ed. Franklin D. Roosevelt & Conservation, 1911-1945, 2 vols., 1. LC 72-2861. (Use & Abuse of America's Natural Resources Ser.). 1342p. 1972. reprint ed. 39.95 (*0-405-04526-3*) Ayer.

— Franklin D. Roosevelt & Conservation, 1911-1945, 2 vols., 2. LC 72-2861. (Use & Abuse of America's Natural Resources Ser.). 1342p. 1972. reprint ed. 44.95 (*0-405-04527-1*) Ayer.

— Franklin D. Roosevelt & Conservation, 1911-1945, 2 vols., Set. LC 72-2861. (Use & Abuse of America's Natural Resources Ser.). 1342p. 1972. reprint ed. 85.95 (*0-405-04525-5*) Ayer.

Nixon, Edgar B., ed. see Roosevelt, Franklin D.

***Nixon, Frank, intro.** Japan Quality Control Circles: Quality Control Circle Case Studies. 3rd ed. (Illus.). 208p. 1984. pap. text ed. 19.75 (*92-833-1022-5*, 310225, Pub. by APO JA) Qual Resc.

Nixon, G. The Geology of Iztaccihuatl Volcano & Adjacent Areas of the Sierra Nevada & Valley of Mexico. (Special Paper Ser.: No. 219). 45p. 1989. pap. 8.00 (*0-8137-2219-5*) Geol Soc.

Nixon, Graham & Honey, John, eds. An Historic Tongue: Studies in English Linguistics in Memory of Barbara Strang. 350p. 1988. lib. bdg. 75.00 (*0-415-00310-5*) Routledge.

Nixon, Herman C. Lower Piedmont Country. LC 78-142685. (Essay Index Reprint Ser.). 1977. 20.95 (*0-8369-2064-3*) Ayer.

An Asterisk (*) at the beginning of an entry indicates that the title is appearing in BIP for the first time.

— Lower Piedmont Country: The Uplands of the Deep South. LC 83-24164. (Library of Alabama Classics). (Illus.). xlvii, 296p. 1984. reprint ed. pap. 14.50 (*0-8173-0214-X*) U of Ala Pr.

Nixon, Howard L., II. Mainstreaming & the American Dream: Sociological Perspectives on Parental Coping with Blind & Visually Impaired Children. LC 91-6866. 256p. 1992. 29.95 (*0-89128-191-6*) Am Foun Blind.

Nixon, Howard L., III. Sport & Social Organization. LC 75-31742. (Studies in Sociology). 64p. 1976. pap. text ed. write for info. (*0-672-61337-9*) Macmillan.

Nixon, Howard L., II. Sport & the American Dream. LC 82-83943. (Illus.). 264p. (Orig.). (C). 1984. pap. 25.00 (*0-88011-112-7*, PNIX0112) Human Kinetics.

***Nixon, Howard L., II & Frey, James H.** A Sociology of Sport. LC 95-15353. 1996. pap. 22.95 (*0-534-24762-8*) Intl Thomson.

Nixon, Howard M., ed. Catalogue of Pepys Library: 6 Bindings. (Illus.). 1970. 171.00 (*0-85991-145-4*) Boydell & Brewer.

Nixon, J. R., ed. see International Symposium on Microencapsulation (2nd: 1974, Chelsea College).

Nixon, Janet J. A Message to the World. 1994. 11.95 (*0-8062-4858-0*) Carlton.

Nixon, Jean L. A Deadly Game of Magic. (J). (gr. 6-12). 1985. mass mkt. 3.99 (*0-440-92102-3*, LFL) Dell.

— A Deadly Game of Magic. LC 83-8379. 148p. (YA). (gr. 7 up). 1983. 13.95 (*0-15-222954-X*, HB Juv Bks) HarBrace.

Nixon, Joan L. And Maggie Makes Three. LC 85-16389. 112p. (J). (gr. 3-7). 1986. 12.95 (*0-15-250355-2*, HB Juv Bks) HarBrace.

— Backstage with a Ghost. LC 94-71793. (Disney Adventures Casebusters Ser.: Bk. 3). (Illus.). 96p. (J). (gr. 2-6). 1995. 13.95 (*0-7868-3048-4*); pap. 3.95 (*0-7868-4025-0*) Disney Pr.

— Beats Me, Claude. (Illus.). (J). (ps-3). 1988. pap. 4.99 (*0-14-050847-3*, Puffin) Puffin Bks.

— Beats Me, Claude. LC 86-5465. (Viking Kestrel Picture Bks.). (Illus.). 32p. (J). (ps-3). 1986. 11.95 (*0-670-80781-8*) Viking Child Bks.

— Before You Were Born. LC 79-91741. (Illus.). 32p. (J). (ps up). 1980. pap. 5.95 (*0-87973-343-8*) Our Sunday Visitor.

— Candidate for Murder. (YA). 1992. pap. 3.99 (*0-440-21212-X*) Dell.

— A Candidate for Murder. large type ed. LC 93-42058. 1994. pap. 15.95 (*0-7862-0142-8*) Thorndike Pr.

— Caught in the Act. (YA). (gr. 7 up). 1989. mass mkt. 3.99 (*0-553-27912-2*, Starfire) Bantam.

— Check in to Danger. LC 94-71794. (Disney Adventures Casebusters Ser.: Bk. 4). (Illus.). 96p. (J). (gr. 2-6). 1995. 13.95 (*0-7868-3049-2*); pap. 3.95 (*0-7868-4026-9*) Disney Pr.

— The Christmas Eve Mystery. Fay, Ann, ed. LC 81-345. (First Read-Alone Mysteries Ser.). (Illus.). 32p. (J). (gr. 1-3). 1981. lib. bdg. 8.95 (*0-8075-1150-1*) A Whitman.

— A Dangerous Promise. LC 94-464. (Orphan Train Adventures Ser.). (J). 1994. 15.95 (*0-385-32073-6*) Delacorte.

— The Dark & Deadly Pool. 196p. (J). (gr. 6 up). 1989. mass mkt. 3.99 (*0-440-20348-1*, LFL) Dell.

— Deadly Promise. (YA). 1993. pap. 3.50 (*0-553-56177-4*) Bantam.

— A Family Apart. (Orphan Train Quartet Ser.: No. 1). 176p. (YA). (gr. 5 up). 1988. mass mkt. 3.99 (*0-553-27478-3*, Starfire) Bantam.

— Fat Chance, Claude. (Illus.). 32p. (J). (ps-3). 1989. pap. 4.99 (*0-14-050679-9*, Puffin) Puffin Bks.

— The Ghosts of Now. 192p. (YA). (gr. 7 up). 1986. pap. 3.50 (*0-440-93115-0*, LFL) Dell.

— The Gift. LC 87-22764. (Illus.). 96p. (J). (gr. 3-7). 1988. reprint ed. pap. 3.95 (*0-689-71217-0*, Aladdin Paperbacks) S&S Childrens.

— The Happy Birthday Mystery. Ann, Fay, ed. LC 79-18362. (First Read-Alone Mysteries Ser.). (Illus.). 32p. (J). (gr. 1-3). 1980. lib. bdg. 8.95 (*0-8075-3150-2*) A Whitman.

— Haunted Island. 128p. (Orig.). (J). (gr. 3-7). 1987. pap. 3.25 (*0-590-43134-X*) Scholastic Inc.

— High Trail To Danger. 1991. 16.00 (*0-553-07314-1*) Bantam.

— High Trail to Danger. (J). (gr. 4-7). 1992. pap. 3.50 (*0-553-29602-7*) Bantam.

— If You Were a Writer. LC 88-402. (Illus.). 32p. (J). (gr. k-3). 1988. text ed. 14.95 (*0-02-768210-2*, Mac Bks Young Read) S&S Childrens.

— In the Face of Danger. (Orphan Train Quartet Ser.: Bk. 3). (YA). (gr. 7 up). 1989. mass mkt. 3.99 (*0-553-28196-8*, Starfire) Bantam.

— The Island of Dangerous Dreams. 196p. (Orig.). (J). (gr. k-12). 1989. pap. 3.50 (*0-440-20258-2*, LFL) Dell.

— Keeping Secrets. LC 94-19682. (Orphan Train Adventures). (J). 1995. 15.95 (*0-385-32139-2*) Delacorte.

— The Kidnapping of Christina Lattimore. 196p. (J). (gr. 7 up). 1992. mass mkt. 3.99 (*0-440-94520-8*, LFL) Dell.

— Land of Dreams. LC 93-8734. (Ellis Island Ser.: Vol. 3). (YA). 1994. 14.95 (*0-385-31170-2*) Delacorte.

— Land of Dreams. (Ellis Island Ser.: No. 3). (YA). 1995. pap. 3.99 (*0-440-21935-3*) Dell.

— Land of Hope. (Ellis Island Novels Ser.: Bk. 1). (YA). 1992. 16.00 (*0-553-08110-1*) Bantam.

— Land of Hope. (Ellis Island Ser.: No. 1). 1993. pap. 3.50 (*0-440-21597-8*) Dell.

— Land of Promise. LC 92-28591. (Ellis Island Novel Ser.: No. 2). (J). (gr. 4-7). 1993. 16.00 (*0-553-08111-X*) Bantam.

— Land of Promise. LC 92-28591. (J). (gr. 5). 1994. mass mkt. 3.99 (*0-440-21904-3*) Dell.

— Legend of Deadman's Mine. LC 94-71792. (Disney Adventures Casebusters Ser.: Bk. 2). (Illus.). 96p. (J). (gr. 2-6). 1995. 13.95 (*0-7868-3047-6*) Disney Pr.

— Legend of Deadman's Mine. LC 94-71792. (Disney Adventures Casebusters Ser.: Bk. 2). (Illus.). 96p. (J). (gr. 2-6). 1995. pap. 3.95 (*0-7868-4019-6*) Disney Pr.

— Maggie, Too. LC 84-19766. 101p. (J). (gr. 3-7). 1985. 11.95 (*0-15-250350-1*, HB Juv Bks) HarBrace.

— The Name of the Game Was Murder. LC 92-8392. (J). 1993. 15.00 (*0-385-30864-7*) Delacorte.

— Name of the Game Was Murder. 1994. mass mkt. 3.99 (*0-440-21916-7*) Dell.

— The Name of the Game Was Murder. large type ed. LC 93-20596. 1993. pap. 15.95 (*1-56054-775-8*) Thorndike Pr.

— The New Year's Mystery. Pacini, Kathy, ed. LC 79-172. (First Read-Alone Mysteries Ser.). (Illus.). 32p. (J). (gr. 1-3). 1979. lib. bdg. 8.95 (*0-8075-5592-4*) A Whitman.

— The Other Side of Dark. (J). 1987. pap. 3.99 (*0-440-96638-8*, LFL) Dell.

— A Place to Belong. (Orphan Train Quartet Ser.: No. 4). (J). 1990. pap. 3.50 (*0-553-28485-1*) Bantam.

— The Seance. 176p. (J). (gr. 7 up). 1981. mass mkt. 3.99 (*0-440-97937-4*, LFL) Dell.

— Secret Silent Screams. (J). (gr. k-8). 1990. pap. 3.99 (*0-440-20539-5*, LFL) Dell.

— Shadowmaker. LC 93-32314. (J). 1994. 14.95 (*0-385-32030-2*) Delacorte.

— Shadowmaker. (YA). (gr. 7 up). 1995. mass mkt. 3.99 (*0-440-21942-6*) Dell.

— Specter. (YA). 1993. pap. 3.99 (*0-440-97740-1*) Dell.

— Spirit Seeker. LC 95-7090. (J). 1995. write for info. (*0-385-32062-0*) Delacorte.

— The Stalker. (J). (gr. 7 up). 1987. mass mkt. 3.99 (*0-440-97753-3*, LFL) Dell.

— Statue Walks at Night. LC 94-71791. (Disney Adventures Casebusters Ser.: Bk. 1). (Illus.). 96p. (J). (gr. 2-6). 1995. 13.95 (*0-7868-3046-8*); pap. 3.95 (*0-7868-4018-8*) Disney Pr.

— The Thanksgiving Mystery. Fay, Ann, ed. LC 79-27346. (First Read-Alone Mysteries Ser.). (Illus.). 32p. (J). (gr. 1-3). 1980. lib. bdg. 8.95 (*0-8075-7820-7*) A Whitman.

— That's the Spirit, Claude. (Illus.). 32p. (J). (gr. k-3). 1994. pap. 4.99 (*0-14-054290-6*) Puffin Bks.

— That's the Spirit, Claude. (Illus.). 32p. (J). (ps-3). 1992. 13.00 (*0-670-83434-3*) Viking Child Bks.

— The Valentine Mystery. Tucker, Kathleen, ed. LC 79-17055. (First Read-Alone Mysteries Ser.). (Illus.). 32p. (J). (gr. 1-3). 1979. lib. bdg. 8.95 (*0-8075-8450-9*) A Whitman.

— The Weekend Was Murder. (YA). 1992. 15.00 (*0-385-30531-1*) Doubleday.

— Weekend Was Murder! (YA). 1994. mass mkt. 3.99 (*0-440-21901-9*) Dell.

— The Weekend Was Murder! large type ed. 225p. 1993. reprint ed. lib. bdg. 15.95 (*1-56054-598-4*) Thorndike Pr.

— When I am Eight. LC 93-20023. (J). (gr. 1-3). 1994. 13.99 (*0-8037-1499-8*) Dial Bks Young.

— When I Am Eight. LC 93-20023. (J). (ps-3). 1994. 14.89 (*0-8037-1500-5*) Dial Bks Young.

— Whispers from the Dead. 192p. (YA). 1991. pap. 3.50 (*0-440-20809-2*, LFL) Dell.

— Will You Give Me a Dream? LC 91-19581. (Illus.). 32p. (J). (ps-1). 1994. text ed. 14.95 (*0-02-768211-0*, Four Winds Pr) S&S Childrens.

— You Bet Your Britches, Claude. (Illus.). 32p. (J). (ps-3). 1991. pap. 3.95 (*0-14-050900-3*, Puffin) Puffin Bks.

Nixon, John S., jt. auth. see Winterowd, W. Ross.

Nixon, Jon. Evaluating the Whole Curriculum. 160p. 1991. 85.00 (*0-335-09457-0*, Open Univ Pr); pap. 32.00 (*0-335-09456-2*, Open Univ Pr) Taylor & Francis.

Nixon, Jon, ed. A Teacher's Guide to Action Research: Evaluation, Enquiry & Development in the Classroom. 209p. 1981. 50.00 (*0-685-11961-0*) Blackwell Pubs.

Nixon, Jon & Ranson, Stewart, eds. Citizenship for Democracy: The Educational Task. 192p. 1994. text ed. 70.00 (*0-304-32765-4*); pap. text ed. 24.95 (*0-304-32764-6*) Cassell.

Nixon, Jude V. Gerald Manley Hopkins & His Contemporaries: Liddon, Newman, Darwin, & Pater. LC 93-28007. (Origins of Modernism Ser.: Vol. 5). 342p. 1993. 51.00 (*0-8153-0386-6*, H1476) Garland.

Nixon, Judith M. Hotel & Restaurant Industries: A Bibliography & Sourcebook. 2nd ed. LC 93-10578. 1993. 44.95 (*0-931682-35-5*) Purdue U Pubns.

— The Hotel & Restaurant Industries: An Information Sourcebook. (Sourcebook Series in Business & Management). 248p. 1988. 43.50 (*0-89774-376-8*) Oryx Pr.

Nixon, Judith M. & Hawbaker, A. Craig, eds. Industry & Company Information: Illustrated Search Strategy & Sources. (Library Research Guide Ser.: No. 10). 1991. pap. 25.00 (*0-87650-287-7*) Pierian.

Nixon, Lois L., jt. auth. see Wear, Delese.

Nixon, Nicholas. People with AIDS. 1991. pap. 25.00 (*0-87923-886-0*) Godine.

Nixon, Nicholas, jt. auth. see Galassi, Peter.

Nixon, P. J. A Glossary of Virginia Words. (Publications of the American Dialect Society: No. 5). 46p. 1946. pap. 4.50 (*0-8173-0605-6*) U of Ala Pr.

Nixon, Pat I. Pat Nixon of Texas: Autobiography of a Doctor. Lang, Herbert H., ed. LC 78-65575. 248p. 1979. 13.50 (*0-89096-072-0*) Tex A&M Univ Pr.

***Nixon, Peter H., ed.** Mantle Xenoliths. fac. ed. LC 86-15705. (Illus.). 895p. 1994. pap. 180.00 (*0-7837-7663-2*, 2047416) Bks Demand.

Nixon, Ralph A., jt. ed. see Banner, Carl D.

Nixon, Regina, jt. auth. see Hill, Robert B.

Nixon, Richard. Beyond Peace. 1994. 23.00 (*0-679-43323-6*) Random.

— Leaders. 1994. lib. bdg. 24.95x (*1-56849-497-1*) Buccaneer Bks.

— Memoirs. 1994. lib. bdg. 39.95x (*1-56849-498-X*) Buccaneer Bks.

— Six Crises. 1994. lib. bdg. 24.95x (*1-56849-499-8*) Buccaneer Bks.

— Speeches. Date not set. write for info. (*0-679-44111-5*) Random.

***Nixon, Richard G.** The Lazy Man's Way to Riche$ 336p. 1995. pap. 14.95 (*0-14-024936-2*, Penguin Bks) Viking Penguin.

— Roadmap to Riches: The Workbook for the Lazy Man's Way to Riches. 143p. 1993. student ed 10.00 (*1-884337-14-7*) F P Pubng.

Nixon, Richard G. & Karbo, Joe. The Lazy Man's Way to Riches: How to Have Everything in the World You Really Want. rev. ed. LC 93-41887. (Illus.). 336p. 1994. pap. 20.00 (*1-884337-11-2*) F P Pubng.

Nixon, Richard M. In the Arena. Rubenstein, Julie, ed. 488p. 1991. reprint ed. pap. 6.99 (*0-671-72934-9*) PB.

— Leaders. (Richard Nixon Library). 1990. pap. 12.95 (*0-671-70618-7*, Touchstone Bks) S&S Trade.

— Nineteen Ninety-Nine: The Global Challenges We Face in the Next Decade. 1988. 100.00 (*0-671-65992-8*) S&S Trade.

— Nineteen Ninety-Nine: Victory Without War. 1989. pap. 10.00 (*0-671-67834-5*) PB.

— Nineteen Ninety-Nine: Victory Without War. 336p. 1988. 19.95 (*0-317-70126-6*) S&S Trade.

— No More Vietnams. 240p. 1986. reprint ed. mass mkt. 4.99 (*0-380-70119-7*) Avon.

— Real Peace - No More Vietnams. (Richard Nixon Library). 1990. pap. 12.95 (*0-671-70620-9*, Touchstone Bks) S&S Trade.

— Real War. (Richard Nixon Library). 1990. pap. 12.95 (*0-671-70617-9*, Touchstone Bks) S&S Trade.

— RN: Memoirs of Richard Nixon. (Richard Nixon Library). 1990. pap. 23.00 (*0-671-70741-8*, Touchstone Bks) S&S Trade.

— Six Crises. 1990. pap. 12.95 (*0-671-70619-5*) S&S Trade.

Nixon, Rob. Homelands, Harlem, & Hollywood: South African Culture & the World Beyond. LC 93-47906. 1994. write for info. (*0-415-90860-4*, Routledge NY); pap. write for info. (*0-415-90861-2*, Routledge NY) Routledge.

— London Calling: V. S. Naipaul, Postcolonial Mandarin. 256p. 1992. 39.95 (*0-19-506717-7*) OUP.

Nixon, Robert. Shades of Autumn. Schmidt, Rosemary J., ed. (Illus.). 36p. (Orig.). (C). 1991. pap. 4.00 (*0-9628611-1-1*) Blue Denim.

Nixon, Robert, jt. auth. see Brown-Nixon, Candace.

Nixon, Sallie. Spiraling: Selected Poems by Sallie Nixon. Campbell, Marybelle, ed. (Persephone Press Poetry Ser.: No. 6). (Illus.). 32p. (Orig.). 1990. pap. 8.95 (*1-879009-00-5*) S P-Persephone Pr.

***Nixon, Tom.** Sell Your Socks Off. 220p. 1995. pap. 14.95 (*1-883629-03-9*) New Mgmt Pub.

Nixon, W. A., et al, eds. Offshore Mechanics & Arctic Engineering 1993, Vol. 4: Arctic-Polar Technology. LC 82-70515. 219p. 1993. pap. 57.50 (*0-7918-0786-X*, G00680) ASME.

Nixon, Wilfred A. Improved Cutting Edges for Ice Removal. 98p. (Orig.). (C). 1993. pap. text ed. 15.00 (*0-309-05605-5*, SHRP-H-346) SHRP.

Nixon, William. Strategic Compromise. 400p. 1990. 19.95 (*1-55972-026-3*, Birch Ln Pr) Carol Pub Group.

Nixson, Frederick, jt. auth. see Colman, David.

Nixson, Frederick, jt. ed. see Cook, Paul.

Niyama, Eisuke. Physical Metallurgy of Cast Iron IV: Conference Proceedings Ser. Ohira, Goro et al, eds. 1990. text ed. 56.00 (*1-55899-090-9*) Materials Res.

Niyekawa, Agnes, jt. auth. see Sikkema, Mildred.

Niyekawa, Agnes M. Minimum Essential Politeness: A Guide to the Japanese Honorific Language. (Illus.). 168p. (Orig.). 1992. pap. text ed. 15.00 (*4-7700-1624-7*) Kodansha.

Niyogi, K. K., jt. ed. see Singh, K. P.

***Nizam-Ud-Din-Wani.** Muslim Rule in Kashmir: 1554 A. D. to 1586 A. D. (C). 1993. 30.00x (*81-7041-831-3*, Pub. by Anmol II) S Asia.

***Nizami.** Haft Paykar: A Medieval Persian Romance. Meisami, Julie S., ed. & tr. by. (World's Classics Ser.). (Illus.). 304p. 1995. pap. 9.95 (*0-19-283184-4*) OUP.

Nizami, Ashraf F. Namaz the Yoga of Islam. (Illus.). xxiii, 46p. 1981. text ed. 5.95 (*0-86590-052-3*, Pub. by Taraporevala II) Apt Bks.

Nizami, Nizam. The Sikandar Nama: E Bara, or Book of Alexander the Great Written AD 1200. Clarke, H. Wilberforce, tr. 857p. reprint ed. text ed. 67.50 (*0-685-13397-4*) Coronet Bks.

Nizamuddin, Mohammed. Contribution to the Marine Algae of Libya Dictyotales. (Bibliotheca Phycologica Ser.: No. 54). (Illus.). 120p. 1982. pap. text ed. 24.00 (*3-7682-1305-6*) Lubrecht & Cramer.

Nizan, Paul. Aden, Arabie. Pinkham, Joan, tr. 159p. 1987. pap. text ed. 12.00 (*0-231-06357-1*) Col U Pr.

— Antoine Bloye: A Novel. LC 72-92034. 255p. reprint ed. pap. 72.70 (*0-7837-3897-8*, 2043745) Bks Demand.

— The Conspiracy. Hoare, Quintin, tr. 256p. 1988. 18.95 (*0-86091-224-8*, Pub. by Verso UK) Routledge Chapman & Hall.

— La Conspiration. (FRE.). 1973. pap. 11.95 (*0-7859-4023-5*) Fr & Eur.

— The Trojan Horse. 1975. reprint ed. 35.00 (*0-86527-317-0*) Fertig.

Nizel & Papas. Nutrition in Clinical Dentistry. 3rd ed. 400p. 1989. pap. text ed. 41.95 (*0-7216-2423-5*) Saunders.

Nizer, Louis. Catspaw: One Man's Ordeal by Trials. 1992. 21.95 (*1-55611-276-9*) D I Fine.

— Catspaw: The Famed Trial Attorney's Heroic Defense of a Man Unjustly Accused. 304p. 1993. pap. 11.95 (*0-88184-956-1*) Carroll & Graf.

— My Life in Court. 1993. reprint ed. lib. bdg. 29.95x (*1-56849-145-X*) Buccaneer Bks.

— New Courts of Industry: Self-Regulation under the Motion Picture Code, Including an Analysis of the Code. LC 70-160243. (Moving Pictures Ser.). 344p. 1971. reprint ed. lib. bdg. 38.95 (*0-89198-044-X*) Ozer.

Nizetic, B. Z., et al, eds. Scientific Approaches to Health & Health Care. 186p. 1986. pap. 9.00 (*92-890-1032-0*) World Health.

Nizetich, Andre. Teaching Hair Coloring: A Step-by-Step Guide to Building Props. LC 92-35110. 1993. pap. text ed. 19.95 (*1-56253-072-0*) Milady Pub.

Nizhny, Vladimir. Lessons with Eisenstein. LC 78-27394. (Quality Paperbacks Ser.). 1979. reprint ed. pap. 9.95 (*0-306-80100-0*) Da Capo.

Niznik. Dopamine Receptors & Transporters, Pharmacology, Structure & Function: Pharmacology, Structure & Function. LC 93-42705. 712p. 1994. 195.00 (*0-8247-9158-4*) Dekker.

Nizolek, Jacquelyn, et al, eds. Retail Tenant Directory, 1989. rev. ed. 1989. 265.00 (*0-911790-12-8*, Pub. by Seaby UK) Numismatic Fine Arts.

Nizri, Osnath, ed. see Pollack, Aharon.

Nizzoli, F, et al, eds. Dynamical Phenomena at Surfaces, Intersurfaces & Superlattices, Vol. 3. (Surface Sciences Ser.: Vol. 3). (Illus.). 350p. 1985. 71.00 (*0-387-15505-8*) Spr-Verlag.

Njaka, E. N. Igbo Political Culture. LC 73-80120. (Studies in Political Culture & National Integration). 187p. reprint ed. pap. 53.30 (*0-8357-9460-1*, 2016077) Bks Demand.

Njama, Karari, jt. auth. see Barnett, Don.

Njegos, Petar P. The Mountain Wreath. Mihailovich, Vasa D., ed. & tr. by. LC 86-21998. xix, 220p. 1986. pap. 22.50 (*1-884445-18-7*) C Schlacks Pub.

Njeri, Itabari. Every Good-Bye Ain't Gone. LC 90-50212. 256p. 1991. pap. 11.00 (*0-679-73242-X*, Vin) Random.

Njeuma, Martin. Introduction to the History of Cameroon: Nineteenth & Twentieth Centuries. LC 89-10420. 224p. 1990. text ed. 55.00 (*0-312-03644-2*) St Martin.

NJIT Staff. Physics Laboratory Manual. 256p. (C). 1993. spiral bd. 19.95 (*0-8403-8875-6*) Kendall-Hunt.

Njogu, A. R., jt. auth. see Tukei, P. M.

***Njoku, John E.** An Allegorical Story of the Restoration of African Democracy: The Strong Versus the Weak. LC 94-25202. (Illus.). 162p. 1995. text ed. 79.95 (*0-7734-8973-8*) E Mellen.

— The Dawn of African Women. LC 77-154067. 96p. reprint ed. pap. 27.40 (*0-317-29160-2*, 2055588) Bks Demand.

— Short Stories of the Traditional People of Nigeria: African Folks, Back Home. LC 91-38739. (Studies in African Literature: Vol. 7). 172p. 1992. lib. bdg. 79.95 (*0-7734-9631-9*) E Mellen.

— Traditionalism vs Modernism at Death: Allegorical Tales of Africa. LC 88-14075. (African Studies: Vol. 11). 150p. 1989. lib. bdg. 69.95 (*0-88946-188-0*) E Mellen.

Njoku, Scholastica I. Dog What? (Ngozi of Africa Ser.: No. 2). (Illus.). 49p. (J). (gr. k up). 1989. per. 6.95 (*0-9617833-1-1*) S I NJOKU.

— The Miracle of a Christmas Doll. (Ngozi of Africa Ser.: No. 1). (Illus.). 29p. (J). (gr. k up). 1986. per. 5.95 (*0-9617833-0-3*) S I NJOKU.

Njolstad, Olav, jt. ed. see Gleditsch, Nils P.

Njozi, Hamza M. The Sources of the Quaran. 96p. 1991. pap. write for info. (*0-318-72150-3*) Wamy Intl.

NK Lawn & Garden Co. Staff. Beautiful Roses. (NK Lawn & Garden Step-by-Step Visual Guides Ser.). (Illus.). 80p. (Orig.). 1992. pap. 6.95 (*0-380-76663-9*) Avon.

— Caring for Lawns. (NK Lawn & Garden Step-by-Step Visual Guides Ser.). (Illus.). 80p. (Orig.). 1992. pap. 6.95 (*0-380-76664-7*) Avon.

— Garden Fresh Vegetables. (NK Lawn & Garden Step-by-Step Visual Guides Ser.). (Illus.). 80p. (Orig.). 1992. pap. 6.95 (*0-380-76662-0*) Avon.

— Improving Garden Soils. (NK Lawn & Garden Step-by-Step Visual Guides Ser.). (Illus.). 80p. (Orig.). 1992. pap. 6.95 (*0-380-76666-3*) Avon.

— Landscape Gardening. (NK Lawn & Garden Step-by-Step Visual Guides Ser.). (Illus.). 80p. (Orig.). 1992. pap. 6.95 (*0-380-76665-5*) Avon.

— My First Garden Book. (NK Lawn & Garden Step-by-Step Visual Guides Ser.). (Illus.). 80p. (Orig.). (J). 1992. pap. 6.95 (*0-380-76667-1*) Avon.

NK Lawn & Garden Staff. Beautiful Roses. (Step-by-Step Visual Guide Ser.). 80p. 1991. pap. 7.95 (*1-880281-01-5*) NK Lawn & Garden.

— Caring for Lawns. (Step-by-Step Visual Guide Ser.). 80p. 1991. pap. 7.95 (*1-880281-04-X*) NK Lawn & Garden.

— Garden Fresh Vegetables. (Step-by-Step Visual Guide Ser.). 80p. 1991. pap. 7.95 (*1-880281-00-7*) NK Lawn & Garden.

— Improving Garden Soils. (Step-by-Step Visual Guide Ser.). 80p. 1991. pap. 7.95 (*1-880281-03-1*) NK Lawn & Garden.

— My First Garden Book. (Step-by-Step Visual Guide Ser.). 80p. 1991. pap. 7.95 (*1-880281-05-8*) NK Lawn & Garden.

— Planning Landscapes. (Step-by-Step Visual Guide Ser.). 80p. 1991. pap. 7.95 (*1-880281-02-3*) NK Lawn & Garden.

NKCA Int. Veld Staff & Altes, A. Korthals. The Forgotten Battle: Overloon & the Maas Salient, 1944-45. (Illus.). 288p. 1995. 24.95 (*1-885119-03-8*) Sarpedon.

Nkemdirim, Bernard. Social Change & Political Violence in Colonial Nigeria. 160p. (C). 1990. 35.00 (*0-7223-0693-8*, Pub. by A H S Ltd UK) St Mut.

N

An Asterisk (*) at the beginning of an entry indicates that the title is appearing in BIP for the first time.

Nketia, J. H. African Music in Ghana. LC 63-8873. (Northwestern University, Evanston, Ill. African Studies: No. 11). (Illus.). 158p. reprint ed. pap. 45.10 (0-8357-5237-2, 2016716) Bks Demand.

Nketia, J. H. & Dje Dje, Jacqueline C., eds. Selected Reports in Ethnomusicology: Studies in African Music, Vol. V. LC 76-640181. (Illus.). xx, 387p. (Orig.). 1984. audio 18.95 (0-88287-017-3) UCLA Dept Ethnom.

Nketia, Joseph H. The Music of Africa. (Illus.). 278p. (C). 1974. pap. text ed. 13.95 (0-393-09249-6) Norton.

Nkjv. Bible-Study New King James Version: Ryrie-Brown. 1986. 35.99 (0-8024-7375-X) Moody.

Nkomo, Mokubung. Student Culture & Activism in Black South African Universities: The Roots of Resistance. LC 84-3819. (Contributions in Afro-American & African Studies: No. 78). (Illus.). xxiii, 209p. 1984. text ed. 55.00 (0-313-24357-3, NSC/) Greenwood.

Nkomo, Mokubung, ed. Pedagogy of Domination: Toward a Democratic Education in South Africa. LC 90-80152. 460p. (C). 1990. 49.95 (0-86543-153-1); pap. 16.95 (0-86543-154-X) Africa World.

Nkomo, Stella M., et al. Applications in Human Resource Management. 2nd ed. 256p. (C). 1992. pap. 30.95 (0-534-92959-1) Intl Thomson.

Nkosi, Lewis. Tasks & Masks: Themes & Styles of African Literature. LC 82-107343. 212p. reprint ed. pap. 60.50 (0-685-20311-5, 2030350) Bks Demand.

Nkotsoe, Mmantho, jt. auth. see Bozzoli, Belinda.

Nkrumah, Kwame. Africa Must Unite. 229p. (C). 1963. pap. 11.95 (0-901787-13-2, Pub. by Panaf Bks UK) Humanities.

— Challenge of the Congo. 304p. (C). 1967. pap. 11.50 (0-901787-10-8, Pub. by Panaf Bks UK) Humanities.

— Class Struggle in Africa. 96p. (C). 1970. text ed. 9.95 (0-901787-12-4, Pub. by Panaf Bks UK); pap. 3.95 (0-901787-32-9, Pub. by Panaf Bks UK) Humanities.

— Consciencism: Philosophy & the Ideology for Decolonization. LC 65-11834. 1970. reprint ed. pap. 8.00 (0-85345-136-2) Monthly Rev.

— Neo-Colonialism: The Last Stage of Imperialism. 280p. (Orig.). (C). 1965. text ed. 25.00 (0-901787-33-7, Pub. by Panaf Bks UK); pap. 11.50 (0-901787-23-X, Pub. by Panaf Bks UK) Humanities.

— The Struggle Continues: Six Panaf Pamphlets. 83p. (C). 1973. pap. 5.95 (0-901787-41-8, Pub. by Panaf Bks UK) Humanities.

— Towards Colonial Freedom: Africa in the Struggle Against World Imperialism. 45p. (C). 1973. pap. 3.95 (0-901787-20-5, Pub. by Panaf Bks UK) Humanities.

— Voice from Conakry. 73p. (C). 1967. pap. 3.95 (0-901787-02-7, Pub. by Panaf Bks UK) Humanities.

NKS-Factory Magazine Staff, ed. Poka-Yoke: Improving Product Quality by Preventing Defects. LC 88-62593. (Illus.). 295p. 1989. 65.00 (0-915299-31-3) Prod Press.

Nkwocha, Oguchi H. Stirring the Dreamer. 52p. 1993. 8.95 (0-533-07984-5) Vantage.

***NLA (Potter) Staff.** Hoover's Water Supply & Treatment. 240p. 1994. 39.95 (0-8403-9625-2) Kendall-Hunt.

— Stabilization of Pavement Subgrades & Base Courses with Lime. 192p. 1994. 39.95 (0-8403-9632-5) Kendall-Hunt.

NLG Central America Task Force. The Illegality of U. S. Intervention: Central America & Caribbean Litigation. 2.00 (0-685-14988-9) Natl Lawyers Guild.

NLG Civil Liberties Committee. Counterintelligence: A Documentary Look at America's Secret Police. 1979. 5.00 (0-685-14938-2) Natl Lawyers Guild.

NLG Delegation to Nicaragua. Freedom of Expression in Nicaragua. 52p. 1985. 4.00 (0-685-14986-2); Five or more copies. 2.50 (0-685-14987-0) Natl Lawyers Guild.

NLG Labor Law Center. Forming a Union: A Worker's Guide. 1980. 2.75 (0-685-14946-3) Natl Lawyers Guild.

NLN Council of Associate Degree Programs Staff. Educational Outcomes of Associate Degree Nursing Programs. 10p. 1990. 4.95 (0-88737-495-6, 23-2348) Natl League Nurse.

NLN Council of Diploma Programs Staff. Role & Competencies of Graduates of Diploma Programs in Nursing. 2nd ed. 4p. 1989. 4.95 (0-88737-474-3, 16-1735) Natl League Nurse.

NLN Council of Practical Nursing Programs Staff. Entry Level Competencies of Graduates of Educational Programs in Practical Nursing. 7p. 1989. 4.95 (0-88737-473-5, 38-1686) Natl League Nurse.

NLN Division of Research Staff. Nurse Educators: Findings from the Faculty Census (1990) Biennial Survey. (Illus.). 62p. (Orig.). (C). 1991. pap. text ed. 21.95 (0-88737-502-2) Natl League Nurse.

NLN Research Division Staff. Nursing Data Source, 1992, I. (Illus.). (Orig.). (C). 1992. pap. text ed. 30.00 (0-88737-557-X, 19-2480) Natl League Nurse.

— Nursing Data Source, 1992, II. (Illus.). (Orig.). (C). 1992. pap. text ed. 30.00 (0-88737-558-8, 19-2481) Natl League Nurse.

— Nursing Data Source, 1992, III. (Illus.). (Orig.). (C). 1992. pap. text ed. 30.00 (0-88737-559-6, 19-2482) Natl League Nurse.

NLN Research Staff. Nursing Data Review, 1992. (Illus.). 288p. 1992. pap. text ed. 32.95 (0-88737-561-8, 19-2484) Natl League Nurse.

NLN Staff. Scholarships & Loans for Nursing Education 1993-1994. 1993. 14.00 (0-88737-580-4, 41-1964) Natl League Nurse.

NLN Staff, ed. Indices of Quality in Long-Term Care: Research & Practice. 192p. 1989. 18.95 (0-88737-454-9) Natl League Nurse.

NLP Comprehensive. NLP, the New Technology of Achievement. LC 94-17712. 1994. 20.00 (0-688-12669-3) Morrow.

NM Magazine Staff & Cameron, Sheila M. More of the Best from New Mexico Kitchens. King, Scottie, ed. LC 82-62076. (Illus.). 164p. 1983. pap. 8.95 (0-937206-02-4) New Mexico Mag.

NMHA Staff. Aiding People in Conflict: A Manual for Law Enforcement. 76p. 1993. pap. text ed. 7.50 (0-8403-8291-X) Kendall-Hunt.

NMSDN (Snell) Staff. An Administrative Manual for Nurse-Midwifery Services. 208p. 1994. per. 29.95 (0-8403-9442-X) Kendall-Hunt.

NMSU Geographics Applications Research Laboratory Staff. Border Atlas New Mexico-Chihuahua. 28p. (Orig.). (C). 1993. pap. text ed. 25.00 (0-937795-17-8) Border Res Inst.

NMSU (Geological Department) Staff. Geology Lab Manual. 112p. (C). 1994. spiral bd. 11.96 (0-8403-9371-7) Kendall-Hunt.

Nmungwun, Aaron F. Video Recording Technology: Its Impact on Media & Home Entertainment. (Communication Ser.). 304p. (C). text ed. 59.95 (0-8058-0360-2); pap. 29.95 (0-8058-0622-9) L Erlbaum Assocs.

***Nnaemeka, Obioma, ed.** Sisterhood, Feminisms, & Power in Africa. 1995. pap. 16.95 (0-86543-439-5) Africa World.

Nnaji, B. O., ed. Transactions, 1992: Robotics Research. 476p. 1992. pap. text ed. 88.00 (0-87263-429-9) SME.

Nnaji, Bartholomew O. Computer-Aided Design, Selection & Evaluation of Robots. (Manufacturing Research & Technology Ser.: No. 2). 292p. 1986. 107.75 (0-444-42614-0) Elsevier.

— Theory of Automatic Robot Assembly & Programming. LC 92-30586. 1992. write for info. (0-442-31663-1) Chapman & Hall.

Nnoli, Okwudiba. Self Reliance & Foreign Policy in Tanzania. LC 73-91415. (Studies in East African Society & History). 1977. text ed. 21.50 (0-88357-014-9); pap. text ed. 8.95 (0-88357-039-4) NOK Pubs.

Nnolim, Charles E., ed. The Role of Education in Contemporary Africa. LC 88-9931. 133p. (Orig.). 1988. pap. 9.99 (0-943852-53-6) Prof World Peace.

No, Yongkyoon & Libucha, Mark, eds. ESCOL '90: Proceedings of the Seventh Eastern States Conference on Linguistics. (Illus.). 363p. (Orig.). (C). 1991. lib. bdg. 12.00 (1-878594-07-9); pap. 10.00 (0-685-48582-X) OSU Dept Linguistics.

NOAA (Nat'l Oceanographic & Atmospheric Administration) Staff. Current & Tide Tables (1991) for Puget Sound, Deception Pass, the San Juans, Gulf Islands & Strait of Juan de Fuca. abr. ed. Island Canoe, Inc. Staff, ed. 96p. 1990. pap. write for info. (0-918439-12-4) Island Canoe.

Noack, Ludwig. Philosophie Geschichtliches Lexikon. 2nd ed. (GER.). 1968. 195.00 (0-8288-6658-9, M-7585, Pub. by Frommann Holzboog) Fr & Eur.

***Noack, Peter, et al, eds.** Psychological Responses to Social Change: Human Development in Changing Environments. (Prevention & Intervention in Childhood & Adolescence Ser.: No. 18). 264p. (C). 1994. lib. bdg. 69.95 (3-11-014343-7) De Gruyter.

Noack, Ruth K. Cadenza. 30p. 1991. vhs 14.95 (0-942229-04-5); spiral bd. 4.95 (0-942229-03-7) Video Album.

Noad, Frederick. The Baroque Guitar. (Illus.). 128p. 1974. pap. 14.95 (0-8256-9951-7, AM35890) Music Sales.

— The Classical Guitar. (Illus.). (Orig.). 1976. pap. 14.95 (0-8256-9952-5) Music Sales.

— Popular Elizabethan Tunes for Recorder & Guitar. (Ensemble Ser.). (Illus.). 1977. pap. 6.95 (0-8256-9963-0, AY15133, Ariel) Music Sales.

— The Renaissance Guitar. (Illus.). 104p. 1974. pap. 14.95 (0-8256-9950-9, AM35882) Music Sales.

Noad, Frederick, sel. One Hundred Graded Classical Guitar Studies. (Illus.). 176p. 1985. pap. 19.95 (0-7119-0612-2, AM38597) Music Sales.

— The Romantic Guitar. (Illus.). 128p. 1974. pap. 14.95 (0-8256-2415-0, AM38993) Music Sales.

Noad, Frederick M. The New Guitar Songbook. 2nd ed. LC 69-16492. (Illus.). 150p. 1985. pap. 16.95 (0-02-872140-3) Schirmer Bks.

— Playing the Guitar. 3rd ed. LC 80-5494. (Illus.). 208p. 1981. pap. 16.95 (0-02-871990-5) Schirmer Bks.

— Solo Guitar Playing, Bk 1. 2nd ed. LC 76-12833. 240p. 1976. pap. 16.95 (0-02-871680-9) Schirmer Bks.

— Solo Guitar Playing, Bk. 2. 2nd ed. LC 77-2529. (Illus.). 160p. 1978. pap. 16.95 (0-02-871690-6) Schirmer Bks.

— Solo Guitar Playing, Book I. 3rd ed. 264p. 1994. pap. 18.00 (0-02-870763-X) Schirmer Bks.

Noad, Peter. VW Beetle in Motorsports: The Illustrated History 1940's to 1990's. (Illus.). 144p. 1993. 29.95 (1-872004-38-5, Pub. by Windrow & Green UK) Motorbooks Intl.

Noah, Harold J. Financing Soviet Schools. LC 66-29416. 318p. reprint ed. pap. 90.70 (0-8357-9600-0, 2016945) Bks Demand.

Noah, Harold J., jt. auth. see Eckstein, Max A.

Noah, Harold J., jt. ed. see Eckstein, Max A.

Noah, Joe. George Preddy: Top Mustang Ace. (Illus.). 192p. 1991. pap. 12.95 (0-87938-531-6) Motorbooks Intl.

Noah, M., tr. Book of Jasher. LC 87-72939. 272p. (C). 1988. reprint ed. pap. 9.00 (0-934666-25-3) Artisan Sales.

Noah, Mordecai. Sampler of Writings of Mordecai Noah. Schuldiner, Michael, ed. (Masterworks of Literature Ser.). 1994. pap. 15.95 (0-685-71559-0) NCUP.

Noah, Raymond E. Mukua Henda, Mona Nzambi. LC 90-30181. 176p. (Orig.). 1990. pap. 9.95 (0-931832-51-9) Fithian Pr.

Noah, Robert. All the Right Answers. 320p. 1988. 17.95 (0-15-104779-0) HarBrace.

Noak, Elsa, ed. Meditations on Marriage: Translated from Hermann Oeser's Original. (C). 1989. pap. 21.00 (0-900657-98-7, Pub. by W Sessions UK) St Mut.

Noakes. Raymond Radiguet. (Coll. Poetes d'aujourd'hui). pap. 14.95 (0-685-37076-3) Fr & Eur.

Noakes, Aubrey. Sportsmen in a Landscape. LC 72-134122. (Essay Index Reprint Ser.). 1977. 26.95 (0-8369-2005-8) Ayer.

Noakes, D. Fertility & Obstetrics in Cattle. 1986. pap. 36.95 (0-632-01581-0) Blackwell Sci.

Noakes, D. L. & Ward, J. A., eds. Ecology & Ethology of Fishes. (Developments in Environmental Biology of Fishes Ser.: No. 1). 144p. 1981. 34.00 (90-6193-896-1) Kluwer Ac.

Noakes, David, tr. see Hodeir, Andre.

Noakes, Ingrid, tr. see Kaeble, Hartmut.

Noakes, J. E., et al, eds. Liquid Scintillation Spectrometry 1992. 520p. 1993. 90.00 (0-9638314-0-2) Radiocarbon.

***Noakes, Keith.** Post War International Frame Makers. (Illus.). 128p. 1995. pap. 24.95 (0-614-07423-1) Motorbooks Intl.

— Successful Composite Techniques. (Illus.). 144p. 1992. pap. 34.95 (1-85532-261-7, Pub. by Osprey Pubng Ltd UK) Motorbooks Intl.

Noakes, Patrick & Savory, Stephen. Tolley's Capital Gains Tax 1993-94. 470p. 1993. 81.00 (0-85459-772-7, Pub. by Tolley Pubng UK) St Mut.

— Tolley's Inheritance Tax 1993-94. 260p. 1993. 72.00 (0-85459-773-5, Pub. by Tolley Pubng UK) St Mut.

Noakes, Patrick, et al. Tolley's Capital Allowances 1993-94. 440p. 1993. 90.00 (0-85459-783-2, Pub. by Tolley Pubng UK) St Mut.

Noakes, Polly, jt. auth. see Kennedy, Fiona.

Noakes, Susan. Timely Reading: Between Exegesis & Interpretation. LC 87-47862. 288p. 1988. 34.95 (0-8014-2144-6) Cornell U Pr.

Noakes, Susan, jt. ed. see Koelb, Clayton.

Noakes, Tim. Lore of Running. (Illus.). 528p. 1989. 45.00 (0-19-570421-5) OUP.

Noakes, Timothy D. Lore of Running. 3rd ed. LC 90-29001. (Illus.). 832p. 1991. text ed. 30.00 (0-88011-437-1, PNOA0437); pap. text ed. 22.95 (0-88011-438-X, PNOA0438) Human Kinetics.

Noakes, Tony, jt. auth. see James, Paul.

Noaks, David, jt. auth. see Lewin, Douglas.

***Noaks, Lesley, et al, eds.** Contemporary Issues in Criminology. 262p. 1995. pap. 28.00 (0-7083-1297-7) Paul & Co Pubs.

Noall, Cyril. Cornish Mine Disasters. (C). 1989. 100.00 (1-85022-032-8, Pub. by Dyllansow Truran UK) St Mut.

— St. Ives Mining District, Vol. 1. (C). 1989. 50.00 (0-907566-33-2, Pub. by Dyllansow Truran UK) St Mut.

— The St. Ives Mining District, Vol. 11. Payton, Philip, ed. (C). 1993. 39.00 (1-85022-067-0, Pub. by Dyllansow Truran UK) St Mut.

Noall, Gyril. Early Lifeboats. (C). 1990. pap. 40.00 (0-85025-317-9, Pub. by Tor Mark Pr UK) St Mut.

— Fishermen. (C). 1989. pap. 24.95 (0-85025-314-4, Pub. by Tor Mark Pr UK) St Mut.

Noam, Eli. Telecommunications in Europe. (Communication & Society Ser.). (Illus.). 496p. 1992. 65.00 (0-19-507052-6, 819) OUP.

Noam, Eli M. Egalitarianism & the Generation of Inequality. (Illus.). 568p. 1991. reprint ed. pap. 29.95 (0-19-828390-3, 10227) OUP.

— Television in Europe. (Communication & Society Ser.). (Illus.). 408p. 1992. 45.00 (0-19-506942-0) OUP.

Noam, Eli M., ed. Video Media Competition: Regulation, Economics & Technology. LC 85-435. (Columbia Studies in Business, Government & Society). 416p. 1985. text ed. 58.00 (0-231-06134-X) Col U Pr.

Noam, Eli M., et al, eds. International Market in Film & Television Programs. (Communication & Information Science Ser.). 216p. (C). 1993. text ed. 45.00 (0-89391-545-9); pap. text ed. 24.50 (0-89391-953-5) Ablex Pub.

Noam, Eli M. & Dennis, Everette, eds. The Cost of Libel: Economic & Policy Implications. (Columbia Studies in Business, Government & Society). 320p. 1989. text ed. 40.00 (0-231-06692-9) Col U Pr.

***Noam, Eli M. & Pogorel, Gerard.** Asymmetric Deregulation: The Dynamics of Telecommunication Policy in Europe & the United States. LC 93-43433. 272p. 1994. pap. 26.00 (1-56750-003-X) Ablex Pub.

Noam, Eli M. & Pogorel, Gerard, eds. Asymmetric Deregulation: The Dynamics of Telecommunications Policy in Europe & the United States. 272p. 1994. 52.50 (0-89391-696-X) Ablex Pub.

Noam, Eli M., et al, eds. Telecommunications in the Pacific Basin: An Evolutionary Approach. LC 92-46617. (Communication & Society Ser.). 544p. 1994. 55.00 (0-19-508421-7) OUP.

***Noam, Gil G. & Borst, Sophie, eds.** Children, Youth, & Suicide: Developmental Perspectives. LC 85-644581. (New Directions for Child Development Ser.: no. 64). 121p. (Orig.). 1994. pap. 17.95 (0-7879-9960-1) Jossey-Bass.

***Noam, Gil G. & Fischer, Kurt W., eds.** Development & Vulnerability in Close Relationships. (Jean Piaget Symposia Ser.). 270p. 1995. text ed. 45.00 (0-8058-1369-1) L Erlbaum Assocs.

Noam, Gil G. & Wren, Thomas E., eds. The Moral Self: Building a Better Paradigm. LC 92-21501. (Illus.). 400p. (C). 1993. 42.50 (0-262-14052-7) MIT Pr.

Noam, Rachel. The View from Above. 200p. (C). 1993. 14.95 (1-56062-178-8) CIS Comm.

Noar, Gertrude. Living with Difference. 16p. 0.75 (0-686-74927-8) ADL.

***Noaro, Pierre, et al.** Dictionnaire Italien D'Aujourd'Hui. 1993. write for info. (0-7859-7872-0, 2-266-02936-3) Fr & Eur.

Noback, C. R. & Harting, J. K. Spinal Cord (Spinal Medulla) Primatologia, Vol. 2, Pt. 2. Hofer, H. et al, eds. (Illus.). 1971. pap. 36.00 (3-8055-1205-8) S Karger.

Noback, C. R. & Montagna, W., eds. The Primate Brain. LC 73-95612. (Advances in Primatology Ser.: Vol. 1). 334p. reprint ed. pap. 95.20 (0-317-26292-0, 2055692) Bks Demand.

Noback, Charles R., et al. The Human Nervous System: Introduction & Review. 4th ed. LC 90-5882. (Illus.). 448p. 1991. text ed. 39.00 (0-8121-1343-8) Williams & Wilkins.

— The Human Nervous System: Introduction & Review. 5th ed. LC 95-10315. (Illus.). 1995. write for info. (0-683-06538-6) Williams & Wilkins.

Nobar, Charles, tr. see Carotenuto, Aldo.

Nobari, Fouad T. & Davidson, Michael E. Data Entry Applications for Microcomputers - 5.25 Version. 176p. 1993. text ed., 5.25 hd write for info. (0-13-203522-7); text ed., 3.5 hd write for info. (0-13-203803-X) P-H.

***Nobari, Nuchine, ed.** Books & Periodicals Online, 1994, 2 vols., Set. 1752p. 1994. 299.00 (0-9630277-2-7) Lib Alliance.

Nobay, A. R., jt. auth. see Johnson, Harry G.

Nobbe, C. F., ed. see Ptolemaeus, Claudius.

Nobbe, Charles, jt. auth. see Kelley, Allen C.

Nobbe, George. North Briton: A Study in Political Propaganda, 1 vol. LC 39-24192. reprint ed. 20.00 (0-404-04779-3) AMS Pr.

***Nobbs, Jack & Hopkins, Ian.** Economics: A Core Text. 4th ed. LC 94-34367. 1994. write for info. (0-07-707916-7) McGraw.

Nobel, A., jt. auth. see Veillon, E.

***Nobel, Albert.** Medizinisches Sachwoerterbuch: German-English-French-Latin. 846p. (ENG, FRE & GER.). 1987. 150.00 (0-7859-6961-6) Fr & Eur.

Nobel, Albert, jt. auth. see Veillon, E.

Nobel, Cascell, jt. auth. see Farrell, H. Clyde.

Nobel, D. & Powell, T., eds. Electrophysiology of Single Cardiac Cells. 252p. 1987. text ed. 104.00 (0-12-520040-4) Acad Pr.

***Nobel, Dodman J.** Whitetail Hunter Education: A Complete Guide to Whitetail Hunting from Scouting to Butchering. LC 94-90454. 184p. (Orig.). 1995. pap. 15.95 (1-56002-489-5, Univ Edtns) Aegina Pr.

Nobel, Erika, ed. see Ryaboy, Vladislav.

Nobel, Erika D., ed. see Ash, Ehiel, et al.

Nobel, Erika D., ed. see Kruglikov, Alexander.

Nobel, Erika D., ed. see Lusnikov, Aleksey.

Nobel Foundation Staff. Nobel Lectures in Peace, 1901-1970, 3 vols., Vol. 1: 1901-1925. 1973. Vol. 1, 1901-1925. 82.00 (0-444-40853-3) Elsevier.

— Nobel Lectures in Peace, 1901-1970, 3 vols., Vol. 2: 1926-1950. 1973. Vol. 2, 1926-1950. 82.00 (0-444-41009-0) Elsevier.

Nobel, John V. Naval Terms Dictionary. 1977. lib. bdg. 75.00 (0-8490-2332-7) Gordon Pr.

Nobel, Milton, ed. Primary Prevention in Mental Health & Social Work: A Sourcebook of Curriculum & Teaching Materials. 8.80 (0-685-35082-7) Coun Soc Wk Ed.

Nobel, Park S. Biophysical Plant Physiology & Ecology. LC 82-20974. (Illus.). 608p. (C). 1995. text ed. write for info. (0-7167-1447-7) W H Freeman.

— Environmental Biology of Agaves & Cacti. (Illus.). 350p. 1988. 79.95 (0-521-34322-4) Cambridge U Pr.

— Physiochemical & Environmental Plant Physiology. 635p. 1991. text ed. 94.00 (0-12-520020-X); pap. text ed. 39.95 (0-12-520021-8) Acad Pr.

— Remarkable Agaves & Cacti. (Illus.). 224p. 1994. 39.95 (0-19-508414-4); pap. 19.95 (0-19-508415-2) OUP.

Nobel, Park S., jt. auth. see Gibson, Arthur C.

Nobel, Peter, ed. Refugees & Development in Africa. (Scandinavian Institute of African Studies: No. 19). 121p. 1987. 42.00x (91-7106-272-6, Pub. by Nordisk Afrikainstitutet SW) Coronet Bks.

Nobel Symposium 84 Staff. Early Life on Earth. Bengtson, Stefan, ed. LC 94-3822. 656p. 1994. 45.00 (0-231-08088-3) Col U Pr.

Nobel Symposium Staff. Substance P. Von Euler, Ulf S. & Pernow, Bengt, eds. LC 76-52600. (Illus.). 358p. reprint ed. pap. 102.10 (0-7837-7103-7, 2046932) Bks Demand.

Nobel, Vicki. Down Is up for Aaron Eagle: A Mother's Spiritual Journey with Downs Syndrome. LC 92-56118. 224p. 1993. 17.00 (0-06-250737-0) Harper SF.

Nobel, W. N., comp. Calendars of Huntingdonshire Wills: 1479-1652. (British Record Society Index Library Ser.: Vol. 42). 1972. reprint ed. pap. 19.00 (0-8115-1487-0) Periodicals Srv.

Nobels, Virginia, ed. see Conner, Tom.

Nobens, C. A. Montgomery's Time Zone. (Illus.). 32p. (J). (ps-3). 1990. lib. bdg. 18.95 (0-87614-398-2, Carolrhoda) Lerner Group.

Nobes, C. W., jt. ed. see Parker, R. H.

Nobes, Christopher. The Baring Securities Guide to International Finance Reporting. 250p. 1991. 56.95 (0-631-17617-9) Blackwell Pubs.

— The Economist Pocket Accountant. (Illus.). 224p. 1987. pap. text ed. 19.95 (0-631-15592-9) Blackwell Pubs.

— Interpreting European Financial Statements. 2nd ed. 192p. 1994. boxed 130.00 (0-406-02882-6, UK) Butterworth Legal Pubs.

— Interpreting U. S. Financial Statements - Towards 1992. 216p. 1990. 120.00 (0-406-51170-5) Butterworth Legal Pubs.

Nobes, Christopher & Alexander, David. A European Introduction to Financial Accounting. LC 93-37958. 1994. write for info. (0-13-030206-6) P-H.

***Nobes, Christopher & Parker, Robert, eds.** Comparative International Accounting. 4th ed. LC 94-21160. 1995. 48.00 (0-13-328733-5) P-H.

An Asterisk (*) at the beginning of an entry indicates that the title is appearing in BIP for the first time.

Nobes, Christopher W. International Classification of Financial Reporting. LC 83-40603. 160p. 1984. text ed. 35.00 (*0-312-41991-0*) St Martin.

— Introduction to Financial Accounting. 3rd ed. (Illus.). 224p. 1992. pap. 26.00 (*0-415-08778-3*, B0107) Routledge.

Nobes, Christopher W. & Parker, R. H., eds. Comparative International Accounting. 2nd ed. LC 85-26110. 399p. 1988. pap. 24.95 (*0-312-02343-X*) St Martin.

Nobes, Christopher W., jt. auth. see James, Simon.

Nobes, Clifford E. Apo Padi: An Autobiography. (Illus.). 168p. (Orig.). (C). 1988. pap. 10.00 (*971-10-0369-4*, Pub. by New Day Pub PH) Cellar.

Nobes, P. Bullseye Special Value Pack, 8 titles, Set: No. 1. (C). 1990. Set. 130.00 (*0-7487-0459-0*, Pub. by S Thornes Pubs UK) St Mut.

Nobile, Peter, jt. auth. see Richards, Ann.

***Nobile, Philip, ed.** Judgement at the Smithsonian. 256p. (Orig.). 1995. pap. 12.95 (*1-56924-841-9*) Marlowe & Co.

Nobile, Philip, jt. auth. see Eichel, Edward.

Nobile, Robert. Guide to Employee Handbooks, 1992: An Annual. 1993. per. 149.00 (*0-7913-1045-0*) Warren Gorham & Lamont.

Nobilt, George, ed. see Corbett, H. Dickson & Wilson, Bruce L.

Nobis, Norbert, intro. Marc Chagall: Arabian Nights: Four Tales from 1001 Arabian Nights. (Illus.). 176p. 1988. 60.00 (*3-7913-0842-4*, Pub. by Prestel) TeNeues.

Nobisso, Joi, jt. auth. see Lehmann, Terry.

Nobisso, Josephine. Grandma's Scrapbook. LC 91-23309. (Illus.). (J). 1991. 12.95 (*0-671-74976-5*, Green Tiger S&S) S&S Childrens.

— Grandpa Loved. (Illus.). 32p. (J). 1991. 12.95 (*0-88138-119-5*, Green Tiger S&S) S&S Childrens.

— Grandpa Loved. 1991. 14.00 (*0-671-75265-0*, Green Tiger S&S) S&S Childrens.

— Shh! The Whale Is Smiling. LC 91-21521. (Illus.). 40p. (J). (ps-1). 1992. 14.00 (*0-671-74908-0*, Green Tiger S&S) S&S Childrens.

Nobisso, Josephine & Krajnc, Anton C. For the Sake of a Cake. LC 92-38391. (Illus.). 28p. (J). 1993. 9.95 (*0-8478-1685-0*) Rizzoli Intl.

Noble. Exercise Physiology. 608p. (C). 1986. 39.95 (*0-8016-3711-2*) Mosby Yr Bk.

— Minds & Machines. 1991. 42.00 (*1-85000-508-7*, Falmer Pr); pap. 20.00 (*1-85000-509-5*, Falmer Pr) Taylor & Francis.

— Physiology of Exercise & Sport, No. 2. (Illus.). 608p. 1991. 37.95 (*0-8016-3342-7*) Mosby Yr Bk.

— Primary Care & General Medicine. 1800p. 1995. 110.00 (*0-8016-7841-2*) Mosby Yr Bk.

Noble, A. Biophysics Progression: Some Physical, Mathematical & Logical Aspects, Vol. 37, No. 1. LC 50-11295. (Illus.). 48p. 1981. pap. 28.00 (*0-08-027133-2*, Pergamon Pr) Elsevier.

— From the Clyde to California: Robert Louis Stevenson's Emigrant Journey. (Illus.). 302p. 1985. text ed. 25.00 (*0-08-032423-1*, R140, K150, P110, Pub. by Aberdeen U Pr) Macmillan.

Noble, Aaron, intro. Flag: Nineteen Ninety Annual Exhibition. (Illus.). 28p. (Orig.). 1990. pap. write for info. (*0-930495-09-8*) San Fran Art Inst.

Noble, Alfredo D. For These Are My Favorite Things, Vol. 1. 76p. (Orig.). 1989. student ed 6.99 (*0-317-93843-6*); spiral bd. 6.99 (*0-317-93842-8*) Papito.

— From Me to You with Love. 42p. (Orig.). 1991. pap. 6.50 (*0-9622849-0-4*) Papito.

— I Will Not Have You Ignorant. Noble, Jean E. et al, eds. (Illus.). 70p. (Orig.). 1992. text ed. 8.95 (*0-9622849-8-X*) Papito.

— A Message to a Black Man. 52p. (Orig.). (C). 1992. pap. 5.95 (*0-9622849-2-0*) Papito.

— Poems for All Occasions. 42p. (Orig.). 1991. pap. 5.70 (*0-9622849-3-9*) Papito.

— These Are My Favorite Things. rev. ed. 56p. (C). 1992. pap. 5.95 (*0-9622849-5-5*) Papito.

Noble, Allen G. Wood, Brick, & Stone: The North American Settlement Landscape; Vol. 1, Houses. LC 83-24110. (Illus.). 168p. 1984. 35.00 (*0-87023-410-2*) U of Mass Pr.

— Wood, Brick, & Stone: The North American Settlement Landscape: Vol. 2, Barns & Farm Structures. LC 83-24110. (Illus.). 192p. 1984. 35.00 (*0-87023-411-0*); pap. 18.95 (*0-87023-518-4*) U of Mass Pr.

Noble, Allen G., ed. To Build in a New Land: Ethnic Landscapes in North America. (Creating the North American Landscape Ser.). (Illus.). 512p. 1992. text ed. 68.00x (*0-8018-4188-7*); pap. text ed. 29.95 (*0-8018-4189-5*) Johns Hopkins.

***Noble, Allen G. & Cleek, Richard K.** The Old Barn: A Field Guide to North American Barns & Other Farm Structures. LC 94-41300. (Illus.). 250p. (C). 1995. text ed. write for info. (*0-614-03256-3*) Rutgers U Pr.

— The Old Barn Book: A Field Guide to North American Barns & Other Farm Structures. LC 91-41300. 1995. pap. 16.95 (*0-8135-2173-4*) Rutgers U Pr.

— The Old Barn Book: A Field Guide to North American Barns & Other Farm Structures. (Illus.). 1995. 32.95 (*0-8135-2172-6*) Rutgers U Pr.

***Noble, Allen G. & Wilhelm, Hubert G., eds.** Barns of the Midwest. (Illus.). 300p. 1995. text ed. 50.00x (*0-8214-1115-2*) Ohio U Pr.

— Barns of the Midwest. (Illus.). 300p. 1995. pap. text ed. 25.00x (*0-8214-1116-0*) Ohio U Pr.

Noble, Ben. Methods Based on the Wiener-Hopf Technique for the Solution of Partial Differential Equations. 2nd ed. LC 88-70741. x, 246p. (C). 1988. text ed. 19.95 (*0-8284-0332-5*, 332) Chelsea Pub.

Noble, Ben & Daniel, James W. Applied Linear Algebra. 3rd ed. (Illus.). 500p. (C). 1987. text ed. write for info. (*0-13-041260-0*) P-H.

Noble, Bill. Conflict, Action & Suspense. (Elements of Fiction Ser.). 176p. 1994. 14.99 (*0-89879-634-2*) Writers Digest.

Noble, Charles. Liberalism at Work: The Rise & Fall of OSHA. (Labor & Social Change Ser.). (Illus.). 304p. 1989. pap. 16.95 (*0-87722-665-2*) Temple U Pr.

— Social Regulation & the State. (Interventions: Theory & Contemporary Politics Ser.). Date not set. 28.00 (*0-8133-0588-8*); pap. 14.95 (*0-8133-0589-6*) Westview.

Noble, Christina & Coram, Robert. Nobody's Child: One Women's Struggle to End the Suffering of Children. 272p. 1995. 22.00 (*0-8021-1551-9*) Grove-Atltic.

Noble, Claudia, ed. see Wanner, Donna T.

Noble, D. Progress in Biophysics & Molecular Biology, Vol. 34. 1979. 76.00 (*0-08-024858-6*, Pergamon Pr) Elsevier.

— Progress in Biophysics & Molecular Biology, Vol. 45. LC 50-11295. (Illus.). 256p. 1986. 102.00 (*0-08-033225-0*, Pub. by PPL UK) Elsevier.

Noble, D. & Blundell, T. L. Progress in Biophysics & Molecular Biology, Vol. 36, Nos. 1-3 Complete. (Illus.). 130p 1981. 83.00 (*0-08-028394-2*, Pergamon Pr) Elsevier.

— Progress in Biophysics & Molecular Biology, Vol. 44. (Illus.). 288p. 1985. 110.00 (*0-08-033210-2*, Pub. by PPL UK) Elsevier.

Noble, D. & Blundell, T. L., eds. Progress in Biophysics & Molecular Biology, Vol. 35. (Illus.). 206p. 1981. 76.00 (*0-08-027122-7*, Pergamon Pr) Elsevier.

— Progress in Biophysics & Molecular Biology, Vol. 37. (Illus.). 229p. 1982. 95.00 (*0-08-029120-1*, Pergamon Pr) Elsevier.

— Progress in Biophysics & Molecular Biology, Vol. 38. (Illus.). 210p. 1982. 94.00 (*0-08-029683-1*, Pergamon Pr) Elsevier.

— Progress in Biophysics & Molecular Biology, Vol. 39. (Illus.). 230p. 1983. 86.00 (*0-08-030015-4*, Pergamon Pr) Elsevier.

— Progress in Biophysics & Molecular Biology, Vol. 41. (Illus.). 260p. 1983. 99.00 (*0-08-031020-6*, Pergamon Pr) Elsevier.

— Progress in Biophysics & Molecular Biology, Vol. 42. LC 50-11295. (Illus.). 202p. 1984. 99.00 (*0-08-031691-3*, Pergamon Pr) Elsevier.

— Progress in Biophysics & Molecular Biology, Vol. 43. (Illus.). 268p. 1985. 110.00 (*0-08-032324-3*, Pergamon Pr) Elsevier.

Noble, D., jt. ed. see Boyd, C. A.

Noble, Daniel. Elements of Psychological Medicine. LC 78-72815. (Brainedness, Handedness, & Mental Abilities Ser.). reprint ed. 32.50 (*0-404-60885-X*) AMS Pr.

— The Human Mind in Its Relations with the Brain & Nervous System. LC 78-72817. (Brainedness, Handedness, & Mental Abilities Ser.). reprint ed. 22.50 (*0-404-60886-8*) AMS Pr.

***Noble, David.** Gallery of Best Resumes for Two Year Degrees. (Orig.). 1996. pap. 16.95 (*1-56370-239-8*) JIST Works.

— Master the Chessmaster. (Illus.). (Orig.). 1992. pap. 16.95 (*0-672-30165-2*) Hayden.

Noble, David, ed. Houses Beneath the Rock: The Anasazi of Canyon de Chelly & Navajo National Monument. 2nd ed. LC 91-78069. (Illus.). 56p. (C). 1993. reprint ed. pap. 8.95 (*0-941270-72-6*) Ancient City Pr.

— Understanding the Anasazi of Mesa Verde & Hovenweep. LC 92-9279. Orig. Title: Tse Ya Kin. (Illus.). 48p. (Orig.). 1992. reprint ed. pap. 8.95 (*0-941270-71-8*) Ancient City Pr.

Noble, David & Course, Charles. Spreadsheets for Agriculture. LC 92-41099. 259p. (Orig.). 1993. pap. text ed. 47.95 (*0-470-22067-8*) Halsted Pr.

Noble, David & Course, Charles, eds. Spreadsheets for Agriculture. LC 92-41099. (Orig.). 1993. write for info. (*0-582-05389-7*) Longman.

Noble, David F. America by Design: Science, Technology, & the Rise of Corporate Capitalism. (Orig.). 1979. pap. 11.95 (*0-19-502618-7*) OUP.

— Forces of Production: A Social History of Industrial Automation. (Illus.). 432p. 1986. pap. 17.95 (*0-19-504046-5*) OUP.

— Forces of Production: A Social History of Machine Tool Automation. LC 83-48867. 416p. 1984. 22.95 (*0-394-51262-6*) Knopf.

— Gallery of Best Resumes: A Display of Professionally Written Resumes for Job Seekers & Career Changers. 400p. (Orig.). 1994. pap. 16.95 (*1-56370-144-8*, GBR) JIST Works.

— Using WordPerfect in Your Job Search. 416p. (Orig.). 1995. pap. 19.95 (*1-56370-177-4*, J1774) JIST Works.

— World Without Women. 1992. pap. 28.00 (*0-394-55650-X*) Knopf.

— A World Without Women: The Christian Clerical Culture of Western Science. LC 92-44613. (C). 1993. pap. 12.95 (*0-19-508435-7*) OUP.

Noble, David G. Ancient Ruins of the Southwest. rev. ed. LC 80-83016. (Illus.). 232p. 1991. pap. 14.95 (*0-87358-530-5*) Northland AZ.

— Pueblos, Villages, Forts, & Trails: A Guide to New Mexico's Past. LC 93-42192. (Coyote Books Ser.). 357p. (C). 1994. 39.95 (*0-8263-1514-3*); pap. 19.95 (*0-8263-1485-6*) U of NM Pr.

Noble, David G., ed. The Hohokam: Ancient People of the Desert. (Illus.). 77p. (Orig.). 1991. pap. 10.95 (*0-933452-29-2*) Schol Am Res.

— New Light on Chaco Canyon. LC 84-10506. (Exploration Ser.). (Illus.). 108p. (Orig.). 1984. pap. 11.95 (*0-933452-10-1*) Schol Am Res.

— Pecos Ruins: Geology, Archaeology, History, & Prehistory. 2nd ed. LC 92-55032. (Illus.). 32p. (C). 1993. reprint ed. pap. 6.95 (*0-941270-76-9*) Ancient City Pr.

— Salinas: Archaeology, History, Prehistory. 2nd ed. LC 92-55035. (Illus.). 40p. (C). 1993. reprint ed. pap. 7.95 (*0-941270-78-5*) Ancient City Pr.

— Santa Fe: History of an Ancient City. (Illus.). 168p. 1989. 29.95 (*0-295-96879-6*); pap. 16.95 (*0-295-96865-6*) U of Wash Pr.

— Wupatki & Walnut Canyon: New Perspectives on History, Prehistory & Rock Art. 2nd ed. LC 92-55034. (Illus.). 48p. (C). 1993. reprint ed. pap. 7.95 (*0-941270-75-0*) Ancient City Pr.

Noble, David G. & Woodbury, Richard, eds. Zuni & el Morro: Past & Present. 2nd ed. LC 92-55033. (Illus.). 40p. (C). 1993. reprint ed. pap. 7.95 (*0-941270-77-7*) Ancient City Pr.

Noble, David G., ed. see Levine, Francis, et al.

Noble, David W. The End of American History: Democracy, Capitalism, & the Metaphor of Two Worlds in Anglo-American Historical Writing, 1880-1980. LC 85-1077. 177p. 1985. pap. text ed. 14.95 (*0-8166-1416-4*) U of Minn Pr.

— Historians Against History: The Frontier Thesis & the National Covenant in American Historical Writing since 1830. LC 65-22811. 205p. reprint ed. pap. 58.50 (*0-8357-8898-9*, 2033276) Bks Demand.

— The Paradox of Progressive Thought. LC 58-8765. 282p. reprint ed. pap. 80.40 (*0-8357-8979-9*, 2033277) Bks Demand.

Noble, David W., jt. auth. see Carroll, Peter N.

Noble, David W., jt. auth. see Carroll, Peter.

Noble, Denis & Earm, Yung E., eds. Ionic Channels & Effect of Taurine on the Heart: Proceedings of the International Symposium on Cardiac Ion Channels & Effects of Taurine on the Heart, Seoul, Korea, 1992. LC 93-9516. (Developments in Cardiovascular Medicine Ser.: Vol. 141). 192p. (C). 1993. Alk. paper. lib. bdg. 85.00 (*0-7923-2199-5*) Kluwer Ac.

Noble, Dennis E. Game. (Illus.). 37p. 1972. pap. 10.00 (*0-88680-063-3*); pap. 3.00 (*0-88680-062-5*) I E Clark.

Noble, Dennis L. The Eagle & the Dragon: The United States Military in China, 1901-1937. LC 90-3146. (Contributions in Military Studies: No. 102). 264p. 1990. text ed. 55.00 (*0-313-27299-9*, NEC, Greenwood Pr) Greenwood.

— Forgotten Warriors: Combat Art from Vietnam. LC 91-44451. 240p. 1992. text ed. 29.95 (*0-275-93868-9*, C3868, Praeger Pubs) Greenwood.

— That Others Might Live: The U. S. Life-Saving Service, 1878-1915. LC 93-37539. (Illus.). 198p. 1994. 27.95 (*1-55750-627-2*) Naval Inst Pr.

Noble, Dennis L. & O'Brien, Mike. U. S. Life-Saving Service 1889-1915, U. S. Coast Guard Service 1915-1989. (Illus.). 24p. (Orig.). (YA). (gr. 8 up). 1989. reprint ed. pap. text ed. 2.00 (*0-935549-12-9*) MI City Hist.

***Noble, Diane.** It's about Time (For Me) LC 95-12361. 208p. (Orig.). 1995. pap. 10.99 (*0-8010-5155-X*) Baker Bk.

Noble, Donald R., ed. The Steinbeck Question: New Essays in Criticism. LC 91-75026. 300p. 1993. 29.50 (*0-87875-424-5*) Whitston Pub.

Noble, Douglas, jt. auth. see Kensek, Karen M.

Noble, Douglas D. The Human Arsenal. 224p. 1991. 80.00 (*1-85000-803-5*, Falmer Pr); pap. 29.00 (*1-85000-804-3*, Falmer Pr) Taylor & Francis.

Noble, Douglas E., jt. auth. see Kenser, Karen M.

Noble, E. Myron. General Procedures & Catalog of the Middle Atlantic Regional Gospel Music Festival. LC 90-23335. (Illus.). 60p. (Orig.). 1991. pap. 4.95 (*1-877971-04-9*) Mid Atl Reg Pr.

— The Gospel of Music: A Key to Understanding a Major Chord of Ministry. LC 85-63559. 159p. (Orig.). 1986. pap. 4.95 (*0-9616056-1-8*) Mid Atl Reg Pr.

— Twentieth Annual Middle Atlantic Regional Gospel Music Festival Journal, 1992. 25p. (Orig.). 1993. pap. 5.00 (*1-877971-06-5*) Mid Atl Reg Pr.

Noble, E. Myron, ed. Constitution & Bylaws & General Procedures of the National Youth Convention of the Apostolic Faith Churches of God, Inc. LC 89-14602. 56p. (Orig.). 1989. pap. 3.95 (*0-9616056-8-5*) Mid Atl Reg Pr.

Noble, E. Myron, intro. Like As of Fire: Newspapers from the Azusa Street World Wide Revival, 1906-1909. rev. ed. 68p. (Orig.). 1994. pap. 16.95 (*1-877971-10-3*) Mid Atl Reg Pr.

***Noble, E. Myron & Taylor, Evelyn M., eds.** Set My Spirit Free: Expressions of Pentecost Selected Papers Presented at the Middle Atlantic Regional Gospel Ministries, 1995 Conference. 100p. (Orig.). 1995. student ed, pap. 100.00 (*1-877971-16-2*) Mid Atl Reg Pr.

— Set My Spirit Free: Expressions of Pentecost: Selected Papers Presented at the Ninth Annual Session, Middle Atlantic Regional Gospel Ministries, Inc., March 16-19, 1995, Inglewood, California. LC 95-13323. 1995. write for info. (*0-614-05427-3*) Mid Atl Reg Pr.

Noble, E. Myron, ed. see Hawkins, M. Elizabeth.

Noble, E. Myron, jt. ed. see Whitaker, Helen L.

Noble, Elizabeth. Essential Exercises for the Childbearing Year: A Guide to Health & Comfort Before & after Your Baby Is Born. (Illus.). 208p. 1988. pap. 12.95 (*0-395-47780-8*) HM.

—Essential Exercises for the Childbearing Year: A Guide to Health & Comfort Before & After Your Baby Is Born. 4th rev. ed. (Illus.). 200p. 1995. pap. 14.95 (*0-9641183-1-9*) New Life Images. ESSENTIAL EXERCISES FOR THE CHILDBEARING YEAR explains why pregnancy creates a need for exercise & explores common discomforts, & problems with the key muscles involved. The functions of the abdominals & pelvic floor during pregnancy, labor, birth & postpartum are detailed to provide a clear rationale for the exercises that follow. Each movement of this preventive program is described & illustrated, from its starting position through various progressions of increasing challenge. Special exercises involve a partner, & skills for relaxation & breathing are offered. Helpful hints are given for various household & work activities. Now in its fourth edition, this guide has helped women for twenty years avoid what many consider inevitable visits to the gynecologist or orthopedic specialist. Sound & safe advice is given on back pain, foot pain, incontinence, & recovery from Cesarean birth. This fully-revised edition includes a chapter for women whose activity level is restricted, & an extended Resources section. These essential exercises emphasize body awareness which leads to a healthier lifestyle in general. They can be started at any time during pregnancy & should be continued throughout life. Elizabeth Noble, a physical therapist from Australia who founded the Section on Women's Health of the American Physical Therapy Association is the author of eight books on women's health & reproduction.

Publisher Provided Annotation.

— Having Twins: A Parent's Guide to Pregnancy, Birth & Early Childhood. 2nd ed. 368p. 1991. pap. 14.95 (*0-395-49338-2*) HM.

— Having Your Baby by Donor Insemination: A Complete Resource Guide. 352p. 1988. pap. 15.95 (*0-395-45395-X*) HM.

— Primal Connections. LC 92-29128. 304p. (Orig.). 1993. pap. 12.00 (*0-671-67851-5*, Fireside) S&S Trade.

Noble, Elizabeth & Sorger, Leo. The Joy of Being a Boy. 15p. (J). (gr. k up). 1994. pap. 4.95 (*0-9641183-0-0*) New Life Images.

Noble, Emily. A Method for the Millions. 38p. 1959. reprint ed. spiral bd. 4.40 (*0-7873-0635-5*) Mokelumne.

Noble, G. Bernard. Christian A. Herter. LC 73-122753. (American Secretaries of State & Their Diplomacy, New Ser. 1925-1961: Vol. 18). 1970. 60.50 (*0-8154-0341-0*) Cooper Sq.

Noble, George. Hazardous Waste & the Public Works Official. (High Tech Waste Management Ser.). (Illus.). 63p. (Orig.). 1984. pap. text ed. 10.00 (*0-917084-50-0*) Am Public Works.

— Siting Landfills & Other LULUs. LC 91-58006. 230p. 1992. text ed. 65.00 (*0-87762-878-5*) Technomic.

Noble, Gil. Black Is the Color of My TV Tube. (Illus.). 1981. 12.00 (*0-8184-0297-0*) Carol Pub Group.

— Black is the Color of My TV Tube. 1991. pap. 9.95 (*0-8184-0538-4*) Carol Pub Group.

Noble, Gilbert W., ed. The Official Catalog of U. S. Bureau Precancels. 64th ed. 1983. 6.00 (*0-685-53039-6*) G W Noble.

Noble, Glen. John Brown & the Jim Lane Trail. (Illus.). 1977. 13.00 (*0-931068-11-8*) Purcells.

Noble, Grant. Children in Front of the Small Screen. LC 75-15432. (Communication & Society Ser.: No. 5). 256p. reprint ed. pap. 73.00 (*0-7837-1116-6*, 2041646) Bks Demand.

— Trader's Edge: Cashing in on the Winning Strategies of Floor Traders, Commercials & Market. 1994. 34.95 (*1-55738-599-8*) Probus Pub Co.

Noble, Gregory W. Flying Apart? Japanese-American Negotiations over the FSX Fighter Plane. LC 92-73489. (Policy Papers in International Affairs Ser.: No. 41). 66p. (Orig.). 1992. pap. text ed. 7.25 (*0-87725-541-5*) U of Cal IAS.

Noble, Holcomb B. Next: The Coming Era in Medicine, Vol. 1. 1988. pap. 9.95 (*0-316-61134-4*) Little.

Noble, Holcomb B., ed. Next: The Coming Era in Science. 192p. 1988. pap. 9.95 (*0-316-61133-6*) Little.

Noble, Hollister. The Winds of Love. (Orig.). 1981. pap. 2.95 (*0-89083-899-2*) Zebra.

Noble, I. R., jt. ed. see Purdie, P. W.

Noble, Ian. Language & Narration in Celine's Writings: The Challenge of Disorder. LC 86-7188. 196p. (C). 1987. text ed. 55.00 (*0-391-03402-2*) Humanities.

Noble, J. World Wide Navigation. (C). 1987. 150.00 (*0-85174-528-8*, Pub. by Brwn Son Ferg) St Mut.

Noble, J. & Lacasas, J. Complete Handbook of Spanish Verbs. (C). 1984. 130.00 (*0-8442-7634-0*, Pub. by S Thornes Pubs UK) St Mut.

Noble, J., jt. ed. see Galasko, C. S.

Noble, J. C. & Bradstock, R. A., eds. Mediterranean Landscapes in Australia: Mallee Ecosystems & Their Management. 1989. 70.00 (*0-643-04985-1*, Pub. by CSIRO AT) Intl Spec Bk.

Noble, J. C., et al. The Mallee Lands: A Conversative Perspective. 340p. 1990. 65.00 (0-643-05105-8, Pub. by CSIRO AT) Intl Spec Bk.
Noble, James P., tr. see **Cotillon, Pierre.**
Noble, Janet, ed. see **Breeden, Terri & Egan, Emalie.**
Noble, Janet, et al. New American Plays Two. 291p. 1992. pap. 15.95 (0-435-08605-7, 8605) Heinemann.
Noble, Jean E., ed. see **Noble, Alfredo D.**
Noble, Jerry. Holding the Harvest Manual. 1992. 34.99 (0-685-55397-3); student ed. pap. 3.99 (0-685-55398-1) Pathway Pr.
***Noble, Joan.** The Wheat-&-Gluten-Free Cookbook: Over 100 Recipes for All the Family. (Illus.). 140p. 1995. pap. 19.95 (0-614-07403-7, Vermillion) Trafalgar.
— The Wheat-&-Gulten-Free Cookbook: Over 100 Recipes for All the Family. (Illus.). 140p. 1995. pap. 19.95 (0-09-177998-7, Vermillion) Trafalgar.
Noble, Joan R., ed. Recollections of Virginia Woolf by Her Contemporaries. 208p. 1994. reprint ed. pap. text ed. 16.95 (0-8214-1105-5) Ohio U Pr.
Noble, John. The Harvard Guide to Careers in Mass Media. 204p. (Orig.). 1989. pap. 7.95 (1-55850-988-7) Adams Pubng.
— The Job Search Handbook: The Basics of a Professional Job Search. 144p. 1988. pap. 6.95 (0-937860-90-5) Adams Pubng.
— The Official Duffer's Rules of Golf. (Illus.). 96p. 1985. reprint ed. pap. 7.95 (0-8092-5144-2) Contemp Bks.
Noble, John, ed. Textbook of General Medicine & Primary Care. 2320p. 1987. text ed. 85.00 (0-317-53603-6, Little Med Div) Little.
Noble, John & Forsyth, Susan. Baltic States & Kaliningrad: A Travel Survival Kit. (Illus.). 448p. (Orig.). 1994. pap. 15.95 (0-86442-183-4) Lonely Planet.
Noble, John & King, John. U. S. S. R. A Travel Survival Kit. (Illus.). 840p. (Orig.). 1991. pap. 21.95 (0-86442-117-6) Lonely Planet.
Noble, John, et al. Sri Lanka: A Travel Survival Kit. 5th ed. (Illus.). 212p. 1993. pap. 13.95 (0-86442-169-9) Lonely Planet.
Noble, John H. The Harvard Guide to Careers in Mass Media. LC 87-21980. 200p. (Orig.). 1987. pap. 12.95 (0-943747-00-7) Harvard OCS.
— I Was a Slave in Russia. 1957. 16.95 (0-8159-5800-5) Devin.
Noble, John H., et al. Emergency Medical Services: Behavioral & Planning Perspectives. LC 73-9940. 595p. 1973. 59.95 (0-87705-117-8) Human Sci Pr.
Noble, Jon, jt. auth. see **Austin, George.**
Noble, Joseph A. From Cab to Caboose: Fifty Years of Railroading. LC 64-11327. (Illus.). 281p. reprint ed. pap. 80.10 (0-317-11166-3, 2016243) Bks Demand.
Noble, Judith. Hispanic Way. 1991. pap. 9.95 (0-8442-7389-9, Natl Textbk) NTC Pub Grp.
Noble, Judith & Lacasa, Jaime. Complete Handbook of Spanish Verbs. 360p. (SPA.). 1991. 19.95 (0-8442-7633-2, Natl Textbk) NTC Pub Grp.
— Complete Handbook of Spanish Verbs. 360p. (C). 1984. 95.00 (0-685-33819-3, Pub. by S Thornes Pubs UK) St Mut.
— They Say - Do It Differently: Seventy-Three Points of Hispanic "Little-c" Culture. LC 89-81229. 150p. (C). 1989. pap. 9.95 (0-9624051-0-8) Hse Enterprises.
***Noble, Judy A.** How to Manage Your Own Rental Property: The Easy Way. 121p. 1995. pap. 24.95 (0-9647366-0-8) Stars End Pubng.
Noble, Julian V. Scientific FORTH: A Modern Language for Scientific Computing. (Illus.). 330p. (Orig.). (C). 1992. pap. text ed. 49.95 (0-9632775-0-2) Mechum Banks.
Noble, June, jt. auth. see **Noble, William.**
Noble, Kate. The Blue Elephant. (Zoo Stories Ser.). (Illus.). 32p. (J). (ps-4). 1995. 14.95 (0-9631798-3-7) Silver Seahorse.
— Bubble Gum. (Africa Stories Ser.). (Illus.). 32p. (J). (ps-4). 1995. 14.95 (0-9631798-0-2) Silver Seahorse.
— Oh Look, It's a Nosserus. (Africa Stories Ser.). (Illus.). 32p. (J). (ps-4). 1995. 14.95 (0-9631798-2-9) Silver Seahorse.
— Pamela's Plan. (Zoo Stories Ser.). (Illus.). 32p. (J). (ps-4). Date not set. 15.95 (0-9631798-4-5) Salmon Run.
***Noble, Kathleen.** The Sound of a Silver Horn: Reclaiming the Heroism in Contemporary Women's Lives. 256p. 1995. pap. 12.00 (0-449-90969-7) Fawcett.
— The Sound of the Silver Horn: Reclaiming the Heroism in Women's Lives. LC 93-14264. 240p. 1994. 20.00 (0-449-90588-8, Columbine) Fawcett.
Noble, Keith A. Changing Doctoral Degrees: An International Perspective. LC 93-14603. 128p. 1993. 85.00 (0-335-19213-0, Open Univ Pr) Taylor & Francis.
***Noble, Keith A., ed. & comp.** The International Education Quotations Encyclopedia. LC 94-36312. 1995. 50.00 (0-335-19394-3, Open Univ Pr) Taylor & Francis.
Noble, Laura. Macintosh Software! Using Microsoft Works! 320p. (C). 1989. text ed. write for info. (0-394-39525-5) Knopf.
Noble, Louis. Course of Empire, Voyage of Life, & Other Pictures of Thomas Cole. 415p. 1993. reprint ed. lib. bdg. 99.00 (0-7812-5281-4) Rprt Serv.
Noble, Louis L. The Life & Works of Thomas Cole. Vesell, Elliot S., ed. LC 64-22725. 401p. reprint ed. pap. 114.30 (0-317-10379-2, 2001644) Bks Demand.
Noble, M. I., jt. ed. see **Ter Keurs, H. E.**
Noble, Margaret. Kali the Mother. 110p. 1985. pap. 1.95 (0-87481-104-X, Pub. by Advaita Ashrama II) Vedanta Pr.
Noble, Margaret, ed. see **Nivedita.**
Noble, Marguerite. Filaree: A Novel of an American Life. 272p. 1980. pap. 3.95 (0-345-28709-6) Ballantine.
— Filaree: A Novel of an American Life. LC 85-1130. (Zia Books Ser.). 249p. 1985. pap. 11.95 (0-8263-0825-2) U of NM Pr.
Noble, Mark I. & Seed, W. A., eds. The Interval-Force Relationship of the Heart: Bowditch Revisited. (Illus.). 300p. (C). 1992. 115.00 (0-521-40022-8) Cambridge U Pr.
Noble, Mark I., jt. ed. see **Drake-Holland, Angela J.**
Noble, Martha L. Statutory Agricultural Liens: Rapid Finder Charts. 174p. 1993. lib. bdg. 35.00 (1-882461-01-0) Natl Ctr Agricult LR&I.
Noble, Mary. You Can Grow Cattleya Orchids. 2nd ed. LC 90-92175. 100p. 1991. pap. 12.95 (0-913928-07-0) McQuerry Orchid.
— You Can Grow Orchids. 5th rev. ed. (Illus.). 128p. 1987. pap. 12.95 (0-913928-06-2) McQuerry Orchid.
— You Can Grow Phalaenopsis Orchids. 2nd rev. ed. (Illus.). 102p. 1994. pap. 12.95 (0-913928-08-9) McQuerry Orchid.
Noble, Mary, jt. ed. see **Hobbs, Anne S.**
Noble, Mary T., tr. see **Pinckaers, Servais.**
***Noble, Maurine.** Machine Quilting Made Easy. Reikes, Ursula, ed. (Joy of Quilting Ser.). (Illus.). 56p. (Orig.). 1994. pap. 9.95 (1-56477-074-5) That Patchwork.
Noble, Nathaniel. Love Me, I'm a Criminal or How to Get Away with Murder. Costa, Gwen, ed. 1990. pap. 14.95 (0-87949-356-9) Ashley Bks.
— Tell Me a Prayer. LC 91-65162. 51p. 1991. pap. 5.95 (1-55523-424-0) Winston-Derek.
Noble, Nicholas, jt. auth. see **Tomsett, Eric.**
Noble, P. B. & Levine, M. D. Computer Assisted Analyses of Cell Locomotion & Chemotaxis. 152p. 1986. 132.00 (0-8493-6342-X, QH647, CRC Reprint) Franklin.
Noble, Park S., jt. auth. see **Gibson, Arthur C.**
Noble, Paul, jt. auth. see **Cooper, Paulette.**
Noble, Peter. Alfred Hitchcock. (Film Ser.). 1979. lib. bdg. 250.00 (0-8490-2862-0) Gordon Pr.
— Anthony Asquith. (Film Ser.). 1979. lib. bdg. 6.95 (0-8490-2866-3) Gordon Pr.
— The Cinema & the Negro: Nineteen Five to Nineteen Forty-Eight. (Film Ser.). 1980. lib. bdg. 69.95 (0-8490-3093-5) Gordon Pr.
— Hollywood Scapegoat: The Biography of Erich Von Stroheim. LC 70-169352. (Arno Press Cinema Program Ser.). (Illus.). 250p. 1975. reprint ed. 20.95 (0-405-03922-0) Ayer.
— Negro in Films. LC 72-124022. (Literature of Cinema, Ser. 1). 1978. reprint ed. 32.95 (0-405-01629-8) Ayer.
Noble, R. Shakespeare's Biblical Knowledge. 1972. 59.95 (0-8490-1039-X) Gordon Pr.
Noble, R. B. Rhythmic Breathings & Olfactory Nerve Influence on Respiration. 1991. lib. bdg. 79.95 (0-8490-4958-X) Gordon Pr.
***Noble, R. D. & Stern, S. A., eds.** Membrane Separations Technology: Principles & Applications. (Membrane Science & Technology Ser.: Vol. 2). 740p. 1995. 340.00 (0-444-81633-X) Elsevier.
Noble, R. Joe & Rothbaum, Donald A., eds. Geriatric Cardiology: Principles & Practice. LC 81-951. (Cardiovascular Clinics Ser.). 238p. 1981. 40.00 (0-8036-6565-2) Davis Co.
Noble, Richard. Language, Subjectivity, & Freedom in Rousseau's Moral Philosophy. LC 91-10201. (Political Theory & Political Philosophy Ser.). 256p. 1991. 20.00 (0-8153-0136-7) Garland.
Noble, Richard, jt. auth. see **Lillo, George.**
Noble, Richard B. Rhythmic Breathing Plus Olfactory Nerve Influence on Respiration. 143p. 1971. reprint ed. spiral bd. 6.60 (0-7873-1026-3) Mokelumne.
Noble, Richard D. & Way, J. Douglas, eds. Liquid Membranes: Theory & Applications. LC 87-18684. (Symposium Ser.: No. 347). (Illus.). ix, 223p. 1987. 54.95 (0-8412-1407-7) Am Chemical.
Noble, Robert D. Continuing Incorporation: Workbook 4. (Welcome in Ser.). 88p. (Orig.). 1987. 10.00 (0-944687-04-0) Gather Family Inst.
— Discovery Weekend Workbook Four. 7th ed. (Reach Out Ser.). (Illus.). 79p. (Orig.). 1994. pap. 20.00 (0-944687-16-4) Gather Family Inst.
— The Facts: Workbook 1. (Reach Out Ser.). 74p. (Orig.). 1987. 10.00 (0-944687-06-7) Gather Family Inst.
— Identify the Fish: Workbook 2. (Reach Out Ser.). (Illus.). 55p. (Orig.). 1987. 10.00 (0-944687-07-5) Gather Family Inst.
— In the Footsteps of John: The Book of Revelation. 49p. (Orig.). 1994. pap. 10.00 (0-944687-15-6) Gather Family Inst.
— Intentional Caring: Workbook 2. (Welcome in Ser.). (Illus.). 57p. (Orig.). 1987. 10.00 (0-944687-02-4) Gather Family Inst.
— Ministries Weekend. rev. ed. 138p. (Orig.). 1993. student ed. pap. 20.00 (0-944687-13-X) Gather Family Inst.
— Organizing for Growth. 51p. 1987. 10.00 (0-944687-10-5) Gather Family Inst.
— Prepare the Bait: Workbook 3. (Reach Out Ser.). 64p. (Orig.). 1987. 10.00 (0-944687-08-3) Gather Family Inst.
— Shepherding: Workbook 3. (Welcome in Ser.). 68p. (Orig.). 1987. 10.00 (0-944687-03-2) Gather Family Inst.
— Spiritual Gifts: Your Portion of Christ's Bounty, Workbook 1. 4th ed. (Welcome in Ser.). 61p. (Orig.). 1985. pap. 10.00 (0-944687-01-6) Gather Family Inst.
— A Study of St. Paul's Letter to the Galatians: The Christian Emancipation Proclamation. 83p. (Orig.). 1993. pap. 10.00 (0-944687-14-8) Gather Family Inst.
Noble, Rudolf E. CD's: A New Concept in Dieting. 100p. 1989. pap. 9.95 (1-885078-03-X) Noble Enter.
— The Soup Diet. 80p. 1993. pap. 9.95 (1-885078-04-8) Noble Enter.
Noble, Sara P., ed. Managing People: One Hundred One Proven Ideas for Making You & Your People More Productive. 191p. (Orig.). 1992. text ed. 24.95 (1-880394-04-9); pap. 12.95 (1-880394-02-2) Inc Pub MA.
— Three Hundred One Great Management Ideas from America's Most Innovative Small Companies. 360p. (Orig.). 1991. 24.95 (0-9626146-5-3); pap. 12.95 (0-9626146-4-5) Inc Pub MA.
Noble, Shiren T. Journey Through the Scriptures: Bible Games & Quizzes for Youth & Adults. 30p. (Orig.). 1994. pap. text ed. 5.95 (1-877971-07-3) Mid Atl Reg Pr.
***Noble-Smith, Dorothy.** Oh, Shenandoah. (Illus.). 336p. 1995. pap. 15.95 (1-57087-078-0) Prof Pr NC.
— Recollections: The People of the Blue Ridge Remember. 96p. 1995. 12.95 (1-57087-162-0) Prof Pr NC.
Noble, Stephanie. Tapping the Wisdom Within: A Guide to Joyous Living. LC 93-79753. 240p. (Orig.). 1994. pap. 10.95 (0-9638088-3-4) Inside Out Bks.
Noble, Stuart G. Forty Years of Public Schools in Mississippi: With Special Reference to the Education of the Negro. LC 73-177109. (Columbia University. Teachers College. Contributions to Education Ser.: No. 94). reprint ed. 37.50 (0-404-55094-0) AMS Pr.
— History of American Education. rev. ed. LC 76-92304. 552p. 1970. reprint ed. text ed. 65.00 (0-8371-2408-5, NOAE, Greenwood Pr) Greenwood.
Noble, Thomas F. & Contreni, John J., eds. Religion, Culture & Society in the Early Middle Ages. LC 87-5709. (Studies in Medieval Culture: No. 23). 1987. 32.95 (0-918720-83-4); pap. 15.95 (0-918720-84-2) Medieval Inst.
Noble, Thomas F. X. The Republic of St. Peter: The Birth of the Papal State, 680-825. LC 83-21870. (Middle Ages Ser.). (Illus.). 412p. 1984. pap. text ed. 19.95 (0-8122-1239-8) U of Pa Pr.
Noble, Trinka H. Apple Tree Christmas. LC 84-1901. (Illus.). 32p. (J). (ps-2). 1984. 14.99 (0-8037-0102-0) Dial Bks Young.
— The Day Jimmy's Boa Ate the Wash. LC 80-15098. (Pied Piper Bks.). (Illus.). 32p. (J). (ps-3). 1980. 14.99 (0-8037-1723-7); lib. bdg. 13.89 (0-8037-1724-5); pap. 4.95 (0-8037-0094-6) Dial Bks Young.
— The Day Jimmy's Boa Ate the Wash. (Illus.). 32p. (J). (ps-3). 1992. pap. 4.99 (0-14-054623-5, Puff Pied Piper) Puffin Bks.
— Day Jimmy's Boa Ate the Wash. enl. ed. (J). (ps-3). 1991. pap. 17.95 (0-8037-1073-9, Puff Pied Piper) Puffin Bks.
— The Day Jimmy's Boa Ate the Wash: Giant Edition. (J). (ps-3). 1993. pap. 18.99 (0-14-054622-7) Viking Penguin.
— Jimmy's Boa & the Big Splash Birthday Bash. LC 88-10933. (Illus.). 32p. (J). (ps-3). 1989. 13.95 (0-8037-0539-5); lib. bdg. 13.89 (0-8037-0540-9) Dial Bks Young.
— Jimmy's Boa & the Big Splash Birthday Bash. (Illus.). 32p. (J). (ps-3). 1993. pap. 4.99 (0-14-054921-8, Puff Pied Piper) Puffin Bks.
— Jimmy's Boa Bounces Back. LC 83-14289. (Pied Piper Bks.). (Illus.). 32p. (J). (ps-3). 1984. 14.99 (0-8037-0049-0); lib. bdg. 13.89 (0-8037-0050-4) Dial Bks Young.
— Jimmy's Boa Bounces Back. (Illus.). 32p. (J). (ps-3). 1992. pap. 4.99 (0-14-054654-5, Puff Pied Piper) Puffin Bks.
— Meanwhile Back at the Ranch. LC 86-11651. (Illus.). 32p. (J). (ps-3). 1987. 14.00 (0-8037-0353-8); lib. bdg. 13.89 (0-8037-0354-6) Dial Bks Young.
— Meanwhile Back at the Ranch. (Illus.). 32p. (J). (ps-3). 1992. pap. 4.99 (0-14-054564-6, Puff Pied Piper) Puffin Bks.
Noble, Trudy V. God Answers Children's Prayers Too. LC 85-217377. (Illus.). 30p. (J). (ps-4). 1990. write for info. (0-9620133-0-7) Joy Deliverance.
Noble, Vicki. Motherpeace: A Way to the Goddess Through Myth, Art, & Tarot. (Illus.). 288p. 1994. reprint ed. pap. 17.00 (0-06-251085-1) Harper SF.
— Shakti Woman: Feeling Our Fire, Healing Our World. 1991. pap. 16.00 (0-06-250667-6) Harper SF.
Noble, Vicki & Tenney, Jonathan. Motherpeace Tarot Playbook. LC 86-1510. (Illus.). 144p. 1986. pap. 19.00 (0-914728-53-9) Wingbow Pr.
Noble, Vicki, jt. auth. see **Vogel, Karen.**
Noble, W. C., ed. The Skin Microflora & Microbial Skin Disease. (Illus.). 500p. (C). 1993. 105.00 (0-521-40198-4) Cambridge U Pr.
Noble, Weston, jt. auth. see **Nesheim, Paul.**
Noble, William. Bookbanning in America: Who Bans Books? - & Why. LC 90-3413. 352p. 1990. 21.95 (0-8397-1080-1) Eriksson.
— Bookbanning in America: Who Bans Books? - & Why. LC 90-3413. 352p. 1992. reprint ed. pap. 14.95 (0-8397-1081-X) Eriksson.
— The Complete Guide to Writers' Conferences & Workshops. 129p. (Orig.). Date not set. pap. 16.95 (0-8397-1840-3) Eriksson.
— Make That Scene: A Writer's Guide to Setting, Mood & Atmosphere. 224p. 1988. 19.95 (0-8397-5708-5) Eriksson.
— Make that Scene: A Writer's Guide to Setting, Mood & Atmosphere. LC 88-19198. 224p. 1991. reprint ed. pap. 12.95 (0-8397-5709-3) Eriksson.
— Show, Don't Tell: A Writer's Guide. 208p. 1991. 19.95 (0-8397-7766-3) Eriksson.
— Show, Don't Tell: A Writer's Guide. LC 91-16580. 224p. 1993. reprint ed. pap. 12.95 (0-8397-7767-1) Eriksson.
— Shut Up! He Explained: A Writer's Guide to the Uses & Misuses of Dialogue. 224p. 1987. 19.95 (0-8397-7777-9) Eriksson.
— Shut up! He Explained: A Writer's Guide to the Uses & Misuses of Dialogue. 2nd ed. LC 87-20053. 224p. 1991. reprint ed. pap. 12.95 (0-8397-7778-7) Eriksson.
— Twenty-Eight Biggest Writing Blunders. 120p. 1992. 12.95 (0-89879-504-4) Writers Digest.
Noble, William & Noble, June. Steal This Plot: A Writer's Guide to Story Structure & Plagiarism. 224p. 1985. 19.95 (0-8397-7880-5) Eriksson.
— Steal This Plot: A Writer's Guide to Story Structure & Plagiarism. 2nd ed. LC 85-6878. 224p. 1991. reprint ed. pap. 12.95 (0-8397-7881-3) Eriksson.
Noble, William, jt. auth. see **Whitehill, Angela.**
Nobleman, Louis R. Second-Hand Dreams. (Illus.). (J). (gr. k-6). 1993. pap. 9.95 (1-56883-010-6) Colonial Pr AL.
Nobleman, Roberta. Fifty Projects for Creative Dramatics. 2nd rev. ed. 34p. 1980. pap. 4.95 (0-932720-22-6) New Plays Inc.
— Mime & Masks. (Illus.). 151p. 1979. pap. 8.95 (0-932720-46-3); write for info. (0-932720-47-1) New Plays Inc.
— Victim, Survivor, Celebrant. LC 94-72394. 240p. 1994. pap. 12.95 (0-87029-249-8) Abbey.
Nobles, Anita K. Dinner Will Be Ready in a Minute: Quick & Easy, So-You-Can-Relax Recipes. 128p. (Orig.). 1994. pap. 12.95 (1-882626-22-2) Impress Ink.
— Dinner Will Be Ready in a Minute: Quick & Easy, So-You-Can-Relax Recipes. (Cookin' Bks.). 128p. (Orig.). 1994. pap. 19.95 (1-882626-25-7) Impress Ink.
— Hey Mom...I'll Cook Dinner: Recipes That Turn a Kid into the Family Chef. 128p. (Orig.). 1994. pap. 12.95 (1-882626-21-4) Impress Ink.
— Hey Mom...I'll Cook Dinner: Recipes That Turn a Kid into the Family Chef. (Cookin' Bks.). 120p. (Orig.). 1994. pap. 19.95 (1-882626-26-5) Impress Ink.
— A Mother's Kiss. 1993. pap. 4.95 (1-882626-13-3) Impress Ink.
— Windows to the Soul. 384p. 1992. pap. 7.95 (1-882626-10-9) Impress Ink.
Nobles, Gregory H., jt. auth. see **Henretta, James A.**
Nobles, M. A. Using Computers to Solve Reservoir Engineering Problems. 2nd ed. LC 84-3759. 562p. 1984. 49.00 (0-87201-899-7) Gulf Pub.
Nobles, Pat, ed. see **Rail, Axel.**
Nobles, Richard. Pensions, Employment, & the Law. (Monographs on Labour Law). 286p. 1993. 55.00 (0-19-825448-2) OUP.
Nobles, Wade W., et al. African-American Families: Issues, Insights & Directions. 1987. 10.00 (0-939205-04-1) Blk Fam Inst Pub.
Nobles, Wade W. African Psychology: Toward its Reclamation, Reascension & Revitalization. 134p. 1986. 10.00 (0-939205-02-5) Blk Fam Inst Pub.
— Africanity & the Black Family: The Development of a Theoretical Model. 116p. 1985. 10.00 (0-939205-01-7) Blk Fam Inst Pub.
Nobles, Wade W. & Goddard, Lawford L. Understanding the Black Family: A Guide for Scholarship & Research. 137p. 1984. 10.00 (0-939205-00-9) Blk Fam Inst Pub.
Nobles, Wade W., et al. The Km Ebit Husia: Authoritative Utterances of Exceptional Insights for the Black Family. 201p. 1985. 15.00 (0-939205-03-3) Blk Fam Inst Pub.
Noblet, Martine, jt. auth. see **Braguet, Anne.**
Noblet, Martine, jt. auth. see **Deltenre, Chantal.**
***Nobli, George W. & Pink, William.** Continuity & Contradiction: The Futures of the Sociology of Education. (Understanding Education & Policy Ser.). 416p. (C). 1995. 26.50 (1-881303-68-3) Hampton Pr NJ.
Noblit, George, ed. see **Corson, David.**
Noblit, George, ed. see **Fox, Thomas.**
Noblit, George W. & Hare, R. Dwight. Meta-Ethnography: Synthesizing Qualitative Studies. (Qualitative Research Methods Ser.: Vol. 11). 96p. (C). 1988. text ed. 21.50 (0-8039-3022-4); pap. text ed. 9.50 (0-8039-3023-2) Sage.
***Noblit, George W. & Pink, William T., eds.** Continuity & Contradiction: The Futures of the Sociology of Education. (Understanding Education & Policy Ser.). 416p. (C). 1995. text ed. 69.50 (1-881303-67-5); pap. text ed. 28.50 (1-881503-68-2) Hampton Pr NJ.
— Schooling in Social Context: Qualitative Studies. LC 86-10890. 352p. (C). 1987. text ed. 55.00 (0-89391-326-X) Ablex Pub.
Noblit, George W., ed. see **Kanpol, Barry.**
Noblit, George W., ed. see **Tesconi, Charles A.**
***Noblitt, James R. & Perskin, Pamela S.** Cult & Ritual Abuse: Its History, Anthropology, & Recent Discovery. LC 95-2492. 240p. 1995. text ed. 55.00 (0-275-95281-9, Praeger Pubs) Greenwood.
Noblitt, James S. Nouveau Point De Vue. (FRE.). 1978. text ed. 31.00 (0-669-96545-6); Wkbk./Lab. manual. student ed 15.00 (0-669-96552-9); Instr.'s guide. teacher ed 2.00 (0-669-00335-2); Cassettes. audio 55.00 (0-669-00250-X); Reels. reel tape 75.00 (0-669-96560-X); Transcripts. write for info. (0-669-01166-5) Heath.
Noblitt, Julia E., ed. see **Burke, Kay.**
Nobo, Jorge L. Whitehead's Metaphysics of Extension & Solidarity. LC 85-25040. 437p. (Orig.). 1986. 74.50 (0-88706-261-X); pap. 24.95 (0-88706-262-8) State U NY Pr.
Nobrega, E., ed. see **Food & Beverage Instrumentation Symposium Staff.**
Nobrega, Jose N., jt. auth. see **Gaito, John.**
Nobs, Malcolm A., jt. auth. see **Hiesey, William.**
Nobuhiko, Maruyama, jt. auth. see **Hayao, Ishimura.**
Nobuka, Yuzuru, tr. see **Takahashi, Masanobu.**
Nobuo Suzuki. Introduction to Building Drawing & Painting. (Easy Start Guide Ser.). (Illus.). 112p. 1992. 36.95 (4-7661-0626-1, Pub. by Graphic Sha JA) Bks Nippan.
***Noce, C., et al.** Superconductivity & Strongly Correlated Electron Systems. 448p. 1994. text ed. 124.00 (981-02-2038-3) World Scientific Pub.
Nocent, Adrian. The Liturgical Year, Vol. 1: Advent, Christmas, Epiphany, Sundays 2-8 in Ordinary Time. 446p. 1977. pap. 10.00 (0-8146-0962-7) Liturgical Pr.
— The Liturgical Year, Vol. 2: Lent & Holy Week. 251p. (C). 1977. pap. 10.00 (0-8146-0963-5) Liturgical Pr.

An Asterisk (*) at the beginning of an entry indicates that the title is appearing in BIP for the first time.

— The Liturgical Year, Vol. 3: Paschal Triduum, Easter Season, & Solemnities of the Lord. 326p. (C). 1977. pap. 10.00 (0-8146-0964-3) Liturgical Pr.

— The Liturgical Year, Vol. 4: Sundays 9-34 in Ordinary Time. 406p. (C). 1977. pap. 10.00 (0-8146-0965-1) Liturgical Pr.

Nocent, Adrien. A Rereading of the Renewed Liturgy. Misrahi, Mary M., tr. LC 94-7253. 168p. (Orig.). (ENG & FRE.). 1994. pap. text ed. 11.95 (0-8146-2299-2, Liturg Pr Bks) Liturgical Pr.

Nocenti, et al. Inhumans. 72p. 1988. 7.95 (0-87135-435-7) Marvel Entmnt.

Nocenti, Ann & Bolton, John. Someplace Strange. Goodwin, Archie, ed. (Limited-Signed Edition Ser.: No. 15). (Illus.). 64p. 1988. 6.95 (0-936211-13-X) Marvel Entmnt.

Nocenti, Ann & Lightle, Steve. Wolverine-Typhoid Mary: Typhoid's Kiss. 64p. 1994. 6.95 (0-7851-0056-3) Marvel Entmnt.

Nocenti, Ann, et al. Longshot. (Illus.). 176p. 1989. pap. 16.95 (0-87135-568-X) Marvel Entmnt.

Nocentini, Alberta. Pasta al Dente: Recipes from All the Regions of Italy. LC 86-22268. (Illus.). 1990. 24.95 (0-87949-264-3) Ashley Bks.

Nocera, Joe, ed. Texas Monthly Bidness. LC 86-14431. 224p. 1986. pap. 12.95 (0-87719-054-2, Lone Star Bks) Gulf Pub.

***Nocera, Joseph.** A Piece of the Action. 1995. pap. 14.00 (0-684-80435-2, Touchstone Bks) S&S Trade.

— A Piece of the Action: How the Middle Class Joins the Money Class. 1994. 25.00 (0-671-66756-4) S&S Trade.

Nocerino, Kathryn. Candles in the Daylight. (Illus.). 46p. 1985. pap. 5.00 (0-942292-03-0) Warthog Pr.

— Death of Plankton Bar & Grill. 88p. 1987. pap. 5.00 (0-89823-092-6) New Rivers Pr.

— Wax Lips. 88p. 1980. pap. 3.00 (0-89823-019-5) New Rivers Pr.

Nocero, Michael A. Transseptal Technique: A Workbook. (Illus.). 112p. 1989. student ed 29.50 (0-87993-351-8) Futura Pub.

Nocetti, D. Fabian & Fleming, Peter J. Parallel Processing in Digital Control. Grimble, M. J. & Johnson, M., eds. LC 92-21882. (Advances in Industrial Control Ser.). (Illus.). xiv, 146p. 1992. 59.00 (0-387-19728-1) Spr-Verlag.

Nochimson, Martha. No End to Her: Soap Opera & the Female Subject. 1993. 40.00 (0-520-07763-6); pap. 15.00 (0-520-07771-7) U CA Pr.

***Nochlin, Linda.** The Body in Pieces: The Fragment As a Metaphor of Modernity. LC 94-61110. (Walter Neurath Memorial Lecture Ser.). (Illus.). 64p. 1995. 14.95 (0-500-55027-1) Thames Hudson.

— Mathis at Colmar: A Visual Confrontation. LC 63-2298. (Illus.). (Orig.). 1963. 5.25 (0-87376-002-6) Red Dust.

— The Politics of Vision: Essays on Nineteenth Century Art & Society. LC 89-45055. (Illus.). 224p. 1991. pap. text ed. 15.00 (0-06-430187-7, Icon Edns) HarpC.

— Realism. (Style & Civilization Ser.). (Orig.). 1972. pap. 10.95 (0-14-021305-8, Penguin Bks) Viking Penguin.

— Women, Art & Power. 1989. pap. 14.00 (0-06-430183-4, Icon Edns) HarpC.

Nochlin, Linda, jt. ed. see Millon, Henry A.

Nochomovitz, Lucien, et al. Atlas of Intraoperative Consultation: A Guide to Smears Imprints & Frozen Sections. LC 89-6936. (Illus.). 160p. 1989. 105.00 (0-89189-279-6) Am Soc Clinical.

Nochomovitz, Lucien E. Bladder Biopsy Interpretation. (Biopsy Interpretation Ser.). 240p. 1992. 86.50 (0-88167-878-3) Raven.

***Nochomovitz, Michael L. & Cherniack, Neil S., eds.** Noninvasive Respiratory Monitoring. fac. ed. LC 85-24275. (Contemporary Issues in Pulmonary Disease Ser.: No. 3). (Illus.). 239p. 1986. reprint ed. pap. 68.20 (0-7837-7824-4, 2047580) Bks Demand.

Nochomovitz, Michael L. & Cherniak, Neil S., eds. Noninvasive Respiratory Monitoring. (Contemporary Issues in Pulmonary Disease Ser.: Vol. 3). (Illus.). 229p. 1986. text ed. 42.00 (0-443-08342-8) Churchill.

Nochomovitz, Micheal L. & Montenegro, Hugo D., eds. Ventilatory Support in Respiratory Failure. (Illus.). 240p. 1987. 45.00 (0-87993-297-X) Futura Pub.

Nock, Albert J. Book of Journeyman, Essays from the New Freeman. LC 67-23253. (Essay Index Reprint Ser.). 1977. 18.95 (0-8369-0744-2) Ayer.

— Free Speech & Plain Language. LC 68-58806. (Essay Index Reprint Ser.). 1977. 19.95 (0-8369-0090-1) Ayer.

— Memoirs of a Superfluous Man. 326p. 1994. pap. 14.95 (0-87319-038-6) Hallberg Pub Corp.

— Memoirs of a Superfluous Man. LC 83-45827. reprint ed. 30.00 (0-404-20192-X) AMS Pr.

— Mr. Jefferson. LC 82-83562. 228p. 1983. pap. 12.95 (0-87319-024-6) Hallberg Pub Corp.

— On Doing the Right Thing & Other Essays. LC 76-128282. (Essay Index Reprint Ser.). 1977. 23.95 (0-8369-2006-6) Ayer.

— Our Enemy, the State. LC 82-83561. 112p. 1983. pap. 9.95 (0-87319-023-8) Hallberg Pub Corp.

— Our Enemy, the State. LC 76-172222. (Right Wing Individualist Tradition in America Ser.). 1979. reprint ed. 23.95 (0-405-00431-1) Ayer.

— Our Enemy, the State: Including "On Doing the Right Thing" xxv, 117p. 1994. 19.95 (0-930073-11-8) Fox & Wilkes.

— Selected Letters of Albert Jay Nock. 1986. lib. bdg. 79.95 (0-8490-3848-0) Gordon Pr.

— Snoring As a Fine Art & Twelve Other Essays. LC 74-121493. (Essay Index Reprint Ser.). 1977. 12.95 (0-8369-2007-4) Ayer.

— The State of the Union: Essays in Social Criticism. LC 90-22412. 342p. (Orig.). 1991. text ed. 18.00 (0-86597-092-0); pap. 7.50 (0-86597-093-9) Liberty Fund.

— Theory of Education in the United States. LC 72-89212. (American Education: Its Men, Institutions & Ideas, Ser. 1). 1971. reprint ed. 16.95 (0-405-01451-1) Ayer.

Nock, Albert J., ed. see Ward, Artemus, pseud.

Nock, Albert J., ed. see Ward, Artemus & Browne, Charles F.

Nock, Ann. Child of the Bay. 1993. 37.50 (1-878901-51-6) Hampton Roads Pub Co.

Nock, Arthur D., ed. see Sallustius, Serenus.

Nock, O. S. One Facet of an Autobiography. 141p. (C). 1989. text ed. 59.00 (1-872795-73-0, Pub. by Pentland Pr UK) St Mut.

Nock, Steven L. The Costs of Privacy: Reputation & Surveillance in America. LC 92-35480. 158p. 1993. lib. bdg. 39.95 (0-202-30454-X); pap. 18.95 (0-202-30455-8) Aldine de Gruyter.

— Sociology of the Family. 2nd ed. 432p. (C). 1991. text ed. 28.00 (0-13-808593-5, 610803) P-H.

Nock, Steven L. & Kingston, Paul W. The Sociology of Public Issues. 256p. (C). 1990. pap. 18.95 (0-534-12096-2) Intl Thomson.

Nockels, Arthur, ed. see Wallraff, Gunter.

Nockles, Peter B. The Oxford Movement in Context: Anglican High Churchmanship, 1760-1857. 365p. (C). 1994. 59.95 (0-521-38162-2) Cambridge U Pr.

Nockolds, Harold. The Coachmakers. 240p. 1990. 60.00 (0-85131-270-5, Pub. by J A Allen & Co UK) St Mut.

Nocks, Elaine C. & Einstein, Gilles O. Learning to Use the SPSS Batch System. (Illus.). 112p. (C). 1986. pap. text ed. 19.00 (0-13-528019-2) P-H.

Nocks, Elaine C., jt. auth. see Einstein, Gilles O.

Nocolis, G., jt. auth. see Prigogine, Ilya.

***Nocon, Gene.** Photographic Printing. (Illus.). 160p. Date not set. pap. 19.95 (0-86369-653-8, London Bridge) Genl Dist Srvs.

Noda, A., jt. ed. see Katayama, T.

Noda, I. & Rubingh, D. N., eds. Polymer Solutions, Blends, & Interfaces: Proceedings of the Procter & Gamble UERP Symposium. LC 92-34493. (Studies in Polymer Science: Vol. 11). 1992. write for info. (0-444-89397-0) Elsevier.

Noda, K., ed. Optical Fiber Transmission. (North-Holland Studies in Telecommunication: No. 6). 316p. 1986. 136.00 (0-444-87685-5, North Holland) Elsevier.

Noda, Mari, jt. auth. see Jorden, Eleanor H.

Noda, Mari, jt. auth. see Jorden, Eleanor Harz.

Noda, Masaki, ed. Cellular & Molecular Biology of Bone. LC 93-14783. (Illus.). 567p. 1993. text ed. 99.00 (0-12-520225-3) Acad Pr.

Noda, Yosiyuki, ed. Introduction to Japanese Law. Angelo, Anthony H., tr. 253p. 1976. 32.50 (0-86008-160-5, Pub. by U of Tokyo JA) Col U Pr.

Nodal, Adolfo V. How the Arts Made a Difference: The MacArthur Park Public Arts Program. Goldstein, Barbara, ed. LC 89-1859. (Illus.). 150p. 1989. pap. 19.95 (0-912158-96-4) Hennessey.

Nodal, Al & De Bretteville, Sheila L. Robert Wilson's Civil Wars: Drawings, Models & Documentation. Belloli, Andrea P., ed. LC 84-6117. (Illus.). 61p. 1984. 15.00 (0-930209-00-1) Otis Art.

Nodal, Al & Frank, Peter. Bob & Bob: Selected Works. (Illus.). 48p. 1986. 10.00 (0-930209-03-6) Otis Art.

Nodal, J. H., jt. ed. see Skeat, W. W.

Nodal, John & Milner, George. A Glossary of the Lancashire Dialect. (English Dialect Society Publications Ser.: No's. 10, 35). 1969. reprint ed. pap. 33.00 (0-8115-0443-3) Periodicals Srv.

Nodar, Carmen M. Abuelita's Paradise. Mathews, Judith, ed. LC 91-42330. (Illus.). 32p. (J). (gr. k-3). 1992. 13.95 (0-8075-0129-8) A Whitman.

— El Paraiso de Abuelita. Mathews, Judith, ed. Mlawer, Teresa, tr. LC 92-3767. (Illus.). 32p. (SPA.). (J). (gr. k-3). 1992. 13.95 (0-8075-6346-3) A Whitman.

Nodar, Carmen S. Abuelita's Paradise. (One World Friends & Neighbors Ser.). (Illus.). (J). (gr. k-4). 1993. 13.95 (0-685-66422-8); audio 11.00 (1-882869-79-6) Varsity Read Servs.

Noddings, Charles R. & Mullett, Gary M. Handbook of Compositions at Thermodynamic Equilibrium. LC 64-14730. (Interscience Library of Chemical Engineering & Processing: No. 5). 629p. reprint ed. pap. 179.30 (0-317-10054-8, 2007394) Bks Demand.

***Noddings Investment Group, Inc. Staff.** The Irwin Yearbook of Convertible Securities: Warrants, Bonds, & Preferred Stocks. 320p. 1995. text ed. 90.00 (0-7863-0432-4) Irwin Prof Pubng.

Noddings, Nel. Caring: A Feminine Approach to Ethics & Moral Education. LC 83-18223. 220p. (C). 1984. 27.50 (0-520-05043-6); pap. 14.00 (0-520-05747-3) U CA Pr.

— The Challenge to Care in Schools: An Alternative Approach to Education. (Advances in Contemporary Educational Thought Ser.). 208p. (C). 1992. text ed. 38.00 (0-8077-3178-1); pap. text ed. 16.95 (0-8077-3177-3) Tchrs Coll.

— Educating for Intelligent Belief or Unbelief. LC 93-19098. (John Dewey Lecture Ser.). 176p. 1993. text ed. 37.00 (0-8077-3272-9); pap. text ed. 17.95 (0-8077-3271-0) Tchrs Coll.

— Philosophy of Education. LC 95-8820. (Dimensions of Philosophy Ser.). 1995. write for info. (0-8133-8429-X) Westview.

— Women & Evil. 293p. 1991. pap. 14.00 (0-520-07413-0) U CA Pr.

Noddings, Nel & Shore, Paul J. Awakening the Inner Eye: Intuition in Education. LC 83-18057. 254p. reprint ed. pap. 72.40 (0-7837-4628-8, 2044351) Bks Demand.

Noddings, Nel, jt. ed. see Witherell, Carol.

Nodel, Maxine. Moral or Less: An Adventure in Addition & Subtraction. (Arithmetic Math Ser.). (Illus.). 32p. (J). (ps-3). 1990. 8.95 (0-922613-25-7); student ed. pap. 6.95 (0-922613-26-5); audio 9.00 (0-922613-28-1); 4.95 (0-922613-27-3) Hachai Pubns.

Nodelman. The Same Place But Different. (J). 1995. 15.00 (0-671-89839-6, S&S Bks Young Read) S&S Childrens.

Nodelman, Perry. The Pleasures of Children's Literature. 260p. (Orig.). (C). 1992. pap. text ed. 26.95 (0-8013-0219-6, 75877) Longman.

— The Same Place but Different. LC 93-29514. (J). Date not set. 15.00 (0-06-024258-2); lib. bdg. 14.89 (0-06-024259-0) HarpC Child Bks.

— Words about Pictures: The Narrative Art of Children's Picture Books. LC 87-38084. (Illus.). 336p. 1990. pap. 15.00 (0-8203-1271-1) U of Ga Pr.

Nodelman, Perry & May, Jill P., eds. Festschrift: A Ten Year Retrospective. 76p. 1983. pap. 6.00 (0-937263-03-6) CHLA Pubns.

Nodelman, Perry, ed. see Children's Literature Association Publications Staff.

Nodelman, Perry, ed. see Children's Literature Association Staff.

Nodelman, Sheldon. The Rothko Chapel Paintings: Form as Meaning in the American Abstract Sublime. (Illus.). 128p. (Orig.). 1995. pap. 23.95 (0-292-77054-5) U of Tex Pr.

Noden & Delahunta. Embryology of Domestic Animals 2. write for info. (0-8016-6434-9) Mosby Yr Bk.

Noden & Vacca. Whole Language in Middle & Secondary Classrooms. (C). 1993. text ed. 29.50 (0-06-500071-4) HarpCollege.

Noden, Alexandra B., jt. auth. see Levitan, Sar A.

Noden, Harry R. & Vacca, Richard. Whole Language in Middle & Secondary Classrooms: Becoming a Classroom Archaeologist. LC 93-31908. 1994. write for info. (0-00-650071-4) HarpCollege.

Nodia, Ghia, jt. ed. see Chavchavadze, N. V.

Nodier, Charles. Fee Aux Miettes & Smarra, Trilby. (Folio Ser.: No. 1420). (FRE.). 1982. pap. 13.95 (2-07-037420-3) Schoenhof.

— History of the Secret Societies of the Army, & of the Military Conspiracies Which Had As Their Object the Destruction of the Government of Bonaparte. LC 78-14740. 1978. reprint ed. 50.00 (0-8201-1318-2) Schol Facsimiles.

— Smarra & Trilby. Landry, Judith, tr. (Dedalus European Classics Ser.). 125p. 1994. pap. 11.95 (0-946626-79-0, Pub. by Dedalus Bks UK) Hippocrene Bks.

Nodine, Barbara F. Psychology by Ludy T. Benjamin Jr. - Study Guide. 3rd ed. (Illus.). 429p. (C). 1994. pap. write for info. (0-02-388071-6) Macmillan.

Nodine, Calvin F. & Fisher, Dennis, eds. Perception & Pictorial Representation. LC 79-4613. (Praeger Special Studies). 448p. 1979. text ed. 38.50 (0-275-90402-4, C0402, Praeger Pubs) Greenwood.

Nodine, John H. & Siegler, Peter E., eds. Animal & Clinical Pharmacologic Techniques in Drug Evaluation. LC 64-19787. 680p. reprint ed. pap. 180.00 (0-8357-5486-3, 2051708) Bks Demand.

Nodine, Richard. The One Million Dollar Desktop Publishing Idea Book. 208p. 1994. pap. 29.95 (0-9641100-0-8) Pacific Lrning.

Nodland, Jory. Americans with a Touch of Greatness, Vol. 1. (Illus.). 64p. (Orig.). 1984. pap. text ed. 4.95 (0-317-93680-8) Nodland Borie.

Nodset, Joan L. Come Here, Cat. LC 92-39005. (Illus.). (J). (ps-3). 1973. lib. bdg. 9.89 (0-06-024558-1) HarpC Child Bks.

— Go Away, Dog. LC 63-11162. (Illus.). 32p. (J). (ps-3). 1963. lib. bdg. 9.89 (0-06-024556-5) HarpC Child Bks.

— Who Took the Farmer's Hat? LC 62-17964. (Illus.). 32p. (J). (gr. k-3). 1963. lib. bdg. 14.89 (0-06-024566-2) HarpC Child Bks.

— Who Took the Farmer's Hat? LC 62-17964. (Trophy Picture Bk.). (Illus.). 32p. (J). (ps-2). 1988. pap. 5.95 (0-06-443174-6, Trophy) HarpC Child Bks.

Nodtuedt, Magnus. Rebirth of Norway's Peasantry: Folk Leader Hans Nielsen Hauge. 305p. 1965. 5.95 (0-685-02327-3) Holmes.

Noe, Courtney, ed. see Puckett, Dale & Dibble, Peter.

Noe, Dennis. A Short Course in Clinical Pharmacokinetics. 225p. (Orig.). (C). 1993. pap. text ed. write for info. (0-915486-19-9) Applied Therapeutics.

Noe, Dennis A. & Rock, Robert C. Laboratory Medicine: The Selection & Interpretation of Clinical Laboratory Studies. (Illus.). 1012p. 1994. 135.00 (0-683-06548-3) Williams & Wilkins.

Noe, Fay. Our Home in the Ozarks. 2nd ed. 1970. pap. 5.50 (0-9600208-5-3) Noe.

Noe, Francis P. & Hammitt, William E., eds. Visual Preferences of Travelers along the Blue Ridge Parkway. LC 88-600093. (Scientific Monograph Ser.: No. 18). (Illus.). (Orig.). (C). 1988. pap. write for info. (0-943475-00-7) Natl Park GA.

Noe, John R. Peak Performance Principles for High Achievers. 192p. 1986. pap. 4.50 (0-425-10150-9) Berkley Pub.

— Peak Performance Principles for High Achievers. 192p. 1984. 14.95 (0-8119-0648-5) LIFETIME.

— People Power. 1988. pap. 4.50 (0-425-10755-8) Berkley Pub.

Noe, Kenneth W. Southwest Virginia's Railroad: Modernization & the Sectional Crisis. LC 93-5632. (Illus.). 232p. 1994. 27.95 (0-252-02070-7) U of Ill Pr.

Noe, Marcia, ed. Exploring the Midwestern Literary Imagination: Essays in Honor of David D. Anderson. LC 92-64472. 234p. 1993. 22.50 (0-87875-430-X) Whitston Pub.

Noe, Marcia & Spelius, Carol, eds. Celebrate the Midwest! Poems & Stories for David D. Anderson. 122p. (Orig.). 1991. pap. 8.95 (0-941363-22-8) Lake Shore Pub.

***Noe, Randolph.** Kentucky Probate Methods. 396p. 1976. 55.00 (0-672-84115-0) Michie Butterworth.

— Kentucky Probate Methods. suppl. ed. 396p. 1976. 55.00 (0-672-82532-5); 25.00 (0-87215-933-7) Michie Butterworth.

Noe, Raymond A., et al. Human Resource Management: Gaining a Competitive Advantage. LC 93-26120. 824p. (C). 1993. text ed. 64.95 (0-256-11349-1) Irwin.

Noe, Raymond A., et al, comps. Readings in Human Resource Management. LC 93-42315. (C). 1994. text ed. 42.95 (0-256-14852-X) Irwin.

Noe, Robert C. MRB Engineering Handbook. LC 93-11421. 250p. 1993. 49.95 (0-87389-199-6) ASQC Qual Pr.

Noe, Robert M., III, jt. auth. see Mondy, R. Wayne.

Noe, Sydney P. Massachusetts Silver Coinage. LC 88-72077. (Illus.). 210p. 1990. 35.00 (0-942666-56-9) S J Durst.

Noe, Sydney P. & Johnston, Ann. The Coinage of Metapontum. (Numismatic Notes & Monographs: Nos. 32 & 47). (Illus.). 165p. 1983. reprint ed. 32.00 (0-89722-202-4) Am Numismatic.

Noe, Sydney P., jt. auth. see Kleiner, Fred S.

***Noe, Tom.** Into the Lion's Den. 190p. (Orig.). 1995. pap. 11.95 (0-937779-29-6) Greenlawn Pr.

Noe, Tom, ed. see Redwood, Ray.

Noe, Virgilio. Prayers to Mary. Buono, Anthony M., ed. 96p. 1988. pap. 3.95 (0-89942-210-1, 210/04) Catholic Bk Pub.

***Noebel, David.** Understanding the Times. LC 94-29314. 1994. 34.99 (1-56507-268-5) Harvest Hse.

***Noebel, David A.** Understanding the Times: The Religious Worldviews of Our Day & the Search for Truth. abr. ed. 1995. pap. write for info. (0-936163-22-4) Summit Pr CO.

***Noebel, David A., et al.** Clergy in the Classroom: The Religion of Secular Humanism. 1995. pap. write for info. (0-936163-27-5) Summit Pr CO.

Noebels, Jeffrey L., jt. ed. see Kellaway, Peter.

Noecker, Duane. Tell Me, Grandpa. 110p. 1994. pap. 6.00 (0-9641678-0-8) D Noecker.

Noehbauer, Hans F. Munich: City of the Arts. 1994. 125.00 (1-55859-865-0) Abbeville Pr.

Noehrenberg, Peter C., jt. auth. see Allen, Patrick D.

Noel, Ann, jt. auth. see Frazee, David.

Noel-Baker, Lord. The First World Disarmament: And Why It Failed. 1979. 64.00 (0-08-023365-1, Pub. by Pergamon Repr UK) Franklin.

Noel-Baker, Philip. The Private Manufacture of Armaments. 11.50 (0-8446-4593-1) Peter Smith.

— The Private Manufacture of Armaments. LC 78-145399. 1971. reprint ed. pap. 9.95 (0-486-22736-7) Dover.

Noel, Barbara. You Must Be Dreaming. 1993. mass mkt. 5.99 (0-449-22268-3) Fawcett.

Noel, Barbara & Watterson, Kathryn. You Must Be Dreaming. LC 92-16265. 1992. 21.00 (0-671-74153-5) S&S Trade.

Noel-Bentley, Peter. Earle Birney: An Annotated Bibliography. 116p. (C). 1983. pap. text ed. 9.00 (0-920763-50-2, Pub. by ECW Press CN) Genl Dist Srvs.

Noel, Bernard. David. (CAL Art Ser.). 1990. 14.95 (0-517-57317-2, Crown) Crown Pub Group.

— Dictionnaire de la Commune, Vol. 1. (FRE.). 1978. pap. 9.95 (0-8288-5177-8, M6428) Fr & Eur.

— Magrihe. 1995. 12.00 (0-517-88414-3) Random.

— Magritte. (CAL Art Ser.). 1989. 14.95 (0-517-53009-0, Crown) Crown Pub Group.

Noel, Chris, et al. Matter of Survival. (Illus.). 1987. 19.95 (0-8283-1903-0) Branden Pub Co.

Noel, Christopher. Rumpelstiltskin. LC 92-4592. (We All Have Tales Ser.). (Illus.). 40p. (J). (gr. k up). 1993. 14.95 (0-88708-279-3, Rabbit); audio 19.95 (0-88708-280-7, Rabbit) S&S Childrens.

Noel, Daniel. Approaching Earth. (Chrysalis Bks.). 192p. (Orig.). 1986. pap. 12.95 (0-916349-12-8) Amity Hse Inc.

Noel, Daniel C. Paths to the Power of Myth: Joseph Campbell & the Study of Religion. 228p. 1994. pap. 12.95 (0-8245-1389-4) Crossroad NY.

Noel, Daniel C., ed. Paths to the Power of Myth: Joseph Campbell & the Study of Religion. 1990. 19.95 (0-8245-1024-0) Crossroad NY.

***Noel, David.** Nuteeriat. 200p. 1989. per., pap. 10.00 (0-9593205-4-7) Bonsall Pub.

Noel, Diana. Five to Seven. 2.95 (0-86072-032-2, Pub. by Quartet UK) Charles River Bks.

Noel, Francoise. The Christie Seigneuries: Estate Management & Settlement in the Upper Richelieu Valley, 1760-1854. (Illus.). 256p. 1992. 44.95 (0-7735-0876-7, Pub. by McGill CN) U of Toronto Pr.

Noel, Gerard E. The Great Lock-Out of Nineteen Twenty-Six. LC 76-372463. 263p. reprint ed. pap. 75.00 (0-317-29894-1, 2019381) Bks Demand.

Noel Hume, Audrey. Archaeology & the Colonial Gardener. LC 73-80008. (Archaeological Ser.: No. 7). (Illus.). 93p. (Orig.). 1974. pap. 5.95 (0-87935-012-1) Colonial Williamsburg.

— Food. LC 78-4683. (Archaeological Ser.: No. 9). (Illus.). 68p. 1978. pap. 5.95 (0-87935-045-8) Colonial Williamsburg.

Noel Hume, Ivor. Archaeology & Wetherburn's Tavern. LC 76-84024. (Archaeological Ser.: No. 3). (Illus.). 47p. (Orig.). 1969. pap. 5.95 (0-910412-08-1) Colonial Williamsburg.

— Digging for Carter's Grove. LC 73-88326. (Archaeological Ser.: No. 8). (Illus.). 61p. (Orig.). 1974. pap. 5.95 (0-87935-016-4) Colonial Williamsburg.

An Asterisk (*) at the beginning of an entry indicates that the title is appearing in BIP for the first time.

— Discoveries in Martin's Hundred. rev. ed. LC 83-1951. (Archaeological Ser.: No. 10). (Illus.). 64p. (Orig.). 1987. pap. 5.95 (*0-87935-069-5*) Colonial Williamsburg.

— Glass in Colonial Williamsburg's Archaeological Collections. LC 79-84022. (Archaeological Ser.: No. 1). (Illus.). 48p. (Orig.). 1969. pap. 5.95 (*0-910412-06-5*) Colonial Williamsburg.

Noel-Hume, Ivor. Historical Archaeology. (Illus.). 1968. 30.00 (*0-394-42848-X*) Knopf.

Noel Hume, Ivor. James Geddy & Sons: Colonial Craftsmen. LC 70-115038. (Archaeological Ser.: No. 5). (Illus.). 45p. (Orig.). 1970. pap. 5.95 (*0-910412-10-3*) Colonial Williamsburg.

Noel-Hume, Ivor. Martin's Hundred. LC 81-48096. (Illus.). 384p. 1982. 25.00 (*0-394-50728-2*) Knopf.

Noel Hume, Ivor. Martin's Hundred. rev. ed. 400p. 1991. pap. 16.50 (*0-8139-1323-3*) U Pr of Va.

Noel, J. The Golden Scarabs & Other Tales. LC 94-70215. (Illus.). 1994. pap. 8.95 (*0-930422-15-5*) Dennis-Landman.

— My Name Is Selah. (Illus.). 22p. 1994. pap. 4.95 (*0-685-75333-6*) Dennis-Landman.

— The Secret of the Seraphims & Other Poems. (Illus.). 28p. Date not set. pap. 4.95 (*0-930422-16-3*) Dennis-Landman.

Noel, James. The Earth Today. Dennison, T. E., ed. (Illus.). 539p. (Orig.). (C). 1988. pap. text ed. 22.00 (*0-923231-11-0*) Mohican Pub.

***Noel, Jan.** Canada Dry: Temperance Crusades Before Confederation. (Illus.). 296p. 1994. 50.00 (*0-8020-0552-7*); pap. 19.95 (*0-8020-6976-2*) U of Toronto Pr.

Noel, John V. Division Officers Guide. 9th ed. LC 88-29130. 344p. 1989. pap. 14.95 (*0-87021-205-2*) Naval Inst Pr.

Noel, John V., Jr., ed. Knight's Modern Seamanship. 18th ed. 624p. 1989. text ed. 64.95 (*0-442-26983-8*) Van Nos Reinhold.

Noel, John V., Jr. & Beach, Edward L. Naval Terms Dictionary. 5th ed. LC 88-18657. 336p. 1988. 24.95 (*0-87021-571-X*) Naval Inst Pr.

Noel, Karen G. Cut & Color Flannel Board Stories, Bk. 1. (Teacher Aid Ser.). 1985. 9.95 (*0-513-01787-9*) Denison.

— Cut & Color Flannel Board Stories, Bk. 2. (Teacher Aid Ser.). 1985. 9.95 (*0-513-01788-7*) Denison.

— Cut & Color Flannel Board Stories, Bk. 3. (Teacher Aid Ser.). 1985. 9.95 (*0-513-01789-5*) Denison.

Noel, Lee, Jr. PageMaker 3 Solutions. (Illus.). (Orig.). 1989. pap. 18.95 (*0-929307-06-2*) GP Pubns.

Noel, Lee, et al. Increasing Student Retention: Effective Programs & Practices for Reducing the Dropout Rate. LC 84-47992. (Higher Education Ser.). 522p. 1985. 49.95x (*0-87589-624-3*) Jossey-Bass.

Noel, Leon & Leon, Marynel. Dictionnaire Marabout des Mots Croises. 508p. 1993. Vol. 2, I-Z. pap. 17.95 (*0-7859-5632-8*, 2501018850) Fr & Eur.

Noel, Linda. Where You First Saw the Eyes of Coyote. 16p. (Orig.). 1983. pap. 2.00 (*0-936574-09-7*) Strawberry Pr NY.

Noel, Lisa, jt. auth. see Kider, Mitchel.

Noel, Lise. Intolerance: The Parameters of Oppression. Bennett, Arnold, tr. LC 93-90589. 288p. (C). 1994. 49.95 (*0-7735-1160-1*, Pub. by McGill CN); pap. text ed. 19.95 (*0-7735-1187-3*, Pub. by McGill CN) U of Toronto Pr.

Noel, Nancy, jt. auth. see Noel, Reuben.

Noel, Octave. Histoire du Commerce du Monde Depuis les Temps les Plus Recules, 3 vols. 1990. reprint ed. 210.00 (*0-8115-3872-9*); reprint ed. pap. 240.00 (*0-685-27124-2*) Periodicals Srv.

Noel, P. Technologie de la Pierre de Taille. 376p. (FRE.). 1968. 49.95 (*0-686-56777-3*, M-6429) Fr & Eur.

Noel, Reuben & Noel, Nancy. Saigon for a Song: The True Story of a Vietnam Gig to Remember. LC 87-16244. (Illus.). 264p. (Orig.). 1987. pap. 6.95 (*0-943247-02-0*) UCS Press.

Noel, Roden B. Life of Lord Byron. LC 72-990. reprint ed. 21.50 (*0-404-07436-7*) AMS Pr.

Noel, Roger. Joufroi de Poitiers: Traduction Critique. (Studies in the Humanities: Literature-Politics-Society: Vol. 7). 219p. (C). 1988. text ed. 36.50 (*0-8204-0376-8*) P Lang Pubs.

Noel, Roger, jt. auth. see Danner, Horace G.

Noel, Roger, jt. auth. see Danner, Horace.

Noel, Ruth S. The Languages of Tolkien's Middle-Earth. 1980. pap. 11.95 (*0-395-29130-5*) HM.

Noel, S. J. Patrons, Clients, Brokers: Ontario Society & Politics, 1791-1896. 328p. 1990. text ed. 45.00 (*0-8020-5858-2*); pap. text ed. 19.95 (*0-8020-6774-3*) U of Toronto Pr.

Noel, Theresa & Joseph, Andre. Developmental Mathematics I: A Workbook. 1984. 10.00 (*0-936264-14-4*) Andres & Co.

— Developmental Mathematics II: A Workbook. 1984. 10.00 (*0-936264-15-2*) Andres & Co.

— Fundamentals of Mathematics: A Workbook. 1984. 12.00 (*0-936264-16-0*) Andres & Co.

Noel, Thomas J. Denver's Larimer Street: Main Street, Skid Row & Urban Renaissance. LC 81-83395. 1981. pap. 14.95 (*0-914248-02-2*) Hist Denver.

— The Golden Gamble: Colorado National Banks, 1862-1987. McLaughlin & Associates, ed. (Illus.). 184p. 1987. text ed. 15.95 (*0-914628-17-8*); pap. text ed. 10.95 (*0-914628-18-6*) Graphic Impress.

Noel, Thomas J. & Norgren, Barbara S. Denver the City Beautiful. LC 87-80609. (Illus.). 256p. 1993. reprint ed. pap. text ed. 22.95 (*0-914628-27-5*) Graphic Impress.

***Noel, Thomas J. & Smith, Duane A.** Colorado: The Highest State. LC 95-2813. (J). 1995. write for info. (*0-87081-373-0*) Univ Pr Colo.

Noel, Thomas J., jt. auth. see Leonard, Stephen J.

Noel, Thomas J., et al. Historical Atlas of Colorado. LC 93-21919. (C). 1993. 29.95 (*0-8061-2555-1*) U of Okla Pr.

— Historical Atlas of Colorado. LC 93-21919. (Illus.). 192p. (C). 1994. pap. 19.95 (*0-8061-2591-8*) U of Okla Pr.

Noel, Thomas S. & Norgren, Barbara J. Denver the City Beautiful. (Illus.). 256p. 1987. 21.95 (*0-914248-04-9*) Hist Denver.

Noel, Yvalth. Symphony. LC 92-70526. 50p. (Orig.). 1992. pap. 6.95 (*0-9631147-1-9*) A S Abrathyn-Arnold.

Noeli, T., jt. auth. see Schoen, T.

Noell, Chuck & Wood, Gary. We are All POWs. LC 75-13032. 96p. reprint ed. pap. 27.40 (*0-685-16035-1*, 2026839) Bks Demand.

Noell, W. K., jt. ed. see Snell, F. M.

Noell, Wilma. Christian Meditations. Date not set. pap. 1.95 (*0-317-05928-9*) Crusade Pubs.

Noelle-Neumann, Elisabeth. The Spiral of Silence: Public Opinion - Our Social Skin. LC 83-18204. (Illus.). 212p. 1986. pap. text ed. 11.95 (*0-226-58933-1*) U Ch Pr.

— The Spiral of Silence: Public Opinion, Our Social Skin. 2nd ed. LC 93-15484. 260p. (ENG & GER.). 1993. lib. bdg. 39.95 (*0-226-58935-8*); pap. text ed. 14.95 (*0-226-58936-6*) U Ch Pr.

Noelle-Neumann, Elisabeth, ed. The Germans: Public Opinions Polls, 1967-1980. rev. ed. LC 81-1075. (Illus.). 552p. 1981. text ed. 59.95 (*0-313-22490-0*, NEG/, Greenwood Pr) Greenwood.

Noelle-Neumann, Elisabeth & Neumann, Erich P., eds. The Germans: Public Opinion Polls 1947-1966. Finan, Gerard, tr. LC 81-1478. (Illus.). xvii, 630p. 1981. reprint ed. text ed. 85.00 (*0-313-22611-3*, NEGE5, Greenwood Pr) Greenwood.

Noels, A., et al. Metal Promoted Selectivity in Organic Synthesis. (C). 1900. lib. bdg. 154.50 (*0-7923-1184-1*) Kluwer Ac.

Noemer, Fred E. The Handbook of Modern Halftone Photography: With Complete Concepts & Practices. 8th enl. rev. ed. (Illus.). 200p. (C). 29.50 (*0-911126-05-8*) Perfect Graphic.

Noepel, Penny. Fast Healthy Way with Vegetables. 1989. pap. 2.95 (*0-88266-521-9*) Storey Comm Inc.

Noer, David M. Healing the Wounds: Overcoming the Trauma of Layoffs & Revitalizing Downsized Organizations. LC 93-13407. (Management Ser.). 215p. 1993. 26.00 (*1-55542-560-7*) Jossey-Bass.

— Healing the Wounds: Overcoming the Trauma of Layoffs & Revitalizing Downsized Organizations. LC 93-13407. (Management Ser.). 288p. 1995. pap. 18.00 (*1-55542-708-1*) Jossey-Bass.

Noer, Deliar. Administration of Islam in Indonesia. (Monograph Ser.: No. 58). 1978. pap. 4.50 (*0-87763-002-X*) Cornell Mod Indo.

Noer, H. Rolf. Navigator's Pocket Calculator Handbook. LC 82-74136. (Illus.). 173p. (Orig.). reprint ed. pap. 49.40 (*0-7837-1212-X*, 2041744) Bks Demand.

Noer, Richard J., jt. auth. see Casper, Barry M.

Noer, Thomas J. Briton, Boer, & Yankee: The United States & South Africa, 1870-1914. LC 78-16749. 206p. reprint ed. pap. 58.80 (*0-7837-0296-5*, 2040617) Bks Demand.

— Cold War & Black Liberation: The United States & White Rule in Africa, 1948-1968. LC 84-19665. 288p. 1985. text ed. 30.00 (*0-8262-0458-9*) U of Mo Pr.

Noerdlinger, Henry S. Moses & Egypt: The Documentation to the Motion Picture "the Ten Commandments" LC 56-12886. 202p. 1956. pap. 1.95 (*0-88474-007-2*) U of S Cal Pr.

Noerper, Norman. Opportunities in Data Processing Careers. 1989. pap. 10.95 (*0-8442-8638-9*, VGM Career Bks) NTC Pub Grp.

Noerper, Norman N. Opportunities in Data Processing. (Illus.). 160p. 1989. 13.95 (*0-8442-8637-0*, VGM Career Bks); pap. 10.95 (*0-8442-6226-9*, VGM Career Bks) NTC Pub Grp.

Noeter, Herman, jt. auth. see Noether, D.

Noethe, Sheryl, jt. auth. see Collom, Jack.

Noether, D. & Noeter, Herman. Encyclopedic Dictionary of Chemical Technology. 297p. 1993. 59.50 (*0-89573-329-3*) VCH Pubs.

Noether, Emiliana P. As Others Saw Us: Italian Views on the United States During the Nineteenth Century. (Transactions Ser.: Vol. 50, Pt. 2). 31p. 1990. pap. 10.50 (*1-878508-01-6*) CT Acad Arts & Sciences.

Noether, Emiliana P., ed. The American Constitution As a Symbol & Reality for Italy. LC 89-14041. (Studies in American History: Vol. 4). 250p. 1989. lib. bdg. 89.95 (*0-88946-095-7*) E Mellen.

Noether, Emmy. Collected Papers. 776p. 1983. 116.00 (*0-387-11504-8*) Spr-Verlag.

Noether, G. E. Introduction to Statistics: The Nonparametric Way. (Texts in Statistics Ser.). (Illus.). 488p. 1990. text ed. 49.50 (*0-387-97284-6*) Spr-Verlag.

Noever, Peter, ed. Aleksandr M. Rodchenko & Varvara F. Stepanova: The Future Is Our Only Goal. (Illus.). 260p. 1991. 65.00 (*3-7913-1134-4*, Pub. by Prestel) TeNeues.

— The Havana Project: Architecture Again. (Illus.). 184p. 1995. pap. 25.95 (*3-7913-1600-1*) Pegasus.

Noever, Peter & Haslinger, Regina, eds. Architecture in Transition: Between Deconstruction & New Modernism. (Illus.). 160p. (Orig.). (C). 1991. pap. 25.95 (*3-7913-1136-0*, Pub. by Prestel) TeNeues.

Noever, Peter, ed. see Himmelblau, Coop, et al.

Noey, Christopher & Temos, Janet. Art of India from the Williams College Museum of Art. LC 93-41492. (Illus.). 136p. (Orig.). 1994. pap. 35.00 (*0-913697-18-4*) Williams Art.

Nof, Shimon Y., ed. Handbook of Industrial Robotics. LC 92-3435. 1376p. (C). 1992. reprint ed. lib. bdg. 165.00 (*0-89464-722-9*) Krieger.

— Integration: Information & Collaboration Models Based on the NATO Advanced Research Workshop, Il Ciocco, Italy, June 6-11, 1993. LC 94-1386. (NATO Advanced Study Institutes Series E, Applied Sciences: Vol. 259). 484p. (C). 1994. lib. bdg. 179.00 (*0-7923-2753-5*) Kluwer Ac.

— Robotics & Material Flow. 206p. 1986. 125.75 (*0-444-42621-3*) Elsevier.

Nof, Shimon Y. & Moodie, C. L., eds. Advanced Information Technologies for Industrial Material Systems. (NATO Asi Series F: Vol. 53). x, 710p. 1989. 133.00 (*0-387-50905-4*) Spr-Verlag.

Nof, Shimon Y., jt. auth. see Dorf, Richard C.

Nofal, Maria B. Absentee Entrepreneurship & the Dynamics of the Motor Vehicle Industry in Argentina. LC 87-15159. 288p. 1989. text ed. 75.00 (*0-275-92607-9*, C2607, Praeger Pubs) Greenwood.

***Noffke, Susan E. & Stevenson, Robert B.** Educational Action Research: Becoming Practically Critical. 240p. (C). 1995. text ed. 46.00x (*0-8077-3441-1*); pap. text ed. 21.95x (*0-8077-3440-3*) Tchrs Coll.

Noffke, Suzanne, ed. Catherine of Siena: The Dialogue. LC 79-56755. (Classics of Western Spirituality Ser.). 416p. 1980. 22.95 (*0-8091-0295-1*); pap. 18.95 (*0-8091-2233-2*) Paulist Pr.

— The Texts & Concordances of the Works of Caterina da Siena: Il Dialogo, Le Orazioni, L'Epistolario. 10p. 1987. text ed. 10.00 (*0-940639-02-5*) Hispanic Seminary.

Noffke, Suzanne, tr. Letters of Catherine of Siena: Vol. One, Letters 1-88. (Medieval & Renaissance Texts & Studies: Vol. 52). (Illus.). 480p. 1988. 30.00 (*0-86698-036-9*) MRTS.

Noffs, David & Noffs, Laurie. The Daily Harold, Bk. 6. (Illus.). 24p. (Orig.). (J). (gr. 6). 1987. student ed 2.50 (*0-929875-07-9*) Noffs Assocs.

— The Daily Harold, Bk. 7. (Illus.). 24p. (Orig.). (J). (gr. 7). 1988. student ed 2.50 (*0-929875-08-7*) Noffs Assocs.

— The Daily Harold, Bk. 8. (Illus.). 24p. (Orig.). (J). (gr. 8). 1991. student ed 2.50 (*0-929875-09-5*) Noffs Assocs.

— Day of the Dinosaur. (Illus.). 24p. (Orig.). (J). (gr. 4-8). 1989. student ed 2.50 (*0-929875-12-5*) Noffs Assocs.

— The Happy Healthy Harold, Bk. 1. (Illus.). 24p. (Orig.). (J). (gr. 1). 1987. student ed 2.50 (*0-929875-02-8*) Noffs Assocs.

— A Happy Healthy Harold, Bk. 2. (Illus.). 24p. (Orig.). (J). (gr. 2). 1987. student ed 2.50 (*0-929875-03-6*) Noffs Assocs.

— Harold: Revista. rev. ed. (Illus.). 24p. (SPA.). (J). 1991. student ed 2.50 (*0-929875-11-7*) Noffs Assocs.

— Harold, Bk. 3: You Are Special. (Illus.). 24p. (Orig.). (J). (gr. 3). 1987. student ed 2.50 (*0-929875-04-4*) Noffs Assocs.

— Harold Magazine, Bk. 4: Let's Be Friends. (Illus.). 24p. (Orig.). (J). (gr. 4). 1987. student ed 2.50 (*0-929875-05-2*) Noffs Assocs.

— Harold Magazine, Bk. 5: Watching the Stars at Night. (Illus.). 24p. (Orig.). (J). (gr. 5). 1987. student ed 2.50 (*0-929875-06-0*) Noffs Assocs.

— Kindergarten - Introductory, Bk. K: The Happy Healthy Harold. (Illus.). 24p. (Orig.). (J). (gr. k). 1987. student ed 2.50 (*0-929875-01-X*) Noffs Assocs.

— Parents' Book. (Illus.). 24p. (Orig.). 1991. student ed 2.50 (*0-929875-10-9*) Noffs Assocs.

Noffs, Laurie, jt. auth. see Noffs, David.

Noffs, Ted. Humanology. 32p. (Orig.). 1988. pap. 3.95 (*0-929875-00-1*) Noffs Assocs.

***Noffsinger, Carol.** Associational WMU Guide. Edwards, Judith, ed. 44p. (Orig.). 1995. pap. text ed. 3.95 (*1-56309-123-2*) Womans Mission Union.

Noffsinger, James P. World War I Aviation Books in English: An Annotated Bibliography. LC 86-26109. (Illus.). 331p. 1987. 32.50 (*0-8108-1951-1*) Scarecrow.

Noffsinger, John S. A Program for Higher Education in the Church of the Brethren. LC 78-177711. (Columbia University. Teachers College. Contributions to Education Ser.: No. 172). (C). reprint ed. 37.50 (*0-404-55172-6*) AMS Pr.

***Nofi.** Civil War Journal. 1995. 6.98 (*0-88394-090-6*) Promntory Pr.

— War Against Hitler: Military Strategy in the West. 1995. pap. text ed. 15.95 (*0-938289-49-7*) Combined Bks.

Nofi, Albert, jt. ed. see Kiraly, Bela K.

Nofi, Albert A. The Alamo: And the Texas War for Independence, 1835-1836. (Illus.). 240p. 1992. 18.95 (*0-938289-10-1*) Combined Bks.

— The Alamo & the Texas War of Independence: Heroes, Myths & History. LC 93-33619. (Illus.). 234p. 1994. reprint ed. pap. 13.95 (*0-306-80563-4*) Da Capo.

— A Civil War Treasury: Being a Miscellany of Arms & Artillery Facts & Figures, Legends & Lore, Etc. (Illus.). 432p. 1992. 24.95 (*0-938289-12-8*) Combined Bks.

— A Civil War Treasury: Being a Miscellany of Arms & Artillery, Facts & Figures, Legends & Lore, Muses & Minstrels, Personalities & People. LC 94-31227. 1995. 15.95 (*0-306-80622-3*) Da Capo.

— The Gettysburg Campaign: June-July, 1863. rev. ed. LC 92-34473. (Great Campaigns Ser.). (Illus.). 240p. 1993. 19.95 (*0-938289-24-1*) Combined Bks.

— The Waterloo Campaign: June 1815. (Illus.). 352p. 1993. 24.95 (*0-938289-29-2*, 7324) Combined Bks.

Nofi, Albert A., ed. The Opening Guns: Fort Sumter to Fredericksburg. (Eyewitness History of the Civil War Ser.). 353p. 1994. pap. 16.95 (*0-938289-41-1*, 7308) Stackpole.

Nofi, Albert A., jt. auth. see Dunnigan, James F.

Nofi, Albert A., jt. auth. see Dunningan, James F.

Nofi, Albert A., jt. ed. see Kiraly, Bela K.

Nofsinger, Ray & Hargrove, Jim. Pigeons & Doves. LC 92-12948. (New True Bks.). (Illus.). 48p. (J). (gr. k-4). 1992. lib. bdg. 12.90 (*0-516-02196-6*) Childrens.

— Pigeons & Doves. LC 92-12948. (New True Bks.). (Illus.). 48p. (J). (gr. k-4). 1993. pap. 4.95 (*0-516-42196-4*) Childrens.

Nofsinger, Robert E. Everyday Conversation. (Interpersonal CommTexts Ser.: Vol. 1). 192p. 1990. 39.95 (*0-8039-3309-6*); pap. 17.95 (*0-8039-3310-X*) Sage.

Noftzger, Richard L., Jr., jt. ed. see Guthrie, David S.

Nofziger, Ed. Animal Cartoons. (How to Draw & Paint Ser.). (Illus.). 32p. (Orig.). 1989. pap. 5.95 (*0-929261-53-4*, HT134) W Foster Pub.

Nofziger, Harold H., illus. And It Was Good. 36p. (J). (ps up). 1993. 12.95 (*0-8361-3634-9*) Herald Pr.

Nofziger, Lyn. Nofziger. LC 92-15908. 352p. 1992. 21.95 (*0-89526-513-3*) Regnery Pub.

— Tackett. LC 93-8244. 192p. 1993. 16.95 (*0-89526-495-1*) Regnery Pub.

— Tackett & the Saloon Keeper. 1994. 16.95 (*0-89526-480-3*) Regnery Pub.

— Tackett & the Teacher. LC 93-45949. 192p. 1994. 16.95 (*0-89526-488-9*) Regnery Pub.

Nofziger, Margaret. Cooperative Method of Natural Birth Control. 4th ed. LC 91-33429. (Illus.). 112p. 1991. pap. 6.95 (*0-913990-84-1*) Book Pub Co.

— Signs of Fertility: The Personal Science of Natural Birth Control. LC 86-90578. (Illus.). 100p. (Orig.). 1988. pap. 6.95 (*0-940847-07-8*) MND Publish.

Noga. Diagnosis & Management of Aquarium Fish Diseases. 300p. 1993. 59.50 (*1-55664-374-8*) Mosby Yr Bk.

Nogab, John W., jt. auth. see Cole, William E.

Nogales, Francisco, ed. The Human Yolk Sac & Yolk Sac Tumors. LC 92-48512. 1993. 298.00 (*0-387-56031-9*) Spr-Verlag.

Nogales, Patti D. Appleworks for Students. LC 90-22741. (Illus.). 464p. (C). 1992. pap. text ed. 34.95 (*0-938661-19-1*) Franklin Beedle.

— Works for Students. LC 91-17145. (Illus.). 628p. (C). 1992. pap. text ed. 37.95 (*0-938661-33-7*) Franklin Beedle.

Nogales, Patti D. & McAllister, Carol H. Appleworks for Teachers. rev. ed. LC 87-14878. (Illus.). 240p. (C). 1992. pap. 23.95 (*0-938661-07-8*) Franklin Beedle.

Nogalski, James. Literary Precursors to the Book of Twelve. (Beiheft zur Zeitschrift fuer die Alttestamentliche Wissenschaft Ser.: Vol. 217). x, 301p. (C). 1993. lib. bdg. 106.15 (*3-11-013702-X*) De Gruyter.

— Redactional Process in the Book of the Twelve. LC 93-37633. (Beiheft zur Zeitschrift fuer die Alttestamentliche Wissenschaft Ser.: Vol. 218). xi, 300p. (C). 1993. lib. bdg. 106.15 (*3-11-013767-4*) De Gruyter.

Nogami, Toyoaki, ed. Dynamic Response of Pile Foundations: Experiment, Analysis & Observation. 192p. 1987. 21.00 (*0-87262-591-5*) Am Soc Civil Eng.

Nogar, N., ed. Laser Photoionization & Desorption Surface Analysis Techniques. 1990. 42.00 (*0-8194-0249-4*, VOL. 1208) SPIE.

Nogay, Beth. The New Drug-Free Workplace Act: The Complete Guide for Federal Contractors & Grantees. LC 89-683. 1989. 75.00 (*1-55871-042-6*) BNA.

Noge, H., jt. auth. see Sakaki, H.

Nogee, Joseph L., ed. Soviet Politics: Russia after Brezhnev. LC 84-26289. 254p. 1985. text ed. 55.00 (*0-275-90148-3*, C0148, Praeger Pubs) Greenwood.

Nogee, Joseph L. & Donaldson, Robert H. Soviet Foreign Policy since World War II. (Policy Studies on International Politics). 300p. 1981. text ed. 43.00 (*0-08-025997-9*, Pergamon Pr); pap. text ed. 12.00 (*0-08-025996-0*, Pergamon Pr) Elsevier.

— Soviet Foreign Policy since World War II. 2nd ed. 400p. 1984. text ed. 47.00 (*0-08-030152-5*, Pergamon Pr); pap. text ed. 13.95 (*0-08-030151-7*, Pergamon Pr) Elsevier.

— Soviet Foreign Policy Since World War II. 3rd ed. 350p. 1988. text ed. write for info. (*0-08-035885-3*, Pergamon Pr); pap. write for info. (*0-08-035886-1*, Pergamon Pr) Elsevier.

Nogee, Joseph L. & Spanier, John W. Peace Impossible - War Unlikely: The Cold War Between the United States & the Soviet Union. (C). 1988. pap. text ed. 19.50 (*0-673-39783-1*) HarpCollege.

Nogg, Sharon M. A Whale Watcher's Cookbook: Views from the Galley. (Illus.). 224p. 1990. reprint ed. pap. 11.95 (*0-939664-66-5*) Actors Etc.

Noggle, Anne. A Dance with Death: Soviet Airwomen in World War II. LC 94-1301. (Illus.). 400p. 1994. 29.95 (*0-89096-601-X*) Tex A&M Univ Pr.

— For God, Country, & the Thrill of It: Women Airforce Service Pilots in World War II. LC 89-20382. (Charles & Elizabeth Prothro Texas Photography Ser.: No. 1). (Illus.). 176p. 1990. 29.95 (*0-89096-401-7*) Tex A&M Univ Pr.

Noggle, Burl. Fleming Lectures, 1937-1990: A Historiographical Essay. LC 92-11948. 104p. (C). 1992. text ed. 19.95 (*0-8071-1780-3*) La State U Pr.

— Teapot Dome: Oil & Politics in the 1920's. LC 80-15396. (Illus.). ix, 234p. 1980. reprint ed. text ed. 59.75 (*0-313-22601-6*, NOTD, Greenwood Pr) Greenwood.

— Working with History: The Historical Records Survey in Louisiana & the Nation, 1936-1942. LC 81-5789. xii, 148p. 1981. text ed. 22.50 (*0-8071-0881-2*) La State U Pr.

Noggle, Dillard & Jeffries, Carolyn. Dillsboro. LC 86-82646. 187p. (Orig.). 1986. pap. 10.00 (*0-931889-05-7*) Epistemology Pubs.

Noggle, Joseph H. Physical Chemistry. 2nd ed. (C). 1989. text ed. 76.50 (*0-673-39817-X*) HarpCollege.

— Physical Chemistry. 3rd ed. LC 95-10742. 1995. write for info. (*0-673-52341-1*) HarpC.

— Practical Curve Fitting & Data Analysis: Software & Self-Instruction for Scientists & Engineers. 192p. 1992. pap. text ed. 67.00 (*0-13-677394-X*) P-H.

— Quickbasic Programming for Scientists & Engineers. 1992. 29.95 (*0-8493-4434-4*, QA76) CRC Pr.

An Asterisk (*) at the beginning of an entry indicates that the title is appearing in BIP for the first time.

***Nogosek, Robert J.** The Enneagram Journey to New Life: Who Am I? What Do I Stand For? 1995. 24.95 (*0-87193-287-3*) Dimension Bks.

— Nine Portraits of Jesus: Discovering Jesus Through the Enneagram. 1987. pap. 11.95 (*0-87193-260-1*) Dimension Bks.

Nogowski, John. Bob Dylan: A Descriptive, Critical Discography & Filmography, 1961-1994. 192p. 1995. pap. 34.50x (*0-89950-785-9*) McFarland & Co.

Nogradi, M. Stereochemistry: Basic Concepts & Applications. 250p. 1981. 128.00 (*0-08-021161-5*, Pub. by Pergamon Repr UK) Franklin.

— Stereoselective Synthesis. 356p. 1986. lib. bdg. 150.00 (*0-89573-494-X*) VCH Pubs.

Nogrady, Thomas. Medicinal Chemistry: A Biochemical Approach. 2nd ed. (Illus.). 496p. 1988. pap. 42.50 (*0-19-505369-9*) OUP.

***Nogrady, Thomas, et al.** Rotifera Vol. 1: Biology, Ecology & Systematics. Dumont, H. J., ed. (Guides to the Identification of the Microinvertebrates of the Continental Waters of the World Ser.: No. 4). (Illus.). 1993. pap. 50.00 (*90-5103-080-0*, Pub. by SPB Acad Pub NE) Koeltz Sci Bks.

Nograsek, A. Ascomyceten auf Gefaesspflanzen der Polsterseggenrasen in den Ostalpen. (Bibliotheca Mycologica Ser.: Vol. 133). (Illus.). 280p. (GER.). 1990. pap. 76.40 (*3-443-59034-9*, Pub. by Cramer-Borntraeger GW) Lubrecht & Cramer.

Noguchi, Isamu. The Isamu Noguchi Garden Museum. (Illus.). 288p. 1987. 39.95 (*0-8109-1374-7*) Abrams.

Noguchi, J. & Ochiai, T. Geometric Function Theory in Several Complex Variables. LC 90-546. (MMONO Ser.: Vol. 80). 282p. 1990. 81.00 (*0-8218-4533-0*, MMONO-80) Am Math.

Noguchi, J. & Ohsawa, T., eds. Prospects in Complex Geometry: Proceedings of the 25th Taniguchi International Symposium Held in Katata, & the Conference held in Kyoto, July 31-August 9, 1989. (Lecture Notes in Mathematics Ser.: Vol. 1468). vii, 421p. 1991. pap. 52.00 (*0-387-54053-9*) Spr-Verlag.

Noguchi, Kaku C. Flowers of the Secret Garden: The Final Episode of the Korean Dynasty of Lee. Briggs, Everett F., tr. 222p. 1988. write for info. (*0-9615976-0-7*) E F Briggs.

— Rajagriha: A Tale of Gautama Buddha. (C). 1992. 15.00 (*81-7023-359-3*, Pub. by Allied II) S Asia.

Noguchi, Paul H. Delayed Departures, Overdue Arrivals: Industrial Familialism & the Japanese National Railways. LC 89-27924. 248p. 1990. text ed. 31.00 (*0-8248-1234-4*); pap. text ed. 14.95 (*0-8248-1288-3*) UH Pr.

Noguchi, Rei R. Grammar & the Teaching of Writing Limits & Possibilities. 140p. 1991. pap. 12.95 (*0-8141-1874-7*) NCTE.

Noguchi, S. & Umeo, H., eds. Transputer - Occam Japan Four: Proceedings of the Fourth T-O International Conference, June 4-5, 1992, Tokyo, Japan. LC 92-53262. (Transputer & Occam Engineering Ser.: Vol. 27). 278p. 1992. pap. 105.00 (*90-5199-093-6*) IOS Press.

Noguchi, S. & Yamamoto, M., eds. Transputer - Occam Japan Five: Proceedings of the 5th Transputer - Occam International Conference 10-11 June 1993, Osaka, Japan. LC 92-63412. (Transputer & Occam Engineering Ser.: Vol. 35). 266p. 1993. pap. 105.00 (*90-5199-125-8*, Pub. by IOS Pr NE) IOS Press.

***Noguchi, S., et al.** Transputer - Occam Japan 6: Proceedings of the 6th International Conference Jun 14-17, 1993, Tokyo, Japan. LC 94-77314. (Transputer & Occam Engineering Ser.: Vol. 39). 330p. 1994. pap. 99.00 (*90-5199-174-6*) IOS Press.

Noguchi, Y. Lafcadio Hearn in Japan. 1973. lib. bdg. 59.95 (*0-8490-0480-2*) Gordon Pr.

Noguchi, Yukio & Poterba, James M., eds. Housing Markets in the United States & Japan. LC 93-48441. (C). 1994. lib. bdg. 40.00 (*0-226-59015-1*) U Ch Pr.

Noguchi, Yukio & Wise, David A., eds. Aging in the United States & Japan: Economic Trends. LC 94-14101. (National Bureau of Economic Research Conference Report Ser.). (Illus.). 208p. 1994. 39.95 (*0-226-59018-6*) U Ch Pr.

Nogueira, Crespo. Glossary of Basic Archival & Library Conservation Terms. 155p. 1988. lib. bdg. 95.00 (*0-8288-3398-2*, F41072) Fr & Eur.

Nogueira, J. & Turover, G. Diccionario Ruso-Espanol: Russian-Spanish Dictionary. deluxe ed. 956p. (RUS & SPA.). 1979. 39.95 (*0-8288-4781-9*, S33593) Fr & Eur.

Noguer More, Jesus. Diccionario Enciclopedico de la Vida Sexual, 5 vols., Set. 792p. (SPA.). 1974. 250.00 (*0-8288-5987-6*, S50029) Fr & Eur.

Noguera, Joseph. Textiles Engineering Experiences. 192p. (C). 1978. pap. text ed. 70.00 (*0-685-36066-0*, Pub. by Textile Institue UK) St Mut.

Nogueras, Amber. Eres Tu una Oveja Herida? (Are You a Wounded Lamb?) (SPA.). 1994. 6.99 (*1-56063-734-X*, 550070) Editorial Unilit.

Nogueira, Carmen C., ed. Glossary of Basic Archival & Library Conservation Terms. (ICA Handbook Ser.: Vol. 4). 151p. (ENG, FRE, GER, ITA, RUS & SPA.). 1988. lib. bdg. 37.50 (*3-598-20276-8*) K G Saur.

Noh, Chin-hwa. Healthful Korean Cooking: Meats & Poultry. LC 85-80450. (Illus.). 64p. 1985. 14.50 (*0-930878-46-9*) Hollym Intl.

— Low-Fat Korean Cooking: Fish, Shellfish & Vegetables. LC 85-80451. (Illus.). 64p. 1985. 14.50 (*0-930878-47-7*) Hollym Intl.

— Practical Korean Cooking. (Illus.). 192p. 1985. 36.50 (*0-930878-37-X*) Hollym Intl.

— Traditional Korean Cooking: Snacks & Basic Side Dishes. (Illus.). 64p. 1985. 14.50 (*0-930878-48-5*) Hollym Intl.

Nohara, Chuck. Patchwork Bags. (Illus.). 96p. (Orig.). 1989. pap. 18.95 (*0-87040-820-8*) Japan Pubns USA.

— Useful Patchwork Gifts. (Illus.). 96p. (Orig.). 1993. pap. 18.95 (*0-87040-907-7*) Japan Pubns USA.

Nohara, Shigeru. A6M Zero. (Aircraft in Action Ser.). (Illus.). 50p. 1983. 8.95 (*0-89747-141-5*) Squad Sig Pubns.

Nohda, Nobuhiko, jt. ed. see Reys, Robert E.

Nohel, John A., ed. Advances in Differential & Integral Equations. (Miscellaneous Bks.: No. 10). xvi, 207p. 1969. 21.50 (*0-89871-037-5*) Soc Indus-Appl Math.

Noher, Ursula R. & Garcia, F. O. Librarian's Puzzle: MARC-CIP-ISBN-ISSN-RLIN. 2nd ed. 130p. 1993. 15.00 (*0-929928-15-6*) Fog Pubns.

Nohl, Frederick. Martin Luther: Hero of Faith. LC 62-14146. (Illus.). (J). (gr. 4-6). 1962. pap. 5.99 (*0-570-03727-1*, 12-2629) Concordia.

Nohl, Louis. Life of Haydn. 1889. reprint ed. 49.00 (*0-403-00343-1*) Scholarly.

— Life of Mozart. Lalor, John J., tr. LC 82-1593. (Music Reprint Ser.). (Illus.). 236p. (GER.). 1982. reprint ed. lib. bdg. 29.50 (*0-306-76171-8*) Da Capo.

Nohl, Ludwig. Life of Haydn. 7th ed. Upton, George P., tr. LC 73-173796. reprint ed. 37.50 (*0-404-04786-6*) AMS Pr.

Nohlen, Klaus & Radt, Wolfgang. Kapikaya: Ein Felsheiligtum Bei Pergamon. (Altertumer Von Pergamon Ser.: Vol. 12). (Illus.). (C). 1978. 107.70 (*3-11-006710-2*) De Gruyter.

Nohmy, Beth J. Federal Funding Guide for Language & International Education. 34p. (Orig.). 1991. pap. text ed. 9.95 (*0-942017-04-8*) Amer Assn Teach German.

Nohowel, Shelley. Portraits of Unique Homes, Vol. 1. Goodwin, Richard A., ed. (Illus.). 224p. 1992. 90.00 (*1-56333-000-8*) Masquerade.

— Portraits of Unique Homes, Vol. 2: A Luxury Perspective. Goodwin, Richard A., ed. (Illus.). 208p. 1993. 90.00 (*1-56333-998-6*) Masquerade.

Nohr, Mary L. UNIX System V Release 4.0 ELF. 200p. 1993. pap. 29.95 (*0-13-091109-7*) P-H.

Nohria, Nitin, ed. see Eccles, Robert G.

Nohria, Nitin, jt. ed. see Eccles, Robert G.

Nohria, Nittin, jt. auth. see Eccles, Robert G., Jr.

Nohring, J. German-English Dictionary of Medicine. 846p. 1987. 124.00 (*3-87144-957-1*) IBD Ltd.

Nohring, Jurgen. Dictionary of Medicine. 1984. 166.75 (*0-444-99641-9*, I-050-84) Elsevier.

— Dictionary of Medicine: German-English. 850p. 1987. 202.75 (*0-444-98982-X*) Elsevier.

— Dictionary of Medicine, German & English. 848p. (ENG & GER.). 1987. 195.00 (*0-8288-0572-5*, M1735) Fr & Eur.

— English & German Dictionary of Medicine. 2nd ed. 708p. (ENG & GER.). 1986. 195.00 (*0-8288-0571-7*, M 14674) Fr & Eur.

Nohrnberg, James. Like Unto Moses: The Constituting of an Interruption. LC 94-18785. (Indiana Studies in Biblical Literature). 368p. 1994. text ed. 39.95 (*0-253-34090-X*) Ind U Pr.

***Nohrnberg, Peter C.** The Book the Poet Makes: Collection & Re-Collection in W. P. Yeats's... LC 95-8401. (The LeBaron Russell Briggs Prize, Honors Essay in English, 1993 Ser.: Vol. 1993). 102p. (Orig.). (C). 1995. pap. text ed. 11.00 (*0-674-07867-5*) HUP.

Noice, Karen, jt. auth. see Ogle, Gini.

Noice, Marshall, jt. auth. see Long, David.

Noin, Daniel & White, Paul. Paris. (World Cities Ser.). 224p. 1994. text ed. 49.95 (*0-470-22012-0*) Halsted Pr.

Noin, Daniel & Woods, Robert, eds. The Changing Population of Europe. LC 92-430003. 288p. 1993. 49.95 (*0-631-17635-7*); pap. 19.95 (*0-631-18972-6*) Blackwell Pubs.

Noiriel, Gerard. Workers in French Society in the 19th & 20th Centuries. McPhail, Helen, tr. LC 89-35885. 288p. 1990. 65.00 (*0-85496-610-2*) Berg Pubs.

Noiriel, Gerard, jt. ed. see Horowitz, Donald L.

Noiset, Marie-Therese, tr. see Badian, Seydou.

Noiseux, Ronald A., jt. auth. see Glass, Robert L.

Noizet, Georges, jt. ed. see Mehler, Jacques.

Noizet, Yvonne, tr. see Mehler, Jacques & Noizet, Georges, eds.

Nojd, R. Swedish-French, French-Swedish Dictionary: Svensk-Fransk-Svensk Ordbok. 450p. (FRE & SWE.). 1986. 49.95 (*0-8288-1681-6*, F57114) Fr & Eur.

Nojd, Ruben. English-Swedish Dictionary. (ENG & SWE.). 39.50 (*0-87557-083-6*, 083-6) Saphrograph.

Noji. Handbook of Toxicologic Emergencies. 880p. 1989. 99.95 (*0-8151-6450-5*, Yr Bk Med Pubs) Mosby Yr Bk.

— Manual of Toxicologic Emergencies. 1989. 99.95 (*0-685-25523-9*, Yr Bk Med Pubs) Mosby Yr Bk.

Nojima, Yasuzo. Yasuzo Nojima & Contemporaries. (Illus.). 176p. 1991. pap. 39.95 (*4-87642-129-3*) Grey Art Gallery Study Ctr.

Nojiri, Kiyohiko, see Jiro Osaragi, pseud..

Nokak, Michael, et al. The New Consensus on Family & Welfare: A Community of Self-Reliance. LC 87-1402. (Illus.). 160p. (Orig.). 1987. pap. 13.00 (*0-8447-3624-4*) U Pr of Amer.

Nokel, K. Temporally Distributed Symptoms in Technical Diagnosis. Siekmann, Joerg H., ed. (Lecture Notes in Artificial Intelligence Ser.: Vol. 517). ix, 164p. 1991. pap. 25.00 (*0-387-54316-3*) Spr-Verlag.

***Nokes, David.** John Gay, a Profession of Friendship: A Critical Biography. (Illus.). 576p. 1995. 39.95 (*0-19-812971-8*) OUP.

— Jonathan Swift, a Hypocrite Reversed: A Critical Biography. (Illus.). 427p. 1986. 35.00 (*0-19-812834-7*) OUP.

— Raillery & Rage: A Study of Eighteenth Century Satire. LC 87-9487. 256p. 1987. text ed. 39.95 (*0-312-00958-5*) St Martin.

Nokes, David & Barron, Janet, eds. An Annotated Critical Bibliography of Augustan Literature. 256p. 1989. text ed. 39.95 (*0-312-01961-0*) St Martin.

Nokes, David, ed. see Fielding, Henry.

Nokes, Jill. How to Grow Native Plants of Texas & the Southwest. LC 85-28831. (Illus.). 288p. 1986. 37.50 (*0-87719-034-8*, Lone Star Bks) Gulf Pub.

Nokleberg, ed. Alaskan Geological & Geophysical Transect. (IGC Field Trip Guidebooks Ser.). 136p. 1989. 28.00 (*0-87590-653-2*, T104) Am Geophysical.

Nokleby, jt. auth. see Riste.

Nola, Robert, ed. Relativism & Realism in Science. (C). 1988. lib. bdg. 111.50 (*90-277-2647-7*) Kluwer Ac.

***Nolan.** A History of Mental Health Nursing. 190p. 1992. pap. 38.25 (*1-56593-029-0*, 0273) Singular Publishing.

— The Pop-Up Buck Rogers: Strange Adventures in the Spider Ship. LC 94-71381. (Illus.). 24p. (J). (gr. 4-7). 1994. 14.95 (*1-55709-236-2*) Applewood.

Nolan & Johnson. Logan's Run. 1976. 16.95 (*0-8488-0102-4*, Amereon Hse) Amereon Ltd.

Nolan, jt. auth. see Lee.

Nolan, Alan T. The Iron Brigade. 2nd ed. (Michigan Heritage Library: Vol. 3). (Illus.). 412p. 1983. reprint ed. 20.00 (*0-915056-16-X*) Hardscrabble Bks.

— The Iron Brigade: A Military History. LC 93-28908. (Illus.). 1994. 35.00 (*0-253-34102-7*); pap. 18.95 (*0-253-20863-7*) Ind U Pr.

— Lee Considered: General Robert E. Lee & Civil War History. LC 90-48296. xii, 231p. (C). 1991. 22.50 (*0-8078-1956-5*) U of NC Pr.

Nolan, Albert. God in South Africa: The Challenge of the Gospel. LC 88-21737. 255p. reprint ed. pap. 72.70 (*0-7837-0523-9*, 2040847) Bks Demand.

— Jesus Before Christianity. rev. ed. LC 92-5604. 142p. (Orig.). 1992. pap. 9.95 (*0-88344-832-7*) Orbis Bks.

— Jesus Before Christianity. LC 78-6708. 168p. (Orig.). reprint ed. pap. 47.90 (*0-7837-5515-5*, 2045285) Bks Demand.

Nolan, B. The Gothic Visionary Perspective. 1977. 45.00 (*0-691-06337-0*) Princeton U Pr.

Nolan, Barbara. Chaucer & the Tradition of the "Roman Antique" (Studies in Medieval Literature: No. 15). 350p. (C). 1992. 69.95 (*0-521-39169-5*) Cambridge U Pr.

— The Gothic Visionary Perspective. LC 76-56241. Date not set. reprint ed. pap. 88.70 (*0-7837-9402-9*, 2060147) Bks Demand.

Nolan, Barbara E, Sr. The Political Theory of Beatrice Webb. LC 87-12592. (Studies in Social History: No. 7). 1988. 47.50 (*0-404-61607-0*) AMS Pr.

***Nolan, Brian & Turbat, Vincent.** Cost Recovery in Public Health Services in Sub-Saharan Africa. LC 95-14406. (EDI Technical Materials Ser.). 1995. write for info. (*0-8213-3240-6*) World Bank.

Nolan, Bryan. Data Analysis: An Introduction. Leigh, Sue, ed. (Illus.). 240p. (C). 1994. text ed. 54.95 (*0-7456-1145-1*); pap. text ed. 22.95 (*0-7456-1146-X*) Blackwell Pubs.

Nolan, Carson Y. & Kederis, Cleves J. Perceptual Factors in Braille Word Recognition. LC 79-9310. (American Foundation for the Blind Research Ser.: No. 20). 192p. reprint ed. pap. 54.80 (*0-7837-0224-8*, 2040532) Bks Demand.

Nolan, Cathal J. The Longman Guide to World Affairs. LC 94-8838. (Illus.). 480p. (C). 1995. pap. text ed. 16.50 (*0-8013-1298-1*) Longman.

— Principled Diplomacy: Security & Rights in U. S. Foreign Policy. LC 92-30006. (Contributions in Political Science Ser.: No. 313). 312p. 1993. text ed. 59.95 (*0-313-28006-1*, NPD/, Greenwood Pr) Greenwood.

Nolan, Cathal J., jt. ed. see Hodge, Carl C.

Nolan, Cecile A. Journey West, on the Oregon Trail. (J). (gr. 5 up). 1993. 16.95 (*0-9633168-2-6*) Rain Dance Pub.

— Oregon: A Feast of Delights. (Illus.). 215p. (Orig.). 1991. pap. 19.95 (*0-9633168-0-X*) Rain Dance Pub.

Nolan, Charles E., jt. auth. see Bulgawicz, Susan L.

Nolan, Charles J., Jr. Aaron Burr & the American Literary Imagination. LC 79-8291. (Contributions in American Studies: No. 45). 210p. 1980. text ed. 55.00 (*0-313-21256-2*, NAB/, Greenwood Pr) Greenwood.

Nolan, Christopher. Dam-Burst of Dreams. LC 81-9669. 96p. 1988. pap. 9.95 (*0-8214-0912-3*) Ohio U Pr.

***Nolan, Cynthia.** Outback & Beyond. 1994. pap. 18.00 (*0-207-18369-4*, Pub. by Angus & Robertson AT) HarpC.

Nolan, D., jt. auth. see Yolen, J.

***Nolan, David.** The Houses of St. Augustine. (Illus.). 112p. 1995. 27.95 (*1-56164-069-7*); pap. 19.95 (*1-56164-075-1*) Pineapple Pr.

— The Ideology of the Sandinistas & the Nicaraguan Revolution. 204p. (Orig.). 1984. pap. 19.95 (*0-935501-01-0*) U Miami N-S Ctr.

Nolan, Dennis. The Castle Builder. LC 86-23784. (Illus.). 32p. (J). (gr. k-3). 1987. text ed. 13.95 (*0-02-768240-4*, Mac Bks Young Read) S&S Childrens.

— The Castle Builder. LC 92-29563. (Illus.). 32p. (J). (gr. k-3). 1993. pap. 4.95 (*0-689-71703-2*, Aladdin Paperbacks) S&S Childrens.

— Dinosaur Dream. LC 89-78208. (Illus.). 32p. (J). (ps-2). 1990. text ed. 14.95 (*0-02-768145-9*, Mac Bks Young Read) S&S Childrens.

— Dinosaur Dream. LC 93-48409. (Illus.). 32p. (J). (gr. k-3). 1994. pap. 4.95 (*0-689-71832-2*, Aladdin Paperbacks) S&S Childrens.

— Wolf Child. LC 88-35955. (Illus.). 40p. (J). (gr. 1-5). 1989. text ed. 14.95 (*0-02-768141-6*, Mac Bks Young Read) S&S Childrens.

***Nolan, Dennis, illus.** William Shakespeare's A Midsummer Night's Dream. LC 94-12600. 1996. 16.99 (*0-8037-1784-9*) Dial Bks Young.

Nolan, Dennis P. Application of HAZOP & What-If Safety Reviews to the Petroleum, Petro-Chemical & Chemical Industries. LC 94-4889. (Illus.). 127p. 1994. 45.00 (*0-8155-1353-4*) Noyes.

Nolan, Dennis R. Labor Arbitration Law & Practice in a Nutshell. LC 79-4316. (Nutshell Ser.). 358p. 1991. reprint ed. pap. text ed. 15.00 (*0-8299-2032-3*) West Pub.

Nolan, Dennis R., jt. auth. see Cooper, Laura J.

Nolan, Donna D. Ending Fatigue & Depression. 1988. write for info. (*0-318-59216-9*); pap. 15.00 (*0-934979-30-8*) James & McCormick Pubs.

Nolan, Edward P. Cry Out & Write: A Feminine Poetics of Revelation. 192p. (C). 1994. 22.50 (*0-8264-0684-X*) Continuum.

— Now Through a Glass Darkly: Specular Images of Being & Knowing from Virgil to Chaucer. 316p. 1990. 39.50 (*0-472-10170-6*) U of Mich Pr.

Nolan, Edward W. Frank Palmer-Scenic Photographer. 32p. 1987. pap. 7.95 (*0-910524-05-X*) Eastern Wash.

— A Guide to the Manuscript Collections in the Eastern Washington State Historical Society. 180p. 1987. pap. 9.95 (*0-910524-06-8*) Eastern Wash.

— A Night of Terror, Devastation, Suffering & Awful Woe: The Spokane Fire of 1889. 64p. 1989. pap. 10.95 (*0-910524-12-2*) Eastern Wash.

Nolan, Emer. James Joyce & Nationalism. LC 94-8223. 192p. 1995. 59.95 (*0-415-10343-6*, B3149) Routledge.

Nolan, Finbarr & Duffy, Martin. Seventh Son of a Seventh Son: The Life Story of a Healer. (Illus.). 192p. 1993. 19.95 (*1-85158-414-5*, Pub. by Mnstream UK) Trafalgar.

***Nolan, Frederick.** Bad Blood: The Life & Times of the Horrel Brothers. LC 94-27503. 1994. 19.95 (*0-935269-16-9*, Barbed Wire Pr) Western Pubns.

— The Lincoln County War: A Documentary History. LC 90-22210. (Illus.). 624p. 1992. 49.95 (*0-8061-2377-X*) U of Okla Pr.

— The Lincoln County War: A Documentary History. LC 90-22210. (Illus.). 624p. 1994. pap. 24.95 (*0-8061-2607-8*) U of Okla Pr.

— A Poet on Broadway: The Life & Lyrics of Lorenz Hart. LC 92-41968. 400p. (C). 1994. 25.00 (*0-19-506837-8*) OUP.

— White Nights, Red Dawn. 1983. pap. 3.95 (*0-8217-1277-2*) Zebra.

***Nolan, Fredrick.** Lorenz Hart: A Poet on Broadway. (Illus.). 416p. 1995. pap. 14.95 (*0-19-510289-4*) OUP.

Nolan, Gwendolyn W., jt. ed. see Nowlan, Robert A.

Nolan-Haley, Jacqueline M. Alternative Dispute Resolution in a Nutshell. (Nutshell Ser.). 298p. 1992. pap. text ed. 15.00 (*0-314-00781-4*) West Pub.

Nolan, Han. If I Should Die Before I Wake. LC 93-30720. (J). 1994. 16.95 (*0-15-238040-X*, HB Juv Bks); pap. write for info. (*0-15-238041-8*, HB Juv Bks) HarBrace.

Nolan, Helen. Early American Dolls in Full Color: The Creative Genius of Unsophisticated America. 32p. 1986. pap. 5.95 (*0-486-25203-5*) Dover.

— Lenci Dolls in Full Color: Toys for the Rich & Famous, 1920-1940. 32p. 1986. pap. 5.95 (*0-486-25204-3*) Dover.

Nolan, Hugh J., ed. Pastoral Letters of the United States Catholic Bishops: 1792-1983, 4 vols. 1890p. 1984. pap. 95.00 (*1-55586-897-5*) US Catholic.

— Pastoral Letters of the United States Catholic Bishops, 1792-1940, Vol. I. 489p. 1984. pap. 24.95 (*1-55586-880-0*) US Catholic.

— Pastoral Letters of the United States Catholic Bishops, 1941-1961, Vol. II. 273p. 1984. pap. 24.95 (*1-55586-885-1*) US Catholic.

— Pastoral Letters of the United States Catholic Bishops, 1962-1974, Vol. III. 511p. 1984. pap. 24.95 (*1-55586-870-3*) US Catholic.

— Pastoral Letters of the United States Catholic Bishops, 1975-1983, Vol. IV. 617p. 1984. pap. 24.95 (*1-55586-875-4*) US Catholic.

Nolan, James. Poet-Chief: The Native American Poetics of Walt Whitman & Pablo Neruda. LC 93-2379. 281p. 1994. 35.00x (*0-8263-1484-8*) U of NM Pr.

Nolan, James & Lipkin, David P. Coronary Care Manual: A Practical Guide to the Management of Acute Cardiac Problems & Their Subsequent Follow-Up. LC 92-49665. (Pocket Medical Reference Ser.). (Illus.). 134p. 1993. 25.95 (*0-19-262315-X*) OUP.

— Coronary Care Manual: A Practical Guide to the Management of Acute Cardiac Problems & Their Subsequent Follow-Up. LC 92-49665. (Pocket Medical Reference Ser.). (Illus.). 134p. 1993. pap. 24.95 (*0-19-262314-1*) OUP.

Nolan, James, tr. see De Biedma, Jaime G.

Nolan, James, jt. auth. see Levin, James.

Nolan, James, tr. see Neruda, Pablo.

Nolan, James B. Lafayette in America Day by Day. LC 72-1709. reprint ed. 38.50 (*0-404-52427-3*) AMS Pr.

Nolan, James I., tr. see Osorio Lizaraza, J. A.

***Nolan, Jane T.** What's So Funny about Getting Old. LC 94-25971. 1994. pap. 6.00 (*0-88166-223-2*, 0671511521) Meadowbrook.

Nolan, Janet A. Ourselves Alone: Women's Emigration from Ireland, 1885-1920. LC 89-35145. 152p. 1989. text ed. 16.00 (*0-8131-1684-8*) U Pr of Ky.

Nolan, Janne E. Trappings of Power: Ballistic Missiles in the Third World. 209p. 1991. 29.95 (*0-8157-6096-5*); pap. 11.95 (*0-8157-6095-7*) Brookings.

Nolan, Janne E., ed. Global Engagement: Cooperation & Security in the 21st Century. 623p. (C). 1994. 39.95 (*0-8157-6098-1*); pap. 19.95 (*0-8157-6097-3*) Brookings.

Nolan, Janne E., jt. auth. see Blechman, Barry M.

Nolan, Jeannette C. La Salle & the Grand Enterprise. LC 90-48978. (American Cavalcade Ser.). (Illus.). 176p. (J). (gr. 6-10). 1991. lib. bdg. 9.95 (*1-55905-087-X*) Marshall Cavendish.

*Nolan, Jerome T.** Almostism in Christianity: A Look at the Lukewarm Christian in Need of Total Commitment. 96p. 1994. per., pap. 9.00 (*0-8059-3629-7*) Dorrance.

Nolan, John, ed. see Collins, Harry.

Nolan, John J. Used Oil: Disposal Options, Management Practices & Potential Liability. 3rd ed. Law Firm of Schmeltzer, Aptaker & Sheppard Staff, ed. 321p. 1991. 69.00 (*0-86587-234-1*) Gov Insts.

Nolan, Joseph, jt. auth. see Noonan, Joseph.

Nolan, Joseph R. Trial Practice Cases & Materials. LC 80-29182. (American Casebook Ser.). 518p. 1981. text ed. 40.00 (*0-8299-2129-X*) West Pub.

*Nolan, Kathleen L.** Gale Directory of Databases, 1995, 4 pts. 1994. pap. 315.00 (*0-8103-5748-8*) Gale.

Nolan, Keith W. The Magnificent Bastards: The Joint Army-Marine Defense of Dong Ha, 1968. LC 94-287. 1994. 24.95 (*0-89141-485-1*) Presidio Pr.

— Operation Buffalo: USMC Fight for the DMZ. 1992. mass mkt. 4.99 (*0-440-21310-X*) Dell.

— Sappers in the Wire: The Life & Death of Firebase Mary Ann. LC 95-12215. (Texas A&M University Military History Ser.: No. 45). (Illus.). 240p. (C). 1995. 24.95 (*0-89096-654-0*) Tex A&M Univ Pr.

Nolan, Kevin C., jt. auth. see Goldman, Ellen F.

Nolan, Leslie, ed. Modern Metropolis: Artists' Images of New York from the Museum of the City of New York. (Illus.). 48p. (Orig.). 1993. pap. 9.95 (*1-56584-066-6*) New Press NY.

*Nolan, Leta A.** County, South Dakota. (Illus.). 481p. 1989. 55.00 (*0-88107-152-8*) Curtis Media.

*Nolan, Madeena B.** The Other Side of the Wall. 1973. 3.00 (*0-87129-397-8*, O21) Dramatic Pub.

*Nolan, Marie T. & Agustine, Sharon M., eds.** Transplantation Nursing. LC 94-31323. 1994. text ed. 47.95 (*0-8385-8989-8*) Appleton & Lange.

Nolan, Mark. The Instant Marketing Plan: Your Simple, Enjoyable, Easy-to-Follow Roadmap to Skyrocket Your Business. Turner, Louise, ed. 250p. Date not set. pap. 15.95 (*0-940673-74-6*) Puma Pub Co.

Nolan, Mark, ed. see Allen, James.

Nolan, Mary. Imagining America, Modernizing Germany: Fordism & Economic Reform in the Weimar Republic. LC 93-20943. 368p. 1994. 45.00 (*0-19-507021-6*); pap. 19.95 (*0-19-508875-1*) OUP.

— Learning Success Kit. 160p. 1995. ring bd. 24.95 (*0-7872-0577-X*) Kendall-Hunt.

Nolan, Mary L. & Nolan, Sidney. Christian Pilgrimage in Modern Western Europe. LC 88-14364. (Studies in Religion). (Illus.). xxii, 422p. (C). 1992. reprint ed. pap. 16.95 (*0-8078-4389-X*) U of NC Pr.

Nolan, Melanie, jt. ed. see Daley, Caroline.

Nolan, Michael & Grant, Gordon, eds. Regular Respite: An Evaluation of a Shoptial Rota Bed Scheme for Elderly People. 312p. (C). 1992. 75.00 (*0-86242-115-2*, Pub. by Age Concern Eng UK) St Mut.

*Nolan, Michael F.** Introduction to the Neurologic Examination. (Illus.). 240p. (C). 1995. pap. text ed. 19. 95 (*0-8036-0017-8*) Davis Co.

Nolan, Michael J. PageMaker 5.0 Design Techniques (Windows Edition) (Illus.). 208p. (Orig.). 1994. pap. 24. 95 (*1-56830-022-0*) Hayden.

— PageMaker 5.0 Expert Techniques (Macintosh Edition) (Illus.). 208p. (Orig.). 1993. pap. 34.95 (*1-56830-017-4*) Hayden.

Nolan, Michael S. Fundamentals of Air Traffic Control. 560p. (C). 1990. text ed. 40.95 (*0-534-12246-9*) Intl Thomson.

— Fundamentals of Air Traffic Control. 2nd ed. 558p. 1994. text ed. 41.95 (*0-534-23058-X*) Intl Thomson.

Nolan, Pat. Drastic Measures. 30p. 1981. pap. 2.00 (*0-916382-25-7*) Telephone Bks.

Nolan, Pat & Ryba, Ken. Assessing Learning with LOGO. 84p. 1986. teacher ed 12.50 (*0-924667-31-1*) Intl Society Tech Educ.

Nolan, Pat, tr. see Soupault, Philippe.

*Nolan, Patrick.** Against the Odds: The True Story of Michele a Cancer Survivor. 256p. 1995. pap. 18.25 (*1-887170-05-7*) Alchemy Pub.

Nolan, Patrick B., jt. auth. see Geibert, Ronald R.

Nolan, Paul. Spirit of Alaska. 1991. 19.99 (*0-517-06592-4*) Random Hse Value.

— Spirit of Ireland. 1992. 19.99 (*0-517-07018-9*) Random Hse Value.

— Spirit of New England. 1991. 19.99 (*0-517-05307-1*) Random Hse Value.

Nolan, Paul T. Folk Tale Plays Round the World. (J). (gr. 3-5). 1982. pap. 13.95 (*0-8238-0253-1*) Plays.

Nolan, Peter & Fureng, D., eds. Market Forces in China: Competition & Small Business: The Wenzhou Debate. LC 89-70608. (Illus.). 208p. (C). 1989. text ed. 49.95 (*0-86232-832-2*, Pub. by Zed Books UK); pap. 17.50 (*0-86232-833-0*, Pub. by Zed Books UK) Humanities.

Nolan, Peter & Fureng, Dong, eds. The Chinese Economy & Its Future: Achievements & Problems of Post-Mao Reform. 250p. (C). 1991. 47.95 (*0-7456-0522-2*) Blackwell Pubs.

Nolan, Peter & Paine, Suzanne, eds. Rethinking Socialist Economics: A New Agenda for Britain. LC 86-6682. 350p. 1986. text ed. 45.00 (*0-312-67806-1*) St Martin.

Nolan, Peter, jt. ed. see Ha-Joon, Chang.

Nolan, Peter J. Fundamentals of College Physics. 1088p. (C). 1992. student ed write for info. (*0-697-12238-7*); student ed write for info. (*0-697-12236-0*) Wm C Brown Pubs.

— Fundamentals of College Physics. 1088p. (C). 1992. text ed. write for info. (*0-697-12145-3*) Wm C Brown Pubs.

— Fundamentals of College Physics, 2 vols. 2nd ed. 48p. (C). 1994. student ed, spiral bd. write for info. (*0-697-25811-4*) Wm C Brown Pubs.

— Fundamentals of College Physics, 2 vols. 2nd ed. 128p. (C). 1995. student ed, spiral bd. write for info. (*0-697-23141-0*) Wm C Brown Pubs.

— Fundamentals of College Physics, 2 vols., Set. 2nd ed. 1136p. (C). 1995. text ed. write for info. (*0-697-23138-0*) Wm C Brown Pubs.

— Fundamentals of College Physics, Vol. I. 2nd ed. 584p. (C). 1994. pap. text ed. write for info. (*0-697-24392-3*) Wm C Brown Pubs.

— Fundamentals of College Physics, Vol. II. 2nd ed. 616p. (C). 1994. pap. text ed. write for info. (*0-697-24393-1*) Wm C Brown Pubs.

Nolan, Peter J. & Bigliani, Raymond. Experiments in Physics. 2nd ed. 416p. (C). 1994. text ed., spiral bd. write for info. (*0-697-24225-0*) Wm C Brown Pubs.

Nolan, Riall. Development Anthropology. (C). 1996. text ed. 37.50 (*0-8133-0983-2*); pap. text ed. 19.95 (*0-8133-0984-0*) Westview.

*Nolan, Riall W.** Ko Conspiracy. 1995. pap. 4.99 (*0-440-21250-2*) Dell.

*Nolan, Richard L. & Crosan, David C.** Creative Destruction: A Six-Stage Process for Transforming the Organization. 1995. 29.95 (*0-87584-498-7*) Harvard Busn.

Nolan, Richard T. & Kirkpatrick, Frank G. Living Issues in Ethics. 388p. (C). 1982. text ed. 31.95 (*0-534-01140-3*) Intl Thomson.

Nolan, Rick, intro. International Electronics Packaging Conference Proceedings, 1993. (Conference Proceedings Ser.: Vol. 13). (Illus.). (Orig.). 1993. pap. text ed. 115.00 (*1-880433-15-X*) Intl Elect Pack.

Nolan, Rita. Cognitive Practices: Human Language & Human Knowledge. 200p. 1994. 44.95 (*0-631-18973-4*); pap. 21.95 (*0-631-18974-2*) Blackwell Pubs.

Nolan, Robert E., et al. Improving Productivity Through Advanced Office Controls. 426p. (C). 1991. reprint ed. lib. bdg. 44.50 (*0-89464-560-9*) Krieger.

Nolan, Robert R., jt. auth. see Deal, Terrence E.

Nolan-Rosager, Sharon, ed. see Behling, Thomas A.

Nolan, Ryan. Miracle Man. 1993. pap. 5.99 (*0-8499-3507-5*) Word Inc.

Nolan, Sidney, jt. auth. see Nolan, Mary L.

*Nolan, Steve.** Winds of Steel. 440p. Date not set. pap. 12. 95 (*0-7610-0253-7*) NW Pub.

Nolan, Thomas J., Jr. Retire Easy! A Blueprint for Building Personal Wealth. (Illus.). 1984. 16.95 (*0-13-778952-1*, Busn); pap. 7.95 (*0-13-778945-9*, Busn) P-H.

Nolan, Thomas L., Jr. Aging Smarter. (Illus.). 156p. (Orig.). 1991. pap. 12.95 (*0-9630727-0-6*) Spring Brook.

Nolan, Timothy M., et al. Applied Strategic Planning: The Consultant's Kit. LC 92-8097. (Illus.). 555p. 1992. ring bd. 495.00 (*0-88390-310-5*) Pfeiffer & Co.

— Plan or Die! Ten Keys to Organizational Success. Padgett, JoAnn, ed. LC 92-51082. (Illus.). 178p. 1993. 29.95 (*0-88390-377-6*); pap. 14.95 (*0-89384-207-9*) Pfeiffer & Co.

Nolan, Tony. A Suggestion of His Climate. 1977. pap. 5.00 (*0-931350-00-X*) Moonlight Pubns.

Nolan, Val, Jr. Ecology & Behavior of the Prairie Warbler Dendroica Discolor. 595p. 1978. 29.50 (*0-943610-26-5*) Am Ornithologists.

Nolan, Virginia E. & Ursin, Edmund, eds. Understanding Enterprise Liability: Rethinking Tort Reform for the 21st Century. LC 94-2881. 272p. (C). 1994. text ed. 39.95 (*1-56639-230-6*) Temple U Pr.

Nolan, Virginia J. & Terry, Phyllis D. Gingerbread & Friends. rev. ed. (Illus.). 22p. (J). 1987. pap. 3.50 (*0-9624497-0-9*) Planet Playmates.

*Nolan, W. C.** Cemetery Inscriptions of Union Parish, Louisiana, Vol. I. 190p. (Orig.). 1988. pap. 16.00 (*1-57088-020-4*) J&W Ent.

— Cemetery Inscriptions of Union Parish, Louisiana, Vol. II. 192p. (Orig.). 1988. pap. 16.00 (*1-57088-021-2*) J&W Ent.

— Cemetery Inscriptions of Union Parish, Louisiana, Vol. III. 200p. (Orig.). 1988. pap. 16.00 (*1-57088-022-0*) J&W Ent.

— Cemetery Inscriptions of Union Parish, Louisiana, Vol. IV. 188p. (Orig.). 1988. pap. 16.00 (*1-57088-023-9*) J&W Ent.

Nolan, William. Urban Horrors. 1992. 19.95 (*0-913165-54-9*) Dark Harvest.

Nolan, William, ed. Shaping of Ireland: The Geographical Perspective. (Illus.). 204p. 1986. pap. 15.95 (*0-85342-765-8*, Pub. by Mercier Pr IE) Dufour.

Nolan, William F. The Black Mask Murders. 224p. 1994. 19.95 (*0-312-10942-3*, Pub. by Thomas Dunne Bks) St Martin.

— Dashiell Hammett: A Casebook. LC 68-8393. 189p. 1969. 18.95 (*0-910278-56-3*) Boulevard.

— Helltracks. 256p. (Orig.). 1991. mass mkt. 4.50 (*0-380-75746-X*) Avon.

— How to Write Horror Fiction. 160p. 1991. 15.95 (*0-89879-442-0*) Writers Digest.

— Legends & Lovers: Fourteen Profiles. LC 88-36791. (Borgo Bioviews Ser.: No. 4). 192p. (C). Date not set. reprint ed. lib. bdg. write for info. (*0-89370-340-0*); reprint ed. pap. write for info. (*0-89370-440-7*) Borgo Pr.

— Look Out for Space. 192p. (Orig.). 1985. pap. 4.95 (*0-930330-20-X*) Intl Polygonics.

— Space for Hire. 200p. 1985. reprint ed. pap. 4.95 (*0-930330-19-6*) Intl Polygonics.

— Three for Space. 1992. 19.95 (*0-936071-32-X*); pap. 9.95 (*0-936071-33-8*) Gryphon Pubns.

— The Work of Charles Beaumont: An Annotated Bibliography & Guide. 2nd ed. Clarke, Boden, ed. LC 90-15043. (Bibliographies of Modern Authors Ser.: No. 6). 92p. 1990. lib. bdg. 25.00x (*0-8095-0517-7*); pap. text ed. 15.00x (*0-8095-1517-2*) Borgo Pr.

Nolan, William F., ed. Max Brand's Best Western Stories, Vol. III. (General Ser.). 366p. 1989. lib. bdg. 17.95 (*0-318-41342-6*) G K Hall.

Nolan, William F. & Greenberg, Martin H., eds. The Bradbury Chronicles: Stories in Honor of Ray Bradbury. 320p. 1991. 19.95 (*0-451-45134-1*, ROC) NAL-Dutton.

— The Bradbury Chronicles: Stories in Honor of Ray Bradbury. 336p. 1992. 5.50 (*0-451-45195-3*, ROC) NAL-Dutton.

— Urban Horrors. 368p. 1993. mass mkt. 5.50 (*0-88677-548-5*) DAW Bks.

Nolan, William F. & Johnson, George C. Logan: A Trilogy. LC 86-62097. (Illus.). 384p. 1986. 16.95 (*0-940776-23-5*) Maclay Assoc.

— Logan's Run. 160p. 1992. reprint ed. lib. bdg. 21.95x (*0-89966-896-8*) Buccaneer Bks.

Nolan, William F., ed. see Bradbury, Ray.

Nolan-Woods, Enid, jt. auth. see Broukal, Milada.

*Noland.** Travels Along the Edge. pap. write for info. (*0-679-76344-9*) Random.

Noland, Aaron. The Founding of the French Socialist Party, 1893-1905. 35.00 (*0-86527-070-8*) Fertig.

Noland, Aaron, jt. ed. see Weiner, Philip P.

*Noland, Brenda.** Wise & Otherwise. (Illus.). 32p. (J). (ps-2). 1996. 13.95 (*1-880092-25-5*) Bright Bks TX.

Noland, Jane & Noland, Mimi. Bear Up: Bear Ways to Cope with Lifes Bumps & Surprises. LC 93-27109. (Illus.). 72p. 1993. pap. 6.95 (*0-89638-323-7*) Hazelden.

— Bearables: Parables of Bear Wisdom for Everyday Living. (Illus.). 72p. (Orig.). 1993. pap. 6.95 (*0-89638-298-2*) Hazelden.

Noland, Jane, ed. see Brinegar, Jerry L.

Noland, Jane, ed. see Wolter, Dwight.

Noland, Jane T. A Day at a Time: Gamblers Anonymous. 384p. (Orig.). 1989. reprint ed. pap. 8.95 (*1-56838-036-4*) Hazelden.

— What's So Funny about Getting Old. 1994. pap. 6.00 (*0-671-51152-1*) S&S Trade.

Noland, Jane T., ed. see Carnes, Patrick.

Noland, Jane T., ed. see F, Dan.

Noland, Jane T., ed. see Keating, Kathleen.

Noland, Jane T., ed. see Ryder, Daniel.

*Noland, Marcus.** Pacific Basin Developing Countries: Prospects for the Future. fac. ed. LC 90-25083. 248p. 1990. reprint ed. pap. 70.70 (*0-7837-8295-0*, 2049077) Bks Demand.

Noland, Marcus, jt. auth. see Balassa, Bela.

Noland, Marcus, jt. auth. see Bergsten, C. Fred.

Noland, Mimi, jt. auth. see Noland, Jane.

Noland, Richard, ed. see Lesser, Simon O.

Noland, Wayland E., ed. Organic Syntheses Collective, Vol. 6. (Organic Syntheses Ser.). 1208p. 1988. text ed. 103.00 (*0-471-85243-0*) Wiley.

Noland, William E. & Bakke, E. Wight. Workers Wanted: Study of Employers' Hiring Policies, Preferences, & Practices in New Haven & Charlotte. Stein, Leon, ed. LC 77-70521. (Work Ser.). (Illus.). 1977. reprint ed. lib. bdg. 23.95 (*0-405-10189-9*) Ayer.

Nolasco-Carrandi, Guadalupe, tr. see Thompson-Peters, Flossie E.

Nolasco, Domingo F. Three Tombs & Other Stories. 97p. (Orig.). (C). 1992. pap. 5.50 (*971-10-0325-2*, Pub. by New Day Pub PH) Cellar.

Nolasco, J. B., jt. auth. see Chua, Philip S.

Nolasquez, Rosinda, jt. auth. see Hill, Jane H.

Nolasquez, Rosinda, jt. ed. see Hill, Jane H.

Nold, James, jt. auth. see Segal, Julie.

Nold, John. Willing Victims. 64p. 1987. 9.95 (*0-920806-89-9*, Pub. by Penumbra Pr CN) U of Toronto Pr.

Nolde, Carol, ed. see Chin-Lee, Cynthia.

Nolde, Eduard. Reise Nach Innerarabien, Kurdistan und Armenien, 1892. (Illus.). xvi, 272p. reprint ed. write for info. (*0-318-71542-2*, Pub. by Georg Olms GW) Lubrecht & Cramer.

Nolde, John. Blossoms from the East: The China Cantos of Ezra Pound. LC 82-61491. (Ezra Pound Scholarship Ser.). 490p. 1983. 35.00 (*0-915032-05-8*); pap. 15.95 (*0-915032-06-6*) Natl Poet Foun.

Noldeke, T. Sketches from Eastern History. 292p. 1985. 220.00 (*1-85077-065-4*, Darf Pubs Ltd) St Mut.

Noldeke, Theodor. Beitrage Zur Kenntnis der Poesie der Alten Araber. xxiv, 244p. 1967. reprint ed. write for info. (*0-318-71540-6*, Pub. by Georg Olms GW) Lubrecht & Cramer.

— Geschichte Des Qorans, 3 vols. in 1. xxxi, 837p. 1981. reprint ed. write for info. (*0-318-71541-4*, Pub. by Georg Olms GW) Lubrecht & Cramer.

— The Quran: An Introductory Essay. Newman, N. A., ed. 1992. 3.95 (*0-944788-93-9*) IBRI.

Nolder, Ann. Dream of Danger. (Orig.). 1981. pap. 1.75 (*0-8439-8030-3*) Dorchester Pub Co.

Nolds, Annrey & Reynolds, Helen A. Unfolding Splendor: A Biography of Laura Ophelia Reynolds Hughes. Carlock, G. M. & Browne, B. Holbrook, eds. (Illus.). 319p. (C). 1992. 29.95 (*1-880926-01-6*) Four Star SC.

Nolen. Computer-Automated Process Planning for World-Class Manufacturing. (Manufacturing Engineering & Materials Processing Ser.: Vol. 29). 448p. 1989. 125.00 (*0-8247-7918-5*) Dekker.

— Healing. 1987. pap. 3.95 (*0-449-21315-3*) Fawcett.

Nolen, Anita L. & Coutts, Mary C., eds. International Directory of Bioethics Organizations. 1993. pap. 35.00 (*1-883913-11-X*) Geo U Kennedy Inst.

Nolen, Ben M. & Narramore, Robert E. Rivers & Rapids: A Very Complete Canoeing, Rafting & Fishing Guide to the Streams & Rivers of Texas, Arkansas & Oklahoma. (Illus.). 144p. 1992. pap. 13.95 (*0-9632403-8-2*) Rivers & Rapids.

*Nolen, Candy L.** The Lectors Sins. 210p. 1995. pap. 8.95 (*1-56901-897-9*) NW Pub.

Nolen, Claude H. The Negro's Image in the South: The Anatomy of White Supremacy. LC 67-17843. 252p. reprint ed. 71.90 (*0-8357-9792-9*, 2011071) Bks Demand.

*Nolen, Elberta.** Pass for Outlaws. 480p. 1995. pap. 9.95 (*1-56901-665-8*) NW Pub.

Nolen, Evelyn T., jt. ed. see Boles, John B.

Nolen, Herman C., jt. auth. see Beckman, Theodore N.

Nolen-Hoeksema, Susan. Sex Differences in Depression. LC 89-27303. 270p. 1990. 39.50 (*0-8047-1640-4*) Stanford U Pr.

— Sex Differences in Depression. 270p. (C). 1993. pap. 13. 95 (*0-8047-2180-7*) Stanford U Pr.

Nolen, Jerdine. Harvey Potter's Balloon Farm. LC 91-38129. (J). (ps-3). 1994. 15.00 (*0-688-07887-7*); 14.93 (*0-688-07888-5*) Lothrop.

Nolen, Willem A., et al. Refractory Depression: Current Strategies & Future Directions. LC 93-49532. 1994. text ed. 74.95 (*0-471-94315-0*) Wiley.

Nolen, William A. The Making of a Surgeon. 2nd ed. 288p. 1990. reprint ed. 17.95 (*0-922811-05-9*) Mid-List.

Noles, bj. Cookbook for a Career Mother. (Illus.). 180p. 1983. pap. 8.95 (*0-9613684-0-3*) BJ Noles.

Noles, Eva. Buffalo Black's Talking Proud. 132p. (Orig.). 1986. pap. 9.95 (*0-9624731-0-3*) Noles Pub.

Noles, Eva M. Black History - A Different Approach. 57p. (Orig.). 1989. pap. 9.95 (*0-9624731-1-1*) Noles Pub.

Nolet, Andree, jt. auth. see Campbell, Carmen.

Nolet, Guust, ed. Seismic Tomography: With Applications in Global Seismology & Exploration Geophysics. (C). 1987. lib. bdg. 124.50 (*90-277-2521-7*) Kluwer Ac.

Noley, Homer. First White Frost: Native Americans & United Methodism. 276p. 1991. pap. 14.95 (*0-687-13051-4*) Abingdon.

Nolf, D. Otolithi Piscium. (Handbook of Paleoichthyology Monograph: Vol. 10). (Illus.). 145p. 1985. pap. text ed. 128.70 (*3-437-30399-6*) Lubrecht & Cramer.

Nolf, Pam, ed. see Kaiser, Hal.

Nolfi, Edward A. Basic Wills, Trusts, & Estates. LC 94-13452. (Legal Studies Ser.). 1994. 30.00 (*0-02-801338-7*) Glencoe.

Nolfi, Edward A. & Tepper, Pamela R. Basic Legal Research & Writing. LC 92-25750. (Legal Studies Ser.). 1992. 45. 00 (*0-02-801276-3*) Glencoe.

Nolfi, Frank V., Jr., ed. Phase Transformations During Irradiation. (Illus.). 363p. 1983. 97.25 (*0-85334-179-6*, Pub. by Elsevier Applied Sci UK) Elsevier.

Nolfi, Kristine. My Experience with Living Food. 23p. 1994. reprint ed. 4.40 (*0-7873-1034-4*) Mokelumne.

— Raw Food Treatment of Cancer & Other Diseases. 8p. 1994. reprint ed. spiral bd. 3.85 (*0-7873-1028-X*) Mokelumne.

Nolfi, Kristine, jt. auth. see Fry, Terry C.

Nolhac, Pierre de, jt. auth. see Du Bellay, Joachim.

Noli, Jean. The Admiral's Wolfpack. (World-at-War Ser.). 1982. pap. 2.50 (*0-89083-630-2*) Zebra.

Nolk, Brian, ed. Fourth International Ferro Alloys Conference Proceedings. 288p. (Orig.). 1985. pap. text ed. write for info. (*0-913333-05-0*) Metal Bulletin.

— Titanium & Superalloys II: Battling the Economics Elements. 188p. 1984. pap. text ed. write for info. (*0-913333-04-2*) Metal Bulletin.

Noll, A. Michael. Introduction to Telecommunication Electronics. 366p. 1988. text ed. 44.00 (*0-89006-228-5*) Artech Hse.

— Introduction to Telephones & Telephone Systems. 2nd ed. (Telecommunications Library). 244p. 1991. text ed. 39.00 (*0-89006-550-0*) Artech Hse.

— Television Technology: Fundamentals & Future Prospects. (Telecommunications Management Library). 200p. 1988. text ed. 53.00 (*0-89006-332-X*) Artech Hse.

Noll, Anna C. Earthly Delights: Garden Imagery in Contemporary Art. LC 88-81964. (Illus.). 46p. (Orig.). 1988. pap. 10.00 (*0-917185-01-3*) Fort Wayne.

— A Point of View: Twentieth-Century Art from a Long Island Collection. LC 90-84052. (Illus.). 48p. (Orig.). 1990. pap. text ed. 9.95 (*1-879195-05-4*) Heckscher Mus.

Noll, Arthur H. From Republic to Empire: The Story of the Struggle for Constitutional Government in Mexico. 1976. lib. bdg. 59.95 (*0-8490-1867-6*) Gordon Pr.

*Noll, Bink.** The House: Poems. fac. ed. LC 84-12590. 64p. 1984. reprint ed. pap. 25.00 (*0-7837-7812-0*, 2047568) Bks Demand.

*Noll, Chuck, intro.** Football Legends, 6 bks., Set. (Illus.). (YA). (gr. 3 up). 1995. lib. bdg. write for info. (*0-7910-2450-4*) Chelsea Hse.

Noll, David. The Age of Dinosaurs. (Arts & Letters Ser.). 44p. 1993. pap. text ed. 3.95 (*1-883515-00-9*) Computer Support.

Noll, Edward. The Basic Guide to VHF-UHF Ham Radio. 86p. (Orig.). 1987. pap. 6.95 (*0-936653-11-6*) Tiare Pubns.

Noll, Greg & Gabbard, Andrea. Da Bull: Life over the Edge. (Illus.). 200p. 1992. reprint ed. pap. 16.95 (*1-55643-143-0*) North Atlantic.

Noll, Greg, et al. Hazardous Materials: Managing the Incident. (Illus.). 206p. (Orig.). (C). 1988. 15.00 (*0-945316-02-X*) IFSTA.

— Hazardous Materials: Managing the Incident. (Illus.). 206p. (Orig.). (C). 1994. student ed 30.00 (*0-945316-01-1*) IFSTA.

Noll, Gregory G., jt. auth. see Hildebrand, Michael S.

*Noll, Gregory G., et al.** Hazardous Materials: Managing the Incident. 2nd ed. Daley, Patricia, ed. (Illus.). 568p. 1994. pap. text ed. 30.00 (*0-87939-111-1*) IFSTA.

Noll, James W. & Kelly, Sam P. Foundations of Education in America: An Anthology of Major Thoughts & Significant Actions. LC 76-95838. 531p. reprint ed. pap. 151.40 (*0-7837-3951-6*, 2043780) Bks Demand.

An Asterisk (*) at the beginning of an entry indicates that the title is appearing in BIP for the first time.

Noll, Joyce E. Company of Prophets: African American Psychics, Healers & Visionaries. LC 91-26482. 308p. (Orig.). 1991. pap. 12.95 (*0-87542-583-6*) Llewellyn Pubns.

Noll, Kenneth E. Adsorption Technology for Air & Water Pollution Control. (Illus.). 420p. 1991. 85.00 (*0-87371-340-0*, TD883) Lewis Pubs.

Noll, Margaret L. Flavor & Fragrance Markets. 135p. 1993. 1,950.00 (*0-945235-68-2*) Lead Edge Reports.

— Industrial Process Control Markets & Technology. 231p. 1991. 1,950.00 (*0-945235-51-8*) Lead Edge Reports.

Noll, Mark, ed. see Dorsett, Lyle W.

Noll, Mark, ed. see Gaustad, Edwin S.

Noll, Mark, ed. see Stout, Harry S.

Noll, Mark A. Between Faith & Criticism: Evangelicals, Scholarship, & the Bible in America. 2nd ed. LC 91-11037. 288p. 1991. pap. text ed. 13.99 (*0-8010-6785-5*) Baker Bk.

— Christians & the American Revolution. LC 77-23354. 195p. reprint ed. pap. 55.60 (*0-8357-9125-4*, 2016042) Bks Demand.

— History of Christianity in the United States & Canada. (Illus.). 544p. 1992. pap. 29.99 (*0-8028-0651-1*) Eerdmans.

— Princeton & the Republic, 1768-1822: The Search for a Christian Enlightenment in the Era of Samuel Stanhope Smith. 320p. (C). 1989. text ed. 45.00 (*0-691-04764-2*) Princeton U Pr.

— The Scandal of the Evangelical Mind. LC 94-18843. x, 256p. 1994. text ed. 19.99 (*0-8028-3715-8*) Eerdmans.

Noll, Mark A., ed. Charles Hodge: The Way of Life & Selected Writings, Vol. 7. (Sources of American Spirituality Ser.). 288p. 1987. 14.95 (*0-8091-0392-3*) Paulist Pr.

— Confessions & Catechisms of the Reformation. LC 90-27535. 224p. (Orig.). 1991. pap. text ed. 14.99 (*0-8010-6784-7*) Baker Bk.

— Religion & American Politics: From the Colonial Period to the 1980s. (Illus.). 416p. (C). 1989. pap. text ed. 17.95 (*0-19-505881-X*) OUP.

Noll, Mark A. & Wells, David F., eds. Christian Faith & Practice in the Modern World: Theology from an Evangelical Point of View. LC 88-3635. 357p. reprint ed. pap. 101.80 (*0-7837-3197-3*, 2042802) Bks Demand.

Noll, Mark A., jt. ed. see Hatch, Nathan O.

Noll, Mark A., ed. see Hodge, Charles.

Noll, Mark A., jt. ed. see Lundin, Roger.

Noll, Mark A., jt. ed. see Rawlyk, George.

Noll, Mark A., et al. The Search for Christian America. 208p. 1989. reprint ed. pap. 14.95 (*0-939443-15-5*) Helmers Howard Pub.

Noll, Mark A., et al, eds. Evangelicalism: Comparative Studies of Popular Protestantism of North America & the British Isles & Beyond, 1700-1900. LC 92-46303. (Religion in America Ser.). 448p. 1994. 55.00 (*0-19-508362-8*); pap. 19.95 (*0-19-508363-6*) OUP.

Noll, Michael A., jt. auth. see Pierce, John R.

Noll, Paul, jt. auth. see Murach, Mike.

Noll, Peter. In the Face of Death. 254p. 1990. 19.95 (*0-685-31397-2*) Viking Penguin.

Noll, Ray R. Christian Ministerial Priesthood: A Search for Its Beginnings in the Primary Documents of the Apostolic Fathers. 275p. 1993. 64.95 (*1-883255-07-4*); pap. 44.95 (*1-883255-00-7*) Intl Scholars.

Noll, Richard. Encyclopedia of Schizophrenia & Psychotic Disorders. 320p. 1991. lib. bdg. 45.00 (*0-8160-2240-2*) Facts on File.

— The Jung Cult: Origins of a Charismatic Movement. LC 94-4831. 1994. 27.95 (*0-691-03724-8*) Princeton U Pr.

— Vampires, Werewolves, & Demons: Twentieth Century Reports in the Psychiatric Literature. LC 91-26933. 272p. (Orig.). 1992. pap. 14.95 (*0-87630-702-0*) Brunner-Mazel.

Noll, Richard & Turkington, Carol. Encyclopedia of Memory & Memory Disorders. LC 94-1590. 280p. 1994. 45.00 (*0-8160-2610-6*) Facts on File.

Noll, Roger, jt. ed. see Cohen, Linda R.

Noll, Roger G. Reforming Regulation: An Evaluation of the Ash Council Proposals. LC 75-179326. (Studies in the Regulation of Economic Activity). 116p. 1971. pap. 7.95 (*0-8157-6107-4*) Brookings.

— Regulatory Policy & the Social Sciences. (California Series on Social Choice & Political Economy: No. 5). 1985. 52.50 (*0-520-05187-4*) U CA Pr.

Noll, Roger G. & Owen, Bruce M. The Political Economy of Deregulation: Interest Groups in the Regulatory Process. LC 83-2638. (AEI Studies: No. 379). 164p. 1983. pap. 11.00 (*0-8447-3519-1*) Am Enterprise.

Noll, Roger G., et al. Economic Aspects of Television Regulation. LC 73-1086. (Studies in the Regulation of Economic Activity). 342p. 1973. 31.95 (*0-8157-6108-2*); pap. 11.95 (*0-8157-6109-0*) Brookings.

Noll, Sally. I Have a Loose Tooth. LC 91-31456. (Illus.). 32p. (J). (ps-4). 1992. 14.00 (*0-688-11191-2*); lib. bdg. 13.93 (*0-688-11192-0*) Greenwillow.

— Jiggle Wiggle Prance. LC 86-18322. (Illus.). 24p. (J). (ps-1). 1987. 11.75 (*0-688-06760-3*); lib. bdg. 11.88 (*0-688-06761-1*) Greenwillow.

— Jiggle, Wiggle, Prance. LC 92-25332. (J). 1993. pap. 3.99 (*0-14-054883-1*) Puffin Bks.

— Lucky Morning. LC 93-18188. (Illus.). 32p. (J). (ps up). 1994. 14.00 (*0-688-12474-7*); lib. bdg. 13.93 (*0-688-12475-5*) Greenwillow.

— That Bothered Kate. LC 90-38488. (Illus.). 32p. (J). (ps up). 1991. 13.95 (*0-688-10095-3*); lib. bdg. 13.88 (*0-688-10096-1*) Greenwillow.

— That Bothered Kate. LC 92-40167. (Illus.). 32p. (J). (ps-3). 1993. pap. 4.99 (*0-14-054885-8*, Puffin) Puffin Bks.

— Watch Where You Go. LC 88-35591. (Illus.). 32p. (J). (ps up). 1990. 12.95 (*0-688-08498-2*); lib. bdg. 12.88 (*0-688-08499-0*) Greenwillow.

— Watch Where You Go. LC 92-25333. (J). 1993. reprint ed. pap. 3.99 (*0-14-054884-X*) Puffin Bks.

Noll, Stephen F. The Intertestamental Period. 92p. 1985. 6.99 (*0-8308-5494-0*) InterVarsity.

***Noll, Steven.** Feeble-Minded in Our Midst: Institutions for the Mentally Retarded in the South, 1900-1940. LC 94-49527. 1995. write for info. (*0-8078-2220-5*); pap. write for info. (*0-8078-4531-0*) U of NC Pr.

Noll, Victor H., et al. Introduction to Educational Measurement. 4th ed. LC 89-5504. (Illus.). 560p. (C). 1989. reprint ed. pap. text ed. 49.50 (*0-8191-7411-4*) U Pr of Amer.

Noll, Walter. Finite-Dimensional Spaces: Algebra, Geometry & Analysis, Vol I. (C). 1900. pap. text ed. 65.00 (*90-247-3582-3*) Kluwer Ac.

— Finite-Dimensional Spaces: Algebra, Geometry & Analysis, Vol I. (C). 1987. lib. bdg. 172.50 (*90-247-3581-5*) Kluwer Ac.

Nolla, Eduardo, ed. Liberty, Equality, Democracy. 320p. (C). 1992. text ed. 45.00 (*0-8147-5774-X*) NYU Pr.

Nolla, Olga. Dulcehombre Prohibido. 150p. 1994. pap. write for info. (*1-56758-052-1*) Edit Cultl.

— La Segunda Hija. 94p. 1993. 11.95 (*0-8477-0176-X*) U of PR Pr.

Nollan, Valerie, tr. see Soloukhin, Vladimir.

Nolland, John. WBC, Vol. 35A: Luke 1: 1-9: 20. 454p. 1990. write for info. (*0-8499-0234-7*) Word Inc.

— Word Biblical Commentary, Vol. 35B: Luke 9: 21-18. 896p. 1993. write for info. (*0-8499-0254-1*) Word Inc.

Nolle, Daniel E., ed. Canada-U. S. Free Trade Agreement: Implications, Opportunities, & Challenges. 208p. 1989. 40.00x (*0-8147-5764-2*) NYU Pr.

Nolle, Johannes. Nundinas Instituere et Habere. (Subsidia Epigraphica Ser.). 172p. 1982. write for info. (*3-487-07259-9*, Pub. by Georg Olms GW) Lubrecht & Cramer.

Nolle, Richard. Chiron: New Planet in the Horoscope. LC 83-70810. 160p. 1983. 12.00 (*0-86690-236-8*, N2281-014) Am Fed Astrologers.

— Critical Astrology: Investigating the Cosmic Connection. LC 80-68779. 204p. 1980. 12.00 (*0-86690-144-2*, N1356-014) Am Fed Astrologers.

— Interpreting Astrology: New Techniques & Perspectives. LC 85-71460. 134p. 1986. 12.00 (*0-86690-292-9*, N2647-014) Am Fed Astrologers.

Nolledo, Wilfrido D. But for the Lovers. LC 94-9184. 325p. 1994. reprint ed. pap. 12.95 (*1-56478-067-8*) Dalkey Arch.

Nollen, Scott A. Boris Karloff: A Critical Account of His Screen, Stage, Radio, Television & Recording Work. LC 90-53515. (Illus.). 487p. 1991. lib. bdg. 43.50x (*0-89950-580-5*) McFarland & Co.

— The Boys: The Cinematic World of Laurel & Hardy. LC 89-42742. 167p. 1989. lib. bdg. 28.50x (*0-89950-383-7*) McFarland & Co.

— Robert Louis Stevenson: Life, Literature & the Silver Screen. (Illus.). 496p. 1994. lib. bdg. 55.00 (*0-89950-788-3*) McFarland & Co.

***Nollen, Stanley.** Exploding the Myth: Is Contingent Labor Cost-Effective? 10p. 1993. 5.00 (*0-614-01661-4*, G-007) New Ways Work.

— New Patterns of Work. (Studies in Productivity: Highlights of the Literature Ser.: Vol. 7). 59p. 55.00 (*0-08-029488-X*, PS7) Work in Amer.

Nollendorfs, Valters, jt. ed. see Lohnes, Walter F.

Nollendorfs, Valters, et al, eds. DAAD - Monatshefte Directory of German Studies: Departments, Programs, & Faculties in the United States & Canada, 1990. xxxviii, 553p. (Orig.). (C). 1991. pap. text ed. 5.00 (*1-880376-00-8*) German Studies.

Noller. Guide to Creative Action. 1981. 18.95 (*0-684-14888-9*, Scribners) S&S Trade.

Noller, B. N. & Chadha, M., eds. Chemistry & the Environment. 334p. 1990. pap. 65.00 (*0-85092-350-6*, Pub. by CSIRO AT) Intl Spec Bk.

Noller, Patricia. Nonverbal Communication & Marital Interaction. (International Series in Experimental Social Psychology: Vol. 9). (Illus.). 250p. 1984. text ed. 96.00 (*0-08-027927-9*, CRC Reprint) Franklin.

Noller, Patricia & Callan, Victor. The Adolescent in the Family. (Adolescence & Society Ser.). 350p. 1991. 72.50 (*0-415-01089-6*, A4928); pap. 16.95 (*0-415-01090-X*, A4932) Routledge.

Noller, Patricia & Fitzpatrick, MaryAnn. Communication in Family Relationships. 352p. (C). 1992. pap. text ed. write for info. (*0-13-301748-6*) P-H.

Noller, Patricia & Fitzpatrick, MaryAnn, eds. Perspectives on Marital Interaction. (Monographs in the Social Psychology of Language). 1988. 99.00 (*0-905028-91-0*, Pub. by Multilingual Matters UK); pap. 39.95 (*0-905028-90-2*, Pub. by Multilingual Matters UK) Taylor & Francis.

Noller, Ruth B. & Frey, Barbara R. Mentoring: An Annotated Bibliography. 80p. (Orig.). 1983. pap. 12.95 (*0-943456-01-0*) Bearly Ltd.

Nolletti, Arthur, Jr. & Desser, David, eds. Reframing Japanese Cinema: Authorship, Genre, History. LC 91-33659. (Illus.). 384p. 1992. 39.95 (*0-253-34108-6*); pap. 18.95 (*0-253-20723-1*, MB-723) Ind U Pr.

Nolling, Wilhelm. Monetary Policy in Europe after Maastricht. LC 93-7294. (ENG & GER.). 1993. text ed. 45.00 (*0-312-09952-5*) St Martin.

Nollius, Henry. The Chymist's Key: The True Doctrine of Corruption & Generation, in Ten Brief Aphorisms Illustrated with the Pure Light of Nature. Vaughan, Henry, tr. reprint ed. pap. 4.95 (*1-55818-187-3*) Holmes Pub.

— Hermetic Physic: or, The Right Way to Preserve & to Restore Health. Holmes, Jefferson D., ed. Vaughan, Henry & Vaughan, Thomas, trs. reprint ed. pap. text ed. 9.95 (*1-55818-273-X*) Holmes Pub.

Nollkaemper, Andre. The Legal Regime for Transboundary Water Pollution: Between Discretion & Constraint. LC 93-31558. (International Environmental Law & Policy Ser.). 408p. (C). 1993. lib. bdg. 134.50 (*0-7923-2476-5*) Kluwer Ac.

Nollman, Jim. Why We Garden. 1994. 25.00 (*0-8050-2719-X*) H Holt & Co.

Nolloth, H. E., ed. see Thoresby, John.

***Nolly, Larry.** Drum Tuning. 2nd ed. 24p. 1988. pap. text ed. 12.95 (*0-9644658-1-7*) Drumstix Pub.

Nolo Press Editors. Fed up with the Legal System? What's Wrong & How to Fix It. 2nd rev. ed. LC 94-974. 1994. pap. 9.95 (*0-87337-242-5*) Nolo Pr.

Nolo Press Editors, jt. auth. see Guerin, Lisa.

***Nolo Press Staff & Guerin, Lisa.** Nolo's Pocket Guide to California Law. 3rd ed. LC 94-36933. 225p. 1995. pap. 10.95 (*0-87337-292-1*) Nolo Pr.

Nolo Press Staff & Legal Star Communications Staff. Legal Research Made Easy: A Roadmap Through the Law Library Maze. 40p. 1990. student ed, vhs 89.95 (*0-87337-138-0*) Nolo Pr.

Nolon, John. Common Walls-Private Homes: Multiresidential Design. 208p. 1990. text ed. 42.00 (*0-07-016819-9*) McGraw.

Nolosco, Marynita A. Physician Heal Thyself: Medical Practitioner of Eighteenth-Century New York. LC 94-13012. (American University Studies, Series IX: History: Vol. 170). 1994. write for info. (*0-8204-2580-X*) P Lang Pubs.

Nolph, K. D., jt. ed. see Mactier, R. A.

Nolph, Karl D., ed. Peritoneal Dialysis. 2nd ed. 1985. lib. bdg. 216.50 (*0-89838-685-3*) Kluwer Ac.

— Peritoneal Dialysis. 3rd ed. (C). 1988. lib. bdg. 207.50 (*0-89838-406-0*) Kluwer Ac.

Nolph, Karl D., jt. ed. see Gokal, Ram.

Nolst-Trenite, G. J. Rhinoplasty: A Practical Guide to Functional & Aesthetic Surgery of the Nose. LC 92-48704. (Illus.). 200p. 1992. lib. bdg. 146.00 (*90-6299-089-4*) Kugler Pubns.

Nolt, Joanne, ed. see Chitra Publications Staff.

Nolt, Joanne S., ed. see Chitra Publications Staff.

Nolt, John E. Informal Logic: Possible Worlds & Imagination. 1984. text ed. write for info. (*0-07-046861-3*) McGraw.

Nolt, John E. & Rohatyn, Dennis A. Schaum's Outline of Logic. 384p. 1988. pap. text ed. 11.95 (*0-07-053628-7*) McGraw.

Nolt, Marilyn, jt. auth. see Peifer, Jane.

Nolt, Steven. A History of the Amish. LC 92-29684. 317p. 1992. 9.95 (*1-56148-072-X*) Good Bks PA.

— What Mennonites Believe about Peace. 1993. pap. 9.95 (*1-56148-102-5*) Good Bks PA.

Nolt, Steven, jt. auth. see Haas, J. Craig.

Nolt, Steven M., jt. auth. see Kraybill, Donald B.

Nolte. Human Brain. 3rd ed. 1993. 47.95 (*0-8016-6861-1*) Mosby Yr Bk.

— The Human Brain: An Introduction to Its Functional Anatomy. 3rd ed. 480p. 1992. pap. 37.95 (*0-8016-7483-2*) Mosby Yr Bk.

— Human Neurobiology. 600p. 1991. 26.95 (*0-8016-3263-3*); International ed. write for info. (*0-318-63392-2*) Mosby Yr Bk.

— Principles of Neurobiology: International Edition. 1991. 20.00 (*0-8016-5501-3*) Mosby Yr Bk.

— Study Guide to Accompany The Human Brain: Introduction to Its Functional Anatomy. 3rd ed. 192p. 1992. pap. 15.95 (*0-8016-6332-6*) Mosby Yr Bk.

Nolte, Claude B. Optimum Pipe Size Selection. (Illus.). 304p. (C). 1978. 60.00 (*0-87849-024-8*, Pub. by Trans Tech GW) LPS Dist Ctr.

***Nolte, David D., ed.** Photorefractive Effects & Materials. LC 95-11662. (International Series in Engineering & Computer Science). 504p. (C). 1995. lib. bdg. 150.00 (*0-7923-9560-3*) Kluwer Ac.

Nolte, Dietrich. Speaking of: Asthma. (Sterling Health & Cure Ser.). 96p. 1989. text ed. 15.95 (*81-207-0840-7*, Pub. by Sterling Pubs II) Apt Bks.

***Nolte, Kristi, ed.** NY Agent Book. 4th ed. 301p. 1995. 17.95 (*1-878355-03-1*) Sweden Pr.

— The Script Is Finished, Now What Do I Do? A Resource Book & Agent Guide for Scriptwriters. 332p. 1993. pap. 15.95 (*1-878355-00-7*) Sweden Pr.

Nolte, Kristi, ed. see K Callan.

Nolte, Lawrence W., jt. auth. see Wilcox, Dennis L.

Nolte, M. Chester. How to Survive As a Principal: The Legal Dimension. LC 83-62499. 256p. (C). 1983. pap. text ed. 17.95 (*0-931028-42-6*) Teach-em.

— How to Survive As a School Board Member: The Legal Dimension. LC 84-50709. 224p. 1984. 19.95 (*0-931028-55-8*) Teach-em.

— How to Survive in Teaching: The Legal Dimension. 3rd ed. LC 78-57206. (Orig.). 1978. pap. text ed. 12.95 (*0-931028-06-X*) Teach-em.

Nolte, Oliver, jt. ed. see Mueller, Erwin.

Nolte, Reginald G. Thunder Monsters over Europe: A History of the 405th Fighter Group in WWII. (Illus.). 160p. 1986. pap. 18.95 (*0-685-11921-1*) Sunflower U Pr.

Nolte, Sharon. Liberalism in Modern Japan: Ishibashi Tanzan & His Teachers, 1905-1960. 1986. 45.00 (*0-520-05707-4*) U CA Pr.

Nolte, Vincent. Fifty Years in Both Hemispheres: or Reminiscences of the Life of a Former Merchant. LC 75-37903. (Select Bibliographies Reprint Ser.). 1977. reprint ed. 29.95 (*0-8369-6741-0*) Ayer.

Nolte, William, jt. auth. see Wilsted, Thomas.

Nolte, William H. H. L. Mencken's Smart Set Criticism. LC 87-23248. 349p. 1987. reprint ed. pap. 10.95 (*0-89526-790-X*) Regnery Pub.

Noltemeier, H., ed. Graphtheoretic Concepts in Computer Science: Proceedings. (Lecture Notes in Computer Science Ser.: Vol. 100). 403p. 1981. pap. 37.00 (*0-387-10291-4*) Spr-Verlag.

Noltemeier, H., jt. ed. see Bieri, H.

Noltemeir, H., ed. Computational Geometry & Its Applications. (Lecture Notes in Computer Science Ser.: Vol. 333). vi, 252p. 1988. pap. 36.00 (*0-387-50335-8*) Spr-Verlag.

Noltensmeier, Lucille. A Country Almanac. (Illus.). 160p. 1982. 10.50 (*0-943782-00-7*, Pantagraph Bks); pap. 5.00 (*0-943782-01-5*, Pantagraph Bks) Evergreen Comm.

***Nolting, Anne.** Dear Future People. (Orig.). (YA). (gr. 7 up). 1995. lib. bdg. write for info. (*0-88092-288-5*); pap. write for info. (*0-88092-287-7*) Royal Fireworks.

Nolting, Frederick. From Trust to Tragedy: The Political Memoirs of Frederick Nolting, Kennedy's Ambassador to Diem's Vietnam. LC 88-15397. 177p. 1988. text ed. 49.95 (*0-275-93080-7*, C3080, Praeger Pubs); pap. text ed. 12.95 (*0-275-93106-4*, B3106, Praeger Pubs) Greenwood.

Nolting, H. P. & Ulrich, R., eds. Integrated Optics. (Optical Sciences Ser.: Vol. 48). (Illus.). x, 242p. 1985. 54.00 (*0-387-15537-6*) Spr-Verlag.

Nolting, Mark. Africa's Top Wildlife Countries: With Mauritius & Seychelles. 1994. pap. 16.95 (*0-939895-05-6*) Global Travel Pubs.

— Travel Journal Africa. 3rd ed. 1994. pap. 12.95 (*0-939895-06-4*) Global Travel Pubs.

Nolting, Mark W. African Safari: The Complete Travel Guide to 10 Top Game Viewing Countries. LC 87-8481. (Illus.). 256p. (Orig.). 1987. pap. 15.95 (*0-939895-00-5*) Global Travel Pubs.

— Travel Journal: Africa. (Illus.). 160p. (Orig.). 1988. pap. 12.95 (*0-939895-01-3*) Global Travel Pubs.

Nolting, Paul D. Math & the Learning Disabled Student: A Practical Guide for Accommodations. 1991. pap. 14.95 (*0-940287-23-4*) Acad Success Pr.

— Successful Math Study Skills: Easy-to-Use Step-by-Step Guide to Higher Math Grades. 1991. pap. 12.95 (*0-940287-18-8*) Acad Success Pr.

— Winning at Math: Your Guide to Learning Mathematics the Quick & Easy Way. 208p. (Orig.). 1988. pap. 12.95 (*0-940287-08-0*) Acad Success Pr.

— Winning at Math: Your Guide to Learning Mathematics Through Successful Study Skills. (Illus.). 248p. (C). 1991. pap. 12.95 (*0-940287-19-6*) Acad Success Pr.

Nolting, S. & Fegler, K. Medical Mycology. 210p. 1987. pap. 29.40 (*0-387-17606-3*) Spr-Verlag.

Nolting, S. & Korting, H. C., eds. Onychomycoses. (Illus.). x, 126p. 1990. pap. 24.00 (*0-387-52132-1*) Spr-Verlag.

Noltingk, B. E. Jones Instrument Technology, Vol. 1: Mechanical Measurements. 4th ed. (Illus.). 180p. 1985. pap. text ed. 52.95 (*0-408-01231-5*) Buttrwrth-Heinemann.

***Noltingk, B. E., ed.** Instrumentation Reference Book. 2nd ed. LC 95-1813. 1000p. 1995. 199.00 (*0-7506-2056-0*, Focal) Buttrwrth-Heinemann.

— Jones' Instrument Technology, Vol. 2. 4th ed. 1985. pap. text ed. 49.95 (*0-408-01232-3*) Buttrwrth-Heinemann.

Noltingk, E., ed. Jones' Instrument Technology: Electrical & Radiation Measurements, Vol. 3. 4th ed. 180p. 1987. 52.95 (*0-408-01233-1*) Buttrwrth-Heinemann.

— Jones' Instrument Technology: Instrumentation Systems, Vol. 4. 4th ed. 186p. 1987. pap. text ed. 52.95 (*0-408-01234-X*) Buttrwrth-Heinemann.

***Noltingk, E. E.** Instrumentation Reference Book. 2nd ed. (Illus.). 1120p. 1995. 199.00 (*0-7506-0906-0*) Buttrwrth-Heinemann.

Nolub, Renata. Antonio Gramsci: Beyond Marxism & Postmodernism. 1992. pap. 16.95 (*0-415-07510-6*, A6855) Routledge.

Nolutshungu, Sam C. Changing South Africa: Political Considerations. 219p. 1982. 19.50 (*0-8419-0807-9*, Africana) Holmes & Meier.

— Limits of Anarchy: Intervention & State Formation in Chad. 392p. (C). 1996. text ed. 39.50 (*0-8139-1628-3*) U Pr of Va.

Noma, Chikako, ed. see Momotani, Yoshihide.

Noma, Chikako, ed. see Takeuchi, Naoko.

Noma, Chikako, ed. see Yamada, Amy.

Noma, Seiroku. Arts of Japan, 2 vols., Vol. I: Ancient & Medieval. Rosenfield, John, tr. LC 65-19186. (Illus.). 305p. 1978. 35.00 (*0-87011-335-6*) Kodansha.

— Arts of Japan, 2 vols., Vol. II: Late Medieval to Modern. Rosenfield, John, tr. LC 65-19186. (Illus.). 326p. 1978. 38.00 (*0-87011-336-4*) Kodansha.

— Arts of Japan, Vol. 2: Late Medieval to Modern. LC 65-19186. (Arts of Japan Ser.). (Illus.). 229p. 1973. 95.00 (*0-87011-050-0*) Kodansha.

Nomad, Ali. Cosmic Consciousness. 310p. 1994. pap. 25.00 (*0-89540-282-3*, SB-282) Sun Pub.

— Cosmic Consciousness: The Man-God Whom We Await. 310p. 1964. reprint ed. spiral bd. 8.25 (*0-7873-0636-3*) Mokelumne.

Nomad, Max. Rebels & Renegades. LC 68-20326. (Essay Index Reprint Ser.). 1977. 23.95 (*0-8369-0745-0*) Ayer.

Nomad Publishers, Ltd. Staff. Atlas of the U. S. A Thematic & Comparative Approach. (Illus.). 128p. 1986. 50.00 (*0-02-922830-1*) Macmillan.

Noman, Omar. Pakistan: Political & Economic History Since 1947. 285p. 1990. pap. 15.95 (*0-7103-0389-0*, A4718, Pub. by Kegan Paul Intl UK) Routledge Chapman & Hall.

— The Political & Economic Development of Pakistan. 260p. 1988. lib. bdg. 55.00 (*0-7103-0211-8*, Pub. by Kegan Paul Intl UK) Routledge Chapman & Hall.

Nomani, Farhad, jt. auth. see Rahnema, Ali.

N

Nomani, Fouad, jt. auth. see Rahnema, Ali.
Nomani, M. M. Meaning & Message of the Traditions, 2 vols., Set. 45.00 (1-56744-132-7) Kazi Pubns.
Nombela, C., ed. Microbial Cell Wall Synthesis & Autolysis: Proceedings of a Symposium Sponsored by the Federation of European Microbiological Societies, Madrid, July 3-6, 1984. 328p. 1985. 121.75 (0-444-80636-9) Elsevier.
Nomberg-Przytyk, Sara. Auschwitz: True Tales from a Grotesque Land. Pfefferkorn, Eli & Hirsch, David, eds. Hirsch, Roslyn, tr. LC 84-17386. xii, 185p. 1985. pap. 9.95 (0-8078-4160-9) U of NC Pr.
Nomenclature & Coding Committee Staff, ed. Orthopaedic ICD-9-CM. 2nd ed. LC 86-72455. 424p. 1991. 40.00 (0-89203-052-6) Amer Acad Ortho Surg.
Nomenclature Committee Staff, et al. The Revised Nomenclature for Museum Cataloging: Robert G. Chenhalls System for Classifying Man-Made Objects. enl. rev. ed. 528p. 1988. 62.00 (0-910050-93-7) AASLH.
Nomikos, Eugenia V. & North, Robert C. International Crisis: The Outbreak of World War I. LC 76-381852. 355p. reprint ed. pap. 101.20 (0-7837-2626-0, 2042976) Bks Demand.
Nomizu, K., tr. see Ise, M., et al.
Nomizu, K., jt. auth. see Kobayashi, Shoshichi.
***Nomizu, Katsumi.** Selected Papers on Number Theory, Algebraic Geometry & Differential Equations. LC 94-26691. (Translations Ser.: 160). 154p. 1994. 75.00 (0-8218-7511-6) Am Math.
***Nomizu, Katsumi, ed.** Selected Papers on Analysis, Probability & Statistics Vol. 161. LC 94-23002. (American Mathematical Society translations ser.). 151p. 1994. 75.00 (0-8218-7512-4) Am Math.
Nomizu, Katsumi & Sasaki, Takeshi. Affine Differential Geometry: Geometry of Affine Immersions. LC 93-46712. (Cambridge Tracts in Mathematics Ser.: Vol. 111). (Illus.). 250p. (C). 1995. 49.95 (0-521-44177-3) Cambridge U Pr.
Nomokov, V. P. & Ganguli, D. K. Theory of Seismic Prospecting Instruments. 2nd rev. ed. 150p. 1967. text ed. 100.00 (0-677-60980-9) Gordon & Breach.
Nomolos, Yaj. Magic Circle. (Illus.). 80p. (Orig.). 1987. pap. 4.95 (0-943832-40-3) Intl Imports.
— The Witches Broomstick Manual. (Illus.). 64p. (Orig.). 1984. pap. 3.95 (0-943832-10-1) Intl Imports.
Nomoto, K., ed. Atmospheric Diagnostics of Stellar Evolution: Chemical Peculiarity, Mass Loss, & Explosion. (Lecture Notes in Physics Ser.: Vol. 305). xiv, 468p. 1988. 58.00 (0-387-19478-9) Spr-Verlag.
Nomura, Gail M., et al, eds. Frontiers of Asian American Studies: Writing, Research, & Commentary. (Association for Asian American Studies Ser.). 341p. 1989. pap. 20.00 (0-87422-063-7) Wash St U Pr.
Nomura, Taka K. Taka Tips: Building Blocks for Parents. 1993. 14.95 (0-533-10518-8) Vantage.
Nomura, Takaaki. Grandpa's Town. Stinchecum, Amanda M., tr. (Illus.). 32p. (J). (ps-3). 1991. 13.95 (0-916291-36-7) Kane-Miller Bk.
— Grandpa's Town. Stinchecum, Amanda M., tr. (Illus.). 32p. (J). (ps-3). 1995. pap. 7.95 (0-916291-57-X) Kane-Miller Bk.
Nomura, Takeo & Furusawa, Shimpei. Essentials of Microscopic Hematology. (Illus.). 1991. pap. 43.50 (0-89640-205-3) Igaku-Shoin.
Nomura, Takeo, ed. see International Symposium on Myelodysplastic Syndromes Staff.
Nomura, Y. Otological Significance of the Round Window. (Advances in Oto-Rhino-Laryngology Ser.: Vol. 33). (Illus.). x, 162p. 1984. 92.00 (3-8055-3806-5) S Karger.
Nomura, Y., jt. ed. see Segawa, M.
Non-Traditional Study Commission. Diversity by Design. LC 73-3772. (Jossey-Bass Higher Education Ser.). 208p. reprint ed. pap. 59.30 (0-317-27219-5, 2023875) Bks Demand.
Nona Gwynn Press. New Insights into Astrology. 448p. (Orig.). 1993. pap. 19.95 (0-935127-12-7) ACS Pubns.
Nona, S., et al, eds. Development & Regeneration of the Nervous System. (Eye & Brain: Biomedical & Clinical Aspects Ser.). (Illus.). 272p. 1992. 170.00 (0-412-40280-7, A9438) Chapman & Hall.
***Nonaka, Ikujiro & Takeuchi, Hiro.** The Knowledge-Creating Company. (Illus.). 240p. 1995. 25.00 (0-19-509269-4) OUP.
Nonas, Elisabeth. Room Full of Women. 256p. 1990. pap. 9.95 (0-941483-69-X) Naiad Pr.
— Staying Home. 320p. 1994. pap. 10.95 (1-56280-076-0) Naiad Pr.
Nonas, Elisabeth, jt. auth. see LeVay, Simon.
Nonas, Michela, tr. see Gimenez, Juan & Dal Pra, Roberto.
Nonell, Juan B., jt. auth. see Collins, George R.
***Nones, Eric J.** Angela's Wings. LC 94-30321. (Illus.). 32p. (J). 1995. 16.00 (0-374-30331-2) FS&G.
— Caleb's Friend. (J). (ps-3). 1993. 15.00 (0-374-31017-3) FS&G.
— Canary Prince. (J). (ps up). 1991. 14.95 (0-374-31029-7) FS&G.
— Wendell. (J). (ps up). 1989. 13.95 (0-374-38266-2) FS&G.
Nonet, Philippe. Administrative Justice: Advocacy & Change in a Government Agency. LC 68-58126. 248p. 1969. 34.95 (0-87154-627-2) Russell Sage.
Nonferrous Metals Society of China Staff, ed. Metallurgy & Materials of Tungsten, Titanium, Rare Earths & Antimony: Proceedings of the 1st International Conference, Changsha, China, 5-8 November 1988. (International Academic Publishers Ser.). (Illus.). 1200p. 1989. 400.00 (0-08-037202-3, Pergamon Pr) Elsevier.
Nong, Phua-Xing. Selected Essays by Teochew Chi. 208p. 1993. pap. text ed. 9.00 (1-879771-05-5) Global Pub NJ.
Nonhebel, G. & Berry, M. Chemical Engineering in Practice. LC 73-77793. (Wykeham Science Ser.: No. 28). 196p. (C). 1973. pap. 18.00 (0-8448-1336-2, Crane Russak) Taylor & Francis.
Nonhebel, Gordon, ed. Gas Purification Processes for Air Pollution Control. 2nd ed. LC 72-193815. (Illus.). 713p. reprint ed. pap. 180.00 (0-317-41697-9, 2025715) Bks Demand.
Nonini, Donald M. British Colonial Rule & the Resistance of the Malay Peasantry, 1900-1957. (Monograph Ser. - Yale University Southeast Asia Studies: No. 38). 350p. 1992. 30.00 (0-938692-48-8); pap. 17.00 (0-938692-47-X) Yale U SE Asia.
Nonis, Michael, tr. see Rabas, Deb, ed.
Nonis, Michela, tr. see Miralles, Ana & Segura, Antonio.
Nonis, Michela, tr. see Serpieri, Paolo E.
***Nonis, Umberto.** Mushrooms & Toadstools of Britain & Europe: A Naturetrek Guide. (Illus.). 232p. 1994. pap. 14.95 (0-7153-0155-1, Pub. by D & C Pub UK) Sterling.
Nonius Marcellus. Dictionary of Republican Latin. Lindsay, W. M., ed. 120p. 1965. reprint ed. write for info. (0-318-72058-2, Pub. by Georg Olms GW) Lubrecht & Cramer.
Nonkin, Lesley J. I Wish My Parents Understood: The Nonkin-Teenage Relationships Survey of Female Relationships. 304p. 1985. 14.95 (0-317-18014-2) Freundlich.
Nonnecke, I. L. Vegetable Production. (Illus.). 448p. (C). 1989. text ed. 72.95 (0-442-26721-5) Chapman & Hall.
Nonneman, A. J., jt. auth. see Woodruff, M. L.
Nonneman, Gerd. Development Administration & Aid in the Middle East. 240p. (C). 1988. lib. bdg. 47.50 (0-415-00104-8) Routledge.
Nonnenmacher, F. F., et al, eds. Fractals in Biology & Medicine. LC 93-44016. 1994. 62.00 (0-8176-2989-0) Birkhauser.
Nonnos. Dionysiaca, 3 vols., 1. (Loeb Classical Library: No. 344, 354, 356). 566p. 1940. 18.95 (0-674-99379-9) HUP.
— Dionysiaca, 3 vols., 2. (Loeb Classical Library: No. 344, 354, 356). 560p. 1940. 18.95 (0-674-99391-8) HUP.
— Dionysiaca, 3 vols., 3. (Loeb Classical Library: No. 344, 354, 356). 530p. 1940. 18.95 (0-674-99393-4) HUP.
Nonte, George. The Home Guide to Cartridge Conversions. rev. ed. 24.95 (0-88227-005-2) Gun Room.
Nonte, George C., Jr. Black Powder Guide. 2nd ed. LC 79-82028. (Illus.). 256p. 1979. pap. 14.95 (0-88317-069-8) Stoeger Pub Co.
— Pistol Guide. (Illus.). 280p. pap. 13.95 (0-88317-095-7) Stoeger Pub Co.
— Pistolsmithing. LC 74-10783. (Illus.). 560p. 1974. 29.95 (0-8117-1265-6) Stackpole.
— Revolver Guide. (Illus.). 288p. pap. 10.95 (0-88317-094-9) Stoeger Pub Co.
Nonte, John, ed. Supercollider 3. (Illus.). 1196p. 1991. 185.00 (0-306-44037-7, Plenum Pr) Plenum.
— Supercollider 4: Proceedings of the Fourth International Industrial Symposium on the Super Collider, Held March 4-6, 1992, in Atlanta, Georgia. LC 92-30221. 1992. 195.00 (0-306-44254-X, Plenum Pr) Plenum.
Nonveiller, E. Grouting, Theory & Practice. (Developments in Geotechnical Engineering Ser.: No. 57). 262p. 1989. 114.25 (0-444-87400-3) Elsevier.
Nonweiler, Terence R. Computational Mathematics: An Introduction to Numerical Approximation. LC 83-12224. (Mathematics & Its Applications Ser.: 1-176). 431p. 1984. pap. 29.95 (0-470-20260-2) P-H.
Nony, D., jt. auth. see Girault, O.
Nony, Daniele & Andre, Alain. Literature Francaise: Histoire et Anthologie. (Illus.). 464p. (FRE.). (C). 1987. text ed. 34.95 (2-218-00976-5, U0976) Hatier Pub.
Nooden, L. D. & Leopold, A. Carl, eds. Senescence & Aging in Plants. 526p. 1988. text ed. 125.00 (0-12-520920-7) Acad Pr.
Noojin, Randy. You Can't Trust the Male. (Orig.). 1991. pap. 2.50 (0-87129-059-6, Y18) Dramatic Pub.
Nool, Richard. Mysteria, Jung & the Ancient Mysteries: Extracts from the Collected Works of C. G. Jung. (C). 1994. pap. 14.95 (0-691-03647-0) Princeton U Pr.
Nooman, Zohair, ed. see Schmidt, Henk G. & Ezzat, Esmat S.
Noomin, Diane, ed. see Doucet, Julie, et al.
Noomin, Diane, ed. see Lay, Carol, et al.
Noomin, Diane, ed. see Lay, Carol & Brown, M. K.
Noon, Alfred. The History of Ludlow, with Biographical Sketches of Leading Citizens, Reminiscences, Genealogies, Etc. 2nd rev. ed. (Illus.). 592p. 1989. reprint ed. lib. bdg. 63.00 (0-8328-0839-3, MA0214) Higginson Bk Co.
***Noon, Jack.** The Big Fish of Barston Falls. (Illus.). 292p. (C). 1995. pap. text ed. 12.95 (0-9642213-3-0) Moose Cntry.
— The Big Fish of Barston Falls. (Illus.). 289p. (C). 1995. 24.00 (0-9642213-2-2) Moose Cntry.
***Noon, Jeff.** Vurt. LC 94-25544. 1995. 22.00 (0-517-59991-0) Crown Pub Group.
Noon, Patrick. English Portrait Drawings & Miniatures. LC 79-63448. (Illus.). 152p. (Orig.). 1979. pap. 10.00 (0-930606-15-9) Yale Ctr Brit Art.
— Richard Parkes Bonington: On the Pleasure of Painting. LC 91-65083. (Illus.). 311p. 1991. pap. 39.95 (0-930606-67-1) Yale Ctr Brit Art.
— Richard Parkes Bonington: On the Pleasures of Painting. (Illus.). 288p. (C). 1991. text ed. 85.00 (0-300-05108-5) Yale U Pr.
Noon, Patrick & Warner, Timothy. Product Design Management: An Annotated Bibliography. 220p. 1988. text ed. 57.00 (0-566-05466-3, Pub. by Gower UK) Ashgate Pub Co.
***Noon, Randall K.** Engineering Analysis of Fires & Explosions. LC 95-3187. 288p. 1995. 59.95 (0-8493-8107-X, 8107) CRC Pr.
— Engineering Analysis of Vehicular Accidents. LC 93-48723. 256p. 1994. 49.95 (0-8493-8104-5) CRC Pr.
Noon, Shereen. Heal Yourself: A Step-by-Step Guide to Self-Healing Through Affirmations. 154p. (Orig.). 1990. pap. 9.95 (0-9624690-0-9) Welcome Home.
Noona, Carol, jt. auth. see Noona, Walter.
Noona, Carol, jt. ed. see Noona, Walter.
Noona, Walter & Noona, Carol. Improv! Bass Patterns & Progressions, Vol. 2: Basic Concepts in Improvisation. (Illus.). 64p. (Orig.). 1992. pap. 8.95 (0-89328-108-5, KM16) Lorenz Corp.
— Improv! Blues & Rock Styles, Vol. 3: Basic Concepts in Improvisation. (Illus.). 64p. (Orig.). 1992. pap. 8.95 (0-89328-106-9, KM21) Lorenz Corp.
— Improv! Follow the Lead, Vol. 1: Basic Concepts in Improvisation. (Illus.). 64p. (Orig.). 1992. pap. 8.95 (0-89328-107-7, KM9) Lorenz Corp.
— New Horizons, Vol. 1: Piano Course for Busy Adults. 96p. (Orig.). 1992. pap. 8.95 (0-89328-109-3, KM152) Lorenz Corp.
— New Horizons, Vol. 2: Piano Course for Busy Adults. 96p. (Orig.). 1992. pap. 8.95 (0-89328-111-5, KM153) Lorenz Corp.
— The Video Pianist, Bk. 1. 48p. (Orig.). 1987. pap. 4.95 (0-89328-100-X, KM121) Lorenz Corp.
Noona, Walter & Noona, Carol, eds. Easy Classics, Piano. 96p. (Orig.). 1989. pap. 9.95 (0-89328-110-7, KK437) Lorenz Corp.
***Noonan.** National Geographic World Wide Lions. 1994. 10.95 (0-7922-2708-5) Random.
— National Geographic World Wild Lions. 1994. 12.95 (0-7922-2707-7) Random.
Noonan, Barry C. Index to Green Bay Newspapers, 1833-1840. 62p. (Orig.). 1987. pap. 8.00 (0-910255-48-2) Wisconsin Gen.
— Index to the Gospel Herald Published at Voree, Racine County, Wisconsin, January 1846-June 6, 1850. 38p. (Orig.). 1988. pap. 5.25 (0-910255-50-4) Wisconsin Gen.
Noonan, Chris. Sales Management: The Complete Marketeer's Guide. (C). 1986. text ed. 49.95 (0-04-658254-1) Routledge Chapman & Hall.
Noonan, D. P. The Catholic Communicators. LC 89-62495. 144p. (Orig.). 1990. pap. 5.95 (0-87973-503-1, 503) Our Sunday Visitor.
Noonan, David. Memoirs of a Caddy. 1993. mass mkt. 4.50 (0-312-95059-4) St Martin.
Noonan, David C. & Curtis, James T. Groundwater Remediation & Petroleum: A Guide for Underground Storage Tanks. (Illus.). 250p. 1990. 79.95 (0-87371-217-X, TD427) Lewis Pubs.
Noonan, Diana. Donkeys. LC 93-28998. (Voyages Ser.). (Illus.). (J). 1994. 4.25 (0-383-03741-7) SRA Schl Grp.
— Fat Cat Tompkin. LC 92-34273. (Voyages Ser.). (Illus.). (J). 1993. 3.75 (0-383-03623-2) SRA Schl Grp.
— The Shepherd Who Planted a Forest. LC 93-11828. (J). 1994. write for info. (0-383-03774-3) SRA Schl Grp.
— Shooting It Straight. LC 93-21248. (J). 1994. 4.25 (0-383-03731-X) SRA Schl Grp.
Noonan, Diane. Houses That Move. LC 92-27085. (Illus.). (J). 1993. 14.00 (0-383-03574-0) SRA Schl Grp.
Noonan, Eileen, comp. Books for Religious Education in Catholic Secondary Schools. 18p. 1986. pap. 5.00 (0-318-41052-4) Cath Lib Assn.
Noonan, Eileen F., comp. Books for Catholic Elementary Schools. 16p. 1987. pap. 5.00 (0-87507-041-8) Cath Lib Assn.
Noonan, Ellen & Spurling, Laurence, eds. The Making of a Counsellor. LC 92-43167. 240p. 1992. pap. 18.95 (0-415-06768-5, A9574) Routledge.
Noonan, Frederick, tr. see Wegeler, Franz & Ries, Ferdinand.
***Noonan, G.** Classification, Cladistics, & Natural History of Native North American Harpalus Latreille. (Thomas Say Monographs: Vol. 13). 310p. 1991. 50.00 (0-938522-35-3) Entomol Soc.
Noonan, Gary P., et al. Guide to Respiratory Protection for the Asbestos Abatement Industry. (Illus.). 193p. 1987. pap. 9.50 (0-16-006442-2, S/N 055-000-00262-2) USGPO.
Noonan, Geoffrey J. Nineteenth-Century Inventors. (American Profiles Ser.). 128p. (YA). (gr. 6-9). 1992. lib. bdg. 16.95 (0-8160-2480-4) Facts on File.
Noonan, George. Classical Scientific Astrology. LC 83-71742. 176p. 1984. 16.00 (0-86690-049-7, N2344-014) Am Fed Astrologers.
— Fixed Stars & Judical Astrology. 1990. pap. 16.00 (0-86690-376-3, 3028-014) Am Fed Astrologers.
— Spherical Astronomy for Astrologers. 64p. 1974. 4.00 (0-86690-134-5, N1357-014) Am Fed Astrologers.
Noonan, Gregory. Brewing Lager Beer. (Illus.). 314p. 1986. pap. 14.95 (0-937381-01-2) Brewers Pubns.
— The New Brewing Lager Beer. Date not set. write for info. (0-937381-46-2) Brewers Pubns.
— Scotch Ale. (Classic Beer Style Ser.). (Illus.). 198p. 1993. pap. 11.95 (0-937381-35-7) Brewers Pubns.
Noonan, Harold, ed. Identity. (International Research Library of Philosophy). 478p. 1993. 129.95 (1-85521-294-3, Pub. by Dartmth Pub UK) Ashgate Pub Co.
— Personal Identity. LC 92-29002. (International Research Library of Philosophy). 560p. 1993. 149.95 (1-85521-299-4, Pub. by Dartmth Pub UK) Ashgate Pub Co.
Noonan, Harold W. Personal Identity. (Problems of Philosophy Ser.). 304p. 1989. 55.00 (0-415-03365-9, A3246) Routledge.
— Personal Identity. (Problems of Philosophy: Their Past & Present Ser.). 304p. 1991. pap. 16.95 (0-415-07047-3, A6284) Routledge.
Noonan, Hugh. Companion to the Clams. (Illus.). 1980. 4.95 (0-8199-0680-8, Frncscn Herld) Franciscan Pr.
Noonan, Janet & Calvert, Jacquelyn. Berries for the Queen. LC 92-32336. (J). (ps-2). 1994. 8.99 (0-7814-0903-9, Chariot Bks) Chariot Family.
— A Crown for Sir Conrad. LC 92-32337. (J). 1994. 8.99 (0-7814-0317-0, Chariot Bks) Chariot Family.
Noonan, Joe, jt. auth. see Mack, John.
Noonan, John T., Jr. The Balanced Budget: The States Call for a Convention. 1984. reprint ed. pap. 2.50 (0-318-02046-7) Natl Taxpayers Union Found.
— Bribes. LC 87-13924. 839p. 1988. pap. 17.00 (0-520-06154-3) U CA Pr.
— Contraception: A History of Its Treatment by the Catholic Theologians & Canonists. 592p. 1986. 45.00 (0-674-16853-4) HUP.
Noonan, John T. Power to Dissolve: Lawyers & Marriages in the Courts of the Roman Curia. LC 75-176044. 510p. reprint ed. pap. 145.40 (0-7837-3959-1, 2043788) Bks Demand.
Noonan, John T., Jr. & Winston, Kenneth I., eds. The Responsible Judge: Readings in Judicial Ethics. LC 92-31841. 416p. 1993. text ed. 75.00 (0-275-94022-5, C4022, Praeger Pubs); pap. text ed. 35.00 (0-275-94023-3, B4023, Praeger Pubs) Greenwood.
Noonan, John T., et al, eds. The Morality of Abortion: Legal & Historical Perspectives. LC 70-129118. 294p. reprint ed. pap. 84.40 (0-7837-2305-9, 2057393) Bks Demand.
Noonan, John T., Jr., et al, eds. The Role & Responsibility of the Moral Philosopher: Proceedings, Vol. 56. LC 81-69068. 214p. 1982. pap. 20.00 (0-918090-16-4) Am Cath Philo.
Noonan, Jon. Captain Cook. LC 92-8231. (Explorers Ser.). (Illus.). 48p. (J). (gr. 5). 1993. text ed. 12.95 (0-89686-709-9, Crstwood Hse) Silver Burdett Pr.
— Ferdinand Magellan. (Explorers Ser.). (Illus.). 48p. (J). (gr. 5). 1993. text ed. 12.95 (0-89686-706-4, Crstwood Hse) Silver Burdett Pr.
— Lewis & Clark. LC 92-9381. (Explorers Ser.). (Illus.). 48p. (YA). (gr. 5). 1993. text ed. 12.95 (0-89686-707-2, Crstwood Hse) Silver Burdett Pr.
— Marco Polo. LC 91-38219. (Explorers Ser.). (Illus.). 48p. (J). (gr. 5). 1993. text ed. 12.95 (0-89686-704-8, Crstwood Hse) Silver Burdett Pr.
Noonan, Joseph & Nolan, Joseph. Gospel Bites: Illustrated Wisdom for Lectionary Cycles A, B, & C. LC 92-23076. (Illus.). 200p. (Orig.). (C). 1992. pap. 10.95 (0-89390-239-X) Resource Pubns.
Noonan, Margaret E. Influence of Summer Vacation on the Abilities of Fifth & Sixth Grade Children. LC 71-177111. (Columbia University. Teachers College. Contributions to Education Ser.: No. 204). reprint ed. 37.50 (0-404-55204-8) AMS Pr.
Noonan, Mary J. & McCormick, Linda. Early Intervention in Natural Environments: Methods & Procedures. LC 92-33628. 1993. pap. 38.95 (0-534-14442-X) Brooks-Cole.
Noonan, Meg, jt. auth. see Kiley, Deborah S.
Noonan, Michael. A Different Drummer: The Story of E. J. Banfield, the Beachcomber of Dunk Island. LC 86-16027. (Illus.). 237p. 1987. pap. 14.95 (0-7022-2027-2, Pub. by Univ Queensland Pr AT) Intl Spec Bk.
— A Grammar of Lango. LC 92-5911. (Mouton Grammar Library: No. 7). xvi, 352p. (C). 1992. lib. bdg. 175.40 (3-11-012992-2) Mouton.
— In with the Tide: Memoirs of a Storyteller. 320p. 1995. pap. 24.95 (0-7022-2710-2, Pub. by Univ Queensland Pr AT) Intl Spec Bk.
Noonan, Michael, ed. The Gentle Art of Beachcombing: A Collection of Writings by E. J. Banfield. 1989. pap. 14.95 (0-7022-2061-2, Pub. by Univ Queensland Pr AT) Intl Spec Bk.
Noonan, Michael, jt. ed. see Downing, Pamela.
Noonan, Michael P., jt. ed. see Hammond, Michael T.
Noonan, Peggy. Life, Liberty & the Pursuit of Happiness. 1994. 23.00 (0-679-40160-1) Random.
— Life, Liberty, & the Pursuit of Happiness. 270p. 1995. pap. 10.95 (1-55850-509-1) Adams Pubng.
— What I Saw at the Revolution: A Political Life in the Reagan Era. 384p. 1991. mass mkt. 5.99 (0-8041-0760-2) Ivy Books.
— What I Saw at the Revolution: A Political Life in the Reagan Era. 1990. 19.95 (0-394-56495-2) Random.
— What I Saw at the Revolution: A Political Life in the Reagan Era. large type ed. (General Ser.). 528p. 1990. 20.95 (0-8161-5047-8, Large Print Bks) G K Hall.
Noonan, R. A. Critters. LC 90-45819. (Tales of Terror Ser.). (Illus.). 48p. (J). (gr. 5-6). 1991. text ed. 13.95 (0-89686-575-4, Crstwood Hse) Silver Burdett Pr.
— Don't Go into the Graveyard! LC 95-1602. (Monsterville U. S. A. Ser.: No. 2). (J). 1995. pap. write for info. (0-689-71864-0, Aladdin Paperbacks) S&S Childrens.
— Enter at Your Own Risk. LC 95-3173. (Monsterville U. S. A. Ser.: No. 1). 1995. write for info. (0-689-71863-2, Mac Bks Young Read) S&S Childrens.
Noonan, Thomas E. Cat's Whiskers. Rockwell, Jeanne, ed. (Illus.). 125p. write for info. (0-9602934-1-8) Noon Rock.
Noonan, Thomas E., jt. ed. see Rockwell, Jeanne.
Noone. Arrhythmia Interpretation. 1992. 24.95 (0-87434-402-6) Springhouse Pub.
— Plastic & Reconstructive Surgery of the Breast. (Illus.). 560p. (C). 1991. 125.00 (1-55664-192-3) Mosby Yr Bk.
Noone, jt. auth. see Gasparis.
Noone, Donald J. Creative Problem Solving. (Business Success Ser.). 112p. 1993. pap. 4.95 (0-8120-1461-8) Barron.
— Great Sales, Great Life: The Hidden Power of "The Ripple Effect" LC 94-45494. 1995. write for info. (0-8144-7889-1) AMACOM.
— Great Sales, Great Life: The Hidden Power of the "Ripple Effect" 240p. 1995. 22.95 (0-8144-0259-3) AMACOM.

*Noone, John. Man Behind the Iron Mask Vol. 1. 1994. pap. 17.95 (0-312-12345-0) St Martin.

*Noone, Judith. The Same Fate As the Poor. rev. ed. 175p. 1995. pap. 12.95 (1-57075-031-9) Orbis Bks.

Noone, Leslie J. The Ability to Risk: Reading Skills for Beginning Students of ESL. (Illus.). 200p. (C). 1985. pap. text ed. 15.75 (0-13-000357-5) P-H.

Noone, Michael, jt. auth. see Kercher, Bruce.

Noone, Richard. Five Five Two-Thousand, Ice: The Ultimate Disaster. (Illus.). 384p. 1988. pap. 14.00 (0-517-56142-5, CPT Corp) Crown Pub Group.

Noone, Suzanne P., jt. auth. see Emery, Leigh.

*Noonon, Joshua. Two Lives...Two Roads. 480p. (Orig.). 1995. pap. 12.95 (0-7610-0116-6) NW Pub.

Noopur, Indira K. Women's Studies in School Education: A New Perspective. 111p. 1989. text ed. 15.95 (81-207-1041-X, Pub. by Sterling Pubs II) Apt Bks.

*Noor, A. K., ed. Buckling & Postbuckling of Composite Structures: 1994 International Mechanical Engineering Congress & Exposition, Chicago, Illinois - November 6-11, 1994. (AD - PVP Ser.: Vol. 41, Vol. 293). 140p. 1994. 60.00 (0-7918-1443-2, G00938) ASME.

— Impact of New Computing Systems on Computational Mechanics. 176p. 1983. pap. text ed. 34.00 (0-317-02625-9, H00275) ASME.

Noor, A. K. & Dwoyer, D. L., eds. Computational Structural Mechanics & Fluid Dynamics: Advances & Trends - Papers Presented at the Symposium Held in Washington DC, U. S. A., 17-19 October 1988. (Computers & Structures Ser.). 466p. 1988. 125.00 (0-08-037197-3, Pergamon Pr) Elsevier.

Noor, A. K. & Housner, J. M., eds. Advances & Trends in Structural & Solid Mechanics: Proceedings of the Symposium, Washington D.C., October 4-7, 1982. 587p. 1983. 180.00 (0-08-029990-3, Pergamon Pr) Elsevier.

Noor, A. K. & McComb, H. G., Jr. Trends in Computerized Structural Analysis & Synthesis, Vol. 10, No. 1-2. 1978. 83.00 (0-08-023261-2, Ed Skills Dallas) Elsevier.

— Trends in Computerized Structural Analysis & Synthesis, Vol. 10, No. 1-2. 1981. pap. 91.00 (0-08-028707-7, Pergamon Pr) Elsevier.

*Noor, A. K. & Needleman, A., eds. Computational Material Modeling: 1994 International Mechanical Engineering Congress & Exposition, Chicago, Illinois - November 6-11, 1994. (AD - PVP Ser.: Vol. 42, Vol. 294). 320p. 1994. 90.00 (0-7918-1444-0, G00939) ASME.

*Noor, A. K. & Reifsnider, K. L., eds. Durability & Damage Tolerance: 1994 International Mechanical Engineering Congress & Exposition, Chicago, Illinois - November 6-11, 1994. (AD Ser.: Vol. 43). 352p. 1994. 96.00 (0-7918-1445-9, G00940) ASME.

*Noor, A. K. & Venneri, S., eds. Computational Structures Technology. (Flight-Vehicle Materials, Structures, & Dynamics Ser.: Vol. 6). 196p. 1995. 100.00 (0-7918-0664-2, 100327) ASME.

Noor, A. K. & Venneri, S. L., eds. Flight Vehicle Materials, Structures, & Dynamics, Vol. 5: Structural Dynamics & Aeroelasticity. 524p. 1993. 105.00 (0-7918-0663-4, I00326) ASME.

*Noor, Ahmed K. & Venneri, Samuel L., eds. Flight-Vehicle Materials, Structures & Dynamics: Assessment & Future Directions, New & Projected Aeronautical & Space Systems, Design Concepts, & Loads. LC 92-52644. 553p. 1994. 100.00 (0-7918-0659-6) ASME.

Noor, Asghar. System Design with the MC68020, MC68030, & MC68040 32-bit Microprocessors. LC 92-12923. 1994. text ed. 59.95 (0-442-31886-3) Van Nos Reinhold.

Noorani, A. G. Indian Affairs: The Constitutional Dimension. 424p. 1990. text ed. 45.00 (81-220-0198-X, Pub. by Konark Pubs Pvt Ltd II) Advent Bks Div.

— Indian Affairs: The Political Dimension. 400p. 1990. text ed. 45.00 (81-220-0199-8, Pub. by Konark Pubs Pvt Ltd II) Advent Bks Div.

— Indian Affairs, the Constitutional Dimension. (C). 1990. 100.00 (0-89771-201-3) St Mut.

— The Presidential System: The Indian Debate. 136p. (C). 1989. 25.00 (0-8039-9610-1) Sage.

Noorani, A. G., ed. The Gulf Wars: Documents & Analysis. xxxvi, 402p. 1992. text ed. 45.00 (81-220-0250-1, Pub. by Konark Pubs Pvt Ltd II) Advent Bks Div.

Noorbergen, Rene. Noah's Ark Found! The End of the Search. LC 86-33162. (Illus.). 192p. 1987. 14.95 (0-688-06456-6) Morrow.

— Nostradamus Predicts the End of the World. 1991. mass mkt. 4.95 (1-55817-545-8, Pinnacle NY) Windsor NY.

— Secrets of the Lost Races. LC 77-76883. (Illus.). 1977. write for info. (0-672-52289-6) Macmillan.

— Shadow of Terror. Wheeler, Gerald, ed. 160p. 1991. pap. 8.95 (0-8280-0576-1) Review & Herald.

Noordam, D. Identification of Plant Viruses: Methods & Experiments. 207p. 1990. 120.00 (81-7089-118-3, Pub. by Intl Bk Distr II) St Mut.

Noordegraaf, Jan, et al, eds. The History of Linguistics in the Low Countries. LC 92-6410. (Studies in the History of the Language Sciences: No. 64). vi, 382p. 1992. 89.00 (1-55619-359-9) Benjamins North Am.

Noordeloos, M. E. Entoloma (Agricales) in Europe: Synopsis & Keys to All Species & a Monograph of the subgenera Trichopilus, Inocephalus, Alboleptonia, Leptonia, Paraleptonia & Omphaliipsis. (Nova Hedwigia Beiheft Ser.: No. 91). (Illus.). 419p. 1987. pap. text ed. 170.00 (3-443-51013-2) Lubrecht & Cramer.

— Entoloma in North America: The Species Described by L. R. Helser, A. H. Smith & S. J. Mazzer. (Cryptogamic Studies: Vol. 2). (Illus.). 164p. 1988. pap. 50.70 (3-457-30506-4) Lubrecht & Cramer.

Noordeloos, Machiel E. Entoloma in North America. (Cryptogamic Studies: Vol. 2). 164p. 1988. pap. text ed. 70.00 (0-89574-276-4, Pub. by Gustav Fischer Verlag); 60.00 (0-685-56002-3, Pub. by Gustav Fischer Verlag) VCH Pubs.

Noordergen, Rene. Treasures of the Lost Races. LC 82-4209. 1982. 13.95 (0-672-52696-4, Bobbs) Macmillan.

Noordergraaf, Abraham. Circulatory System Dynamics. (Bioengineering Ser.). 1979. text ed. 84.00 (0-12-520950-9) Acad Pr.

Noordergraaf, Abraham, et al. Ballistocardiography & Cardiac Performance. LC 67-27246. 156p. 1967. 8.90 (0-87527-062-X) Green.

Noordhoek, C. & De Back, J., eds. Steel in Marine Structures. 954p. 1987. 269.25 (0-444-42805-4) Elsevier.

Noordman, L. G. Inferring from Language. (Language & Communiction Ser.: Vol. 4). (Illus.). 1979. 31.00 (0-387-09386-9) Spr-Verlag.

Noordman-Vonk, W. Retrieval from Semantic Memory. (Language & Communication Ser.: Vol. 5). (Illus.). 1979. 21.00 (0-387-09219-6) Spr-Verlag.

Noordraven, G. Die Fiduzia im Romischen Recht. (Studia Amstelodamensia ad Epigraphicam, Ius Antiquum et Papyrologicam Pertinentia). 300p. 1991. write for info. (90-5063-062-6, Pub. by Egbert Forsten NE) Benjamins North Am.

Noordsy, John L. Food Animal Surgery. 1994. pap. text ed. 44.00 (1-884254-14-4) Vet Lrn Syst.

*Noordung, Hermann & Potocnik, Herman. The Problem of Space Travel: The Rocket Motor. Stuhlinger, Ernst, ed. (NASA History Ser.: 4026). 1995. write for info. (0-615-00279-X) USGPO.

Noordzij, P. C., et al, eds. Alcohol, Drugs & Traffic Safety - T86: Proceedings of the Tenth International Conference, Amsterdam, September 9-12, 1986. (International Congress Ser.: No. 721). 685p. 1987. 190.25 (0-444-80903-1) Elsevier.

Nooren, M. J., jt. ed. see Schouten, M. G.

Noori, Ayatollah Y. Legal & Political Structure of an Islamic State: Implications for Iran & Pakistan. 144p. 1987. 45.00 (0-946706-31-X, Pub. by Royston Ltd) St Mut.

Noori, Hamid. Managing the Dynamics of New Technology: Issues in Manufacturing Management. 352p. 1989. text ed. 65.00 (0-13-551763-X) P-H.

Noori, Hamid & Radford, Russel. Readings & Cases in the Management of New Technology: An Operations Perspective. 400p. 1990. pap. text ed. 43.00 (0-13-552142-4) P-H.

Noori, Y. Finality of Prophethood. 176p. 1985. 25.00 (0-946706-19-0, Pub. by Royston Ltd) St Mut.

— Islamic Government & the Revolution in Iran. 1985. 75.00 (0-946706-25-5, Pub. by Royston Ltd) St Mut.

Noorlun, Lyle J. I Can-Can. 131p. (YA). (gr. 9 up). 1989. 16.95 (1-877616-00-1) Wholeness Intl.

Noory, Samuel. Dictionary of Pronunciation. 4th ed. LC 81-66273. 512p. 1982. 19.95 (0-8453-4722-5, Cornwall Bks) Assoc Univ Prs.

Nooshin, ed. Third International Conference on Space Structures. 1056p. 1984. 246.75 (0-85334-309-8, Pub. by Elsevier Applied Sci UK) Elsevier.

Nooshin, H. Formex Configuration Processing in Structural Engineering. (Illus.). xi, 276p. 1984. 74.00 (0-85334-315-2) Elsevier.

Noot, Jurrien, jt. auth. see Polmar, Norman.

Nooteboom, Cees. Following Story. 1994. 14.95 (0-15-100098-0) HarBrace.

— In the Dutch Mountains. Novel. Dixon, Adrienne, tr. LC 87-3289. 128p. 1987. 14.95 (0-8071-1425-1) La State U Pr.

— Knight Has Died. Novel. Dixon, Adrienne, tr. LC 89-13622. 104p. 1990. 14.95 (0-8071-1544-4) La State U Pr.

— Philip & the Others. Novel. Dixon, Adrienne, tr. LC 88-1394. xi, 107p. 1988. 14.95 (0-8071-1376-X) La State U Pr.

— Rituals. 160p. 1992. pap. 9.00 (0-14-015790-5, Penguin Bks) Viking Penguin.

— Rituals. Novel. Dixon, Adrienne, tr. LC 82-17278. vi, 145p. 1983. 16.95 (0-8071-1081-7) La State U Pr.

— Song of Truth & Semblance. A Novel. Dixon, Adrienne, tr. LC 84-848. Orig. Title: Een Liedvan schijn en wezen. 83p. 1984. 12.95 (0-8071-1176-7) La State U Pr.

Nooter, Mary H. Secrecy: African Art That Conceals & Reveals. LC 92-38495. 1993. pap. 38.50 (0-945802-12-9) Museum African.

Nooter, Mary H., ed. Secrecy: African Art That Conceals & Reveals. (Illus.). 256p. 1993. 70.00 (3-7913-1230-8, Pub. by Prestel) TeNeues.

Nooter, Nancy, jt. auth. see Nooter, Robert.

Nooter, Robert & Nooter, Nancy. The Art of Collecting African Art. Vogel, Susan M., ed. LC 88-7253. (Illus.). 64p. (Orig.). (C). 1988. pap. text ed. 14.50 (0-9614587-9-8) Museum African.

Nooter, Robert, jt. auth. see Brown, Ellen P.

Noothoven van Goor, J. M. & Lefcoe, George, eds. Teleports in the Information Age: Proceedings of the Teleports '86 Congress, Amsterdam, The Netherlands, May 21-23, 1986. 350p. 1987. 107.75 (0-444-70183-4, North Holland) Elsevier.

Nophlin, Barbara, ed. Fun with Math Resource Kit. 1988. teacher ed 299.00 (0-88076-137-7, 17246) Kaplan Pr.

— Manipulative Resource One. 1988. 99.50 (0-88076-128-8, 15645) Kaplan Pr.

— Manipulative Resource Two. 1988. 175.50 (0-88076-129-6, 15646) Kaplan Pr.

Noponen, Helzi, et al, eds. Trading Industries, Trading Regions. (Perspectives on Economic Change Ser.). 290p. 1993. lib. bdg. 40.00 (0-89862-296-4); pap. text ed. 19.95 (0-89862-753-2) Guilford Pr.

Nora. Nora's Operative Surgery: Principles & Techniques. 3rd ed. 1232p. 1989. text ed. 175.00 (0-7216-2134-1) Saunders.

Nora, James. The Upstart Spring. 352p. 1989. 16.95 (0-922811-00-8) Mid-List.

Nora, James J. The New Whole Heart Book. 2nd ed. (Illus.). 350p. 1989. reprint ed. 18.95 (0-922811-02-4); reprint ed. pap. 10.95 (0-922811-03-2) Mid-List.

Nora, James J., jt. auth. see Fraser, F. Clarke.

Nora, James J., et al. Cardiovascular Diseases: Genetics, Epidemiology & Prevention. (Oxford Monographs on Medical Genetics: No. 22). (Illus.). 208p. 1991. 39.95 (0-19-506032-6, 2924) OUP.

— Medical Genetics: Principles & Practice. 4th ed. LC 93-19984. 1993. 42.50 (0-8121-1663-1) Williams & Wilkins.

Nora, Paul F., ed. Professional Liability-Risk Management: A Manual for Surgeons. 240p. (Orig.). 1991. pap. text ed. write for info. (0-9620370-8-7) Am Coll Surgeons.

Nora, Simon & Minc, Alain. The Computerization of Society. 1980. pap. 8.95x (0-262-64020-1) MIT Pr.

Noraas, Margaret. Math Activities for Preschool. 93p. (J). (ps). Date not set. pap. text ed. 12.95 (0-9637985-0-2) Penguin Family.

Norall, Christopher & Renouf, Michael. EC Merger Control. 248p. 1993. U.K. text ed. 147.00 (0-406-11770-5) Butterworth Legal Pubs.

Norall, Frank. Bourgmont: Explorer of the Missouri, 1698-1725. LC 88-4013. (Illus.). x, 192p. 1988. 22.50 (0-8032-3316-7) U of Nebr Pr.

Norang, N., jt. auth. see Goldstein, G.

Noravtov, Yu A., ed. see Galperin, A. M. & Zaytsev, V. S.

Norback, Craig. VGM's Careers Encyclopedia. 3rd ed. LC 90-50726. 464p. (YA). (gr. 7 up). 1991. 39.95 (0-8442-8692-3, VGM Career Bks) NTC Pub Grp.

— VGM's Handbook of Business & Management Careers. 1989. pap. 12.95 (0-8442-8683-4, VGM Career Bks) NTC Pub Grp.

— VGM's Handbook of Scientific & Technical Careers. 1989. pap. 12.95 (0-8442-8684-2, VGM Career Bks) NTC Pub Grp.

Norback, Craig & Norback, Peter. The Must Words: The Six Thousand Most Important Words for a Successful & Profitable Vocabulary. 312p. 1983. pap. text ed. 12.95 (0-07-047141-X) McGraw.

Norback, Craig T. Hazardous Chemicals on File, 3 vols., Set. 756p. 1988. 250.00 (0-8160-2213-5) Facts on File.

— The Hazardous Chemicals on File Collection: 1989 Update. 1989. 50.00 (0-8160-2212-7) Facts on File.

— Human Resource Yearbook, 1989. 750p. 1989. 79.95 (0-318-41473-2) P-H.

— The Human Resources Yearbook. 720p. 1987. text ed. 75.00 (0-13-446378-1) P-H.

— The Human Resources Yearbook, 1989. 784p. 1989. text ed. 79.95 (0-13-448010-4) P-H.

— Human Resources Yearbook, 1990. 768p. 1990. 79.95 (0-13-446212-2) P-H.

Norback, Craig T., ed. The Allergy Encyclopedia. 258p. 1981. pap. 7.95 (0-318-13534-5) Asthma & Allergy.

Norback, Craig T., jt. ed. see Asthma.

Norback, Craig T., jt. auth. see Burrill, Steven G.

Norback, Judith. The Complete Computer Career Guide. 256p. 1987. 19.95 (0-8306-9554-0, 2654, Liberty Hall Pr) TAB Bks.

Norback, Peter, jt. auth. see Norback, Craig.

Norbeck, Carole A., ed. see Osterhoff, Robert J.

Norbeck, Edward. Changing Japan. 2nd ed. (Illus.). 108p. 1984. reprint ed. pap. text ed. 8.50 (0-88133-076-0) Waveland Pr.

— Country to City: The Urbanization of a Japanese Hamlet. LC 77-14737. 381p. reprint ed. pap. 108.60 (0-8357-3272-X, 2039493) Bks Demand.

— Religion in Human Life: Anthropological Views. 74p. (C). 1988. reprint ed. pap. text ed. 6.95 (0-88133-354-9) Waveland Pr.

Norbeck, Edward & Parman, Susan, eds. Study of Japan in the Behavioral Sciences. (Rice University Studies: Vol. 56, No. 4). 309p. (C). 1970. pap. 10.00 (0-89263-206-2) Rice Univ.

Norbeck, Edward, ed. see Lock, Margaret.

Norbeck, Edward, et al. The Anthropological Study of Human Play. (Rice University Studies: Vol. 60, No. 3). (Illus.). 94p. (Orig.). (C). 1974. pap. 10.00 (0-89263-221-6) Rice Univ.

Norbeck, Jack. Encyclopedia of American Steam Traction Engines. Dammann, George, ed. LC 76-5764. (Agricultural Ser.). (Illus.). 320p. 1976. 24.95 (0-912612-09-6) Motorbooks Intl.

Norbeck, Oscar E. Book of Authentic Indian Life Crafts. rev. ed. LC 74-81910. (Illus.). 260p. 1974. 10.95 (0-87874-012-0) Galloway.

Norbelie, Barbro A. Oppressive Narrowness: A Study of the Female Community in George Eliot's Early Writings. (Studia Anglistica Upsaliensia Ser.: No. 80). 163p. (Orig.). 1992. pap. 45.00x (91-554-2982-3, Pub. by Almqv & Wiksell SW) Coronet Bks.

Norbelle, Bernard, tr. see Hedin, Sven.

Norberg, Charles R. Inter-American Commercial Arbitration. 1988. Part of the International Commercial Arbitration Service, Annual Release. ring bd. 125.00 (0-379-10296-X) Oceana.

Norberg, Dag. Syntaktische Forschungen auf dem Gebiet des Spatlateins. (Universitets Arsskrift Ser.: No. 9). 283p. 1990. reprint ed. write for info. (3-487-09347-2, Pub. by Georg Olms GW) Lubrecht & Cramer.

Norberg, Fran, jt. ed. see Ashworth, Sam.

Norberg-Hodge, Helena. Ancient Futures: Learning from Ladakh. LC 91-13868. (Illus.). 224p. 1992. reprint ed. pap. 12.00 (0-87156-643-5) Sierra.

— Ancient Futures - Learning from Ladakh. LC 91-13868. (Illus.). 192p. 1991. 25.00 (0-87156-559-5) Sierra.

Norberg, Jeanne, ed. see Norberg, John.

Norberg, John. Hail Purdue: A Century of Music at Purdue University. Dunscomb, J. Richard & Norberg, Jeanne, eds. LC 86-72652. 240p. 1987. lib. bdg. 40.95 (0-9617991-0-2) All Amer Band Club.

Norberg, Jon. Academic Sportfolio. Gallup, Beth, ed. (Elementary Ser.). (Illus.). 1200p. (J). (gr. 3-6). 1987. 495.00 (0-685-24265-X) Acad Sportfolio.

— Academic Sportfolio: Excuse Notes Are No Excuse. Pranzo, Donard, ed. (Elementary Ser.). (Illus.). (J). (gr. 3-6). 1987. 50.00 (0-924086-00-9) Acad Sportfolio.

Norberg, Kathryn, jt. ed. see Hoffman, Philip T.

*Norberg, Linda. Shale. 250p. 1995. pap. 8.95 (0-7610-0021-6) NW Pub.

Norberg-Schulz, Christian. Architecture: Meaning & Place. LC 87-45387. (Illus.). 256p. 1988. pap. 29.95 (0-8478-0847-5) Rizzoli Intl.

— Baroque Architecture. LC 85-30011. (History of World Architecture Ser.). (Illus.). 220p. 1986. pap. 29.95 (0-8478-0693-6) Rizzoli Intl.

— The Concept of Dwelling. (Illus.). 150p. 1985. pap. 27.50 (0-8478-0590-5) Rizzoli Intl.

— Genius Loci: Towards a Phenomenology of Architecture. LC 79-56612. (Illus.). 216p. 1980. pap. 27.50 (0-8478-0287-6) Rizzoli Intl.

— Intentions in Architecture. (Illus.). 1966. pap. 14.95x (0-262-64002-3) MIT Pr.

— Late Baroque & Rococo Architecture. (History of World Architecture Ser.). (Illus.). 220p. 1985. pap. 29.95 (0-8478-0475-5) Rizzoli Intl.

— Meaning in Western Architecture. LC 80-51173. (Illus.). 236p. 1980. reprint ed. pap. 29.95 (0-8478-0319-8) Rizzoli Intl.

— Nightlands: Nordic Building. McQuillan, Thomas, tr. (Illus.). 224p. 1995. 40.00 (0-262-14057-8) MIT Pr.

Norberg, Tilda, jt. auth. see Webber, Robert D.

Norberg, U. Vertebrate Flight. (Zoophysiology Ser.: Vol. 27). (Illus.). 305p. 1990. 199.00 (0-387-51370-1) Spr-Verlag.

Norbie, D. L. Baptism: The Church's Troubled Water. 1985. pap. 2.50 (0-937396-64-8) Walterick Pubs.

— Danny, a Life Cut Short. 1994. pap. text ed. 5.25 (0-937396-97-4) Walterick Pubs.

Norbie, D. R. Divorce & the Bible. 1971. pap. 3.25 (0-937396-12-5) Walterick Pubs.

Norbie, Don. New Testament Church Organization. 1977. pap. 5.00 (0-937396-28-1) Walterick Pubs.

Norbie, Donald L. First Timothy: Timeless Truths for Today's Church. 1991. pap. 6.00 (0-937396-85-0) Walterick Pubs.

— The Lord's Supper: The Church's Love Feast. 1986. pap. 2.50 (0-937396-67-2) Walterick Pubs.

— Second Timothy & Titus. 1992. pap. 7.00 (0-937396-90-7) Walterick Pubs.

Norborg, Ake. A Handbook of Musical & Other Sound-Producing Instruments from Namibia & Botswana. (Illus.). xxii, 454p. (Orig.). 1987. pap. 78.00x (0-317-89998-8) Coronet Bks.

Norbrook, David. Poetry & Politics in the English Renaissance. 280p. 1984. 32.50 (0-7100-9778-6, RKP) Routledge.

Norbrook, Dominique. Passport to France. rev. ed. LC 93-21188. (Illus.). 48p. (J). (gr. 5-8). 1994. lib. bdg. 14.77 (0-531-14293-0) Watts.

Norbu, Dawa. Culture & the Politics of Third World Nationalism. LC 91-46016. 304p. 1992. 49.95 (0-415-08003-7, A7555) Routledge.

— Red Star over Tibet. 2nd ed. LC 87-80663. 300p. 1988. text ed. 30.00 (0-938719-19-X, Envoy Pr) Apt Bks.

— Red Star over Tibet. 2nd ed. LC 87-80663. 300p. 1988. pap. 14.95 (0-938719-26-2, Envoy Pr) Apt Bks.

Norbu, Jamyang. Warriors of Tibet: The Story of Aten & the Khampa's Fight for the Freedom of Their Country. (Tibet Book - Yellow Ser.). 152p. 1986. pap. 12.95 (0-86171-050-9) Wisdom MA.

Norbu, Namkhai. The Crystal & The Way of Light. 1988. pap. 13.00 (0-14-019314-6, Penguin Bks) Viking Penguin.

— The Cycle of Day & Night: Where One Proceeds Along the Path of the Primordial Yoga; A Basic Tibetan Text on the Practice of Dzogchen. Reynolds, John, ed. & tr. by. LC 87-9953. (Illus.). 128p. 1987. reprint ed. pap. 9.95 (0-88268-040-4) Station Hill Pr.

— Dream Yoga & the Practice of Natural Light. Katz, Michael, ed. LC 92-16147. 128p. (Orig.). 1992. pap. 12.95 (1-55939-007-7) Snow Lion Pubns.

— Dzog Chen & Zen. Lipman, Kennard, ed. Norbu, Namkhai, tr. (Illus.). 48p. (Orig.). 1987. pap. 5.00 (0-931892-08-2) B Dolphin Pub.

Norbu, Namkhai, tr. see Norbu, Namkhai.

Norbu, Thinley. Magic Dance: The Display of the Self-Nature of the Five Wisdom Dakinis. rev. ed. LC 85-59. 166p. (Orig.). 1981. pap. 12.00 (0-9607000-0-5) Jewel Pub Hse.

— The Small Golden Key to the Treasure of the Various Essential Necessities of General & Extraordinary Buddhist Dharma. rev. ed. LC 84-29724. 111p. 1985. pap. 12.00 (0-9607000-2-1) Jewel Pub Hse.

— The Small Golden Key to the Treasure of the Various Essential Necessities of General & Extraordinary Buddhist Dharma. Anderson, Lisa, tr. LC 92-56459. 120p. 1993. reprint ed. pap. 11.00 (0-87773-856-4) Shambhala Pubns.

— White Sail: Crossing the Serene Waves of Ocean Mind to the Serene Continent of the Triple Gems. LC 92-50129. 280p. (Orig.). 1992. pap. 15.00 (0-87773-693-6) Shambhala Pubns.

Norbu, Thubten J. Tibet Is My Country: Autobiography of Thubten Jigme Norbu, Brother of the Dalai Lama. Fitzgerald, Edward, tr. (Tibet Book - Yellow Ser.). 276p. 1986. pap. 16.95 (0-86171-045-2) Wisdom MA.

Norbu, Thubten J., tr. see Blo Bzang, Ye Shes.

N

An Asterisk (*) at the beginning of an entry indicates that the title is appearing in BIP for the first time.

Norburn, C. S. & Norburn, Russell. A New Monetary System. 1979. lib. bdg. 59.95 (0-8490-2977-5) Gordon Pr.

Norburn, Russell, jt. auth. see Norburn, C. S.

Norbury, Betty. Fine Craftsmanship in Wood. LC 90-6336. (Illus.). 200p. 1990. 39.95 (0-941936-18-X) Linden Pub Fresno.

Norbury, Ian. Fundamentals of Figure Carving. LC 93-31545. (Illus.). 256p. 1994. 31.95 (0-941936-26-0) Linden Pub Fresno.

— Projects for Creative Woodcarving. rev. ed. (Illus.). 192p. 1995. pap. 19.95 (0-941936-30-9) Linden Pub Fresno.

— Techniques of Creative Wood Carving. 2nd ed. (Illus.). 160p. 1994. reprint ed. pap. 19.95 (0-941936-29-5) Linden Pub Fresno.

Norbury, J. K. Word Formation in the Noun & Adjective. LC 67-10258. (Studies in the Modern Russian Language: No. 13). 135p. reprint ed. pap. 38.50 (0-317-27313-2, 2024503) Bks Demand.

Norbury, James. Traditional Knitting Patterns from Scandinavia, the British Isles, France, Italy & Other European Countries. LC 73-79490. (Illus.). 240p. 1973. reprint ed. pap. 7.95 (0-486-21013-8) Dover.

Norbury, Paul, ed. The Poetry of Soviet Ukraine's New World: An Anthology - 1917-77. 1985. 75.00 (0-904404-49-8, Pub. by Paul Norbury Pubns UK) Humanities.

— Rosy Glasses. 1985. 45.00 (0-317-39107-0, Pub. by Paul Norbury Pubns UK) Humanities.

Norbury, Paul & Bownas, Geoffrey. Business in Japan: A Guide to Japanese Business Practice & Procedure. 2nd rev. ed. 226p. 1985. 100.00 (0-317-39059-7, Pub. by P Norbury Pubns Ltd UK) St Mut.

Norbury, Rosamond. Behind the Chutes: The Mystique of the Rodeo Cowboy. LC 92-34662. 128p. 1993. 17.00 (0-87842-287-0) Mountain Pr.

Norbury, Rosamond, photos. Guy to Goddess: An Intimate Look at Drag Queens. LC 94-15751. 128p. 1994. 17.95 (0-89815-645-9) Ten Speed Pr.

Norby, Claudia, ed. see Tessmer, Kathryn.

Norby, Jim, et al. The Challenge of Complex School Problems. LC 90-33191. 120p. (Orig.). (C). 1990. pap. text ed. 14.00 (0-89079-242-9, 1436) PRO-ED.

Norbye, Jan. VW Treasures by Karmann. LC 85-15575. (Illus.). 176p. (Orig.). 1985. pap. 16.95 (0-87938-202-3) Motorbooks Intl.

Norbye, Jan P. The Metalcaster's Bible. (Illus.). 434p. 1980. 15.95 (0-8306-9970-8); pap. 19.95 (0-8306-1173-8, 1173) TAB Bks.

Norbye, Jan P. & Dunne, Jim. Buick, 1946-1978: The Classic Postwar Years. LC 92-33314. (MBI Ser.). (Illus.). 200p. 1993. 24.95 (0-87938-727-0) Motorbooks Intl.

— Oldsmobile, 1946-1980: The Classic Postwar Years. LC 92-33784. (MBI Ser.). (Illus.). 200p. 1993. 24.95 (0-87938-731-9) Motorbooks Intl.

— Pontiac, 1946-1978: The Classic Postwar Years. LC 92-33785. (MBI Ser.). (Illus.). 200p. 1993. 24.95 (0-87938-732-7) Motorbooks Intl.

Norbygaard, Elisabeth, jt. ed. see Kristensen, Knud.

Norcliffe, A. & Slater. Mathematics of Software Construction. 200p. 1991. boxed write for info. (0-13-563370-2) P-H.

Norcliffe, Glen B., jt. auth. see Freeman, Donald B.

Norcom, Stanley. Grindstone: An Island World Remembered. Hein, Norvin, ed. 219p. 1995. pap. 17.95 (0-9641529-0-8, TX-3604788) R Edwards Pub.

Norcross, Alastair, jt. ed. see Steinbock, Bonnie.

Norcross, Carl. Townhouses & Condominiums: Residents' Likes & Dislikes; A Special Report. LC 73-82886. (Illus.). 111p. reprint ed. pap. 31.70 (0-8357-3192-8, 2039464) Bks Demand.

Norcross, Carl & Hyson, John. Apartment Communities: The Next Big Market; A Survey of Who Rents & Why. LC 68-57114. (Urban Land Institute, Technical Bulletin Ser.: 61). 83p. reprint ed. pap. 25.00 (0-8357-5653-X, 2023244) Bks Demand.

Norcross, John C. & Goldfried, Marvin R., eds. Handbook of Psychotherapy Integration. LC 92-52740. 416p. 1992. text ed. 55.00 (0-465-02879-9) Basic.

Norcross, John C., jt. auth. see Prochaska, James O.

Norcross, John C., jt. ed. see Saltzman, Nolan.

Nord, B. & Nord, E. Etching & Sandblasting of Glass. (Illus.). 80p. 1980. 10.95 (0-935656-01-4, 101 B); pap. 6.95 (0-685-01090-2) Nords Studio.

Nord, Barry & Nord, Elaine. Glass Etching-Pattern Book I: Fruit, Flowers, & Birds. (Illus.). 50p. (Orig.). 1981. pap. 3.95 (0-935656-02-2, 101C) Nords Studio.

— Glass Etching-Pattern Book II: Wildlife, Alphabets, Geometrics. (Illus.). 50p. (Orig.). 1981. pap. 3.95 (0-935656-03-0, 101D) Nords Studio.

Nord, Barry, ed. see Cottrell, Clayton.

Nord, Barry M. Florida Stock Image Directory. (Illus.). 80p. (Orig.). 1993. pap. 49.95 (0-935656-07-3) Nords Studio.

— One Hundred Years of Citrus: A Glimpse of Citrus. (Illus.). 64p. (Orig.). 1993. vhs 29.95 (0-935656-08-1) Nords Studio.

— One Hundred Years of Citrus: A Glimpse of Citrus, Set. (Illus.). 64p. (Orig.). 1993. pap., vhs 29.95 (0-935656-04-9) Nords Studio.

Nord, Bruce. Mexican Social Policy: Affordability, Conflict & Progress. LC 93-42083. 296p. (C). 1994. pap. text ed. 34.50 (0-8191-9418-2) U Pr of Amer.

Nord, Carl. The Skagway Kids: Alaska Christmas. (J). 1994. 10.95 (0-533-10931-0) Vantage.

Nord, Christine W., jt. auth. see Zill, Nicholas.

Nord, David P. A Guide to Stonefield. (Illus.). 59p. 1977. pap. 1.50 (0-87020-176-X) State Hist Soc Wis.

Nord, Deborah E. The Apprenticeship of Beatrice Webb. LC 89-7272. 304p. 1989. pap. 14.95 (0-8014-9609-8) Cornell U Pr.

— The Apprenticeship of Beatrice Webb. LC 83-18235. 304p. 1985. lib. bdg. 32.50 (0-87023-427-7) U of Mass Pr.

— Walking the Victorian Streets: Women, Representation, & the City. (Illus.). 280p. 1995. 39.95x (0-8014-3196-4); pap. 16.95 (0-8014-8291-7) Cornell U Pr.

Nord, Dennis. Student Handbook Education 164. 68p. (C). 1994. per. 7.95 (0-8403-9335-0) Kendall-Hunt.

Nord, E., jt. auth. see Nord, B.

Nord, Elaine, jt. auth. see Nord, Barry.

Nord, H. Juergen & Brady, Patrick G., eds. Critical Care Gastroenterology. LC 82-12924. (Illus.). 376p. reprint ed. pap. 107.20 (0-7837-2556-6, 2042715) Bks Demand.

***Nord, Philip.** The Republican Moment: The Struggle for Democracy in Nineteenth-Century France. LC 95-10445. 1995. text ed. 49.95 (0-674-76271-1) HUP.

Nord, Philip G. Paris Shopkeepers & the Politics of Resentment. LC 85-42695. (Illus.). 480p. 1986. 65.00x (0-691-05454-1) Princeton U Pr.

— Paris Shopkeepers & the Politics of Resentment. LC 85-42695. Date not set. reprint ed. pap. 159.40 (0-7837-9403-7, 2060148) Bks Demand.

— The Republican Moment: Struggles for Democracy in Nineteenth-Century France. (Illus.). 352p. (C). 1995. text ed. 49.95 (0-614-07251-4) HUP.

Nord, Walter & Tucker, Sharon. Implementing Routine & Radical Innovations: A Comparative Study. LC 84-48504. (Issues in Organization & Management Ser.). 416p. 1986. text ed. 42.95 (0-669-09565-6) Free Pr.

Nord, Walter R., jt. auth. see Brief, Arthur P.

Nord, Warren A. Religion & American Education: Rethinking an American Dilemma. LC 94-4589. (N. Eugene & Lillian Youngs Lehman Ser.). 960p. 1994. text ed. 49.95 (0-8078-2165-9); pap. 19.95 (0-8078-4478-0) U of NC Pr.

Nord World Staff, ed. Winter Safety Handbook. 1975. pap. 2.95 (0-02-499880-X) Macmillan.

Nordal, Sigouur. Hrafnkels Saga Freysgooa: A Study. Thomas, R. George, tr. 81p. 1958. pap. 8.50 (0-7083-0853-8, Pub. by U of Wales UK) Bks Intl VA.

Nordan, Frances. Queen of Darkness. 168p. (Orig.). 1993. pap. 9.95 (1-880365-10-3) Prof Pr NC.

Nordan, Frances M. Night Magic. LC 91-70101. (Orig.). 1991. pap. 11.95 (0-9629135-0-2) Calif Concepts.

— Queen of Darkness. LC 92-70735. (Illus.). (Orig.). 1992. pap. write for info. (0-9629135-1-0) Calif Concepts.

Nordan, Lee, jt. ed. see Maxwell, W. Andrew.

Nordan, Lewis. The All-Girl Football Team. (Contemporaries Ser.). 1989. pap. 5.95 (0-394-75701-7, Vin) Random.

— Music of the Swamp. Ravenel, Shannon, ed. 210p. 1991. 16.95 (0-945575-76-9) Algonquin Bks.

— Music of the Swamp. (Front Porch Paperback Ser.). 191p. 1992. pap. 7.95 (1-56512-016-7) Algonquin Bks.

— The Sharpshooter Blues: A Novel. LC 95-15306. 300p. 1995. write for info. (1-56512-083-3) Algonquin Bks.

— Welcome to the Arrow-Catcher Fair. (Vintage Contemporaries Ser.). 1989. pap. 6.95 (0-679-72164-9, Vin) Random.

— Welcome to the Arrow-Catcher Fair. Stories. LC 83-7888. 127p. 1983. text ed. 15.95 (0-8071-1124-4) La State U Pr.

— Wolf Whistle. 308p. 1995. pap. 9.95 (1-56512-110-4) Algonquin Bks.

— Wolf Whistle: A Novel. LC 93-1011. 1993. 16.95 (1-56512-028-0) Algonquin Bks.

Nordan, Robert. All Dressed up to Die. 224p. 1989. pap. 3.50 (0-449-14576-X, GM) Fawcett.

— Death Beneath the Christmas Tree. (Orig.). 1993. mass mkt. 4.50 (0-449-45258-1, GM) Fawcett.

Nordau, Max. The Conventional Lies of Our Civilization. LC 74-29511. (Modern Jewish Experience Ser.). (ENG.). 1975. reprint ed. 34.95 (0-405-06737-2) Ayer.

— Degeneration. LC 93-8474. xxxvi, 566p. 1993. pap. 18.00 (0-8032-8367-9, Bison Books) U of Nebr Pr.

— The Interpretation of History. 1972. 250.00 (0-8490-0413-6) Gordon Pr.

— Morals & the Evolution of Man. 1976. lib. bdg. 250.00 (0-8490-2280-0) Gordon Pr.

Nordau, Max & Shaw, George Bernard. Degeneration & the Sanity of Art. 1972. 250.00 (0-8490-0015-7) Gordon Pr.

Nordberg, A., et al, eds. Nicotinic Receptors in the CNS: Their Role in Synaptic Transmission. (Progress in Brain Research Ser.: No. 79). 385p. 1989. 195.00 (0-444-81088-9); 157.00 (0-685-32890-2) Elsevier.

***Nordberg, Bengt, ed.** The Sociolinguistics of Urbanization: The Case of the Nordic Countries. (Sociolinguistics & Language Contact Ser.: Vol. 7). viii, 290p. (C). 1994. lib. bdg. 129.25 (3-11-011184-5, 97-94) De Gruyter.

Nordberg, Beverly, jt. auth. see Stewig, John W.

Nordberg, G. F., et al, eds. Cadmium in the Human Environment: Toxicity & Carcinogenicity. (IARC Scientific Publications: No. 118). (Illus.). 496p. 1993. pap. 125.00 (92-832-2118-4) OUP.

Nordberg, H., jt. ed. see Krauss, G.

***Nordberg, Ken.** Do-It-Yourself Black Bear Baiting & Hunting. O'Donnell, M. C. et al, eds. 160p. (Orig.). 1990. pap. 8.95 (1-886422-50-8) Shingle Creek.

— Whitetail Hunter's Almanac: An Introduction to Whitetail Hunting. 150p. 1988. pap. 8.95 (1-886422-01-X) Shingle Creek.

— Whitetail Hunter's Almanac: An Introduction to Whitetail Hunting. 2nd ed. 153p. 1989. pap. 8.95 (1-886422-02-8) Shingle Creek.

— Whitetail Hunter's Almanac: An Introduction to Whitetail Hunting. 3rd ed. 151p. 1990. pap. 8.95 (1-886422-03-6) Shingle Creek.

— Whitetail Hunter's Almanac: An Introduction to Whitetail Hunting. 4th ed. 147p. 1991. pap. 8.95 (1-886422-04-4) Shingle Creek.

— Whitetail Hunter's Almanac: An Introduction to Whitetail Hunting. 5th ed. 166p. 1992. pap. 8.95 (1-886422-05-2) Shingle Creek.

— Whitetail Hunter's Almanac: An Introduction to Whitetail Hunting. 6th ed. 186p. 1993. pap. 8.95 (1-886422-06-0) Shingle Creek.

— Whitetail Hunter's Almanac: First-Seventh Edition. 7th ed. (Illus.). (Orig.). 1994. pap. 62.65 (1-886422-00-1) Shingle Creek.

***Nordberg, Ken & O'Donnell, Jennifer J.** Whitetail Hunter's Almanac: An Introduction to Whitetail Hunting. 7th ed. O'Donnell, M. C. et al, eds. (Illus.). 150p. 1994. pap. 8.95 (1-886422-07-9) Shingle Creek.

Nordberg, Marion, jt. auth. see Jenkins, Lee.

Nordbrant, Henrik. Selected Poems. 2nd ed. Taylor, Alexander, tr. LC 78-1047. (Illus.). 88p. 1978. pap. 9.95 (0-915306-33-6) Curbstone.

Nordbring, F. & Burman, L. G., eds. Urinary Tract Infections. (Illus.). 151p. (Orig.). 1981. pap. text ed. 42.50x (91-22-00455-6, Pub. by Almqv & Wiksell SW) Coronet Bks.

Nordby, Beth D. Love - & Other Things. 1992. 14.95 (0-533-10026-7) Vantage.

Nordby, Gene M., jt. auth. see Andersen, Paul.

Nordby, Judith. Mongolia. (World Bibliographical Ser.). 1993. lib. bdg. 73.00 (1-85109-129-7) ABC-CLIO.

Nordby, Steven, tr. see Christensen, Lars S.

Nordby, Vernon J., jt. auth. see Hall, Calvin S.

Nordby, Will, ed. Seekers of the Horizon: Sea-Kayaking Voyages from Around the World. LC 89-16782. (Illus.). 336p. 1989. 22.95 (0-87106-634-3) Globe Pequot.

Nordbye, Marsha. St. Petersburg: Russia's Imperial City. 2nd ed. 1994. pap. 15.95 (0-8442-9956-1, Passport Bks) NTC Pub Grp.

Nordbye, Masha. Leningrad. (Soviet Guides Ser.). (Illus.). 160p. 1991. pap. 14.95 (0-8442-9678-3, Passport Bks) NTC Pub Grp.

— Moscow. (Soviet Guides Ser.). (Illus.). 256p. 1991. pap. 15.95 (0-8442-9675-9, Passport Bks) NTC Pub Grp.

— Moscow & Leningrad. (Guidebook Ser.). 1991. pap. 9.95 (962-217-117-6) L A Michaux.

— Moscow-Saint Petersburg Handbook: Including the Golden Ring. 2nd ed. LC 92-42317. (Illus.). 250p. 1993. 13.95 (0-918373-91-3) Moon Pubns CA.

***Nordell, John R., Jr.** The Undetected Enemy: French & American Miscalculations at Dien Bien Phu. (Military History Ser.: No. 39). (Illus.). 224p. 1995. 39.50x (0-89096-645-1) Tex A&M Univ Pr.

Nordemann, Wilhelm. Wettbewerbsrecht. 460p. 1990. pap. 44.50 (3-7890-1898-8, Pub. by Nomos Verlags GW) Intl Bk Import.

Nordemann, Wilhelm, et al. International Copyright & Neighboring Rights Law. LC 90-12120. 727p. 1990. text ed. 125.00 (0-89573-412-5) VCH Pubs.

Norden & Gillespie. Infections in Bones & Joints. (Illus.). 400p. 1994. 95.00 (0-86542-273-7) Blackwell Sci.

Norden, Arnold W., et al, eds. Threatened & Endangered Plants & Animals of Maryland. (Maryland Natural Heritage Program Special Publication Ser.). 475p. (C). 1984. pap. 13.00 (0-317-30118-7) MD Dept Natural Res.

Norden, Bengt, jt. ed. see Ramel, Claes.

Norden, C. Christopher. A Comparative Rhetoric of the Contemporary Indigenous Novel. LC 93-47433. (Comparative Cultures & Literatures Ser.: Vol. 6). 1994. write for info. (0-8204-2441-2) P Lang Pubs.

Norden, Carroll R. Deserts. rev. ed. LC 87-23224. (Read about Science Ser.). (Illus.). 48p. (J). (gr. 2-6). 1987. lib. bdg. 10.95 (0-8172-3252-4) Raintree Steck-V.

— The Jungle. rev. ed. LC 87-20820. (Read about Science Ser.). (Illus.). 48p. (J). (gr. 2-6). 1987. lib. bdg. 10.95 (0-8172-3256-7) Raintree Steck-V.

Norden, Deborah, ed. see Gutman, Marta, et al.

Norden, Denis, jt. auth. see Muir, Frank.

Norden, Eduard. Aus Altromischen Priesterbuchern. LC 75-10644. (Ancient Religion & Mythology Ser.). (GER.). 1976. reprint ed. 25.95 (0-405-07019-5) Ayer.

Norden, Heinz, tr. see Schumpeter, Joseph A.

Norden, Hermann. White & Black in East Africa. LC 74-15074. reprint ed. 49.50 (0-404-12124-1) AMS Pr.

Norden, Hugo. The Technique of Canon. 1982. pap. 19.95 (0-8283-1839-5) Branden Pub Co.

Norden, Jan. Yugoslavia, East Europe & the Fourth International: The Evolution of Pabloist Liquidation. Prometheus Research Library Staff, ed. (Prometheus Research Ser.: No. 4). 70p. 1993. 6.00 (0-9633828-2-9) Spartacist Pub.

Norden, John. England: An Intended Guide, for English Travailers. LC 79-84125. (English Experience Ser.: No. 944). 84p. 1979. reprint ed. lib. bdg. 14.00 (90-221-0944-5) Walter J Johnson.

— A Pensive Mans Practise. LC 77-171776. (English Experience Ser.: No. 401). 192p. 1971. reprint ed. 35.00 (90-221-0401-X) Walter J Johnson.

— Speculi Britanniae Pars. Ellis, Henry, ed. (Camden Society, London. Publications, First Ser.: No. 9). reprint ed. 30.00 (0-404-50109-5) AMS Pr.

— Speculi Britanniae; the Description of Hartfordshire. LC 74-171778. (English Experience Ser.: No. 403). 38p. 1971. reprint ed. 20.00 (90-221-0403-6) Walter J Johnson.

— Speculum Britanniae: The First Parte, a Description of Middlesex. LC 70-171777. (English Experience Ser.: No. 402). 58p. 1971. reprint ed. 20.00 (90-221-0402-8) Walter J Johnson.

— The Surveiors Dialogue... for All Men to Peruse, That Have to Do with the Revenues of Land, or the Manurance, Use or Occupation. Third Time Imprinted & Enlarged. LC 79-84126. (English Experience Ser.: No. 945). 280p. 1979. reprint ed. lib. bdg. 26.00 (90-221-0945-3) Walter J Johnson.

Norden, K. Elis. Electronic Weighing: Fundamentals & Applications. LC 93-25908. (Illus.). 208p. 1993. 59.95 (0-7506-1737-3) Buttrwrth-Heinemann.

***Norden, Linda & Morgan, Murray.** Chihuly Baskets. Johnson, Diana, ed. (Illus.). 162p. (C). 1994. 60.00 (0-9608382-0-1) Portland Pr.

Norden, Martin F. The Cinema of Isolation: A History of Physical Disability in the Movies. LC 93-44547. (Illus.). 375p. (C). 1994. text ed. 48.00 (0-8135-2103-3); pap. 16.95 (0-8135-2104-1) Rutgers U Pr.

Norden, Mary. Ethnic Needlepoint: Designs from Asia, Africa & the Americas. (Illus.). 160p. 1993. 35.00 (0-8230-1605-6, Watsn-Guptill) Watsn-Guptill.

— Mary Norden's Needlepoint: Fifty Folk Art Projects for the Home. (Illus.). 160p. 1995. 34.95 (0-297-83265-4, Pub. by Weidenfeld) Trafalgar.

***Norden, Michael.** Beyond Prozac. 1995. 22.00 (0-06-039151-0, HarpT) HarpC.

Norden, Rudolph. Introducing the Books of the Bible: A Devotional Summary. 64p. 1987. pap. 3.95 (0-570-04452-9, 12-3061) Concordia.

Norden, Rudolph F. The Best of Portals of Prayer. 384p. 1990. 19.99 (0-570-03083-8, 06-1198) Concordia.

— Day by Day with Jesus. 400p. (Orig.). 1985. pap. 13.99 (0-570-03971-1, 12-3006) Concordia.

— Each Day with Jesus. 1994. pap. 13.99 (0-570-04655-6) Concordia.

— Radiant Faith. Feucht, Oscar E., ed. 1966. student ed, pap. 2.00 (0-570-03527-9, 14-1330); teacher ed, pap. 2.50 (0-570-03528-7, 14-1331) Concordia.

— Symbols & Their Meaning. 1985. pap. 3.99 (0-570-03949-5, 12-2883) Concordia.

Nordenberg, Mark A. & Sell, W. Edward. Modern Pennsylvania Civil Practice, Vol. I. LC 85-71932. 350p. 1985. ring bd. 59.50 (0-318-20247-6) Bisel Co.

Nordenfeldt, Lennart. On Crime, Punishment & Psychiatric Care: An Introduction to Swedish Philosophy of Criminal Law & Forensic Psychiatry. 87p. (Orig.). 1992. pap. 36.00x (91-22-01487-X, Pub. by Almqv & Wiksell SW) Coronet Bks.

***Nordenfelt, Lennart.** On the Nature of Health: An Action-Theoretic Approach. 2nd ed. LC 95-1945. (Philosophy & Medicine Ser.: Vol. 49). 1995. lib. bdg. 99.00 (0-7923-3369-1) Kluwer Ac.

— Quality of Life, Health & Happiness. 186p. 1993. 54.95 (1-85628-553-7, Pub. by Avebury Pub UK) Ashgate Pub Co.

Nordenfelt, Lennart, ed. Concepts & Measurement of Quality of Life in Health Care. LC 94-14441. (Philosophy & Medicine Ser.: Vol. 47). 292p. (C). 1994. lib. bdg. 87.00 (0-7923-2824-8) Kluwer Ac.

Nordenfelt, Lennart & Lindahl, Ingemar B., eds. Health, Disease, & Causal Explanations in Medicine. 1984. lib. bdg. 79.00 (90-277-1660-9) Kluwer Ac.

Nordenhaug, Joseph, tr. see Blanke, Fritz.

Nordenskiold, Adolf E. Facsimile Atlas to the Early History of Cartography: Reproductions of the Most Important Maps Printed in the Fifteenth & Sixteenth Centuries. (Illus.). 256p. 1973. reprint ed. pap. text ed. 15.95 (0-486-22964-5) Dover.

Nordenskiold, Erik. The History of Biology. 1988. reprint ed. lib. bdg. 89.00 (0-7812-0380-5) Rprt Serv.

— The History of Biology: A Survey. 1935. reprint ed. 85.00 (0-403-01788-2) Scholarly.

Nordenskiold, Erland. The Changes in the Material Culture of Two Indian Tribes Under the Influence of New Surroundings. LC 75-46055. (Comparative Ethnographical Studies: Vol 2). reprint ed. 39.50 (0-404-15142-6) AMS Pr.

— Comparative Ethnographical Studies, 10 vols., Set. reprint ed. 433.00 (0-404-15140-X) AMS Pr.

— The Copper & Bronze Ages in South America. LC 75-46057. (Comparative Ethnographical Studies: Vol. 4). reprint ed. 35.50 (0-404-15144-2) AMS Pr.

— Deductions Suggested by the Geographical Distribution of Some Post-Columbian Words Used by the Indians of South America. LC 75-46058. (Comparative Ethnographical Studies: Vol. 5). 1977. reprint ed. 48.50 (0-404-15145-0) AMS Pr.

— An Ethno-Geographical Analysis of the Material Culture of Two Indian Tribes in the Gran Chaco. LC 75-46054. (Comparative Ethnographical Studies: Vol. 1). reprint ed. 39.50 (0-404-15141-8) AMS Pr.

— The Ethnography of South America Seen from Mojos in Bolivia. LC 75-46056. (Comparative Ethnographical Studies: Vol. 3). reprint ed. 39.50 (0-404-15143-4) AMS Pr.

— An Historical & Ethnological Survey of the Cuna Indians. LC 75-46064. (Comparative Ethnographical Studies: Vol. 10). reprint ed. 72.50 (0-404-15150-7) AMS Pr.

— Modifications in Indian Culture Through Inventions & Loans. LC 75-46062. (Comparative Ethnographical Studies: Vol. 8). reprint ed. 39.50 (0-404-15148-5) AMS Pr.

— Origin of the Indian Civilizations in South America. LC 75-46063. (Comparative Ethnographical Studies: Vol. 9). reprint ed. 39.50 (0-404-15149-3) AMS Pr.

— Picture-Writings & Other Documents by Nele, Paramount Chief of the Cuna Indians, & Ruben Perez Kantule, His Secretary, 2 pts. in 1 vol. LC 75-46061. (Comparative Ethnographical Studies: Vol. 7). reprint ed. 39.50 (0-404-15147-7) AMS Pr.

— The Secret of the Peruvian Quipus, 2 pts. in 1 vol. LC 75-46059. (Comparative Ethnographical Studies: Vol. 6). reprint ed. 39.50 (0-404-15146-9) AMS Pr.

Nordenskiold, Gustaf. From the Far West. Valeri, Renee, tr. LC 92-83788. 90p. (Orig.). Date not set. pap. write for info. (0-937062-20-0) Mesa Verde Museum.

An Asterisk (*) at the beginning of an entry indicates that the title is appearing in BIP for the first time.

— Letters of Gustaf Nordenskiold & Articles from Ymer & the Photographic Times. Diamond, Irving L. & Olson, Daniel M., eds. (Illus.). 99p. (Orig.). 1991. pap. 9.95 (*0-937062-16-2*) Mesa Verde Museum.

Nordenskiold, Gustaf E. The Cliff Dwellers of the Mesa Verde, Southwestern Colorado: Their Pottery & Implements. Morgan, D. Lloyd, tr. LC 72-5006. (Antiquities of the New World Ser.: Vol. 12). (Illus.). reprint ed. 97.50 (*0-404-57312-6*) AMS Pr.

Nordenson, Guy, ed. Harry Wolf. (Illus.). 96p. (ENG & SPA.). 1993. pap. 28.95 (*84-252-1580-3*) Rizzoli Intl.

Nordenstam, Garry & Larson, Steven B. Database Applications: Job-Based Tasks. 160p. (C). 1993. student ed, 5.25 hd 10.95 (*1-56118-394-6*); student ed, 3.5 hd 10.95 (*1-56118-396-2*); teacher ed, 5.25 hd 69.00 (*1-56118-395-4*); teacher ed, 3.5 hd 69.00 (*1-56118-397-0*) Paradigm MN.

Nordenstam, Garry & Otto, Joseph. Mastery Approach to Excel 4.0 for Windows. 448p. 1994. text ed., 3.5 hd 27. 50 (*1-56118-617-1*); teacher ed, 3.5 hd 69.00 (*1-56118-618-X*) Paradigm MN.

Nordenstam, Tore, jt. ed. see Johannessen, Kjell S.

Nordenstreng, Kaarle. Mass Media Declaration of UNESCO. LC 83-25818. (Communication & Information Science Ser.). 496p. (C). 1984. text ed. 75. 00 (*0-89391-077-5*) Ablex Pub.

Nordenstreng, Kaarle & Schiller, Herbert I. Beyond National Sovereignty: International Communications in the 1990s. Dervin, Brenda, ed. (Communication & Information Science Ser.). 483p. (C). 1993. text ed. 85. 00 (*0-89391-959-4*); pap. text ed. 39.95 (*0-89391-960-8*) Ablex Pub.

Nordenstreng, Kaarle & Schiller, Herbert I., eds. National Sovereignty & International Communication: A Reader. LC 78-16046. (Communication & Information Science Ser.). 288p. 1979. 55.00 (*0-89391-008-2*) Ablex Pub.

Nordenstrom, Bjorn E. Biologically Closed Electric Circuits: Clinical, Experimental & Theoretical Evidence for an Additional Circulatory System. (Illus.). 374p. 1983. 247. 50x (*91-970432-0-6*, Pub. by Almqv & Wiksell SW) Coronet Bks.

Nordentoft, Kresten. Kierkegaard's Psychology. Kirmmse, Bruce, tr. LC 77-14423. (Psychological Ser.: Vol. 7). 430p. 1978. pap. 20.00x (*0-8207-0155-6*) Duquesne.

Nordewin, Dr., tr. see Lorber, Jakob.

Nordfors, Jill. Needle Lace & Needleweaving: A New Look at Traditional Stitches. (Illus.). 160p. 1992. reprint ed. pap. 16.95 (*1-879504-00-6*) A Schwartz & Co.

Nordfors, Jill D. Needle Lace & Needleweaving. 2nd ed. LC 85-71196. (Illus.). 160p. 1985. reprint ed. pap. text ed. 16.95 (*0-933877-00-5*) Aardvark.

Nordgaard, M. A. An Historical Survey of Algebraic Methods of Approximating the Roots of Numerical Higher Equations up to the Year 1819. LC 76-177107. (Columbia University. Teachers College. Contributions to Education Ser.: No. 123). reprint ed. 37.50 (*0-404-55123-8*) AMS Pr.

***Nordgaarden, Carol.** Create a Culture. 88p. (YA). (gr. 4-8). 1995. 9.95 (*0-88160-240-X*, LW335) Learning Wks.

***Nordgren, Anders.** Evolutionary Thinking: An Analysis of Rationality, Morality & Religion from an Evolutionary Perspective. (Studia Philosophoae Religionis: No. 17). 244p. (Orig.). 1994. pap. 52.50x (*91-22-01615-5*, Pub. by Almqv & Wiksell SW) Coronet Bks.

***Nordgren, Roger K.** Staffing Commercial Credit Functions: A Survey. Smith, Daphne & Geehr, Shelley, eds. (Illus.). 64p. (Orig.). 1994. pap. text ed. 58.00 (*1-57070-008-7*, 32191) Robt Morris Assocs.

Nordhaus, Jean. A Bracelet of Lies. LC 86-51532. (Series Eleven). 82p. 1987. pap. 7.00 (*0-931846-31-5*) Wash Writers Pub.

— My Life in Hiding. (QRL Poetry Book Ser.: Vol. XXX). 20.00 (*0-614-06432-5*); pap. 10.00 (*0-614-06433-3*) Quarterly Rev.

***Nordhaus, Robert J.** Tipi Rings: A Chronicle of the Jicarilla Apache Land Claim. LC 94-78671. 230p. 1994. 21.95 (*1-885931-00-X*) BowArrow Pubng.

Nordhaus, William, jt. auth. see Samuelson, Paul.

Nordhaus, William B., jt. auth. see Samuelson, Paul A.

Nordhaus, William D. Economics. 14th ed. 1992. text ed. write for info. (*0-07-054879-X*) McGraw.

— The Efficient Use of Energy Resources. LC 79-64225. (Cowles Foundation for Research in Economics at Yale University. Monograph Ser.: No. 26). 186p. reprint ed. pap. 53.10 (*0-7837-4546-X*, 2080334) Bks Demand.

— Managing the Global Commons: The Economics of Climate Change. LC 94-3992. (Illus.). 232p. 1994. 32. 50x (*0-262-14055-1*) MIT Pr.

Nordhaus, William D. & Tobin, James. Economic Research: Retrospect & Prospect, Vol. 5: Economic Growth. (General Ser.: No. 96). 112p. 1972. reprint ed. 29.20 (*0-87014-254-2*) Natl Bur Econ Res.

Nordhaus, William D., jt. auth. see Litan, Robert E.

Nordhauser, Susan L., jt. auth. see Kramer, John L.

Nordhielm, Curt. Reflecting His Image. LC 90-80689. 160p. (Orig.). (C). 1990. pap. 5.99 (*0-89900-357-5*) College Pr Pub.

— Reflecting His Image: Leader's Guide. 32p. (Orig.). 1991. pap. text ed. 2.99 (*0-89900-365-6*) College Pr Pub.

Nordhjem, Bent. What Fiction Means: An Inquiry into the Nature of Fiction with a Study of Three Comic Novels. (University of Copenhagen Dept of English Ser.: No. 15). 144p. (Orig.). 1987. pap. 45.00x (*87-88648-22-2*) Coronet Bks.

Nordhof, Charles. Hawaii-Nei: 1873. Apple, Russell A., ed. (Illus.). 40p. 1977. reprint ed. pap. 3.95 (*0-89646-030-4*) Vistabooks.

Nordhoff, Charles. American Utopias. 1993. pap. 14.95 (*0-936399-53-8*) Berkshire Hse.

— C. P. R. R.-The Central Pacific Railroad. Jones, William R., ed. (Illus.). 32p. 1976. reprint ed. pap. 3.95 (*0-89646-002-9*) Vistabooks.

— California for Travellers & Settlers. 255p. 1992. reprint ed. pap. 7.95 (*0-89815-418-9*) Ten Speed Pr.

— Cape Cod, & All Along Shore: Stories. LC 72-116964. (Short Story Index Reprint Ser.). 1977. 19.95 (*0-8369-3468-7*) Ayer.

— Communistic Societies of the United States: From Personal Visit & Observation. (Illus.). 439p. pap. 9.95 (*0-486-21580-6*) Dover.

— The Communistic Societies of the United States from Personal Visit & Observation. (Illus.). 439p. 1978. reprint ed. 24.00 (*0-87928-092-1*) Corner Hse.

— The Lighthouses of the United States in 1874. Jones, William R., ed. & intro. by. LC 92-18576. (Illus.). 64p. 1981. pap. 5.95 (*0-89646-086-X*) Vistabooks.

— Man-of-War Life. LC 85-4935. (Classics of Naval Literature Ser.). 290p. 1985. reprint ed. 32.95 (*0-87021-349-0*) Naval Inst Pr.

— Northern California, Oregon & the Sandwich Islands. (Illus.). 256p. 1992. reprint ed. pap. 7.95 (*0-89815-419-7*) Ten Speed Pr.

Nordhoff, Charles & Hall, James N. The Bounty Trilogy. 1985. pap. 19.95 (*0-316-61166-2*) Little.

— Falcons of France: A Tale of Youth & the Air. Gilbert, James B., ed. LC 79-7290. (Flight: Its First Seventy-Five Years Ser.). (Illus.). 1980. reprint ed. lib. bdg. 33.95 (*0-405-12198-9*) Ayer.

— Pitcairn's Island. 1989. pap. 10.95 (*0-316-61169-7*) Little.

Nordhoff, Grace, ed. Inside Looking Out: Mental Hospitals Are Overflowing with People Searching for Freedom & Community. (Illus.). 64p. (Orig.). 1989. pap. 5.00 (*0-943810-42-6*) Southern Exposure.

Nordhoff, Grace, ed. see Helms, Jesse.

Nordhoff, Larry S. Whiplash: Mechanisms & Management. LC 92-49445. 608p. 1992. 64.95 (*0-8016-6821-2*) Mosby Yr Bk.

Nordhoff, Nancy S., et al. Fundamental Practices for Success with Volunteer Boards of Non-Profit Organizations. (Fundamental Practices Ser.). 140p. 1982. pap. 16.50 (*0-9609972-0-2*) FunPrax.

Nordholt, E. H. Design of High Performance Negative-Feedback Amplifiers. (Studies in Electric & Electronic Engineering: Vol. 7). 234p. 1983. 84.75 (*0-444-42140-8*) Elsevier.

Nordholt, Henk S. State, Village, & Ritual in Bali: An Historical Perspective. (Comparative Asian Studies: No. 6). 58p. (Orig.). 1992. pap. text ed. 14.50 (*90-5383-023-5*, Pub. by VU Univ Pr NE) Paul & Co Pubs.

***Nordholt, Jan W.** The Myth of the West: America As the Last Empire. Rowen, Herbert H., tr. 224p. 1995. 22.99 (*0-8028-3793-X*) Eerdmans.

Nordhues, Robin, ed. see Evans, Harry.

Nordhues, Robin, ed. see Mitchell, James R.

Nordhues, Robin, ed. see Mitchell, James.

Nordhues, Robin, ed. see Roberts, George & Roberts, Jan.

Nordhues, Robin, ed. see Tegeler, Dorothy.

Nordhuff, Charles. Mutiny on the Bounty. 1976. 24.95 (*0-8488-0597-6*) Amereon Ltd.

Nordhuff, Charles & Hace, James N. The Hurricane. 20.95 (*0-88411-451-1*, Aeonian Pr) Amereon Ltd.

Nordhuff, Charles & Hall, J. Norman. Men Against the Sea. 18.95 (*0-89190-564-2*, Am Repr) Amereon Ltd.

Nordhuff, Charles & Hall, James N. Falcons of France. 17. 95 (*0-89190-232-5*, Am Repr) Amereon Ltd.

Nordic Council of Ministers Staff, ed. The Baltic States: A Survey for Further Industrial Cooperation. 127p. (Orig.). 1991. pap. 47.50x (*91-7996-381-1*, Pub. by Almqv & Wiksell SW) Coronet Bks.

— Transport Between the Nordic Countries & the New Eastern Europe. 100p. (Orig.). 1991. pap. 36.00x (*91-7996-388-9*, Pub. by Almqv & Wiksell SW) Coronet Bks.

— Yearbook of Nordic Statistics 1992. 428p. (Orig.). 1992. pap. 72.50x (*91-7996-411-7*, Pub. by Almqv & Wiksell SW) Coronet Bks.

Nordic, Rolla. Rolla Nordic Tarot. 52p. 1981. 10.00 (*0-913866-38-5*) US Games Syst.

— Tarot Shows the Path. 132p. 1989. 8.95 (*0-939708-25-6*) Magickal Childe.

Nordic World Editors. Snow Camping. LC 74-16796. (Illus.). 128p. 1974. pap. 3.50 (*0-89037-042-7*) Anderson World.

— Winter Safety Handbook. LC 74-16794. (Illus.). 96p. 1975. pap. 2.95 (*0-89037-044-3*) Anderson World.

Nordin, et al. Occupational Orthopaedics. 1994. 125.00 (*0-8016-7984-2*) Mosby Yr Bk.

Nordin, Albert A., jt. auth. see Alder, William H.

Nordin, B. E., ed. Calcium in Human Biology. (ILSI Human Nutrition Reviews Ser.). (Illus.). 480p. 1988. 133.00 (*0-387-17475-3*) Spr-Verlag.

— Metabolic Bone & Stone Disease. 3rd ed. (Illus.). 448p. 1993. text ed. 165.00 (*0-443-04493-7*) Churchill.

— Osteoporosis: Contributions to Modern Management. (Illus.). 96p. 1990. 35.00 (*1-85070-303-5*) Prthnon Pub.

***Nordin, Donna.** Contemporary Southwest: The Cafe Terra Cotta Cookbook. LC 94-37365. (Illus.). 168p. 1995. 26. 95 (*0-9627345-8-6*, Astolat Bks) Harlow & Ratner.

Nordin, Margareta & Frankel, Victor H. Basic Biomechanics of the Musculoskeletal System. 2nd ed. LC 89-2455. (Illus.). 350p. 1989. pap. text ed. 45.00 (*0-8121-1227-X*) Williams & Wilkins.

Nordin, Margareta, jt. auth. see Ozkaya, Nihat.

Nordin, Richard. The Early Hasselblad Cameras. (Illus.). 100p. 1991. write for info. (*1-879561-20-4*); pap. 19.95 (*1-879561-19-0*) Hist Camera Pubns.

Nordkvist, Sven. The Hat Hunt. (Illus.). 28p. 1988. 12.95 (*91-29-59070-1*, Pub. by R & S Bks) FS&G.

Nordland, Eva, jt. ed. see Reardon, Betty A.

Nordland, Gerald. Richard Diebenkorn. LC 87-42688. (Illus.). 248p. 1988. 69.95 (*0-8478-0870-X*) Rizzoli Intl.

Nordland, Gerald, jt. ed. see Pfeiffer, Bruce B.

Nordland, John, II. Heroes, 2 vols., Set. (Illus.). 96p. (Orig.). 1992. pap. 9.90 (*1-883611-00-8*) Blckbird Comics.

— Heroes, 2 vols., Vol. 1. (Illus.). 96p. (Orig.). 1992. pap. 4.95 (*1-883611-01-6*) Blckbird Comics.

— Heroes, Vol. II. (Illus.). 96p. (Orig.). Date not set. pap. 4.95 (*1-883611-02-4*) Blckbird Comics.

***Nordlander, D.** For God & Tsar: A Brief History of Russian America. (Illus.). 28p. 1995. pap. 3.95 (*0-930931-15-7*) Alaska Natural.

Nordlander, David J., tr. see Khlevniuk, Oleg V.

Nordlander, Ingegerd. Real Estate Transfer Deeds in Novgorod 1609-1616: Text & Commentary. (Stockholm Slavic Studies: No. 18). 171p. (Orig.). 1987. pap. text ed. 30.00x (*91-22-00857-8*, Pub. by Almqv & Wiksell SW) Coronet Bks.

Nordlicht, Lillian. I Love to Laugh. LC 80-14399. (Life & Living from a Child's Point of View Ser.). (Illus.). 32p. (J). 1980. 19.97 (*0-8172-1364-3*) Raintree Steck-V.

Nordling, JoAnne. Taking Charge: A Parent & Teacher Guide to Loving Discipline. LC 91-50982. 200p. 1992. pap. 11.95 (*0-88247-906-7*, 906) R & E Pubs.

***Nordling, Lee & Newspaper Features Council Staff.** Your Career in the Comics. 96p. 1995. pap. 9.95 (*0-8362-0748-3*) Andrews & McMeel.

Nordlinger, B. & Jaeck, D., eds. Surgical Treatment of Hepatic Metastases of Colorectal Diseases: Report of the 94th French Congress of Surgery. (Monographs of the French Surgical Association). 140p. 1993. 79.00 (*0-387-55142-5*) Spr-Verlag.

Nordlinger, Eric A. Conflict Regulation in Divided Societies. (Harvard Studies in International Affairs: No. 29). 154p. 1984. reprint ed. pap. text ed. 19.00 (*0-8191-4043-0*) U Pr of Amer.

— Isolationism Reconfigured: American Foreign Policy for a New Century. LC 94-43137. 1995. write for info. (*0-691-04327-2*) Princeton U Pr.

— On the Autonomy of the Democratic State. LC 81-1683. (Center for International Affairs Ser.). (Illus.). 247p. 1981. 32.00 (*0-674-63407-1*) HUP.

— On the Autonomy of the Democratic State. (Center for International Affairs Ser.). 247p. 1982. pap. 13.95 (*0-674-63409-8*) HUP.

Nordloh, David, ed. see Howells, William Dean.

Nordloh, David J., ed. American Literary Scholarship: An Annual, 1989. 523p. 1991. lib. bdg. 48.00 (*0-8223-1139-9*) Duke.

— American Literary Scholarship: An Annual, 1991. LC 65-19450. 540p. 1993. lib. bdg. 45.00 (*0-8223-1315-4*) Duke.

— American Literary Scholarship: An Annual, 1992. 500p. 1994. lib. bdg. 48.00 (*0-8223-1480-0*) Duke.

— American Literary Scholarship, 1986. LC 65-19450. xvii, 522p. (C). 1988. lib. bdg. 48.00 (*0-8223-0802-9*) Duke.

Nordman, Marianne, jt. ed. see Lauren, Christer.

Nordman, Patricia E. & Nordman, Robert F. Minute Meditations. Coffen, Richard W., ed. 32p. 1989. pap. 0.75 (*0-8280-0510-9*) Review & Herald.

Nordman, R., et al, eds. Alcohol Toxicity & Free Radical Mechanism. (Advances in the Biosciences Ser.: Vol. 71). 370p. 1988. 161.00 (*0-08-035586-2*, Pub. by Pergamon Repr UK) Franklin.

Nordman, Robert F., jt. auth. see Nordman, Patricia E.

Nordmann, Alfred, ed. see Wittgenstein, Ludwig.

Nordmann, Martha. Cooking on Your Own: For Newlyweds, College Students or Anyone Who Is. 97p. (Orig.). 1992. spiral bd. 8.50 (*1-882835-24-7*) STA-Kris.

Nordmann, P. I. Tahiti. 1972. 250.00 (*0-8490-1175-2*) Gordon Pr.

Nordmark, Magdalene L. Moss, a Border Collie. (Illus.). 37p. (Orig.). (YA). 1988. pap. 7.00 (*0-685-21901-1*) Willow Run UT.

Nordmeyer, Francis, jt. auth. see Hansen, Lee.

Nordmeyer, U., et al, eds. Anesthesiologische und Intensivmedizinische Aspekte in der Kinderheilkunde. (Beitraege zur Intensiv und Notfallmedizin Ser.: Vol. 6). (Illus.). xi, 208p. 1987. 57.00 (*3-8055-4589-4*) S Karger.

— Grenzbereiche der Anaesthesie und Intensivmedizin. (Beitraege zur Intensiv und Notfallmedizin Ser.: Vol. 7). (Illus.). viii, 190p. 1991. pap. 46.50 (*3-8055-5413-3*) S Karger.

Nordness, Lee. Jack Earl: The Genesis & Triumphant Survival of an Underground Ohio Artist. LC 85-61064. (Illus.). 352p. (Orig.). 1985. pap. 29.95 (*0-937486-03-5*) Perimeter Pr.

Nordness, Lee, ed. The Council House. LC 80-82639. (Illus.). 230p. (C). 1980. 39.00 (*0-937486-01-9*) Perimeter Pr.

Nordoff, Charles & Hall, James N. Mutiny on the Bounty. braille ed. 659p. 1992. vinyl bd. 52.72 (*1-56956-073-0*, BR8669) W A T Braille.

Nordoff, Paul & Robbins, Clive. Music Therapy in Special Education. 2nd rev. ed. (Illus.). 272p. 1983. pap. 17.50 (*0-918812-22-4*, ST 035) MMB Music.

Nordon, Haskell. The Education of a Polish Jew: A Physician's War Memoirs. 314p. 1983. 15.95 (*0-910563-00-4*) D Grossman Pr.

Nordoy, A., ed. Blood Vessel Wall Interactions in Thrombogenesis. (Haemostasis Journal: Vol. 8, Nos. 3-5). 1979. pap. 62.50 (*3-8055-0117-X*) S Karger.

Nordoy, A., ed. see Inserm-International Symposium Staff.

Nordquist, D. L. & Nordquist, G. E. Twana Twined Basketry. (Illus.). 100p. (Orig.). (C). 1983. pap. 19.95 (*0-916552-27-6*) Acoma Bks.

Nordquist, G. E., jt. auth. see Nordquist, D. L.

Nordquist, Gullog C. Middle Helladic Village: Asine in the Argolid. (Uppsala Studies in Ancient Mediterranean & Near Eastern Civilizations: No. 16). (Illus.). 195p. (Orig.). 1987. pap. text ed. 45.00x (*91-554-1971-2*, Pub. by Uppsala Univ Acta Univ Uppsaliensis SW) Coronet Bks.

***Nordquist, Joan.** Feminist Theory: Women of Color: A Bibliography. (Social Theory: A Bibliographic Ser.: No. 40). 72p. (Orig.). (C). 1995. pap. 15.00 (*0-937855-79-0*) Ref Rsch Serv.

— Jacques Derrida II: A Bibliography. (Social Theory: A Bibliographic Ser.: No. 37). 76p. (Orig.). 1995. pap. 15. 00 (*0-937855-73-1*) Ref Rsch Serv.

— Julia Kristeva II: A Bibliography. (Social Theory: A Bibliographic Ser.: No. 39). 72p. (Orig.). (C). 1995. pap. 15.00 (*0-937855-77-4*) Ref Rsch Serv.

— Recent Immigration from Latin America: Social, Economic & Political Aspects: A Bibliography. (Contemporary Social Issues: A Bibliographic Ser.: No. 37). 76p. (Orig.). 1995. pap. 15.00 (*0-937855-72-3*) Ref Rsch Serv.

— Simone Weil: A Bibliography. (Social Theory: A Bibliographic Ser.: No. 38). 76p. (Orig.). 1995. pap. 15. 00 (*0-937855-75-8*) Ref Rsch Serv.

— Women in the United States: Economic Conditions: A Bibliography. (Contemporary Social Issues: A Bibliographic Ser.: No. 38). 76p. (Orig.). 1995. pap. 15. 00 (*0-937855-74-X*) Ref Rsch Serv.

Nordquist, Joan, comp. Glasnost: The Soviet Union Today. (Contemporary Social Issues: A Bibliographic Ser.: No. 13). 60p. (Orig.). 1989. pap. 15.00 (*0-937855-25-1*) Ref Rsch Serv.

— Hannah Arendt: A Bibliography. (Social Theory: A Bibliographic Ser.: No. 14). 60p. (Orig.). (C). 1989. pap. 15.00 (*0-937855-26-X*) Ref Rsch Serv.

— International Debt & the Third World. (Contemporary Social Issues: A Bibliographic Ser.: No. 14). 60p. (Orig.). 1989. pap. 15.00 (*0-937855-27-8*) Ref Rsch Serv.

— Max Weber: A Bibliography. (Social Theory: A Bibliographic Ser.: No. 13). 60p. (Orig.). 1989. pap. 15. 00 (*0-937855-24-3*) Ref Rsch Serv.

Nordquist, Joan, ed. The African American Woman: Social & Economic Conditions: A Bibliography. (Contemporary Social Issues: A Bibliographic Ser.: No. 32). 64p. (Orig.). 1993. pap. 15.00 (*0-937855-62-6*) Ref Rsch Serv.

— African Americans: Social & Economic Conditions: A Bibliography. (Contemporary Social Issues: A Bibliographic Ser.: No. 27). 68p. (Orig.). (C). 1992. pap. 15.00 (*0-937855-52-9*) Ref Rsch Serv.

— AIDS: Political, Social, International Aspects: A Bibliography. (Contemporary Social Issues: A Bibliographic Ser.: No. 10). 60p. (Orig.). 1988. pap. 15. 00 (*0-937855-19-7*) Ref Rsch Serv.

— Animal Rights: A Bibliography. (Contemporary Social Issues: A Bibliographic Ser.: No. 21). 60p. (Orig.). (C). 1991. pap. 15.00 (*0-937855-40-5*) Ref Rsch Serv.

— Antonio Gramsci. (Social Theory: A Bibliographic Ser.: No. 7). 50p. (Orig.). 1987. pap. 15.00 (*0-937855-12-X*) Ref Rsch Serv.

— Biotechnology & Society: A Bibliography. (Contemporary Social Issues: A Bibliographic Ser.: No. 8). 60p. (Orig.). 1987. pap. 15.00 (*0-937855-15-4*) Ref Rsch Serv.

— Claude Levi-Strauss. (Social Theory: A Bibliographic Ser.: No. 6). 1987. pap. 15.00 (*0-937855-10-3*) Ref Rsch Serv.

— Comparable Worth: A Bibliography. (Contemporary Social Issues: A Bibliographic Ser.: No. 2). 1986. pap. 15.00 (*0-937855-03-0*) Ref Rsch Serv.

— Current Central American-U. S. Relations. (Contemporary Social Issues: A Bibliographic Ser.: No. 5). 50p. 1987. pap. 15.00 (*0-937855-09-X*) Ref Rsch Serv.

— Deconstructionism: A Bibliography. (Social Theory: A Bibliographic Ser.: No. 26). 68p. (Orig.). 1992. pap. 15. 00 (*0-937855-51-0*) Ref Rsch Serv.

— Domestic Violence: A Bibliography. (Contemporary Social Issues: A Bibliographic Ser.: No. 4). 50p. 1986. pap. 15.00 (*0-937855-07-3*) Ref Rsch Serv.

— Eating Disorders: Feminist, Historical, Cultural, Psychological Aspects. (Contemporary Social Issues: A Bibliographic Ser.: No. 15). 60p. (Orig.). (C). 1989. pap. 15.00 (*0-937855-29-4*) Ref Rsch Serv.

— The Elderly in America: A Bibliography. (Contemporary Social Issues: A Bibliographic Ser.: No. 23). 60p. (Orig.). (C). 1991. pap. 15.00 (*0-937855-44-8*) Ref Rsch Serv.

— Environment II: Clean Air: A Bibliography. (Contemporary Social Issues: A Bibliographic Ser.: No. 31). 64p. (Orig.). 1993. pap. 15.00 (*0-937855-60-X*) Ref Rsch Serv.

— The Environment One: Clean Water: A Bibliography. (Contemporary Social Issues: A Bibliographic Ser.: No. 28). 68p. (Orig.). (C). 1992. pap. 15.00 (*0-937855-54-5*) Ref Rsch Serv.

— Environmental Issues in the Third World: A Bibliography. (Contemporary Social Issues: A Bibliographic Ser.: No. 22). 60p. (Orig.). (C). 1991. pap. 15.00 (*0-937855-42-1*) Ref Rsch Serv.

— Environmental Racism & the Environmental Justice Movement: A Bibliography. (Contemporary Social Issues: A Bibliographic Ser.: No. 39). 72p. (Orig.). (C). 1995. pap. 15.00 (*0-937855-76-6*) Ref Rsch Serv.

— Ernst Bloch: A Bibliography. (Social Theory: A Bibliographic Ser.: No. 19). 64p. (Orig.). (C). 1990. pap. 15.00 (*0-937855-37-5*) Ref Rsch Serv.

— Felix Guattari & Gilles Deleuze: A Bibliography. (Contemporary Social Issues: A Bibliographic Ser.: No. 26). 68p. (Orig.). 1992. pap. 15.00 (*0-937855-49-9*) Ref Rsch Serv.

— The Feminist Movement: A Bibliography. (Contemporary Social Issues: A Bibliographic Ser.: No. 24). 60p. (Orig.). (C). 1991. pap. 15.00 (*0-937855-46-4*) Ref Rsch Serv.

N

— Feminist Theory: A Bibliography. (Social Theory: A Bibliographic Ser.: No. 28). 68p. (Orig.). (C). 1992. pap. 15.00 (0-937855-55-3) Ref Rsch Serv.

— The Feminization of Poverty. (Contemporary Social Issues: A Bibliographic Ser.: No. 6). 1987. pap. 15.00 (0-937855-11-1) Ref Rsch Serv.

— Food Pollution. (Contemporary Social Issues: A Bibliographic Ser.: No. 20). 64p. (C). 1990. pap. 15.00 (0-937855-38-3) Ref Rsch Serv.

— French Feminist Theory II: Michele le Doeuff, Monique Wittig, Catherine Clement. (Social Theory: A Bibliographic Ser.: No. 31). 64p. (Orig.). 1993. pap. 15.00 (0-937855-61-8) Ref Rsch Serv.

— French Feminist Theory: Luce Irigaray & Helene Cixous: A Bibliography. (Social Theory: A Bibliographic Ser.: No. 20). 64p. (Orig.). (C). 1990. pap. 15.00 (0-937855-39-1) Ref Rsch Serv.

— Georg Lukacs: A Bibliography. (Social Theory: A Bibliographic Ser.: No. 11). 60p. 1988. pap. 15.00 (0-937855-20-0) Ref Rsch Serv.

— The Greenhouse Effect: A Bibliography. (Contemporary Social Issues: A Bibliographic Ser.: No. 18). (Orig.). (C). 1990. pap. 15.00 (0-937855-34-0) Ref Rsch Serv.

— Herbert Marcuse: A Bibliography. (Social Theory: A Bibliographic Ser.: No. 9). 60p. (Orig.). 1988. pap. 15.00 (0-937855-16-2) Ref Rsch Serv.

— The Homeless in America: A Bibliography. (Contemporary Social Issues: A Bibliographic Ser.: No. 12). 60p. (Orig.). 1988. pap. 15.00 (0-937855-23-5) Ref Rsch Serv.

— Investment & Social Responsibility: South Africa A Bibliography. (Contemporary Social Issues: A Bibliographic Ser.: No. 1). 1986. pap. 15.00 (0-937855-01-4) Ref Rsch Serv.

— Jacques Derrida: A Bibliography. (Social Theory: A Bibliographic Ser.: No. 3). 1986. pap. 15.00 (0-937855-02-2) Ref Rsch Serv.

— Jacques Lacan. (Social Theory: A Bibliographic Ser.: No. 5). 50p. 1987. pap. 15.00 (0-937855-08-1) Ref Rsch Serv.

— Jean Baudrillard: A Bibliography. (Social Theory: A Bibliographic Ser.: No. 24). 60p. (Orig.). (C). 1991. pap. 15.00 (0-937855-47-2) Ref Rsch Serv.

— Jean-Francois Lyotard: A Bibliography. (Social Theory: A Bibliographic Ser.: No. 21). 60p. (Orig.). (C). 1991. pap. 15.00 (0-937855-41-3) Ref Rsch Serv.

— Jean-Paul Sartre: A Bibliography. (Social Theory: A Bibliographic Ser.: No. 29). 64p. (Orig.). 1993. pap. 15.00 (0-937855-57-X) Ref Rsch Serv.

— Julia Kristeva: A Bibliography. (Social Theory: A Bibliographic Ser.: No. 16). 60p. (Orig.). (C). 1989. pap. 15.00 (0-937855-30-8) Ref Rsch Serv.

— Jurgen Habermas: A Bibliography. (Social Theory: A Bibliographic Ser.: No. 1). 1986. pap. 15.00 (0-937855-00-6) Ref Rsch Serv.

— Jurgen Habermas: A Bibliography. (Social Theory: A Bibliographic Ser.: No. 22). 60p. (C). 1991. pap. 15.00 (0-937855-43-X) Ref Rsch Serv.

— Latinas in the United States: Social, Economic & Political Aspects: A Bibliography. (Contemporary Social Issues: A Bibliographic Ser.: No. 40). 72p. (Orig.). (C). 1995. pap. 15.00 (0-937855-78-2) Ref Rsch Serv.

— Latinos in the United States: Social Economic & Political Aspects: A Bibliography. (Contemporary Social Issues: A Bibliographic Ser.: No. 34). 72p. (C). 1994. pap. 15.00 (0-937855-66-9) Ref Rsch Serv.

— Louis Althusser: A Bibliography. (Social Theory: A Bibliographic Ser.: No. 3). 50p. 1986. pap. 15.00 (0-937855-04-9) Ref Rsch Serv.

— Martin Heidegger: A Bibliography. (Social Theory: A Bibliographic Ser.: No. 17). 64p. (Orig.). (C). 1990. pap. 15.00 (0-937855-33-2) Ref Rsch Serv.

— Max Horkheimer: A Bibliography. (Social Theory: A Bibliographic Ser.: No. 18). 64p. (Orig.). (C). 1990. pap. 15.00 (0-937855-35-9) Ref Rsch Serv.

— Michel Foucault: A Bibliography. (Social Theory: A Bibliographic Ser.: No. 4). 50p. 1986. pap. 15.00 (0-937855-06-5) Ref Rsch Serv.

— Michel Foucault Two: A Bibliography. (Social Theory: A Bibliographic Ser.: No. 27). 68p. (Orig.). (C). 1992. pap. 15.00 (0-937855-53-7) Ref Rsch Serv.

— Mikhail Bakhtin: A Bibliography. (Social Theory: A Bibliographic Ser.: No. 12). 60p. (Orig.). 1988. pap. 15.00 (0-937855-22-7) Ref Rsch Serv.

— Mikhail Bakhtin Two: A Bibliography. (Social Theory: A Bibliographic Ser.: No. 32). 64p. (Orig.). 1993. pap. 15.00 (0-937855-63-4) Ref Rsch Serv.

— The Multicultural Education Debate in the University: A Bibliography. (Contemporary Social Issues: A Bibliographic Ser.: No. 25). 68p. (Orig.). 1992. pap. 15.00 (0-937855-48-0) Ref Rsch Serv.

— Multinational Corporations & the Environment: A Bibliography. (Contemporary Social Issues: A Bibliographic Ser.: No. 36). 72p. (C). 1994. pap. 15.00 (0-937855-70-7) Ref Rsch Serv.

— Pornography & Censorship. (Contemporary Social Issues: A Bibliographic Ser.: No. 7). 50p. 1987. pap. 15.00 (0-937855-13-8) Ref Rsch Serv.

— Radical Ecological Theory: A Bibliography. (Social Theory: A Bibliographic Ser.: No. 30). 64p. (Orig.). 1993. pap. 15.00 (0-937855-59-6) Ref Rsch Serv.

— Rape: A Bibliography. (Contemporary Social Issues: A Bibliographic Ser.: No. 19). 64p. (Orig.). (C). 1990. pap. 15.00 (0-937855-36-7) Ref Rsch Serv.

— Reproductive Rights: A Bibliography. (Contemporary Social Issues: A Bibliographic Ser.: No. 9). 60p. 1988. pap. 15.00 (0-937855-17-0) Ref Rsch Serv.

— Simone de Beauvoir: A Bibliography. (Social Theory: A Bibliographic Ser.: No. 23). 60p. (Orig.). (C). 1991. pap. 15.00 (0-937855-45-6) Ref Rsch Serv.

— Substance Abuse I: Drug Abuse. (Contemporary Social Issues: A Bibliographic Ser.: No. 16). 64p. (Orig.). (C). 1989. pap. 15.00 (0-937855-31-6) Ref Rsch Serv.

— Substance Abuse II: Alcohol Abuse: A Bibliography. (Contemporary Social Issues: A Bibliographic Ser.: No. 17). 60p. (Orig.). 1990. pap. 15.00 (0-937855-32-4) Ref Rsch Serv.

— Talcott Parsons: A Bibliography. (Social Theory: A Bibliographic Ser.: No. 8). 60p. (Orig.). 1987. pap. 15.00 (0-937855-14-6) Ref Rsch Serv.

— Theodor Adorno: A Bibliography. (Social Theory: A Bibliographic Ser.: No. 10). 60p. (Orig.). 1988. pap. 15.00 (0-937855-18-9) Ref Rsch Serv.

— The Third World Worker in the Multinational Corporation: A Bibliography. (Contemporary Social Issues: A Bibliographic Ser.: No. 30). 64p. (Orig.). 1993. pap. 15.00 (0-937855-58-8) Ref Rsch Serv.

— Toxic Waste: A Bibliography. (Contemporary Social Issues: A Bibliographic Ser.: No. 11). 60p. (Orig.). 1988. pap. 15.00 (0-937855-21-9) Ref Rsch Serv.

— University Research: Social & Political Implications: A Bibliography. (Contemporary Social Issues: A Bibliographic Ser.: No. 3). 1986. pap. 15.00 (0-937855-05-7) Ref Rsch Serv.

— Violence Against Women: A Bibliography. (Contemporary Social Issues: A Bibliographic Ser.: No. 26). 68p. (Orig.). 1992. pap. 15.00 (0-937855-50-2) Ref Rsch Serv.

— Violence in American Society: A Bibliography. (Contemporary Social Issues: A Bibliographic Ser.: No. 33). 72p. (C). 1994. pap. 15.00 (0-937855-64-2) Ref Rsch Serv.

— Walter Benjamin. (Social Theory: A Bibliographic Ser.: No. 15). 60p. (Orig.). (C). 1989. pap. 15.00 (0-937855-28-6) Ref Rsch Serv.

— Women & Aging: A Bibliography. (Contemporary Social Issues: A Bibliographic Ser.: No. 35). 72p. (C). 1994. pap. 15.00 (0-937855-68-5) Ref Rsch Serv.

— Women & AIDS: A Bibliography. (Contemporary Social Issues: A Bibliographic Ser.: No. 29). 64p. (Orig.). 1993. pap. 15.00 (0-937855-56-1) Ref Rsch Serv.

Nordquist, Kay. Dark Gods. Costa, Gwen, ed. LC 90-21747. 166p. (Orig.). 1992. pap. 13.95 (0-87949-322-4) Ashley Bks.

Nordquist, M. & Park, C. H., eds. The Reports of the United States Delegation to the Third United Nations Conference on the Law of the Sea. (Law of the Sea Occasional Papers: No. 33). 689p. 1983. 16.00 (0-911189-07-6) Law Sea Inst.

Nordquist, Myron H., ed. United Nations Convention on the Law of the Sea 1982. 1985. lib. bdg. 214.50 (90-247-3145-3) Kluwer Ac.

— United Nations Convention on the Law of the Sea, 1982: A Commentary Volume II Article 1 to 85 Annexes I & II Final Act, Annex II. 1088p. (C). 1993. lib. bdg. 225.00 (0-7923-2471-4) Kluwer Ac.

— United Nations Convention on the Law of the Sea, 1982, Vol. IV: A Commentary, Articles 192 to 278 Final Act, Annex VI. (C). 1990. lib. bdg. 249.50 (0-7923-0764-X) Kluwer Ac.

***Nordquist, Richard.** Passages: A Beginning Writer's Guide. 3rd ed. 448p. 1995. pap. text ed. 27.27 (0-312-10117-1) St Martin.

Nordquist, Richard F. Writing Exercise: Building, Combing & Revising. 384p. (C). 1985. pap. write for info. (0-02-388220-4) Macmillan.

Nordquist, Sven. Festus & Mercury: Ruckus in the Garden. (Picture Bks.). (Illus.). 24p. (J). (ps-3). 1991. lib. bdg. 18.95 (0-87614-678-7, Carolrhoda) Lerner Group.

— Festus & Mercury: Wishing to Go Fishing. (Picture Bks.). (Illus.). 24p. (J). (ps-3). 1991. lib. bdg. 18.95 (0-87614-658-2, Carolrhoda) Lerner Group.

Nordqvist, Sven. Festus & Mercury Go Camping. LC 92-43181. (J). (ps-3). 1993. 18.95 (0-87614-802-X, Carolrhoda) Lerner Group.

— The Fox Hunt. LC 87-28197. 32p. (J). (ps-2). 1988. 12.95 (0-688-06881-2); lib. bdg. 12.88 (0-688-06882-0) Morrow Jr Bks.

— Merry Christmas, Festus & Mercury. (Illus.). 24p. (J). (ps-3). 1989. lib. bdg. 18.95 (0-87614-383-4, Carolrhoda) Lerner Group.

— Pancake Pie. LC 84-16640. (Illus.). 32p. (J). (ps-3). 1985. 14.00 (0-688-04141-8); lib. bdg. 14.93 (0-688-04142-6) Morrow Jr Bks.

— Porker Finds a Chair. (Carolrhoda Picture Bks.). (Illus.). 24p. (J). (ps-3). 1989. lib. bdg. 13.50 (0-87614-367-2, Carolrhoda) Lerner Group.

— Tomten's Christmas Porridge. Haug, Arden, tr. (Illus.). 28p. (J). (gr. 1-6). 1991. 14.95 (0-9615394-2-9) Skandisk.

Nordskog, John E. Social Reform in Norway. LC 72-13001. 184p. 1973. reprint ed. text ed. 35.00 (0-8371-6736-1, NOSR, Greenwood Pr) Greenwood.

Nordstedt, C. F. Index Desmidiacearum Citationibus Locupletissimus Atque Bibliographia & Suppl. 1978. lib. bdg. 120.00 (3-7682-1171-1) Lubrecht & Cramer.

Nordstein, S. The Genus Crepidotus (Basidiomycotina, Agaricales) 1990. (Synopsis Fungorum Ser.: No. 2). 1990. pap. text ed. 32.50 (82-90724-02-0, Pub. by Fungi-Flora NO) Lubrecht & Cramer.

Nordstran, David E. The Complete Booger Book. Bascom-Haase, Sandra, ed. (Illus.). 104p. (Orig.). 1994. pap. 7.95 (0-9640360-1-0) Guardian Car.

Nordstrom, jt. auth. see Unger.

***Nordstrom, Alison D.** Architectonic Illusion: Photographs by Beatrice Helg. 68p. 1994. pap. text ed. 20.00 (1-887040-09-9) SE Mus Photo.

— Betrayal of Means, Means of Betrayal: Contemporary Art & the Photographic Experience. 27p. 1992. pap. text ed. 10.00 (1-887040-01-3) SE Mus Photo.

— Faces Photographed: The Photographic Portrait. 12p. 1992. pap. text ed. 3.00 (1-887040-00-5) SE Mus Photo.

— Latino America: Photographs by Cecilia Arboleda. 12p. 1993. pap. text ed. 3.00 (1-887040-05-6) SE Mus Photo.

— Nervous Landscapes. 28p. 1994. pap. text ed. 10.00 (1-887040-07-2) SE Mus Photo.

— Re: Photography: Three Exhibitions. 12p. 1994. pap. text ed. 7.00 (1-887040-08-0) SE Mus Photo.

— Victims of Paradox: Photographs by Wallace Wilson. 55p. 1993. pap. text ed. 10.00 (1-887040-03-X) SE Mus Photo.

***Nordstrom, Alison D. & Snavely, Patricia H.** Pro Femina: Images of Women by Women. 32p. 1993. pap. text ed. 8.00 (1-887040-06-4) SE Mus Photo.

***Nordstrom, Alison D. & West, Patricia.** Imag(in)ing the Seminole: Photographs & Their Use since 1880. 44p. 1993. pap. text ed. 10.00 (1-887040-04-8) SE Mus Photo.

***Nordstrom, Alison D. & Zeller, Bob.** Incidents of the War: Alexander Gardner's Antietam Photographs. 28p. 1995. pap. text ed. 10.00 (1-887040-10-2) SE Mus Photo.

Nordstrom, Alison D., jt. auth. see Ely, Deborah.

Nordstrom, Alison D., jt. auth. see Flax, Carol.

Nordstrom, Bengt, et al. Programming in Martin-Lof's Type Theory: An Introduction. (International Series of Monographs on Computer Science: No. 7). 232p. 1990. 52.00 (0-19-853814-6) OUP.

Nordstrom, Byron J., ed. Dictionary of Scandinavian History. LC 83-25204. (Illus.). 724p. 1986. text ed. 89.50 (0-313-22887-6, NCH/, Greenwood Pr) Greenwood.

Nordstrom, Carolyn & Martin, Joanne M., eds. Paths to Domination, Resistance, & Terror. (C). 1992. pap. 15.00 (0-520-07316-9) U CA Pr.

— Paths to Domination, Resistance, & Terror. (C). 1992. 45.00 (0-520-07315-0) U CA Pr.

***Nordstrom, Carolyn & Robben, Antonius C., eds.** Fieldwork under Fire: Contemporary Studies of Violence & Survival. LC 95-6235. 1995. write for info. (0-520-08993-6); pap. write for info. (0-520-08994-4) U CA Pr.

Nordstrom, David E. Inside Secrets of Auto Dealers. 104p. (Orig.). 1994. pap. 19.95 (0-9640360-0-2) Guardian Car.

— Inside Secrets of Auto Dealers. rev. ed. Wulf, Robert, ed. 104p. (Orig.). 1995. pap. 9.95 (0-9640360-2-9) Guardian Car.

Nordstrom, Folke. Goya, Saturn & Melancholy: Studies in the Art of Goya. (Illus.). 239p. 1962. text ed. 46.50x (0-685-14723-1) Coronet Bks.

Nordstrom, Judy. Concord & Lexington. LC 92-23392. (Places in American History Ser.). (Illus.). 72p. (J). (gr. 4 up). 1993. text ed. 14.95 (0-87518-567-3, Dillon Silver Burdett) Silver Burdett Pr.

Nordstrom, Karl, et al. Living with the New Jersey Shore. LC 85-25251. (Living with the Shore Ser.). (Illus.). xvi, 208p. (Orig.). 1986. 37.00 (0-8223-0543-7); pap. 16.95 (0-8223-0698-0) Duke.

Nordstrom, Karl, et al, eds. Coastal Dunes: Form & Process. (Coastal Morphology & Research Ser.). 392p. 1991. text ed. 195.00 (0-471-91842-3) Wiley.

Nordstrom, Lars. Sweden. LC 89-81616. 160p. 1990. 39.95 (1-55868-023-3) Gr Arts Ctr Pub.

— Theodore Roethke, William Stafford, & Gary Snyder: The Ecological Metaphor as Transformed Regionalism. (Studia Anglistica Upsaliensia Ser.: No. 67). 197p. (Orig.). 1989. pap. 42.50x (91-554-2338-8, Pub. by Almqv & Wiksell SW) Coronet Bks.

Nordstrom, Lars, tr. see Aggestam, Rolf.

Nordstrom, Lyle. The Bandora: Its Music & Sources. LC 92-19946. (Detroit Studies in Music Bibliography: No. 66). 1992. 30.00 (0-89990-060-7) Info Coord.

Nordstrom, O., ed. The Dynamics of Vehicles on Roads & on Tracks: Proceedings Ninth IAVSD-Symposium. (Vehicle System Dynamics Ser.: Vol. 15). xii, 656p. 1986. 61.00 (90-265-0710-0, Pub. by Swets Pub Serv NE) Taylor & Francis.

Nordstrom, Oscar L., jt. auth. see Ander, O. F.

Nordstrom, Patricia. Solve Your Child's Math Problem. 1994. pap. 12.00 (0-671-87026-2, Fireside) S&S Trade.

Nordstrom, Robert J. & Clovis, Albert L. Problems & Materials on Commercial Paper. 458p. 1981. reprint ed. write for info. (0-318-57520-5) West Pub.

Nordstrom, Robert J., et al. Sales Problems & Materials. LC 81-16205. (American Casebook Ser.). 515p. (C). 1987. reprint ed. text ed. 37.00 (0-314-62846-0) West Pub.

— Secured Transactions, Problems & Materials. (American Casebook Ser.). 594p. 1986. text ed. 42.50 (0-314-28463-X) West Pub.

Nordstrom, Ursula. Secret Language. LC 60-7701. (Illus.). 192p. (J). (gr. 3-5). 1960. lib. bdg. 12.89 (0-06-024576-X) HarpC Child Bks.

— Secret Language. LC 60-7701. (Trophy Bk.). (Illus.). 192p. (J). (gr. 3-5). 1972. pap. 3.95 (0-06-440022-0, Trophy) HarpC Child Bks.

Nordstrown, Kirk & Munoz, James L. Geochemical Thermodynamics. 2nd ed. LC 93-23633. 574p. 1994. 65.00 (0-86542-274-5) Blackwell Sci.

Nordtvedt, Matilda & Steinkuehler, Pearl. Women's Programs for Every Season. LC 82-6391. 96p. 1982. pap. 5.99 (0-8024-6903-5) Moody.

Nordulen, George & Shields, George W. Faith & Creativity. 256p. (Orig.). 1987. pap. 12.99 (0-8272-1017-5) Chalice Pr.

***Nordunger, Karen & Auxier, Jane.** Marriage, Separation, Divorce & Your Rights: For Wives, Husbands, Children, & Common Law Spouses in B. C.: Canadian Edition. 9th ed. (Legal Ser.). 152p. 1994. 9.95 (0-88908-474-2) Self-Counsel Pr.

Nordwall. Lutoslawski. Date not set. pap. 33.95 (0-685-69089-X, Pub. by Nordiska Pubns DK) Music Sales.

Nordyke, Eleanor C., et al. A Profile of Hawaii's Elderly Population. LC 84-18686. (Papers of the East-West Population Institute: No. 91). vii, 40p. 1984. pap. text ed. 3.00 (0-86638-059-0) EW Ctr HI.

Nordyke, James W. International Finance & New York. Bruchey, Stuart & Bruchey, Eleanor, eds. LC 76-5024. (American Business Abroad Ser.). 1976. 28.95 (0-405-09291-1) Ayer.

Nordyke, Lewis. Cattle Empire: The Fabulous Story of the 3,000,000 Acre XIT. Wilkins, Mira, ed. LC 76-29745. (European Business Ser.). (Illus.). 1977. reprint ed. lib. bdg. 26.95 (0-405-09762-X) Ayer.

Noreen. Public Street Illumination in Washington. 1975. 5.00 (0-318-21771-6) G Washington Univ.

Noreen, Eric. Computer-Intensive Methods for Testing Hypotheses: An Introduction. 229p. 1989. pap. text ed. 69.95 (0-471-61136-0) Wiley.

***Noreen, Eric, et al.** The Theory of Constraints & Its Implications for Management Accounting. Barth, Claire, ed. 188p. 1995. 25.00 (0-614-06484-8, 94300) Inst Mgmt Account.

Noreen, George W. Your First Finch. (YF Ser.). (Illus.). 36p. (Orig.). (YA). 1991. pap. 1.95 (0-86622-062-3, YF-106) TFH Pubns.

Noreen, Sarah P. Public Street Illumination in Washington, DC: An Illustrated History, Vol. M2. 1975. 5.00 (0-317-01771-3) GWU CWAS.

Noreika, Ruta, jt. ed. see Wilkinson, Jane.

Norelius, Eric. The Pioneer Swedish Settlements & Swedish Lutheran Churches in America 1845-1860. Bergendoff, Conrad, tr. LC 84-71391. (Augustana Historical Society Publication Ser.: No. 31). Orig. Title: De Svenska Luterska Forsamlingarnas och Svenska Historia i Amerika. 419p. 1984. 15.00 (0-910184-31-3) Augustana.

Norelius, Theodore A. In the Land of Kichi Saga. (Illus.). 172p. (Orig.). 1973. pap. 8.25 (0-933565-01-1) Porter Pub Co.

Norell, Donna M. Colette: An Annotated Primary & Secondary Bibliography. LC 92-26827. (Reference Library of the Humanities: Vol. 805). (Illus.). 584p. 1992. 87.00 (0-8240-6620-0, H805) Garland.

Norell, Mark. All You Need to Know about Dinosaurs. LC 91-21701. (Illus.). 96p. (J). (gr. 2-9). 1991. 13.95 (0-8069-8396-5) Sterling.

***Norell, Mark, et al.** Discovering Dinosaurs: In the American Museum of Natural History. 1995. 35.00 (0-679-43386-4) Knopf.

Norell, Pia. Native-Speaker Reactions to Swedish Pronunciation Errors in English. (Stockholm Studies in English LXXIX: No. LXXXIX). 181p. (Orig.). 1991. pap. 49.00x (91-22-01435-7, Pub. by Almqv & Wiksell SW) Coronet Bks.

Norell, Staffan, jt. auth. see Ahlbom, Andes.

Norell, Staffan E. A Short Course in Epidemiology. 208p. 1992. 39.50 (0-88167-842-2, 2325) Raven.

— Workbook of Epidemiology. (Illus.). 352p. 1995. 49.95 (0-19-507490-4); pap. 24.95 (0-19-507491-2) OUP.

Norelli-Bachelet, Patrizia. The Gnostic Circle: A Synthesis in the Harmonies of the Cosmos. 2nd ed. (Illus.). 309p. 1994. pap. text ed. 18.00 (0-87728-411-3) Aeon Bks.

— The Hidden Manna. 385p. 1976. text ed. 9.00 (0-945747-99-3) Aeon Bks.

— The Magical Carousel & Commentaries. (Illus.). 153p. 1979. text ed. 19.80 (0-945747-30-6) Aeon Bks.

— The New Way: A Study in the Rise & Establishment of a Gnostic Society, Vols. 1 & 2. (Illus.). 601p. (Orig.). 1981. pap. text ed. 24.00 (0-945747-06-3) Aeon Bks.

— Symbols & the Question of Unity. (Illus.). 157p. 1974. text ed. 6.00 (0-945747-54-3) Aeon Bks.

— The Tenth Day of Victory: An Initiation & Beyond. 300p. (Orig.). 1995. pap. 18.00x (0-945747-33-0) Aeon Bks.

Norelli, Linda K., ed. MicroMash CPA Review Reference 1992-1993, 5 vols., Set. (Orig.). (C). 1992. pap. 35.00 (0-926709-18-6) MicroMash.

— MicroMash CPA Review Reference 1992-1993: Auditing, 5 vols., Set. 216p. (Orig.). (C). 1992. pap. 35.00 (0-926709-20-8) MicroMash.

— MicroMash CPA Review Reference 1992-1993: Business Law, 5 vols., Set. 223p. (Orig.). (C). 1992. pap. 35.00 (0-926709-21-6) MicroMash.

— MicroMash CPA Review Reference 1992-1993: Financial Accounting, 5 vols., Set. 344p. (Orig.). (C). 1992. pap. 35.00 (0-926709-22-4) MicroMash.

— MicroMash CPA Review Reference 1992-1993: Managerial - Governmental - Taxation, 5 vols., Set. 281p. (Orig.). (C). 1992. pap. 35.00 (0-926709-23-2) MicroMash.

— MicroMash CPA Review Reference 1992-1993: The MicroMash Way to Pass, 5 vols., Set. 150p. (Orig.). (C). 1992. pap. 35.00 (0-685-60275-3) MicroMash.

— MicroMash CPA Review Reference 1993-1994, 5 vols., Set. (Orig.). 1993. pap. 35.00 (0-926709-24-0) MicroMash.

— MicroMash CPA Review Reference, 1994-1995, 5 vols., Set. Incl. MicroMash Way to Pass. 160p. 1994. (0-926709-31-3); Auditing (Audit) 208p. 1994. (0-926709-32-1); Business Law (LPR) 264p. 1994. (0-926709-33-X); Financial Accounting (FARE) 352p. 1994. (0-926709-34-8); Managerial - Governmental - Taxation (ARE) 304p. 1994. (0-926709-35-6); (Orig.). (C). 1994. Set pap. 35.00 (0-926709-30-5) MicroMash.

Norelli, Martina R. East Meets West: Chen Chi Watercolors. 88p. 1989. pap. 10.00 (1-882650-02-6) Colmbs Mus GA.

Norelli, Martina R. & Weinke, Jane M. Naturally Drawn: Drawings from the Collection. (Illus.). 48p. (Orig.). 1992. pap. 10.95 (0-685-56518-1) Le Yawkey.

Norelli, Martina R., jt. auth. see Harris, Neil.

Norem, Bonnie L. Psychological Development of Man As Expressed Through Biblical Themes. 1994. 11.95 (0-533-10806-3) Vantage.

An Asterisk (*) at the beginning of an entry indicates that the title is appearing in BIP for the first time.

Noren, Carol. The Woman in the Pulpit. 176p. (Orig.). 1992. pap. 12.95 (*0-687-45893-5*) Abingdon.
Noren, Carol M. What Happens Sunday Morning: A Layperson's Guide to Worship. 112p. (Orig.). 1992. pap. 8.99 (*0-664-25227-3*) Westminster John Knox.
Norena. Studies in Spanish Renaissance Thought. (International Archives of the History of Ideas Ser.: No. 82). 1975. lib. bdg. 99.00 (*90-247-1727-2*) Kluwer Ac.
Norena, Carlos G. Juan Luis Vives & the Emotions. LC 88-36811. (Philosophical Explorations Ser.). 288p. (C). 1989. text ed. 35.00 (*0-8093-1539-4*) S Ill U Pr.
— A Vives Bibliography. LC 89-78313. (Studies in Renaissance Literature: Vol. 5). 88p. 1990. lib. bdg. 49.95 (*0-88946-148-1*) E Mellen.
Norena, Carlos G., tr. see Vives, Juan L.
Noreng, Oystein. The Oil Industry & Government Strategy in the North Sea. LC 80-81590. 1980. 22.00 (*0-918714-02-8*) Intl Res Ctr Energy.
Norevik, Bjarne, jt. auth. see Hjulstad, Havard.
Norfleet, Barbara. Looking at Death. 1993. 40.00 (*0-87923-964-6*); pap. 25.00 (*0-87923-965-4*) Godine.
Norfleet, Barbara P. Killing Time: Photographs by Joe Steinmetz. LC 81-70658. (Illus.). 64p. (Orig.). 1982. pap. 6.95 (*0-9607492-0-9*) Amory & Pugh.
Norfleet-Smith, Violin. Psalms of a Violin. 48p. 1989. 9.95 (*0-930545-10-9*) Maple Hill Pr.
***Norfolk, Donald.** Sex Drive: The Complete Programme for Revitalising Your Sex Life. 320p. 1995. pap. 9.95 (*0-7472-4314-X*, Pub. by Headline UK) Trafalgar.
Norfolk, E. C. Norfolk: Taxation Treatment of Interest. 2nd ed. 1992. pap. 130.00 (*0-406-00285-1*) Butterworth Legal Pubs.
Norfolk, Lawrence. Lempriere's Dictionary. 432p. 1993. pap. 12.50 (*0-345-38423-7*, Ballantine Trade) Ballantine.
— Lempriere's Dictionary. 1994. pap. 5.99 (*0-517-13135-8*) Random Hse Value.
***Norgaard, Corine.** Fundamentals of Management Accounting Study Guide. 2nd ed. (C). 1977. 6.50 (*0-256-01948-7*) Irwin.
Norgaard, Richard B. Development Betrayed: The End of Progress & a Co-Evolutionary Revisioning of the Future. LC 93-24591. 1994. write for info. (*0-415-06861-4*) Routledge.
Norgaard, Rolf. Ideas in Action: A Guide to Critical Thinking & Writing. LC 93-5809. (C). 1993. teacher ed 7.20 (*0-673-46705-8*); text ed. 21.00 (*0-673-46404-0*) HarpCollege.
Norgan, N. G., ed. Physical Activity & Health. (Society for the Study of Human Biology Symposium Ser.: No. 34). (Illus.). 260p. (C). 1993. 69.95 (*0-521-41551-9*) Cambridge U Pr.
Norgan, Susan. Marketing Management: A European Perspective. LC 93-50928. 1994. write for info. (*0-201-54447-4*) Addison-Wesley.
Norgard-Sorensen, Jens. Coherence Theory: The Case of Russian. LC 92-10456. (Trends in Linguistics, Studies & Monographs: Vol. 63). x, 222p. (C). 1992. lib. bdg. 83.10 (*3-11-012911-6*) Mouton.
Norgate, K. England under the Angevin Kings, 2 vols, Set. LC 68-25255. (British History Ser.: No. 30). 1969. reprint ed. lib. bdg. 150.00 (*0-8383-0184-3*) M S G Haskell Hse.
Norgate, Kate. John Lackland. 1972. 75.00 (*0-8490-0455-1*) Gordon Pr.
— John Lackland. LC 71-110740. reprint ed. 19.45 (*0-404-00614-0*) AMS Pr.
Norgate, LeGrys G. The Life of Sir Walter Scott. LC 74-30271. (Sir Walter Scott Ser.: No. 73). 1974. lib. bdg. 63.95 (*0-8383-1927-0*) M S G Haskell Hse.
Norgate, M., tr. see Besedovskii, Grigorii Z.
Norget, Judy, ed. see Bialostok, Steve.
Norgren, Barbara J., jt. auth. see Noel, Thomas S.
Norgren, Barbara S., jt. auth. see Noel, Thomas J.
***Norgren, Jill.** The Cherokee Cases: The Confrontation of Law & Politics. LC 95-13761. 1995. write for info. (*0-07-047191-6*) McGraw.
Norgren, Jill & Davis, Edward, comps. Preliminary Index of Shah-Nameh Illustrations. 1969. pap. text ed. 5.00 (*0-932098-02-9*) UM Ctr MENAS.
Norgren, Jill & Nanda, Serena. American Cultural Pluralism & the Law. LC 88-42540. 265p. 1988. text ed. 55.00 (*0-275-92695-8*, C2695, Praeger Pubs); pap. text ed. 19.95 (*0-275-92696-6*, B2696, Praeger Pubs) Greenwood.
Norgren, Jill, jt. auth. see Shattuck, Petra T.
Norgren, Paul H. & Hill, Samuel E. Toward Fair Employment. LC 64-17756. 296p. 1964. text ed. 54.00 (*0-231-02716-8*) Col U Pr.
***Norgren, William A., ed.** Ecumenism of the Possible: Witness, Theology & the Future Church. 340p. (Orig.). 1994. pap. 10.00 (*0-88028-156-1*, 1280) Forward Movement.
Norgren, William A. & Rusch, William G. Toward Full Communion & Concordat of Agreement: Lutheran-Episcopal Dialogue III. LC 91-12472. 120p. (Orig.). 1992. pap. 4.99 (*0-8066-2578-3*, 9-2578, Augsburg) Augsburg Fortress.
Norgren, William A. & Rusch, William G., eds. Toward Full Communion & Concordat of Agreement. (Lutheran-Episcopal Dialogue Ser.: No. III). 120p. (Orig.). 1991. pap. 5.95 (*0-88028-119-7*, 1119) Forward Movement.
Norgrenand, William A. & Rusch, William G., eds. Implications of the Gospel: Lutheran - Episcopal Dialogue, Ser. III. LC 88-7729. 128p. (Orig.). 1989. pap. 4.99 (*0-8066-2408-6*, 10-2408, Augsburg) Augsburg Fortress.
Norguet, F., ed. Fonctions de Plusieurs Variables Complexes V. (Lecture Notes in Mathematics Ser.: Vol. 1188). vii, 301p. 1986. pap. 48.30 (*0-387-16460-X*) Spr-Verlag.
***Norheim, Carol & McGill, L. Jerome.** Communicating Interpersonally. 192p. (C). 1995. per., pap. text ed. 28.95 (*0-7872-0354-8*) Kendall-Hunt.
Norheim, Karen. Mrs. Preacher. 140p. (Orig.). 1985. pap. 5.95 (*0-89900-204-8*) College Pr Pub.
Nori, Angela, jt. auth. see Greenberg, Ron.
Nori, Don. Secrets of the Most Holy Place. 182p. (Orig.). 1992. pap. 8.99 (*1-56043-076-1*) Destiny Image.
Nori, Donald. His Manifest Presence. 168p. (Orig.). (SPA.). 1992. pap. 7.99 (*1-56043-079-6*) Destiny Image.
Nori, Donald F. His Manifest Presence. 182p. (Orig.). 1991. pap. 7.99 (*0-914903-48-9*) Destiny Image.
— How to Find God's Love. 144p. (Orig.). (SPA.). 1990. pap. 3.99 (*1-56043-024-9*) Destiny Image.
— How to Find God's Love. 108p. (Orig.). 1991. pap. 3.99 (*0-914903-28-4*) Destiny Image.
Nori, K. V., ed. Foundations of Software Technology & Theoretical Computer Science. (Lecture Notes in Computer Science Ser.: Vol. 287). ix, 540p. 1987. pap. 53.00 (*0-387-18625-5*) Spr-Verlag.
Nori, K. V. & Kumar, S., eds. Foundations of Software Technology & Theoretical Computer Science. (Lecture Notes in Computer Science Ser.: Vol. 338). ix, 520p. 1988. pap. 53.00 (*0-387-50517-2*) Spr-Verlag.
Nori, K. V. & Madhavan, C. E., eds. Foundations of Software Technology & Theoretical Computer Science: Proceedings of the Tenth Conference Bangalore, India, December 17-19, 1990. (Lecture Notes in Computer Science Ser.: Vol. 472). x, 420p. 1990. pap. 42.00 (*0-387-53487-3*) Spr-Verlag.
Noriaki Itoh, jt. ed. see Brown, F. C.
***Norian, Nicole A. & Michaud, Paul J.** A Continuous Quality Improvement Approach to Discipline. Date not set. write for info. (*1-878240-42-0*) Coll & U Personnel.
Norian, Todd, jt. ed. see Levitt, JoAnn.
Norich, Anita. The Homeless Imagination in the Fiction of Israel Joshua Singer. LC 90-27480. (Jewish Literature & Culture Ser.). (Illus.). 164p. 1991. 29.95 (*0-253-34109-4*) Ind U Pr.
Norick, Sylvester. Outdoor Life in the Menominee Forest. 1979. 3.95 (*0-8199-0767-7*, Frncscn Herld) Franciscan Pr.
Noricks, Michael L. Dime, Constanza. 142p. 1984. pap. 6.50 (*0-88334-180-8*) Longman.
***Norie, E. W.** The Official Account of Military Operations in China 1900-1901. (Victorian War Ser.: No. 3). (Illus.). 510p. 1995. reprint ed. 59.95 (*0-89839-215-2*) Battery Pr.
Norie, Imray L., jt. auth. see Wilson Ltd. Staff.
Norie, Imray L., jt. ed. see Wilson Ltd. Staff.
Norie, John. Caddy Spoons: An Illustrated Guide. (Illus.). 282p. 1989. 110.00 (*0-7195-4439-4*, Pub. by John Murray UK) Trafalgar.
Noriega, Bienvenido M. Pares-Pares. 238p. (Orig.). 1983. pap. 9.50 (*971-10-0064-4*, Pub. by New Day Pub PH) Cellar.
Noriega, Bienvenido M., Jr. Soltero. Tinio, Roland S., tr. (Illus.). 159p. (Orig.). (ENG & TAG.). 1985. pap. 9.50 (*971-10-0252-3*, Pub. by New Day Pub PH) Cellar.
Noriega, Chon A., ed. Chicanos & Film: Essays on Chicano Representation & Resistance. LC 91-27763. 394p. 1991. 50.00 (*0-8240-7439-4*) Garland.
— Chicanos & Film: Representation & Resistance. (Illus.). 416p. (C). 1992. pap. 19.95 (*0-8166-2218-3*) U of Minn Pr.
***Noriega, Chon A. & Ricci, Steven, eds.** The Mexican Cinema Project. (UCLA Film & Television Archive Studies in History, Criticism & Theory Ser.). (Illus.). 116p. (Orig.). 1995. pap. 16.95 (*0-292-75558-9*) U of Tex Pr.
Noriega-Crespo, Alberto, jt. ed. see Wallerstein, George.
Noriega, Dienvenido, Jr. Bongbong at Kris Batang Pro. (Illus.). 340p. (Orig.). 1987. pap. 12.50 (*971-10-0264-7*, Pub. by New Day Pub PH) Cellar.
Noriega, Irma S., jt. auth. see Kimble, Socorro M.
Noriega-Muro, Antonio E. Nonstationarity & Structural Breaks in Economic Time Series: Asymptotic Theory & Monte Carlo Simulations. 268p. 1993. 59.95 (*1-85628-580-4*, Pub. by Avebury Pub UK) Ashgate Pub Co.
Noriega, Violeta A. Philippine Recipes Made Easy. LC 93-84175. (Illus.). (Orig.). 1993. pap. text ed. 12.95 (*0-9636557-0-1*) Paperworks.
Norihiko Kikumura. Shinran: His Life & Thought. LC 70-172538. 192p. (C). 1972. 12.95 (*0-685-65548-2*) Nembutsu Pr.
Norimatsu, Patricia. Funny Facelift: Facial Exercises for a Fast Facelift. rev. ed. LC 81-83602. Orig. Title: Facemetrics. (Illus.). 46p. 1983. 19.50 (*0-9606890-4-4*) Morris Pub.
Noring, Nina J., jt. auth. see Glennon, John P.
Noring, Nina J., jt. ed. see Glennon, John P.
Norins, A. L., ed. Diapering & Infant Skin Care: Journal, Pediatrician, Supplement 1, 1987, Vol. 14. (Illus.). iv, 52p. 1987. pap. 17.75 (*3-8055-4615-7*) S Karger.
Norins, Hanley. The Young & Rubicam Traveling Creative Workshop. 352p. 1989. 29.95 (*0-13-973116-4*) P-H.
Noris, M. G. The Tom Mix Book. LC 89-40494. (Illus.). 379p. 1989. pap. text ed. 24.95 (*0-936505-11-7*) World Yesterday.
Noris, Michael, tr. see Siro.
Norkin, Cynthia C. & Levangie, Pamela K. Joint Structure & Function: A Comprehensive Analysis. 2nd ed. LC 91-42518. (Illus.). 512p. 1992. 34.95 (*0-8036-6577-6*) Davis Co.
Norkin, Cynthia C. & White, Joyce. Measurement of Joint Motion: A Guide to Goniometry. 2nd ed. (Illus.). 241p. 1994. text ed. 21.95 (*0-8036-6579-2*) Davis Co.
Norkin, John I. The Copper Contacts: A True Account of Extraterrestrial Events. 1994. 15.95 (*0-533-10845-4*) Vantage.
Norkin, S. B. Differential Equations of the Second Order with Retarded Argument: Some Problems of the Theory of Vibrations of Systems with Retardation. Grimm, L. & Schmitt, K., trs. LC 70-37627. (Translations of Mathematical Monographs: Vol. 31). 285p. 1972. 55.00 (*0-8218-1581-4*, MMONO-31) Am Math.
Norkin, Sam. Sam Norkin: Drawings - Stories. 341p. 1994. pap. 29.95 (*0-435-08642-1*) Heinemann.
Norko, Damon. The Glue Factory. 64p. (Orig.). pap. 6.00 (*0-916156-88-5*) Cherry Valley.
Norkunas, Martha K. The Politics of Public Memory: Tourism, History, & Ethnicity in Monterey, California. (SUNY Series in Oral & Public History). 123p. 1993. 49.50 (*0-7914-1483-3*); pap. 16.95 (*0-7914-1484-1*) State U NY Pr.
Norland, Emmalou, jt. auth. see Heimlich, Joe E.
***Norland, Howard B.** Drama in Early Tudor Britain, 1485-1558. 506p. 1995. text ed. 45.00 (*0-8032-3337-X*) U of Nebr Pr.
Norland, Howard B., ed. see Swinburne, Algernon C.
Norland, Kenneth. Just Like You...I've Been There Too: A Journey of Hope & Healing. (Illus.). 80p. 1993. pap. text ed. 11.95 (*1-881116-23-9*, 027) Black Forrest Pr.
Norlen, Paul, tr. see Lagercrantz, Rose & Lagercrantz, Samuel.
Norlev, E. The Way to Danish. 3rd ed. 306p. 1983. pap. 58.00 (*87-16-00998-3*) IBD Ltd.
Norlie, Olaf M. History of the Norwegian People in America. LC 72-1251. (American History & Americana Ser.: No. 47). 1972. reprint ed. lib. bdg. 59.95 (*0-8383-1436-8*) M S G Haskell Hse.
Norlin, Bill. The Business of Woodwork. 326p. 1992. text ed. 75.00 (*0-9635117-7-7*) Woodwork Pr.
***Norlin, Dennis A., et al.** A Directory of Adaptive Technologies to Aid Library Patrons & Staff with Disabilities. LC 94-36089. 1994. write for info. (*0-8389-7754-5*) ALA.
Norlin, George. Fascism & Citizenship. LC 70-180419. (Weil Lectures on American Citizenship). reprint ed. 21.50 (*0-404-56194-2*) AMS Pr.
— Integrity in Education, & Other Papers. LC 74-177964. (Essay Index Reprint Ser.). 1977. reprint ed. 20.95 (*0-8369-2568-8*) Ayer.
— Things in the Saddle. LC 74-80393. (Essay Index Reprint Ser.). 1977. 20.95 (*0-8369-1047-8*) Ayer.
— A Voice from Colorado's Past for the Present: Selected Writings of George Norlin. Ellsworth, Ralph, ed. LC 85-72909. 1986. 17.50 (*0-87081-157-6*) Univ Pr Colo.
Norlin, Julia M., jt. auth. see Chess, Wayne A.
Norling, Bernard. Towards a Better Understanding of History. LC 60-15676. 157p. 1960. pap. 7.95 (*0-268-00284-3*) U of Notre Dame Pr.
Norling, Bernard & Poinsatte, Charles. Understanding History Through the American Experience. LC 76-637. 208p. 1976. pap. 7.95 (*0-268-01911-8*) U of Notre Dame Pr.
Norling, Bernard, jt. auth. see Hunt, Ray C.
Norling, Bernard, jt. auth. see Rinderle, Walter.
Norling, Ernest. Perspective. (How to Draw & Paint Ser.). (Illus.). 32p. (Orig.). 1989. pap. 5.95 (*1-56010-013-3*, HT029) W Foster Pub.
Norling, Thomas B. Auxiliary Tip Party Marking Devices. (ABC Pocket Guide for the Field Ser.). (Illus.). 60p. (Orig.). (C). 1985. pap. 6.95 (*1-56016-036-5*) ABC TeleTraining.
— Precise Tone Plan for End Offices. (ABC Pocket Guide for the Field Ser.). (Illus.). 39p. 1981. pap. 6.95 (*1-56016-033-0*) ABC TeleTraining.
— Principles of Party Line Station Identification. (ABC Pocket Guide for the Field Ser.). (Illus.). 35p. 1982. pap. 6.95 (*1-56016-034-9*) ABC TeleTraining.
Norlund, Irene, et al, eds. Rice Societies: Asian Problems & Prospects. (Studies on Asian Topics (Scandinavian Institute of Asian Studies): No. 10). 322p. (C). 1986. pap. 25.00 (*0-913215-17-1*) Riverdale Co.
— Vietnam in a Changing World. (Scandinavian Institute of Asian Studies Monograph: No. 17). 320p. (C). 1995. text ed. 75.00 (*0-7007-0300-4*, Pub. by Curzon Pr UK); pap. 35.00 (*0-7007-0291-1*, Pub. by Curzon Pr UK) Humanities.
Norma, Eckroate, ed. see Eileen, Rota.
Normal, Henry. Nude Modelling for the Afterlife. 64p. 1994. pap. 12.95 (*1-85224-279-5*, Pub. by Bloodaxe Bks UK) Dufour.
***Norman.** Aircraft Carriers. 1991. pap. 4.95 (*0-516-95136-X*) Childrens.
— Alfred Stieglitz. 1991. 29.95 (*0-89381-429-6*) Aperture.
— A Color Atlas of the Temporomandibular Joint. (SPA.). 1992. write for info. (*0-8151-6430-0*) Mosby Yr Bk.
— Norway Pictures: Stave Churches. pap. 10.00x (*0-85918-604-0*, N604) Vanous.
— PDQ Statistics. 172p. (C). 1987. pap. 15.95 (*0-941158-92-6*) Mosby Yr Bk.
Norman & Sherwood. Logic & Proof. 1991. 24.25 (*0-536-58089-8*) Ginn Pr.
Norman & Streiner. PDQ Statistics. 1986. 13.95 (*0-8016-3840-2*) Mosby Yr Bk.
Norman, jt. ed. see Yoshikawa.
Norman, A. F., ed. & tr. Libanius: Autobiography & Selected Letters, 2 vols., Vol. I. (Loeb Classical Library: Nos. 478 & 479). 529p. 1993. Vol. 1, 478p. 18.95 (*0-674-99527-9*) HUP.
— Libanius: Autobiography & Selected Letters, 2 vols., Vol. 2. (Loeb Classical Library: Nos. 478 & 479). 486p. 1993. 18.95 (*0-674-99528-7*) HUP.
Norman, A. G., ed. Advances in Agronomy, Vols. 1-24. Incl. Vol. 13. 1961. 75.00 (*0-12-000713-4*); write for info. (*0-318-50155-4*) Acad Pr.
Norman, A. Jesse, ed. see Farrell, Martha P. & Farrell, James D.
Norman, A. V. & Pottinger, Don. English Weapons & Warfare: 1449-1660. (Illus.). 250p. 1985. 14.95 (*0-88029-044-7*) Dorset Pr.
Norman, A. W., et al, eds. Vitamin D: Chemical, Biochemical & Clinical Endocrinology of Calcium Metabolism. (Illus.). 1288p. 1982. text ed. 257.70 (*3-11-008864-9*) De Gruyter.
— Vitamin D: Gene Regulation, Structure-Function Analysis & Clinical Application Proceedings of the 8th Workshop on Vitamin D, Paris, France, July 5-10, 1991. (Illus.). xxxviii, 995p. (C). 1991. lib. bdg. 300.00 (*3-11-012638-9*, 261-91) De Gruyter.
— Vitamin D: Molecular, Cellular, & Clinical Endocrinology - Proceedings of the Seventh Workshop on Vitamin D - Rancho Mirage, CA, U. S. A., April 1988. xl, 1072p. (C). 1988. lib. bdg. 300.00 (*0-89925-393-8*) De Gruyter.
— Vitamin D - Chemical, Biochemical & Clinical Update: Proceedings of the 6th Workshop on Vitamin D, Italy, March 1985. (Illus.). xxxxiii, 1249p. 1985. 307.70 (*0-89925-066-1*) De Gruyter.
— Vitamin D - Chemical, Biochemical & Clinical Update: Proceedings of the 6th Workshop on Vitamin D, Italy, March 1985. (Illus.). xxxxiii, 1249p. 1985. 307.70 (*3-11-010181-5*) De Gruyter.
Norman, Adrian R. Electronic Document Delivery: The Artemis Concept. LC 81-20774. (Communications Library). 226p. 1982. lib. bdg. 50.00 (*0-86729-011-0*) G K Hall.
Norman, Adrian R., jt. auth. see Martin, James.
Norman, Albert. The Brittle Middle East: A Political & Internationally Legal Evaluation of Iran & the United States of America, 1979-1980. 190p. 1981. 8.80 (*0-318-00824-6*) A Norman.
— The Falkland Islands, Their Kinship Isles, the Antarctic Hemisphere & the Freedom of the 2 Great Oceans: Discovery & Diplomacy, Law & War, Vol. 3: The 19th Century, to the End of the 20th Century's First World War, 1918 & Vital Principles-Interests of the United States of America & the United Kingdom in the Falklands-Antarctic Regions. 496p. 1989. 31.00 (*0-317-03765-X*) A Norman.
— The Falkland Islands, Their Kinship Isles, the Antarctic Hemisphere, & the Freedom of the 2 Great Oceans, Vol. 2: Discovery & Diplomacy, Law & War. 672p. 1988. 33.00 (*0-317-01605-9*) A Norman.
— Operation Overlord, Design & Reality: The Allied Invasion of Western Europe. LC 73-100252. 230p. 1970. reprint ed. text ed. 35.00 (*0-8371-2985-0*, NOOO, Greenwood Pr) Greenwood.
Norman, Alfred L. Informational Society: An Economic Theory of Discovery, Invention, & Innovation. LC 92-34667. 1992. lib. bdg. 93.50 (*0-7923-9303-1*) Kluwer Ac.
Norman, Andrew & Scharff, Robert. Heavy Duty Truck Systems: Electrical - Powertrain - Steering - Suspension - Brake & Accessory Systems. 864p. 1992. teacher ed 22.95 (*0-8273-4593-3*); text ed. 59.95 (*0-8273-4592-5*); 16.95 (*0-8273-4566-6*) Delmar.
Norman, Ann E. Rapid ECG Interpretation. 1989. pap. text ed. 23.00 (*0-07-105302-6*) Hlth Prof Div.
— Twelve Lead ECG Interpretation: A Self-Teaching Manual. (Illus.). 300p. 1992. pap. text ed. 24.00 (*0-07-105396-4*) Hlth Prof Div.
***Norman, Anthony, et al, eds.** Vitamin D - A Pluripotent Steroid Hormone: Structional Studies, Molecular Endocrinology & Clinical Applications: Proceedings of the Ninth Workshop on Vitamin D, Orlando, Florida (U. S. A.), May 28-June 2, 1994. LC 94-35262. (Proceedings of the 9th Workshop on Vitamin D, Orlando, Florida, May 28-June 2, 1994 Ser.). 1007p. (C). 1994. lib. bdg. 361.55 (*3-11-014157-4*) De Gruyter.
Norman, Anthony W., ed. Vitamin D: Molecular Biology & Clinical Nutrition. LC 80-14327. (Basic & Clinical Nutrition Ser.: No. 2). 818p. reprint ed. pap. 180.00 (*0-7837-3342-9*, 2043300) Bks Demand.
Norman, Anthony W. & Litwack, Gerald. Hormones. 756p. 1987. text ed. 85.00 (*0-12-521440-5*) Acad Pr.
Norman, Arlan D., ed. Inorganic Reactions & Methods, Vol. 8: The Formation of Bonds to N, P, As, Sb, Bi, Pt. 2. 1992. text ed. 220.00 (*0-685-60609-0*) VCH Pubs.
Norman, Arlan D., jt. ed. see Zuckerman, J. J.
Norman, Barbara. Engraving & Decorating Glass: Methods & Techniques. 192p. 1987. reprint ed. pap. 7.95 (*0-486-25304-X*) Dover.
— What Can I Do with My Juicer? 1992. mass mkt. 3.99 (*0-440-21542-0*) Dell.
***Norman, Barry.** Birddog Tape. 1995. 19.95 (*0-312-11753-1*) St Martin.
— The One Hundred Best Films of the Century. LC 93-2520. (Illus.). 280p. 1993. pap. 16.95 (*0-8065-1426-4*, Citadel Pr) Carol Pub Group.
***Norman, Bethany.** Quick Steps to Learning: Windows 3.1. (Illus.). 198p. 1992. spiral bd., pap. 22.95 (*1-56951-000-8*) Sftware Trng.
— Windows 3.1 Beginning. 1993. pap. 22.95 (*1-56951-005-9*) Sftware Trng.
— Word for Windows Version 2.0, Advanced. 1993. pap. 22.95 (*1-56951-013-X*) Sftware Trng.
— Word for Windows Version 2.0, Intermediate. 1993. pap. 22.95 (*1-56951-011-3*) Sftware Trng.
— WordPerfect for Windows 5.1 & 5.2 Beginning. 1993. pap. 22.95 (*1-56951-007-5*) Sftware Trng.
Norman, Beverly. Wildflower Sampler. 100p. 1988. pap. 7.50 (*1-56770-191-4*) S Scheewe Pubns.
Norman, Bruce. Secret Warfare. (Battle Standards Ser.). (Illus.). 192p. 1990. pap. 9.95 (*0-7153-9456-8*, Pub. by D & C Pub UK) Sterling.
— Secret Warfare: Battle of Codes & Ciphers. 1987. 17.95 (*0-88029-160-5*) Dorset Pr.
Norman, Buford. Portraits of Thought: Knowledge, Methods, & Styles in Pascal. 220p. 1989. text ed. 40.00 (*0-8142-0464-3*) Ohio St U Pr.

N

Norman, Buford, jt. auth. see Feldman, Paula R.

Norman, C. A., et al, eds. Stellar Populations. (Space Telescope Science Institute Symposium Ser.: No. 1). 270p. 1987. 54.95 (*0-521-33380-6*) Cambridge U Pr.

Norman, C. J. Aircraft Carriers. LC 85-51452. (Picture Library). (Illus.). 32p. (J). (gr. 3-6). 1989. pap. 4.95 (*0-531-15136-0*) Watts.

— Buques de Guerra. LC 90-71421. (Picture Library). (Illus.). 32p. (SPA.). (J). (gr. k-4). 1991. lib. bdg. 12.60 (*0-531-07921-X*) Watts.

— Tanks. (Picture Library). (Illus.). 32p. (J). (gr. 2 up). 1990. pap. 4.95 (*0-531-15145-X*) Watts.

Norman, C. Lee. Plastic Blow Molding Handbook. 1990. text ed. 95.00 (*0-442-20752-2*) Chapman & Hall.

Norman, C. W. Undergraduate Algebra: A First Course. 400p. 1986. 39.95 (*0-19-853249-0*) OUP.

Norman, Cecilia. The Book of Grilling & Barbecuing. (Book of...Ser.). (Illus.). 120p. (Orig.). 1989. pap. 12.00 (*0-89586-790-7*, HP Books) Berkley Pub.

— Migraine Special Diet Cookbook. 1991. pap. 7.95 (*0-7225-2204-5*) Thorsons SF.

— Veg & Two Veg. (Illus.). 160p. (Orig.). 1992. pap. 13.95 (*0-563-36358-4*, BBC-Parkwest) Parkwest Pubns.

— Vegetarian Microwave Cookbook. (Illus.). 1993. pap. 10.00 (*0-7225-2761-6*) Thorsons SF.

Norman, Cecilia, jt. auth. see Timperley, Carol.

Norman, Charles. The Case of Ezra Pound. 1948. pap. 7.50 (*0-89366-106-6*) Ultramarine Pub.

— Christopher Marlowe: The Muse's Darling. LC 70-142471. 1971. 7.50 (*0-672-51406-0*, Bobbs) Macmillan.

— Portents of the Air. LC 77-187009. 64p. 1973. 5.95 (*0-672-51407-9*, Bobbs) Macmillan.

Norman, Charles J., ed. see Paine, Thomas.

Norman, Chris, ed. see Coale, Phil.

Norman, Colin. The God That Limps: Science & Technology in the Eighties. 1982. pap. 8.95 (*0-393-30026-9*) Norton.

— Knowledge & Power: The Global Research & Development Budget. LC 79-65904. (Worldwatch Papers). 1979. pap. 4.00 (*0-916468-30-5*) Worldwatch Inst.

— Microelectronics at Work: Productivity & Jobs in the World Economy. 1980. pap. write for info. (*0-916468-38-0*) Worldwatch Inst.

— Soft Technologies, Hard Choices. 1978. pap. write for info. (*0-916468-20-8*) Worldwatch Inst.

Norman, Colleen. A Family to Cherish. 1994. mass mkt. 3.50 (*0-373-09894-4*, 5-09894-2) Harlequin Bks.

Norman, D. Dinosaurs. (Spotter's Guides Ser.). (Illus.). 64p. (YA). (gr. 10 up). 1993. pap. 4.95 (*0-86020-458-8*) EDC.

— The Illustrated Encyclopedia of Dinosaurs. (Illus.). 208p. 1985. 19.99 (*0-517-46890-5*) Random Hse Value.

Norman, David. Dinosaur. (Illus.). 192p. 1991. 25.00 (*0-13-218140-1*) P-H Gen Ref & Trav.

— Dinosaur. 1993. pap. 15.00 (*0-671-87472-1*) P-H Gen Ref & Trav.

— Dinosaur Poster Book. 1988. pap. 2.00 (*0-517-65263-3*) Random Hse Value.

— Dinosaurs. (Fact Finders Ser.). (Illus.). 64p. 1989. 7.99 (*0-517-67728-8*) Random Hse Value.

— The Frontier Rakers. (Orig.). 1981. pap. 2.75 (*0-89083-859-3*) Zebra.

— Frontier Rakers, No. 5. (Montana Pass Ser.). (Orig.). 1982. pap. 2.95 (*0-89083-954-9*) Zebra.

— Frontier Rakers, No. 3: Gold Fever. 1981. pap. 2.95 (*0-89083-903-4*) Zebra.

— Gold Fever. (Frontier Rakers Ser.: No. 3). 512p. (Orig.). 1980. pap. 2.50 (*0-89083-621-3*) Zebra.

— Networks for Small Businesses. (Popular Applications Ser.). 160p. (Orig.). 1995. pap. 15.95 (*1-55622-455-9*) Wordware Pub.

— Prehistoric Life. (J). 1994. 30.00 (*0-671-79940-1*) P-H.

— Santa Fe Dream. (Frontier Rakers Ser.: No. 6). 1983. pap. 3.50 (*0-8217-1260-8*) Zebra.

— Silver City. (Frontier Rakers Ser.: No. 4). (Orig.). 1982. pap. 2.95 (*0-89083-921-2*) Zebra.

— When Dinosaurs Ruled the Earth. (J). 1985. 6.98 (*0-671-07522-5*) S&S Trade.

Norman, David & Miller, Angela. Dinosaur. LC 88-27167. (Eyewitness Bks.). (Illus.). 64p. (J). (gr. 5 up). 1989. 16.00 (*0-394-82253-6*); lib. bdg. 16.99 (*0-394-92253-0*) Knopf Bks Yng Read.

Norman, David, jt. ed. see Brant-Zawadzki, Michael.

Norman, Denise. Deni: The Loving Soul of a Woman. LC 84-80373. (Illus.). 72p. pap. 6.95 (*0-930355-00-8*) ELRAMCO Enter.

Norman, Diana. The Morning Gift. large type ed. 544p. 1987. 16.95 (*0-7089-1629-5*) Ulverscroft.

— Road from Singapore. large type ed. 1974. 15.95 (*0-85456-287-7*) Ulverscroft.

— Terrible Beauty. 1988. pap. 12.95 (*1-85371-007-5*) Dufour.

***Norman, Diana, ed.** Sienna, Florence & Padua: Art, Society & Religion 1280-1400, Vol. 1. LC 94-25653. 1995. write for info. (*0-300-06124-2*) Yale U Pr.

Norman, Donald. Things That Make Us Smart: Defending Human Attributes in the Age of the Machine. 304p. 1994. pap. 14.42 (*0-201-62695-0*) Addison-Wesley.

Norman, Donald A. Design of Everyday Things. 1990. pap. 15.00 (*0-385-26774-6*) Doubleday.

— Learning & Memory. LC 82-7441. (Illus.). 129p. (C). 1995. pap. text ed. 15.95 (*0-7167-1300-4*) W H Freeman.

— The Psychology of Everyday Things. LC 87-47782. (Illus.). 288p. 1988. 25.00 (*0-465-06709-3*) Basic.

— Things That Make Us Smart: Cognitive Artifacts As Tools for Thought. (Illus.). 288p. 1993. 22.07 (*0-201-58129-9*) Addison-Wesley.

— Turn Signals Are the Facial Expressions of Automobiles. (Illus.). 224p. 1993. pap. 10.53 (*0-201-62236-X*) Addison-Wesley.

— Turn Signals Are the Facial Expressions of Automobiles: Notes of a Technology Watcher. (Illus.). 1992. 21.11 (*0-201-58124-8*) Addison-Wesley.

Norman, Donald A., ed. Perspectives on Cognitive Science. LC 80-21343. 320p. 1981. 37.50 (*0-89391-071-6*) Ablex Pub.

— Perspectives on Cognitive Science. LC 80-21343. 315p. reprint ed. pap. 89.80 (*0-7837-0201-9*, 2040497) Bks Demand.

Norman, Donald A. & Draper, Stephen. User Centered System Design. (New Perspectives on Human-Computer Interaction Ser.). 544p. (C). 1986. pap. 39.95 (*0-89859-872-9*) L Erlbaum Assocs.

Norman, Donald A., jt. auth. see Lindsay, Peter H.

Norman, Dorothy. Alfred Stieglitz: An American Seer. 1990. pap. 16.95 (*0-89381-425-3*) Aperture.

Norman, Dorothy, comp. Alfred Stieglitz. (Masters of Photography Ser.: Vol. 6). (Illus.). 1989. 22.95 (*0-89381-308-7*); pap. 14.95 (*0-89381-309-5*) Aperture.

Norman, Dwayne, ed. Your Beginning with God. 31p. 1982. pap. 1.95 (*0-88144-063-9*) Christian Pub.

Norman, E., ed. Particle Astrophysics: Forefront Experimental Issues. 388p. (C). 1989. pap. 40.00 (*9971-5-0869-9*) World Scientific Pub.

Norman, E. Herbert. Ando Shoeki & the Anatomy of Japanese Feudalism. LC 79-52922. 340p. 1979. reprint ed. text ed. 75.00 (*0-313-27034-1*, U7034, Greenwood Pr) Greenwood.

— Feudal Background of Japanese Politics... in Preliminary Draft Form. LC 75-30127. (Institute of Pacific Relations Ser.). reprint ed. 49.50 (*0-404-59548-0*) AMS Pr.

— Japan's Emergence As a Modern State. LC 72-9092. 254p. 1973. reprint ed. text ed. 48.50 (*0-8371-6573-3*, NOJE, Greenwood Pr) Greenwood.

— Soldier & Peasant in Japan: The Origins of Conscription. LC 77-4281. (Illus.). 76p. 1977. text ed. 45.00 (*0-8371-9597-7*, NOSP, Greenwood Pr) Greenwood.

— Soldier & Peasant in Japan: The Origins of Conscription. LC 75-33572. (Institute of Pacific Relations Ser.). reprint ed. 29.50 (*0-404-59549-9*) AMS Pr.

Norman, Edward. Roman Catholicism in England from the Elizabethan Settlement to the Second Vatican Council. (Opus Ser.). 160p. 1986. pap. 11.95 (*0-19-281935-6*) OUP.

— The Victorian Christian Socialists. 210p. 1987. 54.95 (*0-521-32515-3*) Cambridge U Pr.

Norman, Edward, jt. auth. see Utley, T. E.

Norman, Edward R., et al. Ethics & Nuclear Arms: European & American Perspectives. LC 85-10304. 1985. pap. 13.50 (*0-89633-095-8*) Ethics & Public Policy.

Norman, Elizabeth. Women at War: The Story of Fifty Military Nurses Who Served in Vietnam. LC 90-34487. (Studies in Health, Illness, & Caregiving). (Illus.). 238p. (Orig.). (C). 1990. pap. 16.95 (*0-8122-1317-3*) U of Pa Pr.

Norman, Enid S., jt. auth. see Norman, Maxwell H.

Norman, Ernest L. The Anthenium. 1964. 8.95 (*0-932642-13-6*) Unarius Acad Sci.

— Cosmic Continuum. 2nd ed. (Illus.). 1960. 16.95 (*0-932642-17-9*) Unarius Acad Sci.

— The Elysium. (Illus.). 1956. 8.95 (*0-932642-14-4*) Unarius Acad Sci.

— Infinite Concept of Cosmic Creation. (Illus.). 1970. 50.00 (*0-932642-05-5*) Unarius Acad Sci.

— Infinite Contact. (Illus.). 1960. 10.95 (*0-932642-11-X*) Unarius Acad Sci.

— Infinite Perspectus. 1962. 19.95 (*0-932642-06-3*) Unarius Acad Sci.

— The Little Red Box. 1968. 6.95 (*0-932642-16-0*); pap. 4.95 (*0-932642-47-0*) Unarius Acad Sci.

— Tempus Interludium, Vol. 1. (Illus.). 1978. 17.95 (*0-932642-09-8*) Unarius Acad Sci.

— Tempus Interludium, Vol. 2. Norman, Ruth E., ed. 251p. 1982. 17.95 (*0-932642-48-9*) Unarius Acad Sci.

— Tempus Invictus. rev. ed. (Illus.). 1965. 17.95 (*0-932642-08-X*) Unarius Acad Sci.

— Tempus Procedium. 1965. 17.95 (*0-932642-07-1*) Unarius Acad Sci.

— The Truth about Mars. (Illus.). 116p. 1956. pap. 4.95 (*0-932642-12-8*) Unarius Acad Sci.

— Voice of Eros, Vol. 2. 2nd ed. (Pulse of Creation Ser.). (Illus.). 1958. 16.95 (*0-932642-01-2*) Unarius Acad Sci.

— Voice of Hermes. (Pulse of Creation Ser.). (Illus.). 1959. 16.95 (*0-932642-02-0*) Unarius Acad Sci.

— Voice of Muse, Unarius, Elysium, Vol. 5. (Pulse of Creation Ser.). 1964. 16.95 (*0-932642-04-7*) Unarius Acad Sci.

— Voice of Orion, Vol. 4. (Pulse of Creation Ser.). 1961. 16.95 (*0-932642-03-9*) Unarius Acad Sci.

Norman, Ernest L., ed. Voice of Venus, Vol. 1. 7th ed. (Pulse of Creation Ser.). (Illus.). 212p. 1956. 19.95 (*0-685-72171-X*) Unarius Acad Sci.

— The Voice of Venus, Vol. 1. 7th ed. (Pulse of Creation Ser.). (Illus.). 212p. 1956. pap. 10.95 (*0-935097-33-3*) Unarius Acad Sci.

Norman, F. Alexander, ed. see Antonovskii, M. Y., et al.

Norman, Floyd. Afro-Classic Folk Tales, Bk. 4: High John. Stewart, Lyn, ed. (Illus.). 28p. (Orig.). (J). (gr. 4-7). 1992. pap. 9.95 (*1-881368-21-1*) Vignette.

— Faster! Cheaper! The Flip Side to the Art of Animation. (Illus.). 128p. (Orig.). 1992. pap. 12.95 (*0-942909-02-X*) Get Animated.

Norman, Floyd & Sullivan, Leo. Afro-Classic Folk Tales, Bk. 6: Work-Let-Me-See. Stewart, Lyn, ed. (Illus.). 28p. (Orig.). (J). (gr. 4-7). 1992. pap. 9.95 (*1-881368-23-8*) Vignette.

Norman, Floyd, jt. auth. see Sullivan, Leo.

Norman, Floyd E. Afro-Classic Folk Tales, Bk. 1: A Rattlesnake Tale. Stewart, Lyn, ed. (Illus.). 28p. (Orig.). (J). (gr. 4-7). 1992. pap. 9.95 (*1-881368-00-9*) Vignette.

Norman, Gene, jt. auth. see Landon, Joyce.

Norman, Geoffrey. Alabama Showdown. 1987. pap. 3.95 (*0-8217-2157-7*) Zebra.

— Blue Chipper. 240p. 1994. mass mkt. 4.99 (*0-380-71911-8*) Avon.

— Bouncing Back. McCarthy, Paul, ed. 256p. 1992. reprint ed. mass mkt. 4.99 (*0-671-74635-9*) PB.

— Deep End. LC 93-37748. 1994. 20.00 (*0-688-11655-8*) Morrow.

— Deep End. 256p. 1995. mass mkt. 4.99 (*0-380-71912-6*) Avon.

— Deep End. large type ed. LC 94-16394. 431p. 1994. 20.95 (*0-7862-0241-6*) Thorndike Pr.

— The Orvis Book of Upland Bird Shooting. LC 85-17780. (Illus.). 160p. 1988. 15.95 (*0-8329-0412-0*) Lyons & Burford.

Norman, Geoffrey, jt. auth. see Ralphs, Lady.

Norman, Geoffrey R. & Streiner, David L. Biostatistics: The Bare Essentials. LC 92-48446. 1993. write for info. (*0-8016-2186-0*) Mosby Yr Bk.

— Biostatistics: The Bare Essentials. 260p. 1994. pap. 32.95 (*1-55664-369-1*) Mosby Yr Bk.

Norman, Geoffrey R., jt. ed. see Neufeld, Victor R.

Norman, Geoffrey R., jt. auth. see Streiner, David L.

Norman, George. Economies of Scale, Transport Costs, & Location. (Studies in Applied Regional Science: Vol. 16). 1979. lib. bdg. 49.50 (*0-89838-017-0*) Kluwer Ac.

Norman, George & La Manna, Manfredi, eds. The New Industrial Economics: Recent Developments in Industrial Organization, Oligopoly & Game Theory. 272p. 1994. pap. 27.95 (*1-85898-127-1*, Pub. by E Elgar Pub UK) Ashgate Pub Co.

Norman, George & LaManna, Manfred, eds. The New Industrial Economics: Recent Developments in Industrial Organization, Oligopoly & Game Theory. 240p. 1992. text ed. 69.95 (*1-85278-139-4*, Pub. by E Elgar Pub UK) Ashgate Pub Co.

Norman, George, ed. see Flanagan, Roger.

Norman, George, jt. auth. see Flanagan, Roger.

Norman, George, jt. ed. see Gee, J. M.

Norman, George, jt. ed. see Greenhut, Melvin L.

Norman, George, jt. ed. see Thisse, Jacques-Francois.

Norman, Geraldine, ed. see Marius.

Norman, Gertrude & Shrifte, Mirian L., eds. Letters of Composers: An Anthology 1603-1945. LC 78-14483. 422p. 1979. reprint ed. text ed. 75.00 (*0-313-20664-3*, NOLC, Greenwood Pr) Greenwood.

Norman, Greg. Greg Norman's Instant Lessons. 1994. pap. 15.00 (*0-671-88425-5*, Fireside) S&S Trade.

Norman, Greg & Peper, George. Greg Norman's Instant Lessons. LC 92-30381. (Illus.). 1993. 25.00 (*0-671-74943-9*) S&S Trade.

— Shark Attack! Greg Norman's Guide to Aggressive Golf. 1989. pap. 14.95 (*0-671-68320-9*, Fireside) S&S Trade.

Norman-Grumbley, Patricia, tr. see Mannino, Marc P. & Mannino, Angelica L.

Norman, Gurney. Divine Right's Trip: A Novel of the Counterculture. 2nd ed. LC 90-80306. 320p. 1990. reprint ed. pap. 14.50 (*0-917788-42-7*) Gnomon Pr.

— Kinfolks: The Wilgus Stories. LC 77-82064. 1989. pap. 10.50 (*0-917788-10-9*) Gnomon Pr.

Norman, H. C., ed. see Dhammapadatthakatha.

Norman, Hans, jt. auth. see Dahlgren, Stellan.

Norman, Hans, jt. ed. see Runblom, Harald.

Norman, Helen, jt. auth. see Annand, Ruth.

Norman, Henry W. Delhi. (Illus.). 400p. (C). 1987. reprint ed. 44.00 (*0-8364-2142-6*, Pub. by Gian Publng Hse II) S Asia.

Norman, Hilary. Fascination. 464p. 1993. pap. 5.99 (*0-451-40378-9*, Onyx) NAL-Dutton.

— Laura. LC 94-9825. 1994. 22.95 (*0-525-93783-8*, Dutton) NAL-Dutton.

— Spellbound. large type ed. LC 93-29305. 1994. 24.95 (*0-7927-1746-5*, Eagle Lrg Print) Chivers N Amer.

— Spellbound. large type ed. LC 93-29305. 1994. pap. 22.95 (*0-7927-1745-7*, Paragon Lrg Print) Chivers N Amer.

— Spellbound. 464p. 1994. reprint ed. pap. 5.99 (*0-451-40458-0*, Onyx) NAL-Dutton.

Norman, Hope J. & Simon, Louise A., eds. Louisiana Entertains: Featured as "a Best Cookbook" by Town & Country Magazine. LC 83-60953. (Illus.). 312p. (Orig.). 1983. pap. 11.95 (*0-9603758-1-3*) Rapides Symphony.

Norman, Howard. Bird Artist. 1994. 20.00 (*0-374-11330-0*) FS&G.

— The Bird Artist. large type ed. LC 95-3156. (Large Print Book Ser.). 1995. pap. 19.95 (*1-56895-094-2*) Wheeler Pub.

— The Bird Artist: A Novel. 320p. 1995. pap. 13.00 (*0-312-13027-9*) St Martin.

— How Glooskap Outwits the Ice Giants: And Other Tales of the Maritime Indians, Vol. 1. (J). 1989. 14.95 (*0-316-61181-6*, Joy St Bks) Little.

— Kiss in the Hotel Joseph Conrad & Other Stories. 160p. 1990. pap. 7.95 (*0-14-013199-X*, Penguin Bks) Viking Penguin.

— The Northern Lights. 240p. 1988. pap. 10.00 (*0-671-65877-8*, WSP) PB.

— The Wishing Bone Cycle: Narrative Poems of the Swampy Cree Indians. Rothenberg, Jerome, ed. (New Wilderness Poetics Ser.). 275p. 1982. pap. 8.95 (*0-915520-44-3*) R-E CA.

Norman, Howard, ed. Northern Tales. (Fairy Tale & Folklore Library). 368p. 1994. pap. 16.00 (*0-679-74036-8*) Pantheon.

Norman, Howard, tr. see Barton, Paule.

Norman, Howard, tr. see Ryunosuke, Akutagawa.

Norman, Howard, ed. see Strauss, Susan.

Norman, J. & Whitwam, J. Topical Reviews in Anaesthesia, Vol. 1. (Topical Reviews Ser.). (Illus.). 271p. 1980. text ed. 49.95 (*0-7236-0539-4*, Pub. by John Wright UK) Buttrwrth-Heinemann.

Norman, J. C. Tropical Vegetable Crops. (C). 1992. text ed. 70.00 (*0-7223-2595-9*, Pub. by A H S Ltd UK) St Mut.

Norman, J. C., jt. auth. see Godfrey-Sam-Aggrey, W.

Norman, Jack & Russell, Jack. The Nashville I Knew. Russell, Jack, ed. LC 84-17950. (Illus.). 264p. 1984. 14.95 (*0-934395-02-0*) Rutledge Hill Pr.

Norman, Jack, jt. auth. see Goldberg, Seymour.

Norman, James. The Obsidian Mirror. LC 77-72806. (Illus.). (Orig.). 1977. pap. 12.50x (*0-914140-03-5*) Carpenter Pr.

— Oregon Main Street: A Rephotographic History. 1994. 29.95 (*0-87595-255-0*); pap. 19.95 (*0-87595-256-9*) Oregon Hist.

— Portland's Architectural Heritage. 172p. 1992. pap. 19.95 (*0-87595-239-9*) Oregon Hist.

Norman, Jane & Beazley, Frank. Big Purr to the Rescue. 24p. (J). (ps-3). 1993. pap. write for info. (*1-883585-11-2*) Pixanne Ent.

— The Case of the Missing Shoes. 24p. (J). (ps-3). 1993. pap. write for info. (*1-883585-07-4*) Pixanne Ent.

— It's Raining Vegetables! 24p. (J). (ps-3). 1993. pap. write for info. (*1-883585-08-2*) Pixanne Ent.

— Maxi's Big Adventure. 24p. (J). (ps-3). 1993. pap. write for info. (*1-883585-04-X*) Pixanne Ent.

— The Mumble Mystery. 24p. (J). (ps-3). 1993. pap. write for info. (*1-883585-12-0*) Pixanne Ent.

— The Mysterious Light. 24p. (J). (ps-3). 1993. pap. write for info. (*1-883585-05-8*) Pixanne Ent.

— The Mystery of the Flying Elephants. 24p. (J). (ps-3). 1993. pap. write for info. (*1-883585-02-3*) Pixanne Ent.

— The Night the Moon Fell. 24p. (J). (ps-3). 1993. pap. write for info. (*1-883585-06-6*) Pixanne Ent.

— The Search for the Peanut Butter King. (Adventures of Tick-i-ty Ted Ser.). 24p. (J). (ps-3). 1993. pap. write for info. (*1-883585-00-7*) Pixanne Ent.

— The Tale of the Tickle Bug. 24p. (J). (ps-3). 1993. pap. write for info. (*1-883585-03-1*) Pixanne Ent.

— Tick-i-ty Ted Joins the Circus. (Adventures of Tick-i-ty Ted Ser.). 24p. (J). (ps-3). 1993. pap. write for info. (*1-883585-01-5*) Pixanne Ent.

— Tick-i-ty Ted Meets the Rude Rabbits. (Adventures of Tick-i-ty Ted Ser.). 24p. (J). (ps-3). 1993. pap. write for info. (*1-883585-09-0*) Pixanne Ent.

— The Voice from Nowhere. 24p. (J). (ps-3). 1993. pap. write for info. (*1-883585-10-4*) Pixanne Ent.

— Who Lives There? 24p. (J). (ps-3). 1993. pap. write for info. (*1-883585-13-9*) Pixanne Ent.

Norman, Jay. Peterson's Directory of College Accommodations: The Low-Cost Alternative for Travelers in the United States & Canada. LC 89-39084. 172p. 1989. pap. 9.95 (*0-87866-869-1*) Petersons Guides.

Norman, Jean & Sylvan, Richard, eds. Directions in Relevant Logic. (Reason & Argument Ser.: No. 1). 466p. 1989. lib. bdg. 158.00 (*0-7923-0386-5*) Kluwer Ac.

Norman, Jeffrey. Laughing Together & Other Ironies. (Illus.). 56p. (Orig.). 1991. pap. write for info. (*0-9628082-0-2*) EyeDea Bks.

— Objects from a Romance. (Illus.). 56p. (Orig.). 1991. pap. write for info. (*0-9628082-1-0*) EyeDea Bks.

Norman, Jeremy M. Morton's Medical Bibliography. 5th ed. 1046p. 1991. text ed. 145.00 (*0-85967-897-0*, Pub. by Scolar Pr UK) Ashgate Pub Co.

Norman, Jeremy M., jt. auth. see Hook, Diana H.

Norman, Jerry. Chinese. (Cambridge Language Surveys Ser.). (Illus.). 310p. 1988. 74.95 (*0-521-22809-3*); pap. 27.95 (*0-521-29653-6*) Cambridge U Pr.

Norman, Jesse, ed. see Barford, Charlotte, et al.

Norman, Jill. Bantam Library of the Culinary Arts, 4 vols. 1989. Boxed set. boxed 23.80 (*0-553-30491-7*) Bantam.

— The Complete Book of Spices: A Practical Guide to Spices & Aromatic Seeds. LC 90-50371. (Illus.). 160p. 1991. 25.00 (*0-670-83437-8*, Viking Studio) Studio Bks.

— The Complete Book of Spices: A Practical Guide to Spices & Aromatic Seeds. (Illus.). 160p. 1995. 14.95 (*0-14-023804-2*, Viking Studio) Studio Bks.

— Dutch Phrase Book. 1972. mass mkt. 4.95 (*0-14-003364-5*, Penguin Bks) Viking Penguin.

— French Phrase Book. 1968. mass mkt. 4.95 (*0-14-002706-8*, Penguin Bks) Viking Penguin.

Norman, Jill & Alvarez, Maria V. Penguin Spanish Phrase Book. 288p. 1988. mass mkt. 6.00 (*0-14-009936-0*, Penguin Bks) Viking Penguin.

Norman, Jill & De Figuerdo, Antonio. Penguin Portuguese Phrase Book. 288p. 1988. mass mkt. 7.00 (*0-14-009937-9*, Penguin Bks) Viking Penguin.

Norman, Jill & Giorgetti, Pietro. Penguin Italian Phrase Book. 272p. 1988. mass mkt. 6.00 (*0-14-009938-7*, Penguin Bks) Viking Penguin.

Norman, Jill & Hitchin, Ute. Penguin German Phrase Book. 272p. (Orig.). 1988. mass mkt. 7.00 (*0-14-009940-9*, Penguin Bks) Viking Penguin.

Norman, Jill & Orteu, Henri. Penguin French Phrase Book. 320p. (Orig.). 1988. mass mkt. 6.00 (*0-14-009942-5*, Penguin Bks) Viking Penguin.

Norman, Jill, jt. auth. see Breman, Paul.

Norman, Jill, jt. auth. see Davidson, Pamela.

Norman, Jill, jt. auth. see Hall, Magda.

Norman, Jill, jt. auth. see Stangos, Nikos.

Norman, Jim. Circle of Fear. 512p. 1993. mass mkt. 4.50 (*1-55817-721-3*, Pinnacle NY) Windsor NY.

Norman, Joanne S. Metamorphoses of an Allegory: The Iconography of the Psychomachia in Medieval Art. (American University Studies: History: Ser. IX, Vol. 29). 359p. 1988. text ed. 52.50 (*0-8204-0445-4*) P Lang Pubs.

Norman, John. Fire Officer's Handbook of Tactics. LC 90-84302. 550p. 1991. 40.00 (*0-87814-922-8*) Fire Eng.

— Fire Officer's Handbook of Tactics Study Guide. 1992. 20.00 (*0-912212-28-4*) Fire Eng.

N

An Asterisk (*) at the beginning of an entry indicates that the title is appearing in BIP for the first time.

— Gor Promotion. Incl. Tarnsman of Gor. 1981. pap. 2.75 (0-345-30284-2); Outlaw of Gor. 1984. pap. 3.95 (0-345-32394-7); Raiders of Gor. 1985. pap. 3.95 (0-345-33109-5); 1973. Set pap. 2.50 (0-686-76992-9) Ballantine.
— Savages of Gor. (Gor Ser.: No. 17). 0192. pap. 3.50 (0-87997-715-9) DAW Bks.
— The Telnarian Histories: The King. 304p. (Orig.). 1993. mass mkt. 4.99 (0-446-36240-9, Questar) Warner Bks.
Norman, John L., jt. ed. see Day, Christopher W.
Norman, John O., ed. New Perspectives on Russian & Soviet Artistic Culture. LC 92-19482. 1994. text ed. 39. 95 (0-312-08558-3) St Martin.
Norman, K. R. Collected Papers, Vol. I. 271p. (C). 1990. 36. 95 (0-86013-295-1, Pub. by Pali Text) Wisdom MA.
— Collected Papers, Vol. II. 271p. 1991. write for info. (0-86013-296-X) Wisdom MA.
— Collected Papers, Vol. III. 271p. 1992. write for info. (0-86013-299-4) Wisdom MA.
— Collected Papers, Vol. IV. 271p. 1993. write for info. (0-86013-306-0) Wisdom MA.
***Norman, K. R., ed.** Pali Text Society Journal, Vol. 16. 185p. (C). 1992. 34.50 (0-86013-304-4) Wisdom MA.
— Pali Text Society Journal, Vol. 17. 224p. (C). 1992. 34.50 (0-86013-305-2) Wisdom MA.
— Pali Text Society Journal, Vol. 18. 185p. (C). 1993. 34.50 (0-86013-307-9) Wisdom MA.
— Pali Text Society Journal, Vol. 19. 224p. (C). 1993. 34.50 (0-86013-309-5) Wisdom MA.
— Pali Text Society Journal, Vol. 20. 240p. (C). 1994. 34.50 (0-86013-314-1) Wisdom MA.
Norman, K. R, tr. Elder's Verses, 2 vols., 1. (C). 1971. 39.00 (0-86013-029-0) Wisdom MA.
— Elder's Verses, 2 vols., 2. (C). 1971. 39.00 (0-86013-031-2) Wisdom MA.
— Elder's Verses, 2 vols., Set. (C). 1971. 65.00 (0-86013-259-5, Pub. by Pali Text) Wisdom MA.
***Norman, K. R., tr.** The Group of Discourses (Sutta-Nipata), Vol. II. 450p. (C). 1992. 53.90 (0-86013-303-6) Wisdom MA.
Norman, K. R., jt. tr. see Davids, C. A.
Norman, K. R., ed. see Geiger, Wilhelm.
Norman, K. R., et al, trs. The Rhinoceros Horn. (C). 1984. pap. 13.00 (0-86013-154-8, Pub. by Pali Text) Wisdom MA.
Norman, Kass-Norman. Successful Reading: Key to Our Dynamic Society. 264p. 1980. pap. text ed. 20.00 (0-03-043126-3) HB Coll Pubs.
Norman, Keith B., jt. auth. see Thomas, James D.
Norman, Kent L. The Psychology of Menu Selection: Designing Cognitive Control at the Human-Computer Interface. Shneiderman, Ben, ed. LC 90-1198. (Human-Computer Interaction Ser.: Vol. 10). 352p. (C). 1990. text ed. 65.00 (0-89391-553-X) Ablex Pub.
Norman, L. C. Mathland: The Expert Version. (Illus.). 80p. (J). 1994. pap. 7.95 (0-521-46802-7) Cambridge U Pr.
— Mathland: The Novice Version. (Illus.). 88p. (J). 1994. pap. 7.95 (0-521-46801-9) Cambridge U Pr.
Norman L. Peterson Memorial Symposium on Oxidation of Metals & Associated Mass Transport Staff. Oxidation of Metals & Associated Mass Transport: Proceedings of a Symposium Sponsored Jointly by the Metallurgical Society of AIME & the MSD-ASM Atomic Transport Activity Held at the TMS-AIME Fall Meeting in Orlando, Florida, October, 6-7, 1986 & Dedicated to the Memory of Norman L. Peterson. Dayananda, M. A. et al, eds. LC 87-14192. 353p. reprint ed. pap. 100.70 (0-7837-2208-7, 2052458) Bks Demand.
Norman, Laura & Cowan, Thomas. Feet First: A Guide to Foot Reflexology. (Illus.). 304p. 1988. pap. 14.00 (0-671-63412-7, Fireside) S&S Trade.
Norman, Liane E. Hammer of Justice: Molly Rush & the Plowshares Eight. LC 89-61406. (Illus.). 280p. 1989. 24. 95 (0-9622766-9-3); pap. 12.95 (0-9622766-8-5) Pittsburgh Peace.
Norman, Lilith. The Paddock: A Story in Praise of the Earth. LC 92-15013. (Illus.). 32p. (J). (ps-3). 1993. 12.00 (0-679-83887-2) Knopf Bks Yng Read.
***Norman, Lisanne.** Fortune's Wheel. 576p. (Orig.). 1995. mass mkt. 4.99 (0-88677-675-9) DAW Bks.
— Turning Point. 256p. (Orig.). 1993. mass mkt. 3.99 (0-88677-575-2) DAW Bks.
Norman, Louise. God's Power Versus Satan's Power: Christian Life Lessons. (BMC Teaching Bks.). (Illus.). 64p. (Orig.). (J). (gr. 1-8). 1985. pap. text ed. 12.50 (0-86508-062-3) BCM Pubn.
***Norman, M. J.T., et al.** The Ecology of Tropical Food Crops. 2nd ed. (Illus.). 370p. (C). 1995. 69.95 (0-521-41062-2); pap. 29.95 (0-521-42264-7) Cambridge U Pr.
Norman, Margaret E. Cooking Atlanta Style: Delicious Recipes from Atlanta's Best Restaurants, Hotels, & Caterers. LC 93-79666. (Illus.). 208p. 1993. pap. 14.95 (1-56352-096-6) Longstreet Pr Inc.
***Norman, Margaret G., et al.** Congenital Malformations of the Brain: Pathological, Embryological, Clinical, Radiological, & Genetic Aspects. (Illus.). 432p. 1995. 95. 00 (0-19-506245-0) OUP.
Norman, Marsha. The Fortune Teller. LC 86-29634. 352p. 1987. 18.95 (0-394-55500-7) Random.
— Four Plays. LC 88-12362. 240p. (C). 1988. pap. 10.95 (0-930452-84-4) Theatre Comm.
— Getting Out. 1979. pap. 4.75 (0-8222-0439-8) Dramatists Play.
— The Holdup. 73p. 1987. pap. 4.75 (0-8222-0524-6) Dramatists Play.
— Night Mother. 1983. pap. 4.75 (0-8222-0821-0) Dramatists Play.
— Night Mother. 1988. pap. 8.95 (0-374-52138-7) FS&G.
— The Secret Garden. LC 92-2562. 120p. 1992. 22.95 (1-55936-048-8); pap. 9.95 (1-55936-047-X) Theatre Comm.
— Third & Oak: The Laundromat. 1980. pap. 2.75 (0-8222-1132-7) Dramatists Play.
— Third & Oak: The Pool Hall. 1985. pap. 2.75 (0-8222-1133-5) Dramatists Play.
— Traveler in the Dark. 1988. pap. 4.75 (0-8222-1168-8) Dramatists Play.
***Norman, Marty.** 101 Uses for a Dead Angel. LC 95-8867. 1995. pap. 6.99 (0-312-13227-1) St Martin.
Norman, Mary Anne. The Texas Economy since World War II. (Texas History Ser.). (Illus.). 38p. (Orig.). 1983. pap. text ed. 3.95x (0-89641-126-5) American Pr.
Norman, Maxwell H. & Norman, Enid S. How to Read & Study for Success in College. 3rd ed. 336p. (C). 1981. pap. text ed. 20.75 (0-03-049621-7) HB Coll Pubs.
Norman, Michael. These Good Men. McCarthy, Paul, ed. 328p. 1991. reprint ed. mass mkt. 4.95 (0-671-73173-4) PB.
Norman, Michael & Edwards, Tim. Micro-Computers in Personnel. 128p. (C). 1984. 47.00 (0-85292-337-6) St Mut.
Norman, Michael & Stoker, Barry. Data Development Analysis: The Assessment of Performance. 262p. 1991. text ed. 79.95 (0-471-92835-6) Wiley.
Norman, Michael, jt. auth. see Scott, Beth.
Norman, Michael E., ed. see Pediatric Nephrology International Symposium Staff.
Norman, Michael J. Annual Cropping Systems in the Tropics: An Introduction. LC 79-10625. (Illus.). 288p. reprint ed. pap. 82.10 (0-7837-4924-4, 2044590) Bks Demand.
Norman, Michael L., jt. ed. see Winkler, Karl-Heinz A.
Norman, N. A. Consecration to the Immaculate Heart of Mary: According to the Spirit of St. Louis De-Montfort's True Devotion to Mary. LC 88-50839. 68p. 1988. reprint ed. pap. 1.50 (0-89555-342-2) TAN Bks Pubs.
Norman, N. Philip, jt. auth. see Rorty, James.
Norman, Naomi. Picture Perfect Patchwork. LC 92-43985. (Designer Ser.). (Illus.). 88p. (Orig.). 1993. pap. 19.95 (1-56477-017-6, B152) That Patchwork.
Norman, Natalie. In the Money: A User-Friendly Guide to Managing Your Money. (Illus.). (Orig.). 1986. pap. 14.95 (0-9617752-0-3) Fealty Weal Pubns.
Norman, Nicholas C. Periodicity & the p-Block Elements. LC 93-37708. (Oxford Chemistry Primers Ser.: Vol. 16). (Illus.). 96p. (C). 1994. text ed. 29.95 (0-19-855764-7); pap. text ed. 9.95 (0-19-855763-9) OUP.
Norman, P. S., ed. Pathology & Physiology of Allergic Reactions. (Journal: International Archives of Allergy & Applied Immunology: Vol. 77, No. 1-2). (Illus.). 280p. 1985. pap. 93.00 (3-8055-4056-6) S Karger.
Norman, Paul, jt. ed. see Connor, Mark.
***Norman, Peter & Ryan, W. F.** The Penguin Russian Dictionary: English-Russian, Russian-English. 1152p. 1995. 50.00 (0-670-82836-X, Viking) Viking Penguin.
Norman, Philip. Elton John. 416p. 1992. 22.50 (0-517-58762-9, Harmony) Crown Pub Group.
— Elton John: The Definitive Biography. (Illus.). 544p. 1993. pap. 13.00 (0-671-79729-8, Fireside) S&S Trade.
— The Life & Good Times of the Rolling Stones. 1989. 12. 99 (0-517-05539-2) Random Hse Value.
— The Stones. 400p. 1994. reprint ed. pap. 10.95 (0-14-017411-7, Penguin Bks) Viking Penguin.
Norman, Philip, jt. auth. see Rorty, James.
Norman, Philip A., jt. auth. see Handscombe, Richard S.
Norman, Philip R. Dancing Dogs. LC 93-2533. (J). 1995. 14.95 (0-316-61208-1) Little.
Norman, R., tr. see Leskov, Nikolai S.
Norman, R. O. & Coxon, James M. Principles of Organic Synthesis. 3rd ed. LC 93-16951. 1993. write for info. (0-7514-0126-9, Pub. by Blackie Acad & Prof UK) Routledge Chapman & Hall.
Norman, Randolph. AIDS: Blunt Talk on How to Avoid It. 32p. 1985. pap. 5.95 (0-86668-057-8) ARCsoft.
Norman, Remington. The Great Domaines of Burgundy: A Guide to the Finest Wine Producers of the Cote D'Or. (Illus.). 288p. 1993. 40.00 (0-8050-2463-8) H Holt & Co.
***Norman, Richard.** Ethics, Killing & War. 266p. (C). 1995. 49.95 (0-521-45539-1); pap. 14.95 (0-521-45553-7) Cambridge U Pr.
— Hegel's Phenomenology: A Philosophical Introduction. (Modern Revivals in Philosophy Ser.). 140p. 1992. 47.50 (0-7512-0015-8, Pub. by Gregg Revivals UK) Ashgate Pub Co.
— The Moral Philosophers: An Introduction to Ethics. 1984. pap. 15.95 (0-19-875059-5) OUP.
Norman, Richard & Sayers, Sean. Hegel, Marx, & Dialectic: A Debate. (Modern Revivals in Philosophy Ser.). 196p. 1993. 50.95 (0-7512-0219-3, Pub. by Gregg Revivals UK) Ashgate Pub Co.
Norman, Rick. Fielder's Choice. 196p. 1992. pap. 9.95 (0-87483-204-7) August Hse.
Norman, Rick J., jt. auth. see Holliday, James S., Jr.
Norman, Robert, tr. The Safeguard of Sailors, or Great Rutter. LC 76-57412. (English Experience Ser.: No. 827). 1977. reprint ed. lib. bdg. 30.00 (90-221-0827-9) Walter J Johnson.
***Norman, Robert A.** The Fax of Life: Jokes, Quotes, & Assorted Wisdom. (Illus.). 80p. (Orig.). 1994. pap. 7.95 (0-9637802-1-2) Medford Sr Citizens.
***Norman, Robert A., ed. & intro.** Where Wisdom Shines. (Illus.). 160p. (Orig.). 1994. pap. text ed. 7.95 (0-9637802-0-4) Medford Sr Citizens.
Norman, Robert W., jt. ed. see Dainty, David A.
***Norman Rockwell Museum at Stockbridge Staff.** Norman Rockwell: The Artist & His Work. LC 95-13523. 1995. write for info. (1-56799-209-9, Friedman-Fairfax) M Friedman Pub Grp Inc.
Norman, Ruth. Beginners Guide to Progressive Evolution. 386p. 1987. 16.95 (0-935097-04-X) Unarius Acad Sci.
— Biographical History of Unarius, Vol. 1. (Illus.). 1985. 17. 95 (0-932642-57-8) Unarius Acad Sci.
— Biographical History of Unarius, Vol. 2. (Illus.). 1985. 17. 95 (0-932642-58-6) Unarius Acad Sci.
— Biography of an Archangel: The Accomplishments of Uriel. (Illus.). 365p. 1989. 24.95 (0-935097-19-8) Unarius Acad Sci.
— Effort to Destroy: The Unarius Mission - "Thwarted" 400p. (Orig.). (C). 1984. pap. 8.95 (0-932642-89-6) Unarius Acad Sci.
— Facts about UFO's. (Illus.). 21p. (Orig.). 1982. pap. 6.95 (0-932642-77-2) Unarius Acad Sci.
— The Grand Design of Life for Man, Vol. 1. 590p. (C). 1984. 18.95 (0-932642-81-0) Unarius Acad Sci.
— Interdimensional Physics: The Mind & the Universe. (Illus.). 332p. (C). 1989. 24.95 (0-935097-15-5) Unarius Acad Sci.
— Man, the Evolutionary Regenerative Spirit, Vol. 1. 325p. (C). 1987. text ed. 17.95 (0-932642-95-0) Unarius Acad Sci.
— My Two Thousand Year Psychic Memory As Mary of Bethany, 13th Disciple to Jesus of Nazareth. 75p. 1987. 7.95 (0-932642-32-2) Unarius Acad Sci.
— New Hope for Drug & Alcohol Abusers. 48p. (Orig.). (C). 1984. pap. 4.95 (0-932642-96-9) Unarius Acad Sci.
— Preparation for the Landing. (Illus.). 493p. 1987. 22.95 (0-935097-07-4) Unarius Acad Sci.
— Preview for the Spacecraft Landing on Earth 2001 A. D. (Illus.). 139p. 1987. 10.95 (0-935097-06-6) Unarius Acad Sci.
— The Proof of the Truth of Past Life Therapy. 200p. 1988. 10.95 (0-935097-13-9) Unarius Acad Sci.
— Ramu of Lemuria Speaks. 430p. 1988. 17.95 (0-935097-08-2) Unarius Acad Sci.
— Satan Is Now a Light Bearer. 24p. (Orig.). (C). 1984. pap. 2.95 (0-932642-88-8) Unarius Acad Sci.
— Unarius Light Magazine. (Illus.). 45p. 1987. pap. text ed. 24.00 (0-317-61768-0) Unarius Acad Sci.
— Visitations: A Saga of Gods & Men, Vol. I. (Illus.). 578p. 1987. text ed. 100.00 (0-932642-84-5) Unarius Acad Sci.
Norman, Ruth, intro. Glowing Moments. 170p. (Orig.). 1982. pap. 6.95 (0-932642-76-4) Unarius Acad Sci.
Norman, Ruth & Adirije, Nwabueze. Man of Earth & His Endless Journey Through the Stars. (Illus.). 72p. (Orig.). 1987. pap. 4.95 (0-935097-02-3) Unarius Acad Sci.
Norman, Ruth & Spaegel, Charles. Communications from Outer Space. 2nd ed. (Illus.). 469p. 1991. 24.95 (0-932642-80-2) Unarius Acad Sci.
— The Interplanetary Confederation. 550p. (C). 1987. pap. 17.95 (0-932642-86-1) Unarius Acad Sci.
— The Joining of Science & Spirit. 336p. 1989. 17.95 (0-935097-17-1) Unarius Acad Sci.
— The Last Inca-Atahualpa: An Eyewitness Account of the Conquest of Peru. Unarius Group, ed. (Illus.). 325p. (C). 1993. 21.95 (0-935097-18-X) Unarius Acad Sci.
— The Psychology of Consciousness: An Intelligent Guide to Psychic Liberation. (Illus.). 725p. (Orig.). (C). 1985. student ed, spiral bd. 65.00 (0-932642-97-7) Unarius Acad Sci.
— The Restoration, Vol. 2. (Illus.). 250p. (Orig.). 1982. pap. 10.95 (0-932642-67-5) Unarius Acad Sci.
Norman, Ruth & Swanson, Jeff. The Restoration, Vol. 1. (Illus.). 250p. (Orig.). 1981. 10.95 (0-932642-66-7) Unarius Acad Sci.
Norman, Ruth, ed. see Dallison, Dennis.
Norman, Ruth, et al. Return to Jerusalem. 286p. (Orig.). 1983. pap. 10.95 (0-932642-78-0) Unarius Acad Sci.
Norman, Ruth E. Bridge to Heaven. 1969. 17.95 (0-932642-10-1) Unarius Acad Sci.
— Celebration of the Millenium: Orbital Mountains & Cities. (Tesla Speaks Ser.: Vol. VI). (Illus.). 1974. pap. 6.95 (0-932642-27-6) Unarius Acad Sci.
— Countdown to Space Fleet Landing. (Tesla Speaks Ser.: Vol. VII). (Illus.). 1974. pap. 7.95 (0-932642-28-4) Unarius Acad Sci.
— The Decline & Destruction of the Orion Empire, Vol. 1. (Illus.). 373p. (Orig.). 1979. pap. 9.95 (0-932642-50-0) Unarius Acad Sci.
— Decline & Destruction of the Orion Empire, Vol. 2. 375p. 1981. pap. 9.95 (0-932642-54-3) Unarius Acad Sci.
— Decline & Destruction of the Orion Empire, Vol. 3. 375p. 1982. pap. 9.95 (0-932642-55-1) Unarius Acad Sci.
— The Epic. (Tesla Speaks Ser.: No. 13). (Illus.). 1977. 17. 95 (0-932642-36-5) Unarius Acad Sci.
— Exploring the Universe with Starship Voyager. 500p. (C). 1986. text ed. 19.95 (0-932642-83-7) Unarius Acad Sci.
— Have You Lived on Other Worlds Before, 2 vols., 2. (Illus.). 1980. pap. 8.95 (0-932642-60-8) Unarius Acad Sci.
— History of the Universe, Vol. 1. 450p. (Orig.). (C). 17.95 (0-932642-71-3) Unarius Acad Sci.
— History of the Universe, Vol. 2. (Illus.). 450p. (Orig.). (C). 1982. 17.95 (0-932642-72-1) Unarius Acad Sci.
— History of the Universe, Vol. 3. (Illus.). 416p. (Orig.). (C). 1983. 17.95 (0-932642-73-X) Unarius Acad Sci.
— Mars Underground Cities Discovered. (Tesla Speaks Ser.: Vol. 12). (Illus.). 1977. 14.95 (0-932642-35-7); pap. 8.95 (0-932642-46-2) Unarius Acad Sci.
— Rainbow Bridge to the Inner Worlds. 400p. (C). 1985. text ed. 17.95 (0-932642-87-X) Unarius Acad Sci.
— A Resume of the Unarius Academy of Science, Vol. 1. (Illus.). 1990. 4.95 (0-935097-24-4) Unarius Acad Sci.
— Thirty-Two Earth Worlds Speak to Planet Earth, 3 parts. Vol. IV. (Illus.). 1974. write for info. (0-318-56275-8) Unarius Acad Sci.
— Thirty-Two Earth Worlds Speak to Planet Earth, 3 parts, Pt. 1. (Tesla Speaks Ser.: Vol. IV). (Illus.). 1974. Part 1. 17.95 (0-932642-23-3) Unarius Acad Sci.
— Thirty-Two Earth Worlds Speak to Planet Earth, 3 parts, Pt. 2. (Tesla Speaks Ser.: Vol. IV). (Illus.). 1974. Part 2. 17.95 (0-932642-24-1) Unarius Acad Sci.
— Thirty-Two Earth Worlds Speak to Planet Earth, 3 parts, Pt. 3. (Tesla Speaks Ser.: Vol. IV). (Illus.). 1974. Part 3. 17.95 (0-932642-25-X) Unarius Acad Sci.
— Twenty-Five Planets Speak to Planet Earth. (Tesla Speaks Ser.: Vol. V). (Illus.). 1975. 12.95 (0-932642-26-8); pap. 8.95 (0-932642-45-4) Unarius Acad Sci.
— Whispers of Love on Wings of Light. (Tesla Speaks Ser.: No. 10). (Illus.). 1975. 17.95 (0-932642-33-0); pap. 8.95 (0-932642-44-6) Unarius Acad Sci.
— Your Encounter with Life, Death & Immortality. (Illus.). 1978. pap. 6.95 (0-932642-43-8) Unarius Acad Sci.
Norman, Ruth E. & Spaegal, Vaughn. Who Is the Mona Lisa. 1973. pap. 7.95 (0-932642-18-7) Unarius Acad Sci.
Norman, Ruth E. & Spaegel, Charles. Principles & Practice of Past Life Therapy. 3rd ed. (Illus.). 411p. 1993. 17.95 (0-932642-34-9) Unarius Acad Sci.
— Return to Atlantis, Vol. 1. 2nd ed. (Illus.). 315p. 1992. reprint ed. 24.95 (0-935097-25-2) Unarius Acad Sci.
— Return to Atlantis, Vol. 3, Pt. 1. (Illus.). 300p. (C). 1982. pap. 8.95 (0-932642-53-5) Unarius Acad Sci.
— Return to Atlantis, Vol. 3, Pt. 2. (Illus.). 300p. 1982. pap. text ed. 9.95 (0-932642-74-8) Unarius Acad Sci.
— Return to Atlantis, Vol. 4. 244p. 1987. text ed. 8.95 (0-932642-70-5) Unarius Acad Sci.
Norman, Ruth E & Spaegel, Vaughn. Uriel & the Masters Speak, Vol. I. (Tesla Speaks Ser.: No. 9). (Illus.). 400p. 1978. 10.95 (0-932642-31-4) Unarius Acad Sci.
Norman, Ruth E., ed. see Norman, Ernest L.
Norman, Ruth E., et al. Lemuria Rising. Incl. Vol. I. 1976. pap. 7.95 (0-932642-37-3); Vol. II. 1976. pap. 7.95 (0-685-63052-8); Vol. IV. 1977. pap. 7.95 (0-932642-40-3); Pt. 1. By Their Fruits (Ye Shall Know Them) 1978. pap. 8.95 (0-932642-41-1); Pt. 2. By Their Fruits (Ye Shall Know Them) 1978. pap. 8.95 (0-932642-42-X); Set pap. write for info. (0-318-56272-3) Unarius Acad Sci.
— The Masters Speak, 2 vols. No. 8. (Illus.). 1975. write for info. (0-318-56273-1) Unarius Acad Sci.
— The Masters Speak, 2 vols., 1. (Tesla Speaks Ser.: No. 8). (Illus.). 1975. 17.95 (0-932642-30-6) Unarius Acad Sci.
— The Masters Speak, 2 vols., 2. (Tesla Speaks Ser.: No. 8). (Illus.). 1975. 17.95 (0-932642-29-2) Unarius Acad Sci.
Norman, Sabrina. Original Monologues for African American Actors. 31p. (Orig.). 1995. pap. 7.95 (0-9627515-8-8) Love Child.
Norman, Susan. Export English, 3 cass., Set. 196p. 1988. audio 49.50 (0-88432-190-8, S32535) Audio-Forum.
Norman, Sylva. Flight of the Skylark: The Development of Shelley's Reputation. LC 54-5932. (Illus.). 338p. reprint ed. 96.40 (0-8357-9726-0, 2010996) Bks Demand.
Norman, Sylva, ed. Contemporary Essays: Nineteen Thirty-Three. LC 68-29235. (Essay Index Reprint Ser.). 1977. reprint ed. 19.95 (0-8369-0746-9) Ayer.
Norman, T. R., ed. see Burrows, G. D., et al.
Norman, Trevor R., jt. ed. see Burrows, Graham D.
Norman, V. D., jt. auth. see Dixit, Avinash K.
Norman, Van. Raven - Johnson: Understanding Biology Test Bank. 512p. 1991. pap. 100.00 (0-8016-4692-8) Mosby Yr Bk.
Norman, W. H., tr. see Akutagawa, Ryunosuke.
Norman, W. J. Taking Freedom Too Seriously? An Essay on Analytic & Post-Analytic Political Philosophy. LC 91-9677. (Political Theory & Political Philosophy Ser.). 200p. 1991. 15.00 (0-8153-0137-5) Garland.
Norman, Wallace, jt. auth. see Chadwick, Annie.
***Norman, William A.** L. A. T. A Multiple Murder Story. 1995. 16.95 (0-533-11459-4) Vantage.
Norman, Winifred L. & Patterson, Lily. Lewis Latimer: Scientist. LC 93-185. (Black Americans of Achievement Ser.). (Illus.). (J). (gr. 5 up). 1994. lib. bdg. 18.95 (0-7910-1977-2, Am Art Analog); pap. write for info. (0-7910-1978-0, Am Art Analog) Chelsea Hse.
Normand, Charles E., ed. see London School of Hygiene & Tropical Medicine Second Annual Public Health Forum Staff.
Normand, Eugene, ed. see Maimon, Sam B.
Normand, Jacques, ed. see National Research Council, Institute of Medicine, Committee on Drug Use in the Workplace Staff.
Normand, Tom. Wyndham Lewis: The Artist: Holding the Mirror up to Politics. (Illus.). 230p. (C). 1993. 79.95 (0-521-41054-1) Cambridge U Pr.
Normandale College, English Composition Dept. Staff, ed. see Stephens, Ted.
***Normandin, Michael.** The Adventures of Captain Morgan & Other Stories & Poems. (J). 1995. 8.95 (0-8062-5267-7) Carlton.
Normandy, Elizabeth, ed. Nigeria: A Bibliography for the Study of Politics, Government, Administration, & International Relations. 188p. 1983. pap. 18.50 (0-918456-36-3, Crossroads) African Studies Assn.
Normann, Francine & Gorman, Maureen. How to Create, Prepare & Deliver Business Presentations. 1987. ring bd. 50.95 (1-55645-438-4) Busn Legal Reports.
Normann, Richard. Management for Growth. LC 77-2839. (Wiley-Interscience Publication Ser.). 216p. reprint ed. pap. 61.60 (0-7837-1888-8, 2042089) Bks Demand.
— Service Management: Strategy & Leadership in Service Business. 2nd ed. 185p. 1991. text ed. 49.95 (0-471-92885-2) Wiley.
Normann, Richard & Ramirez, Rafael. Designing Interactive Strategy: From Value Chain to Value Constellation. LC 94-7850. 1994. text ed. 48.95 (0-471-95086-6) Wiley.
Normann, Richard A. Principles of Bioinstrumentation. 562p. 1988. Net. text ed. write for info. (0-471-60514-X) Wiley.

N

Normano, J. F. The Struggle for South America: Economy & Ideology. 1977. lib. bdg. 59.95 (0-8490-3067-6) Gordon Pr.

Normano, Joao F. Brazil: A Study of Economic Types. LC 67-29551. 1935. 24.00 (0-8196-0208-6) Biblo.

— The Japanese in South America: An Introductory Survey with Special Reference to Peru. LC 75-30075. (Institute of Pacific Relations Ser.). reprint ed. 29.50 (0-404-59550-2) AMS Pr.

Normans. Vigeland Sculpture Park. (Illus.). 1991. 15.00 (82-518-8600-7, N600) Vanous.

***Normansell, David E.** The Principles & Practice of Diagnostic Immunology. LC 94-3583. (Analytical Techniques in Clinical Chemistry & Laboratory Medicine Ser.). 1994. write for info. (1-56081-534-5) VCH Pubs.

Normantoe, T., jt. auth. see Klepsch, E.

Norment, Christopher. In the North of Our Lives: A Year in the Wilderness of Northern Canada. LC 89-50873. (Illus.). 264p. 1989. 21.95 (0-89272-269-X) Down East.

Norment, Lisa. Once upon a Time in Junior High. (J). (gr. 5-7). 1994. pap. 2.95 (0-590-45287-8) Scholastic Inc.

Normile, Patti. Visiting the Sick: A Guide for Parish Ministers. 144p. 1992. 6.95 (0-86716-150-7) St Anthony Mess Pr.

Normington, Susan. Napoleon's Children. LC 92-40834. 1993. 34.00 (0-7509-0203-5) A Sutton Pub.

Norminton, E. J., jt. auth. see Kreyszig, E.

Normot, Tod. The Will: A Modern Day Treasure Hunt. 62p. 1982. 6.95 (0-686-35968-2) Tricore Assoc.

Nornang, Ngawang, jt. ed. see Goldstein, Melvyn C.

Nornes, Abe Mark & Yukio, Fukushima, eds. Dialogue of Violence: Filmmaking in World War II's Pacific Theater. LC 92-40162. (Studies in Film & Video). 1994. pap. text ed. 18.00 (3-7186-0562-7) Gordon & Breach.

Noro, K., ed. Occupational Health & Safety in Automation & Robotics. LC 86-22990. 400p. 1987. 125.00 (0-85066-351-2) Taylor & Francis.

— Productivity in Japan. (Ergonomics Special Issue Ser.: Vol. 28, No. 6). 1985. pap. 23.00 (0-85066-986-3) Taylor & Francis.

— Quality Control in Japan. (Ergonomics Special Issue Ser.: Vol. 27, No. 7). 102p. 1984. pap. 20.00 (0-85066-992-8) Taylor & Francis.

Noro, K. & Brown, O., Jr., eds. Human Factors in Organizational Design & Management, No. 3: Proceedings of the 3rd International Symposium, Kyoto, Japan, 18-21 July, 1990. 514p. 1990. 113.00 (0-444-88784-9, North Holland) Elsevier.

Noro, K. & Imada, A., eds. Participatory Ergonomics. 350p. 1991. 90.00 (0-85066-382-2) Taylor & Francis.

Noro, Kageyu, ed. The Science of Seating. 250p. 1994. 99.00 (0-85066-802-6, Pub. by Tay Francis Ltd UK) Taylor & Francis.

Noronha, Leslie De. The Mango & Tamarind Tree. 6.75 (0-89253-633-0) Ind-US Inc.

— Stories. 8.00 (0-89253-630-6); 4.80 (0-89253-631-4) Ind-US Inc.

Noronha, R. P. A Tale Told by An Idiot. 1976. 9.00 (0-88386-933-0) S Asia.

Noronha, Shonan. Careers in Communications. LC 93-25152. (VGM Professional Careers Ser.). 1993. write for info. (0-8442-4182-2, VGM Career Bks); pap. write for info. (0-8442-4183-0, VGM Career Bks) VCH Pubs.

— Opportunities in Technical Communications. LC 93-20679. (Opportunities in...Ser.). 1994. 13.95 (0-8442-4074-5, VGM Career Bks); pap. 10.95 (0-8442-4075-3, VGM Career Bks) NTC Pub Grp.

— Opportunities in Television & Video Careers. (VGM Career Planner Ser.). (Illus.). 160p. 1988. 13.95 (0-8442-6491-1, VGM Career Bks); pap. 10.95 (0-8442-6493-8, VGM Career Bks) NTC Pub Grp.

— Television & Video. (Opportunities in...Ser.). 1989. pap. 7.95 (0-8442-8682-6, VGM Career Bks) NTC Pub Grp.

Noronha, Shonan F. Careers in Communications. 208p. text ed. 16.95 (0-8442-6115-7, VGM Career Bks); pap. 12.95 (0-8442-6116-5, VGM Career Bks) NTC Pub Grp.

Norpoth, Helmut. Confidence Regained: Economics, Mrs. Thatcher, & the British Voter. 250p. (C). 1992. text ed. 42.50 (0-472-10333-4) U of Mich Pr.

Norpoth, Helmut, jt. auth. see Iversen, Gudmund R.

Norpoth, Helmut, et al, eds. Economics & Politics: The Calculus of Support. 326p. (C). 1991. text ed. 44.50 (0-472-10186-2) U of Mich Pr.

***Norquay, Glenda.** Hear the Call: An Anthology of Writings from the Women's Suffrage Campaign. LC 94-43134. 1995. text ed. write for info. (0-7190-3975-4, Pub. by Manchester Univ Pr UK); text ed. write for info. (0-7190-3976-2) St Martin.

Norquist, Enrest. Our Paradise: A GI's War Diary. LC 88-61934. (Illus.). 385p. 1989. 19.95 (0-9606240-9-0) Pearl-Win.

***Norquist, Grover G.** Rock the House. LC 95-60040. (Illus.). 350p. (Orig.). 1995. pap. 9.65 (0-9645786-0-3) VYTIS Pub.

Norquist, Marilyn. Como Leer y Orar los Evangelios. McPhee, John, ed. Diaz, Olimpia, tr. (Handbook of the Bible Ser.). Orig. Title: Hand. 64p. 1980. pap. 3.95 (0-89243-127-X) Liguori Pubns.

— How to Read & Pray the Gospels. (Handbook of the Bible Ser.). 64p. 1978. pap. 3.95 (0-89243-099-0) Liguori Pubns.

— Jesus' Pattern for a Happy Life: The Beatitudes. LC 80-84870. 112p. 1980. pap. 5.95 (0-89243-136-9) Liguori Pubns.

Norquist, Richard. A Typically Atypical Day. 1985. pap. 2.50 (0-87129-184-3, T60) Dramatic Pub.

Norr, A. K., ed. Adaptive, Multilevel, & Hierarchical Computational Strategies. (AMD Ser.: Vol. 157). 157p. 1992. 72.50 (0-7918-1134-4, G00778) ASME.

Norr, Dieter, jt. auth. see De Robertis, Francesco M.

Norr, Martin. The Taxation of Corporations & Shareholders. 226p. 1982. 42.00 (90-6544-015-1) Kluwer Ac.

Norr, Rita & Tumbarello, Audrey. The Literate Puzzler. LC 94-19668. 128p. 1994. pap. 4.95 (0-8069-0706-1) Sterling.

— The Word Game Power Workout. 192p. 1993. pap. 10.95 (0-399-51836-3, Perigee Bks) Berkley Pub.

Norrander, Barbara. Super Tuesday: Regional Politics & Presidential Primaries. LC 91-31263. (Illus.). 248p. 1992. text ed. 29.00 (0-8131-1773-9) U Pr of Ky.

***Norrbo, Bennet, et al.** Oregon Writers 1994 Anthology. 112p. 1993. pap. 9.95 (1-57555-003-2) Cedar Bay Pr.

Norrbo, Bennett. The Pittock Mansion Through the Ages. 1973. pap. 2.00 (0-911518-24-X) Touchstone Oregon.

Norrby, E., ed. Immunochemistry of AIDS. (Chemical Immunology Ser.: Vol. 56). (Illus.). x, 168p. 1993. 149.00 (3-8055-5655-1) S Karger.

***Norrby, E., et al, eds.** Vaccines 94: Modern Approaches to New Vaccines Including Prevention of AIDS. (Illus.). 403p. (C). 1994. pap. 100.00 (0-87969-434-3) Cold Spring Harbor.

Norrby, S. R., ed. New Antiviral Strategies. (Frontiers of Infectious Diseases Ser.). (Illus.). 288p. 1989. pap. text ed. 53.00 (0-443-04166-0) Churchill.

— New Insights into the Clinical Profile of Norfloxacin: Journal: European Urology, Vol. 17, Suppl. 1. (Illus.). iv, 52p. 1990. pap. 16.00 (3-8055-5198-3) S Karger.

***Norregard-Nielsen, Hans E.** The Golden Age of Danish Art: Drawings from the Royal Museum of Fine Arts, Copenhagen. LC 95-3052. (Illus.). 1995. write for info. (0-88397-115-1) Art Srvc Intl.

Norreklit, Lennart. Concepts: Their Nature & Significance for Metaphysics & Epistemology. (Odense Studies in Philosophy: No. 2). 226p. (Orig.). 1973. pap. 23.50 (87-7492-079-0, Pub. by Odense Universitets Forlag DK) Coronet Bks.

Norrell, Robert J. The Alabama Story: State History & Geography. (Illus.). 304p. (J). (gr. 4). 1993. 22.95 (1-882700-00-7) Yellowhammer.

— James Bowron: The Autobiography of a New South Industrialist. LC 91-9847. (Illus.). xxxiv, 320p. (C). 1991. 45.00 (0-8078-1987-5) U of NC Pr.

— A Promising Field: Engineering at Alabama, 1837-1987. 280p. 1990. 24.95 (0-8173-0478-9) U of Ala Pr.

— Reaping the Whirlwind: The Civil Rights Movement in Tuskegee. LC 85-40845. (Illus.). 272p. 1985. 19.95 (0-394-53688-6) Knopf.

— Reaping the Whirlwind: The Civil Rights Movement in Tuskegee. LC 86-40151. 269p. 1986. pap. 10.36 (0-394-74407-1, Vin) Random.

— We Want Jobs! A Story of the Great Depression. LC 92-18082. (Stories of America Ser.). (Illus.). 40p. (J). (gr. 2-5). 1992. lib. bdg. 22.13 (0-8114-7229-9) Raintree Steck-V.

Norrgard, Lee E. & DeMars, Jo. Making End-of-Life Decisions. (Choices & Challenges Ser.). 200p. 1992. lib. bdg. 45.00 (0-87436-613-5) ABC-CLIO.

Norrick, Neal R. Conversational Joking: Forms & Functions of Humor in Everyday Talk. LC 92-19471. 192p. 1993. 29.95 (0-253-34111-6) Ind U Pr.

— How Proverbs Mean: Semantic Studies in English Proverbs. (Trends in Linguistics Ser.: No. 27). xii, 228p. 1985. 65.40 (0-89925-037-8) Mouton.

— Semiotic Principles in Semantic Theory. (Current Issues in Linguistic Theory Ser.: No. 20). xiii, 252p. 1981. 59.00x (90-272-3513-9) Benjamins North Am.

Norrie, Alan, ed. Closure or Critique: New Directions in Legal Theory. (Edinburgh Law & Society Ser.). 256p. 1993. 60.00 (0-7486-0445-6, Pub. by Edinburgh U Pr UK) Col U Pr.

Norrie, Alan W. Law, Ideology & Punishment: Historical Critique of the Liberal Ideal of Criminal Justice. (C). 1990. lib. bdg. 89.00 (0-7923-1013-6) Kluwer Ac.

Norrie, D. H. & Six, H. W., eds. Computer Assisted Learning: Third International Conference, ICCAL '90 Hagen, FRG, June 11-13, 1990 Proceedings. (Lecture Notes in Computer Science Ser.: Vol. 438). vii, 467p. 1990. pap. 45.10 (0-387-52699-4) Spr-Verlag.

Norrie, Ian & Bohm, Dorothy. Walks Around London: Celebration of the Capital. (Illus.). 160p. 1986. pap. 14.95 (0-233-97853-4, Pub. by A Deutsch UK) Trafalgar.

Norrie, Kenneth M. Family Planning & the Law. 220p. 1991. text ed. 59.95 (1-85521-035-5, Pub. by Dartmth Pub UK) Ashgate Pub Co.

Norrington, A. L. Blackwell's Eighteen Seventy-Nine to Nineteen Seventy-Nine. (Illus.). 191p. 1983. 20.00 (0-946344-00-0, Pub. by B H Blackwell UK) NA Blackwell.

Norris. Adventures of Antar: An Early Arab Epic Approaches to Arabic. 1980. 39.95 (0-85668-161-X, Pub. by Aris & Phillips UK) David Brown.

— Angel in the House. 1976. 15.95 (0-89190-301-1) Amereon Ltd.

— Come Back to Me, Beloved. 1976. 15.95 (0-89190-302-X) Amereon Ltd.

— Hands Full of Living. 1976. 15.95 (0-89190-303-8) Amereon Ltd.

— High Holiday. 1976. 15.95 (0-89190-304-6) Amereon Ltd.

— Immune Mechanisms in Cutaneous Disease. (Immunology Ser.: Vol. 46). 848p. 1989. 215.00 (0-8247-7919-3) Dekker.

— Maiden Voyage. 1976. 15.95 (0-89190-305-4) Amereon Ltd.

— McTeague. Collins, Carvel, ed. 343p. (C). 1950. pap. text ed. 15.00 (0-03-009250-7) HB Coll Pubs.

— Obstetric Anesthesia. (Illus.). 600p. 1992. text ed. 95.00 (0-397-51115-9) Lippincott.

— Pilgrimage of Ahmad: Son of the Little Bird of Paradise. 1991. pap. write for info. (0-85668-057-5, Pub. by Aris & Phillips UK) David Brown.

— Tuaregs: Their Islamic Legacy & Its Diffusion in the Sahel. 1975. pap. 35.00 (0-85668-362-0, Pub. by Aris & Phillips UK) David Brown.

— Women & Politics. (Political Pamphleteer Ser.). (C). 1994. text ed. 3.00 (0-673-99779-0) HarpCollege.

Norris & Fanning. Concepts & Strategies for Lifetime Fitness. 298p. 1989. pap. text ed. 21.95 (0-88725-115-3) Hunter Textbks.

Norris & Pratt. Aging & Sociocognitive Development. 1993. pap. write for info. (0-409-89642-X, Pub. by Buttrwrth Can Acad CN) Buttrwrth-Heinemann.

Norris, jt. auth. see Atkins.

Norris, Ann. On the Go. (Illus.). 32p. (J). 1990. 13.95 (0-688-06336-5); lib. bdg. 13.88 (0-688-06337-3) Lothrop.

Norris, Anne & Douglas, Caroline. Driving. (Illus.). 1990. pap. 21.00 (0-85131-368-X, Pub. by J A Allen & Co UK) St Mut.

Norris, Anne, jt. auth. see Pethick, Nancy.

Norris, Anthony C. Computational Chemistry: An Introduction to Numerical Methods. LC 80-41691. 468p. reprint ed. pap. 133.40 (0-7837-4767-5, 2044521) Bks Demand.

Norris, Bill & Norris, Judy. The Table of Remembrance: Communion Meditations. 104p. (Orig.). 1991. pap. text ed. 6.99 (0-89900-372-9) College Pr Pub.

— What the Bible Says about Growing Old. LC 88-70494. (What the Bible Says Ser.). 304p. 1988. text ed. 13.99 (0-89900-258-7) College Pr Pub.

Norris, C. Paul de Man, Deconstruction & the Critique of Aesthetic Ideology. 1988. pap. 14.95 (0-415-90080-8, Routledge NY) Routledge.

Norris, C. C. William Empson & the Philosophy of Literary Criticism. 222p. (C). 1978. text ed. 36.50 (0-485-11175-6, Pub. by Athlone Pr UK) Humanities.

Norris, Carol. OJT Personnel Clerk Resource Materials. 2nd ed. (Gregg Office Job Training Program Ser.). (Illus.). 112p. 1981. text ed. 9.96 (0-07-047225-4) McGraw.

— OJT Personnel Clerk Training Manual. 2nd ed. (Gregg Office Job Training Program Ser.). (Illus.). 56p. (gr. 11-12). 1981. pap. text ed. 7.56 (0-07-047226-2) McGraw.

Norris, Carolyn. In Our House: Story for Young Children in Sign Language. (Illus.). 32p. (Orig.). (J). (ps-3). 1984. 3.95 (0-916708-11-X) Modern Signs.

— Jeans Christmas Stocking. (Illus.). 24p. (Orig.). (J). (ps-4). 1982. pap. 3.25 (0-916708-10-1) Modern Signs.

Norris, Carolyn B. Island of Silence. 4th ed. LC 83-71342. 238p. 1983. pap. 6.00 (0-933076-04-5) Alinda Pr.

— Signs Unseen, Sounds Unheard. 3rd ed. 173p. 1991. 5.00 (0-933076-02-9) Alinda Pr.

Norris, Charles C. Eastern Upland Shooting. deluxe limited ed. (Illus.). 432p. 1989. 75.00 (0-924357-05-3, 11250-B) Countrysport Pr.

— Eastern Upland Shooting. (Illus.). 432p. 1989. reprint ed. 25.00 (0-924357-01-0, 11250-A) Countrysport Pr.

Norris, Charles G. Salt: Or, the Education of Griffith Adams. A Novel. LC 80-25152. (Lost American Fiction Ser.). 394p. 1981. reprint ed. 19.95 (0-8093-1011-2) S Ill U Pr.

Norris, Charles H., et al. Elementary Structural Analysis. 4th ed. 1991. text ed. write for info. (0-07-065933-8) McGraw.

Norris, Charles R., Jr. Family Addictions: A Guide for Surviving Alcohol & Drug Abuse. 144p. (Orig.). 1990. pap. 7.95 (0-929162-15-3) PIA Pr.

Norris, Charles W. & Waibel-Owen, Jeanne B. Know Your Body: A Family Guide to Sexuality & Fertility. LC 82-60666. (Illus.). 96p. (gr. 6 up). 1982. pap. text ed. 5.95 (0-87973-658-5, 658) Our Sunday Visitor.

Norris, Christofer. The Truth about Postmodernism. LC 92-33828. 1993. 49.95 (0-631-18717-0); pap. 19.95 (0-631-18718-9) Blackwell Pubs.

Norris, Christopher. The Contest of Faculties: Deconstruction, Philosophy & Theory. (Orig.). 1985. 35.00 (0-416-39930-4, 9598); pap. 13.95 (0-416-39940-1, 9599) Routledge Chapman & Hall.

— Deconstruction: Theory & Practice. LC 81-22422. 200p. 1982. pap. 13.95 (0-416-32070-8, NO. 3660) Routledge Chapman & Hall.

— Deconstruction: Theory & Practice. rev. ed. (New Accents Ser.). 216p. 1991. pap. 13.95 (0-415-06174-1, A5676) Routledge.

— Deconstruction & the Interests of Theory. LC 88-40546. (Project for Discourse & Theory Ser.: Vol. 4). 256p. (C). 1992. pap. text ed. 14.95x (0-8061-2388-5) U of Okla Pr.

— The Deconstructive Turn: Essays in the Rhetoric of Philosophy. LC 83-22141. 201p. 1984. pap. 12.95 (0-416-36140-4, NO. 4063) Routledge Chapman & Hall.

— Derrida. LC 87-22922. 272p. 1988. pap. 13.95 (0-674-19824-7) HUP.

— For Truth in Criticism. LC 94-16682. 1995. text ed. 69.95 (0-7190-4452-9) St Martin.

— Paul de Man: Deconstruction & the Critique of Aesthetic Ideology. LC 87-31375. 200p. 1988. pap. text ed. 13.95 (0-416-01971-4) Routledge Chapman & Hall.

— Reclaiming the Truth: Contribution to a Critique of Cultural Relativism. 244p. 1995. pap. 12.99 (0-85315-815-0, Pub. by Lawrence & Wishart UK) Humanities.

— Shostakovich: The Man & His Music. LC 82-4172. 235p. 1983. 25.00 (0-7145-2778-5) M Boyars Pubs.

— Spinoza & the Origins of Modern Critical Theory. 332p. (Orig.). (C). 1991. pap. 21.95 (0-631-17558-X) Blackwell Pubs.

— Uncritical Theory: Postmodernism, Intellectuals, & the Gulf War. LC 92-12147. 224p. 1992. 30.00 (0-87023-817-5); pap. 13.95 (0-87023-818-3) U of Mass Pr.

— What's Wrong with Postmodernism: Critical Theory & the Ends of Philosophy. (Parallax). 256p. 1991. text ed. 48.50x (0-8018-4136-4); pap. text ed. 14.95 (0-8018-4137-2) Johns Hopkins.

Norris, Christopher & Mapp, Nigel, eds. William Empson: The Critical Achievement. 330p. (C). 1993. 59.95 (0-521-35386-6) Cambridge U Pr.

Norris, Christopher M. Sports Injuries: Diagnosis & Management for Physiotherapists. LC 92-22841. 1992. pap. 50.00 (0-7506-0156-6) Buttrwrth-Heinemann.

Norris, Chuck. The Secret of Inner Strength. 1989. pap. 4.50 (1-55773-175-6, Charter Bks) Diamond.

— Winning Tournament Karate. Cocoran, John, ed. LC 75-5497. (Japanese Arts Ser.). (Illus.). 1975. pap. text ed. 14.95 (0-89750-016-4, 121) Ohara Pubns.

Norris, Chuck & Hyams, Joe. The Secret of Inner Strength. (Illus.). 256p. 1988. 16.95 (0-316-61191-3) Little.

Norris, Crystal. The Chocolate War: A Study Guide. (Novel-Ties Ser.). (gr. 7-10). 1987. student ed, teacher ed 15.95 (0-88122-108-2) Lrn Links.

— The Dark Is Rising: A Study Guide. (Novel-Ties Ser.). (gr. 7-11). 1988. student ed, teacher ed 15.95 (0-88122-110-4) Lrn Links.

— A Day No Pigs Would Die: A Study Guide. (Novel-Ties Ser.). (gr. 7-11). 1987. student ed, teacher ed 15.95 (0-88122-111-2) Lrn Links.

— Flowers for Algernon: A Study Guide. (Novel-Ties Ser.). (YA). (gr. 9-11). 1985. teacher ed 15.95 (0-88122-115-5) Lrn Links.

— Great Expectations: A Study Guide. (Novel-Ties Ser.). (YA). (gr. 9-12). 1987. teacher ed 15.95 (0-88122-116-3) Lrn Links.

— I Am the Cheese - Study Guide. Friedland, Joyce & Kessler, Rikki, eds. (Novel-Ties Ser.). (YA). (gr. 7-10). 1993. pap. text ed. 15.95 (0-88122-101-5) Lrn Links.

— Julie of the Wolves - Study Guide. Friedland, Joyce & Kessler, Rikki, eds. (Novel-Ties Ser.). (YA). (gr. 6-9). 1993. pap. text ed. 15.95 (0-88122-099-X) Lrn Links.

— Julius Caesar - Study Guide. Friedland, Joyce & Kessler, Rikki, eds. (Novel-Ties Ser.). (YA). (gr. 9-12). 1993. pap. text ed. 15.95 (0-88122-102-3) Lrn Links.

— The Light in the Forest - Study Guide. Friedland, Joyce & Kessler, Rikki, eds. (Novel-Ties Ser.). (YA). (gr. 6-9). 1993. pap. text ed. 15.95 (0-88122-117-1) Lrn Links.

— One Flew over the Cuckoo's Nest - Study Guide. Friedland, Joyce & Kessler, Rikki, eds. (Novel-Ties Ser.). (YA). (gr. 10-12). 1993. pap. text ed. 15.95 (0-88122-121-X) Lrn Links.

— Ordinary People - Study Guide. Friedland, Joyce & Kessler, Rikki, eds. (Novel-Ties Ser.). (YA). (gr. 9-12). 1993. pap. text ed. 15.95 (0-88122-122-8) Lrn Links.

— The Picture of Dorian Gray - Study Guide. Friedland, Joyce & Kessler, Rikki, eds. (Novel-Ties Ser.). (YA). (gr. 10-12). 1993. pap. text ed. 15.95 (0-88122-123-6) Lrn Links.

— Shane - Study Guide. Friedland, Joyce & Kessler, Rikki, eds. (Novel-Ties Ser.). (YA). (gr. 7-10). 1993. pap. text ed. 15.95 (0-88122-129-5) Lrn Links.

Norris, Curt. Little-Known Mysteries of New England: True Crime Stories from the Past. Johnson, Doris M., ed. LC 92-70661. (Illus.). 160p. (Orig.). 1992. pap. 10.00 (0-9628738-1-0) Jones Riv Pr.

Norris, D. E., et al. Microcomputers in Clinical Practice. LC 84-13020. 159p. 1985. pap. text ed. 44.95 (0-471-90373-6, A R Liss) Wiley.

Norris, D. M., ed. Perception of Behavioral Chemicals. 328p. 1982. 172.00 (0-444-80347-5) Elsevier.

Norris, Dan. Violence Against Social Workers. 144p. 1990. 42.50 (1-85302-041-9, Pub. by J Kingsley Pubs UK) Taylor & Francis.

Norris, David. A Church Planter's Dream. 200p. (Orig.). 1992. pap. 6.95 (1-56722-006-1) Word Aflame.

— Teach Yourself Serbo-Croat. (ENG & SER.). 1993. pap. 18.95 (0-7859-1062-X, 0-340-568038); pap. 29.95 (0-7859-1063-8, 0-340-568046) Fr & Eur.

Norris, David A. Plan to Be Spiritual: The Wonderful Blessing of God's Direction & God's Power. (Illus.). 31p. 1987. pap. 1.95 (0-943177-05-7) Heartland Pr.

Norris, David O. Vertebrate Endocrinology. 2nd ed. LC 84-19425. 517p. reprint ed. pap. 147.40 (0-7837-2734-8, 2043114) Bks Demand.

Norris, David O. & Jones, Richard E., eds. Hormones & Reproduction in Fishes, Amphibians & Reptiles. LC 87-6944. 590p. 1987. 120.00 (0-306-42551-3, Plenum Pr) Plenum.

Norris, Davidson, jt. auth. see Joseph, Peter T.

Norris, Dean M. Advanced Scale Improvisation. 76p. 1991. 14.95 (0-9631368-0-1) Devin Pubns.

— Guitar Chord Studies. (Illus.). 63p. 1992. pap. write for info. (0-9631368-1-X) Devin Pubns.

Norris, Donald. Microcomputers & Local Government. 3rd ed. 130p. (Orig.). 1989. pap. text ed. 24.00 (0-87326-925-X) Intl City-Cnty Mgt.

***Norris, Donald & American Society of Association Executives Staff.** Getting Your Association Hooked on Quality. 100p. 1993. pap. 66.00 (0-88034-074-6) Am Soc Assn Execs.

Norris, Donald F. Microcomputers & Local Government: A Handbook (Instructor's Manual) 174p. (Orig.). 1984. pap. 12.50 (1-55719-012-7) U NE CPAR.

— Microcomputers & Local Government: A Handbook (Participant's Manual) 108p. (Orig.). 1984. pap. 8.00 (1-55719-028-3) U NE CPAR.

Norris, Donald F. & DiMartino, David R. Computers & Small Local Governments: A Survey of Computing in the Plains & Mountain States. 62p. (Orig.). 1983. pap. 4.50 (1-55719-029-1) U NE CPAR.

***Norris, Donald F. & Thompson, Lyke.** The Politics of Welfare Reform. 215p. 1995. text ed. 49.95 (0-8039-5700-9); pap. text ed. 24.95 (0-8039-5701-7) Sage.

N

Norris, Donald M. Market-Driven Management: Lessons Learned from 20 Successful Associations. 128p. (Orig.). 1990. pap. 45.00 (*0-88034-044-4*) Am Soc Assn Execs.

***Norris, Donald M. & Lofton, Marie C.** Winning with Diversity: A Practical Handbook for Creating Inclusive Meetings Events, & Organizations. LC 94-43566. 1994. write for info. (*0-88034-093-2*) Am Soc Assn Execs.

Norris, Dorothy E. & Shiner, Reva P. Keynotes to Modern Dance. LC 69-15426. 237p. (C). reprint ed. 67.60 (*0-8357-9053-3*, 2017316) Bks Demand.

Norris, Dorry B. The Sage Cottage Herb Garden Cookbook: Celebrations, Recipes, & Herb Gardening Tips for Every Month of the Year. LC 91-4193. (Illus.). 320p. (Orig.). 1991. pap. 14.95 (*0-87106-239-9*) Globe Pequot.
— The Sage Cottage Herb Garden Cookbook: Celebrations, Recipes, & Herb Gardening Tips for Every Month of the Year. 2nd ed. LC 95-15669. 1995. write for info. (*1-56440-727-6*) Globe Pequot.

Norris, Edwin, ed. Ancient Cornish Drama, 2 vols. LC 68-56530. 1972. reprint ed. Set. 60.95 (*0-405-08819-1*, Pub. by Blom Pubns UK) Ayer.
— Ancient Cornish Drama, 2 vols., 1. LC 68-56530. 1972. reprint ed. 30.95 (*0-405-08820-5*, Pub. by Blom Pubns UK) Ayer.
— Ancient Cornish Drama, 2 vols., 2. LC 68-56530. 1972. reprint ed. 30.95 (*0-405-08821-3*, Pub. by Blom Pubns UK) Ayer.

Norris, Emilie, jt. auth. see Nisbet, Peter.

Norris, F. Responsibilities of the Novelist & Other Literary Essays. LC 68-26364. (Studies in Fiction: No. 34). 1969. reprint ed. lib. bdg. 75.00 (*0-8383-0269-6*) M S G Haskell Hse.

Norris, Frank. The Argonaut Manuscript: Limited Edition of Frank Norris's Works, 10 vols., Set. (BCL1-PS American Literature Ser.). 1992. reprint ed. lib. bdg. 750.00 (*0-7812-6806-0*) Rprt Serv.
— Blix. LC 74-95150. reprint ed. 37.50 (*0-404-04787-4*) AMS Pr.
— Blix. (BCL1-PS American Literature Ser.). 339p. 1992. reprint ed. lib. bdg. 89.00 (*0-7812-6807-9*) Rprt Serv.
— Deal in Wheat. LC 77-173797. (Illus.). reprint ed. 21.50 (*0-404-04788-2*) AMS Pr.
— A Deal in Wheat: And Other Stories of the New & Old West. (BCL1-PS American Literature Ser.). 272p. 1992. reprint ed. lib. bdg. 79.00 (*0-7812-6808-7*) Rprt Serv.
— Deal in Wheat & Other Stories of the New & Old West. LC 74-131788. (Illus.). 1971. reprint ed. 16.00 (*0-403-00675-9*) Scholarly.
— Frank Norris of the Wave Stories & Sketches from the San Francisco. 1988. reprint ed. lib. bdg. 59.00 (*0-7812-0040-7*) Rprt Serv.
— Man's Woman. LC 71-108125. 1970. reprint ed. 35.00 (*0-404-04789-0*) AMS Pr.
— A Man's Woman. (BCL1-PS American Literature Ser.). 286p. 1992. reprint ed. lib. bdg. 79.00 (*0-7812-6810-9*) Rprt Serv.
— McTeague. 1976. lib. bdg. 18.95 (*0-89968-071-2*, Lghtyr Pr) Buccaneer Bks.
— McTeague. 1964. pap. 4.95 (*0-451-52421-7*, Sig Classics) NAL-Dutton.
— McTeague. 1989. pap. 3.95 (*0-451-52281-8*) NAL-Dutton.
— McTeague. Loving, Jerome, ed. & intro. by. (World's Classics Ser.). 496p. 1996. pap. 9.95 (*0-19-282356-6*) OUP.
— McTeague. Pizer, Donald, ed. LC 77-479. (Critical Editions Ser.). (C). 1978. pap. text ed. 8.95 (*0-393-09136-8*) Norton.
— McTeague: A Story of California. LC 72-184736. 1971. lib. bdg. 20.00 (*0-8376-0406-0*) Bentley.
— McTeague: A Story of San Francisco. Starr, Kevin, ed. (American Library). 1982. pap. 8.95 (*0-14-039017-0*, Penguin Classics) Viking Penguin.
— McTeague: A Story of San Francisco. 496p. 1994. 10.95 (*0-14-018769-3*, Penguin Classics) Viking Penguin.
— McTeague: A Story of San Francisco. (BCL1-PS American Literature Ser.). 442p. 1992. reprint ed. lib. bdg. 99.00 (*0-7812-6809-5*) Rprt Serv.
— Moran of the Lady Letty: A Story of Adventure Off the California Coast. LC 70-104533. 297p. 1979. reprint ed. lib. bdg. 11.50 (*0-8398-1351-1*) Irvington.
— Moran of the Lady Letty: A Story of Adventure off the California Coast. (BCL1-PS American Literature Ser.). 293p. 1992. reprint ed. lib. bdg. 79.00 (*0-7812-6811-7*); reprint ed. pap. text ed. 59.00 (*0-685-51393-9*) Rprt Serv.
— Moran of the Lady Letty, a Story of Adventure off the California Coast. LC 75-144665. reprint ed. 29.50 (*0-404-04790-4*) AMS Pr.
— Novels & Essays. Pizer, Donald, ed. Incl. Vandover & the Brute. LC 85-23133. 1986. (*0-318-62876-7*); McTeague. LC 85-23133. 1986. (*0-318-62877-5*); Octopus. LC 85-23133. 1986. (*0-318-62878-3*); LC 85-23133. 1232p. 1986. 27.50 (*0-940450-40-2*) Library of America.
— Octopus. (Airmont Classics Ser.). (J). (gr. 11 up). 1968. pap. 1.95 (*0-8049-0179-1*, CL-179) Airmont.
— Octopus. 1964. pap. 3.50 (*0-451-51711-3*, CE1711, Sig Classics) NAL-Dutton.
— The Octopus. 1976. lib. bdg. 25.95 (*0-89968-070-4*, Lghtyr Pr) Buccaneer Bks.
— The Octopus. 688p. 1986. pap. 9.95 (*0-14-039040-5*, Penguin Classics) Viking Penguin.
— The Octopus: A Story of California. 496p. 1994. 10.95 (*0-14-018770-7*, Penguin Classics) Viking Penguin.
— The Octopus: A Story of California. (BCL1-PS American Literature Ser.). 361p. 1992. reprint ed. lib. bdg. 89.00 (*0-7812-6812-5*) Rprt Serv.
— The Pit. 1976. lib. bdg. 19.95 (*0-89968-069-0*, Lghtyr Pr) Buccaneer Bks.
— The Pit: A Story of Chicago. 496p. 1994. 10.95 (*0-14-018758-8*, Penguin Classics) Viking Penguin.
— The Pit: A Story of Chicago. (BCL1-PS American Literature Ser.). 421p. 1992. reprint ed. lib. bdg. 99.00 (*0-7812-6813-3*) Rprt Serv.
— The Pit: A Story of Chicago. LC 70-184738. 432p. 1971. reprint ed. lib. bdg. 22.00 (*0-8376-0407-9*) Bentley.
— Vandover & the Brute. (BCL1-PS American Literature Ser.). 354p. 1992. reprint ed. lib. bdg. 89.00 (*0-7812-6814-1*) Rprt Serv.

Norris, Frederick W. The Apostolic Faith: Protestants & Roman Catholics. 206p. (Orig.). 1992. pap. text ed. 14.95 (*0-8146-5029-5*) Liturgical Pr.

Norris, G. M., jt. ed. see Townsend, Frank C.

Norris, Geoffrey. Rachmaninoff. (Master Musicians Ser.). 194p. 1994. text ed. 30.00 (*0-02-870685-4*) Schirmer Bks.

Norris, Geoffrey, jt. auth. see Threltall, Robert.

Norris, George W. Fighting Liberal: The Autobiography of George W. Norris. LC 83-45829. reprint ed. 36.50 (*0-404-20194-6*) AMS Pr.
— Fighting Liberal: The Autobiography of George W. Norris. LC 91-3928. (Illus.). xxx, 419p. 1992. reprint ed. pap. 14.95 (*0-8032-8365-2*, Bison Books) U of Nebr Pr.
— Fighting Liberal, the Autobiography of George W. Norris. (History - United States Ser.). 419p. 1993. reprint ed. lib. bdg. 99.00 (*0-7812-4807-8*) Rprt Serv.

***Norris, Gloria, ed.** The Seasons of Women: An Anthology. 480p. 1995. 25.00 (*0-393-03860-2*) Norton.

Norris, Gregory L. Ghost Kisses: Gothic Gay Romance Stories. 160p. (Orig.). 1994. pap. 15.95 (*0-943595-52-5*) Leyland Pubns.

Norris, Gunilla. Becoming Bread: Meditations on Loving & Transformation. LC 92-19259. (Illus.). 96p. 1993. 15.00 (*0-517-59168-5*, Bell Tower) Crown Pub Group.
— Being Home: A Book of Meditations. (Illus.). 96p. 1991. 16.00 (*0-517-58159-0*, Bell Tower) Crown Pub Group.
— Journeying in Place: Reflections from a Country Garden. LC 93-51088. 1994. 16.00 (*0-517-59762-4*, Bell Tower) Crown Pub Group.
— Learning from the Angel. LC 85-80140. 62p. (Orig.). (YA). (gr. 9-12). 1985. per. 5.00 (*0-916418-59-6*) Lotus.
— Sharing Silence: Meditation Practices & Mindful Living. LC 92-44971. 1993. 13.00 (*0-517-59506-0*, Bell Tower) Crown Pub Group.

Norris, H. T. Arab Conquest of the Western Sahara. 309p. 1986. 42.00 (*0-86685-596-3*) Intl Bk Ctr.
— Berbers in Arabic Literature. 280p. 1982. 42.00 (*0-86685-595-5*) Intl Bk Ctr.
— Berbers in Arabic Literature. 1982. 42.00 (*0-86685-594-7*) Intl Bk Ctr.
— Sufi Mystics of the Niger Desert: Sidi Mahmud & the Hermits of Air. (Illus.). 216p. 1990. 59.00 (*0-19-826538-7*) OUP.

Norris, H. Thomas, ed. Pathology of the Colon, Small Intestine & Anus. 2nd ed. (Contemporary Issues in Surgical Pathology Ser.: Vol. 17). (Illus.). 414p. 1991. text ed. 98.00 (*0-443-08729-6*) Churchill.

Norris, Harold. You Are This Nation. LC 75-27812. 160p. 1976. 7.50 (*0-8187-0020-3*) Harlo Press.

Norris, Harry. Accounting Theory: An Outline of Its Structure with a New Introduction by the Author. Brief, Richard P., ed. LC 80-1512. (Dimensions of Accounting Theory & Practice Ser.). 1980. reprint ed. lib. bdg. 17.95 (*0-405-13537-8*) Ayer.
— Islam in the Balkans: Religion & Society between Europe & the Arab World. LC 93-1637. 1993. 39.95 (*0-87249-977-4*) U of SC Pr.

Norris, Helen. Burning Glass, Stories. LC 91-10557. 192p. 1992. 19.95 (*0-8071-1790-0*) La State U Pr.
— The Christmas Wife: Stories. LC 84-24080. (Illinois Short Fiction Ser.). 144p. 1988. pap. 9.95 (*0-252-06041-5*) U of Ill Pr.
— Walk with the Sickle Moon. Black, Hillel, ed. 176p. 1989. 15.95 (*1-55972-001-8*, Birch Ln Pr) Carol Pub Group.

Norris, Henry H. The Principles of the Jesuits: Developed in a Collection of Extracts from Their Own Authors to Which Are Prefixed a Brief Account of the Origin of the Order & a Sketch of Its Institute. 300p. 1992. pap. 21.00 (*1-56459-292-8*) Kessinger Pub.

Norris, Hoke, ed. We Dissent. LC 73-6210. 211p. 1973. reprint ed. text ed. 55.00 (*0-8371-6889-9*, NOWD, Greenwood Pr) Greenwood.

Norris, J. R., et al, eds. Techniques for Mycorrhizal Research. (Methods in Microbiology Ser.: Vols. 23 & 24). (Illus.). 960p. 1994. 59.95 (*0-12-521490-1*) Acad Pr.

Norris, J. W. & Hachinski, V. C., eds. Prevention of Stroke. (Illus.). 280p. 1991. 108.00 (*0-387-97442-3*) Spr-Verlag.

Norris, Jack. Voyager - the World Flight: The Official Log, Flight Analysis & Narrative Explanation of the Record Around the World Flight of the Voyager Aircraft. LC 88-90609. (Illus.). 72p. (Orig.). 1988. pap. 12.95 (*0-9620239-0-6*) J Norris.

Norris, James. Aladdin & the Wonderful Lamp. (J). 1940. 5.00 (*0-87602-102-X*) Anchorage.
— Robin Hood. (J). (gr. 1-9). 1952. 5.00 (*0-87602-191-7*) Anchorage.

Norris, James D. Advertising. 4th ed. 496p. (C). 1989. pap. text ed. write for info. (*0-13-016056-3*) P-H.
— Advertising & the Transformation of American Society, 1865-1920. LC 90-2760. 224p. 1990. text ed. 45.00 (*0-313-26801-0*, Greenwood Pr) Greenwood.
— R. G. Dun & Co., Eighteen Forty-One to Nineteen Hundred: The Development of Credit-Reporting in the Nineteenth Century. LC 77-95359. (Contributions in Economics & Economic History Ser.: No. 20). (Illus.). 206p. 1978. text ed. 55.00 (*0-313-20326-1*, NDC/) Greenwood.

Norris, James D. & Shaffer, Arthur H., eds. Politics & Patronage in the Gilded Age: The Correspondence of James A. Garfield & Charles E. Henry. LC 70-629850. (Illus.). 304p. 1970. 15.00 (*0-87020-107-7*) State Hist Soc Wis.

Norris, James R., jt. auth. see Deisenhofer, Johann.

Norris, James S. Selling-the How & Why: A Comprehensive Introduction to Salesmanship. (Illus.). 304p. (C). 1982. pap. text ed. write for info. (*0-13-805986-1*) P-H.

Norris, Jane, ed. Daughters of the Elderly: Building Partnerships in Caregiving. LC 87-46246. 236p. (Orig.). 1988. 29.95 (*0-253-31612-X*); pap. 9.95 (*0-253-20484-4*, MB-484) Ind U Pr.

Norris, Jane E. & Norris, Lee G. Written in Water: The Life of Benjamin Harrison Eaton. LC 90-9497. (Illus.). 311p. (C). 1990. text ed. 29.95 (*0-8040-0934-1*) Swallow.

Norris, Janet & Hoffman, Paul. Whole Language Intervention for School-Age Children. LC 92-40679. (School-Age Children Ser.). (Illus.). 361p. (Orig.). (C). 1993. pap. text ed. 45.00 (*1-56593-070-3*) Singular Publishing.

***Norris, Jeffrey A.** Corporate Affirmative Action Practices & the Civil Rights Act of 1991. 35p. 1992. pap. 10.00 (*0-614-06153-9*, 2038-PP-4040) EPF.

***Norris, Jeffrey A. & Perkins, Salvador T.** Developing Effective Affirmative Action Plans. 5th ed. 1995. 125.00 (*0-916559-46-7*, 2017-TM-4045) EPF.

Norris, Jeffrey A. & Shershin, Michael J., Jr. How to Take a Case Before the NLRB. 6th ed. LC 92-16017. 923p. 1992. text ed. 138.00 (*0-87179-750-X*, 0750) BNA.

Norris, Jeffrey A., jt. auth. see Holmes, William F.

Norris, Jeffrey A., jt. auth. see Williams, Robert E.

Norris, Jeremy. The Russian Piano Concerto, Vol. I: The Nineteenth Century. LC 93-11565. (Russian Music Studies). 1994. 35.00 (*0-253-34112-4*) Ind U Pr.

Norris, Jerrie. Presenting Rosa Guy. (United States Authors Ser.: No. 543). 112p. 1988. text ed. 20.95 (*0-8057-8207-9*, TUSAS 543, Twayne) Macmillan.

Norris, Jim. Historical Santa Ynez Valley Coloring Book. 35p. 1989. pap. 6.00 (*0-933380-49-6*) Olive Pr Pubns.
— The Ladies Aid of Santa Ynez: A Cook Book, 1926. Norris, Lynne, ed. 102p. 1983. pap. 5.95 (*0-933380-26-7*) Olive Pr Pubns.
— Manzaha School: A One Room Rural School. (Illus.). 60p. (Orig.). 1995. pap. 5.00 (*0-933380-04-6*) Olive Pr Pubns.

***Norris, Jim & Norris, Lynne.** History of Zaca Lake: La Reata No. 12: Santa Barbara Canal of the Westerners. LC 95-10436. (Reata Ser.: No. 12). (Illus.). xvi, 192p. (Orig.). 1994. pap. 22.00 (*0-933380-09-7*) Olive Pr Pubns.
— Urho Saari: Olympian. LC 88-19538. (Illus.). 200p. (Orig.). 1988. 25.00 (*0-933380-35-6*) Olive Pr Pubns.

Norris, Joan, ed. see Berger, Suzanne E.

Norris, Joan, et al. Psychiatric Mental Health Nursing. 1987. text ed. 47.00 (*0-8273-4324-8*) Delmar.

Norris, Joan, et al, eds. Mental Health Psychiatric Nursing: A Continuum of Care. 1987. teacher ed, pap. text ed. 12.00 (*0-8273-4325-6*); 12.00 (*0-8273-4326-4*) Delmar.

Norris, Joan D. & Forsberg, Barbara. New England. LC 93-49006. (American Food Library). (J). 1994. write for info. (*0-86625-510-9*) Rourke Pubns.

Norris, Joan E. Among Generations: The Cycle of Adult Relationships. LC 93-5972. (C). 1995. text ed. write for info. (*0-7167-2206-2*); pap. text ed. write for info. (*0-7167-2207-0*) W H Freeman.

Norris, Joan E., jt. auth. see Pratt, Michael W.

Norris, Joann, jt. auth. see Norris, John.

Norris, Joel. Arthur Shawcross: The Genesee River Killer. 1992. mass mkt. 4.99 (*1-55817-578-4*, Pinnacle NY); audio 5.99 (*1-55817-592-X*, Pinnacle NY) Windsor NY.
— Henry Lee Lucas. 1991. mass mkt. 5.95 (*0-8217-3564-0*) Zebra.
— Henry Lee Lucas Shocking True. 1991. mass mkt. 4.95 (*0-8217-3530-6*) Zebra.
— Horn of the Goat. 1995. mass mkt. 5.50 (*0-671-79515-5*) PB.
— Jeffrey Dahmer. (Illus.). 320p. 1992. mass mkt. 4.99 (*1-55817-661-6*, Pinnacle NY) Windsor NY.
— Serial Killers: The Growing Menace. 1989. mass mkt. 10.00 (*0-385-26328-7*, Anchor NY) Doubleday.

Norris, John. A Collection of Miscellanies. Wellek, Rene, ed. LC 75-11242. (British Philosophers & Theologians of the 17th & 18th Centuries Ser.). 1978. reprint ed. lib. bdg. 20.00 (*0-8240-1794-3*) Garland.
— An Essay Towards the Theory of the Ideal or Intelligible World, 2 vols. in 1. (Lockeana Ser.). xvi, 1026p. 1974. reprint ed. 154.70 (*3-487-05223-7*, Pub. by Georg Olms GW) Lubrecht & Cramer.

Norris, John & Norris, Joann. Amusement Parks: An American Guidebook. 2nd ed. LC 93-27805. 168p. 1994. pap. 24.95 (*0-89950-789-1*) McFarland & Co.
— The Historic Railroad: A Guide to Museums, Depots & Excursions in the U. S. 200p. 1995. pap. 28.50 (*0-7864-0040-4*) McFarland & Co.

Norris, John R., ed. Methods in Microbiology, Vol. 18. (Serial Publication Ser.). 1985. text ed. 140.00 (*0-12-521518-5*) Acad Pr.

Norris, John R. & Bergan, T. Methods in Microbiology, Vol. 13. LC 68-57745. 1980. text ed. 187.00 (*0-12-521513-4*) Acad Pr.

Norris, John R. & Bergen, T., eds. Methods in Microbiology, Vol. 11. 1979. text ed. 187.00 (*0-12-521511-8*) Acad Pr.

Norris, John R. & Pettipher, G. L., eds. Essays in Agricultural & Food Microbiology. LC 87-2138. 448p. 1987. text ed. 162.95 (*0-471-90987-4*) Wiley.

Norris, John R. & Ribbons, D. W., eds. Methods in Microbiology, Vol. 12. 1979. text ed. 187.00 (*0-12-521512-6*) Acad Pr.

Norris, John R., jt. ed. see Mayer, Frank.

Norris, John R., et al. Methods in Microbiology, 14. 1984. text ed. 140.00 (*0-12-521514-2*) Acad Pr.
— Methods in Microbiology, 15. 1984. text ed. 140.00 (*0-12-521515-0*) Acad Pr.
— Methods in Microbiology, 16. 1985. text ed. 140.00 (*0-12-521516-9*) Acad Pr.

Norris, John R., et al, eds. Methods in Microbiology, Vol. 23: Techniques for the Study of Mycorrhiza. (Illus.). 480p. 1991. text ed. 116.00 (*0-12-521523-1*) Acad Pr.
— Methods in Microbiology, Vol. 24: Techniques for the Study of Mycorrhiza. (Illus.). 450p. 1992. text ed. 110.00 (*0-12-521524-X*) Acad Pr.

Norris, John W., jt. auth. see Hachinski, Vladimir.

Norris, Johnny. Blues Solos for Acoustic Guitar. (Illus.). 1993. pap. 15.95 (*0-7119-2789-8*) Music Sales.
— Super Solos for Acoustic Guitar. (Illus.). 56p. 1989. pap. 15.95 (*0-685-65799-X*, AM75094) Music Sales.

Norris, Joseph E. The Ministry to the Divorced. (Ministry Ser.). 64p. 1990. 1.95 (*0-8146-1923-1*) Liturgical Pr.

Norris, Joye A. & Kennington, Paddy A. Developing Literacy Programs for Homeless Adults. 128p. (Orig.). (C). 1992. 14.50 (*0-89464-679-6*); pap. 10.50 (*0-89464-794-6*) Krieger.

Norris, Judy, jt. auth. see Norris, Bill.

Norris, K. R., jt. auth. see Waterhouse, D. F.

Norris, Kathleen. Baker's Dozen. LC 71-130068. (Short Story Index Reprint Ser.). 1977. 20.95 (*0-8369-3649-3*) Ayer.
— Dakota: A Spiritual Geography. 224p. 1994. pap. 9.95 (*0-395-71091-X*) HM.
— Dakota: A Spiritual Geography. LC 92-30820. 192p. 1993. 19.95 (*0-395-63320-6*) Ticknor & Fields.
— Dakota: A Spiritual Geography. braille ed. 326p. 1994. text ed. 26.08 (*1-56956-414-0*, BR9316) W A T Braille.
— Little Girls in Church. LC 94-44508. (Pitt Poetry Ser.). 88p. 1995. 24.95 (*0-8229-3875-8*) U of Pittsburgh Pr.
— Little Girls in Church. 1995. pap. text ed. (*0-8229-5556-3*) U of Pittsburgh Pr.
— Margaret Yorke. reprint ed. lib. bdg. 15.95 (*0-89190-307-0*, Rivercity Pr) Amereon Ltd.
— Mother. reprint ed. lib. bdg. 15.95 (*0-89190-308-9*, Rivercity Pr) Amereon Ltd.
— Mother, a Story. LC 70-137319. reprint ed. 27.50 (*0-404-04792-0*) AMS Pr.
— Mystery House. reprint ed. lib. bdg. 15.95 (*0-89190-309-7*, Rivercity Pr) Amereon Ltd.
— The Year of Common Things. (Chapbook Ser.: No. 3). 28p. (Orig.). 1988. pap. 4.00 (*0-933573-10-3*) Wayland Pr.

***Norris, Kathleen, ed.** Leaving New York: A Collection. 180p. 1995. 22.00 (*1-886913-00-5*) Hungry Mind.

Norris, Ken. Alphabet of Desire. 70p. (C). 1991. pap. 12.00 (*1-55022-148-5*, Pub. by ECW Press CN) Genl Dist Srvs.
— Autokinesis. 1980. pap. 3.50 (*0-916696-12-X*) Cross Country.
— The Little Magazine in Canada, 1925-80. 220p. (C). 1984. pap. text ed. 15.00 (*0-920802-53-2*, Pub. by ECW Press CN) Genl Dist Srvs.
— Report on the Second Half of the Twentieth Century. 1977. pap. 1.50 (*0-916696-05-7*) Cross Country.
— Under the Skin. 24p. 1976. pap. 1.00 (*0-916696-00-6*) Cross Country.

Norris, Kenneth E. Winning at Work: The Road to Career Success. 126p. (Orig.). 1987. pap. 14.95 (*0-8306-3077-5*, 30077, Liberty Hse) TAB Bks.

Norris, Kenneth S. Dolphin Days: My Life & Times with the Spinners. 1991. 21.95 (*0-393-02945-X*) Norton.
— Dolphin Days: The Life & Times of the Spinner Dolphin. (Illus.). 336p. 1993. reprint ed. pap. 10.00 (*0-380-71965-7*) Avon.
— The Hawaiian Spinner Dolphin. LC 93-38911. 1994. 40.00 (*0-520-08208-7*) U CA Pr.
— The Porpoise Watcher. LC 74-1329. (Illus.). 250p. 1974. 7.95 (*0-393-06385-2*) Norton.

Norris, Kenneth S., jt. ed. see Pryor, Karen.

Norris, Kerstin. Say It in Swedish. LC 72-94755. 1979. pap. 3.50 (*0-486-20812-5*) Dover.

Norris, Lee G., jt. auth. see Norris, Jane E.

Norris, Leslie. Islands off Maine. deluxe ed. (Illus.). 1977. boxed 75.00 (*0-930954-16-5*) Tidal Pr.
— Selected Poems. 1986. pap. 11.95 (*0-907476-60-0*, Pub. by Poetry Wales Pr UK) Dufour.

Norris, Leslie, tr. Rilke's Duino Elegies. (Studies in German Literature, Linguistics & Culture: Vol. 65). (Illus.). 130p. 1993. 49.00 (*1-879751-01-1*) Camden Hse.

Norris, Leslie & Keele, Alan, trs. The Sonnets to Orpheus by Rainer Maria Rilke. LC 88-63602. (Studies in German Literature, Linguistics & Culture: Vol. 42). (Illus.). 88p. (Orig.). (GER.). 1989. 29.95 (*0-938100-65-3*); pap. 12.95 (*0-938100-66-1*) Camden Hse.

Norris, Lynne. Be Careful What You Dream (It Might Come True) LC 84-29619. 200p. (Orig.). 1985. pap. 7.95 (*0-933380-43-7*) Olive Pr Pubns.
— Can a Woman Over Forty? LC 79-12587. 1979. 10.95 (*0-933380-41-0*); pap. 5.95 (*0-933380-47-X*) Olive Pr Pubns.

Norris, Lynne, ed. Smut: American Sex Slang: Over Four Thousand Five Hundred Entries. LC 92-26396. (Illus.). 254p. 1993. 12.00 (*0-933380-22-4*); lib. bdg. 14.00 (*0-933380-23-2*) Olive Pr Pubns.

Norris, Lynne, ed. see Norris, Jim.

Norris, Lynne, jt. auth. see Norris, Jim.

Norris, M. K. & House, Mary A. Organ & Tissue Transplantation: Nursing Care from Procurement Through Rehabilitation. LC 90-14141. 346p. (C). 1991. 39.95 (*0-8036-6587-3*) Davis Co.

Norris, M. W. Local Government in Peninsular Malaysia. 132p. 1980. text ed. 43.95 (*0-566-00283-3*) Ashgate Pub Co.

Norris, Malcolm W. Monumental Brasses: Monumental Brasses. (Illus.). 1987. 79.00 (*0-85115-486-7*) Boydell & Brewer.

Norris, Margaret. Integration of Special Hospital Patients into the Community. LC 84-13733. 180p. 1984. text ed. 63.95 (*0-566-00728-2*) Ashgate Pub Co.

Norris, Margot. Beasts of the Modern Imagination: Darwin, Nietzsche, Kafka, Ernst & Lawrence. LC 84-21320. (Illus.). 279p. reprint ed. pap. 79.60 (*0-7837-4778-0*, 2044533) Bks Demand.

— The Decentered Universe of Finnegans Wake: A Structuralist Analysis. LC 76-25507. 159p. reprint ed. pap. 45.40 (*0-8357-8089-9*, 2034116) Bks Demand.

— Joyce's Web: The Social Unraveling of Modernism. LC 92-15209. (Literary Modernism Ser.). 255p. 1992. 35.00 (*0-292-76537-1*) U of Tex Pr.

Norris, Mark & Rigby, Peter. Software Engineering Explained. 208p. 1992. text ed. 59.95 (*0-471-92950-6*) Wiley.

Norris, Mark, et al. The Healthy Software Project: A Guide to Successful Development & Management. LC 93-10573. 184p. 1994. text ed. 52.95 (*0-471-94042-9*) Wiley.

Norris, Martin J. The Law of Maritime Personal Injuries, 2 vols., Set. 4th ed. LC 90-61399. 1990. 215.00 (*0-685-59891-8*) Clark Boardman Callaghan.

— Law of Seamen, 3 vols., Set. 4th ed. LC 84-52821. 1985. 370.00 (*0-685-59890-X*) Clark Boardman Callaghan.

***Norris, Miles.** Cheffy Baby's Low Fat Gourmet Secrets: Cut the Fat, Not the Flavor. Chaney, Linda, ed. 120p. (Orig.). 1995. pap. text ed. write for info. (*0-9644597-0-1*); pap. text ed., vhs write for info. (*0-9645697-2-8*) Madison Direct.

Norris, Miriam & Spaulding, Patricia J. Blindness in Children. LC 57-6983. 195p. reprint ed. pap. 55.60 (*0-8357-7322-1*, 2020139) Bks Demand.

Norris, Neal A., ed. Community College Futures: From Rhetoric to Reality. 229p. (Orig.). 1989. pap. 16.95 (*0-913507-09-1*) New Forums.

Norris-Newman, Charles L. In Zululand with the British Throughout the War of 1879. 356p. 32.50 (*1-85367-003-0*, 5533) Stackpole.

Norris, Nigel. Understanding in Educational Evaluation. 212p. 1990. text ed. 64.95 (*0-8464-1424-4*) Beekman Pubs.

Norris, Norval, jt. ed. see Tonry, Michael H.

Norris, O. J. Legends of Journeys. (Illus.). 32p. 1988. 14.95 (*0-521-32181-6*) Cambridge U Pr.

Norris, P. About Honey: Nature's Elixir for Health. 1982. pap. 2.95 (*0-87904-043-2*) Lust.

***Norris, Pamela.** Between the Apple-Blossom & the Water: Women Writing about Gardens. (Illus.). 120p. 1994. pap. 17.95 (*0-8212-2139-6*) Bulfinch Pr.

— Come Live with Me & Be My Love: A Pageant of Renaissance Poetry & Painting. (Illus.). 128p. 1993. 16.95 (*0-8212-2044-6*) Bulfinch Pr.

— Through the Glass Window Shines the Sun: An Anthology of Medieval Poetry & Prose. 128p. 1995. 18.95 (*0-8212-2206-6*) Bulfinch Pr.

Norris, Pamela, ed. Sound the Deep Waters: Women's Romantic Poetry in the Victorian Age. (Illus.). 120p. 1992. 16.95 (*0-8212-1895-6*) Bulfinch Pr.

Norris, Pamela, ed. see Austen, Jane.

Norris, Pamela, ed. see Hardy, Thomas.

Norris, Patricia, jt. auth. see Porter, Garrett.

Norris, Patrick. History by Design. 96p. 1984. pap. 8.00 (*0-935260-02-1*) Tex Assn Mus.

Norris, Peter, ed. First Aid to the Battlefront: Life & Letters to Sir Vincent Kennett-Barrington (1844-1903) (Illus.). 224p. 1992. 30.00 (*0-7509-0016-4*) A Sutton Pub.

Norris, Phillip E. The Job Doctor: Good Advice on Getting a Good Job. LC 90-4881. (Illus.). 106p. (Orig.). 1990. pap. 5.95 (*0-942784-43-X*, JD) JIST Works.

Norris, Pippa. British By-Elections: The Volatile Electorate. (Illus.). 280p. 1990. 69.00 (*0-19-827330-4*) OUP.

Norris, Pippa & Lovenduski, Joni. Political Representation & Recruitment: Gender, Race & Class in the British Parliament. (Illus.). 280p. (C). 1995. 59.95 (*0-521-46558-3*); pap. 18.95 (*0-521-46961-9*) Cambridge U Pr.

Norris, Pippa, jt. ed. see Lovenduski, Joni.

Norris, R. C., jt. auth. see Meeske, Milan D.

Norris, Richard A. Understanding the Faith of the Church. (Church's Teaching Ser.: Vol. 4). 288p. 1984. pap. 3.95 (*0-8164-2217-6*) Harper SF.

Norris, Richard A., Jr. & Rusch, William G., eds. The Christological Controversy. LC 79-8890. (Sources of Early Christian Thought Ser.). 176p. 1980. pap. 13.00 (*0-8006-1411-9*, 1-1411, Fortress Pr) Augsburg Fortress.

Norris, Robert. Memoirs of the Reign of Bossa Ahadee King of Dahomey: An Inland Country of Guiney. (Illus.). 186p. 1968. 35.00 (*0-7146-1840-3*, Pub. by F Cass Pubs UK) Intl Spec Bk.

— The People's Will. 80p. (Orig.). 1989. pap. 16.95 (*0-317-93473-2*) Peoples Birmingham.

— A Power of Attorney Handbook. 80p. (Orig.). 1989. pap. 15.95 (*0-317-93474-0*) Peoples Birmingham.

— You Decide: A Power of Attorney Handbook. 80p. (Orig.). 1989. pap. 15.95 (*0-317-93747-2*) Peoples Birmingham.

Norris, Robert, jt. auth. see Buergenthal, Thomas.

Norris, Robert D., et al. Handbook of Bioremediation. LC 93-21172. 1993. 59.95 (*1-56670-074-4*, TD878) Lewis Pubs.

Norris, Robert E. World Regional Geography. LaMarre, ed. 571p. (C). 1990. text ed. 58.25 (*0-314-48133-8*) West Pub.

Norris, Robert E., jt. auth. see Harries, Keith.

Norris, Robert M. & Webb, Robert W. Geology of California. 2nd ed. LC 08-936302. 541p. 1990. Net. text ed. write for info. (*0-471-50980-9*) Wiley.

Norris, Robert S., et al. Nuclear Weapons Databook, Vol. 5: British, French, & Chinese Nuclear Weapons, Vol. 5. LC 93-32975. 1994. text ed. 89.50 (*0-8133-1611-1*) Westview.

— Nuclear Weapons Databook, Vol. 5: British, French, & Chinese Nuclear Weapons, Vol. 5. LC 93-32975. (C). 1994. pap. text ed. 37.95 (*0-8133-1612-X*) Westview.

Norris, Ronald F. Utilizing Task Teams for Profit Improvement. LC 93-46223. 1994. 7.95 (*0-87576-179-8*) Pilot Bks.

Norris, Ronald V. & Sullivan, Colleen. PMS: Pre-Menstrual Syndrome. 50p. 1987. pap. 4.95 (*0-425-10332-3*) Berkley Pub.

Norris, Rosalie N. & Powell, Janet C. Easy-to-Chew & Easy-on-Salt. LC 81-65460. 176p. 1982. 10.95 (*0-8453-4718-7*, Cornwall Bks) Assoc Univ Prs.

Norris, Rosalie N., ed. see Salomone-Marino, Salvatore.

Norris, Ruby T. The Theory of Consumer's Demand. rev. ed. LC 75-39261. (Getting & Spending: the Consumer's Dilemma Ser.). (Illus.). 1976. reprint ed. 23.95 (*0-405-08034-4*) Ayer.

Norris, Sarah, ed. see Johnson, Joe B.

Norris, Scott, ed. Discovered Country: Tourism & Survival in the American West. LC 94-66179. (Illus.). 248p. (Orig.). 1994. pap. 17.95 (*0-9637623-0-3*) Stone Ladder.

Norris, Stephen P. The Generalizability of Critical Thinking: Multiple Perspectives on an Educational Ideal. 248p. (C). 1992. text ed. 44.95 (*0-8077-3173-0*); pap. text ed. 22.95 (*0-8077-3172-2*) Tchrs Coll.

***Norris, Stephen P. & Phillips, Linda M., eds.** Foundations of Literacy Policy in Canada. 278p. (C). 1990. text ed. 19.95x (*1-55059-020-0*) Temeron Bks.

Norris, Thomas, jt. ed. see McGregor, Bede.

Norris, W. One from Seven Hundred: Year in the Life of Parliament. LC 66-22359. 1966. 65.00 (*0-08-013169-7*, Pub. by Pergamon Repr UK) Franklin.

Norris, W. Sonny. How to Tame a One-Eyed Monster: Basic 35mm Photography Course, 2 bks., Bk. 1. (Illus.). 102p. (Orig.). 1988. pap. 24.95 (*0-9619555-0-3*) Son-Ora Photo.

— How to Tame a One-Eyed Monster: Basic 35mm Photography Course, 2 bks., Bk. 2. (Illus.). 48p. (Orig.). 1988. pap. 24.95 (*0-9619555-1-1*) Son-Ora Photo.

Norris, Wayne B. The Big Book of Photocopier Humor: A Treasury of High-Tech Grafitti, Left-Brain Witticisms, & Generic Humor. LC 84-90667. (Illus.). 256p. (Orig.). 1984. reprint ed. pap. 8.96 (*0-685-10088-X*) Norris Assocs Pr.

***Norris, William E. & Strain, Jeris E., eds.** Charles Carpenter Fries: His Oral Approach for Teaching & Learning Foreign Languages. fac. ed. LC 88-33465. (Illus.). 77p. 1989. reprint ed. pap. 25.00 (*0-7837-7783-3*, 2047538) Bks Demand.

Norrisey, Marie C., jt. auth. see Michael, Chester P.

Norrish, Peter. New Tragedy & Comedy in France, 1945-1970. LC 87-11571. 192p. (C). 1988. text ed. 50.00 (*0-389-20746-2*, N8305) B&N Imports.

Norrish, Peter, ed. see Adamov, Arthur & Fernando, Arrabal.

Norrving, B., jt. auth. see Donnan, Geoffrey.

Norse, Elliott A. Ancient Forests of the Pacific Northwest. LC 89-20029. (Illus.). 325p. (C). 1989. 34.95 (*1-55963-017-5*); pap. 19.95 (*1-55963-016-7*) Island Pr.

Norse, Elliott A., ed. Global Marine Biological Diversity: A Strategy for Building Conservation Into Decision Making. LC 93-25350. 350p. 1993. text ed. 50.00 (*1-55963-255-0*); pap. 27.50 (*1-55963-256-9*) Island Pr.

Norse, Harold. Beat Hotel. (Illus.). 78p. (C). 1983. 25.00 (*0-317-11746-7*); pap. 6.95 (*0-912377-00-3*) Atticus Pr.

— Karma Circuit. (Illus.). 70p. (Orig.). 1973. pap. 6.00 (*0-915572-04-4*) Panjandrum.

— Mysteries of Magritte. (Orig.). (C). 1984. pap. 5.00 (*0-912377-07-0*) Atticus Pr.

— Mysteries of Magritte. limited ed. (Orig.). (C). 1984. 15.00 (*0-912377-06-2*) Atticus Pr.

Norse, Harold, tr. see Belli, G. G.

Norse, Harold, jt. auth. see Williams, William Carlos.

Norseng, Mary K. Dagny: Dagny Juel Przybyszewska, the Woman & the Myth. LC 90-30147. (Samuel & Althea Stroum Book Ser.). (Illus.). 240p. 1991. 24.95 (*0-295-96999-7*) U of Wash Pr.

Norseng, Mary K., jt. ed. see Ingwersen, Faith.

Norsett, Syvert P., jt. auth. see Iseries, A.

Norsgaard, E. Jaediker. Nature's Great Balancing Act: In Our Own Backyard. LC 89-38589. (Illus.). 64p. (J). (gr. 4 up). 1990. 14.95 (*0-525-65028-8*, Cobblehill Bks) Dutton Child Bks.

Norsker, Henrik. The Self-Reliant Potter: Clay & Raw Materials. Deutsches Zentrum fur Entwicklungstechnologien GATE In: Deutsche Gesellschaft fur Technische Zusammenarbeit (GTZ) GmbH Staff, ed. (Illus.). 98p. 1990. pap. 17.50 (*3-528-02057-1*, Pub. by Vieweg & Sohn GW) Ballen Bkslr.

— The Self-Reliant Potter Refractories & Kilns. (GATE Ser.). 134p. (Orig.). 1987. pap. 17.50 (*3-528-02031-8*, Pub. by Vieweg & Sohn GW) Ballen Bkslr.

Norskog, Howard. Beyond a Sleeping Prairie. 40p. (Orig.). 1994. pap. 6.00 (*0-9625171-3-5*) H L Norskog.

— High Country Ballads. 40p. (Orig.). 1994. pap. 6.00 (*0-9625171-5-1*) H L Norskog.

— Lonesome, Old Camp Fires. 40p. 1994. pap. 6.00 (*0-9625171-6-X*) H L Norskog.

— Mountains of Thunder. 35p. (Orig.). 1994. pap. 6.00 (*0-685-71206-0*) H L Norskog.

— Sing Me a Mountain. 35p. (Orig.). 1994. pap. 6.00 (*0-9625171-1-9*) H L Norskog.

— Under a Far Away Star. 40p. (Orig.). 1994. pap. 6.00 (*0-9625171-4-3*) H L Norskog.

— Where Wild Rivers Run. 40p. (Orig.). Date not set. pap. 6.00 (*0-9625171-7-8*) H L Norskog.

— Yesterdays Trails. 35p. (Orig.). 1994. pap. 6.00 (*0-9625171-0-0*) H L Norskog.

Norskog, Howard L. High Country Ballads: Cowboy Poetry. (DNA Ser.). 80p. (Orig.). (YA). (gr. 8 up). 1988. pap. 6.99 (*0-685-30409-4*) H L Norskog.

— Yesterdays Trails: Cowboy Poetry. (DNA Ser.). 49p. (YA). (gr. 8 up). 1989. pap. 6.99 (*0-685-30410-8*) H L Norskog.

Norstedt, Johann A. Thomas MacDonagh: A Critical Biography. LC 78-31320. (Illus.). 175p. 1980. 19.50 (*0-8139-0786-1*) U Pr of Va.

Norstedt, Marilyn L., ed. New Scholarship - New Serials: Proceedings of the North American Serials Interest Group, Inc., 8th Annual Conference, June 10-13, 1993, Brown University, Providence, R.I. LC 94-6729. (Serials Librarian Ser.). (Illus.). 284p. 1994. lib. bdg. 24.95 (*1-56024-685-5*) Haworth Pr.

Norster, E. R. Combustion & Heat Transfer in Gas Turbine Systems. (Cranfield International Symposium Ser.: Vol. 11). (Illus.). 1971. 169.00 (*0-08-016524-9*, Pub. by Pergamon Repr UK) Franklin.

Norstrom, Wanda. An American Artist in Africa, 1937: Sketch Book & Diary. (Illus.). 112p. (Orig.). 1991. pap. 19.00 (*0-9630357-0-3*) P Shedding.

Norsworthy, Alex, ed. FRI Prospect Research Resource Directory, Vol. 2. 2nd ed. 491p. 1991. pap. 85.00 (*0-930807-24-3*, 600311) Fund Raising.

— The Nonprofit Computer Sourcebook: The Professional's Guide to Products, Services & Information Sources for Computer Systems. 355p. 1990. pap. 75.00 (*0-914756-97-4*, 600087) Taft Group.

Norsworthy, Gary D. Current Feline Practice. (Illus.). 725p. 1993. text ed. 98.00 (*0-397-51204-X*) Lippincott.

Norsworthy, J. R. & Jang, S. L. Empirical Measurement & Analysis of Productivity & Technological Change: Applications in High-Technology & Service Industries. LC 92-36913. (Contributions to Economic Analysis Ser.: No. 211). 1993. write for info. (*0-444-89002-5*, North Holland) Elsevier.

Norsworthy, Kent & Barry, Tom. Nicaragua: A Country Guide. 2nd ed. 226p. 1990. pap. 9.95 (*0-911213-29-5*) Interhemisp Res Ctr.

North. Handbook of Receptors - Channels. 1993. write for info. (*0-8493-8322-6*) CRC Pr.

— Healthy, Wealthy & Dead. 1994. per. 6.95 (*0-920897-55-X*, Pub. by NeWest Pr CN) InBook.

— Killer. 1995. mass mkt. 3.50 (*0-06-106305-3*, Harp PBks) HarpC.

— Simeon North: First Official Pistol Maker of the United States. reprint ed. 15.95 (*0-88227-001-X*) Gun Room.

North & Hillard, eds. Latin Prose Composition. 310p. (Orig.). (LAT.). (C). 1988. pap. 16.00 (*0-86516-209-3*) Bolchazy-Carducci.

North & Reilly. Raised Intracranial Pressure. 1990. 65.00 (*0-433-00102-X*) Buttrwrth-Heinemann.

North, A. & Bawn, C. Kinetics of Free Radical Polymerization. LC 66-21138. (International Encyclopedia of Physical Chemistry & Chemical Physics Ser.: Vol. 1, TP 17). 1966. 55.00 (*0-08-011850-X*, Pub. by Pergamon Repr UK) Franklin.

North, A. C. & Attwood, Teresa K. Protein Structure. 3rd ed. Head, J. J., ed. (Carolina Biology Readers Ser.: No. 34). (Illus.). 32p. (YA). (gr. 10 up). 1991. pap. 3.00 (*0-89278-434-2*, 45-9634) Carolina Biological.

North, Alan. One Hundred One Atari Computer Programming Tips & Tricks. 128p. (Orig.). 1982. pap. 8.95 (*0-86668-022-5*) ARCsoft.

— Thirty-One New Atari Computer Programs for Home, School & Office. (Illus.). 96p. (Orig.). 1982. pap. 8.95 (*0-86668-018-7*) ARCsoft.

— The Urban Adventure Handbook. (Illus.). 160p. (Orig.). 1990. pap. 11.95 (*0-89815-373-5*) Ten Speed Pr.

North, Alan S. The Urban Adventure Handbook. (Illus.). 160p. (Orig.). 1989. pap. write for info. (*0-318-65889-5*) Adventure Berkeley.

North American Man-Boy Love Association Staff. A Witchhunt Foiled: The FBI vs. NAMBLA. LC 85-72763. (Illus.). 93p. (Orig.). 1985. pap. 5.95 (*0-9615497-0-X*) N Am Man-Boy.

North American Manufacturing Research Conference (14th: 1986: University of Minnesota, Minneapolis) Staff. North American Manufacturing Research Conference Proceedings: May 28-30, 1986, University of Minnesota, Minneapolis, MN - Organized by the University of Minnesota Department of Mechanical Engineering, Minneapolis, MN. LC 76-646280. (Manufacturing Technology Review Ser.: No. 1). (Illus.). 684p. reprint ed. pap. 180.00 (*0-8357-6475-3*, 2035846) Bks Demand.

— North American Manufacturing Research Conference Proceedings, May 19-22, 1985, University of California-Berkeley, Berkeley, CA. LC 76-646280. (Manufacturing Engineering Transactions Ser.: No. 13). (Illus.). 602p. 1985. reprint ed. pap. 171.60 (*0-8357-6505-9*, 2035876) Bks Demand.

— North American Manufacturing Research Conference Proceedings, May 24-26, 1983, University of Wisconsin-Madison, Madison, WI. LC 76-646280. (Manufacturing Engineering Transactions Ser.: No. 11). (Illus.). 504p. 1983. reprint ed. pap. 143.70 (*0-7837-8192-X*, 2047897) Bks Demand.

North American Manufacturing Research Conference (15th: 1987: Bethlehem, PA) Staff. North American Manufacturing Research Conference Proceedings: May 27-29, 1987, Lehigh University, Bethlehem, PA. LC 76-646280. (SME Manufacturing Technology Review Ser.: No. 2). (Illus.). 702p. reprint ed. pap. 180.00 (*0-8357-6507-5*, 2035878) Bks Demand.

North American Metalworking Research Conference Staff. North American Metalworking Research Conference: Proceedings, 7th, May 13-16, 1979, University of Michigan, Ann Arbor, MI. LC 79-63779. (Manufacturing Engineering Transactions Ser.: No. 7). (Illus.). 389p. reprint ed. pap. 110.90 (*0-685-23710-9*, 2032167) Bks Demand.

***North American Nursing Diagnosis Association Staff.** NANDA Nursing Diagnoses: Definitions & Classification 1995-1996. rev. ed. 124p. (C). 1995. pap. 11.00 (*0-9637042-1-4*) N Am Nursing.

North American Prairie Conference Staff. Prairie Peninsula Proceedings, Sixth, Ohio State University, Columbus, Ohio, August 12-17, 1978: In the "Shadow" of Transeau. Stuckey, Ronald L. & Reese, Karen J., eds. LC 81-82059. (Illus.). 1982. text ed. 15.00 (*0-86727-090-X*) Ohio Bio Survey.

North American Rapid Excavation & Tunneling Conference Staff. North American Rapid Evacuation & Tunneling: Proceedings of the Conference, 2nd, San Francisco, CA, June 24-27, 2 vols., 1. LC 74-84644. reprint ed. pap. 160.00 (*0-317-11271-6*, 2005130) Bks Demand.

— North American Rapid Evacuation & Tunneling: Proceedings of the Conference, 2nd, San Francisco, CA, June 24-27, 2 vols., 2. LC 74-84644. reprint ed. pap. 160.00 (*0-317-11272-4*) Bks Demand.

— Proceedings, 1972 Vol. 1. fac. ed. Lane, Kenneth S. & Garfield, Larry A., eds. LC 72-86918. (Illus.). 851p. 1972. reprint ed. pap. 180.00 (*0-7837-7867-8*, 2047625) Bks Demand.

— Proceedings, 1972 Vol. 2. fac. ed. Lane, Kenneth S. & Garfield, Larry A., eds. LC 72-86918. (Illus.). 831p. 1972. reprint ed. pap. 180.00 (*0-7837-7868-6*, 2047625) Bks Demand.

North American Society for the Psychology of Sport & Physical Activity Staff. Psychology of Motor Behavior & Sport, 1976, 2 vols., 1. Christina, Robert W. & Landers, Daniel M., eds. LC 78-641529. reprint ed. pap. 74.00 (*0-317-55475-1*, 2029528) Bks Demand.

— Psychology of Motor Behavior & Sport, 1976, 2 vols., 2. Christina, Robert W. & Landers, Daniel M., eds. LC 78-641529. reprint ed. pap. 70.80 (*0-317-55476-X*) Bks Demand.

— Psychology of Motor Behavior & Sport, 1978. Roberts, Glyn C. & Newell, Karl M., eds. LC 78-641529. 309p. reprint ed. pap. 88.10 (*0-317-55489-1*, 2029531) Bks Demand.

— Psychology of Motor Behavior & Sport, 1979. Nadeau, Claude H., ed. LC 78-641529. 760p. reprint ed. pap. 180.00 (*0-317-55485-9*, 2029530) Bks Demand.

— Psychology of Motor Behavior & Sport, 1980. Roberts, Glyn C. & Landers, Daniel M., eds. LC 78-641529. 220p. reprint ed. pap. 62.70 (*0-317-55496-4*, 2029533) Bks Demand.

North American Spine Society Staff & Fardon, David F., eds. Disorders of the Spine: A Coding System for Diagnoses. LC 91-71142. 132p. (Orig.). 1991. pap. text ed. 27.00 (*1-56053-014-6*) Hanley & Belfus.

North American Symposium on Carbenoxolone Staff. Proceedings of the North American Symposium on Carbenoxolone, Montreal, 1975. Beck, I., ed. (International Congress Ser.: No. 379). 1976. pap. 47.25 (*0-444-15212-1*, Excerpta Medica) Elsevier.

North American Symposium on Family Practice Staff. The Many Dimensions of Family Practice. LC 80-14847. 340p. 1983. 30.00 (*0-87668-427-4*) Aronson.

North American Telecommunication Association Staff. Telecommunications Market Review & Forecast. 279p. 1991. pap. 498.00 (*0-940919-27-3*, 200) NA Telecomm Assn.

North American Telecommunications Association Staff. A Centrex Primer on a Growing Market. 63p. 1991. pap. 40.00 (*0-685-52644-5*, 260) NA Telecomm Assn.

— EuroTelecom, 1992: A Report of Telecommunications in the European Common Market. 225p. 1990. pap. 698.00 (*0-940919-13-3*, 210) NA Telecomm Assn.

— Industry Basics: Introduction to the History, Structure, & Technology of the Telecommunications Industry. 4th ed. 96p. 1991. pap. 40.00 (*0-940919-17-6*, 230) NA Telecomm Assn.

— Safety Resource Manual for the Telecommunications Industry. 125p. 1990. pap. 53.00 (*0-685-52630-5*, 225) NA Telecomm Assn.

— Telecommunications Export Guide: A Directory of International Trade Data & Resources. 3rd ed. Coffman, Mary L., ed. 210p. 1993. pap. 103.00 (*0-940919-31-1*) NA Telecomm Assn.

— Telecommunications Source Book, 1993. 208p. 1993. pap. 53.00 (*0-940919-28-1*) NA Telecomm Assn.

North, Arielle, ed. see Franzwa, Gregory M.

North, Arthur A. Supreme Court: Judicial Process & Judicial Politics. LC 66-17855. (Orig.). 1966. pap. text ed. 8.95 (*0-89197-435-0*) Irvington.

***North, Arthur W.** The Founders & the Founding of Walton, New York. (Illus.). 59p. 1995. reprint ed. pap. 27.00 (*1-887530-02-9*) RSG Pub.

— Walton World War History. (Illus.). 32p. Date not set. reprint ed. pap. write for info. (*1-887530-06-1*) RSG Pub.

North, Audrey. Australia's Fan Heritage. 70p. (C). 1990. 75.00 (*0-86439-001-7*, Pub. by Boolarong Pubns AT) St Mut.

North, B. H., ed. Modern Railway Transportation. 398p. 1993. 115.00 (*0-7844-1973-6*) Am Soc Civil Eng.

North, Barbara. Maid in Taiwan. 1984. pap. 4.95 (*9971-83-773-0*) OMF Bks.

North, Barbara & Crittenden, Penelope. Anti-Stress Workbook. (Illus.). 79p. (Orig.). 1980. pap. 4.95 (*0-938480-00-6*) Healthworks.

North, Barbara, tr. see Duverger, Maurice.

An Asterisk (*) at the beginning of an entry indicates that the title is appearing in BIP for the first time.

North, Barbara B. & Crittenden, Penelope. Cave Time: How to Survive in a Civilized World. rev. ed. Orig. Title: The Anti-Stress Workbook. (Illus.). 49p. pap. 4.95 (*0-938480-02-2*) Healthworks.

North, Bede. Family Prayerbook. 1991. pap. 2.95 (*0-909986-15-0*) Alba.

North Berwick Priory Staff. Carte Monialium De Northberwic. Innes, Cosmo, ed. LC 74-173799. (Bannatyne Club, Edinburgh. Publications: No. 84). reprint ed. 27.50 (*0-404-52809-0*) AMS Pr.

North, Bill & North, Gwen. Best of Britain's Countryside: Northern England & Scotland. LC 90-5455. (Two-Week Traveler Ser.). 272p. (Orig.). 1990. pap. 12.95 (*0-89886-205-1*) Mountaineers.

— The Best of Britain's Countryside: Southern England, a Driving & Walking Itinerary. LC 90-48755. (Illus.). 272p. 1991. pap. 12.95 (*0-89886-264-7*) Mountaineers.

— The Best of Britain's Countryside: The Heart of England & Wales: a Driving & Walking Itinerary. LC 92-41891. (Two-Week Traveler Ser.). 256p. (Orig.). 1993. pap. 12.95 (*0-89886-341-4*) Mountaineers.

North, Bill, et al. Rural America: Prints from the Collection of Steven Schmidt. (Illus.). (Orig.). 1993. pap. 11.95 (*0-913689-37-8*) Spencer Muse Art.

North, Brownlow. The Rich Man & Lazarus. 1979. pap. 4.95 (*0-85151-121-X*) Banner of Truth.

North, C. P. & Prosser, D. J., eds. Characterization of Fluvial & Aeolian Reservoirs. (Geological Society Special Publications: No. 73). (Illus.). 450p. 1993. 108.00 (*0-903317-90-7*, Pub. by Geol Soc Pub Hse UK) AAPG.

North, Carol. Disney Babies: What Does Baby Mickey Find? (Golden Board Bks.). (Illus.). (J). (ps-00). 1991. bds. 1.80 (*0-307-06113-2*, Golden Pr) Western Pub.

— Frosty the Snowman. (Golden Super Shape Bks.). (J). (ps-3). 1990. write for info. (*0-307-10039-1*) Western Pub.

— Hansel & Gretel. (Golden Super Shape Bks.). (J). 1990. pap. write for info. (*0-307-10033-2*, Golden Pr) Western Pub.

— Jungle Book: Mowgli's Noisy Jungle. (J). (ps). 1993. 9.95 (*0-307-06076-4*, Golden Pr) Western Pub.

— Walt Disney's Winnie the Pooh: Pooh Can ... Can You? (Board Bks.). (Illus.). 12p. (J). (ps). 1993. bds. 1.95 (*0-307-06081-0*, 6081, Golden Pr) Western Pub.

North, Carol S. Welcome, Silence: My Triumph over Schizophrenia. 240p. 1989. reprint ed. mass mkt. 4.99 (*0-380-70627-X*) Avon.

North, Carol S., et al. Multiple Personality Disorder: Psychiatric Classification & Media Influence. LC 92-49904. (Oxford Monographs on Psychiatry). (C). 1993. 39.95 (*0-19-508095-5*) OUP.

North Carolina Bar Association Foundation Staff & Blalock, Steven F. Social Security Disability Claims. 1983. write for info. (*0-318-58303-8*) NC Bar Found.

North Carolina Biotechnology Center Institute for Biotechnology Information Staff. Biotechnology in the U. S. Pharmaceutical Industry. 3rd ed. 479p. 1993. pap. 595.00 (*0-945597-20-7*) NC Biotech Ctr.

North Carolina Biotechnology Center Staff. Directory of Biotechnology Centers, 1993. 6th ed. Hafer, Janet E., ed. 65p. 1993. pap. 40.00 (*0-945597-19-3*) NC Biotech Ctr.

— Directory of States' Biotechnology Centers, 1988. rev. ed. 30p. 1988. pap. 10.00 (*0-945597-01-0*) NC Biotech Ctr.

— North Carolina Companies in Biotechnology. 92p. (Orig.). 1988. pap. (*0-945597-00-2*) NC Biotech Ctr.

— North Carolina Companies in Biotechnology 1990 & Biotechnology Related Service Providers. 104p. (Orig.). 1990. pap. text ed. write for info. (*0-945597-10-X*) NC Biotech Ctr.

— North Carolina Companies in Biotechnology, 1992-93: And Biotechnology-Related Service Providers. 5th ed. Hafer, Janet E., ed. 104p. 1992. pap. (*0-945597-18-5*) NC Biotech Ctr.

North Carolina D.A.R. Staff, ed. Roster of Soldiers from North Carolina in the American Revolution. LC 67-28097. 709p. 1988. reprint ed. 35.00 (*0-8063-0091-4*, 4150) Genealog Pub.

North Carolina General Assembly Staff. Colonial Records of North Carolina: 1662-1776, 10 Vols, Set. Saunders, William L., ed. LC 72-130612. reprint ed. 1,800.00 (*0-404-05590-7*) AMS Pr.

— Index to Colonial & State Records of North Carolina, 1662-1790, 4 Vols, Set. Weeks, Stephen B., ed. LC 72-1797. reprint ed. 700.00 (*0-404-07487-1*) AMS Pr.

— State Records of North Carolina, 1777-1790, 16 Vols. Clark, Walter, ed. reprint ed. write for info. (*0-318-50721-8*) AMS Pr.

— State Records of North Carolina, 1777-1790, 16 Vols, Set. Clark, Walter, ed. LC 72-1798. reprint ed. 2,880.00 (*0-404-07470-7*) AMS Pr.

North Carolina Museum of Art Staff, ed. E. L. Kirchner, German Expressionist: A Loan Exhibition. LC 59-2148. (Illus.). 1958. pap. 1.50 (*0-88259-002-2*) NCMA.

***North Carolina School of Science & Mathematics, Department of Mathematics & Computer Science Staff.** Contemporary Calculus Through Applications. 1995. write for info. (*0-614-01932-X*) Janson Pubns.

— Contemporary Precalculus Through Applications: Answer Key. (Illus.). 231p. 1992. pap. 12.95 (*0-939765-55-1*, G149) Janson Pubns.

— Contemporary Precalculus Through Applications: Assessment Resource. 126p. 1993. pap. 19.95 (*0-939765-58-6*, G150) Janson Pubns.

— Contemporary Precalculus Through Applications: Instructor's Guide. 143p. 1993. pap. 19.95 (*0-939765-57-8*, G152) Janson Pubns.

— Data Analysis. LC 88-5305. (New Topics for Secondary School Mathematics: Materials & Software Ser.). (Illus.). 132p. (Orig.). (YA). (gr. 11-12). 1988. pap. 12.00 (*0-87353-263-5*) NCTM.

— Geometric Probability. LC 88-5305. (New Topics for Secondary School Mathematics: Materials & Software Ser.). (Illus.). 40p. (Orig.). (YA). (gr. 11-12). 1988. pap. 11.00 (*0-87353-259-7*) NCTM.

— Matrices. LC 88-5305. (New Topics for Secondary School Mathematics: Materials & Software Ser.). (Illus.). 115p. (Orig.). 1988. pap. 12.00 (*0-87353-270-8*) NCTM.

North Carolina School of Science & Mathematics, Mathematics & Computer Science Dept. Staff. Contemporary Precalculus Through Applications: Supplementary Resource. 79p. 1993. pap. 19.95 (*0-939765-60-8*, G160) Janson Pubns.

North Carolina School of Science & Mathematics, Department of Mathematics & Computer Science Staff, et al. Contemporary Precalculus Through Applications: Functions, Data Analysis & Matrices. (Illus.). 344p. 1992. text ed. 38.50x (*0-939765-54-3*, G148) Janson Pubns.

North Carolina State University, Center for Urban Affairs Community Services Staff, ed. Nineteen Ninety Index of Computer Hardware & Software in Use by North Carolina Local Governments. 525p. (C). 1990. pap. text ed. 25.00 (*1-56011-179-8*) Institute Government.

North Carolina State University Staff. Survey & Evaluation of Factors Affecting Heat Transfer Performance & Cost of Steam Condensers. 93p. 1967. 13.95 (*0-317-34551-6*, 104) Intl Copper.

North Carolina Wildlife Resources Commission Staff. North Carolina Wild Places: A Closer Look. Earley, Lawrence S., ed. LC 92-81998. (Illus.). 82p. (Orig.). (J). (gr. 2-6). 1994. pap. 10.00 (*0-9628949-1-5*) NC Wildlife.

North, Carolyn. Crop Circles: Hoax or Happening. Glaser, Sara, ed. (Fringe Ser.: Vol. 1). (Illus.). 32p. (Orig.). 1992. pap. 3.95 (*0-916147-22-3*) Regent Pr.

— Seven Movements, One Song. 325p. (Orig.). 1991. pap. 14.95 (*0-916147-17-7*) Regent Pr.

North, Carolyn, text. Synchronicity: The Anatomy of Coincidence. LC 94-11735. (Fringe Ser.: Vol. 3). 1994. 3.95 (*0-916147-44-4*) Regent Pr.

North, Catharine M. The History of Berlin, Connecticut. 294p. 1988. reprint ed. lib. bdg. 32.00 (*0-685-22247-0*, CT0001) Higginson Bk Co.

North Central Regional Center for Rural Development. Communities Left Behind: Alternatives for Development. LC 74-11286. 161p. reprint ed. pap. 45.90 (*0-317-55554-5*, 2029622) Bks Demand.

North Central Regional Center for Rural Development Staff. Rural Industrialization: Problems & Potentials. LC 73-20027. 163p. reprint ed. pap. 46.50 (*0-317-55353-4*, 2029164) Bks Demand.

North, Charles. Leap Year. (Illus.). 7.00 (*0-686-65482-X*); pap. 3.50 (*0-686-65483-8*) Kulchur Foun.

— The Year of the Olive Oil. 1989. pap. 8.00 (*0-914610-66-X*); boxed 15.00 (*0-914610-67-8*) Hanging Loose.

North, Charles & Schuyler, James, eds. Broadway Two. 1989. pap. 15.00 (*0-914610-70-8*); boxed, pap. 25.00 (*0-914610-71-6*) Hanging Loose.

North, Christina B. The Autistic Alienated American Misfits. (Contemporary Ser.). (Illus.). 193p. 1982. 9.95 (*0-686-35767-1*) C B North.

— Is a Revolution Necessary? LC 73-89728. (Contemporary Ser.). (Illus.). 141p. 1973. reprint ed. 5.95 (*0-686-32838-8*) C B North.

North, D. C. & Thomas, R. P. The Rise of the Western World: A New Economic History. LC 73-77258. (Illus.). 192p. 1976. pap. 15.95 (*0-521-29099-6*) Cambridge U Pr.

***North, Darian.** Bone Deep. LC 95-12413. 1995. write for info. (*0-525-93849-4*, Dutton) NAL-Dutton.

— Criminal Seduction. 560p. 1994. pap. 5.99 (*0-451-18022-4*, Sig) NAL-Dutton.

North, David. Gerry Healy & His Place in the History of the Fourth International. (Illus.). 117p. (Orig.). (C). 1991. pap. 11.95 (*0-929087-58-5*) Labor Pubns Inc.

— The Heritage We Defend: A Contribution to the History of the Fourth International. 539p. (Orig.). (C). 1988. pap. 18.95 (*0-929087-00-3*) Labor Pubns Inc.

— Perestroika Versus Socialism: Stalinism & the Restoration of Capitalism in the U. S. S. R. 80p. (Orig.). (C). 1989. pap. 7.95 (*0-929087-39-9*) Labor Pubns Inc.

— Trotskyism vs. Stalinism. 33p. 1987. pap. 1.50 (*0-929087-20-8*) Labor Pubns Inc.

— The U. S. S. R. & Socialism: The Trotskyist Perspective. 41p. 1989. pap. 3.00 (*0-929087-45-3*) Labor Pubns Inc.

***North, David S.** Soothing the Establishment: The Impact of Foreign-Born Scientists & Engineers on America. LC 95-3988. 190p. (C). 1995. lib. bdg. 29.50 (*0-8191-9887-0*) U Pr of Amer.

North, Diane M. Samuel Peter Heintzelman & the Sonora Exploring & Mining Company. LC 79-15307. 248p. 1980. 29.95 (*0-8165-0679-5*) U of Ariz Pr.

North, Dick. The Lost Patrol. LC 78-1368. (Illus.). 149p. 1978. pap. 9.95 (*0-88240-106-8*) Alaska Northwest.

— The Mad Trapper of Rat River. (Illus.). 144p. 1991. pap. 5.95 (*0-7736-7307-5*, Pub. by Stoddart Pubng CN) Genl Dist Srvs.

North, Douglass. Washington Whitewater: The Thirty-Four Best Whitewater Rivers. rev. ed. LC 91-39562. (Illus.). 320p. 1992. pap. 16.95 (*0-89886-327-9*) Mountaineers.

North, Douglass C. Institutions, Institutional Change & Economic Performance. (Political Economy of Institutions & Decisions Ser.). 160p. (C). 1990. 39.95 (*0-521-39416-3*); pap. 12.95 (*0-521-39734-0*) Cambridge U Pr.

— Structure & Change in Economic History. (C). 1982. pap. text ed. 9.95 (*0-393-95241-X*) Norton.

North, Douglass C., jt. auth. see Davis, Lance.

North, E. Lee. Fifty-Five West Virginias. 117p. 1985. pap. 18.50 (*0-937058-21-1*) West Va U Pr.

North East London Polytechnic, London, England Staff. The Psychology Readings Catalogue of the North East London Polytechnic, London, England, 2 vols, Set. 1976. lib. bdg. 170.00 (*0-8161-1179-0*, Hall Library) G K Hall.

North East Weld County Book Committee. History of North East Weld County, Colorado. (Illus.). 336p. 1986. 50.00 (*0-88107-064-5*) Curtis Media.

North, Elizabeth. Ancient Enemies. 240p. 1986. reprint ed. pap. 7.95 (*0-89733-214-8*) Academy Chi Pubs.

— Enough Blue Sky. 190p. 1985. 20.00 (*0-89733-150-8*) Academy Chi Pubs.

— Everything in the Garden. 200p. 1984. 20.00 (*0-89733-114-1*) Academy Chi Pubs.

— Pelican Rising. 232p. 1978. reprint ed. 20.00 (*0-915864-94-0*); reprint ed. pap. 7.95 (*0-915864-93-2*) Academy Chi Pubs.

North, F. K. Petroleum Geology. (Illus.). 750p. 1985. text ed. 95.00 (*0-04-553003-3*); pap. text ed. 59.95 (*0-04-553004-1*) Routledge Chapman & Hall.

***North, Freddie.** Cards at Play. (Illus.). 144p. 1995. pap. 16.95 (*0-7134-7644-3*, Pub. by Batsford UK) Trafalgar.

— Conventional Bidding Explained. 144p. 1995. pap. 16.95 (*0-7134-7643-5*, Pub. by Batsford UK) Trafalgar.

North, Freddie & Flint, Jeremy. Tiger Bridge Revisited. 1991. pap. 12.95 (*1-85744-502-3*, Maxwell Macmillan) Macmillan.

North, Gail, jt. auth. see Freudenberger, Herbert J.

North, Gail, jt. auth. see Strauss, Steven C.

North, Gary. Backward, Christian Soldiers? 290p. 1984. pap. 5.95 (*0-930464-01-X*) Inst Christian.

— The Coase Theorum: A Study in Economic Epistemology. LC 91-40767. 128p. 1992. 25.00 (*0-930464-61-3*) Inst Christian.

— Crossed Fingers: How the Liberals Captured the Presbyterian Church. LC 95-194. 1995. 34.95 (*0-930464-74-5*) Inst Christian.

— Dominion & Common Grace. 295p. 1987. pap. 8.95 (*0-930464-09-5*) Inst Christian.

— The Dominion Covenant: Genesis. write for info. (*0-930462-24-6*) Am Bur Eco Res.

— The Dominion Covenant: Genesis. 512p. 1987. reprint ed. 19.95 (*0-930464-03-6*) Inst Christian.

— Entrega Icondicional: Programa de Dios para la Victoria. Howden, Paul, tr. 312p. (SPA.). 1990. pap. 6.95 (*0-930464-34-6*) Inst Christian.

— Government by Emergency. 1983. 19.95 (*0-930462-05-X*) Am Bur Eco Res.

— Heredaran la Tierra: Esquemas Biblicos para la Economia Politica. Howden, Paul, tr. 261p. (SPA.). 1990. pap. 5.95 (*0-930464-26-5*) Inst Christian.

— The Hoax of Higher Criticism. 72p. 1989. pap. 3.95 (*0-930464-30-3*) Inst Christian.

— Honest Money: Biblical Blueprints on Money Making & Banking. write for info. (*0-930462-15-7*) Am Bur Eco Res.

— Inherit the Earth: Biblical Blueprints on Economics. write for info. (*0-930462-56-4*) Am Bur Eco Res.

— Is the World Running Down? Crisis in the Christian Worldview. 345p. 1988. 19.95 (*0-930464-13-3*) Inst Christian.

— The Judeo-Christian Tradition: A Guide for the Perplexed. LC 89-48350. 204p. 1990. 14.95 (*0-930464-28-1*) Inst Christian.

— The Last Train Out. 1983. pap. 6.95 (*0-930462-07-6*) Am Bur Eco Res.

— A Letter to Paul J. Hill. LC 94-37301. 1994. 3.95 (*0-930464-73-7*) Inst Christian.

— Leviticus: An Economic Commentary. LC 94-37832. 1994. 29.95 (*0-930464-72-9*) Inst Christian.

— Liberando la Tierra: Regeneracion O Revolucion? Howden, Paul, tr. 254p. (SPA.). 1989. pap. 5.95 (*0-930464-31-1*) Inst Christian.

— Marx's Religion of Revolution: Regeneration Through Chaos. 280p. 1989. pap. 8.95 (*0-930464-15-X*) Inst Christian.

— Millennialism & Social Theory. LC 90-47609. 393p. 1990. 14.95 (*0-930464-49-4*) Inst Christian.

— Moses & Pharaoh: Dominion Religion vs. Power Religion. 426p. (C). 1985. pap. text ed. 12.50 (*0-930464-05-2*) Inst Christian.

— Political Polytheism: The Myth of Pluralism. LC 89-27431. 771p. 1989. 22.50 (*0-930464-32-X*) Inst Christian.

— Puritan Economic Experiments. 65p. (Orig.). 1989. pap. 5.95 (*0-930464-14-1*) Inst Christian.

— Rapture Fever: Why Dispensationalism is Paralyzed. LC 93-444. 1993. student ed. 25.00 (*0-930464-67-2*); pap. 12.95 (*0-930464-65-6*) Inst Christian.

— La Religion Revolucionaria de Marx: La Regeneracion por Medio del Caos. Howden, Paul & Gonzalez, Jose L., trs. 292p. (SPA.). 1990. pap. 6.95 (*0-930464-37-0*) Inst Christian.

— Salvation Through Inflation: The Economics of Social Credit. LC 93-18285. 1993. 12.95 (*0-930464-64-8*); student ed. 25.00 (*0-930464-66-4*) Inst Christian.

— Seventy-Five Bible Questions Your Instructors Pray You Won't Ask. 238p. (Orig.). (C). 1988. pap. 5.95 (*0-930462-03-3*) Inst Christian.

— The Sinai Strategy: Economics & the Ten Commandments. 368p. (Orig.). 1986. pap. 12.50 (*0-930464-07-9*) Inst Christian.

— Successful Investing in an Age of Envy. 2nd rev. ed. 1983. 19.95 (*0-930462-08-4*) Am Bur Eco Res.

— Tithing & the Church. LC 93-47685. 1994. 25.00 (*0-930464-69-9*); pap. 9.95 (*0-930464-70-2*) Inst Christian.

— Tools of Dominion: The Case Laws of Exodus. LC 90-4054. 1296p. 1989. 29.95 (*0-930464-10-9*) Inst Christian.

— Trespassing for Dear Life: What Is Operation Rescue up To? (Orig.). 1989. pap. 3.95 (*1-55926-125-0*, Dominion) Am Bur Eco Res.

— Unconditional Surrender: God's Program for Victory. 417p. 1988. pap. 5.95 (*0-930464-12-5*) Inst Christian.

— Unholy Spirits: Occultism & New Age Humanism. write for info. (*0-318-62312-9*) Am Bur Eco Res.

— Victim's Rights: The Biblical View of Civil Justice. LC 90-44629. 315p. 1990. 14.95 (*0-930464-17-6*) Inst Christian.

— Westminster's Confession: The Abandonment of Van Til's Legacy. LC 91-7200. 385p. 1991. 14.95 (*0-930464-54-0*) Inst Christian.

— When Justice Is Aborted: Biblical Standards for Non-Violent Resistance. 182p. (Orig.). 1989. pap. 8.95 (*1-55926-124-2*, Dominion) Am Bur Eco Res.

North, Gary, jt. auth. see DeMar, Gary.

North, Gary, jt. auth. see Robinson, Arthur.

North, Gerald. Advanced Amateur Astronomy. 1991. text ed. 50.00 (*0-7486-0253-4*, Pub. by Edinburgh U Pr UK) Col U Pr.

***North, Gerald R., et al, eds.** The Impact of Global Warming on Texas. LC 94-15147. (HARC Global Change Studies). (Illus.). 248p. 1995. 29.95 (*0-292-75555-4*) U of Tex Pr.

North, Gerald R., jt. auth. see Crowley, Thomas J.

North, Grace M. Nan of the Gypsies. 238p. 1989. reprint ed. lib. bdg. 21.95 (*0-89966-649-3*) Buccaneer Bks.

North, Gwen, jt. auth. see North, Bill.

North, H., jt. ed. see Noth.

North, Holly. Dr. Malone, I Presume? large type ed. 291p. 1994. 17.95 (*0-7505-0633-4*, Pub. by Magna Print Bks) Ulverscroft.

— The Invisible Doctor. large type ed. (Magna Romance Ser.). 230p. 1992. 21.95 (*0-7505-0394-7*) Ulverscroft.

— Nurse at Large. large type ed. 245p. 1992. 21.95 (*0-7505-0323-8*, Pub. by Magna Print Bks) Ulverscroft.

— Sister Slater's Secret. large type ed. 271p. 1993. 21.95 (*0-7505-0433-1*) Ulverscroft.

North Iowa Writers Club Staff. Patches of Iowa. Wagner, Catherine et al, eds. 152p. 1988. 6.75 (*0-317-91216-X*) N Iowa Writers.

***North, Ira.** Marching to Zion: A Collection of Ira North's Sermons. 1995. pap. 12.99 (*0-89225-454-8*) Gospel Advocate.

North, J. Mid Nineteenth Century Scientists. LC 68-55957. 1969. 82.00 (*0-08-013238-3*, Pub. by Pergamon Repr UK) Franklin.

North, J. D. Chaucer's Universe. (Illus.). 640p. 1988. 140.00 (*0-19-812668-9*) OUP.

— Measure of the Universe: A History of Modern Cosmology. 1990. pap. 12.95 (*0-486-66517-8*) Dover.

— Stars, Minds & Fate: Essays on Ancient & Medieval Cosmology. 460p. 1989. text ed. 60.00 (*0-907628-94-X*) Hambledon Press.

— The Universal Frame: Historical Essays in Astronomy. 400p. 1989. text ed. 60.00 (*0-907628-95-8*) Hambledon Press.

North, J. J. The Coinages of Edward I & II. 1968. 4.00 (*0-685-51543-5*) S J Durst.

— English Hammered Coinage, Vol. I. 1963. 40.00 (*0-685-51541-9*) S J Durst.

— English Hammered Coinage, Vol. II. 1977. 40.00 (*0-685-51542-7*) S J Durst.

North, Jack. Arnold Schwarzenegger. LC 93-40891. (Taking Part Ser.). (J). 1994. text ed. 14.95 (*0-87518-638-6*, Dillon Silver Burdett) Silver Burdett Pr.

North, Jacquelyne. Perfume, Cologne & Scent Bottles. LC 86-61205. (Illus.). 243p. 1986. 69.95 (*0-88740-072-8*) Schiffer.

North, James. Freedom Rising. 1985. 19.18 (*0-02-589940-6*) Macmillan.

— A History of the Church: From Pentecost to Present. rev. ed. 1991. pap. text ed. 12.99 (*0-89900-371-0*) College Pr Pub.

North, James B. Union in Truth: An Interpretive History of the Restoration Movement. Underwood, Jonathan, ed. 416p. (Orig.). 1994. pap. 17.99 (*0-7847-0197-0*, 30-88577) Standard Pub.

North, James W. History of Augusta, Maine. LC 81-80137. 1120p. 1981. reprint ed. 60.00 (*0-89725-020-6*) Picton Pr.

North, Jane Y., et al. Man in the Narrow Street. (Illus.). 72p. (J). (gr. 4-6). 1994. pap. 6.95 (*1-56721-075-9*) Twnty-Fifth Cent Pr.

— Old Vagabond in the Railroad Yard. (Illus.). 72p. (J). (gr. 4-6). 1994. pap. 6.95 (*1-56721-077-5*) Twnty-Fifth Cent Pr.

— Walls That Spoke. (Illus.). 72p. 1994. pap. 6.95 (*1-56721-073-2*) Twnty-Fifth Cent Pr.

North, John. Astronomy & Cosmology. 1994. 35.00 (*0-393-03656-1*); pap. 18.95 (*0-393-31193-7*) Norton.

North, John, Jr. The Purples. Van Treese, James B., ed. 150p. 1994. pap. 7.95 (*1-56901-187-7*) NW Pub.

North, John. Sherlock Holmes & the Arabian Princess. 124p. 1991. 25.00 (*0-86025-270-1*, Pub. by Ian Henry Pubns UK) Empire Pub Srvs.

— Sherlock Holmes & the German Nanny. 144p. 1991. 25.00 (*0-86025-273-6*, Pub. by Ian Henry Pubns UK) Empire Pub Srvs.

North, John, jt. ed. see Beard, Mary.

North, John, jt. ed. see Sellers, Peter.

North, John S., ed. Waterloo Directory of Irish Newspapers & Periodicals 1800-1900. 838p. (C). 1986. lib. bdg. 300.00 (*0-921075-00-6*) N Waterloo Acad Pr.

— The Waterloo Directory of Scottish Newspapers & Periodicals, 1800-1900, 2 vols., Set. (Illus.). 2199p. (C). 1989. lib. bdg. 640.00 (*0-921075-05-7*) N Waterloo Acad Pr.

N

North, Joseph. The New Masses: An Anthology of the Rebel Thirties. LC 77-93268. (Illus.). 352p. 1980. pap. 2.25 (*0-7178-0355-4*) Intl Pubs Co.
— No Men Are Strangers. LC 58-11504. 300p. 1976. pap. 2.25 (*0-7178-0462-3*) Intl Pubs Co.
— Socialist Cuba: As Seen by a U. S. Communist Delegation. 1970. pap. 0.60 (*0-87898-073-3*) New Outlook.
— What Everyone Should Know about the U. S. S. R. An Eyewitness Report of a Three-Year Visit. 1976. pap. 0.50 (*0-87898-121-7*) New Outlook.
North, Joseph, et al. Gus Hall: the Man & the Message. 1970. pap. 0.50 (*0-87898-060-1*) New Outlook.
North, Joseph H. The Early Development of the Motion Picture, 1887-1909. LC 72-558. (Dissertations on Film Ser.). 316p. 1974. reprint ed. 21.95 (*0-405-04101-2*) Ayer.
North, Julie, jt. auth. see Ruehrwein, Dick.
North, K. Environmental Business Management: An Introduction. (Management Development Ser.: No. 30). v, 194p. (Orig.). 1992. pap. 22.00 (*92-2-107289-4*) Intl Labour Office.
***North, Ken.** Multi-DBMS Programming: Using C++, Visual Basic, ODBC, OLE 2 & Tools for DBMS Projects. Date not set. text ed. 29.95 (*0-471-01778-7*) Wiley.
North, Kenda. Kenda North. (Min Gallery Series of Contemporary American & Japanese Photography). (Illus.). 84p. 1989. pap. 30.00 (*4-906265-21-9*) Aperture.
North, Kendall E. Windows Multi-DBMS Programming: Using C Plus Plus, Visual BASIC, ODBC & Tools for DBMS Projects. 1994. Incl. CD-ROM. cd-rom 59.95 (*0-471-01676-4*); pap. 49.95 (*0-471-01675-6*) Wiley.
North, Larry. Get Fit! The Last Fitness Book You Will Ever Need. Towle, Mike, ed. 240p. 1993. 22.95 (*1-56530-026-2*) Summit TX.
North Light Books Staff. Color on Color: Overprinting Two Colors to Create a New Third Color. 160p. 1993. 34.99 (*1-56496-033-1*, 30467) Rockport Pubs.
North Light Books Staff, ed. Clip Art: Abstract & Geometric Patterns. (Clip Art Ser.). (Illus.). 32p. (Orig.). 1993. pap. 6.95 (*0-89134-521-3*, 30482) North Light Bks.
— Clip Art: Christmas. (Clip Art Ser.). (Illus.). 32p. (Orig.). 1993. pap. 6.95 (*0-89134-525-6*, 30486) North Light Bks.
— Clip Art: Christmas Graphics. (Clip Art Ser.). (Illus.). 32p. (Orig.). 1993. pap. 6.95 (*0-89134-526-4*, 30487) North Light Bks.
— Clip Art: Couples. (Clip Art Ser.). (Illus.). 64p. (Orig.). 1994. pap. 6.95 (*0-89134-557-4*) North Light Bks.
— Clip Art: Creative Backgrounds. (Clip Art Ser.). (Illus.). 64p. (Orig.). 1994. pap. 6.95 (*0-89134-556-6*) North Light Bks.
— Clip Art: Decorative Borders. (Clip Art Ser.). (Illus.). 64p. (Orig.). 1994. pap. 6.95 (*0-89134-555-8*) North Light Bks.
— Clip Art: Families. (Illus.). 64p. (Orig.). 1994. pap. 6.99 (*0-89134-603-1*) North Light Bks.
— Clip Art: Graphic Borders. (Clip Art Ser.). (Illus.). 32p. (Orig.). 1993. pap. 6.95 (*0-89134-523-X*, 30484) North Light Bks.
— Clip Art: Graphic Textures & Patterns. (Clip Art Ser.). (Illus.). 32p. (Orig.). 1993. pap. 6.95 (*0-89134-522-1*, 30483) North Light Bks.
— Clip Art: People at Work. (Clip Art Ser.). (Illus.). 64p. (Orig.). 1994. pap. 6.95 (*0-89134-558-2*, 30578) North Light Bks.
— Clip Art: People from Around the World. (Clip Art Ser.). (Illus.). 64p. (Orig.). 1994. pap. 6.99 (*0-89134-606-6*) North Light Bks.
— Clip Art: Senior Citizens. (Clip Art Ser.). (Illus.). 64p. (Orig.). 1994. pap. 6.99 (*0-89134-604-X*) North Light Bks.
— Clip Art: Spot Illustrations. (Clip Art Ser.). (Illus.). 32p. (Orig.). 1993. pap. 6.95 (*0-89134-524-8*, 30486) North Light Bks.
— Clip Art: Transportation. (Clip Art Ser.). (Illus.). 64p. (Orig.). 1994. pap. 6.99 (*0-89134-605-8*) North Light Bks.
— Clip Art - Animals. (Illus.). 32p. 1992. pap. 6.95 (*0-89134-500-0*, 30446) North Light Bks.
— Clip Art - Food & Drink. (Illus.). 32p. 1992. pap. 6.95 (*0-89134-489-6*, 30448) North Light Bks.
— Clip Art - Holidays. (Illus.). 32p. 1992. pap. 6.95 (*0-89134-487-X*, 30446) North Light Bks.
— Clip Art - Men. (Illus.). 32p. 1992. pap. 6.95 (*0-89134-491-8*, 30450) North Light Bks.
— Clip Art - People Doing Sports. (Illus.). 32p. 1992. pap. 6.95 (*0-89134-490-X*, 30449) North Light Bks.
— Clip Art - Women. (Illus.). 32p. 1992. pap. 6.95 (*0-89134-492-6*, 30451) North Light Bks.
***North Light Staff.** Paint Craft. (Illus.). 144p. 1995. pap. 16.99 (*0-89134-650-3*) North Light Bks.
North, Liisa. Bitter Grounds: Roots of Revolt in El Salvador. rev. ed. LC 85-17632. 144p. (C). 1985. pap. 8.95 (*0-88208-193-4*) L Hill Bks.
North, Lucy, tr. see Taeko, Kono.
North, Luther H. Man of the Plains: Recollections of Luther North, 1856-1882. Danker, Donald F., ed. LC 61-6409. (Pioneer Heritage Ser.: No. 4). 371p. reprint ed. pap. 105.80 (*0-7837-7045-6*, 2046856) Bks Demand.
North, M. Commercial Chicken Production. 1990. text ed. 79.95 (*0-442-31881-2*) Chapman & Hall.
North, M. A. & Hillard, A. E. Greek Prose Composition. 272p. (C). 1989. pap. text ed. 15.95 (*0-89341-564-2*, Longwood Academic) Hollowbrook.
— Key to Greek Prose Composition. 109p. 1990. pap. text ed. 12.50 (*0-89341-733-5*, Longwood Academic) Hollowbrook.
— Key to Latin Prose Composition. 113p. 1990. reprint ed. pap. text ed. 12.50 (*0-89341-623-1*, Longwood Academic) Hollowbrook.
— Latin Prose Composition. LC 89-2646. 300p. (Orig.). 1989. reprint ed. pap. text ed. 15.95 (*0-89341-568-5*, Longwood Academic) Hollowbrook.
North Manhattan Health Action Group & CSS & Center for Health & Human Services. Washington Heights-Inwood Neighborhoods: Assessment of Health Care Needs-Appendices. 175p. (Orig.). 1984. pap. text ed. 15.00 (*0-88156-055-3*) Comm Serv Soc NY.
North Manhattan Health Action Group Report Staff & CCS Center for Health & Human Services Staff. Washington Heights-Inwood Neighborhood: Assessment of Health Care Needs. 129p. (Orig.). 1984. pap. text ed. 12.00 (*0-88156-054-5*) Comm Serv Soc NY.
North, Margie. To Chase a Dream. 418p. (YA). (gr. 8-12). 1989. 14.95 (*0-934188-26-2*) Evans Pubns.
North, Marianne. Recollections of a Happy Life: Being the Autobiography of Marianne North, Vol. 1. Morgan, Susan, ed. LC 93-12326. 400p. 1993. reprint ed. 60.00 (*0-8139-1469-8*); reprint ed. pap. 18.95 (*0-8139-1470-1*) U Pr of Va.
— Vision of Eden. 240p. 1993. 34.95 (*0-11-250088-9*, HM00889, Pub. by HMSO UK) UNIPUB.
North, Mark. Act of Treason: The Role of J. Edgar Hoover in the Assassination of President Kennedy. 672p. 1992. pap. 13.95 (*0-88184-877-8*) Carroll & Graf.
North, Michael. The Final Sculpture: Public Monuments & Modern Poets. LC 84-17011. (Illus.). 264p. (C). 1985. 36.95 (*0-8014-1725-2*) Cornell U Pr.
— Henry Green & the Writing of His Generation. LC 84-3534. 234p. reprint ed. pap. 66.70 (*0-8357-3132-4*, 2039395) Bks Demand.
— The Political Aesthetic of Yeats, Eliot & Pound. 288p. (C). 1992. 54.95 (*0-521-41432-6*) Cambridge U Pr.
North, Michael A. The Dialect of Modernism: Race, Language, & Twentieth-Century Literature. LC 93-36288. (Race & American Culture Ser.). (Illus.). 272p. (C). 1994. 29.95 (*0-19-508516-7*) OUP.
North, Miranda. Desert Slave. 1989. pap. 3.75 (*0-8217-2664-1*) Zebra.
— Forever Paradise. 1990. mass mkt. 4.25 (*0-8217-2997-7*) Zebra.
— Sweet Lies. 1990. mass mkt. 4.50 (*0-8217-3208-0*) Zebra.
***North, Nancy & Berube, Raymond.** You, the Medium: Psychic Development Through Home Circles. 120p. (Orig.). 1995. pap. write for info. (*0-9646600-1-6*) N Ray Publns.
North, Nigel. Continuo Playing on the Lute, Archlute & Theorbo: A Comprehensive Guide for Performers. LC 86-46028. (Music: Scholarship & Performance Ser.). (Illus.). 321p. 1987. 47.95 (*0-253-31415-1*) Ind U Pr.
North, Oliver. Under Fire: An American Story. 1992. mass mkt. 5.99 (*0-06-109056-5*) HarpC.
— Under Fire: An American Story. braille ed. 1032p. 1992. vinyl bd. 82.56 (*1-56956-099-4*, BR8613) W A T Braille.
North, Oliver & Roth, David. One More Mission: Oliver North Returns to Vietnam. (Illus.). 256p. 1993. pap. 22.00 (*0-310-40490-8*) Zondervan.
— One More Mission: Oliver North Returns to Vietnam. 336p. 1994. mass mkt. 5.99 (*0-06-109351-3*) Zondervan.
— One More Mission: Oliver North Returns to Vietnam. 1995. 19.99 (*0-310-40499-1*) Zondervan.
North, Oliver S. Mineral Exploration, Mining, & Processing Patents, 1979. LC 80-66760. (Illus.). 137p. 1980. 5.00 (*0-89520-278-6*) SMM&E Inc.
— Mineral Exploration, Mining, & Processing Patents, 1979. fac. ed. LC 80-66760. (Illus.). 143p. 1980. reprint ed. pap. 40.80 (*0-7837-7850-3*, 2047609) Bks Demand.
— Mineral Exploration, Mining, & Processing Patents, 1980. LC 82-71422. (Illus.). 135p. 1982. 5.00 (*0-89520-294-8*) SMM&E Inc.
— Mineral Exploration, Mining, & Processing Patents, 1980. fac. ed. LC 66-23725. (Illus.). 141p. 1982. reprint ed. pap. 40.20 (*0-7837-7851-1*, 2047610) Bks Demand.
North, P. M., ed. Contract Conflicts: The EEC Convention on the Law Applicable to Contractual Obligations; a Comparative Study. 404p. 1982. 77.00 (*0-444-86446-6*, I-291-82, North Holland) Elsevier.
North, P. M. & Fawcett, J. J., eds. Cheshire & North: Private International Law. 12th ed. 1040p. 1992. U.K. pap. 66.00 (*0-406-53081-5*) Butterworth Legal Pubs.
North, P. M., jt. ed. see Morgan, B. J.
North, P. M., jt. auth. see Morris, J. H.
North, P. M., jt. auth. see Pearce, S. C.
North, Pat. Vehicle Refinishing. (Illus.). 320p. 1993. 29.95 (*1-85532-238-2*, Pub. by Osprey Pubng Ltd UK) Motorbooks Intl.
***North, Percy.** Bernhard Guttman: An American Impressionist. LC 95-15263. 1995. write for info. (*1-55859-611-9*) Abbeville Pr.
— Max Weber: The Cubist Decade, 1910-1920. (Illus.). 120p. 1992. pap. 20.00 (*0-939802-69-4*, 91-75675, U of Wash Pr) High Mus Art.
North, Peter. Essays in Private International Law. 296p. 1993. 55.00 (*0-19-825826-7*) OUP.
— Penetrating Insights: A Guide to Meeting & Dating Beautiful Women. 180p. (Orig.). (C). 1994. pap. write for info. (*1-885591-22-5*) Morris Pubng.
North, Peter M. Principal of Jesus College. 1992. lib. bdg. 106.00 (*0-685-62411-0*) Kluwer Ac.
— Private International Law Problems in Common Law Jurisdictions. LC 92-18236. 1993. lib. bdg. 106.00 (*0-7923-1845-5*) Kluwer Ac.
North, Ph. M., jt. ed. see Lebreton, J. D.
North, Philip M., jt. auth. see Castle, Win M.
North, R. Art of Algebra: Simplified Account Numbers, Equations Groups, Continued Fractions. LC 64-66139. 1965. 98.00 (*0-08-010694-3*, Pub. by Pergamon Repr UK) Franklin.
North, R. A. Cleaning Professional Kitchens. 1986. 75.00 (*0-317-61929-2*, Cresta Pub) St Mut.
— Kitchen Cleaning Manual. 1987. 40.00 (*0-317-61936-5*, Cresta Pub) St Mut.
— Kitchen Cleaning Manuals, 5 vols., Set. 1986. 90.00 (*0-317-61937-3*, Cresta Pub) St Mut.
North, Rachel. Flower of Love. 320p. (Orig.). 1984. pap. 3.25 (*0-8439-2145-5*) Dorchester Pub Co.
North, Rachel V. Work & the Eye. LC 92-22606. 1994. 75.00 (*0-19-262282-X*); pap. 33.00 (*0-19-261885-7*) OUP.
North, Raymond. Night Came to the Farms of the Great Plains. LC 91-71312. 286p. 1991. pap. 17.50 (*0-911311-29-7*) Halcyon Hse.
***North, Richard.** Life on a Modern Planet: Rediscovering Faith in Progress. LC 94-28599. 1995. write for info. (*0-7190-4566-5*, Pub. by Manchester Univ Pr UK); pap. text ed. write for info. (*0-7190-4567-3*, Pub. by Manchester Univ Pr UK) St Martin.
— Schools of Tomorrow: Education As If People Mattered. (Illus.). 148p. (Orig.). 1992. pap. 10.95 (*1-870098-06-4*, Pub. by Green Bks UK) Seven Hills Bk.
North, Richard & Hofstra, Tette, eds. Latin Culture & Medieval Germanic Europe: Proceedings from the First Germania Latina Conference Held at the University of Groningen, 26 May 1989. (Mediaevalia Groningana Ser.: No. 11). 128p. 1992. pap. 34.00x (*90-6980-059-4*, Pub. by Egbert Forsten NE) Benjamins North Am.
North, Rick. Young Astronauts, No. 1, No. 1. (J). 1990. pap. 2.95 (*0-8217-3000-2*) Zebra.
— Young Astronauts, No. 2. (J). 1990. pap. 2.95 (*0-8217-3173-4*) Zebra.
— Young Astronauts, No. 3. (J). 1990. pap. 2.95 (*0-8217-3178-5*) Zebra.
— Young Astronauts, No. 4: Destination Mars. 176p. 1991. pap. 2.95 (*0-8217-3285-4*) Zebra.
— Young Astronauts, No. 5: Space Pioneers. 176p. 1991. pap. 2.95 (*0-8217-3307-9*) Zebra.
— Young Astronauts, No. 6: Citizens of Mars. 160p. 1991. pap. 2.95 (*0-8217-3308-7*) Zebra.
North, Robert, tr. see Duverger, Maurice.
North, Robert, tr. see Randolph, Pascal B.
North, Robert C. Moscow & Chinese Communists. 2nd ed. viii, 310p. 1963. 39.50 (*0-8047-0453-8*); pap. 13.95 (*0-8047-0454-6*) Stanford U Pr.
— War, Peace, Survival: Global Politics & Conceptual Synthesis. 298p. (C). 1990. pap. text ed. 21.50 (*0-8133-0683-3*) Westview.
North, Robert C., jt. auth. see Doolin, Dennis.
North, Robert C., jt. auth. see Eudin, Xenia J.
North, Robert C., jt. auth. see Nomikos, Eugenia V.
North, Robert J., jt. ed. see Steinman, Ralph.

North, Robyn. A Very Mouse Tale. (Illus.). 32p. (J). 1995. 14.95 (*0-9643731-0-6*) Robin Bks. Mr. Mouse is reading the newspaper. The forecast is that bad weather is on the way & the mouse family is almost out of food. He sets out with Mrs. Mouse on a mission to find something to eat. This story is about the adventures they have. A VERY MOUSE TALE will appeal to small children that need to be read to or are attempting to read for themselves. They will be intrigued & delighted with the many intricate illustrations rendered in soft tones on tinted paper. Order from Robin Books, Box 280, Free Union, VA 22940; 804-978-4088.** ***Publisher Provided Annotation.

North, Roche, ed. The Light of Nature. 1985. lib. bdg. 162.50 (*90-247-3165-8*) Kluwer Ac.
***North, Roger.** The Life of the Lord Keeper North. LC 95-2968. (Illus.). 644p. 1995. 129.95 (*0-7734-8972-X*) E Mellen.
— Memoirs of Musick. Rimbault, Edward F., ed. LC 74-24169. reprint ed. 25.00 (*0-404-13073-9*) AMS Pr.
North, Ronald M., et al, eds. Unified River Basin Management: Proceedings of a Symposium Held in Gatlinburg, Tennessee, May 4-7, 1980. LC 81-69176. (American Water Resources Association Technical Publication Ser.: No. TPS-81-3). (Illus.). 666p. reprint ed. pap. 180.00 (*0-8357-3163-4*, 2039426) Bks Demand.
North, S. N. Marriage Laws in the United States, 1887-1906. Allen, Desmond W., ed. 91p. 1994. 24.95 (*0-941765-90-3*); pap. 14.95 (*0-941765-89-X*) Arkansas Res.
North, S. N. D. History & Present Conditions of Newspapers. 446p. 1977. reprint ed. lib. bdg. 38.50 (*0-930342-50-X*, 301100) W S Hein.
North Shuswap Elementary School Students. The Shoe Monster. 32p. (J). (gr. k-3). 1994. pap. 3.50 (*0-87406-687-5*) Willowisp Pr.
***North South Books Staff.** The Bologna Annual Nonfiction '95. 1995. pap. 39.95 (*1-55858-439-0*) North-South Bks NYC.
— Bologna Annual '95. 1995. pap. 39.95 (*1-55858-368-8*) North-South Bks NYC.
North, Stafford. Armageddon Again? A Reply to Hal Lindsey. rev. ed. 124p. (Orig.). 1991. pap. 4.95 (*0-9631138-0-1*) Landmark Bks.
— Handbook on Church Doctrines. 4th ed. 174p. (Orig.). 1990. pap. write for info. (*0-9631138-1-X*) Landmark Bks.
North, Stephen M. The Making of Knowledge in Composition: Portrait of an Emerging Field. 403p. 1987. pap. text ed. 21.00 (*0-86709-151-7*) Boynton Cook Pubs.
North, Sterling. Abe Lincoln: Log Cabin to White House. LC 87-4654. (Landmark Bks.: No. 61). (Illus.). 160p. (J). (gr. 5-9). 1987. pap. 4.99 (*0-394-89179-1*) Random Bks Yng Read.
— Rascal. (J). (gr. 5 up). 1976. pap. 2.75 (*0-380-01518-8*, Flare) Avon.
— Rascal. (J). (gr. 5-9). 1993. 18.00 (*0-8446-6648-3*) Peter Smith.
— Rascal. (Illus.). 192p. (J). (ps up). 1990. pap. 3.99 (*0-14-034445-4*, Puffin) Puffin Bks.
— Rascal: A Memoir of a Better Era. LC 63-13882. (Illus.). (J). (gr. 4 up). 1984. 14.99 (*0-525-18839-8*, DCB) Dutton Child Bks.
— The Wolfling. (Illus.). 224p. (J). (gr. 5-9). 1992. pap. 3.99 (*0-14-036166-9*, Puffin) Puffin Bks.
— The Wolfling. 256p. (J). (gr. 4-6). pap. 2.50 (*0-590-41868-8*) Scholastic Inc.
North Suburban Bethel Sisterhood Staff. Tradition in the Kitchen Two: The Authentic Guide to Kosher Cooking. Frost, Eenie, ed. (Illus.). 328p. 1993. 19.95 (*0-9635594-0-0*) N Suburban BES.
North Sunflower Academy Staff. The Pick of the Crop. (Illus.). 1978. 8.95 (*0-918544-17-3*) Wimmer Bks.
North, T. H., jt. ed. see Olson, D. L.
North, Terrell. How to Turn Your Newspapers into Cash. 42p. 1984. pap. 11.95 (*0-915665-05-0*) Premier Publishers.
North Texas Percussion Press Staff. Drum Set Transcriptions, Vol. 1. 42p. (C). 1991. 7.47 (*1-56870-008-3*) RonJon Pub.
— Drum Set Transcriptions, Vol. 2. 42p. (C). 1991. 7.47 (*1-56870-009-1*) RonJon Pub.
— Drum Set Transcriptions, Vol. 3. 80p. (C). 1991. 8.13 (*1-56870-010-5*) RonJon Pub.
— Mallet Studies. 60p. (C). 1991. 7.89 (*1-56870-011-3*) RonJon Pub.
North, Thomas, tr. see Plutarch.
North, Tony, ed. see Bull, Stephen.
North, W. R. Chinese Themes in American Verse. 1973. 59.95 (*0-87968-857-2*) Gordon Pr.
North, Walter, jt. ed. see Pryor, Timothy R.
North, Wheeler. Underwater California. LC 75-13153. (California Natural History Guides Ser.: No.39). (Illus.). 1976. pap. 12.00 (*0-520-03039-7*) U CA Pr.
North, William G., et al, eds. The Neurohypophysis: A Window on Brain Function. LC 93-25020. (Annals Ser.: Vol. 689). 701p. 1993. text ed. write for info. (*0-89766-773-5*); pap. text ed. 190.00 (*0-89766-774-3*) NY Acad Sci.
Northall, G. English Folk Rhymes. 1972. 59.95 (*0-8490-0110-2*) Gordon Pr.
Northall, G. F. Folk-Phrases of Four Counties: Gloucester, Staffordshire, Warwickshire & Worshestershire: Gathered from Unpublished Manuscripts & Oral Tradition. (English Dialect Society Publications Ser.: No. 73). 1969. reprint ed. pap. 15.00 (*0-8115-0491-3*) Periodicals Srv.
Northall, G. T. A Warwickshire Word-Book Comprising Obsolescent & Dialect Words, Colloquialisms, Etc. (English Dialect Society Publications Ser.: No. 79). 1974. reprint ed. pap. 31.00 (*0-8115-0497-2*) Periodicals Srv.
Northam, Ray M. Urban Geography. 2nd ed. LC 78-12335. (Illus.). 524p. reprint ed. pap. 149.40 (*0-7837-3496-4*, 2057829) Bks Demand.
Northan, Irene. The Hollander's Daughter. large type ed. (Linford Romance Library). 384p. 1992. pap. 14.95 (*0-7089-7134-2*, Trailtree Bookshop) Ulverscroft.
Northbourne, Lord, tr. see Burckhardt, Titus.
Northbrooke, John. Treatise Against Dicing, Dancing, Plays & Interludes. LC 77-149667. reprint ed. 29.50 (*0-404-04793-9*) AMS Pr.
Northcote House Publ. Ltd. Staff. Fred Learns about Computers. 1990. pap. 21.00 (*0-7121-0636-7*, Pub. by Northcote UK) St Mut.
— Fred Learns the New Maths. 1990. pap. 21.00 (*0-7121-0104-7*, Pub. by Northcote UK) St Mut.
Northcote, Hugh. Christianity & Sex Problems. 2nd ed. LC 72-9668. reprint ed. 49.50 (*0-404-57486-6*) AMS Pr.
Northcote, Sydney. The Songs of Henri Duparc: Music Book Index. 122p. 1993. reprint ed. lib. bdg. 69.00 (*0-7812-9595-5*) Rprt Serv.
Northcote, T. G., jt. ed. see Comin, F. A.
Northcott, A. Gary. Sorceror's World. Van Treese, James B., ed. 238p. 1994. pap. 8.95 (*1-56901-156-7*) NW Pub.
Northcott, Bayan, ed. see Keller, Hans.
Northcott, Cecil. South Seas Sailor (John Williams) 1979. 3.95 (*0-87508-622-5*) Chr Lit.
Northcott, Clarence H. Australian Social Development. LC 68-56676. (Columbia University. Studies in the Social Sciences: No. 189). reprint ed. 23.50 (*0-404-51189-9*) AMS Pr.
Northcott, D. G. Multilinear Algebra. 209p. 1984. 64.95 (*0-521-26269-0*) Cambridge U Pr.
Northcott, Deryl. Capital Investment Decision Making. (Advanced Management Accounting & Finance Ser.). (Illus.). 92p. 1992. pap. text ed. 14.95 (*0-12-521685-8*) Acad Pr.
***Northcott, Herbert C.** Aging in Alberta: Rhetoric & Reality. 117p. (Orig.). (C). 1992. pap. text ed. 18.95x (*1-55059-049-9*) Temeron Bks.
***Northcott, Jim.** Britain in Europe in 2010. 200p. (C). 1995. pap. 19.95 (*0-85374-645-1*, Pub. by Pol Studies Inst UK) Brookings.
Northcott, Kenneth J., tr. see Bernhard, Thomas.
Northcott, Kenneth J., tr. see Braunfels, Wolfgang.
Northcott, Kenneth J., tr. see Nissen, Hans J.
Northcott, Kenneth J., tr. see Von Hallberg, Robert.

An Asterisk (*) at the beginning of an entry indicates that the title is appearing in BIP for the first time.

Northcott, Kenneth J., ed. see Von Schiller, Friedrich.

Northcott, Leslie. Molybdenum. LC 57-228. (Metallurgy of the Rarer Metals Ser.: No. 5). 234p. reprint ed. pap. 66. 70 (*0-317-42141-7*, 2025760) Bks Demand.

Northcott, Nancy T., jt. auth. see Quayle, Marilyn T.

Northcott, W. Henry. A Treatise: On Lathes & Turning. LC 87-3618. (Illus.). 328p. 1988. reprint ed. pap. 14.95 (*0-941936-10-4*) Linden Pub Fresno.

Northcott, Winifred H., ed. Curriculum Guide: Hearing-Impaired Children, Birth to Three Years, & Their Parents. LC 76-56634. 1977. pap. text ed. 14.95 (*0-88200-077-2*, D1998) Alexander Graham.

— The Hearing Impaired Child in a Regular Classroom: Preschool, Elementary, & Secondary Years. LC 73-86074. 1973. pap. text ed. 9.95 (*0-88200-064-0*, N7431) Alexander Graham.

Northcraft, Gregory B. & Neale, Margaret A. Organizational Behavior: A Management Challenge. 797p. (C). 1990. text ed. 56.00 (*0-03-020539-5*) Dryden Pr.

— Organizational Behavior: A Management Challenge. 2nd ed. LC 97-72827. 726p. (C). 1994. text ed. 62.75 (*0-03-074611-6*); disk 21.00 (*0-03-074618-3*); disk 21.00 (*0-03-074617-5*); disk 21.00 (*0-03-098053-4*) Dryden Pr.

— Organizational Behavior: A Management Challenge: Teaching Tools & Video Teaching Notes to Accompany. 2nd ed. 385p. (C). 1994. pap. text ed. 28.00 (*0-03-074621-3*) Dryden Pr.

Northcroft, G. J. Sketches of Summerland: Nassau & the Bahama Islands. 1976. lib. bdg. 59.95 (*0-8490-2614-8*) Gordon Pr.

Northcut, Allan, ed. see Knauff, Thomas L.

Northcut, Debbie, ed. see Knauff, Thomas L.

Northcutt, B., jt. auth. see Kittner, M.

Northcutt, Cecilia A. Successful Career Women: Their Professional & Personal Characteristics. LC 90-38415. (Contributions in Women's Studies: No. 120). 144p. 1991. text ed. 39.95 (*0-313-27256-5*, NPY, Greenwood Pr) Greenwood.

Northcutt, J. Duane. Reliable Distributed Real-Time Operating Systems: The Alpha Kernel. (Perspectives in Computing Ser.). 246p. 1987. text ed. 54.00 (*0-12-521690-4*) Acad Pr.

Northcutt, Marjorie. Matilda's Bloomers: Prairie School Stories. Williams, Sue, ed. LC 93-61048. (Illus.). 112p. (Orig.). 1994. pap. text ed. 9.95 (*1-882420-09-8*) Hearth KS.

Northcutt, R. G., ed. Comparative Neurobiology: Problems for a New Decade: 1st Annual Karger Workshop - Journal: Brain, Behavior & Evolution, Vol. 36, Nos. 2 & 3, 1990. 104p. 1990. pap. 120.00 (*3-8055-5319-6*) S Karger.

Northcutt, R. G. & Bemis, W. E. Cranial Nerves of the Coelacanth, Latimeria Chalumnae - Osteichtyes: Sarcoterygii: Actinistia - Comparisons with Other Cranista: Actinistia - Comparisons with Other Craniata. (Journal: Reprint of Brain, Behavior & Evolution: Vol. 42, Suppl. 1, 1993). (Illus.). x, 76p. 1993. 74.50 (*3-8055-5802-3*) S Karger.

Northcutt, Wayne. Mitterrand: A Political Biography. LC 91-29986. 416p. 1993. 34.95 (*0-8419-1295-5*) Holmes & Meier.

Northcutt, Wayne, ed. Historical Dictionary of the French Fourth & Fifth Republics, 1946-1990. LC 91-17387. 544p. 1992. text ed. 89.50 (*0-313-26356-6*, NDF, Greenwood Pr) Greenwood.

Northeast Drama Institute Staff. Full-Color Designs from Chinese Opera Costumes. (Illus.). 1980. reprint ed. pap. 6.95 (*0-486-23979-9*) Dover.

Northeast-Midwest Institute. Education Incorporated: School-Business Cooperation for Economic Growth. LC 87-32591. 218p. 1988. text ed. 55.00 (*0-89930-282-3*, MUE/, Quorum Bks) Greenwood.

Northeast Missouri State University Staff. In Pursuit of Degrees with Integrity: A Value-Added Approach to Undergraduate Assessment. 95p. (Orig.). 1984. pap. text ed. 18.25 (*0-88044-106-2*) AASCU Press.

Northeastern University Center for Labor Market Studies Staff, jt. auth. see Children's Defense Fund Staff.

Northeastern University, Dodge Library, Boston Staff. Selective Bibliography in Science & Engineering. 1970. lib. bdg. 85.00 (*0-8161-0701-7*, Hall Library) G K Hall.

Northedge. Excavations at Ana, Vol. 1: Qala Island Iraq Archaeological Reports. 1989. pap. 75.00 (*0-85668-425-2*, Pub. by Aris & Phillips UK) David Brown.

Northedge, Alastair, et al. Studies on Roman & Islamic Amman: The Excavations of Mrs. C-M Bennett & Other Investigations, Vol. I: History, Site & Architecture. (British Academy Monographs in Archaeology: No. 3). (Illus.). 212p. 1993. 120.00 (*0-19-727002-6*) OUP.

Northedge, F. S., ed. The Use of Force in International Relations. LC 74-10140. 1974. pap. 24.95 (*0-02-923210-4*) Free Pr.

Northedge, F. S. & Donelan, M. D. International Disputes: The Political Aspects. 1971. 20.00 (*0-900362-36-7*) St Mut.

Northen, E. E. & Duckworth, Ruth P. Northern Family in U. S., 1635-1900, & Bridging the Gap, 1900-1960. LC 82-73787. 192p. reprint ed. 40.00 (*0-916497-07-0*); reprint ed. fiche 6.00 (*0-916497-06-2*) Burnett Micro.

Northen, Helen. Clinical Social Work. LC 81-10235. 400p. 1982. text ed. 28.50 (*0-231-03800-3*) Col U Pr.

— Clinical Social Work Knowledge & Skills. 360p. 1994. 37. 50 (*0-231-10110-4*) Col U Pr.

— Clinical Social Work Knowledge & Skills. 2nd ed. 65p. 1994. pap. text ed. write for info. (*0-231-10107-4*) Col U Pr.

— Social Work with Groups. LC 69-19462. (C). 1969. text ed. 37.00 (*0-231-02965-9*) Col U Pr.

— Social Work with Groups. 2nd ed. 452p. 1988. text ed. 31.50 (*0-231-06744-5*) Col U Pr.

Northen, Helen, jt. auth. see Ell, Kathleen.

Northen, Helen, jt. auth. see Roberts, Robert W.

Northen, Henry T. & Northen, Rebecca T. Greenhouse Gardening. 2nd ed. LC 75-190208. (Illus.). 396p. reprint ed. pap. 112.90 (*0-8357-9900-X*, 2055118) Bks Demand.

Northen, Rebecca T. Orchids As House Plants. rev. ed. (Illus.). 160p. 1976. reprint ed. pap. 3.50 (*0-486-23261-1*) Dover.

Northen, Rebecca T., jt. auth. see Northen, Henry T.

Northen, William J., ed. Men of Mark in Georgia: A Complete & Elaborate History of the State from Its Settlement to the Present Time, Vols. 1-7. Incl. Vol. 1. LC 74-2193. 1974. 30.00 (*0-87152-176-8*); Vol. 3. LC 74-2193. 1974. 30.00 (*0-87152-178-4*); Vol. 4. LC 74-2193. 1974. 30.00 (*0-87152-179-2*); Vol. 5. LC 74-2193. 1974. 30.00 (*0-87152-180-6*); Vol. 6. LC 74-2193. 1974. 30.00 (*0-87152-181-4*); Vol. 7. LC 74-2193. 1974. 30.00 (*0-87152-182-2*); LC 74-2193. (Illus.). 3952p. 1974. reprint ed. Set. 197.75 (*0-87152-331-0*) Reprint.

***Northern.** Home Orchid Growing. 4th ed. 1990. 50.00 (*0-671-76327-X*) S&S Trade.

— Study Guide for Handbook of Speech-Language Pathology & Audiology. 446p. 1988. 35.95 (*1-55664-036-6*) Mosby Yr Bk.

***Northern Cartographic Staff.** The Atlas of New Hampshire Trout Ponds. 2nd ed. (Illus.). 164p. Date not set. pap. 14.95 (*0-944187-33-1*) N Cartographic.

Northern, Jerry L., ed. Hearing Disorders. 2nd ed. 331p. (C). 1984. write for info. (*0-205-13539-0*) Allyn.

Northern, Jerry L. & Downs, Marion P. Hearing in Children. 4th ed. (Illus.). 432p. 1991. 49.00 (*0-683-06574-2*) Williams & Wilkins.

Northern, Jerry L., jt. auth. see Hayes, Deborah.

Northern, Jerry L., jt. ed. see Jacobson, John T.

Northern, Jerry L., ed. see Wood, Raymond P.

Northern Pacific Railroad Staff. The Pacific Northwest: Oregon & Washington Territory. (Shorey Historical Ser.). 32p. 1975. reprint ed. pap. 2.95 (*0-8466-0229-6*) Shorey.

Northern, Penny B., jt. ed. see Wall, C. Edward.

Northern, Tamara. The Art of Cameroon. 2nd ed. LC 83-20306. (Illus.). 208p. 1984. pap. 19.95 (*0-86528-026-6*, NOACP) SITES.

— The Sign of the Leopard: Beaded Art of Cameroon. (Illus.). 136p. 1975. write for info. (*0-918386-15-2*) W Benton Mus.

Northern, Tamara & Brown, Wendi-Starr. To Image & to See: Crow Indian Photographs by Edward S. Curtis & Richard Throssel, 1905-1910. LC 93-8625. (Illus.). 1993. 10.00 (*0-944722-14-8*) Hood Mus Art.

Northern Virginia Community College Staff, jt. auth. see JIST Works, Inc. Staff.

Northey, Anthony. Kafka's Relatives: Their Lives & His Writing. 96p. (C). 1991. text ed. 22.00 (*0-300-04585-9*) Yale U Pr.

Northey, Margot. The Haunted Wilderness: The Gothic & Grotesque in Canadian Fiction. LC 76-23329. 139p. reprint ed. pap. 39.70 (*0-8357-8164-X*, 2034007) Bks Demand.

— William Kirby & His Works. (Canadian Author Studies). 26p. (C). 1989. pap. text ed. 9.95 (*1-55022-048-9*, Pub. by ECW Press CN) Genl Dist Srvs.

Northey, Margot, jt. auth. see Fischer, Ann.

Northey, Patrick & Southway, Nigel. Cycle Time Management: The Fast Track to Time-Based Productivity Improvement. LC 92-32449. 1993. 35.00 (*1-56327-015-3*) Prod Press.

Northey, William B. The Land of the Gurkhas. LC 78-179229. (Illus.). reprint ed. 54.00 (*0-404-54856-3*) AMS Pr.

Northfield, T. C., ed. Bile Acids in Health & Disease. (C). 1988. lib. bdg. 104.00 (*0-7462-0076-5*) Kluwer Ac.

— Helicobacter Pylori: Pathophysiology, Epidemiology, & Management. LC 93-38532. 1993. lib. bdg. 60.00 (*0-7923-8825-9*) Kluwer Ac.

Northington, et al. The Botanical World. 2nd ed. (Illus.). 608p. 1991. pap. 37.95 (*0-8016-5169-7*) Mosby Yr Bk.

Northington, David K. Systematic Studies of the Genus Pyrrhopappus (Compositae, Cichorieae) (Special Publications: No. 6). 38p. 1974. pap. 2.00 (*0-89672-031-4*) Tex Tech Univ Pr.

Northington, David K. & Goodin, J. R. The Botanical World. (Illus.). 720p. (C). 1984. 39.95 (*0-8016-1893-2*) Mosby Yr Bk.

Northington, David K., jt. ed. see Goodin, J. R.

***Northington, David K., et al.** Art Study Workbook: The Botanical World. 2nd ed. 128p. (C). 1995. spiral bd. write for info. (*0-697-24279-X*); spiral bd. write for info. (*0-697-27050-5*) Wm C Brown Pubs.

— Art Study Workbook: The Botanical World. 2nd ed. 192p. (C). 1995. student ed write for info. (*0-697-24281-1*) Wm C Brown Pubs.

Northington, Marshall. Managing the Family Business. Gerould, Philip, ed. LC 92-54372. (Small Business & Entrepreneurship Ser.). 175p. (Orig.). 1993. pap. 15.95 (*1-56052-174-0*) Crisp Pubns.

Northman, Phillip. Great Gatsby Notes. 1966. pap. 3.75 (*0-8220-0560-3*) Cliffs.

Northouse, Cameron. Americans Doing Business in Japan: A Resource Book. LC 92-27061. 1992. 21.95 (*0-935061-48-7*) Contemp Res.

— Ishmael Reed: An Interview. LC 93-36204. (Glen Cove Interviews Ser.). 1993. 10.00 (*0-935061-53-3*) Contemp Res.

Northouse, Cameron, ed. Concept: An Anthology of Contemporary Writing. (Orig.). 1979. pap. 9.95 (*0-89683-014-4*) New London Pr.

Northouse, Laurel L., jt. auth. see Northouse, Peter G.

Northouse, Peter G. & Northouse, Laurel L. Health Communication: A Handbook for Health Professionals. 2nd ed. (Illus.). 336p. (C). 1992. pap. text ed. 31.95 (*0-8385-3675-1*, A3675-4) Appleton & Lange.

Northover, Basil J. Electrical Properties of Mammalian Tissues: An Introduction. (Illus.). 160p. 1992. pap. 29.95 (*0-412-46050-5*, A7444) Chapman & Hall.

Northover, John M. & Kettner, Joel D. Bowel Cancer: The Facts. LC 92-12443. 1992. pap. 10.50 (*0-19-262207-2*) OUP.

— Bowel Cancer: The Facts. (Facts Ser.). (Illus.). 184p. 1993. 22.50 (*0-19-261788-5*) OUP.

Northridge, Karen, ed. see Fox, Richard & Fox, Betty.

Northridge, Simon P. Updated World Review of Interactions Between Marine Mammals & Fisheries, Supplement 1. (Fisheries Technical Papers: No. 251). 64p. 1991. pap. 12.00 (*92-5-103054-5*, F0545) UNIPUB.

Northrop & Kelly. Legal Issues in Nursing. (Illus.). 624p. 1987. pap. 34.95 (*0-8016-3720-1*) Mosby Yr Bk.

***Northrop, Albert W. & Schmuhl, Robert A.** Decedents' Estates in Maryland. 500p. 1994. 85.00 (*0-614-05804-X*) Michie Butterworth.

Northrop, Christi M. Skiing with Kids. LC 76-18486. (Illus.). 160p. (Orig.). 1976. pap. 8.95 (*0-85699-136-8*) Chatham Pr.

Northrop, Douglas T., jt. auth. see Chiesa, Giulietto.

Northrop, Emily. The Diminished Anti-Poverty Impact of Economic Growth, the Shift to Services, & the Feminization of Poverty. LC 93-36057. 192p. 1993. 43. 00 (*0-8153-1674-7*) Garland.

Northrop, F. S. The Logic of the Sciences & the Humanities. LC 83-60576. xiv, 402p. 1983. reprint ed. pap. 17.00 (*0-918024-31-5*) Ox Bow.

— The Meeting of East & West: An Inquiry Concerning World Understanding. LC 79-89839. (Illus.). xxii, 531p. 1979. reprint ed. 35.00 (*0-918024-10-2*); reprint ed. pap. 19.95 (*0-918024-11-0*) Ox Bow.

— The Prolegomena to a Nineteen Eighty-Five Philosophiae Naturalis Principia Mathematica. LC 84-27350. xvi, 73p. 1986. 30.00 (*0-918024-35-8*) Ox Bow.

— Science & First Principles. LC 79-89840. 1979. reprint ed. 32.00 (*0-918024-08-0*) Ox Bow.

— The Taming of the Nations: A Study of the Cultural Bases of International Policy. LC 86-28587. xvi, 362p. (C). 1987. reprint ed. 30.00 (*0-918024-45-5*); reprint ed. pap. 16.00 (*0-918024-46-3*) Ox Bow.

Northrop, Filmer S. The Logic of the Sciences & the Humanities. LC 78-21524. 402p. 1979. reprint ed. text ed. 35.00 (*0-313-21161-2*, NOLS, Greenwood Pr) Greenwood.

Northrop, Fyre. The Tempest. (New Penguin Shakespeare Ser.). 1981. mass mkt. 5.50 (*0-14-070713-1*, Penguin Classics) Viking Penguin.

Northrop, Henry D. College of Life or Practical Self Educator. LC 71-79014. (Black Heritage Library Collection). (Illus.). 1977. 54.95 (*0-8369-8638-5*) Ayer.

Northrop, Jo. Country Matters. (Illus.). 208p. 1994. 21.95 (*1-55591-150-1*) Fulcrum Pub.

— Jo Northrop Cooks Country. Ingram, tr. 360p. 1994. pap. 12.95 (*1-880416-99-9*) NW Pub.

Northrop, Marie E. Spanish Mexican Families of Early California, Vol. I: 1769-1850. 2nd ed. (Illus.). 421p. 1987. 30.00 (*0-9617773-0-3*) S CA Geneal Soc.

Northrop, Mildred B. Control Policies of the Reichsbank, 1924-1933. LC 68-58613. (Columbia University. Studies in the Social Sciences: No. 436). reprint ed. 27.50 (*0-404-51436-7*) AMS Pr.

Northrop, Nancy. ABCs for the Child With-in. (Illus.). 30p. 1993. pap. 5.95 (*0-9627894-2-9*) LNR Pubns.

— Mystari. (Illus.). 16p. (J). 1991. spiral bd. 5.95 (*0-9627894-1-0*) LNR Pubns.

— Watch Out for My Nest. (Illus.). 44p. (Orig.). (J). (gr. 1-5). 1994. pap. 5.95 (*0-9627894-3-7*) LNR Pubns.

Northrop, Robert B. Analog Electronic Circuits: Analysis & Applications. (Electrical & Computer Engineering Ser.). (Illus.). 512p. (C). 1990. text ed. 69.95 (*0-201-11656-1*) Addison-Wesley.

Northrop, S. A., et al. Turquoise. (Illus.). 1973. pap. 5.95 (*0-89013-060-4*) Museum NM Pr.

Northrop, Suzane & McLoughlin, Kate. Seance: A Guide for Living. LC 94-17689. 208p. 1994. text ed. 18.00 (*0-9641509-0-5*) Allian Pubng.

***Northrup.** Women's Bodies, Women's Wisdom: Creating Physical & Emotional Health & Healing. 1995. pap. (*0-553-37466-4*) Bantam.

Northrup, A. J. Northrup-Northrop Genealogy; a Record of the Known Descendants of Joseph Northrup, One of the Original Settlers of Milford, Connecticut, in 1639. (Illus.). 473p. 1989. reprint ed. lib. bdg. 79.00 (*0-8328-0906-3*); reprint ed. pap. 71.00 (*0-8328-0907-1*) Higginson Bk Co.

Northrup, Bruce E., jt. ed. see Garfin, Steven R.

Northrup, Christiane. Women's Bodies, Women's Wisdom: Creating Physical & Emotional Health & Healing. LC 94-8357. 1994. 22.95 (*0-553-08120-9*) Bantam.

Northrup, Curt. Los Angeles Survival Guide. LC 92-74429. (City Survival Guides Ser.). 156p. 1992. pap. 10.00 (*0-9634720-0-3*) Arkobaleno.

— New York Survival Guide. LC 93-71212. (City Survival Guides Ser.). 170p. (Orig.). (C). 1993. pap. 7.95 (*0-9634720-1-1*) Arkobaleno.

***Northrup, David.** The Atlantic Slave Trade. (Problems in World History Ser.). 221p. (C). 1994. pap. text ed. write for info. (*0-669-33145-7*) Heath.

— Beyond the Bend in the River: African Labor in Eastern Zaire, 1865-1940. (Monographs in International Studies, Africa Ser.: No. 52). 195p. 1988. pap. text ed. 15.00 (*0-89680-151-9*, Ohio U Ctr Intl) Ohio U Pr.

— Indentured Labor in the Age of Imperialism, 1834-1922. (Studies in Comparative World History). (Illus.). 192p. (C). 1995. 49.95 (*0-521-48047-7*); pap. 14.95 (*0-521-48519-3*) Cambridge U Pr.

***Northrup, Gordon, ed.** Applied Research in Residential Treatment. LC 94-24683. 99p. 1994. 29.95 (*1-56024-687-1*) Haworth Pr.

Northrup, Gordon, intro. The Management of Sexuality in Residential Treatment. LC 93-41273. (Residential Treatment for Children & Youth Ser.). (Illus.). 150p. 1993. lib. bdg. 29.95 (*1-56024-483-6*) Haworth Pr.

— Managing the Residential Treatment Center in Troubled Times. LC 94-17286. (Residential Treatment for Children & Youth Ser.). 111p. 1994. 29.95 (*1-56024-676-6*) Haworth Pr.

Northrup, Gordon & Garfinkel, Barry, eds. Adolescent Suicide: Recognition, Treatment & Prevention. LC 89-19773. (Residential Treatment for Children & Youth Ser.: Vol. 7, No. 1). (Illus.). 116p. 1990. text ed. 29.95 (*0-86656-949-9*) Haworth Pr.

Northrup, Herbert, jt. auth. see Bloom, Gordon F.

Northrup, Herbert R. Black & Other Minority Participation in the All Voluntary Navy & Marine Corps. LC 78-72037. (Pennsylvania University, Wharton School of Finance & Commerce, Industrial Research Unit Study Ser.: No. 57). 265p. reprint ed. pap. 75.60 (*0-8357-7283-7*, 2011212) Bks Demand.

— The Changing Role of Professional Women in Research & Development. LC 88-81113. (Manpower & Human Resources Studies: No. 11A). 78p. 1988. pap. 15.00 (*0-89546-072-6*) U PA Wharton Ctr Human Resc.

— Open Shop Construction Revisited. LC 84-48502. (Major Industrial Research Unit Studies: No. 62). 674p. 1984. 38.00 (*0-89546-047-5*) U PA Wharton Ctr Human Resc.

Northrup, Herbert R. & Larson, John A. The Impact of the AT&T-EEO Consent Decree. LC 79-128190. (Labor Relations & Public Policy Ser.: No. 20). 270p. reprint ed. pap. 77.00 (*0-317-41890-4*, 2025912) Bks Demand.

Northrup, Herbert R. & Malin, Margot E. Personnel Policies for Engineers & Scientists: An Analysis of Major Corporate Practice. LC 85-60642. (Manpower & Human Resources Studies). 331p. 1985. 30.00 (*0-89546-053-X*) U PA Wharton Ctr Human Resc.

Northrup, Herbert R. & Rowan, Richard L. The International Transport Workers' Federation & Flag of Convenience Shipping. (Multinational Industrial Relations Ser.: No. 7c). 251p. (Orig.). 1984. pap. text ed. 18.00 (*0-89546-042-4*) U PA Wharton Ctr Human Resc.

— Multinational Collective Bargaining Attempts: The Record, the Cases, & the Prospects. (Multinational Industrial Relations Ser.: No. 6). 580p. 1979. 27.50 (*0-89546-016-5*) U PA Wharton Ctr Human Resc.

Northrup, Herbert R. & Rowan, Richard L., eds. Employee Relations & Regulation in the '80s: Proceedings of a Conference. LC 81-84823. (Labor Relations & Public Policy Ser.: No. 22). 482p. reprint ed. pap. 137.40 (*0-8357-3154-5*, 2039417) Bks Demand.

Northrup, Herbert R. & Thornton, Amie D. The Federal Government as Employer: The Federal Labor Relations Authority & the PATCO Challenge. LC 87-82880. (Labor Relations & Public Policy Ser.: No. 32). 152p. 1988. pap. 20.00 (*0-89546-068-8*) U PA Wharton Ctr Human Resc.

Northrup, Herbert R., jt. frwd. see Diss-Greis, Theresa.

Northrup, Herbert R., jt. frwd. see Perry, Charles R.

Northrup, Herbert R., jt. auth. see Rowan, Richard L.

Northrup, Herbert R., et al. Doublebreasted Operations & Pre-Hire Agreements in Construction: The Facts & the Law: A Supplement to Open Shop Construction Revisited. LC 87-81475. (Major Industrial Research Unit Ser.: No. 62a). (Illus.). 136p. reprint ed. pap. 38.80 (*0-7837-4334-3*, 2044045) Bks Demand.

— Government Protection of Employees Involved in Mergers & Acquisitions. LC 88-81112. (Labor Relations & Public Policy Ser.: No. 34). 676p. 1989. pap. 45.00 (*0-89546-070-X*) U PA Wharton Ctr Human Resc.

— The Impact of OSHA: A Study of the Effects of the Occupational Safety & Health Act on Three Key Industries - Aerospace, Chemicals, & Textiles. LC 77-95129. (Labor Relations & Public Policy Ser.: No. 17). 592p. reprint ed. pap. 168.80 (*0-317-41884-X*, 2025911) Bks Demand.

— Negro Employment in Land & Air Transport: A Study of Racial Policies in the Railroad, Airline, Trucking, & Urban Transit Industries. LC 70-161216. (Studies of Negro Employment: Vol. 5). 687p. reprint ed. pap. 180. 00 (*0-8357-3156-1*, 2039419) Bks Demand.

— The Objective Selection of Supervisors: A Study of Informal Industry Practice & Two Models for Improved Supervisor Selection. LC 78-61998. (Manpower & Human Resources Studies: No. 8). 247p. 1978. 25.00 (*0-89546-006-8*) U PA Wharton Ctr Human Resc.

Northrup, James P. Old Age, Handicapped & Vietnam-Era Antidiscrimination. rev. ed. LC 80-53990. (Labor Relations & Public Policy Ser.: No. 14). 280p. reprint ed. pap. 79.80 (*0-317-41898-X*, 2025914) Bks Demand.

Northrup, Jim. Walking the Rez Road. 176p. 1993. 15.95 (*0-89658-181-0*) Voyageur Pr.

Northrup, L. W. Encounters with Angels. 112p. 1988. pap. 6.99 (*0-8423-0765-6*) Tyndale.

Northsun, Nila & Sagel, Jim. Small Bones, Little Eyes. Robertson, Kirk, ed. (Windriver Ser.). 72p. (Orig.). (C). 1982. pap. 5.00 (*0-916918-17-3*) Duck Down.

Northup, A. Dale. Frank Lloyd Wright in Michigan. 2nd rev. ed. LC 91-43067. (Michigan Monographs: No. 4). (Illus.). 102p. 1991. pap. text ed. 25.00 (*0-917256-51-4*) Ref Pubns.

N

An Asterisk (*) at the beginning of an entry indicates that the title is appearing in BIP for the first time.

Northup, Arthur. Scenario of the Savior as Sovereign: The Book of Revelation As a Christian World View & Philosophy of History. 345p. 1991. pap. write for info. (*1-881909-18-2*) Advent Christ Gen Conf.

Northup, Bill, jt. auth. see Mollica, Anthony.

Northup, Bill, jt. auth. see Mollica, Tony.

Northup, Charles H. The Japan Vacation Planner: How to Be Your Own Tour Guide - Spend Less, Enjoy More, & Go Anywhere You Want. LC 92-12037. (Illus.). 168p. (Orig.). 1992. pap. 12.95 (*0-9628137-5-3*) Stone Bridge Pr.

Northup, Clark S. Representative Phi Beta Kappa Orations: Second Series. (BCL1-PS American Literature Ser.). 553p. 1992. reprint ed. lib. bdg. 99.00 (*0-7812-6658-0*) Rprt Serv.

Northup, Clark S., ed. Representative Phi Beta Kappa Orations, Ser. 1. 2nd ed. reprint ed. 45.00 (*0-404-04795-5*) AMS Pr.

— Representative Phi Beta Kappa Orations, Ser. 2. LC 74-173800. reprint ed. 45.00 (*0-404-04796-3*) AMS Pr.

Northup, Lesley A. The Eighteen Ninety-Two Book of Common Prayer. LC 93-17882. (Toronto Studies in Theology: Vol. 65). 1993. text ed. write for info. (*0-7734-9322-0*) E Mellen.

Northup, Soloman. Twelve Years a Slave, Eighteen Forty-One to Eighteen Fifty-Three. LC 89-82295. (Jewels from the Past Ser.). (Illus.). 205p. (YA). (gr. 6-12). 1990. lib. bdg. 16.50 (*0-944419-27-5*); pap. text ed. 9.95 (*0-944419-17-8*) Everett Cos Pub.

Northup, Solomon. Twelve Years a Slave. Eakin, Sue & Logsdon, Joseph, eds. LC 68-13454. (Library of Southern Civilization). (Illus.). xxxviii, 274p. 1968. pap. text ed. 11.95 (*0-8071-0150-8*) La State U Pr.

— Twelve Years a Slave: Excerpts from the Narrative of Solomon Northup. abr. ed. Lucas, Alice, ed. (Illus.). 48p. (Orig.). (J). (gr. 5-12). Date not set. pap. text ed. 25.00 (*0-936434-39-2*, Pub. by Zellerbach Fam Fund) SF Study Ctr.

— Twelve Years a Slave: Excerpts from the Narrative of Solomon Northup. abr. ed. Lucas, Alice, ed. (Illus.). 48p. (Orig.). (J). (gr. 5-12). 1992. teacher ed, pap. text ed. 5.00 (*0-936434-59-7*, Pub. by Zellerbach Fam Fund) SF Study Ctr.

Northway, Jeff & Kacalek, Dona, illus. Working Your Way to the Nations: A Guide to Effective Tentmaking. (World Evangelical Fellowship Ser.: No. 1). 208p. (Orig.). 1993. student ed 12.95 (*0-87808-244-1*, WCL244-1) William Carey Lib.

***Northway, Jennifer.** Get Lost, Laura! LC 94-22257. (Illus.). 32p. (J). (ps-2). 1995. 10.95 (*0-307-17520-0*, Artsts Writrs) Western Pub.

***Northwest Environment Watch Staff.** State of the Northwest. (New Report Ser.: 1). 80p. (Orig.). 1994. per., pap. text ed. 8.00 (*1-886093-00-8*) NW Environ Watch.

Northwest Home Designing, Inc. Staff. The Designment Review 1987. Lord, Todd, ed. LC 86-62347. (Illus.). 40p. 1986. pap. 8.00 (*0-936909-02-1*) Northwest Home.

— Designment Review 1988. Lord, Todd, ed. LC 86-657614. (Illus.). 40p. pap. 8.00 (*0-936909-04-8*) Northwest Home.

Northwest Home Designing Inc. Staff. Designment Review '90. Lord, Todd, ed. LC 86-657614. (Pacific Rim Edition Ser.). (Illus.). 40p. (Orig.). (JPN.). (C). 1990. pap. 8.00 (*0-936909-07-2*) Northwest Home.

Northwest Matrix Staff, ed. see Barton, Lois.

Northwest Parent Publishing Staff. Going Places: Family Getaways in the Pacific Northwest. 168p. 1990. pap. 11.95 (*0-9614626-2-0*) NW Parent Pub.

***Northwest Publishing Staff.** Best of Writers at Work 1994. 1994. pap. 12.95 (*1-56901-696-8*) NW Pub.

Northwest Regional Educational Laboratory, Center for Sex Equity Staff. Bibliography of Nonsexist Supplementary Books (K-12) LC 83-42838. 120p. 1984. pap. 32.50 (*0-89774-101-3*) Oryx Pr.

Northwest Regional Educational Laboratory Staff. Advertising Techniques & Consumer Fraud. (Lifeworks Ser.). (Illus.). 1979. text ed. 13.96 (*0-07-047308-0*) McGraw.

— Buying a House, Buying a Mobile Home. (Illus.). 1979. text ed. 13.96 (*0-07-047302-1*) McGraw.

— Buying & Caring for Your Car & Insurance for Your Life, Health & Possessions. (Lifeworks Ser.). (Illus.). 1980. text ed. 13.96 (*0-07-047307-2*) McGraw.

— Comparison Shopping & Caring for Your Personal Possessions. (Lifeworks Ser.). (Illus.). 1980. text ed. 13.96 (*0-07-047309-9*) McGraw.

— Moving on & Getting Utilities & Saving Energy. (Illus.). 1979. text ed. 13.96 (*0-07-047303-X*) McGraw.

— Ordering from Catalogs & Dining Out. (Lifeworks Ser.). (Illus.). 1979. text ed. 13.96 (*0-07-047305-6*) McGraw.

— Understanding Contracts & Legal Documents & Understanding Criminal Law. (Lifeworks Ser.). (Illus.). 1980. text ed. 13.96 (*0-07-060913-6*) McGraw.

— Using Credit & Banking Services & Understanding Income Tax. (Lifeworks Ser.). (Illus.). 1979. text ed. 13.96 (*0-07-047306-4*) McGraw.

Northwest Seafood Consultant Staff, et al. Professional Seafood Demonstrator's Handbook. rev. ed. (Illus.). 48p. (Orig.). 1989. pap. text ed. 5.95 (*0-934363-07-2*) Lance Pubns.

Northwest Seafood Consultants Staff. The Professional Seafood Demonstrator's Handbook. Lane, Jay, ed. (How-to Ser.). (Illus.). 80p. 1988. pap. text ed. 5.00 (*0-934363-06-4*) Lance Pubns.

Northwestern University, School of Commerce Staff. The Ethical Problems of Modern Advertising. Assael, Henry, ed. LC 78-288. (Century of Marketing Ser.). 1979. reprint ed. lib. bdg. 17.95 (*0-405-11169-X*) Ayer.

Northwestern University Staff. Catalog of the Melville J. Herskovits Library of African Studies, Northwestern University, & Africana in Selected Libraries, Evanston, 8 vols., Set. 1972. lib. bdg. 825.00 (*0-8161-0921-4*, Hall Library) G K Hall.

— Catalog of the Transportation Center Library, Northwestern University. 1972. Subject Catalog 9 Vols. lib. bdg. 980.00 (*0-8161-0185-X*, Hall Library); Author-title Catalog. lib. bdg. 1,305.00 (*0-8161-0924-9*, Hall Library) G K Hall.

— Catalog of the Transportation Center Library, Northwestern University, 12 vols., Set. 1972. lib. bdg. write for info. (*0-685-01569-6*, Hall Library) G K Hall.

— Humanities Series, 31 Vols, Set. reprint ed. 737.00 (*0-404-50700-X*) AMS Pr.

— Joint Acquisitions List of Africana: 1978. 1980. lib. bdg. 105.00 (*0-8161-0329-1*, Hall Library) G K Hall.

Northwestern University Traffic Institute Staff. Civil Liability & the Police. LC 83-114221. (Know the Law Ser.: No. 202). 1987. 12.00 (*0-685-07053-0*) Traffic Inst.

***NorthWestNet Staff.** Internet Passport: NorthwestNets Guide to Our World Online. 5th ed. 1995. pap. 29.95 (*0-13-194200-X*) P-H.

Northwood, Arthur, Jr., jt. auth. see Rapport, Leonard.

Northwood, S., jt. auth. see Sekunda, N.

***NorthWord Press, Inc. Staff.** Camp & Cottage Log. (Illus.). 128p. 1995. write for info. (*1-55971-459-X*) NorthWord.

Nortier, J. W. Adjunctive Medical Therapy of Acromegalic Patients. (Clinical Research Ser.: No. 2). x, 91p. (Orig.). (C). 1984. pap. text ed. 23.10 (*3-11-013365-2*) Mouton.

Nortier, Jacomine. Dutch-Moroccan Code Switching among Moroccans in the Netherlands. xiv, 237p. (Orig.). (C). 1990. pap. text ed. 57.70 (*3-11-013102-1*) Mouton.

Nortmann, Ulrich. Deontische Logik Ohne Paradoxien Semantik Und Logik Des Normativen. (Introductiones Ser.). 200p. (GER.). (C). 1989. 50.00 (*3-88405-067-2*) Philosophia Pr.

Norton. Difficult Airway Atlas with Diagnostic & Management Criteria. 200p. 1991. 67.00 (*0-8151-6425-4*, Yr Bk Med Pubs) Mosby Yr Bk.

— Elements of Ceramics. (Illus.). 311p. (C). reprint ed. 40.00 (*1-878907-28-X*) TechBooks.

— Peter N's Guide Question & Answer Mac. Date not set. write for info. (*0-679-79091-8*) Random.

Norton & Meyers. Pet Nor Person, Questions & Answers, No. 4. 1992. pap. write for info. (*0-553-37208-4*) Bantam.

Norton & Pullen. The Attack & Defense of Little Roundtop, Gettysburg, July 2, 1863. 350p. 1983. 25.00 (*0-89029-041-5*) Morningside Bkshop.

Norton & Stuntz. Descriptive Catalog of Hemerocallis Clones, 1893-1948. 100p. 10.00 (*0-930653-02-5*) Intl Bulb Soc.

Norton, jt. auth. see Ellis.

Norton, jt. auth. see St. Paul.

Norton, et al. A People & a Nation, 3 Vols. 3rd ed. (C). 1989. text ed. 51.96 (*0-395-43307-X*) HM.

Norton, A. Banning. A History of Knox Co., Ohio 1779-1862. (Illus.). 424p. 1993. reprint ed. lib. bdg. 45.00 (*0-8328-2998-6*) Higginson Bk Co.

Norton, A. Hollis. How to Make It When You're Cash Poor: The New Strategy for Buying Real Estate with Little or No Cash. rev. ed. 240p. 1986. pap. 9.95 (*0-671-62803-8*, Fireside) S&S Trade.

Norton, Alan. International Handbook of Local & Regional Government: A Comparative Analysis of Advanced Democracies. 576p. 1994. text ed. 119.95 (*1-85278-005-3*, Pub. by Trans Tech SZ) LPS Dist Ctr.

Norton, Andre. Androids at Arms. 240p. 1987. pap. text ed. 2.95 (*0-345-34282-8*, Del Rey) Ballantine.

— Annals of the Witch World, 3 vols. in 1. 528p. 1994. 12.98 (*1-56865-106-6*, GuildAmerica) Dbldy Bk Music.

— Brother to Shadows. LC 93-13971. 1993. 20.00 (*0-380-97229-8*, AvoNova) Avon.

— Brother to Shadows. 320p. 1994. mass mkt. 5.50 (*0-380-77096-2*, AvoNova) Avon.

— Brother to Shadows. 1993. 20.00 (*0-688-12758-4*) Morrow.

— Dare to Go A-Hunting. 1990. pap. 3.95 (*0-8125-4712-8*) Tor Bks.

— Flight in Yiktor. 256p. 1990. reprint ed. pap. 3.95 (*0-8125-1008-9*) Tor Bks.

— Follow the Drum. 224p. 1981. pap. 2.25 (*0-449-24434-2*, Crest) Fawcett.

— Forerunner. 1991. pap. 3.95 (*0-8125-1364-9*) Tor Bks.

— Forerunner Foray. 1992. pap. 4.50 (*0-451-45176-7*, ROC) NAL-Dutton.

— Fur Magic. (Illus.). 1992. 30.00 (*1-880418-20-7*); 65.00 (*1-880418-19-3*) D M Grant.

— Garan the Eternal. 1972. 6.50 (*0-686-02511-3*) Fantasy Pub Co.

— Golden Trillium. 1994. mass mkt. 5.99 (*0-553-56095-6*) Bantam.

— The Hands of Lyr. LC 93-45829. 400p. 1995. mass mkt. 5.50 (*0-380-77097-0*, AvoNova) Avon.

— Hands of Lyr. 1994. 22.00 (*0-688-13417-3*) Morrow.

— Ice Crown. 224p. 1993. pap. 4.99 (*0-451-45248-8*, ROC) NAL-Dutton.

— Imperial Lady. 1990. pap. 3.95 (*0-8125-0722-3*) Tor Bks.

— Iron Cage. 256p. 1992. pap. 4.50 (*0-451-45193-7*, ROC) NAL-Dutton.

— Judgment on Janus. 224p. 1987. 2.95 (*0-345-34365-4*, Del Rey) Ballantine.

— Key Out of Time. 188p. 1978. 25.00 (*0-89366-186-4*) Ultramarine Pub.

— The Magic Books. 1988. pap. 3.95 (*0-451-15232-8*, Sig) NAL-Dutton.

— Mark of the Cat. 1993. mass mkt. 4.99 (*0-441-51971-7*) Ace Bks.

— Mirror of Destiny. LC 94-32818. 1995. 22.00 (*0-688-13988-4*) Morrow.

— Moon Called. (Illus.). (Orig.). 1991. mass mkt. 3.99 (*0-8125-1533-1*) Tor Bks.

— Ralestone Luck. 256p. 1988. pap. 2.95 (*0-8125-4754-3*) Tor Bks.

— Redline the Stars. 304p. 1993. 19.95 (*0-312-85314-9*) Tor Bks.

— Redline the Stars. 304p. 1994. mass mkt. 4.99 (*0-8125-1986-8*) Tor Bks.

— Sea Siege. 224p. 1987. pap. 2.95 (*0-345-34364-6*, Del Rey) Ballantine.

— Star Rangers. 1980. pap. 1.95 (*0-449-24076-2*, Crest) Fawcett.

— Uncharted Stars. 256p. 1993. pap. 4.50 (*0-451-45232-1*, ROC) NAL-Dutton.

— Voodoo Planet. Bd. with Star Hunter. (Solar Queen Ser.: No. 3). 1983. Set pap. 2.75 (*0-441-78196-9*) Ace Bks.

— The Warding of Witch World. (Secrets of the Witch World Ser.: Vol. 3). 1996. write for info. (*0-446-51991-X*) Warner Bks.

— Wheel of Stars. (Orig.). 1991. mass mkt. 3.99 (*0-8125-1678-8*) Tor Bks.

— Witch World. 288p. 1986. pap. 3.50 (*0-441-89708-8*) Ace Bks.

— Wizards' Worlds. 1990. mass mkt. 4.95 (*0-8125-4750-0*) Tor Bks.

— Wraiths of Time. 256p. 1992. mass mkt. 3.99 (*0-8125-4752-7*) Tor Bks.

— The Zero Stone. 256p. 1992. 4.99 (*0-451-45162-7*, ROC) NAL-Dutton.

Norton, Andre, ed. Grand Masters' Choice. 1991. mass mkt. 3.99 (*0-8125-0619-7*) Tor Bks.

— Moon Mirror. 1989. pap. 4.99 (*0-8125-0303-1*) Tor Bks.

Norton, Andre & Adams, Robert. Magic in Ithkar, I. 320p. 1988. pap. 3.95 (*0-8125-4715-2*) Tor Bks.

— Magic in Ithkar III. 1989. pap. 3.95 (*0-8125-4709-8*) Tor Bks.

Norton, Andre & Crispin, A. C. Gryphon's Eyrie. 256p. 1992. mass mkt. 4.99 (*0-8125-3169-8*) Tor Bks.

— Songsmith. 304p. 1992. 19.95 (*0-312-85123-5*) Tor Bks.

— Songsmith. 304p. 1993. mass mkt. 4.99 (*0-8125-1107-7*) Tor Bks.

Norton, Andre & Greenberg, Martin H., eds. Catfantastic III. 320p. (Orig.). 1994. mass mkt. 4.99 (*0-88677-591-4*) DAW Bks.

Norton, Andre & Griffin, P. M. Fire Hand. 224p. 1994. 19.95 (*0-312-85313-0*) Tor Bks.

— Fire Hand. 288p. 1995. mass mkt. 4.99 (*0-8125-1984-1*) Tor Bks.

— Flight of Vengeance. 384p. 1994. mass mkt. 4.99 (*0-8125-0706-1*) Tor Bks.

— Storms of Victory. (Witch World: The Turning Ser.: Vol. 1). 1992. mass mkt. 4.99 (*0-8125-1109-3*) Tor Bks.

Norton, Andre & Hogarth, Grace A. Sneeze on Sunday. 256p. 1992. reprint ed. mass mkt. 4.99 (*0-8125-1697-4*) Tor Bks.

Norton, Andre & Lackey, Mercedes. The Elvenbane. 576p. 1993. mass mkt. 5.99 (*0-8125-1175-1*) Tor Bks.

— The Elvenbane: An Epic High Fantasy of the Halfblood. 1991. 19.95 (*0-312-85106-5*) Tor Bks.

— Elvenblood. 352p. 1995. 22.95 (*0-312-85548-6*) Tor Bks.

— Elvenblood. 352p. 1996. pap. write for info. (*0-614-05548-2*) Tor Bks.

Norton, Andre & McConchie, Lyn. The Key of the Keplian. 304p. 1995. mass mkt. 5.50 (*0-446-60220-5*, Aspect) Warner Bks.

Norton, Andre & Miller, Phyllis. House of Shadows. 256p. 1985. reprint ed. pap. 2.95 (*0-8125-4743-8*) Tor Bks.

***Norton, Andre & Schaub, Mary.** The Magestone. (Secrets of the Witch World Ser.: Vol. 2). (Orig.). 1996. mass mkt. write for info. (*0-446-60222-1*, Aspect) Warner Bks.

Norton, Andre & Shwartz, Susan. Empire of the Eagle. LC 93-26551. 416p. 1993. 22.95 (*0-312-85169-3*) Tor Bks.

— Empire of the Eagle. 416p. 1995. mass mkt. 5.99 (*0-8125-1393-2*) Tor Bks.

Norton, Andre, jt. ed. see Adams, Robert.

Norton, Andre, jt. auth. see Bloch, Robert.

Norton, Andre, et al. Flight of Vengeance. (Witch World: The Turning Ser.: Vol. 2). 384p. 1992. 21.95 (*0-312-85014-X*) Tor Bks.

— On the Wings of Magic: Witch World. (Turning Ser.: Bk. 3). 416p. 1995. mass mkt. 5.99 (*0-8125-0828-9*) Tor Bks.

— On Wings of Magic: Witch World, the Turning, Bk. 3. 448p. 1993. 23.95 (*0-312-85026-3*) Tor Bks.

Norton, Ann. Brooke's Little Lies. (Fifteen - Nickelodeon Bks.: No. 2). 112p. (J). (gr. 4-9). 1992. pap. 2.95 (*0-448-40491-5*, G&D) Putnam Pub Group.

Norton, Ann W. Gods, Saints, & Demons: The Sacred Art of India & Tibet. (Illus.). 24p. 1989. 5.00 (*0-918386-40-3*) W Benton Mus.

Norton, Anne. Reflections on Political Identity. LC 88-45400. (Constitutional Thought Ser.). 192p. 1988. text ed. 35.00 (*0-8018-3694-8*) Johns Hopkins.

— Reflections on Political Identity. (Johns Hopkins Series in Constitutional Thought). 224p. (C). 1993. reprint ed. pap. text ed. 13.95 (*0-8018-4728-1*) Johns Hopkins.

— Republic of Signs: Liberal Theory & American Popular Culture. LC 92-36749. 184p. (C). 1993. lib. bdg. 34.00 (*0-226-59512-9*); pap. text ed. 12.95 (*0-226-59513-7*) U Ch Pr.

Norton, Anthony R. Drift. Axelrod, David B., ed. (Student Chapbook Ser.). (Illus.). 24p. 1987. 10.00 (*0-685-25229-9*); pap. 5.00 (*0-685-25230-2*) Writers Ink Pr.

Norton, Arthur J., tr. see Bryk, Felix.

Norton, Arthur J., et al. Work & Family Patterns of American Women: The Family Life Cycle, 1985; Maternity Leave Arrangements, 1961-85. (Current Population Reports Series P-23, Special Studies: No. 165). (Illus.). 63p. 1990. pap. 3.50 (*0-16-021244-8*) USGPO.

Norton, Arthur O. Readings in the History of Education: Mediaeval Universities. LC 78-173801. reprint ed. 34.50 (*0-404-04797-1*) AMS Pr.

Norton, Arthur O., ed. First State Normal School in America: The Journals of Cyrus Pierce & Mary Swift. LC 76-89213. (American Education: Its Men, Institutions & Ideas, Ser. 1). 1975. reprint ed. 29.95 (*0-405-01452-X*) Ayer.

Norton, Augustus R. Amal & the Shi'a: Struggle for the Soul of Lebanon. (Modern Middle East Ser.: No. 13). (Illus.). 264p. 1987. pap. 12.95 (*0-292-73040-3*) U of Tex Pr.

— Civil Society in the Middle East. LC 94-33780. (Social, Economic, & Political Studies of the Middle East: 50). 1994. 71.50 (*90-04-10037-7*) E J Brill.

Norton, Augustus R. & Weiss, Thomas G. UN Peacekeepers: Soldiers with a Difference. LC 90-82248. (Headline Ser.: No. 292). 64p. 1990. pap. 5.95 (*0-87124-133-1*) Foreign Policy.

Norton, Augustus R., jt. auth. see Muslih, Muhammad.

Norton, B. Efficient Use of Energy in Buildings, No. 11. (C). 1989. 100.00 (*0-685-33089-3*, Pub. by Interntl Solar Energy Soc UK) St Mut.

— Efficient Use of Energy in Buildings (2nd UK-ISES Conference) (C46) 75p. (C). 1986. 120.00 (*0-685-30230-X*, Pub. by Interntl Solar Energy Soc UK) St Mut.

— Linguistic Framework & Ontology. 1977. 51.55 (*3-10-800283-X*) Mouton.

— Solar Energy Technology. (Illus.). xvi, 279p. 1991. 119.00 (*0-387-19583-1*) Spr-Verlag.

Norton, B. & Lockhart-Ball, H. Daylighting Buildings. (C). 1989. 125.00 (*0-685-33097-4*, Pub. by Interntl Solar Energy Soc UK) St Mut.

Norton, B. H. Force Recon Diary, 1969. 1991. mass mkt. 5.99 (*0-8041-0671-1*) Ivy Books.

Norton, B. H., jt. auth. see Hamblen, Donald N.

Norton, Bettina A. Around the Square: An Architectural Hunt in the Environs of Harvard Square. (Neighborhood Trivia Hunt Ser.). (Illus.). 80p. (Orig.). 1992. pap. 11.95 (*0-938357-08-5*) BAN Pub Boston.

— Neighborhood Trivia Hunt for Boston's Back Bay. (Neighborhood Trivia Hunt Ser.). (Illus.). 36p. (Orig.). 1985. pap. 4.95 (*0-938357-01-8*) BAN Pub Boston.

— Neighborhood Trivia Hunt for Boston's Beacon Hill. (Neighborhood Trivia Hunt Ser.). (Illus.). 36p. (Orig.). 1985. pap. 4.95 (*0-938357-00-X*) BAN Pub Boston.

— Neighborhood Trivia Hunt for Boston's Downtown. (Neighborhood Trivia Hunt Ser.). (Illus.). 40p. (Orig.). 1986. pap. 5.95 (*0-938357-03-4*) BAN Pub Boston.

— Neighborhood Trivia Hunt for Concord, Massachusetts. (Neighborhood Trivia Hunt Ser.). (Illus.). 20p. (J). (gr. 7-12). 1985. pap. 4.95 (*0-938357-02-6*) BAN Pub Boston.

— Neighborhood Trivia Hunt for New Haven, Connecticut. (Illus.). 36p. (Orig.). 1986. pap. 4.95 (*0-938357-04-2*) BAN Pub Boston.

— Neighborhood Trivia Hunt for Providence, R. I. (Illus.). 36p. (Orig.). 1987. pap. 4.95 (*0-938357-06-9*) BAN Pub Boston.

— Neighborhood Trivia Hunt for Salem, Massachusetts. (Illus.). 36p. (Orig.). 1986. pap. 4.95 (*0-938357-05-0*) BAN Pub Boston.

— Neighborhood Trivia Hunt on the Salem Heritage Trail for Boys & Girls. (Neighborhood Trivia Hunt Ser.). (Illus.). 16p. (Orig.). 1986. pap. 1.50 (*0-938357-07-7*) BAN Pub Boston.

— Prints at the Essex Institute. Farnam, Anne & Tolles, Bryant F., Jr., eds. LC 78-19448. (E.I. Museum Booklet Ser.). (Illus.). 1978. pap. 5.95 (*0-88389-069-0*, Essx Institute) Peabody Essex Mus.

***Norton, Bob.** The Quality Classroom Manager. 1995. write for info. (*0-614-03980-0*); pap. write for info. (*0-614-03981-9*) Baywood Pub.

Norton, Boyd. The African Elephant: Last Days of Eden. (Illus.). 128p. 1991. 29.95 (*0-89658-156-9*) Voyageur Pr.

— The Art of Outdoor Photography: Techniques for the Advanced Amateur & Professional. LC 92-35905. (Illus.). 152p. 1993. 35.00 (*0-89658-159-4*) Voyageur Pr.

— Backroads of Colorado. LC 95-7222. 1995. write for info. (*0-89658-316-3*) Voyageur Pr.

— Boyd Norton's PhotoJournal. LC 90-30864. (Illus.). 128p. (Orig.). 1990. spiral bd., pap. 2.99 (*0-89658-126-8*) Voyageur Pr.

***Norton, Boyd, photos.** Baikal: Sacred Sea of Siberia. LC 92-3057. (Illus.). 1995. pap. 18.00 (*0-87156-358-4*) Sierra.

Norton, Bruce H. Force Recon Diary, 1970. 1992. mass mkt. 4.99 (*0-8041-0806-4*) Ivy Books.

***Norton, Bruce H. & Jacques, Maurice J.** Sergeant Major, U. S. Marine. 1995. mass mkt. 5.99 (*0-8041-1030-1*) Ivy Books.

Norton, Bryan. The Unity of Environmentalism. (Illus.). 272p. 1991. 29.95 (*0-19-506112-8*) OUP.

Norton, Bryan G. On the Inherent Danger of Undervaluing Species. (Working Papers on the Preservation of Species). 1988. 2.50 (*0-318-33312-0*, PS3) IPPP.

— Toward Unity among Environmentalists. (Illus.). 304p. 1994. reprint ed. pap. 14.95 (*0-19-509397-6*) OUP.

— Why Preserve Natural Variety? 1987. 35.00 (*0-317-05526-7*); pap. 13.95 (*0-317-05216-0*) IPPP.

— Why Preserve Natural Variety? Cohen, Marshall, ed. (Studies in Moral, Political, & Legal Philosophy). 295p. (C). 1987. pap. text ed. 14.95 (*0-691-02507-X*) Princeton U Pr.

Norton, Bryan G., ed. The Preservation of Species: The Value of Biological Diversity. 1986. 45.00 (*0-317-05211-X*); pap. 16.95 (*0-317-05212-8*) IPPP.

— The Preservation of Species: The Value of Biological Diversity. LC 85-42696. 272p. 1986. text ed. 55.00 (*0-691-08389-4*); pap. text ed. 19.95 (*0-691-02415-4*) Princeton U Pr.

N

An Asterisk (*) at the beginning of an entry indicates that the title is appearing in BIP for the first time.

Norton, C. Correspondence Between Goethe & Carlyle. 1972. 59.95 (0-87968-945-5) Gordon Pr.

Norton, Camille, jt. ed. see Robinson, Lou.

***Norton, Carla.** Disturbed Ground. 440p. 1995. mass mkt. 5.50 (0-380-71188-5) Avon.

— Disturbed Ground: The True Story of the Arsenic & Old Lace Case. 1994. 23.00 (0-688-09704-9) Morrow.

Norton, Carla, jt. auth. see McGuire, Christine.

Norton, Carol V. Tapestry Crochet. 1991. pap. 17.95 (0-932394-15-9) Dos Tejedoras.

Norton, Caroline. Caroline Norton's Defense: English Laws for Women in the 19th Century. 208p. 1982. 17.95 (0-915864-87-8); pap. 8.95 (0-915864-88-6) Academy Chi Pubs.

— English Laws for Women in the Nineteenth Century. LC 79-2948. 188p. 1981. reprint ed. 19.50 (0-8305-0111-8) Hyperion Conn.

— Lost & Saved. LC 88-32738. 1989. 60.00 (0-8201-1434-0) Schol Facsimiles.

— A Voice from the Factories. LC 93-46507. (Revolution & Romanticism, 1789-1834 Ser.). 1994. 40.00 (1-85477-169-8, Pub. by Woodstock Bks UK) Cassell.

Norton, Caroline E. Stuart of Dunleath: A Story of Modern Times, 3 vols. in 2, Set. LC 79-8181. reprint ed. 84.50 (0-404-62073-6) AMS Pr.

Norton, Caroline S. Selected Writings of Caroline Norton. LC 78-18828. 1978. 100.00 (0-8201-1312-3) Schol Facsimiles.

Norton, Catherine S. Life Metaphors: Stories of Ordinary Survival. LC 88-17549. 256p. (C). 1989. text ed. 29.95 (0-8093-1427-4) S Ill U Pr.

Norton, Charles E. Historical Studies of Church-Building in the Middle Ages. LC 78-95072. (Select Bibliographies Reprint Ser.). 1977. 24.95 (0-8369-5072-0) Ayer.

— Historical Studies of Church Building in the Middle Ages: Venice, Siena, Florence. 1977. lib. bdg. 39.95 (0-8490-1962-1) Gordon Pr.

— Letters of Charles Eliot Norton with Biographical Comment, 2 Vols, 1. Norton, Sara & Howe, M. A., eds. LC 76-148817. reprint ed. write for info. (0-404-04801-3) AMS Pr.

— Letters of Charles Eliot Norton with Biographical Comment, 2 Vols, 2. Norton, Sara & Howe, M. A., eds. LC 76-148817. reprint ed. write for info. (0-404-04802-1) AMS Pr.

— Letters of Charles Eliot Norton with Biographical Comment, 2 Vols, Set. Norton, Sara & Howe, M. A., eds. LC 76-148817. reprint ed. 125.00 (0-404-04800-5) AMS Pr.

Norton, Charles E., ed. Two Notebooks of Thomas Carlyle: From 23rd March 1822 to 16th May 1832. 1972. reprint ed. 10.00 (0-911858-21-0) Appel.

Norton, Charles E., ed. see Carlyle, Thomas.

Norton, Charles E., ed. see Lowell, James Russell.

Norton, Charles H. Pilgrim. 136p. (Orig.). 1993. pap. 8.95 (1-880451-04-2) Rainbows End.

Norton, Cheryl & Bryant, James E. Racquetball: A Guide for the Aspiring Player. (Illus.). 224p. (C). 1984. pap. text ed. 14.95x (0-89582-112-5) Morton Pub.

Norton, Cheryl, jt. auth. see Bryant, James.

Norton, Christine B., ed. see CGI Staff.

Norton, Christopher & Park, David A., eds. Cistercian Art & Architecture in the British Isles. (Illus.). 448p. 1986. 150.00 (0-521-25475-2) Cambridge U Pr.

Norton, Christopher, et al. Dominican Painting in East Anglia: The Thornham Parva Retable & the Musee De Cluny Frontal. 1987. 79.00 (0-85115-424-7) Boydell & Brewer.

Norton, Colleen K., jt. auth. see Kesten, Karen S.

Norton, Cynthia F. Microbiology. LC 80-23350. (Life Sciences Ser.). (Illus.). 850p. (C). 1981. teacher ed write for info. (0-201-05308-X); text ed. write for info. (0-201-05304-7); student ed write for info. (0-201-05307-1) Addison-Wesley.

— Microbiology. 2nd ed. LC 85-3909. 800p. (C). 1986. 10.75 (0-201-10998-0); text ed. 53.75 (0-201-10997-2); student ed 16.25 (0-201-11037-7); trans. 150.00 (0-201-11038-5) Addison-Wesley.

Norton, D. Early History of Port Moody. Bryce, Herb, ed. 184p. (Orig.). 1987. pap. 12.95 (0-88839-197-8) Hancock House.

— Hospitals & the Long-Stay Patient. 1967. 60.00 (0-08-011053-3, Pub. by Pergamon Repr UK); pap. 64.00 (0-08-011052-5, Pub. by Pergamon Repr UK) Franklin.

Norton, Daniel A. Writing Windows Device Drivers. 1991. pap. 32.95 (0-201-57795-X) Addison-Wesley.

Norton, Daniel S. & Rushton, Peters. Classical Myths in English Literature. LC 70-92305. 444p. 1969. reprint ed. text ed. 41.50 (0-8371-2440-9, NOCM, Greenwood Pr) Greenwood.

Norton, David. History of the Bible As Literature, Vol. 1: From the Beginnings to Jerome, Vol. 1. 408p. (C). 1993. 75.00 (0-521-33398-9) Cambridge U Pr.

— History of the Bible As Literature, Vol. 2: From 1700 to the Present Day. 448p. (C). 1993. 75.00 (0-521-33399-7) Cambridge U Pr.

Norton, David F. David Hume: Common-Sense Moralist, Sceptical Metaphysician. LC 81-47937. 343p. reprint ed. pap. 97.80 (0-7837-6769-2, 2046599) Bks Demand.

Norton, David F., ed. The Cambridge Companion to Hume. LC 92-47406. (Companions to Philosophy Ser.). 448p. (C). 1993. 64.95 (0-521-38273-4); pap. 18.95 (0-521-38710-8) Cambridge U Pr.

Norton, David L. Democracy & Moral Development: A Politics of Virtue. LC 90-37723. 216p. 1991. 30.00 (0-520-07067-4) U CA Pr.

— Democracy & Moral Development: A Politics of Virtue. 1995. pap. 13.95 (0-520-20348-8) U CA Pr.

— Personal Destinies: A Philosophy of Ethical Individualism. 1976. 65.00 (0-691-07215-9); pap. 17.95 (0-691-01975-4) Princeton U Pr.

Norton, David L. & Kille, Mary F., eds. Philosophies of Love. (Helix Bks.: No. 376). 296p. (C). 1983. reprint ed. pap. 20.00 (0-8226-0376-4) Littlefield.

Norton, Delores G. Dual Perspective: Inclusion of Ethnic Minority Content in the Social Work Curriculum. 1978. 3.85 (0-685-21303-X, 78-380-06) Coun Soc Wk Ed.

Norton, Don E., ed. see Nibley, Hugh.

Norton, Donald J. Larry: A Biography of Lawrence D. Bell. LC 80-27791. (Illus.). 280p. 1981. 34.95 (0-88229-615-9) Nelson-Hall.

Norton, Donna E. The Effective Teaching of Language Arts. 4th ed. LC 92-31177. 576p. (C). 1993. write for info. (0-02-388310-3, Merrill Pub Co) Macmillan.

— The Impact of Literature-Based Reading. (Illus.). 464p. (Orig.). (C). 1992. pap. write for info. (0-675-21369-X) Macmillan.

— Through the Eyes of a Child. 4th ed. LC 94-4485. 784p. (C). 1995. write for info. (0-02-388313-8) Macmillan.

— Through the Eyes of a Child: An Intro to Children's Literature. 3rd ed. 784p. (C). 1991. write for info. (0-675-21144-1, Merrill Pub Co) Macmillan.

Norton, Donna E. & Norton, Saundra. Language Arts Activities for Children. 3rd ed. (Illus.). 412p. (C). 1994. pap. write for info. (0-02-388242-5) Macmillan.

Norton, Douglas C., et al. The Economics of Public Issues. 8th ed. 214p. (C). 1990. pap. text ed. 14.00 (0-06-044850-4) HarpCollege.

Norton, E. W., ed. see Gorin, Jules, Club Staff.

Norton, Elliot. Broadway Down East. 1978. 10.00 (0-89073-055-5) Boston Public Lib.

Norton, F. H. Fine Ceramics: Technology & Applications. LC 78-106. 524p. 1978. reprint ed. 55.50 (0-88275-582-X) Krieger.

— Refractories. 4th ed. LC 67-20660. (Illus.). 462p. (C). reprint ed. text ed. 50.00 (1-878907-06-9, RAN) TechBooks.

Norton-Ford, Julian D., jt. auth. see Kendall, Philip C.

Norton, Frances. A Victorian Cup of Tea: A Guide to Victorian Entertaining. 70p. (Orig.). 1992. spiral bd. 9.95 (0-9632938-0-X) F M Norton.

Norton, Frederick J. Printing in Spain, 1501-1520: With a Note on the Early Editions of the "Celestina" LC 65-19156. (Sandars Lectures: 1963). 242p. reprint ed. pap. 69.00 (0-317-10580-9, 2022464) Bks Demand.

Norton, G. & Mumford, J. Decision Tools for Pest Management. 320p. 1993. 71.25 (0-85198-783-4) CAB Intl.

Norton, G. A. & Hollings, C. S., eds. Pest Management: Proceedings of an International Conference, 25-29 October 1976, Laxenburg, Austria. LC 78-40825. 1979. 152.00 (0-08-023427-5, Pub. by Pergamon Repr UK) Franklin.

Norton, G. A. & Pech, R. P., eds. Vertebrate Pest Management. 1989. pap. 30.00 (0-643-04946-0, Pub. by CSIRO AT) Intl Spec Bk.

Norton, George P. Textile Manufacturers' Bookkeeping for the Counting House, Mill & Warehouse. 3rd ed. LC 75-18478. (History of Accounting Ser.). 1979. reprint ed. 25.95 (0-405-07560-X) Ayer.

Norton, George W. Introduction to the Economics of Agricultural Development. 1993. text ed. write for info. (0-07-047922-4) McGraw.

Norton, Glyn P. Montaigne & the Introspective Mind. (Studies in French Literature: No. 22). 219p. 1974. pap. text ed. 42.70 (90-279-3412-6) Mouton.

Norton-Griffiths, M., jt. auth. see Sinclair, A. R.

Norton, Harry N. Biomedical Instrumentation. 1994. write for info. (0-13-067240-8) P-H.

— Electronic Analysis Instruments. 208p. 1991. text ed. 46.00 (0-13-249426-4) P-H.

— Handbook of Transducers. 480p. 1989. text ed. 66.00 (0-13-382599-X) P-H.

Norton, Henry. Computing Procurement. 160p. 1988. 39.95 (0-19-853726-3) OUP.

Norton, Herman A. Religion in Tennessee, 1777-1945. LC 81-1562. (Tennessee Three Star Ser.). (Illus.). 136p. 1981. pap. 4.95 (0-87049-318-3) U of Tenn Pr.

Norton, Hollis. The New Real Estate Game: Building Wealth under the New Tax Laws. 240p. 1988. reprint ed. pap. 11.95 (0-8092-4577-9) Contemp Bks.

Norton, Hugh S. The Quest for Economic Stability: From Roosevelt to Bush. 2nd ed. 361p. (C). 1991. text ed. 39.95 (0-87249-725-9) U of SC Pr.

Norton, J., jt. ed. see King, L.

Norton, J. F., ed. High Temperature Materials Corrosion in Coal Gasification Atmospheres. 152p. 1984. 54.00 (0-85334-241-5, I-522-83, Pub. by Elsevier Applied Sci UK) Elsevier.

Norton, J. J., ed. International Banking Regulation & Supervision: Change & Transformation in the 1990s. (International Banking & Finance Law Ser.). 440p. (C). 1994. lib. bdg. 142.50 (1-85333-998-9, Pub. by Graham & Trotman UK) Kluwer Ac.

Norton, J. J. & Cheng, Chia-Jui, eds. International Banking Operations & Practices: Current Developments. LC 94-2886. (International Banking & Finance Law Ser.). 320p. (C). 1994. lib. bdg. 110.00 (1-85333-997-0, Pub. by Graham & Trotman UK) Kluwer Ac.

Norton, J. J., et al, eds. International Banking Regulation & Supervision: Change & Transformation in the 1990s. LC 94-2887. (International Banking & Finance Law Ser.). 1994. write for info. (1-85333-989-X, Pub. by M Nijhoff) Kluwer Ac.

Norton, J. P. An Introduction to Identification. 1986. text ed. 97.00 (0-12-521730-7); pap. text ed. 49.00 (0-12-521731-5) Acad Pr.

Norton, J. T., et al. Freedom's Gift: Or, Sentiments of the Free. LC 71-83914. (Black Heritage Library Collection). 1977. 13.95 (0-8369-8575-3) Ayer.

***Norton, James.** Global Studies: India & South Asia. 2nd ed. 256p. 1995. pap. text ed. 13.95 (1-56134-379-X) Dushkin Pub.

— Winning Japan for Jesus. 200p. 1988. pap. 9.95 (0-933704-66-6) Dawn Pr.

— You Can Teach Yourself Drums. 1993. 9.95 (1-56222-033-0, 94495); audio 9.98 (1-56222-034-9, 94495); audio 18.95 (1-56222-518-9, 94495) Mel Bay.

Norton, Jane E. Guide to National & Provincial Directories: England & Wales, Excluding London, Published Before 1856. (Royal Historical Society Guides & Handbooks Ser.: No. 5). 247p. 1984. 24.00 (0-86193-102-5) Boydell & Brewer.

Norton, Jed. Corrigan's Range. large type ed. (Linford Western Library). 240p. 1988. pap. 11.95 (0-7089-6607-1, Linford) Ulverscroft.

Norton, Jeni F., jt. auth. see Reckner, Jerald H.

Norton, Jenny, illus. Our Garden Book: The Garden Planner & Record Keeper. 142p. 1988. 14.95 (0-948751-01-0) Interlink Pub.

***Norton, Joan.** The Contracted Marriage. large type ed. 1994. 20.95 (0-7089-3154-5) Ulverscroft.

Norton, John. Abel Being Dead, Yet Speaketh. LC 78-8184. 1978. reprint ed. 50.00 (0-8201-1310-7) Schol Facsimiles.

— The Light at the End of the Bog. 2nd ed. 48p. reprint ed. pap. 8.50 (0-685-61094-2) Black Star.

Norton, John B. The Rebellion in India: How to Prevent Another. (C). 1988. reprint ed. 35.00 (81-7013-059-X, Pub. by Navrang) S Asia.

***Norton, John F. & Wittemore, Joel.** History of Fitzwilliam, from 1752 to 1887, with a Genealogical Record of Many Fitzwilliam Families. (Illus.). 829p. 1995. reprint ed. lib. bdg. 85.00 (0-8328-4624-4) Higginson Bk Co.

Norton, Joseph & Spellman, Paul, eds. Asset Securitization: International Finance & Legal Perspectives. 350p. 1991. 74.95 (0-631-17808-2) Blackwell Pubs.

Norton, Joseph A., ed. Commercial Loan Documentation Guide. 1988. write for info. (0-8205-1376-8) Bender.

***Norton, Joseph J.** Devising International Bank Supervisory Standards. LC 95-1060. (International Banking & Finance Law Ser.: International Banking and Finance Regulation Ser.: Vol. 3). 1995. lib. bdg. 127.00 (1-85966-185-8, Pub. by M Nijhoff) Kluwer Ac.

— Lender Liability Law. 1989. Looseleaf updates available. write for info. (0-8205-1488-8, 488) Bender.

Norton, Joseph J., ed. International Finance in the 1990's: Global Challenges & Opportunities. LC 92-32847. 1993. 64.95 (0-631-18124-5); pap. 29.95 (0-631-18876-2) Blackwell Pubs.

— Public International Law & the Future World Order: Liber Amicorum in Honor of A. J. Thomas, Jr. LC 87-4688. (Illus.). xxxii, 583p. 1987. text ed. 47.50 (0-8377-2510-0) Rothman.

Norton, Joseph J., jt. auth. see Whitley, Sherry C.

Norton, Joseph J., et al. Commercial Finance Guide. 1990. write for info. (0-8205-1395-4, 395) Bender.

Norton, Joy. Furusato: Issa's Journey Home. (Illus.). 176p. 1987. pap. 10.00 (0-933704-58-5) Dawn Pr.

Norton, Judith A., comp. New England Planters in the Maritime Provinces of Canada, 1759-1800: Bibliography of Sources. 512p. 1992. 125.00 (0-8020-2840-3) U of Toronto Pr.

Norton, Kallie, jt. auth. see Parker, Norton.

Norton, Karl K. Numbers with Small Prime Factors & the Least Kth Power Non-Residue. LC 52-42839. (Memoirs Ser.: No. 1/106). 106p. 1971. pap. 16.00 (0-8218-1806-6, MEMO 1/106) Am Math.

Norton, Kay. Normand Lockwood: His Life & Music. LC 93-16889. (Composers of North America Ser.: No. 11). (Illus.). 545p. 1993. 59.50 (0-8108-2683-6) Scarecrow.

Norton, Kingsley & Smith, Samuel P. Problems with Patients: Managing Complicated Transactions. (Illus.). 200p. (C). 1994. 54.95 (0-521-43043-7); pap. 24.95 (0-521-43628-1) Cambridge U Pr.

Norton-Kyshe, J. W. Dictionary of Legal Quotations. 1972. 300.00 (0-8490-0037-8) Gordon Pr.

Norton-Kyshe, James W. Dictionary of Legal Quotations. xxi, 344p. 1984. reprint ed. 47.50 (0-89941-375-7, 303500) W S Hein.

Norton, L., jt. auth. see Cowan, A.

Norton, L., jt. auth. see Sanchez, Tony.

Norton, L. B., jt. auth. see Anderson, Debby.

Norton, L. Charkette, jt. auth. see Puckett, Ruby P.

Norton, L. Charnette, jt. auth. see Hofmeister, Linda R.

Norton, Lawrence, et al. Surgical Decision Making. 3rd ed. (Illus.). 368p. 1992. text ed. 82.95 (0-7216-6598-5) Saunders.

Norton, LoraBeth, ed. see Anderson, Debby.

Norton, LoraBeth, ed. see Dockrey, Emily & Dockrey, Karen.

Norton, LoraBeth, ed. see Hamilton, Kersten.

Norton, LoraBeth, ed. see Littleton, Mark R.

Norton, LoraBeth, ed. see Matthews, Beth, et al.

Norton, LoraBeth, ed. see McEwan, Elaine K.

Norton, LoraBeth, ed. see Tada, Joni E. & Jensen, Steve.

Norton, LoraBeth, ed. see Tada, Joni T. & Jensen, Steve.

Norton, Louis A. & Burstone, Charles J., eds. The Biology of Tooth Movement. 1988. 234.00 (0-8493-4733-5, QP88) CRC Pr.

Norton, Lucy, tr. see Delacroix, Eugene.

Norton, M. D., tr. see Blume, Friedrich.

Norton, M. D., tr. see Rilke, Rainer M.

Norton, M. D., tr. see Rilke, Rainer Maria.

Norton, M. Herter. Art of String Quartet Playing. 1966. pap. 4.95 (0-393-00360-4) Norton.

Norton, M. Herter, tr. see Blume, Friedrich.

Norton, M. Herter, tr. see Haushofer, Albrecht.

Norton, M. Ruth. A Canal for All Seasons: The Romance of Ohio's Canal Era. (Illus.). 85p. (Orig.). Date not set. pap. 4.00 (1-880443-07-4) Roscoe Village.

— A Fine Poor Man's Country: The Life of Ohio's Early Craftsmen. (Illus.). 85p. (Orig.). 1991. pap. 3.95 (1-880443-04-X) Roscoe Village.

— Why Is It Called Whitewoman Street? Roscoe's Pre-Canal History. (Illus.). 80p. (Orig.). 1992. pap. 4.00 (1-880443-06-6) Roscoe Village.

Norton, Margaret. Brantub the Dancing Bear. (Illus.). 32p. (J). (ps-2). 1992. 15.95 (0-370-31409-3, Pub. by Bodley Head UK) Trafalgar.

Norton, Margaret, et al. Student Planned Acquisition of Required Knowledge. Langdon, Danny G., ed. LC 79-23442. (Instructional Design Library). 104p. 1980. 23.95 (0-87778-155-9) Educ Tech Pubns.

Norton, Margaret C. Illinois Census Returns, 1810 (&) 1818. (Illus.). xxxii, 329p. 1993. reprint ed. pap. 29.50 (0-685-65673-X, 4160) Clearfield Co.

Norton, Mark R., jt. ed. see Brown, Robert K.

Norton, Mark R., ed. see Petersen, William J. & Petersen, Randy.

Norton, Martin L., et al, eds. High Intensity Care: Medical, Administrative, & Legal Issues. (Health Care Administration Ser.). 346p. 1988. 65.00 (0-8342-0001-5) Aspen Pub.

Norton, Mary. Are All the Giants Dead? LC 78-6622. (Illus.). 123p. (J). (gr. 3-7). 1978. pap. 9.95 (0-15-607888-0, Voyager Bks) HarBrace.

— Bed-Knob & Broomstick. 229p. (J). (gr. 3-7). 1990. pap. 3.95 (0-15-206231-9, Odyssey) HarBrace.

— Bed-Knob & Broomstick. large type ed. 296p. (J). (gr. 3-7). 1989. 14.95 (0-8161-4786-8, Large Print Bks) Hall.

— Borrowers. LC 53-7870. (Illus.). 180p. (J). (gr. 3 up). 1953. 13.95 (0-15-209987-5, HB Juv Bks) HarBrace.

— Borrowers. (J). (gr. 4-7). 1993. pap. 4.95 (0-15-200086-0) HarBrace.

— The Borrowers. (Illus.). 200p. (J). (gr. 3-7). 1989. pap. 4.95 (0-15-209990-5, Odyssey) HarBrace.

— Borrowers Afield. LC 55-11011. (Illus.). 215p. (J). (gr. 3 up). 1955. 13.95 (0-15-210166-7, HB Juv Bks) HarBrace.

— The Borrowers Afield. 238p. (J). (gr. 5-7). 1990. pap. 4.95 (0-15-210535-2, Odyssey) HarBrace.

— Borrowers Afloat. LC 59-5630. (Illus.). 191p. (J). (gr. 3 up). 1959. 12.95 (0-15-210345-7, HB Juv Bks) HarBrace.

— The Borrowers Afloat. 205p. (J). (gr. 3-7). 1990. pap. 3.95 (0-15-210534-4, Odyssey) HarBrace.

— Borrowers Aloft. LC 61-11751. (Illus.). 192p. (J). (gr. 3 up). 1961. 12.95 (0-15-210524-7, HB Juv Bks) HarBrace.

— The Borrowers Aloft. (Illus.). 196p. (J). (gr. 3-7). 1990. pap. 4.95 (0-15-210533-6, Odyssey) HarBrace.

— The Borrowers Avenged. 365p. (J). (gr. 3-7). 1990. pap. 5.00 (0-15-210532-8, Odyssey) HarBrace.

— The Borrowers Avenged. (J). (gr. 3-6). 1988. 17.75 (0-8446-6358-1) Peter Smith.

— Borrowers Avenged. 1982. 12.95 (0-15-210530-1) HarBrace.

Norton, Mary & Hague, M. The Borrowers. 177p. (J). (ps up). 1991. 22.95 (0-15-209991-3, HB Juv Bks) HarBrace.

Norton, Mary B., ed. American Historical Association's Guide to Historical Literature, 2 vols. 3rd ed. 1728p. 1995. Set. 150.00 (0-19-505727-9) OUP.

— Liberty's Daughters: The Revolutionary Experience of American Women, 1750-1800. (C). 1987. pap. text ed. 29.50 (0-673-39348-8) HarpCollege.

— Major Problems in American Women's History: Documents & Essays. LC 88-80719. (Major Problems in American History Ser.). 461p. (C). 1990. pap. text ed. 15.50 (0-669-14490-8) Heath.

Norton, Mary B., jt. auth. see Berkin, Carol.

Norton, Mary B., jt. ed. see Groneman, Carol.

Norton, Mary B., et al. A People & a Nation: A History of the United States. 2nd ed. LC 85-60316. 1072p. 1985. trans. 84.76 (0-685-12000-7); disk write for info. (0-318-60190-7) HM.

— A People & a Nation: A History of the United States, 1. 2nd ed. LC 85-60316. 1072p. 1985. 27.16 (0-685-11998-X) HM.

— A People & a Nation: A History of the United States, 2. 2nd ed. LC 85-60316. 1072p. 1985. text ed. 27.16 (0-685-11999-8) HM.

— A People & a Nation: Brief Edition, 2 vols., A. 3rd ed. (C). 1991. write for info. (0-395-56298-8); student ed write for info. (0-395-56300-3) HM Soft Schl Col Div.

— A People & a Nation: Brief Edition, 2 vols., B. 3rd ed. (C). 1991. write for info. (0-395-56299-6) HM Soft Schl Col Div.

— A People & a Nation: Brief Edition, 2 vols., B. 3rd ed. (C). 1991. student ed write for info. (0-395-56301-1) HM Soft Schl Col Div.

— A People & a Nation: Brief Edition, Set. 3rd ed. (C). 1991. write for info. (0-395-47302-0) HM Soft Schl Col Div.

Norton, Michael. Blizzard. 368p. (Orig.). 1988. pap. 3.95 (0-8439-2706-2) Dorchester Pub Co.

— Directory of Social Change: Community. 1988. 40.00 (0-7045-0285-2) St Mut.

— Directory of Social Change: Education & Play. 1988. 40.00 (0-7045-0291-7) St Mut.

Norton, Michael, jt. auth. see Corbett, Margery.

Norton, Michael P. Fundamentals of Noise & Vibration Analysis for Engineers. (Illus.). 640p. (C). 1990. 140.00 (0-521-34148-5); pap. 59.95 (0-521-34941-9) Cambridge U Pr.

Norton, Miriam. The Kitten Who Thought He Was a Mouse. (Illus.). 32p. (J). (ps-3). 1993. 11.95 (0-307-17553-7, Artsts Writrs) Western Pub.

Norton, Mortimer, ed. Angling Success, by Leading Outdoor Writers. LC 67-30224. (Essay Index Reprint Ser.). 1977. 23.95 (0-8369-0747-7) Ayer.

Norton, N. P., jt. auth. see Ewing, John S.

N

An Asterisk (*) at the beginning of an entry indicates that the title is appearing in BIP for the first time.

*__Norton, Natascha & Whatmore, Mark.__ Guatemala & Belize. (Cadogan Guides Ser.). (Illus.). 256p. 1994. pap. 14.95 (*0-947754-92-X*) Globe Pequot.

__Norton, Natascha & Whitmore, Mark.__ Central America: Guatemala, Costa Rica, Honduras, Belize, Panama, El Salvador, Nicaragua. (Cadogan Guides Ser.). (Illus.). 400p. (Orig.). 1994. pap. 17.95 (*1-56440-070-0*) Globe Pequot.

__Norton, O. Richard.__ Rocks from Space: Meteorites & Meteorite Hunters. 480p. 1994. pap. 20.00 (*0-87842-302-8*) Mountain Pr.

__Norton, Oliver W.__ Army Letters. 397p. 1990. 30.00 (*0-89029-094-6*) Morningside Bkshop.

— The Attack & Defense of Little Round Top, Gettysburg, July 2, 1863. (Illus.). 350p. 1992. reprint ed. 25.00 (*1-879664-07-0*); reprint ed. pap. 12.95 (*1-879664-08-9*) Stan Clark Military.

__Norton, Penny.__ Earth Watch. (Illus.). 48p. (J). (gr. 7-9). 1992. 13.95 (*0-563-34407-5*, BBC-Parkwest); pap. 7.50 (*0-563-34408-3*, BBC-Parkwest) Parkwest Pubns.

__Norton, Peter.__ Borland C Plus Plus 3.1 Programming. 1992. pap. 29.95 (*0-679-79144-2*) Random.

— Guide to the Norton Utilities. 1991. pap. 24.95 (*0-679-79066-7*) Random.

— Guide to UNIX. 1991. pap. 26.95 (*0-679-79056-X*) Random.

— Inside Norton Desktop for Windows. 2nd ed. 1994. pap. 26.95 (*1-56686-121-7*) Brady Compu Bks.

— Inside the IBM PC: Access to Advanced Features & Programming. 400p. 1985. pap. 19.95 (*0-317-37784-1*) S&S Trade.

— Inside the IBM PC & PS-2. 4th ed. 1991. pap. 24.95 (*0-13-465634-2*) Brady Compu Bks.

— Inside the PC: Everything You Want to Know about Your PC. 5th ed. 1993. pap. 24.95 (*1-56686-097-0*) Brady Compu Bks.

— Official Guide to Norton Utilities Macintosh. 1992. pap. 24.95 (*0-679-79119-1*) Random.

— Outside the Apple Macintosh: Access to New Technology. 1992. pap. 26.95 (*1-56686-015-6*) Brady Compu Bks.

— Outside the IBM PC & PS-2. (Illus.). (Orig.). 1992. pap. 29.95 (*0-13-643586-6*) Brady Compu Bks.

— P. Norton ASM Tandy. 1988. 39.95 (*0-13-661786-7*) P-H.

— PC Programmer's Bible. 1993. pap. 29.95 (*1-55615-555-7*) Microsoft.

— Peter Norton's Advanced DOS 5.0. 1991. pap. 29.95 (*0-13-529645-5*) Brady Compu Bks.

— Peter Norton's Advanced DOS 6.0 Guide. 2nd ed. 1993. pap. 29.95 (*1-56686-046-6*) Brady Compu Bks.

— Peter Norton's Assembly Language Book for the IBM PC. rev. ed. 512p. 1989. pap. 24.95 (*0-13-662453-7*) Brady Compu Bks.

— Peter Norton's Assembly Language for the IBM PC. 3rd ed. 1992. disk 39.95 (*1-56686-016-4*) Brady Compu Bks.

— Peter Norton's DOS 6.0 Guide. 5th ed. 1993. pap. 24.95 (*1-56686-045-8*) Brady Compu Bks.

— Peter Norton's DOS 6.22 Guide, Premier Edition. (Illus.). 1152p. (Orig.). 1994. pap. 29.99 (*0-672-30614-X*) Sams.

— Peter Norton's DosGuide. 4th ed. (Illus.). 1991. pap. 24.95 (*0-13-663048-0*) Brady Compu Bks.

— Peter Norton's Guide to Windows X.0. 1995. pap. 30.00 (*0-679-75588-8*) Random.

— Peter Norton's Inside the PC. 6th ed. 650p. 1995. 35.00 (*0-672-30624-7*) Sams.

— Peter Norton's Inside the Sun 486i & 386i. 1990. pap. 29.95 (*0-13-661612-7*) P-H.

— Peter Norton's Introduction to Computers. LC 93-46202. 1994. pap. 34.95 (*0-02-801318-2*) Glencoe.

— Peter Norton's Introduction to Computers. LC 93-46202. 1994. write for info. (*0-02-801331-X*) Glencoe.

— Peter Norton's Introduction to Computers: Essential Concepts. LC 94-10091. 1994. write for info. (*0-02-802902-X*) Glencoe.

— Peter Norton's Introduction to Computers: With Microsoft Works for Windows. LC 94-25920. 1994. write for info. (*0-02-802896-1*) Glencoe.

— Peter Norton's PC Problem Solver. 2nd ed. (Orig.). 1992. pap. 29.95 (*1-56686-012-1*) Brady Compu Bks.

— Peter Norton's PC Problem Solver: Special Edition, Completely Updated for DOS 6. 1993. pap. 29.95 (*1-56686-094-6*) Brady Compu Bks.

— Peter Norton's QBASIC Programming. (Illus.). (Orig.). 1991. pap. 24.95 (*0-13-663022-7*) Brady Compu Bks.

— Peter Norton's Visual Basic for Windows, Premier Edition. 4th ed. (Illus.). 900p. (Orig.). 1995. pap. 45.00 (*0-672-30615-8*) Sams.

— Users Guide to Windows 3.1. 1993. pap. 27.95 (*0-679-79127-2*) Random.

— Windows 3.1 Power Programming. 1992. pap. 34.95 (*0-679-79108-6*) Random.

__Norton, Peter & Alvernaz, Bill.__ Peter Norton's PC Resource. (Illus.). 400p. 1987. pap. 19.95 (*0-685-18872-8*) P-H.

__Norton, Peter & Gentry, Renee.__ Inside the Norton Desktop for Windows. (Illus.). (Orig.). 1992. pap. 26.95 (*0-13-474503-5*) Brady Compu Bks.

__Norton, Peter & Holzner, Steven.__ Peter Norton's Advanced Assembly. (Illus.). (Orig.). 1991. pap. 24.95 (*0-13-663014-6*); disk 39.95 (*0-13-658774-7*) Brady Compu Bks.

— Peter Norton's Advanced BASIC. (Illus.). (Orig.). 1991. pap. 24.95 (*0-13-663030-8*); disk 39.95 (*0-13-658758-5*) Brady Compu Bks.

__Norton, Peter & Jourdain, Robert.__ Peter Norton's PC Problem Solver. (Illus.). 600p. (Orig.). 1990. pap. 24.95 (*0-13-449133-5*) Brady Compu Bks.

__Norton, Peter & Kent, Peter.__ Peter Norton's Window NT: Tips & Tricks. 414p. 27.00 (*0-679-79200-7*) Random.

__Norton, Peter & Socha, John.__ Peter Norton's Assembly Language Book for the IBM PC: Software Version. rev. ed. (Illus.). 512p. 1990. disk 44.95 (*0-13-662479-0*) Brady Compu Bks.

__Norton, Peter & Wilton, Richard.__ The New Peter Norton Programmer's Guide to the IBM PC & PS-2. 2nd ed. LC 88-21104. 528p. (Orig.). 1988. pap. 22.95 (*1-55615-131-4*) Microsoft.

*__Norton, Peter & Yoa, Paul.__ Windows '95 Power Program Technical Guide. Date not set. 34.00 (*0-679-76188-8*) Random.

__Norton, Peter, jt. auth. see Eckhardt, Robert C.__

__Norton, Peter, jt. auth. see Heid, Jim.__

__Norton, Peter, jt. auth. see Jourdian, Robert.__

__Norton, Peter, Computing Group Staff & Holzner, Steven.__ Advanced Visual BASIC. LC 92-5690. (Illus.). (Orig.). 1992. pap. 39.95 (*1-56686-000-8*) Brady Compu Bks.

— Microsoft C - C Plus Plus 7.0 Programming. (Illus.). (Orig.). 1992. pap. 39.95 (*1-56686-005-9*) Brady Compu Bks.

__Norton, Peter G., ed. see Peace, Sheila M.__

__Norton, Peter G., et al, eds.__ Primary Care Research: Traditional & Innovative Approaches. (Research Methods for Primary Care Ser.: Vol. 1). (Illus.). 272p. (C). 1990. text ed. 49.95 (*0-8039-3870-5*); pap. text ed. 24.00 (*0-8039-3871-3*) Sage.

__Norton, Philip.__ The British Polity. 3rd ed. LC 93-14317. 450p. (C). 1994. pap. text ed. 27.50 (*0-8013-1169-1*, 79663) Longman.

__Norton, Philip, ed.__ Law & Order & British Politics. LC 84-18722. (Illus.). 240p. 1984. text ed. 53.95 (*0-566-00688-X*) Ashgate Pub Co.

— Legislatures. (Oxford Readings in Politics & Government Ser.). (Illus.). 352p. 1990. 55.00 (*0-19-827582-X*); pap. 16.95 (*0-19-827581-1*) OUP.

__Norton, Philip & Wood, David M.__ Back from Westminster: Constituency Service by British Members of Parliament. LC 93-14766. (Comparative Legislative Studies Ser.). 192p. 1993. 29.00 (*0-8131-1834-4*) U Pr of Ky.

__Norton, Philip, jt. ed. see Franklin, Mark N.__

__Norton, Phillip.__ New Directions in British Politics? Essays on the Evolving Constitution. 256p. 1991. text ed. 64.95 (*1-85278-350-8*, Pub. by E Elgar Pub UK) Ashgate Pub Co.

__Norton, Phillip, ed.__ Parliaments in Western Europe. 1990. text ed. 35.00 (*0-7146-3407-7*, Pub. by F Cass Pubs UK) Intl Spec Bk.

__Norton, R. W., Art Gallery Staff.__ America the Beautiful: A Bicentennial Exhibition. LC 75-28257. (Illus.). 40p. 1975. pap. 3.50 (*0-913060-07-0*) Norton Art.

— The American Porcelain Tradition. LC 72-82888. (Illus.). 1972. pap. 3.00 (*0-9600182-8-X*) Norton Art.

— American Sculpture: A Tenth Anniversary Exhibition. LC 76-50425. (Illus.). 1976. pap. 3.50 (*0-913060-11-9*) Norton Art.

— American Silver & Pressed Glass. LC 67-24712. (Illus.). 1967. pap. 3.50 (*0-9600182-0-4*) Norton Art.

— Artistry in Arms: The Art of Gunsmithing & Gun Engraving. LC 75-164699. (Illus.). 1971. pap. 2.50 (*0-9600182-4-7*) Norton Art.

— Artistry in Silver: An Exhibition of Sculpture by Charles M. Russell. LC 78-17945. (Illus.). 1970. pap. 1.00 (*0-9600182-1-2*) Norton Art.

— Bob Timberlake: Paintings & Watercolors. LC 74-5029. (Contemporary Realists Ser.). (Illus.). 1974. pap. 3.50 (*0-913060-04-6*) Norton Art.

— Carolyn Wyeth: A Retrospective Exhibition. LC 75-43579. (Contemporary Realists Ser.). (Illus.). 1976. pap. 2.50 (*0-913060-08-9*) Norton Art.

— Charles M. Russell: 1864-1926: Paintings & Sculpture in the R. W. Norton Art Gallery Collection. LC 78-7115. (Illus.). 1980. pap. 8.50 (*0-913060-15-1*) Norton Art.

— E. C. Prudhomme: Master Gun Engraver. LC 73-78704. (Illus.). 32p. 1973. pap. 3.00 (*0-913060-01-1*) Norton Art.

— Felix Kelly. LC 77-732. (Contemporary Realists Ser.). (Illus.). 1977. pap. 4.50 (*0-913060-12-7*) Norton Art.

— Felix Kelly: A Romantic Realist. LC 72-78863. (Contemporary Realists Ser.). (Illus.). 1972. pap. 2.50 (*0-9600182-7-1*) Norton Art.

— Frederic Remington, Eighteen Sixty-One to Nineteen Hundred Nine: Paintings, Drawings & Sculpture. LC 78-7114. (Illus.). 1979. pap. 8.00 (*0-913060-14-3*) Norton Art.

— John Chumley's Rural America. LC 76-187913. (Contemporary Realists Ser.). (Illus.). 1972. pap. 3.50 (*0-913060-00-3*) Norton Art.

— John McClusky: A Retrospective Exhibition. LC 74-14946. (Contemporary Realists Ser.). (Illus.). 1974. pap. 5.50 (*0-913060-05-4*) Norton Art.

— Medallic Art of the United States, 1800-1972. LC 72-187912. (Illus.). 1972. pap. 3.00 (*0-9600182-9-8*) Norton Art.

— The Old West in Miniature: Sculptures by Don Polland. LC 74-24491. 1974. pap. 2.50 (*0-913060-06-2*) Norton Art.

— The Old West Pictorialized by Joe Ruiz Grandee. LC 79-171014. (Contemporary Realists Ser.). (Illus.). 1971. pap. 1.50 (*0-9600182-5-5*) Norton Art.

— Paintings of the Old West by Frank C. McCarthy. LC 77-7355. (Contemporary Realists Ser.). (Illus.). 1977. pap. 5.50 (*0-913060-13-5*) Norton Art.

— Portrait' Miniatures in Early American History: 1750-1840. LC 76-11634. 1976. pap. 3.50 (*0-913060-09-7*) Norton Art.

— Realism in Retrospect: The Works of James Peter Cost. LC 75-164700. (Contemporary Realists Ser.). (Illus.). 1971. pap. 3.50 (*0-9600182-3-9*) Norton Art.

— Robert William Addison: A Retrospective Exhibition. LC 73-155783. (Contemporary Realists Ser.). (Illus.). 1971. pap. 1.00 (*0-9600182-2-0*) Norton Art.

— Roses in Porcelain by Jean du Tilleux. LC 73-81397. (Illus.). 16p. 1973. pap. 3.50 (*0-913060-02-X*) Norton Art.

— Samuel Kirk & Son: American Silver Craftsmen since Eighteen Fifteen. (Illus.). 32p. 1971. pap. 1.00 (*0-913060-17-8*) Norton Art.

— The Seasonal Transitions of Richard Earl Thompson. LC 82-12437. (Illus.). 76p. 1982. pap. 10.00 (*0-913060-20-8*) Norton Art.

— Stow Wengenroth, Artist-Lithographer: A Retrospective Exhibition. LC 76-26456. (Contemporary Realists Ser.). (Illus.). 1976. pap. 3.00 (*0-913060-10-0*) Norton Art.

— Will Hinds: Artist of the Deep South. LC 79-187911. (Contemporary Realists Ser.). (Illus.). 1972. pap. 2.00 (*0-9600182-6-3*) Norton Art.

— The Works of E. L. Henry: Recollections of a Time Gone by. (Illus.). 56p. 1987. pap. 12.00 (*0-913060-26-7*) Norton Art.

__Norton, Ralph, ed. see IBC-Donoghue, Inc. Staff.__

__Norton, Ralph, ed. see IBC--Donoghue, Inc. Staff.__

__Norton, Ralph G., ed. see IBC Publishing Inc. Staff.__

__Norton, Richard.__ Tonality in Western Culture: A Critical & Historical Perspective. LC 83-43030. (Illus.). 336p. 1984. 35.00 (*0-271-00359-6*) Pa St U Pr.

__Norton, Richard J., jt. ed. see Ricketts, R. Allan.__

__Norton, Richard W., jt. auth. see Bruce, Thomas A.__

__Norton, Rictor H.__ The Homosexual Literary Tradition. 432p. 1974. 250.00 (*0-87700-204-5*) Revisionist Pr.

__Norton, Robert.__ Communicator Style: Theory, Applications, & Measures. LC 83-13720. (Sage Series in Interpersonal Communication: No. 1). (Illus.). 320p. reprint ed. pap. 91.20 (*0-8357-4837-5*, 2037774) Bks Demand.

— The Gunner: Shewing the Whole Practise of Artillerie, No. 617. LC 73-6155. 1973. reprint ed. 70.00 (*90-221-0617-9*) Walter J Johnson.

— The Willow in the Tempest. 324p. (Orig.). 1990. pap. 15.00 (*0-918980-13-5*) St Alban Pr.

__Norton, Robert, ed.__ Types Best Remembered--Types Best Forgotten. (Illus.). 176p. 1994. 16.00 (*1-884606-00-8*); pap. 10.00 (*0-685-71103-X*) Parsimony Pr.

*__Norton, Robert & Brenders, David.__ Communication & Consequences: Laws of Interaction. (LEA's Communication Ser.). 350p. 1995. text ed. 70.00 (*0-8058-2033-7*); pap. 35.00 (*0-8058-2034-5*) L Erlbaum Assocs.

__Norton, Robert, jt. comp. see Wharton, Edith.__

*__Norton, Robert E.__ The Beautiful Soul: Aesthetic Morality in the Eighteenth Century. 336p. 1995. 35.00x (*0-8014-3050-X*) Cornell U Pr.

— Herder's Aesthetics & the European Enlightenment. LC 90-55759. (Illus.). 280p. 1991. 37.95 (*0-8014-2530-1*) Cornell U Pr.

__Norton, Robert E. & Belcher, James O.__ A Guide to Linkages Between Vocational Education & Organized Labor In The United States. 162p. 1984. 12.00 (*0-318-17786-2*, RD252) Ctr Educ Trng Employ.

__Norton, Robert E. & Harrington, Lois G.__ Administrator Competency Study. 114p. 1987. 10.50 (*0-318-35277-X*, RD 268) Ctr Educ Trng Employ.

__Norton, Robert F.__ A Treatise on Deeds. LC 81-83533. 772p. 1981. reprint ed. lib. bdg. 99.00 (*0-912004-17-7*) W W Gaunt.

__Norton, Robert L.__ Design of Machinery: An Introduction to the Synthesis & Analysis of Mechanisms & Machines. 1992. text ed. write for info. (*0-07-047799-X*) McGraw.

__Norton, Robert L. & Leck, Charles F.__ An Annotated Checklist of Birds of the U. S. Virgin Islands. (Illus.). 35p. 1986. pap. text ed. 6.95 (*0-916611-01-9*) Antilles Pr.

__Norton, Robert W., tr. see Ricken, Ulrich.__

__Norton, Roger D. & Leopoldo, Solis M., eds.__ The Book of CHAC: Programming Studies for Mexican Agriculture. LC 80-29366. (World Bank Research Publication Ser.). 622p. reprint ed. pap. 177.30 (*0-7837-5386-1*, 2045150) Bks Demand.

__Norton Rose M5 Group Staff, jt. ed. see Boyle, A.__

__Norton, Russell.__ Stereoviews Illustrated: Fifty Early American, Vol. I. LC 94-92191. (Illus.). 64p. (Orig.). 1994. pap. 18.95 (*0-9641653-0-9*) Stereoviews.

__Norton, S. A., et al, eds.__ Acidic Precipitation. (Advances in Environmental Science Ser.: Vol. 4). (Illus.). xiv, 293p. 1989. 169.00 (*0-387-97026-6*, 2939) Spr-Verlag.

__Norton, Sara, ed. see Norton, Charles E.__

__Norton, Sarah, et al.__ The Bare Essentials: English Writing Skills. 299p. (C). 1983. pap. text ed. 22.00 (*0-03-059821-4*) HB Coll Pubs.

__Norton, Saundra, jt. auth. see Norton, Donna E.__

__Norton-Smith, John.__ A Reader's Guide to Hart Crane's White Buildings. LC 93-18842. 164p. 1993. 79.95 (*0-7734-9257-7*) E Mellen.

__Norton-Smith, John, illus.__ Bodleian Library Manuscript Fairfax 16. (Medieval Manuscripts Ser.). 1979. 275.00 (*0-85967-513-0*, Pub. by Scolar Pr UK) Ashgate Pub Co.

__Norton Staff.__ Official Major League Baseball American League Pocket Almanac 1994. 1994. pap. 2.99 (*0-393-31180-5*) Norton.

— Official Major League Baseball National League Pocket Almanac 1994. 1994. pap. 2.99 (*0-393-31181-3*) Norton.

__Norton Staff & Morgan, Robert P.__ Twentieth-Century Music. (Introduction to Music History Ser.). (C). 1991. text ed. 32.95 (*0-393-95272-X*) Norton.

__Norton, Stephen L.__ Devils Tower: The Story Behind the Scenery. LC 91-60036. (Illus.). 48p. 1991. 6.95 (*0-88714-051-3*) KC Pubns.

*__Norton, Susan J. & Kemp, David T.__ Otoacoustic Emissions: Theory Application & Techniques. 300p. 1995. 45.00 (*1-56593-270-6*, 0592) Singular Publishing.

__Norton, Suza.__ Yoga for People over Fifty: Exercise Without Exhaustion. LC 76-18445. 1977. 15.95 (*0-8159-7404-3*) Devin.

__Norton-Taylor, Duncan, ed.__ For Some, the Dream Came True: The Best from 50 Years of Fortune Magazine. 1981. 15.00 (*0-8184-0317-9*) Carol Pub Group.

__Norton-Taylor, Richard.__ The Accountability of the Security Services. (C). 1988. 21.00 (*0-900137-31-2*, Pub. by NCCL UK) St Mut.

__Norton, Thomas.__ Gorboduc; or, Ferrex & Porres. Cauthen, Irby B., Jr. et al, eds. LC 74-88095. (Regents Renaissance Drama Ser.). 118p. reprint ed. pap. 33.70 (*0-318-39765-X*, 2033139) Bks Demand.

__Norton, Thomas & Sackville, Thomas.__ Ferrex & Porrex. LC 78-133732. (Tudor Facsimile Texts. Old English Plays Ser.: No. 32). reprint ed. 49.50 (*0-404-53332-9*) AMS Pr.

__Norton, Thomas E.__ The Fur Trade in Colonial New York, Sixteen Eighty-Six to Seventeen Seventy-Six. LC 73-2047. 266p. 1974. 37.50 (*0-299-06420-4*) U of Wis Pr.

__Norton, Thomas J.__ Losing Liberty Judicially: Prohibitory & Kindred Laws Examined. xiv, 252p. 1981. reprint ed. lib. bdg. 24.00 (*0-8377-0907-5*) Rothman.

__Norton, Thomas J., jt. ed. see Kalat, James W.__

__Norton, Thomas L.__ Trade Union Policies in the Massachusetts Shoe Industry. LC 78-76630. (Columbia University. Studies in the Social Sciences: No. 372). reprint ed. 27.50 (*0-404-51372-7*) AMS Pr.

__Norton, Tom A., et al.__ The Hanging Tree & Other Clocks. 2nd ed. Uphoff, Joseph A., Jr., ed. (Illus.). 32p. 1986. pap. text ed. 2.00 (*0-943123-02-X*) Arjuna Lib Pr.

__Norton, Virgil J., jt. auth. see Saila, Saul B.__

__Norton, W. W., jt. ed. see Modlin, Charles E.__

__Norton-Wayne, Leonard, jt. auth. see Browne, Arthur.__

__Norton, William.__ Eagle Ventures: With an Introduction by Emil "Bus" Mossbacher, Jr. LC 72-126390. (Illus.). 128p. 1972. 15.00 (*0-87131-022-8*) M Evans.

— Explorations in the Understanding of Landscape: A Cultural Geography. LC 88-21340. (Contributions in Sociology Ser.: No. 77). 213p. 1989. text ed. 47.95 (*0-313-26494-5*, NEX/, Greenwood Pr) Greenwood.

__Norton, William L., Jr., et al.__ Annual Survey of Bankruptcy. LC 93-71459. 1979. 145.00 (*0-685-59826-8*) Clark Boardman Callaghan.

— Norton Banker Forms, 2 vols., Set. LC 81-10028. 1992. ring bd. 195.00 (*0-685-59825-X*) Clark Boardman Callaghan.

— Norton Bankruptcy Code & Rules, 2 vols. LC 81-10028. 1981. pap. 99.75 (*0-685-44923-8*) Clark Boardman Callaghan.

— Norton Bankruptcy Law & Practice, 11 vols. 2nd ed. LC 93-71471. 1993. ring bd. 975.00 (*0-317-11808-0*) Clark Boardman Callaghan.

__Norton, William T., ed.__ Oligodendroglia. (Advances in Neurochemistry Ser.: Vol. 5). 338p. 1984. 89.50 (*0-306-41547-X*, Plenum Pr) Plenum.

__Norton, Yuri E.__ Dear Uncle Dave. (Illus.). 40p. (Orig.). (J). (gr. 1 up). 1993. lib. bdg. 13.95 (*0-9622808-4-4*) S&T Waring.

__Norusis & SPSS.__ Spss for Unix Advanced Statistics Releast 5.0. 1993. pap. text ed. 28.00 (*0-13-107137-8*) P-H.

— Spss for Unix Professional Statistics Release 5.0. 1993. pap. text ed. 28.00 (*0-13-107152-1*) P-H.

__Norusis, Marija J.__ SPSS - PC Plus Advanced Statistics, Version 5.0. LC 92-85165. 592p. 1992. pap. 21.95 (*0-923967-68-0*) SPSS Inc.

— SPSS - PC Plus Base System User's Guide, Version 5.0. LC 92-85164. 800p. 1992. pap. 29.95 (*0-923967-66-4*) SPSS Inc.

— SPSS - PC Plus Professional Statistics, Version 5.0. LC 92-85163. 272p. (Orig.). 1992. pap. 21.95 (*0-923967-67-2*) SPSS Inc.

— SPSS - PC Plus Studentware for Business. SPSS Inc. Staff, ed. LC 91-62550. 604p. (Orig.). 1991. disk 44.95 (*0-923967-30-3*); disk 44.95 (*0-923967-31-1*) SPSS Inc.

— SPSS - PC Plus Studentware Plus. rev. ed. LC 91-62551. 483p. 1991. disk 39.95 (*0-923967-28-1*); disk 39.95 (*0-923967-29-X*) SPSS Inc.

— SPSS for Windows: Advanced Statistics Release 5. LC 92-85019. 400p. (Orig.). Date not set. pap. 24.95 (*0-923967-56-7*) SPSS Inc.

— SPSS for Windows: Base System User's Guide, Release 5.0. SPSS Inc. Staff, ed. LC 91-68310. 768p. 1992. pap. 32.95 (*0-923967-49-4*) SPSS Inc.

— The SPSS Guide to Data Analysis for Release 4. SPSS Inc. Staff, ed. LC 90-63465. (Illus.). 470p. 1991. pap. text ed. 16.95 (*0-923967-08-7*) SPSS Inc.

— The SPSS Guide to Data Analysis for SPSS-X. rev. ed. SPSS Inc. Staff, ed. LC 87-60776. (Illus.). 448p. (C). 1988. pap. text ed. 16.95 (*0-918469-42-2*) SPSS Inc.

— SPSS-PC Plus Studentware. SPSS Inc. Staff, ed. LC 88-80965. 416p. (Orig.). (C). 1988. pap. text ed. 34.95 (*0-918469-73-2*) SPSS Inc.

— SPSS-X Advanced Statistics Guide. 2nd ed. SPSS Inc. Staff, ed. LC 88-61671. 544p. 1988. pap. text ed. 19.95 (*0-918469-81-3*) SPSS Inc.

— SPSS-X Introductory Statistics Guide for SPSS-X Release 3. rev. ed. LC 87-62352. 384p. (C). 1988. pap. text ed. 16.95 (*0-918469-54-6*) SPSS Inc.

__Norusis, Marija J. & SPSS Inc. Staff.__ SPSS for Windows: Professional Statistics User's Guide, Release 5.0. LC 91-68311. 400p. Date not set. pap. 24.95 (*0-923967-50-8*) SPSS Inc.

__Norusis, Marija J., jt. auth. see SPSS Inc. Staff.__

__Norval, Morgan.__ Death in the Desert: The Namibian Tragedy. LC 89-62602. (Illus.). 364p. 1989. 24.95 (*0-944273-03-3*) Selous Found Pr.

— Inside the ANC, Vol. I: The Evolution of a Terrorist Organization. 2nd ed. Kvederas, Robert, ed. LC 90-63074. (Illus.). 263p. 1991. 21.95 (*0-944273-07-6*) Selous Found Pr.

— Politics by Other Means: The ANC's War on South Africa. Krederas, Robert, ed. 350p. 1993. 25.00 (*0-944273-11-4*) Selous Found Pr.

An Asterisk (*) at the beginning of an entry indicates that the title is appearing in BIP for the first time.

— Red Star over Southern Africa. LC 87-51366. 220p. 1988. 18.95 (*0-944273-00-9*); pap. 5.95 (*0-944273-02-5*) Selous Found Pr.

Norval, Morgan, ed. The Militia in Twentieth Century America: A Symposium. 252p. (Orig.). 1985. pap. 9.95 (*0-317-19795-9*) Gun Ownrs Fund.

Norval, Morsan, jt. auth. see Aker, Frank.

Norval, R. A., et al. The Epidemiology of Theileriosis in Africa. (Illus.). 481p. 1991. text ed. 94.00 (*0-12-521740-4*) Acad Pr.

Norvell, Anthony. Astrology, Romance, You & the Stars. 1979. pap. 10.00 (*0-87980-011-9*) Wilshire.

— The Oriental Seven-Day Quick Weight-off Diet. 1975. text ed. 24.95 (*0-13-642116-4*, Parker Publishing Co) P-H.

Norvell, Douglas G., jt. auth. see Branson, Robert E.

Norvell, Nancy & Belles, Dale. Stress Management Training: A Group Leader's Guide. LC 89-62711. 96p. 1990. pap. 15.70 (*0-943158-33-8*, SM-GBP) Pro Resource.

Norvell, Nancy, jt. auth. see Belles, Dale.

Norvelle, Don. Fluid Power Technology. LC 93-46736. 450p. 1994. text ed. 63.00 (*0-314-01218-4*) West Pub.

Norvelle, Joan W. Introduction to Fund Accounting. 5th ed. (Illus.). 270p. 1994. pap. text ed. 20.00 (*0-9623645-6-8*) Thoth Bks.

Norvelle, Joan W., jt. auth. see Nossen, Richard A.

Norvig, Gerda S. Dark Figures in the Desired Country: Blake's Illustrations to the Pilgrim's Progress. 304p. 1993. 70.00 (*0-520-04471-1*) U CA Pr.

Norvig, Peter. Paradigms of Artificial Intelligence Programming; Case Studies in Common LISP. LC 91-39187. 946p. 1992. pap. 49.95 (*1-55860-191-0*, QA76.6) Morgan Kaufmann.

Norvig, Peter, jt. auth. see Russell, Stuart.

Norville, Barbara. Writing the Modern Mystery. 224p. 1992. pap. 13.99 (*0-89879-523-0*) Writers Digest.

Norville, Mary A. Drug Dosages & Solutions: A Workbook. (Illus.). 320p. 1994. pap. text ed. 26.50 (*0-8385-1613-0*, A1613-7) Appleton & Lange.

***Norville, Warren.** Celestial Navigation - Step by Step. 2nd ed. (Illus.). 251p. (C). 1994. pap. text ed. 30.00 (*1-879778-20-3*, BK-203) Marine Educ.

— Celestial Navigation Step by Step. 2nd ed. LC 83-47888. (Illus.). 272p. 1987. pap. text ed. 22.95 (*0-87742-177-3*, C250) Intl Marine.

— Coastal Navigation Step by Step. LC 75-15011. (Illus.). 224p. 1975. 20.00 (*0-87742-056-4*) Intl Marine.

Norvin, W., ed. Olympiodorus Philosophus, In Platonis Gorgiam Commentaria. 250p. 1966. reprint ed. write for info. (*0-318-70988-0*, Pub. by Georg Olms GW) Lubrecht & Cramer.

Norwak, Mary. Book of Crepes & Omelets. Thiesen, Jan, ed. LC 87-17602. (Book of...Ser.). 120p. (Orig.). 1988. pap. 9.95 (*0-89586-669-2*, HP Books) Berkley Pub.

— Book of Preserves: Jams, Chutneys, Pickles, Jellies. Aaron, Patricia J., ed. (Book of...Ser.). 128p. (Orig.). 1986. pap. 11.00 (*0-89586-507-6*, HP Books) Berkley Pub.

— Cooking with Fruit. 1960. 7.95 (*0-685-20569-X*) Transatl Arts.

Norwalk. Cakes & Cookies. 1986. 4.98 (*0-671-07752-X*) S&S Trade.

— Microwave Meals in Minutes. (Getting It Right Ser.). 1995. pap. 3.95 (*0-572-01764-2*, Pub. by Foulsham UK) Atrium Pubs.

Norwalk, Mary. Getting It Right: Microwave Recipes. 1994. pap. 9.95 (*0-572-01773-1*, Pub. by W Foulsham UK) Trans-Atl Phila.

Norway, Nevil S. The Breaking Wave. 22.95 (*0-405-18913-3*) Ayer.

Norwegian-American Historical Association. Norwegian-American Studies & Records, Vol. 14. LC 26-145503. 273p. reprint ed. pap. 77.90 (*0-317-55771-8*, 2029292) Bks Demand.

Norwegian-American Historical Association Staff. Norwegian-American Studies, Vol. 30. LC 87-657088. 352p. reprint ed. pap. 100.40 (*0-7837-0108-X*, 2040385) Bks Demand.

— Studies & Records, Vol. 1: 1926. LC 87-657087. (Illus.). 195p. reprint ed. pap. 55.60 (*0-7837-1650-8*, 2041948) Bks Demand.

Norwegian Institute of Rock Schach Blasting Techniques Staff. Rock Bolting: A Practical Handbook Describing All Aspects of Rock Bolts & Their Application in Rock Engineering. 1979. 37.00 (*0-08-022503-9*, Pub. by Pergamon Repr UK) Franklin.

Norwegian Institute of Technology Staff. North Sea Oil & Gas Reservoirs. (C). 1987. lib. bdg. 165.00 (*0-86010-865-1*, Pub. by Graham & Trotman UK) Kluwer Ac.

Norwegian Petroleum Society (NPF) Staff, ed. Habitat of Hydrocarbons on the Norwegian Continental Shelf. (C). 1986. lib. bdg. 165.00 (*0-86010-833-3*, Pub. by Graham & Trotman UK) Kluwer Ac.

Norwegian Petroleum Society Staff. Geology of the European Countries, 4 vols., Set. Incl. Vol. 1. Geology of the European Countries: Austria, Federal Republic of Germany, Ireland, the Netherlands, Switzerland, United Kingdom. 500p. 1980. lib. bdg. 115.50 (*0-86010-261-0*); Vol. 2. Geology of the European Countries: Denmark, Finland, Iceland, Norway, Sweden. 500p. 1980. lib. bdg. 115.50 (*0-86010-262-9*); Vol. 4. Geologie des Pays Europeens: France, Belgique, Luxembourg. (FRE.). 620p. 1980. lib. bdg. 115.50 (*2-04-011122-0*); 444p. (ENG & FRE.). 1987. Set lib. bdg. 316.50 (*0-86010-919-4*) Kluwer Ac.

— The Petroleum Geology of the North European. 444p. 1984. lib. bdg. 136.50 (*0-86010-486-9*) G & T Inc.

***Norwich.** Shakespeare's History. Date not set. 26.00 (*0-684-81434-X*, Scribners) S&S Trade.

Norwich, Brahm. Reappraising Special Needs Education. Mittler, Peter, ed. (Special Needs in Ordinary Schools Ser.). 208p. 1990. pap. text ed. 22.50 (*0-304-32286-5*) Cassell.

Norwich, John J. Byzantium: The Apogee. 1991. 40.00 (*0-394-53779-3*) Knopf.

— Byzantium: The Early Centuries. 1989. 40.00 (*0-394-53778-5*) Knopf.

— A History of Venice. 1989. pap. 20.00 (*0-679-72197-5*, Vin) Random.

— Sovereign. (Illus.). 128p. 1992. pap. 22.95 (*1-85585-116-4*) Trafalgar.

Norwich, John J., ed. Great Architecture of the World. (Quality Paperbacks Ser.). (Illus.). 288p. 1991. reprint ed. pap. 24.95 (*0-306-80436-0*) Da Capo.

— Oxford Illustrated Encyclopedia, Vol. 5: The Arts. (Illus.). 512p. 1990. 49.95 (*0-19-869137-8*) OUP.

Norwich, John J., jt. auth. see Landon, H. C.

Norwich, Julian, ed. see Hazard, David.

Norwich, Kenneth H. Information, Sensation, & Perception. LC 93-16692. 326p. 1993. text ed. 39.95 (*0-12-521890-7*) Acad Pr.

Norwick, Kenneth H. Molecular Dynamics in Biosystems. 1977. 174.00 (*0-08-020420-1*, Pub. by Pergamon Repr UK) Franklin.

Norwick, Kenneth P. & Chasen, Jerry S. The Rights of Authors, Artists, & Other Creative People: The Basic ACLU Guide to Author & Artist Rights. 2nd rev. ed. LC 91-23721. (ACLU Handbook Ser.). 306p. 1992. pap. 7.95 (*0-8093-1773-7*) S Ill U Pr.

Norwin, W., ed. Olympiodorus Philosophus, In Platonis Phaedonem Commentaria. xi, 272p. 1987. reprint ed. write for info. (*0-318-70989-9*, Pub. by Georg Olms GW) Lubrecht & Cramer.

Norwine, Jim. Climate & Human Ecology. LC 78-52975. (Illus.). 1978. pap. 9.95 (*0-918464-19-6*) D Armstrong.

— A Postmodernist Tao: A Guide to Apprehending Ways of Meaning in Pathless Lands. Winans, Linda F., ed. LC 92-40602. 172p. (Orig.). (C). 1993. lib. bdg. 42.50 (*0-8191-8992-8*); pap. text ed. 16.50 (*0-8191-8993-6*) U Pr of Amer.

Norwine, Jim & Gonzalez, Alfonso, eds. The Third World: States of Mind & Being. (Illus.). 320p. 1988. text ed. 55.00 (*0-04-910106-4*); pap. text ed. 22.95 (*0-04-910121-8*) Routledge Chapman & Hall.

***Norwine, Jim, et al, eds.** The Changing Climate of Texas: Predictability & Implications for the Future. 355p. (C). 1995. pap. 25.00 (*0-9645710-0-5*) TX A&M CGMS.

Norwood, Audrianne. Like Mama Used to Say. LC 92-96895. (Illus.). 208p. (C). 1992. pap. 9.00 (*1-882338-05-7*) Via God Pub.

— Like Mama Used to Say. LC 92-96895. (Illus.). 208p. (C). 1995. 16.00 (*1-882338-13-8*) Via God Pub.

Norwood, Bev, ed. see Dennis, Larry.

Norwood, Bev.

Norwood, Bev, ed. see Dorman, Larry.

Norwood, Bev, ed. see Green, Bob, et al.

Norwood, Bev, ed. see Hopkins, John.

Norwood, Bev, ed. see Mizell, Hubert.

Norwood, Bev, ed. see Nuhn, Gary.

Norwood, Bev, ed. see Parascenzo, Marino.

Norwood, D. Chess Puzzles. (Usborne Guides Ser.). (Illus.). 64p. (J). (gr. 5 up). 1992. lib. bdg. 12.96 (*0-88110-464-7*); pap. text ed. 6.95 (*0-7460-0950-X*) EDC.

Norwood, David. Winning with Modern. (Batsford Chess Library). 1994. pap. 16.95 (*0-8050-3281-9*) H Holt & Co.

Norwood, David, et al, illus. Children's Tour of Red Stick City. 32p. (J). (gr. 1-6). 1980. pap. text ed. 2.00 (*0-9608282-2-2*) YWCO.

Norwood-Fontbonne Home & School Association Staff. Philadelphia Homestyle Cookbook. Wimmer Brothers Books Staff, ed. (Illus.). 288p. (Orig.). 1985. 12.95 (*0-9614938-0-1*) Norwood-Fontbonne.

***Norwood, Frank.** The Burning. LC 94-40987. 1995. 21.95 (*0-385-31380-2*, Dial) Doubleday.

Norwood, Frederick A. The Reformation Refugees As an Economic Force. LC 83-45668. reprint ed. 39.50 (*0-404-19818-X*) AMS Pr.

Norwood, Gilbert. Essays on Euripidean Drama. LC 53-11243. (Scholarly Reprint Ser.). 197p. reprint ed. pap. 56.20 (*0-317-28759-1*, 2055478) Bks Demand.

Norwood, Gus. Washington Grangers Celebrate a Century: History, Fraternal Organization (100th Anniversary), Agriculture. LC 88-50556. (Illus.). (Orig.). 1988. 7.95 (*0-929612-01-9*); pap. 4.95 (*0-929612-02-7*) WA State Grange.

Norwood, James, tr. see Body, Jacques.

***Norwood, James E.** Battle Songs of the Second American Revolution. 1996. write for info. (*0-915854-96-1*) Friend Freedom.

Norwood, James E., et al. The Federalist Papers, No. 86. 1988. pap. 12.00 (*0-915854-87-2*) Friend Freedom.

***Norwood, Janet L.** Organizing to Count: Change in the Federal Statistical System. 150p. (C). 1995. lib. bdg. 43.50 (*0-87766-634-2*); pap. text ed. 22.50 (*0-87766-635-0*) Urban Inst.

Norwood, John. John Norwood's Western Cookbook. LC 85-82339. 76p. 1986. pap. 9.95 (*0-911581-06-5*) Heimburger Hse Pub.

Norwood, John B. Rio Grande Memories. LC 91-71587. (Illus.). 192p. 1991. 41.95 (*0-911581-21-9*) Heimburger Hse Pub.

— Rio Grande Narrow Gauge. Heimburger, Donald J. & Heimburger, Marilyn M., eds. LC 82-84384. (Illus.). 312p. 1983. 44.95 (*0-911581-00-6*) Heimburger Hse Pub.

— Rio Grande Narrow Gauge Recollections. Heimburger, Donald J. & Heimburger, Marilyn M., eds. LC 86-81505. (Illus.). 272p. 1986. 41.95 (*0-911581-07-3*) Heimburger Hse Pub.

Norwood, John H. The Schism in the Methodist Episcopal Church, 1844. LC 76-10284. (Perspectives in American History Ser.: No. 33). 255p. 1976. reprint ed. lib. bdg. 35.00 (*0-87991-357-6*) Porcupine Pr.

Norwood, Ken & Smith, Kathleen. Rebuilding Community in America: Housing for Ecological Living, Personal Empowerment, & the New Extended Family. (Illus.). 432p. 1994. pap. 24.50 (*0-9641346-2-4*) Shared Liv Res.

Norwood, Meredith, jt. auth. see Golden, Larry B.

Norwood, O'Tar T. & Shiell, Richard C. Hair Transplant Surgery. 2nd ed. (Illus.). 356p. (C). 1984. 75.95 (*0-398-04946-7*) C C Thomas.

Norwood, Richard. Fortification, or Architecture Military. LC 72-6019. (English Experience Ser.: No. 545). 1973. reprint ed. 25.00 (*90-221-0545-8*) Walter J Johnson.

— The Sea-Mans Practice. LC 74-28877. (English Experience Ser.: No. 755). 1975. reprint ed. 30.00 (*90-221-0755-8*) Walter J Johnson.

— Trigonometrie, or the Doctrine of Triangles, 2 pts. LC 78-171779. (English Experience Ser.: No. 404). 362p. 1971. reprint ed. 75.00 (*90-221-0404-4*) Walter J Johnson.

Norwood, Rick, ed. see Foster, Hal.

Norwood, Robin. Why Me, Why This, Why Now: A Guide to Answering Life's Toughest Questions. 1994. 22.00 (*0-517-59850-7*, Carol Southern Bks) Crown Pub Group.

***Norwood, Seth W.** Sketches of Brooks History. (Illus.). 454p. 1995. reprint ed. lib. bdg. 46.50 (*0-8328-4666-X*) Higginson Bk Co.

Norwood, Stephen H. Labor's Flaming Youth: Telephone Operators & Worker Militancy, 1878-1923. (Working Class in America History & Women in American History Ser.). (Illus.). 360p. 1990. 34.95 (*0-252-01633-5*) U of Ill Pr.

— Labor's Flaming Youth: Telephone Operators & Worker Militancy, 1878-1923. (Working Class in American History - Women in American History Ser.). (Illus.). 360p. 1991. pap. 12.95 (*0-252-06225-6*) U of Ill Pr.

***Norwood, Sybil, illus. & des.** The Traveler's World: A Dictionary of Industry & Destination Literacy. LC 95-16338. 1995. pap. text ed. 18.00 (*0-13-228651-3*) P-H.

Norwood, Vera. Made from This Earth: American Women & Nature. LC 92-22562. (Gender & American Culture Ser.). (Illus.). xxiv, 368p. (C). 1993. 37.50 (*0-8078-2062-8*); pap. 17.95 (*0-8078-4396-2*) U of NC Pr.

Norwood, Vera & Monk, Janice. The Desert Is No Lady: Southwestern Landscapes in Women's Writing & Art. 288p. (C). 1989. reprint ed. pap. 19.95 (*0-300-04588-3*) Yale U Pr.

Norwood, Victor G. Drums along the Amazon. large type ed. (Non-Fiction Ser.). 1974. 15.95 (*0-85456-269-9*) Ulverscroft.

Norwood, William F. Medical Education in the U. S. Before the Civil War. LC 72-165726. (American Education, Ser, No. 2). 1975. reprint ed. 30.95 (*0-405-03714-7*) Ayer.

Norwood, William I., jt. auth. see Jacobs, Marshall L.

Norworth, Jack. Take Me Out to the Ballgame. LC 91-18555. (Illus.). 40p. (J). (ps up). 1992. lib. bdg. 14.95 (*0-02-735991-3*, Four Winds Pr) S&S Childrens.

Norworthy, Kent. Inside Honduras. 2nd ed. (Illus.). 208p. 1994. pap. 11.95 (*0-911213-49-X*) Interhemisp Res Ctr.

Nosakhere, Moyenda. The Path Toward Liberation: Understanding the Need for Polygamy in the African-American Community. 110p. (Orig.). 1991. pap. 9.95 (*0-685-38399-7*) Imania Pubns.

— The Path Toward Liberation: Understanding the Need for Polygamy in the African-American Community. 110p. (Orig.). 1991. pap. 9.95 (*0-9626613-0-9*) New Nation Bks.

Nosal, Denise, ed. Houston Women: From Suffrage to City Hall. (Illus.). 85p. (Orig.). 1987. pap. text ed. 15.00 (*0-939903-02-4*) LWV Houston Ed Fund.

Nosanchuk, Terry, jt. auth. see Erickson, Bonnie.

Nosay, G., jt. auth. see Nakamura, T.

Nosbisch, Katie. Festival of Dreams: Weekend Retreats for High School People. (Illus.). 150p. (gr. 9-12). 1983. pap. 19.95 (*0-940634-19-8*) Puissance Pubns.

Nosbusch, H. & Mitchell, I. V., eds. Clay-Based Materials for the Ceramics Industry: Proceedings for the Final Contractors' Meeting on Clay-Based Materials for the Ceramics Industry, Organized by the Commission of the European Communities Within the Raw Materials Sector (1982-85), Held in Brussels, Belgium, 11 Dec., 1986. 144p. 1989. 45.00 (*1-85166-315-0*) Elsevier.

— Technical Ceramics: Proceedings of the Final Contractors' Meeitng in the Research Area "Technical Ceramics", Held in Brussels, Belgium, 9-11 Dec. 1986. 354p. 1989. 79.25 (*1-85166-279-0*) Elsevier.

Nosbusch, N., jt. ed. see Mitchell, I. V.

Nosco, Peter. Remembering Paradise: Nativism & Nostalgia in Eighteenth-Century Japan. (Harvard-Yenching Institute Monograph: No. 31). 271p. 1990. 28.00 (*0-674-76007-7*) HUP.

Nosco, Peter, ed. Confucianism & Tokugawa Culture. LC 83-43086. 360p. (C). 1989. pap. text ed. 18.95 (*0-691-00839-6*) Princeton U Pr.

— Confucianism & Tokugawa Culture. LC 83-43086. 301p. 1984. reprint ed. pap. 85.80 (*0-7837-8595-X*, 2049410) Bks Demand.

Nose, jt. ed. see Hori.

Nose, Y., et al, eds. Progress in Artificial Organs-1985: Proceedings from the Fifth International Society for Artificial Organs Congress, Chicago. 110.00 (*0-936022-26-4*); pap. 100.00 (*0-936022-25-6*) ICAOT Pr.

Nose, Y, et al, eds. Therapeutic Apheresis: A Critical Look, Proceedings, Third International Symposium on Therapeutic Apheresis, 1984, Cleveland, Ohio. 70.00 (*0-936022-19-1*); pap. 60.00 (*0-936022-18-3*) ICAOT Pr.

Nose, Yukihiko, jt. ed. see Kambic, Helen E.

Nose, Yukihiko, et al, eds. Plasmapheresis: New Trends in Therapeutic Applications. 60.00 (*0-936022-12-4*); pap. 45.00 (*0-936022-11-6*) ICAOT Pr.

— Plasmapheresis: Therapeutic Applications & New Techniques. fac. ed. LC 82-42896. (Illus.). 462p. Date not set. pap. 131.70 (*0-7837-7187-8*, 2047112) Bks Demand.

Noseda, G. F., et al. Lipoproteins & Coronary Atherosclerosis. (Giovanni Lorenzini Foundation Symposia Ser.: Vol. 13). 450p. 1982. 127.75 (*0-444-80408-0*) Elsevier.

***Nosek, Kathleen.** The Dyslexic Scholar: Helping Your Child Achieve Academic Success. LC 94-45423. 1995. 11.95 (*0-87833-882-9*) Taylor Pub.

Noseworthy, Michelle, jt. auth. see Williams, Larry.

Nosher, John, jt. auth. see Rosen, Robert J.

Noshpitz, Joseph D. & Coddington, R. Dean. Stressors & the Adjustment Disorders. (Series on Personality Processes). 693p. 1990. text ed. 85.00 (*0-471-62186-2*) Wiley.

Noshpitz, Joseph D. & King, Robert. Pathways of Growth: Essentials of Child Psychiatry, 2 vols. 1991. Vol. 1, Introduction to Child Psychiatry, 453p. text ed. 69.95 (*0-471-09917-1*) Wiley.

— Pathways of Growth: Essentials of Child Psychiatry, 2 vols., Vol. 2. 1991. Set. text ed. 145.00 (*0-471-53178-2*) Wiley.

Nosis, George J. Visionary Thinking. LC 86-70664. 120p. 6.95 (*0-910977-02-X*) Avenue Pub.

Nosis, George J., jt. auth. see Pitrone, Jean M.

Noske, Frits. French Song from Berlioz to Duparc. xiv, 454p. 1987. reprint ed. pap. 12.95 (*0-486-25554-9*) Dover.

— Saints & Sinners: The Latin Musical Dialogue in the Seventeenth Century. LC 92-34757. (Illus.). 400p. 1993. 95.00 (*0-19-816298-7*, Old Oregon Bk Store) OUP.

— The Signifier & the Signified. 1977. lib. bdg. 107.50 (*90-247-1995-X*) Kluwer Ac.

— The Signifier & the Signified: Studies in the Operas of Mozart & Verdi. (Illus.). 430p. 1990. 32.00 (*0-19-816201-4*) OUP.

— Sweelinck. (Oxford Studies of Composers: No. 22). 160p. 1990. pap. 18.95 (*0-19-816196-4*) OUP.

Noskowitz, Jack. Mayn Folk (My People) 167p. 1962. pap. 6.50 (*0-318-22121-7*) Workmen's Circle.

Nosofsky, William. Basic Prefix & Root Vocabulary Builder. 2nd ed. 77p. (gr. 7-12). 1984. pap. 8.49 (*0-89026-405-8*) Media Materials.

Nosoh, Yoshiaki & Sekiguchi, Takeshi. Protein Stability & Stabilization Through Protein Engineering. 180p. 1991. text ed. write for info. (*0-13-721788-9*) P-H.

Noson of Breslov. The Fiftieth Gate: Likutey Tefilot (Prayers 1-20), Vol. 1. Greenbaum, Avraham, tr. & intro. by. 609p. 1992. pap. 12.00 (*0-930213-67-X*) Breslov Res Inst.

Nosov, V. R., jt. auth. see Kolmanovski, V. B.

Nosov, Vladimir A. Ultrasonics in the Chemical Industry. LC 64-23248. (Soviet Progress in Applied Ultrasonics Ser.: Vol. 2). 171p. reprint ed. pap. 48.80 (*0-317-10629-5*, 2020692) Bks Demand.

Nosova, L. & Basu, Prabir. Tables of Thomson Functions: Their First Derivatives. LC 61-12445. (Mathematical Tables Ser.). 1961. 177.00 (*0-08-009518-6*, Pub. by Pergamon Repr UK) Franklin.

Noss, David S. A History of the World's Religions. 8th ed. 978p. (C). 1990. text ed. write for info. (*0-02-388480-0*) Macmillan.

Noss, David S. & Noss, John B. A History of the World's Religions. 9th ed. LC 93-3732. 705p. (C). 1993. write for info. (*0-02-388471-1*) Macmillan.

Noss, Elaine M., jt. auth. see Boyd, Alan W.

Noss, John B., jt. auth. see Noss, David S.

Noss, Luther. Paul Hindemith in the United States. LC 88-10694. (Music in American Life Ser.). (Illus.). 248p. 1989. 27.95 (*0-252-01563-0*) U of Ill Pr.

Noss, N. Microworlds - Adventures with Logo. (C). 1985. 54.00 (*0-09-161111-3*, Pub. by S Thornes Pubs UK) St Mut.

Noss, Philip, ed. see Ali, Mushin J.

Noss, Philip A., ed. Grafting Old Rootstock. LC 81-51153. (International Museum of Cultures Publications: No. 14). (Illus.). 246p. (Orig.). 1982. pap. 12.00 (*0-88312-165-4*); fiche 12.00x (*0-88312-990-6*) Summer Instit Ling.

Noss, Reed & Cooperrider, Allen. Saving Nature's Legacy: Protecting & Restoring Biodiversity. 1994. text ed. 48.00 (*1-55963-247-X*); pap. text ed. 27.50 (*1-55963-248-8*) Island Pr.

Noss, Richard, jt. ed. see Dowling, Paul.

Noss, Richard, jt. ed. see Hoyles, Celia.

Noss, Richard, jt. auth. see Nevile, Liddy.

Noss, Richard R. Heavens His Handiwork. (Illus.). 55p. 1962. 2.50 (*0-910840-09-1*) Kingdom.

— Heavens His Handiwork. (Illus.). 55p. 1962. pap. 1.50 (*0-910840-08-3*) Kingdom.

Nossack, Hans E. An Offering for the Dead. Neugroschel, Joachim, tr. LC 90-85935. 124p. 1992. 19.00 (*0-941419-29-0*, Eridanos Library) Marsilio Pubs.

Nossal, G. & Coppel, R. Reshaping Life: Key Issues in Genetic Engineering. 2nd ed. (Illus.). (C). 1990. pap. 16.95 (*0-521-38969-0*) Cambridge U Pr.

Nossal, Kim R. The Politics of Canadian Foreign Policy. 224p. (C). 1985. pap. text ed. write for info. (*0-13-684325-5*) P-H.

— Rain Dancing: Sanctions in Canadian & Australian Foreign Policy. 324p. 1994. 60.00 (*0-8020-0472-5*); pap. 21.95 (*0-8020-7571-1*) U of Toronto Pr.

Nossal, Ralph & Lecar, Harold. Introduction to Cell Physics. (Illus.). 387p. (C). 1991. 49.95 (*0-201-19560-7*, Adv Bk Prog) Addison-Wesley.

N

Nossaman, Allen. Many More Mountains, Vol. 1: Silverton's Roots. (Illus.). 352p. 1989. 39.00 (*0-913582-47-6*) Sundance.

Nosse, Larry & Friberg, Deborah. Management Principles for Physical Therapists. (Illus.). 336p. 1991. 45.00 (*0-683-06576-9*) Williams & Wilkins.

Nosseir, Aida I. Arabic Books Published in Egypt in the Nineteenth Century. 1990. text ed. 50.00 (*0-685-37649-4*, Pub. by Am Univ Cairo Pr UA) Col U Pr.

Nossen, R. A. Advanced Investigative Techniques for Private Financial Records. (Orig.). 1986. lib. bdg. 79.95 (*0-8490-3602-X*) Gordon Pr.

Nossen, Richard A. & Norvelle, Joan W. The Detection, Investigation, & Prosecution of Financial Crimes. 2nd ed. (Illus.). 200p. (Orig.). 1993. pap. text ed. 20.00 (*0-9623645-4-1*) Thoth Bks.

Nossing, Anne F. Heine in Italia nel Secolo Decimonono. 1948. pap. 7.50 (*0-913298-60-3*) S F Vanni.

Nossiter, Adam. Of Long Memory: Mississippi & the Murder of Medgar Evers. LC 94-45. 303p. 1994. 21.15 (*0-201-60844-8*) Addison-Wesley.

— Of Long Memory: Mississippi & the Murder of Medgar Evers. 320p. 1995. pap. 11.54 (*0-201-48339-4*) Addison-Wesley.

Nossiter, Bernard D. The Global Struggle for More: Third World Conflicts with Rich Nations. LC 86-45762. 272p. 1988. 20.00 (*0-318-32651-5*, Icon Edns) HarpC.

***Nossiter, Josh.** Using Excel 5 for Windows. (Illus.). 400p. (Orig.). 1995. pap. 19.99 (*0-7897-0288-6*) Que.

***Nossiter, Josh C.** Using WordPerfect 6.1 for Windows. (Illus.). 400p. (Orig.). 1995. pap. 19.99 (*0-7897-0293-2*) Que.

Nossiter, T. J. Marxist State Government in India: Politics, Economics & Society. (Marxist Regimes Ser.). 250p. 1992. 49.00 (*0-86187-456-0*, Pub. by Pinter Pubs UK) St Martin.

Nossiter, T. J., jt. ed. see Blumler, Jay G.

Nossman, Walter L. & Wyatt, Joseph L. Trust Administration & Taxation, 4 vols. 1966. Updates. ring bd. write for info. (*0-8205-1470-5*) Bender.

Nossum, R. T., ed. Advanced Topics in Artificial Intelligence. (Lecture Notes in Artificial Intelligence Ser.: Vol. 345). vii, 233p. 1989. pap. 34.00 (*0-387-50676-4*) Spr-Verlag.

Noster, M. B. Cuando el Medico Dice: Es Cancer (When the Doctor Says It's Cancer) (SPA.). Date not set. 2.49 (*0-8423-6515-X*, 498042) Editorial Unilit.

Nostlinger, Christine. The Cucumber King. Bell, Anthea, tr. 126p. (J). (gr. 3-7). 1984. 9.95 (*0-930267-01-X*) Bergh Pub.

Nostradamus. Prophecies on World Events by Nostradamus. 4th ed. Robb, Stewart, tr. (Illus.). (Orig.). 1991. pap. 8.95 (*0-87140-220-3*) Liveright.

Nostradamus & Delacroix, Robert. Nostradamus & the Nineties: Prophecies of Nostradamus Pertaining to the 1990's. 150p. 1993. pap. 5.95 (*0-9635358-0-3*) ARS Historica.

Nostrand, Carol A. A Handbook for Improving Your Diet. (Illus.). 363p. 1985. pap. write for info. (*0-9614721-0-3*) Eatongude Pr.

— Junk Food to Real Food: A Blueprint for Healthier Eating. 1994. pap. 16.95 (*0-87983-627-X*) Keats.

Nostrand, Howard L., et al. Savoir Vivre en Francais: Culture et Communication. 196p. 1988. Net. student ed write for info. (*0-471-82725-8*); Net. pap. text ed. write for info. (*0-471-82724-X*); audio write for info. (*0-471-84571-X*) Wiley.

Nostrand, Richard L. The Hispano Homeland. LC 91-50867. (Illus.). 296p. (C). 1992. 32.95 (*0-8061-2414-8*) U of Okla Pr.

Nostrand, Richard L. & Hilliard, Sam B., eds. The American South. LC 88-81746. (Geoscience & Man Ser.: Vol. 25). (Illus.). 174p. (Orig.). (C). 1988. pap. text ed. 25.00 (*0-938909-60-6*) Geosci Pubns LSU.

Nostredame, Jehan D. Les Vies des Plus Celebres et Anciens Poetes Provencaux. 258p. 1971. reprint ed. write for info. (*0-318-71936-3*, Pub. by Georg Olms GW) Lubrecht & Cramer.

Nostwich, T. D., ed. see Dreiser, Theodore.

Noswat, Erd, pseud. MAWS. (Illus.). 36p. (Orig.). 1976. pap. 1.50 (*0-939748-11-8*) Cave Bks MO.

Nosworthy, Brent. Anatomy of Victory: Battle Tactics, 1689-1763. (Illus.). 395p. 1991. pap. 16.95 (*0-87052-014-8*) Hippocrene Bks.

Nosworthy, J. M., ed. see Shakespeare, William.

Nota, John H. Max Scheler: The Man & His Works. 1983. 5.95 (*0-8199-0852-5*, Frncscn Herld) Franciscan Pr.

Notar, Ellen E. Solving the Puzzle: Teaching & Learning with Adults. (Illus.). 1994. pap. text ed. 12.95 (*0-944957-20-X*) Rivercross Pub.

Notari. Biopharmaceutics & Clinical Pharmacokinetics: An Introduction. 4th rev. ed. 440p. 1987. 49.75 (*0-8247-7523-6*) Dekker.

Notarius, Barbara & Brewer, Gail S. Open Your Own Bed & Breakfast. 2nd ed. 272p. 1992. pap. text ed. 14.95 (*0-471-54519-8*) Wiley.

Notarius, Clifford. We Can Work It Out: How to Solve Conflicts, Save Your Marriage & Strenjthen Your Love for Each Other. Markman, Howard, ed. LC 94-14009. 336p. (Orig.). 1994. pap. 12.95 (*0-399-52137-2*, Putnam) Putnam Pub Group.

Notarius, Clifford & Markman, Howard. We Can Work It Out. 288p. 1993. 21.95 (*0-399-13866-8*) Putnam Pub Group.

Notaro, Diane & Notaro, Joe. From the Dragon's Tale, Bk. I: A Door to Watch. LC 93-92776. (Illus.). 96p. (J). (gr. 4 up). 1994. pap. 8.00 (*1-56002-381-3*, AndeLear Pub) Aegina Pr.

Notaro, Joe, jt. auth. see Notaro, Diane.

Notcott, L. A. & Latham, G. C. The African & the Cinema. 1976. lib. bdg. 69.95 (*0-8490-1403-4*) Gordon Pr.

Notcutt, H. Clement. An Interpretation of Keats's Endymion. LC 65-15889. 84p. (C). 1964. text ed. 75.00 (*0-8383-0601-2*) M S G Haskell Hse.

***Notcutt, Michael.** Thai Scene. 1995. pap. 12.95 (*0-85449-224-0*) InBook.

Notehelfer, F. G. American Samurai: Captain L. L. Janes & Japan. LC 84-42896. (Illus.). 381p. 1985. text ed. 55.00x (*0-691-05443-6*) Princeton U Pr.

Notehelfer, F. G., ed. see Hall, Francis.

Notelovitz, M., jt. ed. see Dusitsin, N.

Notelovitz, Morris. Estrogen: Yes or No? 1993. mass mkt. 3.99 (*0-312-95105-1*) St Martin.

— Osteoporosis: Prevention, Diagnosis & Management. 224p. 1994. pap. 17.95 (*1-884735-03-7*) Prof Comms.

Notelovitz, Morris & Tonnessen, Diana. Menopause & Midlife Health. LC 93-679. (Illus.). 480p. 1993. 25.95 (*0-312-09337-3*) St Martin.

— Menopause & Midlife Health. 528p. 1994. pap. 15.95 (*0-312-11314-5*) St Martin.

Notelovitz, Morris, et al. Stand Tall! The Informed Woman's Guide to Preventing Osteoporosis. 2nd ed. (Illus.). 224p. 1995. write for info. (*0-937404-38-1*) Triad Pub FL.

***Noter, Raphael.** Dictionnaire des Synonymes: Repertoire des Mots Francais Usuels Ayant un Sens Sembable, Analogue ou Approche. 140th ed. 283p. (FRE.). 1992. pap. 28.95 (*0-7859-7746-5*, 2130442404) Fr & Eur.

***Noterman, Julie.** Bloodletting. 80p. (Orig.). 1995. pap. 9.95 (*0-9645666-0-5*) Eco Cult Perspect.

Notermans, S. L., ed. Current Practice of Clinical Electromyography. 568p. 1984. 224.75 (*0-444-80567-2*, I-482-84) Elsevier.

Notes, Akwesasne, ed. Basic Call to Consciousness. rev. ed. LC 91-16048. (Illus.). 128p. 1992. 7.95 (*0-913990-23-X*) Book Pub Co.

Notess, Greg R. Internet Access Providers: An International Resource Directory. 350p. 1994. pap. 30.00 (*0-88736-933-2*) Mecklermedia.

Notestein, Lucy. Wooster of the Middle West. 1993. reprint ed. lib. bdg. 89.00 (*0-7812-5394-2*) Rprt Serv.

Notestein, W. A History of Witchcraft in England. 1974. 250.00 (*0-87968-448-8*) Gordon Pr.

Notestein, Wallace. English Folk. LC 72-99643. (Essay Index Reprint Ser.). 1977. 30.95 (*0-8369-1475-9*) Ayer.

— The House of Commons, Sixteen Hundred Four to Sixteen Hundred Ten. LC 72-118733. 612p. reprint ed. pap. 174.50 (*0-8357-8170-4*, 2033844) Bks Demand.

— The Scot in History. LC 76-104225. xvii, 371p. 1970. reprint ed. text ed. 59.75 (*0-8371-3342-4*, NOSH, Greenwood Pr) Greenwood.

Notevitz, M. & Van Keep, P. A., eds. The Climacteric in Perspective. 1986. lib. bdg. 259.50 (*0-85200-919-4*) Kluwer Ac.

Notgrass, Ray. How Is Jesus Good News? 156p. 1992. pap. write for info. (*0-945441-12-6*) Res Pubns AR.

Noth & North, H., eds. Boron Chemistry-3. 1977. 61.00 (*0-08-021206-9*, Pub. by Pergamon Repr UK) Franklin.

Noth, Albrecht & Conrad, Lawrence I. The Early Arabic Historical Tradition: A Source-Critical Study. 2nd rev. ed. Bonner, Michael, tr. LC 94-6798. (Studies in Late Antiquity & Early Islam). 1994. 27.50 (*0-87850-082-0*) Darwin Pr.

Noth, Martin. The Deuteronomistic History. 153p. (C). 1990. 12.50 (*0-905774-30-2*, Pub. by Sheffield Acad UK) CUP Services.

— History of Israel: Biblical History. 2nd ed. LC 58-5195. 1960. 16.95 (*0-06-066310-3*) Harper SF.

Noth, Winfried. Handbook of Semiotics. LC 89-45199. (Advances in Semiotics Ser.). (Illus.). 588p. 1990. text ed. 57.50 (*0-253-34120-5*) Ind U Pr.

— Handbook of Semiotics. LC 89-45199. (Advances in Semiotics Ser.). (Illus.). 588p. 1995. pap. 27.95 (*0-253-20959-5*) Ind U Pr.

Noth, Winfried, ed. Origins of Semiosis: Sign Evolution in Nature & Culture. LC 94-21517. (Approaches to Semiotics Ser.: Vol. 116). x, 480p. 1994. 166.45 (*3-11-014196-5*) Mouton.

Nothdurft, Milton H. Between Two Worlds. 1985. 9.00 (*0-9615415-0-4*) Mtn Valley Pub.

Nothdurft, William. Going to Market: The New Aggressiveness in State Domestic Agricultural Marketing. 6.00 (*0-934842-52-3*) CSPA.

Nothdurft, William E. Going Global: How Europe Helps Small Firms Export. LC 92-22243. 118p. 1992. 26.95 (*0-8157-6204-6*); pap. 9.95 (*0-8157-6203-8*) Brookings.

— Renewing America: Natural Resource Assets & State Economic Development. Dyer, Barbara, ed. LC 84-9190. 190p. 1984. 16.95 (*0-934842-32-9*) CSPA.

— SchoolWorks: Reinventing Public Schools to Create the Workforce for the Future. 104p. 1990. pap. 8.95 (*0-8157-6201-1*) Brookings.

Nothem, Al H. Collective Bargaining in Education: A Casebook. 208p. (C). 1991. text ed. 58.00 (*0-205-13322-3*) Allyn.

Nothmann, Gerhard A. Nonimpact Printing. Destree, Thomas M., ed. LC 89-84486. 1989. pap. text ed. 65.00 (*0-88362-122-3*) Graphic Arts Tech Found.

Nothnagle, John. Pierre Crignon: Poete et Navigateur: Oeuvres en Prose et en Vers. LC 90-70299. (Illus.). 133p. (FRE.). 1990. lib. bdg. 27.95 (*0-917786-80-7*) Summa Pubns.

Nothnagle, John, tr. see Aubigne, Theodore-Agrippa D.

Notholt, A. J. & Jarvis, I., eds. Phosphorite Research & Development. (Geological Society Special Publications: No. 52). (Illus.). 326p. 1990. 115.00 (*0-903317-53-2*, Pub. by Geol Soc Pub Hse UK) AAPG.

Notholt, A. J., et al, eds. Phosphate Deposits of the World, Vol. 2: Phosphate Rock Resources. (Illus.). (C). 1990. 175.00 (*0-521-30509-8*) Cambridge U Pr.

Nothstein, G. Law of Occupational Safety & Health. (Illus.). 832p. 1981. write for info. (*0-318-54249-8*) Free Pr.

Nothstein, Gary Z. Toxic Torts: Litigation of Hazardous Substance Cases. LC 83-27128. (Trial Practice Ser.). 776p. 1984. text ed. 95.00 (*0-07-047454-0*) Shepards-McGraw.

Nothstein, I. O., ed. Selected Documents Dealing with the Organization of the First Congregations & the First Conferences of the Augustana Synod & Their Growth until 1860, Pt. 1. (Augustana Historical Society Publication Ser.: Vol. 10). 195p. 1944. pap. 3.00 (*0-910184-10-0*) Augustana.

— Selected Documents Dealing with the Organization of the First Congregations & the First Conferences of the Augustana Synod & Their Growth until 1860, Pt. 2. (Augustana Historical Society Publication Ser.: Vol. 11). 167p. 1946. pap. 3.00 (*0-910184-11-9*) Augustana.

Nothstein, Ira O., ed. & tr. The Planting of the Swedish Church in America: Graduation Dissertation of Tobias Eric Biorck. LC 43-18182. (Augustana College Library Publication Ser.: No. 19). 39p. 1943. pap. 3.00 (*0-910182-14-0*) Augustana Coll.

Nothstine, William. Influencing Others: A Guide to Positive Pursuasion. Crisp, Michael G., ed. LC 88-92734. (Fifty-Minute Ser.). (Illus.). 96p. (Orig.). 1989. pap. 9.95 (*0-931961-84-X*) Crisp Pubns.

Nothstine, William L., jt. auth. see Cooper, Martha D.

***Nothstine, William L., et al.** Critical Questions: Invention, Creativity, & the Criticism of Discourse & Media. 464p. 1994. pap. text ed. 21.00 (*0-312-08971-6*) St Martin.

Nothstine, William L., et al, eds. Critical Questions: Invention, Creativity, & the Criticism of Discourse & Media. 448p. 1994. text ed. 39.95 (*0-312-09140-0*) St Martin.

Notini, Anja. Made in Sweden: Art Handicrafts Design. (Illus.). 185p. 1988. 45.00 (*0-88736-300-8*) Mecklermedia.

Notini, S., tr. see Celli, L., ed.

Notker, jt. auth. see Einhard.

Notkin, Debbie & Dutcher, Richard F. The Tom Peters Business School in a Box. LC 93-43001. 1995. 50.00 (*0-394-58159-8*) Knopf.

Notkin, Debbie, jt. auth. see Edison, Laurie T.

Notkinds, A. L. & Oldstone, M. B., eds. Concepts in Viral Pathogenesis III. 415p. 1989. 109.00 (*0-387-96974-8*, 2692) Spr-Verlag.

Notkins, A. L. & Oldstone, M. B., eds. Concepts in Viral Pathogenesis. (Illus.). 390p. 1984. 79.00 (*0-387-90982-6*) Spr-Verlag.

— Concepts in Viral Pathogenesis II. (Illus.). 450p. 1986. 85.00 (*0-387-96322-7*) Spr-Verlag.

Notleg, Richard G., jt. auth. see Blandy, J. P.

Notley, Alice. Alice Notley. 1988. write for info. (*0-944521-13-4*) Dia Ctr Arts.

— Alice Ordered Me to Be Made. LC 76-26060. 1976. pap. 2.50 (*0-685-99370-1*) Yellow Pr.

— At Night the States. LC 87-51506. (Illus.). 78p. (Orig.). 1988. pap. 6.95 (*0-916328-18-X*) Yellow Pr.

— Margaret & Dusty. LC 84-27472. 75p. (Orig.). 1985. pap. 8.95 (*0-918273-08-0*) Coffee Hse.

— Selected Poems of Alice Notley. LC 93-30099. 144p. (Orig.). 1993. lib. bdg. 32.95 (*1-883689-03-1*); pap. 11.95 (*1-883689-02-3*) Talisman Hse.

— Waltzing Matilda. 7.00 (*0-317-17176-3*); pap. 3.50 (*0-317-17177-1*) Kulchur Foun.

Notley, Edwin A. A Comparative Grammar of the French, Italian, Spanish & Portuguese Languages. 1977. lib. bdg. 69.95 (*0-8490-1652-5*) Gordon Pr.

Notman, Larry. Ad Kit Four. 5.00 (*0-686-84765-2*) Newspaper Serv.

— Ad Kit Three. (Illus.). 1979. pap. 5.00 (*0-918488-08-7*) Newspaper Serv.

— Advertising Layout Basics: Ad Kit 4. 43p. (C). 1981. pap. 5.00 (*0-918488-09-5*) Newspaper Serv.

— Community Newspaper: Front Office Worker. (Illus.). 1978. pap. 5.00 (*0-918488-06-0*) Newspaper Serv.

— Community Newspaper Advertising Counselor: Getting Started. (Illus.). 1976. pap. 4.00 (*0-918488-01-X*) Newspaper Serv.

— The Community Newspaper Counselor: Professional Ad Sales. (Illus.). 1977. pap. 5.00 (*0-918488-04-4*) Newspaper Serv.

— Community Newspaper Management: Starting Out. 48p. (C). 1981. pap. 10.00 (*0-918488-10-9*) Newspaper Serv.

— Promotions & Sections. (Illus.). 40p. (Orig.). 1983. pap. 5.00 (*0-918488-11-7*) Newspaper Serv.

— Results for Retailers. (Illus.). 1976. pap. 2.50 (*0-918488-02-8*) Newspaper Serv.

— Working Ad Kit. 1976. pap. 5.00 (*0-918488-03-6*) Newspaper Serv.

Notman, Malkah & Nadelson, Carol, eds. Women & Men: New Perspectives on Gender Differences. LC 90-548. (Issues in Psychiatry Ser.). 128p. 1990. pap. text ed. 20.00 (*0-88048-136-6*) Am Psychiatric.

Notman, Malkah T. & Nadelson, Carol C., eds. The Woman Patient Vol. 1: Sexual & Reproductive Aspects of Women's Health Care. (Women in Context Ser.). (Illus.). 376p. 1978. 47.50 (*0-306-31151-8*, Plenum Pr) Plenum.

— The Woman Patient Vol.3: Aggressions, Adaptations, & Psychotherapy. LC 82-5325. (Women in Context Ser.). 326p. 1982. 45.00 (*0-306-40859-7*, Plenum Pr) Plenum.

Noto, Cosimo. Ideal City. LC 70-154454. (Utopian Literature Ser.). 1976. reprint ed. 33.95 (*0-405-03536-5*) Ayer.

Noto, Joanne M. The Use of the Ultrasonic Scaler by the Registered Dental Assistant. 74p. (C). 1987. reprint ed. pap. text ed. 16.95 (*0-942801-00-8*) Apogee Pr.

Noton, B. R., ed. see Metallurgical Society of AIME Staff.

Noton, Bryan R., ed. Composite Materials in Engineering Design: Proceedings of the Sixth St. Louis Symposium Held on 11-12 May, 1972. LC 73-84938. 737p. reprint ed. pap. 180.00 (*0-317-29837-2*, 2051953) Bks Demand.

Noton, M. Modern Control Engineering. LC 72-181056. 288p. 1972. 123.00 (*0-08-016820-5*, Pub. by Pergamon Repr UK) Franklin.

Noton, Thomas A., jt. auth. see Quick, Daniel L.

Notovich, N. The Unknown Life of Jesus Christ. 1973. 250.00 (*0-87968-073-3*) Gordon Pr.

Notovitch, Nicolas. The Unknown Life of Jesus Christ. 2nd rev. ed. Leonardo, Bianca, ed. LC 80-81187. (Illus.). 56p. 1980. pap. 10.00 (*0-9602850-1-6*) Tree Life Pubns.

Notovitch, Nicolas & Loranger, Alexina, trs. The Unknown Life of Jesus Christ. 66p. 1959. reprint ed. spiral bd. 5.50 (*0-7873-0637-1*) Mokelumne.

Notre Dame Conference on Population Staff. Family & Fertility: Proceedings of the Notre Dame Conference on Population, 5th, University of Notre Dame, 1966. Liu, William T., ed. LC 68-6934. 287p. reprint ed. pap. 81.80 (*0-317-42120-4*, 2025943) Bks Demand.

Notrik, Paul, pseud. The Control of Pain in Arthritis in the Knee. LC 84-61283. 32p. (Orig.). 1984. pap. 4.50 (*0-931150-14-0*) Rheumatoid.

Nott, C. S. Teachings of Gurdjieff: A Pupil's Journey. (Illus.). 256p. 1991. pap. 9.95 (*0-14-019156-9*, Arkana) Viking Penguin.

Nott, C. S., tr. see Attar, Farid Ud-Din.

Nott, C. S., ed. see Orage, A. R.

Nott, David, ed. see Vailland, Roger.

Nott, George F., ed. see Howard, Henry & Wyatt, Thomas.

Nott, J. C. & Gliddon, George R. Types of Mankind: Or, Ethnological Researches. LC 76-89386. (Black Heritage Library Collection). (Illus.). 1977. 54.95 (*0-8369-8639-3*) Ayer.

Nott, P. A., jt. auth. see Herbert-Gustan, L. K.

Nott, Susan, jt. auth. see Morgan, Peter.

Nott, Susan M., jt. auth. see Morris, Anne E.

Nottage, James & Carlson, George. George Carlson: Dignity in Art. 1993. pap. 24.95 (*1-882880-00-5*) G Autry Wstrn.

Nottage, W. H. The Calculation & Measurement of Inductance & Capacity: A Handbook for Experimenting with Tesla Coils & Radio. 1991. lib. bdg. 88.95 (*0-8490-4928-8*) Gordon Pr.

Nottale, L. Fractal Space-Time & Microphysics: Towards a Theory of Scale Relativity. 300p. 1993. text ed. 61.00 (*981-02-0878-2*) World Scientific Pub.

Nottebohm, Fernando, ed. Hope for a New Neurology. (Annals Ser.: Vol. 457). 238p. 1985. text ed. 50.00 (*0-89766-309-8*); pap. text ed. 50.00 (*0-89766-310-1*) NY Acad Sci.

Notter, Harley. Postwar Foreign Policy Preparation, 1939-1945. (History - United States Ser.). 726p. 1993. reprint ed. lib. bdg. 109.00 (*0-7812-4920-1*) Rprt Serv.

Notter, Lucille. Essentials of Nursing Research. 4th ed. 208p. (C). 1988. pap. 21.95 (*0-8261-1597-7*) Springer Pub.

Notter, Lucille E. & Hott, Jacqueline R. Essentials of Nursing Research. 5th rev. ed. LC 93-38407. (Illus.). 224p. 1993. pap. text ed. 24.95 (*0-8261-1598-5*) Springer Pub.

Notterman, Joseph M. Forms of Psychological Inquiry. 192p. 1985. text ed. 33.00 (*0-231-05988-4*) Col U Pr.

Notterman, Joseph M. & Drewry, H. N. Psychology & Education: Parallel & Interactive Approaches. LC 93-1257. (Illus.). 262p. (C). 1993. 37.50 (*0-306-44364-3*, Plenum Pr) Plenum.

Nottingham Andragogy Group, ed. Towards a Developmental Theory of Andragogy. (C). 1986. reprint ed. 25.00 (*0-685-50345-3*, Pub. by Univ Nottingham UK) St Mut.

Nottingham Andragogy Group Staff. Towards a Developmental Theory of Andragogy. (C). 1986. 35.00 (*0-685-67269-7*, Pub. by Univ Nottingham UK) St Mut.

— Towards a Developmental Theory of Andragogy. (C). 1988. text ed. 32.00 (*0-685-22137-7*, Pub. by Univ Nottingham UK) St Mut.

Nottingham, Carolyn W. & Hannah, Evelyn. Early History of Upson County, Georgia. 1982. reprint ed. 40.00 (*0-89308-029-2*) Southern Hist Pr.

Nottingham, Ed. It's Not As Bad As It Seems. LC 92-75828. (Illus.). 186p. 1993. pap. 12.95 (*0-916693-16-3*) Castle Bks.

Nottingham, Elizabeth K. Methodism & the Frontier: Indiana Proving Ground. LC 41-19465. reprint ed. 20.00 (*0-404-04798-X*) AMS Pr.

Nottingham, Judith, jt. auth. see Cookson, John.

Nottingham, M. A. Principles for Principals. rev. ed. 220p. (C). 1984. pap. text ed. 22.00 (*0-8191-3571-2*) U Pr of Amer.

Nottingham, Pamela. Batsford Lace Pattern Pack, Bucks Point. (Illus.). 1987. 16.95 (*0-7134-5451-2*) Robin & Russ.

— Bobbin Lace Making. 1983. pap. 14.95 (*0-7134-4132-1*) Robin & Russ.

— Bucks Point Lace-Making. 1985. 18.50 (*0-7134-2234-3*) Robin & Russ.

Nottingham, Rebecca, tr. see Goettmann, Alphonse & Goettmann, Rachel.

Nottingham, Rebecca, tr. see Goettmann, Alphonse.

Nottingham, Stratton. Accomack County, Virginia Certificates & Rights 1663-1709, & Tithables 1663-1695. vi, 230p. (Orig.). 1993. pap. 17.00 (*1-55613-741-9*) Heritage Bk.

— Accomack (Virginia) Land Causes, 1728-1825. 178p. 1990. reprint ed. pap. 17.50 (*1-55613-280-8*) Heritage Bk.

— Certificates & Rights, Accomack County, Virginia, 1663-1709. 491p. 1992. reprint ed. pap. 11.00 (*0-685-60466-7*, 4175) Clearfield Co.

An Asterisk (*) at the beginning of an entry indicates that the title is appearing in BIP for the first time.

— Virginia Land Causes: Lancaster County, 1795-1848 & Northampton County, 1731-1868. vi, 143p. 1991. pap. text ed. 15.00 (*1-55613-438-X*) Heritage Bk.

Nottingham, Stratton, ed. Wills & Administrations of Accomack County, Virginia, 1663-1800. 563p. 1991. reprint ed. pap. 32.50 (*1-55613-405-3*) Heritage Bk.

Nottingham, Ted, et al. Chess for Children. LC 93-24832. (Illus.). 128p. (J). (gr. 3 up). 1993. 14.95 (*0-8069-0452-6*) Sterling.

Nottingham, Theodore, tr. see Goettmann, Alphonse.

Nottingham, Theodore J. Written in Our Hearts: The Practice of Spiritual Transformation. (Illus.). 176p. (Orig.). 1993. pap. 14.95 (*0-9638181-0-4*) Inner Life.

Nottingham, Theodore J., tr. see Goettmann, Alphonse & Goettmann, Rachel.

Nottingham, William J. Practice & Preaching of Liberation. LC 85-18997. 96p. (Orig.). 1986. pap. 9.99 (*0-8272-2931-3*) Chalice Pr.

***Nottle, Trevor.** Growing Old-Fashioned Roses. 2nd ed. (Growing Ser.). (Illus.). 88p. 1995. pap. 13.95 (*0-86417-641-4*) Seven Hills Bk.

— Old Fashioned Gardens. (Illus.). 192p. 1993. 29.95 (*0-86417-436-5*, Pub. by Kangaroo Pr AT) Seven Hills Bk.

Nottonson, Ira. The Secrets to Buying & Selling a Business. Wait, Erin, ed. (Successful Business Library). 300p. (Orig.). 1994. pap. 19.95 (*1-55571-327-0*); ring bd. 39.95 (*1-55571-326-2*) Oasis Pr OR.

Nottridge, Rhoda. Additives. LC 92-33083. (J). 1993. pap. 5.95 (*0-87614-609-4*, Carolrhoda) Lerner Group.

— Adventure Films. LC 91-25839. (Films Ser.). (Illus.). 32p. (J). (gr. 5). 1992. text ed., lib. bdg. 13.95 (*0-89686-718-8*, Crstwood Hse) Silver Burdett Pr.

— Animated Films. LC 91-36041. (Films Ser.). (Illus.). 32p. (J). (gr. 5). 1992. text ed. 13.95 (*0-89686-717-X*, Crstwood Hse) Silver Burdett Pr.

— Apples. (Foods We Eat Ser.). (Illus.). 32p. (J). (gr. 1-4). 1991. lib. bdg. 14.96 (*0-87614-655-8*, Carolrhoda) Lerner Group.

— Care for Your Body. LC 92-13917. (Staying Healthy Ser.). (Illus.). 32p. (J). (gr. 6). 1993. text ed. 13.95 (*0-89686-787-0*, Crstwood Hse) Silver Burdett Pr.

— Fats. LC 92-26758. (J). 1993. pap. 5.95 (*0-87614-606-X*, Carolrhoda) Lerner Group.

— Fats. LC 92-26758. (J). (gr. 2-5). 1993. 14.95 (*0-87614-779-1*, Carolrhoda) Lerner Group.

— Horror Films. LC 91-23328. (Films Ser.). (Illus.). 32p. (J). (gr. 5). 1992. text ed. 13.95 (*0-89686-719-6*, Crstwood Hse) Silver Burdett Pr.

— Our Baby Album. (Illus.). 96p. 1995. 10.98 (*0-8317-6656-5*) Smithmark.

— Sea Disasters. LC 93-6830. (World's Disasters Ser.). 48p. (J). (gr. 4-6). 1993. 15.95 (*1-56847-084-3*) Thomson Lrning.

— Sugar. (Foods We Eat Ser.). (Illus.). 32p. (J). (gr. 1-4). 1990. lib. bdg. 14.96 (*0-87614-418-0*, Carolrhoda) Lerner Group.

— Sugars. LC 92-21414. (J). 1993. pap. 5.95 (*0-87614-611-6*, Carolrhoda) Lerner Group.

— Sugars. LC 92-21414. (J). (gr. 2-5). 1993. lib. bdg. 14.95 (*0-87614-796-1*, Carolrhoda) Lerner Group.

— Vitamins. LC 92-21415. (J). 1993. pap. 5.95 (*0-87614-610-8*, Carolrhoda) Lerner Group.

— Vitamins. LC 92-21415. (J). (gr. 2-5). 1993. lib. bdg. 14. 95 (*0-87614-795-3*, Carolrhoda) Lerner Group.

Nottridge, Robin E., jt. auth. see Marston, John.

Notturno, Francis, jt. auth. see Russ, Fred.

Notturno, M. A. Objectivity, Rationality, & the Third Realm: Justification & the Grounds of Psychologism. 1985. lib. bdg. 45.00 (*0-685-10235-1*); pap. text ed. 14. 95 (*0-318-04250-9*) Kluwer Ac.

Notturno, M. A., ed. Perspectives on Psychologism. LC 89-9849. (Brill's Studies in Epistemology, Psychology & Psychiatry). 504p. 1989. text ed. 128.75 (*90-04-09182-3*) E J Brill.

Notturno, M. A., ed. see Popper, Karl R.

Notturno, M. A., tr. see Popper, Karl R.

Notzing, Baron V. Phenomena of Materialisation. 340p. 1970. reprint ed. spiral bd. 24.75 (*0-7873-0638-X*) Mokelumne.

***Notzon, Francis C.** Proceedings of the International Collaborative Effort on Perinatal & Infant Mortality, Vol. III. (Illus.). 325p. (Orig.). (C). 1994. pap. text ed. 65.00x (*0-7881-1432-8*) Diane Pub.

Notzon, Mark. The Noise of Reason: Scepticism & the Art of Rochester. Lee, Don Y., ed. LC 84-81310. 83p. (C). 1984. 36.50 (*0-939758-09-1*) Eastern Pr.

— Noise of Reason: Scepticism & the Art of Rochester. rev. ed. Lee, Don Y., ed. LC 92-72327. 170p. (C). 1992. 39. 50 (*0-939758-23-7*) Eastern Pr.

Nouas, Nayaso. Survival. 1991. 16.95 (*0-533-09480-1*) Vantage.

Noud, Keith. Courses for Horses. 159p. (C). 1990. pap. 60. 00 (*0-7316-7935-0*, Pub. by Boolarong Pubns AT) St Mut.

Nouet. Shoguns City: A History of Tokyo. (C). 1990. text ed. 35.00 (*0-904404-61-7*, Pub. by Paul Norbury Pubns UK) Humanities.

Noufi, R. Photovolatic Advanced Research & Development. (Conference Proceeding Ser.: No. 268). 560p. 1992. 125. 00 (*1-56396-056-7*) Am Inst Physics.

Noufi, R., jt. ed. see McConnell, R. D.

***Noufi, Rommel & Ullah, Harin S., eds.** NREL Photovoltaic Program Review, 12th: Proceedings... LC 94-70748. (AIP Conference Proceedings Ser.: No. 306). 624p. 1994. text ed. 600.00x (*1-56396-315-9*) Am Inst Physics.

Nougayrol, Pierre, et al. Dictionnaire Elementaire Creole Haitien-Francais. Bentolila, Alain, ed. 511p. (FRE.). 1976. 69.95 (*0-8288-5649-4*, M6430) Fr & Eur.

Nougier, J. P., ed. Microelectronics III-V. LC 91-26281. (European Materials Research Society Monographs: Vol. 2). 514p. 1991. 141.00 (*0-444-88990-6*, TK7874) Elsevier.

***Nouguier, Evariste.** Dictionnaire D'Argot. 2nd ed. 167p. (FRE.). 1993. pap. 32.95 (*0-7859-8197-7*, 2877710173) Fr & Eur.

Noun, Bertic. Georg Brandes. LC 76-2718. (Twayne's World Authors Ser.). 208p. (C). 1976. lib. bdg. 17.95 (*0-8057-6232-9*) Irvington.

Noun, Louise R. Journey to Autonomy: A Memoir. LC 90-4187. (Illus.). 144p. 1990. 21.95 (*0-8138-1899-0*) Iowa St U Pr.

— More Strong-Minded Women: Iowa Feminists Tell Their Stories. LC 92-23124. 318p. 1992. pap. 18.95 (*0-8138-1819-2*) Iowa St U Pr.

— Strong-Minded Women: The Emergence of the Woman-Suffrage Movement in Iowa. LC 86-18597. (Iowa Heritage Collection Ser.). (Illus.). 322p. 1986. reprint ed. pap. 8.95 (*0-8138-1724-2*) Iowa St U Pr.

— Three Berlin Artists of the Weimar Era: Hannah Hoch, Kathe Kollowitz, Jeanne Mammen. LC 94-71498. (Illus.). 48p. 1993. pap. 20.00 (*1-879003-10-4*) Edmundson.

Noun, Louise R., jt. auth. see Demetrion, James T.

Nourie, Alan & Nourie, Barbara, eds. American Mass-Market Magazines. LC 89-17084. (Historical Guides to the World's Periodicals & Newspapers Ser.). 616p. 1990. text ed. 99.50 (*0-313-25254-8*, NMM/, Greenwood Pr) Greenwood.

Nourie, Barbara, jt. ed. see Nourie, Alan.

Nourissier, Francois. Lettre a Mon Chien. (FRE.). 1976. pap. 8.95 (*0-7859-4068-5*) Fr & Eur.

Nourrigat, Jean, jt. auth. see Helffer, Bernard.

Nourse, jt. auth. see Widman.

Nourse, Alan E. Lumps, Bumps, & Rashes: A Look at Kids' Diseases. rev. ed. LC 90-32785. (First Bks.). (Illus.). 64p. (J). (gr. 5-8). 1990. lib. bdg. 13.93 (*0-531-10865-1*) Watts.

— Radio Astronomy. LC 89-32405. (Venture Bks.). (Illus.). 96p. (YA). (gr. 6 up). 1989. lib. bdg. 13.72 (*0-531-10811-2*) Watts.

— Sexually Transmitted Diseases. LC 91-21707. (Illus.). 128p. (YA). (gr. 9-12). 1992. lib. bdg. 15.33 (*0-531-11065-6*) Watts.

— Teen Guide to AIDS Prevention. LC 90-12750. (Teen Guides Ser.). (Illus.). 64p. (YA). (gr. 9-12). 1990. lib. bdg. 14.21 (*0-531-10966-6*) Watts.

— Teen Guide to Birth Control. (Teen Guides Ser.). 1988. lib. bdg. 14.21 (*0-531-10571-7*) Watts.

— Teen Guide to Safe Sex. Kline, Marjory, ed. (Teen Guides Ser.). (Illus.). 64p. (YA). (gr. 6-12). 1988. lib. bdg. 14.21 (*0-531-10592-X*) Watts.

— Teen Guide to Survival. LC 90-12267. (Teen Guides Ser.). (Illus.). 64p. (YA). (gr. 9-12). 1990. lib. bdg. 14.21 (*0-531-10968-2*) Watts.

— The Tooth Book. (J). (gr. 6-p). 1977. 6.95 (*0-679-20376-1*) McKay.

— The Virus Invaders. Mathews, V., ed. LC 91-36650. (Venture Bks.). (Illus.). 96p. (YA). (gr. 9-12). 1992. lib. bdg. 13.72 (*0-531-12511-4*) Watts.

Nourse, Alan E., jt. auth. see Phelps, Janice K.

Nourse, Alan E., jt. auth. see Schaaf, Fred.

Nourse, E., et al. Three Years of the Agricultural Adjustment Administration. LC 79-173654. (FDR & the Era of the New Deal Ser.). 600p. 1971. reprint ed. lib. bdg. 75.00 (*0-306-70365-3*) Da Capo.

Nourse, Edwin G. Price Making in a Democracy. LC 75-39262. (Getting & Spending: the Consumer's Dilemma Ser.). 1976. reprint ed. 46.95 (*0-405-08035-2*) Ayer.

Nourse, Edwin G. & Drury, Horace B. Industrial Price Policies & Economic Progress. (Brookings Institution Reprint Ser.). (Illus.). reprint ed. lib. bdg. 39.50 (*0-697-00177-6*) Irvington.

Nourse, Edwin G., et al. America's Capacity to Produce. (Brookings Institution Reprint Ser.). (Illus.). reprint ed. lib. bdg. 36.00 (*0-697-00176-8*) Irvington.

Nourse, H. S. The Military Annals of Lancaster, 1740-1865. (Illus.). 402p. 1989. reprint ed. lib. bdg. 40.00 (*0-8328-0562-9*) Higginson Bk Co.

Nourse, Henry S. The Birth, Marriage, & Death Register, Church Records & Epitaphs of Lancaster, Massachusetts, 1643-1850. 508p. (Orig.). 1993. reprint ed. pap. text ed. 31.00 (*1-55613-801-6*) Heritage Bk.

— The Military Annals of Lancaster, 1740-1865, Including Lists of Soldiers Serving in the Colonial & Revolutionary Wars. 402p. 1989. reprint ed. lib. bdg. 40.00 (*0-8328-0834-2*, MA0021) Higginson Bk Co.

Nourse, Henry S., ed. The Early Records of Lancaster, Massachusetts, 1643-1725. 364p. (Orig.). 1993. reprint ed. pap. text ed. 24.50 (*1-55613-757-5*) Heritage Bk.

Nourse, Henry S., jt. auth. see Crooker, Lucien B.

Nourse, Hugh O., jt. ed. see Sirmans, C. F.

Nourse, Joan T. Monarch Notes on Cather's My Antonia & Other Works. (Orig.). (C). pap. 3.50 (*0-671-00604-5*, Arco Test) P-H Gen Ref & Trav.

— Monarch Notes on Miller's Crucible & View from the Bridge. (Orig.). (C). pap. 3.95 (*0-671-00687-8*, Arco Test) P-H Gen Ref & Trav.

Nourse, Joseph, jt. auth. see Fitzgerald, Oscar P.

Nourse, Kenneth A. How to Write Your College Application Essay. LC 92-37909. (Opportunities in...Ser.). 1994. 12. 95 (*0-8442-4169-5*, VGM Career Bks) NTC Pub Grp.

Nouryeh, Andrea J., jt. auth. see Vena, Gary.

Nouryeh, Christopher. Translation & Critical Study of Ten Pre-Islamic Odes: Traces in the Sand. LC 93-26256. 264p. 1993. text ed. 89.95 (*0-7734-9319-0*) E Mellen.

Nourzad, Farrokh, jt. auth. see Toumanoff, Peter.

Nouse, C. Dale. Cockpit Quiz Book: Two Hundred Sixty Puzzlers to Amuse, Annoy & Enlighten You & Your Shipmates. 144p. 1989. pap. text ed. 8.95 (*0-915160-97-8*) Seven Seas.

— The Cruising World On-Deck Log. 1984. pap. text ed. 21. 95 (*0-07-157269-4*) McGraw.

Nouse, C. Dale, comp. The Cruising World On-Deck Log: A Complete Log-Keeping System. LC 84-5311. 272p. 1984. 19.95 (*0-915160-73-0*) Seven Seas.

Nouse, Dale. Cruising World On-Deck Log. 1991. 19.95 (*0-8306-5470-4*) TAB Bks.

Nousiainen, Jaakko. The Finnish Political System. Hodgson, John H., tr. LC 76-120320. 464p. reprint ed. pap. 132.30 (*0-7837-2306-7*, 2057394) Bks Demand.

Noussitou, F. M., et al. Leprosy in Children. 1976. pap. 3.60 (*92-4-154053-2*) World Health.

Nouveau, Germain. Germain Nouveau's Symbolist Poetry, 1851-1920: Valentines. Groves, Gerald, tr. LC 88-36513. (Studies in French Literature: Vol. 1). 416p. 1990. lib. bdg. 109.95 (*0-88946-573-8*) E Mellen.

Nouveau, Germain, ed. see De Lautreamont, Isidore.

***Nouvel, Jean & Jodard, Paul, eds.** International Design Yearbook 10. (Illus.). 240p. 1995. 65.00 (*0-7892-0015-5*) Abbeville Pr.

Nouvel, Marcel. Bilingual Dictionary of International Telecommunications, Vol. 1: Antenna Theory. 128p. (ENG & FRE.). 1983. 49.95 (*0-8288-9448-5*) Fr & Eur.

Nouvel, Walter W., jt. auth. see Haskell, Arnold.

Nouvet, Claire, ed. see Yale French Studies Staff.

***Nouwen.** The Nouwen Path Pre-Pack. Date not set. 34.80 (*0-8245-2004-1*) Crossroad NY.

Nouwen, Henri. Gracias! A Latin American Journal. 188p. 1993. reprint ed. pap. 10.95 (*0-88344-851-3*) Orbis Bks.

— Here & Now. 120p. 1994. 14.95 (*0-8245-1409-2*) Crossroad NY.

— Modern Spirituality Series. Garvey, John, ed. 96p. 1990. pap. 4.95 (*0-87243-169-X*) Templegate.

— Return of the Prodigal Son. 1994. pap. 15.00 (*0-385-47307-9*) Doubleday.

— Walk with Jesus: Stations of the Cross. LC 89-27875. (Illus.). 1990. pap. 9.95 (*0-88344-666-9*) Orbis Bks.

Nouwen, Henri, et al. A Dry Roof & a Cow: Dreams & Portraits of Our Neighbours. LC 94-77014. (Illus.). 152p. (Orig.). 1994. pap. 19.95 (*0-9642003-2-5*) Mennonite Central.

Nouwen, Henri J. Behold the Beauty of the Lord: Praying with Icons. LC 86-72698. (Illus.). 80p. (Orig.). 1987. spiral bd. 8.95 (*0-87793-356-1*) Ave Maria.

— Clowning in Rome: Reflections on Solitude, Celibacy, Prayer & Contemplation. LC 78-22423. 110p. 1992. reprint ed. pap. 7.95 (*0-87061-191-7*) Chr Classics.

— Creative Ministry. LC 73-139050. 1991. mass mkt. 8.00 (*0-385-12616-6*, Image Bks) Doubleday.

— A Cry for Mercy: Prayers from the Genesee. LC 93-38555. 125p. (Orig.). 1994. reprint ed. pap. 9.95 (*0-88344-961-7*) Orbis Bks.

— From Resentment to Gratitude. Bd. with Prayer & the Press. (Synthesis Ser.). 1976. 1.95 (*0-685-77512-7*, Frncscn Herld) Franciscan Pr.

— The Genesee Diary: Report from a Trappist Monastery. LC 80-23632. 192p. 1981. mass mkt. 8.95 (*0-385-17446-2*, Image Bks) Doubleday.

— The Genesee Diary: Report from a Trappist Monastery. large type ed. (Large Print Inspirational Ser.). 1985. pap. 12.95 (*0-8027-2500-7*) Walker & Co.

— Heart Speaks to Heart: Three Prayers to Jesus. LC 88-71851. 64p. (Orig.). 1989. pap. 5.95 (*0-87793-388-X*) Ave Maria.

— In Memoriam. LC 79-56690. 64p. 1980. pap. 3.50 (*0-87793-197-6*) Ave Maria.

— In the Name of Jesus: Reflections on Christian Leadership. 2nd ed. 96p. 1993. reprint ed. pap. 7.95 (*0-8245-1259-6*) Crossroad NY.

— Intimacy. LC 80-8906. 160p. 1981. pap. 11.00 (*0-06-066323-5*, RD359) Harper SF.

— Jesus & Mary: Finding Our Sacred Center. 66p. 1993. 3.95 (*0-86716-189-2*) St Anthony Mess Pr.

— Letter of Consolation. 1990. pap. 8.00 (*0-06-066314-6*) Harper SF.

— Letters to Marc about Jesus. 1988. 15.00 (*0-06-066315-4*) Harper SF.

— Letters to Marc about Jesus. 1991. teacher ed, pap. 4.95 (*0-06-066338-3*) Harper SF.

— Life of the Beloved. 144p. 1992. 12.95 (*0-8245-1184-0*) Crossroad NY.

— Lifesigns: Intimacy, Fecundity, & Ecstasy in Christian Perspective. 1989. mass mkt. 7.95 (*0-385-23628-X*) Doubleday.

— Living Reminder. 1984. pap. 4.95 (*0-8164-2355-5*) Harper SF.

— The Living Reminder: Service & Prayer in Memory of Jesus Christ. 80p. 1984. reprint ed. pap. 9.00 (*0-86683-915-1*) Harper SF.

— Making All Things New. large type ed. 1986. pap. 7.95 (*0-8027-2560-0*) Walker & Co.

— Making All Things New: An Invitation to Life in the Spirit. LC 80-8897. 96p. 1981. 15.00 (*0-06-066326-X*) Harper SF.

— Our Greatest Gift: A Meditation on Dying & Caring. LC 93-34310. 144p. 1994. 16.00 (*0-06-066313-8*) Harper SF.

— Our Greatest Gift: A Meditation on Dying & Caring. LC 93-34310. 144p. 1995. pap. 10.00 (*0-06-066355-3*) Harper SF.

— Out of Solitude. (Illus.). 64p. 1974. pap. 3.95 (*0-87793-072-4*) Ave Maria.

— The Path of Freedom. 32p. 1994. pap. 3.95 (*0-8245-2001-7*) Crossroad NY.

— The Path of Peace. 32p. 1994. pap. 3.95 (*0-8245-2002-5*) Crossroad NY.

— The Path of Power. 32p. 1994. pap. 3.95 (*0-8245-2003-3*) Crossroad NY.

— The Path of Waiting. 32p. 1994. pap. 3.95 (*0-8245-2000-9*) Crossroad NY.

— Reaching Out: The Three Movements of the Spiritual Life. LC 86-2901. (Illus.). 168p. 1986. mass mkt. 9.95 (*0-385-23682-4*, Image Bks) Doubleday.

— Road to Daybreak. 1990. mass mkt. 10.00 (*0-385-41607-5*) Doubleday.

— Show Me the Way: Readings for Each Day of Lent. 144p. 1994. reprint ed. pap. 9.95 (*0-8245-1353-3*) Crossroad NY.

— Thomas Merton: Contemplative Critic. LC 90-47991. 168p. 1991. reprint ed. pap. 9.95 (*0-89243-508-9*, Triumph Books) Liguori Pubns.

— The Way of the Heart. (Epiphany Bks.). 1985. mass mkt. 5.99 (*0-345-32959-7*) Ballantine.

— Way of the Heart. 1981. 7.95 (*0-8164-0479-8*) Harper SF.

— With Burning Hearts: A Meditation on the Eucharistic Life. LC 94-14622. 96p. 1994. 15.95 (*0-88344-984-6*) Orbis Bks.

— With Open Hands. 1987. mass mkt. 4.99 (*0-345-35299-8*) Ballantine.

— With Open Hands. rev. ed. LC 94-79358. (Illus.). 136p. 1995. pap. 8.95 (*0-87793-545-9*) Ave Maria.

— The Wounded Healer: Ministry in Contemporary Society. LC 72-186312. 1979. mass mkt. 7.95 (*0-385-14803-8*, Image Bks) Doubleday.

Nouwen, Henri J. & Gaffney, Walter J. Aging: The Fulfillment of Life. LC 74-1773. 160p. 1976. mass mkt. 8.95 (*0-385-00918-6*, Image Bks) Doubleday.

Nouwen, Henri M. Beyond the Mirror: Reflections on Death & Life. 80p. 1991. reprint ed. pap. 5.95 (*0-8245-1130-1*) Crossroad NY.

Nova, Craig. The Book of Dreams. LC 93-23343. 336p. 1994. 22.95 (*0-395-63650-7*) Ticknor & Fields.

— Trombone. 1994. mass mkt. 5.99 (*0-8041-1157-X*) Ivy Books.

— Trombone: A Novel. 1992. 19.95 (*0-8021-1359-1*) Grove-Atltic.

Nova Law Staff. African-American Cemeteries & Their History of Choctaw County, Alabama. (Illus.). 113p. (Orig.). 1993. pap. text ed. 29.95 (*1-882804-01-5*) Legacy Pub AL.

— African-American Genealogy: Workbook for Beginners. 2nd ed. (Illus.). 113p. 1993. 19.95 (*1-882804-02-3*) Legacy Pub AL.

— African-American Genealogy Workbook for Beginners: Tracing Your Ancestry Historically & Genetically. 75p. 1992. 10.95 (*1-882804-00-7*) Legacy Pub AL.

Nova, Lily, ed. see Sams, Margaret, et al.

Nova Scotia Conference on Early Identification of Hearing Loss Staff. Nova Scotia Conference on Early Identification of Hearing Loss, Halifax, Nova Scotia, September 9-11, 1974. Mencher, Georges T., ed. 1976. 39.25 (*3-8055-2296-7*) S Karger.

NOVA Staff. Directory of Victim Assistance Programs & Resources, 1994 Edition. 320p. (C). 1994. pap. text ed., spiral bd. 30.00 (*0-8403-9460-8*) Kendall-Hunt.

— Victim Assistance: Frontiers & Fundamentals. 416p. 1993. per. 34.95 (*0-8403-8971-X*) Kendall-Hunt.

NOVA Staff & Cartlidge-Shearin. Educational Leadership, Vol. 1: Readings for Change. 112p. 1992. per. 13.95 (*0-8403-6539-X*) Kendall-Hunt.

NOVA (Young) Staff. Responding to Communities in Crisis: The Training Manual of the Crisis Response Team. 336p. 1994. spiral bd. 50.00 (*0-8403-9461-6*) Kendall-Hunt.

Novac, L., jt. auth. see Szantay, C.

Novacek, Michael J. & Wheeler, Quentin, eds. Extinction & Phylogeny. (Illus.). 269p. 1992. text ed. 50.00 (*0-231-07438-7*) Col U Pr.

Novack, Barbara, jt. auth. see Ross, George E.

Novack, Cynthia J. Sharing the Dance: Contact Improvisation & American Culture. LC 89-40534. (New Directions in Anthropological Writing Ser.). (Illus.). 272p. (Orig.). 1990. pap. text ed. 16.95 (*0-299-12444-4*) U of Wis Pr.

Novack, George. Democracy & Revolution. LC 74-143807. 286p. 1993. reprint ed. lib. bdg. 50.00 (*0-87348-192-5*); reprint ed. pap. 18.95 (*0-87348-191-7*) Pathfinder NY.

— Empiricism & Its Evolution: A Marxist View. LC 68-59426. 1986. reprint ed. lib. bdg. 40.00 (*0-87348-021-X*); reprint ed. pap. 13.95 (*0-87348-020-1*) Pathfinder NY.

— Genocide Against the Indians. 1992. reprint ed. pap. 3.00 (*0-87348-160-7*) Pathfinder NY.

— How Can the Jews Survive: A Socialist Answer to Zionism. 1970. reprint ed. pap. 2.50 (*0-87348-090-2*) Pathfinder NY.

— Humanism & Socialism. LC 73-77559. 160p. 1980. reprint ed. lib. bdg. 40.00 (*0-87348-308-1*); reprint ed. pap. 13.95 (*0-87348-309-X*) Pathfinder NY.

— Introduction to the Logic of Marxism. 5th rev. ed. LC 76-87909. 1986. reprint ed. lib. bdg. 40.00 (*0-87348-019-8*); reprint ed. pap. 12.95 (*0-87348-018-X*) Pathfinder NY.

— The Long View of History. 3rd ed. 46p. 1993. reprint ed. 3.50 (*0-87348-428-2*) Pathfinder NY.

— The Origins of Materialism: The Evolution of a Scientific View of the World. rev. ed. LC 76-160511. 300p. 1993. reprint ed. pap. 19.95 (*0-87348-022-8*) Pathfinder NY.

— Polemics in Marxist Philosophy. LC 77-70457. 1980. reprint ed. lib. bdg. 55.00 (*0-913460-63-X*); reprint ed. pap. 19.95 (*0-913460-64-8*) Pathfinder NY.

— Pragmatism Versus Marxism: An Appraisal of John Dewey's Philosophy. LC 75-10032. 320p. 1978. reprint ed. lib. bdg. 55.00 (*0-87348-452-5*); reprint ed. pap. 19. 95 (*0-87348-453-3*) Pathfinder NY.

— Revolutionary Dynamics of Women's Liberation. 1973. reprint ed. pap. 2.00 (*0-87348-120-8*) Pathfinder NY.

N

— Understanding History: Marxist Essays. 3rd ed. LC 75-186684. 1992. reprint ed. lib. bdg. 50.00 (0-87348-606-4); reprint ed. pap. 15.95 (0-87348-605-6) Pathfinder NY.

Novack, George, ed. & intro. America's Revolutionary Heritage. rev. ed. LC 76-12292. 1993. reprint ed. lib. bdg. 60.00 (0-87348-464-9); reprint ed. pap. 21.96 (0-87348-465-7) Pathfinder NY.

Novack, George, jt. auth. see Mandel, Ernest.

Novack, Janet. ISO 9000 Documentation Tool Kit. 1994. Incl. disk. disk 79.95 (0-13-124587-2) P-H.

— ISO 9000 Quality Manual Developer. LC 95-13584. 1995. disk, pap. text ed. 49.95 (0-13-215477-3) P-H Gen Ref & Trav.

***Novack, Janet L.** The ISO Nine-Thousand Documentation Toolkit: Nineteen Ninety-Four Revised ISO 9001 Standard. LC 94-31190. 1994. write for info. (0-13-199374-7) P-H.

Novack, Joseph A., jt. ed. see Donini, Antonio O.

Novack, Judith M. The Lilac Bush. LC 89-43228. 108p. 1989. 12.95 (0-88400-137-7) Shengold.

Novack, M., jt. auth. see Korites, B.

Novack, Miriam S. The Bar-Bat Mitzvah Autograph Book. LC 93-13991. 128p. 1994. 20.00 (1-56821-069-8) Aronson.

Novacky, A. J., jt. auth. see Goodman, R. N.

Novak. Contemporary Dental Assisting. 1994. 42.95 (0-8016-7732-7) Mosby Yr Bk.

— Contemporary Dental Assisting: Text & Study Guide. 1994. write for info. (0-8016-7733-5) Mosby Yr Bk.

— Quantitative Analysis by Gas Chromatography. 2nd ed. (Chromatographic Science Ser.: Vol. 41). 360p. 1988. 145.00 (0-8247-7818-9) Dekker.

— Worlds Wisdom. Date not set. pap. 14.00 (0-06-066342-1, PL) HarpC.

Novak, A. Czech Literature. Harkins, W. E., ed. Kussi, P., tr. (Joint Committee on Eastern Europe Publication Ser.: No. 4). 1986. 15.00 (0-930042-64-6) Mich Slavic Pubns.

Novak, Adolph. Store Planning & Design. LC 76-56649. (Illus.). 1977. pap. 28.95 (0-86730-514-2) Lebhar Friedman.

Novak, Alys, ed. see Kaiser, Leland R.

Novak, Alys, jt. auth. see Price, Courtney.

Novak, Anita A. & Jaeger, Ruth A. Cooking Like a Pro. LC 84-90574. 240p. 1985. 15.95 (0-317-19104-7) A A Novak.

Novak, Barbara. American Painting of the Nineteenth Century: Realism, Idealism & the American Experience. LC 79-2093. (Icon Editions Ser.). (Illus.). 1979. reprint ed. text ed. 22.00 (0-06-430099-4, IN99, Icon Edns) HarpC.

— The Ape & the Whale: An Interplay Between Charles Darwin & Herman Melville in Their Own Words. LC 94-77616. (Illus.). 96p. (Orig.). 1994. pap. 12.95 (0-943972-33-7) Homestead WY.

— Nature & Culture: American Landscape & Painting 1825-1875. (Illus.). 1981. pap. 27.50 (0-19-502935-6) OUP.

— Nineteenth-Century American Painting. (Illus.). 332p. 1991. 39.98 (0-89660-026-2, Artabras) Abbeville Pr.

— On Distant Shores. 40p. (Orig.). 1994. pap. text ed. write for info. (1-885206-01-1, Iliad Pr) Cader Pubng.

Novak, Bogdan C. Trieste Nineteen Forty-One to Nineteen Fifty-Four: The Ethnic, Political & Ideological Struggle. LC 73-96068. 1970. lib. bdg. 25.00 (0-226-59621-4) U Ch Pr.

Novak, Dan & Weinberger, Paula. Computer Applications: Programming with SeeLogo: Course Code 194-6. Doheny, Catherine & Schroeder, Bonnie, eds. (Illus.). 36p. (gr. 8). 1989. reprint ed. pap. text ed. 5.95 (0-917531-58-2) CES Compu-Tech.

— Programming with SeeLogo: Lab Pack. Doheny, Catherine & Schroeder, Bonnie, eds. (Illus.). student ed, teacher ed 149.95 (1-56177-051-5, L194-6); disk 15.95 (1-56177-050-7, D194-6) CES Compu-Tech.

Novak, Dan, jt. auth. see Weinberger, Paual.

Novak, Daniel A. The Wheel of Servitude: Black Forced Labor after Slavery. LC 77-76334. 144p. 1978. 15.00 (0-8131-1371-7) U Pr of Ky.

Novak, David. Basic Mathematics. 3rd ed. 680p. (C). 1991. pap. text ed. write for info. (0-669-24691-3); Study guide. student ed write for info. (0-669-24693-X); Instr.'s guide. teacher ed write for info. (0-669-24692-1); Solns. guide. teacher ed write for info. (0-669-24694-8); Test item file. write for info. (0-669-24696-4) Heath.

— Developmental Mathematics. 2nd ed. 947p. (C). 1988. pap. text ed. 28.00 (0-669-17092-5); Student guide to margin exercises. student ed 8.50 (0-669-17096-8); Instr.'s guide. teacher ed 2.00 (0-669-17093-3); Answer key. 2.00 (0-669-17094-1); Topics in basic Mathematics. write for info. (0-669-27651-0) Heath.

— The Election of Israel: The Idea of the Chosen People. 303p. (C). 1991. 54.95 (0-521-41690-6) Cambridge U Pr.

— Halakhah in a Theological Dimension: Essays on the Interpenetration of Law & Theology in Judaism. Neusner, Jacob, ed. LC 84-10661. (Brown Judaic Studies: No. 68). 1985. pap. 17.25 (0-89130-829-6, 14-00-68) Scholars Pr GA.

— The Image of the Non-Jew in Judaism: An Historical & Constructive Study of the Noahide Laws. LC 83-21989. (Toronto Studies in Theology: Vol. 14). 500p. 1984. lib. bdg. 109.95 (0-88946-759-5) E Mellen.

— Jewish Christian Dialogue: A Jewish Justification. 208p. 1989. 37.50 (0-19-505084-3) OUP.

— Jewish-Christian Dialogue: A Jewish Justification. 208p. 1992. pap. 14.95 (0-19-507273-1) OUP.

— Jewish Social Ethics. 272p. 1992. 45.00 (0-19-506924-2) OUP.

— Law & Theology in Judaism. 1974. 20.00 (0-87068-245-8) Ktav.

— Letter to Mom - Letter to Dad. 1994. pap. 6.95 (0-9625261-7-7) Medlicott Pr.

— The Little Ant. 32p. (J). (gr. k-3). 1994. pap. 4.50 (0-87406-689-1) Willowisp Pr.

— The Theology of Nahmanides Systematically Presented. LC 92-35709. (Brown Judaic Studies: No. 271). 149p. 1993. 59.95 (1-55540-802-8, 14 02 71) Scholars Pr GA.

Novak, David & Samuelson, Norbert, eds. Creation & the End of Days - Judaism & Scientific Cosmology: Proceedings of the 1984 Meeting of the Academy for Jewish Philosophy. LC 86-19062. 336p. (Orig.). 1986. 52.00 (0-8191-5524-1, Studies in Judaism) U Pr of Amer.

Novak, David W. Basic Mathematics. 2nd ed. 560p. 1987. 2.00 (0-669-12238-6); pap. text ed. 21.00 (0-669-12235-1); Instr's guide, with test. teacher ed 2.00 (0-669-12236-X); 7.50 (0-669-12237-8) Heath.

Novak, Derry, jt. ed. see Romke, Adam.

Novak, E. Deterministic & Stochastic Error Bounds in Numerical Analysis. (Lecture Notes in Mathematics Ser.: Vol. 1349). 115p. 1988. pap. 28.10 (0-387-50368-4) Spr-Verlag.

Novak, Elaine A. Performing in Musicals. 304p. 1988. text ed. 26.00 (0-02-871731-7) Schirmer Bks.

Novak, F. Surgical Gynecologic Techniques. 422p. 1978. text ed. 112.00 (1-57235-025-3) Piccin NY.

Novak, Frank G., Jr. The Autobiographical Writings of Lewis Mumford: A Study in Literary Audacity. LC 88-50558. (Biography Monographs). 72p. 1988. pap. text ed. 8.95 (0-8248-1189-5) UH Pr.

***Novak, Frank G., Jr., ed.** Lewis Mumford & Patrick Geddes: The Correspondence. LC 94-41551. 1995. 49.95 (0-415-11906-5) Routledge.

Novak, Greg. Over the Top. (Command Decision Ser.). (Illus.). 120p. (Orig.). (YA). (gr. 9-12). 1990. pap. 12.00 (1-55878-012-2) Game Designers.

Novak, Greg, jt. auth. see Chadwick, Frank.

Novak, J., ed. Convergence Structures, Nineteen Eighty-Four. 2545p. (C). 1985. 100.00 (0-685-36901-3, Pub. by Collets) St Mut.

Novak, J., jt. auth. see Karger, A.

Novak, J. P., et al, eds. Liquid-Liquid Equilibria. (Studies in Modern Thermodynamics: No. 7). 320p. 1987. 120.50 (0-444-98975-7) Elsevier.

Novak, James J. Bangladesh: Reflections on the Water. LC 92-41794. (Essential Asia Ser.). 1993. 24.95 (0-253-34121-3) Ind U Pr.

***Novak, Jan.** Commies, Crooks, Gypsies, Spooks, & Poets: Thirteen Books of Prague in the Year of the Great Lice Epidemic. 225p. 1995. 22.00 (1-883642-09-4) Steerforth Pr.

Novak-Jandrey, Mary L., jt. ed. see McKeown, Anthony F.

Novak, Jane. Razor Edge of Balance: A Study of Virginia Woolf. LC 72-85111. 192p. 1973. 9.95 (0-87024-247-4) U of Miami Pr.

Novak, John, ed. Democratic Teacher Education: Programs, Processes, Problems, & Prospects. LC 93-26763. (SUNY Series, Democracy & Education). 288p. 1994. 64.50x (0-7914-1927-4); pap. 21.95x (0-7914-1928-2) State U NY Pr.

Novak, John, jt. auth. see Berry, Fred.

Novak, John J. How to Meditate: A Practical Guide Based on the Teachings of Paramhansa Yogananda & Sri Kriyananda. rev. ed. (Illus.). 111p. 1989. pap. 7.95 (0-916124-55-X, DJN2) Crystal Clarity.

Novak, John M., ed. Advancing Invitational Thinking. 260p. 1992. pap. text ed. 15.95 (1-880192-02-0) Caddo Gap Pr.

Novak, John M., jt. auth. see Purkey, William W.

Novak, Josef F. & McMaster, James H., eds. Frontiers of Osteosarcoma Research: Proceedings of the First International Meeting on Interdisciplinary Research in Osteosarcoma. LC 92-49083. (Illus.). 592p. 1993. 138.00 (0-88937-113-X) Hogrefe & Huber Pubs.

Novak, Joseph D. Improvement of Biology Teaching. LC 75-77822. (C). 1970. pap. write for info. (0-672-60635-6, Bobbs) Macmillan.

— A Theory of Education. LC 77-3123. 296p. 1986. pap. 14.95 (0-8014-9378-1) Cornell U Pr.

Novak, Joseph D. & Gowin, D. Bob. Learning How to Learn. (Illus.). 150p. 1984. 44.95 (0-521-26507-X); pap. 14.95 (0-521-31926-9) Cambridge U Pr.

***Novak, Julie C. & Broom, Betty L.** Ingalls & Salerno's Maternal & Child Health Nursing. 8th ed. LC 94-33454. 1994. write for info. (0-8151-6448-3) Mosby Yr Bk.

Novak, Kate & Grubb, Jeff. Azure Bonds. LC 88-50057. (Forgotten Realms Finder's Stone Trilogy Ser.: Bk. 1). 352p. (Orig.). 1988. pap. 3.95 (0-88038-612-6) TSR Inc.

— Masquerades. (Super Harpers Ser.). 384p. (Orig.). 1995. pap. 5.95 (0-7869-0152-7) TSR Inc.

— Song of the Saurials: Forgotten Realms. LC 90-71497. (Finder's Stone Trilogy Ser.: Bk. 3). 320p. (Orig.). 1991. pap. 4.95 (1-56076-060-5) TSR Inc.

— The Wyvern's Spur. LC 89-51883. (Forgotten Realms Finder's Stone Trilogy Ser.: Bk. 2). 320p. (Orig.). 1990. pap. 4.95 (0-88038-902-8) TSR Inc.

Novak, L., jt. ed. see Dvorak, J.

Novak, Lajos, jt. auth. see Poppe, Laszlo.

Novak, M. Integrated Functional Blocks. (Studies in Electrical & Electronic Engineering: Vol. 3). 388p. 1980. 102.75 (0-444-99759-8) Elsevier.

Novak, M. & Pelikan, E., eds. Theoretical Aspects of Neurocomputing. 300p. (C). 1991. text ed. 118.00 (981-02-0549-X) World Scientific Pub.

Novak, M., ed. see IFAC-IFIP Symposium Staff.

Novak, M. M. Modula-2 in Science & Engineering. 1990. write for info. (0-07-707200-6) Gregg-McGraw.

Novak, Matt. Elmer Blunt's Open House. LC 91-38424. (Illus.). 24p. (J). (ps-1). 1992. 14.95 (0-531-05998-7); lib. bdg. 14.99 (0-531-08598-8) Orchard Bks Watts.

— Gertie & Gumbo. LC 94-45913. (Illus.). 32p. (J). (ps-2). 1995. 14.95 (0-531-09478-2); lib. bdg. 14.99 (0-531-08778-6) Orchard Bks Watts.

— The Last Christmas Present. LC 92-44513. (Illus.). 32p. (J). (ps-1). 1993. 14.95 (0-531-05495-0); lib. bdg. 14.99 (0-531-08645-3) Orchard Bks Watts.

— Mouse TV. LC 93-49399. (Illus.). 32p. (J). (ps-1). 1994. 14.95 (0-531-06856-0); lib. bdg. 14.99 (0-531-08706-9) Orchard Bks Watts.

— Newt. LC 95-13286. (I Can Read Book Ser.). (Illus.). (J). 1996. 14.00 (0-06-024501-8) HarpC.

— Newt. LC 95-13286. (I Can Read Book Ser.). (Illus.). (J). 1996. lib. bdg. 13.89 (0-06-024502-6) HarpC.

Novak, Matt, illus. It's about Time. LC 92-12128. (J). (ps-3). 1993. pap. 14.00 (0-671-78512-5, S&S Bks Young Read) S&S Childrens.

Novak, Maximillian E. Realism, Myth, & History in Defoe's Fiction. LC 82-11141. 199p. reprint ed. pap. 56.80 (0-7837-2087-4, 2042363) Bks Demand.

Novak, Maximillian E., intro. The Merry-Thought: or The Glass-Window & Bog House Miscellany, Pts. II, III, & IV. 2nd ed. LC 92-24240. (Augustan Reprints Ser.: Nos. 221-222 (1983)). reprint ed. 18.50 (0-404-70221-X) AMS Pr.

Novak, Maximillian E., jt. auth. see Defoe, Daniel.

Novak, Maximillian E., jt. ed. see Dudley, Edward J.

Novak, Maximillian E., ed. see Southerne, Thomas.

Novak, Melinda A. & Petto, Andrew J., eds. Through the Looking Glass: Issues of Psychological Well-Being in Captive Nonhuman Primates. 298p. 1991. text ed. 40.00 (1-55798-087-X) Am Psychol.

Novak, Michael. Belief & Unbelief: The Context of Self-Knowledge. 3rd ed. 250p. (C). 1994. pap. 19.95 (1-56000-741-9) Transaction Pubs.

— The Catholic Ethic & the Spirit of Capitalism. 200p. 1993. text ed. 24.95 (0-02-923235-X) Free Pr.

— Catholic Social Thought & Liberal Institutions: Freedom with Justice. 2nd ed. 292p. 1989. pap. text ed. 18.95 (0-88738-763-2) Transaction Pubs.

— Character & Crime: An Inquiry into the Causes of the Virtue of Nations. 152p. (C). 1986. pap. text ed. 18.50 (0-8191-6661-8) U Pr of Amer.

— Choosing Presidents: Symbols of Political Leadership. 2nd ed. 402p. (C). 1991. pap. text ed. 21.95 (1-56000-567-X) Transaction Pubs.

— Confession of a Catholic. LC 85-20367. 232p. 1986. reprint ed. pap. text ed. 24.00 (0-8191-5023-1) U Pr of Amer.

— Free Persons & the Common Good. 175p. 1988. 14.95 (0-8191-6499-2) U Pr of Amer.

— The Glow-in-the-Dark Book of the Human Body. LC 94-47304. (Glowbacks Ser.). (Illus.). (J). 1995. 5.99 (0-679-85646-3) Random Bks Yng Read.

— Human Rights & the New Realism: Strategic Thinking in a New Age. LC 86-7660. (Perspectives on Freedom Ser.). 1986. pap. 10.25 (0-932088-08-2) Freedom Hse.

— The Joy of Sports. rev. ed. 1993. pap. 16.95 (1-56833-009-X) Madison Bks UPA.

— The Spirit of Democratic Capitalism. LC 90-48169. 448p. 1991. 27.95 (0-8191-7822-5); pap. 16.95 (0-8191-7823-3) Madison Bks UPA.

— Story in Politics. LC 73-150866. 1970. pap. 2.00 (0-87641-210-X) Carnegie Ethics & Intl Affairs.

— This Hemisphere of Liberty: A Philosophy for the Americas. 168p. 1990. 24.75 (0-8447-3735-6, AEI Pr) Am Enterprise.

— This Hemisphere of Liberty: A Philosophy of the Americas. 168p. 1992. pap. 12.95 (0-8447-3736-4) Am Enterprise.

— Toward a Theology of the Corporation. rev. ed. 66p. (C). 1990. pap. text ed. 7.25 (0-8447-3744-5) Am Enterprise.

— Unmeltable Ethnics: Politics & Culture in American Life. 385p. (C). 1994. pap. 21.95 (1-56000-773-7) Transaction Pubs.

— Will It Liberate? Questions about Liberation Theology. 330p. (C). 1991. reprint ed. pap. 17.95 (0-8191-8060-2) Madison Bks UPA.

Novak, Michael, ed. Capitalism & Socialism: A Theological Inquiry. 193p. 1979. 38.50 (0-8447-2153-0); pap. 19.50 (0-8447-2154-9) Am Enterprise.

— Democracy & Mediating Structures: A Theological Inquiry. 119p. 1979. 34.00 (0-8447-2175-1); pap. 12.50 (0-8447-2176-X) Am Enterprise.

— Liberation South, Liberation North. 99p. 1981. pap. 13.25 (0-8447-3464-0) Am Enterprise.

Novak, Michael & Cooper, John W., eds. Corporation: A Theological Inquiry. 234p. 1981. 34.00 (0-8447-2203-0); pap. 18.75 (0-8447-2204-9) Am Enterprise.

Novak, Michael & Jackson, Michael P., eds. Latin America: Dependency or Interdependence? 186p. 1985. 34.00 (0-8447-2258-8) Am Enterprise.

Novak, Michael P. A Story to Tell. LC 90-39896. 72p. 1990. 9.50 (0-933532-75-X) BkMk.

Novak, Michael P., jt. ed. see Gillman, Richard.

Novak, Micheal. Taking Glasnost Seriously: Toward an Open Soviet Union. LC 87-34895. 224p. 1988. pap. 9.75 (0-8447-3642-2) Am Enterprise.

Novak, Miroslav M., ed. Fractals in the Natural & Applied Sciences: Proceedings of the Second IFIP Working Conference on Fractals in the Natural & Applied Sciences, London, U. K., 7-10 September 1993. LC 93-48196. (IFIP Transactions A: Computer Science & Technology Ser.: Vol. A-41). 1994. pap. 134.25 (0-444-81628-3, North Holland) Elsevier.

Novak, P. Developments in Hydraulic Engineering, Vol. 1. (Illus.). 240p. 1984. 79.25 (0-85334-227-X, I-338-83, Pub. by Elsevier Applied Sci UK) Elsevier.

Novak, P., ed. Developments in Hydraulic Engineering, Vol. 2. (Illus.). 256p. 1984. 79.25 (0-85334-228-8, I-007-84, Pub. by Elsevier Applied Sci UK) Elsevier.

— Developments in Hydraulic Engineering, Vol. 3. (Illus.). 332p. 1985. 90.00 (0-85334-375-6, Pub. by Elsevier Applied Sci UK) Elsevier.

— Developments in Hydraulic Engineering - 4. 356p. 1987. 84.75 (0-85166-095-9) Elsevier.

— Developments in Hydraulic Engineering - 5. 236p. 1988. 79.25 (1-85166-157-3) Elsevier.

Novak, Paul M. A Baker's Dozen of Daily Breads & More. LC 89-90838. 64p. (Orig.). 1989. Includes soundsheet (flexidisc) with a recording of "Bread Baker's Stomp" by George Winston. pap. 10.95 (0-9622472-1-9) Only Connect.

— A Baker's Dozen of Daily Breads & More. 2nd ed. LC 91-90205. 64p. (Orig.). 1991. pap. 11.95 (0-9622472-2-7) Only Connect.

Novak, Philip. The World's Wisdom: Sacred Texts of the World's Religions. LC 93-43995. 320p. 1994. 22.00 (0-06-066341-3) Harper SF.

***Novak, R., et al, eds.** Proceedings of the Symposium on Contamination Control & Defect Reduction in Semiconductor Manufacturing II. LC 93-70066. (Proceedings Ser.: Vol. 94-03). 364p. 1994. 43.00 (1-56677-065-3) Electrochem Soc.

Novak, R. E., jt. ed. see Ruzyllo, J.

Novak, R. Elizabeth, tr. see Wilson, Paul, ed.

Novak, Ralph M., Jr., jt. auth. see Locke, William H., Jr.

Novak, Richard. Moorhaven Fair. 16p. (Orig.). 1994. pap. 3.00 (0-9640168-0-X) Pirate Writings.

Novak, Robert. At the Splinter House. 1971. 1.00 (0-685-67928-4) Windless Orchard.

— Disappearing Like a Snowman. 1973. 1.00 (0-686-16136-X) Windless Orchard.

— The Hemingway Poems. 1973. 4.00 (0-685-72802-1) Windless Orchard.

— High Afternoon. 1971. 1.00 (0-685-67923-3) Windless Orchard.

— High Afternoon. rev. ed. 1978. 2.00 (0-685-67943-8) Windless Orchard.

— King Tut in America. 1988. 3.00 (0-685-25018-0) Windless Orchard.

— Machines for Loving. 1973. 1.00 (0-686-16137-8) Windless Orchard.

— Shoes. 1975. 1.00 (0-685-67937-3) Windless Orchard.

— Sleeping with Sylvia Plath. 1983. 3.00 (0-686-43216-9) Windless Orchard.

— Things to Do in Fort Wayne. 1973. 1.00 (0-685-67934-9) Windless Orchard.

— The Woman in the Red Skirt. 1971. 1.00 (0-685-67925-X) Windless Orchard.

Novak, Robert, ed. Haiku from the Windless Orchard 1970-1978. 1978. 2.00 (0-685-67940-3) Windless Orchard.

Novak, Slobodan. Gold, Frankincense & Myrrh. Hawkesworth, Celia, tr. (Croatian Literature Ser.: Vol. 4). (Illus.). 244p. (Orig.). 1991. pap. 19.95 (0-948259-88-4, Pub. by Forest Bks UK) Dufour.

Novak, Stan. The Undesirable. 1993. 12.95 (0-533-10417-3) Vantage.

Novak, Steven J. The Rights of Youth: American Colleges & Student Revolt, 1798-1815. LC 76-43109. (Illus.). 230p. reprint ed. pap. 65.60 (0-7837-5939-8, 2045738) Bks Demand.

Novak, Susan, ed. see Wilkerson, Ted & Wilkerson, Evelyn.

Novak, Theodore & Blaesser, Brian W. Condemnation Law: Strategies & Procedures for Winning Just Compensation. (Real Estate Practice Library). 408p. 1994. text ed. 128.00 (0-471-57403-1) Wiley.

Novak, Thomas, ed. see Conference on the Use of Computers in the Coal Industry Staff.

Novak, Thomas, et al, eds. Use of Computers in the Coal Industry Conference, 2nd: Proceedings. LC 85-70438. (Illus.). 475p. 1985. 15.00 (0-89520-437-1, 437-1) SMM&E Inc.

Novak, Tony. Poverty & the State: An Historical Sociology. 192p. 1988. 90.00 (0-335-15545-6, Open Univ Pr); pap. 32.00 (0-335-15540-5, Open Univ Pr) Taylor & Francis.

Novak, V. The Alternative Mathematical Model of Linguistic Semantics. (IFSR International Series on Systems Science: Vol. 8). (Illus.). 230p. (C). 1992. 69.50 (0-306-44269-8, Plenum Pr) Plenum.

— Fuzzy Sets & Their Applications. (Illus.). 190p. 1989. 85.00 (0-85274-583-4) IOP Pub.

Novak, Vilem, et al, eds. Fuzzy Approach to Reasoning & Decision Making. LC 91-24675. (Theory & Decision Library: Vol. 8). 220p. 1992. lib. bdg. 99.00 (0-7923-1358-5) Kluwer Ac.

Novak, Vladimir, et al, eds. Atlas of Insects Harmful to Forest Trees. (Illus.). 126p. 1977. 125.75 (0-444-99874-8) Elsevier.

Novak, W. David. Intermediate Algebra. 2nd ed. 668p. (C). 1987. pap. text ed. 22.00 (0-669-12227-0); Student guide. student ed 7.50 (0-669-12229-7); Instr.'s guide. teacher ed 2.00 (0-669-12228-9); Answer key. 2.00 (0-669-12230-0) Heath.

— Introductory Algebra. 2nd ed. 586p. (C). 1987. pap. text ed. 22.00 (0-669-12231-9); Student guide to margin ex. student ed 7.50 (0-669-12233-5); Instr.'s guide. teacher ed 2.00 (0-669-12232-7); Answer key. 2.00 (0-669-12234-3) Heath.

Novak, Walt. The Haole Substitute. LC 93-41290. 160p. (Orig.). 1994. pap. 12.95 (1-879384-19-1) Cypress Hse.

Novak, William & Waldoks, Moshe. Big Book of Jewish Humor. LC 81-47234. (Illus.). 320p. 1981. pap. 17.00 (0-06-090917-X, CN 917, PL) HarpC.

Novak, William, jt. auth. see Barrows, Sydney B.

Novak, William, jt. auth. see Iacocca, Lee.

Novak, William, jt. auth. see Johnson, Earvin M., Jr.

Novak, William, jt. auth. see O'Neill, Thomas P., Jr.

Novak, William, jt. auth. see Reagan, Nancy.

Novak, William J., jt. auth. see McPartland, Joseph F.

Novakovic, L. The Pseudo-Spin Method in Magnetism & Ferroelectricity. 200p. 1975. 93.00 (0-08-018060-4, Pub. by Pergamon Repr UK) Franklin.

Novakovic, Zoran R. The Principle of Self-Support in Control Systems. LC 92-10012. (Studies in Automation & Control: Vol. 8). 1992. write for info. (0-444-89450-0) Elsevier.

Novakovich, Josip. Apricots from Chernobyl. 224p. (Orig.). 1995. pap. 12.95 (1-55597-212-8) Graywolf.

— Fiction Writer's Workshop. 256p. 1995. 17.99 (1-884910-03-3) Story Pr Ohio.

— Yolk. 224p. 1995. pap. 12.95 (1-55597-229-2) Graywolf.

Novakshonoff, Varlaam, tr. see Khrapovitsky, Antony.

Novalis. Henry Von Ofterdingen: A Novel. Hilty, Palmer, tr. 169p. (C). 1990. reprint ed. pap. text ed. 7.50 (0-88133-574-6) Waveland Pr.

— Hymns to the Night. 3rd rev. ed. LC 87-34706. 55p. 1988. pap. 5.95 (0-914232-90-8) McPherson & Co.

Novalis, pseud. Pollen & Fragments. Versluis, Arthur, tr. 170p. (Orig.). 1989. 25.00 (0-933999-75-5); pap. 14.95 (0-933999-76-3) Phanes Pr.

Novalis, George. The Binding Spell. 224p. (Orig.). 1990. 17.95 (0-9621858-2-5); pap. 9.95 (0-9621858-3-3) Tintagel Assocs.

Novalis, Peter N., et al. Clinical Manual of Supportive Psychotherapy. LC 92-18064. 384p. 1993. spiral bd. 44.00 (0-88048-403-9) Am Psychiatric.

***Novallo, Anette, ed.** Information Industry Directory Supplement. 15th ed. 1994. pap. 365.00 (0-8103-9124-4) Gale.

Novarr, David. The Disinterred Muse: Donne's Texts & Contexts. 264p. 1980. 33.95 (0-8014-1309-5) Cornell U Pr.

— The Lines of Life: Theories of Biography, 1880-1970. LC 85-24562. 202p. 1986. 18.00 (0-911198-79-2) Purdue U Pr.

Novarra, Virginia. Women's Work, Men's Work: The Ambivalence of Equality. LC 79-67452. (Ideas in Progress Ser.). 160p. 1980. 12.00 (0-7145-2680-0); pap. 6.95 (0-7145-2681-9) M Boyars Pubs.

Novas Calvo, Lino, tr. see Faulkner, William.

***Novas, Himalce.** The Hispanic 100: A Ranking of the Latino Men & Women Who Have Most Influenced American Thought & Culture. (Illus.). 556p. 1995. 24.95 (0-8065-1651-8, Citadel Pr) Carol Pub Group.

Novas, Himilce. Everything You Need to Know about Latino History. 272p. 1994. pap. 11.95 (0-452-27100-2, Plume) NAL-Dutton.

Novatny, Fritz & Dobai, Johannes. Gustav Klimt: Catalogue Raisonne of the Paintings. (Illus.). 424p. (GER.). 1975. 550.00 (1-55660-052-6) A Wofsy Fine Arts.

Nove, Alec. An Economic History of the U. S. S. R. rev. ed. 416p. 1972. pap. 7.95 (0-14-021403-8, Penguin Bks) Viking Penguin.

— An Economic History of the U. S. S. R. 1917-1991. 480p. 1993. pap. 12.95 (0-14-015774-3, Penguin Bks) Viking Penguin.

— An Economic History of the U.S.S.R. rev. ed. 1990. pap. 8.95 (0-14-013972-9, Penguin Bks) Viking Penguin.

— The Economics of Feasible Socialism Revisited. 272p. 1991. pap. 18.95 (0-04-446015-5, A8227) Routledge Chapman & Hall.

— Glasnost' in Action: Cultural Renaissance in Russia. 256p. 1989. text ed. 49.95 (0-04-445340-X); pap. text ed. 13.95 (0-04-445440-6) Routledge Chapman & Hall.

— Marxism & "Really Existing Socialism" (Fundamentals of Pure & Applied Economics Ser.: Vol. 8). 64p. 1986. pap. text ed. 21.00 (3-7186-0330-6) Gordon & Breach.

— Political Economy & Soviet Socialism. pap. text ed. 14.95 (0-04-335037-2) Routledge Chapman & Hall.

— Socialism, Economics & Development. 280p. (C). 1986. text ed. 37.95 (0-04-335054-2); pap. text ed. 16.95 (0-04-335055-0) Routledge Chapman & Hall.

— The Soviet Economic System. 3rd ed. 420p. (C). 1986. pap. text ed. 22.95 (0-04-497025-0) Routledge Chapman & Hall.

— Stalinism & After: The Road to Gorbachev. 3rd ed. LC 92-36715. 1992. 19.95 (0-415-09445-3) Routledge.

— Stalinism & After: The Road to Gorbachev. 3rd ed. 1989. pap. 19.95 (0-04-445112-1) Routledge Chapman & Hall.

— Studies in Economics & Russia. LC 89-70362. 270p. 1991. text ed. 49.95 (0-312-04509-3) St Martin.

Nove, Alec, ed. The Stalin Phenomenon. LC 92-41550. 256p. 1993. text ed. 35.00 (0-312-09519-8) St Martin.

Nove, Alec & Thatcher, Ian, eds. Markets & Socialism. (International Library of Critical Writings in Business History: Vol. 39). 576p. 1994. 169.95 (1-85278-842-9, Pub. by E Elgar Pub UK) Ashgate Pub Co.

Nove, I., jt. auth. see Berhard, P.

Noveck, Simon. Creators of the Jewish Experience in Ancient & Medieval Times. 1985. 20.00 (0-910250-02-2) Bnai Brith Intl.

— Creators of the Jewish Experience in the Modern World: B'nai B'rith History of the Jewish. 1985. pap. 12.00 (0-910250-05-7) Bnai Brith Intl.

Noveck, Simon, ed. Contemporary Jewish Thought. (B'nai B'rith History of the Jewish People Ser.: Vol. IV). 392p. (C). 1985. 20.00 (0-910250-09-X); pap. 12.00 (0-685-67343-X, 01-120012) Bnai Brith Intl.

— Creators of the Jewish Experience in Ancient & Medieval Times. (B'nai B'rith History of the Jewish People Ser.: Vol. I). 368p. (C). 1985. 20.00 (0-685-67346-4); pap. 12.00 (0-685-67347-2, 01-120013) Bnai Brith Intl.

— Creators of the Jewish Experience in the Modern World. (B'nai B'rith History of the Jewish People Ser.: Vol. II). 384p. (C). 1985. 20.00 (0-910250-04-9); pap. 12.00 (0-685-67345-6, 01-120014) Bnai Brith Intl.

— Great Jewish Thinkers of the Twentieth Century. (B'nai B'rith History of the Jewish People Ser.: Vol. III). 336p. (C). Date not set. 20.00 (0-910250-07-3); pap. 12.00 (0-685-67349-9, 01-120015) Bnai Brith Intl.

Novell, Cordia. Shades of Womanhood. 1991. 6.95 (0-533-09120-9) Vantage.

Novell Inc. Staff. Netware System Interface Technical Overview. 1990. pap. 32.95 (0-201-57027-0) Addison-Wesley.

Novell Research Department Staff. Novell's Application Notes for Netware 4.01. LC 93-85637. 390p. 1993. pap. 39.99 (0-7821-1375-3) Sybex.

Novell Staff. Novell's Quick Access Guide to NetWare 3.12 Networks. LC 93-84818. 150p. 1993. pap. 14.95 (0-7821-1297-8) Sybex.

Novelli, G. P., ed. Oxygen-Free Radicals in Shock. (Illus.). xii, 248p. 1986. 128.00 (3-8055-4233-X) S Karger.

Novelli, L., jt. ed. see Mattavelli, L.

***Novelli, Norma & Walker, Mike, told to.** The Private Diary of Lyle Menendez (Unauthorized) 1995. mass mkt. 5.99 (0-615-00467-9) Dovebks.

Novelline & Squire. Living Anatomy: A Workbook Using Computed Tomography, Magnetic Resonance, & Angiography. 1986. 35.00 (0-8016-4746-0) Mosby Yr Bk.

Novelline, Robert A. & Squire, Lucy F. Living Anatomy: A Working Atlas Using Computed Tomography, Magnetic Resonance & Angiography Images. LC 86-80893. (Illus.). 117p. (Orig.). 1987. pap. text ed. 39.95 (0-932883-03-6) Hanley & Belfus.

Novelline, Robert A., jt. auth. see Squire, Lucy F.

Novellino, Peter. Advanced Electronic Tune Up. 1984. student ed 6.00 (0-8064-0179-6, 464); audio 219.00 (0-8064-0180-X) Bergwall.

— The Alternator Explained. LC 80-730752. 1980. student ed 6.00 (0-8064-0143-5, 439); audio 319.00 (0-8064-0144-3) Bergwall.

— Auto Standard Transmission. LC 76-732018. 1977. student ed 7.00 (0-8064-0091-9, 413); audio 299.00 (0-8064-0092-7) Bergwall.

— The Automatic Transmission. LC 77-731115. 1978. student ed 6.00 (0-8064-0115-X, 425); audio 279.00 (0-8064-0116-8) Bergwall.

— The Automotive Air Conditioner. LC 81-730758. 1981. student ed 7.00 (0-8064-0149-4, 442); audio 199.00 (0-8064-0150-8) Bergwall.

— Automotive Clutch Assembly. LC 76-731515. 1976. student ed 6.00 (0-8064-0089-7, 412); audio 279.00 (0-8064-0090-0) Bergwall.

— Automotive Pollution Control. LC 81-730757. (C). 1982. student ed 7.00 (0-8064-0157-5, 447); audio 319.00 (0-8064-0158-3) Bergwall.

— Basic Automotive Jobs Explained. student ed 5.00 (0-8064-0159-1, 448); audio 279.00 (0-8064-0160-5) Bergwall.

— Electronic Ignition Tune Up. 1983. student ed 6.00 (0-8064-0175-3, 462); audio 359.00 (0-8064-0176-1) Bergwall.

— Electronic Wheel Balancing. student ed 5.00 (0-8064-0161-3, 449); audio 219.00 (0-8064-0162-1) Bergwall.

— Foreign Car Engine Overhaul: Datsun OHC 4-Cylinder. LC 83-730249. 1984. audio 199.00 (0-8064-0182-6) Bergwall.

— Front Wheel Drive: Transaxle Overhaul. 1984. 6.00 (0-8064-0177-X, 463); audio 319.00 (0-8064-0178-8) Bergwall.

— How to Balance Wheels. LC 76-732022. 1977. student ed 6.00 (0-8064-0099-4, 417); audio 109.00 (0-8064-0100-1) Bergwall.

— How to Overhaul a Carburetor. LC 76-732026. 1977. student ed 7.00 (0-8064-0107-9, 421); audio 159.00 (0-8064-0108-7) Bergwall.

— How to Overhaul a 400 Turbo Hydramatic Transmission. LC 80-730404. 1979. student ed 5.00 (0-8064-0133-8, 434); audio 219.00 (0-8064-0134-6) Bergwall.

— How to Overhaul an Engine. LC 75-735762. 1975. student ed 6.00 (0-8064-0085-4, 410); audio 299.00 (0-8064-0086-2) Bergwall.

— How to Use a Valve & Valve Seat Refacer. LC 76-732029. 1977. student ed 7.00 (0-8064-0103-6, 419); audio 159.00 (0-8064-0104-4) Bergwall.

— How to Use Auto Precision Tools. LC 76-732030. 1977. student ed 7.00 (0-8064-0105-2, 420); audio 199.00 (0-8064-0106-0) Bergwall.

— The Ignition System Explained. LC 73-733984. 1973. student ed 6.00 (0-8064-0067-6, 401); audio 319.00 (0-8064-0068-4) Bergwall.

— Light Beam Alignment. LC 81-730690. 1982. student ed 5.00 (0-8064-0155-9, 446); audio 129.00 (0-8064-0156-7) Bergwall.

— The Operation of the Fuel System. LC 74-734388. 1974. student ed 6.00 (0-8064-0079-X, 407); audio 279.00 (0-8064-0080-3) Bergwall.

— The Problems of the Fuel System. LC 74-734385. 1974. student ed 6.00 (0-8064-0081-1, 408); audio 279.00 (0-8064-0082-X) Bergwall.

— Problems of the Internal Combustion Engine. LC 75-733226. 1975. student ed 6.00 (0-8064-0083-8, 409); audio 219.00 (0-8064-0084-6) Bergwall.

— Problems of the 400 Turbo Hydramatic Transmission Explained. LC 80-730755. 1981. student ed 5.00 (0-8064-0139-7, 437); audio 99.00 (0-8064-0140-0) Bergwall.

— Troubleshooting Electrical Components. (Orig.). 1983. student ed 5.00 (0-8064-0173-7, 461); audio 189.00 (0-8064-0174-5) Bergwall.

— What Your Car Is Trying to Tell You. LC 81-730689. 1982. student ed 5.00 (0-8064-0153-2, 445); audio 179.00 (0-8064-0154-0) Bergwall.

Novello, Adriano A., et al. The Armenians. (Illus.). 288p. 1986. 75.00 (0-8478-0731-2) Rizzoli Intl.

***Novello, Antonia C. & Soto-Torres, Lydia E., eds.** Surgeon General's National Workshop: Implementation Strategies for Improving Hispanic-Latino Health. (Illus.). 51p. (Orig.). (C). 1994. pap. text ed. 25.00x (0-7881-1518-9) Diane Pub.

Novello, Don. Citizen Lazlo! The Lazlo Letters, Vol. 2. LC 92-5483. 160p. 1992. pap. 7.95 (1-56305-182-6, 3182) Workman Pub.

— Lazlo Letters. LC 92-7832. (Illus.). 160p. 1992. pap. 7.95 (1-56305-285-7, 3285) Workman Pub.

Novello, John A. The Contemporary Keyboardist. (Illus.). 551p. (Orig.). 1985. pap. 50.00 (0-9614966-0-6) Source Prods.

Novello, Joseph R. What to Do until the Grownup Arrives: The Art & Science of Raising Teenagers. LC 91-18659. 360p. 1993. 24.50 (0-88937-040-0); write for info. (3-456-81869-6) Hogrefe & Huber Pubs.

Novello, Joseph R., ed. The Short Course in Adolescent Psychiatry. LC 93-74373. 288p. 1994. pap. 27.50 (1-56821-195-3) Aronson.

Novello, M., et al. Cosmology & Gravitation: Proceedings of the 6th Brazilian Sch. 1993. text ed. 103.00 (981-02-0123-0) World Scientific Pub.

Novello, Mary, jt. auth. see Novello, Vincent.

Novello, V. The Armenians. (C). 1990. 500.00 (0-685-34398-7, Pub. by Collets) St Mut.

Novello, Vincent & Novello, Mary. A Mozart Pilgrimage. Meduci, Nerina & Hughes, Rosemary, eds. (Eulenburg Music Ser.). 360p. 1982. reprint ed. pap. text ed. 19.50 (0-903873-10-9) Da Capo.

***Novell's MacIntosh Support Group Staff.** Novell's Guide to Integrating MAC's with Networks. 1995. pap. write for info. (0-7821-1560-8) Sybex.

Novelly, Maria C. Theatre Games for Young Performers. Pijanowski, Kathy & Zapel, Arthur L., eds. LC 85-60572. (Illus.). 160p. (Orig.). (J). (gr. 6-10). 1985. pap. text ed. 10.95 (0-916260-31-3, B-188) Meriwether Pub.

Novembre, A. E., ed. Advances in Resist Technology & Processing IX. 1992. 86.00 (0-8194-0827-1, 1672) SPIE.

Nover, Arno. The Ocular Fundus: Methods of Examination & Typical Findings. 5th ed. 197p. 1987. pap. text ed. 84.00 (0-471-56507-5) Wiley.

Nover, Elizabeth Z. My Land of Israel. (Illus.). 32p. (Orig.). (J). (gr. k-2). 1987. pap. 4.50 (0-87441-447-4) Behrman.

— Reading Workbook for the Hebrew Primer. (Hebrew Primer Ser.). 60p. (J). (gr. 4-7). 1987. pap. 2.95 (0-317-60046-X) Behrman.

Nover, L. Plant Promoters & Transcription Factors. LC 93-29266. (Results & Problems in Cell Differentiation Ser.: Vol. 20). 1994. 198.00 (0-387-57288-0) Spr-Verlag.

Nover, L., et al, eds. Heat Shock & Other Stress Responses in Plants. (Results & Problems in Cell Differentiation Ser.: Vol. 16). (Illus.). 168p. 1990. 58.00 (0-387-51837-1) Spr-Verlag.

Nover, Lutz. Heat Shock Response. (Illus.). 866p. 1991. 236.00 (0-8493-4912-5, QP552) CRC Pr.

Noverr, Douglas A., ed. Film Studies: Introductory Courses Interdisciplinary & Cultural Courses, Courses about Directors & Film & Literature: Selected Course Outlines & Reading Lists. (Selected Course Outlines & Reading Lists from American Colleges & Universities Ser.). 300p. (Orig.). (C). 1989. pap. text ed. 16.95 (1-55876-001-6) Wiener Pubs Inc.

Noverr, Douglas A. & Ziewacz, Lawrence E. The Games They Played: Sports in American History, 1865-1980. LC 83-5647. (Illus.). 432p. 1983. pap. 22.95 (0-88229-819-4) Nelson-Hall.

Noverr, Douglas A., jt. ed. see Huddleston, Eugene L.

Noverr, Douglas A., jt. ed. see Lunde, Erik S.

Noverraz, Ph. Pseudo-Convexite, Convexite Polynomiale et Domaines D'holomorphie En Dimension Infinie. (Mathematics Studies: Vol. 3). 1975. pap. 20.50 (0-444-10692-8, North Holland) Elsevier.

Noverre, Jean G. The Works of Monsieur Noverre, Translated from the French, 3 vols., Set. LC 76-43930. reprint ed. 185.00 (0-404-60110-3) AMS Pr.

Novey. Rapid Access Guide to Physical Examination. 548p. 1988. pap. 27.95 (0-8151-6434-3, Yr Bk Med Pubs) Mosby Yr Bk.

Novey, Donald W., et al. The Guide to Heart Sounds: Normal & Abnormal. 104p. 1988. pap. 46.95 (0-8493-0153-X, RC683) CRC Pr.

Novey, Samuel. The Second Look: The Reconstruction of Personal History in Psychiatry & Psychoanalysis. Chicago Institute for Psychoanalysis Staff, ed. LC 85-10884. (Classics in Psychoanalysis Monograph: No. 3). xiv, 162p. 1986. reprint ed. text ed. 30.00 (0-8236-6022-2, 06022) Intl Univs Pr.

Novey, Theodore B. An Advanced Reference Guide to the Transactional Analysis Literature. 80p. 1987. pap. 12.00 (0-9617020-1-X) TA Assocs.

Novice, Fred M., et al. Handbook of Genetic Skin Disorders. LC 93-25389. (Illus.). 704p. 1994. text ed. 99.95 (0-7216-3803-1) Saunders.

Novich, Martin. Success on the Line: The ABCs of Telephone Selling. LC 89-45454. 192p. 1989. pap. 14.95 (0-8144-7725-9) AMACOM.

Novich, Max M. & Taylor, Buddy. Training & Conditioning of Athletes. 2nd ed. LC 82-17988. (Illus.). 335p. reprint ed. pap. 95.50 (0-8357-7651-4, 2056977) Bks Demand.

***Novich, Michael.** White Lies, White Power: The Face of White Supremacy & Reactionary Violence in the 90's. Bates, Greg, ed. 330p. (C). 1995. lib. bdg. 29.95 (1-56751-051-5); pap. 14.95 (1-56751-050-7) Common Courage.

Novichenko, Leonid. Taras Shevchenko: Poet & Humanitarian. 184p. 1983. 23.00 (0-317-56674-1, Pub. by Collets UK) Pro-Am Music.

Novichkov & Pimenov. Dictionary of Radioelectronics, Laser & Infrared Engineering. (ENG & RUS.). 1984. 125.00 (0-8288-3971-9, F37440) Fr & Eur.

Novick. Surfactant in Lung Injury & Lung Transplantation. (Medical Intelligence Unit Ser.). 110p. 1993. text ed. 89.95 (1-879702-23-1) R G Landes.

— You Can Do Something about Your Allergies. 1995. mass mkt. 5.99 (0-553-57267-9) Bantam.

Novick, Adam. Harmonics for Electric Bass. (Illus.). 80p. (Orig.). 1985. pap. 12.95 (0-8256-9943-6, AM33473) Music Sales.

Novick, Amy R. & Schmidt, Paul W., eds. INS Forms for Applications & Petitions. 400p. 1992. pap. text ed. 50.00 (1-878677-33-0) Amer Immi Law Assn.

Novick, Amy R., jt. ed. see Goldblum, Jane W.

Novick, Andrew, jt. ed. see Resnick, Martin I.

Novick, Andrew C., et al. Stewart's Operative Urology, 2 vols., Set. 2nd ed. (Illus.). 908p. 1989. 225.00 (0-683-06589-0) Williams & Wilkins.

Novick, Barbara & Arnold, Maureen. Why Is My Child Having Trouble at School? A Parent's Guide to Learning Disabilities. LC 90-28508. (Illus.). 256p. 1991. 18.50 (0-394-58509-7, Villard Bks) Random.

Novick, David, ed. Program Budgeting: Program Analysis & the Federal Budget. 2nd ed. LC 68-1604. (Rand Corporation Research Studies). (Illus.). 406p. 1967. 38.50 (0-674-71350-8) HUP.

Novick, David, et al. Wartime Production Controls. LC 76-5795. (FDR & the Era of the New Deal Ser.). 1976. reprint ed. lib. bdg. 49.50 (0-306-70818-3) Da Capo.

Novick, Harold J. Selling Through Independent Reps. 2nd ed. LC 93-20716. 372p. 1993. 69.95 (0-8144-5146-2) AMACOM.

Novick, Julius, ed. see Shaw, George Bernard.

Novick, Laurie B., jt. auth. see Andrews, Laurie J.

Novick, Nelson L. Baby Skin: A Leading Dermatologist's Guide to Infant & Childhood Skin Care. 192p. 1991. pap. 13.00 (0-517-58422-0, C P Pubs) Crown Pub Group.

— Super Skin. (Illus.). 320p. 1991. pap. 13.00 (0-517-58533-2, C P Pubs) Crown Pub Group.

— You Can Do Something about Your Allergies. LC 93-832957. (Lisa Drew Book Ser.). 211p. 1994. text ed. 20.00 (0-02-590785-9) Macmillan.

Novick, Peter. That Noble Dream: The Objectivity Question & the American Historical Profession. (Ideas in Context Ser.). 500p. 1988. 74.95 (0-521-34328-3); pap. 18.95 (0-521-35745-4) Cambridge U Pr.

Novick, Rebecca M., jt. auth. see Brown, David J.

Novick, Richard, ed. Molecular Biology of the Staphylococci. 639p. 1991. lib. bdg. 160.00 (1-56081-032-7) VCH Pubs.

Novick, Richard, jt. ed. see Levy, Stuart B.

Novick, Robert, ed. Thirty Years of Parity Nonconservation: A Symposium Honoring T. D. Lee. 220p. 1987. 44.50 (0-8176-3375-8) Birkhauser.

***Novick, Robert & Novick, Varda U.** Impulse Survey of Focus Facilities 1995. 250p. 1995. pap. 65.00 (1-884301-02-9) Impulse Res.

Novick, Robert & Novick, Verda U., eds. Impulse Survey of Focus Facilities 1992. 129p. 1992. pap. 35.00 (1-884301-00-2) Impulse Res.

— Impulse Survey of Focus Facilities 1993. 232p. 1993. pap. 50.00 (1-884301-01-0) Impulse Res.

Novick, Sheldon M., ed. The Collected Works of Justice Holmes Vols. 1-3: The Complete Public Writings of Oliver Wendell Holmes. 1994. write for info. (0-226-34965-9) U Ch Pr.

Novick, Shimshon, jt. auth. see Lunetta, Vincent N.

Novick, Varda U., jt. auth. see Novick, Robert.

Novick, Verda U., jt. ed. see Novick, Robert.

Novik, Mary & Creeley, Robert, frwds. Robert Creeley: An Inventory, 1945-1970. LC 72-96943. (Serif Series: Bibliographies & Checklists: No. 28). 228p. reprint ed. pap. 65.00 (0-8357-5578-9, 2035205) Bks Demand.

Noviki, H., ed. Africa Policy in Transition. (African American Conferences Ser.). 52p. (Orig.). 1983. pap. 10.00 (0-89192-386-1) Interbk Inc.

— Toward a New Africa. (African-American Conferences Ser.). 36p. (Orig.). 1985. pap. 5.00 (0-89192-388-8) Interbk Inc.

Noviki, Margaret, ed. African Policy in the Eighties. (African-American Conferences Ser.). 40p. (Orig.). 1984. pap. 5.00 (0-89192-387-X) Interbk Inc.

Novikov, B. K., et al. Nonlinear Underwater Acoustics. LC 87-70336. 261p. pap. 30.00 (0-88318-522-9); pap. 25.00 (0-317-05997-1) Acoustical Soc Am.

Novikov, Euvgeny & Bascio, Patrick. Gorbachev & the Collapse of the Soviet Communist Party: The Historical & Theoretical Background. LC 93-24107. (Major Concepts in Politics & Political Theory Ser.: Vol. 4). 238p. (C). 1994. text ed. 32.95 (0-8204-2287-8) P Lang Pubs.

Novikov, I. D., jt. auth. see Zel'dovich, Ya. B.

***Novikov, Igor.** Black Holes & the Universe. (Canto Bk.). (Illus.). 184p. (C). Date not set. pap. 8.95 (0-521-55870-0) Cambridge U Pr.

Novikov, Igor D. Black Holes & the Universe. Kisin, Vitaly I., tr. (Illus.). 200p. (C). 1990. pap. 19.95 (0-521-36683-6) Cambridge U Pr.

Novikov, Igor D., jt. auth. see Sharov, Alexander S.

Novikov, M. P. Dictionary of Atheism. 559p. (RUS.). 1983. 39.95 (0-8288-2316-2, M15213) Fr & Eur.

Novikov, N. V., ed. XI AIRAPT: Selected Soviet Papers from the International High Pressure Conference, July 12-17, 1987, Kiev, U. S. S. R. A Special Issue of the Journal High Pressure Research. ii, 106p. 1989. pap. text ed. 114.00 (2-88124-727-X) Gordon & Breach.

Novikov, P. D., jt. auth. see Egorov, E. V.

Novikov-Priboi, Aleksei S. Tsushima. Paul, E. & Paul, C., trs. LC 75-39005. (Soviet Literature in English Translation Ser.). (Illus.). 407p. 1978. reprint ed. 27.50 (0-88355-408-9) Hyperion Conn.

Novikov, S., et al. Theory of Solitons: The Inverse Scattering Method. Zakharov, V. E., ed. LC 83-21051. (Contemporary Soviet Mathematics Ser.). 288p. 1984. 95.00 (0-306-10977-8, Consultants) Plenum.

Novikov, S. P. Mathematical Physics Reviews, Vol. 7. (Soviet Scientific Reviews Ser.: Section C). 1988. text ed. 300.00 (*3-7186-0455-8*) Gordon & Breach.

— Solitons & Geometry. (Lezione Fermiane Ser.). 55p. (C). 1995. pap. 19.95 (*0-521-47196-6*) Cambridge U Pr.

Novikov, S. P., ed. Mathematical Physics Review, Vol. I, Section C. (Soviet Scientific Reviews Ser.). 222p. 1980. text ed. 342.00 (*3-7186-0019-6*) Gordon & Breach.

— Mathematical Physics Reviews, Vol. 2. (Soviet Scientific Reviews Ser.: Section C). 282p. 1981. text ed. 372.00 (*3-7186-0069-2*) Gordon & Breach.

— Mathematical Physics Reviews, Vol. 3. 324p. 1982. text ed. 320.00 (*3-7186-0107-9*) Gordon & Breach.

— Mathematical Physics Reviews, Vol. 4. Hamermesh, Morton, tr. (Soviet Scientific Reviews Ser.: Section C). 320p. 1984. text ed. 342.00 (*3-7186-0146-X*) Gordon & Breach.

— Mathematical Physics Reviews: Soviet Scientific Reviews, Section C, Vol. 5. 282p. 1985. text ed. 274.00 (*3-7186-0198-2*) Gordon & Breach.

— Mathematical Physics Reviews: Soviet Scientific Reviews Section C, Vol. 6. HAmermesh, Morton, tr. 284p. 1987. text ed. 284.00 (*3-7186-0292-X*) Gordon & Breach.

— Topology & Its Applications: Proceedings of the International Topology Conference, Baku, October 3-8, 1987. LC 93-6106. (Proceedings of the Steklov Institute of Mathematics Ser.: Vol. 193). 1993. pap. 180.00 (*0-8218-3151-8*) Am Math.

Novikov, S. P. & Fomenko, A. T. Basic Elements of Differential Geometry & Topology. (C). 1990. lib. bdg. 177.50 (*0-7923-1009-8*) Kluwer Ac.

Novikov, S. P. & Sinai, Ya G., eds. Integrable Pseudospin Models in Condensed Matter, Vol. 9. (Soviet Scientific Reviews Series, Section D: Biology Reviews: Vol. 9, Pt. 3). 1993. text ed. 130.00 (*3-7186-5378-8*) Gordon & Breach.

Novikov, S. P., jt. ed. see Arnold, V. I.

Novikov, S. P., ed. see Chernikov, A. A., et al.

Novikov, S. P., ed. see Kozlov, V. V.

Novikov, S. P., et al, eds. Discrete Geometry & Topology: On the 100th Anniversary of the Birth of Boris Nikolaevich Delone: Collection of Papers. LC 92-37675. 193p. 1993. 129.00 (*0-8218-3147-X*, STEKLO 196) Am Math.

Novikov, V. M., ed. Handbook of Fishery Technology, Vol. 4. Sharma, B. R., tr. 506p. (C). 1984. text ed. 140.00 (*90-6191-421-3*, Pub. by A A Balkema NE) Ashgate Pub Co.

Novikov, V. V., jt. auth. see Privalko, V. P.

Novikova, Liubov A. Blindness & the Electrical Activity of the Brain: Electroencephalographic Studies of the Effects of Sensory Impairment. Jastzembska, Z. S., ed. Sznycer, B. & Zielinski, L., trs. LC 75-155920. (American Foundation for the Blind Research Ser.: No. 23). 359p. reprint ed. pap. 102.40 (*0-7837-0129-2*, 2040413) Bks Demand.

Novin, D., jt. ed. see Hoebel, B. G.

Novin, Donald, et al, eds. Hunger: Basic Mechanisms & Clinical Implications. LC 75-14563. 510p. 1976. 93.50 (*0-89004-059-1*) Raven.

Novis, Constance, ed. see Dempsey, Michael.

Novisky, Ed, ed. The Mercury Labels, Vol. IV: The 1969-1991 Era & Classical Recordings, Vol. 4. LC 93-15254. (Discographies Ser.: No. 51). 1993. text ed. 95.00 (*0-313-29034-2*, RMG04, Greenwood Pr) Greenwood.

Novit, Mitchell S. Essentials of Personnel Management. 2nd ed. (Illus.). 256p. (C). 1986. pap. text ed. write for info. (*0-13-286626-9*) P-H.

Novit, Renee Z. Alphabet Aa to Zz. (Kidz & Katz Educational Learning Book Ser.). (Illus.). 16p. (J). (ps-00). Date not set. pap. 7.95 (*1-883371-00-7*) Kidz & Katz.

— Counting by Tens & Fives. (Kidz & Katz Educational Learning Book Ser.). (Illus.). 16p. (J). (ps-00). Date not set. pap. 7.95 (*1-883371-02-3*) Kidz & Katz.

— Counting One to Twenty. (Kidz & Katz Educational Learning Book Ser.). (Illus.). 16p. (J). (ps-00). Date not set. pap. 7.95 (*1-883371-01-5*) Kidz & Katz.

Novitch, Miriam. The Passage of the Barbarians. 176p. 1993. 39.00 (*1-870360-10-9*) St Mut.

Novitch, Miriam, ed. Sobibor: Martyrdom & Revolt. (Illus.). 168p. (Orig.). reprint ed. pap. 4.95 (*0-686-95087-9*) ADL.

Novitchkov, Nicolai, jt. auth. see Goursau, Henri.

Novitski, Marya. Auguste Laurent & the Prehistory of Valence. LC 92-23090. (History of Science & Technology Ser.: Vol. 1). 1992. text ed. 58.00 (*3-7186-5235-8*) Gordon & Breach.

Novitsky, A. Sienitieteelinen Sanasto Suomi-Venaja-Latina. 190p. (FIN, LAT & RUS.). 1984. 29.95 (*0-8288-1250-0*, F22445) Fr & Eur.

Novitsky, Ed, ed. The Mercury Labels, 5 vols., Set. LC 93-15254. 4240p. 1993. text ed. 395.00 (*0-313-27371-5*, RMG/, Greenwood Pr) Greenwood.

— The Mercury Labels, Vol. I: The 1945-1956 Era. LC 93-15254. (Discographies Ser.: No. 51). 832p. 1993. text ed. 95.00 (*0-313-29031-8*, RMG01, Greenwood Pr) Greenwood.

— The Mercury Labels, Vol. II: The 1956-1964 Era, Vol. 2. LC 93-15254. (Discographies Ser.: No. 51). 840p. 1993. text ed. 95.00 (*0-313-29032-6*, RMG02, Greenwood Pr) Greenwood.

— The Mercury Labels, Vol. III: The 1964-1969 Era, Vol. 3. LC 93-15254. (Discographies Ser.: No. 51). 768p. 1993. text ed. 95.00 (*0-313-29033-4*, RMG03, Greenwood Pr) Greenwood.

— The Mercury Labels, Vol. V: Record & Artist Indexes, Vol. 5. LC 93-15254. (Discographies Ser.: No. 51). 912p. 1993. text ed. 95.00 (*0-313-29035-0*, RMG05, Greenwood Pr) Greenwood.

Novitt, J. J., jt. auth. see Brown, R. H.

Novitt-Moreno, Anne. How Your Brain Works. (Illus.). (Orig.). 1995. pap. 19.95 (*1-56276-255-9*) Ziff-Davis.

Novitz. Pictures & Their Use in Communication. 1977. pap. text ed. 65.50 (*90-247-1942-9*) Kluwer Ac.

Novitz, David. The Boundaries of Art. 296p. (C). 1992. 44.95 (*0-87722-928-7*) Temple U Pr.

— Knowledge, Fiction & Imagination. LC 86-30048. 304p. 1987. 39.95 (*0-87722-480-3*) Temple U Pr.

Novo, G. Diccionario General de Turismo. (SPA.). 19.50 (*0-7859-0917-6*, S-28710) Fr & Eur.

Novo, S., jt. ed. see Strano, A.

Novo, Salvador. Nuevo Amor. Underwood, E. W., tr. 1977. lib. bdg. 59.95 (*0-8490-2364-5*) Gordon Pr.

— The War of the Fatties & Other Stories from Aztec History. Alderson, Michael, tr. 256p. (C). 1993. text ed. 37.50 (*0-292-79059-7*); pap. 14.95 (*0-292-75554-6*) U of Tex Pr.

Novobilski, Andrew, jt. auth. see Cox, Brad J.

Novogrod, John C., jt. auth. see Hull, Roger H.

Novokshenov, V. Y., jt. auth. see Its, A. R.

Novosad, Garland S. Touchstone for Public Leadership: A Focus on City Government. (Illus.). 150p. 1988. 15.00 (*0-918464-77-3*) D Armstrong.

Novosad, Stanislav & Wagner, Peter, eds. Landslides: Seventh International Conference & Field Workshop. 320p. 1994. 95.00 (*90-5410-302-7*, Pub. by A A Balkema NE) Ashgate Pub Co.

Novoselova, A. V. & Batsanova, L. R. Beryllium. (Analytical Chemistry of the Elements Ser.). 233p. 1970. text ed. 60.00 (*0-7065-0742-8*, Pub. by Keter Pub IS) Coronet Bks.

Novoshilov, K. V., jt. ed. see Fadeev, Iu. N.

Novosti Press Agency Staff. Armenian Earthquake Disaster. (Illus.). 241p. 1989. 19.95 (*0-943071-12-7*) Sphinx Pr.

Novotny, A. J., jt. ed. see Nash, C. E.

Novotny, Ann. Alice's World: The Life & Photography of an American Original: Alice Austen, 1866-1952. LC 76-18489. (Illus.). (J). (gr. 7-9). 1976. 22.50 (*0-85699-128-7*) Chatham Pr.

— Strangers at the Door. (Illus.). 249p. reprint ed. pap. 1.65 (*0-686-95025-9*) ADL.

Novotny, Ann, ed. see Special Libraries Association, Picture Division Staff.

***Novotny, Bruce.** Tales from an Endless Summer: A Novel of the Beach. 208p. 1995. write for info. (*0-945582-30-7*); pap. text ed. write for info. (*0-945582-31-5*) Down the Shore Pub.

Novotny, Donald, jt. auth. see Schmitz, Norbert L.

Novotny, Frantisek. The Posthumous Life of Plato. Svoboda, Ludvik & Barton, J. L., eds. Fabryova, Jana, tr. 1978. lib. bdg. 121.50 (*90-247-2060-5*) Kluwer Ac.

***Novotny, Fritz.** The Great Impressionists. (Illus.). 160p. 1995. 50.00 (*3-7913-1450-5*, Pub. by Prestel) TeNeues.

— Painting & Sculpture in Europe: 1780-1880. (Pelican History of Art Ser.). (Illus.). 483p. (C). 1988. reprint ed. pap. text ed. 25.00 (*0-300-05321-5*) Yale U Pr.

Novotny, George, jt. auth. see Huhtala, Jon.

Novotny, Josef L. English-German Dictionary of American Verbs-Idioms: English-Deutsches Woerterbuch Amerikanischer Zeitwort-Idiome. 464p. (ENG & GER.). 1980. 150.00 (*0-8288-1436-8*, M15480) Fr & Eur.

Novotny, M. V. & Ishii, D., eds. Microcolumn Separations: Columns, Instrumentation & Ancillary Techniques. (Journal of Chromatography Library: Vol. 30). 336p. 1985. 102.75 (*0-444-42429-6*) Elsevier.

Novotny, P., jt. auth. see Sohnel, O.

Novotny, Pamela & Novotny, Patrick. The Joy of Twins & Multiple Births. 1994. pap. 16.00 (*0-517-88071-7*) Crown Pub Group.

Novotny, Pamela P. The Joy of Twins: Having, Raising, & Loving Babies Who Arrive in Groups. (Illus.). 320p. 1988. 22.00 (*0-517-56819-5*, Crown) Crown Pub Group.

Novotny, Pamela P., jt. auth. see Dell Medical Library Staff.

Novotny, Patrick, jt. auth. see Novotny, Pamela.

Novotny, V. Water Quality & Diffuse Pollution. 1994. text ed. 79.95 (*0-442-00559-8*) Van Nos Reinhold.

Novotny, Vladimir, ed. Political Institutional & Fiscal Alternatives for Nonpoint Pollution Abatement Programs. LC 88-61504. 206p. (Orig.). 1988. text ed. 15.00 (*0-87462-499-1*) Marquette.

Novotny, Vladimir, jt. auth. see Krenkel, Peter A.

Novotny, Vladimir, ed. see Symposium on Nonpoint Pollution: Policy, Economy, Management, & Appropriate Technology, 1988 Staff.

Novouspensky, N. The Russian Museum, Leningrad. 193p. 1975. 29.00 (*0-317-14293-3*, Pub. by Collets) St Mut.

Novozhilov, H. M. Fundamental Metallurgy of Gas-Shielded ARC Welding. 410p. 1988. text ed. 222.00 (*2-88124-666-4*) Gordon & Breach.

Novozhilov, K. V. Microbiological Methods for Biological Control of Pests of Agricultural Crops. (C). 1987. 12.50 (*0-8364-2114-0*, Pub. by Oxford IBH II) S Asia.

Novozhilov, K. V., ed. Microbiological Methods for Biological Control of Pests of Agricultural Crops. Nair, Indira, tr. (Russian Translation Ser.: Vol. 51). (Illus.). 91p. (C). 1987. text ed. 55.00 (*90-6191-493-0*, Pub. by A A Balkema NE) Ashgate Pub Co.

Novozhilov, K. V., jt. auth. see Fadeev, I. U.

Novozhilov, V. & Lusher, J. Theory of Elasticity. LC 60-14992. 1961. 187.00 (*0-08-009523-2*, Pub. by Pergamon Repr UK) Franklin.

Novozhilov, Y. V. Elementary Particles. 208p. 1961. text ed. 331.00 (*0-677-20470-1*) Gordon & Breach.

Novozhilov, Y. V. & Tulub, A. V. The Method of Functionals in the Quantum Theory of Fields. (Russian Tracts on the Physical Sciences Ser.). 90p. 1961. text ed. 54.00 (*0-677-20410-8*) Gordon & Breach.

Novozhilov, Yuri V. Introduction to Elementary Particle Theory. Rosner, Jonathon L., tr. 1975. 167.00 (*0-08-017954-1*, Pub. by Pergamon Repr UK) Franklin.

Novrup, Svend. Checkmate. 160p. 1990. pap. write for info. (*0-08-037790-4*, Pub. by CHES UK) Macmillan.

Novshek, William. Mathematics for Economists. LC 93-16696. (Economic Theory, Econometrics & Mathematical Economics Ser.). (Illus.). 308p. 1993. text ed. 59.95 (*0-12-522575-X*) Acad Pr.

Novy, Lubomir & Gabriel, Jiri, eds. Czech Philosophy in the Twentieth Century. LC 93-5986. (Cultural Heritage & Contemporary Change Series VI: Foundations of Moral Education,: Vol. 4). 1993. 45.00 (*1-56518-028-3*); pap. 17.50 (*1-56518-029-1*) Coun Res Values.

Novy, Marianne. Engaging with Shakespeare: Responses of George Eliot & Other Women Novelists. LC 93-4158. 288p. (C). 1994. 50.00 (*0-8203-1596-6*) U of Ga Pr.

— Love's Argument: Gender Relations in Shakespeare. LC 84-3553. reprint ed. pap. 71.00 (*0-7837-9031-7*, 2049782) Bks Demand.

— Women's Re-Visions of Shakespeare. 272p. 1990. 34.95 (*0-252-01698-X*); pap. 15.95 (*0-252-06114-4*) U of Ill Pr.

Novy, Marianne, ed. Cross-Cultural Performances: Differences in Women's Re-visions of Shakespeare. LC 92-44535. 280p. 1993. 49.95 (*0-252-02017-0*); pap. 18.95 (*0-252-06323-6*) U of Ill Pr.

Novy, Marianne L. Love's Argument: Gender Relations in Shakespeare. LC 84-3553. xi, 237p. 1984. 29.95 (*0-8078-1608-6*) U of NC Pr.

Nowab, Hamid, jt. auth. see Oppenheim, A. V.

***Nowacki, Edward.** Janus. 140p. (Orig.). Date not set. pap. 8.95 (*0-7610-0273-1*) NW Pub.

***Nowacki, H., et al, eds.** Computational Geometry for Ships. LC 94-46516. 252p. 1995. text ed. 53.00 (*981-02-2139-8*) World Scientific Pub.

Nowacki, J. P., jt. ed. see Enokizono, M.

Nowacki, Louis J., jt. ed. see Vigo, Tyrone L.

Nowacki, Perry, ed. Oil Shale Technical Data Handbook. LC 80-27547. (Energy Technology Review Series & Chemical Technology Review Ser.: Nos. 63 & 182). (Illus.). 309p. 1981. 48.00 (*0-8155-0835-2*) Noyes.

Nowacki, Wojoiech K. Stress Waves in Non-Elastic Solids. 1978. 104.00 (*0-08-021294-8*, Pub. by Pergamon Repr UK) Franklin.

— Theory of Asymmetrical Elasticity. 2nd ed. 1986. 166.00 (*0-08-027584-2*, Pub. by Pergamon Repr UK) Franklin.

— Thermoelasticity. 2nd ed. 580p. 1986. 239.00 (*0-08-024767-9*) Franklin.

Nowacki, Wojoiech K., ed. see CISM (International Center for Mechanical Sciences), Department for Mechanics of Deformable Bodies Staff.

Nowaczyk, Ronald H. Introductory Statistics for Behavioral Research. 544p. (C). 1988. text ed. 46.75 (*0-03-004043-4*) HB Coll Pubs.

Nowak, A. & Neves, A. C., eds. The Multiple Reciprocity Boundary Element Method. LC 93-74381. (Computational Engineering Ser.). 256p. 1994. 99.00 (*1-56252-201-9*) Computational Mech MA.

Nowak, A. J., jt. auth. see Kurpisz, K.

Nowak, A. J., jt. ed. see Wrobel, L. C.

Nowak, Andrzej. Making Buildings Safer For People During Hurricanes, Earthquakes, & Fires. 1990. text ed. 49.95 (*0-442-26473-9*) Chapman & Hall.

Nowak, Andrzej, jt. ed. see Vallacher, Robin R.

Nowak, Andrzej S., ed. Bridge Evaluation, Repair & Rehabilitation. (C). 1990. lib. bdg. 201.50 (*0-7923-0999-5*) Kluwer Ac.

— Modeling Human Error in Structural Design & Construction. (Workshop Proceedings Ser.). 200p. 1986. 26.00 (*0-87262-558-3*) Am Soc Civil Eng.

Nowak, Barbara. Cook It Right! The Comprehensive Source for Substitutions, Equivalents & Cooking Tips. LC 93-86735. 192p. 1994. pap. text ed. 22.95 (*0-9627756-8-1*) Sandcastle Pub.

Nowak, Bernd. Untersuchungen zur Vegetation Ostliguriens (Italien) (Dissertationes Botanicae Ser.: Vol. 111). (Illus.). 264p. (GER.). 1987. pap. text ed. 86.00 (*3-443-64023-0*) Lubrecht & Cramer.

Nowak, Ed & Yanosey, Robert J. New York Central Color Photography of Ed Nowak, Bk. I. LC 91-67986. (Illus.). 128p. 1992. 45.00 (*1-878887-09-2*) Morning NJ.

— New York Central Color Photography of Ed Nowak, Bk. II. LC 91-67986. (Illus.). 128p. 1992. 49.95 (*1-878887-17-3*) Morning NJ.

— New York Central Color Photography of Ed Nowak, Bk. 3. LC 91-67986. (Illus.). 128p. 1993. 49.95 (*1-878887-24-6*) Morning NJ.

Nowak, G. A. Cosmetic Preparations, Vol. 1. Alexander, Philip, tr. (Illus.). 352p. 1985. 119.00 (*3-87846-118-6*) Micelle Pr.

Nowak, H. Revision der Laubmoosgattung Mitthyridium (Mitten) Robinson Fuer Oreanien (Calymperaceae) (Bryophytorum Bibliotheca Ser.: No. 20). (Illus.). (GER.). 1981. lib. bdg. 36.00 (*3-7682-1236-X*) Lubrecht & Cramer.

Nowak, J. International Colloquium on Diffractive Optical Elements (May 1991, Szklarska Poreba, Poland) 1991. write for info. (*0-8194-0704-6*, 1574) SPIE.

Nowak, Jan. Courier from Warsaw. LC 82-8599. (Illus.). 479p. reprint ed. pap. 136.60 (*0-318-39795-1*, 2033198) Bks Demand.

Nowak, Janie B. The Forty-Seven Hundred: The Story of the Mount Sinai Hospital School of Nursing. LC 81-5202. (Illus.). 160p. 1981. 15.00 (*0-914016-79-2*) Phoenix Pub.

Nowak, Joanna & Rudnicki, Ryszard M. Postharvest Handling & Storage of Cut Flowers, Florist Greens & Potted Plants. LC 89-35490. (Illus.). 208p. 1990. 21.95 (*0-88192-156-4*) Timber.

Nowak, John E. & Rotunda, Ronald D. Treatise on Constitutional Law: Substance & Procedure, 1. 2nd ed. (Practice Ser.: Vols. 1-3). 1992. text ed. write for info. (*0-314-00803-9*) West Pub.

— Treatise on Constitutional Law: Substance & Procedure, 2. 2nd ed. (Practice Ser.: Vols. 1-3). 1992. text ed. write for info. (*0-314-00804-7*) West Pub.

— Treatise on Constitutional Law: Substance & Procedure, 3. 2nd ed. (Practice Ser.: Vols. 1-3). 1992. text ed. write for info. (*0-314-00805-5*) West Pub.

Nowak, John E., jt. auth. see Rotunda, Ronald D.

Nowak, John E., ed. see Story, Joseph.

***Nowak, John F.** Jasiu, or Lumpy Oatmeal & Burnt Toast. 80p. (Orig.). 1995. pap. 8.95 (*0-9644883-0-2*) Ottawa St Pr.

Nowak, Karl F. Versailles. Thomas, Norman M. & Dickes, E. W., trs. LC 76-175705. (Select Bibliographies Reprint Ser.). 1977. reprint ed. 21.95 (*0-8369-6620-1*) Ayer.

— Versailles. Thomas, Norman F. & Dickes, E. W., trs. LC 76-175705. (Select Bibliographies Reprint Ser.). 284p. reprint ed. lib. bdg. 17.50 (*0-8290-0822-5*) Irvington.

Nowak, Laura S. Monetary Policy & Investment Opportunities. LC 92-18366. 232p. 1993. text ed. 45.00 (*0-89930-611-X*, NIO, Quorum Bks) Greenwood.

Nowak, Leszek. Power & Civil Society: Toward a Dynamic Theory of Real Socialism. LC 90-47324. (Contributions in Political Science Ser.: No. 271). 248p. 1991. text ed. 55.00 (*0-313-27505-X*, NDP/, Greenwood Pr) Greenwood.

— Property & Power. 1983. lib. bdg. 121.50 (*90-277-1351-0*); pap. text ed. 55.00 (*90-277-1595-5*) Kluwer Ac.

— The Structure of Idealization: Towards a Systematic Interpretation of the Marxian Idea of Science. (Synthese Library: No. 139). 1979. lib. bdg. 70.00 (*90-277-1014-7*) Kluwer Ac.

Nowak, M. A., et al. Chiral Nuclear Dynamics. 400p. 1995. text ed. 74.00 (*981-02-1000-0*) World Scientific Pub.

Nowak, Margaret C. Two Who Were There: A Biography of Stanley Nowak. LC 88-39057. (Illus.). 270p. 1989. 39.95 (*0-8143-1883-5*); pap. 17.95 (*0-8143-1878-9*) Wayne St U Pr.

Nowak, Michael, jt. auth. see Meyer, Allen.

Nowak, Nancy C., jt. auth. see Furfine, Sandy S.

***Nowak, Pat & Siembieda, Kevin.** Rifts Japan. Marciniszyn, A. et al, eds. (Rifts World Bks.: No. Eight). (Illus.). 200p. (Orig.). (YA). (gr. 8 up). 1995. pap. 19.95 (*0-916211-88-6*) Palladium Bks.

***Nowak, Patrick & Siembieda, Kevin.** Yin-Sloth Jungles. Marcinizyn, A. et al, eds. (Palladium RPG Ser.: Vol. VII). (Illus.). 160p. (Orig.). (YA). (gr. 8 up). 1994. pap. 15.95 (*0-916211-81-9*, 459) Palladium Bks.

Nowak, Paul & Urowsky, Robert. The Complete Non-Authoritative Guide to Japan. (Illus.). 104p. (Orig.). 1994. pap. 9.95 (*0-8048-1948-3*) C E Tuttle.

Nowak, Phil, jt. auth. see Jatich, Alida M.

Nowak, Ronald M. Walker's Bats of the World. (Illus.). 1995. pap. 19.95 (*0-8018-4986-1*) Johns Hopkins.

— Walker's Mammals of the World, 2 vols., Set. 5th rev. ed. LC 91-27011. (Illus.). 1732p. 1991. 95.00 (*0-8018-3970-X*) Johns Hopkins.

Nowak-Solinski, Witold. Krysia. 132p. 1988. 39.00 (*0-85335-242-9*, Pub. by Stuart Titles Ltd UK) St Mut.

***Nowak, Stanley J., Jr.** Institutional Structures & Human Values. (Academic Edition Ser.). 90p. (Orig.). (C). 1988. student ed 68.75 (*1-885886-00-4*) Eikon PA.

— Institutional Structures & Human Values. (Academic Edition UK Ser.). 90p. (Orig.). (C). 1992. student ed write for info. (*1-885886-02-0*) Eikon PA.

— Institutional Structures & Human Values. (Academic Edition Ser.). 100p. (Orig.). (C). 1994. student ed 75.00 (*1-885886-10-1*) Eikon PA.

— Institutional Structures & Human Values. (Professional Edition Ser.). 100p. (Orig.). 1994. student ed 300.00 (*1-885886-11-X*); student ed write for info. (*1-885886-13-6*) Eikon PA.

— Institutional Structures & Human Values. (Academic Edition UK Ser.). 100p. (Orig.). (C). 1994. student ed write for info. (*1-885886-12-8*) Eikon PA.

— Institutional Structures & Human Values: Making Choices. (Employment Edition Ser.). 64p. 1988. student ed 105.00 (*1-885886-01-2*) Eikon PA.

— Institutional Structures & Human Values: Making Choices. (Academic Edition Ser.). 66p. (C). 1993. student ed 55.00 (*1-885886-03-9*) Eikon PA.

— Institutional Structures & Human Values: Making Choices. (Employment Edition Ser.). 64p. 1994. student ed 115.00 (*1-885886-16-0*) Eikon PA.

— Institutional Structures & Human Values: Making Choices. (Academic Edition Ser.). 66p. (C). 1994. student ed 60.00 (*1-885886-15-2*) Eikon PA.

Nowak, Stefan. Methodology of Sociological Research, 2 vols, Vol. 1. Lepa, Maria O., tr. (Synthese Library: No. 82). 1977. lib. bdg. 103.00 (*90-277-0486-4*) Kluwer Ac.

— Understanding & Prediction. (Synthese Library: No. 94). 482p. 1981. pap. text ed. 36.50 (*90-277-1199-2*) Kluwer Ac.

— Understanding & Prediction Essays in the Methodology of Social & Behavioral Theories. LC 75-44179. (Synthese Library: No. 94). 1976. lib. bdg. 126.50 (*90-277-0558-5*) Kluwer Ac.

Nowak, Thomas J. & Handford, A. Gordon. Essentials of Pathophysiology: Concepts & Applications for Health Care Professionals. 688p. (C). 1994. text ed. write for info. (*0-697-13314-1*) Wm C Brown Pubs.

Nowak, W. S. The Marketing of Shellfish. 1978. 50.00 (*0-685-63433-7*) St Mut.

Nowakowska, M. Quantitative Psychology. (Advances in Psychology Ser.: Vol. 15). 1984. 115.50 (*0-444-86708-2, I-232-83*) Elsevier.

Nowakowska, Maria. Cognitive Sciences: Basic Problems, New Perspectives. 1986. pap. text ed. 58.00 (*0-12-522621-7*) Acad Pr.

— Language of Motivation & Language of Actions. LC 72-94491. (Janua Linguarum, Ser. Major: No. 67). (Illus.). 272p. 1973. text ed. 58.70 (*90-279-2385-X*) Mouton.

— Theories of Research. (Systems Inquiry Ser.). 580p. (Orig.). 1984. pap. text ed. 30.50 (*0-914105-20-5*) Intersystems Pubns.

Nowakowski. Pleasing Polish Recipes. 160p. 1989. spiral bd. 5.50 (*0-941016-63-3*) Penfield.

***Nowakowski, Jacek, ed.** Polish-American Ways: Polish Touches. 1995. pap. 9.95 (*1-57216-020-9*) Penfield.

Nowakowski, Jeri. A Handbook of Educational Variables: A Guide to Evaluation. 1984. lib. bdg. 55.50 (*0-89838-161-4*) Kluwer Ac.

Nowakowski, Jeri, ed. The Client Perspective on Evaluation. LC 85-644749. (New Directions for Program Evaluation Ser.: No. PE 36). 1987. 17.95 (*1-55542-942-4*) Jossey-Bass.

Nowakowski, Rodney W. Primary Low Vision Care. LC 94-8438. 1994. 60.00 (*0-8385-7980-9*) Appleton & Lange.

Nowakowski, T., jt. auth. see Kononova, M.

Nowar. History of the Hashemite, Vol. 1. 1991. 60.00 (*0-86372-119-2*, Pub. by Ithaca UK) Paul & Co Pubs.

Nowarra. Fokker Dr. 1 in Action. (Aircraft in Action Ser.). (Illus.). 50p. 1989. pap. 8.95 (*0-89747-229-2*, 1098) Squad Sig Pubns.

***Nowarra, Heinz.** Junkers Ju 52. (Illus.). 48p. 1993. pap. 8.95 (*0-88740-523-1*) Schiffer.

— U-Boat Type VII - Grey Ghosts of the Sea. Force, Edward, tr. (Illus.). 48p. 1992. pap. 7.95 (*0-88740-409-X*) Schiffer.

Nowarra, Heinz J. The Flying Pencil - Dornier Do 17-215. LC 90-60475. (Illus.). 48p. 1990. pap. 6.95 (*0-88740-236-4*) Schiffer.

— Focke-Wulf FW 190-Tal 52: Aircraft & Legend. (Illus.). 160p. 1989. pap. 19.95 (*0-85429-881-9*) Haynes Pubns.

— The Fokker Dr. I & DVII in World War I. Cox, Don, tr. LC 91-62743. (Illus.). 48p. 1991. pap. 7.95 (*0-88740-353-0*) Schiffer.

— Folke-Wulf FW 190: Fighters, Bombers, Ground Attack Aircraft. Cable, James C., tr. LC 91-62744. (Illus.). 48p. 1991. pap. 7.95 (*0-88740-354-9*) Schiffer.

— German Airships - Parseval - Schutte - Lanz - Zeppelin. LC 89-63353. (Illus.). 52p. 1989. pap. 9.95 (*0-88740-199-6*) Schiffer.

— German Dornier DO 335 - "Pfeil" Aircraft. LC 89-84180. (Illus.). 48p. 1989. pap. 6.95 (*0-88740-189-9*) Schiffer.

— German Gliders in World War II. Force, Edward, tr. LC 91-62747. (Illus.). 48p. 1991. pap. 7.95 (*0-88740-358-1*) Schiffer.

— German Guided Missiles. Cox, Don, tr. (Illus.). 48p. (Orig.). 1993. pap. 7.95 (*0-88740-475-8*) Schiffer.

— German Helicopters 1928-1945. LC 90-62988. (Illus.). 48p. 1991. pap. 7.95 (*0-88740-289-5*) Schiffer.

— German "UHU" - He219 Aircraft. LC 89-84179. (Illus.). 48p. 1989. pap. 6.95 (*0-88740-188-0*) Schiffer.

— German "UHU"- He 219 Aircraft. LC 89-84179. (Illus.). 48p. 1989. pap. 6.95 (*0-685-31099-X*) Schiffer.

— Heinkel He 162. Carle, James, tr. (Illus.). 48p. (Orig.). 1993. pap. 7.95 (*0-88740-478-2*) Schiffer.

— Messerschmitt BF 109. LC 91-60857. (Illus.). 48p. 1991. pap. 7.95 (*0-88740-311-5*) Schiffer.

Nowatzki, E. A., jt. auth. see Karafiath, L. L.

***Nowatzki, Richard J.** Memoirs of a Navy Major. (Illus.). 256p. (Orig.). 1995. pap. 10.95 (*0-9645284-0-1*) R J Nowatzki.

Nowell, A. R. & Hollister, C. D., eds. Deep Ocean Sediment Transport: Preliminary Results of the High Energy Benthic Boundary Layer Experiment. 418p. 1985. reprint ed. 128.25 (*0-444-42519-5*) Elsevier.

Nowell, Alexander. A Catechisme, or First Instruction & Learning of Christian Religion. LC 74-23570. 185p. 1975. reprint ed. lib. bdg. 50.00 (*0-8201-1143-0*) Schol Facsimiles.

Nowell, D., jt. auth. see Hills, D. A.

Nowell-Dec, Lisa, ed. see Ojala, William K.

Nowell, Elizabeth. Letters of Thomas Wolfe. (Hudson River Editions Ser.). 1984. text ed. 52.00 (*0-684-18269-6*, Scribners) S&S Trade.

— Thomas Wolfe: A Biography. LC 72-7507. 456p. 1973. reprint ed. text ed. 38.50 (*0-8371-6519-9*, NOTW, Greenwood Pr) Greenwood.

Nowell, Eppler. Sky Scanner. 2nd ed. (Illus.). 17p. (Orig.). 1980. pap. text ed. 4.95 (*0-9611454-0-4*) E Nowell.

Nowell, Gregory P. Mercantile States & the World Oil Cartel, 1900-1939. LC 93-38020. (Cornell Studies in Political Economy). (Illus.). 344p. (C). 1994. 45.00 (*0-8014-2878-5*) Cornell U Pr.

Nowell, Irene. Jonah, Tobit, Judith. (Collegeville Bible Commentary - Old Testament Ser.: Vol. 25). 112p. 1986. pap. 3.95 (*0-8146-1482-5*) Liturgical Pr.

— Sing a New Song: The Psalms in the Sunday Lectionary. 344p. (Orig.). 1993. 17.95 (*0-8146-2043-4*) Liturgical Pr.

Nowell, Iris. Hot Breakfast for Sparrows: My Life with Harold Town. (Illus.). 272p. 1992. 26.95 (*0-7737-2645-4*, Pub. by Stoddart Pubng CN) Genl Dist Srvs.

Nowell, Kristin, jt. ed. see Jackson, Peter.

Nowell, Richard C. & Marshak, Laura E., eds. Understanding Deafness & the Rehabilitation Process. LC 93-50768. 1994. write for info. (*0-205-15628-2*) Allyn.

Nowell-Smith, Geoffrey & Wollen, Tana, eds. After the Wall. (European Media Monograph: No. 1). (Illus.). 96p. 1992. pap. 9.95 (*0-85170-296-1*, Pub. by British Film Inst UK) Ind U Pr.

Nowell-Smith, Geoffrey, ed. see Febvre, Lucien & Martin, Henri-Jean.

Nowell-Smith, Geoffrey, ed. see Gramsci, Antonio.

Nowell-Smith, Simon. Legend of the Master. (BCL1-PS American Literature Ser.). 176p. 1993. reprint ed. lib. bdg. 69.00 (*0-7812-6980-6*) Rprt Serv.

Nowell-Usticke, G. W. Rembrandt's Etchings: States & Values. LC 87-80028. (Illus.). 379p. 1988. reprint ed. lib. bdg. 60.00 (*0-87817-300-5*) Hacker.

Nowell, Vernon L. Fur Rendezvous Remembered, No. 1. (Illus.). 92p. (Orig.). 1991. pap. 9.95 (*0-9628955-0-4*) Blue Star Vid.

Nowels, William, jt. auth. see Bova, Joyce.

Nower, Joyce. Year of the Fires & Other Poems. LC 81-70725. 83p. 1983. pap. 4.75 (*0-9600856-2-9*) Ctr Women's Studies.

Nowick, Arthur S. & Berry, B. S. Anelastic Relaxation in Crystalline Solids. (Materials Science & Technology Ser.). 1972. text ed. 99.00 (*0-12-522650-0*) Acad Pr.

Nowick, Arthur S., jt. ed. see Murch, Graeme E.

Nowicka-Jankowska, T., et al. Comprehensive Analytical Chemistry: Analytical Visible & Ultraviolet Spectrometry. (Wilson & Wilson's Comprehensive Analytical Chemistry Ser.: Vol. 19). 660p. 1986. 282.00 (*0-444-42371-0*) Elsevier.

Nowicki, Dariusz. Gold Medal Mental Workout for Combat Sports: Boxing, Fencing, Judo, Karate, Kick-Boxing, Taekwondo, & Wrestling. (Gold Medal Mental Workout Ser.). 48p. 1993. pap. 21.95 (*0-940149-06-0*) Stadion Pub.

— Gold Medal Mental Workout Fundamentals: A Step-by-Step Program of Mental Exercises to Make You a Winner Every Time. (Gold Medal Mental Workout Ser.). (Illus.). 96p. 1993. pap. 35.95 (*0-940149-05-2*) Stadion Pub.

Nowicki, Dolores A. First Steps in Ritual. 1990. pap. 9.95 (*0-85030-874-7*, Pub. by Aquarian Pr UK) Thorsons SF.

Nowicki, Ed. True Blue: Stories about Real Cops. 1993. mass mkt. 4.99 (*0-312-95061-6*) St Martin.

Nowicki, Ed, comp. Total Survival: A Comprehensive Guide for the Physical, Psychological, Emotional, & Professional Survival of Law Enforcement Officers. LC 92-85340. 1993. pap. 24.95 (*1-879411-18-0*) Perf Dimensions Pub.

Nowicki, Ed, ed. Supervisory Survival: A Practical Guide for the Professional Survival of New, Experienced, & Aspiring Law Enforcement Supervisors. LC 93-4274. 1993. pap. 17.95 (*1-879411-23-7*) Perf Dimensions Pub.

Nowicki, Edward J. True Blue: True Stories about Real Cops. LC 91-66414. 280p. (Orig.). 1992. pap. 14.95 (*1-879411-15-6*) Perf Dimensions Pub.

Nowicki, Edward J. & Ramsey, Dennis A. Street Weapons: An Identification Manual for Improvised, Unconventional, Unusual, Homemade, Disguised & Exotic Personal Weapons. LC 90-92207. (Illus.). 272p. (Orig.). 1991. pap. 19.95 (*1-879411-11-3*) Perf Dimensions Pub.

Nowicki, J. R. & Adam, L. J. Digital Circuits. (Illus.). 320p. 1991. pap. 27.95 (*0-7131-3641-3*, A6451, Pub. by E Arnold UK) Routledge Chapman & Hall.

***Nowicki, Joseph & Meehan, Kerry F.** The Collaborative Social Studies Classroom: A Resource for Teachers. LC 95-13741. 1995. write for info. (*0-205-17391-8*) Allyn.

Nowicki, Maciej. Environment in Poland: Issues & Solutions. 191p. (C). 1993. lib. bdg. 69.50 (*0-7923-2269-X*) Kluwer Ac.

Nowicki, Ron. Warsaw: The Cabaret Years. LC 92-16660. (Illus.). 1992. 30.00 (*1-56279-030-7*) Mercury Hse Inc.

Nowicki, Stephen, Jr. & Duke, Marshall. Helping the Child Who Doesn't Fit In: Clinical Psychologists Decipher the Hidden Dimensions of Social Rejection. (Illus.). 192p. (Orig.). 1992. pap. 14.95 (*1-56145-025-1*) Peachtree Pubs.

Nowicki, Tim. Awake to Wildlife: The Complete Naturalist's Great Lakes Wildlife Almanac. 192p. 1994. pap. 11.95 (*1-881139-08-5*) Glovebox Guidebks.

Nowik, William. War Assets Display Room: A Novel Series of Stories with Photographs, Illustrations, & Music, Vol. 1. Hazem, Beth, ed. (Illus.). 133p. (Orig.). 1993. pap. 20.00 (*0-9636616-8-X*) Blue Buddha.

Nowill, Paul H. Productivity & the Technological Change in Electric Power Generating Plants. Bruchey, Stuart, ed. LC 78-22703. (Energy in the American Economy Ser.). (Illus.). 1979. lib. bdg. 19.95 (*0-405-12005-2*) Ayer.

Nowinski, J. L. Applications of Functional Analysis in Engineering. LC 81-5213. (Mathematical Concepts & Methods in Science & Engineering Ser.: Vol. 22). 320p. 1981. 65.00 (*0-306-40693-4*, Plenum Pr) Plenum.

Nowinski, Joseph K. Becoming Satisfied: A Man's Guide to Sexual Fulfillment. 1980. 12.95 (*0-13-073031-9*, Spectrum Bks) P-H.

— Hungry Hearts: On Men, Intimacy, Self-Esteem, & Addiction. 176p. 1993. text ed. 22.95 (*0-02-923221-X*) Macmillan.

— Lifelong Love Affair. 1989. pap. 7.95 (*0-393-30621-6*) Norton.

— Substance Abuse in Adolescents & Young Adults: A Guide to Treatment. (C). 1990. 29.95 (*0-393-70097-6*) Norton.

Nowinski, Joseph K. & Baker, Stuart. The Twelve-Step Facilitation Handbook: A Systematic Approach to Early Recovery from Alcoholism & Addiction. LC 92-17693. 1992. text ed. 29.95 (*0-02-923225-2*) Free Pr.

Nowinski, Judith. Baron Dominique Vivant Denon, 1747-1825: Hedonist & Scholar in a Period of Transition. LC 78-86651. (Illus.). 280p. 1975. 27.50 (*0-8386-7470-4*) Fairleigh Dickinson.

Nowinsky, Ira. A Beginner's Guide to Snakes. (Illus.). 64p. 1986. 3.95 (*0-86622-313-4*, T-112) TFH Pubns.

Nowinson, Marie. Winds of Change: And Other Stories. 1983. mass mkt. 4.95 (*0-345-31188-4*) Ballantine.

Nowitschkowa, A. L., jt. auth. see Scharow, W. A.

Nowitz, David A., ed. A Taste of College: Summer Programs for High School Students on Campus 1988 Guide. xii, 205p. 1988. pap. 12.95 (*0-944714-00-5*) College Bound.

Nowitz, David A., jt. auth. see Nowitz, Jane E.

Nowitz, Jane E. & Nowitz, David A. A Taste of College: Summer Programs for High School Students on Campus 1988 Guide. rev. ed. LC 88-30244. xiv, 241p. 1989. pap. 12.95 (*0-944714-01-3*) College Bound.

Nowitz, Marilyn, jt. auth. see Caserta, Carmen.

Nowka, Richard H., jt. auth. see Liebson, David J.

***Nowla, Nowlan & Gwend, Robert.** We'll Always Have Paris. 704p. 1995. pap. 20.00 (*0-06-272506-8*, Harper Ref) HarpC.

Nowlan, Alan. Will Ye Let the Mummers In? 164p. 1984. 8.95 (*0-7720-1407-8*, Pub. by Stoddart Pubng CN) Genl Dist Srvs.

Nowlan, Alden. Between Tears & Laughter. 119p. 1971. 3.95 (*0-7720-0630-X*, Pub. by Stoddart Pubng CN) Genl Dist Srvs.

— An Exchange of Gifts: Poems New & Selected. 284p. 1985. 14.95 (*0-7725-1525-5*, Pub. by Stoddart Pubng CN) Genl Dist Srvs.

— Miracle at Indian River. 132p. 1982. pap. 8.95 (*0-7720-1402-7*, Pub. by Stoddart Pubng CN) Genl Dist Srvs.

— What Happened When He Went to the Store for Bread: Poems. Smith, Thomas R., ed. LC 93-14682. 1993. pap. 10.00 (*1-883070-00-7*) Nineties Pr.

— Will Ye Let the Mummers In? 164p. 1984. 14.95 (*0-7720-1451-5*, Pub. by Stoddart Pubng CN) Genl Dist Srvs.

Nowlan, Gwendolyn W., jt. auth. see Nowlan, Robert A.

Nowlan, James D. A New Game Plan for Illinois. (Illus.). 173p. (Orig.). (C). 1989. pap. text ed. 9.95 (*0-9622680-0-3*) Neltnor Hse.

Nowlan, Kevin B. & O'Connell, Maurice R., eds. Daniel O'Connell: Portrait of a Radical. LC 85-80412. 120p. 1885. 24.95 (*0-8232-1140-1*) Fordham.

Nowlan, Robert A. & Nolan, Gwendolyn W., eds. Encyclopedia of Film Festivals, 2 vols. (Foundations in Library & Information Science: Vol. 23). 1987. lib. bdg. 105.00 (*0-89232-734-0*) Jai Pr.

Nowlan, Robert A. & Nowlan, Gwendolyn W. Cinema Sequels & Remakes, 1903-1987. LC 88-42640. (Illus.). 966p. 1988. lib. bdg. 82.00x (*0-89950-314-4*) McFarland & Co.

— Film Quotations: Eleven Thousand Lines Spoken on Screen, Arranged by Subject, & Indexed. LC 92-56673. (Illus.). 756p. 1993. lib. bdg. 75.00 (*0-89950-786-7*) McFarland & Co.

— The Films of the Eighties: A Complete, Qualitative Filmography to over 3400 Feature-Length English Language Films, Theatrical & Video-Only, Released Between Janaury 1, 1980, & December 31, 1989. LC 90-53516. 868p. 1991. lib. bdg. 75.00 (*0-89950-560-0*) McFarland & Co.

— The Name Is Familiar: Who Played Who in the Movies, a Directory of Title Characters. 1016p. 1993. pap. text ed. 75.00 (*1-55570-054-3*) Neal-Schuman.

Nowlen, Kevin, ed. Governments, Ethnic Groups, & Political Representations. (Comparative Studies on Governments & Non-Dominant Ethnic Groups in Europe (1850-1940)). 400p. 1992. text ed. 80.00 (*0-8147-5766-9*) NYU Pr.

Nowlen, Philip. A New Approach to Continuing Education for Business & the Professions. (ACE-Oryx Series on Higher Education). 304p. 1987. 31.95 (*0-02-922740-2*, ACE-Oryx) Oryx Pr.

Nowles, William, jt. auth. see Bova, Joyce.

Nowlin, Barry, jt. ed. see Franklin, Tom.

Nowlin, Barry R., jt. ed. see Franklin, Tom.

Nowlin, James E. Nowlin - Stone Genealogy: Record of the Descendants of James Nowlin, Who Came to Pittsylvania County, Virginia, from Ireland about 1700; Also a Record of the Descendants of George Stone & of James Hoskin Stone Who Was born in Pittsylvania County in 1778. (Illus.). 548p. 1993. reprint ed. lib. bdg. 92.00 (*0-8328-3726-1*); reprint ed. pap. 82.00 (*0-8328-3727-X*) Higginson Bk Co.

Nowlin, James E & Blackburn, J. Vernon. Humanism & Environmentalism: Philosophical Perspectives in Counseling. LC 93-44078. (American University Studies: Language: Ser. XIV, Vol. 24). 1994. write for info. (*0-8204-1109-4*) P Lang Pubs.

Nowlin, Jerry L. Construction Financing to Build Your Own Home. LC 90-92261. 70p. (Orig.). 1990. pap. 19.95 (*0-9628643-0-7*) J L Nowlin.

Nowlin, Susan & Sterling, Mary E. Think & Do Bulletin Boards. (Illus.). 96p. (J). (gr. k-4). 1988. student ed 10.95 (*1-55734-063-3*) Tchr Create Mat.

Nowlin, Susan S. Fall Time Savers. (Illus.). 48p. (J). (gr. k-6). 1989. student ed 6.95 (*1-55734-123-0*) Tchr Create Mat.

— Holiday Crossword Puzzles. (Illus.). 48p. (J). (gr. 2-5). 1988. student ed 6.95 (*1-55734-366-7*) Tchr Create Mat.

— Spring Time Savers. (Illus.). 48p. (J). (gr. k-6). 1989. student ed 6.95 (*1-55734-125-7*) Tchr Create Mat.

— Winter Time Savers. (Illus.). 48p. (J). (gr. k-6). 1989. student ed 6.95 (*1-55734-124-9*) Tchr Create Mat.

— Year-Round Open Worksheets. (Illus.). 48p. (J). (gr. k-6). 1989. student ed 6.95 (*1-55734-126-5*) Tchr Create Mat.

Nowlin, Susan S., jt. auth. see Sterling, Mary E.

Nowlin, William F. Negro in American National Politics. LC 71-173802. reprint ed. 20.00 (*0-404-00204-8*) AMS Pr.

Nowlin, William G., Jr., ed. see Berkman, Alexander.

Nowlin, William G., Jr., ed. see Maximoff, Gregory P.

Nowlis, Elizabeth A., jt. auth. see Ellis, Albert.

Nowlis, Vincent. Companionship Preference & Dominance in the Social Interaction of Young Chimpanzees. (Comparative Psychology Monographs). 1941. pap. 15.00 (*0-527-24920-3*) Periodicals Srv.

Nown, Sylvana. Baby Names & Star Signs. (Family Matters Ser.). (Illus.). 96p. (Orig.). 1990. pap. 4.95 (*0-7063-6801-0*, Pub. by Ward Lock UK) Sterling.

Nownes, Laura. The Best of the Classic Quilt Series. LC 93-7624. 100p. 1993. pap. 21.95 (*0-913327-42-5*) Quilt Digest Pr.

— Grandmother's Flower Garden. (Classic Quilt Ser.). (Illus.). 20p. (Orig.). 1990. pap. text ed. 6.95 (*0-8442-2614-9*) Quilt Digest Pr.

— Log Cabin. (Classic Quilt Ser.). (Illus.). 20p. (Orig.). 1990. pap. 6.95 (*0-8442-2612-2*) Quilt Digest Pr.

— Star of Bethlehem. (Classic Quilt Ser.). (Illus.). 20p. (Orig.). 1990. pap. text ed. 6.95 (*0-8442-2613-0*) Quilt Digest Pr.

Nownes, Laura, jt. auth. see McClun, Diana.

Nowosad, Frank. Ciccimarra: A Biography. LC 88-31037. (Illus.). 253p. 1988. 24.95 (*0-940537-04-4*) Fuller Tech.

Nowotny, A. Basic Exercises in Immunochemistry: A Laboratory Manual. 2nd ed. LC 79-14029. (Illus.). 1979. pap. 39.00 (*0-387-09453-9*) Spr-Verlag.

Nowotny, A., et al, eds. Cellular & Molecular Aspects of Endotoxin Reactions: Proceedings of the 1st Congress of the International Endotoxin Society, San Diego, CA, 9-12 May, 1990. (International Congress Series, No. 923: Endotoxin Research Ser.: Vol. 1). 566p. 1990. 231.25 (*0-444-81365-9*, Excerpta Medica) Elsevier.

Nowotny, Alois, ed. Beneficial Effects of Endotoxins. LC 83-2256. 596p. 1983. 125.00 (*0-306-41147-4*, Plenum Pr) Plenum.

— Biomembranes Vol. 11: Pathological Membranes. LC 82-22343. 494p. 1983. 110.00 (*0-306-41065-6*, Plenum Pr) Plenum.

Nowotny, Franz A., jt. ed. see Jones, Larry W.

Nowotny, Helga & Rose, Hilary, eds. Countermovements in the Sciences. (Sociology of the Sciences Yearbook Ser.: No. 3). 1979. lib. bdg. 70.00 (*90-277-0971-8*); pap. text ed. 36.50 (*90-277-0972-6*) Kluwer Ac.

Nowotny, Helga, jt. ed. see Mendelsohn, Everett I.

Nowotny, J., ed. Diffusion in Solids & High Temperature Oxidations of Metals. 446p. 1992. text ed. 146.00 (*0-87849-626-2*, Pub. by Trans Tech GW) LPS Dist Ctr.

— Electronic Ceramic Materials. 568p. 1992. text ed. 146.00 (*0-87849-627-0*, Pub. by Trans Tech GW) LPS Dist Ctr.

— Interface Segregation & Related Processes in Materials. 460p. 1991. text ed. 168.00 (*0-87849-620-3*, Pub. by Trans Tech GW) LPS Dist Ctr.

— Surface & Near-Surface Chemistry of Oxide Materials. (Materials Science Monographs: Vol. 47). 714p. 1988. 192.50 (*0-444-42954-9*, North Holland) Elsevier.

Nowotny, J. & Weppner, W., eds. Non-Stoichiometric Compounds. (C). 1989. lib. bdg. 190.00 (*0-7923-0225-7*) Kluwer Ac.

Nowotny, J., jt. ed. see Dufour, L. C.

***Nowotny, Janusz & International Workshop on Interfaces of Ceramic Materials Staff, eds.** Science of Ceramic Interfaces II. LC 94-43582. (Materials Science Monographs: Vol. 81). 1995. 234.50 (*0-444-81666-6*) Elsevier.

Nowotny, Karl. Messages from a Doctor in the Fourth Dimension. 128p. (C). 1990. 50.00 (*0-7212-0895-9*, Pub. by Regency Press) St Mut.

Nowotny, Kenneth & Smith, David B., eds. Public Utility Regulation. (C). 1989. lib. bdg. 67.00 (*0-7923-9019-9*) Kluwer Ac.

Nowottny, H., jt. auth. see Arutyunyan, N.

Nowottny, Winifred. The Language Poets Use. 2nd ed. 225p. (C). 1965. pap. 14.95 (*0-485-12009-7*, Pub. by Athlone Pr UK) Humanities.

Nowra, Louis. The Golden Age. 105p. (Orig.). 1990. pap. 4.95 (*0-87129-015-4*, G49) Dramatic Pub.

Nowshadi, Farshad. Managing NetWare. (Data Communications & Networks Ser.). 657p. 1993. pap. 43.25 (*0-201-63194-6*) Addison-Wesley.

Nowzad, Bahram. The IMF & Its Critics. LC 82-958. (Essays in International Finance Ser.: No. 146). 34p. reprint ed. pap. 25.00 (*0-317-30396-1*, 2024749) Bks Demand.

***Noy, David.** Jewish Inscriptions of Western Europe, The City of Rome, Vol. 2. 620p. (C). 1995. 125.00 (*0-521-44202-8*) Cambridge U Pr.

— Jewish Inscriptions of Western Europe, Vol. 1: Italy (Excluding the City of Rome), Spain & Gaul. (Illus.). 407p. (C). 1993. 99.95 (*0-521-44201-X*) Cambridge U Pr.

Noy, David, jt. ed. see Horbury, William A.

Noy, Dov. Studies in Jewish Folklore. 1981. 25.00 (*0-87068-802-2*) Ktav.

Noy, William. The Principal Grounds & Maxims with an Analysis of the Laws of England. 3rd ed. xxviii, 219p. 1980. reprint ed. lib. bdg. 25.00 (*0-8377-0906-7*) Rothman.

Noya, Juan E. Las Palmas Ya No Son Verdes: Analisis y Testimonios de la Tragedia Cubana. LC 85-80134. (Coleccion Cuba y Sus Jueces Ser.). (Illus.). 93p. (Orig.). (SPA.). 1985. pap. 9.95 (*0-89729-368-1*) Ediciones.

Noyan, I. C. & Cohen, J. B. Residual Stress. (Materials Research & Engineering Ser.). (Illus.). 300p. 1987. 79.00 (*0-387-96378-2*) Spr-Verlag.

***Noyce, Gaylord.** Church Meetings That Work. 1995. 9.95 (*1-56699-132-3*, AL153) Alban Inst.

— Twigs: The Absorbing World of Church Education. 1991. pap. 9.50 (*1-877871-28-1*, 4228) Ed Ministries.

Noyce, Ruth M. & Christie, James F. Integrating Reading & Writing Instruction in Grades K-8. 384p. 1989. pap. text ed. 33.00 (*0-205-11815-1*, H18153) Allyn.

N

Noye, B. J. Computational Techniques for Differential Equations. (Mathematical Studies: Vol. 83). 1984. pap. 115.50 (0-444-86783-X, I-446-83, North Holland) Elsevier.

— Computational Techniques for Differential Equations. (North-Holland Mathematical Studies: Vol. 83). 1991. 134.50 (0-685-50935-4) Elsevier.

Noye, B. J., jt. ed. see Brebbia, C. A.

Noye, B. J., jt. ed. see Hogarth, W. L.

***Noye, Dominique.** Dictionnaire Foulfoulde-Francais. 1989. 150.00 (0-7859-7925-5, 2-7053-0484-3) Fr & Eur.

Noye, J. Numerical Solutions of Partial Differential Questions. 648p. 1982. 113.00 (0-444-86356-7, North Holland) Elsevier.

Noye, J., ed. Numerical Modelling: Applications to Marine Systems. 296p. 1987. 73.25 (0-317-67229-0) Elsevier.

Noye, J. & Fletcher, C. A., eds. Computational Techniques & Applications, CTAC - '87: Proceedings of the 1987 International Conference, Sydney, Australia, 24-27 Aug., 1987. 700p. 1988. 179.50 (0-444-70400-0, North Holland) Elsevier.

Noye, J. & May, R., eds. Computational Techniques & Applications CTAC-85: Proceedings of the Conference, University of Melbourne, Australia, August 25-28, 1985. 810p. 1986. 187.25 (0-444-87995-1) Elsevier.

Noyelle, Thierry, ed. Skills, Wages, & Productivity in Service Sector. 244p. (C). 1990. pap. text ed. 66.50 (0-8133-1078-4) Westview.

Noyelle, Thierry J. New Technologies & Services: Impacts on Cities & Jobs. (Urban Studies Monograph Ser.: No. 5). 55p. (Orig.). 1986. pap. text ed. 6.00 (0-913749-03-6) U MD Urban Stud.

***Noyer, Alain-Pierre.** Dictionnaire des Chanteurs Francophones de 1900 a nos Jours. 210p. (FRE.). 1989. pap. 59.95 (0-7859-8082-2, 2853192091) Fr & Eur.

Noyes, Alexander D. Forty Years of American Finance. Bruchey, Stuart, ed. LC 80-1163. (Rise of Commercial Banking Ser.). 1981. reprint ed. lib. bdg. 41.95 (0-405-13672-2) Ayer.

Noyes, Alfred. The Highwayman. (Illus.). 32p. (J). 1987. pap. 7.50 (0-19-272133-X) OUP.

— Highwayman. (Illus.). 28p. (J). (ps-3). 1990. 14.95 (0-15-234340-7) HarBrace.

— The Last Voyage: Book Three of the Torch-Bearers. LC 70-167477. (Granger Index Reprint Ser.). 1977. reprint ed. 18.95 (0-8369-6282-6) Ayer.

— Opalescent Parrot: Essays. (Essay Index Reprint Ser.). 1977. 20.95 (0-8369-0748-5) Ayer.

— Pageant of Letters. LC 68-22935. (Essay Index Reprint Ser.). 1977. reprint ed. 23.95 (0-8369-0749-3) Ayer.

— Watchers of the Sky. 1988. reprint ed. lib. bdg. 59.00 (0-7812-0390-2) Rprt Serv.

— Watchers of the Sky. LC 72-131790. 1971. reprint ed. 29.00 (0-403-00677-5) Scholarly.

— William Morris. LC 70-173176. 1972. reprint ed. 17.95 (0-405-08822-1, Pub. by Blom Pubns UK) Ayer.

— William Morris. LC 72-39201. (Select Bibliographies Reprint Ser.). 1977. reprint ed. 15.95 (0-8369-6803-4) Ayer.

Noyes, Alice D. Metallak, His Legacy. Jordan Associates Staff, ed. & illus. by. 266p. 1988. 18.95 (0-685-25278-7) A D Noyes.

Noyes, Alva. Story of Ajax. LC 67-6837. (Studies in European Literature: No. 56). (C). 1970. lib. bdg. 60.95 (0-8383-1109-1) M S G Haskell Hse.

Noyes, C. P. Noyes-Gilman Ancestry; Being a Series of Sketches with a Chart of the Ancestry of Charles Phelps Noyes & Emily H. (Gilman) Noyes, His Wife. (Illus.). 478p. 1989. reprint ed. lib. bdg. 80.00 (0-8328-0908-X); reprint ed. pap. 72.00 (0-8328-0909-8) Higginson Bk Co.

Noyes, Charlene, jt. auth. see Mellon, Steve.

Noyes, Claudia M., jt. auth. see Lundblad, Roger L.

Noyes, Diane D. & Mellody, Peggy. Beauty & Cancer: A Woman's Guide to Looking Great While Experiencing the Side Effects of Cancer Therapy. LC 88-71039. (Illus.). 200p. (Orig.). 1988. pap. 12.95 (0-929482-01-8) AC Press.

— Beauty & Cancer: Looking & Feeling Your Best. LC 92-14254. (Illus.). 192p. 1992. pap. 12.95 (0-87833-809-8) Taylor Pub.

Noyes, Dorothy. Uses of Tradition: Arts of Italian Americans in Philadelphia. (Illus.). 80p. (Orig.). (C). 1989. pap. 16.95 (0-8122-1387-4) U of Pa Pr.

Noyes, E. The Story of Ferrara. (Mediaeval Towns Ser.: Vol. 2). 1974. reprint ed. pap. 50.00 (0-8115-0844-7) Periodicals Srv.

— The Story of Milan. (Mediaeval Towns Ser.: Vol. 20). 1974. reprint ed. 60.00 (0-8115-0862-5) Periodicals Srv.

Noyes, Edward S., ed. Readings in the Modern Essay. LC 70-121494. (Essay Index Reprint Ser.). 1977. 36.95 (0-8369-2008-2) Ayer.

Noyes, Edward S., ed. see Smollett, Tobias G.

Noyes, Eliot F. Organic Design in Home Furnishings. LC 70-86424. (Museum of Modern Art Publications in Reprint). (Illus.). 1969. reprint ed. 10.95 (0-405-01540-2) Ayer.

Noyes, Florence, tr. see Krasinski, Zygmunt.

Noyes, Frederick B. Noyes' Oral Histology & Embryology. 7th rev. ed. Schour, Isaac, ed. LC 53-9573. 448p. reprint ed. pap. 127.70 (0-317-29248-X, 2055442) Bks Demand.

Noyes, George R., tr. see Asch, Shalom.

Noyes, George R., ed. see Krasinski, Zygmunt.

Noyes, George R., ed. see Ostrovsky, Alexander.

Noyes, George R., ed. see Slowacki, Juliusz.

Noyes, George R., tr. see Zielinski, Thaddeus.

Noyes, George W., ed. Religious Experience of John Humphrey Noyes. 1923. 39.95x (0-8156-8060-0) Syracuse U Pr.

Noyes, George W., ed. see Noyes, John H.

Noyes, Gertrude E., jt. auth. see Starnes, De Witt T.

Noyes, Harriette E. Records of Hampstead, New Hampshire. 60p. 1984. pap. 6.50 (0-912606-23-1) Hunterdon Hse.

Noyes, Henry. China Born: Adventures of a Maverick Bookman. LC 89-60880. 224p. (Orig.). 1989. reprint ed. 19.95 (0-8351-2198-4) China Bks.

— Hand over Fist. LC 80-51041. 322p. 1980. 25.00 (0-89608-026-9); pap. 6.00 (0-89608-025-0) South End Pr.

— Valley of the Sun: Selected Poems. 117p. (Orig.). 1993. pap. 9.95 (0-915117-13-4) New Earth Pubns.

Noyes, James H., jt. ed. see Ahrari, Mohammed E.

Noyes, James L. Artificial Intelligence with Common LISP: Fundamentals of Symbolic & Numeric Processing. 542p. (C). 1992. text ed. write for info. (0-669-19473-5); Instr.'s guide. teacher ed write for info. (0-669-19474-3); Instr.'s diskette 5-1/2". write for info. (0-669-32648-8); Instr.'s diskette 3-1/2". write for info. (0-669-28244-8) Heath.

Noyes, Janet M., jt. ed. see Baber, Christopher.

Noyes, John H. Berean. LC 74-83431. (Religion in America, Ser. 1). 1974. reprint ed. 35.95 (0-405-00256-4) Ayer.

— Home Talks, Vol. 1. Barron, Alfred & Miller, George N., eds. LC 72-2974. reprint ed. 57.50 (0-404-10738-9) AMS Pr.

— Male Continence. 1975. 250.00 (0-87968-231-0) Gordon Pr.

— Male Continence, 4 vols. in 1. Incl. Dixon & His Copyists, a Criticism of the Accounts of the Oneida Community in "New America," "Spiritual Wives," & Kindred Publications. 2nd ed. LC 72-2975. (0-318-50644-0); Essay on Scientific Propagation. LC 72-2975. (0-318-50645-9); Salvation from Sin, the End of Christian Faith. LC 72-2975. (0-318-50646-7); LC 72-2975. reprint ed. 37.50 (0-404-10739-7) AMS Pr.

— Mutual Criticism. 128p. 1975. reprint ed. pap. 9.95 (0-8156-2170-1) Syracuse U Pr.

— Religious Experience of John Humphrey Noyes, Founder of the Oneida Community. Noyes, George W., ed. (Select Bibliographies Reprint Ser.). 1977. reprint ed. 29.95 (0-8369-5750-4) Ayer.

— Salvation from Sin. 1972. 59.95 (0-8490-0990-1) Gordon Pr.

— The Way of Holiness. LC 75-337. (Radical Tradition in America Ser.). 230p. 1975. reprint ed. 21.50 (0-88355-240-X) Hyperion Conn.

Noyes, John S. & Hayat, M. Oriental Mealybug Parasitoids of the Anagyrini. 560p. 1994. 117.00x (0-85198-895-4) CAB Intl.

Noyes, Katherine H., jt. auth. see Ellis, Susan J.

Noyes, Pierrepont. My Father's House. 312p. 1993. reprint ed. lib. bdg. 89.00 (0-7812-5312-8) Rprt Serv.

Noyes, Pierrepont B. My Father's House: An Oneida Boyhood. (American Biography Ser.). 312p. 1991. reprint ed. lib. bdg. 79.00 (0-7812-8300-0) Rprt Serv.

Noyes, R., Jr., et al, eds. Classification, Etiological Factors & Associated Disturbances. (Handbook of Anxiety Ser.: No. 2). 570p. 1989. 288.75 (0-444-90489-1, Excerpta Medica) Elsevier.

— The Treatment of Anxiety. (Handbook of Anxiety Ser.: Vol. 4). 486p. 1990. 275.75 (0-444-81261-X) Elsevier.

Noyes, Ralph. The Crop Circle Enigma: A Range of Viewpoints from the Centre of Crop Circle Studies. (Illus.). 192p. 1995. 19.95 (0-946551-66-9, Pub. by Gateway Bks UK) Atrium Pubs.

Noyes, Richard, ed. Now the Synthesis. 247p. 1991. 30.00 (0-85683-124-7, Pub. by Shepheard-Walwyn Pubs UK) Schalkenbach.

— Now the Synthesis: Capitalism, Socialism & the New Social Contract. 247p. 1991. 32.00 (0-8419-1300-5) Holmes & Meier.

Noyes, Robert, ed. Handbook of Leak, Spill & Accidental Release Prevention Techniques. LC 92-5376. (Illus.). 487p. 1992. 76.00 (0-8155-1296-1) Noyes.

— Handbook of Pollution Control Processes. LC 91-27950. (Illus.). 758p. 1992. 127.00 (0-8155-1290-2) Noyes.

— Pollution Prevention Technology Handbook. LC 92-32508. (Illus.). 683p. 1993. 98.00 (0-8155-1311-9) Noyes.

— Unit Operations in Environmental Engineering. LC 94-1324. (Illus.). 498p. 1994. 76.00 (0-8155-1343-7) Noyes.

Noyes, Robert, jt. auth. see Leekley, Dorothy.

Noyes, Robert G. Ben Jonson on the English Stage, Sixteen Sixty to Seventeen Seventy-Six. LC 65-27916. (Illus.). 1972. 23.95 (0-405-08823-X, Pub. by Blom Pubns UK) Ayer.

— Ben Jonson on the English Stage, 1660-1776. (BCL1-PR English Literature Ser.). 351p. 1992. reprint ed. lib. bdg. 89.00 (0-7812-7258-0) Rprt Serv.

Noyes, Robert W. The Sun, Our Star. LC 82-11733. (Harvard Books on Astronomy). (Illus.). 271p. reprint ed. pap. 77.30 (0-7837-3861-7, 2043683) Bks Demand.

Noyes, Russell. William Wordsworth. (Twayne's English Authors Ser.). 184p. 1991. text ed. 21.95 (0-8057-7002-X, TEAS 118, Pub. by Royal Botanic Garden UK) Macmillan.

— Wordsworth & the Art of Landscape. LC 72-6864. (Studies in Wordsworth: No. 29). 1972. reprint ed. lib. bdg. 75.00 (0-8383-1660-3) M S G Haskell Hse.

Noyes, Russell, ed. English Romantic Poetry & Prose. 1956. 39.95 (0-19-501007-8) OUP.

Noyes, Stanley. Los Comanches: The Horse People, 1751-1845. (Illus.). 393p. 1994. pap. 19.95 (0-8263-1548-8) U of NM Pr.

— The Commander of Dead Leaves. (Poetry Ser.). 80p. (Orig.). 1985. pap. 6.00 (0-940510-10-3) Tooth of Time.

Noyes, William A. Advances in Photochemistry, Vol. 11: 1979. LC 63-13592. (Illus.). 538p. pap. 157.40 (0-8357-5176-7, 2056456) Bks Demand.

Noyle, Ken. What Time's the Midnight Buffet? 2nd ed. LC 81-82179. (Illus.). 72p. (Orig.). 1982. pap. 4.00 (0-940324-00-8) One Thousand Ways.

Noyle, Linda J. Pianists on Playing: Interviews with Twelve Concert Pianists. LC 86-29810. (Illus.). 187p. 1987. 20.00 (0-8108-1953-8) Scarecrow.

Noyori, Kimiharu, et al. Ophthalmic Laser Therapy. (Illus.). 289p. 1992. 170.00 (0-89640-199-5) Igaku-Shoin.

Noyori, Ryoji. Asymmetric Catalysis in Organic Synthesis. (Baker Lecture Ser.). 384p. 1994. text ed. 59.95 (0-471-57267-5) Wiley.

Noz, Marilyn E. & Kim, Y. S., eds. Special Relativity & Quantum Theory: A Collection of Papers on the Poincare Group. (C). 1988. lib. bdg. 157.50 (90-277-2799-6) Kluwer Ac.

Noz, Marilyn E., jt. auth. see Kim, Y. S.

Nozaka, Akiyuki. The Pornographers. Gallagher, Michael, tr. 312p. 1991. pap. 9.95 (0-8048-1378-7) C E Tuttle.

Nozaki, Akihiro & Anno, Mitsumasa. Anno's Hat Tricks. LC 84-18900. (Illus.). 44p. (J). (gr. 3 up). 1985. 15.95 (0-399-21212-4, Philomel Bks) Putnam Pub Group.

Nozaki, H., ed. Current Trends in Organic Synthesis: Proceedings of the Fourth International Conference on Organic Synthesis, Tokyo, Japan, August 22-27, 1982. LC 82-22445. (IUPAC Symposium Ser.). (Illus.). 442p. 1983. 185.00 (0-08-029217-8, Pub. by Pergamon Repr UK) Franklin.

Nozdrev, V. F. Applications of Ultrasonics to Molecular Physics. (Illus.). 542p. 1963. 232.00 (0-685-01944-6) Gordon & Breach.

Nozette, Stewart & Kuhn, Robert L., eds. Commercializing SDI Technologies. LC 87-18333. 256p. 1987. text ed. 59.95 (0-275-92332-0, C2332, Praeger Pubs) Greenwood.

Nozick, jt. auth. see Patt.

Nozick, M., ed. Miguel De Unamuno: The Agony of Belief. 1982. reprint ed. 39.50 (0-691-06498-9); reprint ed. pap. 13.95x (0-691-01366-7) Princeton U Pr.

Nozick, Martin, tr. see De Unamuno, Miguel.

Nozick, Martin, jt. ed. see Kerrigan, Anthony.

Nozick, Martin, jt. ed. see Patt, Beatrice.

Nozick, Robert. Anarchy, State & Utopia. LC 73-91081. 384p. 1977. pap. text ed. 18.00 (0-465-09720-0) Basic.

— The Examined Life: Philosophical Meditations. 1990. pap. 12.00 (0-671-72501-7, Touchstone Bks) S&S Trade.

— The Nature of Rationality. 232p. 1993. 22.95 (0-691-07424-0) Princeton U Pr.

— The Nature of Rationality. 1995. pap. 12.95 (0-691-02096-5) Princeton U Pr.

— The Normative Theory of Individual Choice. (Harvard Dissertations in Philosophy Ser.). 360p. 1990. reprint ed. 30.00 (0-8240-3207-1) Garland.

— Philosophical Explanations. LC 81-1369. 777p. 1981. 42.50 (0-674-66448-5) Belknap Pr.

— Philosophical Explanations. 777p. 1983. pap. text ed. 19.95 (0-674-66479-5) Belknap Pr.

Nozieres, Philippe, jt. auth. see Pines, David.

Nozik, Arthur J., ed. Photoeffects at Semiconductor-Electrolyte Interfaces. LC 80-27773. (Symposium Ser.: No. 146). 1981. 49.95 (0-8412-0604-X) Am Chemical.

Nozik, Robert, jt. auth. see Michelson, Joseph B.

Nozik, Robert A., jt. auth. see Smith, Ronald E.

Nozinski, Michael J. Outrage at Lincheng: China Enters the Twentieth Century. LC 89-80780. (Illus.). 243p. 1990. 19.95 (0-944435-07-6) Glenbridge Pub.

Nozoe, Tetsuo. Seventy Years in Organic Chemistry. Seeman, Jeffrey I., ed. LC 90-876. (Profiles, Pathways, & Dreams Ser.). (Illus.). 267p. 1990. 24.95 (0-8412-1769-6) Am Chemical.

***NPA Staff & ULI Staff.** The Dimensions of Parking. 3rd ed. 335p. 1993. pap. text ed. 34.95 (0-87420-744-4, D85) Urban Land.

***NPC (Randell) National Press Club Staff.** Speeches National Press Club, Vol. 1. 200p. 1995. 34.95 (0-7872-1005-6) Kendall-Hunt.

NPD Group Staff. Consumer Research Study on Book Purchasing, 1991-1992. (Illus.). 138p. 1993. pap. 150.00 (0-940016-40-0) Bk Indus Study.

NPR Staff. Sound Reporting: National Public Radio's Guide to Radio Journalism & Production. 352p. 1992. pap. text ed. 38.95 (0-8403-7202-7) Kendall-Hunt.

***NPS Staff.** Russian Bishop's House. (Illus.). 16p. 1995. pap. 2.95 (0-614-04305-0) Alaska Natural.

NPS Staff, ed. see Gilmore, Jackie.

NPS Staff, ed. see Hayden, Bill & Freillich, Jerry.

NPS Staff, ed. see Salts, Bobbi.

***N.R. Federation Staff, The.** Merchandising & Operating Results of Retail Stores in 1993. 69th ed. (Small Business Editions Ser.). 1994. pap. text ed. 100.00 (0-471-07999-5) Wiley.

NRA Staff. Who's Who Nepal. (C). 1992. 240.00 (0-7855-0220-3, Pub. by Ratna Pustak Bhandar) St Mut.

NREP Board Members Staff. Official Review Guide Book for National Registry of Environmental Manager's Examination. 515p. 1989. 49.95 (0-925760-29-3) SciTech Pubs.

Nrgaard, Ole, et al, eds. The European Community in World Politics. LC 93-5588. 1993. 49.00 (1-85567-147-6, Pub. by Pinter Pubs UK) St Martin.

NRHA Staff. Advance Course Hardware Retailing. 640p. 1992. 49.00 (0-8403-7658-8) Kendall-Hunt.

Nriagu, Jerome O. Biogeochemistry of Lead in the Environment, Vol. I, Pts. A & B: Topics in Environmental Health, Set. 1991. 177.25 (0-685-50936-2) Elsevier.

— Biogeochemistry of Mercury in the Environment. (Topics in Environmental Health Ser.: Vol. 3). 696p. 1980. 217.50 (0-444-80110-3) Elsevier.

— Cadmium in the Environment: Ecological Cycling, Pt. I. LC 79-25087. (Environmental Science & Technology A Wiley-Interscience Ser. of Texts & Monographs). 696p. 1980. 120.00 (0-471-06455-6, Wiley-Interscience) Krieger.

— Cadmium in the Environment: Health Effects, Pt. II. (Environmental Science & Technology Ser.). 920p. 1981. 158.00 (0-471-05884-X, Wiley-Interscience) Krieger.

— Copper in the Environment, 2 pts. Incl. Pt. 1. Ecological Cycling. 536p. 1980. reprint ed. 94.00 (0-471-04778-3); (Environmental Science & Technology Texts & Monographs Ser.). 1980. write for info. (0-318-56422-X, Wiley-Interscience) Krieger.

Nriagu, Jerome O., ed. Environmental Impacts of Smelters. LC 83-21761. (Advances in Environmental Science & Technology Ser.: 2-010). 608p. 1984. text ed. 172.00 (0-471-88043-4) Wiley.

— Gaseous Pollutants: Characterization & Cycling. (Environmental Science & Technology: A Wiley-Interscience Series of Texts & Monographs: No. 1121). 560p. 1992. text ed. 150.00 (0-471-54898-7) Wiley.

— Nickel in the Environment, Pt. 1. LC 80-16600. (Environmental Science & Technology Ser.). 848p. 1980. 140.00 (0-471-05885-8, Wiley-Interscience) Krieger.

Nriagu, Jerome O. & Lakshminarayana, J. S., eds. Aquatic Toxicology & Water Quality Management. LC 88-7282. (Advances in Environmental Science & Technology Ser.). 292p. 1989. text ed. 135.00 (0-471-61551-X) Wiley.

Nriagu, Jerome O. & Moore, P. B., eds. Phosphate Minerals. (Illus.). 470p. 1984. 154.00 (0-387-12757-7) Spr-Verlag.

Nriagu, Jerome O. & Nieboer, Evert, eds. Chromium in the Natural & Human Environments. LC 87-27303. (Advances in Environmental Science & Technology Ser.). 571p. 1988. text ed. 99.00 (0-471-85643-6) Wiley.

Nriagu, Jerome O. & Simmons, Milagros S., eds. Environmental Oxidants. (Advances in Environmental Science & Technology Ser.: Vol. 28). 666p. 1994. text ed. 89.95 (0-471-57928-9) Wiley.

— Food Contamination from Environmental Sources. (Environmental Science & Technology Ser.). 785p. 1990. text ed. 235.00 (0-471-50891-8) Wiley.

Nriagu, Jerome O. & Sprague, John B., eds. Cadmium in the Aquatic Environment. (Advances in Environmental Science & Technology Ser.). 272p. 1987. text ed. 115.00 (0-471-85884-6, Wiley-Interscience) Wiley.

Nriagu, Jerome O., jt. ed. see Nieboer, Evert.

NRMC Staff, jt. ed. see NEBSS Staff.

NRP Staff. AutoCAD, Release 12: The Professional Reference. 2nd ed. Hampe, Kurt et al, eds. LC 93-20218. 1100p. 1993. 42.95 (1-56205-059-1) New Riders Pub.

— Inside FoxPro 2.5 for DOS. 700p. 1993. disk 34.95 (1-56205-143-1) New Riders Pub.

— Three-D Studio Special Effects. 400p. 1994. 50.00 (1-56205-303-5) New Riders Pub.

NRP Staff & Schindler, Esther. New Riders Guide to Modems. LC 94-7720. 369p. 1994. pap. 24.95 (1-56205-302-7) New Riders Pub.

NRP Staff, et al. Inside AutoCAD Release 12. LC 92-19826. (Illus.). 1312p. (Orig.). 1992. pap. 40.00 (1-56205-055-9) New Riders Pub.

***N.S.A.I. Equity Committee Staff.** The Essential Songwriter's Contract Handbook. 120p. (Orig.). (C). 1994. pap. 12.95 (1-886092-00-1) Nashville Songwrit.

Nsamenang, A. Bame. Human Development in Cultural Context: A Third World Perspective. (Cross-Cultural Research & Methodology Ser.: Vol. 16). 320p. (C). 1992. text ed. 46.00 (0-8039-4636-8) Sage.

NSBA Council of School Attorneys Staff. Child Abuse: Legal Issues for Schools. 125p. (Orig.). 1994. pap. 25.00 (0-88364-184-4) Natl Sch Boards.

— Environmental Law: Fundamentals for Schools. (Orig.). 1995. pap. 25.00 (0-88364-194-1) Natl Sch Boards.

— Legal Guidelines for Curbing School Violence. 1995. pap. 25.00 (0-88364-195-X) Natl Sch Boards.

— Protect the Future of Your School District Client. 800p. 1995. pap. 200.00 (0-88364-191-7) Natl Sch Boards.

— Religion, Education & The U. S. Constitution. 140p. (Orig.). 1994. reprint ed. pap. 25.00 (0-88364-183-6) Natl Sch Boards.

— School Law in Review, 1994: 1994. 156p. (Orig.). 1994. pap. 35.00 (0-88364-182-8) Natl Sch Boards.

— School Law in Review 1995. (Orig.). 1995. pap. 28.00 (0-88364-193-3) Natl Sch Boards.

NSCRTA Staff. Iskra - Coursebook One. (C). 1989. text ed. 45.00 (0-7487-0525-2, Pub. by S Thornes Pubs UK) St Mut.

— Iskra - Coursebook Three. (C). 1989. text ed. 50.00 (0-7487-0527-9, Pub. by S Thornes Pubs UK) St Mut.

— Iskra - Coursebook Two. (C). 1989. text ed. 50.00 (0-7487-0526-0, Pub. by S Thornes Pubs UK) St Mut.

NSDAR Youghiogheny Glades Chapter Staff. Maryland's Garrett County Graves. LC 87-50355. (Illus.). 488p. 1987. 29.00 (0-9618240-0-X) N S D A R.

Nsekela, Amon J., ed. Southern Africa: Toward Economic Liberation. (Illus.). 294p. 1981. text ed. 48.00 (0-8476-4741-2) Rowman.

Nskela, Amon J., ed. Southern Africa: Toward Economic Liberation. 274p. 1981. 35.00 (0-86036-154-3) St Mut.

Nsouli, Saleh M., jt. auth. see Zulu, Justin B.

Nsouli, Saleh M., et al. The Path to Convertibility & Growth: The Tunisian Experience. LC 93-45034. (Occasional Paper Ser.: No. 109). 1993. pap. 15.00 (1-55775-357-1) Intl Monetary.

— Resilience & Growth Through Sustained Adjustment: The Moroccan Experience. LC 94-44348. (Occasional Paper Ser.: No. 117). 1995. pap. 15.00 (1-55775-422-5) Intl Monetary.

***NSPS Construction Standards Survey Committee Staff.** Manual on Construction Layout. 40p. 1993. pap. 20.00 (0-614-06108-3, S309) Am Congrs Survey.

***NSSA (Roy) Staff.** Local Leadership for Science Education Reform. 160p. 1994. per., pap. text ed. 13.95 (0-8403-9947-2) Kendall-Hunt.

An Asterisk (*) at the beginning of an entry indicates that the title is appearing in BIP for the first time.

Ntalaja, Nzongola. Class Struggles & National Liberation in Africa. LC 82-81279. 175p. (Orig.). (C). 1982. pap. 6.95 (0-943324-00-9) Omenana.
— The Development of a Marxist Perspective in Africa. Omenana Collective Staff, ed. (Etudes et Analyses Marxistes en Afrique Ser.). 24p. (Orig.). (C). reprint ed. pap. 3.00 (0-686-88663-1) Omenana.
Ntantu, I., jt. auth. see McCoy, R. A.
Ntara, Samuel Y. Headman's Enterprise: An Unexpected Page in Central African History. Young, T. Cullen, tr. & pref. by. (B. E. Ser.: No. 102). 1949. 21.00 (0-8115-3034-5) Periodicals Srv.
— Man of Africa. Young, T. Cullen, tr. (B. E. Ser.: No. 101). 1934. 18.00 (0-8115-3033-7) Periodicals Srv.
NTC Publishing Staff. BBC French Phrase Book. 1994. pap. 5.95 (0-8442-9224-9) NTC Pub Grp.
— BBC German Phrase Book. 1994. pap. 5.95 (0-8442-9225-7) NTC Pub Grp.
— BBC Italian Phrase Book. 1994. pap. 5.95 (0-8442-9227-3) NTC Pub Grp.
— BBC Spanish Phrase Book. 1994. pap. 5.95 (0-8442-9234-6) NTC Pub Grp.
NTIAC Staff. NDE Applications of Magnetic Leakage Field Methods: A State of the Art Survey. 49p. 1980. 68.25 (0-318-21484-9, 443) Am Soc Nondestructive.
Ntiri, Daphne W. Blossoming Trends. (C). 1994. pap. 7.00 (0-911557-06-7) Bedford Publishers.
Ntiri, Daphne W., ed. Consonance & Continuity in Poetry: Detroit Black Writers. 146p. (Orig.). 1988. pap. text ed. 7.00 (0-911557-01-6) Bedford Publishers.
— One Is Not a Woman, One Becomes: The African Woman in a Transitional Society. (Illus.). 143p. (Orig.). 1988. reprint ed. pap. text ed. 10.75 (0-911557-02-4) Bedford Publishers.
Ntumy, Michael A., ed. South Pacific Islands Legal Systems. LC 92-41464. 720p. (C). 1993. text ed. 100.00 (0-8248-1438-X) UH Pr.
Nu, Roland. Early Japanese Painted Crockery & Sculpture. (Illus.). 200p. (JPN.). 1993. reprint ed. pap. 50.00 (0-87556-818-1) Saifer.
NuAge Survival Publishing Editors. How to Prepare for an Earthquake Made Easy: A Planning Workbook for Personal Earthquake Preparedness for California Residents & Visitors. (Illus.). 64p. 1989. 10.00 (0-9622924-0-0) NuAge Survival.
Nuala Ni Dhomhnaill. The Astrakhan Cloak. Muldoon, Paul, tr. LC 92-51047. 112p. 1993. 15.95 (0-916390-55-1); pap. 10.95 (0-916390-54-3) Wake Forest.
— Pharaoh's Daughter. rev. ed. LC 92-51046. 160p. 1993. pap. 10.95 (0-916390-53-5) Wake Forest.
Nualart, D., jt. auth. see Carmona, R. A.
***Nualart, David.** The Malliavin Calculus & Related Topics. LC 94-48195. (Probability & Its Applications Ser.). 1995. write for info. (0-387-94432-X) Spr-Verlag.
Nualart, David & Sole, Marta S., eds. Barcelona Seminar on Stochastic Analysis: St. Feliu de Guixols, 1991. LC 92-45002. (Progress in Probability Ser.: Vol. 32). x, 234p. 1993. 69.00 (0-8176-2833-9) Birkhauser.
***Nuallain, Sean O.** The Search for Mind: A New Foundation for Cognitive Science. (Computational Science Ser.). 1995. write for info. (1-56750-138-9); pap. write for info. (1-56750-139-7) Ablex Pub.
Nuba, Hannah, et al, eds. Resources for Early Childhood: A Handbook. LC 93-5044. (Reference Library of Social Science: Vol. 680). 576p. 1994. 80.00 (0-8240-7395-9, SS680) Garland.
Nuba-Scheffler, Hannah, et al. Infancy: A Guide to Research & Resources. 182p. (C). 1988. reprint ed. pap. text ed. 15.95 (0-8077-2921-3) Tchrs Coll.
NuBer, H. G., jt. ed. see Winter, H.
Nucci, Larry P., ed. Moral Development & Character Education: A Dialogue. LC 88-63921. (National Society for the Study of Education Publication Ser.). 200p. 1989. 27.50 (0-8211-1308-9); text ed. write for info. (0-685-26826-8) McCutchan.
Nucci, N. L., et al, eds. Developments in River Basin Management: Proceedings of an IAWPRC Conference Held in Sao Paulo, Brazil, 13-15 August, 1986. LC 82-645900. (Water Science & Technology Ser.: Vol. 19). (Illus.). 280p. 1988. pap. 77.00 (0-08-035593-5, Pergamon Pr) Elsevier.
Nuccio, Richard. What's Wrong, Who's Right in Central America: A Citizen's Guide. LC 85-31093. (Illus.). 154p. reprint ed. pap. 43.90 (0-318-39769-2, 2033168) Bks Demand.
Nuccio, Richard A. What's Wrong, Who's Right in Central America? 2nd ed. 170p. 1989. pap. 14.95 (0-8419-1177-0) Holmes & Meier.
Nuccitelli, R., et al, eds. Mechanisms of Egg Activation. (Bodega Marine Laboratory Marine Science Ser.). (Illus.). 322p. 1989. 85.00 (0-306-43245-5, Plenum Pr) Plenum.
Nuccitelli, Richard, ed. Methods in Cell Biology, Vol. 40: A Practical Guide to the Study of CA2Plus in Living Cells. (Illus.). 368p. 1994. text ed. 95.00 (0-12-564141-9); spiral bd. 45.00 (0-12-522810-4) Acad Pr.
NUCEA Staff & National University Continuing Education Association Staff. The Foundation of American Distance Education: A Century of Collegiate Correspondence Study. 336p. 1991. pap. text ed. 24.95 (0-8403-7101-2) Kendall-Hunt.
Nucho, Leslie S., ed. Education in the Arab World, Vol. 1. 737p. (Orig.). 1993. pap. 50.00 (0-913957-12-7) AMIDEAST.
Nucho, Leslie S., ed. see Amideast Publications Staff.
Nucius, Nicander. Second Book of the Travels of Nicander Nucius, of Corcyra. Cramer, J. A., tr. (Camden Society, London. Publications, First Ser.: No. 17). reprint ed. 38.50 (0-404-50117-6) AMS Pr.
Nuckolls, B. F. Goodykoontz Family: Extract "Pioneer Settlers of Grayson County, Virginia" 16p. 1994. reprint ed. pap. 5.00 (0-8328-4170-6) Higginson Bk Co.
— Hale Family: Extract "Pioneer Settlers of Grayson County, Virginia" 36p. 1994. reprint ed. pap. 7.00 (0-8328-4169-2) Higginson Bk Co.
— Nuckolls Family: Extract "Pioneer Settlers of Grayson County, Virginia" 32p. 1994. reprint ed. pap. 6.50 (0-8328-4168-4) Higginson Bk Co.
Nuckolls, Benjamin F. Pioneer Settlers of Greyson County, Virginia: With a New Index. 219p. 1994. reprint ed. pap. 23.00 (0-685-75101-5, 4215) Clearfield Co.
Nuckolls, Charles W., ed. Siblings in South Asia: Brothers & Sisters in Cultural Context. LC 92-30076. (Culture & Human Development Ser.). 200p. 1993. lib. bdg. 25.00 (0-89862-146-1) Guilford Pr.
Nuckolls, James L. Interior Lighting for Environmental Designers. 2nd ed. LC 83-1382. 407p. 1983. text ed. 62.95 (0-471-87381-0) Wiley.
Nuckolls, James L., jt. auth. see Gordon, Gary.
***Nuckolls, Janis B.** Sounds Like Life: Sound-Symbolic Grammar, Performance, & Cognition in Pastaza Quechua. (Oxford Studies in Anthropological Linguistics). (Illus.). 352p. 1995. 65.00 (0-19-508985-5) OUP.
Nuckols, C. C. Children in Pain: Helping Chronically Addicted Adolescents. 224p. 1992. pap. 12.95 (0-8306-3768-0, 4096, TAB-Human Servs Inst) TAB Bks.
— Goodbye to the White Lady: Cocaine Addiction & Recovery. 1992. 17.95 (0-07-047455-9); pap. 7.95 (0-07-047456-7) McGraw.
— Goodbye to the White Lady: Cocaine Addiction & Recovery. 154p. 1992. 17.95 (0-8306-3388-X); pap. 7.95 (0-8306-3385-5) TAB Bks.
Nuckols, C. C., et al. Helping Chronically Addictted Adolescents: Problems, Perspectives & Strategies for Recovery. 1993. pap. text ed. 12.95 (0-07-047462-1) McGraw.
Nuckols, Cardwell C. Cocaine: From Dependency to Recovery. 2nd ed. Joiner, Lee M., ed. LC 89-5172. 221p. (Orig.). 1989. pap. 12.95 (0-8306-9203-7, B3409) Sulzburger & Graham Pub.
Nuckols, Marshall L., ed. see American Society of Mechanical Engineers Staff.
Nuclear Instruments & Detectors Committee of the IEEE Nuclear & Plasma Sciences Society, ed. IEEE Standard 960-1989: Revision of IEEE Standard 960-1986 with IEEE Standard 1177-1989. (IEEE Standard Fastbus Modular High-Speed Data Acquisition & Control System & IEEE Fastbus Standard Routines Ser.). (Illus.). 352p. (Orig.). 1990. pap. 54.00 (1-55937-026-2) IEEE Standards.
Nudds, J. R., ed. Directory of British Geological Museums. (Geological Society Misc. Paper Ser.: No. 18). (Illus.). vii, 142p. 1994. 25.00 (1-897799-08-X, Pub. by Geol Soc Pub Hse UK) AAPG.
Nudel, Dov. B., ed. Pediatric Sports Medicine. 442p. 1989. 55.00 (0-89335-305-1) PMA Pub Corp.
Nudel, Ida. A Hand in the Darkness: The Autobiography of a Refusenik. 1990. 22.95 (0-446-51445-4) Warner Bks.
— A Hand in the Darkness: The Autobiography of a Refusenik. Hoffman, Stefani, tr. 336p. 1991. reprint ed. pap. 13.99 (0-446-39325-8) Warner Bks.
Nudell, Mayer & Antokol, Norm. No One a Neutral: Political Hostage-Taking in the Modern World. LC 90-60358. 256p. 1990. pap. 12.95 (0-939427-78-8, 09052); boxed 19.95 (0-939427-59-1, 09051) Alpha Pubns OH.
Nudel'Man, A. A., jt. auth. see Krein, M. G.
Nudelman, Abraham. The Chemistry of Optically Active Sulphur Compounds. 262p. 1984. text ed. 145.00 (0-677-16390-8) Gordon & Breach.
Nudelman, Barry, et al. Federal Taxation of Estates, Gifts, & Trusts. 4th ed. 790p. 1988. text ed. 116.00 (0-8318-0497-1, B497) Am Law Inst.
Nudelman, Dorothea & Willingham, David, eds. Healing the Blues: Drug-Free Psychotherapy of Depression. LC 94-12688. 235p. 1994. 22.00 (0-940168-31-6) Boxwood.
Nudelman, Edward D. Jessie Wilcox Smith: A Bibliography. LC 87-31576. (Illus.). 180p. 1987. 85.00 (0-88289-696-2); 160.00 (0-88289-697-0) Pelican.
— Jessie Wilcox Smith: American Illustrator. LC 89-48273. 144p. 1990. 39.95 (0-88289-786-1) Pelican.
Nudelman, Edward D., frwd. The Jessie Wilcox Smith Mother Goose. LC 90-19903. (Illus.). 192p. (J). (gr. k up). 1991. 24.95 (0-88289-844-2); 75.00 (0-88289-830-2) Pelican.
Nudelman, Jerrold, jt. auth. see Troyka, Lynn Q.
Nudson, Teny. All Through the Night. (Illus.). 36p. (Orig.). 1990. pap. 13.95 (0-935133-38-0) CKE Pubns.
— Dimensions of Christmas. (Illus.). 36p. 1989. pap. 13.95 (0-935133-33-X) CKE Pubns.
Nudson, Teny, jt. auth. see Kyle, Carolyn.
Nuebacher, G. The Frog Prince. (Traditional Fairy Tales Ser.). (Illus.). 32p. (J). (gr. 1-4). 1989. 6.95 (0-88625-216-4) Durkin Hayes Pub.
— Pinocchio. (Traditional Fairy Tales Ser.). (Illus.). 32p. (J). (gr. 1-4). 1989. 6.95 (0-88625-218-0) Durkin Hayes Pub.
— Sleeping Beauty. (Traditional Fairy Tales Ser.). (Illus.). 32p. (J). (gr. 1-4). 1989. 6.95 (0-88625-220-2) Durkin Hayes Pub.
Nuechterlein, Anne M. Families of Alcoholics: A Guide for Healing & Recovery. LC 92-19156. 160p. (Orig.). 1992. pap. 11.99 (0-8066-2615-1, 9-2615, Augsburg) Augsburg Fortress.
Nuechterlein, Donald. America Recommitted: United States National Interests in a Restructured World. LC 91-163. 280p. 1991. 30.00 (0-8131-1746-1) U Pr of Ky.
Nuechterlein, Donald E. America Overcommitted: United States National Interests in the 1980s. LC 84-17409. 248p. 1985. 18.00 (0-8131-1529-9) U Pr of Ky.
— United States National Interests in a Changing World. LC 73-77255. 215p. reprint ed. pap. 61.30 (0-8357-8595-5, 2034969) Bks Demand.
Nuelle, Helen. Surrender to Love. large type ed. LC 93-13682. 1993. 19.95 (0-7927-1688-4, Curley Lrg Print); pap. 17.95 (0-7927-1687-6, Curley Lrg Print) Chivers N Amer.
Nuelle, Helen S. Land Where Our Fathers Died. large type ed. (Linford Mystery Library). 384p. 1992. pap. 14.95 (0-7089-7230-6, Trailtree Bookshop) Ulverscroft.
Nueman, Donald, jt. auth. see Mayesky, Mary E.
Nueman, Mark & Payne, Michael, eds. Self, Sign, & Symbol. LC 86-47606. (Bucknell Review Ser.: Vol. 30, No. 2). 184p. 1987. 22.00 (0-8387-5108-3) Bucknell U Pr.
Nueno, Pedro. Corporate Turnaround: A Practical Guide to Business Survival. 176p. 1993. text ed. 32.95 (0-89397-398-X) Nichols Pub.
Nuerge, W., Jr. Exploiting Single Ticket Discounts. (Illus.). 128p. 1990. student ed 42.50 (1-883555-17-5) Enhance Syst.
— Media Advertising Tips to Turn Around Slow Ticket Sales. (Illus.). 76p. 1992. student ed 28.50 (1-883555-19-1) Enhance Syst.
— Membership Marketing Evaluation & Guide. (Illus.). 168p. 1993. student ed 38.50 (1-883555-14-0) Enhance Syst.
— Organizing Data to Sell Tickets. (Illus.). 92p. 1989. student ed 37.50 (1-883555-18-3) Enhance Syst.
— Overcoming Geographic Barriers to Sell Tickets. 124p. 1989. student ed 39.50 (1-883555-16-7) Enhance Syst.
Nuermberger, Ruth K. Free Produce Movement. LC 73-110135. (Duke University. Trinity College Historical Society. Historical Papers: No. 25). reprint ed. 30.00 (0-404-51775-7) AMS Pr.
***Nuernberg, Susan M.** The Critical Response to Jack London. LC 95-15448. (Critical Responses in Arts & Letters Ser.: No. 19). 352p. 1995. text ed. 59.95 (0-313-28927-1, Greenwood Pr) Greenwood.
Nuernberger, Phil. Freedom from Stress: A Holistic Approach. LC 80-80542. (Illus.). (Orig.). (C). 1981. pap. 10.95 (0-89389-064-2) Himalayan Pubs.
***Nuese, Charles J.** Building the Right Things Right: The New Paradigm for Product & Technology Development. LC 95-14651. 1995. write for info. (0-527-76300-4) Qual Resc.
Nuesse, C. Joseph. The Catholic University of America: A Centennial History. LC 89-29649. 508p. 1990. 39.95 (0-8132-0722-3); pap. 19.95 (0-8132-0736-3) Cath U Pr.
Nuessel, Frank. The Image of Older Adults in the Media: An Annotated Bibliography. LC 92-24259. (Bibliographies & Indexes in Gerontology Ser.: No. 18). 224p. 1992. text ed. 49.95 (0-313-28018-5, NIA, Greenwood Pr) Greenwood.
— The Study of Names: A Guide to the Principles & Topics. LC 92-5424. 176p. 1992. text ed. 49.95 (0-313-28356-7, NSM, Greenwood Pr) Greenwood.
Nueva Cronica Staff, ed. see Fox, Lucia.
Nuevo Herald Staff, jt. auth. see Miami Herald Staff.
Nufer, Doug. Guide to Northwest Minor League Baseball, 1990. Bolotin, Norm, ed. 160p. (Orig.). 1990. pap. 9.95 (0-942381-08-4) Sammamish Pr.
Nuffield Canadian Seminar Staff. Post-Secondary Education in a Technological Society-L'Enseignement Post-Secondaire Dans Ure Societe Technologique. McLeod, T. H., ed. LC 73-79099. (Illus.). 259p. (ENG & FRE.). reprint ed. pap. 73.90 (0-7837-6895-8, 2046725) Bks Demand.
Nuffield, Edward W. The Pacific Northwest. 288p. (Orig.). 1990. pap. 16.95 (0-88839-236-2) Hancock House.
Nuffield, N. Basic Course Home Economics - Masters. (C). 1989. 200.00 (0-09-145581-2, Pub. by S Thornes Pubs UK) St Mut.
— Food Science. (C). 1989. student ed 85.00 (0-09-152881-X, Pub. by S Thornes Pubs UK); teacher ed 120.00 (0-09-152891-7, Pub. by S Thornes Pubs UK); 200.00 (0-09-152901-8, Pub. by S Thornes Pubs UK) St Mut.
— People & Homes. (C). 1989. student ed 55.00 (0-09-152941-7, Pub. by S Thornes Pubs UK); teacher ed 115.00 (0-09-152951-4, Pub. by S Thornes Pubs UK); 200.00 (0-09-152961-1, Pub. by S Thornes Pubs UK) St Mut.
***Nugent, Barb, et al.** 101 Ways to Be an Earth Angel. 112p. 1995. text ed. 18.00 (1-885499-20-5) Angelight.
Nugent, Beth. City of Boys. 1993. pap. 11.00 (0-679-73351-5, Vin) Random.
***Nugent, Christopher.** Masks of Satan: The Demonic in History. 216p. 1984. 22.50 (0-89860-128-2) Eastview.
— Mysticism, Death, & Dying. LC 93-50159. (SUNY Series in Western Esoteric Traditions). 127p. 1994. 39.50 (0-7914-2205-4); pap. 12.95 (0-7914-2206-2) State U NY Pr.
Nugent, Daniel. Spent Cartridges of Revolution: An Anthropological History of Namiquipa, Chihuahua. LC 93-15997. (Illus.). 240p. 1993. pap. text ed. 15.95 (0-226-60742-9) U Ch Pr.
— Spent Cartridges of Revolution: An Anthropological History of Namiquipa, Chihuahua. LC 93-15997. (Illus.). 240p. 1993. lib. bdg. 39.95 (0-226-60741-0) U Ch Pr.
Nugent, Daniel, ed. Rural Revolt in Mexico & U.S. Intervention. fac. ed. (Monograph Ser.: No. 27). 1989. 17.95 (0-935391-80-0, MN-27) UCSD Ctr US-Mex.
Nugent, Daniel, jt. ed. see Joseph, Gilbert M.
Nugent, Donald. Ecumenism in the Age of the Reformation: The Colloquy of Poissy. LC 73-80026. (Historical Studies: No. 89). 296p. 1974. 20.00 (0-674-23725-0) HUP.
Nugent, Frank A. Introduction to the Profession of Counseling. 2nd ed. 592p. (C). 1994. text ed. write for info. (0-02-388581-5, Merrill Pub Co) Macmillan.
Nugent, I., et al. Key Topics in Orthopaedic Surgery. 300p. (Orig.). 1994. pap. 52.50x (1-872748-33-3, Pub. by Bios Scientific UK) Coronet Bks.
Nugent, J. B. & Nabil, M. K., eds. The New Institutional Economics & Development: Theory & Applications to Tunisia. (Contributions to Economic Analysis Ser.: No. 183). 450p. 1989. 75.00 (0-444-87487-9, North Holland) Elsevier.
Nugent, J. Kevin, et al, eds. The Cultural Context of Infancy, Vol.1. LC 88-26059. 416p. 1989. text ed. 65.00 (0-89391-190-9) Ablex Pub.
Nugent, Jeffrey B. Economic Integration in Central America: Empirical Investigations. LC 74-6832. (Illus.). 226p. reprint ed. pap. 64.50 (0-317-09656-7, 2020729) Bks Demand.
***Nugent, Katherine.** Pediatric Nursing. (RN NCLEX Ser.). 300p. (Orig.). (C). 1995. pap. text ed. 18.95 (1-56930-042-9) Skidmore Roth Pub.
Nugent, Kathy, ed. see Rebrovich, Victor E.
Nugent, Kevin, et al, eds. The Cultural Context of Infancy, Vol. 2: Multicultural & Interdisciplinary Approaches to Parent-Infant Relations. 384p. (C). 1991. text ed. 67.50 (0-89391-627-7) Ablex Pub.
Nugent, Madeline. Having Your Baby When Others Say No: Overcoming the Fears about Having Your Baby. LC 90-23287. 240p. (Orig.). 1991. pap. 9.95 (0-89529-438-9) Avery Pub.
Nugent, Margaret L., ed. From Leninism to Freedom: The Challenges of Democratization. 292p. (C). 1992. pap. text ed. 42.00 (0-8133-8524-5) Westview.
Nugent, Nancy, jt. auth. see Prevention Magazine Editors.
Nugent, Neill. The Government & Politics of the European Community. rev. ed. LC 91-14311. 448p. 1991. pap. text ed. 21.95 (0-8223-1193-3) Duke.
— The Government & Politics of the European Community. 2nd rev. ed. LC 91-14311. 448p. 1991. lib. bdg. 52.95 (0-8223-1184-4) Duke.
— The Government & Politics of the European Union. 496p. 1994. pap. text ed. 21.95 (0-8223-1517-3) Duke.
— The Government & Politics of the European Union. 3rd ed. 496p. 1994. lib. bdg. 52.95 (0-8223-1506-8) Duke.
Nugent, Neill, ed. The European Community 1992: Annual Review of Activities. 163p. 1993. pap. 29.95 (0-631-19038-4) Blackwell Pubs.
— The European Union 1993: Annual Review of Activities. (Journal of Common Market Studies). (Illus.). 160p. (C). 1994. pap. text ed. 29.95 (0-631-19284-0) Blackwell Pubs.
***Nugent, Neill & O'Donnell, Rory, eds.** The European Business Environment. LC 94-28903. 1995. write for info. (0-312-12351-5) St Martin.
Nugent, Nell M. Cavaliers & Pioneers: Abstracts of Virginia Land Patents & Grants 1623-1666, Vol. 1. LC 63-23761. (Illus.). 767p. 1991. reprint ed. 40.00 (0-8063-0264-X) Genealog Pub.
Nugent, Nell M. Cavaliers & Pioneers: Abstracts of Virginia Land Patents & Grants, 1695-1732, No. 1. LC 80-141230. iii, 18p. 1980. 4.95 (0-88490-088-6) VA State Lib.
— Cavaliers & Pioneers: Abstracts of Virginia Land Patents & Grants, 1695-1732, Vol. 2. LC 34-42407. xi, 609p. 1992. reprint ed. text ed. 30.00 (0-88490-009-6, F225 N842) VA State Lib.
— Cavaliers & Pioneers: Abstracts of Virginia Land Patents & Grants, 1695-1732, Vol. 3. LC 34-42407. ix, 578p. 1979. 30.00 (0-88490-083-5) VA State Lib.
Nugent, Nell M., contrib. Cavaliers & Pioneers, Vol. I: Abstracts of Virginia Land Patents & Grants, 1623-1666, 1. LC 92-27183. xxxv, 767p. 1992. reprint ed. text ed. 30.00 (0-88490-174-2, F225 N842) VA State Lib.
— Cavaliers & Pioneers, Vol. I: Abstracts of Virginia Land Patents & Grants, 1623-1666, Set. LC 92-27183. xxxv, 767p. 1992. reprint ed. 75.00 (0-88490-175-0) VA State Lib.
Nugent, Nicholas. India. LC 90-25300. (World in View Ser.). (Illus.). 96p. (YA). (gr. 6-12). 1991. lib. bdg. 24.26 (0-8114-2441-3) Raintree Steck-V.
— Pakistan & Bangladesh. LC 92-10765. (World in View Ser.). 96p. (J). 1992. lib. bdg. 24.26 (0-8114-2456-1) Raintree Steck-V.
Nugent, Patricia & Vitale, Barbara. Test Success: Test Taking Techniques for Beginning Nursing Students. (Illus.). 267p. (C). 1993. pap. text ed. 19.95 (0-8036-6598-9) Davis Co.
Nugent, Patricia M., jt. auth. see Vitale, Barbara A.
***Nugent, Paul.** Big Men & Small Boys: Power, Ideology & the Burden of History in Rawlings' Ghana, 1982-1994. LC 95-12503. 1995. write for info. (0-7201-2309-7, Mansell Pub) Cassell.
Nugent, Robert. Paul Elvard. LC 74-4132. (Twayne's World Authors Ser.). (C). 1974. lib. bdg. 17.95 (0-8057-2299-8) Irvington.
— Prayer Journey for Persons with AIDS. 49p. 1989. 3.95 (0-86716-127-2) St Anthony Mess Pr.
Nugent, Robert & Gramick, Jeannine. Building Bridges: Gay & Lesbian Reality & the Catholic Church. LC 91-67051. 224p. (Orig.). 1992. pap. 9.95 (0-89622-503-8) Twenty-Third.
Nugent, Robert, tr. see De Sponde, Jean.
Nugent, Robert, jt. tr. see Lunardi, Egidio.
Nugent, Robert, tr. see Matute, Ana M.
Nugent, Rory. The Search for the Pink-headed Duck: A Journey into the Himalayas & down the Brahmaputra. (Illus.). 240p. 1993. pap. 10.95 (0-395-66994-4) HM.
***Nugent, Stephen.** Big Mouth: The Amazon Speaks. (Illus.). 258p. 1994. 19.95 (1-56313-443-8); pap. 12.95 (1-56313-722-4) BrownTrout Pubs Inc.
Nugent, Stephen L. Amazonian Caboclo Society: An Essay on Invisibility & Peasant Economy. (Explorations in Anthropology Ser.). 304p. 1993. text ed. 54.95 (0-85496-756-7) Berg Pubs.

*__Nugent, Ted.__ Ted Nugent Bloodtrails the Truth about Bowhunting. 147p. (YA). 1991. pap. 10.95 (0-9633699-0-3) South Wind.

Nugent, Thomas, tr. see Burlamaqui, Jean J.

Nugent, Thomas, tr. see Condillac, Etienne B. de.

Nugent, Thomas, tr. see Condillac, Etienne Bonnot de.

Nugent, Thomas, tr. see De Secondat Montesquieu, Charles L.

Nugent, Walter. Crossings: The Great Transatlantic Migrations, 1870-1914. LC 92-7156. (Illus.). 256p. 1995. text ed. 29.95 (0-253-34140-X) Ind U Pr.

— Crossings: The Great Transatlantic Migrations, 1870-1914. LC 92-7156. (Illus.). 256p. 1995. pap. 12.95 (0-253-20953-6) Ind U Pr.

— Structures of American Social History. LC 80-8634. (Illus.). 224p. 1981. pap. 8.95 (0-253-20352-X, MB-352) Ind U Pr.

Nugent, Walter T. Tolerant Populists: Kansas Populism & Nativism. LC 63-13069. 268p. reprint ed. 76.40 (0-8357-9659-0, 2015761) Bks Demand.

Nugent, Walter T., jt. auth. see Juhnke, James C.

Nugent, Ward J. Prejudice: Index of Modern Information with Bibliography. LC 88-47787. 150p. (Orig.). 1988. 44.50 (0-88164-902-3); pap. 39.50 (0-88164-903-1) ABBE Pubs Assn.

Nugent, William A. & Mayer, James M. Metal Ligand Multiple Bonds. LC 88-233. 334p. 1988. text ed. 89.95 (0-471-85440-9) Wiley.

Nugter, A. C. Transborder Flow of Personal Data Within the EC. (Computer - Law Ser.: Vol. 6). 456p. 1990. pap. 94.00 (90-6544-513-7) Kluwer Law Tax Pubs.

Nugues, E., et al. Practical Manual for the Piano & Harmonium Tuner: A Treatise on the Tuning & Repair of These Instruments. (Illus.). vi, 146p. 1913. pap. text ed. 20.00 (0-913746-30-4) Organ Lit.

Nuh Ha Mim Keleer, ed. see Yahya ibn Sharaf Al-Nawawi.

Nuhn, Gary. Eighty Ninth U. S. Open. Norwood, Bev, ed. (Illus.). 64p. 1989. 15.00 (0-9615344-7-8) Intl Merc OH.

— Ninetieth U. S. Open. Norwood, Bev, ed. (Illus.). 64p. 1990. 15.00 (1-878843-00-1) Intl Merc OH.

Nuhn, Roger, ed. New Braunfels, Comal County, Texas: A Pictorial History. LC 93-35505. 1993. write for info. (0-89865-879-9) Donning Co.

Nuhrah, Arthur G., jt. auth. see Aremia, Amelia.

Nuik, Tiina. Selection of Graphic Art of XVI-XIII Century at the Scientific Library of the Tartu State University. 142p. 1981. 55.00 (0-317-14297-6, Pub. by Collets UK) Pro-Am Music.

Nuitter, C. & Thoinan, E. Les Origines de L'opera Francais. LC 77-4106. (Music Reprint Ser.). 1977. reprint ed. lib. bdg. 42.50 (0-306-70895-7) Da Capo.

Nujkamp, Peter, jt. auth. see Cappellin, Riccardo.

Nujssbaumer, H., ed. see Shore, S. N., et al.

Nukayis, Ventris. Last Days? Spiritual Reality & Physical Illusions. 272p. (Orig.). 1991. pap. 9.95 (1-56266-149-3) Anwol.

Nukewatch Staff. Nuclear Heartland: A Guide to the One Thousand Missile Silos of the United States. Day, Samuel H., Jr., ed. (Illus.). 96p. (Orig.). (C). 1988. pap. 12.50 (0-942046-01-3) Prog Found.

— Prisoners on Purpose: A Peacemaker's Guide to Jails & Prisons. Day, Samuel H., Jr., ed. (Illus.). 160p. (Orig.). (C). 1989. pap. 7.50 (0-942046-02-1) Prog Found.

Nuland, Sherwin B. Doctors: The Biography of Medicine. 1989. pap. 15.00 (0-679-72215-7, Vin) Random.

— Doctors: The Biography of Medicine. 1995. pap. 15.00 (0-679-76009-1, Vin) Random.

— How We Die. 1994. write for info. (0-318-70237-1) Knopf.

— How We Die: Reflections on Life's Final Chapter. 1995. pap. 13.00 (0-679-74244-1, Vin) Random.

— How We Die: Reflections on Life's Final Chapter. large type ed. 1994. pap. 23.00 (0-679-75690-6) Random.

— How We Die: Reflections on Life's Final Chapters. 1994. 24.00 (0-679-41461-4) Knopf.

*__Null.__ Allergies & Weight Control. 1995. 16.95 (1-879323-21-4) Sound Horizons AV.

— How to Strengthen Your Immune System. 1995. 16.95 (1-879323-22-2) Sound Horizons AV.

Null & Allen. From Here to Maternity. 6.95 (0-88494-619-3) Bookcraft Inc.

Null & Watts. A Little Bit of Everything Good. 1978. pap. 6.95 (0-89137-619-4) Quality Pubns.

Null, Cheryl J. & Gad, Carol L. The Barnyard Buddies. (Illus.). 32p. (J). (gr. 2-6). 1989. pap. 5.95 (1-880171-00-7) Stardom.

— The Barnyard Buddies in Circus Champions. (Illus.). 36p. (J). (gr. 2-6). 1990. pap. 5.95 (1-880171-01-5) Stardom.

— The Barnyard Buddies in Finders Keepers. (Illus.). 36p. (J). (gr. 2-6). 1992. pap. 5.95 (1-880171-04-X) Stardom.

Null, Gary. Black Hollywood: From Nineteen Seventy to Today. LC 92-37551. 1993. pap. 16.95 (0-8065-1216-4) Carol Pub Group.

— Black Hollywood: The Negro in Motion Pictures. 256p. 1984. pap. 15.95 (0-8065-0908-2, Citadel Pr) Carol Pub Group.

— Change Your Life Now: Get Out of Your Head, Get into Your Life. (Mastering Life Ser.). 180p. 1993. pap. 9.95 (1-55874-290-5) Health Comm.

— Clearer, Cleaner, Safer, Greener: A Blueprint for Detoxifying Your Environment. 1990. 18.95 (0-394-58316-7, Villard Bks) Random.

— Clearer, Cleaner, Safer, Greener: A Blueprint for Detoxifying Your Environment. 1992. pap. 12.00 (0-679-74248-4, Villard Bks) Random.

— The Complete Guide to Sensible Eating: The Egg Project Updated with New & Expanded Chapters on Detoxification, Environmental Medicine, Herbs & Healing. LC 89-71488. (Illus.). 300p. 1990. pap. 14.95 (0-941423-37-9) FWEW.

— Healing Your Body Naturally. 1993. 7.99 (0-517-09301-4) Random Hse Value.

— Healing Your Body Naturally: Alternative Treatments to Illness. LC 91-20385. 330p. (Orig.). 1992. pap. 16.95 (0-941423-66-2) FWEW.

— How to Keep Your Feet & Legs Healthy for a Lifetime: The Complete Guide to Foot & Leg Care with Special Sections for Walkers, Joggers & Runners. LC 89-71438. (Illus.). 168p. (Orig.). 1990. pap. 12.95 (0-941423-36-0) FWEW.

— The New Vegetarian Cookbook. 250p. 1980. pap. 13.95 (0-02-010040-X, Collier S&S) S&S Trade.

— New Vegetarian Cookbook. 1987. pap. 15.95 (0-02-590890-1) Macmillan.

— The Nineties Healthy Body Book: Overcome the Effects of Pollution & Cleanse the Toxins from Your Body. 350p. (Orig.). 1994. pap. 14.95 (1-55874-303-0, 3030) Health Comm.

— No More Allergies: Identifying & Eliminating Allergies & Sensitivity Reactions to Everything in Your Environment. LC 92-50149. 1992. 13.00 (0-679-74310-3, Villard Bks) Random.

— Nutrition & the Mind: Dietary Approaches to Mental Illness from Alcoholism to Migraines. 250p. (Orig.). 1995. pap. 14.95 (1-56858-021-5) FWEW.

— Nutrition Sourcebook for the 80s. 1985. pap. 15.95 (0-02-590900-2) Macmillan.

— Ultimate Training: Gary's Null's Complete Guide to Eating Right, Exercising & Living Longer. LC 92-44033. 1993. pap. 10.95 (0-312-08796-9) St Martin.

— Vegetarian Cooking for Good Health. 320p. 1991. pap. 14.00 (0-02-010050-7, Pub. by Gebrueder Borntraeger GW) Macmillan.

— The Vegetarian Handbook: Eating Right for Total Health. 288p. 1989. pap. 10.95 (0-312-03948-4) St Martin.

Null, Gary & Feldman, Martin. Reverse the Aging Process Naturally: How to Build the Immune System with Antioxidants, the Supernutrients of the Nineties. LC 92-56703. (Gary Null Health Library). 1993. pap. 10.00 (0-679-74509-2, Villard Bks) Random.

Null, Gary & Null, Shelly. The Joy of Juicing Recipe Guide. LC 92-10462. 240p. 1992. pap. 10.95 (0-89529-592-X) Avery Pub.

Null, Gary & Simonson, Richard. How to Turn Your Ideas into Dollars. rev. ed. LC 71-85821. 44p. 1988. pap. 3.95 (0-87576-023-6) Pilot Bks.

Null, Gary, et al. The Complete Question & Answer Book of General Nutrition. LC 79-187997. (Health Library: Vol. 5). 184p. 1972. 9.95 (0-8315-0128-6) Speller.

— The Complete Question & Answer Book of Natural Therapy. LC 75-187996. (Health Library: Vol. 3). 272p. 1972. 9.95 (0-8315-0127-8) Speller.

— The Natural Organic Beauty Book. LC 71-187995. (Health Library: Vol. 4). 168p. 1972. 9.95 (0-8315-0125-1) Speller.

Null, Kathleen C. Where Are We Going Besides Crazy? 8.95 (0-88494-693-2) Bookcraft Inc.

Null, Ralph. The Florist's Guide to Successful Weddings. Hilton, Pat, ed. (Illus.). 130p. 1988. write for info. (0-9620684-0-3) Teleflora.

Null, Ralph, jt. auth. see Hampton, Bob.

Null, Shelly, jt. auth. see Null, Gary.

Nuller, Werner E., ed. see Zahn, Rudolf K.

Nulman, Macy. Encyclopedia of Jewish Prayer: Ashkenazic & Sephardic Rites. LC 92-33637. 464p. 1993. 50.00 (0-87668-370-7) Aronson.

Nulman, Marilyn, ed. see Hagerty, Kevin D.

Nulty, Leslie. The Green Revolution in West Pakistan: Implications of Technological Change. LC 73-170471. (Special Studies in International Economics & Development). 1972. 29.50 (0-89197-779-1) Irvington.

Nulty, William H. Confederate Florida: The Road to Olustee. 1990. pap. 19.95 (0-8173-0748-6) U of Ala Pr.

*__Numa Research Department Staff.__ Het Wereldwijde Boek Van de Familienamen. 95p. 1994. 51.00 (1-885808-05-4); pap. text ed. 46.00 (1-885808-06-2) Numa Corp.

— Il Libro Mondiale di Cognomi. 95p. 1994. 54.00 (1-885808-11-9); pap. text ed. 48.00 (1-885808-12-7) Numa Corp.

— El Libro Mundial de los Apellidos Familiares. 95p. 1994. 54.00 (1-885808-09-7); pap. text ed. 48.00 (1-885808-10-0) Numa Corp.

— Le Livre Mondial de la Famille Patronyme. 95p. 1994. 52.00 (1-885808-07-0); pap. text ed. 46.00 (1-885808-08-9) Numa Corp.

— Das Weltbuch fur Familiennamen. 95p. 1994. 53.00 (1-885808-03-8); pap. text ed. 46.00 (1-885808-04-6) Numa Corp.

— The World Book of Family Surnames. 95p. 1994. 40.00 (1-885808-00-3); pap. text ed. 30.00 (1-885808-01-1) Numa Corp.

Numa, S., ed. Fatty Acid Metabolism & Its Regulation. (New Comprehensive Biochemistry Ser.: Vol. 7). 216p. 1984. 82.75 (0-444-80528-1, I-020-84) Elsevier.

Nu'man, Muhammad A. What Every American Should Know about Islam & the Muslims. 74p. (Orig.). 1985. pap. 5.00 (0-933821-04-2) New Mind Prod.

Nu'Man, Muhammad A. & Nu'man, Muhammad A. Muslim Names & Their Meanings. 20p. (Orig.). reprint ed. pap. 2.50 (0-933821-02-6) New Mind Prod.

Nu'Man, Muhammad A., jt. auth. see Akbar, Na'im.

Nu'man, Muhammad A., jt. auth. see El-Amin, Mustafa.

Nu'man, Muhammad A., jt. auth. see Nu'Man, Muhammad A.

Numani, M. Manzoor. Islamic Faith & Practice. 170p. (C). 1988. 18.50 (1-56744-308-7) Kazi Pubns.

Numani, Shibli. Umar the Great, Vol. II. Saleem, M., tr. 200p. (YA). (gr. 7-12). 1985. 14.50 (1-56744-407-5) Kazi Pubns.

Numano, Fujio, ed. see Saratoga International Conference on Atherosclerosis Staff.

Numata, M., et al, eds. Studies in Conservation of Natural Terrestrial Ecosystems in Japan, Part I: Vegetation & Its Conservation, Vol. 8. (Japan International Biological Program Synthesis Ser.). 157p. 1975. pap. 27.50 (0-86008-218-0, Pub. by U of Tokyo JA) Col U Pr.

— Studies in Conservation of Natural Terrestrial Ecosystems in Japan, Part II: Animal Communities, Vol. 9. (Japan International Biological Program Synthesis Ser.). 91p. 1975. pap. 17.50 (0-86008-219-9, Pub. by U of Tokyo JA) Col U Pr.

Numata, Makoto, ed. Ecology of Grasslands & Bamboolands in the World. 1980. lib. bdg. 103.00 (90-6193-601-2) Kluwer Ac.

Numbers, Ronald L. Almost Persuaded: American Physicians & Compulsory Health Insurance, 1912-1920. LC 77-17254. (Henry E. Sigerist Supplements to the Bulletin of the History of Medicine, New Ser.: No. 1). 173p. reprint ed. pap. 49.40 (0-7837-6425-1, 2046423) Bks Demand.

— The Creationists. LC 91-29562. (Illus.). 448p. 1992. 27.00 (0-679-40104-0) Knopf.

— The Creationists. LC 93-15804. 458p. 1993. pap. 15.00 (0-520-08393-8) U CA Pr.

— Prophetess of Health: Ellen G. White & the Origins of Seventh-Day Adventist Health Reform. LC 91-22807. Orig. Title: Prophetess of Health. (Illus.). 408p. (C). 1992. reprint ed. lib. bdg. 49.95 (0-87049-712-X); reprint ed. pap. text ed. 19.95 (0-87049-713-8) U of Tenn Pr.

*__Numbers, Ronald L., ed.__ The Antievolution Works of Arthur I. Brown. LC 94-45074. (Creationism in Twentieth-Century America Ser.: Vol. 3). 224p. 1995. 55.00 (0-8153-1804-9) Garland.

— Compulsory Health Insurance: The Continuing American Debate. LC 82-6145. (Contributions in Medical History Ser.: No. 11). xv, 172p. 1982. text ed. 49.95 (0-313-23436-1, NHI/, Greenwood Pr) Greenwood.

— Creation-Evolution Debates. LC 94-45074. (Creationism in Twentieth-Century America Ser.: Vol. 2). 520p. 1995. 95.00 (0-8153-1803-0) Garland.

— Early Creationist Journals. LC 94-45522. (Creationism in Twentieth-Century America Ser.: Vol. 9). 650p. 1995. 100.00 (0-8153-1810-3) Garland.

— The Early Writings of Harold W. Clark & Frank Lewis Marsh. LC 94-45067. (Creationism in Twentieth-Century America Ser.: Vol. 8). 560p. 1995. 93.00 (0-8153-1809-X) Garland.

— Medicine in the New World: New Spain, New France, & New England. LC 86-16067. (Illus.). 184p. 1987. text ed. 25.00x (0-87049-517-8) U of Tenn Pr.

— Selected Works of George McCready Price. LC 94-45071. (Creationism in Twentieth-Century America Ser.: Vol. 7). 512p. 1995. 75.00 (0-8153-1808-1) Garland.

Numbers, Ronald L. & Amundsen, Darrel W., eds. Caring & Curing: Historical Essays on Health, Medicine, & the Faith Traditions. 576p. 1986. text ed. 35.00 (0-02-919270-6) Macmillan.

Numbers, Ronald L. & Leavitt, Judith W. Wisconsin Medicine: Historical Perspectives. LC 80-52297. (Illus.). 224p. 1981. 19.95 (0-299-08430-2) U of Wis Pr.

*__Numbers, Ronald L. & Savitt, Todd L., eds.__ Science & Medicine in the Old South. fac. ed. LC 88-32648. (Illus.). 382p. 1989. reprint ed. pap. 108.90 (0-7837-7768-X, 2047524) Bks Demand.

Numbers, Ronald L., jt. ed. see Leavitt, Judith W.

Numbers, Ronald L., jt. ed. see Lindberg, David C.

Numbers, Ronald L., ed. see Patterson, Alexander, et al.

Numbkar, Jai. Come Rain: A Novel. 1993. pap. 8.95 (0-86311-328-1, Pub. by Disha Bks II) Apt Bks.

Numerical Algorithms Group. NAG FORTRAN Library Manual Mark 9. 1981. 35.00 (0-317-52218-3, Pub. by Numer Algo UK) Numer Algorithms.

— NAG Fortran PC50 Handbook - Release 1: Edition 1. 324p. 1983. 30.00 (0-317-52225-6, Pub. by Numer Algo UK) Numer Algorithms.

— NAG FORTRAN PC50 Handbook Release 1: Edition 2. 2nd ed. 324p. 1984. 30.00 (0-317-52226-4, Pub. by Numer Algo UK) Numer Algorithms.

— NAG Graphical Supplement Mark 1. 1981. 40.00 (0-317-52228-0, Pub. by Numer Algo UK) Numer Algorithms.

— NAG Graphical Supplement Mark 2. 1985. 25.20 (0-317-52231-0, Pub. by Numer Algo UK) Numer Algorithms.

Numeroff. Fathers & Mothers. (J). 1997. 15.95 (0-8050-2056-X) H Holt & Co.

*__Numeroff, Laura.__ Chimps Don't Wear Glasses. LC 94-20320. (Illus.). (J). (gr. k-3). 1996. 14.00 (0-671-87007-6, S&S Bks Young Read) S&S Childrens.

— Mouse Cookies: 10 Easy-to-Make Cookie Recipes. (Illus.). 32p. (J). 1995. 10.95 (0-694-00633-5, Festival) HarpC Child Bks.

Numeroff, Laura J. Dogs Don't Wear Sneakers. LC 92-27007. (Illus.). (J). 1993. pap. 14.00 (0-671-79525-2, S&S Bks Young Read) S&S Childrens.

— If You Give a Moose a Muffin. LC 91-2207. (Laura Geringer Bk.). (Illus.). 32p. (J). (ps-2). 1991. 13.95 (0-06-024405-4); lib. bdg. 13.89 (0-06-024406-2) HarpC Child Bks.

— If You Give a Moose a Muffin Big Book. LC 91-2207. (Trophy Picture Bk.). (Illus.). 32p. (J). (ps-2). 1994. pap. 19.95 (0-06-443366-8, Trophy) HarpC Child Bks.

— If You Give a Mouse a Cookie, Book & Tape. LC 84-48343. (Illus.). 32p. (J). (ps-2). 1985. 12.95 (0-06-024586-7); lib. bdg. 12.89 (0-06-024587-5) HarpC Child Bks.

— If You Give a Mouse a Cookie, Book & Tape. (Illus.). 32p. (J). (ps-2). 1994. reel tape, pap. 10.95 (0-694-00630-0, Festival) HarpC Child Bks.

— If You Give a Mouse a Cookie, Book & Tape. (Illus.). (J). (ps-3). 1995. cd-rom 39.95 (0-06-264000-3) HarpC Child Bks.

— If You Give a Mouse a Cookie, Book & Tape. (J). 1993. pap. 19.95 (0-590-71885-1) Scholastic Inc.

— If You Give a Mouse a Cookie Box & Doll. LC 91-46093. (Illus.). 32p. (J). (ps-2). 1992. 16.95 (0-694-00416-2, Festival) HarpC Child Bks.

— Si le das un panecillo a un alce - If You Give a Moose a Muffin. LC 94-37255. (Illus.). 32p. (SPA.). (J). (ps-2). 1995. 14.95 (0-06-025440-8) HarpC Child Bks.

— Si le das una galletita a un raton - If You Give a Mouse a Cookie. LC 94-37254. (Illus.). 32p. (SPA.). (J). (ps-2). 1995. 12.95 (0-06-025438-6) HarpC Child Bks.

— Why a Disguise? LC 93-19025. (Illus.). (J). 1995. pap. 14.00 (0-671-87006-8, S&S Bks Young Read) S&S Childrens.

Numes, Maxine. Backtrack. 1989. pap. 3.95 (0-671-67893-0) PB.

Numez, J. & Dupont, J. E., eds. Hormones & Cell Regulation European Symposium, 11th. (Colloquim Ser.: Vol. 153). 248p. (Orig.). 1987. pap. 63.00 (2-85598-324-X) S M P F Inc.

Nummedal, ed. Cretaceous Shelf Sandstones & Shelf Depositional Sequences, Western Interior Basin, Utah & New Mexico, No. T119. (IGC Field Trip Guidebooks Ser.). 96p. 1989. 21.00 (0-87590-629-X) Am Geophysical.

Nummedal, Dag, et al, eds. Sea-Level Fluctuations & Coastal Evolution. (Special Publications Ser.: No. 41). 276p. 1987. 45.00 (0-918985-71-4) SEPM.

*__Numrich, Carol.__ Consider the Issues: Advanced Listening & Critical Thinking Skills. 1995. audio write for info. (0-201-82533-3) Addison-Wesley.

— Consider the Issues: Advanced Listening & Critical Thinking Skills. 2nd ed. LC 94-33391. 1995. pap. write for info. (0-201-82529-5) Addison-Wesley.

— Raise the Issues: An Integrated Approach to Critical Thinking. LC 93-33842. 1994. pap. text ed. 19.95 (0-8013-1014-8); audio 37.95 (0-8013-1015-6) Longman.

Numrich, Charles. Passion Play. 1983. 5.20 (0-89536-601-0, 1627) CSS OH.

*__Numrich, Paul D.__ Old Wisdom in the New World: Americanization in Two Immigrant Theravada Buddhist Temples. LC 95-4361. 1996. write for info. (0-87049-905-X) U of Tenn Pr.

Numrich, Robert W., ed. Supercomputer Applications. 316p. 1985. 75.00 (0-306-42013-9, Plenum Pr) Plenum.

Numrick, Carol. Face the Issues: Intermediate Listening & Critical Thinking Skills. (Orig.). (YA). (gr. 7 up). 1990. audio 46.50 (0-8013-0535-7, 78411); pap. text ed. 13.95 (0-8013-0300-1, 75950) Longman.

— Face the Issues: Intermediate Listening & Critical Thinking Skills, 2 cass., Set. (Orig.). (YA). (gr. 7 up). 1990. audio 37.95 (0-8013-0301-X, 75951) Longman.

Nunally & Kester. Financial Management: A Practical Approach. 336p. (C). 1993. pap. text ed. 33.95 (0-8403-8380-0) Kendall-Hunt.

Nunamaker, J. A. Rose Genealogy, Including Descendants of Israel Rose, Pioneer of Washington & Oregon, with Additions & Corrections. (Illus.). 71p. 1993. reprint ed. lib. bdg. 26.00 (0-8328-3778-4); reprint ed. pap. 16.00 (0-8328-3779-2) Higginson Bk Co.

Nunan, David. Designing Tasks for the Communicative Classroom. (Cambridge Language Teaching Library). (Illus.). 256p. (C). 1989. pap. 16.95 (0-521-37915-6) Cambridge U Pr.

— The Learner-Centered Curriculum. (Cambridge Applied Linguistics Ser.). (Illus.). 192p. 1988. pap. 16.95 (0-521-35843-4) Cambridge U Pr.

— Research Methods in Language Learning. (Cambridge Language Teaching Library). (Illus.). 304p. (C). 1992. pap. 17.95 (0-521-42968-4) Cambridge U Pr.

— Research Methods in Language Learning. (Cambridge Language Teaching Library). (Illus.). 304p. (C). 1992. 44.95 (0-521-41937-9) Cambridge U Pr.

Nunan, David, ed. Collaborative Language Learning & Teaching. (Cambridge Language Teaching Library). 224p. (C). 1992. 42.95 (0-521-41687-6); pap. 16.95 (0-521-42701-0) Cambridge U Pr.

*__Nunan, David & Lamb, Clarice.__ The Self-Directed Teacher: Managing the Learning Process. (Language Education Ser.). (Illus.). 320p. (C). 1995. write for info. (0-521-49716-7); pap. write for info. (0-521-49773-6) Cambridge U Pr.

*__Nunan, David & Miller, Linsday, eds.__ New Ways in Teaching Listening. 1995. pap. 24.95 (0-939791-58-7) Tchrs Eng Spkrs.

Nunan, David, jt. ed. see Richards, Jack C.

Nunan, J. Carlton, jt. auth. see Masterson, Thomas R.

Nunberg, Barbara. Managing the Civil Service: The Lessons of Reform in Industrial Countries. LC 93-23872. (Discussion Paper Ser.: Vol. 204). 1993. write for info. (0-8213-2498-5) World Bank.

— Public Sector Management Issues in Structural Adjustment. (Discussion Paper Ser.: No. 99). 46p. 1990. 6.95 (0-614-02845-0, 11638) World Bank.

— Public Sector Pay & Employment Reform: A Review of World Bank Experience. (Discussion Paper Ser.: No. 68). 48p. 1989. 6.95 (0-8213-1411-4, 11411) World Bank.

Nunberg, Barbara & Nellis, John. Civil Service Reform & the World Bank. LC 92-12847. (Discussion Paper Ser.: No. 161). 56p. 1993. 6.95 (0-8213-2117-X, 12117) World Bank.

Nunberg, Barbara, jt. ed. see Lindauer, David L.

Nunberg, Geoffrey. The Linguistics of Punctuation. LC 90-1411. (CSLI Lecture Notes Ser.: No. 18). 160p. (C). 1990. 35.00 (0-937073-47-4); pap. 14.95 (0-937073-46-6) Ctr Study Language.

An Asterisk (*) at the beginning of an entry indicates that the title is appearing in BIP for the first time.

Nunberg, Herman. Curiosity. LC 58-9230. (New York Psychoanalytic Institute Freud Anniversary Lecture Ser.). 88p. 1961. text ed. 25.00 (0-8236-1100-0) Intl Univs Pr.

— Practice & Theory of Psychoanalysis, 2 vols., Vol. 1. 218p. 1961. text ed. 30.00 (0-8236-4220-8) Intl Univs Pr.

— Practice & Theory of Psychoanalysis, Vol. 2. 219p. 1961. text ed. 30.00 (0-8236-4240-2) Intl Univs Pr.

— Principles of Psychoanalysis: Their Application to the Neuroses. LC 55-11549. 382p. (Orig.). 1969. reprint ed. text ed. 55.00 (0-8236-4300-X); reprint ed. pap. text ed. 24.95 (0-8236-8198-X, 24300) Intl Univs Pr.

Nunberg, Herman & Federn, Ernst, eds. Minutes of the Vienna Psychoanalytic Society, 4 vols. Incl. Vol. 1. 1906-1908. LC 62-15591. 1963. text ed. 55.00 (0-8236-3380-2); Vol. 2. 1908-1910. LC 62-15591. 1963. text ed. 55.00 (0-8236-3400-0); Vol. 3. 1910-1911. LC 62-15591. 1963. text ed. 55.00 (0-8236-3401-9); Vol. 4. 1912-1918. LC 62-15591. 1963. text ed. 55.00 (0-8236-3402-7); LC 62-15591. 1963. Set text ed. write for info. (0-318-53692-7) Intl Univs Pr.

Nunberg, Margarete, tr. see Meyer, Joachim E.

Nunemacher, Greg. LAN Primer: An Introduction to Local Area Networks. (Illus.). 400p. (Orig.). 1990. pap. 24.95 (1-55851-127-X) M&T Bks.

— LAN Primer: An Introduction to Local Area Networks. 2nd ed. 300p. (Orig.). 1992. pap. 26.95 (1-55851-287-X) M&T Bks.

Nunes, jt. auth. see Fazio.

Nunes, Ana, jt. auth. see Llibre, Jaume.

Nunes, Benedito, ed. see Lispector, Clarice.

Nunes, C. Dicionario de Bolso Russo-Portuguese. 376p. (POR & RUS.). 1976. 9.95 (0-8288-5627-3, M9062) Fr & Eur.

Nunes, Danillo. Judas, Betrayer or Betrayed? 1992. pap. 16.95 (0-533-10065-8) Vantage.

Nunes, Florence I. Songs of Saudades: An Enchanting Journey to the Azores Islands & the Pousadas of Portugal. 176p. 1994. pap. 12.95 (0-929999-02-9) Tzedakah Pubns.

Nunes, Lygia B. My Friend the Painter. Pontiero, Giovanni, tr. 85p. (J). (gr. 3-7). 1991. 13.95 (0-15-256340-7) HarBrace.

Nunes, Maria L. Becoming True to Ourselves: Cultural Decolonization & National Identity in the Literature of the Portuguese-Speaking World. LC 87-8390. (Contributions to the Study of World Literature Ser.: No. 22). 128p. 1987. text ed. 45.00 (0-313-25726-4, NLS/) Greenwood.

— The Craft of an Absolute Winner: Characterization & Narratology in the Novels of Machado de Assis. LC 82-11717. (Contributions in Afro-American & African Studies: No. 71). xii, 158p. 1983. text ed. 47.95 (0-313-23631-3, NCW/) Greenwood.

— A Portuguese Colonial in America: Belmira Nunes Lopes: The Autobiography of a Cape Verdean-American. Miller, Yvette E., ed. LC 82-6569. 224p. 1982. 25.00 (0-935480-08-0); pap. 11.95 (0-935480-07-2) Lat Am Lit Rev Pr.

Nunes, Morris A. Basic Legal Forms for Business. LC 92-33345. 256p. 1993. disk, pap. 37.50 (0-471-59279-X) Wiley.

— Operational Cash Flow Management & Control. 256p. 1982. 34.95 (0-13-637470-0) P-H.

Nunes, Morris A., jt. auth. see Chargar, William.

Nunes, Susan. Coyote Dreams. LC 87-30288. (Illus.). 32p. (J). (ps-3). 1988. text ed. 14.95 (0-689-31398-5, Atheneum Bks Young) S&S Childrens.

— Coyote Dreams. LC 93-22931. (Illus.). 32p. (J). (ps-3). 1994. reprint ed. pap. 4.95 (0-689-71804-7, Aladdin Paperbacks) S&S Childrens.

— A Small Obligation & Other Stories of Hilo. LC 82-72555. 88p. (Orig.). 1982. pap. 5.00 (0-910043-00-0) Bamboo Ridge Pr.

— Tiddalick the Frog. LC 89-1. (Illus.). 32p. (J). (gr. k-3). 1989. lib. bdg. 13.95 (0-689-31502-3, Atheneum Bks Young) S&S Childrens.

— To Find the Way. LC 91-31334. (Illus.). 48p. (J). (gr. 4-8). 1992. 12.95 (0-8248-1376-6) UH Pr.

Nunes, Susan M. The Last Dragon. LC 93-30631. (Illus.). (J). 1995. 14.95 (0-395-67020-9, Clarion Bks) HM.

Nunes, Terezhina, et al. Street Mathematics & School Mathematics. LC 92-23183. (Learning in Doing: Social, Cognitive & Computational Perspectives Ser.). (Illus.). 160p. (C). 1993. 49.95 (0-521-38116-9); pap. 16.95 (0-521-38813-9) Cambridge U Pr.

Nunes-Vais, Al. Vacation Time Sharing: Is It Right for You? (Illus.). 1983. pap. 9.95 (0-910793-02-6) Marlborough Pr.

Nunes, Warren. Jazz Guitar Chord Bible, Vol. 1. (Orig.). 1979. pap. 10.95 (0-89898-167-0) CPP Belwin.

— Jazz Guitar Chord Bible, Vol. 2. (Orig.). 1979. pap. 6.95 (0-89898-168-9) CPP Belwin.

Nunes, Warren, ed. Jazz Guitar Chord Bible. 190p. (Orig.). 1979. pap. 9.95 (0-89705-049-5) Almo Pubns.

Nunez, A. & Fay, D. Hardware & Software Design Automation. 1991. 141.00 (0-444-89256-7) Elsevier.

Nunez, Ana R. Antologia de Poesia Infantil. LC 85-81795. (Coleccion Antologias Ser.). 180p. (Orig.). (SPA.). (J). (gr. 3-12). 1985. pap. 9.95 (0-89729-369-X) Ediciones.

— Homenaje A Dulce Maria Loynaz: Premio Cervantes 1993. LC 92-75732. (Coleccion Clasicos Cubanos Ser.). 415p. (Orig.). (SPA.). 1993. pap. 29.95 (0-89729-669-9) Ediciones.

— Sol de un Solo Dia. LC 92-75884. (Coleccion Espejo de Paciencia Ser.). 93p. (Orig.). (SPA.). 1993. pap. 9.95 (0-89729-658-3) Ediciones.

— Uno Y Veinte Golpes Por America. LC 90-82805. (Coleccion Espejo de Paciencia Ser.). 48p. (Orig.). (SPA.). 1991. pap. 9.00 (0-89729-571-4) Ediciones.

Nunez, Benjamin. Dictionary of Afro-Latin American Civilization. LC 79-7731. (Illus.). xxxv, 525p. 1980. text ed. 69.50 (0-313-21138-8, NAL/, Greenwood Pr) Greenwood.

— Dictionary of Portuguese-African Civilization Vol. 1: From Discovery to Independence, 2 vols. 1060p. 1995. 220.00 (1-873836-70-8, Pub. by H Zell Pubs UK) Bowker-Saur.

— Dictionary of Portuguese-African Civilization Vol. 2: Biographies: From Ancient Kings to Presidents. 500p. 1995. 90.00 (1-873836-65-1) K G Saur.

Nunez Cabeza de Vaca, Alvar. The Journey of Alvar Nunez Cabeza de Vaca & His Companions from Florida to the Pacific, 1528-1536. Bandelier, A. F., ed. Bandelier, Fanny, tr. LC 72-2822. (American Explorers Ser.). reprint ed. 52.50 (0-404-54915-2) AMS Pr.

Nunez-Cedeno, R. A., jt. ed. see Neidle, C.

Nunez, Celia, jt. auth. see Perkins, Michael C.

Nunez, D. R., jt. auth. see Obon De Castro, Comcepcion.

***Nunez, Elizabeth.** Bruised Hibiscus: A Novel. LC 94-32697. 1994. 19.95 (1-56743-065-1) Amistad Pr.

***Nunez, Emilio A.** La Biblia y la Sanidad Divina. 60p. (SPA.). 1976. mass mkt., pap. 3.50 (0-8254-1514-4) Kregel.

— Teologia de la Liberacion: Un Enfoque Evangelico. 266p. (SPA.). 1986. pap. 7.50 (0-89922-242-0) Edit Caribe.

Nunez, Guillermo. Libros de Poemas. LC 78-1444. (UPREX, Poesia Ser.: No. 53). 231p. (SPA.). 1978. pap. 1.50 (0-8477-3225-8) U of PR Pr.

Nunez-Harrell, Elizabeth. When Rocks Dance. 1987. pap. 3.95 (0-345-34771-4) Ballantine.

Nunez, Henry J. Bring Your Own Restaurant Guide. (Orig.). 1992. pap. 9.95 (0-9634741-0-3) Phoenix Comns.

— Bring Your Own Restaurant Guide. 2nd enl. rev. ed. (Orig.). 1993. pap. 9.95 (0-9634741-1-1) Phoenix Comns.

Nunez, J., jt. auth. see Dumont, J. E.

Nunez, J., jt. ed. see Dumont, J. E.

Nunez, Javier F., ed. see Alberti.

Nunez, Luis. Relationships, You - Me - & the Others. 160p. 1994. pap. 8.95 (0-9640457-0-2) Cerebral Impact.

Nunez, Luis M. Santeria: A Practical Guide to Afro-Caribbean Magic. LC 92-24219. 163p. (Orig.). 1992. pap. 16.00 (0-88214-349-2) Spring Pubns.

Nunez, Margaret L., tr. see Baines, John.

Nunez-Melendez, Esteban. Plantas Medicinales de Puerto Rico: Folklore y Fundamentos Cientificos. 2nd abr. rev. ed. LC 82-17321. (Illus.). xii, 498p. (SPA.). 1988. pap. 22.95 (0-8477-2328-3) U of PR Pr.

Nunez, Nemours H. Chien Negre: A Tale of the Vaudoux. LC 72-4645. (Black Heritage Library Collection). 1977. reprint ed. 29.95 (0-8369-9116-8) Ayer.

Nunez, Orlando, jt. auth. see Burbach, Roger.

Nunez, Paul L. Neocortical Dynamics & Human EEG Rhythms. (Illus.). 608p. 1995. 95.00 (0-19-505728-7) OUP.

Nunez-Portuondo, Ricardo. Cuba: La Otra Imagen. LC 94-92123. 232p. (Orig.). (SPA.). 1994. pap. 19.95 (0-9641879-9-X) Cultural Pub.

— Cuban Refugee Program: The Early Years, 1959 - 1965. LC 94-92122. 135p. (Orig.). 1995. pap. 16.50 (0-9641879-7-3) Cultural Pub.

— General Emilio Nunez: Un Procer Cubano. (Illus.). 70p. (Orig.). (SPA.). 1994. pap. 6.00 (0-9641879-8-1) Cultural Pub.

Nunez, Raquel, tr. see Hume, Maggie.

Nunez, Raul. The Lonely Hearts Club. Emery, Ed, tr. (Masks Ser.). 160p. (Orig.). 1990. pap. 10.95 (1-85242-137-1) Serpents Tail.

Nunez, Samuel. The Vision of Daniel Eight: Interpretations from 1700-1800. (Andrews University Seminary Doctoral Dissertation Ser.: Vol. 14). 462p. (Orig.). 1989. pap. 16.95 (0-943872-95-2) Andrews Univ Pr.

***Nunez, Sigrid.** A Feather on the Breath of God: A Novel. LC 94-22766. 1994. 18.00 (0-06-017151-0) HarpC.

Nunez, Wilson P. Foreign Direct Investment & Industrial Development in Mexico. 164p. (Orig.). 1990. pap. 36.00 (92-64-13399-2) OECD.

Nunez-Wormack, Elsa, jt. ed. see Astone, Barbara.

Nunge, Richard J. Flow Through Porous Media. LC 78-146798. 248p. 1970. 15.95 (0-8412-0111-0) Am Chemical.

Nungesser, Lon G. Epidemic of Courage: Facing AIDS in America. (Stonewall Inn Editions Ser.). 272p. 1988. pap. 7.95 (0-312-01560-7) St Martin.

— Homosexual Acts, Actors & Identities. LC 83-17823. 238p. 1983. text ed. 55.00 (0-275-91052-0, C1052, Praeger Pubs) Greenwood.

— One Day at a Time: A Personal Guide to Coping with a Terminal Diagnosis. 1988. write for info. (0-318-61942-3) St Martin.

Nungessor, Lon. Axioms for Survivors. 128p. (C). 1990. reprint ed. lib. bdg. 23.00x (0-8095-6568-4) Borgo Pr.

Nungezer, Edwin. A Dictionary of Actors. LC 75-173803. reprint ed. 27.50 (0-404-04806-4) AMS Pr.

— Dictionary of Actors & of Other Persons Associated with the Public Representation of Plays in England Before 1642. LC 68-57633. 437p. 1969. reprint ed. text ed. 65.00 (0-8371-0593-5, NUDI, Greenwood Pr) Greenwood.

Nunhead, Nancy. Renoir. 1992. 5.98 (1-55521-765-6) Bk Sales Inc.

Nunis & Knill, Harry. Tales of Mexican California. (YA). (gr. 7-12). 1995. pap. 8.95 (0-88388-161-6) Bellerophon Bks.

Nunis, Doyce, Jr., intro. The Bidwell-Bartleson Party, 1841 California Emigrant Adventure: The Documents & Memoirs of the Overland Pioneers. LC 88-51900. (Illus.). 300p. 1991. 19.95 (0-934136-32-7) Western Tanager.

Nunis, Doyce, ed. see Tirsch, Ignacio.

Nunis, Doyce B., Jr. Great Doctors. (Illus.). 64p. (Orig.). (J). (gr. 8). 1991. pap. 3.95 (0-88388-144-6) Bellerophon Bks.

— The Life of Tom Horn Revisited. LC 92-29878. (Keepsake - The Westerners, Los Angeles Corral Ser.: No. 30). 1992. 14.95 (0-87095-107-6) Gldn West Bks.

Nunis, Doyce B. The Mexican War in Baja California: The Memorandum of Captain Henry W. Halleck Concerning His Expeditions in Lower California, 1846-1848. (Baja California Travels Ser.: No. 39). (Illus.). 208p. 1977. 24.00 (0-87093-239-X) Dawsons.

Nunis, Doyce B., Jr., ed. California Diary of Faxon Dean Atherton, 1836-1839. (Illus.). 246p. 1964. 8.95 (0-910312-00-1) Calif Hist.

— Los Angeles & Its Environs in the Twentieth Century. 501p. 1973. 35.00 (0-378-02581-3) Dawsons.

— The Seventeen Sixty-Nine Transit of Venus: The Baja California Observations of Jean-Baptiste Chappe d'Auteroche, Vicente de Doz, & Joaquin Velazquez Cardenas de Leon. Donahue, James et al, trs. LC 82-3548. (Baja California Travels Ser.: No. 46). (Illus.). 185p. 1982. 60.00 (0-938644-18-1) Nat Hist Mus.

Nunis, Doyce B., Jr. & Lothrop, Gloria R., eds. A Guide to the History of California. LC 88-15488. 321p. 1989. text ed. 75.00 (0-313-24970-9, NGC/, Greenwood Pr) Greenwood.

Nunis, Doyce B., ed. see Alric, Abbe H.

Nunis, Doyce B., Jr., ed. see Robinson, W. W.

Nunis, Doyce B., Jr., ed. see Taylor, Raymond G.

Nunley & Bechtel. Infrared Optoelectronics: Devices & Applications. (Optical Engineering Ser.: Vol. 12). 288p. 1987. 110.00 (0-8247-7586-4) Dekker.

Nunley, B. G., jt. auth. see Brand, Neal G.

Nunley, John W. Moving with the Face of the Devil: Art & Politics in Urban West Africa. LC 85-16455. (Illus.). 312p. 1987. 29.95 (0-252-01015-9) U of Ill Pr.

***Nunley, Lovie.** Glutton for Punishment. 1995. 9.95 (0-8062-5254-5) Carlton.

***Nunley, Richard.** The Berkshire Reader. 1995. pap. 16.95 (0-936399-63-5) Berkshire Hse.

— Berkshire Reader: Writings from New England's Secluded Paradise. (Illus.). 1992. 29.95 (0-936399-33-3) Berkshire Hse.

Nunn, Abigail. The Land of Tuppitry. (Illus.). 96p. (J). (gr. 3-4). 1991. reprint ed. pap. 4.95 (0-9620765-3-8) Victory Press.

Nunn, Adrian D., ed. Radiopharmaceuticals: Chemistry & Pharmacology. LC 92-18394. (Drugs & the Pharmaceutical Sciences Ser.: Vol. 55). 460p. 1992. 180.00 (0-8247-8624-6) Dekker.

Nunn, Ancel, jt. auth. see Hale, Leon.

Nunn, Bill. Bill Nunn's Column Book: Essays on the Unbought Graces of Life Everyday. 12.95 (0-915637-00-6) Westphalia Pr.

— Eye of the Eagle: The Outdoor Photography of Don Wooldridge. LC 81-83818. (Illus.). 128p. 1982. 20.00 (0-913504-71-8); pap. 12.95 (0-913504-72-6) Lowell Pr.

— Wrestling with Special Ed: Recollections by Bill Nunn (Written Without Assistance) of His Trials & His Triumphs As a Learning-Disabled Student. Sharkey, Corinne, ed. & illus. by. LC 94-93958. 352p. (Orig.). 1994. 15.00 (0-9644490-0-5) Bill Nunn.

Nunn, Bill, ed. see Ferrier, Grace B.

Nunn, Bill, ed. see Steinhardt, Edward J.

Nunn, C. F. Foreign Immigrants in Early Bourbon Mexico: Seventeen Hundred to Seventeen Sixty. LC 78-1159. (Cambridge Latin American Studies: No. 31). 1979. 74.95 (0-521-22051-3) Cambridge U Pr.

***Nunn, Chris.** Awareness: What It Is, What It Does. LC 95-13966. 1995. write for info. (0-415-13226-6); pap. write for info. (0-415-13227-4) Routledge.

Nunn, Clyde Z., et al. Tolerance for Nonconformity. LC 77-82920. (Jossey-Bass Social & Behavioral Science Ser.). 230p. reprint ed. pap. 65.60 (0-685-23667-6, 2052201) Bks Demand.

Nunn, Curtis. Marguerite Clark: America's Darling of Broadway & the Silent Screen. LC 81-4178. (Illus.). 188p. 1981. pap. 15.00 (0-912646-69-1) Tex Christian.

Nunn, Eric. Books, Books, Everywhere: A Browser's Guide to Bookstores & Libraries in Seattle & Bellevue. LC 93-93613. 68p. 1993. 6.95 (0-9637281-0-5) E Nunn Res.

Nunn, Frederick M. The Time of the Generals: Latin American Professional Militarism in World Perspective. LC 91-39896. xvi, 340p. 1992. 50.00 (0-8032-3334-5) U of Nebr Pr.

— Yesterday's Soldiers: European Military Professionalism in South America, 1890-1940. LC 82-6961. xiv, 365p. 1983. 35.00 (0-8032-3305-1) U of Nebr Pr.

Nunn, G. Raymond. Canada & Asia: A Guide to Archives & Manuscripts. 800p. 1995. text ed. 240.00 (0-7201-2110-8, Mansell Pub) Cassell.

Nunn, George E. The Geographical Conceptions of Colombus: A Critical Consideration of Four Problems. LC 72-8429. (Select Bibliographies Reprint Ser.). 1977. reprint ed. 20.95 (0-8369-6984-7) Ayer.

— The Geographical Conceptions of Columbus: A Critical Consideration of Four Problems. LC 92-71996. (Illus.). 195p. 1992. 15.00 (1-879281-06-6); pap. 8.00 (1-879281-08-2) G Meir Lib.

— Geographical Conceptions of Columbus: A Critical Consideration of Four Problems. (Select Bibliographies Reprint Ser.). reprint ed. lib. bdg. 23.50 (0-8290-0847-0) Irvington.

***Nunn, H. Jack.** Managing for Profits: Lumber Yar Management in the Decades Ahead. 87p. 1995. pap. 150.00 (0-9645680-0-4) CTBMA.

Nunn, J. F. Nunn's Applied Respiratory Physiology. 4th ed. (Illus.). 656p. 1993. 85.00 (0-7506-1336-X) Buttrwrth-Heinemann.

Nunn, J. F., et al. General Anesthesia. 5th ed. (Illus.). 1434p. 1989. text ed. 195.00 (0-407-00693-1) Buttrwrth-Heinemann.

Nunn, Jack H. The Soviet First Strike Threat: The U. S. Perspective. LC 82-344. 304p. 1982. text ed. 55.00 (0-275-90871-2, C0871, Praeger Pubs) Greenwood.

Nunn, Joan. Fashion in Costume. (Illus.). 256p. (C). 1990. reprint ed. pap. 18.95 (0-941533-79-4) New Amsterdam Bks.

Nunn, John. Beating the Sicilian Two: A Complete New Repertoire for White. (Illus.). 160p. 1990. pap. 12.95 (0-7134-6445-3, Pub. by Batsford UK) Trafalgar.

— The Classical King's Indian. 96p. 1990. pap. 14.95 (0-02-035540-8, Collier S&S) S&S Trade.

— John Nunns Best Games. 1995. pap. 26.95 (0-8050-3899-X) H Holt & Co.

— Marshall Attack. 160p. 1990. pap. 14.95 (0-02-035530-0, Collier S&S) S&S Trade.

— New Ideas in the Four Knights. (Batsford Chess Library). 128p. 1993. pap. 16.95 (0-8050-2629-0, Owl) H Holt & Co.

— New Ideas in the Pirc Defence. 144p. 1993. pap. 16.95 (0-8050-2939-7) H Holt & Co.

— Secrets of Grandmaster Play: Tournament Level. Griffiths, Peter, ed. (Chess Library). (Illus.). 176p. 1988. pap. 14.95 (0-02-053130-3, Collier S&S) S&S Trade.

— Secrets of Pawnless Endings. (Batsford Chess Library). 1994. pap. 26.95 (0-8050-3285-1) H Holt & Co.

— Secrets of Rook Endings. (Batsford Chess Library). 320p. 1993. pap. 26.95 (0-8050-2640-1, Owl) H Holt & Co.

Nunn, Kem. Pomona Queen. Sacco, Maryanne, ed. 240p. 1993. reprint ed. pap. 10.00 (0-671-79877-4, WSP) PB.

Nunn, Louie B. The Public Papers of Governor Louie B. Nunn, 1967-1971. Sexton, Robert F., ed. LC 74-18938. (Public Papers of the Governors of Kentucky). 640p. 1975. 40.00 (0-8131-0601-X) U Pr of Ky.

Nunn, M. The Americanismo of Ruben Dario. 1972. 150.00 (0-87968-613-8) Gordon Pr.

Nunn, Michael W. Teach Someone to Read! An Effective How-to Method for Basic Reading & Literacy Programs. (Orig.). 1986. pap. text ed. 12.00 (0-910609-13-6) Gifted Educ Pr.

Nunn, Nancy, jt. auth. see Brett, Jai.

Nunn, Patrick. Oceanic Islands. LC 92-28002. (Natural Environment Ser.). 360p. 1993. pap. 37.95 (0-631-18967-X) Blackwell Pubs.

— Oceanic Islands. LC 92-28002. (Natural Environment Ser.: Vol. 1). 360p. 1993. 84.95 (0-631-17811-2) Blackwell Pubs.

Nunn, Patrick D. Keimami Sa Vakila Na Liga Ni Kalou: Feeling the Hand of God: Human & Nonhuman Impacts on Pacific Island Environments. rev. ed. LC 92-27305. (Occasional Paper Ser.: No. 13). 1992. write for info. (0-86638-154-6) EW Ctr HI.

Nunn, R. Asia & Oceania: A Guide to Archival & Manuscript Sources in the United States, 5 vols., Set. 1985. text ed. 820.00 (0-7201-1713-5, Mansell Pub) Cassell.

Nunn, Rebecca O. Tom's Remembrance. (Illus.). 1987. 10.95 (0-915637-06-5) Westphalia Pr.

Nunn, Richard V. Home Improvement-Home Repair. Horowitz, Shirley M., ed. LC 80-66637. (Illus.). 256p. (Orig.). 1980. pap. 9.95 (0-932944-18-3) Creative Homeowner.

Nunn, Richard V., jt. auth. see Creative Homeowner Press Editors.

Nunn, Robert H. Intermediate Fluid Mechanics. (Illus.). 225p. (C). 1989. text ed. 59.50 (0-89116-647-5); write for info. (0-89116-020-5) Hemisp Pub.

Nunn, Robert R. & Geary, Edward J. The Yourcenar Collection: A Descriptive Catalogue. (Illus.). 1984. pap. 6.00 (0-916606-07-4) Bowdoin Coll.

Nunn, Ron & Marten, Kay. Adventures in Indian Cooking. (Illus.). 61p. (Orig.). 1990. pap. text ed. 5.95 (0-936731-10-9) Devel Self Rel.

Nunn, Sam. Critical Defense Choices. Gulliver, Hal, ed. LC 82-63197. (Papers on International Issues: No. 4). 19p. (Orig.). 1983. pap. text ed. 5.00 (0-935082-03-4) Southern Ctr Intl Stud.

— Nunn Nineteen Ninety: A New Military Strategy. (Significant Issues Ser.: Vol. 12, No. 5). 1990. pap. text ed. 7.95 (0-89206-150-2) CSI Studies.

Nunn, Sam, et al. The CSIS Strengthening of America Commission First Report. 182p. (gr. 13). 1992. pap. text ed. 20.00 (0-89206-211-8) CSI Studies.

Nunn, T. Percy. Anthropomorphism & Physics. 1977. lib. bdg. 59.95 (0-8490-1438-7) Gordon Pr.

Nunn, Trevor, jt. auth. see Caird, John.

Nunn, William C. Escape from Reconstruction. LC 74-9977. (Illus.). 140p. 1974. reprint ed. text ed. 35.00 (0-8371-7611-5, NUER, Greenwood Pr) Greenwood.

— Somervell: Story of a Texas County. LC 75-39912. 267p. reprint ed. pap. 76.10 (0-7837-1240-5, 2041377) Bks Demand.

***Nunnally, Ben & Plath, Tony, eds.** Cases in Finance. LC 94-27736. 400p. (C). 1994. 28.95 (0-256-12338-1) Irwin.

Nunnally, Bennie H. & Kester, George. Financial Management: A Practical Approach. 336p. (C). 1994. per. 27.20 (0-8403-9514-0) Kendall-Hunt.

Nunnally, Bennie H., Jr., et al. Corporate Lease Analysis: A Guide to Concepts & Evaluation. LC 90-45147. 256p. 1991. text ed. 59.95 (0-89930-513-X, NCC, Quorum Bks) Greenwood.

Nunnally, Elam & Moy, Caryl. Communication Basics for Human Service Professionals. (Human Services Guides Ser.: Vol. 56). 172p. (C). 1989. pap. text ed. 17.95 (0-8039-3118-2) Sage.

Nunnally, Jim C. Psychometric Theory. 2nd ed. (McGraw-Hill Psychology Ser.). 1978. text ed. write for info. (0-07-047465-6) McGraw.

N

Nunnally, Jim C. & Bernstein, Ira H. Psychometric Theory. 3rd ed. LC 93-22756. (Series in Social Psychology). 1993. text ed. write for info. (0-07-047849-X) McGraw.

Nunnally, Stephens W. Construction Methods & Management. 3rd ed. 496p. 1992. text ed. 70.00 (0-13-175274-X) P-H.

***Nunnally, Tiina.** Maija. 224p. 1995. 24.00 (0-940242-69-9); pap. 12.00 (0-940242-68-0) Fjord Pr.

Nunnally, Tiina, tr. see Alfredson, Hans.

Nunnally, Tiina, tr. see Andersen Nexo, Martin.

Nunnally, Tiina, tr. see Bang, Herman.

Nunnally, Tiina, tr. see Davidsen, Leif.

Nunnally, Tiina, tr. see Ditlevsen, Tove.

Nunnally, Tiina, tr. see Hamsun, Knut.

Nunnally, Tiina, tr. see Heinesen, William.

Nunnally, Tiina, tr. see Hoeg, Peter.

Nunnally, Tiina, tr. see Jacobsen, Jens P.

Nunnally, Tiina, tr. see Newth, Mette.

Nunnally, Tiina, tr. see Rifbjerg, Klaus.

Nunnally, Tiina, tr. see Sorensen, Villy.

Nunnally, Tiina, tr. see Widerberg, Siv.

Nunneley, Faithe S. Thrums. Bress, Seymour, ed. (Illus.). 149p. 1991. 14.95 (0-9620543-3-X) Flower Valley Pr.

***Nunnelley, Jeanette C.** Developmentally Appropriate Behavior Guidance for Three & Four Year Old Children. 21p. (Orig.). (C). 1994. pap. 4.00 (0-942388-11-9) So Early Childhood Assn.

Nunnelley, L. L. & Arnoldssen, T. C. Noise in Digital Magnetic Recording. 250p. 1992. text ed. 74.00 (981-02-0865-0); pap. text ed. 48.00 (981-02-1025-6) World Scientific Pub.

Nunnelley, William A. Bull Connor. 240p. 1990. pap. 21.95 (0-8173-0495-9) U of Ala Pr.

Nunnenkamp, Peter. The International Debt Crisis of the Third World: Causes & Consequences for the World Economy. LC 85-2008. 208p. 1986. text ed. 45.00 (0-312-42003-X) St Martin.

Nunnery, Gene. I Will Lift up Mine Eyes unto the Hills. 1989. 17.95 (0-916620-83-2) Portals Pr.

— The Old Pro Turkey Hunter. LC 80-80630. (Illus.). 1980. 12.50 (0-916620-48-4) Portals Pr.

Nunnery, Michael Y., jt. auth. see Kimbrough, Ralph B.

Nunney, M. J. Light & Heavy Vehicle Technology. 1988. pap. 32.95 (0-434-91473-8) Buttrwrth-Heinemann.

— Light & Heavy Vehicle Technology. 2nd ed. (Illus.). 528p. 1992. pap. 47.95 (0-7506-0477-8) Buttrwrth-Heinemann.

Nunno, T. J., et al. Toxic Waste Minimization in the Printed Circuit Board Industry. LC 88-22630. (Pollution Technology Review Ser.: No. 162). (Illus.). 162p. 1989. 39.00 (0-8155-1183-3) Noyes.

Nunno, Thomas, et al. International Technologies for Hazardous Waste Site Cleanup. LC 90-30223. (Pollution Technology Review Ser.: No. 183). (Illus.). 283p. 1990. 45.00 (0-8155-1238-4) Noyes.

Nuno, D. Enciclopedia de Poesia Evangelica: Encyclopedia of Evangelical Poetry. 5th ed. 365p. (SPA.). 1983. 19.95 (0-7859-5054-0); pap. 19.25 (0-8288-5220-0, S50573) Fr & Eur.

Nuno, Daniel. Enciclopedia De Poesia Evangelica: Encyclopedia of Evangelical Poetry. (SPA.). 8.95 (0-317-04673-X, 220361, Pub. by Edit Clie SP) TSELF.

— Ofrenda Poetica: Poetic Offering. (SPA.). 5.50 (84-7228-886-2, 222351, Pub. by Edit Clie SP) TSELF.

— Poesias para la Iglesia Cristiana: Poems for the Christian Church. (SPA.). 8.95 (84-7228-271-6, 220700, Pub. by Edit Clie SP) TSELF.

Nunokawa, Jeff. The Afterlife of Property: Domestic Security & the Victorian Novel. LC 93-30912. 1994. 24.95 (0-691-03320-X) Princeton U Pr.

— Oscar Wilde. LC 93-42397. (Lives of Notable Gay Men & Lesbians Ser.). (J). 1994. write for info. (0-7910-2311-7) Chelsea Hse.

— Oscar Wilde. Duberman, Martin, ed. (Lives of Notable Gay Men & Lesbians Ser.). (Illus.). 168p. (YA). (gr. 9 up). 1995. pap. 9.95 (0-7910-2884-4) Chelsea Hse.

Nunrich, C. Consider the Issues: Developing Listening & Critical Thinking Skills. (Illus.). 1987. audio, text ed. 53.08 (0-8013-0137-8, 75801); pap. text ed. 15.34 (0-582-90749-7, 75257); pap. text ed. 43.64 (0-582-90750-0, 75258) Longman.

Nuns of the Monastery of St. Clare, Balsbach, Germany Staff, et al. The Celebration of the Eucharist: The Church's Festival of Love. Smith, David, tr. 1983. 4.00 (0-8199-0866-5, Frncscn Herld) Franciscan Pr.

Nuns of the Visitation Staff, tr. see St. Francis de Sales.

Nunukul, Oodgeroo. Stradbroke Dreamtime. 93p. (Orig.). 1993. pap. 10.00 (0-207-17616-7, Pub. by Angus & Robertson AT) HarpC.

Nunz, Gregory J. Electronics in Our World: A Survey. LC 70-146682. (Illus.). 1972. 39.00 (0-13-252288-8) P-H.

***Nunzio, Rollo R.** Jews, Judaism & the Holocaust: Index of New Information & Current Results of Conditions, Analysis & Progress. 170p. 1995. 44.50 (0-7883-0686-3); pap. 39.50 (0-7883-0687-1) ABBE Pubs Assn.

Nuotio-Antar, Vappu S., jt. auth. see Antar, Basil N.

Nuovo, Gerard J. Cytopathology of the Lower Female Genital Tract: An Integrated Approach. LC 93-9608. (Illus.). 464p. 1994. 165.00 (0-683-06595-5) Williams & Wilkins.

— PCR in Situ Hybridization: Protocols & Applications. 2nd ed. LC 94-4167. 464p. 1994. 80.00 (0-7817-0183-X) Raven.

Nuovo, Gerard J., jt. auth. see Crum, Christopher P.

Nuovo, Victor. Visionary Science: A Translation of Tillich's "On the Idea of a Theology of Culture" with an Interpretive Essay. LC 87-26352. 195p. 1987. 29.95 (0-8143-1940-8) Wayne St U Pr.

Nuovo, Victor, tr. see Tillich, Paul.

NUPE Women's Comittee Northern Ireland Staff. Women's Voices: An Oral History of Women's Health in Northern Ireland. (Illus.). 144p. (Orig.). (C). 1992. pap. 9.99 (1-85594-035-3, Pub. by Attic IE) InBook.

Nuquist, Reidun D., comp. Index to News & Notes & Vermont History News, 1949-1989, Vols. 1-40. 185p. 1993. pap. 34.95 (0-934720-39-8) VT Hist Soc.

— Vermont History Index: The Proceedings of the Vermont Historical Society, 1953-1977, Vols. 21-45. 268p. 1979. pap. 3.75 (0-934720-20-7) VT Hist Soc.

— Vermont History Index, Vols. 46-55: The Proceedings of the Vermont Historical Society, 1978-1987. 136p. 1991. pap. 24.95 (0-934720-34-7) VT Hist Soc.

Nur, Amos & Wang, Zhijing, eds. Seismic & Acoustic Velocities in Reservoir Rocks, Vol. 1: Experimental Studies. (Geophysics Reprint Ser.: No. 10). 420p. (Orig.). 1989. pap. 45.00 (0-931830-70-2, 470) Soc Expl Geophys.

Nur, Amos, jt. ed. see Wang, Zhijing.

Nura Kly, ed. Shelter in the Light: Poetry of the Islamic Awakening. 108p. (Orig.). 1993. pap. 9.95 (0-932863-11-6) Clarity Pr.

NurAhmed, Steven. Love Garden Colors Poetry. 1992. pap. text ed. write for info. (0-9629532-2-9) Black Angels.

Nurbakhsh. Sufi Women. rev. ed. Chittick, William C., ed. Lewisohn, Leonard, tr. 264p. 1990. pap. 11.95 (0-933546-42-4) KNP.

Nurbakhsh, Ali-Reza, tr. see Nurbakhsh, Javad.

Nurbakhsh, Iavad. The Great Satan "EBLIS" Graham, Terry et al, trs. 103p. 1986. pap. 7.95 (0-933546-23-8) KNP.

Nurbakhsh, Javad. Dogs from a Sufi Point of View. Graham, Terry et al, trs. (Illus.). 100p. 1989. pap. 11.95 (0-933546-39-4) KNP.

— In the Paradise of the Sufis. LC 79-83588. 125p. 1979. pap. 8.95 (0-933546-01-7) KNP.

— In the Tavern of Ruin: Seven Essays on Sufism. LC 78-102838. 135p. (Orig.). 1978. pap. 9.95 (0-933546-00-9) KNP.

— Jesus in the Eyes of the Sufis. 1992. pap. 8.95 (0-933546-21-1) KNP.

— Masters of the Path: A History of the Masters of the Nimatullahi Sufi Order. 2nd ed. LC 80-80902. (Illus.). 132p. 1994. pap. 9.95 (0-933546-03-3) KNP.

— The Nurbakhsh Encyclopedia of Sufi Terminology. Graham, Terry et al, trs. (PER.). 1991. write for info. (0-318-68434-9) KNP.

— Psychology of Sufism. 1993. 22.95 (0-933646-49-6) Aries Pr.

— The Psychology of Sufism. 1993. 22.95 (0-933546-49-1) KNP.

— Sufi Symbolism Vol. I: The Nurbakhsh Encyclopedia of Sufi Terminology the Beloved's Body, Wine, Music, Convivial Gatherings. Graham, Terry et al, trs. 190p. 1990. 30.00 (0-933546-40-8) KNP.

— Sufi Symbolism Vol. IV: The Nurbakhsh Encyclopedia of Sufi Terminology the Natural World, Symbolism of Birds & Other Animals in Sufi Poetry. Lewisohn, Leonard & Graham, Terry, trs. 228p. 1986. 30.00 (0-933546-12-2) KNP.

— Sufi Symbolism Vol. V: Veils & Clothing, Government, Economics & Commerce, Medicine & Healing. Graham, Terry, tr. 194p. 1991. 30.00 (0-933546-45-9) KNP.

— Sufi Symbolism Vol. VI: Spiritual Titles & Epithets the Nurbakhsh Encyclopedia of Sufi Terminology. 1993. 25.00 (0-933546-48-3) KNP.

— Sufi Symbolism Vol. VII: Contemplative Disciplines, Teophanies & Visions, Family Relationships, Servants of God, Names of Sufi Orders. Grahom, Terry et al, trs. 208p. 1993. 30.00 (0-933546-52-1) KNP.

— Sufi Symbolism Vol. VIII: Inspirations, Revelations, Lights, Charismatic Powers, Spiritual States & Stations, Praise & Condemnation. Grahom, Terry et al, trs. 167p. 1994. 25.00 (0-933546-53-X) KNP.

— Sufi Symbolism, Vol. II: The Nurbakhsh Encyclopedia of Sufi Terminology. Graham, Terry, tr. 193p. 1987. 30.00 (0-933546-31-9) KNP.

— Sufi Symbolism, Vol. III: The Nurbakhsh Encyclopedia of Sufi Terminology. Graham, Terry et al, trs. 263p. 1988. 30.00 (0-933546-35-1) KNP.

— Sufism I: Meaning, Knowledge, & Unity. Wilson, Peter & Chiltick, William, trs. 111p. (Orig.). 1981. pap. 9.95 (0-933546-05-X) KNP.

— Sufism II: Fear & Hope, Contraction & Expansion, Gathering & Dispersion, Intoxication, & Sobriety, Annihilation & Subsistence. Chittick, William, tr. 126p. (Orig.). 1982. pap. 9.95 (0-933546-07-6) KNP.

— Sufism-III: Submission, Contentment, Absence, Presence, Intimacy. Graham, Terry & Lewisohn, Leonard, trs. 133p. 1985. pap. 11.95 (0-933546-19-X) KNP.

— Traditions of the Prophet, Vol. 2. Lewisohn, Leonard & Graham, Terry, trs. 93p. (ARA, ENG & PER.). 1984. pap. 8.95 (0-933546-10-6) KNP.

— Traditions of the Prophet (Ahadith), Vol. 1. Rothschild, Jeffrey et al, eds. Lewisehn, Leonard & Nurbakhsh, Ali-Reza, trs. 102p. (ARA, ENG & PER.). 1993. reprint ed. pap. 8.95 (0-933546-06-8) KNP.

— The Truths of Love. Lewisohn, Leonard, tr. 1982. pap. 8.95 (0-933546-08-4) KNP.

Nurbaksh, Javad. Divani Nurbakhsh: Sufi Poetry. Rothschild, Jeffrey & Weber, Paul, eds. Godlas, Alan et al, trs. LC 80-84113. 265p. (ENG & PER.). 1980. 30.00 (0-933546-04-1) KNP.

Nurcombe, Barry & Gallagher, Rollin M. The Clinical Process in Psychiatry: Diagnosis & Management Planning. (Illus.). 520p. 1986. pap. 44.95 (0-521-28928-9) Cambridge U Pr.

Nurcombe, Barry & Partlett, David F. Child Mental Health & the Law. LC 93-50557. 1994. text ed. 39.95 (0-02-923245-7) Free Pr.

***Nurcombe, Valerie.** Information Sources in Official Publications. 1996. 95.00 (1-85739-151-9) Bowker-Saur.

***Nurcombe, Valerie, ed.** Information Sources in Architecture and Construction. 2nd ed. 500p. 1995. 90.00 (1-85739-094-6) Bowker-Saur.

Nurcombe, Valerie J. International Real Estate Valuation, Investment & Development: A Select Bibliography. LC 87-14906. (Bibliographies & Indexes in Economics & Economic History Ser.: No. 7). 205p. 1987. text ed. 59.95 (0-313-26082-6, NRE/, Greenwood Pr) Greenwood.

Nuremberg War Trials Staff. Trial of the Major War Criminals Before the International Military Tribunal, 44 vols., Set. LC 70-145536. reprint ed. write for info. (0-404-53650-6) AMS Pr.

Nurge, Ethel. Life in a Leyte Village. LC 65-23916. (American Ethnological Society Monographs: No. 40). (Illus.). 1965. 20.00 (0-295-73829-4) U of Wash Pr.

Nurge, Ethel, ed. The Modern Sioux: Social Systems & Reservation Culture. LC 71-88089. 368p. reprint ed. pap. 104.90 (0-685-17034-9, 2027879) Bks Demand.

Nurick, Aaron J. Participation in Organizational Change: The TVA Experiment. LC 84-26652. 256p. 1985. text ed. 59.95 (0-275-90149-1, C0149, Praeger Pubs) Greenwood.

Nurick, Robert, ed. Nuclear Weapons & European Security. LC 83-40150. (Adelphi Library). 186p. 1984. text ed. 29.95 (0-312-57980-2) St Martin.

Nuriddin, J. & El Hadi, S. The Last Poets: Vibes from the Scribes Selected Poems. LC 91-78312. 92p. 1992. reprint ed. 24.95 (0-86543-316-X); reprint ed. pap. 9.95 (0-86543-317-8) Africa World.

Nurius, Paula S. & Hudson, Walter W. Practice, Evaluation & Computers: A Practical Guide for Today & Beyond. (C). 1993. pap. 47.95 (0-534-15090-X) Brooks-Cole.

Nurius, Paula S., jt. ed. see Hudson, Walter W.

Nurkse, Dennis. Shadow Wars. 1988. pap. 7.00 (0-914610-48-1); boxed 15.00 (0-914610-54-6) Hanging Loose.

— Staggered Lights. 1990. pap. 9.00 (0-937669-42-3) Owl Creek Pr.

— Voices over Water. 96p. 1993. pap. 10.00 (1-55597-188-1) Graywolf.

Nurkse, Dennis & Castelle, Kay. In the Spirit of Peace: A Global Introduction to Children's Rights. (Illus.). 72p. (Orig.). (gr. 5-10). 1990. pap. text ed. 7.95 (0-943965-14-4) DCI USA.

Nurkse, Dennis & Castelle, Kay, eds. Children's Rights: Crisis & Challenge: A Global Report on the Situation of Children in View of the U. N. Convention on the Rights of the Child. 384p. (Orig.). 1990. pap. 25.00 (0-943965-13-6) DCI USA.

Nurland, Patricia. Vietnam. LC 89-43178. (Children of the World Ser.). (Illus.). 64p. (J). (gr. 5-6). 1991. lib. bdg. 21.26 (0-8368-0230-6) Gareth Stevens Inc.

Nurmela, T. Finnish-French Dictionary. 683p. (FIN & FRE.). Date not set. 95.00 (0-7859-0914-1, M-9651) Fr & Eur.

***Nurmi, Debbie, et al.** Greater Lynchburg: The Real Virginia. Gilreath, Lenita & Turner, James E., eds. (Illus.). 170p. 1995. 35.00 (1-885352-16-6) Community Comm.

Nurmi, Hannu. Comparing Voting Systems. (C). 1987. lib. bdg. 80.50 (90-277-2600-0) Kluwer Ac.

Nurmi, Martin. Blake's Marriage of Heaven & Hell. LC 72-6067. (Studies in Blake: No. 3). 1972. reprint ed. lib. bdg. 75.00 (0-8383-1599-2) M S G Haskell Hse.

Nurmi, Martin K., jt. auth. see Bentley, Gerald E.

Nurmi, O., et al, eds. Algorithm Theory - SWAT 92: Third Scandinavian Workshop on Algorithm Theory Helsinki, Finland July 8-10, 1992 Proceedings. LC 92-18643. (Lecture Notes in Computer Science Ser.: Vol. 621). viii, 434p. 1992. pap. 63.00 (0-387-55706-7) Spr-Verlag.

Nurmi, Ruth. A Plain & Easy Introduction to the Harpsichord. LC 86-1875. 262p. 1986. reprint ed. 29.50 (0-8108-1886-8) Scarecrow.

***Nurminen, Mika.** Wild West Country Dancing. LC 95-3836. (Illus.). 128p. 1995. pap. text ed. 20.00 (0-88734-652-9) Players Pr.

Nurnberg, H. W., ed. Electroanalytical Chemistry. LC 73-15061. (Advances in Analytical Chemistry & Instrumentation Ser.: No. 10). 621p. reprint ed. pap. 177.00 (0-685-20644-0, 2030430) Bks Demand.

— Pollutants & Their Ecotoxicological Significance. LC 84-7540. (Wiley-Interscience Publication Ser.). (Illus.). 529p. reprint ed. pap. 150.80 (0-7837-3413-1, 2043380) Bks Demand.

Nurnberg, Maxwell. What to Name Your Baby. 1962. pap. 2.95 (0-02-081020-2) Macmillan.

Nurnberg, Maxwell & Rosenblum, Morris. How to Build a Better Vocabulary. 384p. 1989. mass mkt. 4.50 (0-446-31506-0) Warner Bks.

— What to Name Your Baby: From Adam to Zoe. 2nd ed. 352p. 1984. pap. 4.95 (0-02-081010-5, Pub. by Gebrueder Borntraeger GW) Macmillan.

Nurnberger, G. Approximation by Spline Functions. (Illus.). xi, 243p. 1989. 39.50 (0-387-51618-2, 3491) Spr-Verlag.

Nurnberger, Gunter, jt. auth. see Meinardus, Gunter.

Nurnberger, Lisa, jt. ed. see Lethcoe, Nancy.

***Nurnberger, M. W., et al.** Analysis of a Log-Periodic Folded Slot Antenna Array on Planar & Cylindrical Platforms. fac. ed. (University of Michigan Report: No. 031169-1-T). 61p. 1994. pap. 25.00 (0-7837-7697-7, 2047454) Bks Demand.

Nurock, Max, jt. ed. see Boasson, Charles.

Nurse Assistant Consortium Staff. Handbook for Nurse Assistants: A Pocket Reference. 334p. 1990. 15.95 (0-944132-15-4) Skidmore Roth Pub.

Nurse, Derek & Hinnebusch, Thomas J. Swahili & Sabaki: A Linguistic History. LC 93-4560. (Problems in Linguistics Ser.: Vol. 121). 1993. 82.00 (0-520-09775-0) U CA Pr.

Nurse, Derek & Spear, Thomas. The Swahili: Reconstructing the History & Language of An African Society, 800-1500. LC 84-3659. (Ethnohistory Ser.). (Illus.). 160p. 1985. pap. text ed. 18.95 (0-8122-1207-X) U of Pa Pr.

Nurse, G. T. & Jenkins, T. Health & the Hunter-Gatherer. (Monographs in Human Genetics: Vol. 8). 1976. 41.00 (3-8055-2401-3) S Karger.

Nurse, G. T., et al. The Peoples of Southern Africa & Their Affinities. (Research Monographs on Human Population Biology). (Illus.). 1986. 80.00 (0-19-857541-6) OUP.

Nurse, Lawrence A. Trade Unionism & Industrial Relations in the Commonwealth Caribbean: History, Contemporary Practice & Prospect. LC 91-38212. (Contributions in Legal Studies: No. 40). 168p. 1992. text ed. 45.00 (0-313-28380-X, NTU, Greenwood Pr) Greenwood.

Nurse, M. C. & Serjeantson, R. M., eds. Metallurgical Plantmakers of the World. 3rd ed. 494p. 1989. 167.00 (0-947671-18-8) Metal Bulletin.

Nurse, Milton, ed. Foundry Directory & Register of Forgas Europe. 16th ed. 371p. 1991. 110.00 (0-947671-44-7) Metal Bulletin.

Nurse, P. Corneille: Le Cid. (Bristol French Texts Ser.). (FRE.). 1992. 14.95 (0-685-49971-5, Pub. by Brstl Class Pr UK) Focus Info Gr.

Nurse, Paul & Streiblova, Eva, eds. The Microbial Cell Cycle. 304p. 1984. 191.00 (0-8493-5574-5, QR73, CRC Reprint) Franklin.

Nurse, Peter H., ed. see Corneille, Pierre.

Nurser, Elizabeth, jt. auth. see La Nauze, J. A.

Nursey-Bray, Paul, et al. Anarchist Thinkers & Thought: An Annotated Bibliography. LC 91-33407. (Bibliographies & Indexes in Law & Political Science Ser.: No. 17). 320p. 1992. text ed. 59.95 (0-313-27592-0, NBR, Greenwood Pr) Greenwood.

Nursey-Bray, Rosemary. The Little Mermaid. (Illus.). 56p. 1982. 10.00 (0-88680-377-2); pap. 4.00 (0-88680-113-3); pap. 15.00 (0-88680-114-1) I E Clark.

— Through the Looking Glass & What Alice Found There. (Orig.). (J). (ps up). 1987. 5.50 (0-87602-276-X) Anchorage.

Nursing Council of the Boston Association for Childbirth Education. Breastfeeding Your Baby: A Practical Guide for the New Mother. 3rd ed. LC 89-387. (Illus.). 128p. (Orig.). 1989. pap. 3.95 (0-89529-387-0) Avery Pub.

Nursten, H. E., jt. ed. see Land, D. G.

Nursten, Jean, ed. see Gore, Elizabeth.

Nurul Islam. Development Planning in Bangladesh: A Study in Political Economy. LC 77-77354. 1977. text ed. 29.95 (0-312-19694-6) St Martin.

Nus, Jeff, ed. see Burpee, L. L.

Nusairi, Osman, tr. see El-Saadawi, Nawal.

Nusbaum, D. D., jt. auth. see Zehren, Vincent.

Nusbaum, Howard C., jt. ed. see Goodman, Judith.

Nusbaum, Howard C., jt. auth. see Schwab, Eileen C.

Nusbaum, Marlene & Verdier, Liliane. Parlez sans Peur. (FRE.). 1983. pap. text ed. 24.00 (0-03-058577-5) HB Coll Pubs.

Nusbaum, Rosemary. The City Different & the Palace. LC 78-17591. (Illus.). 1978. pap. 6.95 (0-913270-79-2) Sunstone Pr.

— Tierra Dulce: The Jesse Nusbaum Papers. LC 80-18365. (Illus.). 128p. 1980. pap. 7.95 (0-913270-83-0) Sunstone Pr.

Nusbaumer, Jacques A. Services in the Global Market. (C). 1987. lib. bdg. 64.00 (0-89838-198-3) Kluwer Ac.

Nusberg, Charlotte, ed. Mandatory Retirement: Blessing or Curse? 27p. (Orig.). 1978. pap. text ed. 3.50 (0-910473-06-4) Intl Fed Ageing.

— Self-Determination by the Elderly. LC 82-218. (Orig.). 1981. pap. text ed. 2.50 (0-910473-11-0) Intl Fed Ageing.

Nusberg, Charlotte & Osako, Masako M., eds. The Situation of the Asian-Pacific Elderly. 116p. (Orig.). 1981. pap. text ed. 5.00 (0-910473-10-2) Intl Fed Ageing.

Nusberg, Charlotte & Sokolovsky, Jay, eds. International Directory of Research & Researchers in Comparative Gerontology. rev. ed. 305p. 1990. pap. text ed. 15.00 (0-910473-22-6) Intl Fed Ageing.

Nusberg, Charlotte, jt. auth. see Dunham, Arthur.

Nusberg, Charlotte, jt. ed. see Habib, Jack.

Nusberg, Charlotte, jt. auth. see Peace, Sheila.

Nusberg, Charlotte, et al. Innovative Aging Programs Abroad: Implications for the United States. LC 83-10811. (Contributions to the Study of Aging Ser.: No. 2). (Illus.). xvi, 260p. 1984. text ed. 65.00 (0-313-23684-4, NPE/, Greenwood Pr) Greenwood.

Nuschke, Marie K. The Dam That Could Not Break. (Illus.). 50p. 1961. pap. 3.75 (0-939542-05-6) Leader Pub Co Inc.

Nusom, Lynn. Christmas in Arizona: Recipes, Traditions & Folklore for the Holiday Season. Parker, Steve, tr. LC 92-32251. (Illus.). 128p. 1992. pap. 8.95 (0-914846-65-5) Golden West Pub.

— Christmas in New Mexico: Recipes, Traditions & Folklore for the Holiday Season. LC 91-34113. (Illus.). 144p. (Orig.). 1991. pap. 8.95 (0-914846-59-0) Golden West Pub.

— The Hatch Chile Cookbook: Hot & Spicy Recipes Featuring the World's Finest Chile Peppers. 220p. 1994. 15.95 (1-884374-03-4) Border Bks.

— New Mexico Cook Book. LC 90-3391. 144p. (Orig.). 1990. spiral bd. 5.95 (0-914846-48-5) Golden West Pub.

— The Sizzling Southwestern Cookbook. LC 94-35379. 224p. 1995. 25.00 (1-56565-210-X) Lowell Hse.

— The Tequila Cook Book. LC 93-21428. 128p. 1993. 7.95 (0-914846-89-2) Golden West Pub.

N

Nuss, A. M. Export for Marketing French. 96p. (ENG & FRE.). 1979. pap. 17.95 (0-8288-5456-4, M9208) Fr & Eur.

Nuss, Calvin E. Her Golden Door. LC 85-15333. 163p. 1991. pap. 13.00 (0-9615278-0-3) Am Hist Soc Ger.

Nuss, Ingo. Zur Oekologie der Porlinge, II: Entwicklungsmorphologie der Fruchtkoerper und ihre Beeinflussung durch Klimatische und Andere Faktoren. (Bibliotheca Mycologica Ser.: Vol. 105). (Illus.). 456p. (GER.). 1986. pap. text ed. 112.00 (3-443-59006-3) Lubrecht & Cramer.

Nuss, Shirley, et al. Women in the World of Work: Statistical Analysis & Projections to the Year 2000. (Women, Work & Development Ser.: No. 18). x, 132p. (Orig.). 1989. pap. 16.00 (92-2-106507-3) Intl Labour Office.

Nussbaum, Alan J. Head & Horn in Indo-European. (Studies in Indo-European Language & Culture NF: Vol. 2). xiii, 305p. 1986. 146.15 (0-89925-132-3) De Gruyter.

— Head & Horn in Indo-European. (Studies in Indo-European Language & Culture NF: Vol. 2). xiii, 305p. 1986. 146.15 (3-11-010449-0) De Gruyter.

Nussbaum, Chaim. The Essence of Teshuvah: A Path to Repentance. LC 93-1226. 208p. 1994. 25.00 (1-56821-025-6) Aronson.

— Semblance & Reality. write for info. (0-88125-385-5) Ktav.

Nussbaum, D., jt. ed. see Greer, W. R., Jr.

Nussbaum, Daniel. PL8SPK: California Vanity Plates Retell the Classics. LC 93-14294. 96p. 1993. 15.00 (0-06-258506-1) Harper SF.

Nussbaum, Elaine. Recovery from Cancer: A Personal Story of Sickness & Health. LC 92-3385. 202p. (Orig.). 1992. pap. 9.95 (0-89529-504-0) Avery Pub.

Nussbaum, Eliezer, ed. Pediatric Intensive Care. 2nd ed. (Illus.). 964p. 1989. 150.00 (0-87993-343-7) Futura Pub.

Nussbaum, Felicity & Brown, Laura, eds. The New Eighteenth Century: Theory, Politics, English Literature. 325p. 1987. 35.00 (0-416-01631-6, 1191); pap. 13.95 (0-416-01641-3, 1196) Routledge Chapman & Hall.

Nussbaum, Felicity A. The Autobiographical Subject: Gender & Ideology in Eighteenth-Century England. LC 89-32587. 288p. 1989. text ed. 38.50x (0-8018-3825-8) Johns Hopkins.

— The Autobiographical Subject: Gender & Ideology in Eighteenth-Century England. 288p. 1995. reprint ed. pap. text ed. 16.95x (0-8018-5237-4) Johns Hopkins.

— The Brink of All We Hate: English Satires on Women 1660-1750. LC 83-10181. 192p. 1983. 21.00 (0-8131-1498-5) U Pr of Ky.

— Torrid Zones: Maternity, Sexuality & Empire in Eighteenth Century English Narratives. LC 95-11801. (Parallax). (Illus.). 248p. 1995. text ed. 45.00x (0-8018-5074-6); pap. text ed. 14.95x (0-8018-5075-4) Johns Hopkins.

Nussbaum, Felicity A., intro. Satires on Women. LC 92-24348. (Augustan Reprints Ser.: No. 180 (1976)). reprint ed. 12.00 (0-404-70180-9, PR1195) AMS Pr.

Nussbaum, Frederick L. Commercial Policy in the French Revolution: A Study of the Career of G. J. A. Ducher. LC 79-111782. reprint ed. 41.50 (0-404-04807-2) AMS Pr.

— History of the Economic Institutions of Modern Europe: An Introduction to "Der Moderne Kapitalismus" of Werner Sombart. LC 67-29494. (Reprints of Economic Classics Ser.). (Illus.). xvi, 448p. 1968. reprint ed. 49.50 (0-678-00348-3) Kelley.

Nussbaum, G. Homer's Metre. 44p. 1986. 8.95 (0-86292-172-4, Pub. by Brstl Class Pr UK) Focus Info Gr.

— Vergil's Metre. 104p. 1986. 13.95 (0-86292-173-2, Pub. by Brstl Class Pr UK) Focus Info Gr.

Nussbaum, Gilbert H., ed. Physical Aspects of Hyperthermia: Proceedings of the AAPM Summer School Held at Dartmouth College, Hanover, New Hampshire, August 3-7, 1981. (American Association of Physicists in Medicine Symposium Ser.: No. 8). 650p. 1982. 50.00 (0-88318-414-1) Am Inst Physics.

Nussbaum, Hedda. Animals Build Amazing Homes. LC 79-11326. (Step-up Bks.: No. 29). (Illus.). (J). (gr. 2-5). 1979. 7.95 (0-394-83850-5) Random Bks Yng Read.

— Plants Do Amazing Things. LC 75-36471. (Step-up Bks.: No. 24). (Illus.). 72p. (J). (gr. 2-3). 1977. 11.00 (0-394-83232-9); lib. bdg. 8.99 (0-394-93232-3) Random Bks Yng Read.

Nussbaum, Jack. Punch Line Rhyme. LC 92-96976. 102p. 1992. 13.50 (0-9636110-0-3); pap. 9.50 (0-9636110-1-1) Nut Tree Ent.

***Nussbaum, Jon F. & Coupland, Justine, eds.** Handbook of Communication & Aging Research. (Communication Ser.). 520p. 1995. text ed. 90.00 (0-8058-1453-1) L Erlbaum Assocs.

Nussbaum, Jon F., jt. auth. see Coupland, Nikolas.

Nussbaum, Jon F., et al. Communication & Aging. 275p. (C). 1990. pap. text ed. 21.00 (0-06-046684-7) HarpCollege.

***Nussbaum, Martha & Glover, Jonathon, eds.** Women, Culture, & Development: A Study of Human Capabilities. (WIDER Studies in Development Economics). (Illus.). 376p. 1995. 70.00 (0-19-828917-0); pap. 18.95 (0-19-828964-2) OUP.

Nussbaum, Martha C. Aristotle's "De Motu Animalium" LC 77-72132. 456p. 1985. pap. text ed. 29.95 (0-691-02035-3) Princeton U Pr.

— The Fragility of Goodness: Luck & Ethics in Greek Tragedy & Philosophy. 672p. 1986. 89.95 (0-521-25768-9); pap. 29.95 (0-521-27702-7) Cambridge U Pr.

— Love's Knowledge: Essays on Philosophy & Literature. 432p. 1992. pap. 18.95 (0-19-507485-8) OUP.

— Poetic Justice: The Literary Imagination & Public Life. 128p. (C). 1996. 20.00 (0-8070-4108-4) Beacon Pr.

— The Therapy of Desire: Theory & Practice in Hellenistic Ethics. LC 93-6417. 1994. 29.95 (0-691-03342-0) Princeton U Pr.

Nussbaum, Martha C. & Rorty, Amelie O., eds. Essays on Aristotle's De Anima. 384p. 1992. 55.00 (0-19-824461-4) OUP.

— Essays on Aristotle's De Anima. 448p. 1995. reprint ed. pap. 24.00 (0-19-823600-X) OUP.

Nussbaum, Martha C. & Sen, Amartya K., eds. The Quality of Life. (WIDER Studies in Development Economics). (Illus.). 464p. 1993. pap. 21.00 (0-19-828797-6) OUP.

Nussbaum, Martha C., jt. ed. see Brunschwig, Jacques.

Nussbaum, Max. Max Nussbaum, from Berlin to Hollywood: A Mid-Century Vision of Jewish Life. Nussbaum, Ruth, ed. LC 94-66030. (Illus.). 300p. 1994. 25.00 (0-934710-30-9) J Simon.

***Nussbaum, Melissa M.** I Will Lie down This Night. 48p. (Orig.). 1995. pap. write for info. (1-56854-085-X, NITEPR) Liturgy Tr Pubns.

Nussbaum, Miguel. Building a Deductive Database. Zobrist, George W., ed. (Computer Engineering & Computer Science Ser.). 172p. (C). 1992. text ed. 54.50 (0-89391-768-0) Ablex Pub.

Nussbaum, Nancy & Bigler, Erin D. Identification & Treatment of Attention Deficit Disorder. (Child Guidance Mental Health Ser.). 1990. pap. text ed. 8.00 (0-89079-263-1, 1506) PRO-ED.

Nussbaum, R. Hilbert's Projective Metric & Iterated Nonlinear Maps. LC 88-16693. (MEMO Ser.: No. 75/391). 137p. 1988. pap. 22.00 (0-8218-2454-6, MEMO 75/391) Am Math.

— Iterated Nonlinear Maps & Hilbert's Projective Metric, Pt. 2. LC 89-6590. (MEMO Ser.: No. 79/401). 118p. 1989. pap. 20.00 (0-8218-2465-1, MEMO 79/401) Am Math.

Nussbaum, Roger & Peitgen, Heinz O. Special & Spurious Solutions of X(T) equals -aF(X(T-1)), Vol. 310. LC 84-14568. (Memoirs of the American Mathematical Society Ser.: No. 51/310). 129p. 1984. pap. 21.00 (0-8218-2311-6, MEMO 51/310) Am Math.

Nussbaum, Roger D. Differential-Delay Equations with Two Time Lags. LC 78-16320. (Memoirs of the American Mathematical Society Ser.: No. 205). 62p. reprint ed. pap. 25.00 (0-7837-2035-1, 2042302) Bks Demand.

Nussbaum, Ronald A., et al. Amphibians & Reptiles of the Pacific Northwest. LC 82-60202. (Illus.). 332p. 1983. pap. 24.95 (0-89301-086-3) U of Idaho Pr.

Nussbaum, Ruth, ed. see Nussbaum, Max.

Nussbaumer, H. Fast Fourier Transform & Convolution Algorithms. 2nd ed. (Information Sciences Ser.). (Illus.). 280p. 1990. pap. 49.00 (0-387-11825-X) Spr-Verlag.

Nussbaumer, Henri. Computer Communications Systems, 2 vols. 171p. 1990. Vol. 1: Data Circuits, Error Detection, Data Links, 171p. text ed. 84.95 (0-471-92379-6) Wiley.

— Computer Communications Systems, 2 vols., Vol. 2. 259p. 1990. text ed. 95.00 (0-471-92495-4) Wiley.

Nussberger, J., jt. ed. see Von Mutius, A.

Nussbaum, J. F., ed. Life-Span Communication: Normative Processes. (Communication Textbook Ser.). 392p. 1989. 79.95 (0-8058-0195-2) L Erlbaum Assocs.

Nussdorfer, Laurie. Civic Politics in the Rome of Urban VIII. (Illus.). 296p. 1992. text ed. 45.00 (0-691-03182-7) Princeton U Pr.

***Nusse, H. E.** Dynamics: Numerical Explorations. 1994. pap. 49.95 (0-387-94334-X) Spr-Verlag.

Nussel, Edward, jt. auth. see Kretovics, Joseph.

Nussel, F. E., jt. ed. see Leparsky, E.

Nussenblatt. Uveitis: Fundamental & Clinical Practice. 448p. 1988. 75.00 (0-8151-6457-2, Yr Bk Med Pubs) Mosby Yr Bk.

Nussenblatt & Palestine. Atlas of Uveitis. 1990. 124.95 (0-8151-6445-9, Yr Bk Med Pubs) Mosby Yr Bk.

Nussenblatt, Robert B., jt. auth. see Tabbara, Khalid F.

***Nussenblatt, Robert B., et al, eds.** Advances in Ocular Immunology & Immunopathology of the Eye: Proceedings of the Sixth International Symposium on the Immunology & Immunopathology of the Eye, Bethesda, U. S. A. LC 94-35302. (International Congress Ser.). 479p. 1995. 370.00 (0-444-81742-5) Elsevier.

Nussenzveig, H. M. Diffraction Effects in Semiclassical Light Scattering. (Montroll Memorial Lecture Series in Mathematical Physics). (Illus.). 225p. (C). 1992. 64.95 (0-521-38318-8) Cambridge U Pr.

— Introduction to Quantum Optics. LC 72-80356. (Documents on Modern Physics Ser.). 260p. 1973. pap. text ed. 205.00 (0-677-03900-X) Gordon & Breach.

***Nusser, Alden.** French Fries up Your Nose: 208 Ways to Annoy People. LC 95-6192. 96p. (Orig.). (J). (gr. 3-7). 1995. pap. 3.50 (0-380-77913-7, Camelot) Avon.

Nusser, Richard. Walking after Midnight. 432p. 1990. pap. 3.95 (0-380-70939-2) Avon.

Nussey, Dora, tr. see Male, Emile.

Nussey, Kent. In Christ There Is No East or West. 1993. pap. 11.95 (1-55082-046-X, Pub. by Quarry Pr CN) InBook.

Nustad, Harry L. & Wesner, Terry H. Essentials of Technical Mathematics. 800p. (C). 1983. write for info. (0-697-08551-1); student ed write for info. (0-697-08552-X) Wm C Brown Pubs.

— Principles of Elementary Algebra with Applications. 2nd ed. 640p. (C). 1991. pap. write for info. (0-697-01351-0); student ed write for info. (0-697-11083-4) Wm C Brown Pubs.

— Principles of Intermediate Algebra with Applications. 2nd ed. 736p. (C). 1991. pap. write for info. (0-697-01338-3) Wm C Brown Pubs.

Nustad, Harry L., jt. auth. see Wesner, Terry H.

Nusz, Frieda. The Natural Foods Blender Cookbook. (Pivot Original Health Bks.). 1972. reprint ed. pap. 1.95 (0-87983-022-0) Keats.

Nutall, C. S., jt. auth. see Minkes, A. L.

***Nute, Carol L.** Common Sense to Retailing. rev. ed. (Illus.). 90p. 1995. pap. 9.95 (0-9645328-0-8) Retail Pr.

Nute, Donald. Essential Formal Semantics. LC 81-12114. 200p. (C). 1981. 46.00 (0-8476-7026-0) Rowman.

— Topics in Conditional Logic. (Philosophical Studies in Philosophy Ser.: No. 20). 168p. 1980. lib. bdg. 65.50 (90-277-1049-X) Kluwer Ac.

Nute, Grace L. Caesars of the Wilderness: Medard Chouart, Sieur des Groseilliers & Pierre Esprit Radisson, 1618-1710. LC 78-811. (Publications of the Minnesota Historical Society). 428p. reprint ed. pap. 122.00 (0-8357-3319-X, 2039543) Bks Demand.

— Rainy River Country: A Brief History of the Region Bordering Minnesota & Ontario. LC 71-96385. (Publications of the Minnesota Historical Society). 193p. reprint ed. pap. 55.10 (0-8357-3314-9, 2039538) Bks Demand.

— The Voyageur. LC 55-12180. 289p. 1987. reprint ed. pap. 8.95 (0-87351-213-8) Minn Hist.

— The Voyageur's Highway: Minnesota's Border Lake Land. LC 65-63529. (Illus.). 113p. 1941. pap. 7.95 (0-87351-006-2) Minn Hist.

Nute, Grace Lee. Caesars of the Wilderness: Medard Chouart, Sieur des Groesilliers & Pierre Espirt Radisson, 1618-1710. Wilkins, Mira, ed. LC 76-29750. (European Business Ser.). (Illus.). 1977. reprint ed. lib. bdg. 35.95 (0-405-09766-2) Ayer.

Nute, Kevin. Frank Lloyd Wright & Japan. (Illus.). 244p. 1994. text ed. 59.95 (0-442-30908-2) Van Nos Reinhold.

Nuth, Joan. Wisdom's Daughter: The Theology of Julian of Norwich. 260p. 1991. 24.95 (0-8245-1132-8) Crossroad NY.

Nuti, D. M. V. K. Dmitriev. (Modern Revivals in Economics Ser.). 231p. 1992. 59.95 (0-7512-0095-6, Pub. by Gregg Pub UK) Ashgate Pub Co.

Nutini, H. G. & Bell, B. Ritual Kinship: The Structure & Historical Development of the Compadrazgo System in Rural Tlaxcala. 444p. 1980. pap. 24.95 (0-691-10093-4) Princeton U Pr.

Nutini, Hugo G. Essays on Mexican Kinship. Carrasco, Pedro & Taggart, James M., eds. LC 75-9124. (Pitt Latin American Ser.). 268p. pap. 76.40 (0-317-26654-3, 2025442) Bks Demand.

— Ritual Kinship: Ideological & Structural Integration of the Compadrazgo System in Rural Tlaxcala, Vol. 2. LC 79-3225. 520p. 1984. 79.50x (0-691-07649-9); pap. 27.95 (0-691-10144-2) Princeton U Pr.

— Todos Santos in Rural Tlaxcala: A Syncretic, Expressive, & Symbolic Analysis of the Cult of the Dead. (Illus.). 490p. 1988. text ed. 89.50 (0-691-07755-X) Princeton U Pr.

— Todos Santos in Rural Tlaxcala: A Syncretic, Expressive, & Symbolic Analysis of the Cult of the Dead. LC 87-15173. Date not set. reprint ed. pap. 140.30 (0-7837-9404-5, 2060149) Bks Demand.

— The Wages of Conquest: The Mexican Aristocracy in the Context of Western Aristocracies. 550p. 1995. text ed. 65.00x (0-472-10484-5) U of Mich Pr.

***Nutini, Hugo G. & Bell, Betty.** Ritual Kinship: Ideological & Structural Integration of the Compadrazgo System in Rural Tlaxcala. LC 79-3225. reprint ed. pap. 148.20 (0-7837-9296-4, 2060035) Bks Demand.

Nutini, Hugo G. & Roberts, John M. Bloodsucking Witchcraft: An Epistemological Study of Anthropomorphic Supernaturalism in Rural Tlaxcala. LC 92-34513. 475p. 1993. 40.00 (0-8165-1197-7) U of Ariz Pr.

Nutkins, Terry & Corwin, Marshall. Pets. (Illus.). 48p. (J). (gr. 7-9). 1992. 13.95 (0-563-34523-3, BBC-Parkwest); pap. 6.95 (0-563-34524-1, BBC-Parkwest) Parkwest Pubns.

***Nutley, Joyce.** Advanced Service Techniques. 1993. pap. text ed. 21.95 (0-470-23354-0) Wiley.

Nutman, P. S., ed. Symbiotic Nitrogen Fixation in Plants. LC 75-2732. (International Biological Programme Ser.: No. 7). (Illus.). 652p. 1976. 155.00 (0-521-20645-6) Cambridge U Pr.

Nutman, Philip. Wet Work. 272p. (Orig.). 1993. mass mkt. 4.99 (0-515-11115-5) Jove Pubns.

Nutrinfo Corporation Staff. What's in It? The Busy Cook's Diet & Nutrition Guide to...Chef Paul Prudhomme's Louisiana Kitchen. LC 91-62643. (Orig.). 1991. pap. text ed. 4.95 (1-56503-012-5) Nutrinfo.

— What's in It? The Busy Cook's Diet & Nutrition Guide to. ..Crockery Cookery. LC 91-62644. (Orig.). 1991. pap. text ed. 4.95 (1-56503-013-3) Nutrinfo.

— What's in It? The Busy Cook's Diet & Nutrition Guide to. ..the Frugal Gourmet. LC 91-62631. (Orig.). 1991. pap. text ed. 4.95 (1-56503-000-1); pap. text ed. 4.95 (1-56503-001-X); pap. text ed. 4.95 (1-56503-002-8); pap. text ed. 4.95 (1-56503-003-6); pap. text ed. 4.95 (1-56503-004-4); pap. text ed. 4.95 (1-56503-005-2); pap. text ed. 4.95 (1-56503-006-0); pap. text ed. 4.95 (1-56503-007-9); pap. text ed. 4.95 (1-56503-008-7); pap. text ed. 4.95 (1-56503-009-5); pap. text ed. 4.95 (1-56503-010-9); pap. text ed. 4.95 (1-56503-011-7); pap. text ed. 4.95 (1-56503-014-1) Nutrinfo.

Nutrition Conference for Feed Manufacturers Staff, et al. Recent Advances in Animal Nutrition - 1977: Proceedings of the Nutrition Conference for Feed Manufacturers, 11th, University of Nottingham, 1977. LC 77-30256. (Studies in the Agricultural & Food Sciences). 214p. reprint ed. pap. 61.00 (0-317-41858-0, 2025738) Bks Demand.

Nutrition Education Center Staff, ed. see Gerwick, Clara L.

Nutrition Foundation, jt. auth. see Journal of Nutrition Staff.

Nutrition Services Payment System Committee of the American Dietetic Association Staff. Reimbursement & Insurance Coverage for Nutrition Services. LC 91-26128. 1991. ring bd. 47.00 (0-88091-088-7, 0190) Am Dietetic Assn.

Nutt, A. Fairy Mythology of Shakespeare. LC 68-24913. (Studies in Shakespeare: No. 24). 1969. reprint ed. lib. bdg. 75.00 (0-8383-0929-1) M S G Haskell Hse.

Nutt, Alfred. Studies on the Legend of the Holy Grail with Special Reference to the Hypothesis of Its Celtic Origin. (Folk-Lore Society, London, Monographs: Vol. 23). 1974. reprint ed. pap. 29.00 (0-8115-0510-3) Periodicals Srv.

Nutt, Alfred, ed. see MacInnes, Duncan.

Nutt, Alfred T. Cuchulainn, the Irish Achilles. LC 70-139171. (Popular Studies in Mythology, Romance & Folklore: No. 8). reprint ed. 5.50 (0-404-53508-9) AMS Pr.

— Fairy Mythology of Shakespeare. LC 71-139169. (Popular Studies in Mythology, Romance & Folklore: No. 6). reprint ed. 12.50 (0-404-53506-2) AMS Pr.

— The Fairy Mythology of Shakespeare. (BCL1-PR English Literature Ser.). 40p. 1992. reprint ed. lib. bdg. 59.00 (0-7812-7305-6) Rprt Serv.

— Influence of Celtic Upon Medieval Romance. LC 73-139164. (Popular Studies in Mythology, Romance & Folklore: No. 1). reprint ed. 12.50 (0-404-53501-1) AMS Pr.

— Legends of the Holy Grail. LC 78-139176. (Popular Studies in Mythology, Romance & Folklore: No. 14). reprint ed. 12.50 (0-404-53514-3) AMS Pr.

— Ossian & Ossianic Literature. LC 70-139166. (Popular Studies in Mythology, Romance & Folklore: No. 3). reprint ed. 12.50 (0-404-53503-8) AMS Pr.

Nutt, C. Descendants of George Puffer of Braintree, Mass, 1639-1915. (Illus.). 376p. 1993. reprint ed. lib. bdg. 58.50 (0-8328-3049-6); reprint ed. pap. 48.50 (0-8328-3050-X) Higginson Bk Co.

Nutt, Chas., jt. auth. see Roe, Alfred S.

Nutt, Frances D., ed. An Arizona Alibi: The Desert Humor of Dick Wick Hall Sr. LC 90-91497. 569p. 1990. 29.50 (0-910973-01-6) Arrowhead AZ.

Nutt, Gary J. Centralized & Distributed Operating Systems. 384p. 1991. text ed. 62.00 (0-13-122326-7, 270610) P-H.

— Open Systems. 304p. 1991. text ed. 63.00 (0-13-636234-6, 270703) P-H.

Nutt, Joe. Kernels: Haiku & Senryu, 1968-1989. (Illus.). 100p. (Orig.). 1989. pap. 11.00 (0-9623063-0-4) Nutt Studio.

Nutt, John W. Fragments of a Samaritan Targum. viii, 256p. 1979. reprint ed. 37.70 (3-487-06927-X, Pub. by Georg Olms GW) Lubrecht & Cramer.

Nutt, Karen L. And Baby Makes Four. 172p. 1994. pap. 7.95 (1-56901-278-4) NW Pub.

Nutt, M. C. Metallurgy & Plastics for Engineers. LC 76-19249. 1976. 232.00 (0-08-021684-6, Pub. by Pergamon Repr UK) Franklin.

Nutt, N. A Career Using P. E. (Core Business Studies Ser.). 1990. pap. 21.00 (0-7463-0673-3, Pub. by Northcote UK) St Mut.

Nutt, Paul C. Evaluation Concepts & Methods: Shaping Policy for the Health Administrator. rev. ed. (Health Care Administration: Vol. 14). (Illus.). 364p. 1981. text ed. 32.50 (0-88331-142-9) Luce.

— Making Tough Decisions: Tactics for Improving Managerial Decision Making. LC 88-46079. (Management-Leadership & Management Development Ser.). 648p. 1989. 42.95 (1-55542-138-5) Jossey-Bass.

— Managing Planned Change. (Illus.). 576p. (C). 1991. teacher ed write for info. (0-318-69331-3) Macmillan.

— Managing Planned Change. (Illus.). 576p. (C). 1992. text ed. write for info. (0-02-388685-4) Macmillan.

Nutt, Paul C. & Backoff, Robert W. Strategic Management of Public & Third Sector Organizations: A Handbook for Leaders. LC 91-16608. (Public Administration Ser.). 510p. 1992. 39.95 (1-55542-386-8) Jossey-Bass.

Nutt-Powell, Thomas E. Manufactured Homes: Making Sense of a Housing Opportunity. LC 81-14846. 193p. 1982. text ed. 55.00 (0-86569-086-3, Auburn Hse) Greenwood.

Nutt-Powell, Thomas E., et al. The States & Manufactured Housing. (Illus.). 231p. 1980. pap. 10.00 (0-943142-02-4) St Local Inter.

Nutt, Rick L. Toward Peacemaking: Presbyterians in the South & National Security, 1945-1983. LC 94-4828. 200p. 1994. pap. 19.95 (0-8173-0759-1) U of Ala Pr.

Nuttal, Mark. Arctic Homeland: Kinship, Community, & Development in Northwest Greenland. (Anthropological Horizons Ser.: No. 2). (Illus.). 256p. 1992. 50.00 (0-8020-2886-1); pap. 19.95 (0-8020-7391-3) U of Toronto Pr.

Nuttall, A. D. A New Mimesis: Shakespeare & the Representation of Reality. 232p. (C). 1985. pap. 12.95 (0-416-35870-5, 3947) Routledge Chapman & Hall.

— Openings: Narrative Beginnings from the Epic to the Novel. 250p. 1992. 55.00 (0-19-811741-8) OUP.

— Pope's Essay on Man. LC 83-22298. (Unwin Critical Library). 250p. (C). 1984. text ed. 55.00 (0-04-800017-5) Routledge Chapman & Hall.

— Timon of Athens. (Critical Introductions to Shakespeare Ser.). 150p. 1989. lib. bdg. 20.95 (0-8057-8714-3, Twayne); pap. 13.95 (0-8057-8715-1, Pub. by Royal Botanic Garden UK) Macmillan.

Nuttall, Barbara. Australian Themes. 1994. 17.95 (0-533-10968-X) Vantage.

Nuttall, Brian. Algarve, Travel & Property Guide. (Illus.). 192p. (Orig.). 1990. pap. 19.95 (1-85365-177-X, Pub. by McCarta UK) Seven Hills Bk.

N

An Asterisk (*) at the beginning of an entry indicates that the title is appearing in BIP for the first time.

Nuttall, Christine. Teaching Reading Skills in a Foreign Language. Geddes, Marion & Sturtridge, Gillian, eds. (Practical Language Teaching Ser.). 233p. 1983. pap. text ed. 20.00 (*0-435-28973-X*) Heinemann.

Nuttall, David. Good Lawyer Bad Lawyer. 253p. 1993. pap. 19.95 (*0-88839-315-6*) Hancock House.

— Mooching Salmon. (Illus.). 180p. pap. 16.95 (*0-88839-097-1*) Hancock House.

Nuttall, Desmond L., ed. Assessing Educational Achievement. LC 85-20679. (Contemporary Analysis in Education Ser.: Vol. 10). 190p. 1986. pap. 30.00 (*1-85000-056-5*, Falmer Pr) Taylor & Francis.

Nuttall, Desmond L., jt. ed. see Riley, Katheryn A.

Nuttall, Ena V., et al. Assessing & Screening Preschoolers: Psychological & Educational Dimensions. 512p. (C). 1992. text ed. 51.95 (*0-205-13280-4*, Longwood Div) Allyn.

Nuttall, Geoffrey. Christian Pacifism in History. pap. 1.25 (*0-912018-13-5*) World Without War.

Nuttall, Geoffrey F. The Holy Spirit in Puritan Faith & Experience. 192p. 1992. pap. text ed. 12.95 (*0-226-60941-3*) U Ch Pr.

— Studies in Christian Enthusiasm. (C). 1948. pap. 7.00 (*0-87574-041-3*) Pendle Hill.

— To the Refreshing of the Children of Light. (C). 1959. pap. 3.00 (*0-87574-101-0*) Pendle Hill.

Nuttall, Geoffrey F., ed. Calendar of the Correspondence of Philip Doddridge, D. D., 1702-1751. (Joint Publications Ser.: No. 26). 471p. 1979. 30.00 (*0-11-440067-9*, HM00679, Pub. by HMSO UK) UNIPUB.

Nuttall, Geoffrey F., jt. auth. see Keeble, N. H.

Nuttall, Graeme, jt. auth. see Nelson-Jones, John.

Nuttall, Graeme, jt. auth. see Nelson-Jones, Rodney.

Nuttall, Jeff. Performance Art: Memoirs, Vol. I. (Orig.). 1986. pap. 11.95 (*0-7145-3788-8*) Riverrun NY.

— Performance Art: Scripts, Vol. II. (Orig.). 1986. pap. 11. 95 (*0-7145-3789-6*) Riverrun NY.

Nuttall, Jon. Moral Questions: An Introduction to Ethics. LC 92-19117. 240p. 1993. 49.95 (*0-7456-1039-0*); pap. 17.95 (*0-7456-1040-4*) Blackwell Pubs.

Nuttall, Leonard J. Progress in Adjusting Differences of Amount of Educational Opportunity Offered Under the County Unit Systems of Maryland & Utah. LC 72-177122. (Columbia University, Teachers College. Contributions to Education Ser.: No. 43). reprint ed. 37. 50 (*0-404-55431-8*) AMS Pr.

***Nuttall, Lucy B.** From There to Here. 32p. 1994. pap. 7.00 (*0-8059-3672-6*) Dorrance.

— Looking Back from Eighty Plus. 24p. 1995. per., pap. 6.00 (*0-8059-3622-X*) Dorrance.

Nuttall, Michael. Industrial Relations Strategies. 173p. 1990. text ed. 68.95 (*0-566-05610-0*, Pub. by Avebury Pub UK) Ashgate Pub Co.

Nuttall Ornithological Club Staff. Bulletin of the Nuttall Ornithological Club: A Quarterly Journal of Ornithology, 8 vols. in 3, 1. LC 73-17834. (Natural Sciences in America Ser.). (Illus.). 1826p. 1974. reprint ed. 45.95 (*0-405-05755-9*) Ayer.

— Bulletin of the Nuttall Ornithological Club: A Quarterly Journal of Ornithology, 8 vols. in 3, 2. LC 73-17834. (Natural Sciences in America Ser.). (Illus.). 1826p. 1974. reprint ed. 45.95 (*0-405-05756-3*) Ayer.

— Bulletin of the Nuttall Ornithological Club: A Quarterly Journal of Ornithology, 8 vols. in 3, 3. LC 73-17834. (Natural Sciences in America Ser.). (Illus.). 1826p. 1974. reprint ed. 44.95 (*0-405-05757-1*) Ayer.

— Bulletin of the Nuttall Ornithological Club: A Quarterly Journal of Ornithology, 8 vols. in 3, Set. LC 73-17834. (Natural Sciences in America Ser.). (Illus.). 1826p. 1974. reprint ed. 134.95 (*0-405-05754-7*) Ayer.

Nuttall, P. Austin, ed. see Fuller, Thomas.

Nuttall, Simon J. European Political Co-Operation. 352p. 1992. 65.00 (*0-19-827318-5*) OUP.

Nuttall, Thomas. A Manual of the Ornithology of the United States & Canada, 2 vols., 1. LC 73-17833. (Natural Sciences in America Ser.). 1332p. 1974. reprint ed. 48.95 (*0-405-05752-0*) Ayer.

— A Manual of the Ornithology of the United States & Canada, 2 vols., 2. LC 73-17833. (Natural Sciences in America Ser.). 1332p. 1974. reprint ed. 48.95 (*0-405-05753-9*) Ayer.

— A Manual of the Ornithology of the United States & Canada, 2 vols., Set. LC 73-17833. (Natural Sciences in America Ser.). 1332p. 1974. reprint ed. 96.95 (*0-405-05751-2*) Ayer.

Nuttall, Zelia. Atlatl or Spear-Thrower of the Ancient Mexicans. (HU PMP Ser.: Vol. 1, No. 3). 1972. pap. 14. 00 (*0-527-01185-1*) Periodicals Srv.

— Fundamental Principles of Old & New World Civilization. (HU PMP Ser.: Vol. 2). 1901. 56.00 (*0-527-01190-8*) Periodicals Srv.

— Official Reports on the Towns of Tequizistlan, Tepechpan, Acolman, & San Juan Teotihuacan, Sent to His Majesty Philip Second & the Council of the Indies in 1580. (HU PMP Ser.: Vol. 11, No. 2). 1926. pap. 14. 00 (*0-527-01219-X*) Periodicals Srv.

— Penitential Rite of the Ancient Mexicans. (HU PMP Ser.: Vol. 1, No. 7). 1904. pap. 10.00 (*0-527-01189-4*) Periodicals Srv.

— Standard or Head-Dress? (HU PMP Ser.). 1888. 13.00 (*0-527-01183-5*) Periodicals Srv.

Nuttall, Zelia, ed. The Codex Nuttall. LC 74-83057. (Illus.). 120p. 1975. reprint ed. pap. 11.95 (*0-486-23168-2*) Dover.

— New Light on Drake. (Hakluyt Society Works Ser.: No. 2, Vol. 34). (Illus.). 1974. reprint ed. 75.00 (*0-8115-0350-X*) Periodicals Srv.

Nutter, Carolyn N. The Resume Workbook: A Personal Career File for Job Applications. 5th ed. LC 77-17412. 128p. 1978. 9.95 (*0-910328-00-5*) Sulzburger & Graham Pub.

Nutter, David. Selecting a Developer. McClean, Mary, ed. 20p. (Orig.). 1983. pap. 13.00 (*0-317-04834-1*) Natl Coun Econ Dev.

Nutter, G. Warren. Growth of Government in the West. LC 78-1674. (AEI Studies: No. 185). (Illus.). 104p. reprint ed. pap. 29.70 (*0-8357-4486-8*, 2037338) Bks Demand.

— Political Economy & Freedom: A Collection of Essays. Nutter, Jane C., ed. LC 82-48106. (Illus.). 328p. 1983. 14.00 (*0-86597-024-6*); pap. 5.50 (*0-86597-025-4*) Liberty Fund.

— Some Observations on Soviet Industrial Growth. (Occasional Papers: No. 55). 20p. 1957. reprint ed. 20. 00 (*0-87014-369-7*) Natl Bur Econ Res.

Nutter, G. Warren & Einhorn, Henry. Enterprise Monopoly in the United States, 1899-1958. LC 69-15570. 256p. 1969. text ed. 50.00 (*0-231-02974-8*) Col U Pr.

Nutter, G. Warren, et al. Growth of Industrial Production in the Soviet Union. (General Ser.: No. 75). 735p. 1962. reprint ed. 160.00 (*0-87014-074-4*) Natl Bur Econ Res.

Nutter, Jane C., ed. see Nutter, G. Warren.

Nutter, R. Economics Understood. (C). 1989. 50.00 (*0-09-182259-9*, Pub. by S Thornes Pubs UK) St Mut.

Nutter, Robert S. Economics. Phil, M., ed. 340p. (C). 1991. pap. 60.00 (*1-85352-927-3*, Pub. by HLT Pubns UK) St Mut.

Nutter, W. Yarn Production & Properties. 110p. 1971. 80.00 (*0-686-63812-3*) St Mut.

— Yarn Production & Properties, Vol. 3, No. 2. 110p. (C). 1971. pap. text ed. 75.00 (*0-685-46391-5*, Pub. by Textile Institue UK) St Mut.

***Nuttgens, Patrick.** The Story of Architecture. (Illus.). 288p. (Orig.). 1995. pap. 19.95 (*0-7148-2304-X*, Pub. by Phaidon Press UK) Chronicle Bks.

Nuttgens, Patrick J. The Story of Architecture. (Illus.). 288p. (C). 1983. pap. text ed. 36.95 (*0-13-850131-9*) P-H.

— Understanding Modern Architecture. 220p. 1990. text ed. 45.00 (*0-04-500040-9*) Routledge Chapman & Hall.

Nuttin, Joseph. Future Time Perspective & Motivation: Theory & Research Method. (Louvain Psychology Ser.: Studia Psychologica). 238p. 1985. 49.95 (*0-89859-611-4*) L Erlbaum Assocs.

Nuttin, Joseph R., et al. Motivation, Planning, & Action: A Relational Theory of Behavior Dynamics. 264p. 1984. text ed. 49.95 (*0-89859-332-8*) L Erlbaum Assocs.

Nutting, Adelaide M. A Sound Economic Basis for Schools of Nursing. Reverby, Susan, ed. LC 83-49131. (History of American Nursing Ser.). 372p. 1984. reprint ed. lib. bdg. 15.00 (*0-8240-6519-0*) Garland.

***Nutting, Anthony.** Scramble for Africa: The Great Trek to the Boer War. (Illus.). 454p. 1994. pap. 37.50 (*0-09-473820-3*, Pub. by Constable Pubs UK) Trans-Atl Phila.

Nutting, George L. & Nutting, Ruth E. Chapa's Spring. 268p. (Orig.). 1994. pap. text ed. 6.95 (*0-9612266-3-3*) Numard Bks.

Nutting, Paul A., ed. Community-Oriented Primary Care: From Principle to Practice. LC 90-12627. 572p. 1990. reprint ed. pap. text ed. 22.50 (*0-8263-1230-6*) U of NM Pr.

Nutting, Ruth E., jt. auth. see Nutting, George L.

Nutting, Teresa & Marcy, Michel. Cortina - Holt Traveler's French Dictionary: English-French - French-English. LC 93-3672. 1993. pap. 6.95 (*0-8327-0722-8*) Cortina.

Nutting, W. Checklist of E. A. Reproductions. LC 73-96940. 1969. 4.95 (*0-87282-087-4*) Am Life Foun.

Nutting, Wallace. The Clock Book. 1975. 15.00 (*0-685-56448-7*) Assoc Bk.

— Furniture Treasury, 2 vols., Vol. 3. unabridged ed. (Illus.). 560p. 1949. text ed. 35.00 (*0-02-591040-X*) Macmillan.

— Furniture Treasury, 2 vols., Vols. 1 & 2 in 1. unabridged ed. (Illus.). 1536p. 1954. Vols. 1 & 2 In 1. text ed. 75.00 (*0-02-590980-0*) Macmillan.

— New York Beautiful. 305p. 1993. reprint ed. lib. bdg. 89. 00 (*0-7812-5131-1*) Rprt Serv.

— Wallace Nutting: Supreme Edition, General Catalog. LC 77-608284. 160p. 1978. pap. 10.95 (*0-916838-09-9*) Schiffer.

— The Wallace Nutting Expansible Catalog. Ivankovich, Michael, ed. LC 87-70415. (Illus.). 175p. (Orig.). 1987. reprint ed. pap. 12.95 (*0-9615843-3-5*) Diamond Pr PA.

— Wallace Nutting's Biography. 1976. 22.95 (*0-8488-0599-2*) Amereon Ltd.

— Windsor Handbook. LC 73-77579. (Illus.). 256p. 1973. pap. 14.95 (*0-8048-1105-9*) C E Tuttle.

Nutting, William B., ed. Mammalian Diseases & Arachnids, Vol. I. 288p. 1984. 179.00 (*0-8493-6562-7*, RA641) CRC Pr.

— Mammalian Diseases & Arachnids, Vol. II. 304p. 1984. 179.00 (*0-8493-6563-5*, RA641) CRC Pr.

Nuttleman, Doris. Managing a Nursing Assistant Program. 1990. text ed. 18.95 (*0-8273-4201-2*) Delmar.

Nuttli, Otto. Effects of Earthquakes in the Central United States. (Earthquake Ser.: No. 8). (Illus.). 50p. (Orig.). 1993. reprint ed. pap. 8.95 (*0-934426-50-3*, Gutenberg-Richter) NAPSAC Reprods.

Nutton, Vivian. From Democedes to Harvey: Studies in the History of Medicine. (Collected Studies: No. CS277). (Illus.). 332p. (C). 1990. reprint ed. text ed. 89.95 (*0-86078-225-5*, Pub. by Variorum UK) Ashgate Pub Co.

Nutton, Vivian, ed. Medicine at the Courts of Europe 1500-1837. (Wellcome Institute Series in the History of Medicine). 336p. 1990. 65.00 (*0-415-02264-9*, A4065) Routledge.

Nutzinger, H. G. & Backhaus, J., eds. Codetermination. (Illus.). 320p. 1989. 99.00 (*0-387-50648-9*) Spr-Verlag.

Nuventures Consultants, Inc. Staff. America's Changing Workforce: About You, Your Job & Your Changing Work Environment. McNamara, Ellen, ed. 270p. (Orig.). 1990. pap. 12.95 (*0-9625632-1-8*) NUVENTURES Pub.

Nuwayhid, B. S. Management of the Diabetic Pregnancy. 300p. 1987. 52.50 (*0-444-01198-6*) Elsevier.

***Nuwer, Hank.** How to Write Like an Expert about Anything. 224p. 1995. 17.99 (*0-89879-645-8*) Writers Digest.

— Recruiting in Sports. LC 89-9151. (Illus.). 144p. (YA). (gr. 9 up). 1989. lib. bdg. 14.77 (*0-531-10796-5*) Watts.

— Sports Scandals. LC 93-26317. (Illus.). 196p. (YA). (gr. 9-12). 1994. lib. bdg. 14.77 (*0-531-11183-0*) Watts.

Nuwer, Marc R. Evoked Potential Monitoring in the Operating Room. (Illus.). 256p. 1986. text ed. 58.00 (*0-88167-230-0*) Raven.

Nuyskens, Judith A., et al. Rendezvous: An Invitation to French. 2nd ed. 549p. (C). 1986. student ed 12.95 (*0-394-34265-8*); text ed. 32.95 (*0-394-34267-4*); student ed 12.95 (*0-394-34264-X*) Random.

Nuyts, Jan. Aspects of a Cognitive-Pragmatic Theory of Language: On Cognition, Functionalism & Grammar. LC 91-40002. (Pragmatics & Beyond New Ser.: No. 20). xii, 399p. 1992. 74.00x (*1-55619-288-6*) Benjamins North Am.

Nuyts, Jan & De Schutter, Georges, eds. Getting One's Words into Line: On Word Order & Functional Grammar. (Functional Grammar Ser.). xiv, 218p. (Orig.). (C). 1987. pap. 46.45 (*90-6765-349-7*) Mouton.

Nuyts, Jan, et al, eds. Layers & Levels of Representation in Language Theory: A Functional View. LC 90-33948. (Pragmatics & Beyond New Ser.: No. 13). xii, 348p. 1990. 71.00x (*1-55619-279-7*) Benjamins North Am.

Nuzum, C. The Life of Faith. 96p. 1956. pap. 2.95 (*0-88243-539-6*, 02-0539) Gospel Pub.

Nuzzi, Debra. Herbal Preparations & Natural Therapies: Creating & Using a Home Herbal Medicine Chest. (Illus.). 140p. (Orig.). 1989. student ed. pap. 149.00 (*0-9623812-0-9*) Mrngstar Pubns.

— Pocket Herbal Reference Guide. 144p. (Orig.). 1992. pap. 5.95 (*0-89594-568-1*) Crossing Pr.

Nuzzolo, Luccio & Vellucci, Augusto. Tissue Culture Techniques. LC 67-26015. (Illus.). 256p. 1983. 37.50 (*0-87527-117-0*) Green.

NVision Grafix, Inc. Holusion Art, How & Why It Works. Tucker, Chris, ed. (Illus.). 36p. 1994. 19.99 (*0-9640923-0-1*) NVision Grafix.

NVision Grafix Inc. Staff & Hripko, Thomas. Official Tour Guide to Holusion Art. (Illus.). 40p. 1994. 24.95 (*0-9640923-1-X*) NVision Grafix.

NW Bed & Breakfast Travel Unltd. Staff, ed. West Coast Town B & B's U. S. A. & Canada: Directory of Homes & Inns. 6th ed. (Illus.). 150p. (C). 1989. per. 9.50 (*0-945796-01-3*) NW Bed Breakfast.

Nwabueze, B. O. Constitutionalism in the Emergent States. LC 72-14221. 320p. 1973. 39.50 (*0-8386-1365-9*) Fairleigh Dickinson.

— Judicialism in Commonwealth Africa. LC 76-27553. (C). 1977. text ed. 30.00 (*0-312-44695-0*) St Martin.

— The Presidential Constitution of Nigeria. LC 82-47637. 558p. 1982. text ed. 49.95 (*0-312-64032-3*) St Martin.

— Presidentialism in Commonwealth Africa. LC 74-76990. 480p. (C). 1975. text ed. 39.95 (*0-312-64120-6*) St Martin.

Nwabugwu, Frank. Antalo the Antelope, B-era the Bear, C-esto the Cheetah, D-opicooko the Deer. (Bed Time Stories Ser.). 18p. (J). 1992. write for info. (*1-881687-04-X*); teacher ed write for info. (*1-881687-07-4*); lib. bdg. write for info. (*1-881687-05-8*); pap. write for info. (*1-881687-06-6*) F Nwabugwu.

— Sparo; the Wild & Crazy Pretty Dog. 2nd ed. 26p. (J). (gr. 2-8). 1993. write for info. (*1-881687-08-2*) F Nwabugwu.

Nwachukwu, P. Akujuobi. Towards an Igbo Literary Standard. 200p. 1983. pap. 19.50 (*0-7103-0045-X*, Pub. by Kegan Paul Intl UK) Routledge Chapman & Hall.

Nwachukwu, Richard O. The Agony: The Untold Tale of the Nigerian Society. 118p. (Orig.). 1987. pap. 6.95 (*0-941823-00-8*) Good Hope Enterp.

— The Dark & Bright Continent: Africa in the Changing World. LC 89-80209. 344p. 1989. 17.95 (*0-941823-02-4*); pap. 9.25 (*0-941823-01-6*) Good Hope Enterp.

***Nwaelele, O. Dan.** Health & Safety Risk Management: Guide for Designing an Effective Program. 220p. (Orig.). 1994. pap. text ed. 225.00 (*0-86587-397-6*) Gov Insts.

Nwafor, Azinna. Frelimo & Socialism in Mozambique. Omenana Collective Staff, ed. (Etudes et Analyses Marxistes en Afrique Ser.). 45p. (Orig.). (C). pap. 3.00 (*0-686-88661-5*) Omenana.

— Revolution & Socialism in Ethiopia. Omenana Collective Staff, ed. (Etudes et Analyses Marxistes en Afrique Ser.). 55p. (Orig.). (C). 1983. reprint ed. pap. 3.00 (*0-686-88660-7*) Omenana.

Nwagboso, Christopher, ed. Automotive Sensory Systems. LC 92-47248. (Road Vehicle Automation Ser.). 1993. write for info. (*0-412-45880-2*) Chapman & Hall.

Nwana, Hyacinth S. Mathematical Intelligent Learning Environments. 272p. (Orig.). 1993. pap. text ed. 29.95 (*1-871516-29-3*, Pub. by Intellect Bks UK) Cromland.

Nwangu, Peter, ed. Concepts & Strategies in New Drug Development, Vol.4. LC 83-19248. (Clinical Pharmacology & Therapeutics Ser.). 282p. 1983. text ed. 59.95 (*0-275-91406-2*, C1406, Praeger Pubs) Greenwood.

Nwanna, Gladson I. Americans Traveling Abroad: What You Should Know Before You Go. LC 92-62032. (International Traveler's Guide Ser.). 624p. (Orig.). 1994. pap. 39.99 (*0-9623820-4-3*) Wld Trvl Inst.

Nwanna, Gladson I., ed. Who's Who In Athletics in American Colleges & Universities. 2nd ed. LC 89-85173. 200p. (C). 1992. lib. bdg. 75.00 (*0-9623820-3-5*) AP Amer MD.

— Who's Who in Athletics in American High Schools, 1990-1991. 1991. 50.00 (*0-9623820-2-7*) AP Amer MD.

***Nwanunobi, C.** Soninke. LC 94-45813. (Heritage Library of African Peoples). (J). 1995. write for info. (*0-8239-1978-1*) Rosen Group.

Nwanze, K. F., jt. auth. see Harris, K. M.

Nwapa, Flora. Efuru. (African Writers Ser.). 221p. 1966. pap. 8.95 (*0-435-90026-9*) Heinemann.

— Mammywater. Date not set. pap. 12.00 (*978-2272-00-0*) Three Continents.

— Never Again. 90p. 1992. 24.95 (*0-86543-318-6*); pap. 9.95 (*0-86543-319-4*) Africa World.

— One Is Enough. 157p. 1992. 24.95 (*0-86543-322-4*); pap. 9.95 (*0-86543-323-2*) Africa World.

— This Is Lagos & Other Stories. 140p. 1992. 24.95 (*0-86543-320-8*); pap. 9.95 (*0-86543-321-6*) Africa World.

— Wives at War & Other Stories. 125p. 1992. 24.95 (*0-86543-327-5*); pap. 9.95 (*0-86543-328-3*) Africa World.

— Women Are Different. 144p. 1992. 24.95 (*0-86543-325-9*); pap. 9.95 (*0-86543-326-7*) Africa World.

Nwede, Ken M. Information Seeking & Veterinary Medical Scientists (HVMS) in Africa: Case Study from Borno State, Nigeria. 30p. 1992. 5.00 (*0-685-65163-0*) Indiana Africa.

Nwoga, Donatus I., ed. Critical Perspectives on Christopher Okigbo. LC 80-53349. (Critical Perspectives Ser.). (Illus.). 367p. (C). 1985. 25.00 (*0-89410-258-3*); pap. 16. 00 (*0-89410-259-1*) Three Continents.

***Nwokogba, Isaac E.** Easy Dollars: At the Pick Three - Pick Four Daily Lotto. LC 94-68919. (Illus.). 108p. (Orig.). (YA). 1995. pap. 10.95 (*0-9643342-0-8*) Super-Eagles.

***Nwomonoh, Jonathan.** Education & Development in Africa: Historical, Cultural & Religious Perspectives. (Distinguished Education Ser.). 267p. (C). 1995. 59.95 (*1-57309-011-5*); pap. 39.95 (*1-57309-010-7*) Intl Scholars.

***Nwosu, Peter, et al, eds.** Communication & the Transformation of Society: A Developing Region's Perspectives. LC 95-10746. 1995. Not sold separately (*0-8191-9961-3*) U Pr of Amer.

Nwuga, Vincent C. Manual Treatment of Back Pain. LC 84-3965. 224p. (C). 1986. lib. bdg. 21.50 (*0-89874-753-8*) Krieger.

Nwulia, Moses. Britain & Slavery in East Africa. LC 75-25756. (Illus.). 230p. (Orig.). 1975. 17.00 (*0-914478-11-7*); pap. 9.00 (*0-914478-12-5*) Three Continents.

Nwulia, Moses D. The History of Slavery in Mauritius & the Seychelles, 1810-1875. LC 79-15363. 248p. 1981. 33.50 (*0-8386-2398-0*) Fairleigh Dickinson.

Nwuneli, O. & Opubor, A., eds. The Development & Growth of the Film Industry in Nigeria. (Illus.). 114p. 1980. 19.95 (*0-89388-220-8*); pap. 11.95 (*0-685-59744-X*) Okpaku Communications.

Nwuneli, Onuira E., ed. Communication & Human Needs in Africa. 99p. 1989. pap. 8.95 (*0-940738-13-9*) Lamplight Edits.

NWWA Staff. Annotated Bibliography for Underground Storage Tanks. 207p. 1988. 18.75 (*1-56034-063-0*, K441) Natl Water Well.

— Appraising a Water Well Contracting Firm. 78p. 1988. 6.25 (*1-56034-053-3*, K453) Natl Water Well.

— Conserve Ninety Proceedings. 1310p. 1990. 87.50 (*1-56034-086-X*) Natl Water Well.

— Focus Conference on Eastern Region Ground Water Issues (Held in Kitchener, Ontario, Canada, October 17-19, 1989) Proceedings: Proceedings. 481p. 1989. 43.75 (*1-56034-035-5*) Natl Water Well.

— Fourth National Outdoor Action Conference on Aquifer Restoration, Ground Water Monitoring & Geophysical Methods (May 14-17, 1990) 1317p. 1990. 87.50 (*1-56034-085-1*, P490) Natl Water Well.

— Ground Water Heat Pumps, Vol. I: An Examination of Hydrogeologic, Environmental, Legal & Economic Factors Affecting Their Use. 250p. 1980. 20.00 (*1-56034-057-6*, K021A) Natl Water Well.

— Ground Water Heat Pumps, Vol. II: An Examination of Hydrogeologic, Environmental, Legal & Economic Factors Affecting Their Use. 490p. 1980. 36.00 (*1-56034-058-4*, K021B) Natl Water Well.

— The Handbook of Suggested Practices for the Design & Installation of Ground Water Monitoring Wells. 380p. 1989. 43.75 (*1-56034-061-4*, T479) Natl Water Well.

— Marketing Your Water Well Contracting Business. 26p. 1988. 6.25 (*1-56034-054-1*, K452) Natl Water Well.

— U. S. Cities & Towns: Source of Water Supply. 26p. 1989. 6.25 (*1-56034-055-X*, K500) Natl Water Well.

Nyakatura, J. W. Anatomy of an African Kingdom: A History of Bunyoro-Kitara. LC 73-91729. 282p. 1973. text ed. 19.95 (*0-88357-025-4*) NOK Pubs.

Nyamongo, Issac K., jt. auth. see Kau, Samvit S.

Nyamwaya, David, jt. ed. see Parkin, David.

Nyana, U. The Vipassana Dipani; or the Manual of Insight. LC 78-70107. reprint ed. 22.00 (*0-404-17357-8*) AMS Pr.

Nyanatiloka. Buddhist Dictionary. LC 77-87508. reprint ed. 20.00 (*0-404-16846-9*) AMS Pr.

Nyandoro, Gideon, jt. ed. see Nyangoni, Christopher.

Nyang Oro, Julius E. The State & Capitalist Development in Africa: Declining Political Economies. LC 88-34030. 189p. 1989. text ed. 49.95 (*0-275-93120-X*, C3120, Praeger Pubs) Greenwood.

Nyang, Sulayman S. Islam, Christianity & African Identity. LC 84-72247. 106p. (Orig.). 1985. pap. 6.95 (*0-915597-05-5*) Amana Bks.

Nyang, Sulayman S., jt. ed. see Olupona, Jacob K.

Nyangoni, Christopher & Nyandoro, Gideon, eds. Zimbabwe Independence Movements: Select Documents. LC 79-51834. 456p. 1979. text ed. 46.00 (0-06-495222-3, N6621) B&N Imports.

Nyangoni, Wellington W. Africa in the United Nations System. LC 81-72033. 288p. 1985. 46.50 (0-8386-3118-5) Fairleigh Dickinson.

Nyang'oro, Julius E. & Shaw, Timothy M., eds. Beyond Structural Adjustment in Africa: The Political Economy of Sustainable & Democratic Development. LC 91-47087. 192p. 1992. text ed. 49.95 (0-275-94221-X, C4221, Praeger Pubs) Greenwood.

Nyasaland Economic Symposium Staff. Economic Development in Africa: Proceedings of the Nyasaland Economic Symposium held in Blantyre, 18 to 28 July, 1962. Jackson, Edward F., ed. LC 77-1786. vii, 368p. 1965. 45.00 (0-678-06258-7) Kelley.

Nyazee, Imran, tr. see Rushd, Ibn.

Nybakken, Elizabeth I., ed. The Centinel: Warnings of a Revolution. LC 77-92570. 240p. 1980. 25.00 (0-87413-141-3) U Delaware Pr.

Nybakken, Elizabeth I., jt. ed. see Hawes, Joseph M.

Nybakken, James W. Marine Biology: An Ecological Approach. 446p. (C). 1982. write for info. (0-06-364800-8) HarpCollege.

— Marine Biology: An Ecological Approach. 2nd ed. 514p. (C). 1989. text ed. 31.50 (0-06-044835-0) HarpCollege.

— Marine Biology: An Ecological Approach. 3rd ed. LC 92-20888. (C). 1992. 55.50 (0-06-500822-7) HarpCollege.

Nybakken, Oscar E. Greek & Latin in Scientific Terminology. LC 59-5992. (ENG, GRE & LAT.). 1959. pap. 24.95 (0-8138-0721-2) Iowa St U Pr.

Nyber, D. M. Help for Families with a Problem Child. LC 12-2822. (Trauma Bks.: Ser. 2). 1983. pap. 2.95 (0-570-08259-5) Concordia.

Nyberg. An Ultrasound Atlas of Fetal Malformations. 792p. 1989. 175.00 (0-8151-6439-4, Yr Bk Med Pubs) Mosby Yr Bk.

Nyberg & Boast. Subject Compilations of State Laws: 1979-83 (1984) 75.00 (0-685-53151-1) C Boast & C Nyberg.

Nyberg, Ben & Clift, G. W. Britain 101. (Illus.). 170p. (Orig.). 1989. pap. 8.95 (0-9624608-0-X) Island Pk Bks.

Nyberg, Carl, jt. auth. see Bailey, JoAnne.

Nyberg, Cheryl R. Subject Compilations of State Laws 1983-1985: An Annotated Bibliography. LC 85-73774. 595p. 1986. text ed. 78.00 (0-9616293-0-4) C Boast & C Nyberg.

— Subject Compilations of State Laws, 1985-1988: An Annotated Bibliography. LC 88-93062. 544p. 1989. 83.00 (0-9616293-1-2) C Boast & C Nyberg.

— Subject Compilations of State Laws, 1988-1990: An Annotated Bibliography. 542p. 1991. 98.50 (0-9616293-2-0) C Boast & C Nyberg.

— Subject Compilations of State Laws, 1990-1991: An Annotated Bibliography. 290p. 1992. 100.00 (0-9616293-4-7) C Boast & C Nyberg.

Nyberg, David. The Varnished Truth: Truth Telling & Deceiving in Ordinary Life. LC 92-20637. 256p. (C). 1993. 22.50 (0-226-61051-9) U Ch Pr.

— The Varnished Truth: Truth Telling & Deceiving in Ordinary Life. 244p. 1994. pap. 12.95 (0-226-61052-7) U Ch Pr.

Nyberg, David A. Ultrasound of Fetal Anomalies. 1994. vdisk 700.00 (1-56815-017-2, 10027) Image Premast.

Nyberg, David A., et al. Transvaginal Ultrasound. LC 92-8483. 368p. 1992. 99.00 (0-8016-3709-0) Mosby Yr Bk.

***Nyberg, F., et al, eds.** Neuropeptides in the Spinal Cord. LC 93-11042. (Progress in Brain Research Ser.: Vol. 104). 1995. pap. write for info. (0-444-81719-0) Elsevier.

Nyberg, Jan, ed. Chronic Pain: Finding a Life Worth Living. 1994. 14.95 (0-533-10868-3) Vantage.

Nyberg, Jim, jt. auth. see Nyberg, Tim.

Nyberg, Joan. A Rustling of Wings: An Angelic Guide to the Twin Cities. 2nd ed. LC 94-90051. 200p. (Orig.). 1995. pap. 15.95 (0-9640578-2-4) Wingtip Pr.

***Nyberg, Judy.** Charts for Children: Print Awareness Activities for Young Children. 176p. (Orig.). (J). (ps-k). 1995. pap. 12.95 (0-673-36176-4) GdYrBks.

— Just Pretend! Creating Dramatic Play Centers with Young Children. (Illus.). 104p. (Orig.). (J). (ps-1). 1994. pap. 8.95 (0-673-36116-0) GdYrBks.

Nyberg, Klas, jt. auth. see Eberson, Lennart.

Nyberg, Lennart. The Shakespearean Ideal: Shakespeare Production & the Modern Theatre in Britain. 144p. (Orig.). 1988. pap. 40.00x (91-554-2275-6, Pub. by Uppsala Univ Acta Univ Uppsaliensis SW) Coronet Bks.

Nyberg, O. Impact Use of Expert Systems on Marginal Field Development. 1989. 135.00 (90-6314-502-0, Pub. by Lorne & MacLean Marine) St Mut.

Nyberg, O., ed. Impact Use of Expert Systems on Marginal Field Development. (C). 1989. 95.00 (0-89771-740-6, Pub. by Lorne & MacLean Marine) St Mut.

Nyberg, Richard, jt. auth. see Basmajian, John V.

Nyberg, Sidney L. The Chosen People. LC 74-29512. (Modern Jewish Experience Ser.). 1975. reprint ed. 33.95 (0-405-06738-0) Ayer.

Nyberg, Stanley E., jt. auth. see Zechmeister, Eugene B.

Nyberg, Sten. Honesty, Vanity & Corporate Equity: Four Microeconomic Essays. (Industrial Institute for Economic & Social Research Report Ser.). 73p. (Orig.). 1993. pap. 52.50x (91-7204-418-7, Pub. by Almqv & Wiksell SW) Coronet Bks.

***Nyberg, Tim & Nyberg, Jim.** The Duct Tape Book. (Illus.). 128p. 1994. pap. 6.95 (1-57025-042-1) Pfeifer-Hamilton.

Nyberg, Tore, et al. History & Heroic Tale: A Symposium. 242p. (Orig.). 1985. pap. text ed. 53.00x (87-7492-534-2) Coronet Bks.

Nyblom, Kare, jt. auth. see Jervall, Sverre.

Nybom, Thorsten, ed. Academics & Policy Systems. (Higher Education Policy Ser.: No. 8). 250p. 1999. 56.50 (1-85302-512-7, Pub. by J Kingsley Pubs UK) Taylor & Francis.

Nybom, Thorsten, jt. ed. see Trow, Martin A.

Nyborg, Helmuth. Hormones, Sex & Society: The Science of Physicology. LC 94-8640. (Human Evolution, Behavior, & Intelligence Ser.). 256p. 1994. text ed. 55.00 (0-275-94608-8, Praeger Pubs) Greenwood.

Nyborg, Randell. Analyzing Financial Statements Made Easy. (Illus.). 164p. 1994. 31.95 (1-57002-005-1) Univ Publng Hse.

— Commercial Electroplating, 2 bks. set. (Illus.). 225p. 1990. pap. 39.00 (1-877767-11-5) Univ Publng Hse.

— Commercial Electroplating, 2 bks. set, Set. (Illus.). 225p. 1990. 55.00 (1-877767-12-3) Univ Publng Hse.

— How to Repair Your Copy Machine. (Illus.). (Orig.). 1994. pap. 19.95 (1-877767-84-0) Univ Publng Hse.

— How to Start & Operate a Limousine Service. (Illus.). 85p. (Orig.). 1990. 37.00 (1-877767-14-X) Univ Publng Hse.

— Plastic Injection Molding Made Easy. (Illus.). 100p. (Orig.). 1990. lib. bdg. 30.00 (1-877767-15-8) Univ Publng Hse.

Nyborg, Randell L. Electroplating Fundamentals on Video. (Illus.). 75p. (C). 1990. vhs 29.00 (1-877767-04-2) Univ Publng Hse.

— Hobbyist Electroplating Made Easy. (Illus.). 73p. (Orig.). (C). 1988. pap. 11.50 (1-877767-00-X) Univ Publng Hse.

— How to Start & Operate an Electroplating Shop. (Illus.). 150p. (Orig.). (C). 1988. pap. 35.00 (1-877767-03-4) Univ Publng Hse.

— Powder Coating Made Easy. Taylor, Bob, ed. (Illus.). 101p. 1992. text ed. 32.00 (1-877767-19-0) Univ Publng Hse.

Nyborg, Wesley L. & Ziskin, Marvin C., eds. Biological Effects of Ultrasound. (Clinics in Diagnostic Ultrasound Ser.: Vol. 16). (Illus.). 191p. 1985. text ed. 36.00 (0-443-08314-2) Churchill.

Nyburg, Sidney L. The Chosen People. Sarna, Jonathan D., ed. (Masterworks of Modern Jewish Writing Ser.). 373p. (C). 1986. reprint ed. pap. 9.95 (0-910129-47-9) Wiener Pubs Inc.

Nyce, Ben. Satyajit Ray: A Study of His Films. LC 88-6620. 223p. 1988. text ed. 49.95 (0-275-92666-4, C2666, Praeger Pubs) Greenwood.

Nyce, Dorothy Y. Jesus' Clear Call to Justice. (Peace & Justice Ser.: Vol. 11). 96p. (Orig.). 1990. pap. 5.95 (0-8361-3533-4) Herald Pr.

Nyce, James M. & Kahn, Paul, eds. From Memex to Hypertext: Vannevar Bush & the Mind's Machine. (Illus.). 367p. 1991. text ed. 45.00 (0-12-523270-5) Acad Pr.

Nyczek, Tadeusz, ed. see Karasek, Krzysztof, et al.

Nydahl, Hannah, tr. see Nydahl, Ole.

Nydahl, J. E., jt. auth. see Silver, H. F.

Nydahl, John, jt. auth. see Silver, Howard A.

Nydahl, Ole. Basic Dharma: An Introduction to the Nature of Mind. Clemens, Paul M., ed. 32p. 1988. pap. 5.00 (0-931892-17-1) B Dolphin Pub.

— Entering the Diamond Way: My Path among the Lamas. LC 85-73182. (Illus.). 256p. (Orig.). 1985. pap. 14.95 (0-931892-03-1) B Dolphin Pub.

— Mahamudra: Boundless Joy & Freedom. Nydahl, Hannah, tr. LC 91-26450. (Illus.). 96p. (Orig.). 1991. pap. 9.95 (0-931892-69-4) B Dolphin Pub.

— Ngondro: The Four Foundational Practices of Tibetan Buddhism. (Illus.). 96p. (Orig.). 1990. pap. 9.95 (0-931892-23-6) B Dolphin Pub.

— Riding the Tiger: Twenty Years on the Road: The Risks & Joys of Bringing Tibetan Buddhism to the West. Aronoff, Carol A., ed. LC 92-6605. (Illus.). 512p. (Orig.). 1992. pap. 17.95 (0-931892-67-8) B Dolphin Pub.

— Teachings on the Nature of Mind. (Illus.). 40p. (Orig.). 1993. pap. 5.00 (0-931892-58-9) B Dolphin Pub.

Nydahl, Ole & Aronoff, Carol. Practical Buddhism: The Kagyu Path. 48p. (Orig.). 1989. pap. 5.00 (0-931892-63-5) B Dolphin Pub.

Nydegger, U., jt. ed. see Starsia, Z.

Nydegger, U. E., ed. Immunochemotherapy: A Guide to Intravenous Immunoglobulin Therapy. LC 81-68971. 1982. text ed. 119.00 (0-12-523280-2) Acad Pr.

— Therapeutic Hemapheresis in the 1990s. (Current Studies in Hematology & Blood Transfusion: No. 57). (Illus.). viii, 282p. 1990. 213.75 (3-8055-5166-5) S Karger.

Nydegger, U. E. & Morell, A. Clinical Use of Intravenous Immunoglobulins. 1986. text ed. 105.00 (0-12-523282-9) Acad Pr.

***Nydell, M. K.** Military Phrasebook for Iraqi Arabic. 72p. 1995. pap. text ed. 5.99 (0-9628410-0-5) DLS VA.

***Nydell, M. K. & Ryding, K. C.** Saudi Arabic Familiarization Course. 80p. 1995. pap. text ed. 6.99 (0-9628410-1-3) DLS VA.

Nydell, Margaret, jt. auth. see McGregor, Joy.

***Nydell, Margaret K.** Arabic Dialect Identification Course. 223p. 1995. pap. text ed. 59.95 (0-9628410-9-9) DLS VA.

— From Modern Standard Arabic to the Egyptian Dialect, Conversion Course. 526p. 1995. pap. text ed. 39.95 (0-9628410-2-1) DLS VA.

— From Modern Standard Arabic to the Gulf Dialects, Conversion Course. 335p. 1995. pap. text ed. 39.95 (0-9628410-4-8) DLS VA.

— From Modern Standard Arabic to the Iraqi Dialect, Conversion Course. 324p. 1995. pap. text ed. 39.95 (0-9628410-5-6) DLS VA.

— From Modern Standard Arabic to the Levantine Dialects, Conversion Course. 392p. 1995. pap. text ed. 39.95 (0-9628410-3-X) DLS VA.

— From Modern Standard Arabic to the Maghrebi Dialects, (Libyan & Tunisian), Conversion Course. 405p. 1995. pap. text ed. 39.95 (0-9628410-7-2) DLS VA.

— From Modern Standard Arabic to the Maghrebi Dialects, (Moroccan & Algerian), Conversion Course. 420p. 1995. pap. text ed. 39.95 (0-9628410-6-4) DLS VA.

— Introduction to Colloquial Arabic. 328p. 1995. pap. text ed. 44.95 (0-9628410-8-0) DLS VA.

— Understanding Arabs: A Guide for Westerners. LC 86-83102. 176p. 1987. pap. text ed. 16.95 (0-933662-65-3) Intercult Pr.

Nyden, Philip. Steel Workers Rank & File. LC 83-22462. 192p. 1984. text ed. 45.00 (0-275-91236-1, C1236, Praeger Pubs) Greenwood.

— Steelworkers Rank & File: The Political Economy of a Union Reform Movement. (Illus.). 176p. 1984. text ed. 34.95 (0-03-063370-2, Bergin & Garvey) Greenwood.

Nyden, Philip & Wiewel, Wim. Challenging Uneven Development: An Urban Agenda for the 1990s. LC 90-45221. 275p. (C). 1991. text ed. 37.00 (0-8135-1658-7); pap. text ed. 15.00 (0-8135-1659-5) Rutgers U Pr.

***Nye.** Philosophy & Feminism. 1995. 26.95 (0-8057-9763-7, Twayne); pap. 14.95 (0-8057-9778-5, Twayne) Macmillan.

Nye, jt. auth. see Falconer.

***Nye, Adrian.** X Protocol Reference Manual Vol. 0. 4th ed. 458p. 1995. pap. 34.95 (1-56592-083-X) OReilly & Assocs.

— The X Resource, Issue 4: Practical Journal of the X Window System. (X Window System Ser.). (Illus.). 276p. 1992. pap. 14.95 (0-937175-99-4) OReilly & Assocs.

— Xlib Programming Manual, Vol. 1: For R4-R5. 3rd ed. (X Window System Ser.). (Illus.). 824p. 1992. pap. 34.95 (1-56592-002-3) OReilly & Assocs.

— Xlib Reference Manual, Vol. 2: For R4-R5. 3rd ed. (X Window System Ser.). 1138p. 1992. pap. 34.95 (1-56592-006-6) OReilly & Assocs.

***Nye, Adrian, ed.** Programmer's Supplement for Release 6 of the X Window System. (Illus.). 300p. (Orig.). 1995. 24.95 (1-56592-089-9) OReilly & Assocs.

— Public Review: Public Review Draft: X Image Extension Protocol Reference Manual. (X Window System Ser.: Special Issue C). (Illus.). 202p. 1993. pap. 22.50 (1-56592-034-1) OReilly & Assocs.

— Public Review: Public Review Draft: X Image Extension Protocol Reference Manual. (X Window System Ser.: Special Ed. D). (Illus.). 370p. 1994. pap. 22.50 (1-56592-071-6) OReilly & Assocs.

— The X Resource, Issue 10. 10th ed. (X Window System). (Illus.). 212p. 1994. pap. 14.95 (1-56592-067-8) OReilly & Assocs.

— The X Resource: A Practical Journal of the X Window System, Issue 0. (X Window System Ser.). 253p. (Orig.). 1991. pap. 14.95 (0-937175-79-X) OReilly & Assocs.

— The X Resource: Proceedings of the 6th Annual X Technical Conference, Issue 1. (X Window System Ser.). 240p. (Orig.). 1992. pap. 14.95 (0-937175-96-X) OReilly & Assocs.

— The X Resource: Public Review Draft: PEX Protocol Specification & Encoding. (X Window System Ser.: Speical Issue A). (Illus.). 288p. 1992. pap. 22.50 (1-56592-024-4) OReilly & Assocs.

— The X Resource: Public Review Draft: PEX Protocol Specification & Encoding. (X Window System Ser.: Special Issue B). (Illus.). 500p. 1992. pap. 22.50 (1-56592-050-3) OReilly & Assocs.

— The X Resource, Issue 2: A Practical Journal of the X Window System Series. (X Window System Ser.). 186p. (Orig.). 1992. pap. 22.50 (0-937175-97-8) OReilly & Assocs.

— The X Resource, Issue 3: A Practical Journal of the X Window System Series. (X Window System Ser.). 220p. (Orig.). 1992. pap. 14.95 (0-937175-98-6) OReilly & Assocs.

— The X Resource, Issue 5: Proceedings of the 7th Annual X Technical Conference. (X Window System Ser.). (Illus.). 272p. (Orig.). 1993. pap. 14.95 (1-56592-020-1) OReilly & Assocs.

— The X Resource, Issue 6: A Practical Journal of the X Window System Series. (X Window System Ser.). (Illus.). 234p. (Orig.). 1993. pap. 14.95 (1-56592-021-X) OReilly & Assocs.

— The X Resource, Issue 7. (X Window System Ser.). (Illus.). 150p. 1993. pap. 14.95 (1-56592-022-8) OReilly & Assocs.

— The X Resource, Issue 8. (X Window System Ser.). (Illus.). 176p. 1993. pap. 14.95 (1-56592-023-6) OReilly & Assocs.

— The X Resource, Issue 9: Proceedings of the 8th Annual X Technical Conference. (X Window System Ser.). (Illus.). 256p. 1994. pap. 14.95 (1-56592-066-X) OReilly & Assocs.

Nye, Adrian & O'Reilly, Tim. X Toolkit Intrinsics Programming Manual, Vol. 4: For X11 Release 5 - Standard Edition. 3rd ed. (X Window System Ser.). (Illus.). 616p. 1993. pap. 34.95 (1-56592-003-1) OReilly & Assocs.

— X Toolkit Intrinsics Programming Manual, Vol. 4M: For X11 Release 5 - Motif Edition. 2nd ed. (X Window System Ser.). (Illus.). 714p. 1992. pap. 34.95 (1-56592-013-9) OReilly & Assocs.

Nye, Alan R. How to Stop Paying High Property Taxes in Maine: A Step-by-Step Guide to Reducing Your Tax Bills. 150p. 1991. pap. 19.95 (0-9631045-0-0) Portland Pub.

Nye, Alfred, Jr. Understanding & Managing Your Anger & Aggression: A Book to Help Prevent the Damage Anger Causes You & Your Relationships. LC 92-75756. (Illus.). 253p. (Orig.). 1993. pap. 14.95 (0-9635613-5-9) B C A Pub.

Nye, Alvan C. American Colonial Furniture in Scaled Drawings. 1983. 12.75 (0-8446-6009-4) Peter Smith.

— American Colonial Furniture in Scaled Drawings. (Crafts Ser.). (Illus.). 64p. 1982. reprint ed. pap. 3.95 (0-486-21560-1) Dover.

Nye, Andrea. Feminist Theory & the Philosophies of Man. 256p. 1989. pap. 14.95 (0-415-90204-5, A3889, Routledge NY) Routledge.

— Philosophia: The Thought of Rosa Luxemburg, Simone Weil, & Hannah Arendt. LC 93-10223. 1993. 52.50 (0-415-90830-2, B2299, Routledge NY); pap. 16.95 (0-415-90831-0, B2303, Routledge NY) Routledge.

— Words of Power: A Feminist Reading of the History of Logic. 256p. 1990. 45.00 (0-415-90199-5, A3701, Routledge NY); pap. 14.95 (0-415-90200-2, A3705, Routledge NY) Routledge.

Nye, Bill. The Best of Bill Nye's Humor. Hasley, Louis, ed. (Masterworks of Literature Ser.). 1972. 18.95 (0-8084-0343-5); pap. 14.95x (0-8084-0344-3) NCUP.

— Bill Nye, His Own Life Story. LC 78-124246. (Select Bibliographies Reprint Ser.). 1977. reprint ed. 24.95 (0-8369-5434-3) Ayer.

— Bill Nye the Science Guy's Big Blast of Science. (Illus.). 176p. (YA). 1993. pap. 12.45 (0-201-60864-2) Addison-Wesley.

Nye, D. E., jt. ed. see Gidley, M.

Nye, D. F., ed. see Nye, G. & Best, F.

Nye, David E. American Technological Sublime. 440p. 1994. 35.00x (0-262-14056-X) MIT Pr.

— Christopher Columbus in Philately. (Illus.). 32p. 1992. pap. 6.00 (0-935991-16-6) Am Topical Assn.

— Electrifying America: Social Meanings of a New Technology. (Illus.). 350p. 1990. 40.00x (0-262-14048-9) MIT Pr.

— Electrifying America: Social Meanings of New Technology. (Illus.). 350p. 1992. reprint ed. pap. 18.50x (0-262-64030-9) MIT Pr.

— Image Worlds: Corporate Identities at General Electric, 1890-1930. (Illus.). 250p. 1985. 24.95x (0-262-14038-1) MIT Pr.

Nye, David E. & Thomsen, Christen K., eds. American Studies in Transition: Essays. 234p. (Orig.). 1985. pap. text ed. 43.50 (87-7492-532-6) Coronet Bks.

Nye, Doug. Autocourse History of the Grand Prix Car, 1945-1965. (Illus.). 256p. 1993. 49.95 (1-874557-50-0, Pub. by Hazelton UK) Motorbooks Intl.

— Autocourse History of the Grand Prix 66-91. (Illus.). 304p. 1992. 59.95 (0-905138-94-5, Pub. by Hazelton UK) Motorbooks Intl.

Nye, Doug & Goddard, Geoff. Classic Racers: The Post War Front Engined G.P. Cars. (Illus.). 144p. 1991. 34.95 (0-85429-775-8, Pub. by G T Foulis Ltd) Haynes Pubns.

Nye, Doug & Rudd, Tony. BRM: The Saga of British Racing Motors, Vol. 1: The Front Engined Cars 1945-60. (Illus.). 400p. 1994. 120.00 (0-947981-37-3, Pub. by Motor Racing UK) Motorbooks Intl.

Nye, Edgar W. Bill Nye: His Own Life Story. (BCL1-PS American Literature Ser.). 412p. 1992. reprint ed. lib. bdg. 99.00 (0-7812-6815-X) Rprt Serv.

— Bill Nye & Boomerang. LC 70-166823. 1971. reprint ed. 29.00 (0-403-01449-2) Scholarly.

— Bill Nye's History of the United States. LC 75-96891. (Illus.). reprint ed. lib. bdg. 22.00 (0-8398-1352-X) Irvington.

— Thinks. LC 74-104534. 181p. reprint ed. lib. bdg. 28.00 (0-8398-1354-6) Irvington.

— Thinks. 181p. (C). 1986. reprint ed. pap. text ed. 6.95 (0-8290-2041-1) Irvington.

Nye, Edgar W. & Nye, Frank W. Bill Nye: His Own Life Story. LC 70-145216. (Illus.). 1971. reprint ed. 24.00 (0-403-01133-7) Scholarly.

Nye, F. Ivan. Family Relationships & Delinquent Behavior. LC 73-8562. 168p. 1973. reprint ed. text ed. 38.50 (0-8371-6967-4, NYFR, Greenwood Pr) Greenwood.

Nye, Francis, et al. The Employed Mother in America. LC 76-4503. (Illus.). 406p. 1976. reprint ed. text ed. 35.00 (0-8371-8784-2, NYEM, Greenwood Pr) Greenwood.

Nye, Frank W., jt. auth. see Nye, Edgar W.

Nye, G. & Best, F. Genealogy of the Nye Family. Nye, D. F., ed. (Illus.). 704p. 1989. reprint ed. lib. bdg. 107.00 (0-8328-0910-1); reprint ed. pap. 99.00 (0-8328-0911-X) Higginson Bk Co.

Nye, G. S. Biographical Sketches & Records of the Ezra Olin Family. 441p. 1989. reprint ed. lib. bdg. 78.50 (0-8328-0920-9); reprint ed. pap. 68.50 (0-8328-0921-7) Higginson Bk Co.

Nye, George A. Old Wine in New Skins: Calls to Worship & Other Worship Resources. LC 93-38001. 168p. 1994. pap. 11.95 (1-55673-824-2, 9422) CSS OH.

Nye, Gideon. The Rationale of the China Question. LC 72-79834. (China Library Ser.). 1972. reprint ed. lib. bdg. 14.00 (0-8420-1374-1) Scholarly Res Inc.

Nye, J. F. Physical Properties of Crystals: Their Representation by Tensors & Matrices. 340p. 1985. pap. 35.00 (0-19-851165-5) OUP.

Nye, J. Michael, ed. see Marketing Consultants International Inc. Staff.

Nye, Jamie, jt. auth. see Leinecker, Rick.

Nye, Jim. Aftershock: Poems & Prose from the Vietnam War. LC 91-372302. 80p. (Orig.). 1991. pap. 8.95 (0-938317-14-8) Cinco Puntos.

Nye, Jody L. Higher Mythology. 272p. (Orig.). 1993. mass mkt. 4.99 (0-446-36335-9, Aspect) Warner Bks.

— Magic Touch. (Orig.). 1996. mass mkt. write for info. (0-446-60210-8, Aspect) Warner Bks.

— Medicine Show. 272p. (Orig.). 1994. pap. text ed. 4.99 (0-441-00085-1) Ace Bks.

— Mythology 101. 272p. 1990. mass mkt. 4.95 (0-445-21021-4, Aspect) Warner Bks.

— Taylor's Ark. 288p. (Orig.). 1993. mass mkt. 4.99 (0-441-79974-4) Ace Bks.

N

An Asterisk (*) at the beginning of an entry indicates that the title is appearing in BIP for the first time.

Nye, Jody L. & McCaffrey, Anne. The Dragonlover's Guide to Pern. LC 89-6715. (Illus.). 192p. 1989. 19.95 (*0-345-35424-9*, Del Rey) Ballantine.
— The Dragonlover's Guide to Pern. (Illus.). 192p. 1992. pap. 12.95 (*0-345-37946-2*, Del Rey) Ballantine.
Nye, Jody L., jt. auth. see Anthony, Piers.
Nye, Jody L., jt. auth. see McCaffrey, Anne.
Nye, Jody L., ed. see McCaffrey, Anne.
Nye, Jody L., jt. ed. see Resnick, Mike.
Nye, John. Between the Rivers: A History of United Methodism in Iowa. LC 86-80106. (Illus.). 350p. 1986. 12.95 (*0-9616298-0-0*); pap. 10.95 (*0-9616298-1-9*) IA Conf Com Arch.
Nye, Joseph S., Jr. Bound to Lead: The Changing Nature of American Power. 307p. 1991. pap. 15.00 (*0-465-00744-9*) Basic.
— Ethics & Foreign Policy. 38p. (Orig.). 1985. pap. text ed. 10.50 (*0-8191-5844-5*, Aspen Inst for Humanistic Studies) U Pr of Amer.
Nye, Joseph S., Jr., et al. Global Cooperation after the Cold War: A Reassessment of Trilateralism. (Triangle Papers). 1991. 6.00 (*0-930503-67-8*) Trilateral Comm.
Nye, Joseph S., Jr. Nuclear Ethics. 160p. 1986. 22.95 (*0-02-922460-8*) Free Pr.
— Nuclear Ethics. 130p. 1988. pap. 12.95 (*0-02-923091-8*) Free Pr.
Nye, Joseph S. Pan-Africanism & East African Integration. LC 65-22063. 327p. reprint ed. pap. 93.20 (*0-7837-3845-5*, 2043667) Bks Demand.
— Peace in Parts: Integration & Conflict in Regional Organization. LC 87-10480. (Illus.). 224p. (Orig.). (C). 1987. reprint ed. lib. bdg. 46.00 (*0-8191-6393-7*); reprint ed. pap. text ed. 22.50 (*0-8191-6394-5*) U Pr of Amer.
Nye, Joseph S., Jr. Understanding International Conflict: An Introduction to Theory & History. LC 92-32174. (C). 1992. text ed. 25.00 (*0-06-500720-4*) HarpCollege.
***Nye, Joseph S., ed.** The Making of America's Soviet Policy. LC 83-51295. 379p. 1984. pap. 108.10 (*0-7837-8651-4*, 2082314) Bks Demand.
Nye, Joseph S., Jr. & Rowe, David M., eds. Harness the Rising Sun: An American Strategy for Managing Japan's Rise as a Global Power. LC 93-10863. 1993. 52.00 (*0-8191-9168-X*); pap. 21.50 (*0-8191-9169-8*) U Pr of Amer.
Nye, Joseph S., Jr. & Schear, James A., eds. On the Defensive? The Future of SDI. LC 88-17342. (Aspen Strategy Group Publication Ser.). 222p. (Orig.). (C). 1989. pap. text ed. 20.00 (*0-8191-7021-6*, Aspen Inst for Humanistic Studies) U Pr of Amer.
Nye, Joseph S., Jr. & Shear, James A., eds. Seeking Stability in Space: Anti-Satelite Weapons & the Evolving Space Regime. LC 87-21619. (Illus.). 184p. (Orig.). (C). 1988. pap. text ed. 19.50 (*0-8191-6422-4*) U Pr of Amer.
Nye, Joseph S. & Smith, Roger K., eds. After the Storm: Lessons from the Gulf War. 426p. 1992. 24.95 (*0-8191-8529-9*) Madison Bks UPA.
— After the Storm: Lessons from the Gulf War. 426p. 1993. pap. 14.95 (*1-56833-015-4*) Madison Bks UPA.
Nye, Joseph S., jt. ed. see Hunington, Samuel P.
Nye, Joseph S., jt. auth. see Keohane, Robert O., Jr.
Nye, Joseph S., Jr., jt. ed. see Keohane, Robert O.
Nye, Julie. Every Perfect Gift. Vogt, Carla, ed. (Light Line Ser.). 201p. (Orig.). (YA). (gr. 9 up). 1990. pap. 5.95 (*0-89084-499-2*) Bob Jones Univ Pr.
— In My Uncle's House. (Light Line Ser.). 117p. (Orig.). (J). (gr. 4-6). 1986. pap. 5.95 (*0-89084-349-X*) Bob Jones Univ Pr.
— Scout. (Light Line Ser.). 177p. (Orig.). (J). 1987. pap. 5.95 (*0-89084-413-5*) Bob Jones Univ Pr.
Nye, K. E. & Parkin, J. M. HIV & AIDS. (Medical Perspectives Ser.). 160p. (Orig.). 1994. pap. 42.50x (*1-872748-96-1*, Pub. by Bios Scientific UK) Coronet Bks.
Nye, Kemp B. Ripshin. LC 92-33504. 1992. pap. 12.00 (*0-930095-13-8*) Signal Bks.
— Ripshin. 1993. 16.00 (*0-930095-30-8*) Signal Bks.
— Ripshin. LC 93-42266. 1993. 16.00 (*0-930095-17-0*) Signal Bks.
Nye, Mary J. From Chemical Philosophy to Theoretical Chemistry: Dynamics of Matter & Dynamics of Disciplines, 1800-1950. LC 92-43114. 1993. 50.00 (*0-520-08210-9*) U CA Pr.
Nye, Mary J., et al, eds. The Invention of Physical Science: Intersections of Mathematics, Theology, & Natural Philosophy since the Seventeenth Century: Essays in Honor of Erwin N. Hiebert. LC 92-12520. (Boston Studies in the Philosophy of Science: Vol. 139). 288p. (C). 1992. lib. bdg. 115.50 (*0-7923-1753-X*) Kluwer Ac.
Nye, Mary Jo. Molecular Reality: A Perspective on the Scientific Work of Jean Perrin. LC 70-171234. 1972. lib. bdg. 17.00 (*0-685-52440-X*) Watson Pub Intl.
Nye, Miriam B. But I Never Thought He'd Die: Practical Help for Widows. LC 78-9644. 150p. 1978. pap. 9.99 (*0-664-24208-1*, Westminster) Westminster John Knox.
Nye, Naomi S. Benito's Dream Bottle. LC 93-45675. (Illus.). (J). 1995. text ed. 15.95 (*0-02-768467-9*, Mac Bks Young Read) S&S Childrens.
— Red Suitcase. (American Poets Continuum Ser.: No. 29). 90p. 1994. 20.00 (*1-880238-14-4*); pap. 12.50 (*1-880238-15-2*) BOA Edns.
— Sitti's Secrets. LC 93-19742. (Illus.). 32p. (J). (ps-3). 1994. text ed. 14.95 (*0-02-768460-1*, Four Winds Pr) S&S Childrens.
— This Same Sky: A Collection of Poems from Around the World. LC 92-11617. (Illus.). 224p. (YA). (gr. 5 up). 1992. lib. bdg. 15.95 (*0-02-768440-7*, Four Winds Pr) S&S Childrens.
— Words under the Words: Selected Poems. 160p. (Orig.). 1995. lib. bdg. 22.95 (*0-933377-32-0*); pap. 13.95 (*0-933377-29-0*) Eighth Mount Pr.
Nye, Naomi S., tr. see Al-Maghut, Mohammad.
Nye, Naomi S., tr. see Tuqan, Fadwa, ed.
Nye, Naomi S., et al. The Children of Nigh. 1993. pap. text ed. 5.95 (*1-885405-00-6*) IOC Pr.
Nye, Nelson. Born to Trouble. large type ed. (Nightingale Ser.). 278p. 1991. pap. 14.95 (*0-8161-4831-7*, Nightingale) Hall.
— Come a-Smokin' - Horses, Women & Guns, 2 vols. in 1. 400p. 1994. mass mkt., pap. text ed. 4.99 (*0-8439-3648-7*) Dorchester Pub Co.
— Deadly Companions. 168p. 1987. 16.95 (*0-8027-4069-3*) Walker & Co.
— Desert of the Damned. large type ed. (Linford Western Library). 336p. 1985. pap. 11.95 (*0-7089-6084-7*, Trailtree Bookshop) Ulverscroft.
— The Feud at Sleepy Cat. 1995. 15.95 (*0-7451-4635-X*) Chivers N Amer.
— The Feud at Sleepy Cat. 1979. reprint ed. pap. 1.50 (*0-8439-0611-1*) Dorchester Pub Co.
— Gringo. large type ed. (Linford Western Library). 320p. 1985. pap. 11.95 (*0-7089-6136-3*, Trailtree Bookshop) Ulverscroft.
— Gunfight at the O K Corral. 160p. 1982. pap. 1.95 (*0-8439-1093-3*) Dorchester Pub Co.
— Gunfighter Brand; Breed of the Chaparral; The Kid from Lincoln County, 3 vols. in 1. 432p. 1992. pap. 5.99 (*0-8439-3362-3*) Dorchester Pub Co.
— Gunman, Gunman. large type ed. (Nightingale Ser.). 291p. 1990. pap. 13.95 (*0-8161-4955-0*) G K Hall.
— Guns of Horse Prairie - Wildcats of Tonto Basin, 2 vols. in 1. 336p. 1991. pap. 4.50 (*0-8439-3176-0*) Dorchester Pub Co.
— Gunshot Trail - Texas Tornado. 320p. 1992. pap. 4.50 (*0-8439-3234-1*) Dorchester Pub Co.
— Gunslick Mountain. large type ed. (Linford Western Library). 288p. 1985. pap. 11.95 (*0-7089-6143-6*, Trailtree Bookshop) Ulverscroft.
— Iron Hand. large type ed. (Dales Western Ser.). 265p. 1993. pap. 16.95 (*1-85389-342-0*, Medcom-Trainex) Ulverscroft.
— The Lonely Grass. large type ed. LC 93-25506. 1993. pap. 14.95 (*0-8161-5837-1*) Hall.
— The Lost Padre. 176p. 1993. lib. bdg. 18.00 (*0-7278-4469-5*) Severn Hse.
— The Marshall of Pioche. large type ed. 196p. 1992. pap. 16.95 (*1-85389-340-4*, Dales) Ulverscroft.
— Mule Man. large type ed. (General Ser.). 246p. 1992. text ed. 19.95 (*0-8161-5334-5*) G K Hall.
— The Palominas Pistolero & Smoke Wagon Kid. 1978. pap. 1.95 (*0-89083-418-0*) Zebra.
— The Parson of Gunbarrel Basin. large type ed. LC 93-43546. (General Ser.). 1994. pap. 15.95 (*0-8161-5923-8*, Large Print Bks) Hall.
— The Shootin' Sheriff. 1994. lib. bdg. 15.95 (*0-7451-4605-8*, Gunsmoke) Chivers N Amer.
— The Shootin' Sheriff & The Bandit of Bloody Run. (Two-in One Western Ser.). 1979. pap. 1.95 (*0-89083-444-X*) Zebra.
— Shotgun Law - Hellbound for Ballarat, 2 vols. in 1. 320p. 1993. pap. 4.50 (*0-8439-3397-6*) Dorchester Pub Co.
— The Sure-Fire Kid & Wildcats of Tonto Basin. (Double Barrel Western Ser.: No. 2). 448p. 1987. reprint ed. pap. 3.95 (*0-8439-2474-8*) Harper SF.
— The Texas Gun - Gringo. 320p. 1995. mass mkt. 4.99 (*0-8439-3822-6*) Dorchester Pub Co.
— Thief River. large type ed. (Linford Western Library). 352p. 1986. pap. 11.95 (*0-7089-6199-1*, Linford) Ulverscroft.
— Tornado on Horseback. (Gunsmoke Western Ser.). 160p. 1989. text ed. 12.95 (*0-86220-922-6*, Gunsmoke) Chivers N Amer.
— Trail of Lost Skulls. large type ed. (Nightingale Ser.). 254p. 1991. pap. 14.95 (*0-8161-4832-5*) G K Hall.
— Treasure Trail from Tucson - Feud at Sleepy Cat, 2 vols. in 1. 368p. 1993. pap. 4.99 (*0-8439-3547-2*) Dorchester Pub Co.
— Trigger Talk. large type ed. LC 92-30141. (Nightingale Ser.). 224p. 1993. pap. 14.95 (*0-8161-5631-X*, Nightingale) Hall.
— Wide Loop. large type ed. (General Ser.). 307p. 1990. lib. bdg. 16.95 (*0-8161-4833-3*, Large Print Bks) Hall.
— Wild Horse Shorty - Blood of Kings. 416p. 1995. mass mkt. 4.99 (*0-8439-3751-3*) Dorchester Pub Co.
— Wildcats of Tonto Basin. 1993. 14.95 (*0-7451-4550-7*, Gunsmoke) Chivers N Amer.
— The Wolf That Rode. 224p. (Orig.). 1980. pap. 1.95 (*0-89083-612-4*) Zebra.
Nye, Nelson C. Rafe. large type ed. LC 93-25405. 1993. pap. 17.95 (*0-7927-1774-0*, Curley Lrg Print) Chivers N Amer.
— Speed & the Quarter Horse: A Payload of Sprinters. LC 73-140120. 368p. reprint ed. pap. 104.90 (*0-7837-7136-3*, 2059163) Bks Demand.
Nye, Peter. Hearts of Lions: The Story of American Bicycle Racing. (Illus.). 1989. pap. 12.00 (*0-393-30576-7*) Norton.
Nye, Peter, jt. auth. see Howard, John.
Nye, Robert. Tales I Told My Mother. 171p. 1982. pap. text ed. 12.95 (*0-7145-2741-6*) M Boyars Pubs.
— Tales I Told My Mother. 176p. 1992. 11.95 (*0-7145-2954-0*) M Boyars Pubs.
Nye, Robert A. Crime, Madness & Politics in Modern France: The Medical Concept of National Decline. LC 83-43087. 1984. 52.50 (*0-691-05414-2*) Princeton U Pr.
— Masculinity & Male Codes of Honor in Modern France. (Studies in the History of Sexuality). (Illus.). 336p. 1993. 39.95 (*0-19-504649-8*) OUP.
— The Origins of Crowd Psychology: Gustave LeBon & the Crisis of Mass Democracy in the Third Republic. LC 74-76327. (Sage Studies in 20th Century History: Vol. 2). 226p. reprint ed. pap. 64.50 (*0-317-08777-0*, 2021938) Bks Demand.
Nye, Robert D. The Legacy of B. F. Skinner: Concepts & Perspectives, Controversies & Misunderstandings. LC 91-21644. 176p. (C). 1992. pap. 17.95 (*0-534-16944-9*) Brooks-Cole.
— Three Psychologies: Perspectives from Freud, Skinner & Rogers. 4th ed. LC 91-8546. 176p. (Orig.). (C). 1992. pap. 21.95 (*0-534-16224-X*) Brooks-Cole.
— Three Psychologies: Perspectives from Freud, Skinner, & Rogers. 5th ed. LC 94-42256. 1996. pap. 12.95 (*0-534-26616-9*) Brooks-Cole.
Nye, Robert E. Beowulf. 96p. (YA). (gr. 5 up). 1982. mass mkt. 3.99 (*0-440-90560-5*, LFL) Dell.
Nye, Robert E. & Bergethon, Bjonnar. Basic Music. 6th ed. (Illus.). 256p. (C). 1987. pap. text ed. write for info. (*0-13-065681-X*) P-H.
Nye, Robert E., et al. Music in the Elementary School. 6th ed. 400p. 1992. text ed. 55.33 (*0-13-607722-6*) P-H.
Nye, Robert H. The Patton Mind: The Professional Development of an Extraordinary Leader. LC 92-10490. 224p. 1993. pap. 12.95 (*0-89529-428-1*) Avery Pub.
Nye, Roger H. The Challenge of Command: Reading for Military Excellence. LC 85-30614. (West Point Military History Ser.). 200p. (Orig.). 1986. pap. 9.95 (*0-89529-280-7*) Avery Pub.
Nye, Russel B., ed. see Bancroft, George.
Nye, Russel B., ed. see Franklin, Benjamin.
Nye, Russel B., jt. auth. see McAvoy, Thomas T.
***Nye, Russell.** Simulation Analysis of Capital Structure in a Property Insurance Firm. (C). 1975. 10.50 (*0-256-04607-7*) Irwin.
Nye, Sandra G. Employee Assistance Law Answer Book. 452p. 1991. reprint ed. text ed. 89.00 (*1-878375-12-1*) Panel Pubs.
Nye, Sandra G. & Kaiser, Laura B. Employee Assistance Law Answer Book: 1992 Supplement. 250p. 1991. pap. text ed. 49.00 (*1-878375-54-7*) Panel Pubs.
Nye, W. F., ed. see International Symposium on Boron Staff.
Nye, Wilbur S. Carbine & Lance: The Story of Old Fort Sill. enl. rev. ed. LC 79-13137. (Illus.). 448p. 1983. pap. 17.95 (*0-8061-1856-3*) U of Okla Pr.
— Here Come the Rebels. 1988. 25.00 (*0-89029-080-6*); pap. 14.95 (*0-89029-780-0*) Morningside Bkshop.
— Plains Indian Raiders: The Final Phases of Warfare from the Arkansas to the Red River. LC 67-24624. (Illus.). 438p. 1984. pap. 19.95 (*0-8061-1175-5*) U of Okla Pr.
Nye, Wilbur S., jt. auth. see Betzinez, Jason.
Nyeko, Balaam, jt. auth. see Denoon, Donald.
Nyeko, Balem. Swaziland. (World Bibliographical Ser.: No. 24). 135p. 1983. lib. bdg. 45.00 (*0-903450-35-6*) ABC-CLIO.
Nyeland, Preben. Maxi, the Ultimate Racing Experience. 1990. 50.00 (*0-393-03340-6*) Norton.
***Nyembezi.** Learn Zulu. 264p. (ENG & ZUL.). 1990. pap. 15.95 (*0-7859-7521-7*) Fr & Eur.
— Zulu-English, English-Zulu Dictionary. 2nd ed. 519p. (ENG & ZUL.). 1988. pap. 19.95 (*0-7859-7523-3*) Fr & Eur.
— Zulu Proverbs. rev. ed. (ENG & ZUL.). 1963. pap. 18.95 (*0-7859-7522-5*) Fr & Eur.
Nyembezi, C. L. Learn Zulu. 5th ed. 264p. (ZUL.). 1990. reprint ed. pap. 12.00 (*0-7960-0237-1*) IBD Ltd.
— Zulu Proverbs. rev. ed. 1963. 18.00 (*0-7960-0230-4*) IBD Ltd.
Nyembezi, C. L., jt. auth. see Dent, G. R.
Nyembezi, L. Zulu-English - English-Zulu. 2nd ed. 519p. 1988. pap. 20.00 (*0-7960-0111-1*) IBD Ltd.
Nyenhuis, Jacob E., jt. auth. see Goldman, Norma.
Nyer, Evan. Practical Techniques for Groundwater & Soil Remediation. 1992. 64.95 (*0-87371-731-7*, TD426) Lewis Pubs.
Nyer, Evan K. Groundwater Treatment Technology. 2nd ed. (Illus.). 320p. 1992. text ed. 54.95 (*0-442-00562-8*) Van Nos Reinhold.
***Nyer, Genie.** Mexico Embraces the "Third Age" (Working Paper Ser.: No. 77). 32p. 1994. 5.00 (*0-614-01230-9*) LBJ Sch Pub Aff.
Nyerges, Anton N., tr. & intro. Poems of Attila Josef. (Illus.). 224p. 1987. reprint ed. pap. text ed. 23.25 (*0-8191-6566-2*) U Pr of Amer.
— Poems of Endre Ady. (Illus.). 500p. 1987. reprint ed. lib. bdg. 58.50 (*0-8191-6568-9*) U Pr of Amer.
Nyerges, Anton N., tr. see Ertavy-Barath, Joseph M., ed.
***Nyerges, Timothy L., ed.** Cognitive Aspects of Human-Computer Interaction for Geographic Information Systems: Proceedings of the NATO Advanced Research Workshop, Palma de Mallorca, Spain, March 20-25, 1994. (NATO Advanced Science Institutes Series C). 448p. (C). 1995. lib. bdg. 225.00 (*0-7923-3595-3*) Kluwer Ac.
Nyeste, Zoltan. Recsk - Emberek az embertelensegben (Recsk Man in Inhumanity) LC 82-82973. (Tanuk Korukrol Ser.). (Illus.). 80p. 1982. pap. 6.00 (*0-910539-00-6*) Hungarian Alumni.
Nyffenegger, Eugen. Cristan der Kuchimaister, Nuewe Casus Monasterii Sancti Galli: Edition & Sprachgeschichtliche Einordnung. (Quellen und Forschungen zur Sprach und Kulturgeschichte der Germanischen Voelker Ser.: NF Bd. 60). (GER.). (C). 1974. 153.85 (*3-11-004098-0*) De Gruyter.
Nyfors, E. & Vainikainen, P. Industrial Microwave Sensors. 351p. 1989. 85.00 (*0-89006-397-4*) Artech Hse.
Nygaard, Anita. Earthclock. 1977. reprint ed. pap. 4.95 (*0-8065-0567-2*, Citadel Pr) Carol Pub Group.
Nygaard, Gary & Boone, Thomas H. Coaches Guide to Sport Law. LC 84-25284. 120p. 1985. pap. text ed. 18.00 (*0-931250-94-3*, BNYG0094) Human Kinetics.
Nygaard, K., jt. ed. see Gjessing, S.
Nygaard, Kaare. Knife, Life, & Bronzes: Sculpture & Vignettes. Beeson, Nora, ed. LC 86-90671. (Illus.). 192p. (C). 1986. text ed. 75.00 (*0-9619518-0-X*) Pace Univ Pr.
Nygaard, Oddvar F. & Upton, Arthur C., eds. Anticarcinogenesis & Radiation Protection 2. (Illus.). 458p. 1992. 125.00 (*0-306-44056-3*, Plenum Pr) Plenum.
Nygaard, Reuel & Doud, Guy. Tragedy to Triumph. Horton, Dave, ed. 224p. (Orig.). Date not set. pap. 9.99 (*0-7814-1522-5*, Chariot Bks) Chariot Family.
Nygard, Thomas A., ed. Clyde Aspevig. (Illus.). 36p. 1994. pap. 10.00 (*0-9620327-4-3*) Nygard Pub.
Nygh, Justice. Conflict of Laws in Australia. 5th ed. 1991. Australia. 105.00 (*0-409-30816-1*); Australia. pap. 77.00 (*0-409-30817-X*) Butterworth Legal Pubs.
Nygh, Peter, jt. ed. see McLachlan, Campbell.
Nygren, Anders. Commentary on Romans. Rasmussen, Carl, tr. LC 49-48317. 472p. 1949. reprint ed. pap. 12.00 (*0-8006-1684-7*, 1-1684, Fortress Pr) Augsburg Fortress.
Nygren, David J. & Ukeritis, Miriam D. The Future of Religious Orders in the United States: Transformation & Commitment. LC 93-19088. 344p. 1993. text ed. 59.95 (*0-275-94665-7*, C4665, Praeger Pubs) Greenwood.
Nygren, Edward J., intro. Isaac Cruikshank & the Politics of Parody: Watercolors in the Huntington Collection. LC 94-2794. (Illus.). 162p. (Orig.). 1994. pap. 19.95 (*0-87328-147-0*) Huntington Lib.
Nygren, Edward J. & Marzio, Peter C. Of Time & Place: American Figurative Art from the Corcoran Gallery. 2nd ed. LC 81-607836. (Illus.). 208p. 1981. pap. 10.00 (*0-317-19168-3*, NYTPP) SITES.
Nygren, Malcolm. The Lord of the Four Seasons. 144p. (Orig.). 1986. pap. 7.95 (*0-9617890-1-8*) Doxology Lane.
Nyhan, Elizabeth. Traditional Floral Charted Designs for Borders & Bands. (Needlecraft Ser.). (Illus.). 48p. (Orig.). 1991. pap. 2.95 (*0-486-26696-6*) Dover.
Nyhan, Elizabeth F. Treasury of Patchwork Borders: 92 Foolproof Tricks. 1990. pap. 3.95 (*0-486-26183-2*) Dover.
— Treasury of Patchwork Quilt Sets. LC 94-17258. 1994. write for info. (*0-486-28148-5*) Dover.
Nyhan, Michael, et al. A Snapshot View of Communication Patterns: The New Hampshire Division of Vocational Rehabilitation. 67p. 1982. 7.50 (*0-318-19197-0*, R-55) Inst Future.
Nyhan, Michael J., jt. ed. see Cater, Douglass.
Nyhan, W. L., et al, eds. Purine & Pyrimidine Metabolism in Man V, 2 Vols., Set. LC 85-32557. (Advances in Experimental Medicine & Biology Ser.: Vol. 195). 1986. 195.00 (*0-685-13929-8*, Plenum Pr) Plenum.
— Purine & Pyrimidine Metabolism in Man V, 2 Vols., Vol. A. LC 85-32557. (Advances in Experimental Medicine & Biology Ser.: Vol. 195). 634p. 1986. 120.00 (*0-306-42230-1*, Plenum Pr) Plenum.
— Purine & Pyrimidine Metabolism in Man V, 2 Vols., Vol. B. LC 85-32557. (Advances in Experimental Medicine & Biology Ser.: Vol. 195). 720p. 1986. 125.00 (*0-306-42231-X*, Plenum Pr) Plenum.
Nyhan, William L., ed. Heritable Disorders of Amino Acid Metabolism: Patterns of Clinical Expression & Genetic Variation. LC 74-6255. 783p. reprint ed. pap. 180.00 (*0-317-07890-9*, 2012578) Bks Demand.
Nyhan, William L. & Sakati, Nadia A. Diagnostic Recognition of Genetic Disease. LC 86-21132. 766p. reprint ed. pap. 180.00 (*0-7837-2735-6*, 2043115) Bks Demand.
***Nyhart, Lynn K.** Before Biology: Animal Morphology & the German Universities, 1800-1900. LC 95-3227. (Science & Its Conceptual Foundations Ser.). 1995. lib. bdg. 75.00 (*0-226-61086-1*); pap. text ed. 24.95 (*0-226-61088-8*) U Ch Pr.
Nyhart, Nina. French for Soldiers. LC 86-72478. 72p. (Orig.). (C). 1987. 15.95 (*0-914086-70-7*); pap. 9.95 (*0-914086-71-5*) Alicejamesbooks.
Nyhart, Nina & Lockwood, Margo. Openers & Temper. LC 78-74232. 88p. 1979. pap. 9.95 (*0-914086-26-X*) Alicejamesbooks.
Nyhart, Nina, jt. auth. see Gensler, Kinereth.
Nyhoff, John E., jt. auth. see Labuszewski, John W.
Nyhoff, Larry & Leestama, Sanford. FORTRAN Seventy Seven & Numerical Methods for Engineers & Scientists. LC 94-7462. 740p. (C). 1995. write for info. (*0-02-388741-9*) Macmillan.
Nyhoff, Larry & Leestma, Sanford. Advanced Programming in Pascal with Data Structures. 640p. (C). 1988. pap. write for info. (*0-02-369550-1*) Macmillan.
— Data Structures & Program Design in Modula-2. (Illus.). 675p. (C). 1990. Incl. solns. manual. student ed, text ed. write for info. (*0-02-388621-8*) Macmillan.
— Data Structures & Program Design in Pascal. 2nd ed. (Illus.). 752p. (C). 1992. text ed. write for info. (*0-02-369465-3*) Macmillan.
— FORTRAN 77 for Engineers & Scientists. 3rd ed. (Illus.). 656p. (C). 1992. pap. write for info. (*0-02-388655-2*) Macmillan.
Nyhoff, Larry, jt. auth. see Leestma, Sanford.
Nyhoff, Larry, et al. C Plus Plus: An Introduction to Computing. (Illus.). 900p. (C). 1994. teacher ed write for info. (*0-318-72461-8*); pap. write for info. (*0-02-369402-5*) Macmillan.
Nyholm, Earl, jt. auth. see Nichols, John D.
Nyhuis, Allen W. The Zoo Book: A Guide to America's Best. (Illus.). 288p. (Orig.). 1994. pap. 14.95 (*0-917120-13-2*) Carousel Pr.
***Nyhus.** Surgery Annual 1995. (C). 1995. text ed. 75.00 (*0-8385-7992-2*) Appleton & Lange.
***Nyhus, et al.** Abdominal Pain: Guide to Rapid Diagnosis. (C). 1994. pap. text ed. 19.95 (*0-8385-0068-4*) Appleton & Lange.
Nyhus, Lloyd M. Surgery Annual, 1992, Vol. 24, Pt. 2. (Illus.). 272p. 1992. text ed. 80.00 (*0-8385-8748-8*, A8748-4) Appleton & Lange.
— Surgery Annual, 1993, Pt. 2. (Illus.). 272p. 1993. text ed. 80.00 (*0-8385-8749-6*, A8749-2) Appleton & Lange.

N

An Asterisk (*) at the beginning of an entry indicates that the title is appearing in BIP for the first time.

— Surgery Annual 1993, Vol. 25, Pt. 1. (Illus.). 272p. (C). 1992. text ed. 80.00 (*0-8385-8798-4*, A8798-9) Appleton & Lange.

— Surgery Annual 1994. (Illus.). 288p. 1994. text ed. 80.00 (*0-8385-8531-0*, A8531-4) Appleton & Lange.

Nyhus, Lloyd M., ed. Surgery Annual, 1988, Vol. 20. (Illus.). 384p. 1988. boxed 80.00 (*0-8385-8728-3*, A8728-6) Appleton & Lange.

— Surgery Annual, 1991, Vol. 23, Pt. 1. (Illus.). 242p. (C). 1991. boxed 80.00 (*0-8385-8743-7*, A8743-5) Appleton & Lange.

— Surgery Annual, 1991, Vol. 23, Pt. 2. (Illus.). 194p. (C). 1991. boxed 80.00 (*0-8385-8744-5*, A8744-3) Appleton & Lange.

Nyhus, Lloyd M. & Baker, Robert. Mastery of Surgery, 2 vols., Set. 1540p. 1984. 240.00 (*0-316-61742-3*, Little Med Div) Little.

Nyhus, Lloyd M. & Condon, Robert E. Hernia. 4th ed. (Illus.). 800p. (C). 1994. text ed. 140.00 (*0-397-51286-4*, Lippincott Medical) Lippincott.

Nyhus, Lloyd M., jt. auth. see Barrett, John.

Nyhus, Lloyd M., jt. auth. see Condon, Robert E.

Nyhus, Lloyd M., jt. ed. see Condon, Robert E.

Nyhus, Paul L., tr. see Oberman, Heiko A.

NYIF Staff. Stocks, Bonds, Options, Futures: Investments & Their Markets. (Illus.). 320p. 1987. 27.95 (*0-13-846718-8*) NY Inst Finance.

Nyilas, Jozsef. The World Economy & Its Main Developmental Tendencies. 1982. lib. bdg. 49.50 (*0-686-38405-9*) Kluwer Ac.

Nyingma Centers Art Projects Staff. How to Frame a Thanka: A Guide to Displaying Sacred Art & Constructing Traditional Cloth Mountings. (Illus.). 16p. 1989. pap. 4.95 (*0-89800-203-6*) Dharma Pub.

Nyingpo, Namkhay. Mother of Knowledge: The Enlightenment of Ye-shes Mtsho-Rgyal. Tulku, Tarthang, tr. LC 83-23208. (Translation Ser.: Vol. 12). Orig. Title: Tibetan. (Illus.). 250p. 1983. 30.00 (*0-913546-90-9*); pap. 17.95 (*0-913546-91-7*) Dharma Pub.

Nyiri, Alan. Acadia National Park: Maine's Intimate Parkland. (Illus.). 80p. 1986. pap. 12.95 (*0-89272-219-3*) Down East.

Nyiri, Alan, photos. Cape Cod. LC 91-77669. (Illus.). 112p. 1992. 35.00 (*0-89272-303-3*) Down East.

Nyiri, Alan, photos & text. The White Mountains of New Hampshire. (Illus.). 84p. (Orig.). 1987. pap. 9.95 (*0-89272-241-X*) Down East.

Nyiri, J. C. Tradition & Individuality: Essays. (Synthese Library). 192p. (C). 1992. lib. bdg. 81.50 (*0-7923-1566-9*) Kluwer Ac.

Nyiri, J. C., ed. Karl Wittgenstein: Politico-Economic Writings. (Viennese Heritage Ser.: No. 1). xi, 240p. (GER.). 1984. reprint ed. 62.00x (*90-272-3882-0*); reprint ed. pap. 22.95x (*90-272-3881-2*) Benjamins North Am.

Nyiri, J. C. & Smith, Barry, eds. Practical Knowledge, Tradition & Technique. 224p. 1987. lib. bdg. 62.50 (*0-7099-4477-2*, Pub. by Croom Helm UK) Routledge Chapman & Hall.

Nyiri, J. C., ed. see Masaryk, Thomas G.

Nyiri, J. C., et al, eds. Austrian Philosophy Studies & Texts. (Philosophia Resources Library Ser.). 200p. 1981. lib. bdg. 59.00 (*3-88405-004-4*) Philosophia Pr.

***Nyiri, Janos.** Battlefields & Playgrounds. Brandon, William, tr. LC 95-5389. 536p. 1995. 25.00 (*0-374-10918-4*) FS&G.

Nyiri, Nicolas. The United Nations' Search for a Definition of Aggression. (American University Studies: Political Science: Ser. X, Vol. 22). 412p. (C). 1989. text ed. 53.95 (*0-8204-0869-7*) P Lang Pubs.

***Nyirjesy, Istvan.** Prevention & Detection of Gynecologic & Breast Cancer. 150p. 1994. pap. text ed. write for info. (*0-9642179-0-2*) Intl Fnd Gynecol.

Nyirkos, I. Finnish-Hungarian-Finnish Dictionary (Suomi-Unkari-Suomi) 712p. (FIN & HUN.). 1979. pap. 79.95 (*0-8288-4800-9*, M9642) Fr & Eur.

Nyiroe, L., ed. Literature & Its Interpretation. (De Proprietatibus Litterarum, Ser. Minor: No. 24). 1979. pap. text ed. 34.70 (*90-279-3387-1*) Mouton.

Nyiszli, Miklow. Auschwitz: A Doctor's Eyewitness Account. Kramer, Tibere & Seaver, Richard, trs. 240p. (C). 1993. reprint ed. pap. 10.95 (*1-55970-202-8*) Arcade Pub Inc.

Nykamp, William. Twilight of Orthodoxy in New England. 1987. 175.00 (*0-937048-38-0*) CSUN.

Nykanen, Lalli & Suomalainen, Heikki. Aroma of Beer, Wine & Distilled Alcoholic Beverages. 1983. lib. bdg. 149.50 (*90-277-1553-X*) Kluwer Ac.

Nykanen, Marita & Williams, Esther, trs. The Faith We Hold: Archbishop Paul. LC 80-10404. 96p. 1980. pap. 7.95 (*0-913836-63-X*) St Vladimirs.

Nykiel, Ronald A. Keeping Customers in Good Times & Bad. 1993. pap. 8.95 (*0-425-13875-5*) Berkley Pub.

— Keeping Customers in Good Times & Bad. 160p. 1992. 15.95 (*0-681-41192-9*) Longmeadow Pr.

— Marketing in the Hospitality Industry. 2nd ed. (Illus.). 288p. (C). 1989. 20.95 (*0-442-20579-1*) Van Nos Reinhold.

— You Can't Lose If the Customer Wins: Ten Steps to Growth & Profit. 144p. 1994. reprint ed. pap. 9.00 (*0-425-14144-6*, Berkley Trade) Berkley Pub.

— You Can't Lose If the Customer Wins: Ten Steps to Service Success. 134p. 1990. 14.95 (*0-681-41023-X*) Longmeadow Pr.

Nykl, A. R. Hispano-Arabic Poetry & Its Relations with the Old Provencal Troubadours. 1986. reprint ed. 10.00 (*0-87535-057-7*) Hispanic Soc.

Nykorowitsch, P., ed. Return Passage of Multi-Stage Turbomachinery. 66p. 1983. pap. text ed. 8.00 (*0-317-02644-5*, G00225) ASME.

Nykoruk, Barbara, ed. Business People in the News: A Compilation of News Stories & Feature Articles from American Newspapers & Magazines Covering People in Industry, Finance & Labor, Vol. 1. LC 76-4617. (Illus.). xl, 412p. 1976. 85.00 (*0-8103-0044-3*) Gale.

Nykrog, Per. L' Amour et la Rose: Le Grand Dessein de Jean de Meun. LC 85-73552. (Harvard Studies in Romance Languages: No. 41). 100p. (Orig.) (FRE.). 1986. pap. 10.00 (*0-940940-41-8*) Harvard U Romance Lang & Lit.

— La Recherche du Don Perdu: Points de Repere dans le Roman de Marcel Proust. LC 85-73551. (Harvard Studies in Romance Languages: No. 42). 100p. (Orig.). (FRE.). 1986. pap. 10.00 (*0-940940-42-6*) Harvard U Romance Lang & Lit.

Nylan, Michael. The Canon of Supreme Mystery by Yang Hsiung: A Translation with Commentary of T'ai hsuan ching. LC 92-8631. (Chinese Philosophy & Culture Ser.). 680p. (C). 1993. 74.50 (*0-7914-1395-0*) State U NY Pr.

Nyland, Chris. Reduced Worktime & the Management of Production. (Illus.). 240p. (C). 1989. 49.95 (*0-521-34547-2*) Cambridge U Pr.

Nyland, Scott E. A. I. D. S. & Its Therapy: Index of Modern Information. LC 90-182. 143p. 1990. 39.50 (*1-55914-136-0*); pap. 29.50 (*1-55914-137-9*) ABBE Pubs Assn.

***Nyland, Thomas G. & Mattoon, John S.** Veterinary Diagnostic Ultrasound. 512p. 1995. text ed. 75.00 (*0-7216-2745-5*) Saunders.

Nylander, Jane C. Our Own Snug Fireside: Images of the New England Home, 1760-1860. LC 92-17148. 1993. 30.00 (*0-394-54984-8*) Knopf.

— Our Own Snug Fireside: Images of the New England Home, 1760-1860. (Illus.). 330p. 1994. pap. 16.00 (*0-300-05953-1*) Yale U Pr.

Nylander, Jaye C. Fabrics for Historic Buildings. 4th ed. LC 90-44185. (Historic Interiors Ser.). (Illus.). 303p. 1990. pap. 16.95 (*0-89133-175-1*) Preservation Pr.

Nylander, Richard C. Wallpapers for Historic Buildings. rev. ed. (Historic Interiors Ser.). (Illus.). 224p. (Orig.). 1992. pap. 19.95 (*0-89133-193-X*) Preservation Pr.

Nylander, William. Collected Lichenological Papers. Including a Biography & Bibliography, Vol. 1: Papers 1852-1862. Ahti, Teuvi, ed. 732p. 1990. reprint ed. lib. bdg. 210.00 (*3-443-50013-7*, Pub. by Cramer-Borntraeger GW) Lubrecht & Cramer.

— Collected Lichenological Papers, Vol. 2: Papers 1863-1868 with Addenda Nova ad Lichenographiam Europaeam 1865-1887. Ahti, Teuvi, ed. 801p. (LAT.). 1990. reprint ed. lib. bdg. 210.00 (*3-443-50014-5*, Pub. by Cramer-Borntraeger GW) Lubrecht & Cramer.

— Collected Lichenological Papers, Vol. 3: Papers 1869-1887. Ahti, Teuvi, ed. 560p. (LAT.). 1990. reprint ed. lib. bdg. 210.00 (*3-443-50015-3*, Pub. by Cramer-Borntraeger GW) Lubrecht & Cramer.

— Collected Lichenological Papers, Vol. 4: Papers 1888-1900. Ahti, Teuvi, ed. 826p. 1967. reprint ed. lib. bdg. 90.00 (*3-7682-0434-0*, Pub. by Cramer GW) Lubrecht & Cramer.

— Collected Lichenological Papers, Vol. 5: Synopsis Methodica Lichenum 1958-69 & G. Lindau's Index Nominum Nylanderi Synopsis Lichenum 1907- Ahti, Teuvi, ed. 556p. (LAT.). 1967. reprint ed. lib. bdg. 90.00 (*3-7682-0435-9*, Pub. by Cramer GW) Lubrecht & Cramer.

— Collected Lichenological Papers, Vol. 6: Prodromus Lichenographiae Galliae et Algeriae 1857; Lichenes Scandinaviae 1861; Lichenes Lapponiae Orientalis 1862. Ahti, Teuvi, ed. 636p. (LAT.). 1967. lib. bdg. 90.00 (*3-7682-0436-7*, Pub. by Cramer GW) Lubrecht & Cramer.

Nylen, David W. Advertising: Planning, Implementation, & Control. 4th ed. LC 92-42795. 1993. text ed. 60.95 (*0-538-80918-3*) S-W Pub.

Nylen, Robert A., jt. ed. see Douglass, William A.

Nylen, William R. United States-Grenada Relations, 1979-1983: American Foreign Policy Towards a "Backyard" Revolution. (Pew Case Studies in International Affairs). 50p. (C). 1988. pap. text ed. 2.50 (*1-56927-306-5*) Geo U Inst Dplmcy.

***Nylicek, George, tr.** Ruffo: La Mia Parabola. (Master Singers Ser.). (Illus.). 1995. 35.00 (*1-880909-39-1*) Baskerville.

Nylin, Dawn, jt. auth. see Loehrlein, Myrna.

Nylund, Arabella W. Oriental Learning & Western Knowledge: The Encounter of Educational Traditions in Bengal 1781-1835. (Uppsala Studies in Education: No. 38). 186p. (Orig.). 1991. pap. 39.00x (*91-554-2778-2*, Pub. by Almqv & Wiksell SW) Coronet Bks.

***Nylund, Eric.** Pawn's Dream. 352p. (Orig.). 1995. mass mkt. 4.99 (*0-380-77887-4*, AvoNova) Avon.

Nyman & Tate, eds. The Book of Mormon: First Nephi, the Doctrinal Foundation. (Symposium Ser.: Vol. 2). 10.95 (*0-88494-647-9*) Bookcraft Inc.

— Book of Mormon: Helaman Through 3 Nephi 8, According to Thy Word. 1992. 11.95 (*0-88494-864-1*) Bookcraft Inc.

— The Book of Mormon: Jacob Through Words of Mormon, to Learn with Joy. (Symposium Ser.: Vol. 4). 11.95 (*0-88494-734-3*) Bookcraft Inc.

— The Book of Mormon: Second Nephi, the Doctrinal Structure. (Symposium Ser.: Vol. 3). 11.95 (*0-88494-699-1*) Bookcraft Inc.

Nyman, C. J., jt. ed. see Newton, William E.

Nyman, C. J., et al. Problems for General Chemistry & Qualitative Analysis. 4th ed. LC 79-24489. 342p. 1980. Net. pap. text ed. write for info. (*0-471-05299-X*) Wiley.

Nyman, Elizabeth & Leer, Jeff. Gagiwul.at: Brought Forth to Reconfirm the Legacy of a Taku River Tlingit Clan. LC 93-17399. (Illus.). xxxii, 261p. (Orig.). 1993. pap. 26. 95 (*1-55500-048-7*) Alaska Native.

Nyman, Heikki, ed. see Wittgenstein, Ludwig.

Nyman, Keith O. Re-Entry: How to Turn Your Military Experience into Civilian Success. 2nd rev. ed. LC 89-28850. (Illus.). 192p. 1990. pap. 13.95 (*0-8117-2317-8*) Stackpole.

— Re-Entry from Military Service to Civilian Employment. LC 81-50437. (Illus.). 192p. (Orig.). 1981. pap. 10.00 (*0-9605826-0-6*) Staff Recrters.

— Selecting Business Partners for Success. LC 91-65740. 96p. (Orig.). 1991. pap. text ed. 12.95 (*0-9605826-1-4*) Staff Recrters.

Nyman, Lee R. Making Manufacturing Cells Work. 1993. text ed. 60.00 (*0-07-047977-1*) McGraw.

Nyman, Lee R., ed. Making Manufacturing Cells Work. (Illus.). 388p. 1992. 71.00 (*0-87263-419-1*) SME.

***Nyman, Mary.** When the Leaves Fall. 150p. (Orig.). Date not set. pap. 7.95 (*0-7610-0272-3*) NW Pub.

Nyman, Mattias. Four Colors - One Image. 2nd ed. (Illus.). 84p. 1993. pap. 18.00 (*1-56609-083-0*) Peachpit Pr.

Nyman, Monte S. Great Are the Words of Isaiah. 1993. pap. 6.95 (*0-88494-910-9*) Bookcraft Inc.

— The Most Correct Book: The Book of Mormon. 1991. 10. 95 (*0-88494-798-X*) Bookcraft Inc.

Nyman, Monte S., ed. Isaiah & the Prophets. (Monograph Ser.: Vol. 10). 7.95 (*0-88494-522-7*) Bookcraft Inc.

Nyman, Monte S. & Tate, Charles D., Jr., eds. The Book of Mormon: Alma, the Testimony of the Word. 1992. 11.95 (*0-88494-841-2*) Bookcraft Inc.

Nyman, Monte S., ed. see BYU Religious Studies Center Staff.

Nyman, Richmond C., jt. auth. see Smith, Elliot D.

Nyman, Tore. Guide to the Teaching of Collective Bargaining. 91p. 1991. 4.80 (*92-2-102867-4*) Intl Labour Office.

Nymeyer, Robert. Carlsbad, Caves & a Camera. LC 78-6650. (Illus.). 318p. (Orig.). 1993. pap. 11.95 (*0-939748-36-3*) Cave Bks MO.

Nyoiti, Sakurazawa, pseud. You Are All Sanpaku. 1980. pap. 5.95 (*0-8065-0728-4*, Citadel Pr) Carol Pub Group.

Nyomarkay, Joseph. Charisma & Factionalism in the Nazi Party. LC 67-21015. 165p. reprint ed. pap. 47.10 (*0-318-39683-1*, 2033278) Bks Demand.

Nyoongah, Mudrooroo. Wildcat Falling. 160p. (Orig.). 1993. pap. 10.00 (*0-207-17446-6*, Pub. by Angus & Robertson AT) HarpC.

— Wildcat Screaming. 180p. (Orig.). 1993. pap. 11.00 (*0-207-17712-0*, Pub. by Angus & Robertson AT) HarpC.

Nyquist (CIDR) Staff. Preparing the Professoriate of Tomorrow to Teach Selected Readings in TA Training. 480p. (C). 1990. per. 39.95 (*0-8403-6374-5*) Kendall-Hunt.

Nyquist, Edwin R., jt. ed. see Yocum, Ronald H.

Nyquist, James F. & Kuhatschek, Jack. Leading Bible Discussions. rev. ed. 64p. 1985. pap. 4.99 (*0-8308-1000-5*, 1000) InterVarsity.

Nyquist, Jody D. & Wulff, Donald H., eds. Preparing Teaching Assistants for Instructional Roles in Communication: The Supervisor's Experience. LC 92-61675. 250p. (C). 1992. pap. text ed. 2.50 (*0-944811-10-8*) Speech Commun Assn.

Nyquist, Jody D., et al, eds. Teaching Assistant Training in the 1990s. LC 85-644763. (New Directions for Teaching & Learning Ser.: No. TL 39). 1989. 16.95 (*1-55542-858-4*) Jossey-Bass.

Nyquist, Joy. Travelers Health Handbook: How to Prepare for Carefree Travel. 80p. 1992. per. 7.95 (*1-879899-01-9*) Newjoy Pr.

***Nyquist, M., ed.** Remembering Milton. (C). Date not set. pap. text ed. 29.95 (*0-7870-0003-5*) Digital Print.

Nyquist, Mary, jt. ed. see Ferguson, Margaret.

Nyquist, Ola. Juvenile Justice: A Comparative Study with Special Reference to the Swedish Child Welfare Board & the California Juvenile Court Systems. LC 74-17590. (Cambridge Studies in Criminology Ser.: Vol. 12). (Illus.). 302p. 1974. reprint ed. text ed. 69.50 (*0-8371-7835-5*, NYJJ) Greenwood.

Nyquist, R. A. & Kegel, R. O. Infrared Spectra of Inorganic Compounds. 1971. text ed. 151.00 (*0-12-523450-3*) Acad Pr.

Nyre, G. F., jt. ed. see Rose, Clare.

Nyren, Dorothy, et al, eds. Modern American Literature, Vol. 4: Supplement. LC 76-76599. (Library of Literary Criticism). 622p. 1976. 75.00 (*0-8044-3050-0*, F Ungar Bks) Continuum.

***Nyren, Eve A., tr.** The Bonds of Matrimony Hsing - Shih Yin - Yuan Chuan Vol. 1: A Seventeenth - Century Chinese Novel. LC 94-37609. (Chinese Studies: Vol. 1). 312p. (CHI.). 1995. text ed. 99.95 (*0-7734-9033-7*) E Mellen.

Nyrop, K. The Kiss & Its History. 1973. 250.00 (*0-87968-330-9*) Gordon Pr.

Nyrop, Richard F. Saudi Arabia: A Country Study. 4th ed. LC 84-28460. (Area Handbook Ser.: DA Pam 550-51). (Illus.). 444p. 1984. 15.00 (*0-16-001616-9*, S/N 008-020-01020-1) USGPO.

— Yemens: Country Studies. LC 86-1164. (DA Pam Area Handbook Ser.: No. 550-183). (Illus.). 408p. 1986. 16.50 (*0-16-001649-5*, S/N 008-020-01090-1) USGPO.

Nyrop, Richard F., ed. Guatemala: A Country Study. 2nd ed. LC 84-413. (Area Handbook Ser.: No. 550-78). (Illus.). 287p. 1984. 7.50 (*0-16-001604-5*, 008-020-00987-3) USGPO.

— India: A Country Study. 4th ed. LC 85-18698. (DA Pam Area Handbook Ser.: No. 550-21). (Illus.). 727p. 1986. 20.00 (*0-16-023858-7*, S/N 008-020-01071-5) USGPO.

— Pakistan: A Country Study. 5th ed. (DA Pam Area Handbook Ser.: No. 550-48). (Illus.). 411p. 1984. 14.00 (*0-16-001608-8*, S/N 008-020-01003-1) USGPO.

NYS Department of Motor Vehicles, Division of Vehicle Safety Services Staff. Fuel Injection Systems Training, New York State Edition. LC 92-24673. 1993. pap. text ed. 24.95 (*0-8273-5586-6*) Delmar.

NYS Department of Motor Vehicles Staff & Positano, Nicholas J. Systems Training in Emissions & Performance. LC 92-14877. 1993. pap. text ed. 21.95 (*0-8273-5588-2*) Delmar.

NYS Department of Social Services Staff. Manual de Recursos para el SIDA. 228p. (Orig.). (SPA.). 1993. pap. 17.95 (*0-933681-16-X*) Rockefel Coll.

NYS Ed. Dept. Staff. Teaching Writing to Adults. 1990. text ed. 175.00 (*0-8273-4510-0*) S-W Pub.

Nys, Herman, ed. Medical Law. (International Encyclopedia of Laws Ser.). 1993. ring bd. 115.00 (*0-685-58994-3*) Kluwer Law Tax Pubs.

NYS Task Force on Life & the Law Staff. When Death Is Sought: Assisted Suicide & Euthanasia in the Medical Context. 234p. 1994. pap. 9.00 (*1-881268-01-2*) NYS Task Force.

Nysenholc, Adolphe, ed. Charlie Chaplin: His Reflection in Modern Times. LC 91-25247. (Approaches to Semiotics Ser.: No. 101). xvi, 412p. (C). 1991. lib. bdg. 121.55 (*3-11-012600-1*) Mouton.

Nyssen, Hubert. Lexique du Marketing. 86p. (FRE.). 1971. pap. 7.50 (*0-686-57064-2*, M-6435) Fr & Eur.

Nystrand, Martin. The Structure of Written Communication: Studies in Reciprocity Between Writers & Readers. 1986. text ed. 53.00 (*0-12-523482-1*) Acad Pr.

Nystrand, Martin, ed. What Writers Know: The Language Process & Structure of Written Discourse. 1981. text ed. 53.00 (*0-12-523480-5*) Acad Pr.

Nystrom, Bengt, jt. ed. see Hult, Jan.

Nystrom, Bradley, jt. auth. see Spyridakis, Styliano.

Nystrom, Bradley, jt. auth. see Spyridakis, Stylianos.

Nystrom, Bradley P., tr. The Song of Eros: Ancient Greek Love Poems. LC 90-35758. (Illus.). 120p. (C). 1990. 15. 95 (*0-8093-1640-4*) S Ill U Pr.

Nystrom, Carolyn. Angels & Me. (Children's Bible Basics Ser.). (Illus.). (J). (ps-2). 1984. pap. 4.99 (*0-8024-6150-6*) Moody.

— Angels & Me: Children's Bible Basics. (J). (ps-3). 1994. 5.99 (*0-8024-7863-8*) Moody.

— Before I Was Born. Jones, Stan & Jones, Brenna, eds. (God's Design for Sex Ser.: Bk. 2). (Illus.). 48p. 1995. pap. 9.00 (*0-89109-844-5*, NavPr) NavPress.

— Children's Bible Basics Ser., 11 bks., Set. (Illus.). (J). (ps-2). pap. 54.89 (*0-8024-5988-9*) Moody.

— Emma Says Goodbye. (Lion Care Ser.). (Illus.). 48p. (J). (gr. 4-8). 1990. 7.99 (*0-7459-1826-3*) Lion USA.

— Emma Says Goodbye: A Child's Guide to Bereavement. (J). (gr. 4-7). 1994. pap. 4.99 (*0-7459-2924-9*) Lion USA.

— Finding Contentment. (Christian Character Bible Studies). 64p. (Orig.). 1992. pap. 4.99 (*0-8308-1145-1*, 1145) InterVarsity.

— First & Second Peter & Jude: Compass for a Dark Road. (LifeGuide Bible Studies). 64p. (Orig.). 1992. pap. 3.99 (*0-8308-1019-6*, 1019) InterVarsity.

— Growing Jesus' Way. (Children's Bible Basics Ser.). (J). (ps-2). 1982. 4.99 (*0-8024-6151-4*) Moody.

— Growing Jesus' Way. (J). (ps-3). 1994. 5.99 (*0-8024-7860-3*) Moody.

— The Holy Spirit in Me. (Children's Bible Basics Ser.). 32p. (J). (ps-2). 1980. pap. 4.99 (*0-8024-6152-2*) Moody.

— Holy Spirit in Me: Children's Bible Basics. (J). (ps-3). 1993. 5.99 (*0-8024-7858-1*) Moody.

— Jenny & Grandpa: A Child's Guide to Growing Older. (J). (gr. 4-7). 1994. pap. 3.99 (*0-7459-2922-2*) Lion USA.

— Jesus Is No Secret: Children's Bible Basics. (Children's Bible Basics Ser.). (Illus.). (J). (gr. 3-7). 1994. 5.99 (*0-8024-7865-4*) Moody.

— Jonah & Ruth: A Friend. 96p. 1995. pap. 4.99 (*1-56476-363-3*, 6-3363, Victor Books) SP Pubns.

— Knowing Scripture. (Discipleship Ser.). 64p. 1992. pap. 4.99 (*0-310-54721-0*) Zondervan.

— Living in the World. (Christian Character Bible Studies). 64p. (Orig.). 1992. pap. 4.99 (*0-8308-1144-3*) InterVarsity.

— Loving God. (Christian Character Bible Studies). 64p. (Orig.). 1992. pap. 4.99 (*0-8308-1141-9*, 1141) InterVarsity.

— Loving One Another. (Christian Character Bible Studies). 64p. (Orig.). 1992. pap. 4.99 (*0-8308-1142-7*, 1142) InterVarsity.

— Loving the World. (Christian Character Bible Studies). 64p. (Orig.). 1992. pap. 4.99 (*0-8308-1143-5*, 1143) InterVarsity.

— Mario's Big Question: A Child's Guide Through Adoption. (Lion Care Ser.). (Illus.). 48p. 1987. 7.99 (*0-7459-1087-4*) Lion USA.

— Mario's Big Question: A Child's Guide to Adoption. (J). (gr. 4-7). 1994. pap. 4.99 (*0-7459-2923-0*) Lion USA.

— Meeting with God: A Daily Guide. rev. ed. Orig. Title: Lord, I Want to Have a Quiet Time. 192p. 1991. per., pap. 8.99 (*0-87788-524-9*) Shaw Pubs.

— Mike's Lonely Summer. (Lion Care Ser.). (Illus.). 48p. (J). (gr. 1-6). 1986. 7.99 (*0-7459-1016-5*) Lion USA.

— Mike's Lonely Summer: A Child's Guide to Divorce. (J). (gr. 4-7). 1994. pap. 4.99 (*0-7459-2925-7*) Lion USA.

— New Testament Characters. (LifeGuide Bible Studies). 64p. (Orig.). 1993. pap. 4.99 (*0-8308-1069-2*, 1069) InterVarsity.

— Old Testament Kings. (LifeGuide Bible Studies). 64p. (Orig.). 1993. pap. 4.99 (*0-8308-1070-6*, 1070) InterVarsity.

— Pursuing Holiness. (Christian Character Bible Studies). 64p. (Orig.). 1992. pap. 4.99 (*0-8308-1147-8*, 1147) InterVarsity.

N

— Sharing Your Faith. (Discipleship Ser.). 64p. 1992. pap. 4.99 (0-310-54741-5) Zondervan.
— What Happens When We Die? (Children's Bible Basics Ser.). 32p. (J). (ps-2). 1981. pap. 4.99 (0-8024-6154-9) Moody.
— What Is a Christian? Children's Bible Basics. (J). (ps). 1992. 5.99 (0-8024-7854-9) Moody.
— What Is Prayer? (Children's Bible Basics Ser.). 32p. (J). (ps-2). 1980. pap. 4.99 (0-8024-6156-5) Moody.
— What Is Prayer. (J). (ps-3). 1993. 5.99 (0-8024-7859-X) Moody.
— What Is the Bible? (Children's Bible Basics Ser.). 32p. (J). (ps-2). 1994. 5.99 (0-8024-7864-6) Moody.
— When Jesus Comes Back. (J). (ps-3). 1994. 5.99 (0-8024-7861-1) Moody.
— Who Is God? (Children's Bible Basics Ser.). 32p. (J). (ps-2). 1980. pap. 4.99 (0-8024-6158-1) Moody.
— Who Is God? Children's Bible Basics. 30p. 1992. 5.99 (0-8024-7857-3) Moody.
— Who Is Jesus? (Children's Bible Basics Ser.). 32p. (J). (ps-2). 1980. pap. 4.99 (0-8024-6159-X) Moody.
— Who Is Jesus? Children's Bible Basics. 30p. (J). 1992. 5.99 (0-8024-7856-5) Moody.
— Why Do I Do Things Wrong? (Children's Bible Basics Ser.). 32p. (J). (ps-2). 1994. 5.99 (0-8024-7862-X) Moody.
— A Workshop on David & His Psalms: A Study of the Life & Heart of David. 160p. 1982. pap. 5.99 (0-310-41931-X) Zondervan.
Nystrom, Carolyn & Fromer, Margaret. A Workshop on the Book of James: The Demands of a Practical Faith. 128p. (Orig.). 1980. pap. 5.99 (0-310-41901-8) Zondervan.
Nystrom, Carolyn, et al. Christian Character Bible Study Series, 8 vols., Set. 1992. 39.92 (0-8308-1140-0) InterVarsity.
Nystrom, Debra. A Quarter Turn. LC 90-26317. 60p. (Orig.). 1991. 14.95 (1-878818-02-3); pap. 10.95 (1-878818-00-7) Sheep Meadow.
Nystrom, Dennis C., et al. Instructional Methods in Occupational Education. LC 76-43204. 1977. 15.95 (0-672-97111-9, Bobbs) Macmillan.
Nystrom, Dennis C. Occupation & Career Education Legislation. LC 79-12548. pap. 3.40 (0-672-97133-X, Bobbs); pap. 10.50 (0-685-00789-8, Bobbs) Macmillan.
Nystrom, Fred & Nystrom, Mardi. Special Places: For the Discerning Traveler. 5th ed. Stewart, Beth, ed. 264p. 1992. pap. 15.95 (0-936777-02-8) Special Pl.
Nystrom, Fred & Nystrom, Mardi M. Special Places: For the Discerning Traveler. 4th ed. 272p. 1989. pap. text ed. 14.95 (0-936777-01-X) Special Pl.
Nystrom, Harry. Creativity & Innovation. LC 78-8594. (Illus.). 135p. reprint ed. pap. 38.50 (0-8357-6636-5, 2035289) Bks Demand.
— Technological & Market Innovation: Strategies for Product & Company Development. 307p. 1990. text ed. 100.95 (0-471-92054-1) Wiley.
— Technological & Market Innovation: Strategies for Product & Company Development. 307p. 1993. pap. text ed. 43.50 (0-471-93466-6) Wiley.
Nystrom, Karl R. State D Coaching Course: Workbook. (Illus.). 50p. (Orig.). (C). 1989. pap. 3.50 (1-879397-03-X) Kanvi.
— State D Soccer Coaching Course: Instructor's Manual. 51p. (Orig.). (C). 1989. pap. 3.50 (1-879397-02-1) Kanvi.
Nystrom, Karl R., tr. see Fotbollforbundet, Svenska.
Nystrom, L. E., jt. ed. see Sofer, Gail K.
Nystrom, Lars-Erik, jt. auth. see Sofer, Gail.
Nystrom, Mardi, jt. auth. see Nystrom, Fred.
Nystrom, Mardi M., jt. auth. see Nystrom, Fred.
Nystrom, Nancy J., ed. Latin American Education: A Quest for Identity. (Conference Proceedings Ser.). 253p. pap. 15.00 (0-317-43433-0) Tulane Lat Am Lib.
Nystrom, Nancy J., jt. auth. see O'Connor, Patricia.
Nystrom, P. & Starbuck, William H., eds. Prescriptive Models of Organizations. (TIMS Studies in the Management Sciences: Vol. 5). 190p. 1977. reprint ed. pap. 60.75 (0-7204-0573-4, North Holland) Elsevier.
Nystrom, Paul C. & Starbuck, William H., eds. Handbook of Organizational Design, 2 vols., Set. (Illus.). 1981. 75.00 (0-19-520233-3) OUP.
— Handbook of Organizational Design, Vol. 1: Adapting Organizations & their Environment. (Illus.). 1981. Vol. 1: Adapting Organizations & Their Environments. 45.00 (0-19-827241-3) OUP.
— Handbook of Organizational Design, Vol. 2: Remodeling Orgns. & Their Environments. (Illus.). 1981. Vol. 2: Remodeling Organizations & Their Environments. 45.00 (0-19-827242-1) OUP.
Nystrom, Paul H. Economic Principles of Consumption. LC 75-39263. (Getting & Spending: the Consumer's Dilemma Ser.). (Illus.). 1976. reprint ed. 48.95 (0-405-08036-0) Ayer.
— Economics of Retailing. Assael, Henry, ed. LC 78-246. (Century of Marketing Ser.). (Illus.). 1979. reprint ed. lib. bdg. 41.95 (0-405-11180-0) Ayer.
Nystuen, John D., jt. auth. see Arlinghaus, Sandra L.
Nystul, Michael S. The Art & Science of Counseling & Psychotherapy. 460p. (C). 1993. pap. write for info. (0-675-21212-X, Merrill Pub Co) Macmillan.
Nystul, Mike & Smith, Lester. Mechwarrior. 2nd ed. Ippolito, Donna & Mullvihill, Sharon T., eds. (BattleTech Ser.). (Illus.). 167p. (Orig.). 1991. pap. 15.00 (1-55560-129-4) FASA Corp.
Nythus, Lloyd M., ed. Surgery Annual, 1992, Vol. 24, Pt. 1. 258p. (C). 1992. boxed 80.00 (0-8385-8745-3, A8745-0) Appleton & Lange.
Nyvall. Field Crop Diseases Handbook. 2nd ed. 1989. text ed. 104.95 (0-442-26722-3) Chapman & Hall.
Nyvall, David. My Father's Testament. 1974. pap. 5.95 (0-910452-20-2) Covenant.
Nyvlt. Design of Crystallizers. 1992. 92.00 (0-8493-5072-7, TP156) CRC Pr.
Nyvlt, J., et al. The Kinetics of Industrial Crystallization. (Chemical Engineering Monographs: Vol. 19). 1985. 100.00 (0-444-99610-9) Elsevier.
Nyvlt, J. Solid-Liquid Phase Equilibria. 248p. 1977. 97.50 (0-444-99850-0) Elsevier.
Nyvlt, J. & Zacek, S., eds. Industrial Crystallization '87: Proceeding of the 10th Symposium on Industrial Crystallization, Bechyne, Czechoslovaskia, Sept. 21-25, 1987. 552p. 1989. 184.75 (0-444-98914-5) Elsevier.
Nzongola-Ntalaja. Crisis in Zaire. (C). 1988. 32.00 (0-86543-023-3); pap. 11.95 (0-86543-024-1) Africa World.
Nzongola-Ntalaja, Georges, ed. Conflict in the Horn of Africa. 1991. pap. 15.00 (0-918456-65-7) African Studies Assn.

O

O Baecun Books, Inc. Staff, ed. see Oba Ecun.
O Connor, Fionnuala. In Search of a State: Catholics in Northern Ireland. 400p. 1994. pap. 17.95 (0-85640-509-4, Pub. by Blackstaff Pr IE) Dufour.
O Grada, Cormac, ed. The Economic Development of Ireland since 1870, 2 Vols. (Economic Development of Modern Europe since 1870 Ser.: Vol. 5). 752p. 1994. 199.95 (1-85278-671-X, Pub. by E Elgar Pub UK) Ashgate Pub Co.
O Hehir, Brendan. Harmony from Discords: A Life of Sir John Denham. LC 68-27162. 308p. reprint ed. pap. 87.80 (0-685-23979-9, 2031543) Bks Demand.
O. Henry. Alias Jimmy Valentine. Pauk, Walter & Harris, Raymond, eds. (Classics Ser.). (Illus.). 37p. (gr. 6-12). 1980. teacher ed 5.00 (0-89061-194-7, 411); pap. text ed. 4.00 (0-89061-192-0, 409); audio 13.00 (0-89061-193-9) Jamestown Pubs.
— The Best of O. Henry. LC 91-58651. (Literary Classics Ser.). 176p. 1992. 5.98 (1-56138-111-X) Courage Bks.
— Best of O. Henry. 234p. 1993. pap. text ed. 5.95 (0-460-87339-3, Everyman's Classic Lib) C E Tuttle.
— Best Short Stories. 191p. 1983. reprint ed. lib. bdg. 16.95 (0-89966-446-6) Buccaneer Bks.
— Best Short Stories: O. Henry. 1994. 19.50 (0-679-60122-8, Modern Lib) Random.
— The Best Short Stories of O. Henry. Cerf, Bennett & Cartmell, Van H., eds. LC 45-35106. 340p. 1977. 12.00 (0-394-60423-7, Modern Lib) Random.
— Cabbages & Kings. LC 92-40936. (Twentieth-Century Classics Ser.). 288p. 1993. 10.95 (0-14-018689-1, Penguin Classics) Viking Penguin.
— Collected Stories of O. Henry. 22.95 (0-89190-397-6, Am Repr) Amereon Ltd.
— Collected Stories of O. Henry. 1993. 12.99 (0-517-09340-5) Random Hse Value.
— Collected Stories of O. Henry. rev. ed. Horowitz, P., ed. (Illus.). 1008p. 1986. 12.99 (0-517-61839-7) Random Hse Value.
— Forty-One Stories. 416p. 1986. pap. 5.95 (0-451-52254-0, Sig Classics) NAL-Dutton.
— Four Million & Other Stories. (Airmont Classics Ser.). (J). (gr. 8 up). 1964. pap. 1.25 (0-8049-0025-6, CL-25) Airmont.
— Four Million & Other Stories. 1976. 18.95 (0-8488-1047-3) Amereon Ltd.
— The Gentle Grafter. (Literature of Mystery & Detection Ser.). (Illus.). 1976. reprint ed. 21.95 (0-405-07889-7) Ayer.
— The Gift of the Magi. Pauk, Walter & Harris, Raymond, eds. (Classics Ser.). (Illus.). 35p. (gr. 6-12). 1980. teacher ed 5.00 (0-89061-188-2, 403); pap. text ed. 4.00 (0-89061-186-6, 401); audio 13.00 (0-89061-187-4, 402) Jamestown Pubs.
— The Gift of the Magi. (Illus.). 32p. (J). (gr. 5 up). 1988. pap. 14.00 (0-671-64706-7, Litl Simon S&S) S&S Childrens.
— The Gift of the Magi. LC 82-60896. (Illus.). 32p. 1991. pap. 16.95 (0-907234-17-8, Picture Book Studio) S&S Childrens.
— The Gift of the Magi. LC 92-6632. (Illus.). 28p. (J). 1992. pap. 5.95 (0-88708-276-9, Picture Book Studio) S&S Childrens.
— The Gift of the Magi. LC 91-7313. (Fairy Tale Classics Ser.). 48p. (J). (gr. 1-6). 1991. 9.95 (0-88101-116-9) Unicorn Pub.
— Gift of the Magi. 1986. 13.95 (0-87191-775-0) Creative Ed.
— The Gift of the Magi. LC 78-55660. (Illus.). 1978. reprint ed. write for info. (0-672-52296-9) Macmillan.
— The Gift of the Magi: A Special Christmas Edition. rev. ed. (Creative's Classic Short Stories Ser.). (Illus.). 32p. (J). (gr. 4 up). 1984. lib. bdg. 13.95 (0-87191-954-0) Creative Ed.
— The Gift of the Magi - El Regalo de los Reyes Magos. (SPA.). (J). 16.95 (0-685-65410-9) Santillana.
O Henry. The Gift of the Magi & Other Short Stories. (Thrift Editions Ser.). 96p. (Orig.). 1992. pap. 1.00 (0-486-27061-0) Dover.
O. Henry. The Gift of the Magi & Other Stories. 1993. reprint ed. lib. bdg. 18.95 (1-56849-128-X) Buccaneer Bks.
— The Last Leaf. (Creative's Classic Short Stories Ser.). (Illus.). 32p. (J). (gr. 6 up). 1980. lib. bdg. 13.95 (0-87191-774-2) Creative Ed.
— The Last Leaf. Pauk, Walter & Harris, Raymond, eds. (Classics Ser.). (Illus.). 35p. (gr. 6-12). 1980. teacher ed 4.00 (0-89061-197-1, 415); pap. text ed. 4.00 (0-89061-195-5, 413); digital audio 13.00 (0-89061-196-3, 414) Jamestown Pubs.
— The Last Leaf. rev. ed. (Read-Along Radio Dramas Ser.). (J). (gr. 6-10). 1982. reprint ed. boxed 35.00 (0-685-31126-0) Balance Pub.
— O. Henry Reader. write for info. (0-318-58797-1) S&S Trade.
— O. Henry Stories. 1987. 6.98 (0-671-08619-7) S&S Trade.
— O. Henry's New York. 18.95 (0-89190-313-5, Am Repr) Amereon Ltd.
— O. Henry's Short Stories. 1976. 20.95 (0-8488-0525-9) Amereon Ltd.
— The Pocket Book of O. Henry Short Stories. Hansen, Harry, ed. 256p. 1989. mass mkt. 5.50 (0-671-68861-8, WSP) PB.
— The Ransom of Red Chief. 9.95 (0-89190-342-9, Am Repr) Amereon Ltd.
— The Ransom of Red Chief. (Creative's Classic Short Stories Ser.). (Illus.). 40p. (J). (gr. 4 up). 1980. lib. bdg. 13.95 (0-87191-776-9) Creative Ed.
— The Ransom of Red Chief. Pauk, Walter & Harris, Raymond, eds. (Classics Ser.). (Illus.). 40p. (gr. 6-12). 1980. teacher ed 5.00 (0-89061-191-2, 407); pap. text ed. 4.00 (0-89061-189-0, 405); digital audio 13.00 (0-89061-190-4, 406) Jamestown Pubs.
— Selected Stories. LC 92-39604. 384p. 1993. 11.95 (0-14-018688-3, Penguin Classics) Viking Penguin.
— Stories of O. Henry. 224p. 1989. pap. 2.50 (0-8125-0502-6) Tor Bks.
O. Henry & Gianni, Gary. The Gift of the Magi & Other Stories. (Classics Illustrated Ser.). (Illus.). 52p. (YA). Date not set. pap. 4.95 (1-57209-013-8) Classics Int Ent.
O, Jack. Dealing with Depression in Twelve Step Recovery. LC 90-14047. (Fellow Travelers Ser.). 72p. (Orig.). 1990. pap. 4.95 (0-934125-13-9) Hazelden.
O., M. Holle, jt. auth. see Montes, Alfredo.
O Muirithe, Diarmuid. Wexford Carols. 1982. pap. 14.95 (0-85105-376-9, Pub. by Colin Smythe Ltd UK) Dufour.
O.P. Norton Information Resources Center Staff, jt. auth. see American Society for Industrial Security Staff.
***O., Paul.** There's More to Quitting Drinking Than Quitting Drinking. 1995. pap. 14.95 (0-9644887-4-4) Sabrina Pub.
O Tuama, Sean, ed. The Gaelic League Idea. 109p. 1993. pap. 13.95 (1-85635-046-0, Pub. by Mercier Pr IE) Dufour.
O, Ying-Lie, et al, eds. Shape in Picture: Mathematical Description of Shape in Grey-Level Images. LC 93-48570. (NATO ASI Series F; Computer & Systems Sciences Ser.: Vol. 126). x, 676p. 1994. 155.00 (0-387-57578-2) Spr-Verlag.
O Yong-jin, et al. Wedding Day & Other Korean Plays. The, Korean National Commission for UNESCO, ed. Slettland, G. et al, trs. (Korean Novels, Plays, & Poetry Ser.: No. 2). xiii, 211p. 1983. 20.00 (0-89209-013-8) Pace Intl Res.
Oaczak, Anatoge. Korn Shell User Programming Manual. (C). 1991. pap. text ed. 43.25 (0-201-56548-X) Addison-Wesley.
Oae. Organic Sulphur Chemistry: Biochemical Aspects. 1992. 173.00 (0-8493-4740-8, QP535) CRC Pr.
Oae, Shigeru & Doi, Joyce T. Organic Sulfur Chemistry: Structure & Mechanism. (Illus.). 288p. 1991. 202.00 (0-8493-4739-4, QD412) CRC Pr.
Oae, Shigeru & Furukawa, Naomichi, eds. Sulfilimines & Related Derivatives. LC 83-12220. (ACS Monograph: No. 179). 340p. 1983. lib. bdg. 92.95 (0-8412-0705-4) Am Chemical.
***Oak Associates Staff.** Business Savvy. 160p. 1995. pap. 11.95 (4-89684-244-8, Pub. by Yohan Pubns JA) Weatherhill.
— Getting Acquainted. 160p. 1995. pap. 11.95 (4-89684-243-X, Pub. by Yohan Pubns JA) Weatherhill.
Oak, Henry L. A Visit to the Missions of Southern California in February & March 1874. Axe, Ruth F. et al, eds. LC 81-52830. (Frederick Webb Hodge Publications: No. 11). (Illus.). 87p. 1981. 20.00 (0-916561-66-6) Southwest Mus.
Oak, Jacquelyn. Sotheby's Guide to American Art. 1994. pap. 16.00 (0-671-89950-3, Fireside) S&S Trade.
Oak, Jacquelyn, et al. Face to Face: M. W. Hopkins & Noah North. (Illus.). (Orig.). (C). 1989. pap. text ed. 34.95 (0-9621107-7-9) Scottish Rite Masonic Mus.
Oak, P. N. Tajmahal: The True Story. Orig. Title: The Tajmahal is a Temple Palace. (Illus.). 336p. (Orig.). 1989. pap. 10.95 (0-9611614-4-2) A Ghosh.
Oak Park Historic Preservation Commission Staff. Ridgeland Revealed: Guide to the Architecture of the Ridgeland-Oak Park Historic District. Sanderson, Arlene, ed. (Illus.). 110p. (Orig.). 1993. pap. 7.95 (0-9616915-1-4) Vil Oak Pk.
Oak Ridge National Laboratory, Chemical Assessments Team Staff, ed. see U.S. Department of Energy Staff.
Oak Ridge National Laboratory Staff, et al. Population Exposure from the Nuclear Fuel Cycle: Proceedings of the Topical Meeting, Oak Ridge, Tennessee, September 14-18, 1987 Sponsored by the American Nuclear Society. 372p. 1988. 39.00 (0-318-39936-9) Gordon & Breach.
Oakeley, Hilda D. Greek Ethical Thought: From Homer to the Stoics. LC 76-152999. (Select Bibliographies Reprint Ser.). 1977. reprint ed. 20.95 (0-8369-5751-2) Ayer.
Oakeley, Hilda D., ed. Greek Ethical Thought from Homer to the Stoics. LC 79-173804. (Library of Greek Thought: No. 5). reprint ed. 27.50 (0-404-07804-4) AMS Pr.
Oakenfull. Saponins in Food & Health. 1995. write for info. (0-8493-6867-7) CRC Pr.
Oakes, A. J. Ornamental Grasses & Grasslike Plants. LC 92-42440. 624p. (C). 1993. reprint ed. lib. bdg. 77.50 (0-89464-826-8) Krieger.
Oakes, Baile. Sculpting With the Environment. 256p. 1995. text ed. 59.95 (0-442-01642-5) Van Nos Reinhold.
Oakes, Catherine. The Middle Ages. (Exploring the Past Ser.: Vol. 2). (Illus.). 28p. (J). (gr. 3-7). 1989. 14.95 (0-15-200451-3, Gulliver Bks) HarBrace.
Oakes, Claudia M. United States Women in Aviation 1930-1939. LC 85-600019. Orig. Title: Smithsonian Studies in Air & Space Number 6. (Illus.). 84p. 1991. pap. 9.95 (0-87474-380-X) Smithsonian.
— United States Women in Aviation, 1930-1939. LC 85-600019. (Smithsonian Studies in Air & Science: No. 6). 74p. (Orig.). reprint ed. pap. 25.00 (0-317-41864-5, 2026175) Bks Demand.
Oakes, D. O., jt. auth. see Cox, D. R.
Oakes, Dana. Clinical Practitioners Pocket Guide to Respiratory Care. 3rd ed. (Illus.). 300p. 1994. ring bd. 18.95 (0-932887-05-8) Health Ed Pubns.
— Hemodynamic Monitoring: A Bedside Reference Manual. (Illus.). 300p. (C). 1993. ring bd. 18.95 (0-932887-03-1) Health Ed Pubns.
— Neonatal - Pediatric Respiratory Care: A Critical Care Pocket Guide. 2nd ed. (Illus.). 300p. 1994. ring bd. 18.95 (0-932887-06-6) Health Ed Pubns.
Oakes, Dean. Standard Guide to Small-Sized U. S. Paper Money. LC 93-80100. 1994. pap. 24.95 (0-87341-282-6) Krause Pubns.
Oakes, Dean, jt. auth. see Hickman, John.
Oakes, Donald T. & Scott, Walter H., eds. A Pride of Palaces: Lenox Summer Cottages 1883-1933. LC 81-82277. Orig. Title: The Summer Cottages of Edwin Hale Lincoln. (Illus.). 84p. (Orig.). 1981. pap. 15.00 (0-685-04621-4, Lenox Lib Assn) SnO Pubns.
Oakes, Donald T., ed. see Irving, Washington.
Oakes, Edward, ed. German Essays on Religion. (German Library: Vol. 54). 324p. 1994. 29.50 (0-8264-0734-X); pap. text ed. 14.95 (0-8264-0735-8) Continuum.
Oakes, Edward T. Pattern of Redemption: The Theology of Hans Urs von Balthasar. 300p. (C). 1994. 29.50 (0-8264-0685-8) Continuum.
Oakes, Edward T., tr. see Von Balthasar, Hans U.
Oakes, G. Turn Right at the Fountain. 1981. pap. 11.95 (0-8050-1234-6) H Holt & Co.
Oakes, Ginger, illus. Precious Promises. 32p. 1987. pap. 4.95 (0-929510-01-1) Lewis & Stanley.
Oakes, Guy. The Imaginary War: Civil Defense & American Cold War Culture. LC 93-46098. (Illus.). 224p. 1995. 29.95 (0-19-509027-6) OUP.
— The Soul of the Salesman: The Moral Ethos of Personal Sales. LC 90-31350. 128p. (C). 1990. text ed. 35.00 (0-391-03682-3); pap. 12.50 (0-391-03683-1) Humanities.
— Weber & Rickert: Concept Formation in the Social Sciences. (Studies in Contemporary German Social Thought). 200p. 1988. 24.00 (0-262-15034-4) MIT Pr.
— Weber & Rickert: Concept Formation in the Social Sciences. (Studies in Contemporary German Social Thought). 200p. 1990. reprint ed. pap. 9.95 (0-262-65037-1) MIT Pr.
Oakes, Guy, ed. see Rickert, Heinrich.
Oakes, Guy, tr. see Schmitt, Carl.
Oakes, Guy, tr. see Simmel, Georg.
Oakes, Guy, tr. see Weber, Max M.
Oakes, Ian. Management of Electronics Assembly: Design, Development, Production, Test. 208p. (C). 1992. 62.95 (0-7506-0071-3) Buttrwrth-Heinemann.
Oakes, James. The Oakes Diaries, 1778-1827, Vol. I: Introduction; Diaries 1778-1800. Fiske, Jane, ed. (Suffolk Records Society Ser.: No. 32). (Illus.). 415p. 1991. 39.00 (0-85115-275-9) Boydell & Brewer.
— The Ruling Race: A History of American Slaveholders. LC 83-3472. 336p. 1983. pap. 10.36 (0-394-71639-6, Vin) Random.
— Slavery & Freedom: An Interpretation of the Old South. 1990. 22.95 (0-394-53677-0) Knopf.
— Slavery & Freedom: An Interpretation of the Old South. LC 91-50027. 272p. 1991. pap. 12.00 (0-679-73035-4, Vin) Random.
Oakes, Jeannie. Keeping Track: How Schools Structure Inequality. LC 84-20931. 284p. 1986. pap. 14.00 (0-300-03725-2) Yale U Pr.
Oakes, Jeannie & Lipton, Martin. Making the Best of Schools: A Handbook for Parents, Teachers, & Policymakers. LC 89-39035. 336p. (C). 1990. 27.00 (0-300-04650-2) Yale U Pr.
— Making the Best of Schools: A Handbook for Parents, Teachers, & Policymakers. 336p. (C). 1991. reprint ed. pap. 12.00 (0-300-05123-9) Yale U Pr.
***Oakes, Jeannie & Quartz, Karen H., eds.** Creating New Educational Communities. 275p. 1995. 29.00 (0-226-60166-8) U Ch Pr.
Oakes, Jeannie, jt. ed. see Sirotnik, Kenneth A.
Oakes, Jeannie, et al. Educational Matchmaking: Academic & Vocational Tracking in Comprehensive High Schools. LC 92-15270. 1992. write for info. (0-8330-1244-4, R-4189-NCRVE) Rand Corp.
Oakes, Jill E. Factors Influencing Kamik Production in Arctic Bay, Northwest Territories. (Canadian Museum of Civlization Mercury Series-Canadian Ethnology Service). (Illus.). 63p. 1988. pap. text ed. 9.95 (0-660-10763-5, Pub. by CN Mus Civilization CN) U Ch Pr.
Oakes, John G., ed. In the Realms of the Unreal: "Insane" Writings. LC 90-27390. 254p. 1991. 24.95 (0-941423-52-2); pap. 12.95 (0-941423-57-3) FWEW.
Oakes, John W. Action Amiga: Computer Graphics Animation & Video Production Manual. LC 88-26158. (Illus.). 140p. (Orig.). (C). 1989. pap. text ed. 19.50 (0-8191-7209-X) U Pr of Amer.

An Asterisk (*) at the beginning of an entry indicates that the title is appearing in BIP for the first time.

Oakes, Mary L. & Harris-Oakes, Mary Louise. Motivating Ideas for Teachers, Parents & Students. rev. ed. (Illus.). 20p. 1976. pap. 3.50 (*0-9622843-0-0*) Oakes & Assocs.

Oakes, Maud. Where the Two Came to Their Father: A Navaho War Ceremonial. (Mythos: The Princeton - Bollingen Series in World Mythology: No. I). (Illus.). 72p. 1991. pap. text ed. 14.95 (*0-691-02069-8*) Princeton U Pr.

Oakes, Maud, jt. auth. see Henderson, Joseph L.

Oakes, Michael. Statistical Inference. LC 90-2834. 171p. (Orig.). (C). 1990. pap. text ed. 24.00 (*0-917227-04-2*) Epidemiology.

Oakes, Penelope J., et al. Stereotyping & Social Reality. (Illus.). 272p. 1994. 54.95 (*0-631-18871-1*); pap. 22.95 (*0-631-18872-X*) Blackwell Pubs.

Oakes, Philip. Shopping for Women. 256p. 1994. 24.95 (*0-233-98861-0*, Pub. by A Deutsch UK) Trafalgar.

Oakes, Philip, ed. The Film Addicts Archive: Poetry & Prose of the Cinema. 212p. 1966. 25.00 (*0-8464-1190-3*) Beekman Pubs.

Oakes, Richard T. Ancient Laws & Institutes of Ireland: Introduction to Senchus Mor, & Laws of Distress As Contained in the Harleian Manuscripts. LC 83-82325. xvi, 4p. 1983. reprint ed. lib. bdg. 45.00 (*0-89941-293-9*, 303020) W S Hein.

— Oake's Criminal Practice Guide. (Trial Practice Library Ser.). 928p. 1991. 138.00 (*0-471-55316-6*) Wiley.

— Oake's Criminal Practice Guide. suppl. ed. (Trial Practice Library Ser.). 81p. 1991. 40.00 (*0-471-55421-9*) Wiley.

— Oakes' Criminal Practice Guide: 1989 Supplement. 1991. ring bd. 25.00 (*0-471-57253-5*) Wiley.

Oakes, Sandy, ed. see Lovejoy, Carol.

Oakes, Sherry D. & Kirkham, Robert M. Results of Search for Felt Reports for Selected Colorado Earthquakes. (Information Ser.: No. 23). 89p. (Orig.). 1986. pap. 6.00 (*1-884216-19-6*) Colo Geol Survey.

Oakes, Thomas. Teach Yourself to Ski. 1993. pap. 5.95 (*0-937043-08-7*) K C Terry Assocs.

Oakes, William C. The Falconer's Apprentice: A Guide to Training the Passage Red-Tailed Hawk. rev. ed. (Illus.). 118p. 1994. pap. text ed. 10.00 (*1-885054-01-7*) Eaglewing Pubng.

***Oakeshott, Ewart.** The Archaeology of Weapons: Arms & Armour from Prehistory to the Age of Chivalry. LC 94-40355. (Illus.). 1994. 53.00 (*0-85115-559-6*, Boydell Pr) Boydell & Brewer.

— Records of the Medieval Sword. (Illus.). 288p. 1991. 117.00 (*0-85115-539-1*) Boydell & Brewer.

— The Sword in the Age of Chivalry. (Illus.). 216p. (C). 1994. reprint ed. text ed. 63.00 (*0-85115-362-3*) Boydell & Brewer.

Oakeshott, Gordon B. California's Changing Landscapes. 2nd ed. (Illus.). 1978. text ed. write for info. (*0-07-047584-9*) McGraw.

Oakeshott, J. & Whitten, M. J., eds. Molecular Approaches to Fundamental & Applied Entomology. (Experimental Entomology Ser.). (Illus.). 488p. 1992. 163.00 (*0-387-97814-3*) Spr-Verlag.

Oakeshott, Michael. Experience & Its Modes. (Cambridge Paperback Library). 368p. 1986. pap. 29.95 (*0-521-31179-9*) Cambridge U Pr.

— Morality & Politics in Modern Europe: The Harvard Lectures, 1958. Letwin, Shirley R., ed. 192p. 1993. 22.50 (*0-300-05644-3*) Yale U Pr.

— Rationalism in Politics & Other Essays. LC 91-6951. 584p. (Orig.). 1991. text ed. 21.00 (*0-86597-094-7*); pap. 7.50 (*0-86597-095-5*) Liberty Fund.

— Religion, Politics, & the Moral Life. Fuller, Timothy, ed. 160p. 1993. 22.50 (*0-300-05643-5*) Yale U Pr.

— The Voice of Liberal Learning: Michael Oakeshott on Education. Fuller, Timothy, ed. LC 88-27811. 176p. (C). 1989. text ed. 27.00 (*0-300-04344-9*) Yale U Pr.

— The Voice of Liberal Learning: Michael Oakeshott on Education. Fuller, Timothy, ed. 169p. (C). 1990. reprint ed. pap. 12.00 (*0-300-04753-3*) Yale U Pr.

Oakeshott, R. Ewart. Knight & His Castle. (Illus.). 108p. (J). 1992. 16.95 (*0-8023-1294-2*) Dufour.

Oakeshott, Walter F. Founded upon the Seas. LC 72-10845. (Essay Index Reprint Ser.). 1977. reprint ed. 24.95 (*0-8369-7233-3*) Ayer.

***Oakey, Ray.** High-Technology New Firms: Variable Barriers to Growth. 144p. 1995. 49.95 (*1-85396-239-2*, Pub. by Paul Chapman UK) Taylor & Francis.

***Oakey, Ray, ed.** New Technology-Based Firms in the 1990s. 256p. 1994. 75.00x (*1-85396-274-0*, Pub. by Paul Chapman UK) Taylor & Francis.

Oakey, Raymond P. High Technology Small Firms: Innovation & Regional Development in Britain & the United States. LC 83-40705. 250p. 1984. text ed. 29.95 (*0-312-37239-6*) St Martin.

Oakey, Raymond P., jt. auth. see Thwaites, A. T.

Oakey, Raymond P., et al. The Management of Innovation in High Technology Small Firms: Innovation & Regional Development in Britain & the United States. LC 88-11448. 224p. 1988. text ed. 55.00 (*0-89930-399-4*, OMI/, Quorum Bks) Greenwood.

— New Firms in the Biotechnology Industry: Their Contribution to Innovation & Growth. 224p. 1990. text ed. 49.00 (*0-86187-126-X*, Pub. by Pinter Pubs UK) St Martin.

Oakey, Virginia, jt. auth. see Nash, Constance.

Oakford, Robert V., jt. auth. see Moses, Lincoln E.

OakGrove, Artemis. Dreams of Vengeance. 197p. (Orig.). 1991. reprint ed. pap. 8.95 (*1-55583-306-3*, Lace MA) Alyson Pubns.

— Led Astray. LC 94-8012. 280p. (Orig.). 1994. pap. 9.95 (*1-885084-00-5*) Tickerwick.

— The Raging Peace. 256p. (Orig.). 1991. reprint ed. pap. 8.95 (*1-55583-307-1*, Lace MA) Alyson Pubns.

— Throne of Council. 151p. (Orig.). 1991. reprint ed. pap. 8.95 (*1-55583-308-X*, Lace MA) Alyson Pubns.

— War Clouds Vol. 2: Two of Nighthawk. LC 95-8443. (Nighthawk Ser.: Vol. 2). 240p. (Orig.). 1995. 12.95 (*1-885084-01-3*) Tickerwick.

Oakhill, A., et al. The Supportive Care of the Child with Cancer. (Illus.). 281p. 1988. pap. 45.00 (*0-7236-0745-1*, Pub. by John Wright UK) Buttrwrth-Heinemann.

Oakhill, Jane & Garnham, Alan. Becoming a Skilled Reader. (Illus.). 240p. 1988. pap. text ed. 21.95 (*0-631-15776-X*) Blackwell Pubs.

Oakhill, Jane, jt. auth. see Garnham, Alan.

Oakhill, Jane, jt. auth. see Yuill, Nicola.

Oakie, Jack. Jack Oakie's Double Takes. LC 79-12432. (Illus.). 240p. (Orig.). 1980. pap. 10.95 (*0-89407-019-3*) Strawberry Hill.

Oakie, Victoria H. Jack Oakie's Oakridge. (Illus.). 128p. (Orig.). 1990. pap. 14.95 (*0-89407-102-5*) Strawberry Hill.

Oakie, Victoria H., comp. Dear Jack: Hollywood Birthday Reminiscences to Jack Oakie. (Illus.). 144p. (Orig.). 1994. pap. 9.95 (*0-89407-113-0*) Strawberry Hill.

Oakland, Dennis. Your Planetary Personality: Everything You Need to Make Sense of Your Horoscope. LC 91-47574. (Modern Astrology Library). 580p. 1992. pap. 19.95 (*0-87542-594-1*) Llewellyn Pubns.

Oakland, Don. Northern Lites: A Brave New Wildwoods. (Illus.). 240p. (Orig.). 1990. pap. 7.95 (*0-9615242-2-7*) Oak Pr.

— Wildwoods Dad. (Illus.). 220p. (Orig.). (J). (gr. 5 up). 1987. pap. 6.95 (*0-9615242-1-9*) Oak Pr.

— Wildwoods Weekly Reader. (Illus.). 255p. (Orig.). 1985. pap. 5.95 (*0-9615242-0-0*) Oak Pr.

Oakland, John. British Civilization: An Introduction. 272p. 1989. pap. 12.95 (*0-415-00670-8*, A2673) Routledge.

— British Civilization: An Introduction. 2nd ed. (Illus.). 240p. 1992. pap. 13.95 (*0-415-06475-9*, A6944) Routledge.

— British Civilization: An Introduction. 3rd ed. (Illus.). 368p. 1995. pap. 16.95 (*0-415-12258-9*, C0608) Routledge.

— A Dictionary of British Institutions: A Student's Guide. LC 92-38180. (Illus.). 176p. 1993. 57.50 (*0-415-07109-7*, B0108); pap. write for info. (*0-415-07110-0*) Routledge.

— Total Quality Management. 2nd ed. 316p. (C). 1993. text ed. 37.95 (*0-89397-386-6*) Nichols Pub.

Oakland, John, jt. auth. see Dale, Barrie.

Oakland, John, jt. auth. see Mauk, David.

Oakland, John S. Total Quality Management. 2nd ed. LC 92-40747. 1993. 56.95 (*0-7506-0993-1*) Buttrwrth-Heinemann.

Oakland, John S. & Followell, Roy F. Statistical Process Control. 2nd ed. (Illus.). 431p. 1990. 62.95 (*0-434-91484-3*) Buttrwrth-Heinemann.

***Oakland, John S. & Porter, Les.** Total Quality Management: Student Edition with Cases. 448p. 1995. pap. text ed. 32.95 (*0-7506-2124-9*, Focal) Buttrwrth-Heinemann.

Oakland, John S. & Porter, Leslie J. Cases in Total Quality Management. LC 93-34170. 288p. 1993. 34.95 (*0-7506-1565-6*) Buttrwrth-Heinemann.

***Oakland, Lois.** Bridges of Love. 1995. 16.95 (*0-8062-5299-5*) Carlton.

Oakland, Roger & Wooding, Dan. Let There Be Light. 176p. 1993. pap. write for info. (*0-9637797-0-2*) Oakland Communs.

Oakland, Roger, jt. auth. see Matrisciana, Caryl.

Oakland, T., jt. ed. see Saigh, P. A.

***Oakland, Thomas & Hambleton, Ronald K., eds.** International Perspectives on Academic Assessment. LC 94-38711. (Evaluation in Education & Human Services Ser.). 248p. (C). 1995. lib. bdg. 89.95 (*0-7923-9525-5*) Kluwer Ac.

Oakland, Thomas P. & Terry, Edwin J., Jr. Divorced Fathers: Reconstructing a Quality Life. (Illus.). 201p. 1983. 32.95 (*0-89885-101-7*) Human Sci Pr.

Oakland Tribune Staff. The Bay Area at War: How We Reacted to the Persian Gulf Crisis. 80p. 1991. reprint ed. lib. bdg. 25.00x (*0-8095-4956-5*) Borgo Pr.

Oaklander, L. Nathan. Existentialist Philosophy: An Introduction. 448p. (C). 1991. pap. text ed. 18.00 (*0-13-297219-0*, 660802) P-H.

— Temporal Relations & Temporal Becoming: A Defense of a Russellian Theory of Time. 250p. (Orig.). (C). 1984. lib. bdg. 48.00 (*0-8191-4149-6*); pap. text ed. 22.50 (*0-8191-4150-X*) U Pr of Amer.

***Oaklander, L. Nathan, ed.** Existentialist Philosophy: An Introduction. 2nd ed. LC 95-12632. 1995. pap. write for info. (*0-13-373861-2*) P-H.

Oaklander, L. Nathan & Smith, Quentin. The New Theory of Time. LC 93-47500. 400p. 1994. 37.50 (*0-300-05796-2*) Yale U Pr.

— Time Change & Freedom: An Introduction to Metaphysics. LC 94-34474. (Illus.). 224p. 1995. 55.00x (*0-415-10248-0*, B7014); pap. 16.95 (*0-415-10249-9*, B7018) Routledge.

Oaklander, L. Nathan, jt. ed. see Hoy, Ronald C.

Oaklander, Violet. Windows to Our Children: A Gestalt Therapy Approach to Children & Adolescents. (Illus.). 352p. 1989. reprint ed. pap. 18.50 (*0-939266-06-7*) Gestalt Journal.

Oakleaf, David, ed. Love in Excess: Eliza Haywood. 240p. 1994. 12.95 (*1-55111-016-4*) Broadview Pr.

***Oakley, A. J. Parker & Mellows:** The Modern Law of Trusts. 6th ed. 1994. pap. 44.00 (*0-421-48750-X*, Pub. by Sweet & Maxwll) W W Gaunt.

Oakley, Allen. The Making of Marx's Critical Theory: A Bibliographical Analysis. LC 83-9732. 143p. (Orig.). 1983. pap. 9.95 (*0-7100-9570-8*, RKP) Routledge.

— Schumpeter's Theory of Capitalist Motion: A Critical Exposition & Reassessment. (Illus.). 352p. 1990. text ed. 59.95 (*1-85278-055-X*, Pub. by E Elgar Pub UK) Ashgate Pub Co.

Oakley, Allen, ed. The Political Economics of Democratic Society: Selected Papers of Adolph Lowe. 320p. 1987. 60.00 (*0-8147-6168-2*) NYU Pr.

Oakley, Allen, ed. see Lowe, Adolph.

Oakley, Andy. Eighty-Eight: An Undercover News Reporter's Expose of American Nazis & the Ku Klux Klan. (Illus.). 180p. 1988. 16.95 (*0-944146-00-7*) PO Pub.

— Issues Confronting City & State Governments: A Guide to Improving & Understanding Local Governments of All Shapes & Sizes, from Towns to Counties to State Agencies. LC 93-85469. 224p. 1993. 24.95 (*0-944146-01-5*) PO Pub.

Oakley, Ann. Essays on Women, Medicine & Health. 256p. 1993. 55.00 (*0-7486-0441-3*, Pub. by Edinburgh U Pr UK); pap. 22.00 (*0-7486-0450-2*, Pub. by Edinburgh U Pr UK) Col U Pr.

— Social Support & Motherhood: The Natural History of a Research Project. LC 92-14642. 416p. 1993. 49.95 (*0-631-18273-X*); pap. 24.95 (*0-631-18274-8*) Blackwell Pubs.

Oakley, Ann & Williams, A. S., eds. The Politics of the Welfare State. LC 94-12566. 224p. 1994. 65.00x (*1-85728-205-1*, Pub. by UCL Pr UK); pap. 24.95x (*1-85728-206-X*, Pub. by UCL Pr UK) Taylor & Francis.

Oakley, Annie. Classical Economic Man: Human Agency & Methodology in the Political Economy of Adam Smith & J. S. Mill. (Advances in Economic Methodology Ser.). 352p. 1994. 74.95 (*1-85278-708-2*, Pub. by E Elgar Pub UK) Ashgate Pub Co.

Oakley, Aregood. Chevrolet 55-56 Restoration Guide. (Illus.). 352p. 1992. pap. text ed. 26.95 (*0-87938-581-2*) Motorbooks Intl.

Oakley, Barry. Scribbling in the Dark. LC 85-14090. 160p. 1986. pap. text ed. 14.95 (*0-7022-1939-8*, Pub. by Univ Queensland Pr AT) Intl Spec Bk.

Oakley, Ben. Windsurfing: The Skills of the Game. (Illus.). 128p. 1994. pap. 17.95 (*1-85223-830-5*, Pub. by Crowood Pr UK) Trafalgar.

Oakley, Brian & Owen, Kenneth. Alvey: Britain's Strategic Computing Initiative. 352p. 1990. 44.00x (*0-262-15038-7*) MIT Pr.

Oakley, Bruce & Schafer, Rollie. Neuroanatomy: Dissection of the Sheep Brain. (Illus.). 32p. (C). 1980. pap. text ed. 6.95 (*0-472-08691-X*) U of Mich Pr.

Oakley, Burks, II. Circuit Tutor: Windows Version 1.0. (Illus.). 64p. (C). Date not set. pap. text ed. write for info. (*0-201-51370-6*) Addison-Wesley.

— Circuittutor: By TutorWare. 50p. (C). 1993. pap. text ed. 26.95 (*0-201-52615-8*) Addison-Wesley.

Oakley, Charles A. Men at Work. Stein, Leon, ed. LC 77-70522. (Work Ser.). (Illus.). 1977. reprint ed. lib. bdg. 33.95 (*0-405-10190-2*) Ayer.

Oakley, D. The Phenomenon of Architecture in Cultures in Change. 1970. 162.00 (*0-08-016075-1*, Pub. by Pergamon Repr UK) Franklin.

Oakley, David, jt. auth. see Furnham, Adrian.

Oakley, David A., ed. Brain & Mind. LC 84-29604. (Psychology in Progress Ser.). 320p. 1985. pap. 14.95 (*0-416-31630-1*, 9627) Routledge Chapman & Hall.

Oakley, Derek. The Falklands Military Machine. 192p. (C). 1991. 95.00 (*0-946771-24-3*) St Mut.

Oakley, Diana. Discovering Heirloom Sewing. (Illus.). 72p. 1993. 14.95 (*1-86351-093-1*, Pub. by S Milner AT) Sterling.

Oakley, Don. The Adventure of Christian Fast. LC 88-8001. (Illus.). 279p. (Orig.). (YA). (gr. 9 up). 1989. 12.95 (*0-9619465-1-2*); pap. 8.95 (*0-9619465-2-0*) Eyrie Pr.

— The Creston Creeper. LC 87-82574. 1988. 16.95 (*0-9619465-0-4*) Eyrie Pr.

Oakley, Ed & Krug, Doug. Enlightened Leadership. 1994. pap. 12.00 (*0-671-86675-3*, Fireside) S&S Trade.

— Enlightened Leadership: Getting to the Heart of Change. (Illus.). 256p. 1993. 22.00 (*0-671-86674-5*) S&S Trade.

Oakley, Frances. Understanding the ABCs of Alzheimer's Disease: A Guide for Caregivers. (Illus.). 20p. (Orig.). 1993. pap. 5.50 (*0-910317-94-1*) Am Occup Therapy.

Oakley, Francis. Community of Learning: The American College & the Liberal Arts Tradition. 256p. 1992. 24.00 (*0-19-505199-8*) OUP.

— The Medieval Experience. (Medieval Academy Reprints for Teaching Ser.). 240p. 1988. pap. 9.95 (*0-8020-6707-7*) U of Toronto Pr.

— Omnipotence, Covenant & Order: An Excursion in the History of Ideas from Abelard to Leibniz. LC 83-45945. 166p. 1984. 28.95 (*0-8014-1631-0*) Cornell U Pr.

— The Western Church in the Later Middle Ages. LC 79-7621. 346p. (C). 1985. 41.50 (*0-8014-1208-0*); pap. 13.95 (*0-8014-9347-1*) Cornell U Pr.

Oakley, Gilbert. Old Moore's Dream Book. 96p. 1995. pap. 9.95 (*0-572-01345-0*, Pub. by Foulsham UK) Atrium Pubs.

— Power of Positive Thought: The Key to Attainment. 148p. 1995. pap. 7.95 (*0-572-01536-4*, Pub. by Foulsham UK) Atrium Pubs.

— The Power of Self-Hypnosis: The Key to Confidence. 128p. (Orig.). 1989. pap. text ed. 18.95 (*0-572-01135-0*, Pub. by W Foulsham UK) Trans-Atl Phila.

Oakley, Graham. The Church Mice & the Moon. LC 74-75569. (Illus.). 40p. (J). (gr. k-3). 1974. 13.95 (*0-689-30437-4*, Atheneum Bks Young) S&S Childrens.

— The Church Mice & the Ring. LC 91-45273. (Illus.). 32p. (J). (ps up). 1992. 14.95 (*0-689-31790-5*, Atheneum Bks Young) S&S Childrens.

— The Church Mice in Action. LC 82-11394. (Illus.). 32p. (J). (gr. k-3). 1983. 13.95 (*0-689-30949-X*, Atheneum Bks Young) S&S Childrens.

— The Church Mice Spread Their Wings. LC 75-15102. (Illus.). 40p. (J). (gr. k-3). 1976. 13.95 (*0-689-30496-X*, Atheneum Bks Young) S&S Childrens.

— The Church Mouse. LC 72-75276. (Illus.). 40p. (J). (gr. k-3). 1972. 13.95 (*0-689-30058-1*, Atheneum Bks Young) S&S Childrens.

— Foxbury Force. (J). 1994. 14.95 (*0-689-31898-7*, Atheneum Bks Young) S&S Childrens.

— Hetty & Harriet. LC 81-8024. (Illus.). 32p. (J). (gr. k-3). 1982. text ed. 13.95 (*0-689-30888-4*, Atheneum Bks Young) S&S Childrens.

Oakley, Helen McK. Three Hours for Lunch: The Life & Times of Christopher Morley. LC 75-39492. 1976. 12.00 (*0-88370-005-0*) Watermill Pubs.

Oakley, Hugh. The Buying Guide for Fresh Fruits, Vegetables, Herbs & Nuts. 7th rev. ed. (Illus.). 136p. (C). 1980. pap. text ed. 4.00 (*0-9611512-0-X*) Castle & Cooke.

Oakley, I. Cooper. Comte de St. Germain: The Secret of Kings. 284p. 1985. reprint ed. spiral bd. 16.50 (*0-7873-1265-7*) Mokelumne.

Oakley, J. Ronald. Baseball's Last Golden Age, 1946-1960: The National Pastime in a Time of Glory & Change. LC 93-40432. 384p. 1994. pap. 25.95 (*0-89950-851-0*) McFarland & Co.

— God's Country: America in the Fifties. LC 85-25316. 1990. pap. 10.95 (*0-942637-24-0*, Dembner NY) Barricade Bks.

Oakley, Jane, jt. auth. see Hislop, Bel.

Oakley, Joe, ed. Baptisms, Bk. 4: A Study of the Elementary Principles of Christ. (First Principles Ser.). 1990. student ed 5.00 (*0-923968-04-0*) Shady Grove Ch Pubns.

— Baptisms, Bk. 4: A Study of the Elementary Principles of Christ, Set. (First Principles Ser.). 1990. 28.00 (*0-318-49990-8*) Shady Grove Ch Pubns.

— Faith: A Study of the Elementary Principles of Christ, Bk. 3. (First Principles Ser.). (Orig.). 1990. student ed, pap. 5.00 (*0-923968-03-2*) Shady Grove Ch Pubns.

— Faith: A Study of the Elementary Principles of Christ, Set. (First Principles Ser.). (Orig.). 1990. 28.00 (*0-318-50020-5*) Shady Grove Ch Pubns.

— Laying on of Hands: A Study of the Elementary Principles of Christ, Bk. 5. (First Principles Ser.). (Orig.). 1990. pap. 28.00 (*0-318-50021-3*); student ed, pap. text ed. 5.00 (*0-923968-05-9*) Shady Grove Ch Pubns.

— Repentance, Bk. 2: A Study of the Elementary Principles of Christ. (First Principles Ser.). 1990. student ed 5.00 (*0-685-45027-9*); student ed 5.00 (*0-923968-02-4*); pap. 28.00 (*0-685-32619-5*); 28.00 (*0-318-49989-4*) Shady Grove Ch Pubns.

— Vision, 7 vols. (First Principles Ser.: Vol. 1). 1989. student ed 5.00 (*0-923968-01-6*) Shady Grove Ch Pubns.

— Vision, 7 vols., Set. (First Principles Ser.: Vol. 1). 1989. 28.00 (*0-923968-00-8*) Shady Grove Ch Pubns.

Oakley, John & Perschbacher, Rex. Civil Procedure. Switzer, Robert J., ed. (Law Outlines Ser.). 300p. (Orig.). 1993. pap. text ed. 16.95 (*0-87457-179-0*, 5040) Casenotes Pub.

Oakley, John H. & Sinos, Rebecca H. The Wedding in Ancient Athens. LC 93-17881. (Studies in Classics). (Illus.). 144p. (C). 1993. text ed. 40.00 (*0-299-13720-1*) U of Wis Pr.

Oakley, John W., jt. auth. see Rotroff, Susan I.

Oakley, June. The Gold Chord of God. 200p. 1993. pap. 9.95 (*0-9635904-0-5*) Overcomer Pub.

Oakley, June P., ed. The Charlottesville Collection: Traditional Recipes for Today's Lifestyles. (Illus.). 221p. 1994. write for info. (*0-9641731-0-7*) Feathrstne & Brown.

Oakley, Justin. Morality & the Emotions. 272p. 1991. 55.00 (*0-415-05661-6*, A6185) Routledge.

— Morality & the Emotions. 264p. 1993. pap. 18.95 (*0-415-09341-4*, B0349) Routledge.

Oakley, K. & Richmond, W. A Systematic Approach to Commercial & Clerical Training. 1970. pap. 56.00 (*0-08-015722-X*, Pub. by Pergamon Repr UK) Franklin.

Oakley, Lois F. Georgia Corporations. LC 84-52872. (Georgia Practice Systems Library). 1985. ring bd. 110.00 (*0-318-04601-6*) Lawyers Cooperative.

— Georgia Corporations. suppl. ed. LC 84-52872. (Georgia Practice Systems Library). 1986. Suppl. 1986. 32.00 (*0-317-01014-X*) Lawyers Cooperative.

Oakley, Lucy. Unfaded Pagent: Edwin Austin Abbey's Shakespearean Subjects. LC 94-75803. (Illus.). 104p. (Orig.). 1994. pap. 25.00 (*1-884919-00-6*) Wallach Art Gallery.

Oakley, Lucy, et al. A Brush with Shakespeare: The Bard in Painting, 1780-1910. LC 85-29669. (Illus.). 140p. (Orig.). (ps-12). 1985. pap. 18.00 (*0-89280-024-0*) Montgomery Mus.

Oakley, Meredith L. On the Make: The Rise of Bill Clinton. LC 94-10787. (Illus.). 368p. 1994. 24.95 (*0-89526-493-5*) Regnery Pub.

Oakley, Michael, tr. see Thomas a Kempis.

Oakley, Myrna. Myrna Oakley's Bed & Breakfast Northwest. (Illus.). (Orig.). 1987. pap. 9.95 (*0-932722-14-8*) Solstice Pr.

— Oregon: Off the Beaten Path: A Guide to Unique Places. 2nd ed. LC 94-27159. (Off the Beaten Path Ser.). (Illus.). 208p. 1994. 9.95 (*1-56440-495-1*) Globe Pequot.

Oakley, Obadiah. Expedition to Oregon. 17p. 1967. reprint ed. pap. 2.50 (*0-87770-067-2*) Ye Galleon.

Oakley, P. J., jt. ed. see Crafer, R. C.

Oakley, Peter & Marsden, David. Approaches to Participation in Rural Development. (WEP Study Ser.). x, 91p. (Orig.). 1990. pap. 14.00 (*92-2-103594-8*) Intl Labour Office.

— Evaluating Social Development Projects. 144p. (C). 1990. text ed. 80.00 (*0-85598-146-6*, Pub. by Oxfam Pubns UK); pap. text ed. 32.00 (*0-85598-147-4*, Pub. by Oxfam Pubns UK) St Mut.

Oakley, Peter, et al. Projects with People: The Practice of Participation in Rural Development. xv, 284p. 1991. pap. 26.00 (*92-2-107282-7*) Intl Labour Office.

O

Oakley, Ray, et al. The Diffusion of New Process Technologies in Hungary. LC 92-28351. 1993. 59.00 (0-86187-062-X, Pub. by Pinter Pubs UK) St Martin.

***Oakley, Robert.** Copyright & Preservation: A Serious Problem in Need of a Thoughtful Solution. 58p. 1990. pap. 15.00 (1-887334-04-1) Comm Preserv & Access.

Oakley, Robert, jt. auth. see Hirsch, John.

Oakley, Robert B., jt. auth. see Rasmussen, J. Lewis.

Oakley, Robert B., ed. see Wurmser, David & Beargdyke, Nancy.

Oakley, Ruth. Board & Card Games. LC 88-28710. (Games Children Play Ser.). (Illus.). 48p. (J). (gr. 4-8). 1990. lib. bdg. 9.95 (1-85435-082-X) Marshall Cavendish.

— Chanting Games. LC 88-28774. (Games Children Play Ser.). (Illus.). 48p. (J). (gr. 3-8). 1990. lib. bdg. 9.95 (1-85435-080-3) Marshall Cavendish.

— Games with Papers & Pencils. LC 88-28711. (Games Children Play Ser.). (Illus.). 48p. (J). (gr. 3-8). 1989. lib. bdg. 9.95 (1-85435-083-8) Marshall Cavendish.

— Games with Sticks, Stones & Shells. LC 88-28773. (Games Children Play Ser.). (Illus.). 48p. (J). (gr. 3-8). 1989. lib. bdg. 9.95 (1-85435-079-X) Marshall Cavendish.

Oakley, Stewart P. War & Peace in the Baltic: 1560-1790. LC 92-6571. (War in Context Ser.). 240p. 1992. 69.95 (0-415-02472-2, A7943) Routledge.

Oakley, Thomas P. English Penitential Discipline & Anglo-Saxon Law in Their Joint Influence. LC 71-82243. (Columbia University. Studies in the Social Sciences: No. 242). reprint ed. 20.00 (0-404-51242-9) AMS Pr.

Oakley, Victoria, jt. auth. see Buys, Susan.

Oakman, Douglas E. Jesus & the Economic Questions of His Day. LC 86-23518. (Studies in the Bible & Early Christianity: Vol. 8). 312p. 1986. lib. bdg. 99.95 (0-88946-608-4) E Mellen.

***Oakman, Harry.** What Flowers When. 1995. pap. 29.95 (0-7022-2839-7, Pub. by Univ Queensland Pr AT) Intl Spec Bk.

***Oakman, Robert L.** The Computer Triangle: Hardware, Software & People. LC 94-35441. 336p. 1995. pap. text ed. 40.95 (0-471-53561-3) Wiley.

Oaks, Barbara. The Bannisters. LC 86-61475. (Illus.). 200p. (Orig.). (C). 1986. pap. 7.95 (0-9618582-0-6) Barbara Oaks.

— Prairie Tales & Others. LC 93-92646. (Illus.). 142p. (Orig.). (C). 1993. pap. 7.95 (0-9618582-3-0) Barbara Oaks.

— Queen City of the Plains. LC 91-90347. (Illus.). 175p. (Orig.). (C). 1991. pap. 7.95 (0-9618582-2-2) Barbara Oaks.

— Wild Flowers & How They Grew. Wollman, Robin, tr. (Illus.). 175p. (Orig.). 1995. pap. 7.95 (0-9618582-4-9) Barbara Oaks.

— Woman of the Prairie. LC 88-61831. (Illus.). 215p. (Orig.). (C). 1989. pap. 7.95 (0-9618582-1-4) Barbara Oaks.

Oaks, Dallin H. The Lord's Way. LC 91-30610. x, 259p. 1991. 12.95 (0-87579-578-1) Deseret Bk.

— The Lord's Way. LC 91-30610. x, 259p. 1995. pap. 7.95 (0-87579-960-4) Deseret Bk.

— Pure in Heart. 10.95 (0-88494-650-9) Bookcraft Inc.

Oaks, Dallin H. & Hill, Marvin S. Carthage Conspiracy: The Trial of the Accused Assassins of Joseph Smith. LC 78-1733. 262p. 1979. pap. 9.95 (0-252-00762-X) U of Ill Pr.

***Oaks, Judy & Ezell, Gene.** Dying & Death: Coping, Caring, Understanding. 2nd ed. 1993. pap. text ed. 32.00 (0-89787-623-7) Gorsuch Scarisbrick.

Oaks, Marian. Love Lessons. 480p. 1992. mass mkt. 4.50 (0-8217-3959-X) Zebra.

— My Kind of Love. 512p. 1994. mass mkt. 4.99 (0-8217-4720-7) Zebra.

— To Love Again. 1992. mass mkt. 4.50 (0-8217-3668-X) Zebra.

— To Love Again. large type ed. LC 93-26491. 1993. lib. bdg. 17.95 (0-7862-0019-7) Thorndike Pr.

Oaks, Martha, jt. auth. see Ferguson, Charles B.

Oaks, Ruth, jt. auth. see Borsch, Jennifer C.

Oaks, Sunny & Yorgason, Blaine M. Secrets. LC 92-33959. 504p. 1992. 15.95 (0-87579-657-5) Deseret Bk.

Oaksey, John, jt. auth. see Kidd, Jane.

Oaksford, Michael & Brown, Gordon, eds. Neurodynamics & Psychology. (Illus.). 400p. 1994. text ed. 69.95 (0-12-523515-1) Acad Pr.

Oaksley, John. Oaksey on Racing Thirty Years of Writing & Riding. Magee, Sean, ed. (Illus.). 435p. 1992. 39.95 (0-413-65230-0, Pub. by W Heinemann Ltd) Trafalgar.

Oakum, Peter. Growing Marijuana in New England. rev. ed. (Illus.). 1977. pap. 8.00 (0-89166-008-9) Cobblesmith.

Oamek, George E. Economic & Environmental Impacts of Interstate Water Transfers in the Colorado River Basin. (Illus.). xiv, 197p. (Orig.). 1990. pap. text ed. 10.00 (0-936911-02-6) Ctr Agri & Rural Dev.

Oamggio, Alice C., et al. Kaleidoscope: Grammaire en contexte Deuzieme Edition. 2nd ed. 416p. 1988. student ed 12.95 (0-685-18217-7) McGraw.

Oana. Bobby Bear & the Blizzard. LC 80-82950. (Bobby Bear Ser.). (Illus.). 32p. (J). (ps-1). 1981. lib. bdg. 9.95 (0-87783-151-3) Oddo.

— Bobby Bear Goes to the Beach. LC 80-82951. (Bobby Bear Ser.). (Illus.). 32p. (J). (ps-1). 1981. lib. bdg. 9.95 (0-87783-153-X) Oddo.

— Timmy Tiger & the Butterfly Net. LC 80-82954. (Timmy Tiger Ser.). (Illus.). 32p. (J). (ps-4). 1981. lib. bdg. 9.95 (0-87783-160-2) Oddo.

— Timmy Tiger & the Masked Bandit. LC 80-82955. (Timmy Tiger Ser.). (Illus.). 32p. (J). (ps-4). 1981. lib. bdg. 9.95 (0-87783-161-0) Oddo.

Oana, Katherine. Chirpy Chipmunk. Baird, Tate, ed. LC 88-51854. (Fables for Today Ser.). (Illus.). 16p. (Orig.). (J). (ps). 1989. pap. 5.52 (0-914127-08-X) Univ Class.

— Kippy Koala. Cooper, William, ed. LC 85-51823. (Fables for Today Ser.). (Illus.). 16p. (Orig.). (J). (ps up). 1985. pap. text ed. 4.72 (0-914127-21-7) Univ Class.

— Learning the Words of Color. Baird, Tate, ed. LC 86-50866. (Illus.). 32p. (Orig.). (J). (ps-1). 1986. pap. 3.65 (0-914127-79-9) Univ Class.

— Lori Lamb. Baird, Tate, ed. (Fables for Today Ser.). (Illus.). 16p. (Orig.). (J). (ps-00). 1989. pap. 4.52 (0-914127-09-8) Univ Class.

— Minnie Muskrat. Baird, Tate, ed. LC 88-51856. (Fables for Today Ser.). (Illus.). 16p. (Orig.). (J). (ps-00). 1989. pap. 4.52 (0-914127-10-1) Univ Class.

— Spacebear Lands on Earth. Baird, Tate, ed. (Illus.). 16p. (Orig.). (J). (ps up). 1988. pap. 4.72 (0-614-02537-0) Univ Class.

— The Sporting Way to Reading Comprehension. Cooper, William H., ed. LC 84-51195. (Illus.). 68p. (Orig.). (J). (gr. 3-8). 1984. 6.27 (0-914127-17-9) Univ Class.

— Zippy Zebra, Vol. IV. Baird, Tate, ed. LC 88-51853. (Fables for Today Ser.). (Illus.). 16p. (Orig.). (J). (ps). 1989. pap. 5.52 (0-914127-11-X) Univ Class.

Oana, Katy D. The Little Dog Who Wouldn't Be. LC 77-18351. (Illus.). 32p. (J). (gr. 2-4). 1978. lib. bdg. 9.95 (0-87783-150-5) Oddo.

— Robbie & the Raggedy Scarecrow. LC 77-18349. (Sound Ser.). (Illus.). 32p. (J). (gr. 2-4). 1978. lib. bdg. 9.95 (0-87783-154-8) Oddo.

— Robbie & the Raggedy Scarecrow. LC 77-18349. (Illus.). (J). (gr. k-2). 1978. lib. bdg. 5.95 (0-89508-065-6) Rainbow Bks.

— Shasta & the Shebang Machine. LC 77-18350. (Sound Ser.). (Illus.). 32p. (J). (gr. 2-4). 1978. lib. bdg. 9.95 (0-87783-152-1) Oddo.

— Shasta & the Shebang Machine. LC 77-18350. (Illus.). (J). (gr. k-2). 1978. lib. bdg. 5.95 (0-89508-066-4) Rainbow Bks.

OAS General Secretariat. Aplicacoes da Teoria de Grupos Na Espectroscopia de Raman e do Infravermelho. (Serie de Fisica Monografia: No. 14). 102p. 1980. pap. text ed. 3.50 (0-8270-1126-1) OAS.

— Boletin Estadistico de la OEA: Vol. 2, No. 3 Julio-Septiembre 1980. 212p. (SPA.). (C). 1980. pap. write for info. (0-318-54727-9) OAS.

OAS, General Secretariat. Cromatografia Liquida Alta Presion: Monografia, No. 10. (Serie de Quimica). (Illus.). 72p. (SPA.). (C). 1980. reprint ed. pap. 3.50 (0-8270-1229-2) OAS.

— La Educacion, No. 83. 152p. (POR & SPA.). (C). 1980. pap. 4.00 (0-686-74519-1) OAS.

— Guia de las Fuentes en Hispanoamerica Para el Estudio de la Administracion Virreinal Espanola en Mexico y en el Peru 1535- 1700. 523p. 1980. pap. 15.00 (0-8270-1091-5) OAS.

— Introduccion a la Electroquinica. (Serie de Quimica: No. 22). (Illus.). 136p. (SPA.). (C). 1980. pap. 3.50 (0-8270-1220-9) OAS.

— Recomendaciones e Informes del Comite Jurico Interamericano Documetos Oficiales: Vol. 2, 1974-1977. 675p. (C). 1981. 50.00 (0-8270-1284-5) OAS.

— Revista Interamericana de Bibliografia, Vol. XXX, No. 4, 1980. 150p. (POR & SPA.). (C). 1980. pap. 2.00 (0-686-74520-5) OAS.

— Revista Interamericana de Bibliografia, Vol. 31, No. 1. 196p. (FRE, POR & SPA.). (C). 1981. pap. 3.00 (0-686-75080-2) OAS.

— Revista Interamericana de Bibliografia: (Inter-American Review of Bibliography), Vol. XXX, No. 3. 116p. (ENG & SPA.). 1980. pap. text ed. 2.00 (0-686-69868-1) OAS.

— Tratados y Convenciones Interamerianos. (Serie Sobre Tratados: No. 9). 303p. (C). 1980. 15.00 (0-685-03627-8) OAS.

— Los Virus. (Serie de Biologia: No. 8). 72p. (Orig.). (C). 1980. reprint ed. pap. text ed. 3.50 (0-8270-1169-5) OAS.

— Vocabulario Vial. 368p. (ENG, FRE, POR & SPA.). 1979. text ed. 15.00 (0-8270-1332-9) OAS.

OAS General Secretariat, ed. Boletin Estadistico de la OEA: Enero-Junio 1980, Vol. 2, Nos. 1-2. 221p. 1980. pap. text ed. 4.00 (0-686-69867-3) OAS.

OAS General Secretariat, ed. see Gutilerrez-Vasquez, J. M.

OAS, General Secretariat, Bureau of Legal Affairs Staff. Tratados Sobre el Canal de Panama Suscritos Entre la Republica de Panama y los Estados Unidos de America. (Serie Sobre Tratados: No. 57 & 57a). 157p. (C). 1979. text ed. 9.00 (0-685-03626-X) OAS.

OAS, General Secretariat, Bureau of Legal Affairs Staff, ed. Status of Inter-American Treaties & Conventions. rev. ed. (Treaty Ser.: No. 5). 53p. (C). text ed. 5.00 (0-8270-1147-4) OAS.

OAS, General Secretariat, Department of Scientific & Technological Affairs Staff. Actividad Optica, Dispersion Rotatoria Optica y Dicroismo Circular en Quimica Organica. 2nd ed. (Serie de Quimica: Monografia No. 11). 70p. (SPA.). (C). 1981. pap. 3.50 (0-8270-1418-X) OAS.

OAS, General Secretariat, Department of Technological & Scientific Affairs Staff. Bacteriofagos. 2nd rev. ed. (Serie de Biologia: No. 12). (Illus.). 102p. (SPA.). (C). 1980. pap. 2.00 (0-8270-1301-9) OAS.

OAS, General Secretariat, Department of Material Resources Staff. Catalogo de Informes y Documentos Tecnicos de la OEA: Suplemento 1978. (SG Ser. A: No. III.1). 81p. 1981. pap. text ed. 4.00 (0-8270-1300-0) OAS.

OAS, General Secretariat, Department of Scientific & Technological Affairs Staff. Cinetica de Disolucion de Medicamentos. (Serie de Quimica: Monografia No. 24). 102p. (SPA.). (C). 1981. pap. 3.50 (0-8270-1391-4) OAS.

OAS, General Secretariat, Department of Scientific Affairs Staff. Fisica Cuantica. rev. ed. (Monografias Cientificas (Scientific Monographs)). 62p. (Orig.). (C). 1980. reprint ed. 2.00 (0-8270-1100-8) OAS.

OAS, General Secretariat, Department of Public Information Staff. La OEA y la Evolucion del Sistema Interamericano. 50p. (C). 1982. pap. 5.00 (0-685-05518-3) OAS.

OAS, General Secretariat, Department of Scientific & Technological Affairs Staff. Principios Generales de Microbiologia: Serie de Biologia No. 7. 2nd ed. (Serie de Biologia: No. 7). 143p. (C). 1980. text ed. 3.50 (0-8270-1097-4) OAS.

— Semiconductors. 2nd ed. (Serie de Fisica (Monograph on Physics): No. 6). 63p. (C). 1980. reprint ed. text ed. 3.50 (0-8270-1068-0) OAS.

— A Vida da Celula. (Serie de Biologia: No. 5). (Illus.). 117p. (Orig.). (C). reprint ed. 3.50 (0-8270-1141-5) OAS.

OAS, General Secretariat, Department of Publications Staff, ed. Boletin Estadistico de la OEA. 207p. (C). 4.00 (0-686-68291-2) OAS.

OAS, General Secretariat, Department of Scientific & Technological Affairs Staff, ed. see O'Brien, Horacio H.

OAS General Secretariat Dept. of Cultural Affairs, tr. see Oquli, Ramon & Melendez, Carlos.

OAS, General Secretariat for Juridical Affairs. Anuario Juridico Interamericano, 1980. 339p. 1981. text ed. 50. 00 (0-8270-1399-X) OAS.

— Convencao Interamericana Sobre Extradicao. (Serie Sobre Tratados: No. 60). 16p. (POR.). 1981. pap. 2.00 (0-8270-1331-0) OAS.

— Convencion Interamericana Sobre Extradiction. (Serie Sobre Tratados: No. 60). 16p. (SPA.). (C). 1981. pap. 2.00 (0-8270-1328-0) OAS.

— Convention Interamericaine Sur L'extradition. (Serie Sur les Traites: No. 60). 16p. (FRE.). (C). 1981. pap. 2.00 (0-8270-1330-2) OAS.

— Inter-American Convention on Extradition. (Treaty Ser.: No. 60). 16p. (C). 1981. pap. 2.00 (0-8270-1329-9) OAS.

— Sistema Interamericano a Treaves de Tratados, Convenciones y Otros Documentos: Vol. I, Asuntos Juridicos Politicos. (Sistema Interamericano Ser.). 1040p. (C). 1981. text ed. 60.00 (0-8270-1426-0) OAS.

OAS, General Secretariat for Legal Affairs. Relacion de Acuerdos Bilaterales: OEA Ser. B-II 1, 1949-1980. (Serie Sobre Tratados: No. 59). 74p. (ENG, FRE, POR & SPA.). (C). 1980. 4.00 (0-8270-1283-7) OAS.

— A Statement of the Laws of Honduras in Matters Affecting Business. 4th ed. 292p. (C). 1981. pap. text ed. 10.00 (0-8270-1421-X) OAS.

OAS, General Secretariat for Management. Documentos Oficiales de la Organizacion de los Estados Americanos Lista General de Documentos, Volumen XX: OEA Ser.Z I. 1. Enero-Diciembre de 1979. 144p. (SPA.). (C). 1980. lib. bdg. 9.00 (0-8270-1289-6) OAS.

OAS, General Secretariat, Inter-American Commission of Human Rights. Annual Report of the Inter-American Commission on Human Rights 1979-1980. OAS Staff, tr. (Inter-American Commission on Human Rights Ser.). 153p. (C). 1980. lib. bdg. 6.00 (0-8270-1285-3) OAS.

— Annual Report of the Inter-American Commission on Human Rights, 1980-1981. (OEA Ser.: L/V/II.53 Doc. 9, Rev. 1). 130p. (SPA.). (C). 1981. pap. 5.00 (0-686-81338-3) OAS.

— La Convencion Americana Sobre Derechos Humanos. (Human Rights Ser.). 248p. 1980. 9.00 (0-8270-1222-5) OAS.

— Informe Sobre la Situacion de los Derechos Humanos en Haiti. (Human Rights Ser.). 77p. (C). 1980. text ed. 5.00 (0-8270-1095-8) OAS.

— Informe Sobre la Situacion de los Derechos Humanos en la Republica de Bolivia. (OEA Ser.: L/V/II.53 Doc. 16, Rev. 2). 115p. (SPA.). (C). 1981. pap. 5.00 (0-8270-1423-6) OAS.

— Informe Sobre la Situacion de los Derechos Humanos en la Republica de Colombia. (OEA Ser.: L/V/II 53 Doc. 22. 30 Junio 1981). 222p. 1981. pap. text ed. 9.00 (0-8270-1372-8) OAS.

— Informe Sobre la Situacion de los Derechos Humanos en la Republica de Guatemala. 132p. (C). 1981. pap. 6.00 (0-8270-1422-8) OAS.

— Informe Sobre la Situacion de los Derechos Humanos en la Republica de Nicaragua. (OEA Ser.: L/V/II.53 Doc. 25. 30 Junio 1981). 168p. 1981. pap. 7.00 (0-8270-1369-8) OAS.

— Report on the Situation of Human Rights in the Republic of Bolivia. 117p. (SPA.). (C). 1981. pap. 5.00 (0-685-03623-5) OAS.

— Report on the Situation of Human Rights in the Republic of Colombia. 222p. (SPA.). (C). 1981. pap. 8.00 (0-8270-1374-4) OAS.

— Report on the Situation of Human Rights in the Republic of Guatemala. (OAS Ser.: L/V/II.53 Doc 21, Rev. 3). 133p. (SPA.). (C). 1981. pap. 6.00 (0-8270-1428-7) OAS.

— Report on the Situation of Human Rights in the Republic of Nicaragua. 171p. (SPA.). (C). 1981. pap. 7.00 (0-8270-1373-6) OAS.

OAS, General Secretariat, Inter-American Juridical Committee. Work Accomplished by the Inter-American Juridical Committee During Its Regular Meeting: Held from August 4-29, 1980. (OFA Ser.: No. Q-IV CJI-43). 129p. 1981. pap. text ed. 10.00 (0-8270-1363-9) OAS.

OAS, General Secretariat of Development & Codification of International Law. Recomendaciones e Informes, 1981, Vol. XIII. (Comite Juridico Interamericano Ser.). 125p. (C). 1981. pap. 8.00 (0-8270-1441-4) OAS.

OAS Staff, tr. see OAS, General Secretariat, Inter-American Commission of Human Rights.

Oask, J. A., jt. ed. see Yen, T. S.

Oaten, Edward F. European Travellers in India During the 15th, 16th & 17th Centuries. LC 75-137279. reprint ed. 42.50 (0-404-04808-0) AMS Pr.

Oates. Voices in the Storm. Date not set. 24.95 (0-06-016784-X, HarpT) HarpC.

Oates, A. S. Around Helston in the Old Days. (C). 1989. text ed. 30.00 (0-907566-46-4, Pub. by Dyllansow Truran UK) St Mut.

***Oates, A. S., et al, eds.** Materials Reliability in Microelectronics V. (Symposium Proceedings Ser.: Vol. 391). 1995. text ed. 74.00 (1-55899-294-4) Materials Res.

***Oates, Carol.** Haunted: Tales of the Grotesque. Date not set. 10.95 (0-615-00511-X, Plume) NAL-Dutton.

Oates, Christine. Truro City Trail. (C). 1989. 40.00 (0-907566-16-2, Pub. by Dyllansow Truran UK) St Mut.

Oates, D. Biophysical Ecology. (Advanced Texts in Life Sciences Ser.). (Illus.). 1980. 84.00 (0-387-90414-X) Spr-Verlag.

Oates, Dan, ed. The Hanging Rock Rebel: Lieutenant John Blue's War in West Virginia & the Shenandoah Valley. LC 93-39320. (Illus.). 324p. (C). 1994. 24.95 (0-942597-62-1, Burd St Pr) White Mane Pub.

Oates, David. Earth Rising: Ecological Belief in An Age of Science. LC 88-25468. 264p. 1989. 27.95 (0-87071-358-2); pap. 17.95 (0-87071-357-4) Oreg St U Pr.

— Night of the Potato. (Chapbook Ser.: No. 3). 56p. 1994. pap. 5.00 (1-885912-00-5) Sows Ear Pr.

— Peace In Exile. 1992. pap. 10.00 (0-685-61562-6); audio 22.95 (0-9617481-9-2) Oyster River Pr.

Oates, David, jt. auth. see Barham, Kevin.

Oates, David, jt. auth. see Durcan, Jim.

Oates, Eddie H. Making Music: Six Instruments You Can Create. LC 92-20060. (Illus.). 32p. (J). (gr. 1-5). 1995. 15.00 (0-06-021478-3) HarpC Child Bks.

— Making Music: Six Instruments You Can Create. LC 92-20060. (Illus.). 32p. (J). (gr. 1-5). 1995. lib. bdg. 14.89 (0-06-021479-1) HarpC Child Bks.

Oates, G. C. Aircraft Propulsion Systems Technology & Design. (Educ Ser.). 1989. 57.95 (0-930403-24-X) AIAA.

Oates, Gordon. Aerothermodynamics of Gas Turbine & Rocket Propulsion. enl. rev. ed. (Education Ser.). 1988. 61.95 (0-930403-34-7) AIAA.

Oates, Gordon C., ed. Aerothermodynamics of Aircraft Engine Components. LC 85-13355. (Education Ser.). (Illus.). 450p. 1985. 57.95 (0-915928-97-3) AIAA.

Oates, J. A. Welding & Cutting. (Illus.). 6.00 (0-85344-094-8) Apple Blossom.

Oates, J. C. Cambridge University Library - A History: From the Beginnings to the Copyright Act of Queen Anne. (Illus.). 600p. 1986. 145.00 (0-521-30656-6) Cambridge U Pr.

Oates, Joan C. Babylon. (Ancient Peoples & Places Ser.). (Illus.). 1986. pap. 15.95 (0-500-27384-7) Thames Hudson.

— Phoenix Bird Chinaware, Bk. 1. 2nd ed. (Illus.). 110p. 1989. reprint ed. pap. 15.00 (0-685-25225-6) J Oates.

— Phoenix Bird Chinaware, Bk. 2. (Illus.). 112p. 1985. pap. 14.95 (0-9617047-1-3) J Oates.

— Phoenix Bird Chinaware, Bk. 3. (Illus.). 96p. 1986. pap. 14.50 (0-9617047-2-1) J Oates.

— Phoenix Bird Chinaware, Bk. 4. (Illus.). 100p. 1989. pap. 15.00 (0-9617047-3-X) J Oates.

Oates, John. The Teaching of Tennyson. 1972. 59.95 (0-8490-1181-7) Gordon Pr.

— The Teaching of Tennyson. LC 72-3619. (Studies in Tennyson: No. 27). 1972. reprint ed. lib. bdg. 64.95 (0-8383-1583-6) M S G Haskell Hse.

Oates, John & Sheldon, Sue, eds. Cognitive Development in Infancy. 320p. 1988. 69.95 (0-86377-085-1); pap. text ed. 34.50 (0-86377-086-X) L Erlbaum Assocs.

Oates, John, jt. ed. see Davies, Glyn.

Oates, John A., ed. Prostaglandins & the Cardiovascular System. (Advances in Prostaglandin, Thromboxane, & Leukotriene Research Ser.: Vol. 10). 400p. 1982. 115.00 (0-89004-580-1) Raven.

— Prostaglandins & the Cardiovascular System. LC 82-15035. (Advances in Prostaglandin, Thromboxane, & Leukotriene Research Ser.: No. 10). (Illus.). reprint ed. pap. 114.00 (0-7837-9638-2, 2060391) Bks Demand.

Oates, John A., et al, eds. Interaction of Platelets with the Vessel Wall. (American Physiological Society Book). (Illus.). 180p. 1988. 32.50 (0-19-520688-6) OUP.

Oates, John F., et al. Checklist of Editions of Greek & Latin Papyri, Ostraca & Tablets. 4th ed. LC 92-33810. (Bulletin of the American Society of Papyrologists Supplements Ser.: No. 7). 94p. 1992. 29.95 (1-55540-782-X, 31 11 07) Scholars Pr GA.

— Checklist of Editions of Greek Papyri & Ostraca. LC 85-2027. (Bulletin of the American Society of Papyrologists Supplements Ser.: No. 4). 74p. reprint ed. pap. 25.00 (0-7837-5420-5, 2045184) Bks Demand.

— Yale Papyri in the Beinecke Rare Book & Manuscript Library, Vol. 1. LC 75-81535. (American Studies in Papyrology: No. 2). 320p. reprint ed. pap. 91.20 (0-7837-5485-X, 2045250) Bks Demand.

***Oates, Joyce C.** Haunted: Tales of the Grotesque. 320p. 1995. pap. 10.95 (0-452-27374-9, Plume) NAL-Dutton.

— What I Lived For. 624p. 1995. 14.95 (0-452-27269-6, Plume) NAL-Dutton.

— Wild Nights. deluxe limited ed. 56p. 1985. 45.00 (0-912348-13-5) Croissant & Co.

— Will You Always Love Me? & Other Stories. LC 94-43865. 1996. 22.95 (0-525-93972-5, Dutton) NAL-Dutton.

Oates, Joyce Carol. American Appetites. 1990. pap. 12.00 (0-06-097278-5, PL) HarpC.

An Asterisk (*) at the beginning of an entry indicates that the title is appearing in BIP for the first time.

— The Assignation. 221p. (C). 1988. 16.95 (*0-88001-200-5*) Ecco Pr.

— The Assignation. LC 89-45126. 208p. 1989. reprint ed. pap. 7.95 (*0-06-097246-7*, PL 7246, PL) HarpC.

— Because It Is Bitter, & Because It Is My Heart. 416p. 1991. pap. 11.95 (*0-452-26581-9*, Plume) NAL-Dutton.

— Bellefleur. 1991. pap. 15.95 (*0-452-26794-3*, Plume) NAL-Dutton.

— Black Water. 160p. 1993. pap. 8.00 (*0-452-26986-5*, Plume) NAL-Dutton.

— Black Water. large type ed. LC 92-23384. 1993. pap. 17.95 (*0-7927-1421-0*, Curley Lrg Print) Chivers N Amer.

— Childwold. 288p. 1981. pap. 2.95 (*0-449-23450-9*, Crest) Fawcett.

— Contraries: Essays. 1981. 22.95 (*0-19-502884-8*) OUP.

— Crossing the Border. 1978. pap. 2.50 (*0-449-23751-6*, Crest) Fawcett.

— Expensive People. LC 89-71059. 244p. 1990. reprint ed. pap. 9.95 (*0-86538-069-4*) Ontario Rev NJ.

— The Fabulous Beasts. Poems. LC 74-27198. (Illus.). xii, 86p. 1975. text ed. 13.95 (*0-8071-0153-2*); pap. 6.95 (*0-8071-0285-7*) La State U Pr.

— Foxfire: Confessions of a Girl Gang. 288p. 1993. 21.00 (*0-525-93632-7*, Dutton-W Abrahams Bk) NAL-Dutton.

— Foxfire: Confessions of a Girl Gang. 336p. 1994. pap. 10.95 (*0-452-27231-9*, Dutton-W Abrahams Bk) NAL-Dutton.

— Haunted: Tales of the Grotesque. LC 93-25223. 320p. 1994. 21.95 (*0-525-93655-6*, Dutton-W Abrahams Bk) NAL-Dutton.

— Heat: And Other Stories. (Contemporary Fiction Ser.). 416p. 1992. pap. 12.95 (*0-452-26646-7*, Dutton-W Abrahams Bk) NAL-Dutton.

— I Lock My Door upon Myself. (Fiction on Art Ser.). 112p. (Orig.). 1990. 15.95 (*0-88001-260-9*) Ecco Pr.

— I Lock My Door upon Myself. 112p. (Orig.). 1991. pap. 8.95 (*0-452-26708-0*, Plume) NAL-Dutton.

— New Heaven, New Earth: The Visionary Experience in Literature. 1978. pap. 2.50 (*0-449-23662-5*, Crest) Fawcett.

— On Boxing. 128p. 1988. pap. 3.95 (*0-8217-2370-7*) Zebra.

— On Boxing. LC 94-17428. (Illus.). 1994. reprint ed. 13.00 (*0-88001-385-0*) Ecco Pr.

— The Perfectionist & Other Plays. LC 94-17484. Date not set. 19.00 (*0-88001-400-8*) Ecco Pr.

— The Profane Art: Essays & Reviews. 212p. 1985. reprint ed. pap. 9.95 (*0-89255-095-3*) Persea Bks.

— Reading the Fights. (Spectator Ser.). 1990. pap. 9.95 (*0-685-46179-3*) P-H.

— The Rise of Life on Earth. LC 90-48706. 144p. 1992. 16.95 (*0-8112-1171-1*); pap. 8.95 (*0-8112-1213-0*, NDP746) New Directions.

— Son of the Morning. 1979. pap. 2.75 (*0-449-24073-8*, Crest) Fawcett.

— Them. 1984. mass mkt. 5.95 (*0-449-20692-0*, Crest) Fawcett.

— Three Plays. LC 80-20210. 157p. 1980. reprint ed. 12.95 (*0-86538-001-5*); reprint ed. pap. 7.95 (*0-86538-002-3*) Ontario Rev NJ.

— The Time Traveler. deluxe ed. 36p. 1987. 50.00 (*0-935716-44-0*) Lord John.

— Twelve Plays. 288p. (Orig.). 1991. 24.95 (*0-525-93376-X*, Plume) NAL-Dutton.

— What I Lived For. LC 94-549. 1994. 23.95 (*0-525-93836-2*, Dutton) NAL-Dutton.

— Where Are You Going, Where Have You Been? LC 94-11284. (Women Writers: Texts & Contexts Ser.). 160p. (C). 1995. text ed. 30.00 (*0-8135-2134-3*); pap. text ed. 10.00 (*0-8135-2135-1*) Rutgers U Pr.

— Where Are You Going, Where Have You Been? Selected Early Stories. LC 92-44899. 522p. 1993. 24.95 (*0-86538-077-5*) Ontario Rev NJ.

— Where Are You Going, Where Have You Been? Selected Early Stories. LC 92-44899. 522p. 1994. pap. 12.95 (*0-86538-078-3*) Ontario Rev NJ.

— Where Are You Going, Where Have You Been? Stories of Young America. 352p. 1979. pap. 1.75 (*0-449-30795-6*, Prem) Fawcett.

— Where Is Here? 1992. 18.95 (*0-88001-283-8*) Ecco Pr.

— Where Is Here: Stories. 1993. pap. 10.00 (*0-88001-338-9*) Ecco Pr.

— Will You Always Love Me? 28p. Date not set. 100.00 (*0-9640454-2-7*) J Cahill Pubng.

— Women Whose Lives Are Food, Men Whose Lives Are Money. Poems. LC 77-17220. (Illus.). 80p. 1978. 13.95 (*0-8071-0391-8*) La State U Pr.

— Wonderland. LC 91-41741. 512p. 1992. reprint ed. pap. 12.95 (*0-86538-075-9*) Ontario Rev NJ.

— You Must Remember This. LC 87-46320. 450p. 1988. reprint ed. pap. 13.00 (*0-06-097169-X*, PL-7169, PL) HarpC.

— Zombie. LC 95-8090. 1995. 20.95 (*0-525-94045-6*, Dutton) NAL-Dutton.

Oates, Joyce Carol, ed. First Person Singular: Writers on Their Craft. LC 83-21927. 280p. (C). 1983. pap. 9.95 (*0-86538-045-7*) Ontario Rev NJ.

— The Oxford Book of American Short Stories. 784p. 1992. 25.00 (*0-19-507065-8*) OUP.

— The Oxford Book of American Short Stories. 784p. 1994. reprint ed. pap. 14.95 (*0-19-509262-7*) OUP.

Oates, Joyce Carol & Halpern, Daniel, eds. The Sophisticated Cat: An Anthology. LC 93-803. 416p. 1993. reprint ed. pap. 12.00 (*0-452-27045-6*, Dutton-W Abrahams Bk) NAL-Dutton.

Oates, Joyce Carol, jt. auth. see Litzinger, Boyd.

Oates, Kim. Child Abuse. (Illus.). 320p. 1986. pap. 9.95 (*0-8065-0962-7*, Citadel Pr) Carol Pub Group.

Oates, Kim, ed. Child Abuse & Neglect: What Happens Eventually? LC 84-16968. 225p. 1984. 31.50 (*0-87630-378-5*) Brunner-Mazel.

Oates, Lou. The Complete Book of Ready-to-Finish Furniture. (Illus.). 1984. 21.95 (*0-13-158239-9*, Busn); pap. 12.95 (*0-13-158221-6*, Busn) P-H.

Oates, Marguerite, jt. auth. see Armstrong, Frank H.

Oates, Martha. Death in the School Community: A Handbook for Counselors, Teachers & Administrators. 129p. (C). 1993. pap. 25.95 (*1-55620-099-4*, 72040) Am Coun Assn.

Oates, Mary J. The Catholic Philanthropic Tradition in America. LC 94-13027. (Philanthropic Studies). 1995. 27.95 (*0-253-34159-0*) Ind U Pr.

— The Role of the Cotton Textile Industry in the Economic Development of the American Southeast: 1900-1940. LC 75-4023. (Dissertations in American Economic History Ser.). (Illus.). 1975. 24.95 (*0-405-07211-2*) Ayer.

Oates, MaryLouise. Making Peace. 1991. 19.95 (*0-446-51541-8*) Warner Bks.

Oates, Michael, et al. Entre amis. (C). 1991. write for info. (*0-395-51354-5*); student ed write for info. (*0-395-51356-1*) HM Soft Schl Col Div.

Oates, Nan. Regreening Australia: Caring for Young Trees 2. (Illus.). 76p. 1990. pap. 12.00 (*0-643-05088-4*, Pub. by CSIRO AT) Intl Spec Bk.

Oates, Robert. Creating Heaven on Earth: The Mechanics of the impossible. (Illus.). 191p. 1990. pap. 12.50 (*0-685-35778-3*) Heaven On Earth.

Oates, Robert & Swanson, Gerald. Enlightened Management. (Illus.). 176p. 1989. pap. 11.95 (*0-923569-06-5*) Maharishi Intl U Pr.

***Oates, Robert M., Jr.** The Mechanics of the Impossible. 191p. 1990. write for info. (*0-923569-01-4*) Maharishi Intl U Pr.

Oates, Stephen B. Abraham Lincoln: The Man Behind the Myths. 240p. 1994. reprint ed. pap. 12.00 (*0-06-092472-1*, PL) HarpC.

— Biography as History. LC 90-63742. (Charles Edmondson Historical Lectures). 37p. (Orig.). 1991. pap. text ed. 4.50 (*0-918954-54-1*) Baylor Univ Pr.

— The Confederate Cavalry West of the River. LC 61-10044. (Illus.). 262p. 1992. reprint ed. pap. 12.95 (*0-292-71152-2*) U of Tex Pr.

— The Fires of Jubilee: Nat Turner's Fierce Rebellion. 224p. 1982. pap. 3.95 (*0-451-62308-8*, ME2308, Ment) NAL-Dutton.

— The Fires of Jubilee: Nat Turner's Fierce Rebellion. 192p. (C). 1990. reprint ed. lib. bdg. 29.00x (*0-8095-9010-7*) Borgo Pr.

— The Fires of Jubilee: Nat Turner's Fierce Rebellion. LC 74-1584. 192p. 1990. reprint ed. pap. 12.00 (*0-06-091670-2*, PL) HarpC.

— Let the Trumpet Sound: The Life of Martin Luther King, Jr. (Illus.). 576p. 1994. reprint ed. pap. 15.00 (*0-06-092473-X*, PL) HarpC.

— Our Fiery Trial: Abraham Lincoln, John Brown, & the Civil War Era. LC 78-16286. 160p. 1983. pap. 11.95 (*0-87023-397-1*) U of Mass Pr.

— Portrait of America, 2 vols., 1. 5th ed. (C). 1991. write for info. (*0-395-55427-6*) HM Soft Schl Col Div.

— Portrait of America, 2 vols., 2. (C). 1991. write for info. (*0-395-43354-1*) HM Soft Schl Col Div.

— To Purge This Land with Blood: A Biography of John Brown. 2nd ed. LC 84-2635. (Illus.). 448p. 1984. pap. 19.95x (*0-87023-458-7*) U of Mass Pr.

— William Faulkner: The Man & the Artist. (Illus.). 363p. 1991. 6.99 (*0-517-05345-4*) Random Hse Value.

— With Malice Toward None: The Life of Abraham Lincoln. (Illus.). 1978. pap. 4.95 (*0-451-62314-2*, ME2314, Ment) NAL-Dutton.

— With Malice Toward None: The Life of Abraham Lincoln. (Illus.). 512p. 1994. reprint ed. pap. 15.00 (*0-06-092471-3*, PL) HarpC.

— A Woman of Valor: Clara Barton & the Civil War. LC 93-38830. 1994. text ed. 27.95 (*0-02-923405-0*) Free Pr.

— A Woman of Valor: Clara Barton & the Civil War. 1995. pap. 14.00 (*0-02-874012-2*) Free Pr.

Oates, Stephen B., ed. Biography As High Adventure: Life-Writers Speak on Their Art. LC 85-20847. 160p. (Orig.). 1986. lib. bdg. 22.50 (*0-87023-513-3*); pap. 11.95 (*0-87023-514-1*) U of Mass Pr.

Oates, Stephen B., ed. see Ford, John S.

Oates, Stephen B., jt. auth. see Kendall, Paul M.

Oates, Wallace. Studies in Fiscal Federalism. (Economists of the Twentieth Century Ser.). 480p. 1991. text ed. 79.95 (*1-85278-520-9*, Pub. by E Elgar Pub UK) Ashgate Pub Co.

Oates, Wallace E. The Economics of the Environment. LC 92-20813. (International Library of Critical Writings in Business History: Vol. 20). 592p. 1992. 159.95 (*1-85278-360-5*, Pub. by E Elgar Pub UK) Ashgate Pub Co.

— Fiscal Federalism. (Modern Revivals in Economics Ser.). 272p. 1993. 59.95 (*0-7512-0220-7*, Pub. by Gregg Revivals UK) Ashgate Pub Co.

Oates, Wallace E., ed. The Economics of the Environment. 640p. 1994. pap. 39.95 (*1-85898-002-X*, Pub. by E Elgar Pub UK) Ashgate Pub Co.

Oates, Wallace E., jt. auth. see Baumol, William J.

Oates, Wallace E., jt. auth. see Kelejian, Harry H.

Oates, Wayne. Presence of God in Pastoral Counseling. 132p. 1986. 12.99 (*0-8499-0475-7*) Word Inc.

Oates, Wayne E. Behind the Masks: Personality Disorders in Religious Behavior. LC 87-8221. 140p. (Orig.). 1987. pap. 10.99 (*0-664-24028-3*, Westminster) Westminster John Knox.

— Behind the Masks - Tras las Mascaras. Zorzoli, Alicia, tr. 144p. (SPA.). 1989. pap. 5.95 (*0-311-46116-6*) Casa Bautista.

— The Care of Troublesome People. Date not set. 10.95 (*1-56699-133-1*, AL154) Alban Inst.

— The Christian Pastor. 3rd rev. ed. LC 82-4933. 298p. 1982. pap. 10.99 (*0-664-24372-X*, Westminster) Westminster John Knox.

— Luck: A Secular Faith. LC 94-19996. 128p. (Orig.). 1995. pap. 10.99 (*0-664-25536-1*) Westminster John Knox.

— Pastoral Care & Counseling in Grief & Separation. Clinebell, Howard J. & Stone, Howard W., eds. LC 75-13048. (Creative Pastoral Care & Counseling Ser.). 96p. 1976. pap. 9.00 (*0-8006-0554-3*, 1-554, Fortress Pr) Augsburg Fortress.

— Pastoral Counseling. LC 73-19719. 240p. (C). 1982. reprint ed. pap. 10.99 (*0-664-24405-X*, Westminster) Westminster John Knox.

— Temptation: A Biblical & Psychological Approach. 132p. (Orig.). 1991. pap. 10.99 (*0-664-25113-7*) Westminster John Knox.

— Your Particular Grief. LC 81-3328. 114p. 1981. pap. 9.99 (*0-664-24376-2*, Westminster) Westminster John Knox.

Oates, Whitney. Influence of Simonides of Ceos on Horace. LC 72-122986. (Studies in Comparative Literature: No. 35). 1970. reprint ed. lib. bdg. 29.95 (*0-8383-1119-9*) M S G Haskell Hse.

Oates, Whitney J. Aristotle & the Problem of Value. LC 62-21106. 399p. reprint ed. pap. 113.80 (*0-8357-9493-8*, 2013035) Bks Demand.

Oates, Whitney J., ed. see Augustine.

***Oates, William C.** War Between the Union & the Confederacy. (Illus.). 808p. 1995. 50.00 (*0-89029-017-2*) Morningside Bkshop.

Oatey, M. & Payne, C. COBOL from BASIC: A Short Self-Instructional Course. 144p. (Orig.). (C). 1986. pap. text ed. 25.00 (*0-273-02495-7*) Trans-Atl Phila.

Oatey, Michael & Clare, Chris. Pascal: A Short Self-Instructional Course. 136p. (C). 1985. pap. text ed. 85.00 (*0-273-02203-2*, Pub. by Pitman Pubng UK) St Mut.

Oatey, Michael & Payne, Carl. BASIC: A Short Self-Instructional Course. 94p. (C). 1984. pap. text ed. 60.00 (*0-273-01940-6*, Pub. by Pitman Pubng UK) St Mut.

Oathout, John D. Trademarks. (Illus.). 192p. 1981. 20.00 (*0-685-04569-2*, Scribners) S&S Trade.

Oatis, jt. auth. see Craik.

Oatis, jt. ed. see Craik.

Oatley, Keith. Best Laid Schemes: The Psychology of the Emotions. (Studies in Emotion & Social Interaction). (Illus.). 496p. (C). 1992. 74.95 (*0-521-41037-1*); pap. 34.95 (*0-521-42387-2*) Cambridge U Pr.

Oatley, Mary J., jt. auth. see Harvey, Eliana.

Oatman. The Jungle (Sinclair) (Book Notes Ser.). (C). 1984. pap. 2.50 (*0-8120-3424-4*) Barron.

Oatman, Lorenzo D. & Oatman, Olive A. The Captivity of the Oatman Girls among the Apache & Mohave Indians. LC 94-4747. Orig. Title: Life among the Indians: or the Captivity of the Oatman Girls among the Apache & Mohave Indians. (Illus.). 240p. 1994. reprint ed. pap. 6.95 (*0-486-28078-0*) Dover.

Oatman, Mike. Ol' Mikes Philosophy & Foolishness. (Illus.). 160p. (Orig.). 1993. pap. 14.95 (*0-9638429-0-0*) Hearth KS.

Oatman, Miriam E., jt. auth. see Blachly, Frederick F.

Oatman, Olive A., jt. auth. see Oatman, Lorenzo D.

Oatman, Tamra-Shae. Lone Star Baby: A Consumer Guide for Expectant & New Parents. Van Pilney, Mary, ed. (Orig.). 1988. pap. 8.95 (*0-9620141-0-9*) Oatman-Pilney.

Oatney, Laura, ed. Consumer Approach to Investing: A Teaching Guide. 2nd ed. (Illus.). 180p. 1992. 15.00 (*0-9635157-0-5*) Eastern MI NICE.

Oats, L. B. Emperor's Chambermaids: The Story of the 14th-20th King's Hussars. (Illus.). 518p. (C). 1987. 123.00 (*0-7063-1001-2*, Pub. by Picton UK) St Mut.

Oba Ecun. Addimu: Offerings to the Orichas. O Baecun Books, Inc. Staff, ed. LC 91-90227. 198p. (Orig.). (C). 1992. pap. text ed. 22.00 (*0-926603-07-8*) Obaecun Bks.

Oba-Ecun. Oricha: Metologia De la Religion Yoruba. (Illus.). 423p. (Orig.). 1994. reprint ed. pap. write for info. (*0-926603-11-6*) Obaecun Bks.

***Oba, Sadao.** The Japanese War: London University's WWII Secret Teaching Programme & the "Experts" Sent to Help Beat Japan. Kaneko, Ann, tr. 224p. (C). 1995. text ed. 49.95 (*1-873410-33-6*, Pub. by Curzon Pr UK) Humanities.

Obaba, Al I., ed. Sayings of the Honorable Elijah Muhammad, Vol. II. 49p. (YA). 1991. pap. text ed. 3.95 (*0-916157-86-5*) African Islam Miss Pubns.

— Slave Insurrections "Selected Documents" (Illus.). 176p. (Orig.). 1990. pap. text ed. 15.00 (*0-916157-26-1*) African Islam Miss Pubns.

Obaba, Al I., intro. An Anthology of the Public Utterances. 200p. 1990. pap. text ed. 4.95 (*0-916157-85-7*) African Islam Miss Pubns.

Obaba, Al I., ed. see African Islamic Mission Staff.

Obaba, Al I., ed. see Bode, E. A.

Obaba, Al I., ed. see Budge, E. A.

Obaba, Al I., ed. see Churchward, Albert.

Obaba, Al I., ed. see Deedat, Ahmed.

Obaba, Al I., ed. see Douglass, Frederick.

Obaba, Al I., ed. see Dudley, Dean.

Obaba, Al I., ed. see Foote, G. W. & Wheeler, J. M.

Obaba, Al I., ed. see Houston, Drusilla D.

Obaba, Al I., ed. see Idowu, E. Bqlaji.

Obaba, Al I., ed. see James, George G.

Obaba, Al I., ed. see Lane-Poole, Stanley.

Obaba, Al I., ed. see Massey, Gerald.

Obaba, Al I., ed. see Mufassir, Sulayman.

Obaba, Al I., ed. see Osei, G. K.

Obaba, Al I., ed. see Owaida, Mohammad T.

Obaba, Al I., ed. see Perry, Rufus L.

Obaba, Al I., ed. see Petrie, W. M.

Obaba, Al I., ed. see Sakr, Ahmad.

Obaba, Al I., ed. see Shorter, Alan W.

Obaba, Al I., ed. see Smith, G. Elliot.

Obaba, Al I., ed. see Volney, C. F.

Obaba, Al I., ed. see Westbrook, Henry S.

Obaba, Al I., ed. see Winchell, Alexander.

Obaba, Al-Imam. Adam Clayton Powell, Jr. (Great Nubian Quiz Bks.). (Illus.). 43p. (Orig.). (YA). 1989. pap. 3.95 (*0-916157-06-7*) African Islam Miss Pubns.

— The Aware Pages: Economic Unity a Must. (Illus.). 43p. (Orig.). (J). 1988. pap. text ed. 2.50 (*0-916157-05-9*) African Islam Miss Pubns.

— Dr. Martin Luther King, Jr. (Great Nubian Quiz Bks.). (Illus.). 43p. (Orig.). (YA). 1989. pap. 3.95 (*0-916157-14-8*) African Islam Miss Pubns.

— Emperor Haile Selassie. (Great Nubian Quiz Bks.). (Illus.). 43p. (Orig.). (YA). 1989. pap. 3.95 (*0-916157-07-5*) African Islam Miss Pubns.

— Harriet Tubman Great Nubian Quiz. (Great Nubian Quiz Bks.). (Illus.). 43p. (Orig.). (YA). 1989. pap. 3.95 (*0-916157-09-1*) African Islam Miss Pubns.

— Malcolm X Great Nubian Quiz. (Great Nubian Quiz Bks.). (Illus.). 43p. (Orig.). (YA). 1988. pap. 3.95 (*0-916157-16-4*) African Islam Miss Pubns.

— Marcus Mosiah Garvey, Jr. Great Nubian Quiz. (Great Nubian Quiz Bks.). (Illus.). 43p. (Orig.). (YA). 1989. pap. 3.95 (*0-916157-15-6*) African Islam Miss Pubns.

— Sojourner Truth Great Nubian Quiz. (Great Nubian Quiz Bks.). (Illus.). 43p. (Orig.). (YA). 1989. pap. 3.95 (*0-916157-08-3*) African Islam Miss Pubns.

Obaba, Al-Imam & Abdullah. The Why & How of Burial & Death of a Muslim. (Illus.). 24p. (Orig.). (YA). 1985. pap. 1.50 (*0-916157-03-2*) African Islam Miss Pubns.

Obaba, Al-Imam & Chisa. The Name Book: The One You've Been Waiting For. 48p. (Orig.). (J). 1977. pap. 3.95 (*0-916157-12-1*) African Islam Miss Pubns.

Obaba, Al Imam, ed. see Morgans, William.

Obaba, Al-Iman. The Papyrus Eber: The First Medical Book in the World. (Illus.). 167p. (Orig.). 1927. pap. text ed. 20.00 (*0-916157-17-2*) African Islam Miss Pubns.

Obade, Claire C. Patient Care Decision-Making: A Legal Guide for Providers. LC 91-22470. (Health Law Ser.). 1991. Revised annually. ring bd. 125.00 (*0-87632-819-2*) Clark Boardman Callaghan.

Obaecun Staff. Orisha: Methodology of the Yoruba Religion. (Illus.). 156p. (Orig.). (C). 1990. pap. 45.00 (*0-926603-04-3*) Obaecun Bks.

Obal, F. & Benedek, G., eds. Environmental Physiology: Proceedings of the 28th International Congress of Physiological Sciences, Budapest, 1980 (Including the Satellite Symposium on Sports Physiology) LC 80-42102. (Advances in Physiological Sciences Ser.: Vol. 18). (Illus.). 375p. 1981. 160.00 (*0-08-027339-4*, Pub. by Pergamon Repr UK) Franklin.

Oballa, Michael C. & Shih, Stuart S., eds. Catalytic Hydroprocessing of Petroleum & Distillates: Proceedings of the AIChE Spring National Meeting, Houston, Texas, 1993. LC 94-12079. (Chemical Industries Ser.: Vol. 58). 480p. 1994. 165.00 (*0-8247-9255-6*) Dekker.

Oballa, Michael C., jt. ed. see Shis, Stuart S.

O'Ballance, Edgar. Afghan Wars, 1839-1992: What Britain Gave up & the Soviet Union Lost. (Illus.). 260p. 1993. 30.00 (*0-08-040722-6*, Pub. by Brasseys UK) Brasseys Inc.

— The Arab-Israeli War, Nineteen Forty-Eight. LC 79-2877. (Illus.). 220p. 1983. reprint ed. 24.50 (*0-8305-0045-6*) Hyperion Conn.

— Civil War in Bosnia, 1992-94. LC 94-32534. 1995. write for info. (*0-312-12503-8*) St Martin.

— The Cyanide War: The Tamil Insurrection in Sri Lanka. (Illus.). 139p. 1989. 30.00 (*0-08-036695-3*, 3004, Pub. by Brasseys UK) Brasseys Inc.

— The Gulf War: Nineteen Eighty to Nineteen Eighty-Seven. 232p. 1988. 40.00 (*0-08-034747-9*, Pub. by Brasseys UK) Brasseys Inc.

— The Gulf War 1980-1987. 240p. 1987. 28.01 (*0-317-66337-2*, Pergamon Pr) Elsevier.

— Korea: Nineteen Fifty to Nineteen Fifty-Three. LC 85-14787. 172p. (C). 1985. reprint ed. lib. bdg. 14.00 (*0-89874-885-2*) Krieger.

— No Victor, No Vanquished: The Yom Kippur War. LC 76-58756. (Illus.). 384p. 1979. 24.95 (*0-89141-017-1*) Presidio Pr.

***Obama, Barack.** Dreams from My Father: A Story of Race & Inheritance. 1995. 23.00 (*0-8129-2343-X*, Times Bks) Random.

O'Banion, John D. Reorienting Rhetoric: The Dialectic of List & Story. 312p. 1991. 35.00 (*0-271-00775-3*) Pa St U Pr.

O'Banion, O. Alpine's. (Illus.). 223p. (Orig.). 1994. pap. 8.95 (*0-9637174-2-1*) Two O Bks.

— Means to the End. 297p. (C). 1993. reprint ed. 19.95 (*0-9637174-1-3*) Two O Bks.

— No Longer Alone. (Orig.). 1995. pap. 8.95 (*0-9637174-0-5*) Two O Bks.

O'Banion, Terry. Innovation in the Community College. (ACE-Oryx Series on Higher Education). (Illus.). 320p. 1989. 27.95 (*0-02-897291-0*, ACE-Oryx) Oryx Pr.

O'Bannon, Barbara K., ed. Fisheries of the United States, 1989. (Fishery Statistics Ser.: No. 8900). (Illus.). 127p. 1990. per., pap. 6.00 (*0-16-023064-0*, S/N 003-020-00160-2) USGPO.

O'Bannon, George, et al. Vanishing Jewels: Central Asian Tribal Weavings. Swinney, H. J., ed. LC 90-62705. (Illus.). 128p. (Orig.). 1990. pap. 39.95 (*0-938551-00-0*) Rochester Mus & Sci Ctr.

O'Bannon, George W. Oriental Rugs: A Bibliography. LC 94-11116. 757p. 1994. 79.50 (*0-8108-2899-5*) Scarecrow.

O'Bannon, R. Michael, et al. Honesty & Integrity Testing: A Practical Guide. 227p. (Orig.). 1989. pap. 39.95 (*0-926505-02-5*) Applied Info Rescs.

***O'Bannon, Romonia G.** Zora's House. 1994. 7.95 (*0-533-11056-4*) Vantage.

O'Banyon. Desert Song. 1994. pap. 9.99 (*0-06-108045-4*, PL) HarpC.

O

An Asterisk (*) at the beginning of an entry indicates that the title is appearing in BIP for the first time.

— Highland Love Song. 1994. mass mkt. 5.99 (*0-06-108121-3*, Harp PBks) HarpC.
O'Banyon, Constance. Cheyenne Sunrise. 1990. mass mkt. 4.95 (*0-8217-3088-6*) Zebra.
— Dakota Dreams. 512p. 1991. mass mkt. 4.99 (*0-8217-3677-9*) Zebra.
***Obanyon, Constance.** Desert Song. 1994. pap. 5.99 (*0-06-108290-2*, Harp PBks) HarpC.
O'Banyon, Constance. Ecstasy's Promise. 1982. pap. 3.50 (*0-89083-978-6*) Zebra.
— Enchanted Ecstasy. 496p. 1984. pap. 3.75 (*0-8217-1386-8*) Zebra.
Obanyon, Constance. Enchantress. 1991. mass mkt. 4.95 (*1-55817-527-X*, Pinnacle NY) Windsor NY.
O'Banyon, Constance. Forever My Love. 1992. mass mkt. 5.99 (*0-06-104089-4*, Harp PBks) HarpC.
— Golden Paradise. 512p. 1987. pap. 3.95 (*0-8217-2007-4*) Zebra.
— Highland Love song. 1993. pap. 8.99 (*0-06-108044-6*, Harp PBks) HarpC.
— Lavender Lies. 512p. 1988. pap. 3.95 (*0-8217-2371-5*) Zebra.
— Moontide Embrace. 1987. pap. 3.95 (*0-8217-2182-8*) Zebra.
***Obanyon, Constance.** Moontide Embrace. 1994. pap. 4.50 (*0-8217-2949-7*) Zebra.
— Pirate's Princess. 1989. pap. 3.95 (*0-8217-2726-5*) Zebra.
O'Banyon, Constance. Rebel Temptress. (Orig.). 1983. pap. 3.50 (*0-8217-1215-2*) Zebra.
— Savage Autumn. 1988. pap. 3.95 (*0-8217-1938-6*) Zebra.
— Savage Desire. 1983. pap. 3.50 (*0-8217-1120-2*) Zebra.
— Savage Splendor. 1983. pap. 3.50 (*0-8217-1292-6*) Zebra.
— Savage Spring. 1988. pap. 3.95 (*0-8217-1715-4*) Zebra.
— Savage Summer. 448p. 1986. pap. 3.95 (*0-8217-1922-X*) Zebra.
— Savage Winter. 1988. pap. 3.95 (*0-8217-2372-3*) Zebra.
— September Moon. 1986. pap. 3.95 (*0-8217-1838-X*) Zebra.
— Song of the Nightingale. (J). 1992. pap. 8.99 (*0-06-104122-X*, Harp PBks) HarpC.
— Song of the Nightingale. 1993. mass mkt. 5.99 (*0-06-108003-9*, Harp PBks) HarpC.
— Velvet Chains. 1985. pap. 3.95 (*0-8217-1640-9*) Zebra.
Obar, Robert A., jt. auth. see Dyer, Betsey D.
Obarakpor, Anita M., jt. auth. see Hodgkinson, Harold L.
O'Barr, James. The Crow. 224p. 1993. pap. 15.95 (*0-87816-221-6*) Kitchen Sink.
— Crow Portfolio. (Illus.). 64p. 1993. 24.95 (*1-879450-90-9*) Tundra MA.
— Death. (Crow Ser.: No. 3). (Illus.). 64p. (Orig.). 1992. pap. 4.95 (*1-879450-75-5*) Tundra MA.
— Irony & Despair. (Crow Ser.: No. 2). (Illus.). 64p. 1992. reprint ed. pap. 4.95 (*1-879450-74-7*) Tundra MA.
— Pain & Fear. (Crow Ser.: No. 1). (Illus.). 64p. 1992. reprint ed. pap. 4.95 (*1-879450-73-9*) Tundra MA.
O'Barr, James, jt. ed. see Bergin, John.
O'Barr, Jean & Wyer, Mary, eds. Engaging Feminism: Students Speak up & Speak Out. (Feminist Issues: Practice, Politics, Theory Ser.). (C). 1992. text ed. 29.50 (*0-8139-1386-1*); pap. text ed. 12.95 (*0-8139-1387-X*) U Pr of Va.
O'Barr, Jean F. Feminism in Action: Building Institutions & Community Through Women's Studies. LC 93-33313. xiv, 302p. 1994. text ed. 49.95 (*0-8078-2129-2*); pap. 16.95 (*0-8078-4439-X*) U of NC Pr.
O'Barr, Jean F., ed. Women & a New Academy: Gender & Cultural Contexts. LC 88-40441. 192p. (Orig.). (C). 1989. text ed. 35.00 (*0-299-11930-0*); pap. text ed. 12.95 (*0-299-11934-3*) U of Wis Pr.
O'Barr, Jean F., intro. Perspectives on Power: Women in Africa, Asia, & Latin America. LC 82-50929. 120p. (Orig.). (C). 1991. reprint ed. pap. text ed. 10.00 (*0-685-74439-6*) Ctr Intl Stud Duke.
O'Barr, Jean F., jt. ed. see Harding, Sandra.
O'Barr, Jean F., et al, eds. Ties That Bind: Essays on Mothering & Patriarchy. 296p. 1990. pap. 14.95 (*0-226-61546-4*) U Ch Pr.
— Ties That Bind: Essays on Mothering & Patriarchy. 296p. 1990. lib. bdg. 29.95 (*0-226-61545-6*) U Ch Pr.
O'Barr, William M. Culture & the Ad: Exploring Otherness in the World of Advertising. LC 93-44451. (Institutional Structures of Feeling Ser.). (C). 1994. text ed. 62.00 (*0-8133-2196-4*); pap. text ed. 17.95 (*0-8133-2197-2*) Westview.
— Linguistic Evidence: Language, Power & Strategy in the Courtroom. (Studies on Law & Social Control). 187p. 1982. text ed. 53.00 (*0-12-523520-8*) Acad Pr.
O'Barr, William M. & Conley, John M. Fortune & Folly: The Wealth & Power of Institutional Investing. 240p. 1992. 30.00 (*1-55623-705-7*) Irwin Prof Pubng.
O'Barr, William M. & Jean, F. Languages & Politics. (Contributions to the Sociology of Language Ser.: No. 10). 1977. text ed. 56.95 (*90-279-7761-5*) Mouton.
O'Barr, William M., jt. auth. see Conley, John M.
Obarry, Richard. Beyond the Dolphin Smile. 1991. mass mkt. 5.95 (*0-425-12902-0*) Berkley Pub.
O'Barry, Richard & Coulburn, Keith. Behind the Dolphin Smile. (Illus.). 296p. 1989. 17.95 (*0-912697-79-2*) Algonquin Bks.
Obasanjo, Olusegun. My Command. (African Writers Ser.). (Illus.). xiii, 178p. (C). 1981. reprint ed. pap. 9.95 (*0-435-90249-0*) Heinemann.
Obasanjo, Olusegun, ed. The Challenges of Agricultural Production & Food Security in Africa. 250p. 1992. 42.00 (*0-8448-1724-4*, Crane Russak) Taylor & Francis.
Obasanjo, Olusegun & D'Orville, Hans, eds. Challenges of Leadership in African Government. 200p. 1990. 63.00 (*0-8448-1669-8*, Crane Russak); pap. 35.00 (*0-8448-1670-1*, Crane Russak) Taylor & Francis.
— The Leadership Challenge of Economic Reforms in Africa. 112p. 1991. 40.00 (*0-8448-1680-9*, Crane Russak) Taylor & Francis.
Obasanjo, Olusegun, ed. see De'Orville, Hans.
Obasi, G. P., jt. auth. see Gringof, I. G.
Obasih, K. M., jt. ed. see Eckels, P. W.
***Obata.** Of Lives & Legends: Sketches of Japan. 1995. pap. write for info. (*0-910704-88-0*) Hawley.
Obata, M., ed. Minimal Submanifolds & Geodesics: Proceedings of the Japan-United States Seminar, Tokyo 1977. 292p. 1979. 89.75 (*0-444-85327-8*, North Holland) Elsevier.
— Selected Papers of Yano Kentaro. (North-Holland Mathematics Studies: No. 70). 366p. 1982. 82.00 (*0-444-86495-4*, North Holland) Elsevier.
***Obata, N.** White Noise Calculus & Fock Space. (Lecture Notes in Mathematics: No. 1577). 183p. 1994. pap. text ed. 30.00 (*0-387-57985-0*) Spr-Verlag.
Obayash, Hiroshi, ed. Death & Afterlife: Perspectives of World Religion. LC 91-3876. (Contributions to the Study of Religion Ser.: No. 33). 240p. 1991. text ed. 55.00 (*0-313-27906-3*, ODE, Greenwood Pr); pap. text ed. 17.95 (*0-275-94104-3*, B4104, Greenwood Pr) Greenwood.
Obayashi, Alan W. & Gorgan, Joseph M. Management of Industrial Pollutants by Anaerobic Processes. Patterson, James M., ed. LC 84-23378. (Industrial Waste Management Ser.). (Illus.). 220p. 1985. 112.00 (*0-87371-001-0*, CRC Reprint) Franklin.
Obayashi, Y. Dried BCG Vaccine. (Monograph Ser.: No. 28). 220p. (ENG & FRE.). 1955. 7.20 (*92-4-140028-5*) World Health.
Obayd of Zakan. Kolliyat i Obayd i Zakani: The Complete Works of Obayd of Zakan. Eqbal, 'Abbas, ed. & intro. by. 176p. (Orig.). (PER.). 1986. pap. 10.00 (*0-685-21482-6*) Iran Bks.
Obbagy, William G., jt. auth. see Wood, Edward D.
***Obbard, Elizabeth R.** La Madre: The Life & Spirituality of Teresa of Avila. 160p. 1993. pap. 35.00 (*0-85439-468-0*, Pub. by St Paul Pubns UK) St Mut.
Obbard, Elizabeth R., ed. The Watchful Heart: Daily Reading with Ruth Burrows. 1992. pap. 6.95 (*0-87193-283-0*) Dimension Bks.
Obbink, Dirk, ed. Philodemus & Poetry: Poetic Theory & Practice in Lucretius, Philodemus & Horace. 320p. 1995. 49.95 (*0-19-508815-8*) OUP.
Obbink, Dirk, jt. ed. see Faraone, Christopher A.
Obbink, Dirk, tr. see Gigante, Marcello.
Obbink, Dirk, ed. see Raubitschek, A. E.
Obdam, Jack. The Rape of Britannia. 92p. (C). 1989. text ed. 39.00 (*1-872795-80-3*, Pub. by Pentland Pr UK) St Mut.
Obdidko, V. N., jt. ed. see Stepanov, V. E.
Obe, Arnold F. International Air Traffic Control: Management of the World's Airspace. 2nd ed. (Illus.). 275p. 1985. text ed. 47.00 (*0-08-031312-4*, Pergamon Pr) Elsevier.
Obe, Dorothy M. Hilarious Happenings. 93p. (C). 1989. text ed. 45.00 (*0-685-63533-3*, Pub. by Pentland Pr UK) St Mut.
— Laughter in Khaki. 138p. (C). 1989. text ed. 39.00 (*0-946270-41-4*, Pub. by Pentland Pr UK) St Mut.
— Reflections. 189p. (C). 1989. text ed. 50.00 (*0-946270-55-4*, Pub. by Pentland Pr UK) St Mut.
— Why Forget. 122p. (C). 1989. text ed. 39.00 (*0-946270-54-6*, Pub. by Pentland Pr UK) St Mut.
Obe, Dorothy M., ed. We Simply Had to Laugh. 85p. (C). 1989. text ed. 39.00 (*1-872795-23-4*, Pub. by Pentland Pr UK) St Mut.
Obe, G., ed. Advances in Mutagenesis Research, Vol. 2. (Illus.). 384p. 1991. 128.00 (*0-387-52428-2*) Spr-Verlag.
Obe, G. & Basler, A., eds. Cytogenetics. (Illus.). 415p. 1987. 150.00 (*0-387-18017-6*) Spr-Verlag.
Obe, G. & Natarajan, A. T., eds. Chromosomal Aberrations: Basic & Applied Aspects. (Illus.). xi, 319p. 1990. 128.00 (*0-387-52540-8*) Spr-Verlag.
— Chromosomal Alterations: Origin & Significance. LC 94-8275. 1994. 154.00 (*0-387-57812-9*) Spr-Verlag.
Obe, G., jt. ed. see Sobti, R. C.
Obe, G., et al, eds. Advances in Mutagenesis Research, Vol. 3. (Illus.). ix, 197p. 1991. 149.00 (*0-387-53359-1*) Spr-Verlag.
— Advances in Mutagenesis Research, Vol. 4. (Illus.). x, 241p. 1993. 169.00 (*0-387-55411-4*) Spr-Verlag.
— Advances in Mutagenesis Research, Vol. 5. (Illus.). 240p. 1994. 179.00 (*0-387-56641-4*) Spr-Verlag.
Obear, Katharine T. Through the Years in Old Winnsboro. LC 80-23314. xx, 258p. 1980. reprint ed. 20.00 (*0-87152-344-2*) Reprint.
Obebe, Bolarinde, et al. Caribbean Research Center: Occasional Paper, No. 2. Clarke, Velta, ed. 70p. (Orig.). 1989. pap. text ed. write for info. (*0-318-66547-6*) Caribbean Rsch Ctr.
Obeck, Victor, jt. auth. see Rossman, Isadore.
Obedin, Harry. Peter Penguin & the Polar Sea. LC 88-63171. (Illus.). 32p. (Orig.). (J). (ps-4). 1989. pap. 4.95 (*0-943990-54-8*) Parenting Pr.
Obee, Bruce & Ellis, Graeme. Guardians of the Whales: The Quest to Study Whales in the Wild. LC 92-15419. (Illus.). 188p. 1992. 34.95 (*0-88240-428-8*) Alaska Northwest.
Obeid, Anis I. Echocardiography in Clinical Practice. (Illus.). 384p. 1991. text ed. 125.00 (*0-397-51024-1*) Lippincott.
O'Beirne, H. F. Leaders & Leading Men of the Indian Territory. Goss, Joe R. & Sperry, Phillip A., eds. (Illus.). 326p. 1994. reprint ed. 49.95 (*1-56869-054-1*) Oldbuck Pr.
O'Beirne, Kathleen P. Pass It On! How to Thrive in the Military Lifestyle. LC 91-90191. (Illus.). 528p. (Orig.). 1991. pap. 14.95 (*1-879979-00-4*) Lifescape Enter.
O'Beirne, Martin. Family Tree: Ancestral Record. (Illus.). 30p. (Orig.). 1987. pap. 3.95 (*0-948378-01-8*, Heraldic Art) Irish Bks Media.
O'Beirne, T. H., ed. see Schuh, Fred.
O'Beirne, Thomas. Candid-Impartial Narrative of the Transactions of the Fleet Under the Command of Lord Howe. LC 75-77108. (Eyewitness Accounts of the American Revolution Ser., No. 1). 1969. reprint ed. 11.95 (*0-405-01170-9*) Ayer.
Obejas, Achy. We Came All the Way from Cuba So You Could Dress Like This? Stories. LC 94-18194. 160p. (Orig.). 1994. lib. bdg. 24.95 (*0-939416-92-1*); pap. 10.95 (*0-939416-93-X*) Cleis Pr.
Obel, Borge. Issues of Organizational Design: A Mathematical Programming View of Organizations. LC 81-82093. (Illus.). 273p. 1981. 122.00 (*0-08-025837-9*, Pub. by Pergamon Repr UK) Franklin.
Obel, Borge, jt. auth. see Burton, R. M.
Obelkevich, James, ed. Religion & the People, 800-1700. LC 78-7847. (Illus.). 351p. reprint ed. pap. 100.10 (*0-8357-3889-2*, 2036621) Bks Demand.
Obelkevich, James & Catterall, Peter, eds. Understanding Post-War British Society. LC 94-7263. 224p. 1995. text ed. 55.00x (*0-415-10939-6*, B4686); pap. text ed. 16.95 (*0-415-10940-X*, B4690) Routledge.
Obelkevich, Jim, et al. Disciplines of Faith. 512p. 1987. 59.95 (*0-7102-0750-6*, RKP); pap. 25.00 (*0-7102-0993-2*, RKP) Routledge.
Obello, Albert R. Flowmeters (Rheology) Index of New Information & Medical Research Bible. 150p. 1994. 44.50 (*0-7883-0124-1*); pap. 39.50 (*0-7883-0125-X*) ABBE Pubs Assn.
Oben, Freda M. Edith Stein: Scholar-Feminist-Saint. LC 87-24178. 80p. 1988. pap. 5.95 (*0-8189-0523-9*) Alba.
Oben, Freda M., tr. Edith Stein Vol. 2: Essays on Woman. 304p. (Orig.). 1987. pap. 8.95 (*0-935216-08-1*) ICS Pubns.
Obenaus, W. Handbook of Business English. 380p. (ENG & GER.). 1990. lib. bdg. 95.00 (*0-8288-3887-9*, F107670) Fr & Eur.
Obenchain, Elaine. The Complete Catalog of Ampico Reproducing Piano Rolls. LC 77-22349. 197p. 1987. reprint ed. 30.00 (*0-911572-62-7*) Vestal.
Obenchain, F. D. & Galun, R., eds. The Physiology of Ticks. (Current Themes in Tropical Science Ser.: Vol. 1). (Illus.). 450p. 1982. 216.00 (*0-08-024937-X*, Pub. by Pergamon Repr UK) Franklin.
Obeng, Eddie. The Project Manager's Secret Handbook: Secrets of Successful Change. (Financial Times Management Ser.). 256p. 1994. 75.00x (*0-273-60762-6*, Pub. by Pitman Pubng UK) St Mut.
— Solving Unique Problems: Implementing Strategy Through Projects. (Financial Times Management Ser.). 240p. 1995. 25.00x (*0-273-60265-9*, Pub. by Pitman Pub UK) Natl Bk Netwk.
Obeng, Eddie & Crainer, Stuart. Making Re-Engineering Happen: The Strategic Thinking & Implementation Processes. (Financial Times Management Ser.). 224p. 1994. 75.00x (*0-273-60424-4*, Pub. by Pitman Pubng UK) St Mut.
Obenhaus, Victor. Ethics for an Industrial Age: A Christian Inquiry. LC 73-15317. 338p. 1975. reprint ed. text ed. 35.00 (*0-8371-7189-X*, OBIA, Greenwood Pr) Greenwood.
Obenhaus, Victor, ed. Religion & Ethical Issues: Position Guides for Decision Making. LC 91-73417. 262p. (Orig.). (C). 1991. pap. 11.95 (*0-913552-47-X*) Exploration Pr.
Obenhouse, Susan, jt. auth. see Dunne, Patrick M.
***Obenski, Kenneth S.** Motorcycle Accident Reconstruction: Understanding Motorcycles. LC 94-22972. (Illus.). 296p. 1994. 55.00 (*0-913875-03-1*, 5031) Lawyers & Judges.
Obenski, Kenneth S., jt. auth. see Brown, John F.
Obenzinger, Hilton. Cannibal Eliot & the Lost Histories of San Francisco. LC 93-12722. 256p. (Orig.). 1993. pap. 12.95 (*1-56279-047-1*) Mercury Hse Inc.
— New York on Fire. LC 89-10224. (Illus.). 144p. (Orig.). 1989. 24.95 (*0-941104-40-0*); pap. 12.95 (*0-941104-39-7*) Real Comet.
Ober, jt. auth. see Caller.
Ober, B. Scott, jt. auth. see Grubbs, Robert L.
Ober, C. K., jt. ed. see Weiss, R. A.
Ober, Carol, illus. How Music Came into the World. LC 93-11330. (J). 1994. 14.95 (*0-395-67523-5*) HM.
Ober, Doris, jt. ed. see Kirschman, Richard.
Ober, Doris, ed. see Roads, Michael J.
Ober, Gary J. Operating Techniques for the Tractor-Loader-Backhoe. (Illus.). 175p. 1983. pap. 24.95 (*0-911785-00-0*) Talus Resources.
Ober, J. Hambleton. Writing: Man's Great Invention. (Illus.). 1965. 19.95 (*0-8392-1139-2*) Astor-Honor.
Ober, Josiah. Mass & Elite in Democratic Athens: Rhetoric, Ideology, & the Power of the People. 408p. 1991. text ed. 55.00 (*0-691-09443-8*); pap. text ed. 17.95 (*0-691-02864-8*) Princeton U Pr.
Ober, Josiah, jt. auth. see Strauss, Barry S.
Ober, Kenneth, tr. see Goldschmidt, Meir.
Ober, Kenneth H. Bibliography of Modern Icelandic Literature in Translation: Supplement 1971-1980. LC 89-46232. (Islandica Ser.: No. 47). 325p. 1990. 44.50 (*0-8014-2475-5*) Cornell U Pr.
Ober, Kenneth H., jt. comp. see Mitchell, P. M.
Ober, Norman, ed. see McQueen-Williams, Moryth & Apisson, Barbara.
Ober, Richard, jt. auth. see Dobbs, David.
Ober, Scot. Contemporary Business Communications. (C). 1991. text ed. 50.76 (*0-395-51211-5*) HM.
Ober, Scot, et al. Gregg College Document Processing. LC 92-24928. 1992. write for info. (*0-02-801729-3*) Glencoe.
— Gregg College Document Processing for Microcomputers: Advanced Course. 7th ed. LC 93-16178. (Gregg College Typing Ser.: Series 6). 1993. write for info. (*0-02-801754-4*) Glencoe.
— Gregg College Document Processing for Microcomputers: Intensive Course. 7th ed. LC 92-46513. (Gregg College Typing Ser.). 1993. write for info. (*0-02-801736-6*) Glencoe.
— Gregg College Document Processing for Microcomputers: Intermediate Course. 7th ed. LC 92-30679. 1992. write for info. (*0-02-801753-6*) Glencoe.
— Gregg College Electronic Document Processing: Advanced Course. 7th ed. LC 93-44424. (Gregg College Typing Ser.: Series Six). 1994. write for info. (*0-02-801719-6*) Glencoe.
— Gregg College Keyboarding & Document Processing for Microcomputers, Complete Course. 7th ed. LC 93-25886. (Gregg College Typing Ser.: Series Six). 1993. write for info. (*0-02-801737-4*) Glencoe.
— Gregg College Keyboarding & Electronic Document Processing: Intensive Course. 7th ed. LC 93-44426. (Gregg College Typing Ser.: Series Six). 1994. write for info. (*0-02-801740-4*) Glencoe.
— Gregg College Typing: Series Six, Kit 1 Basic. 160p. 1988. boxed 24.70 (*0-07-038393-6*) McGraw.
— Gregg College Typing, Series 6: Complete Course. 1989. write for info. (*0-07-048124-5*) McGraw.
— Gregg College Typing, Series 6: Intensive Course. 1989. text ed. write for info. (*0-07-048125-3*) McGraw.
— Keyboarding: Adapted from Gregg College Keyboarding & Document Processing. 3rd ed. LC 93-8355. 1993. write for info. (*0-02-801747-1*) Glencoe.
Ober, Scott, et al. Gregg College Typing, Series 6: Keyboarding Course. (C). 1989. teacher ed 5.95 (*0-07-048114-8*) McGraw.
***Ober, Stuart & Richards, Susan.** The Joy of Marriage. LC 95-94028. (Illus.). 70p. 1995. 9.95 (*0-8464-4341-4*) Beekman Pubs.
Ober, Stuart A., ed. Investment Blue Book, 1994. 284p. 1993. pap. 145.00 (*0-8464-4170-5*) Beekman Pubs.
Ober, W. U., ed. Story of the Three Bears. LC 80-28325. 1981. 50.00 (*0-8201-1362-X*) Schol Facsimiles.
Ober, Warren, jt. auth. see Martin, Walter R.
Ober, William B. Bottoms Up! A Pathologist's Essays on Medicine & the Humanities. 1988. pap. 8.95 (*0-685-44374-4*, PL) HarpC.
— Bottoms Up! A Pathologist's Essays on Medicine & the Humanities. LC 87-13125. (Illus.). 356p. 1987. 19.95 (*0-8093-1419-3*) S Ill U Pr.
Oberacker, R., jt. auth. see Thummler, F.
Oberai, A. S. Migration, Urbanisation & Development. (Background Paper for Training in Population, Human Resources & Development Planning Ser.: No. 5). vi, 108p. (Orig.). 1990. pap. 12.00 (*92-2-106129-9*) Intl Labour Office.
Oberai, Amarjit S. Assessing the Demographic Impact of Developmental Projects: Conceptual, Methodological & Policy Issues. (International Labour Organisation Ser.). 128p. 1991. 74.50 (*0-415-06841-X*, A6190) Routledge.
— State Policies & Internal Migration: Studies in Market & Planned Economies. LC 83-40097. 370p. 1983. text ed. 32.50 (*0-312-75630-5*) St Martin.
Oberai, Amarjit S., ed. Land Settlement Policies & Population Redistribution in Developing Countries: Achievements, Problems & Prospects. LC 87-15837. 416p. 1988. text ed. 59.95 (*0-275-92799-7*, C2799, Praeger Pubs) Greenwood.
Oberai, M. M., tr. see Fuentes, Albert.
Obercht, E., jt. ed. see Favini, A.
Oberdieck, Bernard, tr. see Heuck, Sigrid.
Oberdieck, William. America's Prisoner of War 1943-1946. 1995. 9.95 (*0-8062-4981-1*) Carlton.
Oberdiek, Hans, jt. auth. see Tiles, Mary.
Oberdisse, K., ed. Diabetes Mellitus. (Handbuch der Inneren Medigin Ser.: Vol. 7/2). 1977. 327.00 (*0-387-07741-3*) Spr-Verlag.
***Oberdorfer, Bernd.** Geselligkeit und Realisierung von Sittlichkeit: Die Theorieentwicklung Friedrich Schleiermachers bis 1799. (Theologische Bibliothek Toepelmann Ser.: No. 69). 586p. (GER.). (C). 1995. lib. bdg. 191.75 (*3-11-014595-2*) De Gruyter.
Oberdorfer, Don. TET! The Turning Point in the Vietnam War. (Quality Paperbacks Ser.). (Illus.). 400p. 1984. pap. 11.95 (*0-306-80210-4*) Da Capo.
— The Turn: From the Cold War to a New Era. (Illus.). 512p. 1992. pap. 14.00 (*0-671-79230-X*, Touchstone Bks) S&S Trade.
Oberdorfer, E. Pflanzensoziologische Studien in Chile. (Illus.). 1960. 36.00 (*3-7682-0011-6*) Lubrecht & Cramer.
Oberembt, Kenneth, comp. Annual Reports for College Libraries. (CLIP Note Ser.: No. 10). 135p. 1988. 21.95 (*0-8389-7219-5*); 18.75 (*0-685-67652-8*) Assn Coll & Res Libs.
Oberer, Walter & Meinsy, Timothy. Statutory Supplement to Cases & Materials on Labor Law: Collective Bargaining in a Free Society. 4th ed. (American Casebook Ser.). 180p. Date not set. pap. text ed. 12.00 (*0-314-03247-9*) West Pub.
Oberer, Walter E. & Hanslowe, Kurt L. Labor Law: Collective Bargaining in a Free Society, Cases & Materials. 4th ed. Heinsz, Timothy J., ed. (American Casebook Ser.). 859p. 1994. pap. text ed. 46.00 (*0-314-03248-7*) West Pub.
Oberer, Walter E. & Heinsz, Tim. Labor Law: Collective Bargaining in a Free Society, 1991 Case Supplement, Cases & Materials On. 3rd ed. (American Casebook Ser.). 54p. (C). 1991. pap. text ed. 8.00 (*0-314-92861-8*) West Pub.

O

An Asterisk (*) at the beginning of an entry indicates that the title is appearing in BIP for the first time.

***Oberer, Walter E., et al.** Labor Law: Collective Bargaining in Free Society. 4th ed. (American Casebook Ser.). 80p. (C). 1995. teacher ed, pap. text ed. write for info. (*0-314-04826-X*) West Pub.

— Labor Law, Collective Bargaining in a Free Society. 3rd ed. (American Casebook Ser.). 1163p. 1991. reprint ed. text ed. 49.00 (*0-314-25183-9*) West Pub.

— Labor Law, Collective Bargaining in a Free Society, Teacher's Manual to Accompany Cases & Materials On. 3rd ed. (American Casebook Ser.). 95p. (C). 1990. pap. text ed. write for info. (*0-314-80212-6*) West Pub.

— Statutory Supplement to Labor Law: Collective Bargaining in a Free Society. 3rd ed. (American Casebook Ser.). 172p. 1986. pap. text ed. 12.00 (*0-314-25469-2*) West Pub.

Oberg, Alcestis R. Spacefarers of the Eighties & Nineties: The Next Thousand People in Space. (Illus.). 320p. 1985. text ed. 36.50 (*0-231-05906-X*) Col U Pr.

Oberg, Arthur. Anna's Song. Webber, Joan M. & Blessing, Richard, eds. LC 79-4847. 112p. 1980. 15.00 (*0-295-95681-X*) U of Wash Pr.

Oberg, B., jt. auth. see Oxford, John S.

Oberg, Barbara B. & Stout, Harry S., eds. Benjamin Franklin, Jonathan Edwards, & the Representation of American Culture. LC 92-34327. 240p. 1993. 35.00 (*0-19-507775-X*) OUP.

Oberg, Barbara B., ed. see Franklin, Benjamin.

***Oberg, Brent C.** Forensics: The Winner's Guide to Speech Contests. Zapel, Theodore O., ed. 192p. (Orig.). (YA). (gr. 9 up). Date not set. pap. text ed. 12.95 (*1-56608-015-0*) Meriwether Pub.

— Speechcraft: An Introduction to Public Speaking. LC 94-21529. 1994. 12.95 (*1-56608-006-1*) Meriwether Pub.

***Oberg, Charles N., et al. America's Children: Triumph or Tragedy. 94p. 1994. pap. 22.50 (*0-87553-218-7*) Am Pub Health.**
America's children are in a state of crisis. Their representation among the poor & disadvantaged has grown at an unprecedented rate. This book delineates the dimensions of the problem by presenting tragic cases & aggregate data. To foster children's potential for autonomy, the authors propose a solution in the form of an Integrated Children's Network, which consists of six interlocking "gears" necessary for the health of our children: economic security, medical care, shelter, proper nutrition, child care, & early education. Nonmembers: $22.50 APHA Members: $15.75. ***Publisher Provided Annotation.***

Oberg, Charlotte H. A Pagan Prophet, William Morris. LC 77-4730. 199p. reprint ed. pap. 56.80 (*0-8357-3281-9*, 2039504) Bks Demand.

Oberg, Craig J., jt. ed. see Sessions, Gene A.

Oberg, Delroy, comp. Daily Readings with a Modern Mystic: Selections from the Writings of Evelyn Underhill. LC 93-60276. 176p. (Orig.). 1993. pap. 9.95 (*0-89622-566-6*) Twenty-Third.

Oberg, Eric. Machinery's Handbook. 24th ed. 1992. 65.00 (*0-8311-2492-X*); 75.00 (*0-8311-2424-5*) Indus Pr.

Oberg, Erick V. Draftsman's Mathematical Manual. 2nd ed. LC 41-20206. 271p. reprint ed. pap. 77.30 (*0-317-08775-4*, 2001911) Bks Demand.

Oberg, Faye, jt. auth. see Johnson, Dale.

Oberg, James. UFOs & Outer Space Mysteries. LC 81-3193. 1982. pap. 6.95 (*0-89865-102-6*) Donning Co.

Oberg, James E. Red Star in Orbit. (Illus.). 1981. 16.95 (*0-394-51429-7*) Random.

— Uncovering Soviet Disasters. LC 87-42658. (Illus.). 336p. 1988. 19.95 (*0-394-56095-7*) Random.

Oberg, Jan, jt. ed. see Nakarada, Radmila.

Oberg, Kalervo. Indian Tribes of Northern Mato Grosso, Brazil. LC 76-44770. (Smithsonian Institution. Institute of Social Anthropology. Publication Ser.: No. 15). reprint ed. 42.50 (*0-404-15958-3*) AMS Pr.

— The Terena & the Caduveo of Southern Mato Grosso, Brazil. LC 76-44771. (Smithsonian Institution. Institute of Social Anthropology. Publication Ser.: No. 9). reprint ed. 42.50 (*0-404-15959-1*) AMS Pr.

Oberg, Larry R., comp. Human Services in Postrevolutionary Cuba: An Annotated International Bibliography. LC 83-26527. xvi, 433p. 1984. text ed. 59.95 (*0-313-23125-7*, OHS/, Greenwood Pr) Greenwood.

Oberg, P. A., jt. ed. see Shepherd, A. P.

Oberg, Pearl, jt. auth. see Stanley, Samuel.

Oberg, Sture, jt. auth. see Shachar, Arie.

Obergfell, jt. auth. see Shover, B.

***Obergfell, Ann M., ed.** Law & Ethics in Diagnostic Imaging & Therapeutic Radiology: With Risk Management & Safety Applications. LC 95-10278. (Illus.). 208p. 1995. text ed. 29.95 (*0-7216-5062-7*) Saunders.

Obergfoll, Michael. Super Santa of All Space & Beyond Assisted by His Galaxy Elves. (Illus.). 38p. (J). (gr. 2-12). 1988. 2.95 (*0-929052-00-5*) Super Santa Prodns.

— Super Santa of All Space & Beyond Assisted by His Galaxy Elves: Coloring Activity Book. LC 72-847. (Illus.). 34p. (J). (gr. 2-12). 1988. 10.95 (*0-929052-01-3*) Super Santa Prodns.

Oberguggenberger, Michael B. & Rosinger, Elemer E. Solution of Continuous Nonlinear PDEs Through Order Completion. LC 94-19266. (Mathematics Studies: Vol. 181). 1994. 143.00 (*0-444-82035-3*, North Holland) Elsevier.

***Oberhaus, Dorothy H.** Emily Dickinson's Fascicles. (Illus.). 392p. 1995. 40.00 (*0-271-01337-0*) Pa St U Pr.

Oberhaus, Mary A., et al. Computerized Test Bank to Accompany Professional Selling. (C). 1993. teacher ed, disk 20.00 (*0-03-078189-2*) Dryden Pr.

— Professional Selling: A Relationship Process. LC 92-75903. 695p. (C). 1993. pap. text ed. 8.50 (*0-03-097024-5*) Dryden Pr.

— Professional Selling: A Relationship Process. LC 92-75903. 695p. (C). 1993. MacIntosh. disk 20.00 (*0-03-097904-8*) Dryden Pr.

— Professional Selling: A Relationship Process. LC 92-75903. 695p. (C). 1993. text ed. 54.75 (*0-03-032769-5*); trans. 207.50 (*0-03-097051-2*) Dryden Pr.

— Video Manual to Accompany Professional Selling. 48p. (C). 1993. teacher ed, vhs 8.50 (*0-03-098167-0*) Dryden Pr.

Oberheid, K., jt. auth. see Bonnyman, D.

Oberhelman, Harley D. Ernesto Sabato. LC 72-99548. (Twayne's World Authors Ser.). lib. bdg. 17.95 (*0-686-60836-4*) Irvington.

— The Presence of Faulkner in the Writings of Garcia Marquez. (Graduate Studes: No. 22). (Illus.). 43p. 1980. pap. 7.00 (*0-89672-080-2*) Tex Tech Univ Pr.

Oberhelman, Harvey D. Gabriel Garcia Marquez: A Study of the Short Fiction. (Twayne's Studies in Short Fiction: No. 24). 168p. 1991. text ed. 22.95 (*0-8057-8333-4*, Pub. by Royal Botanic Garden UK) Macmillan.

Oberhelman, Steve M., ed. The Oneirocriticon of Achmet: A Medieval Greek & Arabic Treatise on the Interpretation of Dreams. 320p. 1991. 39.00 (*0-89672-262-7*) Tex Tech Univ Pr.

Oberhelman, Steve M., et al, eds. Epic & Epoch: Essays on the Interpretation & History of a Genre. LC 93-33649. (Studies in Comparative Literature: Vol. 24). 320p. (C). 1994. text ed. 30.00 (*0-89672-331-3*) Tex Tech Univ Pr.

Oberhelman, Steven M. Rhetoric & Homiletics in Fourth-Century Christian Literature: Prose Rhythm, Oratorical Style, & Preaching in the Works of Ambrose, Jerome, & Augustine. 199p. 1991. 29.95 (*1-55540-617-3*); pap. 19.95 (*1-55540-618-1*) Scholars Pr GA.

Oberhettinger, F. Fourier Transformations of Distributions & Their Inverses: A Collection of Tables. 1973. text ed. 95.00 (*0-12-523650-6*) Acad Pr.

— Tables of Bessel Transforms. LC 72-88727. 289p. 1972. pap. 34.00 (*0-387-05997-0*) Spr-Verlag.

— Tables of Mellin Transforms. vii, 275p. 1975. pap. 34.00 (*0-387-06942-9*) Spr-Verlag.

Oberhofer, Ed S. & Vermillion, Robert E. Experimental Physics I: A Laboratory Manual. 208p. (C). 1993. pap. text ed., spiral bd. 12.95 (*0-8403-8531-5*) Kendall-Hunt.

Oberhofer, Martin, ed. Advances in Radiation Protection. (C). 1991. lib. bdg. 127.00 (*0-7923-1232-5*) Kluwer Ac.

— Techniques & Management of Personnel Thermoluminescence Dosimetry Services: Based on the Lectures Given During the Eurocourse Techniques & Management of Thermoluminescence Dosimetry Held at the Joint Research Centre, Ispra, Italy, October 19-23, 1992. 446p. (C). 1993. lib. bdg. 165.00 (*0-7923-2436-6*) Kluwer Ac.

Oberholser, Warren L. Mind Aerobics. 176p. 1992. pap. 10.00 (*0-9633500-0-5*) WarVic Prods.

***Oberholtzer, Della.** Katie & the Neighbors. 1995. pap. 3.50 (*0-87813-559-6*) Christian Light.

Oberholtzer, Ellis P. Jay Cooke: Financier of the Civil War, 2 Vols. LC 68-18222. (Library of Money & Banking History). 1968. reprint ed. 95.00 (*0-678-00363-7*) Kelley.

— The Morals of the Movie. LC 74-160244. (Moving Pictures Ser.). 251p. 1971. reprint ed. lib. bdg. 28.95 (*0-89198-045-8*) Ozer.

— The Referendum in America. LC 71-119939. (Select Bibliographies Reprint Ser.). 1977. reprint ed. 20.95 (*0-8369-5382-7*) Ayer.

— The Referendum in America. LC 70-153370. (American Constitutional & Legal History Ser). 1971. reprint ed. lib. bdg. 59.50 (*0-306-70149-9*) Da Capo.

Oberholtzer, Ellsi P. Jay Cooke, Financier of the Civil War, 2 vols., Set. 1993. reprint ed. lib. bdg. 150.00 (*0-7812-5498-1*) Rprt Serv.

— Philadelphia, a History of the City & Its People, 4 vols., Set. 1993. reprint ed. lib. bdg. 300.00 (*0-7812-5499-X*) Rprt Serv.

Oberholtzer, Kenneth E. American Agricultural Problems in the Social Studies. LC 73-177125. (Columbia University. Teachers College. Contributions to Education Ser.: No. 718). reprint ed. 37.50 (*0-404-55718-X*) AMS Pr.

Oberhuber, Konrad. Drawings Defined. 440p. 1987. 69.50 (*0-89835-274-6*) Abaris Bks.

— Poussin - The Early Years in Rome: The Origins of French Classicism. LC 88-9173. (Illus.). 368p. 1988. 65.00 (*1-55595-002-7*); pap. 24.95 (*1-55595-003-5*) Kimbell Art.

Oberhuber, Konrad, ed. Illustrated Bartsch, Vol. 26: The Works of Marcantonio Raimondi. LC 79-50679. 1978. 140.00 (*0-913870-90-0*) Abaris Bks.

— Illustrated Bartsch, Vol. 27: The Works of Marcantonio Raimondi. LC 79-50679. 1978. 140.00 (*0-685-51903-1*) Abaris Bks.

Oberhuber, Konrad & Robinson, William W., eds. Master Drawings & Watercolors: The Hofer Collection. LC 84-1567. (Illus.). 129p. (Orig.). 1984. pap. 12.00 (*0-317-13558-9*) Harvard Art Mus.

Oberhuber, Konrad, tr. see Steiner, Rudolf.

Oberhummer, H. Nuclei in the Cosmos. Birman, J. L. et al, eds. (Graduate Texts in Contemporary Physics Ser.). (Illus.). xii, 236p. 1991. 69.50 (*0-387-54198-5*) Spr-Verlag.

Oberkotter, Mildred, et al, eds. The Possible Dream: Mainstream Experiences of Hearing-Impaired Students. (Centennial Celebration Ser.). 68p. (Orig.). (YA). 1990. pap. text ed. 7.95 (*0-88200-171-X*) Alexander Graham.

Oberlander, Clyde G., ed. see Oberlander, June R.

Oberlander, Cornelia H., jt. auth. see Nadel, Ira B.

Oberlander, June R. Measurable Parameters to Profile Child Development from "Slow & Steady, Get Me Ready" The How-to Book That Grows with the Child. Oberlander, Clyde G., ed. 8p. (Orig.). 1993. pap. 3.95 (*0-9622322-3-8*) Bio-Alpha.

— Parametros Mensurables Para Perfilar el Desarrollo Del Nino de "Slow & Steady, Get Me Ready" El Libro de Instrucciones Que Crece Con el Nino. Oberlander, Clyde G., ed. Roig, Jose G., tr. (Illus.). 8p. (Orig.). (SPA.). (J). (ps). 1994. pap. 3.95 (*0-9622322-6-2*) Bio-Alpha.

— Slow & Steady, Get Me Ready: A How-to Book That Grows with the Child. rev. ed. Oberlander, Clyde G., ed. (Illus.). 344p. (Orig.). 1992. pap. 17.95 (*0-9622322-1-1*) Bio-Alpha.

— Slow & Steady, Get Me Ready - Despacio y Constantemente, Preparenme: El Libro de Instrucciones que Crece Con Su Nino. Sosa, Juan, ed. Roig, Jose G., tr. (Illus.). 344p. (Orig.). (SPA.). 1994. pap. 17.95 (*0-9622322-4-6*) Bio-Alpha.

Oberlander, Theodore M. & Miller, Robert A. Essentials of Physical Geography. 2nd ed. 608p. (C). 1987. text ed. 34.95 (*0-394-36280-2*) Random.

Oberlander, Theodore M. & Muller, Robert A. Essentials of Physical Geography Today. 493p. (C). 1982. text ed. write for info. (*0-394-32543-5*) Random.

— Essentials of Physical Geography Today. 2nd ed. 1987. text ed. write for info. (*0-07-556615-X*) McGraw.

Oberlander, Theodore M., jt. auth. see Muller, Robert A.

Oberle, jt. ed. see Edgley.

Oberle, Joseph G. Anchorage. LC 89-26068. (Downtown America Ser.). (Illus.). 60p. (J). (gr. 3 up). 1990. text ed. 13.95 (*0-87518-420-0*, Dillon Silver Burdett) Silver Burdett Pr.

Oberle, William F. Calculus & the Computer. (C). 1986. pap. text ed. 50.50 (*0-201-15983-X*) Addison-Wesley.

Oberlender, Garold. Project Management for Engineers. 1993. text ed. write for info. (*0-07-048150-4*) McGraw.

Oberlender, Garold D., ed. Earthmoving & Heavy Equipment. (Conference Proceedings Ser.). 201p. 1986. 21.00 (*0-87262-548-6*) Am Soc Civil Eng.

Oberlender, Gary, jt. auth. see Peurifoy, Robert L.

Oberley, Edith T. & Glass, Neal R. Understanding Kidney Transplantation. (Illus.). 160p. (C). 1987. 33.95 (*0-398-05277-8*) C C Thomas.

Oberley, Edith T. & Oberley, Terry D. Understanding Your New Life with Dialysis: A Patient Guide for Physical & Psychological Adjustment. 4th ed. (Illus.). 194p. (C). 1992. pap. text ed. 31.95x (*0-398-05774-5*) C C Thomas.

Oberley, Larry W., ed. Superoxide Dismutase, Vol. I. 168p. 1982. 144.00 (*0-8493-6240-7*, QP603, CRC Reprint) Franklin.

— Superoxide Dismutase, Vol. II. 192p. 1982. 132.00 (*0-8493-6241-5*, CRC Reprint) Franklin.

— Superoxide Dismutase: Pathological States, Vol. III. 280p. 1985. 179.00 (*0-8493-6242-3*, QP603, CRC Reprint) Franklin.

Oberley, Terry D., jt. auth. see Oberley, Edith T.

Oberlin Colloquium in Philosophy Staff. Issues in the Philosophy of Language: Proceedings of the Oberlin Colloquium in Philosophy, 13th, Oberlin College, 1972. MacKay, Alfred F. & Merrill, Daniel D., eds. LC 75-18178. 176p. reprint ed. pap. 50.20 (*0-317-29278-1*, 2022018) Bks Demand.

— Perception & Personal Identity: Proceedings. Care, Norman S. et al, eds. LC 68-9427. 205p. reprint ed. pap. 58.50 (*0-317-08114-4*, 2003253) Bks Demand.

***Oberlin, Loriann H.** Writing for Money: Dozens of Ways to Boost Your Freelance Writing Income. LC 94-27112. 256p. 1995. 17.99 (*0-89879-654-7*) Writers Digest.

Oberlin, Sally, et al. A Quick Course in Windows 3.1. (Quick Course Computer Book Ser.). (Illus.). 144p. (Orig.). 1992. pap. 12.95 (*1-879399-14-8*) Online Pr.

Oberling, Pierre. The Road to Bellapais: The Turkish Cypriot Exodus to Northern Cyprus. (Brooklyn College Studies on Society in Change). 256p. 1982. text ed. 48.00 (*0-88033-000-7*) East Eur Quarterly.

Oberlink, jt. auth. see Butler.

Oberly, James W. Sixty Million Acres: American Veterans & Public Lands Before the Civil War. LC 90-4482. 234p. 1990. 28.00 (*0-87338-421-0*) Kent St U Pr.

Oberly, Jim. Settlement & Survival (Supplement) Building Towns in the Chippewa Valley, 1850-1925, a Case Study. McLeod, Susan, ed. (Illus.). 16p. (Orig.). 1994. 3.00 (*0-9636191-2-8*) Chippewa Val Mus.

Oberly, R. E., et al. General Physics Two Hundred Two: Laboratory Manual. 104p. (C). 1984. pap. text ed. 9.95 (*0-89917-442-6*) Tichenor Pub.

Obermaier, Ernst, jt. auth. see Held, Werner.

Obermaier, Hugo. Fossil Man in Spain. LC 70-121293. reprint ed. 49.50 (*0-404-04809-9*) AMS Pr.

— Fossil Man in Spain. LC 24-25757. (Illus.). 495p. 1969. reprint ed. text ed. 65.00 (*0-8371-1504-3*, OBFM, Greenwood Pr) Greenwood.

Obermaier, Otto G. & Morvillo, Robert G., eds. White Collar Crime: Business & Regulatory Offenses. 800p. 1990. ring bd. 110.00 (*0-317-05403-1*, 00610) NY Law Pub.

Oberman, Albert, et al. Principles & Management of Lipid Disorders: A Primary Care Approach. (Illus.). 368p. 1992. 49.00 (*0-683-06623-4*) Williams & Wilkins.

Oberman, David. The Science of Humanity. 359p. 1985. 59.00 (*0-7212-0716-2*, Pub. by Regency Press) St Mut.

Oberman, Heiko A. The Dawn of the Reformation: Essays in Late Medieval & Early Reformation Thought. 320p. 1986. 35.95 (*0-567-09371-9*, Pub. by T & T Clark UK) Bks Intl VA.

— The Dawn of the Reformation: Essays in Late Medieval & Early Reformation Thought. 320p. (C). 1992. reprint ed. pap. 29.99 (*0-8028-0655-4*) Eerdmans.

— Forerunners of the Reformation: The Shape of Late Medieval Thought, Illustrated by Key Documents: Nyhus, Paul L., tr. LC 81-66518. 347p. reprint ed. pap. 98.90 (*0-685-17052-7*, 2027175) Bks Demand.

— The Harvest of Medieval Theology: Gabriel Biel & Late Medieval Nominalism. LC 82-20896. 512p. (C). 1983. reprint ed. pap. 18.50 (*0-939464-05-5*) Labyrinth Pr.

— The Impact of the Reformation: Essays. LC 93-42559. 256p. (Orig.). (C). 1994. pap. text ed. 19.99 (*0-8028-0732-1*) Eerdmans.

— Luther. 1992. 15.00 (*0-385-42278-4*) Doubleday.

— The Reformation: Roots & Ramifications. 288p. (Orig.). 1994. pap. text ed. 29.99 (*0-8028-0825-5*) Eerdmans.

Oberman, Heiko A. & James, Frank A., III, eds. Via Augustini: Augustine in the Later Middle Ages, Renaissance & Reformation. LC 91-6912. (Studies in Medieval & Reformation Thought: No. 48). 242p. 1991. 65.75 (*90-04-09364-8*) E J Brill.

Oberman, Heiko A., jt. ed. see Dykema, Peter A.

Oberman, Joseph & Bingham, Robert. Planning & Managing the Economy of the City: Policy Guidelines for the Metropolitan Mayor. LC 72-79544. (Special Studies in U. S. Economic, Social & Political Issues). 1972. 29.50 (*0-275-06160-4*) Irvington.

Oberman, Lola. Dial B for Birder: Private Files of a Real Life Bird Detective. Liinder, Greg, ed. 200p. (Orig.). 1992. pap. 12.95 (*1-55971-186-8*) NorthWord.

— The Pleasure of Watching Birds. 224p. 1991. 22.95 (*0-8027-1166-9*); pap. 12.95 (*0-8027-7354-0*) Walker & Co.

Oberman, Sheldon. The Always Prayer Shawl. (Illus.). 32p. (J). (gr. 2 up). 1994. 14.95 (*1-878093-22-3*) Boyds Mills Pr.

— Lion in the Lake - Le Lion dans le Lac. (Illus.). 56p. (ENG & FRE.). (J). (gr. k-3). 1988. 14.95 (*0-920541-36-4*) Peguis Pubs Ltd.

— The White Stone of Casa Loma. LC 93-61791. (Illus.). 24p. (J). (gr. 1-6). 1995. 16.95 (*0-88776-333-2*) Tundra Bks.

Oberman, Wendy. Family of Strangers. large type ed. (Charnwood Romance Ser.). 576p. 1987. 23.95 (*0-7089-8431-2*, Charnwood) Ulverscroft.

Obermann, C. Esco. The History of Vocational Rehabilitation in America. Phillips, William R. & Rosenberg, Janet, eds. LC 79-6919. (Physically Handicapped in Society Ser.). 1980. reprint ed. lib. bdg. 37.95 (*0-405-13128-3*) Ayer.

Obermann, Julian. New Discoveries at Karatepe. (Connecticut Academy of Arts & Sciences Ser., Trans.: Vol. 38). 1949. pap. 39.50 (*0-685-22903-3*) Elliots Bks.

Obermann, Julian, ed. Nissim Ibn Shahin: The Arabic Original of Ibn Shahin's Book of Comfort. LC 78-63561. (Yale Oriental Series: Researches: No. 17). reprint ed. 72.50 (*0-404-60287-8*) AMS Pr.

***Obermann, W. R.** Radiology of Carpal Instability: A Practical Approach. 200p. 1994. 205.75 (*0-444-82080-9*) Elsevier.

Obermayer, et al. Dunlap-Hanna: Pennsylvania Forms, 13 vols. 1985. Updates. ring bd. write for info. (*0-8205-1260-5*) Bender.

Obermayer, A., jt. auth. see Herd, E. W.

Obermayer, Heinz. Diccionario Biblico Manual. 3rd ed. 352p. (SPA.). 1987. pap. 14.95 (*0-7859-4887-2*) Fr & Eur.

— Kleines Stuttgarter-Bibellexikon. 3rd ed. 344p. (GER.). 1976. 24.95 (*0-8288-5719-9*, M7507) Fr & Eur.

Obermayr, Ray. Double You Double You Too. (Illus.). 40p. (Orig.). 1991. pap. 15.00 (*0-931659-11-6*) Limberlost Pr.

Obermeier, Bernhardt & Slaby, Wolfgang. Ilias Latina: Concordantia in Iliadem Latinam. Vol. CXV. 290p. write for info. (*0-318-71962-2*, Pub. by Georg Olms GW) Lubrecht & Cramer.

Obermeier, Bernhardt & Slaby, Wolfgang, eds. Ilias Latina - Concordantia in Iliadem Latinam. Bd. CXV. Date not set. write for info. (*0-318-71152-4*, Pub. by Georg Olms GW) Lubrecht & Cramer.

Obermeier, Klaus. Neural Network Primer: Economics of a New Technology. (Information Technology Ser.). 275p. 1991. pap. 38.00 (*0-13-612821-1*, 330804) P-H.

***Obermeier, Otto-Peter & Schuez, Mathias, eds.** Risk - Paradise Lost or Gained? A Holistic Approach to the Environment. LC 95-6438. (Illus.). 396p. (C). 1995. text ed. write for info. (*0-89876-230-8*) Gardner Pr.

***Obermeyer, Carla M., ed.** Family, Gender, & Population in the Middle East: Policies in Context. 240p. 1995. 35.00 (*977-424-357-9*, Pub. by Am Univ Cairo Pr UA) Col U Pr.

Obermeyer, Nancy J. Bureaucrats, Clients, & Geography: The Bailly Nuclear Power Plant Battle in Northern Indiana. (Research Papers Ser.: No. 216). (Illus.). 140p. 1989. pap. write for info. (*0-89065-121-3*) U Chicago Comm Geo.

Obermeyer, Nancy J. & Pinto, Jeffrey K. Managing Geographic Information Systems. LC 93-47119. 226p. 1994. lib. bdg. 30.00 (*0-89862-005-8*) Guilford Pubns.

Obermeyer, Thomas. Architectural CAD Lab Manual. 216p. 1985. text ed. 15.95 (*0-07-047509-1*) McGraw.

— Architectural Technology. 1976. text ed. 39.95 (*0-07-047496-6*) McGraw.

— Architecture Drawing. 1992. pap. 27.95 (*0-02-800415-9*) Macmillan.

O

— AutoCAD Architectural Lab Manual. 216p. 1987. spiral bd. 17.95 (0-07-047524-5) McGraw.

Obermeyer, Vera & Rifkin, Lori. Finding a Preschool for Your Child in San Francisco. 202p. 1993. pap. 14.95 (0-9635882-0-6) Lrning Assocs.

Obermiller, E. The Doctrine of Prajna-Paramita As Exposed in the Abhisamayalamkara of Maitreya. 153p. 1984. reprint ed. lib. bdg. 22.50 (0-88181-002-9) Canon Pubns.

— Nirvana in Tibetan Buddhism. Sobti, Harcharan S., ed. (C). 1987. 11.50 (81-85132-03-8) S Asia.

Obermiller, E., tr. see Maitreya, Aryasanga.

Obermiller, Philip J., jt. ed. see Borman, Kathryn M.

Obermiller, Phillip J. & Philliber, William W., eds. Appalachia in an International Context. LC 94-6380. 256p. 1994. text ed. 55.00 (0-275-94835-8, Praeger Pubs) Greenwood.

Obermiller, Phillip J., jt. ed. see Borman, Kathryn M.

Obermiller, Phillip J., jt. ed. see Philliber, William W.

Obermire. Selected Examples of the Plant Kingdom. 1980. pap. 14.75 (0-88246-059-5) Oreg St U Bkstrs.

Obern, Jane & Waldron, Valarie, eds. NAHC Wild Game Cookbook, 1987. (Illus.). 192p. (Orig.). 1986. spiral bd., pap. 14.95 (0-914697-11-0) N Amer Outdoor Grp.

Oberndorfer, Anne, jt. auth. see Oberndorfer, Marx.

Oberndorfer, Marx & Oberndorfer, Anne. Noels: A Collection of Christmas Carols. 144p. 1932. 8.50 (0-912222-05-0, R2582751); pap. 4.00 (0-912222-06-9) FitzSimons.

Oberoi, A. S. Support of the Shaken Sangat: Meetings with Three Masters. Perkins, Russell, ed. LC 84-50911. (Illus.). 256p. (Orig.). 1984. pap. 15.00 (0-89142-043-6) Sant Bani Ash.

Oberoi, Harjot. The Construction of Religious Boundaries: Culture, Identity & Diversity in the Sikh Tradition. xxii, 4994p. 1994. pap. text ed. 17.95 (0-226-61593-6) U Ch Pr.

— The Construction of Religious Boundaries: Culture, Identity & Diversity in the Sikh Tradition. xxii, 4994p. 1994. lib. bdg. 49.95 (0-226-61592-8) U Ch Pr.

Oberon, Jake. Snakes As a New Pet. (Illus.). 64p. (Orig.). 1990. pap. 5.95 (0-86622-623-0, TU-015) TFH Pubns.

Oberrecht, Kenn. Angler's Guide to Jigs & Jigging. (Illus.). 342p. 1991. pap. 14.95 (0-88317-161-9) Stoeger Pub Co.

— Driving the Pacific Coast: California: Scenic Driving Tours along the Pacific Coast Highway. 2nd ed. LC 94-854. (Illus.). 272p. (Orig.). 1994. pap. 12.95 (1-56440-400-5) Globe Pequot.

— Driving the Pacific Coast: Oregon & Washington: Scenic Driving Tours along Pacific Coastal Highways. 2nd ed. LC 93-31814. (Voyager Book Ser.). (Illus.). 256p. 1993. pap. 12.95 (1-56440-271-1) Globe Pequot.

— Home Book of Picture Framing: Professional Secrets of Mounting, Matting, Framing, & Displaying Artwork, Photographs, Posters, Collectibles, Carvings, & More. LC 88-15452. (Illus.). 272p. (Orig.). 1988. pap. 19.95 (0-8117-2250-3) Stackpole.

— How to Open & Operate a Home-Based Crafts Business: An Unabridged Guide. LC 94-26657. (Illus.). 224p. 1994. pap. 14.95 (1-56440-485-4) Globe Pequot.

— How to Open & Operate a Home-Based Photography Business: An Unabridged Guide. LC 93-22783. 224p. (Orig.). 1993. pap. 14.95 (1-56440-241-X) Globe Pequot.

O

***Oberrecht, Kenn, ed.** Cabinets & Built-Ins. LC 94-6950. 1995. pap. 14.95 (1-880029-41-3) Creative Homeowner.

Oberreuter, Ray. A Camera Repairman's Guide to Practical Photography. 178p. 1991. pap. 15.95 (0-9630169-0-3) Grassroots.

Oberrheinisches Kardiologen Symposium Staff. Betarezeptoren in der Kardiologie - Probleme aus klinischer Sicht: Proceedings of the Symposium, 1st, Bad Krozingen, October, 1977. Roskamm, H., ed. (Cardiology Journal: Vol. 63, Suppl. 1). (Illus.). (FRE & GER.). 1978. 13.00 (3-8055-2870-1) S Karger.

O'Berry, Little & Fields Staff. Storytime Around the Curriculum: A Comprehensive Early Childhood Curriculum Presented Through Literature. 1992. pap. 29.95 (0-933212-03-8) Partner Pr.

Oberschall, Anthony. Social Movements: Ideologies, Interests & Identities. 402p. (C). 1993. text ed. 39.95 (1-56000-011-2) Transaction Pubs.

Oberschelp, Reinhard, ed. Gesamtverzeichnis des Deutschsprachigen Schrifttums, 1911 to 1965, 150 vols., Set. 77000p. 1981. lib. bdg. 9,300.00 (3-7940-5600-0) U Pubns Amer.

Oberschulte, William, ed. Wood-Frame House Construction. 336p. (Orig.). 1992. pap. 19.75 (0-934041-74-1) Craftsman.

Oberst, B. B. & Long, J. L. Computers in Private Practice Management. (Illus.). 290p. 1987. 79.00 (0-387-96502-5) Spr-Verlag.

Oberst, B. B. & Reid, R. A., eds. Computer Application to Private Office Practices. (Illus.). 145p. 1984. 60.00 (0-387-90933-8) Spr-Verlag.

Oberstone, Joelee. Management Science: Concepts, Insights, & Applications. Perlee, Clyde, ed. 660p. (C). 1990. text ed. 67.50 (0-314-47360-2) West Pub.

Obert, David L. Philippine Defender: A Fighter Pilot's Diary, 1941-1942. LC 92-71109. 175p. (Orig.). 1992. pap. 14.95 (0-927562-12-X) Levite Apache.

Obert, Edward F. Internal Combustion Engines & Air Pollution. 736p. (C). 1990. text ed. 83.50 (0-7002-2183-2) HarpCollege.

Obert, Jessie C. Community Nutrition. 2nd ed. 496p. (C). 1986. text ed. write for info. (0-02-389020-7) Macmillan.

Obert, Leonard & Durall, Wilbur I. Rock Mechanics & the Design of Structures in Rock. LC 66-26753. 669p. reprint ed. pap. 180.00 (0-317-28074-0, 2055766) Bks Demand.

***Obert, Lois C.** Help! Willie's Choking! A Young Child's Introduction to the Heimlich Manuever. Fitting, JanaSue, ed. LC 94-76883. (Illus.). 20p. (J). (ps-3). 1994. teacher ed, spiral bd. 17.95 (0-923889-49-3) Inquisitors Pub.

Oberteuffer, Delbert. Personal Hygiene for College Students. LC 77-177126. (Columbia University. Teachers College. Contributions to Education Ser.: No. 407). (C). reprint ed. 37.50 (0-404-55407-5) AMS Pr.

Oberth, Hermann. Primer for Those Who Would Govern. 320p. 1986. pap. 20.00 (0-914301-06-3) West-Art.

Oberthur, R. C., jt. auth. see Rennie, A. R.

Oberti, Martha, tr. see Schreuder, Sally A.

Oberto, Martino. Anaphilosophia. Salamone, Rosa Maria & Carravetta, Peter, trs. LC 78-58984. (Illus.). 1984. pap. 17.95 (0-915570-10-6) Oolp Pr.

Obertynski, Z., ed. The Cracow Pontifical. (Henry Bradshaw Society Publication Ser.: No. C (100)). 1970. 30.00 (0-907077-17-X) Boydell & Brewer.

Oberwager, Jerome. How to Print Posters (UNESCO) (Education Studies & Documents: No. 3). 1969. reprint ed. pap. 15.00 (0-8115-1327-0) Periodicals Srv.

Oberwinkler, jt. ed. see Hertel, H.

Oberwinkler, F., jt. auth. see Vanky, K.

Obery, Ingrid, jt. ed. see Moss, Glenn.

Obeyd-i-Zakani. Gorby & the Rats. Pound, Omar, tr. LC 89-4754. (Illus.). 60p. 1989. 18.95 (1-55728-100-9); pap. 9.95 (1-55728-101-7) U of Ark Pr.

Obeyesekere, Gananath. The Apotheosis of Captain Cook: European Myth-Making in the Pacific. (Illus.). 272p. 1992. text ed. 39.50 (0-691-05680-3) Princeton U Pr.

— Apotheosis of Captain Cook: European Mythmaking in the Pacific. (C). 1994. pap. 12.95 (0-691-03621-7) Princeton U Pr.

— The Cult of the Goddess Pattini. LC 83-5884. (Illus.). 629p. (C). 1984. lib. bdg. 42.50 (0-226-61602-9) U Ch Pr.

— Medusa's Hair: An Essay on Personal Symbols & Religious Experiences. LC 80-27372. (Illus.). 240p. 1984. pap. text ed. 10.95 (0-226-61601-0) U Ch Pr.

— The Work of Culture: Symbolic Transformation in Psychoanalysis & Anthropology. LC 90-10904. (Lewis Henry Morgan Lectures, 1982). 352p. 1990. pap. text ed. 17.95 (0-226-61599-5) U Ch Pr.

— The Work of Culture: Symbolic Transformation in Psychoanalysis & Anthropology. LC 90-10904. (Lewis Henry Morgan Lectures, 1982). 352p. 1990. lib. bdg. 49.95 (0-226-61598-7) U Ch Pr.

Obeyesekere, Ranjini, tr. see Thera, Dharmasena.

Obeyeskere, Gananth, jt. auth. see Gombrich, Richard.

Obholzer, Anton, et al. The Unconscious at Work: Individual & Organizational Stress in the Human Services. LC 93-44323. 240p. 1994. 59.95x (0-415-10205-7, B4440, Routledge NY); pap. 18.95 (0-415-10206-5, B4444, Routledge NY) Routledge.

Obiakor, Festus E. & Maltby, Gregory M. Pragmatism & Education in Africa: Handbook for Educators & Development Planners. 60p. 1989. spiral bd. 15.95 (0-8403-5450-9) Kendall-Hunt.

Obiakor, Festus E. & Stile, Stephen. Self-Concept of Exceptional Learners: Current Perspectives for Educators. 240p. (C). 1994. per. 39.95 (0-8403-9545-0) Kendall-Hunt.

Obiaya, Joseph O. Mount Zion: The Mystery of God. LC 93-93712. (Illus.). 198p. (C). 1993. lib. bdg. 25.00 (0-9638850-0-6) J O Obiaya. While scientific knowledge is based on tested truths, religion is founded on blind assent to divinely revealed truths. Such is the gap between religion & science. It appears unbridgeable. Or is it? Upon close examination of the Scripture, from Genesis to Revelation, a mystical object (depicting the Kingdom of God) emerges as the central theme of Divine Revelation. Its structural features & attributes are described in different epochs, by different biblical personages. This Hidden Structure - a Cryptogram - is variously portrayed in the Scriptures as a rock or a mountain, & frequently associated with fire (combustion). Through a combustion experiment, the three dimensional picture of this Divine Emblem - a Pictogram - is made manifest. Thus, the authentication of the Scriptures no longer depends on blind faith, but on the systematic verification of this Structure with the testimonies of biblical personages who espied & described it long before the dawn of science. This is the subject matter of: MOUNT ZION: THE MYSTERY OF GOD (Library of Congress Catalog Card Number 93-93712. The Library of Congress dubbed it a REVELATION, in its bibliography; & classified it under Religion & Science.) By virtue of this Pictogram, solutions are provided to, hitherto, challenging theological & philosophical problems. It is 9 1/4 x 6 3/4 hardcover; with a color jacket. For information to order, call or write Joseph O. Obiaya - publisher, P.O. Box 21721 South Euclid, OH 44121; 216-321-1863.

Publisher Provided Annotation.

Obichere, Boniface I., ed. Studies in Southern Nigerian History. 278p. 1982. 40.00 (0-7146-3106-X, Pub. by F Cass Pubs UK) Intl Spec Bk.

Obichkin, G., ed. Lenin, V. I. A Short Biography. (Illus.). 224p. (C). 1983. 30.00 (0-685-31505-3, Pub. by Collets UK) Pro-Am Music.

Obidinski, Eugene & Zand, Helen S. Polish Folkways in America: Community & Family. (Polish Studies: Vol. I). 162p. (Orig.). 1987. lib. bdg. 44.50 (0-8191-5881-X, Polish Am Hist Assn); pap. text ed. 23.00 (0-8191-5882-8, Polish Am Hist Assn) U Pr of Amer.

Obidinski, Eugene E. Ethnic to Status Group: A Study of Polish Americans in Buffalo. Cordasco, Francesco, ed. LC 80-885. (American Ethnic Groups Ser.). 1981. lib. bdg. 26.95 (0-405-13446-0) Ayer.

Obiechina, E. N. Onitsha Market Literature. LC 72-76469. 200p. (C). 1972. 17.50 (0-8419-0122-8, Africana) Holmes & Meier.

Obiechina, Emmanuel. Locusts. 1976. 2.00 (0-912678-23-2, Greenfld Rev Pr) Greenfld Rev Lit.

Obiechina, Emmanuel, ed. Language & Theme: Essays on African Literature. LC 90-34189. 384p. (Orig.). (C). 1990. 26.95 (0-88258-045-0); pap. 14.95 (0-88258-064-7) Howard U Pr.

Obilade, Akintunde O., jt. ed. see Woodman, Gordon R.

Obiols, J., et al, eds. Biological Psychiatry Today: Proceedings of the World Conference, 2nd, Spain, 1978, Set. (Developments in Psychiatry Ser.: Vol. 2). 1979. 218.00 (0-444-80117-0, North Holland) Elsevier.

***Obis, Paul, comp.** America's 365 Best Festivals. 240p. (Orig.). 1995. pap. 12.95 (1-57067-014-5) Book Pub Co.

O'biso Socha, Laura. Birding for the Amateur Naturalist. LC 88-36348. (Illus.). 192p. 1989. reprint ed. pap. 8.95 (0-87106-615-7) Globe Pequot.

Object Management Group Staff. Object Management Architecture Guide. 2nd ed. 1993. pap. text ed. 50.00 (0-471-58792-3) Wiley.

Object Management Group Staff & X-Open Co. Ltd. Staff. The Common Object Request Broker: Architecture & Specification, Revision 1.1. 1993. pap. text ed. 50.00 (0-471-58563-7) Wiley.

Oblander, Ruth. Dresses Cut-to-Fit. Leppert, Mary, ed. LC 76-53237. 1976. 4.95 (0-933956-02-9) Sew-Fit.

— Sewing Without Pins. LC 76-53269. 1986. 4.95 (0-933956-01-0) Sew-Fit.

— Slacks for Perfect Fit: Sew-Fit Method. LC 81-50280. (Illus.). 64p. 1981. pap. 4.95 (0-933956-07-X) Sew-Fit.

Oblander, Ruth, et al. The Sew-Fit Manual. LC 77-84538. (Illus.). (C). 1978. 26.95 (0-933956-03-7) Sew-Fit.

Oblas, Carla. Algebra: Create & Discover. 328p. (C). 1991. pap. text ed. 19.00 (0-89801-021-7) NE Univ Pub.

— Problem Solving & Algebra Too. 4th rev. ed. 496p. (C). 1991. pap. text ed. 20.00 (0-89801-022-5) NE Univ Pub.

***Oblas, Peter B.** Perspectives on Race & Culture in Japanese Society: The Mass Media & Ethnicity. LC 94-38356. 236p. 1995. text ed. 89.95 (0-7734-8986-X) E Mellen.

Obler, Loraine K. & Fein, Deborah, eds. The Exceptional Brain: Neuropsychology of Talent & Special Abilities. LC 86-27136. 522p. 1988. lib. bdg. 45.00 (0-89862-701-X) Guilford Pr.

Obler, Loraine K., jt. auth. see Albert, Martin L.

Obler, Loraine K., jt. ed. see Hyltenstam, Kenneth.

Obler, Loraine K., jt. ed. see Menn, Lise.

Obler, Martin. Moira. LC 92-60567. 304p. 1993. 22.95 (0-88282-120-2) New Horizon NJ.

Obligado, Lilian. The Chocolate Cow. LC 91-27464. (Illus.). 48p. (J). (ps-2). 1993. pap. 14.00 (0-671-73852-6, S&S Bks Young Read) S&S Childrens.

— Guess the Animal! (Golden Sturdy Bks.). (J). 1990. pap. write for info. (0-307-12165-8, Golden Pr) Western Pub.

Oblinger, Carl. Cornwall: The People & Culture of an Industrial Camelot, 1890-1980. (Illus.). 123p. 1984. pap. text ed. 6.95 (0-89271-028-4) Pa Hist & Mus.

— Interviewing the People of Pennsylvania: A Conceptual Guide to Oral History. LC 79-625709. 84p. (Orig.). (C). 1981. pap. 7.95 (0-911124-94-2) Pa Hist & Mus.

Oblinger, Carl D. Divided Kingdom: Work, Community, & the Mining Wars in the Central Illinois Coal Fields During the Great Depression. (Illus.). 273p. (Orig.). 1991. pap. text ed. 12.50 (0-912226-28-5) Ill St Hist Soc.

O'Block, Robert L. Criminal Justice Research Sources. 3rd ed. LC 92-70236. 189p. (C). 1992. pap. text ed. write for info. (0-87084-665-5) Anderson Pub Co.

O'Block, Robert L., et al. Security & Crime Prevention. 2nd ed. 448p. 1991. text ed. 39.95 (0-7506-9007-0) Buttrwrth-Heinemann.

***Obloj, Krzysztof, et al.** Winning: Continuous Improvement Theory in High Performance Organizations. (Series in International Management). 192p. (C). 1995. pap. text ed. 16.95x (0-7914-2522-3) State U NY Pr.

— Winning: Continuous Improvement Theory in High Performance Organizations. (Series in International Management). 192p. (C). 1995. text ed. 49.50x (0-7914-2521-5) State U NY Pr.

Obloj, Krzysztof, jt. auth. see Cavaleri, Steven.

Obminsky, Ernest. Economic Problems of Developing Countries. vi, 87p. 1989. text ed. 15.95 (81-207-0958-6, Pub. by Sterling Pubs II) Apt Bks.

Obminsky, Ernest & Bugrov, Andrei. International Economic Security: A Major Factor of Peace. (C). 1988. 14.00 (0-8364-2394-1, Pub. by Allied II) S Asia.

Obnishi. Membrane Protective Action of Prostaglandin Derivatives. 1995. write for info. (0-8493-8095-2) CRC Pr.

Obojski, Robert. Baseball Bloopers & Baseball Oddities. LC 89-31270. (Illus.). 128p. (YA). 1991. pap. 4.95 (0-8069-6981-4) Sterling.

— Baseball's Strangest Moments. LC 87-33319. (Illus.). 128p. 1989. pap. 4.95 (0-8069-6983-0) Sterling.

— Coin Collector's Price Guide. (Illus.). 128p. (Orig.). 1995. pap. 6.95 (0-8069-3191-4) Sterling.

— A First Stamp Album for Beginners. 1983. pap. 3.50 (0-486-23843-1) Dover.

Obold, Ruth. Prepare for Peace, Pt. I. (Illus.). 40p. (J). (gr. 1-3). 1986. 6.25 (0-87303-116-4) Faith & Life.

— Prepare for Peace, Pt. II. (Illus.). 48p. (J). (gr. 4-6). 1986. 6.25 (0-87303-117-2) Faith & Life.

— Prepare for Peace, Pt. III. (Illus.). 55p. (YA). (gr. 7-8). 1986. 6.25 (0-87303-118-0) Faith & Life.

Obolensky, D., jt. ed. see Auty, R.

Obolensky, Dimitri. The Byzantine Commonwealth: Eastern Europe, 500-1453. LC 82-16970. (Illus.). 552p. 1983. reprint ed. pap. 16.95 (0-913836-98-2) St Vladimirs.

— The Byzantine Inheritance of Eastern Europe. (Collected Studies: No. CS156). (Illus.). 300p. (C). 1982. reprint ed. lib. bdg. 87.95 (0-86078-102-X, Pub. by Variorum UK) Ashgate Pub Co.

— Byzantium & the Slavs. LC 94-25507. 334p. 1994. pap. 18.95 (0-88141-008-X) St Vladimirs.

Obolensky, Dimitri, ed. The Heritage of Russian Verse. LC 75-23893. 544p. 1976. reprint ed. 35.00 (0-253-32735-0); reprint ed. pap. 14.95 (0-253-32736-9) Ind U Pr.

Obolensky, Dmitri. The Bogomils: A Study in Balkan Neo-Manichaeism. LC 77-84712. reprint ed. 39.00 (0-404-16118-9) AMS Pr.

Obolensky, J. & Auty, B. Introduction to Russian Art & Architecture (Companion to Russian Studies) (C). 1990. pap. 150.00 (0-685-34390-1, Pub. by Collets) St Mut.

***Obolensky, Nick.** Practical Business Re-Engineering: Tools & Techniques for Achieving Effective Change. LC 95-12523. 1995. write for info. (0-88415-646-X) Gulf Pub.

Obolensky, S., et al. Spoken Amharic, Bk. 1. 500p. (AMH.). 1980. audio 180.00 (0-87950-654-7) Spoken Lang Serv.

— Spoken Amharic, Bk. 1, Units 1-50. 500p. (AMH.). 1980. pap. text ed. 40.00 (0-87950-650-4); audio 140.00 (0-87950-652-0) Spoken Lang Serv.

— Spoken Amharic, Book 2, Units Fifty-One to Sixty. (Spoken Language Ser.). 500p. (AMH.). 1980. pap. text ed. 40.00 (0-87950-651-2); audio 60.00 (0-87950-653-9) Spoken Lang Serv.

— Spoken Amharic, Book 2, Units Fifty-One to Sixty, Bk. 2. (Spoken Language Ser.). 500p. (AMH.). 1980. digital audio 100.00 (0-87950-655-5) Spoken Lang Serv.

— Spoken Amharic, Book 2, Units Fifty-One to Sixty, Bks. 1 & 2. (Spoken Language Ser.). 500p. (AMH.). 1980. audio 280.00 (0-87950-656-3) Spoken Lang Serv.

Obolensky, Serge. One Man in His Time. (Illus.). 1958. 20.00 (0-8392-1080-9) Astor-Honor.

Obolentsev, R. Chemistry of Organic Sulphur Compounds in Petroleum. 1967. 90.00 (0-7065-0479-8, Pub. by Keter Pub IS) Coronet Bks.

Oboler, Eli M. Defending Intellectual Freedom: The Library & the Censor. LC 79-8585. (Contributions in Librarianship & Information Science Ser.: No. 32). xix, 246p. 1980. text ed. 38.50 (0-313-21472-7, ODF/, Greenwood Pr) Greenwood.

— Ideas & the University Library: Essays of an Unorthodox Academic Librarian. LC 77-11. (Contributions in Librarianship & Information Science Ser.: No. 20). 203p. 1977. text ed. 49.95 (0-8371-9531-4, OIS/, Greenwood Pr) Greenwood.

Oboler, Regina S. Women, Power, & Economic Change: The Nandi of Kenya. LC 83-45345. (Illus.). 368p. 1985. 42.50 (0-8047-1224-7) Stanford U Pr.

***Oboler, Suzanne.** Ethnic Labels, Latino Lives: Identity & the Politics of (Re) Presentation. LC 94-22751. 1995. text ed. 49.95 (0-8166-2284-1); pap. 18.95 (0-8166-2286-8) U of Minn Pr.

***Obon De Castro, Comcepcion & Nunez, D. R.** A Taxonomic Revision of the Section Sideritis (Genus Sideritis) (Labiatae) (Phanerogamarum Monographiae: Tomus XXI, Vol. 22). (Illus.). 640p. 1994. pap. 209.95x (3-443-78003-2, Pub. by Cramer-Borntraeger GW) Lubrecht & Cramer.

Oborne, D. J. & Gruneberg, M. M., eds. The Physical Environment at Work. LC 82-23743. (Wiley Series in Psychology & Productivity at Work). 252p. reprint ed. pap. 71.90 (0-7837-6389-1, 2046102) Bks Demand.

***Oborne, David.** Ergonomics & Human Factors, 2 vols., Set. (International Library of Critical Writings in Psychology: No. 7). 1088p. 1995. 295.00 (0-8147-6187-9) NYU Pr.

Oborne, David J. Computers at Work: A Behavioural Approach. LC 84-17335. (Wiley Series in Psychology & Productivity at Work). 436p. reprint ed. pap. 124.30 (0-7837-3414-X, 2043381) Bks Demand.

— Ergonomics at Work. 2nd ed. 386p. 1991. pap. text ed. 38.95 (0-471-90942-4) Wiley.

— Ergonomics at Work. LC 81-14642. 331p. reprint ed. pap. 94.40 (0-685-20600-9, 2030534) Bks Demand.

Oborne, David J., ed. International Reviews of Ergonomics, Vol. 1. 220p. 1987. 90.00 (0-85066-359-8) Taylor & Francis.

— International Reviews of Ergonomics, Vol. 2. 250p. 1988. 95.00 (0-85066-408-X) Taylor & Francis.

Oborne, David J., et al. Person Centered Ergonomics: A Brantonian View of Human Factors. LC 92-29732. 1993. 80.00 (0-7484-0051-6) Taylor & Francis.

***Oborne, Martine.** Princess Lullaby & Magic Word. (J). 1994. 5.99 (0-517-12014-3) Random Hse Value.

Oborotova, Marina A., jt. ed. see Cross, Sharyl.

An Asterisk (*) at the beginning of an entry indicates that the title is appearing in BIP for the first time.

Obosu-Mensah, Kwaku. Ghana's Volta Resettlement Scheme: The Long-Term Consequences of Post-Colonial State Planning. LC 93-42795. 1994. 64.95 (*1-883255-33-3*); pap. 44.95 (*1-883255-32-5*) Intl Scholars.

O'Bourke, D., ed. French-English Horticultural Dictionary. 2nd ed. 240p. (C). 1989. text ed. 56.00 (*0-85198-626-9*) CAB Intl.

O'Boyle, Edward J., jt. ed. see **Davis, John B.**

O'Boyle, F. J., jt. ed. see **McLoughlin, J.**

O'Boyle, Ita. Gertrud Von le Fort: An Introduction to the Prose Work. LC 64-13378. 128p. reprint ed. pap. 36.50 (*0-7837-0459-3*, 2040782) Bks Demand.

O'Boyle, Lily G. Pacific Crossings: A Philippine Cookbook. LC 93-12794. (Illus.). 192p. 1994. 35.00 (*0-944863-25-6*) Acacia Corp. PACIFIC CROSSINGS is a voyage of rediscovery. This beautiful book offers a closer look at Philippine cuisine, celebrating a new & innovative cookery born out of transoceanic migrations & the transplanting of indigenous food products among many different countries. The recipes presented in this full-color picture filled cookbook are based on a cuisine shaped by the influences of the many countries that have at one time or another occupied this island nation. Four hundred years of Spanish rule, more than half a century of American occupation & the continual presence of Chinese, Malay, Polynesian & Japanese influences have produced a cuisine that is warm, friendly, flavorful, colorful & unique. Ten of the most creative & innovative chefs from the Philippines today are featured in PACIFIC CROSSINGS, along with their favorite dishes. Illustrated with more than fifty stunning color food photographs taken by Bill McConnell, this book includes easy-to-prepare recipes, helpful chef's hints & suggestions on where to find specialty food items. It is 9" X 12", hard bound with dust jacket. Call or write for information to order, Acacia Corporation - Publisher, 459 Columbus Ave. #266, New York, NY 10024. 212-595-4154. *Publisher Provided Annotation.*

O'Boyle, Lily G. & Alejandro, Reynaldo. Philippine Hospitality: A Gracious Tradition of the East. Ner, Sonia & Almario, Lyn, eds. 224p. 1988. 55.00 (*0-944863-00-0*) Acacia Corp.

Obradovic, J., jt. ed. see **Hein, J. R.**

Obradovic, Josip & Dunn, William N., eds. Workers' Self-Management & Organizational Power in Yugoslavia. LC 78-16307. 464p. reprint ed. pap. 132.30 (*0-7837-2145-5*, 2042431) Bks Demand.

Obradovic, Nadezda, ed. African Rhapsody: Short Stories of the Contemporary African Experience. LC 93-21132. 1994. 12.95 (*0-385-46816-4*, Anchor NY) Doubleday.

Obrams, G. I. & Potter, M., eds. Epidemiology & Biology of Multiple Myeloma. (Illus.). xv, 192p. 1991. 44.00 (*0-387-54061-X*) Spr-Verlag.

Obreanu, P. E., jt. ed. see **Gould, S. H.**

Obrebski, Joseph. The Changing Peasantry of Eastern Europe. (Illus.). 100p. 1976. pap. 18.95x (*0-87073-741-4*) Transaction Pubs.

Obrecch, Fred, et al. How to Prepare for the CBEST - California Basic Educational Skill Test. 3rd ed. 352p. 1993. pap. 12.95 (*0-8120-1438-3*) Barron.

Obrecht, Fred. How to Prepare for the California State University Writing Proficiency Exams. 288p. 1992. pap. 11.95 (*0-8120-4962-4*) Barron.

— Minimum Essentials in English. LC 93-22471. 48p. (C). 1993. pap. 6.95 (*0-8120-1522-3*) Barron.

Obrecht, G. & Stark, L. W., eds. Presbyopia Research: From Molecular Biology to Visual Adaptation. (Illus.). 280p. 1990. 75.00 (*0-306-43659-0*, Plenum Pr) Plenum.

Obrecht, J. B. & Dubach, U. C., eds. Medizinische Universitaets Poliklinik Basel, 100 Jahre. (Illus.). 100p. 1975. 24.00 (*3-8055-2280-0*) S Karger.

Obrecht, Jas. Blues Guitar: The Men Who Made the Music. 1991. pap. 19.95 (*0-7935-0074-5*, HL00183632) H Leonard.

Obrecht, Jas, ed. Blues Guitar: The Men Who Made the Music. 2nd ed. (Illus.). 256p. 1993. pap. 19.95 (*0-87930-292-5*) Miller Freeman.

— Masters of Heavy Metal. LC 83-60067. (Illus.). 194p. (Orig.). 1984. pap. 12.95 (*0-688-02937-X*, Quill) Morrow.

Obregon, L. The Streets of Mexico. 1976. lib. bdg. 59.95 (*0-8490-2695-4*) Gordon Pr.

Obregon, Mauricio. The Columbus Papers. (Illus.). 96p. 1991. text ed. 100.00 (*0-02-591045-0*) Macmillan.

O'Brennen, Junius & Smith, Nopal. The Crystal Icon. (Illus.). vii, 200p. 1981. 50.00 (*0-940578-03-4*) Galahand Pr.

O'Brian, ed. Medical Device Packaging Handbook. (Packaging & Converting Technology Ser.: Vol. 2). 376p. 1990. 125.00 (*0-8247-7698-4*) Dekker.

O'Brian, David Z. Thirty Reasons Not to Buy or Start a Business. 201p. 1992. pap. 12.95 (*1-881385-00-0*) New Cent Pubns.

O'Brian, Gayle. Reckless Rapture. 1983. pap. 3.50 (*0-8217-1157-1*) Zebra.

O'Brian, Jim. Doing It Right: The Steelers of Three Rivers & Four Super Bowls Share Their Secrets for Success. (Illus.). 536p. (Orig.). 1991. pap. 14.95 (*0-685-57076-2*) Wolfson.

O'Brian, John. Degas to Matisse: The Maurice Wertheim Collection. (Illus.). 176p. 1988. 39.95 (*0-8109-1138-8*) Abrams.

— Degas to Matisse: The Maurice Wertheim Collection. (Illus.). 176p. 1995. pap. 19.95 (*0-916724-65-4*, 4654) Harvard Art Mus.

O'Brian, John, ed. see **Greenberg, Clement.**

O'Brian, Mark, jt. ed. see **Little, Craig.**

O'Brian, Michael. A Garden of Your Own. 192p. (Orig.). 1993. pap. 3.99 (*0-425-13628-0*) Berkley Pub.

— The Simple Fix It Book. 208p. (Orig.). 1993. pap. 4.50 (*0-425-13713-9*) Berkley Pub.

O'Brian, Patricia, jt. auth. see **Bart, Pauline B.**

***O'Brian, Patrick.** The Aubrey-Maturin Series, 16 vols., Set. (C). 1994. 360.00 (*0-393-03749-5*) Norton.

— The Commodore. (Aubrey - Maturin Ser.). 288p. 1995. 22.50 (*0-393-03760-6*) Norton.

— Desolation Island. 325p. 1991. pap. 10.95 (*0-393-30812-X*) Norton.

— Desolation Island. 1994. 22.50 (*0-393-03705-3*) Norton.

— Far Side. 1994. 22.50 (*0-393-03710-X*) Norton.

— The Far Side of the World. 368p. 1992. pap. 10.95 (*0-393-30862-6*) Norton.

— The Fortune of War. 329p. 1991. pap. 10.95 (*0-393-30813-8*) Norton.

— Fortune of War. 1994. 22.50 (*0-393-03706-1*) Norton.

— The Fortune of War. braille ed. 574p. 1992. vinyl bd. 45. 92 (*1-56956-418-3*, BR8768) W A T Braille.

— Golden Ocean. 1994. 22.50 (*0-393-03630-8*) Norton.

Obrian, Patrick. H. M. S. Surprise. 379p. 1991. pap. 10.95 (*0-393-30761-1*) Norton.

O'Brian, Patrick. H. M. S. Surprise. 1994. 22.50 (*0-393-03703-7*) Norton.

— The Ionian Mission. 368p. 1992. pap. 10.95 (*0-393-30821-9*) Norton.

— Ionian Mission. 1994. 22.50 (*0-393-03708-8*) Norton.

— The Ionian Mission. braille ed. 646p. 1993. vinyl bd. 51. 68 (*1-56956-420-5*, BR8811) W A T Braille.

— Joseph Banks: A Life. 1993. 29.95 (*0-87923-930-1*) Godine.

— Letter of Marque. 1990. 22.50 (*0-393-02874-7*) Norton.

— The Letter of Marque. 288p. 1992. pap. 10.95 (*0-393-30905-3*) Norton.

— The Letter of Marque. braille ed. 521p. 1993. vinyl bd. 41.68 (*1-56956-419-1*, BR8806) W A T Braille.

— Master & Commander. 1990. pap. 10.95 (*0-393-30705-0*) Norton.

— Master & Commander. 1994. 22.50 (*0-393-03701-0*) Norton.

— Master & Commander. braille ed. 739p. 1992. vinyl bd. 59.12 (*1-56956-070-6*, BR8654) W A T Braille.

Obrian, Patrick. Mauritius Command. 1991. pap. 10.95 (*0-393-30762-X*) Norton.

O'Brian, Patrick. Mauritius Command. 1994. 22.50 (*0-393-03704-5*) Norton.

— The Mauritius Command. braille ed. 597p. 1992. vinyl bd. 47.76 (*1-56956-071-4*, BR8742) W A T Braille.

— Men-of-War: Life in Nelson's Navy. LC 95-2297. (Illus.). 96p. 1995. 23.00 (*0-393-03858-0*) Norton.

— The Nutmeg of Consolation. 320p. 1991. 22.50 (*0-393-03032-6*) Norton.

— The Nutmeg of Consolation. 320p. 1993. pap. 10.95 (*0-393-30906-1*) Norton.

— Nutmeg of Consolation. braille ed. 600p. 1993. vinyl bd. 48.00 (*1-56956-422-1*, BR8815) W A T Braille.

— Patrick O'Brian: Critical Essays & a Bibliography. 1994. 23.95 (*0-393-03626-X*) Norton.

— Picasso. 520p. 1994. pap. 14.95 (*0-393-31107-4*) Norton.

— Post Captain. 1990. pap. 10.95 (*0-393-30706-9*) Norton.

— Post Captain. 1994. 22.50 (*0-393-03702-9*) Norton.

— Post Captain. braille ed. 868p. 1992. vinyl bd. 69.44 (*1-56956-080-3*, BR8664) W A T Braille.

— Rendezvous & Other Stories. 240p. 1994. 22.00 (*0-393-03685-5*) Norton.

— The Rendezvous & Other Stories. 256p. 1995. pap. 11.00 (*0-393-31380-8*, Norton Paperbks) Norton.

— The Reverse of the Medal. 288p. 1992. pap. 10.95 (*0-393-30960-6*) Norton.

— Reverse of the Medal. 1994. 22.50 (*0-393-03711-8*) Norton.

— The Surgeon's Mate. 1994. 22.50 (*0-393-03707-X*) Norton.

— The Surgeon's Mate. 384p. 1992. pap. 10.95 (*0-393-30820-0*) Norton.

— The Surgeon's Mate. braille ed. 659p. 1992. vinyl bd. 52. 72 (*1-56956-417-5*, BR8770) W A T Braille.

— Testimonies. LC 92-27426. 224p. 1993. 20.95 (*0-393-03483-6*) Norton.

— Testimonies: A Novel. 224p. 1995. pap. 11.00 (*0-393-31316-6*, Norton Paperbks) Norton.

— Thirteen Gun Salute. 1991. 22.50 (*0-393-02974-3*) Norton.

— The Thirteen Gun Salute. 336p. 1992. pap. 10.95 (*0-393-30907-X*) Norton.

— The Thirteen-Gun Salute. braille ed. 586p. 1993. vinyl bd. 46.88 (*1-56956-421-3*, BR8813) W A T Braille.

— Treason's Harbor. 1994. 22.50 (*0-393-03709-6*) Norton.

— Treason's Harbour. 1992. pap. 10.95 (*0-393-30863-4*) Norton.

— The Truelove. 192p. 1992. 22.50 (*0-393-03109-8*) Norton.

— The Truelove. 256p. 1993. pap. 10.95 (*0-393-31016-7*) Norton.

— The Truelove. braille ed. 482p. 1993. vinyl bd. 38.56 (*1-56956-423-X*, BR9205) W A T Braille.

— The Truelove. large type ed. 418p. 1992. reprint ed. lib. bdg. 17.95 (*1-56054-522-4*) Thorndike Pr.

— The Unknown Shore: A Novel. 288p. 1995. 23.00 (*0-393-03859-9*) Norton.

— The Wine-Dark Sea. LC 93-1521. 1993. 22.50 (*0-393-03558-1*) Norton.

— The Wine-Dark Sea. 272p. 1994. pap. 11.00 (*0-393-31244-5*) Norton.

— The Wine-Dark Sea. large type ed. LC 93-43536. 1994. pap. 18.95 (*0-7862-0133-9*) Thorndike Pr.

O'Brian, Patrick, tr. see **De Beauvoir, Simone.**

O'Brian, Patrick, tr. see **Lacouture, Jean.**

O'Brian, Rita C. White Society in Black Africa: The French of Senegal. LC 74-183533. 320p. reprint ed. pap. 91.20 (*0-317-11345-3*, 2006875) Bks Demand.

O'Brian, Steven. Ulysses S. Grant. (World Leaders - Past & Present Ser.). (Illus.). 112p. (J). (gr. 5 up). 1991. 17.95 (*1-55546-809-8*) Chelsea Hse.

O'Briant, Don. Looking for Tara: The Gone with the Wind Guide to Margaret Mitchell's Atlanta. LC 94-77585. 112p. 1994. pap. 6.95 (*1-56352-172-5*) Longstreet Pr Inc.

O'Briant, Walter H., tr. see **Leibniz, Gottfried W.**

O'Brien. All the Girls. 1983. pap. 3.50 (*0-449-20251-8*) Fawcett.

— Child Pornography. 1987. 13.95 (*0-8403-4403-1*) Kendall-Hunt.

— Industrial Behavior Modification. (C). 1982. 70.95 (*0-205-14428-4*, H4428) Allyn.

***Obrien.** Investments Vol. III: Bond Valuation Using Bond Tutor. (FB-Intro to Finance Ser.). 1995. pap. 36.95 (*0-538-84827-8*) S-W Pub.

***O'Brien.** Managers & the Market. 1995. 26.95 (*0-8057-9834-X*, Twayne); pap. 15.95 (*0-8057-4502-5*) Macmillan.

— Oral Radiology Interpretation. 1991. write for info. (*0-8151-6506-4*, Yr Bk Med Pubs) Mosby Yr Bk.

***Obrien.** Shakespeare Set Free: Teaching Twelfth Night & Othello. 1995. pap. (*0-671-76047-5*, WSP) PB.

O'Brien. Toy Cars & Trucks. 448p. 1994. pap. 22.95 (*0-89689-103-8*) Bks Americana.

O'Brien, ed. Dental Materials: Properties & Selection. 1989. text ed. 68.00 (*0-86715-199-4*, 1994) Quint Pub Co.

***O'Brien & Gere Engineers, Inc.** Innovative Engineering Technologies for Hazardous Waste Remediation. Bellandi, Robert, ed. LC 94-27588. 416p. 1994. text ed. 49.95 (*0-442-01180-6*) Van Nos Reinhold.

O'Brien, Aileen. The Dine: Orgin Myths of the Navaho Indians. 1988. reprint ed. lib. bdg. 75.00 (*0-7812-0065-2*) Rprt Serv.

O'Brien, Alan. Check-Mate: A Pocket-Size Guide to Everyday Spellings for Dyslexics. 64p. 1993. pap. 12.50 (*1-85302-165-2*, Pub. by J Kingsley Pubs UK) Taylor & Francis.

O'Brien, Alice R. Places to Go with Children in the Delaware Valley. 160p. 1989. pap. 9.95 (*0-87701-581-3*) Chronicle Bks.

O'Brien, Anita. A Lab Manual for Desktop Publishing: IBM Version for Beginners. 62p. 1992. 24.95 (*1-881950-01-8*) A OBrien.

— A Lab Manual for Desktop Publishing: IBM Version for Intermediates. 62p. 1992. 22.95 (*1-881950-03-4*) A OBrien.

— A Lab Manual for Desktop Publishing: Macintosh Version for Beginners. 62p. 1992. 24.95 (*1-881950-00-X*) A OBrien.

— A Lab Manual for Desktop Publishing: Macintosh Version for Intermediates. 62p. 1992. 22.95 (*1-881950-02-6*) A OBrien.

O'Brien, Anne. Poverty's Prison: The Poor in New South Wales, 1880-1918. 1988. 34.95 (*0-522-84343-3*) Intl Spec Bk.

O'Brien, Anne S. The Princess & the Beggar: A Korean Folktale. LC 92-11988. (Illus.). 32p. (J). (gr. k-4). 1993. 14.95 (*0-590-46092-7*) Scholastic Inc.

O'Brien, Anne S., jt. auth. see **Knight, Margy B.**

O'Brien, Anthony, jt. auth. see **Thorton, Robert J.**

O'Brien, Bart. Database Decisions: Briefings on the Management of Technology. 288p. (Orig.). 1994. pap. 67.50 (*0-273-60289-6*, Pub. by Pitman Pub Ltd UK) Trans-Atl Phila.

— Information Management Decisions: Briefings & Critical Thinking. 448p. (Orig.). 1994. pap. 72.50 (*0-273-60288-8*, Pub. by Pitman Pub Ltd UK) Trans-Atl Phila.

— Information Technology Strategy: Issues & Logic. 375p. 1992. pap. text ed. 39.00 (*0-13-502691-1*) P-H.

O'Brien, Bartholomew J. The Cure of ARS: Patron Saint of Parish Priests. LC 87-50942. 133p. 1987. reprint ed. pap. 4.50 (*0-89555-324-4*) TAN Bks Pubs.

— The Gift of Celibacy. 48p. (Orig.). 1993. pap. 1.00 (*1-877678-26-0*) Riehle Found.

— An Introduction to: The Promise of Saint Joseph: The Challenge of Teenage Chastity. LC 89-60396. 45p. (Orig.). 1989. pap. 0.50 (*0-9618840-8-8*) Riehle Found.

— Pray: A Mini Course in Spirituality. LC 89-61874. 32p. (Orig.). 1989. pap. 0.50 (*1-877678-02-3*) Riehle Found.

— Primer of Prayer. Faith Publishing Company Staff, ed. LC 91-71541. 124p. (Orig.). 1991. pap. 3.00 (*0-9625975-8-9*) Faith Pub OH.

— Why Be a Priest? Riehle Foundation Staff, ed. 58p. (Orig.). 1993. pap. 0.50 (*0-685-72757-2*) Riehle Found.

O'Brien, Bayne P. The Northumberland County, Virginia, 1850 Census. 118p. (Orig.). 1972. reprint ed. pap. 15.00 (*0-89308-307-0*) Southern Hist Pr.

O'Brien, Bernadette M., jt. auth. see **O'Brien, David.**

O'Brien, Bernard A., jt. auth. see **Mackey, Richard A.**

O'Brien, Bernard M. & Morrison, Wayne A. Reconstructive Microsurgery. (Illus.). 540p. 1987. text ed. 275.00 (*0-443-02557-6*) Churchill.

***O'Brien, Betsy.** The Seoul Food Guide: A Selection of Restaurants. (Illus.). 280p. 1995. pap. 14.95 (*1-56591-040-0*, Pub. by Hollym Bks SK) Weatherhill.

O'Brien, Bonnie B. The Victory of the Lamb. 182p. 1982. pap. 13.50 (*0-311-72280-6*) Casa Bautista.

***O'Brien, Brendan.** The Long War: The IRA & Sinn Fein, 1985 to Today. 1995. 17.95 (*0-8156-0319-3*) Syracuse U Pr.

— Speedy Justice: The Tragic Last Voyage of His Majesty's Vessel Speedy. (Publications of the Osgoode Society). (Illus.). 200p. 1992. 35.00 (*0-8020-2910-8*) U of Toronto Pr.

***O'Brien, C., ed.** Normal & Impaired Motor Development. (Illus.). 272p. 1994. pap. text ed. 49.50 (*1-56593-148-3*, 0460) Singular Publishing.

O'Brien, C., et al, eds. Computer Integrated Manufacturing: Proceedings of the Eighth CIM-EUROPE Annual Conference 27-29 May 1992, Birmingham, UK. (Illus.). 496p. 1992. pap. 179.00 (*0-387-19766-4*) Spr-Verlag.

O'Brien, Carole L. Adult Day Care: A Practical Guide. LC 81-16212. (Nursing-Health Science Ser.). 400p. (C). 1982. 40.00 (*0-8185-0506-0*) Jones & Bartlett.

***O'Brien, Carolyn & Hayes, Alan.** Normal & Impaired Motor Development: Theory into Practice. LC 94-68790. 256p. 1995. pap. 47.75 (*0-412-47890-0*) Chapman.

O'Brien, Charles & Wibmer, Guillermo. Annotated Checklist of the Weevils of North America, Central America, & the West Indies (Coleoptera: Curculionoidea) (Memoir Ser.: No. 34). 382p. 1982. 45. 00 (*1-56665-032-1*) Assoc Pubs FL.

O'Brien, Charles B. One Thousand One Civil War Trivia. (Illus.). 152p. (Orig.). 1991. pap. 12.50 (*1-55613-424-X*) Heritage Bk.

— One Thousand One Civil War Trivia. rev. ed. (Illus.). 156p. (Orig.). 1994. pap. text ed. 8.95 (*0-9637602-0-3*) Neirbo Bks.

O'Brien, Charles F. Sir William Dawson: A Life in Science & Religion. LC 71-153381. (American Philosophical Society, Memoirs Ser.: Vol. 84). 217p. reprint ed. pap. 61.90 (*0-317-20673-7*, 2025140) Bks Demand.

O'Brien, Charles P., ed. see **Association for Research in Nervous & Mental Disease (ARNMD) Staff.**

O'Brien, Charles W., jt. auth. see **Wibmer, Guillermo J.**

O'Brien, Christian. The Megalithic Odyssey: A Search for the Master Builders of the Bodmin Moor Astronomical Complex of Stone Circles in Giant Cairns. LC 87-35773. (Illus.). 176p. (C). 1987. reprint ed. lib. bdg. 27.00x (*0-8095-7012-2*) Borgo Pr.

***O'Brien, Christine.** Butterworths Current Law Digest 1984-1988. 1104p. 1990. boxed write for info. (*0-409-78879-1*, NZ) Butterworth Legal Pubs.

— Butterworths Current Law Digest 1989-1992. 1000p. 1993. boxed 243.00 (*0-408-71356-9*, NZ) Butterworth Legal Pubs.

***O'Brien, Christine & Karunaharan, N.** New Zealand Family Law Reports. Date not set. ring bd. write for info. (*0-409-79037-0*, NZ) Butterworth Legal Pubs.

O'Brien, Christine, jt. ed. see **O'Brien, Maurice.**

***O'Brien, Conor C.** Ancestral Voices: Religion & Nationalism in Ireland. 208p. 1995. pap. 13.95 (*0-226-61652-5*) U Ch Pr.

— Conor: An Anthology. 350p. 1994. 39.95 (*0-8014-3087-9*) Cornell U Pr.

— The Great Melody: A Thematic Biography of Edmund Burke. LC 92-7302. (Illus.). 640p. 1992. 34.95 (*0-226-61650-9*) U Ch Pr.

— The Great Melody: A Thematic Biography of Edmund Burke. lxxvi, 692p. (C). 1993. pap. text ed. 24.95 (*0-226-61651-7*) U Ch Pr.

— The Siege: The Saga of Israel & Zionism. 798p. 1987. pap. 17.00 (*0-671-63310-4*, Touchstone Bks) S&S Trade.

O'Brien, Conor C. & O'Brien, Maire. A Concise History of Ireland. 3rd rev. ed. (Illus.). 1985. pap. 15.95 (*0-500-27379-0*) Thames Hudson.

***O'Brien, D.** The Insiders' Guide to Charlotte. 6th ed. 584p. 1994. pap. 14.95 (*0-9623690-6-3*) Becklyn.

O'Brien, D. P. J. R. McCulloch: A Study in Classical Economics. (Modern Revivals in Economics Ser.). 452p. 1992. 76.95 (*0-7512-0096-4*, Pub. by Gregg Pub UK) Ashgate Pub Co.

— Lionel Robbins. LC 88-3054. 256p. 1988. text ed. 49.95 (*0-312-01998-X*) St Martin.

— Methodology, Money & the Firm: The Collected Essays of D. P. O'Brien, 2 vols., Set. LC 94-3920. (Economists of the Twentieth Century Ser.). 944p. 1994. 149.95 (*1-85278-966-2*, Pub. by E Elgar Pub UK) Ashgate Pub Co.

— Thomas Joplin & Classical Macroeconomics: A Re-Appraisal of Classical Monetary Thought. 352p. 1993. 69.95 (*1-85278-676-0*, Pub. by E Elgar Pub UK) Ashgate Pub Co.

O'Brien, D. P. & Creedy, J. Economic Analysis in Historical Perspective. (Modern Revivals in Economics Ser.). 228p. 1992. 59.95 (*0-7512-0088-3*, Pub. by Gregg Pub UK) Ashgate Pub Co.

O'Brien, D. P. & Presley, John R., eds. Pioneers of Modern Economics in Britain. LC 79-55496. (Illus.). 292p. 1981. text ed. 53.00 (*0-389-20181-2*, N6622) B&N Imports.

O'Brien, Dan. Eminent Domain. LC 86-30846. (Iowa Short Fiction Award Ser.). 145p. 1987. text ed. 19.95 (*0-87745-170-2*) U of Iowa Pr.

— In the Center of the Nation. 384p. 1992. pap. 10.00 (*0-380-71702-6*) Avon.

***O'Brien, Daniel.** Robert Altman: Hollywood Survivor, Vol. 1. LC 94-41864. 144p. 1995. 24.95 (*0-8264-0791-9*) Continuum.

O

O'Brien, Darcy. Dark & Bloody Ground. 1994. mass mkt. 5.99 (0-06-109972-4, Harp PBks) HarpC.
— A Dark & Bloody Ground: Outlaw Love, a Miser's Hoard: Lust, Greed, & Killing from the Beaches of Florida to the Mountains of Kentucky. LC 92-54451. (Illus.). 368p. 1993. 20.00 (0-06-017958-9, HarpT) HarpC.
— Margaret in Hollywood. 320p. 1991. 20.95 (0-688-09169-5) Morrow.
— Murder in Little Egypt. 1990. pap. 4.99 (0-451-40167-0, Onyx) NAL-Dutton.
— Patrick Kavanaugh. (Irish Writers Ser.). 72p. 1975. 8.50 (0-8387-7884-4); pap. 1.95 (0-8387-7985-9) Bucknell U Pr.
— Two of a Kind. 448p. 1990. pap. 4.95 (0-451-16302-8, Onyx) NAL-Dutton.
— Two of a Kind: The Hillside Stranglers. (Illus.). 384p. 1994. 12.99 (1-56865-077-9, GuildAmerica) Dblday Bk Music.
— W. R. Rodgers. LC 70-124646. (Irish Writers Ser.). 103p. 1975. pap. 1.95 (0-8387-7630-2) Bucknell U Pr.
O'Brien, David. California Workers' Compensation Claims & Benefits. 9th ed. 1100p. 1993. ring bd. 125.00 (0-250-47224-4) Michie Butterworth.
O'Brien, David & O'Brien, Bernadette M. California Misconduct Cases. 3rd ed. 520p. 1991. pap. 39.50 (1-55943-121-0) Michie Butterworth.
— California Unemployment & Disability Compensation Programs. 8th ed. 550p. 1991. ring bd. 89.50 (1-55943-119-9) Michie Butterworth.
— California Unemployment & Disability Compensation Programs, No. 1. 8th suppl. ed. 1993. 35.00 (0-685-74366-7) Butterworth Legal Pubs.
O'Brien, David & Shannon, Thomas A., eds. Catholic Social Thought: The Documentary Heritage. LC 92-3185. 1992. 49.95 (0-88344-803-3); pap. 24.95 (0-88344-787-8) Orbis Bks.
O'Brien, David, jt. ed. see Wise, Charles.
O'Brien, David, jt. auth. see Wood, Leon.
O'Brien, David E. Today's Handbook for Solving Bible Difficulties. 450p. 1990. 18.99 (0-87123-814-4) Bethany Hse.
O'Brien, David J. From the Heart of the American Church: Catholic Higher Education & American Culture. 220p. (Orig.). 1994. 34.95 (0-88344-994-3); pap. 14.95 (0-88344-985-4) Orbis Bks.
— Isaac Hecker: An American Catholic. 1992. 25.00 (0-8091-0397-4) Paulist Pr.
— Neighborhood Organization & Interest-Group Processes. LC 75-3468. 276p. reprint ed. pap. 78.70 (0-8357-8966-7, 2033399) Bks Demand.
O'Brien, David J. & Fugita, Stephen S. The Japanese American Experience. LC 90-23961. (Minorities in Modern America Ser.: MB-656). (Illus.). 188p. 1991. 29.95 (0-253-34164-7); pap. 12.95 (0-253-20656-1, MB-656) Ind U Pr.
O'Brien, David J., jt. auth. see Fugita, Stephen S.
O'Brien, David J., et al. A Research Agenda for Studying Rural Public Service Delivery Alternatives in the North Central Region. 76p. 1994. write for info. (0-936913-09-6, RRD 167) NCRCRD.
***O'Brien, David M.** Constitutional Law & Politics Vol. 1: Struggles for Power & Governemtal Accountability. 2nd ed. LC 94-29012. (C). 1994. pap. text ed. 36.95 (0-393-96610-0) Norton.

O

— Constitutional Law & Politics Vol. 2: Civil Rights & Civil Liberties. LC 94-29012. (C). 1994. pap. text ed. 36.95x (0-393-96611-9) Norton.
— Privacy, Law & Public Policy. LC 79-14131. (Praeger Special Studies). 278p. 1979. text ed. 65.00 (0-275-90403-2, C0403, Praeger Pubs) Greenwood.
— The Public's Right to Know: The Supreme Court & the First Amendment. LC 81-988. 218p. 1981. text ed. 55.00 (0-275-90694-9, C0694, Praeger Pubs) Greenwood.
— The Right of Privacy: Its Constitutional & Social Dimensions; a Comprehensive Bibliography. (Legal Bibliography Ser.: No. 21). 55p. (Orig.). 1980. pap. 15.00 (0-935630-04-X) U of Tex Tarlton Law Lib.
— Storm Center: The Supreme Court in American Politics. 404p. (C). 1992. pap. text ed. 15.95 (0-393-96356-X) Norton.
— Storm Center: The Supreme Court in American Politics. 2nd ed. (Illus.). (C). 1990. pap. text ed. 12.95 (0-393-95912-0) Norton.
— Storm Center: The Supreme Court in American Politics. 3rd ed. 404p. (C). 1993. 24.95 (0-393-03521-2) Norton.
— Storm Center: The Supreme Court in American Politics. 4th ed. 1996. write for info. (0-393-96891-X) Norton.
— Supreme Court Watch-1994. (C). 1994. pap. text ed. 9.95x (0-393-96656-9) Norton.
— Supreme Court Watch-1994. 1994. 19.95 (0-393-03681-2) Norton.
— Supreme Court Watch 1995: An Annual Supplement. 1995. pap. write for info. (0-393-96892-8) Norton.
— What Process Is Due? Courts & Science-Policy Disputes. LC 87-43100. 190p. 1988. text ed. 29.95 (0-87154-623-X) Russell Sage.
O'Brien, David M., jt. ed. see Cannon, Mark W.
O'Brien, David M., jt. auth. see Craig, Barbara H.
O'Brien, David W. California Employer-Employee Benefits Handbook: With 1987 Supplement. 6th ed. LC 78-71230. 786p. 1986. pap. text ed. 97.95 (0-9602204-0-2) Winterbrook.
— Misconduct Cases Book. LC 85-51769. 501p. (Orig.). 1985. 49.00 (0-9602204-1-0) Winterbrook.
***O'Brien, Dawn.** Down the Road in the Carolinas: Daytrips & Weekend Vacations. 408p. (Orig.). 1994. pap. 14.95 (0-9623690-8-X) Becklyn.
— North Carolina's Historic Restaurants & Their Recipes. 3rd rev. ed. LC 83-2831. (Illus.). 204p. 1990. 14.95 (0-89587-067-3) Blair.
— Virginia's Historic Restaurants & Their Recipes. 2nd rev. ed. LC 84-2801. (Illus.). 205p. 1990. 14.95 (0-89587-068-1) Blair.
O'Brien, Dawn & Matkov, Becky R. Florida's Historic Restaurants & Their Recipes. rev. ed. (Illus.). 204p. 1994. 14.95 (0-89587-120-3) Blair.
O'Brien, Dawn & Mulford, Karen. South Carolina's Historic Restaurants & Their Recipes. rev. ed. (Illus.). 204p. 1992. 14.95 (0-89587-097-5) Blair.
O'Brien, Dawn & Schenck, Rebecca. Maryland's Historic Restaurants & Their Recipes. LC 85-15108. (Illus.). 206p. 1985. 12.95 (0-89587-048-7) Blair.
O'Brien, Dawn & Spaugh, Jean. Georgia's Historic Restaurants & Their Recipes. LC 87-20951. (Illus.). 204p. 1987. 12.95 (0-89587-056-8) Blair.
O'Brien, Dawn & Walter, Claire. Pennsylvania's Historic Restaurants & Their Recipes. LC 86-3593. (Illus.). 204p. 1986. 12.95 (0-89587-046-0) Blair.
O'Brien, Dean W., ed. Historic Northeast Wisconsin: A Voyageur Guidebook. 160p. 1994. pap. 10.00 (0-9641499-0-7) Brown County Hist.
O'Brien, Dellanna, jt. auth. see Taylor, Larry.
O'Brien, Denis. Empedocles' Cosmic Cycle: A Reconstruction from the Fragments & Secondary Sources. LC 68-10330. 469p. reprint ed. pap. 133.70 (0-317-08858-0, 2013218) Bks Demand.
— Theodicee Plotinienne, Theodicee Gnostique. LC 92-9638. (Philosophia Antiqua Ser.: Vol. 57). 117p. (FRE.). 1993. 45.75 (90-04-09618-3) E J Brill.
O'Brien, Denis, ed. Foundations of Monetary Economics. 1994. 585.00 (1-85196-190-9, Pub. by Pickering & Chatto UK) Ashgate Pub Co.
O'Brien, Denis P. & Swann, D. Information Agreements, Competition & Efficiency. LC 72-83156. 1969. 29.50 (0-678-07000-8) Kelley.
O'Brien, Donal B. & Coulon, Christian, eds. Charisma & Brotherhood in African Islam. (Oxford Studies in African Affairs). 232p. 1989. 55.00 (0-19-822723-X) OUP.
O'Brien, Ed & Sayers, Scott. Sinatra: The Man & His Music: The Recording Artistry of Francis Albert Sinatra, 1939-1992. 312p. 1992. pap. 24.95 (0-934367-24-8); pap. 14.98 (0-685-59669-9) TX St Direct.
O'Brien, Edna. Arabian Days. 15.95 (0-7043-2150-5, Pub. by Quartet UK) Charles River Bks.
— Country Girls Trilogy. 1987. pap. 14.00 (0-452-26394-8, Plume) NAL-Dutton.
— The Country Girls Trilogy: And Epilogue. LC 86-28557. 544p. 1987. pap. 9.95 (0-452-26182-1, Plume) NAL-Dutton.
— Country Girls Trilogy: Second Epilogue. 1989. pap. 8.95 (0-452-25926-6) NAL-Dutton.
— The Country Girls Trilogy & Epilogue. 1986. 18.95 (0-374-13027-2) FS&G.
— An Edna O'Brien Reader. 432p. (Orig.). 1994. pap. 11.99 (0-446-39516-1) Warner Bks.
— A Fanatic Heart. LC 84-13762. 461p. 1984. 17.95 (0-374-15342-6) FS&G.
— A Fanatic Heart: Selected Stories of Edna O'Brien. 480p. 1985. pap. 7.95 (0-452-25752-2, Plume) NAL-Dutton.
— A Fanatic Heart: Selected Stories of Edna O'Brien. LC 85-8935. 480p. 1985. pap. 12.95 (0-452-26116-3, Plume) NAL-Dutton.
— The High Road. 256p. 1988. 18.95 (0-374-29273-6) FS&G.
— House of Splendid Isolation. LC 93-42602. 1994. 21.00 (0-374-17309-5) FS&G.
— House of Splendid Isolation. LC 94-47256. 1995. 10.95 (0-452-27452-4, Plume) NAL-Dutton.
— House of Splendid Isolation. large type ed. LC 94-28267. 314p. 1994. 21.95 (0-8161-7485-7) Hall.
— Lantern Slides. 1990. 18.95 (0-374-18332-5) FS&G.
— Lantern Slides. 240p. 1991. reprint ed. pap. 8.95 (0-452-26628-9, Plume) NAL-Dutton.
— Nights. 1987. pap. 8.00 (0-374-52051-8) FS&G.
— On the Bone. (C). 1990. 35.00 (0-906887-38-0, Pub. by Greville Pr UK) St Mut.
— A Pagan Place. LC 84-81628. 234p. 1984. pap. 8.00 (0-915308-59-2) Graywolf.
— Time & Tide. 1992. 21.00 (0-374-27776-1) FS&G.
— Time & Tide. 336p. 1993. pap. 10.99 (0-446-39510-2) Warner Bks.
— Virginia: A Play. LC 81-7763. 64p. 1981. 7.95 (0-15-193762-1) HarBrace.
— Virginia: A Play. LC 81-7763. 80p. 1985. pap. 4.95 (0-15-693560-0, Harvest Bks) HarBrace.
O'Brien, Edward. Fifty Best American Short Stories, 1915-1939. (BCL1-PS American Literature Ser.). 868p. 1993. reprint ed. lib. bdg. 119.00 (0-7812-6936-9) Rprt Serv.
O'Brien, Edward J. The Advance of the American Short Story. LC 74-145217. 314p. 1972. reprint ed. 29.00 (0-403-01134-5) Scholarly.
O'Brien, Edward J., ed. Elizabethan Tales. LC 70-178452. (Short Story Index Reprint Ser.). 1977. reprint ed. 21.95 (0-8369-4053-9) Ayer.
O'Brien, Edward J., jt. ed. see Lorch, Robert F.
O'Brien, Edward L., et al. Practical Law for Correctional Personnel: A Resource Manual & a Training Curriculum (by the National Street Law Institute) (Illus.). 249p. (C). 1986. reprint ed. pap. text ed. 16.50 (0-8299-1034-4) West Pub.
O'Brien-Eggleston, Bernadette M., jt. auth. see Eggleston, Steven B.
O'Brien, Elaine F. Anita of Rancho del Mar. LC 90-19711. (Illus.). 176p. (Orig.). (YA). (gr. 4-8). 1991. pap. 8.95 (0-931832-79-9) Fithian Pr.
O'Brien, Elmer, tr. The Essential Plotinus: Representative Treatises from The Enneads. (HPC Classics Ser.). 236p. (C). 1975. lib. bdg. 24.95 (0-915144-10-7); pap. 6.95 (0-915144-09-3) Hackett Pub.
O'Brien, Esse. Art & Artists of Texas. 1993. reprint ed. lib. bdg. 75.00 (0-7812-5971-1) Rprt Serv.
O'Brien, Eugene & Dixon, Andrew. Reinforced & Prestressed Concrete Design: The Complete Process. LC 93-40446. 1995. pap. text ed. 59.95 (0-470-23365-6) Halsted Pr.
O'Brien, F. T. Early Solent Steamers. (C). 1987. 82.00 (0-85174-417-6, Pub. by Brwn Son Ferg) St Mut.
O'Brien, Felicity. Not Peace But a Sword: John Henry Newman. 188p. (C). 1990. text ed. 39.00 (0-85439-327-7, Pub. by St Paul Pubns UK) St Mut.
— Saints in the Making. 107p. (Orig.). 1988. pap. 9.95 (1-85390-021-4, Pub. by Veritas Pubns IE) Irish Bks Media.
— Treasure in Heaven Katharine Drexel. 120p. (C). 1990. 45.00 (0-85439-323-4, Pub. by St Paul Pubns UK) St Mut.
O'Brien, Felicity, jt. auth. see Sinclair, Margaret.
O'Brien, Fitz-James. Diamond Lens & Other Stories. LC 70-109502. (Illus.). reprint ed. 26.50 (0-404-00613-2) AMS Pr.
— Diamond Lens & Other Stories. LC 76-131791. (Illus.). 1971. reprint ed. 29.00 (0-403-00678-3) Scholarly.
— The Poems & Stories of Fitz-James O'Brien. 1972. reprint ed. text ed. 24.95 (0-8422-8102-9) Irvington.
O'Brien, Fitz-James, jt. auth. see Twain, Mark.
O'Brien, Flann. At Swim-Two-Birds. 1976. pap. 12.00 (0-452-25913-4, Plume) NAL-Dutton.
— The Dalkey Archive. LC 92-30923. 204p. 1993. reprint ed. pap. 9.95 (1-56478-019-8) Dalkey Arch.
— The Hard Life. 2nd ed. LC 93-21207. 179p. 1994. reprint ed. pap. 9.95 (1-56478-042-2) Dalkey Arch.
— The Third Policeman. 1976. pap. 11.95 (0-452-25912-6, Plume) NAL-Dutton.
O'Brien, Francis P. The High School Failures: A Study of the School Records of Pupils Failing in Academic or Commercial High School Subjects. LC 70-177127. (Columbia University. Teachers College. Contributions to Education Ser.: No. 102). reprint ed. 37.50 (0-404-55102-5) AMS Pr.
O'Brien, Frank. Dime Novels. (Illus.). 99p. reprint ed. pap. 25.00 (0-87556-183-7) Saifer.
O'Brien, Frank J. Stealth Strike. 264p. 1990. 16.95 (0-8306-3472-X, 3472, TAB-Aero) TAB Bks.
O'Brien, Gail W. The Legal Fraternity & the Making of a New South Community, 1848-1882. LC 85-28952. 224p. 1986. 27.50 (0-8203-0849-8) U of Ga Pr.
O'Brien, Gaynell, jt. auth. see O'Brien, H. V.
O'Brien, Gene & O'Brien, Judith T. Couples Praying: A Special Intimacy. 132p. 1986. pap. 5.95 (0-8091-2816-0) Paulist Pr.
O'Brien, Geoffrey. A Book of Maps. LC 88-92340. 48p. 1989. 4.00 (0-87376-061-1) Red Dust.
— The Phantom Empire. LC 93-6824. 1993. 20.00 (0-393-03549-2) Norton.
— The Phantom Empire: Movies in the Mind of the Twentieth Century. (Illus.). 288p. 1995. pap. 12.00 (0-393-31296-8, Norton Paperbks) Norton.
O'Brien, Geoffrey, tr. see Verge, Roger.
O'Brien, Geoffrey, et al, eds. Reader's Catalog: An Annotated Selection of More Than 40,000 of the Best Books in Print in 208 Categories. (Illus.). 1380p. 1989. pap. 24.95 (0-924322-00-4) Readers Catalog.
O'Brien, George. Brian Friel. (Twayne's English Authors Ser.: No. 470). 182p. 1989. text ed. 23.95 (0-8057-6980-3, Twayne) Macmillan.
— Brian Friel: A Reference Guide. LC 94-30903. (Reference Guide to Literature Ser.). 152p. 1995. text ed. 40.00 (0-8161-7273-0) G K Hall.
— The Economic History of Ireland in the 17th Century. 1972. 69.95 (0-8490-0082-3) Gordon Pr.
O'Brien, George, jt. auth. see Morton, Gerald.
O'Brien, George A. The Economic History of Ireland in the Eighteenth Century. LC 77-24245. (Perspectives in European History Ser.: No. 15). (Illus.). 437p. 1977. reprint ed. lib. bdg. 45.00 (0-87991-622-2) Porcupine Pr.
— Essay on Medieval Economic Teaching. LC 67-28412. (Reprints of Economic Classics Ser.). 1967. reprint ed. 35.00 (0-678-00336-X) Kelley.
— Essay on the Economic Effects of the Reformation. LC 68-56556. (Reprints of Economic Classics Ser.). 1970. reprint ed. 29.50 (0-678-00591-5) Kelley.
O'Brien, George D. What to Expect from College: A University President's Guide for Students & Parents. 224p. 1993. pap. 10.95 (0-312-09412-4, Pub. by Thomas Dunne Bks) St Martin.
O'Brien, Gerard. Anglo-Irish Politics in the Age of Grattan & Pitt. 232p. 1987. 39.50 (0-7165-2377-9, Pub. by Irish Acad Pr IE) Intl Spec Bk.
O'Brien, Gerard, ed. Parliament, Politics & People: Essays in Eighteenth Century Irish History. 200p. 1989. 39.50 (0-7165-2421-X, 12421, Pub. by Irish Acad Pr IE) Intl Spec Bk.
O'Brien, Gerard, ed. see Gwynn, Aubrey.
***O'Brien, Geri.** Secrets of a Successful Mom. 366p. 1995. spiral bd., pap. 5.95 (1-56245-173-1) Great Quotations.
***O'Brien, Gordon E.** Psychology of Work & Unemployment. LC 85-29604. (Wiley Series in Psychology & Productivity at Work). 329p. 1986. pap. 93.80 (0-7837-8492-9, 2049299) Bks Demand.
— Psychology of Work & Unemployment. LC 85-29604. (Psychology & Productivity at Work Ser.). 315p. 1986. text ed. 137.00 (0-471-10533-3) Wiley.
O'Brien, Grace. The Golden Age of German Music & Its Origins. LC 78-20485. (Encore Music Editions Ser.). 1980. reprint ed. 22.00 (0-88355-861-0) Hyperion Conn.
O'Brien, Grant. Ruckers: A Harpsichord & Virginal Building Tradition. (Cambridge Musical Texts & Monographs). (Illus.). 360p. (C). 1990. 130.00 (0-521-36565-1) Cambridge U Pr.
***O'Brien, Greg, ed.** A Guide to Nature on Cape Cod & the Islands. expanded rev. ed. (Illus.). 272p. 1995. pap. 13.95 (0-940160-61-7) Parnassus Imprints.
O'Brien, H. V. & O'Brien, Gaynell. Painting for Freedom. LC 87-50148. (Illus.). 160p. 1987. 12.95 (0-9618480-0-6) Times Pub TX.
O'Brien, Henry. Atlantis in Ireland: Round Towers of Ireland. LC 73-94419. (Illus.). 536p. 1989. reprint ed. pap. 18.00 (0-89345-245-9, Steinerbks) Garber Comm.
O'Brien, Horacio H. Estructuras Algebraicas III (Grupos Finitos) OAS, General Secretariat, Department of Scientific & Technological Affairs Staff, ed. (Serie de Matematica-Monografia: No. 14). 138p. (C). 1981. pap. text ed. 2.00 (0-8270-1298-5) OAS.
***O'Brien, Howard.** All Things Considered. (American Autobiography Ser.). 345p. 1995. reprint ed. lib. bdg. 89.00 (0-7812-8601-8) Rprt Serv.
O'Brien, J. E. & Dallman, R. J., eds. Phase Change Heat Transfer, 1993. LC 91-55579. 109p. 1993. pap. 40.00 (0-7918-1008-9) ASME.
O'Brien, J. J., jt. auth. see Angel, M. V.
O'Brien, J. J., jt. ed. see Angel, M. V.
O'Brien, J. J., jt. ed. see Lerche, Ian.
O'Brien, J. R. & Verstraete, M., eds. Ciclopidine. (Journal: Haemostasis: Vol. 13, Suppl. 1). (Illus.). ii, 54p. 1983. pap. 38.50 (3-8055-3816-2) S Karger.
O'Brien, J. S., jt. ed. see Durand, P.
O'Brien, J. Stephen. An Urgent Task: What Bishops & Priests Say about Religious Education Programs. 90p. (Orig.). 1989. pap. 8.00 (1-55833-020-8) Natl Cath Educ.
O'Brien, Jack. British Brutality in Ireland. LC 89-50971. (Illus.). 178p. 1989. pap. 15.95 (0-85342-879-4, Pub. by Mercier Pr IE) Dufour.
— The Complete Job Search Organizer. 1995. 9.95 (0-938721-41-0) Kiplinger Bks.
— The Job Search Organizer. (Illus.). 85p. (C). 1990. 14.95 (0-9617524-8-3) Miranda Assocs.
— The Job Search Organizer. LC 90-91686. (Illus.). 55p. (C). 1990. 24.95 (0-9617524-7-5) Miranda Assocs.
— Kiplinger's Career Starter. Date not set. pap. 12.00 (0-8129-2657-9, Times Bks) Random.
— Kiplinger's Career Starter: Your Game Plan for a Successful Job Search. LC 93-3017. 1993. pap. 10.95 (0-938721-25-9) Kiplinger Bks.
— The Return of Silver Chief. 19.95 (0-89190-398-4, Amereon Hse) Amereon Ltd.
— Silver Chief: Dog of the North. 250p. 1991. reprint ed. lib. bdg. 20.95 (0-89966-823-2) Buccaneer Bks.
— The Unionjacking of Ireland. 192p. 1994. pap. 15.95 (1-85635-038-X, Pub. by Mercier Pr IE) Dufour.
O'Brien, Jacqueline & Guinness, Desmond. Dublin: A Grand Tour. LC 94-262. 1994. write for info. (0-8109-3216-4) Abrams.
— Great Irish Houses & Castles. (Illus.). 264p. 1992. 65.00 (0-8109-3365-9) Abrams.
***O'Brien, Jacqueline W. & Wasserman, Steven R., eds.** Statistics Sources: A Subject Guide to Data on Industrial, Business, Social, Educational, Financial & Other Topics for the United States & Internationally, 2 Vols. 19th ed. (Statistics Sources Ser.). 3000p. 1995. text ed. 385.00 (0-8103-9091-4) Gale.
O'Brien, Jacqueline W., jt. ed. see Wasserman, Steven R.
O'Brien, James. Akutagawa & Dazai: Instances of Literary Adaptation. LC 88-70040. (Arizona State University Center for Asian Studies Monograph Ser.: No. 21). 150p. 1988. pap. 10.00 (0-939252-18-X) ASU Ctr Asian.
— Introduction to Information Systems: An End User - Enterprise Perspective, Alternate. LC 94-31626. 525p. (C). 1994. text ed. 58.95 (0-256-16221-2) Irwin.
— Introduction to Information Systems in Business Management. 7th ed. 224p. (C). 1993. student ed, text ed. 20.50 (0-256-11888-4) Irwin.
— Management Information Systems: A Managerial End-User Perspective. (C). 1990. text ed. 57.95 (0-256-07862-9) Irwin.
— Management Information Systems, International: Managerial End User Perspective. 2nd ed. 728p. (C). 1992. text ed. 35.50 (0-256-10830-7) Irwin.
— Music in World Cultures: Understanding Multiculturalism Through the Arts. 400p. (C). 1994. per., pap. text ed. 36.95 (0-8403-9122-6) Kendall-Hunt.
O'Brien, James, tr. Muro Saisei: Three Works. (Cornell East Asia Ser.: No. 38). 131p. 1985. 9.00 (0-939657-38-4) Cornell East Asia Pgm.
O'Brien, James, tr. see Dazai, Osamu.
O'Brien, James A. Computer Concepts & Applications. 3rd ed. 640p. (C). 1988. pap. text ed. 42.95 (0-256-07001-6) Irwin.
— Introduction to Information Systems. 7th ed. LC 93-24018. 534p. (C). 1993. text ed. 58.95 (0-256-11884-1) Irwin.
— Introduction to Information Systems in Business Management. 6th ed. (Illus.). 608p. (C). 1990. text ed. 53.95 (0-256-08855-1, 14-1108-06) Irwin.
— Liam O'Flaherty. LC 78-126291. (Irish Writers Ser.). 124p. 1975. 8.50 (0-8387-7772-4); pap. 1.95 (0-8387-7773-2) Bucknell U Pr.
— Management Information Systems: A Managerial End User Perspective. 2nd ed. LC 92-17554. 704p. (C). 1992. text ed. 64.95 (0-256-10346-1) Irwin.
— The Nature of Computers. LC 92-71117. 464p. (C). 1993. pap. text ed. 37.25 (0-15-500048-9) Dryden Pr.
— The Nature of Computers. LC 92-71117. 464p. (C). 1993. trans. 76.25 (0-15-500787-4) Dryden Pr.
— The Nature of Computers. 3rd ed. LC 92-71117. 464p. (C). 1994. 36.25 (0-03-098354-1) Dryden Pr.
— The Nature of Computers: With Productivity Software Guides. LC 92-71117. 840p. (C). 1993. pap. text ed. 48.00 (0-15-500489-1) Dryden Pr.

An Asterisk (*) at the beginning of an entry indicates that the title is appearing in BIP for the first time.

O'Brien, James A. & Kain, Richard M. George Russell-AE. (Irish Writers Ser.). 93p. 1976. 8.50 (0-8387-1101-4); pap. 1.95 (0-8387-1206-1) Bucknell U Pr.

O'Brien, James A., jt. auth. see Kaye, Harvey.

O'Brien, James C. & Drenowatz, Claire. Blueprint for Fundraising. (Illus.). 800p. 1991. student ed 295.00 (0-9628823-0-5) Money Magnet.

O'Brien, James F. How to Design by Accident: A Book of Accidental Effects for Artists & Designers. (Illus.). 215p. (Orig.). 1968. pap. 9.95 (0-486-21942-9) Dover.

***O'Brien, James J.** Construction Documentation. 3rd ed. LC 95-1088. (Construction Law Library). 1995. text ed. 110.00 (0-471-11041-8) Wiley.

— CPM in Construction Management. 4th ed. LC 92-24367. 1993. text ed. 71.00 (0-07-047921-6) McGraw.

— Preconstruction Estimating: Budget Through Bid. 1994. text ed. 49.00 (0-07-047928-3) McGraw.

O'Brien, James J., ed. Lawrence D. Miles: Recollections. (Illus.). 124p. 1988. 17.50 (0-9619440-0-5) Value Found.

O'Brien, James P. The Listening Experience: Elements, Forms, & Styles in Music. (Illus.). 558p. (C). 1987. pap. 28.00 (0-02-872130-6) Schirmer Bks.

— The Listening Experience: Elements, Forms, & Styles in Music. (Illus.). 558p. (C). 1987. audio 48.00 (0-02-872131-4) Schirmer Bks.

— The Listening Experience: Elements, Forms, & Styles in Music. 2nd ed. (C). 1995. teacher ed write for info. (0-02-872134-9); pap. 35.00 (0-02-872139-X); audio 45.00 (0-02-872138-1); cd-rom 70.00 (0-02-872135-7); 25.00 (0-02-872137-3); 50.00 (0-02-872136-5); write for info. (0-02-872133-0) Schirmer Bks.

— The Listening Experience: Elements, Forms, & Styles in Music, Set. (Illus.). 558p. (C). 1987. lp 48.00 (0-02-872630-8) Schirmer Bks.

— Teaching Music. 362p. (C). 1983. pap. text ed. 34.00 (0-03-057718-7) HB Coll Pubs.

O'Brien, James W. Science Policy, Biotechnology, & American State Government: Recommendations for State Action. (Studies in Technology & Social Change: No. 12). 76p. (Orig.). (C). 1989. pap. 8.00 (0-945271-17-4) ISU-TSCP.

O'Brien, Jane. Alien. (Tales of Terror Ser.). (Illus.). 48p. (J). (gr. 5-6). 1991. text ed. 13.95 (0-89686-573-8, Crstwood Hse) Silver Burdett Pr.

O'Brien, Jay & Roseberry, William, eds. Golden Ages, Dark Ages: Imagining the Past in Anthropology & History. 348p. 1991. 35.00 (0-520-07018-6) U CA Pr.

O'Brien, Jay, jt. auth. see O'Neill, Norman.

O'Brien, Jerry, ed. see Stanley, Charles A.

***O'Brien, Jim.** Maz & the Sixty Bucs: When Pittsburgh & Its Pirates Went All the Way. (Pittsburgh Proud Ser.). (Illus.). 512p. 1993. 24.95 (0-916114-12-0); pap. 14.95 (0-916114-13-9) J P OBrien.

— Penguin Profiles: Pittsburgh's Boys of Winter. (Pittsburgh Proud Ser.). (Illus.). 448p. 1994. 24.95 (0-916114-16-3); pap. 14.95 (0-916114-17-1) J P OBrien.

— Remember Roberto: Clemente Recalled by Teammates, Family, Friends & Fans. (Pittsburgh Proud Ser.). (Illus.). 448p. 1994. 24.95 (0-916114-14-7); pap. 14.95 (0-916114-15-5) J P OBrien.

— Whatever It Takes: The Continuing Saga of the Pittsburgh Steelers II. (Pittsburgh Proud Ser.). (Illus.). 486p. 1992. 24.95 (0-916114-10-4); pap. 14.95 (0-916114-11-2) J P OBrien.

O'Brien, Jim, jt. auth. see Wolfson, Marty.

O'Brien, Joan. State of Religion Atlas. (Illus.). 1993. pap. 16.00 (0-671-79376-4, Touchstone Bks) S&S Trade.

O'Brien, Joan & Major, Wilfred. In the Beginning: Creation Myths from Ancient Mesopotamia, Israel, & Greece. LC 81-21311. (American Academy of Religion Academy Ser.). (C). 1985. pap. 19.95 (0-89130-559-9, 010311) Scholars Pr GA.

O'Brien, Joan V. Bilingual Selections from Sophocles' Antigone: An Introduction to the Text for the Greekless Reader. LC 76-50116. 136p. 1977. 6.95 (0-8093-0826-6) S Ill U Pr.

O'Brien, Joanne & Kwok Man Ho. The Elements of Feng Shui. (Illus.). 144p. 1990. pap. 9.95 (1-85230-220-8) Element MA.

O'Brien, Joanne, jt. ed. see Man Ho, Kwok.

O'Brien, Joanne, tr. see Man Ho, Kwok & O'Brien, Joanne, eds.

O'Brien, Jodi, jt. auth. see Kolluck, Peter.

***O'Brien, John.** Break a Leg. 1983. 5.00 (0-87129-489-3) Dramatic Pub.

— Daniel Mannix: Builder of the Australian Church. 1989. pap. 22.00 (1-85390-042-7, Pub. by Veritas IE) St Mut.

— High Water. Date not set. pap. write for info. (0-394-56451-0) Knopf.

— Leaving Las Vegas. 206p. 1991. 19.50 (0-922820-12-0) Watermark Pr.

— Memory. 1981. 2.50 (0-87129-232-7, M52) Dramatic Pub.

— Milan Kundera & Feminism: Dangerous Intersections. LC 94-46777. 1995. text ed. 39.95 (0-312-12206-3) St Martin.

— Mirrors. 1982. 3.00 (0-87129-540-7, M53) Dramatic Pub.

Obrien, John. Night Before Christmas Coloring Book. (Illus.). (J). (gr. k-3). 1990. pap. 2.95 (0-486-24169-6) Dover.

***O'Brien, John.** Please Don't Go Back Where You Came From. 1994. 5.00 (0-87129-434-6, P75) Dramatic Pub.

— Polish Robbin' Hoods: A Virtual Primer on Crime - The Exploits of the Country's Most Inept. 342p. 1992. 19.95 (0-929387-85-6) Bonus Books.

— Sam & Spot. (Illus.). 32p. (Orig.). (J). (gr. 1-4). 1995. pap. 4.99 (1-56790-501-3) Cool Hand Comms.

— Sam & Spot: A Silly Story. LC 94-26643. (Illus.). 32p. (J). (gr. 1-4). 1995. 14.95 (1-56790-500-5, Cool Kids Pr) Cool Hand Comms.

— Softy. 18p. 1991. pap. 2.50 (0-87129-098-7, S94) Dramatic Pub.

— Success. 43p. 1984. pap. 2.50 (0-87129-100-2, S70) Dramatic Pub.

— Theology & the Option for the Poor. (Theology & Life Ser.: Vol. 22). 167p. (Orig.). 1992. pap. text ed. 14.95 (0-8146-5787-7) Liturgical Pr.

— The Twelve Days of Christmas. (Illus.). 32p. (J). 1993. 14.95 (1-56397-142-9) Boyds Mills Pr.

O'Brien, John, et al, eds. Children of the World: England. LC 89-4462. (Illus.). 64p. (J). (gr. 5-6). 1989. lib. bdg. 21.26 (1-55532-211-5) Gareth Stevens Inc.

O'Brien, John & Baumann, Edward W. The Chicago Heist. LC 81-68394. (Illus.). 280p. (Orig.). 1981. pap. 6.95 (0-89708-053-X) And Bks.

***O'Brien, John & Srivastava, Sanjay.** Modern Portfolio Theory. 1994. write for info. (0-538-84809-X) S-W Pub.

— Option Valuation. LC 94-44758. 1995. write for info. (0-538-84810-3) S-W Pub.

O'Brien, John & Travers, Pauric. The Irish Emigrant Experience in Australia. 279p. 1991. pap. 26.00 (1-85371-129-2, Pub. by Poolbeg Pr IE) Dufour.

O'Brien, John, jt. auth. see Baumann, Ed.

O'Brien, John, jt. auth. see Baumann, Edward.

O'Brien, John, et al, eds. Psychotherapies with Children & Adolescents: Adapting the Psychodynamic Process. LC 91-44051. 368p. 1992. text ed. 46.50 (0-88048-406-3) Am Psychiatric.

O'Brien, John A. The Faith of Millions. rev. ed. LC 74-82119. 416p. 1974. pap. 9.95 (0-87973-830-8) Our Sunday Visitor.

O'Brien, John C. & Goldman, Roger L. Federal Criminal Trial Evidence. LC 89-61440. 726p. 1989. text ed. 15.00 (0-685-45800-8, C1-1184) PLI.

***O'Brien, John C., et al.** Missouri Evidentiary Foundations. 400p. 1994. 75.00 (1-55834-177-3) Michie Butterworth.

O'Brien, John E. Refreshed by the Word: Cycle C. 144p. 1994. pap. 10.95 (0-8091-3506-X) Paulist Pr.

O'Brien, John J. Defending DWI Cases in Connecticut. 149p. (Orig.). 1992. pap. 50.00 (1-878698-13-3) Atlantic Law.

Obrien, John J. A Turn of the Verse. 1991. 2.00 (0-9628932-0-X) J Obrien.

***O'Brien, John M.** Alexander the Great: The Invisible Enemy. (Illus.). 360p. 1994. pap. 16.95 (0-415-10617-6, B3961) Routledge.

— Alexander the Great: The Invisible Enemy: A Biography. LC 91-37212. (Illus.). 336p. 1992. 29.95 (0-415-07254-9, A7501) Routledge.

— Medieval Church. (Quality Paperback Ser.: No. 227). 120p. (Orig.). 1968. pap. 11.00 (0-8226-0227-X) Littlefield.

O'Brien, John T., Jr. From Bondage to Citizenship. LC 90-33971. (Dissertations in Nineteenth-Century American Political & Social History). 528p. 1990. reprint ed. 35.00 (0-8240-0047-1) Garland.

O'Brien, Joseph & Kurins, Andris. Boss of Bosses. large type ed. 607p. 1992. reprint ed. lib. bdg. 22.95 (1-56054-284-5) Thorndike Pr.

— Boss of Bosses. large type ed. 607p. 1992. reprint ed. pap. 14.95 (1-56054-945-9) Thorndike Pr.

O'Brien, Joseph F. Boss of Bosses: The FBI & Paul Castellano. 1992. mass mkt. 5.99 (0-440-21229-4) Dell.

O'Brien, Joseph V. Dear, Dirty Dublin: A City in Distress 1899-1916. LC 79-64662. (Illus.). 416p. 1982. 50.00 (0-520-03965-3) U CA Pr.

— William O'Brien & the Course of Irish Politics, 1881-1918. LC 74-22970. (Illus.). 287p. reprint ed. pap. 81.80 (0-685-23978-0, 2031542) Bks Demand.

***O'Brien, Judith.** Ashton's Bride. Marrow, Linda, ed. 352p. (Orig.). 1995. mass mkt. 5.50 (0-671-87149-8) PB.

— Rhapsody in Time. Marrow, Linda, ed. 304p. (Orig.). 1994. mass mkt. 5.50 (0-671-87148-X) PB.

O'Brien, Judith T., jt. auth. see O'Brien, Gene.

O'Brien, Julia. Priest & Levite in Malachi. (Society of Biblical Literature Dissertation Ser.). 310p. 1991. 22.95 (1-55540-438-3, 062121); pap. 14.95 (1-55540-439-1, 062121) Scholars Pr GA.

***O'Brien, Julia M. & Horton, Fred L., Jr., eds.** The Yahweh-Baal Confrontation & Other Studies in Biblical Literature & Archaeology: Essays in Honour of Emmett Willard Hamrick. LC 95-1377. (Studies in Bible & Early Christianity: Vol. 35). (Illus.). 194p. 1995. text ed. 79.95 (0-7734-2426-1, Mellen Biblical Pr) E Mellen.

O'Brien, Justin. The Wellness Tree: The Dynamic Six-Step Program for Rejuvenating Health & Creating Optimal Wellness. 2nd ed. LC 93-10357. (Illus.). 200p. (Orig.). (C). 1993. pap. 16.00 (0-936663-08-1) Yes Intl.

O'Brien, Justin, jt. auth. see Bates, Charles.

O'Brien, Justin, tr. see Camus, Albert.

O'Brien, Justin, tr. see Gide, Andre.

O'Brien, Justin, ed. see Gide, Andre.

O'Brien, K. & Gorenberg, Steve, eds. Electric Boys - Groovus Maximus. pap. 19.95 (0-89524-728-3) Cherry Lane.

O'Brien, Kate. The Ante-Room. 306p. 1992. pap. 10.95 (0-86068-825-9, Pub. by Virago Pr UK) Trafalgar.

— Last of Summer. (Virago Modern Classic Ser.). 243p. 1993. reprint ed. pap. 10.95 (1-85381-165-3, Pub. by Virago Pr UK) Trafalgar.

— Talk of Angels. 300p. 1995. 19.95 (0-7868-6191-6) Hyperion.

— Teresa of Avila. 96p. 1993. pap. 11.95 (1-85635-054-1, Pub. by Mercier Pr IE) Dufour.

O'Brien, Katherine, jt. ed. see Nasr, Seyyed H.

O'Brien, Kathleen. The Colorado Ski Industry: Highlights of the 1986-87 Season. rev. ed. 27p. 1987. pap. text ed. 15.00 (0-89478-000-X) U CO Busn Res Div.

— Colorado Travel & Tourism Statistics. 67p. 1986. pap. text ed. 25.00 (0-89478-110-3) U CO Busn Res Div.

— Cost of Recreation & Leisure Activities. 1988. pap. text ed. 25.00 (0-89478-056-5) U CO Busn Res Div.

— A Forgotten Magic. (Presents Ser.). 1994. mass mkt. 2.99 (0-373-11642-X, 1-11642-5) Harlequin Bks.

— Memory Lapse. (Temptation Ser.: No. 522). 1995. pap. 3.25 (0-373-25626-4, 1-25626-2) Harlequin Bks.

— Michael's Silence. 1994. mass mkt. 2.99 (0-373-11698-5, 1-11698-7) Harlequin Bks.

— When Dragons Dream. (Presents Plus Ser.). 1993. mass mkt. 2.99 (0-373-11600-4, 1-11600-3) Harlequin Bks.

O'Brien, Kathleen, ed. see Brock, Jim, et al.

O'Brien, Kathleen, jt. auth. see Gamon, David.

O'Brien, Kathryn. The Great & the Gracious. (Illus.). 292p. 1987. reprint ed. pap. 22.50 (0-932052-56-8) North Country.

O'Brien, Keith T. Computer Modeling for Extrusion & Other Continuous Polymer Processes. 552p. (C). 1992. text ed. 125.00 (1-56990-068-X) Hanser-Gardner.

***O'Brien, Kenneth P. & Parsons, Lynn H., eds.** The Home-Front War: World War II & American Society. LC 95-3803. (Contributions in American History Ser.: Vol. 161). 224p. 1995. text ed. 55.00 (0-313-29211-6, Greenwood Pr) Greenwood.

O'Brien, Kevin & Corn, David. Energy Conservation: A Campus Guide. 33p. 1981. 5.00 (0-936758-04-X) Ctr Responsive Law.

O'Brien, Kevin, tr. see Vertov, Dziga.

O'Brien, Kevin J. Reform Without Liberalization: China's National People's Congress & the Politics of Institutional Change. (Illus.). 324p. (C). 1990. 54.95 (0-521-38086-3) Cambridge U Pr.

O'Brien, Kevin J., jt. auth. see Walkow, Richard A.

O'Brien, Kevin T., ed. Composite Materials, Vol. 3: Fatigue & Fracture. (Illus.). 845p. 1991. text ed. 148.00 (0-685-52360-8, 04-011100-33) ASTM.

O'Brien, Kieran D. Ireland: An Illustrated Yearbook. (Illus.). 112p. 1994. 22.95 (0-86281-509-6, Pub. by Appletree Pr IE) Irish Bks Media.

O'Brien, Larry. Exploring Artificial Life in C Plus Plus. 1994. disk, pap. 39.95 (1-55851-391-4) M&T Bks.

— Introducing Quantitative Geography: Measurement, Method & Generalised Linear Models. LC 91-28683. (Geography & Environment Ser.). 340p. (C). 1992. 67.50 (0-415-00465-9, A2528); pap. 35.00 (0-415-07558-0, A6852) Routledge.

O'Brien, Larry & Harris, Frank. Retailing: Shopping, Society & Space. 224p. (C). 1990. lib. bdg. 38.95 (0-8464-1515-1) Beekman Pubs.

O'Brien, Laurie. Rogues Codes. 100p. 1993. pap. 12.00 (0-916092-24-0) Tex Ctr Writers.

O'Brien, Lee. American Jewish Organizations & Israel: Arabic Edition. Institute for Palestine Studies Staff, tr. 393p. (Orig.). (C). 1987. pap. 10.00 (0-88728-198-2) Inst Palestine.

O'Brien, Linda, tr. see De Heusch, Luc.

O'Brien, Lucy. Annie Lennox: Sweet Dreams Are Made of This. (Illus.). 224p. (Orig.). 1993. pap. 13.95 (0-312-09740-9) St Martin.

O'Brien, Lynn. Strengthening of Skills: Advanced Teacher's Manual. 206p. 1991. teacher ed 199.00 (1-56602-044-1); student ed 69.95 (1-56602-045-X) Research Better.

— Strengthening of Skills: Basic Teacher's Manual. 3rd ed. 221p. 1991. teacher ed 199.00 (1-56602-042-5); student ed 69.95 (1-56602-043-3) Research Better.

O'Brien, M. Divorce: Facing the Issues. 1993. 64.00 (1-85594-077-9, Pub. by Attic Pr IE) St Mut.

O'Brien, M. A. New Russian-English & English-Russian Dictionary. pap. 8.95 (0-486-20208-9) Dover.

O'Brien, M. J. Archaeology of the Central Salt River Valley: An Overview of the Prehistoric Occupation, Vol. 46. (Missouri Archaeologist Ser.). 1985. 8.00 (0-943414-66-0) MO Arch Soc.

O'Brien, M. J., jt. auth. see Majewski, T.

***O'Brien, Maas, ed.** Divorce: Facing the Issues. 160p. (Orig.). 1995. pap. 11.99 (1-85594-195-3) InBook.

O'Brien, Maire, jt. auth. see O'Brien, Conor C.

O'Brien, Margaret. Discovering Your Light: Common Journeys of Young Adults. Teutschman, Emilie, ed. LC 90-66455. 64p. (Orig.). 1991. student ed 6.95 (1-878718-09-6) Resurrection.

— My Diary. (American Autobiography Ser.). 117p. 1995. reprint ed. lib. bdg. 69.00 (0-7812-8602-6) Rprt Serv.

O'Brien, Margaret, jt. ed. see Lewis, Charles.

O'Brien, Margaret, jt. auth. see Shepherd, Ursula L.

O'Brien, Marie, jt. auth. see Kearns, Kimberly.

O'Brien, Marion, jt. ed. see Horowitz, Frances D.

O'Brien, Marion, jt. ed. see Horowitz, Frances Degen.

O'Brien, Mark. High Tech Jobs for Non-Tech Grads. 1986. 15.50 (0-13-387911-9) S&S Trade.

— The MBA Answer Book: A Career Guide for the Person Who Means Business. (Illus.). 240p. 1984. 15.50 (0-13-566779-8) P-H.

O'Brien, Mark A., jt. auth. see Campbell, Anthony F.

***O'Brien, Mark S., ed.** Pediatric Neurological Surgery - Sponsored by the Subcommittee on Continuing Education II (Expanded Program), American Association of Neurological Surgeons, & Congress of Neurological Surgeons. fac. ed. LC 78-3005. (Seminars in Neurological Surgery Ser.). (Illus.). 216p. Date not set. pap. 61.60 (0-7837-7277-7, 2047029) Bks Demand.

O'Brien, Mary. Reproducing the World: Essays in Feminist Theory. (Feminist Theory & Politics Ser.). 306p. (C). 1989. pap. text ed. 20.95 (0-8133-0760-0) Westview.

O'Brien, Mary & Christie, Clare, eds. Single Women: Affirming Our Spiritual Journey. LC 92-39121. 232p. 1993. text ed. 49.95 (0-89789-321-2, H321, Bergin & Garvey) Greenwood.

O'Brien, Mary, ed. see Christie, Clare.

***O'Brien, Mary B.** Jeannette Rankin: Bright Star in the Big Sky. (Illus.). 80p. (Orig.). Date not set. pap. 7.95 (1-56044-360-X) Falcon Pr MT.

— Jeannette Rankin: Bright Star in the Big Sky. (Illus.). 80p. (Orig.). 1994. 10.95 (1-56044-265-4) Falcon Pr MT.

O'Brien, Mary B., jt. auth. see McCarney-Muldoon, Eileen.

***O'Brien, Mary E.** The AIDS Challenge: Breaking Through the Boundaries. LC 94-43170. 176p. 1995. text ed. 49.95 (0-86569-247-5, Auburn Hse) Greenwood.

— In Sickness & in Health--What Every Man Should Know about the Woman He Loves. LC 90-4408. (Illus.). 208p. (Orig.). 1991. pap. 14.95 (0-929173-05-8) Health Press.

— Living with HIV: Experiment in Courage. LC 91-44130. 248p. 1992. text ed. 55.00 (0-86569-040-5, T040, Auburn Hse); pap. text ed. 18.95 (0-86569-203-3, R203, Auburn Hse) Greenwood.

O'Brien, Mary E., jt. ed. see Luteyn, James L.

***O'Brien, Mary J.** Implementation Plan & Recommendations for Integrated Service Networks (ISNs) & a Regulated All-Payer Option (RAPO) Minnesota Care. 62p. (Orig.). (C). 1994. pap. text ed. 45.00x (0-7881-1375-5) Diane Pub.

O'Brien, Mary L. Netsuke: A Guide for Collectors. LC 65-11837. (Illus.). 246p. 1965. 45.00 (0-8048-0423-0, TR84-1) C E Tuttle.

***O'Brien, Maryann.** Gambler's Desire. 288p. (Orig.). Date not set. pap. text ed. 6.50 (0-515-11658-0) Jove Pubns.

— Night Train. 272p. 1994. pap. 4.99 (0-7865-0058-1) Diamond.

O'Brien, MaryEllen, jt. auth. see Keller, Hans J.

***O'Brien, Maureen.** Deadly Reflection. 288p. 1995. pap. 11.95 (0-7472-4374-3, Pub. by Headline UK) Trafalgar.

— Who's Got the Ball? (& Other Nagging Questions about Team Life) A Player's Guide for Work Teams. LC 94-23535. (Management Ser.). 224p. 1995. 22.00 (0-7879-0057-5) Jossey-Bass.

O'Brien, Maureen, jt. auth. see Bloom, Bernard M.

O'Brien, Maureen C. A History of the Burke - Bourke Clan. (Illus.). 300p. 1991. 55.00 (0-9629074-0-5) Clan Pubns.

— In Support of Liberty: European Paintings at the 1883 Pedestal Fund Art Loan Exhibition. LC 86-60099. (Illus.). 180p. (C). 1986. pap. 20.00 (0-943526-14-0) Parrish Art.

O'Brien, Maureen C. & Mandel, Patricia C. The American Painter-Etcher Movement. LC 84-60411. (Illus.). 62p. 1984. pap. 15.00 (0-943526-11-6) Parrish Art.

— Nineteenth Century American Etchings in the Collection of The Parrish Art Museum. LC 87-61051. 108p. 1987. pap. 15.00 (0-943526-16-7) Parrish Art.

O'Brien, Maurice & O'Brien, Christine, eds. New Zealand Law Reports, 6 pts., Set. 1993. write for info. (0-318-72510-X) Butterworth Legal Pubs.

***O'Brien, Mauryeen.** New Day Facilitator's Guide. 38p. 1993. 14.95 (0-89944-265-X) Don Bosco Multimedia.

— New Day Journal: A Journey from Grief to Healing. 92p. 1993. 12.95 (0-89944-264-1) Don Bosco Multimedia.

O'Brien, Meg. Thin Ice. LC 93-8460. 1993. 18.50 (0-385-42572-4) Doubleday.

— Thin Ice. 1995. mass mkt. 4.99 (0-553-56962-7) Bantam.

O'Brien, Michael. Cat Monsters & Head Pots: The Archaeology of Missouri's Pemiscot Bayou. (Illus.). 472p. 1994. 39.95 (0-8262-0969-6) U of Mo Pr.

— A Character of Hugh Legare. LC 85-3207. 372p. 1985. text ed. 40.00x (0-87049-471-6) U of Tenn Pr.

— The Floor & the Breath. 72p. 1994. pap. 7.50 (1-886044-03-1) Cairn Editions.

— The Idea of the American South: 1920-1941. LC 78-12250. 1979. text ed. 42.50x (0-8018-2166-5) Johns Hopkins.

— The Idea of the American South, 1920-1941. LC 89-43551. 296p. 1990. reprint ed. pap. text ed. 16.95 (0-8018-4017-1) Johns Hopkins.

— McCarthy & McCarthyism in Wisconsin. LC 80-16792. 288p. 1981. 32.00 (0-8262-0319-1) U of Mo Pr.

— Phil Hart: The Conscience of the Senate. 250p. 1996. 29.95 (0-87013-407-8) Mich St U Pr.

— Rethinking the South: Essays in Intellectual History. LC 87-32482. 304p. 1988. text ed. 42.50x (0-8018-3617-4) Johns Hopkins.

— Rethinking the South: Essays in Intellectual History. LC 92-21424. (Brown Thrasher Bks.). (Illus.). 288p. 1993. reprint ed. pap. 19.95 (0-8203-1525-7) U of Ga Pr.

— The Ruin. 32p. 1986. pap. 4.00 (1-886044-02-3) Cairn Editions.

— Veil, Hard Rain. 48p. 1986. pap. 4.00 (1-886044-01-5) Cairn Editions.

— Vince: A Personal Biography of Vince Lombardi. LC 87-12980. 352p. 1989. pap. 9.95 (0-688-09204-7, Quill) Morrow.

O'Brien, Michael, ed. All Clever Men, Who Make Their Way: Critical Discourse in the Old South. LC 92-17539. (Brown Thrasher Bks.). 480p. 1992. reprint ed. pap. 19.95 (0-8203-1490-0) U of Ga Pr.

— An Evening When Alone: Four Journals of Single Women in the South, 1827-67. LC 92-39514. (Publications of the Southern Texts Society). 512p. (C). 1993. 35.00 (0-8139-1440-X) U Pr of Va.

O'Brien, Michael & Moltke-Hansen, David, eds. Intellectual Life in Antebellum Charleston. LC 85-15022. (Illus.). 488p. 1986. text ed. 47.50 (0-87049-484-8) U of Tenn Pr.

O'Brien, Michael, jt. auth. see McLagan, Patricia.

O'Brien, Michael F. & Sibley, Norman. Photographic Eye: Learning to See with a Camera. rev. ed. LC 93-74644. (Illus.). 288p. 1995. 23.96 (0-87192-283-5) Davis Mass.

O'Brien, Michael J. Grassland, Forest, & Historical Settlement: An Analysis of Dynamics in Northeast Missouri. LC 84-3660. (Studies in North American Archaeology). (Illus.). 367p. reprint ed. pap. 104.60 (0-7837-6890-7, 2046720) Bks Demand.

— A Hidden Phase of American History: Ireland's Part in America's Struggle for Liberty. LC 76-165648. (Select Bibliographies Reprint Ser.). 1977. reprint ed. 42.95 (0-8369-5957-4) Ayer.

O

An Asterisk (*) at the beginning of an entry indicates that the title is appearing in BIP for the first time.

— Irish Settlers in America: A Consolidation of Articles from the Journal of the American Irish Historical Society, 2 vols., Set. LC 78-78381. 1282p. 1993. reprint ed. 75.00 (*0-8063-0837-0*) Genealog Pub.
— Pioneer Irish in New England. 325p. 1988. reprint ed. pap. 18.00 (*1-55613-106-2*) Heritage Bk.
O'Brien, Michael J. & Clarke, J. I. A Hidden Phase of American History. LC 76-165648. (Illus.). 533p. reprint ed. lib. bdg. 17.50 (*0-8290-0493-9*) Irvington.
O'Brien, Michael J. & Lewarch, Dennis E., eds. Plowzone Archeology: Contributions to Theory & Technique. (Publications in Anthropology: No. 27). 214p. 1981. pap. 12.15 (*0-935462-18-X*) Vanderbilt Pubns.
***O'Brien, Michael J. & Shook, Larry.** Profit from Experience: How to Make the Most of Your Learning & Your Life. 192p. 1995. 24.95 (*1-885167-12-1*); pap. 14. 95 (*1-885167-06-7*) Bard & Stephen.
O'Brien, Michael J., et al. A Late Formative Irrigation Settlement below Monte Albán: Survey & Excavation on the Xoxocotlan Piedmont, Oaxaca, Mexico. (Institute of Latin American Studies Special Publication). (Illus.). 254p. 1982. text ed. 27.50 (*0-292-74628-8*) U of Tex Pr.
O'Brien, Mike, jt. auth. see Noble, Dennis L.
O'Brien, Mollie M. A Pilgrim Wind. LC 85-60237. 64p. (Orig.). 1985. pap. 5.95 (*0-89390-062-1*) Resource Pubns.
O'Brien-Moore, A. Madness in Ancient Literature. 1973. 69. 95 (*0-8490-0575-2*) Gordon Pr.
O'Brien, N. R. & Slatt, R. M. Argillaceous Rock Atlas. (Illus.). xv, 141p. 1990. 79.00 (*0-387-97306-0*) Spr-Verlag.
O'Brien-Nabors, Lyn & Gelardi, Robert C., eds. Alternative Sweetners. 2nd ed. (Food Science & Technology Ser.: Vol. 48). 480p. 1991. 160.00 (*0-8247-8475-8*) Dekker.
O'Brien, Nancy P. Test Construction: A Bibliography of Selected Resources. LC 87-25119. 320p. 1988. text ed. 59.95 (*0-313-23435-3*, CTC/, Greenwood Pr) Greenwood.
O'Brien, Nancy P. & Fabiano, Emily S. Core List of Books & Journals in Education. 136p. 1991. 39.95 (*0-89774-559-0*) Oryx Pr.
O'Brien, Nellie. We Made the West Wild. Van Treese, James B., ed. 148p. 1994. pap. 7.95 (*1-56901-160-5*) NW Pub.
O'Brien, Niall. Seeds of Injustice: Reflections on the Murder Frame-up of the Negros. 200p. 1985. pap. 8.95 (*0-86278-091-8*, Pub. by OBrien Pr IE) Dufour.
O'Brien, Niall. Island of Tears, Island of Hope: Living the Gospel in a Revolutionary Situation. LC 93-23776. 175p. (Orig.). 1993. pap. 12.95 (*0-88344-927-7*) Orbis Bks.
O'Brien, Niall, jt. auth. see Gill, Denis.
O'Brien, P. J. Will Rogers: Ambassador of Good Will. 1976. 21.95 (*0-8488-1114-3*) Amereon Ltd.
O'Brien, P. K., intro. The Industrial Revolution in Europe, Vol. 1. LC 93-40550. (Industrial Revolutions Ser.: Vols. 4-5). 1994. write for info. (*0-631-18073-7*) Blackwell Pubs.
— The Industrial Revolution in Europe, Vol. 2. LC 93-40550. (Industrial Revolutions Ser.: Vols. 4-5). 1994. write for info. (*0-631-18145-8*) Blackwell Pubs.
O'Brien, P. M. The Promoter: His Life & Times. (Illus.). 118p. (YA). (gr. 10-12). 1988. pap. 5.65 (*0-9620540-0-3*) P M O'Brien.
***O'Brien, P. T.** Gospel & Mission in the Writings of Paul: An Exegetical & Theological Analysis. 161p. 1995. reprint ed. pap. 9.99 (*0-8010-2052-2*) Baker Bk.
O'Brien, Paddy. A Gentler Strength: The Yoga Book for Women. (Illus.). 1992. pap. 12.00 (*0-7225-2536-2*) Thorsons SF.
— Positive Management: Assertiveness for Managers. 166p. 1993. pap. 14.95 (*0-89384-240-0*) Pfeiffer & Co.
O'Brien-Palmer, Michelle. Book-Talk: Exciting Literature Experience for Kids. (Illus.). 160p. (J). (gr. k-6). 1993. pap. 16.95 (*1-879235-02-1*) MicNik Pubns.
— Book-Write: A Creative Bookmaking Guide for Young Authors. LC 91-68412. (Illus.). 128p. (J). (gr. k-6). 1992. pap. 16.95 (*1-879235-01-3*) MicNik Pubns.
— I Love to Read: Fun Reading Projects Recommended by Kids. (J). (gr. 1-7). 1995. pap. 16.95 (*1-879235-06-4*) MicNik Pubns.
— Read & Write: Fun Literature & Writing Connections for Kids. (Illus.). 160p. (J). (gr. k-6). 1994. pap. 16.95 (*1-879235-04-8*) MicNik Pubns.
O'Brien, Pat. The Finding. 1994. 16.95 (*0-533-10710-5*) Vantage.
O'Brien, Pat A. Outwitting the Hun; My Escape from a German Prison Camp. (American Biography Ser.). 283p. 1991. reprint ed. lib. bdg. 69.00 (*0-7812-8301-9*) Rprt Serv.
O'Brien, Patricia. The Candidate's Wife. 1993. reprint ed. mass mkt. 5.99 (*0-312-95021-7*) St Martin.
— Ladies Lunch. 1994. 22.00 (*0-671-78906-6*) S&S Trade.
— The Promise of Punishment: Prisons in Nineteenth-Century France. LC 81-47143. (Illus.). 348p. 1981. 49. 50 (*0-691-05339-1*) Princeton U Pr.
— The Woman Alone. LC 72-94650. 288p. 1974. write for info. (*0-8129-0344-7*, Times Bks) Random.
O'Brien, Patricia H., jt. auth. see Bart, Pauline B.
O'Brien, Patricia J. Archeology in Kansas. (Public Education Ser.: No. 9). (Illus.). vii, 144p. (Orig.). 1984. pap. 12.95 (*0-89338-020-2*) U of KS Mus Nat Hist.
O'Brien, Patricia J., jt. ed. see Brown, James A.
O'Brien, Patrick G., comp. Herbert Hoover: A Bibliography. LC 92-29467. (Bibliographies of the Presidents of the United States Ser.: No. 30). 416p. 1992. text ed. 69.50 (*0-313-28188-2*, AP30, Greenwood Pr) Greenwood.
O'Brien, Patrick G. & Peak, Kenneth J. Kansas Bootleggers. (Illus.). 135p. (Orig.). 1991. pap. 14.95 (*0-89745-139-2*) Sunflower U Pr.
O'Brien, Patrick K. & Quinault, Roland E., eds. The Industrial Revolution & British Society. LC 92-9649. 300p. (C). 1993. 59.95 (*0-521-43154-9*); pap. 18.95 (*0-521-43744-X*) Cambridge U Pr.
O'Brien, Paul, jt. ed. see Long, Robert L.
O'Brien, Paul E., jt. ed. see Garner, Andrew.
O'Brien, Peggy. Shakespeare Set Free: Teaching Romeo & Juliet, Macbeth, & A Midsummer Night's Dream. 304p. (Orig.). 1993. pap. 18.00 (*0-671-76046-7*, WSP) PB.
O'Brien, Peggy & Rosenman, Jane, eds. Teaching Hamlet & Henry IV, Pt. 1. (Shakespeare Set Free Ser.). 272p. (Orig.). 1994. pap. 18.00 (*0-671-76048-3*, WSP) PB.
O'Brien, Penny. How to Select the Best Child-Care Option for Your Employees. LC 86-22178. 101p. (Orig.). (C). 1987. pap. 11.95 (*0-930256-15-8*) Almar.
O'Brien, Peter. Quick Reference Bible Topic, Colossians, Philemon. 132p. 1991. pap. 6.99 (*0-8499-3246-7*) Word Inc.
O'Brien, Peter & Karmokolias, Yannis. Radical Reform in the Automotive Industry: Policies in Emerging Markets. LC 94-8112. (IFC Discussion Paper Ser.: No. 21). 58p. 1994. write for info. (*0-8213-2806-9*) World Bank.
O'Brien, Peter T. The Epistle to the Philippians: A Commentary on the Greek Text. Gasque, W. Ward & Marshall, I. Howard, eds. (New International Greek Testament Commentary Ser.). xl, 560p. 1991. 39.99 (*0-8028-2392-0*) Eerdmans.
— WBC, Vol. 44: Colossians - Philemon. 328p. 1982. write for info. (*0-8499-0243-6*) Word Inc.
O'Brien, Philip. T. E. Lawrence: A Bibliography. (Reference Bks.). 416p. 1988. text ed. 65.00 (*0-8161-8945-5*, Hall Reference); lib. bdg. 60.00 (*0-318-32523-3*, Hall Reference) Macmillan.
O'Brien, R. L. Plasma Arc Metalworking Processes (PMP) 160p. 1967. 10.00 (*0-685-65957-7*) Am Welding.
O'Brien, Raymond J. American Sublime: Landscape & Scenery of the Lower Hudson Valley. LC 80-21827. (Illus.). 353p. 1981. text ed. 40.00 (*0-231-04778-9*) Col U Pr.
***O'Brien, Richard.** Collecting Toy Seven: A Collector's Identification & Value Guide. 6th rev. ed. (Collecting Toys Ser.). (Illus.). 600p. 1995. pap. 22.95 (*0-89689-114-3*) Bks Americana.
— Collecting Toy Soldiers. 2nd ed. 512p. 1992. 29.95 (*0-89689-089-9*) Bks Americana.
— Collecting Toy Trains. 3rd ed. 360p. 1991. 22.95 (*0-89689-084-8*) Bks Americana.
— Global Financial Integration: The End of Geography. 128p. 1992. pap. 14.95 (*0-87609-123-0*) Coun Foreign.
— Life of Charles Stewart Parnell, 1846-1891, 2 Vols, Set. LC 68-25256. (English Biography Ser.: No. 31). 1969. reprint ed. lib. bdg. 150.00 (*0-8383-0167-3*) M S G Haskell Hse.
Obrien, Richard. Never Tell Him You're Alone. 1992. mass mkt. 4.50 (*0-312-92826-2*) St Martin.
O'Brien, Richard. Rocky Horror Picture Show. (Illus.). 72p. 1991. pap. 15.95 (*0-7119-2764-2*, AM86101) Music Sales.
— The Story of American Toys. (Illus.). 252p. 1993. 24.98 (*0-89660-029-7*, Artabras) Abbeville Pr.
— When God Spoke. 1995. 13.95 (*0-8062-5179-4*) Carlton.
***O'Brien, Richard, ed.** Finance & the International Economy Vol. 8: The AMEX Bank Review Prize Essays. (Illus.). 100p. 1995. pap. text ed. 18.95 (*0-19-828962-6*) OUP.
— Finance & the International Economy, No. 5: The AMEX Bank Review Prize Essays, 1991. (Illus.). 144p. 1992. pap. 19.95 (*0-19-828766-6*) OUP.
— Finance & the International Economy 7: The AMEX Bank Review Prize Essays 1993. (Illus.). 176p. 1994. pap. 14.95 (*0-19-828879-4*) OUP.
O'Brien, Richard & Hewin, Sarah, eds. Finance & the International Economy: The AMEX Bank Review Prize Essays, 1990. (Illus.). 200p. 1991. pap. 19.95 (*0-19-828740-2*) OUP.
O'Brien, Richard & Iverson, Ingrid, eds. Finance & the International Economy 3: The AMEX Bank Review Prize Essays. (Illus.). 208p. 1990. 38.00 (*0-19-829008-X*) OUP.
O'Brien, Richard, jt. ed. see Calverley, John.
O'Brien, Richard C. Dental Radiography: An Introduction for Dental Hygienists & Assistants. 4th ed. (Illus.). 296p. 1982. text ed. 43.95 (*0-7216-6887-9*) Saunders.
O'Brien, Richard J. A Descriptive Grammar of Ecclesiastical Latin Based on Modern Structural Analysis. LC 65-25149. (Georgetown University Latin Ser.). 283p. reprint ed. pap. 80.70 (*0-8357-8566-1*, 2034932) Bks Demand.
— Georgetown University Round Table: Selected Papers on Linguistics, 1961-1965. LC 68-57729. 507p. reprint ed. pap. 144.50 (*0-7837-6348-4*, 2046060) Bks Demand.
O'Brien, Richard J., ed. see Georgetown University Round Table on Languages & Linguistics Staff.
O'Brien, Richard L., ed. see International Leucocyte Culture Conference, 15th: 1982: Asilomar, Pacific Grove, CA.
O'Brien Riley, Miles. Promises to Keep: People, Places & Parables in Communications from Around the World. (Orig.). 1991. write for info. (*0-9620554-1-7*) Perfect Page Pub.
O'Brien, Rita C., ed. The Political Economy of Underdevelopment: Dependence in Senegal. LC 78-27183. (Sage Series on African Modernization & Development: No. 3). 277p. reprint ed. pap. 79.00 (*0-8357-8502-5*, 2034779) Bks Demand.
O'Brien, Robert. The Encyclopedia of New England. (Illus.). 400p. 1985. 29.95 (*0-87196-759-6*) Facts on File.
— This Is San Francisco: A Classic Portrait of the City. LC 94-4578. (Illus.). 372p. 1994. 12.95 (*0-8118-0578-6*) Chronicle Bks.
***O'Brien, Robert & Chafetz, Morris, eds.** The Encyclopedia of Alcoholism. Date not set. reprint ed. pap. 113.50 (*0-7837-9268-9*, 2060004) Bks Demand.
O'Brien, Robert & Martin, Harold H., eds. The Encyclopedia of the South. LC 82-12098. (Illus.). 591p. reprint ed. pap. 168.50 (*0-8357-4237-7*, 2037024) Bks Demand.
O'Brien, Robert C. Mrs. Frisby & the Rats of NIMH. LC 74-134818. (Illus.). 240p. (J). (gr. 3-7). 1971. text ed. 15. 95 (*0-689-20651-8*, Atheneum Bks Young) S&S Childrens.
— Mrs. Frisby & the Rats of NIMH. 248p. (J). (gr. 3-7). 1986. reprint ed. pap. 3.95 (*0-689-71068-2*, Aladdin Paperbacks) S&S Childrens.
— Secret of Nimh. (J). 1988. pap. 2.75 (*0-590-41708-8*) Scholastic Inc.
— The Silver Crown. LC 88-2837. 272p. (YA). (gr. 7 up). 1988. pap. 3.95 (*0-02-044651-9*, Collier Bks Young) S&S Childrens.
— Z for Zachariah. LC 74-76736. 256p. (YA). (gr. 7 up). 1975. text ed. 15.95 (*0-689-30442-0*, Atheneum Bks Young) S&S Childrens.
— Z for Zachariah. LC 86-23228. 256p. (YA). (gr. 7 up). 1987. reprint ed. pap. 3.95 (*0-02-044650-0*, Collier Bks Young) S&S Childrens.
O'Brien, Robert F. School Songs of America's Colleges & Universities: A Directory. LC 91-11337. 208p. 1991. text ed. 42.95 (*0-313-27890-3*, OSS/, Greenwood Pr) Greenwood.
O'Brien, Robert J., jt. ed. see Dunnette, David A.
O'Brien, Robert M. Crime & Victimization Data. LC 84-29835. (Law & Criminal Justice Ser.: No. 4). 127p. reprint ed. pap. 36.20 (*0-7837-4579-6*, 2044108) Bks Demand.
O'Brien, Robert W. The Brown Thrush. 1977. text ed. 12.95 (*0-8369-9247-4*, 9101) Ayer.
O'Brien, Robert W. & Daniels, Roger. The College Nisei. LC 78-54829. (Asian Experience in North America Ser.). (Illus.). 1979. reprint ed. lib. bdg. 15.95 (*0-405-11286-6*) Ayer.
O'Brien, Ron. Ron O'Brien's Diving for Gold. LC 91-28668. (Illus.). 200p. 1992. pap. 19.95 (*0-88011-448-7*, POBR0448) Human Kinetics.
***O'Brien-Rothe, Linda, ed.** Molokan Singing. 60p. (Orig.). 1994. pap. 29.95 (*1-57205-756-4*) Rector Pr.
O'Brien, Rourke M. & Thomas, John B. The Quick & Easy Guide to Driveway Detailing. LC 89-85081. (Practice Ring Ser.). (Illus.). 80p. (Orig.). 1993. pap. 9.95 (*0-929758-05-6*) Beeman Jorgensen.
O'Brien, S. Peachtree Accounting Made Easy for DOS. 1990. pap. text ed. 21.95 (*0-07-881611-4*) Osborne-McGraw.
O'Brien, Sean. The Frighteners. LC 88-70226. 64p. (Orig.). 1987. pap. 10.95 (*1-85224-013-X*, Pub. by Bloodaxe Bks UK) Dufour.
— Ghost Train. 72p. 1995. pap. 11.95 (*0-19-283007-4*) OUP.
— HMS Glasshouse. 64p. 1991. pap. 10.95 (*0-19-282835-5*) OUP.
— Indoor Park. 64p. 1983. pap. 12.95 (*0-906427-49-5*, Pub. by Bloodaxe Bks UK) Dufour.
O'Brien, Seumas. Duty & Other Irish Comedies. LC 77-89724. (One-Act Plays in Reprint Ser.). 1977. reprint ed. 16.50 (*0-8486-2029-1*) Roth Pub Inc.
O'Brien, Sharon. American Indian Tribal Governments. LC 89-4791. (Civilization of the American Indian Ser.: Vol. 192). (Illus.). 380p. 1989. 34.95 (*0-8061-2199-8*) U of Okla Pr.
— American Indian Tribal Governments. LC 89-4791. (C). 1993. pap. 17.95 (*0-8061-2564-0*) U of Okla Pr.
— Willa Cather. LC 93-43244. (Lives of Notable Gay Men & Lesbians Ser.). (Illus.). 1994. 19.95 (*0-7910-2302-8*, Am Art Analog); pap. write for info. (*0-7910-2877-1*, Am Art Analog) Chelsea Hse.
— Willa Cather. (Illus.). 144p. (YA). (gr. 7 up). Date not set. 19.95 (*0-615-00738-4*); pap. 9.95 (*0-615-00739-2*) Chelsea Hse.
— Willa Cather: The Emerging Voice. 1988. pap. 12.95 (*0-449-90283-8*, Columbine) Fawcett.
— Willa Cather: The Emerging Voice. (Illus.). 576p. 1986. 35.00 (*0-19-504132-1*) OUP.
O'Brien, Sharon, ed. Later Novels: Willa Cather: Incl. A Lost Lady; The Professor's House; Death Comes for the Archbishop; Shadows on the Rock; Lucy Gayheart; Sapphira & the Slave Girl. LC 89-64130. 988p. 1990. 32. 50 (*0-940450-52-6*) Library of America.
— The Stories of Willa Cather. 1988. mass mkt. 9.95 (*0-452-00874-3*, Mer) NAL-Dutton.
O'Brien, Sharon, ed. see Cather, Willa.
O'Brien, Shirley. Child Abuse: A Crying Shame. LC 80-23708. 184p. 1980. 9.95 (*0-8425-1829-0*) BYU Scholarly.
— Child Abuse & Neglect: Everyone's Problem. Martin, Lwey P., ed. LC 84-20351. 32p. 1984. 7.50 (*0-87173-106-1*) ACEI.
— Child Pornography. 208p. 1992. per. 22.95 (*0-8403-7845-9*) Kendall-Hunt.
— Victims of Child Sexual Exploitation. 140p. 1992. per. 15. 95 (*0-8403-7886-6*) Kendall-Hunt.
O'Brien, Stephen. Genetic Maps. 5th ed. (Illus.). 1156p. 1990. 150.00 (*0-87969-338-X*) Cold Spring Harbor.
O'Brien, Stephen, ed. Genetic Maps, Bk. I: Viruses. (Illus.). 181p. 1990. pap. 27.00 (*0-87969-342-8*) Cold Spring Harbor.
— Genetic Maps, Bk. II: Bacteria, Protozoa & Algae. (Illus.). 134p. 1990. pap. 27.00 (*0-87969-343-6*) Cold Spring Harbor.
— Genetic Maps, Bk. III: Lower Eukaryotes. (Illus.). 201p. 1990. pap. 27.00 (*0-87969-344-4*) Cold Spring Harbor.
— Genetic Maps, Bk. IV: Nonhuman Vertebrates. (Illus.). 175p. 1990. pap. 27.00 (*0-87969-345-2*) Cold Spring Harbor.
— Genetic Maps, Bk. V: Human Maps. (Illus.). 257p. 1990. pap. 27.00 (*0-87969-346-0*) Cold Spring Harbor.
— Genetic Maps, Bk. VI: Plants. (Illus.). 147p. 1990. pap. 27.00 (*0-87969-347-9*) Cold Spring Harbor.
O'Brien, Stephen J., ed. Genetic Maps: Locus Maps of Complex Genomes, 6 vols., Bk. 1: Viruses. 6th ed. (Illus.). 205p. (C). 1993. pap. text ed. 35.00 (*0-87969-415-7*) Cold Spring Harbor.
— Genetic Maps: Locus Maps of Complex Genomes, 6 vols., Bk. 2: Bacteria, Algae, & Protozoa. 6th ed. (Illus.). 181p. (C). 1993. pap. text ed. 35.00 (*0-87969-416-5*) Cold Spring Harbor.
— Genetic Maps: Locus Maps of Complex Genomes, 6 vols., Bk. 3: Lower Eukaryotes. 6th ed. (Illus.). 318p. (C). 1993. pap. text ed. 40.00 (*0-87969-417-3*) Cold Spring Harbor.
— Genetic Maps: Locus Maps of Complex Genomes, 6 vols., Bk. 4: Nonhuman Vertebrates. 6th ed. (Illus.). 342p. (C). 1993. pap. text ed. 40.00 (*0-87969-418-1*) Cold Spring Harbor.
— Genetic Maps: Locus Maps of Complex Genomes, 6 vols., Bk. 5: The Human Maps. 6th ed. (Illus.). 310p. (C). 1993. pap. text ed. 40.00 (*0-87969-419-X*) Cold Spring Harbor.
— Genetic Maps: Locus Maps of Complex Genomes, 6 vols., Bk. 6: Plants. 6th ed. (Illus.). 261p. (C). 1993. pap. text ed. 40.00 (*0-87969-420-3*) Cold Spring Harbor.
— Genetic Maps: Locus Maps of Complex Genomes, 6 vols., Set. 6th ed. (Illus.). 1620p. (C). 1993. text ed. 195. 00 (*0-87969-414-9*) Cold Spring Harbor.
O'Brien, Stephen K. Turbo Pascal Six: The Complete Reference, Second Edition. 2nd ed. (Programming Ser.). 1008p. 1991. pap. text ed. 29.95 (*0-07-881703-X*) Osborne-McGraw.
O'Brien, Stephen K. & Nameroff, Steven. Turbo Pascal Seven: The Complete Reference. 864p. 1992. pap. text ed. 29.95 (*0-07-881793-5*) Osborne-McGraw.
O'Brien, Steve. Alexander Hamilton. (World Leaders - Past & Present Ser.). (Illus.). 112p. (YA). (gr. 5 up). 1989. 17. 95 (*1-55546-810-1*) Chelsea Hse.
O'Brien, Steven. Pancho Villa: Mexican Revolutionary. LC 93-37890. (Hispanics of Achievement Ser.). (Illus.). 112p. (J). (gr. 6-12). 1994. lib. bdg. 18.95 (*0-7910-1257-3*, Am Art Analog); lib. bdg. write for info. (*0-7910-1284-0*, Am Art Analog) Chelsea Hse.
O'Brien, Steven, et al, eds. American Political Leaders. 473p. 1991. lib. bdg. 65.00 (*0-87436-570-8*) ABC-CLIO.
O'Brien, Sue M., comp. The Register of Americans of Prominent Descent, Vol. I. LC 81-69243. 545p. 1982. 35.00 (*0-686-36318-3*) Morten Pub.
O'Brien, T. Kevin, ed. Long-Term Behavior of Composites -STP 813. LC 82-73765. 300p. 1983. 42.00 (*0-8031-0252-6*, 04-813000-33) ASTM.
O'Brien, Terence. The Moonlight War. large type ed. (Non-Fiction Ser.). 1990. 21.95 (*0-7089-2176-0*) Ulverscroft.
— Out of the Blue: A Pilot with the Chindits. large type ed. (Non-Fiction Ser.). 480p. 1985. 15.95 (*0-7089-1392-X*) Ulverscroft.
O'Brien, Terence P. The Prehistory of Uganda Protectorate. LC 76-44772. reprint ed. 34.50 (*0-404-15874-9*) AMS Pr.
O'Brien, Teresa. Memories. LC 90-46155. (J). 1985. 5.95 (*0-685-52310-1*) Childs Play.
O'Brien, Theresa. Animals of the Jungle. (First Flaps First Facts Ser.). (Illus.). (J). (gr. 1-3). 1994. reprint ed. pap. 4.50 (*1-884628-06-0*) Flying Frog.
— Animals of the Ocean. (First Flaps First Facts Ser.). (Illus.). (J). (gr. 1-3). 1994. reprint ed. pap. 4.50 (*1-884628-08-7*) Flying Frog.
— Little Fish in a Big Pond. LC 90-46519. (J). (ps-3). 1990. 7.95 (*0-85953-390-5*); pap. 3.95 (*0-85953-391-3*) Childs Play.
O'Brien, Thomas. Lab & Field Guide for Ocean Sciences. 2nd ed. (Illus.). 351p. (C). 1994. student ed 25.00 (*0-685-75075-2*) Whittier Pubns.
Obrien, Thomas C. Puzzle Tables: Number Problems with Computational Skills. (J). (gr. 4-7). 1980. pap. 8.95 (*0-201-48011-5*) Addison-Wesley.
O'Brien, Thomas C. Wollygoggles & Other Creatures: Problems for Developing Thinking Skills. 64p. (J). (gr. 3-12). 1980. pap. text ed. 8.95 (*0-914040-85-5*) Cuisenaire.
Obrien, Thomas C. Woolygoggles & Other Creatures: Problems for Developing Thinking Skills. (J). (gr. 4-7). 1992. pap. 8.95 (*0-201-48018-2*) Addison-Wesley.
O'Brien, Thomas C., ed. see International Committee on English in the Liturgy.
O'Brien, Thomas G., III. Connecticut Corporation Law & Practice. (National Corporation Law Ser.). 1992. 126.00 (*0-13-297623-4*) Aspen Law.
— Florida Law of Corporations & Business Organizations. Date not set. 110.00 (*0-13-295007-3*) Aspen Law.
— Florida Law of Corporations & Business Organizations. 1992. ring bd. 126.00 (*0-13-288226-4*) Aspen Law.
***O'Brien, Thomas G. & Charlton, Samuel G., eds.** Handbook of Human Factors Testing & Evaluation. 600p. 1995. text ed. 120.00 (*0-8058-1724-7*) L Erlbaum Assocs.
— Handbook of Human Factors Testing & Evaluation. 1995. pap. 60.00 (*0-8058-1725-5*) L Erlbaum Assocs.
O'Brien, Thomas J., jt. auth. see Mandell, Lewis.
O'Brien, Tim. The Amusement Park Guide: Fun for the Whole Family at More Than 250 Amusement Parks from Coast to Coast. LC 91-7421. (Illus.). 320p. (Orig.). 1991. pap. 12.95 (*0-87106-300-X*) Globe Pequot.
— Going after Cacciato. 1989. pap. 11.95 (*0-385-28349-0*, Delta) Dell.
— Going after Cacciato. 1992. mass mkt. 6.99 (*0-440-21439-4*) Dell.

O

An Asterisk (*) at the beginning of an entry indicates that the title is appearing in BIP for the first time.

— If I Die in a Combat Zone. 252p. 1992. mass mkt. 5.99 (*0-440-34311-9*, LE) Dell.
— In the Lake of the Wood. 320p. 1995. 10.95 (*0-14-025094-8*, Penguin Bks) Viking Penguin.
— In the Lake of the Woods. 320p. 1994. 21.95 (*0-395-48889-3*, Seymour Law) HM.
— The Nuclear Age. 1993. mass mkt. 5.99 (*0-440-21586-2*, LE) Dell.
— Tennessee: Off the Beaten Path. 2nd ed. LC 92-31223. (Voyager Book Ser.). (Illus.). 144p. (Orig.). 1993. pap. 9.95 (*1-56440-143-X*) Globe Pequot.
— The Things They Carried. (Contemporary American Fiction Ser.). 288p. 1991. pap. 10.95 (*0-14-014773-X*) Viking Penguin.
— Where the Animals Are: A Guide to the Best Zoos, Aquariums, & Wildlife Attractions in North America. LC 92-20081. (Illus.). 320p. (Orig.). 1993. pap. 12.95 (*1-56440-077-8*) Globe Pequot.
O'Brien, Tom. Marine Biology. 2nd ed. (Illus.). 280p. (Orig.). 1993. 20.00 (*1-878045-20-2*) Whittier Pubns.
— Ocean Sciences Lab & Field Guide. (Illus.). 351p. (C). 1994. student ed 25.00 (*1-878045-60-1*) Whittier Pubns.
O'Brien, Tom, jt. auth. see Cunningham, Vance.
O'Brien, W. J., ed. Toolik Lake: Ecology of an Aquatic Ecosystem in Arctic Alaska. LC 92-26746. (Developments in Hydrobiology Ser.: Vol. 78). (C). 1992. lib. bdg. 181.00 (*0-7923-1952-4*) Kluwer Ac.
O'Brien, W. M., ed. Fenbufen. (Journal: Pharmacology: Vol. 25, Suppl. 1). (Illus.). iv, 96p. 1982. pap. 41.75 (*3-8055-3542-2*) S Karger.
O'Brien, William. When We Were Boys. LC 79-8182. reprint ed. 44.50 (*0-404-62077-9*) AMS Pr.
O'Brien, William B. & Henican, Ellis. You Can't Do It Alone: The Daytop Way to Make Your Child Drug-Free. LC 93-22051. 288p. 1993. 20.00 (*0-671-72837-7*) S&S Trade.
O'Brien, William J., ed. The Labor of God: An Ignatian View of Church & Culture. LC 91-24720. 120p. (Orig.). 1991. pap. 8.95 (*0-87840-527-5*) Georgetown U Pr.
— Minding the Time, 1492-1992: Jesuit Education & Issues in American Culture. LC 93-23150. 135p. 1992. pap. 10.00 (*0-87840-533-X*) Georgetown U Pr.
— Riding Time Like a River: The Catholic Moral Tradition since Vatican II. LC 93-4394. 192p. 1993. 36.00 (*0-87840-542-9*) Georgetown U Pr.
— Splendor & Wonder: Jesuit Character, Georgetown Spirit, & Liberal Education. LC 88-24652. 120p. (Orig.). reprint ed. pap. 34.20 (*0-7837-6703-X*, 2046335) Bks Demand.
O'Brien, William V. The Conduct of a Just & Limited War. LC 81-11883. 512p. 1981. text ed. 50.95 (*0-275-90693-0*, C0693, Praeger Pubs) Greenwood.
— Law & Morality in Israel's War with the P.L.O. 352p. 1991. 45.00 (*0-415-90300-9*, A4350, Routledge NY); pap. 15.95 (*0-415-90301-7*, A4354, Routledge NY) Routledge.
O'Brien, Wm. Arctander. Novalis: Signs of Revolution. (Post-Contemporary Interventions Ser.). 384p. 1994. lib. bdg. 49.95 (*0-8223-1509-2*); pap. text ed. 18.95 (*0-8223-1519-X*) Duke.
O'Bries, Thomas C. Puzzle Tables. 64p. (J). (gr. 3-8). 1980. pap. text ed. 8.95 (*0-914040-83-9*) Cuisenaire.
Obringer, John W. & Tillinghast, Henry S., Jr., eds. Biotechnology for Aerospace Applications. (Advances in Applied Biotechnology Ser.: Vol. 3). (Illus.). 288p. (C). 1989. 55.00 (*0-943255-05-8*) Portfolio Pub.
Obrink, K. J. & Flemstrom, G., eds. Gastric Ion Transport. (Illus.). 434p. (Orig.). 1978. pap. text ed. 35.00x (*91-22-00254-5*) Coronet Bks.
Obrinsky, Mark. Profit Theory & Capitalism. LC 82-40482. (Illus.). 176p. 1983. pap. text ed. 19.95 (*0-8122-1147-2*) U of Pa Pr.
Obrist, Barbara. Constantine of Pisa: The Book of the Secrets of Alchemy. LC 90-37150. (Collection de Travaux de l'Academie Internationale d'Histoire des Sciences: Vol. 34). x, 339p. (ENG & LAT.). 1990. 85.75 (*90-04-09288-9*) E J Brill.
Obrist, Hans-Ulrich, ed. see Richter, Gerhard.
Obrist, Paul A. Cardiovascular Psychophysiology: A Perspective. LC 80-28582. 246p. 1981. 45.00 (*0-306-40599-7*, Plenum Pr) Plenum.
Obrizok, Robert. A Garden of Conifers: Introduction & Selection Guide. LC 93-71498. (Illus.). 120p. (Orig.). 1994. pap. 24.95 (*0-913643-08-4*) Capabilitys.
Obroslinski, Lisa A. A Bridge to Understanding: Listening, Speaking, Thinking, the Differences Between Men & Women. 104p. 1992. pap. 12.95 (*0-9633649-4-4*) L A Obroslinski.
***O'Bryan, Aileen.** Dine: Origin Myths of the Navaho Indians. (Bureau of American Ethnology Bulletins Ser.). 187p. 1995. lib. bdg. 79.00 (*0-7812-4163-4*) Rprt Serv.
O'Bryan, Aileen, tr. Navaho Indian Myths. LC 93-9688. (Illus.). 208p. 1993. reprint ed. pap. 5.95 (*0-486-27592-2*) Dover.
O'Bryant, D. C. Graphics for Engineers: Visualization, Communication, & Design. (Illus.). 620p. (C). 1991. pap. text ed. 41.80 (*0-87563-361-7*) Stipes.
O'Bryant, D. C., jt. auth. see Hartley, T. C.
O'Bryant, D. C., et al. Problems in Engineering Graphics, No. 87. (Engineering Graphics Ser.: Vol. 87). 90p. (C). 1987. student ed 13.80 (*0-87563-292-0*) Stipes.
O'Bryant, Harold S., jt. auth. see Stone, Michael H.
O'Bryant, M. C. Making It As a Sports Official. (Illus.). 90p. (Orig.). 1991. pap. text ed. 9.95 (*0-88314-520-0*) AAHPERD.
O'Bryant-Puentes, Nancy. First Aid for Family Quilts. (Illus.). 34p. (Orig.). 1986. pap. 5.95 (*0-9602970-6-5*) Leman Pubns.
O'Bryne, Seamus, ed. Be Reconciled! 113p. 1989. pap. 30.00 (*0-86217-235-7*, Pub. by Veritas IE) St Mut.
Obrzut, John E. & Hynd, George W. Child Neuropsychology, Vol. 1. (Perspectives in Neurolinguistics, Neuropsychology & Psycholinguistics Ser.). 1986. text ed. 75.00 (*0-12-524041-4*); pap. text ed. 49.00 (*0-12-524043-0*) Acad Pr.
— Child Neuropsychology, Vol. 2. (Perspectives in Neurolinguistics, Neuropsychology & Psycholinguistics Ser.). 1986. text ed. 75.00 (*0-12-524042-2*); pap. text ed. 49.00 (*0-12-524044-9*) Acad Pr.
Obrzut, John E. & Hynd, George W., eds. Neuropsychological Foundations of Learning Disabilities: A Handbook of Issues, Methods & Practice. 833p. 1991. text ed. 182.00 (*0-12-524040-6*) Acad Pr.
Obrzut, John E., jt. ed. see Hynd, George W.
Observer Staff. Chernobyl: The End of the Nuclear Dream. LC 86-22462. 256p. 1986. pap. 4.95 (*0-394-75107-8*, Vin) Random.
— Observer Profiles. Brown, Ivor, ed. LC 78-117330. (Biography Index Reprint Ser.). 1977. reprint ed. 23.95 (*0-8369-8022-0*) Ayer.
Obshey, G., jt. auth. see Tenzin, K. S.
Obshey, O., jt. auth. see Tenzin, K. S.
Obst, Peter, tr. see Kurski, Jaroslaw.
Obstbaum. Atlas of Glaucoma Surgery. (Illus.). 210p. (C). 1991. boxed 125.00 (*0-8385-3270-5*, A3270-4) Appleton & Lange.
***Obstfeld.** Spectacle Frames & Their Dispensing. 1995. write for info. (*0-7506-2061-7*, Focal) Buttrwrth-Heinemann.
Obstfeld, jt. auth. see Krugman, Paul R.
Obstfeld, H., tr. see Aust, W.
Obstfeld, Maurice, jt. auth. see Krugman, Paul R.
Obstfeld, Raymond. Joker & the Thief. 1994. mass mkt. 3.99 (*0-440-21909-4*) Dell.
Obstfelder, Sigbjorn. A Priest's Diary. McFarlane, James, tr. & intro. by. LC 87-63149. (Series B: No. 1). 75p. (Orig.). 1987. pap. 9.95 (*1-870041-01-1*, Pub. by Norvik Pr UK) Dufour.
O'Buachalla, Seamas. Education Policy in Twentieth Century Ireland. (Illus.). 434p. 1988. 55.00 (*0-86327-146-4*, Pub. by Wolfhound Pr IE) Dufour.
— Education Policy in Twentieth Century Ireland. (Illus.). 434p. 1990. pap. 30.00 (*0-86327-255-X*, Pub. by Wolfhound Pr IE) Dufour.
O'Buachalla, Seamas, ed. The Letters of P. H. Pearse. 1980. 50.00 (*0-901072-87-7*, Pub. by Colin Smythe Ltd UK) Dufour.
Obuchov, V., jt. auth. see Loqinov, V.
Obuchowski, Chester W. Franco-Phonics, Etc. 156p. 1989. pap. 15.00 (*0-8191-7535-8*) U Pr of Amer.
Obudho, Constance E. Black-White Racial Attitudes: An Annotated Bibliography. LC 75-35351. 180p. 1976. text ed. 42.95 (*0-8371-8582-3*, OBW/, Greenwood Pr) Greenwood.
Obudho, Constance E., comp. Human Nonverbal Behavior: An Annotated Bibliography. LC 79-7586. 196p. 1979. text ed. 59.95 (*0-313-21094-2*, OBH/, Greenwood Pr) Greenwood.
Obudho, Constance E., ed. Black Marriage & Family Therapy. LC 82-20967. (Contributions in Afro-American & African Studies: No. 72). (Illus.). xv, 269p. 1983. text ed. 59.95 (*0-313-22119-7*, OBM/, Greenwood Pr) Greenwood.
Obudho, Robert A., comp. Demography, Urbanization, & Spatial Planning in Kenya: A Bibliographical Survey. LC 84-19805. (African Special Bibliographic Ser.: No. 7). xix, 285p. 1985. text ed. 55.00 (*0-313-24420-0*, OBD/, Greenwood Pr) Greenwood.
Obudho, Robert A. & El-Shakhs, Salah S., eds. Development of Urban Systems in Africa. LC 78-19766. 432p. 1979. text ed. 65.00 (*0-275-90404-0*, C0404, Praeger Pubs) Greenwood.
Obudho, Robert A. & Mhlanga, Constance C., eds. Slum & Squatter Settlements in Sub-Saharan Africa: Toward a Planning Strategy. LC 87-11705. 448p. 1988. text ed. 75.00 (*0-275-92309-6*, C2309, Praeger Pubs) Greenwood.
Obudho, Robert A. & Scott, Jeannine B. Afro-American Demography & Urban Issues: A Bibliography. LC 85-17752. (Bibliographies & Indexes on Afro-American & African Studies Ser.: No. 8). xl, 433p. 1985. text ed. 65.00 (*0-313-24656-4*, OAA/) Greenwood.
Obudho, Robert A. & Waller, P. P. Periodic Markets, Urbanization, & Regional Planning: A Case Study from Western Kenya. LC 75-23867. (Contributions in Afro-American & African Studies: No. 22). (Illus.). 289p. 1976. text ed. 55.00 (*0-8371-8375-8*, OPM/) Greenwood.
Obudhowski, jt. auth. see Kassakowski.
***Obukhov, Y. N. & Sardanashvily, G. A.** Connections in Classical & Quantum Field Theory. 400p. 1995. text ed. 86.00 (*981-02-2013-8*) World Scientific Pub.
Obukhov, Yu N., jt. ed. see Pronin, P. I.
O'Byrne, ed. Asthma As an Inflammatory Disease. (Allergic Disease & Therapy Ser.: Vol. 2). 336p. 1990. 140.00 (*0-8247-8220-8*) Dekker.
O'Byrne, Cathal. From Green Hills of Galilee. LC 71-167464. (Short Story Index Reprint Ser.). 1977. reprint ed. 17.95 (*0-8369-3990-5*) Ayer.
O'Byrne, F. D. Reichenbach's Letters on OD & Magnetism (1852) 119p. 1964. reprint ed. spiral bd. 9.90 (*0-7873-0639-8*) Mokelumne.
O'Byrne, John, ed. see Levy, David H.
O'Byrne, John C. & Davenport, Charles. Doane's Tax Guide for Farmers. (Illus.). 333p. (Orig.). 1988. pap. 29.95 (*0-932250-28-9*) Red Wing Busn.
***O'Byrne, Lorraine.** What Is It? A Gallery of Historic Phrases. 48p. 1995. pap. 2.95 (*0-919822-19-3*, Pub. by Stoddart Publng CN) Pubs Dist MI.
O'Byrne, P., jt. auth. see Masson, H. C.
O'Byrne-Pelham, Fran & Balcer, Bernadette. The Search for the Atocha Treasure. LC 88-20201. (Illus.). 128p. (J). (gr. 4 up). 1988. text ed. 14.95 (*0-87518-399-9*, Dillon Silver Burdett) Silver Burdett Pr.
O'Byrne-Pelham, Fran, jt. auth. see Balcer, Bernadette.
***O'Byrne, Roscoe C.** Roster of Soldiers & Patriots of the American Revolution Buried in Indiana. 407p. 1994. pap. 32.50 (*0-614-00897-2*, 4260) Clearfield Co.
O'Byrne, Seamus, ed. Challenge or Crisis? Texts by John Paul II on Religious Life. Romano, Osservatore, tr. 312p. (Orig.). 1987. pap. 17.95 (*0-86217-238-1*, Pub. by Veritas Publns IE) Ignatius Pr.
Oc, Taner, jt. auth. see Trench, Sylvia.
Oc, Taner, jt. ed. see Trench, Sylvia.
OCA Staff. A Place Called Chinese America. 2nd ed. 208p. 1993. per. 22.95 (*0-8403-8589-7*) Kendall-Hunt.
O'Cadhain, Mairtin. Road to Brightcity. 112p. 1981. pap. 8.95 (*0-905169-47-6*, Pub. by Poolbeg Pr IE) Dufour.
O'Cain, Raymond, jt. ed. see Davis, Boyd H.
O'Cain, Raymond K., jt. auth. see McDavid, Raven I., Jr.
Ocallachan, John. Bit of the Blarney. 1992. pap. 6.95 (*1-882255-00-3*) Hot To Trot.
***O'Callaghan, A. J. & Leigh, M.** Object Technology Transfer: Meeting the Training Needs of Software Development. 300p. Date not set. 65.00 (*1-872474-14-4*, Pub. by Alfred Waller UK) Paul & Co Pubs.
O'Callaghan, Bryn. History of the Twentieth Century. 1987. pap. text ed. 17.25 (*0-582-33172-2*, 72065) Longman.
O'Callaghan, Chris, jt. auth. see Stephenson, Terence.
O'Callaghan, D., jt. ed. see Roche, J. F.
O'Callaghan, E. B. Calendar of Historical Manuscripts in the Office of the Secretary of State, Albany, NY. 423p. 1994. reprint ed. lib. bdg. 45.00 (*0-8328-3803-9*) Higginson Bk Co.
O'Callaghan, E. B., comp. Calendar of N. Y. Colonial Manuscripts: Indorsed Land Papers, 1643-1803. LC 87-14830. 1090p. 1987. reprint ed. 59.50 (*0-916346-59-5*) Picton Pr.
***O'Callaghan, Edmund B.** The Documentary History of the State of New York, 4 vols. 4356p. Date not set. write for info. (*1-886103-00-3*) Fine Books.
— Lists of Inhabitants of Colonial New York. LC 79-52062. 331p. 1989. reprint ed. 20.00 (*0-8063-0847-8*) Genealog Pub.
O'Callaghan, Evelyn, ed. Woman Version: Theoretical Approaches to West Indian Fiction by Women. LC 93-14204. (Warwick University Caribbean Studies). 1993. text ed. 45.00 (*0-312-10218-6*) St Martin.
O'Callaghan, Gary. The Structure & Operation of the World Gold Market. LC 93-22746. (Occasional Paper Ser.: No. 105). 60p. 1993. 15.00 (*1-55775-281-8*) Intl Monetary.
O'Callaghan, J. Brien. School-Based Collaboration with Families: Constructing Family-School-Agency Partnerships That Work. LC 93-6573. (Social & Behavioral Sciences Ser.). 224p. 1993. 26.95 (*1-55542-527-5*) Jossey-Bass.
***O'Callaghan, J. M.** Taxation of Estates: The Law in Ireland. 1993. pap. text ed. 91.00 (*1-85475-621-4*, IE) Butterworth Legal Pubs.
— Taxation of Trusts: The Law in Ireland. 1993. pap. text ed. 91.00 (*1-85475-616-8*, IE) Butterworth Legal Pubs.
O'Callaghan, Jerry. The Red Book: The Hanrahan Case Against Merck, Sharp & Dohme. 228p. (Orig.). 1992. pap. 15.95 (*1-85371-167-5*, Pub. by Poolbeg Pr IE) Dufour.
O'Callaghan, Jerry A. The Disposition of the Public Domain in Oregon. Bruchey, Stuart, ed. LC 78-53563. (Development of Public Land Law in the U. S. Ser.). 1979. reprint ed. lib. bdg. 15.95 (*0-405-11382-X*) Ayer.
O'Callaghan, Joseph F. A History of Medieval Spain. LC 74-7698. 736p. 1983. pap. 22.95 (*0-8014-9264-5*) Cornell U Pr.
— The Learned King: The Reign of Alfonso X of Castile. LC 93-13417. (Middle Ages Ser.). (Illus.). 408p. (C). 1993. text ed. 49.95 (*0-8122-3226-7*) U of Pa Pr.
O'Callaghan, Joseph F., ed. Heresies of the Early Christian & Medieval Era, 67 titles in 92 vols. (AMS Reprint Ser.). 1965. reprint ed. write for info. (*0-404-16090-5*) AMS Pr.
O'Callaghan, Joseph F., tr. The Autobiography of St. Ignatius of Loyola, with Related Documents. LC 92-32959. x, 113p. 1993. reprint ed. pap. 15.00 (*0-8232-1480-X*) Fordham.
O'Callaghan, Julie. Edible Anecdotes. 1983. pap. 9.95 (*0-85105-414-5*, Pub. by Colin Smythe Ltd UK) Dufour.
— What's What. 77p. (Orig.). 1991. pap. 15.95 (*1-85224-161-6*, Pub. by Bloodaxe Bks UK) Dufour.
***O'Callaghan, Karen & Londesborough, Kate.** Finding Food. (Fight for Survival Ser.). 40p. (J). 1994. 4.98 (*1-85854-140-9*) Brimax Bks.
— Growing Up. (Fight for Survival Ser.). 40p. (J). 1994. 4.98 (*1-85854-141-7*) Brimax Bks.
— Safety in Numbers. (Fight for Survival Ser.). 40p. (J). 1994. 4.98 (*1-85854-142-5*) Brimax Bks.
— Somewhere to Sleep. (Fight for Survival Ser.). 40p. (J). 1994. 4.98 (*1-85854-143-3*) Brimax Bks.
***O'Callaghan, Margaret.** British High Politics & a Nationalist Ireland: Criminality, Land, & the Law Under Forster & Balfour. 220p. 1994. 55.00 (*0-312-12497-X*) St Martin.
O'Callaghan, Maxine. Set-Up: A Delilah West Mystery. 208p. 1991. 18.95 (*0-312-06462-4*) St Martin.
O'Callaghan, Myrnie. A Boy Called Mish Mash. LC 91-92177. 100p. (Orig.). (J). (gr. 5-8). 1991. pap. 9.95 (*0-9630075-0-5*) Creole Connect.
O'Callaghan, P. O. An Eastern Orthodox Response to Evangelical Claims. 1984. pap. 2.95 (*0-937032-35-2*) Light&Life Pub Co MN.
O'Callaghan, P. W. Building for Energy Conservation. 1978. 105.00 (*0-08-022120-3*, Pub. by Pergamon Repr UK) Franklin.
— Design & Management for Energy Conservation. 1981. 150.00 (*0-08-027287-8*, Pub. by Pergamon Repr UK) Franklin.
O'Callaghan, P. W., ed. Energy for Industry. LC 78-41102. (Illus.). 1979. 177.00 (*0-08-022704-X*, Pub. by Pergamon Repr UK) Franklin.
O'Callaghan, Patricia. Andrew a Fable of Flight. LC 94-60117. (Illus.). 44p. (J). (gr. k-3). 1994. 6.95 (*1-55523-686-3*) Winston-Derek.
Ocallaghan, Paul. Energy Management. 1993. text ed. 55.00 (*0-07-707678-8*) McGraw.
O'Callaghan, Phyllis, ed. A Clashing of Symbols: Method & Meaning in Liberal Studies. LC 87-29950. 164p. 1988. pap. 7.95 (*0-87840-468-6*) Georgetown U Pr.
O'Callaghan, Sean. Down by the Glenside. 1992. pap. 14.95 (*1-85635-004-5*) Dufour.
***O'Callaghan, Timothy J.** Henry Ford's Airport & Other Aviation Interests 1909-1954. (Illus.). v, 160p. 1995. 24.00 (*1-882792-07-6*) Proctor Pubns.
Ocallahan. The Dance. audio 18.00 (*1-877954-22-5*) Artana Prodns.
O'Callahan, D. B. The United States Since 1945. 1983. pap. text ed. 9.75 (*0-582-22181-1*, 70893) Longman.
O'Callahan, J. F., ed. Studies in Cistercian Medieval History: Presented to Jeremiah F. O'Sullivan. LC 77-152486. (Cistercian Studies: No. 13). 1971. 7.95 (*0-87907-813-8*) Cistercian Pubns.
***O'Callahan, Jay.** Herman & Marguerite: An Earth Story. LC 94-47561. (Illus.). (J). 1995. 15.95 (*1-56145-103-7*) Peachtree Pubs.
— Orange Cheeks. LC 92-43509. (Illus.). 40p. (J). (ps-3). 1983. 15.95 (*1-56145-073-1*) Peachtree Pubs.
— Tulips. LC 91-41704. (Illus.). 28p. (J). (gr. k up). 1992. pap. 14.95 (*0-88708-223-8*, Picture Book Studio) S&S Childrens.
Ocampo de Gomez, Aurora & Prado Velazquez, Ernesto. Diccionario de Escritores Mexicanos. (SPA.). 69.95 (*0-7859-0713-0*, S-6745) Fr & Eur.
Ocampo, Estela. Diccionario de Terminos Artisticos y Arqueologicos. 240p. 1988. pap. 24.95 (*0-7859-6247-6*, 8476390769) Fr & Eur.
Ocampo, Jose A. & Steiner, Roberto, eds. Foreign Capital in Latin America. 240p. (Orig.). 1994. pap. text ed. 18.50x (*0-940602-77-6*) IADB.
Ocampo, Juan, jt. auth. see Rosenthal, James.
***Ocana, Maria T.** Picasso: Landscapes 1890-1912: From the Academy to the Avant-Garde. 342p. 1995. 75.00 (*0-8212-2239-2*) Bulfinch Pr.
Ocana, Maria T., jt. ed. see Weiss, Evelyn.
O'Canainn, Tomas. Traditional Music in Ireland. (Illus.). 1978. pap. 13.95 (*0-7100-0021-9*, RKP) Routledge.
O'Caoimh, Thomas. Beginning to Pray: Prayer for Young People & Those Who Would Like to Start Again. 112p. (Orig.). 1992. pap. 8.95 (*1-85607-055-7*, Pub. by Columba Pr IE) Twenty-Third.
Ocariz, Fernando. Opus Dei in the Church. 380p. 1994. 19.95 (*0-933932-72-3*, Pub. by Four Courts Pr EIRE) Scepter Pubs.
Ocariz, Fernando, et al. The Canonical Path of Opus Dei. 656p. 1994. 29.95 (*0-933932-70-7*) Scepter Pubs.
O'Carroll, Cian, ed. see Dowd, James.
O'Carroll, Ide. Models for Movers: Irish Women's Emigration to America. (Illus.). 176p. (Orig.). (C). 1990. pap. 13.99 (*1-85594-008-6*, Pub. by Attic IE) InBook.
O'Carroll, Michael. Corpus Christi: An Encyclopedia of the Eucharist. LC 88-45354. (Illus.). 232p. 1988. 42.00 (*0-8146-5687-0*) Liturgical Pr.
— Medjugorje: Facts, Documents, Theology. 4th ed. 224p. (Orig.). 1989. pap. 13.95 (*1-85390-073-7*, Pub. by Veritas Publns IE) Ignatius Pr.
— Medjugorje Facts Documents Theology. 265p. 1989. 24.00 (*1-85390-141-5*, Pub. by Veritas IE) St Mut.
— Theotokos: A Theological Encyclopedia of Mary. LC 82-82382. 400p. 1982. pap. 24.95 (*0-8146-5268-9*) Liturgical Pr.
— Trinitas: A Theological Encyclopedia of the Holy Trinity. LC 86-45326. 232p. (Orig.). 1986. 35.00 (*0-8146-5595-5*) Liturgical Pr.
— Verbum Caro: An Encyclopedia on Jesus, the Christ. 216p. (Orig.). 1993. pap. text ed. 35.00 (*0-8146-5017-1*, M Glazier) Liturgical Pr.
O'Carroll, Michael, ed. Veni Creator Spiritus: An Encyclopedia of the Holy Spirit. 235p. 1990. 29.95 (*0-8146-5785-0*) Liturgical Pr.
O'Casey, Sean. Blasts & Benedictions: Articles & Stories. Ayling, Ronald, ed. LC 75-8487. 314p. 1976. reprint ed. text ed. 45.00 (*0-8371-8158-5*, OCBB, Greenwood Pr) Greenwood.
— Cock-a-Doodle Dandy. LC 90-41574. (Irish Dramatic Texts Ser.). 119p. 1991. 24.95 (*0-8132-0741-X*) Cath U Pr.
— Drums under the Windows. adapted ed. 1961. pap. 4.75 (*0-8222-0336-7*) Dramatists Play.
— The Harvest Festival: A Play in Three Acts. 1979. 25.00 (*0-87104-273-8*) NY Pub Lib.
— I Knock at the Door. adapted ed. 1958. pap. 4.75 (*0-8222-0547-5*) Dramatists Play.
— The Letters of Sean O'Casey, 1959-64, Vol. 4. Krause, David, ed. LC 74-11442. (Illus.). 610p. 1992. 49.95 (*0-8132-0678-2*) Cath U Pr.
— Niall. 96p. 1992. 28.95 (*0-7145-4196-6*) Riverrun NY.
— Purple Dust. 1957. pap. 4.75 (*0-8222-0922-5*) Dramatists Play.
— Story of the Irish Citizen Army. (C). 1980. pap. text ed. 14.50 (*0-904526-50-X*, Pub. by Pluto Pr UK) Westview.
— Three Plays: Juno & the Paycock, The Shadow of a Gunman, & The Plough & the Stars. 218p. 1969. pap. 6.95 (*0-312-80290-0*, Papermac) St Martin.
O'Cathain, Seamas. Bedside Book of Irish Folklore. 127p. 1988. pap. 9.95 (*0-85342-853-0*, Pub. by Mercier Pr IE) Dufour.

O

Occamore, David. Essex Potpourri. 1993. pap. 15.00 (*0-86025-271-X*, Pub. by Ian Henry Pubns UK) Empire Pub Srvs.

OCCC Montage Staff, ed. see OCCC Press Staff, Students & Friends.

OCCC Press Staff, Students & Friends. Montage, 1990: Anthology of Oregon Coast Community College. OCCC Montage Staff, ed. 56p. (Orig.). 1990. pap. 6.00 (*0-9623452-5-3*) Oregon Coast Cmnty Col.

Occeli, Mario L., ed. Fluid Catalytic Cracking: Role in Modern Refining. LC 88-22151. (Symposium Ser.: No. 375). (Illus.). xii, 356p. 1988. 79.95 (*0-8412-1534-0*) Am Chemical.

Occelli, M. & Anthony, Rayford, eds. Hydrotreating Catalysts - Preparation, Characterization & Performance: Proceedings of the Annual International AIChE Meeting, Washington, DC, Nov. 27 to Dec. 2, 1988. (Studies in Surface Science & Catalysis: Vol. 50). 296p. 1989. 151.50 (*0-444-88032-1*) Elsevier.

Occelli, Mario & Robson, Harry, eds. Synthesis of Microporous Materials, 2 vols., Set, Vols. 1-2. (Illus.). 932p. 1992. Set. 199.95 (*0-442-01116-4*) Chapman & Hall.

— Synthesis of Microporous Materials, 2 vols., Vol. 1: Molecular Sieves. (Illus.). 932p. 1992. text ed. 124.95 (*0-442-00661-6*) Chapman & Hall.

— Synthesis of Microporous Materials, 2 vols., Vol. 2: Expanded Clays & Other Microporous Solids. (Illus.). 932p. 1992. text ed. 124.95 (*0-442-00662-4*) Chapman & Hall.

Occelli, Mario L., ed. Fluid Catalytic Cracking Two: Concepts in Catalyst Design. LC 90-23463. (ACS Symposium Ser.: No. 452). (Illus.). 384p. 1991. 79.95 (*0-8412-1908-7*) Am Chemical.

***Occelli, Mario L. & O'Connor, Paul, eds.** Fluid Catalytic Cracking Vol. III: Materials & Processes. LC 94-33553. (Symposium Ser.: No. 571). (Illus.). 400p. 1994. text ed. 99.95 (*0-8412-2996-1*) Am Chemical.

Occelli, Mario L. & Robson, Harry E., eds. Zeolite Synthesis. LC 89-6884. (Symposium Ser.: No. 398). (Illus.). xi, 653p. 1989. 139.95 (*0-8412-1632-0*) Am Chemical.

Occhiello, Ernesto, jt. ed. see Garbassi, Fabio.

***Occhiogrosso, James.** CA-Clipper Developer's Library. 1995. pap. text ed. 44.95 (*0-07-911883-6*, Windcrest) TAB Bks.

— Clipper Developer's Library: Version 5.2. 3rd ed. Leventhal, Lance A., ed. LC 93-15438. (Lance A. Leventhal Microtrend Ser.). 624p. (Orig.). 1993. pap. 44.95 (*0-915391-82-1*, Microtrend) Slawson Comm.

— Clipper Power Utilities. 1993. Incl. disk. disk, pap. text ed. 39.95 (*0-07-047483-4*) McGraw.

— Clipper Power Utilities. 1993. pap. 39.95 (*0-8306-4507-1*, Windcrest) TAB Bks.

***Occhiogrosso, James J.** Mastering Visual Objects. 350p. 1995. pap. 42.95 (*0-442-02015-5*) Van Nos Reinhold.

Occhiogrosso, Jim. Clipper Developer's Library: Version 5.01. 2nd ed. Leventhal, Lance A., ed. (Lance A. Leventhal Microtrend Ser.). 624p. (Orig.). 1992. pap. 44.95 (*0-915391-69-4*, Microtrend) Slawson Comm.

Occhiogrosso, Michael G. & Frankel, Martin R. Arbitron Replication II: A Study of the Reliability of Radio Ratings. (Illus.). 148p. (Orig.). 1982. 3.00 (*0-942720-02-4*); pap. 1.50 (*0-942720-03-2*) Fishergate.

Occhiogrosso, Peter. The Joy of Sects. LC 93-48492. 1994. 24.95 (*0-385-42564-3*) Doubleday.

Occhiogrosso, Peter, jt. auth. see Zappa, Frank.

Occidental College Staff. Of Excellence & Equity: The 1990 Report of the Occidental College Strategic Planning Steering Committee. (Illus.). 102p. 1991. pap. write for info. (*0-940349-02-7*) Occi Coll ERC.

OCCP Health Ser. Staff. Pestline, 2 vols., 1. 1991. text ed. write for info. (*0-442-00697-7*) Van Nos Reinhold.

— Pestline, 2 vols., 2. 1991. text ed. write for info. (*0-442-00698-5*) Van Nos Reinhold.

Occupational Health - Safety Programs Accreditation Committee Staff. Standards, Interpretations & Audit Criteria for Performance of Occupational Health Programs. 218p. 1976. 50.00 (*0-932627-15-3*) Am Indus Hygiene.

***Occupational Safety & Health Administration Staff.** OSHA Field Inspection Reference Manual. 144p. 1995. pap. text ed. 59.00 (*0-86587-426-3*) Gov Insts.

— OSHA Technical Manual. 3rd ed. 300p. Date not set. pap. text ed. 75.00 (*0-86587-366-6*) Gov Insts.

— Process Safety Management Standard Inspection Manual. 120p. 1994. pap. text ed. 65.00 (*0-86587-427-1*) Gov Insts.

Occupational Safety & Health Administration Staff, ed. Hazard Communication Standard Inspection Manual. 4th ed. 180p. 1993. pap. text ed. 69.00 (*0-86587-365-8*) Gov Insts.

Occupational Safety & Health Administration U. S. Department of Labor Staff. OSHA Regulated Hazardous Substances: Health, Toxicity, Economic & Technological Data, 2 vols., Set. LC 90-6751. (Illus.). 2294p. 1990. 185.00 (*0-8155-1240-6*) Noyes.

Occupational Therapy Roles Task Force Staff & Use Document Task Force Staff. Occupational Roles & Career Exploration & Development: A Companion Guide to the Occupational Roles Document. 60p. 1994. pap. text ed. write for info. (*1-56900-013-1*) Am Occup Therapy.

OCDE Staff. Energy Glossary: Glossaire de l'Energie. 354p. (ENG & FRE.). 1983. pap. 65.00 (*0-7859-4868-6*) Fr & Eur.

— Glossaire de l'Agriculture: Anglais-Francais. 262p. (ENG & FRE.). 1982. pap. write for info. (*0-7859-4908-9*) Fr & Eur.

— Glossaire De l'Economie: Glossary of the Economy: English - French. 616p. (ENG & FRE.). 1992. 195.00 (*0-8288-9195-8*, 9264237453) Fr & Eur.

— Glossaire De l'Energie Nucleaire: Glossary of Nuclear Energy: English - French. 914p. (ENG & FRE.). 1992. 195.00 (*0-8288-9196-6*, 9264237461) Fr & Eur.

Ocean County College Staff. Ocean County College Student Resource Manual. 3rd ed. 264p. 1992. pap. 13.95 (*0-8016-7287-2*) Mosby Yr Bk.

Ocean, Joan. Dolphin Connection: Interdimensional Ways of Living. LC 89-81370. (Illus.). 144p. (Orig.). 1989. pap. 11.95 (*0-9625058-9-7*) Dolphin Connection.

Ocean Studies Board, National Research Council Staff. The Ocean's Role in Global Change. 96p. (Orig.). (C). 1994. pap. text ed. 25.00 (*0-309-05043-X*) Natl Acad Pr.

Oceanic Society & Earthtrust Staff. Field Guide to the Humpback Whale. (Sasquatch Field Guide Ser.). (Illus.). 48p. 1993. pap. 5.95 (*0-912365-93-5*) Sasquatch Bks.

Oceanic Society Staff. Field Guide to the Gray Whale. (Sasquatch Field Guide Ser.). (Illus.). 50p. 1989. reprint ed. pap. 5.95 (*0-912365-25-0*) Sasquatch Bks.

Oceano. Enciclopedia General Basica Visual, 5 vols., Set. 1983. 595.00 (*0-7859-2020-1*, S39879) Fr & Eur.

***Oceano Staff.** Diccionario Enciclopedico Exito, 8 vols. 4044p. 1990. write for info. (*0-7859-5044-3*) Fr & Eur.

— Diccionario Enciclopedico Exito, Vol. 1. 456p. 1990. 250.00 (*0-7859-6311-1*, 8477644683) Fr & Eur.

— Diccionario Enciclopedico Exito, Vol. 2. 435p. 1991. 250.00 (*0-7859-6299-9*, 8477640467) Fr & Eur.

— Diccionario Enciclopedico Exito, Vol. 3. 458p. 1991. 250.00 (*0-7859-6300-6*, 8477640475) Fr & Eur.

— Diccionario Enciclopedico Exito, Vol. 4. 468p. 1991. 250.00 (*0-7859-6301-4*, 8477640483) Fr & Eur.

— Diccionario Enciclopedico Exito, Vol. 5. 480p. 1991. 250.00 (*0-7859-6302-2*, 8477640491) Fr & Eur.

— Diccionario Enciclopedico Exito, Vol. 6. 736p. 1990. 250.00 (*0-7859-6496-7*) Fr & Eur.

— Diccionario Enciclopedico Exito, Vol. 8. 508p. 1990. 250.00 (*0-7859-6313-8*, 8477644756) Fr & Eur.

— Diccionario Enciclopedico Oceano, 5 vols., Set. 1990. 695.00 (*0-7859-6303-0*, 8477640998) Fr & Eur.

— Diccionario Enciclopedico Oceano, Vol. 1. 424p. 1990. 150.00 (*0-7859-6304-9*, 8477641005) Fr & Eur.

— Diccionario Enciclopedico Oceano, Vol. 2. 424p. 1990. 150.00 (*0-7859-6305-7*, 8477641013) Fr & Eur.

— Diccionario Enciclopedico Oceano, Vol. 3. 424p. 1990. 150.00 (*0-7859-6495-9*); 150.00 (*0-7859-6306-5*, 8477641021) Fr & Eur.

— Diccionario Enciclopedico Oceano, Vol. 5. 364p. 1990. 150.00 (*0-7859-6307-3*, 8477641048) Fr & Eur.

— Diccionario Espanol-Ingles, Ingles-Espanol, 2 vols., Set. 1989. 195.00 (*0-7859-6308-1*, 8477644454) Fr & Eur.

— Diccionario Espanol-Ingles, Ingles-Espanol, Vol. 2. 484p. 1989. 105.00 (*0-7859-6310-3*, 8477644470) Fr & Eur.

— Enciclopedia de la Ciencia y de la Tecnica, 8 vols. 3rd ed. 3191p. (SPA.). 1987. 695.00 (*0-7859-5073-7*) Fr & Eur.

— Enciclopedia de la Ciencia y de la Tecnica: Encyclopedia of Science & Technology, 4 vols. 3063p. (SPA.). 1982. 175.00 (*0-7859-5052-4*) Fr & Eur.

Ochart, Yvonne. El Fuego de Las Cosas. LC 90-36240. 173p. (Orig.). (SPA.). 1990. pap. 7.50 (*0-8477-3619-9*) U of PR Pr.

Ochberg, Frank M. Post-Traumatic Therapy & Victims of Violence. LC 87-26877. (Psychosocial Stress Ser.: No. 11). 384p. 1988. 43.95 (*0-87630-490-0*) Brunner-Mazel.

Ochberg, Richard L. Psychobiography & Life Narratives. McAdams, Dan P. & Ochberg, Richard L., eds. LC 88-21922. 325p. 1988. pap. 23.95 (*0-8223-0892-4*) Duke.

Ochberg, Richard L., ed. see Ochberg, Richard L.

Ochberg, Richard L., jt. ed. see Rosenwald, George C.

***Ocheltree, C. J.** Night Before Halloween House. (Illus.). 24p. (J). (gr. 1 up). 1995. pap. 8.95 (*0-8431-3914-5*) Price Stern.

Ochesli, Matt. Winning the Inner Game of Selling. 1991. 24.50 (*1-877723-76-2*, 29002) Rough Notes.

Ochester, Ed. Changing the Name to Ochester. LC 87-71455. (Poetry Ser.). 1988. 16.95 (*0-88748-068-3*); pap. 9.95 (*0-88748-069-1*) Carnegie-Mellon.

— Dancing on the Edges of Knives: Poems. LC 73-85458. (Breakthrough Bks.). 64p. 1973. 14.95 (*0-8262-0153-9*) U of Mo Pr.

— Miracle Mile. LC 83-72900. 1984. 16.95 (*0-915604-88-4*); pap. 9.95 (*0-915604-89-2*) Carnegie-Mellon.

— Weehawken Ferry. (W.N.J. Ser.: No. 21). 1985. pap. 7.00 (*1-55780-070-7*) Juniper Pr WI.

— Weehawken Ferry. deluxe ed. (W.N.J. Ser.: No. 21). 1985. Signed Edition. 20.00 (*1-55780-088-X*) Juniper Pr WI.

Ochester, Ed & Oresick, Peter, eds. The Pittsburgh Book of Contemporary American Poetry. LC 92-50846. (Poetry Ser.). (Illus.). 416p. (Orig.). (C). 1993. text ed. 29.95 (*0-8229-3752-2*); pap. 15.95 (*0-8229-5506-7*) U of Pittsburgh Pr.

Ochi, Michel K. Applied Probability & Stochastic Processes in Engineering & the Physical Sciences. (Probability & Mathematical Statistics Ser.). 499p. 1990. text ed. 114.00 (*0-471-85742-4*) Wiley.

Ochiai. Mechanical Properties of Metallic Composites. (Materials Engineering Ser.: Vol. 7). 808p. 1994. 195.00 (*0-8247-9116-9*) Dekker.

Ochiai, Ei-Ichiro. General Principles of Biochemistry of the Elements. LC 87-20236. (Biochemistry of the Elements Ser.: Vol. 7). (Illus.). 482p. 1987. 110.00 (*0-306-42647-1*, Plenum Pr) Plenum.

Ochiai, Hidetoshi, et al, eds. Earth Reinforcement Practice: Proceedings of the International Symposium on Earth Reinforcement Practice Fukuoka, Kyushu, Japan 11-13 November 1992, 2 vols., Set. (Illus.). 1200p. (C). 1992. text ed. 160.00 (*90-5410-093-1*, Pub. by A A Balkema NE) Ashgate Pub Co.

Ochiai, Hidy. The Essence of Self-Defense. 1979. pap. 15.95 (*0-8092-7377-2*) Contemp Bks.

— Hidy Ochiai's Complete Book of Self-Defense. (Illus.). 352p. (Orig.). 1991. pap. 16.95 (*0-8092-4055-6*) Contemp Bks.

Ochiai, K., et al, eds. Endocrine Correlates of Reproduction. (Illus.). xii, 320p. 1984. 79.00 (*0-387-13514-6*) Spr-Verlag.

Ochiai, Kingo, tr. see Mori, Ogai.

Ochiai, T., jt. auth. see Noguchi, J.

Ochieng, William R. People of the South-Western Highlands: Gusii. (Kenya People Ser.). (Illus.). 34p. (YA). (gr. 6-9). 1991. pap. 4.95 (*0-237-49898-7*, Pub. by Evans Bros Ltd UK) Trafalgar.

— People Round the Lake: Luo. (Kenya People Ser.). (Illus.). 32p. (YA). (gr. 6-9). 1991. pap. 4.95 (*0-237-50924-5*, Pub. by Evans Bros Ltd UK) Trafalgar.

Ochman, Myron S., jt. auth. see Mc Allister, Lee.

Ochmanek, David A., jt. auth. see Warner, Edward L., III.

Ochner, Nobuko M., jt. ed. see Toyama, Jean Y.

Ochnio, Constance M., jt. auth. see Shea, Jonathan D.

Ochnio, Constance M., et al. Cemetery Inscriptions, St. Stanislaus Kostka Cemetery, Dabrowa Bialostocka, Poland. LC 89-61487. (Illus.). 130p. 1989. write for info. (*0-945440-02-2*) Pol Geneal CT.

Ochoa, Anna, jt. auth. see Engle, Shirley H.

Ochoa, Carlos M. The Potatoes of South America: Bolivia. Ugent, Donald, tr. (Illus.). 450p. (C). 1991. 155.00 (*0-521-38024-3*) Cambridge U Pr.

Ochoa, George. The Fall of Mexico City. (Turning Points in American History Ser.). (Illus.). 64p. (J). (gr. 5 up). 1989. lib. bdg. 14.95 (*0-382-09836-6*); pap. 7.95 (*0-382-09853-6*) Silver Burdett Pr.

— The Fall of Quebec & the French & Indian War. (Turning Points in American History Ser.). (Illus.). 64p. (J). (gr. 5 up). 1990. lib. bdg. 14.95 (*0-382-09954-0*); pap. 7.95 (*0-382-09950-8*) Silver Burdett Pr.

— Let's Visit a Bicycle Factory. LC 89-35714. (Let's Visit Ser.). (Illus.). 32p. (J). (gr. 2-4). 1990. lib. bdg. 10.79 (*0-8167-1739-7*); pap. text ed. 2.95 (*0-8167-1740-0*) Troll Assocs.

***Ochoa, George & Corey, Melinda.** The Timeline Book of Science. (Illus.). 464p. (Orig.). 1995. pap. 12.00 (*0-345-38265-X*) Ballantine.

— The Timeline Book of the Arts. (Illus.). 464p. (Orig.). 1995. pap. 12.00 (*0-345-38264-1*) Ballantine.

Ochoa, George & Osier, Jeffrey. The Writer's Guide to Creating a Science Fiction Universe. 336p. 1993. 18.95 (*0-89879-536-2*) Writers Digest.

Ochoa, George, jt. auth. see Corey, Melinda.

Ochoa, George, ed. see King, Stephen.

Ochoa, George. The Assassination of Julius Caesar. (Turning Points in World History Ser.). (Illus.). 64p. (YA). (gr. 7 up). 1991. lib. bdg. 14.95 (*0-382-24130-4*); pap. 7.95 (*0-382-24136-3*) Silver Burdett Pr.

Ochoa, Holly B., jt. ed. see Palmer, Beverly W.

Ochoa, Jose L., jt. auth. see Rosenbaum, Richard B.

Ochoa, O. O. & Reddy, J. N. Finite Element Analysis of Composite Laminates. LC 92-26602. (Solid Mechanics & Its Applications Ser.: Vol. 7). (C). 1992. lib. bdg. 109.50 (*0-7923-1125-6*) Kluwer Ac.

Ochojski, Paul M. Monarch Notes on Dickens' Hard Times. (Orig.). (C). pap. 3.95 (*0-671-00823-4*, Arco Test) P-H Gen Ref & Trav.

Ocholla-Ayayo, A. B. Luo Culture: A Reconstruction of the Material Culture Patterns of a Traditional African Society. (Illus.). 225p. (Orig.). 1980. pap. 62.50x (*3-515-02925-7*) Coronet Bks.

Ochorowicz, Julien. Mental Dominance: Classics of Personal Magnetism & Hypnotism. 300p. 1991. reprint ed. 29.98x (*0-941683-04-4*) Instant Improve.

Ochorowicz-Monatowa, Marja. Polish Cookery. Karsavina, Jean, ed. & tr. by. (International Cookbook Ser.). 1968. 12.00 (*0-517-50526-6*, Crown) Crown Pub Group.

Ochosa, Orlino A. The Tinio Brigade: Anti-American Resistance in Ilocos Provinces, 1899-1901. 286p. (Orig.). (C). 1989. pap. 14.50 (*971-10-0340-6*, Pub. by New Day Pub PH) Cellar.

Ochowicz, Jim, jt. auth. see Alexander, Don.

Ochroch, Ruth, ed. The Diagnosis & Treatment of Minimal Brain Dysfunction in Children: A Clinical Approach. LC 80-15858. 303p. 1981. 45.95 (*0-87705-503-3*) Human Sci Pr.

Ochs & Slobin, eds. Variation & Error: A Sociolinguistic Approach to Language Acquisition in Samoa. (Crosslinguistic Study of Language Acquisition Ser.). 1986. pap. 14.95 (*0-89859-847-8*) L Erlbaum Assocs.

Ochs, Bill. The Clarke Learn to Play Tin Whistle Set. (Illus.). 80p. (Orig.). (J). (gr. 3 up). 1988. pap. 6.95 (*0-9623456-0-1*); audio, pap. 14.95 (*0-9623456-5-2*); Incl. tin whistle & cassette in blister package. pap. 24.95 (*0-9623456-2-8*) Pnnywhstlrs Pr.

Ochs, Carol. The Noah Paradox: Time As Burden, Time As Blessing. LC 90-50969. (C). 1991. text ed. 19.95 (*0-268-01470-1*) U of Notre Dame Pr.

— Song of the Self: Biblical Spirituality & Human Holiness. LC 94-4924. 112p. (Orig.). (C). 1994. pap. 11.00 (*1-56338-096-X*) TPI PA.

— Women & Spirituality. LC 83-3397. (New Feminist Perspectives Ser.). 166p. (C). 1983. 42.00 (*0-8476-7232-8*) Rowman.

Ochs, Carol P. Moose on the Loose. (Illus.). 32p. (J). (ps-3). 1991. lib. bdg. 18.95 (*0-87614-448-2*, Carolrhoda) Lerner Group.

— When I'm Alone. (J). (ps-3). 1993. 18.95 (*0-87614-752-X*, Carolrhoda) Lerner Group.

— When I'm Alone. (J). (ps-3). 1993. pap. 6.95 (*0-87614-620-5*, Carolrhoda) Lerner Group.

Ochs, Donovan J. Consolatory Rhetoric: Grief, Symbol, & Ritual in the Greco-Roman Era. LC 93-16393. (Studies in Rhetoric-Communication). (C). 1993. 29.95 (*0-87249-885-9*) U of SC Pr.

Ochs, Donovan J., et al. A Brief Introduction to Speech. 2nd ed. 240p. (C). 1983. pap. text ed. 18.75 (*0-15-505585-2*); pap. text ed. 2.00 (*0-15-505586-0*) HB Coll Pubs.

Ochs, Elinor. Culture & Language Developement: Language Acquisition & Language Socialization in a Samoan Village. (Social & Cultural Foundations of Language Ser.: No. 6). 272p. 1988. pap. 21.95 (*0-521-34894-3*) Cambridge U Pr.

Ochs, Elinor, ed. Developmental Pragmatics. LC 78-20047. 1979. text ed. 59.00 (*0-12-524550-5*) Acad Pr.

Ochs, Elinor, jt. auth. see Capps, Lisa.

Ochs, Elinor, jt. ed. see Schieffelin, Bambi B.

Ochs, Linnea L. Webster's New World Legal Word Finder. 352p. 1987. pap. 10.95 (*0-13-947300-9*) P-H.

Ochs, Linnea L. & Van Der Reyden, Susan, eds. Secretarial Word Finder. LC 83-8640. 540p. 1983. 19.95 (*0-13-798157-0*, Busn) P-H.

Ochs, Martin. The African Press. 155p. 1987. pap. 17.50 (*977-424-128-2*, Pub. by Am Univ Cairo Pr UA) Col U Pr.

Ochs, Peter, ed. The Return to Scripture in Judaism & Christianity: Essays in Postcritical Scriptural Interpretation. LC 93-24518. (Theological Inquiries Ser.). 384p. (Orig.). 1993. pap. 18.95 (*0-8091-3425-X*) Paulist Pr.

Ochs, Stephen J. Desegregating the Altar: The Josephites & the Struggle for Black Priests, 1871-1960. LC 89-48219. (C). 1993. pap. 16.95 (*0-8071-1859-1*) La State U Pr.

Ochs, Vanessa. Words on Fire: One Woman's Journey into the Sacred. 1990. 22.95 (*0-15-198380-1*) HarBrace.

— Words on Fire: One Woman's Journey into the Sacred. 1992. pap. 12.00 (*0-15-698363-X*, Harvest Bks) HarBrace.

***Ochs, Vanessa L.** Safe & Sound: Protecting Your Child in an Unpredictable World. LC 94-45521. 216p. (Orig.). 1995. pap. 10.95 (*0-14-017880-5*, Penguin Bks) Viking Penguin.

Ochs, Walter J. & Bishay, Bishay G. Drainage Guidelines. LC 92-40966. (Technical Paper Ser.: No. 195). 193p. 1992. 11.95 (*0-8213-2312-1*, 12312) World Bank.

Ochse, Orpha. The History of the Organ in the United States. LC 73-22644. (Illus.). 512p. 1975. 39.95 (*0-253-32830-6*); pap. 18.95 (*0-253-20495-X*, MB-495) Ind U Pr.

Ochse, Orpha, jt. auth. see Duncan, James L.

Ochse, Orpha C. Organists & Organ Playing in Nineteenth-Century France & Belgium. LC 94-2589. 1994. 29.95 (*0-253-34161-2*) Ind U Pr.

Ochse, R. A. Before the Gates of Excellence: The Determinants of Creative Genius. (Illus.). 300p. (C). 1990. 59.95 (*0-521-37557-6*); pap. 19.95 (*0-521-37699-8*) Cambridge U Pr.

***Ochsendorf, Falk R. & Fuchs, Jurgen, eds.** Oxidative Stress in Male Infertility. 1995. 129.95 (*0-8493-4798-X*, 4798) CRC Pr.

***Ochsenius, Claudio & Gruhn, Ruth, eds.** Taima-Taima. 138p. 1992. pap. 10.00 (*1-55889-874-3*) Ctr Study First Am.

Ochsenwald, William. The Hijaz Railroad. LC 80-10505. (Illus.). 187p. reprint ed. pap. 53.30 (*0-8357-3137-5*, 2039400) Bks Demand.

— Religion, Society, & the State in Arabia: The Hijaz under Ottoman Control, 1840-1908. LC 84-7498. (Illus.). 257p. 1984. 42.50 (*0-8142-0366-3*) Ohio St U Pr.

Ochsenwald, William L., jt. auth. see Fisher, Sydney N.

Ochshorn, Judith. The Female Experience & the Nature of the Divine. LC 81-47012. 286p. reprint ed. pap. 81.60 (*0-685-16314-8*, 2056237) Bks Demand.

***Ochshorn, Judith & Cole, Ellen, eds.** Women's Spirituality, Women's Lives. LC 95-11386. 227p. 1995. 29.95 (*1-56024-722-3*); pap. 14.95 (*1-56023-065-7*) Haworth Pr.

Ochshorn, Kathleen. The Heart's Essential Landscape: Bernard Malamud's Hero. LC 90-35147. (American University Studies: American Literature: Ser. XXIV, Vol. 3). 336p. (C). 1990. text ed. 55.95 (*0-8204-1269-4*) P Lang Pubs.

Ochshorn, Susan, jt. auth. see Logan, William B.

Ochsman, R. B., jt. ed. see Whitney, P.

Ochsner, et al. Tobacco & Marijuana. 1976. per. 12.00 (*0-88252-048-2*) Paladin Hse.

Ochsner, Florence M., jt. auth. see Peck, Janice L.

Ochsner, George H. The Rape of God. Ochsner, Virginia, ed. LC 90-84940. 396p. (Orig.). 1990. pap. 12.95 (*0-945201-16-8*) Gannam-Kubat.

Ochsner, Jeffery K. H. H. Richardson: Complete Architectural Works. (Illus.). 424p. 1982. pap. 37.50x (*0-262-65015-0*) MIT Pr.

Ochsner, Jeffrey K., ed. Shaping Seattle Architecture: A Historical Guide to the Architects. LC 94-17618. (Illus.). 446p. 1994. 40.00x (*0-295-97365-X*); pap. 19.95 (*0-295-97366-8*) U of Wash Pr.

Ochsner, Othon H., II. Ochsner Pocket Guide to the Finest Restaurants in the World. 10th ed. (Illus.). 248p. 1993. pap. 20.00 (*1-881546-01-2*) Ochsner Intl.

— Ochsner Pocket Guide to the Finest Restaurants in the World 1992-93. 9th ed. (Illus.). 199p. (Orig.). 1992. pap. write for info. (*1-881546-00-4*) Ochsner Intl.

Ochsner, Robert S. Physical Eloquence & the Biology of Writing. LC 89-38062. (Literacy, Culture, & Learning: Theory & Practice Ser.). 223p. 1990. 59.50 (*0-7914-0313-0*); pap. 19.95 (*0-7914-0314-9*) State U NY Pr.

— Rhythm & Writing. LC 87-50836. 150p. 1989. 18.50 (*0-87875-347-8*) Whitston Pub.

Ochsner, Virginia, ed. see Ochsner, George H.

O

An Asterisk (*) at the beginning of an entry indicates that the title is appearing in BIP for the first time.

Ochtrup, Monica. Pieces from the Long Afternoon: Prose Poems. 1991. pap. 6.00 (*0-89823-125-6*) New Rivers Pr.
— What I Cannot Say - I Will Say. 80p. 1984. pap. 3.50 (*0-89823-059-4*) New Rivers Pr.
Ochwadt, Curd. Voltaire und die Grafen zu Schaumburg-Lippe. 1990. reprint ed. pap. 32.00 (*3-87447-230-2*) Periodicals Srv.
Ochwat, John, jt. auth. see Kaun, David.
Ociepka, Bob, jt. auth. see Ratermann, Dale.
OCIME Staff, jt. auth. see ICS Staff.
OCIMF. Safe Navigation Symposium Papers Washington, D. C. 1978. 198.00 (*0-317-61463-0*, Pub. by Witherby & Co UK) St Mut.
OCIMF Staff. Anchoring Systems & Procedures for Large Tankers. (C). 1988. 80.00 (*0-900886-73-0*, Pub. by Witherby & Co UK) St Mut.
— Buoy Mooring Forum SPM Hose Ancillary Equipment Guide. 1975. 45.00 (*0-317-61154-2*, Pub. by Witherby & Co UK) St Mut.
— Buoy Mooring Forum SPM Hose System Design Commentary. (C). 1975. 75.00 (*0-685-22646-8*, Pub. by Witherby & Co UK) St Mut.
— Design & Construction Specification for Marine Loading Arms. 1986. 310.00 (*0-317-61172-0*, Pub. by Witherby & Co UK) St Mut.
— Design & Construction Specification for Marine Loading Arms. (C). 1987. 315.00 (*0-685-36231-0*, Pub. by Witherby & Co UK) St Mut.
— Design & Construction Specification for Marine Loading Arms. 1993. 120.00 (*1-85609-071-X*, Pub. by Witherby & Co UK) St Mut.
— Disabled Tankers: Report of Studies on Drift & Towage. 1981. 450.00 (*0-900886-63-3*, Pub. by Witherby & Co UK) St Mut.
— Drift Characteristics of Fifty Thousand to Seventy Thousand DWT Tankers. 1982. 180.00 (*0-900886-67-6*) St Mut.
— Drift Characteristics of Fifty Thousand to Seventy Thousand DWT Tankers. (C). 1982. 175.00 (*0-685-31785-4*, Pub. by Witherby & Co UK) St Mut.
— Effect on the Operation of Tanker Terminals Following International Tanker Safety & Pollution Prevention Standards. (C). 1981. 24.00 (*0-900886-59-5*, Pub. by Witherby & Co UK) St Mut.
— Effective Mooring. (C). 1989. 75.00 (*0-948691-88-3*, Pub. by Witherby & Co UK) St Mut.
— Guide for the Handling, Storage Inspection & Testing of Hoses in the Field. Orig. Title: Buoy Mooring forum Hose Guide. 1993. text ed. 150.00 (*1-85609-070-1*, Pub. by Witherby & Co UK) St Mut.
— Guide on Marine Terminal Fire Protection & Emergency Evacuation. (C). 1987. 200.00 (*0-948691-28-X*, Pub. by Witherby & Co UK) St Mut.
— Guide on Terminal Fire Protection & Emergency Evacuation. (C). 1987. 200.00 (*0-948691-30-1*, Pub. by Witherby & Co UK) St Mut.
— Guidelines & Recommendations for Safe Mooring of Large Ships at Piers & Sea Islands. 1993. 180.00 (*1-85609-041-8*, Pub. by Witherby & Co UK) St Mut.
— Guidelines & Recommendations for the Safe Mooring of Large Ships at Piers & Sea Islands. (C). 1978. 160.00 (*0-900886-33-1*, Pub. by Witherby & Co UK) St Mut.
— Hawser Guidelines, Vol. 1: Guide to Purchasing Hawsers. 1987. 110.00 (*0-948691-31-X*, Pub. by Witherby & Co UK) St Mut.
— Hawser Guidelines, Vol. 2: Procedures for Quality Control & Inspection During Production of Hawsers. (C). 1987. 80.00 (*0-948691-34-4*, Pub. by Witherby & Co UK) St Mut.
— Hawser Guidelines, Vol. 3: Prototype Rope Testing. (C). 1987. 80.00 (*0-948691-35-2*, Pub. by Witherby & Co UK) St Mut.
— Hawser Test Report. 1982. 250.00 (*0-900886-68-4*, Pub. by Witherby & Co UK) St Mut.
— Hose Standards. (C). 1988. 100.00 (*0-900886-37-4*, Pub. by Witherby & Co UK) St Mut.
— Hose Standards. (C). 1990. 195.00 (*0-948691-98-0*, Pub. by Witherby & Co UK) St Mut.
— Inspection Guidelines for Bulk Oil Carriers. (C). 1989. 110.00 (*0-948691-92-1*, Pub. by Witherby & Co UK) St Mut.
— Inspection Guidelines for Bulk Oil Carriers. 1993. 48.00 (*1-85609-059-0*, Pub. by Witherby & Co UK) St Mut.
— Marine & Terminal Operations Survey Guidelines. (C). 1983. 65.00 (*0-900886-86-2*, Pub. by Witherby & Co UK) St Mut.
— Marine Terminal Survey Guidelines. 1993. 60.00 (*1-85609-062-0*, Pub. by Witherby & Co UK) St Mut.
— Mooring Equipment Guidelines. (C). 1991. 150.00 (*1-85609-018-3*, Pub. by Witherby & Co UK) St Mut.
— Prediction of Wind & Current Loads on VLCCs. (C). 1977. 400.00 (*0-685-36229-9*, Pub. by Witherby & Co UK) St Mut.
— Prediction of Wind & Current Loads on VLCCS. 1993. 240.00 (*1-85609-042-6*, Pub. by Witherby & Co UK) St Mut.
— Predictions of Wind & Current Loads on VLCC's. 1977. 360.00 (*0-317-61263-8*, Pub. by Witherby & Co UK) St Mut.
— Recomendations on Equipment for the Towing of Disabled Tankers. 1981. 150.00 (*0-317-61454-1*, Pub. by Witherby & Co UK) St Mut.
— Recommendation for Manifolds Refrigerated Liquefied Natural Gas Carriers, LNG. 1994. 60.00 (*1-85609-066-3*, Pub. by Witherby & Co UK) St Mut.
— Recommendations for Equipment Employed in the Mooring of Ships at Single Point Moorings. (C). 1988. 80.00 (*0-948691-56-5*, Pub. by Witherby & Co UK) St Mut.
— Recommendations for Equipment Employed in the Mooring of Ships at Single Point Moorings. (C). 1991. 170.00 (*1-85609-020-5*, Pub. by Witherby & Co UK) St Mut.
— Recommendations for Manifolds for Refrigerated Liquefied Gas Carriers for Cargoes from 0'C to Minus 104'C. (C). 1988. 80.00 (*0-685-36228-0*, Pub. by Witherby & Co UK) St Mut.
— Recommendations for Manifolds for Refrigerated Liquified Gas Carriers for Cargos from 0 C to Minus 104 C. (C). 1987. 80.00 (*0-685-31792-7*, Pub. by Witherby & Co UK) St Mut.
— Recommendations for Oil Tanker Manifolds & Associated Equipment. (C). 1991. 110.00 (*1-85609-017-5*, Pub. by Witherby & Co UK) St Mut.
— Recommendations on Equipment for the Towing of Disabled Tankers. (C). 1981. 160.00 (*0-900886-65-X*, Pub. by Witherby & Co UK) St Mut.
— Safety Guide for Terminals Handling Ships Carrying Liquefied Gases in Bulk. (C). 1982. 210.00 (*0-900886-72-2*, Pub. by Witherby & Co UK) St Mut.
— Safety Guide for Terminals Handling Ships Carrying Liquefied Gases in Bulk. 1993. 72.00 (*1-85609-057-4*, Pub. by Witherby & Co UK) St Mut.
— Safety Inspection Guidelines & Terminal Safety Check List for Gas Carriers. (C). 1979. 60.00 (*0-900886-43-9*, Pub. by Witherby & Co UK) St Mut.
— Ship Information Questionnaire for Bulk Oil Carriers. (C). 1989. 80.00 (*0-948691-91-3*, Pub. by Witherby & Co UK) St Mut.
— Single Point Mooring Maintenance & Operations Guide. (C). 1985. 200.00 (*0-900886-95-1*, Pub. by Witherby & Co UK) St Mut.
— Single Point Mooring Maintenance & Operations Guide. 1993. 80.00 (*1-85609-072-8*, Pub. by Witherby & Co UK) St Mut.
— Single Point Morning: Maintenance & Operations Guide. 1985. 162.00 (*0-317-61479-7*, Pub. by Witherby & Co UK) St Mut.
— SPM Hose Ancillary Equipment Guide. (C). 1987. 100.00 (*0-948691-54-9*, Pub. by Witherby & Co UK) St Mut.
— SPM Hose System Design Commentary. 1993. 60.00 (*1-85609-027-2*, Pub. by Witherby & Co UK) St Mut.
— Standardisation of Manifolds for Refrigerated Liquefied Gas Carriers (LNG) (C). 1979. 55.00 (*0-685-26148-4*, Pub. by Witherby & Co UK) St Mut.
— Standards for Equipment Employed in the Mooring & Ships at Single Point Moorings. 1978. 36.00 (*0-317-61485-1*, Pub. by Witherby & Co UK) St Mut.
— Standards for Oil Tanker Manifolds & Associated Equipment. (C). 1981. 95.00 (*0-900886-64-1*, Pub. by Witherby & Co UK) St Mut.
OCIMF Staff, ed. Buoy Mooring Forum Hose Guide. (C). 1974. 75.00 (*0-685-31788-9*, Pub. by Witherby & Co UK) St Mut.
OCIMF Staff & IPIECA Staff. Oil Spills, Their Fate & Impact on the Marine Environment. 1980. 50.00 (*0-900886-49-8*, Pub. by Witherby & Co UK) St Mut.
OCIMF Staff & SIGGTO Staff. Prevention of Wind Loads on Large Liquified Gas Carriers. (C). 1985. 600.00 (*0-685-31795-1*, Pub. by Witherby & Co UK) St Mut.
OCIMF Staff & SIGTTO Staff. Inspection Guidelines for Ships Carrying Liquefied Gases in Bulk. (C). 1990. 195.00 (*0-948691-96-4*, Pub. by Witherby & Co UK) St Mut.
— Prediction of Wind Loads on Large Liquefied Gas Carriers. (C). 1985. 600.00 (*0-900886-97-8*, Pub. by Witherby & Co UK) St Mut.
— Ship Information Questionnaire for Liquefied Gas Carriers. (C). 1990. 125.00 (*0-948691-99-9*, Pub. by Witherby & Co UK) St Mut.
OCIMF Staff & SSIGTTO Staff. Predictions of Wind Loads on Large Liquified Gas Carrers. 1987. 540.00 (*0-317-61267-0*, Pub. by Witherby & Co UK) St Mut.
OCIMF Staff, jt. auth. see ICS Staff.
Ockel, Gerhard. Guilt. (C). 1951. pap. 3.00 (*0-87574-061-8*) Pendle Hill.
Ockelton, Mark. Medicine, Ethics & Law. 111p. (Orig.). 1987. pap. 42.50x (*3-515-04935-5*) Coronet Bks.
— Trusts for Accountants. 1987. U.K. pap. 34.00 (*0-406-50090-8*) Butterworth Legal Pubs.
Ockelton, Mark, ed. see Heydon, J. D.
***Ocken, Rebecca L.** The Relationship Between Site Design & Travel Behavior. LC 95-3538. (CPL Bibliography Ser.: Vol. 312). (Illus.). 1995. write for info. (*0-86602-312-7*) Am Plan Assn.
Ocken, Stanley. Parametrized Knot Theory. LC 76-3641. (Memoirs Ser.: No. 5/170). 114p. 1976. pap. 22.00 (*0-8218-1870-8*, MEMO 5/170) Am Math.
***Ockenden, Jonathan & Franklin, Michael.** The Future of European Agricultural Policy. LC 95-15800. Orig. Title: European Agriculture. 1995. pap. write for info. (*0-87609-180-X*) Coun Foreign.
Ockenden, Michael & Jones, Timothy. Around Town: Situational Conversation Practice. (English As a Second Language Bk.). 1982. audio, pap. text ed. 37.95 (*0-582-79798-5*, 75052); pap. text ed. 13.74 (*0-582-79769-1*, 75023); pap. text ed. 28.69 (*0-582-79772-1*, 75026) Longman.
Ockendon, H. & Taylor, A. B. Inviscid Fluid Flows. (Applied Mathematical Sciences Ser.: Vol. 43). (Illus.). 146p. 1983. pap. 43.00 (*0-387-90824-2*) Spr-Verlag.
Ockendon, Hilary & Ockendon, John. Viscous Flow. (Texts in Applied Mathematics Ser.: No. 13). (Illus.). 130p. (C). 1995. 49.95 (*0-521-45244-9*); pap. 19.95 (*0-521-45881-1*) Cambridge U Pr.
Ockendon, John, jt. auth. see Ockendon, Hilary.
Ockene, Ira S. & Ockene, Judith, eds. Prevention of Coronary Heart Disease. LC 92-10336. 1992. 85.00 (*0-316-62214-1*) Little.
Ockene, Judith, jt. ed. see Ockene, Ira S.
Ockenfels, R. A., et al. Pronghorn Home Ranges, Movements, & Habitat Selection in Central Arizona: Arizona Game & Fish Department Technical Report, No. 13. (Illus.). 80p. (Orig.). 1994. pap. (*0-917563-18-2*) AZ Game & Fish.
Ockenga, Earl & Rucker, Walt. Money. (Elementary Mathematics Ser.). (Illus.). 16p. (J). (gr. 1). 1990. pap. text ed. 1.25 (*1-56281-125-8*, M125) Extra Eds.
— Place Value to One Hundred. (Elementary Mathematics Ser.). (Illus.). 16p. (J). (gr. 1). 1990. pap. text ed. 1.25 (*1-56281-115-0*, M115) Extra Eds.
— Subtracting from Eighteen or Less. (Elementary Mathematics Ser.). (Illus.). 16p. (J). (gr. 1). 1990. pap. text ed. 1.25 (*1-56281-135-5*, M135) Extra Eds.
— Subtracting from Ten or Less. (Elementary Mathematics Ser.). (Illus.). 16p. (J). (gr. 1). 1990. pap. text ed. 1.25 (*1-56281-110-X*, M110) Extra Eds.
— Sums Through Eighteen. (Elementary Mathematics Ser.). (Illus.). 16p. (J). (gr. 1). 1990. pap. text ed. 1.25 (*1-56281-130-4*, M130) Extra Eds.
— Sums Through Ten. (Elementary Mathematics Ser.). (Illus.). 16p. (J). (gr. 1). 1990. pap. text ed. 1.25 (*1-56281-105-3*, M105) Extra Eds.
— Telling Time. (Elementary Mathematics Ser.). (Illus.). 16p. (J). (gr. 1). 1990. pap. text ed. 1.25 (*1-56281-120-7*, M120) Extra Eds.
Ockenga, Starr. On Women & Friendship: A Collection of Victorian Keepsakes & Traditions. LC 92-27152. (Illus.). 208p. 1993. 35.00 (*1-55670-242-6*) Stewart Tabori & Chang.
Ocker, Christopher. Johannes Klenkok: A Friar's Life, c. 1310-1374. LC 93-71200. (Transactions Ser.: Vol. 83, Pt. 5). 115p. 1993. pap. 15.00 (*0-87169-835-8*, M825-OCC) Am Philos.
Ocker, Christopher, ed. see Sluga, Hans.
Ocker, Jim, et al. Fishing the Mississippi Pools, 15-17. (Mississippi River Ser.). (Illus.). 80p. 1990. pap. 9.95 (*0-939314-28-2*) Fishing Hot.
— Fishing the Mississippi Pools 18-19. (Mississippi River Ser.). (Illus.). 84p. 1991. pap. 9.95 (*0-939314-29-0*) Fishing Hot.
Ocker, Lewis B. Growing up in the Catskills. 1994. 8.95 (*0-8062-4898-X*) Carlton.
Ockerman, Herbert. Food Science Sourcebook, 2 vols., 1. enl. rev. ed. (Illus.). 1600p. 1991. text ed. write for info. (*0-442-00776-0*) Chapman & Hall.
— Food Science Sourcebook, 2 vols., 2. enl. rev. ed. (Illus.). 1600p. 1991. text ed. write for info. (*0-442-00777-9*) Chapman & Hall.
— Food Science Sourcebook, 2 vols., Set. 2nd enl. rev. ed. (Illus.). 1600p. 1991. text ed. 215.00 (*0-442-23388-4*) Chapman & Hall.
— Sausage & Processed Meat Formulations. 1989. text ed. 74.95 (*0-442-23436-8*) Chapman & Hall.
Ockerman, Herbert W. Illustrated Chemistry Laboratory Terminology. 280p. 1991. 32.95 (*0-8493-0152-1*, QD51) CRC Pr.
Ockershausen, Jane. The Georgia One-Day Trip Book: A New Way to Explore the State's Romantic Past, Vibrant Present & Olympian Future. LC 93-5351. (Illus.). 415p. (Orig.). 1993. pap. 14.95 (*0-939009-71-4*) EPM Pubns.
— The New Washington One-Day Trip Book: One Hundred One Offbeat Excursions in & Around the Nation's Capital. 4th ed. LC 91-46710. 271p. 1992. pap. 9.95 (*0-939009-59-5*) EPM Pubns.
— The North Carolina One-Day Trip Book: 150 Excursions in the Land of Dramatic Diversity. LC 90-34997. (Illus.). 304p. (Orig.). 1990. pap. 11.95 (*0-939009-38-2*, F252-3-035) EPM Pubns.
— The Pennsylvania One-Day Trip Book. (Illus.). 400p. (Orig.). Date not set. pap. 14.95 (*0-939009-88-9*) EPM Pubns.
Ockert, Carl E. Compassion & Common Sense. LC 79-92791. (Illus.). 172p. (Orig.). 1980. 6.95 (*0-9603926-0-2*); pap. 4.95 (*0-9603926-1-0*) MCP Bks.
***Ockham, William.** A Letter to the Friars Minor & Other Writings. Kilcullen, John & McGrade, Arthur S., eds. (Cambridge Texts in the History of Political Thought Ser.). (Illus.). 400p. (C). 1992. write for info. (*0-521-35243-6*) Cambridge U Pr.
— Opera Politica IV. Offler, H. S., ed. (Auctores Britannici Medii Aevi XIV British Academy). 336p. 1995. 125.00 (*0-19-726127-2*) OUP.
— A Short Discourse on Tyrannical Government. Kilcullen, John & McGrade, Arthur S., eds. (Cambridge Texts in the History of Political Thought Ser.). (Illus.). 400p. (C). 1995. pap. 15.95 (*0-521-35804-3*) Cambridge U Pr.
Ockham, William Of. Quddlibetal Questions, 2 vols., Set. Freddoso, Alfred J. & Kelley, Francis E., eds. (Yale Library on Medieval Philosophy: No. 1). 728p. 1991. text ed. 110.00 (*0-300-04832-7*) Yale U Pr.
— Quddlibetal Questions, Vol. 1: Quolibets 1-4. Freddoso, Alfred J. & Kelley, Francis E., eds. 728p. 1991. write for info. (*0-318-68384-9*) Yale U Pr.
— Quddlibetal Questions, Vol. 2: Quolibets 5-7. Freddoso, Alfred J. & Kelley, Francis E., eds. 728p. 1991. write for info. (*0-318-68385-7*) Yale U Pr.
Ockinga. Two Ramesside Tombs at Mashayakh, No. II. pap. 70.00 (*0-85668-566-6*, Pub. by Aris & Phillips UK) David Brown.
Ockinga, ed. Two Ramesside Tombs at El Mashayikh, Vol. 1: The Tomb of Anhurmose The Outer Room. 1988. pap. 70.00 (*0-85668-453-8*, Pub. by Aris & Phillips UK) David Brown.
Ockleford, C. D. & Whyte, A., eds. Coated Vesicles. LC 79-17280. 400p. reprint ed. pap. 114.00 (*0-685-16174-9*, 2027260) Bks Demand.
Ockley, S., jt. auth. see Gibbon, E.
Ockley, Simon, tr. see Ibn-Tufail, Abu-Bakr M.
***Ockman, Carol.** Ingres's Eroticized Bodies: Retracing the Serpentine Line. LC 94-34311. (Publications in the History of Art). 1995. 40.00 (*0-300-05961-2*) Yale U Pr.
Ockman, Joan, ed. Architecture Culture 1943-1968: A Documentary Anthology. LC 91-38729. (Readers in Twentieth Century Thought Ser.). (Illus.). 464p. 1993. 50.00 (*0-8478-1511-0*); pap. 35.00 (*0-8478-1522-6*) Rizzoli Intl.
Ocko, Jonathan K. Bureaucratic Reform in Provincial China: Ting Jih-ch'ang in Restoration Kiangsu, 1867-1870. (East Asian Monographs: No. 103). 316p. 1983. 28.00 (*0-674-08617-1*) HUP.
Ocko, Judy Y., ed. The Retail Advertising Manual. (Illus.). 400p. 1987. 89.95 (*0-934590-18-4*) Retail Report.
Ocko, Judy Y. & Rosenblum, M. L. Your Secret Ingredient: Advertising Handbook for Retail Merchants. rev. ed. 125p. pap. 10.00 (*0-87102-073-4*, 60-1651) Natl Ret Merch.
***Ocko, Stephanie.** Adventure Vacations: A 50-State Guide to Rock Climbing, Horseback Riding, Spelunking, Whitewater Rafting, Snorkeling, Hang Gliding & Ballooning. (Illus.). 256p. 1995. pap. 14.95 (*0-8065-1632-1*, Citadel Pr) Carol Pub Group.
— Environmental Vacations: Volunteer Projects to Save the Planet. 2nd ed. 248p. (Orig.). 1992. pap. 16.95 (*1-56261-033-3*) John Muir.
— Water: Almost Enough for Everyone. LC 94-34743. (J). 1995. write for info. (*0-615-00137-8*, Atheneum S&S) S&S Trade.
— Water: Almost Enough for Everyone. (J). (gr. 5-9). 1995. 15.00 (*0-689-31797-2*, Atheneum Bks Young) S&S Childrens.
O'Clair, Rita M., et al. Nature of Southeast Alaska: A Guide to Plants, Animals & Habitats. 256p. (Orig.). 1992. pap. 17.95 (*0-88240-419-9*) Alaska Northwest.
O'Clair, Robert, jt. ed. see Ellmann, Richard.
OCLC Online Computer Library Center, Inc. Staff. U. S. Newspaper Program: National Union List. 3rd ed. 1989. fiche 275.00 (*0-685-25894-7*) OCLC Online Comp.
OCLC Staff. USNP National Unionfest 1989. 3rd ed. 2000p. 1989. fiche 275.00 (*1-55653-074-9*) OCLC Online Comp.
O'Cleary, Helen. Athgreany Stone Circle - The Stones of Time. (Illus.). 203p. (Orig.). 1991. pap. 38.00 (*0-9626761-0-1*) Al H Morrison.
O'Cleireacain, Seamus. Third World Debt & International Public Policy. LC 89-16019. 262p. 1990. text ed. 59.95 (*0-275-92520-X*, C2520, Praeger Pubs) Greenwood.
O'Cleirich, Nellie. Carrickmacross Lace. 1985. pap. 11.95 (*0-85105-436-6*, Pub. by Colin Smythe Ltd UK) Dufour.
O'Clery, Conor. America, a Place Called Hope? 222p. 1993. pap. 18.95 (*0-86278-342-9*, Pub. by OBrien Pr IE) Dufour.
O'Clery, Helen. Zodiacal Archetypes in Celtic Myths. Morrison, Al H., ed. (Illus.). 48p. (Orig.). 1993. pap. 11.00 (*0-9626761-2-8*) Al H Morrison.
Ocneanu, Adrian. Actions of Discrete Amenable Groups on von Neumann Alegbras. (Lecture Notes in Mathematics Ser.: Vol. 1138). v, 115p. 1985. pap. 46.20 (*0-387-15663-1*) Spr-Verlag.
Ocoboc, Ed, jt. auth. see Guenther, Jeff.
***O'Cofaigh, E., et al.** The Climatic Dwelling: An Introduction to Climate-Responsive Residential Architecture. (Illus.). 176p. (Orig.). 1994. pap. 50.00 (*1-873936-39-7*, Pub. by J & J Sci Pubs UK) Bks Intl VA.
— The Climatic Dwelling: An Introduction to Climate-Responsive Residential Architecture. (Illus.). 40p. (Orig.). (C). 1994. 240.00 (*1-873936-35-4*, Pub. by J & J Sci Pubs UK) Bks Intl VA.
***O'Collins, Gerald.** Christology: A Biblical, Historical, & System. 352p. 1995. text ed. 56.00 (*0-19-875501-5*); pap. 14.95 (*0-19-875502-3*) OUP.
— Experiencing Jesus. 128p. (Orig.). (C). 1995. pap. 6.95 (*0-8091-3543-4*) Paulist Pr.
— Finding Jesus: Living Through Lent with John's Gospel. 64p. 1984. pap. 3.95 (*0-8091-2565-X*) Paulist Pr.
— Fundamental Theology. LC 80-82809. 288p. (Orig.). 1981. pap. 12.95 (*0-8091-2347-9*) Paulist Pr.
— Interpreting Jesus. 1983. pap. 12.95 (*0-8091-2572-2*) Paulist Pr.
— The Resurrection of Jesus Christ. (Pere Marquette Lectures). 1993. 10.00 (*0-87462-548-3*) Marquette.
— Retrieving Fundamental Theology: The Three Styles of Contemporary Theology. LC 93-28251. 240p. (Orig.). (C). 1993. pap. 14.95 (*0-8091-3418-7*) Paulist Pr.
O'Collins, Gerald & Farrugia, Edward G. Concise Dictionary of Theology. LC 91-7187. 272p. 1991. pap. 14.95 (*0-8091-3235-4*) Paulist Pr.
O'Collins, Gerald & Marconi, Gilberto, eds. Luke & Acts. O'Connell, Matthew J., tr. LC 92-35226. 320p. 1993. pap. 10.95 (*0-8091-3360-1*) Paulist Pr.
O'Collins, Gerald, et al. Believing: Understanding the Creed. 1991. pap. 8.95 (*0-8091-3282-6*) Paulist Pr.
O'Collins, Gerald S. J. Interpreting the Resurrection: Examine the Major Problems in the Stories of Jesus' Resurrection. 1989. 8.95 (*0-8091-0425-3*) Paulist Pr.
O'Con, Robert & Carr, Richard. Advanced Oxyacetlene Flame Cutting. (Series 910). (Orig.). 1985. 8.00 (*0-8064-0387-X*); audio 459.00 (*0-8064-0388-8*) Bergwall.
— Metal Fabrication: A Practical Guide. (Illus.). 400p. (C). 1985. text ed. 46.00 (*0-13-577685-6*) P-H.
O'Con, Robert, jt. auth. see Carr, Richard.
O'Con, Robert, jt. auth. see Hunter, Richard.
O'Conaire, Padraic. Finest Stories of Padraic O'Conaire. 210p. 1982. pap. 8.95 (*0-905169-54-9*, Pub. by Poolbeg Pr IE) Dufour.
Ocone, D., jt. ed. see Karatzas, I.
O'Connell, jt. auth. see Engelmeier.
O'Connell, jt. auth. see Kaye, M. P.

C

An Asterisk (*) at the beginning of an entry indicates that the title is appearing in BIP for the first time.

O'Connell, Agnes & Russo, Nancy F. Models of Achievement Vol. 2: Reflections of Eminent Women in Psychology. 400p. (C). 1988. 79.95 (*0-8058-0083-2*); pap. text ed. 36.00 (*0-8058-0322-X*) L Erlbaum Assocs.

O'Connell, Agnes N. & Russo, Nancy F., eds. Women in Psychology: A Bio-Bibliographic Sourcebook. LC 89-25787. 424p. 1990. text ed. 55.00 (*0-313-26091-5*, OWP/, Greenwood Pr) Greenwood.

O'Connell, Alison. Shopping Twin Cities & More. 1992. pap. 12.95 (*0-9631192-0-6*) Chamberlin Pub.

O'Connell, Ann B., jt. auth. see O'Connell, Brian.

O'Connell, Anne. First Cancer then Lupus: The Courageous Story of One Woman's Journey Through Illness, Chemotherapy, Steroids & Pain Control. 145p. 1992. pap. 14.95 (*0-9627274-2-3*) A O'Connell.

— In Love & Honor: A Novel of a Navy Nurse. 2nd ed. 328p. 1990. reprint ed. pap. 16.95 (*0-9627274-1-5*) A O'Connell.

O'Connell, April & O'Connell, Vincent. Choice & Change: The Psychology of Holistic Growth, Adjustment & Creativity. 4th ed. 496p. (C). 1991. pap. text ed. write for info. (*0-13-132754-2*) P-H.

O'Connell, Avice M. & Leone, Norma L. Your Child & X-Rays: A Parent's Guide to Radiation, X-Rays & Other Imaging Procedures. LC 87-37854. (Illus.). 104p. (Orig.). 1989. pap. 8.95 (*0-936635-05-3*) Lion Pr & Vid.

O'Connell, Bill. Foreign Student Education at Two-Year Colleges. 164p. 1994. pap. write for info. (*0-912207-66-3*) NAFSA Washington.

— On the Map to Your Life. 27p. 1992. pap. 5.00 (*0-933292-20-1*, Dytiscid Pr) Arts End.

O'Connell, Bonnie. The Anti-Warhol Museum Proposals for the Socially Responsible Disposal of Warholia. (Illus.). 1993. 15.00 (*0-932526-48-9*) Nexus Pr.

O'Connell, Brian. America's Voluntary Spirit. 460p. 1983. 14.95 (*0-87954-081-8*) Ind Sector.

— America's Voluntary Spirit: A Book of Readings. LC 83-81223. 461p. 1983. 19.95 (*0-87954-079-6*) Foundation Ctr.

— The Board Member's Book: Making a Difference in Voluntary Organizations. 2nd ed. LC 93-26639. 208p. (Orig.). 1993. 24.95 (*0-87954-502-X*) Foundation Ctr.

— The Comedy of Boards. (Nonprofit Sector Ser.). 1995. 22.95 (*0-7879-0179-2*) Jossey-Bass.

— Effective Leadership in Voluntary Organizations. LC 81-69289. 1981. 5.95 (*0-8027-7188-2*) Walker & Co.

— Our Organization. 1987. pap. 12.95 (*0-8027-1006-9*) Walker & Co.

— People Power: Service, Advocacy, Empowerment : Selected Writings of Brian O'Connell. limited ed. LC 94-23368. 1994. pap. 24.95 (*0-87954-563-1*) Foundation Ctr.

O'Connell, Brian & O'Connell, Ann B. Volunteers in Action. LC 89-1472. 1989. 24.95 (*0-87954-291-8*); pap. 19.95 (*0-87954-292-6*) Foundation Ctr.

O'Connell, Carol. How to Start a School-Business Partnership. LC 85-61795. (Fastback Ser.: No. 226). 50p. (Orig.). 1985. pap. 1.25 (*0-87367-226-7*) Phi Delta Kappa.

— Mallory's Oracle. 336p. 1995. pap. text ed. 5.99 (*0-515-11647-5*) Jove Pubns.

— Mallory's Oracle. LC 94-2234. 288p. 1994. 21.95 (*0-399-13975-3*, Putnam) Putnam Pub Group.

— The Man Who Cast Two Shadows. LC 94-43797. 1995. 22.95 (*0-399-14064-6*, Putnam) Putnam Pub Group.

O'Connell, Caroline. Every Woman's Guide to Romance in Paris. LC 95-25589. (Illus.). 192p. (Orig.). 1992. pap. 9.95 (*0-89529-437-0*) Avery Pub.

O'Connell, Caroline & Brada, Debra. Best Places to Kiss in Southern California: A Romantic Travel Guide. 3rd ed. Bulmer, Miriam, ed. (Best Places to Kiss Ser.). 300p. 1994. pap. 12.95 (*1-877988-13-8*) Beginning Pr.

O'Connell, Catherine. Skins. LC 92-54469. 1993. 20.00 (*1-55611-343-9*) D I Fine.

O'Connell, Charles F. Compensating United States Employees Abroad. (International Business Portfolios Ser.). 1988. write for info. (*0-8205-1953-7*) Bender.

— First Fighter: A History of America's First Team, 1918-1983. (Illus.). 183p. 1987. 20.00 (*0-16-002232-0*, S/N 008-070-00595-6) USGPO.

O'Connell, Colette, jt. auth. see Shupe, Barbara.

O'Connell, Colette, et al, eds. Directory of Microcomputer Software for Mechanical Engineering Design. LC 85-1540. 431p. reprint ed. pap. 122.90 (*0-7837-4320-3*, 2044006) Bks Demand.

O'Connell, Colin B. A Study of Heinrich Ott's Theological Development: His Hermeneutical & Ontological Programme. LC 91-16572. (American University Studies: Theology & Religion: Ser. VII, Vol. 107). 262p. (C). 1992. text ed. 45.95 (*0-8204-1569-3*) P Lang Pubs.

O'Connell, D., ed. Nuclei of Galaxies. 1971. 92.50 (*0-444-10095-4*) Elsevier.

O'Connell, D. C. Critical Essays on Language Use & Psychology. xx, 351p. 1988. pap. 41.00 (*0-387-96703-6*) Spr-Verlag.

O'Connell, Daniel. The Opposition Critics: The Antisymbolist Reaction in the Modern Period. LC 73-80108. (De Proprietatibus Litterarum, Ser. Minor: No. 14). 172p. 1974. pap. text ed. 32.35 (*90-279-3422-3*) Mouton.

O'Connell, Daniel J. The Appraisal of Apartment Buildings. 184p. 1989. text ed. 69.95 (*0-471-50955-8*) Wiley.

O'Connell, Daniel M., comp. A Cardinal Newman Prayerbook: Kindly Light. 352p. 1985. pap. 14.95 (*0-87193-220-2*) Dimension Bks.

O'Connell, Daniel M., ed. see Newman, John H.

***O'Connell, David.** Francois Mauriac Revisited. rev. ed. (Twayne's World Author Ser.: No. 844). 208p. 1994. text ed. 22.95 (*0-8057-4302-2*, Twayne) Macmillan.

— Managing the Dually Diagnosed. 1992. pap. 14.95 (*0-86656-978-2*) Haworth Pr.

— Michel de Saint Pierre: A Catholic Novelist at the Crossroads. LC 89-52103. 189p. 1990. lib. bdg. 27.95 (*0-917786-76-9*) Summa Pubns.

O'Connell, Donald W., ed. Public Sector Labor Relations in Maryland: Issues & Prospects. LC 72-92069. (PSLRCB Publication Ser.: No. 1). (Illus.). (Orig.). 1972. pap. 7.50 (*0-913400-00-9*) Pub Sect Lab Rel.

O'Connell, E. Patrick, tr. see De La Touche, Louise M.

***O'Connell, Eileen M., ed.** Rockhurst Review - 1991 Vol. IV: A Fine Arts Journal. 75p. 1991. pap. 5.00 (*1-886761-03-5*) Rockhurst Col.

O'Connell, Fergus. How to Run Successful Projects. 1994. pap. text ed. 26.25 (*0-685-70921-3*) P-H.

— How to Run Successful Projects. LC 93-33567. (BCS Practitioner Ser.). 300p. 1994. pap. text ed. 37.00 (*0-13-138793-6*) P-H Gen Ref & Trav.

O'Connell, Frances H. Giving & Growing: A Student's Guide for Service Projects. Stamschror, Robert P., ed. (Illus.). 79p. (Orig.). (YA). (gr. 7-12). 1990. teacher ed 3.95 (*0-88489-225-5*); text ed. 3.50 (*0-88489-224-7*) St Marys.

O'Connell, Francis A. Plant Closings: Worker Rights, Management Rights, & the Law. (Studies in Social Philosophy & Policy: No. 7). 313p. 1987. 32.95 (*0-912051-07-8*); pap. 19.95 (*0-912051-08-6*) Transaction Pubs.

O'Connell, Frank. Farewell to the Farm. LC 61-11875. 198p. 1962. 4.50 (*0-87004-113-4*) Caxton.

O'Connell, Geoffrey. The Boat Owner's Maintenance Book. 164p. 1989. 17.95 (*0-87201-221-2*) Gulf Pub.

— Southwick: The D-Day Village That Went to War. 1995. 8.95 (*1-85253-299-8*) Cimino Pub Grp.

O'Connell, Helen. Dedicated Lives. (C). 1993. pap. text ed. 35.00 (*0-85598-197-0*, Pub. by Oxfam Pubns UK) St Mut.

O'Connell, Helen, ed. Women & the Family. LC 94-2289. (Women & World Development Ser.). (Illus.). 144p. (C). 1994. text ed. 49.95 (*1-85649-105-6*, Pub. by Zed Books UK); pap. 17.50 (*1-85649-106-4*, Pub. by Zed Books UK) Humanities.

O'Connell, J, tr. see Tamez, Elsa.

O'Connell, J. Thomas. Mount Zion Field. 101p. 1990. 24.50 (*0-916379-39-6*) Scripta.

***O'Connell, J. W. & Korff, Anne, eds.** The Book of the Burren. (Illus.). 228p. 1991. pap. 23.95 (*1-873821-00-X*, Pub. by Tir Eolas IE) Irish Bks Media.

— The Book of the Burren. (Illus.). 228p. 1991. 35.95 (*1-873821-03-4*, Pub. by Tir Eolas IE) Irish Bks Media.

O'Connell, Jack. Box Nine. LC 91-52863. 272p. 1992. 17.95 (*0-89296-472-3*) Mysterious Pr.

— Box Nine. 336p. 1993. mass mkt. 4.99 (*0-446-40100-5*, Mysterious Paperbk) Warner Bks.

— The Skin Palace. 1996. write for info. (*0-89296-547-9*) Mysterious Pr.

— Wireless. 416p. 1993. 19.95 (*0-89296-546-0*) Mysterious Pr.

— Wireless. 416p. 1995. mass mkt. 5.99 (*0-446-40356-3*, Mysterious Paperbk) Warner Bks.

O'Connell, James. Meaning of Irish Place Names. 90p. 1979. pap. 5.95 (*0-685-25952-8*, Pub. by Blackstaff Pr IE) Dufour.

— Meaning of Irish Place Names. 1986. pap. 5.95 (*0-85640-175-7*) Dufour.

***O'Connell, James C., ed.** The Pioneer Valley Reader: Prose & Poetry from New England's Literary Heartland. LC 95-8414. (Illus.). 1995. 24.95 (*0-936399-71-6*) Berkshire Hse.

O'Connell, James F., jt. ed. see Madsen, David B.

O'Connell, Jeffrey. Ending the Lottery: A Consumer Proposal for Medical Malpractice Reform. 16p. (Orig.). 1987. pap. text ed. write for info. (*0-910073-11-2*) HALT DC.

— The Lawsuit Lottery: Only the Lawyers Win. LC 79-7579. 1979. 22.95 (*0-02-923280-5*) Free Pr.

O'Connell, Jeffrey & Kelly, C. Brian. The Blame Game: Injury, Insurance & Injustice. LC 85-45027. 176p. 1986. text ed. 29.95 (*0-669-11129-5*) Free Pr.

O'Connell, Jeffrey & Wilson, Wallace H. Car Insurance & Consumer Desires. LC 78-85554. (Illus.). 123p. reprint ed. pap. 35.10 (*0-8357-6047-2*, 2034456) Bks Demand.

***O'Connell, Joanna.** Prospero's Daughter: The Prose of Rosario Castellanos. LC 95-3795. (The Texas Pan American Ser.). 1995. write for info. (*0-292-76041-8*) U of Tex Pr.

O'Connell, John. Doctor John: Crusading Doctor & Politician. (Illus.). 175p. 1989. pap. 9.95 (*1-85371-025-3*, Pub. by Poolbeg Pr IE) Dufour.

— Welfare Economic Theory. LC 82-1760. 206p. (C). 1982. text ed. 35.00 (*0-86569-087-1*, Auburn Hse); pap. text ed. 15.00 (*0-86569-074-X*, Auburn Hse) Greenwood.

— Where in the World Is the Coverage? Extraterritorial Coverages in United States Insurance Policies. (Orig.). (C). 1990. pap. text ed. 10.00 (*1-878204-15-7*) APIS Inc.

O'Connell, John F. Remedies in a Nutshell. LC 84-19705. (Nutshell Ser.). 320p. 1992. reprint ed. pap. text ed. 15.00 (*0-314-85066-X*) West Pub.

O'Connell, Joseph. Twenty Innovative Electronics Projects for Your Home. (Illus.). 256p. 1988. 21.95 (*0-8306-0947-4*); pap. 13.95 (*0-8306-2947-5*) TAB Bks.

O'Connell, Joseph J., jt. auth. see Rounds, Stowell.

O'Connell, Joseph T., et al. Sikh History & Religion in the Twentieth Century. (C). 1988. reprint ed. 34.00 (*0-9692907-4-8*, Pub. by Ctre South Asian CN) S Asia.

O'Connell, June. His & Hers. (Sweet Dreams Ser.: No. 201). (YA). 1993. pap. 2.99 (*0-553-29980-8*) Bantam.

— Why Must I Choose? 143p. (J). (gr. 5-8). 1992. pap. 2.75 (*0-87406-631-X*) Willowisp Pr.

***O'Connell, Kathleen R.** Bruised by Life: Turn Life's Wounds into Gifts. 1994. pap. 10.95 (*0-925190-32-2*) Fairview Press.

— End of the Line: Quitting Cocaine. LC 85-7135. 120p. 1985. pap. 9.99 (*0-664-24669-9*, Westminster) Westminster John Knox.

O'Connell, Kerrill. A Guide for Writing Formal Papers. 2nd ed. 80p. (C). 1988. 7.95 (*0-8403-4696-4*) Kendall-Hunt.

O'Connell, Kevin G., jt. ed. see Dahlberg, Bruce T.

O'Connell, Kevin J., jt. auth. see Levy, David N.

O'Connell, Kevin J., jt. ed. see Wade, Robert G.

O'Connell, Lenahan & Ryan, James W. Able, Active & Aggressive: History of the O'Connell Family of Massachusetts. (Illus.). 327p. 1994. 35.00 (*0-9641376-0-7*) Elizabeth-James.

O'Connell, Lily H., et al. Nutrition in a Changing World: Grade Five. (Illus.). 152p. (Orig.). (J). (gr. 5). 1981. pap. text ed. 11.95 (*0-8425-1916-5*) BYU Scholarly.

O'Connell, M. J., tr. see Calvez, Jean Y.

O'Connell, Margaret. The Magic Cauldron: Witchcraft for Good & Evil. LC 75-26757. (Illus.). 256p. (J). (gr. 9-12). 1975. 33.95 (*0-87599-187-4*) S G Phillips.

O'Connell, Margaret J. Pennington Profile. 2nd ed. (Illus.). 452p. 1986. 25.00 (*0-9617592-1-6*); 50.00 (*0-9617592-0-8*) Pennington Lib.

O'Connell, Marvin R. Critics on Trial: An Introduction to the Catholic Modernist Crisis. LC 93-41850. 464p. 1994. 59.95 (*0-8132-0799-1*) Cath U Pr.

— Critics on Trial: An Introduction to the Catholic Modernist Crisis. LC 93-41850. 464p. 1995. pap. write for info. (*0-8132-0800-9*) Cath U Pr.

— John Ireland & the American Catholic Church. (Illus.). 610p. 1988. 34.95 (*0-87351-230-8*) Minn Hist.

— The Oxford Conspirators: A History of the Oxford Movement 1833-45. 478p. (C). 1991. reprint ed. pap. text ed. 38.00 (*0-8191-8074-2*) U Pr of Amer.

***O'Connell, Mary.** Updike & the Patriachal Dilemma: Masculinity in the Rabbit Novels. 1995. write for info. (*0-615-00323-0*) S Ill U Pr.

— Updike & the Patriachal Dilemma: Masculinity in the Rabbit Novels. LC 94-39038. 288p. (C). 1995. 34.95x (*0-8093-1949-7*) S Ill U Pr.

O'Connell, Mathew J., tr. see Horkheimer, Max.

O'Connell, Mathew J., tr. see Sobrino, Jon.

O'Connell, Matthew, tr. see Cabie, Robert, et al.

O'Connell, Matthew, tr. see Di Sante, Carmine.

O'Connell, Matthew, tr. see Gutierrez, Gustavo.

O'Connell, Matthew, tr. see Parazzoli, Ferruccio.

O'Connell, Matthew, tr. see Possidius.

O'Connell, Matthew, tr. see St. Augustine.

O'Connell, Matthew, tr. see Tabori, Fabio.

O'Connell, Matthew, tr. see Vaillancourt, Raymond.

O'Connell, Matthew J., tr. see Alberigo, Giuseppe, et al, eds.

O'Connell, Matthew J., tr. see Back, Siegfried.

O'Connell, Matthew J., tr. see Belo, Fernando.

O'Connell, Matthew J., tr. see Berger, Rupert & Hollerweger, Hans, eds.

O'Connell, Matthew J., tr. see Bugnini, Annibale.

O'Connell, Matthew J., tr. see Danneels, Godfried C.

O'Connell, Matthew J., tr. see De Orozco, Alonso.

O'Connell, Matthew J., tr. see Deiss, Lucien.

O'Connell, Matthew J., tr. see Echegaray, Hugo.

O'Connell, Matthew J., tr. see Gonzalez Ruiz, Jose M.

O'Connell, Matthew J., tr. see Gutierrez, Gustavo.

O'Connell, Matthew J., tr. see Martimort, A. G., et al.

O'Connell, Matthew J., tr. see Metz, Rene & Schlick, Jean, eds.

O'Connell, Matthew J., tr. see O'Collins, Gerald & Marconi, Gilberto, eds.

O'Connell, Matthew J., tr. see Ratzinger, Joseph C.

O'Connell, Matthew J., tr. see St. Augustine.

O'Connell, Matthew J., tr. see Tamez, Elsa.

O'Connell, Matthew J., tr. see Wa Ilunga, Bakole.

***O'Connell, Maureen.** Reach for the Heart. 1995. 17.95 (*0-8034-9093-3*, 094621) Bouregy.

O'Connell, Maurice. Daniel O'Connell: The Man & His Politics. 160p. (C). 1990. 29.50 (*0-7165-2446-5*, Pub. by Irish Acad Pr IE) Intl Spec Bk.

O'Connell, Maurice R. Irish Politics & Social Conflict in the Age of the American Revolution. LC 76-2388. (Illus.). 444p. 1976. reprint ed. lib. bdg. 30.00 (*0-8371-8758-3*, OCIP, Greenwood Pr) Greenwood.

O'Connell, Maurice R., jt. ed. see Nowlan, Kevin B.

O'Connell, Michael. Mirror & Veil: The Historical Dimension of Spenser's "Faerie Queene" LC 77-1733. 234p. reprint ed. pap. 66.70 (*0-7837-3754-8*, 2043571) Bks Demand.

— Robert Burton. (Twayne English Authors Ser.: No. 426). 152p. (C). 1986. lib. bdg. 25.95 (*0-8057-6919-6*, Twayne) Macmillan.

— Shadows: An Album of the Irish People. 132p. 1985. pap. 19.95 (*0-86278-101-9*, Pub. by OBrien Pr IE) Dufour.

O'Connell, Michael, jt. auth. see Huxley, Phil.

O'Connell, Michael, jt. ed. see Huxley, Phil.

O'Connell, Michael A., et al. Working with Sex Offenders: Practical Guidelines for Therapist Selection. 132p. (C). 1990. text ed. 38.95 (*0-8039-3754-7*); pap. text ed. 19.50 (*0-8039-3763-6*) Sage.

O'Connell, Mitch. Good Taste Gone Bad: The "Art" of Mitch O'Connell. 2nd ed. (Illus.). 88p. (Orig.). 1993. pap. 12.95 (*0-9639762-0-6*) Good Taste.

O'Connell, Nancy. Take a Camel to Lunch: And Other Adventures for Mature Travelers. (Mature Reader Ser.). (Illus.). 228p. (Orig.). 1991. pap. 8.95 (*1-55867-024-6*) Bristol Pub Ent CA.

O'Connell, Nicholas. At the Field's End: Interviews with Twenty Pacific Northwest Writers. LC 87-7053. 336p. 1987. pap. 12.95 (*0-88089-026-6*) Madrona Pubs.

— Beyond Risk: Conversation with Climbers. LC 93-22723. (Illus.). 256p. 1993. 19.95 (*0-89886-296-5*) Mountaineers.

O'Connell, P. Edna, jt. ed. see Bowles, David S.

O'Connell, P. J. Robert Drew & the Development of Cinema Verite in America. LC 91-39992. 312p. (C). 1992. 34.95 (*0-8093-1779-6*) S Ill U Pr.

O'Connell, Patrick. The Origin & Early History of Man. 72p. 1986. reprint ed. pap. 2.50 (*0-317-54409-8*) Stella Maris Bks.

— Original Sin in the Light of Modern Science. 128p. 1973. pap. 3.00 (*0-912414-15-4*) Lumen Christi.

— Science of Today & the Problems of Genesis. LC 90-71913. 382p. 1993. pap. 16.50 (*0-89555-438-0*) TAN Bks Pubs.

O'Connell, Patrick, ed. Life & Work of Mother Louise Margaret. LC 86-51579. 230p. 1987. reprint ed. pap. 10.00 (*0-89555-311-2*) TAN Bks Pubs.

O'Connell, Patrick & Carty, Charles. The Holy Shroud & Four Visions: The Holy Shroud New Evidence Compared with the Visions of St. Bridget of Sweden, Maria d'Agreda, Anne Catherine Emmerich, & Teresa Neumann. (Illus.). 1974. reprint ed. pap. 2.00 (*0-89555-102-0*) TAN Bks Pubs.

O'Connell, Patrick, tr. see Croiset, J.

O'Connell, Patrick, tr. see Margaret Louise Margaret Cloret de la Touche.

O'Connell, Patrick, tr. see St. Joseph Cafasso.

O'Connell, Paul, jt. auth. see Conroy, Larry.

O'Connell, Peggy. Aim for a Job As a Waiter or Waitress. LC 79-15014. (Arco's Career Guidance Ser.). (Illus.). 1980. lib. bdg. 7.95 (*0-668-04767-4*, Arco Test); pap. 4.50 (*0-668-04771-2*, Arco Test) P-H Gen Ref & Trav.

O'Connell, Peter. Greg's Mill. 60p. (C). 1988. text ed. 39.00 (*0-947818-09-X*, Pub. by Old Vicarage UK) St Mut.

O'Connell, R. J. & Fyfe, W. S., eds. Evolution of the Earth. (Geodynamics Ser.: Vol. 5). 282p. 1981. 25.00 (*0-87590-506-4*) Am Geophysical.

O'Connell, Richard. Battle Poems. 1977. pap. 2.50 (*0-686-17592-1*) Atlantis.

— Battle Poems. 1987. pap. 10.00 (*0-318-32928-X*) Atlantis Edns.

— Brazilian Happenings. 1966. pap. 10.00 (*0-685-62617-2*) Atlantis Edns.

— Brazilian Poems. 1928. 35.00 (*0-87556-226-4*) Saifer.

— The Caliban Poems. 1992. pap. 10.00 (*0-685-55467-8*) Atlantis Edns.

— Cries of Flesh & Stone. 1962. pap. 10.00 (*0-685-62608-3*) Atlantis Edns.

— Deaths & Distances. 1965. pap. 10.00 (*0-685-62613-X*) Atlantis Edns.

— Hanging Tough. 1986. pap. 10.00 (*0-317-56161-8*) Atlantis Edns.

— Hudson's Fourth Voyage. 1978. pap. 10.00 (*0-685-87717-5*) Atlantis Edns.

— Lives of the Poets. 1990. pap. 10.00 (*0-685-38406-3*) Atlantis Edns.

— New Poems & Translations. 1963. pap. 10.00 (*0-685-62610-5*) Atlantis Edns.

— Poems & Epigrams. 1929. pap. 25.00 (*0-87556-227-2*) Saifer.

— RetroWorlds: Selected Poems by Richard O'Connell. 1993. pap. 25.00 (*3-7052-0804-7*) Atlantis Edns.

— Selected Epigrams. 1990. pap. 10.00 (*0-685-38407-1*) Atlantis Edns.

— Simulations, Selected Translations. 1993. pap. 25.00 (*3-7052-0625-7*) Atlantis Edns.

— Temple Poems. 1985. pap. 6.00 (*0-317-38870-3*) Atlantis Edns.

O'Connell, Richard, ed. Apollo's Day: Seventeenth Century Songs. 1969. pap. 10.00 (*0-685-62618-0*) Atlantis Edns.

O'Connell, Richard, illus. Thirty Epigrams. 1971. pap. 6.00 (*0-685-62619-9*) Atlantis Edns.

O'Connell, Richard, tr. The Epigrams of Luxorius. 1984. pap. 10.00 (*0-317-17736-2*) Atlantis Edns.

— Irish Monastic Poems. 1984. pap. 10.00 (*0-317-07621-3*) Atlantis Edns.

— Middle English Poems. 1976. pap. 10.00 (*0-685-62624-5*) Atlantis Edns.

— New Epigrams from Martial. 1991. pap. 10.00 (*0-685-55466-X*) Atlantis Edns.

— One Hundred Epigrams: From the Greek Anthology. 1977. pap. 10.00 (*0-685-63924-X*) Atlantis Edns.

O'Connell, Richard, ed. see Martialis, Marcus V.

O'Connell, Richard L., tr. see Garcia Lorca, Federico.

O'Connell, Richard L., tr. see Lorca, Federico G.

O'Connell, Richard T., jt. auth. see Bowerman, Bruce L.

OConnell, Richard T.

***O'Connell, Rick M.** Three Hundred & Sixty-Five Easy Italian Recipes. 1994. pap. 5.99 (*0-06-109345-9*, Harp PBks) HarpC.

— Three Hundred Sixty-Five Easy Italian Recipes. (Three Hundred Sixty-Five Ways Ser.). 1991. 17.95 (*0-06-016310-0*, HarpT) HarpC.

O'Connell, Robert. Imagination & Metaphysics in St. Augustine. LC 85-82595. (Aquinas Lectures). 70p. 1986. 10.00 (*0-87462-227-1*) Marquette.

O'Connell, Robert J. Art & the Christian Intelligence in St. Augustine. LC 78-546. 272p. 1978. 32.00 (*0-674-04675-7*) HUP.

— Images of Conversion in St. Augustine's Confessions. 320p. 1995. 35.00 (*0-8232-1598-9*) Fordham.

— The Origin of the Soul in St. Augustine's Later Works. LC 86-82222. xvi, 363p. (C). 1987. 40.00 (*0-8232-1172-X*) Fordham.

— Plato on the Human Paradox. LC 84-73309. vi, 217p. 1987. pap. 9.95 (*0-8232-1186-X*) Fordham.

— Saint Augustine's Confessions: The Odyssey of Soul. LC 69-12731. 200p. 1989. pap. 19.95 (*0-8232-1265-3*) Fordham.

— Soundings in St. Augustine's Imagination. LC 93-11257. 309p. 1994. 40.00 (*0-8232-1347-1*); pap. 19.95 (*0-8232-1348-X*) Fordham.

An Asterisk (*) at the beginning of an entry indicates that the title is appearing in BIP for the first time.

— St. Augustine's Early Theory of Man, A. D. 386-391. LC 68-21981. 323p. 1969. reprint ed. pap. 92.10 (*0-7837-4173-1*, 2059022) Bks Demand.

— Teilhard's Vision of the Past: The Making of a Method. LC 82-71279. x, 205p. 1982. 30.00 (*0-8232-1090-1*); pap. 15.00 (*0-8232-1091-X*) Fordham.

— William James on the Courage to Believe. LC 83-83319. xiv, 141p. 1984. 30.00 (*0-8232-1108-8*) Fordham.

O'Connell, Robert L. Of Arms & Men: A History of War, Weapons, & Aggression. (Illus.). 384p. 1989. reprint ed. 29.95 (*0-19-505359-1*) OUP.

— Of Arms & Men: A History of War, Weapons, & Aggression. (Illus.). 384p. 1990. reprint ed. pap. 12.95 (*0-19-505360-5*) OUP.

— Ride of the Second Horseman: The Birth & Death of War. (Illus.). 320p. 1995. 25.00 (*0-19-506460-7*) OUP.

— Sacred Vessels: The Cult of the Battleship & the Rise of the U. S. Navy. LC 92-25712. (C). 1993. pap. 15.95 (*0-19-508006-8*) OUP.

— Sacred Vessels: The Cult of the Battleship & the Rise of the U. S. Navy. 409p. 1991. text ed. 30.50 (*0-8133-1116-0*) Westview.

O'Connell, Sandra E. The Manager As Communicator. LC 79-17821. (Continuing Management Education Ser.). reprint ed. pap. 51.50 (*0-317-28118-6*, 2022506) Bks Demand.

— The Manager As Communicator. (Illus.). 206p. (C). 1986. reprint ed. pap. text ed. 21.50 (*0-8191-5402-4*) U Pr of Amer.

O'Connell, Sean, jt. auth. see King-Farlow, John.

O'Connell, Shaun. Imagining Boston: A Literary Landscape. 424p. 1992. pap. 15.00 (*0-8070-5103-9*) Beacon Pr.

— Remarkable, Unspeakable New York: A Literary History. LC 94-36415. 400p. 1995. 27.50 (*0-8070-5002-4*) Beacon Pr.

O'Connell, Timothy. Vatican II & Its Documents. (Theology & Life Ser.: Vol. 15). 260p. 1985. pap. 14.95 (*0-8146-5537-8*) Liturgical Pr.

***O'Connell, Tom.** Addicted? A Guide to Understanding Addiction. LC 90-91803. 210p. (Orig.). 1990. pap. text ed. 19.00 (*0-9620318-0-1*) Sanctuary Comns.

— Danny the Prophet: A Fantastic Adventure. LC 94-92421. 220p. (Orig.). 1995. pap. 12.95 (*0-9620318-4-4*) Sanctuary Comns.

— Improving Intimacy: Ten Powerful Strategies. LC 93-92664. 56p. (Orig.). 1993. pap. text ed. 7.00 (*0-9620318-2-8*) Sanctuary Comns.

— The Odd Duck: A Story for Odd People of All Ages. LC 93-84633. 60p. (Orig.). 1993. pap. 7.00 (*0-9620318-3-6*) Sanctuary Comns.

O'Connell, Victoria M., jt. auth. see Kramer, Donald E.

O'Connell, Vincent, jt. auth. see O'Connell, April.

O'Connell, Walter E. Action Therapy & Adlerian Theory: Selected Papers. LC 75-16932. 253p. (Orig.). 1975. pap. text ed. 8.00 (*0-918560-06-3*) Adler Sch Prof Psy.

O'Connell, William. Graphic Communication in Architecture. 148p. 1985. text ed. 19.80 (*0-87563-275-0*) Stipes.

O'Connell, William B. America's Money Trauma: How Washington Blunders Crippled the U. S. Financial System. 176p. (Orig.). 1992. pap. 14.95 (*0-9634395-0-2*) Conversation Pr.

O'Conner, Daniel J. Airplanes & Income Tax. 6th ed. 75p. 1994. pap. 12.95 (*0-9613218-5-7*) Aviation.

O'Conner, David. Old Delaware County in Postcards. (Illus.). 160p. (Orig.). 1984. pap. 8.95 (*0-931308-15-1*) Molly Yes.

O'Conner, David, jt. auth. see Silverman, David P.

***O'Conner, Edward.** Importance of Apparitions. 96p. Date not set. pap. 2.95 (*1-882972-45-7*) Queenship Pub.

O'Conner, Edwin. Benjy: A Ferocious Fairy Tale. LC 88-46131. (Pocket Paragon Ser.). (Illus.). 128p. (J). (gr. 4-7). 1995. pap. 11.95 (*0-87923-795-3*) Godine.

O'Conner, Fr. J., tr. see Claudel, Paul.

O'Conner, Frederick. Express Yourself in Written English. 1990. pap. 11.95 (*0-8442-7692-8*, Natl Textbk) NTC Pub Grp.

O'Conner, J. & Smiltens, J. Silicon Carbide High Temperature Semiconductor: Proceedings of the Conference on Silicon Carbide, Boston, Mass. April, 1959. LC 60-7402. 1960. 217.00 (*0-08-009304-3*, Pub. by Pergamon Repr UK) Franklin.

***O'Conner, Karen.** Junk-Food Finders. (J). (ps-3). 1994. pap. 1.99 (*0-570-04769-2*) Concordia.

— Service with a Smile. (J). (ps-3). 1994. pap. 3.99 (*0-570-04772-2*) Concordia.

O'Conner, Kathleen & Prothero, Joyce, eds. The Alzheimer's Caregiver: Strategies for Support. LC 85-40979. (Illus.). 150p. 1987. 25.00 (*0-295-96385-9*) U of Wash Pr.

O'Conner, Madeline A. Small Sips of Water: Understanding Dissociation in Recovery. LC 91-19755. (Illus.). 56p. (Orig.). 1991. pap. 5.95 (*1-877872-03-2*) Launch Pr.

O'Conner, Margaret A. Soft Coated Wheaten Terriers. (Illus.). 160p. 1989. 11.95 (*0-86622-684-2*, KW-177) TFH Pubns.

O'Conner, Michael & Gray, David. Crime in a Rural Community. 150p. 1989. pap. 26.00 (*0-685-51048-4*, Pub. by Federation Pr AU) W W Gaunt.

O'Conner, Michelle, ed. see Bachand, Robert G.

O'Conner, N. & Tizard, J. Social Problem of Mental Deficiency. 1956. 78.00 (*0-08-009045-1*, Pub. by Pergamon Repr UK) Franklin.

O'Conner, Pat. Friendships Between Women: A Critical Review. LC 92-13770. (Series on Personal Relationships). 228p. 1992. lib. bdg. 44.95 (*0-89862-976-4*); pap. text ed. 17.95 (*0-89862-981-0*) Guilford Pr.

O'Conner, Patricia. In Search of Therese. LC 86-45343. (Way of the Christian Mystics Ser.: Vol. 3). 184p. 1987. pap. 9.95 (*0-8146-5596-3*) Liturgical Pr.

O'Conner, Rebecca, pseud. Jenny Mitchel: Young Irelander, a Biography. LC 85-90519. 453p. (Orig.). (C). 1988. pap. 21.95 (*0-9602768-2-3*) O Conner Trust.

O'Conner, Richard. Invincible Sheridan. 1994. 12.98 (*0-914427-97-0*) W S Konecky Assocs.

O'Conner, Robert, jt. auth. see Flores, Tom.

O'Conner, Rosann, ed. see Kone, Linda.

O'Conner, Varley. Like China. 1991. 19.95 (*0-688-09444-9*) Morrow.

***O'Connor.** Dining & the Opera: In Manhattan. LC 94-78254. 1994. 24.95 (*1-883914-04-3*) Menus & Music.

— Dinners for Two. 1994. 24.95 (*1-883914-07-8*) Menus & Music.

— A Good Man Is Hard to Find. 1992. 15.95 (*0-15-136504-0*) HarBrace.

— Holidays. 1994. 24.95 (*1-883914-05-1*) Menus & Music.

— Picnics: Picnic Recipes from Summer Music Festivals. LC 94-75888. 1994. 24.95 (*1-883914-08-6*) Menus & Music.

O'Connor, Alan, ed. see Williams, Raymond.

O'Connor, Andrea B. Nursing Staff Development & Continuing Education. (C). 1986. text ed. 21.00 (*0-673-39366-6*) HarpCollege.

O'Connor, Ann, ed. Congress A to Z: A Ready Reference Encyclopedia. 2nd ed. LC 93-25926. 560p. 1993. 125.00 (*0-87187-826-7*) Congr Quarterly.

***O'Connor, Anna T. & Callahan-Young, Sheila.** Seven Windows to a Child's World: 100 Ideas for the Multiple Intelligences Classroom - Grades Pre-K - 3. LC 94-78533. 256p. 1994. pap. 19.95 (*0-932935-77-X*, NB1261) IRI-Skylght.

O'Connor, Anthony. Poverty in Africa: A Geographical Approach. 184p. 1992. pap. text ed. 23.95 (*0-470-21897-5*) Halsted Pr.

— Poverty in Africa: A Geographical Approach. 184p. 1992. pap. text ed. 23.95 (*1-85293-088-8*, Pub. by Pinter Publishers UK) Wiley.

— Poverty in Africa: A Geographical Approach. 1993. pap. text ed. 34.95 (*0-471-94738-5*) Wiley.

O'Connor, Anthony M. The African City. LC 83-10648. (Illus.). 360p. (C). 1983. 32.50 (*0-8419-0881-8*); pap. 17.50 (*0-8419-0882-6*) Holmes & Meier.

O'Connor, B. T., et al. Bone Grafts & Derivatives. (Illus.). 456p. 1994. 135.00 (*0-7506-1369-6*) Buttrwrth-Heinemann.

O'Connor, Barbara. Barefoot Dancer: The Story of Isadora Duncan. LC 93-14312. (Trailblazers Ser.). (J). (gr. 4-7). 1994. 17.50 (*0-87614-807-0*, Carolrhoda) Lerner Group.

— Mammolina: A Story about Maria Montessori. LC 92-415. (Creative Minds Ser.). (J). (gr. 3-6). 1993. lib. bdg. 15.95 (*0-87614-743-0*, Carolrhoda); pap. 5.95 (*0-87614-602-7*, Carolrhoda) Lerner Group.

O'Connor, Barbara H. A Color Atlas & Instruction Manual of Peripheral Blood Morphology. (Illus.). 316p. (C). 1984. pap. text ed. 45.00 (*0-683-06624-2*) Williams & Wilkins.

O'Connor, Basilides A., ed. see Henri D'Arci.

O'Connor, Bernard, ed. see Stanbrook, et al.

O'Connor, Bernard F. A Dialogue Between Philosophy & Religion: The Perspective of Karl Jaspers. LC 87-34685. 228p. (Orig.). (C). 1988. pap. text ed. 22.00 (*0-8191-6863-7*) U Pr of Amer.

O'Connor, Bill. The Trekking Peaks of Nepal. (Illus.). 224p. 1989. pap. 24.95 (*0-938567-28-4*) Cloudcap.

O'Connor, Bob, jt. auth. see Flores, Tom.

O'Connor, Bonnie B. Healing Traditions: Alternative Medicine & the Health Professions. (Studies in Health, Illness, & Caregiving). (Illus.). 288p. (Orig.). (C). 1995. text ed. 36.95 (*0-8122-3184-8*); pap. text ed. 16.95 (*0-8122-1398-X*) U of Pa Pr.

O'Connor, Brendan D., jt. ed. see Keegan, Brendan F.

O'Connor, Brian P., et al. The Role of the Minister in Caring for the Dying Patient & the Bereaved. 18.95 (*0-405-12504-6*) Ayer.

O'Connor, Brian P., et al, eds. The Pastoral Role in Caring for the Dying & Bereaved: Pragmatic & Ecumenical. LC 86-545. (Foundation of Thanatology Ser.: Vol. 7). 245p. 1986. text ed. 69.50 (*0-275-92153-0*, C2153, Praeger Pubs) Greenwood.

O'Connor, Bridget. Here Comes John. (Illus.). 170p. 1994. pap. 17.95 (*0-224-03218-6*, Pub. by Jonathan Cape UK) Trafalgar.

O'Connor, Bridget N., jt. auth. see Regan, Elizabeth A.

O'Connor, C., ed. Extrusion Technology for the Food Industry: Proceedings of the European Conference Held at the Institute for Industrial Research & Standards (IIRS), Dublin, December 9-10, 1986. 178p. 1987. 52.25 (*1-85166-129-8*, Pub. by Elsevier Applied Sci UK) Elsevier.

O'Connor, C. J. Research Frontiers in Magnetochemistry. LC 93-16991. 424p. 1993. text ed. 109.00 (*981-02-1246-1*) World Scientific Pub.

O'Connor, Candace, ed. see Rockwell, Gray.

O'Connor, Candace, ed. see Van Ravenswaay, Charles.

O'Connor, Carol A. The Handbook for Organizational Change: Strategy & Skill for Trainers & Developers. LC 93-21715. (Training Ser.). 1993. write for info. (*0-07-707693-1*) McGraw.

— The Professional's Guide to Successful Management: The Eight Essentials for Running Your Firm, Practice or Partnership. LC 94-27726. 1994. write for info. (*0-07-707999-X*) McGraw.

— A Sort of Utopia: Scarsdale, 1891-1981. LC 82-5855. (Illus.). 283p. 1983. 59.50 (*0-87395-659-1*); pap. 19.95 (*0-87395-660-5*) State U NY Pr.

O'Connor, Charles A. Perspective Drawing & Applications. (Illus.). 80p. (C). 1984. pap. text ed. 40.00 (*0-13-660382-3*) P-H.

O'Connor, Charles J. & Lirtzman, Sidney I., eds. Handbook of Chemical Industry Labeling. LC 83-22108. (Illus.). 487p. 1984. 64.00 (*0-8155-0965-0*, Noyes Pubns) Noyes.

O'Connor, Christine, jt. auth. see O'Connor, Robert.

O'Connor, Clairr. Belonging. 224p. (Orig.). (C). 1991. pap. 13.99 (*1-85594-014-0*, Pub. by Attic IE) InBook.

O'Connor, Colin. Design of Bridge Superstructures. LC 76-121912. (Illus.). 563p. reprint ed. pap. 160.50 (*0-7837-3460-3*, 2057786) Bks Demand.

— Roman Bridges. LC 92-30900. (Illus.). 200p. (C). 1994. 105.00 (*0-521-39326-4*) Cambridge U Pr.

O'Connor, Colleen. They Bury Their Mistakes: How to Survive Your Hospitalization. 100p. (Orig.). 1994. pap. 10.95 (*0-9641088-3-6*) Valverde Pubns.

O'Connor, Colleen M., jt. ed. see Flemion, Jess.

O'Connor, D. & Fairall, P. A. Criminal Defences. 2nd ed. 1988. Australia. 76.00 (*0-409-49276-0*) Butterworth Legal Pubs.

O'Connor, D., jt. auth. see Eckenfelder, W. Wesley.

O'Connor, D. E., jt. auth. see French, T. W.

***O'Connor, D. J.** Crime at El Escorial: The 1892 Child Murder, the Press & Spanish Justice. (Iberian Studies in History, Literature & Culture). 1995. pap. text ed. 39.95x (*1-883255-90-2*) Intl Scholars.

— Crime at El Escorial: The 1892 Child Murder, the Press & Spanish Justice. (Iberian Studies in History, Literature & Culture). 264p. (C). 1995. text ed. 59.95x (*1-883255-96-1*) Intl Scholars.

— An Introduction to the Philosophy of Education. (Modern Revivals in Philosophy Ser.). 156p. 1994. 51.95 (*0-7512-0307-6*, Pub. by Gregg Revivals UK) Ashgate Pub Co.

O'Connor, D. J., ed. A Critical History of Western Philosophy. (C). 1985. pap. 17.95 (*0-02-923840-4*) Free Pr.

O'Connor, D. J., et al, eds. Surface Analysis Methods in Materials Science. (Surface Sciences Ser.: Vol. 23). (Illus.). 480p. 1992. text ed. 79.00 (*0-387-53611-6*) Spr-Verlag.

O'Connor, Dagmar. How to Make Love to the Same Person for the Rest of Your Life. 256p. 1986. 5.50 (*0-553-26099-5*) Bantam.

O'Connor, Daniel J. Airplanes & Income Tax. 3rd rev. ed. Ebersole, Michael J., ed. 85p. 1984. spiral bd. 14.95 (*0-685-46436-9*) GCBA.

— Airplanes & Income Tax. 4th ed. Ebersole, Michael J., ed. 85p. 1985. spiral bd. 14.95 (*0-9613218-1-4*) GCBA.

— Airplanes & Income Tax. 5th ed. Ebersole, Michael J., ed. 85p. 1986. spiral bd. 12.95 (*0-9613218-3-0*) GCBA.

O'Connor, Darlene, jt. auth. see Lowy, Louis.

O'Connor, David. Ancient Egyptian Society. LC 89-85824. (Illus.). 48p. (Orig.). (C). 1990. pap. text ed. 7.95 (*0-911239-17-0*) Carnegie Mus.

— The Metaphysics of G. E. Moore. 1982. lib. bdg. 74.50 (*90-277-1352-9*) Kluwer Ac.

— My Father's Diary: A Ghost Story. 66p. (Orig.). 1978. pap. 2.50 (*0-931308-00-3*) Molly Yes.

— Old Chenango County in Postcards. (Illus.). 168p. (Orig.). 1983. pap. 8.95 (*0-931308-14-3*) Molly Yes.

— A Short History of Ancient Egypt. LC 89-85826. (Illus.). 48p. (Orig.). (C). 1990. pap. text ed. 7.95 (*0-911239-16-2*) Carnegie Mus.

— Walking Tour of Historic Cooperstown. (Illus.). 48p. (Orig.). 1983. pap. 2.95 (*0-931308-13-5*) Molly Yes.

O'Connor, David, jt. auth. see Brown, Sarah.

O'Connor, David, jt. auth. see Ernst, Dieter.

O'Connor, David, jt. ed. see Lord, Carnes.

O'Connor, David, tr. see Speltz, Alexander.

O'Connor, David E. & Soderlind, Arthur E. The Swedes: In Their Homeland, in America, in Connecticut. (Peoples of Connecticut Ser.). 238p. 1983. 8.00 (*0-685-09449-9*) I N Thut World Educ Ctr.

O'Connor, Denis. Glue Sniffing & Volatile Substance Abuse: Case Studies of Children & Young Adults. LC 83-16464. 103p. 1983. text ed. 55.00 (*0-566-00641-3*) Ashgate Pub Co.

O'Connor, Dennis J. & Bueso, Alberto T. Personal Financial Management: A Forecasting & Control Approach. (Illus.). 560p. (C). 1983. text ed. 36.00 (*0-13-657940-X*) P-H.

O'Connor, Diane V. Guide to Photographic Collections at the Smithsonian Institution, Vol. II. LC 89-60016. (Illus.). 256p. (Orig.). (C). 1991. pap. text ed. 49.95 (*1-56098-033-8*) Smithsonian.

— Guide to Photographic Collections at the Smithsonian Institution, Vol. III. LC 89-600116. (Illus.). 336p. (Orig.). (C). 1992. pap. text ed. 49.95 (*1-56098-188-1*) Smithsonian.

— Guide to Photographic Collections at the Smithsonian Institution, Vol. 1: National Museum of American History. LC 89-600116. (Illus.). 528p. (C). 1989. 49.95 (*0-87474-927-1*) Smithsonian.

O'Connor, Edmund. Darwin. Yapp, Malcolm et al, eds. (World History Ser.). (Illus.). 32p. (YA). (gr. 6-11). 1980. reprint ed. pap. text ed. 3.45 (*0-89908-022-7*) Greenhaven.

— Education. Yapp, Malcolm, ed. (World History Ser.). (Illus.). 32p. (YA). (gr. 6-10). 1980. reprint ed. pap. text ed. 3.45 (*0-89908-122-3*) Greenhaven.

— Japan's Modernization. Yapp, Malcolm & Killingray, Marget, eds. (World History Ser.). (Illus.). (YA). (gr. 6-11). 1980. reprint ed. pap. text ed. 4.35 (*0-89908-207-6*) Greenhaven.

— Roosevelt. Yapp, Malcolm & Killingray, Margaret, eds. (World History Ser.). (Illus.). 32p. (YA). (gr. 6-11). 1980. reprint ed. pap. text ed. 4.35 (*0-89908-100-2*) Greenhaven.

— The Wealth of Japan. Yapp, Malcolm et al, eds. (World History Ser.). (Illus.). 32p. (YA). (gr. 6-11). 1980. reprint ed. pap. text ed. 4.35 (*0-89908-212-2*) Greenhaven.

O'Connor, Edmund, ed. see Doncaster, Islay.

O'Connor, Edmund, ed. see Killingray, David & Killingray, Margaret.

O'Connor, Edmund, ed. see Killingray, Margaret.

O'Connor, Edmund, ed. see Yapp, Malcolm.

O'Connor, Edward D. The Catholic Vision. LC 91-66667. 480p. 1992. 24.95 (*0-87973-418-3*, 418) Our Sunday Visitor.

— The Catholic Vision. LC 91-66667. 480p. 1994. pap. 19.95 (*0-87973-736-0*, 736) Our Sunday Visitor.

O'Connor, Edwin. The Edge of Sadness. 1991. lib. bdg. 21.95 (*1-56849-061-5*) Buccaneer Bks.

— The Edge of Sadness. 1991. 17.95 (*0-88347-259-7*) Thomas More.

— I Was Dancing. 1966. pap. 4.75 (*0-8222-0552-1*) Dramatists Play.

— The Last Hurrah. 448p. 1985. reprint ed. pap. 12.95 (*0-316-62659-7*) Little.

O'Connor, Egan, jt. auth. see Gofman, John W.

O'Connor, Elizabeth. Journey Inward, Journey Outward. LC 75-9313. 192p. 1975. pap. 11.00 (*0-06-066332-4*, RD100) Harper SF.

— Servant Leaders, Servant Structures. (Illus.). 96p. (Orig.). 1991. pap. 7.95 (*1-883639-03-4*) Servant Ldrship.

O'Connor, Elizabeth R., jt. auth. see Cass, Patricia J.

O'Connor, Ellen. Within Ourselves. 91p. 1982. 7.95 (*0-9613897-0-2*) Valen Pub.

O'Connor, Ellen M., ed. Myrtilla Miner. LC 79-89384. (Black Heritage Library Collection). 1977. 16.95 (*0-8369-8640-7*) Ayer.

O'Connor, Ellen M. & Miner, Myrtilla. Myrtilla Miner: A Memoir. Bd. with School for Colored Girls in Washington, D. C. LC 73-92235. LC 73-92235. (American Negro, Ser. 3). 1970. reprint ed. 18.95 (*0-405-01933-5*) Ayer.

***O'Connor, Emily & Fenelon, Mary, comps.** Business Directory & Buyer's Guide: Orange County, NY. 400p. (Orig.). Date not set. pap. write for info. (*0-945965-02-8*) Centers Composition.

O'Connor, Eugene Michael, tr. see Epicurus.

O'Connor, Feargus, et al.

O'Connor, Finbarr W., jt. ed. see Klockars, Carl B.

O'Connor, Flannery. Les Braves Gens Ne Courent Pas les Rues. (FRE.). 1981. pap. 10.95 (*0-7859-4144-4*) Fr & Eur.

— Collected Works. Fitzgerald, Sally, ed. Incl. Wise Blood. LC 87-37829. 1988. (*0-318-62912-7*); Good Man Is Hard to Find. LC 87-37829. 1988. (*0-318-62913-5*); Violent Bear It Away. LC 87-37829. 1988. (*0-318-62914-3*); Everything That Rises Must Converge. LC 87-37829. 1988. (*0-318-62915-1*); LC 87-37829. 1281p. 1988. 35.00 (*0-940450-37-2*) Library of America.

— The Complete Stories. LC 72-171492. 572p. 1971. 35.00 (*0-374-12752-2*); pap. 12.00 (*0-374-51536-0*) FS&G.

— Everything That Rises Must Converge. 269p. 1965. pap. 11.00 (*0-374-50464-4*) FS&G.

— A Good Man Is Hard to Find. LC 77-3306. 251p. 1977. pap. 7.95 (*0-15-636465-4*, Harvest Bks) HarBrace.

— A Good Man Is Hard to Find. LC 92-39505. (Women Writers: Text & Contexts Ser.). 1993. text ed. 30.00 (*0-8135-1976-4*); pap. text ed. 10.00 (*0-8135-1977-2*) Rutgers U Pr.

— The Habit of Being. Fitzgerald, Sally, ed. & intro. by. LC 78-11559. 639p. 1979. 30.00 (*0-374-16769-9*); pap. 18.00 (*0-374-52104-2*) FS&G.

— Mystery & Manners: Occasional Prose. Fitzgerald, Robert & Fitzgerald, Sally, eds. LC 69-15409. 237p. 1969. pap. 9.00 (*0-374-50804-6*) FS&G.

— Three by Flannery O'Connor: Wise Blood, the Violent Bear It Away, a Good Man Is Hard to Find. 1986. pap. 4.95 (*0-451-52101-3*, Sig Classics) NAL-Dutton.

— The Violent Bear It Away. 243p. 1960. pap. 10.00 (*0-374-50524-1*) FS&G.

— Wise Blood. 232p. 1962. pap. 9.00 (*0-374-50584-5*) FS&G.

O'Connor, Flannery, jt. auth. see Westarp, Karl-Heinz.

O'Connor, Francine M. The ABCs Lessons of Love: Sermon on the Mount for Children. (Illus.). 48p. (J). (gr. 6-8). 1991. pap. text ed. 4.95 (*0-89243-345-0*) Liguori Pubns.

— The ABC's of Christmas. LC 94-76021. (Illus.). 48p. (J). (ps-3). 1994. 14.95 (*0-89243-581-X*) Liguori Pubns.

— The ABCs of Prayer...for Children. (Illus.). 32p. (J). (gr. 1-5). 1989. pap. 3.95 (*0-89243-317-5*) Liguori Pubns.

— ABCs of the Mass...for Children. (Illus.). 32p. (Orig.). (J). (ps-4). 1988. pap. 3.95 (*0-89243-291-8*) Liguori Pubns.

— ABCs of the Old Testament...for Children. (Illus.). 32p. (J). (gr. 1-5). 1989. pap. 3.95 (*0-89243-310-8*) Liguori Pubns.

— ABCs of the Sacraments...for Children. (Illus.). 32p. (J). (gr. k-3). 1989. pap. 3.95 (*0-89243-298-5*) Liguori Pubns.

— My Lenten Walk with Jesus. 1992. teacher ed 9.95 (*0-89243-666-2*) Liguori Pubns.

— My Lenten Walk with Jesus. (Cycle C Ser.). (Illus.). 32p. (J). (gr. 1-3). 1992. pap. 2.50 (*0-89243-421-X*); teacher ed, pap. 9.95 (*0-89243-420-1*) Liguori Pubns.

— My Lenten Walk with Jesus. (Illus.). 1993. teacher ed, audio 9.95 (*0-89243-454-6*) Liguori Pubns.

— My Lenten Walk with Jesus, Cycle A. (Illus.). 32p. 1993. pap. 2.50 (*0-89243-453-8*) Liguori Pubns.

— My Lenten Walk with Jesus, Cycle B. 32p. 1991. pap. 2.50 (*0-89243-665-4*) Liguori Pubns.

— Wait & Wonder. (Cycle C Ser.). (Illus.). 16p. (J). (gr. 1-3). 1991. pap. 1.95 (*0-89243-419-8*) Liguori Pubns.

— Wait & Wonder, Cycle C. (Cycle C Ser.). (Illus.). 16p. (J). (gr. 1-3). 1991. 9.95 (*0-89243-418-X*) Liguori Pubns.

— Wait & Wonder, Cycle A. (Illus.). 16p. 1992. 1.95 (*0-89243-447-3*) Liguori Pubns.

— Wait & Wonder, Cycle A. (Illus.). 1992. teacher ed 9.95 (*0-89243-448-1*) Liguori Pubns.

— Wait & Wonder, Cycle B. 16p. 1993. 1.95 (*0-89243-663-8*) Liguori Pubns.

— Wait & Wonder, Cycle B. 1993. teacher ed 9.95 (*0-89243-664-6*) Liguori Pubns.

— You & God: Friends Forever - A Faith Book for Catholic Children. (Illus.). 64p. (J). (gr. 1-4). 1993. pap. text ed. 2.95 (*0-89243-515-1*) Liguori Pubns.

O

O'Connor, Francine M. & Boswell, Kathryn. The ABCs of the Rosary. (Illus.). 32p. (J). (gr. 1-4). 1984. pap. 3.95 (*0-89243-221-7*) Liguori Pubns.
— ABCs of the Ten Commandments. (Illus.). 32p. (Orig.). (J). (gr. 1-4). 1980. pap. 3.95 (*0-89243-125-3*) Liguori Pubns.
O'Connor, Francis B. Like Bread, Their Voices Rise! Global Women Challenge the Church. LC 93-77734. 208p. (Orig.). 1993. pap. 9.95 (*0-87793-509-2*) Ave Maria.
***O'Connor, Francis V., ed.** Jackson Pollock: Supplement Number One to a Catalogue Raisonne of Paintings, Drawings, & Other Works. 114p. 1995. write for info. (*0-9644639-0-3*) Pollock-Krasner Found.
O'Connor, Frank. Art of the Theatre. LC 74-6483. (Studies in Drama: No. 39). (C). 1974. lib. bdg. 49.95 (*0-8383-1909-2*) M S G Haskell Hse.
— Big Fellow. 221p. 1979. reprint ed. pap. 9.95 (*0-905169-84-0*, Pub. by Poolbeg Pr IE) Dufour.
— Collected Stories. LC 81-1253. 702p. 1981. 20.00 (*0-394-51602-8*) Knopf.
— Collected Stories. LC 82-40039. 736p. 1982. pap. 18.00 (*0-394-71048-7*, Vin) Random.
— First Confession. (Creative's Classic Short Stories Ser.). 32p. (J). (gr. 3 up). 1986. 13.95 (*0-88682-058-8*) Creative Ed.
— Guests of the Nation. 1987. reprint ed. pap. 10.95 (*0-905169-89-1*, Pub. by Poolbeg Pr IE) Dufour.
— Jackson Pollock: The Black Pourings, 1951-1953. (Illus.). 1980. pap. 5.00 (*0-910663-25-4*) ICA Inc.
— Kings, Lords & Commons: Irish Poems from the Seventh to Seventeenth Century. 188p. 1989. reprint ed. pap. 11.95 (*0-926689-00-2*) Ford & Bailie Pubs.
— The Midnight Court. LC 74-6477. (English Literature Ser.: No. 33). 1974. lib. bdg. 75.00 (*0-8383-1896-7*) M S G Haskell Hse.
— Mirror in the Roadway. LC 77-117886. (Select Bibliographies Reprint Ser.). 1977. 24.95 (*0-8369-5339-8*) Ayer.
— My Oedipus Complex. LC 85-32526. (Creative's Classic Short Stories Ser.). 40p. (J). (gr. 4 up). 1986. lib. bdg. 13.95 (*0-88682-062-6*) Creative Ed.
— Saint & Mary Kate. 301p. 1990. reprint ed. pap. 11.95 (*0-85640-445-4*, Pub. by Blackstaff Pr IE) Dufour.
— Three Hand Reel: Three One Act Plays Based on Short Stories by Frank O'Connor. adapted ed. 1967. pap. 4.75 (*0-8222-1138-6*) Dramatists Play.
— Towards an Appreciation of Literature. LC 74-6482. (Studies in Comparative Literature: No. 35). 1974. lib. bdg. 75.00 (*0-8383-1907-6*) M S G Haskell Hse.
O'Connor, Frank, ed. Classic Irish Short Stories. 352p. 1990. pap. 11.95 (*0-19-281918-6*) OUP.
— Kings, Lords & Commons. LC 72-75716. (Granger Index Reprint Ser.). 1977. 19.95 (*0-8369-6034-3*) Ayer.
O'Connor, Frank & Hunt, Hugh. The Invincibles. (Abbey Theatre Ser.). 1980. pap. 2.95 (*0-912262-67-2*) Proscenium.
— Moses' Rock. Sherry, Ruth, ed. LC 82-23478. (Irish Dramatic Texts Ser.). 110p. 1983. 15.95 (*0-8132-0584-0*); pap. 6.95 (*0-8132-0585-9*) Cath U Pr.
O'Connor, Frank, tr. see Merriman, Brian.
O'Connor, Frederick. English Inc. Functional English for Japanese Business People. 128p. 1991. pap. text ed. 15.75 (*0-13-107905-0*) P-H.
O'Connor, Frederick, jt. auth. see Mejia, Elizabeth A.
O'Connor, Garry. Mahabharata: Peter Brook's Epic in the Making. LC 89-12203. (Illus.). 192p. 1990. 24.95 (*0-916515-73-7*) Mercury Hse Inc.
O'Connor, Genevieve A. The Admiral & the Deck Boy: One Boy's Journey with Christopher Columbus. LC 91-17978. (Illus.). 168p. (J). (gr. 10 up). 1991. 12.95 (*1-55870-218-0*) Shoe Tree Pr.
O'Connor, Gerald G., jt. auth. see Martin, Patricia Y.
O'Connor, Greg. The Aikido Student Handbook. LC 93-25763. (Illus.). 108p. (Orig.). 1993. pap. 9.95 (*1-883319-04-8*) Frog CA.
O'Connor, Harold. The Flexibleshaft Machine-Jewelry Techniques. LC 83-70022. (Illus.). 1983. 12.95 (*0-918820-05-7*) Dunconor Bks.
— The Jeweler's Bench Reference. LC 76-53236. (Illus.). (C). 1978. student ed 11.95 (*0-918820-03-0*) Dunconor Bks.
O'Connor, Harvey. The Guggenheims: The Making of an American Dynasty. Bruchey, Stuart & Bruchey, Eleanor, eds. LC 76-5026. (American Business Abroad Ser.). (Illus.). 1976. reprint ed. 45.95 (*0-405-09292-X*) Ayer.
***O'Connor, Helen K. & Teixeira, Rozalyn K.** Waianae Diet Book on Hawaiian Foods & Recipes. 96p. 1995. pap. text ed. 10.00 (*0-9646023-2-6*) Waianae Coast CHC.
O'Connor, Helen K., jt. auth. see Beckham, Sheila.
***O'Connor, Helene A.** The Spying Tree. 60p. 1995. pap. 7.95 (*1-56901-724-7*) NW Pub.
O'Connor, Hyla. Cooking on Your Wood Stove. (Illus.). 78p. (Orig.). 1982. pap. 5.95 (*0-9608050-0-1*) Turkey Hill Pr.
O'Connor, J. The Big Game Rifle. (Illus.). 370p. 1994. 37.50 (*1-57157-000-4*) Safari Pr.
— Sheep & Sheep Hunting. (Illus.). 398p. 1992. 35.00 (*0-940143-73-9*) Safari Pr.
O'Connor, J. & Ruddle, H., eds. Business Matters. (C). 1989. 39.00 (*0-946211-87-6*, Pub. by Attic Pr IE) St Mut.
O'Connor, J. D. Better English Pronunciation. 2nd ed. LC 79-41438. (Cambridge English Language Learning Ser.). (Illus.). 1981. pap. 11.95 (*0-521-23152-3*) Cambridge U Pr.
O'Connor, J. E. Hydrology, Hydraulics, & Geomorphology of the Bonneville Flood. LC 92-42641. (Special Paper Ser.: No. 274). 1993. pap. 27.75 (*0-8137-2274-8*) Geol Soc.
O'Connor, J. F. The Banking Crisis & Recovery under the Roosevelt Administration. LC 73-171696. (FDR & the Era of the New Deal Ser.). 168p. 1971. reprint ed. lib. bdg. 27.50 (*0-306-70366-1*) Da Capo.
— Good Faith in English Law. 200p. 1990. text ed. 48.95 (*1-85521-017-7*, Pub. by Dartmth Pub UK) Ashgate Pub Co.
O'Connor, J. J. Practical Fire & Arson Investigation. (Practical Aspects of Criminal & Forensic Investigations Ser.). 400p. 1986. 44.95 (*0-444-00874-8*) CRC Pr.
O'Connor, J. Regis, jt. auth. see Capps, Randall.
O'Connor, Jack. Jack O'Connor's Gun Book. 1992. 26.00 (*1-879356-11-2*) Wolfe Pub Co.
O'Connor, James. The Father's Son. LC 84-11377. 324p. (C). 1984. pap. 10.95 (*0-8198-2622-7*) Pauline Bks.
— Works of James O'Connor, the Deaf Poet, with a Biography Sketch of the Author. 1972. 59.95 (*0-8490-1330-5*) Gordon Pr.
O'Connor, James, jt. auth. see Hart, Norman A.
O'Connor, James T. The Hidden Manna: A Theology of the Eucharist. LC 88-82477. 390p. (Orig.). 1989. 29.95 (*0-89870-288-7*); pap. 17.95 (*0-89870-225-9*) Ignatius Pr.
O'Connor, Jane. Amy's (Not So) Great Camp-Out. LC 92-45881. (Here Come the Brownies, Brownie Girl Scout Bks.: No. 4). (Illus.). 64p. (J). (gr. 1-4). 1993. 7.99 (*0-448-40167-3*, G&D); pap. 3.95 (*0-448-40166-5*, G&D) Putnam Pub Group.
— Corrie's Secret Pal. LC 92-35602. (Here Come the Brownies, Brownie Girl Scout Bks.). (Illus.). 64p. (J). (gr. 1-4). 1993. 7.99 (*0-448-40161-4*, G&D); pap. 3.95 (*0-448-40160-6*, G&D) Putnam Pub Group.
— Eek! Stories to Make You Shriek. (All Aboard Reading Bks.). (Illus.). 48p. (J). (gr. 1-3). 1992. lib. bdg. 7.99 (*0-448-40383-8*, G&D); pap. 3.50 (*0-448-40382-X*, G&D) Putnam Pub Group.
— Kate Skates. LC 94-45101. (All aboard Reading Ser.). (Illus.). (J). 1995. lib. bdg. write for info. (*0-448-40936-4*, G&D); pap. 3.50 (*0-448-40935-6*, G&D) Putnam Pub Group.
— Lauren & the New Baby. (Here Come the Brownies, Brownie Girl Scout Bks.: No. 6). (Illus.). 64p. (J). (gr. 1-4). 1994. 7.99 (*0-448-40468-0*, G&D); pap. 3.95 (*0-448-40467-2*, G&D) Putnam Pub Group.
— Lulu & the Witch Baby. LC 85-45832. (Harper I Can Read Bk.). (Illus.). 64p. (J). (gr. k-3). 1986. lib. bdg. 14.89 (*0-06-024627-8*) HarpC Child Bks.
— Lulu & the Witch Baby. LC 85-45832. (Trophy I Can Read Bk.). (Illus.). 64p. (J). (gr. k-3). 1989. pap. 3.50 (*0-06-444130-X*, Trophy) HarpC Child Bks.
— Lulu Goes to Witch School. LC 87-37. (Trophy I Can Read Bk.). (Illus.). 64p. (J). (gr. k-3). 1990. pap. 3.50 (*0-06-444138-5*, Trophy) HarpC Child Bks.
— Make up Your Mind, Marsha! LC 92-45880. (Here Come the Brownies, Brownie Girl Scout Bks.: No. 3). (Illus.). 64p. (J). (gr. 1-4). 1993. 7.99 (*0-448-40165-7*, G&D); pap. 3.95 (*0-448-40164-9*, G&D) Putnam Pub Group.
— Molly the Brave & Me. LC 89-10864. (Step into Reading Bks.). (Illus.). 48p. (Orig.). (J). (gr. 1-3). 1990. pap. 3.50 (*0-394-84175-1*) Random Bks Yng Read.
— Molly the Brave & Me. LC 89-10864. (Step into Reading Bks.). (Illus.). 48p. (Orig.). (J). (gr. 1-3). 1990. lib. bdg. 7.99 (*0-394-94175-6*) Random Bks Yng Read.
— Nina, Nina, Ballerina. LC 92-24465. (All Aboard Reading Ser.). (Illus.). 32p. (J). (ps-1). 1993. lib. bdg. 7.99 (*0-448-40512-1*, G&D); pap. 3.50 (*0-448-40511-3*, G&D) Putnam Pub Group.
— Sarah's Incredible Idea. LC 92-36803. (Here Come the Brownies, Brownie Girl Scout Bks.). (Illus.). 64p. (J). (gr. 1-4). 1993. 7.99 (*0-448-40163-0*, G&D); pap. 3.95 (*0-448-40162-2*, G&D) Putnam Pub Group.
— Sir Small & the Dragonfly. LC 87-35309. (Step into Reading Bks.). (Illus.). 32p. (Orig.). (J). (ps-1). 1988. pap. 3.50 (*0-394-89625-4*) Random Bks Yng Read.
— Splat! LC 93-34127. (All Aboard Reading Ser.). (Illus.). 32p. (J). (ps-1). 1994. 7.99 (*0-448-40220-3*, G&D); pap. 3.50 (*0-448-40219-X*, G&D) Putnam Pub Group.
— Think, Corrie, Think! (Here Come the Brownies, Brownie Girl Scout Bks.: No. 5). (Illus.). 64p. (J). (gr. 1-4). 1994. 7.99 (*0-448-40466-4*, G&D); pap. 3.95 (*0-448-40465-6*, G&D) Putnam Pub Group.
O'Connor, Jane & O'Connor, Jim. The Ghost in Tent Nineteen. LC 87-82372. (Stepping Stone Bks.). (Illus.). 64p. (Orig.). (J). (gr. 2-4). 1988. lib. bdg. 6.99 (*0-394-99800-6*); pap. 2.50 (*0-394-89800-1*) Random Bks Yng Read.
O'Connor, Jane & O'Connor, Robert. Super Cluck. LC 90-32832. (I Can Read Bk.). (Illus.). 64p. (J). (ps-3). 1991. 11.95 (*0-06-024594-8*); lib. bdg. 14.89 (*0-06-024595-6*) HarpC Child Bks.
— Super Cluck. LC 90-32832. (Trophy I Can Read Bk.). (Illus.). 64p. (J). (gr. k-3). 1993. pap. 3.50 (*0-06-444162-8*, Trophy) HarpC Child Bks.
O'Connor, Jane, jt. auth. see O'Connor, Jim.
O'Connor, Jerome M. Becoming Human Together: The Pastoral Anthropology of St. Paul, Vol. 2. 242p. 1989. pap. 24.00 (*0-89453-075-5*, Pub. by Veritas IE) St Mut.
— Paul the Letter-Writer: His World, His Options, His Skills. LC 94-11566. (Good News Studies: No. 41). 160p. (Orig.). 1995. pap. text ed. 11.95 (*0-8146-5845-8*, M Glazier) Liturgical Pr.
O'Connor, Jessie L., et al. Harvey & Jessie: A Couple of Radicals. LC 87-21737. (Illus.). 288p. (C). 1988. 34.95 (*0-87722-519-2*); pap. 14.95 (*0-87722-659-8*) Temple U Pr.
O'Connor, Jill. Sweet Nothings: The Art of Light & Luscious Desserts. LC 92-25616. (Illus.). 112p. 1993. pap. 12.95 (*0-8118-0289-2*) Chronicle Bks.
O'Connor, Jim. The Blizzard. (Survive! Ser.). (Illus.). 160p. (J). (gr. 3-7). 1994. pap. 3.50 (*0-448-40435-4*, G&D) Putnam Pub Group.
— Comeback! Four True Stories. LC 91-25028. (Step into Reading Bks.). (Illus.). 48p. (Orig.). (J). (gr. 2-4). 1992. pap. 3.50 (*0-679-82666-1*) Random Bks Yng Read.
— Jackie Robinson & the Story of All-Black Baseball. LC 88-18466. (Step into Reading Bks.). (Illus.). 48p. (Orig.). (J). (gr. 2-4). 1989. pap. 3.50 (*0-394-82456-3*) Random Bks Yng Read.
— Jackie Robinson & the Story of All-Black Baseball. LC 88-18466. (Step into Reading Bks.). (Illus.). 48p. (Orig.). (J). (gr. 2-4). 1989. lib. bdg. 7.99 (*0-394-92456-8*) Random Bks Yng Read.
O'Connor, Jim & O'Connor, Jane. Slime Time. LC 89-77324. (Stepping Stone Bks.). (Illus.). 64p. (Orig.). (J). (gr. 2-4). 1990. pap. 2.50 (*0-679-80714-4*) Random Bks Yng Read.
O'Connor, Jim, jt. auth. see O'Connor, Jane.
O'Connor, Joan. John Alden Carpenter: A Bio-Bibliography. LC 93-45943. (Bio-Bibliographies in Music Ser.). 54p. 1994. text ed. 65.00 (*0-313-26430-9*, Greenwood Pr) Greenwood.
***O'Connor, Joey.** You're Grounded for Life: And 49 Other Crazy Things That Parents Say. LC 94-31929. (Illus.). 192p. (Orig.). (YA). (gr. 8-11). 1995. pap. 7.99 (*0-8007-5549-9*) Revell.
O'Connor, John. The Workhouses of Ireland. (Illus.). 160p. (Orig.). 1994. pap. 13.95 (*0-937702-15-3*) Irish Bks Media.
— Writing with PC Write. 48p. (C). 1988. 3.95 (*0-8403-4860-6*) Kendall-Hunt.
O'Connor, John, tr. see Biver, Paul.
O'Connor, John, jt. ed. see Cohen, Gary.
O'Connor, John, jt. auth. see Langlois, Bill.
O'Connor, John, jt. auth. see Lewis, Hilary.
O'Connor, John, ed. see Shanghai College of Traditional Medicine Staff.
O'Connor, John, jt. auth. see Wiesel, Elie.
O'Connor, John B. Chapters in the History of Actors & Acting in Ancient Greece. LC 65-21095. (Studies in Drama: No. 39). (C). 1969. reprint ed. lib. bdg. 75.00 (*0-8383-0602-0*) M S G Haskell Hse.
***O'Connor, John C., ed.** On Being Catholic: Reflections Addressed to Youth. LC 94-30653. 176p. (Orig.). (J). 1994. pap. 8.95 (*0-8189-0718-5*) Alba.
O'Connor, John C., intro. Essential Catholic Handbook: With References to the Catechism of the Catholic Church. rev. ed. LC 94-75245. 192p. 1994. 14.95 (*0-89243-672-7*) Liguori Pubns.
— Manual Catolico Esencial: Con Referencias al Catecismo de la Iglisia Catolica. rev. ed. LC 94-75248. 192p. (SPA.). 1994. 14.95 (*0-89243-694-8*) Liguori Pubns.
— Manual Para el Catolico de Hoy: Con Referencias Al Catecismo de la Iglesia Catolica. rev. ed. LC 94-75246. 112p. (SPA.). 1994. pap. 2.95 (*0-89243-673-5*) Liguori Pubns.
O'Connor, John C. & Koch, Edward I. His Eminence & Hizzoner: A Candid Exchange. 352p. 1989. mass mkt. 4.95 (*0-380-70715-2*) Avon.
O'Connor, John C., jt. auth. see Murphy, Matthew F.
O'Connor, John E. Image As Artifact: The Historical Analysis of Film & Television. LC 88-13854. 356p. (Orig.). 1990. pap. 32.50 (*0-89464-313-4*) Krieger.
— Teaching History with Film & Television. (Discussions on Teaching Ser.: No. 2). 86p. 1987. pap. 6.00 (*0-87229-040-9*) Am Hist Assn.
— William Paterson, Lawyer & Statesman, 1745-1806. LC 79-15966. 367p. 1979. reprint ed. pap. 104.60 (*0-7837-5679-8*, 2059107) Bks Demand.
O'Connor, John E., ed. I Am a Fugitive from a Chain Gang. LC 81-50823. (Warner Bros. Screenplay Ser.). (Illus.). 200p. (Orig.). 1981. 19.95 (*0-299-08750-6*); pap. 9.95 (*0-299-08754-9*) U of Wis Pr.
O'Connor, John F. The Adobe Book. LC 72-95653. (Illus.). 160p. 1973. lib. bdg. 29.95 (*0-941270-06-8*); pap. 15.95 (*0-941270-19-X*) Ancient City Pr.
— Good Faith in International Law. 144p. 1991. text ed. 55.95 (*1-85521-197-1*, Pub. by Dartmth Pub UK) Ashgate Pub Co.
O'Connor, John F., tr. see Leo.
O'Connor, Joseph. Not Pulling Strings. rev. ed. 176p. 1989. reprint ed. pap. 9.95 (*1-55552-000-6*) Metamorphous Pr.
***O'Connor, Joseph & Prior, Robin.** Successful Selling with NLP: Neuro-Linguistic Programming--The Way Forward in the New Bazaar. 1995. pap. 16.00 (*0-7225-2978-3*) Harper SF.
O'Connor, Joseph & Seymour, John. Introducing Neuro-Linguistic Programming: The New Psychology of Personal Excellence. 240p. 1993. reprint ed. pap. 15.00 (*1-85538-344-6*, Pub. by Aquarian Pr UK) Thorsons SF.
— Training with NLP: Neurolinguistic Programming. (Illus.). 224p. 1994. pap. 16.00 (*0-7225-2853-1*) Thorsons SF.
O'Connor, June. The Quest for Political & Spiritual Liberation: A Study in the Thought of Sri Aurobindo Ghose. LC 75-5249. 153p. (C). 1976. 16.50 (*0-8386-1734-4*) Fairleigh Dickinson.
O'Connor, June E. The Moral Vision of Dorothy Day: A Feminist Perspective. 200p. 1991. 16.95 (*0-8245-1080-1*) Crossroad NY.
O'Connor, K., tr. see Bulgakov, Mikhail.
***O'Connor, Karen.** American Government: Readings & Cases. LC 94-38283. 1994. pap. text ed. 23.00 (*0-02-388900-4*) Allyn.
— Dan Thuy's New Life in America. (In My Shoes Ser.). (Illus.). 40p. (J). (gr. 4-8). 1992. lib. bdg. 18.95 (*0-8225-2555-0*, Lerner Publctns) Lerner Group.
— The Feather Book. LC 90-2959. (Illus.). 60p. (J). (gr. 4 up). 1991. text ed. 14.95 (*0-87518-445-6*, Dillon Silver Burdett) Silver Burdett Pr.
— French Toast & Dutch Chocolate. (J). (ps-3). 1994. pap. 3.99 (*0-570-04771-4*) Concordia.
— Garbage. LC 89-9382. (Overview Ser.: Our Endangered Planet). (Illus.). 96p. (J). (gr. 5-8). 1989. lib. bdg. 16.95 (*1-56006-100-6*) Lucent Bks.
— The Green Team: The Adventures of Mitch & Molly. LC 92-24643. (God's Green Earth Ser.: Bk. 1). (Illus.). 80p. (Orig.). (J). (gr. 1-4). 1993. pap. 4.99 (*0-570-04726-9*) Concordia.
— The Herring Gull. LC 91-40856. (Remarkable Animals Ser.). (Illus.). 60p. (J). (gr. 4 up). 1992. text ed. 13.95 (*0-87518-506-1*, Dillon Silver Burdett) Silver Burdett Pr.
— Homeless Children. LC 89-37553. (Overview Ser.). (Illus.). 96p. (J). (gr. 5-8). 1989. lib. bdg. 16.95 (*1-56006-109-X*) Lucent Bks.
— How To Be a (Great!) Grandparent. LC 95-10024. 1995. write for info. (*0-570-04824-9*) Concordia.
— Little-Kids' Olympics. (J). (ps-3). 1994. pap. 3.99 (*0-570-04770-6*) Concordia.
— San Diego. (Downtown America Ser.). (Illus.). 60p. (J). (gr. 3 up). 1990. text ed. 13.95 (*0-87518-439-1*, Dillon Silver Burdett) Silver Burdett Pr.
— The Water Detectives: The Adventures of Mitch & Molly. LC 92-24649. (God's Green Earth Ser.: Bk. 2). (Illus.). 80p. (Orig.). (J). (gr. 1-4). 1993. pap. 4.99 (*0-570-04727-7*) Concordia.
O'Connor, Karen & Epstein, Lee. Public Interest Law Groups: Institutional Profiles. LC 88-37382. 278p. 1989. text ed. 69.50 (*0-313-24787-0*, OPI, Greenwood Pr) Greenwood.
O'Connor, Karen & Sabato, Larry J. American Government: Roots & Reform. LC 92-17330. 752p. (C). 1993. write for info. (*0-02-388887-3*) Macmillan.
— American Government: Roots & Reform. abr. ed. 625p. (C). 1994. pap. write for info. (*0-02-388883-0*) Macmillan.
O'Connor, Karen, jt. ed. see Griggs, Francis E., Jr.
O'Connor, Karen, jt. auth. see McGlen, Nancy E.
O'Connor, Katherine. My Sister-Life. 200p. 1989. 32.50 (*0-88233-778-5*) Ardis Pubs.
O'Connor, Kathleen. The Confessions of Jeremiah: Their Interpretation & Their Role in Chapters 1-25. LC 86-29803. (Society of Biblical Literature Ser.). 199p. 1988. pap. 11.95 (*1-55540-001-9*, 06 01 94) Scholars Pr GA.

—Robert Musil & the Tradition of the German Novelle. (Studies in Austrian Literature, Culture, & Thought). 192p. 1992. 28.00 (*0-929497-45-7*) Ariadne CA.

— The Way It Happens in Novels. 1989. mass mkt. 5.95 (*0-345-35970-4*, Available Pr) Ballantine.
— The Way It Happens in Novels. 1992. mass mkt. 4.99 (*0-345-37369-3*) Ballantine.
— Wisdom Literature. (Message of Biblical Spirituality Ser.: Vol. 5). 199p. 1988. 12.95 (*0-8146-5555-6*); pap. 9.95 (*0-8146-5571-8*) Liturgical Pr.
***O'Connor, Kathleen S.** The Son of a Nobody. 416p. (Orig.). 1995. pap. 11.99 (*1-85594-156-2*) InBook.
O'Connor, Kevin. Melbourne. (World Cities Ser.). 256p. 1994. text ed. 49.95 (*0-470-22013-9*) Halsted Pr.
O'Connor, Kevin, jt. auth. see Kofler, Marilyn.
O'Connor, Kevin E. & Bucaro, Frank C. When All Else Fails: Finding Solutions to Your Most Persistent Management Problems. 154p. 1992. 19.95 (*0-9631170-4-1*) Ritmar Pub.
O'Connor, Kevin J. The Play Therapy Primer: In Integration of Theories & Techniques. (Series on Personality Processes). 371p. 1991. text ed. 49.95 (*0-471-52543-X*) Wiley.
***O'Connor, Kevin J. & Schaefer, Charles E., eds.** Handbook of Play Therapy Vol. 2: Advances & Innovations, Vol. 2. 1994. text ed. 59.95 (*0-471-58463-0*) Wiley.
O'Connor, Kevin J., jt. auth. see Schaefer, Charles E.
O'Connor, Kieron, jt. auth. see Fewtrell, David.
O'Connor, Leo F. The Protestant Sensibility in the American Novel: An Annotated Bibliography. LC 91-38034. 224p. 1991. 28.00 (*0-8240-4605-6*, H1082) Garland.
Oconnor, Letitia. Exploring Cultural Resources in Los Angeles. 1990. pap. 12.95 (*0-9619095-3-6*) LA Times.
O'Connor, Letitia B. Spectacular America. (Illus.). 132p. 1994. 75.00 (*0-88363-394-9*) H L Levin.
O'Connor, Linda J. & Gourley, Rebecca J. Obstetric & Gynecologic Care in Physical Therapy. LC 89-43071. 363p. 1990. pap. 35.00 (*1-55642-139-7*) SLACK Inc.
O'Connor, Lindsey. Working at Home: A Dream That's Becoming a Trend. 192p. (Orig.). 1990. pap. 6.99 (*0-89081-799-5*) Harvest Hse.
***O'Connor, Lisa C.** The Newspaper: A Subscription for Success. Drolet, Cindy & Gilles-Brown, C., eds. (Language for Living Ser.). 140p. (Orig.). 1992. pap. text ed. 31.00 (*0-9609464-8-9*) Imaginart Pr.
O'Connor, Lois. Earth Is a Seedbed. 2nd rev. ed. Martin, Diane, ed. LC 86-63215. 56p. 1986. pap. 7.95 (*0-931485-26-6*) Scriptorium Pr.
— Of Tarragon, Thyme & Tauvrig: Delectable Cooking with Herbs & Spices. 2nd rev. ed. 1987. pap. 14.95 (*0-931485-08-8*) Scriptorium Pr.
O'Connor, Loretto, Sr. Shared Harvest: Prose of Medieval England in Modern Version. LC 81-43629. (Illus.). 184p. (Orig.). 1982. pap. text ed. 23.50 (*0-8191-2128-2*) U Pr of Amer.
O'Connor, Louis, jt. ed. see Evans, Roy.
O'Connor, Luke J. & Seberry, Jennifer. Cryptographic Significance of the Knapsack Problem: Plus Exercises & Solutions. 186p. (Orig.). (C). 1988. lib. bdg. 42.30 (*0-89412-151-0*); pap. 32.80 (*0-89412-150-2*) Aegean Park Pr.
O'Connor, M., jt. ed. see Meyers, Carol L.
O'Connor, M., jt. auth. see Waltke, Bruce K.

An Asterisk (*) at the beginning of an entry indicates that the title is appearing in BIP for the first time.

O'Connor, M. E., et al, eds. Emerging Electromagnetic Medicine. (Illus.). xiii, 307p. 1990. pap. 54.00 (*0-387-97224-2*) Spr-Verlag.

O'Connor, Maeve. Writing Successfully in Science. 200p. (C). 1992. text ed. 49.95 (*0-04-445805-3*, A8245); pap. text ed. 14.95 (*0-04-445806-1*, A8246) Routledge Chapman & Hall.

O'Connor, Maeve, ed. The Scientist As Editor. LC 78-60428. 224p. 1979. 22.50 (*0-471-04932-8*) Wiley.

***O'Connor, Mallory M.** Lost Cities of the Ancient Southeast. LC 94-39265. (Illus.). 192p. 1995. lib. bdg. 49.95 (*0-8130-1350-X*) U Press Fla.

O'Connor, Margaret. Tears in the Lion's Heart. Balliett, Bev, ed. LC 88-84155. 292p. (Orig.). 1989. pap. 7.95 (*0-317-93748-0*) Po Kuan Pr.

O'Connor, Marion. William Poel & the Elizabethan Stage Society. (Theatre in Focus Ser.). 120p. 1987. pap. 105.00 (*0-85964-164-3*) Chadwyck-Healey.

O'Connor, Marion, jt. ed. see Howard, Jean E.

O'Connor, Mark, jt. ed. see Phillips, Stacy.

O'Connor, Martha, ed. see Columbia University, Legislative Drafting Research Fund Staff.

O'Connor, Martha, jt. ed. see Grad, Frank.

O'Connor, Martin. Air Aces of the Austro-Hungarian Empire, 1914-1918. LC 86-8237. (Illus.). 336p. 1994. reprint ed. 49.95 (*0-9637110-1-6*) Flying Machines.

— The New Zealand European Connection. 172p. (C). 1988. 65.00 (*1-86934-018-3*, Pub. by Grantham Hse NZ) St Mut.

O'Connor, Martin, ed. Is Capitalism Sustainable? Political Economy & the Politics of Ecology. LC 94-11689. (Democracy & Ecology Ser.). 260p. 1994. lib. bdg. 40.00 (*0-89862-127-5*, C2127); pap. text ed. 17.95 (*0-89862-594-7*, C2594) Guilford Pr.

O'Connor, Mary A. The NPM Reference to Prayers We Have in Common: Musical Settings of the ICET Texts - A Catalog, Collection, & Evaluation. 243p. (Orig.). 1990. pap. 30.00 (*0-912405-71-6*) Pastoral Pr.

O'Connor, Mary C. Topics in Northern Pomo Grammar. LC 92-13239. (Outstanding Dissertations in Linguistics Ser.). 360p. 1992. 82.00 (*0-8153-0700-4*) Garland.

O'Connor, Mary I. Study of the Sources of Han D'Islande & Their Significance in the Literary Development of Victor Hugo. LC 76-115357. (Catholic University Romance Languages Ser.: No. 24). reprint ed. 37.50 (*0-404-50324-1*) AMS Pr.

O'Connor, Mary L., ed. see Orr, Margaret T.

O'Connor, Maura. Call of Kolea. Wong, Keola, tr. 24p. 1993. pap. text ed. write for info. (*1-882163-08-7*) Moanalua Grdns Fnd.

— Flowing to the Sea. Wong, Keola, tr. (J). (gr. 4-6). 1994. text ed. write for info. (*1-882163-19-2*) Moanalua Grdns Fnd.

— The Hummingbird Graveyard. 18p. (Orig.). 1992. pap. 3.00 (*0-929730-35-6*) Zeitgeist Pr.

O'Connor, Maureen. Generation to Generation: Older People As an Educational Resource. 96p. 1993. text ed. 50.00 (*0-304-32682-8*); pap. text ed. 16.95 (*0-304-32588-0*) Cassell.

— Secondary Education. Wragg, C. E., ed. (Education Matters Ser.). 112p. 1990. text ed. 50.00 (*0-304-31951-1*); pap. text ed. 17.95 (*0-304-31956-2*) Cassell.

O'Connor, Michael. Hebrew Verse Structure. LC 80-68370. xvii, 629p. 1980. 30.00 (*0-931464-02-1*) Eisenbrauns.

O'Connor, Michael F. For White Boys Who Have Contemplated Monasteries After Being Dumped on Once Too Often. (Illus.). 1980. write for info. (*0-318-51091-X*) Blarney Bks.

O'Connor, Michael J., jt. auth. see Kennedy, Malcolm J.

O'Connor, Michael P. Pandary. LC 89-11763. 47p. 1990. per. 8.95 (*0-934332-50-9*) LEpervier Pr.

O'Connor, Michael P. & Erickson, Becky. The MNM Team Building Process for Printers. LC 91-90250. 250p. 1991. pap. 39.95 (*0-9629366-7-7*) Old Stone Pub.

— The Team Building Book: How to Build Your Staff into a High Performance Team. 250p. (Orig.). 1992. pap. 23.95 (*0-9629366-3-4*) Old Stone Pub.

O'Connor, Michael P. & Freedman, David N. Backgrounds for the Bible. LC 87-13592. xii, 369p. 1987. text ed. 29.50 (*0-931464-30-7*) Eisenbrauns.

O'Connor, Micheal G., jt. auth. see Moss, Thomas C.

O'Connor, Michol. O'Connor's Texas Rules: Civil Trial 1991. Burns, Tracie M., ed. (Texas Lawyer Litigation Ser.). 760p. (Orig.). (C). 1991. pap. 49.95 (*1-879590-00-X*) Amer Law Media.

— O'Connor's Texas Rules Civil Appeals, 1993. (O'Connor's Litigation Ser.). 882p. 1993. pap. 49.95 (*1-884554-02-4*) J McClure Pubng.

— O'Connor's Texas Rules Civil Trials, 1994. (O'Connor's Litigation Ser.). 900p. 1994. pap. 49.95 (*1-884554-00-8*) J McClure Pubng.

— O'Connor's Texas Rules Civil Trials 1995. (O'Connor's Litigation Ser.). 900p. 1995. pap. 49.95 (*1-884554-03-2*) J McClure Pubng.

O'Connor, Mike. The Basin: Life in a Chinese Province Poems & Translations. 127p. 1989. 15.00 (*0-912887-21-4*); pap. 10.00 (*0-912887-20-6*) Empty Bowl.

— The Rainshadow. 100p. 1989. ring bd. 6.95 (*0-912887-03-6*) Empty Bowl.

O'Connor, N., ed. Present Day Russian Psychology. 1967. 92.00 (*0-08-012099-7*, Pub. by Pergamon Repr UK) Franklin.

— Recent Soviet Psychology. (C). 1961. text ed. 9.50 (*0-87140-864-3*) Liveright.

Oconnor, N. & Hermelin, B. Speech & Thought in Severe Subnormality: Experimental Study. LC 62-21782. 1963. 54.00 (*0-08-009786-3*, Pub. by Pergamon Repr UK) Franklin.

Oconnor, N. & Kirsch, R. Recent Soviet Psychology. LC 60-16487. 146.00 (*0-08-009575-5*, Pub. by Pergamon Repr UK) Franklin.

O'Connor, N., jt. auth. see Hermelin, B.

O'Connor, Nancy. Growing up When You're a Grown-up: A Guide to Personal Growth, Balance, & Maturity in Adulthood. 170p. 1991. 27.50 (*1-879041-11-1*); pap. 14.95 (*1-879041-10-3*) Sigo Pr.

— Letting Go with Love: The Grieving Process. LC 84-61538. 186p. (C). 1985. 22.95 (*0-9613714-1-2*); Incl. cass. audio 15.95 (*0-9613714-3-9*); pap. 12.95 (*0-9613714-0-4*) La Mariposa.

— Paterson & Zderad: Humanistic Nursing Theory. (Notes on Nursing Theories Ser.: Vol. 7). (Illus.). 64p. (C). 1992. text ed. 18.95 (*0-8039-4798-4*); pap. text ed. 8.95 (*0-8039-4489-6*) Sage.

O'Connor, Nancy D. How to Grow up When You're Grown Up: Using Growth to Achieve Balance in Adulthood. 353p. 1994. 24.95 (*0-9613714-6-3*); pap. 14.95 (*0-9613714-5-5*) La Mariposa.

O'Connor, Nancy F., intro. Fred E. Miller: Photographer of the Crows. (Illus.). 164p. (Orig.). 1985. pap. 25.00 (*0-9615029-0-8*) U of MT Sch Arts.

O'Connor, Nancy J., jt. ed. see Bissette, Stephen R.

O'Connor, Nancy L., jt. auth. see Wenzlik, Virginia C.

O'Connor, Neal W. The Aviation Awards of Imperial Germany in World War I & the Men Who Earned Them Vol. IV: The Aviation Awards of Wurttemberg, Vol. 1. (Illus.). 288p. (Orig.). (C). 1995. 34.95 (*0-9619867-0-0*) Fndtn Aviation.

O'Connor, Noreen & Ryan, Joanna. Wild Desires & Mistaken Identities: Lesbianism & Psychoanalysis. LC 93-43814. (Between Men - Between Women Ser.). 1994. write for info. (*0-231-10022-1*) Col U Pr.

O'Connor, P., jt. auth. see Healy, G.

O'Connor, P. J. Brendan Behan's 'The Scarperer' (Adaptations Ser.). 1978. 6.95 (*0-685-04179-4*); pap. 2.95 (*0-912262-56-7*) Proscenium.

O'Connor, P. J., jt. auth. see Kavanagh, Patrick.

O'Connor, Patricia. Hitting the Nail on the Head. Trotter, Candace L., ed. 112p. (Orig.). (YA). (gr. 8 up). 1991. reprint ed. pap. text ed. 9.95 (*0-9622684-0-2*) Nugget Pub.

— Therese of Lisieux: A Biography. LC 83-63169. 168p. 1984. pap. 6.95 (*0-87973-607-0*, 607) Our Sunday Visitor.

O'Connor, Patricia & Nystrom, Nancy J. Siestas & Fiestas: Images of Latin America in U. S. History Textbooks. 30p. 1985. pap. 2.00 (*0-317-43430-6*) Tulane Lat Am Lib.

O'Connor, Patricia W. Gregorio & Maria Martinez Sierra. LC 76-45170. (Twayne's World Authors Ser.). 155p. (C). 1977. lib. bdg. 17.95 (*0-8057-6252-3*) Irvington.

— Plays of the New Democratic Spain (1975-1990) 500p. (Orig.). (C). 1992. lib. bdg. 74.00 (*0-8191-8441-1*); pap. text ed. 35.50 (*0-8191-8442-X*) U Pr of Amer.

O'Connor, Patricia W., tr. see Halsey, Martha T., ed.

O'Connor, Patrick. Don't Look Back: A Memoir. 140p. 1993. 18.95 (*1-55921-098-2*) Moyer Bell.

O'Connor, Patrick D. Practical Reliability Engineering. 3rd ed. 409p. 1991. text ed. 79.95 (*0-471-92696-5*) Wiley.

— The Practice of Engineering Management. LC 93-31656. 1994. text ed. 39.95 (*0-471-93974-9*) Wiley.

O'Connor, Patrick D., ed. Reliability Engineering. (Arab School of Science & Technology Ser.). 305p. 1987. 67.00 (*0-89116-684-X*) Hemisp Pub.

O'Connor, Patrick J. Understanding Digital Electronics: How Microcomputers & Microprocessors Work. LC 83-21206. (Illus.). 266p. (C). 1984. 18.50 (*0-13-936964-3*) P-H.

O'Connor, Patrick J., jt. auth. see Gurrie, Michael.

***O'Connor, Paul.** Eskimo Parish. (American Autobiography Ser.). 134p. 1995. reprint ed. lib. bdg. 69.00 (*0-7812-8603-4*) Rprt Serv.

— Grimtooth's Traps Lite. Loomis, Rick, ed. (Illus.). 80p. (Orig.). 1992. pap. 9.95 (*0-940244-87-X*) Flying Buffalo.

— Lensman: Birth of a Lensman. (Illus.). 75p. 1991. pap. 5.95 (*0-944735-86-X*) Malibu Graphics.

— Lensman: The Secret of the Lens. (Illus.). 98p. 1991. pap. 5.95 (*0-944735-87-8*) Malibu Graphics.

— Loom-Controlled Double Weave from the Notebook of a Double Weaver. 1992. pap. 18.95 (*0-932394-18-3*) Dos Tejedoras.

O'Connor, Paul, ed. Grimtooth's Traps. (Illus.). 1981. 9.95 (*0-940244-75-6*) Flying Buffalo.

— Grimtooth's Traps Ate. 1989. 9.95 (*0-940244-84-5*) Flying Buffalo.

O'Connor, Paul, jt. ed. see Occelli, Mario L.

O'Connor, Paul, et al, eds. Grimtooth's Traps Too. (Illus.). 1982. 9.95 (*0-940244-78-0*) Flying Buffalo.

O'Connor, Peter. Dreams & the Search for Meaning. 264p. 1987. pap. 8.95 (*0-8091-2870-5*) Paulist Pr.

— Using Computers in Hospitality & Tourism. LC 95-10738. (Illus.). 256p. 1995. 60.00 (*0-304-33296-8*); pap. 22.50 (*0-304-33299-2*) Cassell.

O'Connor, Peter D., jt. auth. see Wyne, Marvin D.

O'Connor, Philip, tr. see Mommsen, Hans.

O'Connor, Philip F. Old Morals, Small Continents, Darker Times: The 1971 Iowa Short Fiction Award. LC 70-158043. (Iowa Short Fiction Award Ser.). 198p. 1971. pap. 12.95 (*0-87745-023-4*) U of Iowa Pr.

***O'Connor, Philip F., et al.** Human Anatomy: Three Fictions. 9.95 (*0-614-03735-2*) Bottom Dog Pr.

— Human Anatomy - Three Fictions: Martin's World by Philip F. O'Connor; A Well of Living Water by Annabel Thomas; Moonless by Jack Matthews. Smith, Larry, ed. (Contemporary Midwest Fiction Ser.). 208p. (Orig.). Date not set. pap. 9.95 (*0-933087-27-6*) Bottom Dog Pr.

O'Connor, Raymond G. Diplomacy for Victory: FDR & Unconditional Surrender. LC 70-155986. (Essays in American History Ser.). (Illus.). (C). 1971. pap. text ed. 7.95 (*0-393-09765-X*) Norton.

— Origins of the American Navy: Sea Power in the Colonies & the New Nation. LC 93-17839. 134p. (C). 1993. lib. bdg. 34.50 (*0-8191-9161-2*) U Pr of Amer.

O'Connor, Raymond J. The Growth & Development of Birds. LC 84-3724. 315p. 1984. text ed. 159.95 (*0-471-90345-0*) Wiley.

O'Connor, Raymond J. & Shrubb, Michael. Farming & Birds. (Illus.). (C). 1990. pap. 24.95 (*0-521-38973-9*) Cambridge U Pr.

O'Connor, Richard. Invincible Sheridan. 1994. 12.98 (*0-8317-2440-4*) Smithmark.

O'Connor, Riley. Greenberg's Model Railroading with Marklin Z. 96p. 1990. 24.95 (*0-89778-161-9*, 10-7170LE); pap. 14.95 (*0-89778-137-6*, 10-7170) Greenberg Bks.

O'Connor, Robert. Buffalo Soldiers. LC 93-43487. 1994. pap. 12.00 (*0-679-74203-4*, Vin) Random.

— Buffalo Soldiers: A Novel. 1993. 22.00 (*0-679-41508-4*) Knopf.

O'Connor, Robert & O'Connor, Christine. Thinking Life Through: Then Making Intelligent Choices for Our Health. 2nd ed. 296p. 1992. per. 33.95 (*0-8403-7473-9*) Kendall-Hunt.

O'Connor, Robert, jt. auth. see O'Connor, Jane.

O'Connor, Robert F., ed. Texas Myths. LC 85-40743. (Published for the Texas Committee for the Humanities). 264p. 1986. 17.95 (*0-89096-264-2*) Tex A&M Univ Pr.

O'Connor, Robert H., intro. Henry William Bunbury's Tales of the Devil. LC 93-49334. 96p. 1994. 49.95 (*0-7734-9429-4*) E Mellen.

O'Connor, Robert T., ed. Instrumental Analysis of Cotton Cellulose & Modified Cotton Cellulose. LC 72-78243. (Fiber Science Ser.: Vol. 3). 504p. reprint ed. pap. 143.70 (*0-685-15814-4*, 2027811) Bks Demand.

O'Connor, Roger, ed. see Fisher, James J.

O'Connor, Ronald W. Health Care in Muslim Asia: Development & Disorder in Wartime Afghanistan. LC 94-2655. (Illus.). 312p. (C). 1994. lib. bdg. 61.00 (*0-8191-9444-1*); pap. 24.50 (*0-8191-9445-X*) U Pr of Amer.

O'Connor, Rosanne, ed. see Daniels, Rhonda L.

O'Connor, Rosanne, ed. see Kilpatrick, John A.

O'Connor, S., ed. Calendar of the Carularies of Adam Fraunceys & John Pyel, Mayors & Merchants of London. (Royal Historical Society: Camden Fifth Ser.: Vol. 2). 256p. (C). 1993. text ed. 35.00 (*0-86193-137-8*, Royal Historical Soc) Boydell & Brewer.

O'Connor, S., jt. auth. see Talley, N. J.

***O'Connor, S. J., ed.** A Calendar of the Cartularies of John Pyel & Adam Fraunceys. (Camden Fifth Ser.: No. 5). 486p. (C). 1995. 54.95 (*0-521-55160-9*) Cambridge U Pr.

O'Connor, Sally. Common Sense Dressage: An Illustrated Guide. LC 90-5375. (Illus.). 178p. 1990. 24.95 (*0-939481-21-9*) Half Halt Pr.

— Practical Eventing. LC 80-51298. 165p. 1987. reprint ed. pap. 8.00 (*0-9617826-1-7*) USCTA.

O'Connor, Sally, ed. The USCTA Book of Eventing: The Official Handbook of the United States Combined Training Association, Inc. 2nd ed. LC 86-51445. (Illus.). 288p. 1987. reprint ed. 18.95 (*0-9617826-0-9*) USCTA.

O'Connor, Sara & Myers, Sherrill. Working Space: The Milwaukee Repertory Theater Builds a Home. LC 91-20250. (Illus.). 144p. (Orig.). 1992. pap. 16.95 (*1-55936-033-X*) Theatre Comm.

O'Connor, Sara, tr. see Feydeau, Georges.

O'Connor, Sean. Sexual Secrets: A Lover's Guide to Sexual Ecstasy. Brastow, Scott, ed. (Sexual Enrichment Ser.). (Illus.). 128p. (Orig.). 1987. pap. 14.95 (*0-917181-08-5*) Media Pr.

O'Connor, Sharon H., jt. ed. see Cohen, Morris L.

O'Connor, Shaun & Chwalek, Kazimierz. MIC - Marians of the Immaculate Conception: Sources of Marian History & Spirituality. Bukowicz, John & Gorski, Thaddeus, eds. 300p. 1988. write for info. (*0-318-62733-7*); text ed. write for info. (*0-944203-09-4*); pap. text ed. write for info. (*0-944203-10-8*) Marian Pr.

O'Connor, Sheila. Tokens of Grace: A Novella in Stories. LC 90-5438. 128p. 1990. pap. 9.95 (*0-915943-47-6*) Milkweed Ed.

***O'Connor, Sheila, ed.** Come Home Before Dark. (Illus.). 149p. (Orig.). 1993. pap. 9.00 (*0-927663-21-X*) COMPAS.

***O'Connor, Sifu R. Tai Chi Beginner: Yang Style of Shaolin Chi Mantis(TM) McCarty, Michelle, ed. (Shaolin Chi Mantis (TM) Tai Chi Ser.). (Illus.). 208p. (Orig.). (YA). 1995. pap. 18.88 (*1-885910-00-2*) Shaolin Commns. This quintessential book recombines Tai Chi Chuan with its original martial arts heritage of "Silk Reel Boxing." Sparring is forbidden & replaced with self-awareness, chi energy control, & a mind-body balance that reduces stress & builds self-esteem. Complete with illustrations that teach the entire Yang Style Tai Chi Short Form, this book is more than a training guide. Class discussion topics are included such as "Judgement," "Doing Well," & "Meditation." They provide a comprehensive understanding of Tai Chi principles, history, fighting techniques, chi energy flow basics, as well as mental & emotional development concepts. Sifu O'Connor is also an instructor of Shaolin Kung Fu & Praying Mantis Kung Fu. His instructor, Dr. Kam Yuen, was the technical advisor, stuntman, & monk on the original KUNG FU TV series starring David Carradine. This marriage of Tai Chi & Shaolin Kung Fu & Buddhist concepts has been widely acclaimed in California & Utah where Sifu O'Connor has taught in youth prisons, rehab centers & the YWCA. TAI CHI BEGINNER includes perspectives & wisdoms that have benefitted youths in prison & senior citizens recovering from cancer surgeries. To order, call: Baker & Taylor or dial 801-595-1123 or write: Shaolin Communications, P.O. Box 58547, Salt Lake City, UT 84158.**

Publisher Provided Annotation.

O'Connor, Simon, jt. auth. see Talley, Nicholas J.

O'Connor, Stanley J., jt. auth. see Harrisson, Tom.

O'Connor, Susan L., jt. auth. see Shaner, Dale L.

O'Connor, Terrence M. Winning Negotiations in Federal Contracting. 291p. 1992. 139.00 (*1-56726-004-7*) Holbrook & Kellogg.

O'Connor, Terrence M., ed. Contract Administration. 2nd ed. (Complete Contractor Ser.). 177p. 1993. ring bd. write for info. (*1-56726-019-5*) Holbrook & Kellogg.

— Identifying Markets. (Complete Contractor Ser.). 120p. 1993. ring bd. write for info. (*1-56726-018-7*) Holbrook & Kellogg.

— Negotiating Internal & External Policies, Procedures, & Agreements. (Complete Contractor Ser.). 121p. 1993. ring bd. write for info. (*1-56726-017-9*) Holbrook & Kellogg.

O'Connor, Thomas. Lotton Art Glass. 1993. 49.95 (*0-915410-45-1*) McGraw.

O'Connor, Thomas A. Myth & Mythology in the Theater of Pedro Calderon de la Barca. 365p. 35.00 (*0-939980-21-5*) Trinity U Pr.

***O'Connor, Thomas A., ed.** El Encanto Es La Hermosura Y El Hechizo Sin Hechizo - La Segunda Celestina. 224p. 1994. pap. 8.00 (*0-86698-134-9*) MRTS.

— El Encanto Es La Hermosura Y El Hechizo Sin Hechizo - La Segunda Celestina. 224p. 1994. 30.00 (*0-86698-135-7*, MR128) MRTS.

O'Connor, Thomas F., ed. Building Sealants: Materials, Properties, & Performance. LC 90-937. (Special Technical Publication (STP) Ser.: STP 1069). (Illus.). 362p. 1990. text ed. 45.00 (*0-8031-1282-3*) ASTM.

O'Connor, Thomas H. Bibles, Brahmins & Bosses: A Short History of Boston. (Illus.). 1976. 5.00 (*0-89073-049-0*) Boston Public Lib.

— Bibles, Brahmins, & Bosses: A Short History of Boston. 3rd rev. ed. (Illus.). 271p. (Orig.). (YA). 1991. 12.00 (*0-89073-082-2*) Boston Public Lib.

— The Boston Irish: A Political History. (Illus.). 288p. 1995. 24.95 (*1-55553-220-9*) NE U Pr.

— Building a New Boston: Politics & Urban Renewal, 1950-1970. 328p. 1993. text ed. 24.95 (*1-55553-161-X*) NE U Pr.

— South Boston, My Home Town: The History of an Ethnic Neighborhood. LC 93-43535. 272p. (C). 1994. reprint ed. pap. 14.95 (*1-55553-188-1*) NE U Pr.

O'Connor, Thomas P., jt. ed. see Wolfe, Douglas A.

O'Connor, Thomas P., et al, eds. Physicochemical Processes & Wastes in the Ocean: Oceanic Processes in Marine Pollution, Vol. 2. LC 84-29746. 252p. (C). 1987. lib. bdg. 54.50 (*0-89874-811-9*) Krieger.

O'Connor, Timothy E. The Engineer of Revolution: L. B. Krasin & the Bolsheviks, 1870-1926. 322p. (C). 1992. text ed. 66.00 (*0-8133-7684-X*) Westview.

— The Politics of Soviet Culture: Anatolii Lunacharskii. LC 83-18231. (Studies in the Fine Arts: The Avant-Garde: No. 42). (Illus.). 211p. reprint ed. pap. 60.20 (*0-8357-1468-3*, 2070566) Bks Demand.

O'Connor, Timothy W. Agents, Causes, & Events: Essays on Indeterminism & Free Will. 288p. (C). 1995. pap. text ed. 18.95 (*0-685-72943-5*) OUP.

— Agents, Causes, & Events: Essays on Indeterminism & Free Will. 288p. (C). 1995. 39.95 (*0-19-509156-6*) OUP.

O'Connor, Ulick. Biographers & the Art of Biography: To Tell Or Not to Tell. 1990. 28.00 (*0-685-38821-2*, Pub. by Wolfhound Pr IE) Dufour.

— Biographers & the Art of Biography: or To Tell or Not to Tell: To Tell or Not to Tell. 130p. 1990. 28.00 (*0-86327-253-3*, Pub. by Wolfhound Pr IE) Dufour.

— Biographers & Their Art. 200p. 1990. pap. 19.95 (*0-86327-259-2*, Pub. by Wolfhound Pr IE) Dufour.

— Oliver St. John Gogarty. (Illus.). 316p. (C). 1991. pap. 11.95 (*0-685-63018-8*, A0576, Pub. by Mandarin UK) Heinemann.

— Sputnik & Other Poems. (Orig.). pap. 3.50 (*0-8159-6822-1*) Devin.

— Times I've Seen. (Illus.). 1964. 19.95 (*0-8392-1119-8*) Astor-Honor.

O'Connor, Vincent D. Nearly Departed. 1984. pap. 6.00 (*0-88734-212-4*) Players Pr.

O'Connor, W. F. Folk Tales from Tibet. (Illus.). 176p. (C). 1982. reprint ed. 65.00 (*0-89771-114-9*, Pub. by Ratna Pustak Bhandar) St Mut.

O'Connor, W. J. British Physiologists Eighteen Eighty-Five to Nineteen Fourteen: A Biographical Dictionary. LC 90-8666. 400p. 1991. text ed. 90.00 (*0-7190-3282-2*, Pub. by Manchester Univ Pr UK) St Martin.

***O'Connor, Walter F.** Accounting & Taxation. (Business Library). 320p. 1990. pap. 16.95 (*0-8120-4154-2*) Barron.

— An Inquiry into the Foreign Tax Burdens of U. S. Based Multinational Corporations. Bruchey, Stuart, ed. LC 80-586. (Multinational Corporations Ser.). 1981. lib. bdg. 49.95 (*0-405-13377-4*) Ayer.

O'Connor, William. Sense & Sensibility in Modern Poetry. (BCL1-PS American Literature Ser.). 278p. 1993. reprint ed. lib. bdg. 79.00 (*0-7812-6586-X*) Rprt Serv.

O'Connor, William B. & Lubin, Bernard. Ecological Approaches to Clinical & Community Psychology. LC 89-8224. 420p. (C). 1990. reprint ed. lib. bdg. 47.50 (*0-89464-391-6*) Krieger.

***O'Connor, William E.** An Introduction to Airline Economics. 5th ed. LC 94-37883. 256p. 1995. text ed. 45.00 (*0-275-94863-3*, Praeger Pubs) Greenwood.

O'Connor, William J. & Toohey, Phillip S. Regulation Z Truth-in-Lending: Comprehensive Compliance Manual. rev. ed. 524p. 1991. disk 254.00 (*0-685-62690-3*) Am Bankers.

O'Connor, William J., jt. auth. see American Bankers Association Staff.

O'Connor, William R. Natural Desire for God. (Aquinas Lectures). 1948. 10.00 (*0-87462-113-5*) Marquette.

O'Connor, William V. Ezra Pound. LC 63-62712. (University of Minnesota Pamphlets on American Writers Ser.: No. 26). 48p. (Orig.). reprint ed. pap. 25.00 (*0-7837-2870-0*, 2057585) Bks Demand.

— Joyce Cary. LC 66-19552. (Columbia Essays on Modern Writers Ser.: No. 16). 47p. (Orig.). (C). 1966. pap. text ed. 7.50 (*0-231-02680-3*) Col U Pr.

— Seven Modern American Novelists: An Introduction. LC 64-18175. 308p. reprint ed. pap. 87.80 (*0-317-29452-0*, 2055894) Bks Demand.

— William Faulkner. LC 59-63269. (University of Minnesota Pamphlets on American Writers Ser.: No. 3). 47p. reprint ed. pap. 25.00 (*0-317-29465-2*, 2055928) Bks Demand.

O'Connor, William V., ed. see Beach, Joseph W.

***O'Conor, Charles.** Letters of Charles O'Conor of Belanagare: A Catholic Voice in Eighteenth-Century Ireland. Ward, Robert E. et al, eds. LC 87-32563. reprint ed. pap. 162.80 (*0-7837-9104-6*, 2049906) Bks Demand.

O'Conor, John F., tr. see Sokolov, Nicolai.

O'Conor, Norreys J. Battles & Enchantments Retold from Early Gaelic Literature. LC 71-124247. (Select Bibliographies Reprint Ser.). 1977. reprint ed. 17.95 (*0-8369-5435-1*) Ayer.

O'Conor, William A. Essays in Literature & Ethics. 1977. 17.95 (*0-8369-7234-1*, 8033) Ayer.

OCork, Shannon. How to Write Mysteries. 144p. 1989. 14.95 (*0-89879-372-6*) Writers Digest.

O'Corrain, Donncha, jt. ed. see Mac Curtain, Margaret.

OCP Publications Staff, ed. see Walsh, Eugene A.

Ocran, Emanuel B. Energy Costs & Costing: A Selected, Annotated Bibliography. LC 83-8610. 213p. 1983. 22.50 (*0-8108-1631-8*) Scarecrow.

O'Crohan, Sean. A Day in Our Life. Enright, Tim, tr. LC 92-30092. 160p. 1993. 9.95 (*0-19-283119-4*) OUP.

O'Crohan, Thomas. Island Cross-Talk. Enright, Tim, tr. (Illus.). 192p. 1986. pap. 9.95 (*0-19-281909-7*) OUP.

— The Islandman. Flower, Robin, tr. 248p. 1978. reprint ed. pap. 9.95 (*0-19-281233-5*) OUP.

O'Croinin, Connacha, jt. auth. see Dillon, Myles.

***O'Croinin, Daibhi, ed.** Early Medieval Ireland, A.D. 400-1200. LC 94-43307. (History of Ireland Ser.). (C). 1995. text ed. 52.95 (*0-582-01566-9*, Pub. by Longman UK); pap. text ed. 22.95 (*0-582-01565-0*, Pub. by Longman UK) Longman.

OCS Marine Staff. Coal-Fired Ships, 3 vols. (C). 1989. text ed. 395.00 (*0-906314-39-9*, Pub. by Lorne & MacLean Marine) St Mut.

— COW - IGS Conference Papers & Proceedings. (C). 1989. text ed. 195.00 (*0-906314-00-3*, Pub. by Lorne & MacLean Marine) St Mut.

— COW - IGS Manual. (C). 1989. text ed. 235.00 (*0-906314-15-1*, Pub. by Lorne & MacLean Marine) St Mut.

— Dry Dock Planning Manual. (C). 1989. text ed. 720.00 (*0-906314-16-X*, Pub. by Lorne & MacLean Marine) St Mut.

— English - Portuguese Marine Engineering Glossary. (C). 1989. text ed. 325.00 (*0-906314-11-9*, Pub. by Lorne & MacLean Marine) St Mut.

— Inert Gas Systems Manual. (C). 1989. text ed. 225.00 (*0-906314-10-0*, Pub. by Lorne & MacLean Marine) St Mut.

— International Manual or Maritime Safety. (C). 1989. text ed. 290.00 (*0-906314-14-3*, Pub. by Lorne & MacLean Marine) St Mut.

— Manual de Controle de Incendio de Buques. (SPA.). (C). 1989. text ed. 195.00 (*0-685-63530-9*, Pub. by Lorne & MacLean Marine) St Mut.

— Marginal Oilfield Development Manual. (C). 1989. text ed. 350.00 (*0-906314-35-6*, Pub. by Lorne & MacLean Marine) St Mut.

— Operacion y Seguridad en Buques Tanqueros (Tanker Safety Manual) (SPA.). (C). 1989. text ed. 395.00 (*0-906314-04-6*, Pub. by Lorne & MacLean Marine) St Mut.

— S. O. S. (Ship Operational Safety) Manual. (C). 1989. text ed. 425.00 (*0-906314-09-7*, Pub. by Lorne & MacLean Marine) St Mut.

— Ship Squat Manual. (C). 1989. text ed. 290.00 (*0-906314-07-0*, Pub. by Lorne & MacLean Marine) St Mut.

— Shipowners Guide to Yard Repairs. (C). 1989. text ed. 310.00 (*0-906314-29-1*, Pub. by Lorne & MacLean Marine) St Mut.

— Ships Fire-Fighting Manual. (C). 1989. text ed. 195.00 (*0-906314-03-8*, Pub. by Lorne & MacLean Marine) St Mut.

— Steering Gear Systems. (C). 1989. text ed. 120.00 (*0-685-63531-7*) St Mut.

— Survival Techniques. (C). 1989. text ed. 110.00 (*0-906314-01-1*, Pub. by Lorne & MacLean Marine) St Mut.

OCS Publishing Group Staff. Subsea Production Systems - Can Engineering Reduce Pipeline Costs? 1989. 125.00 (*90-6314-562-4*, Pub. by Lorne & MacLean Marine) St Mut.

Octagon Museum Staff & American Architectural Foundation Staff. The Grand American Avenue, 1850-1920. (Illus.). 360p. 1994. 45.00 (*1-56640-680-3*); pap. 29.95 (*1-56640-679-X*) Pomegranate Calif.

October Ventures, Inc., Staff. Handbook of Practical Knowledge. 236p. 1989. 24.95 (*0-9625913-0-0*) October Ventures.

***Octogram Publishing Staff.** MAC-graphics Interactive Workshop. 290p. 1995. cd-rom, pap. 79.95 (*0-201-88365-1*) Peachpit Pr.

Octopus, Conran, jt. auth. see Burnett, Sarah.

Octrue, Michel. A New Method for Designing Worm-Gear. (Fall Technical Meeting Papers 88FTM6). (Illus.). 5p. 1988. pap. text ed. 30.00 (*1-55589-511-5*) AGMA.

O'Cuilleanain, C. & Haywood, E., eds. Italian Storytellers. 216p. 1989. 39.50 (*0-7165-2389-2*, Pub. by Irish Acad Pr IE) Intl Spec Bk.

***O'Cuinn, Gerard, ed.** Metabolism of Brain Peptides. 272p. 1995. 110.00 (*0-8493-7665-3*, 7665) CRC Pr.

***O'Cuinneagain, Mel, et al.** Butterworths Ireland Tax Guide 1993-94. 1993. pap. text ed. 99.00 (*1-85475-626-5*, IE) Butterworth Legal Pubs.

Ocvirk, Otto, et al. Art Fundamentals: Theory & Practice. 7th ed. 320p. 1994. pap. write for info. (*0-697-12545-9*) Brown & Benchmark.

Oda, Hidetomo. Animals of the Seashore. LC 85-28192. (Nature Close-Ups Ser.). (Illus.). 32p. (J). (gr. 3-7). 1986. lib. bdg. 10.95 (*0-8172-2543-9*) Raintree Steck-V.

— Butterflies. Pohl, Kathy, ed. LC 85-28196. (Nature Close-Ups Ser.). (Illus.). 32p. (J). (gr. 3-7). 1986. text ed. 10.95 (*0-8172-2531-5*) Raintree Steck-V.

— The Diving Beetle. Pohl, Kathy, ed. LC 85-28300. (Nature Close-Ups Ser.). (Illus.). 32p. (J). (gr. 3-7). 1986. lib. bdg. 10.95 (*0-8172-2533-1*) Raintree Steck-V.

— Dragonflies. Pohl, Kathy, ed. LC 85-28197. (Nature Close-Ups Ser.). (Illus.). 32p. (J). (gr. 3-7). 1986. text ed. 10.95 (*0-8172-2534-X*) Raintree Steck-V.

— Insect Hibernation. Pohl, Kathy, ed. LC 85-2892. (Nature Close-Ups Ser.). (Illus.). 32p. (Orig.). (J). (gr. 3-7). 1986. text ed. 10.95 (*0-8172-2526-9*) Raintree Steck-V.

— Insects & Flowers. Pohl, Kathy, ed. LC 85-28206. (Nature Close-Ups Ser.). (Illus.). 32p. (J). (gr. 3-7). 1986. text ed. 10.95 (*0-8172-2527-7*) Raintree Steck-V.

— Insects & Their Homes. Pohl, Kathleen, ed. LC 85-28226. (Nature Close-Ups Ser.). (Illus.). 32p. (J). (gr. 3-7). 1986. lib. bdg. 10.95 (*0-8172-2528-5*) Raintree Steck-V.

— Insects in the Pond. Pohl, Kathy, ed. LC 85-28227. (Nature Close-Ups Ser.). (Illus.). 32p. (J). (gr. 3-7). 1986. text ed. 10.95 (*0-8172-2529-3*) Raintree Steck-V.

— The Ladybug. Pohl, Kathy, ed. LC 85-28199. (Nature Close-Ups Ser.). (Illus.). 32p. (J). (gr. 3-7). 1986. text ed. 10.95 (*0-8172-2538-2*) Raintree Steck-V.

— Observing Bees & Wasps. Pohl, Kathy, ed. LC 85-28195. (Nature Close-Ups Ser.). (Illus.). 32p. (J). (gr. 3-7). 1986. lib. bdg. 10.95 (*0-8172-2540-4*) Raintree Steck-V.

— Snails. LC 85-28211. (Nature Close-Ups Ser.). (Illus.). 32p. (J). (gr. 3-7). 1986. lib. bdg. 10.95 (*0-8172-2544-7*) Raintree Steck-V.

— The Swallowtail Butterfly. Pohl, Kathy, ed. LC 85-28229. (Nature Close-Ups Ser.). (Illus.). 32p. (J). (gr. 3-7). 1986. lib. bdg. 10.95 (*0-8172-2542-0*) Raintree Steck-V.

— The Tadpole. Pohl, Kathy, ed. LC 85-28202. (Nature Close-Ups Ser.). (Illus.). 32p. (J). (gr. 3-7). 1986. lib. bdg. 10.95 (*0-8172-2545-5*) Raintree Steck-V.

— The Tree Frog: Annual. annuals Pohl, Kathy, ed. LC 85-28194. (Nature Close-Ups Ser.). (Illus.). 32p. (J). (gr. 3-7). 1986. lib. bdg. 10.95 (*0-8172-2546-3*) Raintree Steck-V.

— The Turtle. Pohl, Kathy, ed. LC 85-28234. (Nature Close-Ups Ser.). (Illus.). 32p. (J). (gr. 3-7). 1986. lib. bdg. 10.95 (*0-8172-2547-1*) Raintree Steck-V.

Oda, Hiroshi. Japanese Law. 1992. U.K. pap. 80.00 (*0-406-66921-X*) Butterworth Legal Pubs.

Oda, Hiroshi, ed. Japanese Commercial Law in an Era of Internationalization. LC 93-44889. 328p. (C). 1994. lib. bdg. 120.00 (*1-85333-786-2*, Pub. by Graham & Trotman UK) Kluwer Ac.

— Law & Politics of West-East Technology Transfer. (C). 1991. lib. bdg. 115.00 (*0-7923-0990-1*) Kluwer Ac.

Oda, Hiroshi & Grice, Geoffrey, eds. Japanese Banking, Securities & Anti-Monopoly Law. 170p. 1988. boxed 85.00 (*0-88063-264-X*) Butterworth Legal Pubs.

Oda, Makoto. The Bomb. Whittaker, D. H., tr. 192p. 1990. 18.95 (*0-87011-981-8*) Kodansha.

— H: A Hiroshima Novel. Whittaker, D. H., tr. Orig. Title: The Bomb. 218p. 1995. pap. 10.00 (*4-7700-1947-5*) Kodansha.

Oda, Mayumi. Goddesses. enl. rev. ed. LC 88-190. (Illus.). 74p. 1988. pap. 14.95 (*0-912078-82-0*, Kazan Bks) Volcano Pr.

— Happy Veggies. 1990. pap. 12.50 (*0-938077-14-7*) Parallax Pr.

Oda, N. & Takayanagi, Kazuo, eds. Electronic & Atomic Collisions: Invited Papers-11th International Conference on Physics of Electricity & Atomic Collisions, Kyoto, Japan, August 1979. 1980. 202.75 (*0-444-85434-7*) Elsevier.

Oda, Osamu. Compound Semiconductor Bulk Materials & Characterizations. 250p. 1995. text ed. 59.00 (*981-02-1728-5*) World Scientific Pub.

Oda, Patsy. Mi Primer Amor. 128p. (Orig.). (SPA.). 1991. pap. 3.95 (*0-88113-059-1*) Edit Betania.

Oda, Shigeru. International Control of Sea Resources. rev. ed. (C). 1989. reprint ed. lib. bdg. 94.50 (*90-247-3800-8*) Kluwer Ac.

— International Law of the Resources of the Sea. 144p. 1979. reprint ed. lib. bdg. 37.50 (*90-286-0399-9*) Kluwer Ac.

Oda, Shigeru, et al, eds. The Practice of Japan in International Law, 1961-1970. 470p. 1982. 82.50 (*0-86008-301-2*, Pub. by U of Tokyo JA) Col U Pr.

Oda, Stephanie. Hope Lines Journal, No. H40. 1991. 15.95 (*0-8378-2042-1*) Gibson.

***Oda, Stephanie & Schoen, Clare.** Trade Book Publishing 1995: Review, Forecast & Segment Analysis. (Illus.). 288p. 1995. write for info. (*0-88709-085-0*) Simba Info Inc.

Oda, Stephanie C. My Nighttime Book. (Good Little Books for Good Little Children). 12p. (J). (ps). 1986. 3.25 (*0-8378-5091-6*) Gibson.

Oda, Stephanie C., ed. In Sympathy. (Illus.). 1992. 9.50 (*0-8378-2500-8*) Gibson.

Oda, T., ed. Therapeutic Plasmapheresis (VII) Proceeding of the Seventh Symposium on Therapeutic Plasmapheresis, Tokyo, June 5-6, 1987. LC 87-82168. 51.25 (*0-936022-32-9*) ICAOT Pr.

Oda, T., et al, eds. The First International Congress of the World Apheresis Association - Proceedings: Therapeutic Plasmapheresis (VI). In Conjunction with the Sixth Symposium on Therapeutic Plasmapheresis, Tokyo, May 1986. LC 87-82168. 60.00 (*0-936022-31-0*) ICAOT Pr.

Oda, Tadao. Algebraic Geometry: Sendai, Nineteen Eighty-Five. (Advanced Studies in Pure Mathematics: Vol. 10). 794p. 1988. 231.00 (*0-444-70313-6*, North Holland) Elsevier.

— Convex Bodies & Algebraic Geometry. (Ergebnisse der Mathematik und Ihrer Grenzgebiete Ser.: Vol. 15, 3 Folge). (Illus.). 280p. 1987. 89.00 (*0-387-17600-4*) Spr-Verlag.

— Internal Medicine: Today & Tomorrow. Hamaguchi, K. et al, eds. 506p. 1986. 176.00 (*0-444-80755-1*, Excerpta Medica) Elsevier.

Oda, Tadao, et al, eds. Recent Advances in Traditional Medicine in East Asia. (International Congress Ser.: No. 693). 387p. 1986. 141.75 (*0-444-80713-6*, Excerpta Medica) Elsevier.

Oda, Tadao & Tygstrup, N. Hepatotrophic Agent Malotilate. (Current Clinical Practice Ser.: Vol. 10). 1984. 77.50 (*0-444-39210-6*, I-197-84) Elsevier.

Oda, Takayuki. Periods of Hilbert Modular Surfaces. (Progress in Mathematics Ser.: Vol. 19). 1982. text ed. 32.50 (*0-8176-3084-8*) Birkhauser.

Odabasi, Halis & Akyuz, O., eds. Topics in Mathematical Physics: Papers Presented at an International Symposium held July 28-August 2, 1975 at Bogazici University, Istanbul, Turkey. LC 77-84853. (Illus.). 291p. reprint ed. pap. 83.00 (*0-8357-5511-8*, 2035126) Bks Demand.

Odabasi, Halis, jt. ed. see Brittin, Wesley E.

Odabasi, Halis, ed. see Conference on International Implications of Environmental Problems Staff.

Odaet, Cooper F. Implementing Educational Policies in Uganda. (Discussion Paper Ser.: No. 89). 40p. 1990. 6.95 (*0-685-74580-5*, 11586) World Bank.

O'Daffer, Phares G., ed. Problem Solving: Tips for Teachers. LC 88-17870. (Illus.). 80p. 1988. pap. 8.50 (*0-87353-264-3*) NCTM.

O'Daffer, Phares G. & Clemens, Stanley R. Geometry: An Investigative Approach. 2nd ed. (Illus.). 600p. (C). 1992. text ed. 51.75 (*0-201-21795-3*) Addison-Wesley.

Odagiri, Hiroyuki. Growth Through Competition, Competition Through Growth: Strategic Management & the Economy in Japan. 384p. 1994. reprint ed. pap. 24.95 (*0-19-828873-5*) OUP.

— The Theory of Growth in a Corporate Economy: Management Preference, Research & Development & Economic Growth. LC 80-23494. (Illus.). 256p. 1981. 64.95 (*0-521-23132-9*) Cambridge U Pr.

Odahl, C. Early Christian Latin Literature: Readings from the Ancient Texts. (Illus.). 209p. (Orig.). (LAT.). (C). 1993. pap. text ed. 30.00 (*0-89005-515-7*) Ares.

Odahl, Charles M. Catilinarian Conspiracy. 1972. 14.95 (*0-8084-0032-0*); pap. write for info. (*0-8084-0033-9*) NCUP.

Odajnyk, V. Walter. Gathering the Light: A Psychology of Meditation. LC 92-56446. (C. G. Jung Foundation Bks.). 264p. (Orig.). 1993. pap. 14.00 (*0-87773-684-7*) Shambhala Pubns.

Odaka, Konosuke, et al. The Automobile Industry in Japan: A Study of Ancillary Firm Development. (Hitotsubashi University Economic Research Ser.: No. 26). 356p. 1988. 79.00 (*4-314-00487-8*) OUP.

Odaka, Kunio. Japanese Management: A Forward Looking Analysis. 85p. 1986. 15.25 (*0-685-55861-4*, 0077, Pub. by APO JA); pap. 11.50 (*0-685-55862-2*, 0075, Pub. by APO JA) Qual Resc.

— Toward Industrial Democracy: Management & the Workers in Modern Japan. LC 74-82575. (East Asian Monographs: No. 80). 272p. 1975. 18.50 (*0-674-89816-8*) HUP.

O'Daly, Gerard. The Poetry of Boethius. LC 90-2528. xii, 252p. (C). 1991. 45.00 (*0-8078-1989-1*) U of NC Pr.

O'Daly, William, tr. see Neruda, Pablo.

Odam, Joyce. Women of Bones Come off the Mountain. 1991. write for info. (*0-943787-03-3*) Hibiscus Pr.

Odamtten, Vincent O. The Art of Ama Ata Aidoo: Polylectics & Reading Against Neocolonialism. LC 93-35009. (Illus.). 216p. (C). 1994. lib. bdg. 32.95 (*0-8130-1276-7*); pap. 16.95 (*0-8130-1277-5*) U Press Fla.

Odanaka, T. Dynamic Management Decision & Stochastic Control Processes. 240p. (C). 1990. text ed. 41.00 (*981-02-0092-7*) World Scientific Pub.

O'Daniel, H. Edward, Jr., text. Kentucky Workers' Compensation Law, 1987. 250p. 1988. pap. 38.00 (*0-8322-0219-3*) Banks-Baldwin.

O'Daniel, Therman B., ed. James Baldwin: A Critical Evaluation. LC 74-30006. 1981. pap. 9.95 (*0-88258-091-4*) Howard U Pr.

— Jean Toomer: A Critical Evaluation. 576p. 1988. 22.95 (*0-88258-111-2*) Howard U Pr.

Odarty, Bill. A Safari of African Cooking. LC 72-115155. 1971. pap. 12.00 (*0-910296-63-4*) Broadside Pr.

Odate, Gyoju. Japan's Financial Relations with the United States. LC 78-57574. (Columbia University. Studies in the Social Sciences: No. 224). reprint ed. 20.00 (*0-404-51224-0*) AMS Pr.

Odate, Toshio. Japanese Woodworking Tools: Their Tradition, Spirit & Use. LC 83-50679. (Illus.). 200p. (C). 1984. 23.95 (*0-918804-19-1*) Taunton.

Odawara, G., ed. CAD Systems Using AI Techniques: Proc. of the IFIP TC10-WG10.2 Working Conf., Tokyo, Japan, 6-7 June 1989. 230p. 1989. 64.00 (*0-444-88319-3*, North Holland) Elsevier.

O'Day, Alan. The English Face of Irish Nationalism: Parnellite Involvement in British Politics, 1880-86. (Modern Revivals in History Ser.). 212p. 1994. 55.95 (*0-7512-0240-1*, Pub. by Gregg Revivals UK) Ashgate Pub Co.

— Reactions to Irish Nationalism, 1865-1914. 422p. 1987. text ed. 55.00 (*0-907628-85-0*) Hambledon Press.

O'Day, Alan, ed. Dimensions of Irish Terrorism. LC 93-38372. (International Library of Terrorism: No. 2). 428p. 1994. text ed. 45.00 (*0-8161-7338-9*) G K Hall.

— Government & Institutions in the Post-1832 United Kingdom. LC 94-38867. (Studies in British History: Vol. 34). 420p. 1995. text ed. 109.95 (*0-7734-8980-0*) E Mellen.

— A Survey of the Irish in England (1872) 174p. 1990. boxed 45.00 (*1-85285-010-8*) Hambleden Press.

— Terrorism's Laboratory: The Case of Northern Ireland. LC 95-3902. 1995. write for info. (*1-85521-457-1*, Pub. by Dartmth Pub UK) Ashgate Pub Co.

O'Day, Alan & Alexander, Yonah, eds. Irish Terrorist Trauma. 288p. 1989. 39.95 (*0-685-23482-7*) St Martin.

O'Day, Alan & Stevenson, John, eds. Irish Historical Documents Since 1800. 300p. (C). 1992. text ed. 72.50 (*0-389-20971-6*) B&N Imports.

O'Day, Alan, jt. auth. see Alexander, Yonah.

O'Day, Alan, jt. ed. see Alexander, Yonah.

O'Day, Alan, jt. ed. see Boyce, D. George.

O'Day, Anita & Eells, George. High Times Hard Times. LC 88-17896. (Illus.). 349p. 1989. reprint ed. Incl. updated discography. pap. 15.00 (*0-87910-118-0*) Limelight Edns.

O'Day, Bonnie. Preventing Sexual Abuse of Persons with Disabilities. 175p. 1985. pap. text ed. 19.95 (*0-941816-23-0*) ETR Assocs.

O'Day, Danton H., ed. Calcium As an Intracellular Messenger in Eucaryotic Microbes. (Illus.). 418p. 1990. 49.00 (*1-55581-023-3*) Am Soc Microbio.

— Signal Transduction During Biomembrane Fusion. (Cell Biology Ser.). (Illus.). 270p. 1993. text ed. 85.00 (*0-12-524155-0*) Acad Pr.

O'Day, Danton H. & Horgen, Paul A., eds. Eucaryotic Microbes As Model Developmental Systems. LC 76-28079. (Microbiology Ser.: No. 2). (Illus.). 456p. reprint ed. pap. 130.00 (*0-8357-6107-X*, 2034558) Bks Demand.

O'Day-Flannery, Constance. The Gift. 400p. 1994. mass mkt. 5.99 (*0-8217-4648-0*) Zebra.

— Once in a Lifetime. 1994. mass mkt. 5.99 (*0-8217-4795-9*) Zebra.

— Seasons. 416p. (Orig.). 1995. mass mkt. 6.50 (*0-446-60107-1*) Warner Bks.

— Second Chances. 400p. 1992. mass mkt. 5.99 (*0-8217-3950-6*) Zebra.

— Sunsets. (Orig.). 1996. mass mkt. write for info. (*0-446-60307-4*) Warner Bks.

— This Time Forever. 1990. mass mkt. 4.95 (*0-8217-3557-8*) Zebra.

— Time for Love. 448p. 1991. mass mkt. 4.95 (*0-8217-3295-1*) Zebra.

— Time Kept Promises. 1994. mass mkt. 4.95 (*0-8217-3554-3*) Zebra.

— Time Kissed Destiny. 1991. mass mkt. 4.99 (*0-8217-4023-7*) Zebra.

— Timeless Passion. 1991. mass mkt. 4.99 (*0-8217-3683-3*) Zebra.

— Timeswept Lovers. 496p. 1987. pap. 3.95 (*0-8217-2057-0*) Zebra.

O'Day-Flannery, Constance, et al. Secret Loves. 304p. (Orig.). 1994. pap. text ed. 4.99 (*0-425-14124-1*) Berkley Pub.

O'Day, Gabrielle. The Matter of Shiva. 226p. 1991. 24.95 (*0-8191-8202-8*) U Pr of Amer.

Oday, Gail R. Proclamation Five: Epiphany, Series C. 1994. pap. 4.50 (*0-8006-4194-9*, Fortress Pr) Augsburg Fortress.

O'Day, Gail R. & Long, Thomas G., eds. Listening to the Word: Studies in Honor of Fred B. Craddock. LC 92-38030. 256p. (Orig.). 1993. pap. 15.95 (*0-687-37062-0*) Abingdon.

Oday, Kate. Waite Group's Discovering Ms-Dos. 2nd ed. 1991. pap. 19.95 (*0-672-22772-X*, Bobbs) Macmillan.

O'Day, Kate, jt. auth. see Waite Group Staff.

O'Day, Kate, et al. The Waite Group's Understanding MS-DOS. 2nd ed. (Understanding Ser.). 384p. 1989. pap. 19.95 (0-672-27298-9) Sams.
O'Day, Rosemary. The Debate on the English Reformation. 217p. 1986. pap. text ed. 12.95 (0-416-72680-1, 9802) Routledge Chapman & Hall.
— The Family & Family Relationships, 1500-1900: England, France, & the United States of America. LC 94-19509. 1994. write for info. (0-312-12271-3); pap. write for info. (0-312-12272-1) St Martin.
— The Longman Companion to the Tudor Age. LC 94-9970. (Longman Companions to History Ser.). 336p. (C). 1995. text ed. 49.95 (0-582-06725-1, 77010, Pub. by Longman UK); pap. text ed. 19.95 (0-582-06724-3, 77009, Pub. by Longman UK) Longman.
O'Day, Rosemary & Englander, David. Mr. Charles Booth's Inquiry: Life & Labour of the People in London Reconsidered. LC 93-356. 256p. 1993. Alk. paper. boxed 55.00 (1-85285-079-5) Hambledon Press.
O'Day, Rosemary, jt. ed. see Englander, David.
Odber de Baubeta, Patricia A. Anticlerical Satire in Medieval Portuguese Literature. LC 92-23339. 356p. 1992. text ed. 99.95 (0-7734-9607-6) E Mellen.
Odden, Allan R. Education Policy Implementation. LC 90-43395. (SUNY Series, Educational Leadership). 383p. (C). 1991. 74.50 (0-7914-0665-2); pap. 24.95 (0-7914-0666-0) State U NY Pr.
Odden, Allan R., ed. Rethinking School Finance: An Agenda for the 1990s. LC 92-11512. (Education-Higher Education Ser.). 384p. 1992. 32.95 (1-55542-451-1) Jossey-Bass.
***Odden, Allan R. & Odden, Eleanor R.** Educational Leadership for America's Schools. 1995. pap. text ed. write for info. (0-07-047489-3) McGraw.
Odden, Allan R. & Picus, Lawrence O. School Finance: A Policy Perspective. 1992. text ed. write for info. (0-07-047486-9) McGraw.
Odden, D., ed. Current Approaches to African Linguistics, Vol. 4. (Publications in African Languages & Linguistics). x, 428p. 1987. pap. 113.85 (3-11-013103-X) Mouton.
***Odden, David.** The Phonology & Morphology of Kimatuumbi. (Phonology of the World's Languages Ser.). 200p. 1995. 49.95 (0-19-823503-8) OUP.
Odden, Eleanor R., jt. auth. see Odden, Allan R.
***Oddenina, Michael L.** Putting Kids First: Walking Away from a Marriage Without Walking over the Kids. (Illus.). 151p. Date not set. 16.95 (1-884862-03-9) Fmly Connect.
Oddenino, Kathy. Bridges of Consciousness. 300p. (Orig.). 1989. pap. 14.95 (0-923081-01-1) Joy Pubns MD.
— Healing Ourself: Growing Beyond the True Cause of Disease. 636p. (Orig.). 1994. pap. 24.95 (0-923081-04-6) Joy Pubns MD.
— The Joy of Health: A Spiritual Concept of Integration & the Practicalities of Living. 300p. (Orig.). 1989. pap. 14.95 (0-923081-00-3) Joy Pubns MD.
— Love, Truth & Perception. 262p. (Orig.). (C). 1993. pap. 14.95 (0-923081-03-8) Joy Pubns MD.
— Sharing: Self Discovery in Relationships. 300p. (Orig.). 1990. pap. 14.95 (0-923081-02-X) Joy Pubns MD.
Oddey, Alison. Devising Theatre: A Practical & Theoretical Handbook. (Illus.). 256p. 1992. 59.95 (0-415-04899-0, A7963); pap. 15.95 (0-415-04900-8, A7967) Routledge.
Oddi, Marcia, ed. Indiana Environmental Air Rules, 1992. (Orig.). 1992. pap. 39.95 (1-880182-03-3) CEM.
— Indiana Environmental Solid & Hazardous Waste Rules, 1992. (Orig.). 1992. pap. 39.95 (1-880182-05-X) CEM.
— Indiana Environmental Statutes, 1992. (Orig.). 1992. pap. 39.95 (1-880182-06-8) CEM.
— Indiana Environmental Water Rules, 1992. (Orig.). 1992. pap. 39.95 (1-880182-04-1) CEM.
Oddi, Marcia J., ed. Indiana Environmental Rules, 1991, Vol. I. 1991. 39.95 (1-880182-00-9) CEM.
— Indiana Environmental Rules, 1991, Vol. II. 1991. 39.95 (1-880182-01-7) CEM.
— Indiana Environmental Statutes, 1991. 1991. 39.95 (1-880182-02-5) CEM.
Oddi, Marsha, ed. Indiana Criminal Law 1989 Edition. 187p. (Orig.). 1990. pap. 10.00 (1-878760-02-5) Graphics Ltd IN.
— Indiana Motor Vehicle Laws 1989 Edition. 287p. (Orig.). 1990. pap. 10.00 (1-878760-01-7) Graphics Ltd IN.
Oddie, C., et al, eds. Butterworths County Court Precedents & Pleadings. U.K. ring bd. 370.00 (0-406-29211-6) Butterworth Legal Pubs.
Oddie, G. A. Social Protest in India: British Protestant Missionaries & Social Reforms, Eighteen Fifty to Nineteen Hundred. 1979. 17.50 (0-8364-0195-6) S Asia.
Oddie, G. A., ed. Religion in South Asia. 204p. 1988. 22.95 (0-318-37152-9) Asia Bk Corp.
— Religion in South Asia: Religious Conversion & Revival Movements in South Asia in Medieval & Modern Times. (C). 1991. text ed. 24.00 (0-945921-18-7, Pub. by S Asia Pubs II) S Asia.
Oddie, Geoffrey A. Hindu & Christian in South-East Asia: Aspects of Religious Continuity & Change, 1800-1900. (London Studies on South Asia: No. 6). (Illus.). 304p. (C). 1992. text ed. 60.00 (0-7007-0224-5, Pub. by Curzon Pr UK) Humanities.
Oddie, Graham. Likeness to Truth. 1986. lib. bdg. 85.50 (90-277-2238-2) Kluwer Ac.
Oddie, Graham & Perrett, Roy W., eds. Justice, Ethics, & New Zealand Society. 252p. 1993. pap. 35.00 (0-19-558241-1) OUP.
Oddie, William. What Will Happen to God? Feminism & the Reconstruction of Christian Belief. LC 88-81091. 179p. 1988. pap. 9.95 (0-89870-211-9) Ignatius Pr.
Oddo Editorial Staff. Oddo-Matic Teacher Manual. 1977. ring bd. 26.60 (0-87783-140-8) Oddo.
Oddo, Eileen, jt. auth. see Patella, Chris.
Oddo, Frank. Street Rodder's Handbook: How to Build a Street Rod. Sessions, Ron, ed. LC 86-81201. (Illus.). 208p. 1986. pap. 14.95 (0-89586-369-3, HP Books) Berkley Pub.
Oddo, Genevieve, ed. see Moore, Silas.
Oddo, Paul C., jt. auth. see Harding, Robert G.
Oddo, Richard J. Sharing of the Heart. LC 89-92801. (Illus.). 320p. (Orig.). (C). 1990. pap. text ed. 10.00 (0-945637-02-0) Spirit Warrior Pr.
— Within a Miraculous Realm. (Illus.). 320p. (Orig.). (C). 1988. pap. 9.95 (0-945637-00-4) Spirit Warrior Pr.
Oddo, Victor R., Jr. Kansas City Attractions. 100p. (Orig.). 1993. pap. 9.95 (1-883562-00-7) Natl Pub MO.
— St. Louis Attractions. 108p. (Orig.). 1994. pap. 9.95 (1-883562-01-5) Natl Pub MO.
Oddo, Vincent. Playing & Teaching the Strings. 189p. (C). 1979. Spiralbound. pap. 24.95 (0-534-00614-0) Intl Thomson.
— Playing & Teaching the Strings. 2nd ed. LC 94-35620. (Illus.). 190p. 1995. pap. 24.95 (0-534-22971-9) Intl Thomson.
Oddou, Gary, jt. auth. see Mendenhall, Mark.
Oddou, Gary, jt. ed. see Mendenhall, Mark.
Odds. Candida & Candidosis. 2nd ed. 448p. 1988. text ed. 105.00 (0-7020-1265-3) Saunders.
***Odds, Geoffrey.** Fear & Fascination: The 100 Best Rock Climbs in England & Wales. (Illus.). 160p. 1995. 39.95 (1-85223-607-8) Trafalgar.
Oddsson, Gisli. Annalium in Islandia Farrago, & De Mirabilibus Islandiae. Hermannsson, Halldor, ed. (Islandica Ser.: Vol. 10). 1917. 15.00 (0-527-00340-9) Periodicals Srv.
Oddy, Andrew, ed. The Art of the Conservator. LC 92-60302. (Illus.). 208p. 1992. 39.95 (1-56098-229-2) Smithsonian.
Oddy, Derek, jt. ed. see Burnett, John.
Oddy, Derek J., jt. ed. see Burnett, John.
***Oddy, Russell.** For Sale by Owner: Sell Your Own Home & Save Thousands: Canadian Edition. 5th ed. (Legal Ser.). 144p. 1994. 9.95 (0-88908-519-6) Self-Counsel Pr.
Ode, David. Of Eagles & Other Truths. LC 87-50265. 50p. 1987. 6.95 (1-55523-076-8) Winston-Derek.
O'Dea, Desmond J. The Cyclical Timing of Labor Market Indicators in Great Britain & the United States. (Explorations in Economic Research Two Ser.: No. 2). 36p. 1975. reprint ed. 35.00 (0-685-61379-8) Natl Bur Econ Res.
O'Dea-Evans, Pat. Leisure Education for Addicted Persons. LC 90-92064. (Illus.). 111p. (Orig.). (C). 1990. student ed 5.00 (1-879078-03-1); pap. text ed. 29.00 (1-879078-04-X) Pea Pod IL.
O'Dea, J., jt. auth. see Fee, Derek A.
***O'Dea, John.** History of the Ancient Order of Hibernians & Ladies' Auxiliary. (C). 1995. text ed. 49.95x (0-268-01108-7); pap. text ed. 29.95x (0-268-01109-5) U of Notre Dame Pr.
O'Dea, Judith L., jt. auth. see Taguchi, Dorothy M.
Odea, Mark. Red Bud Women-Four Dramatic Episodes. LC 76-40391. (One-Act Plays in Reprint Ser.). 1976. 15.00 (0-8486-2006-2) Roth Pub Inc.
***O'Dea, Michael.** Jean-Jacques Rousseau: Music, Illusion, & Desire. LC 94-45305. 1995. write for info. (0-312-12570-4) St Martin.
O'Dea, Thomas F. Mormons. LC 57-6984. 1964. pap. text ed. 11.00 (0-226-61744-0, P162) U Ch Pr.
O'Dea, Thomas F. & Aviad, Janet O. The Sociology of Religion. 144p. (C). 1983. text ed. 26.00 (0-13-821066-7); pap. text ed. write for info. (0-13-821058-6) P-H.
Oded, Arye. Africa & the Middle East Conflict. LC 87-9576. 244p. 1987. lib. bdg. 40.00 (1-55587-057-0) Lynne Rienner.
Odegaard, Charles E. Dear Doctor: A Personal Letter to a Physician. 172p. (Orig.). 1987. pap. text ed. 3.00 (0-318-23186-7) H J Kaiser.
Odegaard, Charles E., et al. Man & Learning in Modern Society. LC 59-15076. (Illus.). 203p. 1959. 20.00 (0-295-73835-9) U of Wash Pr.
Odegaard, H., ed. Small Wastewater Treatment Plants. (Water Science & Technology Ser.: No. 22). (Illus.). 392p. 1990. pap. 155.00 (0-08-040764-1, Pergamon Pr) Elsevier.
Odegaard, H., ed. see Second International Conference on Design & Operation of Small Wastewater Treatment Plants Staff.
Odegaard, Thomas A. Study Guide to Accompany Green, "Macroeconomics: Analysis & Applications" 293p. (C). 1993. pap. text ed. 21.00 (0-03-043632-X) Dryden Pr.
— Study Guide to Accompany Green, "Macroeconomics: Analysis & Applications" 293p. (C). 1993. pap. text ed. 28.00 (0-03-043633-8) Dryden Pr.
Odegard, Gordon. Modeling the Clinchfield Railroad in N Scale. (Illus.). 64p. 9.95 (0-89024-544-4) Kalmbach.
Odegard, Knut. Bee Buzz, Salmon Leap. Johnston, George, tr. 48p. 1988. 9.95 (0-921254-01-6, Pub. by Penumbra Pr CN) U of Toronto Pr.
Odegard, Peter H. & Helms, E. Allen. American Politics: A Study in Political Dynamics. LC 73-19164. (Politics & People Ser.). 900p. 1974. reprint ed. 69.95 (0-405-05886-1) Ayer.
Odeh & Owen. Attribute Sampling Plans, Tables of Tests & Confidence Limits for Proportions. (Statistics: Textbooks & Monographs: Vol. 49). 384p. 1983. 125.00 (0-8247-7136-2) Dekker.
Odeh, H. S. Impact of Inflation on the Level of Economic Activity. 112p. 1964. text ed. 62.00 (0-677-61565-5) Gordon & Breach.
Odeh, R., jt. auth. see Shah, B. K.
Odeh, R., et al, eds. Pocket Book of Statistical Tables. (Statistics: Textbooks & Monographs: Vol. 22). 184p. 1977. 49.75 (0-8247-6515-X) Dekker.
Odeh, Robert E. & Fox, Martin. Sample Size Choice: Charts for Experiments with Linear Models. LC 75-10347. (Statistics, Textbooks & Monographs: No. 14). 204p. reprint ed. pap. 58.20 (0-8357-3524-9, 2052302) Bks Demand.
Odeh, Robert E. & Owen, D. B. Tables for Normal Tolerance Limits, Sampling Plans & Screening. LC 79-27905. (Statistics, Textbooks & Monographs: No. 32). 332p. reprint ed. pap. 94.70 (0-7837-7135-5, 2052529) Bks Demand.
Odekon, Mehmet, jt. ed. see Nas, Tevfik F.
Odel, G. C. Annals of New York Stage. 1993. reprint ed. lib. bdg. 89.00 (0-7812-5282-2) Rprt Serv.
***Odelain, Olivier.** Dictionnaire des Noms Propres de la Bible. 536p. (FRE.). 1978. 115.00 (0-7859-7761-9, 2204011630) Fr & Eur.
Odell, Allen, jt. auth. see Hohensee, Donald.
O'Dell, Amanda. Kentucky Fire. 1990. mass mkt. 4.25 (0-8217-2999-3) Zebra.
Odell, Bill. When a Chip Was off the Old Block: A Time of Rutabagas & Childhood - And Beyond. 216p. 1990. 13.95 (0-533-08482-2) Vantage.
O'Dell, Carla S., jt. auth. see Grayson, C. Jackson, Jr.
Odell, Catherine M. Father Solanus: The Story of Solanus Casey, O. F. M. Cap. LC 87-62387. 1988. pap. 7.95 (0-87973-486-8, 486) Our Sunday Visitor.
Odell, Daniel, jt. auth. see Reynolds, John, III.
O'Dell, De Forest. The History of Journalism Education in the United States. LC 78-177129. (Columbia University. Teachers College. Contributions to Education Ser.: No. 653). reprint ed. 37.50 (0-404-55653-1) AMS Pr.
Odell, E. & Rosenthal, H. P., eds. Functional Analysis: Proceedings, the University of Texas at Austin, 1987. (Lecture Notes in Mathematics Ser.: Vol. 1470). viii, 199p. 1991. pap. 32.00 (0-387-54206-X) Spr-Verlag.
Odell, Eric. Robinson Crusoe's Return. Reginald, R. & Menville, Douglas, eds. LC 75-46298. (Supernatural & Occult Fiction Ser.). 1976. reprint ed. lib. bdg. 17.95 (0-405-08158-8) Ayer.
O'Dell, Felicity, jt. auth. see Lane, David.
Odell, G. & Segel, Lee A. Biograph: Software & Software Manual for Modeling Dynamic Phenomena in Molecular & Cellular Biology. (Illus.). 96p. 1987. pap. 64.95 (0-521-33973-1) Cambridge U Pr.
Odell, G. V., jt. ed. see Ownby, C. L.
Odell, George C. Annals of the New York Stage, 15 Vols, Set. LC 77-116018. reprint ed. 1,425.00 (0-404-07830-3) AMS Pr.
— Shakespeare-from Betterton to Irving, 2 vols., 1. LC 63-23277. (Illus.). 1972. reprint ed. 30.95 (0-405-08825-6) Ayer.
— Shakespeare-from Betterton to Irving, 2 vols., 2. LC 63-23277. (Illus.). 1972. reprint ed. 30.95 (0-405-08826-4) Ayer.
— Shakespeare-from Betterton to Irving, 2 vols., Set. LC 63-23277. (Illus.). 1972. reprint ed. 60.95 (0-405-08824-8) Ayer.
Odell, George H., jt. ed. see Henry, Donald O.
***O'Dell, Gracie.** Gracie's Story: Tales of a Sharecropper's Daughter. (Illus.). 120p. (Orig.). 1995. pap. 10.00 (1-885480-03-2) Pioneer Pubng.
Odell, J. W., jt. auth. see Cawson, R. A.
Odell, James. An Essay on the Elements, Accents, & Prosody of the English Language. (Anglistica & Americana Ser.: No. 47). vii, 205p. 1969. reprint ed. 44.20 (0-685-66496-1, 05102590, Pub. by Georg Olms GW) Lubrecht & Cramer.
Odell, James J., jt. auth. see Martin, James.
O'Dell, James P., ed. see Nee, Watchman.
O'Dell, James R. Crises in Midwifery. 50p. (Orig.). 1989. pap. write for info. (0-933865-17-1) Doris Pubns.
— Crises in Midwifery. LC 88-82207. 33p. (Orig.). 1988. pap. text ed. 5.00 (0-933856-17-2) Green Rvr Writers.
Odell, Jay S., jt. auth. see Goodway, Martha.
O'Dell, Jennifer. Meditations for Success. Ramsden, Francis, ed. 112p. (Orig.). Date not set. pap. 7.95 (0-9637428-0-9) Visions Unltd.
O'Dell, Jerry W., jt. auth. see Karson, Samuel.

***O'Dell, John. The River to River Trail Guide in Southern Illinois. (Illus.). 52p. 1995. pap. 19.95x (0-9646435-0-2) River to River Trl Soc.**
THE RIVER TO RIVER TRAIL GUIDE describes the route of the River to River Trail from historic Battery Rock on the Ohio River to equally historic Devil's Backbone Park at Grand Tower on the Mississippi. The trail is 146 miles mostly through the Shawnee National Forest for hikers, equestrians & some mountain bikes & goes through seven wilderness areas & several National Scenic Attractions. The trail is described in detail through a narrative & then shown on topographic maps alongside. There are plenty of vistas, deep forests, rock monuments & history noted in the trail guide. The trail is part of the southern leg of the American Discovery Trail that extends coast to coast & is considered one of the best trails in the country. Order from River to River Trail Society, 1142 Winkleman, Harrisburg, IL 62946, 618-252-6789. ***Publisher Provided Annotation.***

Odell, John, jt. auth. see Dibble, Anne.
Odell, John, jt. auth. see Lang, David.
Odell, John, jt. auth. see Matzinger-Tchakerian, Margit.
Odell, John P., jt. auth. see Clark, John S.
Odell, John S. & Willett, Thomas D., eds. International Trade Policies: Gains from Exchange Between Economics & Political Science. LC 90-32073. (Studies In International Trade Policy). 296p. (C). 1993. text ed. 47.50 (0-472-10153-6); pap. text ed. 19.95 (0-472-08197-7) U of Mich Pr.
Odell, Karen, jt. auth. see Porrazzo, Ed.
***O'Dell, Kathleen.** Concepts in Nutrition. (RN NCLEX Ser.). 300p. (Orig.). (C). 1995. pap. text ed. 18.95 (1-56930-017-8) Skidmore Roth Pub.
Odell, Kerry A. Capital Mobilization & Regional Financial Markets: The Pacific Coast States, 1850-1920. rev. ed. LC 92-27793. (Financial Sector of the American Economy Ser.). 240p. 1992. 60.00 (0-8153-0959-7) Garland.
Odell, Lee, ed. Theory & Practice in the Teaching of Writing: Rethinking the Discipline. LC 92-40547. 352p. (C). 1993. 39.95 (0-8093-1755-9); pap. 19.95 (0-8093-1947-0) S Ill U Pr.
Odell, Lee & Goswami, Dixie, eds. Writing in Nonacademic Settings. (Guilford Perspectives in Writing Research Ser.). 553p. 1986. lib. bdg. 50.00 (0-89862-252-2); pap. text ed. 24.95 (0-89862-906-3) Guilford Pr.
Odell, Marcia L. Divide & Conquer. Bruchey, Stuart, ed. LC 78-56681. (Management of Public Lands in the United States Ser.). 1979. lib. bdg. 42.95 (0-405-11347-1) Ayer.
O'Dell, Mary. Bridesongs. Xavier Oone' Juaseaux, pseud., ed. 43p. (Orig.). 1989. 6.50 (0-9623666-0-9) Green Rvr Writers.
O'Dell, Mary, ed. see Miller, Jim W.
O'Dell, Mary E., ed. see Gatus, Tomas W.
O'Dell, Mary E., ed. see Pennington, Lee.
Odell, Michael E. A Layman's Gold Investment Manual: A Book on Picking & Choosing. Palmquist, Joe, ed. (Illus.). 192p. (Orig.). (C). 1989. pap. 17.95 (0-924380-00-4) Veritas Rsch Pub.
— Silver Investments Volatility & Boredon for the Enduring. Palmquist, Joe, ed. (Illus.). 176p. (C). 1989. pap. text ed. 14.95 (0-924380-01-2) Veritas Rsch Pub.
Odell, P. L., jt. auth. see Newman, T. C.
O'Dell, Peter. Ham Radio Horizons: The Book: What Ham Radio Is All about & How to Get Started. (Illus.). 120p. (Orig.). 1995. pap. 12.95 (0-943016-03-7) CQ Commns Inc.
— Ham Radio Horizons: The Book: What Ham Radio Is All about & How to Get Started. (Orig.). 1995. vhs 19.95 (0-614-05116-9) CQ Commns Inc.
Odell, Peter R. & Preston, David A. Economies & Societies in Latin America: A Geographical Interpretation. 2nd ed. LC 77-12400. 307p. reprint ed. pap. 87.50 (0-318-34860-8, 2031025) Bks Demand.
Odell, Rice, jt. auth. see Rodes, Barbara K.
O'Dell, Richard F. Marquette on a Vanishing Frontier. (Illus.). 16p. 1978. pap. 2.50 (0-938746-09-X) Marquette Cnty.
— Reaching Out: A History of the Rotary Club of Marquette, Michigan 1916-1981. Duerfeldt, Pryse H., ed. LC 82-60037. (Illus.). 254p. 1982. 13.00 (0-9609764-0-X) Rotary Club.
O'Dell, Ruth W. Over the Misty Blue Hills: The Story of Cocke County, Tennessee. 436p. 1982. reprint ed. 37.50 (0-89308-276-7, TN 53) Southern Hist Pr.
Odell, Sandra J., jt. ed. see O'Hair, Mary J.
Odell, Sandra J., jt. auth. see O'Hair, Mary.
O'Dell, Scott. Alexandra. 1987. pap. 3.50 (0-449-70290-1) Fawcett.
— The Black Pearl. 96p. (gr. 7 up). 1977. mass mkt. 3.99 (0-440-90803-5, LFL) Dell.
— Black Pearl. LC 67-23311. (Illus.). 160p. (J). (gr. 7 up). 1967. 14.95 (0-395-06961-0) HM.
— Black Star, Bright Dawn. 112p. 1989. mass mkt. 3.99 (0-449-70340-1, Juniper) Fawcett.
— Black Star, Bright Dawn. LC 87-35351. 144p. (J). (gr. 5-9). 1988. 14.95 (0-395-47778-6) HM.
— The Captive. 244p. (J). (gr. 7 up). 1979. 14.95 (0-395-27811-2) HM.
— Carlota. LC 77-9468. (Illus.). 176p. (J). (gr. 5-9). 1977. 14.95 (0-395-25487-6) HM.
— Carlotta. 144p. (J). (gr. k-12). 1989. mass mkt. 3.99 (0-440-90928-7, LFL) Dell.
— The Castle in the Sea. 160p. (YA). (gr. 7 up). 1984. pap. 3.50 (0-449-70123-9, Juniper) Fawcett.
— The Castle in the Sea. 192p. (J). (gr. 7-p). 1983. 13.95 (0-395-34831-5) HM.
— The Hawk That Dare Not Hunt by Day. (Light Line Ser.). (Illus.). 192p. (J). (gr. 4-6). 1986. reprint ed. pap. 5.95 (0-89084-368-6) Bob Jones Univ Pr.
— Janey. (YA). (gr. 7-12). 1986. write for info. (0-318-60130-3) HM.
— King's Fifth. (Illus.). (J). (gr. 7-10). 1966. 15.95 (0-395-06963-7) HM.
— My Name Is Not Angelica. (J). (gr. k-6). 1990. mass mkt. 3.99 (0-440-40379-0, YB) Dell.
— My Name Is Not Angelica. 144p. (J). (gr. 5-9). 1989. 14.95 (0-395-51061-9) HM.
— Representative Photoplays Analyzed. 1972. 44.95 (0-8490-0947-2) Gordon Pr.
— The Road to Damietta. 240p. (J). 1987. mass mkt. 3.99 (0-449-70233-2, Juniper) Fawcett.
— Sarah Bishop. (J). (gr. 7 up). 1980. 14.95 (0-395-29185-2) HM.
— Sarah Bishop. 240p. (J). (gr. 7-p). 1991. pap. 3.25 (0-590-44651-7, Point) Scholastic Inc.
— The Serpent Never Sleeps: A Novel of Jamestown & Pocahontas. (YA). (gr. 8 up). 1988. mass mkt. 3.99 (0-449-70328-2, Juniper) Fawcett.

O

An Asterisk (*) at the beginning of an entry indicates that the title is appearing in BIP for the first time.

— The Serpent Never Sleeps: A Novel of Jamestown & Pocahontas. (Illus.). 240p. (J). (gr. 5 up). 1987. 16.95 (*0-395-44242-7*) HM.

— Sing down the Moon. 138p. (gr. 5 up). 1976. mass mkt. 3.99 (*0-440-97975-7*, LFL) Dell.

— Sing Down the Moon. 144p. (J). (gr. 5 up). 1992. mass mkt. 3.99 (*0-440-40673-0*, YB) Dell.

— Sing Down the Moon. LC 71-98513. (J). (gr. 5 up). 1970. 14.95 (*0-395-10919-1*) HM.

— Spanish Smile. 1983. pap. 3.50 (*0-449-70094-1*, Juniper) Fawcett.

— Streams to the River, River to the Sea. 176p. 1987. mass mkt. 3.99 (*0-449-70244-8*, Juniper) Fawcett.

— Streams to the River, River to the Sea: A Novel of Sacagawea. (YA). 1986. 14.95 (*0-395-40430-4*) HM.

— Streams to the River, River to the Sea: A Novel of Sacagawea. large type ed. 312p. (J). (gr. 7 up). 1989. lib. bdg. 14.95 (*0-8161-4811-2*, Large Print Bks) Hall.

— Thunder Rolling in the Mountains. (J). 1993. mass mkt. 3.99 (*0-440-40879-2*) Dell.

— Zia. 144p. (J). (gr. 4 up). 1978. mass mkt. 3.99 (*0-440-99904-9*, LFL) Dell.

— Zia. LC 75-44156. (Illus.). 224p. (J). (gr. 4-8). 1976. 14.95 (*0-395-24393-9*) HM.

***Odell, Scott.** Zia. (J). (gr. 4-7). 1995. pap. 3.99 (*0-440-41001-0*) Dell.

O'Dell, Scott & Hall, Elizabeth. Thunder Rolling in the Mountains. (Illus.). 144p. (J). (gr. 5-9). 1992. 14.95 (*0-395-59966-0*) HM.

O'Dell, Scott, jt. auth. see Hall, Elizabeth.

Odell-Scott, David W. A Post-Patriarchal Christology. (American Academy of Religion Academy Ser.). 280p. (C). 1991. 29.95 (*1-55540-657-2*, 010178); pap. 19.95 (*1-55540-658-0*, 010178) Scholars Pr GA.

O'Dell, T. H. Circuits for Electronic Instrumentation. (Illus.). 200p. (C). 1991. 84.95 (*0-521-40428-2*) Cambridge U Pr.

— Electronic Circuit Design: Art & Practice. 200p. 1988. pap. 29.95 (*0-521-35858-2*) Cambridge U Pr.

***O'Dell, Tom H.** Inventions & Official Secrecy: A History of Secret Patents in the U. K. (Illus.). 220p. 1995. 39.95 (*0-19-825942-5*) OUP.

O'Dell, Tommy. The Search for the King. (Adventures of Zor Ser.). 182p. (Orig.). 1992. pap. 9.99 (*1-56043-650-6*) Destiny Image.

O'Dell, William F. Effective Business Decision Making: And the Educated Guess. LC 90-13489. (Illus.). 130p. 1993. 27.95 (*0-8442-3289-0*, NTC Busn Bks); pap. 14.95 (*0-8442-3291-2*, NTC Busn Bks) NTC Pub Grp.

Odelstad, J. Invariance & Structural Dependence. (Lecture Notes in Economics & Mathematical Systems Ser.: Vol. 380). (Illus.). xii, 245p. 1992. pap. 50.00 (*0-387-55260-X*) Spr-Verlag.

***Odem, Mary E.** Delinquent Daughters: Protecting & Policing Adolescent Female Sexuality in the United States, 1885-1920. LC 95-13185. (Gender & American Culture Ser.). 1995. write for info. (*0-8078-2215-9*); pap. write for info. (*0-8078-4528-0*) U of NC Pr.

O'Dempsey, F., tr. see Pilnyak, Boris, pseud.

Oden & Owen. Parts Per Million Values for Estimating Quality Levels. (Statistics: Vol. 87). 360p. 1988. 135.00 (*0-8247-7950-9*) Dekker.

Oden, Amy, ed. In Her Words: Women's Writings in the History of Christian Thought. LC 93-23624. 384p. (Orig.). 1994. pap. 18.95 (*0-687-45979-2*) Abingdon.

Oden, Bertil & Othman, Haroub, eds. Regional Cooperation in Southern Africa: A Post-Apartheid Perspective. (Scandinavian Institute of African Studies). 243p. 1989. 59.00x (*91-7106-298-X*, Pub. by Almqv & Wiksell SW) Coronet Bks.

***Oden, Bertil, et al.** The South African Tripod: Studies on Economics, Politics & Conflict. (Scandinavian Institute of African Studies). 281p. (Orig.). 1994. pap. 49.50x (*91-7106-341-2*, Pub. by Almqv & Wiksell SW) Coronet Bks.

Oden, Chester W., Jr., jt. auth. see MacDonald, W. Scott.

Oden, Fay G. Where Is Calvin? (Illus.). 48p. (Orig.). (J). (gr. 2-6). 1994. pap. text ed. 6.95 (*0-9638946-0-9*) Tennedo Pubs.

Oden, Howard W., et al. Handbook of Material & Capacity Requirements. LC 93-14719. 1993. Acid-free paper. text ed. 59.50 (*0-07-047909-7*) McGraw.

Oden, J. T., jt. auth. see Kikuchi, N.

Oden, J. Tinsley, ed. Reliability in Computational Mechanics: Proceedings of the Workshop, Austin, TX, 26-28 Oct., 1989. 388p. 1990. reprint ed. 192.25 (*0-444-88560-9*, North Holland) Elsevier.

Oden, J. Tinsley & Becker, E. B. Computational Methods in Nonlinear Mechanics Structures. 1981. pap. 56.00 (*0-08-026153-1*, Pergamon Pr) Elsevier.

Oden, J. Tinsley, ed. see Carey, Graham F., et al.

Oden, J. Tinsley, ed. see International Conference on Computational Methods in Nonlinear Mechanics Staff.

Oden, J. Tinsley, jt. auth. see Rabier, P. J.

O'Den, Jeff & Sexton, John. Secret Thoughts of Men: Why Men Won't Talk. 480p. 1992. pap. 19.95 (*0-9631291-0-4*) Intl Assn Men.

Oden, Melita H., jt. auth. see Terman, Lewis M.

Oden, R. A. Studies in Lucian's De Syria Dea. LC 76-54988. (Harvard Semitic Monographs: No. 15). (Illus.). 189p. reprint ed. pap. 53.90 (*0-7837-5412-4*, 2045176) Bks Demand.

Oden, Richard L., ed. see Dryden, John & Shadwell, Thomas.

Oden, Robert A., Jr., jt. auth. see Attridge, Harold W.

Oden, Robert A.

Oden, S., et al. Challenging the Potential: Programs for Talented Disadvantaged Youth. LC 91-35023. 400p. 1991. pap. 29.00 (*0-929816-35-8*) High-Scope.

Oden, Sherri & Weikart, David P. Workshops. LC 94-17644. (Program Guidebooks Ser.). 1994. write for info. (*0-929816-83-8*) High-Scope.

Oden, Thomas. The Transforming Power of Grace. 224p. (Orig.). 1993. pap. 16.95 (*0-687-42260-4*) Abingdon.

Oden, Thomas C. After Modernity... What? 1992. pap. 16.99 (*0-310-75391-0*) Zondervan.

— Becoming a Minister. (Classical Pastoral Care Ser.). 192p. 1994. reprint ed. pap. 10.99 (*0-8010-6763-4*) Baker Bk.

— Corrective Love: The Power of Communion Discipline. LC 95-4150. (Scholarship Today Ser.). 1995. write for info. (*0-570-04803-6*) Concordia.

— Crisis Ministries. (Classical Pastoral Care Ser.). 278p. 1994. reprint ed. pap. 12.99 (*0-8010-6766-9*) Baker Bk.

— First & Second Timothy, Titus. (Interpretation: A Bible Commentary for Teaching & Preaching Ser.). 192p. 1989. 20.00 (*0-8042-3143-5*, John Knox) Westminster John Knox.

— John Wesley's Scriptural Christianity. 400p. 1994. pap. 22.99 (*0-310-75321-X*) Zondervan.

— Life in the Spirit: Systematic Theology: Vol. 3. LC 90-55805. 560p. 1994. reprint ed. pap. text ed. 22.00 (*0-06-066362-6*) Harper SF.

— The Living God: Systematic Theology, Vol. 1. LC 85-45720. 416p. 1992. reprint ed. pap. text ed. 20.00 (*0-06-066363-4*) Harper SF.

— Ministry Through Word & Sacrament. (Classical Pastoral Care Ser.). 232p. 1994. reprint ed. pap. 10.99 (*0-8010-6764-2*) Baker Bk.

— Pastoral Counsel. (Classical Pastoral Care Ser.: Vol. 3). 224p. 1989. 19.95 (*0-8245-0935-8*) Crossroad NY.

— Pastoral Counsel. (Classical Pastoral Care Ser.). 297p. 1994. reprint ed. pap. 12.99 (*0-8010-6765-0*) Baker Bk.

— Pastoral Theology: Essentials of Ministry. LC 82-47753. 456p. (Orig.). 1983. pap. text ed. 21.00 (*0-06-066353-7*, RD 415) Harper SF.

— Requiem: A Lament in Three Movements. LC 94-38524. 176p. 1995. 16.95 (*0-687-01160-4*) Abingdon.

— Two Worlds: Notes on the Death of Modernity in America & Russia. LC 91-37117. 168p. (Orig.). 1992. pap. 9.99 (*0-8308-1763-8*, 1763) InterVarsity.

— The Word of Life: Systematic Theology, Vol. 2. LC 88-46011. 512p. 1992. reprint ed. pap. text ed. 23.00 (*0-06-066364-2*) Harper SF.

Oden, Thomas C., ed. Parables of Kierkegaard. (Illus.). 212p. (C). 1989. pap. text ed. 9.95 (*0-691-02053-1*) Princeton U Pr.

— Phoebe Palmer: Selected Writings. (Sources of American Spirituality Ser.). 384p. 1988. 24.95 (*0-8091-0405-9*) Paulist Pr.

Oden, ViAnn. Dialogue with a Dolphin: A Journey in Self-Awareness. Hartloff, Paul M. & Reid, Tanya, eds. (Illus.). (Orig.). 1991. pap. 10.95 (*0-944474-28-4*) Anvipa Pr.

— A New Approach to Christmas Greetings. (Christmas Ease Ser.). (Illus.). (Orig.). 1988. pap. 9.95 (*0-944474-27-6*) Anvipa Pr.

***Odenbach, Ginny & Osborn, Linda.** Sunblade. Kolsen, Wendy S., ed. (Illus.). 54p. (Orig.). (J). (gr. 3-8). 1995. pap. 3.50 (*1-885101-12-0*) Writers Pr Srv.

Odencrantz, Louise C. Italian Women in Industry: Study of Conditions in New York City. Stein, Leon, ed. LC 77-70523. (Work Ser.). (Illus.). 1977. reprint ed. lib. bdg. 33.95 (*0-405-10191-0*) Ayer.

Odendaal, Andre, ed. see Forman, Lionel.

Odendaal, P. E., ed. Mine Water Pollution, No. 2. (Water Science & Technology Ser.: Vol. 15). (Illus.). 180p. 1983. pap. 44.00 (*0-08-030423-0*, Pergamon Pr) Elsevier.

Odendahl, Teresa, ed. America's Wealthy & the Future of Foundations: A Study of Private Philanthropy in America. LC 87-7397. 325p. 1987. 34.95 (*0-87954-197-0*); pap. 24.95 (*0-87954-194-6*) Foundation Ctr.

Odendahl, Teresa, pref. Conference Proceedings, Vol. II: Second Annual Women's Policy Research Conference. LC 91-75395. 325p. (Orig.). (C). 1991. pap. text ed. 30.00 (*1-878428-04-7*) Inst Womens Policy Rsch.

Odendahl, Teresa & O'Neill, Michael, eds. Women & Power in the Nonprofit Sector. LC 93-47558. (Nonprofit Sector-Public Administration Ser.). 260p. 1994. 32.95 (*1-55542-650-6*) Jossey-Bass.

Odenheimer, Micha, tr. see Shapira, Kalonymus K.

Odenheimer, William H. Jerusalem & Its Vicinity: Familiar Lectures on the Sacred Localities Connected with the Week Before the Resurrection. Davis, Moshe, ed. (America & the Holy Land Ser.). (Illus.). 1977. reprint ed. lib. bdg. 23.95 (*0-405-10272-0*) Ayer.

Odens, James A. Submitting to Christ: Living in Light of His Lordship. 214p. (Orig.). 1990. pap. 6.95 (*0-9627088-0-1*) J A Odens.

Odens, Peter. Picacho: Life & Death of a Great Gold Mining Camp. (Illus.). 44p. 1982. reprint ed. lib. bdg. 3.50 (*0-9609484-4-9*) P R Odens.

Odens, Peter R. Along the Butterfield Trail. (Illus.). 46p. (Orig.). 1982. pap. 3.50 (*0-9609484-0-6*) P R Odens.

— Along the Cactus Border. (Illus.). 110p. 1978. pap. 3.50 (*0-9609484-1-4*) P R Odens.

— Ben Hulse: From Mountain Boy to State Senator. LC 84-158219. (Illus.). 56p. 1984. pap. 3.50 (*0-9609484-7-3*) P R Odens.

— The Desert Trackers: Men of the Border Patrol. (Illus.). 70p. (Orig.). 1972. reprint ed. per., pap. 5.00 (*0-9609484-9-X*) P R Odens.

— The Desert's Edge. 5th ed. (Illus.). 102p. 1982. reprint ed. pap. 3.50 (*0-916428-19-2*) P R Odens.

— Dreamers, Adventurers & Storytellers of the American West. (Illus.). 1988. pap. 5.00 (*0-9609484-8-1*) P R Odens.

— Father Garces: The Maverick Priest. (Illus.). 1980. pap. 3.50 (*0-9609484-3-0*) P R Odens.

— Outlaws, Heroes & Jokers of the Old Southwest. (Illus.). 77p. 1975. reprint ed. pap. 3.50 (*0-9609484-6-5*) P R Odens.

Odenstedt, Bengt. On the Origin & Early History of the Runic Script: Typology & Graphic Variation in the Older Futbark. (Acta Academiae Regiae Gustavi Adolphi Ser.: No. 59). 181p. (Orig.). 1990. pap. 50.00x (*91-85352-20-9*, Pub. by Almqv & Wiksell SW) Coronet Bks.

Odenstedt, Bengt & Persson, Gunnar, eds. Instead of Flowers: Papers in Honour of Mats Rydén. (Umea Studies in the Humanities: No. 90). 316p. (Orig.). 1989. pap. 52.50x (*91-7174-416-9*, Pub. by Umea U Bibl SW) Coronet Bks.

***Odent, Michel.** Birth Reborn. rev. ed. (Illus.). 123p. 1994. pap. 17.95 (*0-9642036-9-3*) Birth Works.

— The Nature of Birth & Breastfeeding. LC 91-44076. 160p. 1992. text ed. 16.95 (*0-89789-287-9*, H287, Bergin & Garvey) Greenwood.

Odent, Michel, jt. auth. see Johnson, Jessica.

***Odenwald, Neil & Turner, James.** Identification, Selection, & Use of Southern Plants for Landscape Design. 1987. 39.95 (*0-87511-817-8*) Claitors.

Odenwald, Neil, et al. Attracting Birds to Southern Gardens. LC 93-7572. 176p. 1993. 24.95 (*0-87833-830-6*) Taylor Pub.

Odenwald, Neil G. & Feltwell, John. Live Oak Splendor: Gardens of the Mississippi from Natchez to New Orleans. LC 92-13054. (Illus.). 192p. 1992. 35.00 (*0-87833-807-1*) Taylor Pub.

Odenwald, Sylvia B. Global Training: How to Design a Program for the Multinational Corporation. LC 93-18101. 225p. 1993. text ed. 30.00 (*1-55623-986-6*) Irwin Prof Pubng.

Odenweller, Arthur L. Predicting the Quality of Teaching: The Predictive Value of Certain Traits for Effectiveness in Teaching. LC 72-177130. (Columbia University. Teachers College. Contributions to Education Ser.: No. 676). reprint ed. 37.50 (*0-404-55676-0*) AMS Pr.

Oderman, Kevin. Ezra Pound & the Erotic Medium. LC 86-11471. xv, 160p. 1986. text ed. 27.00 (*0-8223-0672-7*) Duke.

Oderman, Stuart. Roscoe "Fatty" Arbuckle: A Biography of the Silent Film Comedian, 1887-1933. LC 92-56674. 255p. 1994. lib. bdg. 29.95 (*0-89950-872-3*) McFarland & Co.

Odes, S. H., jt. auth. see Madar, Z.

Odessey, R. Problems & Potential of Branched Chain Amino Acids in Physiology & Medicine. 356p. 1987. 162.00 (*0-444-80775-6*) Elsevier.

Odessky, Anatoly. Medical Hypnosis & Methods for Self-Control. 1990. 18.95 (*0-533-09081-4*) Vantage.

Odetola, Olatunde. Military Regimes & Development: A Comparative Analysis in African Societies. 240p. (C). 1982. pap. text ed. 16.95 (*0-04-301154-3*) Routledge Chapman & Hall.

Odetola, Theophilus O. Military Politics in Nigeria: Economic Development & Political Stability. LC 76-58232. (Illus.). 180p. 1978. 34.95 (*0-87855-100-X*) Transaction Pubs.

Odetola, Theophilus O., et al. Man & Society in Africa: An Introduction to Sociology. LC 82-23975. (Illus.). 176p. reprint ed. pap. 50.20 (*0-8357-2967-2*, 2039229) Bks Demand.

Odets, Clifford. The Big Knife. 1963. pap. 4.75 (*0-8222-0115-1*) Dramatists Play.

— The Country Girl. 1953. pap. 4.75 (*0-8222-0243-3*) Dramatists Play.

— The Flowering Peach. 1973. pap. 4.75 (*0-8222-0411-8*) Dramatists Play.

— Golden Boy. 1948. pap. 4.75 (*0-8222-0456-8*) Dramatists Play.

— Waiting for Lefty. 1989. pap. 2.75 (*0-8222-1215-3*) Dramatists Play.

— Waiting for Lefty: And Other Plays. LC 93-2795. 418p. 1993. pap. 14.00 (*0-8021-3220-0*) Grove-Atltic.

***Odets, Walt.** In the Shadow of the Epidemic: Being HIV-Negative in the Age of AIDS. LC 95-1311. (Series Q). 1995. write for info. (*0-8223-1626-9*) Duke.

***Odets, Walt & Shernoff, Michael, eds.** The Second Decade of AIDS: A Mental Health Practice Handbook. LC 94-40679. 320p. 1995. 29.95 (*1-886330-00-X*) Hatherleigh.

— The Second Decade of AIDS: A Mental Health Practice Handbook. LC 94-40679. 320p. (Orig.). 1995. pap. 19.95 (*1-886330-01-8*) Hatherleigh.

Odette, Lou. Intelligent Embedded Systems with Disk. 1990. 24.75 (*0-201-51753-1*) Addison-Wesley.

Odgaard, Ole. Private Enterprises in Rural China: A Study of Their Impact on Agriculture & Social Stratification. 210p. 1992. 68.95 (*1-85628-405-0*, Pub. by Avebury Pub UK) Ashgate Pub Co.

Odgen, Annegret S. The Great American Housewife: From Helpmate to Wage Earner, 1776-1986. LC 85-9935. (Contributions in Women's Studies: No. 61). (Illus.). 279p. 1986. text ed. 55.00 (*0-313-24752-8*, OGH/, Greenwood Pr) Greenwood.

Odgen, Edith B. The Ferns of Maine. LC 78-7982. 128p. 1978. reprint ed. pap. 6.95 (*0-89621-016-2*) U Maine Pr.

Odgen, Ellen E. Growing & Using Basil. 1990. pap. 2.95 (*0-88266-630-4*) Storey Comm Inc.

Odgen, Jack. Ancient Jewellery. 1992. pap. 11.00 (*0-520-08030-0*) U CA Pr.

Odgen, Sharon C. Optical Illusions Quilt Designs. LC 93-32469. (Design Library). 1994. write for info. (*0-486-27932-4*) Dover.

Odgers, F. J. & McClintock, F. H. Sexual Offences: A Report. Radzinowicz, L., ed. (Cambridge Studies in Criminology: Vol. 9). 1974. reprint ed. pap. 43.00 (*0-8115-0423-9*) Periodicals Srv.

Odgers, J. & Kretschmer, D. Gas Turbine Fuels & Their Influence on Combustion. LC 85-15633. (Energy & Engineering Science Ser., Abacus Bks.). 181p. 1986. text ed. 90.00 (*0-85626-342-7*) Gordon & Breach.

Odgers, Merle M. Latin Parens, Its Meanings & Uses. (Language Dissertations Ser.: No. 3). 1928. pap. 16.00 (*0-527-00749-8*) Periodicals Srv.

Odgers, O. Purchasing, Costing & Control. (C). 1985. 110.00 (*0-948315-00-8*, Pub. by S Thornes Pubs UK) St Mut.

Odgers, Peter. Purchasing, Costing & Control for Hotel & Catering Operations. 272p. (Orig.). 1985. pap. 33.50 (*0-7487-0324-1*, Pub. by Stanley Thornes UK) Trans-Atl Phila.

Odgers, Sally F. Dog Went for a Walk. LC 92-27100. (Illus.). (J). (gr. 3 up). 1993. 2.50 (*0-383-03564-3*) SRA Schl Grp.

— Mrs. Honey's List. LC 93-6572. (J). 1994. write for info. (*0-383-03703-4*) SRA Schl Grp.

— Tasmania: A Guide. (Illus.). 224p. 1992. reprint ed. pap. 12.95 (*0-86417-236-2*, Pub. by Kangaroo Pr AT) Seven Hills Bk.

— Up the Stairs. LC 92-21395. (Voyages Ser.). (Illus.). (J). 1993. 4.25 (*0-383-03601-1*) SRA Schl Grp.

— Wiz. LC 92-31952. (Voyages Ser.). (Illus.). (J). 1993. 3.75 (*0-383-03608-9*) SRA Schl Grp.

Odgvist, Folke K. Mathematical Theory of Creep & Creep Ruptures. 2nd ed. LC 75-306213. (Oxford Mathematical Monographs). (Illus.). 213p. reprint ed. pap. 60.80 (*0-317-08339-2*, 2051834) Bks Demand.

Odham, Goran, et al, eds. Gas Chromatography-Mass Spectroscopy: Applications in Microbiology. LC 83-16102. 460p. 1984. 110.00 (*0-306-41314-0*, Plenum Pr) Plenum.

***Odhiambo, Atieno.** The Luo. (Heritage Library of African Peoples Ser.). 64p. 1995. 15.95 (*0-8239-1758-4*) Rosen Group.

Odhiambo, E. S., jt. auth. see Cohen, David W.

Odhner, C. Th, tr. see Swedenborg, Emanuel.

Odhner, Carl T. Michael Servetus, His Life & Teachings. LC 83-45626. reprint ed. 18.50 (*0-404-19844-9*) AMS Pr.

Odhner, Hugo L. The Human Mind. (Illus.). 127p. 1988. reprint ed. 9.95 (*0-915221-66-7*) Swedenborg Sci Assn.

— The Moral Life. 142p. 1985. reprint ed. 3.75 (*0-910557-08-X*) Acad New Church.

Odhner, Hugo L., jt. ed. see Pitcairn, Harold F.

Odhner, Hugo Lj. Principles of the New Philosophy. 2nd rev. ed. 36p. 1986. reprint ed. pap. 4.00 (*0-915221-13-6*) Swedenborg Sci Assn.

Odhner, Hugo Lj., tr. see Swedenborg, Emanuel.

Odhner, J. Durban. Alpha & Omega. 63p. (Orig.). 1978. pap. 3.00 (*0-915221-27-6*) Swedenborg Sci Assn.

Odhner, John. Light Burden: Easier Ways to Shun Evils. 48p. (Orig.). 1987. pap. 1.00 (*0-910557-16-0*) Acad New Church.

Odhner, John D., ed. see Swedenborg, Emanuel.

***Odhner, Philip N.** The Formation of the Church in Man. 184p. 1994. 17.50 (*1-883270-00-6*) Swedenborg Assn.

— The Lord's Prayer. 77p. 1994. 12.50 (*1-883270-01-4*) Swedenborg Assn.

— Reflections on the Book, "The Doctrine of Nova Hierosolyma Concerning the Sacred Scripture" 86p. 1987. 12.50 (*1-883270-07-3*) Swedenborg Assn.

ODI Staff. Making Teams Work: A Guide to Creating & Managing Teams. 142p. 1993. write for info. (*0-9636723-0-4*) ODI.

Odiaga, Lola, tr. see Rephann, Ricahrd T.

O'Diam, Eva. Love & Justice. (Covenant Bible Study Ser.). 48p. 1990. pap. 3.95 (*0-87178-543-9*) Brethren.

Odian, George. Principles of Polymerization. 3rd ed. 800p. 1991. text ed. 69.95 (*0-471-61020-8*) Wiley.

— Schaum's Outline of General, Organic, & Biological Chemistry. 1994. pap. text ed. 14.95 (*0-07-047609-8*) McGraw.

***O'Diear, James.** Season of the Tigers: A Novel of Pre-Pearl Harbor Espionage & Counter-Espionage. Hall, Kathryn, ed. (Illus.). 320p. Date not set. pap. text ed. 12.95 (*1-57090-015-9*) Alexander Bks.

***Odier, Antoine.** Dictionnaire des Telecommunications. 352p. (FRE.). 1992. pap. 17.95 (*0-7859-7898-4*, 2501016742) Fr & Eur.

Odier, Charles. Anxiety & Magic Thinking: The Psychogenetic Analysis of Phobia & the Neurosis of Abandonment. Schoelly, Marie-Louise & Sherfey, Mary J., trs. LC 56-9335. 316p. 1956. text ed. 38.00 (*0-8236-0400-4*) Intl Univs Pr.

Odier, Daniel. Nirvana-Tao: The Secret Meditation Techniques of the Taoist & Buddhist Masters. (Illus.). 208p. (Orig.). 1986. pap. 12.95 (*0-89281-045-9*) Inner Tradit.

Odier, Daniel, see Delacorta, pseud..

Odier, Georges. A Revolutionary Approach to Successful Fly Fishing: Swimming Flies. LC 83-51086. (Illus.). 222p. 1984. 19.95 (*0-913276-48-0*) Stone Wall Pr.

Odier, Pierre. The Rock: A History of Alcatraz, the Fort - The Prison. (Illus.). 260p. 1982. 17.00 (*0-9611632-0-8*) Odier CA.

Odievre, Michel, jt. auth. see Alagille, Daniel.

Odifreddi, P. G. Classical Recursion Theory: The Theory Functions & Sets of Natural Numbers. (Studies in Logic & the Foundations of Mathematics: No. 125). 668p. 1989. 107.75 (*0-444-87295-7*, North Holland) Elsevier.

Odifreddi, Piergiorgio, ed. Logic & Computer Science. (APIC Studies in Data Processing). 430p. 1990. text ed. 66.00 (*0-12-524220-4*) Acad Pr.

Odifreddi, Piergiorgio, ed. see Homer, S., et al.

Odijk, E., et al, eds. PARLE 'Eighty-Nine Parallel Architectues & Languages Europe, Vol. II: Parallel Languages. (Lecture Notes in Computer Science Ser.: Vol. 366). xiii, 442p. 1989. pap. 44.00 (*0-387-51285-3*) Spr-Verlag.

— PARLE Eighty-Nine Parallel Architectures & Languages Europe, Vol. I: Parallel Architectures. (Lecture Notes in Computer Science Ser.: Vol. 365). xiii, 478p. 1989. pap. 51.00 (*0-387-51284-5*) Spr-Verlag.

Odijk, Pamela. The Ancient World, 12 bks., Set. (Illus.). 48p. (J). (gr. 5-8). 1991. lib. bdg. 179.40 (*0-382-09883-8*) Silver Burdett Pr.

— The Ancient World, 12 bks., Set, 48pg. ea. (Illus.). (J). (gr. 5-8). 1991. pap. 95.40 (*0-382-24258-0*) Silver Burdett Pr.

— The Aztecs. (Ancient World Ser.). (Illus.). 48p. (J). (gr. 5-8). 1990. pap. 7.95 (*0-382-24262-9*) Silver Burdett Pr.

— The Aztecs. (Ancient World Ser.). (Illus.). 48p. (J). (gr. 5-8). 1990. lib. bdg. 14.95 (*0-382-09887-0*) Silver Burdett Pr.

— The Chinese. (Ancient World Ser.). (Illus.). 48p. (J). (gr. 5-8). 1991. lib. bdg. 14.95 (*0-382-09894-3*) Silver Burdett Pr.

— The Chinese. (Ancient World Ser.). (Illus.). 48p. (J). (gr. 5-8). 1991. teacher ed 4.50 (*0-382-24285-8*); pap. 7.95 (*0-382-24271-8*) Silver Burdett Pr.

— The Egyptians. (Ancient World Ser.). (Illus.). 48p. (J). (gr. 5-8). 1989. teacher ed 4.50 (*0-382-24276-9*); pap. 7.95 (*0-382-24261-0*) Silver Burdett Pr.

— The Egyptians. (Ancient World Ser.). (Illus.). 48p. (J). (gr. 5-8). 1989. lib. bdg. 14.95 (*0-382-09886-2*) Silver Burdett Pr.

— The Greeks. (Ancient World Ser.). (Illus.). 48p. (J). (gr. 5-8). 1989. teacher ed 4.50 (*0-382-24274-2*); pap. 7.95 (*0-382-24259-9*) Silver Burdett Pr.

— The Greeks. (Ancient World Ser.). (Illus.). 48p. (J). (gr. 5-8). 1989. lib. bdg. 14.95 (*0-382-09884-6*) Silver Burdett Pr.

— The Incas. (Ancient World Ser.). (Illus.). 48p. (J). (gr. 5-8). 1990. 7.95 (*0-382-24264-5*); teacher ed 4.50 (*0-382-24279-3*); lib. bdg. 14.95 (*0-382-09889-7*) Silver Burdett Pr.

— The Israelites. (Ancient World Ser.). (Illus.). 48p. (J). (gr. 5-8). 1990. 7.95 (*0-382-24263-7*); teacher ed 4.50 (*0-382-24278-5*); lib. bdg. 14.95 (*0-382-09888-9*) Silver Burdett Pr.

— The Japanese. (Ancient World Ser.). (Illus.). 48p. (J). (gr. 5-8). 1991. 7.95 (*0-382-24272-6*); teacher ed 4.50 (*0-382-24286-6*); lib. bdg. 14.95 (*0-382-09898-6*) Silver Burdett Pr.

— The Mayas. (Ancient World Ser.). (Illus.). 48p. (J). (gr. 5-8). 1990. 7.95 (*0-382-24265-3*); teacher ed 4.50 (*0-382-24280-7*); lib. bdg. 14.95 (*0-382-09890-0*) Silver Burdett Pr.

— The Phoenicians. (Ancient World Ser.). (Illus.). 48p. (J). (gr. 5-8). 1989. 7.95 (*0-382-24266-1*); 4.50 (*0-382-24281-5*); lib. bdg. 14.95 (*0-382-09891-9*) Silver Burdett Pr.

— The Romans. (Ancient World Ser.). (Illus.). 48p. (J). (gr. 5-8). 1989. 7.95 (*0-382-24260-2*); teacher ed 4.50 (*0-382-24275-0*); lib. bdg. 14.95 (*0-382-09885-4*) Silver Burdett Pr.

— The Sumerians. (Ancient World Ser.). (Illus.). 48p. (J). (gr. 5-8). 1990. 7.95 (*0-382-24268-8*); 4.50 (*0-382-24282-3*); lib. bdg. 14.95 (*0-382-09892-7*) Silver Burdett Pr.

— The Vikings. Easton, Emily, ed. (Ancient World Ser.). (Illus.). 48p. (J). (gr. 5-8). 1990. 7.95 (*0-382-24269-6*); teacher ed 4.50 (*0-382-24283-1*); lib. bdg. 14.95 (*0-382-09893-5*) Silver Burdett Pr.

Odin, Dexter, jt. auth. see Odin, Paula.

Odin, G. S., ed. Green Marine Clays: Oolitic Ironstone Facies, Verdine Facies, Glaucony Facies & Caledonite - Bearing Rock Facies - A Comparative Study. (Developments in Sedimentology Ser.: No. 45). 445p. 1988. 107.75 (*0-444-87120-9*) Elsevier.

Odin, Gilles S., ed. Numerical Dating in Stratigraphy, Pt. 1. LC 81-14792. (Wiley-Interscience Publication Ser.). 658p. reprint ed. pap. 177.70 (*0-7837-3198-1*, 2043245) Bks Demand.

— Numerical Dating in Stratigraphy, Pt. 2. LC 81-14792. (Wiley-Interscience Publication Ser.). 438p. reprint ed. pap. 124.90 (*0-7837-3199-X*) Bks Demand.

Odin, Paula & Odin, Dexter. Yachtsman's Legal Guide to Co-Ownership. 166p. 1981. 4.95 (*0-8286-0104-6*, 60765) J De Graff.

Odin, Steve. Process Metaphysics & Hua-Yen Buddhism: A Critical Study of Cumulative Penetration vs. Interpretation. LC 81-9388. 242p. (C). 1983. 59.50 (*0-87395-568-4*); pap. 19.95 (*0-87395-569-2*) State U NY Pr.

— The Social Turn in Zen & American Pragmatism. LC 94-33404. (Constructive Postmodern Thought Ser.). 384p. 1995. text ed. 74.50x (*0-7914-2491-X*); pap. text ed. 24.95x (*0-7914-2492-8*) State U NY Pr.

Odingo, Lumumba & Khalifah, H. Khalif. Bumpy Johnson & Lumumba Odingo: Two Uncompromised Black Men in the Slavery Society Called the United States of America. (Illus.). 82p. (Orig.). Date not set. pap. 7.95 (*1-56411-013-3*) Untd Bros & Sis.

Odintsov, V. A., jt. auth. see Kondrat'ev, N. Y.

Odio, Elena B., tr. see Delannoy, Luc.

Odio, Elena B., tr. see Zech, Paul.

Odiorne & Rummler. Training & Development: A Guide for Professionals. 472p. 1988. 55.00 (*0-685-67146-1*, 5287) Commerce.

Odiorne, George S. Green Power: The Corporation & the Urban Crisis. 208p. reprint ed. text ed. 27.50 (*0-8290-0290-1*) Irvington.

— How Managers Make Things Happen. 2nd ed. 1987. 9.95 (*0-13-400557-0*) P-H.

— The Human Side of Management. LC 86-46314. 256p. 1987. text ed. 27.95 (*0-669-15350-8*) Free Pr.

— Human Side of Management. 1990. pap. 14.95 (*0-669-24826-6*) Free Pr.

— Management Decisions by Objectives. 1968. 17.95 (*0-13-548529-0*) P-H.

— Management Decisions by Objectives. 1986. 6.95 (*0-13-548172-4*, Reward) P-H.

— Performance Driven Sales Management. 260p. 1991. ring bd. 91.50 (*0-85013-189-8*) Dartnell Corp.

— Personal Effectiveness: A Strategy for Success. LC 79-88613. (Orig.). 1979. pap. 11.95 (*0-9602950-0-3*) MBO Inc.

— Sales Management by Objectives. 260p. 1991. pap. 34.95 (*0-85013-183-9*) Dartnell Corp.

— Strategic Management of Human Resources: A Portfolio Approach. LC 84-47993. (Management Ser.). 376p. 1984. 39.95 (*0-87589-625-1*) Jossey-Bass.

Odiorne, George S., jt. auth. see Brooks, Earl.

Odishelidze, Alexander. Dollars Making It...&...Keeping It: The Common Sense Guide to Financial Wellbeing. 208p. 1993. 22.95 (*0-9633405-0-6*) Employ Benefits.

Odlaug, Theron O. & Chiasson, Robert B. Laboratory Anatomy of the Fetal Pig. 10th ed. 160p. (C). 1994. spiral bd. write for info. (*0-697-15984-1*) Wm C Brown Pubs.

Odle, Joe T. Church Member's Handbook. pap. 1.50 (*0-8054-9401-4*) Broadman.

Odlin, Terence. Language Transfer: Cross-Linguistic Influence in Language Learning. (Cambridge Applied Linguistics Ser.). 192p. (C). 1989. pap. 17.95 (*0-521-37809-5*) Cambridge U Pr.

Odlin, Terence, ed. Perspectives on Pedagogical Grammar. (Applied Linguistics Ser.). (Illus.). 240p. (C). 1994. 42.95 (*0-521-44530-2*); pap. 19.95 (*0-521-44990-1*) Cambridge U Pr.

Odlozilik, Otaker. Rembrandt's Polish Nobleman. 32p. 1963. 3.00 (*0-685-25019-9*) Polish Inst Art & Sci.

Odlum, Floyd, jt. auth. see Cochran, Jacqueline.

Odlum, Hortense. A Women's Place. Baxter, Annette K., ed. LC 79-8804. (Signal Lives Ser.). 1980. reprint ed. lib. bdg. 33.95 (*0-405-12850-9*) Ayer.

Odmark, John, ed. Language, Literature & Meaning I: Problems of Literary Theory. (Linguistic & Literary Studies in Eastern Europe: No. 1). x, 467p. 1979. 97.00x (*90-272-1502-2*) Benjamins North Am.

— Language, Literature & Meaning II: Current Trends in Literary Research. (Linguistic & Literary Studies in Eastern Europe: No. 2). x, 569p. 1980. 124.00x (*90-272-1503-0*, 2) Benjamins North Am.

Odo, Franklin. Pictorial History of the Japanese in Hawaii 1885-1924. 1989. pap. 19.95 (*0-930897-07-2*) Bishop Mus.

Odo of Tournai. On Original Sin & A Disputation with the Jew, Leo, Concerning the Advent of Christ, the Son of God: Two Theological Treatises. Resnick, Irven M., tr. LC 94-16217. (Middle Ages Ser.). 168p. (Orig.). (C). 1994. text ed. 29.95 (*0-8122-3288-7*); pap. text ed. 12.95 (*0-8122-1540-0*) U of Pa Pr.

***O'Dochartaigh, Fionnbarra.** Ulster's White Negroes. 136p. (Orig.). 1994. pap. 8.95 (*1-873176-67-8*, AK Pr San Fran) AK Pr Dist.

Odoevsky, Vladimir F. Russian Nights. Koshansky-Olienikov, Olga & Matlaw, Ralph E., trs. 265p. Date not set. reprint ed. pap. 14.95 (*0-8101-1087-3*) Northwestern U Pr.

— The Salamander & Other Gothic Tales. Cornwell, Neil, ed. & tr. by. 250p. (Orig.). 1992. pap. 15.95 (*0-8101-1062-8*) Northwestern U Pr.

O'Dogherty, Laura. Central Americans in Mexico City: Uprooted & Silenced. 75p. (Orig.). 1989. pap. text ed. 7.50 (*0-924046-11-2*) Ctr EPRA.

O'Doherty, Brian. Inside the White Cube: The Ideology of the Gallery Space. LC 85-81090. (Illus.). 91p. (Orig.). 1986. 25.95 (*0-932499-14-7*); pap. 15.95 (*0-932499-05-8*) Lapis Pr.

— Joseph Cornell: Dovecotes, Hotels & Other White Spaces. (Illus.). 48p. 1989. pap. write for info. (*1-878283-01-4*) PaceWildenstein.

— The Strange Case of Mademoiselle P. 240p. 1993. pap. 10.00 (*0-14-017926-7*, Penguin Bks) Viking Penguin.

— William Scharf: Essay. (Illus.). 12p. 1993. pap. 3.00 (*0-685-72255-4*) Michigan Mus.

***O'Doherty, Brian, text.** John Chamberlain: Recent Sculpture. 460p. 1994. pap. write for info. (*1-878283-47-2*) PaceWildenstein.

***O'Doherty, Dermot P., ed.** Globalisation, Networking & Small Firm Innovation. LC 95-13903. 1995. write for info. (*1-85966-189-0*) G & T Inc.

O'Doherty, E. F. Helping Disturbed Religious. McNamee, Fintan, ed. (Synthesis Ser.). pap. 1.95 (*0-8199-0393-0*, L38268, Frncscn Herld) Franciscan Pr.

— Helping Disturbed Religious. McNamee, Fintan, ed. (Synthesis Ser.). Date not set. pap. 1.95 (*0-8199-0234-9*, L38268, Frncscn Herld) Franciscan Pr.

O'Doherty, Eamonn, jt. auth. see Feldman, Allen.

O'Doherty, Michael & Griffin, Tim. Bio-Energy Healing. 1991. pap. 18.95 (*0-86278-244-9*) Dufour.

O'Doherty, N. Atlas of the Newborn. 1985. lib. bdg. 82.00 (*0-85200-924-0*) Kluwer Ac.

— Inspecting the Newborn Baby's Eyes. (Atlases of Childhood Ser.). 1986. lib. bdg. 204.50 (*0-85200-857-0*) Kluwer Ac.

— The Neurological Examination of the Newborn. 1986. lib. bdg. 82.00 (*0-85200-877-5*) Kluwer Ac.

Odom. Current Therapy in Dermatology. 350p. Date not set. 55.00 (*1-55664-383-7*) Mosby Yr Bk.

— The Integrated Preschool Curriculum. 1988. student ed 75.00 (*0-295-96664-5*) U of Wash Pr.

Odom, jt. auth. see LaForte.

Odom, Guy R. Mothers, Leadership, & Success. LC 89-23027. 358p. 1990. 9.95 (*0-9624006-0-2*) Polybius Pr.

Odom, J. M., et al, eds. The Sulfate-Reducing Bacteria: Contemporary Perspective. LC 92-2311. (Contemporary Bioscience Ser.). (Illus.). 264p. 1992. 76.00 (*0-387-97865-8*) Spr-Verlag.

Odom, Judy. Blossom, Stalk & Vine. Tickle, Phyllis, ed. 96p. 1990. pap. 8.95 (*0-918518-89-X*) Iris Pr.

***Odom, Keith.** Only in Louisiana: A Guide for the Adventurous Traveler. 128p. (Orig.). 1994. pap. 6.95 (*0-937552-56-9*) Quail Ridge.

Odom, M. Mega Score. 1994. mass mkt. 3.99 (*0-06-100617-3*, Harp PBks) HarpC.

***Odom, Mel.** Freelancers. 320p. (Orig.). 1995. pap. 4.95 (*0-7869-0113-6*) TSR Inc.

— Lethal Interface. 384p. (Orig.). 1992. pap. 5.50 (*0-451-45154-6*, ROC) NAL-Dutton.

— Omega Blue. 1993. mass mkt. 3.99 (*0-06-100616-5*, Harp PBks) HarpC.

— Stalker Analog. 352p. (Orig.). 1993. pap. 5.50 (*0-451-45257-7*, ROC) NAL-Dutton.

Odom, Melissa. A Medal for Murphy. LC 86-25369. (Illus.). 32p. (J). (gr. 1-6). 1987. 12.95 (*0-88289-635-0*) Pelican.

Odom, Melissa W. No Regard Beauregard & the Golden Rule. LC 87-36118. (Illus.). 132p. (J). (gr. k-6). 1988. 12.95 (*0-88289-686-5*) Pelican.

***Odom, Richmond.** Circle of Death: Clinton's Climb to the Presidency. 1995. pap. 10.99 (*1-56384-089-8*) Huntington Hse.

Odom, Richmond C. New Gods for a New Age. LC 93-80620. 224p. 1994. pap. 9.99 (*1-56384-062-6*) Huntington Hse.

Odom, Robert, Jr. Smoke of Signal Dreams. Mallory, Lee, ed. (Poetry Ser.). 1989. write for info. (*0-9626168-3-4*) Prometh Pr CA.

Odom, Robert. Your Companion to Twelve Step Recovery. LC 94-10243. 192p. 1994. pap. 8.95 (*1-56170-098-3*, 161) Hay House.

Odom, Robert, Jr., ed. see Mallory, Lee.

Odom, Robert, Jr., ed. see Rafel, Lisa.

Odom, Samuel L., et al, eds. Social Competence of Children with Disabilities: Nature, Development, & Intervention. 352p. (Orig.). (C). 1992. pap. text ed. 32.00 (*1-55766-085-9*) P H Brookes.

Odom, Thomas P. Dragon Operations: Hostage Rescues in the Congo, 1964-1965. LC 87-36503. (Leavenworth Papers: No. 14). (Illus.). 236p. 1988. per., pap. 9.50 (*0-16-001695-9*, S/N 008-020-011) USGPO.

Odom, W. E. Trial after Triumph: East Asia after the Cold War. 151p. (Orig.). (C). 1992. pap. text ed. 12.95 (*1-55813-042-X*) Hudson Instit IN.

Odom, William. German for Singers: A Textbook of Diction & Phonetics. LC 80-5493. (Illus.). 170p. (Orig.). (C). 1981. pap. 15.00 (*0-02-871750-3*) Schirmer Bks.

Odom, William E. America's Military Revolution: Strategy & Structure after the Cold War. LC 93-9704. 186p. (C). 1993. lib. bdg. 22.95 (*1-879383-15-2*) Am Univ Pr.

— On Internal War: American & Soviet Approaches to Third World Clients & Insurgents. LC 91-18572. 280p. 1991. text ed. 31.95 (*0-8223-1182-8*) Duke.

— The Soviet Volunteers: Modernization & Bureaucracy in a Public Mass Organization. LC 72-6517. 336p. 1973. 57.50 (*0-691-08718-0*) Princeton U Pr.

— Soviet Volunteers: Modernization & Bureaucracy in a Public Mass Organization. LC 72-6517. Date not set. reprint ed. pap. 107.20 (*0-7837-9406-1*, 2060151) Bks Demand.

— Unreasonable Sufficiency? Assessing the New Soviet Strategy. (C). 1990. 35.00 (*0-907967-13-2*, Pub. by Inst Euro Def & Strat UK) St Mut.

Odom-Winn, Danni & Dunagan, Dianne E. PreNatally Exposed Kids. Dodson, J. Lynne & Dow, Rosalie, eds. LC 91-77184. (Illus.). 120p. (Orig.). 1991. pap. 14.95 (*0-7925-1867-5*, B302) Ed Activities.

Odoms Tennessee Pride Staff. Cooking with Pride: Celebrating Fifty Years. LC 93-70328. 1993. 12.95 (*0-87197-366-9*) Favorite Recipes.

O'Donahue, William & Gear, James H., eds. Handbook of Sexual Dysfunctions: Assessment & Treatment. 576p. Date not set. write for info. (*0-318-71705-0*) Allyn.

O'Donaill. Focloir Gaeilge Bearla (Irish-English Dictionary) (ENG & IRI.). 1992. 60.00 (*1-85791-038-9*) Colton Bk.

O'Donaill, Niall. Focloir Gaeige-Bearla: Irish-English Dictionary. 533p. (ENG & IRI.). 1986. pap. 19.95 (*0-8288-1708-1*, M6303) Fr & Eur.

O'Donald, Peter. Genetic Models of Sexual Selection. LC 78-73249. (Illus.). 1980. 64.95 (*0-521-22533-7*) Cambridge U Pr.

O'Donell, et al. Beginning WordPerfect 6.0 for DOS. 1994. pap. text ed. write for info. (*0-07-070387-6*) McGraw.

Odoni, A. R., et al, eds. Flow Control of Congested Networks. (NATO Asi Series F: Vol. 38). x, 355p. 1987. 87.00 (*0-387-18398-1*) Spr-Verlag.

Odoni, Amedeo R., ed. see Bianco, Lucio.

Odoni, Amedeo R., jt. ed. see Bianco, Lucio.

O'Donnchadha, Diarmuid. Irish Phrase-Book: An Raleabhar Gaeilge. 1990. pap. 7.95 (*0-85342-752-6*) Dufour.

O'Donnel, Hugh, ed. see Dodin, Andre.

O'Donnel, Peggy, jt. auth. see Shaevel, Evelyn.

O'Donnell. Automobile Insurance in Ontario. 472p. 1991. 90.00 (*0-409-89361-7*) Butterworth Legal Pubs.

— Financial Management Workbook. 80p. 1991. spiral bd. 7.50 (*0-8403-6874-7*) Kendall-Hunt.

— Pediatric Urology. 3rd ed. 1995. 295.00 (*0-7506-1365-3*, Focal) Buttrwrth-Heinemann.

O'Donnell, et al. Advanced WordPerfect 6.0 for DOS. 1994. pap. text ed. write for info. (*0-07-070413-9*) McGraw.

O'Donnell, A., jt. auth. see Willet, C. F.

O'Donnell, A. G., jt. ed. see Goodfellow, Michael.

O'Donnell, Aidan, jt. auth. see Willett, Chris.

O'Donnell, Amy & O'Donnell, Charles. Increase Your Child's Learning Potential. (Illus.). 415p. 1992. 39.95 (*1-882761-00-6*) Spectrum MA.

O'Donnell, Anthony G., jt. ed. see Goodfellow, Michael.

O'Donnell, Asta & Lipton, June. Keeping Fit with Asta O'Donnell: An Exercise Program for Problem Backs. (Illus.). 103p. (Orig.). 1983. pap. 12.50 (*0-9610564-0-1*) J L Prods.

O'Donnell, Bernard. The Old Bailey & Its Trials. LC 78-2732. (Illus.). 226p. 1978. reprint ed. text ed. 67.50 (*0-313-20362-8*, ODOB, Greenwood Pr) Greenwood.

O'Donnell, Bob, jt. auth. see Daly, Dan.

***O'Donnell, Brennan.** The Passion of Meter: A Study of Wordsworth's Metrical Art. LC 94-30735. 340p. 1995. text ed. 35.00x (*0-87338-510-1*) Kent St U Pr.

O'Donnell, C. James. One, Two, Three, You're Hired. 160p. 1992. pap. 9.95 (*0-912495-14-6*) San Diego Pub Co.

O'Donnell, C. Patrick, Jr., ed. see Spenser, Edmund.

O'Donnell, Cara, ed. see Remakus, Bernard L.

O'Donnell, Carlotta, tr. see Brazinsky, Terri C. & Bowden, Kathi, eds.

O'Donnell, Charles, jt. auth. see O'Donnell, Amy.

O'Donnell, Charles P., ed. see Simon, Yves R.

O'Donnell, Chris. The New Superfund Program: Redefining the Federal-State Partnership. Glass, Karen, ed. 32p. (Orig.). 1988. pap. text ed. 7.50 (*1-55877-009-7*) Natl Governor.

O'Donnell, Christine & Thompson, Paul. A State Guide to Cleanup & Compliance Issues at Federal Facilities. Feinstein, Gerry & Miller, Mark, eds. 195p. (Orig.). 1991. pap. text ed. 15.00 (*1-55877-095-X*) Natl Governor.

O'Donnell, Christopher. Commodity Price Stabilization: An Empirical Analysis. 157p. 1993. 59.95 (*1-85628-497-2*, Pub. by Avebury Pub UK) Ashgate Pub Co.

O'Donnell, Chuck. Job Hunter's Workbook: A Complete System for Career Planning & Job Hunting. (Illus.). 200p. 1984. 10.00 (*0-9613166-0-8*) C O'Donnell Pub.

O'Donnell, Craig. Cool Mac Sounds. 2nd ed. (Illus.). 176p. (Orig.). 1993. disk, pap. 24.95 (*1-56830-067-0*) Hayden.

— MAC Sound Tools, Set. (Illus.). 350p. 1995. cd-rom, pap. write for info. (*0-12-524225-5*) Acad Pr.

O'Donnell, Desmond. To Stay a Believer: The Challenge of Christians in the Age of Technology. LC 90-71271. 128p. (Orig.). 1990. pap. 7.95 (*0-89622-462-7*) Twenty-Third.

O'Donnell, E. E. Annals of Dublin Fair City. (Illus.). 237p. 1987. 32.00 (*0-86327-149-9*, Pub. by Wolfhound Pr IE) Dufour.

— The Genius of Father Browne: Ireland's Photographic Discovery. 1990. 40.00 (*0-86327-265-7*, Pub. by Wolfhound Pr IE) Dufour.

O'Donnell, E. E., ed. Father Browne's Dublin: Photographs from the Francis Browne Collection 1920-1950. (Illus.). 96p. 1994. 35.00 (*0-86327-366-1*, Pub. by Wolfhound Pr IE) Dufour.

— Father Browne's Ireland: Remarkable Images of People & Places. LC 89-82287. 144p. 1990. 39.95 (*0-86327-200-2*, Pub. by Wolfhound Pr IE) Dufour.

O'Donnell, Elizabeth L. Are You Flying, Charlie Duncan? LC 92-39876. (Illus.). 96p. (J). (gr. 4 up). 1993. 14.00 (*0-688-09027-3*) Morrow Jr Bks.

— I Can't Get My Turtle to Move. LC 88-22046. (Illus.). 32p. (J). (ps-1). 1989. 11.95 (*0-688-07323-9*); lib. bdg. 11.88 (*0-688-07324-7*) Morrow Jr Bks.

— Maggie Doesn't Want to Move. LC 86-23684. (Illus.). 32p. (J). (gr. k-3). 1987. text ed. 13.95 (*0-02-768830-5*, Four Winds Pr) S&S Childrens.

— Maggie Doesn't Want to Move. LC 89-18207. (Illus.). 32p. (J). (gr. k-3). 1990. pap. 3.95 (*0-689-71375-4*, Aladdin Paperbacks) S&S Childrens.

— Patrick's Day. LC 92-27421. (Illus.). 32p. (YA). (gr. k up). 1994. 15.00 (*0-688-07853-2*); lib. bdg. 14.93 (*0-688-07854-0*) Morrow Jr Bks.

— Sing Me a Window. LC 92-10719. (J). (ps up). 1993. 15.00 (*0-688-09500-3*); lib. bdg. 14.93 (*0-688-09501-1*) Morrow Jr Bks.

— The Twelve Days of Summer. LC 89-35161. (Illus.). 32p. (J). (ps up). 1991. 15.00 (*0-688-08202-5*); lib. bdg. 14.93 (*0-688-08203-3*) Morrow Jr Bks.

O'Donnell, Elliot. The Sorcery Club. Reginald, R. & Menville, Douglas, eds. LC 75-46295. (Supernatural & Occult Fiction Ser.). (Illus.). 1976. reprint ed. lib. bdg. 29.95 (*0-405-08156-1*) Ayer.

— Strange Disappearances. 1990. pap. 9.95 (*0-8065-1140-0*, Citadel Pr) Carol Pub Group.

O'Donnell, Elliott. Strange Disappearances. 1972. 7.95 (*0-8216-0155-5*, Univ Bks) Carol Pub Group.

O'Donnell, Gabriel & Maas, Robin. Spiritual Traditions for the Contemporary Church. 464p. (Orig.). 1993. pap. 24.95 (*0-687-39233-0*) Abingdon.

O'Donnell, Gail & Travolta, Michele, eds. Making It in Hollywood: Behind the Success of 50 of Today's Favorite Actors, Screenwriters, Producers & Directors. LC 94-18450. 1994. 24.95 (*1-57071-015-5*) Sourcebks.

O'Donnell, Guillermo. Bureaucratic Authoritarianism: Argentina, 1966-1973 - In Comparative Perspective. 1988. 52.50 (*0-520-04260-3*) U CA Pr.

O'Donnell, Guillermo & Schmitter, Philippe C., eds. Transitions from Authoritarian Rule: Tentative Conclusions about Uncertain Democracies. LC 86-2714. 96p. 1986. pap. text ed. 8.95 (*0-8018-2682-9*) Johns Hopkins.

O'Donnell, Guillermo, et al, eds. Transitions from Authoritarian Rule: Comparative Perspectives. LC 86-2710. 240p. 1986. pap. text ed. 13.50x (*0-8018-3192-X*) Johns Hopkins.

— Transitions from Authoritarian Rule: Latin America. LC 86-2711. 272p. 1986. pap. text ed. 13.50x (*0-8018-3188-1*) Johns Hopkins.

— Transitions from Authoritarian Rule: Southern Europe. LC 86-2713. 232p. 1986. pap. text ed. 13.50x (*0-8018-3190-3*) Johns Hopkins.

O'Donnell, Guillermo A. & Apter, David E. Modernization & Bureaucratic-Authoritarianism: Studies in South American Politics. LC 73-620029. (Politics of Modernization Ser.: No. 9). (Illus.). xvi, 226p. 1973. pap. 15.00 (*0-87725-209-2*) U of Cal IAS.

O'Donnell, Harold K. & Weihrich, Heinz. Management: A Book of Readings. 5th ed. (Illus.). 736p. 1980. text ed. write for info. (*0-07-035418-9*) McGraw.

O'Donnell, J. D. Free Will Baptist Doctrines. 1974. pap. 6.95 (*0-89265-019-2*) Randall Hse.

— Handbook for Deacons. 1973. pap. 6.95 (*0-89265-011-7*) Randall Hse.

— The Preacher & His Preaching. 1974. pap. 6.95 (*0-89265-018-4*) Randall Hse.

— A Survey of Church History. 1973. pap. 6.95 (*0-89265-009-5*) Randall Hse.

O'Donnell, J. D. & Hampton, Ralph, Jr. A Survey of the Books of History. 1976. pap. 3.95 (*0-89265-032-X*) Randall Hse.

— A Survey of the Books of Poetry. 1976. pap. 2.95 (*0-89265-033-8*) Randall Hse.

O'Donnell, J. D. & Melvin, Billy A. Faith for Today. LC 65-29130. (Sunday School Workers Training Course Ser.: No. 5). 1974. pap. 6.95 (*0-89265-000-1*) Randall Hse.

O'Donnell, J. D., jt. auth. see Outlaw, Stanley.

O'Donnell, J. T., ed. see Van Rijsbergen, C. J.

***O'Donnell, James.** Statistics: Elementary Units. 304p. (C). 1995. pap. text ed., ring bd. 27.95 (*0-7872-0982-1*) Kendall-Hunt.

O'Donnell, James H. Southern Indians in the American Revolution. LC 76-146662. 185p. reprint ed. pap. 52.80 (*0-317-28845-8*, 2020630) Bks Demand.

O'Donnell, James J. Augustine. LC 84-28133. (World Authors Ser.: No. 759). 168p. 1985. text ed. 23.95 (*0-8057-6609-X*, Twayne) Macmillan.

— Boethius Consolatio Philosophiae. (Latin Commentaries Ser.). 273p. (Orig.). (C). 1984. pap. text ed. 10.00 (*0-929524-37-3*) Bryn Mawr Commentaries.

— Statistics: Elementary Study Units. 288p. (C). 1994. spiral bd. 24.95 (*0-8403-9231-1*) Kendall-Hunt.

O'Donnell, James J. & Hall, Bryan D., eds. Penetrance & Variability in Malformation Syndromes. LC 79-5115. (Alan R. Liss Ser.: Vol. 15, No. 5b). 1979. 50.00 (*0-685-03295-7*) March of Dimes.

O'Donnell, James J. & Reichmanis, Elsa. The Effects of Radiation on High-Technology Polymers. LC 88-39298. (Symposium Ser.: No. 381). (Illus.). xi, 272p. 1988. 54.95 (*0-8412-1558-8*) Am Chemical.

O'Donnell, James J., ed. see St. Augustine.

O'Donnell, Jeff. Blood on the Republican. LC 91-29076. (Novel of the West Ser.). 192p. 1992. 16.95 (*0-87131-665-X*) M Evans.

— Luther North, Frontier Scout. 1994. pap. 19.95 (*0-934904-10-3*) J & L Lee.

O'Donnell, Jeff & Oliver, Kevin. Starkweather: A Story of Mass Murder on the Great Plains. (Illus.). 208p. (Orig.). 1993. pap. 10.00 (*0-934904-31-6*) J & L Lee.

O'Donnell, Jeffrey P. Insurance Smart: How to Buy the Right Insurance at the Right Price. 236p. 1991. pap. text ed. 12.95 (*0-471-52711-4*) Wiley.

O'Donnell, Jennifer J., jt. auth. see Nordberg, Ken.

O

***O'Donnell, Jim. The Day John Met Paul: An Hour-by-Hour Account of How the Beatles Began. LC 99-77840. 164p. (Orig.). 1994. pap. 9.95 (*0-9636905-6-6*) Hall Fame Bks.**

THE DAY JOHN MET PAUL is the remarkable hour-by-hour account of the day the Beatles began: July 6, 1957. On that day in northwest England, teenagers John Lennon & Paul McCartney met & exchanged guitar licks. Jim O'Donnell, a journalist & author of three rock music books, goes further back than the Hamburg of the "Backbeat" movie to unearth this amazing close-up portrait. O'Donnell reconstructs the events of that single July day, from pre-dawn to near-midnight, with each chapter containing a group of hours. During his eight years of research, O'Donnell gained the unprecedented cooperation of many of the day's major figures, including most of Lennon's band, the Quarry Men. Includes extensive bibliography. According to Ray Coleman, best-selling writer of John Lennon's authorized biography, "This is one of the best Beatle books ever written! It's a crucial book to understanding the Beatle story." Colin Hanton, the Quarry Man who played drums behind Lennon that day, said: "THE DAY JOHN MET PAUL is brilliant! I can't fault it." To order direct: send $12.95 ($9.95 plus $3 s&h) to Hall of Fame Books, Box 232, 61 East 8th St., New York, NY 10003.

Publisher Provided Annotation.

— Wonderful Tonight: Eric Clapton, Les Paul & Queen in Concert. LC 93-78190. 104p. 1993. 9.95 (*0-9636905-0-7*) Hall Fame Bks.

O'Donnell, Joan K., ed. see Dillingham, Rick & Elliott, Melinda.

***O'Donnell, Jodi.** Daddy Was a Cowboy: (Stetsons & Lace) (Sil Romance Ser.). 1995. mass mkt. 2.99 (*0-373-19080-8*, 1-19080-0) Silhouette.

— The Farmer Takes a Wife. (Silhouette Romance Ser.). 1994. pap. 2.75 (*0-373-08992-9*, 5-08992-5) Silhouette.

— Still Sweet on Him: Premiere. (Romance Ser.). 1993. pap. 2.75 (*0-373-08969-4*, 5-08969-3) Silhouette.

O'Donnell, Joe & Reuse, Ruth B. Birmingham: Magic City Renaissance. Turner, James E. & Hughes, Mary S., eds. LC 92-73285. 1992. text ed. 45.00 (*0-9630029-3-7*) Community Comm.

O'Donnell, Joe, jt. auth. see Doherty, Jim.

O'Donnell, John H. The Catholic Hierarchy of the United States, 1790-1922. LC 73-3558. (Catholic University of America. Studies in Romance Languages & Literatures: No. 4). reprint ed. 39.50 (*0-404-57754-7*) AMS Pr.

O'Donnell, John J. The Mystery of the Triune God. 1989. pap. 8.95 (*0-8091-3112-9*) Paulist Pr.

O'Donnell, John R. Trumped! Rubenstein, Julie, ed. (Illus.). 392p. 1992. reprint ed. mass mkt. 5.99 (*0-671-73818-6*) PB.

O'Donnell, Joseph D., jt. auth. see Aycock, Johnnie R.

O'Donnell, Joseph F., et al. Oncology for the House Officer. (Illus.). 352p. 1992. 20.00 (*0-683-06626-9*) Williams & Wilkins.

***O'Donnell, Joseph M.** Hometown Hero: An Action Guide for the Solo Practice. LC 94-48595. 1995. write for info. (*0-87814-435-8*) PennWell Bks.

O'Donnell, Kate. Defy the Wind. 368p. (Orig.). 1987. pap. 3.95 (*0-380-75396-0*) Avon.

— Frontier Enchantress. 1992. mass mkt. 4.25 (*0-8217-3674-4*) Zebra.

O'Donnell, Kelly, ed. Missionary Care: Counting the Cost for World Evangelization. LC 92-72009. 560p. (Orig.). (C). 1992. pap. text ed. 13.95 (*0-87808-233-6*, WCL233-6) William Carey Lib.

O'Donnell, Lewis B., et al. Announcing: Broadcast Communicating Today. 2nd ed. 437p. (C). 1992. text ed. 46.95 (*0-534-14958-8*) Intl Thomson.

— Modern Radio Production. 3rd ed. 347p. (C). 1993. text ed. 29.95 (*0-534-19080-4*) Intl Thomson.

— Radio Station Operations: Management & Employee Perspectives. 409p. (C). 1989. pap. 32.95 (*0-534-09540-2*) Intl Thomson.

O'Donnell, Lillian. Aftershock. 1982. pap. 2.50 (*0-449-24479-2*) Fawcett.

— Casual Affairs. large type ed. 377p. 1991. reprint ed. lib. bdg. 20.95 (*1-56054-134-2*) Thorndike Pr.

— Falling Star. large type ed. LC 90-45873. 333p. 1990. reprint ed. lib. bdg. 20.95 (*1-56054-061-3*) Thorndike Pr.

— Lady Killer. 240p. 1985. pap. 2.95 (*0-449-20744-7*, Crest) Fawcett.

— Lockout. 240p. 1994. 19.95 (*0-399-13921-4*, Putnam) Putnam Pub Group.

— Lockout. 1995. pap. 5.99 (*0-449-22329-9*) Fawcett.

— Lockout. large type ed. LC 94-25459. (Cloak & Dagger Ser.). 353p. 1994. 20.95 (*0-7862-0294-7*) Thorndike Pr.

— No Business Being a Cop. 1987. pap. 2.95 (*0-449-21322-6*) Fawcett.

— No Business Being a Cop. large type ed. LC 92-33704. 346p. 1993. reprint ed. lib. bdg. 17.95 (*1-56054-372-8*) Thorndike Pr.

— Other Side of Door. 1988. pap. 2.95 (*0-449-21598-9*) Fawcett.

— A Private Crime. large type ed. (General Ser.). 333p. 1992. text ed. 21.95 (*0-8161-5277-2*, Large Print Bks) Hall.

— Pushover. large type ed. 343p. 1992. reprint ed. lib. bdg. 20.95 (*1-56054-416-3*) Thorndike Pr.

— The Raggedy Man. LC 95-3925. 240p. 1995. 19.95 (*0-399-14019-0*, Putnam) Putnam Pub Group.

— Used to Kill. 1994. mass mkt. 4.99 (*0-449-22249-7*, Crest) Fawcett.

— Used to Kill. 240p. 1993. 19.95 (*0-399-13782-3*, Putnam) Putnam Pub Group.

— Used to Kill. large type ed. LC 93-17005. 1993. 20.95 (*1-56054-736-7*) Thorndike Pr.

— Wicked Designs. 224p. 1987. pap. 2.95 (*0-449-21532-6*, Crest) Fawcett.

— Wicked Designs: A Mici Anhalt Mystery. large type ed. LC 92-19379. 341p. 1992. reprint ed. lib. bdg. 17.95 (*1-56054-373-6*) Thorndike Pr.

— A Wreath for the Bride. 224p. 1991. pap. 4.99 (*0-449-21867-8*, Expression) Fawcett.

— A Wreath for the Bride. large type ed. LC 90-10938. 334p. 1990. reprint ed. lib. bdg. 20.95 (*1-56054-024-9*) Thorndike Pr.

***O'Donnell, M.** Developing Health Promotional Programs: HP 620. 102p. (C). 1989. student ed write for info. (*0-931657-14-8*) Learning Proc Ctr.

O'Donnell, M. C., ed. see Nordberg, Ken & O'Donnell, Jennifer J.

O'Donnell, M. C., ed. see Nordberg, Ken.

O'Donnell, Mark. Fables for Friends. 1984. pap. 4.75 (*0-8222-0377-4*) Dramatists Play.

— The Nice & the Nasty. 1987. pap. 4.75 (*0-8222-0815-6*) Dramatists Play.

— Strangers on Earth. (Illus.). 96p. 1993. 5.99 (*1-56865-067-1*, GuildAmerica) Dblday Bk Music.

— Strangers on Earth. 1993. 4.75 (*0-8222-1350-8*) Dramatists Play.

— That's It, Folks! 1983. pap. 4.75 (*0-8222-1128-9*) Dramatists Play.

— Vertigo Park: And Other Tall Tales. 160p. 1994. pap. 9.95 (*0-312-11363-3*) St Martin.

— Vertigo Park: The Whom of Kaboom & Other Tall Tales. LC 92-20673. 1993. 18.00 (*0-679-40040-0*) Knopf.

O'Donnell, Mark, tr. see Besset, Jean-Marie.

O'Donnell, Martin J. Annual Reports in Organic Synthesis, Vol. 11. Wade, L. G., Jr., ed. (Serial Publication Ser.). 1981. pap. text ed. 106.00 (*0-12-040811-2*) Acad Pr.

O'Donnell, Martin J. & Scriven, F. V., eds. Annual Reports in Organic Synthesis, 1985. 513p. 1986. pap. text ed. 92.00 (*0-12-040816-3*) Acad Pr.

O'Donnell, Martin J., jt. ed. see Wade, L. G., Jr.

O'Donnell, Mary. The Light-Makers. 193p. 1993. pap. 28.00 (*1-85371-177-2*, Pub. by Poolbeg Pr IE) Dufour.

— Strong Pagans & Other Stories. 258p. 1991. pap. 12.95 (*1-85371-123-3*, Pub. by Poolbeg Pr IE) Dufour.

***Odonnell, Michael.** Finding Contentment for the Restless Heart. 1994. 16.99 (*0-8499-1142-7*) Word Inc.

O'Donnell, Michael. The Long Walk Home. large type ed. (Adventure Suspense Ser.). 1989. 17.95 (*0-7089-2061-6*) Ulverscroft.

— The Marketing Plan - Step-by-Step. Gjovig, Bruce, ed. 150p. (Orig.). 1991. pap. 29.95 (*0-930204-30-1*) Lord Pub.

— Review for the CLEP General Mathematics Examination. (Illus.). 192p. (C). 1994. pap. text ed. 12.95 (*1-56030-000-0*) Comex Systs.

— Writing Business Plans That Get Results: A Step-by-Step Guide. 128p. (Orig.). 1991. pap. 12.95 (*0-8092-4007-6*) Contemp Bks.

O'Donnell, Michael & Morris, Michelle. Heart of the Warrior: A Battle Plan for Fathers to Reclaim Their Families. 1993. 15.95 (*0-89112-234-6*); pap. 10.95 (*0-89112-233-8*) Abilene Christ U.

O'Donnell, Michael A. Home from Oz: Finding Contentment in the Sacredness of the Family. 1994. pap. 10.99 (*0-8499-3599-7*) Word Inc.

O'Donnell, Michael J. Equational Logic As a Programming Language. (Foundations of Computing Ser.). (Illus.). 250p. 1985. 42.50x (*0-262-15028-X*) MIT Pr.

— Lift up Your Hearts Year A: Eucharistic Prayers Based on the Revised Common Lectionary. rev. ed. Crouch, Timothy J., ed. 1504p. 1995. spiral bd. 19.95 (*1-878009-23-0*) Order St Luke Pubns.

— Lift up Your Hearts - Year B: Eucharistic Prayers Based on the Revised Common Lectionary. rev. ed. Crouch, Timothy J., ed. 148p. 1993. spiral bd. 19.95 (*1-878009-16-8*, OSL Pubns) Order St Luke Pubns.

— Lift up Your Hearts - Year C: Eucharistic Prayers Based on the Revised Common Lectionary. rev. ed. Crouch, Timothy J., ed. 148p. 1994. spiral bd. 19.95 (*1-878009-20-6*, OSL Pubns) Order St Luke Pubns.

O'Donnell, Michael J., ed. see Holien, Kim B.

O'Donnell, Michael J., ed. see Keim, Lon W., et al.

O'Donnell, Michael J., jt. auth. see Sylvia, Stephen W.

O'Donnell, Michael P. & Harris, Jeffrey S. Health Promotion in the Workplace. 2nd ed. LC 93-676. 554p. 1993. text ed. 44.95 (*0-8273-4940-8*) Delmar.

O'Donnell, Michael P. & Wood, Margo. Becoming a Reader: A Developmental Approach to Reading Instruction. 300p. (C). 1991. pap. text ed. write for info. (*0-205-12826-2*) Allyn.

O'Donnell, Micheal J., jt. auth. see Sylvia, Stephen W.

O'Donnell, Michele L., ed. Helping Missionaries Grow: Readings in Mental Health & Missions. LC 88-71334. (Illus.). 592p. (Orig.). 1988. pap. 17.95 (*0-87808-217-4*) William Carey Lib.

O'Donnell, Mike, ed. see Pistole, Larry M.

O'Donnell, Monica M., ed. Contemporary Theatre, Film, & Television, Vol. 4. 450p. 1987. 128.00 (*0-8103-2067-3*) Gale.

— Contemporary Theatre, Film, & Television, Vol. 5. (Illus.). 1988. 128.00 (*0-8103-2068-1*) Gale.

— Contemporary Theatre, Film & Television 1984, Vols. 1-3. Incl. Vol 1. 554p. 1984. 128.00 (*0-8103-2064-9*); Vol. 2. 396p. 1985. 128.00 (*0-8103-0241-1*); Vol. 3. 1986. 128.00 (*0-8103-2066-5*); (Illus.). 500p. write for info. (*0-318-58316-X*) Gale.

O'Donnell, Nina S., ed. see Sazer, Victor.

O'Donnell, O., jt. auth. see Caffarella, C.

O'Donnell, Owen, ed. Contemporary Theatre, Film, & Television, Vol. 8. LC 84-649371. (Illus.). 558p. 1990. text ed. 128.00 (*0-8103-2071-1*) Gale.

O'Donnell, Owen, ed. see Gale Research, Inc. Staff.

O'Donnell, Owen, jt. ed. see Hubbard, Linda S.

O'Donnell, Pat D., ed. Geriatric Urology. (Illus.). 608p. 1994. 132.00 (*0-316-63003-9*) Little.

O'Donnell, Patrick. Echo Chambers: Figuring Voice in Modern Narrative. LC 92-3841. 236p. 1992. text ed. 32.95 (*0-87745-375-6*) U of Iowa Pr.

— Passionate Doubts: Designs of Interpretation in Contemporary American Fiction. LC 85-28865. 213p. 1986. 27.95 (*0-87745-138-9*) U of Iowa Pr.

O'Donnell, Patrick, ed. New Essays on "The Crying of Lot 49" (American Novel Ser.). 150p. (C). 1992. 27.95 (*0-521-38163-0*); pap. 11.95 (*0-521-38833-3*) Cambridge U Pr.

O'Donnell, Patrick & Davis, Robert C., eds. Intertextuality & Contemporary American Fiction. LC 88-46066. 352p. 1989. text ed. 48.50x (*0-8018-3773-1*) Johns Hopkins.

O'Donnell, Peadar. The Big Windows. (Classic Irish Fiction Ser.). 212p. 1984. 15.95 (*0-8159-5117-5*) Devin.

— Big Windows. 211p. 1988. pap. 7.95 (*0-86278-090-X*, Pub. by OBrien Pr IE) Dufour.

— Islanders. 124p. 1988. pap. 9.95 (*0-85342-851-4*, Pub. by Mercier Pr IE) Dufour.

— Knife. LC 81-670153. (Illus.). 288p. 1980. reprint ed. pap. 11.95 (*0-906462-03-7*, Pub. by Irish Humanities IE) Dufour.

— Proud Island. 128p. 1988. pap. 8.95 (*0-86278-093-4*, Pub. by OBrien Pr IE) Dufour.

O'Donnell, Peggy. Public Library Development Program: Manual for Trainers. (Illus.). 154p. reprint ed. pap. 43.90 (*0-7837-5908-8*, 2045706) Bks Demand.

O'Donnell, Peggy, jt. auth. see Ingram, Anne.

O'Donnell, Peggy, jt. auth. see Phelps, Thomas C.

O'Donnell, Peter. Carnegie's Excuse. LC 92-17617. (Illus.). 32p. (J). (ps-3). 1993. 14.95 (*0-590-46435-3*) Scholastic Inc.

— Dead Man's Handle. (Modesty Blaise Adventure Ser.). 1986. 15.95 (*0-89296-245-3*); pap. 3.95 (*0-445-40587-2*) Mysterious Pr.

— Dizzy. (Illus.). (J). (ps up). 1992. 14.95 (*0-590-45475-7*, 021, Scholastic Hardcover) Scholastic Inc.

— Modesty Blaise: Death in Slow Motion; The Alternative Man; Sweet Caroline. Yronwode, Catherine, ed. (Comic Strip Ser.). (Illus.). 72p. (Orig.). 1986. pap. 5.95 (*0-912277-30-0*) K Pierce Inc.

— Modesty Blaise: The Head Girls; The Black Pearl; The Magnified Man. Yronwode, Catherine, ed. & intro. by. (Comic Strip Ser.). (Illus.). 64p. (Orig.). 1983. pap. 5.95 (*0-912277-10-6*) K Pierce Inc.

— Modesty Blaise: The Jericho Caper; The Killing Ground; Bad Suki. Yronwode, Catherine, ed. (Comic Strip Ser.). (Illus.). 56p. (Orig.). 1982. pap. 5.95 (*0-912277-09-2*) K Pierce Inc.

— Modesty Blaise: The Lady Killer; Garvin's Travels; The Scarlet Maiden. Yronwode, Catherine, ed. & intro. by. (Comic Strip Ser.). (Illus.). 72p. 1984. pap. 5.95 (*0-912277-25-4*) K Pierce Inc.

— Modesty Blaise: The Mind of Mrs. Drake; Uncle Happy. Yronwode, Catherine, ed. (Comic Strip Ser.). (Illus.). 64p. (Orig.). 1981. pap. 5.95 (*0-912277-08-4*) K Pierce Inc.

— Modesty Blaise: The Moon Man; A Few Flowers for the Colonel; The Balloonatic. Yronwode, Catherine, ed. (Comic Strip Ser.). (Illus.). 72p. (Orig.). 1985. pap. 5.95 (*0-912277-28-9*) K Pierce Inc.

— Modesty Blaise: The Return of the Mammoth; Plato's Republic; The Sword of the Bruce. Yronwode, Catherine, ed. (Comic Strip Ser.). (Illus.). 72p. (Orig.). 1986. pap. 5.95 (*0-912277-33-5*) K Pierce Inc.

— Modesty Blaise: Top Traitor; The Vikings. Yronwode, Catherine, ed. & intro. by. (Comic Strip Ser.). (Illus.). 64p. (Orig.). 1981. pap. 5.95 (*0-912277-07-6*) K Pierce Inc.

— The Night of Morningstar. 272p. 1987. reprint ed. 15.95 (*0-89296-222-4*) Mysterious Pr.

— Pieces of Modesty. 192p. 1986. reprint ed. 15.95 (*0-89296-172-4*) Mysterious Pr.

— Pinkie Leaves Home. (J). 1992. 13.95 (*0-590-45485-4*, Scholastic Hardcover) Scholastic Inc.

O'Donnell, R. M. Keynes: Philosophy, Economics & Politics: The Philosophical Foundations of Keynes's Thought & Their Influence on His Economics. LC 89-32732. 256p. 1989. text ed. 55.00 (*0-312-03578-0*) St Martin.

O'Donnell, R. M., ed. Keynes As Philosopher-Economist: The Ninth Keynes Seminar Held at the University of Kent at Canterbury, 1989. LC 91-16172. 190p. 1991. text ed. 49.95 (*0-312-06667-8*) St Martin.

O'Donnell, Randall L. Nurturing Leadership. LC 92-34531. 80p. 1992. 6.95 (*0-87483-296-9*) August Hse.

O'Donnell, Red. Country Gentleman: Biography Chet Atkins. 1976. 19.95 (*0-8488-1115-1*) Amereon Ltd.

***O'Donnell, Robert A.** Hooked on Philosophy. (Orig.). 1996. pap. write for info. (*0-8189-0740-1*) Alba.

O'Donnell, Rory. Adam Smith's Theory of Value & Distribution. LC 89-70271. 250p. 1990. text ed. 49.95 (*0-312-04508-5*) St Martin.

O'Donnell, Rory, jt. ed. see Nugent, Neill.

O'Donnell, S. & Persson, C. G. Directions for New Anti-Asthma Drugs. (Agents & Actions Supplements Ser.: No. 23). 246p. 1988. 82.00 (*0-8176-1957-7*) Birkhauser.

O'Donnell, Terence. An Arrow in the Earth: General Joel Palmer & the Indians of Oregon. (Illus.). 560p. 1991. pap. 14.95 (*0-87595-156-2*) Oregon Hist.

— Garden of the Brave in War: Recollections of Iran. xvi, 216p. 1988. pap. text ed. 12.95 (*0-226-61764-5*) U Ch Pr.

— That Balance So Rare: The Story of Oregon. (Illus.). 144p. (Orig.). 1988. pap. 8.95 (*0-87595-202-X*) Oregon Hist.

O'Donnell, Terence, ed. Talking on Paper: An Anthology of Oregon Letters & Diaries. (Oregon Literature Ser.: Vol. 6). (Illus.). 352p. (Orig.). 1994. text ed. 35.95 (*0-87071-377-9*); pap. 21.95 (*0-87071-378-7*) Oreg St U Pr.

O'Donnell, Teresa D. & Paiva, Judith L. Independent Writing. 2nd ed. 1993. pap. 20.95 (*0-8384-4206-4*) Heinle & Heinle.

O'Donnell, Terrence P. DOS 6: A Tutorial Accompany Peter Norton's Introduction to Computers. LC 93-44147. 1994. write for info. (*0-02-801328-X*) Glencoe.

— Lotus 1-2-3, Release 2.4: A Tutorial to Accompany Peter Norton's Introduction to Computers. LC 93-38995. 1994. write for info. (*0-02-801326-3*) Glencoe.

O'Donnell, Thomas A. Superacids & Acidic Melts As Inorganic Chemical Reaction Media. LC 92-15542. 243p. 1992. 110.00 (*1-56081-035-1*) VCH Pubs.

O'Donnell, Thomas F., jt. auth. see Franchere, Hoyt C.

O'Donnell, Thomas F., ed. see Frederic, Harold.

O'Donnell, Thomas F., jt. auth. see Jackson, Harry F.

O'Donnell, Thomas F., ed. see Paulding, James K.

O'Donnell, Thomas F., ed. see Van Der Donck, Adriaen.

O'Donnell, Thomas J. The Confessions of T. E. Lawrence: The Romantic Hero's Presentation of Self. LC 77-92257. x, 196p. 1979. 18.95 (*0-8214-0370-2*) Ohio U Pr.

— Medicine & Christian Morality. 2nd enl. rev. ed. LC 91-6673. 331p. 1991. pap. 16.95 (*0-8189-0609-X*) Alba.

O'Donnell, Timothy S. World Quality Life Indicators. (World Facts & Figures Ser.). 1991. lib. bdg. 40.00 (*0-87436-657-7*) ABC-CLIO.

O'Donnell, Timothy T. Heart of the Redeemer. LC 91-76070. (Illus.). 301p. 1992. reprint ed. pap. 14.95 (*0-89870-396-4*) Ignatius Pr.

An Asterisk (*) at the beginning of an entry indicates that the title is appearing in BIP for the first time.

***O'Donnell, Vivette & Campaign Against Bullying Staff.** Bullying: A Guide for Counsellers, Managers, Teachers & Parents. 192p. (Orig.). 1995. pap. 16.99 (1-85594-175-9, Pub. by Attic IE) InBook.

O'Donnell, W. R. & Todd, Loreto. Variety in Contemporary English. 192p. (Orig.). 1991. pap. 16.95 (0-04-445737-5, A8213) Routledge Chapman & Hall.

— Variety in Contemporary English. 2nd ed. LC 92-30151. (Orig.). 1992. write for info. (0-415-08437-7, Routledge NY) Routledge.

O'Donnell, William F. Mother Santa Clauss Stories. (J). 1976. 16.95 (0-8488-1116-X) Amereon Ltd.

O'Donnell, William H. A Guide to the Prose Fiction of W. B. Yeats. LC 83-3639. (Studies in Modern Literature: No. 12). 190p. reprint ed. pap. 54.20 (0-8357-1421-7, 2070567) Bks Demand.

O'Donnell, William H., ed. The Collected Works of W. B. Yeats Vol. V: Later Essays, Vol. 5. 296p. 1994. text ed. 35.00 (0-02-632702-3, Scribners) S&S Trade.

— The Collected Works of W. B. Yeats, Vol. 6: Prefaces & Introductions, Vol. 6. 370p. 1990. text ed. 35.00 (0-02-592551-2) Macmillan.

O'Donnell, William H., ed. see Yeats, William Butler.

O'Donnol, Dion. Listen-No Echo. (Destiny Ser). pap. 5.00 (0-686-00949-5) Wagon & Star.

O'Donnol, Shirley M. American Costume, 1915-1970: A Source Book for the Stage Costumer. LC 81-48390. (Illus.). 286p. (C). 1982. 35.00 (0-253-30589-6); pap. 15.00 (0-253-20543-3, MB-543) Ind U Pr.

***O'Donoghue, B.** Black Tides: The Alaska Oil Spill. (Illus.). 40p. 1995. pap. 4.95 (0-930931-05-X) Alaska Natural.

***ODonoghue, Bernard.** Seamus Heaney & the Language of Poetry. 1994. pap. text ed. 19.95 (0-13-320763-3) P-H.

O'Donoghue, Bernard. The Weakness. 80p. 1992. pap. 13.95 (0-7011-3859-9, Pub. by Chatto & Windus UK) Trafalgar.

O'Donoghue, D. J. The Poets of Ireland. 1972. 59.95 (0-8490-0867-0) Gordon Pr.

O'Donoghue, D. J., ed. see Mangan, James C.

O'Donoghue, David J. The Humour of Ireland, Selected. LC 75-28833. (Illus.). reprint ed. 54.00 (0-404-13823-3) AMS Pr.

O'Donoghue, Florence. No Other Law. 368p. (Orig.). 1986. reprint ed. pap. 11.95 (0-947962-12-3, Pub. by Anvil Bks Ltd IE) Irish Bks Media.

O'Donoghue, Gerard, et al. Clinical ENT: An Illustrated Textbook. (Illus.). 320p. 1992. 98.00 (0-19-262226-9); pap. 49.95 (0-19-261667-6) OUP.

O'Donoghue, Heather, ed. see Woolf, Rosemary.

O'Donoghue, Jo. Brian Moore: A Critical Study. 280p. (C). 1991. text ed. 44.95 (0-7735-0850-3, Pub. by McGill CN) U of Toronto Pr.

O'Donoghue, Jo, ed. Taisce Duan: A Treasury of Irish Poems with Translations in English. 270p. (Orig.). 1993. pap. 19.95 (1-85371-118-7, Pub. by Poolbeg Pr IE) Dufour.

O'Donoghue, John, jt. ed. see Weiss, Bernard.

O'Donoghue, John L., ed. Neurotoxicity of Industrial & Commercial Chemicals, 2 vols., Vol. I. 232p. 1985. 156.00 (0-8493-6454-X, RC347) CRC Pr.

— Neurotoxicity of Industrial & Commercial Chemicals, 2 vols., Vol. II. 224p. 1985. 156.00 (0-8493-6455-8) CRC Pr.

O'Donoghue, Mary X. Mother Vincent Whitty: Woman & Educator in a Masculine Society. 189p. 1972. 29.95 (0-522-84017-5) Intl Spec Bk.

O'Donoghue, Maureen. Jedder's Land. large type ed. (Charnwood Romance Ser.). 592p. 1985. 23.95 (0-7089-8249-2, Trail West Pubs) Ulverscroft.

O'Donoghue, Michael. Identifying Man-Made Gems. (Illus.). 221p. 1983. 37.50 (0-7198-0111-7, Pub. by NAG Press UK) Antique Collect.

— Illustrated Guide to Rocks & Minerals. (Illus.). 192p. 1992. 24.98 (0-8317-6389-2) Smithmark.

— Rocks & Minerals. (American Nature Guide Ser.). 1992. 9.98 (0-8317-6964-5) Smithmark.

— Socks Goes to Washington: The Diary of America's First Cat. 1993. pap. 6.95 (1-56566-042-0) Thomasson-Grant.

O'Donoghue, Michael, jt. auth. see Rowland-Entwistle, Theodore.

O'Donoghue, Noel D. Heaven in Ordinarie. 1979. 14.95 (0-87243-085-5) Templegate.

— The Mountain Behind the Mountain: Aspects of the Celtic Tradition. 1993. text ed. 29.95 (0-567-09652-1, Pub. by T & T Clark UK) Bks Intl VA.

— Mystics for Our Time. 159p. (Orig.). 1990. pap. text ed. 14.95 (0-8146-5783-4) Liturgical Pr.

O'Donoghue, Patrick. Decision-Related Research on the Organization of Service Delivery Systems in Metropolitan Areas: Public Health. LC 79-83820. 1979. write for info. (0-89138-984-9) ICPSR.

O'Donohoe, Niall V. Epilepsies of Childhood. 3rd ed. 320p. 1994. 70.00 (0-7506-1598-2) Buttrwrth-Heinemann.

O'Donohoe, Nick. The Magic & the Healing. 352p. (Orig.). 1994. pap. text ed. 5.99 (0-441-00053-3) Ace Bks.

— Too, Too Solid Flesh. LC 88-51731. (TSR Bks.). 352p. (Orig.). (J). 1989. pap. 3.95 (0-88038-767-X) TSR Inc.

— Under the Healing Sun. 352p. (Orig.). 1995. pap. text ed. 4.99 (0-441-00180-7) Ace Bks.

O'Donohue, John, tr. see Renault, Francois.

O'Donohue, W. T. & Geer, J. H., eds. The Sexual Abuse of Children, 2 vols., Set. 1992. text ed. 150.00 (0-8058-0956-2); pap. 60.00 (0-8058-0957-0) L Erlbaum Assocs.

— The Sexual Abuse of Children, 2 vols., Vol. I. 424p. 1991. pap. 36.00 (0-8058-0340-8) L Erlbaum Assocs.

— The Sexual Abuse of Children, 2 vols., Vol. I. 424p. (C). 1991. 79.95 (0-8058-0339-4) L Erlbaum Assocs.

— The Sexual Abuse of Children, 2 vols., Vol. II. 544p. 1991. pap. 39.95 (0-8058-0955-4) L Erlbaum Assocs.

— The Sexual Abuse of Children, Vol. II. 544p. (C). 1991. 89.95 (0-8058-0954-6) L Erlbaum Assocs.

***O'Donohue, Walter J., Jr., ed.** Long Term Oxygen Therapy: Scientific Basis & Clinical Application. LC 94-48767. (Lung Biology in Health & Disease Ser.: Vol. 81). 1995. text ed. write for info. (0-8247-9499-0) Dekker.

O'Donohue, William. Handbook of Psychological Skills Training: Clinical Techniques & Applications. 1994. 69.95 (0-205-15261-9, Longwood Div) Allyn.

O'Donohue, William & Geer, James H., eds. Handbook of Sexual Dysfunction: Assessment & Treatment. LC 92-48984. 1993. 69.95 (0-205-14787-9, Longwood Div) Allyn.

***O'Donohue, William & Krasner, Leonard, eds.** Theories of Behavior Therapy: Exploring Behavior Change. 600p. 1995. text ed. 69.95 (1-55798-265-1) Am Psychol.

O'Donohue, William, jt. ed. see Geer, James H.

O'Donovan, Daniel, tr. Bernard of Clairvaux, Treatises III: On Grace & Free Choice, in Praise of the New Knighthood. (Cistercian Studies: No. 3). 1977. 10.95 (0-87907-119-2); pap. 4.95 (0-87907-719-0) Cistercian Pubns.

O'Donovan, Dermot. Silas Rat & the Nuclear Tail. (Illus.). 125p. (J). 1988. reprint ed. pap. 7.95 (0-947962-22-0, Pub. by Childrens Pr IE) Irish Bks Media.

O'Donovan, Donal. The Rock from Which You Were Hewn. (Illus.). 224p. (Orig.). 1989. pap. 12.50 (0-9623863-0-8) D ODonovan.

O'Donovan, Edmond. Merv Oasis: Travels & Adventures East of the Caspian During the Years 1879-80-81. LC 71-115570. (Russia Observed Ser., No. 1). 1970. reprint ed. 56.95 (0-405-03053-3) Ayer.

O'Donovan, James. McPherson: The Law of Company Liquidation. 3rd ed. lxxxii, 501p. 1987. 110.50 (0-455-20741-0, Pub. by Law Bk Co) W W Gaunt.

— McPherson's Law of Company Liquidation. 250p. 1994. pap. 39.00 (0-455-21232-5, Pub. by Law Bk Co) W W Gaunt.

— Winding up & Receivership: Under the Companies Act 1981. xix, 48p. 1982. pap. 18.50 (0-455-20443-8, Pub. by Law Bk Co) W W Gaunt.

O'Donovan, James & Phillips, John C. The Modern Contract of Guarantee. xcvi, 675p. 1985. 113.50 (0-455-20349-0, Pub. by Law Bk Co) W W Gaunt.

O'Donovan, Jeremiah. Irish Immigration in the United States. LC 69-18786. (American Immigration Collection Ser., No. 1: No. 1). 1969. reprint ed. 18.95 (0-405-00534-2) Ayer.

O'Donovan, Joan. Dangerous Worlds. LC 72-75783. (Short Story Index Reprint Ser.). 1977. 17.95 (0-8369-3008-8) Ayer.

O'Donovan, Joan E. George Grant & the Twilight of Justice. 208p. 1984. pap. 13.95 (0-8020-6538-4) U of Toronto Pr.

O'Donovan, Joan L. The Theology of Law & Authority in the English Reformation. 421p. 1991. 39.95 (1-55540-628-9); pap. 24.95 (1-55540-629-7) Scholars Pr GA.

O'Donovan, John. Antiquities of the Country of Kerry. 1983. pap. 39.95 (0-946645-01-9) Dufour.

— Genealogies, Tribes & Customs of Hy-Fiachrach in Ireland. (Old Ireland Ser.). (Illus.). xii, 530p. 1993. reprint ed. lib. bdg. 129.00 (0-940134-38-1) Irish Genealog.

— Jonathan, Jack, & GBS: Four Plays about Irish History & Literature. Hogan, Robert T., ed. LC 91-51141. (Illus.). 232p. 1993. 35.00 (0-87413-452-8) U Delaware Pr.

— Tribes & Customs of Hy Many Commonly Called O'Kellys Country. (Old Ireland Ser.). (Illus.). vi, 221p. 1992. reprint ed. lib. bdg. 100.00 (0-940134-39-X) Irish Genealog.

O'Donovan, John, ed. Annals of the Four Masters, 7 Vols, Set. LC 70-15820. reprint ed. 875.00 (0-404-04820-X) AMS Pr.

O'Donovan, K. Sexual Divisions in Law. (Law in Context Ser.). xii, 242p. 1985. 30.00 (0-297-78664-4) Rothman.

O'Donovan, Katherine. Family Law Matters. LC 93-18373. 138p. 1993. pap. 17.95 (0-7453-0507-5, Pub. by Pluto Pr UK) Westview.

— Family Law Matters. LC 93-18373. 138p. (C). 1993. text ed. 50.00 (0-7453-0506-7) Westview.

O'Donovan, Leo J., ed. Cooperation Between Theologians & the Ecclesiastical Magisterium: A Report of the Joint Committee of the Canon Law Society of America & the Catholic Theological Society of America. 200p. (Orig.). 1982. pap. 5.00 (0-943616-12-3) Canon Law Soc.

***O'Donovan, Margaret & Dare, Angela.** A Practical Guide to Working with Babies 0-1. 128p. (C). 1994. pap. 30.00x (0-7478-1743-X, Pub. by S Thornes Pubs UK) St Mut.

O'Donovan, Mary A. Anglo-Saxon Charters, Vol. 3: Charters of Sherborne. (British Academy Ser.). (Illus.). 182p. 1988. 74.00 (0-19-726051-9) OUP.

O'Donovan, Michael. The Road to Stratford. 1988. reprint ed. lib. bdg. 39.00 (0-7812-0091-1) Rprt Serv.

— The Road to Stratford. reprint ed. 29.00 (0-403-04239-9) Somerset Pub.

O'Donovan, Oliver. Peace & Certainty: A Theological Essay on Deterrence. 1989. pap. 8.99 (0-8028-0414-4) Eerdmans.

— The Problem of Self-Love in St. Augustine. LC 80-5397. 229p. reprint ed. pap. 65.30 (0-8357-8285-9, 2033846) Bks Demand.

— Resurrection & Moral Order: An Outline for Evangelical Ethics. rev. ed. 320p. (C). 1994. pap. 22.99 (0-8028-0692-9) Eerdmans.

O'Donovan, Thomas M. G. P. S. S. Simulation Made Simple. LC 79-40520. (Wiley Computing Ser.). 127p. 1980. text ed. 68.95 (0-471-27614-6, Wiley-Interscience) Wiley.

— GPSS Simulation Made Simple. LC 79-40520. (Wiley Series in Computing). 139p. 1979. pap. 39.70 (0-7837-4011-5, 2043841) Bks Demand.

— VisiCalc Made Simple. LC 84-3680. 165p. reprint ed. pap. 47.10 (0-685-23443-6, 2032696) Bks Demand.

O'Donovan, Valentine, jt. auth. see Kudsia, Chandra M.

O'Dooley, Patrick. Flight Plan for Living: The Art of Self-Encouragement. LC 92-18245. 1992. 17.95 (0-942361-55-5) MasterMedia Ltd.

Odor, Harold & Odor, Ruth. Becoming a Christian. (Illus.). 16p. (J). (gr. 3-7). 1985. 0.99 (0-87239-901-X, 3301) Standard Pub.

— Sharing Your Faith. (Illus.). 16p. (J). (gr. 3-7). 1985. 0.75 (0-87239-902-8, 3302) Standard Pub.

***Odor, Kent & Ingmeier, Mark.** Creative Groups Guide: Faith's Fundamentals. Mack, Michael C., ed. 96p. (Orig.). 1995. student ed. pap. 12.99 (0-7847-0391-4, 11-40311) Standard Pub.

Odor, Ruth, jt. auth. see Odor, Harold.

Odor, Ruth S. A Child's Book of Manners. Beegle, Shirley, ed. (Happy Day Bks.). (Illus.). 24p. (J). (ps-3). 1994. reprint ed. pap. 1.89 (0-7847-0252-7) Standard Pub.

— Followers of Jesus. LC 91-67210. (Turn-the-Page-&-See Ser.). (Illus.). 32p. (J). (gr. 5-7). 1992. 5.99 (0-87403-933-9, 24-03563) Standard Pub.

— Glad. LC 79-26076. (What Does It Mean? Ser.). (Illus.). (J). (ps-2). 1980. lib. bdg. 18.50 (0-89565-114-9) Childs World.

— God Answers Prayers. LC 91-67209. (Turn-the-Page-&-See Ser.). (Illus.). 32p. (J). (gr. 5-7). 1992. 5.99 (0-87403-932-0, 24-03562) Standard Pub.

— God Keeps His Promises. LC 91-67212. (Turn-the-Page-&-See Ser.). (Illus.). 32p. (J). (gr. 5-7). 1992. 5.99 (0-87403-931-2, 24-03561) Standard Pub.

— Jesus Loves Us. LC 91-67211. (Turn-the-Page-&-See Ser.). (Illus.). 32p. (J). (gr. 5-7). 1992. 5.99 (0-87403-934-7, 24-03564) Standard Pub.

— Please. LC 79-25319. (What Does It Mean? Ser.). (Illus.). (J). (ps-2). 1980. lib. bdg. 18.50 (0-89565-115-7) Childs World.

— Thanks. LC 79-23926. (What Does It Mean? Ser.). (Illus.). (J). (ps-2). 1980. lib. bdg. 18.50 (0-89565-113-0) Childs World.

— The Very Special Visitors. (Happy Day Bks.). (Illus.). 28p. (J). (ps). 1992. 2.50 (0-87403-955-X, 24-03595) Standard Pub.

O'Dorisio, T. M., ed. Sandostatin in the Treatment of GEP Endrocine Tumors. 170p. 1989. 42.00 (0-387-50715-9) Spr-Verlag.

O'Dougherty, Patrick. Walden III: A Catholic America. 92p. (C). 1991. lib. bdg. 10.99 (0-9626665-1-3) Hellenist Amer Co.

O'Dougherty, Patrick A. An Existential Approach to American History: Patrick's "Unfinished" 60p. (C). 1989. lib. bdg. 5.99 (0-9626665-0-5) Hellenist Amer Co.

— Reinventing Physics: Logic & Physics, a Dialectical Approach to Physics. 144p. (C). 1993. lib. bdg. 10.99 (0-9626665-2-1) Hellenist Amer Co.

— Shaking up Shakespeare: His Dreamwork & Personality: Shakespeare: Dreamwork, Personality & Complexity. (Illus.). 169p. (C). 1994. lib. bdg. 19.99 (0-9626665-4-8) Hellenist Amer Co.

O'Dowd, Anne. Spalpeens & Tattie Hokers: History & Folklore of the Irish Migratory Agricultural Worker in Ireland & Britain. (Illus.). 456p. 45.00 (0-7165-2450-3, Pub. by Irish Acad Pr IE) Intl Spec Bk.

O'Dowd, Karen. Quick-&-Easy Heart Motif Quilts: Instructions & Full-Size Templates for Applique Projects. 48p. (Orig.). 1986. pap. 3.95 (0-486-25136-5) Dover.

O'Dowd, M. J., jt. ed. see Philipp, E. E.

O'Dowd, Mary, jt. ed. see MacCurtain, Margaret.

O'Dowda, Brendan. The World of Percy French. 2nd ed. (Illus.). 192p. 1992. pap. 21.00 (0-85640-482-9, Pub. by Blackstaff Pr IE) Dufour.

Odozor, Paulinus I. Richard A. McCormick & the Renewal of Moral Theology. LC 94-15941. (C). 1995. text ed. 34.95 (0-268-01648-8) U of Notre Dame Pr.

O'Drago, Alicia S. Radio Dial. LC 88-70857. 133p. (Orig.). 1988. pap. 9.95 (0-929273-00-1) AMP Publishing.

O'Driscoll, Ciaran, ed. The Poet & His Shadow. (C). 1990. 25.00 (0-948268-73-5, Pub. by Dedalus Pr IE); pap. 15.00 (0-948268-72-7, Pub. by Dedalus Pr IE) St Mut.

O'Driscoll, Donal. Alaska's Factory Fishing Boom: A Career & Job Opportunity Guide to the New Alaskan Goldrush. LC 90-80753. (Illus.). 150p. 1990. pap. 9.95 (1-878587-18-8) Global Fishing Pubns.

O'Driscoll, Gerald P., Jr., ed. Adam Smith & Modern Political Economy: Bicentennial Essays on the Wealth of Nations. LC 78-10181. 197p. reprint ed. pap. 56.20 (0-8357-6757-4, 2035414) Bks Demand.

— An Economic Perspective on the Southwest: Defining the Decade: Proceedings of the 1990 Conference on the Southwest Economy Sponsored by the Federal Reserve Bank of Dallas. 176p. (C). 1991. lib. bdg. 49.50 (0-7923-9221-3) Kluwer Ac.

— Free Trade Within North America: Expanding Trade for Prosperity, Proceedings of the 1991 Conference on the Southwest Economy Sponsored by the Federal Reserve Bank of Dallas. LC 92-33253. 1992. lib. bdg. 73.00 (0-7923-9291-4) Kluwer Ac.

O'Driscoll, Gerald P., Jr. & Brown, Stephen P., eds. The Southwest Economy in the Nineteen Nineties: A Different Decade. 224p. 1990. lib. bdg. 52.00 (0-7923-9092-X) Kluwer Ac.

***O'Driscoll, Gerald P., Jr. & Rizzo, Mario J.** The Economics of Time & Ignorance. 2nd ed. (Foundations of the Market Economy Ser.). 288p. 1995. pap. 19.95 (0-415-12120-5, C0408) Routledge.

O'Driscoll, Herbert. A Certain Life: Contemporary Meditations on the Way of Christ. large type ed. 192p. (Orig.). 1985. reprint ed. pap. 8.95 (0-8027-2491-4) Walker & Co.

— Emmanuel: Encountering Jesus as Lord. LC 92-24293. 110p. 1992. pap. 9.95 (1-56101-059-6) Cowley Pubns.

— For All the Saints: Homilies for Saints' & Holy Days. 168p. 1995. pap. 10.95 (1-56101-111-8) Cowley Pubns.

— The Leap of the Deer: Memories of a Celtic Childhood. LC 93-41744. 120p. 1994. 21.95 (1-56101-093-6); pap. 10.95 (1-56101-086-3) Cowley Pubns.

— Portrait of a Woman. 96p. (Orig.). 1981. pap. 4.95 (0-8164-2332-6) Harper SF.

— Prayers for the Breaking of Bread: Reflections on the Collects of the Church Year. LC 91-19446. 184p. 1991. pap. 9.95 (1-56101-045-6) Cowley Pubns.

— A Year of the Lord. LC 86-23835. 143p. (Orig.). 1987. pap. 8.95 (0-8192-1400-0) Morehouse Pub.

O'Driscoll, James E., ed. English Language & Orientation Programs in the United States. 214p. 1988. pap. 21.95 (0-87206-161-2) Inst Intl Educ.

O'Driscoll, Kenneth F., ed. see Sawada, Hideo.

O'Driscoll, Kenneth F., jt. ed. see Tsuruta, Teiji.

O'Driscoll, Mary, ed. see Saint Catherine of Siena.

O'Driscoll, Robert, ed. The Celtic Consciousness. LC 82-1269. (Illus.). 642p. 1982. 40.00 (0-8076-1041-0) Braziller.

— The Celtic Consciousness. LC 82-1269. (Illus.). 642p. 1985. reprint ed. pap. 27.95 (0-8076-1136-0) Braziller.

O'Driscoll, Robert, ed. see Seminar in Irish Studies (2nd: 1968: University of Toronto) Staff.

O'Driscoll, Sally, tr. see Clement, Catherine.

Oduba, Rebecca E., ed. see Koger, Dorothy P.

O'Duffy & Kokmen, eds. Behcet's Disease: Basic & Clinical Aspects. (Inflammatory Disease & Therapy Ser.: Vol. 8). 696p. 1991. 215.00 (0-8247-8476-6) Dekker.

O'Duffy, E. Crusade in Spain. 1972. 69.95 (0-87968-972-2) Gordon Pr.

***O'Duigneain, Prionnsios.** North Leitrim: The Land War & the Fall of Parnell. (North Leitrim History Ser.). (Illus.). 77p. (Orig.). 1988. pap. 6.95 (1-873437-06-4, Pub. by Drumlin Pubns Ltd IE) Irish Bks Media.

***O'Duignean, Prionnsias.** North Leitrim in Famine Times 1840-1850. (North Leitrim History Ser.). (Illus.). 56p. 1986. pap. 6.95 (1-873437-03-X, Pub. by Drumlin Pubns Ltd IE) Irish Bks Media.

— North Leitrim in Land League Times 1880-1884. (North Leitrim History Ser.). (Illus.). 52p. Date not set. pap. 6.95 (1-873437-04-8, Pub. by Drumlin Pubns Ltd IE) Irish Bks Media.

O'Duignean, Prionnsias, ed. see Duibhir, Ciaran O.

O'Duinn, Sean. Forbhais Droma Damhghaire: The Siege of Knocklong. 112p. (ENG & IRI.). 1993. pap. 15.95 (1-85635-021-5, Pub. by Mercier Pr IE) Dufour.

***Odukoya, Adebola T.** Let Your Works Speak for You: New Voices from American Pulpits. 90p. (Orig.). Date not set. pap. write for info. (1-885591-99-3) Morris Pubng.

O'Dulaing, Donncha. Voices of Ireland. 176p. 1984. 17.95 (0-86278-063-2, Pub. by OBrien Pr IE); pap. 8.95 (0-86278-065-9, Pub. by OBrien Pr IE) Dufour.

Odulate, Olu. Make Yourself Profitable for Yourself & Your Company. 160p. (C). 1989. pap. 65.00 (0-948353-50-3, Pub. by Oldcastle Bks UK) St Mut.

Odulphi Van Den Eynde, jt. ed. see Damiani Van Den Eynde.

Odum, Eugene P. Basic Ecology. 613p. (C). 1983. text ed. 53.25 (0-03-058414-0) SCP.

— Ecology: The Link Between the Natural & the Social Sciences. 2nd ed. LC 74-34189. (Modern Biology Ser.). 256p. (C). 1975. pap. text ed. 24.00 (0-03-004771-4) SCP.

— Ecology & Our Endangered Life-Support Systems. 2nd rev. ed. LC 92-40107. (Illus.). 320p. (C). 1993. pap. text ed. 21.95x (0-87893-634-3) Sinauer Assocs.

— Fundamentals of Ecology. 3rd ed. LC 76-81826. (Illus.). (C). 1971. text ed. 51.25 (0-7216-6941-7) Saunders.

Odum, Eugene P., ed. see Brimley, Herbert H.

Odum, H., jt. contrib. see Blissett, M.

Odum, Harry. The Vital Singles Ministry. (Effective Church Ser.). 144p. 1992. pap. 11.95 (0-687-43800-4) Abingdon.

Odum, Howard T. Ecological & General Systems: An Introduction to Systems Ecology. rev. ed. LC 93-46846. (Illus.). 664p. (C). 1994. pap. text ed. 39.95 (0-87081-320-X) Univ Pr Colo.

— Environmental Accounting: Energy & Environmental Decision Making. LC 95-11683. 1995. text ed. 79.95 (0-471-11442-1) Wiley.

— Systems Ecology: An Introduction. LC 82-8650. reprint ed. pap. 178.80 (0-7837-2809-3, 2057663) Bks Demand.

Odum, Howard T., ed. see AEC Technical Information Center Staff.

Odum, Howard T., jt. auth. see Beyers, Robert J.

Odum, Howard T., jt. ed. see Carter Ewel, Katherine.

Odum, Howard W. An American Epoch: Southern Portraiture in the National Picture. (BCL1 - United States Local History Ser.). 379p. 1991. reprint ed. lib. bdg. 89.00 (0-7812-6292-5) Rprt Serv.

— American Social Problems. LC 70-128283. (Essay Index Reprint Ser.). 1977. 44.95 (0-8369-1839-8) Ayer.

— Social & Mental Traits of the Negro. LC 68-56677. (Columbia University. Studies in the Social Sciences: No. 99). reprint ed. 29.50 (0-404-51099-X) AMS Pr.

Odum, Howard W., ed. Southern Pioneers in Social Interpretation. LC 67-23254. (Essay Index Reprint Ser.). 1977. 19.95 (0-8369-0750-7) Ayer.

Odum, Howard W. & Johnson, Guy B. Negro & His Songs: A Study of Typical Negro Songs in the South. LC 68-55902. 306p. 1969. reprint ed. text ed. 59.75 (0-8371-0596-X, ODS&, Negro U Pr) Greenwood.

O

— Negro Workaday Songs. LC 78-89050. 278p. 1970. reprint ed. text ed. 52.50 (0-8371-1938-3, ODW&, Negro U Pr) Greenwood.
— Negro Workaday Songs. 278p. 1990. reprint ed. lib. bdg. 69.00 (0-7812-9123-2) Rprt Serv.
***Odum, Jack K., et al.** High-Resolution, Shallow, Seismic Reflection Surveys of the Northwest Reelfoot Rift Boundary Near Marston, Missouri. LC 94-43970. (Professional Papers: Investigations of the New Madrid Seismic Zone: Vol. 1538-P). 1996. write for info. (0-614-03401-9) US Geol Survey.
O'Dunn & Sill. Exploring Geology: Introductory Laboratory Activities. 292p. (C). 1988. pap. text ed. write for info. (0-13-295668-3) P-H.
***Oduyoye, Mercy A.** Daughters of Anowa: African Women & Patriarchy. 226p. (Orig.). 1995. pap. 16.95 (0-88344-999-4) Orbis Bks.
— Hearing & Knowing: Theological Reflections on Christianity in Africa. LC 85-29873. 176p. (Orig.). 1986. pap. 16.95 (0-88344-258-2) Orbis Bks.
Oduyoye, Mercy A. & Kanyoro, Musimbi R., eds. The Will to Arise: Women, Tradition & the Church in Africa. LC 91-45847. 1992. 16.95 (0-88344-782-7) Orbis Bks.
Oduyoye, Mercy A., jt. ed. see Fabella, Virginia.
Odwin, Charles, et al. Appleton & Lange Review of Ultrasonography. 2nd ed. (Illus.). 556p. (C). 1993. pap. text ed. 54.95 (0-8385-9073-X, A9073-6) Appleton & Lange.
O'Dwyer, Barry W., tr. Letters from Ireland, 1228-1229. (Cistercian Fathers Ser.: No. 28). Orig. Title: Registrum epistolarum Stephani de Lexinton abbatis de Stanlegia et de Saviagnaco. 1982. 24.95 (0-87907-428-0) Cistercian Pubns.
O'Dwyer, George. Irish Catholic Genesis of Lowell. 80p. 1981. pap. 4.95 (0-942472-02-0) Lowell Museum.
O'Dwyer, J. R. O'Dwyer's Directory of Corporate Communications: 1991 Edition. 400p. (Orig.). 1990. pap. 110.00 (0-941424-22-7) J R ODwyer.
— O'Dwyer's Directory of Corporate Communications, 1982. 260p. (Orig.). 1982. pap. 70.00 (0-941424-01-4) J R ODwyer.
— O'Dwyer's Directory of Corporate Communications, 1984. 300p. (Orig.). 1984. pap. 80.00 (0-941424-06-5) J R ODwyer.
— O'Dwyer's Directory of Public Relations Executives, 1983. 310p. (Orig.). 1983. pap. 70.00 (0-941424-02-2) J R ODwyer.
— O'Dwyer's Directory of Public Relations Executives, 1986 Edition. 400p. 1986. pap. 70.00 (0-941424-10-3) J R ODwyer.
— O'Dwyer's Directory of Public Relations Firms: 1991 Edition. 400p. (Orig.). 1990. pap. 110.00 (0-941424-23-5) J R ODwyer.
— O'Dwyer's Directory of Public Relations Firms, 1984. 300p. (C). 1984. pap. 70.00 (0-941424-05-7) J R ODwyer.
— O'Dwyer's Directory of Public Relations Firms, 1986 Edition. 400p. 1986. text ed. 90.00 (0-317-38197-0); pap. 90.00 (0-941424-09-X) J R ODwyer.
O'Dwyer, J. R., Co., Inc. Staff. O'Dwyer's Directory of Corporate Communications, 1986-87. 320p. 1986. 90.00 (0-941424-11-1) J R ODwyer.
O'Dwyer, Jack. O'Dwyer's Directory of Corporate Communication, 1988. 450p. 1988. 110.00 (0-317-62319-2) J R ODwyer.
— O'Dwyer's Directory of Public Relations Executives, 1986. 300p. 1986. 70.00 (0-317-62316-8) J R ODwyer.
***O'Dwyer, Jack, ed.** O'Dwyer's Washington, D. C. Public Relations Directory. 216p. (Orig.). 1994. pap. 49.50 (0-941424-32-4) J R ODwyer.
O'Dwyer, Jade. O'Dwyer's Directory of Public Relations Firms, 1987. 400p. 1987. text ed. 90.00 (0-317-52438-0); pap. 90.00 (0-941424-12-X) J R ODwyer.
O'Dwyer, James F. The Art of the Matador. LC 87-72377. (Illus.). 87p. 1988. 19.95 (0-87062-183-1) A H Clark.
O'Dwyer, John R. O'Dwyer's Directory of Corporate Communications, 1983. annuals 260p. (Orig.). 1983. pap. 70.00 (0-941424-04-9) J R ODwyer.
— O'Dwyer's Directory of Corporate Communications, 1985. 300p. (Orig.). 1985. pap. 90.00 (0-941424-08-1) J R ODwyer.
O'Dwyer, Margaret M. The Papacy in the Age of Napoleon & the Restoration: Pius VII, 1800-1823. 296p. (Orig.). 1985. pap. text ed. 24.00 (0-8191-4826-1) U Pr of Amer.
***O'Dwyer, Michael.** Drowning the Hullaballoo Blues. 256p. (Orig.). 1995. pap. 11.99 (1-85594-151-1) InBook.
O'Dwyer, Paul, ed. see O'Dwyer, William.
O'Dwyer, R. & Le Page, R. B. Glossary of Modern Art. pap. 1.45 (0-685-19403-5, 99, Citadel Pr) Carol Pub Group.
O'Dwyer, William. Beyond the Golden Door. O'Dwyer, Paul, ed. LC 86-62415. 457p. 1987. 18.95 (0-87075-575-7) St Johns.
Ody, Anthony. Rural Enterprise Development in China, 1986-90. LC 92-12836. (Discussion Paper Ser.: Vol. 162). 61p. 1992. pap. 6.95 (0-8213-2118-8, 12118) World Bank.
Ody, Penelope. The Complete Medicinal Herbal. LC 92-53451. (Illus.). 144p. 1993. 29.95 (1-56458-187-X) Dorling Kindersley.
— Home Herbal. LC 94-26719. (Illus.). 144p. 1995. 19.95 (1-56458-863-7) Dorling Kindersley.
Odyniec, M. Solid State Microwave Oscillators. 1987. text ed. write for info. (0-442-23708-1) Van Nos Reinhold.
Odyniec, W. & Lewicki, G. Minimal Projections in Banach Spaces: Problems of Existence & Uniqueness & Their Application. (Lecture Notes in Mathematics Ser.: Vol. 1449). (Illus.). viii, 168p. 1990. pap. 27.00 (0-387-53197-1) Spr-Verlag.
***Odyssey Group Staff.** The ZEV (Zero Emissions Vehicle) Book. (Illus.). 30p. (J). 1995. pap. text ed. 4.00 (1-57074-248-0) Greyden Pr.
Odzer, Cleo. Patpong Sisters: Prostitution in Bangkok. (Illus.). 320p. 1994. 24.95 (1-55970-281-8) Arcade Pub Inc.
— Where Did the Hippies Go? They Went to Goa. (Illus.). 1995. 15.95 (1-56201-059-X) Blue Moon Bks.
Odzer, Esther. Miss Rogan Poems. (Illus.). 96p. (Orig.). 1984. pap. 4.76 (0-9613572-0-7) E Odzer.
***Oe, Kenzaburo.** An Echo of Heaven. Mitsutani, Magaret, tr. 240p. Date not set. 22.00 (4-7700-1986-6) FS&G.
— Hiroshima Notes. Swain, David L. & Yonezawa, Toshi, trs. 168p. (JPN.). 1995. 22.95 (0-7145-3007-7) M Boyars Pubs.
— Japan, the Ambiguous & Myself: The Nobel Prize Speech & Other Lectures. (Illus.). 130p. 1995. 18.00 (4-7700-1980-7) Kodansha.
— Nip the Buds, Shoot the Kids. Mackintosh, Paul S. & Sugiyama, Maki, trs. 1995. 22.95 (0-7145-2997-4) M Boyars Pubs.
— A Personal Matter. Nathan, John, tr. 214p. 1991. pap. 7.95 (0-8021-5061-6) Grove-Atltic.
— The Pinch Runner Memorandum: Oe Kenzaburo. Wilson, Michiko N. & Wilson, Michael K., trs. LC 94-26114. 265p. 1994. text ed. 39.95 (1-56324-183-8, East Gate Bk); pap. text ed. 17.95 (1-56324-184-6, East Gate Bk) M E Sharpe.
— The Silent Cry. Shaw, S., ed. 288p. 1994. 25.00 (4-7700-0450-8); pap. 11.00 (4-7700-1965-3) Kodansha.
— Teach Us to Outgrow Our Madness. Nathan, John, tr. LC 76-54582. 261p. 1977. 11.00 (0-8021-5185-X) Grove-Atltic.
Oe, Kenzaburo, et al. The Catch & Other War Stories. LC 80-84420. 156p. 1981. pap. 9.00 (0-87011-457-3, L46) Kodansha.
OECD, CERI Staff. Environment, School & Active Learning. 146p. (Orig.). 1991. pap. 30.00 (92-64-13569-3) OECD.
OECD-CERI Staff. Information Technologies in Education: The Quest for Quality Software. 126p. (Orig.). 1989. pap. 17.00 (92-64-13287-2) OECD.
OECD-IEA Staff. Collaboration in Energy Technology, 1987-1990. 238p. (Orig.). 1992. pap. 44.00 (92-64-13661-4) OECD.
OECD-NEA Staff. Nuclear Energy Data 1992. 45p. (Orig.). 1992. pap. 14.00 (92-64-03680-6) OECD.
OECD, Nuclear Energy Agency Staff. Advanced Water-Cooled Reactor Technologies: Rationale, State of Progress & Outlook - Report by an Expert Group. 103p. (Orig.). 1989. pap. 28.00 (92-64-13302-X) OECD.
— Gas Generation & Release from Radioactive Waste Repositories: Proceedings 23-26 Sept 1991. 438p. (Orig.). (ENG & FRE.). 1992. pap. 78.00 (92-64-03691-1) OECD.
— Good Performance in Nuclear Projects: Proceedings of an International Symposium, April 1989. 786p. (Orig.). (ENG & FRE.). 1989. pap. 95.00 (92-64-03239-8) OECD.
— Probabilistic Safety Assessment in Nuclear Power Plant Management. 112p. (Orig.). 1990. pap. 25.00 (92-64-13318-6) OECD.
OECD Staff. Access to Taxis. 224p. (Orig.). 1992. pap. 27.00 (92-821-1166-0) OECD.
— Accounting Reform in Central & Eastern Europe. 160p. (Orig.). 1992. pap. 28.00 (92-64-13609-6) OECD.
— Achieving Nuclear Safety: Improvements in Reactor Safety Design & Operation. 96p. (Orig.). 1993. pap. 19.00 (92-64-13833-1) OECD.
— Adjustment & Equity in Cote D'Ivoire. 172p. (Orig.). 1992. pap. 31.00 (92-64-13654-1) OECD.
— Adjustment & Equity in Developing Countries: A New Approach. 112p. (Orig.). 1992. pap. 31.00 (92-64-13664-9) OECD.
— Adjustment & Equity in Ecuador. 174p. (Orig.). 1991. pap. 31.00 (92-64-13539-1) OECD.
— Adjustment & Equity in Ghana. 164p. (Orig.). 1992. pap. 31.00 (92-64-13757-2) OECD.
— Adjustment & Technology: The Case of Rice. 160p. (Orig.). 1993. pap. 24.00 (92-64-13942-7) OECD.
— Advanced Emission Controls for Power Plants. 236p. (Orig.). 1993. pap. 40.00 (92-64-03865-5) OECD.
— Advanced Logistics & Road Freight Transport. 184p. (Orig.). 1992. pap. 64.00 (92-64-13730-0) OECD.
— Advanced Materials: Policies & Technological Challenges. 188p. (Orig.). 1990. pap. 40.00 (92-64-13255-4) OECD.
— Agricultural & Environmental Policies: Opportunities for Integration. 200p. (Orig.). Date not set. pap. text ed. 22.00 (92-64-13127-2, 97-88-04-1) OECD.
— Agricultural & Environmental Policy Integration: Recent Progress & New Directions. 112p. (Orig.). 1993. pap. 24.00 (92-64-13820-X) OECD.
OECD Staff, et al. Agricultural Developments in Africa & Supply of Manufactured Goods. 130p. (Orig.). 1989. pap. 24.00 (92-64-13273-2) OECD.
OECD Staff. Agricultural Policies, Markets & Trade: Monitoring & Outlook 1993. 380p. (Orig.). 1993. pap. 52.00 (92-64-13902-8) OECD.
— Agricultural Policies, Markets & Trade: Monitoring & Outlook, 1994. 365p. (Orig.). 1994. pap. 50.00 (92-64-14140-5) OECD.
— Agricultural Policies, Markets & Trade in the Central & East European Countries, the New Independent States & China. 150p. (Orig.). 1993. pap. 22.00 (92-64-13916-8) OECD.
— Agricultural Trade Liberalisation & India. 120p. (Orig.). 1993. pap. 23.00 (92-64-13851-X) OECD.
— Agriculture & the Consumer. 58p. (Orig.). 1990. pap. 14.00 (92-64-13411-5) OECD.
— Agriculture & the Environment in the Transition to a Market Economy (CCET) 290p. (Orig.). 1994. pap. 33.00 (92-64-14137-5) OECD.
— Agriculture & the Policy Environment: Tanzania & Kenya. 104p. (Orig.). 1993. pap. 19.00 (92-64-13906-0) OECD.
— Agriculture, Liberalisation, & Economic Growth in Ghana & Cote D'Ivoire. 144p. (Orig.). 1993. pap. 27.00 (92-64-13936-2) OECD.
— Alternatives to Universities. 85p. (Orig.). 1991. pap. 22.00 (92-64-13530-8) OECD.
— The Apple Market in OECD Countries. (Orig.). Date not set. pap. text ed. 30.00 (92-64-13590-1, 51-91-05-1) OECD.
— Applying Economic Instruments to Environmental Policies in OECD & Dynamic Non-Member Countries. 260p. (Orig.). 1994. pap. 30.00x (92-64-14212-6) OECD.
— Apprenticeship: Which Way Forward? 160p. (Orig.). 1994. pap. 38.00x (92-64-14294-0) OECD.
— Aquaculture: A Review of Recent Experience. (Aquaculture Ser.). 331p. (Orig.). 1989. pap. 52.50 (92-64-13218-X) OECD.
— Aquaculture: Developing a New Industry. 126p. (Orig.). 1989. pap. 34.00 (92-64-13206-6) OECD.
— Aquatic Biotechnology & Food Safety. 100p. (Orig.). 1994. pap. 18.00 (92-64-14063-8) OECD.
— Assessing Investment Opportunities in Economies in Transition. 186p. (Orig.). 1994. pap. 52.00x (92-64-24252-X) OECD.
— Assessing the Effects of the Uruguay Round. 38p. (Orig.). 1993. pap. 11.00 (92-64-14017-4) OECD.
— Asset & Liability Management by Banks. (Trends in Banking Structure & Regulation in OECD Countries Ser.). 176p. (Orig.). 1987. pap. 20.00 (92-64-13009-8) OECD.
— Astronomy. 150p. (Orig.). 1993. pap. 40.00 (92-64-13928-1) OECD.
— Automobile Insurance & Road Accident Prevention. 128p. (Orig.). 1990. pap. 32.00 (92-64-13409-3) OECD.
— Bank Profitability: Financial Statements of Banks - Statistical Supplement 1981-1990. 194p. (Orig.). (ENG & FRE.). 1992. pap. 37.00 (92-64-03531-1) OECD.
— Bank Profitability: Financial Statements of Banks 1983-1992. 190p. (Orig.). 1994. pap. 39.00 (92-64-04114-1) OECD.
— Bank Profitability Statistical Supplement: Financial Statements of Banks 1982-1991. 200p. (Orig.). 1993. pap. 42.00 (92-64-03719-5) OECD.
— Banks under Stress. 172p. (Orig.). 1992. pap. 35.00 (92-64-13631-2) OECD.
— Barriers to Trade with the Economies in Transition. 46p. (Orig.). 1994. pap. 7.00x (92-64-14206-1) OECD.
— Basic Science & Technology Statistics. 377p. (Orig.). (ENG & FRE.). 1991. pap. 60.00 (92-64-03501-X) OECD.
— Basic Science & Technology Statistics: 1993 Edition. 334p. (Orig.). (ENG & FRE.). 1993. pap. 60.00 (92-64-04896-0) OECD.
— Behavioural Adaptations to Changes in the Road Transport System. 123p. (Orig.). 1990. pap. 26.00 (92-64-13389-5) OECD.
— Benefits Estimates & Environment Decision-Making. 64p. (Orig.). 1992. pap. 14.00 (92-64-13751-3) OECD.
— Benefits of Different Transport Modes: Round Table, No. 93. 105p. (Orig.). 1994. pap. 18.00 (92-821-1189-X) OECD.
— The Benefits of Free Trade: East Asia & Latin America. 228p. (Orig.). 1994. pap. 49.00 (92-64-14110-3) OECD.
— Biofuels. 80p. (Orig.). 1994. pap. 28.00x (92-64-14233-9) OECD.
— Biotechnology: Economic & Wider Impacts. 110p. (Orig.). 1989. pap. 20.00 (92-64-13196-5) OECD.
— Biotechnology, Agriculture & Food. 220p. (Orig.). 1992. pap. 43.00 (92-64-13725-4) OECD.
— Biotechnology & the Changing Role of Government. 125p. (Orig.). 1988. pap. 20.00 (92-64-13072-1) OECD.
— Biotechnology for a Clean Environment: Prevention, Detection & Remediation. 204p. (Orig.). 1994. pap. 68.00x (92-64-14257-6) OECD.
— Bridge Management. (Road Transport Research Ser.). 126p. (Orig.). 1992. pap. 43.00 (92-64-13617-7) OECD.
— Bridge Rehabilitation & Strengthening. (Road Transport Research Ser.). 104p. 1983. pap. 15.00 (92-64-12528-0) OECD.
— Broad Economic Impact of Nuclear Power. 244p. (Orig.). 1992. pap. 62.00 (92-64-13789-0) OECD.
— Bulgaria: An Economic Assessment. 152p. (Orig.). 1992. pap. 23.00 (92-64-13753-X) OECD.
— Business & Jobs in the Rural World: Local Initiatives for Job Creation. 203p. (Orig.). 1992. pap. 41.00 (92-64-13630-4) OECD.
— Canada 1994. (Development Cooperation Review Ser.: No. 5). 64p. (Orig.). 1994. pap. 9.00x (92-64-14221-5) OECD.
— Caring for Frail Elderly People: New Directions in Care. 143p. (Orig.). 1994. pap. 27.00x (92-64-14160-X) OECD.
— Cars & Climate Change. 350p. (Orig.). 1993. pap. 60.00 (92-64-13804-8) OECD.
— Changes in Cereals & Dairy Policies in OECD Countries: A Model-Based Analysis. 170p. (Orig.). 1991. pap. text ed. 33.00 (92-64-13582-0, 51-91-6-1) OECD.
— The Changing Course of International Migration. 272p. (Orig.). 1993. pap. 72.00 (92-64-13827-7) OECD.
— The Changing Public Policies in Information Technology: Canada, the Netherlands, & Sweden. 156p. 1992. pap. 19.00 (92-64-03694-6) OECD.
— The Changing Role of Government Research Laboratories. 74p. (Orig.). 1989. pap. 15.00 (92-64-13181-7) OECD.
— Charging for the Use of Urban Roads. 174p. (Orig.). 1994. pap. 39.00x (0-614-02756-X) OECD.
— China's Long March to an Open Economy. 120p. (Orig.). 1994. pap. 19.00x (92-64-14290-8) OECD.
— Choosing Priorities in Science & Technology. 91p. (Orig.). 1991. pap. 24.00 (92-64-13499-9) OECD.
— Cities & New Technologies. 289p. (Orig.). 1992. pap. 80.00 (92-64-13591-X) OECD.
— Cities for the 21st Century. 204p. (Orig.). 1994. pap. 39.00x (92-64-14287-8) OECD.
— Clean & Efficient Use of Coal & Ignite. 1186p. (Orig.). 1994. pap. 150.00x (92-64-14243-6) OECD.
— Climate: Designing a Practical Tax System. 276p. (Orig.). 1992. pap. text ed. 35.00 (92-64-13776-9, 02-92-07-1) OECD.
— Climate Change: Designing a Tradeable Permit System. 282p. (Orig.). 1992. pap. 31.00 (92-64-13731-9) OECD.
— Climate Change: Policy Initiatives. 184p. (Orig.). 1992. pap. 37.00 (92-64-13754-8) OECD.
— Climate Change Policy Initiatives 1994 Vol. 1: Update. 217p. (Orig.). 1994. pap. 53.00x (92-64-14142-1) OECD.
— Co-Ordinated Urban Transport Pricing. (Road Transport Research Ser.). 152p. (Orig.). 1985. 22.00 (92-64-12692-9) OECD.
— Coal Information Nineteen Ninety-Two. 542p. (Orig.). 1992. pap. 125.00 (92-64-13679-7) OECD.
— Coal Information, 1992: 1993 Edition. 500p. (Orig.). 1993. pap. 125.00 (92-64-13941-9) OECD.
— Coal Information 1993. 605p. (Orig.). 1994. pap. 125.00x (92-64-14185-5) OECD.
— Coastal Zone Management: Integrated Policies. 148p. (Orig.). 1993. pap. 36.00 (92-64-13826-9) OECD.
— Coastal Zone Management: Selected Case Studies. 312p. (Orig.). 1993. pap. 37.00 (92-64-03715-2) OECD.
— Code of Liberalisation of Capital Movements: 1993 Edition. 143p. (Orig.). 1993. pap. text ed. 30.00 (92-64-13969-9, 21-93-11-1) OECD.
— Code of Liberalisation of Capital Movements 1992. 142p. (Orig.). 1992. pap. 31.00 (92-64-13658-4) OECD.
— Code of Liberalisation of Current Invisible Operations: 1992 Edition. 124p. (Orig.). 1992. pap. 31.00 (92-64-13659-2) OECD.
— Code of Liberalisation of Current Invisible Operations: 1993 Editions. 121p. (Orig.). 1993. pap. text ed. 30.00 (92-64-13968-0, 21-93-08-1) OECD.
— Communications Outlook, 1990. 54p. (Orig.). 1990. pap. 32.00 (92-64-03336-X) OECD.
— Communications Outlook, 1993. 164p. (Orig.). 1993. pap. 40.00 (92-64-13841-2) OECD.
— Competition & Economic Development. 268p. (Orig.). 1991. pap. 34.00 (92-64-03347-5) OECD.
— Competition Policy & Intellectual Property Rights. 122p. (Orig.). 1989. pap. 19.00 (92-64-13242-2) OECD.
— Competition Policy & the Deregulation of Road Transport. 78p. (Orig.). 1990. pap. 16.00 (92-64-13428-X) OECD.
— Competition Policy & Vertical Restraints: Franchising Agreements. 241p. (Orig.). 1994. pap. 42.00 (92-64-14053-0) OECD.
— Competition Policy in OECD Countries: 1989-1990. 324p. (Orig.). 1992. pap. 40.00 (92-64-13728-9) OECD.
— Competition Policy in OECD Countries, 1990-1991. 370p. (Orig.). 1993. pap. 45.00 (92-64-14023-9) OECD.
— Competition Policy in OECD Countries 1991-1992. 456p. (Orig.). 1994. pap. 49.00x (92-64-14227-4) OECD.
— Conference on Energy & Environment in European Economies in Transition: Priorities & Opportunities for Cooperation & Integration. 256p. (Orig.). 1992. pap. 53.00 (92-64-13813-7) OECD.
— Congestion Control & Demand Management. 144p. (Orig.). 1994. pap. 38.00x (92-64-14315-7) OECD.
— Consumer Policy in OECD Countries, 1987-1988. 248p. (Orig.). 1990. pap. 32.00 (92-64-13351-8) OECD.
— Consumer Policy in OECD Member Countries 1989-1990. 260p. (Orig.). 1993. pap. 39.00 (92-64-13835-8) OECD.
— Consumer Price Indices: Sources & Methods. 86p. (Orig.). (ENG & FRE.). 1994. pap. 9.00 (92-64-04113-3) OECD.
— The Contribution of Amenities to Rural Development. 91p. (Orig.). 1994. pap. 18.00x (92-64-14164-2) OECD.
— Control & Management of Government Expenditures. 192p. (Orig.). 1987. pap. 27.00 (92-64-12995-2) OECD.
— Control Strategies for Photochemical Oxidants Across Europe. 116p. (Orig.). 1990. pap. 26.00 (92-64-13401-8) OECD.
— Convention on Climate Change: Economic Aspects of Negotiations. 98p. (Orig.). 1992. pap. 23.00 (92-64-13668-1) OECD.
— Convergence Between Communications Technologies: Case Studies from North America & Europe. (Information Computer Communications Policy Ser.: No. 28). 148p. (Orig.). 1992. pap. 37.00 (92-64-13633-9) OECD.
— Corporate Bankruptcy & Reorganization Procedures in OECD & Central & Eastern European Countries. 144p. (Orig.). 1994. pap. 26.00x (92-64-14192-8) OECD.
— The Cost of High-Level Waste Disposal in Geological Repositories: An Analysis of Factors Affecting Cost Estimates. 136p. (Orig.). 1993. pap. 36.00 (92-64-13914-1) OECD.
— The Costs of Cutting Carbon Emissions: Results from Global Models. 160p. (Orig.). 1993. pap. 19.00 (92-64-03875-2) OECD.
— The Costs of Restricting Imports: The Automobile Industry. 174p. (Orig.). 1988. pap. 18.00 (92-64-13037-3) OECD.
— Creating Rural Indicators for Shaping Territorial Policy. 85p. (Orig.). 1994. pap. 18.00 (92-64-14112-X) OECD.

An Asterisk (*) at the beginning of an entry indicates that the title is appearing in BIP for the first time.

— Credit Reporting System Gazette: Quarterly Report on Individual Aid Commitments Oct. 1994-Feb. 1995. 50p. (Orig.). 1995. pap. 12.00x (*0-614-04183-X*) OECD.
— Creditor Reporting System Gazette: Individual Aid Commitments Reports July to October 1994. 128p. (Orig.). 1994. pap. 12.00x (*92-64-04268-7*) OECD.
— Curriculum Reform: Assessment in Question. 148p. (Orig.). (ENG & FRE.). 1993. pap. 19.00 (*92-64-03863-9*) OECD.
— Curtailing Usage of De-Icing Agents in Winter Maintenance. (Road Transport Research Ser.). 124p. (Orig.). 1989. pap. 24.00 (*92-64-13280-5*) OECD.
— Dairy Sector Indicators. 228p. (Orig.). (ENG & FRE.). 1994. pap. 36.00x (*92-64-04264-4*) OECD.
— Debt Stocks, Debt Flows, & the Balance of Payment. 156p. (Orig.). 1994. pap. 36.00x (*92-64-14258-4*) OECD.
— Decommissioning of Nuclear Facilities: An Analysis of the Variability of Decommissioning Cost Estimates. 130p. (Orig.). 1991. pap. 33.00 (*92-64-13552-9*) OECD.
— Decommissioning Policies for Nuclear Facilities: Proceedings 2-4 Oct 1991 in Paris. 398p. (Orig.). (ENG & FRE.). 1992. pap. 82.00 (*92-64-03689-X*) OECD.
— Deep Drilling. 135p. (Orig.). 1993. pap. 40.00 (*92-64-13956-7*) OECD.
— Delinquency & Vandalism in Public Transport. (ECMT Round Table Ser.: No. 77). 164p. (Orig.). 1989. pap. 20.00 (*92-821-1126-1*) OECD.
— Demand Side Management: Opportunities & Perspectives in the Asia-Pacific Region with Emphasis on the Gas & Electricity Sectors. 308p. (Orig.). 1994. pap. 42.00 (*0-317-05753-7*) OECD.
— Demand-Side Management: Opportunities & Perspectives in the Asia-Pacific Region, with Emphasis on the Gas & Electricity Sectors. 308p. (Orig.). 1994. pap. text ed. 42.00 (*92-64-14060-3*, 61-94-03-1) OECD.
— Deregulation of Freight Transport. (ECMT Round Table Ser.: No. 84). 132p. (Orig.). 1991. pap. 32.00 (*92-821-1154-7*) OECD.
— Development Cooperation Review Series: France. 40p. (Orig.). 1994. pap. 9.00x (*92-64-14162-6*) OECD.
— Development Cooperation Review Series: Spain 1994. 40p. (Orig.). 1994. pap. 9.00x (*92-64-14215-0*) OECD.
— Development Cooperation Review Series: United Kingdom 1994. 50p. (Orig.). 1994. pap. 9.00x (*92-64-14125-1*) OECD.
— The Diffusion of Advanced Telecommunications in Developing Countries. 111p. (Orig.). 1991. pap. 19.00 (*92-64-13578-2*) OECD.
— Directory - French Research Development Databases: An Overview. 126p. (Orig.). 1994. pap. 20.00x (*92-64-04262-8*) OECD.
— Directory of Development Research & Training Institutes in Africa. 248p. (Orig.). 1992. pap. 40.00 (*92-64-03539-7*) OECD.
— Directory of Development Research & Training Institutes in Europe. 237p. (Orig.). (ENG & FRE.). 1991. pap. 40.00 (*92-64-03505-2*) OECD.
— Directory of Non-Governmental Environment & Development Organisations in OECD Member Countries. 410p. (Orig.). 1992. pap. 68.00 (*92-64-03536-2*) OECD.
— Directory of Research & Training Institutes in Latin America. 154p. (Orig.). 1993. pap. 27.00 (*92-64-03705-5*) OECD.
— Disabled Youth: From School to Work. 70p. (Orig.). 1991. pap. 16.00 (*92-64-13448-4*) OECD.
— Disabled Youth & Employment. 135p. (Orig.). 1994. pap. 13.00x (*92-64-14152-9*) OECD.
— Disposal of Radioactive Waste: Review of Safety Assessment Methods. 77p. (Orig.). 1991. pap. 23.00 (*92-64-13493-X*) OECD.
— Durability of Concrete Road Bridges. (Road Transport Research Ser.). 136p. (Orig.). 1989. pap. 23.50 (*92-64-13199-X*) OECD.
— Dynamic Loading of Pavements. 188p. (Orig.). 1992. pap. 80.00 (*92-64-13762-9*) OECD.
— ECMT Thirty-Ninth Annual Report, 1992: Resolutions of the Council of Ministers & Reports Approved in 1992. 320p. (Orig.). 1993. pap. 53.00 (*92-821-1186-5*) OECD.
— ECMT 40th Annual Report: Resolutions of the Council of Ministers Approved in 1993. 200p. (Orig.). 1994. pap. 59.00x (*92-64-11196-4*) OECD.
— Economic Accounts for Agriculture, 1976-1989. 237p. (Orig.). 1992. pap. 40.00 (*92-64-03521-4*) OECD.
— Economic & Trade Issues in the Computerised Database Market. 216p. (Orig.). 1993. pap. 42.00 (*92-64-13830-7*) OECD.
— Economic Instruments for Environmental Management in Developing Countries. 101p. (Orig.). 1993. pap. 11.00 (*92-64-13952-4*) OECD.
— Economic Instruments for Environmental Protection. 132p. (Orig.). 1989. pap. 23.50 (*92-64-13251-1*) OECD.
— Economic Integration, Dynamic Asian Economies, & Central & Eastern European Countries. 136p. (Orig.). 1993. pap. 35.00 (*92-64-13840-4*) OECD.
— The Economics of Climate Change: Proceedings of an OECD - IEA Conference. 320p. (Orig.). 1994. pap. 40.00 (*92-64-14138-3*) OECD.
— The Economics of the Nuclear Fuel Cycle. 190p. (Orig.). 1994. pap. 46.00x (*92-64-14154-5*) OECD.
— Economies in Transition: Structural Adjustment in OECD Countries. 216p. (Orig.). 1989. pap. 34.00 (*92-64-13204-X*) OECD.
— Education & the Economy in a Changing Society. 117p. (Orig.). 1989. pap. 17.00 (*92-64-13176-0*) OECD.
— Education at a Glance: OECD Indicators. 148p. (Orig.). 1992. pap. 28.00 (*92-64-03692-X*) OECD.
— Education at a Glance: 1993 Edition. 260p. (Orig.). 1993. pap. text ed. 30.00 (*92-64-03894-9*, 96-93-03-3) OECD.
— Education in OECD Countries 1987-1988: A Compendium of Statistical Information, 1990 Special Edition. 146p. (Orig.). 1991. pap. 30.00 (*92-64-13425-5*) OECD.
— Educational Facilities for Special Needs. 32p. (Orig.). 1994. pap. 9.00 (*92-64-14098-0*) OECD.
— The Educational Infrastructure in Rural Areas. 36p. (Orig.). 1994. pap. 9.00x (*92-64-14189-8*) OECD.
— Electric Vehicles: Technology, Performance, & Potential. 201p. (Orig.). 1994. pap. text ed. 53.00 (*92-64-14015-8*, 61-93-20-1) OECD.
— Electricity in European Economies in Transition. 260p. (Orig.). 1994. pap. 70.00 (*92-64-14133-2*) OECD.
— Electricity Information. 292p. (Orig.). 1992. pap. 60.00 (*92-64-13795-5*) OECD.
— Electricity Information, 1992: 1993 Edition. 340p. (Orig.). 1993. pap. 58.00 (*92-64-13961-3*) OECD.
— Electricity Information 1993: (1994 Edition) 500p. (Orig.). 1994. pap. 64.00x (*92-64-14184-7*) OECD.
— Electricity Supply Industry: Structure, Ownership & Regulation. 350p. (Orig.). 1994. pap. 113.00x (*92-64-14222-3*) OECD.
— Electronic Funds Transfer: Plastic Cards & the Consumer. 136p. (Orig.). 1989. pap. text ed. 17.00 (*92-64-13179-5*) OECD.
— Emergency Planning in Case of Nuclear Accident: Proceedings of NEA-CEC Workshop. 400p. (Orig.). (ENG & FRE.). 1990. pap. 47.00 (*92-64-03291-6*) OECD.
— Emergency Preparedness for Nuclear Powered Satellites. 104p. (Orig.). 1990. pap. 19.00 (*92-64-13352-6*) OECD.
— Emerging Bond Markets in the Dynamic Asian Economies. 240p. (Orig.). 1993. pap. 59.00 (*92-64-13846-3*) OECD.
— Employment & Development: A New Review of Evidence. 280p. (Orig.). 1993. pap. 47.00 (*92-64-13842-0*) OECD.
— Employment & Unemployment in Economies in Transition: Conceptual & Measurement Issues. 129p. (Orig.). 1993. pap. 26.00 (*92-64-13910-9*) OECD.
— Employment Outlook: July 1992. 284p. (Orig.). 1992. pap. 52.00 (*92-64-13720-3*) OECD.
— Employment Outlook, July 1994. 220p. (Orig.). (ENG & FRE.). 1994. pap. 52.00x (*92-64-14166-9*) OECD.
— Energy Balances of OECD Countires, 1960-1979. 740p. (Orig.). 1991. pap. text ed. 105.00 (*92-64-03515-X*, 61-91-17-3) OECD.
— Energy Balances of OECD Countries 1980-1989. 450p. (Orig.). 1991. pap. 60.00 (*92-64-03500-1*) OECD.
— Energy Balances of OECD Countries, 1989-1990. 215p. (Orig.). (ENG & FRE.). 1992. pap. 37.00 (*92-64-03535-4*) OECD.
— Energy Balances of OECD Countries 1990-1991. 240p. (Orig.). 1993. pap. 42.00 (*92-64-03860-4*) OECD.
— Energy Balances of OECD Countries, 1991-1992. 230p. (Orig.). (ENG & FRE.). 1994. pap. 40.00 (*92-64-04041-2*) OECD.
— Energy Efficiency & the Environment. 240p. (Orig.). 1991. pap. text ed. 48.00 (*92-64-13561-8*, 61-91-15-1) OECD.
— Energy Efficiency in Asian Countries. 164p. (Orig.). 1993. pap. 33.00 (*92-64-13852-8*) OECD.
— Energy in Developing Countries: A Sectoral Analysis. 130p. (Orig.). 1994. pap. 42.00x (*92-64-14135-9*) OECD.
— Energy in Non-OECD Countries: Selected Topics, 1991. 125p. (Orig.). 1991. pap. 24.00 (*92-64-13482-4*) OECD.
— Energy Policies: The Czech & Slovak Federal Republic. 200p. (Orig.). 1992. pap. 46.00 (*92-64-13786-6*) OECD.
— Energy Policies in the Republic of Korea. 123p. (Orig.). 1993. pap. 38.00 (*92-64-13805-6*) OECD.
— Energy Policies of IEA Countries: 1991 Review. 467p. (Orig.). 1992. pap. 120.00 (*92-64-13739-4*) OECD.
— Energy Policies of IEA Countries: 1992 Review. 520p. (Orig.). 1993. pap. 110.00 (*92-64-13946-X*) OECD.
— Energy Policies of IEA Countries (Yr.) Review 1993. 608p. (Orig.). 1994. pap. 112.00x (*92-64-14199-5*, ECD1995, Pub. by Econ & Coop Dev FR) UNIPUB.
— Energy Policies of the Czech Republic 1994 Survey. 200p. (Orig.). 1994. pap. 45.00x (*92-64-14207-X*) OECD.
— Energy Policies, Poland: 1990 Survey. 162p. (Orig.). 1991. pap. 34.00 (*92-64-13483-2*) OECD.
— Energy Statistics & Balances of Non-OECD Countries, 1989-1990. 432p. (Orig.). 1992. pap. 90.00 (*92-64-03693-8*) OECD.
— Energy Statistics & Balances of Non-OECD Countries 1990-1991. 445p. (Orig.). 1993. pap. 95.00 (*92-64-03877-9*) OECD.
— Energy Statistics & Balances of Non-OECD Countries, 1991-1992. 480p. (Orig.). (ENG & FRE.). 1994. pap. 95.00x (*92-64-04177-X*) OECD.
— Energy Statistics of OECD Countries, 1960-1979. 1300p. (Orig.). 1991. pap. text ed. 168.00 (*92-64-03516-8*, 61-91-18-3) OECD.
— Energy Statistics of OECD Countries 1980-1989. 721p. (Orig.). (ENG & FRE.). 1991. pap. 84.00 (*92-64-03299-1*) OECD.
— Energy Statistics of OECD Countries 1990-1991. 256p. (Orig.). 1993. pap. 54.00 (*92-64-03861-2*) OECD.
— Energy Statistics of OECD Countries 1991-92. 238p. (Orig.). (ENG & FRE.). 1994. pap. 52.00 (*92-64-04040-4*) OECD.
— Energy Technologies for Reducing Emissions of Greenhouse Gases, 2 vols., Set. (Orig.). 1989. pap. 84.00 (*92-64-13267-8*) OECD.
— Energy Technologies to Reduce CO2 Emissions in Europe: Prospects, Competition, Synergy. 200p. (Orig.). 1995. pap. 51.00x (*92-64-14308-4*) OECD.
— Energy Technology Policy for Sustainable Development: Comparing Long-Term Approaches. 257p. (Orig.). 1993. pap. 49.00 (*92-64-13901-X*) OECD.
— English-French Glossary of the Environment: Glossaire de l'Environnement Anglais-Francais. 300p. (ENG & FRE.). 1981. 35.00 (*0-8288-0940-2*, M14216) Fr & Eur.
— Environment & Transport Infrastructures ECMT Round Table 79. 158p. (Orig.). 1989. pap. 24.00 (*92-821-1141-5*) OECD.
— Environmental Degradation from Mining & Mineral Processing in Developing Countries: Corporate Responses & National Policies. 92p. (Orig.). 1994. pap. 11.00 (*92-64-14131-6*) OECD.
— Environmental Education: An Approach to Sustainable Development. 260p. (Orig.). 1993. pap. 30.00 (*92-64-13771-8*) OECD.
— Environmental Effects of Automotive Transport: The OECD Compass Project. 172p. 1986. pap. 20.00 (*92-64-12862-X*) OECD.
— The Environmental Effects of Trade. 210p. (Orig.). (ENG & FRE.). 1994. pap. 44.00 (*92-64-14094-8*) OECD.
— Environmental Indicators: OECD Core Set. 170p. (Orig.). 1994. pap. 22.00x (*92-64-04263-6*) OECD.
— Environmental Labelling in OECD Countries. 133p. (Orig.). 1991. pap. 32.00 (*92-64-13538-3*) OECD.
— Environmental Policies & Industrial Competitiveness. 180p. (Orig.). 1993. pap. 20.00 (*92-64-03886-8*) OECD.
— Environmental Policies in Turkey. 176p. (Orig.). 1992. pap. 35.00 (*92-64-13749-1*) OECD.
— Environmental Policy Benefits: Monetary Valuation. 82p. (Orig.). 1989. pap. text ed. 20.00 (*92-64-13182-5*, 97-88-07-1) OECD.
— European Conference of Ministers of Transport: 38th Annual Report, 1991, Activities of the Conference. 300p. (Orig.). 1992. pap. 62.00 (*92-821-1167-9*) OECD.
— Eutrophication of Waters: Monitoring, Assessment, & Control. 154p. 1982. pap. 11.50 (*92-64-12298-2*) OECD.
— Evaluating Innovations in Environmental Education. 282p. (Orig.). 1994. pap. 27.00x (*92-64-12411-X*) OECD.
— Evaluating Investment in Transport Infrastructure. (ECMT Round Table Ser.: No. 86). 112p. (Orig.). 1992. pap. 28.00 (*92-821-1160-1*) OECD.
— Evaluating Labour Market & Social Program: The State of a Complex Art. 173p. (Orig.). 1991. pap. 37.00 (*92-64-13537-5*) OECD.
— Evaluation & the Decision Making Process in Higher Education: French, German, & Spanish Experiences. 204p. (Orig.). 1995. pap. 20.00x (*92-64-14303-3*) OECD.
— Evaluation of Research: A Selection of Current Practices. 78p. (Orig.). 1987. pap. 11.00 (*92-64-12981-2*) OECD.
— Excavation Response in Geological Repositories for Radioactive Waste. 538p. (Orig.). (ENG & FRE.). 1988. pap. 59.00 (*92-64-03148-0*) OECD.
— Exchanging Control Policy. 90p. (Orig.). 1993. pap. 18.00 (*92-64-13945-1*) OECD.
— Explanatory Report on the Convention on Mutual Administrative Assistance in Tax Matters. 96p. (Orig.). 1989. pap. text ed. 8.50 (*0-317-05950-5*, 23-88-10-1) OECD.
— The Export Credit Financing Systems in OECD Member Countries. 4th ed. 315p. (Orig.). 1990. pap. 32.00 (*92-64-13358-5*) OECD.
— External Debt: Definition, Statistical Coverage & Methodology. 180p. (Orig.). 1988. pap. 12.00 (*92-64-13039-X*) OECD.
— External Debt Statistics: The Debt & Other External Liabilities of Developing, Central & Eastern European & Certain Other Countries. 30p. (Orig.). 1992. pap. 26.00 (*92-64-13766-1*) OECD.
— External Debt Statistics: The Debt & Other External Liabilities of Developing, Central & Eastern European, & Certain Other Countries at End-Dec. 1993 & End-Dec. 1992. 33p. (Orig.). 1994. pap. 23.00x (*92-64-14276-2*) OECD.
— Farm Employment & Economic Adjustment in OECD Countries. 252p. 1994. pap. 22.00 (*92-64-14084-0*) OECD.
— Field Releases of Transgenic Plants, 1986-1992: Analysis. 48p. (Orig.). 1994. pap. 12.00 (*92-64-14046-8*) OECD.
— Fighting Noise in the Nineteen Nineties. 120p. (Orig.). 1991. pap. 21.00 (*92-64-13457-3*) OECD.
— Financial Conglomerates. 130p. (Orig.). 1993. pap. 24.00 (*92-64-13925-7*) OECD.
— Financial Opening: Policy Issues & Experiences in Developing Countries. 272p. (Orig.). 1993. pap. 23.00 (*92-64-03862-0*) OECD.
— Financing & External Debt of Developing Countries: 1991 Survey. 220p. (Orig.). 1992. pap. 43.00 (*92-64-13741-6*) OECD.
— Financing & External Debt of Developing Countries: 1992 Survey. 200p. (Orig.). 1993. pap. 38.00 (*92-64-14007-7*) OECD.
— Financing & External Debt of Developing Countries, 1990 Survey. 212p. (Orig.). 1991. pap. 36.00 (*92-64-13494-8*) OECD.
— Financing Higher Education: Current Patterns. 100p. (Orig.). 1990. pap. 21.00 (*92-64-13422-0*) OECD.
— Fisheries: Trade & Access to Resources. 322p. (Orig.). 1989. pap. 52.50 (*92-64-13246-5*) OECD.
— Fisheries Enforcement Issues. 253p. (Orig.). 1994. pap. 30.00x (*92-64-14165-0*) OECD.
— Flexible Personnel Management in the Public Service. 100p. (Orig.). 1990. pap. 19.00 (*92-64-13353-4*) OECD.
— Flows & Stocks of Fixed Capital 1976-1992. 52p. (Orig.). (ENG & FRE.). 1994. pap. 24.00 (*92-64-04120-6*) OECD.
— Food Consumption Statistics 1979-1988. 588p. (Orig.). (ENG & FRE.). 1991. pap. 100.00 (*92-64-03513-3*) OECD.
— Foreign Direct Investment: OECD Countries & Dynamic Economies of Asia & Latin America. 190p. (Orig.). 1995. pap. 55.00 (*92-64-14382-3*, Pub. by Econ & Coop Dev FR) OECD.
— Foreign Direct Investment in Brazil: Impact on Industrial Restructuring. 155p. (Orig.). 1991. pap. 33.00 (*92-64-13547-2*) OECD.
— Foreign Direct Investment Relations Between the OECD & the Dynamic Asian Countries: The Bangkok Workshop. 200p. (Orig.). 1993. pap. 35.00 (*92-64-13850-1*) OECD.
— Freight Transport & the Environment. (ECMT Round Table Ser.). 172p. (Orig.). 1991. pap. 28.00 (*92-821-1156-3*) OECD.
— From Higher Education to Employment: Australia, Austria, Belgium, Germany, Vol. 1. 224p. (Orig.). 1992. pap. 15.00 (*92-64-03524-9*) OECD.
— From Higher Education to Employment: Canada, Denmark, Spain, United States, Vol. 2. 242p. (Orig.). (ENG & FRE.). 1992. pap. 15.00 (*92-64-03525-7*) OECD.
— From Higher Education to Employment: Synthesis Report. 152p. (Orig.). 1993. pap. 35.00 (*92-64-13825-0*) OECD.
— From Higher Education to Employment, Vol. IV: Portugal, United Kingdom, Sweden, Switzerland. 242p. (Orig.). 1992. pap. 15.00 (*92-64-03695-4*) OECD.
— From Higher Education to Employment, Vol. Three: Finland, France, Italy, Japan, Netherlands, Norway. 370p. (Orig.). 1992. pap. 15.00 (*92-64-03529-X*) OECD.
— From Marshall Plan to Global Interdependence: New Challenges for the Industrialized Nations. 246p. (Orig.). 1978. pap. 17.50 (*92-64-11767-9*) OECD.
— From Reform to Growth: China & Other Countries in Transition in Asia & Central & Eastern Europe. 286p. (Orig.). 1994. pap. 27.00 (*92-64-04118-4*) OECD.
— Fuel Efficiency of Passenger Cars. 91p. 1991. pap. 21.00 (*92-64-13463-8*) OECD.
— The Future of Migration. 320p. (Orig.). 1987. pap. 20.00 (*92-64-12949-9*) OECD.
— Geographical Distribution of Financial Flows to Developing Countries 1988-1991. 356p. (Orig.). (ENG & FRE.). 1993. pap. 68.00 (*92-64-03717-9*) OECD.
— Geographical Distribution of Financial Flows to Developing Countries, 1989-1992. 332p. (Orig.). 1994. pap. 63.00 (*92-64-04034-X*) OECD.
— Geographical Distributions of Financial Flows to Developing Countries, 1987-1990. 336p. (Orig.). 1992. pap. 66.00 (*92-64-03526-5*) OECD.
— Germany. (Environmental Performance Reviews Ser.). 227p. (Orig.). 1993. pap. 29.00 (*92-64-13917-6*) OECD.
— Global Energy: The Changing Outlook. 204p. (Orig.). 1992. pap. 40.00 (*92-64-13618-5*) OECD.
— Global Methane & the Coal Industry. 70p. (Orig.). 1994. pap. 24.00x (*92-64-14203-7*) OECD.
— Globalisation of Industrial Acitivities: Four Case Studies - Auto Parts, Chemicals, Construction, & Semiconductors. 160p. (Orig.). 1992. pap. text ed. 36.00 (*92-64-13627-4*, 70-92-01-1) OECD.
— Glossaire De l'Economie Anglais - Francais. 616p. (Orig.). 1992. pap. 115.00 (*92-64-23645-7*) OECD.
— Glossaire de l'Energie Nucleaire. 924p. (Orig.). (FRE.). 1992. pap. 135.00 (*92-64-23746-1*) OECD.
— Glossary of Industrial Organisation Economics & Competition Law. 90p. (Orig.). 1993. pap. 20.00 (*92-64-13793-9*) OECD.
— Government Securities & Debt Management in the 1990s. 220p. (Orig.). 1993. pap. 42.00 (*92-64-14011-5*) OECD.
— Guidelines for Renewable Energy Technology Applications. 171p. (Orig.). 1991. pap. 44.00 (*92-64-13481-6*) OECD.
— Health Care Systems in Transition: The Search for Efficiency. 204p. (Orig.). 1990. pap. 30.00 (*92-64-13310-0*) OECD.
— Health Quality & Choice. (Health Policy Studies: No. 4). 124p. (Orig.). 1994. pap. 28.00x (*92-64-14213-4*) OECD.
— Heterogeneity of Groundwater Flow & Site Evaluation. 334p. (Orig.). (ENG & FRE.). 1991. pap. 48.00 (*92-64-03346-7*) OECD.
— High Speed Trains. (ECMT Round Table Ser.: No. 87). 102p. (Orig.). 1992. pap. 28.00 (*92-821-1161-X*) OECD.
— Higher Education & Employment: The Case of Humanities & Social Sciences. 128p. (Orig.). 1993. pap. 14.00 (*92-64-13844-7*) OECD.
— Human Resources & Corporate Strategy: Technological Change in Banks & Insurance Companies. 88p. (Orig.). 1988. pap. text ed. 15.50 (*92-64-13096-9*, 96-88-02-1) OECD.
— IEA - OECD Scoping Study on Energy & Environmental Technologies to Respond to Global Climate Change Concerns. 336p. (Orig.). 1994. pap. 79.00x (*92-64-14224-X*) OECD.
— Implementing Change: Entrepreneurship & Local Initiative. (Local Initiatives for Employment Creation Ser.). 88p. (Orig.). 1990. pap. 15.00 (*92-64-13360-7*) OECD.
— Improvements in Main International Piggyback Links. 128p. (Orig.). 1992. pap. 38.00 (*92-821-1163-6*) OECD.
— Improving Road Safety by Attitude Modification. 96p. (Orig.). 1994. pap. 30.00x (*92-64-14147-2*) OECD.
— In-Core Instrumentation & Reactor Assessment: Proceedings 1-4 Oct 1991. 398p. (Orig.). 1992. pap. 67.00 (*92-64-03682-2*) OECD.
— In Situ Experiments Associated with the Disposal of Radioactive Waste. (Proceedings Stripa Project Ser.). 329p. (Orig.). (ENG & FRE.). 1990. pap. 45.00 (*92-64-03333-5*) OECD.

— Industrial Energy Efficiency: Policies & Programmes. 340p. (Orig.). 1994. pap. 75.00x (92-64-14304-1) OECD.
— Industrial Policy in OECD Countries: Annual Review, 1993. 200p. (Orig.). 1993. pap. 30.00 (92-64-14000-X) OECD.
— Industrial Policy in OECD Countries: Annual Review 1994. 200p. (Orig.). 1994. pap. 49.00x (92-64-14295-9) OECD.
— Industrial Structure Statistics, 1989-1990. 312p. (Orig.). 1992. pap. 52.00 (92-64-03528-1) OECD.
— Industrial Structure Statistics, 1991. 316p. (Orig.). (ENG & FRE.). 1993. pap. 57.00 (92-64-03866-3) OECD.
— Industrial Structure Statistics 1992. 364p. (Orig.). (ENG & FRE.). 1994. pap. 55.00 (92-64-04035-8) OECD.
— Industrial Subsidies: A Reporting Manual. 76p. (Orig.). 1995. pap. 23.00x (92-64-14318-1) OECD.
— Industry & University: New Forms of Cooperation & Communication. 70p. (Orig.). 1984. pap. 7.00 (92-64-12607-4) OECD.
— Industry Attitudes to Combined Cycle Clean Coal Technologies: Current Status & Survey. 40p. (Orig.). 1994. pap. 13.00x (92-64-14231-2) OECD.
— Industry in the Czech & Slovak Republics. 140p. (Orig.). 1994. pap. 20.00x (92-64-14187-1) OECD.
— Industry Training in Australia, Sweden & the United States. 118p. (Orig.). 1993. pap. 31.00 (92-64-13905-2) OECD.
— The Influence of Seasonal Conditions on the Radiological Consequences of a Nuclear Accident. 186p. (Orig.). (ENG & FRE.). 1989. pap. 28.00 (92-64-03232-0) OECD.
— Information Systems for Urban Management. 110p. (Orig.). 1993. pap. 12.00 (92-64-13935-4) OECD.
— Information Technology Outlook 1994. 82p. (Orig.). 1994. pap. 30.00x (92-64-14289-4) OECD.
— Information to the Medical Profession on Ionising Radiation: Proceedings of an International Seminar in Grenoble, France. 368p. (Orig.). (ENG & FRE.). 1993. pap. 59.00 (92-64-03718-7) OECD.
— Infrastructure Policies for the 1990s. 110p. (Orig.). 1993. pap. 25.00 (92-64-13963-X) OECD.
— Inland Waterway Transport in ECMT Countries to the Year 2000: A New Dimension. 123p. (Orig.). 1990. pap. 24.00 (92-821-1148-2) OECD.
— Insurance Statistics Yearbook, 1983-1990. 220p. (Orig.). 1993. pap. 57.00 (92-64-03881-7) OECD.
— Insurance Statistics Yearbook, 1984-1991. 232p. (Orig.). 1994. pap. text ed. 55.00 (92-64-04027-7, 21-94-01-3) OECD.
— Insurance Statistics Yearbook, 1985-1992. 240p. (Orig.). (ENG & FRE.). 1994. pap. 55.00 (92-64-04123-0) OECD.
— INT Conference on Coal, the Environment & Development: Technologies to Reduce Greenhouse Emissions. 904p. (Orig.). 1992. pap. 82.00 (92-64-13657-6) OECD.
— INT Standardisation of Fruit & Vegetables: Kiwifruit. 68p. (Orig.). 1992. pap. 30.00 (92-64-03697-0) OECD.
— Integrated Traffic Safety Management in Urban Areas. (Road Transport Research Ser.). 122p. (Orig.). 1990. pap. 25.00 (92-64-13317-8) OECD.
— Integrating Emerging Market Economices into the International Trading System. 106p. (Orig.). 1994. pap. 24.00 (92-64-14064-6) OECD.
— Intelligent Vehicle Highway Systems: Review of Field Trials. 104p. (Orig.). 1992. pap. 40.00 (92-64-13769-6) OECD.
— The Interface in Nuclear Safety & Public Health (NEA) 249p. (Orig.). 1991. pap. 48.00 (92-64-03349-1) OECD.
— Intermediate Energy Nuclear Data: Models & Codes. 420p. (Orig.). 1994. pap. 59.00x (92-64-14278-9) OECD.
— Internalising the Social Costs of Transport. 192p. (Orig.). 1992. pap. 44.00 (92-64-14141-3) OECD.
— International Air Transport: The Challenge Ahead. 118p. (Orig.). 1993. pap. 29.00 (92-64-13797-1) OECD.
— International Conference on Emerging Natural Gas Technologies: Implications & Applications. 219p. (Orig.). 1993. pap. 47.00 (92-64-13919-2) OECD.
— International Direct Investment: Policies & Trends in the 1990s. 145p. (Orig.). 1992. pap. 44.00 (92-64-13799-8) OECD.
— International Direct Investment & the New Economic Environment: The Tokyo Roundtable. 130p. (Orig.). 1989. pap. text ed. 21.00 (92-64-13289-9, 21-89-03-1) OECD.
— International Direct Investment Statistics Yearbook, 1993. 299p. (Orig.). 1993. pap. 52.00 (92-64-03887-6) OECD.
— International Direct Investment Statistics Yearbook 1994. 315p. (Orig.). 1994. pap. 58.00x (92-64-04180-X) OECD.
— International Economic Instruments & Climate Change. 101p. (Orig.). 1993. pap. text ed. 25.00 (92-64-13937-0, 97-93-09-1) OECD.
— International Energy Conference on Demand-Side Management: A Current & Future Resource. 332p. (Orig.). 1992. pap. 34.00 (92-64-13649-5) OECD.
— International Mergers & Competition Policy. 118p. (Orig.). 1988. pap. text ed. 20.00 (92-64-03143-X, 24-88-03-3) OECD.
— International Standardisation of Fruit & Vegetables: Garlic. rev. ed. (Illus.). 50p. 1992. pap. text ed. 12.00 (92-64-02098-5, 51-80-07-3) OECD.
— International Standardisation of Fruit & Vegetables: Strawberries. rev. ed. (Illus.). 32p. 1980. pap. text ed. 7.50 (92-64-02051-9, 51-80-02-3) OECD.
— International Standardisation of Fruit & Vegetables: Table Grapes. rev. ed. (Illus.). 38p. 1980. pap. text ed. 8.00 (92-64-01997-9, 51-80-01-3) OECD.
— International Standardisation of Fruit & Vegetables: Tomatoes. 2nd rev. ed. (Illus.). 66p. 1988. pap. text ed. 24.50 (92-64-03063-8, 51-88-01-3) OECD.
— International Standardisation of Fruit & Vegetables: Unshelled Sweet Almonds, Unshelled Hazelnuts. (Illus.). 84p. (Orig.). 1981. pap. text ed. 18.00 (92-64-02230-9, 51-81-09-3) OECD.
— International Standardization of Fruit & Vegetables: Apples & Pears (Revision) (Illus.). 109p. (Orig.). 1983. pap. 19.00 (92-64-02413-1) OECD.
— International Standardization of Fruit & Vegetables: Aubergines. 55p. (Orig.). 1987. pap. 15.00 (92-64-02930-3) OECD.
— International Standardization of Fruit & Vegetables: Onions. rev. ed. 50p. 1984. pap. 14.00 (92-64-02495-6) OECD.
— International Standardization of Fruit & Vegetables: Witloof Chicories. 84p. (Orig.). 1994. pap. 20.00x (92-64-04117-6) OECD.
— International Standardization of Fruits & Vegetables: Sweet Peppers. 48p. 1982. pap. 13.00 (92-64-02321-6) OECD.
— International Telecommunication Tariffs: Charging Practices & Procedures. 115p. (Orig.). 1994. pap. 30.00x (92-64-14197-9) OECD.
— International Trade in Services: Audiovisual Works. 46p. (Orig.). 1986. pap. 10.00 (92-64-12860-3) OECD.
— International Trade in Services: Securities. 126p. (Orig.). 1987. pap. 11.00 (92-64-12956-1) OECD.
— Introduction to the OECD Codes of Liberalisation. 42p. (Orig.). 1987. pap. 10.00 (92-64-12978-2) OECD.
— Investing In Energy Efficiency: The Role of Third Party Financing. 150p. (Orig.). 1994. pap. 40.00x (92-64-14208-8) OECD.
— Investment Guide for Belarus. 186p. (Orig.). 1994. pap. 27.00x (92-64-14201-0) OECD.
— Investment Guide for Ukraine. 142p. (Orig.). 1993. pap. 27.00 (92-64-13957-5) OECD.
— Investment in Transport Infrastructure in the 1980s. (ECMT Round Table Ser.). 350p. (Orig.). 1992. pap. 68.00 (92-821-1162-8) OECD.
— Investment Incentives & Disincentives: Effects on International Direct Investment. (Orig.). 1989. pap. 17.00 (92-64-13216-3) OECD.
— The Iron & Steel Industry in 1991. 54p. (Orig.). (ENG & FRE.). 1993. pap. 19.00 (92-64-03713-6) OECD.
— The Iron & Steel Industry in 1992. 50p. (Orig.). (ENG & FRE.). 1994. pap. 22.00x (92-64-04266-0, ECD4266, Pub. by Econ & Coop Dev FR) UNIPUB.
— Issues in Education in Asia & the Pacific: An International Perspective. Huges, Philip, ed. 196p. (Orig.). 1994. pap. 24.00 (92-64-14095-6, 96-94-02-1) OECD.
— Labour Force Statistics, 1970-1990. 500p. (Orig.). 1992. pap. 98.00 (92-64-03685-7) OECD.
— Labour Force Statistics, 1972-1992. 496p. (Orig.). (ENG & FRE.). 1994. pap. 96.00x (92-64-04173-7) OECD.
— The Labour Market in Poland. 130p. (Orig.). 1994. pap. 22.00 (92-64-14048-4) OECD.
— The Labour Market in the Netherlands. 124p. (Orig.). 1993. pap. 14.00 (92-64-13855-2) OECD.
— Labour Market Policies for the 1990s. 100p. (Orig.). 1990. pap. 23.00 (92-64-13363-1) OECD.
— Liability & Compensation for Nuclear Damage: An International Overview. 204p. (Orig.). 1995. pap. 49.00x (92-64-14280-0) OECD.
— Liberalisation of Capital Movements & Financial Services in the OECD Area. 125p. (Orig.). 1990. pap. 26.00 (92-64-13430-1) OECD.
— Life-Cycle Analysis of Energy Systems, Methods, & Experience. 370p. (Orig.). 1993. pap. text ed. 49.00 (92-64-13992-3, 61-93-18-1) OECD.
— Life-Cycle Management & Trade. 205p. (Orig.). 1994. pap. 23.00x (92-64-14148-0) OECD.
— Light Rail Transit Systems. 300p. (Orig.). 1994. pap. 60.00x (92-64-14299-1) OECD.
— List of Descriptors in Transport Economics. 4th ed. 355p. (Orig.). (ENG, FRE & GER.). 1989. pap. 94.50 (92-821-0135-5) OECD.
— Lone-Parent Families: The Economic Challenge. (Social Policy Studies: No. 8). 252p. (Orig.). 1990. pap. 34.00 (92-64-13303-8) OECD.
— Long-Term Observation of the Geological Environment: Needs & Techniques. 220p. (Orig.). 1993. pap. 43.00 (92-64-03970-8) OECD.
— Long-Term Prospects for the World Economy. 193p. (Orig.). 1992. pap. 34.00 (92-64-13675-4) OECD.
— The Macro-Economic Impact of Environmental Expenditure. 120p. (Orig.). 1985. pap. 15.00 (92-64-12716-X) OECD.
— Main Developments in Trade 1993. 75p. (Orig.). (ENG & FRE.). 1994. pap. 13.00 (92-64-14104-9) OECD.
— Main Economic Indicators - Historical Statistics, 1969-1988. 766p. (Orig.). (ENG & FRE.). 1990. pap. 90.00 (92-64-03296-7) OECD.
— Main Economic Indicators Historical Statistics: Prices, Labour, & Wages 1962-1991. 300p. (Orig.). 1993. pap. 58.00 (92-64-03873-6) OECD.
— Major R & D Programmes for Information Technology, ICCP, No. 20. 212p. (Orig.). 1989. pap. 42.00 (92-64-13253-8) OECD.
— Management of Water Projects: Decision Making & Investment Appraisal. 254p. (Orig.). 1985. pap. 24.00 (92-64-12695-3) OECD.
— Managing & Financing Urban Services. 94p. (Orig.). 1987. pap. 11.00 (92-64-12951-0) OECD.
— Managing Technological Change in Less-Advanced Developing Countries. 86p. (Orig.). 1991. pap. 17.00 (92-64-13570-7) OECD.
— Managing the Environment: The Role of Economic Instruments. 192p. (Orig.). 1994. pap. 34.00 (92-64-14136-7) OECD.
— Managing the Environment with Rapid Industrialisation: Lessons from the East Asian Experience. 218p. (Orig.). 1994. pap. 27.00x (92-64-14181-2) OECD.
— Managing with Market-Type Mechanisms. 108p. (Orig.). 1993. pap. 16.00 (92-64-14010-7) OECD.
— Maritime Transport, 1991. 158p. (Orig.). 1993. pap. 48.00 (92-64-13822-6) OECD.
— Maritime Transport, 1992. 174p. (Orig.). 1993. pap. text ed. 43.00 (92-64-13997-4, 76-93-02-1) OECD.
— Market & Government Failures in Environmental Management: Wetlands & Forests. 82p. (Orig.). 1992. pap. 24.00 (92-64-13610-X) OECD.
— The Marketing of Traffic Safety. 120p. (Orig.). 1993. pap. 35.00 (92-64-13903-6) OECD.
— The Measurement of Scientific & Technical Activities: Proposed Standard Practice for Surveys of Research & Development - Frascati Manual, 1993. 5th ed. 262p. (Orig.). 1994. pap. 58.00x (92-64-14202-9) OECD.
— Measures Used by OECD Countries to Measure Stocks of Fixed Capital. 68p. (Orig.). 1993. pap. 26.00 (92-64-03708-X) OECD.
— Meat Balances in OECD Countries, 1985-1991. 146p. (Orig.). 1993. pap. 36.00 (92-64-03878-7) OECD.
— Meat Balances in OECD Countries 1986-1992. 143p. (Orig.). (ENG & FRE.). 1994. pap. 37.00x (92-64-04178-8) OECD.
— Megascience & Its Background. 53p. (Orig.). 1993. pap. 17.00 (92-64-13926-5) OECD.
— Merger Cases in the Real World: A Study of Merger Control Procedures. 190p. (Orig.). 1994. pap. 39.00 (92-64-14100-6) OECD.
— Methods of Privatising Large Enterprises. 208p. (Orig.). 1993. pap. 36.00 (92-64-03709-8) OECD.
— Micro-Enterprises & the Institutional Framework in Developing Countries. 250p. (Orig.). 1994. pap. 30.00x (92-64-14195-2) OECD.
— Migration & Development: New Partnerships for Cooperation. 305p. (Orig.). 1994. pap. 75.00x (92-64-14200-2) OECD.
— Minimizing Conflicting Requirements: Approaches of Moderation & Restraints. (International Investment & Multinational Enterprises Ser.). 47p. (Orig.). 1987. pap. 11.00 (92-64-13031-4) OECD.
— Mobilising International Investment for Latin America. Bradford, Colin, Jr., ed. 252p. (Orig.). 1993. pap. 44.00 (92-64-13837-4) OECD.
— Model Tax Convention: Attribution of Income to Permanent Establishments. 50p. (Orig.). 1994. pap. 11.00 (92-64-14058-1) OECD.
— Model Tax Convention: Four Related Studies. 104p. (Orig.). 1992. pap. 24.00 (92-64-13801-3) OECD.
— Model Tax Convention on Income & on Capital. 460p. (Orig.). 1992. pap. 120.00 (92-64-13735-1) OECD.
— Model Tax Convention on Income & on Capital: September 1992. 224p. (Orig.). 1993. Condensed ver. pap. 47.00 (92-64-13915-X) OECD.
— Multicultural Education. 350p. (Orig.). 1987. pap. 25.00 (92-64-12989-8) OECD.
— Multilingual Dictionary of Fish & Fish Products. (Fishing News Bks.). 480p. 1994. (0-85238-216-2) Blackwell Sci.
— Multilingual Dictionary of Fish & Fish Products. 1990. pap. 69.95 (0-8288-7920-6) Fr & Eur.
— Multilingual Dictionary of Fish & Fish Products. 1990. 175.00 (0-685-63442-6) St Mut.
— Multinational Enterprises & Disclosure of Information: Clarification of the OECD Guidelines. 46p. (Orig.). 1988. pap. 15.50 (92-64-03080-8) OECD.
— National Accounts Detailed Tables, Vol. 2: 1978-1990. 590p. (Orig.). 1992. pap. 120.00 (92-64-03683-0) OECD.
— National Accounts for Hungary: Sources, Methods & Estimates. 204p. (Orig.). 1994. pap. 45.00x (92-64-14229-0) OECD.
— National Accounts for the Former Soviet Union. 152p. (Orig.). 1993. pap. 35.00 (92-64-13856-0) OECD.
— National Accounts Main Aggreates, Vol. 1: 1960-1992. 155p. (Orig.). 1994. pap. 33.00 (92-64-03976-7) OECD.
— National Accounts, Vol. I: Main Aggregates, 1960-1990. 158p. (Orig.). 1992. pap. 35.00 (92-64-03522-2) OECD.
— National Accounts, Vol. I: Main Aggregates, 1960-1991. 158p. (Orig.). 1993. pap. 38.00 (92-64-03707-1) OECD.
— National Accounts, Vol. Two: Detailed Tables 1979-1991. 590p. (Orig.). (ENG & FRE.). 1993. pap. 125.00 (92-64-03876-0) OECD.
— National & International Tourism Statistics, 1974-1985. 726p. (Orig.). 1989. pap. text ed. 80.00 (92-64-03221-5, 78-89-01-3) OECD.
— National Policies & Agricultural Trade: Finland. 168p. (Orig.). 1989. pap. text ed. 15.00 (92-64-13240-6, 51-89-04-1) OECD.
— National Policies & Agricultural Trade: Norway. 166p. (Orig.). 1990. pap. 20.00 (92-64-13384-4) OECD.
— National Policies & Agricultural Trade: Switzerland. 174p. (Orig.). 1990. pap. 20.00 (92-64-13385-2) OECD.
— National Policies & Agricultural Trade: Turkey. 248p. (Orig.). 1994. pap. 40.00x (92-64-14238-X) OECD.
— National Treatment for Foreign-Controlled Enterprises, 1993: 92-64-13923-0. 185p. (Orig.). 1993. pap. 43.00 (0-317-05618-2) OECD.
— Natural Gas Prospects & Policies. 242p. (Orig.). 1991. pap. 52.00 (92-64-13567-7) OECD.
— Natural Gas Technologies: Energy Security, Environment, & Economic Development. 1008p. (Orig.). 1994. pap. 130.00x (92-64-14234-7) OECD.
— Natural Gas Transportation: Organization & Regulation. 345p. (Orig.). 1994. pap. 96.00x (92-64-14097-2) OECD.
— Natural Resource Management: Crude Oil Sector. 435p. (Orig.). 1993. pap. text ed. 80.00 (92-64-13924-9, 61-93-12-1) OECD.
— The Netherlands 1994. (Development Cooperation Review Ser.). 48p. (Orig.). 1994. pap. 9.00x (92-64-14223-1) OECD.
— Netron Beams & Synchrotron Radiation Sources. 130p. (Orig.). 1994. pap. 44.00x (92-64-14249-5) OECD.
— New Directions in Donor Assistance to Microenterprises. 80p. (Orig.). 1993. pap. text ed. 17.00 (92-64-13991-5, 43-93-02-1) OECD.
— New Directions in Work Organization: The Industrial Relations Response. 266p. (Orig.). 1992. pap. 48.00 (92-64-13667-3) OECD.
— New Economic Partners: Dynamic Asian Economies & Central & Eastern European Countries. 160p. (Orig.). 1994. pap. 22.00x (92-64-14246-0) OECD.
— New Electricity Twenty-One: Power Industry Technology & Management Strategies for the Twenty-First Century. 992p. (Orig.). 1994. pap. 95.00 (92-64-14073-5) OECD.
— New Financial Instruments. (Accounting Standards Harmonization Ser.: No. 6). 36p. (Orig.). 1991. pap. 16.00 (92-64-03508-7) OECD.
— New Financial Instruments: Disclosure & Accounting. 232p. (Orig.). 1988. pap. text ed. 33.00 (92-64-13159-0, 21-88-06-1) OECD.
— New Home Shopping Technologies. 52p. (Orig.). 1992. pap. 13.00 (92-64-13738-6) OECD.
— New Man-Machine Interfaces in Nuclear Power Plants. 132p. (Orig.). 1995. pap. 36.00x (92-64-14329-7) OECD.
— The New Paradigm of Systemic Competitiveness: Toward More Integrated Policies in Latin America. 272p. 1994. pap. 29.00x (92-64-14259-2) OECD.
— New Technologies in the Nineteen Nineties: A Socio-Economic Strategy. 130p. (Orig.). 1989. pap. text ed. 19.00 (92-64-13180-9, 81-88-07-1) OECD.
— New Technology & Its Impact on Educational Buildings. 52p. (Orig.). 1992. pap. 11.00 (92-64-13756-4) OECD.
— New Trends in Rural Policymaking. 162p. (Orig.). 1988. pap. 18.00 (92-64-13135-3) OECD.
— New Ways of Managing Infrastructure Provision. 200p. (Orig.). 1994. pap. 23.00x (92-64-14306-8) OECD.
— New Ways of Managing Services in Rural Areas. 114p. (Orig.). 1991. pap. text ed. 24.00 (0-317-05951-3, 42-91-02-1) OECD.
— The New World Trading System: Readings. 240p. (Orig.). 1994. pap. 29.00x (92-64-14245-2) OECD.
— Nineteen Ninety-Three Issues: The OECD Response. 80p. (Orig.). 1993. pap. 12.00 (92-64-13944-3) OECD.
— Non-Governmental Organisations & Governments: Stakeholders for Development. 364p. (Orig.). (ENG & FRE.). 1993. pap. 35.00 (92-64-03899-X) OECD.
— Nuclear Accidents Liabilities & Guarantees: The Helsinki Symposium. 602p. (Orig.). 1993. pap. 105.00 (0-317-05593-3) OECD.
— Nuclear Energy: Communication with the Public. 92p. (Orig.). 1991. pap. 20.00 (92-64-13456-5) OECD.
— Nuclear Energy Data, 1991. 45p. (Orig.). 1991. pap. 13.00 (92-64-03297-5) OECD.
— Nuclear Energy Data 1993. 48p. (Orig.). 1993. pap. 17.00 (92-64-03871-X) OECD.
— Nuclear Energy Data 1994. 48p. (Orig.). 1994. pap. 17.00 (92-64-04122-2) OECD.
— Nuclear Power Economics & Technology: An Overview. 120p. (Orig.). 1993. pap. 36.00 (92-64-13798-X) OECD.
— Nuclear Safety Research in OECD Countries. 89p. (Orig.). 1994. pap. 29.00x (92-64-14248-7) OECD.
— Obstacles to Trade & Competition. 116p. (Orig.). 1993. pap. 30.00 (92-64-13838-2) OECD.
— Oceanography. 170p. (Orig.). 1994. pap. 31.00x (92-64-14205-3) OECD.
— The OECD - Loft Project: Achievements & Significant Results: Proceedings, Open Forum 1990. 424p. (Orig.). (ENG & FRE.). 1991. pap. 47.00 (92-64-03339-4) OECD.
— The OECD Declaration & Decisions on International Investment & Multinational Enterprises, '91 Rev. 120p. (Orig.). 1992. pap. 18.00 (92-64-13629-0) OECD.
— OECD Economic Surveys: By Country, 1993-1994 Korea. 139p. 1994. pap. 27.00 (92-64-14129-4, ECD4129, Pub. by Econ & Coop Dev FR) UNIPUB.
— OECD Economic Surveys: 1993-1994 United States. 139p. 1994. pap. 20.00 (92-64-14292-4, ECD4292, Pub. by Econ & Coop Dev FR) UNIPUB.
— OECD Employment Outlook, July 1993. 260p. (Orig.). 1993. pap. 54.00 (92-64-13938-9) OECD.
— OECD Environmental Data Compendium 1991. 338p. (Orig.). 1991. pap. 56.00 (92-64-03512-5) OECD.
— OECD Environmental Data Compendium 1993. 330p. (Orig.). 1993. pap. 60.00 (92-64-03882-5) OECD.
— OECD Environmental Performance Review: Japan. 210p. (Orig.). 1994. pap. 29.00 (92-64-24085-3) OECD.
— OECD Environmental Performance Review: United Kingdom. 212p. (Orig.). 1994. pap. 29.00x (92-64-14260-6) OECD.
— OECD Environmental Performance Reviews: Iceland. 127p. (Orig.). 1993. pap. text ed. 29.00 (92-64-13920-6, 97-93-04-1) OECD.
— OECD Environmental Performance Reviews: Norway. 150p. (Orig.). 1993. pap. text ed. 29.00 (92-64-14002-6, 97-93-06-1) OECD.
— OECD Environmental Performance Reviews: Portugal. 108p. (Orig.). 1993. pap. text ed. 29.00 (92-64-14003-4, 97-93-13-1) OECD.
— The OECD Guidelines for Multinational Enterprises, 1994. 81p. (Orig.). 1994. pap. 15.00 (92-64-14109-X) OECD.
— OECD Guidelines for Testing of Chemicals, 2 vols., Set. (Orig.). 1994. ring bd., pap. 199.00 (92-64-14018-2) OECD.

— OECD Guidelines for Testing of Chemicals: 3rd Supplement. 114p. (Orig.). 1987. 40.00 (92-64-12900-6); pap. text ed. 80.00 (92-64-12221-4) OECD.
— OECD Health Systems: Facts & Trends, 1960-1991, 2 vols., Set. (Orig.). 1993. pap. 89.00 (92-64-13800-5) OECD.
— The OECD International Education Indicators. 118p. (Orig.). 1992. pap. 23.00 (92-64-13726-2) OECD.
— The OECD Jobs Study: Evidence & Explanations. 400p. (Orig.). 1994. pap. 60.00x (92-64-14241-X) OECD.
— OECD Reviews of Foreign Direct Investment: Greece. 53p. (Orig.). 1994. pap. 20.00x (92-64-14153-7) OECD.
— OECD Reviews of Foreign Direct Investment: Ireland. 73p. (Orig.). 1994. pap. 20.00 (92-64-14149-9) OECD.
— OECD Reviews of Foreign Direct Investment: Italy. 70p. (Orig.). 1994. pap. 20.00x (92-64-14217-7) OECD.
— OECD Reviews of Foreign Direct Investment: Portugal. 81p. (Orig.). 1994. pap. 20.00 (92-64-14130-8) OECD.
— OECD Reviews on Foreign Direct Investment: New Zealand. 70p. (Orig.). 1993. pap. 20.00 (92-64-13848-X) OECD.
— OECD Reviews on Foreign Direct Investment: Sweden. 48p. (Orig.). 1993. pap. 20.00 (92-64-13849-8) OECD.
— OECD Societies in Transition: The Future of Work & Leisure. 128p. (Orig.). 1994. pap. 33.00x (92-64-14256-8) OECD.
— The OECD Stan Database for Industrial Analysis, 1972-1991. 240p. (Orig.). (ENG & SPA.). 1994. pap. 59.00 (92-64-04121-4) OECD.
— Off-Site Nuclear Emergency Exercises. 196p. (Orig.). (ENG & FRE.). 1993. pap. 42.00 (92-64-03716-0) OECD.
— Oil & Gas Information 1989-1991. 584p. (Orig.). 1992. pap. 125.00 (92-64-03684-9) OECD.
— Oil & Gas Information, 1992. 585p. (Orig.). 1993. pap. 120.00 (92-64-03872-8) OECD.
— Oil & Gas Information, 1993. 600p. (Orig.). 1994. pap. 125.00x (92-64-04168-0) OECD.
— One School, Many Cultures. 78p. (Orig.). 1989. pap. 15.00 (92-64-13195-7) OECD.
— One World or Several? Emmerij, Louis, ed. 314p. (Orig.). 1989. pap. text ed. 34.00 (92-64-13249-X, 41-89-04-1) OECD.
— Operating Results of Insurance Companies: Current Practices in OECD Countries. (Accounting Standards Harmonisation Ser.: No. 4). 72p. (Orig.). 1988. pap. text ed. 13.50 (92-64-03067-0, 21-88-02-3) OECD.
— Paleohydrogeological Methods & Their Applications for Radioactive Waste Disposal. 170p. (Orig.). 1993. pap. text ed. 48.00 (92-64-03892-2, 66-93-10-3) OECD.
— Partnerships: The Key to Job Creation: Experiences from OECD Countries. 138p. (Orig.). 1993. pap. 26.00 (92-64-14013-1) OECD.
— Partnerships for Rural Development. 156p. (Orig.). 1990. pap. 24.00 (92-64-13380-1) OECD.
— Pathways for Learning: Education & Training from 16 to 19. 123p. (Orig.). 1989. pap. 19.00 (92-64-13175-2) OECD.
— Pay Flexibility in the Public Sector. 240p. (Orig.). 1993. pap. 41.00 (92-64-13949-4) OECD.
— Performance Indicators for Public Telecommunications Operators. (Information Computer Communications Policy Ser.: No. 22). 208p. (Orig.). 1990. pap. 38.00 (92-64-13403-4) OECD.
— Performance Measurement in Government: Issues & Illustrations. 93p. (Orig.). 1994. pap. 17.00x (92-64-14302-5) OECD.
— Performance of Foreign Affiliates in OECD Countries. 174p. (Orig.). 1994. pap. 45.00x (92-64-14220-7) OECD.
— The Personal Income Tax Base: A Comparative Study. 267p. (Orig.). 1990. pap. 40.00 (92-64-13368-2) OECD.
— Policy Issues in Insurance. 301p. (Orig.). 1993. pap. 49.00 (92-64-03889-2) OECD.
— Policy Reform, Economic Growth & China's Agriculture. 128p. (Orig.). 1993. pap. 23.00 (92-64-13907-9) OECD.
— Population & Development Directory of Non-Governmental Organisations in OECD Countries. 360p. (Orig.). 1994. pap. 73.00x (92-64-04171-0) OECD.
— Possibilities & Limitations of Combined Transport. 140p. (Orig.). 1993. pap. 21.00 (92-821-1183-0) OECD.
— Power Generation Choices: Costs, Risks, & Externalities. 470p. (Orig.). 1994. pap. 60.00x (92-64-14236-3) OECD.
— Power Generation Management & Structures in East & West. 459p. (Orig.). 1991. pap. text ed. 72.00 (92-64-13586-3, 61-91-19-1) OECD.
— Predatory Pricing. 100p. (Orig.). 1989. pap. 15.00 (92-64-13245-7) OECD.
— Pricing of Water Services. 146p. 1987. 17.00 (92-64-12921-9) OECD.
— Private & Public Investment in Transport. (ECMT Round Table Ser.: No. 81). 109p. (Orig.). 1990. pap. 17.00 (92-821-1146-6) OECD.
— Private Pay for Public Work: Performance-Related Pay for Public Sector Managers. 236p. (Orig.). 1993. pap. 28.00 (92-64-13823-4) OECD.
— Private Pensions & Public Policy. 160p. (Orig.). 1992. pap. 35.00 (92-64-13790-4) OECD.
— Private Pensions in OECD Countries: New Zealand. 92p. (Orig.). 1993. pap. 20.00 (92-64-13803-X) OECD.
— Private Pensions in OECD Countries: The United States. 100p. (Orig.). 1993. pap. 22.00 (92-64-13802-1) OECD.
— Privatisation of Railways. 164p. (Orig.). 1993. pap. 30.00 (92-821-1182-2) OECD.
— Probabilistic Accident Consequence Assessment Codes: Second International Comparison Overview Report. 104p. (Orig.). 1994. pap. 27.00 (92-64-14101-4) OECD.
— Producer Price Indices: Sources & Methods. 68p. (Orig.). (ENG & FRE.). 1994. pap. 9.00 (92-64-04037-4) OECD.
— Progress in Structural Reform: An Overview. 112p. (Orig.). 1992. pap. 28.00 (92-64-13763-7) OECD.
— Project & Policy Appraisal: Integrating Environment & Economics. 346p. (Orig.). 1994. pap. 40.00 (92-64-14107-3) OECD.
— Projected Costs of Generating Electricity, 1992. 200p. (Orig.). 1993. pap. 50.00 (92-64-14020-4) OECD.
— Promoting Foreign Direct Investment in Developing Countries. 100p. (Orig.). 1993. pap. 24.00 (92-64-13964-8) OECD.
— Promoting Private Enterprise in Developing Countries. 128p. (Orig.). 1990. pap. 19.00 (92-64-13359-3) OECD.
— Promoting Regional Transport: ECMT Round Table, No. 82. 69p. (Orig.). 1990. pap. 17.00 (92-821-1149-0) OECD.
— Prospects for East-West European Transport. 561p. (Orig.). 1991. pap. 74.00 (92-821-1153-9) OECD.
— The Public Employment Service in Japan, Norway, Spain & the United Kingdom. 136p. (Orig.). 1993. pap. 24.00 (92-64-14021-2) OECD.
— Public Information on Nuclear Energy: Proceedings of NEA Workshop Paris 1990. 335p. (Orig.). (ENG & FRE.). 1991. pap. 32.00 (92-64-03341-6) OECD.
— Public Management: OECD Country Profiles. 470p. (Orig.). 1993. pap. 80.00 (92-64-13809-9) OECD.
— Public Management Developments: Survey, 1993. 280p. (Orig.). 1993. pap. text ed. 42.00 (92-64-13966-4, 42-93-03-1) OECD.
— Public Management Developments: Update 1994. 136p. (Orig.). 1994. pap. 32.00x (92-64-14244-4) OECD.
— Public Management Developments Update 1991. 92p. (Orig.). 1991. pap. 21.00 (92-64-13546-4) OECD.
— Public Management Developments, Update 1992. 110p. (Orig.). 1992. pap. 22.00 (92-64-13729-7) OECD.
— Public Participation in Nuclear Decision-Making. 400p. (Orig.). (ENG & FRE.). 1993. pap. 55.00 (92-64-03975-9) OECD.
— Public Service Pay Determination & Pay Systems in OECD Countries. 92p. (Orig.). 1994. pap. 14.00x (92-64-14159-6) OECD.
— The Pulp & Paper Industry, 1990. 102p. (Orig.). 1993. pap. 34.00 (92-64-03870-1) OECD.
— The Pulp & Paper Industry 1991. 100p. (Orig.). 1994. pap. 31.00 (92-64-04028-5) OECD.
— Purchasing Power Parities & Real Expenditures for Canada & the United States 1990 (GK Results) 60p. (Orig.). 1993. pap. 18.00 (92-64-03711-X) OECD.
— Purchasing Power Parities & Real Expenditures for Nordic Countries. 69p. (Orig.). 1992. pap. 18.00 (92-64-03533-8) OECD.
— Purchasing Power Parities & Real Expenditures, 1990, Vol. 2: GK Results. 96p. (Orig.). (ENG & FRE.). 1993. pap. 22.00 (92-64-03897-3) OECD.
— Purchasing Power Parity & Real Expenditures, EKS Results: 1990, Vol. 1. 68p. (Orig.). 1992. pap. 26.00 (92-64-03686-5) OECD.
— Qualified Manpower & Equipment for the Nuclear Industry. 267p. (Orig.). (ENG & FRE.). 1993. pap. 56.00 (92-64-03973-2) OECD.
— Qualified Manpower for the Nuclear Industry: An Assessment of Demand & Supply. 90p. (Orig.). 1993. pap. 30.00 (92-64-13932-X) OECD.
— Quality in Teaching. 130p. (Orig.). 1994. pap. 23.00x (92-64-14242-8) OECD.
— R & D, Production, & Diffusion of Technology. (Science & Technology Indicators Ser.: No. 3). 132p. (Orig.). 1989. pap. text ed. 42.00 (92-64-13217-1, 92-89-03-1) OECD.
— R & D Statistics & Output Measurement in the Higher Education Sector "Frascati Manual" Supplement. (Measurement of Scientific & Technical Activities Ser.). 72p. (Orig.). 1989. pap. 12.00 (92-64-13193-0) OECD.
— Radiation Protection on the Threshold of the 21st Century. 324p. (Orig.). 1993. pap. 56.00 (92-64-03971-6) OECD.
— Radionuclide Sorption from the Safe Evaluation Perspective. 296p. (Orig.). (ENG & FRE.). 1992. pap. 46.00 (92-64-03700-4) OECD.
— Rail Network Co-Operation in the Age of Information Technology & High Speed. (ECMT Round Table Ser.). 116p. (Orig.). 1989. pap. 31.50 (92-821-1129-6) OECD.
— Redefining the State in Latin America. 273p. (Orig.). 1994. pap. 42.00 (92-64-14089-1) OECD.
— Reducing Environmental Pollution: Looking Back, Thinking Ahead. 48p. (Orig.). 1994. pap. 9.00x (92-64-14214-2) OECD.
— The Reform of Health Care Systems: A Review of Seventeen OECD Countries. 344p. (Orig.). 1994. pap. 86.00x (92-64-14250-9) OECD.
— Reforming Agricultural Policies: Quantitative Restrictions on Production Direct Income Support. 86p. (Orig.). 1990. pap. 24.00 (92-64-13414-X) OECD.
— Reforming Public Pensions. 154p. (Orig.). 1988. pap. 29.00 (92-64-13123-X) OECD.
— Regional Development Problems & Policies in Canada. 67p. (Orig.). 1994. pap. 20.00x (92-64-14193-6) OECD.
— Regional Development Problems & Policies in Poland. 84p. (Orig.). 1993. pap. 15.00 (92-64-13807-2) OECD.
— Regional Development Problems & Policies in the United Kingdom. 90p. (Orig.). 1994. pap. 20.00x (92-64-14194-4) OECD.
— Regional Integration & Developing Countries. 96p. (Orig.). 1993. pap. 28.00 (92-64-13909-5) OECD.
— Regional Policies in Germany. 52p. (Orig.). 1990. pap. 11.00 (92-64-13307-0) OECD.
— Regional Policy, Transport Networks & Communications. (ECMT Round Table Ninety Four Ser.). 140p. (Orig.). 1994. pap. 22.00 (92-821-1191-1) OECD.
— Register of Development Research Projects in Africa. 360p. (Orig.). 1992. pap. 58.00 (92-64-03699-7) OECD.
— Register of Development Research Projects in Asia & the Pacific. 358p. (Orig.). (ENG & FRE.). 1989. pap. 53.00 (92-64-03237-1) OECD.
— Register of Development Research Projects in Latin America. 455p. (Orig.). 1993. pap. 75.00 (92-64-03076-X) OECD.
— Register of Development Research Projects in Selected European Countries. 362p. (Orig.). (ENG & FRE.). 1992. pap. 58.00 (92-64-03532-X) OECD.
— The Regulation of Nuclear Trade, Vol. I: International Aspects. 262p. (Orig.). 1988. pap. 60.00 (92-64-13120-5) OECD.
— The Regulation of Nuclear Trade, Vol. II: National Regulations. 325p. (Orig.). 1988. pap. 60.00 (92-64-13121-3) OECD.
— Regulatory Cooperation in an Interdependent World. 250p. (Orig.). 1994. pap. 50.00x (92-64-14196-0) OECD.
— Regulatory Reform, Privatisation & Competition Policy. 134p. (Orig.). 1992. pap. 31.00 (92-64-13666-5) OECD.
— Renewable Natural Resources: Economic Incentives for Improved Management. 156p. (Orig.). 1989. pap. 20.00 (92-64-13194-9) OECD.
— Research Manpower: Managing Supply & Demand. 70p. (Orig.). 1989. pap. 19.00 (92-64-13272-4) OECD.
— Research on Transport Economics: ECMT Annual Information Bulletin, Nov. 1991, Vol. XXIII. 644p. (Orig.). (ENG & FRE.). 1992. pap. 100.00 (92-821-0172-X) OECD.
— Research on Transport Economics Vol. XXVI. 440p. (Orig.). (ENG & FRE.). 1994. pap. 100.00x (92-821-0194-0) OECD.
— Research on Transport Economics Vol. XXVI, Vol. XXIV. 407p. (Orig.). 1993. pap. text ed. 110.00 (92-821-0175-4, 74-92-02-3) OECD.
— Research on Transport Economics Vol. XXVI, Vol. XXV. 360p. (Orig.). 1993. pap. text ed. 90.00 (92-821-0185-1, 74-93-01-3) OECD.
— Resources for Tomorrow's Transport: ECMT 11th International Symposium. 524p. (Orig.). 1989. pap. 47.00 (92-821-1142-3) OECD.
— Revenue Statistics of OECD Countries 1965-1992. 264p. (Orig.). 1993. pap. 50.00 (92-64-03885-X) OECD.
— Revenue Statistics of OECD Member Countries 1965-1993. 255p. (Orig.). (ENG & FRE.). 1994. pap. 50.00x (92-64-04176-1) OECD.
— Review of Agricultural Policies: Hungary. 222p. (Orig.). 1994. pap. 49.00 (92-64-14055-7) OECD.
— Review of Fisheries in OECD Member Countries, 1990. 340p. (Orig.). 1993. pap. 96.00 (92-64-13810-2) OECD.
— Reviews of National Policies for Education: Belgium. 133p. (Orig.). 1993. pap. text ed. 29.00 (92-64-13989-3, 91-93-03-1) OECD.
— Reviews of National Policies for Education: Higher Education in California. 167p. (Orig.). 1990. pap. 30.00 (92-64-13412-3) OECD.
— Reviews of National Policies for Education: Ireland. 156p. (Orig.). 1991. pap. 31.00 (92-64-13488-3) OECD.
— Reviews of National Policies for Education: Netherlands. 148p. (Orig.). 1992. pap. 31.00 (92-64-13608-8) OECD.
— Reviews of National Policies for Education: Norway. 116p. (Orig.). 1990. pap. 19.00 (92-64-13315-1) OECD.
— Reviews of National Policies for Education: Switzerland. 214p. (Orig.). 1992. pap. 46.00 (92-64-13603-7) OECD.
— Reviews of National Policies for Education: Turkey. 113p. (Orig.). 1989. pap. 20.00 (92-64-13207-4) OECD.
— Reviews of National Science & Technology Policy: Czech & Slovak Federal Republic. 204p. (Orig.). 1992. pap. 44.00 (92-64-13796-3) OECD.
— Reviews of National Science & Technology Policy: Italy. 163p. (Orig.). 1992. pap. 25.00 (92-64-13614-2) OECD.
— Reviews of National Science & Technology Policy: Portugal. 180p. (Orig.). 1993. pap. 22.00 (92-64-24042-X) OECD.
— Reviews of National Science & Technology Policy: Switzerland. 144p. (Orig.). 1989. pap. 21.00 (92-64-13283-X) OECD.
— Reviews of National Science & Technology Policy by Country: Mexico. 197p. (Orig.). 1994. pap. 24.00x (92-64-14232-0, ECD4232, Pub. by Econ & Coop Dev FR) UNIPUB.
— Reviews of National Science Policy: United States. Cohen, I. Bernard, ed. LC 79-7979. (Three Centuries of Science in America Ser.). 1980. reprint ed. lib. bdg. 55.95 (0-405-12561-5) Ayer.
— Risk Management in Financial Services. 104p. (Orig.). 1992. pap. 24.00 (92-64-13727-0) OECD.
— Risks Associated with Human Intrusion at Radioactive Waste Disposal Sites: Proceedings of an NEA Workshop. 246p. (Orig.). (ENG & FRE.). 1990. pap. 32.00 (92-64-03292-4) OECD.
— Road Maintenance & Rehabilitation: Funding & Allocation Strategies. 159p. (Orig.). 1994. pap. 36.00x (92-64-14277-0) OECD.
— Road Maintenance Management Systems in Developing Countries. 208p. (Orig.). 1995. pap. 49.00x (92-64-14300-9) OECD.
— Road Monitoring for Maintenance Management: Road Transport Research, 2 vols., Set. 204p. (Orig.). 1990. pap. 22.95 (92-64-13309-7) OECD.
— Road Safety Education for Young Children & Teenagers: Fourth Joint ECMT - Council of Europe Conference. 250p. (Orig.). 1994. pap. 42.00 (0-317-06261-1) OECD.
— Road Safety, First & Foremost a Matter of Responsibility. (ECMT Round Table Ser.). 160p. (Orig.). 1989. pap. 20.00 (92-821-1128-8) OECD.
— Road Strengthening in Central & Eastern European Countries. (Road Transport Research Ser.). 150p. (Orig.). 1993. pap. text ed. 27.00 (92-64-13988-5, 77-93-03-1) OECD.
— Road Transport Research Outlook: 25th Anniversary. 100p. (Orig.). 1993. pap. 19.00 (92-64-13900-1) OECD.
— The Role of IEA Governments in Energy: A Survey. 304p. (Orig.). 1992. pap. 72.00 (92-64-13740-8) OECD.
— The Role of Nuclear Reactor Containment in Severe Accidents. 27p. (Orig.). 1989. pap. 11.00 (92-64-13263-5) OECD.
— The Role of Technology in Iron & Steel Developments. 69p. (Orig.). 1989. pap. 21.00 (92-64-13252-X) OECD.
— The Role of the State in a Deregulated Transport Market: Round Table, No. 83. 141p. (Orig.). 1991. pap. 28.00 (92-821-1151-2) OECD.
— Romania: An Economic Assessment. 125p. (Orig.). 1993. pap. 24.00 (92-64-13939-7) OECD.
— Route Guidance & In-Car Communications Systems. (Road Transport Research Ser.). 104p. (Orig.). 1988. pap. 16.50 (92-64-13046-2) OECD.
— Rural Public Management. 86p. (Orig.). 1986. pap. 10.00 (92-64-12858-1) OECD.
— Russian Energy Prices, Taxes & Costs, 1993. 100p. (Orig.). 1994. pap. 23.00x (92-64-14158-8) OECD.
— Safety Assessment of Radioactive Waste Repositories: Proceedings of Paris Symposium, October 1989. 1023p. (Orig.). 1990. pap. 112.00 (92-64-03334-3) OECD.
— Safety Evaluation of Foods Derived by Modern Biotechnology: Concepts & Principles. 72p. (Orig.). 1993. pap. 19.00 (92-64-13859-5) OECD.
— School: A Matter of Choice. 184p. (Orig.). 1994. pap. 22.00 (92-64-14087-5) OECD.
— Schools & Quality: An International Report. 140p. (Orig.). 1989. pap. 20.00 (92-64-13254-6) OECD.
— Science & Mathematics Education in the United States: Eight Innovations. 180p. (Orig.). 1993. pap. text ed. 28.00 (92-64-13918-4, 96-93-01-1) OECD.
— Science & Technology Policy: Review & Outlook, 1991. 262p. (Orig.). 1992. pap. 60.00 (92-64-13626-6) OECD.
— Science & Technology Policy: Review & Outlook 1994. 250p. (Orig.). 1994. pap. 46.00x (92-64-14237-1) OECD.
— Science Responds to Environmental Threats: Country Studies. 455p. (Orig.). 1992. pap. 58.00 (92-64-03688-1) OECD.
— Science Responds to Environmental Threats: Synthesis Report. 142p. (Orig.). 1992. pap. 18.00 (92-64-03687-3) OECD.
— Science, Technology, & Innovation Policies: Hungary. 168p. (Orig.). 1993. pap. text ed. 31.00 (92-64-13834-X, 14-93-04-1) OECD.
— Science, Technology & Innovation Policies: Iceland. 200p. (Orig.). 1993. pap. 34.00 (92-64-23947-2) OECD.
— Science, Technology & Innovation Policies, Federation of Russia Vol. II: Background Report. 260p. (Orig.). 1995. pap. 35.00x (92-64-14239-8) OECD.
— Segmented Financial Information. 82p. (Orig.). 1990. pap. 16.00 (92-64-13410-7) OECD.
— Seminar on East-West Energy Trade: Proceedings Vienna, 3-4 October 1991. 308p. (Orig.). 1992. pap. 50.00 (92-64-13621-5) OECD.
— Services: Statistics on International Transactions, 1970-1991. 500p. (Orig.). (ENG & FRE.). 1993. pap. 64.00 (92-64-03883-3) OECD.
— Short-Distance Passenger Travel. (ECMT Round Table Ser.: 96). 135p. (Orig.). 1994. pap. 27.00x (92-821-1193-8) OECD.
— Short Sea Shipping. 128p. (Orig.). 1993. pap. 21.00x (92-821-1181-4) OECD.
— Short-Term Economic Indicators Central & Eastern Europe: Sources & Definitions. 127p. (Orig.). 1993. pap. 9.00 (92-64-03864-7) OECD.
— Short-Term Economic Statistics: Commonwealth of Independent States. 176p. (Orig.). 1993. pap. text ed. 35.00 (92-64-03888-4, 14-93-11-3) OECD.
— Skills Acquisitions in Microenterprises: Evidence from West Africa. 92p. (Orig.). 1994. pap. 11.00x (92-64-14182-0) OECD.
— South-South Cooperation in a Global Perspective. 272p. (Orig.). 1994. pap. 33.00 (92-64-04033-1) OECD.
— The Soviet Agro-Food System & Agricultural Trade: Prospects for Reform. 224p. (Orig.). 1992. pap. 61.00 (92-64-13602-9) OECD.
— Spin-Off Technologies Developed Through Nuclear Activities. 114p. (Orig.). 1993. pap. 20.00 (92-64-13965-6) OECD.
— Statistical Report on Road Accidents in 1988, EMCT. 73p. (Orig.). 1990. pap. 20.00 (92-821-0137-1) OECD.
— Statistical Report on Road Accidents in 1990. 80p. (Orig.). 1992. pap. 27.00 (92-821-0174-6) OECD.
— Statistical Report on Road Accidents in 1991. 81p. (Orig.). (ENG & FRE.). 1993. pap. 23.00 (92-821-0176-2) OECD.
— Statistical Reports on Road Accidents in 1992. 68p. (Orig.). 1994. pap. 25.00x (92-64-04267-9) OECD.
— Statistical Sources on Public Sector Employment. 180p. (Orig.). 1994. pap. 35.00x (92-64-14235-5) OECD.
— Statistical Trends in Transport 1965-1988. 152p. (Orig.). 1992. pap. 38.00 (92-821-0173-8) OECD.
— Statistical Trends in Transport, 1965-1989. 181p. (Orig.). 1993. pap. 38.00 (92-821-0187-8) OECD.
— Statistics for a Market Economy: CCEET. 200p. (Orig.). 1991. pap. 36.00 (92-64-13486-7) OECD.
— Statistics on Military Expenditure in Developing Countries: Concepts, Methodological Problems, & Sources. 76p. (Orig.). 1994. pap. 12.00x (92-64-14230-4) OECD.
— Status of Near Field Modelling. 360p. (Orig.). (ENG & FRE.). 1993. pap. 59.00 (92-64-03974-0) OECD.
— The Steel Market in Nineteen Ninety-Two & the Outlook for 1993. 40p. (Orig.). 1993. pap. 29.00 (92-64-13930-3) OECD.
— The Steel Market in 1991 & the Outlook for 1992. 36p. (Orig.). 1992. pap. 27.00 (92-64-13677-0) OECD.

O

— The Steel Market in 1993 & the Outlook for 1994 & 1995. 40p. (Orig.). 1994. pap. 26.00x (*92-64-14288-6*) OECD.
— Strategic Industries in a Global Economy: Policy Issues for the 1990s. 106p. (Orig.). 1991. pap. 20.00 (*92-64-13559-6*) OECD.
— Strengthening Environmental Co-Operation with Developing Countries. 146p. (Orig.). 1989. pap. 19.00 (*92-64-13262-7*, ECD2627) OECD.
— Structural Change & Industrial Performance: A Seven Country Growth Decomp. Study. 170p. 1992. pap. 28.00 (*92-64-13722-X*) OECD.
— Structural Changes in Population & Impact on Passenger Transport. (ECMT Round Table Ser.: No. 88). 160p. (Orig.). 1992. pap. 35.00 (*92-821-1164-4*) OECD.
— Structure & Organization of Multinational Enterprises. (International Investment & Multinational Enterprises Ser.). 59p. (Orig.). 1987. 13.00 (*92-64-13030-6*) OECD.
— A Study of the Soviet Economy, 3 vols., Set. 1170p. (Orig.). 1991. pap. 100.00 (*92-64-13468-9*) OECD.
— System of National Accounts 1993. 711p. (Orig.). 1994. pap. 85.00 (*92-1-161352-3*) OECD.
— Systemic Risks in Securities Markets. 64p. (Orig.). 1991. pap. 21.00 (*92-64-13454-9*) OECD.
— Systems of Road Infrastructure Cost Coverage: ECMT Round Table, No. 80. 185p. (Orig.). 1990. pap. 28.00 (*92-821-1144-X*) OECD.
— Tax Aspects of Transfer Pricing Within Multinational Enterprises: The United States Proposed Regulations. 80p. (Orig.). 1993. pap. 9.00 (*92-64-13821-8*) OECD.
— Tax-Benefit Position of Production Workers, 1989-1992. 253p. (Orig.). 1993. pap. text ed. 44.00 (*92-64-03898-1*, 23-93-05-3) OECD.
— Tax-Benefits Position of Production: Workers Annual Report 1990-1993. 392p. 1994. pap. 49.00x (*92-64-04175-3*) OECD.
— Tax Consequences of Foreign Exchange Gains & Losses, No. 3. (Issues in International Taxation Ser.). 71p. (Orig.). 1988. pap. 22.00 (*92-64-13124-8*) OECD.
— Tax Information Exchange Between OECD Member Countries: A Survey of Current Practices. 54p. (Orig.). 1994. pap. 15.00 (*92-64-04039-0*) OECD.
— Taxation & Household Saving. 308p. (Orig.). 1994. pap. 60.00x (*92-64-14251-7*) OECD.
— Taxation & Household Savings: Country Surveys. 212p. (Orig.). 1994. pap. 24.00x (*92-64-04265-2*) OECD.
— Taxation & International Capital Flows: A Symposium of OECD & Non-OECD Countries, June, 1990. 283p. (Orig.). 1990. pap. 36.00 (*92-64-13426-3*) OECD.
— Taxation & Investment Flows: An Exchange of Experiences Between the OECD & the Dynamic Asian Economies. 264p. (Orig.). 1994. pap. 45.00x (*92-64-14309-2*) OECD.
— Taxation & the Environment: Complementary Policies. 88p. (Orig.). 1993. pap. 22.00 (*92-64-13839-0*) OECD.
— Taxation in OECD Countries. 116p. (Orig.). 1993. pap. 36.00 (*92-64-13815-3*) OECD.
— The Taxation of Fringe Benefits. 104p. (Orig.). 1988. pap. 13.20 (*92-64-13054-3*) OECD.
— Taxation of New Financial Instruments. 111p. (Orig.). 1994. pap. 16.00x (*92-64-14161-8*) OECD.
— Taxing Consumption. 288p. (Orig.). 1988. pap. text ed. 37.50 (*92-64-13160-4*, 23-88-09-1) OECD.
— Taxing Energy: Why & How. 152p. (Orig.). 1993. pap. 39.00 (*92-64-13806-4*) OECD.
— Taxing Profits in a Global Economy: Domestic & International Issues. 470p. (Orig.). 1992. pap. 84.00 (*92-64-13596-0*) OECD.
— Taxpayers Rights & Obligations: A Survey of the Legal Situation in OECD Countries. 105p. (Orig.). 1990. pap. 21.00 (*92-64-13390-9*) OECD.
— Teachers & Nuclear Energy. 312p. (Orig.). (ENG & FRE.). 1994. pap. 42.00 (*92-64-04036-6*) OECD.
— Technical Engineering Services. 124p. (Orig.). 1990. pap. 17.00 (*92-64-13367-4*) OECD.
— Technology & Developing Country Agriculture: The Impact of Economic Reform. 136p. (Orig.). 1993. pap. 24.00 (*92-64-13931-1*) OECD.
— Technology & Productivity: The Challenge for Economic Policy. 588p. (Orig.). 1991. pap. 129.00 (*92-64-13549-9*) OECD.
— Technology & the Economy: The Key Relationships - TEP Programme. 328p. (Orig.). 1992. pap. 60.00 (*92-64-13622-3*) OECD.
— The Technology-Economy Programme (TEP) International Conference Cycle. 97p. (Orig.). 1991. pap. 36.00 (*92-64-13489-1*) OECD.
— Technology Fusion: A Path to Innovation: The Case of Optoelectronics. 109p. (Orig.). 1994. pap. 27.00 (*92-64-14043-3*) OECD.
— Technology in a Changing World: The Technology - Economy Programme. 157p. (Orig.). 1992. pap. 42.00 (*92-64-13598-7*) OECD.
— Technology Responses to Global Environmental Challenges. 974p. (Orig.). 1994. pap. 100.00 (*92-64-14072-7*) OECD.
— Telecommunication Network-Based Services: Policy Implications. (Information Computer Communications Policy Ser.: No. 18). 276p. (Orig.). 1989. pap. 42.00 (*92-64-13205-8*) OECD.
— Telecommunications Equipment: Changing Markets & Rate Structures. (Information Computer Communications Policy Ser.: No. 24). 78p. (Orig.). 1991. pap. 19.00 (*92-64-13553-7*) OECD.
— Telecommunications Type Approval: Policies & Procedures for Market Access. (Information Computer Communications Policy Ser.: No. 27). 166p. (Orig.). 1992. pap. 37.00 (*92-64-13615-0*) OECD.
— Telematics in Goods Transport: ECMT Round Table 78. 115p. (Orig.). 1989. pap. 17.00 (*92-821-1140-7*) OECD.
— Territorial Development & Structural Change: A New Perspective on Adjustment & Reform. 57p. (Orig.). 1993. pap. 9.00 (*92-64-14014-X*) OECD.
— Third Party Liability: Nuclear Energy Agency. 280p. (Orig.). 1990. pap. 45.00 (*92-64-13421-2*) OECD.
— Third World Debt & Financial Innovation: The Experiences of Chile & Mexico. 148p. (Orig.). 1991. pap. 31.00 (*92-64-13496-4*) OECD.
— Three Mile Island Pressure Vessel Investigation Project: Achievements & Significant Results. 404p. (Orig.). 1994. pap. 42.00x (*92-64-14134-0*) OECD.
— Tourism Policy & International Tourism in OECD Member Countries 1990. 196p. (Orig.). 1990. pap. 42.00 (*92-64-13424-7*) OECD.
— Tourism Policy & International Tourism in OECD Member Countries 1990-1991. 320p. (Orig.). 1993. pap. 42.00 (*92-64-13829-3*) OECD.
— Tourism Policy & International Tourism in OECD Member Countries, 1992. 310p. (Orig.). 1992. pap. 38.00 (*92-64-13734-3*) OECD.
— Tourism Policy & International Tourism in OECD Countires, 1991-1992. 1,994th ed. 240p. (Orig.). 1994. pap. 42.00 (*92-64-14091-3*) OECD.
— Toward Clean & Fuel Efficient Automobiles. 620p. (Orig.). 1993. pap. 64.00 (*92-64-03869-8*) OECD.
— Towards Sustainable Agricultural Production: Cleaner Technologies. 100p. (Orig.). 1994. pap. 14.00x (*92-64-14188-X*) OECD.
— Trade & Competition Policies: Comparing Objectives & Methods. 40p. (Orig.). 1994. pap. 7.00x (*92-64-14157-X*) OECD.
— Trade & Environment: Processes & Production Methods (PPMS) 168p. (Orig.). 1994. pap. 23.00x (*92-64-14319-X*) OECD.
— Trade & Investment: Transplants. 178p. (Orig.). 1994. pap. 44.00x (*92-64-14156-1*) OECD.
— Trade in Information, Computer & Communication Service. (Information Computer Communications Policy Ser.: No. 21). 56p. (Orig.). 1990. pap. 13.00 (*92-64-13327-5*) OECD.
— Trade in Services & Developing Countries. 128p. (Orig.). 1989. pap. 15.00 (*92-64-13278-3*) OECD.
— Trade Investment & Technology in the 1990s. 129p. 1991. 30.00 (*92-64-13480-8*) OECD.
— Trade Liberalisation: Global Economic Implications. 242p. (Orig.). 1993. pap. 43.00 (*92-64-13962-1*) OECD.
— Traditional Crop Breeding Practices: An Historical Review to Serve As a Baseline for Assessing the Role of Modern Biotechnology. 236p. (Orig.). 1994. pap. 60.00 (*92-64-14047-6*) OECD.
— Traffic Management & Safety at Highway Work Zones. (Road Transport Research Ser.). 144p. (Orig.). 1989. pap. 30.00 (*92-64-13281-3*) OECD.
— Transfer Pricing & Multinational Enterprises: Three Taxation Issues. 92p. (Orig.). 1984. pap. 20.00 (*92-64-12626-0*) OECD.
— Transfer Pricing Guidelines for Multinational Enterprises & Tax Administrations Pt. 1: Discussion Draft. 140p. (Orig.). 1994. pap. 14.00x (*92-64-04170-2*) OECD.
— Transformation of Planned Economies: Property Rights, Reform & Macroeconomic Stability. 136p. (Orig.). 1991. pap. 30.00 (*92-64-13491-3*) OECD.
— Transformation of the Banking System: Portfolio Restructuring, Privatisation & the Payment System. 219p. (Orig.). 1993. pap. 40.00 (*92-64-03880-9*) OECD.
— Transfrontier Movements of Hazardous Waste Statistics, 1989-90. 18p. (Orig.). 1993. pap. 9.00 (*92-64-13943-5*) OECD.
— Transfrontier Movements of Hazardous Wastes: 1991 Statistics. 20p. (Orig.). 1994. pap. 9.00x (*92-64-14191-X*) OECD.
— Transition to a Market Economy, 2 vols. 700p. (Orig.). (ENG & FRE.). 1992. pap. 72.00 (*92-64-03520-6*) OECD.
— Transport & Spatial Distribution of Activities. (ECMT Round Table Ser.: No. 85). 143p. (Orig.). 1992. pap. 30.00 (*92-821-1159-8*) OECD.
— Transport for Disabled People: A Review of Provisions & Standards for Journey Planning & Pedestrian Access. 115p. (Orig.). 1990. pap. 17.00 (*92-821-1145-8*) OECD.
— Transport Growth in Question. 653p. (Orig.). 1993. pap. 80.00 (*92-821-1180-6*) OECD.
— Transport Infrastructure & Systems for a New Europe. 130p. (Orig.). 1994. pap. 25.00x (*92-821-1192-X*) OECD.
— Transport Policy & Global Warming. 245p. (Orig.). 1994. pap. 45.00 (*92-821-2188-7*) OECD.
— Trends in International Migration: Sopemi. 157p. (Orig.). 1992. pap. 37.00 (*92-64-13663-0*) OECD.
— Trends in Public Sector Pay: A Study of Nine OECD Countries 1985-1990. 130p. (Orig.). 1994. pap. 18.00x (*92-64-14143-X*) OECD.
— The U. S. & the Regionalization of the World Economy. 52p. (Orig.). 1992. pap. 7.00 (*92-64-13671-1*) OECD.
— United States Energy Policy: An IEA Review, 1993-1994. 42p. (Orig.). 1994. pap. 10.00 (*0-614-00076-9*) OECD.
— Universal Service & Rate Restructuring in Telecommunications. (Information Computer Communications Policy Ser.: No. 23). 193p. (Orig.). 1991. pap. 52.00 (*92-64-13497-2*) OECD.
— Universities under Scrutiny. 114p. (Orig.). 1987. pap. 18.00 (*92-64-12922-7*) OECD.
— Uranium, Resources Production & Demand, 1989. 359p. (Orig.). 1990. pap. 52.00 (*92-64-13364-X*) OECD.
— Uranium Resources, Production & Demand, 1993. 314p. (Orig.). 1994. pap. 59.00 (*92-64-14019-0*) OECD.
— The Urban Electric Vehicle: Policy Options, Technological Trends, & Market Prospects. 508p. (Orig.). 1992. pap. 72.00 (*92-64-13752-1*) OECD.
— Urban Infrastructure: Finance & Management. 92p. (Orig.). 1991. pap. 22.00 (*92-64-13584-7*) OECD.
— Urban Policies for Ageing Populations. 160p. (Orig.). 1992. pap. 37.00 (*92-64-13758-0*) OECD.
— Usage Indicators: A New Foundation for Information Technology Policies. 132p. (Orig.). 1993. pap. 24.00 (*92-64-13814-5*) OECD.
— Use of Individual Quotas in Fisheries Management. 224p. (Orig.). 1993. pap. 26.00 (*92-64-13940-0*) OECD.
— Validation of Geosphere Flow & Transport Models (Geoval) Proceedings, Stockholm 1990. 668p. (Orig.). (ENG & FRE.). 1991. pap. 88.00 (*92-64-03343-2*) OECD.
— Valuation & Privatisation. 120p. (Orig.). 1993. pap. 24.00 (*92-64-13818-8*) OECD.
— Visitor Centres at Nuclear Facility Sites. 250p. (Orig.). 1993. pap. text ed. 41.00 (*92-64-03972-4*, 66-93-12-3) OECD.
— Vocational Education & Training for Youth: Towards Coherent Policy & Practice. 180p. (Orig.). 1994. pap. 41.00x (*92-64-14285-1*) OECD.
— Vocational Training in Germany: Modernisation & Responsiveness. 120p. (Orig.). 1994. pap. 29.00x (*92-64-14301-7*) OECD.
— Vocational Training in the Netherlands Modernisation & Responsiveness. 215p. (Orig.). 1994. pap. 48.00x (*92-64-14298-3*) OECD.
— Voluntary Aid for Development: The Role of Non-Governmental Organizations. 154p. (Orig.). 1988. pap. text ed. 20.00 (*92-64-13153-1*, 43-88-05-1) OECD.
— The Welfare State in Crisis. 274p. (Orig.). 1981. pap. text ed. 17.50 (*92-64-12192-7*) OECD.
— What Future for Our Countryside? A Rural Development Policy. 84p. (Orig.). 1993. pap. 20.00 (*92-64-13808-0*) OECD.
— Work Management in Occupational Dose Control. 344p. (Orig.). 1993. pap. 70.00 (*92-64-13819-6*) OECD.
— World Cereal Trade: What Roles for Developing Countries? 104p. (Orig.). 1994. pap. 25.00 (*92-64-14025-5*) OECD.
— World Energy Outlook, 1994. 230p. (Orig.). 1994. pap. 61.00 (*92-64-14074-3*) OECD.
— The World Oilseed Market: Policy Impacts & Market Outlook. 62p. (Orig.). 1994. pap. 15.00x (*92-64-14247-9*) OECD.
OECD Staff & Anderson, K. Changing Comparative Advantages in China: Effects on Food, Feed & Fibre Markets. 118p. (Orig.). 1990. pap. 25.00 (*92-64-13354-2*) OECD.
OECD Staff & Aziz, Sartaj. Agricultural Policies for the Nineteen Nineties. 136p. (Orig.). 1990. pap. 25.00 (*92-64-13350-X*) OECD.
OECD Staff & Bloom, Martin. Technological Change in the Korean Electronics Industry. 133p. (Orig.). 1992. pap. 30.00 (*92-64-13670-3*) OECD.
OECD Staff & Erocal, D. Environmental Management in Developing Countries. 417p. (Orig.). 1991. pap. 52.00 (*92-64-03503-6*) OECD.
OECD Staff & Healey, Derek. Japanese Capital Exports & Asian Economic Development. 256p. (Orig.). 1991. pap. 48.00 (*92-64-13484-0*) OECD.
OECD Staff & IEA Staff. Substitute Fuels for Road Transport: A Technology Assessment. 114p. (Orig.). 1990. pap. 27.00 (*92-64-13324-0*) OECD.
— World Energy Outlook. 71p. (Orig.). 1993. pap. 28.00 (*92-64-13904-4*) OECD.
OECD Staff & Jepma, Catrinus J. The Tying of Aid. 80p. (Orig.). 1991. pap. 12.00 (*92-64-13459-X*) OECD.
OECD Staff & Maddison, Angus. The World Economy in the Twentieth Century. 147p. (Orig.). 1989. pap. 30.00 (*92-64-13274-0*) OECD.
OECD Staff & NEA. The Radiological Impact of the Chernobyl Accident in OECD Countries. 184p. (Orig.). 1988. pap. 31.00 (*92-64-13043-8*) OECD.
OECD Staff & NEA Staff. Living Probabilistic Safety Assessment for Nuclear Power Plant Management. 82p. (Orig.). 1992. pap. 31.00 (*92-64-13611-8*) OECD.
— The Safety of the Nuclear Fuel Cycle. 248p. (Orig.). 1993. pap. 65.00 (*92-64-13824-2*) OECD.
— Sealing of Radioacative Waste Repositories. 388p. (Orig.). (ENG & FRE.). 1989. pap. 47.00 (*92-64-03290-8*) OECD.
— Systematic Approaches to Scenario Development: Safety Assessment of Radioactive Waste. 76p. (Orig.). 1992. pap. 38.00 (*92-64-13605-3*) OECD.
OECD Staff & Oman, Charles. Globalisation & Regionalisation: The Challenge for Developing Countries. 128p. (Orig.). 1994. pap. 19.00 (*92-64-14106-5*) OECD.
OECD Staff & Raynould, Andre C. Financing Exports to Developing Countries. 116p. (Orig.). 1992. pap. 24.00 (*92-64-13673-8*) OECD.
OECD Staff & Robson, Mark. Taxation & Small Businesses. 126p. (Orig.). 1994. pap. 20.00 (*92-64-14093-X*, 23-94-02-1) OECD.
OECD Staff & Sun-Taik Han. European Integration: The Impact on Asian Newly Industrialising Economices. 54p. (Orig.). 1992. pap. 9.50 (*92-64-13672-X*) OECD.
OECD Staff & Tucker, G. Privacy & Data Protection Issues & Challenges. 72p. (Orig.). 1994. pap. 11.00 (*92-64-14096-4*, 93-94-03-1) OECD.
OECD Staff & World Bank Staff. Agricultural Trade Liberalization: Implications for Developing Countries. (Orig.). 1990. pap. 32.95 (*92-64-13366-6*) OECD.
OECD Staff, ed. see Brunhes, Bernhard, et al.
OECD Staff, ed. see Dore, Ronald, et al.
OECD Staff, ed. see Ernst, Dieter & O'Connor, David.
OECD Staff, ed. see Polak, Jacques J.
OECD Staff, ed. see Skilbeck, Malcolm.
OECD Staff, et al. The Informal Sector Revisited. Turnham, D. et al, eds. 226p. (Orig.). 1990. pap. 27.50 (*92-64-13328-3*) OECD.
— Modelling Economy-Wide Reforms. 296p. (Orig.). 1994. pap. 50.00 (*92-64-14080-8*, 41-93-12-1) OECD.
— The Political Feasibility of Adjustment in the Philippines. Morrisson, Christian, ed. 88p. (Orig.). 1994. pap. 22.00 (*92-64-14105-7*) OECD.
— Seminar on Energy in East & West: The Polish Case. 624p. (Orig.). 1990. pap. 48.00 (*92-64-13431-X*) OECD.
Oechel, Walter C., jt. ed. see Moreno, Jose M.
Oechsle, Robert. Ducky, Ucky & Mucky. (Illus.). 40p. (J). (ps). 1985. pap. 7.95 (*0-9603376-0-1*) Flourtown Pub.
***Oechsli.** Home Sweet Home. 1995. pap. text ed. (*0-8114-8403-3*) Raintree Steck-V.
Oechsli, Helen & Oechsli, Kelly. In My Garden: A Child's Gardening Book. LC 84-21285. (Illus.). 32p. (J). (ps-2). 1985. lib. bdg. 12.95 (*0-02-768510-1*, Mac Bks Young Read) S&S Childrens.
Oechsli, Kelly. Mice at Bat. LC 85-45266. (Trophy I Can Read Bk.). (Illus.). 64p. (J). (gr. k-3). 1990. pap. 3.50 (*0-06-444139-3*, Trophy) HarpC Child Bks.
Oechsli, Kelly, jt. auth. see Oechsli, Helen.
Oechsli, Wilhelm. History of Switzerland, Fourteen Ninety-Nine to Nineteen Fourteen. Paul, Eden & Paul, Cedar, trs. LC 83-45627. reprint ed. 49.50 (*0-404-19845-7*) AMS Pr.
Oechsner, H., ed. Thin-Film & Depth-Profile Analysis. (Topics in Current Physics Ser.: Vol. 37). (Illus.). 225p. 1984. 61.00 (*0-387-13320-8*) Spr-Verlag.
Oecumenical Synod Seventh, jt. auth. see Damascene, John.
Oedo, Yusuke, ed. Ranka Yearbook, 1991: The Bulletin of the International Go Federation. Power, John, tr. (Illus.). 96p. (Orig.). 1991. pap. text ed. 4.00 (*0-685-50760-2*, RY91) Ishi Pr Intl.
OEF International Staff, ed. see Mermel, Anita & Simons, Judy.
***Oeffner, Barbara.** CHIEF - Champion of the Everglades: A Biography of Seminole Chief James Billie. LC 95-67410. (Illus.). 256p. 1995. 24.95 (*0-9645266-0-3*) Cape Cod Writers.
Oefinger, Judy F. The Saddlebred - America's Horse of Distinction. Strode, William & Butler, William, eds. (Illus.). 160p. 1991. 45.00 (*0-916509-79-6*) Harmony Hse Pub LO.
Oegerle, W., et al, eds. Clusters of Galaxies. (Space Telescope Science Institute Symposium Ser.). (Illus.). 408p. (C). 1990. 59.95 (*0-521-38462-1*) Cambridge U Pr.
Oeglin, Erhart. Liederbuch von 1512. Eitner, Robert & Maier, Jul. J., eds. (Publikation aelterer praktischer und theoretischer Musikwerke Ser.: Vol. 9). (Illus.). (GER.). 1966. reprint ed. lib. bdg. 75.00 (*0-8450-1709-8*) Broude.
Oehler. QED 3.04. (C). 1995. text ed. write for info. (*0-7167-2253-4*) W H Freeman.
— User's Guide 3.04. (C). 1995. text ed. write for info. (*0-7167-2254-2*) W H Freeman.
Oehler, Charles M. Jumping Spiders (Araneae: Salticidae) in the Cincinnati Region of Ohio Including Butler, Clermont, Hamilton, & Warren Counties. (Biological Notes Ser.: No. 13). 1982. 5.00 (*0-86727-087-X*) Ohio Bio Survey.
Oehler, Dottlieb & Smith, David Z. Description of a Journey & Visit to the Pawnee Indians. 32p. 1974. 7.50 (*0-87770-140-7*); pap. 4.95 (*0-87770-134-2*) Ye Galleon.
Oehler, Mike. The Fifty Dollar & up Underground House Book with Supplements. (Illus.). 1978. per., pap. 13.95 (*0-442-27311-8*) Mole Pub Co.
— One Mexican Sunday. LC 80-82949. (Illus.). 112p. 1981. 8.50 (*0-9604464-1-9*) Mole Pub Co.
Oehler, Paul & Minor, William. Natural Counterpoint. (Illus.). 64p. (Orig.). 1985. pap. 4.95 (*0-9612914-1-9*) Betty's Soup.
Oehlerts, Donald E. Books & Blueprints: Building America's Public Libraries. LC 91-3233. (Contributions in Librarianship & Information Science Ser.: No. 69). 200p. 1991. text ed. 47.95 (*0-313-26570-4*, OBB, Greenwood Pr) Greenwood.
Oehling, A., ed. see International Congress of Allergology Staff.
Oehlschlaeger, Fritz, ed. & tr. Old Southwest Humor from the St. Louis Reveille, 1844-1850. 304p. 1990. text ed. 27.00 (*0-8262-0741-3*) U of Mo Pr.
Oehlschlaeger, Fritz & Hendrick, George, eds. Toward the Making of Thoreau's Modern Reputation: Selected Correspondence of S. A. Jones, A. W. Hosmer, H. S. Salt, H. G. O. Blake & D. Ricketson. LC 79-12831. (Illus.). 433p. 1980. 39.95 (*0-252-00725-5*) U of Ill Pr.
Oehlschlaeger, Fritz H., jt. auth. see Graham, Peter W.
Oehme. Toxicity of Heavy Metals, Pt. 1. (Hazardous & Toxic Substances Ser.: Vol. 2). 528p. 1978. 155.00 (*0-8247-6718-7*) Dekker.
— Toxicity of Heavy Metals in the Environment, Pt. 2. (Hazardous & Toxic Substances Ser.: Vol. 2). 472p. 1979. 170.00 (*0-8247-6719-5*) Dekker.
Oehme, P., jt. ed. see Jordan, C. C.
***Oehme, S., ed.** Annual Directory, 1994-1995. 290p. (GER.). 1994. 80.00 (*0-86640-051-6*) German Am Chamber.
Oehmich-Russcol, Nancy, jt. auth. see Russcol, Herbert.
Oehmke, Thomas. Dr. Death: Murder or Mercy? Jack Kevorkian's Rx: Death: The Trials of Jack Kevorkian. 1993. pap. 12.95 (*0-8119-0782-1*) LIFETIME.
— International Arbitration. annuals rev. suppl. ed. LC 90-60910. (International Business & Law Ser.). 1990. Revised annually with supplement. 145.00 (*0-685-59808-X*) Clark Boardman Callaghan.
Oehmke, Thomas, jt. auth. see Brovins, Joan.
Oehmke, Thomas H. Construction Arbitration. LC 88-81923. (Real Property-Zoning Ser.). 1988. Revised annually with supplement. 135.00 (*0-685-59798-9*) Clark Boardman Callaghan.
***Oehring, Connie.** Meeting the Bear & Other Poems. 1995. write for info. (*0-9646009-0-0*) P S Press.

O

An Asterisk (*) at the beginning of an entry indicates that the title is appearing in BIP for the first time.

Oehrlein, Bill. One Hundred Ninety-Three Days to Summer. 1993. 13.95 (*0-533-10567-6*) Vantage.

Oehser, Paul H. Sons of Science: The Story of the Smithsonian Institution & Its Leaders. LC 69-10144. (Illus.). 220p. 1969. reprint ed. text ed. 59.75 (*0-8371-0185-9*, OESI, Greenwood Pr) Greenwood.

***Oei, Hong L.** Genes & Politics: The Recombinant DNA Debate. (Orig.). 1995. pap. 24.95 (*1-57420-050-X*) Chatelaine.

Oein, E. Mac, et al, eds. Third International Conference on Minority Languages: Celtic Papers. 1987. 59.00 (*0-905028-64-3*, Pub. by Multilingual Matters UK) Taylor & Francis.

Oelbaum, Freda. Creation: You Can't Beat the Bible - the Book & Game about the Bible, Incl. game. 224p. 1990. 10.95 (*0-944007-15-5*) Sure Sellers.

Oelbermann, Maren, jt. auth. see Milburn, Michael.

Oelerich, Jeanne. Just Marvelous Florence Walking Guide. rev. ed. (Illus.). 16p. 1994. pap. text ed. 9.95 (*1-882546-05-9*) Just Marvelous.

— Just Marvelous Paris Walking Guide. rev. ed. (Illus.). 20p. 1994. pap. text ed. 9.95 (*1-882546-03-2*) Just Marvelous.

— Just Marvelous Rome Walking Tours. rev. ed. (Illus.). 16p. 1994. pap. text ed. 9.95 (*1-882546-04-0*) Just Marvelous.

— Just Marvelous Venice Walking Guide. (Illus.). 16p. 1994. pap. text ed. 9.95 (*1-882546-06-7*) Just Marvelous.

Oelerich, Jeanne B. Just Marvelous Florence: City Guide, 1993. 16p. 1992. pap. text ed. 10.00 (*1-882546-02-4*) Just Marvelous.

— Just Marvelous Paris: City Guide, 1993. 20p. 1992. pap. text ed. 10.00 (*1-882546-00-8*) Just Marvelous.

— Just Marvelous Rome Walking Guide, 1993. 16p. 1992. pap. text ed. 10.00 (*1-882546-01-6*) Just Marvelous.

Oelerich, Marjorie, ed. see Sandell, Elizabeth.

Oelert, W., jt. auth. see Hadjimichael, E.

Oelke, Harry. Die Konfessionsbildung Des Sixteen: Jahrunderts in Spiegel Illustrierter Flugblatter. (Arbeiten zur Kirchengeschichte Ser.: Bd. 5). x, 477p. (GER.). (C). 1992. lib. bdg. 136.95 (*3-11-012912-4*) De Gruyter.

Oellerich, Michael, ed. Tobramycin Profile. 30p. 1988. pap. text ed. 20.00 (*0-89573-870-8*, Pub. by Deutsche Forschungsgemeinschaft) VCH Pubs.

Oellers-Frahm, K., et al, eds. Dispute Settlement in Public International Law: Texts & Materials. 930p. 1985. 179.00 (*0-387-13190-6*) Spr-Verlag.

Oelman, Timothy, ed. & tr. Marrano Poets of the Seventeenth Century: An Anthology. (Littman Library of Jewish Civilization). (Illus.). 296p. 1982. 20.00 (*0-19-710047-3*, Pub. by Littman Lib Jew UK) Bnai Brith Bk.

Oelman, Timothy, ed. see Gomez, Antonio E.

Oelofse, A. N. Suid-Afrikaanse Valutabeheerwetgewing. 190p. 1991. pap. write for info. (*0-7021-2547-4*, Pub. by Juta SA) W W Gaunt.

Oelofse, A. N., jt. auth. see Malan, F. R.

Oelrich, Ivan. Conventional Arms Control: The Limits & Their Verification. (Occasional Papers: No. 8). (Illus.). 92p. (C). 1990. lib. bdg. 38.50 (*0-8191-7833-0*); pap. text ed. 19.00 (*0-8191-7834-9*) U Pr of Amer.

Oelschlaeger, Max. The Idea of Wilderness: From Prehistory to the Age of Ecology. 488p. (C). 1993. reprint ed. pap. text ed. 18.00 (*0-300-05370-3*) Yale U Pr.

— The Wilderness Condition: Essays on Environment & Civilization. LC 91-37949. 356p. 1992. 30.00 (*0-87156-642-7*) Sierra.

Oelschlaeger, Max, ed. After Earth Day: Continuing the Conservation Effort. LC 92-922. (Philosophy & the Environment Ser.: No. 1). 264p. 1992. text ed. 24.50 (*0-929398-44-0*); pap. text ed. 15.95 (*0-929398-40-8*) UNTX Pr.

— The Company of Others: Essays in Celebration of Paul Shepard. 352p. (C). 1995. 34.95 (*1-882308-24-7*) Kivaki Pr.

— Postmodern Environmental Ethics. LC 94-32139. 288p. (C). 1995. text ed. 59.50x (*0-7914-2547-9*) State U NY Pr.

— Postmodern Environmental Ethics. LC 94-32139. 288p. (C). 1995. pap. text ed. 19.95x (*0-7914-2548-7*) State U NY Pr.

— The Wilderness Condition: Essays on Environment & Civilization. LC 92-52649. 343p. 1992. reprint ed. pap. 16.00 (*1-55963-190-2*) Island Pr.

Oelschlager, H., jt. ed. see Murphy, G. P.

Oelschlager, Max. Caring for Creation: An Ecumenical Approach to the Environmental Crisis. LC 93-23215. 296p. Date not set. 30.00 (*0-300-05817-9*) Yale U Pr.

Oelschlegel, F. Change of Sight: Classical German Surgery & Pathology As Mirrored in the Fine Arts. (Illus.). 215p. (C). Date not set. pap. 29.50 (*0-930329-42-2*) KABEL Pubs.

Oelsner, G. H. Handbook of Weaves. Dale, Samuel S., ed. 1915. pap. 9.95 (*0-486-23169-0*) Dover.

Oelsner, O. & Hazzard, B. J. Atlas Most Important Ore Paragenese under Microscope. LC 65-15381. 1966. 131.00 (*0-08-011201-3*, Pub. by Pergamon Repr UK) Franklin.

Oeltgen, P. R., jt. auth. see Chien.

Oeltjen, Jody, jt. auth. see Palmer, Elsie.

Oelwein, Patricia, jt. ed. see Dmitriev, Valentine.

Oelwein, Patricia L. Teaching Reading to Children with Down Syndrome: A Guide for Parents & Teachers. (Topics in Down Syndrome Ser.). (Illus.). 392p. (Orig.). (C). 1995. pap. 16.95 (*0-933149-55-7*) Woodbine House.

Oemler, Marie S., ed. Principles of Life & Health Insurance Student Guide. 2nd ed. (FLMI Insurance Education Program Ser.). 263p. 1988. student ed, pap. text ed. 10.00 (*0-915322-99-4*) LOMA.

Oenen, K. & Diehm, C., eds. Beta-Blockers in the Treatment of Hypertension in the 90s: Experience with Tertatolol. (Journal: Cardiology: Vol. 83, Suppl. 1, 1993). (Illus.). iv, 72p. 1993. pap. 21.75 (*3-8055-5869-4*) S Karger.

Oengus the Culdee. Felire of Oengus the Culdee. Stokes, Whitley, tr. pap. 12.50 (*0-89981-025-X*) Eastern Orthodox.

— Saltair na Rann. MacCarthy, B., tr. 1987. reprint ed. pap. 9.95 (*0-89979-036-4*) British Am Bks.

Oenslager, Donald. The Theatre of Donald Oenslager. LC 77-16026. (Illus.). 194p. reprint ed. pap. 55.30 (*0-685-23378-2*, 2032491) Bks Demand.

Oeren, T. I., et al, eds. Simulation & Model-Based Methodologies: An Integrative View. (NATO ASI Series F: Computer & Systems Sciences, Special Programme AET: No. 10). xiv, 651p. 1984. 118.00 (*0-387-12884-0*) Spr-Verlag.

Oeric, O. N., jt. auth. see Oss, O. T.

Oerlemans, J., ed. Glacier Fluctuations & Climatic Change. (C). 1989. lib. bdg. 137.00 (*0-7923-0110-2*) Kluwer Ac.

Oerlemans, J., jt. auth. see Van der Veen, C. J.

Oermann, Marilyn, jt. auth. see Reilly, Dorothy.

Oermann, Marilyn H. Professional Nursing Practice: A Conceptual Approach. (Illus.). 330p. 1990. text ed. 28.95 (*0-397-54851-6*) Lippincott.

— Trends & Issues in Nursing. 1993. write for info. (*0-397-54919-9*) Lippincott.

Oermann, Marilyn H., jt. auth. see Reilly, Dorothy E.

Oermann, R., jt. auth. see Bupwack, M.

Oermann, Robert K., jt. auth. see Bufwack, Mary A.

***Oertel, Gerhard.** Stress & Deformation: A Handbook on Tensors in Geology. (Illus.). 272p. 1995. text ed. 62.50 (*0-19-509503-0*) OUP.

Oertel, Gunter. Polyurethane Handbook. 649p. (C). 1985. text ed. 195.50 (*1-56990-069-8*) Hanser-Gardner.

Oertel, Gunter, ed. Polyurethane Handbook. 2nd ed. LC 93-33469. 664p. (C). 1993. text ed. write for info. (*1-56990-157-0*) Hanser-Gardner.

Oertel, H. & Korner, H., eds. Orbital Transport - Technical, Meteorological & Chemical Aspects: Third Aerospace Symposium Braunschweig 26-28 August, 1991. (Illus.). 492p. 1993. 179.00 (*0-387-56318-0*) Spr-Verlag.

Oertel, H., jt. ed. see Zierep, J.

Oertling, Sewall J., II. Calligraphy & Painting in the Wu-tsa-tsu: Conservative Aesthetics in Seventeenth Century China. (Michigan Monographs in Chinese Studies: No. 66). 1994. write for info. (*0-89264-098-7*); pap. write for info. (*0-89264-099-5*) Ctr Chinese Studies.

Oervik, Nils. Europe's Northern Cap & the Soviet Union. LC 73-38763. (Harvard University. Center for International Affairs. Occasional Papers in International Affairs: No. 6). reprint ed. 22.50 (*0-404-54606-4*) AMS Pr.

***Oesch, Herbert.** Finland: The Color & Printing Identification of the 1875 Issues: A New Approach, 2 vols., Set. Aro, Kauko I., tr. (Illus.). 672p. (C). Date not set. text ed. 85.00 (*0-936493-17-8*) Scand Philatelic.

— Finland: The Color & Printing Identification of the 1875 Issues: A New Approach, Vol. II. Aro, Kauko I., tr. (Illus.). iv, 450p. (C). 1994. text ed. 50.00 (*0-936493-16-X*) Scand Philatelic.

— Finland: The Color & Printing Identification of the 1875 Issues Vol. I: A New Approach. Aro, Kauko I., tr. (Illus.). x, 108p. (C). 1994. pap. text ed. 40.00 (*0-936493-15-1*) Scand Philatelic.

Oesch, Ronald D., jt. auth. see Parmalee, Paul W.

Oeschger, H., jt. ed. see Eddy, J. A.

Oeser, Oscar, tr. see Buhler, Karl.

Oeser, Oscar, ed. see Jaensch, Erich.

Oeser, Oscar, tr. see Vossler, Karl.

Oest, O. N., jt. ed. see Bjorner, B.

Oester, Dave R., jt. auth. see Gill, Sharon A.

Oesterby, M., ed. Dictionary of the Russian Academy, 7 vols., Set. (RUS.). 1981. reprint ed. 1,100.00 (*0-915346-76-1*) A Wofsy Fine Arts.

Oestereicher, Emil. Thinking, Feeling, & Doing. Hughes, Patrick M., ed. 208p. (Orig.). 1992. pap. 10.00 (*0-9605008-9-8*) Hermes Hse.

Oesterle, Dale A. Mergers, Acquisitions & Reorganizations, The Law Of. (American Casebook Ser.). 1096p. 1991. text ed. 55.50 (*0-314-85043-0*) West Pub.

— Mergers, Acquisitions, & Reorganizations, the Law Of. (American Casebook Ser.). 265p. (C). 1992. pap. text ed. 16.50 (*0-314-01045-9*) West Pub.

Oesterle, Jean T., tr. Aristotle: On Interpretation. Incl. Commentary by St. Thomas & Cajetan. 1962. (*0-318-54284-6*); (Medieval Philosophical Texts in Translation Ser.). 288p. 1962. Set pap. 20.00 (*0-87462-211-5*) Marquette.

Oesterle, Jean T., tr. see St. Thomas Aquinas.

Oesterle, John A. Logic: The Art of Defining & Reasoning. 2nd ed. 1963. pap. text ed. write for info. (*0-13-539999-8*) P-H.

Oesterle, John A., tr. see Aquinas, St. Thomas.

Oesterle, John A., tr. see St. Thomas Aquinas.

Oesterley, Hermann. Wegweiser Durch die Literatur der Urkundensammlungen, 2 vols., Set. vi, 997p. 1969. reprint ed. write for info. (*0-318-71849-9*, Pub. by Georg Olms GW) Lubrecht & Cramer.

Oesterley, William O. The Jewish Background of the Christian Liturgy. 1925. 11.75 (*0-8446-1329-0*) Peter Smith.

Oesterlin, Pauline J. New Hampshire Marriage Licenses & Intentions, 1709-1961. 265p. (Orig.). 1992. pap. 20.00 (*1-55613-530-0*) Heritage Bk.

— New Hampshire 1742 Estate List. (Illus.). 432p. 1995. text ed. 31.00 (*0-7884-0129-7*) Heritage Bk.

Oesterlin, Pauline J., jt. auth. see Longver, Phyllis O.

Oesterreich, T. K. Possession: Demoniacal & Other. 400p. 1974. reprint ed. pap. 4.95 (*0-8065-0436-6*, Citadel Pr) Carol Pub Group.

Oesterreich, Traugott K. Possession. 1966. 10.00 (*0-8216-0138-5*, Univ Bks) Carol Pub Group.

Oesterreicher, John M. Walls Are Crumbling. (Illus.). 10.00 (*0-8159-7201-6*) Devin.

***Oesterreicher, Michel.** Pioneer Family: Life on Florida's 20th-Century Frontier. LC 95-15202. 1996. write for info. (*0-8173-0783-4*) U of Ala Pr.

***Oesterreicher-Mollwo, Marianne.** Dictionnaire des Symboles. 312p. (FRE.). 1992. pap. 59.95 (*0-7859-7903-4*, 2503502458) Fr & Eur.

Oesting, Heather H. Hidden Assets: The Guide to the Best Catalogs. LC 81-90554. 91p. (Orig.). 1982. pap. 6.95 (*0-941552-00-4*) Hidden Assets.

Oestmann, Cord. Lordship & Community: The Lestrange Family & the Village of Hunstanton, Norfolk, in the First Half of the Sixteenth Century. (Illus.). 288p. (C). 1993. text ed. 63.00 (*0-85115-351-8*) Boydell & Brewer.

Oestmann, J. W., jt. auth. see Greene, R.

Oestmann, R. English for Military Leaders. 128p. (ENG & GER.). 1987. lib. bdg. 65.00 (*0-8288-3405-9*, F55110) Fr & Eur.

Oestreich, A. E. How to Measure Angles from Foot Radiographs. (Illus.). 65p. 1989. pap. 28.00 (*0-387-97107-6*) Spr-Verlag.

Oestreich, Daniel K., jt. auth. see Ryan, Kathleen D.

***Oestreich, Nathan.** Federal Taxation 1994. 7th ed. (C). 1993. student ed, text ed. 21.50 (*0-256-12168-0*) Irwin.

— Individual Taxation 1994. 7th ed. (C). 1993. student ed, text ed. 20.95 (*0-256-12143-5*) Irwin.

Oestreich, Nelson, jt. auth. see Perkins, James A.

Oestreicher, H. L. & Moore, D. R., eds. Cybernetic Problems in Bionics. 916p. 1968. text ed. 549.00 (*0-677-11450-8*) Gordon & Breach.

Oestreicher, James. Choice Adventures: Monumental Discovery. 160p. (J). 1992. pap. 4.99 (*0-8423-5030-6*) Tyndale.

Oestreicher, Joy & Singer, Richard, eds. Air Fish: An Anthology of Speculative Writing. LC 93-70458. (Illus.). 320p. (Orig.). 1993. pap. 16.95 (*0-9631755-2-1*) Omega Cat Pr.

Oestreicher, Richard. Solidarity & Fragmentation: Working People & Class Consciousness in Detroit, 1875-1900. LC 85-1030. (Working Class in American History Ser.). (Illus.). 296p. 1990. pap. 12.95 (*0-252-06120-9*) U of Ill Pr.

Oeter, D. Herder-Lexikon Medizin. 35.00 (*0-8288-7921-4*, M7446) Fr & Eur.

— Herder-Lexikon Medizin. 2nd ed. 240p. (GER.). pap. 35.00 (*0-686-56479-0*, M-7446) Fr & Eur.

Oetinger, Annis. Snow Job. (Illus.). 192p. (Orig.). 1992. pap. 10.95 (*0-9634757-0-3*) A Oetinger.

***Oetinger, Friedrich.** Biblisches und Emblematisches Woerterbuch. 930p. (GER.). 1994. 650.00 (*0-7859-8267-1*, 3110049031) Fr & Eur.

Oetinger, Friedrich C. Biblisches und Emblematisches Worterbuch. 880p. (GER.). 1988. reprint ed. write for info. (*3-487-02345-8*, Pub. by Georg Olms GW) Lubrecht & Cramer.

Oetker. Garnishing Book & Tool Set. 1989. 24.99 (*0-517-69600-2*) Random Hse Value.

Oetker, D. Garnishing. 1989. pap. 12.99 (*0-517-68792-5*) Random Hse Value.

Oetliker, O., jt. ed. see Rossi, E.

Oets, Pim. MS-DOS & PC-DOS: A Practical Guide. 2nd ed. (Computer Science Ser.). (Illus.). 216p. (C). 1988. pap. text ed. 35.00 (*0-333-45440-5*, Pub. by Macmill Press UK) Scholium Intl.

Oetteking, Bruno. Craniology of the North Pacific Coast. LC 73-3533. (Jessup North Pacific Expedition. Publications: No. 11). reprint ed. 82.50 (*0-404-58111-0*) AMS Pr.

— Skeletal Remains from Santa Barbara, California: I. Craniology. LC 76-43795. (MAI. Indian Notes & Monographs: No. 39). reprint ed. 49.50 (*0-404-15651-7*) AMS Pr.

— The Skeleton from Mesa House. (Illus.). 48p. 1970. reprint ed. pap. 3.50 (*0-916561-61-5*) Southwest Mus.

Oetter, R. G., jt. auth. see Vickers, G. W.

Oettgen, H. F., ed. Gangliocides & Cancer. LC 88-33916. 366p. 1989. lib. bdg. 170.00 (*0-89573-877-5*) VCH Pubs.

Oettgen, Herbert F., jt. ed. see Mitchell, Malcolm S.

Oetting. The Chieftain of Chaucer. LC 73-87806. (Sound Ser.). (Illus.). 32p. (J). (gr. 2-5). 1974. lib. bdg. 9.95 (*0-87783-137-8*) Oddo.

— The Chieftain of Chaucer. deluxe ed. LC 73-87806. (Sound Ser.). (Illus.). 32p. (J). (gr. 2-5). 1974. pap. 3.94 (*0-87783-138-6*) Oddo.

— The Gray Ghosts of Gotham. LC 73-87804. (Sound Ser.). (Illus.). 32p. (J). (gr. 2-5). 1974. lib. bdg. 9.95 (*0-87783-135-1*) Oddo.

— The Gray Ghosts of Gotham. deluxe ed. LC 73-87804. (Sound Ser.). (Illus.). 32p. (J). (gr. 2-5). 1974. pap. 3.94 (*0-87783-136-X*) Oddo.

— Keiki of the Islands. LC 71-108728. (Illus.). 96p. (J). (gr. 3 up). 1970. lib. bdg. 10.95 (*0-87783-018-5*) Oddo.

— Keiki of the Islands. deluxe ed. LC 71-108728. (Illus.). 96p. (J). (gr. 3 up). 1970. pap. 3.94 (*0-87783-096-7*) Oddo.

Oetting, E. R., jt. auth. see Drake, Lewis E.

Oetting, R. Orderly Cricket. LC 68-16395. (Illus.). 32p. (J). (gr. 2-3). 1967. lib. bdg. 9.95 (*0-87783-028-2*) Oddo.

— Prairie Dog Town. LC 68-56829. (Illus.). 48p. (J). (gr. 2-5). 1968. lib. bdg. 10.95 (*0-87783-030-4*) Oddo.

— Prairie Dog Town. deluxe ed. LC 68-56829. (Illus.). 48p. (J). (gr. 2-5). 1968. pap. 3.94 (*0-87783-157-2*) Oddo.

— Quetico Wolf. LC 71-190274. (Illus.). 48p. (J). (gr. 4 up). 1972. lib. bdg. 9.95 (*0-87783-059-2*) Oddo.

— Quetico Wolf. deluxe ed. LC 71-190274. (Illus.). 48p. (J). (gr. 4 up). 1972. pap. 3.94 (*0-87783-103-3*) Oddo.

— When Jesus Was a Lad. LC 68-56816. (Illus.). 32p. (J). (gr. 2-3). 1968. lib. bdg. 9.95 (*0-87783-047-9*) Oddo.

Oetting, Rae. Bobby Bear's Birthday. LC 87-62508. (Bobby Bear Ser.). (Illus.). 32p. (J). (ps-1). 1988. lib. bdg. 11.45 (*0-87783-220-X*) Oddo.

— Timmy Tiger & the Elephant. LC 73-108730. (Timmy Tiger Ser.). (Illus.). 32p. (J). (ps-2). 1970. lib. bdg. 9.95 (*0-87783-041-X*); audio 7.94 (*0-87783-277-3*) Oddo.

— Timmy Tiger & the Elephant. deluxe ed. LC 73-108730. (Timmy Tiger Ser.). (Illus.). 32p. (J). (ps-2). 1970. pap. 3.94 (*0-87783-111-4*) Oddo.

— Timmy Tiger to the Rescue. LC 70-108733. (Timmy Tiger Ser.). (Illus.). 32p. (J). (ps-4). 1970. lib. bdg. 9.95 (*0-87783-043-6*); audio 7.94 (*0-87783-229-3*) Oddo.

— Timmy Tiger to the Rescue. deluxe ed. LC 70-108733. (Timmy Tiger Ser.). (Illus.). 32p. (J). (ps-4). 1970. pap. 3.94 (*0-87783-112-2*) Oddo.

— Timmy Tiger's New Coat. LC 74-108734. (Timmy Tiger Ser.). (Illus.). 32p. (J). (ps-2). 1970. lib. bdg. 9.95 (*0-87783-044-4*); audio 7.94 (*0-87783-230-7*) Oddo.

— Timmy Tiger's New Coat. deluxe ed. LC 74-108734. (Timmy Tiger Ser.). (Illus.). 32p. (J). (ps-2). 1970. pap. 3.94 (*0-87783-113-0*) Oddo.

— Timmy Tiger's New Friend. LC 77-108732. (Timmy Tiger Ser.). (Illus.). (J). (ps-2). 1970. lib. bdg. 9.95 (*0-87783-042-8*); audio 7.94 (*0-87783-231-5*) Oddo.

— Timmy Tiger's New Friend. deluxe ed. LC 77-108732. (Timmy Tiger Ser.). (Illus.). (J). (ps-2). 1970. pap. 3.94 (*0-87783-114-9*) Oddo.

— Wrongway Santa. LC 90-62546. (Illus.). 32p. (J). 1991. lib. bdg. 15.95 (*0-87783-254-4*) Oddo.

Oettinger, Anthony, jt. ed. see Ernst, Martin L.

Oettinger, Anthony, jt. auth. see Weinhaus, Carol.

Oettinger, Anthony G. Run, Computer, Run: The Mythology of Educational Innovation. LC 71-78522. (Illus.). 323p. reprint ed. pap. 92.10 (*0-7837-5940-1*, 2045739) Bks Demand.

— Telling Ripe from Hype in Multimedia: The Ecstasy & the Agony. 32p. (Orig.). 1994. pap. text ed. write for info. (*1-879716-14-3*, I94-2) Ctr Info Policy.

Oettinger, Anthony G., ed. see Horowitz, Barry M., et al.

Oettinger, Anthony G., ed. see Horton, Frank B., et al.

Oettinger, Bob, ed. see Webb, Michael.

Oettinger, Elizabeth N., jt. ed. see Kenny, Dennis E.

Oettinger, Marion, Jr. Discovering the Folk Art of Latin America: Visiones del Pueblo. LC 92-52861. (Illus.). 112p. 1992. 30.00 (*0-525-93435-9*, Dutton Studio); pap. 19.00 (*0-525-48599-6*, Dutton Studio) Studio Bks.

— Folk Treasures of Mexico: The Nelson A. Rockefeller Collection. (Illus.). 224p. 1990. 60.00 (*0-8109-1182-5*) Abrams.

Oettli, Peter H. Tradition & Creativity: The Engelhard of Konrad von Wurzburg - Its Strucutre & its Sources. (Australian & New Zealand Studies in German Language & Literature: Vol. 14). 194p. 1986. text ed. 20.55 (*0-8204-0302-4*) P Lang Pubs.

Oettli, W. & Pallaschke, D., eds. Advances in Optimization: Proceedings of the 6th French-German Colloquium on Optimization, Held at Lambrecht, FRG, June 2-8, 1991. LC 92-5741. (Lecture Notes in Economics & Mathematical Systems Ser.: Vol. 382). 1992. write for info. (*3-540-55446-7*) Spr-Verlag.

Oettli, W., et al, eds. Advances in Optimization: Proceedings of the 6th French-German Colloquium on Optimization, Held at Lambrecht, FRG, June 2-8, 1991. (Lecture Notes in Economics & Mathematical Systems Ser.: Vol. 382). (Illus.). x, 527p. 1992. pap. 78.00 (*0-387-55446-7*) Spr-Verlag.

Oettmeier, Timothy N., jt. auth. see Pekar, George M.

Oetzel, James L., jt. auth. see Chester, Sharon R.

Oewn, Wanda. Texas Wildfire. 1984. pap. 3.75 (*0-8217-1337-X*) Zebra.

Oey, Eric. Java: Garden of the East. (Passport's Regional Guides of Indonesia Ser.). (Illus.). 272p. 1990. pap. 15.95 (*0-8442-9903-0*, Passport Bks) NTC Pub Grp.

— Java: Garden of the East. 2nd ed. 1994. pap. 17.95 (*0-8442-9947-2*, Passport Bks) NTC Pub Grp.

Oey, Eric, ed. Bali. 272p. 1991. pap. 37.50 (*0-945971-32-X*) Periplus.

— Bali. 3rd ed. 312p. 1995. pap. 19.95 (*962-593-028-0*) Periplus.

— Bali: Eiland der Goden. Pessissiron, Sylvia, tr. (Indonesie Reisbibliotheek Ser.). (Illus.). 272p. (DUT.). 1990. 19.95 (*0-945971-17-6*) Periplus.

— Java. 2nd ed. 416p. (DUT.). 1995. pap. 19.95 (*962-593-013-2*) Periplus.

— Sumatra. 2nd ed. 332p. 1995. pap. 19.95 (*962-593-017-5*) Periplus.

Oey, Eric, ed. see Muller, Kal.

Oey, Thomas G. Everyday Indonesian. (Illus.). 192p. 1994. pap. write for info. (*0-945971-92-3*) Periplus.

— Everyday Indonesian: Phrasebook & Dictionary. 198p. 1992. pap. 11.95 (*0-945971-58-3*) Periplus.

— Indonesissch Fur Reise und Alltag. 200p. 1993. pap. write for info. (*0-945971-85-0*) Periplus.

— Pocket Dictionary: Dutch - Indonesian. (Illus.). 1994. pap. write for info. (*0-945971-94-X*) Periplus.

— Pocket Dictionary: English-Indonesian - Indonesian-English. 72p. (Orig.). 1992. pap. 3.95 (*0-945971-66-4*) Periplus.

Oey, Thomas G. & Hutton, Wendy. Everyday Malay: Phrasebook & Dictionary. 192p. 1994. pap. 14.95 (*0-945971-83-4*) Periplus.

Oey, Thomas G., jt. auth. see Hutton, Wendy.

Oezisik, M. Necati. Heat Conduction. LC 79-990. 687p. 1980. text ed. 79.95 (*0-471-05481-X*) Wiley.

O'Fahey, R. S. State & Society in Dar Fur. LC 80-13372. 1980. text ed. 35.00 (*0-312-75606-2*) St Martin.

O'Fahey, R. S. & Salim, M. I. Land in Dar Fur: Charters & Related Documents from the Dar Fur Sultanate. LC 82-4186. (Fontes Historiae Africanae, Series Arabica: No. 3). (Illus.). 176p. 1983. 44.95 (*0-521-24643-1*) Cambridge U Pr.

O

O'Fahey, R. S., jt. ed. see Hunwick, J. O.

O'Faolain, Eileen. Irish Sagas & Folk Tales. 1986. reprint ed. pap. 10.95 (0-905169-71-9, Pub. by Poolbeg Pr IE) Dufour.

— Little Black Hen. 128p. 1990. pap. 6.95 (1-85371-053-9, Pub. by Poolbeg Pr IE); pap. 7.95 (1-85371-049-0) Dufour.

O'Faolain, Julia. No Country for Young Men. 416p. 1986. pap. 8.95 (0-88184-354-7) Carroll & Graf.

— The Obedient Wife. LC 85-17145. 230p. (Orig.). 1985. 17.95 (0-88184-197-8) Carroll & Graf.

O'Faolain, Sean. And Again? Richardson, Stewart, ed. 290p. 1989. 16.95 (1-55972-003-4, Birch Ln Pr) Carol Pub Group.

— Irish: A Character Study. 1979. pap. 12.95 (0-8159-5812-9) Devin.

— The Man Who Invented Sin. (Illus.). 1974. reprint ed. 12.95 (0-8159-6212-6) Devin.

Ofaolain, Sean. Nest of Simple Folk. 1990. 17.95 (1-55972-041-7, Birch Ln Pr) Carol Pub Group.

O'Faolain, Sean. The Short Story. pap. 9.95 (0-8159-6814-0) Devin.

— Short Story. 1989. pap. 19.95 (0-85342-860-3) Dufour.

— A Summer in Italy. 9.95 (0-8159-6831-0) Devin.

— Vanishing Hero. LC 71-142686. (Essay Index Reprint Ser.). 1977. 18.95 (0-8369-2065-1) Ayer.

— The Vanishing Hero. 1991. reprint ed. lib. bdg. 21.95 (1-56849-074-7) Buccaneer Bks.

O'Faolain, Sean, comp. Silver Branch. LC 68-58822. (Granger Index Reprint Ser.). 1977. 15.95 (0-8369-6035-1) Ayer.

O'Faolin, Sean. The Great O'Neill: A Biography of Hugh O'Neill, Earl of Tyrone, 1550-1616. 284p. 1993. reprint ed. pap. 16.95 (0-85342-769-0, Pub. by Mercier Pr IE) Dufour.

O'Farrell, Clare. Foucault: Historian or Philosopher? LC 89-33424. 180p. 1990. text ed. 45.00 (0-312-03463-6) St Martin.

O'Farrell, Kathleen. The Fiddler of Kilbroney. 352p. (Orig.). 1994. pap. 15.95 (0-86322-177-7, Pub. by Brandon Bk Pubs IE) Irish Bks Media.

— Kilbroney. 352p. (Orig.). 1992. pap. 11.95 (0-86322-141-6, Pub. by Brandon Bk Pubs IE) Irish Bks Media.

O'Farrell, Kevin, jt. auth. see Johanson, Donald.

***O'Farrell, Lawrence.** Education & the Art of Drama. 69p. (C). 1994. 40.00x (0-7300-1799-0, Pub. by Deakin Univ AT) St Mut.

O'Farrell, M. Brigid, ed. see National Research Council, Panel on Employer Policies & Working Families Staff.

***O'Farrell, Padraic.** Ancient Irish Legends. (Illus.). 96p. (Orig.). 1995. pap. 7.95 (0-614-06647-6, Pub. by Gill & MacMill IE) Irish Bks Media.

— The Burning of Brinsley MacNamara. (Illus.). 176p. 1990. pap. 11.95 (0-946640-56-4, Pub. by Lilliput Pr Ltd IE) Irish Bks Media.

— By Rail Through the Heart of Ireland. (Illus.). 1990. pap. 16.95 (0-85342-948-0, Pub. by Mercier Pr IE) Dufour.

— How the Irish Speak English. rev. ed. 128p. 1994. pap. 12.95 (1-85635-055-X, Pub. by Mercier Pr IE) Dufour.

— Humorous Folktales of Ireland. LC 89-81673. 91p. 1990. pap. 9.95 (0-85342-895-6, Pub. by Mercier Pr IE) Dufour.

— Irish Proverbs & Sayings. 1990. pap. 9.95 (0-85342-846-8) Dufour.

— Irish Rogues, Rascals & Scoundrels. 120p. 1993. pap. 12.95 (1-85635-006-1, Pub. by Mercier Pr IE) Dufour.

— Irish Toasts, Curses & Blessings. LC 94-40340. 128p. 1995. pap. 5.95 (0-8069-0872-6) Sterling.

— Superstitions of the Irish Country People. 1991. pap. 9.95 (0-85342-891-3, Pub. by Mercier Pr IE) Dufour.

O'Farrell, Padraic, ed. Before the Devil Knows You're Dead: Irish Blessings, Toasts & Curses. 117p. 1993. pap. 11.95 (1-85635-033-9, Pub. by Mercier Pr IE) Dufour.

— Green, Chaste & Foolish: Irish Literary & Theatrical Anecdotes. 256p. (Orig.). 1994. pap. 19.95 (0-7171-2106-2, Pub. by Gill & MacMill IE) Irish Bks Media.

O'Farrell, Patrick. The Irish in Australia. (Illus.). 342p. (C). 1989. text ed. 32.95 (0-268-01164-8) U of Notre Dame Pr.

— Letters from Irish Australia, 1825-1925. 244p. 1990. pap. 24.95 (0-86840-235-4, Pub. by New South Wales Univ Pr AT) Intl Spec Bk.

— Vanished Kingdoms: Irish in Australia & New Zealand. 1990. 39.95 (0-86840-148-X, Pub. by New South Wales Univ Pr AT) Intl Spec Bk.

O'Farrell, R. C. Seafood Fishing for Amateur & Professional. 1978. 25.00 (0-685-63452-3) St Mut.

O'Farrell, Timothy J., ed. Treating Alcohol Problems: Marital & Family Interventions. (Substance Abuse Ser.). 446p. 1993. lib. bdg. 36.95 (0-89862-195-X) Guilford Pr.

***O'Farrell, Valerie.** Manual of Canine Behaviour. 2nd ed. (Illus.). 132p. 1995. pap. 46.95 (0-905214-17-X) Iowa St U Pr.

***O'Farrell, Valerie & Neville, Peter.** Manual of Feline Behaviour. Ross, Christopher S., ed. (Illus.). 84p. 1995. pap. 26.95 (0-905214-24-2) Iowa St U Pr.

O'Farrell, William. Repeat Performance. LC 87-82446. 248p. 1987. reprint ed. pap. 4.95 (0-930330-71-4) Intl Polygonics.

Ofcansky, Thomas, ed. Ethiopia Country Studies: Area Handbook. 4th ed. LC 92-507. (Area Handbook Ser.: Vol. 550-28). 412p. 1993. 27.50 (0-8444-0739-9) Lib Congress.

Ofcansky, Thomas P. Paradise Lost: A History of Game Preservation in East Africa. (Illus.). 1993. write for info. (0-937058-29-7) West Va U Pr.

— Uganda: Tarnished Pearl of Africa. LC 95-13468. (Nations of the Modern World Ser.). 1995. write for info. (0-8133-1059-8) Westview.

Ofek, Itzhak, jt. auth. see Doyle, Ronald J.

Ofek, Uriel. Beware! Ducks Crossing. Kriss, David, tr. (Hippy Ser.). (Illus.). 24p. (Orig.). (J). (ps). 1992. pap. text ed. 3.00 (1-56134-145-2) Dushkin Pub.

— Cuidado! Patos Cruzando. Writer, C. C. & Nielsen, Lisa C., trs. (Hippy Ser.). (Illus.). 24p. (Orig.). (SPA.). (J). (ps). 1992. pap. text ed. 3.00 (1-56134-155-X) Dushkin Pub.

Ofeoegbu, Charles O., ed. The Benue Through: Structure & Evolution. (Earth Evolution Sciences Ser.). vi, 362p. (C). 1989. 142.00 (3-528-06376-9, Pub. by Vieweg & Sohn GW) Ballen Bkslr.

Ofer, Dalia. Escape from the Holocaust: Illegal Immigration to Israel, 1939-1944. (Studies in Jewish History). (Illus.). 432p. 1991. 39.95 (0-19-506340-6) OUP.

Ofer, Gur. The Service Sector in Soviet Economic Growth: A Comparative Study. LC 72-87775. (Russian Research Center Studies, No. 71, Economic Studies: No. 141). (Illus.). 216p. 1973. 16.50 (0-674-80180-6) HUP.

Ofer, Gur & Vinokur, Aaron. The Soviet Household under the Old Regime: Economic Conditions & Behaviour in the 1970s. (Illus.). 450p. (C). 1992. 79.95 (0-521-38398-6) Cambridge U Pr.

Ofer, Gur, jt. ed. see Bosworth, Barry P.

Ofer, Gur, jt. auth. see De Melo, Martha.

Ofer, Gur, jt. ed. see Keren, Michael.

O'Ferrall, More G., ed. Beef Production from Different Dairy Breeds & Dairy Beef Crosses. 1982. lib. bdg. 126.50 (90-247-2759-6) Kluwer Ac.

Offe, Claire & Heinze, Rolf G. Beyond Employment: Time, Work & the Informal Economy. Braley, Alan, tr. 248p. 1992. 44.95 (0-87722-951-1) Temple U Pr.

Offe, Claus. Contradictions of the Welfare State. Keane, John B., ed. (German Social Thought Ser.). 304p. (Orig.). (C). 1984. pap. 16.95 (0-262-65014-2) MIT Pr.

— Disorganized Capitalism: Contemporary Transformations of Work & Politics. Keane, John B., tr. (German Social Thought Ser.). 280p. 1985. 30.00 (0-262-15029-8) MIT Pr.

Offederal, E., jt. ed. see Bjerkholt, O.

***Offen.** European Feminism. Date not set. 24.95 (0-8057-8608-2, Twayne) Macmillan.

— VLSI Image Processing. 1986. text ed. 40.00 (0-07-047771-X) McGraw.

Offen, Hilda. As Quiet As a Mouse. (Illus.). 32p. (J). (ps-2). 1994. 12.99 (0-525-45309-1, DCB) Dutton Child Bks.

— Elephant Pie. (Illus.). 32p. (J). (ps-2). 1993. 13.99 (0-525-45123-4, DCB) Dutton Child Bks.

— Favorite Fairy Tales. 1989. 3.99 (0-517-67166-2) Random Hse Value.

— A Fox Got My Socks. LC 92-7380. (J). (ps-2). 1993. 10.00 (0-525-44991-4, DCB) Dutton Child Bks.

— Nice Work, Little Wolf! LC 91-23741. (Illus.). 32p. (J). (ps-2). 1992. 14.00 (0-525-44880-2, DCB) Dutton Child Bks.

— The Sheep Made a Leap. (Illus.). 32p. (J). (ps-2). 1994. 10.99 (0-525-45174-9, DCB) Dutton Child Bks.

Offen, Hilda, illus. Beauty & the Beast & Other Stories. LC 93-5772. (Little Library). (J). 1994. 3.95 (1-85697-967-9, Kingfisher LKC) LKC.

— Cinderella & Other Stories. LC 93-5770. (Little Library). (J). 1994. 3.95 (1-85697-968-7, Kingfisher LKC) LKC.

Offen, HIlda, illus. Goldilocks & Other Stories. LC 93-5771. (Little Library). (J). 1994. 3.95 (1-85697-969-5, Kingfisher LKC) LKC.

Offen, Hilda, illus. Little Red Riding Hood & Other Stories. LC 93-5768. (Little Library). 32p. (J). (ps-00). 1994. 3.95 (1-85697-970-9, Kingfisher LKC) LKC.

— My Favorite Nursery Rhymes. (J). (ps-5). 1987. pap. 12.95 (0-671-64705-9, S&S Bks Young Read) S&S Childrens.

— Sleeping Beauty & Other Stories. LC 93-5769. (Little Library). (J). 1994. 3.95 (1-85697-971-7, Kingfisher LKC) LKC.

Offen, HIlda, illus. Snow White & Other Stories. LC 93-5767. (Little Library). (J). 1994. 3.95 (1-85697-972-5, Kingfisher LKC) LKC.

Offen, Hilda, illus. A Treasury of Bedtime Stories. 160p. (J). (ps-3). 1981. pap. 13.00 (0-671-44463-8, S&S Bks Young Read) S&S Childrens.

— A Treasury of Mother Goose. (J). (gr. 1 up). 1984. pap. 13.00 (0-671-50118-6, S&S Bks Young Read) S&S Childrens.

Offen, Karen. Paul De Cassagnac & the Authoritarian Tradition in Nineteenth-Century France. rev. ed. LC 91-23151. 416p. 1991. 90.00 (0-8153-0479-X) Garland.

Offen, Karen M., jt. ed. see Bell, Susan G.

Offen, Karen M., et al, eds. Writing Women's History: International Perspectives. LC 90-49155. 596p. 1991. 37.50 (0-253-34160-4); pap. 17.50 (0-253-20651-0, MB-651) Ind U Pr.

***Offen, Ron, ed.** The Starving Poets' Cookbook. LC 94-90594. 68p. 1994. per., pap. 10.00 (0-9643296-0-3) Free Lunch.

Offenbach, Jacques. Offenbach in America: Notes of a Travelling Musician. LC 74-24172. reprint ed. 12.50 (0-404-13076-3) AMS Pr.

***Offenbacher, Ami.** The Dragonfly. LC 94-60832. (Illus.). 44p. (J). (gr. k-3). 1995. 6.95 (1-55523-712-6) Winston-Derek.

Offenberg, A. K. A Choice of Corals. Facets of Fifteenth Century Hebrew Printing. (Illus.). 263p. 1992. 87.50 (90-6004-421-5, Pub. by B De Graaf NE) Coronet Bks.

Offenberg, A. K. & Van Walraven, C. Moed, comps. Hebrew Incunabula in Public Collections: A First International Census. 300p. 1990. lib. bdg. 77.50 (90-6004-404-5, Pub. by B De Graaf NE) Coronet Bks.

***Offenberg, A. K., et al.** Bibliotheca Rosenthaliana: Treasures of Jewish Booklore: Marketing the 200th Anniversary of the Birth of Leeser Rosenthal, 1794-1994. 130p. 1994. 39.50 (90-5356-088-2) IBD Ltd.

Offenberger, Niels. Zur Modernen Deutung der Aristotelischen Logik, Bd. IV: Niels Offenberger, Zur Vorgeschichte der Mehrwertigen Logik in der Antike. viii, 172p. (GER.). 1990. write for info. (3-487-09350-2, Pub. by Georg Olms GW) Lubrecht & Cramer.

Offenberger, Niels, jt. auth. see Menne, Albert.

Offenburger, Chuck. Ah, You Iowans! At Home, at Work, at Play, at War. LC 92-20994. (Illus.). 316p. 1992. pap. 14.95 (0-8138-1833-8) Iowa St U Pr.

— Babe: An Iowa Legend. LC 88-37461. (Illus.). 174p. 1989. 12.95 (0-8138-0269-5) Iowa St U Pr.

— Iowa Boy: Ten Years of Columns by Chuck Offenburger. LC 87-17269. (Illus.). 250p. (Orig.). 1987. pap. 12.95 (0-8138-0039-0) Iowa St U Pr.

Offenburger, Chuck, intro. Iowa: A Photographic Celebration. (Illus.). 96p. (Orig.). 1990. pap. 12.95 (0-938314-85-8) Am Wrld Geog.

Offenburger, Jeffrey & Constant, Nancy. Mind Matters in Selling. 20p. 1982. audio 49.50 (0-88432-175-4, S29600) Audio-Forum.

Offer, Avner. The First World War: An Agrarian Interpretation. (Illus.). 480p. 1991. reprint ed. pap. 29.95 (0-19-820279-2) OUP.

— Property & Politics 1870-1914: Ideology & Urban Development in England. (Modern Revivals in History Ser.). 445p. 1992. 69.95 (0-7512-0066-2, Pub. by Gregg Revivals UK) Ashgate Pub Co.

Offer, Daniel, jt. ed. see Strozier, Charles B.

Offer, Daniel, et al. The Teenage World: Adolescents' Self-Image in Ten Countries. LC 88-4127. (Illus.). 288p. 1988. 45.00 (0-306-42747-8, Plenum Med Bk) Plenum.

Offer, Daniel, et al, eds. Patterns of Adolescent Self-Image. LC 83-82733. (New Directions for Mental Health Services Ser.: No. MHS 22). 1984. 17.95 (0-87589-779-7) Jossey-Bass.

Offer, John, ed. see Spencer, Herbert.

Offerhaus, J. P., ed. see Verzijl, J. H.

Offerman-Zuckerberg, J., ed. Critical Psychophysical Passages in the Life of a Woman. LC 88-12615. (Illus.). 310p. 1988. 45.00 (0-306-42639-0, Plenum Med Bk) Plenum.

— Gender in Transition: A New Frontier. (Illus.). 326p. 1989. 49.50 (0-306-43132-7, Plenum Med Bk) Plenum.

— Politics & Psychology: Contemporary Psychodynamic Perspectives. (Illus.). 360p. 1991. 49.50 (0-306-43864-X, Plenum Pr) Plenum.

Offermann, Lynn R. & Gowing, Marilyn K., eds. Organizational Psychology. (Special Issue of American Psychologist Ser.: Vol. 45, No. 2). 224p. 1990. pap. 16.00 (1-55798-092-6) Am Psychol.

Office de la Langue Francaise Staff. Vocabulary of Banking & Currency. 39p. (ENG & FRE.). 1974. pap. 14.95 (0-8288-9388-8) Fr & Eur.

— Vocabulary of Paper Industry Materials: Vocabulaire du Materiel Papetier. 144p. (ENG & FRE.). 1983. 75.00 (0-8288-4419-4, M7573) Fr & Eur.

Office Depot Staff, jt. auth. see Allen, Kathleen.

Office Depot Staff, jt. auth. see Lund, Bonnie.

Office for Standards in Education HMSO Staff. Handbook for the Inspection of Schools. 524p. 1993. ring bd. 30.00 (0-11-350017-3, HM00173, Pub. by HMSO UK) UNIPUB.

Office for the Pastoral Care of Migrants & Refugees, United States Catholic Conference Staff. Catholic Shrines & Places of Pilgrimage. 176p. 1992. pap. 9.95 (1-55586-821-5) US Catholic.

Office International des Epizooties Staff. Dictionary of Animal Health Terminology in English, French, Spanish, German & Latin. Mack, Roy, ed. 426p. (ENG, FRE, GER, LAT & SPA.). 1992. 250.00 (0-8288-9215-6) Fr & Eur.

Office Lighting Committee Staff. Office Lighting. rev. ed. (Recommended Practices Ser.). (Illus.). 64p. 1993. pap. 18.00 (0-87995-021-8, RP-2-85) Illum Eng.

— VDT Lighting. (Recommended Practices Ser.). 25p. 1989. pap. 35.00 (0-87995-031-5, RP-24-89) Illum Eng.

***Office of Commissioner Federal Judicial Affairs Staff.** Federal Court Reports: Consolidated Index 1989-1992. Rankin, William J., ed. 287p. 1993. 162.50x (0-660-58036-5, Pub. by Canada Commun Grp CN) Accents Pubns.

Office of Disease Prevention & Health Promotion Staff, jt. auth. see American Dietetic Association Staff.

Office of Economic Affairs Staff, comp. Economic Fact Book for Psychiatry. 2nd ed. 216p. 1987. pap. text ed. 21.00 (0-88048-158-7, 8158) Am Psychiatric.

Office of International Affairs, National Research Council Staff. U. S.-Japan Strategic Alliances in the Semiconductor Industry: Technology Transfer, Competition, & Public Policy. 126p. (C). 1992. pap. text ed. 19.00 (0-309-04779-X) Natl Acad Pr.

Office of Juvenile Justice & Delinquency Prevention Staff, jt. auth. see American Correctional Association Staff.

Office of Management & Budget Staff. Managing Federal Assistance in the 1980s, 3 vols., Set. 1982. reprint ed. 145.00 (0-89941-223-8, 201560) W S Hein.

Office of Population Censuses & Surveys Staff. Communicable Disease Statistics MB2 1990. (Office of Population Censuses & Surveys Reference Series AB: No. 17). 73p. 1992. pap. 19.00 (0-11-691445-9, HM14459, Pub. by HMSO UK) UNIPUB.

— Communicable Disease Statistics (OPCS Series MB2) 1992, No. 19. 66p. 1994. pap. 19.00 (0-11-691572-2, HM15722, Pub. by HMSO UK) UNIPUB.

— Communicable Disease Statistics, 1991 MB2. (Office of Population Censuses & Surveys Reference Series AB: No. 18). 66p. 1993. pap. 19.00 (0-11-691531-5, HM15315, Pub. by HMSO UK) UNIPUB.

Office of Research & Policy, Radio Marti Program Staff. Cuba Annual Report 1985. 400p. 1987. 79.95 (0-88738-146-4) Transaction Pubs.

Office of Research & Policy Staff. Cuba Annual Report 1986. 800p. 1989. 79.95 (0-88738-191-X) Transaction Pubs.

Office of Research & Policy Staff, et al. Cuba Annual Report, 1987. 800p. 1989. 79.95 (0-88738-273-8) Transaction Pubs.

Office of Scientific & Engineering Personnel, National Research Council, ed. Climbing the Ladder: An Update on the Status of Doctoral Women Scientists & Engineers. 112p. (C). 1983. pap. text ed. 14.95 (0-309-03341-1) Natl Acad Pr.

Office of South Carolina Court Administration Staff. South Carolina Bench Book for Magistrates & Municipal Court Judges. 2nd ed. 1988. ring bd. 90.00 (0-943856-02-7, 410) SC Bar CLE.

Office of State-Federal Relations Staff. Summary of the One Hundred First Congress First Session (1989), Vol. 2, No. 11. (State-Federal Issue Brief Ser.: Vol. 2, No. 11). 10p. 1989. pap. text ed. 6.50 (1-55516-881-7, 8500-0211) Natl Conf State Legis.

Office of Technology Assessment, Congress of the United States Staff. Technology & Handicapped People. 224p. 1983. 29.95 (0-8261-4510-8) Springer Pub.

Office of Technology Assessment (OTA) Staff. Police Body Armor Standards & Testing. 114p. 1993. 49.50 (0-912702-79-6) Global Eng Doc.

Office of Technology Assessment Staff. Identifying & Regulating Carcinogens. 272p. 1989. 99.75 (0-8247-8070-1) Dekker.

— Intellectual Property Rights in an Age of Electronics & Information. LC 86-20874. 320p. 1987. reprint ed. 29.50 (0-89874-972-7) Krieger.

— New Developments in Biotechnology: Patenting Life. 208p. 1989. 79.75 (0-8247-8317-4) Dekker.

— Ocean Incineration: Its Role in Managing Hazardous Waste. LC 87-3649. 232p. (C). 1988. 27.50 (0-89464-212-X) Krieger.

— Technologies & Management Strategies for Hazardous Waste Control. LC 87-3546. 416p. 1988. lib. bdg. 39.50 (0-89464-217-0) Krieger.

— Technologies for Prehistoric & Historic Preservation. LC 87-3304. 210p. 1988. reprint ed. lib. bdg. 25.50 (0-89464-219-7) Krieger.

— Transportation of Hazardous Materials: State & Local Activities. LC 87-3555. 100p. 1988. reprint ed. lib. bdg. 19.50 (0-89464-218-9) Krieger.

Office of Technology Assessment Staff, comp. Wastes in Marine Environments. LC 66-65012. 320p. 1987. 67.00 (0-89116-793-5) Hemisp Pub.

Office of Technology Assessment Task Force Staff, ed. Life-Sustaining Technologies & the Elderly. LC 65-20241. 450p. 1988. text ed. 39.95 (0-397-53024-2) Lippincott.

Office of the Chief of Engineers, U. S. Army Staff, ed. Laws of the United States Relating to the Improvement of Rivers & Harbors from August 11, 1790 to June 29, 1938, 3 vols., 1. LC 73-5434. reprint ed. write for info. (0-404-11191-2) AMS Pr.

— Laws of the United States Relating to the Improvement of Rivers & Harbors from August 11, 1790 to June 29, 1938, 3 vols., 2. LC 73-5434. reprint ed. write for info. (0-404-11192-0) AMS Pr.

— Laws of the United States Relating to the Improvement of Rivers & Harbors from August 11, 1790 to June 29, 1938, 3 vols., 3. LC 73-5434. reprint ed. write for info. (0-404-11193-9) AMS Pr.

— Laws of the United States Relating to the Improvement of Rivers & Harbors from August 11, 1790 to June 29, 1938, 3 vols., Set. LC 73-5434. reprint ed. 125.00 (0-404-11190-4) AMS Pr.

Office of the Commissioner of Official Languages Staff. Keeping up Your Skills & More in French. 42p. (Orig.). 1993. pap. 6.75 (0-660-14995-8, Pub. by Canada Commun Grp CN) Accents Pubns.

Office of the Comptroller of the Currency Staff. Foreign Acquisition of U. S. Banks. 1983. 54.95 (0-8359-2083-6, Reston) P-H.

Office of the Federal Register, National Archives & Records Administration Staff. United States Government Manual, 1993-94. (Illus.). 1000p. 1993. reprint ed. lib. bdg. 30.00 (0-89059-019-2); reprint ed. pap. 30.00 (0-89059-016-8) Bernan Pr.

— The United States Government Manual 1994-95. (Illus.). 1000p. 1994. reprint ed. pap. 29.95 (0-89059-031-1) Bernan Pr.

Office of the Primate of the Ecumenical Catholic Church Staff & Shirilau, Mark S. Canon Law of the Ecumenical Catholic Church. 2nd rev. ed. 32p. 1992. pap. 5.00 (1-881568-01-6) Healing Spirit.

Office of the Sesquicentennial Fordham University Staff. As I Remember Fordham: Selections from the Sesquicentennial Oral History Project. LC 91-61628. 208p. 1991. 20.00 (0-8232-1338-2) Fordham.

Office of Water Resources Research Staff, comp. Algae Abstracts: A Guide to the Literature, 3 vols. Incl. Vol. 1. To 1969. 586p. 1973. 95.00 (0-306-67181-6); Vol. 2. 1970 to 1972. 694p. 1973. 95.00 (0-306-67182-4); Vol. 3. 1972 to 1974. 890p. 1976. 95.00 (0-306-67183-2); write for info. (0-318-53513-0, IFI-Plenum) Plenum.

Office Staff of International Affairs, National Research Council, ed. Microlivestock: Little-Known Small Animals with a Promising Economic Future. 472p. 1991. pap. 29.95 (0-309-04295-X) Natl Acad Pr.

Officer, Charles & Page, Jake. Tales of the Earth. LC 92-28320. 1993. 26.00 (0-19-507785-7) OUP.

— Tales of the Earth. (Illus.). 246p. 1994. reprint ed. pap. 10.95 (0-19-509048-9) OUP.

An Asterisk (*) at the beginning of an entry indicates that the title is appearing in BIP for the first time.

Officer, Charles B. Introduction to the Theory of Sound Transmission, with the Application to the Ocean. LC 58-6693. (McGraw-Hill Series in the Geological Sciences). 292p. reprint ed. pap. 83.30 (*0-317-08768-1*, 2051899) Bks Demand.

Officer, James E. Hispanic Arizona, 1536-1856. LC 87-18783. 462p. 1990. pap. 19.95 (*0-8165-1152-7*) U of Ariz Pr.

Officer, Lawrence A., ed. International Economics. (C). 1987. lib. bdg. 67.00 (*0-89838-196-7*) Kluwer Ac.

Officer, Lawrence H. Econometric Model of Canada under the Fluctuating Exchange Rate. LC 68-14270. (Economic Studies: No. 130). (Illus.). 331p. 1968. 22.50 (*0-674-22500-7*) HUP.

— Purchasing Power Parity & Exchange Rates: Theory, Evidence, & Relevance. LC 81-81650. (Contemporary Studies in Economic & Financial Analysis: Vol. 35). 361p. 1982. 73.25 (*0-89232-229-2*) Jai Pr.

Officer, Lawrence H., et al. So You Have to Write an Economics Term Paper. LC 80-80313. x, 149p. (Orig.). 1985. reprint ed. pap. 5.95 (*0-87013-229-6*) Mich St U Pr.

Officer, Robyn, illus. Mother Goose's Nursery Rhymes. (Children's Classics Ser.). 32p. (J). (ps-3). 1992. 6.95 (*0-8362-4907-0*) Andrews & McMeel.

***Officer X.** Ten-Eight: A Cop's Honest Look at Life on the Street. LC 94-68989. 240p. (Orig.). 1994. pap. 14.95 (*0-935878-13-0*) Calibre Pr.

Officers of the U.S. Army Ordnance Dept. Staff. Small Arms Eighteen Fifty-Six: Reports of Experiments with Small Arms for the Military Service. (Illus.). 168p. (C). 1984. reprint ed. 14.95 (*0-939631-01-6*) Thomas Publications.

Official Board of Ballroom Dancing Staff. Modern & Latin Sequence Dances. (Ballroom Dance Ser.). 1986. lib. bdg. 79.00 (*0-8490-3252-0*) Gordon Pr.

— Modern & Latin Sequence Dances. (Ballroom Dance Ser.). 1985. lib. bdg. 79.00 (*0-87700-691-1*) Revisionist Pr.

Officials of the National Oceanic & Atmospheric Administration Staff. Climates of the States, 2 vols., Set. LC 73-93482. (Illus.). 1004p. 1974. 75.00 (*0-912394-09-9*) Water Info.

Offinoski, Steve. Jesse Jackson: A Voice for Change. ("Great Lives" Biography Ser.). (Illus.). 128p. 1989. mass mkt. 4.99 (*0-449-90402-4*, Columbine) Fawcett.

Offiong, Daniel O. Imperialism & Dependency: Obstacles to African Development. LC 82-15833. 304p. 1982. pap. 9.95 (*0-88258-127-9*) Howard U Pr.

Offit, Avodah. Virtual Love. LC 93-36227. 1994. 22.00 (*0-671-87436-5*) S&S Trade.

***Offit, Avodah K.** Night Thoughts: Reflections of a Sex Therapist. rev. ed. LC 94-45758. 256p. 1995. pap. 17.50 (*1-56821-458-8*) Aronson.

— The Sexual Self. 320p. 9.95 (*0-86553-079-3*) Congdon & Weed.

— The Sexual Self. 320p. 1992. pap. 47.88 (*0-312-92766-5*) Congdon & Weed.

— The Sexual Self: How Character Shapes Sexual Experience. 1995. pap. write for info. (*1-56821-548-7*) Aronson.

***Offit, Sidney.** Memoir of the Bookie's Son. 176p. 1995. 18.95 (*0-312-13140-2*, Pub. by Thomas Dunne Bks) St Martin.

Offitzer, Karen, comp. The Learning Annex Guide to Starting Your Own Import-Export Business. 108p. 1992. pap. 8.95 (*0-8065-1321-7*, Citadel Pr) Carol Pub Group.

Offler, H. S., ed. see Ockham, William.

Offner, Arnold A. The Origins of the Second World War: American Foreign Policy & World Politics, 1917-1941. LC 85-23928. 288p. (C). 1986. reprint ed. text ed. 23.50 (*0-89874-924-7*); reprint ed. pap. 19.50 (*0-89464-320-7*) Krieger.

Offner, Hazel. The Fruit of the Spirit. (LifeGuide Bible Studies). 64p. 1987. pap. 4.99 (*0-8308-1058-7*, 1058) InterVarsity.

Offner, Herman L. Administrative Procedures for Changing Curriculum Patterns for Selected State Teachers Colleges. LC 76-177131. (Columbia University. Teachers College. Contributions to Education Ser.: No. 898). reprint ed. 37.50 (*0-404-55898-4*) AMS Pr.

Offner, Jerome A. Law & Politics in Aztec Texcoco. LC 82-4368. (Cambridge Latin American Studies: No. 44). (Illus.). 334p. 1984. 69.95 (*0-521-23475-1*) Cambridge U Pr.

Offner, John L. An Unwanted War: The Diplomacy of the United States & Spain over Cuba, 1895-1898. LC 91-48198. (Illus.). xiv, 306p. (C). 1992. 39.95 (*0-8078-2038-5*); pap. 14.95 (*0-8078-4380-6*) U of NC Pr.

Offner, Richard. Italian Primitives at Yale University. (Illus.). 1927. 100.00 (*0-685-89760-5*) Elliots Bks.

Offner, Richardson R. A Critical & Historical Corpus of Florentine Painting Section IV. Final Vol. 70.00 (*0-685-71750-X*) J J Augustin.

— A Critical & Historical Corpus of Florentine Painting Section IV, IV. write for info. (*0-685-71749-6*) J J Augustin.

Offor, George, ed. see Bunyan, John.

Offord, Carl R. The White Face. LC 73-18596. reprint ed. 32.50 (*0-404-11407-5*) AMS Pr.

Offord, D. C., jt. ed. see Leatherbarrow, William J.

Offord, Derek. Portraits of Early Russian Liberals: A Study of the Thought of T. N. Granovsky, V. P. Botkin, P. V. Annenkov, A. V. Druzhinin, & K. D. Kavelin. (Cambridge Studies in Russian Literature). 306p. 1985. 69.95 (*0-521-30550-0*) Cambridge U Pr.

— The Russian Revolutionary Movement in the 1880s. (Illus.). 230p. 1986. 59.95 (*0-521-32723-7*) Cambridge U Pr.

Offord, Derek, ed. The Golden Age of Russian Literature & Thought. LC 92-4307. (Selected Papers from the Fourth World Congress for Soviet & East European Studies, Harrogate, 1990). 192p. 1992. text ed. 45.00 (*0-312-08043-3*) St Martin.

Offord, Kenneth, jt. auth. see Colligan, Robert C.

Offord, Malcolm H., jt. auth. see Batchelor, R. E.

Offord, R. M., ed. Jerry McAuley, an Apostle to the Lost. LC 75-124248. (Select Bibliographies Reprint Ser.). (Illus.). 1977. reprint ed. 21.95 (*0-8369-5436-X*) Ayer.

Offord, Robin, jt. auth. see Yudkin, Michael.

Offord, Robin E. Semisynthetic Proteins. LC 79-40521. (Illus.). 247p. reprint ed. pap. 70.40 (*0-685-20601-7*, 2030535) Bks Demand.

Offredi, Mariola, ed. Literature, Language & the Media in India. (C). 1992. text ed. 30.00 (*81-85425-75-2*, Pub. by Manohar II) S Asia.

Offsey, Sol. Edifice & Other Stories. 56p. 1985. pap. 5.00 (*0-940584-08-5*) Gull Bks.

Offshore Mechanics, Arctic Engineering, Deepsea Systems Symposium Staff. Proceedings of the First Offshore Mechanics, Arctic Engineering, Deepsea Systems Symposium: Presented at Energy-Sources Technology Conference & Exhibition, New Orleans, Louisiana, March 7-10, 1982, 2 vols., Vol. 1. Chung, Jin S. et al, eds. LC 82-70515. (Illus.). 254p. reprint ed. pap. 72.40 (*0-8357-2838-2*, 2039074) Bks Demand.

— Proceedings of the First Offshore Mechanics, Arctic Engineering, Deepsea Systems Symposium: Presented at Energy-Sources Technology Conference & Exhibition, New Orleans, Louisiana, March 7-10, 1982, 2 vols., Vol. 2. Chung, Jin S. et al, eds. LC 82-70515. (Illus.). 300p. reprint ed. pap. 85.50 (*0-8357-2839-0*, 2039074) Bks Demand.

Offut, Andrew. The Shadow of Sorcery. 240p. (Orig.). 1993. mass mkt. 4.99 (*0-441-76026-0*) Ace Bks.

Offutt, A. J. Swords Against Darkness, No. 1. 1990. pap. 3.95 (*0-8217-2972-1*) Zebra.

Offutt, Andrew J., ed. Swords Against Darkness, No. 4. 1981. pap. 2.50 (*0-89083-784-8*) Zebra.

— Swords Against Darkness, No. 5. 1981. pap. 2.50 (*0-89083-839-9*) Zebra.

Offutt, Chris. Kentucky Straight. LC 91-5806. 1992. pap. 10.00 (*0-679-73886-X*, Vin) Random.

— The Same River Twice: A Memoir. 192p. 1993. 18.00 (*0-671-78734-9*) S&S Trade.

— The Same River Twice: A Memoir. 192p. 1994. pap. 9.95 (*0-14-023253-2*, Penguin Bks) Viking Penguin.

— The Same River Twice: A Memoir. braille ed. 332p. 1994. text ed. 26.56 (*1-56956-476-0*, BR9329) W A T Braille.

Offutt, George. The Electromodel of the Auditory System. 196p. (Orig.). 1984. pap. 15.00 (*0-9614983-0-7*) GoLo Press.

Offutt, Jane S. Bluegrass Secrets: A Resource Guide for the Home & Garden. (Illus.). 192p. (Orig.). Date not set. pap. text ed. 12.95 (*1-883554-01-2*) City Secrets.

Offutt, Jane S., jt. auth. see Hodges, Renee.

Offutt, Nelson T. More Than a Cookbook. LC 79-93281. 192p. spiral bd., pap. 6.95 (*0-89709-019-5*) Liberty Pub.

***Offutt, William M.** Bethesda, a Social History. (Illus.). 784p. (Orig.). 1995. pap. 25.00 (*0-9643819-0-7*) Innovat Game.

***Offutt, William M., Jr.** Of "Good Laws" & "Good Men" A Law & Society in the Delaware Valley, 1680-1710. 1995. write for info. (*0-252-02152-5*) U of Ill Pr.

Offutt, William M., ed. see Cartwright, William H. & Goeden, Louise E.

O'Fiannachta, Padraig, ed. Saltair: Prayers from the Irish Tradition. Forristal, Desmond, tr. 96p. (Orig.). 1988. pap. 7.95 (*0-948183-65-9*, Pub. by Columba Pr IE) Twenty-Third.

O'Flaherty, Brendan. Rational Commitment: A Foundation for Macroeconomics. LC 85-13161. (Duke Press Policy Studies). (Illus.). x, 230p. 1985. 41.95 (*0-8223-0454-6*) Duke.

O'Flaherty, C. A. Highways: Highway Engineering, Vol. 2. 3rd ed. 704p. (C). 1988. pap. text ed. 75.00 (*0-7131-3596-4*, Pub. by E Arnold UK) Routledge Chapman & Hall.

O'Flaherty, C. A., jt. auth. see Tough, J. M.

O'Flaherty, Eamon, tr. see Vovelle, Michel.

O'Flaherty, James C. Hamann's Socratic Memorabilia: A Translation & Commentary. LC 67-12424. 240p. 1967. 35.00 (*0-8018-0493-0*) Johns Hopkins.

— The Quarrel of Reason with Itself: Essays on Hamann, Michaelis, Lessing & Nietzsche. LC 87-70862. (Studies in German Literature, Linguistics & Culture: Vol. 35). (Illus.). 230p. 1988. 35.00 (*0-938100-56-4*) Camden Hse.

— Unity & Language: A Study in the Philosophy of Johann Georg Hamann. LC 52-4007. (North Carolina. University. Studies in the Germanic Languages & Literatures: No. 6). reprint ed. 27.00 (*0-404-50906-1*) AMS Pr.

O'Flaherty, James C., et al, eds. Studies in Nietzsche & the Judaeo-Christian Tradition. LC 84-11963. (Germanic Languages & Literatures Ser.: No. 103). 424p. (C). 1985. 40.00 (*0-8078-8104-X*) U of NC Pr.

O'Flaherty, Joseph S. An End & a Beginning: The South Coast & Los Angeles 1850-1887. 2nd ed. LC 92-81269. (Illus.). 323p. 1992. 24.95 (*0-914421-05-0*) Hist Soc So CA.

— Those Powerful Years: The South Coast & Los Angeles 1887-1917. 2nd ed. LC 92-81270. (Illus.). 357p. 1992. 29.95 (*0-914421-06-9*) Hist Soc So CA.

O'Flaherty, Joseph T. & Ramwell, Peter W., eds. Platelet-Activating Factor Antagonists: New Developments for Clinical Application. (Advances in Applied Biotechnology Ser.: Vol. 9). (Illus.). 256p. (C). 1990. 55.00 (*0-943255-13-9*) Portfolio Pub.

O'Flaherty, Liam. All Things Come of Age & the Test of Courage. (Illus.). 39p. 1984. pap. 5.95 (*0-86327-044-1*, Pub. by Wolfhound Pr IE) Dufour.

— Assassin. 286p. 1988. reprint ed. pap. 8.95 (*0-86327-006-9*, Pub. by Wolfhound Pr IE) Dufour.

— Famine. 1989. pap. 12.95 (*0-86327-043-3*, Pub. by Wolfhound Pr IE) Dufour.

— Famine. LC 81-7161. (Non Pareil Ser.). 458p. 1995. reprint ed. pap. 13.95 (*0-87923-434-2*) Godine.

— The Informer. LC 79-26156. 188p. 1980. reprint ed. pap. 7.95 (*0-15-644356-2*, Harvest Bks) HarBrace.

— Insurrection. 254p. 1988. pap. 7.95 (*0-86327-135-9*, Pub. by Wolfhound Pr IE) Dufour.

— Joseph Conrad: An Appreciation. LC 72-6945. (Studies in Conrad: No. 8). 1972. reprint ed. lib. bdg. 75.00 (*0-8383-1642-5*) M S G Haskell Hse.

— Mountain Tavern, & Other Stories. LC 73-178453. (Short Story Index Reprint Ser.). 1980. reprint ed. 18.95 (*0-8369-4054-7*) Ayer.

— Mr. Gilhooley. 288p. (Orig.). 1991. pap. 10.95 (*0-86327-289-4*, Pub. by Wolfhound Pr IE) Dufour.

— Short Stories: The Pedlar's Revenge. 224p. 1989. pap. 7.95 (*0-905473-51-5*, Pub. by Wolfhound Pr IE) Dufour.

— Short Stories: The Pedlar's Revenge. 1991. pap. 9.95 (*0-86327-225-8*) Dufour.

— Skerrett. 287p. 1988. reprint ed. pap. 8.95 (*0-905473-11-6*, Pub. by Wolfhound Pr IE) Dufour.

— Spring Sowing. LC 72-10748. (Short Story Index Reprint Ser.). 1977. reprint ed. 21.95 (*0-8369-4221-3*) Ayer.

— Thy Neighbour's Wife. 1992. pap. 12.95 (*0-86327-328-9*, Pub. by Wolfhound Pr IE) Dufour.

***O'Flaherty, Patrick.** Benny's Island: A Novel. 64p. 1995. pap. 9.95 (*1-55081-102-9*) Paul & Co Pubs.

— The Rock Observed: Studies in the Literature of Newfoundland. rev. ed. (Illus.). 304p. 1992. 40.00 (*0-8020-2807-1*); pap. 18.95 (*0-8020-7683-1*) U of Toronto Pr.

— The Rock Observed: Studies in the Literature of Newfoundland. LC 80-475278. 254p. reprint ed. pap. 72.40 (*0-685-15820-9*, 2026370) Bks Demand.

O'Flaherty, Patrick, jt. ed. see Neary, Peter.

***O'Flaherty, Terrence.** Masterpiece Theatre: Silver Anniversary Album. Sharpe, Karen, ed. (Illus.). 224p. (Orig.). 1995. pap. 24.95 (*0-912333-74-X*) KQED.

O'Flaherty, Thomas J., ed. Software Engineering Strategies. 132.00 (*0-685-69692-8*, SONE) Warren Gorham & Lamont.

O'Flaherty, Tom. Aranmen All. 192p. 1991. reprint ed. pap. 9.95 (*0-86322-123-8*, Pub. by Brandon Bk Pubs IE) Irish Bks Media.

O'Flaherty, W. D. Dreams, Illusions & Other Realities. 382p. 1987. 39.95 (*0-318-37018-2*) Asia Bk Corp.

O'Flaherty, Wendy D. Dreams, Illusion & Other Realities. LC 83-17944. (Illus.). xvi, 384p. 1984. 25.00 (*0-226-61854-4*) U Ch Pr.

— Dreams, Illusion & Other Realities. LC 83-17944. (Illus.). xvi, 384p. 1986. pap. text ed. 17.95 (*0-226-61855-2*) U Ch Pr.

— The Origins of Evil in Hindu Mythology. (Hermeneutics: Studies in the History of Religions: No. 6). 1977. pap. 16.00 (*0-520-04098-8*) U CA Pr.

Oflaherty, Wendy D. Other People's Myths. 1990. pap. 14.95 (*0-02-897295-3*) Macmillan.

O'Flaherty, Wendy D. Other People's Myths: The Cave of Echoes. 192p. 1988. 19.95 (*0-02-896041-6*) Macmillan.

— Other People's Myths: The Cave of Echoes. xiv, 226p. 1995. pap. 13.95x (*0-226-61857-9*) U Ch Pr.

— Rig Veda. (Classics Ser.). 1982. pap. 9.95 (*0-14-044402-5*, Penguin Classics) Viking Penguin.

— Siva: The Erotic Ascetic. (Illus.). 1981. reprint ed. pap. 14.95 (*0-19-520250-3*) OUP.

— Tales of Sex & Violence: Folklore, Sacrifice & Danger in the Jaiminya Brahmana. LC 84-16393. (Illus.). 128p. 1985. 16.95 (*0-226-61852-8*) U Ch Pr.

— Women, Androgynes, & Other Mythical Beasts. LC 79-16128. 1980. lib. bdg. 27.50 (*0-226-61849-8*) U Ch Pr.

— Women, Androgynes, & Other Mythical Beasts. LC 79-16128. 1982. pap. text ed. 17.95 (*0-226-61850-1*) U Ch Pr.

O'Flaherty, Wendy D., ed. Karma & Rebirth in Classical Indian Traditions. LC 79-64475. 400p. 1980. 48.00 (*0-520-03923-8*) U CA Pr.

O'Flaherty, Wendy D., ed. & tr. Textual Sources for the Study of Hinduism. Gold, Daniel H. et al, trs. (Sources for the Textual Study of Religion Ser.). xii, 212p. 1990. pap. text ed. 14.95 (*0-226-61847-1*) U Ch Pr.

O'Flaherty, Wendy D., tr. Hindu Myths. (Classics Ser.). 360p. 1975. pap. 9.95 (*0-14-044306-1*, Penguin Classics) Viking Penguin.

O'Flaherty, Wendy D., tr. see Aeschylus.

O'Flanagan, J. Roderick. Lives of the Lord Chancellors & Keepers of the Great Seal of Ireland, 2 Vols. 1971. reprint ed. 50.00 (*0-8377-2500-3*) Rothman.

— Lives of the Lord Chancellors & Keepers of the Great Seal of Ireland, 2 vols., Set. LC 71-112406. 1971. reprint ed. 95.00 (*0-678-04540-2*) Kelley.

***O'Flanagan, Rory.** Dictionary of Personnal & Educational Terms: English-German, German-English. 263p. (ENG & GER.). 1991. 95.00 (*0-7859-7111-4*) Fr & Eur.

O'Flannery, Patsy. Hash & Rehash. 32p. 1994. pap. 4.95 (*1-883849-05-5*) Nine Hund Forty Six Pr.

O'Flynn, Grainne. World Survival. 128p. 1984. pap. 11.95 (*0-86278-041-1*, Pub. by OBrien Pr IE) Dufour.

O'Flynn, Joseph P. Nautical Dictionary: Over Three Thousand Eight Hundred Maritime Terms Defined. (Illus.). 112p. (Orig.). 1992. pap. 9.95 (*0-937360-16-3*) Harbor Hse MI.

O'Flynn, Kathryn K., jt. auth. see Joseph, Mark L.

O'Flynn, Mark. Captain Cook. 143p. (C). 1990. 30.00 (*0-947087-05-2*, Pub. by Pascoe Pub AT) St Mut.

O'Flynn, Michael F. & Moriarity, Gene M. Linear Systems: Time Domain & Transform Analysis. 448p. 1986. Net. text ed. write for info. (*0-471-60373-2*) Wiley.

O'Flynn, Silvester. Gather in My Name. 118p. (Orig.). 1993. pap. 7.95 (*1-85607-070-0*) Twenty-Third.

— Good News of Luke's Year: Reflections for Year C. 270p. (Orig.). 1991. pap. 10.95 (*1-85607-038-7*, Pub. by Columba Pr IE) Twenty-Third.

— The Good News of Mark's Year. 288p. (Orig.). 1990. pap. 10.95 (*1-85607-001-8*, Pub. by Columba Pr IE) Twenty-Third.

— Good News of Matthew's Year. 272p. (Orig.). 1989. pap. 10.95 (*0-948183-89-6*, Pub. by Columba Pr IE) Twenty-Third.

Ofoegbu, Charles O., ed. Groundwater & Mineral Resources of Nigeria. vi, 159p. 1988. 60.00 (*3-528-06324-6*, Pub. by Vieweg & Sohn GW) Ballen Bkslr.

Ofonagoro, W. I. Trade & Imperialism in Southern Nigeria, 1881-1929. LC 78-64521. 263p. 1979. text ed. 23.95 (*0-88357-049-1*) NOK Pubs.

Ofosu-Appiah, L. H. People in Bondage. (YA). (gr. 5 up). 1992. 17.50 (*0-8225-3150-X*, Lerner Publctns) Lerner Group.

— People in Bondage: African Slavery in the Modern Era. (History Ser.). (Illus.). 132p. (J). (gr. 5-12). 1993. lib. bdg. 19.95 (*0-8225-1437-0*, Lerner Publctns) Lerner Group.

Ofosu-Appiah, L. H., ed. see Abraham, Arthur, et al.

Ofosu-Appiah, L. H., et al. The Encyclopaedia Africana Dictionary of African Biography: Ethiopia-Ghana, Vol. 1. Irvine, Keith, ed. LC 76-17954. (Illus.). 1977. 75.00 (*0-917256-01-8*) Ref Pubns.

O'Frank, Milo. How to Get Your Point Across in 30 Seconds or Less. 1990. pap. 8.00 (*0-671-72752-4*) PB.

— How to Have a Successful Meeting in Half the Time. Rubenstein, Julie, ed. 160p. 1990. reprint ed. pap. 9.00 (*0-671-72601-3*) PB.

Ofsanko, Frank J. & Napier, Nancy K., eds. Effective Human Resource Measurement Techniques - A Handbook for Practitioners. 109p. 1990. pap. 15.00 (*0-685-54590-3*, PB18) Soc Human Resc Mgmt.

Ofshe, Lynne & Ofshe, Richard. Utility & Choice in Social Interaction. LC 70-101539. (Illus.). 1970. 39.50 (*0-13-939645-4*) Irvington.

Ofshe, Richard & Watters, Ethan. Making Monsters: False Memories, Psychotherapy, & Sexual Hysteria. 1994. 23.00 (*0-684-19698-0*) S&S Trade.

Ofshe, Richard, jt. auth. see Ofshe, Lynne.

Ofstedal, Paul. Daily Readings from Spiritual Classics. LC 89-30976. 408p. 1990. pap. 21.99 (*0-8066-2424-8*, 9-2424) Augsburg Fortress.

Ofsthun, N. J., et al, eds. Lymphatic & Non-Lymphatic Fluid Loss from the Peritoneal Cavity. (Journal: Blood Purification: Vol. 10, Nos. 3-4, 1992). (Illus.). 132p. 1993. pap. 81.75 (*3-8055-5769-8*) S Karger.

Ofuatey-Kodjoe, W. The Principle of Self-Determination in International Law. 250p. 1977. text ed. 26.50 (*0-8290-1569-8*) Irvington.

O'Gaea, Ashleen. The Family Wicca Book: The Craft for Parents & Children. LC 92-12569. (Modern Witchcraft Ser.). (Illus.). 240p. 1993. pap. 9.95 (*0-87542-591-7*) Llewellyn Pubns.

Ogai, Mori. The Historical Fiction of Mori Ogai. Dilworth, David & Rimer, J. Thomas, eds. LC 91-2350. 448p. 1991. reprint ed. pap. text ed. 16.95 (*0-8248-1366-9*) UH Pr.

— Saiki Koi & Other Stories. Dilworth, David & Rimer, J. Thomas, eds. Rimer, J. Thomas, tr. LC 77-4455. 1977. text ed. 14.95 (*0-8248-0454-6*) UH Pr.

— The Wild Goose (Gan) Watson, Burton, tr. (Michigan Monograph Series in Japanese Studies: No. 14). 1995. write for info. (*0-939512-70-X*); pap. write for info. (*0-939512-71-8*) U MI Japan.

— Youth & Other Stories. Rimer, J. Thomas, ed. LC 93-38737. (SHAPS Library of Translations). 576p. 1994. text ed. 38.00 (*0-8248-1600-5*) UH Pr.

Ogaki, Tetsuya. Top Shopping in Japan. Iwakiri, Yutaka et al, eds. Maene, Ayako & Motoyoshi, Hiroko, trs. (Illus.). 304p. (Orig.). 1984. pap. 19.95 (*0-8048-1477-5*) C E Tuttle.

Ogali, Ogali. Veronica My Daughter & Other Onitsha Plays & Stories. Sander, Reinhard W. & Ayers, Peter K., eds. LC 80-80886. 376p. (Orig.). 1980. 18.00 (*0-914478-61-3*); pap. 10.00 (*0-914478-62-1*) Three Continents.

O'Gallagher, Liam. Planet Noise. (Nova Broadcast Ser.: No. 4). (Illus.). 43p. (Orig.). 1969. pap. 3.50 (*0-89366-022-1*) Ultramarine Pub.

Ogan, Beverly J., jt. auth. see Rottier, Jerry.

Ogan, Guy D. Can Anyone Help my Child? Therapies & Treatment for Attention Deficit & Other Learning & Behavioral Disorders in Children, Adolescents, & Adults. rev. ed. 186p. (Orig.). 1991. pap. 9.95 (*0-9631880-1-1*) Faith Pub & Media.

Ogan, Lew. History of Vinton County, Ohio. 314p. 1994. reprint ed. lib. bdg. 37.50 (*0-8328-3627-3*) Higginson Bk Co.

***Oganessian, Yu T., et al, eds.** Heavy Ion Physics: Proceedings of International School Held at Jinr (Dubna, Russia) 10-15 May 1993, 2 vols., Set, Vols. I & II. (Illus.). 1085p. (C). 1995. text ed. 110.00 (*0-614-05122-3*) Hadronic Pr Inc.

Oganesyan, O. V., jt. auth. see Volkov, M. V.

Oganov, Raphael G., jt. ed. see Chazov, Eugeni.

O'Gara, Geoffrey. The Western Alphabet. LC 83-51556. (Illus.). 64p. (Orig.). 1983. pap. 3.95 (*0-915333-00-7*) Trotevale.

O'Gara, Gordon C. Theodore Roosevelt & the Rise of the Modern Navy. LC 69-14016. 138p. 1970. reprint ed. text ed. 38.50 (*0-8371-1480-2*, OGTR, Greenwood Pr) Greenwood.

— Theodore Roosevelt & the Rise of the Modern Navy. (History - United States Ser.). 138p. 1993. reprint ed. lib. bdg. 69.00 (*0-7812-4858-2*) Rprt Serv.

O'Gara, Margaret. Triumph in Defeat: Infallibility, Vatican I, & the French Minority Bishops. LC 87-17889. 296p. 1988. 48.95 (*0-8132-0641-3*) Cath U Pr.

O'Gara, W. H. A Black Hills Lady. Meyers, Jean O., ed. (Illus.). (Orig.). 1990. pap. 8.95 (*0-934904-12-X*) J & L Lee.

— In All Its Fury: A History of the Blizzard of January 12, 1888. 3rd ed. Clement, Ora A., ed. (Illus.). 344p. 1988. reprint ed. pap. 9.95 (*0-934904-04-9*) J & L Lee.

O'Gara, William W. Foster's & Nobody Else's: The N. C. Foster Enterprises. (Illus.). 72p. (Orig.). 1988. pap. 8.95 (*0-9622213-0-9*) MCRHSI.

O'Garden, Irene. Fat Girl: One Woman's Way Out. LC 92-54663. 96p. 1993. 12.00 (*0-06-250727-3*) Harper SF.

— The Fat Girl Companion. (Illus.). 1994. pap. 12.00 (*0-685-68145-9*) Harper SF.

— The Fat Girl Companion. LC 93-20952. 1994. pap. 10.00 (*0-06-250854-7*, PL) HarpC.

Ogarkov, N. Military Encylopaedic Dictionary. 865p. (RUS.). (C). 1984. 150.00 (*0-685-56242-5*, Pub. by Collets) St Mut.

Ogasapian, John. Church Organs: A Guide to Selection & Purchase. (Illus.). 144p. (Orig.). 1991. reprint ed. pap. 6.95 (*0-913499-06-4*) Organ Hist Soc.

— English Cathedral Music in New York: Edward Hodges of Trinity Church. (Illus.). x, 244p. 1994. 29.95 (*0-913499-12-9*) Organ Hist Soc.

— Henry Erben: Portrait of a Nineteenth Century Organ Builder. (Illus.). 72p. 1980. pap. 15.00 (*0-913746-13-4*) Organ Lit.

— Organ Building in New York City, 1700 to 1900. LC 78-300889. (Illus.). 1977. pap. text ed. 30.00 (*0-913746-10-X*) Organ Lit.

***Ogasawara, Frances.** History of the American Lung Association. 172p. Date not set. 12.50 (*0-915116-19-7*) Am Lung Assn.

Ogata, Katsuhiko. Designing Linear Control Systems with MATLAB. LC 93-34429. 1993. pap. text ed. 33.40 (*0-13-293226-1*) P-H.

— Discrete-Time Control Systems. (Illus.). 928p. 1986. text ed. 76.00 (*0-13-216102-8*) P-H.

— Discrete Time-Control Systems. 2nd ed. LC 94-19896. 1994. text ed. 74.00 (*0-13-034281-5*) P-H.

— Modern Control Engineering. 2nd ed. (Electrical Engineering Ser.). 960p. 1990. text ed. 74.00 (*0-13-589128-0*) P-H.

— System Dynamics. 2nd ed. 656p. 1992. text ed. 78.00 (*0-13-855941-4*) P-H.

Ogata, Masana, jt. ed. see Fiserova-Bergerova, Vera.

Ogata, S., jt. auth. see Ichimaru, S.

Ogata, Sadako. Normalization with China: A Comparative Study of U. S. & Japanese Processes. (Research Papers & Policy Studies: No. 30). xii, 109p. (Orig.). (C). 1989. pap. text ed. 15.00 (*1-55729-013-X*) IEAS.

Ogata, Sadako N. Defiance in Manchuria: The Making of Japanese Foreign Policy, 1931-1932. LC 84-543. xvi, 259p. (C). 1984. reprint ed. text ed. 41.50 (*0-313-24428-6*, OGDM, Greenwood Pr) Greenwood.

Ogata, Shijuro, et al. International Financial Integration: The Policy Challenges. (Triangle Papers: No. 37). 36p. (Orig.). 1989. pap. 6.00 (*0-930503-07-4*) Trilateral Comm.

Ogata, Sohaku, tr. The Transmission of the Lamp: Early Masters. rev. ed. LC 89-8125. 475p. 1990. pap. 19.95 (*0-89341-565-0*, Longwood Academic) Hollowbrook.

Ogawa. Electron Microscopic Cytochemistry in Biomedicine. 1992. 282.00 (*0-8493-6012-9*, RB46) CRC Pr.

— Vortex Flow. 1992. 219.00 (*0-8493-5782-9*, QA925) CRC Pr.

Ogawa, ed. Bonsai. (Postcard Book Ser.). (Illus.). 56p. 1994. pap. 9.00 (*4-7700-1805-3*) Kodansha.

Ogawa & Katayama, eds. Animal Fables. (Nihongo Folktales Ser.). (Illus.). 32p. (J). 1994. pap. 7.00 (*4-7700-1794-4*) Kodansha.

— Beautiful Kyoto. (Postcard Book Ser.). (Illus.). 56p. 1994. 8.00 (*4-7700-1674-3*) Kodansha.

— Cinderella. (Nihongo Folktales Ser.). (Illus.). 32p. (J). 1994. pap. 7.00 (*4-7700-1796-0*) Kodansha.

— Hokusai. (Postcard Book Ser.). (Illus.). 56p. 1994. 8.00 (*4-7700-1803-7*) Kodansha.

— The Story of Snow White. (Nihongo Folktales Ser.). (Illus.). 32p. (J). 1994. pap. 7.00 (*4-7700-1795-2*) Kodansha.

Ogawa & Pockell, eds. Grandfather Cherry Blossom. LC 93-18301. (Children's Classics Ser.: Vol. 5). (Illus.). 48p. (J). 1993. 13.00 (*4-7700-1759-6*) Kodansha.

— The Inch-High Samurai. LC 93-16310. (Children's Classics Ser.: No. 4). (Illus.). 48p. (J). 1993. 14.95 (*4-7700-1758-8*) Kodansha.

— The Moon Princess. LC 93-18300. (Children's Classics Ser.: Vol. 2). (Illus.). 48p. (J). 1993. 13.00 (*4-7700-1756-1*) Kodansha.

Ogawa, ed. see Kodansha International Staff.

Ogawa, ed. see McCarthy, Ralph F.

Ogawa, ed. see Oka, Isaburo.

Ogawa, ed. see Quackenbuch, Hiroko C.

Ogawa, ed. see Sumida, Atsuki.

Ogawa, Akira. Separation of Particles from Air & Gases, Vol. I. 168p. 1984. 97.00 (*0-8493-5787-X*, TH7692, CRC Reprint) Franklin.

— Separation of Particles from Air & Gases, Vol. II. 200p. 1984. 111.00 (*0-8493-5788-8*, CRC Reprint) Franklin.

Ogawa, Brian. Walking on Eggshells: Practical Counsel for Women in or Leaving a Violent Relationship. LC 89-51441. (Illus.). 68p. (Orig.). 1989. pap. 10.00 (*0-9621260-1-2*) VWAP.

Ogawa, Brian K., et al. To Tell the Truth. LC 88-51256. (Illus.). 40p. (J). (gr. 4-6). 1988. text ed. write for info. (*0-9621260-0-4*) VWAP.

Ogawa, Dennis M. Jan Ken Po: The World of Hawaii's Japanese Americans. LC 78-9513. (Illus.). 196p. 1978. pap. 6.95 (*0-8248-0398-1*) UH Pr.

— Kodomo No Tame Ni - For the Sake of the Children: The Japanese American Experience in Hawaii. LC 77-18368. 639p. 1980. reprint ed. pap. 16.95 (*0-8248-0730-8*) UH Pr.

Ogawa, Dennis M. & Grant, Glen. Kodomo No Tame Ni - For the Sake of the Children: The Japanese American Experience in Hawaii. LC 77-18368. 1978. text ed. 17.50 (*0-8248-0528-3*) UH Pr.

***Ogawa, Eiji.** Modern Production Management: A Japanese Experience. 132p. 1984. 21.70 (*92-833-1071-3*, Pub. by APO JA); pap. text ed. 17.95 (*92-833-1072-1*, Pub. by APO JA) Qual Resc.

— Small Business Management Today. (Productivity Ser.: No. 25). (Illus.). 119p. 1994. pap. text ed. 7.50 (*92-833-1715-7*, 317157, Pub. by Asian Productvty Org JA) Qual Resc.

Ogawa, H., jt. auth. see Nakajima, H.

Ogawa, Hirohide. Enlightenment Through the Art of Basketball. Taniguchi, H. et al, trs. (Illus.). 1979. 13.50 (*0-900891-36-X*); pap. 12.50 (*0-900891-35-1*) Oleander Pr.

Ogawa, Hiroshi. The Potter Wasp. Pohl, Kathy, ed. (Nature Close-Ups Ser.). (Illus.). 32p. (J). (gr. 3-7). 1986. lib. bdg. 10.95 (*0-8172-2541-2*) Raintree Steck-V.

***Ogawa, J. M., et al.** Compendium of Stone Fruit Diseases. (Disease Compendium Ser.). 128p. 1995. 30.00 (*0-89054-174-4*) Am Phytopathol Soc.

Ogawa, Joseph M. & English, Harley. Diseases of Temperate Zone Tree Fruit & Nut Crops. LC 91-65409. (Illus.). 464p. 1991. 55.00 (*0-931876-97-4*, 3345) ANR Pubns CA.

Ogawa, Joshua K. Unlimited Purpose. 1986. pap. 4.95 (*9971-972-46-8*) OMF Bks.

Ogawa, Junjiro. Statistical Theory of the Analysis of Experimental Designs. LC 73-90769. (Statistics, Textbooks & Monographs: Vol. 8). 475p. reprint ed. pap. 135.40 (*0-685-15685-0*, 2027339) Bks Demand.

Ogawa, M., et al. Chemotherapy of Hepatic Tumors. (International Congress Ser.: Vol. 659). 1984. 98.50 (*4-900392-27-8*) Elsevier.

Ogawa, M., et al, eds. Adriamycin. (International Congress Ser.: Vol. 629). 1985. 238.50 (*4-900392-22-7*, I-345-84) Elsevier.

Ogawa, Makoto, jt. ed. see Tsuruo, Takashi.

Ogawa, Naohiro, jt. auth. see Hodge, Robert W.

Ogawa, Naohiro, et al, eds. Human Resources in Development along the Asia-Pacific Rim. (South-East Asia Social Science Monographs). 350p. 1993. 55.00 (*0-19-588596-1*) OUP.

Ogawa, Tomoko & Davies, James. The Endgame. (Elementary Go Ser.: Vol. 6). 1990. reprint ed. pap. 14.95 (*4-87187-015-4*, G15) Ishi Pr Intl.

Ogawa, Yujiro, jt. ed. see Taira, Asahiko.

Ogbaa, Kalu. Gods, Oracles & Divination: Folkways in Chinua Achebe's Novels. LC 91-72278. 320p. 1992. 49.95 (*0-86543-256-2*); pap. 14.95 (*0-86543-257-0*) Africa World.

— Igbo. LC 94-36608. (Heritage Library of African Peoples). (J). 1994. 15.95 (*0-8239-1977-3*) Rosen Group.

Ogbaa, Kalu, ed. The Gong & the Flute: African Literary Development & Celebration. LC 94-16121. (Contributions in Afro-American & African Studies: No. 173). 224p. 1994. text ed. 49.95 (*0-313-29281-7*, Greenwood Pr) Greenwood.

***Ogbankwa, Michelle.** All the Right Men. 503p. 1995. pap. 22.95 (*0-9644230-5-7*) Diamond Pubng.

***Ogboajah, Frank O., ed.** Mass Communication, Culture & Society in West Africa. 335p. 1985. 50.00 (*0-905450-18-3*, Pub. by H Zell Pubs UK) Bowker-Saur.

Ogbondah, Chris W. Military Regimes & the Press in Nigeria, 1966-1993: Human Rights & National Development. 200p. (Orig.). (C). 1994. lib. bdg. 46.50 (*0-8191-8834-4*); pap. text ed. 28.50 (*0-8191-8835-2*) U Pr of Amer.

Ogbondah, Chris W., comp. The Press in Nigeria: An Annotated Bibliography. LC 90-3676. (African Special Bibliographic Ser.: No. 12). 144p. 1990. text ed. 42.95 (*0-313-26521-6*, OPN/, Greenwood Pr) Greenwood.

Ogbor, Wisdom O. King Zugo's Clan. (Wisdom's Writings Ser.). 175p. (Orig.). 1985. pap. 6.95 (*0-933889-00-3*) Ashiedu Pubns.

— This Young World. (Wisdom's Writings Ser.). 250p. (Orig.). 1985. write for info. (*0-933889-01-1*) Ashiedu Pubns.

Ogborn, Jane, ed. see Twain, Mark.

Ogborn, Jon, jt. ed. see Jennison, Brenda.

Ogborne, Chris. Stillwater Trout Fishing: Expert Advice for Beginners. (Illus.). 1992. pap. 13.95 (*1-85223-495-4*, Pub. by Crowood Pr UK) Trafalgar.

***Ogbru, Irene.** I'm Born a Woman, Not Daddy's Son. 1995. 11.95 (*0-8062-5159-X*) Carlton.

Ogbru, Irene O. The Power of Women. 104p. (Orig.). 1993. pap. 10.95 (*1-880365-49-9*) Prof Pr NC.

Ogbu, John U., jt. ed. see Gibson, Margaret A.

Ogburn, Charlton. The Marauders. LC 82-16149. 307p. 1982. reprint ed. pap. 6.25 (*0-688-01625-1*, Quill) Morrow.

— The Mysterious William Shakespeare: The Myth & the Reality. 2nd ed. LC 92-31513. (Illus.). 892p. 1992. 37.50 (*0-939009-67-6*) EPM Pubns.

Ogburn, Charlton, Jr. The Winter Beach. 336p. 1966. pap. 7.95 (*0-688-07785-4*) Parnassus Imprints.

Ogburn, Jacqueline K. Masked Maverick. LC 92-1669. (Illus.). (J). 1994. write for info. (*0-688-11049-5*); lib. bdg. write for info. (*0-688-11050-9*) Lothrop.

— Noise Lullaby. LC 93-37417. (J). (gr. 2 up). 1994. write for info. (*0-688-10452-5*); write for info. (*0-688-10453-3*) Lothrop.

— Scarlett Angelina Wolverton-Manning. LC 92-41930. (Illus.). (J). 1994. 14.99 (*0-8037-1376-2*); lib. bdg. 14.89 (*0-8037-1377-0*) Dial Bks Young.

Ogburn, Joyce L., jt. ed. see Rice, Patricia O.

Ogburn, William F. Social Characteristics of Cities: A Basis for New Interpretations of the Role of the City in American Life. LC 73-11940. (Metropolitan America Ser.). 80p. 1979. reprint ed. 18.95 (*0-405-05409-2*) Ayer.

Ogburn, William F., ed. American Society in Wartime. LC 72-2380. (FDR & the Era of the New Deal Ser.). 237p. 1972. reprint ed. lib. bdg. 29.50 (*0-306-70484-6*) Da Capo.

— Social Changes During Depression & Recovery. LC 72-2381. (FDR & the Era of the New Deal Ser.). 117p. 1974. reprint ed. lib. bdg. 22.50 (*0-306-70483-8*) Da Capo.

Ogburn, William F. & Bettelheim, Bruno. The Wolf Boy of Agra & Feral Children & Autistic Children. (Reprint Series in Social Sciences). (C). 1993. reprint ed. pap. text ed. 1.90x (*0-8290-2709-2*, S-608) Irvington.

Ogburn, William F. & Goldenweiser, Alexander. The Social Sciences & Their Interrelations. LC 73-14173. (Perspectives in Social Inquiry Ser.). 518p. 1974. reprint ed. 33.95 (*0-405-05516-1*) Ayer.

Ogburn, William F., jt. auth. see Groves, Ernest R.

Ogden. Skeletal Injury in the Child. 2nd ed. 960p. 1989. text ed. 205.00 (*0-7216-2955-5*) Saunders.

Ogden, August R. The Dies Committee: A Study of the Special House Committee for the Investigation of Un-American Activities, 1938-1944. LC 84-10736. vi, 318p. 1984. reprint ed. text ed. 59.75 (*0-313-24567-3*, OGDC, Greenwood Pr) Greenwood.

— Dies Committee, a Study of the Special House Committee for the Investigation of Un-American Activities, 1938-1944. (History - United States Ser.). 318p. 1993. reprint ed. lib. bdg. 89.00 (*0-7812-4816-7*) Rprt Serv.

Ogden, Betina, illus. Hello, Zoo Babies! (Pudgy Board Bks.). 18p. (J). (ps). 1994. bds. 2.95 (*0-448-40582-2*, G&D) Putnam Pub Group.

— The Ugly Duckling. (Pudgy Pals Ser.). 18p. (J). (ps). 1994. bds. 3.95 (*0-448-40184-3*, G&D) Putnam Pub Group.

Ogden, Bradley. Bradley Ogden's Breakfast, Lunch & Dinner. 1991. 27.50 (*0-394-55802-2*) Random.

Ogden, C. K., tr. see Wittgenstein, Ludwig.

Ogden, Charles K. & Richards, Ivor A. The Meaning of Meaning. 363p. 1989. pap. 8.95 (*0-15-658446-8*, Harvest Bks) HarBrace.

Ogden, Christopher. Life of the Party: The Biography of Pamela Digby Churchill Hayward Harriman. LC 93-44379. 1994. 24.95 (*0-316-63376-3*) Little.

— Life of the Party: The Biography of Pamela Digby Churchill Hayward Harriman. (Illus.). 592p. 1995. pap. 6.50 (*0-446-60264-7*, Warner Vision) Warner Bks.

Ogden, Clint. Heller from Green Valley. large type ed. 220p. 1992. pap. 16.95 (*1-85389-359-5*, Medcom-Trainex) Ulverscroft.

Ogden, D. J. Re-Manufacturing the American Dream. 1994. 18.95 (*0-533-10945-0*) Vantage.

Ogden, D. Kelly. Where Jesus Walked: The Land & Culture of New Testament Times. LC 91-11411. 171p. 1991. 16.95 (*0-87579-530-7*) Deseret Bk.

Ogden, Dale. Hoosier Sports Heroes. LC 90-84308. (Hoosier Heritage Ser.). (Illus.). 192p. (YA). 1990. 19.95 (*1-878208-01-2*) Guild Pr IN.

Ogden, Daniel M., Jr. & Bone, Hugh A. Washington Politics: Published under the Auspices of the Citizenship Clearing House. LC 80-25647. (Illus.). vi, 77p. 1981. reprint ed. text ed. 35.00 (*0-313-22803-5*, OGWP, Greenwood Pr) Greenwood.

Ogden, David, jt. auth. see Jamison, Lynette.

Ogden, David W., jt. auth. see Jacobs, Jerald A.

Ogden, Donald I. Natural Care of Pets. 65p. 1993. reprint ed. spiral bd. 6.60 (*0-7873-0640-1*) Mokelumne.

Ogden, Dunbar H., tr. The Italian Baroque Stage: Documents by Giulio Troili, Andrea Pozzo, Ferdinando Galli-Bibiena, & Baldassare Orsini. LC 75-7197. 1978. 55.00 (*0-520-03006-0*) U CA Pr.

Ogden, Eugene C. & Mitchell, Richard S. Identification of Plants with Fleshy Fruits. (Bulletin Ser.: No. 467). (Illus.). 97p. (Orig.). (C). 1990. pap. text ed. 12.95 (*0-685-48715-6*) NYS Museum.

Ogden, Evelyn H. Completing Your Doctoral Dissertation or Master's Thesis: In Two Semesters or Less. 2nd ed. LC 93-60088. 157p. 1993. pap. text ed. 22.00 (*1-56676-035-3*) Technomic.

Ogden, Evelyn H. & Germinario, Vito. The At-Risk Student: A Practical Guide for Educators. LC 87-51632. 192p. 1988. 28.00 (*0-87762-573-5*) Technomic.

— The Nation's Best Schools: Blueprints for Excellence Vol. 2: Middle & Secondary Schools. LC 94-60605. 445p. 1995. text ed. 39.00 (*1-56676-278-2*) Technomic.

— The Nation's Best Schools: Blueprints for Excellence, Vol. 1: Elementary & Middle Schools. LC 94-60605. 365p. 1994. 39.00 (*1-56676-148-4*) Technomic.

Ogden, Frederic D., ed. see Johnson, Keen.

Ogden, Gary. Biology 2A Syllabus. 72p. 1993. spiral bd. 10.95 (*0-8403-8385-1*) Kendall-Hunt.

Ogden, Gina. Everywoman's Guide to Understanding Sexual Style & Creating Intimacy. 176p. (Orig.). 1992. pap. 8.95 (*1-55874-220-4*) Health Commn.

— Women Who Love Sex. Silvestro, Denise, ed. 288p. 1994. 21.00 (*0-671-86550-1*) PB.

— Women Who Love Sex. Silvestro, Denise, ed. 320p. 1995. mass mkt. 5.99 (*0-671-86551-X*) PB.

Ogden, Graham, et al. A Promise of Hope-A Call to Obedience: Joel & Malachi. Holmgren, Fredrick C. & Knight, George, eds. (International Theological Commentary Ser.). 160p. (Orig.). 1987. pap. 10.99 (*0-8028-0093-9*) Eerdmans.

Ogden, Greg. The New Reformation: Returning the Ministry to the People of God. 224p. 1991. pap. 10.99 (*0-310-31021-0*) Zondervan.

Ogden, Hugh. Looking for History. (Red Hill Ser.). 64p. 1991. pap. 8.95 (*1-879969-00-9*) Catskill Reading.

— Two Roads & This Spring. (Red Hill Ser.). 88p. (Orig.). 1993. pap. 9.95 (*1-879969-03-3*) Catskill Reading.

Ogden, Jack, jt. auth. see Williams, Dyfri.

Ogden, James, ed. see Wycherley, William.

Ogden, James R. The Essentials of Advertising. rev. ed. 128p. 1994. pap. text ed. 5.95 (*0-87891-906-6*) Res & Educ.

Ogden, Jane. Fat Chance! The Myth of Dieting Explained. LC 91-44109. 176p. 1992. pap. 12.95 (*0-415-07371-5*, A7167) Routledge.

Ogden, Joan M. & Williams, Robert H. Solar Hydrogen: Moving Beyond Fossil Fuels. 100p. (Orig.). 1989. pap. 10.00 (*0-915825-38-4*) World Resources Inst.

Ogden, John, jt. ed. see Davis, Steve.

Ogden, John A. The Medibears Guide to the Doctor's Exam: For Children & Parents. (Illus.). (J). (gr. k-5). 1991. 11.95 (*0-8130-1082-9*) U Press Fla.

Ogden, Julie, ed. see Coupe, Stuart.

Ogden, K. W. Urban Goods Movement: A Guide to Policy & Planning. 256p. 1991. 74.95 (*1-85742-029-2*, Pub. by Avebury Pub UK) Ashgate Pub Co.

Ogden, Lawrence, jt. auth. see Lounsbury, John F.

Ogden, M. R., jt. ed. see Wedemeyer, D. J.

Ogden, Margaret S., ed. Liber de Diversis Medicinis. (EETS, OS Ser.: Vol. 207). 1969. reprint ed. 17.00 (*0-8115-3383-2*) Periodicals Srv.

Ogden-Niemeyer, Linda, jt. auth. see Jacobs, Karen.

Ogden, Paul. Chelsea: The Story of a Signal Dog. 1993. mass mkt. 4.99 (*0-449-22200-4*) Fawcett.

— Chelsea: The Story of Signal Dog. 1992. 18.95 (*0-316-63375-5*) Little.

Ogden, Peggy, ed. see Vrooman, Christine W.

Ogden, Peter S. Traits of American Indian Life. 1987. 19.95 (*0-87770-389-2*) Ye Galleon.

— Traits of American Indian Life & Character. (Illus.). 128p. 1995. pap. text ed. 6.95 (*0-486-28436-0*) Dover.

— Traits of American Indian Life & Character. 2nd ed. reprint ed. 34.50 (*0-404-07149-X*) AMS Pr.

Ogden, Philip E. & White, Paul E., eds. Migrants in Modern France. 320p. 1989. text ed. 75.00 (*0-04-301209-4*) Routledge Chapman & Hall.

Ogden, R. High Technology Design. 1993. text ed. write for info. (*0-442-01347-7*) Van Nos Reinhold.

Ogden, R. M. Hearing. 1973. 59.95 (*0-8490-0287-7*) Gordon Pr.

Ogden, Richard E. Green Knight, Red Mourning. 1985. pap. 3.50 (*0-8217-1626-3*) Zebra.

Ogden, Richard H. How to Succeed in Business & Marriage. LC 78-15072. 169p. reprint ed. pap. 48.20 (*0-317-19933-1*, 2023574) Bks Demand.

Ogden, Richard W. Manage Your Plant for Profit & Your Promotion. LC 78-2540. 204p. reprint ed. pap. 58.20 (*0-317-20770-9*, 2023905) Bks Demand.

Ogden, Robert M. Hearing. LC 75-124248. (Select Bibliographies Reprint Ser.). 1977. 31.95 (*0-8369-5137-9*) Ayer.

Ogden, Rollo, tr. see Isaacs, Jorge.

Ogden, Russell. A Capsule View of the Bible. 1979. pap. 1.50 (*0-88469-045-8*) BMH Bks.

Ogden, S. Step by Step Organic Flowers. 1995. 25.00 (*0-06-016996-6*, HarpT) HarpC.

Ogden, Schubert M. Christ Without Myth: A Study Based on the Theology of Rudolf Bultmann. LC 79-10284. 192p. 1991. reprint ed. pap. text ed. 9.95 (*0-87074-172-1*) SMU Press.

— Is There Only One True Religion or Are There Many? LC 91-52781. 114p. 1992. text ed. 22.50x (*0-87074-328-7*); pap. text ed. 12.95x (*0-87074-329-5*) SMU Press.

— On Theology. LC 91-52782. 176p. 1992. reprint ed. pap. text ed. 12.95x (*0-87074-330-9*) SMU Press.

— The Point of Christology. LC 91-52783. 206p. 1992. reprint ed. pap. text ed. 12.95x (*0-87074-331-7*) SMU Press.

— The Reality of God & Other Essays. LC 90-52663. 238p. 1992. reprint ed. pap. text ed. 12.95x (*0-87074-318-X*) SMU Press.

Ogden, Schubert M., ed. see Bultmann, Rudolf.

Ogden, Scott. Garden Bulbs for the South. LC 94-7931. 200p. 1994. 22.95 (*0-87833-861-6*) Taylor Pub.

— Gardening Success with Difficult Soils: Limestone, Alkaline Clay, & Caliche Soils. LC 91-33679. 272p. (Orig.). 1992. pap. 18.95 (*0-87833-741-5*) Taylor Pub.

Ogden, Sharon C. Irish Chain Quilts: Single, Double & Triple. Orig. Title: Double Irish Chain. (Illus.). 32p. 1992. reprint ed. pap. 3.50 (*0-486-26962-0*) Dover.

***Ogden, Sheila J.** Radcliff & Ogden's Calculation of Drug Dosages: An Interactive Workbook. 5th ed. LC 94-32094. 1994. write for info. (*0-8151-7002-5*) Mosby Yr Bk.

Ogden, Shepherd. Step by Step Organic Vegetable Gardening. rev. ed. (Illus.). 320p. 1994. reprint ed. pap. 14.00 (*0-06-092225-7*, PL) HarpC.

Ogden, Sherelyn, ed. Preservation of Library & Archival Materials: A Manual. LC 92-61755. (Illus.). 155p. 1992. write for info. (*0-9634685-0-2*) NE Document.

— Preservation of Library & Archival Materials: A Manual. expanded rev. ed. LC 94-67348. 241p. 1994. 35.00 (*0-9634685-1-0*) NE Document.

Ogden, Suzanne. China's Unresolved Issues: Politics, Development, & Culture. 2nd ed. 400p. (C). 1991. pap. text ed. write for info. (*0-13-132747-X*) P-H.
— China's Unresolved Issues: Politics, Development, & Culture. 3rd ed. LC 94-30959. 352p. 1994. pap. text ed. write for info. (*0-13-178591-5*) P-H.
— Global Studies: China. 5th ed. 256p. 1995. pap. text ed. 13.95 (*1-56134-378-1*) Dushkin Pub.
Ogden, Suzanne, et al, eds. China's Search for Democracy: The Student & Mass Movement of 1989. LC 91-26768. 488p. 1992. 57.95 (*0-87332-723-3*); pap. text ed. 20.95 (*0-87332-724-1*) M E Sharpe.
Ogden, Thomas. Subjects of Analysis. LC 93-43113. 240p. 1994. 40.00 (*1-56821-185-6*) Aronson.
***Ogden, Thomas E. & Goldberg, Israel A.** Research Proposals: A Guide to Success. 2nd ed. 396p. 1995. 49.00 (*0-7817-0313-1*) Raven.
Ogden, Thomas H. The Matrix of the Mind: Object Relations & the Psychoanalytic Dialogue. LC 85-13404. 288p. 1994. reprint ed. pap. 30.00 (*1-56821-051-5*) Aronson.
— The Primitive Edge of Experience. LC 89-6878. 256p. 1989. 25.00x (*0-87668-982-9*) Aronson.
— The Primitive Edge of Experience. LC 89-6878. 256p. 1993. pap. 30.00x (*0-87668-290-5*) Aronson.
— Projective Identification & Psychotherapeutic Technique. LC 81-67124. 256p. 1982. 30.00x (*0-87668-446-0*) Aronson.
— Projective Identification & Psychotherapeutic Technique. LC 81-67124. 256p. 1993. pap. 25.00x (*0-87668-542-4*) Aronson.
Ogden, ThomasH. The Matrix of the Mind: Object Relations & the Psychoanalytic Dialogue. LC 85-13404. 288p. 1990. 30.00 (*0-87668-742-7*) Aronson.
Ogden, Tom. Two Hundred Years of the American Circus. LC 92-31880. (Illus.). 402p. 1993. 50.00 (*0-8160-2611-4*) Facts on File.
Ogden, W. K., ed. Combination Vehicles: A Special Issue of the Journal of Transportation Planning & Technology. 82p. 1989. pap. text ed. 154.00 (*0-677-25900-X*) Gordon & Breach.
Ogden, William, jt. auth. see Schreiber, Richard.
Ogdin, Carol A. Software Design for Microcomputers. LC 78-5801. (Illus.). 1978. 32.00 (*0-13-821744-0*) P-H.
Ogdon, Donald P. Handbook of Psychological Signs, Symptoms, & Syndromes. LC 81-52961. (Professional Handbook Ser.). 102p. 1981. pap. 37.50x (*0-87424-173-1*, W-173) Western Psych.
— Psychodiagnostics & Personality Assessment: A Handbook. 2nd ed. LC 66-29866. (Professional Handbook Ser.). 144p. (C). 1967. pap. 39.50x (*0-87424-095-6*, W-95) Western Psych.
Ogelman, H. & Van Den Heuvel, E. P., eds. Timing Neutron Stars. (C). 1989. lib. bdg. 239.00 (*0-7923-0101-3*) Kluwer Ac.
Ogen, Gregory L. CA Public Agency Practice, 3 vols. 1988. ring bd. write for info. (*0-8205-1141-2*) Bender.
Ogesan, T. The Beginning. 1993. 12.95 (*0-533-10600-1*) Vantage.
Ogg, David. Ioannis Seldeni Ad Fletam Dissertatio. LC 85-48160. (Cambridge Studies in English Legal History). 270p. 1986. reprint ed. 64.00 (*0-912004-30-4*) W W Gaunt.
Ogg, Frederic. Opening of the Mississippi: A Struggle for Supremacy in the American Interior. LC 68-24990. (American History & Americana Ser.: No. 47). (Illus.). 1969. reprint ed. lib. bdg. 59.95 (*0-8383-0223-8*) M S G Haskell Hse.
Ogg, Frederic A. Economic Development of Modern Europe. rev. ed. 1968. reprint ed. 79.00 (*0-403-00126-9*) Scholarly.
— The Old Northwest: A Chronicle of the Ohio Valley & Beyond. (BCL1 - United States Local History Ser.). 220p. 1991. reprint ed. lib. bdg. 79.00 (*0-7812-6563-0*) Rprt Serv.
— The Opening of the Mississippi: A Struggle for Supremacy in the American Interior. (BCL1 - United States Local History Ser.). 670p. 1991. reprint ed. text ed. 109.00 (*0-7812-6304-2*) Rprt Serv.
Ogg, George. Chronology of the Public Ministry of Jesus. 1980. lib. bdg. 75.00 (*0-8490-3142-7*) Gordon Pr.
Ogg, Harold C. Introduction to the Use of Computers in Libraries: A Textbook for the Non-Technical Student. 200p. 1994. pap. 39.50 (*0-88736-876-X*) Learned Info.
Ogg, R., jt. auth. see Browning, N.
Ogg, Wilson R. Love's Cradle: Selected Poems by Wilson Reid Ogg. (Illus.). 75p. (Orig.). 1988. pap. 5.00 (*0-929707-01-X*) Pinebrook CA.
— My Escaping Self: Poems by Wilson Reid Ogg. (Illus.). 250p. (Orig.). 1988. pap. 8.50 (*0-929707-03-6*) Pinebrook CA.
— Suns Without End: Selected Poems by Wilson Reid Ogg. (Illus.). 95p. 1988. pap. 5.00 (*0-929707-00-1*) Pinebrook CA.
— We Hatch Our Embryo: Selected Poems by Wilson Reid Ogg. (Illus.). 70p. (Orig.). 1988. pap. 5.00 (*0-929707-02-8*) Pinebrook CA.
Oggel, L. Terry. Edwin Booth: A Bio-Bibliography. LC 92-8910. (Bio-Bibliographies in the Performing Arts Ser.: No. 28). 320p. 1992. text ed. 55.00 (*0-313-26195-4*, OEB, Greenwood Pr) Greenwood.
Oggel, L. Terry, ed. The Letters & Notebooks of Mary Devlin Booth. LC 87-130. (Contributions in Drama & Theatre Studies: No. 23). 200p. 1987. text ed. 49.95 (*0-313-25468-0*, OCE/, Greenwood Pr) Greenwood.
Oggins, Robin S. Castles & Fortresses. LC 94-9454. 1994. write for info. (*1-56799-095-9*, MetroBooks) M Friedman Pub Grp Inc.
Oggins, Virginia, jt. ed. see Szarmach, Paul E.
Oghigian, Haig. Law of Commerce in Japan. 1993. 24.95 (*0-13-524836-1*) P-H.
Oghlukian, Abel. The Deaconess in the Armenian Church. Cowe, S. Peter, tr. LC 94-65849. (Illus.). 68p. 1994. pap. 10.00 (*1-885011-00-8*) St Nersess.
Ogibalov, P. M., ed. Structural Polymers, 2 vols., Set. 618p. 1973. text ed. 143.50 (*0-7065-1338-X*, Pub. by Keter Pub IS) Coronet Bks.
Ogibenin, B. L. Structure d'un Mythe Vedique: Le Mythe Cosmogonique dans le Rgveda. (Approaches to Semiotics Ser.: No. 30). 1973. 56.95 (*90-279-2404-X*) Mouton.
Ogier, James M., tr. see Madsen, Svend A.
Ogilby, John. The Fables of Aesop Paraphrased in Verse, 1668. LC 92-24824. (Augustan Reprints Ser.: No. 1 (1965)). 1992. 50.00 (*0-404-70101-9*) AMS Pr.
Ogilive, Marilyn B. Women in Science - Antiquity Through the Nineteenth Century: A Biographical Dictionary with Annotated Bibliography. (Illus.). 272p. 1990. reprint ed. pap. 14.95 (*0-262-65038-X*) MIT Pr.
Ogilive, R. M., ed. see Tacitus.
***Ogilvie.** Silent Strength. 1994. 4.99 (*0-517-13634-1*) Random Hse Value.
Ogilvie, Charlot. Love Song on a Chinese Flute. 560p. 1987. mass mkt. 4.50 (*0-8217-2006-6*) Zebra.
Ogilvie, Colin. Chamberlain's Symptoms & Signs in Clinical Medicine. 11th ed. (Illus.). 608p. 1987. 60.00 (*0-7236-0864-4*) Buttrwrth-Heinemann.
Ogilvie, Colin & Earls, J. E. Questions & Answers for Symptoms & Signs in Clinical Medicine. (Illus.). 268p. 1987. pap. 19.95 (*0-7236-0865-2*, Pub. by John Wright UK) Buttrwrth-Heinemann.
Ogilvie, Elisabeth. Answer in the Tide. 1976. 21.95 (*0-8488-1117-8*) Amereon Ltd.
— An Answer in the Tide. 288p. 1991. reprint ed. pap. 12.95 (*0-89272-311-4*) Down East.
— Bellwood. 1976. 18.95 (*0-8488-1118-6*) Amereon Ltd.
— Blueberry Summer. reprint ed. lib. bdg. 18.95 (*0-88411-327-2*, Aeonian Pr) Amereon Ltd.
— Call Home the Heart. reprint ed. lib. bdg. 20.95 (*0-88411-328-0*, Aeonian Pr) Amereon Ltd.
— The Ebbing Tide. LC 85-72649. 280p. 1985. reprint ed. pap. 9.95 (*0-89272-218-5*) Down East.
— High Tide at Noon. LC 85-72647. 400p. 1985. reprint ed. pap. 10.95 (*0-89272-216-9*) Down East.
— Jennie about to Be. LC 94-14450. 352p. 1994. pap. 13.95 (*0-89272-345-9*) Down East.
— Jennie Glenroy. LC 93-12684. (Jennie Trilogy Ser.: Bk. 3). 512p. 1993. 24.95 (*0-89272-326-2*) Down East.
— Jenny Glenroy. 1994. pap. 15.95 (*0-89272-350-5*) Down East.
— My World Is an Island. LC 90-80510. (Illus.). 288p. 1990. reprint ed. pap. 10.95 (*0-89272-288-6*) Down East.
— Storm Tide. LC 85-72648. 368p. 1985. reprint ed. pap. 9.95 (*0-89272-217-7*) Down East.
— Until the End of Summer. 17.95 (*0-8488-1119-4*) Amereon Ltd.
— When the Music Stopped. large type ed. LC 89-77193. 560p. 1990. lib. bdg. 18.95 (*0-89621-966-6*) Thorndike Pr.
— The World of Jennie G. LC 94-14449. 368p. 1994. reprint ed. pap. 13.95 (*0-89272-346-7*) Down East.
Ogilvie, Elizabeth. Becky's Island. reprint ed. lib. bdg. 18.95 (*0-88411-326-4*, Aeonian Pr) Amereon Ltd.
— Ceiling of Amber. reprint ed. text ed. 17.95 (*0-88411-329-9*, Aeonian Pr) Amereon Ltd.
— Dawning of the Day. 1976. reprint ed. lib. bdg. 22.95 (*0-88411-186-5*, Aeonian Pr) Amereon Ltd.
— The Dreaming Swimmer. reprint ed. lib. bdg. 21.95 (*0-88411-189-X*, Aeonian Pr) Amereon Ltd.
— Ebbing Tide. 1976. reprint ed. lib. bdg. 22.95 (*0-88411-185-7*, Aeonian Pr) Amereon Ltd.
— The Fabulous Year. reprint ed. lib. bdg. 19.95 (*0-88411-330-2*, Aeonian Pr) Amereon Ltd.
— The Face of Innocence. reprint ed. lib. bdg. 20.95 (*0-88411-188-1*, Aeonian Pr) Amereon Ltd.
— High Tide at Noon. 1976. reprint ed. lib. bdg. 25.95 (*0-88411-183-0*, Aeonian Pr) Amereon Ltd.
— How Wide the Heart. reprint ed. lib. bdg. 18.95 (*0-88411-332-9*, Aeonian Pr) Amereon Ltd.
— Image of a Lover. reprint ed. lib. bdg. 23.95 (*0-88411-187-3*, Aeonian Pr) Amereon Ltd.
— Masquerade at Sea House. reprint ed. lib. bdg. 17.95 (*0-88411-333-7*, Aeonian Pr) Amereon Ltd.
— My World Is an Island. reprint ed. lib. bdg. 21.95 (*0-88411-334-5*, Aeonian Pr) Amereon Ltd.
— No Evil Angel. reprint ed. lib. bdg. 21.95 (*0-88411-335-3*, Aeonian Pr) Amereon Ltd.
— The Pigeon Pair. reprint ed. lib. bdg. 17.95 (*0-88411-336-1*, Aeonian Pr) Amereon Ltd.
— Rowan Head. 1976. reprint ed. lib. bdg. 22.95 (*0-88411-181-4*, Aeonian Pr) Amereon Ltd.
— The Seasons Hereafter. reprint ed. lib. bdg. 22.95 (*0-88411-337-X*, Aeonian Pr) Amereon Ltd.
— The Silent Ones. 23.95 (*0-89190-399-2*, Am Repr) Amereon Ltd.
— Storm Tide. 1976. reprint ed. lib. bdg. 23.95 (*0-88411-184-9*, Aeonian Pr) Amereon Ltd.
— A Theme for Reason. 25.95 (*0-89190-394-1*, Am Repr) Amereon Ltd.
— There May Be Heaven. reprint ed. lib. bdg. 23.95 (*0-88411-338-8*, Aeonian Pr) Amereon Ltd.
— Turn Around Twice. reprint ed. lib. bdg. 16.95 (*0-88411-339-6*, Aeonian Pr) Amereon Ltd.
— Whistle for a Wind: Maine 1820. reprint ed. lib. bdg. 20.95 (*0-88411-340-X*, Aeonian Pr) Amereon Ltd.
— Witch Door. 1976. reprint ed. lib. bdg. 17.95 (*0-88411-182-2*, Aeonian Pr) Amereon Ltd.
— The Young Islanders. reprint ed. lib. bdg. 16.95 (*0-88411-341-8*, Aeonian Pr) Amereon Ltd.
Ogilvie, Elizabeth & Baum, Vicki. Honeymoon. reprint ed. lib. bdg. 16.95 (*0-88411-331-0*, Aeonian Pr) Amereon Ltd.
***Ogilvie, Gregory K. & Moore, Antony.** Managing the Veterinary Cancer Patient: A Practice Manual. 540p. 1995. pap. write for info. (*1-884254-20-9*) Vet Lrn Syst.
Ogilvie, John. An Essay on the Lyric Poetry of the Ancients: (From Poems on Several Subjects. To Which is Prefix'd, an Essay on the Lyric Poetry of the Ancients; in Two Letters) LC 92-24823. (Augustan Reprints Ser.: No. 139 (1969)). reprint ed. 12.00 (*0-404-70139-6*, PA3020) AMS Pr.
— Philosophical & Critical Observations on the Nature, Characters, & Various Species of Composition, 2 vols. (Anglistica & Americana Ser.: No. 27). 1968. reprint ed. 128.70 (*0-685-66497-X*, 05102142, Pub. by Georg Olms GW) Lubrecht & Cramer.
— The Theology of Plato: Compared with the Principles of Oriental & Grecian Philosophers. xxiii, 205p. 1976. reprint ed. 37.70 (*3-487-05710-7*, Pub. by Georg Olms GW) Lubrecht & Cramer.
Ogilvie, John S. Life & Death of Jay Gould & How He Made His Millions. Bruchey, Stuart, ed. LC 80-1336. (Railroads Ser.). (Illus.). 1981. reprint ed. lib. bdg. 20.95 (*0-405-13809-1*) Ayer.
Ogilvie, John W. Advanced C Structured Programming: Data Structure Design & Implementation in C. 432p. 1990. pap. text ed. 26.95 (*0-471-51943-X*); write for info. (*0-471-53580-X*) Wiley.
Ogilvie, John W. L. Modula 2 Programming. 1985. 30.00 (*0-07-047770-1*) McGraw.
Ogilvie, L. J. Autobiography of God. Fung, Man-chong, tr. (CHI.). 1983. pap. write for info. (*0-941598-06-3*) Living Spring Pubns.
Ogilvie, Lloyd. Climbing the Rainbow. 224p. 1993. 15.99 (*0-8499-0762-4*) Word Inc.
— Communicator's Commentary, Vol. 5: Acts. 369p. 1991. reprint ed. pap. 10.99 (*0-8499-3278-5*) Word Inc.
— Turning Your Struggles into Steppingstones. LC 93-38209. 1993. 12.99 (*0-8499-3530-X*) Word Pub.
Ogilvie, Lloyd J. Ask Him Anything. (QP Proven-Word Ser.). 269p. 1984. write for info. (*0-8499-2982-2*) Word Inc.
— Autobiography of God. LC 78-53355. 324p. (C). 1981. pap. 8.99 (*0-8307-0791-3*, 5415106) Regal.
— CC, NT, Vol. 5: Acts. 369p. 1983. write for info. (*0-8499-0158-8*) Word Inc.
— CC, OT, Vol. 20: Hosea, Joel, Amos, Obadiah, Jonah. 1991. 19.99 (*0-8499-0426-9*) Word Inc.
— Conversation with God. 1993. pap. 9.99 (*1-56507-048-8*) Harvest Hse.
— L' Ecole des Psaumes. Cosson, Annie L., ed. Rousseau, Marie-Andre, tr. 208p. (FRE.). 1985. pap. 7.95 (*0-8297-0700-X*) Life Pubs Intl.
— God's Best for My Life. LC 81-82390. 390p. (Orig.). 1981. 12.99 (*0-89081-293-4*) Harvest Hse.
— The Greatest Counselor in the World. 200p. 1994. 16.99 (*0-89283-817-5*, Vine Bks) Servant.
— The Greatest Counselor in the World: A Fresh New Look at the Holy Spirit. 208p. 1995. pap. 10.99 (*0-89283-909-0*, Vine Bks) Servant.
— The Heart of God: Daily Meditations on the Goodness of God. Woodward, Virginia, ed. LC 94-27433. 336p. 1994. 12.99 (*0-8307-1656-4*, 5112438) Regal.
— Jesus the Healer. 192p. 1984. pap. 8.99 (*0-8007-5247-3*) Revell.
— Lord of the Impossible. LC 84-333. 224p. (Orig.). 1984. pap. 11.95 (*0-687-22710-0*) Abingdon.
— The Magnificent Vision. LC 91-31726. 164p. (C). 1992. reprint ed. pap. 8.99 (*0-89283-754-3*, Vine Bks) Servant.
— Silent Strength for My Life: God's Wisdom for Daily Living. 1990. 14.99 (*0-89081-829-0*) Harvest Hse.
— Twelve Steps to Living Without Fear. 224p. 1990. pap. write for info. (*0-8499-3241-6*) Word Inc.
— You Are Loved & Forgiven. rev. ed. LC 86-10186. 192p. 1986. pap. text ed. 7.99 (*0-8307-1110-4*, S412117) Regal.
— La Zarza Sique Ardiendo. Orig. Title: The Bush Is Still Burning. 336p. (SPA.). 1986. 6.95 (*0-8297-1094-9*) Life Pubs Intl.
Ogilvie, Lloyd J., ed. CCOT Mastering the Old Testament, Vol. 1. LC 93-39330. 1993. 12.99 (*0-8499-3540-7*) Word Pub.
Ogilvie, Lloyd J., jt. auth. see Chafin, Kenneth L.
Ogilvie, M. A. Wild Geese. LC 77-94181. (Illus.). 1978. 35.00 (*0-931130-00-X*) Harrell Bks.
Ogilvie, Mardel, jt. auth. see Eisenson, Jon.
Ogilvie, Mary G., ed. see Stephen, Caroline.
Ogilvie, R. M. Roman Literature & Society. 304p. 1980. mass mkt. 6.95 (*0-14-022081-X*, Penguin Bks) Viking Penguin.
— Romans & Their Gods in the Age of Augustus. (Ancient Culture & Society Ser.). (Illus.). (C). 1970. pap. text ed. 10.95 (*0-393-00543-7*) Norton.
Ogilvie, R. M., ed. see Tacitus.
Ogilvie, Robert, jt. ed. see Harsh, John.
Ogilvie, Robert D. Sleep, Arousal, & Performance. Broughton, Roger J., ed. (Illus.). xvi, 286p. 1991. 94.50 (*0-8176-3518-1*) Birkhauser.
Ogilvie, Sheila A., tr. see Folz, Robert.
Ogilvie, T. Francis. Oscillating Pressure Fields on a Free Surface. (University of Michigan, Dept. of Naval Architecture & Marine Engineering, Report Ser.: No. 30). 64p. reprint ed. pap. 25.00 (*0-317-27206-3*, 2023868) Bks Demand.
— Wave Resistance: The Low Speed-Limit. (University of Michigan, Dept. of Naval Architecture & Marine Engineering, Report Ser.). 34p. reprint ed. pap. 25.00 (*0-317-28265-4*, 2022627) Bks Demand.
Ogilvie-Thompson, S. J., ed. The Index of Middle English Prose Handlist VIII: Oxford College Libraries. (Index of Middle English Prose Ser.). 256p. (C). 1991. text ed. 70.00 (*0-85991-296-5*) Boydell & Brewer.
Ogilvie, William. Birthright in Land: An Essay on the Right of Property in Land. LC 68-57110. (Reprints of Economic Classics Ser.). 1970. reprint ed. 49.50 (*0-678-00597-4*) Kelley.
— Early Days on the Yukon & the Story of Its Gold Finds, Vol. 15. LC 74-356. (Illus.). 306p. 1974. reprint ed. 24.95 (*0-405-05917-5*) Ayer.
Ogilvie, William E. Pioneer Agricultural Journalists: Brief Biographical Sketches of Some of the Early Editors in the Field of Agricultural Journalism. LC 72-89071. (Rural America Ser.). 1973. reprint ed. 16.00 (*0-8420-1492-6*) Scholarly Res Inc.
Ogilvy, C. Stanley. Excursions in Geometry. 1990. pap. 5.95 (*0-486-26530-7*) Dover.
— Excursions in Mathematics: Excursions in Mathematics. LC 94-24696. (Illus.). 192p. 1994. pap. text ed. 6.95 (*0-486-28283-X*) Dover.
— Excursions in Number Theory. 1988. pap. 5.95 (*0-486-25778-9*) Dover.
Ogilvy, Carol & Tinkham, Trudy. Classy Christmas Concerts. 112p. (J). (gr. k-7). 1986. student ed 10.95 (*0-86653-349-4*, GA 795) Good Apple.
— Primary Christmas Concerts. 112p. (J). (gr. k-3). 1989. 10.95 (*0-86653-485-7*, GA1091) Good Apple.
Ogilvy, David. Confessions of an Advertising Man. 172p. 1987. 11.00 (*0-8442-3711-6*, NTC Busn Bks) NTC Pub Grp.
— Confessions of an Advertising Man. 2nd ed. 180p. 1989. pap. 11.00 (*0-689-70800-9*, Atheneum S&S) S&S Trade.
— DH 88: The Story of the DeHaviland Racing Comet. LC 84-73107. (Illus.). 174p. 1985. 19.95 (*0-911139-02-8*) Flying Bks.
— Ogilvy on Advertising. 1985. pap. 20.00 (*0-394-72903-X*, Vin) Random.
— Old Aeroplanes. 1989. pap. 25.00 (*0-7478-0107-X*, Pub. by Shire UK) St Mut.
— UK Airspace: Is It Safe. (Illus.). 136p. 1990. pap. 16.95 (*0-85429-726-X*, Pub. by J H Haynes & Co UK) Motorbooks Intl.
Ogilvy, Graham. The River Tay & Its People. (Illus.). 224p. 1994. 34.95 (*1-85158-406-4*, Pub. by Mnstream UK) Trafalgar.
Ogilvy, J. A. Theory of Wave Scattering from Random Rough Surfaces. (Illus.). 292p. 1991. 85.00 (*0-7503-0063-9*) IOP Pub.
Ogilvy, J. D. & Baker, Donald C. Reading "Beowulf" An Introduction to the Poem, Its Background, & Its Style. LC 83-47835. (Illus.). 240p. 1986. reprint ed. pap. 14.95 (*0-8061-2019-3*) U of Okla Pr.
Ogilvy, James. Living Without a Goal: Finding the Freedom to Live a Creative, Innovative & Fulfilled Life. 1995. 22.95 (*0-385-41799-3*) Doubleday.
Ogilvy, James, ed. Revisioning Philosophy. LC 91-30803. (SUNY Series in Philosophy). 318p. 1991. 59.50 (*0-7914-0989-9*); pap. 19.95 (*0-7914-0990-2*) State U NY Pr.
Ogilvy, James A. Self & World: Readings in Philosophy. 2nd ed. 507p. (C). 1981. pap. text ed. 22.75 (*0-15-579628-3*) HB Coll Pubs.
Ogino. Catalysis & Surface Properties of Liquid Metals & Liquid Alloys. (Chemical Industries Ser.: Vol. 29). 224p. 1987. 125.00 (*0-8247-7699-2*) Dekker.
Ogino & Abe. Mixed Surfactant Systems. (Surfactant Science Ser.: Vol. 46). 472p. 1993. 165.00 (*0-8247-8796-X*) Dekker.
Ogintz. Northern California: Everything That's Fun to Do & See for Kids - & Parents Too! (Taking the Kids Ser.). 96p. 1994. pap. 9.95 (*0-06-258547-9*) Harper SF.
Ogintz, Eileen. The Great American Southwest: Everything That's Fun to Do & See for Kids - & Parents Too! (Taking the Kids Ser.). (Illus.). 96p. (Orig.). 1994. pap. 9.95 (*0-06-258534-7*) HarpC West.
— Sunny Southern California: Everything That's Fun to Do & See for Kids - & Parents Too! (Taking the Kids Ser.). (Illus.). 96p. (Orig.). (J). 1994. pap. 9.95 (*0-06-258542-8*) HarpC West.
— Taking the Kids to the Pacific Northwest: Everything That's Fun to Do & See for Kids. 1995. pap. 9.95 (*0-06-258580-0*) Harper SF.
Ogiwara, Noriko. Dragon Sword & Wind Child. Hirano, Cathy, tr. LC 92-7970. 1993. 17.00 (*0-374-30466-1*) FS&G.
Oglander, John. A Royalist's Notebook: The Commonplace Book of Sir John Oglander. Bamford, Francis, ed. LC 72-174427. (Illus.). 1972. reprint ed. 19.95 (*0-405-08827-2*) Ayer.
Ogle, Anna C., see Ashford Owen, pseud..
Ogle, Deborah, tr. see Botermans, Jack.
Ogle, George B. South Korea: Dissent Within the Economic Miracle. LC 90-21221. 192p. (C). 1990. text ed. 49.95 (*1-85649-002-5*, Pub. by Zed Books UK); pap. 19.95 (*1-85649-003-3*, Pub. by Zed Books UK) Humanities.
Ogle, Gini & Noice, Karen. Souvenirs: A Feast of Local Color & Home Cooking. 205p. 1993. 18.95 (*0-9640623-0-5*) Echo Designs.
Ogle, Henry. Ogle - Bertram, Ogle & Bothal: History of the Baronies of Ogle, Bothal & Hepple, & of the Families of Ogle & Bertram Who Held Possession of Those Baronies in Northumberland, to Which Is Added Accounts of Several Branches bearing the Name of Ogle. (Illus.). 496p. 1993. reprint ed. lib. bdg. 85.00 (*0-8328-3728-8*); reprint ed. pap. 75.00 (*0-8328-3729-6*) Higginson Bk Co.
Ogle, Kenneth N., et al. Oculomotor Imbalance in Binocular Vision & Fixation Disparity. LC 67-19139. 384p. reprint ed. pap. 109.50 (*0-317-26696-9*, 2056005) Bks Demand.
Ogle, Laurence T. & Alsalam, Nabeel. Condition of Education, 1990, Vol. 1: Elementary & Secondary Education. 250p. 1990. per., pap. 9.00 (*0-16-022853-0*, S/N 065-000-003) USGPO.

An Asterisk (*) at the beginning of an entry indicates that the title is appearing in BIP for the first time.

Ogle, Lucille & Thoburn, Tina. The Golden Picture Dictionary. (Deluxe Golden Bks.). (Illus.). (J). (ps-3). 1989. write for info. (*0-307-17861-7*, Golden Bks) Western Pub.

Ogle, Madeline B. From Problems to Profits: Madson Management System for Pet Grooming Salons. (Illus.). 325p. 1989. 189.95 (*0-942383-07-9*) Manor Hse Pub.

Ogle, Marbury B., ed. see Tortarius, Rudolphus.

Ogle, Patrick, ed. Facets African-American Video Guide. (Illus.). 230p. 1993. pap. 10.95 (*0-89733-402-7*) Academy Chi Pubs.

Ogle, T. P., tr. see Andenaes, Johannes.

Oglesbee, Maggie. Maggie's Fax-a-Gram. Parker, Diane, ed. LC 92-50867. (Illus.). 60p. 1993. spiral bd. 7.95 (*0-88247-964-4*) R & E Pubs.

***Oglesbee, Rollo B. & Hale, Albert.** History of Michigan City. (Illus.). 201p. 1995. reprint ed. lib. bdg. 29.50 (*0-8328-4645-7*) Higginson Bk Co.

***Oglesby, Arthur.** Fly Fishing for Salmon & Sea Trout. (Illus.). 320p. 1995. 45.00 (*1-85223-840-2*, Pub. by Crowood UK) Trafalgar.

Oglesby, Carl. JFK Assassination: The Facts & the Theories. 1992. pap. 4.99 (*0-451-17476-3*, Sig) NAL-Dutton.

— Who Killed JFK? (Real Story Ser.). 1992. pap. 5.00 (*1-878825-10-0*) Odonian Pr.

Oglesby, Carl, jt. auth. see Melanson, Philip.

Oglesby, Carole A., ed. Women & Sport: From Myth to Reality. LC 77-19255. (Illus.). 268p. reprint ed. pap. 76.40 (*0-7837-1492-0*, 2057188) Bks Demand.

Oglesby, Catharine. Modern Primitive Arts of Mexico, Guatemala & the Southwest. LC 75-90670. (Essay Index Reprint Ser.). 1977. 18.95 (*0-8369-1215-2*) Ayer.

Oglesby, Clarkson H. & Hicks, Russell G. Highway Engineering. 4th ed. LC 81-12949. 844p. 1982. Net. text ed. write for info. (*0-471-02936-X*) Wiley.

Oglesby, Clarkson H., et al. Successful Techniques for Improving Productivity in On-Site Construction. (Illus.). 512p. 1988. text ed. write for info. (*0-07-047802-3*) McGraw.

***Oglesby, Dee.** Inside Looking Out. 82p. (YA). (gr. 7-12). 1995. pap. write for info. (*1-57515-053-0*) PPI Pubng.

***Oglesby, Dee, told to.** Lost Love of a Child. 36p. (YA). (gr. 7-12). 1995. pap. write for info. (*1-57515-052-2*) PPI Pubng.

Oglesby, Enoch H. Born in the Fire: Case Studies in Christian Ethics & Globalization. LC 90-43875. 192p. (Orig.). (C). 1990. pap. 14.95 (*0-8298-0849-3*) Pilgrim OH.

— God's Divine Arithematic. Jones, Amos, Jr., ed. LC 84-54498. 150p. (Orig.). 1986. pap. write for info. (*0-910683-06-9*) Townsnd-Pr.

Oglesby, Francis C. An Examination of a Decision Procedure. LC 52-42839. (Memoirs Ser.: No. 1/44). 148p. 1971. reprint ed. pap. 18.00 (*0-8218-1244-0*, MEMO 1/44) Am Math.

Oglesby, Lloyd S. The Chemistry of Glitter. (Illus.). 90p. 1989. pap. 19.95 (*0-929931-01-7*) Amer Fireworks.

Oglesby, Mira-Lani. Athena Louise Replies. (Morning Chapbook Ser.). 16p. (Orig.). 1989. pap. 7.50 (*0-918273-62-5*) Coffee Hse.

Oglesby, Richard E. Manuel Lisa & the Opening of the Missouri Fur Trade. LC 63-9956. (Illus.). 246p. (Orig.). 1963. pap. 13.95 (*0-8061-1860-1*) U of Okla Pr.

Oglesby, Robert, Jr., jt. auth. see Cope, Mike.

Oglesby, Stuart R. Prayers for All Occasions. 180p. 1983. reprint ed. pap. 8.99 (*0-8042-2485-4*, John Knox) Westminster John Knox.

Oglesby, William B., Jr. Biblical Themes for Pastoral Care. 1983. pap. 15.95 (*0-687-03447-7*) Abingdon.

— With Wings As Eagles: Toward Personal Christian Maturity. LC 87-51654. 194p. (C). 1987. text ed. 24.95 (*1-55605-035-6*); pap. text ed. 14.95 (*1-55605-036-4*) Wyndhall Pr.

Oglethorpe, James E. Some Account of the Design of the Trustees for Establishing Colonys in America. Baine, Rodney M. & Spalding, Phinizy, eds. LC 89-20639. 60p. 1990. 25.00 (*0-8203-1237-1*) U of Ga Pr.

Oglethorpe, Jean, ed. see Martin, Olive.

***Ogletree, Madema & Lamb County History Book Comm. Staff.** Lamb County, Texas. (Illus.). 549p. 1992. 65.00 (*0-88107-195-1*) Curtis Media.

Ogletree, Roberta J., et al. The Consumer's Guide to School-Based Sexuality Education Curricula. LC 93-46042. 1994. write for info. (*1-56071-354-2*) ETR Assocs.

***Ogley, Adrian.** Principles of International Tax: A Multinational Perspective. 1993. 95.00 (*0-9520442-0-X*, Pub. by Interfisc Pub UK) Intl Info Srvcs Inc.

Ogley, Bob. Doodlebugs & Rockets: The Battle of the Flying Bombs. (Illus.). 208p. 1993. pap. 24.95 (*1-872337-21-X*, Pub. by AMCD Pubs UK) Motorbooks Intl.

Ogley, Brian. Exporting: Step by Step to Success. 160p. (C). 1987. 32.00 (*0-317-93201-2*, Pub. by P Chapman Pub UK) St Mut.

Ogley, Roderick. Internationalizing the Seabed. LC 83-20555. 264p. 1984. text ed. 52.95 (*0-566-00629-4*) Ashgate Pub Co.

Ogley, Roderick C. Conflict under the Microscope: An Inter-Disciplinary Diagnosis. 750p. 1991. text ed. 68.95 (*1-85628-023-3*, Pub. by Avebury Pub UK) Ashgate Pub Co.

Ogliaruso, Michael A. & Wolfe, James F. Synthesis of Lactones & Lactams. Patai, Saul E. & Rappoport, Zvi, eds. LC 92-28932. (Updates from the Chemistry of Functional Groups Ser.). 1085p. 1993. text ed. 570.00 (*0-471-93734-7*) Wiley.

Ogliaruso, Michael A., jt. auth. see Wolfe, James F.

Ogloff, James R., ed. Law & Psychology: The Broadening of the Discipline. LC 92-71726. 420p. (C). 1992. lib. bdg. 45.00 (*0-89089-475-2*) Carolina Acad Pr.

O'Glove, Thornton. Quality of Earnings: The Investor's Guide to How Much Money a Company Is Really Making. 200p. 1987. text ed. 32.95 (*0-02-922630-9*) Free Pr.

Ognibene, Peter J. The Big Byte. 320p. (Orig.). 1984. pap. 2.95 (*0-345-31418-2*) Ballantine.

***Ogniedou, Altan.** Phantasmagoria: A Book of Poems. Probstein, Ian E., ed. 80p. 1993. pap. text ed. 6.00 (*0-9635200-0-8*) R E M Pr.

Ognyov, Nikolai, pseud. Diary of a Communist Undergraduate. Werth, Alexander, tr. LC 72-90304. (Soviet Literature in English Translation Ser.). 288p. 1973. reprint ed. 21.50 (*0-88355-015-6*) Hyperion Conn.

***Ogo, Christine & Wolfe, Leslie R.** Midlife & Older Women & HIV-AIDS: Executive Summary & Recommendations from the Report on the Seminar. 11p. 1994. 3.50 (*1-877966-22-3*) Ctr Women Policy.

Ogoltsev, V. Common Russian Similes. (Illus.). 174p. (C). 1984. 30.00 (*0-685-39364-X*, Pub. by Collets) St Mut.

***Ogonowski, Lawrence.** The Plutonian. 300p. 1996. pap. 9.95 (*0-7610-0470-X*) NW Pub.

Ogorkiewicz, R., ed. Tank Technology. (Illus.). 500p. 1991. 99.00 (*0-7106-0595-1*) Janes Info Group.

Ogorkiewicz, R. M., ed. Engineering Properties of Thermoplastics. LC 72-83219. 330p. reprint ed. pap. 94.10 (*0-8357-9885-2*, 2051614) Bks Demand.

O'Gorman, Angie, ed. The Universe Bends Towards Justice: A Reader on Christian Nonviolence in the U. S. 288p. 1990. 39.95 (*0-86571-177-1*); pap. 14.95 (*0-86571-178-X*) New Soc Pubs.

O'Gorman, Edmund. St. Francis for Today. 1987. pap. 7.95 (*0-85244-130-4*, Pub. by Gracewing UK) Morehouse Pub.

O'Gorman, Edmund, tr. The Little Flowers of Saint Clare. LC 92-37755. (Illus.). 176p. 1993. reprint ed. 6.99 (*0-89283-823-X*, Charis) Servant.

O'Gorman, Edmundo. The Invention of America. LC 72-6203. 177p. 1972. reprint ed. text ed. 35.00 (*0-8371-6470-2*, OGIA, Greenwood Pr) Greenwood.

O'Gorman, F. P. Rationality & Relativity: The Quest for Objective Knowledge. (Avebury Series in Philosophy). 160p. 1989. text ed. 68.95 (*0-566-07035-9*, Pub. by Avebury Pub UK) Ashgate Pub Co.

O'Gorman, Frank. Voters, Patrons, & Parties: The Unreformed Electorate of Hanoverian England 1734-1832. (Illus.). 464p. 1989. 89.00 (*0-19-820056-0*) OUP.

O'Gorman, Gerald, ed. Marcus Tullius Ciceroes Thre Bokes of Duties. Grimalde, Nicolas, tr. LC 86-46408. (Renaissance English Text Society Ser.: No. 12). (Illus.). 272p. 1990. 37.50 (*0-918016-93-2*) Folger Bks.

O'Gorman, Hubert J. Lawyers & Matrimonial Cases: Study of Informal Pressures in Private Professional Practice. Zuckerman, Harriet & Merton, Robert K., eds. LC 79-3754. (Dissertations on Sociology Ser.). 1980. lib. bdg. 23.95 (*0-405-12986-6*) Ayer.

O'Gorman, Hubert J., ed. see Klassen, Albert D., et al.

O'Gorman-Hughes, D. W., jt. auth. see Gupta, J. M.

O'Gorman, J. F., et al. Architecture of Frank Furness. LC 87-11339. (Illus.). 215p. (Orig.). 1987. pap. 18.95 (*0-87633-015-4*) Phila Mus Art.

O'Gorman, James F. H. H. Richardson: Architectural Forms for an American Society. LC 86-19223. (Illus.). xvi, 172p. (C). 1987. 24.95 (*0-226-62069-7*) U Ch Pr.

— H. H. Richardson: Architectural Forms for an American Society. LC 86-19223. (Illus.). 188p. 1990. pap. text ed. 12.95 (*0-226-62070-0*) U Ch Pr.

— On the Boards: Drawings by Nineteenth Century Boston Architects. LC 88-27850. (Illus.). 162p. (C). 1989. text ed. 41.95x (*0-8122-8170-5*, Wellesley Coll Mus) U of Pa Pr.

— On the Boards: Drawings by Nineteenth-Century Boston Architects. LC 88-27850. (Illus.). 162p. (Orig.). (C). reprint ed. pap. 25.95 (*0-8122-1287-8*, Wellesley Coll Mus) U of Pa Pr.

— Three American Architects: Richardson, Sullivan, & Wright, 1865-1915. LC 90-10957. (Illus.). 168p. 1991. 24.95 (*0-226-62071-9*) U Ch Pr.

— Three American Architects: Richardson, Sullivan, & Wright, 1865-1915. LC 90-10957. (Illus.). 190p. 1992. pap. 12.95 (*0-226-62072-7*) U Ch Pr.

O'Gorman, James F., intro. Portrait of a Place, Some American Landscape Painters in Gloucester. (Illus.). 1973. 8.95 (*0-930352-03-3*) Nelson B Robinson.

O'Gorman, Jodie. The Tremaine Site Complex: Oneota Occupation In the La Crosse Locality, Wisconsin. LC 93-38782. 1993. write for info. (*0-87020-273-1*) State Hist Soc Wis.

O'Gorman, Kathleen, ed. Charles Tomlinson: Man & Artist. LC 87-19076. (Illus.). 268p. 1988. text ed. 24.00 (*0-8262-0656-5*) U of Mo Pr.

***O'Gorman, Lawrence & Kasturi, Rangachar, eds.** Document Image Analysis. LC 94-32859. 536p. 1994. text ed. 48.00 (*0-8186-6547-5*, BP06547) IEEE Comp Soc.

O'Gorman, Paschal F., jt. auth. see Boylan, Thomas A.

O'Gorman, Patricia. Dancing Backwards in High Heels: How Women Master the Art of Resilience. LC 94-18598. 208p. (Orig.). 1994. pap. 12.00 (*0-89486-998-1*) Hazelden.

— Patios & Gardens of Mexico. 1994. reprint ed. 40.00 (*0-8038-0210-2*) Archit CT.

O'Gorman, Patricia A. & Oliver-Diaz, Philip. Self-Parenting 12-Step Workbook: Windows to Your Child. 1990. pap. 9.95 (*1-55874-052-X*) Health Comm.

O'Gorman, Patricia W. Tradition of Craftsmanship in Mexican Homes. (Illus.). 272p. 1988. 37.50 (*0-8038-0047-9*) Archit CT.

O'Gorman, Thomas, ed. An Advent Sourcebook. (Seasonal Sourcebook Ser.). 1990. 24.95 (*0-929650-32-8*); pap. 12.95 (*0-930467-82-5*) Liturgy Tr Pubns.

O'Gorman, Thomas & Sincoe, Mary A. Presentation Set: Advent Sourcebook - Christmas Sourcebook, 2 vols., Set. (Seasonal Sourcebook Ser.). 1990. 49.95 (*0-929650-34-4*) Liturgy Tr Pubns.

O'Gormand, Patricia & Oliver-Diaz, Philip. Twelve Steps to Self Parenting for Adult Children. 1988. pap. 7.95 (*0-932194-68-0*) Health Comm.

Ogorzaly, Michael A. Waldo Frank, Prophet of Hispanic Regeneration. LC 92-55007. (C). 1994. write for info. (*0-8387-5233-0*) Bucknell U Pr.

Ogorzaly, Molly C., jt. auth. see Simpson, Beryl B.

Ogoshi, S. & Okada, A., eds. Parenteral & Enteral Hyperalimentation: Proceedings of the International Symposium on Parenteral & Enteral Nutrition, Kochi, Japan 16-17, November 1984. (International Congress Ser.: No. 649). 392p. 1985. 177.00 (*0-444-80625-3*, Excerpta Medica) Elsevier.

Ogot, B. A., ed. General History of Africa, Vol. V: Africa from the Sixteenth to the Eighteenth Century. LC 78-57321. (Illus.). 1076p. (C). 1992. 45.00 (*0-520-03916-5*) U CA Pr.

Ogot, Bethwell A., ed. War & Society in Africa. 276p. 1972. pap. 17.50 (*0-7146-4009-3*, Pub. by F Cass Pubs UK) Intl Spec Bk.

Ogra, Pearay, et al, eds. Handbook of Mucosal Immunology. LC 93-11197. (Illus.). 766p. 1994. text ed. 195.00 (*0-12-524730-3*) Acad Pr.

Ogra, Pearay L., jt. ed. see Bernstein, Joel M.

***O'Grada, Cormac.** Ireland: A New Economic History, 1780-1939. (Illus.). 560p. 1995. pap. 24.95 (*0-19-820598-8*) OUP.

— Ireland Before & After the Famine: Explorations in Economic History, 1800-1925. 2nd ed. 224p. 1993. text ed. 59.95 (*0-7190-4034-5*, Pub. by Manchester Univ Pr UK); text ed. 19.95 (*0-7190-4035-3*, Pub. by Manchester Univ Pr UK) St Martin.

O'Grady. Early Phase Drug Evaluation in Man. 1990. 103.95 (*0-8493-7708-0*, RM301) CRC Pr.

O'Grady, jt. auth. see Porter.

O'Grady, Chris. Love Song to a Long Gone Time: Memoirs of a Moviegoer from Way Back. LC 86-90178. 258p. 1991. 15.00 (*0-9631753-0-0*) C-C OGrady.

O'Grady, Deirdre. The Last Troubadours: Poetic Drama in Italian Opera 1597-1887. 272p. 1990. 74.50 (*0-415-05459-1*, A4908) Routledge.

***O'Grady, Dennis.** Taking the Fear out of Changing. LC 94-28764. 1994. pap. 14.95 (*1-55850-408-7*) Adams Pubng.

O'Grady, Dennis E. Taking the Fear Out of Changing: Guidelines for Getting Through Tough Life Transitions. (Illus.). 480p. (Orig.). 1992. pap. 14.95 (*0-9628476-0-7*) New Insights.

O'Grady, Desmond. Alexandrian Notebook. 32p. 1990. pap. 7.95 (*1-85186-064-9*) Dufour.

— Caesar, Christ & Constantine: A History of the Early Church in Rome. LC 90-61060. (Orig.). 1991. pap. 7.95 (*0-87973-456-6*, 456) Our Sunday Visitor.

— Gododdin. 1970. 47.50 (*0-85105-310-6*, Pub. by Colin Smythe Ltd UK) Dufour.

O'Grady, Donald J., jt. ed. see Wester, William C.

O'Grady, F. Prediction & Assessment of Antibiotic Clinical Efficacy. (Beecham Colloquia Ser.). 203p. 1987. text ed. 80.00 (*0-12-524755-9*) Acad Pr.

O'Grady, Francis, jt. ed. see Lambert, Harold P.

O'Grady, Francis T., ed. Individual Health Insurance. LC 88-6439. 200p. 1988. text ed. 35.00 (*0-938959-00-X*) Soc Actuaries.

O'Grady, G. W. & O'Rourke, K. J. Ryan's Manual of the Law of Income Tax in Australia. 7th ed. xliv, 513p. 1989. 68.00 (*0-455-20906-5*, Pub. by Law Bk Co); pap. 42.50 (*0-455-20907-3*, Pub. by Law Bk Co) W W Gaunt.

O'Grady, J., jt. ed. see Ayer, A. J.

O'Grady, J. P., ed. Obstetrics: Psychological & Psychiatric Syndromes. (Current Topics in Obstetrics & Gynecology Ser.). 352p. 1991. 65.00 (*0-444-01620-1*) Elsevier.

***O'Grady, J. P., et al.** Modern Vacuum Extraction: Instruments, Operations, Risks & Benefits. LC 94-49184. (Illus.). 1995. 27.95 (*1-85070-665-4*) Prthnon Pub.

O'Grady, Jim. Dorothy Day: With Love for the Poor. (Unsung Americans Ser.). (Illus.). 115p. (J). (gr. 4 up). 1993. lib. bdg. 14.95 (*0-9623380-2-8*); pap. 10.95 (*0-9623380-6-0*) Ward Hill Pr.

O'Grady, Joan. Heresy: Heretical Truth or Orthodox Error? A Study of Early Christian Heresies. 164p. 1990. 17.95 (*0-906540-75-5*, Pub. by Element Bks UK) Element MA.

— Prince of Darkness. 1993. pap. 12.95 (*1-85230-056-6*, Pub. by Element Bks UK) Element MA.

O'Grady, John. Catholic Charities in the United States: History & Problems. LC 71-137180. (Poverty U. S. A. Historical Record Ser.). 1977. reprint ed. 35.95 (*0-405-03118-1*) Ayer.

O'Grady, John, jt. ed. see Lewis, Peter J.

O'Grady, John F. Disciples & Leaders: The Origins of Christian Ministry in the New Testament. 1991. pap. 9.95 (*0-8091-3269-9*) Paulist Pr.

— Four Gospels & the Jesus Tradition. 1989. pap. 12.95 (*0-8091-3085-8*) Paulist Pr.

— Models of Jesus Revisited. LC 94-11962. 256p. 1994. pap. 14.95 (*0-8091-3474-8*) Paulist Pr.

— Pillars of Paul's Gospel: Galatians & Romans. LC 91-45556. 192p. 1992. pap. 9.95 (*0-8091-3327-X*) Paulist Pr.

O'Grady, John P. Modern Instrumental Delivery. (Illus.). 288p. 1989. 39.00 (*0-683-06632-3*) Williams & Wilkins.

— Pilgrims to the Wild: Everett Ruess, Henry David Thoreau, John Muir, Clarence King, Mary Austin. LC 92-29783. 184p. (Orig.). 1993. pap. 16.95 (*0-87480-412-4*) U of Utah Pr.

***O'Grady, John P., et al, eds.** Operative Obstetrics. LC 95-8734. 1995. write for info. (*0-683-06633-1*) Williams & Wilkins.

O'Grady, Joseph P. Irish-Americans & Anglo-American Relations, 1880-1888. LC 76-6360. (Irish Americans Ser.). 1976. 29.95 (*0-405-09353-5*) Ayer.

O'Grady, Kevin F., et al, eds. Case Management Resource Guide, Set. 2nd ed. 2500p. 1991. pap. 240.00 (*0-9624105-4-3*) Ctr CHI.

— Case Management Resource Guide, Set. 4th ed. 3300p. 1993. pap. 225.00 (*1-880874-05-9*) Ctr CHI.

— Case Management Resource Guide, Vol. 1: Eastern U. S. 2nd ed. 2500p. 1991. Vol. 1:Eastern U.S. pap. 75.00 (*0-9624105-5-1*) Ctr CHI.

— Case Management Resource Guide, Vol. 1: Eastern U. S. 4th ed. 3300p. 1993. Vol. 1: Eastern U.S. pap. 60.00 (*1-880874-06-7*) Ctr CHI.

— Case Management Resource Guide, Vol. 2: Southern U. S. 2nd ed. 2500p. 1991. Vol. 2: Southern U.S. pap. 75.00 (*0-9624105-6-X*) Ctr CHI.

— Case Management Resource Guide, Vol. 2: Southern U. S. 4th ed. 3300p. 1993. Vol. 2: Southern U.S. pap. 60.00 (*1-880874-07-5*) Ctr CHI.

— Case Management Resource Guide, Vol. 3: Midwestern U. S. 2nd ed. 2500p. 1991. Vol. 3: Midwestern U.S. pap. 75.00 (*0-9624105-7-8*) Ctr CHI.

— Case Management Resource Guide, Vol. 3: Midwestern U. S. 4th ed. 3300p. 1993. Vol. 3: Midwestern U.S. pap. 60.00 (*1-880874-08-3*) Ctr CHI.

— Case Management Resource Guide, Vol. 4: Western U. S. 2nd ed. 2500p. 1991. Vol. 4: Western U.S. pap. 75.00 (*0-9624105-8-6*) Ctr CHI.

— Case Management Resource Guide, Vol. 4: Western U. S. 4th ed. 3300p. 1993. Vol. 4: Western U.S. pap. 60.00 (*1-880874-09-1*) Ctr CHI.

O'Grady, Kieran G., jt. auth. see Morgan, John W.

***O'Grady, Lauren.** Sunrise. 260p. 1996. pap. 8.95 (*0-7610-0465-3*) NW Pub.

***O'Grady, Lois F.** A Practical Approach to Breast Cancer. LC 94-26205. 1994. 49.95 (*0-316-63377-1*) Little.

O'Grady, O. M. The Beasts of the Apocalypse: Two Thousand Years of Jewish History. 1991. lib. bdg. 62.00 (*0-8490-4461-8*) Gordon Pr.

O'Grady, Pat B. The Poverty Survival Handbook. LC 86-62681. (Illus.). 72p. (Orig.). 1986. pap. 5.00 (*0-9601846-3-5*) PM Ent.

O'Grady, Patricia. A Recipe for Happy Days. (Illus.). 65p. (Orig.). 1982. pap. 4.25 (*0-9601846-2-7*) PM Ent.

O'Grady, Patrick. The Politics of Dancing. abr. ed. 380p. 1995. pap. 9.95 (*1-56901-433-7*) NW Pub.

O'Grady, Paul. Henry the Eighth & the Conforming Catholics. 186p. (C). 1990. pap. 11.95 (*0-8146-5781-8*) Liturgical Pr.

O'Grady, Rohan. Curse of the Montrolfes. 230p. 1983. reprint ed. 22.00 (*0-933256-43-4*) Second Chance.

O'Grady, Ron. Bread & Freedom: Understanding & Acting on Human Rights. LC 81-470289. (Risk Book Ser.: No. 4). (Illus.). 87p. reprint ed. pap. 25.00 (*0-7837-5996-7*, 2045806) Bks Demand.

— Tourism in the Third World: Christian Reflections. LC 82-8227. 91p. (Orig.). reprint ed. pap. 26.00 (*0-8357-4076-5*, 2036766) Bks Demand.

O'Grady, Ron, jt. auth. see Takenaka, Masao.

O'Grady, Standish. Bog of Stars, & Other Stories & Sketches of Elizabethan Ireland. LC 74-125234. (Short Story Index Reprint Ser.). 1977. 16.95 (*0-8369-3601-9*) Ayer.

O'Grady, Standish J. The Flight of the Eagle. LC 79-8428. reprint ed. 44.50 (*0-404-62078-7*) AMS Pr.

O'Grady, Terence J. The Beatles: A Musical Revolution. LC 82-21288. (Music Ser.). (Illus.). 208p. 1983. text ed. 20.95 (*0-8057-9453-0*, Twayne) Macmillan.

***O'Grady, Tom.** Carvings of the Moon: A Cycle of Poems. 16p. (Orig.). 1992. pap. 9.95 (*0-940475-00-6*) Dolphin-Moon.

— In the Room of the Just Born. 72p. (Orig.). 1989. pap. 7.95 (*0-940475-89-8*) Dolphin-Moon.

— Shaking the Tree: A Book of Works & Days. (Illus.). 197p. (Orig.). 1993. pap. 10.95 (*0-614-05294-7*) Dolphin-Moon.

O'Grady, Tom, intro. The Hampden-Sydney Poetry Review Anthology (1975-1990) 328p. (Orig.). 1990. pap. 12.95 (*0-940475-91-X*) Dolphin-Moon.

O'Grady, Tom, tr. see Seifert, Jaroslav.

O'Grady, W. E., ed. see Electrocatalysis of Fuel Cell Reactions Workshop Staff.

O'Grady, William. Categories & Case: The Sentence Structure of Korean. LC 90-42137. (Current Issues in Linguistic Theory Ser.: Vol. 71). vii, 294p. 1990. 65.00x (*1-55619-127-8*) Benjamins North Am.

— Principles of Grammar & Learning. LC 86-11402. 248p. (C). 1987. 27.50 (*0-226-62074-3*) U Ch Pr.

O'Grady, William, et al. Contemporary Linguistics: An Introduction. 2nd ed. LC 92-50040. 492p. (Orig.). (C). 1993. pap. text ed. 24.50 (*0-312-06780-1*) St Martin.

Ogram, Ernest W. The Emerging Pattern of the Multinational Corporation. LC 65-64947. (Georgia State University College of Business Administration Research Monograph Ser.: No. 31). 39p. reprint ed. pap. 25.00 (*0-317-28484-3*, 2019054) Bks Demand.

Ogren, Kathy J. The Jazz Revolution: Twenties America & the Meaning of Jazz. (Illus.). 232p. 1992. pap. 11.95 (*0-19-507479-3*) OUP.

Ogretir, Cemil & Csizmadia, Imre G., eds. Computational Advances in Organic Chemistry: Molecular Structure & Reactivity. (NATO Advanced Science Institutes Series C: Mathematical & Physical Sciences). 432p. 1991. lib. bdg. 144.00 (*0-7923-1064-0*) Kluwer Ac.

Ogrin, Dusan. A World Heritage of Gardens. LC 93-60427. (Illus.). 396p. 1993. 40.00 (*0-500-23666-6*) Thames Hudson.

O'Griofa, Mairtin. Irish Folk Wisdom. LC 92-45750. (Illus.). 128p. 1994. pap. 5.95 (*0-8069-0379-1*) Sterling.

An Asterisk (*) at the beginning of an entry indicates that the title is appearing in BIP for the first time.

O'Griofa, Mairtin, ed. Celtic Tales of Terror. LC 94-3394. 144p. 1994. pap. 5.95 (*0-8069-0868-8*, Sterling-Main St) Sterling.
— Famous Irish Ghost Stories. LC 93-44263. (Illus.). 144p. 1994. pap. 5.95 (*0-8069-0708-8*, Sterling-Main St) Sterling.
— The Leprechaun Book. LC 94-26080. 128p. 1994. pap. 5.95 (*0-8069-0829-7*) Sterling.
Ogrizek, Dore, ed. Winter Book of Switzerland. (Illus.). 383p. 1957. 5.00 (*0-686-75372-0*) Bookfinger.
Ogrizovich, Dorothy M., ed. Sins & Secrets. 115p. (Orig.). (C). 1994. pap. 6.95 (*0-9639229-0-4*) Plautz Enter.
*__Ogrodzki, Jan.__ Circuit Simulation Methods & Algorithms. 496p. 1994. 69.95 (*0-8493-7894-X*, 7894) CRC Pr.
Ogston, D. & Bennett, B., eds. Haemostasis: Biochemistry, Physiology, & Pathology. LC 76-44231. 539p. reprint ed. pap. 153.70 (*0-317-55729-7*, 2029270) Bks Demand.
Ogston, Derek. Antifibrinolytic Drugs: Chemistry, Pharmacology, & Clinical Usage. LC 84-13099. (Wiley-Medical Publication Ser.). (Illus.). 194p. reprint ed. pap. 55.30 (*0-8357-8642-0*, 2035066) Bks Demand.
— The Physiology of Hemostasis. (Illus.). 390p. (C). 1983. 42.50 (*0-674-66660-7*) HUP.
— Venous Thrombosis: Causation & Prediction. LC 87-8146. (Wiley-Medical Publication Ser.). 258p. reprint ed. pap. 73.60 (*0-8357-3473-0*, 2039735) Bks Demand.
Ogston, R., jt. auth. see Harty, F. J.
*__Ogu, Lawrence.__ Echi's Steps to Solve World Problems. 1995. 9.95 (*0-8062-5302-9*) Carlton.
Oguchi, Hakuro. Rarefied Gas Dynamics, 2 vols., Set. 1130p. 1985. 165.00 (*0-86008-383-7*, Pub. by U of Tokyo JA) Col U Pr.
Oguchi, T., et al, eds. Electronic Properties & Mechanisms of High TC Superconductors: Proceedings of the International Workshop on Electronic Properties & Mechanisms of High TC Superconductors, Tsukuba, Japan, 29-31 July 1991. LC 92-14448. 1992. write for info. (*0-444-89345-8*, North Holland) Elsevier.
*__Oguhebe, Festus S.__ The "How to Write" Book. (YA). Date not set. write for info. (*0-9636510-0-5*); pap. write for info. (*0-9636510-1-3*) Hebes Intl.
O'Guiheen, Michael. A Pity Youth Does Not Last: Reminiscences of the Last of the Great Blasket Island's Poets & Storytellers. Enright, Tim, tr. (Paperbacks Ser.). (Illus.). 160p. 1982. pap. 9.95 (*0-19-281320-X*) OUP.
O'Guin, C. M. Basic Homelitical Studies. 127p. 1967. pap. 5.95 (*1-882449-16-9*) Messenger Pub.
Oguin, Michael. Activity Based Costing. 1991. 69.95 (*0-13-853318-0*, Busn) P-H.
Ogul, Morris S. Congress Oversees the Bureaucracy: Studies in Legislative Supervision. LC 75-33546. 250p. (C). 1976. pap. 15.95 (*0-8229-5288-2*) U of Pittsburgh Pr.
Ogul, Morris S., jt. auth. see Keefe, William J.
Ogumbi, O., ed. see International Conference GIAM Staff.
Ogumefu, M. I. Yoruba Legends. LC 78-63217. (Folktale Ser.). 96p. 1985. reprint ed. 20.00 (*0-404-16153-7*) AMS Pr.
*__Ogun, Funmi.__ Bobo & the Greedy Tito. (Illus.). 16p. (Orig.). (J). 1994. pap. 14.95 (*1-882188-09-8*) Magnolia Mktg.
*__Ogunade, Taiwo.__ Igbo Wise Sayings, Ibo Proverbs & Greetings. 46p. 1995. lib. bdg. 4.95 (*1-881549-06-2*) Oluweri Pubns.
— Jeffries, Putting Fire into Whities Ass. 150p. 1995. lib. bdg. 12.50 (*1-881549-09-7*) Oluweri Pubns.
— Nigerian Musical Styles, Africa's Rhythm of Unity. LC 92-90729. 78p. 1991. lib. bdg. 11.95 (*1-881549-01-1*) Oluweri Pubns.
— This Side of Harlem, Short Stories about Us. 85p. 1995. lib. bdg. 4.95 (*1-881549-08-9*) Oluweri Pubns.
*__Ogunade, Taiyewo.__ Asose Aworo Onile, a Yoruba Fortune Teller (English) 4p. 1992. 3.50 (*1-881549-00-3*) Oluweri Pubns.
— Asose Aworo Onile, Oraculo Yoruba. 4p. (SPA.). 1992. 3.50 (*1-881549-02-X*) Oluweri Pubns.
— Yoruba Religious Worship, Traditional God Worship, Belief & Practice. LC 92-91208. 182p. 1995. lib. bdg. 19.95 (*1-881549-03-8*) Oluweri Pubns.
Ogunbadejo, Oye. The International Politics of Africa's Strategic Minerals. LC 85-951. (Contributions in Afro-American & African Studies: No. 88). ix, 213p. 1985. text ed. 49.95 (*0-313-24803-6*, OGI/, Greenwood Pr) Greenwood.
*__Ogundijo, Bayo, ed.__ Yoruba Popular Theatre: Three Plays by the Oyin Adejobi Company. Barter, Karin, tr. LC 94-29997. 1994. 35.00 (*0-918456-70-3*) African Studies Assn.
Ogundipe, Femi, ed. see Onuzo, Okey.
Ogundipe-Leslie, Molara. Re-Creating Ourselves: African Women & Critical Transformations. LC 93-43967. 250p. 1994. 49.95 (*0-86543-411-5*); pap. 16.95 (*0-86543-412-3*) Africa World.
Ogundipe-Leslie, Molara, jt. ed. see Davies, Carole B.
Ogungbesan, Kolawole. The Writing of Peter Abrahams. LC 78-26133. 156p. (C). 1979. 29.50 (*0-8419-0472-3*, Africana); 17.50 (*0-8419-0480-4*, Africana) Holmes & Meier.
Ogunnaike, Babatund A., jt. auth. see Ray, Harmon.
*__Ogunnaike, Babatunde A. & Ray, W. Harmon.__ Process Dynamics, Modeling, & Control. (Topics in Chemical Engineering Ser.). (Illus.). 1280p. (C). 1994. text ed. 79.95 (*0-19-509119-1*) OUP.
Ogunremi, G. O. The Counting the Camels: The Economics of Transportation in Pre-Industrial Nigeria. LC 79-88989. (Illus.). 1982. 21.50 (*0-88357-092-0*) NOK Pubs.
Ogunsanwo, Alaba. China's Policy in Africa, Nineteen Fifty-Eight to Nineteen Seventy-One. LC 72-89810. (International Studies). 329p. reprint ed. pap. 93.80 (*0-317-27987-4*, 2025593) Bks Demand.
Oguntoyinbo, J., jt. auth. see Hayward, D.
Oguntoyinbo, J. S., et al. Nigeria in Maps. Barbour, K. M. et al, eds. 160p. 1982. 49.50 (*0-8419-0763-3*) Holmes & Meier.
*__Ogunyemi, Chikwenye O.__ Africa Wo/Man Palava: The Nigerian Novel by Women. (Women in Culture & Society Ser.). 336p. 1995. 37.50 (*0-226-62084-0*); pap. 15.95 (*0-226-62085-9*) U Ch Pr.
Ogura, F. & Aso, Y. Design of Novel Chalcogen-Containing Organic Metals: Extensively Conjugated Electron Donors & Acceptors with Reduced On-site Coulomb Repulsion. (Sulfur Report Ser.). 1992. pap. text ed. 99.00 (*3-7186-5295-1*) Gordon & Breach.
Ogura, Haruo, et al, eds. Carbohydrates: Synthetic Methods & Applications in Medicinal Chemistry. LC 92-49258. 408p. 1993. 140.00 (*1-56081-701-1*) VCH Pubs.
Ogura, K., jt. ed. see Okimura, H.
Ogura, Takeshi, jt. ed. see Takaku, Fumimaro.
Ogura, Y. & Kisara, K. Trends in Pharmacological Research on Platelet Activating Factor (PAF) in Japan. (Illus.). 208p. 1988. 28.00 (*0-912791-67-5*) Ishiyaku Euro.
Ogura, Yasuyuki, jt. photos see Anzai, Shigeo.
Oguro, Y., jt. ed. see Joffe, S. N.
Oguro, Yanao & Takagi, Kunio, eds. Endoscopic Approaches to Cancer Diagnosis & Treatment. (Gann Monograph on Cancer Research Ser.: No. 37). 172p. 1990. 125.00 (*0-7484-0016-8*, Pub. by Tay Francis Ltd UK) Taylor & Francis.
Ogus, A. I. & Barendt, E. M. The Law of Social Security. 3rd ed. 1988. 124.00 (*0-406-63372-X*); pap. 61.00 (*0-406-63370-3*) Butterworth Legal Pubs.
— The Law of Social Security. 3rd suppl. ed. 1991. Latest suppl. 1991. 20.00 (*0-406-00189-8*, U.K.) Butterworth Legal Pubs.
Ogus, Anthony I. Regulation: Legal Form & Economic Theory. (Clarendon Law Ser.). 350p. 1994. 65.00 (*0-19-825443-1*); pap. 29.95 (*0-19-825934-4*) OUP.
Ogus, Arthur, jt. auth. see Berthelot, Pierre.
Ogus, Hugh D. & Toller, Paul A. Common Disorders of the Temporomandibular Joint. 2nd ed. (Dental Practitioners' Handbook Ser.: No. 26). (Illus.). 123p. 1986. 37.50 (*0-7236-0874-1*) Buttrwrth-Heinemann.
Ogut, A., jt. ed. see Rohatgi, U. S.
Oh, Bonnie B., ed. see Spence, Jonathan D., et al.
Oh, Jae K., et al. The Echo Manual. (Illus.). 336p. 1993. 85.00 (*0-316-63374-7*) Little.
Oh, Jai K., ed. see Gold, Joseph.
Oh, John. International Financial Management: Problems, Issues & Experiences. Altman, Edward I. & Walter, Ingo, eds. LC 81-81655. (Contemporary Studies in Economic & Financial Analysis: Vol. 34). 300p. 1981. 73.25 (*0-89232-228-4*) Jai Pr.
Oh, Kongdan, jt. auth. see Fukuyama, Francis.
Oh, Kook S., et al. Practical Gamuts & Differential Diagnosis in Pediatric Radiology. LC 81-19832. 243p. reprint ed. pap. 69.30 (*0-8357-7597-6*, 2056918) Bks Demand.
Oh, Lin. Fitness for the Busy Executive in Only Ten Minutes a Day: A Lifetime Program to Stay in Shape for Your Best Top Level Performance. (Life Management Ser.). 1994. 14.95 (*0-89896-247-1*) Larksdale.
— Stock Pickers, Pocket Pickers: How to Invest in Wall Street. Williamson, Mary M., ed. 160p. (Orig.). 1993. pap. 14.95 (*0-89896-201-3*, Better Life Bks) Larksdale.
Oh, S. Prevention of Head Injuries in Skiing. (Illus.). viii, 164p. 1985. pap. 39.25 (*3-8055-3978-9*) S Karger.
Oh, Shin J. Clinical Electromyography: Nerve Conduction Studies. 2nd ed. LC 92-48896. (Illus.). 720p. 1993. 120.00 (*0-683-06644-7*) Williams & Wilkins.
Oh, Teik E. Intensive Care Manual. 3rd ed. 700p. 1990. pap. text ed. 49.95 (*0-409-30170-1*) Buttrwrth-Heinemann.
Oh, Timothy T., jt. ed. see Schmitz, Robert L.
Oh, William, jt. auth. see Tsang, Reginald.
*__Oh, Yisok.__ Microwave Polarimetric Backscattering from Natural Rough Surfaces. fac. ed. (University of Michigan Report: No. RL904). 249p. 1994. pap. 71.00 (*0-7837-7699-3*, 2047456) Bks Demand.
Ohadike, Don C. Animoa: A Social History of the Western Igbo People. LC 93-31029. (Illus.). 272p. (C). 1994. text ed. 39.95 (*0-8214-1072-5*); pap. text ed. 17.95 (*0-8214-1073-3*) Ohio U Pr.
— The Ekumeku Movement: Western Igbo Resistance to the British Conquest of Nigeria, 1883-1914. LC 90-23998. (Illus.). 215p. (C). 1991. text ed. 29.95 (*0-8214-0985-9*) Ohio U Pr.
— The Ekumeku Movement: Western Igbo Resistance to the British Conquest of Nigeria, 1883-1914. LC 90-23998. 215p. (C). 1991. reprint ed. pap. text ed. 16.95 (*0-8214-0992-1*) Ohio U Pr.
Ohaegbulam, Festus U. Towards an Understanding of the African Experience from Historical & Contemporary Perspectives. 298p. (Orig.). (C). 1990. lib. bdg. 47.00 (*0-8191-7940-X*) U Pr of Amer.
O'Hagan. Benediction at the Savoia. 1992. 21.95 (*0-15-111810-8*) HarBrace.
— Trees Are Lonely Company. (NFS Canada Ser.). 1994. pap. 15.95 (*0-88922-327-0*, Pub. by Talonbooks CN) InBook.
*__O'Hagan, Anthony.__ Kendall's Advanced Theory of Statistics: Bayesian Inference, Vol. 2. (Kendall's Advanced Theory of Statistics: 2). 1994. text ed. 59.95 (*0-470-23381-8*) Wiley.
— Probability: Methods & Measurements. 300p. 1988. text ed. 65.00 (*0-412-29530-X*); pap. text ed. 30.00 (*0-412-29540-7*) Chapman & Hall.
O'Hagan, David. The Polyketides Metabolites. 250p. 1991. text ed. 99.00 (*0-13-683269-5*) P-H.
O'Hagan, Derek T., ed. Novel Delivery Systems for Oral Vaccines. LC 93-40167. 288p. 1994. 169.95 (*0-8493-4866-8*, 4866) CRC Pr.
O'Hagan, James P., ed. Growth & Adjustment in National Agricultures: Four Case Studies & an Overview. LC 77-84411. 200p. 1978. text ed. 38.50 (*0-916672-90-5*) Rowman.
O'Hagan, John T. High Rise Fire & Life Safety. (Illus.). 1977. 22.00 (*0-912212-08-X*) Fire Eng.
O'Hagan, Kieran. Emotional & Psychological Abuse of Children. LC 92-23834. 160p. (C). 1992. 88.00 (*0-335-09889-4*); pap. 32.50 (*0-335-09884-3*) U of Toronto Pr.
— Emotional & Psychological Abuse of Children. LC 92-23834. 167p. 1993. pap. 19.95 (*0-8020-7446-4*) U of Toronto Pr.
— Working with Child Sexual Abuse: A Post-Cleveland Guide to Effective Principles & Practice. 192p. 1989. 90.00 (*0-335-15598-7*, Open Univ Pr); pap. 32.00 (*0-335-15597-9*, Open Univ Pr) Taylor & Francis.
*__O'Hagan, Kieran & Dillenburger, Karola.__ The Abuse of Women in Childcare Work. LC 95-3097. 160p. 1995. 79.00 (*0-335-19261-0*, Open Univ Pr); pap. 24.95 (*0-335-19260-2*, Open Univ Pr) Taylor & Francis.
O'Hagan, Michael. Guide to the General Budget of the Commission of the European Communities, 1989: And the Other Community Institutions. 224p. 1989. pap. text ed. 129.95 (*1-85521-043-6*, Pub. by Dartmth Pub UK) Ashgate Pub Co.
O'Hagan, Robert E., jt. auth. see Besterfield, Dale H.
O'Hagan, Thomas. Essays on Catholic Life. LC 67-22106. (Essay Index Reprint Ser.). 1977. 19.95 (*0-8369-1333-7*) Ayer.
O'Hagan, Timothy. Revolution & Enlightenment in Europe. (Enlightenment Rights & Revolution Ser.). 160p. 1991. pap. 37.90 (*0-08-040920-2*, Pub. by Aberdeen U Pr) Macmillan.
O'Hagan, Timothy, tr. see Poulantzas, Nicos.
O'Hair, Dan & Kreps, Gary L., eds. Applied Communication Theory & Research. 392p. (C). 1990. text ed. 79.95 (*0-8058-0400-5*); pap. 39.95 (*0-8058-0915-5*) L Erlbaum Assocs.
O'Hair, Dan, jt. ed. see Kreps, Gary L.
*__O'Hair, Dan, et al.__ Competent Communication. 512p. 1995. pap. text ed. 30.59 (*0-312-04057-1*) St Martin.
O'Hair, Henry D. & Friedrich, Gustav. Strategic Communication in Business & the Professions. (C). 1991. pap. 30.36 (*0-395-51539-4*) HM.
O'Hair, J. Millions Now Dying Will Never Live: A Scriptural Investigation of Russellism As Propagated by the International Bible Students. 22p. 1988. reprint ed. pap. 1.95 (*1-883858-52-6*) Witness CA.
O'Hair, J. S., et al. Australian Company Law. LC 85-226602. 1984. write for info. (*0-07-452033-4*) McGraw.
O'Hair, Madalyn. All about Atheists. LC 87-30815. (American Atheist Radio Ser.: Vol. 3). 407p. (Orig.). 1988. pap. 8.00 (*0-910309-44-2*, 5097) Am Atheist.
— Atheist Epic. 2nd ed. LC 89-28711. 302p. 1989. pap. 10.00 (*0-910309-89-2*, 5376) Am Atheist.
— An Atheist Speaks. (American Atheist Radio Ser.: Vol. 2). 322p. (Orig.). 1986. pap. 8.00 (*0-910309-27-2*, 5098) Am Atheist.
— The Atheist World. LC 91-22920. (American Atheist Radio Ser.: Vol. 5). 358p. (Orig.). 1991. pap. 8.00 (*0-910309-69-8*, 5094) Am Atheist.
— Atheists: The Last Minority. LC 90-41448. 24p. (Orig.). 1990. 3.00 (*0-910309-66-3*, 5402) Am Atheist.
— Atheists: Their Dilemma. 11p. (Orig.). 1993. pap. 3.00 (*0-910309-73-6*, 5408) Am Atheist.
— O'Hair on Prayer. 12p. (Orig.). 1980. 1.00 (*0-910309-30-2*) Am Atheist.
— Our Constitution: The Way It Was. rev. ed. 70p. 1988. 4.00 (*0-910309-41-8*, 5400) Am Atheist.
— Why I Am an Atheist, Including a History of Materialism. 2nd rev. ed. LC 91-26426. 56p. 1991. pap. 6.00 (*0-910309-98-1*, 5416) Am Atheist.
O'Hair, Madalyn, jt. auth. see Murray, Jon.
O'Hair, Madalyn M. Atheist Heroes & Heroines. LC 91-42408. (American Atheist Radio Ser.: Vol. 4). 370p. (Orig.). 1992. pap. 8.00 (*0-910309-57-4*, 5414) Am Atheist.
— Atheist Magazines: A Sampling, 1927-1970. LC 72-171441. (Atheist Viewpoint Ser.). 554p. 1978. reprint ed. 41.95 (*0-405-03812-7*) Ayer.
— Atheist Primer: Did You Know All the Gods Came from the Same Place? (Illus.). 30p. (Orig.). (J). (gr. 2-4). 1978. 4.00 (*0-911826-10-6*, 5372) Am Atheist.
— What on Earth Is an Atheist! LC 71-88701. (Fifty-Two Programs from the American Atheist Radio Ser.). 288p. 1969. pap. 8.00 (*0-911826-00-9*, 5412) Am Atheist.
— What on Earth Is an Atheist. LC 74-161339. (Atheist Viewpoint Ser.). 288p. 1976. reprint ed. 20.95 (*0-405-03802-X*) Ayer.
— Women & Atheism: The Ultimate Liberation. 26p. 1979. 3.50 (*0-911826-17-3*, 5420) Am Atheist.
O'Hair, Madalyn M., ed. The Atheist Viewpoint, 25 bks., Set. 1972. 498.00 (*0-405-03620-5*) Ayer.
O'Hair, Mary & Odell, Sandra J. Diversity & Teaching. 320p. (C). 1993. pap. text ed. write for info. (*0-15-500498-0*) HB Coll Pubs.
O'Hair, Mary J. & Odell, Sandra J., eds. Diversity & Teaching: Teacher Education Yearbook I. 1993. pap. 18.75 (*0-685-74809-X*) Assn Tchr Ed.
— Educating Teachers for Leadership & Change: Teacher Education Yearbook III. (ATE Yearbook Ser.: Vol. 3). 416p. 1995. 50.00 (*0-8039-6216-9*) Corwin Pr.
— Educating Teachers for Leadership & Change: Teacher Education Yearbook III. (ATE Yearbook: Vol. 3). 416p. 1995. pap. 25.00 (*0-8039-6217-7*) Corwin Pr.
O'Hair, Michael T., ed. see Engineering Technology Centennial Committee.
O'Haire, Daniel, jt. auth. see Connor, Cathy.
Ohajunwa, Emeka. India-U. S. Security Relations, 1947-1990. (C). 1992. 18.00 (*81-7001-090-X*, Pub. by Chanakya II) S Asia.
Ohala, John J. & Jaeger, Jeri J. Experimental Phonology. 1986. text ed. 79.00 (*0-12-524940-3*); pap. text ed. 44.00 (*0-12-524941-1*) Acad Pr.
Ohalla, N. S., ed. Methods in Studying Cardiac Membranes, Vol. I. 1984. 156.00 (*0-8493-5995-3*, QP114, CRC Reprint) Franklin.
O'Halloran, Aideen, jt. auth. see Cohen, Robert.
O'Halloran, D., et al, eds. Geological & Landscape Conservation: Proceedings of the Malvern International Conference, 1993. (Illus.). 544p. 1994. 117.00 (*1-897799-09-8*, Pub. by Geol Soc Pub Hse UK) AAPG.
O'Halloran, James. Signs of Hope: Developing Small Christian Communities. LC 90-46180. 1991. pap. 9.95 (*0-88344-730-4*) Orbis Bks.
O'Halloran, Kerry. Adoption in the Two Jurisdictions of Ireland: A Comparative Study. 256p. 1994. 59.95 (*1-85628-904-4*, Pub. by Avebury Pub UK) Ashgate Pub Co.
O'Halloran, M. Sean. Focus on Eating Disorders. (Teenage Perspectives Ser.). 297p. 1993. lib. bdg. 39.50 (*0-87436-692-5*) ABC-CLIO.
*__O'Halloran, Maura.__ Pure Heart, Enlightened Mind: The Zen Journal & Letters of Maura "Shoshin" O'Halloran. 1995. 13.00 (*1-57322-503-7*) Riverhead Bks.
O'Halloran, Maura S. Pure Heart, Enlightened Mind: The Zen Journal & Letters of Maura Soshin O'Halloran. (Illus.). 192p. (Orig.). 1994. pap. 18.00 (*0-8048-1977-7*) C E Tuttle.
O'Halloran, Sharyn. Politics, Process & American Trade Policy. 200p. 1994. text ed. 39.50x (*0-472-10516-7*) U of Mich Pr.
*__O'Halloran, Susan.__ The Hunt for Spring. (Illus.). 32p. (J). (gr. k-3). 1995. pap. 4.50 (*0-87406-740-5*) Willowisp Pr.
O'Halloran, Susan & Delattre, Susan. The Woman Who Lost Her Heart: A Tale of ReAwakening. Butler, Ruth, ed. LC 92-8661. (Women's Ser.). (Illus.). 96p. (Orig.). 1992. pap. 10.95 (*0-931055-91-1*) LuraMedia.
O'Halloran, Terence P. Mountains out of Molehills. 250p. (C). 1993. 95.00 (*1-85609-048-5*, Pub. by Witherby & Co UK) St Mut.
— You Sign. 100p. 1992. 75.00 (*1-85609-038-8*, Pub. by Witherby & Co UK) St Mut.
O'Halloran, Tim. Know Your Numbers. (Illus.). 38p. (J). (ps-1). 1983. 10.95 (*0-88625-045-5*) Durkin Hayes Pub.
— Words Around Us. (Illus.). 48p. (J). (ps-00). 1985. 10.95 (*0-88625-124-9*) Durkin Hayes Pub.
— Words Around Us in French. (Illus.). 48p. (FRE.). (J). (ps-00). 1985. 10.95 (*0-88625-125-7*) Durkin Hayes Pub.
O'Halpin, Eunan. The Decline of the Union: British Government in Ireland, 1892-1920. (Irish Studies). (Illus.). 260p. (C). 1988. text ed. 33.00 (*0-8156-2425-5*) Syracuse U Pr.
Ohama, Gary. Determining Your First Step to Success. 48p. 1988. pap. 2.95 (*0-88144-119-8*) Christian Pub.
Ohama, Yoshihiko. Handbook of Polymer-Modified Mortars & Concrete: Properties & Process Technology. LC 94-15235. (Illus.). 236p. 1995. 64.00 (*0-8155-1358-5*) Noyes.
Ohanesian, C., jt. auth. see White, P.
Ohanesian, Consuelo, jt. auth. see White, Pauline.
*__Ohanesian, Diane.__ Benjamin's Beach Trip. LC 95-61142. (Illus.). 24p. (Orig.). (J). Date not set. pap. write for info. (*0-9641089-3-3*) VanderWyk & Burnham.
— Let's Pretend Bunny. (Playtime Pals Ser.). (Illus.). 12p. (J). (ps). 1993. Incl. bunny. bds. 9.95 (*0-89577-451-8*, Random) RD Assn.
— Let's Pretend Teddy. (Playtime Pals Board Book Ser.). (Illus.). 12p. (J). (ps). 1992. boxed 9.95 (*0-89577-450-X*, Random) RD Assn.
— Oh, No, Simon! LC 95-61144. (Illus.). 24p. (Orig.). (J). Date not set. pap. write for info. (*0-9641089-5-X*) VanderWyk & Burnham.
— Penny's Quilt. LC 95-61143. (Illus.). 24p. (Orig.). (J). Date not set. pap. write for info. (*0-9641089-4-1*) VanderWyk & Burnham.
Ohanian, C. M. The Vegetarian Traveler's Guide to North America. 80p. 1993. pap. 8.95 (*1-883138-00-0*) Cold Sprng.
Ohanian, Edward J. What Price Mink? (Illus.). 240p. (Orig.). 1983. pap. 9.95 (*0-317-13105-2*) Ohanian.
Ohanian, Hans C. Modern Physics. (Illus.). 640p. (C). 1986. text ed. 72.00 (*0-13-596123-8*) P-H.
— Modern Physics. 2nd ed. LC 94-38687. 1995. text ed. 70.00 (*0-13-124439-6*) P-H.
— Physics, 1. (C). 1989. text ed. 41.95 (*0-393-95748-9*) Norton.
— Physics, 2. (C). 1989. text ed. 57.95 (*0-393-95750-0*); text ed. 41.95 (*0-393-95786-1*) Norton.
— Physics, Vols. I & II. (C). 1985. Solutions manual. teacher ed write for info. (*0-318-58340-2*); Tranparencies. trans. write for info. (*0-318-58341-0*) Norton.
— Physics, Vols. I & II. (C). 1989. student ed, pap. text ed. 18.95 (*0-393-95752-7*) Norton.
— Physics, Vols. I & II. (C). 1989. Transparencies. student ed, trans. write for info. (*0-393-95763-2*) Norton.
— Physics, Vols. I & II. (C). 1990. Solutions manual. student ed, teacher ed write for info. (*0-393-95754-3*) Norton.
— Physics, Vols. I & II. (C). 1990. Answer key. student ed, pap. text ed. 4.95 (*0-393-95756-X*) Norton.
— Physics, Vols. I & II. 2nd ed. (C). 1989. text ed. 55.95 (*0-393-95746-2*) Norton.
— The Principles of Physics. (C). 1994. pap. text ed. 69.95 (*0-393-95773-X*); pap. text ed. 21.95 (*0-393-95780-2*) Norton.
— The Principles of Physics. (C). 1994. pap. text ed. write for info. (*0-393-96336-5*); write for info. (*0-318-69460-3*) Norton.

O

An Asterisk (*) at the beginning of an entry indicates that the title is appearing in BIP for the first time.

— Principles of Quantum Mechanics. 384p. (C). 1989. Casebound. text ed. 72.00 (*0-13-712795-2*) P-H.

Ohanian, Hans C. & Rufkin, Reno. Gravitation & Spacetime. 2nd ed. LC 93-34408. (Illus.). 500p. (C). 1994. text ed. 49.95x (*0-393-96501-5*) Norton.

Ohanian, Nancy K. The American Pulp & Paper Industry, 1900-1940: Mill Survival, Firm Structure, & Industry Relocation. LC 92-18362. (Contributions in Economics & Economic History Ser.: No. 140). 240p. 1993. text ed. 52.95 (*0-313-27366-9*, KPJ, Greenwood Pr) Greenwood.

Ohanian, Susan. All about Bears. LC 93-28988. (Illus.). (J). 1994. 4.25 (*0-383-03735-2*) SRA Schl Grp.

— From Pumpkin Time to Valentines: Sneaking Language Arts Strategies into Holiday Celebrations. 120p. 1994. pap. 17.50 (*1-56308-171-7*) Teacher Ideas Pr.

— Garbage Pizza, Patchwork Quilts, & Math Magic: Stories About Teachers Who Love to Teach & Children Who Love to Learn. LC 92-26094. 1995. text ed. write for info. (*0-7167-2360-3*) W H Freeman.

O'Hanian, Susan. Garbage Pizzas, Patchwork Quilts & Math Magic: Stories about Teachers Who Love to Teach. 256p. 1995. pap. text ed. 10.95 (*0-7167-2584-3*) W H Freeman.

***Ohanian, Susan.** Math at A Glance: A Month-by-Month Celebration of the Numbers Around Us. LC 94-46723. 115p. 1995. pap. 13.95 (*0-435-08364-3*, 08364) Heinemann.

— Who's in Charge? A Teacher Speaks Her Mind. LC 94-5586. 352p. 1994. pap. 19.95 (*0-86709-339-0*) Boynton Cook Pubs.

— Wolves. LC 93-28973. (Voyages Ser.). (Illus.). (J). 1994. 4.25 (*0-383-03742-5*) SRA Schl Grp.

Ohanian, Thomas A. Digital Nonlinear Editing: New Approaches to Editing Film & Video. LC 92-32378. (Illus.). 304p. 1993. 49.95 (*0-240-80175-X*, Focal) Buttrwrth-Heinemann.

O'Hanlan, Katherine, jt. auth. see Perry, Susan.

O'Hanlan, Katherine A., jt. auth. see Perry, Susan.

***O'Hanley, David S.** Serpentinites: Recorders of Tectonic & Petrological History. (Oxford Monographs on Geology & Geophysics: No. 34). (Illus.). 256p. 1995. 89.95 (*0-19-508254-0*) OUP.

O'Hanlon, Alvin M. Reflections, Sharing Thoughts: One-on-One. LC 86-61409. 1986. 17.50 (*0-9616898-0-3*) Phoenix Pr FL.

O'Hanlon, Bill & Hudson, Pat. Love Is A Verb: How to Stop Analyzing Your Relationship, Start Making It Great! 160p. 1995. 19.95 (*0-393-03734-7*) Norton.

O'Hanlon, Bill & Wilk, James. Shifting Contexts: The Generation of Effective Psychotherapy. LC 86-26986. 289p. 1987. lib. bdg. 33.00 (*0-89862-677-3*) Guilford Pr.

O'Hanlon, Christine. Special Education Integration in Europe. 192p. 1993. pap. 32.00 (*1-85346-236-5*, Pub. by D Fulton UK) Taylor & Francis.

O'Hanlon, Daniel P., tr. Macer's Virtue of Herbs. Orig. Title: Macer Floridus De Viribus Herbarum. 125p. (C). 10.00 (*0-89744-243-1*) Auromere.

O'Hanlon, Gerard F. The Immutability of God in the Theology of Hans Urs von Balthasar. 246p. (C). 1990. 64.95 (*0-521-36649-6*) Cambridge U Pr.

O'Hanlon, J. F., jt. ed. see De Gier, J. J.

O'Hanlon, John F. A User's Guide to Vacuum Technology. 2nd ed. 481p. 1989. text ed. 69.95 (*0-471-81242-0*) Wiley.

***O'Hanlon, Joseph.** Beginning the Bible. 122p. 1994. pap. 29.00 (*0-85439-496-6*, Pub. by St Paul Pubns UK) St Mut.

— The Dance of the Merrymakers. 255p. (C). 1990. 39.00 (*0-85439-331-5*, Pub. by St Paul Pubns UK) St Mut.

— Mark My Words. 316p. 1994. pap. 39.00 (*0-85439-472-9*, Pub. by St Paul Pubns UK) St Mut.

O'Hanlon, Lynne. Introduction to Computer Programming Logic. 720p. (C). 1992. spiral bd. 35.16 (*0-8403-7840-8*) Kendall-Hunt.

***O'Hanlon, Michael.** Defense Planning for the Late 1990's: Beyond the Desert Storm Framework. 150p. (C). 1995. pap. 12.95x (*0-8157-6449-9*) Brookings.

— Reading the Skin: Adornment, Display & Society among the Wahgi. (Illus.). 164p. 1989. 44.95 (*0-7141-1596-7*, Pub. by British Mus Pubns UK) U of Pa Pr.

O'Hanlon, Michael, jt. ed. see Hirsch, Eric.

O'Hanlon, Michael E. The Art of War in the Age of Peace: U. S. Military Posture for the Post-Cold War World. LC 91-47086. 176p. 1992. text ed. 45.00 (*0-275-94259-7*, C4259, Praeger Pubs) Greenwood.

***O'Hanlon, Michael E., et al.** Enhancing U.S. Security Through Foreign Aid. (Illus.). 90p. (Orig.). (C). (gr. 12 up). 1994. pap. text ed. 40.00 (*0-7881-0831-X*) Diane Pub.

O'Hanlon, Redmond. In Trouble Again. LC 89-40563. (Vintage Departures Ser.). 288p. 1990. pap. 11.00 (*0-679-72714-0*, Vin) Random.

— Into the Heart of Borneo. LC 87-40084. (Vintage Departures Ser.). 204p. 1987. pap. 11.00 (*0-394-75540-5*, Vin) Random.

O'Hanlon, Rosalind. Caste, Conflict & Ideology: Mahatma Jotirao Phule & Low Caste Protest in Nineteenth-Century Western India. LC 84-9419. (Cambridge South Asian Studies: No. 30). (Illus.). 352p. 1985. 69.95 (*0-521-26615-7*) Cambridge U Pr.

— A Comparison Between Women & Men: Tarabai Shinde & the Critique of Gender Relations in Colonial India. 147p. 1994. 14.95 (*0-19-563266-4*) OUP.

***O'Hanlon, Tim.** Accessing Federal Adoption Subsidies after Legalization. (Orig.). 1995. pap. text ed. 14.95 (*0-87868-569-3*) Child Welfare.

O'Hanlon, W. M. Walks Among the Poor of Belfast. 1971. reprint ed. 22.00 (*0-8464-0961-5*) Beekman Pubs.

O'Hanlon, William H. Taproots: Underlying Principles of Milton Erickson's Therapy & Hypnosis. (Professional Bks.). 1987. 22.95 (*0-393-70031-3*) Norton.

— Uncommon Casebook. 1990. 34.95 (*0-393-70101-8*) Norton.

O'Hanlon, William H. & Martin, Michael. Solution-Oriented Hypnosis: An Ericksonian Approach. LC 92-16410. 180p. (C). 1992. 22.95 (*0-393-70149-2*); text ed. 22.95 (*0-685-59449-1*) Norton.

O'Hanlon, William H. & Weiner-Davis, Michele. In Search of Solutions: Creating a Context for Change. 1988. 22.95 (*0-393-70061-5*) Norton.

O'Hanlon, William H., jt. auth. see Cade, Brian.

O'Hanlon, William H., jt. auth. see Hudson, Patricia O.

Ohannessian, Sirarpi & Kashoki, Mubanga E., eds. Language in Zambia. LC 78-325190. (Ford Foundation Language Surveys Ser.). 471p. reprint ed. pap. 134.30 (*0-8357-3022-0*, 2057109) Bks Demand.

Ohannessian, Sirarpi, et al, eds. Language Surveys in Developing Nations: Papers & Reports on Sociolinguistic Surveys. LC 75-7584. 234p. reprint ed. pap. 66.70 (*0-8357-3369-6*, 2039610) Bks Demand.

Ohaodha, M. & Robinson, Lennox. Pictures at the Abbey: The Collection of the Irish National Theatre. 1983. 21.00 (*0-85105-418-8*, Pub. by Colin Smythe Ltd UK); pap. 11.95 (*0-85105-399-8*, Pub. by Colin Smythe Ltd UK) Dufour.

***OhAodha, Michael.** Siobhan: A Memoir of an Actress. (Illus.). 190p. Date not set. 31.95 (*0-86322-188-2*, Pub. by Brandon Bk Pubs IE) Irish Bks Media.

O'Hara. Practical Artwork for the Media. 1991. pap. write for info. (*0-434-91486-X*) Buttrwrth-Heinemann.

O'Hara & Gardner, eds. Write to One Million: Turn Your Dreams into Dollars. (Illus.). 162p. (Orig.). 1990. pap. 15.00 (*0-9625725-0-0*) Cat Tale Pr.

O'Hara, jt. auth. see Harawi.

O'Hara, Albert R. The Position of Woman in Early China: According to the Lieh Nu Chuan, "The Biographies of Eminent Chinese Women" LC 79-2949. 301p. 1984. reprint ed. 23.00 (*0-8305-0112-6*) Hyperion Conn.

— Research on Changes of Chinese Society. (Asian Folklore & Social Life Monographs: No. 20). 1971. 19.00 (*0-89986-022-2*) Oriental Bk Store.

O'Hara, Arnold. As Burns Said.... (C). 1988. 30.00 (*0-907526-30-6*, Alloway Pub) St Mut.

O'Hara, Carol, et al, eds. Seasons & Seasonings: Recipes from Yesterday, for Today, & for Tomorrow, Vol. II: All Pieces of a Legacy. (Illus.). 156p. (Orig.). 1994. pap. 12.00 (*0-9625725-3-5*) Cat Tale Pr.

O'Hara, Catherine L. Tarleton Blackwell: The Greatest Show of Hogs. (Illus.). 44p. (Orig.). 1993. pap. 12.00 (*0-915577-25-9*) Taft Museum.

O'Hara, Catherine L. & Meyer, Ruth K. Tyrone Geter: Images of Africa & Recent Works. (Illus.). 20p. (Orig.). 1989. pap. 5.00 (*0-915577-18-6*) Taft Museum.

O'Hara, Charles E. & O'Hara, Gregory L. Fundamentals of Criminal Investigation. 6th ed. LC 93-26172. (Illus.). 1010p. (C). 1994. text ed. 49.95x (*0-398-05889-X*) C C Thomas.

O'Hara, Christiane C. & Harrell, Minnie. Rehabilitation with Brain Injury Survivors: An Empowerment Approach. LC 90-1040. 528p. 1990. 110.00 (*0-8342-0180-1*) Aspen Pub.

***O'Hara, Craig.** Philosophy of Punk: More Than Noise. (Illus.). 148p. (Orig.). 1995. pap. 8.00 (*1-873176-43-0*) AK Pr Dist.

O'Hara, Daniel T. Lionel Trilling: The Work of Liberation. LC 87-37178. 332p. (Orig.). (C). 1988. text ed. 40.00 (*0-299-11310-8*); pap. text ed. 17.50 (*0-299-11314-0*) U of Wis Pr.

— Radical Parody: American Culture & Critical Agency after Foucault. 264p. 1992. text ed. 37.50 (*0-231-07692-4*) Col U Pr.

— The Romance of Interpretation: Visionary Criticism from Pater to de Man. LC 85-477. 256p. 1985. text ed. 36.00 (*0-231-06068-8*) Col U Pr.

— Tragic Knowledge: Yeat's Autobiography & Hermeneutics. LC 80-26825. 224p. 1981. text ed. 46.00 (*0-231-05204-9*) Col U Pr.

O'Hara, Daniel T., ed. Why Nietzsche Now? LC 84-48455. (Illus.). 460p. 1985. 29.95 (*0-253-36530-9*) Ind U Pr.

O'Hara-Devereaux, Mary & Johansen, Robert. Globalwork: Bridging Distance, Culture & Time. LC 94-4431. (Business-Management Ser.). (Illus.). 480p. 1994. 29.00 (*1-55542-602-6*) Jossey-Bass.

O'Hara-Devereaux, Mary, et al, eds. Eldercare: A Practical Guide to Clinical Geriatrics. (Illus.). 368p. 1981. text ed. 46.50 (*0-8089-1285-2*, 793190, Grune) Saunders.

O'Hara, Edgar, jt. ed. see Ramos-Garcia, Luis A.

O'Hara, Edwin V. The Church & the Country Community. 1978. 17.95 (*0-405-10846-X*, 11849) Ayer.

O'Hara, Elizabeth. The Hiring Fair. 162p. (J). (gr. 5-9). 1994. pap. 8.95 (*1-85371-275-2*, Pub. by Poolbeg Pr IE) Dufour.

— Singles. 288p. 1994. pap. 11.99 (*1-85594-057-4*) InBook.

O'Hara, Evone. The Hartes of Roebuck. (Illus.). 368p. 1985. 19.95 (*0-900068-92-2*, Pub. by Anvil Bks Ltd IE) Irish Bks Media.

O'Hara, F., tr. see Leger, E., et al.

O'Hara, F. M., Jr., ed. see Hirst, Eric, et al.

O'Hara, Frank. Art Chronicles, 1954-1966. LC 74-77526. 1990. pap. 14.95 (*0-8076-0756-8*) Braziller.

— Biotherm. limited ed. (Illus.). 1990. 2,750.00 (*0-685-56696-X*) Arion Pr.

— Lunch Poems. LC 64-8689. (Pocket Poets Ser.: No. 19). (Orig.). 1964. pap. 5.95 (*0-87286-035-3*) City Lights.

— Selected Poems. Allen, Donald, ed. 1974. pap. 17.00 (*0-394-71973-5*, V-973, Vin) Random.

— Standing Still & Walking in New York. Allen, Donald, ed. LC 74-75455. 192p. 1983. reprint ed. pap. 6.95 (*0-912516-12-7*) Grey Fox.

— Today in American Drama. (BCL1-PS American Literature Ser.). 277p. 1993. reprint ed. lib. bdg. 79.00 (*0-7812-6588-6*) Rprt Serv.

O'Hara, Frank H. Invitation to the Theater. LC 76-109299. xi, 211p. 1971. reprint ed. text ed. 55.00 (*0-8371-3842-6*, OHIT, Greenwood Pr) Greenwood.

— Today in American Drama. LC 40-666. (Illus.). 277p. 1969. reprint ed. text ed. 35.00 (*0-8371-0600-1*, OHAD, Greenwood Pr) Greenwood.

O'Hara, Frederic J. A Guide to Publications of the Executive Branch. LC 78-66368. 1979. 39.50 (*0-87650-072-6*); pap. 24.50 (*0-87650-088-2*) Pierian.

O'Hara, Frederic J., ed. Informing the Nation: A Handbook of Government Information for Librarians. LC 90-34263. 584p. 1990. text ed. 65.00 (*0-313-27267-0*, OHG, Greenwood Pr) Greenwood.

O'Hara, Frederick M., Jr. & Sicignano, Robert. Handbook of United States Economic & Financial Indicators. LC 84-22469. vii, 224p. 1985. text ed. 42.95 (*0-313-23954-1*, SHK/, Greenwood Pr) Greenwood.

O'Hara, Georgina & Donovan, Carrie. The Encyclopaedia of Fashion. (Illus.). 272p. 1986. 34.95 (*0-8109-0882-4*) Abrams.

O'Hara, Gregory, jt. auth. see Hamel, William.

O'Hara, Gregory L., jt. auth. see O'Hara, Charles E.

O'Hara, James. John Cheever: A Study of the Short Fiction. (Twayne's Studies in Short Fiction: No. 9). 168p. 1989. text ed. 22.95 (*0-8057-8310-5*, Pub. by Royal Botanic Garden UK) Macmillan.

O'Hara, James J. Death & the Optimistic Prophecy in Vergil's AENEID. 228p. 1990. text ed. 37.50 (*0-691-06815-1*) Princeton U Pr.

O'Hara, James T., et al. Corporate Taxation. 1360p. 1992. text ed., ring bd. 165.00 (*0-07-172176-2*) Shepards-McGraw.

O'Hara, Jean, jt. auth. see Rebert, Jo.

O'Hara, Jim & Walle, Grace. Collage; A Resource Book for Christian Youth Groups. 86p. (Orig.). 1976. pap. 4.00 (*0-9608124-5-8*) Marianist Com Ctr.

O'Hara, Joe, jt. auth. see McCormack, Vincent.

O'Hara, John. Appointment in Samarra. LC 82-40029. 256p. 1982. pap. 10.00 (*0-394-71192-0*) Random.

— Appointment in Samarra. 1994. 13.50 (*0-679-60110-4*, Modern Lib) Random.

— Appointment in Samarra. 1993. reprint ed. lib. bdg. 89.00 (*0-7812-5481-7*) Rprt Serv.

— Butterfield Eight. 1976. 21.95 (*0-8488-1441-X*) Amereon Ltd.

— Butterfield Eight. 300p. 1991. reprint ed. lib. bdg. 22.95 (*0-89966-871-2*) Buccaneer Bks.

— Butterfield Eight, No. 8. 1994. pap. 10.00 (*0-679-75580-2*) Random.

— Collected Stories of John O'Hara. MacShane, Frank, ed. LC 84-42661. 1985. 19.95 (*0-394-54083-2*) Random.

— Forty-Nine Stories. 26.95 (*0-89190-393-3*, Am Repr) Amereon Ltd.

— From the Terrace. 981p. 1993. pap. 7.95 (*0-88184-971-5*) Carroll & Graf.

— Gibbsville, PA. Bruccoli, Matthew J., ed. 512p. 1992. 27.95 (*0-88184-899-9*) Carroll & Graf.

— Gibbsville, PA. Bruccoli, Matthew J., ed. 864p. 1994. pap. 17.95 (*0-7867-0082-3*) Carroll & Graf.

— Hope of Heaven. 182p. 1985. pap. 3.95 (*0-88184-149-8*) Carroll & Graf.

— The Lockwood Concern. 432p. 1986. pap. 4.95 (*0-88184-217-6*) Carroll & Graf.

— The Novellas of John O'Hara. 1995. 18.00 (*0-679-60167-8*) Random.

— A Rage to Live. 542p. 1986. reprint ed. pap. 4.95 (*0-88184-216-8*) Carroll & Graf.

— The Second Ewings: A Facsimile of the Manuscript. 1977. boxed 60.00 (*0-89723-012-4*) Bruccoli.

— Sermons & Soda Water. 336p. 1986. pap. 4.95 (*0-88184-271-0*) Carroll & Graf.

— Sermons & Soda-Water, 3 Vols, Set. 1960. 12.50 (*0-394-44480-9*) Random.

— Ten North Frederick. 408p. 1985. pap. 4.50 (*0-88184-173-0*) Carroll & Graf.

O'Hara, John M., tr. see De Heredia, Jose M.

O'Hara, Kathryn J. & Iudicello, Suzanne. A Citizen's Guide to Plastic in the Ocean: More Than a Litter Problem. (Illus.). 140p. (Orig.). 1988. pap. write for info. (*0-9615294-2-3*) Ctr Env Educ.

O'Hara, Kevin, jt. auth. see Walters, Annette.

O'Hara, Kirk B., jt. auth. see Backer, Thomas E.

***O'Hara, Larry.** Turning up the Heat: MI5 after the Cold War. 96p. (Orig.). 1994. pap. 10.95 (*0-948984-29-5*, Pub. by Phoenix Pr UK) AK Pr Dist.

Ohara, Leander L. Jurisprudence & Organ Procurements: Index of Authors & Subjects. 180p. 1993. 49.50 (*1-55914-938-8*); pap. 39.50 (*1-55914-939-6*) ABBE Pubs Assn.

O'Hara, Liz, jt. auth. see Schettino, John.

***O'Hara, M. W. & Alloy, L. B.** Postpartum Depression: Causes & Consequences. (Series in Psychopathology). 256p. 1994. 69.00 (*0-387-94261-0*) Spr-Verlag.

***O'Hara, Mark.** The Composer's Dream. 32p. 1995. pap. 5.50 (*0-9647127-2-5*) Coreopsis Bks.

O'Hara, Mary. The Catch Colt. 1964. pap. 4.75 (*0-8222-0190-9*) Dramatists Play.

— The Devil Enters by a North Window. Orig. Title: The Son of Adam Wyngate. 440p. 1990. reprint ed. pap. 9.95 (*0-89733-354-3*) Academy Chi Pubs.

— My Friend Flicka. LC 87-45654. 272p. (YA). (gr. 7 up). 1988. reprint ed. mass mkt. 5.50 (*0-06-080902-7*, P-902, PL) HarpC.

— Thunderhead. LC 87-45653. 320p. (YA). (gr. 7 up). 1988. reprint ed. pap. 7.00 (*0-06-080903-5*, P-903, PL) HarpC.

***O'Hara, Maureen.** Market Microstructure Theory. (Illus.). 225p. (C). 1994. text ed. 44.95 (*1-55786-443-8*) Blackwell Pubs.

***O'Hara, Michael, et al, eds.** Psychological Aspects of Women's Reproductive Health. 320p. 1995. 43.95 (*0-8261-8660-2*) Springer Pub.

O'Hara, Michael W. Postpartum Depression: Causes & Consequences. LC 94-7180. 1994. write for info. (*0-387-94861-9*) Spr-Verlag.

O'Hara, Nancy. Find a Quiet Corner: A Simple Guide to Self-Peace. 128p. (Orig.). 1995. pap. 8.99 (*0-446-67111-8*) Warner Bks.

O'Hara, Pat. Wilderness Scenario: Peaceful Images from the Wild. (Illus.). 132p. 1991. 45.00 (*1-56037-005-X*) Am Wrld Geog.

O'Hara, Pat, jt. auth. see Smithson, Michael.

O'Hara, Patrick, jt. auth. see Iaconetti, Joan.

O'Hara, Patrick D. Computerizing a Small Business. LC 92-14972. 272p. 1993. pap. text ed. 19.95 (*0-471-57869-X*) Wiley.

— Computerizing a Small Business. LC 92-14972. 272p. 1993. text ed. 59.95 (*0-471-57870-3*) Wiley.

— SBA Loans: A Step-by-Step Guide. 2nd ed. 304p. 1994. 65.00 (*0-471-30332-1*); pap. text ed. 19.95 (*0-471-30331-3*) Wiley.

— The Total Business Plan: How to Write, Rewrite & Revise. 288p. 1990. text ed. 65.00 (*0-471-52450-6*); disk 85.00 (*0-471-54778-6*) Wiley.

— The Total Business Plan: How to Write, Rewrite, & Revise. 2nd ed. LC 94-17935. 1994. 49.95 (*0-471-07829-8*) Wiley.

— The Total Marketing & Sales Plan. 304p. 1992. 75.00 (*0-471-57114-8*) Wiley.

O'Hara, Peg, ed. see Baker, Amy J.

O'Hara, R. A. Guide to Highway Law for Architects, Engineers, Surveyors & Contractors. 136p. 1991. write for info. (*0-419-17330-7*, E & FN Spon) Routledge Chapman & Hall.

O'Hara, R. Philip, tr. see Bultmann, Rudolf.

O'Hara, Robert C. Language & Meaning. 224p. (C). 1993. per. 27.95 (*0-8403-8600-1*) Kendall-Hunt.

O'Hara, S. C., jt. ed. see Corner, E. D.

O'Hara, Scott R. Operation : Air Traffic Controller: Secrets of Air Traffic Controller Exam. 290p. (Orig.). 1991. pap. 14.95 (*0-9629713-0-8*) Intercntl News.

***O'Hara, Shelley.** The Complete Idiot's Guide to Buying & Selling a Home. 384p. 1994. 16.95 (*1-56761-510-4*) Alpha Bks IN.

— Easy AMI Pro. (Easy Ser.). (Illus.). 224p. (Orig.). 1992. pap. 19.95 (*0-88022-977-2*) Que.

— Easy DOS 6. (Illus.). 256p. 1993. pap. 16.95 (*1-56529-095-X*) Que.

— Easy Excel. 2nd ed. (Illus.). 256p. (Orig.). 1993. pap. 16.95 (*1-56529-540-4*) Que.

— Easy Harvard Graphics. (Easy Ser.). (Illus.). (Orig.). 1992. pap. 19.95 (*0-88022-942-X*) Que.

— Easy OS-2. (Illus.). 256p. 1993. pap. 16.95 (*1-56529-145-X*) Que.

— Easy Quattro Pro for Windows. (Easy Ser.). (Illus.). (Orig.). 1992. pap. 19.95 (*0-88022-993-4*) Que.

— Easy QuattroPro. 2nd ed. (Easy Ser.). (Illus.). 224p. (Orig.). 1993. pap. 16.95 (*1-56529-225-1*) Que.

— Easy Quicken. (Easy Ser.). (Illus.). 208p. (Orig.). 1992. pap. 19.95 (*0-88022-821-0*) Que.

— Easy Windows: 3.1 Edition. (Easy Ser.). (Illus.). (Orig.). 1992. pap. 19.95 (*0-88022-985-3*) Que.

Ohara, Shelley. Easy Windows 3.1. 2nd ed. 1994. pap. 19.95 (*1-56529-641-9*) Que.

O'Hara, Shelley. Easy Word for Windows. (Easy Ser.). (Illus.). (Orig.). 1992. pap. 19.95 (*0-88022-922-5*) Que.

— Easy Word for Windows. 2nd ed. 256p. (Orig.). 1993. pap. 19.95 (*1-56529-444-0*) Que.

— Easy WordPerfect. 2nd ed. (Easy Ser.). (Illus.). 200p. 1991. pap. 19.95 (*0-88022-797-4*) Que.

— Easy WordPerfect for Windows Version 6. (Easy Ser.). (Illus.). 256p. (Orig.). 1993. pap. 19.95 (*1-56529-230-8*) Que.

— Easy WordPerfect 6. 256p. (Orig.). 1993. pap. 16.95 (*0-685-70409-2*) Que.

— Easy Works for Windows. (Easy Ser.). (Illus.). 1992. pap. 19.95 (*1-56529-063-1*) Que.

— Easy 1-2-3. 2nd ed. (Easy Ser.). (Illus.). 1992. pap. 19.95 (*1-56529-022-4*) Que.

— Easy 1-2-3 for Windows. (Easy Ser.). (Illus.). 256p. (Orig.). 1993. pap. 16.95 (*0-88022-954-3*) Que.

— 10 Minute Guide to ACT! for Windows. (Illus.). 160p. (Orig.). 1995. pap. text ed. 10.99 (*1-56761-539-2*) Alpha Bks IN.

— Ten Minute Guide to Buying a Computer. 160p. 1994. 12.99 (*1-56761-500-7*) Alpha Bks IN.

O'Hara, Shelley, jt. auth. see Miller, Mike.

***O'Hara, Shelly.** Easy DOS. 3rd ed. 1994. pap. 19.95 (*1-56529-640-0*) Que.

— Excel 5.0 Cheat Sheet. 1994. pap. 19.95 (*1-56761-473-6*) Alpha Bks IN.

— Word for Windows 6.0 Cheat Sheet. 1994. pap. 19.99 (*1-56761-471-X*) Alpha Bks IN.

O'Hara, Susan P. & Graves, Gregory. Saving California's Coast: Army Engineers at Oceanside & Humboldt Bay. (Western Lands & Waters Ser.: No. 16). (Illus.). 278p. 1991. 38.50 (*0-87062-201-3*) A H Clark.

***O'Hara, Thomas E.** Taking Control of Your Financial Future: Making Smart Investment Decisions With Stocks & Mutual Funds. LC 94-25001. 272p. 1994. 25.00 (*0-7863-0139-2*) Irwin Prof Pubng.

O'Hara, Tom. At Home with the Spirit: On Retreat in Daily Life. LC 93-27210. 160p. (Orig.). 1994. pap. 5.95 (*0-8091-3460-8*) Paulist Pr.

O'Hara, Valerie. The Fitness Option: Five Weeks to Healing Stress. 2nd ed. (Illus.). 192p. (C). 1993. reprint ed. pap. 13.95 (*0-9627298-0-9*) Dawn CA.

— Wellness at Work: Building Resilience to Job Stress. 210p. (Orig.). 1995. text ed. 29.95 (*1-57224-031-8*); pap. 14.95 (*1-57224-030-X*) New Harbinger.

An Asterisk (*) at the beginning of an entry indicates that the title is appearing in BIP for the first time.

O'Hara, Walter J. Mariner's Gyro-Navigation Manual for Masters, Mates, Marine Engineers. LC 51-7444. (Illus.). 192p. reprint ed. pap. 54.80 (*0-317-08235-3*, 2011305) Bks Demand.

O'Hara, William T. & Hill, John T., Jr. The Student, the College, the Law. LC 72-87116. 234p. reprint ed. pap. 66.70 (*0-317-41886-6*, 2026049) Bks Demand.

O'Hare. Artificial Recharge. 1986. 59.95 (*0-87371-050-9*, TD404, CRC Reprint) Franklin.

O'Hare & Terry. Discharge Planning: Assuring the Continuity of Care. 196p. 1987. 65.00 (*0-87189-895-0*, 89895) Aspen Pub.

O'Hare, Carol. Cycling the San Francisco Bay Area: Thirty Rides to Historic Sites & Scenic Places. LC 93-83823. (Illus.). 272p. 1993. pap. 12.95 (*0-933201-57-5*) Bicycle Books.

O'Hare, Carol, ed. see Stevens, Doris.

O'Hare, Carol, ed. see Willard, Frances E.

O'Hare, David & Roscoe, Stanley. Flightdeck Performance: The Human Factor. LC 89-19904. (Illus.). 308p. 1990. pap. 19.95 (*0-8138-0173-7*) Iowa St U Pr.

O'Hare, Dermot, jt. ed. see Bruce, Duncan W.

O'Hare, Frank & Kline, Edward A. The Modern Writer's Handbook. 3rd ed. (Illus.). 736p. (C). 1992. pap. write for info. (*0-02-389170-X*) Macmillan.

O'Hare, Frank & Memering, W. Dean. The Writer's Work: A Guide to Effective Composition. 3rd ed. 592p. (C). 1989. Casebound. text ed. write for info. (*0-13-969635-0*) P-H.

O'Hare, G., jt. auth. see Tivy, Joy.

O'Hare, Jeff. Globe Probe: Exciting Geographical Adventures All Around the World. 32p. (J). (gr. 4-7). 1993. 10.95 (*1-56397-037-6*) Boyds Mills Pr.

— Hanukkah, Happy Hanukkah: Crafts, Recipes, Games, Puzzles, Songs, & More for the Joyous... LC 93-73302. (Illus.). 32p. (J). (ps-5). 1994. pap. 4.95 (*1-56397-369-3*) Boyds Mills Pr.

— Searchin' Safari: Looking for Camouflaged Creatures. LC 91-72974. (Illus.). 32p. (J). (ps-3). 1992. 8.95 (*1-56397-016-3*) Boyds Mills Pr.

O'Hare, Jeff, ed. Cat & Dog Mysteries: Fourteen Exciting Mini-Mysteries with Hidden Pictures. (Illus.). 32p. (Orig.). (J). (gr. 2-7). 1993. pap. 4.95 (*1-56397-291-3*) Boyds Mills Pr.

— Knee Slappers, Side Splitters & Tummy Ticklers: A Book of Riddles & Jokes. LC 91-76204. (Illus.). 48p. (J). (ps-7). 1992. pap. 6.95 (*1-56397-019-8*) Boyds Mills Pr.

O'Hare, Julianna. Heroes. 450p. 1994. pap. 14.95 (*0-9640345-9-X*) Bk Factory.

O'Hare, Kate R. In Prison. LC 76-7793. (American Library: No. 30). 150p. 1977. reprint ed. 25.00 (*0-295-95451-5*) U of Wash Pr.

— Kate Ricards O'Hare, Selected Writings & Speeches. fac. ed. Foner, Philip S. & Miller, Sally M., eds. LC 81-15667. 371p. 1982. reprint ed. pap. 105.80 (*0-7837-7732-9*, 2047488) Bks Demand.

O'Hare, Martin, jt. ed. see Drysdale, Peter.

O'Hare, O. Introduction to Documentary Credits. (C). 1989. 90.00 (*0-85297-264-4*, Pub. by Inst Bankers UK) St Mut.

***O'Hare, Padraic.** Busy Life, Peaceful Center: A Book of Meditating. 192p. (Orig.). 1995. pap. 9.95 (*0-88347-291-0*) Thomas More.

— Way of Faithfulness: Contemplation & Formation in the Church. LC 93-22668. 1993. pap. 13.50 (*1-56338-066-8*) TPI PA.

O'Hare, Patrick F. The Facts about Luther. LC 87-50945. 378p. 1987. reprint ed. pap. 13.50 (*0-89555-322-8*) TAN Bks Pubs.

***O'Hare, Sheila & Atterwill, Chris K., eds.** In Vitro Toxicity Testing Protocols. LC 95-3384. (Methods in Molecular Biology Ser.: Vol. 43). (Illus.). 352p. 1995. 69.50 (*0-89603-282-5*) Humana.

O'Hare, Thomas & Schlossnagle, Sherry, eds. Disability Income Insurance. 41p. (Orig.). 1993. pap. text ed. write for info. (*1-879143-23-2*) Health Ins Assn Am.

O'Hare, William P. Wealth & Economic Status: A Perspective on Racial Inequity. 38p. 1983. pap. 12.25 (*0-941410-35-8*) Jt Ctr Pol Studies.

O'Harra, Marjorie L. Southern Oregon: Short Trips into History. (Illus.). 200p. 1985. pap. 11.95 (*0-943388-06-6*) South Oregon.

Ohashi, Haruzo. Japanese Gardens of the Modern Era. LC 87-45213. (Illus.). 100p. 1987. 29.95 (*0-87040-743-0*) Japan Pubns USA.

Ohashi, Kenzaburo, ed. Melville & Melville Studies in Japan. LC 92-36613. (Contributions in American Studies: No. 103). 272p. 1993. text ed. 59.95 (*0-313-28622-1*, OMS, Greenwood Pr) Greenwood.

Ohashi, Kenzaburo, et al, eds. Faulkner Studies in Japan. LC 84-16391. 232p. 1985. 25.00 (*0-8203-0745-9*) U of Ga Pr.

Ohashi, Pamela, jt. ed. see Bleuthmann, Horst.

Ohashi, Tadahiko, jt. ed. see Klass, Donald L.

Ohashi, Watari. Do-It-Yourself Shiatsu. Lindner, Vicki, ed. 1976. pap. 9.95 (*0-525-47416-1*, Dutton) NAL-Dutton.

— Do It Yourself Shiatsu. 1993. reprint ed. pap. 13.95 (*0-14-019351-0*, Arkana) Viking Penguin.

Ohashi, Watari & Lindner, Vicki. Do-It-Yourself Shiatsu. 1976. pap. 10.95 (*0-525-48312-8*, Dutton) NAL-Dutton.

Ohashi, Watari & Monte, Tom. Reading the Body: Ohashi's Book of Oriental Diagnosis. 156p. (Orig.). 1991. pap. 15.00 (*0-14-019362-6*, Arkana) Viking Penguin.

***Ohashi, Wataru.** The Ohashi Bodywork Book: Beyond Shiatsu with the Ohashiatsu Method. De Angelis, Paul, ed. (Illus.). 160p. 1996. pap. 20.00 (*1-56836-096-7*) Kodansha.

Ohashi, Wataru, jt. auth. see Masunaga, Shizuto.

Ohashi, Yuji, ed. Reactivity in Molecular Crystals. LC 93-42020. 1993. 130.00 (*1-56081-857-3*) VCH Pubs.

Ohayon, jt. auth. see Morand.

Ohayon, R., jt. auth. see Crolet, J. M.

Ohba, Hideaki & Malla, Samal B., eds. The Himalayan Plants, Vol. 1. 1988. 225.00 (*0-86008-427-2*, Pub. by U of Tokyo JA) Col U Pr.

Ohba, Hideaki & Malla, Sarah B. The Himalayan Plants, Vol. 2. (Illus.). 360p. 1990. text ed. 227.50 (*0-86008-459-0*, Pub. by U of Tokyo JA) Col U Pr.

Ohba, Y., ed. Intelligent Sensor Technology. LC 92-18809. (Series in Measurement Science & Technology). 167p. 1993. text ed. 59.95 (*0-471-93423-2*) Wiley.

Ohba, Yoko, jt. auth. see Tsuyuki, Hiroshi.

Ohde, Ralph. Phonetic Analysis of Normal & Abnormal Speech. 400p. (C). 1991. write for info. (*0-675-20681-2*, Merrill Pub Co) Macmillan.

Ohdomari, I., ed. see First International Symposium Staff.

Ohe, S. Vapor-Liquid Equilibrium Data. (Physical Sciences Data Ser.: No. 37). 742p. 1989. 254.00 (*0-444-98876-9*) Elsevier.

— Vapor-Liquid Equilibrium Data at High Pressure. (Physical Sciences Data Ser.: No. 42). 356p. 1990. 202.75 (*0-444-98797-5*) Elsevier.

O'Healy, Aine, tr. see De Marinis, Marco.

O'Healy, Anne-Marie. Cesare Pavese. (Twayne World Authors Ser.: No. 785). 192p. (C). 1988. text ed. 26.95 (*0-8057-8242-7*, 398, Twayne) Macmillan.

O'Hear, Ann, ed. see Carnegie, David W.

O'Hear, Anthony. Education, Society & Human Nature: An Introduction to the Philosophy of Education. 192p. (C). 1981. pap. 13.95 (*0-7100-0748-5*, RKP) Routledge.

— The Element of Fire: Science, Art & the Human World. 192p. 1988. 34.50 (*0-415-00618-X*) Routledge.

— Experience, Explanation & Faith: A Study in the Philosophy of Religion. (Modern Revivals in Philosophy Ser.). 285p. 1992. 56.95 (*0-7512-0052-2*, Pub. by Gregg Pub UK) Ashgate Pub Co.

— Experience, Explanation & Faith: An Introduction to the Philosophy of Religion. LC 83-15957. 266p. (Orig.). 1984. pap. 13.95 (*0-7100-9768-9*, RKP) Routledge.

— An Introduction to the Philosophy of Science. 256p. (C). 1989. pap. 15.95 (*0-19-824813-X*) OUP.

O'Hear, Michael D. Empty Beds. (Lewiston Poetry Ser.: Vol. 12). (Illus.). 64p. 1989. lib. bdg. 24.95 (*0-88946-893-1*) E Mellen.

O'Hear, Philip & White, John, eds. Assessing the National Curriculum. 128p. 1993. pap. 27.00 (*1-85396-232-5*, Pub. by Paul Chapman UK) Taylor & Francis.

***Ohearn.** Hercules the Harbor Tug. 1995. 6.95 (*0-08-810688-8*, Pub. by Aberdeen U Pr) Macmillan.

O'Hearn, Bill. From the Heart of a Child & Other Lessons to Live By. LC 91-72584. 144p. (Orig.). 1991. pap. 11.95 (*0-9626161-0-9*) Entheos Pub.

O'Hearn, Carolyn. Writing, Grammar, & Usage. 433p. (C). 1988. pap. write for info. (*0-02-389130-0*) Macmillan.

O'Hearn, Frank, tr. see Dent, Robert L.

O'Hearn, Michael. Hercules the Harbor Tug. (Illus.). 32p. (J). (ps-4). 1995. pap. 6.95 (*0-88106-888-8*) Charlesbridge Pub.

O'Heffernan, Patrick. Mass Media & American Foreign Policy: Insider Perspectives on Global Journalism & the Foreign Policy Process. 288p. 1991. text ed. 45.00 (*0-89391-728-1*); pap. text ed. 24.50 (*0-89391-729-X*) Ablex Pub.

Oheh, Robert & Fox, M. Sample Size Choice: Charts for Experiments with Linear Models. 2nd ed. (Statistics Ser.: Vol. 122). 216p. 1991. 75.00 (*0-8247-8600-9*) Dekker.

O'Hehir, Brendan & Dillon, John M. A Classical Lexicon for Finnegans Wake: A Glossary of the Greek & Latin in the Major Works of Joyce, Including Finnegans Wake, the Poems, Dubliners, Stephen Hero, a Portrait of the Artist as a Young Man, Exiles, & Ulysses. LC 77-372235. 675p. reprint ed. pap. 180.00 (*0-7837-4691-1*, 2044438) Bks Demand.

O'Hehir, Diana. Summoned: Poems. LC 76-16011. (Breakthrough Bks.). 64p. 1976. 14.95 (*0-8262-0204-7*) U of Mo Pr.

O'Heigeartaigh, M., et al, eds. Combinatorial Optimization: Annotated Bibliographies. LC 84-5081. 212p. reprint ed. pap. 60.50 (*0-7837-6391-3*, 2046104) Bks Demand.

O'Heithir, Breandan. Lead Us into Temptation. 1991. pap. 10.95 (*1-85371-120-9*) Dufour.

— Pocket History of Ireland. LC 89-82005. 144p. 1990. pap. 7.95 (*0-86278-188-4*, Pub. by OBrien Pr IE) Dufour.

Oheneba-Sakyi, Yaw, ed. Family Planning & Reproductive Health Services in Ghana: An Annotated Bibliography. LC 94-10358. (African Special Bibliographic Ser.: No. 18). 176p. 1994. text ed. 55.00 (*0-313-28900-X*, Greenwood Pr) Greenwood.

O.Henry. The Gift of the Magi. LC 94-4571. (Illus.). 32p. 1994. 14.95 (*1-57102-003-9*, Ideals Child) Hambleton-Hill.

***O'Hern, T. J., ed.** Cavitation & Gas-Liquid Flow in Fluid Machinery & Devices. LC 94-71579. (Fluid Engineering Division Conference Ser.: Vol. 190). 343p. 1994. pap. text ed. 55.00 (*0-7918-1373-8*) ASME.

O'Herron, Paul. An Alembic of Philosophy. 192p. (C). 1994. pap. 15.00 (*0-9641821-0-6*) Okapi Press.

O'Herron, Thomas F., ed. Terms of Trade: The Language of International Trade Law, Policy & Diplomacy. 110p. (C). 1989. pap. 12.00 (*0-9624861-1-6*) Intl Advisory Serv.

O'Higgins. Determinism & Freewill. (International Archives of the History of Ideas Ser.: No. 18). 1976. pap. text ed. 51.50 (*90-247-1776-0*) Kluwer Ac.

— A Taste of Old Cuba. 1994. 25.00 (*0-06-016964-8*, HarpT) HarpC.

O'Higgins, Harvey J. From the Life: Imaginary Portraits of Some Distinguished Americans. LC 75-130069. (Short Story Index Reprint Ser.). 1977. 20.95 (*0-8369-3650-7*) Ayer.

— Silent Sam, & Other Stories of Our Day. 1977. 23.95 (*0-8369-4251-5*, 6061) Ayer.

— The Smoke Eaters: The Story of a Fire Crew. 1977. 21.95 (*0-8369-4249-3*, 6059) Ayer.

— Some Distinguished Americans: Imaginary Portraits. LC 78-144166. (Short Story Index Reprint Ser.). 1977. reprint ed. 23.95 (*0-8369-3781-3*) Ayer.

O'Higgins, James. Yves de Vallone: The Making of an Espirit-Fort. 1982. lib. bdg. 74.50 (*90-247-2520-8*) Kluwer Ac.

O'Higgins, Michael & Downes, John. Beating the Dow: A High Return, Low-Risk Method for Investing in the Dow Jones Industrial Stocks with As Little As 5,000 Dollars. LC 89-46551. 288p. 1992. reprint ed. pap. 13.00 (*0-06-098404-X*, PL) HarpC.

O'Higgins, Nuala, jt. auth. see O'Higgins, Paul.

O'Higgins, P. & Partington, M. Social Security Law in Britain & Ireland: A Bibliography. 446p. 1986. text ed. 120.00 (*0-7201-1794-1*, Mansell Pub) Cassell.

O'Higgins, Patrick J. Basic Instrumentation, Industrial Measurement. 1966. text ed. 45.95 (*0-07-047649-7*) McGraw.

O'Higgins, Paul. Bibliography of Irish Trials & Other Legal Proceedings. 1986. U.K. text ed. 111.00 (*0-86205-080-4*) Butterworth Legal Pubs.

— Labour Law in Great Britain & Ireland, 1979-1990: A Bibliography. 320p. 1994. text ed. 90.00 (*0-7201-1850-6*, Mansell Pub) Cassell.

O'Higgins, Paul & O'Higgins, Nuala. Fresh Bread: Manna for Kingdom Living Today. (Orig.). 1987. pap. text ed. 4.95 (*0-944795-02-1*) Recon Outreach.

O'Higgins, Paul, ed. see Creighton, W. B.

O'Higgins, Paul, ed. see Elias, Patrick & Ewing, K. D.

O'Higgins, Paul, ed. see Fredman, Sandra & Morris, Gillian S.

O'Higgins, Paul, jt. auth. see Hepple, B. A.

O'Higgins, Paul, ed. see Hepple, B.

O'Higgins, Paul, ed. see Morris, G. S.

O'Higgins, Paul, ed. see Szyszczak, Erika M.

O'Higgins, Paul, ed. see Von Prondzynski, F.

O'Higgins, R., jt. ed. see McEldowney, J.

Ohio Adjutant General's Department Staff. Roster of Ohio Soldiers in the War of 1812. 157p. 1989. reprint ed. 16.00 (*0-685-60357-1*, 4300) Clearfield Co.

Ohio, Denise. Blue. LC 93-29091. 192p. 1993. pap. 12.00 (*0-929701-30-5*) McPherson & Co.

— End of the Empire. 160p. 1993. 16.95 (*0-312-09282-2*) St Martin.

— End of the Empire. 160p. 1994. pap. 8.95 (*0-312-10975-X*, Stonewall Inn) St Martin.

— The Finer Grain. 216p. 1988. pap. 8.95 (*0-941483-11-8*) Naiad Pr.

***Ohio Genealogical Society (Hamilton Co. Chapter) Staff.** Hamilton Co., Ohio, Burial Records Vol. 7: Springfield Township Cemeteries. Remter, Mary H., ed. (Illus.). 402p. (Orig.). 1994. pap. text ed. 50.00 (*0-614-02754-3*) Heritage Bk.

Ohio Genealogical Society Staff. Ohio Cemeteries. 1988. reprint ed. 29.50 (*0-935057-52-8*) OH Genealogical.

Ohio Historical Society Staff. Union Bibliography of Ohio Printed State Documents, 1803-1970. 750p. 1973. 20.00 (*0-318-03190-6*) Ohio Hist Soc.

Ohio Historical Society Staff & Kitchen, Judith L. Old Building Owner's Manual. 86p. 1983. spiral bd. 9.95 (*0-87758-016-2*) Ohio Hist Soc.

Ohio Judicial Conference. Ohio Jury Instructions 1968-1985, 4 vols. 1987. 325.00 (*0-317-57018-8*) Anderson Pub Co.

— Ohio Jury Instructions 1968-1985, 4 vols., 4. 1987. 125.00 (*0-317-57020-X*) Anderson Pub Co.

— Ohio Jury Instructions 1968-1985, Set, Vols. 1-3. 1987. Set. 400.00 (*0-317-57017-X*); Set. 325.00 (*0-317-57019-6*) Anderson Pub Co.

Ohio Judicial Conference, Jury Instruction Committee Staff. Ohio Jury Instructions, 4 vols., Set. 1987. ring bd. write for info. (*0-87084-675-2*) Anderson Pub Co.

***Ohio Math Project, Inc. Staff.** Introduction to Algebra & Statistics. Anthony, Edward F., ed. (Illus.). 456p. (YA). (gr. 8-10). 1993. teacher ed 68.00 (*1-880251-11-6*); text ed. 37.30 (*1-880251-10-8*) EFA & Assocs.

— Mathematics across the Curriculum. Anthony, Edward F., ed. (Illus.). 575p. (YA). (gr. 8-10). 1992. teacher ed 70.00 (*1-880251-08-6*); text ed. 37.80 (*1-880251-06-X*) EFA & Assocs.

Ohio Otterbein College Staff, ed. see Humesky, Assya & Shamraj, Ruth.

Ohio Otterbein College Staff, ed. see Kuruoglu, Guliz.

Ohio Staff & Case Western Reserve University. Center for Criminal Justice Staff. Criminal Justice: Constitutional Provisions, Criminal Code with Comment, Juvenile Court Statutes, Controlled Substances, Rules of Criminal Procedure, Rules of Juvenile Procedure, Ohio Rules of Evidence, with Annotations & Complete Analysis of Elements of Crimes in Ohio. LC 83-174489. 1985. 35.00 (*0-317-00848-X*) Case Western.

Ohio State Board of Pharmacy Staff, ed. Drug Laws of Ohio: 1993 Official Edition. 1142p. 1993. ring bd. 64.00 (*0-8322-0380-7*) Banks-Baldwin.

Ohio State Grange Staff. The Ohio State Grange Cookbook. LC 92-20292. 1992. write for info. (*0-87197-339-1*) Favorite Recipes.

Ohio State University, Department of Home Economics Education Faculty. Home Economics Education: A Review & Synthesis of the Research. 5th ed. 55p. 1986. 7.00 (*0-317-01422-6*, IN 313) Ctr Educ Trng Employ.

Ohio State University, Department of Linguistics Staff. Language Files: Materials for an Introduction to Language & Linguistics. 6th ed. 480p. (C). 1994. pap. 35.00x (*0-8142-0645-X*) Ohio St U Pr.

Ohio State University Research Foundation Staff. Toilet Training: Help for the Delayed Learner. (Illus.). 1978. text ed. 19.36 (*0-07-047681-0*) McGraw.

Ohio State University Staff. Laboratory Manual for Geological Sciences 100. 148p. (C). 1994. per. 16.80 (*0-8403-9457-8*) Kendall-Hunt.

***Ohio University Staff.** University Experience. 320p. (C). 1994. per., pap. text ed. 19.98 (*0-8403-9987-1*) Kendall-Hunt.

— University Experience. 320p. (C). 1995. pap. text ed. 28.50 (*0-7872-0814-0*) Kendall-Hunt.

Ohio Veterinary Medical Association Staff. A Century of Caring. Flournoy & Gibbs, Inc. Staff, ed. (Illus.). 132p. 1984. 30.00 (*0-9613273-0-8*) Ohio Vet.

Ohiorhenuan, John F. Capital & the State in Nigeria. LC 88-7710. (Contributions in Afro-American & African Studies). 280p. 1989. text ed. 59.95 (*0-313-26460-0*, OCN, Greenwood Pr) Greenwood.

Ohira, Goro, ed. see Niyama, Eisuke.

Ohira, Nine-Dan S. Appreciating Famous Games. Fairbairn, John, tr. 1977. 13.95 (*4-87187-025-1*, G25) Ishi Pr Intl.

Ohishi, Hiroshi. Photometric Determination of Traces of Metals: Individual Metals Magnesium to Zirconium, Pt. 2B. 4th ed. 848p. 1989. text ed. 345.00 (*0-471-84694-5*) Wiley.

Ohkawa, Kazushi & Key, Bernard, eds. Asian Socioeconomic Development: A National Accounts Approach. 326p. 1981. text ed. 27.50 (*0-8248-0743-X*) UH Pr.

Ohkawa, Kazushi & Kohama, Hirohisa. Lectures on Economic Development: Japan's Experience & Its Relevance. 380p. 1989. 57.50 (*0-86008-438-8*, Pub. by U of Tokyo JA) Col U Pr.

Ohkawa, Kazushi & Rosovsky, Henry. Japanese Economic Growth: Trend Acceleration in the Twentieth Century. LC 72-97203. (Studies of Economic Growth in Industrialized Countries). 352p. 1973. 42.50 (*0-8047-0833-9*) Stanford U Pr.

Ohkawa, Kazushi, ed. see International Conference on Economic Growth Staff.

Ohkawa, Kazushi, jt. ed. see Maunder, Aller.

Ohkawa, Kazushi, et al. Growth Mechanism of Developing Economies: Investment, Productivity, & Employment. LC 92-33578. 524p. 1992. pap. 24.95 (*1-55815-193-1*) ICS Pr.

Ohkawa, Kazushi, et al, eds. Patterns of Japanese Economic Development: A Quantitative Appraisal. LC 78-23317. (Economic Growth Center, Yale University, & the Council on East Asian Studies, Yale University Publication Ser.). (Illus.). 428p. reprint ed. pap. 122.00 (*0-8357-8261-1*, 2033847) Bks Demand.

Ohkawara, Akira & McGuire, Joseph, eds. The Biology of the Epidermis: Molecular & Functional Aspects: Proceedings of the Fifth Japan-United States Symposium on the Biology of the Epidermis, Niseko, Hokkaido, 21-25 July 1991. LC 92-22112. 1992. write for info. (*0-444-89232-X*) Elsevier.

Ohki. Membrane Fusion. 1995. write for info. (*0-8493-5078-6*) CRC Pr.

Ohki, S., ed. Cell & Model Membrane Interactions. (Illus.). 284p. 1992. 89.50 (*0-306-44097-0*, Plenum Pr) Plenum.

Ohkusu, M. Advances in Marine Hydrodynamics. (Advances in Fluid Mechanics Ser.). 300p. 1995. 118.00 (*1-56252-211-6*) Computational Mech MA.

Ohl, Dana A., jt. auth. see Lechtenberg, Richard.

Ohl, John F., jt. auth. see Parrish, Carl.

Ohl, John K. Hugh S. Johnson & the New Deal. (Illus.). 374p. 1985. 30.00 (*0-87580-110-2*) N Ill U Pr.

— Supplying the Troops: General Somervell & American Logistics in WW II. LC 93-39869. (Illus.). 325p. 1994. lib. bdg. 32.00 (*0-87580-185-4*) N Ill U Pr.

Ohl, S. S., et al. Guide to Modern Meals. 4th ed. 640p. 1985. student ed, text ed. 30.12 (*0-07-047513-X*) McGraw.

Ohlander, Stephen. Dramatic Suspense in Euripides' & Seneca's "Medea" (American University Studies: Classical Languages & Literature: Ser. XVII, Vol. 6). 345p. (C). 1989. text ed. 49.50 (*0-8204-0873-5*) P Lang Pubs.

Ohlander, U. Studies on Co-Ordinate Expressions in Middle English. (Lund Studies in English: Vol. 5). 1974. reprint ed. pap. 25.00 (*0-8115-0548-0*) Periodicals Srv.

Ohlbach, Hans J., ed. GWAI-92 - Advances in Artificial Intelligence: Proceedings of the 16th German Conference on Artificial Intelligence, Bonn Germany, August 31-September 3, 1992. LC 93-15233. (Lecture Notes in Computer Science Ser.: Vol. 671). 1993. 60.00 (*0-387-56667-8*) Spr-Verlag.

Ohlbach, Hans J., jt. auth. see Gabbay, Dov M.

Ohlbach, Hans J., jt. ed. see Gabbay, Dov M.

***Ohle, Nancy & Morley, Cindy L.** How to Solve Typical School Problems. LC 94-38880. 1994. pap. 6.95 (*0-87120-235-2*) Assn Supervision.

Ohle, Waldemar, ed. The Ecology of Aquatic Micro-Organisms. Wareing, Helen, tr. (Binnengewaesser Ser.: Vol. XXVIII). (Illus.). 252p. 1983. lib. bdg. 87.50 (*3-510-40039-9*, Pub. by E Schweizerbartsche GW) Lubrecht & Cramer.

Ohlendorf, Barbara, ed. Integrated Pest Management for Apples & Pears. (Illus.). 216p. (Orig.). 1991. pap. 30.00 (*0-931876-94-X*, 3340) ANR Pubns CA.

Ohlendorf, Barbara & Flint, Mary L. UC Integrated Pest Management Guidelines. 737p. 1990. ring bd. 80.00 (*0-931876-92-3*, 3339) ANR Pubns CA.

Ohlendorf, Sheila & Wittliff, William D., eds. The Horsemen of the Americas: An Exhibition from the Hall of the Horsemen of the Americas. (Illus.). 1968. pap. 5.00 (*0-87959-028-9*) U of Tex H Ransom Ctr.

Ohlendorf, Sheila M., ed. see Berlandier, Jean L., et al.

Ohlens, Rosemary C., et al. Did Your Granny Have a Hammer? A History of the Irish Women's Suffrage Movement. (Illus.). (C). 1989. pap. 7.95 (*0-946211-14-0*, Pub. by Attic IE) InBook.

Ohler, Annemarie. Studying the Old Testament: From Tradition to Canon. 400p. 39.95 (*0-567-09335-2*, Pub. by T & T Clark UK) Bks Intl VA.

— Studying the Old Testament: From Tradition to Canon. Cairns, David, tr. 400p. 1989. pap. 25.95 (*0-567-29166-9*, Pub. by T & T Clark UK) Bks Intl VA.

Ohler, C. P., comp. Paine: Ancestors & Descendants of David Paine & Abigail Shepard of Ludlow, MA, 1463-1913. (Illus.). 252p. 1993. reprint ed. lib. bdg. 49.50 (*0-8328-3730-X*); reprint ed. pap. 39.50 (*0-8328-3731-8*) Higginson Bk Co.

Ohler, Frederick. Better Than Nice & Other Unconventional Prayers. 120p. 1989. 14.00 (*0-664-21880-6*) Westminster John Knox.

Ohler, Norbert. The Medieval Traveller. (Illus.). 272p. (C). 1989. 45.00 (*0-85115-490-5*) Boydell & Brewer.

***Ohler, Norman.** Medieval Traveller. (Illus.). 264p. 1995. pap. 22.00 (*0-85115-607-X*) Boydell & Brewer.

Ohlert, Konrad. Rathsel und Gesellschaftsspiele der Alten Griechen. vii, 252p. 1979. reprint ed. write for info. (*3-487-06850-8*, Pub. by Georg Olms GW) Lubrecht & Cramer.

Ohles, Frederik. Germany's Rude Awakening: Censorship in the Land of the Brothers Grimm. LC 92-826. 240p. 1992. lib. bdg. 35.00 (*0-87338-460-1*) Kent St U Pr.

Ohles, John F., ed. Biographical Dictionary of American Educators, 3 vols. LC 77-84750. 1978. text ed. 195.00 (*0-8371-9893-3*, OHB/) Greenwood.

— Biographical Dictionary of American Educators, 3 vols., 1. LC 77-84750. 1978. text ed. 85.00 (*0-8371-9894-1*, OHB/1) Greenwood.

— Biographical Dictionary of American Educators, 3 vols., Vol. 2. LC 77-84750. 1978. text ed. 85.00 (*0-8371-9895-X*, OHB/2) Greenwood.

— Biographical Dictionary of American Educators, 3 vols., Vol. 3. LC 77-84750. 1978. text ed. 85.00 (*0-8371-9896-8*, OHB/3) Greenwood.

Ohles, John F. & Ohles, Shirley M. The Greenwood Encyclopedia of American Institutions, No. 6: Private Colleges & Universities, 2 vols., 1. LC 81-13238. x, 1619p. 1982. text ed. 95.00 (*0-313-23323-3*, OHP/01, Greenwood Pr) Greenwood.

— The Greenwood Encyclopedia of American Institutions, No. 6: Private Colleges & Universities, 2 vols., Set. LC 81-13238. x, 1619p. 1982. text ed. 175.00 (*0-313-21416-6*, OHP/, Greenwood Pr) Greenwood.

— The Greenwood Encyclopedia of American Institutions, No. 6: Private Colleges & Universities, 2 vols., Vol. 2. LC 81-13238. x, 1619p. 1982. text ed. 95.00 (*0-313-23324-1*, OHP/02, Greenwood Pr) Greenwood.

— Public Colleges & Universities. LC 85-17725. (Encyclopedia of American Institutions Ser.: No. 9). 1024p. 1986. text ed. 115.00 (*0-313-23257-1*, OHC/, Greenwood Pr) Greenwood.

Ohles, Judith K. & McDaniel, Julie A. Training Paraprofessionals for Reference Service: A How-to-Do-It Manual for Librarians. (How-to-Do-It Ser.). 184p. 1993. pap. 39.95 (*1-55570-084-5*) Neal-Schuman.

Ohles, Shirley M., jt. auth. see Ohles, John F.

Ohlgren, Thomas, ed. Anglo-Saxon Textual Illustration: Photographs of Sixteen Manuscripts with Description & Index. (Illus.). 1992. boxed 75.00 (*1-879288-10-9*) Medieval Inst.

Ohlgren, Thomas H., comp. Insular & Anglo-Saxon Illuminated Manuscripts: An Iconographic Catalogue c. A.D. 625 to 1100. LC 85-20446. (Illus.). 480p. 1986. 88.00 (*0-8240-8651-1*) Garland.

Ohlig, Adelheid. Luna Yoga: Vital Fertility & Sexuality. Liebenstein, Meret, tr. (Best of Europe Ser.). (Illus.). 224p. (Orig.). 1995. pap. 11.95 (*0-9614620-6-X*) Ash Tree.

Ohlig, Hayley, tr. see Burian, Peter K. & Richter, Gunter.

Ohlig, Hayley, tr. see Huber, Michael & Meehan, Joseph.

Ohlig, Hayley, tr. see Huber, Michael & Peterson, B. Moose.

Ohlig, Hayley, tr. see Richter, Gunter & Burian, Peter K.

Ohliger, J. Listening Groups: Mass Media in Adult Education. 1967. 2.50 (*0-317-18228-5*, REP 119) Syracuse U Cont Ed.

— The Mass Media in Adult Education. LC 73-80717. (Occasional Papers: No. 18). 1968. pap. text ed. 2.00 (*0-685-76689-6*, OCP 18) Syracuse U Cont Ed.

Ohlin, Bertil. The Course & Phases of the World Economic Depression: Report Presented to the Assembly of the League of Nations. LC 72-4284. (World Affairs Ser.: National & International Viewpoints). 342p. 1972. reprint ed. 23.95 (*0-405-04577-8*) Ayer.

Ohlin, Bertil, jt. ed. see Hechscher, Eli F.

Ohlin, Bertil, et al, eds. The International Allocation of Economic Activity. LC 77-11048. 572p. 1978. 65.00 (*0-8419-0342-5*) Holmes & Meier.

Ohlin, Goran, tr. see Heckscher, Eli F.

Ohlin, Lloyd & Tonry, Michael H., eds. Family Violence. LC 88-17386. (Studies in Crime & Justice: A Review of Research Ser.: Vol. 11). 480p. 1990. pap. 19.95 (*0-226-80807-6*) U Ch Pr.

Ohlin, Lloyd E. Selection for Parole. (Russell Sage Foundation Reprint Ser.). reprint ed. lib. bdg. 34.50 (*0-697-00207-1*) Irvington.

Ohlin, Lloyd E., ed. Prisoners in America: Perspectives on Our Correctional System. LC 73-1221. (American Assembly Guides Ser.). 224p. 1973. 6.95 (*0-13-710822-2*); pap. 2.45 (*0-13-710814-1*) Am Assembly.

Ohlin, Lloyd E. & Remington, Frank J., eds. Discretion in Criminal Justice: The Tension Between Individualization & Uniformity. LC 92-30233. (SUNY Series in New Directions in Crime & Justice Studies). 365p. (C). 1993. 64.50 (*0-7914-1563-5*); pap. 21.95 (*0-7914-1564-3*) State U NY Pr.

Ohlin, Per G. The Positive & the Preventive Check: A Study of the Rate of Growth of Pre-Industrial Populations. Bruchey, Stuart, ed. LC 80-2819. (Dissertations in European Economic History Ser.). (Illus.). 1981. lib. bdg. 54.95 (*0-405-14003-7*) Ayer.

Ohlin, Peter. Agee. 1965. 19.95 (*0-8392-1146-5*); pap. 7.95 (*0-8392-5011-8*) Astor-Honor.

Ohlinger, John & McCarthy, Colleen. Lifelong Learning or Lifelong Schooling: A Tentative View of the Ideas of Ivan Illich. LC 70-164120. (Occasional Papers: No. 24). 1971. text ed. 2.25 (*0-87060-044-3*, OCP 24) Syracuse U Cont Ed.

Ohlman, Jim, jt. auth. see Green, J. D.

Ohlmann, G., et al, eds. Catalysis & Adsorption by Zeolites: Proceedings of the ZEOCAT 90, Leipzig, FRG, Aug. 20-23, 1990. (Studies in Surface Science & Catalysis: No. 65). 718p. 1991. 225.75 (*0-444-89088-2*) Elsevier.

Ohlmeyer, Jane H. Civil War & Restoration in the Three Stuart Kingdoms: The Career of Randal MacDonnell, Marquis of Antrim, 1609-1683. LC 92-8873. (Cambridge Studies in Early Modern British History). (Illus.). 336p. (C). 1993. 69.95 (*0-521-41978-6*) Cambridge U Pr.

***Ohlmeyer, Jane H., ed.** Ireland from Independence to Occupation, 1641-1660. (Illus.). 300p. (C). 1995. 59.95 (*0-521-43479-3*) Cambridge U Pr.

***Ohlms, David L.** Cocaine. rev. ed. GWC, Inc. Staff, ed. & intro. by. 22p. (Orig.). 1988. pap. 2.50 (*1-56168-028-1*, B104) GWC Inc.

— Disease of Alcoholism. rev. ed. GWC, Inc. Staff, ed. & intro. by. (Illus.). 30p. (Orig.). 1994. pap. 2.50 (*1-56168-025-7*, B101) GWC Inc.

— Marijuana. rev. ed. GWC, Inc. Staff, ed. & intro. by. 17p. (Orig.). 1988. pap. 2.50 (*1-56168-030-3*, B106) GWC Inc.

— Pot. rev. ed. GWC, Inc. Staff, ed. & intro. by. (Orig.). 1988. pap. 2.50 (*1-56168-026-5*, B102) GWC Inc.

— Prescription Trap. rev. ed. GWC, Inc. Staff, ed. & intro. by. 20p. (Orig.). 1988. pap. 2.50 (*1-56168-027-3*, B103) GWC Inc.

Ohloff, Gunther. Scent & Fragrances: The Fascination of Odors & Their Chemical Perspectives. Pickenhagen, W., tr. LC 93-44959. (Illus.). 260p. 1994. 88.00 (*0-387-57108-6*) Spr-Verlag.

Ohlott, Patricia J., jt. auth. see Ruderman, Marian N.

***Ohlrich, Warren.** Columbia Running Routes: 84 Measured Courses in Columbia, Maryland, for Runners, Walkers, & Bikers. LC 95-60455. (Illus.). 88p. 1995. pap. 12.95 (*0-614-04503-7*); pap. 12.95 (*1-882426-03-7*) W H O Pr.

Ohlrich, Warren H. Aspen & Central Colorado Trails. LC 93-93820. (Illus.). 100p. (Orig.). 1993. pap. 9.95 (*0-9620046-9-3*) W H O Pr.

— Aspen in Color. LC 90-90323. (Illus.). 112p. 1990. 34.95 (*0-9620046-5-0*) W H O Pr.

— Aspen-Snowmass Cross Country Ski Trails. LC 89-51494. 56p. (Orig.). 1989. pap. 5.95 (*0-9620046-2-6*) W H O Pr.

— Aspen-Snowmass Downhill Ski Trails. LC 89-90419. 104p. (Orig.). 1990. pap. 7.95 (*0-9620046-3-4*) W H O Pr.

— Aspen-Snowmass Trails: A Hiking Trail Guide. LC 87-92228. 52p. (Orig.). 1988. pap. 7.95 (*0-9620046-0-X*) W H O Pr.

Ohlrich, Warren H., ed. Aspen, Portrait of a Rocky Mountain Town. LC 92-90947. (Illus.). 112p. 1993. 29.95 (*1-882426-00-2*) W H O Pr.

Ohlrich, Warren H., jt. auth. see Barlow-Perez, Sally.

Ohlrich, Warren H., ed. see Dawson, Louis W., Jr.

Ohlrich, Warren H., ed. see Photographers Aspen Staff.

Ohlrich, Warren H., ed. see Rankin, Joyce.

Ohls, James C. & Beebout, Harold. The Food Stamp Program: Design Tradeoffs, Policy, & Impacts. A Mathematics Policy Research Study. LC 93-7222. (Illus.). 230p. (Orig.). (C). 1993. lib. bdg. 57.00 (*0-87766-576-1*); pap. text ed. 24.00 (*0-87766-577-X*) Urban Inst.

Ohlschlager, George W. & Mosgofian, Peter T. Law for the Christian Counselor. Collins, Gary R., ed. (Contemporary Christian Counseling Ser.: Vol. 6). 1992. 15.99 (*0-8499-0889-2*) Word Inc.

Ohlschlager, George W., jt. auth. see Mosgofian, Peter T.

Ohlsen, G. G., et al, eds. Polarization Phenomena in Nuclear Physics, 1980: Fifth International Symposium, Santa Fe. (AIP Conference Proceedings Ser.: No. 69). 1536p. 1981. lib. bdg. 84.00 (*0-88318-168-1*) Am Inst Physics.

Ohlsen, Merle M., et al. Group Counseling. 3rd ed. LC 87-17599. 432p. (C). 1988. text ed. 38.75 (*0-03-008464-4*) HB Coll Pubs.

Ohlsen, Woodrow. Perspectives on Old Testament Literature. LC 77-91012. (Illus.). 450p. (C). 1978. pap. text ed. 20.00 (*0-15-570484-2*) HB Coll Pubs.

Ohlson, J. A. The Theory of Financial Markets & Information. 362p. 1987. 42.75 (*0-444-01161-7*) P-H.

Ohlson, Lori. Whimsical Critters. 100p. 1990. pap. 7.50 (*1-56770-228-7*) S Scheewe Pubns.

Ohlson, N. G. & Wester, I., eds. Swedish Symposium on Classical Fatigue. (Illus.). 418p. 1985. text ed. 108.00x (*91-22-00770-9*, Pub. by Almqv & Wiksell SW) Coronet Bks.

Ohlson, Olof. Helpful Information for Watchmakers. LC 84-16877. (Illus.). 104p. 1987. reprint ed. pap. 11.95 (*0-930163-21-4*) Arlington Bk.

Ohlson, Philip A. Economic Consequences of Financial Accounting Standards: Selected Papers. LC 78-67861. (Financial Accounting Standards Board Research Report Ser.). (Illus.). 278p. (Orig.). 1978. pap. 10.00 (*0-910065-04-7*) Finan Acct Found.

Ohlson, Thomas, ed. Arms Transfer Limitations & Third World Security. (SIPRI Ser.). (Illus.). 272p. 1988. 55.00 (*0-19-829124-8*) OUP.

Ohlson, Thomas, jt. auth. see Brzoska, Michael.

Ohlson, Thomas, et al. The New Is Not Yet Born: Conflict Resolution in Southern Africa. 322p. (C). 1994. 36.95x (*0-8157-6452-9*); pap. 15.95x (*0-8157-6451-0*) Brookings.

Ohlsson, Leif, ed. Regional Case Studies of Water Conflicts. (Illus.). 140p. (Orig.). 1992. pap. 36.50x (*91-87380-25-0*, Pub. by Almqv & Wiksell SW) Coronet Bks.

***Ohlsson, Leif, et al, eds.** Hydropolitics: Conflicts over Water As a Development Constraint. LC 95-13681. 256p. (C). 1995. text ed. 59.95 (*1-85649-331-8*, Pub. by Zed Books UK); pap. 25.00 (*1-85649-332-6*, Pub. by Zed Books UK) Humanities.

***Ohlsson, R., et al, eds.** Genomic Imprinting: Causes & Consequences. (Illus.). 380p. (C). 1995. write for info. (*0-521-47243-1*) Cambridge U Pr.

***Ohlsson, Ragnar.** Morals Based on Needs. 164p. (C). 1995. lib. bdg. 34.50 (*0-8191-9853-6*) U Pr of Amer.

Ohly, Friedrich. The Damned & the Elect: Guilt in Western Culture. Archibald, Linda, tr. (Illus.). 215p. (C). 1992. 54.95 (*0-521-38250-5*) Cambridge U Pr.

OHM Staff. OHM's Dictionary of Computers, English-Japanese-English. 256p. (ENG & JPN.). 1985. 95.00 (*0-8288-0252-1*, F17250) Fr & Eur.

***Ohmachi, T. & Kuwano, J., eds.** Dynamic Safety of Earth & Rockfill Dams: Proceedings of a Course, New Delhi, August 1993. (Illus.). 160p. (C). 1994. text ed. 55.00 (*90-5410-265-9*) Ashgate Pub Co.

Ohmae, Kenichi. The Borderless World: Power & Strategy in the Interlinked Economy. LC 90-56432. 224p. 1991. reprint ed. pap. 12.00 (*0-06-097412-5*, PL) HarpC.

— The End of the Nation State: The Rise of Regional Economies. 256p. 1995. 25.00 (*0-02-923341-0*) Free Pr.

— The Mind of the Strategist: The Art of Japanese Business. LC 81-18630. (Illus.). 304p. 1991. text ed. 29.95 (*0-07-047595-4*); pap. text ed. 12.95 (*0-07-047904-6*) McGraw.

— Triad Power: The Coming Shape of Global Competition. LC 84-26068. 192p. (C). 1985. 32.95 (*0-02-923470-0*) Free Pr.

Ohman, A., jt. ed. see Birbaumer, N.

Ohman, Arne & Ohngren, Bo, eds. Two Faces of Swedish Psychology, Vol. 1: An Evaluation of Swedish Research in Cognitive Psychology. 168p. (Orig.). 1991. pap. 35.00x (*91-86362-16-X*, Pub. by Almqv & Wiksell SW) Coronet Bks.

Ohman, Arne, jt. ed. see Magnusson, David.

Ohman, Jack. Fear of Fly-Fishing: Do Trout Exist? And Other Facts of Reel Life. (Illus.). 144p. 1988. pap. 9.00 (*0-671-66151-5*, Fireside) S&S Trade.

— Fishing Bass-Ackwards. (Illus.). 142p. 1995. reprint ed. pap. 9.95 (*1-57223-030-4*, WCP) Outlook Pubng.

— Fishing Bass-Ackwards: Coming down the Pike with Off-the-Walleye Humor. (Illus.). 144p. (Orig.). 1991. pap. 7.95 (*0-671-68624-0*, Fireside) S&S Trade.

— Why Johnny Can't Putt... 1994. 9.00 (*0-671-87298-2*, Fireside) S&S Trade.

Ohman, Marian, jt. auth. see Budds, Michael.

Ohman, Marian M. Encyclopedia of Missouri Courthouses. LC 80-54474. (Illus.). 230p. 1981. pap. 10.00 (*0-933842-01-5*) Extension Div.

— The History of Missouri Capitols. (Illus.). 120p. 1982. pap. 10.00 (*0-933842-02-3*) Extension Div.

— A History of Missouri's Counties, County Seats & Courthouse Squares. (Illus.). 146p. 1983. 15.00 (*0-933842-03-1*) Extension Div.

— Twenty Towns: Their Histories, Town Plans, & Architecture. (Illus.). 260p. 1985. pap. 6.00 (*0-933842-04-X*) Extension Div.

Ohman, R., et al, eds. Interaction Between Mental & Physical Illness. (Illus.). 185p. 1989. 79.00 (*0-387-50161-4*) Spr-Verlag.

Ohman, Sven, jt. ed. see Kanger, Stig.

Ohman, Sven, jt. ed. see Lindblom, Bjorn.

Ohman, Y., ed. Mass Motions in Solar Flares & Related Phenomena: Proceedings of the Nobel Symposium, Ninth. 245p. (Orig.). 1968. text ed. 30.50 (*0-685-13808-9*, Pub. by Keter Pub IS) Coronet Bks.

***Ohmann, Richard.** English in America: A Radical View of the Profession. 416p. (C). 1995. pap. 17.95 (*0-8195-6293-9*, Wesleyan Univ Pr) U Pr of New Eng.

Ohmann, Richard M. Politics of Letters. LC 87-2152. (Illus.). 336p. 1988. text ed. 35.00 (*0-8195-5175-9*, Wesleyan Univ Pr); pap. 16.95 (*0-8195-6213-0*, Wesleyan Univ Pr) U Pr of New Eng.

Ohmart, Ben, tr. see De Sade, Marquis.

Ohmberger, D. Bamboos of the World: A Preliminary Study of the Names & Distribution of the Herbaceous & Woody Bamboos. 1112p. 1990. 1,500.00 (*81-7089-115-9*, Pub. by Intl Bk Distr II) St Mut.

Ohme, Heinz. Das Concilium Quinisextum und Seine Bischofsliste: Studien zum Konstantinopeler Konzil von 692. (Arbeiten zur Kirchengeschichte Ser.: Band 756). xii, 423p. (C). 1990. lib. bdg. 104.65 (*3-11-012432-7*) De Gruyter.

Ohme, Herman. Foreign Language Grammatical Glossary. rev. ed. Ohme, Jean, ed. (Illus.). 80p. 1989. pap. 6.00 (*0-936047-07-0*) CA Educ Plan.

— Learn How to Learn Study Skills. rev. ed. Ohme, Jean, ed. (Illus.). 256p. 1989. pap. 12.00 (*0-936047-00-3*) CA Educ Plan.

— Motivation & Concentration. rev. ed. Ohme, Jean, ed. (Illus.). 48p. 1989. pap. 5.00 (*0-685-49850-6*) CA Educ Plan.

— Organization & Time Management. rev. ed. Ohme, Jean, ed. (Illus.). 48p. 1989. pap. 5.00 (*0-936047-03-8*) CA Educ Plan.

— Parent Guide to Study Skills. rev. ed. Ohme, Jean, ed. (Illus.). 48p. 1989. pap. 5.00 (*0-936047-06-2*) CA Educ Plan.

— Teacher Guide to "Learn How to Learn" Study Skills. rev. ed. Ohme, Jean, ed. (Illus.). 24p. 1989. pap. 5.00 (*0-936047-02-X*) CA Educ Plan.

— Test Taking. rev. ed. Ohme, Jean, ed. (Illus.). 54p. 1989. pap. 5.00 (*0-936047-05-4*) CA Educ Plan.

Ohme, Herman & Ohme, Jean. Notetaking & Report Writing. rev. ed. (Illus.). 56p. 1989. pap. 5.00 (*0-936047-11-9*) CA Educ Plan.

Ohme, Jean, ed. see Ohme, Herman.

Ohme, Jean, jt. auth. see Ohme, Herman.

Ohme, Jean, ed. see Ohme, Herman.

Ohmi. Ultra-Clean Technology Handbook Vol. 1: Ultra-Pure Water. 968p. 1993. 215.00 (*0-8247-8753-6*) Dekker.

***Ohmori, Koichiro.** Over the Himalaya. (Illus.). 110p. 1994. 40.00 (*0-938567-37-3*) Cloudcap.

Ohnami, Masateru, ed. Fracture & Society. LC 92-53265. 420p. 1992. 105.00 (*90-5199-092-8*, Pub. by IOS Pr NE) IOS Press.

Ohnesorg, Aenne. Inselionische Marmordaecher. Deutsches Archaeologisches Institut Staff, ed. (Denkmaeler Antiker Architecktur, Vol. 18, 2: Architektur Auf Naxos und Paros Ser.: No. II). (Illus.). xvi, 160p. (GER.). (C). 1993. lib. bdg. 186.15 (*3-11-013718-6*) De Gruyter.

Ohnesorg, Karel, ed. Colloquium Paedolinguisticum. (Janua Linguarum, Ser. Minor: No. 133). 1972. pap. text ed. 45.50 (*90-279-2315-9*) Mouton.

Ohngren, Bo, jt. ed. see Ohman, Arne.

Ohnishi. Malignant Hyperthermia Membrane-Linked Diseases, Vol. III. 1994. 129.95 (*0-8493-8093-6*, RD82) CRC Pr.

— Membrane Associated Abnormalities - Sickle Cell Diseases - Membrane Linked Diseases, Vol. II. 1994. 95.00 (*0-8493-8092-8*, RC641) CRC Pr.

Ohnishi, S. Tsuyoshi & Ohnishi, Tomoko, eds. Central Nervous System Trauma Research Techniques, Vol. 4. (Membrane-Linked Diseases Ser.). 560p. 1995. 149.95 (*0-8493-8094-4*, 8094) CRC Pr.

Ohnishi, Tomoko, jt. ed. see Ohnishi, S. Tsuyoshi.

Ohno, A. Solidification. (Illus.). 130p. 1987. pap. 53.00 (*0-387-18233-0*) Spr-Verlag.

Ohno, Eiichi, et al. Introduction to Power Electronics. (Monographs in Electrical & Electronic Engineering: No. 20). (Illus.). 304p. 1988. 95.00 (*0-19-859338-4*) OUP.

Ohno, K. & Morokuma, K. Quantum Chemistry Literature Data Base: Bibliography of AB Initio Calculations for 1978-80. (Physical Sciences Data Ser.: Vol. 12). 460p. 1982. 156.50 (*0-444-42074-6*) Elsevier.

Ohno, M., jt. ed. see Lukacs, Gabor.

***Ohno, Noriko.** Ikebana in Modern Life: 48 Stylish Arrangements. 132p. Date not set. 28.00 (*4-7700-2020-1*) FS&G.

Ohno, Shuho. Modern Senryu in English. (Illus.). 256p. (C). 1988. 18.50 (*0-9620359-0-4*) Hokubei Intl.

Ohno, Susumu. Animal Cytogenetics, Vol. 4: Chordata, Pt. 1: Protochordata, Cyclostomata, & Pisces. (Illus.). 100p. 1974. text ed. 33.50 (*3-443-26001-2*, Pub. by Gebruder Borntraeger GW) Lubrecht & Cramer.

Ohno, T. & Yamamoto, R., eds. Multilayers: Materials Research Society International Symposium Proceedings-IMAM, No. 10. 619p. 1989. text ed. 85.00 (*1-55899-039-9*) Materials Res.

Ohno, Taiichi. Toyota Production System: Beyond Large-Scale Production. LC 87-43172. (Illus.). 162p. 1988. 45.00 (*0-915299-14-3*) Prod Press.

— Workplace Management. LC 87-43173. (Illus.). 164p. 1988. 40.00 (*0-318-32669-8*) Prod Press.

Ohno, Taiichi & Mito, Setsuo. Just-In-Time for Today & Tomorrow. LC 88-42624. (Illus.). 160p. 1988. 40.00 (*0-915299-20-8*) Prod Press.

Ohno, Y., ed. Distributed Environments: Software Paradigms & Workstations. (Illus.). xi, 322p. 1991. 117.00 (*0-387-70075-7*) Spr-Verlag.

— Requirements Engineering Environments: Proceedings of the International Symposium on Current Issues of Requirements Engineering Environments, Sept. 20-21, 1982, Kyoto, Japan. 174p. 1983. 72.00 (*0-444-86533-0*, North Holland) Elsevier.

Ohno, Yutaka, jt. auth. see Matsumoto, Yoshihio.

Ohnsorg, jt. auth. see Rothenberger.

Ohnstad, Bob. Scissors & Comb Haircutting: A Cut-by-Cut Guide for Home Haircutters. LC 84-90072. (Illus.). 186p. (Orig.). 1985. pap. 15.95 (*0-916819-01-9*) You Can Pub.

Ohnuki-Tierney, Emiko. The Ainu of the Northwest Coast of Southern Sakhalin. (Illus.). 127p. (C). 1984. reprint ed. pap. text ed. 8.95 (*0-88133-092-2*) Waveland Pr.

— Culture Through Time: Anthropological Approaches. LC 90-36662. 344p. 1991. 45.00 (*0-8047-1792-3*); pap. 14.95 (*0-8047-1791-5*) Stanford U Pr.

— Illness & Culture in Contemporary Japan: An Anthropological View. LC 83-14415. 320p. 1984. 64.95 (*0-521-25982-7*); pap. 17.95 (*0-521-27786-8*) Cambridge U Pr.

— Illness & Healing among the Sakhalin Ainu: A Symbolic Interpretation. LC 80-24268. 261p. reprint ed. pap. 74.40 (*0-318-34830-6*, 2031701) Bks Demand.

— The Monkey As Mirror. LC 87-45530. (Illus.). 280p. 1987. text ed. 49.50 (*0-691-09434-9*) Princeton U Pr.

— The Monkey As Mirror: Symbolic Transformations in Japanese History & Ritual. 286p. 1989. pap. text ed. 14.95 (*0-691-02846-X*) Princeton U Pr.

— Rice as Self: Japanese Identities Through Time. LC 92-43711. (Illus.). 200p. 1993. text ed. 19.95 (*0-691-09477-2*) Princeton U Pr.

Ohnuki, Y. Unitary Representations of the Poincare Group & Relativistic Wave Equations. 228p. (C). 1988. text ed. 54.00 (*9971-5-0250-X*) World Scientific Pub.

Ohnuki, Y. & Kamefuchi, S. Quantum Field Theory & Parastatistics. (Illus.). 489p. 1982. 120.00 (*0-387-11643-5*) Spr-Verlag.

An Asterisk (*) at the beginning of an entry indicates that the title is appearing in BIP for the first time.

Ohnuma, Toshiro. Radiation Phenomena in Plasmas. 326p. 1994. text ed. 74.00 (*981-02-1840-0*) World Scientific Pub.

Ohnysty, James. Aids to Ethics & Professional Conduct for Student Radiologic Technologists. 2nd ed. 176p. 1979. spiral bd., pap. 27.95x (*0-398-01419-1*) C C Thomas.

Oho, Kenkichi. Practical Fiberoptic Bronchoscopy. 2nd ed. LC 84-3836. (Illus.). 240p. 1984. 92.00 (*0-89640-103-0*) Igaku-Shoin.

Oholo Biological Conference Staff. Skin: Drug Application & Evaluation of Environmental Hazards, Proceedings of the Oholo Biological Conference, 22nd, Ma'alot, March 1977. Mali, J. W. et al, eds. (Current Problems in Dermatology Ser.: Vol. 7). (Illus.). 1977. 79.25 (*3-8055-2797-7*) S Karger.

O'Holohan, John. My Pocket Prayer Book. 96p. (Orig.). 1988. pap. 4.95 (*1-85390-017-6*, Pub. by Veritas Pubns IE) Irish Bks Media.

O'Holohan, John, comp. Pocket Prayer Book. Orig. Title: My Pocket Prayer Book. 96p. 1993. reprint ed. 5.99 (*0-89283-837-X*, Charis) Servant.

O'Hooper, David. The Peace Tree: A Modern Christmas Fable. (Illus.). 32p. (J). (gr. k-8). 1994. 12.50 (*0-9640684-3-5*) Pixie Dust.

Ohotin, Nicholas A., tr. see Soloveichik, Svetlana A.

Ohr, Karlfriedrich. Die Basilika In Pompeji: Unter Mitarbeit von Jurgen J. Rasch. (Denkmaeler Antiker Architektur Ser.: Vol. 17). (Illus.). x, 87p. (GER.). (C). 1991. lib. bdg. 152.35 (*3-11-012283-9*) De Gruyter.

***Ohrbach, Barbara M.** All Things Are Possible - Pass the Word. LC 94-37344. (J). 1995. pap. 7.00 (*0-517-88426-7*, Clarkson Potter) Crown Bks Yng Read.

— Antiques at Home. 1989. 27.50 (*0-517-56986-8*, C P Pubs) Crown Pub Group.

— A Bouquet of Flowers: Sweet Thoughts, Recipes, & Gifts from the Garden, with "The Language of Flowers" (Illus.). 1990. 9.95 (*0-517-57428-4*, C P Pubs) Crown Pub Group.

— A Cheerful Heart: A Collection of Thoughts, Poems, Sentiments, & Recipes to Share with Those You Love. (Illus.). 64p. 1991. 3.50 (*0-517-58181-7*, C P Pubs) Crown Pub Group.

— Memories of Childhood: Old-Fashioned Rhymes, Poems, Lullabies, & Thoughts to Share with Children. (Illus.). 64p. 1988. 9.95 (*0-517-57021-1*, C P Pubs) Crown Pub Group.

— Merry Christmas: Festive Stories, Songs, Poems, Recipes, & Gift Ideas for the Holidays. (Illus.). 64p. 1992. 10.00 (*0-517-58626-6*, C P Pubs) Crown Pub Group.

— The Scented Room: Cherchez's Book of Dried Flowers, Fragrance, & Potpourri. 1986. 18.00 (*0-517-56081-X*, C P Pubs) Crown Pub Group.

— The Scented Room Gardening Notebook. LC 89-7993. (Illus.). 519p. 1990. 15.95 (*0-517-57577-9*, C P Pubs) Crown Pub Group.

— Spirit of America: A Collection of Favorite American Quotes, Poems, Songs & Recipes. 1992. 10.00 (*0-517-58627-4*, C P Pubs) Crown Pub Group.

— A Token of Friendship: A Collection of Sentiments, Thoughts, Gift Ideas, & Recipes for Special Friends. (Illus.). 64p. 1987. 10.00 (*0-517-56657-5*, C P Pubs) Crown Pub Group.

— Token of Friendship Notepads. 1993. pap. 6.00 (*0-517-88095-4*, Ebury Pr Stationery) Random Hse Value.

Ohrbach, Barbara M., comp. Happy Birthday! LC 93-25256. 1994. 10.00 (*0-517-58625-8*, C P Pubs) Crown Pub Group.

Ohrbach, K. H. The Parat Dictionary of Ecology: English-German, German-English. 330p. (ENG & GER.). 1991. text ed. 89.00 (*0-89573-989-5*) VCH Pubs.

***Ohrbach, Karl-Heinz.** Parat Dictionary of Ecology: English-German, German-English. 330p. (ENG & GER.). 1991. 175.00 (*0-7859-6955-1*) Fr & Eur.

Ohren, Margaret, ed. Taking Time Out: Managing Employment Breaks. 160p. (C). 1991. pap. text ed. 65.00 (*0-85292-460-7*, Pub. by IPM Hse UK) St Mut.

Ohrenstein, Roman A. & Gordon, Barry. Economic Analysis in Talmudic Literature: Rabbinic Thought in the Light of Modern Economics. LC 91-41392. (Studia Post-Biblica Ser.: No. 40). (Illus.). xviii, 152p. 1992. 43.00 (*90-04-09540-3*) E J Brill.

Ohri, Sushel, jt. auth. see Radical Statistics Race Group (BAHT) Staff.

Ohri, Vishwa C. On the Origins of the Pahari Painting. (C). 1991. 25.00 (*81-85182-53-1*, Pub. by Motilal Banarsidass II) S Asia.

Ohri, Vishwa C., ed. History & Culture of the Chamba State. (C). 1988. 110.00 (*81-85016-25-9*, Pub. by Bks & Bks IA) S Asia.

Ohring, G. & Bolle, H. J., eds. Space Observations for Climate Studies: Proceedings of Symposium 4 of the COSPAR Twenty-Fifth Plenary Meeting Held in Graz Austria, 25 June-7 July 1984. (Illus.). 404p. 1985. pap. 54.00 (*0-08-033195-5*, Pub. by PPL UK) Elsevier.

***Ohring, Milton.** Engineering Materials Science. (Illus.). 800p. 1995. boxed write for info. (*0-12-524995-0*) Acad Pr.

— The Materials Science of Thin Films. (Illus.). 704p. 1991. text ed. 74.95 (*0-12-524990-X*) Acad Pr.

Ohrlin, Glenn. Hell-Bound Train: A Cowboy Songbook. 312p. 1989. pap. 14.95 (*0-252-06071-7*) U of Ill Pr.

— The Hellbound Train: A Cowboy Songbook. LC 72-88808. (Music in American Life Ser.). 311p. reprint ed. pap. 88.70 (*0-317-09635-4*, 2022774) Bks Demand.

***Ohrn, Deborah, ed.** Herstory: Women Who Changed the World. (Illus.). 288p. (YA). 1995. 19.95 (*0-670-85434-4*, Viking) Viking Penguin.

Ohrn, Steven G. Cataloguing in Context: The African Studies Program Slide Archives. 49p. 1975. pap. 2.00 (*0-941934-16-0*) Indiana Africa.

Ohrnberger, D. Bamboos of the World: A Preliminary Study of the Names & Distribution of the Herbaceous & Woody Bamboos (Bambusoideae Nees V. Esenb) 1112p. (C). 1990. 160.00 (*0-685-61463-8*, Pub. by Intl Bk Distr II) St Mut.

Ohrt, Wallace. The Accidental Missionaries: How a Vacation Turned into a Vocation. LC 90-48587. 190p. (Orig.). 1990. pap. 9.99 (*0-8308-1741-7*, 1741) InterVarsity.

Ohry, Abraham, jt. auth. see Kossoy, Edward.

Ohsawa, George. The Art of Peace. Rothman, Sandy, ed. Gleason, William, tr. LC 90-82077. 152p. (Orig.). 1990. pap. 7.95 (*0-918860-50-4*) G Ohsawa.

— Gandhi: The Eternal Youth. Burns, Kenneth G., tr. & intro. by. LC 86-80512. 142p. (Orig.). (FRE.). 1986. pap. 6.95 (*0-918860-45-8*) G Ohsawa.

— Macrobiotic Guidebook for Living. rev. ed. 130p. 1985. pap. 7.95 (*0-918860-41-5*) G Ohsawa.

— Macrobiotics: An Invitation to Health & Happiness. 77p. 1984. reprint ed. pap. 5.95 (*0-918860-02-4*) G Ohsawa.

— Macrobiotics: The Way Healing. 2nd ed. Aihara, Herman, ed. 162p. 1984. pap. 8.95 (*0-918860-38-5*) G Ohsawa.

— Order of the Universe. Poggi, Jim, ed. (Illus.). 103p. (Orig.). 1986. pap. 7.95 (*0-918860-46-6*) G Ohsawa.

— Philosophy of Oriental Medicine: Key to Your Personal Judging Ability. Aihara, Herman & Rothman, Sandy, eds. LC 91-76486. 153p. (Orig.). 1991. pap. 7.95 (*0-918860-52-0*) G Ohsawa.

Ohsawa, George, see Sakurazawa Nyoiti, pseud..

Ohsawa, George, Macrobiotic Foundation Staff. The First Macrobiotic Cookbook. rev. ed. Ruggles, Laurel, ed. (Illus.). 134p. 1985. 9.95 (*0-918860-42-3*) G Ohsawa.

Ohsawa, Georges. Clara Shumann, Dialectic of Education. 1992. pap. 9.50 (*0-685-57010-X*) Happiness Pr.

Ohsawa, Georges & De Langre, Jacques. But I Love Fruits. (Illus.). 1993. pap. 4.50 (*0-916508-32-3*) Happiness Pr.

Ohsawa, Junko, jt. tr. see Levy, Howard S.

Ohsawa, T., jt. ed. see Noguchi, J.

Ohsberg, H. Oliver. Church & Persons with Handicaps. LC 82-80342. 128p. 1982. pap. 7.95 (*0-8361-1996-7*) Herald Pr.

Ohshima, Tsutomu, tr. see Funakoshi, Gichin.

Ohshiro, Toshio & Calderhead, R. Glen. Low Level Laser Therapy: A Practical Introduction. 250p. 1988. text ed. 135.00 (*0-471-91956-X*) Wiley.

— Low Reactive Level Laser Therapy: Practical Application. 242p. 1991. text ed. 125.95 (*0-471-92845-3*, Wiley-Liss) Wiley.

— Progress in Laser Therapy: Selected Papers from the October 1990 ILTA Congress. 232p. 1991. text ed. 120.00 (*0-471-93154-3*, Wiley-Liss) Wiley.

Ohshiro, Y., jt. ed. see Yoshida, Z.

Ohsuga, S., et al, eds. Information Modelling & Knowledge Bases III. LC 91-77697. (Frontiers in Artificial Intelligence & Applications Ser.: Vol. 13). 712p. 1992. 135.00 (*90-5199-073-1*, Pub. by IOS Pr NE) IOS Press.

Ohta, Hiroshi. Spatial Price Theory of Imperfect Competition. LC 87-22333. (Economics Ser.: No. 8). (Illus.). 254p. 1988. lib. bdg. 34.50 (*0-89096-372-X*) Tex A&M Univ Pr.

Ohta, Hiroshi & Thisse, Jacques-Francois, eds. Does Economic Space Matter? Essays in Honour of Melvin L. Greenhut. LC 93-3. 1993. text ed. 75.00 (*0-312-09640-2*) St Martin.

Ohta, Kaoru. Japanese Grammar & Usage: A Companion to Modern Japanese, A Basic Reader. 416p. (JPN.). (C). 1991. pap. text ed. 29.95 (*0-88710-163-1*) Yale Far Eastern Pubns.

Ohta, M. & Remand, B. Tours Symposium on Nuclear Physics. 364p. 1992. text ed. 102.00 (*981-02-0892-8*) World Scientific Pub.

Ohta, Masahiro. Japanese Guide to the Grand Canyon. LC 82-82562. (Illus.). 26p. 1982. pap. 6.95 (*0-938216-18-X*) GCNHA.

Ohta, Naohisa. Packet Video: Modeling & Signal Processing. LC 93-38080. 207p. 1994. 69.00 (*0-89006-519-5*) Artech Hse.

***Ohta, Naohisa, et al.** Super-High Definition Images: Beyond HDTV. LC 94-49709. 1995. text ed. write for info. (*0-89006-674-4*) Artech Hse.

Ohta, T. Evolution & Variation of Multigene Families. (Lecture Notes in Biomathematics Ser.: Vol. 37). 131p. 1980. pap. 26.00 (*0-387-09998-0*) Spr-Verlag.

Ohta, T., ed. Solar-Hydrogen Energy System: An Authoritative Review of Water-Splitting Systems by Solar Beam & Solar Heat; Hydrogen Production, Storage & Utilization. LC 79-40694. (Illus.). 1979. 111.00 (*0-08-022713-9*, Pub. by Pergamon Repr UK) Franklin.

Ohta, T. & Aoki, K., eds. Population Genetics & Molecular Evolution. 400p. 1986. 94.00 (*0-387-15584-8*) Spr-Verlag.

Ohta, Tokio. Energy Technology: Sources, Systems, & Frontier Conversion. LC 94-11525. 1994. text ed. 65.00 (*0-08-042132-6*, Pergamon Pr) Elsevier.

Ohta, Y., ed. Color Vision Deficiencies. LC 90-5233. (Illus.). 267p. 1990. lib. bdg. 67.50 (*90-6299-063-0*, Pub. by Kugler NE) Kugler Pubns.

Ohta, Yuichi. Knowledge-Based Interpretation of Outdoor Natural Color Scenes. (Research Notes in Artificial Intelligence Ser.). 1985. 29.95 (*0-273-08673-1*) Morgan Kaufmann.

Ohtaishi, N. & Sheng, H. L., eds. Deer of China: Biology & Management: Proceedings of the International Symposium on Deer of China, Held in Shanghai, China, 21-23 November 1992. LC 93-33240. (Developments in Animal & Veterinary Science Ser.: Vol. 26). 1993. 177.25 (*0-444-81540-6*) Elsevier.

Ohtake, Noriko. Creative Sources for the Music of Toru Takemitsu. LC 92-28294. 160p. 1993. 44.95 (*0-85967-954-3*, Pub. by Scolar Pr UK) Ashgate Pub Co.

Ohtaki, H. & Yamatera, H., eds. Structure & Dynamics of Solutions. LC 92-16273. (Studies in Physical & Theoretical Chemistry: Vol. 79). 1992. write for info. (*0-444-89651-1*) Elsevier.

Ohtani, R., et al, eds. High Temperature Creep Fatigue. (Illus.). 280p. 1988. 118.00 (*1-85166-135-2*) NACE Intl.

Ohtsu, Motoichi. Coherent Quantum Optics & Technology. LC 92-38956. (Advances in Optoelectronics Ser.: Vol. 5). 250p. (C). 1993. lib. bdg. 125.00 (*0-7923-2079-4*) Kluwer Ac.

— Highly Coherent Semiconductor Lasers. (Optoelectronics Library). 352p. 1991. text ed. 79.00 (*0-89006-462-8*) Artech Hse.

Ohtsuka, E., ed. Fifteenth Symposium on Nucleic Acids Chemistry, Japan: September 19-21, 1988. (Nucleic Acids Symposium Ser.: No. 20). 160p. 1988. pap. 60.00 (*1-85221-106-7*, IRL Pr) OUP.

Ohtsuka, Ryutaro. Oriomo Papuans: Ecology of Sago-Eaters in Lowland Papua. (Illus.). 197p. 1983. 30.00 (*0-86008-327-6*, Pub. by U of Tokyo JA) Col U Pr.

Ohtsuka, Ryutaro & Suzuki, Tsuguyoshi, eds. Population Ecology of Human Survival. 300p. 1990. text ed. 52.50 (*0-86008-456-6*, Pub. by U of Tokyo JA) Col U Pr.

Ohtsuka, Ryutaro, jt. ed. see Suzuki, Tsuguyoshi.

Ohtsuka, Yasunori & Matsumoto, Kenichi. Protecting Intellectual Property in Japan. (Illus.). 75p. 1992. 98.20 (*0-9632832-1-9*) Wrld Res Assocs.

Ohtsuki, H. Y., ed. Recent Theoretical (Computational) Developments in Atomic Collisions in Solids: Proceedings of a Conference, Strasbourg, France, July 14-16, 1981. 162p. 1983. 46.00 (*9971-950-33-2*) World Scientific Pub.

Ohtsuki, T., ed. Layout Design & Verification. (Advances in CAD for VLSI Ser.: Vol. 4). 348p. 1986. 57.50 (*0-444-87894-7*, North Holland) Elsevier.

Ohtsuki, Y. H., ed. Charged Beam Interaction with Solids. 260p. (C). 1983. 90.00 (*0-8002-3083-3*) Taylor & Francis.

O'Huigin, Sean. The Ghost Horse of the Mounties. LC 87-46287. (Illus.). (J). (gr. 4-6). 1991. 14.95 (*0-87923-721-X*) Godine.

— King of the Birds. (Illus.). 36p. (J). (ps-5). 1992. pap. 4.95 (*0-88753-168-7*, Pub. by Black Moss Pr CN) Firefly Bks Ltd.

Ohya, Masanori & Petz, Denes. Quantum Entropy & Its Use. LC 92-29580. (Texts & Monographs in Physics). 1993. 98.00 (*0-387-54881-5*) Spr-Verlag.

Ohye, C., ed. see Annual Meeting of the Japanese Society for Stereotactic & Functional Neurosurgery Staff.

Ohye, C., et al, eds. Motor Thalamus. (Journal: Stereotactic & Functional Neurosurgery: Vol. 60, Nos. 1-3, 1993). (Illus.). 156p. 1993. pap. 101.00 (*3-8055-5756-6*) S Karger.

Ohzu, Hitoshi, ed. see International Conference on Optics within Life Sciences Staff.

Oi, Jean C. State & Peasant in Contemporary China: The Political Economy of Village Government. 1989. 42.00 (*0-520-06105-5*) U CA Pr.

— State & Peasant in Contemporary China: The Political Economy of Village Government. (Illus.). 308p. 1991. reprint ed. pap. 14.00 (*0-520-07637-0*) U CA Pr.

***Oida, Yoshi.** An Actor Adrift. 188p. 1995. pap. 19.95 (*0-413-65840-6*, A0741) Heinemann.

***Oifer, Jessica.** Hidden Pictures Coloring Book: Jungle Animals. (Illus.). 1995. pap. 2.95 (*1-56565-246-0*) Lowell Hse Juvenile.

Oikawa, jt. auth. see Kobayashi.

Oike, Yasaburo & Kanazawa, Takemichi, eds. The Third International Conference on Nutrition in Cardio-Cerebrovascular Diseases. LC 92-48405. (Annals Ser.: Vol. 676). 1993. write for info. (*0-89766-775-1*); pap. write for info. (*0-89766-776-X*) NY Acad Sci.

Oikkonen, J. & Vaananen, J., eds. Logic Colloquium '90: ASL Summer Meeting in Helsinki. (Lecture Notes in Logic Ser.: Vol. 2). (Illus.). vii, 305p. 1994. pap. 54.00 (*0-387-57094-2*) Spr-Verlag.

Oikonomides, A., ed. see Mueller, L., et al.

Oikonomides, Al. N. Abbreviations in Greek: Inscriptions, Papyri, Manuscripts & Early Printed Books. 214p. (Orig.). 1986. 25.00 (*0-89005-049-X*) Ares.

Oikonomides, Al N. Mithraic Art. 95p. 1975. 15.00 (*0-89005-081-3*) Ares.

Oikonomides, Al N., ed. Supplementum Inscriptionum Atticarum I. 1976. 45.00 (*0-89005-126-7*) Ares.

— Supplementum Inscriptionum Atticarum II. 1978. 45.00 (*0-89005-249-2*) Ares.

Oikonomides, Al. N., ed. Supplementum Inscriptionum Atticarum III. 1979. 45.00 (*0-89005-275-1*) Ares.

Oikonomides, Al N., ed. Supplementum Inscriptionum Atticarum IV. 1980. 45.00 (*0-89005-377-4*) Ares.

— Supplementum Inscriptionum Atticarum V. 1984. 45.00 (*0-89005-531-9*) Ares.

Oikonomides, Al N., ed. see Hanno the Carthaginian.

Oikonomides, Nicolas. Byzantine Lead Seals. (Byzantine Collection Publications Ser.: No. 7). (Illus.). 28p. (Orig.). 1985. pap. 6.00 (*0-88402-144-0*) Dumbarton Oaks.

— Byzantium from the Ninth Century to the Fourth Crusade: Studies, Texts, Monuments. (Collected Studies: Vol. CS369). 350p. 1992. 97.95 (*0-86078-321-9*, Pub. by Variorum UK) Ashgate Pub Co.

— A Collection of Dated Byzantine Lead Seals. LC 86-6191. (Illus.). 176p. (Orig.). 1986. pap. text ed. 15.00 (*0-88402-150-5*, OIDLP) Dumbarton Oaks.

Oikonomides, Nicolas, ed. Studies in Byzantine Sigillography. LC 87-22266. 128p. 1988. pap. 18.00 (*0-88402-171-8*) Dumbarton Oaks.

— Studies in Byzantine Sigillography, No. 2. LC 90-33600. (Illus.). 328p. 1990. pap. 45.00 (*0-88402-188-2*, OBS2P, Dumbarton Rsch Lib) Dumbarton Oaks.

— Studies in Byzantine Sigillography, No. 3. (Illus.). 244p. 1993. pap. 25.00 (*0-88402-218-8*) Dumbarton Oaks.

— Studies in Byzantine Sigillography Vol. 4. LC 94-5393. 1995. pap. write for info. (*0-88402-229-3*, Dumbarton Rsch Lib) Dumbarton Oaks.

Oikonomides, Nicolas, jt. ed. see Nesbitt, John.

***Oikonomidse, Nicolas, ed.** Studies in Byzantine Sigillography, Vol. 4. (Illus.). 216p. 1995. pap. 24.00x (*0-614-06259-4*) Dumbarton Oaks.

Oil & Colour Chemists' Association of Australia Staff. Surface Coatings, Vol. 1: Raw Materials & Their Usage. 2nd ed. LC 83-7262. 388p. 1983. 75.00 (*0-412-25660-6*, NO. 6860) Chapman & Hall.

Oil & Gas Journal Energy Database Staff. OGJ Energy Statistics Sourcebook. 8th ed. 475p. 1993. 185.00 (*0-685-71330-X*, E1293) PennWell Bks.

— OGJ International Energy Statistics Sourcebook. 3rd ed. 650p. 1993. 185.00 (*0-685-71331-8*, E1283) PennWell Bks.

Oil & Gas Journal Staff, ed. International Petroleum Encyclopedia, 1990. 400p. 1990. 110.00 (*0-87814-337-8*, 19001) PennWell Bks.

OIL Symposia Staff. Orbital International Laboratory: Proceedings of the OIL Symposia, 3rd, 1970 & 4th, 1971. Steinhoff, Ernst A., ed. (Science & Technology Ser.: Vol. 33). 322p. 1974. lib. bdg. 30.00 (*0-87703-068-5*, Pub. by Am Astro Soc) Univelt Inc.

Oilfield Publications Ltd. Staff. Anchor Handling Tugs & Supply Vessels of the World. 349p. (C). 1993. 515.00 (*1-870945-00-X*, Pub. by Oilfield Pubns UK) St Mut.

— Construction Vessels of the World: 1993-94. (C). 1993. 790.00 (*0-685-67243-3*, Pub. by Oilfield Pubns UK) St Mut.

— An Introduction to Offshore Maintenance. 256p. (C). 1993. 290.00 (*1-870945-21-2*, Pub. by Oilfield Pubns UK) St Mut.

— Mobile Drilling Units of the World. 800p. (C). 1993. 780.00 (*1-870945-29-8*, Pub. by Oilfield Pubns UK) St Mut.

— The North Sea & N62 Atlas 1992-3 Edition. (C). 1993. 300.00 (*1-870945-35-2*, Pub. by Oilfield Pubns UK) St Mut.

— North Sea Facts. 2nd ed. 340p. (C). 1993. 300.00 (*0-685-67241-7*, Pub. by Oilfield Pubns UK) St Mut.

— The North Sea Field Development Guide: 1993-4 Edition. 1400p. (C). 1993. 900.00 (*1-870945-28-X*, Pub. by Oilfield Pubns UK) St Mut.

— The North Sea Subsea Atlas 1993-94 Edition. (C). 1993. 300.00 (*1-870945-34-4*, Pub. by Oilfield Pubns UK) St Mut.

— Offshore Production Concepts. 200p. (C). 1993. 315.00 (*0-685-67242-5*, Pub. by Oilfield Pubns UK) St Mut.

— ROV Review 1993-4 Edition. 223p. (C). 1993. 360.00 (*1-870945-66-2*, Pub. by Oilfield Pubns UK) St Mut.

— Russia & the Commonwealth of Independent States Oil & Gas Industry Guide. 480p. (C). 1993. 3,800.00 (*1-870945-31-X*, Pub. by Oilfield Pubns UK) St Mut.

— Single Point Moorings of the World: The World's Only Complete Reference to Every SPM, CALM, SALM, SAL, ALP & Turret Type Installation. 300p. (C). 1993. 580.00 (*1-870945-30-1*, Pub. by Oilfield Pubns UK) St Mut.

— South East Asia Atlas. (C). 1993. 1,000.00 (*1-870945-36-0*, Pub. by Oilfield Pubns UK) St Mut.

— Standby Vessels of the World. (C). 1993. 380.00 (*1-870945-24-7*, Pub. by Oilfield Pubns UK) St Mut.

— Survey Vessels of the World. 350p. (C). 1993. 500.00 (*1-870945-37-9*, Pub. by Oilfield Pubns UK) St Mut.

— West Africa Atlas. (C). 1993. 900.00 (*1-870945-12-3*, Pub. by Oilfield Pubns UK) St Mut.

— The World Offshore Field Development Guide Series, Vol. 1: Mediterranean, Middle East & Africa. 750p. (C). 1993. 780.00 (*1-870945-22-0*, Pub. by Oilfield Pubns UK) St Mut.

— The World Offshore Field Development Guide Series, Vol. 2: Asia, Indian Sub-Continent, Australasia & Far East. 750p. (C). 1993. 780.00 (*1-870945-25-5*, Pub. by Oilfield Pubns UK) St Mut.

— The World Offshore Field Development Guide Series, Vol. 3: North & South America. (C). 1993. 780.00 (*1-870945-11-5*, Pub. by Oilfield Pubns UK) St Mut.

Oilfield Publications Ltd. Staff & Williams, Paul. An Introduction to Diving Operations Offshore. 300p. (C). 1993. 260.00 (*1-870945-33-6*, Pub. by Oilfield Pubns UK) St Mut.

Oinas, Felix. Basic Course in Estonian. 3rd rev. ed. LC 66-63527. (Uralic & Altaic Ser.: Vol. 54). 393p. 1968. reprint ed. 39.00 (*0-87750-018-5*) Res Inst Inner Asian Studies.

Oinas, Felix J. Studies in Finnic Folklore. LC 84-80930. (Uralic & Altaic Ser.: Vol. 147). 219p. (Orig.). (C). 1985. pap. 30.00 (*0-933070-15-2*) Res Inst Inner Asian Studies.

Oinas, Felix J., ed. Heroic Epic & Saga: An Introduction to the World's Great Folk Epics. LC 77-9637. 381p. reprint ed. pap. 109.20 (*0-8357-3948-1*, 2057043) Bks Demand.

Oinas, Felix J. & Soudakoff, Stephen. The Study of Russian Folklore. (Indian Univ. Folklore Ser.: No. 25). 341p. 1975. text ed. 64.00 (*90-279-3147-X*) Mouton.

Oir, Gregory, tr. see Volkova, Bronislava, et al.

Oiringel, I. M., jt. ed. see Tsytovich, V. N.

Oishi, Sabine, jt. auth. see Simons, Jeanne.

Oishi, Shinsaburo, jt. auth. see Nakane, Chie.

Oisteanu, Valery. Do Not Defuse. 1980. pap. 2.50 (*0-9601870-2-2*) Pass.

— Pasport to Eternal Life. 68p. 1990. pap. 8.00 (*0-685-46237-4*) Pass.

— Passport to Eternal Life: Poetry 1980-1990. Sheinman, Allen J., ed. (Illus.). 72p. (Orig.). 1990. pap. text ed. 8.00 (*0-685-45645-5*) Pass.

Oistenau, Valery. Underground Shadows. 1977. pap. 1.50 (*0-9601870-0-6*) Pass.

Oister, Lisa, ed. see Fowler, Raymond E.

O

Oiticica, Helio. Helio Oiticica. 280p. 1992. pap. 45.00 (*90-73362-18-0*, Pub. by Witte De With CFCA NE) Dist Art Pubs.

Oivardi, Anne & Philpot, Graham. My First Picture Dictionary. (Illus.). 64p. (J). (gr. 1-3). 1989. 7.95 (*0-8120-5961-1*) Barron.

Oizerman, T., jt. auth. see Bobomolov, A.

***Oizumi, Aklo.** A Complete Concordance to the Works of Geoffrey Chaucer, Vol. 11. (Alpha-Omega Series C. English Authors C: Suppl. 1). 555p. 1994. lib. bdg. 340.00 (*3-487-09821-0*, Pub. by Georg Olms GW) Lubrecht & Cramer.

Oizumi, Aklo, ed. A Complete Concordance to the Works of Geoffrey Chaucer, 10 vols., Set. (Alpha-Omega Series C. English Authors: Vol. 1). 9510p. 1992. lib. bdg. 3,400.00 (*3-487-09412-6*, Pub. by Georg Olms GW) Lubrecht & Cramer.

***Oizzumi, Aklo, ed.** A Complete Concordance to the Works of Geoffrey Chaucer, Vol. 12. (Alpha-Omega Series C: Suppl. 2). 767p. 1994. lib. bdg. 340.00 (*3-487-09822-9*, Pub. by Georg Olms GW) Lubrecht & Cramer.

Oja, Carol, ed. Stravinsky in Modern Music. LC 82-1473. (Music Reprint Ser.). 1982. reprint ed. 39.50 (*0-306-76108-4*) Da Capo.

Oja, Carol J. Colin McPhee: Composer in Two Worlds. LC 89-600387. (Studies of American Musicians). (Illus.). 376p. 1990. 39.95 (*0-87474-732-5*) Smithsonian.

Oja, Carol J., ed. American Music Recordings: A Discography of 20th-Century U. S. Composers. LC 82-83008. 368p. (Orig.). 1982. pap. 60.00 (*0-914678-19-1*) Inst Am Music.

Oja, P. & Telama, R., eds. Sport for All: Proc. of the World Congress, Held in Tampere, Finland, 3-7 June, 1990. 696p. 1991. 189.75 (*0-444-81450-7*) Elsevier.

Oja, Sharon N. & Smulyan, Lisa, eds. Collaborative Action Research: A Developmental Process. (Social Research & Educational Studies). 240p. 1989. 70.00 (*1-85000-520-6*, Falmer Pr); pap. 32.00 (*1-85000-521-4*, Falmer Pr) Taylor & Francis.

Ojai Symposium Staff. Neural Theory & Modeling: Proceedings of the 1962 Ojai Symposium. Reiss, Richard F., ed. (Illus.). viii, 427p. 1964. 47.50 (*0-8047-0194-6*) Stanford U Pr.

Ojaide, Tanure. The Blood of Peace: And Other Poems. (African Writers Ser.). 128p. (Orig.). 1991. pap. 8.95 (*0-435-91193-7*) Heinemann.

— Children of Iroko. 1973. per. 3.00 (*0-912678-09-7*, Greenfld Rev Pr) Greenfld Rev Lit.

— The Eagle's Vision. LC 87-46316. 104p. (Orig.). (YA). (gr. 9-12). 1987. per., pap. 8.00 (*0-916418-66-9*) Lotus.

— Labyrinths of the Delta. 1986. 9.95 (*0-912678-67-4*, Greenfld Rev Pr) Greenfld Rev Lit.

***Ojakanga, Beatrice.** Beatrice Ojakanga Light Baking Book. Date not set. write for info. (*0-517-70134-0*) Random.

Ojakangas, Beatrice. Best of Gourmet Recipes for Two. 1993. pap. 5.95 (*0-934860-99-8*) Adventure Pubns.

— Best of Honey Recipes. 1991. 5.95 (*0-934860-68-8*) Adventure Pubns.

— The Best of Pancake & Waffle Recipes. 102p. (Orig.). 1990. pap. 5.95 (*0-934860-59-9*) Adventure Pubns.

— The Best of the Liberated Cook. 96p. 1991. spiral bd. 9.95 (*0-9609408-0-4*) Adventure Pubns.

— The Best of the Liberated Cook. 96p. spiral bd. 9.95 (*0-685-49578-7*) Gloria Pubs.

— The Best of Wild Rice Recipes. 1989. 5.95 (*0-934860-56-4*); 13.95 (*0-934860-58-0*) Adventure Pubns.

— The Best of Wild Rice Recipes. 1991. Gift Pack, Hand-Picked, incl. rice & wood crate. 17.95 (*0-934860-71-8*) Adventure Pubns.

— The Book of Regional American Cooking: Heartland. 120p. 1992. pap. 11.95 (*1-55788-073-5*, HP Books) Berkley Pub.

Ojakangas, Beatrice, ed. Fantastically Finnish: Recipes & Traditions. LC 85-61029. (Illus.). 88p. 1985. pap. 7.95 (*0-941016-22-6*) Penfield.

Ojakangas, Beatrice A. Beatrice Ojakangas' Great Holiday Baking Book. 1994. 25.00 (*0-517-59330-0*, Clarkson Potter) Crown Bks Yng Read.

— Finnish Cook Book. (International Cookbook Ser.). 1964. 12.00 (*0-517-50111-2*, Crown) Crown Pub Group.

— The Great Scandinavian Baking Book. 1988. 24.95 (*0-316-63372-0*) Little.

— Great Whole Grain Breads. (Cookbook Classic Ser.). (Illus.). 368p. 1993. pap. 13.00 (*0-671-77045-4*, Fireside) S&S Trade.

— Pot Pies: Forty Savory Suppers. LC 92-16447. 112p. 1992. 11.00 (*0-517-58573-1*, C P Pubs) Crown Pub Group.

— Quick Breads: Sixty-Three Recipes for Bakers in a Hurry. (Illus.). 128p. 1991. 12.00 (*0-517-58013-6*, C P Pubs) Crown Pub Group.

Ojakangas, R. Schaum's Outline of Introductory Geology. (Schaum Outline Ser.). 1991. pap. text ed. 12.95 (*0-07-047704-3*) McGraw.

Ojakangas, Richard W., ed. see International Conference on Basement Tectonics Staff.

Ojakangas, Richards W. & Matsch, Charles L. Minnesota's Geology. LC 81-14709. (Illus.). 267p. (C). 1982. pap. 26.95 (*0-8166-0953-5*) U of Minn Pr.

***Ojakargas, Beatrice.** Light Muffins: 60 Recipes for Sweet & Savory Low-Fat Muffins & Spreads. LC 94-42664. 96p. 1995. 12.00 (*0-517-70066-2*, C P Pubs) Crown Pub Group.

Ojala, Jeanne A. Auguste de Colbert: Aristocratic Survival in an Era of Upheaval, 1793-1809. LC 79-4872. 213p. reprint ed. pap. 60.80 (*0-8357-5883-4*, 2027169) Bks Demand.

Ojala, Jeanne A. & Ojala, William T. Madame de Sevigne: A Seventeenth-Century Life. LC 89-37007. (Women's Ser.). 234p. 1990. 46.00 (*0-85496-169-0*) Berg Pubs.

***Ojala, Marydee.** Business Online Searching: The Basics & Beyond. 250p. 1996. pap. 39.95 (*0-910965-16-1*) Online.

Ojala, William K. Motoring Tips: How-to-Improve the Safety, Comfort, Utility & Convenience of Your Vehicle. Nowell-Dec, Lisa, ed. (Illus.). (Orig.). 1986. pap. 10.95 (*0-938877-00-3*) Practical Tech.

Ojala, William T., jt. auth. see Ojala, Jeanne A.

Ojalvo, Morris. Thin-Walled Bars with Open Profiles. Straw, Richard, ed. LC 90-60103. (Illus.). 208p. (C). 1990. lib. bdg. 27.50 (*0-9627025-0-1*) Olive Press.

Ojeda, Almerindo E. Linguistic Individuals. LC 92-5935. (Center for the Study of Language & Information-Lecture Notes Ser.: No. 31). 200p. (Orig.). (C). 1992. text ed. 45.00 (*0-937073-85-7*); pap. text ed. 17.95 (*0-937073-84-9*) Ctr Study Language.

Ojeda, Almerindo E., jt. ed. see Huck, Geoffrey J.

Ojeda, Almerindo E., jt. ed. see Kreiman, Jody.

Ojeda, Enriave. Jorge Carrera Andrade: Introduccion a Su Vida. 1972. 16.95 (*0-88303-003-9*); pap. 12.95 (*0-685-73209-6*) E Torres & Sons.

Ojeda, Felix. Programa para Todo el Pueblo. (SPA.). 1966. pap. 0.25 (*0-87898-013-X*) New Outlook.

Ojeda, Felix, ed. Vito Marcantonio y Puerto Rico. 156p. 1978. pap. 5.95 (*0-940238-40-3*) Ediciones Huracan.

Ojeda, Graciela Y., tr. see U. S. A. Gymnastics Staff.

Ojeda, Linda. Exclusively Female: A Nutrition Guide for Better Menstrual Health. 2nd rev. ed. LC 83-81702. (Illus.). 160p. 1983. pap. 5.95 (*0-89793-032-0*) Hunter Hse.

— Exclusively Female: A Nutrition Guide for Better Menstrual Health. LC 85-22387. xx, 138p. 1985. reprint ed. lib. bdg. 23.00x (*0-89370-589-6*) Borgo Pr.

— Menopause Without Medicine. 2nd rev. ed. LC 91-44103. (Illus.). 304p. (Orig.). 1992. pap. 12.95 (*0-89793-097-5*) Hunter Hse.

— Menopause Without Medicine. 3rd ed. LC 87-22531. (Orig.). 1995. 23.95 (*0-89793-178-5*); pap. 13.95 (*0-89793-177-7*) Hunter Hse.

— Menopause Without Medicine: Feel Healthy, Look Younger, Live Longer. 2nd ed. 304p. 1991. reprint ed. lib. bdg. 33.00x (*0-8095-6320-7*) Borgo Pr.

— Safe Dieting for Teens. LC 92-26432. 116p. (Orig.). (YA). (gr. 7-12). 1992. pap. 7.95 (*0-89793-113-0*) Hunter Hse.

— Safe Dieting for Teens. (Illus.). 105p. (Orig.). (C). 1992. reprint ed. lib. bdg. 23.00x (*0-8095-6333-9*) Borgo Pr.

***Ojeda, Oscar R.** The New American House: Innovations in Residential Design & Construction. (Illus.). 264p. 1995. pap. 55.00 (*0-8230-3163-2*) Watsn-Guptill.

Ojeda, Oscar. Moore, Ruble & Yudell: Houses & Housing. 192p. 1993. 39.95 (*1-55835-122-1*) AIA Press.

Ojeda, Sergio R., jt. auth. see Griffin, James E.

Ojemann, George A., jt. auth. see Calvin, William H.

***Ojemann, Robert G., et al.** Surgical Management of Neurovascular Disease. 3rd ed. LC 94-40513. (Illus.). 1995. write for info. (*0-683-06629-3*) Williams & Wilkins.

Ojetti, Ugo. As They Seemed to Me. Furst, H., tr. LC 68-54364. (Essay Index Reprint Ser.). 1977. 20.95 (*0-8369-0751-5*) Ayer.

Ojha, Ashutosh. Hindi Self-Taught. (Orient Paperbacks Ser.). 315p. 1973. pap. 4.95 (*0-88253-245-6*) Ind-US Inc.

***Ojha, Brahm S. & Singh, Jasbir.** Resource Planning Atlas. (C). 1993. text ed. 50.00 (*81-85135-73-8*) S Asia.

Ojha, D. C., jt. ed. see Sharma, C. D.

Ojha, Divakar & Kumar, Ashok. Panchakrma Therapy in Ayurveda. 219p. 1979. text ed. 12.00 (*0-89744-057-9*) Auromere.

Ojha, G. K. Predictive Astrology of the Hindus. (Illus.). 347p. 1988. 19.95 (*0-318-36380-1*) Asia Bk Corp.

Ojha, Pandit G., et al. Aspects in Vedic Astrology. 180p. 1993. pap. 13.95 (*1-878423-15-0*) Morson Pub.

Ojha, Puran C. Asvattha in Everyday Life as Related in Puranas. 1991. 27.00 (*0-685-48712-1*, Pub. by Sundeep II) S Asia.

Ojha, Purana C. Asvattha in Every Day Life as Related in Puranas. (C). 1991. 30.00 (*81-85067-64-3*, Pub. by Sundeep II) S Asia.

Ojha, R. R. & Bir, Avnita R. Introduction to Economic Theory. 240p. 1991. text ed. 25.00 (*81-207-1235-8*, Pub. by Sterling Pubs II) Apt Bks.

Ojha, R. R., et al. National Income Accounting. vi, 139p. 1989. text ed. 18.95 (*81-207-0992-6*, Pub. by Sterling Pubs II) Apt Bks.

***Ojha, S. K.** Introduction to Aircraft Performance. LC 95-4456. (Education Ser.). 1995. write for info. (*1-56347-113-2*) AIAA.

Ojha, Shiva K. Riding the Storm: A Play on Mahatma Gandhi. 96p. 1989. text ed. 15.95 (*81-207-0953-5*, Pub. by Sterling Pubs II) Apt Bks.

Oji, Apollos O. Longing for Home. 1991. 13.95 (*0-533-08239-0*) Vantage.

Ojiambo, Joseph B., ed. see Tallman, Julie I.

Ojima, I, jt. auth. see Nakanishi, N.

Ojima, Iwao, ed. Catalytic Asymmetric Synthesis. LC 93-19389. 476p. 1993. 110.00 (*1-56081-532-9*) VCH Pubs.

Ojo-Ade, Femi. Analytical Index of Presence Africaine (1948-1972) LC 77-71232. (Illus.). 1977. boxed 22.00 (*0-914478-92-3*) Three Continents.

— Rene Maran: The Black Frenchman: A Biocritical Study. LC 81-51663. (Illus.). 277p. 1984. 32.00 (*0-914478-93-1*); pap. 12.00 (*0-914478-94-X*) Three Continents.

Ojo-Igbinoba, M. E. The Practice of Conservation of Library Materials in Sub-Saharan Africa. 61p. 1993. 7.00 (*0-941934-65-9*) Indiana Africa.

Oka, H. I., ed. Origin of Cultivated Rice: Developments in Crop Science. 254p. 1988. 95.00 (*0-444-98919-6*) Elsevier.

Oka, Hideyuki. How to Wrap Five More Eggs: Traditional Japanese Packaging. LC 74-23690. (Illus.). 216p. 1975. 39.95 (*0-8348-0108-6*) Weatherhill.

Oka, Isaburo. Hiroshige: Japan's Great Landscape Artist. Lancet & Ogawa, eds. 96p. 1992. 32.00 (*4-7700-1658-1*) Kodansha.

Oka, K. Collected Papers. 245p. 1984. 119.00 (*0-387-13240-6*) Spr-Verlag.

Oka, Melvin S. & Rupp, Randall G., eds. Cell Biology & Biotechnology: Novel Approaches to Increased Cellular Productivity. LC 92-37369. 176p. 1993. 99.00 (*0-387-97951-4*) Spr-Verlag.

Oka, Sheoten. Cardiovascular Hemorheology. LC 80-41338. 220p. reprint ed. pap. 62.70 (*0-318-34831-4*, 2031702) Bks Demand.

Oka, Takashi. Prying Open the Door: Foreign Workers in Japan. LC 94-20944. (Contemporary Issue Papers: Vol. 2). 60p. (C). 1994. pap. 9.95 (*0-87003-053-1*) Carnegie Endow.

Oka, Yasu & Goldiner, Paul L. Transesophageal Echocardiography. (Illus.). 300p. 1992. text ed. 150.00 (*0-397-51158-2*) Lippincott.

Oka, Yasu & Konstadt, Steven N. Transesophageal Echocardiography: A Teaching File. (Illus.). 300p. 1994. 95.00 (*0-397-51426-3*) Lippincott.

Okabe, Atsuyuki, et al. Spatial Tessellations: Concepts & Applications of Voroni Diagrams. (Series in Probability & Mathematics). 532p. 1992. text ed. 115.00 (*0-471-93430-5*) Wiley.

Okabe, H., et al. Endoscopic Surgery: Proceedings of the International Symposium-Satellite Symposium for the 25th Annual Meeting of Japan Gastroenterological Endoscopy Society, Tokyo, Japan, 18 November 1983. (International Congress Ser.: Vol. 638). 160p. 1984. 96.50 (*0-444-80616-4*, Excerpta Medica) Elsevier.

Okabe, Hideo. Photochemistry of Small Molecules. LC 78-6704. (Illus.). 445p. reprint ed. pap. 127.40 (*0-685-20443-X*, 2056455) Bks Demand.

Okabe, Mitsuaki, jt. ed. see Suzuki, Yoshio.

***Okabe, S. & Takeuchi, K., eds.** International Conference on Ulcer Research, 8th Meeting, Kyoto-Japan, November 1994: Abstracts. (Journal: Digestion: Vol. 55, Supplement 2, 1994). (Illus.). ii, 62p. 1994. pap. 25.75 (*3-8055-6069-9*) S Karger.

Okada, A., jt. ed. see Ogoshi, S.

Okada, A., jt. ed. see Tanaka, T. M.

Okada, Amina. Indian Miniatures of the Mughal Court. LC 92-15417. 1992. 95.00 (*0-8109-3461-2*) Abrams.

— Taj Mahal. 1993. 65.00 (*1-55859-617-8*) Abbeville Pr.

Okada, Barbara T. & Neill, Mary G. Real & Imaginary Beings: The Netsuke Collection of Joseph & Edith Kurstin. LC 79-67298. (Illus.). 135p. 1980. 30.00 (*0-89467-012-3*) Yale Art Gallery.

Okada, Barbara T. & Okada, Nancy T. Do's & Don't's for the Japanese Businessman Abroad. 130p. (C). (gr. 10 up). 1973. pap. text ed. 4.75 (*0-88345-208-1*, 18133) Prentice ESL.

Okada, Florence, tr. see Kikudri, Shigeo.

Okada, H. Richard. Figures of Resistance: Language, Poetry, & Narrating in The Tale of the Genji & Other Mid-Heian Texts. LC 91-13312. (Post-Contemporary Interventions Ser.). 400p. 1991. lib. bdg. 52.95 (*0-8223-1185-2*); pap. text ed. 23.95 (*0-8223-1192-5*) Duke.

Okada, Jo, jt. auth. see Shiraichi, Masami.

Okada, John. No-No Boy. LC 79-55834. 176p. 1980. reprint ed. pap. 12.95 (*0-295-95525-2*) U of Wash Pr.

Okada, K., et al, eds. Alkali-Aggregate Reaction: Eighth International Conference, Kyob, Japan, 17-20 July 1989. 890p. 1990. 176.50 (*1-85166-417-3*) Elsevier.

Okada, Miyo. Language of Courtesy: Honorific Speech of Japanese. 97p. 1954. 8.95 (*0-88710-041-4*) Yale Far Eastern Pubns.

Okada, Mokichi. Health & the New Civilization. LC 91-60112. 96p. (Orig.). 1991. pap. 3.75 (*0-9629183-0-X*) Johrei Fellow.

Okada, Nancy T., jt. auth. see Okada, Barbara T.

Okada, Shintaro, et al. Biochemical Basis of Inherited Human Disease. 1973. 29.50 (*0-8422-7087-6*) Irvington.

Okada, T. S. Transdifferentiation: Flexibility in Cell Differentiation. (Illus.). 248p. 1991. 98.00 (*0-19-854281-X*) OUP.

Okada, Toshimi & Iwai, Akira. Natural VLF Radio Waves. 174p. 1988. text ed. 155.00 (*0-471-91954-3*) Wiley.

Okada, Yasue. Public Lands & Pioneer Farmers, Gage County, Nebraska, 1850-1900. Bruchey, Stuart, ed. LC 78-56687. (Management of Public Lands in the U. S. Ser.). (Illus.). 1979. reprint ed. lib. bdg. 18.95 (*0-405-11348-X*) Ayer.

Okada, Yoshio, jt. ed. see Seno, Satimaru.

Okagaki, Alan & Benson, Jim. County Energy Plan Guidebook. 2nd ed. (Illus.). 200p. (Orig.). (C). 1979. pap. text ed. 10.00 (*0-937786-01-2*) Inst Ecological.

Okagaki, Lynn & Sternberg, Robert J., eds. Directors of Development: Influences on the Development of Children's Thinking. 304p. 1991. text ed. 59.95 (*0-8058-0627-X*); pap. 29.95 (*0-8058-0628-8*) L Erlbaum Assocs.

Okagaki, Lynn, jt. ed. see Luster, Tom.

Okaichi, T., et al, eds. Red Tides: Biology, Environmental Science, & Toxicology. 489p. 1988. 97.50 (*0-444-01343-1*) P-H.

Okakura, Kakuzo. Book of Tea. Bleiler, Everett F., ed. 1906. pap. 2.95 (*0-486-20070-1*) Dover.

— The Book of Tea. 144p. 1991. reprint ed. pap. 8.00 (*4-7700-1542-9*) Kodansha.

— The Book of Tea. LC 92-50737. (Illus.). 200p. 1993. reprint ed. pap. 6.00 (*0-87773-918-8*, Sham Pocket Class) Shambhala Pubns.

Okakura, Y. The Japanese Spirit. 1972. 250.00 (*0-8490-0436-5*) Gordon Pr.

— The Japanese Spirit. 1972. lib. bdg. 79.95 (*0-87968-549-2*) Krishna Pr.

Okal, Emile A., ed. Advances in Volcanic Seismology. 248p. 1988. reprint ed. 41.00 (*0-8176-1927-5*) Birkhauser.

— Aspects of Pacific Seismicity. 200p. 1991. reprint ed. pap. 27.50 (*0-8176-2589-5*) Spr-Verlag.

Okali, Christine. Cocoa & Kinship in Ghana: The Matrilineal Akan of Ghana. 200p. 1983. pap. 25.00 (*0-7103-0041-7*, Pub. by Kegan Paul Intl UK) Routledge Chapman & Hall.

Okali, Christine, et al. Farmer Participatory Research: Rhetoric & Reality. 156p. (Orig.). 1994. pap. 17.50 (*1-85339-252-9*, Pub. by Intermed Tech UK) Women Ink.

Okami, Paul. Goju Ryu Karate Do. LC 85-52272. (Orig.). 1986. pap. write for info. (*0-86568-074-4*, 315) Unique Pubns.

Okamoto, jt. auth. see Lovece.

Okamoto, H., ed. Phase Diagrams of Binary Iron Alloys. LC 93-70331. (Monograph Series on Alloy Phase Diagrams). (Illus.). 480p. 1993. 301.00 (*0-87170-469-2*) ASM.

Okamoto, H. & Massalski, T. B., intros. Phase Diagrams of Binary Gold Alloys. (Monograph Series on Alloy Phase Diagrams). (Illus.). 343p. (C). 1987. text ed. 256.00 (*0-87170-249-5*) ASM.

Okamoto, H., jt. auth. see White, C. E.

Okamoto, Hiroshi, ed. Molecular Biology of the Islets of Langerhans. (Illus.). 375p. (C). 1990. 99.95 (*0-521-36204-0*) Cambridge U Pr.

Okamoto, K., ed. Group Representations & Systems of Differential Equations: Proceedings of the Symposium Tokyo, Japan, 20-27 Dec. 1982. (Advanced Studies in Pure Mathematics: Vol. 4). 498p. 1985. 205.25 (*0-444-87710-X*, North Holland) Elsevier.

***Okamoto, Kanoko.** The House Spirit: And Other Stories. 160p. (Orig.). 1995. pap. 10.95 (*0-88496-392-6*) Capra Pr.

— The House Spirit & Other Stories. Sugisaki, Kenzuko, tr. 160p. 1995. lib. bdg. 29.00 (*0-8095-4131-9*) Borgo Pr.

Okamoto, Kiyosato & Oshima, T., eds. Representation of Lie Groups. (Advances Studies in Pure Mathematics: Vol. 14). 660p. 1989. text ed. 140.00 (*0-12-525100-9*) Acad Pr.

Okamoto, Lorina R., jt. auth. see Huff, Helen E.

Okamoto, M., jt. ed. see Tajima, T.

***Okamoto, Naomi.** Japanese Ink Painting: The Art of Sumi-e. LC 94-40844. (Illus.). 96p. (ENG & GER.). 1995. 19.95 (*0-8069-0832-7*) Sterling.

Okamoto, Osamu. Sam Okamoto's Incredible Vegetables. LC 94-8520. 1993. 19.95 (*1-56554-025-5*) Pelican.

Okamoto, Rai Y. & Williams, Frank E. Urban Design Manhattan. (Illus.). 130p. (C). 1969. text ed. 10.00 (*0-318-19021-4*) Regional Plan Assn.

Okamoto, S., jt. ed. see Copley, A.

Okamoto, Shumpei. Impressions of the Front: Woodcuts of the Sino-Japanese War, 1894-95. LC 83-4096. (Illus.). 56p. (Orig.). 1983. pap. 7.50 (*0-87633-049-9*) Phila Mus Art.

— The Japanese Oligarchy & the Russo-Japanese War. LC 74-114259. (Studies of the East Asian Institute). 355p. 1971. text ed. 52.50 (*0-231-03404-0*) Col U Pr.

— The Japanese Oligarchy & the Russo-Japanese War. LC 74-114259. 372p. reprint ed. pap. 106.10 (*0-8357-3728-4*, 2036450) Bks Demand.

Okamoto, Shumpei, tr. see Yoshitake, Oka.

Okamoto, Shunzo. Introduction to Earthquake Engineering. 629p. 1985. reprint ed. 89.50 (*0-86008-361-6*, Pub. by U of Tokyo JA) Col U Pr.

Okamoto, Shunzo, et al, eds. Static & Dynamic Behavior of Kurobe Dam. 550p. 1988. 144.50 (*0-86008-425-6*, Pub. by U of Tokyo JA) Col U Pr.

Okamoto, Yoshitomo. The Namban Art of Japan. LC 72-78597. (Heibonsha Survey of Japanese Art Ser.: Vol. 19). (Illus.). 158p. 1972. 20.00 (*0-8348-1008-5*) Weatherhill.

Okamoto, Yukari, jt. auth. see Case, Robbie.

Okamura, Arthur. Rabbit Magic. 64p. 1990. pap. 12.00 (*0-918395-11-9*) Poltroon Pr.

Okamura, Arthur, jt. auth. see Kowit, Steve.

Okamura, Hajime, jt. ed. see Meyer, Christian.

Okamura, Kichiemon, jt. auth. see Muraoka, Kageo.

Okamura, S. History of Electron Tubes. LC 93-80285. 230p. 1994. 79.00 (*90-5199-145-2*) IOS Press.

Okamura, S., ed. Recent Trends in Radiation Polymer Chemistry. (Advances in Polymer Science Ser.: Vol. 105). (Illus.). 166p. 1993. 109.00 (*0-387-55812-8*) Spr-Verlag.

Okamura, William H., jt. ed. see Dawson, Marcia I.

***Okanagan Native Band Staff.** How Food Was Given: An Okanagan Legend. (Kou-Skelowh Ser.). (Illus.). 28p. (Orig.). (J). (gr. 1-4). 1991. pap. 10.95 (*0-919441-22-X*, Pub. by Theytus Bks Ltd CN) Orca Bk Pubs.

— How Names Were Given: An Okanagan Legend. (Kou-Skelowh Ser.). (Illus.). 28p. (Orig.). (J). (gr. 1-4). 1991. pap. 10.95 (*0-919441-24-6*, Pub. by Theytus Bks Ltd CN) Orca Bk Pubs.

— How Turtle Set the Animals Free: An Okanagan Legend. (Kou-Skelowh Ser.). (Illus.). 28p. (Orig.). (J). (gr. 1-4). 1993. pap. 10.95 (*0-919441-16-5*, Pub. by Theytus Bks Ltd CN) Orca Bk Pubs.

Okanakan. IFA: Antigua Sabiduria. Ecun, Oba, tr. & intro. by. (Illus.). 185p. (Orig.). Date not set. pap. write for info. (*0-926603-10-8*) Obaecun Bks.

Okandan, Ender, ed. Geothermal Reservoir Engineering. (C). 1988. lib. bdg. 125.50 (*90-247-3751-6*) Kluwer Ac.

— Heavy Crude Oil Recovery. 1984. lib. bdg. 122.50 (*90-247-2951-3*) Kluwer Ac.

O'Kane, Bernard. Timurid Architecture in Khurasan. LC 85-43494. (Islamic Art & Architecture Ser.: Vol. 3). (Illus.). 520p. 1987. lib. bdg. 55.00 (*0-685-11887-8*) Mazda Pubs.

An Asterisk (*) at the beginning of an entry indicates that the title is appearing in BIP for the first time.

O'Kane, Hugh P. & O'Kane, Monica. The Nolan Family Tree. (Illus.). 253p. 1983. 25.00 (*0-9609198-2-1*) Diction Bks.
O'Kane, J., tr. see Al-Rabghuzi.
O'Kane, J. Philip, ed. Advances in Theoretical Hydrology: A Tribute to Jim Dooge. LC 92-35090. (European Geophysical Society Series in Hydrological Sciences: Vol. 1). 1992. write for info. (*0-444-89831-X*) Elsevier.
O'Kane, James M. The Crooked Ladder: Gangsters, Ethnicity, & the American Dream. 185p. (C). 1992. 34.95 (*1-56000-021-X*) Transaction Pubs.
O'Kane, John, tr. The Ship of Sulaiman. LC 70-186605. 250p. (C). 1972. text ed. 46.50 (*0-231-03654-X*) Col U Pr.
O'Kane, John, tr. see Bozorg Alavi.
O'Kane, John, tr. see Monavvar, Mohammad E.
O'Kane, John, tr. see Vilhjalmsson, Thor.
O'Kane, Monica, jt. auth. see O'Kane, Hugh P.
O'Kane, Monica L. Hey, Mom, I'm Home Again! Strategies for Parents & Grown Children Who Live Together. 216p. 1992. pap. 14.95 (*0-943400-68-6*) Marlor Pr.
O'Kane, Richard H. Clear the Bridge. 1989. 24.95 (*0-89141-346-4*) Presidio Pr.
— Wahoo: The Patrols of America's Most Famous W. W. II Submarine. (Illus.). 380p. 1987. 18.95 (*0-89141-301-4*) Presidio Pr.
O'Kane, Rosemary. Likelihood of Coups. 160p. 1987. text ed. 49.95 (*0-566-05006-4*) Ashgate Pub Co.
O'Kane, Rosemary H. The Revolutionary Reign of Terror: The Role of Violence in Political Change. 336p. 1991. text ed. 63.95 (*1-85278-082-7*, Pub. by E Elgar Pub UK) Ashgate Pub Co.
O'Kane, Walter C. The Intimate Desert. LC 71-76989. 143p. 1985. reprint ed. pap. 8.50 (*0-8165-0938-7*) U of Ariz Pr.
— Sun in the Sky. LC 50-7404. (Civilization of the American Indian Ser.: No. 30). (Illus.). 274p. reprint ed. 78.10 (*0-8357-9742-2*, 2016245) Bks Demand.
Okano, I. & Sato, T. Vital Judo: Throwing Techniques. pap. 14.95 (*0-685-38458-6*) Wehman.
Okano, Isai. Vital Judo: Grappling Techniques. pap. 14.95 (*0-685-70712-1*) Wehman.
Okano, Kaori. School to Work Transition in Japan: An Ethnographic Study. LC 92-20817. (Language & Education Library: No. 3). 1992. 99.00 (*1-85359-163-7*, Pub. by Multilingual Matters UK) Taylor & Francis.
Okantah, Mwatabu. Collage. LC 83-82776. 68p. 1984. per., pap. 5.00 (*0-916418-56-1*) Lotus.
Okantah, Mwatabu S. Afreeka Brass. 28p. (Orig.). 1983. pap. 3.50 (*0-914946-41-2*) Cleveland St Univ Poetry Ctr.
Okara, Gabriel. The Voice. LC 76-90298. (C). 1970. pap. text ed. 12.95 (*0-8419-0015-9*, Africana) Holmes & Meier.
***Okas, John.** Free Wayfarers' Book of the Dead. LC 94-31751. 320p. 1995. 24.00 (*1-877946-60-5*) Permanent Pr.
— Routes. LC 93-27528. 225p. 1994. 22.00 (*1-877946-43-5*) Permanent Pr.
Okasaki-Ward, Lola. Management, Education & Training in Japan: Background & Practice. LC 93-22622. 640p. (C). 1993. lib. bdg. 180.00 (*1-85333-781-1*, Pub. by Graham & Trotman UK) Kluwer Ac.
***O'Kash, Alex.** Stop in the Name of the Law. 1994. pap. 9.95 (*1-886028-00-1*) Savage Pr.
Okasha. Arabic Encyclopaedic Dictionary of Cultural Terms. 1990. 48.00 (*0-86685-500-9*) Intl Bk Ctr.
Okasha, Elisabeth. Corpus of Early Christian Inscribed Stones. LC 93-9951. (Studies in the Early History of Britain). 256p. 1993. 95.00 (*0-7185-1475-0*, Pub. by Leicester Univ Pr) St Martin.
Okawa, Essei. The Adventures of the One Inch Boy. Ooka, D. T., tr. (Japanese Fairy Tale Ser.: No. 4). (Illus.). 32p. (J). (gr. k-6). 1985. 11.95 (*0-89346-258-6*) Heian Intl.
— The Fisherman & the Grateful Turtle. Ooka, D. T., tr. (Japanese Fairy Tale Ser.: No. 3). (Illus.). 32p. (J). (gr. k-6). 1985. 11.95 (*0-89346-257-8*) Heian Intl.
Okawa, Naomi. Edo Architecture: Katsura & Nikko. Woodhull, Alan & Miyamoto, Akito, trs. LC 74-23786. (Heibonsha Survey of Japanese Art Ser.: Vol. 20). (Illus.). 164p. 1975. 20.00 (*0-8348-1027-1*) Weatherhill.
Okawara, M., et al. Organic Colorants: A Handbook of Data of Selected Dyes for Electro-Optical Applications. (Physical Sciences Data Ser.: No. 35). 504p. 1989. 231.00 (*0-444-98884-X*) Elsevier.
Okawara, Nobuo, jt. auth. see Katzenstein, Peter J.
Okawara, Yoshio. To Avoid Isolation: An Ambassador's View of the U. S. - Japanese Relations. 192p. 1990. 34.95 (*0-87249-646-5*) U of SC Pr.
Okayama, J., jt. auth. see Ergas, H.
Okayama, Kotaro. Zur Grundlegung Christlicher Ethik Theologische Konzeptionen der Gegenwart im Lichte des Analogie-Problems. (Theologische Bibliothek Toepelmann Ser.: Vol. 30). (C). 1977. 75.40 (*3-11-005812-X*) De Gruyter.
Okazaki, Chieko. Cat's Cradle. 1993. 12.95 (*0-88494-904-4*) Bookcraft Inc.
— Shared Motherhood. 1994. pap. 1.95 (*0-88494-932-X*) Bookcraft Inc.
***Okazaki, Chieko N.** Aloha! 1995. 14.95 (*0-87579-979-5*) Deseret Bk.
— Lighten Up! Finding Real Joy in Real Life. LC 92-40396. 232p. 1993. 12.95 (*0-87579-668-0*) Deseret Bk.
Okazaki, Haruo. Fundamentals of Neuropathology. 2nd ed. LC 89-2048. (Illus.). 328p. 1989. 79.00 (*0-89640-156-1*) Igaku-Shoin.
Okazaki, Renji, jt. auth. see Inagaki, Yoshio.
Okazawa-Rey, Margo, et al, eds. Teachers, Teaching, & Teacher Education. LC 87-80233. (Reprint Ser.: No. 19). 488p. 1987. pap. 19.95 (*0-916690-21-0*) Harvard Educ Rev.
***Oke.** Canadian West Saga. 1995. 12.98 (*0-88486-112-0*) Arrowood Pr.
***Oke, Barbara & Oke, Deborah.** The Oke Family Cookbook: Favorite Recipes of Janette's Family. LC 94-37627. 208p. 1994. 9.99 (*1-55661-529-9*) Bethany Hse.
Oke, Deborah, jt. auth. see Oke, Barbara.
Oke, Isaiah & Wright, Joe. Blood Secrets: The True Story of Demon Worship & Ceremonial Murder. 1991. pap. 4.95 (*0-425-12852-0*) Berkley Pub.
— Blood Secrets: The True Story of Demon Worship & Ceremonial Murder. 235p. 1989. text ed. 23.95 (*0-87975-568-7*) Prometheus Bks.
***Oke, Janette.** The Bluebird & the Sparrow. 240p. 1995. pap. 8.99 (*1-55661-612-0*); pap. 12.99 (*1-55661-613-9*) Bethany Hse.
— A Bride for Donnigan. 224p. (Orig.). (YA). 1993. pap. 7.99 (*1-55661-327-X*) Bethany Hse.
— A Bride for Donnigan. large type ed. 224p. (Orig.). (YA). 1993. pap. 9.99 (*1-55661-328-8*) Bethany Hse.
— A Bride for Donnigan. large type ed. LC 93-48240. (Orig.). 1994. 20.95 (*0-8161-5958-0*, Large Print Bks) Hall.
— The Calling of Emily Evans. LC 89-78543. 224p. (Orig.). 1990. pap. 7.99 (*1-55661-118-8*) Bethany Hse.
— The Calling of Emily Evans. large type ed. 222p. (Orig.). 1990. 9.99 (*1-55661-121-8*) Bethany Hse.
— Canadian West Gifset, 4 bks., Set. (Orig.). 1986. pap. 27.99 (*0-87123-972-8*) Bethany Hse.
— A Cote of Many Colors. (Illus.). 128p. (Orig.). (J). (gr. 3 up). 1987. pap. 4.99 (*0-934998-27-2*) Bethel Pub.
— Ducktails. (Illus.). 131p. (J). (gr. 3 up). 1985. pap. 4.99 (*0-934998-20-5*) Bethel Pub.
— Faithful Father: Selected Readings from the Women of the West Series for Meditations And. 1993. 10.99 (*1-55661-361-X*) Bethany Hse.
— The Father of Love. (Illus.). 208p. 1989. text ed. 10.99 (*1-55661-064-5*) Bethany Hse.
— Father of My Heart. 1990. 10.99 (*1-55661-155-2*) Bethany Hse.
— The Father Who Calls. LC 88-22128. (Illus.). 192p. (Orig.). 1988. text ed. 10.99 (*1-55661-043-2*) Bethany Hse.
— Heart of the Wilderness. 1993. 9.99 (*1-55661-363-6*); pap. 7.99 (*1-55661-362-8*) Bethany Hse.
— Hey, Teacher! 79p. (Orig.). 1982. pap. 3.99 (*0-934998-06-X*) Bethel Pub.
— The Impatient Turtle. Peterson, Pete, ed. (Illus.). 110p. (Orig.). (J). (gr. 3-6). 1986. pap. 4.99 (*0-934998-24-8*) Bethel Pub.
— Janette Oke's Reflections on the Christmas Story. LC 94-39586. 96p. 1994. 10.99 (*1-55661-528-0*) Bethany Hse.
— Julia's Last Hope. 224p. (Orig.). (YA). (gr. 8 up). 1990. pap. 7.99 (*1-55661-153-6*) Bethany Hse.
— Julia's Last Hope. large type ed. 224p. (Orig.). (YA). (gr. 8 up). 1990. pap. 9.99 (*1-55661-157-9*) Bethany Hse.
— Love Comes Softly. LC 79-16421. 192p. (Orig.). 1979. pap. 6.99 (*0-87123-342-8*) Bethany Hse.
— Love Comes Softly. large type ed. 188p. (Orig.). (J). (gr. 4 up). 1985. pap. 8.99 (*0-87123-828-4*) Bethany Hse.
— Love Comes Softly, 4 bks., Set, Vols. 1-4. (Orig.). (YA). 1993. Set. 27.99 (*1-55661-777-1*) Bethany Hse.
— Love Comes Softly, 4 bks., Set, Vols. 5-8. (Orig.). (YA). 1993. Set. 27.99 (*1-55661-778-X*) Bethany Hse.
— Love Finds a Home. large type ed. (Love Comes Softly Ser.). 224p. (Orig.). (J). 1989. Large type. pap. 8.99 (*1-55661-093-9*); pap. 6.99 (*1-55661-086-6*) Bethany Hse.
— Love Finds a Home. large type ed. LC 94-42034. 1995. 22.95 (*0-7838-1207-8*) Hall.
— Love Takes Wing. 224p. (Orig.). 1988. pap. 5.95 (*0-685-51994-5*) Bethany Fellow.
— Love Takes Wing. LC 88-19276. (Love Comes Softly Ser.). 224p. (Orig.). (YA). (gr. 8 up). 1988. pap. 6.99 (*1-55661-035-1*) Bethany Hse.
— Love Takes Wing. large type ed. LC 88-19276. (Love Comes Softly Ser.). 224p. (Orig.). 1988. pap. 7.99 (*1-55661-045-9*) Bethany Fellow.
— Love Takes Wing. large type ed. LC 94-43842. (Love Comes Softly Ser.: Vol. 7). 322p. (Orig.). 1995. 21.95 (*0-7838-1206-X*, Large Print Bks) Hall.
— Love's Abiding Joy. LC 83-15503. (Love Comes Softly Ser.). 224p. (Orig.). 1983. pap. 6.99 (*0-87123-401-7*) Bethany Hse.
— Love's Abiding Joy. (Paperback Ser.). 312p. (Orig.). 1991. pap. 13.95 (*0-8161-5093-1*) G K Hall.
— Love's Abiding Joy. large type ed. 224p. (Orig.). 1983. pap. 8.99 (*0-87123-854-3*) Bethany Hse.
— Love's Enduring Promise. LC 80-22993. (Love Comes Softly Ser.). 206p. (Orig.). 1980. pap. 6.99 (*0-87123-345-2*) Bethany Hse.
— Love's Enduring Promise. large type ed. 206p. (Orig.). 1980. pap. 8.99 (*0-87123-829-2*) Bethany Hse.
— Love's Long Journey. 1985. pap. 7.99 (*0-87123-315-0*) Bethany Fellow.
— Love's Long Journey. (Paperback Ser.). 302p. 1990. pap. 13.95 (*0-8161-5019-2*) G K Hall.
— Love's Long Journey. large type ed. LC 82-9469. 207p. 1985. pap. 8.99 (*0-87123-853-5*) Bethany Hse.
— Love's Unending Legacy. LC 84-18412. 224p. (Orig.). 1984. pap. 6.99 (*0-87123-616-8*) Bethany Hse.
— Love's Unending Legacy. 362p. (Orig.). 1991. pap. 14.95 (*0-8161-5161-X*) G K Hall.
— Love's Unending Legacy. large type ed. LC 84-18412. (Love Comes Softly Ser.). 224p. (Orig.). (J). (gr. 4 up). 1985. pap. 8.99 (*0-87123-855-1*) Bethany Hse.
— Love's Unfolding Dream. LC 87-15780. (Love Comes Softly Ser.). 224p. 1987. pap. 6.99 (*0-87123-979-5*) Bethany Hse.
— Love's Unfolding Dream. large type ed. 224p. 1987. pap. 9.99 (*0-87123-980-9*) Bethany Fellow.
— Love's Unfolding Dream. large type ed. 1991. pap. 14.95 (*0-8161-5174-1*, Large Print Bks) Hall.
— Maury Had a Little Lamb. (Illus.). 137p. (Orig.). (J). (gr. 3 up). 1989. pap. 4.99 (*0-934998-34-5*) Bethel Pub.
— The Measure of a Heart. 224p. (Orig.). 1992. pap. 7.99 (*1-55661-296-6*) Bethany Hse.
— The Measure of a Heart. large type ed. LC 93-36155. (Orig.). 1994. 19.95 (*0-8161-5850-9*, Large Print Bks) Hall.
— Measure of a Heart. large type ed. 1992. pap. 9.99 (*1-55661-297-4*) Bethany Hse.
— New Kid in Town. (Illus.). 125p. (Orig.). (J). (gr. 3 up). 1983. pap. 4.99 (*0-934998-16-7*) Bethel Pub.
— Once upon a Summer. LC 81-10183. 203p. (Orig.). 1981. pap. 6.99 (*0-87123-413-0*) Bethany Hse.
— Once upon a Summer. large type ed. LC 81-10183. (Orig.). (YA). (gr. 7 up). 1987. pap. 8.99 (*0-87123-981-7*) Bethany Hse.
— Pioneer Love Stories Gifset, 8 bks., Set. (Love Comes Softly Ser.). (Orig.). 1990. pap. 55.99 (*1-55661-757-7*) Bethany Hse.
— Pordy's Prickly Problem. (Illus.). (J). 1993. pap. 4.99 (*0-934998-50-7*) Bethel Pub.
— Prairie Dog Town. (Illus.). 140p. (J). (gr. 3 up). 1988. pap. 4.99 (*0-934998-31-0*) Bethel Pub.
— The Prodigal Cat. 160p. (Orig.). (J). (gr. 3). 1984. pap. 4.99 (*0-934998-19-1*) Bethel Pub.
— La Promesa de Amor. 224p. (Orig.). (SPA.). 1989. pap. 4.95 (*0-88113-254-3*) Edit Betania.
— Quiet Places, Warm Thoughts. 112p. 1983. pap. 5.99 (*0-934998-15-9*) Bethel Pub.
— Roses for Mama. 224p. (Orig.). 1991. pap. 7.99 (*1-55661-185-4*) Bethany Hse.
— Roses for Mama. large type ed. 224p. (Orig.). 1991. pap. 9.99 (*1-55661-199-4*) Bethany Hse.
— Seasons of the Heart. 1993. 10.98 (*0-88486-088-4*) Arrowood Pr.
— Seasons of the Heart Giftset, 4 bks., Set. (Orig.). 1990. pap. 27.99 (*1-55661-756-9*) Bethany Hse.
— Spring's Gentle Promise. LC 89-22. (Seasons of the Heart Ser.). 224p. (Orig.). (J). (gr. 4 up). 1989. pap. 6.99 (*1-55661-059-9*) Bethany Hse.
— Spring's Gentle Promise. large type ed. (Seasons of the Heart Ser.). 224p. (Orig.). (J). 1989. pap. 8.99 (*1-55661-074-2*) Bethany Hse.
— Spunky's Diary. 99p. (J). (gr. 5-12). 1982. pap. 4.99 (*0-934998-11-6*) Bethel Pub.
— They Called Her Mrs. Doc. (Women of the West Ser.). 224p. (YA). 1992. pap. 7.99 (*1-55661-246-X*) Bethany Hse.
— They Called Her Mrs. Doc. large type ed. (Women of the West Ser.). 224p. (J). 1992. pap. 9.99 (*1-55661-247-8*) Bethany Hse.
— This Little Pig. (Illus.). 145p. (Orig.). (J). (gr. 1-6). 1991. pap. 4.99 (*0-934998-43-4*) Bethel Pub.
— Too Long a Stranger. 1994. pap. 8.99 (*1-55661-456-X*); pap. 13.99 (*1-55661-457-8*) Bethany Hse.
— Too Long a Stranger. large type ed. LC 94-33675. 1995. 21.95 (*0-7838-1158-6*, Large Print Bks) Hall.
— Trouble in a Fur Coat. (Illus.). 152p. (Orig.). (J). (gr. 1-6). 1990. pap. 4.99 (*0-934998-38-8*) Bethel Pub.
— When Breaks the Dawn. LC 86-3405. (Canadian West Ser.). 250p. (Orig.). (J). (gr. 4 up). 1986. pap. 6.99 (*0-87123-882-9*) Bethany Hse.
— When Breaks the Dawn. large type ed. (Canadian West Ser.). 219p. (Orig.). (J). (gr. 4 up). 1986. pap. 8.99 (*0-87123-895-0*) Bethany Hse.
— When Calls the Heart. LC 82-24451. 221p. (Orig.). 1983. pap. 6.99 (*0-87123-611-7*) Bethany Hse.
— When Calls the Heart. large type ed. LC 82-24451. (Canadian West Ser.). 221p. (Orig.). 1986. pap. 8.99 (*0-87123-885-3*) Bethany Hse.
— When Calls the Heart. large type ed. (General Ser.). 322p. (Orig.). 1992. pap. 15.95 (*0-8161-5366-3*, Large Print Bks) Hall.
— When Comes the Spring. LC 85-11261. 224p. (Orig.). (J). (gr. 6). 1985. pap. 6.99 (*0-87123-795-4*) Bethany Hse.
— When Comes the Spring. large type ed. LC 85-11261. (Canadian West Ser.). 253p. (Orig.). 1986. pap. 8.99 (*0-87123-884-5*) Bethany Hse.
— When Comes the Spring. large type ed. LC 92-22425. (General Ser.). 375p. (Orig.). 1993. lib. bdg. 19.95 (*0-8161-5395-7*) G K Hall.
— When Hope Springs New. LC 86-13664. (Canadian West Ser.). 224p. (Orig.). (J). (gr. 4 up). 1986. pap. 6.99 (*0-87123-657-5*) Bethany Hse.
— When Hope Springs New. large type ed. (Canadian West Ser.). 216p. (Orig.). (J). (gr. 4 up). 1986. pap. 8.99 (*0-87123-675-3*) Bethany Hse.
— Who's New at the Zoo. (Illus.). (J). 1994. pap. 4.99 (*0-934998-55-8*) Bethel Pub.
— Winds of Autumn. LC 86-34299. 1987. pap. 6.99 (*0-87123-946-9*) Bethany Hse.
— The Winds of Autumn. large type ed. 1987. pap. 8.99 (*0-87123-982-5*) Bethany Hse.
— Winter Is Not Forever. large type ed. LC 88-2882. 224p. (J). (gr. 4 up). 1988. 6.99 (*1-55661-002-5*); pap. 8.99 (*1-55661-008-4*) Bethany Hse.
— A Woman Named Damaris. (Illus.). 224p. (Orig.). 1991. pap. 7.99 (*1-55661-225-7*) Bethany Hse.
— A Woman Named Damaris. large type ed. 224p. (Orig.). (YA). (gr. 9 up). 1991. pap. 9.99 (*1-55661-226-5*) Bethany Hse.
— Women of the West I: Calling of Emily Evans, Julias Last Hope, Roses for Mama, Woman Named Damaris. 1991. pap. 31.99 (*1-55661-761-5*) Bethany Hse.
Oke, Oluremilekun A. Reminiscences on Psychosomatics. 1993. 15.00 (*0-533-10441-6*) Vantage.
Oke, T. R. Boundary Layer Climates. 2nd ed. (Illus.). 416p. 1988. lib. bdg. 99.00 (*0-416-04422-0*, A1481); pap. text ed. 35.00 (*0-416-04432-8*, A1485) Routledge Chapman & Hall.
***Oke, Timothy & Wynn, Graeme, eds.** Vancouver & Its Region. 351p. 1992. pap. 29.95 (*0-7748-0421-1*) U of Wash Pr.
O'Keafe, Cynthia, jt. auth. see Crawley, Amy.
Okeay, T. The Story of Venice. (Mediaeval Towns Ser.: Vol. 31). 1974. reprint ed. 60.00 (*0-8115-0873-0*) Periodicals Srv.
OKechukwu, A. On Communitarian Divinity: An African Interpretation of the Trinity. LC 94-12161. 140p. 1994. 29.95 (*1-55778-704-2*) Paragon Hse.
Okediji, Florence A. The Cattle Industry in Northern Nigeria, 1900-1939. (African Humanities Ser.). (Illus.). (Orig.). 1973. pap. text ed. 2.00 (*0-941934-07-1*) Indiana Africa.
O'Keef, Richard D. How to Make More Money Babysitting: What Works, What Doesn't, & Why. LC 91-92960. (Illus.). 136p. (Orig.). (YA). (gr. 6-10). 1992. pap. 8.95 (*0-9630531-3-2*) Diamond Bks UT.
O'Keefe, Brendan. Medicine at War. (Official History of Australia's Involvement in Southeast Asian Conflicts Ser.: Vol. III). (Illus.). 536p. 1994. 59.95 (*1-86373-301-9*, Pub. by Allen Unwin AT) Paul & Co Pubs.
O'Keefe, Candace. Texas Women - A Celebration of History: A Multicultural Instructional Guide. (Illus.). 60p. (J). (gr. 4 up). 1991. pap. 8.95 (*0-9606256-2-3*) Hendrick-Long.
O'Keefe, Claudia. Gawkers. 1995. 20.95 (*0-312-85574-5*) Tor Bks.
O'Keefe, Constance, jt. auth. see Kanno, Eiji.
O'Keefe, Daniel, Jr. & Spiegel, Robert A. An Analytical Legislative History of the Medical Device Amendments of 1976: An Amendment to the Federal Food, Drug, & Cosmetic Act. (Food & Drug Law Institute Ser.). 323p. 1976. pap. write for info. (*1-885259-03-4*) Food & Drug Law.
O'Keefe, David, jt. auth. see Curtin, Deirdre.
O'Keefe, Donna. Linn's Philatelic Gems, No. 4. (Illus.). 167p. 1989. pap. 9.95 (*0-940403-12-9*) Linns Stamp News.
— Philatelic Gems, No. 3. (Illus.). 168p. 1987. reprint ed. pap. 9.95 (*0-940403-04-8*) Linns Stamp News.
— Philatelic Gems, No. 4. (Illus.). 168p. 1989. 30.00 (*0-940403-17-X*) Linns Stamp News.
— Philatelic Gems, No. 5. (Illus.). 168p. 1991. 30.00 (*0-940403-45-5*); pap. 9.95 (*0-940403-44-7*) Linns Stamp News.
— Philatelic Gems Set, Vols. 1-5. 1989. pap. 55.00 (*0-940403-16-1*) Linns Stamp News.
— Philatelic Gems, Three. (Illus.). 168p. (Orig.). 1987. pap. 9.95 (*0-940403-02-1*) Linns Stamp News.
— Philatelic Gems, Two. (Illus.). 168p. 1985. reprint ed. pap. 9.95 (*0-940403-03-X*) Linns Stamp News.
O'Keefe, Donna, ed. Linn's Stamp Identifier. LC 93-2693. 144p. (Orig.). 1993. pap. 9.95 (*0-940403-52-8*) Linns Stamp News.

O'Keefe, Edward J. & Berger, Donna S. Self-Management for College Students: The ABC Approach. rev. ed. LC 93-85780. (Illus.). (C). 1993. pap. write for info. (*0-9637801-0-7*) Partridge Hill. A holistic approach to self-management provides a comprehensive framework for attaining academic & personal goals. Students learn to manage time, motivation, study habits, procrastination, assertiveness, & self-esteem by managing their Affect, Behavior & Cognition. Seemingly disparate skills are integrated through common ABC principles & methods. The central role of the ABCs to developing & applying skills in all of these areas transforms otherwise complex topics such as motivation & self-esteem into skills that students can understand & manage. Basic feelings, behaviors, & thoughts that help or hinder achievement are discussed along with methods for change & improvement. These principles are then applied to each of the topic areas. A useful self-help book for high school seniors or college bound students, its focus on life skills is relevant to everyone. With plenty of exercises that can be done independently or in a classroom setting, the book is an excellent resource for student success courses, freshman seminars, or any program emphasizing self-reliance. The foreword by John Gardner, Director of the University of South Carolina's Freshman Year Experience, urges students to read carefully its "all-powerful message." Teacher's guide is also available. Contact Partridge Hill Publishers, FAX/Phone: 914-229-6672. Price $19.95. ***Publisher Provided Annotation.***

O

An Asterisk (*) at the beginning of an entry indicates that the title is appearing in BIP for the first time.

*__O'Keefe, Eric.__ The Texas Monthly Guidebooks: West Texas & the Big Bend. (The Texas Monthly Guidebooks Ser.). 1995. write for info. (*0-87719-250-2*) Gulf Pub.

O'Keefe, Georgia. Georgia O'Keefe: Paintings. LC 94-20417. (Illus.). 1994. pap. 4.99 (*0-517-11923-4*, Pub. by Wings Bks) Random Hse Value.

Okeefe-Gravalos, Mary E. & Pulin, Carol. Bertha Lum. (American Printmakers Ser.). 1991. pap. 19.95 (*1-56098-008-7*) Smithsonian.

O'Keefe, Herbert. Southern Redwood Co., Set. 5th ed. 56p. (C). 1991. Manual practice set. student ed, pap. text ed. 20.95 (*0-256-09254-0*, 36-1345-05) Irwin.

*__O'Keefe, J. A. & Farrand, W. L.__ Introduction to New Zealand Law. 4th ed. 650p. 1986. pap. 63.00 (*0-409-65537-6*, NZ) Butterworth Legal Pubs.

O'Keefe, Jack. Reading to Writing: Form & Meaning. 352p. (C). 1990. pap. text ed. 20.00 (*0-15-575784-9*) HB Coll Pubs.

O'Keefe, Jack V. Flyin' Ain't What It Used to Be. (Illus.). 84p. 1993. pap. 8.95 (*0-8059-3382-4*) Dorrance.

O'Keefe, Jacquelyn, ed. see Thompson, J. Clay.

*__O'Keefe, James H., Jr. & Hammill, Stephen C.__ ECG Board Review & Study Guide: Criteria Definitions, 2 pts. LC 94-29343. (Illus.). 144p. 1994. 35.00 (*0-87993-600-2*) Futura Pub.

OKeefe, JoAnna. Come to the Garden: An Invitation to Serenity. Mitchell, Julie, ed. (Illus.). 1992. 6.50 (*0-8378-2502-4*) Gibson.

O'Keefe, John. Shimmer & Other Texts. LC 89-20312. 72p. (Orig.). 1989. pap. 6.95 (*1-55936-002-X*) Theatre Comm.

— What Color Is Your Swimming Pool? The Guide to Trouble-Free Pool Maintenance. Clarkson, Sarah M., ed. LC 85-61479. 120p. (Orig.). 1987. pap. 9.95 (*0-88266-408-5*, Storey Pub) Storey Comm Inc.

O'Keefe, John J., jt. auth. see Allsopp, Michael E.

O'Keefe, John M. Water-Conserving Gardens & Landscapes. Oxley, Constance, ed. LC 91-51124. (Down-to-Earth Book Ser.). (Illus.). 160p. 1992. pap. 12.95 (*0-88266-786-6*, Garden Way Pub) Storey Comm Inc.

O'Keefe, Katherine O. Old English Shorter Poems: Basic Readings. LC 94-10194. (Reference Library of the Humanities; Basic Readings on Anglo-Saxon England Ser.: Vol. 3; Vol. 1432). 456p. 1994. 67.00 (*0-8153-0097-2*, H1432) Garland.

— Visible Song: Transitional Literacy in Old English Verse. (Cambridge Studies in Anglo-Saxon England: No. 4). (Illus.). 220p. (C). 1990. 64.95 (*0-521-37550-9*) Cambridge U Pr.

O'Keefe, Laura K., ed. Records of the National Council of Women of the United States, Inc., 1988-ca. 1970: A Guide to the Microfiche Edition. 41p. 1988. pap. 15.00 (*0-8357-0799-7*) Univ Microfilms.

O'Keefe, Lawrence P. Technology Assessment for State & Local Government: A Guide to Decision Making. LC 82-71314. 222p. reprint ed. pap. 63.30 (*0-317-26718-3*, 2023520) Bks Demand.

O'Keefe, M. & Hyde, B. G. Symmetry & Structures of Crystals. 600p. 1995. text ed. 97.00 (*981-02-1701-3*) World Scientific Pub.

O'Keefe, M., jt. ed. see Krakow, W.

O'Keefe, M. Timothy. Caribbean Afoot! A Walking & Hiking Guide to Twenty-Nine of the Caribbean's Best Islands. (Illus.). 224p. 1993. pap. 14.95 (*0-89732-110-3*) Menasha Ridge.

— Diving to Adventure. LC 92-74327. (Diving Ser.). 160p. (Orig.). (C). 1992. pap. text ed. 9.95 (*0-936513-30-6*) Larsens Outdoor.

— The Hiker's Guide to Florida. (Illus.). 257p. (Orig.). 1993. pap. 12.95 (*1-56044-168-2*) Falcon Pr MT.

— Manatees - Our Vanishing Mermaids. LC 93-79803. (Illus.). 128p. (Orig.). 1993. pap. text ed. 8.95 (*0-936513-43-8*) Larsens Outdoor.

— Sea Turtles: The Watchers Guide. LC 95-75545. (Illus.). 128p. (Orig.). 1993. pap. text ed. 8.95 (*0-936513-47-0*) Larsens Outdoor.

O'Keefe, M. Timothy, jt. auth. see Larsen, Larry.

O'Keefe, Martin D. Known from the Things That Are: Fundamental Theory of the Moral Life. LC 87-16496. 348p. 1987. pap. 12.95 (*0-685-31935-0*) Ctr Thomistic.

— Known from the Things That Are: Fundamental Theory of the Moral Life. LC 87-16496. 348p. (C). 1987. pap. text ed. 12.95 (*0-268-01228-8*) U of Notre Dame Pr.

O'Keefe, Martin D., tr. Oremus: Speaking with God in the Words of the Roman Rite. LC 93-61062. (Series V: No. 2). viii, 390p. 1993. 24.95 (*1-880810-05-0*) Inst Jesuit.

O'Keefe, Martin D., tr. see McCarthy, John L., ed.

O'Keefe, Michael, ed. see Minerals, Metals & Materials Society Staff.

*__O'Keefe, P. J.__ And Then There Was One. DHP, Inc. Staff, ed. 160p. 1994. write for info. (*1-885531-54-0*) Doghouse Pubng.

O'Keefe, P. J. & Prott, Lyndel V. Law & the Cultural Heritage, Vol. I: Discovery & Excavation. U.K. pap. 80.00 (*0-86205-065-0*) Butterworth Legal Pubs.

— Law & the Cultural Heritage, Vol. II: Creation & Preservation. 1992. U.K. text ed. 112.00 (*0-406-12070-6*) Butterworth Legal Pubs.

— Law & the Cultural Heritage, Vol. III: Movement. U.K. text ed. 159.00 (*0-406-12071-4*) Butterworth Legal Pubs.

— Law & the Cultural Heritage, Vol. IV: Monuments & Sites. 1992. U.K. text ed. 112.00 (*0-406-12072-2*) Butterworth Legal Pubs.

— Law & the Cultural Heritage, Vol. V: Principles. 1992. U.K. text ed. 112.00 (*0-406-12073-0*) Butterworth Legal Pubs.

O'Keefe, Phil & Wisner, Ben, eds. Landuse & Development. LC 78-308975. (African Environment: Special Report Ser.: Vol. 5). 242p. reprint ed. pap. 69.00 (*0-8357-3023-9*, 2057110) Bks Demand.

O'Keefe, Philip. The New Forester. 128p. (Orig.). 1994. pap. 15.50 (*1-85339-232-4*, Pub. by Intermed Tech UK) Women Ink.

O'Keefe, Richard A. The Craft of Prolog. (Logic Programming Ser.). 408p. 1990. 47.50 (*0-262-15039-5*) MIT Pr.

*__O'Keefe, Richard R.__ Mythic Archetypes in Ralph Waldo Emerson: A Blakean Reading. LC 95-1707. 256p. 1995. text ed. 35.00x (*0-87338-518-7*) Kent St U Pr.

O'Keefe, Rip. Sober Living Workbook. 240p. 1980. pap. 11.00 (*0-89486-093-3*, 1098A) Hazelden.

*__O'Keefe, Roger.__ Trusted Faces Violating Private Places: Teaching Your Children How to Protect Themselves from Sexual Assault. (Illus.). 150p. (Orig.). 1995. pap. 14.95 (*0-942963-56-3*) Distinctive Pub.

O'Keefe, Ruth A. Starter One Hundred One, Bk. 8. AEVAC, Inc. Staff, ed. (Structured Beginning Reading Program Ser.). 96p. student ed 3.50 (*0-913356-14-X*) AEVAC.

*__O'Keefe, Susan H.__ Countdown to Christmas: Advent Thoughts, Prayers & Activities. LC 95-16257. (Illus.). 80p. (Orig.). (J). (gr. 4-8). 1995. pap. 4.95 (*0-8091-6628-3*) Paulist Pr.

— One Hungry Monster: A Counting Book in Rhyme. (Illus.). 32p. (J). (ps-3). 1989. 12.95 (*0-316-63385-2*, Joy St Bks) Little.

— One Hungry Monster: A Counting Book in Rhyme. (Illus.). 32p. (J). (ps-3). 1992. mass mkt. 4.95 (*0-316-63388-7*, Joy St Bks) Little.

— Who Will Miss Me If I Don't Go to Church? LC 92-28347. 32p. (J). 1993. pap. 3.95 (*0-8091-6608-9*) Paulist Pr.

O'Keefe, Susan H., ed. see Stroman, J. & Wilson, K.

O'Keefe, Ted, jt. auth. see Degrelle, Leon.

O'Keefe, Theodore J., ed. Journal of Historical Review, Vol. 10, Nos. 1-4: 1990 Index. 519p. 1991. 35.00 (*0-939484-42-0*) Inst Hist Rev.

— Journal of Historical Review, Vol. 11, Nos. 1-4: 1991 Index. 544p. 1992. 35.00 (*0-939484-43-9*) Inst Hist Rev.

— Journal of Historical Review, Vol. 7, Nos. 1-4: 1987 Index. 544p. 1988. 25.00 (*0-939484-48-X*) Inst Hist Rev.

— The Journal of Historical Review, Vol. 8, Nos. 1-4: 1988 Index. 522p. 1989. 25.00 (*0-939484-34-X*) Inst Hist Rev.

— Journal of Historical Review, Vol. 9, Nos. 1-4: 1989 Index. 545p. 1990. 35.00 (*0-939484-41-2*) Inst Hist Rev.

O'Keefe, Theodore J., jt. auth. see App, Austin J.

O'Keefe, Timothy J., ed. & intro. Columbus, Confrontation, Christianity: The European-American Encounter Revisited. (Illus.). 256p. (Orig.). 1994. pap. 19.95 (*0-9636059-1-7*) Forbes Mill.

O'Keefe, Timothy J., jt. auth. see Walsh, James P.

O'Keefe, Tom. The Art of Ray Swanson: Celebrating People & Lifestyles. Westheimer, Mary et al, eds. LC 92-82070. (Illus.). 208p. 1994. 75.00 (*0-9638565-0-2*) Old Paint.

O'Keefe, Vincent T., ed. see O'Malley, John W. & Padberg, John W.

*__O'Keefe, Virginia.__ Speaking to Think - Thinking to Speak. LC 94-45175. 180p. 1995. pap. text ed. 22.50 (*0-86709-358-7*) Boynton Cook Pubs.

O'Keeffe, B. Emer, jt. ed. see Harris, Ruth-Ann.

*__O'Keeffe, D. J.__ Truancy in English Secondary Schools - a Report Prepared for the DFE. 134p. 1994. pap. 19.00 (*0-11-270870-6*, HM08706, Pub. by HMSO UK) UNIPUB.

O'Keeffe, Daniel. Book of Irish Wit & Humour. 120p. 1989. pap. 9.95 (*0-85342-873-5*, Pub. by Mercier Pr IE) Dufour.

*__O'Keeffe, David & Twomey, Patrick M., eds.__ Legal Issues of the Maastricht Treaty. 1994. text ed. 85.00 (*0-471-94199-9*) Wiley.

O'Keeffe, Georgia. Georgia O'Keeffe. 1993. 18.95 (*0-394-58182-2*); pap. 12.00 (*0-679-72703-5*) Knopf.

— Georgia O'Keeffe. (Illus.). 1977. 75.00 (*0-670-33710-2*); pap. 29.95 (*0-14-004677-1*, Penguin Bks) Viking Penguin.

— Georgia O'Keeffe: One Hundred Flowers. 1989. pap. 45.00 (*0-679-72408-7*) Knopf.

— Georgia O'Keeffe: One Hundred Flowers. 1990. Gift ed. pap. 9.95 (*0-679-73323-X*) Knopf.

— Poppy, Nineteen Twenty-Seven. (Fine Art Jigsaw Puzzles Ser.). 1989. 9.95 (*0-317-93249-7*) Battle Rd Pr.

— Some Memories of Drawings. LC 74-14986. 1974. 250.00 (*0-686-17542-5*, Archway) PB.

O'Keeffe, Janet, jt. ed. see Bruyere, Susanne M.

O'Keeffe, John. Recollections of the Life of John O'Keeffe, 2 vols. in 1. LC 70-89711. 1972. 48.95 (*0-405-08828-0*) Ayer.

O'Keeffe, Katherine O'Brien, jt. ed. see Ezell, Margaret J. M.

O'Keeffe, Michael & Navrotsky, Alexandra, eds. Structure & Bonding in Crystals, Vol. 2. LC 81-7924. 1981. text ed. 134.00 (*0-12-525102-5*) Acad Pr.

— Structure & Bonding in Crystals, Vol. 1. LC 81-7924. 1981. text ed. 134.00 (*0-12-525101-7*) Acad Pr.

O'Keeffe, Peter & Simington, Tom. Irish Stone Bridges: History & Heritage. (Illus.). 356p. 1992. text ed. 47.50 (*0-7165-2465-1*, Pub. by Irish Acad Pr IE) Intl Spec Bk.

Okell, John. Burmese: An Introduction to the Literary Style. (Southeast Asian Language Text Ser.). Date not set. write for info. (*1-877979-44-9*) North Ill U Ctr SE Asian.

— Burmese: An Introduction to the Script. (Southeast Asian Language Text Ser.). Date not set. write for info. (*1-877979-43-0*) North Ill U Ctr SE Asian.

— Burmese: An Introduction to the Spoken Language, Bk. 1. (Southeast Asian Language Text Ser.). Date not set. write for info. (*1-877979-41-4*) North Ill U Ctr SE Asian.

— Burmese: An Introduction to the Spoken Language, Bk. 2. (Southeast Asian Language Text Ser.). Date not set. write for info. (*1-877979-42-2*) North Ill U Ctr SE Asian.

O'Kelley, Joyce. Love Letters to God. 1989. 7.95 (*0-86544-053-0*) Salv Army Suppl South.

O'Kelley, Mattie L. Moving to Town. (Illus.). (J). (ps-3). 1991. 15.95 (*0-316-63805-6*) Little.

O'Kelly, Bernard & Jarrott, Catherine A. L. John Colet's Commentary on First Corinthians. LC 82-12403. (Medieval & Renaissance Texts & Studies: Vol. 21). (Illus.). 352p. 1985. 24.00 (*0-86698-056-3*) MRTS.

O'Kelly De Galway, A. O. Tigran Petrosian - World Champion. 1965. 60.00 (*0-08-011013-4*, Pergamon Pr); pap. 45.00 (*0-08-011012-6*, Pergamon Pr) Elsevier.

O'Kelly, M. E., jt. auth. see Fotheringham, A. S.

O'Kelly, Michael J. Early Ireland: An Introduction to Irish Prehistory. 350p. 1989. pap. 32.95 (*0-521-33687-2*) Cambridge U Pr.

— Here Kitty, Kitty: Here Kiddy, Kiddy. (Illus.). 565p. (C). 1989. 29.95 (*0-685-26324-X*); text ed. 24.95 (*0-685-26325-8*); pap. text ed. 9.95 (*0-685-26326-6*) M J OKelly.

— Newgrange: Archaeology, Art & Legend. LC 81-86413. (New Aspects of Antiquity Ser.). (Illus.). 1983. 29.95 (*0-500-39015-0*) Thames Hudson.

— Newgrange: Archaeology, Art & Legend. LC 81-86413. (New Aspects of Antiquity Ser.). (Illus.). 240p. 1995. pap. 22.50 (*0-500-27371-5*) Thames Hudson.

O'Kelly, Seamus. Weaver's Grave. 128p. 1989. reprint ed. pap. 8.95 (*0-86278-152-3*, Pub. by OBrien Pr IE) Dufour.

O'Kelly, Seumas. Waysiders: Stories of Connacht. LC 73-150480. (Short Story Index Reprint Ser.). 1977. reprint ed. 19.95 (*0-8369-3821-6*) Ayer.

*__O'Kelly, Sile P. & Ronan, Johanna.__ Nursing Law & Practice. 1994. pap. text ed. 66.00 (*1-85475-315-0*, IE) Butterworth Legal Pubs.

Okely, Judith & Callaway, Helen, eds. Anthropology & Autobiography. LC 91-32485. (ASA Monographs: No. 29). (Illus.). 244p. 1992. pap. 16.95 (*0-415-05189-4*, A5912) Routledge.

Oken, Alan. Alan Oken's Complete Astrology. rev. ed. LC 87-47885. (Illus.). 640p. 1988. pap. 15.95 (*0-553-34537-0*) Bantam.

*__Okenfuss, Max J.__ The Rise & Fall of Latin Humanism in Early-Modern Russia: Pagan Authors, Ukrainians, & the Resiliency of Muscovy. (Brill's Studies in Intellectual History: No. 64). (Illus.). 312p. 1995. 90.50 (*90-04-10331-7*) E J Brill.

Okenfuss, Max J., tr. see Tolstoi, Peter.

*__Okeragori.__ Totems of the Kisii. 1995. 14.95 (*9966-884-74-2*) Nocturnal Sun.

*__Okere, Theophilus, ed.__ Identity & Change: Nigerian Philosophical Studies I. LC 94-40762. (Cultural Heritage & Contemporary Change, Ser. II, Africa: Vol. 3). 1995. 45.00 (*1-56518-071-2*); pap. 17.50 (*1-56518-072-0*) Coun Res Values.

Okerlund, Twila. Stepping Toward Control: A Book for People Who Live with Diabetes. Allen, Susan D. & Holloran, Colleen A., eds. (Illus.). 64p. Date not set. pap. text ed. 3.75 (*0-916999-15-7*) HERC Inc.

Okerman, Lieve. Diseases of Domestic Rabbits. 2nd ed. Sundahl, Richard, tr. LC 93-29982. (Library of Veterinary Practice). 1994. write for info. (*0-632-03804-7*, Pub. by Blckwell Sci Pubns UK) Blackwell Sci.

Okerstrom, Dennis & Morgan, Sarah J. The Peace & War Reader. 512p. (C). 1993. pap. text ed. 22.00 (*0-205-13603-6*) Allyn.

Okerstrom, Dennis, jt. auth. see Morgan, Sarah J.

*__Okeson, Jeffrey P.__ Bell's Orofacial Pains. 5th ed. LC 95-1313. 500p. 1995. text ed. 68.00 (*0-86715-293-1*) Quint Pub Co.

— Management of Temporomandibular Disorders & Occlusion, No. 3. 624p. 1992. 57.95 (*0-8016-6548-5*) Mosby Yr Bk.

Okey Onuzo. Pathway to Conversational Prayer. 1990. 14.95 (*0-533-08719-8*) Vantage.

Okey, Robin. Eastern Europe 1740-1985: Feudalism to Communism. 2nd ed. LC 86-11319. (Illus.). 264p. (C). 1986. pap. text ed. 15.95 (*0-8166-1561-6*) U of Minn Pr.

Okey, T. The Story of Paris. (Mediaeval Towns Ser.: Vol. 15). 1974. reprint ed. 60.00 (*0-8115-0857-9*) Periodicals Srv.

Okhi, S., et al, eds. Molecular Mechanisms of Membrane Fusion. LC 87-29163. (Illus.). 598p. 1988. 125.00 (*0-306-42773-7*, Plenum Pr) Plenum.

*__Okholm, Dennis L. & Phillips, Timothy R., eds.__ More Than One Way? Four Views on Salvation in a Pluralistic World. 224p. 1995. pap. 14.99 (*0-310-20116-0*) Zondervan.

Okholm, Dennis L., jt. ed. see Phillips, Timothy R.

Okhubo, Hitoshi, tr. see Fukuda, Tadashi.

Okhuereigbe, Andy, et al. How to Promote Your Business & Increase Sales. Tyner, Harry & Aina, Justin, eds. 120p. (C). 1983. 19.95 (*0-912305-01-0*); pap. 11.95 (*0-912305-00-2*) Unltd Mktg Pubns.

Okhuijsen, G. & Van Opzeeland, C. In Heaven There Are No Thunderstorms: Celebrating the Liturgy with Developmentally Disabled People. 136p. (Orig.). 1992. pap. text ed. 7.95 (*0-8146-1999-1*) Liturgical Pr.

Oki, Michinori. Applications of Dynamic NMR Spectroscopy to Organic Chemistry. LC 84-20844. (Methods in Stereochemical Analysis Ser.: Vol. 4). 423p. 1985. lib. bdg. 140.00 (*0-89573-120-7*) VCH Pubs.

Oki, Michinori & Ito, Sho. The Chemistry of Rotational Isomers. LC 92-37400. (Reactivity & Structure Ser.: Vol. 30). 1993. 145.00 (*0-387-56193-5*) Spr-Verlag.

Oki, Morihiro, photos. India: Fairs & Festivals. 160p. 1989. 29.95 (*0-87040-823-2*) Japan Pubns USA.

Oki, T., jt. ed. see Henein, H.

Okidi, C. O. Regional Control of Ocean Pollution: Legal & Institutional Problems & Prospects. 292p. 1978. lib. bdg. 90.50 (*90-286-0367-0*) Kluwer Ac.

Okie, Laird. Augustan Historical Writing: Histories of England in the English Enlightenment. 248p. (C). 1991. lib. bdg. 46.00 (*0-8191-8050-5*) U Pr of Amer.

Okie, Susan, jt. auth. see Ride, Sally.

O'Kieff. Home Care Documentation: An Integrated System. Date not set. 99.95 (*0-8016-3713-9*) Mosby Yr Bk.

O'Kieffe, Charley. Western Story: The Recollections of Charley O'Kieffe, 1884-1898. LC 60-5381. (Pioneer Heritage Ser.: Vol. 2). (Illus.). xvi, 223p. 1960. pap. 5.50 (*0-8032-5796-1*) U of Nebr Pr.

Okigbo, Christopher. Labyrinths with "Path of Thunder" LC 72-90297. (Illus.). 72p. 1971. 12.50 (*0-8419-0045-0*, Africana); pap. 8.50 (*0-8419-0016-7*, Africana) Holmes & Meier.

Okigbo, P. N. National Development Planning in Nigeria, 1900-1992. 229p. 1989. text ed. 40.00 (*0-435-08039-3*, 08039) Heinemann.

— Nigerian Public Finance. LC 65-15473. (Northwestern University African Studies Ser.: No. 15). 259p. reprint ed. pap. 73.90 (*0-317-27584-4*, 2014855) Bks Demand.

Okigbo, Pius N. Africa & the Common Market. LC 67-18007. 199p. reprint ed. pap. 56.80 (*0-8357-5223-2*, 2016718) Bks Demand.

— Nigeria's Financial System. LC 82-158952. 300p. reprint ed. pap. 85.50 (*0-8357-2969-9*, 2039231) Bks Demand.

Okihiro, Gary Y. Cane Fires: The Anti-Japanese Movement in Hawaii, 1865-1945. 1992. pap. 19.95 (*0-87722-945-7*) Temple U Pr.

— Margins & Mainstreams: Asians in American History & Culture. LC 93-44382. 222p. (C). 1994. 25.00 (*0-295-97338-2*); pap. 12.95 (*0-295-97339-0*) U of Wash Pr.

*__Okihiro, Gary Y., ed.__ In Resistance: Studies in African, Caribbean, & Afro-American History. LC 85-28874. 240p. Date not set. reprint ed. pap. 68.40 (*0-7837-9205-0*, 2049955) Bks Demand.

Okihiro, Gary Y., intro. Ethnic Studies, Vol. I: Cross-Cultural, Asian, & Afro-American Studies. LC 88-39578. (Selected Course Outlines & Reading Lists from American Colleges & Universities Ser.). 270p. (Orig.). (C). 1989. pap. text ed. 16.95 (*1-55876-004-0*) Wiener Pubs Inc.

— Ethnic Studies, Vol. II: Chicano & Native American Studies. LC 88-39578. (Selected Course Outlines & Reading Lists from American Colleges & Universities Ser.). 146p. (Orig.). (C). 1989. pap. text ed. 16.95 (*1-55876-005-9*) Wiener Pubs Inc.

Okihiro, Gary Y., et al, eds. Reflections on Shattered Windows: Promises & Prospects for Asian American Studies. LC 87-31725. (Association for Asian American Studies Ser.). 238p. (C). 1988. pap. 20.00 (*0-87422-039-4*) Wash St U Pr.

Okihiro, Norman, jt. auth. see Waller, Irvin.

Okiji, A. & Kawakami, N., eds. Correlation Effects in Low-Dimensional Electron Systems: Proceedings of the 16th Taniguchi Symposium, Kashkojima, Japan, October 25-29, 1993. LC 94-8947. (Springer Series in Solid-State Sciences: Vol. 118). 1994. 79.00 (*0-387-57878-1*) Spr-Verlag.

Okilo, Melford. The Law of Life. 250p. 1991. text ed. 15.00 (*1-879605-03-1*) U Sci & Philos.

Okimoto, Daniel I. Between MITI & the Market: Japanese Industrial Policy for High Technology. LC 88-39837. (ISIS Studies in International Policy). 288p. 1989. 37.50 (*0-8047-1298-0*); pap. 13.95 (*0-8047-1812-1*) Stanford U Pr.

Okimoto, Daniel I. & Rohlen, Thomas P., eds. Inside the Japanese System: Readings on Contemporary Society & Political Economy. LC 87-18820. xiv, 286p. 1988. 39.50 (*0-8047-1425-8*); pap. 14.95 (*0-8047-1423-1*) Stanford U Pr.

Okimoto, Daniel I. & Yoshikawa, Aki. Japan's Health System: Efficiency & Effectiveness in Universal Care. Lee, Amy K., ed. (International Health Policy Ser.). (Illus.). 266p. Date not set. pap. text ed. 95.00 (*1-881393-14-3*) Faulkner & Gray.

Okimoto, Daniel I., jt. ed. see Inoguchi, Takashi.

Okimoto, Daniel I., et al. The Semiconductor Competition & National Security. (Special Report of the Northeast Asia-United States Forum on International Policy, Stanford University Ser.). 87p. (Orig.). 1987. pap. 12.00 (*0-935371-16-8*) CFISAC.

Okimoto, Daniel I., et al, eds. Competitive Edge: The Semiconductor Industry in the U. S. & Japan. LC 83-40107. (ISIS Studies in International Policy). xviii, 275p. 1984. 37.50 (*0-8047-1225-5*) Stanford U Pr.

Okimoto, Jean D. Blumpoe Grumpoe Meets Arnold C, Vol. 1. (J). (ps-3). 1990. 13.95 (*0-316-63811-0*, Joy St Bks) Little.

— Jason's Women. LC 85-28655. 210p. (J). (gr. 7-p). 1986. 14.95 (*0-316-63809-9*, 638099, Joy St Bks) Little.

— Molly by Any Other Name. (J). 1993. pap. 2.95 (*0-590-42994-9*) Scholastic Inc.

— No Dear, Not Here: The Marbled Murrelets' Quest for a Nest in the Pacific Northwest. (Illus.). 32p. (J). (ps-2). 1995. 14.95 (*1-57061-019-3*) Sasquatch Bks.

— A Place for Grace. (Illus.). 32p. (J). (gr. 1 up). 1993. 14.95 (*0-912365-73-0*) Sasquatch Bks.

— Take a Chance, Gramps!, Vol. 1. (J). (gr. 4-7). 1990. 15.95 (*0-316-63812-9*, Joy St Bks) Little.

— Talent Night. LC 93-34591. (YA). 1995. 14.95 (*0-590-47809-5*) Scholastic Inc.

Okimura, H. & Ogura, K., eds. Fracture Mechanics. 282p. 1991. 116.00 (*1-85166-547-1*) Elsevier.

Okin, Louis, jt. ed. see Burstein, Stanley.

*__Okin, Milton, ed.__ From the Heart Easy Piano. 64p. (YA). Date not set. pap. 9.95 (*0-89524-885-9*) Cherry Lane.

Okin, Susan M. Justice, Gender, & the Family. LC 89-42519. 224p. 1991. pap. 13.00 (*0-465-03703-8*) Basic.

O

An Asterisk (*) at the beginning of an entry indicates that the title is appearing in BIP for the first time.

— Women in Western Political Thought. LC 79-84004. 384p. 1992. pap. text ed. 16.95 (*0-691-02191-0*) Princeton U Pr.

Okin, Susan M. & Mansbridge, Jane, eds. Feminism, 2 vols. (Schools of Thought in Politics Ser.: Vol. 6). 864p. 1994. 247.95 (*1-85278-565-9*, Pub. by E Elgar Pub UK) Ashgate Pub Co.

Okita, Dwight. Crossing with the Light. 60p. 1992. pap. 6.95 (*0-9624287-9-5*) Tia Chucha Pr.

Okita, Saburo. The Developing Economics of Japan. 284p. 1981. 32.50 (*0-86008-271-7*, Pub. by U of Tokyo JA) Col U Pr.

— Essays on Japan & Asian Economic Cooperation: Japan's Structural Adjustment, Asian Economic Growth, & the Transition to Market Economies. LC 92-43432. (Occasional Papers: No. 39). 1993. pap. 6.95 (*1-55815-253-9*) ICS Pr.

— Japan in the World Economy of the 1980's. 270p. 1990. text ed. 37.50 (*0-86008-451-5*, Pub. by U of Tokyo JA) Col U Pr.

— Postwar Reconstruction of the Japanese Economy. 200p. 1991. text ed. 37.50 (*0-86008-478-7*, Pub. by U of Tokyo JA) Col U Pr.

Okita, Yoshihiro & Hollenberg, J. Leland. The Miniature Palms of Japan: Cultivating Kannonchiku & Shurochiku. LC 81-387. (Illus.). 166p. 1981. 19.95 (*0-8348-0160-4*) Weatherhill.

Okkema, Kathleen. Cognition & Perception in the Stroke Patient: A Guide to Functional Outcomes in Occupational Therapy. LC 92-48191. (Rehabilitation Institute of Chicago Publication Ser.). 250p. 1993. boxed 59.00 (*0-8342-0362-6*, 20362) Aspen Pub.

Okken, P. A., et al, eds. Climate & Energy: The Feasibility of Controlling CO2 Emissions. (C). 1989. lib. bdg. 105.50 (*0-7923-0519-1*) Kluwer Ac.

Okker, Patricia. Out Sister Editors: Sarah J. Hale & the Tradition of Nineteenth-Century American Women Editors. LC 94-15269. (Illus.). 280p. 1995. 40.00 (*0-8203-1686-5*) U of Ga Pr.

Okkonen, Marc. Baseball Memories 1930-1939: A Complete Pictorial History of the "Hall of Fame" Decade. LC 94-20698. (Illus.). 256p. 1994. 24.95 (*0-8069-0574-3*) Sterling.

— Baseball Memories, 1950-1959: An Illustrated Scrapbook of Baseball's Fabulous 50's: All the Players, Managers, Cities & Ballparks. LC 93-4749. (Illus.). 240p. 1993. 30.00 (*0-8069-0427-5*) Sterling.

— Baseball Uniforms of the Twentieth Century: The Official Major League Baseball Guide. (Illus.). 288p. 1993. pap. 19.95 (*0-8069-8491-0*) Sterling.

— Federal League. 64p. 1989. pap. 12.00 (*0-910137-37-4*) Soc Am Baseball Res.

Okkonen, Mark. Baseball Memories: 1900-1909. LC 92-20532. (Illus.). 240p. 1992. 30.00 (*0-8069-8728-6*) Sterling.

Okladnikov, Aleksei P. Ancient Population of Siberia & Its Cultures. Maurin, Vladimir M., tr. LC 76-38729. (Harvard University. Peabody Museum of Archaeology & Ethnology. Antiquities of the New World Ser.: Vol. 1, No. 1). reprint ed. 47.50 (*0-404-52641-1*) AMS Pr.

Okladnikov, Alekseui P. Yakutia Before Its Incorporation into the Russian State. LC 71-102976. (Arctic Institute of North America-Anthropology of the North; Translation from Russian Sources Ser.: No. 8). (Illus.). 541p. reprint ed. pap. 154.20 (*0-7837-1171-9*, 2041700) Bks Demand.

Oklahoma Department of Libraries Staff. Directory of Oklahoma: State Almanac. 43th ed. Vesely, Marilyn & Lester, Patricia, eds. (Illus.). 792p. 1991. pap. 12.00 (*1-880438-00-3*) OK Dept Lib.

Oklahoma Department of Libraries Staff, et al, eds. Oklahoma Almanac. 44th ed. 792p. 1993. pap. 12.00 (*1-880438-01-1*) OK Dept Lib.

***Oklahoma Department of Wildlife Conservation Staff.** Oklahoma Watchable Wildlife Viewing Guide. 84p. Date not set. pap. 7.95 (*0-614-06141-5*) Falcon Pr MT.

Oklahoma Four-H Staff. Discover Oklahoma Cookin' LC 93-72517. 1993. write for info. (*0-87197-388-X*) Favorite Recipes.

Oklahoma Future Homemakers of America Staff. Oklahoma Recipe Roundup. LC 92-20293. 1992. write for info. (*0-87197-340-5*) Favorite Recipes.

Oklahoma West Publishing Company Staff. Wildlife Laws of Oklahoma: Oklahoma Statutes: Title 29, Game & Fish, & Title 22, Double Section Symbol 1111 Through 1113 As Amended Through Laws of the 1984 Regular Session of the Legislature. 1984. write for info. (*0-318-59005-0*) West Pub.

Okninski, Jan, ed. Semigroup Algebras. (Pure & Applied Mathematics Ser.: Vol. 138). 376p. 1991. 125.00 (*0-8247-8356-5*) Dekker.

***Oknuki-Tierney.** Rice As Self: Japanese Identies Through Time. 1995. pap. (*0-691-02110-4*) Princeton U Pr.

Oko, R. J., jt. auth. see Barth, A. D.

Okochi, Akio & Inoue, Tadakatsu, eds. Overseas Business Activities: The International Conference on Business History, 9. 296p. 1983. 37.50 (*0-86008-325-X*, Pub. by U of Tokyo JA) Col U Pr.

Okochi, Akio & Shimokawa, Koichi S., eds. The Development of Marketing in the Automobile Industry. (International Conferences on Business History Ser.: No. 7). 303p. 1981. 42.50 (*0-86008-288-1*, Pub. by U of Tokyo JA) Col U Pr.

Okochi, Akio & Uchida, Hoshimi, eds. The International Conferences on Business History: Development & Diffusion of Technology, Electrical & Chemical Industries, No. 6. 236p. 1980. 42.50 (*0-86008-270-9*, Pub. by U of Tokyo JA) Col U Pr.

Okochi, Akio & Yasuoka, Shigeaki, eds. Family Business in the Era of Industrial Growth. (International Conferences on Business History Ser.: No. 10). 318p. 1984. 42.50 (*0-86008-346-2*, Pub. by U of Tokyo JA) Col U Pr.

Okochi, Akio & Yonekawa, Shin-ichi, eds. The International Conferences on Business History: The Textile Industry & Its Business Climate, No. 8. 299p. 1982. 42.50 (*0-86008-298-9*, Pub. by U of Tokyo JA) Col U Pr.

Okoko, Don. The Kingdom of the Vampires. 1994. 11.95 (*0-533-10924-8*) Vantage.

Okoko, K. A. Socialism & Self-Reliance in Tanzania. 200p. 1985. 65.00 (*0-7103-0269-X*, Pub. by Kegan Paul Intl UK) Routledge Chapman & Hall.

Okolicsanyi, L., ed. see Familial Disorders of Hepatic Bilirubin Metabolism Workshop Staff.

Okolie, Charles. International Law Perspectives of the Developing Countries. LC 74-81841. 1978. 24.95 (*0-88357-011-4*); pap. 9.95 (*0-88357-042-4*) NOK Pubs.

Okolie, Charles C. International Law of Satellite Remote Sensing & Outer Space. 224p. 1989. boxed 39.95 (*0-8403-5288-3*) Kendall-Hunt.

Okolo, ed. Health Research & Design. 1990. 133.00 (*0-8493-4627-4*, R850) CRC Pr.

Okolo, Julius E., jt. ed. see Shaw, Timothy W.

Okolov, Vladislav, jt. auth. see Samarin, Viktor.

Okolowicz, John. The Radio - TV Finder: An Index to Nearly 7000 Pictures of Collectable Radios & TVs in 24 Popular Books. 100p. (Orig.). 1992. pap. 13.95 (*0-9632440-0-0*) Antique Elect.

Okon, Yaacov, ed. Azospirillum - Plant Associations. LC 93-26203. 1993. 149.95 (*0-8493-4925-7*, QR82) CRC Pr.

Okoneck, Christian, et al. Vector Bundles on Complex Projective Spaces. (Progress in Mathematics Ser.: No. 3). 396p. 1980. 49.00 (*0-8176-3000-7*) Birkhauser.

Okonek, Christian, et al. Vector Bundles on Complex Projective Spaces. (Progress in Mathematics Ser.: Vol. 3). 414p. 1988. 54.50 (*0-8176-3385-5*) Spr-Verlag.

Okongwu, Anne, jt. ed. see Mencher, Joan.

Okonjo, I. M. British Administration in Nigeria, 1900-1950: A Nigerian View. LC 73-84372. (Library of African Affairs). 390p. 1974. text ed. 21.50 (*0-88357-002-5*) NOK Pubs.

***Okonkwo, Rina.** Protest Movements in Lagos, 1908-1930. LC 94-33462. (African Studies: Vol. 37). 134p. 1995. text ed. 69.95 (*0-7734-9049-3*) E Mellen.

***Okonowicz, Ed.** Pulling Back the Curtain Vol. I. (Spirits Between the Bays Ser.). (Illus.). 64p. (Orig.). 1994. pap. 8.95 (*0-9643244-0-7*) Myst & Lace.

— Stairway over the Brandywine: A Love Story. 24p. (Orig.). 1995. pap. 5.00 (*0-9643244-2-3*) Myst & Lace.

***Okonowicz, Kathleen, illus.** Opening the Door, Vol. II. (Spirits Between the Bays Ser.). 96p. (Orig.). 1995. pap. 8.95 (*0-9643244-3-1*) Myst & Lace.

O'Konski, Chester, ed. Molecular Electro-Optics Pt. 1: Theory & Method. (Electro-Optics Ser.: Vol. 1). 544p. 1976. 195.00 (*0-8247-6395-5*) Dekker.

— Molecular Electro-Optics Pt. 2: Applications to Biopolymers. (Electro-Optics Ser.: Vol. 1). 352p. 1978. 170.00 (*0-8247-6402-1*) Dekker.

Okonta, Ike. Nietzsche: The Politics of Power. LC 91-31790. (American University Studies: Philosophy: Ser. V, Vol. 132). 192p. (C). 1993. text ed. 38.95 (*0-8204-1727-0*) P Lang Pubs.

Okoroche, Cyril C. Meaning of Religious Conversion: The Case of the Igbo of Nigeria. (Avebury Series in Philosophy). 354p. 1987. text ed. 105.00 (*0-566-05030-7*, Pub. by Avebury Pub UK) Ashgate Pub Co.

***Okos, Martin R. & Renkowitz, Marshall.** Environmentally Responsible Food Processing. LC 94-28115. 1994. 75.00 (*0-8169-0651-3*, S-300) Am Inst Chem Eng.

Okos, Martin R., jt. ed. see Barbosa-Canovas, Gustavo V.

Okoshi, Takanori. Planar Circuits. (Electroyphysics Ser.: Vol. 18). (Illus.). 220p. 1985. 79.00 (*0-387-13853-6*) Spr-Verlag.

Okoshi, Takanori & Kikuchi, K. Coherent Optical Fiber Communications. (C). 1988. lib. bdg. 172.00 (*90-277-2677-9*) Kluwer Ac.

Okosun, T. Y. How Much Longer? Racism, Broken Children, African Americans & Anti-Human Churches. LC 93-73406. 155p. 1993. pap. 9.00 (*0-9637979-0-5*) T Y Okosun.

— Violence, Values & Inner-City Children. (Orig.). 1994. pap. 8.00 (*0-9637979-2-1*) T Y Okosun.

Okot, Kotber B., jt. ed. see Watson, J. A.

Okoye, Mokwugo. African Responses. 420p. 1987. 40.00 (*0-7223-0018-2*, Pub. by A H S Ltd UK) St Mut.

— The Beard of Prometheus. 220p. 1985. 35.00 (*0-317-39407-X*, Pub. by A H S Ltd UK) St Mut.

— The Beard of Prometheus. 220p. 1987. 35.00 (*0-7223-9988-X*, Pub. by A H S Ltd UK) St Mut.

Okpako, D. T. Principles of Pharmacology: A Tropical Approach. (Illus.). 544p. (C). 1991. 170.00 (*0-521-34095-0*) Cambridge U Pr.

Okpaku, Joseph, Sr. Nigeria: Hundred Questions & Answers. 100p. 1992. 19.95 (*0-89388-226-7*); pap. 9.95 (*0-89388-227-5*) Okpaku Communications.

Okpaku, Joseph. Superfight No. II: The Story Behind the Fights Between Muhammad Ali & Joe Frazier. LC 74-74429. 1974. 20.00 (*0-89388-165-1*) Okpaku Communications.

— Verdict: The Exclusive Picture Story of the Trial of the Chicago 8. LC 79-129568. (Illus.). 160p. 1970. 30.00 (*0-89388-008-6*); pap. 20.00 (*0-89388-009-4*) Okpaku Communications.

Okpaku, Joseph, Sr., ed. Nigeria & the Organisation of African Unity: In Search of an African Reality. LC 91-67250. 446p. 1991. 50.00 (*0-685-59746-6*) Okpaku Communications.

— Nigeria at the United Nation: Partnership for a Better World. LC 91-67251. 742p. 60.00 (*0-89388-211-9*) Okpaku Communications.

Okpaku, Joseph, ed. Nigeria, Dilemma of Nationhood: An African Analysis of the Biafran Conflict. LC 78-111266. (Contributions in Afro-American & African Studies: No. 12). 426p. (C). 1970. text ed. 47.95 (*0-8371-4668-2*, OKN/, Greenwood Pr) Greenwood.

— Nigeria-Dilemma of Nationhood: An African Analysis of the Biafran Conflict. LC 73-83162. 426p. 1974. reprint ed. pap. 15.95 (*0-89388-088-4*) Okpaku Communications.

Okpaku, Joseph O., ed. New African Literature & the Arts, Vol. 3. LC 76-109903. 224p. 1973. 29.95 (*0-685-29060-3*); pap. 14.95 (*0-89388-083-3*) Okpaku Communications.

Okpaku, Samuel O. Mental Health in Africa & the Americas Today. 507p. (C). 1993. pap. text ed. 49.95 (*0-916085-01-5*) Chrisolith Bks.

— Sex, Orgasm & Depression: Their Inner Relationship in a Changing Society. LC 83-63524. 160p. (Orig.). 1984. 12.95 (*0-916085-00-7*) Chrisolith Bks.

Okpara, Mzee L. Life Sentences: Freeing Black Relationships. 85p. 1993. pap. 8.00 (*0-88378-146-8*) Third World.

Okpewho, Isidore. African Oral Literature: Backgrounds, Character, & Continuity. LC 91-25671. (Illus.). 408p. 1992. text ed. 45.00 (*0-253-34167-1*); pap. text ed. 18.95 (*0-253-20710-X*, MB-710) Ind U Pr.

— The Epic in Africa. 312p. 1991. pap. text ed. 17.00 (*0-231-04401-1*) Col U Pr.

— The Epic in Africa: Towards a Poetics of the Oral Performance. LC 78-12893. 240p. 1979. text ed. 40.50 (*0-231-04400-3*) Col U Pr.

— Myth in Africa: A Study of its Aesthetic & Cultural Relevance. LC 82-19756. 305p. 1983. 74.95 (*0-521-24554-0*) Cambridge U Pr.

Okpewho, Isidore, ed. The Heritage of African Poetry. (Illus.). 256p. (C). 1985. pap. text ed. 22.95 (*0-582-72704-9*, 74743) Longman.

***Okpi.** Love Changes Everything. 1994. pap. text ed. (*0-7910-2934-4*) Chelsea Hse.

Okrand, Marc. The Klingon Dictionary. Stern, Dave, ed. 192p. 1992. pap. 10.00 (*0-671-74559-X*) PB.

***Okrant, Mark J.** Judson's Island. (Illus.). 131p. (Orig.). (C). 1995. pap. text ed. 13.95 (*0-9646061-1-9*) Wayfarer Pr.

***Okrent.** Legal Terminology. 96p. 1995. pap. text ed. 14.00 (*0-8273-6522-5*) Delmar.

Okrent, Cathy. Civil Litigation for the Paralegal New York State Student Pocket Part. 1992. student ed 9.95 (*0-8273-5294-8*) Delmar.

***Okrent, Cathy J.** Legal Terminology with Flashcards. LC 94-38109. 384p. 1994. pap. text ed. 26.95 (*0-8273-6521-7*) Delmar.

Okrent, Daniel. Baseball Book. pap. write for info. (*0-318-61607-6*, Penguin Bks) Viking Penguin.

— Nine Innings: The Anatomy of a Baseball Game. 288p. 1994. pap. 9.95 (*0-395-71040-5*) HM.

Okrent, Daniel & Lewine, Harris, eds. The Ultimate Baseball Book. rev. ed. (Illus.). 384p. 1991. pap. 22.95 (*0-395-59697-1*) HM.

Okrent, Daniel & Wulf, Steve. Baseball Anecdotes. 368p. 1989. 21.95 (*0-19-504396-0*) OUP.

Okrent, Daniel & Wulf, Steve. Baseball Anecdotes. 352p. 1993. reprint ed. pap. 13.00 (*0-06-273206-4*, Harper Ref) HarpC.

Okrent, David. Nuclear Reactor Safety: On the History of the Regulatory Process. LC 80-53958. 392p. (C). 1981. 45.00 (*0-299-08350-0*) U of Wis Pr.

Okrent, Hummel. Reactivity Coefficients in Large Fast Power Reactors. LC 73-119000. (ANS Monographs). 386p. 1970. 18.40 (*0-89448-006-5*, 300002) Am Nuclear Soc.

Okrent, Mark. Heidegger's Pragmatism: Understanding, Being, & the Critique of Metaphysics. LC 87-26014. 320p. 1988. 37.95 (*0-8014-2094-6*) Cornell U Pr.

— Heidegger's Pragmatism: Understanding, Being, & the Critique of Metaphysics. LC 87-26014. 320p. 1991. reprint ed. pap. 14.95 (*0-8014-9962-3*) Cornell U Pr.

Okri, Ben. Songs of Enchantment. LC 93-17198. 1993. 21.00 (*0-385-47154-8*, N A Talese) Doubleday.

— Songs of Enchantment. LC 94-19767. 1994. pap. 12.00 (*0-385-47157-2*, Anchor NY) Doubleday.

— Stars of the New Curfew. 208p. 1990. pap. 10.00 (*0-14-011602-8*, Penguin Bks) Viking Penguin.

Okroi, Loren J. Galbraith, Harrington, Heilbroner: Economics & Dissent in an Age of Optimism. 280p. 1988. text ed. 45.00 (*0-691-07771-1*) Princeton U Pr.

Okruhlik, Kathleen & Brown, James R., eds. The Natural Philosophy of Leibniz. 1985. lib. bdg. 105.50 (*90-277-2145-9*) Kluwer Ac.

Okruhlik, Kathleen, jt. ed. see Harvey, Elizabeth D.

***Oks, Eugen A.** Plasma Spectroscopy: The Influence of Microwave & Laser Fields. LC 94-35448. (Series on Atoms & Plasmas: Vol. 9). 1995. write for info. (*0-387-54100-4*) Spr-Verlag.

Oksana, Chrystine. Safe Passage to Healing: A Guide to Survivors of Ritual Abuse. 352p. (Orig.). 1994. pap. 15.00 (*0-06-096996-2*, PL) HarpC.

Oksas, Richard M., jt. auth. see Pallasch, Thomas J.

Oksche & Pevet, Paul. Pineal Organ: Photobiology, Biochronometry & Endocrinology. (Developments in Endocrinology Ser.: Vol. 14). 366p. 1982. 94.50 (*0-444-80387-4*) Elsevier.

Oksche, A. & Vollrath, L., eds. Teeth. (Handbook of Microscopic Anatomy Ser.: Vol. V/6). (Illus.). 605p. 1988. 387.00 (*0-387-19331-6*) Spr-Verlag.

Oksche, A., et al, eds. The Subcommissural Organ: An Ependymal Brain Gland. LC 93-9609. 1993. Alk. paper. 150.00 (*0-387-56336-9*) Spr-Verlag.

Oksenberg, ed. see Rorty, Amelie O.

Oksenberg, et al. Polymerase Chain Reaction & the Analysis of the T Cell Receptor Repertoire. (Medical Intelligence Ser.). 125p. 1992. text ed. 89.95 (*1-879702-47-9*) R G Landes.

Oksenberg, Micheal, jt. auth. see Jacobson, Harold K.

Oksenberg, Michel & Henderson, Gail. Research Guide to People's Daily Editorials, 1949-1975. LC 82-4408. 212p. (Orig.). 1982. pap. 8.50 (*0-89264-949-6*) Ctr Chinese Studies.

Oksenberg, Michel, jt. auth. see Lieberthal, Kenneth.

Oksenberg, Michel, et al, eds. Beijing Spring, 1989: Confrontation & Conflict: the Basic Documents. LC 90-8077. 448p. (C). 1990. 57.95 (*0-87332-683-0*); pap. text ed. 20.95 (*0-87332-684-9*) M E Sharpe.

Oksendal, B. Stochastic Differential Equations. (Universitext Ser.). xiii, 205p. 1985. pap. 29.00 (*0-387-15292-X*) Spr-Verlag.

— Stochastic Differential Equations. 2nd ed. (Universitext Ser.). 208p. 1989. pap. 29.95 (*0-387-51740-5*) Spr-Verlag.

— Stochastic Differential Equations: An Introduction with Applications. 3rd ed. (Universitext Ser.). 224p. (C). 1993. pap. text ed. 32.00 (*0-387-53335-4*) Spr-Verlag.

Oksendal, B., jt. ed. see Lund, D.

Okshansky, Robert B. Landslide Hazard in the United States: Case Studies in Planning & Policy Development. LC 90-43660. (Environment: Problems & Solutions Ser.). 192p. 1990. 50.00 (*0-8240-0472-8*) Garland.

Oktavec, Eileen, photos. Great Walks of Acadia National Park & Mount Desert Island. (Great Walks Ser.: No. 1). (Illus.). 176p. 1994. pap. 8.95 (*1-879741-00-8*) Great Walks.

— Great Walks of Big Bend National Park. (Great Walks Ser.: No. 3). (Illus.). 44p. (Orig.). 1991. pap. 3.95 (*1-879741-03-2*) Great Walks.

— Great Walks of Sequoia & Kings Canyon National Parks. (Great Walks Ser.: No. 6). (Illus.). 208p. (Orig.). 1994. pap. 8.95 (*1-879741-06-7*) Great Walks.

— Great Walks of Southern Arizona. (Great Walks Ser.: No. 2). (Illus.). 46p. (Orig.). 1990. pap. 3.95 (*1-879741-02-4*) Great Walks.

— Great Walks of the Great Smokies. (Great Walks Ser.: No. 4). (Illus.). 120p. (Orig.). 1992. pap. 5.95 (*1-879741-04-0*) Great Walks.

— Great Walks of Yosemite National Park. (Great Walks Ser.: No. 5). (Illus.). 192p. (Orig.). 1993. pap. 8.95 (*1-879741-05-9*) Great Walks.

Oktavec, Frank L. The Professional Education of Special Men Teachers of Physical Education in Prussia. LC 73-177133. (Columbia University. Teachers College. Contributions to Education Ser.: No. 369). reprint ed. 37.50 (*0-404-55369-9*) AMS Pr.

Oktay, Julianne & Walter, Carolyn, eds. Breast Cancer in the Life Course: Women's Experiences. (Social Work Ser.: Vol. 20). 232p. 1991. 28.95 (*0-8261-7110-9*) Springer Pub.

Oktay, Julianne S., jt. ed. see Palley, Howard A.

Oku, Hachiro. Plant Pathogenesis & Disease Resistance. 1993. 75.00 (*0-87371-727-9*, SB731) Lewis Pubs.

***Oku, Milton, ed.** Roxette for Easy Piano. 48p. (YA). Date not set. pap. 9.95 (*0-89524-889-1*, 02505509) Cherry Lane.

Okubo. Differential Geometry. (Pure & Applied Mathematics Ser.: Vol. 112). 816p. 1987. 199.00 (*0-8247-7700-X*) Dekker.

Okubo, Akira. Oceanic Mixing. LC 73-133442. 151p. 1970. 19.00 (*0-403-04523-1*) Scholarly.

***Okubo, Derek.** Governance & Diversity: Findings from Los Angeles. 1994. write for info. (*0-916450-48-1*) Nat Civic League.

Okubo, Mine. Citizen 13660. LC 82-20221. (Illus.). 226p. (Orig.). 1983. pap. 14.95 (*0-295-95989-4*) U of Wash Pr.

***Okubo, Susumo.** Introduction to Octonion & Other Non-Associative Algebras in Physics. (Montroll Memorial Lecture Series in Mathermatical Physics: No. 2). (Illus.). 170p. (C). 1995. write for info. (*0-521-47215-6*) Cambridge U Pr.

Okubo, Toshiteru, jt. ed. see Reich, Michael R.

Okubo, Y., jt. auth. see Goris, R. C.

Okuda, Denise, jt. auth. see Okuda, Michael.

Okuda, K., ed. International Congress on Clinical Enzymology, Osaka, 7th, September 1988, Abstracts. (Journal: Enzymology: Vol. 40, Suppl. 1, 1988). ii, 66p. 1988. pap. 19.25 (*3-8055-4915-6*) S Karger.

Okuda, Kunio, ed. The Sixth International Symposium on Quality Control: Osaka. (Current Clinical Practice Ser.: No. 47). 486p. 1989. pap. 154.00 (*90-219-1685-1*, Excerpta Medica) Elsevier.

Okuda, Kunio & Benhamou, J. P., eds. Portal Hypertension: Clinical & Physiological Aspects. (Illus.). 592p. 1991. 298.00 (*0-387-70054-4*) Spr-Verlag.

Okuda, Kunio & Ishak, K. G. Neoplasms of the Liver. (Illus.). 500p. 1987. 348.00 (*0-387-70020-X*) Spr-Verlag.

Okuda, Kunio & Omata, Masao, eds. Idiopathic Portal Hypertension. 606p. 1984. 100.00 (*0-86008-353-5*, Pub. by U of Tokyo JA) Col U Pr.

Okuda, Michael, ed. The Star Trek Encyclopedia. (Illus.). 1994. 28.00 (*0-671-88684-3*); pap. 18.00 (*0-671-86905-1*) PB.

Okuda, Michael & Okuda, Denise. Star Trek Chronology: The History of the Future. Stern, Dave, ed. (Orig.). 1993. pap. 14.00 (*0-671-79611-9*) PB.

Okuda, Michael, jt. auth. see Sternbach, Rick.

Okuda, Minoru. Progress in Allergy & Clinical Immunology: Kyoto, Vol. 2. Miyamoto, Terumasa, ed. LC 92-53196. (Illus.). 747p. 1992. text ed. 50.00 (*0-88937-087-7*) Hogrefe & Huber Pubs.

Okuda, S., et al, eds. Extreme Land Forming Events. (Annals of Gemorphology Supplement Ser.: No. 46). (Illus.). 169p. (Orig.). 1983. pap. text ed. 70.00 (3-443-21046-5, Pub. by Gebruder Borntraeger GW) Lubrecht & Cramer.

***Okuda, Setsuo, et al, eds.** The Physical Processes of Lake Biwa, Japan. LC 95-1870. (Coastal & Estuarine Studies: Vol. 48). 1995. write for info. (0-87590-262-6) Am Geophysical.

Okuda, Ted. Grand National, Producers Releasing Corporation, & Screen Guild-Lippert: Complete Filmographies & Studio Histories. LC 89-42743. 255p. 1989. lib. bdg. 38.50x (0-89950-384-5) McFarland & Co.

— The Monogram Checklist: The Films of Monogram Pictures Corporation, 1931-1958. LC 86-43089. 399p. 1987. lib. bdg. 49.95x (0-89950-286-5) McFarland & Co.

Okuda, Ted & Watz, Edward. The Columbia Comedy Shorts: Two-Reel Hollywood Film Comedies, 1933-1958. LC 84-43241. (Illus.). 272p. 1986. lib. bdg. 38.50x (0-89950-181-8) McFarland & Co.

Okuda, Ted, jt. auth. see Neibaur, James L.

Okudaira, Hideo. Narrative Picture Scrolls. Rosenfield, John, ed. Ten Grotenhuis, Elizabeth, tr. LC 73-9619. (Arts of Japan Ser.: Vol. 5). (Illus.). 152p. 1973. 15.00 (0-8348-2710-7) Weatherhill.

Okudzhava, Bulat. Songs: Bulat Okudzhava, Vol. II. Frumkin, Vladimir, ed. Wolfson, Tanya et al, trs. 117p. (ENG & RUS.). 1986. pap. text ed. 11.95 (0-87501-022-9) Ardis Pubs.

Okuguchi, K. & Szidarovszky, Ferenc. The Theory of Oligopoly with Multi-Product Firms. (Lecture Notes in Economics & Mathematical Systems Ser.: Vol. 342). v, 167p. 1990. pap. 29.90 (0-387-52567-X) Spr-Verlag.

Okuizumi, Kaori, et al, eds. The U. S.-Japan Economic Relationship in East & Southeast Asia: A Policy Framework for Asia-Pacific Economic Cooperation. (Significant Issues Ser.: Vol. XIV, No. 1). 281p. (Orig.). 1992. pap. text ed. 16.95 (0-89206-184-7) CSI Studies.

***Okulicz, Karen.** Try: A Survival Guide to Unemployment. 60p. 1995. pap. 10.00 (0-9644260-0-5) K Slaw.

Okuma, Augustine I. Awakening to Prayer. Hiraki, Theresa K. & Yamato, Albert M., trs. LC 93-33061. 1994. pap. 8.95 (0-935216-22-7) ICS Pubns.

Okuma, Thomas M. Angola in Ferment: The Background & Prospects of Angolan Nationalism. LC 73-17929. (Illus.). 137p. 1974. reprint ed. text ed. 49.75 (0-8371-7272-1, OKAF, Greenwood Pr) Greenwood.

Okumiya, Masatake, jt. auth. see Fuchida, Mitsuo.

Okumiya, Masatake, et al. Zero: The Air War in the Pacific in World War II, from the Japanese Viewpoint. LC 79-20670. reprint ed. 25.00 (0-89201-082-7) Zenger Pub.

Okumu, Washington. Lumumba's Congo. 1962. 12.95 (0-8392-1062-0) Astor-Honor.

Okumura, Nobuyoshi, tr. see Shimomura, Kojin, ed.

Okumura, Shohaku, tr. see Leighton, Taigen D., ed. & tr.

Okumura, Shohaku, tr. see Uchiyama, Kosho.

Okumura, Toshie, ed. Theoretical & Applied Mechanics: Proceedings of the Japan National Congress for Applied Mechanics, Vol. 22. 528p. 1974. 69.50 (0-86008-117-6, Pub. by U of Tokyo JA) Col U Pr.

— Theoretical & Applied Mechanics: Proceedings of the Japan National Congress for Applied Mechanics, Vol. 23. 560p. 1975. 74.50 (0-86008-138-9, Pub. by U of Tokyo JA) Col U Pr.

Okun, Arthur M. Equality & Efficiency: The Big Tradeoff. LC 75-5162. 124p. 1975. pap. 8.95 (0-8157-6475-8) Brookings.

— The Political Economy of Prosperity. LC 76-108835. 122p. 1970. 14.95 (0-8157-6478-2) Brookings.

— Prices & Quantities: A Macroeconomic Analysis. LC 80-70076. 367p. 1981. pap. 14.95 (0-8157-6479-0) Brookings.

Okun, Arthur M. & Perry, George L., eds. Brookings Papers on Economic Activity: No. 1-1978. LC 74-129564. 238p. reprint ed. pap. 67.90 (0-8357-7442-2, 2025394) Bks Demand.

— Brookings Papers on Economic Activity: No. 2-1979. LC 74-129564. 226p. reprint ed. pap. 64.50 (0-8357-7444-9, 2025396) Bks Demand.

— Brookings Papers on Economic Activity: No. 3-1978. LC 74-129564. 370p. reprint ed. pap. 105.50 (0-8357-7443-0, 2025395) Bks Demand.

— Curing Chronic Inflation. LC 78-11859. 311p. reprint ed. pap. 88.70 (0-317-26328-5, 2025393) Bks Demand.

Okun, Arthur M., jt. auth. see Baily, Martin.

Okun, Barbara F. Effective Helping: Interviewing & Counseling Techniques. 4th ed. 320p. (C). 1992. pap. 26.95 (0-534-14544-2) Brooks-Cole.

— Seeking Connections in Psychotherapy. LC 90-4738. (Social & Behavioral Science Ser.). 475p. 1990. 34.95 (1-55542-261-6) Jossey-Bass.

Okun, Barbara F., jt. ed. see Kantor, David.

Okun, D. A. & Ponghis, G. Community Wastewater Collection & Disposal. 1975. pap. 16.80 (92-4-156045-2) World Health.

Okun, Daniel & Ernst, Walter. Community Piped Water Supply Systems in Developing Countries: A Planning Manual. (Technical Paper Ser.: No. 60). 262p. 1987. 17.95 (0-8213-0896-3, BK0896) World Bank.

Okun, Daniel A. Regionalization of Water Management: A Revolution in England & Wales. (Illus.). 377p. 1977. 74.00 (0-85334-738-7, Pub. by Elsevier Applied Sci UK) Elsevier.

Okun, Daniel A., jt. auth. see Fair, Gordon M.

Okun, L. B. Leptons & Quarks. (North-Holland Personal Library: Vol. 2). 362p. 1985. reprint ed. pap. 32.50 (0-444-86924-7, North Holland) Elsevier.

— Particle Physics: The Quest for Substance of Substance. (Contemporary Concepts in Physics Ser.: Vol. 2). 223p. 1985. text ed. 82.00 (3-7186-0228-8); pap. text ed. 22.00 (3-7186-0229-6) Gordon & Breach.

— A Primer in Particle Physics, Alpha, Beta, Gamma...Z. 120p. 1987. text ed. 32.00 (3-7186-0374-8); pap. text ed. 14.00 (3-7186-0405-1) Gordon & Breach.

— The Relations of Particles, Vol. 42: Lecture Notes in Physics. 160p. 1991. text ed. 48.00 (981-02-0453-1); pap. text ed. 23.00 (981-02-0454-X) World Scientific Pub.

— Weak Interaction of Elementary Particles. 1965. 129.00 (0-08-011122-X, Pub. by Pergamon Repr UK) Franklin.

Okun', L. B. Weak Interaction of Elementary Particles. 184p. 1965. text ed. 52.50 (0-7065-0563-8, Pub. by Keter Pub IS) Coronet Bks.

O'Kun, Lan, jt. auth. see Lewis, Shari.

Okun, Lewis. Woman Abuse: Facts Replacing Myths. LC 84-26912. 298p. 1985. 64.50 (0-88706-077-3); pap. 21.95 (0-88706-079-X) State U NY Pr.

Okun, M., ed. see Dylan, Bob.

Okun, Milt & Phillips, Mark, eds. Bruce Hornsby & the Range - Scenes from the Southside (Piano - Vocal) (Illus.). 63p. (Orig.). 1990. pap. text ed. 12.95 (0-89524-385-7) Cherry Lane.

Okun, Milton. New York Times Country Music's Greatest Songs. LC 78-58169. 1980. pap. 19.95 (0-8129-6312-1) Cherry Lane.

Okun, Milton, ed. Ain't Broadway Grand - A Brand New 1948 Musical. pap. 14.95 (0-89524-747-X) Cherry Lane.

— Andre Motion Picture Soundtrack Songbook. (Illus.). 55p. (YA). 1994. pap. 14.95 (0-89524-876-X, 02502155) Cherry Lane.

— The Authentic Guitar Style of Harry Chapin. (Illus.). 55p. (Orig.). 1990. pap. text ed. 10.95 (0-89524-384-9) Cherry Lane.

— Barbra Streisand: Back to Broadway. (Illus.). 96p. (Orig.). 1995. pap. 19.95 (0-89524-806-9, HL02502132) Cherry Lane.

— Barbra Streisand: The Concert. 1995. pap. 17.95 (0-614-03545-7) Cherry Lane.

— Barbra Streisand - A Collection: Greatest Hits...& More. pap. 16.95 (0-89524-504-3) Cherry Lane.

— Barbra Streisand - Till I Loved You (Piano - Vocal) (Illus.). 56p. (Orig.). 1990. pap. text ed. 14.95 (0-89524-421-7) Cherry Lane.

— Best of American Music Awards. pap. 19.95 (0-89524-669-4) Cherry Lane.

— The Best of Contemporary Folk. (Illus.). 120p. (Orig.). (YA). 1995. pap. 17.95 (0-89524-861-1, HL02502122) Cherry Lane.

— The Best of Huey Lewis & the News: Piano - Vocal. (Illus.). 158p. (Orig.). 1990. pap. text ed. 17.95 (0-89524-341-5) Cherry Lane.

— Best of John Denver for Easy Guitar. 64p. (YA). Date not set. pap. 9.95 (0-89524-913-8) Cherry Lane.

— Best of John Denver for Easy Piano. 63p. Date not set. pap. 9.95 (0-89524-910-3) Cherry Lane.

— Best of Lenny Kravitz. 1994. pap. 12.95 (0-89524-829-8) Cherry Lane.

— Best of Richard Marx. 63p. (YA). 1994. per., pap. 12.95 (0-89524-828-X, 02502136) Cherry Lane.

— The Best of Roxette. 1994. pap. 12.95 (0-89524-827-1) Cherry Lane.

— Best of Steve Wariner. pap. 14.95 (0-89524-672-4) Cherry Lane.

— Bonnie Raitt - Longing in Their Hearts (Piano-Vocal-Guitar) 71p. (Orig.). (YA). Date not set. pap. 16.95 (0-89524-844-1, 02502139) Cherry Lane.

— Bonnie Raitt - Luck of the Draw. pap. 14.95 (0-89524-646-5) Cherry Lane.

— Bonnie Raitt - Nick of Time. pap. 14.95 (0-89524-440-3) Cherry Lane.

— Boston - Third Stage: Piano - Vocal. (Illus.). 63p. (Orig.). 1990. pap. text ed. 10.95 (0-89524-333-4) Cherry Lane.

— The Bottom Line 20th Anniversary Songbook. (Illus.). 149p. (Orig.). (YA). Date not set. pap. 19.95 (0-89524-852-2, 02502038) Cherry Lane.

— Broadway Today. 1994. pap. 14.95 (0-89524-814-X) Cherry Lane.

— Bruce Hornsby & the Range - A Night on the Town. pap. 14.95 (0-89524-580-9) Cherry Lane.

— Bruce Hornsby & the Range - Five of the Best. pap. 7.95 (0-89524-539-6) Cherry Lane.

— Cherry Lane Chartbusters. pap. 12.95 (0-89524-590-6) Cherry Lane.

— The Cherry Lane Gospel Songbook. pap. 16.95 (0-89524-703-8) Cherry Lane.

— Christine Lavin Songbook. pap. 17.95 (0-89524-712-7) Cherry Lane.

— Classic Country. pap. 14.95 (0-89524-595-7) Cherry Lane.

— Classic Country Encore. pap. 14.95 (0-89524-755-0) Cherry Lane.

— Classic Love Songs: Piano - Vocal. rev. ed. (Illus.). 128p. (Orig.). 1990. pap. text ed. 12.95 (0-89524-377-6) Cherry Lane.

— Classic Standards: Piano - Vocal - Guitar. (Illus.). 111p. (Orig.). 1990. pap. text ed. 12.95 (0-89524-365-2) Cherry Lane.

— Concrete Blonde- Bloodletting. pap. 12.05 (0-89524-624-4) Cherry Lane.

— Contemporary Christian Today. pap. 14.95 (0-89524-793-3) Cherry Lane.

— Contemporary Folk - Five of the Best. pap. 7.95 (0-89524-637-6) Cherry Lane.

— Country Chartbusters - Five of the Best. pap. 6.95 (0-89524-641-4) Cherry Lane.

— Country Ladies. (Illus.). 128p. (Orig.). 1995. pap. 12.95 (0-89524-819-0, HL02502129) Cherry Lane.

— Dancin' with Country. 1994. pap. 9.95 (0-89524-818-2) Cherry Lane.

— Deck the Halls: Fifty Beloved Traditional & Contemporary Christmas Favorites. 143p. (Orig.). (YA). 1994. pap. 12.95 (0-89524-858-1) Cherry Lane.

— Dick Clark's American Bandstand Gold Vol. 1: 1955-1965. pap. 16.95 (0-89524-713-5) Cherry Lane.

— Dick Clark's American Bandstand Gold Vol. 2: 1965-1975. 142p. (Orig.). (YA). 1994. pap. 16.95 (0-89524-815-8, 02502123) Cherry Lane.

— Eric Andersen Selected Songs (Piano - Vocal) (Illus.). 96p. (Orig.). (YA). 1993. pap. text ed. 17.95 (0-89524-733-X) Cherry Lane.

— Erroll Garner for Easy Piano. (Illus.). 31p. (YA). Date not set. pap. 10.95 (0-89524-860-3, 02505504) Cherry Lane.

— Follow That Road: Martha's Vineyard II Songbook. 92p. (Orig.). (YA). Date not set. pap. 22.95 (0-89524-875-1, 02506919) Cherry Lane.

— From a Distance & Thirty-Three More Easy Listening Classics. 1994. pap. 14.95 (0-89524-813-1) Cherry Lane.

— From a Distance & Twenty-Four Other Easy Listening Favorites for Easy Piano. 119p. (Orig.). (YA). Date not set. pap. 12.95 (0-89524-871-9, 02505508) Cherry Lane.

— From the Heart - 30 Love Songs. 117p. (Orig.). (YA). Date not set. pap. 14.95 (0-89524-864-6, 02502146) Cherry Lane.

— The Giant Book of Children's Songs. 280p. (Orig.). (J). pap. 19.95 (0-89524-821-2, HL02507977) Cherry Lane.

— Grand Hotel - The Musical. pap. 10.95 (0-89524-603-1) Cherry Lane.

— Great Songs of the Eighties. pap. 16.95 (0-89524-792-5) Cherry Lane.

— Great TV Themes - Five of the Best. pap. 5.95 (0-89524-636-8) Cherry Lane.

— Guns n' Roses - Appetite for Destruction: Piano - Vocal. (Illus.). 112p. (Orig.). 1990. pap. text ed. 16.95 (0-89524-417-9) Cherry Lane.

— Guns n' Roses for Easy Piano. 1994. pap. 9.95 (0-89524-808-5) Cherry Lane.

— Hal Ketchum - Past the Point of Rescue. pap. 14.95 (0-89524-719-4) Cherry Lane.

— Hal Ketchum - Sure Love. 1994. pap. 14.95 (0-89524-739-9) Cherry Lane.

— Harry Chapin Tribute: Piano - Vocal. (Illus.). 103p. (Orig.). 1990. pap. text ed. 17.95 (0-89524-418-7) Cherry Lane.

— Heavy Metal Bass Lines: Play-it-Like-It-Is Bass, Vol. 2. pap. 14.95 (0-89524-444-6) Cherry Lane.

— Heavy Metal Guitar, Vol. 1. (Illus.). 127p. (Orig.). 1990. pap. text ed. 14.95 (0-89524-221-4) Cherry Lane.

— Highlights from Jekyll & Hyde: Piano - Vocal - Guitar. (Illus.). 64p. (Orig.). 1990. pap. text ed. 9.95 (0-89524-531-0) Cherry Lane.

— Indian Runner - Soundtrack. pap. 12.95 (0-89524-648-1) Cherry Lane.

— Jekyll & Hyde: Revised Vocal Selections. rev. ed. 109p. (YA). 1995. pap. 16.95 (0-89524-899-9) Cherry Lane.

— John Denver - Aerie. pap. 10.95 (0-89524-004-1) Cherry Lane.

— John Denver - Authentic Guitar Style. pap. 12.95 (0-89524-376-8) Cherry Lane.

— John Denver - Autograph: Piano - Vocal. (Illus.). 63p. (Orig.). 1990. pap. text ed. 12.95 (0-89524-085-8) Cherry Lane.

— John Denver - Dreamland Express. pap. 10.95 (0-89524-306-7) Cherry Lane.

— John Denver - Five of the Best. pap. 6.95 (0-89524-638-4) Cherry Lane.

— John Denver - Flower That Shattered the Stone. pap. 12.95 (0-89524-615-5) Cherry Lane.

— John Denver - Greatest Hits, Vol. 3: Piano - Vocal. (Illus.). 67p. (Orig.). 1990. pap. text ed. 9.95 (0-89524-294-X) Cherry Lane.

— John Denver - Higher Ground (Piano - Vocal) (Illus.). 53p. (Orig.). 1990. pap. text ed. 12.95 (0-89524-410-1) Cherry Lane.

— John Denver - It's about Time: Piano - Vocal. (Illus.). 72p. (Orig.). 1990. pap. text ed. 12.95 (0-89524-196-X) Cherry Lane.

— John Denver - JD. pap. 10.95 (0-89524-051-3) Cherry Lane.

— John Denver - Rocky Mountain Christmas: Piano - Vocal. (Illus.). 63p. (Orig.). 1990. pap. text ed. 10.95 (0-89524-006-8) Cherry Lane.

— John Denver - Rocky Mountain High: Piano - Vocal. (Illus.). 79p. (Orig.). 1990. pap. text ed. 10.95 (0-89524-118-8) Cherry Lane.

— John Denver - Spirit. pap. 10.95 (0-89524-005-X) Cherry Lane.

— John Denver - Windsong. pap. 10.95 (0-89524-000-9) Cherry Lane.

— John Denver - 25 Years. (Living Legends Ser.). 1995. 24.95 (0-614-03543-0); pap. 16.95 (0-614-03542-2) Cherry Lane.

— John Denver's Greatest Hits, Vols. 1-3. 152p. (YA). Date not set. pap. 16.95 (0-89524-914-6) Cherry Lane.

— John Hiatt - Slow Turning. pap. 12.95 (0-89524-422-5) Cherry Lane.

— John Hiatt Songbook (Piano - Vocal) (Illus.). 64p. (Orig.). 1990. pap. text ed. 14.95 (0-89524-479-9) Cherry Lane.

— Johnny Cash - A Man & His Music. 1994. pap. 16.95 (0-89524-778-X) Cherry Lane.

— Kenny Rogers: Gideon. 1980. 6.95 (0-89898-011-9) Almo Pubns.

— Lenny Kravitz - Are You Gonna Go My Way. 1994. pap. 14.95 (0-89524-776-3) Cherry Lane.

— Lenny Kravitz - Mama Said. pap. 14.95 (0-89524-634-1) Cherry Lane.

— Leslie Bricusse Theatre Book. 224p. (YA). Date not set. per., pap. 24.95 (0-89524-882-4, 02502148) Cherry Lane.

— Linda Ronstadt - Cry Like a Rainstorm, Howl Like the Wind: Piano - Vocal. (Illus.). 52p. (Orig.). 1990. pap. text ed. 14.95 (0-89524-501-9) Cherry Lane.

— Linda Ronstadt - Five of the Best. pap. 6.95 (0-89524-639-2) Cherry Lane.

— Lionel Richie - Can't Slow Down. pap. 9.95 (0-89524-194-3) Cherry Lane.

— Lionel Richie - Complete: Piano - Vocal. (Illus.). 264p. (Orig.). 1990. pap. text ed. 19.95 (0-89524-370-9) Cherry Lane.

— Lionel Richie - Dancing on the Ceiling: Piano - Vocal. (Illus.). 61p. (Orig.). 1990. pap. text ed. 9.95 (0-89524-324-5) Cherry Lane.

— Lionel Richie - Love Ballads. pap. 12.95 (0-89524-355-5) Cherry Lane.

— Lionel Richie Greatest Hits: Ez Piano. (Illus.). 72p. (Orig.). 1990. pap. text ed. 10.95 (0-89524-292-3) Cherry Lane.

— Little Feat - Let It Roll - (Piano - Vocal) (Illus.). 64p. (Orig.). 1990. pap. text ed. 12.95 (0-89524-425-X) Cherry Lane.

— Liz Story: Escape of the Circus Ponies - Solo Piano. 62p. (YA). 1995. pap. 14.95 (0-89524-868-9) Cherry Lane.

— Liz Story: Piano Solo, Vol. 1. 88p. 1995. pap. 17.95 (0-89524-837-9, HL02503608) Cherry Lane.

— Liz Story: Piano Solo, Vol. 2. pap. 17.95 (0-89524-838-7) Cherry Lane.

— The Love Ballads of Lionel Richie (Piano - Vocal) (Illus.). 95p. (Orig.). 1990. pap. text ed. 14.95 (0-89524-343-1) Cherry Lane.

— Lucinda Williams - Sweet Old World. pap. 14.95 (0-89524-744-5) Cherry Lane.

— Magic of Music: Christmas Songs: Piano - Vocal. (Illus.). 56p. (Orig.). 1988. pap. text ed. 9.95 (0-89524-457-8) Cherry Lane.

— Magic of Music - Children's Song: Piano - Vocal. (Illus.). 80p. (Orig.). (J). 1988. pap. text ed. 9.95 (0-89524-372-5) Cherry Lane.

— Magic of Music - Dances from Around the World: Piano - Vocal. (Illus.). 80p. (Orig.). 1988. pap. text ed. 9.95 (0-89524-423-3) Cherry Lane.

— Magic of Music - Holiday Songs: Piano - Vocal. (Illus.). 63p. (Orig.). 1990. pap. text ed. 7.95 (0-89524-380-6) Cherry Lane.

— Mary Chapin Carpenter: Stones in the Road. (Illus.). 92p. (Orig.). (YA). Date not set. pap. 16.95 (0-89524-901-4) Cherry Lane.

— Maury Yeston - December Songs. pap. 16.95 (0-89524-679-1) Cherry Lane.

— Molly Hatchet. (Illus.). 160p. 1983. pap. 14.95 (0-89524-185-4, 9952) Cherry Lane.

— Music of Bruce Hornsby. pap. 9.95 (0-89524-339-3) Cherry Lane.

— The Music of John Denver Made Easy for Guitar. pap. 9.95 (0-89524-018-1) Cherry Lane.

— The Music of Richard Marx (Easy Piano) (Illus.). 56p. (Orig.). 1990. pap. text ed. 10.95 (0-89524-478-0) Cherry Lane.

— The New York Times Great Songs of the Seventies. 19.95 (0-8129-0727-2); pap. 11.95 (0-8129-6311-3) Cherry Lane.

— New York Times Great Songs of the Sixties, Vol. 1. pap. 19.95 (0-8129-6201-X) Cherry Lane.

— Nine. pap. 17.95 (0-89524-820-4) Cherry Lane.

— Of Love & Hope - Selections from "Beauty & the Beast" pap. 12.95 (0-89524-484-5) Cherry Lane.

— Ozzy Ozbourne Songbook: Guitar - Vocal. (Illus.). 175p. (Orig.). 1990. pap. text ed. 24.95 (0-89524-237-0) Cherry Lane.

— Patty Loveless: Only What I Feel. 57p. (Orig.). (YA). Date not set. pap. 14.95 (0-89524-898-0) Cherry Lane.

— Patty Loveless: When Fallen Angels Fly. 70p. (Orig.). (YA). Date not set. pap. 14.95 (0-89524-897-2, 02502161) Cherry Lane.

— The Perfect Wedding Songbook. (Illus.). 232p. (Orig.). 1995. pap. 14.95 (0-89524-633-3, HL02507950) Cherry Lane.

— Peter, Paul & Mary - Holiday Concert. pap. 17.95 (0-89524-609-0) Cherry Lane.

— Phantom - The American Musical Sensation. pap. 12.95 (0-89524-727-5) Cherry Lane.

— Pixies - Bossanova. pap. 12.95 (0-89524-608-2) Cherry Lane.

— Pixies - Trompe le Monde. pap. 14.95 (0-89524-709-7) Cherry Lane.

— Pop Songs for the Wedding. 1994. pap. 14.95 (0-89524-822-0) Cherry Lane.

— Richard Marx - Five of the Best. pap. 6.95 (0-89524-538-8) Cherry Lane.

— Richard Marx - Repeat Offender. pap. 14.95 (0-89524-441-1) Cherry Lane.

— Richard Marx - Rush Street. pap. 14.95 (0-89524-692-9) Cherry Lane.

— Richard Marx (Piano - Vocal) (Illus.). 63p. (Orig.). 1990. pap. text ed. 12.95 (0-89524-346-6) Cherry Lane.

— Ricky Lee Jones - Flying Cowboys: Piano - Vocal. (Illus.). 67p. (Orig.). 1990. pap. text ed. 14.95 (0-89524-505-1) Cherry Lane.

— Roberta Flack - Oasis. pap. 12.95 (0-89524-428-4) Cherry Lane.

— Roxette - Five of the Best. pap. 6.95 (0-89524-540-X) Cherry Lane.

— Roxette - Joyride. pap. 14.95 (0-89524-673-2) Cherry Lane.

— Roxette - Look Sharp. pap. 14.95 (0-89524-473-X) Cherry Lane.

— Roxette - Tourism. pap. 16.95 (0-89524-729-1) Cherry Lane.

— Scrooge - The Musical. pap. 14.95 (0-89524-726-7) Cherry Lane.

— Shawn Colvin - Cover Girl. 32p. (Orig.). (YA). Date not set. pap. 12.95 (0-89524-867-0, 02506918) Cherry Lane.

— Shawn Colvin - Steady On: Piano - Vocal. (Illus.). 55p. (Orig.). 1990. pap. text ed. 14.95 (0-89524-516-7) Cherry Lane.
— Sherlock Holmes. pap. 19.95 (0-89524-745-3) Cherry Lane.
— Skid. pap. 14.95 (0-89524-667-8); pap. 18.95 (0-89524-578-7); pap. 14.95 (0-89524-579-5); pap. 9.95 (0-89524-656-2); pap. 16.95 (0-89524-601-5) Cherry Lane.
— Songs of John Denver. pap. 9.95 (0-89524-019-X) Cherry Lane.
— Statler Brothers Anthology. pap. 14.95 (0-89524-044-0) Cherry Lane.
— Steve Morse - Songbook: Guitar. (Illus.). 103p. (Orig.). 1990. pap. text ed. 18.95 (0-89524-323-7) Cherry Lane.
— Super Groups Bass Lines. pap. 9.95 (0-89524-219-2) Cherry Lane.
— Suzanne Vega - Days of Open Hand. pap. 14.95 (0-89524-545-0) Cherry Lane.
— Suzanne Vega - Solitude Standing. pap. 12.95 (0-89524-345-8) Cherry Lane.
— Today's Country Hits. 1994. pap. 12.95 (0-89524-789-5) Cherry Lane.
— Today's Country Hits: Easy Piano. pap. 14.95 (0-89524-801-8) Cherry Lane.
— Tom Chapin: Zag Zig. (Illus.). 45p. (Orig.). (YA). Date not set. pap. 14.95 (0-89524-905-7) Cherry Lane.
— Tom Paxton - Authentic Guitar Style. pap. 12.95 (0-89524-448-9) Cherry Lane.
— Tom Paxton - Politics. pap. 9.95 (0-89524-435-7) Cherry Lane.
— Tom Paxton-Wearing the Time. 63p. (YA). Date not set. pap. 14.95 (0-89524-881-6, 02502157) Cherry Lane.
— Twin Peaks. pap. 12.95 (0-89524-613-9) Cherry Lane.
— Van Halen - 1984. pap. 12.95 (0-89524-606-6); pap. 19.95 (0-89524-642-2) Cherry Lane.
— Van Halen - 5150. P/V/G. pap. 12.95 (0-89524-450-0); Play-It-Like-It-Is Guitar. pap. 19.95 (0-89524-387-3); Play-It-Like-It-Is Bass. pap. 14.95 (0-89524-460-8) Cherry Lane.

Okun, Milton & Fox, Dan, eds. Donald Fagen: The Nightfly. (Illus.). 64p. 1983. pap. 12.95 (0-89524-176-5) Cherry Lane.
— John Denver: Some Days Are Diamonds. (Illus.). 71p. 1981. pap. 10.95 (0-89524-143-9, 9016) Cherry Lane.
— John Denver Anthology: Easy Guitar. (Illus.). 255p. 1981. pap. 17.95 (0-89524-142-0, 9091) Cherry Lane.
— Kenny Rogers: Greatest Hits Easy Piano. 48p. 1980. pap. 9.95 (0-89524-105-6) Cherry Lane.
— Lionel Richie. (Illus.). 64p. 1982. pap. 9.95 (0-89524-175-7) Cherry Lane.

Okun, Milton, ed. see Alger, Pat.
Okun, Milton, ed. see Blonde, Concrete.
Okun, Milton, ed. see Bricusse, Leslie.
Okun, Milton, ed. see Burgie, Irving.
Okun, Milton, ed. see Chapin, Harry.
Okun, Milton, ed. see Chapin, Tom.
Okun, Milton, ed. see Denver, John.
Okun, Milton, ed. see Guns N' Roses.
Okun, Milton, ed. see Huey Lewis & the News.
Okun, Milton, ed. see Koller, Fred.
Okun, Milton, ed. see Kravitz, Lenny.
Okun, Milton, ed. see McBroom, Amanda.
Okun, Milton, ed. see Overstreet, Paul.
Okun, Milton, ed. see Waller, Robert J.
Okun, Milton, ed. see Wheeler, Cheryl, et al.

Okun, Milton R., et al. Gross & Microscopic Pathology of the Skin, 2 vols., Set. 2nd ed. LC 87-71751. (Illus.). 1988. 375.00 (0-9618536-0-3) Derma Found Pr.

Okun, Mitchell. Fair Play in the Marketplace: The First Battle for Pure Food & Drugs. LC 85-25921. 1986. 27.50 (0-87580-115-3) N Ill U Pr.

Okun, Tema & Wood, Peter, eds. Through the Hoop. (Southern Exposure Ser.). (Illus.). 128p. (Orig.). (C). 1979. pap. 4.00 (0-943810-07-8) Inst Southern Studies.

O'Kunewick, James P. & Meredith, Ruby F., eds. Graft vs. Leukemia in Man & Animal Models. 288p. 1981. 143.00 (0-8493-5745-4, RC643) CRC Pr.

Okuno, T., ed. Biometry - Clinical Trials & Related Topics: Proceedings of the ISI Satellite Meeting Held in Osaka, Japan, 21st Sept., 1987. (International Congress Ser.: No. 787). 132p. 1988. 72.00 (0-444-81009-9, Excerpta Medica) Elsevier.

Okunor, Shiame. Politics, Misunderstandings, Misconceptions: The History of Colonial Universities. LC 90-22144. (American University Studies: Education: Ser. XIV, Vol. 26). 190p. (C). 1991. text ed. 34.95 (0-8204-1176-0) P Lang Pubs.

Okura, Nagatsune. Seiyu Roku: Oil Manufacturing in Japan in 1836. Ariga, Eiko, tr. LC 74-6761. (Illus.). 79p. 1974. 25.00 (0-917526-01-5) Olearius Edns.

Okure, Teresa. Johannine Approach to Mission: A Contextual Study of John 4: 1-42. 370p. 1987. lib. bdg. 63.50 (3-16-145049-3, Pub. by J C B Mohr GW) Coronet Bks.

Okuyama, Shinichi & Mishina, Hitoshi. Evolution of Cancer. 1990. text ed. 67.50 (0-685-37650-8, Pub. by U of Tokyo JA) Col U Pr.

Okuyama, Y. Absolute Summability of Fourier Series & Orthogonal Series. (Lecture Notes in Mathematics Ser.: Vol. 1067). vi, 118p. 1984. pap. 28.10 (0-387-13355-0) Spr-Verlag.

Okwumabua, Theresa M., jt. ed. see Morgan, Sam B.

Okyayuz-Baklouti, I., jt. ed. see Stefanovich, V.

Ola, R. O. Public Administration in Nigeria. 220p. 1984. pap. 24.50 (0-7103-0044-1, Pub. by Kegan Paul Intl UK) Routledge Chapman & Hall.

Ola, S. Tropical Soils of Nigeria in Engineering Practice. 336p. (C). 1983. text ed. 140.00 (90-6191-264-4, Pub. by A A Balkema NE) Ashgate Pub Co.

Ola, Virginia U. The Life & Works of Bessie Head. LC 94-20128. 108p. 1994. text ed. 59.95 (0-7734-9018-3) E Mellen.

Oladeji, Niyi. Two Contemporary African Plays. 144p. (C). 1991. pap. text ed. 19.95 (0-8403-6880-1) Kendall-Hunt.

***Oladipo, Caleb O.** The Development of the Doctrine of the Holy Spirit in the Yoruba (African) Indigenous Christian Movement. LC 94-35601. (American University Studies, Ser. VII: Vol. 185). 1994. write for info. (0-8204-2708-X) P Lang Pubs.

***Olaf, Erwin, photos.** Chessman. (Illus.). 72p. 1995. pap. 29.95 (90-72216-40-7) Dist Art Pubs.

Olafioye, Tayo. Politics in African Poetry. 148p. (Orig.). (C). 1984. pap. 15.00 (0-916765-00-8) PCA Enterp.

Olafson, Frederick A. The Dialectic of Action: A Philosophical Interpretation of History & the Humanities. LC 79-10316. 303p. reprint ed. pap. 86.40 (0-685-23838-5, 2056619) Bks Demand.
— Heidegger & the Philosophy of Mind. LC 86-11180. 320p. 1987. text ed. 32.00 (0-300-03727-9) Yale U Pr.
— Principles & Persons: An Ethical Interpretation of Existentialism. LC 67-16038. 276p. reprint ed. pap. 78.70 (0-7837-6426-X, 2046424) Bks Demand.
— What Is a Human Being? A Heideggerian View. (Modern European Philosophy Ser.). 304p. (C). 1995. 59.95 (0-521-47395-0); pap. 18.95 (0-521-47937-1) Cambridge U Pr.

***Olafson, Peter.** Final Fantasy III: Players Guide. (Illus.). 192p. (Orig.). 1994. pap. 12.95 (1-57280-039-9) IFTW Bks.

Olafsson, Olaf. Absolution. 272p. 1994. 20.00 (0-679-42891-7) Pantheon.

Olafsson, R., jt. auth. see Pau, L. F.

Olagoke, D. Olu. The Incorruptible Judge. (Evans Africa Plays Ser.). 48p. 1991. pap. 4.50 (0-237-49522-8, Pub. by Evans Bros Ltd UK) Trafalgar.
— The Iroko-Man & the Wood-Carver. (Evans Africa Plays Ser.). 44p. 1991. pap. 4.50 (0-237-49523-6, Pub. by Evans Bros Ltd UK) Trafalgar.

Ola'h, G. M. A New Way to Grow Edible Mushrooms: White Pleurotus. (Illus.). 88p. 1981. pap. text ed. 9.75 (2-7637-6963-2) Lubrecht & Cramer.

Olah, George, et al. Nitration: Methods & Mechanisms. LC 89-16582. (Organic Nitro Chemistry Ser.). 330p. 1989. lib. bdg. 75.00 (0-89573-144-4) VCH Pubs.

Olah, George A. Halonium Ions. LC 75-16417. 206p. 1975. 22.50 (0-471-65329-2) Wiley.

Olah, George A., ed. Cage Hydrocarbons. 432p. 1990. text ed. 99.95 (0-471-62292-3) Wiley.

***Olah, George A. & Molnar, Arpad.** Hydrocarbon Chemistry. LC 94-31442. 1995. text ed. 69.95 (0-471-11359-X) Wiley.

Olah, George A. & Squire, David R., eds. Chemistry of Energetic Materials. (Illus.). 212p. 1991. text ed. 79.00 (0-12-525440-7) Acad Pr.

Olah, George A., et al. Synthetic Fluorine Chemistry. 416p. 1992. text ed. 117.00 (0-471-54370-5) Wiley.

Olah, George A., et al, eds. Electron Deficient Boron & Carbon Clusters. 379p. 1991. text ed. 88.00 (0-471-52795-5) Wiley.

Olah, J. Fish, Pathogens & Environment in European Polyculture. 266p. 1984. 112.00 (0-569-08804-6, Pub. by Collets UK) Pro-Am Music.
— Fish, Pathogens & Environments in European Polyculture: Proceedings of an International Seminar, Szarvar, Hungary, June 23-27, 1981. 264p. (C). 1984. 72.00x (963-05-3614-5, Pub. by Akad Kiado HU) St Mut.

Olah, Suzann M. My Phone Book. 18p. (J). (ps-2). 1991. pap. 6.95 (0-9630985-0-0) RJB Enter.

Olaitan, Samson O. & Agusiobo, Obiora N. Introduction to the Teaching of Home Economics. LC 80-40288. (Education in Africa Ser.). 341p. reprint ed. pap. 97.20 (0-8357-6941-0, 2039000) Bks Demand.

Olajide, Michael, Jr. & Berger, Phil. Aerobox: A High Performance Fitness Program. 192p. (Orig.). 1995. pap. 12.99 (0-446-67116-9) Warner Bks.

Olaleve, Isaac. Bitter Bananas. LC 93-73306. (Illus.). 32p. (J). (ps-3). 1994. 14.95 (1-56397-039-2) Boyds Mills Pr.

***Olaleye, Isaac.** Distant Talking Drum: Poems from Nigeria. (Illus.). (J). (gr. 3-6). 1995. 14.95 (1-56397-095-3, Wordsong) Boyds Mills Pr.

Olaleye, Isaac O. Did God Make Them Black? LC 88-51961. 262p. 1990. 14.95 (1-55523-223-X) Winston-Derek.

Olaloku, F. Akin, et al. The Structure of the Nigerian Economy. LC 78-14765. 1980. text ed. 29.95 (0-312-76777-3) St Martin.

Olalquiaga, Celeste. Megalopolis: Contemporary Cultural Sensibilities. LC 91-12383. (Illus.). 136p. (C). 1992. 34.95 (0-8166-1998-0); pap. 13.95 (0-8166-1999-9) U of Minn Pr.

***Olamigoke, Olumide K.** How to Reduce Crime Rates in America. (Illus.). 80p. (Orig.). 1994. pap. 8.95 (1-56167-162-2) Am Literary Pr.

Olan, jt. auth. see Allen.

Olan, Susan. Earth Remembers. LC 88-51732. (TSR Bks.). 320p. 1990. pap. 3.95 (0-88038-778-5) TSR Inc.

Oland, Pamela P. You Can Write Great Lyrics. 184p. 1989. pap. 17.95 (0-89879-363-7) Writers Digest.

Olander, Donald R. Fundamental Aspects of Nuclear Reactor Fuel Elements, 2 vols., Vol. 1. LC 76-6485. (ERDA Technical Information Center Ser.). 625p. 1976. pap. 23.50 (0-87079-031-5, TID-26711-P1); fiche 9.00 (0-685-01475-4, TID-26711-P2) DOE.
— Fundamental Aspects of Nuclear Reactor Fuel Elements, 2 vols., Vol. 2. LC 76-6485. (ERDA Technical Information Center Ser.). 565p. 1976. pap. 22.00 (0-685-01474-6, TID-26711-P2); fiche 9.00 (0-87079-467-1, TID-26711-P2) DOE.

***Olander, Doug.** Gyotaku Fish Impressions: The Art of Japanese Fish Printing. (Illus.). 64p. 1994. pap. 17.95 (1-878175-83-1) F Amato Pubns.
— Northwest Coastal Fishing Guide. (Illus.). 230p. (Orig.). 1991. reprint ed. pap. 24.95 (0-936608-99-4) F Amato Pubns.

Olander, Folke, ed. European Consumer Policy after Maastricht. LC 94-7632. 344p. (C). 1994. lib. bdg. 105.00 (0-7923-2770-5) Kluwer Ac.

Olander, Folke, jt. ed. see Grunert, Klaus G.

Olander, Joseph D., et al, eds. School & Society Through Science Fiction. LC 81-40587. (Illus.). 404p. 1982. reprint ed. pap. text ed. 31.00 (0-8191-1997-0) U Pr of Amer.

Olander, William. Holzer, Kruger, Prince. Barendse, Henry, ed. (Illus.). 38p. 1984. 7.50 (0-915427-03-6) Spirit Sq Ctr.

Olander, William & Debavpatnaik, P. Contemporary Afro-American Photography. LC 83-72603. (Illus.). 32p. 1983. pap. 3.00 (0-942946-03-0) Ober Coll Allen.

Olander, William & Grundberg, Andy. Drawings: After Photography. LC 89-82028. (Illus.). 48p. 1984. 10.00 (0-916365-12-3) Ind Curators.

Olaniyan, Richard, ed. African History & Culture. (Illus.). 259p. (Orig.). (C). 1982. pap. text ed. 23.95 (0-582-64369-4, 74594) Longman.

***Olaniyan, Tejumola.** Scars of Conquest - Masks of Resistance: The Invention of Cultural Identities in African, African-American, & Caribbean Drama. 224p. 1995. 39.95 (0-19-509405-0); pap. 15.95 (0-19-509406-9) OUP.

Olano, Pamela J., jt. auth. see McNaron, Toni A.

Olanon, Katy H. Medical Technology: Subject Analysis Index with Research Bibliography. LC 85-47569. 150p. 1987. 37.50 (0-88164-312-2); pap. 34.50 (0-88164-313-0) ABBE Pubs Assn.

***Olanow, C. W. & Zesiewicz, T. A.** Parkinson's Disease: Questions & Answers. (Illus.). 140p. 1995. pap. 32.95 (1-873413-01-7) Merit Pub Intl.

Olanow, Charles W. & Lieberman, Abraham, eds. The Scientific Basis for the Treatment of Parkinson's Disease. (Illus.). 250p. 1992. 68.00 (1-85070-355-8) Prthnon Pub.

Olanrewaju, S. A., jt. ed. see Falola, Toyin.

Olaru, Victor, tr. see Chufu, Gabriel.

Olasiji, Dele, ed. Who's Who Among International Students in American Universities & Colleges: 1989-90. 2nd ed. 228p. 1990. write for info. (0-929336-01-1) Rsch Servs USA.
— Who's Who in Oklahoma. (Orig.). 1990. write for info. (0-318-65539-X) Rsch Servs USA.

Olasiji, Thompson, jt. auth. see Henderson, George.

***Olasky, Marvin.** Abortion Rites: A Social History of Abortion in America. 336p. 1995. reprint ed. pap. 14.95 (0-89526-723-3) Regnery Pub.
— Central Ideas in the Development of American Journalism: A Narrative History. 208p. 1990. text ed. 36.00 (0-8058-0893-0) L Erlbaum Assocs.
— Fighting for Liberty & Virtue: Political & Cultural Wars in Eighteenth-Century America. LC 95-8446. (American Experience Ser.: Bk. 1). 224p. 1995. 25.00 (0-89107-848-7) Crossway Bks.
— The Press & Abortion, 1838-1988. (Communication Ser.). 208p. (C). pap. 27.50 (0-8058-0485-4) L Erlbaum Assocs.
— Prodigal Press: The Anti-Christian Bias of the American News Media. LC 87-72951. (Turning Point Christian Worldview Ser.). 256p. (Orig.). 1988. pap. 12.99 (0-89107-476-7) Crossway Bks.
— The Tragedy of American Compassion. 320p. (Orig.). 1992. 21.99 (0-89107-654-9) Crossway Bks.
— The Tragedy of American Compassion. 320p. (Orig.). 1995. pap. 14.99 (0-89107-863-0) Crossway Bks.
— The Tragedy of American Compassion. 299p. 1995. pap. 14.95 (0-89526-725-X) Regnery Pub.

Olasky, Marvin, jt. auth. see Olasky, Susan.

Olasky, Marvin, jt. auth. see Schlossberg, Herbert.

Olasky, Marvin, et al. Freedom, Justice & Hope: Toward a Strategy for the Poor & the Oppressed. LC 87-72955. (Turning Point Christian Worldview Ser.). 1988. pap. 12.99 (0-89107-478-3) Crossway Bks.

Olasky, Marvin N. Abortion Rites: A Social History of Abortion in America. LC 92-12118. 320p. (Orig.). 1992. pap. 13.99 (0-89107-687-5) Crossway Bks.
— Corporate Public Relations: A New Historical Perspective. 192p. 1987. pap. 36.00 (0-8058-0052-2) L Erlbaum Assocs.

***Olasky, Susan.** Annie Henry & the Birth of Liberty. LC 94-45739. (Adventures of the American Revolution Ser.: Vol. 2). 128p. (Orig.). (J). (gr. 4-6). 1995. pap. 4.99 (0-89107-842-8) Crossway Bks.
— Annie Henry & the Secret Mission. LC 94-38671. (Adventures of the American Revolution Ser.). 128p. (Orig.). (J). (gr. 3-7). 1995. pap. 4.99 (0-89107-830-4) Crossway Bks.

Olasky, Susan & Olasky, Marvin. More Than Kindness: A Compassionate Approach to Crisis Childbearing. LC 90-80625. 224p. (Orig.). 1990. pap. 12.99 (0-89107-584-4) Crossway Bks.

Olatunji, Sunday. Free Money in America & How to Get It. 200p. (Orig.). (C). 1989. pap. text ed. write for info. (0-318-64799-0) Olatunji Bks.

***O'Laughlin.** Families of Co. Clare, Ireland, Past & Present. (Illus.). 250p. 1995. 27.95 (0-940134-37-3) Irish Genealog.
— Families of Co. Cork, Ireland, Past & Present. (Illus.). 250p. 1995. 27.95 (0-940134-35-7) Irish Genealog.

O'Laughlin, Jay, jt. auth. see Cubbage, Frederick W.

***O'Laughlin, M., ed.** Master Book of Irish Maps. (Illus.). Date not set. 29.95 (0-940134-34-9) Irish Genealog.

O'Laughlin, Michael. The Book of "Irish Families" Great & Small. 320p. 1992. 28.00 (0-940134-08-X) Irish Genealog.

O'Laughlin, Michael C. Beginners Guide to Irish Genealogy. (Common Sense Guide Ser.). (Illus.). 50p. 1988. pap. 12.95 (0-940134-03-9) Irish Genealog.
— The Complete Book of Irish Family Names. 311p. 1987. 15.00 (0-940134-41-1) Irish Genealog.
— Families of Co. Kerry, Ireland: Past & Present. (Illus.). 272p. 1994. 27.95 (0-940134-36-5) Irish Genealog.
— The Flaherty Book. (Irish Family Histories Ser.). (Illus.). 40p. (ENG & GAE.). 1983. 15.00 (0-940134-22-5) Irish Genealog.
— Irish Settlers on the American Frontier, Vol. 1: Gateway West. Donahue, P. J., ed. (Irish West of the Mississippi Ser.). (Illus.). 250p. 1983. lib. bdg. 34.50 (0-940134-25-X) Irish Genealog.
— The Kelly Book. (Irish Family Histories Ser.). (Illus.). 50p. 1981. 15.00 (0-940134-19-5) Irish Genealog.
— The Murphy Book. (Irish Family Histories Ser.). (Illus.). 15.00 (0-940134-20-9) Irish Genealog.
— The O'Donaghue Book. (Irish Family Histories Ser.). 50p. 1981. 15.00 (0-940134-16-0) Irish Genealog.
— The O'Laughlin Book. (Irish Family Histories Ser.). 50p. 1981. 15.00 (0-940134-17-9) Irish Genealog.
— The O'Reilly Book. (Irish Family Histories Ser.). (Illus.). 50p. 1981. 15.00 (0-940134-21-7) Irish Genealog.
— The O'Sullivan Book. (Irish Family Histories Ser.). (Illus.). 50p. 1981. 15.00 (0-940134-18-7) Irish Genealog.

O'Laughlin, Michael C., ed. & intro. The Irish Book of Arms. (Illus.). 328p. (C). 1988. 45.00 (0-940134-07-1) Irish Genealog.

O'Laughlin, Michael C., ed. Master Book of Irish Placenames: Master Atlas & Book of Irish Placenames. (Illus.). 270p. 1994. 23.95 (0-940134-33-0) Irish Genealog.
— Master Book of Irish Surnames: (Locations, Origins & Ethnicity) (Illus.). 304p. 1993. 23.95 (0-940134-32-2) Irish Genealog.

O'Laughlin, Robert J., jt. auth. see Bukowski, Richard W.

Olaus, Murie J. A Field Guide to Animal Tracks. 2nd ed. LC 74-6294. (Peterson Field Guide Ser.). 1975. 24.95 (0-395-19978-6); pap. 15.95 (0-395-18323-5) HM.

Olausson, Eric & Cato, Ingemar, eds. Chemistry & Biogeochemistry of Estuaries. LC 79-41211. (Illus.). 462p. reprint ed. pap. 131.70 (0-685-20648-3, 2030434) Bks Demand.

O'Laverty, H. Mother of God & Her Glorious Feasts. LC 87-50580. (Illus.). 200p. 1987. pap. 9.00 (0-89555-317-1) TAN Bks Pubs.

Olayiwola, Peter O. Petroleum & Structural Change in a Developing Country: The Case of Nigeria. LC 86-21216. 225p. 1986. text ed. 55.00 (0-275-92115-8, C2115, Praeger Pubs) Greenwood.

Olazagasti-Segovia, Elena. Sopresas: Antologia de Cuentos Hispanicos. 242p. (SPA.). 1993. pap. text ed. write for info. (0-03-054823-3) HB Coll Pubs.

Olbrechts-Tyteca, L., jt. auth. see Perelman, Chaim.

Olbrich, Emil. Development of Sentiment on Negro Suffrage to 1860. Fish, Carl R., ed. LC 72-154085. (Black Heritage Library Collection). 1977. 17.95 (0-8369-8796-9) Ayer.

Olbrich, Freny. Desouza in Stardust. large type ed. (Mystery Ser.). 384p. 1983. 15.95 (0-7089-0951-5) Ulverscroft.
— Desouza Pays the Price. large type ed. (Mystery Ser.). 352p. 1982. 15.95 (0-7089-0844-6) Ulverscroft.

Olbricht, Thomas H. Message of the New Testament-Ephesians & Colossians. LC 82-74323. (Way of Life Ser.: No. 170). 91p. 1983. pap. 6.95 (0-89112-170-6) Abilene Christ U.

Olby, R. Early Nineteenth Century European Scientists. LC 66-29597. 1967. 78.00 (0-08-012035-0, Pub. by Pergamon Repr UK) Franklin.
— Late Eighteenth Century European Scientists. LC 66-238563. 1966. 96.00 (0-08-011983-2, Pub. by Pergamon Repr UK); 96.00 (0-08-011984-0, Pub. by Pergamon Repr UK) Franklin.

Olby, Robert. The Path to the Double Helix: The Discovery of DNA. (Illus.). 544p. 1994. reprint ed. pap. 12.95 (0-486-68117-3) Dover.

Olby, Robert, et al, eds. Companion to the History of Modern Science. 992p. 1989. 89.95 (0-415-01988-5, A3891) Routledge.

Olby, Robert C. The Origins of Mendelism. LC 84-2491. (Illus.). xviii, 310p. 1985. pap. text ed. 14.95 (0-226-62592-3) U Ch Pr.

***Olcen, Mehmet A.** Vetluga Memoir: A Turkish Prisoner of War in Russia, 1916-1918. Leiser, Gary, ed. & tr. by. LC 94-48881. (Illus.). 264p. 1995. lib. bdg. 39.95 (0-8130-1353-4) U Press Fla.

Olcheski, Bill. One Hundred Trivia Quizzes for Stamp Collectors. 130p. 1982. pap. 4.95 (0-933580-09-6) Am Philatelic Society.

Olcott, Anthony. Murder at the Red October. (Academy First Mystery Ser.). 320p. 1990. reprint ed. pap. 5.95 (0-89733-327-6) Academy Chi Pubs.
— Rough Beast: A Novel by the Author of Murder at the Red October. 320p. 1992. text ed. 20.00 (0-684-19406-6, Scribners) S&S Trade.

Olcott, Anthony, tr. see Malashenko, Alexei.

Olcott, Anthony, tr. see Markish, Shimon.

Olcott, Anthony, tr. see Moscovit, Andrei, pseud.

Olcott, Charles, comp. Two Lectures on the Subjects of Slavery & Abolition. LC 71-164391. (Black Heritage Library Collection). 1977. reprint ed. 17.95 (0-8369-8850-7) Ayer.

Olcott, Charles S. Life of William McKinley, 2 vols., 1. LC 79-128946. (American Statesmen Ser.: Nos. 38, 39). reprint ed. write for info. (0-404-50888-X) AMS Pr.

O

An Asterisk (*) at the beginning of an entry indicates that the title is appearing in BIP for the first time.

— Life of William McKinley, 2 vols., 2. LC 79-128946. (American Statesmen Ser.: Nos. 38, 39). reprint ed. write for info. (*0-404-50889-8*) AMS Pr.

— Life of William McKinley, 2 vols., Set. LC 79-128946. (American Statesmen Ser.: Nos. 38, 39). reprint ed. 90.00 (*0-404-50893-6*) AMS Pr.

Olcott, Frances J. Good Stories for Anniversaries. LC 89-43342. (Tower Bks.). (Illus.). 264p. 1990. reprint ed. 48.00 (*0-8103-3910-2*); reprint ed. lib. bdg. 48.00 (*1-55888-876-4*) Omnigraphics Inc.

Olcott, Frances J., comp. Story-Telling Poems. LC 77-128155. (Granger Index Reprint Ser.). 1977. 21.95 (*0-8369-6182-X*) Ayer.

Olcott, H. S., ed. see D'Assier, Adolphe.

Olcott, Henry S. The Golden Rules of Buddhism Compiled from the Bana Books. 1992. pap. 3.00 (*1-56459-256-1*) Kessinger Pub.

— Old Diary Leaves, I. 1973. 9.50 (*0-8356-7106-2*) Theos Pub Hse.

— Old Diary Leaves, II. 1973. 9.50 (*0-8356-7123-2*) Theos Pub Hse.

— Old Diary Leaves, III. 1973. 9.50 (*0-8356-7480-0*) Theos Pub Hse.

— Old Diary Leaves, IV. 1973. 9.50 (*0-8356-7484-3*) Theos Pub Hse.

— Old Diary Leaves, V. 1973. 9.50 (*0-8356-7487-8*) Theos Pub Hse.

— Old Diary Leaves, VI. 1973. 9.50 (*0-8356-7491-6*) Theos Pub Hse.

— People from the Other World. 492p. 1972. reprint ed. spiral bd. 24.75 (*0-7873-0641-X*) Mokelumne.

— Theosophy: Religion & Occult Theosophy. 384p. 1993. reprint ed. pap. 24.95 (*1-56459-390-8*) Kessinger Pub.

***Olcott, Martha B.** Central Asia's New States: Independence, Foreign Policy, & Regional Security. (Orig.). 1995. pap. text ed. write for info. (*1-878379-51-8*) US Inst Peace.

— The Kazakhs. 2nd ed. (Studies of Nationalities). (Illus.). 390p. (C). 1995. 38.95 (*0-614-03535-X*) Hoover Inst Pr.

— The Kazakhs. 2nd ed. (Studies of Nationalities). (Illus.). 390p. (C). 1995. pap. 20.95 (*0-8179-9352-5*) Hoover Inst Pr.

Olcott, Martha B., ed. see Poliakov, Sergei P.

Olcott, Martha B., et al, eds. The Soviet Multinational State: Readings & Documents. LC 88-36747. (USSR in Transition: Readings & Documents Ser.). 616p. 1990. text ed. 62.95 (*0-87332-389-0*) M E Sharpe.

Olcott, Martha Brill. The Kazakhs. (Publication Series: Studies of Nationalities in the U. S. S. R.). (C). 1987. pap. 15.95 (*0-8179-8382-1*) Hoover Inst Pr.

Olcott, Nick, tr. see Lehmann, Rudolf.

Olcott, W. T. Sun Lore of All Ages. 1991. lib. bdg. 79.95 (*0-8490-4271-2*) Gordon Pr.

Olcott, William T. Star Lore of All Ages. 452p. 1985. reprint ed. spiral bd. 30.25 (*0-7873-1096-4*) Mokelumne.

Olczak, Anatole. The Bourne Shell Quick Reference Guide. 44p. (Orig.). 1991. pap. text ed. 9.95 (*0-935739-22-X*) A System Pubns.

— C Reference Card. (Orig.). 1985. pap. 3.95 (*0-935739-01-7*) A System Pubns.

— Complete C Reference Guide. (Orig.). pap. text ed. 9.95 (*0-935739-08-4*) A System Pubns.

— CSH Reference Guide. (Orig.). 1986. pap. 7.95 (*0-935739-06-8*) A System Pubns.

— Korn Shell Quick Reference Guide. 1991. pap. 9.95 (*0-935739-21-1*) A System Pubns.

— NetNews Reference Manual. 2nd ed. 206p. 1990. pap. 19.95 (*0-935739-18-1*) A System Pubns.

— SCCS Reference Card. 2nd ed. 8p. 1991. pap. 4.95 (*0-935739-04-1*) A System Pubns.

— The UNIX Reference Guide for BSD. 80p. (Orig.). 1987. pap. 14.95 (*0-935739-09-2*) A System Pubns.

— The UNIX Reference Guide For System V. 4th ed. 240p. (Orig.). 1989. pap. 19.95 (*0-935739-00-9*) A System Pubns.

— UNIX System Administrative Guide for System V. 4th ed. 130p. (Orig.). pap. 14.95 (*0-935739-03-3*) A System Pubns.

— UNIX System V Quick Reference Guide. 237p. 1992. pap. text ed. 14.95 (*0-935739-25-4*) A System Pubns.

— VI-ED Reference Card. 2nd ed. (Orig.). 1990. pap. 4.95 (*0-935739-02-5*) A System Pubns.

Olczak, Paul L., jt. auth. see Grosch, James.

Old California Preservation Society Staff, ed. California Historic Sites. (Illus.). 1986. pap. 4.95 (*0-913290-69-6*) Camaro Pub.

— Historic Restaurants of California. (Illus.). 1986. pap. 4.95 (*0-913290-60-2*) Camaro Pub.

***Old Coyote, Lloyd M. & Smith, Helene.** Visions of Wisdom. LC 93-81241. (Illus.). 244p. 1995. pap. 24.95 (*0-945437-13-7*) MacDonald-Sward.

Old, David. Twenty-Two Days in Japan: The Itinerary Planner. (Illus.). 136p. (Orig.). 1987. pap. 7.95 (*0-912528-73-7*) John Muir.

Old-House Journal Editors. Old-House Journal Catalog, 1989: A Buyer's Guide for the Pre-1939 House. 248p. 1988. pap. 15.95 (*0-942202-19-8*) Old Hse Journ Corp.

— The Old-House Journal 1980 Yearbook: A One-Volume Compilation of All the Editorial Pages Printed in the Old-House Journal in 1980. Poore, Patricia & Labine, Clem, eds. (Yearbook Ser.). (Illus.). 212p. (Orig.). 1981. pap. 18.00 (*0-942202-04-X*) Old Hse Journ Corp.

— The Old-House Journal 1982 Yearbook. (Yearbook Ser.). (Illus.). 274p. 1982. pap. 18.00 (*0-942202-06-6*) Old Hse Journ Corp.

— Old-House Journal 1987 Yearbook. Poore, Patricia & Labine, Clem, eds. (Yearbook Ser.). (Illus.). 314p. 1988. pap. 15.95 (*0-942202-18-X*) Old Hse Journ Corp.

— Restoration Manual No. 9: Old-House Journal 1984 Yearbook. Poore, Patricia & Labine, Clem, eds. (Illus.). 256p. 1983. pap. 16.00 (*0-942202-09-0*) Old Hse Journ Corp.

— Restoration Manual No. 10: Old-House Journal 1985 Yearbook. Poore, Patricia & Labine, Clem, eds. (Yearbook Ser.). (Illus.). 240p. 1986. pap. 16.00 (*0-942202-14-7*) Old Hse Journ Corp.

— Restoration Manual No. 11: Old-House Journal 1986 Yearbook. Poore, Patricia & Labine, Clem, eds. (Yearbook Ser.). (Illus.). 240p. 1987. pap. 15.95 (*0-942202-17-1*) Old Hse Journ Corp.

Old, Hughes O. Guides to the Reformed Tradition: Worship. LC 83-19616. 194p. 1984. pap. 12.99 (*0-8042-3252-0*, John Knox) Westminster John Knox.

— Leading in Prayer: A Workbook for Worship. 320p. (Orig.). 1995. pap. 19.99 (*0-8028-0821-2*) Eerdmans.

— The Shaping of the Reformed Baptismal Rite in the Sixteenth Century. 352p. 1992. text ed. 44.99 (*0-8028-3699-2*) Eerdmans.

— Themes & Variations for a Christian Doxology: A Theology of Worship. 148p. 1992. pap. 10.99 (*0-8028-0614-7*) Eerdmans.

***Old Joe.** The Grouch with the Pouch. (Illus.). 40p. (J). 1995. pap. 9.95 (*0-8059-3683-1*) Dorrance.

***Old, John & Shafto, Tony.** Introduction to Business Economics. 320p. (C). 1990. 59.00x (*0-7578-0412-8*, Pub. by S Thornes Pubs UK) St Mut.

Old Northwest Genealogical Quarterly Staff. Ohio Cemetery Records Extracted from the "Old Northwest" Genealogical Quarterly. LC 84-80083. 495p. 1989. 30.00 (*0-8063-1071-5*) Genealog Pub.

Old, O. & Shafto, S. Introduction to Business Economics. (C). 1990. 120.00 (*0-7487-0412-4*, Pub. by S Thornes Pubs UK) St Mut.

Old, O., jt. auth. see Shafto, S.

Old, R., jt. auth. see Worssam, B.

Old, R. A. Geology of the Country Around Redditch. 90p. 1991. pap. 55.00 (*0-11-884477-6*, HM7674) UNIPUB.

Old, R. W. & Primrose, S. B. Principles of Gene Manipulation: An Introduction to Genetic Engineering. 4th ed. (Illus.). 414p. 1990. pap. text ed. 39.95 (*0-632-02608-1*) Blackwell Sci.

Old Slave Mart Museum & Library Staff. Catalog of the Old Slave Mart Museum & Library. 1978. lib. bdg. 145.00 (*0-8161-0073-X*, Hall Library) G K Hall.

Old Time Publications Staff, ed. see Goss, Carrie F.

Old-Time Publications Staff, ed. see Williams, Ernestine C.

Old Vicarage Publications Staff. Antiqvarivm Forense. (C). 1982. pap. text ed. 34.00 (*0-685-22058-3*, Pub. by Old Vicarage UK) St Mut.

— Athens. (C). 1982. pap. text ed. 50.00 (*0-9508635-5-6*, Pub. by Old Vicarage UK) St Mut.

— Baths of Diocletian. 280p. (C). 1982. pap. text ed. 34.00 (*0-685-22053-2*, Pub. by Old Vicarage UK) St Mut.

— Capri. (C). 1982. pap. text ed. 60.00 (*0-685-22065-6*, Pub. by Old Vicarage UK) St Mut.

— Cave of Tiberius. 66p. (C). 1982. pap. text ed. 60.00 (*0-685-22061-3*, Pub. by Old Vicarage UK) St Mut.

— Corinth-Mycenae-Nauplion-Tiryns-Epidauros. 50p. (C). 1982. pap. text ed. 33.00 (*0-9508635-7-2*, Pub. by Old Vicarage UK) St Mut.

— Crete. (C). 1982. pap. text ed. 33.00 (*0-9508635-4-8*, Pub. by Old Vicarage UK) St Mut.

— Delphi. 96p. (C). 1982. pap. text ed. 33.00 (*0-947818-01-4*, Pub. by Old Vicarage UK) St Mut.

— Florence & Environs. 236p. (C). 1982. pap. text ed. 40.00 (*0-685-44230-6*, Pub. by Old Vicarage UK) St Mut.

— Herculaneum. 135p. (C). 1982. pap. text ed. 34.00 (*0-685-44229-2*, Pub. by Old Vicarage UK) St Mut.

— M Sixty-Three - Motorway Through a Town. 80p. (C). 1982. pap. text ed. 39.00 (*0-9508635-0-5*, Pub. by Old Vicarage UK) St Mut.

— Ostia. (C). 1982. pap. text ed. 34.00 (*0-685-44228-4*, Pub. by Old Vicarage UK) St Mut.

— Paestum. (C). 1982. pap. text ed. 60.00 (*0-685-22066-4*, Pub. by Old Vicarage UK) St Mut.

— The Palatine. 94p. (C). 1982. pap. text ed. 34.00 (*0-685-22059-1*, Pub. by Old Vicarage UK) St Mut.

— Phlegraean Fields. 168p. (C). 1982. pap. text ed. 45.00 (*0-685-22056-7*, Pub. by Old Vicarage UK) St Mut.

— Piazza Armerina Imperial Villa. 92p. (C). 1982. pap. text ed. 65.00 (*0-685-22060-5*, Pub. by Old Vicarage UK) St Mut.

— The Quincentenary Year of Stockport Grammar School. 128p. (C). 1988. pap. text ed. 39.00 (*0-947818-10-3*, Pub. by Old Vicarage UK) St Mut.

— The Roman Forum. 104p. (C). 1982. pap. text ed. 34.00 (*0-685-44227-6*, Pub. by Old Vicarage UK) St Mut.

— Rome & Environs. 240p. (C). 1982. pap. text ed. 45.00 (*0-685-22067-2*, Pub. by Old Vicarage UK) St Mut.

— Tivoli Hadrian's Villa & Villa d'Este. 70p. (C). 1982. pap. text ed. 65.00 (*0-685-22054-0*, Pub. by Old Vicarage UK) St Mut.

— Tres Nationes. 80p. (C). 1982. pap. text ed. 45.00 (*0-900269-16-2*, Pub. by Old Vicarage UK) St Mut.

— Vatican City. 136p. (C). 1982. pap. text ed. 50.00 (*0-685-22063-X*, Pub. by Old Vicarage UK) St Mut.

— Venice Archaeological Museum. (C). 1982. pap. text ed. 50.00 (*0-685-22055-9*, Pub. by Old Vicarage UK) St Mut.

Old, W. Gorn. The Yoga of Yama. 64p. 1970. reprint ed. spiral bd. 3.85 (*0-7873-1169-3*) Mokelumne.

***Old, Wendie.** Marian Wright Edelman: Fighting for Children's Rights. (People to Know Ser.). (Illus.). 112p. (YA). (gr. 6 up). 1995. lib. bdg. 17.95 (*0-89490-623-2*) Enslow Pubs.

— Stacy Had a Little Sister: A Concept Book. Grant, Christy, ed. (Illus.). 32p. (J). (ps-3). 1994. lib. bdg. 13.95 (*0-8075-7598-4*) A Whitman.

***Old World Wisconsin Staff.** Taste of Tradition: Old World Wisconsin Cooking. Larson, Carolyn, ed. & pref. by. (Illus.). 208p. (Orig.). 1988. 12.50 (*0-9620365-0-1*) Friends Old World WI.

***Oldach, Mark.** Creativity for Graphic Designers. (Illus.). 144p. 1995. 29.99 (*0-89134-583-3*) North Light Bks.

Oldal, E., jt. auth. see Redl, E.

Oldale, Robert. Cape Cod & the Islands: The Geologic Story. (Orig.). 1992. pap. 12.95 (*0-940160-53-6*) Parnassus Imprints.

Oldani, Robert W., jt. auth. see Emerson, Caryl.

Oldcorn, Anthony, tr. see Goldoni, Carlo.

Oldcorn, Roger. Accounting for Managers. LC 92-39190. 1993. 12.95 (*0-415-00230-3*, Routledge NY) Routledge.

***Oldcorn, Roger & Parker, David.** The Strategic Investment Decision: Evaluating Investment Opportunities. (Financial Times Management Ser.). 300p. 1995. 72.50 (*0-273-61779-6*, Pub. by Pitman Pub Ltd UK) Trans-Atl Phila.

Oldcoyote, Sally, ed. Teepees are Folded: American Indian Poetry. (J). (gr. 4 up). 1991. pap. 5.95 (*0-89992-133-7*) Coun India Ed.

***Olde, Peter & Marriott, Neil.** The Grevillea Book Vols. 1-3, 3 vols., Set. (Illus.). 1995. 149.85 (*0-88192-308-7*) Timber.

Oldekoeft, jt. auth. see Maekawa, M.

Oldelsted, Jan, jt. ed. see Needham, Paul.

Oldeman, R. A. Forests: Elements of Silvology. (Illus.). 640p. 1990. 161.00 (*0-387-51883-5*) Spr-Verlag.

Olden, Anthony & Wise, Michale, eds. Information & Libraries in the Developing World, No. 3: Arab States. 272p. 1994. 90.00 (*1-85604-085-2*, LAP0852, Pub. by Lib Assn Pub UK) UNIPUB.

Olden, Anthony, jt. auth. see Wise, Michale.

Olden, Diana J. & Smith, Vicki. Pendleton Pennywise Presents the Money Book - Just for You: A Budget Book for Children. 44p. (J). (gr. 3-5). 1991. spiral bd. 11.95 (*0-9630463-0-6*) S & D.

Olden, Marc. Gossip. 1979. pap. 2.50 (*0-449-14260-4*, GM) Fawcett.

— Kisaeng. 1991. 21.95 (*1-55611-247-5*) D I Fine.

— Kisaeng. 416p. 1992. reprint ed. mass mkt. 5.99 (*0-8217-3897-6*) Zebra.

***Olden, Roger C.** Victims. LC 95-68400. 204p. 1995. lib. bdg. 50.00x (*0-923687-35-1*) Celo Valley Bks.

Oldenberg, H. Dipavamsa. 232p. 1986. reprint ed. 20.00 (*0-8364-1747-X*, Pub. by Manohar II) S Asia.

Oldenberg, H., ed. The Dipavamsa: An Ancient Buddhist Historical Record. LC 78-72428. (ENG & PLI.). reprint ed. 27.00 (*0-404-17289-X*) AMS Pr.

Oldenberg, H., jt. auth. see Muller, F. Max.

Oldenberg, Hermann. Buddha: His Life, His Doctrine & His Order. 1972. 59.95 (*0-87968-800-9*) Gordon Pr.

— The Dipavamsa: An Ancient Buddhist Historical Record. (C). 1982. 17.00 (*0-8364-2831-5*, Pub. by Asian Educ Servs II) S Asia.

— The Doctrine of the Upanisads & the Early Buddhism. (C). 1991. 26.00 (*81-208-0830-4*, Pub. by Motilal Banarsidass II) S Asia.

— The Religion of the Veda. Shrotri, Shridhar B., tr. (C). 1988. 42.50 (*81-208-0392-2*, Pub. by Motilal Banarsidass II) S Asia.

Oldenberg, Otto & Rasmussen, Norman C. Modern Physics for Engineers. (Illus.). 477p. (C). reprint ed. 50.00 (*1-878907-47-6*) TechBooks.

***Oldenberg, Philip, ed.** India Briefing: Staying the Course. (Asia Society Country Briefing Ser.). 250p. 1995. 55.00 (*1-56324-609-0*); pap. 18.95 (*1-56324-610-4*) M E Sharpe.

***Oldenbourg, Lennart.** Engelsk-Svensk Affarsordbok: English-Swedish Business Dictionary. 376p. (ENG & SWE.). 1994. write for info. (*0-7859-8582-4*, 9127570576) Fr & Eur.

Oldenbourg, Rudolf C. & Sartorius, Hans. The Dynamics of Automatic Controls. Mason, H. L., ed. LC 49-2386. 276p. reprint ed. pap. 78.70 (*0-317-08004-0*, 2051945) Bks Demand.

Oldenbourg, Zoe. Argile et Cendres, Tome I. 1979. pap. 15.95 (*0-7859-4126-6*) Fr & Eur.

— Les Brules. (FRE.). 1975. pap. 13.95 (*0-7859-4043-X*, 2070366855) Fr & Eur.

— Les Cites Charnelles. (FRE.). 1983. pap. 20.95 (*0-7859-4189-4*) Fr & Eur.

— La Joie des Pauvres, Tome I. (FRE.). 1981. pap. 13.95 (*0-7859-4153-3*) Fr & Eur.

— La Joie des Pauvres, Tome II. (FRE.). 1981. pap. 13.95 (*0-7859-4154-1*) Fr & Eur.

— La Joie-Souffrance, Tome I. (FRE.). 1985. pap. 20.95 (*0-7859-4226-2*) Fr & Eur.

— La Joie-Souffrance, Tome II. (FRE.). 1985. pap. 20.95 (*0-7859-4227-0*) Fr & Eur.

— Massacre at Montsegur: A History of the Albigensian Crusade. Green, Peter, tr. (Dorset Reprints Ser.). 420p. 1990. 19.95 (*0-88029-477-9*) Marboro Bks.

— La Pierre Angulaire. (FRE.). 1972. pap. 17.95 (*0-7859-3986-5*) Fr & Eur.

— Reveilles de la Vie. (FRE.). 1974. pap. 11.95 (*0-7859-4035-9*) Fr & Eur.

— Visages d'un Autoportrait. 409p. (FRE.). 1988. pap. 17.95 (*0-7859-4284-X*, 2070379167) Fr & Eur.

Oldenburg. Great Good Place. 1994. pap. 14.95 (*1-56924-907-5*) Marlowe & Co.

Oldenburg, Claes & Van Bruggen, Coosje. Large-Scale Projects: Claes Oldenburg Coosje van Bruggen. LC 94-76579. (Illus.). 584p. 1994. 95.00 (*1-885254-04-0*) Monacelli Pr.

Oldenburg, Don, jt. ed. see Hackman, Peggy.

Oldenburg, Douglas W., jt. auth. see Whittall, Kenneth P.

Oldenburg, Joseph. A Genealogical Guide to the Burton Historical Collection. (Illus.). 128p. 1988. 10.95 (*0-916489-33-7*) Ancestry.

Oldenburg, Kirsten U., jt. auth. see Hirschhorn, Joel S.

Oldenburg, Philip, ed. India Briefing, 1991. 220p. (C). 1991. pap. text ed. 15.85 (*0-8133-8254-8*) Westview.

— India Briefing 1993. 252p. (C). 1993. pap. text ed. 15.85 (*0-8133-8772-8*) Westview.

Oldenburg, Rick. Conducting the Phonothon. (Illus.). 44p. (Orig.). 1991. pap. 6.00 (*1-55833-109-3*) Natl Cath Educ.

Oldenburg, Veena T. The Making of Colonial Lucknow, 1856-1877. 320p. 1990. 11.95 (*0-19-562473-4*) OUP.

— The Making of Colonial Lucknow, 1856-1877. LC 83-16008. Date not set. reprint ed. pap. 89.50 (*0-7837-9407-X*, 2060152) Bks Demand.

— Say It in Hindi. (Say It Ser.). 192p. (Orig.). 1981. pap. 3.50 (*0-486-23959-4*) Dover.

Oldenburg, Veena Talwar. The Making of Colonial Lucknow, 1856-1877. (Illus.). 304p. 1984. 47.50 (*0-691-06590-X*) Princeton U Pr.

Oldendorf, Donna, ed. see Commire, Anne.

Oldendorf, Walter P., jt. ed. see Rud, Anthony G., Jr.

Oldendorf, William & Oldendorf, William, Jr. MRI Primer. 240p. 1991. 53.50 (*0-88167-769-8*) Raven.

Oldendorf, William, Jr., jt. auth. see Oldendorf, William.

Oldendorf, William H. The Quest for an Image of Brain: Computerized Tomography in the Perspective of Past & Future Imaging Methods. 167p. 1980. text ed. 55.50 (*0-89004-429-5*) Raven.

Oldendorp, C. G. A Caribbean Mission. Bossard, Johann J., ed. Highfield, Arnold R. & Barac, Valdimir, trs. 1987. 30.00 (*0-89720-075-6*) Karoma.

Oldenquist, Andrew. The Non-Suicidal Society. LC 85-45804. (Illus.). 280p. (C). 1986. 25.00 (*0-253-34107-8*) Ind U Pr.

Oldenquist, Andrew & Rosner, Menachem, eds. Alienation, Community, & Work. LC 91-6282. (Contributions in Sociology Ser.: No. 96). 224p. 1991. text ed. 49.95 (*0-313-27541-6*, OAL, Greenwood Pr) Greenwood.

Oldenquist, Andrew G. Moral Philosophy: Text & Readings. 2nd ed. 415p. (C). 1984. reprint ed. pap. text ed. 19.95 (*0-88133-104-X*) Waveland Pr.

Oldenquist, Andrew G., jt. ed. see Garner, Richard T.

Oldenverg, Herman. Buddha: His Life, His Doctrine, His Order. (C). 1992. 27.00 (*81-7062-177-1*, Pub. by Lancer II) S Asia.

Older, Anne, et al. In & Around Albany, Schenectady & Troy. 3rd ed. (Illus.). 368p. 1992. pap. 14.95 (*1-881324-00-1*) Wash Park.

Older, Cora M. Love Stories of Old California. LC 75-167465. (Short Story Index Reprint Ser.). 1977. reprint ed. 26.95 (*0-8369-3991-3*) Ayer.

***Older, Cora M. B.** Love Stories of Old California. LC 94-43777. 320p. 1995. pap. 15.95 (*1-55709-400-4*) Applewood.

Older, Fremont. My Own Story: New Edition. rev. ed. (BCL1 - United States Local History Ser.). 340p. 1991. reprint ed. lib. bdg. 89.00 (*0-7812-6343-3*) Rprt Serv.

— William Randolph Hearst, American. LC 72-7195. (Select Bibliographies Reprint Ser.). 1977. reprint ed. 42.95 (*0-8369-6951-0*) Ayer.

Older, John, ed. Bone Implant Grafting. LC 92-2327. xviii, 226p. 1992. write for info. (*3-540-19720-6*); 198.00 (*0-387-19720-6*) Spr-Verlag.

Older, Jules. Ben & Jerry...The Real Scoop! LC 92-39649. (Illus.). 80p. (Orig.). (J). (gr. 3-8). 1993. pap. 6.95 (*1-881527-04-2*) Chapters Pub.

— Ski Vermont! A Complete Guide to the Best Vermont Skiing. LC 91-16650. (Illus.). 160p. 1990. pap. 14.95 (*0-930031-44-X*) Chelsea Green Pub.

Older, Julia. Endometriosis. (Illus.). 240p. 1985. pap. 10.95 (*0-684-18505-9*, Scribners) S&S Trade.

— Higher Latitudes. LC 95-79509. 61p. (Orig.). 1995. pap. 8.00 (*0-9627162-3-5*) Appledore Bks.

— The Island Queen: Celia Thaxter of the Isles of Shoals. LC 94-70760. 185p. (Orig.). 1994. pap. 11.00 (*0-9627162-2-7*) Appledore Bks.

— A Little Wild. (Illus.). 40p. 1987. 26.00 (*0-930126-19-X*) Typographeum.

— Oonts & Others. 72p. 1982. 17.50 (*0-87775-150-1*); pap. 8.95 (*0-87775-151-X*) Unicorn Pr.

Older, Julia & Sherman, Steve. Grand Monadnock: Exploring the Most Popular Mountain in America. LC 90-83104. (Illus.). 112p. (Orig.). 1990. pap. 15.95 (*0-9627162-1-9*) Appledore Bks.

— Nature Walks in Southern New Hampshire: An AMC Nature Walks Book. 1994. pap. 10.95 (*1-878239-35-X*) AMC Books.

— The Ultimate Soup Book: Two Hundred Fifty Soups for Appetizers, Entrees, & Desserts. (Illus.). 224p. (Orig.). 1991. pap. 11.00 (*0-452-26609-2*, Plume) NAL-Dutton.

Older, Julia, jt. auth. see Sherman, Steve.

Older, Julia, ed. see Vian, Boris.

Older, Ricki, jt. auth. see Reynolds, Dona.

Olderman, Raymond M. Beyond the Waste Land: A Study of the American Novel in the Nineteen-Sixties. LC 73-182210. 269p. reprint ed. pap. 76.70 (*0-8357-8042-2*, 2033848) Bks Demand.

Olderog, E. R. Nets, Terms & Formulas: Three Views of Concurrent Processes & Their Relationship. (Tracts in Theoretical Computer Science Ser.: No. 23). 250p. (C). 1991. 54.95 (*0-521-40044-9*) Cambridge U Pr.

***Olderog, Ernst R., ed.** Programming Concepts, Methods & Calculi: Proceedings of the IFIP TC2/WG2.1/WG2.2/WG2.3 Working Conference on Programming Concepts, Methods, & Calculi (PROCOMET '94), San Miniato, Italy, 6-10 June 1994. LC 94-36660. (IFIP Transactions & Computer Science & Technology Ser.). 1994. write for info. (*0-444-82020-5*) Elsevier.

Olderog, F. R., jt. auth. see Apt, Krzystof R.

Olderr, Steven. Mystery Index: Subjects, Settings, & Sleuths of 10,000 Mystery Novels. LC 87-1294. 448p. 1987. text ed. 20.00 (*0-8389-0461-0*) ALA.

O

An Asterisk (*) at the beginning of an entry indicates that the title is appearing in BIP for the first time.

— Olderr's Fiction Subject Headings: A Supplement & Guide to the LC Thesaurus. LC 91-8679. 160p. (C). 1991. pap. text ed. 35.00 (*0-8389-0562-5*) ALA.

— Reverse Symbolism Dictionary: Symbols Listed by Subject. LC 90-53517. 191p. 1992. lib. bdg. 32.50x (*0-89950-561-9*) McFarland & Co.

Olderr, Steven, comp. Symbolism: A Comprehensive Dictionary. LC 85-42833. 159p. 1986. lib. bdg. 28.50x (*0-89950-187-7*) McFarland & Co.

Olderr, Steven, ed. Olderr's Fiction Index, 1987. 350p. 1988. 60.00 (*0-912289-85-6*) St James Pr.

— Olderr's Fiction Index, 1988. 1989. 60.00 (*1-55862-028-1*) St James Pr.

— Olderr's Fiction Index, 1989. 450p. 1990. lib. bdg. 60.00 (*1-55862-057-5*) St James Pr.

— Olderr's Fiction Index 1990. 557p. 1992. lib. bdg. 60.00 (*1-55862-090-7*, 200143) St James Pr.

— Olderr's Young Adult Fiction Index, 1988. 1989. 61.00 (*1-55862-020-6*) St James Pr.

— Olderr's Young Adult Fiction Index, 1989. 250p. 1990. lib. bdg. 61.00 (*1-55862-058-3*) St James Pr.

— Olderr's Young Adult Fiction Index 1990. 310p. 1991. lib. bdg. 61.00 (*1-55862-091-5*, 200144) St James Pr.

Oldershaw, Callie. Oceans. LC 91-45079. (Our Planet Ser.). (Illus.). 32p. (J). (gr. 4-6). 1993. lib. bdg. 11.59 (*0-8167-2753-8*); pap. text ed. 3.95 (*0-8167-2754-6*) Troll Assocs.

Oldershaw, Paul, jt. ed. see Sutton, Martin S.

Oldertz, Carl & Tidefelt, Eva, eds. Compensation for Personal Injury in Sweden & 17 Other Countries. 408p. 1988. 109.00x (*91-7598-197-1*) Coronet Bks.

Oldfather, W. A. A Bibliography of Epictetus. 177p. 1952. 20.00 (*0-685-02325-7*) Holmes.

Oldfather, William A. Contributions Toward a Bibliography of Epictetus: A Supplement. Harman, Marion, ed. LC 28-2296. 197p. reprint ed. pap. 56.20 (*0-317-10227-3*, 2020870) Bks Demand.

Oldfather, William A., et al. Index Apuleianus. (American Philological Association Philological Monographs). 1984. 47.00 (*0-89130-703-6*, 40-00-03) Scholars Pr GA.

— Index Verborum Ciceronis Epistularum. 583p. 1965. reprint ed. write for info. (*0-318-72059-0*, Pub. by Georg Olms GW) Lubrecht & Cramer.

— Index Verborum Quae in Senecae Fabulis Necnon in Octavia Praetexta Reperiuntur. Vol. IV, 2-4. 272p. 1964. reprint ed. write for info. (*0-318-72060-4*, Pub. by Georg Olms GW) Lubrecht & Cramer.

— Index Verborum Quae in Senecae Fabulis Necnon in Octavia Praetexta Reperiuntur. (University of Illinois Studies in Language & Literature: Vol. IV, 2-4). 272p. 1983. reprint ed. write for info. (*3-487-00658-8*, Pub. by Georg Olms GW) Lubrecht & Cramer.

Oldfather, Wiilliam A., et al. Index Verborum Ciceronis Epistularum. 583p. 1988. reprint ed. write for info. (*3-487-00880-7*, Pub. by Georg Olms GW) Lubrecht & Cramer.

Oldfeather, William A., et al. Index Apuleianus. li, 490p. 1979. reprint ed. lib. bdg. 89.70 (*3-487-06678-5*, Pub. by Georg Olms GW) Lubrecht & Cramer.

Oldfield, Adrian. Citizenship & Community: Civic Republicanism & the Modern World. 224p. 1990. 62.50 (*0-415-04875-3*, A4705) Routledge.

Oldfield, Audrey. Woman Suffrage in Australia: A Gift or a Struggle? (Studies in Australian History). (Illus.). 272p. (C). 1993. 64.95 (*0-521-40380-4*); pap. 22.95 (*0-521-43611-7*) Cambridge U Pr.

Oldfield, Barney & Moriarty, John J. Amphibians & Reptiles Native to Minnesota. LC 93-45018. (C). 1994. 25.95 (*0-8166-2384-8*) U of Minn Pr.

Oldfield, Charles. Single in New York. 1977. pap. 1.50 (*0-8439-0426-7*, LB426DK) Dorchester Pub Co.

***Oldfield, Elisabeth.** Backlash. large type ed. (Magna Large Print Ser.). 1994. 18.95 (*0-7505-0667-9*, Pub. by Magna Print Bks) Ulverscroft.

Oldfield, Elizabeth. Beloved Stranger. large type ed. (Magna Romance Ser.). 1992. 17.95 (*0-7505-0401-3*, Pub. by Magna Print Bks) Ulverscroft.

— Bodycheck. large type ed. 264p. 1993. 21.95 (*0-7505-0555-9*, Pub. by Magna Print Bks) Ulverscroft.

— Close Proximity. large type ed. (Magna Large Print Ser.). 1994. 18.95 (*0-7505-0739-X*, Pub. by Magna Print Bks) Ulverscroft.

— Dark Victory. large type ed. 1995. 18.95 (*0-263-13940-9*) Thorndike Pr.

— Designed to Annoy. (Presents Ser.). 1994. mass mkt. 2.99 (*0-373-11636-5*, 1-11636-7) Harlequin Bks.

— Fighting Lady. large type ed. 305p. 1993. 21.95 (*0-7505-0474-9*) Ulverscroft.

— Final Surrender. (Presents Ser.). 1995. mass mkt. 3.25 (*0-373-11747-7*, 1-11747-2) Harlequin Bks.

— The Final Surrender. large type ed. (Romance Ser.). 1993. 17.95 (*0-263-13200-5*, Pub. by Mills & Boon Ltd UK) Chivers N Amer.

— Living Dangerously. large type ed. 255p. 1992. 21.95 (*0-7505-0317-3*, Pub. by Magna Print Bks) Ulverscroft.

— Love's Prisoner. large type ed. (Traditional Romance Ser.). 1994. 17.95 (*0-263-13897-6*, Pub. by Mills & Boon Ltd UK) Chivers N Amer.

— Love's Prisoner (Presents Plus) 1995. mass mkt. 3.25 (*0-373-11773-6*) Harlequin Bks.

— Sudden Fire. large type ed. (Harlequin Ser.). 1994. 18.95 (*0-263-13778-3*) Thorndike Pr.

Oldfield, George S., Jr. Implications of Regulation on Bank Expansion: A Simulation Analysis. Altman, Edward I. & Walter, Ingo, eds. LC 76-10399. (Contemporary Studies in Economic & Financial Analysis: Vol. 10). 1980. lib. bdg. 73.25 (*0-89232-015-X*) Jai Pr.

Oldfield, Harry, jt. auth. see Coghill, Roger.

Oldfield, J. E., jt. auth. see Kains, M. G.

Oldfield, J. R. Alexander Crummell (Eighteen Nineteen to Eighteen Ninety-Eight) & the Creation of an African-American Church in Liberia. LC 90-31353. (Studies in the History of Missions: Vol. 6). 180p. 1990. lib. bdg. 79.95 (*0-88946-074-4*) E Mellen.

Oldfield, Jenny. Misfits & Rebels. 112p. (YA). (gr. 8-11). 1991. pap. 9.95 (*1-85381-155-6*, Pub. by Virago Pr UK) Trafalgar.

***Oldfield, John, ed.** Civilization & Black Progress: Selected Writings of Alexander Crummell on the South. 320p. (C). 1995. text ed. 38.50 (*0-8139-1602-X*) U Pr of Va.

***Oldfield, John R.** Popular Politics & British Anti-Slavery: The Mobilisation of Public Opinion Against the Slave Trade, 1787-1807. LC 94-26468. 1995. text ed. write for info. (*0-7190-3856-1*, Pub. by Manchester Univ Pr UK) St Martin.

Oldfield, John V. & Dorf, Richard C. Field-Programmable Gate Arrays: Reconfigurable Logic for Rapid Prototyping of Digital Systems. LC 94-20839. 327p. 1995. text ed. 59.95 (*0-471-55665-3*) Wiley.

Oldfield, Josiah. Eat Nature's Food & Live Long. 84p. 1960. reprint ed. spiral bd. 5.50 (*0-7873-0642-8*) Mokelumne.

Oldfield, Margaret J. Costumes & Customs of Many Lands. (Illus.). (J). (gr. k-3). 1982. reprint ed. pap. 2.95 (*0-934876-19-3*) Creative Storytime.

— Fat Cat & Ebenezer Geezer: The Teeny Tiny Mouse. 2nd ed. (Illus.). (J). (gr. k-2). 1980. pap. 3.00 (*0-934876-13-4*) Creative Storytime.

— Finger Puppets & Finger Plays. (Illus.). (J). (ps-3). 1982. reprint ed. pap. 3.00 (*0-934876-18-5*) Creative Storytime.

— Lots More Tell & Draw Stories. (Illus.). (J). (ps-3). 1973. lib. bdg. 11.95 (*0-934876-07-X*); pap. 6.95 (*0-934876-03-7*) Creative Storytime.

— More Tell & Draw Stories. (Illus.). (J). (ps-3). 1969. lib. bdg. 11.95 (*0-934876-06-1*); pap. 6.95 (*0-934876-02-9*) Creative Storytime.

— Tell & Draw Paper Bag Puppet Book. 2nd ed. (Illus.). (J). (gr. k-2). 1981. pap. 5.95 (*0-934876-16-9*) Creative Storytime.

— Tell & Draw Paper Cut-Outs. (Illus.). (Orig.). (J). (gr. k-2). 1988. pap. 3.50 (*0-934876-23-1*, 23) Creative Storytime.

Oldfield, Mary. Please Communicate. 1956. pap. 4.75 (*0-8222-0900-4*) Dramatists Play.

***Oldfield, Maurice.** Tolley's Understanding Occupational Pension Schemes. 5th ed. Orig. Title: Tolley's Understanding Pension Schemes. 150p. (C). 1994. 60. 00x (*1-85190-878-1*, Pub. by Tolley Pubng UK) St Mut.

— Understanding Occupational Pension Schemes. 5th ed. 170p. 1994. pap. 100.00 (*0-85459-878-2*, Pub. by Tolley Pubng UK) St Mut.

— Understanding Pension Schemes. 4th ed. 182p. 1992. 45. 00 (*1-85190-168-X*, Pub. by Tolley Pubng UK) St Mut.

Oldfield, Pamela. An Embarrassment of Riches. large type ed. 389p. 1994. 19.95 (*0-7505-0534-6*, Pub. by Magna Print Bks) Ulverscroft.

— The Gooding Girl. large type ed. 929p. 1994. 19.95 (*0-7505-0535-4*, Pub. by Magna Print Bks) Ulverscroft.

— The Rich Earth. large type ed. (Magna Large Print Ser.). 1994. 26.95 (*0-7505-0619-9*, Pub. by Magna Print Bks) Ulverscroft.

— String of Blue Beads. large type ed. LC 94-45926. 509p. 1995. reprint ed. 20.95 (*0-7838-1240-X*) Hall.

— Summer Song. large type ed. 767p. 1993. 21.95 (*0-7505-0536-2*) Ulverscroft.

Oldfield, Phyllis, jt. auth. see Chirgwin, F. John.

Oldfield, R. A., jt. auth. see Laird, MacGregor.

Oldfield, Sybil & Purvis, June, eds. This Working Day World: A Social, Political, & Cultural History of Women's Lives, 1914-1945. LC 93-41225. (Gender & society Series: Feminist Perspectives on the Past & Present). 224p. 1994. 75.00 (*0-7484-0107-5*, Pub. by Tay Francis Ltd UK); pap. 27.50 (*0-7484-0108-3*, Pub. by Tay Francis Ltd UK) Taylor & Francis.

Oldfield, Wendy, jt. auth. see Davies, Kay.

***Oldford-Matchim, Joan.** Help Your Child Become a Reader: A Guide for Reading Conversations, Activities & Games. (Illus.). 120p. (Orig.). 1995. pap. text ed. 13. 50 (*1-887176-01-2*) Globl Age Pub.

Oldford, R. W., jt. ed. see Cheeseman, P.

Oldgate, Karl. Karate. rev. ed. (Play the Game Ser.). (Illus.). 80p. (YA). (gr. 10-12). 1993. pap. 7.95 (*0-7137-2410-2*, Pub. by Blandford Pr UK) Sterling.

Oldham, Bruce, ed. Footprints: Following Jesus for Junior Highers. 144p. (Orig.). (YA). (gr. 7-9). 1983. pap. 4.50 (*0-8341-0863-1*) Beacon Hill.

Oldham, C. E., jt. ed. see Temple, R. C.

Oldham, D., ed. Engineering Design for TEC, Level Three. (C). 1981. 90.00 (*0-85950-303-8*, Pub. by S Thornes Pubs UK) St Mut.

Oldham, Dale. Badlands Drifter. 1979. pap. 1.50 (*0-8439-0629-4*) Dorchester Pub Co.

— The Sudden Land. 192p. (Orig.). 1985. reprint ed. pap. 2.25 (*0-8439-2233-8*) Dorchester Pub Co.

Oldham, Elizabeth, ed. see Miller, Richard F. & Mooney, Robert F.

Oldham, Eric. The Nineteen Fifties: Steam in the Countryside. LC 94-3170. (Illus.). 160p. 1994. 33.00 (*0-7509-0556-5*) A Sutton Pub.

Oldham, Frank, Jr. Job Descriptions in Banking: The Complete Guide to Planning, Writing, & Using Job Descriptions. 2nd ed. Seglin, Jeffrey L., ed. 337p. 1989. 55.00 (*1-55520-046-X*, TE7473) Probus Pub Co.

Oldham, G. The Future of Research: SHRE Leverhulme IV. 220p. 1982. pap. 28.00 (*0-900868-86-4*) Taylor & Francis.

Oldham, Gabriella. First Cut: Conversations with Film Editors. 1992. 35.00 (*0-520-07586-2*) U CA Pr.

— First Cut: Conversations with Film Editors. 1995. pap. 14. 95 (*0-520-07588-9*) U CA Pr.

— Keaton's Silent Shorts: Beyond the Laughter. LC 95-13970. (C). 1995. write for info. (*0-8093-1951-9*); pap. write for info. (*0-8093-1952-7*) S Ill U Pr.

***Oldham, George E.** Dictionary of Business & Finance Terms. 1993. pap. 9.95 (*1-882912-01-2*) Sunrise TN.

Oldham, Glenna. Cherish the Memories. (Illus.). 1990. 9.95 (*0-685-51754-3*, D1028) Warner Pr.

Oldham, Greg R., jt. auth. see Hackman, J. Richard.

Oldham, J. H., jt. auth. see Hooft, W. A.

Oldham, J. Thomas. Texas Marital Property Rights. 2nd ed. 588p. (Orig.). 1992. pap. 55.00 (*0-916081-30-3*) J Marshall Pub Co.

Oldham, Jack, jt. auth. see Goldstein, Bernard.

Oldham, James. The Mansfield Manuscripts & the Growth of English Law in the Eighteenth Century, 2 vols. (C). 1992. Vol. I: xxxvi, 772p. write for info. (*0-318-69357-7*); Vol. II: xxi, 914p. write for info. (*0-318-69358-5*) U of NC Pr.

— The Mansfield Manuscripts & the Growth of English Law in the Eighteenth Century, 2 vols., Set. LC 91-46199. (Studies in Legal History). (C). 1992. 150.00 (*0-8078-2052-0*) U of NC Pr.

Oldham, James B. Blind Panels of English Binders. (History of Bookbinding & Design Ser.). (Illus.). 144p. 1990. reprint ed. 80.00 (*0-8240-4048-1*) Garland.

— English Blind-stamped Bindings. LC 52-9808. (Sanders Lectures: 1949). 212p. reprint ed. pap. 60.50 (*0-317-27543-7*, 2024507) Bks Demand.

— English Blind-Stamped Bindings, Vol. 18. Huttner, Sidney F., ed. (History of Bookbinding & Design Ser.). (Illus.). 160p. 1990. 109.00 (*0-8240-4047-3*) Garland.

— Shrewsbury School Library Bindings, Vol. 17. Huttner, Sidney F., ed. (History of Bookbinding & Design Ser.). (Illus.). 296p. 1990. reprint ed. 140.00 (*0-8240-4046-5*) Garland.

Oldham, John. The Poems of John Oldham. Seldon, Raman & Brooks, Harold F., eds. (Illus.). 760p. 1987. 125.00 (*0-19-812456-2*) OUP.

— Selected Poems. Robinson, Ken, ed. 88p. 1980. pap. 10.95 (*0-906427-12-6*, Pub. by Bloodaxe Bks UK) Dufour.

— Works of Mr. John Oldham. LC 79-26304. 1980. reprint ed. 90.00 (*0-8201-1337-9*) Schol Facsimiles.

Oldham, John, ed. Personality Disorders: New Perspectives on Diagnostic Validity. LC 89-18135. (Progress in Psychiatry Ser.). 200p. 1990. text ed. 30.00 (*0-88048-113-7*) Am Psychiatric.

Oldham, John & Morris, Lois B. The Personality Self-Portrait: Why You Feel, Think, Work, Love & Act the Way You Do. 448p. 1991. pap. 11.95 (*0-553-35336-5*) Bantam.

Oldham, John, jt. auth. see Oldham, Ray.

Oldham, John M. & Bone, Stanley, eds. Paranoia: New Psychoanalytic Perspectives. 166p. 1994. text ed. 27.50 (*0-8236-3985-1*) Intl Univs Pr.

Oldham, John M. & Liebert, Robert S. The Middle Years: New Psychoanalytic Perspectives. 304p. (C). 1990. 35.00 (*0-300-04418-6*) Yale U Pr.

***Oldham, John M. & Morris, Lois B.** New Personality Self-Portrait: Why You Think, Work, Love & Act the Way You Do. rev. ed. LC 95-12233. Orig. Title: The Personality Self-Portrait. 1995. pap. write for info. (*0-553-37393-5*) Bantam.

***Oldham, John M. & Riba, Michelle B., eds.** American Psychiatric Press Review of Psychiatry, Vol. 14. 992p. 1995. boxed 59.95 (*0-88048-441-1*, 8441) Am Psychiatric.

— American Psychiatric Press Review of Psychiatry, Vol. 13. 1994. boxed 59.95 (*0-88048-440-3*, 8440) Am Psychiatric.

Oldham, John M. & Russakoff, L. Mark. Dynamic Therapy in Brief Hospitalization. LC 87-12629. 235p. 1987. 30. 00x (*0-87668-965-9*) Aronson.

Oldham, John M., et al, eds. American Psychiatric Press Review of Psychiatry, Vol. 12. 1993. 59.95 (*0-88048-439-X*) Am Psychiatric.

Oldham, Joseph H. Christianity & the Race Problem. LC 73-75534. 280p. 1969. reprint ed. text ed. 52.50 (*0-8371-1112-9*, OLC&, Negro U Pr) Greenwood.

Oldham, June. Little Rattle in the Air. 238p. 1991. pap. 11. 95 (*1-85381-152-1*, Pub. by Virago Pr UK) Trafalgar.

Oldham, K. G., jt. ed. see Evans, E. A.

Oldham, K. M. Accounting Systems & Practice in Europe. 3rd ed. 335p. 1987. text ed. 89.95 (*0-566-02612-0*) Ashgate Pub Co.

Oldham, Keith B. & Myland, Jan C. Fundamentals of Electrochemical Science. (Illus.). 496p. 1993. text ed. 49. 95 (*0-12-525545-4*) Acad Pr.

Oldham, Keith B., jt. auth. see Spanier, Jerome.

Oldham, Kenneth. Steam in Wartime Britain. LC 92-45036. 1993. 30.00 (*0-7509-0325-2*) A Sutton Pub.

***Oldham, Lea L.** Teaching Techniques for Non-Credit & Continuing Education of Adults & Seniors. Greive, Donald, ed. 34p. (Orig.). (C). 1995. pap. text ed. 4.95 (*0-940017-20-2*) Info Tec OH.

Oldham, Lea L., jt. auth. see Allen, Nancy.

Oldham, Linda, jt. auth. see Lee, Nancy.

Oldham-Merrill, J. & Reed-Scott, J. Preservation Planning Program: An Assisted Self-Study Manual for Libraries. 1,993th ed. 138p. 1993. pap. 40.00 (*0-918006-69-4*) ARL.

Oldham, Mika. Blackstone's Statutes on Family Law. 2nd ed. pap. 32.00 (*1-85431-220-0*, Pub. by Blackstone Pr UK) W W Gaunt.

— Blackstone's Statutes on Family Law, Vol. 1. 3rd ed. 385p. 1994. pap. text ed. 28.00 (*1-85431-346-0*, Blckstone AT) W W Gaunt.

Oldham, Neild. Studying Smart: Thinking & Study Skills for School & the Workplace. 260p. 1993. teacher ed 8.00 (*1-56118-529-9*); pap. text ed. 15.95 (*1-56118-528-0*) Paradigm MN.

Oldham, Neild B., jt. auth. see Fruehling, Rosemary T.

Oldham, R., jt. ed. see Finter, N. B.

Oldham, Ray & Oldham, John. Western Heritage: A Study of the Colonial Architecture of Perth, Western Australia. LC 79-670392. 1979. 15.00 (*0-85564-134-7*, Pub. by Univ of West Aust Pr AT) Intl Spec Bk.

— Western Heritage Part 2: George Temple-Pool, Architect of the Golden Years 1885-1897. 227p. 1981. 35.00 (*0-85564-173-8*, Pub. by Univ of West Aust Pr AT) Intl Spec Bk.

Oldham, Robert K. The Cure. LC 90-92322. 343p. (Orig.). (YA). 1991. pap. write for info. (*0-9628850-0-2*) Media Amer.

Oldham, Robert K., ed. Principles of Cancer Biotherapy. (Illus.). 512p. 1988. text ed. 109.50 (*0-88167-364-1*) Raven.

— Principles of Cancer Biotherapy. 2nd rev. ed. 696p. 1991. 165.00 (*0-8247-8504-5*) Dekker.

Oldham, Thomas J. Divorce, Separation & the Distribution of Property. 400p. 1987. ring bd. 65.00 (*0-318-23153-0*, 00604) Law Journal.

— Divorce, Separation & the Distribution of Property. ring bd. 98.00 (*0-318-23686-9*) NY Law Pub.

Oldham, Tim. World Cup U. S. A., 1994. 1994. mass mkt. 4.99 (*0-06-100847-8*, Harp PBks) HarpC.

Oldham, Tom, jt. auth. see Alderman, Richard.

Oldham, W. G., jt. auth. see Schwarz, Stephen E.

Oldham, William G., jt. auth. see Schwarz, Steven E.

Olding, Alan. Modern Biology & Natural Theology. (Illus.). 224p. (C). 1991. text ed. 65.00 (*0-415-04971-7*, A4744) Routledge.

Oldis, Daniel. Albert. LC 85-91094. 1986. 12.95 (*0-87212-196-8*) Libra.

Oldknow, Adrian, jt. auth. see Griffiths, H.

***Oldknow, Antony.** Wanderers: Selected Poems & Translations. 80p. 1994. 8.00 (*1-881604-19-5*) Scopcraeft.

***Oldknow, Antony & Swan, Jesse.** Book of Literary Terms. 70p. (C). 1995. 8.00 (*1-881604-17-9*) Scopcraeft.

Oldknow, Antony, jt. ed. see Hendershot, Cynthia.

Oldknow, Antony, tr. see Jammes, Francis.

Oldman, Mark. Princeton Review Student Access Guide: America's Top 100 Internships, Counselors, Employers. 1994. pap. 16.00 (*0-679-74960-8*, Villard Bks) Random.

— Student Access Guide to America's Top 100 Internships, 1995. 1994. pap. 17.00 (*0-679-75655-8*) Random.

Oldman, Oliver, jt. ed. see Bird, Richard M.

Oldman, Oliver, jt. auth. see Popkin, William D.

Oldman, Oliver S., et al. Financing Urban Development in Mexico City: A Case Study of Property Tax, Land Use, Housing, & Urban Planning. Herrman, Lawrence M. & Lee, Lawrence D., trs. LC 67-20878. 374p. reprint ed. pap. 106.60 (*0-7837-2307-5*, 2057395) Bks Demand.

Oldmixon, John. The Arts of Logick & Rhetorick: Interpreted & Explain'd by ... Bouhours. (Anglistica & Americana Ser.: No. 163). xxxii, 418p. 1976. reprint ed. 76.70 (*3-487-05926-6*, Pub. by Georg Olms GW) Lubrecht & Cramer.

Oldridge, Les. Basic Benchwork. (Workshop Practice Ser.: No. 18). (Illus.). 128p. (Orig.). 1988. pap. 18.50x (*0-85242-920-7*, Pub. by Argus Books UK) Trans-Atl Phila.

Oldridge, N. B., et al, eds. Clinical Exercise Programs: Theory & Practice. (Illus.). 300p. 1988. pap. 24.95 (*0-317-59354-4*) Mouvement Pubns.

Oldring, P. & Hayward, G. Resins for Surface Coatings. (C). 1989. 305.00 (*0-685-36806-8*, Pub. by Fuel Metallurgical Jrnl UK); 900.00 (*0-86108-200-1*, Pub. by Fuel Metallurgical Jrnl UK) St Mut.

Oldring, P., jt. ed. see Holman, R.

Oldring, P. K. & Hayward, G. Resins for Surface Coatings, Vol. 1. 2nd ed. (Illus.). 230p. 1989. text ed. 85.00 (*0-947798-04-8*, Pub. by SITA Tech UK) Scholium Intl.

Oldring, P. K., ed. see Castle, Roger & Standen, C.

Oldring, P. K., jt. auth. see Lowe, C.

Oldring, Peter, ed. see Braithwaite, M., et al.

Oldring, Peter, ed. see Dietliker, K. K.

Oldring, Peter, ed. see Dufour, P. & Knight, R. E.

Oldrizzi, L., ed. The Progressive Nature of Renal Diseases: Myths & Facts. (Contributions to Nephrology Ser.: Vol. 75). (Illus.). viii, 218p. 1989. 143.25 (*3-8055-5021-9*) S Karger.

Oldroyd, David. The Arch of Knowledge. (C). 1990. pap. 24. 95 (*0-86840-049-1*, Pub. by New South Wales Univ Pr AT) Intl Spec Bk.

Oldroyd, David & Hall, Valerie. Managing Staff Development: A Handbook for Secondary Schools. 144p. (C). 1991. pap. text ed. 34.00 (*1-85396-112-4*, Pub. by P Chapman Pub UK) Taylor & Francis.

Oldroyd, David R. The Highlands Controversy: Constructing Geological Knowledge Through Fieldwork in Nineteenth-Century. LC 89-20610. (Science & Its Conceptual Foundations Ser.). (Illus.). 528p. 1990. pap. text ed. 29.95 (*0-226-62635-0*) U Ch Pr.

— The Highlands Controversy: Constructing Geological Knowledge Through Fieldwork in Nineteenth-Century. LC 89-20610. (Science & Its Conceptual Foundations Ser.). (Illus.). 528p. 1990. lib. bdg. 65.00 (*0-226-62634-2*) U Ch Pr.

Oldroyd, David R. & Langham, Ian G. The Wilder Domain of Evolutionary Thought. 1983. lib. bdg. 117.00 (*90-277-1477-0*) Kluwer Ac.

Oldroyd, George. The Technique & Spirit of Fugue: An Historical Study. LC 85-27089. viii, 228p. 1986. reprint ed. text ed. 59.75 (*0-313-25052-9*, OLTS, Greenwood Pr) Greenwood.

Oldroyd, Ida S. The Marine Shells of the West Coast of North America, 4 vols., Set. (Illus.). 1530p. 1927. 139.50 (*0-8047-0987-4*) Stanford U Pr.

Oldroyd, Mike, jt. auth. see Hatton, Angela.

Oldroyd, Osborn H. The Assassination of Abraham Lincoln: Flight, Pursuit, Capture, & Punishment of the Conspirators. (Illus.). 332p. 1990. reprint ed. pap. 22.50 (*1-55613-360-X*) Heritage Bk.

Oldroyd, Stephen & Stoffers, Kenneth. Hypodermics. 48p. 1980. 45.00 (*0-88014-022-4*) Mosaic Pr OH.

Olds, Arthur F. It's No Bull! The True Story of the Taming of Northeast Pinellas County. 300p. 1992. pap. 18.50 (*0-9632576-3-3*) Boot Ranch Pub.

***Olds, Bruce.** Raising Holy Hell: A Novel. LC 95-9707. 320p. 1995. 22.50 (*0-8050-3856-6*) H Holt & Co.

Olds, Carl D. Continued Fractions. LC 61-12185. (New Mathematical Library: No. 9). 162p. 1963. pap. 12.00 (*0-88385-609-3*) Math Assn.

Olds, Clifton C., jt. auth. see Hall, Donald.

Olds, Edward C., jt. auth. see Freeman, Leon L.

Olds, Elizabeth F. Women of the Four Winds. (Illus.). 263p. 1985. pap. 13.95 (*0-395-39584-4*) HM.

Olds-Ellingson, Alice. The Devil Won't Let Me In. 64p. (Orig.). 1990. pap. 6.95 (*0-916397-11-4*) Manic D Pr.

Olds, Henry F. The Computer As an Educational Tool. LC 86-3132. (Computers in the Schools Ser.: Vol. 3, No. 1). 99p. 1986. text ed. 29.95 (*0-86656-559-0*) Haworth Pr.

Olds, James. Drives & Reinforcements: Behavioral Studies of Hypothalamic Functions. LC 75-31480. 148p. 1977. pap. 27.00 (*0-89004-087-7*) Raven.

Olds, Jennifer. Rodeo & the Mimosa Tree. LC 91-74038. 80p. 1991. pap. 9.95 (*0-9627501-4-X*) Event Horizon.

Olds, Linda E. Metaphors of Interrelatedness: Toward a Systems Theory of Psychology. LC 91-18490. (SUNY Series, Alternatives in Psychology). 217p. (C). 1992. 49.50 (*0-7914-1011-0*); pap. 16.95 (*0-7914-1012-9*) State U NY Pr.

Olds, Marshall. Analysis of the Interchurch World Movement Report on the Steel Strike. LC 70-172223. (Right Wing Individualist Tradition in America Ser.). 1972. reprint ed. 35.95 (*0-405-00432-X*) Ayer.

— Analysis of the Interchurch World Movement Report on the Steel Strike. LC 73-139199. (Civil Liberties in American History Ser.). 1971. reprint ed. lib. bdg. 65.00 (*0-306-70082-4*) Da Capo.

— Desire Seeking Expression: Mallarme's Prose pour des Esseintes. LC 82-82431. (French Forum Monographs: No. 42). 129p. (Orig.). 1983. pap. 10.95 (*0-917058-41-0*) French Forum.

Olds, Marshall C., ed. Essays in European Literature: For Walter A. Strauss. (STCL Monographs: No. 1). (Illus.). (Orig.). (C). 1990. pap. text ed. 12.00 (*0-685-30124-9*) Studies Twentieth.

Olds, Marshall C., ed. see Rogers, Peter S.

Olds, Robert. Helldiver Squadron: The Story of Carrier Bombing Squadron 17 with Task Force 58. LC 79-16872. reprint ed. 17.95 (*0-89201-054-1*) Zenger Pub.

Olds, S., tr. see Szymborska, Wislawa.

Olds, Sally B. Maternal Newborn Nursing. 4th ed. Cleary, Patti, ed. 1328p. (C). 1992. teacher ed 10.75 (*0-8053-5582-0*); text ed. 63.50 (*0-8053-5580-4*); student ed, pap. text ed. 21.50 (*0-8053-5584-7*); trans. 193.75 (*0-8053-5583-9*); 18.75 (*0-8053-5581-2*) Addison-Wesley.

Olds, Sally B., et al. Maternal-Newborn Nursing: A Family-Centered Approach. 2nd ed. 1168p. 1984. write for info. (*0-201-12797-0*, Health Sci) Addison-Wesley.

— Maternal-Newborn Nursing Care: A Workbook. 2nd ed. 1984. pap. write for info. (*0-201-12799-7*) Addison-Wesley.

Olds, Sally W., jt. auth. see Eiger, Marvin S.

Olds, Sally W., jt. auth. see Papalia, Diane E.

Olds, Sally W., jt. auth. see Simon, Sidney B.

Olds, Sarah E. Twenty Miles from a Match: Homesteading in Western Nevada. LC 78-13766. (Illus.). 200p. 1990. reprint ed. pap. 12.95 (*0-87417-052-4*) U of Nev Pr.

Olds, Sharon. The Dead & the Living. LC 83-47780. (Poetry Ser.: No. 12). 96p. 1984. pap. 13.00 (*0-394-71563-2*) Knopf.

— Father. 1992. pap. 11.00 (*0-679-74002-3*) Knopf.

— Father. 1992. 19.50 (*0-679-41127-5*) Knopf.

— The Gold Cell. 1987. 16.95 (*0-394-55699-2*); pap. 13.00 (*0-394-74770-4*) Knopf.

— Satan Says. LC 79-24300. (Poetry Ser.). 1980. 19.95 (*0-8229-3413-2*); pap. 10.95 (*0-8229-5314-5*) U of Pittsburgh Pr.

— The Wellspring. LC 95-15835. 1996. write for info. (*0-679-44592-7*); pap. write for info. (*0-679-76560-3*) Knopf.

Oldsberg, Jim. The Flip Side, Vol. One: An Illustrated History of Rock & Roll Music - Southern Minnesota. (Illus.). 256p. (Orig.). 1994. pap. 19.95 (*0-911007-30-X*) Prairie Hse.

Oldsey, Bernard. Hemingway's Hidden Craft: The Writing of "A Farewell to Arms" LC 79-743. (Illus.). 1979. 30.00 (*0-271-00213-1*) Pa St U Pr.

Oldsey, Bernard, ed. British Novelists, 1930-1959, 2 vols., Set. (Dictionary of Literary Biography Ser.: Vol. 15). 713p. 1983. pap. 238.00 (*0-8103-1637-4*, 006392-M99348) Gale.

— British Novelists, 1930-1959, 2 Vols., Vol. 15. (Dictionary of Literary Biography Ser.: Vol. 15). (Illus.). 376p. 1983. Set. 250.00 (*0-8103-0938-6*) Gale.

Oldsfield, Wendy, jt. auth. see Davis, Kay.

Oldson, William O. The Historical & Nationalistic Thought of Nicolae Iorga. (East European Monographs: No. 5). 181p. 1974. text ed. 47.50 (*0-231-03747-3*) East Eur Quarterly.

— A Providential Anti-Semitism: Nationalism & Polity in Nineteenth-Century Romania. LC 90-56109. (Memoirs Ser.: Vol. 193). (Illus.). 177p. (Orig.). (C). 1991. pap. 20.00 (*0-87169-193-0*, M193-OLW) Am Philos.

Oldstone, M. B., ed. Molecular Mimicry. (Current Topics in Microbiology & Immunology Ser.: Vol. 145). (Illus.). 145p. 1989. 73.00 (*0-387-50929-1*) Spr-Verlag.

Oldstone, M. B. & Koprowski, Hilary, eds. Retroviruses Infections of the Nervous System. (Current Topics in Microbiology & Immunology Ser.: Vol. 160). (Illus.). 176p. 1990. 88.00 (*0-387-51939-4*) Spr-Verlag.

Oldstone, M. B., jt. ed. see Haase, A. T.

Oldstone, M. B., jt. ed. see Notkinds, A. L.

Oldstone, M. B., jt. ed. see Notkins, A. L.

Oldstone, Michael B., ed. Animal Virus Pathogenesis: A Practical Approach. (Practical Approach Ser.). (Illus.). 192p. 1990. 70.00 (*0-19-963100-X*, IRL Pr); pap. 39.00 (*0-19-963101-8*, IRL Pr) OUP.

Oldt, Franklin T., ed. History of Dubuque County, Iowa. (Illus.). 943p. 1993. reprint ed. lib. bdg. 92.50 (*0-8328-2950-1*) Higginson Bk Co.

***Oldt, Linda.** Mad Money: How to Preserve, Protect & Multiply Your Personal Injury Lawsuit Settlement. Oldt, Thomas R., ed. LC 94-96293. 160p. (Orig.). 1994. pap. 24.95 (*0-9642868-0-7*) Invest Informat.

Oldt, Thomas R., ed. see Oldt, Linda.

Olea, Ricardo A., ed. Geostatistical Glossary & Multilingual Dictionary. (International Association for Mathematical Geology: Studies in Mathematical Geology: No. 3). (Illus.). 192p. 1991. 45.00 (*0-19-506689-8*) OUP.

Olearius, Adam. The Travels of Olearius in Seventeenth-Century Russia. Baron, Samuel H., ed. & tr. by. (Illus.). xvi, 352p. 1967. 49.50 (*0-8047-0219-5*) Stanford U Pr.

O'Leary. Classroom Management. (C). 1977. 63.95 (*0-205-14430-6*, H4430) Allyn.

— Fistful of Art & Craft Ideas: Autumn-Halloween. 1987. pap. 4.95 (*0-86278-126-4*, Pub. by OBrien Pr IE) Dufour.

— Fistful of Art & Craft Ideas: Spring. 1987. pap. 4.95 (*0-86278-128-0*, Pub. by OBrien Pr IE) Dufour.

— Fistful of Art & Craft Ideas: Summer. 1987. pap. 4.95 (*0-86278-125-6*, Pub. by OBrien Pr IE) Dufour.

— Fistful of Art & Craft Ideas: Winter-Christmas. 1987. pap. 4.95 (*0-86278-127-2*, Pub. by OBrien Pr IE) Dufour.

O'Leary, jt. tr. see De Lacey.

***O'Leary, Alice M.** Pigs on the Links: Hidden Hazards for the Woman Golfer. LC 94-77832. (Illus.). 104p. (Orig.). 1994. pap. 11.95 (*0-936485-09-4*) Lkng Glass Pubns.

O'Leary, Arthur F. Construction Administration in Architectural Practice. 288p. 1992. text ed. 48.00 (*0-07-047903-8*) McGraw.

O'Leary, Barrie. A Field Guide to Australian Opals. (Illus.). 159p. 1984. 36.50 (*0-7270-0387-9*, Pub. by NAG Press UK) Antique Collect.

O'Leary, Brendan & McGarry, John. Politics of Antagonism: Explaining Northern Ireland. LC 92-26103. (Conflict & Change in Britain - A New Audit Ser.). 240p. (C). 1993. text ed. 60.00 (*0-485-80003-9*, Pub. by Athlone Pr UK); pap. 19.95 (*0-485-80103-5*, Pub. by Athlone Pr UK) Humanities.

O'Leary, Brendan, jt. auth. see Dunleavy, Patrick.

O'Leary, Brendan, jt. ed. see McCarry, John.

O'Leary, Brendan, jt. auth. see McGarry, John.

O'Leary, Brendan, jt. ed. see McGarry, John.

O'Leary, Brian. Exploring Inner & Outer Space: A Scientist's Perspective on Personal & Planetary Transformation. (Illus.). 240p. (Orig.). 1989. pap. 12.95 (*1-55643-068-X*) North Atlantic.

— The Second Coming of Science: An Intimate Report on the New Science. (Orig.). Date not set. pap. 12.95 (*1-55643-152-X*) North Atlantic.

O'Leary, Brian, ed. Space Industrialization, Vol. I. 176p. 1982. 110.00 (*0-8493-5890-6*, TL797, CRC Reprint) Franklin.

— Space Industrialization, Vol. II. 240p. 1982. 156.00 (*0-8493-5891-4*, CRC Reprint) Franklin.

O'Leary, Cornelius, et al. The Northern Ireland Assembly. LC 88-26420. 280p. 1988. text ed. 45.00 (*0-312-02714-1*) St Martin.

O'Leary, D. L. How Greek Science Passed to the Arabs. 196p. 1979. 20.00 (*0-89005-282-4*) Ares.

O'Leary, Daniel. Audit & Security Issues with Expert Systems. LC 92-28385. (Information Technology Division Research Report Ser.). 1992. write for info. (*0-87051-124-6*) Am Inst CPA.

O'Leary, Daniel E. & Watkins, Paul R. Expert Systems & Artificial Intelligence in Internal Auditing. (Rutgers Series in Accounting Research). 320p. (C). 1994. text ed. 49.95 (*1-55876-086-5*) Wiener Pubs Inc.

— Expert Systems & Artificial Intelligence in Internal Auditing. (Rutgers Series in Accounting Research). 370p. (C). 1995. text ed. 49.95x (*1-66876-086-X*) Wiener Pubs Inc.

O'Leary, Daniel J. Year of the Heart: A Spirituality for Lovers. LC 89-9233. 224p. 1989. pap. 8.95 (*0-8091-3081-5*) Paulist Pr.

O'Leary, De Lacy. Coptic Hymns-Fragments from the Wadi n Narrun, Pt. 1, Translation. pap. 3.95 (*0-89979-008-9*) British Am Bks.

O'Leary, De Lacy E. Arabia Before Muhammad. LC 74-180373. (Illus.). reprint ed. 39.50 (*0-404-56313-9*) AMS Pr.

— Arabic Thought & Its Place in History. rev. ed. LC 80-1917. 1981. reprint ed. 35.00 (*0-404-18982-2*) AMS Pr.

— Islam at the Cross Roads: A Brief Survey of the Present Position & Problems of the World of Islam. LC 80-1916. 1981. reprint ed. 26.50 (*0-404-18983-0*) AMS Pr.

O'Leary, Donal. Creative Crisis: A Spiritual Guide for Mid-Life Men. LC 90-70992. 80p. (Orig.). 1990. pap. 7.95 (*0-89622-450-3*) Twenty-Third.

O'Leary, Donal & Sallnow, Teresa. Religious Education & Young Adults. (C). 1988. 50.00 (*0-85439-229-7*, Pub. by St Paul Pubns UK) St Mut.

***O'Leary, E.** Counseling the Older Patient. 160p. 1995. 41.50 (*1-56593-281-1*, 0605) Singular Publishing.

O'Leary, Eleanor. Gestalt Therapy: Theory, Practice, & Research. LC 92-17085. 1992. write for info. (*1-56593-036-3*) Singular Publishing.

O'Leary, James, Jr., ed. see Jwing-Ming, Yang.

O'Leary, James, ed. see Katchmer, George A., Jr.

O'Leary, James A. Shoulder Dystocia & Birth Injury: Prevention & Treatment. (Illus.). 200p. 1992. pap. text ed. 42.00 (*0-07-105393-X*) Hlth Prof Div.

O'Leary, James J. Stagnation or Healthy Growth? The Economic Challenge to the United States in the Nineties. 162p. (C). 1992. lib. bdg. 34.50 (*0-8191-8839-5*) U Pr of Amer.

O'Leary, James L. & Goldring, Sidney. Science & Epilepsy: Neuroscience Gains in Epilepsy Research. LC 75-21860. 303p. 1976. 62.00 (*0-89004-072-9*) Raven.

O'Leary, Jenifer. Write Your Own Curriculum: A Complete Guide to Planning, Organizing & Documenting Homeschool Curriculums. Ebel, Maureen, ed. LC 93-60801. (Illus.). 130p. (Orig.). 1993. pap. 12.95 (*1-883947-24-3*) Whole Life.

— Write Your Own Curriculum: A Complete Guide to Planning, Organizing & Documenting Homeschool Curriculums, Family. LC 93-60801. (Illus.). 130p. (Orig.). 1994. 29.95 (*1-883947-23-5*) Whole Life.

— Write Your Own Curriculum: A Complete Guide to Planning, Organizing & Documenting Homeschool Curriculums, High School. LC 93-60801. (Illus.). 130p. (Orig.). 1994. student ed 29.95 (*1-883947-22-7*) Whole Life.

— Write Your Own Curriculum: A Complete Guide to Planning, Organizing & Documenting Homeschool Curriculums, Middle Grades. LC 93-60801. (Illus.). 130p. (Orig.). 1994. student ed 29.95 (*1-883947-21-9*) Whole Life.

— Write Your Own Curriculum: A Complete Guide to Planning, Organizing & Documenting Homeschool Curriculums, Primary. LC 93-60801. (Illus.). 130p. (Orig.). 1994. student ed 29.95 (*1-883947-20-0*) Whole Life.

O'Leary, Joan, et al. Winning Strategies for Nursing Managers. (Illus.). 165p. 1986. text ed. 16.95 (*0-397-54541-X*, Lippincott Nursing) Lippincott.

O'Leary, Joanne, jt. auth. see Martinson, Linda.

O'Leary, Joseph, tr. see Dumoulin, Heinrich.

O'Leary, Joseph S., tr. see Dumoulin, Heinrich.

O'Leary, K. D. Assessment of Marital Discord: An Integration for Research & Practice. 392p. 1987. text ed. 79.95 (*0-89859-901-6*) L Erlbaum Assocs.

O'Leary, K. Daniel. Mommy, I Can't Sit Still: Coping with Hyperactive & Aggressive Children. Dunphy, Joan, ed. 132p. 1989. 13.95 (*0-88282-000-1*); pap. 8.95 (*0-88282-055-9*) New Horizon NJ.

O'Leary, K. Daniel & Wilson, G. Terence. Behavior Therapy: Application & Outcome. (Social Learning Theory Ser.). (Illus.). 480p. 1975. write for info. (*0-13-073890-5*) P-H.

— Behavior Therapy: Applications & Outcome. 2nd ed. (Illus.). 512p. (C). 1986. text ed. 44.25 (*0-13-073875-1*) P-H.

O'Leary, K. Daniel, jt. auth. see Wilson, G. Terence.

O'Leary, Lacy E. Arabia Before Mohammed. 1973. 59.95 (*0-87968-651-0*) Gordon Pr.

O'Leary, Lawrence R. Interviewing for the Decisionmaker. LC 75-44322. 144p. 1976. 26.95 (*0-88229-215-3*) Nelson-Hall.

O'Leary, Liam. Rex Ingram: Master of the Silent Cinema. (Illus.). 224p. 1994. pap. 23.95 (*0-85170-443-3*, Pub. by British Film Inst UK) Ind U Pr.

O'Leary, Linda I. & O'Leary, Timothy J. Lotus 1-2-3 for Windows. 208p. 1993. pap. text ed. write for info. (*0-07-048879-7*) McGraw.

— WordPerfect for Windows. 176p. 1993. pap. text ed. write for info. (*0-07-048878-9*) McGraw.

O'Leary, Linda I., jt. auth. see O'Leary, Timothy J.

O'Leary, Linda I., et al. Excel 4.0 for Windows. 208p. 1993. pap. text ed. write for info. (*0-07-048883-5*) McGraw.

— Paradox 4.0. 208p. 1993. pap. text ed. write for info. (*0-07-048882-7*) McGraw.

O'Leary, Linda L., jt. auth. see O'Leary, Timothy J.

O'Leary, Michael. B-17 Flying Fortress. (Osprey Colour Library). (Illus.). 128p. 1992. pap. 15.95 (*1-85532-197-1*, Pub. by Osprey Pubng Ltd UK) Motorbooks Intl.

— Bombing Twins: Allied Medium Bombers. (OCL Ser.). (Illus.). 128p. 1994. 15.95 (*1-85532-312-5*, Pub. by Osprey Pubng Ltd UK) Motorbooks Intl.

— California High: Warbirds of the West Coast. (Wings Ser.: No. 3). (Illus.). 96p. (Orig.). 1992. pap. 17.95 (*1-872004-37-7*) Specialty Pr.

— Douglas C-47 & DC-3 Gooney Birds. (Illus.). 128p. 1992. pap. 19.95 (*0-87938-543-X*) Motorbooks Intl.

— En Route: Label Art from the Golden Age of Air Travel. LC 92-12167. 1992. pap. 14.95 (*0-8118-0045-8*) Chronicle Bks.

— High VIZ U. S. Military Aircraft 1954-1964. (Color Library). (Illus.). 128p. 1994. pap. 15.95 (*1-85532-450-4*, Pub. by Osprey Pubng Ltd UK) Motorbooks Intl.

— Thunderbolt & Lightning. (Osprey Color Library Ser.). (Illus.). 128p. 1995. pap. 15.95 (*1-85532-519-5*) Motorbooks Intl.

O'Leary, Michael & Schulzinger, Eric. SR-71. (Illus.). 128p. 1991. pap. 19.95 (*0-87938-541-3*) Motorbooks Intl.

O'Leary, Michael K., jt. auth. see Coplin, William D.

***O'Leary, Mick.** The Online 100: Online Magazine's Field Guide to the 100 Most Important Online Databases. 256p. 1995. pap. 22.95 (*0-910965-14-5*, Pembrtn Pr Bks) Online.

O'Leary, Minnie, et al. Songs of Self-Esteem. (Illus.). 23p. 1981. pap. 4.95 (*0-9603656-2-1*); audio 10.95 (*0-686-79640-3*); 6.95 (*0-686-79639-X*) Whitenwife Pubns.

O'Leary, Pat W., jt. auth. see Dishon, Dee.

***O'Leary, Patrick.** Door Number Three. 1995. 23.95 (*0-312-85872-8*) Tor Bks.

— Sir James Mackintosh: The Whig Cicero. 224p. 1989. text ed. 29.95 (*0-08-034531-X*, Pub. by Aberdeen U Pr) Macmillan.

O'Leary, Patrick F., jt. auth. see Camins, Martin B.

O'Leary, Patrick F., jt. ed. see Camins, Martin B.

O'Leary, Patrick J. The Physiologic Basis of Surgery. Capote, Lea R., ed. LC 93-17306. (Illus.). 672p. 1993. 95.00 (*0-683-06634-X*) Williams & Wilkins.

***O'Leary, Patsy B.** The Chinaberry Tree. LC 95-1666. (J). 1995. write for info. (*0-395-70557-6*) Ticknor & Flds Bks Yng Read.

O'Leary, Philip. The Prose Literature of the Gaelic Revival, 1881-1921: Ideology & Innovation. LC 92-47013. 544p. (C). 1994. 75.00 (*0-271-01063-0*); pap. 25.00 (*0-271-01064-9*) Pa St U Pr.

O'Leary, Rosemary. Emergency Planning: Local Government & the Community Right-to-Know Act. (Special Report Ser.). 56p. 1993. 21.95 (*0-87326-092-9*) Intl City-Cnty Mgt.

— Environmental Change: Federal courts & the EPA. LC 93-6637. 272p. 1993. Alk pbk. pap. 34.95 (*1-56639-095-8*) Temple U Pr.

O'Leary, Sean C. Christmas Wonder: From Ireland - For Children: Craftwork, Lore, Poems, Songs & Stories. LC 89-50972. (Illus.). 98p. (Orig.). (J). 1989. pap. 12.95 (*0-86278-177-9*, Pub. by OBrien Pr IE) Dufour.

— Whizz Quiz: Quiz & Puzzle Book. (Illus.). 92p. (J). (gr. 2-6). 1993. pap. 7.95 (*0-86278-287-2*, Pub. by OBrien Pr IE) Dufour.

O'Leary, Stephen D. Arguing the Apocalypse: A Theory of Millennial Rhetoric. 336p. 1994. 35.00 (*0-19-508045-9*) OUP.

O'Leary, Timothy, jt. auth. see Murdock, George P.

O'Leary, Timothy J., et al. DOS 5.0: With Introduction to Labs. 1993. pap. text ed. write for info. (*0-07-048877-0*) McGraw.

O'Leary, Timothy J. Ethnographic Bibliography of South America. LC 63-20695. (Bibliographies Ser.). 414p. 1978. pap. 35.00 (*0-87536-224-9*) HRAFP.

— Lotus 1-2-3 Release 2.2. 3rd ed. 1991. text ed. write for info. (*0-07-048808-8*) McGraw.

— MS Works on IBM PC, Release 2.0. 1991. pap. text ed. write for info. (*0-07-048807-X*) McGraw.

O'Leary, Timothy J., et al. Quattro Pro 4.0. 1993. pap. text ed. write for info. (*0-07-048881-9*) McGraw.

O'Leary, Timothy J. Tutorial Guide to Lotus 1-2-3: Release 2.2. 1991. 24.75 (*0-201-50625-4*) Addison-Wesley.

— Tutorial Guide to the Student Edition of Lotus 1-2-3, Release 2.3. (C). 1992. pap. 27.95 (*0-201-50694-7*) Addison-Wesley.

O'Leary, Timothy J., et al. WordStar 4.0. 1992. pap. text ed. write for info. (*0-07-048856-8*) McGraw.

O'Leary, Timothy J., ed. Ethnographic Bibliography of North America: Supplement to the 1975 Edition, 3 vols. (Bibliographies Ser.). 2331p. 1990. text ed. 395.00 (*0-87536-254-0*) HRAFP.

O'Leary, Timothy J. & O'Leary, Linda I. DBASE III Plus. rev. ed. 1993. pap. text ed. write for info. (*0-07-048898-3*) McGraw.

— DOS 6.0. 1994. pap. text ed. write for info. (*0-07-048996-3*) McGraw.

— Lotus 1-2-3, Release 2.2. rev. ed. 1993. pap. text ed. write for info. (*0-07-048897-5*) McGraw.

— Lotus 1-2-3, Release 2.4. 1994. pap. text ed. write for info. (*0-07-048994-7*) McGraw.

— McGraw-Hill Microcomputing Labs: Edition B. 1993. pap. text ed. write for info. (*0-07-048904-1*) McGraw.

— Microcomputing Labs: Edition C, DOS 3.3 - 6.0, WordPerfect 6.0 for DOS, Lotus 1-2-3, Release 2.4, dBASE IV, Version 2.0. 1994. pap. text ed. write for info. (*0-07-048982-3*) McGraw.

— Microcomputing, 1994-1995: DOS 3.3 6.0, WordPerfect 6.0 for DOS, Lotus 1-2-3, Release 2.4, dBASE IV, Version 2.0. 1994. pap. text ed. write for info. (*0-07-048980-7*) McGraw.

— Microsoft Access 1.1. 1994. pap. text ed. write for info. (*0-07-048992-0*) McGraw.

— Microsoft Works 3.0 for DOS. 1994. pap. text ed. write for info. (*0-07-048988-2*) McGraw.

— Paradox for Windows. 1993. pap. text ed. write for info. (*0-07-048892-4*) McGraw.

— WordPerfect 5.1. rev. ed. 1994. pap. text ed. write for info. (*0-07-048896-7*) McGraw.

— WordPerfect 6.0 for DOS. 1994. pap. text ed. write for info. (*0-07-048998-X*) McGraw.

— WordPerfect 6.0 for Windows. 1994. pap. text ed. write for info. (*0-07-049000-7*) McGraw.

O'Leary, Timothy J. & O'Leary, Linda L. The Student Edition of Lotus 1-2-3 Release 2.4. 524p. (C). disk 44.99 (*0-8053-1352-4*); disk 44.99 (*0-8053-1353-2*); disk 44.99 (*0-685-73067-0*) Benjamin-Cummings.

O'Leary, Timothy J. & Williams, Brian K. Computers & Information Systems. 2nd ed. (Illus.). 800p. (C). 1989. teacher ed 11.95 (*0-8053-6944-9*); teacher ed 9.95 (*0-685-44109-1*); student ed 10.95 (*0-8053-6939-2*); teacher ed 11.95 (*0-8053-6948-1*); text ed. 41.95 (*0-8053-6942-2*); student ed, pap. text ed. 11.95 (*0-8053-6946-5*); trans. write for info. (*0-8053-6949-X*) Benjamin-Cummings.

O'Leary, Timothy J., jt. ed. see Levinson, David.

O'Leary, Timothy J., jt. auth. see Murdock, George P.

O'Leary, Timothy J., jt. auth. see O'Leary, Linda I.

O'Leary, Timothy J., jt. ed. see Sweet, Louise E.

O'Leary, Timothy J., et al. DBASE IV, Release 1.1. 1992. pap. text ed. write for info. (*0-07-048814-2*) McGraw.

— Lotus 1-2-3, Release 2.3. 1992. pap. text ed. write for info. (*0-07-048818-5*) McGraw.

— Mc-Graw Hill Microcomputing Labs, 1992-1993. 1992. text ed. write for info. (*0-07-048837-1*) McGraw.

— McGraw-Hill Computing Essentials, 1993-1994. 1993. pap. text ed. write for info. (*0-07-048868-1*) McGraw.

— McGraw-Hill Microcomputing Labs: Annual Edition, 1990. 1990. 7.14 (*0-07-047882-1*) McGraw.

— McGraw-Hill Microcomputing Labs, 1993-1994. 1993. pap. text ed. write for info. (*0-07-048867-3*) McGraw.

— McGraw-Hill Microcomputing, 1993-1994. 1993. pap. text ed. write for info. (*0-07-048866-5*) McGraw.

— Quattro. 1992. text ed. write for info. (*0-07-048839-8*) McGraw.

— SuperCalc IV: Spreadsheet Software, 1990. (Microcomputing Labs Ser.). 1990. pap. write for info. (*0-07-047868-6*) McGraw.

— VP-Planner: Spreadsheet Software, 1990. (Microcomputing Labs Ser.). 1990. pap. write for info. (*0-07-047869-4*) McGraw.

— Windows 3.0. 1992. pap. text ed. write for info. (*0-07-048854-1*) McGraw.

— Windows 3.1. 1993. pap. text ed. write for info. (*0-07-048880-0*) McGraw.

O'Leary, Tomas. The Devil Take a Crooked House. LC 88-1214. 1990. 15.95 (*0-89924-063-1*); pap. 8.00 (*0-89924-055-0*) Lynx Hse.

— Fool at the Funeral. 66p. 1975. pap. 7.00 (*0-89924-001-1*) Lynx Hse.

O'Leary, Vincent, jt. auth. see National Council on Crime.

O'Leary, Virginia, jt. auth. see Lie, Suzanne S.

O'Leary, Virginia, et al, eds. Women, Gender & Social Psychology. 400p. (C). 1985. text ed. 79.95 (*0-89859-447-2*) L Erlbaum Assocs.

***O'Leary, Wayne M.** The Tancook Schooners: An Island & It's Boats. (Illus.). 304p. 1994. 44.95 (*0-7735-1172-5*, Pub. by McGill CN); pap. 17.95 (*0-7735-1206-3*, Pub. by McGill CN) U of Toronto Pr.

O'Leary, William, ed. Practical Handbook of Microbiology. 704p. 1989. 72.95 (*0-8493-3704-6*, QR72) CRC Pr.

Olech. Proceedings of the International Congress of Mathematicians, 2 vols., 1. 1730p. 1985. write for info. (*0-444-86659-0*) Elsevier.

— Proceedings of the International Congress of Mathematicians, 2 vols., 2. 1730p. 1985. write for info. (*0-444-86660-4*) Elsevier.

— Proceedings of the International Congress of Mathematicians, 2 vols., Set, Vols. 1 & 2. 1730p. 1985. Set. 215.50 (*0-444-86661-2*) Elsevier.

Olechno-Huszcza, Gillian, et al, eds. Polish Music Literature (1515-1990) A Selected Annotated Bibliography. (Polish Music History Ser.: No. 4). 240p. 1991. 25.00 (*0-916545-04-0*, ML 120 P6 1991) Friends of Pol Mus.

***Olechowska, Elzbieta & Aster, Howard, eds.** Challenges for International Broadcasting Vol. III: Identity, Economics, Integration. (Illus.). 300p. 1995. lib. bdg. 48.00 (*0-8095-4886-0*) Borgo Pr.

Olechowski, Andrzej, ed. La Ronda Uruguay: Manual Para las Negociaciones Comerciales Multilaterales. Orig. Title: The Uruguay Round: a Handbook for the Multilateral Trade Negotiations. 262p. 1989. 22.95 (*0-8213-1152-2*); Spanish. write for info. (*0-318-65017-7*, BK1152); English. write for info. (*0-318-65018-5*, BK0975); French. write for info. (*0-8213-1151-4*, BK1151) World Bank.

Olechowski, Andrzej, jt. ed. see Finger, J. Michael.

Olechowski, Andrzej, jt. auth. see Finger, Michael.

Oleck, Howard. Law for Living. 1967. 11.95 (*0-685-92669-9*); pap. 8.00 (*0-685-92670-2*) Prof Bks Serv.

Oleck, Howard L. Cumulative Supplement to Nonprofit Corporations, Organizations & Associations. 5th ed. 250p. 1990. pap. 39.95 (*0-13-626946-X*) P-H.

— Debtor-Creditor Law: A Treatise. (Business Enterprises Reprint Ser.). xi, 474p. 1986. reprint ed. lib. bdg. 47.50 (*0-89941-480-X*, 304080) W S Hein.

— Lion of Islam. (Orig.). 1980. pap. 1.95 (*0-89083-615-9*) Zebra.

— Non-Profit Corporations, Organizations, & Associations. 4th ed. 1251p. 1980. 59.95 (*0-685-03913-7*, Busn) P-H.

— Nonprofit Corporations, Organizations, & Associations. 5th ed. 1216p. 1988. 79.95 (*0-13-623380-5*) P-H.

— Parliamentary Law for Nonprofit Organizations. 160p. 1979. pap. 5.00 (*0-317-31049-6*, B229) Am Law Inst.

— Trends in Nonprofit Organizations Law. 176p. 1977. pap. 5.00 (*0-317-31050-X*, B227/B228) Am Law Inst.

Oleck, Howard L. & Green, Cami. Parliamentary Law & Practice for Nonprofit Organizations. 2nd ed. LC 91-72549. 180p. 1991. pap. 50.00 (*0-8318-0598-6*, B598) Am Law Inst.

Oleck, Howard L. & Steart, Martha E. Nonprofit Corporations, Organizations & Associations. 6th ed. LC 93-47544. 1994. 99.95 (*0-13-121310-5*) P-H.

Oleck, Jack. The Villagers. 5.95 (*0-8184-0117-6*) Carol Pub Group.

Olefsky, Jerrold M. & Robbins, Richard J., eds. Prolactinomas. (Contemporary Issues in Endocrinology & Metabolism Ser.: Vol. 2). (Illus.). 230p. 1985. text ed. 42.00 (*0-443-08406-8*) Churchill.

Olefsky, Jerrold M. & Sherwin, Robert S., eds. Diabetes Mellitus: Management & Complications. (Contemporary Issues in Endocrinology & Metabolism Ser.: Vol. 1). (Illus.). 399p. 1985. text ed. 50.00 (*0-443-08379-7*) Churchill.

— Diabetes Mellitus: Management & Complications. fac. ed. LC 84-29258. (Contemporary Issues in Endocrinology & Metabolism Ser.). (Illus.). 413p. 1985. reprint ed. pap. 117.80 (*0-7837-7899-6*, 2047655) Bks Demand.

Olefsky, Jerrold M., jt. ed. see Manolagas, Stavros C.

Olefsky, Jerrold M., jt. ed. see Manolagas, Stavros.

Olefsky, Jerrold M., jt. ed. see Steinberg, Daniel.

Oleinick, Peter N. Parallel Algorithms on a Multiprocessor. LC 82-4954. (Computer Science: Systems Programming Ser.: No. 4). 124p. reprint ed. pap. 35.40 (*0-685-20847-8*, 2070079) Bks Demand.

Oleinik, O. A., ed. Topics in Modern Mathematics: Petrovskii Seminar, No. 5. LC 84-14291. (Contemporary Soviet Mathematics Ser.). 346p. 1985. 110.00 (*0-306-10980-8*, Consultants) Plenum.

Oleinik, O. A., et al. Mathematical Problems in Elasticity & Homogenization. LC 92-15390. (Studies in Mathematics & Its Applications: Vol. 26). 1992. write for info. (*0-444-88441-6*, North Holland) Elsevier.

***Oleinik, Olga.** Some Asymptotic Problems in the Theory of Partial Differential Equations. (Lezioni Lincee Lectures). 176p. (C). 1995. write for info. (*0-521-48083-3*); pap. write for info. (*0-521-48537-1*) Cambridge U Pr.

Olejniczak, Verena. Wirkungsstrukturen in Ausgewahlten Texten T. S. Eliots und Virginia Woolfs. (Anglistische und Amerikanistische Texte und Studien Ser.: No. 3). 385p. 1987. write for info. (*3-487-07885-6*, Pub. by Georg Olms GW) Lubrecht & Cramer.

Olejnik, Irena, ed. see Riggs, Anne & Farmer, Bev.

Olejnik, Renee M. & Masters, Marie, eds. Rules for Inboard, Inboard Endurance & Unlimited Racing, 1989. 98p. 1990. 10.00 (*0-318-41009-5*) Am Power Boat.

— Rules for Offshore Racing, 1989. 62p. 1990. 10.00 (*0-318-41010-9*) Am Power Boat.

— Rules for Stock Outboard, PRO Outboard, Modified Outboard, & Outboard Performance Craft, 1989. 86p. 1990. 5.00 (*0-318-41011-7*) Am Power Boat.

Oleksa, Michael. Alaskan Missionary Spirituality. (Sources of American Spirituality Ser.: Vol. 6). 416p. 1987. 18.95 (*0-8091-0386-9*) Paulist Pr.

Oleksa, Michael J. Orthodox Alaska: A Theology of Mission. LC 92-37026. 1993. 10.95 (*0-88141-092-6*) St Vladimirs.

Oleksak, Mary A., jt. auth. see Oleksak, Michael M.

Oleksak, Michael M. & Oleksak, Mary A. Beisbol: Latin Americans & the Grand Old Game. LC 91-10697. (Illus.). 320p. 1991. 22.95 (*0-940279-35-5*) Masters Pr IN.

Oleksiw, Andrew. A Guide to Analyzing Foreign Banks. Burke, Sarah A., ed. LC 88-23611. 64p. (Orig.). 1988. pap. text ed. 37.00 (*0-936742-57-7*, 34041) Robt Morris Assocs.

***Oleksiw, Susan.** Family Album: Mellingham Mystery. LC 94-19679. Date not set. 20.00 (*0-684-19731-6*, Scribners) S&S Trade.

— Readers Guide to Classic British Mysteries. 1989. 19.95 (*0-89296-968-7*) Mysterious Pr.

Oleksiw, Susan P. Double Take: A Mellingham Mystery. 256p. 1994. text ed. 20.00 (*0-684-19656-5*, Scribners) S&S Trade.

— Murder in Mellingham: A Mystery Introducing Joe Silva. 288p. 1993. text ed. 20.00 (*0-684-19528-3*, Scribners) S&S Trade.

— A Reader's Guide to the Classic British Mystery. 300p. 1988. text ed. 35.00 (*0-8161-8787-8*, Hall Reference) Macmillan.

Oleksowicz, Ruth J., jt. auth. see Blair, Jane.

Oleksy, Elzbieta. Plight in Common: Hawthorne & Percy. LC 92-4487. (American University Studies: American Literature: Ser. XXIV, Vol. 34). 244p. (C). 1993. text ed. 35.95 (*0-8204-1848-X*) P Lang Pubs.

Oleksy, Elzbieta, jt. ed. see Lawson, Lewis A.

***Oleksy, Elzbieta, ed.** American Cultures: Assimilation & Multiculturalism. 1995. pap. 39.95 (*1-57309-012-3*) Intl Scholars.

— American Cultures: Assimilation & Multiculturalism. 264p. 1995. 64.95 (*1-57309-013-1*) Intl Scholars.

Oleksy, Walter. Entertainers. (Faces of America Ser.). (Illus.). 128p. (J). (gr. 3-6). Date not set. 19.95 (*1-56065-120-2*) Capstone Pr.

— Experiments with Heat. LC 85-30860. (New True Bks.). (Illus.). 48p. (J). (gr. k-4). 1986. lib. bdg. 12.90 (*0-516-01277-0*); pap. 4.95 (*0-516-41277-9*) Childrens.

— Inventors. (Faces of America Ser.). (Illus.). 128p. (J). (gr. 3-6). Date not set. 19.95 (*1-56065-118-0*) Capstone Pr.

— Mikhail Gorbachev: A Leader for Soviet Change. LC 88-36960. (People of Distinction Ser.). (Illus.). 152p. (J). (gr. 4 up). 1989. lib. bdg. 14.40 (*0-516-03265-8*) Childrens.

— Military Leaders of World War II. LC 93-33641. (American Profiles Ser.). (Illus.). 128p. (YA). (gr. 4-11). 1994. 16.95 (*0-8160-3008-1*) Facts on File.

— Musicians. (Faces of America Ser.). (Illus.). 128p. (J). (gr. 3-6). Date not set. 19.95 (*0-685-57489-X*) Capstone Pr.

— The Old Country Cookbook: Recipes from Thirty-One Countries. LC 73-81082. 416p. 1974. 27.95 (*0-88229-105-X*) Nelson-Hall.

— Science & Medicine. (Information Revolution Ser.). (Illus.). 128p. (J). (gr. 5-12). 1995. 17.95x (*0-8160-3076-6*) Facts on File.

— Sports Legends. (Faces of America Ser.). (Illus.). 128p. (J). (gr. 3-6). Date not set. 19.95 (*1-56065-121-0*) Capstone Pr.

Oleksy, Walter, jt. auth. see Emerson, Larry.

Oleksy, Walter, jt. auth. see Kozlowski, Joseph G.

Oleksy, Wieslaw, ed. Contrastive Pragmatics. LC 88-7613. (Pragmatics & Beyond New Ser.: Vol. 3). xiii, 282p. (C). 1989. 83.00x (*1-55619-050-6*) Benjamins North Am.

Oleksy, Wieslaw & Swan, Oscar E. W Labiryncie (Labyrinth of Life) An Advanced Polish Course. (Illus.). xiv, 378p. (Orig.). (C). 1993. pap. text ed. 22.95 (*0-89357-242-X*) Slavica.

Olem, H., ed. Diffuse Pollution. (Water Science & Technology Ser.: Vol. 28). 722p. 1993. pap. 335.00 (*0-08-042345-0*) Elsevier.

Olem, Harvey. Liming Acidic Surface Waters. (Illus.). 200p. 1990. 89.95 (*0-87371-243-9*, TD427) Lewis Pubs.

Olema, A. History of Evangelical Christianity in Russia. 7.00 (*1-56632-082-8*) Revival Lit.

Olemskoi, Al, jt. ed. see Katsnel'son, A. A.

Olen, Dale R. Accepting Yourself: Liking Yourself All of the Time. (Illus.). 64p. (Orig.). 1992. pap. 5.95 (*1-56583-005-9*) Life Skills WI.

— Being Intimate: Achieving Union with Others Without Losing Yourself. (Illus.). 60p. (Orig.). 1992. pap. 5.95 (*1-56583-008-3*) Life Skills WI.

— Communicating: Speaking & Listening to End Misunderstanding & Promote Friendship. (Illus.). 60p. (Orig.). 1992. pap. 5.95 (*1-56583-007-5*) Life Skills WI.

— Defeating Depression: Lifting Yourself from Sadness into Joy. (Illus.). 60p. (Orig.). 1992. pap. 5.95 (*1-56583-011-3*) Life Skills WI.

— Managing Stress: Learning to Pace Your Chase Through Life. 64p. (Orig.). 1992. pap. write for info. (*1-56583-003-2*) Life Skills WI.

— Overcoming Fear: Reaching for Your Dreams & Knowing Peace of Mind. (Illus.). 62p. (Orig.). 1992. pap. 5.95 (*1-56583-010-5*) Life Skills WI.

— Parenting for the First Time. 1994. pap. 8.95 (*1-56583-015-6*) Life Skills WI.

— Reducing Anger: Harnessing Passion & Fury to Work for You - Not Against Others. (Illus.). 64p. (Orig.). 1992. pap. text ed. 5.95 (*1-56583-009-1*) Life Skills WI.

— Resolving Conflict: Learning How You Both Can Win & Keep Your Relationship. (Illus.). 60p. (Orig.). 1992. pap. text ed. 5.95 (*1-56583-012-1*) Life Skills WI.

— The Thoughtful Art of Discipline: Teaching Responsibility When Your Child Misbehaves. (Life Skills Parenting Ser.). (Illus.). 128p. (Orig.). 1994. pap. 8.95 (*1-56583-014-8*) Life Skills WI.

Olen, Dale R., illus. Meeting Life Head On: Moving into Life with Courage - Not Backing Away in Fear. 60p. (Orig.). 1992. pap. 5.95 (*1-56583-006-7*) Life Skills WI.

— Thinking Reasonably: Reaching Emotional Peace Through Mental Toughness. 60p. (Orig.). 1992. pap. 5.95 (*1-56583-004-0*) Life Skills WI.

Olen, Jeffrey. Moral Freedom. LC 88-15916. 149p. (C). 1988. 27.95 (*0-87722-578-8*) Temple U Pr.

— Persons & Their World: An Introduction to Philosophy. 608p. (C). 1983. text ed. write for info. (*0-07-554311-7*) McGraw.

Olen, Jeffrey & Barry, Vincent. Applying Ethics: A Text with Readings. 4th ed. 470p. (C). 1992. pap. 34.95 (*0-534-16470-6*) Intl Thomson.

— Applying Ethics: A Text with Readings. 5th ed. LC 95-11852. 1996. pap. 35.95 (*0-534-26316-X*) Intl Thomson.

Olen, Stephanie, jt. auth. see Giangrande, Patricia.

Olenchak, F. Richard. Digging Through Archaeology. (Triad Prototype Ser.). 36p. 1989. pap. 8.95 (*0-936386-49-5*) Creative Learning.

Olencki, Mark, jt. auth. see Gould, Scott.

Olender, Maurice. The Languages of Paradise: Race, Religion, & Philology in the Nineteenth Century. Goldhammer, Arthur, tr. 193p. (C). 1992. 32.00 (*0-674-51052-6*) HUP.

Olendorf. Something about the Author, Vol. 63. 1991. 87.00 (*0-8103-2273-0*) Gale.

— Something about the Author, Vol. 64. 1991. 87.00 (*0-8103-2274-9*) Gale.

Olendorf, Bill. Paris Sketchbook: An American Retrospective of a Beautiful City. (Sketchbook Ser.). (Illus.). 144p. 1990. 40.00 (*0-923078-02-9*) Olendorf Graph.

Olendorf, Donna, ed. Something about the Author, Vol. 65. 1991. 87.00 (*0-8103-2275-7*) Gale.

— Something about the Author, Vol. 66. 1991. 87.00 (*0-8103-2276-5*) Gale.

Olendorf, Donna, ed. see Commire, Anne.

Olendorf, Donna, jt. ed. see McMurray, Emily J.

Olendzenski, Lorraine, jt. ed. see Margulis, Lynn.

Olenick, Arnold & Olenick, Phil, eds. Making the Non-Profit Organization Work: A Legal & Accounting Guide for Administrators. LC 83-12885. 416p. 1983. 49.95 (*0-87624-354-5*, Inst Busn Plan) P-H.

Olenick, Arnold J. Managing to Have Profits: The Secrets Japan Learned but the U. S. Forgot. (Illus.). xii, 210p. 1992. reprint ed. 24.95 (*1-880561-00-X*); reprint ed. pap. 14.95 (*0-685-44092-3*) CashFlow.

Olenick, Arnold J. & Olenick, Philip R. Nonprofit Organization Operating Manual: Planning for Survival & Growth. LC 91-12292. (Orig.). 1991. pap. text ed. 29.95 (*0-87954-293-4*) Foundation Ctr.

Olenick, Phil, jt. ed. see Olenick, Arnold.

Olenick, Philip R., jt. auth. see Olenick, Arnold J.

Olenick, Rhoda & Prarie, Arleen. The Developing Child. rev. ed. 110p. 1991. student ed 18.50 (*1-55740-186-1*) Magna Systems.

Olenick, Susan. The Real Estate License Examination Review Program for the ASI Exam. 62p. 1990. pap. text ed. 50.00 (*0-13-291733-5*) P-H.

Oler, J. W. & Jordan, D. P. GRPHX: A High-Level System of Graphics Rountines Version 1.6. (Illus.). (C). 1989. pap. 9.95 (*0-89672-195-7*) Tex Tech Univ Pr.

Olerich, Henry. Cityless & Countryless World: An Outline of Practical Cooperative Individualism. LC 73-154455. (Utopian Literature Ser.). 1976. reprint ed. 35.95 (*0-405-03537-3*) Ayer.

Olerud, Lesley A., jt. auth. see Morse, Jerome G.

Olerup, A., et al, eds. Women, Work & Computerization: Opportunities & Disadvantages: Proceedings of the IFIP WG9.1 First Working Conference on Women, Work & Computerization, Riva del Sole, Tuscany, Italy, Sept. 17-21, 1984. 372p. 1986. 69.25 (*0-444-87864-5*, North Holland) Elsevier.

Oles, Carole. Coming into the United Society of Believers. (Sansfolio Ser.: 2). (Illus.). (Orig.). 1978. pap. 1.75 (*0-913282-13-8*) Seven Woods Pr.

— The Loneliness Factor. LC 78-24746. 82p. 1979. 7.95 (*0-89672-072-1*) Tex Tech Univ Pr.

— Night Watches: Inventions on the Life of Maria Mitchell. LC 85-70621. 72p. 1985. 15.95 (*0-914086-56-1*); pap. 9.95 (*0-914086-57-X*) Alicejamesbooks.

Oles, Carole S. The Deed: Poems by Carole Simmons Oles. LC 91-3931. 72p. 1991. text ed. 14.95 (*0-8071-1701-3*); pap. 7.95 (*0-8071-1702-1*) La State U Pr.

Oles, James. South of the Border: Mexico in the American Imagination, 1914-1947. LC 92-41507. (Illus.). 352p. 1993. 75.00 (*1-56098-294-2*); pap. 29.95 (*1-56098-295-0*) Smithsonian.

Oles, James, tr. see Debroise, Olivier.

Olesen, Asta. Afghan Craftsmen: The Cultures of Three Itinerant Communities. LC 94-60295. (Carlsberg Nomad Ser.). (Illus.). 320p. 1994. 50.00 (*0-500-01612-7*) Thames Hudson.

— Islam & Politics in Afghanistan. 350p. (C). 1995. text ed. 75.00 (*0-7007-0299-7*, Pub. by Curzon Pr UK) Humanities.

— Islam & Politics in Afghanistan. (Scandinavian Institute of Asian Studies Monograph: No. 67). 350p. (C). 1995. pap. 37.50 (*0-7007-0296-2*, Pub. by Curzon Pr UK) Humanities.

Olesen, Dave. Cold Nights, Fast Trails. 224p. 1989. 16.95 (*1-55971-041-1*, 0184) NorthWord.

Olesen, David. North of Reliance: A Personal Story of Living Beyond the Wilderness. (Illus.). 176p. 1994. pap. write for info. (*1-55971-433-6*) NorthWord.

***Olesen, Eric.** The Little Sailboat & the Big Storm. LC 94-70627. (Illus.). 40p. (J). (gr. k-3). 1994. 17.95 (*0-9636274-5-7*) Coming Age Pr.

***Olesen, Erik.** The Little Sailboat & the Big Storm. LC 94-70627. (Illus.). 40p. (J). (gr. k-3). 1994. pap. 8.95 (*1-885340-04-4*) Coming Age Pr.

— Mastering the Winds of Change: Peak Performers Reveal How to Stay on Top in Times of Turmoil. Orig. Title: Twelve Steps to Mastering the Winds of Change. 272p. 1994. reprint ed. pap. 12.00 (*0-88730-692-6*) Harper Busn.

— Twelve Steps to Mastering the Winds of Change: Peak Performers Reveal How to Stay on Top in Times of Turmoil. LC 92-39486. 251p. 1993. text ed. 20.00 (*0-89256-357-5*, Rawson Assocs) Macmillan.

Olesen, J. & Edvinsson, Lars, eds. Basic Mechanisms of Headache: Pain Research & Clinical Management, 2, 1988. 508p. 1988. 192.50 (*0-444-80955-4*) Elsevier.

Olesen, Jens. Snail. LC 86-10084. (Stopwatch Ser.). (Illus.). 25p. (J). (gr. k-4). 1986. 6.95 (*0-382-09304-6*); lib. bdg. 9.95 (*0-382-09289-9*); pap. 3.95 (*0-382-24019-7*) Silver Pr.

Olesen, Jes. Migraine & Other Headaches: The Vascular Mechanisms. (Frontiers in Headache Research Ser.: Vol. 1). 368p. 1991. 99.50 (*0-88167-795-7*) Raven.

Olesen, Jes, ed. Headache Classification & Epidemiology. LC 94-15738. (Frontiers in Headache Research Ser.: Vol. 4). 416p. 1994. 89.00 (*0-7817-0195-3*) Raven.

***Olesen, Jes & Moskowitz, Michael A., eds.** Experimental Headache Models. LC 95-12054. (Frontiers in Headache Research Ser.: Vol. 5). 1995. write for info. (*0-7817-0330-1*) Raven.

Olesen, Jes & Saxena, Pramod R., eds. Five-Hydroxytryptamine Mechanisms in Primary Headaches. LC 92-17140. (Frontiers in Headache Research Ser.: Vol. 2). 384p. 1992. 100.00 (*0-88167-927-5*) Raven.

Olesen, Jes & Schoenen, Jean, eds. Tension-Type Headache: Classification, Mechanisms, & Treatment. LC 93-19572. (Frontiers in Headache Research Ser.: Vol. 3). 1993. 100.00 (*0-7817-0070-1*) Raven.

Olesen, Jes, et al, eds. The Headaches. LC 93-19517. 928p. 1993. 173.50 (*0-7817-0069-8*) Raven.

Olesen, Sigrid. Summer Is from Winter Until Winter. (Illus.). 80p. (C). 1980. 4.95 (*0-936748-02-8*); pap. 3.50 (*0-685-01610-2*) Fade In.

Olesen, Virginia & Woods, Nancy F., eds. Culture, Society & Menstruation. LC 66-55252. 186p. 1986. 41.00 (*0-89116-557-6*) Hemisp Pub.

Olesen, Virginia L. & Whittaker, Elvi W. The Silent Dialogue: A Study in the Social Psychology of Professional Socialization. LC 68-21320. (Jossey-Bass Behavioral Science Ser.). 328p. reprint ed. pap. 93.50 (*0-317-41981-1*, 2025678) Bks Demand.

Olesha, Yury. Envy. Berczynski, Thomas, tr. (Orig.). 1979. pap. 9.95 (*0-88233-091-8*) Ardis Pubs.

***Oleske, Denise M., ed.** Epidemiology & the Delivery of Health Care Services: Methods & Applications. 230p. 1995. 45.00 (*0-306-44968-4*) Plenum.

Olesker, Jack. Confessional. 368p. (Orig.). 1990. pap. 3.95 (*0-8439-2949-9*) Dorchester Pub Co.

***Olesker, Michael.** Michael Olesker's Baltimore: If You Live Here, You're Home. 176p. 1995. 22.95 (*0-8018-5203-X*) Johns Hopkins.

Oleski, Frank. World Sports Cars. (Illus.). 468p. 1990. 195.00 (*3-907004-02-7*, 3-AQ-0060) Auto Quarterly.

Olesko, Kathryn M. Physics As a Calling: Discipline & Practice in the Konigsberg Seminar for Physics. LC 90-55717. (History of Science Ser.). (Illus.). 496p. 1991. 46.50 (*0-8014-2248-5*) Cornell U Pr.

Olesky, J. & Rutkowski, George B. Microprocessor & Digital Computer Technology. 1981. text ed. 54.00 (*0-13-581116-3*) P-H.

***Olesky, Rio.** Astrology & Consciousness. (Illus.). 384p. (Orig.). 1995. pap. 14.95 (*1-56184-123-4*) New Falcon Pubns.

Olesky, Walter. Boston Tea Party. LC 92-26247. (First Bks.). (Illus.). 64p. (J). (gr. 4-6). 1993. lib. bdg. 13.93 (*0-531-20147-3*) Watts.

— Education & Learning. LC 94-45246. 128p. 1995. 17.95 (*0-8160-3074-X*) Facts on File.

An Asterisk (*) at the beginning of an entry indicates that the title is appearing in BIP for the first time.

O

Oleson, Alexandra & Brown, Sanborn C., eds. The Pursuit of Knowledge in the Early American Republic: American Scientific & Learned Societies from Colonial Times to the Civil War. LC 75-36941. 400p. reprint ed. pap. 114.00 (*0-8357-8294-8*, 2034117) Bks Demand.

Oleson, Alexandra & Voss, John, eds. The Organization of Knowledge in Modern America, 1860-1920. LC 78-20521. 503p. reprint ed. pap. 143.40 (*0-317-51974-3*, 2027375) Bks Demand.

Oleson, Amy. Love & Memory. LC 91-214292. 224p. (Orig.). 1991. pap. 9.95 (*0-933216-85-8*) Spinsters Ink.

Oleson, Emery. How to Create/Market/Operate a Mini Storage Complex. rev. ed. LC 93-92654. (Illus.). 84p. 1993. vinyl bd. write for info. (*0-9636920-0-3*) Ole & Co.

Oleson, John P. Greek & Roman Mechanical Water-Lifting Devices: The History of Technology. (Phoenix Supplementary Volumes Ser.: Vol. 16). (Illus.). 624p. 1984. 95.00 (*0-8020-5597-4*) U of Toronto Pr.

Oleson, Terry. Auriculotherapy Manual: Chinese & Western Systems of Ear Acupuncture. (Illus.). 178p. 1990. pap. 35.00 (*0-9629415-0-6*) Hlth Care Altern.

Oleson, Trygovi J. The Witenagemot in the Reign of Edward the Confessor: A Study in the Constitutional History of Eleventh-Century England. LC 80-2217. 1981. reprint ed. 32.50 (*0-404-18769-2*) AMS Pr.

Oleson, W. B., jt. auth. see Stevens, John L.

Oleszczuk, Thomas. Political Justice in the Soviet Union: Dissent & Repression in Lithuania, 1969-1987. (East European Monographs: No. 247). 240p. 1988. text ed. 45.00 (*0-88033-144-5*) East Eur Quarterly.

Oleszek, Walter. Congressional Procedures: The Policy Process. 3rd ed. 330p. 1988. 35.95 (*0-87187-487-3*); pap. 23.95 (*0-87187-477-6*) Congr Quarterly.

Oleszek, Walter J., jt. auth. see Davidson, Roger H.

***Oleszewski, Wes.** Ghost Ships, Gales & Forgotten Tales. LC 95-79791. (Illus.). 1995. pap. 12.95 (*0-932212-83-2*) Avery Color.

— Ice Water Museum. (Illus.). 152p. 1993. 11.95 (*0-932212-78-6*) Avery Color.

— Sounds of Disaster. LC 92-75915. (Illus.). 144p. 1993. pap. 11.95 (*0-932212-76-X*) Avery Color.

Oleszowksi, Wes. Stormy Seas. 2nd ed. LC 90-86206. 1991. pap. 11.95 (*0-932212-67-0*) Avery Color.

Olev, Kulno. English-Estonian-Russian Maritime Dictionary. 560p. (ENG, EST & RUS.). 1981. 70.00 (*0-686-82322-2*, Pub. by Collets UK) St Mut.

— Maritime Dictionary. 560p. (ENG, EST & RUS.). 1981. 50.00 (*0-686-44731-X*, Pub. by Collets UK) Pro-Am Music.

— Maritime Dictionary English-Estonian-Russian. 560p. (ENG, EST & RUS.). 1981. 35.00 (*0-8288-0430-3*, M 15461) Fr & Eur.

***Olevianus, Caspar.** A Firm Foundation: An Aid to Interpreting the Heidelberg Cathechism. Bierma, Lyle D., ed. & tr. by. LC 95-12360. (Texts & Studies in Reformation & Post-Reformation Thought: Vol. 1). 178p. 1995. pap. 16.99 (*0-8010-2022-0*) Baker Bk.

O'Levin, Marcia. Baby's First Year. 1992. 8.99 (*0-517-07010-3*) Random Hse Value.

— The Bride's Book. 1992. 8.99 (*0-517-07008-1*) Random Hse Value.

***Olevitch, Barbara A.** Cognitive Approaches to the Seriously Mentally Ill: Dialogue Across the Barrier. LC 95-6348. 192p. 1995. text ed. 55.00 (*0-275-95244-4*, Praeger Pubs) Greenwood.

Olevnik, Peter P. American Higher Education: A Guide to Reference Sources. LC 93-25015. (Bibliographies & Indexes in Education Ser.: No. 12). 232p. 1993. text ed. 55.00 (*0-313-27749-4*, OHU/, Greenwood Pr) Greenwood.

Olexy, Ronald T., et al. Cantus - An Aquitanian Antiphoner: Toledo, Biblioteca Capitular, 44.2. (Wissenschaftliche Abhandlungen-Musicological Studies: Vol. 55, Pt. 1). 185p. 1992. 80.00 (*0-931902-71-1*) Inst Mediaeval Mus.

***Oleynik, Igor S.** Russian Regional Investment & Business Guide: Stategic Information & Data for Corporate Executives on Russia. 1995. pap. 59.00 (*0-9646241-1-7*) Russ Info & Busn Ctr.

Oleynik, Nick, jt. auth. see Chiarella, Don.

Oleynikol, Nikolai. Fronichiskie Stikhi: Fronical Verses. 2nd ed. Poliak, Gregory, ed. (Illus.). 96p. (Orig.). (RUS.). pap. 8.00 (*0-940294-04-4*) Silver Age Pub.

Olf, Lillian. Their Name Is Pius. LC 74-107729. (Essay Index Reprint Ser.). 1977. 30.95 (*0-8369-1768-5*) Ayer.

***Olfe, Daniel B.** Computer Graphics for Design: From Algorithms to AutoCAD. LC 94-28190. 544p. 1995. text ed. 52.00 (*0-13-159583-0*) P-H.

Olfe, Julie T., ed. see Andrews, Lawrence F.

Olff, M., et al, eds. Quantification of Human Defense Mechanisms. (Recent Research in Psychology Ser.). (Illus.). vi, 327p. 1991. pap. 59.00 (*0-387-53821-6*) Spr-Verlag.

Olford, A. Stephen. A Graca de Dar. Orig. Title: The Grace of Giving. 128p. (POR.). 1986. 3.95 (*0-8297-1602-5*) Life Pubs Intl.

Olford, Stephen. The Secret of Soul Winning. 126p. (Orig.). 1994. pap. 7.99 (*1-56043-800-2*) Destiny Image.

Olford, Stephen F. Believing Our Beliefs: Preaching on the Foundations & Evidence for New Life. (Stephen Olford Biblical Preaching Library). 112p. 1991. pap. 6.99 (*0-8010-6720-0*) Baker Bk.

— Biblical Answers to Personal Problems. (Olford Biblical Preaching Library). 112p. 1991. pap. 6.99 (*0-8010-6718-9*) Baker Bk.

— Committed to Christ & His Church. (Olford Biblical Preaching Library). 144p. 1991. pap. 6.99 (*0-8010-6717-0*) Baker Bk.

— Fresh Lessons from Former Leaders. (Olford Biblical Preaching Library). 128p. 1991. pap. 6.99 (*0-8010-6719-7*) Baker Bk.

— The Grace of Giving: Biblical Expositions. 2nd rev. ed. 119p. 1990. pap. 7.95 (*1-879028-00-X*) Encounter Minist.

— Living Words & Loving Deeds: Messages on Christ's Claims & Miracles in the Gospel of John. (Stephen Olford Biblical Preaching Library). 128p. 1991. pap. 6.99 (*0-8010-6721-9*) Baker Bk.

— Not I, But Christ. LC 94-41421. 192p. 1995. 14.99 (*0-89107-801-0*) Crossway Bks.

— The Pulpit & the Christian Calendar. (Olford Biblical Preaching Library). 128p. 1991. pap. 6.99 (*0-8010-6716-2*) Baker Bk.

— The Pulpit & the Christian Calendar, No. 2. (Stephen Olford Biblical Preaching Library). 128p. 1991. pap. 6.99 (*0-8010-6722-7*) Baker Bk.

— The Pulpit & the Christian Calendar, No. 3. (Stephen Olford Biblical Preaching Library). 128p. 1991. pap. 6.99 (*0-8010-6723-5*) Baker Bk.

— The Tabernacle: Camping with God. LC 78-173686. 1971. 14.99 (*0-87213-675-2*) Loizeaux.

Olga, J. S. Passengers on My Train: Three Journeys. 144p. 1993. pap. 7.95 (*1-883683-00-9*) Metropolis Pubs.

— Remnants of Receding Tears: Narrative Poems. 58p. 1993. pap. 5.95 (*1-883683-99-8*) Metropolis Pubs.

— What Was & Could Be: Narrative Poems. 48p. 1993. pap. 5.95 (*1-883683-06-8*) Metropolis Pubs.

Olgaard, P. L. & Petersen, R. Interpretation of Borehold Logging Data by Use of Theoretical Models for the..., No. EUR 12534. 55p. 1990. pap. 6.00 (*92-826-1012-8*, CD-NA-12534-EN-) UNIPUB.

Olgin, M. J., ed. see Trotsky, Lev D.

Ol'gin, Olgert, jt. auth. see Krivitch, Mikhail.

Olgivie-Gordon, Maria M., tr. see Von Zittel, K. A.

Olgyay. Safety Symbols. 1994. pap. 49.95 (*0-442-01844-4*) Van Nos Reinhold.

Olgyay, Aladar. Solar Control & Shading Devices. LC 57-5455. (Illus.). 208p. reprint ed. pap. 59.30 (*0-8357-3703-9*, 2036428) Bks Demand.

Olgyay, Victor. Design with Climate: A Bioclimatic Approach to Architectural Regionalism. (Illus.). 200p. 1992. pap. 29.95 (*0-442-01110-5*) Van Nos Reinhold.

Olhausen, Pam, jt. auth. see Russo, Ron.

Olhoff, N., jt. ed. see Eschenauer, H. A.

Olhovych, Orest, ed. An Interview with Political Prisoners in a Soviet Perm Camp. 2nd ed. Drozd, Taras, tr. (Documents of Ukrainian Samvydav Ser.: No. 2). 1978. 1.00 (*0-686-58232-2*) Smoloskyp.

Olhovych, Orest, jt. ed. see Harasowska, Marta.

Oli, G. C., jt. ed. see Devoto, G.

Olian, Helen. The Aliens: Cartoons by Olian. LC 92-30135. (Illus.). 1992. 5.95 (*0-926524-21-6*, Wild Flower Pr) Blue Wtr Pubng.

Olian, Joanne. Everyday Fashions of the Forties As Pictured in Sears Catalogs. (Illus.). 1991. pap. 9.95 (*0-486-26918-3*) Dover.

Olian, JoAnne, ed. Authentic French Fashions of the Twenties. 144p. 1990. pap. 7.95 (*0-486-26187-5*) Dover.

— Everyday Fashions, 1910-1920, as Pictured in Sears Catalogs. (Illus.). 144p. 1995. pap. 11.95 (*0-486-28628-2*) Dover.

— Wedding Fashions, 1860-1912: Three Hundred Eighty Designs from "La Mode Illustree" (Illus.). 96p. 1994. reprint ed. pap. text ed. 10.95 (*0-486-27882-4*) Dover.

Olian, JoAnne, intro. Children's Fashions, 1860-1912: One Thousand Sixty-Five Costume Designs from "La Mode Illustree" (Illus.). 1993. pap. write for info. (*0-486-27615-5*) Dover.

Olian, Judy D., et al. Pension Plans: The Human Resource Management Perspective. LC 85-2758. (Key Issues Ser.: No. 28). 56p. 1985. pap. 6.00 (*0-87546-121-2*) ILR Pr.

Olidort, Baila. Just Like Mommy. LC 92-20591. 1992. write for info. (*0-8266-0359-9*) Kehot Pubn Soc.

Oliemans, R. V., ed. Computational Fluid Dynamics for the Petrochemical Process Industry. 242p. (C). 1991. lib. bdg. 115.50 (*0-7923-1360-7*) Kluwer Ac.

Olien, Charles R. & Smith, Myrtle N. Analysis & Improvement of Plant Cold Hardiness. 224p. 1981. 132. 00 (*0-8493-5397-1*, SB781, CRC Reprint) Franklin.

Olien, Diana D., jt. auth. see Olien, Roger M.

Olien, Roger M. From Token to Triumph: The Texas Republicans since 1920. LC 81-13589. (Illus.). 320p. 1982. 15.00 (*0-87074-180-2*) SMU Press.

Olien, Roger M & Olien, Diana D. Easy Money: Oil Promoters & Investors in the Jazz Age. LC 90-50011. xi, 216p. (C). 1990. 32.50 (*0-8078-1928-X*); pap. 12.95 (*0-8078-4291-5*) U of NC Pr.

Olien, Roger M. & Olien, Diana D. Oil Booms: Social Change in Five Texas Towns. LC 81-11686. (Illus.). 238p. reprint ed. pap. 67.90 (*0-7837-4668-7*, 2044395) Bks Demand.

***Oliensis, Adam.** Ring of Men. Date not set. 2.75 (*0-8222-1468-7*) Dramatists Play.

Oliff, Douglas B. Mastiff & Bullmastiff Handbook. 1988. 25. 95 (*0-85115-485-9*) Howell Bk.

Oliff, Michael. Intelligent Manufacturing: The First International Conference on Expert Systems & the Leading Edge in Production Planning & Control. 350p. (C). 1988. text ed. 49.50 (*0-8053-3820-9*) Benjamin-Cummings.

Oliger, Joseph, jt. ed. see Golub, Gene H.

Oligny, Paul J., tr. see Lekeux, Martial.

Oliker, I., ed. see American Society of Mechanical Engineers Staff.

Oliker, Stacey J. Best Friends & Marriage: Exchange among Women. 1989. 22.50 (*0-520-06392-9*) U CA Pr.

Oliker, Vladimir & Treibergs, Andrejs, eds. Geometry & Nonlinear Partial Differential Equations. LC 92-4421. (Contemporary Mathematics Ser.: Vol. 127). 154p. 1992. 36.00 (*0-8218-5135-7*, CONM/127C) Am Math.

O'Lill, Ruth. A Consumer's Guide to Hope: Where to Find It & How to Keep It. 199p. 1994. pap. 11.95 (*0-87604-313-9*, 384) ARE Pr.

***Olimpio, Sal.** Taxpayer, Dragonslayer: The Consumer's Guide to Solving IRS Problems. Donovan, Jim, ed. 336p. 1995. pap. 17.95 (*1-880925-06-0*) Equitable Media.

Olimpo Staff, ed. see Delgado, Joaquin J.

Olin. Construction: Principle Matters & Methods. 6th ed. 1994. text ed. 59.95 (*0-442-00605-5*) Van Nos Reinhold.

— Drug Facts & Comparisons. 49th ed. 1994. 99.50 (*0-932686-95-8*) Facts & Comparisons.

Olin, Bernie R., ed. see Billups, Norman A.

Olin, Bernie R., jt. auth. see Tatro.

Olin, Bernie R., et al. Patient Drug Facts. (C). 59.95 (*0-03-268636-6*) Lippincott.

Olin, Bernie R., et al, eds. Patient Drug Facts, 1993: Professional's Guide to Patient Drug Facts. 922p. 1993. ring bd. 65.95 (*0-932686-36-2*) Facts & Comparisons.

Olin, Caroline & Dutton, Bertha P. Southwest Indians, Bk. 1: (Navajo, Pima, Apache), Bk. 1. (Illus.). (J). (gr. 5). 1978. pap. 3.95 (*0-88388-049-0*) Bellerophon Bks.

Olin, Doris, ed. William James "Pragmatism" in Focus. LC 91-35744. (Philosophers in Focus Ser.). 256p. 1992. 69. 95 (*0-415-04056-6*, A7475); pap. 16.95 (*0-415-04057-4*, A7479) Routledge.

Olin, George. House in the Sun: A Natural History of the Sonoran Desert. 2nd ed. LC 93-86936. 230p. (YA). (gr. 8-12). 1994. pap. 12.95 (*1-877856-39-8*) SW Pks Mnmts.

— Mammals of the Southwest Desert. rev. ed. Houk, Rose et al, eds. LC 81-86094. (Illus.). 100p. 1982. pap. 5.95 (*0-911408-60-6*) SW Pks Mnmts.

***Olin, Harold.** Construction Principles, Materials & Methods. 5th ed. (Architecture Ser.). 1990. text ed. 64. 95 (*0-442-00431-1*) Van Nos Reinhold.

***Olin, Harold & Schmidt, John.** Construction: Principles, Materials & Methods. 6th ed. (Building Construction Ser.). 1995. pap. 19.95 (*0-442-01576-3*) Van Nos Reinhold.

Olin, Jacqueline S., jt. ed. see Fitzhugh, William W.

Olin, John C. Catholic Reform from Cardinal Ximenes to the Council of Trent, 1495-1563: An Essay with Illustrative Documents & a Brief Study of St. Ignatius Loyola. LC 90-80702. (Illus.). xv, 190p. 1990. 35.00 (*0-8232-1280-7*) Fordham.

— Catholic Reform from Cardinal Ximenes to the Council of Trent, 1495-1563: An Essay with Illustrative Documents & a Brief Study of St. Ignatius Loyola. LC 90-80702. (Illus.). xv, 190p. 1990. pap. 17.50 (*0-8232-1281-5*) Fordham.

— Christian Humanism & the Reformation: Selected Writings of Erasmus. 3rd ed. LC 65-10218. (Illus.). x, 221p. 1987. pap. 15.00 (*0-8232-1192-4*) Fordham.

— Six Essays on Erasmus & a Translation of Erasmus' Letter to Carondelet 1523. LC 76-18467. (Illus.). xiv, 125p. 1977. pap. 17.50 (*0-8232-1024-3*) Fordham.

Olin, John C., comp. The Catholic Reformation: Savonarola to Ignatius Loyola: Reform in the Church. LC 92-29865. xxiv, 218p. (C). 1993. reprint ed. write for info. (*0-8232-1477-X*); reprint ed. pap. 17.00 (*0-8232-1478-8*) Fordham.

Olin, John C., ed. Interpreting Thomas More's Utopia. LC 89-80149. (Illus.). 98p. 1989. 27.50 (*0-8232-1233-5*) Fordham.

Olin, John C., intro. Essays on Erasmus & the Outreach of Humanism. 96p. 1994. text ed. 25.00 (*0-8232-1600-4*); pap. text ed. 15.95 (*0-8232-1601-2*) Fordham.

Olin, John C., ed. see Erasmus, Desiderius.

Olin, John C., tr. see Erasmus, Desiderius.

Olin, John C., et al, eds. Luther, Erasmus & the Reformation: A Catholic-Protestant Reappraisal. LC 68-8749. 160p. reprint ed. pap. 45.60 (*0-7837-0460-7*, 2040783) Bks Demand.

— Luther, Erasmus & the Reformation: A Catholic-Protestant Reappraisal. LC 82-15500. x, 150p. 1982. reprint ed. text ed. 49.75 (*0-313-23652-6*, OLLE, Greenwood Pr) Greenwood.

Olin, Margaret. Forms of Representation in Alois Riegl's Theory of Art. (Illus.). 272p. 1992. text ed. 42.50 (*0-271-00777-X*) Pa St U Pr.

Olin Metals Research Laboratories Staff. Corrosion Testing of Welded Copper-Nickel Clad Steel. 49p. 1977. 7.35 (*0-317-34504-4*, 227) Intl Copper.

Olin Metals Research Laboratory Staff. Forming Limit Analysis for Enchanced Fabrication. (INCRA Monograph). 137p. 1983. 30.00 (*0-943642-09-4*) Intl Copper.

Olin, Phillip S. Treasure, the Business & Technology. (Illus.). 188p. (Orig.). 1991. pap. 19.95 (*1-880502-00-3*) Omicron Grp.

Olin, R. F., jt. auth. see Conway, J. B.

Olin, Spencer C., Jr. California Politics, Eighteen Forty-Six to Nineteen Twenty: The Emerging Corporate State. Hundley, Norris, Jr. & Schutz, John A., eds. (Golden State Ser.). (Illus.). 96p. 1981. pap. 10.00 (*0-87835-114-0*) MTL.

Olin, Spencer C. California's Prodigal Sons: Hiram Johnson & the Progressives, 1911-1917. LC 68-11968. 267p. reprint ed. pap. 76.10 (*0-8357-7975-0*, 2031309) Bks Demand.

Olin, Spencer C., jt. auth. see Nelson, Keith L.

Olin, Stephen. Travels in Egypt, Arabia Petraea &the Holy Land, 2 vols. in one. Davis, Moshe, ed. LC 77-70727. (America & the Holy Land Ser.). 1977. lib. bdg. 81.95 (*0-405-10273-9*) Ayer.

Olin, Walter E., et al. Writing That Works: Effective Communication in Business. 4th ed. LC 90-71635. 624p. (C). 1992. pap. text ed. 0.55 (*0-312-06792-5*) St Martin.

— Writing That Works: Effective Communication in Business. 4th ed. LC 90-71635. 624p. (C). 1992. pap. text ed. 22.00 (*0-312-04829-7*) St Martin.

Olinde, Garrett. How Many Lives? abr. ed. 526p. 1994. pap. 12.95 (*1-56901-333-0*) NW Pub.

Olinde, Kacoo, jt. ed. see Olinde, Ralph.

Olinde, Ralph & Olinde, Kacoo, eds. Ralph & Kacoo, a Taste of Louisiana. 2nd ed. (Illus.). 348p. 1988. reprint ed. 13.95 (*0-9613196-0-7*) Cajun Bayou.

Olinekova, Gayle. Winning Without Steroids. (Sports & Fitness Library). (Illus.). 40p. (Orig.). (C). 1988. pap. 2.95 (*0-87983-480-3*) Keats.

Oliner, Arthur A., ed. see Phased Array Antenna Symposium (1970: Polytechnic Institute of Brooklyn.

Oliner, Marion M. Cultivating Freud's Garden in France. LC 87-31908. 332p. 1988. 40.00 (*0-87668-995-0*) Aronson.

Oliner, Pearl, jt. auth. see Oliner, Samuel P.

***Oliner, Pearl M. & Oliner, Samuel P.** Toward a Caring Society: Ideas into Action. LC 95-3339. 256p. 1995. text ed. 59.95 (*0-275-95198-7*, Praeger Pubs) Greenwood.

Oliner, Pearl M., et al, eds. Embracing the Other: Philosophical, Psychological, & Historical Perspectives on Altruism. 450p. (C). 1992. 55.00 (*0-8147-6175-5*) NYU Pr.

— Embracing the Other: Philosophical, Psychological, & Historical Perspectives on Altruism. 450p. 1995. pap. 19. 95 (*0-8147-6190-9*) NYU Pr.

Oliner, Samuel P. Altruistic Personality: Rescuers of Jews in Nazi Europe. 1992. pap. 14.95 (*0-02-923829-3*) Free Pr.

— Restless Memories: Recollections of the Holocaust Years. 2nd rev. ed. LC 85-82084. 215p. (Orig.). 1986. pap. 9.95 (*0-943376-28-9*) Magnes Mus.

Oliner, Samuel P. & Oliner, Pearl. The Altruistic Personality: Rescuers of Jews in Nazi Europe. LC 87-33223. 432p. 1988. text ed. 27.95 (*0-02-923830-7*) Free Pr.

Oliner, Samuel P., jt. auth. see Oliner, Pearl M.

Olinger, Paula. Images of Transformation in Traditional Hispanic Poetry. Lathrop, Thomas et al, eds. 185p. 1985. 16.50 (*0-936388-21-8*) Juan de la Cuesta.

Olinick, Michael. Introduction to Mathematical Models in the Social & Life Sciences. LC 77-77758. (Illus.). 1978. text ed. 38.36 (*0-201-05448-5*) Addison-Wesley.

Olinick, Stanley L. The Psychotherapeutic Instrument. LC 80-620. 216p. 1980. 25.00 (*0-87668-403-7*) Aronson.

***Olinka, Sharon.** A Face Not My Own. 65p. (Orig.). 1995. pap. 8.95 (*0-931122-82-1*) West End.

Olins, Wally. Corporate Identity: Making Business Strategy Visible Through Design. 224p. (C). 1992. pap. 24.95 (*0-87584-368-9*) Harvard Busn.

— Corporate Identity: Making Business Strategy Visible Through Design. 1990. text ed. 50.00 (*0-07-103301-7*); pap. text ed. 39.95 (*0-07-103300-9*) McGraw.

— Corporate Identity: Making Business Strategy Visible Through Design. 1992. pap. text ed. 24.95 (*0-07-103378-5*) McGraw.

— Corporate Identity: Making Business Strategy Visible Through Design. 224p. 1992. reprint ed. 50.00 (*0-87584-250-X*) Harvard Busn.

— The Wolff Olins Guide to Corporate Identity. rev. ed. (Illus.). 80p. (C). 1990. pap. 16.95 (*0-85072-260-8*, Pub. by Design Council Bks UK) Ashgate Pub Co.

Olinser, Chauncey G., Jr., jt. ed. see Kuhn, James W.

Olinto, Antonio. The Water House. 416p. 1985. pap. 9.95 (*0-88184-229-X*) Carroll & Graf.

Oliphant. Stories of the Seen & the Unseen. 316p. 1971. reprint ed. spiral bd. 8.25 (*0-7873-0643-6*) Mokelumne.

Oliphant, B. J. Dead in the Scrub. 240p. 1990. mass mkt. 4.95 (*0-449-14653-7*, GM) Fawcett.

— Death & the Delinquent. (Southwest Mysteries Ser.). (Orig.). 1992. mass mkt. 4.50 (*0-449-14718-5*, GM) Fawcett.

— Death Served up Cold. (Orig.). 1994. mass mkt. 5.99 (*0-449-14896-3*, GM) Fawcett.

— Deservedly Dead, No. 1. 1992. mass mkt. 3.99 (*0-449-14717-7*) Fawcett.

— The Unexpected Corpse. 224p. (Orig.). 1990. mass mkt. 4.99 (*0-449-14674-X*, GM) Fawcett.

Oliphant, Dave. Austin. 160p. (Orig.). 1985. lib. bdg. 13.95 (*0-933384-16-5*); pap. 9.95 (*0-933384-15-7*) Prickly Pear.

— Civilization & Barbarism: A Guide to the Teaching of Latin American Literature. (Latin American Curriculum Units for Junior & Community Colleges Ser.). v, 94p. (Orig.). (C). 1979. pap. text ed. 4.95 (*0-86728-002-6*) U TX Inst Lat Am Stud.

— Footprints: Poems. 1978. 10.00 (*0-914476-84-X*); pap. 5.00 (*0-914476-85-8*) Thorp Springs.

— On a High Horse: Views Mostly of Latin American & Texan Poetry. 1983. lib. bdg. 13.95 (*0-933384-12-2*); pap. 9.95 (*0-933384-11-4*) Prickly Pear.

Oliphant, Dave, ed. The Bebop Revolution in Words & Music. (Illus.). 227p. 1994. pap. 20.00 (*0-87959-131-5*) U of Tex H Ransom Ctr.

— Conservation & Preservation of Humanities Research Collections. (Illus.). 166p. 1989. pap. 17.95 (*0-87959-109-9*) U of Tex H Ransom Ctr.

— Hopkins Lives: An Exhibition & Catalogue. (Illus.). 187p. 1989. 25.00 (*0-87959-115-3*); pap. 17.95 (*0-87959-110-2*) U of Tex H Ransom Ctr.

— Perspectives on Australia. (Illus.). 204p. 1988. pap. 18.95 (*0-87959-108-0*) U of Tex H Ransom Ctr.

Oliphant, Dave, intro. Nahuatl to Rayuela: The Latin American Collection at Texas. (Illus.). 160p. 1992. 15.00 (*0-87959-128-5*) U of Tex H Ransom Ctr.

— Rossetti to Sexton: Six Women Poets at Texas. (Illus.). 237p. (Orig.). (C). 1992. pap. 20.00 (*0-87959-127-7*) U of Tex H Ransom Ctr.

O

Oliphant, Dave & Carver, Larry, eds. New Directions in Textual Studies. (Illus.). 185p. 1990. pap. 20.00 (0-87959-111-0) U of Tex H Ransom Ctr.

Oliphant, Dave & Dagel, Gena, eds. Lawrence, Jarry, Zukofsky: A Triptych. (Manuscript Collections at the Harry Ransom Humanities Research Center). (Illus.). 1986. pap. 20.00 (0-87959-106-4) U of Tex H Ransom Ctr.

Oliphant, Dave & Ramos-Garcia, Luis, eds. Washing the Cow's Skull: Texas Poetry in Translation. 400p. (ENG & SPA.). (C). 1981. pap. 15.00 (0-933384-05-X) Prickly Pear.

Oliphant, Dave & Zigal, Thomas, eds. Joyce at Texas. (Illus.). 172p. 1983. pap. 20.00 (0-87959-099-8) U of Tex H Ransom Ctr.

— Perspectives on Music. (Illus.). 235p. 1984. pap. 16.95 (0-87959-102-1) U of Tex H Ransom Ctr.

— WCW & Others. (Illus.). 128p. 1984. pap. 16.95 (0-87959-103-X) U of Tex H Ransom Ctr.

Oliphant, Dave, ed. see Barney, William.

Oliphant, Dave, ed. see Behlen, Charles.

Oliphant, Dave, ed. see Murphey, Joseph C.

Oliphant, Dave, et al, eds. New Poetry from a New Spain: The Generation of 1970: A Bilingual Anthology. Sulllivan, Constance et al, trs. (Poiesis Ser.: No. 8). (Illus.). 400p. (C). 1993. 15.95 (0-934840-15-6) Studia Hispanica.

Oliphant, David, ed. see Lynn, Sandra.

Oliphant, Eleana. The Haunting at Lost Lake. 224p. (Orig.). 1985. pap. 2.50 (0-8439-2191-9) Dorchester Pub Co.

Oliphant, Ernest H. Plays of Beaumont & Fletcher. LC 73-126657. reprint ed. 37.50 (0-404-04814-5) AMS Pr.

— Plays of Beaumont & Fletcher. LC 70-93250. 968p. 1970. reprint ed. 75.00 (0-87753-030-0) Phaeton.

— Plays of Beaumont & Fletcher: An Attempt to Determine Their Respective Shares & the Shares of Others. 1971. reprint ed. 10.00 (0-403-01138-8) Scholarly.

— The Plays of Beaumont & Fletcher: An Attempt to Determine Their Respective Shares & the Shares of Others. (BCL1-PR English Literature Ser.). 553p. 1992. reprint ed. lib. bdg. 99.00 (0-7812-7236-X) Rprt Serv.

Oliphant, Herman & Hope, Theodore S. A Study of Day Calendars. 1979. 15.95 (0-405-10618-1) Ayer.

Oliphant, J. Orin, ed. see Jackson, William E.

Oliphant, James. Victorian Novelists. LC 02-26320. reprint ed. 29.50 (0-404-04816-1) AMS Pr.

Oliphant, John. Brother Twelve: The Incredible Story of Canada's False Prophet. (Illus.). 400p. 1992. pap. 17.99 (0-7710-6849-2, Pub. by McClelland & Stewart CN) Firefly Bks Ltd.

Oliphant, Laurence. Altiora Peto. LC 79-8183. reprint ed. 44.50 (0-404-62079-5) AMS Pr.

— Russian Shores of the Black Sea: In the Autumn of 1852 with a Voyage Down the Volga, & a Tour Through the Country of the Don Cossacks. LC 75-115571. (Russia Observed, Series I). 1970. reprint ed. 19.95 (0-405-03054-1) Ayer.

***Oliphant, Lawrence.** A Journey to Katmandu: With the Camp of Jung Bahadoor. (C). 1994. text ed. 17.50 (81-206-0941-7, Pub. by Asian Educ Servs II) S Asia.

Oliphant, M. Jerusalem, the Holy City. 600p. 1985. 350.00 (1-85077-083-2) St Mut.

Oliphant, Margaret. A Beleaguered City. (BCL1-PR English Literature Ser.). 267p. 1992. reprint ed. lib. bdg. 79.00 (0-7812-7610-1) Rprt Serv.

— The Earliest Civilizations. (Illustrated History of the World Ser.). (Illus.). 80p. (J). (gr. 2-6). 1993. 17.95 (0-8160-2785-4) Facts on File.

Oliphant, Margaret O. Annals of a Publishing House: William Blackwood & His Son, Their Magazine & Friends, 3 Vols, 1. LC 70-148282. reprint ed. write for info. (0-404-07731-5) AMS Pr.

— Annals of a Publishing House: William Blackwood & His Son, Their Magazine & Friends, 3 Vols, 2. LC 70-148282. reprint ed. write for info. (0-404-07732-3) AMS Pr.

— Annals of a Publishing House: William Blackwood & His Son, Their Magazine & Friends, 3 Vols, 3. LC 70-148282. reprint ed. write for info. (0-404-07733-1) AMS Pr.

— Annals of a Publishing House: William Blackwood & His Son, Their Magazine & Friends, 3 Vols, Set. LC 70-148282. reprint ed. 205.00 (0-404-07730-7) AMS Pr.

— The Atlas of the Ancient World: Charting the Great Civilizations of the Past. (Illus.). 220p. 1992. 40.00 (0-671-75103-4) S&S Trade.

— The Autobiography of Margaret Oliphant: The Complete Text. Jay, Elisabeth, ed. 208p. 1990. 39.95 (0-19-818615-0) OUP.

— Beleaguered City. LC 79-98862. 267p. 1970. reprint ed. text ed. 55.00 (0-8371-3137-5, OLBC, Greenwood Pr) Greenwood.

— The Greatest Heiress in England, 3 vols. in 2, 1. LC 79-8184. reprint ed. write for info. (0-404-62083-3) AMS Pr.

— The Greatest Heiress in England, 3 vols. in 2, 2. LC 79-8184. reprint ed. write for info. (0-404-62084-1) AMS Pr.

— The Greatest Heiress in England, 3 vols. in 2, Set. LC 79-8184. reprint ed. 84.50 (0-404-62082-5) AMS Pr.

— Literary History of England in the End of the Eighteenth & Beginning of the Nineteenth Century, 3 Vols, Set. LC 76-121021. reprint ed. 45.00 (0-404-04830-7) AMS Pr.

— Makers of Venice: Doges, Conquerors, Painters & Men of Letters. LC 77-173809. (Illus.). reprint ed. 39.50 (0-404-04815-3) AMS Pr.

— Memoir of the Life of Laurence Oliphant & of Alice Oliphant, His Wife. LC 75-36915. (Occult Ser.). 1976. reprint ed. 35.95 (0-405-07970-2) Ayer.

— The Minister's Wife, 3 vols. in 2, 1. LC 79-8185. reprint ed. write for info. (0-404-62099-X) AMS Pr.

— The Minister's Wife, 3 vols. in 2, 2. reprint ed. write for info. (0-318-50664-5) AMS Pr.

— The Minister's Wife, 3 vols. in 2, Set. LC 79-8185. reprint ed. 84.50 (0-404-62098-1) AMS Pr.

— Stories of the Seen & the Unseen. LC 72-113682. (Short Story Index Reprint Ser.). 1977. 36.95 (0-8369-3411-3) Ayer.

Oliphant, Pat. Ban This Book! LC 82-72414. (Illus.). 180p. 1982. pap. 6.95 (0-8362-1251-7) Andrews & McMeel.

— But Seriously, Folks! (Orig.). 1983. pap. 6.95 (0-8362-1199-5) Andrews & McMeel.

— Fashions for the New World Order. (Illus.). 176p. (Orig.). 1991. pap. 9.95 (0-8362-1879-5) Andrews & McMeel.

— Just Say No! More Cartoons by Pat Oliphant. 160p. (Orig.). 1992. pap. 9.95 (0-8362-1700-4) Andrews & McMeel.

— Make My Day. 1992. pap. 8.95 (0-8362-2072-2) Andrews & McMeel.

— Nothing Basically Wrong. (Illus.). 176p. (Orig.). 1988. pap. 8.95 (0-8362-1833-7) Andrews & McMeel.

— Oliphant's Presidents: Twenty-Five Years of Caricature. (Illus.). 96p. (Orig.). 1990. pap. 12.95 (0-8362-1813-2) Andrews & McMeel.

— Waiting for the Other Shoe to Drop. 1994. pap. 9.95 (0-8362-1765-9) Andrews & McMeel.

— What Those People Need Is a Puppy! More Cartoons by Pat Oliphant. (Illus.). 180p. (Orig.). 1989. pap. 8.95 (0-8362-1857-4) Andrews & McMeel.

— Why Do I Feel Uneasy? (Illus.). 160p. (Orig.). 1993. pap. 9.95 (0-8362-1719-5) Andrews & McMeel.

— The Year of Living Perilously. 1992. pap. 6.95 (0-8362-2056-0) Andrews & McMeel.

Oliphant, Patrick. Between Rock & a Hard Place. (Illus.). 176p. (Orig.). 1986. pap. 8.95 (0-8362-2084-6) Andrews & McMeel.

— Oliphant: The New World Order in Drawing & Sculpture, 1983-1993. LC 94-2147. 1994. pap. 12.95 (0-8362-1755-1) Andrews & McMeel.

— Up to There in Alligators. (Illus.). 176p. (Orig.). 1987. pap. 8.95 (0-8362-2095-1) Andrews & McMeel.

Oliphant, Robert. Harley Latin-Old English Glossary. (Janua Linguarum, Ser. Practica: No. 20). (ENG & LAT.). 1966. pap. text ed. 48.00 (90-279-0639-4) Mouton.

Oliphant, Robert, ed. see Younger, Irving.

Oliphant, Robert E. Deposition Tactics & Considerations. 2nd ed. 186p. 1988. 16.95 (1-55681-180-2, FBA0180) Natl Inst Trial Ad.

Oliphant, Susan, ed. see Frederickson, Jeanette A. & Holton, Court C.

***Oliphint, K. Scott & Ferguson, Sinclair B.** If I Should Die Before I Wake: Help for Those Who Hope for Heaven. LC 94-30849. 128p. (Orig.). 1995. pap. 7.99 (0-8010-6767-7) Baker Bk.

Olishey, O., jt. auth. see Tenzin, T.

Olishifski, Julian B., ed. see National Safety Council Staff.

Olitsky, Matis, jt. auth. see Mlotek, Joseph.

Olitzki, A. Enteric Fevers. Causing Organisms & Host's Reactions. Grumbach, A., ed. (Bibliotheca Microbiologica Ser.: Vol. 10). 1972. pap. 116.00 (3-8055-1237-6) S Karger.

— Immunological Methods in Brucellosis Research: Procedures, Pt. 2. (Bibliotheca Microbiologica Ser.: Vol 9). 1970. pap. 85.00 (3-8055-0149-8) S Karger.

Olitzky, Kerry, et al. Explaining Reform Judaism. 96p. (J). (gr. 6-8). 1985. By Kerry Olitzky. teacher ed 14.95 (0-87441-436-9) Behrman.

Olitzky, Kerry, jt. auth. see Isaacs, Ron.

Olitzky, Kerry M. Eight Nights, Eight Lights. (Illus.). 64p. (Orig.). (C). Date not set. pap. 6.95 (1-881283-09-7) Alef Design.

— One Hundred Blessings Every Day: Daily Twelve Step Recovery Affirmations & Exercises for Personal Growth & Renewal. LC 93-9090. 432p. (Orig.). 1993. pap. 14.95 (1-879045-30-3) Jewish Lights.

— Recovery from Codependence: A Jewish 12-Step Guide to Healing Your Soul. LC 93-20051. (Illus.). 160p. (Orig.). 1993. 21.95 (1-879045-27-3); pap. 13.95 (1-879045-32-X) Jewish Lights.

— Renewed Each Day, Vols. 1 & 2: Daily Twelve Step Recovery Meditations Based on the Bible, 2 vols., Set. LC 92-8517. (Illus.). 1992. boxed 27.90 (1-879045-21-4) Jewish Lights.

— Renewed Each Day, Vols. 1 & 2: Daily Twelve Step Recovery Meditations Based on the Bible, Vol. 1. LC 92-8517. (Illus.). 224p. 1992. pap. 12.95 (1-879045-12-5) Jewish Lights.

— Renewed Each Day, Vols. 1 & 2: Daily Twelve Step Recovery Meditations Based on the Bible, Vol. 2. LC 92-8517. (Illus.). 256p. 1992. pap. 14.95 (1-879045-13-3) Jewish Lights.

Olitzky, Kerry M., aft. The Safe Deposit & Other Stories About Grandparents, Old Lovers & Crazy Old Men. 364p. 1992. pap. 12.95 (1-55876-062-8) Wiener Pubs Inc.

Olitzky, Kerry M., ed. In Celebration: An American Jewish Perspective on the Bicentennial of the United States Constitution. LC 88-27867. 142p. (Orig.). (C). 1989. lib. bdg. 41.00 (0-8191-7221-9); pap. text ed. 19.50 (0-8191-7222-7) U Pr of Amer.

— Interfaith Ministry to the Aged: A Survey of Models, A Special Issue of Journal of Aging & Judaism. 58p. 1988. pap. 14.95 (0-89885-432-6) Human Sci Pr.

Olitzky, Kerry M. & Isaacs, Ronald H. A Glossary of Jewish Life. LC 91-12399. 264p. 1992. 40.00 (0-87668-547-5) Aronson.

— The How-to-Handbook for Jewish Living. LC 93-14594. 1993. 24.95 (0-88125-294-8); pap. 12.95 (0-88125-290-5) Ktav.

Olitzky, Kerry M. & Stevens, Joel, eds. An Index to the Sound Recordings Collection of the American Jewish Archives. (Publications of the American Jewish Archives: No. 13). 74p. 1980. pap. 7.50 (0-87820-009-6) Hebrew Union Coll Pr.

Olitzky, Kerry M., jt. ed. see Isaacs, Ronald H.

Olitzky, Kerry M., jt. auth. see Kasakove, David P.

Olitzky, Kerry M., jt. ed. see Kravitz, Leonard S.

Olitzky, Kerry M., jt. ed. see Kravitz, Leonard.

Olitzky, Kerry M., tr. see Kravitz, Leonard & Olitzky, Kerry M., eds.

Olitzky, Kerry M., jt. auth. see Kushner, Lawrence S.

Olitzky, Kerry M., et al. Twelve Jewish Steps to Recovery: A Personal Guide to Turning from Alcoholism & Other Addictions. LC 91-25346. (Illus.). 136p. (Orig.). 1992. 19.95 (1-879045-08-7); pap. 12.95 (1-879045-09-5) Jewish Lights.

— When Your Jewish Child Asks Why: Answers for Tough Questions. LC 92-37176. 1992. 19.95 (0-685-66225-X, BookWorld Dist); pap. 12.95 (0-88125-451-7, BookWorld Dist) Ktav.

Olitzky, Kerry M., et al, eds. Reform Judaism in America: A Biographical Dictionary & Sourcebook. LC 92-25794. (Jewish Denominations in America Ser.). 384p. 1993. text ed. 75.00 (0-313-24628-9, SUJ, Greenwood Pr) Greenwood.

***Oliu, Walter E., et al.** Writing that Works: Effective Communication in Business. 608p. 1995. pap. text ed. 28.60 (0-312-10376-X) St Martin.

Oliva. Basic Electricity. 1986. 24.95 (0-672-27023-4, Bobbs) Michie Butterworth.

— Developing the Curriculum. 3rd ed. (C). 1992. text ed. 59.50 (0-673-52195-8) HarpCollege.

Oliva & Buxton, A. English Catalan Dictionary: Bilingual General Dictionary. 2nd rev. ed. 1107p. (CAT & ENG.). 1989. 69.95 (0-685-52395-0, S39887) Fr & Eur.

Oliva, Bonita M., jt. auth. see Oliva, Leo E.

Oliva, Cesar, ed. see Del Valle-Inclan, Ramon.

Oliva, Juan, contrib. A Portolan Atlas of the Mediterranean Sea & Western European Waters, with a World Map. LC 87-675334. 12p. 1987. 15.95 (0-8444-0572-8) Lib Congress.

Oliva, Judy L. David Hare: Theatricalizing Politics. LC 89-27751. (Theatre & Dramatic Studies: No. 66). 216p. (C). reprint ed. 61.60 (0-8357-2048-9, 2070747) Bks Demand.

Oliva, L. & Veiga-Pires, J. A., eds. Intervention Radiology: Proceedings, 2nd International Symposium, Venice-Lido, Italy, September 27 - October 1, 1981, No. 2. (International Congress Ser.: No. 575). 366p. 1982. 95. 00 (0-444-90252-X, Excerpta Medica) Elsevier.

Oliva, Lawrence. Partners, Not Competitors: The Age of Teamwork & Technology. LC 90-82962. 250p. (C). 1992. pap. text ed. 32.95 (1-878289-09-8) Idea Group Pub.

Oliva, Leo E. Fort Hays, Frontier Army Post, 1865-1889. LC 80-82227. (Illus.). 66p. 1980. pap. 3.50 (0-87726-020-6) Kansas St Hist.

— Fort Larned on the Santa Fe Trail. LC 82-80495. (Illus.). 84p. 1982. pap. 3.50 (0-87726-024-9) Kansas St Hist.

— Fort Scott on the Indian Frontier. LC 84-81183. (Illus.). 78p. 1984. pap. 3.50 (0-87726-027-3) Kansas St Hist.

— Woodston: The Story of a Kansas Country Town. (Illus.). viii, 237p. (Orig.). 1985. pap. 15.00 (0-685-66152-0) Western Bks.

Oliva, Leo E., ed. Adventure on the Santa Fe Trail. LC 88-50922. (Illus.). 127p. 1988. pap. 7.95 (0-87726-033-8) Kansas St Hist.

Oliva, Leo E. & Oliva, Bonita M. Santa Fe Trail Trivia. 2nd ed. iv, 56p. (Orig.). 1987. pap. 1.95 (0-685-66153-9) Western Bks.

— Santa Fe Trail Trivia. 3rd ed. viii, 68p. (Orig.). 1989. pap. 2.95 (0-938463-04-7) Western Bks.

Oliva, Max. Free to Pray, Free to Love. 1994. pap. 39.00 (1-85390-275-6, Pub. by Veritas IE) St Mut.

— Free to Pray, Free to Love: Growing in Prayer & Compassion. LC 93-74040. 160p. (Orig.). 1994. pap. 7.95 (0-87793-521-1) Ave Maria.

— Praying the Beatitudes: A Retreat on the Sermon on the Mount. 126p. 1989. pap. 22.00 (1-85390-039-7, Pub. by Veritas IE) St Mut.

Oliva, Peter F. Developing the Curriculum. 2nd ed. (C). 1988. text ed. 35.75 (0-673-39742-4) HarpCollege.

— Supervision for Today's Schools. 4th ed. 640p. (C). 1993. text ed. 50.95 (0-8013-0778-3, 78807) Longman.

Oliva, Peter R. Developing the Curriculum. (C). 1982. text ed. 24.95 (0-316-64995-3) Little.

***Oliva-Rasbich.** Viva la Mediterranean: A Cultural Feast from Healthmark. 1994. 21.95 (0-9624784-2-3) HealthMark.

Oliva, S. & Buxton, A. Catalan-English Dictionary. 842p. 1989. 46.00 (84-85194-39-X) IBD Ltd.

— English-Catalan Dictionary. 2nd ed. 1107p. 1989. 46.00 (0-88431-048-5) IBD Ltd.

Olivar, Celia B. Aristocracy of the Mind, a Precious Heritage: A Biography of Jorge Bocobo. (Illus.). 124p. 1981. pap. 6.50 (0-686-32580-X, Pub. by New Day Pub PH) Cellar.

Olivares, Angelina S., tr. see Fisher, J., et al.

Olivares, Jose, jt. auth. see Dejene, Alemneh.

Olivares, Julian. The Love Poetry of Francisco de Quevedo: An Aesthetic & Existential Study. LC 82-14702. (Cambridge Iberian & Latin American Studies). 200p. 1983. 49.95 (0-521-24362-9) Cambridge U Pr.

Olivares, Julian, ed. Cuentos Hispanos de los Estado Unidos. LC 92-21056. 350p. 1993. pap. 15.00 (1-55885-045-7) Arte Publico.

— Decade II: A Twentieth Anniversary Anthology. LC 92-35458. 256p. (Orig.). 1993. pap. 12.00 (1-55885-062-7) Arte Publico.

— International Studies in Honor of Tomas Rive ra. LC 84-72306. 200p. (Orig.). 1985. pap. 11.00 (0-934770-60-3) Arte Publico.

— Tomas Rivera: The Complete Works. LC 91-12328. 448p. 1992. 38.95 (1-55885-039-2) Arte Publico.

Olivares, Julian, ed. see Rivera, Tomas.

Olivares, Rafael A. Using the Newspaper to Teach ESL Learners. LC 93-988. 104p. 1993. pap. 9.00 (0-87207-237-1) Intl Reading.

Olivarez, Anna, ed. The Adventures of Connie & Diego Audiocassette. (ENG & SPA.). (J). 1989. 8.95 (0-89239-051-4) Childrens Book Pr.

— Brother Anansi & the Cattle Ranch Read-Along. (ENG & SPA.). (J). (ps-7). 1989. audio 22.95 (0-89239-063-8) Childrens Book Pr.

— How We Came to the Fifth World Read-Along. (ENG & SPA.). (J). (gr. 2-7). 1987. 22.95 (0-89239-038-7) Childrens Book Pr.

— Uncle Nacho's Hat Read-Along. (ENG & SPA.). (J). (ps-7). 1990. 22.95 (0-89239-061-1) Childrens Book Pr.

Olivari, Mariolina. Giovanni Bellini. Brierley, Anthony, tr. (Library of Great Masters). (Illus.). 80p. (Orig.). 1990. pap. 12.99 (1-878351-09-5) Riverside NY.

Olivart, Jose-Maria A. Diccionari de Noms de Persona. 6th ed. 368p. (CAT.). 1991. 39.95 (0-7859-5877-0, 8429715738) Fr & Eur.

Olivas, Michael A. The Law & Higher Education: Cases & Materials on Colleges in Court. LC 89-62027. 1056p. 1989. lib. bdg. 80.00 (0-89089-364-0) Carolina Acad Pr.

— The Law & Higher Education: Cases & Materials on Colleges in Court. suppl. ed. 1056p. 1989. write for info. (0-318-65578-0) Carolina Acad Pr.

Olivas, Michael A., ed. Latino College Students. (Bilingual Education Ser.). 384p. 1986. text ed. 28.95 (0-8077-2798-9) Tchrs Coll.

Olivastro, Dominic. Ancient Puzzles: Classic Brainteasers & Other Timeless Mathematical Games of the Last Ten Centuries. LC 93-3985. 1993. pap. 12.95 (0-553-37297-1) Bantam.

Olive, D., jt. ed. see Goddard, P.

Olive, David. Business Babble: A Cynic's Dictionary of Corporate Jargon. 192p. 1991. text ed. 14.95 (0-471-54789-1) Wiley.

— Genderbabble: The Dumbest Things Men Ever Said about Women. LC 93-773. (Illus.). 192p. 1993. 14.95 (0-399-51821-5, Perigree Bks) Berkley Pub.

— Political Babble: The One Thousand Dumbest Things Ever Said by Politicians. 256p. 1992. text ed. 16.95 (0-471-57710-3) Wiley.

***Olive, Diane.** Think Before You Eat: Smarter Food Choices for You & Your Family. 1994. pap. 12.95 (1-882180-25-9) Griffin CA.

Olive, G. & Boissier, J. Drug Action Modifications in Comparative Pharmacology: Proceedings of the 7th International Congress of Pharmacology, Paris 1978. LC 78-41031. (Advances in Pharmacology & Therapeutics Ser.: Vol. 8). 1979. 150.00 (0-08-023198-5, Pub. by Pergamon Repr UK) Franklin.

Olive, G., et al, eds. International Colloquium of Developmental Pharmacology, 4th, Paris, May 1983. (Journal: Developmental Pharmacology & Therapeutics: Vol. 7, Suppl. 1). (Illus.). viii, 224p. 1984. pap. 56.00 (3-8055-3997-5) S Karger.

***Olive, J. Fred.** The Educational Technology Profession: A Bibliographic Overview of a Profession in Search of Itself; a Selected Bibliography. LC 94-27747. (Educational Technology Selected Bibliography Ser.: Vol. 12). 1995. 19.95 (0-87778-277-6) Educ Tech Pubns.

Olive, J. P., et al. Acoustics of American English Speech: A Dynamic Approach. LC 92-44839. 408p. 1993. 59.00 (0-387-97984-0) Spr-Verlag.

Olive, John. Killers. 1990. pap. 4.75 (0-8222-0612-9) Dramatists Play.

— Minnesota Moon. 48p. (Orig.). 1990. 5.95 (0-317-91359-X) Playsmith.

— Standing on My Knees. 1983. pap. 4.75 (0-8222-1071-1) Dramatists Play.

Olive, John H. & Smith, Kenneth R. Benthic Macroinvertebrates As Indexes of Water Quality in the Scioto River Basin, Ohio. 1975. 10.00 (0-86727-077-2) Ohio Bio Survey.

Olive, Martin-Maria. Praxedes: Wife, Mother, Widow, & Lay Dominican. LC 87-50548. 203p. 1987. pap. 10.00 (0-89555-309-0) TAN Bks Pubs.

Olive, Pat. Be Just & Fear. abr. ed. 266p. 1994. pap. 8.95 (1-56901-388-8) NW Pub.

Olive, S., ed. see Shutov, F. A.

Olive, Teresa. Joseph & His Brothers. (Arch Bks.). (Illus.). 24p. (Orig.). (J). (ps-4). 1993. pap. 1.99 (0-570-09030-X) Concordia.

— Life after TV: Slaying the One-Eyed Monster. (Contemporary Christian Living Ser.). 51p. (Orig.). 1992. 1.99 (0-87509-470-8) Chr Pubns.

Oliveira, Americo B. The Philosophy of the Ecological Conscience: A Post-Cartesian Worldview. 1994. 17.95 (0-533-10774-1) Vantage.

Oliveira, Armando, ed. Hypermedia Courseware: Structures of Communication & Intelligent Help. LC 92-35693. x, 241p. 1992. 84.00 (0-387-55810-1) Spr-Verlag.

Oliveira, David. Storytelling. 12p. (Orig.). 1993. pap. 5.00 (0-9638843-0-1) Mille Grazie.

Oliveira, David B. Immunological Aspects of Renal Disease. (Reviews in Clinical Immunology Ser.: No. 2). 220p. (C). 1992. 64.95 (0-521-40174-7) Cambridge U Pr.

Oliveira, David J., jt. auth. see Tarantino, John A.

Oliveira, Fernanda A. R., jt. ed. see Singh, R. Paul.

Oliveira, Joao & Rumble, Greville, eds. Vocational Education at a Distance: International Perspectives. (New Developments in Vocational Education Ser.). 208p. 1992. 57.00 (0-7494-0550-3, Pub. by Kogan Page Educ UK) Taylor & Francis.

O

Oliveira, Joao B., jt. ed. see Farrell, Joseph P.

Oliveira, Jura. Living Portuguese: Conversational Manual. rev. ed. (Complete Living Language Course Ser.). (ENG & POR.). 1993. pap. 6.00 (*0-517-59035-2*, Living Language) Crown Pub Group.

— Living Portuguese: Dictionary. (Complete Living Language Course Ser.). (ENG & POR.). 1993. pap. 5.00 (*0-517-59036-0*, Living Language) Crown Pub Group.

— Living Portuguese (Brazilian) rev. ed. (Complete Living Language Course Ser.). (ENG & POR.). 1993. 20.00 (*0-517-59032-8*, Living Language) Crown Pub Group.

— Living Portuguese (Continental) rev. ed. (Complete Living Language Course Ser.). (ENG & POR.). 1993. 20.00 (*0-517-59033-6*, Living Language) Crown Pub Group.

Oliveira, Marques A. A History of Portugal. 2nd ed. 1976. pap. text ed. 39.50 (*0-231-08353-X*) Col U Pr.

— A History of Portugal, Vol. 1. 1972. text ed. 54.00 (*0-231-03159-9*) Col U Pr.

— A History of Portugal, Vol. 2. 2nd ed. 1976. text ed. 50.00 (*0-231-04162-4*) Col U Pr.

Oliveira, Nuno. Reflections on Equestrian Art. 130p. 1990. write for info. (*0-85131-461-9*, Pub. by J A Allen & Co UK) St Mut.

Oliveira, P. R. & Almeida, S. A., eds. Use of Soil for Treatment & Final Disposal Effluents & Sludge: Proceedings of an IAWPRC Seminar Held in Salvador, Brazil, 13-15 August 1986. LC 82-645900. (Water Science & Technology Ser.: Vol. 19). (Illus.). 214p. 1988. pap. 61.00 (*0-08-035590-0*, Pergamon Pr) Elsevier.

Oliveira, Paulo de, jt. auth. see Cohen, Steve.

***Oliveira, R., et al, eds.** 7th International Congress International Association of Engineering Geology, Lisbon, Portugal, 5-9 September 1994, 6 vols. (Illus.). 5240p. (C). 1994. text ed. 490.00 (*90-5410-503-8*, Pub. by A A Balkema NE) Ashgate Pub Co.

Olivella, Manuel Z. Chambacu: Black Slum. Tittler, Johnathan, tr. LC 89-12406. 128p. 1989. pap. 12.95 (*0-935480-39-0*) Lat Am Lit Rev Pr.

Olivelle, Patrick. The Asrama System: The History & Hermeneutics of a Religious Institution. LC 92-38998. 288p. (C). 1993. 49.95 (*0-19-508327-X*) OUP.

— Rule & Regulatioms of Brahmanical Asceticism. LC 94-36124. (Religion Ser.). 458p. 1994. pap. 18.95 (*0-7914-2284-4*) State U NY Pr.

— Rule & Regulatioms of Brahmanical Asceticism. LC 94-36124. (Religion Ser.). 458p. 1994. 57.50 (*0-7914-2283-6*) State U NY Pr.

— The Samnyasa Upanisads: Hindu Scriptures on Asceticism & Renunciation. 320p. (C). 1992. pap. text ed. 18.95 (*0-19-507045-3*) OUP.

Oliver. Ankylosaurus. (Dinosaur Library: Set II). (Illus.). 24p. (J). 1984. lib. bdg. 14.00 (*0-86592-212-8*) Rourke Enter.

— Archaeopteryx. (Dinosaur Library: Set II). (Illus.). 24p. (J). 1984. lib. bdg. 14.00 (*0-86592-209-8*) Rourke Enter.

— Brachiosaurus. (Dinosaur Library: Set III). (Illus.). 24p. (J). 1986. lib. bdg. 14.00 (*0-86592-219-5*) Rourke Enter.

— Chasmosaurus. (Dinosaur Library: Set III). (Illus.). 24p. (J). 1986. lib. bdg. 14.00 (*0-86592-218-7*) Rourke Enter.

— Deinonychus. (Dinosaur Library: Set II). (Illus.). 24p. (J). 1984. lib. bdg. 14.00 (*0-86592-213-6*) Rourke Enter.

— Dilophosaurus. (Dinosaur Library: Set III). (Illus.). 24p. (J). 1986. lib. bdg. 14.00 (*0-86592-215-2*) Rourke Enter.

— Dimetrodon. (Dinosaur Library: Set II). (Illus.). 24p. (J). 1984. lib. bdg. 14.00 (*0-86592-210-1*) Rourke Enter.

— Dimorphodon. (Dinosaur Library: Set III). (Illus.). 24p. (J). 1986. lib. bdg. 14.00 (*0-86592-217-9*) Rourke Enter.

— Dinosaur Library, 6 bks., Set III. (Illus.). 144p. (J). 1986. Set. lib. bdg. write for info. (*0-86592-214-4*) Rourke Enter.

— Five-Minute Pasta Sauce. Date not set. write for info. (*0-517-70154-5*) Random Hse Value.

— Mamenchisaurus. (Dinosaur Library: Set III). (Illus.). 24p. (J). 1986. lib. bdg. 14.00 (*0-86592-220-9*) Rourke Enter.

— Plesiosaurus. (Dinosaur Library: Set II). (Illus.). 24p. (J). 1984. lib. bdg. 14.00 (*0-86592-211-X*) Rourke Enter.

— Protoceratops. (Dinosaur Library: Set III). (Illus.). 24p. (J). 1986. lib. bdg. 14.00 (*0-86592-216-0*) Rourke Enter.

Oliver, ed. Iguanodon. (Dinosaur Library: Set II). (Illus.). 24p. (J). 1984. lib. bdg. 14.00 (*0-86592-207-1*) Rourke Enter.

— Nothosaurus. (Dinosaur Library: Set II). (Illus.). 24p. (J). 1984. lib. bdg. 14.00 (*0-86592-208-X*) Rourke Enter.

Oliver & Wilson. Dinosaur Library, 13 bks., Set II. (Illus.). 312p. (J). 1984. Set. lib. bdg. write for info. (*0-86592-200-4*) Rourke Enter.

Oliver, jt. auth. see Wright.

Oliver, A. Richard. Charles Nodier, Pilot of Romanticism. LC 64-8670. (Illus.). 1964. 39.95x (*0-8156-2073-X*) Syracuse U Pr.

Oliver, Andrew. The Portraits of John Marshall. LC 76-13648. (Illus.). 233p. reprint ed. pap. 66.50 (*0-7837-4355-6*, 2044065) Bks Demand.

— Portraits of John Quincy Adams & His Wife. LC 70-128349. (Adams Papers Ser.: No. 4, Adams Family Portraits). (Illus.). 335p. 1970. 39.95 (*0-674-69152-0*) HUP.

Oliver, Andrew, ed. Journal of Samuel Curwen, Loyalist, 2 vols., Set. LC 72-180150. (Illus.). 1972. 49.95 (*0-88389-096-8*, Essx Institute) Peabody Essex Mus.

Oliver, Andrew & Tolles, Bryant F., Jr. Windows on the Past: Portraits at the Essex Institute. LC 80-70017. (E.I. Museum Booklet Ser.). (Illus.). 64p. (Orig.). 1981. pap. 5.95 (*0-88389-079-8*, Essx Institute) Peabody Essex Mus.

Oliver, Andrew, ed. see Curwen, Samuel.

Oliver, Andrew, et al. Portraits in the Massachusetts Historical Society. LC 88-2936. (Illus.). 163p. 1988. 50.00 (*0-934909-26-1*) Mass Hist Soc.

Oliver, Annette. Italian Greyhounds Today. (Illus.). 160p. 1993. 25.95 (*0-87605-191-3*) Howell Bk.

Oliver, Anthony. Cover-Up. 1988. mass mkt. 4.99 (*0-449-21466-4*, Crest) Fawcett.

— The Elberg Connection. 1986. pap. 3.95 (*0-449-21093-6*, Crest) Fawcett.

***Oliver, Anthony M.** Hawaii Fact & Reference Book: Recent & Historical Facts & Events in the Fiftieth State. 300p. 1995. pap. 12.95 (*0-614-05582-2*) Mutual Pub HI.

Oliver, Barbara. Mission Stories for Young Children. 48p. (Orig.). (J). (gr. 1-3). 1990. pap. 2.95 (*0-936625-93-7*, New Hope AL) Womans Mission Union.

Oliver, Barbara & Utain, Marsha. The Healing Relationship: A Gifted Therapist Answers the Plea for Help from a Survivor of Child Abuse. (Orig.). 1991. pap. 11.95 (*1-55874-187-9*) Health Comm.

Oliver, Barry D. SDA Organizational Structure, Vol. 15: Past, Present, & Future. (Andrews University Seminary Doctoral Dissertation Ser.: Vol. 15). 446p. (Orig.). 1989. pap. 16.95 (*0-943872-97-9*) Andrews Univ Pr.

Oliver, Benjamin L. The Rights of an American Citizen. LC 76-119940. (Select Bibliographies Reprint Ser.). 1977. reprint ed. 25.95 (*0-8369-5383-5*) Ayer.

Oliver, Bernard J., Jr. Marriage & You. 1964. 14.95 (*0-8084-0211-0*); pap. 16.95x (*0-8084-0212-9*) NCUP.

— Sexual Deviation in American Society: A Social-Psychological Study of Sexual Nonconformity. 1967. pap. 18.95x (*0-8084-0277-3*) NCUP.

Oliver-Bever, B. Medicinal Plants in Tropical West Africa. (Illus.). 366p. 1986. 105.00 (*0-521-26815-X*) Cambridge U Pr.

Oliver, Beverly. Nightmare in Dallas: The "Babushka Lady" 304p. 1994. 19.95 (*0-914984-60-8*) Starburst.

Oliver, Bob, jt. auth. see Oliver, Helen.

Oliver Brachfeld, F. Inferiority Feelings in the Individual & the Group. Gabain, Marjorie, tr. LC 70-169849. 301p. 1973. reprint ed. text ed. 59.75 (*0-8371-6245-9*, OLIF, Greenwood Pr) Greenwood.

Oliver, Brett. Extending Clipper 5: Includes Version 5.01. 1992. pap. write for info. (*0-201-56783-0*) Addison-Wesley.

Oliver, C. Herbert. Cadmus & Europa. 1994. pap. 10.95 (*0-533-10989-2*) Vantage.

Oliver, Caroline. Western Women in Colonial Africa. LC 81-24194. (Contributions in Comparative Colonial Studies: No. 12). xv, 201p. 1982. text ed. 49.95 (*0-313-23388-8*, OWA/, Greenwood Pr) Greenwood.

Oliver, Carolyn C. & McCormick, Ellen R. A Good Teacher. (Illus.). 112p. 1992. pap. 9.95 (*0-9629972-6-9*) Meredith VA.

Oliver, Celia. Fifty-Five Famous Quilts from the Shelburne Museum in Full Color. 1990. pap. 9.95 (*0-486-26474-2*) Dover.

Oliver, Chad. Another World. 1993. reprint ed. lib. bdg. 18.95 (*0-89968-356-8*, Lghtyr Pr) Buccaneer Bks.

— Cannibal Owl. 1994. 4.99 (*0-553-29656-6*) Bantam.

— Shadows in the Sun. 1993. reprint ed. lib. bdg. 18.95 (*0-89968-357-6*, Lghtyr Pr) Buccaneer Bks.

Oliver, Charles. How to Take Standardized Tests. 215p. (Orig.). (gr. 10-12). 1981. pap. text ed. 5.50 (*0-89285-155-4*) ELS Educ Servs.

— How to Take Standardized Tests. 215p. (Orig.). (YA). (gr. 10-12). 1981. audio 16.95 (*0-89285-157-0*) ELS Educ Servs.

Oliver, Charles M., ed. A Moving Picture Feast: A Filmgoer's Hemingway. LC 88-32292. 202p. 1989. text ed. 55.00 (*0-275-93146-3*, C3146, Praeger Pubs) Greenwood.

***Oliver, Charly.** Front Range Ski Mountaineering. (Illus.). 180p. (Orig.). 1995. pap. write for info. (*0-614-05456-7*) Chockstone Pr.

Oliver, Clifford. Operations Manual for Machine Tool Technology. LC 82-13489. 272p. (C). 1982. pap. text ed. 29.95 (*0-471-04744-9*) P-H.

Oliver, Clinton F., jt. ed. see Sills, Stephanie.

***Oliver, Constance, ed.** Cell Biology of Trauma. LC 94-30688. 1995. write for info. (*0-8493-2453-X*) CRC Pr.

Oliver, Cookie D. Come Comet Come Cupid. LC 91-65161. (Illus.). 44p. (J). (gr. k-3). 1991. 6.95 (*1-55523-426-7*) Winston-Derek.

Oliver, Cordelia. Glasgow Citizens' Theatre, Robert David MacDonald & German Drama. 24p. 1984. 32.00 (*0-906474-42-6*, Pub. by Third Eye Centre UK) St Mut.

— Jack Knox: Paintings & Drawings 1960-1983. 64p. 1983. 40.00 (*0-685-16973-1*, Pub. by Third Eye Centre UK) St Mut.

— James Cowie. (Scottish Painters Ser.: No. 7). (Illus.). 80p. 1980. 18.00 (*0-85224-384-7*, Pub. by Edinburgh U Pr UK) Col U Pr.

— Joan Eardley, RSA. (Illus.). 120p. 1993. 34.95 (*1-85158-166-9*, Pub. by Mnstream UK) Trafalgar.

— A Pictorial History of the Citizens Theatre. 128p. 1986. 60.00 (*0-906474-57-4*, Pub. by Third Eye Centre UK) St Mut.

Oliver, Covey T., et al. The International Legal System, Cases & Materials. 4th ed. (University Casebook Ser.). 1771p. 1995. text ed. 52.95 (*1-56662-135-6*) Foundation Pr.

Oliver, D. L. Studies in the Anthropology of Bougainville, Solomon Islands. (HU PMP Ser.). 1974. reprint ed. 26.00 (*0-527-01274-2*) Periodicals Srv.

Oliver, D. R., ed. Third European Rheology Conference & Golden Jubilee Meeting of the British Society of Rheology: Proceedings of the Golden Jubilee Meeting, Edinburgh, U. K., 3-7 Sept. 1990. 568p. 1990. 108.00 (*1-85166-538-2*) Elsevier.

Oliver, Dale D. Your Guide to Financial Success! A Do-It-Yourself Guide to No-Load & Low-Load Mutual Funds. LC 92-60501. (Illus.). 160p. (Orig.). 1992. pap. 14.95 (*0-938041-09-6*) Arc Pr AR.

Oliver, Dana M. California Game Book. Oliver, Rice D., ed. (Illus.). 32p. (YA). (gr. 4-12). 1993. pap. 7.00 (*0-936778-69-5*) Calif Weekly.

Oliver, Dave. Lead On: A Practical Approach to Leadership. 1992. pap. 9.95 (*0-89141-427-4*) Presidio Pr.

Oliver, David. MIG Dynasty. 1990. pap. 17.95 (*0-87938-489-1*) Motorbooks Intl.

— The Shaggy Steed of Physics: Mathematical Beauty in the Physical World. LC 93-33015. (Illus.). 320p. 1994. 44.50 (*0-387-94163-0*) Spr-Verlag.

Oliver, David, jt. ed. see Feskens, Theo.

Oliver, David B. & Tureman, Sally, eds. The Human Factor in Nursing Home Care. LC 87-36625. (Activities, Adaptation & Aging Ser.: Vol. 10, Nos. 3 & 4). (Illus.). 202p. 1988. text ed. 39.95 (*0-86656-715-1*); pap. text ed. 14.95 (*0-86656-732-1*) Haworth Pr.

Oliver, Dawn. The Foundations of Citizenship. 272p. 1994. pap. text ed. 37.95 (*0-13-302738-4*) P-H.

— Government in the United Kingdom: The Search for Accountability, Effectiveness & Citizenship. 224p. 1991. 90.00 (*0-335-15640-1*, Open Univ Pr); pap. 34.00 (*0-335-15639-8*, Open Univ Pr) Taylor & Francis.

Oliver, Dawn, jt. ed. see Freeman, M. D.

Oliver, Dawn, jt. ed. see Jowell, Jeffrey.

Oliver, Derek, jt. auth. see Jasper, Tony.

Oliver, Diana. Annie's Rainbow. (McCracken's Class Ser.). 120p. (Orig.). (J). (gr. 3-7). 1993. pap. 3.50 (*0-679-85006-6*, Bullseye Bks) Random Bks Yng Read.

— Get Lost, Sylvie! (McCracken's Class Ser.: Vol. 1). (Orig.). (J). (gr. 3-7). 1993. pap. 3.50 (*0-679-84988-2*, Bullseye Bks) Random Bks Yng Read.

— John Jerome for President. (McCracken's Class Ser.). 132p. (Orig.). (J). (gr. 3-7). 1995. pap. 3.99 (*0-679-86844-5*) Random Bks Yng Read.

— Lucy on Strike. (McCracken's Class Ser.). 132p. (Orig.). (J). (gr. 3-7). 1994. pap. 3.99 (*0-679-86843-7*, Bullseye Bks) Random Bks Yng Read.

— Sam the Spy. LC 93-85236. (McCracken's Class Ser.: No. 7). 132p. (Orig.). (J). (gr. 3-7). 1994. pap. 3.50 (*0-679-85698-6*) Random Bks Yng Read.

— Sasha's Secret Boyfriend. (McCracken's Class Ser.). 132p. (Orig.). (J). (gr. 3-7). 1994. pap. 3.99 (*0-679-86564-0*, Bullseye Bks) Random Bks Yng Read.

— Sharon Plays It Cool. LC 93-85235. (McCracken's Class Ser.: No. 6). 132p. (Orig.). (J). (gr. 3-7). 1994. pap. 3.50 (*0-679-85476-2*) Random Bks Yng Read.

— Tough Luck, Ronnie. (McCracken's Class Ser.). 132p. (J). (gr. 3-5). 1994. pap. 3.50 (*0-679-85475-4*, Bullseye Bks) Random Bks Yng Read.

Oliver-Diaz, Philip, jt. auth. see O'Gorman, Patricia A.

Oliver-Diaz, Philip, jt. auth. see O'Gormand, Patricia.

Oliver, Dick. Fractals: Not Just a Pretty Picture. (Illus.). (Orig.). 1992. pap. 39.95 (*0-672-30248-9*) Sams.

— Tricks of the Graphics Gurus. 1993. pap. 49.95 (*0-672-30308-6*) Sams.

Oliver, Dick & Hoviss. Fractal Magic for Windows. 500p. 1993. 39.95 (*0-672-30347-7*) Sams.

Oliver, Donald. Auditioning for the Musical Theater. 96p. Date not set. pap. 11.95 (*1-880399-58-X*) Smith & Kraus.

Oliver, Donald W. Education, Modernity, & Fractured Meaning: Toward a Process Theory of Teaching & Learning. LC 88-20990. (SUNY Series, Philosophy of Education). 261p. (C). 1989. 64.50 (*0-88706-941-X*); pap. 21.95 (*0-88706-942-8*) State U NY Pr.

Oliver, Douglas. Black Islanders: A Personal Perspective of Bougainville, 1937-1991. LC 91-57969. (Illus.). 348p. (C). 1992. pap. text ed. 19.95 (*0-8248-1434-7*) UH Pr.

— Kind: Collected Poems. (Illus.). 192p. (Orig.). 1987. 24.00 (*0-907954-04-9*) SPD-Small Pr Dist.

— Kind: Collected Poems. (Agneau 2 Paperbook Ser.: No. 3). (Illus.). 192p. (Orig.). 1987. Agneau 2 Paperbook Ser.: No. 3. pap. 12.00 (*0-907954-05-7*) SPD-Small Pr Dist.

— Poetry & Narrative in Performance. 196p. 1989. text ed. 39.95 (*0-312-03221-8*) St Martin.

Oliver, Douglas L. Native Cultures of the Pacific Islands. LC 88-20625. (Illus.). 184p. (C). 1989. pap. text ed. 12.95 (*0-8248-1182-8*) UH Pr.

— Oceania: The Native Cultures of Australia & the Pacific Islands, 2 vols., Set. LC 88-29551. (Illus.). 1264p. 1988. text ed. 90.00 (*0-8248-1019-8*) UH Pr.

— The Pacific Islands. 3rd ed. LC 88-38668. (Illus.). 336p. (C). 1989. pap. text ed. 14.95 (*0-8248-1233-6*) UH Pr.

— Return to Tahiti: Bligh's Second Breadfruit Voyage. LC 88-14298. (Illus.). 306p. 1988. text ed. 40.00 (*0-8248-1184-4*) UH Pr.

Oliver, Dub. Ostrich Ranching in America: Big Birds Bring Big Bucks! LC 92-75008. (Illus.). 300p. 1993. per., pap. 24.95 (*0-9634566-0-1*) Oliver Comms.

Oliver, E. Eugene. Greece: A Study of the Educational System of Greece & a Guide to the Academic Placement of Students in Educational Institutions of the United States. LC 81-20595. (World Education Ser.). (Illus.). 134p. reprint ed. pap. 38.20 (*0-8357-3115-4*, 2039372) Bks Demand.

— Saudi Arabia: A Study of the Educational System of Saudi Arabia & a Guide to the Academic Placement of Students in Educational Institutions of the United States. LC 87-1204. (World Education Ser.). 132p. reprint ed. pap. 37.70 (*0-8357-8660-9*, 2035108) Bks Demand.

Oliver, Egbert S. Homes in the Oregon Forest: Settling Columbia County, 1870-1920. (Illus.). 230p. (Orig.). 1983. pap. 12.95 (*0-934784-37-X*) Calapooia Pubns.

Oliver, Eileen Iscoff. Crossing the Mainstream: Multicultural Perspectives in Teaching Literature. 235p. (Orig.). 1994. pap. 19.95 (*0-8141-0972-1*) NCTE.

***Oliver, Elizabeth.** Pagan Dreams. (Orig.). 1995. pap. text ed. 5.95 (*1-56333-295-7*) Masquerade.

— The SM Murder. (Orig.). 1995. pap. text ed. 5.95 (*1-56333-353-8*) Masquerade.

Oliver, Elizabeth M. Black Mother Goose Book. 2nd ed. LC 81-83427. (Illus.). 48p. 1981. 7.95 (*0-912444-12-6*) DARE Bks.

— Black Mother Goose Book. 2nd ed. LC 81-83427. (Illus.). 48p. (J). (gr. k-3). 1994. reprint ed. 12.95 (*0-912444-35-5*) DARE Bks.

Oliver, Elma, jt. auth. see Schwartz, Anna J.

Oliver, Eloise M., jt. auth. see Bryant, Rosalie.

Oliver, Eric. The Human Factor at Work: A Guide to Self-Reliance & Consumer Protection for the Mind. Beacon, Ursula, ed. (Orig.). 1993. pap. 14.95 (*0-9636980-0-1*) Metasystems.

Oliver, Eric & Wilson, John. Security Manual. 6th ed. (Illus.). 250p. (Orig.). 1994. pap. 15.95 (*0-566-07443-5*, Pub. by Gower UK) Ashgate Pub Co.

Oliver, Eric, et al. Practical Security in Commerce & Industry. 576p. 1988. text ed. 74.95 (*0-566-02716-X*, Pub. by Gower UK) Ashgate Pub Co.

Oliver, Eric G., jt. auth. see Lisnek, Paul M.

Oliver, Ethel R. Favorite Eskimo Tales Retold. Ingram, Jan, ed. (Alaskana Book Ser.: No. 46). (Illus.). 96p. (Orig.). 1992. pap. 9.95 (*0-935094-17-2*) Alaska Pacific.

***Oliver, Everett W.** Chop, Chop Chick: or We Are Not Our Own. 1994. 13.95 (*0-533-11053-X*) Vantage.

Oliver, F. W., ed. The Natural History of Plants, 2 vols., Set. (C). 1988. text ed. 800.00 (*0-685-22102-4*, Scientific) St Mut.

Oliver, Fitch E., ed. see Pynchon, William.

Oliver, Frederick S. Endless Adventure. LC 78-123762. reprint ed. 165.00 (*0-404-04840-4*) AMS Pr.

Oliver, G. Marketing Today. 425p. (C). 1988. 100.00 (*0-685-29268-1*, Inst Pur & Supply) St Mut.

— Marketing Today. 425p. (C). 1990. 200.00 (*0-685-39812-9*, Inst Pur & Supply) St Mut.

Oliver, G., ed. Marketing Today. 425p. (C). 1989. 173.00 (*0-685-36142-X*, Inst Pur & Supply) St Mut.

Oliver, Gary. Low Limit Seven-Card Stud. 28p. (Orig.). 1991. pap. 6.95 (*0-9635909-1-X*) Poker Tips Pr.

— Masculinity at the Crossroads. (Men of Integrity Ser.). 1993. pap. 2.99 (*0-8024-3712-5*) Moody.

— Poker Humor. 100p. 1993. pap. 5.95 (*0-9635909-0-1*) Poker Tips Pr.

— Will I Ever Get It Right? 1995. 15.99 (*1-56476-486-9*, 6-3486, Victor Books) SP Pubns.

Oliver, Gary, jt. auth. see Wright, H. Norman.

Oliver, Gary D. Enigma at Tumacacori Arizona. 112p. 1992. pap. 9.95 (*0-9633813-0-X*) G D Oliver.

Oliver, Gary J. Real Men Have Feelings Too: Regaining a Male Passion for Life. (Men of Integrity Ser.). 1993. 16.99 (*0-8024-7125-0*) Moody.

***Oliver, Gary J. & Wright, H. Norman.** Good Women Get Angry: A Woman's Guide to Handling Her Anger, Depression, Anxiety, & Stress. 320p. 1995. 16.99 (*0-89283-935-X*, Vine Bks) Servant.

— Pressure Points: Women Speak Out about Their Anger at Life's Demands. 192p. 1993. 16.99 (*0-8024-6320-7*) Moody.

— Women Facing Life's Demands: A Workbook for Handling the Pressure Points in Your Life. 144p. 1993. student ed 12.99 (*0-8024-6321-5*) Moody.

Oliver, Gary J., jt. auth. see Wright, H. Norman.

Oliver, George. The Antiquities of Freemasonry Comprising Illustrations of the Five Grand Periods of Masonry from the Creation of the World to the Dedication of King Solomon's Temple. 250p. 1993. reprint ed. pap. 16.95 (*1-56459-398-3*) Kessinger Pub.

— The History of Initiation in Twelve Lectures Comprising a Detailed Account of the Rites & Ceremonies, Doctrines & Discipline of All the Secret & Mysterious Institutions of the Ancient World. 236p. 1993. pap. 17.00 (*1-56459-301-0*) Kessinger Pub.

— Motor Trials & Tribulations - A History of Scottish Vehicle Manufacture. 96p. 1993. pap. 19.95 (*0-11-495171-3*, HM51713, Pub. by HMSO UK) UNIPUB.

— Revelations of a Square Exhibiting a Graphic Display of the Savings & Doings or Eminent Free & Accepted Masons, from the Revival in 1717 by Dr. Desauguliers, to the Reunion in 1813 by Their R.H. The Duke of Kent & Sussex. 330p. 1995. reprint ed. pap. 24.95 (*1-56459-477-7*) Kessinger Pub.

— Signs & Symbols Illustrated & Explained in a Course of Twelve Lectures on Freemasonry. 210p. 1993. pap. 17.00 (*1-56459-302-9*) Kessinger Pub.

— Widdershins. Reginald, R. & Manville, Douglas, eds. LC 75-46297. (Supernatural & Occult Fiction Ser.). 1976. reprint ed. lib. bdg. 25.95 (*0-405-08157-X*) Ayer.

Oliver, George R. Pythagorean Triangle: The Science of Numbers. 260p. 1993. pap. 17.95 (*1-56459-372-X*) Kessinger Pub.

Oliver, Gerald. Stewardship: Lessons from the Bible. LC 84-62421. write for info. (*0-9614316-0-1*) Natl Inst Phil.

***Oliver, Gordon.** Marketing Today. 4th ed. LC 94-45430. 1995. pap. text ed. 55.00 (*0-13-203001-2*) P-H.

Oliver, Graham J., jt. auth. see Bennett, Henry.

***Oliver, H.** Merry Wives of Windsor. 1993. pap. 8.95 (*0-415-02698-9*) Routledge Chapman & Hall.

Oliver, H. J., ed. see Shakespeare, William.

Oliver, Harold H. Relatedness: Essays in Metaphysics & Theology. LC 84-1152. xvi, 178p. 1984. 14.50 (*0-86554-141-8*, MUP/H132) Mercer Univ Pr.

— A Relational Metaphysics. (Studies in Philosophy & Religion: No. 4). 224p. 1981. lib. bdg. 80.00 (*90-247-2457-0*) Kluwer Ac.

Oliver, Harold H, tr. see Buri, Fritz.

Oliver, Harry R., III. Business Persons' Guide to Taxation in the 90's: Starting & Running Your Business. 212p. 1990. 19.95 (*0-9622569-1-9*) El Dorado Pr.

Oliver, Heddy, ed. see Jones, Mark.

An Asterisk (*) at the beginning of an entry indicates that the title is appearing in BIP for the first time.

Oliver, Helen & Oliver, Bob. Trillium Basal Math-Ware: Apple Diskette. (gr. 1-6). 1985. pap. 29.99 (*0-89824-080-8*) Trillium Pr.

Oliver, Henry M. Economic Opinion & Policy in Ceylon. LC 57-13023. (Commonwealth Studies Center: No. 6). 160p. reprint ed. 45.60 (*0-8357-9103-3*, 2017920) Bks Demand.

Oliver, I. Madsin, ed. Algebraic Topology, Aarhus 1982: Proceedings of a Conference Held in Aarhus, August 1-7, 1982. (Lecture Notes in Mathematics Ser.: Vol. 1051). x, 665p. (FRE & GER.). 1984. pap. 56.90 (*0-387-12902-2*) Spr-Verlag.

Oliver, J. David & Rogers, Ian T., eds. Permanent Establishment as a Basis for Tax - A Case Study. 208p. 1991. pap. text ed. 75.00 (*1-56423-003-1*) Ntl Ctr Tax Ed.

Oliver, J. L. The Development & Structure of the Furniture Industry. 1966. 97.00 (*0-08-011460-1*, Pub. by Pergamon Repr UK) Franklin.

Oliver, J. P., jt. ed. see King, R. B.

Oliver, J. P., et al, eds. Mental Health Casework: Illuminations & Reflections. 1991. text ed. 16.95 (*0-7190-2360-2*, Pub. by Manchester Univ Pr UK) St Martin.

Oliver, Jack. The Incomplete Guide to the Art of Discovery. (Illus.). 232p. 1991. text ed. 45.00 (*0-231-07620-7*); pap. 17.95 (*0-231-07621-5*) Col U Pr.

Oliver, James, tr. see Kersten, Felix.

Oliver, James E. Educational Interest Inventory Answer Sheet, Profile & Interpretation Guide. 9p. (Orig.). (YA). (gr. 12). 1989. student ed, pap. write for info. (*0-933510-84-5*) Wintergrn-Orchard Hse.

— Educational Interest Inventory Booklet. 12p. (Orig.). (YA). (gr. 12). 1989. student ed, pap. 3.00 (*0-933510-83-7*) Wintergrn-Orchard Hse.

Oliver, James E., des. Career Guidance Inventory. enl. rev. ed. 1989. 3.00 (*0-933510-85-3*); 35.00 (*0-933510-86-1*) Wintergrn-Orchard Hse.

— Educational Interest Inventory & Career Guidance Inventory, Set. enl. rev. ed. 1989. Specimen set. 10.00 (*0-685-53405-7*) Wintergrn-Orchard Hse.

Oliver, James H. The Civic Tradition & Roman Athens. LC 82-16180. 182p. reprint ed. pap. 51.90 (*0-7837-0338-4*, 2040657) Bks Demand.

— Demokratia, the Gods, & the Free World. Vlastos, Gregory, ed. LC 78-19378. (Morals & Law in Ancient Greece Ser.). (Illus.). (ENG, GRE & LAT.). 1979. reprint ed. lib. bdg. 18.95 (*0-405-11564-4*) Ayer.

— Greek Constitutions of Early Roman Emperors from Inscriptions & Papyri. LC 86-72884. (American Philosophical Society, Memoirs Ser.: No. 178). (Illus.). 670p. reprint ed. pap. 180.00 (*0-7837-6704-8*, 2046337) Bks Demand.

— Greek Constitutions of Early Roman Emperors from Inscriptions & Papyri. Clinton, Kevin, ed. LC 86-72884. (American Philosophical Society, Memoirs Ser.: No. 178). (Illus.). 670p. reprint ed. pap. 180.00 (*0-7837-6805-2*, 2046637) Bks Demand.

— Marcus Aurelius: Aspects of Civic & Cultural Policy in the East, No. 13. LC 72-22588. (Hesperia Supplement Ser.: No. 13). (Illus.). xv, 160p. 1970. pap. 15.00 (*0-87661-513-2*) Am Sch Athens.

Oliver, James K., jt. auth. see Nathan, James A.

***Oliver, James S., et al, eds.** Early Hominid Behavioural Ecology: New Looks at Old Questions. (Illus.). 328p. 1994. pap. text ed. 30.00 (*0-12-525660-4*) Acad Pr.

Oliver, Jane. Blue Heaven Bends over All: A Novel of the Life of Sir Walter Scott. 384p. (Orig.). 1993. pap. 12.95 (*0-85640-450-0*, Pub. by Blackstaff Pr IE) Dufour.

Oliver, Jean. Back Care: An Illustrated Guide. (Illus.). 192p. 1994. pap. 34.95 (*0-7506-0191-4*) Buttrwrth-Heinemann.

Oliver, Jean & Middleditch, Alison. Functional Anatomy of the Spine. (Illus.). 304p. 1991. text ed. 42.95 (*0-7506-0052-7*) Buttrwrth-Heinemann.

Oliver, Jeffery. How to Identify a Housengiger. 160p. (Orig.). 1993. pap. text ed. 13.95 (*1-884638-03-1*) Black Impact.

Oliver, John E., Jr. & Lorenz, Michael D. Handbook of Veterinary Neurology. 2nd ed. LC 92-22000. (Illus.). 416p. 1993. pap. text ed. 49.95 (*0-7216-6968-9*) Saunders.

Oliver, John E., jt. auth. see Fairbridge, Rhodes W.

Oliver, John E., jt. auth. see Hidore, John J.

Oliver, John W. History of American Technology. LC 56-6269. 686p. reprint ed. pap. 180.00 (*0-317-10652-X*, 2012521) Bks Demand.

Oliver, John W. & Roberts, Arthur O., eds. J. Walter Malone: The Autobiography of an Evangelical Quaker. LC 93-2204. (Illus.). 122p. (Orig.). (C). 1993. lib. bdg. 49.50 (*0-8191-9207-4*); pap. text ed. 27.50 (*0-8191-9208-2*) U Pr of Amer.

***Oliver, Joseph.** Quality of Life & Mental Health Services. LC 95-14468. 1996. write for info. (*0-415-11603-1*) Routledge.

Oliver, Joseph R. Eleven Twenty Handbook. 600p. 1988. 49.95 (*0-13-635129-8*, Busn) P-H.

— Preparing the Consolidated Return, 1992. 360p. 1992. 54.95 (*0-7811-0004-6*, Maxwell Macmillan) Macmillan.

— Preparing the 1120 Return, 1992. 580p. 1992. 54.95 (*0-7811-0002-X*, Maxwell Macmillan) Macmillan.

— Preparing the 1120 Return, 1993. rev. ed. LC 88-60292. (Professional Tax Advisor's Guide Ser.). (Illus.). 1992. pap. text ed. 56.00 (*0-7811-0060-7*) Res Inst Am.

Oliver, Julia. Goodbye to the Buttermilk Sky. 176p. 1994. 18.00 (*1-881320-18-9*) Black Belt Pr.

— Goodbye to the Buttermilk Sky. 192p. 1995. 10.95 (*0-452-27425-7*, Plume) NAL-Dutton.

— Seventeen Times As High As the Moon: Stories by Julia Oliver. LC 92-37457. 1993. 18.00 (*1-881320-04-9*) Black Belt Pr.

Oliver, June. Polysymetrics: The Art of Making Geometric Patterns. (Illus.). 32p. (J). (gr. 5-9). 1986. pap. 7.50 (*0-906212-09-X*, Pub. by Tarquin UK) Parkwest Pubns.

— Polysymetrics: The Art of Making Geometric Patterns. 40p. 1982. pap. 3.95 (*0-685-05678-3*) P-H.

***Oliver, Kelly.** The Complete Idiot's Pocket Guide to MS-DOS 6.2. 130p. 1993. pap. 5.99 (*1-56761-417-5*) Alpha Bks IN.

— Complete Idiot's Pocket Guide to WordPerfect for Windows. 1993. pap. 5.99 (*1-56761-371-3*) Alpha Bks IN.

— One Minute Reference Excel 5. 1993. pap. 7.95 (*1-56761-316-0*) Alpha Bks IN.

— Reading Kristeva: Unraveling the Double-Bind. LC 92-9543. 240p. (C). 1993. 35.00 (*0-253-34173-6*); pap. 14.95 (*0-253-20761-4*, MB-761) Ind U Pr.

— Womanizing Nietzsche: Philosophy's Relation to "the Feminine" 224p. 1994. 55.00 (*0-415-90681-4*, A9541); pap. 16.95 (*0-415-90682-2*, A9545) Routledge.

Oliver, Kelly, ed. Ethics, Politics, & Difference in Julia Kristeva's Writings: A Collection of Essays. LC 92-47482. 1993. 49.95 (*0-415-90703-9*, A9779, Routledge NY); pap. 15.95 (*0-415-90704-7*, A9783, Routledge NY) Routledge.

Oliver, Kenneth. The Way English Works: How to Understand It & Use It. 288p. (Orig.). 1994. pap. 19.95 (*1-56883-036-X*) Colonial Pr AL.

Oliver, Kenneth G. Basic Industrial Electricity: A Training & Maintenance Manual. 300p. (C). 1990. pap. text ed. 32.95 (*0-8311-3006-7*) Indus Pr.

— Industrial Boiler Management: An Operator's Guide. (Illus.). 412p. 1989. 32.95 (*0-8311-3018-0*) Indus Pr.

— Under the Southern Cross: A Petty Officer's Chronicle of the U.S.S. Octans, Banana Boat Become World War II Supply Ship for the Southern Pacific Fleet. (Illus.). 304p. 1995. lib. bdg. 25.95 (*0-89950-999-1*) McFarland & Co.

Oliver, Kevin, jt. auth. see O'Donnell, Jeff.

Oliver, Lawrence J. Brander Matthews, Theodore Roosevelt, & the Politics of American Literature, 1880-1920. LC 91-24627. 272p. (C). 1992. text ed. 31.00x (*0-87049-738-3*) U of Tenn Pr.

***Oliver, Lawrence J., ed.** The Letters of Theodore Roosevelt & Brander Matthews. LC 94-18766. 1995. write for info. (*0-87049-894-0*) U of Tenn Pr.

Oliver, Leonard P. Study Circles: Coming Together for Personal Growth and Social Change. LC 87-12874. (Illus.). 165p. (Orig.). 1987. pap. 9.95 (*0-932020-47-X*) Seven Locks Pr.

Oliver, Lewis. Estiyut Omayat: Creek Writing. 17p. 1985. pap. 2.00 (*0-940392-16-X*) Indian U Pr OK.

Oliver, Libbey H. Colonial Williamsburg Decorates for Christmas: Step-by-Step Illustrated Instructions for Christmas Decorations That You Can Make for Your Home. LC 81-10103. (Illus.). 80p. 1981. 15.95 (*0-87935-056-3*); pap. 10.95 (*0-87935-058-X*) Colonial Williamsburg.

Oliver, Lilian H. Some Boone Descendants & Kindred of the St. Charles District. LC 84-70107. 442p. 1984. pap. 47.00 (*0-939052-02-4*) Dean Pubns.

Oliver, Lin, jt. auth. see Mooser, Stephen.

Oliver, Lloyd F. Houses of Strother Descendants of William Strother I King George County, Virginia, Vol. I: William Strother II (CA. 1653-1726) & His Descendants. (Orig.). 1993. pap. write for info. (*0-9637624-0-0*) W Strother Soc.

Oliver, Louis. Caught in a Willow Net. LC 83-80757. (American Indian Poetry Ser.). 88p. 1983. 5.00 (*0-912678-57-7*, Greenfld Rev Pr) Greenfld Rev Lit.

— Horned Snake. Barken, Stanley H., ed. (Cross-Cultural Chapbook: No. 15). 16p. 1981. 15.00 (*0-89304-839-9*, CCC142); pap. 5.00 (*0-89304-814-3*) Cross-Cultrl NY.

Oliver, Louis L. Chasers of the Sun: Creek Indian Thoughts, Poems & Stories. 105p. 1990. 9.95 (*0-912678-70-4*) Greenfld Rev Lit.

Oliver, Lucy. The Meditator's Guidebook: Pathways to Greater Awareness & Creativity. 160p. (Orig.). 1991. pap. 8.95 (*0-89281-360-1*) Inner Tradit.

Oliver, M. Agent Arthur's Arctic Adventure. (Puzzle Adventures Ser.). (Illus.). 48p. (J). 1990. lib. bdg. 11.96 (*0-88110-408-6*); pap. 4.95 (*0-7460-0145-2*) EDC.

— Agent Arthur's Desert Challenge. (Puzzle Adventure Ser.). (Illus.). 48p. (J). (gr. 2-7). 1994. lib. bdg. 11.96 (*0-88110-696-8*, Usborne); pap. 4.95 (*0-7460-1406-6*, Usborne) EDC.

— Agent Arthur's Jungle Journey. (Puzzle Adventures Ser.). (Illus.). 48p. (J). 1989. lib. bdg. 11.96 (*0-88110-334-9*); pap. 4.95 (*0-7460-0141-X*) EDC.

— The Intergalactic Bus Trip. (Puzzle Adventures Ser.). (Illus.). 48p. (J). (gr. 3-5). 1988. lib. bdg. 11.96 (*0-88110-301-2*); pap. 4.95 (*0-7460-0151-7*) EDC.

— Search for the Sunken City. (Puzzle Adventures Ser.). (Illus.). 48p. (J). 1989. lib. bdg. 11.96 (*0-88110-409-4*); pap. 4.95 (*0-7460-0304-8*) EDC.

Oliver, M. & Waters, G. Agent Arthur's Puzzle Adventures. (Puzzle Adventures Ser.). (Illus.). (J). 1990. pap. 9.95 (*0-7460-0147-9*) EDC.

Oliver, M., jt. auth. see Fischel, E.

Oliver, M. A., jt. auth. see Webster, R.

Oliver, M. C. & Barrister, M. A. The Private Company in Germany: A Translation & Commentary. LC 85-23769. (International Corporate Law Ser.: No. 2). 1986. 54.00 (*90-6544-244-8*) Kluwer Law Tax Pubs.

Oliver, M. C. & Marshall, E. A. Company Law. 485p. (C). 1987. 100.00 (*0-685-39833-1*, Inst Pur & Supply) St Mut.

Oliver, M. F., et al. Intensive Coronary Care. 1974. 4.80 (*92-4-154046-X*) World Health.

Oliver, M. F., jt. ed. see Riemersma, R. A.

Oliver, M. R., jt. auth. see Reid, G. S.

Oliver, Mae T. Nuthin' Much. 1989. pap. 14.95 (*0-932298-76-1*) Tri-State Pr Corp.

Oliver, Marcy S. Miracles Do Happen. 1994. 10.95 (*0-8062-4859-9*) Carlton.

Oliver, Margo. Margo Oliver's Cookbook for Seniors: Nutritious Recipes for One- Two- or More. (Retirement Ser.). 272p. 1989. pap. 9.95 (*0-88908-695-8*) Self-Counsel Pr.

— Margo Oliver's Good Food for One: Easy Recipes for Today's Busy Singles. (Reference Ser.). 280p. (Orig.). 1990. pap. 9.95 (*0-88908-889-6*) Self-Counsel Pr.

Oliver, Maria-Antonia. Antipodes. McNerney, Kathleen, tr. LC 89-10199. (International Women's Crime Ser.). 224p. (Orig.). 1989. reprint ed. pap. 8.95 (*0-931188-82-2*) Seal Pr Feminist.

— Study in Lilac. McNerney, Kathleen, tr. LC 87-20516. (International Women's Crime Ser.). 161p. (Orig.). 1987. pap. 8.95 (*0-931188-52-0*) Seal Pr Feminist.

Oliver, Marilyn T. Gangs: Trouble in the Streets. LC 94-34619. (Issues in Focus Ser.). (Illus.). 128p. (YA). (gr. 6 up). 1995. lib. bdg. 17.95 (*0-89490-492-2*) Enslow Pubs.

— Natural Crafts: Seventy-Two Easy Projects. (Illus.). 245p. 1994. pap. 16.95 (*0-8117-2564-2*) Stackpole.

Oliver, Marina. The Baron's Bride. large type ed. (Linford Romance Library). 1991. pap. 13.95 (*0-7089-7107-5*, Linford) Ulverscroft.

— Campaign for a Bride. 320p. 1994. 20.95 (*0-7089-3117-0*) Ulverscroft.

— Cavalier Courtship. large type ed. (Romance Ser.). 1991. 21.95 (*0-7089-2466-2*) Ulverscroft.

— Highland Destiny. large type ed. (Historical Romance Ser.). 1991. 21.95 (*0-7089-2411-5*) Ulverscroft.

— Lord Hugo's Bride. large type ed. (Linford Romance Library). 1991. pap. 13.95 (*0-7089-7101-6*, Linford) Ulverscroft.

— Lord Hugo's Wedding. large type ed. (Linford Romance Library). 320p. 1993. pap. 14.95 (*0-7089-7459-7*, Linford) Ulverscroft.

— Masquerade for the King. large type ed. (Historical Ser.). 272p. 1992. 21.95 (*0-7089-2679-7*) Ulverscroft.

— Player's Wench. large type ed. (Dales Large Print Ser.). 1994. pap. 16.95 (*1-85389-511-3*, Pub. by Magna Print Bks) Ulverscroft.

— Runaway Hill. large type ed. (Historical Romance Ser.). 288p. 1992. 21.95 (*0-7089-2592-8*) Ulverscroft.

Oliver, Mark A., jt. auth. see Talbot, Steven R.

Oliver, Mark E. Modern Communications. 3rd ed. (Illus.). 176p. (C). 1988. 21.00 (*0-317-64538-2*) P-H.

Oliver, Martha H. Cooking with Vitamins: How to Get the Most Out of Food You Cook. LC 80-84432. 200p. 1982. 8.95 (*0-87983-157-X*) Keats.

Oliver-Martin, Felix. L' Organisation Corporative de la France d'Ancien Regime. xiii, 565p. reprint ed. write for info. (*0-318-71385-3*, Pub. by Georg Olms GW) Lubrecht & Cramer.

Oliver, Marvin E. Word Identification for Teachers. rev. ed. Gibson, Victoria L., ed. LC 86-82262. 80p. (C). 1992. pap. text ed. 9.95 (*0-935435-00-X*) High Impact Pr.

— Writing Student Papers. (Illus.). (Orig.). 1994. pap. 7.95 (*0-935435-10-7*) High Impact Pr.

Oliver, Mary. Dream Work. LC 86-7656. 90p. 1986. pap. 10.95 (*0-87113-069-6*) Grove-Atltic.

— House of Light. LC 89-46059. 96p. 1992. pap. 12.00 (*0-8070-6811-X*) Beacon Pr.

— New & Selected Poems. LC 92-7767. 272p. 1993. 25.00 (*0-8070-6818-7*) Beacon Pr.

— New & Selected Poems. LC 92-7767. 272p. 1993. pap. 15.00 (*0-8070-6819-5*) Beacon Pr.

— A Poetry Handbook. LC 93-49676. 1994. pap. 9.00 (*0-15-672400-6*, Harvest Bks) HarBrace.

— Provincetown. Wheatcroft, John, ed. (Bucknell University Fine Editions: Series in Contemporary Poetry). (Illus.). 40p. 1987. 120.00 (*0-916375-06-4*) Press Alley.

— Twelve Moons. LC 79-10428. 1979. pap. 10.95 (*0-316-65000-5*) Little.

— White Pine: Poems & Prose Poems. LC 94-20112. 1994. 20.00 (*0-15-100131-6*); pap. 12.00 (*0-15-600120-9*) HarBrace.

Oliver, Mary A. Conjugal Spirituality: The Primacy of Mutual Love in Christian Tradition. 176p. (Orig.). (C). 1994. pap. 12.95 (*1-55612-312-4*) Sheed & Ward MO.

Oliver, Mary M. & Surovell, Edward, eds. Story of an Ordinary Woman: The Extraordinary Life of Florence Cushman Milner. (Illus.). 135p. 1989. 15.00 (*0-9614344-3-0*) Historical Soc MI.

Oliver, Matt. Paradox for Windows Handbook. 1993. pap. 27.00 (*0-679-79107-8*) Random.

***Oliver, Melvin L. & Shapiro, Thomas M.** Black Wealth/White Wealth: A New Perspective on Racial Inequality. LC 95-17000. 1995. write for info. (*0-415-91375-6*) Routledge.

Oliver, Merle J., jt. auth. see Fay, Jessica B.

Oliver, Michael. Alden Nowlan & His Works. 58p. (C). 1990. pap. text ed. 9.95 (*1-55022-067-5*, Pub. by ECW Press CN) Genl Dist Srvs.

— Igor Stravinsky. (20th Century Composers Ser.). (Illus.). 240p. 1995. pap. 19.95 (*0-7148-3158-1*, Pub. by Phaidon Press UK) Chronicle Bks.

— The Politics of Disablement: A Sociological Approach. LC 90-8133. 168p. 1990. text ed. 29.95 (*0-312-04658-8*) St Martin.

Oliver, Michael, ed. Social Work: Disabled People & Disabling Environments. 160p. 1991. 57.00 (*1-85302-042-7*, Pub. by J Kingsley Pubs UK) Taylor & Francis.

— Social Work: Disabled People & Disabling Environments. 208p. 1992. pap. 27.50 (*1-85302-178-4*, Pub. by J Kingsley Pubs UK) Taylor & Francis.

Oliver, Michael, ed. see Workshop on Strategies for Screening for Risk of Coronary Heart Disease Staff.

Oliver, Michael, et al, eds. Screening for Risk of Coronary Heart Disease. 193p. 1987. text ed. 44.95 (*0-471-91191-7*) Wiley.

Oliver, Michael J. Hegel's Revenge. LC 83-8834. 1987. pap. 13.95 (*0-87949-236-8*) Ashley Bks.

Oliver, Mona A., ed. see Savage, Gary.

***Oliver, Narelle.** The Best Beak in Boonaroo Bay. LC 95-8075. (Illus.). 32p. (J). 1995. 15.95 (*1-55591-227-3*) Fulcrum Pub.

— Leaf Tail. (Illus.). 32p. (Orig.). (J). (gr. k-3). 1995. pap. 6.95 (*0-85091-653-4*, Pub. by Lothian Pub AT) Seven Hills Bk.

***Oliver, Nick & Wilkinson, Barry.** Japanization of British Industry. (Illus.). 256p. 1992. pap. write for info. (*0-631-18676-X*) Blackwell Pubs.

Oliver, O., jt. auth. see Allwright, A. D.

Oliver, Owen L. Colorado Real Estate Transactions. LC 85-80619. (Practice Systems Library Manual). 1985. 120.00 (*0-318-18298-X*); Suppl. 1993. 67.50 (*0-317-03274-7*) Lawyers Cooperative.

Oliver, P. Black Music in Britain. 1990. 90.00 (*0-335-15298-8*, Open Univ Pr); pap. 32.00 (*0-335-15297-X*, Open Univ Pr) Taylor & Francis.

Oliver, Pam D., ed. Subject Bibliographies of Government Publications: A Compilation of Books, Reports, & Pamphlets Available from the U. S. Government Printing Office at the Time of Their Publication. 932p. 1989. 85.00 (*1-55888-813-6*) Omnigraphics Inc.

Oliver, Pamela, jt. auth. see Marwell, Gerald.

***Oliver, Patricia.** An Immodest Proposal. (Regency Romance Ser.). 224p. 1995. pap. 3.99 (*0-451-18094-1*, Sig) NAL-Dutton.

— Lord Gresham's Lady. 224p. (Orig.). 1994. pap. 3.99 (*0-451-18092-5*) NAL-Dutton.

— Miss Drayton's Downfall. (Signet Regency Romance Ser.). 224p. (Orig.). 1994. pap. 3.99 (*0-451-18019-4*, Sig) NAL-Dutton.

— Roses for Harriet. (Regency Romance Ser.). 224p. (Orig.). 1995. mass mkt. 3.99 (*0-451-18093-3*, Sig) NAL-Dutton.

— The Runaway Duchess. (Regency Romance Ser.). 224p. 1993. pap. 3.99 (*0-451-17730-4*, Sig) NAL-Dutton.

Oliver, Paul. Blackwell Guide to Blues Records. 1991. pap. 15.95 (*0-631-18301-9*) Blackwell Pubs.

— Blues off the Record: Thirty Years of Blues Commentary. (Quality Paperbacks Ser.). (Illus.). 1988. reprint ed. pap. 13.95 (*0-306-80321-6*) Da Capo.

— Dwellings: The House across the World. (Illus.). 256p. 1987. 40.00 (*0-292-71554-4*); pap. 27.50 (*0-292-71555-2*) U of Tex Pr.

— Screening the Blues: Aspects of the Blues Tradition. (Quality Paperbacks Ser.). (Illus.). 302p. 1989. reprint ed. pap. 11.95 (*0-306-80344-5*) Da Capo.

— Songsters & Saints: Vocal Traditions on Race Records. (Illus.). 339p. 1984. pap. 19.95 (*0-521-26942-3*) Cambridge U Pr.

Oliver, Paul, comp. Early Blues Songbook. (Illus.). 192p. 1982. pap. 21.95 (*0-86001-942-X*, AM29083) Music Sales.

Oliver, Paul, ed. Shelter, Sign & Symbol. LC 77-77089. (Illus.). 1980. 40.00 (*0-87951-068-4*); pap. 16.95 (*0-87951-112-5*) Overlook Pr.

Oliver, Paul & Hayward, Richard. Invitation to Architecture: An Invitation. (Illus.). 256p. 1990. text ed. 29.95 (*0-631-16129-5*) Blackwell Pubs.

Oliver, Paul & Wright, Richard, frwds. Blues Fell This Morning: Meaning in the Blues. 2nd ed. (Canto Bk.). (Illus.). 372p. (C). 1994. pap. 11.95 (*0-521-47738-7*) Cambridge U Pr.

***Oliver, Paul, et al.** Dunroamin' The Suburban Semi & Its Enemies. (Illus.). 224p. 1995. pap. 22.95 (*0-7126-6029-1*, Pub. by Pimlico) Trafalgar.

— The New Grove Gospel, Blues & Jazz. (New Grove Composer Biography Ser.). (Illus.). 1987. pap. 16.95 (*0-393-30100-1*) Norton.

O

*Oliver, Peter. Bicycling: A Complete Guide. LC 95-5526. (Trailside Series Guide). 1995. pap. 17.95 (0-393-31337-9) Norton.
— G. Howard Ferguson: Ontario Tory. (Ontario Historical Studies). 1977. 27.50 (0-8020-3346-6) U of Toronto Pr.
— Insider's Guide to the Best Skiing in New England. (Illus.). 192p. (Orig.). 1991. pap. 10.95 (0-941283-09-7) Western Eye Pr.
— Insider's Guide to the Best Skiing in New England. rev. ed. (Illus.). 192p. (Orig.). 1994. pap. 12.95 (0-89732-154-5) Menasha Ridge.
— Peter Oliver's "Origin & Progress of the American Rebellion" A Tory View. Adair, Douglass & Schutz, John A., eds. xxiv, 176p. 1961. 24.50 (0-8047-0599-2); pap. 10.95 (0-8047-0601-8) Stanford U Pr.
— The Puritan Commonwealth. LC 75-31127. reprint ed. 41.50 (0-404-13606-0) AMS Pr.
— Saints of Chaos. LC 67-23255. (Essay Index Reprint Ser.). 1977. 19.95 (0-8369-0752-3) Ayer.
*Oliver, Peter, adapt. Myths & Legends. 144p. (J). 1994. 9.98 (0-86112-639-4) Brimax Bks.
— The Odyssey. 144p. (J). 1994. 9.98 (0-86112-781-1) Brimax Bks.
— Timeless Myths. 64p. (J). 1995. 5.98 (0-86112-984-9) Brimax Bks.
Oliver, Philip M. The Oliver System--Using the Factor Ranking-Benchmark-Guidechart Evaluation Plan, 2 vols. LC 84-90567. (Illus.). 267p. 1984. 90.00 (0-9617464-2-4) P M Oliver.
— The Oliver System--Using the Factor Ranking-Benchmark-Guidechart Evaluation Plan, 2 vols., Set. LC 84-90567. (Illus.). 267p. 1984. 90.00 (0-9617464-0-8) P M Oliver.
Oliver, R. Whitehead Groups of Finite Groups. (London Mathematical Society Lecture Note Ser.: 132). 360p. 1988. pap. 47.95 (0-521-33646-5) Cambridge U Pr.
Oliver, R. & Taylor, L. Logarithmic Descriptions of Whitehead Groups & Class Groups for P-Groups. LC 88-22226. (MEMO Ser.: No. 76/392). 97p. 1988. pap. 16.00 (0-8218-2455-4, MEMO 76/392) Am Math.
Oliver, R. A., jt. ed. see Fage, J. D.
Oliver, R. M. & Smith, J. Q., eds. Influence Diagrams, Belief Nets & Decision Analysis. 465p. 1990. text ed. 139.00 (0-471-92381-8) Wiley.
*Oliver, R. T., et al, eds. Preventing Prostate Cancer: Screening Versus Chemoprevention. (Cancer Surveys Ser.: Vol. 23). (Illus.). 350p. (C). 1995. text ed. 75.00 (0-87969-466-1) Cold Spring Harbor.
Oliver, R. W., ed. HPLC of Macromolecules. (Practical Approach Ser.). (Illus.). 254p. (C). 1989. text ed. 70.00 (0-19-963020-8, IRL Pr); pap. 39.00 (0-19-963021-6, IRL Pr) OUP.
Oliver, R. W. & Allwright, A. D. Terms & Conditions of Contract. 125p. 1989. 45.00 (0-317-43795-X, Inst Pur & Supply) St Mut.
Oliver, R. W., jt. auth. see Allwright, A. D.
*Oliver, Raylynn. Contraceptive Use in Ghana: The Role of Service Availability, Quality & Price, 111. LC 94-31691. (LSMS Working Papers). 1994. write for info. (0-8213-3020-9) World Bank.
Oliver, Regina M., jt. auth. see Meehan, Bridget M.
Oliver, Revilo P. Conspiracy or Degeneracy. 1984. lib. bdg. 79.95 (0-87700-590-7) Revisionist Pr.
— Is There Intelligent Life on Earth? 1984. lib. bdg. 79.95 (0-87700-589-3) Revisionist Pr.
— Mrcchakatika the Little Clay Cart: A Drama in Ten Acts. LC 74-14116. 1975. text ed. 55.00 (0-8371-7789-8, SULC, Greenwood Pr) Greenwood.
Oliver, Rice D. California Student Resource File. (Explorer Ser.). (Illus.). 158p. (J). (gr. 4). 1993. 25.00 (0-936778-66-0) Calif Weekly.
— Lone Woman of Ghalas-hat. (Illus.). 32p. (J). (gr. 4-8). 1993. lib. bdg. 12.00 (0-936778-52-0); pap. 6.00 (0-936778-51-2) Calif Weekly.
— Lone Woman of Ghalas-Hat: The True Story of the Island of the Blue Dolphins. (Illus.). 48p. (J). (gr. 4-8). 1986. lib. bdg. 9.95 (0-936778-96-2); pap. 3.95 (0-936778-95-4) Calif Weekly.
— Student Atlas of California. (Illus.). 66p. (J). (gr. 4-8). 1993. teacher ed 13.00 (0-936778-64-4) Calif Weekly.
— Student Atlas of California. 3rd ed. (Illus.). 72p. (J). (gr. 4 up). 1988. 7.95 (0-936778-98-9); teacher ed 8.95 (0-936778-99-7) Calif Weekly.
— Student Atlas of California. 4th rev. ed. (Illus.). 66p. (J). (gr. 4-8). 1993. pap. text ed. 11.00 (0-936778-63-6) Calif Weekly.
Oliver, Rice D., ed. see Oliver, Dana M.
Oliver, Richard, jt. auth. see Cotton, Bob.
Oliver, Richard L., jt. ed. see Rust, Roland T.
Oliver, Richard R., jt. auth. see Kain, Roger J.
Oliver, Rick, ed. see Conway, Gerry.
Oliver, Rick, ed. see Koike, Kazuo.
Oliver, Rick, ed. see Moorcock, Michael & Thomas, Roy.
Oliver, Rick, ed. see Shanower, Eric.
Oliver, Rick, ed. see Thomas, Roy & Moorcock, Michael.
Oliver, Rick, ed. see Truman, Timothy.
Oliver, Robert. Career Unrest: A Source of Creativity. 1981. text ed. 20.00 (0-685-09088-4) CU Ctr Career Res.
— A Photographic Guide to Stable Management. (Illus.). 160p. 1994. 29.95 (0-7153-0084-9, Pub. by David & Charles UK) Trafalgar.
Oliver, Robert & Langrish, Bob. A Photographic Guide to Conformation. 250p. 1990. 68.00 (0-85131-522-4, Pub. by J A Allen & Co UK) St Mut.
Oliver, Robert, ed. see Fesmire, Robert H.
Oliver, Robert, jt. auth. see Stafford, Christine.
Oliver, Robert A. & Johnson, Dewayne J. Beginning Swimming. (Illus.). 52p. (C). 1982. pap. text ed. 5.95x (0-89641-075-7) American Pr.
Oliver, Robert A., jt. auth. see Johnson, Dewayne J.
Oliver, Robert M., jt. auth. see Marshall, Kneale T.
Oliver, Robert M., jt. auth. see Potts, Renfrey B.
Oliver, Robert S. The Complete Sketch. (Illus.). 256p. 1989. pap. 34.95 (0-442-26685-5) Van Nos Reinhold.
Oliver, Robert T. Communication & Culture in Ancient India & China. LC 73-151717. 1971. 29.95 (0-8156-0082-8) Syracuse U Pr.
— Four Who Spoke Out. LC 75-101831. (Biography Index Reprint Ser.). 1977. 21.95 (0-8369-8005-0) Ayer.
— History of Public Speaking in America. LC 78-13428. 566p. 1978. reprint ed. text ed. 47.50 (0-313-21152-3, OLPS, Greenwood Pr) Greenwood.
— A History of the Korean People in Modern Times: 1800 to the Present. LC 92-50486. (C). 1993. 49.50 (0-87413-477-3) U Delaware Pr.
— The Influence of Rhetoric in the Shaping of Great Britain: From the Roman Invasion to the Early Nineteenth Century. LC 85-40519. 320p. 1986. 50.00 (0-87413-289-4) U Delaware Pr.
— Leadership in Asia: Persuasive Communication in the Making of Nations, 1850-1950. 1989. 47.50 (0-87413-353-X) U Delaware Pr.
— Public Speaking in the Reshaping of Great Britain. LC 86-40355. (Illus.). 248p. 1987. 40.00 (0-87413-315-7) U Delaware Pr.
— Syngman Rhee. LC 72-13864. (Illus.). 380p. 1973. reprint ed. text ed. 65.00 (0-8371-6759-0, OLSR, Greenwood Pr) Greenwood.
Oliver, Robert W. George Woods & the World Bank. LC 94-8738. 228p. 1994. lib. bdg. 30.00 (1-55587-503-3) Lynne Rienner.
*Oliver, Roger W., ed. Ingmar Bergman: An Artist's Journey. LC 94-46211. (Illus.). 192p. 1995. pap. 17.95 (1-55970-295-8) Arcade Pub Inc.
Oliver, Roland. The African Experience. (Illus.). 304p. 1992. pap. 15.00 (0-06-430218-0, PL) HarpC.
Oliver, Roland & Atmore, A. African Middle Ages: 1400-1800. (Illus.). 245p. 1981. pap. 19.95 (0-521-29894-6) Cambridge U Pr.
Oliver, Roland & Fagan, Brian M. Africa in the Iron Age. LC 74-25639. (Illus.). 300p. 1975. pap. 19.95 (0-521-09900-5) Cambridge U Pr.
Oliver, Roland & Fage, J. D. A Short History of Africa. 304p. 1988. mass mkt. 6.95 (0-14-022759-8, Penguin Bks) Viking Penguin.
Oliver, Roland, jt. auth. see Atmore, Anthony.
Oliver, Ronald. A Primer in Electrocardiography with Technical & Some Evaluative Values. 1991. 10.95 (0-533-08413-X) Vantage.
— A Primer in Electrocardiography with Technical & Some Evaluative Values. 2nd ed. 1995. 12.50 (0-533-10221-9) Vantage.
Oliver, Rose & Bock, Frances. Coping with Alzheimer's: A Caregiver's Emotional Survival Guide. 1989. pap. 10.00 (0-87980-424-6) Wilshire.
Oliver, Rupert. Brontosaur. (J). (gr. 4-7). 1991. 4.95 (0-8167-1303-0) Troll Assocs.
— Tyrannosaurus. (J). (gr. 4-7). 1991. 4.95 (0-8167-1305-7) Troll Assocs.
— Whales & Giants of the Deep. 1989. 4.99 (0-517-69061-6) Random Hse Value.
Oliver, S. G., jt. auth. see Gull, K.
Oliver, S. G., jt. ed. see Tuite, Mick F.
Oliver, S. Pasfield. Pendennis & St. Mawes: An Historical Sketch of Two Cornish Castles. (C). 1989. 70.00 (0-907566-90-1, Pub. by Dyllansow Truran UK) St Mut.
*Oliver, Sandra L. Saltwater Foodways: New Englanders & Their Food, at Sea & Ashore, in the Nineteenth Century. (Illus.). xiii, 442p. 1995. 39.95 (0-913372-72-2) Mystic Seaport.
Oliver-Smith, Anthony. The Martyred City: Death & Rebirth in the Andes. rev. ed. LC 85-20974. (Illus.). 280p. (C). 1992. reprint ed. pap. text ed. 10.50x (0-88133-674-2) Waveland Pr.
Oliver, Stephen, photos. Clothes. LC 90-23999. (My First Look At Ser.). (Illus.). 24p. (J). (ps-00). 1991. 7.00 (0-679-81806-5) Random Bks Yng Read.
— Counting. LC 90-8577. (My First Look At Ser.). (Illus.). 24p. (J). (ps-00). 1991. 7.00 (0-679-81163-X) Random Bks Yng Read.
— Home. LC 89-63092. (My First Look At Ser.). (Illus.). 24p. (J). (ps-00). 1990. 7.00 (0-679-80622-9) Random Bks Yng Read.
— My First Look at Colors. LC 89-63091. (Illus.). 24p. (J). (ps-00). 1990. 9.00 (0-679-80535-4) Random Bks Yng Read.
— My First Look at Numbers. LC 89-63088. (Illus.). 24p. (J). (ps-00). 1990. 8.00 (0-679-80533-8) Random Bks Yng Read.
— My First Look at Shapes. LC 89-63087. (Illus.). 24p. (J). (ps-00). 1990. 8.00 (0-679-80534-6) Random Bks Yng Read.
— My First Look at Sizes. LC 89-63086. (Illus.). 24p. (J). (ps-00). 1990. 9.00 (0-679-80532-X) Random Bks Yng Read.
— Nature. LC 90-23568. (My First Look At Ser.). (Illus.). 24p. (J). (ps-00). 1991. 9.00 (0-679-81805-7) Random Bks Yng Read.
— Noises. LC 90-8587. (My First Look At Ser.). (Illus.). 24p. (J). (ps-00). 1991. 6.95 (0-679-81161-3) Random Bks Yng Read.
— Opposites. LC 89-63093. (My First Look At Ser.). (Illus.). 24p. (J). (ps-00). 1990. 7.00 (0-679-80620-2) Random Bks Yng Read.
— Seasons. LC 89-63094. (My First Look At Ser.). (Illus.). 24p. (J). (ps-00). 1990. 7.00 (0-679-80621-0) Random Bks Yng Read.
— Shopping. LC 90-23567. (My First Look At Ser.). (Illus.). 24p. (J). (ps-00). 1991. 7.00 (0-679-81803-0) Random Bks Yng Read.
— Sorting. LC 90-8575. (My First Look At Ser.). (Illus.). 24p. (J). (ps-00). 1991. 6.95 (0-679-81162-1) Random Bks Yng Read.
— Time. LC 90-8576. (My First Look At Ser.). (Illus.). 24p. (J). (ps-00). 1991. 6.95 (0-679-81164-8) Random Bks Yng Read.
— Touch. LC 89-63095. (My First Look At Ser.). (Illus.). (J). (ps-00). 1990. 6.95 (0-679-80623-7) Random Bks Yng Read.

***Oliver, Steve. Clueless in Seattle. (Illus.). 137p. (Orig.). 1995. pap. 10.95 (0-9644138-6-8) OffByOne. Simon, in the title story, was very proud of his personals ad. The only problem was that it took over 700 words to describe him & his needs. Simon is only one of the typically angst-ridden middle-class men in this wonderful collection of tongue-in-cheek short stories, mostly set in rainy, latte-addicted Seattle. Other stories feature a terribly tall man given to relationships with incredibly short women, a military robot who is converted into a cybernetic chimp named Bonzo, & Milo & his too-silent girlfriends. Tongue-in-cheek, hilarious stories, these will tickle your funnybone every time. Oliver's offbeat characters are lovingly nerdy (sometimes just plain nerdy!) guys suffering through the male-female relationship pains of unrequited (or occasionally incorrectly requited) love. Copies may be ordered by sending either check or money order for $10.95 plus $3.00 shipping to: OffByOne Press, 9594 1st Avenue N.E. #322, Seattle, WA 98115-2012. Phone: (206) 528-0185; FAX: (206) 528-0147.** *Publisher Provided Annotation.*

Oliver, Thomas W. The United Nations in Bangladesh. LC 77-85554. 1978. 39.50x (0-691-07593-X) Princeton U Pr.
— The United Nations in Bangladesh. LC 77-85554. Date not set. reprint ed. pap. 72.20 (0-7837-9408-8, 2060153) Bks Demand.
Oliver, Tony. Touring Bikes: A Practical Guide. (Illus.). 176p. 1991. 39.95 (1-85223-339-7, Pub. by Crowood Pr UK) Trafalgar.
*Oliver, Vere L. Monumental Inscriptions: Tombstones of the Island of Barbados. LC 94-36625. (Stokvis Studies in Historical Chronology & Thought: No. 13). viii, 224p. 1995. lib. bdg. 33.00x (0-89370-811-9, Sidewinder Press); pap. 23.00x (0-89370-911-5, Sidewinder Press) Borgo Pr.
— More Monumental Inscriptions: Tombstones of the British West Indies. LC 93-90. (Stokvis Studies in Historical Chronology & Thought: No. 14). 267p. 1993. reprint ed. lib. bdg. 35.00x (0-89370-322-2, Sidewinder Press); reprint ed. pap. 25.00x (0-89370-422-9, Sidewinder Press) Borgo Pr.
Oliver, Vere L., jt. auth. see Christian College Coalition Staff.
Oliver, Vickie. Kalyn's Life Adventures: Not Even in a Book. 32p. (J). (gr. 4-10). 1991. 4.95 (1-877610-07-0) Sea Island.
Oliver, Virginia H. Apocalypse of Green: A Study of Emily Dickinson's Eschatology. (American University Studies: American Literature: Ser. XXIV, Vol. 4). 252p. 1989. text ed. 38.00 (0-8204-0887-5) P Lang Pubs.
Oliver, W. C., et al, eds. Thin Films: Stresses & Mechanical Properties II: Symposium Proceedings Ser., Vol. 188. 1990. text ed. 48.00 (1-55899-077-1) Materials Res.
Oliver, W. R. Genus Coprosma. (BMB Ser.: No. 132). 1969. reprint ed. 35.00 (0-527-02238-1) Periodicals Srv.
Oliver, Wendy, ed. Focus on Dance, Twelve: Dance in Higher Education. (Illus.). 128p. (Orig.). (C). 1992. pap. text ed. 24.15 (0-88314-521-9) AAHPERD.
Oliver, William. The Violent Social World of Black Men. LC 93-48216. 1994. text ed. 24.95 (0-669-27952-8) Free Pr.
Oliver, William, ed. Pigs, Peccaries & Hippos: An Action Plan for the Suiformes. (C). 1995. pap. text ed. 25.00 (2-8317-0057-4, Pub. by IUCN SZ) Island Pr.
Oliver, William I., ed. & tr. Voices of Change in the Spanish American Theater: An Anthology. (Texas Pan American Ser.). 312p. 1971. 20.00 (0-292-70123-3) U of Tex Pr.
Olivera, Antonio J. Desert Visions. 1993. 10.95 (0-533-10594-3) Vantage.
Olivera, Francisco E. Internship & Residency: Research Index with Bibliography. LC 88-47576. 150p. 1988. 44.50 (0-88164-648-2); pap. 39.50 (0-88164-649-0) ABBE Pubs Assn.
Olivera, Otto. Bibliografia de la Literatura Dominicana (1960-1982) LC 83-51004. 86p. 1984. pap. 18.00 (0-89295-027-7) Society Sp & Sp-Am.
— La Literatura en Periodicos & Revistas de Puerto Rico: Siglo XIX. LC 85-1143. (Comunicacion Ser.: No. 74). 410p. (SPA.). 1987. pap. 10.00 (0-8477-0074-7) U of PR Pr.
— La Literatura en Publicaciones Periodicas de Guatemala: Siglo XIX, Vol. 5. 273p. 1974. pap. 7.00 (0-912788-04-6) Tulane Romance Lang.
Olivera, Ruth R. & Crete, Liliane. Life in Mexico under Santa Ana, 1822-1855. LC 90-50693. (Illus.). 280p. 1991. 26.95 (0-8061-2320-6) U of Okla Pr.
Oliveri, Ernest J. Latin American Debt & the Politics of International Finance. LC 91-30394. 256p. 1992. text ed. 55.00 (0-275-94123-X, C4123, Praeger Pubs) Greenwood.
Oliveri, Francesco, jt. ed. see Donato, Andrea.
Oliveri, Gianluigi, jt. ed. see McGuinness, Brian.
Oliveri Lopez, Angel M. Key to an Enigma: British Sources Disprove British Claims to the Falkland-Malvinas Islands. LC 94-31531. 160p. 1994. lib. bdg. 30.00 (1-55587-521-1) Lynne Rienner.
Oliveri, Mario. The Representatives: The Real Nature & Function of Papal Legates. LC 81-108272. 192p. (Orig.). (C). 1981. reprint ed. pap. 4.95 (0-905715-20-9) Wanderer Pr.
Oliverio, Mary E., jt. auth. see Newman, Bernard H.
Olivero, Federico. Edgar Allan Poe. LC 79-144666. (ITA.). reprint ed. 42.50 (0-404-04818-8) AMS Pr.
Olivero, Michael J. Honor, Violence, & Upward Mobility: A Case Study of Chicago Gangs During the 1970s & 1980s. (Illus.). 186p. (Orig.). (C). 1991. pap. text ed. 12.95 (0-938738-10-0) U TX Pan Am Pr.
Olivero, Raymond. Robert Kushner: Paintings. (Illus.). 15p. 1989. pap. 1.00 (0-939324-41-5) Wichita Art Mus.
Oliveroff, Andre. Flight of the Swan: A Memory of Anna Pavlova. LC 79-17902. (Series in Dance). 1979. reprint ed. 29.50 (0-306-79580-9) Da Capo.
Oliveros, Chuck. The Pterodactyl in the Wilderness. 56p. (Orig.). 1983. pap. 3.00 (0-911757-00-7) Dead Angel.
Oliveros, Gumersindo, jt. auth. see Dillon, K. Burke.
Oliveros, Pauline & Cohen, Becky. Initiation Dream. (Illus.). 50p. (Orig.). 1981. pap. 10.00 (0-937122-07-6) Astro Artz.
Oliverus. The Capture of Damietta. Gavigan, John J., tr. LC 78-63353. (Crusades & Military Orders Ser.: Second Series). reprint ed. 34.50 (0-404-17026-9) AMS Pr.
Olivetti. English-Spanish Dictionary of Computer Science. 11th ed. 270p. 1992. pap. 24.00 (84-283-1230-3) IBD Ltd.
— Olivetti English-Spanish Computer Dictionary (Diccionario de Informatica Olivetti Ingles-Espanol) 10th ed. 271p. (ENG & SPA.). 1991. pap. 39.95 (0-7859-4873-2) Fr & Eur.
Olivetti Staff. Diccionario de Informatica Ingles-Espanol. 272p. (ENG & SPA.). 1989. pap. 39.95 (0-685-53860-5, S50364) Fr & Eur.
Olivey, Captain. Sea Stories. (C). 1989. text ed. 59.00 (1-85821-031-3, Pub. by Pentland Pr UK) St Mut.
*Olivi, Jan. Complete Book of Cat Care. 1994. 14.98 (0-7858-0133-2) Bk Sales Inc.
— Complete Book of Dog Care. 1994. 14.98 (0-7858-0132-4) Bk Sales Inc.
Olivi, Terry, jt. ed. see Petofi, Janos S.
Olivia. Olivia. LC 75-12342. (Homosexuality Ser.). 1975. reprint ed. 13.95 (0-405-07382-8) Ayer.
Olivia Kennedy Lab Staff. Under the Portico. (Orig.). Date not set. pap. write for info. (1-881542-24-6) Blue Star Prodns.
Olivie, Jean-Luc, jt. ed. see Petrova, Sylva.
Olivier, A., et al, eds. American Society for Stereotactic & Functional Neurosurgery, Montreal, Quebec, June 1987: Journal: Applied Neurophysiology, Vol. 50, Nos. 1-6, 1987. xii, 512p. 1987. pap. 189.00 (3-8055-4756-0) S Karger.
Olivier, B., et al, eds. Animal Models in Psychopharmacology. (Advances in Pharmacological Sciences Ser.). 476p. 1991. 112.00 (0-8176-2503-8) Spr-Verlag.
— Ethopharmacology of Agonistic Behaviour in Animals & Humans. (Topics in the Neurosciences Ser.). (C). 1987. lib. bdg. 117.00 (0-89838-972-0) Kluwer Ac.
Olivier, Bernard V. The Implementation of China's Nationality Policy in the Northeastern Provinces. LC 93-539. 340p. 1993. text ed. 99.95 (0-7734-2228-5) E Mellen.
Olivier, Christine. Jocasta's Children. 192p. 1989. 39.95 (0-415-01434-4); pap. 13.95 (0-415-01435-2) Routledge.
Olivier, D. Luther's Faith: The Cause of the Gospel in the Church. LC 12-2961. 1982. pap. 13.95 (0-570-03868-5) Concordia.
Olivier, Daniel D., jt. auth. see Grew, James H.
Olivier, Fernande. In Love with Picasso: A Memoir. 1995. 30.00 (0-679-43694-4) Random.
Olivier, Laurence. On Acting. 1987. pap. 12.00 (0-671-64562-5, Touchstone Bks) S&S Trade.
— On Acting. deluxe limited ed. (Illus.). 368p. 1986. 100.00 (0-685-16699-6) S&S Trade.
Olivier-Martin, R., jt. ed. see Pichot, P.
Olivier, N. J., jt. auth. see Delport, H. J.
Olivier, N. J., et al. Law of Property: Students' Handbook. 2nd ed. 337p. 1993. pap. write for info. (0-7021-2937-2, Pub. by Juta SA) W W Gaunt.
— Sakereg Studentehandboek. 2nd ed. 355p. 1993. pap. write for info. (0-7021-2938-0, Pub. by Juta SA) W W Gaunt.
— Statutere Sakereg. 700p. 1988. ring bd. write for info. (0-7021-1994-6, Pub. by Juta SA) W W Gaunt.
Olivier, P. A. & Van Den Berg, G. P. Praktiese Boedelbeplanning. 307p. 1991. pap. write for info. (0-7021-2623-3, Pub. by Juta SA) W W Gaunt.
Olivier, Pierre & Wessels, Florence. My Body. (Young World Ser.). (Illus.). 128p. (J). (ps-3). 1993. lib. bdg. 11.99 (0-679-94160-6) Random Bks Yng Read.
*Olivier, Rejean. Dictionnaire Biographique des Createurs de la Region de Joli. 1975. write for info. (0-7859-8255-8, 2-920249-28-2) Fr & Eur.
Olivier, Richard. Olivier at Work. 1990. pap. 13.95 (0-87830-096-1, Theatre Arts Bks) Routledge Chapman & Hall.
Olivier, Robert L. Tidoon. LC 70-18934. 83p. 1972. 9.95 (0-911116-62-1) Pelican.

O

An Asterisk (*) at the beginning of an entry indicates that the title is appearing in BIP for the first time.

— Tinonc: Son of the Cajun Teche. (Illus.). 122p. 1974. 9.95 (0-88289-054-9) Pelican.

Olivier, Sydney H. The Anatomy of African Misery. LC 74-38017. (Black Heritage Library Collection). 1977. reprint ed. 21.95 (0-8369-8984-8) Ayer.

Olivier, Tarquin. My Father Laurence Olivier. (Illus.). 271p. 1993. 22.95 (0-7472-0611-2, Pub. by Headline UK); pap. 13.95 (0-7472-3988-6, Pub. by Headline UK) Trafalgar.

Olivier, William P. Videodiscs in Vocational Educational. 35p. 1985. 4.75 (0-317-01301-7, IN299) Ctr Educ Trng Employ.

Oliviera, John & DeLisa, Douglas J. Baseball from the Ground Up. (Illus.). 1993. 12.95 (0-533-10411-4) Vantage.

Olivieri, A., jt. auth. see Arangio-Ruis, V.

Olivieri, D., ed. Interstitial Lung Disease & Bronchial Hyperreactivity: Selected Papers from the Meeting of the Italian Chapter of ACCP, Parma, May 1987, Journal: Respiration, Vol. 54, Supplement 1. iv, 122p. 1988. pap. 36.00 (3-8055-4891-5) S Karger.

Olivieri, D. & Bianco, S., eds. Airway Obstruction & Inflammation: Present Status & Perspectives. (Progress in Respiration Research Ser.: Vol. 24). (Illus.). viii, 288p. 1990. 223.25 (3-8055-5006-5) S Karger.

Olivieri, D. & Nadel, J. A., eds. Chronic Bronchitis in the 90's, Vol. 58, Supplement 1: Journal: Respiration. (Illus.). vi, 58p. 1991. pap. 25.75 (3-8055-5452-4) S Karger.

Olivieri, D., et al, eds. Asthma Treatment: A Multidisciplinary Approach. (NATO ASI Series A, Life Sciences: Vol. 299). (Illus.). 296p. (C). 1992. 85.00 (0-306-44215-9, Plenum Pr) Plenum.

Olivieri, Francesca. Muppet Babies: Baby Farm Animals. (Golden Board Bks.). (Illus.). 12p. (J). 1994. write for info. (0-307-06087-X, Golden Bks) Western Pub.

— Muppet Babies Noisy Book. (Little Nugget Bks.). (Illus.). 28p. (J). 1994. write for info. (0-307-12544-0, Golden Bks) Western Pub.

Olivieri, Joseph. How to Design Heating-Cooling Comfort Systems. 4th ed. LC 85-31387. 316p. 1987. 17.00 (0-912524-36-7) Busn News.

***Oliviero, Jamie.** The Day Sun Was Stolen. LC 94-19374. (Illus.). 32p. (J). (ps-3). 1995. 14.95 (0-7868-0031-3); lib. bdg. 14.89 (0-7868-2026-8) Hyprn Child.

— The Fish Skin. LC 92-85509. (Illus.). 40p. (J). (ps-2). 1993. 14.95 (1-56282-401-5); lib. bdg. 14.89 (1-56282-402-3) Hyprn Child.

— Som See & the Magic Elephant. large type ed. LC 94-1164. (Illus.). 32p. (J). (ps-3). 1995. 14.95 (0-7868-0025-9) Hyprn Child.

— Som See & the Magic Elephant. large type ed. LC 94-1164. (Illus.). 32p. (J). (ps-3). 1995. lib. bdg. 14.89 (0-7868-2020-9) Hyprn Child.

Oliviero, Jeffrey. Motion Picture Players' Credits: Worldwide Performers of 1967 Through 1980 with Filmographies of Their Entire Careers, 1905-1983. LC 89-13644. 1023p. 1991. lib. bdg. 145.00 (0-89950-315-2) McFarland & Co.

Olivio, Eddie. Soul Dance. 24p. 1993. 6.95 (0-8059-3412-X) Dorrance.

Olivo, C. T. & Marsh, R. W. Principles of Refrigeration. 3rd ed. LC 76-14089. 1979. 35.95 (0-8273-3557-1) Delmar.

Olivo, C. T., jt. auth. see Olivo, T.

Olivo, C. Thomas. Advanced Machine Tool Technology & Manufacturing Processes. Putnam, H. G., ed. LC 89-64000. (Illus.). 608p. (C). 1991. 39.95 (0-938561-04-9); teacher ed 15.95 (0-938561-06-5); student ed 9.95 (0-938561-05-7) C T Olivo.

— Basic Technical Mathematics Simplified: Instructor's Guide. 1992. 12.00 (0-8273-4642-5) Delmar.

— Basic Vocational Technical Mathematics. 5th ed. Olivo, Thomas P., ed. 448p. (C). teacher ed 12.00 (0-8273-2228-3); text ed. 38.95 (0-8273-2226-7); pap. text ed. 32.95 (0-8273-2225-9) Delmar.

— Fundamentals of Machine Tool Technology & Manufacturing Processes. Putnam, H. G., ed. LC 89-64001. (Illus.). 544p. (C). 1991. 34.95 (0-938561-00-6); teacher ed 15.95 (0-938561-02-2); teacher ed 9.95 (0-938561-01-4) C T Olivo.

— Machine Tool Technology & Manufacturing Processes. Putnam, H. G., ed. LC 86-18216. (Illus.). 640p. 1987. 29.95 (0-938561-08-1); teacher ed 15.95 (0-938561-10-3); 8.95 (0-938561-09-X) C T Olivo.

Olivo, C. Thomas & Olivo, Thomas P. Basic Blueprint Reading & Sketching. 6th ed. 1993. trans. 99.00 (0-8273-5924-1) Delmar.

— Basic Technical Mathematics. 6th ed. 694p. 1992. text ed. 38.95 (0-8273-4666-2) Delmar.

— Basic Technical Mathematics Fundamentals. 6th ed. 384p. 1992. pap. 21.95 (0-8273-4958-0) Delmar.

— Basic Vocational-Technical Mathematics: Fundamentals Edition. 5th ed. LC 84-23257. 352p. (C). 1985. pap. text ed. 19.95 (0-8273-2227-5) Delmar.

— Industrial Drawings Supplement for Basic Blueprint Reading & Sketching. 6th ed. 1993. 16.95 (0-8273-5923-3) Delmar.

— Teacher's Resource Guide to Accompany Basic Blueprint Reading & Sketching. 6th ed. 154p. 1993. teacher ed 22.00 (0-8273-5921-7) Delmar.

Olivo, C. Thomas, jt. auth. see Olivo, Thomas P.

Olivo, C. Thomas, et al. Basic Blueprint Reading & Sketching. 5th ed. (Illus.). 196p. 1988. pap. text ed. 21.95 (0-8273-3084-7) Delmar.

— Basic Blueprint Reading & Sketching. 6th ed. LC 92-35367. 199p. 1993. pap. 23.95 (0-8273-5740-0) Delmar.

Olivo, Rey. Healthy Heart Cookbook. 53p. (Orig.). 1989. pap. 3.00 (0-16-002266-5, S/N 008-070-00632-4) USGPO.

Olivo, T. & Olivo, C. T. Fundamentals of Applied Physics. 3rd ed. LC 83-71503. 440p. (C). 1984. teacher ed 20.00 (0-8273-2160-0); text ed. 44.95 (0-8273-2159-7); student ed 19.95 (0-8273-2161-9) Delmar.

Olivo, Thomas C. Basic Machine Technology. 1980. 21.95 (0-672-97171-2, Bobbs) Macmillan.

Olivo, Thomas P. Blueprint Reading & Technical Sketching for Industry: Instructor's Guide. 2nd ed. 1992. 12.00 (0-8273-5078-3) Delmar.

Olivo, Thomas P. & Olivo, C. Thomas. Basic Vocational Technical Math. 6th ed. 1992. pap. text ed. 32.95 (0-8273-4641-7) Delmar.

— Blueprint Reading & Technical Sketching for Industry. LC 83-26174. 464p. (C). 1985. teacher ed 12.00 (0-8273-2206-2); pap. text ed. 33.95 (0-8273-2205-4) Delmar.

Olivo, Thomas P., jt. auth. see C. Thomas Olivo.

Olivo, Thomas P., jt. auth. see Olivo, C. Thomas.

Olivo, Thomas P., ed. see Olivo, C. Thomas.

Olivo, Thomas P., jt. auth. see Olivo, C. Thomas.

Olivova, Vera. The Doomed Democracy: Czechoslovakia in a Disrupted Europe, 1914-38. Theiner, George, tr. LC 78-189266. 294p. reprint ed. pap. 83.80 (0-7837-1018-6, 2041329) Bks Demand.

Olk, R. Joseph & Lee, Carol M. Diabetic Retinopathy: Practical Management. LC 92-48876. 1993. 89.50 (0-397-51167-1) Lippincott.

Olken, Charles E., jt. auth. see Roby, Norman S.

Olken, Charles E., et al. The Connoisseurs' Handbook of California Wines. 3rd ed. LC 84-47864. (Illus.). 256p. 1984. pap. 6.95 (0-685-08624-0) Knopf.

Olken, Hyman. The High-Tech Industry Manual: Conversion of U. S. Industry to High Technology Through Technology Transfer. 144p. 1986. pap. 20.00 (0-934818-02-9) Olken Pubns.

— Memory: The Physiological Mechanism of Memory in the Human Center. (Illus.). 87p. 1990. 12.00 (0-685-47603-0) Olken Pubns.

— Opening the Door to the Brain: Granular Cell Neuron Masses. (Illus.). 30p. (Orig.). Date not set. pap. 12.00 (0-934818-05-3) Olken Pubns.

— The Technical Communicator's Handbook of Technology Transfer. 144p. 1980. pap. 12.50 (0-934818-01-0) Olken Pubns.

— Technology Transfer: How to Make It Work, a Management Handbook. 92p. 1972. pap. 7.00 (0-934818-00-2) Olken Pubns.

Olken, Ilene T. With Pleated Eye & Garnet Wing: Symmetries of Italo Galvino. 168p. (C). 1984. text ed. 34.50 (0-472-10044-0) U of Mich Pr.

Olken, Ilene T. & Mazzola, Claudio. Racconti Del Novecento: Realta Regionali. 320p. (C). 1990. pap. text ed. write for info. (0-13-750001-7) P-H.

Olker, J. Florida Attorney's - Secretary's Handbook, 1993. 1992. 59.00 (1-880919-02-8) Namar Comms.

— Florida Attorney's - Secretary's Handbook, 1994. 1993. 59.00 (1-880919-05-2) Namar Comms.

— Illinois Attorney's - Secretary's Handbook: 1992 Edition. 650p. 1991. ring bd. 63.00 (1-880919-00-1) Namar Comms.

— Illinois Attorney's - Secretary's Handbook, 1993. 1993. 63.00 (1-880919-03-6) Namar Comms.

— Illinois Attorney's - Secretary's Handbook, 1994. 1994. 63.00 (1-880919-06-0) Namar Comms.

— Wisconsin Attorney's - Secretary's Handbook, 1993-94. 1993. 59.00 (1-880919-04-4) Namar Comms.

— Wisconsin Attorney's - Secretary's Handbook, 1994-95. 1994. 59.00 (1-880919-07-9) Namar Comms.

Olkes, Cheryl, jt. auth. see Stoller, Paul.

Olkhovsky, Andrey. Music under the Soviets: The Agony of an Art. LC 74-20341. (Studies of the Research Program of the U. S. S. R.: No. 11). 427p. 1975. reprint ed. text ed. 72.50 (0-8371-7856-8, OLMS, Greenwood Pr) Greenwood.

Olkhovsky, Yuri. Vladimir Stasov & Russian National Culture. LC 83-3528. (Russian Music Studies: No. 6). (Illus.). 207p. reprint ed. pap. 59.00 (0-8357-1412-8, 2070515) Bks Demand.

Olkin, Ingram, ed. see Berger, M. A. & Fienberg, Stephen E.

Olkin, Ingram, ed. see Finkelstein, Michael O. & Levin, B.

Olkin, Ingram, jt. auth. see Hedges, Larry V.

Olkin, Ingram, ed. see Jobson, J. D.

Olkin, Ingram, ed. see Karr, Alan F.

Olkin, Ingram, jt. auth. see Marshall, Albert.

Olkin, Ingram, ed. see Sen, A. & Srivastava, M.

Olkin, Ingram, ed. see Whittle, P.

Olkin, Ingram, et al. Probability Models & Applications. (Illus.). (C). 1980. text ed. write for info. (0-02-389230-7) Macmillan.

— Probability Models & Applications. 2nd ed. LC 93-22412. (Illus.). 672p. (C). 1994. text ed. write for info. (0-02-389220-X) Macmillan.

Olkin, Ingram, et al, eds. Contributions to Probability & Statistics: Essays in Honor of Harold Hotelling. x, 517p. 1960. 62.50 (0-8047-0596-8) Stanford U Pr.

Olkin, Sylvia K. Positive Parenting Fitness: The Parents Resource Guide to Nutrition, Stress Reduction, Total Exercise, & Practical Information. LC 91-28933. (Illus.). 344p. (Orig.). 1992. pap. 12.95 (0-89529-481-8) Avery Pub.

— Positive Pregnancy Fitness: A Guide to a More Comfortable Pregnancy & Easier Birth Through Exercise & Relaxation. LC 87-18844. 272p. 1987. pap. 9.95 (0-89529-373-0) Avery Pub.

Olkowski, Dorothea, jt. ed. see Boundas, Constantin V.

Olkowski, Thomas T. & Parker, Lynn. Helping Children Cope with Moving. 20p. 1992. 2.95 (1-56456-070-8, 269) W Gladden Found.

— Moving with Children: A Parent's Guide to Moving with Children. LC 93-19123. (Illus.). 196p. (Orig.). 1993. pap. 12.95 (1-880197-08-1) Gylantic Pub.

Olkowski, William, et al. Common-Sense Pest Control. Timmons, Christine, ed. 512p. (C). 1991. 39.95 (0-942391-63-2) Taunton.

Olla, Bori L., jt. ed. see Burger, Joanna.

Olla, Bori L., jt. auth. see Winn, Howard E.

Ollagnier, J. Moulin. Ergodic Theory & Statistical Mechanics. (Lecture Notes in Mathematics Ser.: Vol. 1115). vi, 147p. 1985. pap. 31.10 (0-387-15192-3) Spr-Verlag.

Ollapally, Deepa M. Confronting Conflict: Domestic Factors & U. S. Policymaking in the Third World. LC 92-45073. (Contributions in Political Science Ser.: No. 324). 232p. 1993. text ed. 55.00 (0-313-28824-0, GM8824, Greenwood Pr) Greenwood.

Ollard, Eric A. Installation & Maintenance in Electroplating Shops. (C). 1988. 160.00 (0-85218-021-7, Pub. by Fuel Metallurgical Jrnl UK) St Mut.

Ollard, Richard. The Image of the King: Charles the First & Charles the Second. (Illus.). 211p. 1994. pap. 16.95 (0-7126-5698-7, Pub. by Pimlico) Trafalgar.

Ollard, Sidney. The Anglo-Catholic Revival. 1973. 59.95 (0-87968-634-0) Gordon Pr.

Ollason, Robert J. Penguin Parade. LC 94-6433. (Illus.). 40p. (J). (gr. 4-6). 1994. lib. bdg. 19.95 (0-8225-1491-5, Lerner Publctns) Lerner Group.

Ollawa, Patrick E. Participatory Democracy in Zambia. 520p. 1985. 39.00 (0-317-39410-X, Pub. by A H S Ltd UK); pap. 25.00 (0-317-39411-8, Pub. by A H S Ltd UK) St Mut.

— Participatory Democracy in Zambia. 520p. (C). 1990. 60.00 (0-685-49136-6, Pub. by A H S Ltd UK); pap. 40.00 (0-7223-1214-8, Pub. by A H S Ltd UK) St Mut.

Olle, James G. A Guide to Sources of Information in Libraries. LC 84-4066. 178p. 1984. text ed. 54.95 (0-566-03477-8) Ashgate Pub Co.

Olle, T. William. The CODASYL Approach to Data Base Management. LC 77-12375. 307p. reprint ed. pap. 87.50 (0-685-44427-9, 2032663) Bks Demand.

— Information System Methodologies: A Framework for Understanding. 2nd ed. (C). 1991. pap. text ed. 36.75 (0-201-54443-1) Addison-Wesley.

— Information Systems Methodologies: A Framework for Understanding. (Illus.). 190p. (C). 1988. pap. text ed. 34.50 (0-201-41610-7) Addison-Wesley.

Olle, T. William, ed. Information Systems Design Methodologies: Improving the Practice. 318p. 1986. 69.25 (0-444-70014-5, North Holland) Elsevier.

Olle, T. William, jt. ed. see Verrijn-Stuart, A. A.

Olle, T. William, et al, eds. Computerized Assistance During the Information Systems Life Cycle: Proc. of the IFIP WG8.1 Conf. CRIS 88, Egham, Surrey, UK, 19-22 Sept., 1988. 540p. 1988. 113.00 (0-444-70512-0, North Holland) Elsevier.

— Information Systems Design Methodologies: A Comparative Review. 648p. 1982. 97.50 (0-444-86407-5, I-301-82, North Holland) Elsevier.

— Information Systems Design Methodologies - A Feature Analysis: Proceedings of the IFIP WG 8.1 Working Conference on Feature Analysis of Information Systems Design Methodologies, York, U. K., July 5-7, 1983. 230p. 1984. 54.00 (0-444-86705-8, I-459-83, North Holland) Elsevier.

Ollenberger, Ben C., et al, eds. The Flowering of Old Testament Theology: A Reader in Twentieth-Century Old Testament Theology, 1930-1990. LC 91-24963. (Sources for Biblical & Theological Study Ser.: Bk. 1). xii, 547p. 1992. 29.50 (0-931464-62-5) Eisenbrauns.

Ollenburger, Ben C., ed. So Wide a Sea: Essays on Biblical & Systematic Theology. (Text-Reader Ser.: No. 4). 145p. (Orig.). 1991. pap. text ed. 10.00 (0-936273-18-6) Inst Mennonite.

Ollenburger, Ben C., jt. auth. see Kraftchick, Steven J.

Ollenburger, Jane & Moore, Helan. A Sociology of Women: The Intersection of Patriarchy, Capitalism & Colonization. 240p. (C). 1991. pap. text ed. 19.00 (0-13-818766-5, 610702) P-H.

Ollendick, T. H., et al, eds. International Handbook of Phobic & Anxiety Disorders in Children & Adolescents. (Issues in Clinical Child Psychology Ser.). (Illus.). 435p. (C). 1994. text ed. 75.00 (0-306-44759-2, Plenum Pr) Plenum.

Ollendick, Thomas H. & Cerny, Jerome A. Clinical Behavior Therapy with Children. LC 81-17891. (Applied Clinical Psychology Ser.). 364p. (C). 1981. 49.50 (0-306-40774-4, Plenum Pr) Plenum.

Ollendick, Thomas H. & Hersen, M., eds. Handbook of Child Psychopathology. 2nd ed. (Illus.). 570p. 1989. 85.00 (0-306-42975-6, Plenum Pr) Plenum.

Ollendick, Thomas H. & Hersen, Michael, eds. Handbook of Child & Adoloscent Assessment. 528p. 1992. 61.95 (0-205-14592-2, Longwood Div) Allyn.

Ollendick, Thomas H. & Prinz, Ronald J., eds. Advances in Clinical Child Psychology, Vol. 15. (Illus.). 365p. (C). 1993. 69.50 (0-306-44273-6, Plenum Pr) Plenum.

— Advances in Clinical Child Psychology, Vol. 16. 1994. 69.50 (0-306-44552-2, Plenum Pr) Plenum.

— Advances in Clinical Child Psychology, Vol. 17. LC 77-643411. 406p. 1995. 79.50 (0-306-44799-1) Plenum.

Oller, John W., Jr. Coding Information in Natural Languages. LC 74-182465. (Janua Linguarum, Ser. Minor: No. 123). (Illus.). 120p. (Orig.). 1971. pap. text ed. 15.40 (3-10-800282-1) Mouton.

— Language & Bilingualism: More Tests of Tests. LC 90-55874. 192p. 1991. 32.50 (0-8387-5210-1) Bucknell U Pr.

— Language Tests at School: A Pragmatic Approach. (Applied Linguistics & Language Study Ser.). (Illus.). 1979. pap. text ed. 27.95 (0-582-55294-X, 74360) Longman.

— Methods That Work: Ideas for Language Teachers. 2nd ed. 1994. pap. 28.95 (0-8384-4271-4) Heinle & Heinle.

Oller, John W. & Jonz, Jon. Cloze & Coherence. LC 94-11856. 1994. write for info. (0-8387-5303-5) Bucknell U Pr.

Ollerenshaw, Chris & Ritchie, Ron. Primary Science: Making it Work. (Primary Curriculum Ser.). 192p. 1993. pap. 32.00 (1-85346-199-7, Pub. by D Fulton UK) Taylor & Francis.

Ollerenshaw, Chris & Triggs, Pat. Electricity. LC 94-4883. (Toy Box Science Ser.). (Illus.). 32p. (J). (gr. 3 up). 1994. lib. bdg. 17.27 (0-8368-1119-4) Gareth Stevens Inc.

— Gears. LC 94-4884. (Toy Box Science Ser.). (Illus.). 32p. (J). (gr. 3 up). 1994. lib. bdg. 17.27 (0-8368-1120-8) Gareth Stevens Inc.

— Levers. LC 94-4886. (Toy Box Science Ser.). (Illus.). 32p. (J). (gr. 3 up). 1994. lib. bdg. 17.27 (0-8368-1121-6) Gareth Stevens Inc.

— Toy Box Science, 4 vols., Set. (Illus.). (J). (gr. 3 up). 1994. lib. bdg. 69.08 (0-8368-1118-6) Gareth Stevens Inc.

— Wind-Ups. LC 94-4885. (Toy Box Science Ser.). (Illus.). 32p. (J). (gr. 3 up). 1994. lib. bdg. 17.27 (0-8368-1122-4) Gareth Stevens Inc.

Ollerenshaw, Philip G. Banking in Nineteenth-Century Ireland: The Belfast Banks, 1825-1914. (Illus.). 275p. 1989. reprint ed. text ed. 27.95 (0-7190-2277-0, Pub. by Manchester Univ Pr UK) St Martin.

— Banking in Nineteenth-Century Ireland: The Belfast Banks, 1825-1914. 288p. 1988. text ed. 75.00 (0-7190-2276-2, Pub. by Manchester Univ Pr UK) St Martin.

Ollerenshaw, Philip G., jt. ed. see Kennedy, Liam.

Ollero, A. & Camacho, E. F., eds. Intelligent Components & Instruments for Control Applications: Selected Papers from the IFAC Symposium, Malaga, Spain, 20-22 May, 1992. LC 92-44354. (IFAC Symposia Ser.). 1993. 200.00 (0-08-041899-6, Pergamon Pr) Elsevier.

Olleros, Angel Rodriguez. Canto a la Raza: Composicion Sangvinea De Estudiantes De la Universidad De Puerto Rico. 94p. 1974. 2.00 (0-8477-2314-3) U of PR Pr.

Ollerton, E., jt. ed. see Hyde, T. H.

Olley, John W. Righteousness in the Septuagint of Isaiah: A Contextual Study. LC 78-3425. (Society of Biblical Literature. Septuagint & Cognate Studies: No. 8). 201p. reprint ed. pap. 57.30 (0-7837-5438-8, 2045203) Bks Demand.

Olley, Peter M., jt. ed. see Coceani, Flavio.

Ollie. Suzann Says, Vol. I. (Illus.). 48p. (Orig.). 1992. pap. 5.95 (0-9624100-6-3) Bell Buckle.

Ollier, C. D. Ancient Landforms. 240p. 1992. text ed. 59.00 (1-85293-074-8, Pub. by Pinter Pubs UK) St Martin.

— Weathering. rev. ed. LC 75-320198. (Geomorphology Texts Ser.). (Illus.). 304p. (C). 1975. pap. text ed. 22.95 (0-582-30103-3) Wiley.

Ollier, C. D., ed. Morphotectonics of Passive Continental Margins. (Annals of Gemorphology Supplement Ser.: No. 54). (Illus.). 121p. (Orig.). 1985. pap. text ed. 46.50 (3-443-21054-6, Pub. by Gebruder Borntraeger GW) Lubrecht & Cramer.

Ollier, Claude. Disconnection. Di Bernardi, Dominic, tr. LC 89-35215. 130p. 1989. 19.95 (0-916583-47-3) Dalkey Arch.

— Law & Order. Molinaro, Ursule, tr. LC 76-133248. Orig. Title: Le Maintien De L'ordre. 126p. 1971. 4.95 (0-87376-015-8) Red Dust.

— Mise-en-Scene. LC 87-73069. 240p. 1988. 20.00 (0-916583-26-0) Dalkey Arch.

Ollier, Cliff. Volcanoes. (Illus.). 240p. 1988. pap. text ed. 32.95 (0-631-15977-0) Blackwell Pubs.

Ollier, Francois. La Mirage Spartiate Part 1: Etude sur l'Idealisation de Sparte dans l'Antiquite Greque de ' Origine Jusqu'aux Cyniques, 2 vols. in 1. Bd. with Mirage Spartiate Part 2: Etude sur l'Idealisation de Sparte dans "Antiquite Greque du Debut de l'Ecole Cynique Jusqu'a la Fin de la Cite. LC 72-7903. LC 72-7903. (Greek History Ser.). (FRE.). 1979. reprint ed. 53.95 (0-405-04799-1) Ayer.

Ollier, Susan, jt. auth. see Davies, Robert J.

Ollila, Dale G., jt. auth. see Renes, Robert M.

Ollila, Lloyd O., ed. The Kindergarten Child & Reading. LC 77-4318. 88p. (Orig.). reprint ed. pap. 25.10 (0-8357-8198-4, 2034083) Bks Demand.

Ollila, Lloyd O. & Mayfield, Margie I. Emergent Literacy: Preschool, Kindergarten, & Primary Grades. 320p. (C). 1991. pap. text ed. 29.00 (0-205-13216-2, H3216) Allyn.

***Ollin, Ros & Tucker, Jenny.** The NVQ & GNVQ Assessor Handbook: A Practical Guide to Achieving Units D32, D33, D34, D36. 128p. 1994. pap. 29.00x (0-7494-1356-5, Pub. by Kogan Page Educ UK) Taylor & Francis.

Olling, G. J. & Deng, Z., eds. Information Technology for Advanced Manufacturing Systems: Proceedings of the IFIP TC5 - WG5.3 International Conference on Information Technology for Advanced Manufacturing Systems, Nanjing, Jiangsu, P. R. China, 17-19 September 1991. LC 92-11567. (IFIP Transactions B: Applications in Technology Ser.: Vol. B-1). 1992. pap. write for info. (0-444-89308-3, North Holland) Elsevier.

Olling, G. J. & Kimura, F., eds. Human Aspects in Computer Integrated Manufacturing: Proceedings of the IFIP TC5 - WG5.3 Eighth International PROLAMAT Conference, Man in CIM, Tokyo, Japan, 24- 26 June 1992. LC 92-14799. (IFIP Transactions B: Applications in Technology Ser.). 1992. write for info. (0-444-89465-9, North Holland) Elsevier.

Olling, G. J., jt. ed. see Kochan, D.

Olling, G. J., jt. ed. see Sata, T.

Olling, Gustav, jt. ed. see Wozny, Michael J.

Ollinger, Michael. Organizational Form & Business Strategy in the U. S. Petroleum Industry. LC 92-41876. 166p. (C). 1993. lib. bdg. 35.00 (0-8191-8990-1) U Pr of Amer.

Olliphant, Jo A. Total Physical Fun: Strategies & Activities for Teaching & Learning Language Through Cooperative Play. (Illus.). 168p. 1991. pap. text ed. 24.95 (1-879725-00-2) Sahmarsh Pub.

O

Ollis, David F. & Al-Ekabi, Hussain, eds. Photocatalytical Purification & Treatment of Water & Air: Proceedings of the First International Conference on TiO2 Photocatalytical Purification & Treatment of Water & Air, London, Ontario, Canada, 8-13 November, 1992. LC 93-20734. (Trace Metals in the Environment Ser.: Vol. 3). 820p. 1993. 257.25 (0-444-89855-7) Elsevier.

Ollis, David F., jt. auth. see Bailey, James.

Ollis, W. Recent Developments of Chemistry of Natural Phenolic Compounds: Proceedings of the Plant Phenolics Group Symposium. LC 61-10648. 1961. 107.00 (0-08-009489-9, Pub. by Pergamon Repr UK) Franklin.

Ollis, W. D., jt. ed. see Barton, Derek H.

Ollivant. Bob Son of Battle. pap. 2.95 (0-89375-780-2) Troll Assocs.

Ollivant, Alfred. Bob, Son of Battle. (Airmont Classics Ser.). (Illus.). (J). (gr. 5 up). 1967. pap. 2.50 (0-8049-0141-4, CL-141) Airmont.

— Bob, Son of Battle. 22.95 (0-8488-0137-7, Amereon Hse) Amereon Ltd.

— Bob, Son of Battle. (Illus.). 306p. (J). (gr. 5 up). 1988. 19.95 (0-9616844-2-9) Greenhouse Pub.

— Bob, Son of Battle. Hinkle, Don, ed. LC 87-15477. (Illus.). 48p. (J). (gr. 3-6). 1988. lib. bdg. 12.89 (0-8167-1211-5); pap. text ed. 3.95 (0-8167-1212-3) Troll Assocs.

Olliver, Jane, ed. Doubleday Children's Atlas. LC 86-67523. (Illus.). 96p. (J). (gr. k-6). 1987. pap. 14.00 (0-385-23760-X) Doubleday.

— A Treasury of Animal Stories. LC 92-53110. (Treasury of Stories Ser.). (Illus.). 160p. (Orig.). (J). (gr. k-5). 1992. pap. 5.95 (1-85697-831-1, Kingfisher LKC) LKC.

— A Treasury of Giant & Monster Stories. LC 92-53112. (Treasury of Stories Ser.). (Illus.). 160p. (Orig.). (J). (gr. k-5). 1992. pap. 5.95 (1-85697-832-X, Kingfisher LKC) LKC.

— A Treasury of Spooky Stories. LC 92-53111. (Treasury of Stories Ser.). (Illus.). 160p. (Orig.). (J). (gr. k-5). 1992. pap. 5.95 (1-85697-830-3, Kingfisher LKC) LKC.

Ollivier, Emile. The Franco-Prussian War & Its Hidden Causes. Ives, George B., tr. LC 71-140369. (Select Bibliographies Reprint Ser.). 1977. reprint ed. 31.95 (0-8369-5612-5) Ayer.

Ollivier, Eric. L' Orphelin de Mer, Ou, Les Memoires de Monsieur Non. (FRE.). 1984. pap. 10.95 (0-7859-4200-9) Fr & Eur.

Ollivier, Jacqueline. Grammaire Francaise. 454p. (FRE.). (C). 1979. pap. text ed. 29.50 (0-15-529675-2) HB Coll Pubs.

— Grammaire Francaise. 2nd ed. 480p. (FRE.). (C). 1993. pap. text ed. 4.50 (0-15-501032-8) HB Coll Pubs.

— Grammaire Franciase. 2nd ed. 486p. (FRE.). 1993. lib. bdg. write for info. (0-15-500661-4) HB Coll Pubs.

Ollivier, Jacqueline, et al. Appel: Initiation Au Francais D'Jourd'Hui. 2nd ed. 557p. (C). 1988. pap. text ed. 44.75 (0-15-502927-4); teacher ed. pap. text ed. 14.50 (0-15-502929-0); pap. text ed. 27.75 (0-15-502928-2); audio 83.50 (0-15-502926-6) HB Coll Pubs.

Ollivier, John. Fun with Nursery Rhymes: Or What Was the Real Ending of Humpty Dumpty? (Illus.). 72p. (Orig.). 1990. pap. text ed. 9.95 (0-9626821-0-1) J Ollivier.

Ollivier, John J. Fun with Irish Myths: For Every Irishman.. .or Those Who Have to Live with One. Powell, Judith & Van Horn, Carol, eds. LC 91-11422. (Illus.). 230p. 1991. pap. 11.95 (1-56087-014-1) Top Mtn Pub.

— The Wisdom of African Mythology. Nguyen, Alina, ed. LC 91-35050. (Illus.). 256p. (Orig.). 1994. pap. 14.95 (1-56087-023-0) Top Mtn Pub.

— Wisdom of American Indian Mythology. 272p. 1995. pap. 17.95 (1-56087-049-4) Top Mtn Pub.

Ollivier, Louis, jt. ed. see Straszewska, Sophie.

Ollman, Arthur & Perez, Nissan N. Revelaciones: The Art of Manuel Alvarez Bravo. LC 90-62301. 143p. 1992. pap. 32.50 (0-8263-1397-3) U of NM Pr.

Ollman, B. Alienation. 2nd ed. LC 76-4234. (Studies in the History & Theory of Politics). 1977. pap. 22.95 (0-521-29083-X) Cambridge U Pr.

Ollman, Bertell. Dialectical Investigations. 192p. 1992. 49.95 (0-415-90679-2, A9542, Routledge NY); pap. 14.95 (0-415-90680-6, A9546, Routledge NY) Routledge.

— Marxism: An Uncommon Introduction. 128p. 1990. text ed. 22.50 (81-207-1197-1, Pub. by Sterling Pubs II) Apt Bks.

— Social & Sexual Revolution: Essays on Marx & Reich. LC 78-71204. 228p. 1979. 20.00 (0-89608-081-1); pap. 7.50 (0-89608-080-3) South End Pr.

Ollman, Bertell & Birnbaum, Jonathan, eds. U. S. Constitution: Two Hundred Years of Anti-Federalist, Abolitionist, Feminist, Muckraking, Progressive, & Especially Socialist Criticism. 416p. 1990. 50.00 (0-8147-6169-0); pap. 18.50 (0-8147-6170-4) NYU Pr.

Ollman, Bertell & Vernoff, Edward, eds. The Left Academy: Marxist Scholarship on American Campuses, Vol. 2. LC 81-12365. 202p. (Orig.). (C). 1984. text ed. 59.95 (0-275-91237-X, C12372, Praeger Pubs) Greenwood.

— The Left Academy: Marxist Scholarship on American Campuses, Vol. 3. LC 86-9321. 192p. (Orig.). 1986. text ed. 55.00 (0-275-92116-6, C21163, Praeger Pubs) Greenwood.

— The Left Academy: Marxist Scholarship on American Campuses, Vol. 3. LC 86-9321. 192p. (Orig.). 1986. pap. text ed. 14.95 (0-275-92117-4, B21173, Praeger Pubs) Greenwood.

Ollman, John, ed. see Fitzpatrick, Tony.

Ollman, John E., ed. Joseph Yoakum: Animistic Landscapes. (Illus.). 56p. (Orig.). 1989. pap. 15.00 (0-9621506-1-4) J Fleisher Gallery.

Ollson, Thomas. Swedish Lotto Systems: Guaranteed & Tested Strategies. (LOMAP Ser.: Vol. 4). (Illus.). 80p. 1986. pap. 9.95 (0-317-47680-7) Intergalactic NJ.

Ollswang, Jeffrey, jt. auth. see Ambrose, James.

Ollus, M. Digital Image Processing in Industrial Applications: Proceedings of the IFAC Workshop, Espoo, Finland, 10-12 June 1986. (IFAC Publication). 178p. 1987. 82.00 (0-08-034346-5, Pub. by Pergamon Repr UK) Franklin.

Olm, Kenneth & Eddy, George. Entrepreneurship & Venture Management. 528p. (C). 1985. write for info. (0-675-20097-0, Merrill Pub Co) Macmillan.

Olman, John M. The Squire: The Legendary Golfing Life of Gene Sarazen. LC 87-5714. (Illus.). 176p. 1987. 29.95 (0-942117-00-X) Market St Pr.

— The Squire: The Legendary Golfing Life of Gene Sarazen. deluxe limited ed. LC 87-5714. (Illus.). 176p. 1987. ring bd. 140.00 (0-942117-01-8) Market St Pr.

Olman, John M. & Olman, Morton W. Golf Antiques: And Other Treasures of the Game. abr. rev. ed. LC 93-78337. (Illus.). 312p. 1993. pap. 19.95 (0-942117-16-6) Market St Pr.

— Olmans' Guide to Golf Antiques: And Other Treasures of the Game. (Illus.). 280p. 1992. 24.95 (0-942117-02-6) Market St Pr.

— St. Andrews & Golf; With Illustrations by Authur Weaver. LC 93-78338. (Illus.). 208p. (Orig.). 1995. 55.00 (0-942117-20-4) Market St Pr.

Olman, Morton W., jt. auth. see Olman, John M.

Olmedo, Alfonso, tr. see Augsburger, David.

Olmedo, Alfonso, tr. see Benko, Stephen.

Olmedo, Esteban L. & Walker, Verna R., eds. Hispanics in the United States: Abstracts of the Psychological & Behavioral Literature, 1980-1989. LC 90-1218. (PsycINFO Bibliographies in Psychology Ser.: No. 8). 318p. (Orig.). 1990. pap. 27.50 (1-55798-103-5) Am Psychol.

Olmedo, Teofilo E., tr. see Synowiec, Bertie Ryan.

Olmert, Michael. Official Guide to Colonial Williamsburg. LC 85-3729. (Illus.). 160p. (Orig.). 1985. pap. 4.78 (0-87935-111-X) Colonial Williamsburg.

— The Smithsonian Book of Books. LC 91-39590. (Illus.). 320p. 1992. 49.95 (0-89599-030-X) Smithsonian Bks.

— The Smithsonian Book of Books. LC 95-14441. 1995. 24.99 (0-517-14725-4, Pub. by Wings Bks) Random.

***Olmi, M.** The Dryinidae & Embolemidae (Hymenoptera:Chrysidoidea) of Fennoscandia & Denmark. (Fauna Entomologica Scandinavica Ser.: 30). 1994. 40.00 (90-04-10224-8) E J Brill.

— Revision of the Dryinidae (Hymenoptera), 2 vols. (Memoir Ser.: No. 37). (Illus.). 1938p. 1984. 130.00 (1-56665-035-6) Assoc Pubs FL.

Olmo, Ettore. A. Reptilia. (Animal Cytogenetics Ser.: Vol. 4: Chordata 3). (Illus.). 100p. 1986. pap. text ed. 54.60 (0-685-59739-3, Pub. by Gebrueder Borntraeger GW) Lubrecht & Cramer.

— Animal Cytogenetics, Vol. 4: Chordata, Pt. 3: Reptilia. (Illus.). 104p. 1986. text ed. 62.50 (0-685-55889-4, Pub. by Gebrueder Borntraeger GW) Lubrecht & Cramer.

— Cytogenetics of Amphibians & Reptiles. (Advances in Life Sciences Ser.). 280p. 1990. 64.50 (0-8176-2358-2) Birkhauser.

***Olmo, Lauro.** Camisa English Spoken - S. Garcia. 3rd ed. 234p. 1986. pap. 9.95 (0-7859-5184-9) Fr & Eur.

Olmos, Dan, ed. see Cirincione, Diane V.

Olmos, Dan, ed. see Dean, Amy E.

Olmos, Dan, ed. see Fox, Arnold & Fox, Barry.

Olmos, Dan, ed. see Hay, Louise L.

Olmos, Dan, ed. see Hay, Louise L. & Tomchin, Linda C.

Olmos, Dan, ed. see Peterson, Wilferd A.

Olmos, Dan, ed. see Scolastico, Ron.

Olmos, Dan, ed. see Shultz, J. Kennedy.

Olmos, Margarite F. & Paravisini-Gebert, Lizabeth, eds. Pleasure in the Word: Erotic Writing by Latin American Women. 288p. 1994. pap. 10.95 (0-452-27104-5, Plume) NAL-Dutton.

Olmos, Vicente-Juan B. A Catalogue of Two Hundred Type-I UFO Events in Spain & Portugal. (Illus.). 91p. (C). 1976. pap. 6.00 (0-929343-50-6) J A Hynek Ctr UFO.

Olmstead. Small Animal Orthopedics. (Illus.). 700p. 1991. 55.00 (0-8016-5874-8) Mosby Yr Bk.

Olmstead, Albert T. History of Assyria. LC 23-17167. (Midway Reprint Ser.). 727p. reprint ed. pap. 180.00 (0-317-20694-X, 2024061) Bks Demand.

Olmstead, Andrea, ed. Conversations with Roger Sessions. (Illus.). 224p. 1987. text ed. 30.00 (1-55553-010-9) NE U Pr.

— The Correspondence of Roger Sessions. 550p. 1992. text ed. 60.00 (1-55553-122-9) NE U Pr.

Olmstead, Arthur T. History of the Persian Empire. LC 48-7317. (Illus.). 1959. pap. 22.95 (0-226-62777-2, P36) U Ch Pr.

***Olmstead, Cresencia & Olmstead, Dale.** Mission Santa Ines: The Hidden Gem. 24p. (Orig.). 1995. pap. 6.00 (0-9646858-0-9) Old Mission Santa Ines.

Olmstead, Dale, jt. auth. see Olmstead, Cresencia.

Olmstead, Earl P. Blackcoats among the Delaware: David Zeisberger on the Ohio Frontier. LC 90-47576. (Illus.). 296p. 1991. 29.00 (0-87338-422-9); pap. 17.50 (0-87338-434-2) Kent St U Pr.

Olmstead, Esther R. Beta: A Novel. 1994. 15.95 (0-533-10771-7) Vantage.

Olmstead, Frederick L. A Journey in the Back Country. 394p. 1972. reprint ed. 24.00 (0-87928-032-8) Corner Hse.

— The Yosemite Valley & the Mariposa Big Trees: A Preliminary Report, 1865. LC 93-22909. (Illus.). 1995. write for info. (0-939666-68-5); pap. write for info. (0-939666-69-3) Yosemite Assn.

Olmstead, Gerald W. The Best of the Sierra Nevada: Lake Tahoe - Reno - Sequoia - Kings Canyon - Yosemite - The Gold Country. (Illus.). 288p. 1991. pap. 14.00 (0-517-57467-5, Crown) Crown Pub Group.

Olmstead, Jean E. Itinerant Teaching: Tricks of the Trade for Teachers of Blind & Visually Impaired Students. LC 91-8392. 136p. 1991. 24.95 (0-89128-190-8) Am Foun Blind.

Olmstead, Marty, jt. auth. see Ritz, Stacy.

Olmstead, Marty, et al. San Francisco & the Bay Area: California Gateway to the Future. (Illus.). 224p. 1992. 32.95 (0-89781-443-6) Preferred Mktg.

Olmstead, Robert. America by Land. LC 92-50511. 1993. 20.00 (0-679-41130-5) Random.

— America by Land. braille ed. 314p. 1994. text ed., vinyl bd. 25.12 (1-56956-530-9, BR9526) W A T Braille.

— A Trail of Heart's Blood Wherever We Go. 1990. 19.95 (0-394-57539-3) Random.

— A Trail of Heart's Blood Wherever We Go. 416p. 1992. reprint ed. pap. 11.00 (0-380-71548-1) Avon.

Olmstead & Williams. Chemistry: The Molecular Science. 992p. 1993. 52.00 (0-8016-7485-9) Mosby Yr Bk.

— General Chemistry Lab Manual. 1993. 16.00 (0-8016-5072-0) Mosby Yr Bk.

***Olmsted, Barney & Smith, Suzanne.** Creating a Flexible Workplace: How to Select & Manage Alternative Work Options. 2nd ed. LC 94-28096. 384p. 1994. 59.95 (0-8144-0214-3) AMACOM.

Olmsted, Bernie A. Injection Molding Basics. 47p. 1990. pap. 96.95 (0-929870-05-0) Advanstar Commns.

Olmsted, Cheryl. Alphabet Cooking Cards. (J). (gr. k-1). 1990. pap. 11.99 (0-8224-0454-0) Fearon Teach Aids.

Olmsted, D. L. Out of the Mouth of Babes: Earliest Stages in Language Learning. LC 70-17001. (Janua Linguarum, Ser. Minor: No. 117). (Illus.). 260p. (Orig.). 1971. pap. text ed. 39.70 (90-279-1892-9) Mouton.

Olmsted, Denison. Memoir of Eli Whitney, Esq. LC 72-5065. (Technology & Society Ser.). 90p. 1977. reprint ed. 19.95 (0-405-04716-9) Ayer.

Olmsted, Frederick L. The Cotton Kingdom. Powell, Lawrence et al, eds. (Modern Library College Editions). 708p. (C). 1983. pap. text ed. write for info. (0-07-554413-X) McGraw.

— Journey in the Seaboard Slave States, with Remarks on Their Economy. LC 68-55903. (Illus.). 723p. 1969. reprint ed. text ed. 35.00 (0-8371-0601-X, OLJ&, Negro U Pr) Greenwood.

— Journey Through Texas. 1993. reprint ed. lib. bdg. 75.00 (0-7812-5891-X) Rprt Serv.

— A Journey Through Texas: or, A Saddle-Trip on the Southwestern Frontier. (American Biography Ser.). 516p. 1991. reprint ed. lib. bdg. 99.00 (0-7812-8302-7) Rprt Serv.

Olmsted, Frederick L., Jr. Public Parks & the Enlargement of Towns. LC 76-112564. (Rise of Urban America Ser.). 1973. reprint ed. 15.95 (0-405-02469-X) Ayer.

Olmsted, Frederick L., Jr. & Kimball, Theodora. Frederick Law Olmsted, Landscape Architect: 1822-1903, 2 vols in 1. LC 68-57756. (Illus.). 1972. reprint ed. 38.95 (0-405-08829-9) Ayer.

Olmsted, Gerald W. The Best of the Pacific Coast: San Francisco to British Columbia: A Guide for the Curious Traveler. 1989. pap. 16.00 (0-517-57159-5, Crown) Crown Pub Group.

— A Rambler's Guide to the Trails of the East Bay Hills: Central Section Including Redwood, Chabot, Las Trampas, Sibley & Joaquin Miller Parks & Lands of East Bay MUD. (Illus.). 1987. 5.95 (0-941969-00-2) Olmsted Bros Map.

Olmsted, Henry K. & Ward, George K. Olmsted Family in America. LC 93-79946. (Illus.). 550p. 1994. reprint ed. 60.00 (1-55787-046-2) Hrt of the Lakes.

Olmsted, J. M. Francois Magendie. Cohen, I. Bernard, ed. LC 80-2139. (Illus.). 1981. reprint ed. lib. bdg. 30.95 (0-405-13894-6) Ayer.

Olmsted, J. M., jt. auth. see Gelbaum, B. R.

Olmsted, James F., jt. auth. see Whitney, Philip R.

Olmsted, John C., ed. Victorian Painting, Vol. 1: Essays & Reviews, 1832-1848. LC 80-65711. 688p. 1980. 12.00 (0-8240-2742-6) Garland.

Olmsted, John M. Second Course in Calculus. LC 68-14041. (Century Mathematics Ser.). (Illus.). 336p. (C). 1968. 39.50 (0-89197-395-8) Irvington.

Olmsted, Merle. The Three Hundred Fifty-Seventh over Europe: The 357th Fighter Group in World War II. Lambert, John W., ed. LC 94-65589. (Illus.). 164p. (C). 1994. 27.95 (1-883809-02-9) Phalanx Pub.

Olmsted, Merle C. Yoxford Boys. Rust, Kenn, ed. LC 77-135044. (Orig.). 1971. pap. 7.95 (0-8168-9766-2, 29766, TAB-Aero) TAB Bks.

Olmsted, Michael S. & Hare, A. Paul. The Small Group. 2nd ed. 1978. pap. text ed. write for info. (0-07-553607-2) McGraw.

Olmsted, Nancy. To Walk with a Quiet Mind: Hikes in the Woodlands, Parks & Beaches of the San Francisco Bay Area. LC 75-1053. (Totebook Ser.). (Illus.). 256p. 1975. pap. 9.95 (0-87156-125-5) Sierra.

Olmsted, P. & Weikart, D. P. How Nations Serve Young Children: Profiles of Care & Education in 14 Countries. LC 89-35026. 480p. (C). 1989. pap. text ed. 29.95 (0-929816-07-2, R1029) High-Scope.

Olmsted, Patricia P., jt. ed. see Weikart, David P.

Olmsted, Patricia P., et al. Parent Education: The Contributions of Ira J. Gordon. Sunderlin, Sylvia, ed. LC 80-12211. (Illus.). 64p. (Orig.). 1980. 4.75 (0-87173-094-4) ACEI.

Olmsted, Robert. The Shotgun. 16p. 1991. pap. 1.50 (0-89754-077-8) Dan River Pr.

Olmsted, Robert, ed. see Diamond, Olivia.

Olmsted, Robert W. Wild Strawberries at 3000 Feet. LC 86-60424. 64p. (Orig.). 1986. 19.95 (0-89002-245-3); pap. 6.95 (0-89002-244-5) Am Hist Pr.

Olmsted, S. L., jt. auth. see Holum, John R.

Olmsted, Sterling. Motions of Love: Woolman as Mystic & Activist. LC 93-85961. (Orig.). 1993. pap. 3.00 (0-87574-312-9) Pendle Hill.

Olmus, Margarite F. & Pavruisini-Gebert, Lizabeth, eds. Remaking & Lost Harmony: Stories from the Hispanic Caribbean. (Dispatches Ser.: Vol. 3). 250p. (Orig.). 1995. pap. 17.00 (1-877727-36-9) White Pine.

Olness, Frederick I., jt. auth. see Zimmerman, Robert L.

Olney, Clarke, jt. ed. see Hoge, James O.

Olney, Claude. Bucks Start Here: How to Turn Your Hidden Assets into Money. 1992. pap. 10.00 (0-688-11607-8, Quill) Morrow.

Olney, Claude W. How to Get Better Grades in College: Where There's a Will There's an "A" (Illus.). 22p. (Orig.). 1986. 29.95 (0-9617886-0-7) Olney A Seminar.

Olney, Don. The Little Book of Tops. LC 93-83462. (Miniature Editions Ser.). (Illus.). 96p. 1993. 4.95 (1-56138-310-4) Running Pr.

— The Tops Discovery Kit. LC 93-87365. (Discovery Kit Ser.). (Illus.). 64p. (J). (gr. 3 up). 1994. 17.95 (1-56138-389-9) Running Pr.

***Olney, J.** Modern Geography As of 1828. (Illus.). 200p. 1994. pap. 25.00 (0-87556-789-4) Saifer.

Olney, James. The Language(s) of Poetry: Walt Whitman, Emily Dickinson, Gerard Manley Hopkins. LC 92-12564. (Georgia Southern University Jack N. & Addie D. Averett Lecture Ser.: No. 2). 176p. 1993. 27.50 (0-8203-1485-4) U of Ga Pr.

— Metaphors of Self: The Meaning of Autobiography. LC 71-173758. 358p. reprint ed. pap. 102.10 (0-7837-1412-2, 2041766) Bks Demand.

— The Rhizome & the Flower: The Perennial Philosophy--Yeats & Jung. 1980. 50.00 (0-520-03748-0) U CA Pr.

Olney, James, ed. Afro-American Writing Today: An Anniversary Issue of the Southern Review. LC 88-39021. (Illus.). 328p. 1989. text ed. 34.95 (0-8071-1482-0) La State U Pr.

— T. S. Eliot: Essays from the Southern Review. (Illus.). 368p. 1988. 76.50 (0-19-818575-8) OUP.

Olney, Judith. The Joy of Chocolate. 208p. 1989. pap. 13.95 (0-8120-4279-4) Barron.

— Joy of Chocolate. LC 82-1356. 1982. 15.95 (0-8120-5435-0) Barron.

Olney, Marguerite, jt. ed. see Flanders, Helen H.

Olney, Martha L. Buy Now, Pay Later: Advertising, Credit, & Consumer Durables in the 1920s. LC 90-49565. xx, 424p. (C). 1991. 49.95 (0-8078-1958-1) U of NC Pr.

Olney, P. J., et al, eds. Creative Conservation: Interactive Management of Wild & Captive Animals. LC 93-33949. 1993. 94.95 (0-412-49570-8, Chap & Hall NY) Chapman & Hall.

Olney, R. J. & Melvin, Julia, eds. Wellington II: Political Correspondence, November 1834 - April 1835. (Prime Ministers' Papers Ser.). 669p. 1986. 50.00 (0-11-440201-9, HM02019, Pub. by HMSO UK) UNIPUB.

Olney, Rich. Lulu's Provencal Table. 448p. 1994. 30.00 (0-06-016922-2, HarpT) HarpC.

***Olney, Richard.** Romanee Conti. (Illus.). 208p. 1995. 30.00 (0-8478-1927-2) Rizzoli Intl.

— Simple French Food. LC 73-80755. (Illus.). 1977. pap. 10.95 (0-689-70546-8, 229, Atheneum S&S) S&S Trade.

— Simple French Food. (Illus.). 448p. 1992. reprint ed. pap. 13.00 (0-02-010060-4, Pub. by Gebrueder Borntraeger GW) Macmillan.

— Ten Vineyard Lunches. LC 88-21936. (Ten Menus Ser.). (Illus.). 128p. 1988. Cookery Book. 19.95 (0-940793-23-7) Interlink Pub.

Olney, Ross R. The Farm Combine. LC 84-5288. (Inventions That Changed Our Lives Ser.). (Illus.). 64p. (J). (gr. 4 up). 1984. lib. bdg. 10.85 (0-8027-6568-8) Walker & Co.

Olney, Ross R., jt. auth. see Sorrentino, Amedeo J.

Olney, Sandra S. Passengers on the "Lion" from England to Boston, 1632. 821p. (Orig.). 1992. pap. 53.00 (1-55613-706-0) Heritage Bk.

Olney Street Group Staff. The Olney Street Anthology. LC 88-92293. 120p. (Orig.). 1988. pap. 5.00 (0-9621084-0-5) Olney St Pr.

Oloff, Lawrence M., ed. Musculoskeletal Disorders of the Lower Extremities. LC 93-7250. 1994. text ed. 125.00 (0-7216-3716-7) Saunders.

***Olofsdotter, Marie.** Frej the Fearless: (The Secret World of Frej) Espeland, Pamela, ed. LC 95-2125. (Illus.). 32p. (J). (gr. k up). 1995. 14.95 (0-915793-86-5) Free Spirit Pub.

— Sofia & the Heartmender. LC 92-46200. (Illus.). 32p. (J). (gr. k up). 1993. 14.95 (0-915793-50-4) Free Spirit Pub.

Olofsson, Staffan. God is My Rock: A Study of Translation Technique & Theological Exegesis in the Septuagint. (Coniectanea Biblica. Old Testament Ser.: N. 31). 208p. (Orig.). 1990. pap. 46.50x (91-22-01394-6, Pub. by Almqv & Wiksell SW) Coronet Bks.

— The LXX Version: A Guide to the Translation Technique of the Septuagint. (Coniectanea Biblica. Old Testament Ser.: No. 30). 105p. (Orig.). 1990. pap. 31.00x (91-22-01392-X, Pub. by Almqv & Wiksell SW) Coronet Bks.

Olofsson, Tommy. Elemental Poems. Pearson, Jean, tr. 72p. 1991. 9.00 (1-877727-09-1) White Pine.

Olomucki, Martin. The Chemistry of Life. Leonard, Isabel A., tr. LC 92-14287. (McGraw-Hill Horizons of Science Ser.). 1992. pap. text ed. 11.95 (0-07-047929-1) McGraw.

Oloniyo, N. Living by Faith. 204p. 1993. pap. 5.95 (0-88172-201-4) Believers Bkshelf.

***O'Looney, John.** Economic Development & Environmental Control: Balancing Business & Community in Age of NIMBYS & LULUS. LC 94-45283. 368p. 1995. text ed. 69.50 (0-89930-940-2, Quorum Bks) Greenwood.

An Asterisk (*) at the beginning of an entry indicates that the title is appearing in BIP for the first time.

Olorenshaw, R. Teach Yourself French, Further. (Teach Yourself Ser.). 1992. 15.95 (0-8288-8328-9); 45.00 (0-8288-8329-7) Fr & Eur.

Olorode, Omotoye. Taxonomy of West African Flowering Plants. (Illus.). 176p. 1984. text ed. 25.95 (0-582-64429-1) Longman.

O'Loughlin, Anne, jt. auth. see Plagman, Bernard K.

Oloughlin, C. Economics of Sea Transport. LC 66-29598. 1967. 96.00 (0-08-012295-7, Pub. by Pergamon Repr UK) Franklin.

O'Loughlin, C. National Economic Accounting. 1971. 88.00 (0-08-016395-5, Pub. by Pergamon Repr UK) Franklin.

O'Loughlin, Edward T., ed. Hearst & His Enemies. LC 76-125710. (American Journalists Ser.). 1974. reprint ed. 16.95 (0-405-01691-3) Ayer.

O'Loughlin, Geoffrey, intro. International Symposium on Urban Stormwater Management. (Illus.). 460p. (Orig.). 1992. pap. 72.00 (0-85825-547-2, Pub. by Inst Engrs Aust-EA Bks AT) Accents Pubns.

O'Loughlin, John, ed. Dictionary of Geopolitics. LC 93-25072. 304p. 1993. text ed. 69.50 (0-313-26313-2, ODG/, Greenwood Pr) Greenwood.

— The New Political Geography of Eastern Europe. 1993. text ed. 69.95 (0-471-94812-8) Wiley.

O'Loughlin, John & Van der Wusten, Herman. The New Political Geography of Eastern Europe. 280p. 1993. text ed. 65.00 (0-470-21933-5) Halsted Pr.

O'Loughlin, John, jt. ed. see Glebe, Gunther.

O'Loughlin, John, et al, eds. War & Its Consequences: Lessons from the Persian Gulf Conflict. LC 93-34027. (C). 1994. 14.50 (0-06-502260-2) HarpCollege.

***O'Loughlin, Luanne.** Free Stuff from CompuServe. 1995. pap. 19.99 (1-883577-26-8) Coriolis Grp.

***O'Loughlin, Luannr S.** Free Stuff from America Online. 1994. pap. 19.99 (1-883577-17-9) Coriolis Grp.

O'Loughlin, Michale, tr. see Achterberg, Gerrit.

O'Loughlin, Micheal, ed. see Kuhn, Deanna & Amsel, Eric.

O'Loughlin, Raphael. Basilian Leaders from Texas. Whitebird, J., ed. (Texas-Church History Ser.). (Illus.). 112p. (Orig.). 1992. pap. 20.00 (0-685-50819-6) Wings Pr.

O'Loughlin, Sean, jt. auth. see Muir, Kenneth.

O'Loughlin, Thomas. Cardinal Newman: Seeker of Truth. 1989. pap. 22.00 (1-85390-096-6, Pub. by Veritas IE) St Mut.

Olovsson, Paul, jt. ed. see Klevmarken, Anders.

Olowofoyeku, Abimbola. Suing Judges: A Study of Judicial Immunity. 256p. 1994. 45.00 (0-19-825793-7) OUP.

Olowomeye, Richard. The Management of Solid Waste in Nigerian Cities. LC 90-27893. (Environment: Problems & Solutions Ser.). 224p. 1991. 20.00 (0-8240-9274-0) Garland.

Oloyede, Olajide. Coping under Recession: Workers in a Nigerian Factory. (Studia Sociologica Upsaliensia: No. 34). 177p. (Orig.). 1991. pap. 45.00x (91-554-2801-0, Pub. by Almqv & Wiksell SW) Coronet Bks.

Olozak, Anatole, jt. auth. see Waechter, Parker.

Olpin, Robert S., ed. see Harwood, James T.

Olrik, Axel. Principles for Oral Narrative Research. Wolf, Kirsten & Jensen, Jody, trs. LC 88-46034. (Folklore Studies in Translation). 240p. 1992. text ed. 29.95 (0-253-34175-2) Ind U Pr.

***Olry, Regis.** Dictionary of Anatomical Eponyms. LC 94-23697. 1994. write for info. (1-56081-407-1) VCH Pubs.

Olsa, Aaron C., tr. see Hutchinson, Hanna.

Olsav Lautenschlaeger, Susan J. Blooming Discoveries: Fun Language Activities to Explore Everyday Wonders Based on Bloom's Taxonomy. 80p. (J). (gr. k-5). 1991. pap. 15.95 (1-55999-206-9) LinguiSystems.

Olsavsky, Mary A. New Work Systems Network: A Compendium of Selected Work Innovation Cases. (BLMR Ser.: No. 136). (Illus.). 499p. 1990. boxed, pap. 25.00 (0-16-019802-X, S/N 029-011-000) USGPO.

Olsby, Gary. Bible History Overview: Old Testament. (Orig.). 1989. pap. 13.99 (0-89900-440-7); student ed 5.99 (0-89900-441-5) College Pr Pub.

— Bible History Overview - New Testament. 1991. student ed 5.99 (0-89900-443-1); student ed, pap. 13.99 (0-89900-442-3) College Pr Pub.

Olscamp, Paul J. An Introduction to Philosophy. LC 77-144104. 523p. reprint ed. pap. 149.10 (0-317-08892-0, 2012522) Bks Demand.

Olscamp, Paul J., tr. see Malebranche, Nicolas.

Olschak, Blanche, et al. Himalayas. (Illus.). 288p. 1988. 40. 00 (0-8160-1994-0) Facts on File.

Olschewski, Andreas, jt. auth. see Groth, Wolfgang.

Olsder, G. J., jt. auth. see Basar, T.

Olsen, et al. Alemany Press Teacher Resource Sampler. 1992. pap. write for info. (0-13-063736-X) P-H.

Olsen. Electronics: A Course Book for Students: 2nd. 1982. pap. text ed. 24.95 (0-408-00491-6) Buttrwrth-Heinemann.

— Fundamentals of Nursing. (Nursetest: A Review Ser.). 1991. 19.95 (0-87434-302-X) Springhouse Pub.

— A Killer Is Waiting. (Gunsmoke Western Ser.). 12.95 (0-86220-958-7, C0499, Gunsmoke) Chivers N Amer.

Olsen, ed. Tectonic, Depositional, & Paleoecological History of Early Mesozoic Rift Basins, Eastern North America, No. T351. (IGC Field Trip Guidebooks Ser.). 184p. 1989. 35.00 (0-87590-658-3) Am Geophysical.

Olsen & Murray. Dosage Calculations. (Nursetest: A Review Ser.). 1991. 19.95 (0-87434-301-1) Springhouse Pub.

Olsen, Afton S., ed. see McFarland, Minnie B.

Olsen, Alan. Fundamentals of Microanalytical Entomology: A Practical Guide to Detecting & Identifying Filth in Foods. 320p. 1995. 89.95 (0-8493-8925-9, 8925) CRC Pr.

Olsen, Alexandra H. Betwene Ernest & Game: The Literary Artistry of the Confessio Amantis. LC 89-133292. (American University Studies: English Language & Literature: Ser. IV, Vol. 110). 130p. 1990. text ed. 31.50 (0-8204-1141-8) P Lang Pubs.

Olsen, Alexandra H., jt. ed. see Damico, Helen.

Olsen, Alfa-Betty & Efron, Marshall. Gabby the Shrew. LC 92-31902. (Illus.). (J). 1994. lib. bdg. write for info. (0-679-94467-2) Random.

Olsen, Alfa-Betty, jt. auth. see Efron, Marshall.

Olsen, Allison, tr. see Tonnessen, Tor I.

***Olsen, Anders, et al.** Systems Engineering Using SDL-92. LC 94-31557. 1994. write for info. (0-444-89872-7, North Holland) Elsevier.

Olsen, Andrea. Bodystories. 1991. pap. 19.95 (0-88268-106-0) Station Hill Pr.

Olsen, Ardath, et al. Christmas Journeys with Howard Shuler. Smith, Bernadine, ed. 102p. 1987. 15.00 (0-940696-16-9) Monroe County Lib.

Olsen, Bernard A. Upon the Tented Field. LC 93-80311. (Illus.). 336p. 1993. 34.95 (0-9638729-0-7) Historic Proj.

Olsen, Bjorn R., jt. ed. see Nimni, Marcel E.

Olsen, Bruce, tr. see Cho Chikun Nine-Dan.

Olsen, Bruce L., jt. auth. see Garrison, Marc S.

Olsen, Carol. Left-Over Louie. (Illus.). 169p. (Orig.). (J). 1993. 29.95 (1-883078-75-X) Gig Harbor Pr.

— Left-Over Louie. 2nd ed. (Illus.). 168p. (Orig.). (J). (gr. 2 up). 1993. pap. 11.95 (1-883078-76-8) Gig Harbor Pr.

— Slime: Slugs Have Feelings Too. (Left-over Louie Ser.: 1). (Illus.). 26p. (Orig.). (J). (k-6). 1994. pap. 6.95 (1-883078-80-6) Gig Harbor Pr.

Olsen, Catherine. Index Theory in Von Neumann Algebras. LC 83-22519. (Memoirs Ser.: No. 47/294). 71p. 1984. pap. 15.00 (0-8218-2295-0, MEMO 47/294) Am Math.

***Olsen, Charles M.** Transforming Church Boards into Communities of Spiritual Leaders. 1995. 15.25 (1-56699-148-X, AL158) Alban Inst.

***Olsen, Christina.** The Art of Tarot. LC 95-15102. 1995. write for info. (0-7892-0016-3) Abbeville Pr.

Olsen, Claudia, jt. auth. see Allred, Jacki.

Olsen, Clifford C., jt. auth. see Townsend, Thomas H.

Olsen, Cynthia B. El Aceita de Arbol de Te Australiano (Australian Tea Tree Oil Handbook) 101 Maneras de Usar el Aceite de Arbol Dete. Gerlach, Chris, ed. Isberg, Kathleen B., tr. (Illus.). 48p. (Orig.). (SPA.). 1991. pap. 3.50 (0-9628882-2-2) Kali Pr.

— Australian Tea Tree Oil. (Illus.). 40p. (Orig.). 1989. pap. text ed. 3.95 (0-9628882-0-6) Kali Pr.

— Australian Tea Tree Oil Guide. 2nd ed. LC 91-220651. 80p. 1991. pap. 6.95 (0-9628882-1-4) Kali Pr.

Olsen, D. H. & Straub, B. E. Delaware Bay Fishing Guide: Delaware Edition. 128p. 1991. pap. 9.95 (0-9629749-0-0) Vayu Pr.

— Delaware Bay Fishing Guide: New Jersey Edition. 128p. (Orig.). 1991. pap. 9.95 (0-9629749-1-9) Vayu Pr.

Olsen, Dale & Olsen, Dale A. Music of Many Cultures: Study Guide & Workbook. 272p. (C). 1994. per., pap. text ed. 19.95 (0-8403-8596-X) Kendall-Hunt.

Olsen, Dale A., jt. auth. see Olsen, Dale.

Olsen, Dan R. User Interface Management Systems; Models & Algorithms. LC 91-41076. (Morgan Kaufmann Series in Computer Graphics & Geometric Modeling). 231p. 1992. 49.95 (1-55860-220-8, QA76.9) Morgan Kaufmann.

Olsen, David. Socio-Economic Survey of Recreational Boating & Fishing in the U. S. Virgin Islands. (Illus.). 80p. 1979. 12.00 (0-318-14618-5) Isl Resources.

— Two Thousand Plus Creative Dates: Dating Ideas & Activities. Akens, Jean et al, eds. (Illus.). 52p. (Orig.). 1991. pap. 5.95 (0-925685-99-2) Canyon Country Pubns.

— Words You Should Know. 260p. 1991. pap. 6.95 (1-55850-018-9) Adams Pubng.

Olsen, David C. Integrative Family Therapy. LC 92-44125. (Creative Pastoral Care & Counseling Ser.). 96p. 1993. 10.00 (0-8006-2638-9, 1-2638, Fortress Pr) Augsburg Fortress.

Olsen, David C., ed. Atkins - Knopfler: Neck & Neck. 132p. 1991. pap. text ed. 16.95 (0-89898-635-4) CPP Belwin.

— The Great Songs of Country Music. rev. ed. (New Home Library). 112p. (Orig.). (YA). 1995. reprint ed. pap. text ed. 9.95 (0-89724-630-6) Warner Brothers.

— The Greatest Songs of 1890-1920. 112p. (Orig.). (YA). 1990. pap. text ed. 9.95 (0-89898-599-4) CPP Belwin.

— The Greatest Songs of 1940-1960. 112p. (Orig.). (YA). 1990. pap. text ed. 9.95 (0-89898-601-X) CPP Belwin.

— The Greatest Songs of 1975-1990. 112p. (Orig.). (YA). 1993. pap. text ed. 9.95 (0-89898-603-6) CPP Belwin.

— Life of the Christmas Party. 160p. (Orig.). (YA). 1988. pap. text ed. 19.95 (0-89898-645-1) CPP Belwin.

— One Hundred Seventy Christmas Songs & Carols. 232p. (Orig.). (YA). 1987. pap. text ed. 19.95 (0-89898-644-3) CPP Belwin.

— Songs of Judy Garland. 80p. (Orig.). (YA). 1990. pap. text ed. 11.95 (0-89898-611-7) CPP Belwin.

— The World's Best Piano. 280p. (Orig.). (YA). 1991. pap. text ed. 19.95 (0-89898-598-6) CPP Belwin.

Olsen, David C., ed. see Charles, Ray.

Olsen, David C., jt. auth. see Grosch, William N.

Olsen, Donald J. The City As a Work of Art: London, Paris, Vienna. LC 85-24639. 360p. 1986. text ed. 55.00 (0-300-02870-9) Yale U Pr.

— The City As a Work of Art: London, Paris, Vienna. LC 85-24639. 360p. (C). 1988. reprint ed. 22.50 (0-300-04212-4) Yale U Pr.

— Town Planning in London: The Eighteenth & Nineteenth Centuries. LC 82-50440. (Illus.). 246p. 1982. pap. 22.00 (0-300-02915-2, Y-443) Yale U Pr.

Olsen, E. A. Adrift on a Raft. LC 68-16397. (Oceanography Ser.). (Illus.). 48p. (J). (gr. 3 up). 1970. lib. bdg. 10.95 (0-87783-000-2); audio 10.60 (0-87783-176-9) Oddo.

— Adrift on a Raft. deluxe ed. LC 68-16397. (Oceanography Ser.). (Illus.). 48p. (J). (gr. 3 up). 1970. pap. 3.94 (0-87783-078-9) Oddo.

— Killer in the Trap. LC 68-16399. (Oceanography Ser.). (Illus.). 48p. (J). (gr. 3 up). 1970. lib. bdg. 10.95 (0-87783-019-3); audio 10.60 (0-87783-190-4) Oddo.

— Killer in the Trap. deluxe ed. LC 68-16399. (Oceanography Ser.). (Illus.). 48p. (J). (gr. 3 up). 1970. pap. 3.94 (0-87783-097-5) Oddo.

— Lobster King. LC 68-16400. (Oceanography Ser.). (Illus.). 48p. (J). (gr. 3 up). 1970. lib. bdg. 10.95 (0-87783-024-X); audio 10.60 (0-87783-192-0) Oddo.

— Lobster King. deluxe ed. LC 68-16400. (Oceanography Ser.). (Illus.). 48p. (J). (gr. 3 up). 1970. pap. 3.94 (0-87783-099-1) Oddo.

— Mystery at Salvage Rock. LC 68-16401. (Oceanography Ser.). (Illus.). 48p. (J). (gr. 3 up). 1970. lib. bdg. 10.95 (0-87783-027-4); audio 10.60 (0-87783-195-5) Oddo.

— Mystery at Salvage Rock. deluxe ed. LC 68-16401. (Oceanography Ser.). (Illus.). 48p. (J). (gr. 3 up). 1970. pap. 3.94 (0-87783-101-7) Oddo.

Olsen, E. G. Atlas of Cardiovascular Pathology. 1987. lib. bdg. 177.50 (0-85200-866-X) Kluwer Ac.

Olsen, E. G., jt. ed. see Goodwin, J. F.

Olsen, E. G., jt. ed. see Sekiguchi, Morie.

Olsen, Eddie, jt. auth. see Patterson, Jerry L.

Olsen, Edward A. U. S. - Japan Strategic Reciprocity: A Neo-Internationalist View. (Publication Ser.: No. 307). xiii, 194p. 1985. 24.95 (0-8179-8071-7); pap. 10.95 (0-8179-8072-5) Hoover Inst Pr.

— U. S. Policy & the Two Koreas. 115p. (C). 1988. pap. text ed. 27.00 (0-8133-0593-4) Westview.

Olsen, Edward J. Meteorites: The Poor Man's Space Probe. LC 73-163905. (Augustana College Library Occasional Papers, Wallin Lecture: No. 11). 18p. 1973. pap. 1.00 (0-910182-34-5) Augustana Coll.

Olsen, Elise A. Disorders of Hair Growth: Diagnosis & Treatment. (Illus.). 448p. 1994. 115.00 (0-07-047934-8) Hlth Prof Div.

Olsen, Ellyn. God's Blueprint for Mankind: As Revealed in the Feasts of the Lord. LC 83-72382. (Illus.). 96p. 1983. pap. 3.95 (0-913961-00-0) Bless Israel.

Olsen, Eric. On the Right Track: A Spectator's Guide to the Olympic Running Events. 1984. pap. write for info. (0-672-52807-X) Macmillan.

Olsen, Eve C., jt. auth. see Strang, Paul D.

***Olsen, Frances, ed.** Feminist Legal Theory Vol. I: Foundations & Outlooks. 574p. 1995. pap. 29.50 (0-8147-6185-2) NYU Pr.

— Feminist Legal Theory Vol. II: Positioning Feminist Theory Within the Law. 593p. 1995. pap. 29.50 (0-8147-6186-0) NYU Pr.

***Olsen, Frances E., ed.** Feminist Legal Theory, 2 vols. Incl. Vol. 1. Feminist Legal Theory, 2 vols. LC 94-30376. 1994. (0-8147-6179-8); Vol. 2. Feminist Legal Theory, 2 vols. LC 94-30376. 1994. (0-8147-6180-1); LC 94-30376. (International Library of Essays in Law & Legal Theory, Schools: Vol. 15). 250.00 (0-8147-6177-1) NYU Pr.

Olsen, Fred. Indian Creek. LC 74-5959. (Illus.). 100p. 1975. pap. 7.95 (0-8061-1208-5) U of Okla Pr.

Olsen, Fred A., ed. Technology: A Reign of Benevolence & Destruction. LC 73-16385. 1974. 29.50 (0-8422-5130-8) Irvington.

Olsen, Frederick. The Kiln Book. 2nd ed. LC 81-71090. 312p. (C). 1983. 35.00 (0-8019-7071-7) Chilton.

Olsen, Frederick I., et al. Frederick Layton & His World, 1888. Tilendis, Robert M., ed. LC 87-61767. (Illus.). 283p. (Orig.). 1988. pap. 19.95 (0-944110-23-1) Milwauk Art Mus.

Olsen, Gary. Getting Started in Computer Graphics. rev. ed. (Illus.). 160p. 1993. pap. 27.95 (0-89134-468-3, 30469) North Light Bks.

Olsen, George H. The Beginner's Handbook of Electronics. 1980. 17.95 (0-13-074211-2) P-H.

Olsen, Gerald W., intro. & notes. Religion & Revolution in Early-Industrial England: The Halevy Thesis & Its Critics. LC 89-36361. 252p. (Orig.). (C). 1990. lib. bdg. 40.75 (0-8191-7554-4); pap. text ed. 24.00 (0-8191-7555-2) U Pr of Amer.

Olsen-Gisel, H. Developments in Stamens of Viola Odorata. (Dissertationes Botanicae Ser.: Vol. 70). (Illus.). 192p. 1983. pap. text ed. 48.00 (3-7682-1362-5) Lubrecht & Cramer.

Olsen, Glenda P. Birds of Prey. LC 93-2670. (Naturebooks Ser.). (J). (gr. 2-6). 1993. lib. bdg. 22.79 (1-56766-059-2) Childs World.

Olsen, Gregg. Abandoned Prayers. 1990. mass mkt. 4.95 (0-445-21076-1) Warner Bks.

— Bitter Almonds: The True Story of Mothers, Daughters & the Seattle Cyanide Murders. 552p. (Orig.). 1993. mass mkt. 6.99 (0-446-36359-6) Warner Bks.

— Mockingbird: A Mother, a Child, a Tragedy. 344p. 1995. mass mkt. 5.99 (0-446-60095-4) Warner Bks.

Olsen, Gregg M. The Struggle for Economic Democracy in Sweden. 159p. 1992. 68.95 (1-85628-298-8, Pub. by Avebury Pub UK) Ashgate Pub Co.

Olsen, H. N., et al. Temperature Measurements in Seeded Air & Nitrogen Plasmas. LC 79-131016. 133p. 1970. 19. 00 (0-403-04524-X) Scholarly.

Olsen, Hans C. The Work of Boards of Education. LC 77-177134. (Columbia University. Teachers College. Contributions to Education Ser.: No. 213). reprint ed. 37.50 (0-404-55213-7) AMS Pr.

Olsen, Harry, ed. see Riekes, Linda & Ackerly, Sally M.

Olsen, Harvet W. The Signature Man: Tales of a Detached Rear. 1993. pap. 11.95 (0-533-10126-3) Vantage.

Olsen, Ib S. The Grown-up Trap. LC 91-35251. (Illus.). 32p. (J). (ps-4). 1990. 6.98 (0-934738-96-3) Thomasson-Grant.

Olsen, J. L., ed. see Dederichs, P. H., et al.

Olsen, Jack. Charmer. LC 94-3320. 1994. write for info. (0-688-10903-9) Morrow.

— Cold Kill. 1988. mass mkt. 5.95 (0-440-20212-4) Dell.

— Doc. 1990. mass mkt. 5.95 (0-440-20668-5) Dell.

— Give a Boy a Gun: The True Story of Law & Disorder in the American West. 1986. mass mkt. 4.99 (0-440-13168-5) Dell.

— The Misbegotten Son. 1993. mass mkt. 5.99 (0-440-21646-X) Dell.

— Predator: Rape, Madness, & Injustice in Seattle. 1992. mass mkt. 5.99 (0-440-21192-1) Dell.

— Son: A Psychopath & His Victims. 544p. (Orig.). 1985. mass mkt. 5.95 (0-440-18148-8) Dell.

***Olsen, James S., et al.** U. S. in the 20th Century: America since 1945, 2 vols., Vol. 2. 430p. 1995. pap. text ed. 19. 29 (0-312-08437-4) St Martin.

Olsen, Jean, tr. see Paludan, Lis.

Olsen, Johan P., jt. auth. see March, James G.

Olsen, Johann, jt. auth. see Brunsson, Nils.

Olsen, John B. & Eadie, Douglas C. The Game Plan: Governance with Foresight. Walter, Susan, ed. LC 82-7378. 176p. 1982. 16.95 (0-934842-20-5) CSPA.

Olsen, John W. Vertebrate Faunal Remains from Grasshopper Pueblo, Arizona. LC 90-6183. (Anthropological Papers: No. 83). (Illus.). xvi, 200p. (Orig.). 1990. pap. 15.00 (0-915703-21-1) U Mich Mus Anthro.

Olsen, John W. & Rukang, Wu, eds. Palaeoanthropology & Palaeolithic Archaeology in the People's Republic of China. 1985. text ed. 49.00 (0-12-601720-4) Acad Pr.

Olsen, Jorgen L. Electron Transport in Metals. LC 61-17893. (Interscience Tracts on Physics & Astronomy Ser.: No. 12). 129p. reprint ed. pap. 36.80 (0-317-08470-4, 2011962) Bks Demand.

Olsen, Jorn. Searching for Causes of Work-Related Diseases: An Introduction to Epidemiology at the Work Site. 100p. 1991. pap. 19.95 (0-19-261819-9) OUP.

Olsen, Judy E., ed. Communication-Starters & Other Activities for the ESL Classroom. (Illus.). 129p. 1977. teacher ed 19.95 (0-13-155656-8) Alemany Pr.

***Olsen, June L., et al.** Medical Dosage & Calculations. 6th ed. LC 94-33488. (C). 1995. pap. text ed. 26.95 (0-8053-5605-3) Benjamin-Cummings.

Olsen, June L. Medical Dosage Calculations. 4th ed. 1987. pap. text ed. 14.36 (0-201-19185-7) Addison-Wesley.

— Medical Dosage Calculations. 5th ed. 246p. (C). 1991. pap. text ed. 26.95 (0-8053-5603-7) Addison-Wesley.

Olsen, Karen, jt. auth. see Enkelis, Liane.

Olsen, Karen, jt. auth. see Ross, Ann.

Olsen, Karen D. The Mentor Teacher Role: Owner's Manual. 5th ed. (Illus.). 150p. (Orig.). 1989. Tchr.'s ed. teacher ed 16.95 (0-9624475-0-1) Bks Educators.

Olsen, Karen D., jt. auth. see Kovalik, Susan J.

Olsen, Karen D., jt. auth. see Ross, Ann.

Olsen, Kathy. Silent Pain. LC 91-67288. 252p. (Orig.). 1992. pap. 10.00 (0-89109-659-0) NavPress.

Olsen, Ken, et al. Cross-Country Skiing Yellowstone Country. (Illus.). 164p. (Orig.). 1993. pap. 10.95 (1-56044-191-7) Falcon Pr MT.

Olsen, Kenneth R., tr. see Ingarden, Roman.

Olsen, Kent J. Chamorro. Van Treese, James B., ed. Ingram, tr. 212p. 1994. pap. 8.95 (1-56901-126-5) NW Pub.

Olsen, Kirstin. Chronology of Women's History. LC 93-50542. 528p. 1994. text ed. 39.95 (0-313-28803-8) Greenwood.

— Quilter's Pattern Workbook: Creating Dramatically Different Designs with Color. (Illus.). 112p. 1993. pap. 12.95 (0-8069-0477-1) Sterling.

— Remember the Ladies: A Woman's Book of Days. LC 93-16868. (C). 1993. 17.95 (0-8061-2558-6) U of Okla Pr.

***Olsen, Klaus M. & Larsson, Hans.** Terns of Europe & North America. LC 94-39312. 1995. write for info. (0-691-04387-6) Princeton U Pr.

Olsen, Lance. Elipse of Uncertainty: An Introduction to Postmodern Fantasy. LC 86-22789. (Contributions to Postmodern Fantasy Ser.: No. 26). 145p. 1987. text ed. 45.00 (0-313-25511-3, OEU, Greenwood Pr) Greenwood.

— Lolita: A Janus Text. LC 94-24562. (Twayne's Masterwork Studies: Vol. 153). 1995. lib. bdg. 22.95x (0-8057-8355-5, Twayne); pap. 12.95 (0-8057-8593-0, Twayne) Macmillan.

— Tonguing the Zeitgeist. 192p. (Orig.). 1994. pap. 11.95 (1-882633-04-0) Permeable.

— William Gibson. LC 93-201910. (Starmont Reader's Guide Ser.: Vol. 58). vii, 131p. 1992. 27.00x (1-55742-199-4); pap. 17.00x (1-55742-198-6) Borgo Pr.

***Olsen, Lance, ed.** Surfing Tomorrow: Essays on the Future of American Fiction. 105p. 1995. per. 9.95 (1-884754-22-8) Potpourri Pubns.

Olsen, Lance, jt. auth. see Worley, Jeff.

Olsen, Larry & Mahoney, Beverly, eds. Health Education Teacher Resource Handbook. 400p. (Orig.). (C). 1993. pap. text ed. 19.95 (0-527-20811-6) Kraus Intl.

Olsen, Larry D. Outdoor Survival Skills. 1990. pap. 5.99 (0-671-72298-0) S&S Trade.

— Outdoor Survival Skills. rev. ed. (Illus.). (J). (gr. 6 up). 1988. pap. 9.95 (0-9620429-0-0) Salmon Falls Pub.

— Outdoor Survival Skills. 5th ed. LC 89-49670. (Illus.). 240p. 1990. pap. 11.95 (1-55652-084-0) Chicago Review.

Olsen, Larry K., et al. Health Today. 656p. (C). 1986. teacher ed write for info. (0-318-59089-1) Macmillan.

— Health Today. 2nd ed. 656p. (C). 1986. pap. write for info. (0-02-389260-9) Macmillan.

***Olsen, Lars.** ndom Geometrically Graph Directed Self-Similar Multifractals. (Pitman Research Notes in Mathematics). 1994. pap. text ed. 59.95 (0-470-23442-3) Halsted Pr.

Olsen, Lauri A., jt. auth. see Kutten, L. J.

An Asterisk (*) at the beginning of an entry indicates that the title is appearing in BIP for the first time.

***Olsen, Laurie.** Bridges: Promising Programs for the Education of Immigrant Children. 176p. 1989. pap. 17.00 (*1-887039-01-5*) Calif Tomorrow.

***Olsen, Laurie & Chen, Marcia T.** Crossing the Schoolhouse Border: Immigrant Students & the California Public Schools. 128p. 1988. pap. 16.00 (*1-887039-00-7*) Calif Tomorrow.

***Olsen, Laurie & Mullen, Nina A.** Embracing Diversity: Teachers' Voices from California's Classrooms. 115p. 1990. pap. 20.00 (*1-887039-03-1*) Calif Tomorrow.

***Olsen, Laurie & Raffel, Lisa, eds.** California Perspectives Vol. 4: An Anthology from California Tomorrow Special Issue: Community Canons. 110p. 1994. pap. 17.00 (*1-887039-11-2*) Calif Tomorrow.

***Olsen, Laurie, et al.** The Unfinished Journey: Restructuring Schools in a Diverse Society. 362p. 1994. pap. 27.00 (*1-887039-09-0*) Calif Tomorrow.

Olsen, Leslie A. Technical Writing & Professional Communication. 2nd ed. 1991. pap. text ed. write for info. (*0-07-047823-6*) McGraw.

Olsen, Leslie A., ed. see Skinner, Ernest M. & Skinner, Richmond H.

Olsen, Lester P. Cybernetics - Come of Age. (Illus.). 173p. (Orig.). (C). 1992. write for info. (*0-9632625-0-5*) Winchester NE.

Olsen, M. Menu Planning & Nutrition in Foodservice. 1990. text ed. write for info. (*0-442-00287-4*) Van Nos Reinhold.

Olsen, M., ed. Financial Management. 50p. 1984. pap. 23.00 (*0-08-031290-X*, Pergamon Pr) Elsevier.

Olsen, Mahlon E. History of the Origin & Progress of Seventh-Day Adventists. LC 76-134375. reprint ed. 67.50 (*0-404-08423-0*) AMS Pr.

Olsen, Margaret A. & Matthews, Alison F. The Gold Book: A Guide to Commonly Traded Gold Bullion Coins & Bars. (Illus.). (Orig.). 1992. pap. 19.95 (*0-9630498-4-4*) Westminster CO.

Olsen, Marilyn A., ed. Libro del Caballero Cifar. (Spanish Ser.: No. 15). (Illus.). 1984. fiche 25.00 (*0-942260-42-2*) Hispanic Seminary.

Olsen, Mark. The Golden Buddha Changing Masks: Essays on the Spiritual Dimension of Acting. LC 89-1409. (Illus.). 210p. (Orig.). 1990. pap. 12.50 (*0-89556-058-5*, Empire Pub Srvs) Gateways Bks & Tapes.

Olsen, Mark & Avital, Samuel. The Conception Mandala: Creative Techniques for Inviting a Child into Your Life. (Illus.). 96p. (Orig.). 1992. pap. 8.95 (*0-89281-356-3*) Inner Tradit.

Olsen, Marvin E. Participatory Pluralism: Political Participation & Influence in the United States & Sweden. LC 82-2263. 324p. (C). 1982. text ed. 35.95 (*0-88229-711-2*) Nelson-Hall.

Olsen, Marvin E. & Marger, Martin N., eds. Power in Modern Societies. LC 92-28612. 328p. (C). 1992. pap. text ed. 21.50 (*0-8133-1289-2*) Westview.

— Power in Modern Societies. LC 92-28612. 328p. (C). 1993. text ed. 72.00 (*0-8133-1288-4*) Westview.

Olsen, Marvin E. & Micklin, Michael, eds. Handbook of Applied Sociology: Frontiers of Contemporary Research. LC 81-5891. 640p. 1981. text ed. 85.00 (*0-275-90695-7*, C0695, Praeger Pubs) Greenwood.

Olsen, Mary L. Creative Connections: Literature & the Reading Program, Grades 1-3. LC 87-29665. xix, 250p. 1987. pap. 23.50 (*0-87287-651-9*) Libs Unl.

— More Creative Connections: Literature & the Reading Program, Grades 4-6. (Illus.). 225p. 1993. pap. text ed. 24.00 (*1-56308-027-3*) Teacher Ideas Pr.

Olsen, Mary M. & Harris, Kenneth R. Color Vision Deficiency & Color Blindness. 62p. (Orig.). 1988. pap. 8.50 (*0-9615332-2-6*) Fern Ridge Pr.

Olsen, Maryann & Berrey, Henry. Pictorial Guide to Yosemite. Stock, Edith, tr. (Illus.). 22p. 1981. pap. 2.95 (*0-939666-35-9*) Yosemite Assn.

— A Pictorial Guide to Yosemite. (Illus.). 22p. (Orig.). 1981. pap. 2.95 (*0-939666-37-5*) Yosemite Assn.

Olsen, Maryann, et al. Guia Ilustrada de Yosemite. (Illus.). 22p. 1987. pap. 2.95 (*0-939666-48-0*) Yosemite Assn.

— Guide Illustre de Yosemite. Billot, Michel & Tech-Tran, Agnew, trs. Orig. Title: Pictorial Guide to Yosemite. (Illus.). 22p. (Orig.). 1979. pap. 2.95 (*0-939666-36-7*) Yosemite Assn.

Olsen, Michael D. Strategic Management in the Hospitality Industry. 1992. text ed. 44.95 (*0-442-00246-7*) Van Nos Reinhold.

Olsen, Michael D., jt. ed. see Teare, Richard.

Olsen, Nancy. Starting a Mini-Business: A Guidebook for Seniors. rev. ed. LC 88-81194. (Illus.). 144p. 1988. pap. 8.95 (*0-933271-02-6*) Fair Oaks CA.

Olsen, O. & Bergman, L., eds. Economic Modeling in the Nordic Countries. LC 92-30304. (Contributions to Economic Analysis Ser.: Vol. 210). xvi, 298p. 1992. write for info. (*0-444-89653-8*, North Holland) Elsevier.

Olsen, O. Wilford. Animal Parasites: Their Life Cycles & Ecology. xii, 564p. 1986. reprint ed. pap. text ed. 19.95 (*0-486-65126-6*) Dover.

Olsen, Ole, jt. auth. see Speirs, Mike.

Olsen, Otto H. Carpetbagger's Crusade: The Life of Albion Winegar Tourgee. LC 65-13522. (Illus.). 413p. reprint ed. pap. 117.80 (*0-685-23485-1*, 2027900) Bks Demand.

Olsen, Paul. Comprehensive Psychotherapy, 3. 183p. 1984. pap. 79.00 (*0-677-16369-X*) Gordon & Breach.

— Comprehensive Psychotherapy, Vol. 4. 183p. 1984. pap. text ed. 117.00 (*0-677-16539-0*) Gordon & Breach.

Olsen, Paul, ed. Comprehensive Psychotherapy, Vol. 1. viii, 176p. 1980. 63.00 (*0-685-37404-1*) Gordon & Breach.

— Comprehensive Psychotherapy, Vol. 2. vi, 122p. 1981. pap. 75.00 (*0-685-01948-9*) Gordon & Breach.

Olsen, Paul, jt. auth. see Cornet, Bruce.

Olsen, Paul, jt. auth. see Murrell, Sandra.

Olsen, Paul T., ed. Emotional Flooding: An Official Publication of the National Institute for the Psychotherapies. LC 74-12620. (New Directions in Psychotherapy Ser.: Vol. I). 270p. 1976. 35.95 (*0-87705-239-5*) Human Sci Pr.

Olsen, Paul T., jt. ed. see Grayson, Henry.

Olsen, Penny. Falcons & Hawks. LC 92-11986. (Great Creatures of the World Ser.). (Illus.). 72p. (J). (gr. 5 up). 1992. lib. bdg. 17.95 (*0-8160-2843-5*) Facts on File.

Olsen, Penny, jt. ed. see Newton, Ian.

Olsen, Phyllis J., jt. auth. see Coombs, Gary B.

Olsen, Phyllis Jean, jt. auth. see Coombs, Gary B.

Olsen, R. W., jt. ed. see Lunt, G. G.

Olsen, Richard G., ed. Feline Leukemia. 184p. 1981. 92.95 (*0-8493-6070-6*, SF986, CRC Reprint) Franklin.

Olsen, Richard G., et al, eds. Comparative Pathobiology of Viral Diseases. 232p. 1985. Vol. I, 232 p. 156.00 (*0-8493-5945-7*, SF780, CRC Reprint); Vol. II, 232p. 156.00 (*0-8493-5946-5*, SF780, CRC Reprint) Franklin.

Olsen, Robert. Handgun Muzzle Flash Tests. (Illus.). 144p. 1993. pap. 20.00 (*0-87364-705-X*) Paladin Pr.

Olsen, Robert D., Sr. Scott's Fingerprint Mechanics. (Illus.). 480p. 1978. 73.95 (*0-398-03730-2*) C C Thomas.

— Scott's Fingerprint Mechanics. (Illus.). 480p. 1978. pap. 39.95 (*0-398-06308-7*) C C Thomas.

Olsen, Roberta J. Fire & Ice: A History of Comets in Art. LC 85-7295. (Illus.). 134p. 1985. 24.95 (*0-8027-0855-2*); pap. 14.95 (*0-8027-7283-8*) Walker & Co.

Olsen, Rodney D. Dancing in Chains: The Youth of William Dean Howells. (American Social Experience Ser.). (Illus.). 320p. 1991. text ed. 50.00x (*0-8147-6172-0*) NYU Pr.

— Dancing in Chains: The Youth of William Dean Howells. (American Social Experience Ser.). 288p. (C). 1992. pap. text ed. 18.50 (*0-8147-6178-X*) NYU Pr.

Olsen, Roger E., ed. see Seward, Bernard.

Olsen, Roger E., ed. see Stricherz, Gregory.

Olsen, S., jt. auth. see Johansen, P.

Olsen, S., jt. ed. see Johansen, P.

Olsen, Solveig, ed. Computer-Aided Instruction in the Humanities. LC 85-13740. (Technology & the Humanities Ser.: No. 2). xviii, 266p. 1985. pap. text ed. 19.75 (*0-87352-553-1*) Modern Lang.

Olsen, Sondra S. Traps. LC 91-19062. (Iowa Short Fiction Award Ser.). 159p. 1991. 22.95 (*0-87745-346-2*) U of Iowa Pr.

Olsen, Stanley J. Origins of the Domestic Dog: The Fossil Record. LC 85-1024. (Illus.). 132p. reprint ed. pap. 37.70 (*0-7837-5052-8*, 2044730) Bks Demand.

Olsen, Steen. Tumors of the Kidney & Urinary Tract. (Illus.). 291p. 1985. text ed. 121.00 (*0-7216-1588-0*) Saunders.

Olsen, Stein H. The End of Literary Theory. LC 86-20692. 240p. 1987. 74.95 (*0-521-33326-1*) Cambridge U Pr.

Olsen, Stein H., jt. auth. see Lamarque, Peter.

Olsen, Stephen, et al. Atacames Special Area Management Plan: Atacames-Sua Muisne. 68p. 1994. write for info. (*1-885454-01-5*) Coastal Res.

Olsen, Susan, ed. see Hiader, Hubert.

Olsen, T. Canyon of the Gun. 1983. pap. 2.95 (*0-449-13943-3*) Fawcett.

Olsen, T. V. Bitter Grass. large type ed. LC 93-30322. 1994. 18.95 (*0-7927-1871-2*, Roundup Lrg Print Westerns); pap. 16.95 (*0-7927-1870-4*, Roundup Lrg Print Westerns) Chivers N Amer.

— Blizzard Pass. 1995. 15.95 (*0-7451-4630-9*) Chivers N Amer.

— Blizzard Pass. 160p. 1982. pap. 2.95 (*0-449-12360-X*, GM) Fawcett.

— Blizzard Pass. large type ed. (Linford Western Library). 1991. pap. 13.95 (*0-7089-7040-0*, Linford) Ulverscroft.

— Blood of the Breed. large type ed. 1985. 15.95 (*0-7089-1262-1*) Ulverscroft.

— Brand of Star. large type ed. (Linford Western Library). 1990. pap. 12.95 (*0-7089-6859-7*, Linford) Ulverscroft.

— Break the Young Land. 224p. 1988. pap. 2.75 (*0-380-75290-5*) Avon.

— Canyon of the Gun - Haven of the Hunted, 2 vols. in 1. 304p. 1993. pap. 4.99 (*0-8439-3545-6*) Dorchester Pub Co.

— The Golden Chance. large type ed. LC 93-27028. (Orig.). 1993. 17.95 (*0-8161-5861-4*) Hall.

— Gunswift. 1994. 14.95 (*0-7451-4588-4*, Gunsmoke) Chivers N Amer.

— Gunswift. large type ed. (Linford Western Library). 1991. pap. 13.95 (*0-7089-6967-4*, Trailtree Bookshop) Ulverscroft.

— The Hard Men. large type ed. LC 93-50789. 1994. 18.95 (*0-7927-2007-5*, Roundup Lrg Print Westerns); pap. 16.95 (*0-7927-2006-7*, Roundup Lrg Print Westerns) Chivers N Amer.

— High Lawless. large type ed. 1977. 15.95 (*0-85456-515-9*) Ulverscroft.

— High Lawless - Savage Sierra. 336p. 1993. pap. 4.99 (*0-8439-3524-3*) Dorchester Pub Co.

— A Man Called Brazos. large type ed. (Linford Western Library). 1991. pap. 13.95 (*0-7089-7015-X*, Linford) Ulverscroft.

— A Man Called Brazos - Brand of the Star. 320p. 1994. mass mkt. 4.99 (*0-8439-3688-6*) Dorchester Pub Co.

— The Man from Nowhere. large type ed. (Linford Western Library). 1990. pap. 12.95 (*0-7089-6946-1*, Linford) Ulverscroft.

— The Man from Nowhere - Bitter Grass: Bitter Grass. 336p. 1995. mass mkt. 4.99 (*0-8439-3728-9*) Dorchester Pub Co.

— A Man Named Yuma. large type ed. LC 93-19805. 1993. 18.95 (*0-7927-1711-2*, Roundup Lrg Print Westerns); pap. 16.95 (*0-7927-1710-4*, Roundup Lrg Print Westerns) Chivers N Amer.

— McGivern - The Hard Men. 320p. 1994. pap. 4.99 (*0-8439-3612-6*) Dorchester Pub Co.

— Mission to the West. large type ed. LC 93-30362. 1994. 19.95 (*0-7927-1865-8*, Roundup Lrg Print Westerns); pap. 17.95 (*0-7927-1864-X*, Roundup Lrg Print Westerns) Chivers N Amer.

— Red Is the River. 416p. (Orig.). 1983. pap. 3.50 (*0-449-12407-X*, GM) Fawcett.

— Run to the Mountain. large type ed. 1994. 19.95 (*0-7927-2081-4*, Roundup Lrg Print Westerns); pap. 18.95 (*0-7927-2080-6*, Roundup Lrg Print Westerns) Chivers N Amer.

— Run to the Mountain. large type ed. LC 94-5719. 1994. write for info. (*0-7929-2081-3*, Roundup Lrg Print Westerns); pap. write for info. (*0-7929-2080-5*, Roundup Lrg Print Westerns) Chivers N Amer.

— Run to the Mountains. 192p. 1989. mass mkt. 3.99 (*0-449-13089-4*, GM) Fawcett.

— Savage Sierra. (Gunsmoke Western Ser.). 184p. 1990. reprint ed. text ed. 12.95 (*0-86220-938-2*, Gunsmoke) Chivers N Amer.

— Starbuck's Brand. large type ed. LC 92-19929. (Nightingale Ser.). 311p. 1992. pap. 14.95 (*0-8161-5594-1*, Nightingale) Hall.

— There Was a Season. 448p. 1994. reprint ed. mass mkt., pap. text ed. 4.99 (*0-8439-3652-5*) Dorchester Pub Co.

— Track the Man Down. large type ed. LC 92-42101. (Nightingale Ser.). 1993. write for info. (*0-8161-5722-7*) G K Hall.

— Under the Gun. 160p. 1989. pap. 2.95 (*0-449-14621-9*, GM) Fawcett.

— Under the Gun. LC 94-1037. 1994. write for info. (*0-8161-5823-0*) G K Hall.

***Olsen, T. V., et al.** Red Is the River. (Illus.). 416p. (Orig.). 1995. mass mkt., pap. text ed. 4.99 (*0-8439-3747-5*) Dorchester Pub Co.

***Olsen, Terry.** My Father, My Hero: Becoming Your Child's Best Friend. (Illus.). 208p. (Orig.). (C). 1995. pap. 9.95 (*1-883831-35-0*) Winepress Pub.

Olsen, Tillie. Silences. 1979. pap. 12.95 (*0-385-28893-X*, Delta) Dell.

— Silences. 1984. 22.00 (*0-8446-6091-4*) Peter Smith.

— Tell Me a Riddle. 1971. pap. 10.95 (*0-385-29010-1*, Delta) Dell.

— Tell Me a Riddle. 1984. 21.00 (*0-8446-6090-6*) Peter Smith.

— Yonnondio. 1984. 21.00 (*0-8446-6089-2*) Peter Smith.

Olsen, Tillie, ed. Mother to Daughter, Daughter to Mother: A Daybook & Reader. LC 84-21038. 312p. 1984. 19.95 (*1-55861-008-1*); pap. 10.95 (*0-935312-37-4*) Feminist Pr.

Olsen, Tillie, ed. see Davis, Rebecca H.

Olsen, V. Norskov. Man, the Image of God. Woolsey, Raymond H., ed. 192p. 1988. 11.95 (*0-8280-0418-8*) Review & Herald.

— The New Relatedness for Man & Woman in Christ: A Mirror of the Divine. LC 93-13440. 1993. 9.95 (*1-881127-01-X*) LLU Ctr Christ Bio.

— The New Testament Logia on Divorce. vi, 161p. 1994. pap. 36.50 (*3-16-131441-7*, Pub. by J C B Mohr GW) Coronet Bks.

— Papal Supremacy & American Democracy. LC 87-83037. 190p. (Orig.). 1988. pap. 10.95 (*0-944450-01-6*) La Sierra U Pr.

Olsen, V. Norskov, et al, eds. The Advent Hope in Scripture & History. 272p. (Orig.). 1987. 29.95 (*0-8280-0311-4*) Review & Herald.

Olsen, Victoria. Emily Dickinson. (American Women of Achievement Ser.). (Illus.). 112p. (YA). (gr. 5 up). 1990. 17.95 (*1-55546-649-4*) Chelsea Hse.

Olsen, W. Scott. Meeting the Neighbors: Sketches of Life on the Northern Prairie. LC 93-12827. 1993. 9.95 (*0-87839-080-4*) North Star.

Olsen, W. Scott, ed. Just This Side of Fargo. 128p. (Orig.). Date not set. pap. 12.95 (*1-877628-15-8*) Ironwood Winona.

Olsen, Wallace C. Agricultural Economics & Rural Sociology: The Contemporary Core Literature. 304p. 1991. 53.95 (*0-8014-2677-4*) Cornell U Pr.

Olsen, Wallace C., ed. The Literature of Animal Science & Health. 400p. 1993. 79.95 (*0-8014-2886-6*) Cornell U Pr.

— The Literature of Crop Science. (Literature of the Agricultural Sciences Ser.). (Illus.). 544p. 1995. 79.95x (*0-8014-3138-7*) Cornell U Pr.

Olsen, Wallace C., jt. ed. see Brogdon, Jennie L.

Olsen, Wallace C., jt. ed. see Hall, Carl W.

Olsen, Warren & Rinden, David. Explanation of Luther's Small Catachism. 128p. (J). (gr. 7-8). 1988. text ed. 7.95 (*0-943167-12-4*) Faith & Fellowship Pr.

Olsen, Warren & Rinden, David, eds. Explanation of Luther's Small Catechism. 2nd ed. 128p. (J). (gr. 7-8). 1992. text ed. 7.95 (*0-943167-20-5*) Faith & Fellowship Pr.

Olsen, William. The Hand of God & a Few Bright Flowers. Poems. LC 87-24507. (National Poetry Ser.). 80p. 1988. pap. 9.95 (*0-252-06001-6*) U of Ill Pr.

Olsen, Winnifred L. For the Record: A History of the Tacoma Public Schools, 1869-1984. Huyler, Jean W., ed. LC 85-12652. 232p. (Orig.). 1985. pap. 13.95 (*0-941554-05-8*) EdCom.

Olsenius, Richard. Distant Shores: Music & Photographs from Lake Superior & Lake Michigan. 112p. (Orig.). 1990. audio, pap. 19.95 (*0-9609064-4-4*); pap. 14.95 (*0-9609064-5-2*); audio 9.95 (*0-9609064-6-0*) Bluestem Prod.

— Distant Shores: Music & Photographs from Lake Superior & Lake Michigan. 112p. (Orig.). 1993. cd-rom, pap. 24.95 (*0-9609064-8-7*) Bluestem Prod.

— Distant Shores: Music & Photographs from Lake Superior & Lake Michigan. (Orig.). 1993. cd-rom 14.95 (*0-9609064-7-9*) Bluestem Prod.

— Minnesota Travel Companion: A Unique Guide to the History Along Minnesota's Highway. 5th ed. LC 82-72658. (Illus.). 260p. (Orig.). 1981. pap. 14.95 (*0-9609064-0-1*) Bluestem Prod.

Olsgaard, John N., ed. Principles & Applications of Information Science for Library Professionals. LC 88-36876. 152p. reprint ed. pap. 43.40 (*0-7837-5922-3*, 2045721) Bks Demand.

Olshaker, Bennett. The Child As a Work of Art. 1985. reprint ed. pap. 6.95 (*0-9617697-0-X*) Marko Bks.

Olshan. Nightswimmer. 1994. 20.00 (*0-671-88580-4*) S&S Trade.

Olshan, A. F., jt. ed. see Mattison, D. R.

Olshan, Al. My Life, My Way. 300p. (Orig.). 1992. pap. write for info. (*0-9632134-0-7*) Al Olshan.

Olshan, Marc A., jt. ed. see Kraybill, Donald B.

Olshan, Neal H. Golden Handcuffs: How Women Can Break Free of Financial Dependence in Their Intimate Relationships. 208p. 1993. 17.95 (*1-55972-202-9*, Birch Ln Pr) Carol Pub Group.

Ol'shanskii, A. Yu. Geometry of Defining Relations in Groups. 544p. (C). 1991. lib. bdg. 219.00 (*0-7923-1394-1*) Kluwer Ac.

Olshansky, Beth. Portfolio of Illustrated Step-by-Step Art Projects for Young Children. 192p. 1990. pap. 24.95 (*0-87628-639-2*) Ctr Appl Res.

Olshansky, Joanne. The Pizza Boogie Songbook. (Illus.). 33p. (Orig.). (J). (gr. k-6). 1990. pap. 9.95 (*0-9626239-0-3*) JHO Music.

***Olshausen, Hans-Gustav.** VDI-Lexikon Bauingenieurwesen. 649p. (GER.). 1991. 250.00 (*0-7859-8287-6*, 3184008975) Fr & Eur.

Olshavsky, Richard W., ed. see Attitude Research Conference Staff.

Olshen, Barry N. & Feldman, Yael, eds. Approaches to Teaching the Hebrew Bible As Literature in Translation. LC 89-32332. (Approaches to Teaching World Literature Ser.: No. 25). x, 156p. 1989. text ed. 37.50 (*0-87352-523-X*, AP25C); pap. 18.00x (*0-87352-524-8*, AP25P) Modern Lang.

Olshen, Richard A., jt. ed. see Le Cam, Lucien M.

Olshevsky, Moshe, et al. The Manual of Natural Therapy. 1990. pap. 12.95 (*0-8065-1202-4*, Citadel Pr) Carol Pub Group.

— Manual of Natural Therapy: A Succint Catalog of Complementary Treatments. LC 88-24410. (Illus.). 384p. reprint ed. pap. 109.50 (*0-7837-6694-7*, 2046311) Bks Demand.

Olshine, David. Staying on Top: How to Know God in an Upside-down World. Clark, Brian & Reeves, Dale, eds. (Illus.). 80p. 1994. reprint ed. pap. 12.99 (*0-7847-0100-8*) Standard Pub.

Olshine, David, jt. auth. see Habermas, Ron.

Olshtain, Elite, jt. auth. see Dubin, Fraida.

Olshtain, Elite, et al. The Junior Files, File 1: English for Today & Tomorrow. rev. ed. Berman, Aaron & Chapman, Charles, eds. (Illus.). 270p. (YA). (gr. 6-10). 1991. pap. write for info. (*1-878598-02-3*) Alta Bk Co Pubs.

Olson. Virus Infections: Modern Concepts & Status. (Microbiology Ser.: Vol. 6). 304p. 1982. 125.00 (*0-8247-1859-3*) Dekker.

— When Do I Start? 1994. pap. 4.99 (*0-517-13448-9*) Random.

Olson & Hanratty. Key Factor to Motivation. LC 81-66054. 64p. 1981. 5.00 (*0-86690-008-X*, O1359-014) Am Fed Astrologers.

— Your Motive Factor. 24p. 1981. 4.00 (*0-86690-218-X*, O1361-014) Am Fed Astrologers.

Olson, jt. auth. see Ferno.

Olson, jt. auth. see Lockerbie.

Olson, et al. Handbook of Symptom Oriented Neurology. 2nd ed. 525p. 1994. pap. 26.95 (*0-8016-7779-3*) Mosby Yr Bk.

Olson, Adolf. A Centenary History As Related to the Baptist General Conference of America. Ganstad, Edwin S., ed. LC 79-52602. (Baptist Tradition Ser.). (Illus.). 1980. reprint ed. lib. bdg. 61.95 (*0-405-12467-8*) Ayer.

Olson, Alan M. Hegel & the Spirit: Philosophy as Pneumatology. 176p. 1992. text ed. 29.95 (*0-691-07411-9*) Princeton U Pr.

— The Seven Matrices: The Forest of Fecundity. LC 90-72009. 134p. (Orig.). 1992. pap. 10.00 (*1-56002-090-3*, Univ Edtns) Aegina Pr.

— Transcendence & Hermeneutics. (Studies in Philosophy & Religion: No. 2). 1979. pap. text ed. 74.50 (*90-247-2092-3*) Kluwer Ac.

Olson, Alan M., ed. Heidegger & Jaspers. LC 93-9674. 192p. (C). 1994. 44.95 (*1-56639-114-8*); pap. 19.95 (*1-56639-115-6*) Temple U Pr.

Olson, Alan M. & Rouner, Leroy S., eds. Transcendence & the Sacred. LC 81-50456. (Boston University Studies in Philosophy & Religion: Vol. 2). 256p. (C). 1981. text ed. 29.95x (*0-268-01841-3*) U of Notre Dame Pr.

— Transcendence & the Sacred. LC 81-50456. (Boston University Studies in Philosophy & Religion: Vol. 2). (C). 1994. reprint ed. pap. text ed. 10.95 (*0-268-01888-X*) U of Notre Dame Pr.

Olson, Alan M., et al, eds. Video Icons & Values. LC 89-49240. (SUNY Series in Speech Communication). 189p. 1990. 59.50 (*0-7914-0411-0*); pap. 19.95 (*0-7914-0412-9*) State U NY Pr.

Olson, Alan P. Archaeology of the Arizona Public Service 345 KV Line. (Bulletin Ser.). 71p. 1971. pap. 2.50 (*0-685-14710-X*, BS-46) Mus Northern Ariz.

Olson, Alan P., jt. auth. see Ambler, J. Richard.

Olson, Alison G. Making the Empire Work: London & American Interest Groups, 1690-1790. 272p. 1992. 44.50 (*0-674-54318-1*) HUP.

O

An Asterisk (*) at the beginning of an entry indicates that the title is appearing in BIP for the first time.

Olson, Allen M. Exercise by Walking: Index of New Information for the Young & Old for Health Saving & Promotion. (Illus.). 150p. 1994. 44.50 (0-7883-0020-2); pap. 39.50 (0-7883-0021-0) ABBE Pubs Assn.

Olson, Alton T. Mathematics Through Paper Folding. LC 75-16115. (Illus.). 64p. 1975. pap. 6.50 (0-87353-076-4) NCTM.

Olson, Ann S., ed. see Tampa Museum of Art Staff.

Olson, Annette, ed. Alternatives to the Peace Corps: A Directory of Third World & U. S. Volunteer Opportunities. 6th ed. 88p. 1994. reprint ed. pap. 6.95 (0-935028-62-5) Inst Food & Develop.

Olson, Arielle N. Hurry Home, Grandma! LC 84-1529. (Unicorn Paperbacks Ser.). (Illus.). 32p. (J). (ps-1). 1990. pap. 3.95 (0-525-44650-8, DCB) Dutton Child Bks.

— The Lighthouse Keeper's Daughter. (Illus.). 32p. (J). (ps-3). 1987. 14.95 (0-316-65057-9) Little.

— Noah's Cats & the Devil's Fire. LC 91-17408. (Illus.). 32p. (J). (ps-2). 1992. 16.95 (0-531-05984-7); lib. bdg. 16.99 (0-531-08584-8) Orchard Bks Watts.

Olson, Arnold T. The Significance of Silence. LC 80-70698. (Heritage Ser.: Vol. 2). 208p. 1981. 8.95 (0-685-01674-9) Free Church Pubns.

— Stumbling Toward Maturity. LC 81-66943. (Heritage Ser.: Vol. 3). 208p. 1981. 8.95 (0-911802-50-9) Free Church Pubns.

Olson, Arnold T., ed. The Search for Identity. LC 80-66030. (Heritage Ser.: Vol. 1). 160p. 1980. 8.95 (0-911802-46-0); pap. 6.95 (0-685-42119-8) Free Church Pubns.

Olson, Audrey L. St. Louis Germans, 1850-1920: The Nature of an Immigrant Community & Its Relation to the Assimilation Process. Cordasco, Francesco, ed. LC 80-886. (American Ethnic Groups Ser.). 1981. lib. bdg. 42.95 (0-405-13447-9) Ayer.

***Olson, B. G.** Umbrella Guide to Interior Alaska: Including Fairbanks & Denali Park. Ummel, Christine, ed. (Illus.). 160p. 1995. pap. 12.95 (0-945397-39-9, Umbrella Bks) Epicenter Pr.

Olson, B. G., ed. see Nelson, Ted & Nelson, Sharlene.

Olson, B. G., ed. see Simpson, Sherry.

Olson, B. G., jt. auth. see Stockley, Tom.

Olson, B. H., jt. ed. see Jenkins, D.

Olson, B. Kaye. Energy Secrets for Tired Mothers on the Run. 260p. 1993. pap. 11.95 (1-55874-250-6) Health Comm.

Olson, Betty. Cat Lovers Against the Bomb: Nineteen Ninety-Five Wall Calendar. (Illus.). 32p. 1994. 7.95 (0-86571-299-9) New Soc Pubs.

Olson, Beverly & Lazzara, Judy. Country Flower Drying. LC 87-26705. (Illus.). 132p. 1988. pap. 9.95 (0-8069-6746-3) Sterling.

Olson, Bjorn. The Family Guide to Training Your Dog. LC 91-3871. (Illus.). 128p. 1991. pap. 14.95 (0-8069-8497-X) Sterling.

Olson, Bruce. Bruchko. LC 73-81494. 208p. (Orig.). 1973. pap. 8.99 (0-88419-133-8, Creation Hse) Strang Comms Co.

Olson, Bruce H., jt. auth. see Marple, Elliot.

Olson, C. Gordon. What in the World Is God Doing? The Essentials of Global Missions. (Illus.). 320p. (Orig.). (C). 1989. pap. 9.95 (0-685-30119-2) Global Gospel Pubs.

— What in the World is God Doing? The Essentials of Global Missions. 2nd rev. ed. (Illus.). 320p. (C). 1993. pap. text ed. 11.95 (0-9624850-1-2) Global Gospel Pubs.

— What in the World is God Doing? The Essentials of Global Missions. 3rd ed. (Illus.). 320p. 1994. pap. text ed. 11.95 (0-9624850-2-0) Global Gospel Pubs.

Olson, C. L. & Schumacher, U. Collective Ion Acceleration. (Tracts in Modern Physics Ser.: Vol. 84). (Illus.). 1979. 46.00 (0-387-09066-5) Spr-Verlag.

Olson, Carl. Book of the Goddess. 264p. 1985. pap. 15.95 (0-8245-0689-8) Crossroad NY.

— The Mysterious Play of Kali: An Interpretive Study of Ramakrishna. 140p. 1990. 29.95 (1-55540-339-5); pap. 19.95 (1-55540-340-9) Scholars Pr GA.

Olson, Carl R., jt. ed. see Hanson, Stephen J.

Olson, Carol, jt. ed. see Doss, Cheryl.

Olson, Carol B. Practical Ideas for Teaching Writing As a Process. (Illus.). 224p. 1987. pap. 8.00 (0-8011-0671-0) Calif Education.

— Reading, Thinking, & Writing about Multicultural Literature. 704p. (Orig.). (YA). (gr. 6-12). 1995. pap. 29.95 (0-673-36296-5) GdYrBks.

Olson, Carol T. The Life of Illness: One Woman's Journey. LC 91-33457. (SUNY Series, The Body in Culture, History, & Religion). 203p. (C). 1992. 49.50 (0-7914-1199-0); pap. 16.95 (0-7914-1200-8) State U NY Pr.

Olson, Charles. Call Me Ishmael. (BCL1-PS American Literature Ser.). 119p. 1993. reprint ed. lib. bdg. 69.00 (0-7812-6991-1) Rprt Serv.

— The Collected Poems of Charles Olson. Butterick, George F., ed. LC 86-14652. 609p. 1987. 60.00 (0-520-05764-3) U CA Pr.

— Maximus to Gloucester: The Letters & Poems of Charles Olson to the Editor of the Gloucester Daily Times, 1962-1969. Anastas, Peter, ed. (Illus.). 161p. (Orig.). 1992. pap. 15.00 (0-938459-07-4) Ten Pound Isl Bk.

— A Nation of Nothing but Poetry: Supplementary Poems. LC 88-36879. 226p. (Orig.). (C). 1989. pap. 12.50 (0-87685-750-0) Black Sparrow.

— The Post Office. LC 74-75456. (Illus.). 66p. 1975. pap. 4.95 (0-912516-14-3) Grey Fox.

— Reading at Berkeley. 1966. 15.00 (0-685-80372-4) SPD-Small Pr Dist.

— Selected Poems. Creeley, Robert, ed. LC 92-23838. 1993. 25.00 (0-520-07528-5) U CA Pr.

— Selected Writings. Creeley, Robert, ed. LC 66-27613. (Orig.). 1967. pap. 10.95 (0-8112-0128-7, NDP231) New Directions.

Olson, Charles & Creeley, Robert. Charles Olson & Robert Creeley: The Complete Correspondence, Vol. 1. Butterick, George F., ed. LC 80-12222. (Illus.). 184p. (Orig.). 1980. 20.00 (0-87685-400-5); pap. 10.00 (0-87685-399-8) Black Sparrow.

— Charles Olson & Robert Creeley: The Complete Correspondence, Vol. 2. Butterick, George F., ed. LC 80-12222. (Illus.). 184p. (Orig.). 1980. 20.00 (0-87685-441-2); pap. 10.00 (0-87685-440-4) Black Sparrow.

— Charles Olson & Robert Creeley: The Complete Correspondence, Vol. 3. Butterick, George F., ed. LC 80-12222. (Illus.). 175p. (Orig.). (C). 1981. 20.00 (0-87685-483-8); pap. 10.00 (0-87685-482-X) Black Sparrow.

— Charles Olson & Robert Creeley: The Complete Correspondence, Vol. 3, signed ed. deluxe ed. Butterick, George F., ed. LC 80-12222. (Illus.). 175p. (Orig.). (C). 1981. 30.00 (0-87685-484-6) Black Sparrow.

— Charles Olson & Robert Creeley: The Complete Correspondence, Vol. 4. Butterick, George F., ed. LC 80-12222. (Illus.). 158p. (Orig.). (C). 1982. 20.00 (0-87685-486-2); pap. 10.00 (0-87685-485-4) Black Sparrow.

— Charles Olson & Robert Creeley: The Complete Correspondence, Vol. 4, signed ed. deluxe ed. Butterick, George F., ed. LC 80-12222. (Illus.). 158p. (Orig.). (C). 1982. 30.00 (0-87685-487-0) Black Sparrow.

— Charles Olson & Robert Creeley: The Complete Correspondence, Vol. 6. LC 80-12222. (Illus.). 247p. (Orig.). 1985. 20.00 (0-87685-586-9); pap. 12.50 (0-87685-585-0) Black Sparrow.

— Charles Olson & Robert Creeley: The Complete Correspondence, Vol. 6, signed ed. deluxe ed. LC 80-12222. (Illus.). 247p. (Orig.). 1985. 30.00 (0-87685-587-7) Black Sparrow.

— Charles Olson & Robert Creeley: The Complete Correspondence, Vol. 7. Butterick, George F., ed. LC 80-12222. (Illus.). 286p. (Orig.). 1987. 20.00 (0-87685-690-3); pap. 12.50 (0-87685-689-X) Black Sparrow.

— Charles Olson & Robert Creeley: The Complete Correspondence, Vol. 7, signed ed. deluxe ed. Butterick, George F., ed. LC 80-12222. (Illus.). 286p. (Orig.). 1987. 30.00 (0-87685-691-1) Black Sparrow.

— Charles Olson & Robert Creeley: The Complete Correspondence, Vol. 8. LC 80-12222. (Illus.). 284p. (Orig.). (C). 1987. 20.00 (0-87685-705-5); pap. 12.50 (0-87685-704-7) Black Sparrow.

— Charles Olson & Robert Creeley: The Complete Correspondence, Vol. 8, signed ed. deluxe ed. LC 80-12222. (Illus.). 284p. (C). 1987. 30.00 (0-87685-706-3) Black Sparrow.

— Charles Olson & Robert Creeley: The Complete Correspondence, Vol. 9. Blevins, Richard, ed. LC 80-12222. (Illus.). 346p. (Orig.). (C). 1990. 25.00 (0-87685-782-9); pap. 15.00 (0-87685-781-0) Black Sparrow.

— Charles Olson & Robert Creeley: The Complete Correspondence, Vol. 9, signed ed. deluxe ed. Blevins, Richard, ed. LC 80-12222. (Illus.). 346p. (Orig.). (C). 1990. 35.00 (0-87685-783-7) Black Sparrow.

Olson, Charles & Den Boer, James. Olson-Den Boer: a Letter. 1977. pap. 6.00 (0-87922-051-1) Christophers Bks.

Olson, Charles, et al. Charles Olson & Robert Creeley: The Complete Correspondence, Vol. 5. Butterick, George F., ed. LC 80-12222. (Illus.). 222p. (Orig.). (C). 1983. 20.00 (0-87685-561-3); pap. 10.00 (0-87685-560-5) Black Sparrow.

— Charles Olson & Robert Creeley: The Complete Correspondence, Vol. 5, signed ed. deluxe ed. Butterick, George F., ed. LC 80-12222. (Illus.). 222p. (Orig.). (C). 1983. 30.00 (0-87685-562-1) Black Sparrow.

Olson, Charles J., jt. auth. see Olson, William H.

Olson, Charles L., et al. Consumer & Business Arithmetic. LC 79-57434. 1981. teacher ed 5.96 (0-02-831240-6); 9.32 (0-02-831230-9); text ed. 22.64 (0-02-831220-1) Glencoe.

Olson, Charles L. Lighthouse. 1987. 16.95 (0-316-65053-6) Little.

— Thinking-Writing: Fostering Critical Thinking Through Writing. (C). 1991. text ed. 29.00 (0-673-46346-X) HarpCollege.

Olson, Charles L., jt. auth. see Roberts.

Olson, Charles L., jt. auth. see Striker.

Olson, Chester L. Essentials of Statistics: Data. 1987. teacher ed write for info. (0-697-06945-1) Wm C Brown Pubs.

***Olson, Christine, ed.** The Multimedia Home Companion for Parents & Kids. 240p. (Orig.). 1995. pap. 19.99 (0-446-67168-1) Warner Bks.

***Olson, Christine A.** Libraries Through the Seasons Vol. 3, Pt. 2: Spring. (Olson's Library Clip Art). (Illus.). 16p. (Orig.). 1995. pap. text ed. 33.00 (1-56984-009-1) C Olson & Assocs.

***Olson, Christine A., ed.** Libraries Through the Seasons Vol. 3: Winter, Spring, Summer & Fall. (Olson's Library Clip Art). (Illus.). 64p. (Orig.). 1995. pap. text ed. 112.00 (1-56984-020-2) C Olson & Assocs.

— Libraries Through the Seasons Vol. 3, Pt. 1: Winter. (Olson's Library Clip Art). (Illus.). 16p. (Orig.). 1995. pap. text ed. 33.00 (1-56984-008-3) C Olson & Assocs.

— Libraries Through the Seasons Vol. 3, Pt. 3: Summer. (Olson's Library Clip Art). (Illus.). 16p. (Orig.). 1995. pap. text ed. 33.00 (1-56984-010-5) C Olson & Assocs.

— Libraries Through the Seasons Vol. 3, Pt. 4: Fall. (Olson's Library Clip Art). (Illus.). 16p. (Orig.). 1995. pap. text ed. 33.00 (1-56984-011-3) C Olson & Assocs.

— Olson's Book of Library Clip Art, Vol. 1: 200 Graphics for All Types of Libraries. (Illus.). 30p. (Orig.). 1992. pap. text ed. 48.00 (0-9632754-0-2) C Olson & Assocs.

Olson, Clair C., ed. see Rickert, Edith.

Olson, Colleen M. Domestic Relations Law for Paralegals. LC 93-72661. 270p. (C). 1993. pap. text ed. write for info. (0-87084-681-7) Anderson Pub Co.

Olson, Cory, jt. auth. see Olson, Diane.

Olson, D. H., jt. auth. see Meier, W. M.

Olson, D. L. & North, T. H., eds. Ferrous Alloy Weldments. 422p. 1992. text ed. 136.00 (0-87849-544-4, Pub. by Trans Tech GW) LPS Dist Ctr.

Olson, D. L., et al, eds. Welding: Theory & Practice. (Material Processing Theory & Practice Ser.: No. 8). 384p. 1990. 141.00 (0-444-87427-5, North Holland) Elsevier.

Olson, D. V. Badges & Distinctive Insignia of the Saudi Arabian National Guard (SANG), Vol. 3. (Illus.). 50p. (Orig.). 1984. pap. 10.00 (0-9609690-3-9) Regt QM.

— Badges & Distinctive Insignia of the Syrian Armed Forces. (Illus.). 51p. (Orig.). 1989. pap. 10.00 (0-929757-20-3) Regt QM.

— Badges, Medals & Distinctive Insignia of the United Nations Peace Keeping Forces, 1947-1989. (Illus.). 67p. (Orig.). 1989. pap. 15.00 (0-929757-17-3) Regt QM.

— U. S. Army Officer & Enlisted Rank Insignia, 1924-1989. (Illus.). 50p. (Orig.). 1988. pap. 15.00 (0-929757-15-7) Regt QM.

***Olson, Dale P.** Modern Civil Practice in West Virginia. 697p. 1984. 55.00 (0-614-05907-0) Michie Butterworth.

Olson, Dale W. Knowing Your Intuitive Mind. Scholze, Elizabeth et al, eds. (Illus.). 177p. (Orig.). 1990. pap. text ed. 14.95 (1-879246-00-7) Crystalline Pubns.

Olson, Daniel, ed. Canons to the Theotokos for Compline. Lambertsen, Isaac E., tr. 160p. (Orig.). 1994. spiral bd. 35.00 (0-912927-58-5, D016) St John Kronstadt.

Olson, Daniel M., ed. see Nordenskiold, Gustaf.

Olson, Dave. Exploiting Chaos: Cashing in on the Realities of Software Development. LC 92-14997. 1993. pap. 39.95 (0-442-01112-1) Van Nos Reinhold.

Olson, David, jt. auth. see Jewell, Malcolm.

***Olson, David A.** The Cost of Select Recreation & Leisure Activities 1993. 78p. 1994. pap. text ed. 25.00 (0-614-06283-7) U CO Busn Res Div.

Olson, David H. Family Perspectives in Child & Youth Services. LC 88-32006. (Child & Youth Services Ser.: Vol. 11, No. 1). (Illus.). 211p. 1989. text ed. 39.95 (0-86656-850-6) Haworth Pr.

Olson, David H., ed. Two Thousand One: Preparing Families for the Future: NCFR Presidential Report. (Illus.). 40p. (Orig.) (C). 1990. pap. text ed. 8.00 (0-916174-26-3) Natl Coun Family.

***Olson, David H. & DeFain, John.** Instructor's Manual for Marriage & the Family: Diversity & Strengths. 736p. 1994. teacher ed, pap. write for info. (1-55934-338-9) Mayfield Pub.

— Marriage & the Family: Diversity & Strengths, Testbank. 1994. disk write for info. (0-614-02714-4) Mayfield Pub.

Olson, David H. & DeFrain, John. Marriage & the Family: Diversity & Strengths. LC 93-6051. (Illus.). 701p. 1994. text ed. 48.95 (1-55934-094-0) Mayfield Pub.

— Study Guide for Marriage & the Family: Diversity & Strengths. (Illus.). 1994. student ed, text ed. 15.95 (1-55934-293-5) Mayfield Pub.

Olson, David H., jt. ed. see Miller, Brent C.

Olson, David H., et al. Families: What Makes Them Work. 316p. (C). 1989. 42.00 (0-8039-2011-3); pap. text ed. 22.50 (0-8039-2854-8) Sage.

Olson, David H., et al, eds. Circumplex Model: Systemic Assessment & Treatment of Families. LC 88-30151. (Journal of Psychotherapy & the Family: Vol. 4, Nos. 1 & 2). (Illus.). 296p. 1989. text ed. 49.95 (0-86656-776-3) Haworth Pr.

— Inventory of Marriage & Family Literature, 7 vols., Vol. 4. LC 67-63014. 648p. reprint ed. pap. 180.00 (0-8357-4838-3, 2037775) Bks Demand.

— Inventory of Marriage & Family Literature, 7 vols., Vol. 5. LC 67-63014. 498p. reprint ed. pap. 142.00 (0-8357-4839-1, 2037775) Bks Demand.

— Inventory of Marriage & Family Literature, 7 vols., Vol. 6. LC 67-63014. 402p. reprint ed. pap. 114.60 (0-8357-4840-5, 2037775) Bks Demand.

— Inventory of Marriage & Family Literature, 7 vols., Vol. 7. LC 67-63014. 520p. reprint ed. pap. 148.20 (0-8357-4841-3, 2037775) Bks Demand.

— Inventory of Marriage & Family Literature, 7 vols., Vol. 8. LC 67-63014. 510p. reprint ed. pap. 145.40 (0-8357-4842-1, 2037775) Bks Demand.

— Inventory of Marriage & Family Literature, 7 vols., Vol. 9. LC 67-63014. 509p. reprint ed. pap. 145.10 (0-8357-4843-X, 2037775) Bks Demand.

— Inventory of Marriage & Family Literature, 7 vols., Vol. 10. LC 67-63014. 392p. reprint ed. pap. 111.80 (0-8357-4844-8, 2037775) Bks Demand.

Olson, David J., jt. ed. see Gardiner, John A.

Olson, David J., jt. auth. see Lipsky, Michael.

Olson, David L., ed. see Daly, Lawrence W.

Olson, David L., et al, eds. ASM Handbook, Vol. 6: Welding, Brazing & Soldering. rev. ed. LC 90-115. (Illus.). 1299p. 1993. 147.00 (0-87170-382-3, 6480U) ASM.

Olson, David M. Democratic Legislative Institutions: A Comparative View. LC 94-18913. (Comparative Politics Ser.). (Illus.). 200p. 1994. text ed. 47.50 (1-56324-314-8); pap. text ed. 19.95 (1-56324-315-6) M E Sharpe.

Olson, David M. & Franks, C. E., eds. Representation & Policy Formation in Federal Systems: Canada & the United States. LC 93-19575. 325p. 1993. pap. 24.95 (0-87772-340-0) UCB IGS.

Olson, David M. & Mezey, Michael L., eds. Legislatures in the Policy Process: The Dilemmas of Economic Policy. (Advances in Political Science Ser.). (Illus.). 256p. (C). 1991. 59.95 (0-521-38103-7) Cambridge U Pr.

Olson, David R. The World on Paper: The Conceptual & Cognitive Implications of Writing & Reading. (Illus.). 304p. (C). 1994. 24.95 (0-521-44311-3) Cambridge U Pr.

Olson, David R. & Bialystok, Ellen. Spatial Cognition: The Structure & Development of Mental Representations of Spatial Relations. 296p. 1983. text ed. 69.95 (0-89859-252-6) L Erlbaum Assocs.

Olson, David R. & Torrance, Nancy, eds. Literacy & Orality. (Illus.). 304p. (C). 1991. 59.95 (0-521-39217-9); pap. 21.95 (0-521-39850-9) Cambridge U Pr.

Olson, David R., ed. see Astington, Janet W., et al.

Olson, David R., jt. ed. see Van Holthoon, Frits.

Olson, David R., et al, eds. Literacy, Language & Learning: The Nature & Consequences of Reading & Writing. (Illus.). 420p. 1985. pap. 29.95 (0-521-31912-9) Cambridge U Pr.

Olson, David V. Badges & Distinctive Branch Insignia of the U. S. Army Quartermaster Corps, 1775-1995. (Illus.). 60p. (Orig.). 1994. pap. 15.00 (0-929757-16-5) Regt QM.

— Badges & Distinctive Insignia of the Arab Republic of Egypt (A. R. E.) (Illus.). 50p. 1987. pap. 10.00 (0-9609690-8-X) Regt QM.

— Badges & Distinctive Insignia of the Israeli Defense Forces (IDF) (Illus.). 50p. 1986. pap. 10.00 (0-9609690-7-1) Regt QM.

— Badges & Distinctive Insignia of the Kingdom of Jordan. (Illus.). 50p. 1987. pap. 10.00 (0-9609690-5-5) Regt QM.

— Badges & Distinctive Insignia of the Kingdom of Saudi Arabia: Para-Military Forces, Vol. 5. (Illus.). 50p. 1987. pap. 10.00 (0-9609690-4-7) Regt QM.

— Badges & Distinctive Insignia of the Kingdom of Saudi Arabia: Royal Saudi Air Force, Vol. 2. (Illus.). 55p. 1984. pap. 10.00 (0-9609690-1-2) Regt QM.

— Badges & Distinctive Insignia of the Kingdom of Saudi Arabia: Saudi Arabian Army, Vol. 1. (Illus.). 192p. 1981. pap. 10.00 (0-9609690-0-4) Regt QM.

— Badges & Distinctive Insignia of the Multinational Force & Observers (MFO) (Illus.). 85p. 1986. pap. 15.00 (0-9609690-6-3) Regt QM.

— Badges & Distinctive Insignia of the Royal Saudi Navy (RSNF), Vol. 4. (Illus.). 50p. 1985. pap. 10.00 (0-9609690-2-0) Regt QM.

Olson, David V., jt. auth. see G-1 Military Affairs, MODA Staff.

Olson, David V., jt. auth. see Republic of Egypt, Cabinet of the Grand Chamberlain Staff.

Olson, Dean. Industrial Arts for the General Shop. 4th ed. 1973. text ed. 24.28 (0-13-459131-3) P-H.

Olson, Dean, jt. auth. see Carey, Omer.

***Olson, Dennis L.** Shared Spirits: The Native American Kinship with Wildlife. (Illus.). 144p. 1995. write for info. (1-55971-474-3) NorthWord.

— Way of the Whitetail: Magic & Mystery. (Illus.). 160p. 1994. 35.00 (1-55971-427-1) NorthWord.

Olson, Dennis T. The Death of the Old & the Birth of the New: Framework of the Book of Numbers & the Pentateuch. (Brown Judaic Studies). (C). 1985. pap. 23.95 (0-89130-886-5) Scholars Pr GA.

— Deuteronomy & the Death of Moses: A Theological Reading. LC 94-12729. 1994. pap. 14.00 (0-8006-2639-7, Fortress Pr) Augsburg Fortress.

Olson, Diane & Olson, Cory. Black Diamond: Mining the Memories. LC 88-83375. (Illus.). 236p. 1988. pap. 12.95 (0-939116-19-7) Frontier OR.

Olson, Don. Movie. 1990. pap. 8.95 (0-8216-2008-8, Univ Books) Carol Pub Group.

Olson, E. Van. Retiree Nonpension Benefits: Management Guidelines. (Current Issues Ser.: No. 2). 32p. 1993. reprint ed. 5.50 (0-89215-137-4) U Cal LA Indus Rel.

Olson, Edna M., jt. auth. see Sperandio, Richard G.

Olson, Edward C., jt. ed. see Christoffersen, Ralph E.

Olson, Elder. Aristotle's Poetics & English Literature: A Collection of Critical Essays. LC 65-24430. (Gemini Bks: Patterns of Literary Criticism). 264p. reprint ed. pap. 75.30 (0-8357-5734-X, 2026737) Bks Demand.

— Last Poems. LC 84-136. 64p. (C). 1984. pap. 6.95 (0-226-62898-1) U Ch Pr.

— Tragedy & Theory of Drama. 1961. pap. 5.95 (0-8143-1149-0) Wayne St U Pr.

Olson, Eleanor. Wayne Estes: A Hero's Legacy. (Illus.). (YA). (gr. 7-12). 1991. pap. text ed. 6.00 (0-9628317-0-0) E Olson.

Olson, Eleonora & Olson, Ethel. Yust for Fun. (Illus.). 60p. 1979. reprint ed. pap. 2.50 (0-9602914-1-5) Eggs Pr.

***Olson, Elizabeth A., ed.** Dollars for College: The Quick Guide to Financial Aid for Business & Related Fields, Vol. 1. LC 95-1364. (Dollars for College Ser.). 76p. (Orig.). 1995. pap. 6.95 (1-880774-10-0) Garrett Pk.

— Dollars for College: The Quick Guide to Financial Aid for Journalism & Mass Communications. LC 95-1364. (Dollars for College Ser.). 76p. (Orig.). 1995. pap. 6.95 (1-880774-11-9) Garrett Pk.

— Dollars for College: The Quick Guide to Financial Aid for Liberal Arts: Humanities & Social Science. LC 95-1364. (Dollars for College Ser.). 84p. (Orig.). 1995. pap. 6.95 (1-880774-18-6) Garrett Pk.

— Dollars for College: The Quick Guide to Financial Aid for Science. LC 95-1364. (Dollars for College Ser.). 80p. (Orig.). 1995. pap. 6.95 (1-880774-14-3) Garrett Pk.

— Dollars for College: The Quick Guide to Financial Aid for Women in All Fields. LC 95-1364. (Dollars for College Ser.). 80p. (Orig.). 1995. pap. 6.95 (1-880774-20-8) Garrett Pk.

Olson, Elizabeth A., jt. auth. see Young, Rosalie F.

O

An Asterisk (*) at the beginning of an entry indicates that the title is appearing in BIP for the first time.

***Olson, Ellen, et al, eds.** Controversies in Ethics in Long-Term Care. 184p. 1994. 34.95 (*0-8261-8600-9*) Springer Pub.

Olson, Eric & Kelso, Susan. Horrorscope: It's Written in the Stars. (Illus.). (Orig.). 1991. pap. 5.95 (*0-681-41165-1*) Longmeadow Pr.

— Horrorscope: More Bad News. LC 92-15327. 1992. 5.95 (*0-681-41603-3*) Longmeadow Pr.

Olson, Ernest W. & Lawson, Evald B. Augustana Book Concern & Christine Nilsson's Visit to Brockton, Mass. in November, 1870. (Augustana Historical Society Publication Ser.: Vol. 3). 96p. 1933. pap. 3.00 (*0-910184-03-8*) Augustana.

Olson, Ernst W., et al. History of the Swedes of Illinois, 2 vols., Set. Scott, Franklyn D., ed. LC 78-15844. (Scandinavians in America Ser.). (Illus.). 1979. reprint ed. lib. bdg. 101.95 (*0-405-11656-X*) Ayer.

Olson, Esther E. Let's Make Up. 1945. pap. 2.75 (*0-8222-0653-6*) Dramatists Play.

Olson, Ethel, jt. auth. see Olson, Eleonora.

Olson, Everett C. The Other Side of the Medal: A Paleobiologist Reflects on the Art & Serendipity of Science. LC 90-5612. (Illus.). xiv, 182p. 1990. 29.95 (*0-939923-13-0*) M & W Pub Co.

Olson, Everett C., jt. ed. see Czerkas, Sylvia J.

Olson, F. W., et al, eds. Symposium on Small Hydropower & Fisheries. LC 85-72260. 497p. 1985. text ed. 25.50 (*0-913235-37-7*, 85-72260) Am Fisheries Soc.

Olson-Fallon & Tarvers, Josephine K. The Writer's Library, Vol. 2: Growing up, Growing Old. (C). 1992. text ed. 8.50 (*0-06-501123-6*) HarpCollege.

Olson-Fallon, Judith, jt. auth. see HarperCollins Editors.

Olson, Frederick I., jt. auth. see Anderson, Harry H.

Olson, G. Keith. Counseling Teenagers. 528p. 1984. pap. 21.99 (*0-931529-67-0*) Group Pub.

Olson, Gail A. & Robbins, Michael J. Scars & Stripes: Healing the Wounds of War. 1992. 17.95 (*0-07-047906-2*); pap. 8.95 (*0-07-047905-4*) McGraw.

— Scars & Stripes: Healing the Wounds of War. 210p. 1992. 17.95 (*0-8306-3946-2*, 3979, TAB-Human Servs Inst); pap. 8.95 (*0-8306-3088-0*, 3979, TAB-Human Servs Inst) TAB Bks.

Olson, Gary. Hartford Whalers. LC 93-48433. (NHL Today Ser.). 32p. (J). 1995. 14.95 (*0-88682-676-4*) Creative Ed.

— Quebec Nordiques. LC 93-48453. (NHL Today Ser.). 32p. (J). 1995. 14.95 (*0-88682-685-3*) Creative Ed.

Olson, Gary, et al, eds. Empirical Studies of Programmers: Second Workshop. LC 87-25942. (Human-Computer Interaction Ser.: Vol. 7). 272p. 1987. text ed. 55.00 (*0-89391-461-4*); pap. text ed. 22.50 (*0-89391-462-2*) Ablex Pub.

Olson, Gary A., ed. Philosophy, Rhetoric, Literary Criticism: Inter-Views. LC 93-38349. 264p. (C). 1994. 24.95 (*0-8093-1908-X*) S Ill U Pr.

Olson, Gary A. & Dobrin, Sidney I., eds. Composition Theory for the Postmodern Classroom. 360p. (C). 1994. text ed. 59.50 (*0-7914-2305-0*); pap. text ed. 19.95 (*0-7914-2306-9*) State U NY Pr.

Olson, Gary A. & Gale, Irene, eds. Interviews: Cross-Disciplinary Perspectives on Rhetoric & Literacy. LC 91-17653. 200p. 1991. 19.95 (*0-8093-1737-0*) S Ill U Pr.

Olson, Gary A., jt. auth. see Ashton-Jones, Evelyn.

Olson, Gary A., et al. Style in Technical Writing. (C). 1984. pap. text ed. write for info. (*0-07-554380-X*) McGraw.

Olson, Gene. Basic Spanish for Idiots: An Anti-Textbook. 64p. 1993. pap. 6.95 (*0-913366-10-2*) Windyridge.

— Skunk River Anthology. (Illus.). 166p. 1992. pap. 9.95 (*1-878488-59-7*) Quixote Pr IA.

— Southern Oregon Revealed: From Climate to Culture Shock. 56p. (Orig.). 1990. pap. 3.95 (*0-913366-09-9*) Windyridge.

— Sweet Agony Two: A Writing Book of Sorts. 194p. 1983. pap. 7.97 (*0-913366-07-2*) Windyridge.

Olson, Gene, jt. auth. see Olson, Joan.

Olson, Georgine N. & Allen, Barbara, eds. Cooperative Collective Management: The Conspectus Approach. LC 94-20036. 1994. write for info. (*1-55570-200-7*) Neal-Schuman.

Olson, Gerald, ed. Advances in Consumer Research: Proceedings of 1979 Meeting, Vol. 7. 802p. 1980. pap. 29.00 (*0-915552-05-1*) Assn Consumer Res.

Olson, Gerald W. Soils & the Environment: A Guide to Their Applications. 191p. 1982. pap. 19.95 (*0-412-23760-1*, 6587) Chapman & Hall.

Olson, Glending. Literature As Recreation in the Later Middle Ages. LC 82-2462. 246p. 1982. 37.50 (*0-8014-1494-6*); pap. 14.95 (*0-8014-9368-4*) Cornell U Pr.

Olson, Glending, ed. see Chaucer, Geoffrey.

Olson, Gordon L. A Grand Rapids Sampler. LC 92-72735. (Illus.). 240p. (C). 1992. 29.95 (*0-9617708-3-X*) GRMI Hist Comm.

Olson, Grant A., tr. see Payutto, Phra P.

***Olson, Gregory A.** Mansfield & Vietnam: A Study in Rhetorical Adaptation. 1995. 39.95 (*0-87013-386-1*) Mich St U Pr.

Olson, H. W. The Earthworms of Ohio. (Bulletin Ser.: No. 17). 1928. 2.00 (*0-86727-016-0*) Ohio Bio Survey.

Olson, Harry A. Power Strategies of Jesus Christ: Principles of Leadership from the Greatest Motivator of All Time. LC 91-11891. 192p. 1991. reprint ed. pap. 9.95 (*0-89243-505-4*, Triumph Books) Liguori Pubns.

Olson, Harry F. Music, Physics, & Engineering. enl. rev. ed. (Illus.). 1966. pap. 9.95 (*0-486-21769-8*) Dover.

***Olson, Helen, ed.** Please Listen... 144p. Date not set. pap. text ed. 4.95 (*1-882972-52-X*) Queenship Pub.

Olson, Helen, jt. auth. see Olson, Virgil J.

Olson, Hilary C., jt. ed. see Graham, Stephan A.

Olson, J. M., et al, eds. Green Photosynthetic Bacteria. LC 88-12419. (Illus.). 338p. 1988. 85.00 (*0-306-42920-9*, Plenum Pr) Plenum.

Olson, Jack, jt. auth. see Bragg, Bernard.

Olson, Jack, jt. auth. see Price, Wilson.

Olson, James. Clinical Pharmacology Made Ridiculously Simple. (Illus.). 162p. (C). 1994. pap. text ed. 17.95 (*0-940780-17-8*) MedMaster.

Olson, James, jt. auth. see Roberts, Randy.

Olson, James C. Red Cloud & the Sioux Problem. LC 65-10048. (Illus.). xii, 401p. 1965. reprint ed. pap. 12.50 (*0-8032-5817-8*) U of Nebr Pr.

— Serving the University of Missouri: A Memoir of Campus & System Administration. (Illus.). 232p. 1993. text ed. 34.95 (*0-8262-0924-6*) U of Mo Pr.

Olson, James C. & Olson, Vera B. The University of Missouri: An Illustrated History. LC 88-1158. (Illus.). 312p. 1988. 29.95 (*0-8262-0678-6*) U of Mo Pr.

Olson, James D. Minnesota Residential Real Estate. suppl. ed. 1994. ring bd. 45.00 (*0-318-68686-4*) Butterworth Legal Pubs.

— Minnesota Residential Real Estate, 2 vols., Set. 980p. 1994. ring bd. 165.00 (*0-88063-862-1*) Michie Butterworth.

Olson, James E., et al, eds. Historical Dictionary of the British Empire. LC 94-871. 1995. text ed. write for info. (*0-313-27917-9*) Greenwood.

— Historical Dictionary of the British Empire, 1. LC 94-871. 1995. text ed. write for info. (*0-313-29366-X*) Greenwood.

— Historical Dictionary of the British Empire, Vol. 2. LC 94-871. 1995. text ed. write for info. (*0-313-29367-8*) Greenwood.

Olson, James M. & Zanna, Mark P., eds. Self-Inference Processes Vol. VI: The Ontario Symposium on Personality & Social Psychology. 336p. (C). 1990. text ed. 69.95 (*0-8058-0551-6*) L Erlbaum Assocs.

Olson, James M., jt. ed. see Roese, Neal J.

Olson, James M., jt. ed. see Zanna, Mark P.

Olson, James M., et al, eds. Relative Deprivation & Social Comparison: The Ontario Symposium on Personality & Social Psychology, Vol. 4. (Ontario Symposia on Personality Ser.). 272p. (C). 1986. text ed. 49.95 (*0-89859-704-8*) L Erlbaum Assocs.

Olson, James N., jt. auth. see Pfeiffer, Kenneth.

Olson, James S. Catholic Immigrants in America. 260p. 1986. 31.95 (*0-8304-1037-6*) Nelson-Hall.

— Dictionary of United States Economic History. LC 91-32193. 680p. 1992. text ed. 85.00 (*0-313-26532-1*, OEH/, Greenwood Pr) Greenwood.

— The Ethnic Dimension in American History. 2nd ed. 384p. 1994. pap. text ed. 17.00 (*0-312-08934-1*) St Martin.

— Historical Dictionary of the Nineteen Twenties: From World War I to the New Deal, 1919-1933. LC 87-29987. 432p. 1988. text ed. 65.00 (*0-313-25683-7*, OHD/, Greenwood Pr) Greenwood.

— The History of Cancer: An Annotated Bibliography. LC 89-2174. (Bibliographies & Indexes in Medical Studies: No. 3). 434p. 1989. text ed. 89.50 (*0-313-25889-9*, OHY/, Greenwood Pr) Greenwood.

— The Indians of Latin America: An Ethnohistorical Dictionary. LC 90-47503. 528p. 1991. text ed. 75.00 (*0-313-26387-6*, OIL/, Greenwood Pr) Greenwood.

— Saving Capitalism: The Reconstruction Finance Corporation & the New Deal, 1933-1940. 315p. 1988. text ed. 39.50 (*0-691-04749-9*) Princeton U Pr.

— Slave Life in America: A Historiography & Selected Bibliography. 128p. (Orig.). (C). 1983. lib. bdg. 47.50 (*0-8191-3285-3*) U Pr of Amer.

— The Vietnam War: Handbook of the Literature & Research. LC 92-25626. 536p. 1993. text ed. 85.00 (*0-313-27422-3*, OVA, Greenwood Pr) Greenwood.

Olson, James S., ed. Dictionary of the Vietnam War. LC 87-12023. 593p. 1988. text ed. 75.00 (*0-313-24943-1*, OVW/, Greenwood Pr) Greenwood.

— The Great Depression 1929-1941. 200p. (Orig.). (C). 1994. pap. text ed. 9.56 (*1-881089-27-4*) Brandywine Press.

— Historical Dictionary of the New Deal: From Inauguration to Preparation for War. LC 84-19792. viii, 611p. 1985. text ed. 75.00 (*0-313-23873-1*, ODN/, Greenwood Pr) Greenwood.

***Olson, James S. & Olson, Judith E.** The Cuban Americans. LC 94-34365. (Immigrant Heritage of America Ser.). 1995. lib. bdg. 26.95x (*0-8057-8430-6*, Twayne); pap. 15.95 (*0-8057-8439-X*, Twayne) Macmillan.

Olson, James S. & Roberts, Randy. Where the Domino Fell: America & Vietnam, 1945-1990. LC 89-63924. 310p. (Orig.). (C). 1990. pap. text ed. 14.00 (*0-312-03263-3*) St Martin.

Olson, James S. & Wilson, Raymond. Native Americans in the Twentieth Century. (Illus.). 248p. 1986. pap. 11.95 (*0-252-01285-2*) U of Ill Pr.

Olson, James S., jt. auth. see Roberts, Randy.

Olson, James S., et al. An Ethnohistorical Dictionary of the Russian & Soviet Empires. LC 93-18149. 848p. 1994. text ed. 125.00 (*0-313-27497-5*, OEA/, Greenwood Pr) Greenwood.

— U. S. in the 20th Century: America, 1900-1945, 2 vols., Vol. 1. 430p. 1995. pap. text ed. 19.29 (*0-312-10104-X*) St Martin.

Olson, James S., et al, eds. Historical Dictionary of European Imperialism. LC 90-38413. 804p. 1991. text ed. 105.00 (*0-313-26257-8*, OIM, Greenwood Pr) Greenwood.

— Historical Dictionary of the Spanish Empire, 1402-1975. LC 91-8250. 720p. 1991. text ed. 89.50 (*0-313-26413-9*, OSR, Greenwood Pr) Greenwood.

Olson, Janet L. Envisioning Writing: Toward an Integration of Drawing & Writing. LC 92-7322. 176p. 1992. pap. text ed. 19.50 (*0-435-08700-2*, 08700) Heinemann.

Olson, Jeannine E. Calvin & Social Welfare: Deacons & the Bourse Francaise. LC 86-43234. (Illus.). 344p. 1989. 60.00 (*0-941664-85-6*) Susquehanna U Pr.

— Deacons & Deaconesses Through the Centuries: One Ministry - Many Roles. LC 92-30071. (Scholarship Today Ser.). 1992. 21.95 (*0-570-04596-7*) Concordia.

Olson, Jeff, ed. The Vermont Almanac. (Illus.). 528p. (Orig.). 1989. pap. 19.95 (*0-9622690-0-X*) Reg Facts.

— The Vermont Almanac: 1991. 2nd ed. (Illus.). 528p. (Orig.). 1990. pap. 24.95 (*0-9622690-1-8*) Reg Facts.

Olson, Jeff & Swift, Tammy. Bismarck - Mandan: The Cities & the People. (Illus.). 112p. (Orig.). 1995. pap. 14.95 (*1-56037-069-6*) Am Wrld Geog.

Olson, Jerry C. & Sentis, Keith, eds. Advertising & Consumer Psychology, Vol. 3. LC 86-12219. 302p. 1986. text ed. 55.00 (*0-275-92154-9*, C21543, Praeger Pubs) Greenwood.

Olson, Jerry C., jt. auth. see Peter, J. Paul.

Olson, Jim. Environmental Law: A Citizens Guide in the 1980's. 344p. 1981. pap. 21.95 (*0-943806-01-1*) Neahtawanta Pr.

— The Reindeer & the Easter Bunny. Van Vleck, Jane & Olson, Sally, eds. (Illus.). 18p. (Orig.). (J). (gr. 1-4). 1981. pap. 4.95 (*0-943806-00-3*) Neahtawanta Pr.

Olson, Jim & Kozar, Elaine. Half Headed People. (Green Legend Ser.). (Illus.). 80p. (Orig.). pap. 5.95 (*0-943806-04-6*) Neahtawanta Pr.

Olson, Jim, jt. auth. see Olson, Lori.

Olson, Joan & Olson, Gene. Silver Dust & Spanish Wine: A Bilingual History of Mexico. De Gutierrez, Frances A., tr. LC 78-55885. (Illus.). (gr. 9 up). 1979. pap. text ed. 10.97 (*0-913366-05-6*) Windyridge.

— Silver Dust & Spanish Wine: A History of Mexico. LC 80-51869. (Illus.). 336p. (Orig.). (gr. 9 up). 1980. pap. text ed. 9.47 (*0-913366-06-4*) Windyridge.

Olson, John. Building an H-O Model Railroad with Personality. Hayden, Bob, ed. (Illus.). 68p. (Orig.). 1983. pap. 8.95 (*0-89024-042-6*) Kalmbach.

— Understanding Teaching: Beyond Expertise. (Developing Teachers & Teaching Ser.). 160p. 1991. 90.00 (*0-335-09289-6*, Open Univ Pr); pap. 32.00 (*0-335-09288-8*, Open Univ Pr) Taylor & Francis.

***Olson, John E.** Anywhere - Anytime. (Illus.). 238p. Date not set. 13.50 (*0-9644432-2-8*) J E Olson.

— The Guerrilla & the Hostage. (Illus.). 256p. (Orig.). Date not set. pap. 13.50 (*0-9644432-0-1*) J E Olson.

— O'Donnell, Andersonville of the Pacific: Extermination Camp of American Hostages in the Philippines. (Illus.). 194p. (Orig.). Date not set. pap. 12.95 (*0-9644432-1-X*) J E Olson.

— Twenty-First Virginia Cavalry. (Virginia Regimental Histories Ser.). (Illus.). 91p. 1989. 19.95 (*0-930919-81-5*) H E Howard.

Olson, John F., jt. ed. see Goodman, Amy L.

Olson, John F., jt. auth. see Johnston, Joseph J.

Olson, John R. Collecting the Mercedes-Benz SL, 1954-1993. 235p. 1993. 19.95 (*0-9635394-0-X*); pap. 16.95 (*0-9635394-1-8*) SL Mkt Letter.

— Make Money Owning Your Car (& Enjoy Every Minute) rev. ed. (Illus.). 184p. 1976. 9.95 (*0-686-09315-1*) Electronic Flea.

Olson, Jon, ed. Minnesota Business Almanac: The Most Comprehensive Reference Guide Anywhere for Minnesota Job Seekers, Investors, Sales People & Researchers. (Illus.). 628p. 1994. pap. write for info. (*0-9641908-5-0*) MSP Communs.

Olson, Joseph. Federal Taxation of Intellectual Property Transfers. 400p. ring bd. 70.00 (*0-318-21432-6*, 00597) NY Law Pub.

Olson, Joseph E. Federal Taxation of Intellectual Property Transfers. 500p. 1986. ring bd. 85.00 (*0-317-05389-2*, 00597) NY Law Pub.

Olson, Joubert W. Craps: There Are No Secrets to This Game! How Craps Is Played. 156p. 1994. pap. 19.95 (*1-883067-24-3*) South Shore.

Olson, Joyce A. & McCauley, Janet. ECO Workshop Leader's Manual. 64p. 1989. teacher ed 19.95 (*1-55990-020-2*) Special Pr TX.

Olson, Judith E., jt. auth. see Olson, James S.

Olson, Karen, jt. ed. see Brown, Cheryl L.

Olson, Karla. Creative Embroidery. 1992. pap. 9.95 (*0-937769-86-X*) Mark Inc CA.

— Creative Quilting. 1992. pap. 9.95 (*0-937769-87-8*) Mark Inc CA.

— My First Kitten. (J). 1994. 9.95 (*0-8362-4232-7*) Andrews & McMeel.

— My First Puppy. (J). 1994. 9.95 (*0-8362-4233-5*) Andrews & McMeel.

Olson, Keith G. The Art of Steve Hanks: Poised Between Heartbeats. (Illus.). 128p. 1994. 69.95 (*0-9618978-2-1*) Hadley Hse.

— The Art of Steve Hanks: Poised Between Heartbeats. deluxe limited ed. (Illus.). 128p. 1994. 200.00 (*0-9618978-3-X*) Hadley Hse.

— The Art of Terry Redlin: Opening Windows to the Wild. 4th deluxe limited ed. (Illus.). 132p. 1991. ring bd. 400.00 (*0-9618978-1-3*) Hadley Hse.

— The Art of Terry Redlin: Opening Windows to the Wild. 4th ed. (Illus.). 132p. 1991. 65.00 (*0-9618978-0-5*) Hadley Hse.

Olson, Keith W. Biography of a Progressive: Franklin K. Lane, 1864-1920. LC 78-57766. (Contributions in American History Ser.: No. 78). 233p. 1979. text ed. 59.95 (*0-313-20613-9*, OBP/, Greenwood Pr) Greenwood.

Olson, Kenfield, ed. Collected Memoirs of Central School: Kirkland, Washington, 1890-1980. 67p. (Orig.). (YA). (gr. 9-12). 1982. pap. 5.00 (*0-685-28866-8*) Marymoor Mus.

Olson, Kenneth B. One Doctor Learns to Be a Patient. Wills, Susan E., ed. LC 93-83044. (Illus.). 320p. 1993. 29.00 (*1-883122-00-7*) Pearce Pub.

Olson, Kenneth E. Music & Musket: Bands & Bandsmen of the American Civil War. LC 79-6195. (Contributions to the Study of Music & Dance Ser.: No. 1). (Illus.). xx, 299p. 1981. text ed. 59.95 (*0-313-22112-X*, OMM/, Greenwood Pr) Greenwood.

Olson, Kenneth R. An Essay on Facts. LC 86-72171. (Center for the Study of Language & Information-Lecture Notes Ser.: No. 6). 160p. 1987. 23.95 (*0-937073-07-5*); pap. text ed. 11.95 (*0-937073-08-3*) Ctr Study Language.

Olson, Kent C., jt. auth. see Cohen, Morris L.

Olson, Kent R. Poisoning & Drug Overdose. 2nd ed. (Illus.). 592p. 1994. pap. text ed. 28.95 (*0-8385-1108-2*, A1108-8) Appleton & Lange.

Olson, Kristin. Legal Aspects of Asbestos Abatement. 1986. 6.95 (*1-56534-008-6*) NOLPE.

Olson, Kyle, jt. ed. see Morel, Benoit.

Olson, Lance. Circus of the Mind in Motion: Postmodernism & the Comic Vision. LC 89-39857. 172p. (C). 1990. text ed. 34.95 (*0-8143-2132-1*) Wayne St U Pr.

Olson, Laura K. The Political Economy of Aging: The State, Private Power, & Social Welfare. LC 82-1315. 288p. 1982. text ed. 45.00 (*0-231-05450-5*, King's Crown Paperbacks) Col U Pr.

Olson, Laura K., ed. The Graying of the World: Who Will Care for the Frail Elderly? LC 92-1661. (Illus.). 320p. 1994. lib. bdg. 69.95 (*1-56024-363-5*) Haworth Pr.

Olson, Laura K., jt. ed. see Browne, William P.

Olson, Laurie S. He Was Still My Daddy: Coming to Terms with Mental Illness. LC 94-65716. 157p. 1994. pap. 12.95 (*0-9640680-0-1*) Ogden Hse.

Olson, Lawrence. The Ambivalent Moderns: Portraits in Japanese Cultural Identity. 200p. (C). 1992. text ed. 52.00 (*0-8476-7738-9*); pap. text ed. 17.95 (*0-8476-7739-7*) Rowman.

Olson, Lawrence A. Japan in Postwar Asia. LC 79-101674. 302p. reprint ed. pap. 86.10 (*0-317-08407-0*, 2002954) Bks Demand.

Olson, Lee. Marmalade & Whiskey: British Remittance Men in the West. LC 92-54762. 260p. (Orig.). 1993. pap. 16.95 (*1-55591-110-2*) Fulcrum Pub.

Olson, Lester C. Emblems of American Community in the Revolutionary Era: A Study in Rhetorical Iconology. LC 90-24923. (Illus.). 328p. (C). 1991. text ed. 40.00 (*1-56098-066-4*) Smithsonian.

Olson, Linda L. & Bywater, Tim. Guide to Exploring Grand Teton National Park. rev. ed. LC 90-61339. (Illus.). 176p. (Orig.). 1995. pap. 10.95 (*0-9621511-1-4*) RNM Pr.

Olson, Linus. You Can Grow Roses in Florida. (Illus.). 1978. pap. 5.95 (*0-8200-0407-3*) Great Outdoors.

***Olson, Lori & Olson, Jim.** Norsk Hostfest. (Illus.). (Orig.). 1995. pap. 14.95 (*0-614-02589-3*) Am Wrld Geog.

Olson, Lynette. Early Monasteries in Cornwall. (Studies in Celtic History: No. XI). (Illus.). 160p. 1989. 79.00 (*0-85115-478-6*) Boydell & Brewer.

Olson, Lynn. Sculpting with Cement: Direct Modeling in a Permanent Medium. LC 81-708. (Illus.). 109p. (Orig.). (C). 1995. reprint ed. pap. 24.95 (*0-9605678-0-1*) Steelstone.

Olson, Lynn F. Exploring More Piano Literature. (Illus.). 1980. pap. 6.50 (*0-8258-0057-9*, 0-5082) Fischer Inc NY.

— Exploring Piano Literature. (Illus.). 48p. 1978. pap. 6.95 (*0-8258-0056-0*, 0-5041) Fischer Inc NY.

Olson, Lynn F., jt. auth. see Hilley, Martha.

Olson, Lynn F., jt. auth. see Reilly, Mary L.

Olson, M. Genevieve. From Ax & Plow to Here & Now. (Illus.). 188p. (Orig.). 1991. pap. 13.50 (*0-9629033-1-0*) Farmstead MN.

Olson, M. H., ed. Technological Support for Work Group Collaboration. (John Seely Brown Ser.). 208p. 1989. 24.95 (*0-8058-0304-1*) L Erlbaum Assocs.

Olson, M. H., jt. auth. see Davis, Gordon B.

Olson, Mancur, Jr. The Logic of Collective Action: Public Goods & the Theory of Groups. (Economic Studies: Vol. No. 124). 186p. (C). 1965. pap. 12.95 (*0-674-53751-3*) HUP.

— Logic of Collective Action: Public Goods & the Theory of Groups. rev. ed. LC 65-19826. (Economic Studies: No. 24). 1965. pap. 6.95 (*0-674-03751-0*) HUP.

Olson, Mancur. The Rise & Decline of Nations: Economic Growth, Stagflation, & Social Rigidities. LC 82-40163. 287p. 1982. 37.00 (*0-300-02307-3*) Yale U Pr.

— The Rise & Decline of Nations: Economic Growth, Stagflation, & Social Rigidities. LC 82-40163. 287p. 1984. reprint ed. pap. 14.00 (*0-300-03079-7*, Y-487) Yale U Pr.

Olson, Mancur, ed. New Approach to the Economics of Health Care. 502p. 1981. 48.50 (*0-8447-2212-X*); pap. 26.00 (*0-8447-2213-8*) Am Enterprise.

Olson, Mancur, Jr. & Landsberg, Hans H., eds. The No-Growth Society. 259p. (C). 1974. text ed. 10.00 (*0-393-01111-9*) Norton.

Olson, Mancur L., Jr. Economics of Wartime Shortages: A History of British Food Supplies in the Napoleonic War & in World War I & World War II. LC 63-17328. 160p. reprint ed. 45.60 (*0-8357-9104-1*, 2017917) Bks Demand.

Olson, Margaret J. Aloysious Alligator. 2nd ed. (Illus.). (J). (gr. k-2). 1980. pap. 3.00 (*0-934876-14-2*) Creative Storytime.

— Tell & Draw Animal Cut-outs. 3rd ed. (J). (gr. k-2). 1963. pap. 3.00 (*0-934876-15-0*) Creative Storytime.

— Tell & Draw Stories. (Illus.). (J). (ps-3). 1963. lib. bdg. 11.95 (*0-934876-05-3*); pap. 6.95 (*0-934876-01-0*) Creative Storytime.

Olson, Margot & Forrest, Mary. Shared Meaning: An Introduction to Speech Communication. 304p. (C). 1994. per. 29.95 (*0-8403-9290-7*) Kendall-Hunt.

Olson, Margrethe H., jt. auth. see Davis, Gordon B.

An Asterisk (*) at the beginning of an entry indicates that the title is appearing in BIP for the first time.

Olson, Marian. Facing the Wind. 108p. 1990. write for info. (*0-9625862-1-8*) Raven Pr CA.

Olson, Marie M. A Bibliography on the Germans from Russia: Material Found in the New York Public Library, 1970. 29p. 1976. 7.00 (*0-914222-21-X*) Am Hist Soc Ger.

Olson, Marie M. & Reisbick, Anna M., eds. Norka: A German Village in Russia. 2nd rev. ed. 49p. 1986. 9.00 (*0-914222-22-8*) Am Hist Soc Ger.

Olson, Marilynn S. Ellen Raskin. (Twayne's United States Authors Ser.: No. 579). 152p. 1991. text ed. 20.95 (*0-8057-7627-3*, Pub. by Royal Botanic Garden UK) Macmillan.

Olson, Mark. Galatians in Defense of Love: A Study Guide. 102p. (Orig.). 1994. pap. 8.95 (*1-880837-86-2*) Smyth & Helwys.

— Innerer Klang. (Illus.). 28p. 1981. 25.00 (*0-939622-20-3*); pap. 5.00 (*0-939622-19-X*) Four Zoas Night Ltd.

— The Woodcutter. (Chickadee Ser.: No. 4). 1992. pap. 7.00 (*1-55780-117-7*) Juniper Pr WI.

Olson, Mark, jt. ed. see Bridwell-Bowles, Lillian.

Olson, Mark, ed. see Ganguli, Aparna B. & Henry, Richard.

Olson, Mark, ed. see Homstad, Torild & Thorson, Helga.

Olson, Mark, ed. see Kassner, Linda A. & Collins, Terence.

Olson, Mark, ed. see Nereson, Sally.

Olson, Mark, ed. see Schmitz, James.

Olson, Mark D. Go Public - Thirty Days: The Comprehensive Course on Regulation D. (Illus.). (C). 1989. 225.00 (*0-685-24733-3*) C Counsel Inc.

Olson, Mark J. Irenaeus, the Valentinian Gnostics, & the Kingdom of God (A.H. Book V) LC 92-29432. (Mellen Biblical Press Ser.). 164p. 1992. text ed. 79.95 (*0-7734-2352-4*) E Mellen.

Olson, Marr, ed. see Henderson, Zenna.

Olson, Mary W., ed. Opening the Door to Classroom Research. 166p. 1990. 8.75 (*0-87207-746-2*) Intl Reading.

Olson, Mary W. & Homan, Susan P., eds. Teacher to Teacher: Strategies for the Elementary Classroom. 256p. 1993. pap. 20.00 (*0-87207-382-3*) Intl Reading.

Olson, Mary W. & Miller, Samuel D. Reading & Language Arts Programs: A Guide to Evaluation. (Essential Tools for Educators Ser.). 115p. 1993. pap. 16.95 (*0-8039-6042-5*) Corwin Pr.

Olson, Matthew H., jt. auth. see Hergenhahn, B. R.

Olson, May E., jt. ed. see Arndt, Karl J.

***Olson, Melfried & Rosene, Candace.** Mathematics Activities for Elementary Teachers. 176p. (C). 1994. pap. text ed., spiral bd. 14.36 (*0-8403-9930-8*) Kendall-Hunt.

Olson, Michael. MetroFarm: The Guide to Growing for Big Profit on a Small Parcel of Land. (Illus.). 576p. 1995. pap. 29.95 (*0-9637876-0-8*) T S Bks.

Olson, Michelle. The Adventures of Eggbert Egghead. Van Treese, James B., ed. Ingram, tr. (Illus.). (J). 1993. 9.95 (*1-880416-27-1*) NW Pub.

Olson, Milton C. & Haber, F. Barry. Business Mathematics. 1981. write for info. (*0-672-97328-6*); pap. write for info. (*0-672-97327-8*) Macmillan.

Olson, Miriam M., ed. Women's Health & Social Work: Feminist Perspectives. LC 94-3951. (Social Work in Health Care Ser.: Vol. 19, Nos. 3-4). 175p. 1994. 32.95 (*1-56024-683-9*) Haworth Pr.

Olson, Myrle, jt. auth. see Metcalfe, Kathy.

Olson, Myrna R. Women's Journeys Through Crisis. LC 88-60778. (Illus.). (Orig.). 1988. pap. 8.95 (*0-9620254-0-2*) Nathan Star Pr.

Olson, Myrna R. & Mangold, Sally S. Guidelines & Games for Teaching Efficient Braille Reading. LC 81-14906. (Illus.). 116p. 1981. pap. 16.95 (*0-89128-105-3*) Am Foun Blind.

Olson, Nancy. Garvarni's Carnival Lithographs. (Illus.). 1979. pap. 1.00 (*0-89467-009-3*) Yale Art Gallery.

— Patterngrams: How to Copy Designs at Home. 2nd ed. LC 72-78471. (Illus.). 1979. pap. 10.00 (*0-87005-312-4*) Fairchild.

Olson, Nancy B. Audiovisual Material Glossary. (Library, Information, & Computer Science Ser.: No. 7). (Illus.). 56p. (Orig.). 1988. pap. text ed. 8.50 (*1-55653-026-9*) OCLC Online Comp.

— Cataloger's Guide to MARC Coding & Tagging for Audio Visual Materials. 29.50 (*0-933474-49-0*) Media Mktg Group.

— Cataloging Computer Files. (Minnesota AACR 2 Trainers Ser.: No. 2). 1992. 30.00 (*0-936996-47-1*) Soldier Creek.

— Cataloging Microcomputer Software. 263p. 1989. lib. bdg. 33.00 (*0-87287-513-X*) Libs Unl.

— Cataloging Motion Pictures & Videorecordings. (Minnesota AACR 2 Trainers Ser.: No. 1). 1991. pap. 30.00 (*0-936996-38-2*) Soldier Creek.

— Cataloging of Audiovisual Materials: A Manual Using AACR 2. 3rd ed. 300p. 1991. lib. bdg. 55.00 (*0-933474-48-2*) Media Mktg Group.

Olson, Nancy B., comp. Cataloging Service Bulletin Index: Index to Bulletins 1-62 (Summer 1978-Winter 1993) annuals 1994. 30.00 (*0-936996-65-X*) Soldier Creek.

Olson, Nancy B., jt. ed. see Olson, Susan.

Olson, Nathanael. Como Ganar a Tu Familia Para Cristo. Villarello, Ildefonso, tr. 182p. 1987. reprint ed. pap. 2.75 (*0-311-13801-2*) Casa Bautista.

Olson, Nels. Time in Many Places. 218p. 1980. 9.00 (*0-87839-036-7*) North Star.

Olson, Norman. I Can Read About Trucks & Cars. LC 72-96957. (Illus.). (J). (gr. 2-4). 1973. pap. 2.50 (*0-89375-055-7*) Troll Assocs.

Olson, O. Charles. Diagnosis & Management of Diabetes Mellitus. 2nd ed. 352p. 1988. text ed. 41.00 (*0-88167-287-4*) Raven.

— Diagnosis & Management of Diabetes Mellitus: A Clinical Manual for Medical Students, Residents, & Primary Care Physicians. LC 80-27025. (Illus.). 308p. reprint ed. pap. 87.80 (*0-8357-7652-2*, 2056978) Bks Demand.

— Prevention of Football Injuries: Protecting the Health of the Student Athlete. LC 70-157472. 136p. reprint ed. 38. 80 (*0-8357-9413-X*, 2014569) Bks Demand.

Olson, O. N. A. J. Lindstrom. LC 58-2906. (Augustana Historical Society Publication Ser.: Vol. 16). 47p. 1957. pap. 3.00 (*0-910184-16-X*) Augustana.

Olson, Oscar N. Olof Christian Telemak Andren, Ambassador of Good Will. LC 55-2674. (Augustana Historical Society Publication Ser.: Vol. 14). 103p. 1954. pap. 3.00 (*0-910184-14-3*) Augustana.

— Sward & Johnston, Biographical Sketches of Augustana Leaders. LC 56-5870. (Augustana Historical Society Publication Ser.: No. 15). 80p. 1955. pap. 3.00 (*0-910184-15-1*) Augustana.

Olson, Pamela, jt. auth. see Marx, Pamela.

Olson, Patricia S. And Suddenly They're Gone: What Parents Need to Know about the Empty Nest. LC 92-61770. 237p. (Orig.). 1993. pap. 14.00 (*0-9634523-0-4*) Tiffany Pr CO.

— Study Skills: The Parent Connection. Hess, Karen M., ed. (Illus.). 50p. 1988. pap. text ed. 7.50 (*0-929168-00-3*) Milestone Pub.

***Olson, Paul.** The Journey to Wisdom: Self-Education in Patristic & Medieval Literature. LC 95-3042. 352p. 1995. text ed. 40.00 (*0-8032-3562-3*) U of Nebr Pr.

Olson, Paul, ed. The Struggle for the Land: Indigenous Insight & Industrial Empire in the Semiarid World. LC 89-22422. (Illus.). x, 317p. 1990. 40.00 (*0-8032-3555-0*) U of Nebr Pr.

Olson, Paul & Olson, Susan. Communication in the Work Place. 200p. 1991. 29.95 (*0-913690-16-3*) Aloray.

Olson, Paul A. The Canterbury Tales & the Good Society. (Illus.). 320p. 1987. text ed. 49.50x (*0-691-06693-0*) Princeton U Pr.

Olson, Paul R. Circle of Paradox: Time & Essence in the Poetry of Juan Ramon Jimenez. LC 67-21581. 248p. reprint ed. pap. 70.70 (*0-317-28736-2*, 2020730) Bks Demand.

Olson, Paul W. Beyond the Blue Ridge. (Illus.). (Orig.). 1990. pap. write for info. (*1-879077-50-7*) Olson Pub Co.

Olson, Phillip. The Discipline of Freedom: A Kantian View of the Role of Moral Precepts in Zen Practice. LC 91-26526. (SUNY Series in Buddhist Studies). 217p. (C). 1993. 59.50 (*0-7914-1115-X*); pap. 19.95 (*0-7914-1116-8*) State U NY Pr.

Olson, Priscilla, ed. see Henderson, Zenna.

Olson, R. A. & Frey, K. J. Nutritional Quality of Cereal Grains: Genetic & Agronomic Improvement. 512p. 1987. 37.50 (*0-89118-092-3*) Am Soc Agron.

Olson, R. E., jt. auth. see Pascale, J.

Olson, R. K., et al, eds. The Response of Western Forests to Air Pollution. LC 92-21992. (Ecological Studies: Vol. 97). (Illus.). xii, 532p. 1992. 87.00 (*0-387-97895-X*) Spr-Verlag.

Olson, Rachel. Twas the Night Before: A Picture-Story of the Nativity. Wray, Rhonda, ed. LC 93-26740. (Illus.). 24p. (Orig.). (J). (gr. k-3). 1993. 14.95 (*0-916260-85-2*, B143) Meriwether Pub.

Olson, Randy. Spring Wildflowers. (Field Guide Ser.). (Illus.). 156p. 1993. pap. 9.95 (*1-55109-050-3*, Pub. by Nimbus Publishing Ltd CN) Chelsea Green Pub.

Olson, Randy M. Views of the Present...Visions of the Past. Kremer, William N., ed. (Illus.). 225p. (Orig.). 1984. pap. text ed. 22.50 (*0-318-03518-9*) Gazette Print.

***Olson-Raymer, Gayle.** Historical & Contemporary Perspectives on Terrorism. 220p. (Orig.). (C). 1995. pap. text ed. 30.00 (*0-9606960-9-1*, Crimnal Justce) Willow Tree NY.

Olson, Raymond E. & Paul, Anthony M., eds. Contemporary Philosophy in Scandinavia. LC 70-148242. 520p. reprint ed. pap. 148.20 (*0-318-34950-7*, 2030747) Bks Demand.

Olson, Reuben M. & Wright, Steven J. Essentials of Engineering Fluid Mechanics. 5th ed. 624p. (C). 1989. text ed. 87.50 (*0-06-044926-8*) HarpCollege.

Olson, Reuel L. The Colorado River Compact. LC 26-15594. xxiv, 527p. 1983. reprint ed. lib. bdg. 53.00x (*0-89370-777-5*) Borgo Pr.

Olson, Richard. The Emergence of the Social Sciences, 1642-1792. (Studies in Intellectual & Cultural History). 260p. 1993. text ed. 26.95 (*0-8057-8607-4*, Pub. by Royal Botanic Garden UK); pap. 14.95 (*0-8057-8632-5*, Pub. by Royal Botanic Garden UK) Macmillan.

— Emergence of the Social Sciences, 1642-1792. 1992. pap. 13.95 (*0-8057-8617-1*, Twayne) Macmillan.

— Science Deified & Science Defied: The Historical Significance of Science in Western Culture: Vol 1, From the Bronze Age to the Beginnings of the Modern Era ca. 3500 B. C. to ca. A. D. 1640. LC 82-40093. (Illus.). 375p. 1982. pap. 15.00 (*0-520-04716-8*) U CA Pr.

— Science Deified & Science Defied: The Historical Significance of Science in Western Culture: Vol 1, From the Bronze Age to the Beginnings of the Modern Era ca. 3500 B. C. to ca. A. D. 1640. LC 82-40093. 448p. 1990. 45.00 (*0-520-06846-7*) U CA Pr.

— Science Deified & Science Defied: The Historical Significance of Science in Western Culture Vol. 2: From the Early Modern Age Through the Early Romantic Era ca.1640-ca.1820. (Illus.). 445p. 1995. pap. 17.00x (*0-520-20167-1*) U CA Pr.

Olson, Richard F. When Do I Start? A Nine-Point Strategy for Getting the Job You Want. (Illus.). 224p. 1992. 15. 00 (*0-688-11245-5*) Morrow.

— When Do I Start? A Nine-Point Strategy for Getting the Job You Want. 1995. pap. 10.00 (*0-688-14073-4*, Quill) Morrow.

Olson, Richard K. Wisconsin Divorce: Practice Systems Library Manual. LC 79-91167. 97.50 (*0-317-00435-2*) Lawyers Cooperative.

— Wisconsin Divorce: Practice Systems Library Manual. suppl. ed. LC 79-91167. 1982. Suppl. 1982. 22.00 (*0-317-00436-0*) Lawyers Cooperative.

Olson, Richard K., jt. ed. see Poincelot, Raymond P.

Olson, Richard P. The Practical Dreamer & Other Stories to Tell at Christmas. LC 89-51766. 128p. (Orig.). 1990. pap. 8.95 (*0-8358-0611-1*) Upper Room Bks.

***Olson, Richard P. & Froyd, Helen E.** Discoveries: Expanding Your Child's Vocational Horizons. (Illus.). (Orig.). 1995. pap. 14.95 (*0-8298-1106-0*) Pilgrim OH.

Olson, Richard P. & Leonard, Joe, Jr. Ministry with Families in Flux. 192p. (Orig.). 1990. pap. 13.99 (*0-664-25082-3*) Westminster John Knox.

Olson, Richard S., et al. The Politics of Earthquake Prediction. 204p. 1989. text ed. 27.50 (*0-691-07798-3*) Princeton U Pr.

Olson, Robert. Art Direction for Film & Video. (Illus.). 160p. 1993. pap. 19.95 (*0-240-80189-X*, Focal) Buttrwrth-Heinemann.

— The Emergence of Kurdish Nationalism & the Sheikh Said Rebellion, 1880-1925. 251p. 1989. text ed. 35.00 (*0-292-77619-5*) U of Tex Pr.

— The Emergence of Kurdish Nationalism, 1880-1925. 251p. 1989. reprint ed. pap. 14.95 (*0-292-72085-8*) U of Tex Pr.

Olson, Robert, ed. Islamic & Middle Eastern Societies. 293p. (Orig.). 1987. pap. 9.95 (*0-915597-46-2*) Amana Bks.

Olson, Robert, jt. ed. see Rothkrug, Paul.

Olson, Robert A. & Thiel, Charles C., Jr., eds. Earthquake Damage Mitigation for Computer Systems: Workshop Proceedings, July 12, 1983. 128p. 1983. 12.00 (*0-685-14421-6*) Earthquake Eng.

Olson, Robert C. Motto, Context, Essay: The Classical Background of Samuel Johnson's "Rambler" & "Adventurer" Essays. 398p. (Orig.). 1985. lib. bdg. 57.00 (*0-8191-4235-2*); pap. text ed. 32.00 (*0-8191-4236-0*) U Pr of Amer.

Olson, Robert E., ed. Annual Review of Nutrition, Vol. 7. (Illus.). 1987. text ed. 43.00 (*0-8243-2807-8*) Annual Reviews.

— Annual Review of Nutrition, Vol. 13. (Illus.). 1993. text ed. 45.00 (*0-8243-2813-2*) Annual Reviews.

— Perspectives in Biological Chemistry. LC 78-103834. (Illus.). 298p. reprint ed. pap. 85.00 (*0-7837-0960-9*, 2041265) Bks Demand.

Olson, Robert E., et al, eds. Annual Review of Nutrition, Vol. 5. (Illus.). (C). 1985. text ed. 43.00 (*0-8243-2805-1*) Annual Reviews.

— Annual Review of Nutrition, Vol. 6. (Illus.). 1986. text ed. 43.00 (*0-8243-2806-X*) Annual Reviews.

— Annual Review of Nutrition, Vol. 8. (Illus.). 1988. text ed. 43.00 (*0-8243-2808-6*) Annual Reviews.

— Annual Review of Nutrition, Vol. 9. 1989. text ed. 43.00 (*0-8243-2809-4*) Annual Reviews.

— Annual Review of Nutrition, Vol. 10. 1990. 43.00 (*0-8243-2810-8*) Annual Reviews.

— Annual Review of Nutrition, Vol. 11. 1991. text ed. 43.00 (*0-8243-2811-6*) Annual Reviews.

— Annual Review of Nutrition, Vol. 12. 1992. text ed. 45.00 (*0-8243-2812-4*) Annual Reviews.

— Annual Review of Nutrition, Vol. 14. (Illus.). 1994. text ed. 48.00 (*0-8243-2814-0*) Annual Reviews.

Olson, Robert G. Ethics: A Short Introduction. 1977. pap. text ed. 10.50 (*0-394-32033-6*) McGraw.

— Introduction to Existentialism. (Orig.). 1962. pap. text ed. 5.95 (*0-486-20055-8*) Dover.

Olson, Robert L., jt. ed. see Bezold, Clement.

Olson, Robert L., jt. auth. see Bonnett, Thomas W.

Olson, Robert W. The Ba'th & Syria, 1947-1982, the Evolution of Party & State: From the French Withdrawal to the Era of Hafiz Al-Asad. (Leaders, Politics, & Social Change in the Islamic World Ser.: Vol. 1). 235p. 1982. 19.00 (*0-940670-18-6*) Kingston Pr.

— Stepping Out Within: The Ennegram & Essence. (Illus.). 276p. (Orig.). 1993. pap. 14.95 (*0-9634860-0-4*) Awakened Pr.

Olson, Roberta. Italian Renaissance Sculpture. LC 91-65310. (World of Art Ser.). (Illus.). 216p. (Orig.). 1992. pap. 12. 95 (*0-500-20253-2*) Thames Hudson.

Olson, Roberta A., jt. ed. see Seibert, Jeffrey M.

Olson, Roberta A., et al, eds. The Sourcebook of Pediatric Psychology. 438p. 1994. 69.95 (*0-205-15182-5*, Longwood Div) Allyn.

Olson, Roberta J. Ottocento: Romanticism & Revolution in Nineteenth-Century Italian Painting. LC 92-30898. (Illus.). 296p. 1992. 67.95 (*0-917418-94-8*); pap. 39.95 (*0-685-72532-4*) Am Fed Arts.

— Ottocento: Romanticism & Revolution in 19th-Century Italian Painting. LC 92-30898. (Illus.). 296p. (C). 1993. text ed. 67.95 (*0-8122-3207-0*, Pub. by Centro Di IT) U of Pa Pr.

Olson, Roger E., jt. auth. see Grenz, Stanley J.

Olson, Ron. Half Life. LC 84-70678. (Orig.). 1984. pap. 3.95 (*0-916027-01-5*) Bannack Pub Co.

— Three for the Bobcat. LC 84-70024. 187p. (Orig.). 1984. pap. 2.95 (*0-916027-00-7*) Bannack Pub Co.

Olson, Ronald, jt. auth. see Voight, Randall L.

Olson, S. Dean, ed. see Kale, W. Wilford.

Olson, S. Douglas. Aristophanes' "Plutus" (Greek Commentaries Ser.). 101p. (Orig.). (C). 1989. pap. text ed. 7.00 (*0-929524-63-2*) Bryn Mawr Commentaries.

— Blood & Iron: Story & Storytelling in Homer's Odyssey. LC 94-45655. (Mnemosyne, Bibliotheca Classica Batava Ser.: Vol. 145). 1995. write for info. (*90-04-10251-5*) E J Brill.

Olson, Sally, ed. see Olson, Jim.

Olson, Sandra, ed. Career Counseling of Older Adults: Pioneers & Prophets - A Special Issue of Journal of Career Development. 69p. 1987. pap. 14.95 (*0-89885-347-8*) Human Sci Pr.

Olson, Sandra S. Dental Radiology Laboratory Manual. LC 94-8369. (Illus.). 256p. 1994. pap. text ed. 23.95 (*0-7216-6455-5*) Saunders.

Olson, Sharon. Into the Light: For Women Experiencing the Transformative Nature of Grief. 64p. 1993. 24.45 (*0-9638984-0-X*) Seasons.

Olson, Sheldon R. Issues in the Sociology of Criminal Justice. LC 74-31261. (Studies in Sociology). 58p. 1975. pap. text ed. 2.50 (*0-672-61348-4*, Bobbs) Macmillan.

Olson, Sherry H. Baltimore: The Building of an American City. LC 79-21950. (Illus.). 446p. reprint ed. pap. 127.20 (*0-8357-4334-9*, 2037134) Bks Demand.

— Depletion Myth: A History of Railroad Use of Timber. LC 70-148940. 246p. 1971. 25.00 (*0-674-19820-4*) HUP.

Olson, Sheryl L., jt. auth. see Thorpe, Geoffrey L.

Olson, Sigurd. The Hidden Forest. LC 90-40374. (Illus.). 128p. 1990. 27.95 (*0-89658-133-0*) Voyageur Pr.

— Songs of the North. 288p. 1995. pap. 11.95 (*0-14-025218-5*, Penguin Bks) Viking Penguin.

Olson, Sigurd F. Listening Point. (Illus.). 1958. 25.00 (*0-394-43358-0*) Knopf.

— Reflections from the North Country. (Illus.). 1976. 23.00 (*0-394-40265-0*) Knopf.

— Runes of the North. 1963. 24.00 (*0-394-44348-9*) Knopf.

— The Singing Wilderness. (Illus.). 1956. 24.95 (*0-394-44560-0*) Knopf.

Olson, Stan, ed. Foundation Directory, Pt. 2: A Guide to Grant Programs 50,000 Dollars-200,000 Dollars. (Orig.). 1994. pap. 170.00 (*0-87954-547-X*) Foundation Ctr.

— Foundation Directory Supplement, 1994. 1994. pap. 110. 00 (*0-87954-555-0*) Foundation Ctr.

Olson, Stan, ed. see Foundation Center Staff.

Olson, Stanley, ed. see Foundation Center Staff.

Olson, Steve. Biotechnology: An Industry Comes of Age. LC 85-28442. (Illus.). 128p. (Orig.). reprint ed. pap. 36. 50 (*0-8357-4214-8*, 2036996) Bks Demand.

Olson, Steve & Gerstein, Dean R. Alcohol in America: Taking Action to Prevent Abuse. LC 85-13667. (Illus.). 125p. 1985. 14.95 (*0-309-03449-3*) Natl Acad Pr.

Olson, Steven. The Prairie in Nineteenth-Century American Poetry. LC 93-32550. (Illus.). 224p. 1994. 29.95 (*0-8061-2600-0*) U of Okla Pr.

— The Prairie in Nineteenth-Century American Poetry. LC 93-325506. (Illus.). 224p. 1995. pap. 14.95 (*0-8061-2640-X*) U of Okla Pr.

Olson, Stuart A. Cultivating the Chi. 2nd ed. (Chen Kung Ser.: Vol. 1). (Illus.). 164p. (CHI.). 1992. pap. 16.95 (*0-938045-08-3*) Dragon Door.

— Cultivating the Ch'i: The Secrets of Energy & Vitality. 3rd ed. (Chen Kung Ser.). (Illus.). 164p. (Orig.). 1993. pap. 12.95 (*0-938045-11-3*) Dragon Door.

— Imagination Becomes Reality: The Teachings of Master T. T. Liang, A Complete Guide to the 150 Posture Solo Form. rev. ed. (Illus.). 292p. 1992. pap. 19.95 (*0-938045-09-1*) Dragon Door.

— The Intrinsic Energies of T'ai Chi Ch'uan. (Chen Kung Ser.: Vol. 2). 192p. (Orig.). 1995. pap. 12.95 (*0-938045-13-X*) Dragon Door.

— The Jade Emperor's Mind Seal Classic: A Taoist Guide to Health, Longevity & Immortality. (Illus.). 124p. (Orig.). 1992. pap. 10.95 (*0-938045-10-5*) Dragon Door.

Olson, Susan & Olson, Nancy B., eds. The Butterfield Family History & Recipe Book. 200p. 1989. 6.95 (*0-685-72978-8*) Apple Blossom.

Olson, Susan, jt. auth. see Olson, Paul.

Olson, Susan C., jt. auth. see Colvin, Robert H.

Olson, Susan M. Clients & Lawyers: Securing the Rights of Disabled Persons. LC 83-11724. (Contributions in Legal Studies: No. 28). (Illus.). xv, 236p. 1984. text ed. 55.00 (*0-313-24105-8*, OCL/, Greenwood Pr) Greenwood.

Olson, Tamara, jt. auth. see Squibb, Ronald.

Olson, Theodore. Millennialism, Utopianism, & Progress. 1981. 45.00 (*0-8020-5506-0*) U of Toronto Pr.

Olson, Therese M. We'll Make It: A Devotional Diary for the Improving Reader. 48p. (Orig.). 1991. pap. 5.99 (*0-8066-2582-1*, 10-25821) Augsburg Fortress.

Olson, Tillie. Tell Me a Riddle. Rosenfelt, Deborah S., ed. (Women Writers: Texts & Contexts Ser.). 200p. (C). 1995. text ed. 32.00 (*0-8135-2136-X*); pap. text ed. 12. 00 (*0-8135-2137-8*) Rutgers U Pr.

Olson, Tim J. Portland Rock Climbs: A Climber's Guide to Northwest Oregon. Walker, Terri et al, eds. (Illus.). 192p. (Orig.). 1993. pap. write for info. (*0-9635660-0-8*) T J Olson.

Olson, Toby. At Sea. LC 92-42395. 256p. 1993. 19.00 (*0-671-73641-8*) S&S Trade.

— Changing Appearance. 1975. pap. 10.00 (*0-87924-021-0*) Membrane Pr.

— Home. 1976. pap. 5.00 (*0-87924-035-0*) Membrane Pr.

— The Life of Jesus: An Apocryphal Novel. LC 76-8210. 1976. 8.50 (*0-8112-0613-0*); pap. 3.95 (*0-8112-0614-9*, NDP417) New Directions.

— Seaview. LC 88-22359. 288p. 1982. 15.95 (*0-8112-0828-1*); pap. 6.95 (*0-8112-0829-X*, NDP532) New Directions.

— Unfinished Building. LC 93-15299. 96p. (Orig.). 1993. pap. 11.95 (*1-56689-009-8*) Coffee Hse.

— Vectors. 1972. pap. 3.00 (*0-87924-017-2*) Membrane Pr.

— We Are the Fire: A Selection of Poems. LC 84-4772. 128p. 1984. 14.95 (*0-8112-0913-X*); pap. 7.50 (*0-8112-0914-8*, NDP580) New Directions.

Olson, Toby, jt. ed. see Siegel, Muffy E.

Olson, V. M., jt. auth. see Stadelman, W. J.

Olson, Vera B., jt. auth. see Olson, James C.

Olson, Virgil J. & Olson, Helen. Capitol Reef: The Story Behind the Scenery. rev. ed. LC 90-60036. (Illus.). 48p. 1990. pap. 6.95 (*0-88714-043-2*) KC Pubns.

O

Olson, W. & Groves, M., eds. Aseptic Pharmaceutical Manufacturing: Technology for the 1990s. 430p. 1987. 116.00 (*0-935184-06-6*) Interpharm.

Olson, W., et al. Handbook of Symptom-Oriented Neurology. (Illus.). 432p. 1989. pap. 32.95 (*0-8151-6534-X*, Yr Bk Med Pubs) Mosby Yr Bk.

Olson, W. K., et al, eds. Structure & Expression: DNA Bending & Curvature, Vol. 3. (Structure & Expression Ser.). (Illus.). 280p. 1988. lib. bdg. 100.00 (*0-940030-23-3*) Adenine Pr.

— Structure & Expression: From Proteins to Ribosomes; DNA & Its Drug Complexes; DNA Bending & Curvature, 3 vols. (Illus.). 1988. Vol. 3, 280p. write for info. (*0-318-64593-9*) Adenine Pr.

— Structure & Expression: From Proteins to Ribosomes; DNA & Its Drug Complexes; DNA Bending & Curvature, 3 vols., Set. (Illus.). 1988. lib. bdg. 300.00 (*0-940030-24-1*) Adenine Pr.

Olson, W. P., ed. Quantitative Modeling of Magnetospheric Processes. (Geophysical Monograph Ser.: Vol. 21). (Illus.). 655p. 1979. 30.00 (*0-87590-021-6*, GM2100) Am Geophysical.

Olson, W. T., jt. ed. see Hawthorne, William R.

Olson, Waldemar. Methods of Teaching Elementary School Mathematics. LC 68-56887. 281p. reprint ed. pap. 80.10 (*0-317-08671-5*, 2003474) Bks Demand.

***Olson, Wallace.** Search for the Northwest Passage: A Bicentennial Exhibition on the Alaska Voyages of George Vancouver. (Illus.). 16p. (YA). 1994. pap. text ed. 5.00 (*0-614-00854-9*) AK State Musms.

Olson, Wallace M., anno. & intro. The Alaska Travel Journal of Archibald Menzies, 1793-1794. LC 93-1334. xvi, 247p. (C). 1993. pap. 17.50 (*0-912006-70-6*) U of Alaska Pr.

Olson, Walter K. The Litigation Explosion: Understanding the Legal Revolution Around Us. 400p. 1992. pap. 13.00 (*0-452-26824-9*, Plume-Truman Talley Bks) NAL-Dutton.

Olson, Warren E., jt. auth. see Hertzke, Eugene R.

***Olson, Wayne, ed.** Automated Microbiological Identification & Quantification. (Illus.). 450p. 1995. 179.00 (*0-935184-82-1*) Interpharm.

Olson, Wayne, ed. see Schwartz, Frederick J.

***Olson, Wayne P., ed.** Separations Technology: Pharmaceutical & Biotechnology Applications. 450p. 1995. 161.00 (*0-935184-72-4*) Interpharm.

Olson, Willard C. The Measurement of Nervous Habits in Normal Children, Vol. 3. LC 73-9228. 97p. 1970. reprint ed. text ed. 45.00 (*0-8371-6991-7*, CWOH, Greenwood Pr) Greenwood.

Olson, William, jt. auth. see Burns, Robert.

Olson, William C. Congressional Power in International Relations. (C). 1929. text ed. 65.00 (*0-8133-1060-1*); pap. text ed. 19.95 (*0-8133-1061-X*) Westview.

Olson, William C. & Groom, A. J. International Relations Then & Now: Origins & Trends in Interpretation. LC 92-22900. 1992. write for info. (*0-415-09080-6*, Routledge NY) Routledge.

— International Relations Then & Now: Origins & Trends in Interpretation. 384p. 1991. 49.95 (*0-04-445101-6*, A8224); pap. 18.95 (*0-04-445102-4*, A8223) Routledge Chapman & Hall.

Olson, William C. & Howell, Llewellyn D., eds. International Education: The Unfinished Agenda. LC 84-52254. (ITT Key Issues Lecture Ser.). 160p. (Orig.). 1984. pap. text ed. write for info. (*0-932431-00-3*) White River.

***Olson, William H.** Island Verse. 61p. (Orig.). 1995. 3.99 (*0-9640210-2-1*) Jackson Harbor.

— Island Verse. 61p. (Orig.). 1995. pap. 3.99 (*1-85312-393-5*) Jackson Harbor.

— North of Death's Door. LC 92-3505. (Illus.). vi, 66p. 1992. 10.00 (*0-940473-25-9*) Wm Caxton.

Olson, William H. & Olson, Charles J. Washington Island Guidebook. 52p. 1994. pap. 4.98 (*0-9640210-0-5*) Jackson Harbor.

Olson, William J. Anglo-Iranian Relations During the First World War. 305p. 1986. 35.00 (*0-7146-3178-7*, Pub. by F Cass Pubs UK) Intl Spec Bk.

Olson, Yvonne. A Letter to Someone I Love: And Other Poems. Shaw, Thelma, ed. LC 85-63772. (Illus.). 1986. pap. 8.00 (*0-933829-07-8*) Ponce Pr.

Olsson, jt. auth. see Barger.

Olsson, Anders. The Swedish Wage Negotiation System. 220p. 1990. text ed. 52.95 (*1-85521-203-X*, Pub. by Dartmth Pub UK) Ashgate Pub Co.

Olsson, Anders G., jt. ed. see Carlson, Lars A.

Olsson, Axel A. Neogene Mollusks from Northwestern Ecuador. (Illus.). 258p. 1964. 12.00 (*0-87710-367-4*) Paleo Res.

Olsson, Birger, jt. ed. see Hartman, Lars.

Olsson, Birgur. Structure & Meaning in the Fourth Gospel: A Text-Linguistic Analysis of John. (New Testament Ser.: No. 6). 328p. 1974. pap. 53.00x (*91-40-03344-9*, Pub. by LiberUtbildning SW) Coronet Bks.

Olsson, C. & McLaughlin, R., eds. American-Swedish Handbook. 11th rev. ed. 200p. 1992. pap. 8.50 (*0-9609620-2-6*) Swedish Council.

Olsson, Carl A., ed. Oncogenes & Molecular Genetics of Urological Tumours. (International Society of Urology Report Ser.). (Illus.). 304p. 1993. text ed. 99.00 (*0-443-04646-8*) Churchill.

Olsson, David E. Management by Objectives. LC 67-21207. (Illus.). 1968. 12.95x (*0-87015-168-1*) Pacific Bks.

Olsson, David L. & Raphael, Harold J. Packaging Science. (Opportunities in...Ser.). (Illus.). 160p. 1989. 13.95 (*0-8442-6587-X*, Natl Textbk) NTC Pub Grp.

Olsson, David L., jt. auth. see Raphael, Harold J.

Olsson, Gosta, ed. Research & Results in Plant Breeding. (Illus.). 292p. (Orig.). 1986. pap. text ed. 58.00x (*91-36-88705-6*, Pub. by LTs Forlag A B SW) Coronet Bks.

Olsson, Gunnar. Lines of Power - Limits of Language. (Illus.). 144p. (C). 1991. text ed. 24.95 (*0-8166-1949-2*) U of Minn Pr.

Olsson, Gunnar, jt. ed. see Gale, Stephen.

Olsson, Gustaf & Piani, Gianguido. Computer Systems for Automation & Control. 450p. 1992. pap. text ed. 42.00 (*0-13-457581-4*) P-H.

Olsson, Hagar. Woodcarver & Death. Schoolfield, George C., tr. (Nordic Translation Ser.). 176p. 1965. 17.50 (*0-299-03731-2*) U of Wis Pr.

Olsson, Karl A. By One Spirit. (Illus.). 1962. pap. 12.95 (*0-910452-10-5*) Covenant.

— A Family of Faith. 157p. 1975. pap. 5.45 (*0-910452-24-5*) Covenant.

— Into One Body...by the Cross, Vol. 1. 1985. pap. 8.95 (*0-910452-64-4*) Covenant.

— Into One Body...By the Cross, Vol. 2. 1986. pap. 8.95 (*0-910452-62-8*) Covenant.

Olsson, Kurt. John Gower & the Structures of Conversion: A Reading of the Confessio Amantis. (Piers Plowman Studies: Vol. 4). 256p. (C). 1992. text ed. 70.00 (*0-85991-314-7*) Boydell & Brewer.

Olsson, Martin G., jt. auth. see Barger, Vernon D.

Olsson, Nils W. Swedish Passenger Arrivals in New York 1820-1850. LC 67-21056. 392p. 1967. 15.00 (*0-318-03677-0*) Swedish-Am.

— Swedish Passenger Arrivals in U. S. Ports 1820-1850, Except New York. 1979. 15.00 (*0-318-03678-9*) Swedish-Am.

Olsson, Nils W., ed. A Pioneer in Northwest America 1841-1858, 2 vols. LC 60-11209. 1960. 16.00 (*0-318-03680-0*) Swedish-Am.

Olsson, O. Roentgen Diagnosis of the Urogenital System. LC 73-14486. (Encyclopedia of Medical Radiology Ser.: Vol. 13, Pt. 1). (Illus.). 690p. 1974. 251.00 (*0-387-06514-8*) Spr-Verlag.

Olsson, O., jt. ed. see Nielzen, S.

Olsson, Paula, jt. auth. see Saunders, Richard.

Olsson, Rolf, jt. ed. see Tygstrup, Niels.

Olsson, Ron, jt. auth. see Andrews, Gregory R.

Olsson, S. Bertil, et al. Atrial Fibrillation: Mechanisms & Therapeutic Strategies. LC 94-4682. (Illus.). 432p. 1994. 79.00 (*0-87993-587-1*) Futura Pub.

Olsson-Seffer, Pehr. Genesis & Development of Sand Formations on Marine Coasts, & The Sand Strand Flora of Marine Coasts. LC 11-22544. (Augustana College Library Publication Ser.: No. 7). 183p. 1910. pap. 1.00 (*0-910182-04-3*) Augustana Coll.

***Olsson, Sigrid, illus.** Going for a Visit. 10p. (J). (ps). 1993. 11.95 (*1-881445-19-4*) Sandvik Pub.

Olsson, Sten E. The Radiological Diagnosis in Canine & Feline Emergencies: An Atlas of Thoracic & Abdominal Changes. LC 71-146031. reprint ed. pap. 58.00 (*0-685-20938-5*, 2056522) Bks Demand.

Olsson, Suzann, ed. The Gender Factor: Women in New Zealand Organizations. (Orig.). 1992. pap. 35.00 (*0-86469-167-X*) Intl Spec Bk.

Olsson, Sven E., ed. Social Policy & Welfare State in Sweden. 2nd ed. (Lund Studies in Social Welfare: No. 3). 348p. (Orig.). 1992. pap. 70.00x (*91-7924-053-4*, Pub. by Almqv & Wiksell SW) Coronet Bks.

***Olsten, Judi.** Sensational Desserts. 93p. 1994. write for info. (*1-57215-001-7*) World Pubns.

Olster, David M. The Politics of Usurpation in the Seventh Century: Rhetoric & Revolution in Byzantium. vii, 209p. 1993. pap. 57.00 (*90-256-1010-2*, Pub. by A M Hakkert NE) Benjamins North Am.

— Roman Defeat, Christian Response, & the Literary Construction of the Jew. LC 93-42841. (Middle Ages Ser.). 224p. (C). 1994. text ed. 32.95 (*0-8122-3152-X*) U of Pa Pr.

Olster, Stacey. Reminiscence & Re-Creation in Contemporary American Fiction. 350p. (C). 1989. 49.95 (*0-521-36383-7*) Cambridge U Pr.

Olswang, Steven G. & Lee, Barbara A. Faculty Freedoms & Institutional Accountability: Interactions & Conflicts. Fife, Jonathan D., ed. LC 84-73305. (ASHE-ERIC Higher Education Report Ser.: No. 5, 1984). 92p. (Orig.). 1985. pap. 7.50 (*0-913317-14-4*) GWU Schl E&HD.

Olswanger, Anna, ed. The Memphis Music of Berl Olswanger. 82p. (Orig.). 1985. pap. 12.95 (*0-9614598-3-2*) Anna Olswanger.

Olszak, W., ed. Thin Shell Theory: New Trends & Applications. (CISM Courses & Lectures Ser.: Vol. 240). (Illus.). 301p. 1981. pap. 46.00 (*0-387-81602-X*) Spr-Verlag.

Olszak, W. & Sawczuk, A. Inelastic Behavior in Shells. 122p. 1967. text ed. 136.00 (*0-677-61350-4*) Gordon & Breach.

Olszer, Krystyna, ed. Informator Dla Nowoprzybytych Z Polski: Guide for Newcomers from Poland. 84p. 1983. 4.00 (*0-940962-48-9*) Polish Inst Art & Sci.

Olszewska, E. S., jt. tr. see Turville-Petre, G.

Olszewski & Schiavo. Readings in Environmental Studies. 416p. (C). 1992. pap. text ed. 24.95 (*0-8403-7324-4*) Kendall-Hunt.

Olszewski, Daryl. Balloons! Candy! Toys! & Other Parables for Storytellers. LC 85-60241. 104p. (Orig.). 1986. reprint ed. pap. 8.95 (*0-89390-069-9*) Resource Pubns.

— Everyday Theology for Catholic Adults. LC 89-80060. 144p. (Orig.). 1989. pap. 6.95 (*0-937997-13-7*) Hi-Time Pub.

Olszewski, Deborah I. & Dibble, Harold L., eds. The Paleolithic Prehistory of the Zagros-Taurus. LC 93-12382. (University Museum Monographs: Vol. 83). (C). 50.00 (*0-924171-24-3*) U PA Mus Pubns.

Olszewski-Kubilius, Paula, jt. ed. see VanTassel-Baska, Joyce.

Olszewski, Lema J., ed. see Ward, Fred & Ward, Betty.

Olszewski, W. Handbook of Microsurgery, Vol. 1. LC 83-15087. 1984. 268.00 (*0-8493-3920-0*, CRC Reprint) Franklin.

— Handbook of Microsurgery, Vol. 2. LC 82-15087. 1984. 295.00 (*0-8493-3921-9*, CRC Reprint) Franklin.

Olszewski, W. L., ed. see European Society for Surgical Research Staff.

Olszewski, Waldemar L. Lymph Stasis: Pathophysiology, Diagnosis, & Treatment. (Illus.). 592p. 1991. 236.00 (*0-8493-6499-X*, RC646) CRC Pr.

— Peripheral Lymph: Formation & Immune Function. 176p. 1985. 144.00 (*0-8493-6137-0*, QP115, CRC Reprint) Franklin.

Olszewsky, J. & Baxter, D. Cytoarchitecture of the Human Brain Stem. 2nd ed. (Illus.). 200p. 1981. 223.25 (*3-8055-2210-X*) S Karger.

Olszowka, Albert J., et al. Blood Gases: Hemoglobin, Base Excess & Maldistribution; Nomograms for Normal & Abnormal Bloods, Effects of Maldistribution. LC 72-12923. 179p. reprint ed. pap. 51.10 (*0-8357-7327-2*, 2055439) Bks Demand.

Olthuis, James. I Pledge You My Troth: Marriage, Family, Friendship. LC 74-25695. 160p. 1975. 7.95 (*0-06-066394-4*, RD-155) Harper SF.

Olthuis, James H., et al. A Hermeneutics of Ultimacy: Peril or Promise? (Christian Studies Today). 90p. (Orig.). (C). 1987. lib. bdg. 35.50 (*0-8191-5800-3*) U Pr of Amer.

Oltjenbruns, Kevin A., jt. auth. see Cook, Alicia S.

Oltman, Debra O. & Lackritz, James R. Statistics for Business & Economics. LC 90-2148. 984p. (C). 1991. text ed. 62.95 (*0-534-14430-6*) Intl Thomson.

***Oltmanns, Thomas F. & Emery, Robert E.** Abnormal Psychology. LC 94-35274. 704p. 1994. text ed. write for info. (*0-13-007295-8*) P-H.

Oltmanns, Thomas F. & Maher, Brendan A., eds. Delusional Beliefs. LC 87-25328. (Personality Processes Ser.). 352p. 1988. text ed. 55.00 (*0-471-83635-4*) Wiley.

Oltmanns, Thomas F., jt. auth. see Davison, Gerald C.

Oltmanns, Thomas F., et al. Case Studies in Abnormal Psychology. 3rd ed. 341p. 1991. Net. pap. text ed. write for info. (*0-471-53106-5*) Wiley.

— Case Studies in Abnormal Psychology. 4th ed. LC 94-42723. 1995. text ed. write for info. (*0-471-00581-9*) Wiley.

Olton, Charles S. Artisans for Independence: Philadelphia Mechanics & the American Revolution. (Illus.). 182p. 1975. 29.95x (*0-8156-0111-5*) Syracuse U Pr.

Olton, D., jt. ed. see Kesner, R.

Olton, Roy, jt. auth. see Plano, J. P.

Olton, Roy, jt. auth. see Plano, Jack C.

Oltrogge, David & Rensch, Calvin. Two Studies in Middle American Comparative Linguistics. (Publications in Linguistics: No. 55). 108p. 1977. fiche 8.00x (*0-88312-474-2*) Summer Instit Ling.

Olu Easmon, Carol. Bisi & the Golden Disc. LC 89-77347. (Illus.). 32p. (J). 1990. 13.95 (*0-940793-56-3*, Crocodile Bks) Interlink Pub.

Olu, Yaounde. Quantum Man: Introduction to Uniphysics, the Science of Synthesis. (Illus.). 50p. 1985. pap. 7.00 (*0-9615454-0-2*) Astropoint Res.

Oluer-Zimmerman, Joelle, jt. auth. see LesPes, Claudine.

Olufs, Dick, jt. auth. see Schuman, David.

Olufs, Dick W., jt. auth. see Schuman, David F., III.

Olufs, Dick W., III, jt. auth. see Schuman, David F.

Olufs, Dick W., III, jt. auth. see Schuman, David.

O'Luing, Sean. The Catalpa Rescue. 184p. 1965. 13.95 (*0-900068-89-2*, Pub. by Anvil Bks Ltd IE); pap. 4.95 (*0-900068-84-1*) Irish Bks Media.

Olujic, Grozdana. Rose of Mother-of-Pearl. Kessler, Jascha, tr. LC 83-18254. (Illus.). 19p. (Orig.). (CRO & SER.). (J). (gr. 4 up). 1983. pap. 6.00 (*0-915124-90-4*, Toothpaste) Coffee Hse.

Olukoshi. Politics of Structural Adjustment in Nigeria. (C). 1993. text ed. 50.00 (*0-435-08072-5*, 08072) Heinemann.

Olum, Paul. Invariants for Effective Homotopy Classification & Extension of Mappings. LC 52-42839. (Memoirs Ser.: No. 1/37). 69p. 1989. reprint ed. pap. 22.00 (*0-8218-1237-8*, MEMO 1/37) Am Math.

— Invariants for Effective Homotopy Classification & Extension of Mappings. (Memoirs of the American Mathematical Society Ser.: No. 37). 75p. reprint ed. pap. 25.00 (*0-7837-7000-6*, 2046813) Bks Demand.

Olupona, J. K. Kingship, Religion & Rituals in a Nigerian Community: A Phenomenological Study of Ondo Yoruba Festivals. (Stockholm Studies in Comparative Religion: No. 28). (Illus.). 195p. (Orig.). 1991. pap. 47.50x (*91-22-01382-2*, Pub. by Almqv & Wiksell SW) Coronet Bks.

Olupona, Jacob K., intro. African Traditional Religion in Contemporary Society. LC 89-77137. 212p. 1991. pap. 12.95 (*0-89226-079-3*, New Era Bks) Paragon Hse.

Olupona, Jacob K. & Nyang, Sulayman S., eds. Religious Plurality in Africa: Essays in Honour of John S. Mbiti. LC 93-7392. (Religion & Society Ser.: No. 32). xxi, 455p. (C). 1993. lib. bdg. 152.00 (*3-11-012220-0*) Mouton.

Oluwasanmi, H. A. & Knowles, John H. The Roles of the University in a Post-Colonial World. 1975. 3.00 (*0-685-74440-X*) Ctr Intl Stud Duke.

Olver, A. D., jt. auth. see Clarricoats, P. J.

Olver, A. David. Microwave & Optical Transmission. 389p. 1992. text ed. 98.00 (*0-471-93478-X*) Wiley.

Olver, Graham. A French-English Dictionary of Legal & Commercial Terms. xi, 170p. (ENG & FRE.). 1988. reprint ed. lib. bdg. 26.00 (*0-8377-2515-1*) Rothman.

Olver, Michael L. Bascomb's Rogue. LC 93-93775. 184p. 1994. pap. 4.95 (*1-56002-310-4*, Univ Edtns) Aegina Pr.

Olver, Peter J. Applications of Lie Groups to Differential Equations. (Graduate Texts in Mathematics Ser.: Vol. 107). (Illus.). 495p. 1986. 54.00 (*0-387-96250-6*) Spr-Verlag.

— Applications of Lie Groups to Differential Equations. 2nd ed. LC 92-44573. 513p. 1994. 59.00 (*0-387-94007-3*) Spr-Verlag.

— Equivalence, Invariants, & Symmetry. (Illus.). 350p. (C). 1995. 39.95 (*0-521-47811-1*) Cambridge U Pr.

Olver, Peter J., ed. Solitons in Physics, Mathematics, & Nonlinear Optics. (IMA Volumes in Mathematics & Its Applications Ser.: Vol. 25). (Illus.). xiii, 215p. 1990. 36.00 (*0-387-97309-5*) Spr-Verlag.

Olver, Peter J., jt. ed. see Kamran, Niky.

Olwell, Carol. Gardening from the Heart: Why Gardeners Garden. (Illus.). 240p. (Orig.). 1990. 24.95 (*0-917946-04-9*) Antelope Island.

Olweny, Ch. L., et al, eds. Kaposi's Sarcoma. (Antibiotics & Chemotherapy Ser.: Vol. 29). (Illus.). xii, 104p. 1981. 71.25 (*3-8055-2076-X*) S Karger.

Olweus, Dan. Bullying at School: What We Know & What We Can Do. (Understanding Children's Worlds Ser.). (Illus.). 136p. 1994. 34.95 (*0-631-19239-5*); pap. 14.95 (*0-631-19241-7*) Blackwell Pubs.

Olwig, Karen F. Cultural Adaptation & Resistance on St. John: Three Centuries of Afro-Caribbean Life. LC 85-13414. (Illus.). 240p. (Orig.). 1985. pap. 24.95 (*0-8130-0818-2*) U Press Fla.

— Global Culture, Island Identity: Continuity & Change in the Afro-Caribbean Community. LC 92-35262. (Studies in Anthropology & History: No. 8). 1993. text ed. 54.00 (*3-7186-5329-X*) Gordon & Breach.

***Olwig, Karen F., ed.** Small Islands, Large Questions: Society, Culture & Resistance in the Post-Emancipation Caribbean. LC 95-14437. (Studies in Slave & Post-Slave Societies & Cultures). 1995. write for info. (*0-7146-4576-1*, Pub. by F Cass Pubs UK) Intl Spec Bk.

Olwig, Kenneth R. Nature's Ideological Landscape. (London Research Series in Geography: No. 5). (Illus.). 144p. 1984. text ed. 60.00 (*0-04-710002-8*) Routledge Chapman & Hall.

Olyan, jt. auth. see Anderson.

Olyan, Saul. Asherah & the Cult of Yahweh in Israel. LC 88-19168. (Society of Biblical Literature Monographs). 144p. 1988. 20.95 (*1-55540-253-4*, 06 00 34); pap. 13.95 (*1-55540-254-2*, 06 00 34) Scholars Pr GA.

Olyan, Saul M. A Thousand Thousands Served Him: Exegesis & the Naming of Angels in Ancient Judaism. (Texte und Studien zum Antiken Judentum Ser.: No. 36). 148p. 1993. 97.50 (*3-16-146063-4*, Pub. by J C B Mohr GW) Coronet Bks.

Olyanova, Nadya. Handwriting Tells. 1976. pap. 7.00 (*0-87980-046-1*) Wilshire.

— Psychology of Handwriting. (Illus.). 1978. pap. 7.00 (*0-87980-128-X*) Wilshire.

Olyff, Clotilde. 123... LC 94-1238. (Illus.). 22p. (J). (ps-3). 1994. 13.95 (*0-395-70736-6*) Ticknor & Fields.

Olympia, Daniel, et al. Homework Teams: Homework Management Strategies for the Classroom. (Homework Partners Ser.). (Illus.). 104p. 1993. teacher ed 14.95 (*0-944584-50-0*, 44TEAM) Sopris.

Olympia, Peter L. Dbase Power: Building & Using Programming Tools. 1988. 29.95 (*0-13-198805-0*) P-H.

— Developing Foxpro Applications. 1990. pap. 24.95 (*0-201-55070-9*) Addison-Wesley.

— Developing Foxpro Applications. 2nd ed. 1991. pap. 26.95 (*0-201-56786-5*) Addison-Wesley.

Olympic Mountain Rescue Staff. Climber's Guide to the Olympic Mountains. 3rd ed. LC 88-17636. (Illus.). 260p. (Orig.). 1988. pap. 12.95 (*0-89886-154-3*) Mountaineers.

Olympiodorus. Commentary on the First Alcibiades of Plato. 220p. 1987. lib. bdg. 52.50 (*0-317-54447-0*, Pub. by A M Hakkert SP) Coronet Bks.

Olympus Press Staff, ed. California State Parks Guide. (Illus.). 232p. (Orig.). 1987. pap. 12.95 (*0-934161-01-1*) Olympus Pr.

Olyniec, James H., ed. Transition in the Nuclear Industry: Proceedings of a Symposium Sponsored by the Construction & Energy Division. 237p. 1985. 26.00 (*0-87262-443-9*) Am Soc Civil Eng.

Olynyk, M., tr. see Zinkewych, Osyp & Hula, Volodymyr.

***Olyott, Stuart.** Alive in Christ. 1994. pap. 8.99 (*0-85234-315-9*, Pub. by Evangel Pr UK) Presby & Reformed.

— Son of Mary, Son of God. 1984. pap. 7.99 (*0-85234-189-X*, Pub. by Evangel Pr UK) Presby & Reformed.

— The Three Are One. 1979. pap. 3.99 (*0-85234-138-5*, Pub. by Evangel Pr UK) Presby & Reformed.

— You Might Have Asked. 1983. pap. 7.99 (*0-85234-175-X*, Pub. by Evangel Pr UK) Presby & Reformed.

Olyott, Stuart J. Gospel As It Really Is (Romans) (Welwyn Commentary Ser.). 1979. pap. 8.99 (*0-85234-124-5*, Pub. by Evangel Pr UK) Presby & Reformed.

— A Life Worth Living: Ecclesiastes & Song of Solomon. (Welwyn Commentary Ser.). 1983. pap. 8.99 (*0-85234-173-3*, Pub. by Evangel Pr UK) Presby & Reformed.

Olzak, Susan. The Dynamics of Ethnic Competition & Conflict. 288p. (C). 1992. 32.50 (*0-8047-2028-2*) Stanford U Pr.

— Dynamics of Ethnic Competition & Conflict. 1994. pap. 14.95 (*0-8047-2337-0*) Stanford U Pr.

Olzak, Susan & Nagel, Joane. Competitive Ethnic Relations. 1986. text ed. 54.00 (*0-12-525890-9*) Acad Pr.

Olzendam, Roderic M. & Keith, Gordon. It Came to Pass in the San Juan Islands. LC 78-73807. (Illus.). 152p. 1978. 7.95 (*0-8323-0318-6*); pap. 4.95 (*0-8323-0319-4*) Binford Mort.

Olzog, Gunther, jt. auth. see Vinz, Curt.

O

An Asterisk (*) at the beginning of an entry indicates that the title is appearing in BIP for the first time.

***OM Association, Inc. Staff.** Creativity Around Us. 1995. vdisk 64.95 (*0-7872-0972-4*) Kendall-Hunt.

Om, Hari. Muslims of Jammu & Kashmir: A Study in the Spread of Education & Consciousness, 1857-1925. 156p. 1986. 12.00 (*0-685-58187-X*, Pub. by Archives Pubs II) Nataraj Bks.

Om, R. Hari. Muslims of Jammu & Kashmir. 160p. 1986. 150.00 (*0-317-61969-1*, Pub. by Archives Pubs II) St Mut.

Om-Ra-Zeti, Khafra K. World Economic Collapse: The Last Decade & the Global Depression. (Illus.). 288p. (Orig.). 1994. pap. text ed. 18.95 (*0-9635645-0-1*) KMT Pubns.

Omachanu, Vincent & Ross, Joel. Principles of Total Quality. LC 93-46439. 250p. (C). 1994. text ed. 44.00 (*0-9634030-6-0*) St Lucie Pr.

Omachonu, Vincent K. Total Quality & Productivity Management in Health Care Organizations. LC 91-21753. 1991. 49.95 (*0-89806-113-X*) Ind Eng Mgmt Pr.

Omae, I. Organometallic Intramolecular-Coordination Compounds. (Journal of Organometallic Chemistry Library: No. 18). 402p. 1986. 138.50 (*0-444-42584-5*) Elsevier.

— Organotin Chemistry. (Journal of Organometallic Chemistry Library: No. 21). 356p. 1989. 138.50 (*0-444-87456-9*) Elsevier.

***Omae, Kenichi.** The Evolving Global Economy: Making Sense of the New World Order. LC 95-2910. (Review Bks.). 1995. write for info. (*0-87584-640-8*) Harvard Busn.

Omae, Kinjiro & Tachibana, Yuzuru. The Book of Sushi. LC 81-80658. 128p. 1988. pap. 15.00 (*0-87011-866-8*) Kodansha.

— The Book of Sushi. 180p. Date not set. 9.95 (*4-7700-1954-8*) FS&G.

Omaggi, Alice C., et al. Kaleidoscope: Grammaire en Contexte. 3rd ed. LC 92-25063. 1993. pap. text ed. write for info. (*0-07-047319-6*) McGraw.

Omaggio, Alice C., ed. Proficiency, Curriculum, Articulation: The Ties That Bind. (Reports of the Northeast Conference on the Teaching of Foreign Languages). 220p. 1985. pap. 10.95 (*0-915432-85-4*) NE Conf Teach Foreign.

Omaggio, Alice C., et al. Second-Year French. 416p. (FRE.). (C). 1984. 10.50 (*0-07-554567-5*) McGraw.

O'Mahoney, Patrick D. The Fantasy of Human Rights. 192p. 1978. pap. 6.50 (*0-85597-256-4*) Attic Pr.

O'Mahoney, R. & Doggett, R. Leisure Environment. (C). 1990. 90.00 (*0-7487-0416-7*, Pub. by S Thornes Pubs UK) St Mut.

O'Mahoney, Rose, jt. auth. see Doggett, Rosalyn.

O'Mahony, Bernadette, ed. see O'Mahony, Kieran.

***O'Mahony, Charles.** Blue Battlefields. Frisque, Tom, ed. (Illus.). 153p. 1994. 39.95 (*0-9623080-6-4*) Aviation Usk.

O'Mahony, Christopher, ed. & tr. St. Therese of Lisieux: By Those Who Knew Her. 287p. (Orig.). 1975. pap. 14.95 (*0-901810-84-3*, Pub. by Veritas Publns IE) Ignatius Pr.

O'Mahony, Ciaran, ed. see Crossland, Stewart C.

O'Mahony, Felicity, ed. Book of Kells: Proceedings of a Conference at Trinity College, Dublin, 1994. LC 94-38638. (Illus.). 640p. 1994. 129.95 (*0-85967-967-5*, Pub. by Scolar Pr UK) Ashgate Pub Co.

O'Mahony, Gerald. Abba! Father! (C). 1988. 39.00 (*0-85439-194-0*, Pub. by St Paul Pubns UK) St Mut.

— The Cup That I Drink. (C). 1988. 39.00 (*0-85439-240-8*, Pub. by St Paul Pubns UK) St Mut.

— Living & Believing, 4 bks. (C). 1988. write for info. (*0-318-63951-3*, Pub. by St Paul Pubns UK) St Mut.

— Living & Believing, 4 bks., Bk. 1. (C). 1988. 50.00 (*0-85439-163-0*, Pub. by St Paul Pubns UK) St Mut.

— Living & Believing, 4 bks., Bk. 2. (C). 1988. 50.00 (*0-85439-174-6*, Pub. by St Paul Pubns UK) St Mut.

— Living & Believing, 4 bks., Bk. 3. (C). 1988. 50.00 (*0-85439-175-4*, Pub. by St Paul Pubns UK) St Mut.

— Living & Believing, 4 bks., Bk. 4. (C). 1988. 50.00 (*0-85439-176-2*, Pub. by St Paul Pubns UK) St Mut.

O'Mahony, John, tr. see Keating, Geoffrey.

O'Mahony, Kieran. The Dictionary of Geographical Literacy: The Complete Geography Reference. O'Mahony, Bernadette, ed. (Illus.). 380p. (Orig.). (C). 1993. pap. 19.95 (*0-944638-08-2*) EduCare Pr.

— Geographical Literacy: What Every American Needs to Know about Geography. (Illus.). (Orig.). 1992. pap. 14.95 (*0-944638-06-6*) EduCare Pr.

— Geography & Education. 250p. (C). 1988. text ed. 24.95 (*0-944638-00-7*) EduCare Pr.

O'Mahony, Kieran, ed. see Brinn, Ross.

O'Mahony, Kieran, ed. see Jacobson, Sheldon A.

O'Mahony, M. J., jt. auth. see Spirit, D. M.

O'Mahony, Mary, jt. auth. see Oulton, Nicholas.

O'Mahony, Michael. Sensory Evaluation of Food: Statistical Methods & Procedure. (Food Science & Technology Ser.: Vol. 16). 512p. 1986. 165.00 (*0-8247-7337-3*) Dekker.

O'Mahony, Patrick J. A Question of Life: Its Beginning & Transmission. 253p. 1990. pap. 19.95 (*0-87061-175-5*) Chr Classics.

O'Mahony, Paul. Crime & Punishment in Ireland. 240p. 1993. lib. bdg. 24.50 (*1-85800-024-6*, Pub. by Round Hall) Intl Spec Bk.

O'Mahony, T. P. Lynch Years. 1986. pap. 10.95 (*0-85105-449-8*, Pub. by Colin Smythe Ltd UK) Dufour.

Omalia, Michael. Beginners Guide to Window Cleaning. Bradley, Austin, ed. & illus. by. (Orig.). 1992. pap. 9.95 (*0-9633996-9-1*) Ready Bks.

O'Malley. Artificial Intelligence Project for Commodore. 1991. 19.95 (*0-8306-6420-3*) TAB Bks.

***Omalley.** Roller Coaster. 1995. (*0-688-13972-8*) Lothrop.

O'Malley, jt. auth. see Daley.

O'Malley, Anne E. & Radke, Ellie. Miracle of Iniki. 64p. 1993. pap. 14.95 (*1-880188-55-4*) Bess Pr.

O'Malley, Bert W., jt. ed. see Gotto, Antonio M., Jr.

O'Malley, Bert W., jt. auth. see Means, Anthony R.

O'Malley, Bert W., jt. auth. see Tsai, M. J.

O'Malley, Brendan, ed. A Welsh Pilgrim's Manual. 147p. (C). 1989. pap. 20.00x (*0-86383-583-X*, Pub. by Gomer Pr UK) St Mut.

O'Malley, Brian. Secret of the Mountains. 28p. (J). (gr. 2-5). 1993. 14.95 (*0-7634-4460-X*) Westcliffe Pubs Inc.

— The Secret of the Mountains. 40p. (J). (gr. 1-6). 1993. 14.95 (*0-9634446-0-3*) Spirit of Advent.

O'Malley, C. D. Andreas Vesalius of Brussels (1514-1564) Saunders, John M., tr. Bd. with Andreas Vesalius Bruxellensis: The Bloodletting Letter of 1539. Date not set. reprint ed. write for info. (*0-930405-55-2*) Norman SF.

O'Malley, C. D., ed. The History of Medical Education. LC 72-85449. (UCLA Forum in Medical Sciences Ser.: No. 12). (Illus.). 1970. 75.00 (*0-520-01578-9*) U CA Pr.

O'Malley, C. D., jt. auth. see Clarke, Edwin.

O'Malley, Charles D., tr. see Da Vinci, Leonardo.

***O'Malley, Charles T.** Low Bridges & High Water. (Illus.). 284p. 1991. pap. 19.95 (*0-925168-38-6*) North Country.

O'Malley, Claire, ed. Computer Supported Collaborative Learning. LC 94-40220. (NATO ASI F Computer & Systems Sciences Ser.: Vol. 128). x, 305p. 1994. 76.00 (*0-387-57740-8*) Spr-Verlag.

— Computer Supported Collaborative Learning. LC 94-40220. (NATO ASI F, Computer & Systems Sciences Ser.: Vol. 128). x, 305p. 1995. write for info. (*3-540-57740-8*) Spr-Verlag.

O'Malley, Colleen, jt. auth. see Wincek, Jean.

O'Malley, Cormac, jt. auth. see English, Richard.

O'Malley, Emanuela. Cloud of Darkness. LC 89-51087. 208p. 1990. pap. 9.95 (*1-55523-246-9*) Winston-Derek.

O'Malley, Ernie. On Another Man's Wound. 343p. 1979. reprint ed. pap. 15.95 (*0-947962-31-X*, Pub. by Anvil Bks Ltd IE) Irish Bks Media.

— Prisoners: The Civil War Letters of Ernie O'Malley. 1992. pap. 15.95 (*1-85371-140-3*) Dufour.

— Raids & Rallies. 208p. 1985. pap. 6.95 (*0-900068-63-9*, Pub. by Anvil Bks Ltd IE) Irish Bks Media.

O'Malley, Ilene V. The Myth of the Revolution: Hero Cults & the Institutionalization of the Mexican State, 1920-1940. LC 85-30488. (Contributions to the Study of World History Ser.: No. 1). 211p. 1986. text ed. 42.95 (*0-313-25184-3*, OMR/, Greenwood Pr) Greenwood.

O'Malley, J. Michael & Chamot, Anna U. Learning Strategies in Second Language Acquisition. (Cambridge Applied Linguistics Ser.). (Illus.). 272p. (C). 1990. pap. 17.95 (*0-521-35837-X*) Cambridge U Pr.

— Turning Points Placement Test Package. (Turning Points Ser.). (Illus.). 80p. 1989. pap. text ed. 34.50 (*0-201-52169-5*) Addison-Wesley.

O'Malley, J. Michael, jt. auth. see Chamot, Anna U.

O'Malley, J. Steven. Pilgrimage of Faith: The Legacy of the Otterbeins. LC 73-5684. (American Theological Library Association Monograph: No. 4). 226p. 1973. 22.50 (*0-8108-0626-6*) Scarecrow.

O'Malley, Jan. The Politics of Community Action. 180p. (C). 1988. 60.00 (*0-85124-184-0*, Bertrand Russell Soc); pap. 35.00 (*0-85124-183-2*, Bertrand Russell Soc) St Mut.

O'Malley, John. Fifth Week. LC 75-43583. 216p. 1976. 2.95 (*0-8294-0248-9*) Loyola Univ Pr.

— Schaum's Outline of Basic Circuit Analysis. 2nd ed. (Schaum Outline Ser.). 448p. 1992. pap. text ed. 12.95 (*0-07-047824-4*) McGraw.

O'Malley, John W. The First Jesuits. 471p. (C). 1993. 37.50 (*0-674-30312-1*) HUP.

— The First Jesuits. (Illus.). 471p. 1995. pap. 16.95 (*0-674-30313-X*, OMAFIX) HUP.

— Religious Culture in the Sixteenth Century: Preaching, Rhetoric, Spirituality, & Reform. (Collected Studies: No. CS 404). 294p. 1993. 82.95 (*86078-369-3*, Pub. by Variorum UK) Ashgate Pub Co.

— Tradition & Transition: Historical Perspectives on Vatican Two. (Theology & Life Ser.: Vol. 26). 191p. 1989. pap. 14.95 (*0-8146-5769-9*) Liturgical Pr.

O'Malley, John W., ed. Catholicism in Early Modern History: A Guide to Research. (Reformation Guides to Research Ser.: Vol. II). 346p. 1988. 29.50 (*0-910345-02-3*) Center Reform.

— Humanity & Divinity in Renaissance & Reformation: Essays In Honor of Charles Trinkaus. LC 93-14242. (Studies in the History of Christian Thought: Vol. 51). 325p. 1993. 91.50 (*90-04-09804-6*) E J Brill.

— Spiritualia. (Collected Works of Erasmus: No. 66). 406p. 1988. 80.00 (*0-8020-2656-7*) U of Toronto Pr.

O'Malley, John W. & Padberg, John W. Jesuit Spirituality: A Now & Future Resource. O'Keefe, Vincent T., ed. LC 90-39457. 77p. (Orig.). 1990. pap. 5.50 (*0-8294-0699-9*) Loyola Univ Pr.

O'Malley, John W., ed. see Martin, Francis X.

O'Malley, Joseph, ed. see Marx, Karl.

O'Malley, Joseph, ed. see Rubel, Maximilien.

O'Malley, K. & Waddington, J. L., eds. Therapeutics in the Elderly: Scientific Foundations & Clinical Practice. (International Congress Ser.: No. 677). 236p. 1985. 110.25 (*0-444-80711-X*, Excerpta Medica) Elsevier.

O'Malley, Kathleen, jt. auth. see Crispin, A. C.

***O'Malley, Kevin.** Carl Caught a Flying Fish. LC 95-1756. (J). 1996. 12.00 (*0-689-80098-3*, S&S Bks Young Read) S&S Childrens.

— Who Killed Cock Robin? LC 92-40340. (Illus.). (J). (gr. k-3). 1993. write for info. (*0-688-12430-5*); lib. bdg. write for info. (*0-688-12431-3*) Lothrop.

***O'Malley, Kevin, illus.** There Was a Crooked Man. (J). (ps). 1995. 9.95 (*0-671-89477-3*, Litl Simon S&S) S&S Childrens.

O'Malley, L. S. Hinduism: The Religion of the Masses. 1986. 175.00 (*0-317-62262-5*, Scientific) St Mut.

— Indian Civil Service, 1601-1930. 310p. 1965. 35.00 (*0-7146-2023-8*, Pub. by F Cass Pubs UK) Intl Spec Bk.

O'Malley, M. Hinduism: The Religion of the Masses. (C). 1985. text ed. 100.00 (*81-85046-21-2*, Pub. by Scientific Pubs II) St Mut.

O'Malley, Martin J. The Lun Yu of Kung Fu. LC 75-19749. 20p. 1975. pap. 1.00 (*0-9606610-0-X*) M J O'Malley.

— The Tao of Mao Tse-Tung. 1977. pap. 1.00 (*0-9606610-1-8*) M J O'Malley.

***O'Malley, Michael, Jr.** The Family Business: How to Work with Your Family & Still Enjoy Sunday Dinner. (Illus.). 127p. (Orig.). Date not set. pap. 8.95 (*0-9639548-0-6*) Family Busn.

***O'Malley, Nancy.** Sailing South. LC 94-68046. 1994. 17.95 (*1-877978-68-X*, FLF Pr) Woldt.

— Suicide on Campus: Caring & Coping. 24p. (C). 1987. pap. 9.95 (*0-912150-18-1*) Magna Pubns.

O'Malley, Padraig. Biting at the Grave: The Irish Hunger Strikes & the Politics of Despair. LC 89-43076. 344p. 1991. pap. 14.00 (*0-8070-0209-7*) Beacon Pr.

— Homelessness: New England & Beyond: A Special Issue of the New England Journal of Public Policy. 816p. 1992. pap. 27.95 (*0-87023-825-6*) U of Mass Pr.

— The Uncivil Wars: Ireland Today. LC 90-52592. 532p. 1991. pap. 18.00 (*0-8070-0215-1*) Beacon Pr.

O'Malley, Padraig, ed. AIDS: A Special Issue of the New England Journal of Public Policy. 526p. 1988. pap. 20.95x (*0-87023-657-1*) U of Mass Pr.

— The AIDS Epidemic: Private Rights & the Public Interest. LC 88-47890. 566p. 1989. pap. 16.00 (*0-8070-0601-7*) Beacon Pr.

O'Malley, Pam, jt. ed. see Boyd-Barrett, Oliver.

O'Malley, Penelope. Takeoffs Are Optional, Landings Are Mandatory. LC 93-10889. 224p. (Orig.). 1993. 24.95 (*0-8138-2414-1*) Iowa St U Pr.

O'Malley, R. E., Jr. Singular Perturbation Methods for Ordinary Differential Equations. John, F. et al, eds. (Applied Mathematical Sciences Ser.: Vol. 89). (Illus.). 248p. 1991. 42.00 (*0-387-97556-X*) Spr-Verlag.

O'Malley, Robert E., Jr., ed. Asymptotic Methods & Singular Perturbations: New York, April 1976. LC 76-27872. (SIAM-AMS Proceedings Ser.: Vol. 10). 154p. 1976. 42.00 (*0-8218-1330-7*, SIAMS-10) Am Math.

— ICIAM 91: Proceedings of the Second International Conference on Industrial & Applied Mathematics. (Proceedings in Applied Mathematics Ser.: No. 61). xvii, 391p. 1992. text ed. 61.50 (*0-89871-302-1*) Soc Indus-Appl Math.

O'Malley, Sarah & Eimer, Robert. Come, Let Us Celebrate! LC 86-60168. 104p. 1986. pap. 9.95 (*0-89390-082-6*) Resource Pubns.

— Mary from Nazareth. Basile, Deana, tr. (Illus.). 32p. (Orig.). (J). (gr. 2-5). 1994. pap. 0.95 (*0-8198-4771-2*) Pauline Bks.

O'Malley, Sarah, jt. auth. see Eimer, Robert D.

O'Malley, Sarah, jt. auth. see Eimer, Robert.

O'Malley, Sarah A. & Eimer, Robert D. Journey of Decision: A Way of the Cross. 32p. (Orig.). 1991. pap. text ed. 1.95 (*0-8146-2016-7*) Liturgical Pr.

O'Malley, Sarah A., jt. auth. see Eimer, Robert D.

***O'Malley, Steven.** Early German-American Evangelicalism: Influential Sources on Discipleship & Sanctification, 7 Vols., Vol. 7. LC 94-21622. (Pietist & Wesleyan Studies: 7). 1995. write for info. (*0-8108-2873-1*) Scarecrow.

O'Malley, Suzanne, jt. auth. see Greenburg, Dan.

O'Malley, T. J. Artillery: Guns & Rocket Systems. LC 94-13570. (Military Manuals Ser.). 160p. 1994. 19.95 (*1-85367-188-6*, 5404) Stackpole.

— Fighting Vehicles: Armoured Personnel Carriers & Infantry Fighting Vehicles. LC 95-15140. (Military Manuals Ser.). (Illus.). 144p. 1995. 19.95 (*1-85367-211-4*, Pub. by Greenhill Bks UK) Stackpole.

— Military Transport: Trucks & Transporters. LC 94-41840. (Greenhill Military Manuals Ser.: Vol. 3). (Illus.). 160p. 1995. 19.95 (*1-85367-202-5*, Pub. by Greenhill Bks UK) Stackpole.

O'Malley, Terry, jt. auth. see Fulmer, Terry.

O'Malley, Therese & Trieb, Marc, eds. Regional Garden Design in the United States. LC 93-23720. 1995. write for info. (*0-88402-223-4*) Dumbarton Oaks.

O'Malley, Thomas. The Round Hall Guide to the Sources of Law: An Introduction to Legal Research & Writing. 218p. (C). 1993. pap. text ed. 29.95 (*1-85800-003-3*, Pub. by Round Hall) Intl Spec Bk.

O'Malley, Tom. Closedown? The BBC & Government Broadcasting Policy 1979-92. LC 94-18521. (C). 1994. text ed. 49.95 (*0-7453-0570-9*, Pub. by Pluto Pr UK) Westview.

O'Malley, Victoria, jt. ed. see Brickman, Patti.

***O'Malley, Vincent J., ed.** Saintly Companions. LC 95-3115. (Orig.). 1995. pap. 9.95 (*0-8189-0693-6*) Alba.

O'Malley, William. Converting the Baptized: A Survival Manual for Parents, Teachers, & Pastors. 265p. (Orig.). 1991. pap. 9.40 (*1-55924-490-9*, 22038) Tabor Pub.

— Young People & ... You Know What: Eroding the New Paganism. (Spirit Life Ser.). 40p. (Orig.). 1993. pap. 3.50 (*1-878718-13-4*) Resurrection.

O'Malley, William D., jt. auth. see Howe, Robert D.

O'Malley, William J. Becoming a Catechist: Ways to Outfox Teenage Skepticism. LC 92-14192. 208p. 1992. pap. 9.95 (*0-8091-3323-7*) Paulist Pr.

— Building Your Own Conscience. 311p. 1992. 14.50 (*0-7829-0112-3*, 22045) Tabor Pub.

— Clever Foxes & Lucky Klutzes. 169p. 1993. 12.95 (*0-7829-0364-9*, 22055) Tabor Pub.

— Daily Prayers for Busy People. Koch, Carl, ed. (Illus.). 192p. (Orig.). 1990. pap. 7.95 (*0-88489-242-5*); spiral bd. 9.95 (*0-88489-248-4*) St Marys.

— Dangerous Prayer: Being Vulnerable to God. 160p. 1995. pap. 6.95 (*0-89243-787-1*) Liguori Pubns.

— Matthew, Mark, Luke, & You. (Orig.). Date not set. pap. 10.95 (*0-88347-286-4*, 7286) Thomas More.

— Matthew, Mark, Luke, & You. 256p. (Orig.). 1995. pap. 10.95 (*0-88347-293-7*) Thomas More.

— Meeting the Living God. 2nd rev. ed. (C). 1983. pap. 11.95 (*0-8091-9565-8*) Paulist Pr.

— Sacraments: Rites of Passage. 288p. (Orig.). 1995. pap. 10.95 (*0-614-06510-0*) Thomas More.

— Why Be Catholic? LC 93-17605. 169p. (Orig.). 1993. pap. 11.95 (*0-8245-1362-2*) Crossroad NY.

— Why Not? Daring to Live the Challenge of Christ. LC 86-14059. 169p. (Orig.). 1986. pap. 6.95 (*0-8189-0504-2*) Alba.

— Yielding: Prayers for Those in Need of Hope. LC 91-76677. 176p. (Orig.). 1992. pap. 7.95 (*0-89243-422-8*) Liguori Pubns.

O'Malley, William J., et al. What Makes a School Catholic? 47p. (Orig.). 1991. pap. 5.00 (*1-55833-102-6*) Natl Cath Educ.

O'Malley, William T., comp. Anglo-Irish Literature: A Bibliography of Dissertations, 1873-1989. LC 89-78163. (Bibliographies & Indexes in World Literature Ser.: No. 26). 312p. 1990. text ed. 75.00 (*0-313-27303-0*, ODL/, Greenwood Pr) Greenwood.

Oman, Anne. Twenty-Five Bicycle Tours in Maryland: From the Allegheny Mountains to the Atlantic Ocean. LC 93-45462. (Bicycle Tours Ser.). (Illus.). 200p. (Orig.). 1994. pap. 12.00 (*0-88150-287-1*, Backcountry) Countryman.

Oman, Anne C., jt. auth. see Churchman, Deborah.

Oman, Anne H. Twenty-Five Bicycle Tours in & Around Washington, D. C. LC 90-26986. 144p. 1991. pap. 10.00 (*0-88150-190-5*, Backcountry) Countryman.

Oman, C. W. History of England from the Accession of Richard Second to the Death of Richard Third: Thirteen Seventy-Seven to Fourteen Eighty-Five. (Political History of English Ser.: Vol. 4). 1969. reprint ed. 45.00 (*0-527-00849-4*) Periodicals Srv.

Oman, Carl & Culler, Ida M. Carl Oman Remembers: Early Episodes for Sharing. (Illus.). 229p. 1987. 14.95 (*0-87770-422-8*) Ye Galleon.

Oman, Charles. Great Revolt of Thirteen Eighty-One. LC 68-25257. (British History Ser.: No. 30). 1969. reprint ed. lib. bdg. 75.00 (*0-8383-0224-6*) M S G Haskell Hse.

— The Great Revolt of 1381. 232p. 35.00 (*1-85367-045-6*, 5515) Stackpole.

— A History of the Art of War in the Middle Ages, Vol. 2: 1278-1485. 506p. 45.00 (*1-85367-105-3*, 5463) Stackpole.

— A History of the Art of War in the Middle Ages, Vol. 1: 378-1278 AD. 576p. 45.00 (*1-85367-100-2*, 5462) Stackpole.

— A History of the Art of War in the Sixteenth Century. 810p. 1989. 50.00 (*0-947898-69-7*, 5454) Stackpole.

— History of the Peninsular War, 7 vols., Set. Incl. Vol. 1. From the Treaty of Fontainebleau to the Battle of Corunna, 1807-1809. LC 77-93687. (*0-404-16961-9*); Vol. 2. From the Battle of Corunna to the End of the Talavera, Jan.-Sept. 1809. LC 77-93687. 49.50 (*0-404-16962-7*); Vol. 3. Ocana, Cadiz, Bussaco, Torres Vedras, Sept.-Dec. 1810. LC 77-93687. 49.50 (*0-404-16963-5*); Vol. 4. Massena's Retreat, Fuentes de Onoro, Albuera, Tarragona, Dec. 1810-Dec. 1811. LC 77-93687. 49.50 (*0-404-16964-3*); Vol. 5. Valencia, Ciudad Rodrigo, Badajos, Salamanca, Madrid, Oct. 1811-Aug. 31, 1812. LC 77-93687. 49.50 (*0-404-16965-1*); Vol. 6. Siege of Burgos, the Retreat from Burgos the Campaign of Vittoria, the Battles of the Pyrennes, Sept. 1, 1812-Aug. 5, 1813. LC 77-93687. 49.50 (*0-404-16966-X*); Vol. 7. Capture of St. Sebastian, Wellington's Invasion of France, Battles of Nivelle, the Nive Orthez & Toulouse, Aug. 1813-Apr. 1814. LC 77-93687. (*0-404-16967-8*); LC 77-93687. (Illus.). 345.00 (*0-404-16960-0*) AMS Pr.

— A History of the Peninsular War, January to September 1809 Vol. 2: From the Battle of Corunna to the End of the Talavera Campaign. (Illus.). 720p. 1995. 59.95 (*1-85367-215-7*, Pub. by Greenhill Bks UK) Stackpole.

— A History of the Peninsular War, 1807-1809 Vol. 1: From the Treaty of Fontainebleau to the Battle of Corunna. (Illus.). 704p. 1995. 59.95 (*1-85367-214-9*, Pub. by Greenhill Bks UK) Stackpole.

— Wellington's Army, 1809-1814. 440p. 1986. 40.00 (*0-947898-41-7*) Stackpole.

Oman, Charles, jt. auth. see OECD Staff.

Oman, Charles, et al. New Forms of Investment in Developing Country Industries: Mining, Petrochemicals, Automobiles, Textiles, Food. 276p. 1989. 48.50 (*92-64-13188-4*) OECD.

Oman, Charles P. & Wignaraja, Ganeshan. The Postwar Evolution of Development Thinking. LC 91-27768. 288p. 1991. text ed. 55.00 (*0-312-07186-8*); pap. 19.95 (*0-312-07185-X*) St Martin.

Oman, Charles W. The Art of War in the Middle Ages: A.D. 378-1515. rev. ed. Beeler, John H., ed. (Illus.). 194p. 1960. pap. 9.95 (*0-8014-9062-6*) Cornell U Pr.

— British Castles. 1989. pap. 11.95 (*0-486-26086-0*) Dover.

— Great Revolt of Thirteen Eighty-One. LC 69-14020. 219p. 1969. reprint ed. text ed. 35.00 (*0-8371-1860-3*, OMGR, Greenwood Pr) Greenwood.

— History of England. LC 71-39469. (Select Bibliographies Reprint Ser.). 1977. reprint ed. 37.95 (*0-8369-9920-7*) Ayer.

— History of England from the Accession of Richard Second to the Death of Richard Third. LC 71-5632. (Political History of England Ser.: No. 4). reprint ed. 45.00 (*0-404-50774-3*) AMS Pr.

— A History of the Art of War in the Sixteenth Century. LC 75-41204. reprint ed. 67.50 (*0-404-14579-5*) AMS Pr.

— Seven Roman Statesmen of the Later Republic. LC 75-156699. (Essay Index Reprint Ser.). 1977. reprint ed. 30.95 (*0-8369-2288-3*) Ayer.

O

— The Sixteenth Century. LC 75-25517. 247p. 1976. reprint ed. text ed. 59.75 (0-8371-8118-6, OMSIC, Greenwood Pr) Greenwood.

— Warwick the Kingmaker. LC 79-137383. (Select Bibliographies Reprint Ser.). 1977. reprint ed. 18.95 (0-8369-5584-6) Ayer.

Oman, Frydman R. & Phelps, E. Individual Forecasting & Aggregate Outcomes: "Rational Expectations Examined" (Illus.). 250p. 1987. pap. 22.95 (0-521-31095-4) Cambridge U Pr.

Oman, J. C. The Mystics, Ascetics & Saints of India: A Study of Sadhmaism with an Account of the Yogis, Sanyasis, Bairagis, & other Strange Hindu Sectarians. 308p. 1984. text ed. 38.50 (0-89563-650-6) Coronet Bks.

Oman, John, tr. see Schleiermacher, Friedrich.

Oman, John C. The Brahmans, Theists & Muslims of India. LC 76-179231. (Illus.). reprint ed. 49.50 (0-404-54858-X) AMS Pr.

— Cults, Customs, & Superstitions of India: Being a Revised & Enlarged Edition of Indian Life, Religious & Social. LC 70-179232. (Illus.). reprint ed. 36.00 (0-404-54859-8) AMS Pr.

— Great Indian Epics: The Stories of the Ramayana & the Mahabharata with Notes Appendices & Illustrations. (C). 1995. reprint ed. 17.50x (81-206-0994-8, Pub. by Asian Educ Servs II) S Asia.

Oman, John W. The Natural & the Supernatural. LC 79-39696. (Select Bibliographies Reprint Ser.). 1977. reprint ed. 22.95 (0-8369-9941-X) Ayer.

***Oman, Mark.** Golf Astrology: Your Pars Are in the Stars! Your Astrological Guide to Better Golf. (Illus.). 168p. (Orig.). 1995. pap. 9.95 (0-917346-06-8) Golfaholics Anon.

— Golf Lovers' Diet: How to Lose Your Handicap Without Losing Your Mind. LC 93-91467. (Illus.). 112p. (Orig.). 1993. pap. 8.95 (0-917346-04-1) Golfaholics Anon.

— The Nine Commandments of Golf...According to the Pro Upstairs. LC 88-81603. (Illus.). 112p. (Orig.). 1988. pap. 6.95 (0-917346-07-6) Golfaholics Anon.

— The Sensuous Golfer. LC 76-19347. (Illus.). 1976. pap. 6.95 (0-917346-01-7) Golfaholics Anon.

Oman, Mark & Gevertz, Hal. World's Greatest Golf Excuses: All the Good Reasons for Playing So Bad in the 1990's. LC 89-81851. (Illus.). 112p. (Orig.). 1990. pap. 9.95 (0-917346-03-3) Golfaholics Anon.

Oman, Mary, jt. auth. see Favazza, Armando R.

Oman, P. W., et al. Leafhoppers (Cicadellidae) A Bibliography, Generic Check-list & Index to the World Literature, 1956-1985. 384p. 1990. text ed. 98.00 (0-85198-690-0) CAB Intl.

Oman, Paul. Pursuing the Ten Million Dollar Dream, 3 vols., Set. 1991. pap. text ed. 30.00 (1-879317-05-2) Success Info Mktg.

— Pursuing the Ten Million Dollar Dream, No. 1: The Lifestyle. 114p. (Orig.). 1991. pap. text ed. 10.00 (1-879317-02-8) Success Info Mktg.

— Pursuing the Ten Million Dollars Dream: A Field Guide for All Entrepreneurs. (Illus.). 156p. (Orig.). 1990. pap. 21.95 (1-879317-00-1) Success Info Mktg.

Oman, Paul, ed. Pursuing the Ten Million Dollar Dream, No. 2: Tips & Tricks. 119p. (Orig.). 1991. pap. text ed. 10.00 (1-879317-03-6) Success Info Mktg.

— Pursuing the Ten Million Dollar Dream, No. 3: How to - How Come. 118p. 1991. pap. text ed. 10.00 (1-879317-04-4) Success Info Mktg.

***Oman, Paul W.** Progamming Style Analysis. (Computer Engineering & Computer Science Ser.). (Illus.). 272p. 1995. 65.00 (0-89391-935-7) Ablex Pub.

Oman, Paul W. & Lewis, Ted G. Milestones in Software Evolution. LC 90-33878. 328p. 1990. 10.95 (0-8186-9033-X, 2033) IEEE Comp Soc.

Oman, R. M., jt. auth. see Masters, Richard.

Oman, Ray, et al. Management Analysis in Public Organizations: History, Concepts, & Techniques. LC 91-25533. 224p. 1992. text ed. 55.00 (0-89930-403-6, OMA, Quorum Bks) Greenwood.

Oman, Robert M. The Easy Way to Higher Grades. 40p. (C). 1978. pap. 2.95 (0-931660-01-7) R Oman Pub.

— Graphing Algebraic Functions. (C). 1979. pap. 2.95 (0-931660-02-5) R Oman Pub.

O'Manique, John & Lerner, Michael. World Leadership & International Development. 138p. 1984. pap. 20.00 (0-86346-011-9, Tycooly Pub) Weidner & Sons.

Omans, Donald J., jt. auth. see Omans, Nancy W.

Omans, Glen A. Passion in Poe: The Development of a Critical Term. 1986. pap. 2.95 (0-910556-22-9) Enoch Pratt.

Omans, Nancy W. & Omans, Donald J. Marriages of Montgomery County, Maryland 1798-1875. vii, 293p. (Orig.). 1988. pap. 15.00x (0-935931-35-X) Borgo Pr.

— Marriages of Montgomery County, Maryland 1798-1875. vii, 293p. (C). 1988. reprint ed. lib. bdg. 37.00x (0-8095-8236-8) Borgo Pr.

Omanson, Roger L. & Ellington, John. A Handbook on Paul's Second Letter to the Corinthians. LC 93-4494. (UBS Handbook Ser.). viii, 272p. 1993. 14.00 (0-8267-0162-0, 105034) Untd Bible Soc.

O'Maolmorda, Sheila. Matthew Moss-the Man & the Artist. Moss, Matthew, tr. LC 82-72263. (Illus.). 100p. 1983. 50.00 (0-943884-00-4) Conserv Pr.

Omar, Ariffin. Bangsa Melayu: Malay Concepts of Democracy & Community, 1945-1950. LC 92-40292. (South-East Asian Historical Monographs). 276p. 1993. 49.95 (0-19-588613-5) OUP.

Omar, B. K. Human Radiological Anatomy. (C). 1989. 60.00 (0-89771-358-3, Current Dist) St Mut.

— Normal Radiographic Anatomy. 1983. 70.00 (0-317-39486-X, Current Dist) St Mut.

Omar, H. A. The Great Warriors. 1984. pap. 30.00 (0-7212-0631-X, Pub. by Regency Press) St Mut.

— The Human Perfection. 96p. (C). 1988. 40.00 (0-7212-0701-4, Pub. by Regency Press) St Mut.

— The Paragon of Human Perfection. 85p. 1984. 25.00 (0-7212-0566-6, Pub. by Regency Press) St Mut.

Omar, Ishak H. Market Power, Vertical Linkages, & Government Policy: The Fish Industry in Peninsular Malaysia. (South-East Asian Social Science Monographs). 232p. 1995. 49.95 (967-65-3056-5) OUP.

Omar, Ka. Wolof Phonology & Morphology. LC 93-30604. 160p. (Orig.). (C). 1993. pap. text ed. 28.50 (0-8191-9288-0) U Pr of Amer.

Omar, Khayyam. Ruba'iyat of Omar Khayyam. Saidi, Ahmad & Nasr, Seyyed H., trs. LC 91-20526. 304p. (Orig.). 1991. 60.00 (0-89581-897-3, Asian Human Pr); pap. 20.00 (0-89581-898-1, Asian Human Pr) Jain Pub Co.

Omar, M. Ali. Elementary Solid State Physics: Principles & Applications. LC 73-10593. (C). 1975. text ed. 61.25 (0-201-05482-5) Addison-Wesley.

Omar, Margaret K. The Acquisition of Egyptian Arabic As a Native Language. 1973. pap. text ed. 58.75 (90-279-2468-6) Mouton.

— Saudi Arabic Basic Course: Urban Hajazi Dialect. 288p. (Orig.). 1994. 14.95 (0-7818-0257-1) Hippocrene Bks.

Omar, N. Bradley. My Toy Box. (Chubby Board Bks.). 16p. (J). 1980. pap. 2.95 (0-671-41343-0) S&S Trade.

Omar, Rdean. Death on Your Doorstep: One Hundred One Weapons in the Average Home. (Illus.). 75p. 1992. pap. 7.95 (0-939427-85-0) Alpha Pubns OH.

Omar, Saleh Beshara. Ibn-Al-Haytham's Optics: A Study of the Origins of Experimental Science. LC 76-42611. (Studies in Islamic Philosophy & Science). (Illus.). 1977. 30.00 (0-88297-015-1) Bibliotheca.

Omar, Samira A S, et al, eds. Range Management in Arid Zones: Proceedings of the Second International Conference on Range Management in the Arabian Gulf. LC 93-37668. 1994. write for info. (0-7103-0472-2, Pub. by Kegan Paul Intl UK) Routledge Chapman & Hall.

Omar, Sydney. My World of Astrology. 1976. pap. 7.00 (0-87980-103-4) Wilshire.

— Thought Dial. 1975. pap. 7.00 (0-87980-164-6) Wilshire.

O'Mara, B., ed. see Electrochemical Society Staff.

***O'Mara, Carmel.** Good Morning, Good Night. (J). 1996. write for info. (0-15-200672-9) HarBrace.

***Omara, Ed L.** Classic Erotic Tales. 1994. 8.98 (0-7858-0198-7) Bk Sales Inc.

***O'Mara, Jacqueline.** Shooting Moonbeams. 180p. 1995. pap. 7.95 (1-56901-751-4) NW Pub.

O'Mara, Julie. Diversity Activities & Training Designs. LC 94-65469. (Illus.). 416p. 1994. ring bd. 149.00 (0-88390-436-5) Pfeiffer & Co.

O'Mara, Julie, jt. auth. see Jamieson, David.

O'Mara, Lesley. Best Dog Stories. 256p. 1991. reprint ed. 8.99 (0-517-06498-7) Random Hse Value.

— Best Horse Stories. (Illus.). 256p. 1992. reprint ed. 8.99 (0-517-07251-3) Random Hse Value.

— Great Cat Tales. (Illus.). 224p. 1990. pap. 9.95 (0-88184-645-7) Carroll & Graf.

Omara, Lesley. Great Cat Tales. 1991. 7.98 (1-55521-757-5) Bk Sales Inc.

O'Mara, Lesley, ed. Best Cat Stories. 256p. 1992. reprint ed. 8.99 (0-517-07391-9, Pub. by Wings Bks) Random Hse Value.

— Classic Animal Stories. (Illus.). 160p. (J). (gr. 1 up). 1991. 18.95 (1-55970-143-9) Arcade Pub Inc.

O'Mara, Michael. Tales of Old Ireland. 1994. 8.98 (0-7858-0087-5) Bk Sales Inc.

O'Mara, Michael, ed. Tales of Old Ireland. 247p. 1994. 42.50 (1-85479-981-9, Pub. by Pan Books UK) Trans-Atl Phila.

Omara-Otunnu, Amii. Politics & the Military in Uganda, 1890-1985. 208p. 1987. text ed. 39.95 (0-312-00046-4) St Martin.

O'Mara, Patrick F. Egyptian Hieroglyphics: An Easy Introduction for History & Art Students. 2nd ed. (Illus.). 55p. (Orig.). (C). 1976. pap. text ed. 9.50 (0-686-30248-6) Paulette Pub.

— The Palermo Stone & the Archaic Kings of Egypt. (Studies in the Structural Archaeology of Ancient Egypt: Vol. I). (Illus.). xvi, 208p. (Orig.). 1979. pap. 22.00 (0-686-30249-4) Paulette Pub.

O'Mara, Peggy. Way Back Home. 1993. pap. 14.95 (0-914257-09-9) Mothering Magazine.

O'Mara, Peggy, intro. Vaccinations: Mothering Special Edition. rev. ed. Orig. Title: Mothering Special Edition Immunizations. (Illus.). 54p. 1989. pap. 7.00 (0-914257-07-2) Mothering Magazine.

O'Mara, Veronica J. & O'Reilly, Fionnauala. A Trifle, A Coddle, A Fry: An Irish Literary Cookbook. (Illus.). 192p. 1993. 18.95 (1-55921-081-8); pap. 12.95 (1-55921-084-2) Moyer Bell.

O'Mara, W. Paul & Casazza, John A. Office Development Handbook. LC 82-50078. (Community Builders Handbook Ser.). (Illus.). 272p. 1982. 64.95 (0-87420-607-3, OD1) Urban Land.

O'Mara, W. Paul, et al. Adaptive Use: Development Economics, Process, & Profiles. LC 78-56054. (Illus.). 246p. (C). 1978. 43.95 (0-87420-582-4, A08) Urban Land.

— Rental Housing. LC 84-51908. 167p. reprint ed. pap. 47.60 (0-7837-1008-9, 2041318) Bks Demand.

O'Mara, William C. Liquid Crystal Flat Panel Display: Manufacturing Science & Technology. LC 92-43119. 1993. text ed. 59.95 (0-442-01428-7) Van Nos Reinhold.

O'Mara, William C., et al, eds. Handbook of Semiconductor Silicon Technology. LC 89-77167. (Illus.). 795p. 1990. 96.00 (0-8155-1237-6) Noyes.

Omarbetade, T. Prisma Modern Swedish-English Dictionary. 394p. (ENG & SWE.). 1980. 24.95 (0-8288-1678-6, M9450) Fr & Eur.

Omari, C. K. Socio-Cultural Factors in Modern Family Planning Methods in Tanzania. LC 88-9352. (Studies in African Health & Medicine: Vol. 3). 250p. 1989. lib. bdg. 89.95 (0-88946-189-9) E Mellen.

Omari, C. K., jt. ed. see Creighton, Colin.

O'Marie, Carol A. Advent of Dying. 1987. mass mkt. 3.99 (0-440-10052-6) Dell.

— Death Goes on Retreat. LC 95-8458. 1995. write for info. (0-385-31047-1) Delacorte.

— The Missing Madonna. 1989. reprint ed. mass mkt. 4.99 (0-440-20473-9) Dell.

Omarie, Carol A. Murder in Ordinary Time: A Sister Mary Helen Mystery. 1992. mass mkt. 4.99 (0-440-21353-3) Dell.

O'Marie, Carol A. Murder Makes a Pilgrimage. LC 93-9984. 1993. 19.95 (0-385-31050-1) Delacorte.

***Omarie, Carol A.** Murder Makes a Pilgrimage. 1994. pap. 4.99 (0-440-21613-3) Dell.

O'Marie, Carol A. Murder Makes a Pilgrimage. large type ed. LC 93-48607. 1994. 20.95 (0-8161-5951-3, Large Print Bks) Hall.

— A Novena for Murder. 1986. mass mkt. 3.99 (0-440-16469-9) Dell.

O'Marie, Carol A. & O'Marie, Carol Anne. Murder in Ordinary Time. large type ed. LC 92-18774. (General Ser.). 352p. 1992. lib. bdg. 20.95 (0-8161-5425-2); pap. 16.95 (0-8161-5426-0) G K Hall.

O'Marie, Carol Anne. The Missing Madonna. large type ed. (General Ser.). 371p. 1990. 20.95 (0-8161-4814-7, Large Print Bks) Hall.

O'Marie, Carol Anne, jt. auth. see O'Marie, Carol A.

Omark, jt. ed. see Chance, Michael R.

***Omarr, Sydney.** Answer in the Sky, Almost: Confessions of an Astrologer. 240p. (Orig.). 1995. pap. 10.95 (1-57174-028-7) Hampton Roads Pub Co.

— Aquarius, 1987. 1987. pap. 2.95 (0-317-47657-2, Sig) NAL-Dutton.

— Astrology: Off the Top. 128p. 1975. 6.50 (0-86690-135-3, O1362-014) Am Fed Astrologers.

— Sydney Omarr - Horoscope 1993: Aquarius. 1992. pap. 3.99 (0-451-17296-5, Sig) NAL-Dutton.

— Sydney Omarr - Horoscope 1993: Aries. 1992. pap. 3.99 (0-451-17286-8, Sig) NAL-Dutton.

— Sydney Omarr - Horoscope 1993: Cancer. 1992. pap. 3.99 (0-451-17289-2, Sig) NAL-Dutton.

— Sydney Omarr - Horoscope 1993: Capricorn. 1992. pap. 3.99 (0-451-17295-7, Sig) NAL-Dutton.

— Sydney Omarr - Horoscope 1993: Gemini. 1992. pap. 3.99 (0-451-17288-4, Sig) NAL-Dutton.

— Sydney Omarr - Horoscope 1993: Leo. 1992. pap. 3.99 (0-451-17290-6, Sig) NAL-Dutton.

— Sydney Omarr - Horoscope 1993: Libra. 1992. pap. 3.99 (0-451-17292-2, Sig) NAL-Dutton.

— Sydney Omarr - Horoscope 1993: Pisces. 1992. pap. 3.99 (0-451-17297-3, Sig) NAL-Dutton.

— Sydney Omarr - Horoscope 1993: Sagittarius. 1992. pap. 3.99 (0-451-17294-9, Sig) NAL-Dutton.

— Sydney Omarr - Horoscope 1993: Scorpio. 1992. pap. 3.99 (0-451-17293-0, Sig) NAL-Dutton.

— Sydney Omarr - Horoscope 1993: Taurus. 1992. pap. 3.99 (0-451-17287-6, Sig) NAL-Dutton.

— Sydney Omarr - Horoscope 1993: Virgo. 1992. pap. 3.99 (0-451-17291-4, Sig) NAL-Dutton.

— Sydney Omarr Aquarius, 1994. 1993. pap. 3.99 (0-451-17655-3, Sig) NAL-Dutton.

— Sydney Omarr Aquarius, 1995. 1994. pap. 3.99 (0-451-18117-4) NAL-Dutton.

— Sydney Omarr Aries, 1994. 1993. pap. 3.99 (0-451-17661-8, Sig) NAL-Dutton.

— Sydney Omarr Aries, 1995. 1994. pap. 3.99 (0-451-18120-4) NAL-Dutton.

— Sydney Omarr Cancer, 1994. 1993. pap. 3.99 (0-451-17659-6, Sig) NAL-Dutton.

— Sydney Omarr Cancer, 1995. 1994. pap. 3.99 (0-451-18119-0) NAL-Dutton.

— Sydney Omarr Capricorn, 1994. 1993. pap. 3.99 (0-451-17654-5, Sig) NAL-Dutton.

— Sydney Omarr Capricorn, 1995. 1994. pap. 3.99 (0-451-18116-6) NAL-Dutton.

— Sydney Omarr Gemini, 1994. 1993. pap. 3.99 (0-451-17658-8, Sig) NAL-Dutton.

— Sydney Omarr Gemini, 1995. 1994. pap. 3.99 (0-451-18115-8) NAL-Dutton.

— Sydney Omarr Leo, 1994. 1993. pap. 3.99 (0-451-17662-6, Sig) NAL-Dutton.

— Sydney Omarr Leo, 1995. 1994. pap. 3.99 (0-451-18121-2) NAL-Dutton.

— Sydney Omarr Libra, 1994. 1993. pap. 3.99 (0-451-17665-0, Sig) NAL-Dutton.

— Sydney Omarr Libra, 1995. 1994. pap. 3.99 (0-451-18124-7) NAL-Dutton.

— Sydney Omarr Pisces, 1994. 1993. pap. 3.99 (0-451-17656-1, Sig) NAL-Dutton.

— Sydney Omarr Pisces 1995. 1994. pap. 3.99 (0-451-18118-2, Sig) NAL-Dutton.

— Sydney Omarr Sagittarius, 1994. 1993. pap. 3.99 (0-451-17664-2, Sig) NAL-Dutton.

— Sydney Omarr Sagittarius, 1995. 1994. pap. 3.99 (0-451-18123-9) NAL-Dutton.

— Sydney Omarr Scorpio, 1995. 1994. pap. 3.99 (0-451-18122-0) NAL-Dutton.

— Sydney Omarr Taurus, 1994. 1993. pap. 3.99 (0-451-17653-7, Sig) NAL-Dutton.

— Sydney Omarr Taurus, 1995. 1994. pap. 3.99 (0-451-18113-1) NAL-Dutton.

— Sydney Omarr Virgo, 1994. 1993. pap. 3.99 (0-451-17652-9, Sig) NAL-Dutton.

— Sydney Omarr Virgo, 1995. 1994. pap. 3.99 (0-451-18112-3) NAL-Dutton.

— Sydney Omarr's Astrological Guide for You in 1995. 288p. (Orig.). 1994. pap. 4.50 (0-451-18163-8, Sig) NAL-Dutton.

— Sydney Omarr's Astrological Guide for You in 1996. 288p. (Orig.). 1995. mass mkt. 4.99 (0-451-18495-5, Sig) NAL-Dutton.

Omartian, S. Llaves De la Salud Emocional (Stormie-Keys to Emotional Health) (SPA.). Date not set. 1.99 (1-56063-161-9, 498123) Editorial Unilit.

Omartian, Stormie. Better Body Management. LC 93-23876. 1993. 10.95 (0-917143-25-6) Sparrow TN.

— Can I Afford Time for Friendship? Answers to Questions Women Ask about Friends. 1994. pap. 8.99 (1-55661-517-5) Bethany Hse.

— Greater Health God's Way. 208p. 1984. pap. 5.95 (0-917143-00-0) Sparrow TN.

— The Power of the Praying Parent. (Orig.). 1995. pap. 9.99 (1-56507-354-1) Harvest Hse.

— Stormie. LC 86-80704. 224p. (Orig.). 1986. pap. 7.99 (0-89081-556-9) Harvest Hse.

— Stormie. (Orig.). 1995. mass mkt. 4.99 (1-56507-400-9) Harvest Hse.

O'Mary, Barbara. This Woman: Poetry of Love & Change. LC 72-95283. (Illus.). 64p. (Orig.). 1973. pap. 3.25 (0-87810-024-5) Times Change.

Omata, Masao, jt. ed. see Okuda, Kunio.

O'Mathuna, Diarmuid. Mechanics, Boundary Layers & Function Spaces. 240p. 1989. 57.50 (0-8176-3464-9) Birkhauser.

O'Mathuna, Sean P. William Bathe, S. J., 1564-1614: A Pioneer in Linguistics. LC 86-11791. (Studies in the History of Language Sciences: Vol. 37). (Illus.). iv, 211p. 1986. 55.00x (90-272-4520-7) Benjamins North Am.

Omatu, Sigeru & Seinfeld, John H. Distributed Parameter Systems: Theory & Applications. (Oxford Mathematical Monographs). (Illus.). 448p. 1989. 95.00 (0-19-853295-4) OUP.

***Omaye, Stanley T. & Bidlak, Wayne, eds.** Natural Protectants & Natural Toxicants in Food, Vol. 1. LC 94-61655. 137p. 1994. pap. text ed. 65.00 (1-56676-206-5) Technomic.

Ombaaka, Oki, jt. auth. see Truchelvam, Neelan.

Omchery, Leela. Studies in Indian Music & Applied Arts. 1990. 180.00 (0-317-99586-3, Pub. by Sundeep II) S Asia.

***Omdahl, Becky.** Cognitive Appraisal, Emotion, & Empathy. 288p. 1995. text ed. 59.95 (0-8058-1479-5) L Erlbaum Assocs.

Omdahl, Lloyd, jt. auth. see Grant, Daniel R.

Omdra 6 Staff. Dreamrise. 2nd ed. 1977. pap. 2.95 (0-930472-00-4) G Stempien.

— Elltradonnic City. 1979. pap. 3.95 (0-930472-02-0) G Stempien.

O'Meally, Robert. History & Memory in African American Culture. Fabre, Genevieve, ed. (Illus.). 336p. 1994. 39.95 (0-19-508396-2) OUP.

— Lady Day: The Many Faces of Billie Holiday. (Illus.). 208p. (C). 1993. reprint ed. pap. 17.95 (1-55970-200-1) Arcade Pub Inc.

O'Meally, Robert, jt. ed. see Fabre, Genevieve.

O'Meally, Robert G., ed. New Essays on "Invisible Man" (American Novel Ser.). 200p. 1988. pap. 11.95 (0-521-31369-4) Cambridge U Pr.

O'Meara, Barry E. Napoleon in Exile, 2 Vols, 1. LC 74-106520. reprint ed. write for info. (0-404-00611-6) AMS Pr.

— Napoleon in Exile, 2 Vols, 2. LC 74-106520. reprint ed. write for info. (0-404-00612-4) AMS Pr.

— Napoleon in Exile, 2 Vols, Set. LC 74-106520. reprint ed. 57.50 (0-404-00610-8) AMS Pr.

O'Meara, Dan. Volkskapitalisme: Class, Capital & Ideology in the Development of Afrikaner Nationalism, 1934-1948. LC 82-9504. (African Studies: No. 34). (Illus.). 352p. 1983. 74.95 (0-521-24285-1) Cambridge U Pr.

O'Meara, Daniel P. Protecting the Growing Number of Older Workers: The Age Discrimination in Employment Act. LC 88-80365. (Labor Relations & Public Policy Ser.: No. 33). 384p. 1989. pap. 35.00 (0-89546-069-6) U PA Wharton Ctr Human Resc.

O'Meara, Dominic J. Plotinus: An Introduction to the Enneads. LC 92-24776. (C). 1993. 39.95 (0-19-875121-4, Clarendon Pr) OUP.

— Plotinus: An Introduction to the Enneads. 158p. 1995. pap. 15.95 (0-19-875147-8) OUP.

— Pythagoras Revived: Mathematics & Philosophy in Late Antiquity. 264p. 1991. reprint ed. pap. 28.00 (0-19-823913-0) OUP.

O'Meara, Dominic J., ed. Neoplatonism & Christian Thought. LC 81-5272. (Studies in Neoplatonism: Ancient & Modern: Vol. 3). 297p. 1981. 59.50 (0-87395-492-0); pap. 19.95 (0-87395-493-9) State U NY Pr.

— Studies in Aristotle. LC 81-4381. (Studies in Philosophy & the History of Philosophy: No. 9). 321p. reprint ed. pap. 91.50 (0-7837-1000-3, 2041307) Bks Demand.

O'Meara, Donna D., jt. auth. see O'Meara, Stephen J.

O'Meara, Jan. Alaska Backyard Wines. (Illus.). 60p. (Orig.). 1988. pap. 6.50 (0-9621543-1-8) Wizard Works.

— Alaska Backyard Wines. (Illus.). 64p. (Orig.). 1988. pap. 7.95 (0-9621543-5-0) Wizard Works.

— Alaska Dictionary & Pronunciation Guide. (Illus.). 156p. (Orig.). 1988. pap. 8.50 (0-9621543-0-X) Wizard Works.

— Kids' Guide to Common Alaska Critters. (Illus.). 32p. (Orig.). (J). 1995. pap. text ed. 7.95 (0-9621543-3-4) Wizard Works.

O'Meara, Jan, ed. Flights of Fancy: Alaska Birds in Verse. (Illus.). 64p. (Orig.). 1994. pap. 8.95 (0-9621543-4-2) Wizard Works.

O'Meara, Jim, jt. auth. see Levi, Steven.

O'Meara, John. Otherworldly Hamlet: Four Essays. 112p. 1991. pap. 12.00 (0-920717-50-0) SPD-Small Pr Dist.

O

An Asterisk (*) at the beginning of an entry indicates that the title is appearing in BIP for the first time.

— Studies in Augustine & Eriugena. Halton, Thomas P., ed. LC 92-7188. 362p. 1993. text ed. 59.95 (*0-8132-0768-1*) Cath U Pr.

O'Meara, John J., tr. Voyage of St. Brendan. 1981. pap. 9.95 (*0-85105-384-X*, Pub. by Colin Smythe Ltd UK) Dufour.

O'Meara, John J., tr. see Gerald of Wales.

O'Meara, John J., tr. see Giraldus, Cambrensis.

O'Meara, Maurice A., tr. & intro. Elegies par Guillevic: Bilingual Edition. LC 75-26931. 139p. 1976. 8.95 (*0-8093-0737-5*) S Ill U Pr.

Omeara, Meghan. World Business Directory: Private - Public WW, 2 vols. 3rd ed. 1994. 495.00 (*0-8103-8053-6*) Gale.

— World Trade Centers Assoc. World Business Directory, 4 vols. 2nd ed. (Business Directory Worldwide Ser.). 1993. 450.00 (*0-8103-8056-0*) Gale.

— World Trade Centers Assoc. World Business Directory 2, Vol. 1. 2nd ed. (Business Directory Worldwide Ser.). 1993. write for info. (*0-8103-8057-9*) Gale.

— World Trade Centers Assoc. World Business Directory 2, Vol. 2. 2nd ed. (Business Directory Worldwide Ser.). 1993. write for info. (*0-8103-8058-7*) Gale.

— World Trade Centers Assoc. World Business Directory 3, Vol. 1. 3rd ed. 1994. write for info. (*0-8103-8054-4*) Gale.

— World Trade Centers Assoc. World Business Directory 3, Vol. 2. 3rd ed. 1994. write for info. (*0-8103-8055-2*) Gale.

— World Trade Resources Guide One. 1991. 169.00 (*0-8103-8404-3*) Gale.

O'Meara, O. T. Lectures on Linear Groups. LC 74-8773. (CBMS Regional Conference Series in Mathematics: No. 22). 87p. 1988. reprint ed. pap. 19.00 (*0-8218-1672-1*, CBMS-22) Am Math.

O'Meara, O. T., jt. auth. see Hahn, Alexander J.

O'Meara, O. Timothy. Symplectic Groups. LC 78-19101. (Mathematical Surveys Ser.). 122p. 1982. reprint ed. pap. 49.00 (*0-8218-1516-4*, SURV 16) Am Math.

***O'Meara, Patrick.** K. F. Ryleev: A Political Biography of the Decembrist Poet. LC 83-24658. Date not set. reprint ed. pap. 108.60 (*0-7837-9405-3*, 2060150) Bks Demand.

— K. S. Ryleev. 392p. 1984. 55.00 (*0-691-06602-7*) Princeton U Pr.

O'Meara, Patrick, jt. ed. see Carter, Gwendolen M.

O'Meara, Patrick, jt. ed. see Carter, Gwendolyn M.

O'Meara, Patrick, jt. ed. see Martin, Phyllis M.

O'Meara, Stephen J. & O'Meara, Donna D. Volcanoes: Passion & Fury. LC 93-47387. (Illus.). 96p. (J). 1994. 16.95 (*0-933346-70-0*) Sky Pub.

O'Meara, Thomas F. Church & Culture: German Catholic Theology, 1860-1914. LC 90-50971. (C). 1992. text ed. 35.95 (*0-268-00783-7*) U of Notre Dame Pr.

— Fundamentalism: A Catholic Perspective. 96p. 1990. pap. 5.95 (*0-8091-3133-1*) Paulist Pr.

— Theology of Ministry. LC 82-60588. 1983. pap. 12.95 (*0-8091-2487-4*) Paulist Pr.

O'Meara, Tim. Samoan Planters: Tradition & Economic Development in Polynesia. 200p. (C). 1990. pap. text ed. 13.50 (*0-03-022847-6*) HB Coll Pubs.

O'Meara, Walter. Guns at the Forks. LC 79-4000. (Illus.). 280p. 1979. pap. 15.95 (*0-8229-5309-9*) U of Pittsburgh Pr.

— Spanish Bride. 224p. Date not set. 12.95 (*0-491-10802-8*) Museum NM Pr.

— The Spanish Bride. 224p. (Orig.). 1990. reprint ed. pap. 12.95 (*0-941108-02-3*) Friends Palace Pr.

— We Made It Through the Winter. (Illus.). 128p. 1987. pap. 7.95 (*0-87351-212-X*) Minn Hist.

O'Meara, William E., et al. The Continuing Quest: Introductory Readings in Philosophy. 232p. (C). 1994. per., pap. text ed. 22.95 (*0-8403-3121-5*) Kendall-Hunt.

Omedo, Teofilo E., tr. see Synowiec, Bertie Ryan.

Omelchenko, William, ed. see Doroshenko, Dmytro.

Omelchuck, Kathryn. The Parachute Pages. 176p. (Orig.). 1991. pap. text ed. write for info. (*0-9607814-8-X*) AeroGraphics.

O'Melia, Charles R., ed. Environmental Engineering. LC 90-881. 940p. 1990. pap. text ed. 78.00 (*0-87262-768-3*) Am Soc Civil Eng.

Omenana Collective Research Group Staff. Intulogy: An African Theory of "Being With" (Laying the Foundations into the Heart Ser.). 60p. (Orig.). (C). 1985. pap. 5.95 (*0-943324-20-3*) Omenana.

— Maatics: African Ethical Foundations. (Laying the Foundations into the Heart Ser.). 60p. (Orig.). 1985. pap. 5.95 (*0-943324-21-1*) Omenana.

— Nyalogy: African Epistemetadynaminological Foundations. (Laying the Foundations into the Heart Ser.). 60p. (Orig.). 1985. pap. 5.95 (*0-943324-22-X*) Omenana.

Omenana Collective Staff, ed. see Gibrill, Hashim.

Omenana Collective Staff, ed. see Ntalaja, Nzongola.

Omenana Collective Staff, ed. see Nwafor, Azinna.

Omenana Staff. Buna-Kima or Theologia Africana, Vol. I. 200p. (Orig.). 1982. pap. 9.95 (*0-943324-03-3*) Omenana.

— Corporate Class Ethics & Apartheid. 120p. (Orig.). 1982. pap. 3.95 (*0-943324-04-1*) Omenana.

Omenetto, P., jt. ed. see Boissonnas, J.

Omenka, Nicholas I. The School in the Service of Evangelization: The Catholic Educational Impact in Eastern Nigeria 1886-1950. LC 88-37555. (Studies on Religion in Africa - Supplements to the Journal of Religion in Africa: Vol. 6). xv, 317p. 1989. 73.25 (*90-04-08632-3*) E J Brill.

***Omenn, Gilbert S., ed.** Annual Review of Pubic Health, Vol. 16. 1995. lib. bdg. 52.00 (*0-8243-2716-0*) Annual Reviews.

— Environmental Biotechnology: Reducing Risks from Environmental Chemicals Through Biotechnology. LC 88-17886. (Basic Life Sciences Ser.: Vol. 45). (Illus.). 520p. 1988. 125.00 (*0-306-42984-5*, Plenum Pr) Plenum.

Omenn, Gilbert S. & Gelboin, Harry V., eds. Genetic Variability in Responses to Chemical Exposure. LC 84-4947. (Banbury Report Ser.: No. 16). 433p. reprint ed. pap. 123.50 (*0-7837-2011-4*, 2042285) Bks Demand.

Omenn, Gilbert S. & Hollaender, Alexander, eds. Genetic Control of Environmental Pollutants. LC 82-26942. (Basic Life Sciences Ser.: Vol. 28). 418p. 1984. 95.00 (*0-306-41624-7*, Plenum Pr) Plenum.

Omenn, Gilbert S. & Teich, Albert H., eds. Biotechnology & the Environment: Research Needs. LC 86-18181. (Illus.). 169p. 1987. 36.00 (*0-8155-1105-1*) Noyes.

Omenn, Gilbert S., jt. auth. see Lave, Lester B.

Omenn, Gilbert S., et al, eds. Annual Review of Public Health, Vol. 12. 1991. text ed. 45.00 (*0-8243-2712-8*) Annual Reviews.

— Annual Review of Public Health, Vol. 13. 1992. text ed. 49.00 (*0-8243-2713-6*) Annual Reviews.

— Annual Review of Public Health, Vol. 14. (Illus.). 1993. 49.00 (*0-8243-2714-4*) Annual Reviews.

— Annual Review of Public Health, Vol. 15. (Illus.). 1994. text ed. 52.00 (*0-8243-2715-2*) Annual Reviews.

Omer-Cooper, J. D. History of Southern Africa. 2nd ed. LC 93-40500. 322p. (Orig.). 1994. pap. 22.50 (*0-435-08095-4*, Pub. by Heinemann Educ Bks UK) Heinemann.

Omer, Devora. The Teheran Operation: The Rescue of Jewish Children from the Nazis. Rubin, Riva, tr. 426p. Date not set. 29.95 (*0-685-67828-8*); pap. 15.95 (*0-685-67829-6*, 01-1300-18) Bnai Brith Intl.

Omer, Devorah. The Gideonites. 256p. 1968. 3.50 (*0-88482-750-X*) Hebrew Pub.

— Once There Was a Hassid. (Illus.). 28p. (J). (gr. 4 up). 1987. 9.95 (*0-915361-73-6*) Modan-Adama Bks.

— Path Beneath the Sea. 192p. 1969. 3.50 (*0-88482-744-5*) Hebrew Pub.

Omer, Elhaj B. Danagla Traders of Northern Sudan. (Sudan Studies: No. 10). 105p. 1985. 25.00 (*0-685-14919-6*, Pub. by Ithaca UK) Evergreen Dist.

Omer, Haim. Critical Interventions in Psychotherapy. 192p. 1994. 23.00 (*0-393-70182-4*) Norton.

Omer-Man, Jonathan, jt. ed. see Wiener, Shohama H.

Omerod, Henry. Piracy in the Ancient World: An Annotated History of the Mediterranean Covering All of the Countries to 250 A. D. 1977. lib. bdg. 69.95 (*0-8490-2445-5*) Gordon Pr.

O'Merry, Rory. Dr. Smog's Used Car Lemon Check: The Used Car Buying Guide for Smart People. 96p. (Orig.). 1995. reprint ed. pap. 12.95 (*0-9625048-4-X*) Dr Smogs Clean Air.

— My Wife in Bangkok: AIDS & Prostitution in Thailand. (Illus.). 184p. (Orig.). (C). 1990. pap. 9.95 (*0-9625048-0-7*) Asia Pr.

***Omery, Anna, et al.** In Search of Nursing Science. 328p. 1995. text ed. 48.00 (*0-8039-5093-4*); pap. text ed. 22.95 (*0-8039-5094-2*) Sage.

Ometrics. First Steps Beyond. 1976. 11.95 (*0-89190-964-8*, Rivercity Pr) Amereon Ltd.

***OMG Staff.** OMG Specification Set. pap. text ed. 129.00 (*0-471-11146-5*) Wiley.

Omi, Michael & Winant, Howard. Racial Formation in the United States: 1960-1990. LC 93-336254. 1994. write for info. (*0-415-90904-X*, Routledge NY); pap. write for info. (*0-415-90864-7*, Routledge NY) Routledge.

Omi, Michael & Winant, Howard A. Racial Formation in the United States from the 1960's to the 1980's. 224p. 1986. pap. 13.95 (*0-7102-0970-3*, 09703, RKP) Routledge.

OMI Staff, et al. O Blessed Night: Theological Underpinnings for Recovery from Addiction. LC 90-19635. 204p. (Orig.). 1991. pap. 9.95 (*0-8189-0587-5*) Alba.

Omichinski, Linda. You Count, Calories Don't. 312p. 1993. pap. 14.95 (*1-895569-12-5*, Pub. by Tamos Bks CN) Sterling.

***Omichinski, Linda & Hildebrand, Heather W.** Tailoring Your Tastes. (Illus.). 176p. 1995. pap. 14.95 (*1-895569-34-6*, Pub. by Tamos Bks CN) Sterling.

Omidvar, Omid M., ed. Progress in Neural Networks, Vol. 1. 240p. (C). 1990. text ed. 45.00 (*0-89391-610-2*) Ablex Pub.

— Progress in Neural Networks, Vol. 2. (Progress in Neural Networks Ser.). 256p. (C). 1993. pap. text ed. write for info. (*0-89391-946-2*) Ablex Pub.

— Progress in Neural Networks, Vol. 2. (Progress in Neural Networks Ser.). 448p. (C). 1995. text ed. 75.00 (*0-89391-735-4*) Ablex Pub.

— Progress in Neural Networks Vol. 3. (Illus.). 440p. 1995. 75.00 (*0-89391-965-9*) Ablex Pub.

Omidvar, Omid M., ed. see Bolle, Ruud M., et al.

Omidvar, Omid M., ed. see Lehar, Steven M., et al.

Omilian, Susan. Sex-Based Employment Discrimination. 1990. 130.00 (*0-685-46258-7*) Clark Boardman Callaghan.

Omilian, Susan M. What Every Employer Should Be Doing About Sexual Harassment. 1986. pap. 24.95 (*1-55645-443-0*) Busn Legal Reports.

Ominde, S. H., ed. Kenya's Population Growth & Development to the Year 2000. 160p. 1989. text ed. 29.95 (*0-8214-0915-8*) Ohio U Pr.

Ominsky, Alan, jt. auth. see Kane, Lucile M.

Omissi, David E. Air Power & Colonial Control: The Royal Air Force 1919-1939. LC 90-40817. (Studies in Imperialism). 288p. 1990. text ed. 79.95 (*0-7190-2960-0*, Pub. by Manchester Univ Pr UK) St Martin.

Omiya, James K., jt. auth. see Gutierrez, Jorge A.

***Omiyi, Ben E.** City of Lagos. 1995. 12.50 (*0-533-11088-2*) Vantage.

***Omland, Erling O.** Hill Echoes. 528p. 1995. 34.95 (*0-8338-0223-2*) M Jones.

Omland, Omar K. The Third Mile: A Biblical View of Codependency. 105p. (Orig.). 1992. pap. 8.95 (*0-943167-11-6*) Faith & Fellowship Pr.

***Omlor, Georg.** Isolated Hyperthermic Limb Perfusion. Vaupel, Peter & Alexander, Cristof, eds. (Medical Intelligence Unit Ser.). 120p. 1995. write for info. (*1-57059-178-4*) R G Landes.

Omlor, J. Dennis. Efficiency Analysis of File Organization & Information. LC 81-11693. (Computer Science: Distributed Database Systems Ser.: No. 10). 124p. reprint ed. pap. 35.40 (*0-685-20868-0*, 2070161) Bks Demand.

Ommagio-Hadley. Teaching Language in Context. 2nd ed. 1993. pap. 30.95 (*0-8384-4067-3*) Heinle & Heinle.

— Teaching Language in Context. 2nd ed. 1993. student ed, pap. 17.95 (*0-8384-4068-1*) Heinle & Heinle.

Ommanney, Francis D. The Shoals of Capricorn. LC 74-15555. (Illus.). 322p. 1975. reprint ed. text ed. 59.75 (*0-8371-7823-1*, OMSC, Greenwood Pr) Greenwood.

Ommanney, K. A. & Schanker, Harry H. The Stage & the School. 5th ed. 1982. text ed. 29.76 (*0-07-047671-3*) McGraw.

Ommen, Thomas B. The Hermeneutic of Dogma. LC 75-29493. (American Academy of Religion. Dissertation Ser.: No. 11). 262p. reprint ed. pap. 74.70 (*0-7837-5468-X*, 2045233) Bks Demand.

Ommer, Rosemary E. From Outpost to Outport: A Structural Analysis of the Jersey-Gaspe Cod Fishery, 1767-1886. 264p. (C). 1991. text ed. 49.95 (*0-7735-0730-2*, Pub. by McGill CN) U of Toronto Pr.

Omnes, Roland. The Interpretation of Quantum Mechanics. LC 93-47445. (Physics Ser.). (C). 1994. 95.00 (*0-691-03336-6*); pap. 39.50 (*0-691-03669-1*) Princeton U Pr.

***Omni, Phyllis.** The Brandiad. 1994. 18.95 (*0-533-11040-8*) Vantage.

Omnik, Tukummiq C. & Lowenstein, Tom, trs. The Things That Were Said of Them: Shaman Stories & Oral Histories of the Tikigaq People. 285p. 1992. 30.00 (*0-520-06569-7*) U CA Pr.

Omo-Osagie, Solomon I., II. Native Voices. 108p. 1995. pap. 6.50 (*0-9647217-0-8*) S I Omo-Osagie. NATIVE VOICES is a book of poetry written out of a traditional African perspective. The voices of our loved ones who have passed on (Ancestors), are the words for the living. These words constitute the centerpiece of our human existence. Knowing the past is crucial to dealing with the future. The first part of this book addresses this belief. A traditional maxim says when the "frog" falls into a hole, the rest in line must take notice. Have we learned from the events of the past so that we do not fall into a hole? The second part of the book deals with the appreciation of the sentimental gifts of nature. We spend an inordinate amount of time "investigating" the origins of the things of this life, & very little time appreciating them. The final part of this book has pride at its theme. The path to life could sometimes be "chokish." When you have survived the choking, you ought to beat your chest, & stomp your feet. It is good for the soul. This book will motivate you! To order, call (410) 687-9894, or write Mr. Solomon Iyobosa Omo-Osagie II, P.O. Box 34223, Baltimore, MD 21221.** ***Publisher Provided Annotation.

Omodt, Jimm. The Chronicles of Caroltune: Scherzo Finds a Home. Omodt, Mary, ed. & illus. by. 40p. (Orig.). (J). (gr. 3-8). 1993. pap. text ed. 10.00 (*1-881026-05-1*) Scherzo Pub.

Omodt, Jimm A. How to Buy a Used Piano. rev. ed. (Illus.). 50p. 1987. pap. text ed. 6.95 (*1-881026-04-3*) Scherzo Pub.

— The Huge Hairy Horse & Other Songs from A to Z. 36p. (ps-5). 1991. pap. 12.95 (*1-881026-00-0*) Scherzo Pub.

— The Huge Hairy Horse Comes Back with Twenty-Six More. Omodt, Mary, ed. & illus. by. 40p. (Orig.). (J). (ps-5). 1993. pap. text ed. 10.00 (*1-881026-03-5*); pap. text ed. 20.00 (*1-881026-02-7*) Scherzo Pub.

Omodt, Mary, ed. see Omodt, Jimm A.

Omodt, Mary, ed. see Omodt, Jimm.

Omohundro, Gary. Fatal Recall. Van Treese, James B., ed. 220p. 1994. pap. 8.95 (*1-56901-053-6*) NW Pub.

Omohundro, John T. & Goodman, Kathleen. Mystery Fossil: A Physical Anthropology Laboratory Exercise for the MacIntosh. (C). 1990. disk, pap. 19.95 (*1-55934-019-3*) Mayfield Pub.

— Mystery Fossil 1: A Physical Anthropology Laboratory Exercise for the Macintosh. (Mystery Fossil Ser.). (C). 1993. pap. text ed. 18.95 (*1-55934-264-1*) Mayfield Pub.

— Mystery Fossil 2: A Physical Anthropology Laboratory Exercise for the Macintosh. (Mystery Fossil Ser.). (C). 1993. pap. text ed. 18.95 (*1-55934-275-7*) Mayfield Pub.

Omohundro, S. M. Geometric Perturbation Theory in Physics. 584p. 1986. text ed. 77.00 (*9971-5-0136-8*) World Scientific Pub.

Omoigui, Sota. Anesthesia Drugs Handbook. LC 92-12908. 352p. 1992. pap. 29.95 (*0-8016-6898-0*) Mosby Yr Bk.

— The Pain Drugs Handbook. LC 94-32993. 1994. write for info. (*0-8151-6505-6*) Mosby Yr Bk.

***Omoike, Isaac I.** Euthanasia, Right or Wrong? (Or Tell-Tale Signs of Murders) LC 94-90564. 169p. (Orig.). (C). 1995. pap. text ed. 19.95 (*0-9632236-3-1*) I Omoike Bks.

— Genocide: The Ultimate Threat of the Next Milleniums. LC 91-70487. 228p. (Orig.). 1991. pap. text ed. 16.99 (*0-9632236-0-7*) I Omoike Bks.

Omolade, Barbara. It's a Family Affair: The Real Lives of Black Single Mother. (Freedom Organizing Pamphlet Ser.). 16p. (Orig.). 1987. pap. 3.50 (*0-913175-10-2*) Kitchen Table.

— The Rising Song of African American Women. LC 94-4752. 1994. 55.00 (*0-415-90760-8*); pap. 16.95 (*0-685-71484-5*) Routledge.

— Rising Song of African American Women. 1994. pap. 16.95 (*0-415-90761-6*, Pub. by Tavistock UK) Routledge Chapman & Hall.

Omolke, Isaac I. Insider America. LC 91-90721. 106p. (Orig.). 1993. pap. 11.00 (*0-9632236-1-5*) I Omoike Bks.

Omond, James. Orkney Eighty Years Ago: With Special Attention to Evie. LC 77-87683. reprint ed. 14.50 (*0-404-16479-X*) AMS Pr.

Omond, T. S. English Metrists: Being a Sketch of English Prosidical Criticism from Elizabethan Times to the Present Days. LC 68-15694. 336p. 1968. reprint ed. 60.00 (*0-87753-031-9*) Phaeton.

Omond, Thomas S. The Romantic Triumph. LC 74-38364. (Select Bibliographies Reprint Ser.). 1977. reprint ed. 25.95 (*0-8369-6781-X*) Ayer.

Omonde, Lois G., jt. auth. see Mattaliano, Jane.

Omondi, Amos R. Computer Arithmetic Systems: Algorithms, Architecture, & Implementation. LC 93-46281. (Prentice-Hall International Series in Computer Science). 520p. 1994. 52.00 (*0-13-334301-4*) P-H Intl.

O'Mongain, Eon & O'Toole, C. P., eds. Physics in Industry: Proceedings of an International Conference, Dublin, 1976. LC 76-17504. 1976. 250.00 (*0-08-020922-X*, Pub. by Pergamon Repr UK) Franklin.

Omont, Henri A. Facsimiles De Manuscrits Grecs Des XVe et XVIe Siecles. 65p. 1974. reprint ed. write for info. (*3-487-05259-8*, Pub. by Georg Olms GW) Lubrecht & Cramer.

O'Moore, R. R., et al. Medical Informatics Europe, 1990, Vol. 40: Proceedings Glasgow, Scotland, August 20-23, 1990. Rienhoff, O. & Lindberg, D. A., eds. (Lecture Notes Ser.). xxv, 820p. 1990. pap. 118.00 (*0-387-52936-5*) Spr-Verlag.

O'Morain. Ulcerative Colitis. 1991. 119.00 (*0-8493-5498-6*, RC862) CRC Pr.

O'More, Peggy. Love's Inner Beauty. large type ed. (Linford Romance Library). 1991. pap. 13.95 (*0-7089-6984-4*, Linford) Ulverscroft.

— Marta. large type ed. 1994. 20.95 (*0-7089-3205-3*) Ulverscroft.

— No Place for Love. large type ed. (Linford Romance Library). 320p. 1993. pap. 14.95 (*0-7089-7410-4*, Linford) Ulverscroft.

— Pixie. large type ed. (Romance Library). 256p. 1995. pap. 14.95 (*0-7089-7664-6*, Linford) Ulverscroft.

— Vacation with Love. large type ed. (Linford Romance Library). 1990. pap. 12.95 (*0-7089-6917-8*, Trailtree Bookshop) Ulverscroft.

O'More, Peggy A. Mary Contrary. large type ed. 212p. 1994. pap. 16.95 (*1-85389-437-0*, Dales) Ulverscroft.

Omori, Annie S. & Kochi, Doi, trs. Diaries of Court Ladies of Old Japan. LC 72-111775. reprint ed. 29.50 (*0-404-04819-6*) AMS Pr.

Omori, Makoto & Tsutomu, Ikeda. Methods in Marine Zooplankton Ecology. LC 91-24425. 348p. (C). 1992. reprint ed. lib. bdg. 59.95 (*0-89464-653-2*) Krieger.

Omori, Rotaishi S. Zen & Budo. Wong, Brenda, ed. Tanouye, Tenshin, tr. (Illus.). 23p. (Orig.). 1989. pap. 5.00 (*1-877982-02-4*) Daihonzan Chozen-ji.

O'Morrow, Gerald & Reynolds, Ron. Study Guide for National Certification in Therapeutic Recreation. LC 90-71335. 89p. 1990. 11.95 (*0-910251-38-X*) Venture Pub PA.

O'Morrow, Gerald S. & Reynolds, Ronald P. Therapeutic Recreation. 3rd ed. 352p. 1988. text ed. 59.00 (*0-13-914896-5*) P-H.

O'Morrow, Gerald S., jt. auth. see Reynolds, Ronald P.

Omotani, Les M. Konnichi Wa, Japan: Middle School Through High School. 120p. (JPN.). (YA). (gr. 7-12). 1993. pap. 15.95 (*0-8442-8497-1*, Natl Textbk) NTC Pub Grp.

Omoto, Sadayoshi, intro. & pref. Early Michigan Paintings. (Illus.). 130p. (Orig.). 1976. pap. 4.00 (*1-879147-02-5*) Kresge Art Mus.

Omoto, Sadayoshi & Van Liere, Eldon N. The Michigan Experience. (Illus.). 176p. (Orig.). 1986. pap. 7.00 (*1-879147-08-4*) Kresge Art Mus.

Omotoso, Kole. Achebe or Soyinka? A Re-Interpretation & a Study in Contrasts. (New Perspectives on African Literature Ser.: No. 3). 240p. 1995. lib. bdg. 70.00 (*0-905450-38-8*, Pub. by H Zell Pubs UK) Bowker-Saur.

Omowale, Hassan. Book of the Living Dead: Essays for African-American Awareness. LC 90-84513. (Illus.). 250p. 1991. pap. 13.95 (*0-9627633-0-6*) Amen-Ra.

Omoyajowo, J. A. Cherubim & Seraphim: The History of an African Independent Church. LC 78-64624. 256p. (Orig.). 1982. 21.50 (*0-88357-068-8*); pap. 8.95 (*0-88357-069-6*) NOK Pubs.

Omran, Abdel R. Egypt: Population Problems & Prospects. 448p. 1973. pap. 6.50 (*0-89055-106-5*) Carolina Pop Ctr.

O

Omran, Abdel R., ed. Family Planning in the Legacy of Islam. LC 92-11914. 288p. (C). 1992. 74.00 (0-415-05541-5, A5591) Routledge.
— Liberalization of Abortion Laws: Implications. LC 75-42005. 305p. 1976. pap. 5.00 (0-89055-115-4) Carolina Pop Ctr.
Omrcanin, Ivo. Anglo-American Croatian Rapprochement. 650p. 1989. 25.00 (0-9613814-6-9) Ivor Pr.
— Boljsevici Kolju Sami Sebe. 72p. (CRO.). 1995. pap. 7.00 (0-614-06282-9) Ivor Pr.
— Croatia Rediviva. 72p. (CRO.). 1995. pap. 10.00 (0-614-06281-0) Ivor Pr.
— Diplomatische und Politische Geschichte Kroatiens. rev. ed. 416p. 1990. 25.00 (1-878716-03-4) Ivor Pr.
— Diplomatska i Politicka Povijest Hrvatske, 4 vols., Set. 298p. (CRO.). 1992. pap. 25.00 (1-878716-06-9) Ivor Pr.
— Diplomatska i Politicka Povijest Hrvatske, Vol. 1. 272p. (CRO.). 1991. pap. 20.00 (0-614-03039-0) Ivor Pr.
— Diplomatska i Politicka Povijest Hrvatske, Vol. 2. 303p. (CRO.). 1991. pap. 20.00 (0-685-59169-7) Ivor Pr.
— Hrvatska Backa. 104p. (Orig.). (CRO.). 1995. pap. write for info. (1-878716-19-0) Ivor Pr.
— Hrvatska 1944. 500p. 1990. pap. 25.00 (1-878716-01-8) Ivor Pr.
— Hrvatska, 1945. 400p. (Orig.). (CRO.). 1992. pap. 25.00 (1-878716-05-0) Ivor Pr.
— Hrvatski Boljsevici (su) Srpski Drek. 104p. (CRO.). 1993. pap. 10.00 (1-878716-10-7) Ivor Pr.
— Hrvatski Srijem. 160p. (Orig.). (CRO.). 1944. pap. write for info. (1-878716-18-2) Ivor Pr.
— Hrvatsko Kraljevstvo Slavnikovica. (Illus.). 104p. (Orig.). (CRO.). 1994. pap. 10.00 (1-878716-16-6) Ivor Pr.
— Hrvatsko Kraljevstvo Slavnikovica (The Slavnik Kingdom of Croatia) 104p. (CRO.). 1994. pap. 10.00 (1-878716-14-X) Ivor Pr.
— Ime Pobjede Krscanstvo Hrvata: Name Victories Christianity of Croatians. 24p. (CRO.). 1993. pap. write for info. (1-878716-12-3) Ivor Pr.
— L' Influence du Droit Canonique sur le Droit Coutumier Croate. 100p. (FRE.). 1990. 5.00 (1-878716-00-X) Ivor Pr.
— Mi i Drugi u Sedmom Stoljecu: Us & Others in the Seventh Century. (Illus.). 160p. (CRO.). 1993. pap. write for info. (1-878716-13-1) Ivor Pr.
— Mit Bogova u Predpovijesti Hrvatske. 158p. (Orig.). (CRO.). 1993. pap. 10.00 (1-878716-09-3) Ivor Pr.
— Ratna Povijest Hrvatske (Military History of Croatia), 4 vols., Set. (CRO.). 1993. pap. 5.00 (1-878716-08-5) Ivor Pr.
— Spasio Sam Ustastvo. 104p. (CRO.). 1994. pap. 10.00 (1-878716-17-4) Ivor Pr.
— Stvaranje Krscanstva u Hrvata. 104p. (CRO.). 1994. pap. 10.00 (0-685-72633-9) Ivor Pr.
— Ubijaj Boljsevicke Lazi i Zlocine - Kill Bolshevik Lies & Crimes. 104p. (CRO.). 1993. pap. 10.00 (1-878716-11-5) Ivor Pr.
— Velika Hrvatska. 104p. (CRO.). 1994. pap. 10.00 (1-878716-15-8) Ivor Pr.
Omrcanin, Margaret. Goodbye - Zbogom Srbijo. 126p. (CRO.). 1991. write for info. (1-878716-04-2) Ivor Pr.
Omrcanin, Margaret S. Margaret Thatcher's Doctrine on Recognition of Croatia. 82p. (Orig.). 1992. pap. 5.00 (1-878716-07-7) Ivor Pr.
— Los Von Serbien: Kroatien und das Skandinavische Modell. 2nd ed. Rullman, Hans P., tr. 100p. (GER.). 1990. pap. 7.00 (1-878716-02-6) Ivor Pr.
Omstead, Daniel R., ed. Computer Control of Fermentation Processes. 320p. 1989. 216.00 (0-8493-5496-X, TP156) CRC Pr.
O'Muircheartaigh, Colm A. & Payne, Clive, eds. The Analysis of Survey Data, 2 vols., 1. LC 76-951. (Illus.). 289p. reprint ed. pap. 75.20 (0-8357-8798-2, 2033620) Bks Demand.
— The Analysis of Survey Data, 2 vols., 2. LC 76-951. (Illus.). 289p. reprint ed. pap. 77.30 (0-8357-8799-0) Bks Demand.
O'Mulgreavey, Seamus. Bonkie the Great Bank Blagger. 264p. (C). 1990. 39.00 (1-86305-003-5, Pub. by Pascoe Pub AT) St Mut.
***Omura, et al.** AutoCad 13 Instant Reference. 1995. 12.99 (0-614-05127-4) Sybex.
Omura, George. Mastering AutoCAD Release 12. LC 92-82600. 1142p. 1992. 34.95 (0-7821-1134-3) Sybex.
— Mastering AutoCAD Release 12 for Windows. LC 92-82017. 1155p. 1993. disk, pap. 34.95 (0-7821-1221-8) Sybex.
— Mastering AutoCAD Rel.x for DOS. LC 94-69307. 1200p. 1994. pap. 37.99 (0-7821-1475-X) Sybex.
— Mastering AutoCAD Rel.x for Windows. 2nd ed. 1200p. 1995. disk, pap. 37.99 (0-7821-1476-8) Sybex.
— Mastering AutoCAD 13 for DOS. 1995. 39.99 (0-614-04790-0) Sybex.
— Mastering AutoCAD 13 for Windows. 1995. 39.99 (0-614-05123-1) Sybex.
Omura, George & Callori, B. Robert. AutoCAD Release 12 for Windows Instant Reference. LC 93-83694. 321p. 1993. pap. 12.95 (0-7821-1222-6) Sybex.
— AutoCAD Release 12 Instant Reference. LC 92-61598. 305p. 1992. 12.95 (0-7821-1167-X) Sybex.
***Omura, George, et al.** AutoCad Rel.X (WIN & DOS) LC 94-68874. 350p. 1995. pap. 12.99 (0-7821-1474-1) Sybex.
Omura, James K., jt. auth. see Viterbi, Andrew J.
Omura, S., ed. The Search for Bioactive Compounds from Microorganisms. (Contemporary Bioscience Ser.). (Illus.). 376p. 1992. 69.00 (0-387-97755-4) Spr-Verlag.
Omura, Satoshi, ed. Macrolide Antibiotics: Chemistry, Biology & Practice. 1984. text ed. 190.00 (0-12-526450-X) Acad Pr.
Omura, Tsuneo, et al, eds. Cytochrome P-450. 2nd ed. LC 92-48499. 300p. 1993. 130.00 (1-56081-710-0) VCH Pubs.
Omura, Tsuneo, jt. ed. see Tagashira, Yusaku.
***O'Murchu, Diarmuid.** Reframing Religious Life: An Expanded Vision for the Future. 160p. 1994. pap. 39.00 (0-85439-499-0, Pub. by St Paul Pubns UK) St Mut.
— Religious Life: A Prophetic Vision: Hope & Promise for Tomorrow. LC 91-72859. 264p. (Orig.). 1991. pap. 9.95 (0-87793-463-0) Ave Maria.
Omvedt, Gail. Dalits & the Democratic Revolution: Dr. Ambedkar & the Dalit Movement in Colonial India. LC 93-11778. 352p. (C). 1994. text ed. 36.00 (0-8039-9139-8) Sage.
— Reinventing Revolution: New Social Movements & the Socialist Tradition in India. LC 92-46911. (Socialism & Social Movements Ser.). 384p. (C). 1993. 57.95 (0-87332-784-5); pap. text ed. 20.95 (0-87332-785-3) M E Sharpe.
— We Will Smash This Prison: Indian Women in Struggle. 189p. 1979. 19.95 (0-318-37315-7) Asia Bk Corp.
On, Danny & Sumner, David, photos. Along the Trail: A Photographic Essay of Glacier National Park & the Northern Rockies. LC 79-53223. (Illus.). 128p. 1980. 20.00 (0-913504-53-X); pap. 12.95 (0-913504-54-8) Lowell Pr.
On, Danny, jt. auth. see Shaw, Richard J.
On Demand Data, Inc. Staff. The Corporate Tree: Directory of Corporate Linkage in the U. S. 1231p. (Orig.). 1989. 369.00 (0-9625174-1-0) On Demand Data.
— The Corporate Tree: Directory of Corporate Linkage in the U. S. Ward-Waller, Patti, ed. 1180p. (Orig.). 1990. pap. 369.00 (0-9625174-0-2) On Demand Data.
ON Health Care Systems Staff, et al. Being a Long-Term Care Nursing Assistant. 3rd ed. 416p. 1991. pap. 23.50 (0-89303-101-1) P-H.
O'N, Kathleen, jt. auth. see Gear, Michael.
On-Line Publishing Staff. Wu Style Tai Chi Practitioners of North America. (Illus.). 48p. (Orig.). 1993. pap. 9.95 (0-9635087-2-5) On-Line Pub.
***On Wheels Staff.** Arizona & New Mexico on Wheels. 448p. 1995. pap. 13.95 (0-02-860144-0) Macmillan.
— California & Nevada on Wheels. (New Ser.). 448p. 1995. pap. 13.00 (0-02-860146-7) Macmillan.
— Florida on Wheels. 304p. 1995. pap. 13.00 (0-02-860145-9) Macmillan.
— Middle Atlantic on Wheels. 384p. 1995. pap. 13.95 (0-02-860143-2) Macmillan.
Onacewicz, Wlodzimierz. Empires by Conquest, 2 vols. (Illus.). (C). 1986. 25.00 (0-685-73673-3) NOVA Pubns.
— Empires by Conquest, 2 vols., Set. (Illus.). (C). 1986. 25.00 (0-915979-04-7) NOVA Pubns.
Onaga, Christine Y., jt. auth. see Niesen, Karen L.
O'Nan, Michael & Enderton, Herbert B. Linear Algebra. 3rd ed. 461p. (C). 1989. pap. text ed. 2.75 (0-15-551009-6) SCP.
— Linear Algebra. 3rd ed. 461p. (C). 1990. text ed. 55.00 (0-15-551008-8) SCP.
O'Nan, Stewart. In the Walled City. (Drue Heinz Literature Prize Ser.). 184p. (C). 1993. text ed. 22.50 (0-8229-3768-9) U of Pittsburgh Pr.
— Snow Angels. 320p. 1995. pap. 10.95 (0-14-025096-4, Penguin Bks) Viking Penguin.
***Onan, Stewart.** Snow Angels: A Novel. 1994. 20.00 (0-385-47574-8) Doubleday.
O'Nan, Stewart. Transmission. 2nd ed. LC 87-30635. (Illus.). 26p. 1987. pap. text ed. 2.00 (0-943123-04-6) Arjuna Lib Pr.
O'Nan, Stewart, ed. see Gardner, John.
O'Nan, Stewart, jt. auth. see Gardner, John.
Onate, Andres D. Chairman Mao & the Chinese Communist Party. LC 78-11049. (Illus.). 316p. 1979. 33.95 (0-88229-250-1) Nelson-Hall.
Onate, E., jt. ed. see Chenot, J. L.
Onate, E., jt. ed. see Kratzig, W. B.
Onate, E., et al, eds. The Finite Element Method in the Nineteen Ninety's: A Book Dedicated to O.C. Zienkiewicz. (Illus.). 650p. 1992. 158.00 (0-387-54930-7) Spr-Verlag.
***Once Upon a Planet, Inc. Staff.** Let's Hug! (Illus.). 32p. (Orig.). 1994. 2.50 (0-88009-071-5) Planet Bks.
Onchi, Koshiro, et al. Onchi: Prints of Onchi (Koshiro) (Illus.). 327p. 1975. 210.00 (0-8150-0776-0) Wittenborn.
Oncina, J., jt. ed. see Carrasco, R. C.
Oncken, William, Jr. Managing Management Time: Who's Got the Monkey? 260p. 1989. 9.95 (0-13-551086-4) P-H.
Oncken, William, Jr., jt. auth. see Blanchard, Kenneth H.
Oncken, William Jr. Managing Management Time: Who's Got the Monkey? 238p. 1986. 19.95 (0-13-550690-5, Busn) P-H.
Oncology Nursing Society Staff. Guidelines for Oncology Nursing Practice. 2nd ed. 1991. pap. text ed. 47.95 (0-7216-3419-2) Saunders.
— Instructor's Resource Manual for the ONS Core Curriculum for Oncology Nursing. McMillan, Susan C. & Holley, Sandra, eds. (Illus.). 823p. 1995. text ed. write for info. (0-7216-4724-3) Saunders.
***Ondaatje & Tostevin, trs.** Elimination Dance - La Danse Eliminatoire. (NFS Canada Ser.). Date not set. pap. 8.50 (0-919626-55-6, Pub. by Brick Bks CN) InBook.
Ondaatje, Elizabeth H. Policy Options for Army Involvement in Youth Development. LC 93-21331. 1993. 15.00 (0-8330-1460-9, MR-352) Rand Corp.
Ondaatje, Michael. Cinnamon Peeler. 1991. pap. 18.50 (0-679-40260-8) McKay.
— The Cinnamon Peeler. LC 90-53557. 208p. 1992. pap. 14.00 (0-679-74272-7) Knopf.
— The Collected Works of Billy the Kid. 112p. 1984. pap. 10.00 (0-14-007280-2, Penguin Bks) Viking Penguin.
— Coming Through Slaughter. 160p. 1984. pap. 10.95 (0-14-007281-0, Penguin Bks) Viking Penguin.
— The English Patient. LC 92-53089. 1992. 22.00 (0-679-41678-1) Knopf.
— English Patient. Date not set. pap. 10.50 (0-394-28013-X) Knopf.
— The English Patient: A Novel. LC 93-10492. 1993. pap. 11.00 (0-679-74520-3, Vin) Random.
— In the Skin of a Lion. 256p. 1988. pap. 10.95 (0-14-011309-6, Penguin Bks) Viking Penguin.
— Running in the Family. LC 93-10494. 1993. pap. 10.00 (0-679-74669-2, Vin) Random.
Ondar, O., ed. Correspondence Between A. A. Markov & A. A. Chuprov on the Theory of Probability & Mathematical Statistics. 192p. 1981. pap. 79.00 (0-387-90585-5) Spr-Verlag.
Ondeck, Deborah A., jt. auth. see Gingerich, Barbara S.
Onderdonk, A., jt. auth. see Onderdonk, E.
Onderdonk, E. & Onderdonk, A. Genealogy of the Onderdonk Family in America. (Illus.). 374p. 1989. reprint ed. lib. bdg. 64.00 (0-8328-0922-5); reprint ed. pap. 56.00 (0-8328-0923-3) Higginson Bk Co.
Ondori. An Embroidery Sampler. (Illus.). 102p. 1988. pap. 12.95 (0-87040-758-9) Japan Pubns USA.
Ondori Publishing Company Editors. American Patchwork Quilt Designs. (Illus.). 78p. (Orig.). 1987. pap. 13.95 (0-87040-744-9) Japan Pubns USA.
— Basic Patchwork with Patterns. (Illus.). 72p. (Orig.). 1990. pap. 13.95 (0-87040-818-6) Japan Pubns USA.
— The Book of Christmas Decorations. LC 88-80143. (Illus.). 72p. (Orig.). 1988. pap. 9.95 (0-87040-753-8) Japan Pubns USA.
— Full Color Illustrated Basic Knit. (Illus.). 40p. (Orig.). 1987. pap. 9.95 (0-87040-745-7) Japan Pubns USA.
— My Lace. (Illus.). 94p. 1987. pap. 11.95 (0-87040-736-8) Japan Pubns USA.
— New Embroidery for Beginners. (Illus.). 48p. 1986. pap. 11.95 (0-87040-702-3) Japan Pubns USA.
— Quilting & Applique All Around the House. (Illus.). 120p. 1986. 13.95 (0-87040-703-1) Japan Pubns USA.
— Small Embroidery Gifts. (Illus.). 124p. (Orig.). 1989. pap. 13.95 (0-87040-819-4) Japan Pubns USA.
Ondori Publishing Company Staff. Attractive Cross Stitch Designs. LC 81-80834. (Illus.). 104p. (Orig.). 1981. pap. 13.95 (0-87040-501-2) Japan Pubns USA.
— Basic Knit Sweaters: Step-by-Step. (Illus.). 64p. 1986. pap. 11.95 (0-87040-654-X) Japan Pubns USA.
— Collections of Designs for Cross Stitches. LC 80-81038. (Illus.). 1980. pap. 11.95 (0-87040-486-5) Japan Pubns USA.
— Creative Embroidery Designs. (Illus.). 1979. pap. 15.95 (0-87040-452-0) Japan Pubns USA.
— Crochet Lace with Complete Diagrams. (Ondori Needlecraft Ser.). (Illus.). 1979. pap. 14.95 (0-87040-415-6) Japan Pubns USA.
— Cross Stitch: Three Hundred Motifs. LC 81-84804. (Illus.). 100p. 1982. pap. 13.95 (0-87040-506-3) Japan Pubns USA.
— Cross Stitch Designs. (Ondori Handicrafts Ser.). (Illus.). 96p. 1979. pap. 13.95 (0-87040-366-4) Japan Pubns USA.
— Cross Stitch for Your Home. (Illus.). 134p. (Orig.). 1986. pap. 11.95 (0-87040-734-1) Japan Pubns USA.
— Cross Stitch in Small Designs. LC 79-66300. (Illus.). 1980. pap. 10.95 (0-87040-464-4) Japan Pubns USA.
— Danish Cross-Stitch. (Illus.). 112p. 1985. pap. 14.95 (0-87040-627-2) Japan Pubns USA.
— Easy Cross-Stitch. (Illus.). 124p. (Orig.). 1984. pap. 15.95 (0-87040-604-3) Japan Pubns USA.
— Easy Embroidery. rev. ed. (Illus.). 96p. (Orig.). 1984. pap. 12.95 (0-87040-608-6) Japan Pubns USA.
— Elegant Cross-Stitch Embroidery. (Illus.). 100p. (Orig.). 1983. pap. 15.95 (0-87040-538-1) Japan Pubns USA.
— Embroidery & Cross-Stich for Framing. (Illus.). 100p. (Orig.). 1983. pap. 13.95 (0-87040-537-3) Japan Pubns USA.
— Fine Patchwork & Quilting. (Illus.). 80p. 1983. pap. 11.95 (0-87040-557-8) Japan Pubns USA.
— Floral Designs in Cross Stitch. LC 82-81055. (Illus.). 112p. 1982. pap. 12.95 (0-87040-520-9) Japan Pubns USA.
— Gorgeous Crochet Laces for Interior Decoration. LC 80-81039. 1980. pap. 14.95 (0-87040-487-3) Japan Pubns USA.
— Handcraft for Baby: Cotton Wares up to Two Years Old. (Illus.). 96p. (Orig.). 1993. pap. 14.95 (0-87040-606-X) Japan Pubns USA.
— Lovely Embroidery Patterns. LC 79-66301. (Illus.). 1980. pap. 12.95 (0-87040-465-2) Japan Pubns USA.
— Modern Patchwork. LC 81-84806. (Illus.). 108p. 1982. 12.95 (0-87040-507-1) Japan Pubns USA.
— A New Look for Needlework, Embroidery & Cross Stitch. (Illus.). 112p. (Orig.). 1984. pap. 13.95 (0-87040-568-3) Japan Pubns USA.
— Patchwork & Quilting Book. LC 81-80836. (Illus.). 104p. (Orig.). 1981. pap. 12.95 (0-87040-498-9) Japan Pubns USA.
— White Crochet Lace. (Illus.). 96p. 1982. pap. 11.95 (0-87040-521-7) Japan Pubns USA.
Ondori Staff. Classic Quilting of Sashiko. 1990. pap. 16.95 (0-87040-854-2) Japan Pubns USA.
— Glass Bead Artistry: Over 200 Playful Designs. (Illus.). 48p. (Orig.). 1992. pap. 12.95 (0-87040-890-9) Japan Pubns USA.
— Home Embroidery. (Illus.). 64p. (Orig.). 1993. pap. 15.95 (0-87040-927-1) Japan Pubns USA.
— Living with Cross-Stitch. (Illus.). 96p. (Orig.). 1988. pap. 11.95 (0-87040-760-0) Japan Pubns USA.
— Patchwork Made Perfect. 1990. pap. 15.95 (0-87040-855-0) Japan Pubns USA.
— Playful Patchwork: Great Gift Ideas for Children. (Illus.). 84p. (Orig.). 1993. pap. 14.95 (0-685-70058-5) Kodansha.
— Simple Patchwork. (Illus.). 64p. (Orig.). 1993. pap. 15.95 (0-87040-928-X) Japan Pubns USA.
— Simple Tiny Cross-Stitch. (Illus.). 72p. (Orig.). 1990. pap. 12.95 (0-87040-864-X) Japan Pubns USA.
Ondori Staff & Onoue, Masano. The World of Cross Stitch. (Illus.). 100p. (Orig.). 1983. pap. 11.95 (0-87040-558-6) Japan Pubns USA.
Ondorisha. The Patchwork Pattern Book. (Illus.). 106p. 1981. pap. 11.50 (0-525-47681-4, Dutton) NAL-Dutton.
Ondrackova, Jana. The Physiological Activity of the Speech Organs: An Analysis of the Speech-Organs During the Phonation of Sung, Spoken, & Whispered Czech Vowels on the Basis of X-Ray Methods. Short, D., tr. LC 72-94494. (Illus.). 105p. 1973. text ed. 40.00 (90-279-2374-4) Mouton.
Ondrey, Patrick, jt. auth. see Avanzini, John.
Ondrich, Jan & Wasylenko, Michael. Foreign Direct Investment in the United States: Issues, Magnitudes & Location Choice of New Manufacturing Plants, 1978 to 1987. LC 93-32159. 160p. 1993. text ed. 23.00 (0-88099-140-2); pap. text ed. 13.00 (0-88099-139-9) W E Upjohn.
Ondryas, I. S. & Fransson, T. H., eds. Nineteen-Ninety ASME COGEN-TURBO: International Symposium on Gas Turbines in Cogeneration, Repowering, & Peak-Load Power Generation, 4th, Held in New Orleans, Louisiana, August 27-29, 1990. LC 90-195623. (IGTI Ser.: Vol. 5). 264p. reprint ed. pap. 75.30 (0-7837-1448-3, 2052423) Bks Demand.
One Hundred & Third Ohio Volunteer Infantry Members. Personal Reminiscences & Experiences. 444p. 1984. reprint ed. 25.00 (0-9613625-0-2) OH Volunteer.
One Hundred First Airborne Division. Vietnam Odyssey: 101st Airborne Division. (Illus.). 112p. 1986. reprint ed. write for info. (0-917231-06-6) Ferguson Comns Pubs.
O'Neal. Come Follow Me. 1992. 6.99 (0-7814-0031-7, Chariot Bks) Chariot Family.
— God's Gift to Mary. 1992. 6.99 (0-7814-0030-9, Chariot Bks) Chariot Family.
— Shaq Attaq! 6.99 (0-517-13653-8) Random Hse Value.
O'Neal, Bill. The American Association: A Baseball History, 1902-1991. LC 91-24176. 400p. (Orig.). 1992. pap. 17.95 (0-89015-812-6) Sunbelt Media.
— The Arizona Rangers. Eakin, Edwin M., ed. (Illus.). 288p. 1988. pap. 15.95 (0-89015-610-7) Sunbelt Media.
— Cattleman vs. Sheepherders: Violence in the West, 1880-1920. 1989. 16.95 (0-89015-665-4) Sunbelt Media.
— Encyclopedia of Western Gunfighters. LC 78-21380. (Illus.). 1979. 34.95 (0-8061-1508-4) U of Okla Pr.
— Encyclopedia of Western Gunfighters. LC 78-21380. (Illus.). 400p. 1991. pap. 18.95 (0-8061-2335-4) U of Okla Pr.
— Fighting Men of the Indian Wars: A Biographical Encyclopedia of the Mountain Men, Soldiers, Cowboys, & Pioneers Who Took up Arms During America's Westward Expansion. (Illus.). 272p. 1992. 26.95 (0-935269-07-X) Western Pubns.
— The International League: A Baseball History, 1884-1991. 452p. (Orig.). 1992. pap. 17.95 (0-89015-856-8) Sunbelt Media.
— Pacific Coast League, Nineteen Hundred Three to Nineteen Eighty-Eight. Roberts, Melissa, ed. (Illus.). 356p. 1990. 17.95 (0-89015-776-6) Sunbelt Media.
— The Southern League: Baseball in Dixie, 1885-1994. LC 93-47554. 1994. 17.95 (0-89015-952-1) Sunbelt Media.
O'Neal, Charles. Developing a Winning Just-in-time Marketing Strategy: The Industrial Marketer's Guide. 1990. text ed. 31.67 (0-13-205303-9) P-H.
— Three Wishes for Jamie. 1976. 20.95 (0-8488-0184-9) Amereon Ltd.
— Three Wishes for Jamie. large type ed. LC 93-42059. 1994. 17.95 (0-7862-0140-1) Thorndike Pr.
— Three Wishes for Jamie. LC 79-66116. 256p. 1980. reprint ed. 22.00 (0-933256-08-6); reprint ed. pap. text ed. 16.00 (0-933256-09-4) Second Chance.
O'Neal, Christopher. Frankenstein. 52p. 1980. pap. 4.00 (0-88680-056-0) I E Clark.
O'Neal, Daisy E. Man in the Kitchen Texas Style! 150p. (Orig.). 1990. pap. 9.95 (0-9626482-0-5) Star-Daze Prodns.
***O'Neal, Dan, et al, eds.** The Transient & Permanent in Liberal Religion: Reflections from the UUMA Convocation on Ministry. 1995. pap. 16.00 (1-55896-330-8) Unitarian Univ.
O'Neal, Debbie T. Before & after Christmas: Activities & Ideas for Advent & Epiphany. LC 91-9988. (Illus.). 64p. pap. 8.99 (0-8066-2534-1) Augsburg Fortress.
— Before & After Easter: Activities & Ideas for Lent to Pentecost. LC 92-32415. (Illus.). 64p. 1993. pap. 9.99 (0-8066-2604-6, 9-2604) Augsburg Fortress.
— The Big Bedtime Book of Stories & Prayers. 64p. 1995. 9.95 (0-687-00126-9) Abingdon.
— Christmas Is Coming: Sixteen Fun Things to Make. (Illus.). 20p. 1993. pap. 6.99 (0-8010-6755-3) Baker Bk.
— Come Hear the Story: Christmas Program Resource. 48p. (Orig.). 1992. pap. 4.99 (0-8066-2598-8, 10-25988) Augsburg Fortress.
— Easter Is Coming: Thirteen Fun Things to Make. (Illus.). 20p. (Orig.). (J). (ps). 1993. pap. 6.99 (0-8010-6759-6) Baker Bk.
— An Easter People: Family Devotional Activities for Lent & Easter. 32p. (Orig.). 1986. pap. 6.99 (0-8066-2255-5, 10-1990, Augsburg) Augsburg Fortress.
— Family Time: One Hundred One Ideas for Sunday Afternoons. LC 93-5065. 144p. (Orig.). 1994. pap. 11.00 (0-687-38507-5) Dimen for Liv.

An Asterisk (*) at the beginning of an entry indicates that the title is appearing in BIP for the first time.

— Family Fun: 104 Easy Ways to Make the Most of Busy Days. 160p. (Orig.). 1995. pap. 9.00 (*0-687-01023-3*) Dimen for Liv.

Oneal, Debbie T. More Than Glue & Glitter: Classroom Guide for Volunteer Teachers. LC 91-47157. 96p. 1992. pap. 11.99 (*0-8066-2561-9*, 9-2561) Augsburg Fortress.

O'Neal, Debbie T. My Read-&-Do Bible Storybook. LC 89-15184. (Illus.). 128p. (Orig.). (J). (gr. 3-8). 1989. kivar, pap. 14.99 (*0-8066-2431-0*, 9-2431) Augsburg Fortress.

— Now I Lay Me down to Sleep: Action Prayers, Poems, & Songs for Bedtime. LC 94-71213. 1994. pap. 5.99 (*0-8066-2602-X*, 9-2602, Augsburg) Augsburg Fortress.

— 101 Things to Do for Christmas. LC 94-46532. 1995. pap. write for info. (*0-8066-2792-1*) Augsburg Fortress.

— Thank You for This Food: Action Prayers, Songs, & Blessings for Mealtime. LC 94-78747. (J). (ps). 1994. pap. 5.99 (*0-8066-2603-8*, Augsburg) Augsburg Fortress.

O'Neal, Debbie T. & Rosato, Amelia. The Lost Coin. LC 92-46610. (Illus.). 14p. (J). 1993. 7.00 (*0-8170-1194-3*) Judson.

— The Lost Sheep. LC 92-46612. (Illus.). 14p. (J). 1993. 7.00 (*0-8170-1193-5*) Judson.

O'Neal, Esther. Knowing Christ. (Illus.). 64p. (J). (gr. k-6). 1962. pap. text ed. 8.99 (*1-55976-026-5*) CEF Press.

O'Neal, F., ed. Corporate Practice Commentator, 1966-1990, 25 vols. (*0-318-61075-2*); 135.00 (*0-685-14553-0*) Clark Boardman Callaghan.

— Corporate Practice Commentator, 1966-1990, 25 vols., Set. LC 68-3938. 515.00 (*0-685-14552-2*) Clark Boardman Callaghan.

O'Neal, F. & Hazen, Thomas L. O'Neal & Hazen on Corporations. 1989. write for info. (*0-318-63271-3*) Little.

O'Neal, F. Hodge & Thompson, Robert B. O'Neal Close Corporations: Law & Practice, 2 vols., No. 12. 1990. 200.00 (*0-685-33314-0*); Suppl. 1987. write for info. (*0-318-66850-5*); Suppl. 1986. write for info. (*0-318-66851-3*) Clark Boardman Callaghan.

— O'Neal's Oppression of Minority Shareholders, 2 vols. 3rd ed. LC 85-7867. 1990. 230.00 (*0-318-42412-6*); write for info. (*0-318-65004-5*) Clark Boardman Callaghan.

O'Neal, Glenn. Make the Bible Live. pap. 3.50 (*0-88469-020-2*) BMH Bks.

O'Neal, James. Commercial General Liability Coverages. 1991. 39.50 (*1-56461-007-1*, 46020) Rough Notes.

— Hitch in Hell. 1995. 13.95 (*0-8062-5128-X*) Carlton.

— Workers in American History. 32th ed. LC 78-156437. (American Labor Ser., No. 2). 1977. reprint ed. 19.95 (*0-405-02935-7*) Ayer.

O'Neal, Jim. Confessions of a Mass Murderer. 117p. (Orig.). 1993. pap. text ed. 10.95 (*1-883457-02-5*) Mouseion Pub.

— Dumferling Castle & Other Plays. 235p. 1993. pap. 11.95 (*1-883457-03-3*) Mouseion Pub.

— Poems Especially for You. 24p. 1993. pap. 9.95 (*1-883457-32-7*) Mouseion Pub.

— Professor Rubin. 118p. (Orig.). 1993. pap. text ed. 10.95 (*1-883457-00-9*) Mouseion Pub.

— The Wretch. 318p. (Orig.). 1993. pap. text ed. 12.95 (*1-883457-01-7*) Mouseion Pub.

O'Neal, John C. Seeing & Observing: Rousseau's Rhetoric of Perception. (Stanford French & Italian Studies: Vol. 41). 160p. 1985. pap. 46.50 (*0-915838-55-9*) Anma Libri.

O'Neal, John R. Foreign Policy Making in Times of Crisis. LC 81-22489. 368p. 1982. 49.50 (*0-8142-0339-6*) Ohio St U Pr.

O'Neal, John T. Osha Bloodborne Pathogen Standard: A Pragmatic Approach. 1994. text ed. 49.95 (*0-442-01779-0*) Van Nos Reinhold.

O'Neal, Jon T. A Practical Guide to the Blood Borne Pathogens Standard. 325p. 1995. 49.95 (*0-685-75061-2*) Van Nos Reinhold.

O'Neal, Katherine. Princess of Thieves. 1993. mass mkt. 5.50 (*0-553-56066-2*, Fanfare) Bantam.

O'Neal, Kathleen, jt. auth. see Polette, Nancy.

O'Neal, Kathleen M. Redemption of Light. (Powers of Light Ser.: Bk. 3). 1991. mass mkt. 4.99 (*0-88677-470-5*) DAW Bks.

O'Neal, L. Thomas. Maya in Sankara: Measuring the Immeasurable. 1980. 16.00 (*0-8364-0611-7*) S Asia.

O'Neal, Lulu R. A Peculiar Piece of Desert: The Story of California's Morongo Basin. LC 81-50577. (Illus.). 1981. 9.95 (*0-930704-06-1*) Sagebrush Pr.

O'Neal, Malinda K., jt. auth. see Franklin, Gordon T.

O'Neal, Mary L., jt. auth. see Hildebrand, Lee.

O'Neal, Michael. The Assassination of Abraham Lincoln: Opposing Viewpoints. LC 91-13682. (Great Mysteries Ser.). (Illus.). 112p. (J). (gr. 5-8). 1991. lib. bdg. 16.95 (*0-89908-092-8*) Greenhaven.

— Haunted Houses. LC 93-4330. (Great Mysteries Ser.). (YA). 1994. 14.95 (*1-56510-095-6*) Greenhaven.

— King Arthur: Opposing Viewpoints. LC 92-11421. (Great Mysteries Ser.). (Illus.). 112p. (J). (gr. 5-8). 1992. 16.95 (*0-89908-095-2*) Greenhaven.

— President Truman & the Atomic Bomb: Opposing Viewpoints. LC 90-35611. (Great Mysteries Ser.). (Illus.). 112p. (J). (gr. 5-8). 1990. lib. bdg. 16.95 (*0-89908-079-0*) Greenhaven.

— Pyramids: Opposing Viewpoints. (Great Mysteries Ser.). (Illus.). 128p. (J). (gr. 5-9). 1994. lib. bdg. 16.95 (*1-56510-216-9*, 2169) Lucent Bks.

O'Neal, Norma. Formal Feeling. 1985. pap. 2.95 (*0-449-70181-6*) Fawcett.

***O'Neal, Norman.** Sqwidget. 100p. Date not set. pap. 7.95 (*0-7610-0398-3*) NW Pub.

O'Neal, P. Language of Gold Fish. 1987. pap. 2.95 (*0-449-70300-2*) Fawcett.

O'Neal, Patrick H., jt. ed. see McElligott, Mary E.

O'Neal, R. D. A Fire in the Sea. 240p. 1985. pap. 10.95 (*0-930096-80-0*) G Gannett.

***O'Neal, Regan.** Fallon Blood. 1995. write for info. (*0-312-85973-2*) Forge NYC.

O'Neal, Regina. And Then the Harvest: Three T.V. Plays. 1975. 6.00 (*0-910296-90-1*) Broadside Pr.

O'Neal, Scott. Theory on the Major Scales. (Illus.). 64p. (J). 1993. pap. 6.95 (*0-8059-3414-6*) Dorrance.

O'Neal, Sean, jt. auth. see Tunzi, Joseph A.

O'Neal, Shaquille. Shaq Attaq! (Illus.). 224p. 1994. pap. 9.95 (*0-7868-8076-7*) Hyperion.

O'Neal, Virginia. Beecher. Chirich, Nancy, ed. LC 90-31496. 224p. 1991. pap. 9.95 (*0-912761-31-8*) Cliffhanger Pr.

— Beecher. large type ed. LC 93-34590. 1993. pap. 17.95 (*0-7862-0078-2*) Thorndike Pr.

O'Neal, William. The Life & History of William O'Neal: The Man Who Sold His Wife. 2nd ed. Eakin, Sue, ed. LC 89-80326. (Illus.). 212p. 1990. reprint ed. pap. text ed. 9.95 (*0-944419-07-0*) Everett Cos Pub.

O'Neal, William B. Jefferson's Fine Arts Library: His Selections for the University of Virginia Together with His Own Architectural Books at Monticello. LC 75-33229. (Illus.). 409p. 1976. 35.00 (*0-8139-0282-7*) U Pr of Va.

O'Neal, William B. & Weeks, Christopher. The Work of William Lawrence Bottomley in Richmond. LC 84-20800. (Illus.). xxiv, 262p. 1989. 42.95 (*0-8139-1046-3*) U Pr of Va.

— The Work of William Lawrence Bottomley in Richmond. LC 84-20800. (Illus.). 286p. Date not set. reprint ed. pap. 81.60 (*0-7837-9230-1*, 2049981) Bks Demand.

O'Neal, Zibby. Grandma Moses. (J). 1987. pap. 4.99 (*0-14-032220-5*, Puffin) Puffin Bks.

— Grandma Moses: Painter of Rural America. (Women of Our Time Ser.). (Illus.). (J). (gr. 2-6). reprint ed. pap. 3.50 (*0-317-62289-7*, Puffin) Puffin Bks.

— In Summer Light. LC 85-50806. 180p. (J). (gr. 7 up). 1985. pap. 12.95 (*0-670-80784-2*) Viking Child Bks.

Oneal, Zibby. Language of Goldfish. (J). 1990. pap. 3.99 (*0-14-034540-X*, Puffin) Puffin Bks.

— A Long Way to Go. (Once Upon America Ser.). (Illus.). 64p. (J). (gr. 2-6). 1990. pap. 11.95 (*0-670-82532-8*) Viking Child Bks.

— A Long Way to Go: A Story of Women's Right to Vote. (Once Upon America Ser.). (Illus.). 64p. (J). (gr. 2-6). 1992. pap. 4.99 (*0-14-032950-1*, Puffin) Puffin Bks.

O'Neale, Sondra. Jupiter Hammon & the Biblical Beginnings of African-American Literature. LC 91-38904. (American Theological Library Association Monograph: No. 28). 303p. 1993. 37.50 (*0-8108-2479-5*) Scarecrow.

O'Neall, John B. Biographical Sketches of the Bench & Bar of South Carolina, 2 vols., Set. Incl. Vol. 1. LC 75-1159. 470p. 1975. 22.50 (*0-87152-198-9*); Vol. 2. LC 75-1159. 620p. 1975. 22.50 (*0-87152-199-7*); LC 75-1159. 1975. reprint ed. 45.00 (*0-87152-300-0*) Reprint.

O'Neall, John B. & Chapman, John A. The Annals of Newberry, South Carolina, Historical Biographical & Anecdotal: Also Religious Medical & Literary, 2 vols., Set. iii, 890p. 1993. reprint ed. pap. text ed. 51.00 (*1-55613-772-9*) Heritage Bk.

Oneda, S., ed. Hadron Spectroscopy - 1985, (International Conference, University of Maryland. LC 85-72537. (AIP Conference Proceedings Ser.: No. 132). 504p. 1985. lib. bdg. 49.75 (*0-88318-331-5*) Am Inst Physics.

Oneda, S. & Koide, Y. Asymptotic Symmetry & Its Implication in Elementary Particle Physics. 300p. 1991. text ed. 61.00 (*981-02-0498-1*) World Scientific Pub.

Oneda, S., jt. ed. see Peaslee, D. C.

O'Neeall, Parris, et al. Caribbean Family Planning Guide: A Self Instruction Manual for Health Professionals. 432p. 1990. 25.00 (*0-916683-24-9*) Intl Plan Parent.

Onega, Susana. Form & Meaning in the Novels of John Fowles. LC 89-4700. (Challenging the Literary Canon Ser.). 220p. 1991. 50.00 (*0-8357-1949-9*) Univ Rochester Pr.

Oneglia, Mario F. Contemporary Conducting Techniques. LC 79-66924. (Illus.). (Orig.). 1979. spiral bd. 15.00 (*0-9603470-0-3*) Tritone Music.

Oneida Community Staff. Annual Report: 1848-1851, 3 vols. in 1. LC 78-72358. (Free Love in America Ser.). reprint ed. 18.50 (*0-404-60982-1*) AMS Pr.

— Bible Communism: A Compilation from the Annual Reports & Other Publications of the Oneida Association & Its Branches. LC 72-2978. reprint ed. 27.50 (*0-404-10742-7*) AMS Pr.

— Hand-book of the Oneida Community, with a Sketch of Its Founder, & an Outline of Its Constitution & Doctrines, 3 vols in 1. Incl. Hand-Book of the Oneida Community, Containing a Brief Sketch of Its Present Condition, Internal Economy & Leading Principles. LC 72-2977. (*0-318-50597-5*); Mutual Criticism. LC 72-2977. (*0-318-50598-3*); LC 72-2977. reprint ed. 47.50 (*0-404-10741-9*) AMS Pr.

***Oneida County Historical Society Staff.** Focus on the Fifties: Utica & Vicinity. (Illus.). 1995. pap. write for info. (*0-925168-43-2*) North Country.

O'Neil & Brown. Adopting a Child. (Changing Behavior Through Understanding Ser.). 20p. (Orig.). 1991. pap. text ed. 2.95 (*1-56456-046-5*) W Gladden Found.

— Child Incest. (Changing Behavior Through Understanding Ser.). 20p. (Orig.). 1991. pap. text ed. 2.95 (*1-56456-052-X*) W Gladden Found.

— Kids Who Kill. 20p. 1995. 2.95 (*1-56456-092-9*) W Gladden Found.

— Sleep Disturbances in Early Childhood. 20p. 1993. 2.95 (*1-56456-085-6*, 283) W Gladden Found.

O'Neil, ed. see Barretto.

O'Neil, ed. see Grant & Wagner.

O'Neil, jt. auth. see Keyser.

O'Neil, ed. see Wagner, M.

O'Neil, et al. Shadow: Hitler's Astrologer. 64p. 1988. 12.95 (*0-87135-341-5*) Marvel Entmnt.

— The Shadow: Hitler's Astrologer. (Illus.). 64p. 1990. reprint ed. pap. 10.95 (*0-87135-664-3*) Marvel Entmnt.

O'Neil, A. W. & Palmer, Paul C. A Checklist of the Birds of Brooks County, Texas. 6p. (Orig.). 1988. pap. 0.50 (*0-9611604-4-6*) C Del Grullo.

O'Neil, Alice A., jt. auth. see O'Neil, Thomas E.

O'Neil, Amanda. Biblical Times. (Historical Facts Ser.). 1992. 12.99 (*0-517-06560-6*) Random Hse Value.

— Complete Book of the Dog. 19.98 (*1-55521-492-4*) Bk Sales Inc.

***O'Neil, Amanda & Hillyard, Paul.** I Wonder Why Spiders Spin Webs: And Other Questions about Creepy Crawlies. LC 94-45121. (I Wonder Why Ser.). (J). 1995. 8.95 (*1-85697-581-9*, Kingfisher LKC) LKC.

O'Neil, Barbara T. & Foreman, George C. The Prairie Print Makers. 2nd ed. Ellington, Howard W., ed. (Illus.). 60p. 1984. reprint ed. pap. 10.00 (*0-9614307-0-2*) Gallery Ellington.

O'Neil, Brian. Acting As a Business: Strategies for Success. LC 93-9183. 1993. pap. 13.95 (*0-435-08623-5*, 08623) Heinemann.

O'Neil, Brian, jt. auth. see Cohen, Elizabeth R.

O'Neil, Bryan H. Castles & Cannon. LC 74-30843. (Illus.). 121p. 1975. reprint ed. text ed. 35.00 (*0-8371-7933-5*, ONCC, Greenwood Pr) Greenwood.

***O'Neil, Buck & Wulf, Steve.** I Was Right on Time. 1996. 22.00 (*0-684-80305-4*) S&S Trade.

***O'Neil, Carle F.** Child Pornography. 20p. 1993. 2.95 (*1-56456-084-8*, 282) W Gladden Found.

O'Neil, Carle F. & Brown, Waln K. Blending Families with Children. 20p. 1992. 2.95 (*1-56456-069-4*, 268) W Gladden Found.

— Planning & Building a Step-Family. 20p. 1991. 2.95 (*1-56456-013-9*, 243) W Gladden Found.

O'Neil, Charles. Integrated Science Laboratory Manual. 128p. (C). 1992. spiral bd. 12.95 (*0-8403-8259-6*) Kendall-Hunt.

O'Neil, Charles J. Imprudence in Saint Thomas Aquinas. LC 55-9017. (Aquinas Lectures). 1955. 10.00 (*0-87462-120-8*) Marquette.

O'Neil, Christopher, ed. see DiMona, Joseph.

***O'Neil, D.** Batman: Forever Movie Adaptation. Peterson, ed. (Illus.). 64p. 1995. pap. 5.95 (*1-56389-199-9*) DC Comics.

— Batman - Punisher: Lake of Fire. Goodwin, A., ed. (Illus.). 48p. 1994. pap. 4.95 (*1-56389-161-1*) DC Comics.

O'Neil, D., ed. see Grant, A. & Dixon, C.

O'Neil, D., ed. see Harris, J. C.

O'Neil, D., ed. see Lusterbader, Eric.

O'Neil, D., ed. see Miller, Frank.

O'Neil, D., ed. see Moench, D., et al.

O'Neil, D., ed. see Moench, D.

***O'Neil, Daniel X.** Boilerplate: Koreshians, Potential Rioters, & Bureaucratic Complicity in American Self-Destruction: Being a List of Eight Ways in Which the Dead at Waco Were a Lot Like the Rest of Us. 32p. 1994. pap. 5.00 (*0-9646137-1-9*) Juggernaut.

— Bricks: A New Book of Poems by Daniel X. O'Neil. 53p. 1992. pap. 10.00 (*0-9646137-0-0*) Juggernaut.

—Memo to All Employees: Poetry by Daniel X. O'Neil. (Illus.). 48p. 1995. 12.00 (*0-9646137-2-7*) Juggernaut. MEMO TO ALL EMPLOYEES is the second book of poetry by Daniel X. O'Neil, a nationally-known performance poet based in Chicago. O'Neil bridges the printed gap between the thriving Spoken Word poetry movement & the publishing world. O'Neil draws his immediate, gripping style from the daily newspaper & his use of cultural figures from pop art. His performance moniker is "The Worldwide Entertainment Juggernaut of the 21st Century." Through superior graphic design he reduces a sweeping, grand performance style to the page in an electrifying way. Pre-World War I Futurism has helped shape his poetic mission, which places the poet at the center of society instead of on the freaky, inconsequential fringe. This volume has love poems, narrative portraits, & experiments in the Beat Breath. It also contains a verse drama & a poetic essay on the 1993 government raid on the Koreshians in Waco, Texas. Many poems have "stage directions" which set the tone & open up new levels of meaning. The result is a lively, highly literary, & gigantically entertaining volume of poetry that destroys the concept that poetry is a "tough sell." This book is dedicated to the public library. All book orders are taken directly through Juggernaut, P.O. Box 3824, Chicago, IL 60654-0824, or call 312-907- 8947. ***Publisher Provided Annotation.***

O'Neil, Dennis. Batman: Birth of the Demon. Goodwin, Archie, ed. 112p. 1993. pap. 12.95 (*1-56389-081-X*) DC Comics.

Oneil, Dennis. Batman: Knightfall. 1994. 19.95 (*0-553-09673-7*) Bantam.

O'Neil, Dennis. Batman: Shaman. Kahan, Bob, ed. 136p. 1992. pap. 12.95 (*1-56389-083-6*) DC Comics.

— Batman: Sword of Azrael. Kahan, Bob, ed. (Illus.). 112p. 1993. pap. 9.95 (*1-56389-100-X*) DC Comics.

— Batman: Tales of the Demon. Levitz, Paul et al, eds. (Illus.). 208p. (YA). 1991. pap. 17.95 (*0-930289-94-3*) DC Comics.

— Batman: Venom. Kahan, Bob, ed. (Illus.). 136p. (YA). 1993. pap. 9.95 (*1-56389-101-8*) DC Comics.

— Batman - Green Arrow: The Poison Tomorrow. Goodwin, Archie, ed. 64p. 1992. pap. 5.95 (*0-930289-15-3*) DC Comics.

— Green Lantern - Green Arrow: Hard Traveling Heroes, Vol. 1. Hill, Michael, ed. 176p. 1992. pap. 12.95 (*1-56389-038-0*) DC Comics.

— Green Lantern - Green Arrow: Hard Traveling Heroes, Vol. 2. Kahan, Bob, ed. 168p. 1993. pap. 12.95 (*1-56389-086-0*) DC Comics.

O'Neil, Dennis, ed. see Augustyn, Brian.

O'Neil, Dennis, ed. see Barr, Mike.

O'Neil, Dennis, ed. see Brennert, Alan.

O'Neil, Dennis, ed. see Byrne, John.

O'Neil, Dennis, ed. see Chaykin, H. & Moore, J. F.

O'Neil, Dennis, ed. see Maggin, Elliot S.

O'Neil, Dennis, ed. see Milligan, Peter.

O'Neil, Dennis, ed. see Moench, Doug.

O'Neil, Dennis, ed. see Moore, Alan.

O'Neil, Dennis, ed. see Newell, Mindy.

O'Neil, Dennis, ed. see Niven, Larry & Byrne, John.

O'Neil, Dennis, ed. see Ostrander, John.

O'Neil, Dennis, ed. see Starlin, Jim.

O'Neil, Dennis, ed. see Wagner, John & Grant, Alan.

O'Neil, Dennis, ed. see Wagner & Grant.

O'Neil, Dennis, et al. Batman: Shaman. 136p. 1993. 12.99 (*0-446-39522-6*) Warner Bks.

O'Neil, Denny, ed. see Moench, D.

O'Neil, Doris C. Life: The Sixties. (Illus.). 1989. 35.00 (*0-8212-1752-6*) Little.

O'Neil, Doris C., ed. see Eisenstaedt, Alfred.

O'Neil, Elizabeth M., ed. The Last Word: Letters Between Marcia Nardi & William Carlos Williams. LC 93-20999. (Illus.). 290p. 1994. text ed. 34.95 (*0-87745-445-0*); pap. 16.95 (*0-87745-461-2*) U of Iowa Pr.

***O'Neil, Eugene.** Long Voyage Home & Other Plays. (Thrift Editions Ser.). 1995. pap. 1.00 (*0-486-28755-6*) Dover.

O'Neil, Floyd A., ed. see Lyman, Stanley D.

O'Neil, Floyd A., jt. ed. see Milner, Clyde A., II.

O'Neil, Gerard. The High Frontier: Human Colonies in Space. (Illus.). 326p. 1989. pap. 9.95 (*0-9622379-0-6*) SSIP.

O'Neil, Gisela, ed. see Steiner, Rudolf.

O'Neil, Gladys, jt. ed. see Helfrich, G. W.

O'Neil, Harold & Drillings, Michael, eds. Motivation: Theory & Research. 328p. 1994. text ed. 69.95 (*0-8058-1286-5*); pap. 29.95 (*0-8058-1287-3*) L Erlbaum Assocs.

O'Neil, Harold F., Jr., ed. Learning Strategies. (Educational Technology Ser.). 1978. text ed. 43.00 (*0-12-526650-2*) Acad Pr.

— Procedures for Instructional Systems Development. LC 79-12002. (Educational Technology Ser.). 1979. text ed. 52.00 (*0-12-526660-X*) Acad Pr.

O'Neil, Harold F. & Baker, Eva L., eds. Technology Assessment, 2 vols., Vol. II. 296p. 1994. 59.95 (*0-8058-1248-2*) L Erlbaum Assocs.

O'Neil, Harold F., Jr. & Spielberger, Charles D., eds. Cognitive & Affective Learning Strategies. LC 79-18162. (Educational Technology Ser.). 1979. text ed. 52.00 (*0-12-526680-4*) Acad Pr.

O'Neil, Harold F., jt. ed. see Baker, Eva L.

O'Neil, Isabel. The Art of the Painted Finish for Furniture & Decoration. LC 70-151928. (Illus.). 1980. reprint ed. pap. 18.45 (*0-688-06070-6*, Quill) Morrow.

O'Neil, J. J. The Prodigal Genius: The Life & Mind of Nikola Tesla. (Nikola Tesla Ser.). 1986. lib. bdg. 79.95 (*0-8490-3839-1*) Gordon Pr.

O'Neil, James. Qwik-Sane: Topological Puzzle. 1970. 3.00 (*0-911624-10-4*) Wffn Proof.

O'Neil, James B. Workers Compensation & Employers. 1991. 39.50 (*1-56461-036-5*, 46090) Rough Notes.

O'Neil, James L. The Origins & Development of Ancient Greek Democracy. (Greek Studies: Interdisciplinary Approaches). 195p. 1994. lib. bdg. 54.50 (*0-8476-7956-X*); pap. 22.95 (*0-8476-7957-8*) Rowman.

O'Neil, James M., jt. ed. see Conyne, Robert K.

O'Neil, John. Plato's Cave. 224p. 1991. text ed. 35.00 (*0-89391-722-2*); pap. 22.50 (*1-56750-080-3*) Ablex Pub.

— Raising Our Sights: Improving U. S. Mathematics & Science Achievement. LC 91-32235. 40p. 1991. pap. 6.50 (*0-87120-187-9*, 611-91170) Assn Supervision.

O'Neil, John R. Paradox of Success: Personal & Organizational Renewal for Leaders. 240p. 1994. pap. 12.95 (*0-685-74801-4*) J P Tarcher.

— The Paradox of Success: Personal & Organizational Renewal for Leaders. 240p. 1993. 19.95 (*0-87477-707-0*) J P Tarcher.

O'Neil, Karen E. Health & Medicine Projects for Young Scientists. LC 92-42745. (Projects for Young Scientists Ser.). (Illus.). 128p. (J). (gr. 8-9). 1993. lib. bdg. 14.77 (*0-531-11050-8*) Watts.

— Health & Medicine Projects for Young Scientists. LC 92-42745. (Projects for Young Scientists Ser.). (Illus.). 128p. (YA). (gr. 8-9). 1993. pap. 6.95 (*0-531-15668-0*) Watts.

O'Neil, Kevin. American Buddhist Directory. 2nd ed. 116p. (Orig.). 1985. pap. 20.00 (*0-685-11198-9*) Crises Res Pr.

— The American Buddhist Directory, 1982. 96p. 1982. pap. 7.00 (*0-86627-003-5*) Crises Res Pr.

O

— Awakening of Faith in Mahayana. (Orig.). 1984. pap. 14.95 (*0-685-09623-8*) Crises Res Pr.

— Basic Buddhism. 41p. (Orig.). 1981. pap. 5.00 (*0-86627-006-X*) Crises Res Pr.

— The Diamond Sutra. 1978. pap. 5.00 (*0-86627-004-3*) Crises Res Pr.

— How to Protect Your Family from Terrorists. 106p. 1979. pap. 15.00 (*0-86627-007-8*) Crises Res Pr.

— An Introduction to Nichiren Shoshu Buddhism. 111p. 1980. pap. 5.00 (*0-86627-002-7*) Crises Res Pr.

— Realm of Totality. 49p. (Orig.). 1984. pap. 6.00 (*0-86627-011-6*) Crises Res Pr.

O'Neil, Kevin, ed. The Sutra Spoken by Vimilakirti. pap. 6.00 (*0-86627-009-4*) Crises Res Pr.

O'Neil, Kevin R. What to Tell Your Children about Cults. 52p. (Orig.). 1982. pap. 9.95 (*0-86627-001-9*) Crises Res Pr.

O'Neil, Kevin R., ed. American Buddhist Newsletter: 1981-82, Vol. I. 136p. (Orig.). 1982. pap. 35.00 (*0-86627-000-0*) Crises Res Pr.

O'Neil, Kitty & Libby, Bill. Kitty: A Story of Triumph in a Soundless World. LC 81-9664. (Illus.). 256p. Date not set. write for info. (*0-688-00355-9*) Morrow.

O'Neil, Laurie A. Little Rock: The Desegregation of Central High. LC 93-29057. (Spotlight on American History Ser.). (Illus.). 64p. (J). (gr. 4-6). 1994. lib. bdg. 15.40 (*1-56294-354-5*) Millbrook Pr.

O'Neil, Marie H. The Whispering Winds of Chapel Road. LC 91-77625. (Illus.). 114p. (Orig.). 1993. pap. 6.50 (*1-56002-184-5*) Aegina Pr.

O'Neil, Mike. Power to Choose: Twelve Steps to Wholeness. 209p. 1991. pap. 19.95 (*0-9633454-0-0*) Sonlight Pub.

***O'Neil, Mike & Nightingale, Peggy, eds.** Achieving Quality in Higher Education. 220p. 1994. pap. 42.00x (*0-7494-1325-5*, Pub. by Kogan Page Educ UK) Taylor & Francis.

***O'Neil, Mike S. & Newbold, Charles E., Jr.** Boundary Power: How I Treat You, How I Let You Treat Me, How I Treat Myself. 190p. (Orig.). 1995. pap. 19.95 (*0-9633454-2-7*) Sonlight Pub.

— The Church As a Healing Community: Setting up Shop to Deal with the Pain of Life-Controlling Problems. 177p. (Orig.). 1995. pap. 19.95 (*0-9633454-1-9*) Sonlight Pub.

O'Neil, P. Fundamental Concepts of Topology. 336p. 1972. text ed. 190.00 (*0-677-03420-2*) Gordon & Breach.

O'Neil, Pat. Explore Cape Breton: A Field Guide to Adventure. (Illus.). 176p. 1994. pap. 10.95 (*1-55109-085-6*, Pub. by Nimbus Publishing Ltd CN) Chelsea Green Pub.

— What Now? 60p. (Orig.). 1989. pap. text ed. 7.95 (*0-9627243-0-0*) Pat Pubns.

— What Now?! (This Book Is User Friendly) 61p. 1991. Tchr's. ed. teacher ed 7.95 (*0-9627243-1-9*) Pat Pubns.

O'Neil, Patricia. Robert Browning & Twentieth-Century Criticism. (Studies in English & American Literature, Linguistics, & Culture). 180p. 1995. 54.95 (*1-879751-92-5*) Camden Hse.

O'Neil, Patrick. Database Systems: Principles, Programming & Performance. LC 94-26710. 873p. 1994. 54.95 (*1-55860-219-4*) Morgan Kaufmann.

***O'Neil, Patrick B.** The Cosmology of John Ross. LC 94-61226. 136p. (Orig.). 1995. 10.00 (*1-884570-14-3*) Research Triangle.

O

O'Neil, Paul. The Expert Salesperson. (Illus.). 80p. (Orig.). 1989. pap. write for info. (*0-9623451-0-5*) P ONeil.

O'Neil, Peter V. Advanced Engineering Mathematics. 3rd ed. 1460p. (C). 1991. text ed. 79.95 (*0-534-13584-6*) PWS Pubs.

— Advanced Engineering Mathematics. 4th ed. LC 94-35425. 1248p. 1995. text ed. 79.95 (*0-534-94320-9*) PWS Pubs.

O'Neil, R., et al. New Dimensions: Advanced Level. (Illus.). 1993. teacher ed 18.95 (*0-8013-0921-2*); student ed 7.95 (*0-8013-0927-1*); pap. text ed. 13.95 (*0-8013-0607-8*); audio 24.95 (*0-8013-0926-3*) Longman.

O'Neil, Robert M. The Courts, Government, & Higher Education. LC 72-90171. 40p. 1972. pap. 1.00 (*0-87186-237-9*) Comm Econ Dev.

— Discriminating Against Discrimination: Preferential Admissions & the DeFunis Case. LC 75-3888. 282p. reprint ed. pap. 80.40 (*0-685-20431-6*, 2056433) Bks Demand.

— The Rights of Public Employees: The Basic ACLU Guide to the Rights of Public Employees. rev. ed. LC 93-17474. (American Civil Liberties Union Handbook Ser.). 163p. (C). 1993. pap. 7.95 (*0-8093-1928-4*) S Ill U Pr.

— The Rights of Public Employees: The Basic ACLU Guide to the Rights of Public Employees. 2nd rev. ed. LC 93-17474. (American Civil Liberties Union Handbook Ser.). 163p. (C). 1993. 24.95x (*0-8093-1927-6*) S Ill U Pr.

O'Neil, Robert M., et al. No Heroes, No Villains: New Perspectives on Kent State & Jackson State. LC 72-6044. (Jossey-Bass Higher Education Ser.). 189p. reprint ed. pap. 53.90 (*0-317-42369-X*, 2052162) Bks Demand.

O'Neil, Rosanna M. Total Quality Management in Libraries: A Sourcebook. 125p. 1994. pap. text ed. 25.00 (*1-56308-247-0*) Libs Unl.

O'Neil, Sally M., jt. auth. see Cassingham, Barbee J.

O'Neil, Sharon L. Information Systems. 3rd ed. 1989. teacher ed (*0-07-047819-8*); pap. 23.60 (*0-07-047818-X*) McGraw.

O'Neil, Sharon L., jt. auth. see Robbins, Stephen P.

O'Neil, Thomas. Sex with God. rev. ed. LC 93-61845. (Illus.). 168p. (Orig.). 1994. pap. 6.95 (*0-9622398-1-X*) Indulgence Pr.

O'Neil, Thomas E. & O'Neil, Alice A. The Custers in Monroe. (Illus.). 21p. (Orig.). 1991. pap. text ed. write for info. (*0-940696-25-8*) Monroe County Lib.

O'Neil, Thomas J., ed. Application of Computers & Operations Research in the Mineral Industry: 16th International Symposium. LC 79-52273. (Illus.). 651p. 1979. text ed. 10.00 (*0-89520-261-1*) SMM&E Inc.

O'Neil, Thomas J., ed. see Society of Mining Engineers of AIME Staff.

***O'Neil, Vincent.** Things My Mother Tried to Teach Me. (Illus.). 89p. 1994. 9.95 (*0-9644938-0-2*) RVON Enter.

— Who Am I? The Mysterious Search for My Identity. (Illus.). 182p. 1994. 19.95 (*0-9644938-1-0*) RVON Enter.

O'Neil, William J. How to Make Money in Stocks: A Winning System in Good Times or Bad. 256p. 1988. text ed. 22.95 (*0-07-047760-4*); audio 9.95 (*0-07-047791-4*) McGraw.

— How to Make Money in Stocks: A Winning System in Good Times or Bad. rev. ed. 224p. 1991. pap. text ed. 9.95 (*0-07-047893-7*) McGraw.

— How to Make Money in Stocks: A Winning System in Good Times or Bad. 2nd ed. LC 94-28192. 1994. pap. text ed. 10.95 (*0-07-048017-6*) McGraw.

— How to Make Money in Stocks: A Winning System in Good Times or Bad. 2nd ed. LC 94-28192. 1994. 22.95 (*0-07-048059-1*) McGraw.

O'Neil, William L. American High: The Years of Confidence, 1945-1960. 1987. 27.95 (*0-02-923680-0*) Free Pr.

O'Neill. Farewell to the Gipper. (Illus.). 1990. pap. 12.95 (*0-913035-52-1*) Eclipse Bks.

O'Neill, jt. auth. see Mills.

***O'Neill, Aidan & Coppel, Jason.** EC Law for U. K. Lawyers: The Domestic Impact of EC Law in the U. K. 278p. 1994. pap. text ed. 40.00 (*0-406-02459-6*, UK) Butterworth Legal Pubs.

***O'Neill, Aidan & Vaughan, David.** Decisions of the European Court of Justice & Their National Implications. 315p. 1994. pap. text ed. 193.00 (*0-406-02896-6*, UK) Butterworth Legal Pubs.

O'Neill, Alan, ed. Dynamics, Transport & Photochemistry in the Middle Atmosphere of the Southern Hemisphere. (NATO Advanced Science Institutes Series C: Mathematical & Physical Sciences). 268p. 1990. lib. bdg. 99.50 (*0-7923-0977-4*) Kluwer Ac.

O'Neill, Alexis. Syracuse: The Heart of New York. 1988. 34.95 (*0-89781-275-1*, 5219) Preferred Mktg.

O'Neill, Amanda, jt. auth. see Stanford, Maureen.

O'Neill, Ana Maria. Psicologia de la Comunicacion. 541p. (SPA.). 1987. reprint ed. 11.75 (*0-8477-2907-9*) U of PR Pr.

O'Neill, Ana Maria, et al. Etica Comercial: Una Filosofia para la Libre Empresa. (C). 1986. reprint ed. pap. 6.00 (*0-8477-2624-X*) U of PR Pr.

O'Neill, Angus, jt. ed. see Bernard, Leo.

O'Neill, Ann M. Quimper Pottery. LC 94-65615. (Illus.). 160p. (Orig.). 1994. pap. 16.95 (*0-88740-650-5*) Schiffer.

***O'Neill, Arthur.** Enemies Within & Without. Date not set. pap. 24.95 (*1-86324-413-1*, Pub. by LaTrobe Univ AT) Intl Spec Bk.

O'Neill, Audrey M. Clinical Inference: How to Draw Meaningful Conclusions from Psychological Tests. LC 92-52846. 1992. pap. 24.95 (*0-88422-117-2*) Clinical Psych.

O'Neill, B. E. Insurgency & Terrorism: Inside Modern Revolutionary Warfare. 181p. 1990. 22.00 (*0-08-037456-5*) Brasseys Inc.

O'Neill, Barbara. Saving on a Shoestring. 224p. 1994. pap. 15.95 (*0-7931-1118-8*, 568009-01) Dearborn Finan.

O'Neill, Barrett. Elementary Differential Geometry. 1966. text ed. 61.00 (*0-12-526750-9*) Acad Pr.

— The Geometry of Kerr Black Holes. LC 93-21643. (Illus.). 430p. (C). 1995. text ed. 79.95 (*1-56881-019-9*) AK Peters.

— Semi-Riemannian Geometry: With Applications to Relativity. (Pure & Applied Mathematics Ser.). 1983. text ed. 84.00 (*0-12-526740-1*) Acad Pr.

O'Neill, Basil, jt. ed. see Gowland, David.

O'Neill, Bertram L. Descendants of Joshua Ballinger Lippincott & Josephine Craige of Philadelphia: A Line Chart, 1813-1992. 90p. 1992. 45.00 (*0-9631783-0-X*) B L ONeill.

O'Neill, Blane, jt. auth. see Wolter, Allan B.

O'Neill, Brian. Half a Wing, Three Engines & a Prayer: B-17s over Germany. 1989. pap. text ed. 18.95 (*0-07-156533-7*) McGraw.

O'Neill, Brian, ed. Let's Write about It: The Indiana Experience. x, 124p. (Orig.). 1989. pap. 10.95 (*0-9624180-0-5*) Stone Hills Area Lib Servs.

O'Neill, Brian D. Half a Wing, Three Engines & a Prayer: B-17s over Germany. (Illus.). 224p. 1989. pap. 16.95 (*0-8306-8385-2*, 22385, TAB-Aero) TAB Bks.

O'Neill, Brian F., ed. Let's Write about It, Vol. 2: The Indiana Experience. 170p. (Orig.). 1991. pap. 10.95 (*0-9624180-2-1*) Stone Hills Area Lib Servs.

O'Neill, Brian J. Social Inequality in a Portuguese Hamlet: Land, Late Marriage, & Bastardy, 1870-1978. (Cambridge Studies in Social & Cultural Anthropology: No. 63). (Illus.). 464p. 1987. 79.95 (*0-521-32284-7*) Cambridge U Pr.

O'Neill-Butler, Marjorie & Sonnichsen, Ingrid, eds. The Source: The Greater Boston Theatre Resource Guide. (Orig.). 1989. spiral bd. 19.95 (*0-685-29415-3*) StageSource.

O'Neill, C., jt. auth. see Johnson, L.

O'Neill, Catherine. Amazing Mysteries of the World. Crump, Donald J., ed. LC 83-13444. (Books for World Explorers Series 5: No. 1). 104p. (J). (gr. 3-8). 1983. lib. bdg. 12.50 (*0-87044-502-2*) Natl Geog.

— The Daffodil Farmer. LC 79-63168. (Series Four). 44p. 1979. pap. 7.00 (*0-931846-09-9*) Wash Writers Pub.

— Dogs on Duty. LC 88-15933. (Books for World Explorers Series 9: No. 4). (Illus.). 104p. (J). (gr. 4 up). 1988. lib. bdg. 12.50 (*0-87044-664-9*) Natl Geog.

— Focus on Alcohol. (Drug-Alert Ser.). (Illus.). 56p. (J). (gr. 2-4). 1991. lib. bdg. 14.98 (*0-941477-96-7*) TFC Bks NY.

— Let's Visit a Chocolate Factory. LC 87-3460. (Illus.). 32p. (J). (gr. 2-4). 1988. lib. bdg. 10.79 (*0-8167-1161-5*); pap. text ed. 2.95 (*0-8167-1162-3*) Troll Assocs.

— Let's Visit a Printing Plant. LC 87-3484. (Illus.). 32p. (J). (gr. 2-4). 1988. lib. bdg. 10.79 (*0-8167-1163-1*); pap. text ed. 2.95 (*0-8167-1164-X*) Troll Assocs.

— Natural Wonders of North America. Crump, Donald J., ed. LC 84-16614. (Books for World Explorers Series 6: No. 1). (Illus.). 104p. (J). (gr. 3-8). 1984. 8.95 (*0-87044-514-6*); lib. bdg. 12.50 (*0-87044-519-7*) Natl Geog.

***O'Neill, Cecily.** Drama Worlds: A Framework for Process Drama. LC 95-8111. (Dimensions of Drama Ser.). 169p. 1995. pap. text ed. 19.50 (*0-435-08671-5*) Heinemann.

O'Neill, Cecily & Lambert, Alan. Drama Structures: A Practical Handbook for Teachers. 244p. (Orig.). 1982. pap. 36.50 (*0-7487-0191-5*, Pub. by Stanley Thornes UK) Trans-Atl Phila.

O'Neill, Cecily, et al. Drama Guidelines. 75p. (C). 1977. pap. text ed. 15.00 (*0-435-18670-1*) Heinemann.

O'Neill, Charles E. Viel: Louisiana's Firstborn Author with Evandre, the First Literary Creation of a Native of the Mississippi Valley. LC 90-84994. 96p. (FRE.). (C). 1991. 10.00 (*0-940984-65-2*) U of SW LA Ctr LA Studies.

***O'Neill, Cherry B.** Dear Cherry: Questions & Answers on Eating Disorders. 144p. 1987. pap. 8.95 (*0-8264-0387-5*) Crossroad NY.

— Starving for Attention: A Young Woman's Struggle with & Triumph over Anorexia Nervosa. 2nd rev. ed. Unseth, Nathan, ed. 240p. 1992. pap. 12.95 (*0-89638-274-5*) Hazelden.

O'Neill, Cherry B., jt. auth. see O'Neill, Dan.

O'Neill, Christine, ed. see Senn, Fritz.

O'Neill, Colman. Meeting Christ in the Sacraments. LC 90-25917. 328p. 1991. pap. 16.95 (*0-8189-0598-0*) Alba.

O'Neill, Craig & Ritter, Kathleen. Coming Out Within: Stages of Spiritual Awakening for Lesbians & Gay Men. LC 91-55287. 256p. 1992. pap. 11.00 (*0-06-250706-0*) Harper SF.

O'Neill, Dan. The Return. 146p. (Orig.). (C). 1984. pap. 2.50 (*0-931660-05-X*) R Oman Pub.

O'Neill, Dan & O'Neill, Cherry B. Living on the Border of Disorder. 224p. (Orig.). 1992. pap. 7.99 (*1-55661-262-1*) Bethany Hse.

O'Neill, Dan & Wagner, Donald E. The Peace Accord: How Does It Fit into God's Plan? LC 93-39357. 112p. 1993. pap. 7.99 (*0-310-44401-2*) Zondervan.

O'Neill, Dan, jt. auth. see Talbot, John M.

O'Neill, Daniel J. Menopause & Its Effects on the Family. LC 81-43827. 66p. (Orig.). 1982. pap. text ed. 15.00 (*0-8191-2500-8*) U Pr of Amer.

— Public Speaking: Planning, Patterning & Presenting. 164p. (Orig.). (C). 1992. pap. text ed. 12.95x (*0-89641-205-9*) American Pr.

O'Neill, Daniel J., jt. auth. see Damron, O. Rex.

O'Neill, Daniel T. The Firecracker Boys. 384p. 1994. 24.95 (*0-312-11183-5*) St Martin.

O'Neill, Dave M., jt. auth. see O'Neill, June E.

O'Neill, Deirdre, jt. auth. see Afford, John.

O'Neill, Dell. Only the Wind & the Sea Were My Friends. 160p. (C). 1989. text ed. 65.00 (*1-872795-99-4*, Pub. by Pentland Pr UK) St Mut.

O'Neill, Dorothy P. Beyond Endearment. 1993. 13.95 (*0-8034-9037-2*) Bouregy.

— Change of Heart. 1993. 13.95 (*0-8034-8983-8*) Bouregy.

— Heart's Choice. 1993. 13.95 (*0-8034-9013-5*) Bouregy.

O'Neill, Eamonn P., jt. auth. see McGinley, Ken.

O'Neill, Edward L. Introduction to Statistical Optics. rev. ed. LC 92-23179. (Illus.). 179p. 1992. reprint ed. pap. text ed. 6.95 (*0-486-67328-6*) Dover.

O'Neill, Edward N., jt. auth. see Hock, Ronald F.

O'Neill, Elizabeth S. Mountain Sage - The Life Story of Carl Sharsmith, Yosemite Ranger - Naturalist. (Illus.). 220p. (Orig.). 1988. pap. 7.95 (*0-939666-47-2*) Yosemite Assn.

O'Neill, Erin & Morgan, Ella J. When Women Dive: A Female's Guide to Both Diving & Snorkeling. 1992. pap. 12.95 (*0-922769-11-7*) Watersport Pub.

O'Neill, Eugene. Anna Christie. Bd. with Emperor Jones. LC 72-4211.; Hairy Ape. LC 72-4211. LC 72-4211. 1972. Set pap. 8.00 (*0-394-71855-0*, Vin) Random.

— Beyond the Horizon. 1948. pap. 4.75 (*0-8222-0112-7*) Dramatists Play.

— Beyond the Horizon. 1994. lib. bdg. 21.95x (*1-56849-514-5*) Buccaneer Bks.

— Children of the Sea. Atkinson, Jennifer, ed. 1972. 25.00 (*0-910972-14-1*) Bruccoli.

— Children of the Sea. limited ed. Atkinson, Jennifer, ed. 1972. 50.00 (*0-910972-15-X*) Bruccoli.

— Chris Christophersen: A Play in Three Acts. LC 82-40135. 150p. 1982. 15.00 (*0-394-52531-0*) Random.

— Collected Plays of Eugene O'Neill, Vol. II. 1986. pap. 17.95 (*0-452-26358-1*, Plume) NAL-Dutton.

— Complete Plays, 3 vols. Bogard, Travis, ed. 1988. Vol. I, 1913-1920. 35.00 (*0-940450-48-8*); Vol. II, 1920-1931. 35.00 (*0-940450-49-6*); Vol. III, 1932-1943. 35.00 (*0-940450-50-X*) Library of America.

— Hughie. 1982. pap. 2.75 (*0-8222-0543-2*) Dramatists Play.

— Hughie. 1982. pap. 5.95 (*0-300-02881-4*, Y-431) Yale U Pr.

— Iceman Cometh. 1957. pap. 8.00 (*0-394-70018-X*) Random.

— Later Plays. 1988. pap. 7.25 (*0-394-30991-X*) Random.

O'Neill, Eugene, Jr. The Later Plays. Bogard, Travis, ed. 1967. pap. text ed. write for info. (*0-07-553664-1*) McGraw.

O'Neill, Eugene. Long Day's Journey into Night. 1950. 18.50 (*0-300-04600-6*) Yale U Pr.

— Long Day's Journey into Night. 1962. pap. 8.00 (*0-300-04601-4*) Yale U Pr.

— Long Day's Journey into Night. braille ed. 264p. 1993. vinyl bd. 21.12 (*1-56956-437-X*, BR9137) W A T Braille.

— Long Day's Journey into the Night. 17.95 (*0-89190-370-4*, Am Repr) Amereon Ltd.

— The Long Voyage Home: Seven Plays of the Sea. 19.95 (*0-89190-369-0*, Am Repr) Amereon Ltd.

— Lost Plays of Eugene O'Neill. 160p. 1993. reprint ed. pap. text ed. 6.95 (*0-486-27796-8*) Dover.

— Moon for the Misbegotten. LC 74-5218. 1974. pap. 7.00 (*0-394-71236-6*, Vin) Random.

— More Stately Mansions. abr. ed. Gallup, Donald, ed. (Illus.). (Orig.). 1964. pap. 11.00 (*0-300-00177-0*, Y101) Yale U Pr.

— More Stately Mansions: The Unexpurgated Edition. Bower, Martha, ed. (Illus.). 328p. 1988. 42.00 (*0-19-505364-8*) OUP.

— Nine Plays. 1993. 20.00 (*0-679-60045-0*, Modern Lib) Random.

— Nine Plays of Eugene O'Neill. LC 46-45216. 1977. 14.95 (*0-394-60416-4*, Modern Lib) Random.

— The Plays of Eugene O'Neill, 3 vols., I. LC 83-42952. 1983. 10.95 (*0-394-60807-0*, Modern Lib) Random.

— The Plays of Eugene O'Neill, 3 vols., II. LC 83-42952. 1983. 10.95 (*0-394-60805-4*, Modern Lib) Random.

— The Plays of Eugene O'Neill, 3 vols., III. LC 83-42952. 1983. 10.95 (*0-394-60806-2*, Modern Lib) Random.

— Selected Letters of Eugene O'Neill. Bogard, Travis & Bryer, Jackson, eds. (Illus.). (C). 1988. 48.00 (*0-300-04374-0*) Yale U Pr.

— Seven Plays of the Sea. 199p. 1972. pap. 9.00 (*0-394-71856-9*, Vin) Random.

— Six Plays. 1976. 22.95 (*0-8488-0600-X*) Amereon Ltd.

— Ten "Lost" Plays. 320p. 1995. pap. text ed. 8.95 (*0-486-28367-4*) Dover.

— The Theatre We Worked for: The Letters of Eugene O'Neill to Kenneth Macgowan. Bryer, Jackson R., ed. LC 81-299. (Illus.). 292p. (C). 1982. 37.00 (*0-300-02583-1*) Yale U Pr.

— A Touch of the Poet. 1973. reprint ed. pap. 4.75 (*0-8222-1393-1*) Dramatists Play.

— The Unknown O'Neill: Unpublished & Unfamiliar Writings of Eugene O'Neill. Bogard, Travis, ed. LC 87-24637. 352p. (C). 1988. 48.00 (*0-300-03985-9*) Yale U Pr.

O'Neill, Eugene, Jr., ed. Seven Famous Greek Plays. 1950. pap. text ed. write for info. (*0-07-553629-3*) McGraw.

O'Neill, Eugene S., ed. The Psychiatric Emergency: Its Recognition & Management. LC 85-21986. (Emergency Health Services Review Ser.: Vol. 3, No. 1). 128p. 1986. text ed. 39.95 (*0-86656-518-3*) Haworth Pr.

O'Neill, Evelyn. Aussie Soft Toys. (Lothian Australian Craft Ser.). (Illus.). 64p. (Orig.). 1995. pap. 14.95 (*0-85091-483-3*, Pub. by Lothian Pub AT) Seven Hills Bk.

— Easy Ribbon Embroidery. (Lothian Australian Craft Ser.). (Illus.). 64p. (Orig.). 1995. pap. 14.95 (*0-85091-561-9*, Pub. by Lothian Pub AT) Seven Hills Bk.

O'Neill, Francis. Irish Minstrels & Musicians: Story of Irish Music. 497p. 1987. pap. 30.00 (*0-85342-801-8*, Pub. by Mercier Pr IE) Dufour.

— O'Neill's Irish Music. 1987. pap. 21.00 (*0-85342-800-X*) Dufour.

O'Neill, Frank Q., jt. ed. see Greene, Harlan.

O'Neill, George & O'Neill, Nena. Open Marriage: A New Lifestyle for Couples. LC 75-164550. 300p. (C). 1975. reprint ed. pap. 8.95 (*0-87131-438-X*) M Evans.

O'Neill, Gerard & Lehr, Dick. The Underboss: The Rise & Fall of a Mafia Family. (Illus.). 1989. mass mkt. 4.95 (*0-312-91731-7*) St Martin.

O'Neill, Gerard K., ed. Space-Based Manufacturing from Nonterrestrial Materials. LC 77-15130. (PAAS Ser.: Vol. 57). (Illus.). 177p. 1977. 34.95 (*0-915928-21-3*) AIAA.

O'Neill, Harold F. Effects of Stress on State Anxiety & Performance in Computer-Assisted Learning. LC 79-136729. 1970. 25.00 (*0-403-04525-8*) Scholarly.

O'Neill, Helen, ed. Third World Debt: How Sustainable Are Current Strategies & Solutions? 1990. text ed. 32.00 (*0-7146-3409-3*, Pub. by F Cass Pubs UK) Intl Spec Bk.

***O'Neill, Holly A. & AACRAO-AID Project Staff.** Afghanistan. LC 95-15772. (OIES Country Guide Ser.). 1995. write for info. (*0-929851-39-0*) Am Assn Coll Registrars.

O'Neill, Hugh. Creating Opportunity: Strategies for Reducing Poverty Through Economic Development. LC 85-5931. 207p. 1985. 16.95 (*0-934842-41-8*) CSPA.

— Police Officer. 1994. pap. 14.00 (*0-671-89231-2*) P-H.

— Woodturning: A Guide to Advanced Techniques. (Illus.). 192p. 1995. 39.95 (*1-85223-836-4*, Pub. by Crowood UK) Trafalgar.

— Woodturning: A Manual of Techniques. (Illus.). 192p. 1993. pap. 24.95 (*1-85223-723-6*, Pub. by Crowood Pr UK) Trafalgar.

O'Neill, Hugh B. Companion to Chinese History. 416p. 1987. 27.50 (*0-87196-841-X*) Facts on File.

— Companion to Chinese History. 416p. 1988. pap. 14.95 (*0-8160-1825-1*) Facts on File.

O'Neill, Hugh E., et al. Police Officer. 11th ed. (Illus.). 464p. 1992. pap. 14.00 (*0-13-678624-3*, Arco Test) P-H Gen Ref & Trav.

O'Neill, Hugh M., jt. auth. see Hoffman, Alan N.

O'Neill, I. K., jt. ed. see Fishbein, L.

An Asterisk (*) at the beginning of an entry indicates that the title is appearing in BIP for the first time.

O'Neill, I. K., et al, eds. Environmental Carcinogens: Methods of Analysis & Exposure Measurement, Vol. 9- Passive Smoking. (IARC Scientific Publications: No. 81). (Illus.). 414p. 1988. 80.00 (*92-832-1181-2*) OUP.
— Relevance to Human Cancer of N-Nitroso Compounds, Tobacco Smoke & Mycotoxins. (IARC Scientific Publications: No. 105). (Illus.). 642p. 1991. pap. 150.00 (*92-832-2105-2*) OUP.

O'Neill, J. The Ultimate Test of Television Trivia. 1994. pap. 9.99 (*0-06-100627-0*, PL) HarpC.

O'Neill, J. C. The Bible's Authority: A Portrait Gallery of Thinkers from Lessing to Bultmann. 312p. 1991. pap. 29. 95 (*0-567-29189-8*, Pub. by T & T Clark UK) Bks Intl VA.

***O'Neill, J. Michael, ed.** Table Mountain Quartzite & Moose Formation (New Names) & Associated Rocks of the Middle Proterozoic Belt Supergroup, Highland Mountains, Southwestern Montana. LC 95-3665. (Belt Supergroup in the Highland Mountains & Probable Equivalent Rocks in the Pioneer & Anaconda Ranges Bulletin Ser.: Vol. 2121). 1995. write for info. (*0-615-00519-5*) US Geol Survey.

O'Neill, Jack. Stress Busters: Twenty-One Thoughts for Your Emotional Wellness. 160p. 1993. pap. 9.95 (*1-883000-00-9*) Derrymore West.

O'Neill, Jaime. What Do You Know? An All New Test of Common (& Not So Common) Knowledge, Vol. 2. 1992. pap. 11.00 (*0-553-35436-1*) Bantam.
— What Do You Know? The Ultimate Test of Common (& Not So Common) Knowledge. 272p. 1990. pap. 10.00 (*0-553-34880-9*) Bantam.

***O'Neill, James.** Terror on Tape: A Complete Guide to Over 2,000 Horror Movies on Video. LC 94-25496. 400p. 1994. pap. 16.95 (*0-8230-7612-1*, Billboard Bks) Watsn-Guptill.

O'Neill, James A., Jr., jt. ed. see Dean, Richard H.

O'Neill, James E. & Krauskopf, Robert, eds. World War II: An Account of Its Documents. LC 74-34112. (National Archives Conference Ser.: Vol. 8). (Illus.). 1976. 19.50 (*0-88258-053-1*) Howard U Pr.

O'Neill, James Milton. Religion & Education Under the Constitution. LC 72-171389. (Civil Liberties in American History Ser.). 338p. 1972. reprint ed. lib. bdg. 39.50 (*0-306-70228-2*) Da Capo.

O'Neill, James P. The Mystic Policeman. Chirich, Nancy, ed. LC 87-6589. 208p. (Orig.). 1987. pap. 6.95 (*0-912761-08-3*) Cliffhanger Pr.

O'Neill, Joan. Daisy Chain War. (Bright Sparks Ser.). 256p. (Orig.). (YA). 1990. pap. 9.99 (*1-85594-004-3*, Pub. by Attic IE) InBook.
— Promised. 352p. (Orig.). (C). 1991. pap. 9.99 (*1-85594-025-6*, Pub. by Attic IE) InBook.

O'Neill, John. The Communicative Body: Studies in Communicative Philosophy, Politics & Sociology. (Studies in Phenomenology & Existential Philosophy). 264p. 1989. pap. 15.95 (*0-8101-0802-X*) Northwestern U Pr.
— Critical Conventions: Interpretation in the Literary Arts & Sciences. LC 91-50868. (Project for Discourse & Theory Ser.: Vol. 8). (Illus.). 352p. 1992. 34.95 (*0-8061-2378-8*) U of Okla Pr.
— Critical Conventions: Interpretation in the Literary Arts & Sciences. LC 91-50868. (Project for Discourse & Theory Ser.: Vol. 8). (Illus.). 354p. 1992. pap. text ed. 14.95 (*0-8061-2445-8*) U of Okla Pr.
— Ecology, Policy, & Politics: Human Well-Being & the Natural World. LC 93-16367. (Environmental Philosophies Ser.). 240p. 1994. 59.95 (*0-415-07299-9*, B2474, Routledge NY); pap. 15.95 (*0-415-07300-6*, B2478, Routledge NY) Routledge.
— Five Bodies: The Human Shape of Modern Society. LC 84-22947. (Illus.). 184p. 1985. 32.50 (*0-8014-1727-9*); pap. 12.95 (*0-8014-9455-9*) Cornell U Pr.
— For Marx Against Althusser & Other Essays. LC 82-17353. (Current Continental Research Ser.). (Illus.). 192p. (Orig.). 1983. pap. text ed. 19.50 (*0-8191-2816-3*) U Pr of Amer.
— Hegel's Dialectic of Recognition & Desire: Texts & Commentary. LC 95-5523. (SUNY Series in the Philosophy of the Social Sciences). 1995. pap. text ed. write for info. (*0-7914-2714-5*) State U NY Pr.
— The Missing Child in Liberal Theory: Towards a Covenant Theory of Family, Community Welfare & the Civic State. 136p. 1994. 40.00 (*0-8020-0627-2*); pap. 14. 95 (*0-8020-7586-X*) U of Toronto Pr.
— Perception, Expression, & History: The Social Phenomenology of Maurice Merleau-Ponty. (Studies in Phenomenology & Existential Philosophy). 101p. 1970. 12.95 (*0-8101-0299-4*) Northwestern U Pr.
— The Poverty of Postmodernism. LC 94-7260. (Social Futures Ser.). 240p. (Orig.). 1994. 55.00x (*0-415-11686-4*, B4742) Routledge.
— The Poverty of Postmodernism. LC 94-7260. (Social Futures Ser.). (Orig.). 1994. pap. 16.95 (*0-415-11687-2*, B4746) Routledge.
— Worlds Without Content: Against Formalism. 176p. 1992. 49.95 (*0-415-06791-X*, A6515) Routledge.

***O'Neill, John, ed.** Hegel's Dialectic of Recognition & Desire: Texts & Commentary. LC 95-5523. (SUNY Series in the Philosophy of the Social Sciences). 1995. write for info. (*0-7914-2713-7*) State U NY Pr.
— On Critical Theory. 270p. (C). 1989. reprint ed. pap. text ed. 25.00 (*0-8191-7514-5*) U Pr of Amer.

O'Neill, John & O'Neill, Pat. Concerned Intervention: When Your Loved One Won't Quit Alcohol or Drugs. 2nd ed. (Illus.). 190p. (Orig.). (C). 1993. text ed. 24.95 (*1-879237-37-7*); pap. text ed. 11.95 (*1-879237-36-9*) New Harbinger.

O'Neill, John, ed. see De Villena, Enrique.

O'Neill, John, tr. see Merleau-Ponty, Maurice.

O'Neill, John J. Management of Industrial Construction Projects. 285p. 1990. 49.95 (*0-89397-357-2*) Nichols Pub.
— Prodigal Genius: The Life of Nikola Tesla. 326p. reprint ed. 12.00 (*0-913022-40-3*); reprint ed. pap. 6.00 (*0-913022-39-X*) Angriff Pr.
— Prodigal Genius, the Life of Nikola Tesla. 328p. 1994. pap. 12.00 (*0-914732-33-1*) Bro Life Inc.

O'Neill, John P. Barnett Newman: Selected Writings & Interviews. 1992. pap. 15.00 (*0-520-07817-9*) U CA Pr.
— Just for Today, Lord. 192p. (Orig.). 1993. pap. 10.00 (*0-9637937-0-5*) DEO Bks.
— Metropolitan Cats. LC 81-9590. (Illus.). 112p. 1981. 16. 95 (*0-87099-276-7*) Metro Mus Art.

O'Neill, John R. The Paradox of Success: When Winning at Work Means Losing at Life: A Book of Renewal for Leaders. 272p. 1994. pap. 12.95 (*0-87477-772-0*, J P T-Putnam) Putnam Pub Group.

O'Neill, Joseph. Land under England. LC 80-14273. 312p. 1985. reprint ed. 22.50 (*0-87951-117-6*); reprint ed. pap. 9.95 (*0-87951-218-0*) Overlook Pr.
— This Is the Life. 224p. 1991. 18.95 (*0-374-27590-4*) FS&G.

O'Neill, Joseph E., ed. Fifty Years of Thought: Representative Selections. LC 30-22096. 630p. reprint ed. pap. 179.60 (*0-7837-5585-6*, 2045377) Bks Demand.

O'Neill, Judith. Transported to Van Diemen's Land. (Cambridge Introduction to World History Topic Bks.). (Illus.). 48p. (YA). (gr. 7 up). 1977. pap. 7.95 (*0-521-21231-6*) Cambridge U Pr.

O'Neill, Judith, ed. Critics on Blake. LC 75-142198. (Readings in Literary Criticism Ser.: No. 7). 1970. 10.95 (*0-87024-189-3*) U of Miami Pr.
— Critics on Charlotte & Emily Bronte. LC 68-54477. (Readings in Literary Criticism Ser.: No. 2). 1979. pap. 10.95 (*0-87024-098-6*) U of Miami Pr.
— Critics on Jane Austen. LC 69-15928. (Readings in Literary Criticism Ser.: No. 5). 1970. 10.95 (*0-87024-117-6*) U of Miami Pr.
— Critics on Marlowe. LC 69-15927. (Readings in Literary Criticism Ser.: No. 4). 1970. 10.95 (*0-87024-121-4*) U of Miami Pr.
— Critics on Pope. LC 68-54478. (Readings in Literary Criticism Ser.: No. 3). (C). 1968. 10.95 (*0-87024-099-4*) U of Miami Pr.

O'Neill, June. Work & Welfare in Massachusetts: An Evaluation of the ET Program. (Pioneer Paper Ser.: No. 3). 114p. (Orig.). 1990. pap. 10.00 (*0-929930-03-7*) Pioneer Inst.

O'Neill, June E. & O'Neill, Dave M. The Employment & Distributional Effects of Mandated Benefits. (Studies in Health Reform). 35p. (Orig.). 1994. pap. 9.95 (*0-8447-7021-3*, AEI Pr) Amer Enterprise.

O'Neill, K., jt. auth. see Laskin, D.

O'Neill, Kent. Small Business Development: Some Current Issues. 280p. 1987. text ed. 59.95 (*0-566-05382-9*, Pub. by Avebury Pub UK) Ashgate Pub Co.

O'Neill, Kevin. Family & Farm in Pre-Famine Ireland: The Parish of Killashandra. LC 84-40154. (Illus.). 256p. 1985. text ed. 25.00 (*0-299-09840-0*) U of Wis Pr.

O'Neill, Kevin, tr. see Finkielkraut, Alain.

O'Neill, Kevin, jt. auth. see Mills, Pat.

O'Neill, Kevin M., jt. auth. see Evans, Howard E.

O'Neill, Kitty. Snack Attack: How to Stick to a Diet, Eat Lots of Snacks, & Still Lose Weight. LC 94-60670. 100p. (Orig.). 1994. pap. 12.95 (*0-9641463-4-7*) Ctr for Design.

O'Neill, Laura. No More Little Miss Perfect. (Fifteen - Nickelodeon Bks.: No. 1). 112p. (J). (gr. 4-9). 1992. pap. 2.95 (*0-448-40490-7*, G&D) Putnam Pub Group.

O'Neill, Laurie. Wounded Knee: Death of a Dream. LC 92-12998. (Spotlight on American History Ser.). (Illus.). 64p. (J). (gr. 4-6). 1993. 15.40 (*1-56294-253-0*); pap. 5.95 (*1-56294-748-6*) Millbrook Pr.

***O'Neill, Laurie A.** The Shawnees: People of the Eastern Woodlands. LC 94-42234. (Native Americans Ser.). (Illus.). 64p. (J). (gr. 4-6). 1995. lib. bdg. 15.40 (*1-56294-533-5*) Millbrook Pr.

O'Neill, Lois D., ed. The Women's Book of World Records & Achievements. (Quality Paperbacks Ser.). (Illus.). xiii, 800p. 1983. reprint ed. pap. 14.95 (*0-306-80206-6*) Da Capo.

O'Neill, Luke, jt. ed. see Murphy, Michael P.

O'Neill, Margaret. Doctor on Skye. large type ed. 1993. 16. 95 (*0-263-13155-6*, MB082, Pub. by Mills & Boon Ltd UK) Chivers N Amer.
— Handful of Dreams. large type ed. 1994. 17.95 (*0-263-13848-8*, Pub. by Mills & Boon Ltd UK) Chivers N Amer.
— A Question of Honour. large type ed. (Medical Romance Ser.). 1992. 16.95 (*0-263-13149-1*, Pub. by Mills & Boon Ltd UK) Chivers N Amer.
— Seeds of Love. large type ed. (Medical Romance Ser.). 1993. 17.95 (*0-263-13527-6*, Pub. by Mills & Boon Ltd UK) Chivers N Amer.

O'Neill, Margaret R. The Life of Mother Clare: Out from the Shadow of the Upas Tree. 221p. (Orig.). 1990. pap. 9.95 (*0-910303-16-9*) Writers Pub Serv.

O'Neill, Marnie, jt. ed. see Carter, David.

O'Neill, Marnie H., jt. ed. see Carter, David S.G.

O'Neill, Martha, ed. see Chamberlain, Valerie M., et al.

O'Neill, Martha, ed. see Shand, Dorothy E., et al.

O'Neill, Martha, ed. see Snyder, Thomas F.

O'Neill, Martha, jt. auth. see Snyder, Thomas F.

O'Neill, Martha, ed. see Tsumura, Ted K. & Jones, Lorraine H.

O'Neill, Mary. Air Scare. LC 89-49626. (SOS Planet Earth Ser.). (Illus.). 32p. (J). (gr. 3-6). 1991. lib. bdg. 12.89 (*0-8167-2082-7*); pap. text ed. 3.95 (*0-8167-2083-5*) Troll Assocs.
— Dinosaur Mysteries. LC 89-4789. (Illus.). 32p. (J). (gr. 3-7). 1989. lib. bdg. 12.89 (*0-8167-1635-8*); pap. text ed. 3.95 (*0-8167-1636-6*) Troll Assocs.
— A Family of Dinosaurs. LC 89-4792. (Illus.). 32p. (J). (gr. 3-7). 1989. lib. bdg. 12.89 (*0-8167-1633-1*); pap. text ed. 3.95 (*0-8167-1634-X*) Troll Assocs.
— Hailstones & Halibut Bones. 1990. mass mkt. 6.95 (*0-385-41078-6*) Doubleday.
— Hailstones & Halibut Bones: Adventures in Color. (Illus.). (J). 1989. 12.95 (*0-385-24484-3*) Doubleday.
— Life after the Dinosaurs. LC 89-31164. (Illus.). 32p. (J). (gr. 3-7). 1989. lib. bdg. 12.89 (*0-8167-1639-0*); pap. text ed. 3.95 (*0-8167-1640-4*) Troll Assocs.
— Nature in Danger. LC 90-37437. (SOS Planet Earth Ser.). (Illus.). 32p. (J). (gr. 3-6). 1991. lib. bdg. 12.89 (*0-8167-2285-4*); pap. text ed. 3.95 (*0-8167-2286-2*) Troll Assocs.
— Power Failure. LC 90-11148. (SOS Planet Earth Ser.). (Illus.). 32p. (J). (gr. 3-6). 1991. lib. bdg. 12.89 (*0-8167-2288-9*); pap. text ed. 3.95 (*0-8167-2289-7*) Troll Assocs.
— Water Squeeze. LC 89-77456. (SOS Planet Earth Ser.). (Illus.). 32p. (J). (gr. 3-6). 1989. lib. bdg. 12.89 (*0-8167-2080-0*); pap. text ed. 3.95 (*0-8167-2081-9*) Troll Assocs.
— What Is Orange? (J). (gr. k-2). 1993. audio 8.95 (*0-7608-0500-8*); 21.95 (*0-88741-932-1*); pap. 4.95 (*0-88741-933-X*) Sundance Pub.
— Where Are All the Dinosaurs? LC 89-31165. (Illus.). 32p. (J). (gr. 2-6). 1989. lib. bdg. 12.89 (*0-8167-1637-4*); pap. text ed. 3.95 (*0-8167-1638-2*) Troll Assocs.

O'Neill, Mary, jt. ed. see Correard, Marie-Helene.

O'Neill, Mary, tr. see Harnoncourt, Nikolaus.

O'Neill, Maura. Women Speaking, Women Listening: Women in Interreligious Dialogue. LC 90-35123. (Faith Meets Faith Ser.). 1990. 39.95 (*0-88344-698-7*) Orbis Bks.

O'Neill, Michael. The Human Mind's Imaginings: Conflict & Achievement in Shelley's Poetry. (Illus.). 232p. 1989. 55. 00 (*0-19-811748-5*) OUP.
— Percy Bysshe Shelley: A Literary Life. LC 89-34864. (Literary Lives Ser.). 280p. 1989. text ed. 39.95 (*0-312-03248-X*) St Martin.
— The Third America: The Emergence of the Nonprofit Sector in the United States. LC 89-33760. (Nonprofit Sector-Public Administration Ser.). 236p. 1989. 27.95x (*1-55542-165-2*) Jossey-Bass.
— Zoobabies. LC 91-50271. (Illus.). 64p. 1991. 16.50 (*0-679-40698-0*, Villard Bks) Random.

O'Neill, Michael, ed. The Bodelian Shelley Manuscripts. LC 86-4746. (Bodleian Shelley Manuscripts Ser.). 548p. 1994. 195.00 (*0-8153-1155-9*) Garland.

O'Neill, Michael, intro. Shelley. (Longman Critical Readers Ser.). (C). 1994. pap. text ed. 67.50 (*0-582-08668-X*) Longman.

O'Neill, Michael & Young, Dennis R., eds. Educating Managers of Nonprofit Organizations. LC 87-25869. 190p. 1988. text ed. 49.95 (*0-275-92609-5*, C2609, Praeger Pubs) Greenwood.

O'Neill, Michael, jt. auth. see Gallegos, Herman E.

O'Neill, Michael, jt. ed. see Odendahl, Teresa.

O'Neill, Michael J. The Roar of the Crowd: How Television & People are Changing the World. LC 92-56836. 1993. 21.00 (*0-8129-2078-3*, Times Bks) Random.
— Terrorist Spectaculars: Should TV Coverage Be Curbed? - A Twentieth Century Fund Paper. 109p. (Orig.). (C). 1986. pap. text ed. 7.50 (*0-87078-202-9*) TCFP-PPP.

O'Neill, Michael T. A. P. Richardson: The Ethics of a Humanist, Original Anthology. Brief, Richard P., ed. LC 80-1461. (Dimensions of Accounting Theory & Practice Ser.). 1980. lib. bdg. 31.95 (*0-405-13483-5*) Ayer.

O'Neill, Michael W., ed. Drilled Piers & Caissons. LC 81-69227. 159p. 1981. 19.00 (*0-87262-285-1*) Am Soc Civil Eng.

O'Neill, Michael W. & Dobry, Ricardo, eds. Dynamic Response of Pile Foundations: Analytical Aspects. LC 80-69151. 118p. 1980. pap. 13.00 (*0-87262-257-6*) Am Soc Civil Eng.

O'Neill, Michelle L. Creative Childbirth: The Leclaire Method of Easy Birthing Through Hypnosis & Rational-Intuitive Thought. LC 92-81691. (Illus.). 105p. (Orig.). 1993. pap. 11.95 (*0-9633087-3-4*) Papyrus Pr.

O'Neill, Molly. Feast of Irish Cooking. 1986. pap. 7.95 (*0-85105-450-1*, Pub. by Colin Smythe Ltd UK) Dufour.
— New York Cookbook. LC 92-50280. 1992. 27.95 (*1-56305-337-3*, 3337); pap. 17.95 (*0-89480-698-X*, 1698) Workman Pub.
— A Well-Seasoned Appetite. LC 94-43961. 464p. 1995. 24. 95 (*0-670-85574-X*, Viking) Viking Penguin.

O'Neill, Nancy G., jt. auth. see Klingner, Donald E.

O'Neill, Nena, jt. auth. see O'Neill, George.

O'Neill, Nick & Handley, Robin. Retreat from Injustice: Human Rights in Australian Law. 544p. 1994. pap. 59. 00 (*1-86287-121-3*, Pub. by Federation Pr AU) W W Gaunt.

O'Neill, Norman. Capitalism, Socialism & the Development Crisis in Tanzania. (Illus.). 295p. 1990. text ed. 78.95 (*0-566-05598-8*) Ashgate Pub Co.

O'Neill, Norman & O'Brien, Jay. Economy & Class in Sudan. 331p. 1988. text ed. 76.95 (*0-566-05604-6*, Pub. by Avebury Pub UK) Ashgate Pub Co.

O'Neill, Onora. Constructions of Reason: Explorations of Kant's Practical Philosophy. 300p. (C). 1990. 64.95 (*0-521-38121-5*); pap. 19.95 (*0-521-38816-3*) Cambridge U Pr.

O'Neill, P., jt. ed. see Fielden, E. M.

O'Neill, P. A. Industrial Compressors. (Illus.). 360p. 1993. 110.00 (*0-7506-0870-6*) Buttrwrth-Heinemann.

O'Neill, P. G. Early Noh Drama: Its Background, Character, & Development, 1300-1450. LC 73-21264. (Illus.). 223p. (C). 1974. reprint ed. text ed. 47.50 (*0-8371-6104-5*, ONND, Greenwood Pr) Greenwood.
— Japanese Kana Workbook. 1973. pap. 10.00 (*0-87011-039-X*) Kodansha.
— Japanese Kana Workbook. LC 94-48166. 128p. 1995. pap. 9.95 (*0-8348-0337-2*) Weatherhill.
— A Reader of Handwritten Japanese. (Illus.). 232p. 1992. pap. 24.95 (*4-7700-1663-8*) Kodansha.

O'Neill, P. G., ed. Tradition & Modern Japan. 320p. 1985. 35.00 (*0-904404-36-6*, Pub. by Paul Norbury Pubns UK) Humanities.

O'Neill, Pat, jt. auth. see O'Neill, John.

O'Neill, Patrick. The Comedy of Entropy: Humour, Narrative, Reading. 320p. 1990. text ed. 50.00 (*0-8020-2737-7*) U of Toronto Pr.
— Fictions of Discourse: Reading Narrative Theory. (Theory-Culture Ser.). 190p. 1994. 35.00 (*0-8020-0468-7*) U of Toronto Pr.
— Gunter Grass: A Bibliography, 1955-1975. LC 76-17278. 116p. reprint ed. pap. 33.10 (*0-317-27004-4*, 2023657) Bks Demand.
— Ireland & Germany: A Study in Literary Relations. LC 84-48081. (Canadian Studies in German Language & Literature: Vol. 33). 352p. (Orig.). (C). 1985. text ed. 27. 40 (*0-8204-0173-0*) P Lang Pubs.

O'Neill, Patrick, ed. Critical Essays on Gunter Grass. (Critical Essays on World Literature Ser.). 208p. 1987. text ed. 45.00 (*0-8161-8830-0*) G K Hall.

O'Neill, Patrick I. & Trickett, Edison J. Community Consultation. LC 82-48062. (Jossey-Bass Social & Behavioral Science Ser.). 307p. reprint ed. pap. 87.50 (*0-8357-4914-2*, 2037844) Bks Demand.

O'Neill, Peter. Environmental Chemistry. (Illus.). 176p. (C). 1985. text ed. 60.00 (*0-04-551085-7*); pap. text ed. 19.95 (*0-04-551086-5*) Routledge Chapman & Hall.
— Environmental Chemistry. 2nd ed. LC 92-46390. 1993. pap. write for info. (*0-412-48490-0*) Chapman & Hall.

O'Neill, Philip. Dunfermline College of Physical Education. (C). 1989. 45.00 (*1-85098-148-5*, Pub. by Jordanhill College UK) St Mut.
— Wilkie Collins: Women, Property & Propriety. 1988. 50. 00 (*0-389-20771-3*) Rowman.

O'Neill, Pierre-George. Too Good to Be True: The Perils & Pitfalls of Work-at-Home Programs. 128p. (Orig.). 1990. pap. 12.95 (*0-9693942-0-9*, Pub. by Factfinder CN) Quality Bks IL.

O'Neill, R., et al. New Dimensions: Intermediate Level. (Illus.). 1993. teacher ed 18.95 (*0-8013-0852-6*); student ed 7.95 (*0-8013-0851-8*); pap. text ed. 13.95 (*0-8013-0459-8*); audio 24.95 (*0-8013-0856-9*) Longman.

O'Neill, R. H. & Boretz, N. M. The Director As Artist: Play Direction Today. 352p. (C). 1987. text ed. 34.75 (*0-03-064146-2*) HB Coll Pubs.

O'Neill, R. V., jt. ed. see Innis, G. S.

O'Neill, R. V., et al. A Hierarchical Concept of Ecosystems. (Monographs in Population Biology: No. 23). (Illus.). 272p. 1986. text ed. 59.50 (*0-691-08436-X*); pap. text ed. 17.95 (*0-691-08437-8*) Princeton U Pr.

O'Neill, Reginald F. Theories of Knowledge: With a New Preface. 242p. 1980. reprint ed. text ed. 29.50 (*0-8290-0227-8*); reprint ed. pap. text ed. 18.95 (*0-8290-0386-X*) Irvington.

O'Neill, Reginald F., ed. Readings in Epistemology. LC 61-18427. 1979. reprint ed. pap. text ed. 14.95 (*0-89197-604-3*) Irvington.

O'Neill, Richard. Suicide Squads of WW II. (Reprints Ser.). 304p. 1989. 24.95 (*0-88029-299-7*) Dorset Pr.

O'Neill, Robert, et al. American Kernel Lessons: Advanced Student Book. (Illus.). 142p. (Orig.). 1981. pap. 12.95 (*0-582-79741-1*, 74995); audio 8.95 (*0-582-79764-0*, 75018) Longman.
— American Kernel Lessons: Advanced Student Book, No. 1. (Illus.). 142p. (Orig.). 1981. audio 39.95 (*0-582-79765-9*, 75019) Longman.
— American Kernel Lessons: Advanced Student Book, No. 2. (Illus.). 142p. (Orig.). 1981. audio write for info. (*0-582-79766-7*, 75020) Longman.

O'Neill, Robert. The Cavalry Battles of Aldie, Middleburg & Upperville: Small but Important Riots, June 10 - 27, 1863. (Virginia Civil War Battles & Leaders Ser.). 1994. 19.95 (*1-56190-052-4*) H E Howard.

O'Neill, Robert, ed. Security in East Asia. LC 83-40156. (Adelphi Library). 208p. 1984. text ed. 29.95 (*0-312-70916-1*) St Martin.

O'Neill, Robert & Markstein, Linda. American Kernel Lessons: Advanced Student's Tests. (Orig.). 1982. pap. text ed. 8.95 (*0-582-79807-8*, 75057) Longman.

O'Neill, Robert & Vincent, R. J., eds. The West & the Third World: Essays in Honour of J. D. B. Miller. LC 89-70079. 256p. 1990. text ed. 55.00 (*0-312-04096-2*) St Martin.

O'Neill, Robert, jt. auth. see Brunelle, Wallace.

O'Neill, Robert, jt. ed. see Heuser, Beatrice.

O'Neill, Robert, jt. auth. see LaPorte, Penny.

O'Neill, Robert, et al. American Kernel Lessons: Beginning Level. (English As a Second Language Bk.). 1981. teacher ed 18.95 (*0-582-79779-9*, 75033); student ed 8.95 (*0-582-79899-X*, 75132); student ed, pap. text ed. 12.95 (*0-582-79734-9*, 74990); audio 8.95 (*0-582-78342-9*, 74909); audio 8.95 (*0-582-78341-0*, 74908) Longman.
— American Kernel Lessons: Beginning Level, No. 1. (English As a Second Language Bk.). 1981. teacher ed, audio 39.95 (*0-582-79778-0*, 75032) Longman.
— American Kernel Lessons: Beginning Level, No. 2. (English As a Second Language Bk.). 1981. audio 69.95 (*0-582-79800-0*, 75054) Longman.

O

An Asterisk (*) at the beginning of an entry indicates that the title is appearing in BIP for the first time.

O'Neill, Robert, Jr., et al. American Kernel Lessons: Intermediate Level. (English As a Second Language Bk.). (Illus.). 1978. teacher ed 18.95 (0-582-79707-1, 74974); student ed 8.95 (0-582-90624-5, 75196); student ed, pap. text ed. 12.95 (0-582-79706-3, 74973); teacher ed 8.95 (0-582-79708-X, 74975); audio 8.95 (0-582-79709-8, 74976) Longman.

— American Kernel Lessons: Intermediate Level, Set 1. (English As a Second Language Bk.). (Illus.). 1978. audio 24.95 (0-582-79715-2, 74978) Longman.

— American Kernel Lessons: Intermediate Level, Set 2. (English As a Second Language Bk.). (Illus.). 1978. audio 39.95 (0-582-79716-0, 74979) Longman.

— American Kernel Lessons: Intermediate Level, Set 3. (English As a Second Language Bk.). (Illus.). 1978. audio 69.95 (0-582-79710-1, 74977) Longman.

O'Neill, Robert, et al. Functional Analysis of Problem Behavior: A Practical Assessment Guide. Repp, Alan C. & Singh, Nirbhay N., eds. 85p. (C). 1990. pap. text ed. 21.95 (0-9625233-2-1) Sycamore Pub.

O'Neill, Robert K., comp. English-Language Dictionaries, Sixteen Hundred Four - Nineteen Hundred: The Catalog of the Warren N. & Suzanne B. Cordell Collection. LC 87-35947. (Bibliographies & Indexes in Library & Information Science: No. 1). 512p. 1988. text ed. 135.00 (0-313-25522-9, OEL/) Greenwood.

O'Neill, Rosary H. The Actor's Checklist. 256p. (C). 1992. pap. text ed. 12.00 (0-03-073142-9) HB Coll Pubs.

O'Neill, Rowan. The Making of a Seaman. 3rd ed. (Illus.). 164p. 1982. pap. 2.95 (0-933704-45-3) Dawn Pr.

— Making of a Seaman. 4th ed. (Illus.). 164p. 1988. pap. 5.95 (0-933704-53-4) Dawn Pr.

O'Neill, Sharman D., jt. ed. see Bennett, Alan B.

O'Neill, Sharon G. Lurning: One Hundred & Forty-Seven Inspiring Thoughts for Learning on the Job. 1993. pap. 7.95 (0-89815-536-3) Ten Speed Pr.

O'Neill, Suzannah. Innismere. 1991. mass mkt. 4.50 (0-06-100212-7, Harp PBks) HarpC.

— Return to Innismere. (Orig.). 1991. mass mkt. 4.50 (0-06-104073-8, Harp PBks) HarpC.

O'Neill, Suzanne B. & Sparkman, Catherine G. From Law School to Law Practice: The New Associate's Guide. LC 89-80281. 286p. 1989. text ed. 83.00 (0-8318-0593-5, B593) Am Law Inst.

O'Neill, Tania D. Ukrainian Embroidery Techniques. LC 84-52257. (Illus.). 158p. (ENG & UKR.). 1985. text ed. 35.00 (0-9614540-0-8) STO Pub.

O'Neill, Teresa, ed. Immigration: Opposing Viewpoints. LC 92-21794. (American History Ser.). 288p. (YA). 1992. lib. bdg. 19.95 (1-56510-007-7); pap. 11.55 (1-56510-006-9) Greenhaven.

O'Neill, Teresa, jt. ed. see Dudley, William.

O'Neill, Terry. The Homeless: Distinguishing Between Fact & Opinion. LC 90-45283. (Opposing Viewpoints Juniors Ser.). (Illus.). 32p. (J). (gr. 3-6). 1990. lib. bdg. 11.55 (0-89908-605-5) Greenhaven.

— Zoos: Identifying Propaganda Techniques. LC 90-3247. (Opposing Viewpoints Juniors Ser.). (Illus.). 32p. (J). (gr. 3-6). 1990. pap. text ed. 11.95 (0-89908-600-4) Greenhaven.

O'Neill, Terry, ed. Biomedical Ethics: Opposing Viewpoints. LC 93-7260. 1994. lib. bdg. 19.95 (1-56510-062-X); pap. 11.55 (1-56510-061-1) Greenhaven.

— Paranormal Phenomena: Opposing Viewpoints. LC 90-24081. (Opposing Viewpoints Ser.). (Illus.). 240p. (YA). (gr. 10 up). 1991. lib. bdg. 19.95 (0-89908-487-7); pap. 11.55 (0-89908-462-1) Greenhaven.

O'Neill, Terry & Swisher, Karin, eds. Economics in America: Opposing Viewpoints. LC 91-42802. (Illus.). 264p. (YA). (gr. 10 up). 1992. lib. bdg. 19.95 (0-89908-187-8); pap. text ed. 11.55 (0-89908-162-2) Greenhaven.

O'Neill, Terry R. Life Insurance Kit. 249p. (Orig.). 1993. pap. 19.95 (0-7931-0362-2, 1919-01) Dearborn Finan.

O'Neill, Thomas. Lakes, Peaks, & Prairies: Discovering the United States-Canadian Border. Crump, Donald J., ed. LC 84-22775. (Special Publications Series 19: No. 3). (Illus.). 200p. 1984. 12.95 (0-87044-478-6); lib. bdg. 12.95 (0-87044-483-2) Natl Geog.

O'Neill, Thomas & Hymel, Gary. All Politics is Local & Other Rules of the Game. LC 93-29988. 1993. 15.00 (0-8129-2297-2, Times Bks) Random.

O'Neill, Thomas J., jt. auth. see Gentry, Donald W.

O'Neill, Thomas P., Jr. & Novak, William. Man of the House: The Life & Political Memoirs of Speaker Tip O'Neill. 480p. 1988. mass mkt. 4.95 (0-312-91191-2) St Martin.

— Man of the House: The Life & Political Memoirs of Speaker Tip O'Neill. limited ed. (Illus.). 400p. 1987. 100.00 (0-394-56505-3) Random.

***O'Neill, Tim.** Airy Plumeflights: A Beginner's Guide to Celtic Script & Design. (Illus.). 48p. (Orig.). 1994. pap. 11.95 (1-874675-35-X, Pub. by Lilliput Pr Ltd IE) Irish Bks Media.

O'Neill, Timothy. Irish Hand: Scribes & Their Manuscripts from the Earliest Times. 1984. 40.00 (0-85105-411-0, Pub. by Colin Smythe Ltd UK) Dufour.

— Merchants & Mariners in Medieval Ireland. (Illus.). 164p. 1987. 25.00 (0-7165-2398-1, Pub. by Irish Acad Pr IE) Intl Spec Bk.

O'Neill, Timothy J. Bakke & the Politics of Equality: Friends & Foes in the Classroom of Litigation. LC 83-26122. (Illus.). 344p. 1987. pap. 17.95 (0-8195-6199-1, Wesleyan Univ Pr) U Pr of New Eng.

***O'Neill, Tip & Hymel, Gary.** All Politics Is Local: And Other Rules of the Game. 1995. pap. 7.95 (1-55850-470-2) Adams Pubng.

O'Neill, Tom, ed. The Shared Horizon. 216p. 1989. 39.50 (0-7165-2414-7, Pub. by Irish Acad Pr IE) Intl Spec Bk.

O'Neill, William. The Ethics of Our Climate: Hermeneutics & Ethical Theory. 160p. 1994. 40.00 (0-87840-565-8) Georgetown U Pr.

O'Neill, William, ed. see Doggett, Martha.

O'Neill, William F. Educational Ideologies: Contemporary Expressions of Educational Philosophy. 448p. (C). 1990. per. 39.95 (0-8403-5877-6) Kendall-Hunt.

— With Charity Toward None: An Analysis of Ayn Rand's Philosophy. (Quality Paperback Ser.: No. 179). 233p. 1977. reprint ed. pap. 7.95 (0-8226-0179-6) Littlefield.

O'Neill, William G. & Schrage, Elliot. Haiti: A Human Rights Nightmare. 80p. (Orig.). 1992. 8.00 (0-934143-56-0) Lawyers Comm Human.

O'Neill, William G., jt. auth. see Lawyers Committee for Human Rights Staff.

O'Neill, William G., ed. see Ross, James D.

O'Neill, William J., Jr., ed. see Campbell, John H.

O'Neill, William L. American High: The Years of Confidence, 1945-1960. 336p. 1989. pap. 12.95 (0-02-923679-7) Free Pr.

— A Better World: Stalinism & the American Intellectuals. 464p. 1989. pap. 21.95 (0-88738-631-8) Transaction Pubs.

— Coming Apart: An Informal History of America in the 1960's. LC 79-152098. (Illus.). 480p. 1974. reprint ed. write for info. (0-8129-0190-8, Times Bks); reprint ed. pap. 13.00 (0-8129-6223-0, Times Bks) Random.

— A Democracy at War: America's Fight at Home & Abroad in World War II. 400p. (Orig.). 1993. text ed. 24.95 (0-02-923678-9) Free Pr.

— A Democracy at War: America's Fight at Home & Abroad in World War II. (Illus.). 496p. (Orig.). (C). 1995. pap. 16.95 (0-674-19737-2) HUP.

— Divorce in the Progressive Era. LC 67-24507. 309p. reprint ed. pap. 88.10 (0-317-09686-9, 2022025) Bks Demand.

— Feminism in America: A History. 2nd rev. ed. 408p. 1994. pap. 21.95 (0-88738-761-6) Transaction Pubs.

— The Great Schism: Stalinism & the American Intellectuals. (Illus.). 447p. 17.95 (0-686-43340-8) S&S Trade.

— The Last Romantic: A Life of Max Eastman. 350p. (C). 1990. pap. 19.95 (0-88738-859-0) Transaction Pubs.

— Women at Work. LC 72-182506. 384p. 1972. pap. 4.95 (0-8129-6237-0, Times Bks) Random.

O'Neill, William L., ed. Echoes of Revolt: The Masses 1911-1917. (Illus.). 304p. 1989. reprint ed. pap. 18.95 (0-929587-15-4, Elephant Paperbacks) I R Dee.

O'Neill, Ynez V. Speech & Speech Disorders in Western Thought Before 1600. LC 79-7361. (Contributions in Medical History Ser.: No. 3). 246p. 1980. text ed. 55.00 (0-313-21058-6, OSD/, Greenwood Pr) Greenwood.

Onenko, S. N. Nanaisk-Russian Dictionary. (RUS.). 1980. 24.95 (0-8288-1627-1, F47740) Fr & Eur.

Onerheim, Margaret O. Threads of Memory: A Memoir of the 1920s. LC 93-12733. (Illus.). 146p. (Orig.). 1993. pap. 14.95 (0-8138-0902-9) Iowa St U Pr.

O'Nes, D. The Guide to Legally Obtaining a Foreign Passport: The Easy Way to Get Additional Citizenships. 192p. pap. 9.95 (0-944007-93-7) Sure Sellers.

Ones, Gwyneth. Flowerdust. 1995. 20.95 (0-685-75366-2) Tor Bks.

Onesti, Gaddo & Brest, Albert N. Hypertension: Mechanisms, Diagnosis & Treatment. LC 77-25888. (Cardiovascular Clinics Ser.: Vol. 9, No. 1). (Illus.). 333p. 1978. text ed. 35.00 (0-8036-6630-6) Davis Co.

Onesti, Marco, jt. auth. see Arbola, Savi.

***Onet, Ionel.** ABC de Esperanto. 15p. 1994. pap. 1.00 (1-882251-08-3) Eldonejo Bero.

— Primii Pasi in Esperanto. 68p. 1993. pap. text ed. 5.00 (1-882251-03-2) Eldonejo Bero.

Onet, Ionel, tr. see Brancusi, Constantin.

Onet, Ionel, tr. see Canache, George, et al.

***Onetti.** Cuando Ya No Importe: When It Matters No More. 1995. pap. 14.95 (0-679-76094-6, Vin) Random.

Onetti, Juan C. Body Snatcher. Adam, Alfred M., tr. LC 91-58061. 1992. pap. 13.00 (0-679-73887-8, Vin) Random.

— Brief Life. 1994. pap. 15.99 (1-85242-301-3) Serpents Tail.

— Goodbyes & Stories. Balderston, Daniel, tr. (Texas Pan American Ser.). 190p. (Orig.). 1990. text ed. 22.50 (0-292-72743-7); pap. 10.95 (0-292-72746-1) U of Tex Pr.

— Shipyard. 1993. pap. 14.95 (1-85242-191-6) Serpents Tail.

Oney, Steve, jt. auth. see Tartikoff, Brandon.

***Ong.** The Practice of Health Services Research. 174p. 1993. pap. 54.25 (1-56593-214-5, 0567) Singular Publishing.

***Ong, A., et al, eds.** Proceedings of the UNESCO Conference: Lipids, Nutrition, Health & Disease. 1995. write for info. (0-935315-64-0) AOCS Pr.

Ong, A. S. & Packer, L., eds. Lipid-Soluble Antioxidants: Biochemistry & Clinical Applications. LC 92-49649. (Molecular & Cell Biology Updates Ser.). xii, 640p. 1992. 139.50 (0-8176-2667-0, Pub. by Birkhauser Vlg SZ) Birkhauser.

Ong, Aihwa. Spirits of Resistance & Capitalist Discipline: Factory Women in Malaysia. LC 86-22980. (Anthropology of Work Ser.). 268p. 1987. 59.50 (0-88706-380-2); pap. 19.95 (0-88706-381-0) State U NY Pr.

Ong, Bie N., jt. ed. see Alaszewski, Andy.

Ong, Cristina, illus. The Little Engine That Could: Let's Sing ABC. (Lift-the-Flap Alphabet Book Ser.). 24p. (J). (ps). 1993. 9.95 (0-448-40509-1, Platt & Munk Pubs) Putnam Pub Group.

— The Little Engine That Could: Little Library, 3 bks., Set. (J). (ps). 1992. boxed 7.95 (0-448-40261-0, Platt & Munk Pubs) Putnam Pub Group.

— The Little Engine That Could ABC. (Wee Pudgy Board Bks.). 20p. (J). (ps-3). 1994. bds. 2.95 (0-448-40262-9, Platt & Munk Pubs) Putnam Pub Group.

— The Little Engine That Could Colors. (Wee Pudgy Board Bks.). 20p. (J). (ps-3). 1994. bds. 2.95 (0-448-40264-5, Platt & Munk Pubs) Putnam Pub Group.

— The Little Engine That Could Numbers. (Wee Pudgy Board Bks.). 20p. (J). (ps-3). 1994. bds. 2.95 (0-448-40263-7, Platt & Munk Pubs) Putnam Pub Group.

Ong, DeWitt. UNIX Operating System: A Menu-Driven Book. 224p. 1993. pap. 12.95 (0-9634874-1-8) Calligraph Pr.

Ong, Helen, illus. Amal & the Letter from the King: Adapted from a Play by Rabindranath Tagore. LC 91-77712. 40p. (J). 1992. lib. bdg. 14.95 (1-56397-120-8) Boyds Mills Pr.

Ong, Henry. Madame Mao's Memories. LC 92-25273. 1993. pap. 10.00 (0-89410-756-9) Three Continents.

Ong, I. K., jt. ed. see Loh, C. Y.

Ong, L. S., jt. auth. see Cheung, J. S.

Ong, Paul & Hee, Suzanne. Losses in the Los Angeles Civil Unrest, April 29-May 1, 1992: Lists of the Damaged Properties & Korean Merchants & the L. A. Riot - Rebellion. 138p. 1993. pap. 6.95 (1-883191-00-9) U CA Ctr Pac Rim.

Ong, Paul, et al, eds. The New Asian Immigration in Los Angeles & Global Restructuring. LC 93-49863. (Asian American History & Culture Ser.). 336p. (C). 1994. text ed. 49.95 (1-56639-217-9); pap. text ed. 22.95 (1-56639-218-7) Temple U Pr.

Ong, W. J., ed. see Ramus, Petrus.

Ong, Walter J. American Catholic Crossroads: Religious-Secular Encounters in the Modern World. LC 80-29660. xi, 160p. 1981. reprint ed. text ed. 49.75 (0-313-22467-6, ONAM, Greenwood Pr) Greenwood.

— Faith & Contexts, Vol. 1: Selected Essays & Studies, 1952-1991. LC 92-34277. (USF-Rochester-Saint Louis Studies on Religion & the Social Order: Vol. 1-2). 238p. 1992. 74.95 (1-55540-766-8, 24 50 01) Scholars Pr GA.

— Faith & Contexts, Vol. 2: Supplemntary Studies, 1946-1989. LC 92-34277. (USF-Rochester-Saint Louis Studies on Religion & the Social Order: Vol. 1-2). 255p. 1992. Vol. 2: Supplementary Studies, 1946-1989; 255p. 74.95 (1-55540-767-6, 24 50 02) Scholars Pr GA.

— Fighting for Life: Contest, Sexuality, & Consciousness. LC 80-66968. (Illus.). 240p. 1981. 32.95 (0-8014-1342-7) Cornell U Pr.

— Fighting for Life: Contest, Sexuality, & Consciousness. LC 89-4743. 238p. (C). 1989. reprint ed. pap. 15.95x (0-87023-679-2) U of Mass Pr.

— Hopkins, the Self, the God. 194p. 1986. text ed. 32.50 (0-8020-5688-1); pap. 17.95 (0-8020-7413-8) U of Toronto Pr.

— Orality & Literacy: The Technologizing of the World. 280p. 1982. pap. 13.95 (0-415-02796-9, NO. 6526) Routledge Chapman & Hall.

— The Presence of the Word: Some Prolegomena for Cultural & Religious History. LC 81-3017. xvi, 360p. (C). 1981. reprint ed. pap. text ed. 14.95 (0-8166-1043-6) U of Minn Pr.

— Ramus, Method, & the Decay of Dialogue: From the Art of Discourse to the Art of Reason. 432p. 1983. pap. 14.95 (0-674-74802-6) HUP.

Ong, William A. Target Luftwaffe. LC 80-83828. (Illus.). 384p. 1981. 19.95 (0-913504-60-2) Lowell Pr.

Ongkeko, Lourdes A., jt. ed. see Munoz, Alfredo N.

Ongong'a, Jude J. & Gray, Kenneth R., eds. Bottlenecks to National Identity: Ethnic Co-Operation Towards Nation Building. 142p. 1989. pap. text ed. 10.95 (9966-835-24-5) Prof World Peace.

***Onguard.** Hazardous Materials Emergency Response Handbook. 1995. pap. 69.95 (0-614-03568-6) Van Nos Reinhold.

OnGuard Staff. Fire Attack: Strategy & Tactics of Initial Company Response: Student Textbook. 237p. 1987. teacher ed 34.95 (1-56916-002-3); pap. text ed. 12.95 (1-56916-001-5) OnGuard.

— Making a Difference: The Fire Officer's Role: Student Textbook. 226p. 1988. student ed 12.95 (1-56916-110-0); teacher ed 34.95 (1-56916-111-9) OnGuard.

— Silent War: Infection Control for Emergency Responders. (Student Textbook Ser.). 232p. 1995. pap. text ed. 12.95 (1-56916-403-7) R G Landes.

— Silent War: Infection Control for Emergency Responsers. 177p. 1992. teacher ed 34.95 (1-56916-402-9); pap. text ed. 12.95 (1-56916-401-0) OnGuard.

— Silent War: Infection Control for Law Enforcement: Post-Incident Procedures. (Illus.). 50p. (Orig.). 1993. teacher ed 19.95 (1-56916-709-5); pap. text ed. 3.50 (1-56916-708-7) OnGuard.

— Silent War: Infection Control for Law Enforcement: Reducing Your Risk. (Illus.). 50p. (Orig.). 1993. teacher ed 19.95 (1-56916-706-0); pap. text ed. 3.50 (1-56916-705-2) OnGuard.

— Silent War: Infection Control for Law Enforcement: Understanding Contagious Diseases. (Illus.). 60p. (Orig.). 1993. teacher ed 19.95 (1-56916-703-6); pap. text ed. 3.50 (1-56916-702-8) OnGuard.

— The Volunteer Firefighter: A Breed Apart Resource Manual. 261p. 1993. student ed 15.95 (1-56916-057-0) OnGuard.

Ongwamuhana, Kibuta. The Taxation of Income from Foreign Investments: A Tax Study of Developing Countries. 156p. 1991. pap. 40.00 (90-6544-542-0) Kluwer Law Tax Pubs.

Oni, Sauda. What Kwanzaa Means to Me. (Illus.). 36p. (J). (gr. k-3). 1992. pap. 3.95 (0-912444-38-X) DARE Bks.

Onians, John. Bearers of Meaning: The Classical Orders in Antiquity, the Middle Ages, & the Renaissance. (Illus.). 400p. (Orig.). 1990. 85.00 (0-691-04043-5); pap. text ed. 27.50 (0-691-00219-3) Princeton U Pr.

— Sight & Insight: Essays on Art & Culture in Honor of E. H. Gombrich at 85. (Illus.). 420p. (C). 1994. 49.95 (0-7148-2971-4, Pub. by Phaidon Press UK) Chronicle Bks.

Onians, Richard B. The Origins of European Thought About the Body, the Mind, the Soul, the World, Time, & Fate. LC 72-9298. (Philosophy of Plato & Aristotle Ser.). 1980. reprint ed. 43.95 (0-405-04853-X) Ayer.

— The Origins of European Thought about the Body, the Mind, the Soul, the World, Time, & Fate: New Interpretations of Greek, Roman, & Kindred Evidence, Also of Some Basic Jewish & Christian Beliefs. 2nd ed. (Illus.). 580p. 1988. pap. 29.95 (0-521-34794-7) Cambridge U Pr.

Onicescu, O. Invariantive Mechanics. (International Centre for Mechanical Sciences Ser.: No. 218). 1976. pap. 23.00 (0-387-81349-7) Spr-Verlag.

Onida, Fabrizio & Viesti, Gianfranco, eds. The Italian Multinationals. (International Business Ser.). 192p. 1988. lib. bdg. 69.95 (0-7099-1966-2, Pub. by Croom Helm UK) Routledge Chapman & Hall.

O'Niel, Charles J., ed. An Etienne Gilson Tribute. LC 59-8092. 355p. reprint ed. pap. 101.20 (0-317-09021-6, 2012015) Bks Demand.

O'Niell, John, ed. Modes of Individualism & Collectivism. (Modern Revivals in Philosophy Ser.). 368p. 1992. 69.95 (0-7512-0050-6, Pub. by Gregg Pub UK) Ashgate Pub Co.

Oniell, Laura. The Ski Trip. (Nickelodeon Fifteen Ser.: No. 5). 128p. (Orig.). (J). (gr. 3-9). 1993. pap. 2.95 (0-448-40494-X, G&D) Putnam Pub Group.

O'Niell, Lin, ed. His & Hers: The Anatomy of a Marriage. rev. ed. 160p. 1993. reprint ed. pap. 10.00 (0-931104-36-X) Sunflower Ink.

Onieva. Diccionario Multiple. 4th ed. (SPA.). 1987. write for info. (0-7859-3678-5, 8428304009) Fr & Eur.

Onieva, Antonio. Lengua Espanola. 299p. 1969. 9.95 (0-8288-7480-8) Fr & Eur.

Onieva Morales, Juan L. Curso de Comunicacion Activa: Desarrollo de las Destrezas Basicas del Espanol. 5th ed. (SPA.). (C). 1991. reprint ed. pap. text ed. 12.95 (1-56328-009-4) Edit Plaza Mayor.

Onieva-Morales, Juan L. Intercomunicacion, No. 1: Curso Basico Para el Aprendizaje Activo del Espanol. 4th ed. (Textbook Ser.). 260p. (Orig.). (SPA.). (C). 1991. reprint ed. pap. text ed. 12.95 (1-56328-001-9) Edit Plaza Mayor.

— Intercomunicacion, No. 2: Curso Basico Para el Aprendizaje Activo del Espanol. 2nd ed. (Textbook Ser.). 216p. (Orig.). (SPA.). (C). 1991. reprint ed. pap. text ed. 12.95 (1-56328-002-7) Edit Plaza Mayor.

— Introduccion a los Generos Literarios a Traves del Comentario de Textos. 372p. (SPA.). (C). 1993. pap. text ed. 14.95 (1-56328-036-1) Edit Plaza Mayor.

Onik, Gary, et al. Percutaneous Prostate Cryoblation. LC 94-34029. 1994. 75.00 (0-942219-66-X) Quality Med Pub.

***Onion, Daniel.** The Little Black Book of Primary Care: Pearls & References. 2nd ed. 600p. (C). 1995. write for info. (0-393-71024-6) Norton.

Onion, Daniel K. The Little Black Book of Primary Care: Pearls & References. 600p. (C). 1993. 29.95 (0-393-71014-9) Norton.

Onion, Meredith, jt. auth. see Dennis, Leslie.

***Onion, Susan.** Beverly Cleary. (Favorite Authors Ser.). (Illus.). 1994. 10.95 (1-55734-457-4) Tchr Create Mat.

— The Cricket in Times Square: A Literature Unit. (Literature Units Ser.). (Illus.). 48p. (Orig.). 1993. student ed, pap. 6.95 (1-55734-419-1) Tchr Create Mat.

***Onion, Susan, et al.** Survival. (Interdisciplinary Units Ser.). 1995. pap. text ed. 14.95 (1-55734-604-6) Tchr Create Mat.

Onions, A. H., jt. ed. see Smith, D.

Onions, Charles T. A Shakespeare Glossary. enl. rev. ed. Eagleson, Robert D., ed. 360p. 1986. pap. 16.95 (0-19-812521-6) OUP.

Onions, Charles T., et al, eds. Oxford Dictionary of English Etymology. 1966. 60.00 (0-19-861112-9) OUP.

Onions, H. S., jt. auth. see Smith, D.

Onions, John. English Fiction & Drama of the Great War. LC 89-70290. 230p. 1990. text ed. 45.00 (0-312-04507-7) St Martin.

Onions, Oliver. A Case in Camera. 320p. 1980. reprint ed. lib. bdg. 19.95 (0-89968-205-7, Lghtyr Pr) Buccaneer Bks.

— The First Book of Ghost Stories: Widdershins. LC 77-20545. 1978. reprint ed. pap. 5.95 (0-486-23608-0) Dover.

— Widdershins. 1993. reprint ed. lib. bdg. 18.95 (0-89968-438-6, Lghtyr Pr) Buccaneer Bks.

Onipko, Alexander I., tr. see Ostapenko, N. I., et al.

Onis, Ziya & Riedel, James. Economic Crisis & Long-Term Growth in Turkey. LC 93-18167. (Comparative Macroeconomic Studies). 152p. 1993. 8.95 (0-8213-2298-2, 12298) World Bank.

Onischchik, A. L. & Vinberg, E. B., eds. Lie Groups & Lie Algebra Three: Structure of Lie Groups & Lie Algebras. LC 93-33446. (Encyclopaedia of Mathematical Sciences Ser.: Vol. 41). 1994. 98.00 (0-387-54683-9) Spr-Verlag.

Onischenko, George T., tr. see Blinkov, Samuil Mikha'ilovich & Smirnov, N. A.

***Onish, Liane.** Dinosaur's Busy Day. (Doll Book Ser.). (Illus.). 8p. (J). (ps-2). 1995. bds. 4.95 (1-56293-802-9) McClanahan Bk.

— Hooray for Little Kitten. (Doll Book Ser.). (Illus.). 8p. (J). (ps-2). 1995. bds. 4.95 (1-56293-804-5) McClanahan Bk.

Onishchik, A. L., ed. Lie Groups & Lie Algebras I. LC 92-21600. (Encyclopaedia of Mathematical Sciences Ser.: Vol. 20). 1993. 89.00 (0-387-18697-2) Spr-Verlag.

Onishenko, Gary, jt. auth. see Roberts, Edmund B.

An Asterisk (*) at the beginning of an entry indicates that the title is appearing in BIP for the first time.

Onishi, Hiroshi. On a Riverboat Journey: A Handscroll by Ito Jakuchu, with Poems by Daiten. LC 89-62484. (Illus.). 180p. 1990. boxed 45.00 (*0-8076-1229-4*) Braziller.

— Photometric Determination of Trace Metals: Individual Metals, Aluminum to Lithium, Vol. 1, Pt. 2A. 4th ed. 885p. 1986. text ed. 250.00 (*0-471-86139-1*) Wiley.

— Photometric Determination of Traces of Metals, Set, Vol. 1, Pts. 2A & 2B. 4th ed. 1989. Set. text ed. 464.00 (*0-471-52748-3*) Wiley.

Onishi, Hiroshi, jt. auth. see Sandell, Ernest B.

Onishi, K., jt. auth. see Ninomiya, H.

Onishi, Katsuhito. The Bonsai Art of Kimura. Palmer, W. John, ed. Cullen, Margaret, tr. (Illus.). 176p. (Orig.). 1992. pap. 24.95 (*0-9634423-0-9*) Stone Lantern.

Onissi, T. R. Elsevier's Dictionary of the Cement Industry. 520p. (ENG, FRE, GER, JPN & SPA.). 1987. 350.00 (*0-8288-9285-7*, M1535) Fr & Eur.

— Elsevier's Dictionary of the Cement Industry: In English, French, German, Spanish, & Japanese. 520p. 1987. 192.50 (*0-444-42629-9*) Elsevier.

Onizuka, Richard, jt. auth. see Glodava, Mila.

Onken, U., jt. auth. see Gmehling, J.

onks of New Skete, M. Exaltation of the Holy Cross. Mancuso, Laurence, tr. (Liturgical Music Series I: Great Feasts: Vol. 4). 60p. 1986. pap. text ed. 15.00 (*0-935129-05-7*) Monks of New Skete.

Onkvisit, Sak & Shaw. International Marketing: Analysis & Strategy. 848p. (C). 1989. write for info. (*0-675-20556-5*, Merrill Pub Co) Macmillan.

Onkvisit, Sak & Shaw, John J. Consumer Behavior: Strategy & Analysis. LC 93-34137. (Illus.). 640p. (C). 1994. text ed. write for info. (*0-02-389353-2*) Macmillan.

— International Marketing: Analysis & Strategy. 2nd ed. LC 92-83811. 960p. (C). 1993. text ed. write for info. (*0-02-389343-5*) Macmillan.

— Product Life Cycles & Product Management. LC 88-26509. 172p. 1989. text ed. 49.95 (*0-89930-319-6*, OKV, Quorum Bks) Greenwood.

Onley, David C. Shuttle. (Orig.). 1982. pap. 3.25 (*0-89083-951-4*) Zebra.

Onley, Elaine H. Crying on Sunday. LC 94-14018. 76p. (Orig.). 1994. pap. 6.95 (*1-880837-47-1*) Smyth & Helwys.

***Online Press Inc. Staff, ed.** A Quick Course Instructor's Guide for Microsoft Office. (Illus.). 90p. 1995. teacher ed, ring bd. 19.95 (*1-879399-45-8*) Online Pr.

— A Quick Course Instructor's Guide for Microsoft Works 3 for Windows. (Illus.). 90p. 1995. teacher ed, ring bd. 19.95 (*1-879399-43-1*) Online Pr.

— A Quick Course Workbook for Microsoft Office. (Illus.). 72p. (Orig.). 1995. student ed, pap. 7.50 (*1-879399-46-6*) Online Pr.

— A Quick Course Workbook for Microsoft Works 3 for Windows. (Illus.). 72p. (Orig.). 1995. student ed, pap. 7.50 (*1-879399-44-X*) Online Pr.

Onn, Gerald, tr. see Von Rauch, Georg.

Onnerfors, Alf, ed. see Plinius.

Onnerfors, Alf, et al, eds. Bibliotheca Graeca et Latina Suppletoria, Bd. II: Physica Plinii Bambergensis. 174p. 1976. write for info. (*0-318-70725-X*, Pub. by Georg Olms GW) Lubrecht & Cramer.

Onnes, Keike K. Through Measurement to Knowledge: The Selected Papers of Heike Hamerlingh Onnes, 1853-1926. Gavroglu, Kostas & Goudaroulis, Yorgos, eds. (C). 1990. lib. bdg. 167.50 (*0-7923-0825-5*) Kluwer Ac.

Ono, Hiroko, tr. see Kamimura, Ikuro.

Ono, J., et al, eds. Vitamin D & Calcium Metabolism in the Renal Diseases. (Contributions to Nephrology Ser.: Vol. 22). (Illus.). vi, 122p. 1980. 56.00 (*3-8055-0389-X*) S Karger.

Ono, K., jt. ed. see Uchida, A.

Ono, K., et al. Introduction to Color & Composition. (Easy Start Guide Ser.). (Illus.). 112p. 1992. 36.95 (*4-7661-0629-6*, Pub. by Graphic Sha JA) Bks Nippan.

Ono, K., et al, eds. Lumbar Fusion & Stabilization. LC 92-46674. 1993. 145.00 (*0-387-70116-8*) Spr-Verlag.

Ono, K. A., jt. auth. see Trillmich, F.

***Ono, Kaoru, illus.** The Bee & the Dream: A Japanese Tale. LC 94-43784. (J). 1996. 14.99 (*0-525-45287-7*, DCB) Dutton Child Bks.

Ono, Koichi. Little Panda Bear. (Shaggies Ser.). (Illus.). 12p. (J). (ps-2). 1982. 4.95 (*0-671-42549-8*, Litl Simon S&S) S&S Childrens.

Ono, Michio. Atlas of the Cerebral Sulci. (Illus.). 232p. 1990. text ed. 173.00 (*0-86577-362-9*) Thieme Med Pubs.

Ono, R. Dana. Business of Biotechnology: From the Bench to the Street. 384p. 1991. text ed. 56.95 (*0-7506-9119-0*) Buttrwrth-Heinemann.

Ono, Shuichi. Sino-Japanese Economic Relationships: Trade, Direct Investment, & Future Strategy. (Discussion Paper Ser.: No. 146). 83p. 1992. 7.95 (*0-8213-1993-0*, 11993) World Bank.

Ono, Sokyo. Shinto: The Kami Way. (Illus.). 144p. 1994. pap. 8.95 (*0-8048-1960-2*) C E Tuttle.

Ono, T. An Introduction to Algebraic Number Theory. LC 90-30155. (University Series in Mathematics). (Illus.). 234p. 1990. 45.00 (*0-306-43436-9*, Plenum Pr) Plenum.

— Variations on a Theme of Euler: Quadratic Forms, Elliptic Curves & Hopf Maps. (University Series in Mathematics). (Illus.). 344p. (C). 1994. 79.50 (*0-306-44789-4*, Plenum Pr) Plenum.

Ono, Taketoshi, et al, eds. Brain Mechanisms of Perception & Memory: From Neuron to Behavior. LC 92-49789. (Illus.). 722p. 1993. 95.00 (*0-19-507770-9*) OUP.

***Ono, Yoko.** Grapefruit. LC 94-36990. 1995. 13.95 (*0-312-11816-3*) St Martin.

Ono, Yoshiyasu. Money, Interest, & Stagnation: Dynamic Theory & a Monetary Economy. (Illus.). 208p. 1994. 45.00 (*0-19-828837-9*) OUP.

Onoda, George Y., Jr. & Hench, Larry L., eds. Ceramic Processing Before Firing. LC 77-10553. 490p. 1978. text ed. 144.00 (*0-471-65410-8*, Wiley-Interscience) Wiley.

Onodera, T. & Kawai, S. A Formal Model of Visualization in Computer Graphics Systems. (Lecture Notes in Computer Science Ser.: Vol. 421). x, 100p. 1990. pap. 24.50 (*0-387-52395-2*) Spr-Verlag.

Onofrey. Clinical Optometric Pharmacology & Therapeutics: Clinical Text, Annual New. (Illus.). 170p. 1992. ring bd. 115.00 (*0-397-52133-2*) Lippincott.

Onofri, M. & Tesei, A. Fluid Dynamical Aspects of Combustion Theory. (Pitman Research Notes in Mathematics Ser.: No. 1775). 364p. 1992. pap. text ed. 63.95 (*0-470-21589-5*) Halsted Pr.

Onoh, J. K. Money & Banking in Africa. LC 82-15266. 224p. reprint ed. pap. 63.90 (*0-8357-2968-0*, 2039230) Bks Demand.

Onokerhoraye, A. G. Social Services in Nigeria: An Introduction. LC 82-17156. 354p. 1983. pap. 18.50 (*0-7103-0042-5*, Pub. by Kegan Paul Intl UK) Routledge Chapman & Hall.

Onon, Urgunge. The History & the Life of Chinggis Khan: The Secret History of the Mongols. LC 90-2136. xix, 183p. 1990. 54.50 (*90-04-09236-6*) E J Brill.

Onon, Urgunge, ed. Mongolian Heroes of the Twentieth Century. LC 76-23980. (Asian Studies: No. 1). (Illus.). 1976. lib. bdg. 32.50 (*0-404-15402-6*) AMS Pr.

Onopa, Sally, illus. The Weekend Woodworker: Projects for the Home Craftsman: Cabinets & Chests, Tables & Chairs, Kitchen Projects, Accents, Outdoor Projects, Toys. LC 92-32816. 1993. pap. 14.95 (*0-87596-575-X*) Rodale Pr Inc.

Onorato, Michael P. Forgotten Heroes: Japan's Imprisonment of American Civilians in the Phillipines, 1942-1945. LC 89-13402. (Oral History Ser.). 344p. 1989. text ed. 75.00 (*0-313-28084-3*, OFH/, Greenwood Pr) Greenwood.

Onorato, Michael P., ed. Another Time, Another World: Coney Island Memories. 1988. 25.00 (*0-930046-09-9*) CSUF Oral Hist.

Onorato, Michael P., jt. ed. see Cariaga-Barden, Regina.

Onorato, Richard J. Character of the Poet: Wordsworth in The Prelude. LC 74-131126. 1971. 65.00 (*0-691-06049-5*) Princeton U Pr.

— The Character of the Poet: Wordsworth in the Prelude. LC 74-131126. Date not set. reprint ed. pap. 127.40 (*0-7837-9409-6*, 2060154) Bks Demand.

Onorato, Ronald. Maria Nordman: Trabajos en la Ciudad de Ondas. LC 85-80104. (Illus.). 20p. 1985. 5.00 (*0-934418-23-3*) Mus Contemp Art.

— Wendy Edwards: Paintings & Drawings. (Illus.). 16p. (Orig.). 1989. pap. 5.00 (*0-933519-18-4*) D W Bell Gallery.

Onorato, Ronald J. Douglas Huebler. LC 88-81414. 52p. 1988. pap. text ed. 14.00 (*0-934418-30-6*) Mus Contemp Art.

Onorato, Ronald J., jt. auth. see Davies, Hugh M.

Onorato, Ronald J., et al. Satellite Intelligence: Boston-San Diego New Art Exchange. LC 90-61071. (Illus.). 36p. (Orig.). 1990. pap. 10.00 (*0-934418-35-7*) Mus Contemp Art.

Onore, Cynthia S., jt. auth. see Lester, Nancy B.

Onosko, Tim. Funland U. S. A. 1978. 15.95 (*0-405-11151-7*) Ayer.

Onoue, Masano, jt. auth. see Ondori Staff.

Onoura, Lesley I., jt. ed. see Haubold, Hans J.

***Onselen, Charles van.** Kas Maine, Son of Shield & Plow: The Life & Times of an African Sharecropper. 480p. Date not set. 27.50 (*0-8090-9603-X*) FS&G.

Onslow-Ford, Gordon. Creation. (Illus.). 123p. 1978. text ed. 35.00 (*0-9612760-0-2*) Bishop Pine.

***Onsrud, Harlan J. & Cook, David W., eds.** Geographic & Land Information Systems for Practicing Surveyors. 219p. 1990. pap. 45.00 (*0-614-06118-0*, L293) Am Congrs Survey.

Onsrud, Harlan J. & Rushton, Gerard, eds. Sharing Geographic Information. LC 94-19192. (Illus.). 528p. (C). 1995. 44.95 (*0-88285-152-7*) Ctr Urban Pol Res.

Onsrud, Harlan J., jt. ed. see Masser, Ian.

Onstad, Esther. Courage for Today Hope for Tomorrow. LC 75-2829. 144p. 1993. pap. 10.99 (*0-8066-2651-8*, 9-2651) Augsburg Fortress.

O'nstein, Allan. Institutionalized Learning in America. 248p. 1990. 34.95 (*0-88738-331-9*) Transaction Pubs.

Onstine, Burton W. Oregon Votes: 1858-1972. LC 73-88980. 395p. 1973. pap. 9.95 (*0-87595-043-4*) Oregon Hist.

Onstott, Kyle. The Falconhurst Fancy. 1978. lib. bdg. 14.30 (*0-89966-248-X*) Buccaneer Bks.

— Mandingo. 1987. mass mkt. 4.95 (*0-449-13226-9*) Fawcett.

Onstott, T. G. Pioneers of Menard & Mason Cos., Illinois. 404p. 1987. reprint ed. lib. bdg. 19.95 (*1-877869-08-2*) Mason Cnty Hist Proj.

Ontario Science Center Staff. Foodworks: Over One Hundred Science Activities & Fascinating Facts That Explore the Magic of Food. LC 87-1796. 96p. (J). (gr. 7-12). 1987. pap. 9.57 (*0-201-11470-4*) Addison-Wesley.

— Science Express. 1991. 14.38 (*0-201-57773-9*); pap. 8.61 (*0-201-57725-9*) Addison-Wesley.

— Scienceworks: Sixty-Five Experiments That Introduce the Fun & Wonder of Science. (Illus.). (J). (gr. 2-7). 1986. pap. 9.57 (*0-201-16780-8*) Addison-Wesley.

Ontario Science Centre Staff. Sportsworks: More Than Fifty Fun Games & Activities That Explore the Science of Sports. 1989. pap. 9.57 (*0-201-15296-7*) Addison-Wesley.

***Ontario Symposium on Personality & Social Psychology Staff.** Consistency in Social Behavior. Zanna, Mark P. et al, eds. LC 82-11489. (Ontario Symposium Ser.: No. 2). (Illus.). reprint ed. pap. 93.50 (*0-7837-9050-3*, 2049801) Bks Demand.

Ontiueros, Erlinda. San Ramon Chapel Pioneers & Their California Heritage. LC 90-7934. 572p. (Orig.). 1990. 50.00 (*0-933380-06-2*) Olive Pr Pubns.

Ontiveros, Suzanne R. Global Terrorism: A Historical Bibliography. (ABC-Clio Research Guides Ser.: No. 16). 168p. 1986. lib. bdg. 49.50 (*0-87436-453-1*) ABC-CLIO.

Ontiveros, Suzanne R., ed. The Dynamic Constitution: A Historical Bibliography. (ABC-Clio Research Guides Ser.: No. 19). 343p. 1986. lib. bdg. 49.50 (*0-87436-470-1*) ABC-CLIO.

Ontko, Andrew G. Thunder over the Ochoco, Vol. I, Pts. 1 & 2. LC 93-18698. (Illus.). 400p. (Orig.). 1993. pap. 16.95 (*0-89288-232-8*) Maverick.

Ontko, Gale. Thunder over the Ochco: Distant Thunder, Vol. II. 400p. 1994. pap. 16.95 (*0-89288-248-4*) Maverick.

Ontza, J. Diccionarios del Saber Moderno: La Politica en Su Entorno Historico Actual. 671p. (SPA.). 1980. 45.00 (*0-8288-2269-7*, S35606) Fr & Eur.

Onuf, Nicholas G. World of Our Making: Rules & Rule in Social Theory & International Relations. Kegley, Charles W., Jr. & Puchala, Donald, eds. (Studies in International Relations). 352p. 1989. text ed. 39.95 (*0-87249-626-0*); pap. 21.95 (*0-87249-680-5*) U of SC Pr.

Onuf, Nicholas G., ed. Law Making in the Global Community. LC 80-68078. 214p. 1982. lib. bdg. 29.95 (*0-89089-169-9*) Carolina Acad Pr.

Onuf, Nicholas G., jt. auth. see Onuf, Peter S.

Onuf, Peter, ed. American Culture, 1776-1815. LC 91-15465. (New American Nation, 1775-1820 Ser.: Vol. 12). 508p. 1991. 80.00 (*0-8153-0447-1*) Garland.

— American Society, 1776-1815. LC 91-13745. (New American Nation, 1775-1820 Ser.: Vol. 11). 550p. 1991. 90.00 (*0-8153-0446-3*) Garland.

— Patriots, Redcoats, & Loyalists. LC 91-15282. (New American Nation, 1775-1820 Ser.: Vol. 2). 544p. 1991. 85.00 (*0-8153-0437-4*) Garland.

Onuf, Peter S. The Revolution in American Thought. LC 91-13170. (New American Nation, 1775-1820 Ser.: Vol. 1). 376p. 1991. 70.00 (*0-8153-0436-6*) Garland.

— Statehood & Union: A History of the Northwest Ordinance. LC 86-43046. (Midwestern History & Culture Ser.). (Illus.). 224p. 1987. 29.95 (*0-253-35482-X*) Ind U Pr.

— Statehood & Union: A History of the Northwest Ordinance. LC 86-43046. (Midwestern History & Culture Ser.). 224p. 1992. reprint ed. pap. 10.95 (*0-253-20758-4*, MB-758) Ind U Pr.

Onuf, Peter S., ed. America & the World: Diplomacy, Politics, & War. LC 91-15487. (New American Nation, 1775-1820 Ser.: Vol. 9). 472p. 1991. 80.00 (*0-8153-0444-7*) Garland.

— Congress & the Confederation. LC 91-13165. (New American Nation, 1775-1820 Ser.: Vol. 4). 460p. 1991. 80.00 (*0-8153-0439-0*) Garland.

— Establishing the New Regime: The Washington Administration. LC 91-3515. (New American Nation, 1775-1820 Ser.: Vol. 7). 476p. 1991. 80.00 (*0-8153-0442-0*) Garland.

— The Federal Constitution. LC 91-13164. (New American Nation, 1775-1820 Ser.: Vol. 5). 626p. 1991. 95.00 (*0-8153-0440-4*) Garland.

— Federalists & Republicans. LC 91-15475. (New American Nation, 1775-1820 Ser.: Vol. 8). 400p. 1991. 70.00 (*0-8153-0443-9*) Garland.

— Jeffersonian Legacies. 528p. (C). 1993. pap. 18.95 (*0-8139-1463-9*) U Pr of Va.

Onuf, Peter S., intro. Ratifying, Amending, & Interpreting the Constitution. LC 91-3502. (New American Nation, 1775-1820 Ser.: Vol. 6). 536p. 1991. 85.00 (*0-8153-0441-2*) Garland.

— The Revolution in the States. LC 91-14591. (New American Nation, 1775-1820 Ser.: Vol. 3). 552p. 1991. 85.00 (*0-8153-0438-2*) Garland.

— State & Local Politics in the New Nation. LC 91-15466. (New American Nation, 1775-1820 Ser.: Vol. 10). 600p. 1991. 95.00 (*0-8153-0445-5*) Garland.

Onuf, Peter S. & Onuf, Nicholas G. Federal Union, Modern World: The Law of Nations in an Age of Revolutions, 1776-1814. 250p. 1994. 29.95 (*0-945612-34-6*) Madison Hse.

Onuf, Peter S., jt. auth. see Cayton, Andrew R.

Onuf, Peter S., ed. see Dulany, Daniel.

Onuf, Peter S., jt. auth. see Matson, Cathy D.

Onuki, A. & Kawasaki, K., eds. Dynamics & Patterns in Complex Fluids: New Aspects of the Physics-Chemistry Interface: Proceedings of the 4th Nishinomiya-Yukawa Memorial Symposium Nishinomiya City, Japan, October 26-27, 1989. (Proceedings in Physics Ser.: Vol. 52). (Illus.). x, 223p. 1990. 68.00 (*0-387-53051-7*) Spr-Verlag.

Onuki, Yoshio, jt. auth. see Terada, Kazuo.

Onuma, Hideharu, et al. Kyudo: The Essence & Practice of Japanese Archery. LC 92-30473. (Illus.). 160p. 1993. 32.00 (*4-7700-1734-0*) Kodansha.

Onuma, Tadayoshi, tr. see Yoshioka, Minoru & Iijima, Koichi.

Onuma, Yasuaki & Crawford, James, eds. A Normative Approach to War: Peace, War, & Justice in Hugo Grotius. LC 92-2466. 426p. 1993. 69.00 (*0-19-825709-0*, Clarendon Pr) OUP.

Onuoha, Everest C. & Alden, Richard A. The Fundamental English Handbook & Rhetoric. 269p. (C). 1988. pap. text ed. 27.30 (*0-943437-45-8*) CT Pub.

Onuska, Francis I. & Karasek, Francis W. Open Tubular Column Gas Chromatography in Environmental Sciences. LC 84-4806. 294p. 1984. 75.00 (*0-306-41589-5*, Plenum Pr) Plenum.

Onuzo, Okey. The Convert & the Counsellor. Ogundipe, Femi, ed. 120p. (Orig.). (C). 1990. pap. 5.00 (*978-30915-0-6*) Life Link.

— The Convert & the Counsellor: Following up New Christians. 2nd ed. Ndego, Anne, ed. 122p. 1992. pap. text ed. 6.99 (*1-880608-00-6*) Life Link.

— Dimensions of Faith. Ogundipe, Femi, ed. 168p. (Orig.). 1992. pap. text ed. 17.50 (*1-880608-01-4*) Life Link.

— From Everlasting to Everlasting (in Search of Truth) 1992. 15.95 (*0-533-09680-4*) Vantage.

— You May Kiss the Bride: Choice, Engagement, Courtship, Marriage, Divorce, Remarriage, Polygamy...& the Christian. Ndego, Anne, ed. 209p. (Orig.). 1992. pap. text ed. 8.50 (*1-880608-02-2*) Life Link.

Onvural, R. O., ed. Political Science Abstracts. (Illus.). 2086p. (C). 1993. 625.00 (*0-685-68782-1*, Plenum Pr) Plenum.

Onvural, R. O. & Nilsson, A., eds. Local Area Network Interconnection. (Illus.). 370p. 1994. 89.50 (*0-685-68781-3*, Plenum Pr) Plenum.

Onvural, Raif O. Asynchronous Transfer Mode Networks: Performance Issues. LC 93-30130. 260p. 1993. 65.00 (*0-89006-662-0*) Artech Hse.

Onvural, Raif O. & Akyildiz, Ian F., eds. Queuing Networks with Finite Capacity: Proceedings of the Second Interantional Conference on Queueing Networks with Finite Capacity, May 28-29, 1992 & September 28-30, 1992, Research Triangle Park, NC. LC 92-39977. 1992. write for info. (*0-444-89772-0*, North Holland) Elsevier.

Onvural, Raif O. & Nilsson, Arne, eds. Local Area Network Interconnection. LC 93-6370. 358p. 1993. 89.50 (*0-306-44630-8*, Plenum Pr) Plenum.

Onvural, Raif O., jt. ed. see Viniotis, Yannis.

OnWord Press Development Staff. One Minute HP-UX Manager. 112p. 1993. pap. 14.95 (*0-934605-26-2*, OnWord Pr) High Mtn.

— Pro-Engineer Exercise Book: Real Life Training That Builds Pro-Engineer Skills. 152p. 1994. 39.95 (*1-56690-037-9*, OnWord Pr) High Mtn.

OnWord Press Development Staff & Burns, Margaret. One Minute SunSoft Solaris Manager. 112p. 1993. pap. 14.95 (*0-934605-81-5*, OnWord Pr) High Mtn.

Onword Press Development Staff & Rice, Jim. HP-UX Quick Reference. 210p. 1994. pap. 18.95 (*0-934605-23-8*, OnWord Pr) High Mtn.

***OnWord Press Development Team.** MicroStation 5.X Productivity Book: Using MicroStation's Advanced Tools. (Illus.). 500p. 1995. pap. 49.95 (*1-56690-077-8*, 1436, OnWord Pr) High Mtn.

— SunSoft Solaris 2.X for Windows Users. 256p. 1994. pap. 24.95 (*1-56690-004-2*, OnWord Pr) High Mtn.

OnWord Press Development Team & Hicks, Clint. The SunSoft Solaris 2.0 Quick Reference. 256p. 1993. pap. 18.95 (*0-934605-76-9*, OnWord Pr) High Mtn.

OnWord Press Development Team & Kimery, Sam. The SunSoft Solaris 2.0 User's Guide. 304p. 1994. pap. 29.95 (*0-934605-74-2*, OnWord Pr) High Mtn.

OnWord Press Development Team & Rice, Jim. HP-UX User's Guide. (Illus.). 350p. 1995. pap. 29.95 (*0-934605-21-1*, 5088, OnWord Pr) High Mtn.

***OnWord Press Development Team, et al.** Inside Pro - Jr. LC 95-1000. (Illus.). 672p. 1995. pap. 49.95 (*1-56690-082-4*, 1915, OnWord Pr) High Mtn.

OnWord Press Staff & Hicks, Cliff. Five Steps to SunSoft Solaris 2. 196p. 1993. disk, pap. 24.95 (*0-934605-80-7*, OnWord Pr) High Mtn.

Onwuanibe, Richard C. A Critique of Revolutionary Humanism: Frantz Fanon. 168p. 1983. 15.50 (*0-87527-296-7*) Green.

Onwueme, I. C. The Tropical Tuber Crops: Yam, Cassava, Sweet Potato, Cocoyams. LC 77-20932. 248p. reprint ed. 70.70 (*0-8357-9996-4*, 2051823) Bks Demand.

Onwueme, Tess A. Three Plays: "The Broken Calabash," "Parables for a Season," & "The Reign of Wazobia" LC 92-47582. (African American Life Ser.). 174p. 1993. text ed. 29.95 (*0-8143-2444-4*); pap. text ed. 16.95 (*0-8143-2445-2*) Wayne St U Pr.

Onwueme, Tess O. Go Tell It to Women: An Epic Drama for Women. LC 92-72594. 350p. (C). 1992. 10.00 (*0-9628864-3-2*); pap. text ed. 5.00 (*0-9628864-0-8*) Afri Her Pr.

Onwuka, Ralph A., et al, eds. African Development, OAU-ECA & Lagos Plan of Action. LC 85-70677. (Illus.). 242p. 1985. 21.50 (*0-931494-58-3*); pap. 12.50 (*0-931494-57-5*) Brunswick Pub.

Onwuka, Ralph I. & Aluko, Olajide, eds. The Future of Africa & the New International Economic Order. LC 85-30277. 325p. 1986. text ed. 39.95 (*0-312-31412-4*) St Martin.

Onwuka, Ralph I. & Sesay, Amadu. The Future of Regionalism in Africa. LC 84-40335. 288p. 1985. text ed. 35.00 (*0-312-31482-5*) St Martin.

Onyefulu, Ifeoma. A Is for Africa. LC 92-39964. (Illus.). 32p. (J). (ps-3). 1993. 14.99 (*0-525-65147-0*, Cobblehill Bks) Dutton Child Bks.

— Emeka's Gift: An African Counting Story. LC 94-30700. 32p. (J). 1995. 14.99 (*0-525-65205-1*, Cobblehill Bks) Dutton Child Bks.

Onyemelukwe, Clement C. Economic Underdevelopment: An Inside View. LC 75-302086. (Illus.). 127p. reprint ed. pap. 36.20 (*0-8357-6101-0*, 2034497) Bks Demand.

Onyemelukwe, J. O. Industrialization in West Africa. LC 83-40175. 226p. 1984. text ed. 29.95 (*0-312-41574-5*) St Martin.

Onyenorah, Edith. The Gorgeous Black Prince. 1987. 24.00 (*0-7223-2173-2*, Pub. by A H S Ltd UK) St Mut.

O

***Onyett.** Case Management Mental Health. 1992. 44.95 (*1-56593-018-5*, 0261) Singular Publishing.

Onyett, Gail, jt. auth. see Onyett, Lloyd.

Onyett, Lloyd & Onyett, Gail. Essentials of Lotus 1-2-3 Release 2.2. (Illus.). 272p. (C). 1991. teacher ed write for info. (*1-56527-022-3*); pap. text ed. 17.95 (*1-878748-69-6*); disk 44.95 (*1-878748-67-X*); disk 44.95 (*1-878748-68-8*) Course Tech.

— Essentials of Lotus 1-2-3 Release 2.3. (Illus.). 384p. (C). 1992. teacher ed write for info. (*0-318-69235-X*); pap. text ed. 19.95 (*1-878748-91-2*); disk 49.95 (*1-878748-89-0*); disk 49.95 (*1-878748-90-4*) Course Tech.

Onyett, Lloyd C. Advanced Structured BASIC Using MicroSoft's BASIC & QuickBASIC. 345p. (C). 1988. pap. text ed. 25.00 (*0-669-15442-3*); Instr.'s guide. teacher ed 2.00 (*0-669-15441-5*) Heath.

Onyiah, Leonard. Statistical Design - Analysis of Experiments: An App. Approach. 1995. write for info. (*0-8493-8632-2*) CRC Pr.

Onyschuk, Motria, tr. The Cat & the Rooster. LC 94-14505. (Illus.). (ENG.). (J). (gr. 2 up). 1995. 15.00 (*0-679-86964-6*); pap. 15.99 (*0-679-96964-0*) Knopf.

Onyszkiewicz, Janusz, jt. auth. see Marek, Wiktor.

Onzuka-Anderson, Roberta, jt. ed. see Browne, Colette.

***Oo, N. K.** The Book of Leo: An Enchiridion, Vol. 1. (Enchiridions Ser.: Vol. 1 of 12). 80p. 1995. 14.95 (*1-56313-461-6*) BrownTrout Pubs Inc.

— The Book of Scorpio: An Enchiridion, Vol. 2. (Enchiridions Ser.: Vol. 2 of 12). 80p. 1995. 14.95 (*1-56313-639-2*) BrownTrout Pubs Inc.

***Oodgeroo.** Dreamtime: Aboriginal Stories. LC 93-79375. (J). (gr. 4-7). 1994. 16.00 (*0-688-13296-0*) Lothrop.

Oody, T. Eugene. The Bible Goes to Kruka Town. (Illus.). 74p. (Orig.). 1994. pap. 5.00 (*0-9640888-0-0*) T E Oody.

Ooi, B. C. Efficient Query Processing in Geographic Information Systems. (Lecture Notes in Computer Science Ser.: Vol. 471). viii, 208p. 1990. pap. 29.00 (*0-387-53474-1*) Spr-Verlag.

Ooi, B. C., jt. ed. see Abel, D.

Ooi, B. C., jt. auth. see Lu, H. J.

Ooi Jin Bee. Development Problems of an Open-Access Resource: The Fisheries of Peninsular Malaysia. 61p. 1990. pap. text ed. 10.00 (*981-3035-46-3*, Pub. by Inst SE Asian Studies SI) Ashgate Pub Co.

Ooi, Jin-Bee. Peninsular Malaysia. LC 75-42166. (Geographies for Advances Study Ser.). 453p. reprint ed. pap. 129.20 (*0-685-16389-X*, 2027710) Bks Demand.

Ooka, D. T., tr. see Horio, Seishi.

Ooka, D. T., tr. see Okawa, Essei.

Ooka, D. T., tr. see Shibano, Tamizo.

Ooka, D. T., tr. see Watanabe, Yuichi.

Ooka, D. T., tr. see Yazaki, Setsuo.

Ooka, Diane, tr. see Masui, Mitsuko.

Ooka, Dianne, ed. see Ger, Lily.

Ooka, Dianne, tr. see Kawahata, Aiyoshi.

Ooka, Dianne, tr. see Nakano, Toru.

Ooka, Makoto, et al. What the Kite Thinks: A Linked Poem. 88p. 1994. pap. text ed. 10.95 (*0-8248-1599-8*) UH Pr.

Ooka, Shohei. Fires on the Plain. Morris, Ivan, tr. 254p. 1957. pap. 12.95 (*0-8048-1379-5*) C E Tuttle.

— Fires on the Plain. Morris, Ivan, tr. LC 78-16916. 246p. 1978. reprint ed. text ed. 38.50 (*0-313-20567-1*, OOFP, Greenwood Pr) Greenwood.

***Oomen.** My Friends. (Peephole Board Bks). (J). 1995. 2.95 (*0-689-80260-9*, Mac Bks Young Read) S&S Childrens.

— My House. (Peephole Board Bks). (J). 1995. 2.25 (*0-689-80261-7*, Mac Bks Young Read) S&S Childrens.

— My Toys. (Peephole Board Bks). (J). 1995. 2.25 (*0-689-80262-5*, Mac Bks Young Read) S&S Childrens.

— My World. (J). 1995. 2.25 (*0-689-80263-3*, Mac Bks Young Read) S&S Childrens.

Oomen, T. K. State & Society in India: Studies in Nation Building. 210p. (C). 1990. text ed. 26.00 (*0-8039-9656-X*) Sage.

Oomen, T. K. & Mukherji, P. N., eds. Indian Sociology: Reflections & Introspections. (C). 1986. 28.00 (*0-86132-133-2*, Pub. by Popular Prakashan II) S Asia.

Oomen, T. K. & Venugopal, C. N. Sociology. (C). 1988. 80.00 (*0-685-25674-X*) St Mut.

Oomi, G., et al, eds. Transport & Thermal Properties of f-Electron Systems. 1993. 89.50 (*0-306-44531-X*, Plenum Pr) Plenum.

Oommen, M. A. Economics of Indian Cinema. (C). 1991. 17.50 (*81-204-0575-7*, Pub. by Oxford IBH II) S Asia.

— Issues in Teaching of Economics in Indian Universities. (C). 1987. 18.50 (*81-204-0203-0*, Pub. by Oxford IBH II) S Asia.

Oommen, M. A., jt. ed. see Ramachandran, P.

Oommen, T. K. From Mobilization to Institutionalization: The Dynamics of Agrarian Movement in Twentieth Century Kerala. 1985. 27.50 (*0-8364-1407-1*, Pub. by Popular Prakashan II) S Asia.

— Protest & Change: Studies in Social Movements. 304p. (C). 1990. text ed. 32.50 (*0-8039-9652-7*) Sage.

Oommen, T. K., ed. Sociological Literature South Asia, Vol. 1: 1992. (C). 1993. 62.00 (*81-900333-0-1*, Pub. by Deep) S Asia.

Oommen, T. K. & Venugopal, C. N. Sociology for Law Students. (C). 1993. 32.50 (*81-7012-375-5*, Pub. by Eastern Book II) St Mut.

Ooms, Emily G. Women & Millenarian Protest in Meiji, Japan: Deguchi Nao & Omotokyo. (Cornell East Asia Ser.: No. 61). 164p. (Orig.). (C). 1993. pap. 10.00 (*0-939657-61-9*) Cornell East Asia Pgm.

Ooms, Herman. Tokugawa Ideology: Early Constructs, 1570-1680. LC 84-42897. (Illus.). 350p. (C). 1989. pap. text ed. 18.95 (*0-691-00838-8*) Princeton U Pr.

Ooms, L. A. & Degryse, A. D., eds. Physiological & Pharmacological Aspects of the Reticulo-rumen. (Current Topics in Veterinary Medicine & Animal Science Ser.). (C). 1987. lib. bdg. 144.00 (*0-89838-878-3*) Kluwer Ac.

Ooms, Marius. Empirical Vector Autoregressive Modeling. LC 93-46882. (Lecture Notes in Economics & Mathematical Systems Ser.: Vol. 407). (Illus.). xiv, 380p. 1994. pap. 64.00 (*0-387-57707-6*) Spr-Verlag.

Ooms, Theodora J., jt. ed. see Lerman, Robert I.

Oomura, Y., ed. Emotions. (Illus.). xiv, 446p. 1986. 214.50 (*3-8055-4405-7*) S Karger.

Oonk, H. A. Phase Theory: The Thermodynamics of Heterogeneous Equilibria. (Studies in Modern Thermodynamics: Vol. 3). 270p. 1981. 105.25 (*0-444-42019-3*) Elsevier.

Oorde, Willem V. Lexikon Aetherianum. viii, 219p. 1963. reprint ed. write for info. (*0-318-72061-2*, Pub. by Georg Olms GW) Lubrecht & Cramer.

Oordt, Kari van, tr. see Steiner, Rudolf.

Oorschot, D. E. & Jones, D. G. Axonal Regeneration in the Mammalian Central Nervous System. (Advances in Anatomy, Embryology & Cell Biology Ser.: Vol. 119). (Illus.). 128p. 1990. 58.00 (*0-387-51757-X*) Spr-Verlag.

Oort, J., jt. auth. see Baak, J. P.

Oort, Marianne, tr. see Vetter, Tilmann.

Oosawa, F., et al, eds. Transmembrane Signaling & Sensation. (Taniguchi Symposia on Brain Sciences Ser.: No. 7). 278p. 1984. lib. bdg. 112.00 (*90-6764-041-7*, Pub. by VSP NE) Coronet Bks.

Oosawa, Fumio. Polyelectrolytes. LC 70-134786. (Illus.). 167p. reprint ed. pap. 47.60 (*0-317-07976-X*, 2055010) Bks Demand.

Oost, Stewart I. Roman Policy in Epirus & Acarnania in the Age of the Roman Conquest of Greece. LC 75-7333. (Roman History Ser.). 1975. reprint ed. 12.95 (*0-405-07050-0*) Ayer.

Oost, W. A., jt. ed. see Komen, G. J.

Oostendorp, Cora. The Bryophytes of the Palaeozoic & Mesozoic. (Bryophytorum Bibliotheca Ser.: Vol. 34). (Illus.). 208p. 1987. pap. 78.25 (*3-443-62006-X*) Lubrecht & Cramer.

Oostendorp, Eric, jt. auth. see Munnik, Josha.

***Oosterbaan, Amanda.** Freddy the Fire Truck. LC 94-94353. (Illus.). 32p. (Orig.). (J). (ps-2). 1994. text ed. 166.95 (*0-9643138-8-X*); pap. 8.95 (*0-9643138-9-8*) Chldrns Pubng.

Oosterhaven, Jan, jt. auth. see Folmer, Hendrik.

Oosterhof, Albert C. Classroom Applications of Educational Measurement. 2nd ed. 544p. (C). 1994. text ed. write for info. (*0-02-389350-8*, Merrill Pub Co) Macmillan.

Oosterhouse, Kenneth, et al. Born of a Glorious Thunder: Real Life Accounts of Foreign Christian Work. Kortenhoeven, Helen, tr. 304p. (Orig.). 1986. pap. 6.95 (*0-318-22002-4*) West Indies Pub.

Oosterhuis, D. M., jt. ed. see Miley, W. N.

Oosterhuis, Hans J., jt. ed. see De Baets, Marc H.

Oosterhuis, Harry, ed. Homosexuality & Male Bonding in Pre-Nazi Germany: the Youth Movement, the Gay Movement & Male Bonding Before Hitler's Rise: Original Transcripts from "Der Eigene", the First Gay Journal in the World. LC 91-27666. (Journal of Homosexuality). 297p. 1991. lib. bdg. 39.95 (*1-56024-164-0*) Haworth Pr.

— Homosexuality & Male Bonding in the Pre-Nazi Germany: the Youth Movement, the Gay Movement & Male Bonding Before Hitler's Rise: Original Transcripts from "Der Eigene", the First Gay Journal in the World. LC 91-27388. (Journal of Homosexuality). 297p. 1991. lib. bdg. 14.95 (*1-56023-008-8*) Haworth Pr.

Oosterhuis, Huub. The Children of the Poor Man. Kaan, Fred, tr. LC 84-240947. (Risk Book Ser.: No. 7). (Illus.). 60p. reprint ed. pap. 25.00 (*0-7837-5998-3*, 2045808) Bks Demand.

— Your Word Is Near. Carmody, John, tr. 112p. 1994. pap. 7.95 (*0-8358-0714-2*) Upper Room Bks.

— Your Word is Near: Contemporary Christian Prayers. Smith, N. D., tr. LC 68-20848. 164p. reprint ed. pap. 46.80 (*0-8357-4631-3*, 2037560) Bks Demand.

Oosterhuis, J. W., et al, eds. Pathobiology of Human Germ Cell Neoplasia. (Recent Results in Cancer Research Ser.: Vol. 123). (Illus.). 192p. 1991. 97.00 (*0-387-53928-X*) Spr-Verlag.

Oosterhuis, Jendo A., ed. Ophthalmic Tumours. (Monographs in Ophthalmology). 1985. lib. bdg. 154.00 (*90-6193-528-8*) Kluwer Ac.

Oosterlinck, ed. see Tescher.

Oosterlinck, A., jt. ed. see Hutzler, P.

Oosterling, Henk. Denken Unterwegs: Philosophie im Kratefeld Sozialen und Politischen Engagements. Festschrift fur Heinz Kimmerle Zu Seinem 60. Geburstag. DeJong, Frans, ed. (Schriften Zur Philosophie der Differenz Ser.: No. 4). xxii, 436p. 1990. 83.00 (*90-6032-317-3*, Pub. by B R Gruener NE) Benjamins North Am.

Oosterman, Margaret A., et al, eds. Earth Science Investigations. (Illus.). 238p. (Orig.). 1990. pap. 34.95 (*0-922152-07-1*) Am Geol.

Oosterveen, Karla, tr. see Mitterauer, Michael & Sieder, Reinhard.

Oosterveld-Egas, jt. auth. see Raparaz, M. C.

Oosterveld, Wilhelmus J., ed. Meniere's Disease: A Comprehensive Appraisal. LC 83-5962. (Wiley-Medical Publication Ser.). 145p. reprint ed. pap. 41.40 (*0-8357-7878-9*, 2036296) Bks Demand.

— Otoneurology. LC 84-3717. (Wiley-Medical Publication Ser.). (Illus.). 284p. reprint ed. pap. 81.00 (*0-8357-7929-7*, 2052329) Bks Demand.

Oosterwegel, Annerieke & Oppenheimer, Louis. The Self-System: Developmental Changes Between & Within Self-Concepts. 208p. 1993. text ed. 39.95 (*0-8058-1216-4*) L Erlbaum Assocs.

Oosthoek, Hans. Education from the Multi-Level Perspective. (Special Aspects of Education Ser.: Vol. 4). 295p. 1984. text ed. 63.00 (*0-677-06450-0*) Gordon & Breach.

Oosthout, Henri. Modes of Knowledge & the Transcendental: An Introduction to Plotinus Ennead 5.3 (49) with a Commentary & Translation. LC 91-23974. (Bochumer Studien zur Philosophie Ser.: Vol. 17). 1992. 65.00x (*90-6032-319-X*, Pub. by Gruner NE) Benjamins North Am.

Oosthuizen. Physiology Workbook. (C). 1983. pap. text ed. 14.95 (*0-409-08631-2*) Buttrwrth-Heinemann.

***Oosthuizen, G. C. & Becken, H. J., eds.** Afro-Christianity at the Grassroots: Bits Dynamics & Strategies. LC 94-26023. (Studies of Religion in Africa: 9). 1994. 74.50 (*90-04-10035-0*) E J Brill.

Oosthuizen, G. C. & Hexham, Irving, eds. Afro-Christian Religion at the Grassroots in Southern Africa. LC 91-10173. (African Studies: Vol. 19). 440p. 1991. lib. bdg. 109.95 (*0-88946-226-7*) E Mellen.

— Empirical Studies of African Independent- Indigenous Churches. LC 92-22083. 356p. 1992. text ed. 99.95 (*0-7734-9588-6*) E Mellen.

Oosthuizen, G. C., et al. Religion, Intergroup Relations, & Social Change in South Africa. LC 88-15430. (Contributions in Ethnic Studies: No. 24). 249p. 1988. text ed. 49.95 (*0-313-26360-4*, HSG/, Greenwood Pr) Greenwood.

Oosthuizen, G. C., et al, eds. Afro-Christian Religion & Healing in Southern Africa. LC 88-8894. (African Studies: Vol. 8). 450p. 1989. lib. bdg. 109.95 (*0-88946-282-8*) E Mellen.

Oosthuizen, Gerhardus C. The Healer-Prophet in Afro-Christian Churches. LC 92-15125. (Studies in Christian Mission: Vol. 3). (Illus.). xxvii, 200p. 1992. 57.25 (*90-04-09468-7*) E J Brill.

Oosthuizen, P. H., jt. ed. see Ebadian, M. A.

Oota, Kunio & Otsu, Syoichi, eds. Pathology of Extreme Aged, Vol. 1. (Pathology of the Extreme Aged Ser.: Vol. 1). (Illus.). 200p. 1984. pap. 22.50 (*0-912791-10-1*) Ishiyaku Euro.

Oothoudt, Michael, jt. ed. see Lillberg, John.

Oots, Kent L. A Political Organization Approach to Transnational Terrorism. LC 85-17030. (Contributions to Political Science Ser.: No. 141). (Illus.). 184p. 1986. text ed. 49.95 (*0-313-25105-3*, OPO/, Greenwood Pr) Greenwood.

Op De Beeck, Bart, jt. auth. see Callewaert, Winand M.

Op den Kamp, J. A., ed. Dynamics of Membrane Assembly. (NATO ASI Series H: Cell Biology: Vol. 63). (Illus.). 393p. 1992. 189.00 (*0-387-53149-1*) Spr-Verlag.

Op Den Kamp, J. A., ed. Membrane Biogenesis. (NATO ASI Series H: Vol. 16). (Illus.). viii, 477p. 1988. 167.00 (*0-387-18566-6*) Spr-Verlag.

Op den Kamp, J. A., et al, eds. Lipids & Membranes: Past, Present & Future: In Honour of Laurens L. M. van Deenen. 380p. 1987. 147.25 (*0-444-80743-8*) Elsevier.

Op den Kamp, Jos A. F., ed. Biological Membranes: Structure, Biogenesis & Dynamics. LC 94-2915. (NATO ASI Series H: Cell Biology: Vol. 82). (Illus.). 366p. 1994. 154.00 (*0-387-57731-9*) Spr-Verlag.

Op den Velde, W., jt. ed. see De Loos, W. S.

Op Ten Berg, M., jt. ed. see Newton, J. R.

Opachak, Mark, ed. Industrial Fluids: Controls, Concerns & Costs. LC 82-60442. (Manufacturing Update Ser.). 276p. reprint ed. pap. 78.70 (*0-318-35020-3*, 2030897) Bks Demand.

Opalenik, Andrea, jt. auth. see Khalsa, Baba S.

Opalski, Magdalena & Bartal, Israel. Poles & Jews: A Failed Brotherhood, The Tauber Institute for the Study of European Jew. LC 92-53865. (Tauber Institute for the Study of European Jewry Ser.: Vol. 13). 205p. (C). 1992. text ed. 40.00 (*0-87451-601-3*); pap. 16.95 (*0-87451-602-1*) U Pr of New Eng.

Oparil, Suzanne, jt. auth. see Snider, Arthur J.

Oparka, K. J., jt. ed. see Harris, N.

Opas, Susan R., jt. auth. see Servonsky, Jane.

Opatoshu, Joseph. A Day in Regensburg: Short Stories. Sloan, Jacob, tr. LC 68-15788. 252p. reprint ed. pap. 71.90 (*0-685-17854-4*, 2029213) Bks Demand.

Opatrny, Josef. Historical Pre-Conditions of the Origin of the Cuban Nation. LC 92-32972. 264p. 1993. text ed. 89.95 (*0-7734-2304-4*) E Mellen.

— U. S. Expansionism & Cuban Annexationism in the 1850s. LC 93-15343. 324p. 1993. text ed. 99.95 (*0-7734-2308-7*) E Mellen.

Opatz, Joseph P., ed. Health Promotion Evaluation: Measuring the Organizational Impact. (Illus.). (Orig.). 1987. pap. 22.95 (*0-940981-00-9*) Natl Wellness Inst.

Opatz, Joseph P., ed. see Association for Worksite Health Promotion Staff.

Opdahl, Keith. Novels of Saul Bellow: An Introduction. LC 67-16197. 1967. 28.50 (*0-271-73118-4*) Pa St U Pr.

Opdam, Paul, jt. ed. see Vos, Claire C.

Opdycke, John B. Harper's English Grammar. 288p. 1983. mass mkt. 4.50 (*0-446-31184-7*) Warner Bks.

Opdyke, C. W. Opdyke: Genealogy, Containing the Opdyck-Opdycke-Updike American Descendants of the Wesel & Holland Families. 499p. 1991. reprint ed. lib. bdg. 87.50 (*0-8328-1824-0*); reprint ed. pap. 77.50 (*0-8328-1825-9*) Higginson Bk Co.

Opdyke, D. L., ed. Monographs on Fragrance Raw Materials. (Illus.). 1979. 300.00 (*0-08-023775-4*, Pub. by Pergamon Repr UK) Franklin.

Opdyke, George. Treatise on Political Economy. LC 68-56559. (Reprints of Economic Classics Ser.). 1973. reprint ed. 45.00 (*0-678-00802-7*) Kelley.

Opdyke, Irene G. & Elliot, Jeffrey M. Into the Flames: The Life Story of a Righteous Gentile. Burgess, Mary A., ed. LC 91-41355. (Studies in Judaica & the Holocaust: No. 8). (Illus.). 176p. 1993. reprint ed. lib. bdg. 29.00x (*0-89370-375-3*); reprint ed. pap. 19.00x (*0-89370-475-X*) Borgo Pr.

Opechowski, W. Crystallographic & Metacrystallographic Groups. 640p. 1986. 197.50 (*0-444-86955-7*) Elsevier.

O'Pecko, Michael T. & Hofstetter, Eleanore O. The Twentieth-Century German Novel: A Bibliography of English Language Criticism, 1945-1986. LC 89-10872. 816p. 1989. 65.00 (*0-8108-2262-8*) Scarecrow.

Opeka, Kay. Keep Them Thinking, Level 1: A Handbook of Model Lessons. 2nd ed. LC 91-61813. (Illus.). 80p. (Orig.). 1991. pap. text ed. 17.95 (*0-932935-34-6*) IRI-Skylght.

Opeka, Kay, jt. auth. see Fogarty, Robin.

Opeke, Lawrence K. Tropical Tree Crops. LC 81-11501. 330p. reprint ed. pap. 94.10 (*0-685-23670-6*, 2027895) Bks Demand.

Opekola, Pauline N. Advertising & Medicine: Guidebook for Reference & Research. LC 83-46107. 150p. 1984. 39.50 (*0-88164-148-0*); pap. 34.50 (*0-88164-149-9*) ABBE Pubs Assn.

Opel, Adolf, ed. Relationships: An Anthology of Contemporary Austrian Prose. (Studies in Austrian Literature, Culture, & Thought. Translation Ser.). 362p. 1991. pap. 25.00 (*0-929497-05-8*) Ariadne CA.

Opelima, Ecniv. God Unveiled & Demystified: The Master Key Revealed for Happiness, Love, Wisdom & Power. (Illus.). 192p. (Orig.). 1994. pap. 19.95 (*1-884767-00-1*) Celestial Lodge.

Opelka, Gregg, jt. auth. see Boyd, Jane.

Opella, S. J. & Lu, P., eds. NMR & Biochemistry: A Symposium Honoring Mildred Cohn. LC 79-19485. (Illus.). 448p. reprint ed. pap. 127.70 (*0-7837-0618-9*, 2040963) Bks Demand.

Opello, Walter C., Jr. Portugal: From Monarchy to Pluralist Democracy. (Profiles - Nations of Contemporary Western Europe Ser.). 177p. 1991. text ed. 48.00 (*0-8133-0488-1*) Westview.

Opelt, James R. Organizing & Managing the High School Theatre Program. 276p. 1991. text ed. 46.95 (*0-205-12820-3*, H28202) Allyn.

***Open.** OSF DCE Administration Guide: Extended Services (Release 1.0.3) (Illus.). 1024p. (C). 1994. pap. text ed. 57.00 (*0-13-186743-1*) P-H.

Open, jt. auth. see Rzevski.

Open Framework Staff. Application Development: UNIX. 132p. (C). 1993. pap. text ed. 22.00 (*0-13-630484-2*) P-H.

— Availability. 72p. (C). 1993. pap. text ed. 16.00 (*0-13-630948-8*) P-H.

— Distributed Application Services. 195p. (C). 1993. pap. text ed. 22.00 (*0-13-630518-0*) P-H.

— Information Management. 150p. (C). 1993. pap. text ed. 20.00 (*0-13-630500-8*) P-H.

— Networking Services: UNIX. 180p. (C). 1993. pap. text ed. 22.00 (*0-13-630393-5*) P-H.

— Performance. 98p. (C). 1993. pap. text ed. 18.00 (*0-13-630666-7*) P-H.

— Platforms. 172p. (C). 1993. pap. text ed. 20.00 (*0-13-630385-4*) P-H.

— Potential for Change. 130p. (C). 1993. pap. text ed. 20.00 (*0-13-630617-9*) P-H.

— The Systems Architecture: An Introduction. 160p. (C). 1993. pap. text ed. 20.00 (*0-13-560186-X*) P-H.

— Systems Management. 150p. (C). 1993. pap. text ed. 20.00 (*0-13-630450-8*) P-H.

— Transaction Management. 148p. (C). 1993. pap. text ed. 20.00 (*0-13-630377-3*) P-H.

— Usability. 170p. (C). 1993. pap. text ed. 20.00 (*0-13-630930-5*) P-H.

— User Interface. 222p. (C). 1993. pap. text ed. 24.00 (*0-13-630591-1*) P-H.

Open Path Staff. Namgyal Rinpoche: Unfolding Through Art. Wongmo, Karma C., ed. (Illus.). 157p. (Orig.). (C). 1982. text ed. 75.00 (*0-9602722-2-4*); pap. text ed. 25.00 (*0-685-07078-6*) Open Path.

Open Petrotechnical Staff. POSC E&P User Interface Style Guide. 1993. text ed. 95.00 (*0-13-100728-9*) P-H.

— POSC Epicentre Data Model, 3 Volumes, 3 Vols. Incl. Vol. 1. Tutorial. 1993. (*0-13-102666-6*); Vol. 2. Entity Dictionary. 1993. (*0-13-102674-7*); Vol. 3. Properties, Reference Entities, & DataTy. 1993. (*0-13-102682-8*); (Software Integration Platform Specifications Ser.). 1993. Set text ed. 495.00 (*0-13-100702-5*) P-H.

— POSC Exchange Format. 1994. text ed. 75.00 (*0-13-100710-6*) P-H.

Open, Software. Motif Online Library. 1994. Incl. disk. disk 105.00 (*0-13-108945-5*) P-H.

Open Software Foundation Staff. Application Environment Specification (AES) User Environment Volume Revision C. 880p. 1992. pap. text ed. 53.00 (*0-13-043621-6*) P-H.

— Design of the OSF-1 Operating System. 1993. pap. text ed. 47.00 (*0-13-202813-1*) P-H.

— Motif Widget Writing. 1995. disk, pap. 36.00 (*0-13-143141-2*) P-H.

— OSF - Motif Programmer's Guide Release 1.2. 576p. 1992. pap. text ed. 45.00 (*0-13-643107-0*) P-H.

— OSF - Motif Programmer's Reference Release 1.2. 1260p. 1992. pap. text ed. 55.00 (*0-13-643115-1*) P-H.

— OSF - MOTIF Programmer's Reference Release 1.2, Vol. 2. 1992. pap. 28.00 (*0-13-012790-6*) P-H.

— OSF - MOTIF User's Guide Release 1.2. 176p. 1992. pap. text ed. 30.00 (*0-13-643131-3*) P-H.

— OSF - One: 1.1 User's Guide. 1993. pap. text ed. 42.00 (*0-13-014291-3*) P-H.

— OSF DCE Administration Guide: Core Components. (C). 1993. pap. text ed. 42.00 (*0-13-176553-1*) P-H.

— OSF DCE Administration Guide: Extended Services. (C). 1993. pap. text ed. 51.00 (*0-13-176561-2*) P-H.
— OSF DCE Administration Guide: Introduction. 1993. pap. text ed. 40.00 (*0-13-176546-9*) P-H.
— OSF DCE Administration Reference. 740p. 1993. pap. text ed. 48.00 (*0-13-643818-0*) P-H.
— OSF DCE Application Development Guide. 1025p. 1993. pap. text ed. 55.00 (*0-13-643826-1*) P-H.
— OSF DCE Applicaton Development Reference. 1246p. 1993. pap. text ed. 53.00 (*0-13-643834-2*) P-H.
— OSF DCE User's Guide & Reference. 208p. 1992. pap. text ed. 30.00 (*0-13-643842-3*) P-H.
— OSF-1 Command Reference. 928p. 1991. pap. text ed. 52.00 (*0-13-643628-5*, 270512) P-H.
— OSF-1 Programmer's Reference. 1248p. 1991. pap. text ed. 56.00 (*0-13-643610-2*, 270513) P-H.
— OSF-1 System & Network Administrator's Reference. 633p. 1991. pap. text ed. 50.00 (*0-13-643602-1*, 270511) P-H.
— OSF 1 1.2 Network Applications Programmers Guide. 1993. pap. 36.00 (*0-13-030461-1*) P-H.
— OSF 1 1.2 Programmers Reference. 1120p. 1994. pap. text ed. 51.00 (*0-13-020561-3*) P-H.
— OSF 1 1.2 Programmer's Reference. 1632p. 1994. pap. text ed. 66.00 (*0-13-020579-6*) P-H.
— OSF 1 1.2 System & Network Administrators Reference. 1993. pap. 41.00 (*0-13-020587-7*) P-H.
Open University Course Team Staff, ed. Ocean Chemistry & Deep-Sea Sediments, Vol. 5. (Illus.). 128p. 1989. pap. text ed. 24.95 (*0-08-036373-3*, Pergamon Pr) Elsevier.
— Ocean Circulation. (Open University Oceanography Ser.: Vol. 3). (Illus.). 190p. 1989. pap. text ed. 27.00 (*0-08-036369-5*, Pergamon Pr) Elsevier.
Open University Health & Disease Course Team Staff. The Biology of Health & Disease. (Health & Disease Ser.). 168p. 1985. pap. text ed. 32.00 (*0-335-15053-5*, Open Univ Pr) Taylor & Francis.
— Birth to Old Age: Health & Disease in Transition. (Health & Disease Ser.). 204p. 1985. pap. 32.00 (*0-335-15054-3*, Open Univ Pr) Taylor & Francis.
— Caring for Health: Dilemmas & Prospects. 148p. 1985. pap. 32.00 (*0-335-15057-8*, Open Univ Pr) Taylor & Francis.
— Medical Knowledge: Doubt & Certainty. (Health & Disease Ser.). 112p. 1985. pap. 32.00 (*0-335-15051-9*, Open Univ Pr) Taylor & Francis.
— Studying Health & Disease. (Health & Disease Ser.). 112p. 1985. pap. 32.00 (*0-335-15050-0*, Open Univ Pr) Taylor & Francis.
Open University Staff, et al. The Welsh & Their Country: Selected Readings in the Social Sciences. 365p. (C). 1986. pap. 30.00x (*0-86383-245-8*, Pub. by Gomer Pr UK) St Mut.
Opendall, Francois. Challenging the Amazon: The Ultimate Adventure. 203p. (Orig.). 1993. pap. 5.99 (*1-56171-208-6*, S P I Bks) Sure Sellers.
***Openframework Staff.** Services. (Illus.). 130p. 1994. pap. write for info. (*0-13-101213-4*) P-H.
OpenGL Architecture Review Staff. OpenGL Reference Manual: The Official Reference Document for OpenGl, Release 1. 1992. pap. 32.95 (*0-201-63276-4*) Addison-Wesley.
OpenInventor Architecture Group Staff. OpenInventor C Plus Plus Reference Manual: The Official Reference Document for OpenInventor Release 2. 1994. pap. 26.95 (*0-201-62493-1*); pap. 40.95 (*0-201-62491-5*) Addison-Wesley.
Openo, Woodard D. Tugboats on the Piscataqua: A Brief History of Towing on One of America's Toughest Rivers. (Illus.). 184p. 1992. 25.00 (*0-915819-17-1*) Portsmouth Marine Soc.
Openo, Woodward D. The Sarah Mildred Long Bridge: The History of the Maine-New Hampshire Interstate Bridge. (Portsmouth Marine Society Ser.: No. 13). (Illus.). 130p. 1989. 30.00 (*0-915819-12-0*) Portsmouth Marine Soc.
Openshaw, Gene, jt. auth. see Steves, Rick.
Openshaw, Harry T. Laboratory Manual of Qualitative Organic Analysis. 3rd ed. 1976. pap. 15.95 (*0-521-29112-7*) Cambridge U Pr.
Openshaw, Howard. Race & Residence: An Analysis of Property Values in Transitional Areas, Atlanta, Georgia, 1960-1971. LC 74-620726. (Research Monograph: No. 53). 132p. 1973. spiral bd. 19.95 (*0-88406-019-5*) GA St U Busn Pr.
Openshaw, Jennifer, ed. see UCLA Students.
Openshaw, K. Cost & Financial Accounting in Forestry. 1980. reprint ed. text ed. 94.00 (*0-08-021456-8*, CRC Reprint) Franklin.
Openshaw, Keith, jt. auth. see Barnes, Douglas F.
Openshaw, Stan. Nuclear Power: Siting & Safety. (Illus.). 337p. 1986. text ed. 45.00 (*0-7102-0183-4*, RKP) Routledge.
***Openshaw, Stanley, ed.** Census User's Handbook. 1995. pap. text ed. 47.95 (*0-470-23481-4*) Halsted Pr.
Opera Guild Staff. Intermission. (Illus.). 222p. 1992. 15.95 (*0-9637382-0-8*) Sprngfld Reg.
Opera Society of Fort Lauderdale. Libretto: Opera Society Menu Cookbook. Camp, Melanie & Gamble, Marion, eds. 192p. 1987. 17.95 (*0-9618686-0-0*) Opera Soc Ft Lauderdale.
Operation Smile International Staff. A Smile is the Beginning: Operation Smile International the First Ten Years. 196p. 1993. 35.00 (*0-9635271-0-X*) Oper Smile Intl.
Operations Evaluation Department Staff. Evaluation Results for 1990. 159p. 1992. 9.95 (*0-8213-2105-6*, 12105) World Bank.
— Evaluation Results for 1991. (Operations Evaluation Study Ser.). 160p. 1993. 9.95 (*0-8213-2400-4*, 12400) World Bank.
Operations Evaluation Department Staff, World Bank. New Lessons from Old Projects: The Workings of Rural Development in Northeast Brazil. LC 93-14543. (Operations Evaluation Study Ser.). 126p. 1993. 7.95 (*0-8213-2512-4*, 12512) World Bank.
Operkola, Pauline N. Philately & Health Sciences: Index of Modern Information. LC 88-47615. 150p. 1988. 37.50 (*0-88164-846-9*); pap. 34.50 (*0-88164-847-7*) ABBE Pubs Assn.
— Stamps & Philately Honors in Science & Medicine: Index of Modern Authors & Subjects with Guide for Rapid Research. LC 90-56321. 170p. 1991. 44.50 (*1-55914-436-X*); pap. 39.50 (*1-55914-437-8*) ABBE Pubs Assn.
Opeschowski, Charles. Guide to Environmental Law in Washington, D. C. 236p. 1990. pap. 28.00 (*0-911937-37-4*) Environ Law Inst.
Opfell, Olga S. The Lady Laureates: Women Who Have Won the Nobel Prize. 2nd ed. LC 85-19670. 334p. 1986. 32.50 (*0-8108-1851-5*) Scarecrow.
— Queens, Empresses, Grand Duchesses & Regents: Women Rulers of Europe, A.D. 1328-1989. LC 88-43484. (Illus.). 296p. 1989. lib. bdg. 32.50x (*0-89950-385-3*) McFarland & Co.
— Special Visions: Profiles of Fifteen Women Artists from the Renaissance to the Present Day. LC 90-53603. (Illus.). 231p. 1991. lib. bdg. 29.95x (*0-89950-603-8*) McFarland & Co.
— Women Prime Ministers & Presidents. LC 92-56675. (Illus.). 237p. (YA). (gr. 9-12). 1993. lib. bdg. 29.95 (*0-89950-790-5*) McFarland & Co.
Ophee, Matanya. Luigi Boccherini's Guitar Quintets - New Evidence. LC 82-181560. (Studies in Guitar History Ser.). (Illus.). 88p. (Orig.). 1981. pap. 15.00 (*0-936186-06-2*) Edit Orphee.
Ophee, Matanya, intro. Dictionary of Guitarists: A Biographical-Bibliographical-Historical-Critical Dictionary of Guitars (Related Instruments), Guitarists (Teachers-Composers-Performers-Luthiers-Amateurs), Guitar-Makers (Luthiers), Dances & Songs - Terminology. LC 86-80463. 488p. (SPA.). 1988. reprint ed. 135.00 (*0-936186-18-6*); reprint ed. pap. 95.00 (*0-685-17660-6*) Edit Orphee.
Ophee, Matanya, ed. see Chaine, Jacques.
Ophee, Matanya, ed. see Johnson, John.
Ophee, Matanya, ed. see Pujol, Emilio.
Opheij, Wilfrid, jt. ed. see Keuning, Doede.
Opheim, Edward N., Sr. The Day the Meadowlark Sang. 1994. pap. 7.95 (*0-533-10756-3*) Vantage.
Opheim, Teresa. AIDS: Distinguishing Between Fact & Opinion. LC 89-12006. (Opposing Viewpoints Juniors Ser.). (Illus.). 32p. (J). (gr. 3-6). 1990. lib. bdg. 11.95 (*0-89908-633-0*) Greenhaven.
O'Phelan, Cesar A., jt. ed. see Barkin, Jamie S.
O'Phelan, Cesar A., jt. auth. see Barkin, Jamie.
Ophiel. Art & Practice of Astral Projection. 124p. (Orig.). 1974. pap. 8.95 (*0-87728-246-3*) Weiser.
— Art & Practice of Getting Material Things Through Creative Visualization. rev. ed. 120p. 1975. pap. 8.95 (*0-87728-279-X*) Weiser.
Ophir, Adi. Plato's Republic & the Space of Discourse. 300p. (C). 1990. text ed. 62.00 (*0-389-20930-9*) Rowman.
Ophthalmic Microsurgery Study Group Staff. Surgery of the Iris & the Ciliary Body: Proceedings of the Ophthalmic Microsurgery Study Group, 4th, Lund, Sweden, July 4-7, 1972. Palm, E. & Mackensen, G., eds. (Advances in Ophthalmology Ser.: Vol. 30). 300p. 1975. 158.50 (*3-8055-1844-7*) S Karger.
Ophthalmic Microsurgery Study Group Symposium Staff. Microsurgery of Cataract, Vitreous & Astigmatism: Proceedings of the Ophthalmic Microsurgery Study Group Symposium, 5th, London, June 1974. Kersley, J. & Pierse, D., eds. (Advances in Ophthalmology Ser.: Vol.33). 400p. 1976. 143.25 (*3-8055-2323-8*) S Karger.
***Ophthalmology Annual Staff.** Ophthalmology Annual, 1988. Reinecke, Robert D., ed. LC 85-646190. (Illus.). 256p. 1988. pap. 73.00 (*0-7837-8356-6*, 2049146) Bks Demand.
Ophuls, Marcel. Hotel Terminus: The Life & Times of Klaus Barbie. 1993. 18.95 (*0-671-68703-4*) S&S Trade.
Ophuls, William. Ecology & the Politics of Scarcity Revisited: The Unraveling of the American Dream. LC 91-46535. (C). 1995. pap. text ed. write for info. (*0-7167-2313-1*) W H Freeman.
Opie, A., jt. auth. see Brown, G.
***Opie, Amelia.** Adeline Mowbray. LC 94-44529. (Revolution & the Age of Romanticism, 1789-1834, Ser.). 1995. 85.00 (*1-85477-188-4*, Pub. by Woodstock Bks UK) Cassell.
Opie, Amelia A. Memorials of the Life of Amelia Opie. LC 79-37711. reprint ed. 67.50 (*0-404-56774-6*) AMS Pr.
— The Works of Mrs. Amelia Opie, 3 vols., Set. LC 70-37706. (Women of Letters Ser.). reprint ed. 270.00 (*0-404-56796-7*) AMS Pr.
Opie, Anne, et al. There's Nobody There: Community Care of Confused Older People. (Studies in Health, Illness, & Caregiving). 232p. (Orig.). (C). 1992. pap. text ed. 19.95 (*0-8122-1419-6*) U of Pa Pr.
Opie, Brenda & McAvinn, Douglas. Effective Language Arts Techniques for Middle Grades (4-8) An Integrated Approach. (Illus.). 84p. (Orig.). (J). (gr. 4-8). 1989. pap. text ed. 7.95 (*0-685-26803-9*) Masterminds Pubns.
***Opie, Brenda & McKenzie, Douglas.** Effective Language Arts Techniques for Middle Grades: An Integrated Approach. (Illus.). 96p. (Orig.). (J). (gr. 4-8). 1995. pap. text ed. 9.95 (*0-614-01841-2*) Incentive Pubns.
***Opie, Brenda, et al.** Masterminds Addition, Subtraction, Place Value, & Other Numeration Systems: Reproducible Skill Builders & Higher Order Thinking Activities Based on NCTM Standards. (Illus.). 96p. (Orig.). 1995. pap. text ed. 9.95 (*0-86530-303-7*) Incentive Pubns.
— Masterminds Decimals, Percentages, Metric System, & Consumer Math: Reproducible Skill Builders & Higher Order Thinking Activities Based on NCTM Standards. (Illus.). 96p. (Orig.). 1995. pap. text ed. 9.95 (*0-86530-301-0*) Incentive Pubns.
— Masterminds Fractions, Ratio, Probability, & Standard Measurement: Reproducible Skill Builders & Higher Order Thinking Activities Based on NCTM Standards. (Illus.). 96p. (Orig.). 1995. pap. text ed. 9.95 (*0-86530-302-9*) Incentive Pubns.
— Masterminds Geometry & Graphing: Reproducible Skill Builders & Higher Order Thinking Activities Based on NCTM Standards. (Illus.). 96p. (Orig.). 1995. pap. text ed. 9.95 (*0-86530-305-3*) Incentive Pubns.
— Masterminds Multiplication & Division: Reproducible Skill Builders & Higher Order Thinking Activities Based on NCTM Standards. (Illus.). 96p. (Orig.). 1995. pap. text ed. 9.95 (*0-86530-304-5*) Incentive Pubns.
Opie, C. Interfacing the BBC Microcomputer. 208p. 1984. write for info. (*0-07-084724-X*) McGraw.
Opie, I. & Opie, P. Tail Feathers from Mother Goose: The Opie Rhyme Book. (Illus.). 124p. (J). 1991. 7.99 (*0-517-05555-4*) Random Hse Value.
Opie, Iona. The People in the Playground. LC 92-12172. (Illus.). 256p. 1993. 25.00 (*0-19-811265-3*) OUP.
— The People in the Playground. LC 93-32898. (Illus.). 254p. (C). 1994. reprint ed. pap. 10.95 (*0-19-285301-5*) OUP.
Opie, Iona & Opie, Peter. Children's Games in Street & Playground. (Illus.). (C). 1985. reprint ed. pap. 10.95 (*0-19-281489-3*) OUP.
— The Classic Fairy Tales. (Illus.). 1980. pap. 11.95 (*0-19-520219-8*) OUP.
— The Classic Fairy Tales. (Illus.). 256p. 1992. 30.00 (*0-19-211559-6*) OUP.
— The Lore & Language of Schoolchildren. (Illus.). 448p. 1987. pap. 10.95 (*0-19-282059-1*) OUP.
— A Nursery Companion. (Illus.). 1980. 29.95 (*0-19-212213-4*) OUP.
— The Singing Game. 544p. 1988. pap. 10.95 (*0-19-284019-3*) OUP.
Opie, Iona & Opie, Peter, eds. The Oxford Book of Children's Verse. 448p. (J). 1995. reprint ed. pap. text ed. 14.95 (*0-19-282349-3*) OUP.
— Oxford Dictionary of Nursery Rhymes. (Illus.). (J). (ps-3). 1951. 47.50 (*0-19-869111-4*) OUP.
— Oxford Nursery Rhyme Book. (Illus.). 1312p. (J). (ps-3). 1964. 29.95 (*0-19-869112-2*) OUP.
Opie, Iona & Tatem, Moira, eds. A Dictionary of Superstitions. 510p. 1989. 39.95 (*0-19-211597-9*) OUP.
— A Dictionary of Superstitions. 512p. 1992. pap. 14.95 (*0-19-282916-5*) OUP.
Opie, Iona, jt. auth. see Opie, Peter.
Opie, Iona, jt. comp. see Opie, Peter.
Opie, Iona, jt. ed. see Opie, Peter.
***Opie, Iona, et al.** The Treasures of Childhood: Books, Toys & Games from the Opie Collection. (Illus.). 192p. 1995. pap. 24.95 (*1-85793-624-8*, Pub. by Pavilion UK) Trafalgar.
***Opie, James.** Collecting Toy Soldiers. (Pincushion Press Collectibles Ser.). 144p. Date not set. pap. 19.95 (*1-872727-76-X*) Pincushion Pr.
— The Great Book of Britains: 100 Years of Britains Toy Soldiers 1893-1993. (Illus.). 640p. Date not set. 95.00 (*1-872727-32-8*, Pub. by New Cavendish UK) Pincushion Pr.
— Opie's Pocket Price Guide to Britains Hollowcast Toy Soldiers. 128p. Date not set. 12.95 (*1-872727-82-4*, Pub. by New Cavendish UK) Pincushion Pr.
— Toy Soldiers. 1989. pap. 25.00 (*0-85263-632-6*, Pub. by Shire UK) St Mut.
— Tribal Rugs: Nomadic & Village Weavers from the Near East & Central Asia. Gill, Spencer & Collins, Sophie, eds. LC 92-72906. (Illus.). 328p. 1992. 95.00 (*0-9633689-0-7*) Tolstoy Pr.
— Tribal Rugs of Southern Persia. LC 81-90582. 223p. text ed. 90.00 (*0-9611144-0-1*) J Opie Oriental.
Opie, Jamesnce. Collector's Guide to Twentieth Century Toys. 1990. 12.98 (*1-55521-544-0*) Bk Sales Inc.
Opie, John. The Law of the Land: Two Hundred Years of American Farmland Policy. LC 86-30860. xxii, 231p. 1987. 30.00 (*0-8032-3553-4*) U of Nebr Pr.
— The Law of the Land: Two Hundred Years of American Farmland Policy. (Illus.). xxii, 231p. 1987. reprint ed. pap. text ed. 12.00 (*0-8032-8607-4*, Bison Books) U of Nebr Pr.
— Ogallala: Water for a Dry Land. LC 92-26718. (Our Sustainable Future Ser.: Vol. 1). (Illus.). xxi, 412p. 1993. 35.00 (*0-8032-3557-7*) U of Nebr Pr.
Opie, L., jt. ed. see Sugimoto, T.
***Opie, L. H., ed.** Myocardial Protection by Calcium Antagonists. 1994. pap. text ed. 34.95 (*0-471-07669-4*) Wiley.
Opie, L. H. & Sabino, F., eds. Heart Failure Today. (Journal: Cardiology: Vol. 75, Suppl. 1, 1988). (Illus.). iv, 160p. 1988. pap. 45.00 (*3-8055-4929-6*) S Karger.
***Opie, Lionel H.** Angiotensin Converting Enzyme Inhibitors. 2nd ed. Date not set. pap. text ed. 34.95 (*0-471-11195-3*) Wiley.
— Angiotension - Converting Enzyme Inhibitors: Scientific Basis for Clinical Use. 320p. (Orig.). 1992. text ed. 37.95 (*0-471-58836-9*) Wiley.
— Clinical Use of Calcium Antagonist Drugs. (C). 1989. lib. bdg. 97.00 (*0-7923-0155-2*) Kluwer Ac.
— Drugs for the Heart. 4th ed. 336p. 1995. pap. text ed. 29.95 (*0-7216-5943-8*) Saunders.
— The Heart: Physiology & Metabolism. 2nd ed. (Illus.). 528p. 1991. 89.50 (*0-88167-751-5*) Raven.
Opie, Lionel H., ed. Stunning, Hibernation, & Calcium in Myocardial Ischemia & Reperfusion. LC 92-17257. (C). 1992. pap. text ed. 88.50 (*0-7923-1793-9*) Kluwer Ac.
Opie, Lionel H., jt. auth. see Ferrari, Roberto.
Opie, Lionel H., jt. ed. see Thadani, Udho.
***Opie, Mary-Jane.** Eyewitness Art: Sculpture. 1994. 16.95 (*1-56458-613-8*) Dorling Kindersley.
— Sculpture. LC 94-2593. (Eyewitness Art Ser.). (Illus.). 64p. 1994. 16.95 (*1-56458-495-X*) Dorling Kindersley.
Opie, P., jt. auth. see Opie, I.
Opie, Peter, ed. The Oxford Book of Narrative Verse. LC 82-2294. 432p. 1983. reprint ed. 29.95 (*0-19-214131-7*) OUP.
— The Oxford Book of Narrative Verse. LC 82-2294. 432p. 1989. reprint ed. pap. 12.95 (*0-19-282243-8*) OUP.
Opie, Peter & Opie, Iona. I Saw Esau. LC 91-71845. (Illus.). 160p. (J). (ps up). 1992. 19.95 (*1-56402-046-0*) Candlewick Pr.
Opie, Peter & Opie, Iona, comps. The Opie Collection of Children's Literature: A Guide to the Microfiche Collection, Unit 1. v, 79p. 1992. pap. 20.00 (*0-8357-2151-5*) Univ Microfilms.
— The Opie Collection of Children's Literature: A Guide to the Microfiche Collection, Unit 2. v, 65p. 1992. pap. 20.00 (*0-8357-2152-3*) Univ Microfilms.
Opie, Peter & Opie, Iona, eds. The Oxford Book of Children's Verse. (Illus.). 1973. 29.95 (*0-19-812140-7*) OUP.
Opie, Peter, jt. auth. see Opie, Iona.
Opie, Peter, jt. ed. see Opie, Iona.
Opie, Redvers, tr. see Schumpeter, Joseph A.
Opie, William. Shenandoah Spector. 120p. (Orig.). (YA). 1989. pap. write for info. (*0-318-65487-3*) Opie Pub.
Opiela, Kenneth S. & Stammer, Robert E., eds. Microcomputer Applications in Transportation III. LC 90-716. 1320p. 1990. pap. text ed. 96.00 (*0-87262-757-8*) Am Soc Civil Eng.
Opies, Redvers, tr. see Schumpeter, Joseph A.
Opik, Helgi, jt. auth. see Street, H. E.
Opila, R. L., et al, eds. Polymer - Inorganic Interfaces. (Symposium Proceedings Ser.: Vol. 304). 1993. text ed. 63.00 (*1-55899-200-6*) Materials Res.
Opinion Research Corporation Staff. Implementation & Enforcement Codes of Ethics in Corporations & Associations. (Opinion Research Corporation Study Ser.: No. 65334). 256p. 1980. 17.50 (*0-916152-05-7*) Ethics Res Ctr.
Opio, Aba J. Casting Shadows. 24p. 1991. 3.00 (*1-877610-04-6*) Sea Island.
Opitz, ed. see Pfaffenberger.
Opitz, Bruce K., ed. Geographic Information Systems in Government, 2 vols., Set. 968p. 1986. 94.00 (*0-937194-20-4*) A Deepak Pub.
Opitz, Edmund A. Religion & Capitalism: Allies, Not Enemies. 2nd ed. 318p. 1992. reprint ed. pap. 24.95 (*0-910614-81-4*) Foun Econ Ed.
Opitz, Glenn, ed. Dictionary of Contemporary Artists in America. 1989. write for info. (*0-938290-12-6*) Apollo.
Opitz, Glenn B., ed. Dictionary of American Sculptors: Eighteenth Century to the Present. (Illus.). 656p. 85.00 (*0-938290-03-7*) Apollo.
— Mantle Fielding's Dictionary of American Painters, Sculptors & Engravers. 2nd rev. ed. 1081p. 1986. 95.00 (*0-938290-04-5*) Apollo.
Opitz, H. A Classification System to Describe Workpieces, Classification System, Set. Taylor, R. A., tr. LC 71-112891. 1970. 97.00 (*0-08-015758-0*, Pub. by Pergamon Repr UK) Franklin.
Opitz, H. & Schmid, F. Enciclopedia Pediatrica, 12 vols., Set. 13429p. (SPA.). 1974. 1,495.00 (*0-8288-6036-X*, S50558) Fr & Eur.
— Enciclopedia Pediatrica, Vol. 1, Pt. 1: Historia De. 960p. 1973. 275.00 (*0-7859-6113-5*, 8471121352) Fr & Eur.
— Enciclopedia Pediatrica, Vol. 1, Pt. 2: Fisio-Patologia del Recien. 570p. 1974. 275.00 (*0-7859-6115-1*, 8471121433) Fr & Eur.
— Enciclopedia Pediatrica, Vol. 2, Pt. 2: Terapeutica Pediatrica. 806p. 1971. 275.00 (*0-7859-6117-8*, 8471121875) Fr & Eur.
— Enciclopedia Pediatrica, Vol. 3: Immunologia. Pediatria Social. 1366p. 1969. 295.00 (*0-7859-6118-6*, 8471121883) Fr & Eur.
— Enciclopedia Pediatrica, Vol. 4: Metabolismo, Nutricion, Digestion. 1376p. 1967. 295.00 (*0-7859-6119-4*, 8471121891) Fr & Eur.
— Enciclopedia Pediatrica, Vol. 5: Enfermedades Infecciosas. 1398p. 1967. 295.00 (*0-7859-6120-8*, 8471121905) Fr & Eur.
— Enciclopedia Pediatrica, Vol. 6: Enfermedades de los Tejidos De. 1353p. 1970. 295.00 (*0-7859-6121-6*, 8471121913) Fr & Eur.
— Enciclopedia Pediatrica, Vol. 7: Enfermedades del Aparato Respirato. 1450p. 1968. 295.00 (*0-7859-6122-4*, 8471121921) Fr & Eur.
— Enciclopedia Pediatrica, Vol. 8, Pt. 1: Neurologia, Psicologia. 1136p. 1971. 275.00 (*0-7859-6481-9*) Fr & Eur.
— Enciclopedia Pediatrica, Vol. 8, Pt. 2: Tumores en la Infancia. 840p. 1974. 275.00 (*0-7859-6114-3*, 8471121417) Fr & Eur.
— Enciclopedia Pediatrica, Vol. 9: Ojos, Nariz, Dientes, Piel. 997p. 1972. 295.00 (*0-7859-6112-7*, 8471121174) Fr & Eur.

***Opitz, Helmut & Richter, Elisabeth, eds. World Guide to Special Libraries, 2 Vols. 3rd ed. 1258p. 1994. 325.00**

O

(*3-598-22234-3*) K G Saur. "All Saur reference works are splendid, & this is no exception...a veritable tour de force of information gathering."-- WORLD AFFAIRS REPORT. Incorporating virtually every type of special library--from university medical libraries to independent archives focusing on a single discipline, such as music or art--the third edition of this directory categorizes over 35,000 libraries in 183 countries under 750 subject headings. Since libraries may appear under multiple subjects, the main section contains over 47,000 entries, Listings are arranged by subject, then alphabetically by country, & then by library. Additionally, the INDEX TO LIBRARIES in Volume 2 cumulates all libraries world-wide in a single alphabetical sequence with references to the main entry number.
Publisher Provided Annotation.

Opitz, John M. Blastogenesis: Normal & Abnormal. 424p. 1993. text ed. 185.95 (*0-471-59789-9*, Wiley-Liss) Wiley.
Opitz, May, et al, eds. Showing Our Colors: Afro-German Women Speak Out. Adams, Anne V., tr. LC 91-17061. (Illus.). 272p. (C). 1991. lib. bdg. 40.00 (*0-87023-759-4*); pap. 16.95 (*0-87023-760-8*) U of Mass Pr.
Opitz, O., ed. Conceptual & Numerical Analysis of Data. (Illus.). 560p. 1989. pap. 109.00 (*0-387-51641-7*, 3488) Spr-Verlag.
Opitz, Otto, et al, eds. Information & Classification: Concepts, Methods, & Applications: Proceedings of the 16th Annual Conference of the "Gesellschaft Fur Klassifikation E. V." University of Dortmund, April 1-3, 1992. LC 93-5237. (Studies in Classification, Data Analysis, & Knowledge Organization). (Illus.). xii, 517p. 1993. pap. 110.00 (*0-387-56736-4*) Spr-Verlag.
Opland, Jeff. Anglo-Saxon Oral Poetry: A Study of the Traditions. LC 79-24202. 301p. reprint ed. pap. 85.80 (*0-8357-3754-3*, 2036480) Bks Demand.
Opler, M. E. Childhood & Youth in Jicarilla Apache Society. (Frederick Webb Hodge Publications: No. 5). (Illus.). xii, 170p. 1964. reprint ed. pap. 5.00 (*0-916561-13-5*) Southwest Mus.
Opler, Morris E. Apache Life-Way. LC 65-23533. 500p. reprint ed. 47.25 (*0-8154-0168-X*) Cooper Sq.
— Apache Odyssey: A Journey Between Two Worlds. Spindler, George & Spindler, Louise, eds. LC 82-23355. (Case Studies in Cultural Anthropology). (Illus.). 320p. 1983. reprint ed. pap. text ed. 16.95 (*0-8290-1267-2*) Irvington.
— Childhood & Youth in Jicarilla Apache Society. LC 76-43797. reprint ed. 21.00 (*0-404-15653-3*) AMS Pr.
— Dirty Boy: A Jicarilla Tale of Raid & War. LC 39-14218. (American Anthropological Association Memoirs Ser.). 1938. 15.00 (*0-527-00551-7*) Periodicals Srv.
— Myths & Tales of the Chiricahua Apache Indians. LC 94-12396. (Studies in American Indian Oral Literature). 144p. 1994. pap. 6.95 (*0-8032-8602-3*, Bison Books) U of Nebr Pr.
— Myths & Tales of the Jicarilla Apache Indians. unabridged ed. 406p. 1994. pap. text ed. 9.95 (*0-486-28324-0*) Dover.
— Myths & Tales of the Jicarilla Apache Indians. LC 38-22477. (American Folklore Society Memoirs Ser.). 1974. reprint ed. 40.00 (*0-527-01083-9*) Periodicals Srv.
— Myths & Tales of the Jicarilla Apache Indians. (Studies in American Indian Oral Literature). 448p. 1994. reprint ed. pap. 14.95 (*0-8032-8603-1*, Bison Books) U of Nebr Pr.
Opler, Morris E., jt. ed. see Basso, Keith H.
Opler, Morris E., ed. see Goodwin, Grenville.
Opler, Morris E., jt. auth. see Hoijer, Harry.
Opler, Pat. At Home on the Range Cooking School Cookbook. (Illus.). 208p. (Orig.). 1992. pap. 15.95 (*0-87905-465-4*, Peregrine Smith) Gibbs Smith Pub.
Opler, Paul. Butterflies East & West: A Book to Color. (Illus.). 96p. (Orig.). (J). (gr. 1-6). 1993. pap. 8.95 (*1-879373-45-9*) R Rinehart.
Opler, Paul & Strawn, Susan. Butterflies of Eastern North America: A Coloring Album & Activity Book. (Illus.). (J). (gr. 1-6). 1989. pap. 4.95 (*0-911797-53-X*) R Rinehart.
Opler, Paul A. A Field Guide to Eastern Butterflies. (Illus.). 512p. 1992. 24.95 (*0-395-36452-3*, Field Guides); pap. 16.95 (*0-395-63279-X*, Field Guides) HM.
— Peterson First Guide to Butterflies & Moths. LC 93-5751. (Illus.). 1994. pap. 4.95 (*0-395-67072-1*) HM.
Opler, Paul A. & Krizek, George O. Butterflies East of the Great Plains: An Illustrated Natural History. LC 83-6197. (Illus.). 312p. 1984. 49.50 (*0-8018-2938-0*) Johns Hopkins.
Oplinger, Carl S. & Halma, J. Robert. The Poconos: An Illustrated Natural History Guide. (Illus.). 280p. (C). 1988. text ed. 37.00 (*0-8135-1293-X*); pap. 13.95 (*0-8135-1294-8*) Rutgers U Pr.
Oplinger, Jon. The Politics of Demonology: The European Witchcraze & the Mass Production of Deviance. LC 89-43149. 312p. 1990. 44.50 (*0-945636-11-3*) Susquehanna U Pr.
— Quang Tri Cadence: Memoir of a Rifle Platoon Leader in the Mountains of Vietnam. LC 92-56676. (Illus.). 220p. 1993. pap. 19.95x (*0-89950-873-1*) McFarland & Co.
Opoku, Kofi A., et al. Healing for God's World: Remedies from Three Continents. (Orig.). 1991. pap. 10.95 (*0-377-00229-1*) Friendship Pr.
Opolka, H., jt. auth. see Scharlau, W.
Opolot, James. Contemporary American Local Jails. 165p. (C). 1993. pap. text ed. 25.00 (*1-884028-01-2*) SL Pubs.
Opower, H., ed. CO2 Lasers & Applications II. 1990. 70.00 (*0-8194-0323-7*, VOL. 1276) SPIE.
Oppedisano-Reich, Marie, jt. auth. see Cohen, Lily.
***Oppel, Ed.** Fish & Seafood Cooking. 1994. 12.98 (*0-7858-0195-2*) Bk Sales Inc.
Oppel, F. Limericks, Limericks, Limericks, Limericks. 1992. 7.98 (*1-55521-783-4*) Bk Sales Inc.
— Tales of Alaska & the Yukon. 1992. 8.98 (*1-55521-119-4*) Bk Sales Inc.
— Tales of the Great Lakes. 1992. 8.98 (*1-55521-120-8*) Bk Sales Inc.
— Tales of the West. 1992. 7.98 (*0-89009-796-8*) Bk Sales Inc.
— True Tales of the West. 1994. 8.98 (*0-89009-874-3*) Bk Sales Inc.
— Winning System. 1993. 12.98 (*1-55521-966-7*) Bk Sales Inc.
Oppel, Frances N. Mask & Tragedy: Yeats & Nietzsche, 1902-10. LC 86-24652. 267p. reprint ed. pap. 76.10 (*0-7837-4366-1*, 2044076) Bks Demand.
Oppel, Frank. Tales of Old Florida. 1988. 8.98 (*1-55521-225-5*) Bk Sales Inc.
Oppel, Kenneth. Dead Water Zone. LC 92-37282. (J). 1993. 14.95 (*0-316-65102-8*, Joy St Bks) Little.
Oppelland, H. J., jt. ed. see Kaiser, K. M.
Oppelt, Norman T. Earth, Water, & Fire: The Prehistoric Pottery of Mesa Verde. LC 91-75686. (Illus.). 100p. 1991. pap. 12.95 (*1-55566-085-1*) Johnson Bks.
— Guide to Prehistoric Ruins of the Southwest. 2nd ed. (Illus.). 208p. (Orig.). 1989. pap. 12.95 (*0-87108-783-9*) Pruett.
— Southwestern Pottery: An Annotated Bibliography & List of Types & Wares. LC 88-6424. (Illus.). 333p. 1988. 45.00 (*0-8108-2119-2*) Scarecrow.
— The Tribally Controlled Indian College. 1990. pap. 20.00 (*0-912586-67-2*) Navajo Coll Pr.
Oppen, George. Collected Poems. LC 75-6965. 1976. pap. 10.95 (*0-8112-0615-7*, NDP418) New Directions.
— Of Being Numerous. LC 68-15882. 1965. 5.25 (*0-8112-0336-0*) New Directions.
— Primitive. 36p. 1979. 10.00 (*0-87685-415-3*) Black Sparrow.
Oppen, Mary. Meaning a Life. LC 78-6223. (Illus.). 214p. 1990. reprint ed. 25.00 (*0-87685-375-0*); reprint ed. pap. 12.50 (*0-87685-374-2*) Black Sparrow.
Oppen, William A. The Riel Rebellions: A Cartographic History (Le Recit Cartographique des Affaires Riel) LC 80-453679. (Illus.). 119p. reprint ed. pap. 34.00 (*0-8357-4000-5*, 2036701) Bks Demand.
Oppeneer, P. M., jt. auth. see Kubler, J.
Oppenheim. Consumer Skills. rev. ed. (gr. 9-12). 1982. text ed. 19.00 (*0-02-663080-X*) Bennett IL.
— Listening to American Jews. 1987. 16.95 (*1-55774-004-6*) Modan-Adama Bks.
— Living Today. (gr. 9-12). 1981. teacher ed 9.60 (*0-02-664890-3*); text ed. 17.80 (*0-02-664860-1*); student ed 7.00 (*0-02-664870-9*) Bennett IL.
— Rob-Pat Act, 1. 1971. 47.00 (*0-316-65090-0*) Little.
— Rob-Pat Act, 2. 1971. 47.00 (*0-316-65091-9*) Little.
— Rob-Pat Act, 3. 1971. 47.00 (*0-316-65092-7*) Little.
— Rob-Pat Act, 4. 1971. 47.00 (*0-316-65093-5*) Little.
Oppenheim, A. K. Impact of Aerospace Technology on Studies of the Earth's Atmosphere. LC 74-5410. 1974. 104.00 (*0-08-018131-7*, Pub. by Pergamon Repr UK) Franklin.
Oppenheim, A. Leo. Ancient Mesopotamia: Portrait of a Dead Civilization. 2nd rev. ed. LC 64-19847. (Illus.). 1977. pap. text ed. 16.95 (*0-226-63187-7*) U Ch Pr.
Oppenheim, A. Leo, ed. The Assyrian Dictionary of the Oriental Institute of the University of Chicago, Vol. 5, G. LC 56-58292. (AKK & ENG.). 1956. lib. bdg. 20.00 (*0-918986-11-7*) Orientl Inst Pr IT.
— The Assyrian Dictionary of the Oriental Institute of the University of Chicago, Vol. 6, H. LC 56-58292. (AKK & ENG.). 1956. lib. bdg. 25.00 (*0-918986-12-5*) Orientl Inst Pr IT.
Oppenheim, A. Leo & Reiner, Erica, eds. The Assyrian Dictionary of the Oriental Institute of the University of Chicago, Vol. 1, A, Pt. 1. LC 56-58292. (AKK.). 1964. lib. bdg. 40.00 (*0-918986-06-0*) Orientl Inst Pr IT.
— Assyrian Dictionary of the Oriental Institute of the University of Chicago, Vol. 1, A, Pt. 2. LC 56-58292. (AKK.). 1989. reprint ed. lib. bdg. 60.00 (*0-918986-07-9*) Orientl Inst Pr IT.
— Assyrian Dictionary of the Oriental Institute of the University of Chicago, Vol. 3, D. (AKK.). 1989. reprint ed. lib. bdg. 25.00 (*0-918986-09-5*) Orientl Inst Pr IT.
— Assyrian Dictionary of the Oriental Institute of the University of Chicago, Vol. 4, E. (AKK.). 1974. reprint ed. lib. bdg. 45.00 (*0-918986-10-9*) Orientl Inst Pr IT.
— Assyrian Dictionary of the Oriental Institute of the University of Chicago, Vol. 7, I/J. (AKK.). 1989. reprint ed. lib. bdg. 40.00 (*0-918986-13-3*) Orientl Inst Pr IT.
— Assyrian Dictionary of the Oriental Institute of the University of Chicago, Vol. 9, L. (AKK.). 1978. reprint ed. lib. bdg. 35.00 (*0-918986-15-X*) Orientl Inst Pr IT.
— Assyrian Dictionary of the Oriental Institute of the University of Chicago, Vol. 10, M, Pts. 1 & 2. LC 56-58292. (AKK.). 1991. reprint ed. lib. bdg. 110.00 (*0-918986-16-8*) Orientl Inst Pr IT.
— Assyrian Dictionary of the Oriental Institute of the University of Chicago, Vol. 16, S. LC 56-58292. (AKK.). 1989. reprint ed. lib. bdg. 30.00 (*0-918986-18-4*) Orientl Inst Pr IT.
— The Assyrian Dictionary of the Oriental Institute of the University of Chicago, Vol. 21, Z. LC 56-58292. 1961. lib. bdg. 20.00 (*0-918986-19-2*) Orientl Inst Pr IT.
Oppenheim, A. Leo, et al, eds. The Assyrian Dictionary of the Oriental Institute of the University of Chicago, Vol. 2, B. LC 56-58292. (AKK.). 1966. lib. bdg. 35.00 (*0-918986-08-7*) Orientl Inst Pr IT.
— The Assyrian Dictionary of the Oriental Institute of the University of Chicago, Vol. 8, K. LC 56-58292. 1971. lib. bdg. 65.00 (*0-918986-14-1*) Orientl Inst Pr IT.
Oppenheim, A. V. & Nowab, Hamid. Symbolic & Knowledge-Based Signal Processing. 384p. 1992. text ed. 70.00 (*0-13-880444-3*) P-H.
Oppenheim, Alan V. Applications of Digital Signal Processing. LC 77-8547. 1977. text ed. 94.00 (*0-13-039115-8*) P-H.
Oppenheim, Alan V. & Schafer, Ronald W. Digital Signal Processing. LC 74-17280. (Illus.). 608p. 1975. text ed. 76.00 (*0-13-214635-5*) P-H.
— Discrete-Time Signal Processing. 640p. 1988. text ed. 75.00 (*0-13-216292-X*) P-H.
Oppenheim, Alan V., jt. auth. see Lim, Joe S.
Oppenheim, Alan V., et al. Signals & Systems. (Illus.). 464p. 1982. text ed. 76.00 (*0-13-809731-3*) P-H.
Oppenheim, Carolyn T., ed. Listening to American Jews. 210p. 1988. pap. 13.95 (*1-55774-002-X*) Modan-Adama Bks.
Oppenheim, Charles, ed. CD ROM: From Fundamentals to Application. (Illus.). 416p. 1988. text ed. 99.95 (*0-408-00746-X*) Buttrwrth-Heinemann.
Oppenheim, D. E., jt. auth. see Freud, Sigmund.
Oppenheim, E. Phillips. The Golden Beast. reprint ed. lib. bdg. 21.95 (*0-89190-411-5*, Rivercity Pr) Amereon Ltd.
— The Great Impersonation. 1990. reprint ed. lib. bdg. 19.95x (*0-89968-542-0*) Buccaneer Bks.
— The Great Impersonation. LC 77-20546. (Illus.). 1978. reprint ed. pap. 5.95 (*0-486-23607-2*) Dover.
— The Great Impersonation - Illustrated. 1976. reprint ed. lib. bdg. 19.95 (*0-89190-412-3*, Rivercity Pr) Amereon Ltd.
— Murder at the Monte Carlo. reprint ed. lib. bdg. 22.95 (*0-89190-413-1*, Rivercity Pr) Amereon Ltd.
— The Oppenheim Secret Service Omnibus, 2 vols., Vol. 1. (Spies & Intrigues Ser.: No. 1). 525p. 1984. pap. 8.95 (*0-918172-13-6*) Leetes Isl.
— The Oppenheim Secret Service Omnibus, 2 vols., Vol. 2. (Spies & Intrigues Ser.: No. 1). 440p. 1984. pap. 8.95 (*0-918172-14-4*) Leetes Isl.
— Pawns Count. 22.95 (*0-8488-0304-3*) Amereon Ltd.
— The Spy Paramount. reprint ed. lib. bdg. 21.95 (*0-89190-414-X*, Rivercity Pr) Amereon Ltd.
— Treasure House of Martin Hews. reprint ed. lib. bdg. 24.95 (*0-89190-415-8*, Rivercity Pr) Amereon Ltd.
— The Vanished Messenger. reprint ed. lib. bdg. 23.95 (*0-89190-416-6*, Rivercity Pr) Amereon Ltd.
Oppenheim, Edward P. Advice Limited. LC 74-134972. (Short Story Index Reprint Ser.). 1977. 20.95 (*0-8369-3703-1*) Ayer.
— Ask Miss Mott. LC 79-128745. (Short Story Index Reprint Ser.). 1977. 19.95 (*0-8369-3636-1*) Ayer.
— The Ex-Detective. LC 77-150481. (Short Story Index Reprint Ser.). 1977. reprint ed. 19.95 (*0-8369-3822-4*) Ayer.
— Seven Conundrums. LC 78-134973. (Short Story Index Reprint Ser.). (Illus.). 1977. 20.95 (*0-8369-3704-X*) Ayer.
***Oppenheim, Emilie, ed.** The Paintings of Samuel Edmund Oppenheim. LC 94-73957. (Illus.). 80p. 1994. 35.00 (*0-9643447-0-X*) E W Oppenheim.
Oppenheim, Felix E. The Place of Morality in Foreign Policy. (Issues in World Politics Ser.). 128p. 1991. text ed. 27.95 (*0-669-21450-7*); pap. 14.95 (*0-669-21452-3*) Free Pr.
— Political Concepts: A Reconstruction. LC 80-23846. 240p. 1981. pap. text ed. 5.50 (*0-226-63185-0*) U Ch Pr.
Oppenheim, Frank M. Royce's Mature Ethics. LC 92-53531. (C). 1993. text ed. 36.95 (*0-268-01642-9*) U of Notre Dame Pr.
— Royce's Mature Philosophy of Religion. LC 87-12458. 432p. 1987. text ed. 34.95 (*0-268-01633-X*) U of Notre Dame Pr.
— Royce's Voyage Down Under: A Journey of the Mind. LC 79-4007. 136p. reprint ed. pap. 38.80 (*0-7837-5786-7*, 2045452) Bks Demand.
Oppenheim, Frank M., ed. The Reasoning Heart: Toward a North American Theology. LC 86-4655. 159p. (Orig.). reprint ed. pap. 45.40 (*0-7837-6336-0*, 2046048) Bks Demand.
Oppenheim, Garrett & Oppenheim, Gwen. The Golden Handicap: A Polio Victim Asks, "Why?" & Turns His Life Around. 237p. 1993. pap. 11.95 (*0-87604-306-6*, 382) ARE Pr.
Oppenheim, Gary S., jt. auth. see Richards, Regina.
Oppenheim, Gwen, jt. auth. see Oppenheim, Garrett.
Oppenheim, Israel. The Struggle of Jewish Youth for Productivization. 240p. 1989. text ed. 42.00 (*0-88033-170-4*) East Eur Quarterly.
Oppenheim, J., jt. auth. see Beattie, J. A.
Oppenheim, J. J., et al. Cellular Functions in Immunity & Inflammation. 1984. pap. 51.25 (*0-444-00951-5*) Elsevier.
Oppenheim, James. The Nine-Tenths. LC 68-57543. (Muckrakers Ser.). 1979. reprint ed. lib. bdg. 26.00 (*0-8398-1453-4*) Irvington.
— Pay Envelopes: Tales of the Mill, the Mine & the City Street, Vol. 1. LC 72-3288. (Short Story Index Reprint Ser.). (Illus.). 1977. reprint ed. 18.95 (*0-8369-4158-6*) Ayer.
Oppenheim, Janet. The Other World: Spiritualism & Psychical Research in England, 1850-1914. (Illus.). 580p. 1985. 69.95 (*0-521-26505-3*) Cambridge U Pr.
— The Other World: Spiritualism & Psychical Research in England, 1850-1914. (Illus.). 580p. 1988. pap. 19.95 (*0-521-34767-X*) Cambridge U Pr.
— Shattered Nerves: Doctors, Patients, & Depression in Victorian England. 400p. 1991. 30.00 (*0-19-505781-3*) OUP.
Oppenheim, Joanne. Black Hawk, Frontier Warrior. LC 78-18049. (Illus.). 48p. (J). (gr. 4-6). 1979. lib. bdg. 10.59 (*0-89375-157-X*); pap. 3.50 (*0-89375-147-2*) Troll Assocs.
— Could It Be - Bank Street. (J). (ps-3). 1990. mass mkt. 3.99 (*0-553-34924-4*, Little Rooster) Bantam.
— Do You Like Cats? LC 92-14113. (Bank Street Ready-to-Read Ser.). (Illus.). (J). 1993. 9.99 (*0-553-09116-6*, Little Rooster); 3.99 (*0-553-37107-X*, Little Rooster) Bantam.
— Eency Weency Spider. (J). (ps-3). 1991. pap. 9.99 (*0-553-07316-8*); mass mkt. 3.99 (*0-553-35304-7*) Bantam.
— Floratorium. LC 92-17886. (Bank Street Museum Bks.). (Illus.). (J). (gr. 1-4). 1994. pap. 15.95 (*0-553-09365-7*); mass mkt. 9.95 (*0-553-37145-2*) Bantam.
— Follow That Fish. 1990. pap. 3.99 (*0-553-34850-7*) Bantam.
— Have You Seen Birds? (J). (ps-2). 1988. pap. 2.95 (*0-590-40890-9*) Scholastic Inc.
— Have You Seen the Birds? (Illus.). (J). (ps-3). 1988. pap. 2.95 (*0-590-27030-3*) Scholastic Inc.
— Have You Seen Trees? LC 94-14585. (J). 1995. 14.95 (*0-590-46691-7*) Scholastic Inc.
— Left & Right. LC 87-22939. (Illus.). 153p. (J). (ps-3). 1989. 13.95 (*0-15-200505-6*, Gulliver Bks) HarBrace.
— Money. LC 94-12740. (United Nations Bookshelf Ser.). (J). 1994. text ed. 14.95 (*0-689-31910-X*, Atheneum S&S) S&S Trade.
— The Not Now! Said the Cow-Bank Street. (J). (ps-3). 1989. 3.99 (*0-553-34691-1*) Bantam.
— One Gift Deserves Another. (Illus.). 32p. (J). (ps-1). 1992. 13.00 (*0-525-44975-2*, DCB) Dutton Child Bks.
— Osceola, Seminole Warrior. LC 78-60116. (Illus.). 48p. (J). (gr. 4-6). 1979. lib. bdg. 10.59 (*0-89375-158-8*); pap. 3.50 (*0-89375-148-0*) Troll Assocs.
— Row, Row, Row Your Boat. LC 92-29015. (Bank Street Ready-to-Read Ser.). (Illus.). (J). 1993. mass mkt. 9.99 (*0-553-09498-X*) Bantam.
— Sequoyah, Cherokee Hero. LC 78-60117. (Illus.). 48p. (J). (gr. 4-6). 1979. lib. bdg. 10.59 (*0-89375-159-6*); pap. 3.50 (*0-89375-149-9*) Troll Assocs.
— The Story Book Prince. LC 85-31745. (Illus.). 32p. (J). (ps-3). 1987. 12.95 (*0-15-200590-0*, Gulliver Bks) HarBrace.
— Uh-oh! Cawed the Crow. LC 92-1629. (Bank Street Ready-to-Read Ser.). (Illus.). (J). 1993. pap. 3.50 (*0-553-37186-X*, Little Rooster); mass mkt. 9.99 (*0-553-09387-8*, Little Rooster) Bantam.
— Wake Up, Baby. (Bank Street Ready-to-Read Ser.). (J). (ps-3). 1990. lib. bdg. 9.99 (*0-685-54065-0*, Little Rooster); pap. 3.50 (*0-685-46039-8*, Little Rooster) Bantam.
— Wake up, Baby! (Illus.). (J). (ps-3). 1990. mass mkt. 3.99 (*0-553-34914-7*) Bantam.
***Oppenheim, Joanne & Oppenheim, Stephanie.** The Best Toys, Books & Videos for Kids, 1995: A Guide to One Thousand Plus Kid-Tested, Classic & New Products for Ages 0-10. (Illus.). 352p. (Orig.). 1994. pap. 12.00 (*0-06-273315-X*, Harper Ref) HarpC.
— The Best Toys, Books and Videos for Kids 1996. (Illus.). 384p. 1995. pap. 13.00 (*0-06-273379-6*) HarpC.
Oppenheim, Joost J. & Shevach, Ethan M., eds. Immunophysiology: The Role of Cells & Cytokines in Immunity & Inflammation. (Illus.). 448p. 1991. reprint ed. pap. 59.95 (*0-19-507064-X*) OUP.
Oppenheim, Joost J., et al, eds. Clinical Applications of Cytokines: Role in Pathogenesis, Diagnosis, & Therapy. LC 92-49062. 1993. 150.00 (*0-19-507129-8*) OUP.
Oppenheim, Leo. The Interpretation of Dreams in the Ancient Near East. LC 78-72754. (Ancient Mesopotamian Texts & Studies). reprint ed. 40.00 (*0-404-18198-8*) AMS Pr.
Oppenheim, Lois. Directing Beckett. LC 94-13121. (Illus.). 469p. 1994. 42.50 (*0-472-10535-3*) U of Mich Pr.
— Intentionality & Intersubjectivity: A Phenomenological Study of Butor's La Modification. LC 79-53399. (French Forum Monographs: No. 16). 187p. (Orig.). 1980. pap. 12.95 (*0-917058-15-1*) French Forum.
Oppenheim, Lois H. Politics in Chile: Democracy, Authoritarianism, & the Search for Development. LC 93-29887. 260p. (C). 1993. text ed. 58.00 (*0-8133-8210-6*); pap. text ed. 19.95 (*0-8133-8211-4*) Westview.
Oppenheim, M., ed. see Helps, Arthur.
Oppenheim, Micha F., jt. auth. see Cutter, Charles.
Oppenheim, Michael. A Doctor's Guide to the Best Medical Care: A Practical, No-Nonsense Evaluation of Your Treatment Options for over 100 Conditions & Diseases. LC 91-4973. 288p. 1991. 24.95 (*0-87857-982-6*, 05-995-0) Rodale Pr Inc.
— A Doctor's Guide to the Best Medical Care: A Practical, No-Nonsense Evaluation of Your Treatment Options for over 100 Conditions & Diseases. LC 91-4973. 336p. 1992. pap. 14.95 (*0-87596-108-8*, 05-995-1) Rodale Pr Inc.
— Mutual Upholding: Fashioning Jewish Philosophy Through Letters. LC 91-36045. (Revisioning Philosophy Ser.: Vol. 9). 186p. (C). 1992. text ed. 36.95 (*0-8204-1685-1*) P Lang Pubs.
— What Does Revelation Mean for the Modern Jew? LC 85-18929. (Symposium Ser.: Vol. 17). 152p. 1985. lib. bdg. 79.95 (*0-88946-708-0*) E Mellen.
Oppenheim, Mike. The Man's Health Book. LC 94-4872. 1994. write for info. (*0-13-880550-4*) P-H.

O

An Asterisk (*) at the beginning of an entry indicates that the title is appearing in BIP for the first time.

— One-Hundred Drugs That Work. 348p. 1995. pap. 15.00 (*1-56565-214-2*) Lowell Hse.
— One Hundred Drugs That Work: A Guide to Prescription & Non-Prescription Drugs. 348p. 1994. 22.95 (*1-56565-115-4*) Lowell Hse.
Oppenheim, Norbert. Urban Travel Demand Modeling: From Individual Choices to General Equilibrium. LC 94-13852. 1995. text ed. 64.95 (*0-471-55723-4*) Wiley.
Oppenheim, Peter. The Language of International Finance in English: Money & Banking. (English for Careers Ser.). (Illus.). (C). (gr. 10 up). 1976. pap. text ed. 4.25 (*0-88345-272-3*, 18504) Prentice ESL.
Oppenheim, Peter K. International Banking. 400p. 1991. 51.00 (*0-89982-369-6*, 050290) Am Bankers.
Oppenheim, Phillip. Japan Without Blinders: Coming to Terms with Japan's Economic Success. 448p. 1992. 24.95 (*4-7700-1682-4*) Kodansha.
Oppenheim, Rosalind C. Effective Teaching Methods for Autistic Children. 124p. 1977. 28.95 (*0-398-02858-3*) C C Thomas.
— Effective Teaching Methods for Autistic Children. 124p. 1977. pap. 15.95 (*0-398-06309-5*) C C Thomas.
Oppenheim, Samuel. Early History of the Jews in New York. 96p. 1993. reprint ed. lib. bdg. 69.00 (*0-7812-5313-6*) Rprt Serv.
***Oppenheim, Shulamith.** The Hundredth Name. LC 94-72255. (Illus.). 32p. (J). (ps-3). 1995. 14.95 (*1-56397-183-6*, Wordsong) Boyds Mills Pr.
Oppenheim, Shulamith L. Appleblossom. Yolen, Jane, ed. (Illus.). 28p. (J). (gr. 1-7). 1991. 14.95 (*0-15-203750-0*, HB Juv Bks) HarBrace.
— Fireflies for Nathan. LC 93-29568. (Illus.). (J). 1994. 15.00 (*0-688-12147-0*, Tambourine Bks); lib. bdg. 14.93 (*0-688-12148-9*, Tambourine Bks) Morrow.
— I Love You, Bunny Rabbit. (Illus.). 32p. (J). (ps-2). 1995. 14.95 (*1-56397-322-7*) Boyds Mills Pr.
— Iblis: An Islamic Tale. LC 92-15060. (Illus.). (J). (gr. 1 up). 1994. 15.95 (*0-15-238016-7*) HarBrace.
— The Lily Cupboard. LC 90-38592. (Charlotte Zolotow Bk.). (Illus.). 32p. (J). (gr. 1-3). 1992. lib. bdg. 14.89 (*0-06-024670-7*) HarpC Child Bks.
— Lily Cupboard: A Story of the Holocaust. LC 90-38592. (Charlotte Zolotow Bk.: A Trophy Picture Bk.). (Illus.). 32p. (J). (gr. 1-3). 1995. pap. 4.95 (*0-06-443393-5*, Trophy) HarpC Child Bks.
— Waiting for Noah. LC 89-35561. (Charlotte Zolotow Bk.). (Illus.). 32p. (J). (ps-2). 1990. 12.95 (*0-06-024633-2*) HarpC Child Bks.
Oppenheim, Stephanie, jt. auth. see Oppenheim, Joanne.
***Oppenheim, Vicki A. & Sierra, Luis F.** Building Blocks: Community-Based Strategies to Counteract Housing Disinvestment & Abandonment in New York City. 236p. (Orig.). 1994. pap. 15.00 (*0-88156-158-4*) Comm Serv Soc NY.
Oppenheimer. Names & Local Habitations: Selected Poems. 1990. 30.00 (*0-912330-66-X*) Jargon Soc.
— The Other Mrs. Kennedy. 1995. pap. 6.99 (*0-312-95600-2*) St Martin.
Oppenheimer, Andres. Castro's Final Hour. 1993. pap. 13.00 (*0-671-87299-0*, Touchstone Bks) S&S Trade.
Oppenheimer, Andrew, ed. European Community Law & National Law: Cases on Their Relationship. 850p. (C). 1995. 200.00 (*0-521-47296-2*) Cambridge U Pr.
Oppenheimer, Bruce I., jt. ed. see Dodd, Lawrence C.
Oppenheimer, Carl H., ed. see Kuznetsov, S. I.
Oppenheimer, Catherine, jt. ed. see Jacoby, Robin.
Oppenheimer, D., jt. auth. see Esiri, M.
Oppenheimer, David, ed. see Englefield, Ronald.
Oppenheimer, David B. Rowe v. Pacific Quad, Inc. 44p. 1987. teacher ed 6.00 (*1-55681-138-1*, FBA0138) Natl Inst Trial Ad.
— Rowe v. Pacific Quad, Inc. 2nd ed. 110p. 1987. 12.75 (*1-55681-137-3*, FBA0137) Natl Inst Trial Ad.
Oppenheimer, Ernest J. Balancing the Federal Budget: The Cure for U. S. Wealth Dissipation. LC 90-62918. 181p. 1991. 20.00 (*0-9603982-6-0*) Pen & Podium.
— Gasoline Tax Advantages. 90p. (Orig.). 1987. pap. 10.00 (*0-9603982-5-2*) Pen & Podium.
— Natural Gas, the Best Energy Choice. LC 89-63205. 188p. 1990. 22.50 (*0-9603982-7-9*) Pen & Podium.
— A Realistic Approach to U. S. Energy Independence. (Orig.). 1980. pap. 5.00 (*0-9603982-0-1*) Pen & Podium.
— Solving the U. S. Energy Problem. 50p. (Orig.). 1984. pap. 5.00 (*0-9603982-4-4*) Pen & Podium.
***Oppenheimer, Evelyn.** A Book Lover in Texas. 176p. 1995. 16.95 (*0-929398-89-0*) UNTX Pr.
— Gilbert Onderdonk: The Nurseryman of Mission Valley, Pioneer Horticulturist. LC 90-28231. (Illus.). 176p. 1991. pap. 12.95 (*0-929398-23-8*) UNTX Pr.
— Heroes of Texas. (Illus.). 1964. 20.00 (*0-87244-001-X*) Texian.
— Oral Book Reviewing to Stimulate Reading: A Practical Guide in Technique for Lecture & Broadcast. LC 80-20006. 168p. 1980. 20.00 (*0-8108-1352-1*) Scarecrow.
— Tilli Comes to Texas. LC 86-3089. (Illus.). 40p. (J). (gr. k-3). 1986. lib. bdg. 9.95 (*0-937460-21-4*) Hendrick-Long.
Oppenheimer, Evelyn, ed. see Tolbert, Frank.
Oppenheimer, Francis J. Ezekiel to Einstein: Israel's Gifts to Science & Invention. LC 70-167398. (Essay Index Reprint Ser.). 1977. reprint ed. 12.95 (*0-8369-2438-X*) Ayer.
Oppenheimer, Franz. Selected Writings. 1973. 300.00 (*0-8490-1022-5*) Gordon Pr.
— The State. 1984. lib. bdg. 250.00 (*0-87700-647-4*) Revisionist Pr.
— State: Its History & Development Viewed Sociologically. Gitterman, John M., tr. LC 73-172224. (Right Wing Individualist Tradition in America Ser.). 1978. reprint ed. 25.95 (*0-405-00433-8*) Ayer.
Oppenheimer, George, jt. auth. see Kober, Arthur.
Oppenheimer, Gerald M., jt. ed. see Bayer, Ronald.
Oppenheimer, Heinrich. Rationale of Punishment: With Intro. & Index Added. LC 72-172579. (Criminology, Law Enforcement, & Social Problems Ser.: No. 167). 1975. 24.00 (*0-87585-167-3*) Patterson Smith.
***Oppenheimer, Helen.** Helping Children Find God: A Book for Parents, Teachers, & Clergy. 206p. Date not set. reprint ed. pap. 12.95 (*0-8192-1650-X*) Morehouse Pub.
— The Hope of Heaven: What Happens When We Die? LC 87-33120. 160p. (Orig.). 1988. pap. 7.95 (*0-936384-56-5*) Cowley Pubns.
Oppenheimer, J. R. Lectures on Electrodynamics. (Documents on Modern Physics Ser.). 174p. 1970. text ed. 81.00 (*0-677-40130-2*) Gordon & Breach.
Oppenheimer, J. Robert. Atom & Void: Essays on Science & Community. (Science Library). 164p. (C). 1989. text ed. 29.95 (*0-691-08547-1*); pap. text ed. 9.95 (*0-691-02434-0*) Princeton U Pr.
— Uncommon Sense. Metropolis, N. et al, eds. LC 84-439. 195p. 1984. 25.00 (*0-8176-3165-8*) Birkhauser.
Oppenheimer, James. Poems. 1972. 69.95 (*0-8490-0847-6*) Gordon Pr.
Oppenheimer, Jane M., ed. Autobiography of Dr. Karl Ernst von Baer. LC 86-1924. 1986. 25.00 (*0-88135-079-6*) Watson Pub Intl.
Oppenheimer, Jane M., tr. see Groeben, Christiane, ed. & tr.
Oppenheimer, Jerry. Barbara Walters. 1991. mass mkt. 5.95 (*0-312-92387-2*) St Martin.
— The Other Mrs. Kennedy: Ethel Skakel Kennedy - an American Drama of Power, Privilege & Politics. (Illus.). 512p. 1994. 25.95 (*0-312-11040-5*) St Martin.
Oppenheimer, Joachim. Take Your Brother by the Hand. LC 91-71463. (Illus.). 186p. (Orig.). 1991. pap. 17.95 (*0-9629401-0-0*) J Oppenheimer.
Oppenheimer, Joan. Rattlesnakes & Roses. LC 86-63269. 161p. (Orig.). 1987. pap. 8.95 (*0-9602676-5-4*) Persevrnce Pr.
Oppenheimer, Joan L. Trouble at the Gabourys' 1987. 16.95 (*0-8027-0981-8*) Walker & Co.
Oppenheimer, Joe A., jt. auth. see Frohlich, Norman.
Oppenheimer, Joel. The Ghost Lover. 16p. 1993. pap. 3.00 (*0-9632962-0-5*) A Mann Kaye.
— The Ghost Lover. limited ed. 16p. 1993. 10.00 (*0-9632962-1-3*) A Mann Kaye.
— Just Friends: Friends & Lovers, Poems, 1959-1962. LC 70-83559. 1980. 15.00 (*0-912330-26-0*); pap. 7.50 (*0-912330-27-9*) Jargon Soc.
— New Spaces: Poems, 1975-1983. LC 85-9060. 151p. (Orig.). 1985. pap. 8.50 (*0-87685-640-7*) Black Sparrow.
— Pan's Eyes. LC 74-77760. (Haystack Bks.). 64p. 1974. pap. 3.50 (*0-685-46899-2*) Mulch Pr.
— Poetry: The Ecology of the Soul. Landrey, David & Maloney, Dennis, eds. 1983. pap. 7.50 (*0-934834-36-9*) White Pine.
— Poetry: The Ecology of the Soul. deluxe ed. Landrey, David & Maloney, Dennis, eds. 1983. 25.00 (*1-877727-49-0*) White Pine.
— Why Not. 1987. 7.00 (*0-685-67621-8*) White Pine.
— The Woman Poems. LC 74-17641. 128p. 1975. 7.95 (*0-672-52025-7*, Bobbs); pap. 4.95 (*0-672-52026-5*, Bobbs) Macmillan.
Oppenheimer, L., ed. The Self-Concept: European Perspectives on Its Development, Aspects, & Applications. (Recent Research in Psychology Ser.). (Illus.). viii, 160p. 1990. pap. 38.00 (*0-387-52371-5*) Spr-Verlag.
Oppenheimer, L. & Valsiner, Jaan, eds. The Origins of Action: Interdisciplinary & International Perspectives. (Illus.). xv, 265p. 1991. 54.00 (*0-387-97510-1*) Spr-Verlag.
Oppenheimer, Lillian & Epstein, Natalie. Decorative Napkin Folding for Beginners. (Illus.). 1980. pap. 2.50 (*0-486-23797-4*) Dover.
— More Decorative Napkin Folding. (Cookery, Wine, Nutrition Ser.). 48p. 1984. pap. 2.50 (*0-486-24673-6*) Dover.
— Napkin Folding for Everyone, 2 bks. 96p. (Orig.). 1986. pap. 5.00 (*0-486-25146-2*) Dover.
Oppenheimer, Lillian, jt. auth. see Lewis, Shari.
Oppenheimer, Lillian, jt. auth. see Montroll, John.
Oppenheimer, Louis, jt. auth. see Oosterwegel, Annerieke.
Oppenheimer, Martin. White Collar Politics. 288p. 1985. 26.00 (*0-85345-659-3*); pap. 12.00 (*0-85345-660-7*) Monthly Rev.
Oppenheimer, Martin, ed. The American Military. LC 73-78698. (Society Bks.). 180p. (C). 1971. reprint ed. 29.95 (*0-87855-056-9*); reprint ed. pap. text ed. 17.95 (*0-87855-549-8*) Transaction Pubs.
Oppenheimer, Martin, et al, eds. Radical Sociologists & the Movement: Experiences, Lessons, & Legacies. 256p. 1990. 29.95 (*0-87722-745-4*) Temple U Pr.
Oppenheimer, Mary, jt. auth. see Fitch, Robert B.
***Oppenheimer, Max, Jr.** Pedro Balderon de la Barca's The Fake Astrologer: A Critical Spanish Text & English Translation. LC 93-12701. (Iberica Ser.: Vol. 9). 250p. (C). 1994. text ed. 48.95 (*0-8204-2166-9*) P Lang Pubs.
Oppenheimer, Max, Jr., tr. see De Molina, Tirso.
Oppenheimer, Norman J., et al, eds. Methods in Enzymology, Vol. 177: Nuclear Magnetic Resonance, Pt. B: Structure & Mechanism. 550p. 1989. text ed. 104.00 (*0-12-182078-5*) Acad Pr.
Oppenheimer, Paul. The Birth of the Modern Mind: Self, Consciousness, & the Invention of the Sonnet. (Illus.). 224p. 1989. 42.00 (*0-19-505692-2*) OUP.
***Oppenheimer, Paul, tr.** Till Eulenspiegel: His Adventures. (World's Classics Ser.). (Illus.). 256p. 1995. pap. 8.95 (*0-19-282343-4*) OUP.
Oppenheimer, Peter. Mirror by the Road: A Transforming Journey of Spirituality in Everyday Life. (Illus.). 208p. (Orig.). 1988. pap. 12.95 (*0-945925-03-4*) Inner Wealth Pr.
Oppenheimer, Richard, ed. see Schuyler, Arlene A.
Oppenheimer, Robert. Robert Oppenheimer: Letters & Recollections. Smith, Alice K. & Weiner, Charles, eds. LC 80-10106. (Harvard Paperbacks Ser.). 387p. 1980. text ed. 37.50 (*0-674-77605-4*) HUP.
— Robert Oppenheimer: Letters & Recollections. Smith, Alice K. & Weiner, Charles, eds. LC 80-10106. (Harvard Paperbacks Ser.). 387p. 1981. pap. text ed. 12.50 (*0-674-77606-2*) HUP.
Oppenheimer, Samuel. Survey of Electronics. 500p. (C). 1990. text ed. 40.00 (*0-03-020842-4*) SCP.
***Oppenheimer, Steve.** SoundBlaster Book. 1995. pap. write for info. (*0-7821-1699-X*) Sybex.
Oppenheimer, Steve, jt. auth. see Petersen, George.
Oppenheimer, Steven B., ed. Cancer: A Biological & Clinical Introduction. 262p. 1985. boxed 35.00 (*0-86720-062-6*) Jones & Bartlett.
Oppenheimer, Steven B. & Lefevre, George, Jr. Introduction to Embryonic Development. 3rd enl. rev. ed. 500p. 1988. pap. text ed. write for info. (*0-205-11708-2*, H17080) P-H.
Oppenheimer, Valerie K. The Female Labor Force in the United States, Vol. 5. LC 76-4536. (Population Monograph Ser.: No. 5). (Illus.). 197p. 1976. reprint ed. text ed. 25.00 (*0-8371-8829-6*, OPFL, Greenwood Pr) Greenwood.
— Work & the Family: A Study in Social Demography. (Studies in Population). 1982. text ed. 55.00 (*0-12-527580-3*) Acad Pr.
***Oppenheimer, William.** El Dorado: Lament for the Gold Double Eagle. LC 94-77949. 152p. 1994. 23.00 (*0-913559-25-3*); pap. 14.00 (*0-913559-24-5*) Birch Brook Pr.
Oppenhelm, Joanne. Donkey's Tale. (J). (ps-3). 1991. pap. 3.99 (*0-553-35208-3*) Bantam.
Oppenlander & Poser. Business Cycle Analysis by Means of Economic Surveys, Pt. 1: Papers Presented at the 20th CIRET Conference Proceedings, Budapest 1991. 453p. 1992. 93.95 (*1-85628-260-0*, Pub. by Avebury Pub UK) Ashgate Pub Co.
Oppenlander, Ann. Dickens' All Year Round: An Index. LC 82-50403. 752p. 1985. 55.00 (*0-87875-252-8*) Whitston Pub.
Oppenlander, K. H. & Poser, G. Business Cycle Surveys in the Assessment of Economic Activity: Papers Presented at the 17th Ciret Conference Proceedings Vienna 1985. 674p. 1986. text ed. 99.95 (*0-566-05108-7*) Ashgate Pub Co.
Oppenlander, Karl H. & Poser, Gunter. Business Cycle Analysis by Means of Economic Surveys, Pt. II: Papers Presented at the 20th CIRET Conference Proceedings, Budapest 1991. 480p. 1993. 75.95 (*1-85628-429-8*, Pub. by Avebury Pub UK) Ashgate Pub Co.
— Business Cycle Surveys with Special Reference to the Pacific Basin Economies: Papers Presented at the 19th CIRET Conference Proceedings, OSaka, 1989. (CIRET Conference Proceedings Ser.). 761p. 1990. text ed. 119.95 (*1-85628-123-X*, Pub. by Avebury Pub UK) Ashgate Pub Co.
— Contributions of Business Cycle Surveys to Empirical Economics: Proceedings of the CIRET Conference, 18th, Zurich, 1987. 692p. 1988. text ed. 102.95 (*0-566-05629-1*, Pub. by Avebury Pub UK) Ashgate Pub Co.
Oppenlander, Karl H. & Poser, Gunter, eds. The Explanatory Powers of Business Cycle Surveys: Papers Presented at the 21st Ciret Conference Proceedings, Stellenbosch, 1993. 738p. 1994. 118.95 (*1-85628-575-8*, Pub. by Avebury Pub UK) Ashgate Pub Co.
— Leading Indicators & Business Cycle Surveys. LC 84-9981. 500p. 1984. text ed. 45.00 (*0-312-47645-0*) St Martin.
Oppenneer, Betsy. Betsy's Breads. rev. ed. (Illus.). 70p. (YA). (gr. 8 up). 1991. pap. 7.95 (*0-9627665-2-6*) Breadworks.
— The Bread Book: More Than Two Hundred Recipes & Techniques for Baking & Shaping Perfect Breads, Sweet & Savory, Muffins, Rolls, Buns, Biscuits, & Pizzas. (Illus.). 416p. 1994. 27.50 (*0-06-016716-5*, HarpT) HarpC.
— Perfect Bread: How to Conquer Bread Baking. 1991. vhs 29.95 (*0-9627665-1-8*) Breadworks.
Opper, Frederick B. Happy Hooligan: First Collection in Full Continuity of Two Complete Years from the Sunday Strip, 1904. Blackbeard, Bill, ed. LC 76-53052. (Classic American Comic Strips Ser.). (Illus.). 1977. 16.50 (*0-88355-659-6*); pap. 10.00 (*0-88355-658-8*) Hyperion Conn.
Opper, Jacob. Science & the Arts: A Study in Relationships from 1600-1900. LC 70-178042. 226p. 1973. 32.50 (*0-8386-1054-4*) Fairleigh Dickinson.
Opper, S., jt. ed. see Husen, Torsten.
Opper, Susan, et al. The Impact on Study Abroad Programmes on Students & Graduates, Vol. 2. (Higher Education Policy Ser.: No. 11). 250p. 1990. 45.00 (*1-85302-523-2*, Pub. by J Kingsley Pubs UK) Taylor & Francis.
Opper, Susanna & Fersko-Weiss, Henry. Technology for Teams. (Illus.). 225p. 1992. pap. 34.95 (*0-442-23928-9*) Van Nos Reinhold.
Opper, Sylvia. Hong Kong's Young Children: Their Preschools & Families. 232p. (Orig.). 1992. pap. 34.50 (*962-209-307-8*, Pub. by Hong Kong Univ Pr HK) Coronet Bks.
Opper, Sylvia, jt. auth. see Ginsburg, Herbert P.
Opperheimer-Dekker, A., jt. ed. see Van Mierop, L. H.
Opperman, Hal. Jean-Baptiste Oudry Sixteen Eighty-Six to Seventeen Fifty-Five. 250p. 1983. pap. 24.95 (*0-912804-12-2*) Kimbell Art.
— Jean-Baptiste Oudry Sixteen Eighty-Six to Seventeen Fifty-Five. LC 82-84544. 226p. (C). 1983. 50.00 (*0-295-96014-0*); pap. 24.95 (*0-295-96015-9*) U of Wash Pr.
Opperman, Henry J. Career Challenge. LC 84-73103. 300p. (Orig.). 1988. 27.95 (*0-318-03059-4*) BJIS Pub.
— The No Illusions Philatelic Numismatic Combinations Catalog. LC 84-73102. 417p. (Orig.). 1985. pap. 21.95 (*0-318-03055-1*) BJIS Pub.
Opperman, K., jt. ed. see Kroner, W.
Oppermann, Alfred. Dictionary of Dataprocessing. 2nd ed. (ENG & GER.). 1973. pap. 55.00 (*0-8288-6244-3*, M-7116) Fr & Eur.
— Dictionary of Electronics, Vol. 1. 1987p. (ENG & GER.). 195.00 (*0-8288-0294-7*, M 15118) Fr & Eur.
— Dictionary of Electronics, Vol. 2. 800p. (ENG & GER.). 1987. 225.00 (*0-8288-0293-9*, M8702) Fr & Eur.
— Dictionary of Modern Technology: English-German, 2 vols., Vol. 1. 2nd ed. 1935p. (ENG & GER.). 1990. 375.00 (*0-8288-0631-4*, M6982) Fr & Eur.
— Dictionary of Modern Technology: English-German, 2 vols., Vol. 2. 2044p. (GER.). 1987. 375.00 (*0-8288-0632-2*) Fr & Eur.
— Woerterbuch der Modernen Technik. (ENG & GER.). 350.00 (*0-685-01777-X*, M-6982) Fr & Eur.
— Woerterbuch Kybernetik: Dictionary of Cybernetics. (ENG & GER.). 1969. pap. 22.50 (*3-7940-3258-6*, M-6915) Fr & Eur.
Oppermann, Helga. Das Engelsmuster - Zur Theorie und Geschichte, Analyse und Interpretation eines Kulturellen Deutungsmusters Des Weiblichen. (Anglistische und Amerikanistische Texte und Studien Ser.: No. 2). xvi, 518p. 1986. write for info. (*3-487-07747-7*, Pub. by Georg Olms GW) Lubrecht & Cramer.
Oppermann, Reinhard, ed. Adaptive User Support: Ergonomic Design of Manually & Automatically Adaptable Software. (Computers, Cognition, & Work Ser.). 272p. 1994. text ed. 49.95 (*0-8058-1655-0*) L Erlbaum Assocs.
Oppersdorff, Mathias, photos. Adirondack Faces. LC 90-28862. (Illus.). 136p. 1991. 34.95 (*0-8156-0260-X*) Syracuse U Pr.
Oppert, Gustav. On the Original Inhabitants of Bharatavarsa or India. Bolle, Kees W., ed. (Mythology Ser.). 1978. reprint ed. lib. bdg. 60.95 (*0-405-10557-6*) Ayer.
Oppian.
Oppianus. Index in Halieutica Oppiani Cilicis et in Cynegetica Poetae Apameensis. James, A. W., ed. Bd. IV. 132p. 1970. write for info. (*0-318-70990-2*, Pub. by Georg Olms GW) Lubrecht & Cramer.
Oppitz, Joseph, ed. Alphonsus Liguori: The Redeeming Love of Christ. 136p. (Orig.). 1992. pap. 8.95 (*0-911782-97-4*) New City.
Oppl, Hubert, jt. ed. see Radke, Dietmar.
Oppl, Hubert, jt. auth. see Von Kardorff, Ernst.
Opplt, J. J., jt. ed. see Lewis, L. A.
Oppold, Robert S. Iowa Bankruptcy: 1984-1992. 420p. 1992. ring bd. 105.00 (*0-86678-370-9*) Michie Butterworth.
Oppolzer, H., jt. ed. see Bastard, Gerald.
Oppong, C., ed. Female & Male in West Africa. 280p. (C). 1983. pap. text ed. 47.95 (*0-04-301158-6*) Routledge Chapman & Hall.
Oppong, Christine, ed. Sex Roles, Population & Development in West Africa. LC 87-27386. xiii, 242p. 1988. text ed. 40.00 (*0-435-08022-9*) Heinemann.
Oppong, Christine & Abu, Katharine. Seven Roles of Women: Impact of Education, Migration & Employment on Ghanian Mothers. (Women, Work & Development Ser.: No. 13). xi, 127p. (Orig.). (C). 1987. pap. 16.00 (*92-2-105858-1*) Intl Labour Office.
Oppong, Christine, jt. auth. see Adepoju, Aderanti.
O'Pray, Michael, ed. Andy Warhol: The Film Factory. (Illus.). 196p. 1990. 45.00 (*0-85170-250-3*, Pub. by British Film Inst UK); pap. 19.95 (*0-85170-243-0*, Pub. by British Film Inst UK) Ind U Pr.
Oprea, A. G., jt. auth. see Cuculescu, I.
Opremack, E. Mitchell. Uveitis: A Clinical Manual for Ocular Inflammation. LC 94-13826. 1994. 120.00 (*0-387-94247-5*) Spr-Verlag.
Oprendek, Donald V., jt. auth. see Davis, Patricia A.
***O'Prey, Kevin P.** The Arms Export Challenge: Cooperative Approaches to Export Management & Defense Conversion. 75p. (C). 1995. pap. 9.95x (*0-8157-6499-5*) Brookings.
— Russian Defense Conversion: The Need for a Strategic Partnership. 120p. (C). 1995. pap. 9.95x (*0-87078-375-0*) TCFP-PPP.
O'Prey, Paul, ed. see Conrad, Joseph.
Oprey, Paul, ed. see Graves, Robert.
O'Prey, Paul
O'Prey, Philip, tr. see Tubiana, Joseph.
Opromolla, Diltor V., jt. ed. see Hastings, Robert C.
Opsal, Knut. Business Strategy & Ethnic Identity. (Bergen Studies in Social Anthropology: No. 44). 127p. (Orig.). 1989. pap. text ed. 13.95 (*0-936508-73-6*) Barber Pr.
Opschoor, A. Conformations of Polyethylene & Polypropylene. x, 68p. 1966. 50.00 (*0-685-47151-9*) Gordon & Breach.
Opschoor, J. B., ed. Persistent Pollutants. (Economy & Environment Ser.). (C). 1991. lib. bdg. 112.50 (*0-7923-1168-X*) Kluwer Ac.
Opschoor, J. B. & Turner, R. K., eds. Economic Incentives & Environmental Policies: Principles & Practice. LC 93-41913. 312p. (C). 1994. lib. bdg. 120.00 (*0-7923-2601-6*) Kluwer Ac.

O

Opsomer, Carmelia. Opsomer, Carmelia: Index de la Pharmacopee Latine du Ler Au Xe Siecle, 2 vols., Set. (Alpha-Omega, Reihe A Ser.: Bd. CV). lxxxviii, 824p. (GER.). 1989. write for info. (*3-487-09190-9*, Pub. by Georg Olms GW) Lubrecht & Cramer.

Opstelten, George E., Jr. Older Adults: A Unique Population at Risk for Alcoholism & Drug Abuse Problems. Visconte, Pasquale J. & Hance, Emilie, eds. (Illus.). 70p. 1983. pap. text ed. 3.95 (*0-9612426-0-4*) Aging Alcoholism.

Optical Data Staff. Bar Code Manual. 1991. 25.00 (*0-8016-7055-1*) Mosby Yr Bk.

Optical Society of America, Committee on Colorimetry. The Science of Color. LC 52-7039. (Illus.). 385p. 1963. 50.00 (*0-9600380-1-9*) Optical Soc.

Optical Society of America Staff. Handbook of Optics. 1978. text ed. 129.50 (*0-07-047710-8*) McGraw.

— Handbook of Optics, Vol. 1. 2nd ed. 1994. text ed. 99.50 (*0-07-047740-X*) McGraw.

— Handbook of Optics, Vol. 2. 2nd ed. 1993. text ed. 99.50 (*0-07-047974-7*) McGraw.

— Optics Index, 1974-1979. LC 81-81242. 1980. 30.00 (*0-9600380-2-7*) Optical Soc.

— Optics Index, 1980-1984. LC 85-61256. 1981. 30.00 (*0-9600380-3-5*) Optical Soc.

Optical Spectrometric Measurements of High Temperatures Symposium Staff. Optical Spectrometric Measurements of High Temperatures. Dickerman, Philip J., ed. LC 61-5607. 397p. reprint ed. pap. 113.20 (*0-317-08417-8*, 2005139) Bks Demand.

Options, Inc. Staff & Robbins, Wendy H. The Job Seekers Guide to the Delaware Valley: A Source Book Linking People to Jobs. LC 92-40246. (Illus.). 162p. (Orig.). 1993. pap. 11.95 (*0-940159-22-8*) Camino Bks.

Options Institute Staff. Options: Essential Concepts & Trading Strategies. 2nd ed. 430p. 1994. text ed. 55.00 (*0-7863-0272-0*) Irwin Prof Pubng.

Opton, Frank. Liberal Religion: Principles & Practices. LC 81-81129. (Library of Liberal Religion). 295p. 1981. 30.95x (*0-87975-155-X*) Prometheus Bks.

Opton, Frank G. Decedents' Estates, Wills & Trusts in the USA. 188p. 1987. 71.00 (*90-6544-271-5*) Kluwer Law Tax Pubs.

Opubor, A., jt. ed. see Nwuneli, O.

***Opus Communications Staff.** Focus on JCAHO Video Series Workbook. 104p. 1994. student ed write for info. (*1-885829-12-4*) Opus Communs.

Opuszynski, Karol & Shireman, Jerome V. Herbivorous Fish: Culture & Use For Weed Management. LC 94-13708. 1994. write for info. (*0-8493-4988-5*) CRC Pr.

Oputa, C. A. Conduct at the Bar & the Unwritten Laws of the Legal Profession. LC 81-85780. xiv, 69p. 1982. reprint ed. lib. bdg. 28.00 (*0-912004-20-7*) W W Gaunt.

— Modern Bar Advocacy. LC 81-85779. 224p. 1982. reprint ed. lib. bdg. 47.00 (*0-912004-19-3*) W W Gaunt.

Oquendo de Amat, Carlos. Five Meters of Poems. Guss, David M., tr. & intro. by. (Illus.). 1986. 75.00 (*0-918824-53-2*) Turkey Pr.

O'Quinn, Garland. Developmental Gymnastics, Pt. I: Building Physical Skills for Children. LC 77-91498. (Illus.). 125p. 1978. 18.00 (*0-292-71514-5*) U of Tex Pr.

O'Quinn, Garland, Jr. & Hickman, E. Jessica. Teaching Developmental Gymnastics: Skills to Take Through Life. (Illus.). 224p. 1990. 39.95 (*0-292-78101-6*); pap. 24.95 (*0-292-78104-0*) U of Tex Pr.

***O'Quinn, Kevin B.** The Oracle & the Well. 400p. 1995. pap. 9.95 (*0-7610-0048-8*) NW Pub.

Oquist, Paul. Violence, Conflict, & Politics in Colombia. LC 79-6778. (Studies in Social Discontinuity). 1980. text ed. 43.00 (*0-12-527750-4*) Acad Pr.

Oquli, Ramon & Melendez, Carlos. Escritos de Jose Cecilio del Valle: Una Seleccion. OAS General Secretariat Dept. of Cultural Affairs, tr. 255p. (C). 1982. pap. text ed. 20.00 (*0-8270-1271-3*) OAS.

Oraa, Jaime. Human Rights in States of Emergency in International Law. (Oxford Monographs in International Law). 320p. 1992. 69.00 (*0-19-825710-4*) OUP.

Orage, A. R. Commentaries on G. I. Gurdjieff's All & Everything. Nott, C. S., ed. 100p. 1985. 14.95 (*0-89756-015-9*) Two Rivers.

— The Gospel According to A. R. Orage. Holmes, J. D. et al, eds. (Illus.). 1995. pap. 15.95 (*1-55818-322-1*) Holmes Pub.

— Nietzsche in Outline & Aphorism. 1974. 250.00 (*0-8490-0733-X*) Gordon Pr.

— On Love: Freely Adapted from the Tibetan. 1989. reprint ed. pap. 4.95 (*1-55818-156-3*) Holmes Pub.

— Political & Economic Writings. 1973. 250.00 (*0-8490-0872-7*) Gordon Pr.

Orage, Alfred R. Political & Economic Writings from the New English Weekly, 1932-1934. LC 67-28762. (Essay Index Reprint Ser.). 1977. 19.95 (*0-8369-0753-1*) Ayer.

— Psychological Exercises & Essays. LC 72-181083. (Orig.). 1974. pap. 12.50 (*0-87728-265-X*) Weiser.

— Readers & Writers. LC 72-99714. (Essay Index Reprint Ser.). 1977. 19.95 (*0-8369-1367-1*) Ayer.

— Selected Essays & Critical Writings. Read, Herbert E. & Saurat, D., eds. LC 67-30225. (Essay Index Reprint Ser.). 1977. 19.95 (*0-8369-0754-X*) Ayer.

O'Rahilly. Irish Dialects: Past & Present. 1988. reprint ed. 40.00 (*0-901282-55-3*) Colton Bk.

O'Rahilly, Aodhogan. Winding the Clock: O'Rahilly & the 1916 Rising. (Illus.). 240p. 1991. 31.95 (*0-946640-65-3*, Pub. by Lilliput Pr Ltd IE) Irish Bks Media.

O'Rahilly, Egan. The Poems of Egan O'Rahilly: To Which Are Added Miscellaneous Pieces Illustrating Their Subjects & Language. Dinneen, Patrick S., ed. LC 75-28837. reprint ed. 30.00 (*0-404-13826-8*) AMS Pr.

O'Rahilly, Ronan & Muller, Fabiola. Developmental Stages in Human Embryos. LC 87-70669. (Illus.). 320p. 1987. 52.00 (*0-87279-666-3*, 637) Carnegie Inst.

— The Embryonic Brain: An Atlas of Developmental Stages. LC 93-33438. (Illus.). 1994. text ed. 134.95 (*0-471-58845-8*, Wiley-Liss) Wiley.

— Human Embryology & Teratology. 328p. 1992. text ed. 185.00 (*0-471-56186-X*, Wiley-Liss) Wiley.

O'Rahilly, Thomas F. Danfhocail: Irish Epigrams in Verse. LC 75-28834. reprint ed. 29.50 (*0-404-13824-1*) AMS Pr.

O'Rahilly, Thomas F., comp. Danta Gradha: An Anthology of Irish Love Poetry (A.D. 1350-1750) 2nd rev. ed. LC 75-28836. reprint ed. 24.00 (*0-404-13825-X*) AMS Pr.

O'Raifeartaigh, Lochlainn. Group Structure of Gauge Theories. (Cambridge Monographs on Mathematical Physics). 174p. 1988. pap. 18.95 (*0-521-34785-8*) Cambridge U Pr.

***Oral History Association Staff.** Oral History Evaluation Guidelines. (Pamphlet Ser.: Vol. 3). (Orig.). 1992. pap. text ed. 5.00 (*0-615-00636-1*) Oral Hist.

Oral History Task Force Staff. Extended Roots: From Hawaii to New York, Migraciones Puertorriquenas a los Estados Unidos. (Illus.). 86p. (Orig.). 1986. pap. 7.00 (*1-878483-04-8*) Hunter Coll CEP.

Oral, O., ed. see Sahin, I.

***Oram.** Badger's Bring Something Party. 1995. (*0-688-14082-3*) Lothrop.

Oram, Allan E., jt. auth. see Gellinas, Ulric J., Jr.

Oram, Andrew, jt. auth. see Talbot, Steve.

Oram, Andy, ed. see Jameson, Kevin.

Oram, Andy, ed. see Kirch, Olaf.

Oram, Andy, ed. see Schwartz, Randal L.

Oram, Andy, ed. see Shirley, John, et al.

Oram, Andy, ed. see Welsh, Matt & Kaufman, Lar.

Oram, Barbara, jt. auth. see Maclean, Heather.

Oram, Helen, jt. auth. see Oram, Tom.

Oram, Hiawyn. A Boy Wants a Dinosaur. (J). (ps-3). 1991. bds. 13.95 (*0-374-30939-6*) FS&G.

— Boy Wants a Dinosaur. (J). (ps-3). 1993. pap. 4.95 (*0-374-40889-0*) FS&G.

— Creepy Crawly Song Book. (J). (ps-3). 1993. 17.00 (*0-374-31639-2*) FS&G.

— In the Attic. LC 84-15570. (Illus.). 32p. (J). (ps-2). 1985. 13.95 (*0-8050-0779-2*, Bks Young Read) H Holt & Co.

— In the Attic. LC 84-15570. (Illus.). 32p. (J). (ps-2). 1988. pap. 4.95 (*0-8050-0780-6*, Bks Young Read) H Holt & Co.

— Mine! (Illus.). 16p. (J). (ps-00). 1992. 12.95 (*0-8120-6303-1*); pap. 5.95 (*0-8120-4905-5*) Barron.

— Ned & the Joybaloo. (Illus.). 28p. (J). (ps up). 1989. 11.95 (*0-374-35501-0*) FS&G.

— Ned & the Joybaloo. 1990. pap. 3.95 (*0-374-45492-2*) FS&G.

— Out of the Blue: Poems about Color. LC 92-55044. (Illus.). 64p. (J). (gr. 1-5). 1993. 18.95 (*1-56282-469-4*); lib. bdg. 18.89 (*1-56282-470-8*) Hyprn Child.

— Reckless Ruby. LC 91-20124. (Illus.). 32p. (J). (ps-2). 1992. 12.00 (*0-517-58744-0*) Crown Bks Yng Read.

— The Second Princess. LC 94-1658. (Illus.). 32p. (J). 1994. 13.95 (*0-307-17513-8*, Artsts Writrs) Western Pub.

Oram, Hiawyn & Baird, Daniel. Just Like Us. (Illus.). 32p. (J). (gr. 2-4). 1988. 12.95 (*0-8192-1472-8*) Morehouse Pub.

Oram, Hugh. All about Ireland: Facts & Figures. (Pocket Guide Ser.). (Illus.). 72p. (Orig.). 1990. pap. 7.95 (*0-86281-231-3*, Pub. by Appletree Pr IE) Irish Bks Media.

Oram, Liz & Baker, R. Robin. Bird Migration. LC 91-12120. (Migrations Ser.). (Illus.). 48p. (J). (gr. 4-8). 1992. lib. bdg. 22.80 (*0-8114-2925-3*) Raintree Steck-V.

— Insect Migration. LC 91-12776. (Migrations Ser.). (Illus.). 48p. (J). (gr. 4-8). 1992. lib. bdg. 22.80 (*0-8114-2926-1*) Raintree Steck-V.

— Mammal Migration. LC 91-12181. (Migrations Ser.). (Illus.). 48p. (J). (gr. 4-8). 1992. lib. bdg. 22.80 (*0-8114-2927-X*) Raintree Steck-V.

— Migration in the Sea. LC 91-12765. (Migrations Ser.). (Illus.). 48p. (J). (gr. 4-8). 1992. lib. bdg. 22.80 (*0-8114-2928-8*) Raintree Steck-V.

Oram, R. B. Cargo Handling in a Modern Port. 1964. pap. 82.00 (*0-08-011305-2*, Pub. by Pergamon Repr UK) Franklin.

Oram, R. B., jt. auth. see Course, A. G.

Oram, R. N., ed. Register of Australian Herbage Plant Cultivars. 3rd ed. 300p. 1990. pap. 50.00 (*0-643-05054-X*, Pub. by CSIRO AT) Intl Spec Bk.

***Oram, Tom & Oram, Helen.** Book Sales in America: The Guide to Used Book Sales Throughout the U. S. A., 1995-1996. 384p. (Orig.). 1995. pap. 14.95 (*0-9640950-3-3*) Baysys Pubng.

— The Guide to Book Sales in the Central States. (Orig.). 1995. pap. write for info. (*0-9640950-4-1*) Baysys Pubng.

— The Guide to Book Sales in the Northeast: 1995-1996 Edition. (Orig.). 1995. pap. write for info. (*0-9640950-9-2*) Baysys Pubng.

— The Guide to Book Sales in the South. (Orig.). 1995. pap. write for info. (*0-9640950-6-8*) Baysys Pubng.

— A Guide to Book Sales in the West: 1995-1996 Edition. (Orig.). 1995. pap. write for info. (*0-9640950-2-5*) Baysys Pubng.

Oram, William A., ed. see Spenser, Edmund.

Oran, Daniel. Law Dictionary for Non-Lawyers. 2nd ed. 337p. 1984. pap. text ed. 13.75 (*0-314-85283-2*) West Pub.

— Law Dictionary for Non-Lawyers. 3rd ed. 303p. 1991. pap. 15.50 (*0-314-87532-8*) West Pub.

— Oran's Dictionary of the Law. 2nd ed. 500p. 1991. pap. text ed. 24.00 (*0-314-84690-5*) West Pub.

Oran, Daniel & Tosti, Mark. Law Dictionary for Non-Lawyers. 3rd ed. 303p. 1991. pap. text ed. 18.50 (*0-314-87535-2*) West Pub.

Oran, E. S. & Boris, J. P. Numerical Simulation of Reactive Flow. 550p. 1987. 59.75 (*0-444-01251-6*) P-H.

Oran, Elaine S. & Boris, Jay P., eds. Numerical Approaches to Combustion Modeling. (PAAS Ser.: Vol. 135). (Illus.). 900p. 1991. 109.95 (*1-56347-004-7*) AIAA.

O'Rand, Angela M., jt. ed. see Osterbind, Carter C.

O'Rand, M. G., jt. ed. see Dunbar, Bonnie S.

Orange, Charlotte, ed. see Mungin, Horace.

Orange, Charlotte, ed. see Tevis, Nova.

Orange County Association Staff. Frases Fundamentales para Comunicarse. (J). (gr. k-12). 1975. 5.15 (*0-89075-200-1*) Bilingual Ed Serv.

Orange County Genealogical Committee Members & Hovemeyer, Gretchen A., eds. Early Records of the St. James Episcopal Church of Goshen, New York: Baptisms, Marriages, & Funerals, 1799-1911. 140p. (Orig.). 1985. pap. 20.00 (*0-9604116-4-X*) Orange County Genealog.

Orange County Genealogical Society Staff. Amity Cemetery Family Plot Map, 1938. 1986. pap. text ed. 0.50 (*0-937135-01-1*) Orange County Genealog.

— Beers Atlas Ulster County, 1875. 80p. 1986. lib. bdg. 30.00 (*0-685-12121-6*) Orange County Genealog.

— Cemeteries of Montgomery, Orange County, New York. (Orange County, New York Cemeteries Ser.). (Orig.). 1986. pap. write for info. (*0-9604116-5-8*) Orange County Genealog.

— Cemeteries of Town of Minisink: Names & Dates. (Orange County, New York Cemeteries Ser.: No. 3). 1988. 10.00 (*0-937135-00-3*) Orange County Genealog.

— Diagram & List of Goshen Presbyterian Church Pews, 1796. 1986. pap. text ed. 0.50 (*0-937135-02-X*) Orange County Genealog.

— Eighteen Hundred Fifty Census: Town & Village of Warwick, New York. 1986. pap. text ed. 9.00 (*0-937135-03-8*) Orange County Genealog.

— Eighteen Sixty French's New York Gazeteer. 1986. lib. bdg. 22.00 (*0-937135-04-6*, 86-43) Orange County Genealog.

— Index from J. J. Nutts Eighteen Ninety-One History of Newburgh. 16p. 1986. 4.00 (*0-937135-05-4*) Orange County Genealog.

— Index to the History of Orange County, New York (1881 Ruttenber & Clark) LC 79-84908. 262p. 1980. 20.00 (*0-9604116-1-5*) Orange County Genealog.

— List of Freeholders, Albany, New York, 1720. 1986. pap. text ed. 0.50 (*0-937135-07-0*) Orange County Genealog.

— List of Inhabitants in Dutchess County, 1714. 1986. pap. text ed. 0.50 (*0-937135-08-9*) Orange County Genealog.

— List of Inhabitants of Orange County, 1702. 1986. pap. text ed. 0.50 (*0-937135-09-7*) Orange County Genealog.

— Port Jervis Diamond Jubilee Journal History, 1982. 140p. 1986. 5.00 (*0-937135-16-X*) Orange County Genealog.

— Port Jervis Industrial Record, 1902. 42p. 1986. 4.00 (*0-937135-17-8*, 86-47) Orange County Genealog.

— Researchers' Guide to Genealogical & Historical Records in Orange County, New York. (Orig.). 1985. write for info. (*0-9604116-6-6*) Orange County Genealog.

— Thomas Burt's "Bellvale Rising Star Newspaper", 1889. 1986. pap. text ed. 3.50 (*0-937135-18-6*) Orange County Genealog.

— The Whig Press: Marriages, 1851-1865, Names & Dates. 1986. 22.00 (*0-9604116-9-0*) Orange County Genealog.

Orange County Genealogical Society Staff, et al. Orange County New York Atlas. 85p. (Orig.). 1984. reprint ed. lib. bdg. 30.00 (*0-9604116-7-4*) Orange County Genealog.

— Ulster County, New York Atlas. 130p. 1984. reprint ed. lib. bdg. 30.00 (*0-9604116-8-2*) Orange County Genealog.

Orange County Guild of American Paralysis Association Staff. Melange: Taste of Orange County. 225p. 1992. 13.95 (*0-9631784-0-7*) OC Guild Am Paralysis.

Orange County Pioneer Council Staff. Centennial Cookbook, 1889-1989: Second Printing with Historical Vignettes. (Illus.). 134p. 1989. 12.00 (*0-943480-69-8*) Friis-Pioneer Pr.

— Centennial Cookbook, 1889-1989: With Historical Vignettes. (Illus.). 134p. 1988. 12.00 (*0-943480-68-X*) Friis-Pioneer Pr.

Orange County Register Staff. Inferno. 1993. pap. 12.95 (*0-8362-8063-6*) Andrews & McMeel.

Orange, Cynthia. Addicts & Families in Recovery. 20p. (Orig.). 1986. pap. 1.55 (*0-89486-403-3*, 5215B) Hazelden.

Orange, Donna M. Peirce's Conception of God: A Developmental Study. LC 84-80516. (Peirce Studies). 106p. 1984. 24.95 (*0-936842-02-4*) Ind U Pr.

Orange Frazer Press Editors. The Ohio Sports Almanac: An Encyclopedia of Indispensable Information about Ohio's Sporting Universe. (Illus.). 225p. (Orig.). 1992. pap. 10.95 (*0-9619637-8-6*) Orange Frazer.

— Particular Places: A Traveler's Guide to Inner Ohio, Vol. I. LC 90-61654. (Illus.). 264p. (Orig.). 1990. pap. 14.95 (*0-9619637-4-3*) Orange Frazer.

— Particular Places: A Traveler's Guide to Inner Ohio, Vol. 2. LC 90-61654. (Illus.). 320p. (Orig.). 1993. pap. 14.95 (*0-9619637-9-4*) Orange Frazer.

Orange, John. Ernest Buckler: An Annotated Bibliography. 56p. (C). 1981. pap. text ed. 9.00 (*0-920763-51-0*, Pub. by ECW Press CN) Genl Dist Srvs.

— Ernest Buckler & His Works. (Canadian Author Studies). 56p. (C). 1990. pap. text ed. 9.95 (*1-55022-028-4*, Pub. by ECW Press CN) Genl Dist Srvs.

— Farley Mowat: A Biography. (Illus.). 112p. (Orig.). 1993. pap. 9.95 (*1-55022-186-8*, Pub. by ECW Pr CN) InBook.

— Orpheus in Winter: Morley Callaghan's The Loved & the Lost. (Canadian Fiction Studies: No. 22). 120p. (C). 1993. pap. text ed. 14.95 (*1-55022-123-X*, Pub. by ECW Press CN) Genl Dist Srvs.

— P. K. Page & Her Works. (Canadian Author Studies). 53p. (C). 1989. pap. text ed. 9.95 (*1-55022-011-X*, Pub. by ECW Press CN) Genl Dist Srvs.

Orange, Linwood E. English: The Preprofessional Major. 4th ed. LC 85-31962. 31p. 1986. pap. text ed. 1.85 (*0-87352-148-X*) Modern Lang.

Orange, Tom. Scripture Bulletin Boards. (Bulletin Board Ser.). 96p. (J). (gr. 2-7). 1987. 10.95 (*0-86653-397-4*, SS1826, Shining Star Pubns) Good Apple.

Orange, Tom & McClure, Nancee. Bulletin Boards That Bless. (Helping Hand Ser.). 48p. (YA). (gr. 4-8). 1984. student ed 7.95 (*0-86653-201-3*, SS 821, Shining Star Pubns) Good Apple.

***Orange, Vincent.** Ensor's Endeavour: A Biography of Wing Commander Mick Ensor DSO & BAR, DFC & BAR, AFC RNZAF & RAF. (Illus.). 208p. 1994. 29.95 (*1-898697-04-3*) Seven Hills Bk.

Orange, Vincent, jt. auth. see Marshal Sir Kenneth Bing Cross.

Orans, Martin. The Santal: A Tribe in Search of a Great Tradition. LC 65-12595. 168p. reprint ed. 47.90 (*0-685-16243-5*, 2027605) Bks Demand.

Orans, Muriel. Houseplants & Indooor Landscaping. (Illus.). 1984. pap. 5.95 (*0-88453-000-0*) Countryside Bks.

Orant, Neil. Five Hundred Questions & Answers about the Bible. 1988. 7.99 (*0-517-66472-0*) Random Hse Value.

***Oranzon, Bo G., ed.** Skill, Technology, & Enlightenment: On Practical Philosophy. LC 94-43443. (Artificial Intelligence & Society Ser.). 1994. write for info. (*3-540-19920-9*) Spr-Verlag.

Oras, Ants. Blank Verse & Chronology in Milton. LC 66-63667. (University of Florida Humanities Monographs: No. 20). (Illus.). 86p. reprint ed. pap. 25.00 (*0-7837-4921-X*, 2044586) Bks Demand.

— Milton's Editors & Commentators. LC 67-31494. (Studies in Milton: No. 22). 1969. reprint ed. lib. bdg. 75.00 (*0-8383-0604-7*) M S G Haskell Hse.

— Pause Patterns in Elizabethan & Jacobean Drama: An Experiment in Prosody. LC 60-62779. (University of Florida Humanities Monographs: No. 3). 96p. reprint ed. pap. 27.40 (*0-7837-4920-1*, 2044585) Bks Demand.

Orasanu, Judith, ed. see Garner, Ruth.

Orasanu, Judith, ed. see Goldman, Susan & Trueba, Henry.

Orasanu, Judith, et al, eds. Language, Sex & Gender. (Annals Ser.: Vol. 327). (Orig.). 1979. pap. 22.00 (*0-89766-021-8*) NY Acad Sci.

Orasanu, Judith M., ed. Reading Comprehension: From Research to Practice. 408p. (C). 1985. text ed. 79.95 (*0-89859-528-2*); pap. 36.00 (*0-89859-798-6*) L Erlbaum Assocs.

***Orason, Roy.** Five Iron. 300p. (Orig.). 1994. pap. 6.95 (*0-9642392-3-X*) Orason.

— Plight of a Flight Attendant. 325p. (Orig.). 1994. pap. 6.95 (*0-9642392-2-1*) Orason.

Oratofsky, Paul. The Bee. limited ed. (Illus.). 8p. 1992. 22.00 (*1-880392-03-8*) Flockophobic Pr.

Oratz, Ephraim. And Nothing but the Truth: Insights, Anecdotes & Stories from Rabbi Menachem Mendel of Kotzk. 1989. 13.95 (*0-910818-81-9*) Judaica Pr.

Oratz, Ephraim, ed. Samuel: Hebrew Text, English Translation & Commentary Digest. 2nd rev. ed. LC 93-14555. (Books of the Bible Ser.). 1995. 14.95 (*1-871055-90-3*) Soncino Pr.

Orav, Endel J., jt. auth. see Lewis, Peter A.

Oravas, G. A., ed. see Duhem, Pierre M.

Oravecz, Imre. When You Became She. Berlind, Bruce, tr. LC 93-6265. xii, 113p. 1994. lib. bdg. 20.00x (*1-879378-10-8*); pap. 10.00x (*1-879378-09-4*) Xenos Riverside.

Oravetz, Jules, Sr. Gardening, Landscaping & Grounds Maintenance: Lawns, Vegetables, Flowers, Trees, & Shrubs. 3rd ed. LC 74-28650. 1985. text ed. 15.95 (*0-672-23417-3*, 23229, Audel) Macmillan.

— Questions & Answers for Plumbers Examinations. 2nd ed. LC 73-85726. (Illus.). 1985. pap. 10.95 (*0-8161-1703-9*, Audel) Macmillan.

— Questions & Answers for the Plumbers Examination. 3rd ed. 272p. 1991. pap. 14.95 (*0-02-593510-0*, Audel) Macmillan.

Oravez, David L. Woodcut: Step-by-Step Lessons in Designing, Cutting, & Printing the Woodblock. (Illus.). 128p. (Orig.). 1992. pap. 18.95 (*0-8230-5851-4*, Watsn-Guptill) Watsn-Guptill.

Orawski, Arthur T. TAICHI: A Personal Learning Experience. (Illus.). 1277p. 1992. lib. bdg. 196.00 (*0-9633995-0-0*) TIPRAC.

Orayevskiy, A. N., ed. Research on Chemical Lasers. (Proceedings of Lebedev Physics Institute Ser.: Vol. 193). 169p. 1992. 105.00 (*1-56072-053-0*) Nova Sci Pubs.

— Research on Laser Theory. (Proceedings of the Lebedev Physics Institute Ser.: Vol. 171). 288p. (C). 1988. text ed. 115.00 (*0-941743-06-3*) Nova Sci Pubs.

Orazem, Frank, jt. auth. see Doll, John P.

***Orbach.** The Hidden Mind: Unconscious Processes & Psychological Models. Date not set. text ed. 42.95 (*0-471-95578-7*) Wiley.

Orbach, Barbara M. Simply Flowers: Beautiful Ideas & Practical Advice for Creating Flower Filled Rooms. LC 92-29768. (Illus.). 1993. 22.50 (*0-517-58183-3*, C P Pubs) Crown Pub Group.

Orbach, Harold L., ed. see Michigan University Conference on Aging Staff.

Orbach, Israel. Children Who Don't Want to Live: Understanding & Treating the Suicidal Child. LC 87-46338. (Social & Behavioral Science Ser.). 282p. 1988. 31.95x (*1-55542-076-1*) Jossey-Bass.

Orbach, Julian. Victorian Architecture in Britain. (Blue Guides Ser.). 1988. pap. 24.95 (*0-393-30070-6*) Norton.

***Orbach, Larry & Smith, Vivien O.** Soaring Underground: A Young Fugitive's Life in Nazi Berlin. (Illus.). 300p. 1995. 24.95 (*0-929590-15-5*) Howells Hse.

Orbach, R. L., ed. Condensed Matter Physics. (Illus.). 210p. 1987. 66.00 (*0-387-96528-9*) Spr-Verlag.

Orbach, Susie. Fat Is a Feminist Issue. (Learn to Control Stress Ser.). 1987. pap. 4.95 (0-425-09920-2) Berkley Pub.
— Fat Is a Feminist Issue. 240p. 1994. pap. 9.00 (0-425-14145-4, Berkley Trade) Berkley Pub.
— Fat Is a Feminist Issue II: The Anti-Diet Guide to Permanent Weight Loss. 192p. 1987. pap. 4.95 (0-425-10351-X) Berkley Pub.
— Hunger Strike: The Anorectic's Struggle as a Metaphor for Our Age. 272p. 1988. mass mkt. 4.50 (0-380-70393-9) Avon.
Orbach, Susie, jt. auth. see Eichenbaum, Luise.
Orbach, William W. The American Movement to Aid Soviet Jews. LC 78-19696. 256p. 1979. 30.00x (0-87023-267-3) U of Mass Pr.
— To Keep the Peace: The United Nations Condemnatory Resolution. LC 75-41989. 165p. reprint ed. pap. 47.10 (0-7837-5793-X, 2045459) Bks Demand.
Orbaker, Douglas & Blake, Robert A. Day of Redemption. Sherer, Michael L., ed. (Orig.). 1987. pap. 2.35 (0-89536-848-X, 7807) CSS OH.
Orban, G. A. Neuronal Operations in the Visual Cortex. (Studies of Brain Function: Vol. 11). (Illus.). 385p. 1984. 85.00 (0-387-11919-1) Spr-Verlag.
Orban, G. A. & Nagel, H. H., eds. Artificial & Biological Vision Systems. LC 92-33976. (ESPRIT Basic Research Ser.). 1992. 98.00 (0-387-56012-2) Spr-Verlag.
Orban, Guy A. & Singer, W., eds. Cognitive Neuroscience: Research Directions in Cognitive Science. 192p. 1991. text ed. 45.00 (0-86377-114-9) L Erlbaum Assocs.
***Orban, John, III.** Money in the Ground: Insider's Guide to Oil & Gas Deals. 300p. (Orig.). 1995. pap. 39.50 (0-9615776-6-5) Meridian Oklahoma.
— Oil in YOUR Backyard! (Illus.). 128p. (Orig.). 1987. pap. 17.00 (0-9615776-3-0) Meridian Oklahoma.
— Oil Talk! Your Key to Oil Patch Lingo. (Illus.). 120p. (Orig.). 1989. pap. 10.00 (0-9615776-2-2) Meridian Oklahoma.
— Sekiyu Tooshi No Kagi: Key to Oil & Gas Investment. The, Japan Connection of Oklahoma City, tr. (Illus.). 168p. (Orig.). (JPN.). 1988. pap. 50.00 (0-9615776-4-9) Meridian Oklahoma.
Orban, Nancy, ed. Fiberarts Design Book IV. LC 91-11695. (Illus.). 208p. 1993. pap. 21.95 (0-937274-71-2) Lark Books.
Orban, Nancy, jt. auth. see Batchelder, Ann.
Orban, Otto. The Blood of the Walsungs: Selected Poems. 94p. 1994. pap. 13.95 (1-85224-203-5, Pub. by Bloodaxe Bks UK) Dufour.
— Journey of Barbarus. Berlind, Bruce, ed. Berlind, John, tr. 148p. (ENG & HUN.). 1995. 24.00 (0-89410-810-7); pap. 15.00 (0-89410-811-5) Three Continents.
Orban-Szontagh, Madeleine. Japanese Floral Patterns & Motifs. 1990. pap. 3.95 (0-486-26330-4) Dover.
— North American Indian Designs Iron-on Transfer Patterns. (Illus.). 48p. (Orig.). pap. 2.95 (0-486-26883-7) Dover.
— North American Indian Stickers. (Illus.). (J). (gr. k-3). 1991. pap. 1.00 (0-486-26821-7) Dover.
— Northwest Coast Indian Designs. LC 94-19490. 1994. pap. write for info. (0-486-28179-5) Dover.
— Southwestern Indian Designs. 1992. pap. 3.95 (0-486-26985-X) Dover.
— Traditional Animal Designs & Motifs for Artists & Craftspeople. LC 92-43113. (Pictorial Archive Ser.). 1993. pap. write for info. (0-486-27485-3) Dover.
— Two Hundred Sixty-One North American Indian Designs. LC 93-11145. 1993. pap. write for info. (0-486-27718-6) Dover.
Orban-Szontagh, Madeline. Traditional Korean Designs. 1991. pap. 3.95 (0-486-26646-X) Dover.
Orbanes, Philip. The Monopoly Companion. 216p. 1988. pap. 5.95 (1-55850-950-X) Adams Pubng.
Orbanz, Eva, et al. Journey to a Legend & Back: The British Realistic Film. 1981. pap. 9.95 (3-920889-51-7) Baseline Bks.
Orbeck, Anders, tr. see Larsen, Hanna A., ed.
Orbelian, George. Essential Surfing. 3rd ed. (Illus.). 247p. 1987. pap. 12.95 (0-9610548-2-4) Orbelian Arts.
Orbeliani, Sulkhan-Saba. The Book of Wisdom & Lies. Vivian, Katherine, tr. 1982. 22.00 (0-317-03152-X, Pub. by Octagon Pr UK) ISHK Bk Service.
Orbell, John, jt. auth. see Pressnell, L. S.
Orbell, John, et al. From Cape to Cape: This History of Lyle Shipping. (Illus.). 1978. 30.00 (0-8464-0433-8) Beekman Pubs.
Orbell, Margaret & McLean, Mervyn. Traditional Songs of the Maori. 324p. 1991. pap. 36.00 (1-86940-048-8) OUP.
Orbell, Margaret, jt. ed. see Finnegan, Ruth.
Orben, Robert. Joke-Teller's Handbook or 1,999 Belly Laughs. 1976. reprint ed. pap. 7.00 (0-87980-323-1) Wilshire.
— Twenty-Five Hundred Jokes to Start 'em Laughing. 1987. 10.00 (0-87980-387-8) Wilshire.
— Two Thousand Four Hundred Jokes to Brighten Your Speeches. 1989. pap. 7.00 (0-87980-425-4) Wilshire.
— Two Thousand New Laughs for Speakers. 1980. pap. 7.00 (0-87980-382-7) Wilshire.
— Two Thousand One Hundred Laughs for All Occasions. LC 82-45448. 240p. 1986. mass mkt. 8.95 (0-385-23488-0) Doubleday.
— Two Thousand Sure Fire Jokes for Speakers & Writers. LC 86-24240. 240p. 1986. mass mkt. 8.95 (0-385-23465-1) Doubleday.
Orber, Linda, jt. auth. see Roslak, Deborah.
Orberg, Hans H. Lingua Latina: Colloqvia Personarvm. 96p. 1994. pap. 7.00 (87-88073-75-0, Pub. by Mus Tusculanum DK) Paul & Co Pubs.
— Lingua Latina: Exercitia Latina. 154p. 1994. pap. 9.00 (87-88073-77-7, Pub. by Mus Tusculanum DK) Paul & Co Pubs.
— Lingua Latina: Grammatica Latina. 38p. 1994. pap. 6.00 (87-88073-07-6, Pub. by Mus Tusculanum DK) Paul & Co Pubs.
— Lingua Latina Pt. 1: Familia Romana. 328p. 1994. pap. 34.00 (87-7289-139-4, Pub. by Mus Tusculanum DK) Paul & Co Pubs.
— Lingua Latina Pt. II: Roma Aeterna. 424p. 1994. pap. 55.00 (87-7289-107-6, Pub. by Mus Tusculanum DK) Paul & Co Pubs.
Orbigny, A. D'. Foraminiferes Fossiles du Bassin Tertiaire de Vienne. 1963. reprint ed. 25.00 (0-934454-39-6) Lubrecht & Cramer.
— Memoire sur les Foraminiferes de la Craie Blanche du Bassin de Paris. 1964. reprint ed. pap. 5.00 (0-934454-63-9) Lubrecht & Cramer.
Orbis Direct Staff. How to Quit: The National Wellness Stop Smoking Campaign. Date not set. 59.95 (0-9640449-0-0) Orbis Direct.
***Orbis Staff.** Woerterbuch der Synonyme. 352p. (GER.). 1993. 29.95 (0-7859-8437-2, 3572006309) Fr & Eur.
***Orbitz.** Six Days to Better Golf. 1995. 7.98 (0-88365-896-8) Galahad Bks.
Orbuch, T. L., ed. Close Relationship Loss: Theoretical Approaches. (Illus.). xvi, 233p. 1992. 83.00 (0-387-97727-9) Spr-Verlag.
Orbuch, Terri L., jt. auth. see Cohen, Bruce J.
Orchard, Andy. The Poetic Art of Aldhelm. (Cambridge Studies in Anglo-Saxon England: No. 8). (Illus.). 355p. (C). 1994. 59.95 (0-521-45090-X) Cambridge U Pr.
— Pride & Prodigies: Studies in the Monsters of the Beowulf-Manuscript. 176p. (C). 1995. text ed. 63.00 (0-85991-456-9, DS Brewer) Boydell & Brewer.
Orchard, Bernard & Riley, Harold. The Order of the Synoptics: Why Three Synoptic Gospels? LC 87-5593. 384p. 1987. 38.95 (0-86554-222-8, MUP H-199) Mercer Univ Pr.
Orchard, Bernard, tr. see Vanhoye, Albert.
Orchard, D. F. Concrete Technology: Properties & Testing of Aggregates. 3rd ed. (Concrete Technology Ser.: Vol. 3). 1976. 65.00 (0-85334-654-2, Pub. by Elsevier Applied Sci UK) Elsevier.
Orchard, David. Techniques of Wood Sculpture. (Illus.). 144p. 1994. 27.50 (0-7134-7262-6, Pub. by Batsford UK) Trafalgar.
Orchard, G., ed. Neural Computing Research & Applications: Proceedings of the Second Irish Neural Networks Conference, Queen's University, Belfast, Northern Ireland, 25-26 June, 1992. 311p. 1993. 127.00 (0-7503-0259-3) IOP Pub.
Orchard, G. A. & Phillips, W. A. Neural Computation: A Beginner's Guide. 1991. pap. 24.95 (0-86377-235-8) L Erlbaum Assocs.
Orchard, G. Edward, ed. see Bussow, Conrad.
Orchard, Harry F. Charles Lanman: Landscapes & Nature Studies. (Illus.). 28p. 1983. pap. 4.00 (0-9613046-0-X) Morris Mus.
Orchard, Harry F., et al. Julian Rockmore: The American Scene...Then & Now. (Illus.). 40p. 1984. pap. 4.00 (0-9613046-1-8) Morris Mus.
Orchard, Hugh. Old Orchard Farm. LC 87-34488. (Iowa Heritage Collection). (Illus.). 252p. 1988. reprint ed. pap. 7.95 (0-8138-0084-6) Iowa St U Pr.
Orchard, Jan. Lighting for a Beautiful Home. (Beautiful Home Ser.). 160p. 1990. 19.95 (0-8120-6169-1) Barron.
— Microwave Cooking Times: The Safe Cooking Times for 500, 600, 650 & 700 Watt Microwaves. 1994. pap. 9.95 (0-572-01400-7, Pub. by W Foulsham UK) Trans-Atl Phila.
Orchard, Janet, jt. auth. see Perry, Garry P.
***Orchard, Jeff.** Gold, Gold? in New Hampshire. 2nd ed. (Illus.). 74p. 1995. pap. text ed. 8.95 (0-9645890-0-1) Gold in NH.
Orchard, Lionel & Dare, Robert. Market Morals & Public Policy. 240p. 1989. pap. 41.00 (1-86287-624-X, Pub. by Federation Pr AU) W W Gaunt.
Orchard, Thomas N. Astronomy of Milton's Paradise Lost. LC 68-4178. (Studies in Milton: No. 22). (Illus.). 1969. reprint ed. lib. bdg. 75.00 (0-8383-0672-1) M S G Haskell Hse.
Orchard, Vance. Just Rambling Around Blue Mountain Country. 184p. 1981. 15.95 (0-936546-03-4); pap. 10.95 (0-936546-04-2) Pioneer Pr Bks.
— Life on the Dry Side: A Nostalgic Journey Down the Backroads of the Inland Northwest. 192p. 1984. 15.95 (0-936546-09-3) Pioneer Pr Bks.
Orchard, W. G. A Dictionary of Cornish Mining Terms. (C). 1989. pap. 35.00 (1-85022-053-0, Pub. by Dyllansow Truran UK) St Mut.
Orchard, W. R. & Sherratt, A. F., eds. Combined Heat & Power: Whole City Heating, Planning Tomorrow's Energy Economy. LC 80-41444. 248p. reprint ed. pap. 70.70 (0-317-27696-4, 2025214) Bks Demand.
Orchard, William A. Music in Australia. LC 74-24174. reprint ed. 14.50 (0-404-13078-X) AMS Pr.
Orchard, William C. The Technique of Porcupine Quill Decoration among the Indians of North America. Smith, Monte, ed. (Illus.). 88p. 1982. reprint ed. per. 8.95 (0-943604-00-1) Eagles View.
Orcutt, Ben A. Science & Inquiry in Social Work Practice. 256p. 1990. text ed. 39.00 (0-231-07040-3) Col U Pr.
Orcutt, Ben A., et al, eds. Social Work & Thanatology. LC 79-22448. 300p. 1980. lib. bdg. 27.95 (0-405-12621-2) Ayer.
Orcutt, David M., jt. auth. see Hale, Maynard G.
Orcutt, Fred. The Traffic Signal Book. 176p. 1992. text ed. 66.00 (0-13-926957-6) P-H.
Orcutt, G., et al, eds. Microanalytic Simulation Models to Support Social & Financial Policy. (Information Research & Resource Reports Ser.: Vol. 7). 568p. 1986. 102.75 (0-444-87876-9, North Holland) Elsevier.
Orcutt, Georgia. Massachusetts: Portrait of the Land & Its People: Today. (Massachusetts Geographic Ser.: No. 2). (Illus.). 104p. 1988. pap. 15.95 (0-938314-42-4) Am Wrld Geog.
— Massachusetts: Portrait of the Land & Its People-Yesterday. (Massachusetts Geographic Ser.: No. 1). (Illus.). 104p. (Orig.). 1988. pap. 15.95 (0-938314-45-9) Am Wrld Geog.
— The Old Farmer's Almanac: Gardener's Companion. 1994. 2.95 (0-89909-272-1) Random.
— Old Farmer's Almanac Hearth & Home Companion 1995. 1994. pap. 2.95 (0-89909-280-2) Random.
Orcutt, Georgia & Taylor, Sandra, eds. Flavor of New England: Breads, Rolls & Pastries. LC 81-50147. (Illus.). 144p. 1981. pap. 9.95 (0-911658-28-9, 80-151-1) Yankee Bks.
Orcutt, Guy H., et al. Policy Exploration Through Microanalytic Simulation. 370p. (Orig.). 1976. 71.00 (0-87766-170-7); pap. text ed. 28.00 (0-87766-169-3) Urban Inst.
Orcutt, John. Betty & Pansy's Severe Queer Review of San Francisco. 2nd ed. (Illus.). 1992. pap. text ed. 8.95 (0-9633048-0-1) Bedpan Prods.
Orcutt, S. A History of the Old Town of Stratford & the City of Bridgeport, Connecticut, Pt. I. (Illus.). 692p. 1988. reprint ed. lib. bdg. 70.00 (0-8328-0014-7, CT0014) Higginson Bk Co.
Orcutt, S. & Beardsley, A. History of the Old Town of Derby, Connecticut, 1642-1880: With Biographies & Genealogies. (Illus.). 843p. 1988. reprint ed. lib. bdg. 85.00 (0-8328-0001-5, CT0002) Higginson Bk Co.
Orcutt, Samuel. A History of the Old Town of Stratford & the City of Bridgeport, Connecticut, Pt. II. (Illus.). 700p. 1988. reprint ed. lib. bdg. 70.00 (0-8328-0015-5, CT0015) Higginson Bk Co.
— History of the Town of Wolcott, Connecticut, from 1731 to 1874. 608p. 1992. reprint ed. lib. bdg. 60.00 (0-8328-2270-1) Higginson Bk Co.
— History of the Towns of New Milford & Bridgewater, 1703-1882. 909p. 1992. reprint ed. lib. bdg. 90.00 (0-8328-2265-5) Higginson Bk Co.
— History of Torrington, Connecticut: From Its First Settlement in 1737 with Biographies & Genealogies. (Illus.). 817p. 1988. reprint ed. lib. bdg. 85.00 (0-8328-0016-3, CT0024) Higginson Bk Co.
***Orcutt, Ted.** No Beggars Just Balloons: A Practical Approach to Self-Transformation. 248p. 1989. 19.95 (0-9623434-2-0) Global Village.
***Orcutt, Ted L.** Magicians of the Soul: Exploring the World of Paranormal & Mystical Experience. LC 95-94237. 264p. 1995. 35.00 (0-9623434-4-7) Global Village.
Orcutt, Ted L. & Prell, Jan R. Integrative Paradigms of Psychotherapy. 288p. 1994. 39.95 (0-205-14823-9, Longwood Div) Allyn.
Orcutt, William D. Celebrities off Parade. LC 79-93369. (Essay Index Reprint Ser.). 1977. 23.95 (0-8369-1424-4) Ayer.
— In Quest of the Perfect Book. LC 74-121495. (Essay Index Reprint Ser.). 1977. 28.95 (0-8369-1769-3) Ayer.
— Magic of the Book. LC 79-107730. (Essay Index Reprint Ser.). 1977. 36.95 (0-8369-2009-0) Ayer.
— Mary Baker Eddy & Her Books. (Twentieth-Century Biographers Ser.). (Illus.). 224p. 1992. 14.95 (0-87510-274-3) Christian Sci.
— The Stradivari Memorial. LC 76-58561. (Music Reprint Ser.). 1977. reprint ed. lib. bdg. 21.50 (0-306-70865-5) Da Capo.
Orczy, Baroness. Scarlet Pimpernel. 18.95 (0-8488-0601-8) Amereon Ltd.
— The Scarlet Pimpernel. (Illustrated Classics Collection 4). 64p. 1994. pap. 3.60 (1-56103-606-4) Lake Pub Co.
— The Scarlet Pimpernel Readalong. (Illustrated Classics Collection 4). 64p. 1994. audio 13.50 (1-56103-608-0) Lake Pub Co.
— Way of the Scarlet Pimpernel. 22.95 (0-8488-1442-8) Amereon Ltd.
Orczy, Emmuska. Adventures of the Scarlet Pimpernel. 321p. 1983. reprint ed. lib. bdg. 24.95 (0-89966-459-8) Buccaneer Bks.
— Beau Brocade. 275p. (J). (gr. 4 up). 1980. reprint ed. lib. bdg. 13.95 (0-89968-194-8, Lghtyr Pr) Buccaneer Bks.
— Blue Eyes & Gray. 1976. lib. bdg. 14.75 (0-685-03051-2, Lghtyr Pr) Buccaneer Bks.
— Eldorado. 435p. 1980. reprint ed. lib. bdg. 27.95 (0-89968-195-6, Lghtyr Pr) Buccaneer Bks.
— The Elusive Pimpernel. 1976. lib. bdg. 27.95x (0-89968-073-9, Lghtyr Pr) Buccaneer Bks.
— The Elusive Pimpernel. 419p. 1984. lib. bdg. 27.95x (0-89966-488-1) Buccaneer Bks.
— Emperor's Candlesticks. 1976. lib. bdg. 13.75 (0-89968-075-5, Lghtyr Pr) Buccaneer Bks.
— Lady Molly of Scotland Yard. LC 75-32771. (Literature of Mystery & Detection Ser.). 1976. reprint ed. 25.95 (0-405-07890-0) Ayer.
— The Laughing Cavalier. 1976. lib. bdg. 18.50 (0-89968-076-3, Lghtyr Pr) Buccaneer Bks.
— The League of the Scarlet Pimpernel. 238p. 1981. reprint ed. lib. bdg. 24.95 (0-89966-286-2) Buccaneer Bks.
— Lord Tony's Wife. (J). 1986. reprint ed. lib. bdg. 29.95x (0-89966-553-5) Buccaneer Bks.
— Old Man in the Corner. 340p. 1980. reprint ed. lib. bdg. 15.95 (0-89968-196-4, Lghtyr Pr) Buccaneer Bks.
— The Old Man in the Corner: Twelve Mysteries by the Baroness Orczy. Bleiler, E. G., ed. (Orig.). 1980. pap. 4.50 (0-486-23972-1) Dover.
— Pimpernel & Rosemary. 341p. 1983. reprint ed. lib. bdg. 24.95 (0-686-47487-2) Buccaneer Bks.
— Scarlet Pimpernel. (Airmont Classics Ser.). (J). (gr. 7 up). 1964. pap. 2.95 (0-8049-0028-0, CL-28) Airmont.
— Scarlet Pimpernel. 1992. mass mkt. 4.50 (0-553-21402-0, Bantam Classics) Bantam.
— The Scarlet Pimpernel. 1976. lib. bdg. 21.95 (0-89968-072-0, Lghtyr Pr) Buccaneer Bks.
— The Scarlet Pimpernel. 256p. (J). (gr. 7). 1974. pap. 4.95 (0-451-52315-6, Sig Classics) NAL-Dutton.
— The Scarlet Pimpernel. Farr, Naunerle, ed. (Now Age Illustrated IV Ser.). (Illus.). (gr. 4-12). 1978. student ed 1.25 (0-88301-345-2); pap. text ed. 2.95 (0-88301-321-5) Pendulum Pr.
— The Scarlet Pimpernel. (Classics Ser.). 256p. (J). (gr. 5 up). 1989. pap. 4.99 (0-14-035056-X, Puffin) Puffin Bks.
— The Scarlet Pimpernel. 256p. 1984. reprint ed. lib. bdg. 21.95 (0-89966-508-X) Buccaneer Bks.
— The Triumph of the Scarlet Pimpernel. 321p. 1983. reprint ed. lib. bdg. 27.95 (0-89966-460-1) Buccaneer Bks.
— The Way of the Scarlet Pimpernel. 318p. 1983. reprint ed. lib. bdg. 27.95 (0-89966-461-X) Buccaneer Bks.
***Ord, Alan J.** Songs for Bass Voice: An Annotated Guide to Works for Bass Voice. 228p. 1994. 32.50 (0-8108-2897-9) Scarecrow.
Ord, Alison, et al, eds. Localization of Deformation in Rocks & Metals. LC 92-22431. (PAGEOPH Reprint from Pure & Applied Geophysics Ser.: Vol. 137). v, 150p. 1992. 58.00 (3-7643-2772-3, Pub. by Birkhauser Vlg SZ); pap. 20.50 (0-8176-2772-3, Pub. by Birkhauser Vlg SZ) Birkhauser.
Ord, David, jt. auth. see Coote, Robert B.
Ord, David R. & Coote, Robert B. Is the Bible True? Understanding the Bible Today. LC 93-37570. 100p. (Orig.). 1994. pap. 9.95 (0-88344-948-X) Orbis Bks.
Ord, Hubert W. Chaucer & the Rival Poet in Shakespeare's Sonnets, a New Theory. LC 71-173810. reprint ed. 21.50 (0-404-07829-X) AMS Pr.
***Ord-Hume, Arthur W.** The Musical Box. (Illus.). 336p. 1995. 79.95 (0-88740-764-1) Schiffer.
— Perpetual Motion: The History of an Obsession. LC 76-10560. 1980. pap. 6.95 (0-312-60131-X) St Martin.
— Pianola: The History of the Self-Playing Piano. (Illus.). 360p. 1984. 70.00 (0-04-789009-6) Routledge Chapman & Hall.
— Restoring Pianolas & Other Self Playing Pianos. (Illus.). 160p. 1983. 45.00 (0-04-789008-8) Routledge Chapman & Hall.
Ord-Hume, Arthur W. J. G. Harmonium: The History of the Reed Organ & its Makers. (Illus.). 256p. 1986. 24.95 (0-911572-57-0) Vestal.
Ord, Irene. Bolero. large type ed. (Linford Romance Library). 288p. 1993. pap. 14.95 (0-7089-7320-5, Linford) Ulverscroft.
— Desert Romance. large type ed. (Linford Romance Library). 352p. 1988. pap. 11.95 (0-7089-6553-9, Linford) Ulverscroft.
— Flower of the Desert. large type ed. (Linford Romance Library). 1990. pap. 12.95 (0-7089-6826-0, Trailtree Bookshop) Ulverscroft.
— The Fragrance of Love. large type ed. (Romance Ser.). 304p. 1988. 15.95 (0-7089-1853-0) Ulverscroft.
— The Hawk & the Angel. large type ed. (Linford Romance Library). 304p. 1988. pap. 11.95 (0-7089-6583-0, Linford) Ulverscroft.
— Midnight Melody. large type ed. (Linford Romance Library). 1988. pap. 11.95 (0-7089-6474-5, Linford) Ulverscroft.
— Not the Marrying Kind. large type ed. (Linford Romance Library). 1991. pap. 13.95 (0-7089-7119-9, Linford) Ulverscroft.
— Passion in Paradise. large type ed. (Linford Romance Library). 272p. 1989. pap. 11.95 (0-7089-6705-1, Linford) Ulverscroft.
— Stand-In for Love. large type ed. (Linford Romance Library). 1989. pap. 11.95 (0-7089-6787-6, Trailtree Bookshop) Ulverscroft.
Ord, J. K. Families of Frequency Distributions. (Griffin's Statistical Monographs: No. 30). 231p. 1972. 21.50 (0-85264-137-0) Lubrecht & Cramer.
Ord, J. K., jt. ed. see Cormack, R. M.
Ord, J. K., et al, eds. Statistical Distributions in Ecological Work. (Statistical Ecology Ser.: Vol. 4). 1979. 45.00 (0-89974-001-4) Intl Co-Op.
Ord, J. Keith, jt. auth. see Kendall, Maurice.
Ord, Keith J, jt. auth. see Stuart, Alan.
Ord, M. J., et al, eds. The Use of Computers & Statistics in Toxicology, Vol. 10. 102p. 1985. 32.00 (0-85066-977-4) Taylor & Francis.
Ord-Smith, R. J. & Stephenson, J. Computer Simulation of Continuous Systems. LC 74-12957. (Cambridge Computer Science Texts Ser.: No. 3). 333p. reprint ed. pap. 95.00 (0-318-34832-2, 2031703) Bks Demand.
Ordan, Dena, tr. see David, Abraham, ed.
***Ordaz, Amado N.** Poemas. 7th ed. 1983. pap. 9.95 (0-7859-5191-1) Fr & Eur.
Ordaz, Luis, jt. auth. see Neglia, Erminio.
***Orde, A. J.** Dead on Sunday. (Southwest Mysteries Ser.). 1994. mass mkt. 5.99 (0-449-22282-9, Crest) Fawcett.
— Death & the Dogwalker. 1993. mass mkt. 4.50 (0-449-22027-3, Crest) Fawcett.
— Death for Old Times' Sake. 1993. mass mkt. 4.50 (0-449-22193-8, Crest) Fawcett.
— A Little Neighborhood Murder. 1992. mass mkt. 4.50 (0-449-22026-5, Crest) Fawcett.
— A Little Neighbourhood Murder. large type ed. (Linford Mystery Library). 448p. 1992. pap. 14.95 (0-7089-7163-6, Linford) Ulverscroft.
— A Long Time Dead. 1995. mass mkt. 5.50 (0-449-22359-0, Crest) Fawcett.
— Looking for the Aardvark: A Jason Lynx Mystery. LC 92-42100. 1993. 17.00 (0-385-41942-2) Doubleday.

O

An Asterisk (*) at the beginning of an entry indicates that the title is appearing in BIP for the first time.

Orde, Anne. British Policy & European Reconstruction after the First World War. (Illus.). 360p. (C). 1990. 69.95 (*0-521-37150-3*) Cambridge U Pr.

Orde-Browne, Granville S. The African Labourer. LC 33-28584. reprint ed. pap. 67.00 (*0-8357-3024-7*, 2057-111) Bks Demand.

Orde, H. L., tr. see Ebbinghaus, H. D., et al.

Orde, Julian. Conjurors. (C). 1990. 35.00 (*0-906887-25-9*, Pub. by Greville Pr UK) St Mut.

Orde, Lewis. By Blood Divided. 480p. 1991. 19.95 (*0-8217-3287-0*) Zebra.

— By Blood Divided. 1992. mass mkt. 5.99 (*0-8217-3655-8*) Zebra.

— Deadfall. 464p. 1984. pap. 3.95 (*0-8217-1400-7*) Zebra.

— Dreams of Gold. 532p. 1993. 20.00 (*0-8217-4015-6*) Zebra.

— Dreams of Gold. 576p. 1993. mass mkt. 4.99 (*0-8217-4395-3*) Zebra.

— Eagle & the Dove. 1989. mass mkt. 4.95 (*0-8217-2832-6*) Zebra.

— Eagles. 1984. pap. 3.95 (*0-8217-1500-3*) Zebra.

— Heritage. 1982. pap. 3.75 (*0-8217-1100-8*) Zebra.

— The Lion's Way. 1982. mass mkt. 4.50 (*0-8217-2087-2*) Zebra.

— Munich Ten. 1983. pap. 3.95 (*0-8217-1300-0*) Zebra.

— The Proprietor's Daughter. 1988. 18.95 (*0-316-67340-4*) Little.

— The Tiger's Heart. 720p. 1987. mass mkt. 4.50 (*0-8217-2086-4*) Zebra.

Ordelheide, Dieter & Pfaff, Dieter. European Financial Reporting: Germany. (Illus.). 1993. 74.50 (*0-415-06775-8*, B0276) Routledge.

Orden, J. Hannah. In Real Life. LC 92-31359. 192p. (YA). (gr. 7 up). 1993. pap. 3.99 (*0-14-034039-4*) Puffin Bks.

Order-Disorder Transformations in Alloys International Symposium Staff. Proceedings of the Order-Disorder Transformations in Alloys International Symposium, Tubinger, Germany, September 1973. Warlimont, H., ed. (Reine Uno Angewandte Metallkunde in Einzel-Darstellungen Ser.: Vol. 24). (Illus.). viii, 556p. 1974. 79. 00 (*0-387-06766-3*) Spr-Verlag.

Order of Buddhist Contemplatives Monks Staff & Kennett, Jiyu. Serene Relfection Meditation. 1989. pap. 5.95 (*0-930066-11-1*) Shasta Abbey.

Order of Mercy, Mt. St. Joseph Seminary Staff, tr. A Year with the Saints. 2nd ed. LC 88-50638. (Illus.). 364p. 1988. reprint ed. pap. 15.00 (*0-89555-339-2*) TAN Bks Pubs.

Order of the Secret Chief of the Rosicrucian Order. The Book of the Goetia: The Lesser Key of Solomon the King. 82p. 1976. reprint ed. spiral bd. 7.70 (*0-7873-0644-4*) Mokelumne.

Order, S. E. & Donaldson, S. Radiation Therapy of Benign Diseases. (Medical Radiology, Diagnostic Imaging & Radiation Oncology Ser.). viii, 213p. 1991. 104.00 (*0-387-50901-1*) Spr-Verlag.

Ordericus Vitalis Staff. Ecclesiastical History of England & Normandy, 4 Vols, Set. Forrester, T., tr. LC 68-57872. (Bohn's Antiquarian Library). reprint ed. 185.00 (*0-404-50040-4*) AMS Pr.

Ordeshook, Peter C. Game Theory & Political Theory: An Introduction. (Illus.). 528p. 1986. 74.95 (*0-521-30612-4*); pap. 27.95 (*0-521-31593-X*) Cambridge U Pr.

— A Political Theory Primer. (Illus.). 272p. 1992. 55.00 (*0-415-90240-1*, A4112, Routledge NY); pap. 17.95 (*0-415-90241-X*, A4116, Routledge NY) Routledge.

Ordeshook, Peter C., ed. Models of Strategic Choice in Politics. 1989. 52.50 (*0-472-10122-6*) U of Mich Pr.

Ordeshook, Peter C., et al. The Balance of Power: Stability & Instability in International Systems. (Illus.). (C). 1989. 64.95 (*0-521-37471-5*) Cambridge U Pr.

Ordesky, Maxine. Complete Home Organizer: A Guide to Functional Storage Space for All the Rooms in Your Home. 1993. pap. 19.95 (*0-8021-3340-1*) Grove-Atltic.

Ordet, Stephen M. & Grand, Leonard S. Dynamics of Clinical Rehabilitative Exercise: Dynamics of Clinical Rehabilitative Exercise. (Illus.). 304p. 1992. 55.00 (*0-683-06654-4*) Williams & Wilkins.

Ordidge, Paul D. Simple Case Books for Small Businesses. 96p. (Orig.). 1990. pap. 14.95 (*0-8464-1379-5*) Beekman Pubs.

Ordin, Robert L. Contesting Confirmation: A Creditor's Perspective. 524p. 1993. 110.00 (*0-13-296955-6*) Aspen Law.

— Contesting Confirmation: A Creditor's Perspective. LC 93-7740. 1993. 150.00 (*0-13-359183-2*) P-H Gen Ref & Trav.

Ordinary Differential Equations Symposium Staff. Proceedings of the Ordinary Differential Equations Symposium, Minneapolis, May 1972. Harris, W. A., Jr. & Sibuya, Y., eds. LC 72-97022. (Lecture Notes in Mathematics Ser.: Vol. 312). (Illus.). 204p. 1973. pap. 29.00 (*0-387-06146-0*) Spr-Verlag.

Ordish, George. The Living Garden. 1993. 21.50 (*0-8446-6714-5*) Peter Smith.

Ordish, T. P. Shakespeare's London. 1972. 59.95 (*0-8490-1043-8*) Gordon Pr.

Ordiz, Javier, ed. see Fuentes, Carlos.

Ordman, Kathryn A. & Ralli, Mary P. What People Say. 5th ed. LC 76-6143. 1976. pap. text ed. 10.95 (*0-88200-073-X*, B0990) Alexander Graham.

***Ordnance Survey Staff.** Brecon Beacons & Glamorgan Walks. (Pathfinder Guides Ser.). (Illus.). 80p. (Orig.). 1994. pap. 12.95 (*0-7117-0671-9*) Seven Hills Bk.

Ordog, G., ed. Management of Gunshot Wounds. 480p. 1988. 97.00 (*0-8385-5713-9*) Appleton & Lange.

Ordon, Edmund, ed. Ten Contemporary Polish Stories. LC 74-2842. 252p. 1974. reprint ed. text ed. 47.50 (*0-8371-7436-8*, ORPS, Greenwood Pr) Greenwood.

Ordonez, Elizabeth J. Voices of Their Own: Contemporary Spanish Narrative by Women. LC 90-55690. 256p. 1991. 42.50 (*0-8387-5203-9*) Bucknell U Pr.

Ordonez, Francisco. Del Odio al Amor. 1991. reprint ed. pap. 2.80 (*0-311-08223-8*) Casa Bautista.

— Repertorio de Navidad. 80p. 1986. reprint ed. pap. 2.95 (*0-311-08211-4*) Casa Bautista.

Ordonez, Hernan, jt. auth. see Cadavid, Gilberto.

Ordonez-Hernandez, Maria. English for Progress. Smith, Daniel D. et al, eds. LC 87-71460. (Illus.). 304p. (Orig.). 1987. pap. write for info. (*0-942995-02-3*) Casa Blanca Pr.

Ordonez, Maria A., jt. auth. see Ferre, Rosario.

Ordonez, Maria A., jt. auth. see Pico, Fernando.

Ordonez y Montalvo, Jose A., ed. The Pictorial History of St. Paul's School. 242p. 1991. 155.00 (*0-9630522-0-9*) St. Pauls Sch.

***Ordovensky, Pat.** College Planning for Dummies. 1995. pap. 16.99 (*1-56884-382-8*) IDG Bks.

— U. S. A. Today Financial Aid for College. LC 94-26614. 160p. 1994. 8.95 (*1-56079-377-5*) Petersons Guides.

— U. S. A. Today's Getting into College: A Quick Guide to Everything You Need to Know. 160p. (Orig.). 1995. pap. 8.95 (*1-56079-463-1*, Petersons Pacesetter) Petersons Guides.

Ordovensky, Pat & Thornton, Robert. Opening College Doors: How to Make the Admission Process Work for You. LC 92-52848. 324p. (Orig.). 1992. pap. 13.00 (*0-06-463737-9*, Harper Ref) HarpC.

Ordovensky, Pat, jt. auth. see Marx, Gary.

Ordover, Abraham P. Flinders v. Mismo. 5th ed. 66p. 1988. 10.00 (*1-55681-166-7*, FBA0166); teacher ed 5.00 (*1-55681-184-5*, FBA0184) Natl Inst Trial Ad.

— Fordyce v. Harris & Felson. 5th ed. 82p. 1988. 10.00 (*1-55681-167-5*, FBA0167); teacher ed 5.00 (*1-55681-185-3*, FBA0185) Natl Inst Trial Ad.

***Ordover, Eileen L. & Boundy, Kathleen B.** Educational Rights of Children with Disabilities. 120p. 1991. pap. 12. 50 (*0-912585-06-4*) Ctr Law & Ed.

Ordover, John, ed. Warchild. (Star Trek: Deep Space Nine Ser.: No. 7). 288p. (Orig.). 1994. mass mkt. 5.50 (*0-671-88116-7*) PB.

Ordover, John, ed. see Archer, Nathan.

Ordover, John, ed. see Graf, L. A.

Ordover, John, ed. see Hambly, Barbara.

Ordover, John, ed. see Hugh, Dafyddab.

Ordover, John, ed. see Johnson, Kij.

Ordover, John, ed. see Schofield, Sandy.

Ordover, John, ed. see Scott, Melissa.

Ordover, John, ed. see Thompson, W. R.

Ordover, John, ed. see Vornholt, John.

Ordover, John, ed. see Weinstein, Howard.

Ordowski, Charles. Echoes & Images. LC 88-81605. (Illus.). 50p. (Orig.). 1988. pap. 5.95 (*0-929412-00-1*) Gray Shadow Pr.

Ordronaux, John. Hints on the Preservation of Health in Armies: Bound with: Manual of Instructions for Military Surgeons. (American Civil War Medical Ser.: No. 1). 238p. 1990. reprint ed. 45.00 (*0-930405-34-X*) Norman SF.

— Jurisprudence in Medicine in Relation to the Law. LC 73-5158. (Mental Illness & Social Policy; the American Experience Ser.). 1973. reprint ed. 26.95 (*0-405-05239-1*) Ayer.

Ordubadi, M. H. The Dilemma of Longevity. Van Treese, James B., ed. 144p. 1993. pap. 8.95 (*1-56901-034-X*) NW Pub.

Ordway, Frederick I., III, ed. History of Rocketry & Astronautics. LC 57-43769. (American Astronautical Society History Ser.: Vol. 9). (Illus.). 330p. 1989. lib. bdg. 50.00 (*0-87703-309-9*, Pub. by Am Astro Soc); pap. text ed. 35.00 (*0-87703-310-2*, Pub. by Am Astro Soc) Univelt Inc.

Ordway, Frederick I., III & Lieberman, Randy, eds. Blueprint for Space: Science Fiction to Science Fact. LC 91-3160. (Illus.). 320p. (C). 1992. text ed. 60.00 (*1-56098-072-9*); pap. text ed. 24.95 (*1-56098-073-7*) Smithsonian.

Ordway, Frederick I., III, jt. auth. see Stuhlinger, Ernst.

***Ordway, Jerry.** The Power of Shazam! Carlin, Mike, ed. (Illus.). 96p. 1994. pap. 9.95 (*1-56389-153-0*) DC Comics.

Ordway, N. Real Estate Math Made Easy: A Step-by-Step Instructional Approach. 2nd ed. 1985. pap. text ed. 37. 00 (*0-8359-6485-X*) P-H.

Ordway, Nicholas O., jt. auth. see Friedman, Jack P.

Ordway, Nicholas O., jt. auth. see Tosh, Dennis S., Jr.

***Ordys, A. W., et al.** Modelling & Simulation of Power Generation Plants. LC 94-27489. (Advances in Industrial Control Ser.). 1994. 59.00 (*0-387-19907-1*) Spr-Verlag.

Ore, Oystein. Graphs & Their Uses. rev. ed. (New Mathematical Library: No. 34). 160p. 1990. pap. 19.00 (*0-88385-635-2*) Math Assn.

— Invitation to Number Theory. LC 67-20607. (New Mathematical Library: No. 20). 129p. 1967. pap. 18.50 (*0-88385-620-4*) Math Assn.

— Niels Hendrik Abel, Mathematician Extraordinary. LC 73-14693. (Illus.). viii, 277p. 1974. reprint ed. text ed. 19.95 (*0-8284-0274-4*) Chelsea Pub.

— Number Theory & Its History. (Illus.). 380p. 1988. reprint ed. pap. text ed. 8.95 (*0-486-65620-9*) Dover.

— Theory of Graphs. LC 61-15687. (Colloquium Publications: Vol. 38). 270p. 1987. reprint ed. pap. 37.00 (*0-8218-1038-3*, COLL-38) Am Math.

Ore, Rebecca. Alien Bootlegger & Other Stories. 1993. mass mkt. 3.99 (*0-8125-1278-2*) Tor Bks.

— Alien Bootlegger & Other Stories. 320p. 1993. 19.95 (*0-312-85549-4*) Tor Bks.

— Alien Bootlegger & Other Stories. 1995. pap. 14.95 (*0-312-89030-3*) Tor Bks.

— Becoming Alien. 1989. pap. 3.95 (*0-8125-0313-9*) Tor Bks.

— Gaia's Toys. 320p. 1995. 22.95 (*0-312-85781-0*) Tor Bks.

— Human to Human. 1990. pap. 3.95 (*0-8125-0045-8*) Tor Bks.

— Illegal Rebirth of Billy the Kid. 1991. pap. 3.95 (*0-8125-0672-3*) Tor Bks.

— Slow Funeral. 320p. 1994. 21.95 (*0-312-85201-0*) Tor Bks.

— Slow Funeral. 320p. 1995. mass mkt. 4.99 (*0-8125-1604-4*) Tor Bks.

O'Rear, C. E. & Llewellyn, G. C., eds. Biodeterioration Research: General Biodeterioration, Degradation, Mycotoxins, Biotoxins, & Wood Decay, Vol. 2. (Illus.). 720p. 1989. 135.00 (*0-306-43229-3*, Plenum Pr) Plenum.

O'Rear, C. E., jt. ed. see Llewellyn, G. C.

***O'Rear, Charles.** Napa Valley. (Illus.). 170p. 1995. 39.95 (*0-9625227-1-6*) Papillon CA.

— Napa Valley: Land of Vines & Wines. (Illus.). 192p. 1989. 39.50 (*0-9625227-2-4*) Papillon CA.

Orear, Elizabeth, jt. auth. see Orear, Gordon.

Orear, Gordon & Orear, Elizabeth. The Pottery of John Foster: Form & Meaning. LC 89-38978. (Great Lakes Bks.). (Illus.). 147p. (C). 1990. text ed. 29.95 (*0-8143-2003-1*) Wayne St U Pr.

— Sarkis. (Illus.). 160p. 1995. text ed. 27.95 (*0-8143-2517-3*, Great Lks Bks) Wayne St U Pr.

O'Rear, Jan. Such a Deal! rev. ed. 96p. 1993. reprint ed. pap. 8.95 (*1-878686-14-3*) Two Lane Pr.

Orear, Leslie F., ed. On the Job in Illinois, Then & Now. (Illus.). 1976. 8.00 (*0-916884-04-X*); pap. 3.50 (*0-916884-02-3*) Ill Labor Hist Soc.

O'Rear, Sybil J. Charles Goodnight: Pioneer Cowman. LC 89-48652. (Illus.). 69p. (J). (gr. 5-8). 1990. 10.95 (*0-89015-741-3*) Sunbelt Media.

Orebaugh, Walter W. & Jose, Carol. The Consul. 2nd rev. ed. LC 94-70993. (Illus.). 336p. 1994. pap. 9.95 (*1-878398-08-3*) Blue Note Pubns.

— Guerilla in Striped Pants: A U. S. Diplomat Joins the Italian Resistance. LC 91-32212. 264p. 1992. text ed. 49. 95 (*0-275-94149-3*, C4149, Praeger Pubs) Greenwood.

Orecchia, Ferruccio & Chiantini, Luca, eds. Zero-Dimensional Schemes: Proceedings of the International Conference held in Ravello, Italy, June 8-13, 1992. LC 94-20654. vii, 339p. (C). 1994. lib. bdg. 98. 95 (*3-11-013934-0*) De Gruyter.

Oredson, Olivia, jt. auth. see Kushi, Michio.

***Orefjaerd, Curth.** Bhagavan Sri Sathya Sai Baba, My Divine Teacher. (C). 1995. 14.00x (*81-208-1269-7*, Pub. by Motilal Banarsidass II); pap. 14.00x (*81-208-1270-0*, Pub. by Motilal Banarsidass II) S Asia.

O'Regan, Brendan. Spontaneous Remission: An Anotated Bibliography. LC 93-19749. 737p. 1995. 49.00 (*0-943951-17-8*) Inst Noetic Sci.

O'Regan, Cyril. The Heterodox Hegel. (SUNY Series in Hegelian Studies). 517p. 1994. 74.50 (*0-7914-2005-1*); pap. 24.95 (*0-7914-2006-X*) State U NY Pr.

O'Regan, Daphne. Rhetoric, Comedy, & the Violence of Language in Aristophanes' Clouds. 432p. 1992. 49.95 (*0-19-507017-8*) OUP.

O'Regan, Donal. Theory of Singular Boundary Value Problems. 168p. 1994. text ed. 48.00 (*981-02-1760-9*) World Scientific Pub.

O'Regan, J. K. & Levy-Schoen, A., eds. Eye Movements: From Physiology to Cognition: Proceedings of the European Conference, 3rd, Dourdan, France, September, 1985. 678p. 1987. 120.50 (*0-444-70113-3*, North Holland) Elsevier.

O'Regan, Marie B., jt. auth. see Detty, Michael R.

O'Regan, R. G., jt. ed. see Acker, H.

O'Regan, R. S. New Essays on the Australian Criminal Codes. xxii, 125p. 1988. pap. 39.00 (*0-455-20797-6*, Pub. by Law Bk Co) W W Gaunt.

***O'Regan, R.G., et al, eds.** Arterial Chemoreceptors: Cell to System, 360. (Advances in Experimental Medicine & Biology Ser.). (Illus.). 370p. (C). 1994. 95.00 (*0-306-44824-6*, Plenum Pr) Plenum.

O'Regan, Tom, jt. auth. see Moran, Albert.

O'Regan, Vivienne. The Pillar of Isis: A Practical Manual on the Mysteries of the Goddess. 1993. pap. 15.00 (*1-85538-236-9*, Pub. by Aquarian Pr UK) Thorsons SF.

Oregon Business Professionals. The Gold Book: Starting & Mining Success in Business. Smith, R. G., ed. (Illus.). 160p. (Orig.). 1988. pap. 7.95 (*0-944312-01-2*) Minds Ink Pub.

Oregon Historical Society Staff. One Average Day: Oregon Project Dayshoot Photographs - 15 July 1983. (Illus.). 152p. (Orig.). 1984. pap. 21.95 (*0-87595-132-5*); pap. 14. 95 (*0-87595-133-3*) Oregon Hist.

***Oregon Nikkei Endowment Staff.** Touching the Stones. 112p. Date not set. 34.95 (*0-9644806-0-3*); pap. 19.95 (*0-9644806-1-1*) OR Nikkei Endow.

Oregon State Bar Committee on Continuing Legal Education. Land Use, 1982 & Supplement, 1988, 2 Vols. LC 82-82129. 135.00 (*0-317-00353-4*) OR Bar CLE.

Oregon State Bar Committee on Uniform Criminal Jury Instructions. Oregon Jury Instructions for Criminal Cases. 1,984th ed. 1984. write for info. (*0-318-59235-5*) Oregon St Bar.

Oreier, John C., ed. The Alliance for Progress: Problems & Perspectives. LC 62-18508. 166p. reprint ed. pap. 47.40 (*0-8357-5319-0*, 2020765) Bks Demand.

O'Reilley, Mary. The Peaceable Classroom: Essays Toward a Pedagogy of Nonviolence. LC 93-17781. 160p. 1993. pap. text ed. 18.50 (*0-86709-328-5*, 0328) Boynton Cook Pubs.

***O'Reilly.** Travelers Tales Hong Kong. 1995. pap. text ed. 17.95 (*1-885211-03-1*) Trvlers Tale.

O'Reilly, jt. auth. see Watson, Philippa.

O'Reilly, et al. Diagnostic Techniques in Urology. (Illus.). 640p. 1990. text ed. 210.00 (*0-7216-3116-9*) Saunders.

***O'Reilly & Associates Staff.** The X Companion CD for R6. 80p. (Orig.). 1994. text ed. 29.95 (*1-56592-084-8*) OReilly & Assocs.

O'Reilly & Associates Staff, ed. see Gilly, Daniel.

O'Reilly & Assocs. & Cutler, Ellie. SCO UNIX in a Nutshell. 590p. 1994. pap. 9.95 (*1-56592-037-6*) OReilly & Assocs.

O'Reilly, A. J. The Martyrs of the Coliseum with Historical Records of the Great Amphitheater of Ancient Rome. LC 82-50595. 450p. 1987. reprint ed. pap. 16.50 (*0-89555-192-6*) TAN Bks Pubs.

O'Reilly, Anthony. The Complete Cookery Manual. 608p. (Orig.). 1993. pap. 57.50 (*0-273-03387-5*, Pub. by Pitman Pub Ltd UK) Trans-Atl Phila.

O'Reilly, Barbi L., ed. Manhattan Dance School Directory. LC 78-10411. (Dance Program Ser.: Vol. 13). 191p. reprint ed. pap. 54.50 (*0-685-15854-3*, 2027815) Bks Demand.

O'Reilly, Betty. The Magic of Food: For Our Darling Children - & Their Children Too. 149p. (Orig.). (C). 1990. pap. write for info. (*1-878968-01-7*) Better ID.

— The Magic of McCall: Footsteps Across a Century, 1890-1990. (Illus.). 63p. (Orig.). (C). 1989. pap. 8.50 (*1-878968-00-9*) Better ID.

***O'Reilly, Ciaron.** Bomber Grounded, Runway Closed: Prison Letters & Court Notes of a Gulf War Resister. Sprong, Michael, ed. 175p. (Orig.). 1994. pap. 9.95 (*0-9636224-2-0*) Rose Hill Bks.

***O'Reilly, Daragh & Gibas, Julian.** Business to Business Marketing. (Pitman Marketing Ser.). 250p. 1995. pap. 47.50 (*0-273-61692-7*, Pub. by Pitman Pub Ltd UK) Trans-Atl Phila.

O'Reilly, David, et al. Baculovirus Expression Vectors: A Laboratory Manual. LC 93-43895. (Illus.). 364p. (C). 1993. 49.95 (*0-19-509131-0*) OUP.

O'Reilly, Diane. Retard. LC 88-83478. 200p. 1989. 18.95 (*0-944435-05-X*) Glenbridge Pub.

***O'Reilly, Donal.** The Supermarket Shopper's Guide to Fat Free Foods. 55p. (Orig.). (YA). Date not set. pap. 3.95 (*0-9643726-6-5*) Onomy Hse.

O'Reilly, E. Heroic Spain. 1976. lib. bdg. 59.95 (*0-8490-1948-6*) Gordon Pr.

O'Reilly, Edward. Brown Pelican at the Pond. LC 78-58689. (Illus.). (J). (gr. k-4). 1979. 7.95 (*0-931644-01-1*) Manzanita Pr.

— An Irish-English Dictionary. (ENG & IRI.). 1973. 75.00 (*0-8490-0424-1*) Gordon Pr.

O'Reilly, Fionnauala, jt. auth. see O'Mara, Veronica J.

O'Reilly, Frank A. The Fredericksburg Campaign "Stonewall" Jackson at Fredericksburg: The Battle of Prospect Hill. (Virginia Civil War Battles & Leaders Ser.). (Illus.). 243p. 1993. 19.95 (*1-56190-050-8*) H E Howard.

O'Reilly, Harry T. Practical Burglary Investigation. (Illus.). 90p. (C). 1991. pap. text ed. 8.00 (*0-942511-37-9*) OICJ.

O'Reilly, Henry. Settlement in the West. 468p. 1993. reprint ed. lib. bdg. 99.00 (*0-7812-5193-1*) Rprt Serv.

O'Reilly, J. Multivariable Control for Industrial Applications. (Control Engineering Ser.: No. 32). 466p. 1987. 99.00 (*0-86341-117-7*, CE032) Inst Elect Eng.

O'Reilly, J. A. International Marketing. 208p. (Orig.). 1985. pap. text ed. 27.50 (*0-317-01019-0*) Trans-Atl Phila.

O'Reilly, J. J., jt. ed. see Cattermole, K. W.

***O'Reilly, Jacqueline.** Banking on Flexibility: A Comparison of Flexible Employment Strategies in the Retail Banking Sector in Britain & France. 310p. 1994. 59.95 (*1-85628-549-9*) Ashgate Pub Co.

***O'Reilly, James.** Travelers' Tales India. 1995. pap. 17.95 (*1-885211-01-5*) Trvlers Tale.

— Travelers' Tales Mexico. 1994. pap. 17.95 (*1-885211-00-7*) Trvlers Tale.

O'Reilly, James & Habegger, Larry, eds. Travelers' Tales Thailand. 405p. 1993. pap. 15.95 (*1-56592-900-4*) OReilly & Assocs.

— Travelers' Tales Thailand. rev. ed. (Travelers' Tales Ser.). (Illus.). 404p. 1994. pap. 17.95 (*1-885211-05-8*) Trvlers Tale.

***O'Reilly, James, et al, eds.** Travelers' Tales France. (Travelers' Tales Ser.). (Illus.). 430p. (Orig.). 1995. pap. 17.95 (*1-885211-02-3*) Trvlers Tale.

O'Reilly, James M., ed. Structure & Mobility in Molecular & Atomic Glasses, Vol. 371. LC 81-14226. 354p. 1981. pap. 76.00 (*0-89766-132-X*) NY Acad Sci.

O'Reilly, James T. Adminstrative Rulemaking. 480p. 1983. text ed. 95.00 (*0-07-047738-8*) Shepards-McGraw.

— American Environmental Liability Risks. (International Environmental Law & Policy Ser.). 256p. (C). 1995. lib. bdg. 90.00 (*1-85966-093-2*, Pub. by Graham & Trotman UK) Kluwer Ac.

— Federal Information Disclosure. 2nd ed. 1990. text ed. 200.00 (*0-07-172197-5*) McGraw.

— Federal Information Disclosure: Procedures, Forms, & the Law, 2 vols. LC 77-21381. 1344p. 1977. 200.00 (*0-07-047825-2*) Shepards-McGraw.

— Food & Drug Administration. 2nd rev. ed. LC 93-32386. 1993. text ed. 250.00 (*0-07-172376-5*) Shepards-McGraw.

— Food & Drug Administration Regulatory Manual, 2 vols. LC 79-21246. (Regulatory Manual Ser.). 1494p. 1979. text ed. 180.00 (*0-07-047724-8*) Shepards-McGraw.

— Ohio Public Employee Collective Bargaining. 300p. 1984. 47.50 (*0-87084-667-1*) Anderson Pub Co.

— Ohio Public Employee Collective Bargaining. suppl. ed. 300p. 1989. Suppl., 1989. 27.50 (*0-685-42882-6*) Anderson Pub Co.

— Ohio Public Employee Collective Bargaining Law. (Anderson's Ohio Practice Manual Ser.). 1991. pap. write for info. (*0-87084-668-X*) Anderson Pub Co.

— Toxic Torts Practice Guide. 2nd ed. LC 92-39224. 1158p. 1993. text ed. 180.00 (*0-07-172430-3*) Shepards-McGraw.

O'Reilly, James T. & Aronson, Jodi C. Unions' Rights to Company Information. rev. ed. LC 85-82257. (Labor Relations & Public Policy Ser.). 300p. 1987. pap. 30.00 (*0-89546-060-2*) U PA Wharton Ctr Human Resc.

O'Reilly, James T. & Simon, Gale P. Unions' Rights to Company Information. LC 80-53300. (Labor Relations & Public Policy Ser.: No. 21). 292p. reprint ed. pap. 83.30 (*0-317-41895-5*, 2025913) Bks Demand.

***O'Reilly, James T., et al.** Clean Air Permitting Manual. LC 94-47499. (Environmental Law Ser.). 1995. write for info. (*0-07-172590-3*) Shepards-McGraw.

— Federal Regulation of the Chemical Industry. LC 80-11488. (Regulatory Manual Ser.). 1184p. 1980. text ed. 95.00 (*0-07-047728-0*) Shepards-McGraw.

— RCRA & Superfund: A Practice Guide with Forms. 2nd ed. LC 93-40258. 1993. write for info. (*0-07-172535-0*) McGraw.

O'Reilly, John. Boater's Guide to the Upper Florida Keys: Jewfish Creek to Long Key. LC 70-125659. (Illus.). 64p. 1970. spiral bd., pap. 7.95 (*0-87024-175-3*) U of Miami Pr.

O'Reilly, John, ed. Observers for Linear Systems. (Mathematics in Science & Engineering Ser.). 1983. text ed. 99.00 (*0-12-527780-6*) Acad Pr.

O'Reilly, John, ed. see DeCesare, Ruth.

O'Reilly, John B., comp. The Poetry & Song of Old Ireland. (Illus.). 852p. 1985. 45.00 (*0-940134-43-8*) Irish Genealog.

O'Reilly, John L. The Smoldering Wick: Never Too Late for New Life. (Illus.). 144p. (Orig.). 1990. write for info. (*0-9625748-0-5*); write for info. (*0-9625748-1-3*); teacher ed write for info. (*0-9625748-6-4*); student ed write for info. (*0-9625748-7-2*); student ed write for info. (*0-9625748-8-0*); write for info. (*0-9625748-9-9*); text ed. write for info. (*0-9625748-3-X*); lib. bdg. write for info. (*0-9625748-2-1*); pap. 12.00 (*0-9625748-4-8*); pap. text ed. write for info. (*0-9625748-5-6*) J L OReilly.

O'Reilly, Kenneth. Black Americans: The FBI Files. Gallen, David, ed. 512p. 1994. 24.95 (*0-7867-0010-6*); pap. 14.95 (*0-7867-0027-0*) Carroll & Graf.

Oreilly, Kenneth. Racial Matters: The FBI's Secret File on Black America. 1991. pap. 14.95 (*0-02-923682-7*) Free Pr.

O'Reilly, Kenneth. Racial Matters: The FBI's Secret File on Black America, 1960-1972. 400p. 1989. text ed. 29.95 (*0-02-923681-9*) Free Pr.

O'Reilly, Marjorie I., jt. auth. see O'Reilly, Robert C.

***O'Reilly, Maureen.** Current Concepts in Pediatrics. (Newsletter Ser.: No. 2). 4p. (Orig.). 1994. write for info. (*0-944036-99-6*) Medicine Grp USA.

— Current Concepts in Pediatrics, Vol. 1, No. 1. 4p. (Orig.). 1994. write for info. (*0-944036-97-X*) Medicine Grp USA.

***O'Reilly, Maureen, ed.** The Challenges in Studying the Socio-Economic Dimensions in Cancer Therapy. 88p. (Orig.). 1995. write for info. (*1-57130-013-9*) Medicine Grp USA.

O'Reilly, Pat. The Skills Development Handbook for Busy Managers. LC 92-45730. 1993. write for info. (*0-07-707682-6*) McGraw.

— Tactical Fly Fishing: For Trout & Sea Trout on River & Stream. (Illus.). 272p. 1991. 45.00 (*1-85223-294-3*, Pub. by Crowood Pr UK) Trafalgar.

O'Reilly, Pat & Hoskin, Derek. An Introduction to Fly Tying. (Illus.). 112p. 1993. 29.95 (*1-85223-747-3*, Pub. by Crowood Pr UK) Trafalgar.

— An Introduction to Fly Tying. (Illus.). 112p. 1993. 29.95 (*1-85223-647-7*, Pub. by Crowood Pr UK) Trafalgar.

***O'Reilly, Peter.** Trout & Salmon Rivers of Ireland: An Angler's Guide. (Fly Fishing International Ser.). (Illus.). 336p. 1995. 24.95 (*0-8117-1758-5*) Stackpole.

O'Reilly, Peter, tr. see Maritain, Jacques.

O'Reilly, Peter J., jt. auth. see Hammond, Joseph L.

O'Reilly, Priscilla. Preservation Guide 3: Paintings. LC 84-106237. (Illus.). ii, 14p. 1986. pap. 3.95 (*0-917860-22-5*) Historic New Orleans.

***O'Reilly, Priscilla & Lord, Allyn, eds.** Basic Condition Reporting: A Handbook. 2nd expanded rev. ed. LC 88-62138. 56p. 1988. pap. 9.45 (*0-9621348-0-5*) SERA LA.

— Basic Condition Reporting: A Handbook. 2nd rev. ed. LC 88-62138. 1988. pap. 7.95 (*0-685-44324-8*) SERA LA.

O'Reilly, Richard, jt. ed. see Nahmias, Andre J.

O'Reilly, Robert C. & Green, Edward T. School Law for the Practitioner. LC 82-11982. (Contributions to the Study of Education Ser.: No. 6). (Illus.). xiv, 314p. 1983. text ed. 36.95 (*0-313-23639-9*, ORS/, Greenwood Pr) Greenwood.

— School Law for the 1990s: A Handbook. LC 91-27237. 320p. 1992. text ed. 49.95 (*0-313-27817-2*, OSL/, Greenwood Pr) Greenwood.

O'Reilly, Robert C. & O'Reilly, Marjorie I. Librarians & Labor Relations: Employment Under Union Contracts. LC 80-1049. (Contributions in Librarianship & Information Science Ser.: No. 35). xiv, 191p. 1981. text ed. 49.95 (*0-313-22485-4*, OLL/) Greenwood.

O'Reilly, Sean. In the Image of God. 92p. 1982. 2.95 (*0-8198-3607-9*, MS0308) Pauline Bks.

O'Reilly, Susan M. On Track: The Railway Mail Service in Canada. (Illus.). 100p. 1993. pap. 14.95 (*0-660-14005-5*, Pub. by CN Mus Civilization CN) U Ch Pr.

O'Reilly, Susie. Batik & Tie-Dye. LC 92-43264. (Arts & Crafts Ser.). 32p. (J). (gr. 4-6). 1993. 14.95 (*1-56847-064-9*) Thomson Lrning.

— Batik & Tie-Dye. (Arts & Crafts Ser.). (Illus.). 32p. (J). (gr. 4-6). 1995. reprint ed. pap. 5.95 (*1-56847-300-1*) Thomson Lrning.

— Block Printing. LC 92-43263. (Arts & Crafts Ser.). 32p. (J). (gr. 4-6). 1993. 14.95 (*1-56847-065-7*) Thomson Lrning.

— Block Printing. (Arts & Crafts Ser.). (Illus.). 32p. (J). (gr. 4-6). 1995. reprint ed. pap. 5.95 (*1-56847-301-X*) Thomson Lrning.

— Knitting & Crochet. (Arts & Crafts Ser.). (Illus.). 32p. (J). (gr. 4-6). 1994. 14.95 (*1-56847-221-8*) Thomson Lrning.

— Modeling. LC 93-7517. (Arts & Crafts Ser.). (Illus.). 32p. (J). (gr. 4-6). 1993. 14.95 (*1-56847-066-5*) Thomson Lrning.

— NeedleCraft. (Arts & Crafts Ser.). (Illus.). 32p. (J). (gr. 4-6). 1994. 14.95 (*1-56847-220-X*) Thomson Lrning.

— Papermaking. LC 93-24397. (Arts & Crafts Ser.). (Illus.). 32p. (J). (gr. 4-6). 1994. 14.95 (*1-56847-069-X*) Thomson Lrning.

— Stencils & Screens. LC 93-28349. (Arts & Crafts Ser.). (Illus.). 32p. (J). (gr. 4-6). 1994. 14.95 (*1-56847-068-1*) Thomson Lrning.

— Weaving. LC 93-18935. (Arts & Crafts Ser.). (Illus.). 32p. (J). (gr. 4-6). 1993. 14.95 (*1-56847-067-3*) Thomson Lrning.

O'Reilly, Tim & Todino, Grace. Managing UUCP & Usenet. 10th ed. (Nutshell Handbook Ser.). 368p. 1992. pap. 27.95 (*0-937175-93-5*) OReilly & Assocs.

O'Reilly, Tim, ed. see Costales, Bryan, et al.

O'Reilly, Tim, jt. auth. see Dougherty, Dale.

O'Reilly, Tim, ed. see Flanagan, David.

O'Reilly, Tim, ed. see Frey, Donnalyn & Adams, Rick.

O'Reilly, Tim, ed. see Libes, Don.

O'Reilly, Tim, ed. see Mui, Linda & Pearce, Eric.

O'Reilly, Tim, ed. see Mui, Linda & Quercia, Valerie.

O'Reilly, Tim, jt. auth. see Nye, Adrian.

O'Reilly, Tim, ed. see Peek, Jerry.

O'Reilly, Tim, jt. auth. see Quercia, Valerie.

O'Reilly, Tim, jt. auth. see Ridley, Elizabeth.

O'Reilly, Tim, ed. see Todino, Grace, et al.

O'Reilly, Tim, ed. see Todino, Grace.

O'Reilly, Victor. Games of the Hangman. 512p. 1992. pap. text ed. 5.99 (*0-425-13456-3*) Berkley Pub.

— Rules of the Hunt. LC 94-32242. 416p. 1995. 23.95 (*0-399-13869-2*, Putnam) Putnam Pub Group.

O'Reilly, Vincent M., et al. The Coopers & Lybrand SEC Manual. 6th ed. LC 93-23569. 1993. write for info. (*0-13-300427-9*) P-H.

— Montgomery's Auditing. 11th ed. 1150p. 1990. text ed. 145.00 (*0-471-50522-6*); write for info. (*0-471-59241-2*) Wiley.

O'Reilly, W. International Directory of Geophysical Research. 122p. 1986. pap. 48.75 (*0-444-42591-8*) Elsevier.

O'Reilly, W., ed. Magnetism, Planetary Rotation, & Convention in the Solar System: Retrospect & Prospect, Vol. 7. (Geophysical Surveys Ser.: Nos. 1, 2 & 3). 1985. lib. bdg. 113.00 (*90-277-2050-9*) Kluwer Ac.

O'Reily, Emily. Candidate: The Truth Behind the Presidential Campaign. 160p. (Orig.). (C). 1991. pap. 13.99 (*1-85594-021-3*, Pub. by Attic IE) InBook.

— masterminds of the Right. 160p. (C). 1992. pap. 15.99 (*1-85594-044-2*, Pub. by Attic IE) InBook.

***O'Reily, Kenneth.** Nixson's Piano: Presidents & the Politics of Race from Washington to Clinton. 1995. 27.50 (*0-02-923685-1*) Free Pr.

Orejas, F., jt. auth. see Diaz, J.

Orejas, Fernando, jt. ed. see Ehrig, Hartmut.

Orel, Harold. Critical Essays on Sir Arthur Conan Doyle. (Critical Essays on British Literature Ser.). 250p. 1992. text ed. 45.00 (*0-8161-8865-3*, Hall Reference) Macmillan.

— Critical Essays on Thomas Hardy's Poetry. LC 94-27561. (Critical Essays on British Literature Ser.). 208p. 1994. lib. bdg. 42.00x (*0-8161-8768-1*, Twayne) Macmillan.

— The Historical Novel from Scott to Sabatini: Changing Attitudes Toward a Literary Genre, 1814-1920. LC 94-34636. 1995. write for info. (*0-312-12473-2*) St Martin.

— A Kipling Chronology. (Chronologies-Reference Ser.). 1990. text ed. 38.50 (*0-8161-9090-9*, Hall Reference) Macmillan.

— Popular Fiction in England, 1914-1918. LC 91-36651. 256p. 1992. lib. bdg. 28.00 (*0-8131-1789-5*) U Pr of Ky.

— Thomas Hardy's Epic-Drama: A Study of the Dynasts. LC 69-14022. 122p. 1969. reprint ed. text ed. 45.00 (*0-8371-0602-8*, ORTD, Greenwood Pr) Greenwood.

— The Unknown Thomas Hardy: Lesser Known Aspects of Hardy's Life & Career. LC 86-4653. 256p. 1987. text ed. 39.95 (*0-312-00538-5*) St Martin.

— Victorian Literary Critics: George Henry Lewes, Walter Bagehot, Richard Holt Hutton, Leslie Stephen, Andrew Lang, George Saintsbury, & Edmund Gosse. LC 83-11093. (Illus.). 240p. 1984. text ed. 35.00 (*0-312-84304-6*) St Martin.

— The Victorian Short Story: Development & Triumph of a Literary Genre. (Illus.). 224p. 1986. 74.95 (*0-521-25899-5*) Cambridge U Pr.

Orel, Harold, ed. Critical Essays on Rudyard Kipling. (Critical Essays on British Literature Ser.). 248p. 1989. text ed. 45.00 (*0-8161-8767-3*) G K Hall.

— Gilbert & Sullivan: Interviews & Recollections. LC 93-60769. 232p. 1994. text ed. 29.95x (*0-87745-442-6*) U of Iowa Pr.

— Gilbert & Sullivan: Interviews & Recollections. LC 93-60769. 232p. 1995. pap. 14.95 (*0-87745-476-0*) U of Iowa Pr.

— Sir Arthur Conan Doyle: Interviews & Recollections. LC 90-44945. 296p. 1991. text ed. 45.00 (*0-312-05374-6*) St Martin.

— Victorian Short Stories 2: The Trials of Love. 287p. 1991. pap. 8.95 (*0-460-87007-6*, Everyman's Classic Lib) C E Tuttle.

— World of Victorian Humor. LC 61-8018. (Goldentree Books in English Literature). (Illus.). (Orig.). 1961. pap. text ed. 12.95 (*0-89197-474-1*) Irvington.

Orel, Harold, ed. see Hardy, Thomas.

Orel, Sara E., ed. Death & Taxes in the Ancient Near East. LC 92-4673. (Illus.). 256p. 1992. lib. bdg. 89.95 (*0-7734-9512-6*) E Mellen.

***Orel, Vitezslav.** Gregor Mendel: The First Geneticist. (Illus.). 256p. 1995. 38.95 (*0-19-854774-9*) OUP.

***Orel, Vladimir E. & Stolbova, Olga V.** Hamito-Semitic Etymological Dictionary: Materials for Reconstruction. LC 94-32911. (Handbuch der Orientalistik, Erste Abteilung, Nahe und Mittlere Osten Ser.). 652p. 1994. 200.00 (*90-04-10051-2*) E J Brill.

Orell, R. Svente, et al. Manual & Atlas of Fine Needle Aspiration Cytology. 2nd ed. (Illus.). 341p. 1992. text ed. 219.00 (*0-443-04239-X*) Churchill.

***Orellana, Juan, et al.** Color Atlas of Ocular Manifestations of AIDS: Diagnosis & Management. LC 94-33155. 105p. 1995. 98.50 (*0-89640-273-8*) Igaku-Shoin.

Orellana, Juan & Friedman, Alan H. Clinico-Pathological Atlas of Congenital Fundus Disorders. LC 92-49529. 1993. 150.00 (*0-387-97936-0*) Spr-Verlag.

Orellana, M. Spanish-English - English-Spanish Glossary of Selected Terms Used in International Organizations. 3rd ed. 645p. 1993. pap. 36.00 (*0-88431-149-X*) IBD Ltd.

Orellana, Marina. International Glossary for Translators, Spanish-English, English-Spanish. 3rd ed. 648p. (ENG & SPA.). 1993. pap. 95.00 (*0-8288-9422-1*) Fr & Eur.

Orellana, Sandra L. The Tzutujil Mayas: Continuity & Change, 1250-1630. LC 83-47837. (Civilization of the American Indian Ser.: Vol. 162). (Illus.). 320p. 1984. 39.95 (*0-8061-1739-7*) U of Okla Pr.

Orelli, J. C. & Baiter, J. G. Onomasticon Tullianum, 3 vols. Vols. VI-VIII. 1965. reprint ed. Set. write for info. (*0-318-72062-0*, Pub. by Georg Olms GW) Lubrecht & Cramer.

Orelove, Frank P., jt. auth. see Garner, Howard G.

Orelove, Fred P. & Sobsey, Dick. Educating Children with Multiple Disabilities: A Transdisciplinary Approach. 2nd ed. LC 91-12364. 496p. (Orig.). (C). 1991. pap. text ed. 29.00 (*1-55766-077-8*, 0778) P H Brookes.

Orem, Dorothea E. Nursing: Concepts of Practice. (Illus.). 400p. 1990. pap. 31.95 (*0-8016-6064-5*) Mosby Yr Bk.

— Nursing: Concepts of Practice. 2nd ed. (Illus.). 1980. text ed. 24.95 (*0-07-047718-3*) McGraw.

— Nursing: Concepts of Practice. 3rd ed. 288p. 1985. text ed. 29.95 (*0-07-047525-3*) McGraw.

— Nursing: Concepts of Practice. 5th ed. LC 94-47916. 1995. write for info. (*0-8151-6552-8*) Mosby Yr Bk.

Orem, Howard & Snyder, Suzen. Country Land & Its Uses. LC 74-22154. (Illus.). 310p. 1975. 16.95 (*0-87961-031-X*); pap. 8.95 (*0-87961-030-1*) Naturegraph.

Orem, J. & Barnes, C. D., eds. Physiology in Sleep. (Research Topics in Physiology Ser.). (C). 1980. text ed. 103.00 (*0-12-527650-8*) Acad Pr.

Orem, Reginald C., jt. auth. see Amos, William E.

Orem, Sara & Demarest, Larry. Living Simply. 200p. (Orig.). 1994. pap. 9.95 (*1-55874-321-9*, 3219) Health Comm.

Orem, Sue D. & Brue, Deborah F., eds. Practical Programming in Continuing Professional Education: Examples for Understanding & Improving Practice. 1991. 13.95 (*0-88379-050-5*) A A A C E.

Oremland, Jerome. Interpretation & Interaction: Psychoanalysis or Psychotherapy? 192p. 1991. text ed. 29.95 (*0-88163-127-2*) Analytic Pr.

Oremland, Jerome D. Michelangelo's Sistine Ceiling: A Psychoanalytic Study of Creativity. (Applied Psychoanalysis Monographs: No. 2). (Illus.). 337p. 1989. text ed. 42.50 (*0-8236-3364-0*) Intl Univs Pr.

***Oremland, R. S.** Biogeochemistry of Global Change: Radiatively Active Trace Gases. LC 93-19052. 879p. 1993. 99.50 (*0-412-04141-3*) Routledge.

Oremland, Ronald S., ed. The Biogeochemistry of Global Change: Radiatively Active Trace Gases. LC 93-19052. 1993. write for info. (*0-04-120304-6*) Routledge Chapman & Hall.

Oren. Annotated Bibliographies of Simulation. 132p. 1976. 36.00 (*0-685-66776-6*, SS04-1) Soc Computer Sim.

Oren, Aras. Please, No Police: A Novella. Sipahigil, Teoman, tr. LC 92-75236. (Modern Middle East Literature in Translation Ser.). 174p. 1992. pap. 8.95 (*0-292-76038-8*, Pub. by Ctr Mid East Stud) U of Tex Pr.

Oren, Dan A. Joining the Club: A History of Jews & Yale. LC 85-14252. (Yale Scene, University Ser.: No. 4). 448p. 1986. 48.00 (*0-300-03330-3*) Yale U Pr.

— Joining the Club: A History of Jews & Yale. 448p. (C). 1988. reprint ed. pap. 20.00 (*0-300-04384-8*) Yale U Pr.

Oren, Dan A., et al. How to Beat Jet Lag: A Practical Guide for Air Travelers. LC 93-17190. (Illus.). 144p. 1993. pap. 14.95 (*0-8050-2687-8*) H Holt & Co.

Oren, Israel. Taberna Pauperum: The Development of a New Background to the Nativity of Christ in the Fourteenth & Fifteenth Centuries in the North. LC 93-31501. (Hermeneutics of Art Ser.: Vol. 3). 1994. write for info. (*0-8204-2073-5*) P Lang Pubs.

Oren, John W., jt. auth. see Brown, Ronald.

Oren, Michael B. The Origins of the Second Arab-Israel War: Egypt, Israel & the Great Powers, 1952-56. 199p. 1993. 40.00 (*0-7146-3430-1*, Pub. by F Cass Pubs UK) Intl Spec Bk.

Oren, Nissan. Bulgarian Communism: The Road to Power 1934-1944. LC 84-25247. xiv, 290p. (C). 1985. reprint ed. text ed. 69.50 (*0-313-24741-2*, ORBC, Greenwood Pr) Greenwood.

— Prudence in Victory: The Dynamics of Post-War Settlements. 16p. (Orig.). 1977. pap. text ed. 11.00 (*0-8191-5830-5*, Aspen Inst for Humanistic Studies) U Pr of Amer.

— Revolution Administered: Agrarianism & Communism in Bulgaria. LC 72-8831. (Integration & Community Building in Eastern Europe Ser.: EE8). 224p. reprint ed. pap. 63.90 (*0-317-39640-4*, 2023108) Bks Demand.

Oren, Nissan, ed. Images & Reality in International Politics. LC 83-40613. 247p. 1985. text ed. 22.50 (*0-312-40917-6*) St Martin.

— When Patterns Change: Turning Points in International Politics. LC 83-40614. 250p. 1985. text ed. 29.95 (*0-312-86666-6*) St Martin.

Oren, Rony. The Animated Haggadah (1990 Edition) (Illus.). 54p. (J). 1990. 14.95 (*0-944007-43-0*) Sure Sellers.

Oren, Shmuel S. & Smith, Stephen A., eds. Service Opportunities for Electric Utilities: Creating Differentiated Products. LC 92-44559. (Topics in Regulatory Economics & Policy Ser.). 352p. (C). 1993. lib. bdg. 79.95 (*0-7923-9319-8*) Kluwer Ac.

Oren, Simon. BBQ & All the Fixins. LC 93-22437. (Illus.). 144p. 1994. pap. 13.00 (*0-02-074575-3*, Collier S&S) S&S Trade.

Oren, Tuncer I., ed. Advances in Artificial Intelligence in Software Engineering, Vol. 1. 1991. 73.25 (*0-89232-854-1*) Jai Pr.

— Advances in Modelling & Simulation, Vol. 1. 1989. write for info. (*0-89232-873-8*) Jai Pr.

Oren, Yizhak. The Imaginary Number. Knight, Max, ed. 130p. 1986. pap. 9.95 (*0-917883-01-7*) Benmir Bks.

Orenstein. The Immune System. 1989. pap. 2.50 (*0-87983-506-0*) Keats.

Orenstein, Alex & Stern, Raphael. Developments in Semantics. LC 83-83299. (Language, Logic & Linguistics Ser.). 402p. (C). 1984. 65.00 (*0-930586-34-4*); pap. text ed. 29.00 (*0-930586-13-1*) Haven Pubns.

Orenstein, Arbie. Ravel: Man & Musician. 1991. pap. 9.95 (*0-486-26633-8*) Dover.

— A Ravel Reader: Correspondence, Articles, Interviews. 1990. text ed. 49.00 (*0-231-04962-5*) Col U Pr.

Orenstein, Aviel, ed. Mishnah Berurah, Vol. 2B: Covering Chapters 157-201 of the Shulchan Aruch Orach Chaim. 570p. (HEB.). 1988. 22.95 (*0-87306-445-3*) Feldheim.

— Mishnah Berurah, Vol. 2B: Covering Chapters 157-201 of the Shulchan Aruch Orach Chaim. large type ed. 570p. (HEB.). 1988. 27.95 (*0-87306-444-5*) Feldheim.

Orenstein, Aviel, tr. Mishnah Berurah, Vol. 1A: Laws of Daily Conduct. 1993. 18.95 (*0-87306-604-9*) Feldheim.

— Mishnah Berurah, Vol. 1A: Laws of Daily Conduct. large type ed. 1993. 23.95 (*0-87306-603-0*) Feldheim.

— Mishnah Berurah, Vol. 1B: Laws of Tefillin. 1993. 20.95 (*0-87306-623-5*) Feldheim.

— Mishnah Berurah, Vol. 1B: Laws of Tefillin. large type ed. 1993. 24.95 (*0-87306-624-3*) Feldheim.

— Mishnah Berurah, Vol. 1C: Laws of Daily Prayer. 1991. 21.95 (*0-87306-552-2*) Feldheim.

— Mishnah Berurah, Vol. 1C: Laws of Daily Prayer. large type ed. 1991. 26.95 (*0-87306-551-4*) Feldheim.

— Mishnah Berurah, Vol. 1D: Laws of Daily Prayer. 1991. 19.95 (*0-87306-554-9*) Feldheim.

— Mishnah Berurah, Vol. 1D: Laws of Daily Prayer. large type ed. 1991. 24.95 (*0-87306-553-0*) Feldheim.

Orenstein, Aviel, tr. see Chaim-Chofet.

Orenstein, Aviel, tr. see Ha-Cohen, Yisroel Meir.

Orenstein, David M. Cystic Fibrosis: A Guide for Patient & Family. 253p. 1989. 21.00 (*0-88167-486-9*, 1952) Raven.

— The Sociological Quest: Principles of Sociology. (Illus.). 415p. 1985. pap. text ed. 35.75 (*0-314-77938-8*) West Pub.

Orenstein, Debra, ed. Lifecycles Vol. 1: Jewish Women on Life Passages & Personal Milestones, Vol. 1. LC 94-14799. 480p. 1994. 24.95 (*1-879045-14-1*) Jewish Lights.

— Lifecycles Vol. 2: Jewish Women on Life Themes & Cycles of Meaning. 250p. 1996. 24.95 (*1-879045-15-X*) Jewish Lights.

— Lifecycles Vol. 3: Jewish Women on Holy Days & Communal Celebrations. 300p. Date not set. 24.95 (*1-879045-18-4*) Jewish Lights.

Orenstein, Eugene, tr. see Mahler, Raphael.

Orenstein, Frank. A Vintage Year for Dying. 256p. 1994. 20.95 (*0-312-10442-1*, Pub. by Thomas Dunne Bks) St Martin.

Orenstein, Glenn S. & Orenstein, Ruth M. CompuServe Companion: Finding Newspapers & Magazines Online. 204p. (Orig.). 1994. pap. 29.95 (*1-879258-10-2*) BiblioData.

Orenstein, Gloria, jt. auth. see Diamond, Irene.

Orenstein, Gloria F. Multi-Cultural Celebrations: The Paintings of Betty LaDuke. LC 92-62861. (Illus.). 141p. 1993. 35.00 (*1-56640-600-5*); pap. 25.00 (*1-56640-452-5*) Pomegranate Calif.

— The Reflowering of the Goddess. (Athene Ser.). 256p. (C). text ed. 47.50 (*0-8077-6243-1*); pap. text ed. 17.95 (*0-8077-6242-3*) Tchrs Coll.

— The Reflowering of the Goddess: Contemporary Journeys & Cycles of Empowerment. (Athene Ser.). (Illus.). 250p. 1990. text ed. 47.50 (*0-08-035179-4*, 2707, Pub. by PPI UK); pap. text ed. 17.95 (*0-08-035178-6*, Pub. by PPI UK) Elsevier.

Orenstein, Harold & Sinacore-Guinn, David. Entertainment Law & Business, 1989-1993: A Guide to the Law & Business Practices of the Entertainment Industry. 1991. ring bd. 180.00 (*0-88063-163-5*) Michie Butterworth.

— Entertainment Law & Business, 1989-1993: A Guide to the Law & Business Practices of the Entertainment Industry. suppl. ed. 1991. 55.00 (*1-56257-152-4*) Butterworth Legal Pubs.

Orenstein, Harold S. Soviet Documents on the Use of War Experiences, Vol. 3: Military Operations, 1941-1942. LC 91-11452. 224p. 1993. 45.00 (*0-7146-3402-6*, Pub. by F Cass Pubs UK) Intl Spec Bk.

O

Orenstein, Harold S., tr. Soviet Documents on the Use of War Experience, Vol. 1: The Initial Period of War 1941. 83p. 1991. text ed. 37.50 (*0-7146-3392-5*, Pub. by F Cass Pubs UK) Intl Spec Bk.

— Soviet Documents on the Use of War Experience, Vol. 2: The Winter Campaign 1941-1942. 255p. 1991. text ed. 37.50 (*0-7146-3393-3*, Pub. by F Cass Pubs UK) Intl Spec Bk.

Orenstein, Henry. Gaon: Conflict & Cohesion in an Indian Village. LC 65-12991. (Illus.). 349p. reprint ed. pap. 99.50 (*0-8357-4397-7*, 2057067) Bks Demand.

Orenstein, Herta. Die Refrainformen im Chansonnier de L'Arsenal. (Wissenschaftliche Abhandlungen-Musicological Studies: Vol. 19). 120p. (GER.). 1972. lib. bdg. 54.00 (*0-912024-89-5*) Inst Mediaeval Mus.

Orenstein, Jeffrey. United States Railroad Policy: Uncle Sam at the Throttle. 186p. 1990. lib. bdg. 26.95 (*0-8304-1205-0*) Nelson-Hall.

Orenstein, Jeffrey R., jt. auth. see Fowler, Robert B.

Orenstein, Neil S. & Bingham, Sarah L. Food Allergies. 160p. 1988. pap. 9.95 (*0-399-51383-3*, Perigree Bks) Berkley Pub.

Orenstein, Peggy. School Girls: Young Women, Self-Esteem, & the Confidence Gap. LC 94-9883. 1994. 23.50 (*0-385-42575-9*) Doubleday.

Orenstein, Robert, jt. auth. see Burke, James.

Orenstein, Ronald. Elephants: The Deciding Decade. LC 91-15254. (Illus.). 160p. 1991. 35.00 (*0-87156-565-X*) Sierra.

— How on Earth? A Question & Answer Book about How Our Planet Works. LC 94-43967. (J). 1995. write for info. (*0-89658-269-8*) Voyageur Pr.

— How on Earth? A Question-&-Answer Book about Life on Our Planet. LC 94-13927. (Illus.). 96p. (J). 1994. 15.95 (*0-89658-257-4*) Voyageur Pr.

***Orenstein, Ruth M., ed.** Fulltext Sources Online. 430p. (Orig.). 1996. pap. text ed. 105.00 (*1-879258-15-3*) BiblioData.

— Fulltext Sources Online: For Periodicals, Newspapers, Newsletters, Newswires & TV-Radio Transcripts. 13th ed. 390p. 1995. pap. text ed. 105.00 (*1-879258-13-7*) BiblioData.

Orenstein, Ruth M., jt. auth. see Orenstein, Glenn S.

Orenstein, Vik. Creative Techniques for Photographing Children. 144p. 1993. pap. 24.95 (*0-89879-543-5*, 10358) Writers Digest.

Orenstein, Walter. The Cantor's Manual of Jewish Law. LC 94-9953. 200p. 1994. pap. 24.95 (*1-56821-258-5*) Aronson.

— Letters to My Daughter: A Father Writes about Torah & the Jewish Woman. LC 94-45801. 1995. text ed. write for info. (*1-56821-387-5*) Aronson.

Orenstein, Walter & Frankel, Hertz. The Passover Haggadah. 197p. 1962. 3.50 (*0-88482-364-4*) Hebrew Pub.

Orent, Sander. Stress & the Heart: Storm in a Bottle. LC 87-7540. 256p. 1989. text ed. 24.95 (*0-89876-139-5*) Gardner Pr.

Oreopoulos, Dimitrious G., et al, eds. Nephrology & Urology in the Aged Patient. LC 92-48668. 1993. lib. bdg. 269.00 (*0-7923-2019-0*) Kluwer Ac.

Oreovicz, Frank S., jt. auth. see Wankat, Phillip C.

Oresick, Peter. Definitions. LC 90-12346. 72p. (C). 1990. 18.95 (*0-931122-59-7*); pap. 8.95 (*0-931122-58-9*) West End.

— Other Lives. 2nd ed. 48p. 1985. pap. 4.00 (*0-938566-29-6*) Adastra Pr.

Oresick, Peter & Coles, Nicholas, eds. Working Classics: Poems on Industrial Life. 304p. 1990. 34.95 (*0-252-01730-7*); pap. 13.95 (*0-252-06133-0*) U of Ill Pr.

Oresick, Peter, jt. ed. see Coles, Nicholas.

Oresick, Peter, ed. see Dobler, Patricia.

Oresick, Peter, ed. see Ignatow, David.

Oresick, Peter, jt. ed. see Ochester, Ed.

Oreskes, Irwin, jt. auth. see Spiera, Harry.

Oresman, Janice C. New Vistas: Contemporary American Landscapes. (Illus.). 55p. (Orig.). 1984. pap. 4.75 (*0-943651-20-4*) Hudson Riv.

— Twentieth Century American Watercolor. (Illus.). 56p. 1983. 15.00 (*0-934483-03-5*) Gal Assn NY.

Oresme, Nicole. Livre du Ciel & du Monde. 2nd ed. Menut, Albert D. & Denomy, Alexander J., eds. LC 67-11061. (Medieval Science Publications: No. 11). (Illus.). 792p. 1968. 45.00 (*0-299-04670-2*) U of Wis Pr.

— Nicole Oresme & the Medieval Geometry of Qualities & Motions: A Treatise on the Uniformity & Difformity of Intensities Known As Tractatus de Configurationibus Qualitatum et Motuum. Clagett, Marshall, ed. LC 68-14031. (University of Wisconsin Publications in Medieval Science). (Illus.). 736p. reprint ed. pap. 180.00 (*0-7837-5901-0*, 2045692) Bks Demand.

Orest. ONE. LC 76-47223. (Orig.). 1977. pap. 4.95 (*0-89407-002-9*) Strawberry Hill.

Orevkov, V. P. Complexity of Proofs & Their Transformations in Axiomatic Theories. Louvish, David, ed. Bochman, Alexander, tr. LC 93-11139. (ENG.). 1993. write for info. (*0-8218-4576-4*) Am Math.

Orevkov, V. P. & Sanin, N. A., eds. Problems in the Constructive Trend in Mathematics: Part VI. LC 75-11951. (Proceedings of the Steklov Institute of Mathematics Ser.: No. 129). 272p. 1976. 135.00 (*0-8218-3029-5*, STEKLO 129) Am Math.

Orevkov, V. P., ed. see Steklov Institute of Mathematics, Academy of Sciences, U. S. S. R. Staff.

***Orey, Maureen.** Successfully Staffing a Diverse Workplace: A Practical Guide to Building an Effective & Diverse Staff. (Workplace Diversity Ser.). (Illus.). 120p. 1995. pap. 12.95 (*1-883553-67-9*) R Chang Assocs.

Orfalea, Gregory. Before the Flames: A Quest for the History of Arab Americans. (Illus.). 408p. 1988. 24.95 (*0-292-70748-7*) U of Tex Pr.

— The Capital of Solitude. LC 87-81729. (Ithaca House Ser.). 84p. 1988. pap. 9.95 (*0-87886-129-7*, Greenfld Rev Pr) Greenfld Rev Lit.

— U. S. - Arab Relations: The Literary Dimension, No. 2. 44p. (Orig.). 1984. pap. 4.00 (*0-916729-01-X*) Natl Coun Arab.

Orfalea, Gregory & Elmusa, Sharif, eds. Grape Leaves: A Century of Arab American Poetry. LC 88-19041. (Illus.). 330p. reprint ed. pap. 94.10 (*0-7837-5537-6*, 2045310) Bks Demand.

Orfali. Client Server Program with OS-2 2.1. 3rd ed. (Computer Science Ser.). 1993. pap. 39.95 (*0-442-01833-9*) Van Nos Reinhold.

— Client Server Survival Guide with OS-2. 1994. pap. 24.95 (*0-442-01818-5*) Van Nos Reinhold.

Orfali, J. Sebastian, jt. auth. see Potter, Beverly A.

Orfali, J. Sebastian, jt. auth. see Potter, Beverly.

Orfali, Jacob G. An Armenian from Jerusalem: Tales of Hagop. (Illus.). 128p. 1987. 9.95 (*0-914171-09-7*) Ronin Pub.

— Everywhere You Go, People Are the Same. 176p. 1995. pap. 14.95 (*0-914171-75-5*) Ronin Pub.

Orfali, Robert & Harkey, Dan. Client Server Programming with OS 2, 2.1. 3rd ed. 1993. write for info. (*0-318-72440-5*) Van Nos Reinhold.

Orfali, Robert & Harkey, Daniel. A Client Server Survival Guide with OS 2. (Illus.). 352p. 1994. pap. 39.95 (*0-442-01798-7*) Van Nos Reinhold.

Orfali, Robert, et al. Essential Client/Server Survival Guide. LC 94-20084. 527p. 1994. pap. 24.95 (*0-442-01941-6*) Van Nos Reinhold.

Orfali, Sebastian, ed. see Potter, Beverly.

Orfali, Sebastian, ed. see Stafford, Peter.

Orfali, Sebstain, ed. Computer Comics. (Illus.). 96p. (Orig.). 1984. pap. 5.95 (*0-914171-03-8*) Ronin Pub.

Orfali, Stephanie. A Jewish Girl in the Weimar Republic. (Illus.). 192p. 1987. 9.95 (*0-914171-10-0*) Ronin Pub.

Orfanidi. Optimal Signal Processing. 1985. 34.95 (*0-02-949860-0*) Macmillan.

Orfanidis, Sophocles J. Optimum Signal Processing: An Introduction. 2nd ed. 1989. 49.00 (*0-07-047794-9*) McGraw.

Orfanos, C. E., ed. Recent Developments in Clinical Research. (Current Problems in Dermatology Ser.: Vol. 13). (Illus.). viii, 192p. 1984. 131.25 (*3-8055-3928-2*) S Karger.

Orfanos, C. E. & Happle, R., eds. Hair & Hair Diseases. (Illus.). 1070p. 1990. 225.00 (*0-387-50960-7*) Spr-Verlag.

Orfanos, C. E. & Schuppli, R., eds. Oral Retinoids in Dermatology Workshop Held on the 15th International Congress of Dermatology, Mexico City, October 1977. 1978. pap. 21.00 (*3-8055-2950-3*) S Karger.

Orfeuil, Maurice. Electric Process Heating: Technologies, Equipment, Applications. LC 86-3531. 832p. 1987. 95.00 (*0-935470-26-3*) Battelle.

Orff, Carl. The Schulwerk, Vol. 3. Murray, Margaret, tr. (Carl Orff Documentation Ser.). 1978. pap. 25.00 (*0-930448-06-5*, STAP065) Eur-Am Music.

Orfield, Gary. Turning Back the Clock: The Reagan-Bush Retreat for Civil Rights in Higher Education. 150p. (C). 1992. lib. bdg. 42.00 (*0-941410-86-2*); pap. text ed. 14.50 (*0-941410-85-4*) Jt Ctr Pol Studies.

Orfield, Gary & Ashkinaze, Carole. The Closing Door: Conservative Policy & Black Opportunity. LC 90-48542. (Illus.). 232p. 1991. 22.50 (*0-226-63272-5*) U Ch Pr.

— The Closing Door: Conservative Policy & Black Opportunity. LC 90-48542. (Illus.). xx, 254p. 1993. pap. 11.95 (*0-226-63273-3*) U Ch Pr.

***Orfield, Gary & Eaton, Susan E.** Dismantling Desegregation: The Quiet Reversal of Brown vs. Board of Education. 496p. 1996. 30.00 (*1-56584-305-3*) New Press NY.

***Orfield, Gary & Monfort, Franklin.** Status of School Desegregation: The Next Generation. 39p. (Orig.). 1992. pap. 25.00 (*0-88364-174-7*) Natl Sch Boards.

Orfield, Gary, jt. auth. see Ford Foundation Staff.

Orfield, Gary, jt. auth. see Monfort, Franklin.

***Orfield, Gary, et al.** The Growth of Segregation in American Schools: Changing Patterns of Separation & Poverty since 1968. 34p. (Orig.). 1993. pap. 15.00 (*0-88364-179-8*) Natl Sch Boards.

— Status of School Desegregation 1968-1986: Segregation, Integration, & Public Policy: National, State, & Metropolitan Trends in Public Schools. 31p. (Orig.). 1989. pap. text ed. 10.00 (*0-88364-171-2*) Natl Sch Boards.

Orfield, Lester B. Amending of the Federal Constitution. LC 74-146151. (American Constitutional & Legal History Ser). (Illus.). 1971. reprint ed. lib. bdg. 29.50 (*0-306-70094-8*) Da Capo.

— The Amending of the Federal Constitution. LC 42-36735. (Michigan Legal Publications). xxvii, 242p. 1984. reprint ed. lib. bdg. 37.50 (*0-89941-324-2*, 303160) W S Hein.

***Orfila, E. F.** Glimpses Beyond Time. LC 94-90159. (Illus.). 128p. (Orig.). 1995. pap. 8.00 (*1-56002-453-4*, Univ Edtns) Aegina Pr.

***Orford, J.** Excessive Appetites: A Psychological View of Addiction. 1995. pap. text ed. 45.00 (*0-471-93613-8*) Wiley.

Orford, Jim. Community Psychology: Theory & Practice. 292p. 1992. pap. text ed. 36.95 (*0-471-93810-6*) Wiley.

Orford, Jim, ed. Treating the Disorder, Treating the Family. LC 87-3159. 304p. 1987. text ed. 45.00 (*0-8018-3536-4*) Johns Hopkins.

Orford, Jim, jt. auth. see Otto, Shirley.

Orford, Margaret. The King's Daughter. large type ed. (Linford Romance Library). 1991. pap. 13.95 (*0-7089-7108-3*) Ulverscroft.

Org, jt. auth. see Frank-Stromb.

Orga, Ates. Beethoven. (Illustrated Lives of the Great Composers Ser.). (Illus.). 176p. 1987. pap. 14.95 (*0-7119-0251-8*, OP42373) Omnibus NY.

— Chopin. (Illustrated Lives of the Great Composers Ser.). (Illus.). 144p. pap. 14.95 (*0-7119-0247-X*, OP42332) Omnibus NY.

Organ, Allan J. Thermodynamic Design of the Stirling Cycle Machine. (Illus.). 375p. (C). 1992. 125.00 (*0-521-41363-X*) Cambridge U Pr.

Organ, Claude H., Jr. & Smith, R. Stephen. Gasless Laparoscopy with Conventional Instruments: The Next Phase in Minimally Invasive Surgery. LC 93-26738. (Illus.). 153p. 1993. 98.00 (*0-930405-61-7*) Norman SF.

Organ, Dennis M. Tennyson's Dramas: A Critical Study. (Graduate Studies: No. 17). 125p. 1979. pap. 7.00 (*0-89672-066-7*) Tex Tech Univ Pr.

Organ, Dennis W. Organizational Citizenship Behavior: The Good Soldier Syndrome. LC 85-45471. (Issues in Organization & Management Ser.). 160p. 1988. text ed. 27.95 (*0-669-11788-9*) Free Pr.

Organ, Dennis W., ed. The Applied Psychology of Work Behavior: A Book of Readings. 4th ed. 528p. (C). 1991. pap. text ed. 33.95 (*0-256-08275-8*) Irwin.

Organ, Dennis W. & Bateman, Thomas S. Organizational Behavior. 4th ed. 720p. (C). 1990. text ed. 62.95 (*0-256-06667-1*, 08-1206-04) Irwin.

Organ, James A. A Manual for the Biology of the Vertebrates. (Illus.). 180p. (C). 1977. 13.95 (*0-89529-009-X*) Avery Pub.

Organ, L. W., ed. see Toronto University, Dept. of Physiology Staff.

Organ, Sue. Salt Dough Models. (Illus.). 48p. (YA). 1993. pap. 12.95 (*0-85532-756-1*, Pub. by Search Pr UK) A Schwartz & Co.

Organ, Troy W. Hindu Quest for the Perfection of Man. LC 73-81450. x, 439p. 1970. pap. 21.95 (*0-8214-0575-6*) Ohio U Pr.

— Index to Aristotle. LC 66-19085. 181p. 1966. reprint ed. 75.00 (*0-87752-079-8*) Gordian.

— The One: East & West. 464p. (Orig.). (C). 1991. lib. bdg. 52.00 (*0-8191-7877-2*) U Pr of Amer.

— Philosophy & the Self: East & West. LC 86-62506. 240p. 1987. 42.50 (*0-941664-80-5*) Susquehanna U Pr.

— Philosophy for the Left Hand. (Revisioning Philosophy Ser.: Vol. 3). 398p. (C). 1990. text ed. 54.95 (*0-8204-1308-9*) P Lang Pubs.

— Radhakrishnan & the Ways of Oneness of East & West. LC 89-9397. 120p. 1989. lib. bdg. 22.95 (*0-8214-0936-0*) Ohio U Pr.

— The Self in Its Worlds: East & West. LC 87-42799. 256p. 1988. 36.50 (*0-941664-88-0*) Susquehanna U Pr.

— Third Eye Philosophy: Essays in East-West Thought. LC 86-12597. 200p. 1986. text ed. 26.95 (*0-8214-0851-8*) Ohio U Pr.

Organic Gardening Magazine Staff, ed. Q & A: Hundreds of Can-Do Answers to a Gardener's Toughest Questions. LC 88-29982. (Illus.). 336p. 1989. 21.95 (*0-87857-800-5*, 01-461-0) Rodale Pr Inc.

Organic Gardening Staff. Rodale's Gardening Questions & Answers. Date not set. 9.99 (*0-517-09304-9*) Random Hse Value.

Organick, Elliot I. A Programmer's View of the Intel 432 System. 432p. 1983. text ed. 40.00 (*0-07-047719-1*) McGraw.

Organick, Elliot I., jt. auth. see Meissner, Loren P.

Organisation for Economic Cooperation & Development, CERI Staff. Adult Illiteracy & Economic Performance. 88p. (Orig.). 1992. pap. 24.00 (*92-64-13597-9*) OECD.

Organisation for Economic Cooperation & Development Staff. Advanced Technologies for Electric Demand-Side Management, 3 vols., Set. (Orig.). 1991. pap. 118.00 (*92-64-13563-4*) OECD.

— Climate Change: Evaluating the Socio-Economic Impacts. 110p. (Orig.). 1991. pap. 27.00 (*92-64-13462-X*) OECD.

— Environmental Policy: How to Apply Economic Instruments. 130p. (Orig.). 1991. pap. 28.00 (*92-64-13568-5*) OECD.

— Greenhouse Gas Emissions: The Energy Dimension. 200p. (Orig.). 1991. pap. 40.00 (*92-64-13444-1*) OECD.

— Information Technology Standards: The Economic Dimension. (Information Computer Communications Policy Ser.: No. 25). 108p. (Orig.). 1991. pap. 21.00 (*92-64-13564-2*) OECD.

— Integration of Developing Countries into the International Trading System. 137p. (Orig.). 1992. pap. 33.00 (*92-64-13616-9*) OECD.

— Licensing Systems & Inspection of Nuclear Installations, 1991. 144p. (Orig.). 1991. pap. 50.00 (*92-64-13574-X*) OECD.

— Managing Manpower for Advanced Manufacturing Technology. 150p. (Orig.). 1991. pap. 36.00 (*92-64-13467-0*) OECD.

— Rebalancing the Public & Private Sectors: Developing Country Experience. 270p. (Orig.). 1991. pap. 32.00 (*92-64-13440-9*) OECD.

— Reforming the Economies of Central & Eastern Europe. 119p. (Orig.). 1992. pap. 21.00 (*92-64-13613-4*) OECD.

— Restoring Financial Flows to Latin America. Emmerij, Louis & Iglesias, Enrique V., eds. 251p. (Orig.). 1991. pap. 31.00 (*92-64-13476-X*) OECD.

— Short-Term Economic Statistics: Central & Eastern Europe. 390p. (Orig.). 1992. pap. 32.00 (*92-64-03523-0*) OECD.

— Transport for People with Mobility Handicaps: Information & Communication. 152p. (Orig.). 1991. pap. 17.00 (*92-821-1157-1*) OECD.

— Transport for People with Mobility Handicaps: Public Transport by Bus. 110p. (Orig.). 1991. pap. 16.00 (*92-821-1152-0*) OECD.

— Utility Pricing & Access: Competition for Monopolies. 45p. (Orig.). 1991. pap. 16.00 (*92-64-13464-6*) OECD.

Organisation for Economic Cooperation & Development Staff & Lubell, Harold. The Informal Sector in the 1980s & 1990s. 128p. (Orig.). 1991. pap. 21.00 (*92-64-13475-1*) OECD.

Organisation for Economic Cooperation & Development Staff & Pickett, J. Economic Development in Ethiopia: Agriculture, the Market & the State. 198p. (Orig.). 1991. pap. 36.00 (*92-64-13572-3*) OECD.

Organisation for Economic Cooperation & Development Staff, et al. Financial Systems & Development: What Role for the Formal & Informal Financial Sectors? 253p. (Orig.). 1991. pap. 34.00 (*92-64-13472-7*) OECD.

Organization for Economic Co-Operation & Development Staff. Challenge & Opportunities for Tomorrow. (Road Transport Research 20th Anniversary Seminar Ser.). 180p. (Orig.). 1989. pap. 21.00 (*92-64-13208-2*) OECD.

Organization for Economic Co-Operation & Development, Transborder Data Flow Symposium Staff. Transborder Data Flows: Proceedings of an OECD Conference Held December 1983. Gassmann, Hans P., ed. LC 85-1482. 504p. 1985. 102.75 (*0-444-87700-2*, North Holland) Elsevier.

Organization for Economic Cooperation & Development Staff. The Automobile & the Environment: An International Perspective. (Transportation Studies). 1978. 55.00 (*0-262-07070-7*) MIT Pr.

— The Economy of the U. S. S. R. IMF-WB-OECD-ERBD. 51p. (Orig.). 1991. pap. 15.95 (*92-64-13453-0*) OECD.

— Enterprising Women: Local Initiatives for Job Creation. 100p. (Orig.). 1991. pap. 20.00 (*92-64-13436-0*) OECD.

— Environmental Policies for Cities in the 1990s. 91p. (Orig.). 1991. pap. 21.00 (*92-64-13435-2*) OECD.

— Migration: The Demographic Aspects, Demographic Change & Public Policy. 78p. (Orig.). 1991. pap. 26.00 (*92-64-13439-5*) OECD.

— Multilingual Dictionary of Fish & Fish Products. 3rd ed. 464p. 1990. 69.95 (*0-85238-164-6*) Blackwell Sci.

— The Teacher Today. 140p. (Orig.). 1991. pap. 20.00 (*92-64-13413-1*) OECD.

Organization for Obstetric, Gynecologic & Neonatal Nurses Staff. Core Curriculum for Maternal-Newborn Nursing. Mattson, Susan & Smith, Judy E., eds. (Illus.). 816p. 1992. pap. text ed. 54.50 (*0-7216-3122-3*) Saunders.

— Core Curriculum for Neonatal Intensive Care Nursing. Beachy, Patricia O. & Deacon, Jane, eds. (Illus.). 746p. 1992. pap. text ed. 55.50 (*0-7216-3121-5*) Saunders.

Organization of American States - Bogota Staff. American Treaty of Peaceful Settlement: Pact of Bogota. rev. ed. (Treaty Ser.: No. 17). (ENG, FRE, POR & SPA.). 1978. pap. 1.00 (*0-8270-0355-2*) OAS.

Organization of American States Editors. Index to Latin American Periodical Literature, 1929-1960, 8 Vols, Set. 1970. lib. bdg. 595.00 (*0-8161-0501-4*, Hall Library) G K Hall.

— Index to Latin American Periodical Literature, 1961-1965, 2 Vols, Set. 1970. lib. bdg. 240.00 (*0-8161-0768-8*, Hall Library) G K Hall.

— Index to Latin American Periodical Literature, 1966-1970. 1980. lib. bdg. 220.00 (*0-8161-0314-3*, Hall Library) G K Hall.

— Index to Latin American Periodicals Literature, 1961, Set. 1970. 90.00 (*0-685-01809-1*, Hall Library) G K Hall.

— Index to Latin American Periodicals Literature, 1961, Vol. 1. 1970. lib. bdg. 100.00 (*0-8161-0502-2*, Hall Library) G K Hall.

— Index to Latin American Periodicals Literature, 1961, Vol. 2. 1970. lib. bdg. 95.00 (*0-8161-0236-8*, Hall Library) G K Hall.

Organization of American States General Secretariat, Dept. of Echnological & Scientific Affairs Staff. Biogeografia de America Latina. 2nd ed. (Serie de Biologia: No. 13). (Illus.). 122p. (SPA.). (C). 1980. pap. 3.50 (*0-8270-1233-0*) OAS.

Organization of American States General Secretariat Staff, ed. see Piscoya, Francisco M.

Organization of American States Staff. Charter of the Organization of American States, Bogota, 1948. (Treaty Ser.: No. 1). (ENG, FRE, POR & SPA.). 1948. pap. 1.00 (*0-8270-0245-9*) OAS.

— Sectoral Study of Transnational Enterprises in Latin America: The Banana Industry. 1978. reprint ed. pap. text ed. 5.00 (*0-685-03624-3*); reprint ed. Span. Ed. write for info. (*0-8270-3310-9*) OAS.

Organization of Peace Commission. Building Peace: Reports of the Commission to Study the Organization of Peace, 1939-1972, 2 vols, Set. LC 73-4845. 1973. reprint ed. 65.00 (*0-8108-0621-5*) Scarecrow.

Organization of Peace Commission & Holcombe, Arthur N. Strengthening the United Nations. LC 74-7536. 276p. 1976. reprint ed. text ed. 65.00 (*0-8371-7579-8*, HOUN, Greenwood Pr) Greenwood.

Organization of the Petroleum Exporting Countries Seminar Staff. OPEC & Future Energy Markets: Proceedings of the OPEC Seminar, Vienna, Austria, October 1979. 300p. 1981. text ed. 39.95 (*0-312-58611-6*) St Martin.

Organization of the Petroleum Exporting Countries Staff. Selected Documents of the International Petroleum Industry: 1966-1978 (with Pre-1966 Reports), 15 bks., Set. 1983. reprint ed. 465.00 (*0-89941-291-2*, 201610) W S Hein.

Organization of the Petroleum Exporting Countries, Vienna, Austria Staff. OPEC Official Resolutions & Press Releases, 1960-1983. 226p. 1984. pap. 99.00 (*0-08-031122-9*, Pub. by Pergamon Repr UK) Franklin.

Organizations for Professional Women Staff, jt. auth. see American Psychological Association, Women.

O

An Asterisk (*) at the beginning of an entry indicates that the title is appearing in BIP for the first time.

Organizers Against Deportation & Refugees in Oakdale CA. On Loving Neighbors & Aliens. (Common Ground Ser.: Vol. II). (Illus.). 24p. (Orig.). 1986. pap. 5.00 (*1-884478-01-8*) Common Grnd.

Organos, Minnie, ed. Catalog of the Dental School Library, 8 vols., Set. 1978. lib. bdg. 825.00 (*0-8161-0239-2*, Hall Library) G K Hall.

Organski, A. F. The Thirty Six Billion Dollar Bargain. 315p. 1991. pap. text ed. 15.00 (*0-231-07197-3*) Col U Pr.

Organski, A. F. & Kugler, Jacek. The War Ledger. LC 79-23366. (Illus.). 1981. pap. text ed. 11.95 (*0-226-63280-6*) U Ch Pr.

Organski, A. F., et al. Births, Deaths, & Taxes: The Demographic & Political Transitions. LC 83-17989. 144p. (C). 1984. lib. bdg. 20.00 (*0-226-63281-4*) U Ch Pr.

Organski, A. F. K. Hose & Tubing Markets P-122. 123p. 1990. 1,950.00 (*0-685-45625-0*) BCC.

— The Thirty-Six Billion Dollar Bargain: Strategy & Politics in U. S. Assistance to Israel. 1990. text ed. 39.50 (*0-231-07196-5*) Col U Pr.

Orgebin Crist, M. C. & Danzo, B. J., eds. Cell Biology of the Testis & Epididymis. (Annals Ser.: Vol. 513). (Illus.). 622p. 1987. 155.00 (*0-89766-422-1*) NY Acad Sci.

***Orgel, Dorio.** The Devil in Vienna. 1995. 17.75 (*0-8446-6797-8*) Peter Smith.

Orgel, Doris. Ariadne, Awake! LC 93-24123. (Illus.). 80p. (J). (ps-3). 1994. lib. bdg. 15.99 (*0-670-85158-2*) Viking Child Bks.

— Button Soup. LC 93-14087. (Bank Street Ready-to-Read Ser.). (Illus.). (J). 1994. 10.95 (*0-553-09045-3*); mass mkt. 3.99 (*0-553-37341-2*) Bantam.

— Crack in the Heart. (YA). (gr. 7 up). 1989. pap. 2.95 (*0-449-70204-9*, Juniper) Fawcett.

— Devil in Vienna. (J). 1988. pap. 4.99 (*0-14-032500-X*, Puffin) Puffin Bks.

— The Flower of Sheba. LC 92-33477. (Bank Street Ready-to-Read Ser.). (J). (ps-3). 1994. 10.95 (*0-553-09041-0*) Bantam.

— The Mouse Who Wanted to Marry. LC 92-10741. (J). 1993. mass mkt. 9.99 (*0-553-09235-9*); mass mkt. 3.99 (*0-553-37143-6*) Bantam.

— Nobodies & Somebodies. 160p. (J). (gr. 3-7). 1993. pap. 3.99 (*0-14-034098-X*, Puffin) Puffin Bks.

— Sarah's Room. LC 63-13675. (Illus.). (J). (gr. k-3). 1963. 11.95 (*0-06-024605-7*) HarpC Child Bks.

— Sarah's Room. LC 63-13675. (Illus.). 48p. (J). (gr. k-3). 1963. lib. bdg. 14.89 (*0-06-024606-5*) HarpC Child Bks.

— The Spaghetti Party. LC 94-9788. (Bank Street Ready-to-Read Ser.). (J). 1995. pap. 12.95 (*0-553-09052-6*); mass mkt. 3.99 (*0-553-37571-7*) Bantam.

— Two Crows Counting. LC 94-32240. (Bank Street Ready-to-Read Ser.). (Illus.). 1995. mass mkt. 3.99 (*0-553-37573-3*) Bantam.

— Two Crows Counting. LC 94-32240. (Bank Street Ready-to-Read Ser.). (Illus.). (J). 1995. pap. 13.95 (*0-553-09741-5*) Bantam.

Orgel, Doris & Schecter, Ellen. The Flower of Sheba. LC 92-33477. (Bank Street Ready-to-Read Ser.). (Illus.). (J). 1994. 3.50 (*0-553-37235-1*, Little Rooster) Bantam.

Orgel, Irene. Odd Tales of Irene Orgel. LC 67-14531. 116p. 1966. 30.00 (*0-87130-015-X*) Eakins.

Orgel, Shelly & Fine, Bernard D., eds. Clinical Psychoanalysis. LC 79-51910. (Downstate Psychoanalytic Institute Twenty-Fifth Anniversary Ser: Vol. III). 360p. 1979. 45.00 (*0-87668-368-5*) Aronson.

Orgel, Stephen. Christopher Marlowe: The Complete Poems & Translation. (Poetry Library). 1980. pap. 9.95 (*0-14-042267-6*, Penguin Classics) Viking Penguin.

— The Illusion of Power: Political Theater in the English Renaissance. 95p. 1991. reprint ed. pap. 13.00 (*0-520-02741-8*) U CA Pr.

— The Jonsonian Masque. LC 81-6174. (Morningside Bk.). (Illus.). 240p. 1981. reprint ed. text ed. 43.50 (*0-231-05370-3*); reprint ed. pap. text ed. 18.00 (*0-231-05371-1*) Col U Pr.

Orgel, Stephen & Goldberg, Jonathan, eds. John Milton. (Poetry Library). 352p. 1994. pap. 7.95 (*0-19-282304-3*) OUP.

Orgel, Stephen, ed. see Cole, Phyllis.

Orgel, Stephen, ed. see Gordon, D. J.

Orgel, Stephen, ed. see Jonson, Ben.

Orgel, Stephen, jt. ed. see Lytle, Guy F.

Orgel, Stephen, ed. see Milton, John.

Orgel, Stephen, ed. see Shakespeare, William.

Orgel, Stephen, ed. see Wharton, Edith.

Orgelfinger, Gail, ed. The Hystorye of Olyuer of Castylle. LC 88-7223. (Medieval Texts Ser.: Vol. 14). 291p. 1988. lib. bdg. 20.00 (*0-8240-8500-0*, 746) Garland.

Orgill, Andrew. The Falklands War: Background, Conflict, Aftermath: An Annotated Bibliography. 128p. 1993. text ed. 60.00 (*0-7201-2130-2*, Mansell Pub) Cassell.

— The Nineteen Ninety-Ninety One Gulf War: Crisis, Conflict, Aftermath: An Annotated Bibliography. LC 94-28447. 1995. 80.00 (*0-7201-2174-4*, Mansell Pub) Cassell.

Orgill, Douglas. The Gothic Line. 352p. 1986. pap. 3.95 (*0-8217-1916-5*) Zebra.

Orgogozo, J. M. & Dyken, M., eds. Advances in Stroke Prevention: Sanofi-Winthrop Symposium, Second European Stroke Conference, Lausanne, June 1992. (Journal: Cerebrovascular Diseases: Vol. 3, Suppl. 1, 1993). (Illus.). iv, 44p. 1993. pap. 19.25 (*3-8055-5787-6*) S Karger.

Orgogozo, J. M. & Gottfries, C. G., eds. Progress in Dementia Research. (New Trends in Clinical Neurology Ser.). (Illus.). 144p. 1990. 65.00 (*1-85070-319-1*) Prthnon Pub.

***Orgogozo, J. M. & Lenzi, G. L., eds.** Assessment of Stroke Outcome: Round Table. (Journal: Cerebrovascular Diseases Ser.: Vol. 4, Suppl. 2, 1994). (Illus.). iv, 30p. 1994. pap. 13.75 (*3-8055-6064-8*) S Karger.

Orhbach, Frank, jt. auth. see Hughes, Megan.

Orhelein, Ann, ed. see Perez, Ramon.

Orhon, D., et al, eds. Waste Management Problems in Agro-Industries: Proceedings of an IAWPRC Symposium Held in Istanbul, Turkey, 25-27 September 1989. (Water Science & Technology Ser.: WST 22). 1990. pap. 130.00 (*0-08-040778-1*, Pergamon Pr) Elsevier.

— Waste Management Problems in Agro-Industries 1992. (Water Science & Technology Ser.). 286p. 1993. pap. 110.00 (*0-08-042349-3*, Pergamon Pr) Elsevier.

***Orhon, Derin & Artan, Nazik.** Modelling of Activated Sludge Systems. (Illus.). 585p. 1994. 95.00 (*1-56676-101-8*) Technomic.

Ori, Kan, jt. auth. see Benjamin, Roger.

Oria, Tomas G. Marti y el Krausismo. LC 86-63038. 176p. (SPA.). 1987. pap. 30.00 (*0-89295-047-1*) Society Sp & Sp-Am.

Oriani, Richard A., et al, eds. Hydrogen Degradation of Ferrous Alloys. LC 85-4932. (Illus.). 886p. 1985. 84.00 (*0-8155-1027-6*) Noyes.

Orianne, Andre, tr. see Levinas, Emmanuel.

Orians, Betty, ed. see University of Washington, Faculty Auxiliary Staff.

Orians, Gordon H. Blackbirds of the Americas. LC 85-40352. (Illus.). 164p. 1985. 35.00 (*0-295-96253-4*) U of Wash Pr.

— Some Adaptations of Marsh-Nesting Blackbirds. LC 79-84005. (Monographs in Population Biology: No. 14). (Illus.). 1980. 49.50 (*0-691-08236-7*); pap. 17.95 (*0-691-08237-5*) Princeton U Pr.

Orians, Gordon H., et al, eds. The Preservation & Valuation of Biological Resources. LC 90-12118. 304p. 1990. 40.00 (*0-295-97004-9*) U of Wash Pr.

Orians, Thomas, jt. ed. see Leopold, Kathleen.

Oriard, Michael. Dreaming of Heroes. LC 81-16877. 384p. 1982. 33.95 (*0-88229-588-8*) Nelson-Hall.

— Reading Football: How the Popular Press Created an American Spectacle. LC 92-42840. (Cultural Studies of the United States). xxviii, 320p. (C). 1993. 29.95 (*0-8078-2083-0*) U of NC Pr.

— Sporting with the Gods: The Rhetoric of Play & Game in American Literature. (Cambridge Studies in Latin American LIterature & Culture: No. 45). (Illus.). 500p. (C). 1991. 59.95 (*0-521-39113-X*) Cambridge U Pr.

Oribe, Jose. The Fine Guitar. 96p. 1985. 19.95 (*0-9615906-1-0*) Vel-or Co.

Oribello, William. Sacred Magic. 100p. 6.95 (*0-938294-26-1*) Glob Comm-Inner Lght.

— The Sealed Magical Book of Moses. (Illus.). 96p. 5.00 (*0-938294-68-7*) Glob Comm-Inner Lght.

Oribello, William A. Candle Burning Magic with the Psalms. 100p. 1988. pap. 5.00 (*0-938294-58-X*) Glob Comm-Inner Lght.

Orichowski, Rose M., jt. auth. see Johnson, Rachel P.

***Orie, Sandra.** Did You Hear Wind Sing Your Name? (Illus.). 32p. (J). 1995. 14.95 (*0-8027-8350-3*); lib. bdg. 15.85 (*0-8027-8351-1*) Walker & Co.

Oriel, Charles. Writing & Inscription in Golden Age Drama. LC 92-26368. (Studies in Romance Literatures). 200p. 1992. 26.00 (*1-55753-019-X*) Purdue U Pr.

— Writing & Inscription in Golden Age Drama. LC 92-26368. (Studies in Romance Literatures). 200p. 1992. reprint ed. pap. 18.95 (*1-55753-074-2*) Purdue U Pr.

Oriel, D., et al, eds. Chlamydial Infections. 595p. 1986. 99.95 (*0-521-32453-X*) Cambridge U Pr.

Oriel, J. D. The Scars of Venus: A History of Venereology. LC 93-34554. vii, 248p. 1994. 98.00 (*0-387-19844-X*) Spr-Verlag.

***O'Rielly, Terence.** From Ignatius to John of the Cross. (Collected Studies: Vol. CS484). 300p. 1995. 80.95 (*0-86078-459-2*, Pub. by Variorum UK) Ashgate Pub Co.

Orient, Grand. The Book of Destiny & the Art of Reading Therein. 277p. 1986. spiral bd. 19.25 (*0-7873-0647-9*) Mokelumne.

— A Handbook of Cartomancy: Fortune-Telling & Occult Divination. 114p. 1966. reprint ed. spiral bd. 4.95 (*0-7873-0645-2*) Mokelumne.

— A Manual of Cartomancy, Fortune-Telling & Occult Divination. 278p. 1969. reprint ed. spiral bd. 7.15 (*0-7873-0646-0*) Mokelumne.

— The Occult Science of Jewels: The Symbolism of Precious Stones. Holmes, J. D., ed. Date not set. pap. 6.95 (*1-55818-316-7*, Sure Fire) Holmes Pub.

Orient, Jane M. Your Doctor Is Not In: Healthy Skepticism about National Health Care. LC 93-38180. 1994. 23.00 (*0-517-59011-5*, Crown) Crown Pub Group.

Orient, Jane M., jt. auth. see Sapira, Joseph D.

Oriental Division of the New York Public Library Staff, jt. auth. see LC Marc Tapes Staff.

Oriental Institute Staff. The Nineteen Hundred Five - Nineteen Hundred Seven Breasted Expeditions to Egypt & the Sudan: A Photographic Study, 2 vols., Vol. 1. LC 76-22621. (Illus.). 1976. fiche, lib. bdg. 12.50 (*0-226-69471-2*) U Ch Pr.

— The Nineteen Hundred Five - Nineteen Hundred Seven Breasted Expeditions to Egypt & the Sudan: A Photographic Study, 2 vols., Vol. 2. LC 76-22621. (Illus.). 1976. fiche, lib. bdg. 12.50 (*0-226-69472-0*) U Ch Pr.

— The Nineteen Nineteen to Nineteen Twenty Breasted Expedition to the Near East. LC 77-2731. 1978. Incl. 2 black & white fiches. fiche, lib. bdg. 17.00 (*0-226-69473-9*) U Ch Pr.

— Persepolis & Ancient Iran. LC 76-7942. 1976. lib. bdg. 55.00 (*0-226-69493-3*) U Ch Pr.

— Studies in Honor of John A. Wilson. LC 76-81081. 1969. pap. text ed. 9.00 (*0-226-62408-0*, SAOC35) U Ch Pr.

Oriental Institute Staff & Nasgowitz, David. Ptolemais Cyrenaica. LC 80-26769. (Illus.). 75p. 1981. lib. bdg. 50.00 (*0-226-69474-7*) U Ch Pr.

Orieux, Jean. L' Aigle de Fer. (FRE.). 1985. pap. 17.95 (*0-7859-4234-3*) Fr & Eur.

Oriev, Uri. Island on Bird Street. (J). (gr. 4-7). 1992. pap. 4.95 (*0-395-61623-9*) HM.

Origen. Commentary on the Gospel According to John, Bks. 1-10. Heine, Ronald E., tr. LC 88-20406. (Fathers of the Church Ser.: Vol. 80). 344p. 1989. 34.95 (*0-8132-0080-6*) Cath U Pr.

— Commentary on the Gospel According to John, Books 13-32. Heine, Ronald, tr. LC 88-20406. (Fathers of the Church Ser.: Vol. 89). 432p. 1993. 34.95 (*0-8132-0089-X*) Cath U Pr.

— Homilies on Genesis & Exodus. LC 82-4124. (Fathers of the Church Ser.: Vol. 71). 422p. (C). 1982. 29.95 (*0-8132-0071-7*) Cath U Pr.

— Homilies on Leviticus. LC 89-78173. (Fathers of the Church Ser.: Vol. 83). 294p. 1990. 31.95 (*0-8132-0083-0*) Cath U Pr.

— On First Principles: Being Koetschau's Text of the De Principiis. Butterworth, G. W., tr. 14.00 (*0-8446-2685-6*) Peter Smith.

— The Philocalia of Origen. LC 80-2359. reprint ed. 39.50 (*0-404-18911-3*) AMS Pr.

Origen, et al. The Pilgrim Road. Roberts, Alexnder et al, trs. 192p. (Orig.). 1991. pap. 7.95 (*0-924722-04-5*) Scroll Pub.

Origenes. Hexaplorum Quae Supersunt, 2 vols., Set. ci, 1918p. 1964. reprint ed. write for info. (*0-318-70992-9*, Pub. by Georg Olms GW) Lubrecht & Cramer.

Original Publications, tr. Helping Yourself With Selected Prayers. 1984. pap. 4.95 (*0-942272-01-3*) Original Pubns.

Origo, Iris. War in Val d'Orcia: An Italian War Diary, 1943-1944. LC 82-49344. 256p. 1984. pap. 13.95 (*0-87923-476-8*) Godine.

Orihara, Kei. Children of the World: Thailand. LC 88-21050. (Illus.). 64p. (J). (gr. 5-6). 1988. lib. bdg. 21.26 (*1-55532-223-9*) Gareth Stevens Inc.

Orihel, jt. auth. see Ash, Lawrence.

Orihel, Thomas & Ash, Lawrence. Parasites in Human Tissues. (Illus.). 300p. 1995. 165.00 (*0-89189-379-2*) Am Soc Clinical.

Orihel, Thomas C., jt. auth. see Ash, Lawrence R.

Oriji, John N. Traditions of Igbo Origin: A Study of Pre-Colonial Population Movements in Africa. rev. ed. LC 93-43268. (Am. Univ. Studies, XI: Vol. 48). 234p. (C). 1994. pap. text ed. 24.95 (*0-8204-2481-1*) P Lang Pubs.

***O'Riley, Ronald P.** Electrical Grounding: Bringing Grounding Back to Earth. 4th ed. LC 95-13272. 1996. write for info. (*0-8273-6657-4*) Delmar.

— Electrical Grounding: Bringing Grounding Back to Earth, Based on the 1933 National Electric Code. 3rd ed. LC 92-36735. 278p. 1993. pap. text ed. 23.95 (*0-8273-5248-4*) Delmar.

— Illustrated Changes in the National Electrical Code, 1993. LC 92-17310. 1992. pap. text ed. 20.95 (*0-8273-5304-9*) Delmar.

— Illustrated Changes in the 1993 National Electrical Code: Instructor's Guide. 1993. teacher ed 12.00 (*0-8273-5616-1*); trans. 225.00 (*0-8273-5615-3*) Delmar.

— Illustrated Changes in the 1996 National Electrical Code. LC 95-7607. (Illus.). 1995. write for info. (*0-8273-6773-2*) Delmar.

Orilia, Lawrence S. Structured BASIC. 384p. 1984. text ed. 34.95 (*0-07-047839-2*) McGraw.

Orimalade, Adeyinka. Petroleum Refining in Africa: Origin, Growth & Prospects. (C). 1989. 22.00 (*81-7023-211-2*, Pub. by Allied II) S Asia.

***Orimo, H., ed.** Fifth Symposium by the Nine Winners of the Grants from Sandoz Foundation for Gerontological Research: Annual Meeting of the Japan Gerontological Society, Sapporo, Japan, September 1993, No. 40. (Journal: Gerontology: Supplement 2, 1994). (Illus.). iv, 72p. 1994. pap. 30.50 (*3-8055-6044-3*) S Karger.

— The First Symposium by the Six Winners of the Grants from Sandoz Foundation for Gerontological Research: Annual Meeting of the Japan Gerontological Society, Nagoya, Japan, November 1989 - Journal: Gerontology, Vol. 36, Suppl. 1, 1990. (Illus.) vi, 50p. 1990. pap. 22.50 (*3-8055-5240-8*) S Karger.

— Fourth Symposium by the Five Winners of the Grants from Sandoz Foundation for Gerontological Research, Annual Meeting of the Japan Gerontological Society, Kanazawa, Japan, November 1992. (Journal: Gerontology: Vol. 39, Suppl. 1, 1993). (Illus.). vi, 38p. 1993. pap. 13.00 (*3-8055-5823-6*) S Karger.

— The Second Symposium by the Eight Winners of the Grants from Sandoz Foundation for Gerontological Research: Annual Meeting of the Japan Gerontological Society, Kochi-Japan, November 1990 - Journal: Gerontology, Vol. 37, Suppl. 1, 1991. (Illus.). iv, 64p. 1991. pap. 19.25 (*3-8055-5473-7*) S Karger.

— Third Symposium by the Seven Winners of the Grants from Sandoz Foundation for Gerontological Research, Annual Meeting of the Japan Gerontological Society, Yokohama, November 1991. (Journal: Gerontology: Vol. 38, Suppl. 1, 1992). (Illus.). vi, 50p. 1992. pap. 16.00 (*3-8055-5661-6*) S Karger.

Oring, Elliott. Folk Groups & Folklore Genres: An Introduction. (Illus.). 258p. (Orig.). 1986. pap. text ed. 19.95 (*0-87421-128-X*) Utah St U Pr.

— Humor & the Individual. LC 84-70061. (Orig.). 1984. pap. 8.95 (*0-914563-02-5*) CA Folklore Soc.

— Israeli Humor: The Content & Structure of the Chizbat of the Palmah. LC 80-25483. (SUNY Series in Modern Jewish Literature & Culture). 295p. 1981. 64.50 (*0-87395-512-9*); pap. 21.95 (*0-87395-513-7*) State U NY Pr.

— Jokes & Their Relations. LC 91-35254. 184p. 1992. text ed. 23.00 (*0-8131-1774-7*) U Pr of Ky.

Oring, Elliott, ed. Folk Groups & Folklore Genres: A Reader. 384p. 1989. pap. text ed. 19.95 (*0-87421-140-9*) Utah St U Pr.

Oring, Stuart A. Understanding Pictures: Theories, Exercises, & Procedures. enl. rev. ed. LC 91-75593. (Illus.). 233p. 1992. reprint ed. teacher ed 7.00 (*0-685-71434-9*); reprint ed. spiral bd. 33.00 (*0-9630896-0-9*) ISIS Visual.

Oringel, Robert. Television Operations Handbook. LC 84-10140. (Illus.). 208p. (Orig.). (C). 1984. pap. 26.95 (*0-240-51734-2*, Focal) Buttrwrth-Heinemann.

Oringel, Robert S. Audio Control Handbook. 6th ed. (Illus.). 304p. 1989. pap. 34.95 (*0-240-80015-X*, Focal) Buttrwrth-Heinemann.

— Audio Control Handbook: For Radio & Television Broadcasting. 5th enl. rev. ed. LC 83-6131. (Communication Arts Bks.). (Illus.). 380p. 1983. pap. text ed. 16.00 (*0-8038-0550-0*) Hastings.

Oriol, William, et al. Preparing for an Aging Society: Changes & Challenges. 68p. 1992. 7.50 (*0-910883-63-7*) Natl Coun Aging.

Oriol, William E. Aging in All Nations: A Special Report on the United Nations World Assembly on Aging. Incl. Aging in North America. 1982. (*0-318-56805-5*); 200p. 1982. Set pap. 14.00 (*0-910883-00-9*, 4166) Natl Coun Aging.

Oriol, William E., comp. Federal Public Policy on Aging since 1960: An Annotated Bibliography. LC 87-8343. (Bibliographies & Indexes in Gerontology Ser.: No. 5). 141p. 1987. text ed. 55.00 (*0-313-25286-6*, OPP/, Greenwood Pr) Greenwood.

Orion Agency, Inc. Staff. Obtaining Your Private Investigator's License. 64p. (Orig.). 1986. pap. 10.00 (*0-87364-390-9*) Paladin Pr.

Orion, Dave. The Ethereal Corridors: Power of the Crystal. Ingram, tr. 310p. 1995. pap. 9.95 (*1-56901-237-7*) NW Pub.

Orion, Gertrude. Pronouncing American English: Sounds, Stress, & Intonation. 321p. (C). 1987. pap. 22.95 (*0-8384-2699-9*, Newbury); teacher ed, pap. 8.95 (*0-8384-2696-4*, Newbury); audio 200.00 (*0-8384-2697-2*, Newbury) Heinle & Heinle.

Orion, Janice, tr. see Calame, Claude.

***Orion, Loretta.** Never Again the Burning Times: Paganism Revived. (Illus.). 322p. (Orig.). (C). 1995. pap. text ed. 11.95x (*0-88133-835-4*) Waveland Pr.

Orion Research Corporation Staff, comp. Orion Office Equipment Blue Book, 1991. 192p. 1992. 200.00 (*0-932089-43-7*) Orion Res.

Orion Research Corporation Staff, ed. Orion Computer Blue Book, 1991. 732p. 1991. 200.00 (*0-932089-50-X*) Orion Res.

***Oriordan.** Perceiving Environmental Risks. 1995. pap. text ed. 24.95 (*0-12-527840-3*) Acad Pr.

O'Riordan, Brian, jt. auth. see Meyer, Bruce.

O'Riordan, J., et al. Essentials of Endocrinology. 2nd ed. 1988. pap. 37.95 (*0-632-02112-8*) Blackwell Sci.

***O'Riordan, T.** Perceiving Environmental Risks. (Readings in Environmental Psychology Ser.). (Illus.). 256p. 1995. boxed 24.95 (*0-614-01339-9*) Acad Pr.

— Perceiving Environmental Risks. (Readings in Environmental Psychology Ser.). (Illus.). 320p. 1995. boxed 24.95 (*0-614-05261-0*) Acad Pr.

O'Riordan, Timothy, ed. Environmental Science for Environmental Management. LC 94-8529. 1994. pap. text ed. 39.95 (*0-470-23407-5*) Halsted Pr.

— Progress in Resource Management & Environmental Planning, 4 vols., Vol. 1. LC 80-646092. 335p. reprint ed. pap. 87.10 (*0-8357-4623-2*, 2037555) Bks Demand.

— Progress in Resource Management & Environmental Planning, 4 vols., Vol. 2. LC 80-646092. 256p. reprint ed. pap. 73.00 (*0-8357-4624-0*) Bks Demand.

— Progress in Resource Management & Environmental Planning, 4 vols., Vol. 3. LC 80-646092. 340p. reprint ed. pap. 96.90 (*0-8357-4625-9*) Bks Demand.

— Progress in Resource Management & Environmental Planning, 4 vols., Vol. 4. LC 80-646092. 322p. reprint ed. pap. 91.80 (*0-8357-4626-7*) Bks Demand.

O'Riordan, Timothy & Sewell, W. R., eds. Project Appraisal & Policy Review. LC 80-40847. (Wiley Series on Studies in Environmental Management & Resource Development). (Illus.). 316p. reprint ed. pap. 90.10 (*0-8357-4622-4*, 2037554) Bks Demand.

O'Riordan, Timothy & Turner, K., eds. An Annotated Reader in Environmental Planning & Management. LC 82-7569. (Urban & Regional Planning Ser.: Vol. 30). (Illus.). 484p. 1983. 196.00 (*0-08-024669-9*, Pub. by Pergamon Repr UK) Franklin.

O'Riordan, Timothy & Weale, Albert. The New Politics of Pollution. (Issues in Environmental Politics Ser.). (Illus.). 208p. 1992. text ed. 49.95 (*0-7190-3066-8*, Pub. by Manchester Univ Pr UK); pap. 14.95 (*0-7190-3067-6*, Pub. by Manchester Univ Pr UK) St Martin.

O'Riordan, Timothy, jt. auth. see Cameron, James.

O'Riordan, Timothy, ed. see Kemp, Ray.

O'Riordan, Timothy, ed. see Robinson, Mike.

O'Riordan, Timothy, jt. ed. see Watson, J. Wreford.

O'Riordan, Timothy, ed. see Wiesenthal, Helmut.

Oriowski, S. & Schaller, K. H. Objectives, Standards & Criteria for Radioactive Waste Disposal in the E.C., No. EUR 12570. 89p. 1990. pap. 9.00 (*92-826-0994-4*, CD-NA-12570-EN-C) UNIPUB.

Orishagbemi, Babatudne. In Front of Lincoln. 1991. 13.95 (*0-533-09002-4*) Vantage.

Orishimo, I., et al, eds. Information Technology: Social & Spatial Perspectives. (Lecture Notes in Economics & Mathematical Systems Ser.: Vol. 315). vi, 268p. 1988. pap. 38.70 (*0-387-50158-4*) Spr-Verlag.

O

Orishimo, Isao. Urbanization & Environmental Quality. (Studies in Applied Regional Science). 192p. 1982. lib. bdg. 49.50 (*0-89838-080-4*) Kluwer Ac.
Oritz-Franco, Luis, et al, eds. Discrimination & Prejudice: An Annotated Bibliography. LC 92-11244. 312p. 1992. 89.95 (*0-942259-03-3*); pap. 59.95 (*0-942259-02-5*) Westerfield Enter.
Oritz, Simon J. From Sand Creek. 96p. (Orig.). 1981. pap. 6.95 (*0-938410-00-8*) Thunders Mouth.
Orizet, Jean. Tiers of Survival: Selected Poems. DeWees, Aletha, tr. Orig. Title: Niveaux de Survie. 120p. (Orig.). 1984. pap. 8.00 (*0-939378-03-5*) Mundus Artium.
Orjuela, Hector, ed. see Silva, Jose A.
Orkand, Robert, jt. auth. see Bogot, Howard.
Orkeny, Istvan. The Flower Show-The Toth Family. Heim, Michael & Gyorgyey, Clara, trs. LC 81-22373. 160p. 1982. 14.95 (*0-8112-0836-2*); pap. 6.95 (*0-8112-0837-0*, NDP536) New Directions.
— Unuminutaj Noveloj. Ertl, Istvan, ed. 120p. 1995. pap. 7.95 (*1-882251-06-7*) Eldonejo Bero.
Orkin. Can You Win? (C). 1995. pap. text ed. write for info. (*0-7167-2155-4*) W H Freeman.
Orkin & Maibach. Cutaneous Infestations & Insect Bites. LC 84-22977. (Dermatology Ser.: Vol. 4). 368p. 1985. 140.00 (*0-8247-7273-3*) Dekker.
Orkin, M. Mark & Bickerstaff, Isaac. Conserve Tuvs, Eh? (Illus.). 96p. 1986. pap. 9.95 (*0-7737-5077-0*, Pub. by Stoddart Pubng CN) Genl Dist Srvs.
Orkin, Mark. Disinvestment, the Struggle, & the Future: What Black South Africans Really Think. 78p. 1986. pap. text ed. 7.95 (*0-86975-305-3*, Pub. by Ravan Pr ZA) Ohio U Pr.
Orkin, Mark, ed. Sanctions Against Apartheid. LC 89-28795. 256p. 1990. text ed. 55.00 (*0-312-04143-8*) St Martin.
Orkin, Mark M. Speaking Canadian English: An Informal Account of the English Language in Canada. 276p. 1970. 7.95 (*0-7736-0014-0*, Pub. by Stoddart Pubng CN) Genl Dist Srvs.
Orkin, Martin. Drama & the South African State. Dollimore, Jonathan & Sinfield, Alan, eds. LC 90-6556. (Cultural Politics Ser.). 192p. 1991. text ed. 59.95 (*0-7190-2576-1*, Pub. by Manchester Univ Pr UK); text ed. 16.95 (*0-7190-2577-X*, Pub. by Manchester Univ Pr UK) St Martin.
Orkin, Michael, jt. auth. see Hoffman, Laurence D.
Orkin, Milton, et al. Dermatology. (Illus.). 696p. (C). 1991. pap. text ed. 37.95 (*0-8385-1288-7*, A1288-8) Appleton & Lange.
Orkow, Ben. The First Actress. 1976. pap. 4.75 (*0-8222-0401-0*) Dramatists Play.
Orlady, Harry W., ed. see Hawkins, Frank H.
Orlan, Pierre M. A Bord de l'Etoile Matutine. (FRE.). 1983. pap. 10.95 (*0-7859-4188-6*) Fr & Eur.
— Le Bal du Pont du Nord Suivi d'Entre Deux Jours. (FRE.). 1984. pap. 11.95 (*0-7859-4208-4*) Fr & Eur.
— La Cavaliere Elsa. (FRE.). 1980. pap. 10.95 (*0-7859-4136-3*) Fr & Eur.
— Mademoiselle Bambu, Filles et Ports d'Europe-Pere Barbancon. (FRE.). 1982. pap. 10.95 (*0-7859-4163-0*) Fr & Eur.
— La Venus Internationale suivi de Dinah Miami. (FRE.). 1981. pap. 11.95 (*0-7859-4160-6*) Fr & Eur.
Orland, Henri, jt. auth. see Negele, John W.
Orland, Leonard. Prisons: Houses of Darkness. LC 75-8428. (Illus.). 1978. pap. 14.95 (*0-02-923420-4*) Free Pr.
***Orland, Leonard, ed.** Corporate & White Collar Crime: An Anthology. LC 95-11892. 1995. write for info. (*0-87084-870-4*) Anderson Pub Co.
Orland, Ted. Scenes of Wonder & Curiosity. LC 88-45333. (Illus.). 128p. 1988. 35.00 (*0-87923-768-6*) Godine.
Orland, Ted, jt. auth. see Bayles, David.
Orland, Ted, jt. auth. see Mazza, Cris.
Orland, Ted N. Man & Yosemite: A Photographer's View of the Early Years. (Illus.). 96p. (Orig.). 1985. 19.95 (*0-9614547-0-9*); pap. 10.95 (*0-9614547-1-7*) Image Continuum.
Orlandello, John. O'Neill on Film. LC 80-70627. 192p. 1982. 32.50 (*0-8386-2291-7*) Fairleigh Dickinson.
Orlandi, Camillo, et al, eds. Recent Advances in Prenatal Diagnosis: Proceedings of the First International Symposium on Recent Advances in Prenatal Diagnosis, Bologna, September 15-16, 1980. LC 81-198305. (Illus.). 344p. reprint ed. pap. 98.10 (*0-317-58634-3*, 2029638) Bks Demand.
Orlandi, F., jt. auth. see Tygstrup, N.
Orlandi, Mario, et al. Substance Abuse. (Encyclopedia of Health Ser.). (YA). (gr. 5 up). 1989. 18.95 (*0-8160-1669-0*) Facts on File.
— Exercise. (Encyclopedia of Good Health Ser.). (Illus.). 128p. 1988. 18.95 (*0-8160-1671-2*) Facts on File.
— Human Sexuality. (Encyclopedia of Good Health Ser.). (Illus.). 128p. (YA). 1989. 18.95 (*0-8160-1666-6*) Facts on File.
— Maintaining Good Health. (Encyclopedia of Health Ser.). 128p. (YA). (gr. 5 up). 1989. 18.95 (*0-8160-1667-4*) Facts on File.
— Nutrition. (Encyclopedia of Good Health Ser.). (Illus.). 128p. (YA). 1988. 18.95 (*0-8160-1670-4*) Facts on File.
— Stress & Mental Health. (Encyclopedia of Good Health Ser.). (Illus.). 128p. 1988. 18.95 (*0-8160-1668-2*) Facts on File.
Orlandi, Pellegrino A. Abcedario Pittorico. (Documents of Art & Architectural History Ser.: Vol. 6). (Illus.). 447p. (ITA.). 1981. reprint ed. lib. bdg. 50.00 (*0-89371-106-3*) Broude Intl Edns.
Orlandini, Paolo, jt. auth. see Lucci, Robert.
Orlandis, Jose. A Short History of the Catholic Church. Adams, Michael, tr. 163p. 1992. pap. 9.95 (*0-906127-86-6*, Pub. by Four Courts Pr EIRE) Scepter Pubs.
Orlando, tr. see Fisher, J., et al.
Orlando, A., ed. Cost 212: Human Factors in Information Services, EUR 13189. 125p. 1991. pap. 16.00 (*92-826-2020-4*, CD-NA-13189-EN-C) UNIPUB.
— Cost 212 Human Factors in Information Services, EUR 14277. 175p. 1992. 25.00 (*92-826-4132-5*, CG-NA-14277-EN-C, Pub. by Europ Com) UNIPUB.
Orlando, Dennis, jt. auth. see Erdos, Dawn.
Orlando, Francesco. Toward a Freudian Theory of Literature: With an Analysis of Racine's Phedre. Lee, Charmaine, tr. LC 78-7577. 224p. reprint ed. pap. 63.90 (*0-8357-6622-5*, 2035267) Bks Demand.
Orlando, Frank & Orlando, Regina. How to Own a New Home & Save Thousands: The Modular Home Manual. (Illus.). 113p. (Orig.). 1993. pap. 29.95 (*0-9642015-0-X*) Proven Methods.
Orlando, Jordon. The Object Lesson: A Novel. LC 93-12145. 560p. 1993. 23.00 (*0-671-66978-8*) S&S Trade.
Orlando, Joseph. The San Francisco Waterfront Cookbook. (Illus.). 144p. 1991. reprint ed. pap. 9.95 (*0-89087-652-5*) Celestial Arts.
Orlando, Joseph A. Cogeneration Planner's Handbook. 1991. 74.00 (*0-88173-111-0*) Fairmont Pr.
Orlando, Lou. The Ultimate Phillies Trivia Quiz. 80p. (Orig.). 1994. write for info. (*0-9641936-0-4*) Rockford Assocs.
Orlando, Regina, jt. auth. see Orlando, Frank.
Orlando, S., jt. auth. see Meyer, A.
Orlando, Terry P. & Delin, Kevin A. Foundations of Applied Superconductivity. (Electrical Engineering Ser.). (Illus.). 650p. (C). 1991. text ed. 72.25 (*0-201-18323-4*) Addison-Wesley.
Orlans, Barbara F. In the Name of Science: Issues in Responsible Animal Experimentation. LC 92-39344. (Illus.). 312p. 1993. 39.95 (*0-19-507043-7*) OUP.
Orlans, F. Barbara, ed. Field Research Guidelines: Impact on Animal Care & Use Committees. (Illus.). 23p. (Orig.). 1988. pap. text ed. 5.00 (*0-9620700-0-9*) Scientists Ctr.
Orlans, F. Barbara, jt. ed. see Dodds, W. Jean.
Orlans, Harold. Contracting for Atoms. LC 80-58. (Illus.). xvii, 242p. 1980. reprint ed. text ed. 69.50 (*0-313-22287-8*, ORCA, Greenwood Pr) Greenwood.
— Stevenage: A Sociological Study of a New Town. LC 71-139142. 313p. (C). 1971. reprint ed. text ed. 55.00 (*0-8371-5758-7*, ORST, Greenwood Pr) Greenwood.
Orlans, Harold, ed. Adjustment to Adult Hearing Loss. (Illus.). 204p. (C). 1991. reprint ed. pap. text ed. 29.95 (*1-879105-47-0*, A056) Singular Publishing.
Orlans, Harold, ed. see Lawrence, T. E.
Orlansky, Michael D., jt. auth. see Heward, William L.
Orlean, Rene, jt. auth. see Cooke, Barclay.
Orlean, Susan. Saturday Night. 1990. 19.95 (*0-317-99650-9*) Knopf.
— Saturday Night. 1991. mass mkt. 5.99 (*0-449-22001-X*) Fawcett.
Orleans, C. Tracy & Slade, John, eds. Nicotine Addiction: Principles & Management. LC 92-29443. (Illus.). 456p. 1993. 55.00 (*0-19-506441-0*) OUP.
Orleans, Charlotte-Elisabeth. A Woman's Life in the Court of the Sun King: Letters of Liselotte von der Pfalz, Elisabeth Charlotte, Duchesse d'Orleans, 1652-1722. Forster, Elborg, tr. & intro. by. LC 84-5718. 349p. reprint ed. pap. 99.50 (*0-7837-3391-7*, 2043349) Bks Demand.
Orleans, Ellen. Can't Keep a Straight Face: A Lesbian Looks & Laughs At Life. (Illus.). 128p. (Orig.). 1993. pap. 7.50 (*0-9632526-1-5*) Laugh Lines.
— Who Cares If Its a Choice? Snappy Answers to 101 Nosey, Intrusive & Highly Personal Questions about Lesbians & Gays. 96p. (Orig.). 1994. pap. 7.50 (*0-9632526-4-X*) Laugh Lines.
Orleans, Henri P. Around Tonkin & Siam. Pitman, C. B., tr. LC 77-87071. (Illus.). reprint ed. 24.00 (*0-404-16847-7*) AMS Pr.
Orleans, Jacob & Jacobson, Edmund. The Scrabble Brand Word Guide. 112p. 1990. pap. 6.95 (*0-399-51645-X*, Perigree Bks) Berkley Pub.
Orleans, Jacob S. A Study of the Nature of Difficulty. LC 74-177136. (Columbia University. Teachers College. Contributions to Education Ser.: No. 206). reprint ed. 37.50 (*0-404-55206-4*) AMS Pr.
Orleans, Leo A. Chinese Students in America: Policies, Issues & Numbers. 156p. 1988. pap. 14.95 (*0-309-03886-3*) Natl Acad Pr.
— Every Fifth Child: The Population of China. LC 70-190527. 192p. 1972. 29.50 (*0-8047-0819-3*) Stanford U Pr.
Orleans, Leo A., ed. Chinese Approaches to Family Planning. LC 79-64372. 232p. 1979. 49.95 (*0-87332-139-1*) M E Sharpe.
— Science in Contemporary China. LC 79-65178. 640p. 1980. 72.50 (*0-8047-1078-3*) Stanford U Pr.
Orleans, Peter & Ellis, William R., Jr., eds. Race, Change & Urban Society. LC 70-127992. (Urban Affairs Annual Reviews Ser.: Vol. 5). 640p. reprint ed. pap. 180.00 (*0-317-08723-1*, 2021939) Bks Demand.
***Orlebar, Christopher.** The Concorde Story. (Illus.). 144p. 1994. 17.95 (*0-600-58515-8*, Pub. by Osprey Pubng Ltd UK) Motorbooks Intl.
Orlebar, John. A Midshipman's Journal on Board H. M. S. Seringapatam During the Year 1830. LC 76-11241. (Illus.). 1976. reprint ed. pap. 3.95 (*0-914488-10-4*) Rand-Tofua.
Orlebeke, Charles J. Federal Aid to Chicago. LC 82-74097. 80p. 1983. pap. 8.95 (*0-8157-6649-1*) Brookings.
***Orleck, Annalise.** Common Sense & a Little Fire: Women & Working-Class Politics in the United States, 1900-1965. LC 94-24544. (Gender & American Culture Ser.). (Illus.). 410p. 1995. text ed. 39.95x (*0-8078-2199-3*) U of NC Pr.
— Common Sense & a Little Fire: Women & Working-Class Politics in the United States, 1900-1965. LC 94-24544. (Gender & American Culture Ser.). (Illus.). 410p. 1995. pap. 15.95x (*0-8078-4511-6*) U of NC Pr.
Orledge, R. Charles Koechlin (Eighteen Sixty-Seven to Nineteen Fifty) His Life & Works. (Contemporary Music Studies: Vol. 1). xxvi, 458p. 1989. pap. text ed. 128.00 (*3-7186-4898-9*) Gordon & Breach.
Orledge, Robert. Gabriel Faure. (Eulenburg Music Ser.). (Illus.). 367p. 1982. reprint ed. pap. text ed. 22.50 (*0-903873-41-9*) Da Capo.
— Satie Remembered. (Illus.). 180p. 1995. 29.95 (*1-57467-000-X*, Amadeus Pr); pap. 19.95 (*1-57467-001-8*, Amadeus Pr) Timber.
— Satie the Composer. (Music in the Twentieth Century Ser.: No. 1). (Illus.). 275p. (C). 1990. 79.95 (*0-521-35037-9*) Cambridge U Pr.
Orlemann, Clinton & Stevenson, Hollis. Cincinnati: Paintings & Sketches. (Illus.). 116p. reprint ed. 24.95 (*0-9618069-1-5*) C Orlemann.
***Orlemann, Eric.** Giant Earth Moving Equipment. (Illus.). 128p. 1995. 14.98 (*0-7603-0032-1*) Motorbooks Intl.
Orlen, Steve. The Bridge of Sighs: Poems. LC 92-8418. (Miami University Press Poetry Ser.). 60p. (C). 1992. 15. 95 (*1-881163-00-8*); pap. 9.95 (*1-881163-01-6*) Miami Univ Pr.
Orlev, Uri. The Island on Bird Street. Halkin, Hillel, tr. 176p. (J). (gr. 5 up). 1984. 14.95 (*0-395-33887-5*, 5-92515) HM.
— Lady with the Hat. (YA). 1995. 14.95 (*0-395-69957-6*) HM.
— Lydia: Queen of Palestine. Halkin, Hillel, tr. LC 93-12488. (J). 1993. 13.95 (*0-395-65660-5*) HM.
— Lydia, Queen of Palestine. Halkin, Hillel, tr. LC 94-30188. 176p. (J). 1995. pap. 3.99 (*0-14-037089-7*) Puffin Bks.
— The Man from the Other Side. Halkin, Hillel, tr. LC 90-47898. 144p. (J). (gr. 5 up). 1991. 13.95 (*0-395-53808-4*) HM.
— The Man from the Other Side. Halkin, Hillel, tr. LC 94-30189. 192p. (J). (gr. 1-8). 1995. pap. 3.99 (*0-14-037088-9*) Puffin Bks.
***Orley, J. & Kuyken, W., eds.** Quality of Life Assessment - International Perspectives: Proceedings of the Joint Meeting Organized by the World Health Organization & the Foundation IPSEN in Paris, July 2-3,1993. LC 94-26934. 1994. 67.00 (*0-387-58205-3*) Spr-Verlag.
***Orliac, Catherine & Orliac, Michel.** Easter Island: Mystery of the Stone Giants. Bahn, Paul G., tr. (Discoveries Ser.). (Illus.). 144p. 1995. pap. 12.95 (*0-8109-2834-5*) Abrams.
Orliac, Michel, jt. auth. see Orliac, Catherine.
Orlich, Donald C., et al. Teaching Strategies: A Guide to Better Instruction. 3rd ed. LC 89-84051. 408p. (Orig.). (C). 1990. pap. text ed. 25.00 (*0-669-20160-X*); Instr.'s guide/test item file. teacher ed 2.00 (*0-669-20161-8*) Heath.
— Teaching Strategies: A Guide to Better Instruction. 4th ed. 400p. (Orig.). (C). 1994. pap. text ed. write for info. (*0-669-34960-7*) Heath.
Orlick, Terry. Coaches Training Manual to Psyching for Sport. LC 85-31837. 104p. (Orig.). 1986. pap. 13.95 (*0-88011-274-3*, PORL0274) Human Kinetics.
— The Cooperative Sports & Games Book: Challenge Without Competition. LC 77-88771. 1978. pap. 14.00 (*0-394-73494-7*) Pantheon.
— In Pursuit of Excellence: How to Win in Sport & Life Through Mental Training. 2nd ed. LC 89-39657. (Illus.). 208p. 1990. pap. 14.95 (*0-88011-380-4*, PORL0380) Human Kinetics.
— Psyching for Sport: Mental Training for Athletes. LC 85-23293. 216p. (Orig.). 1986. pap. 15.95 (*0-88011-273-5*, PORL0273) Human Kinetics.
— Psyching for Sport: Mental Training for Athletes & Coaches Training Manual to Psyching for Sport, 2 vols., Set. 1986. pap. 26.95 (*0-88011-275-1*, PORL0275) Human Kinetics.
— The Second Cooperative Sports & Games Book: Over 200 Brand-New Noncompetitive Games for Kids & Adults Both. 255p. 1982. 11.95 (*0-394-74813-1*) NASCO.
Orlick, Terry & Botterill, Cal. Every Kid Can Win. LC 74-19385. 202p. 1975. 27.95 (*0-88229-194-7*); pap. 18.95 (*0-88229-471-7*) Nelson-Hall.
Orlicz, W. Linear Functional Analysis. Lee Peng Yee, tr. (Series in Real Analysis: Vol. 4). 220p. 1992. text ed. 48. 00 (*9810-02-0853-7*) World Scientific Pub.
Orlik, Deborah K. Ethics for the Legal Assistant. 2nd ed. 250p. (C). 1992. teacher ed write for info. (*0-9633276-1-5*); pap. text ed. 15.95 (*0-9633276-0-7*) Marlen Hill Pub.
***Orlik, Deborah K., ed.** Ethics for the Legal Assistant Unauthorized Practice of Law. (Illus.). 1994. teacher ed, disk write for info. (*0-9633276-3-1*) Marlen Hill Pub.
— Ethics for the Legal Assistant Unauthorized Practice of Law. (Illus.). 1994. vdisk 149.95 (*0-9633276-4-X*) Marlen Hill Pub.
— Ethics for the Legal Assistant Unauthorized Practice of Law. 3rd rev. ed. (Illus.). 360p. (C). 1994. pap. text ed. 19.95 (*0-9633276-2-3*) Marlen Hill Pub.
Orlik, P. Introduction to Arrangements. LC 89-14893. (CBMS Regional Conference Series in Mathematics: No. 72). 110p. 1989. pap. 21.00 (*0-8218-0723-4*, CBMS-72) Am Math.
Orlik, P. P. & Terao, H. Arrangements of Hyperplanes. Berger, M. et al, eds. (Grundlehren der Mathematischen Wissenschaften Ser.: Vol. 300). (Illus.). xvii, 325p. 1992. 79.00 (*0-387-55259-6*) Spr-Verlag.
Orlik, Peter, ed. Singularities: Proceedings of Symposia in Pure Mathematics, Pt. 1. LC 83-2529. (Proceedings of Symposia in Pure Mathematics Ser., Humboldt State University, Arcata, CA, July 29-August 16, 1974: Vol. 40). 676p. 1983. text ed. 80.00 (*0-8218-1450-8*, PSPUM 40.1) Am Math.
— Singularities: Proceedings of Symposia in Pure Mathematics, Pt. 2. LC 83-2529. (Proceedings of Symposia in Pure Mathematics Ser., Humboldt State University, Arcata, CA, July 29-August 16, 1974: Vol. 40). 680p. 1983. text ed. 80.00 (*0-8218-1466-4*, PSPUM 40.2) Am Math.
— Singularities: Proceedings of Symposia in Pure Mathematics, Set. LC 83-2529. (Proceedings of Symposia in Pure Mathematics Ser., Humboldt State University, Arcata, CA, July 29-August 16, 1974: Vol. 40). 1356p. 1983. text ed. 138.00 (*0-8218-1443-5*, PSPUM-40) Am Math.
Orlik, Peter B. Broadcast-Cable Copywriting. 5th ed. LC 93-27113. 540p. 1993. text ed. 50.00 (*0-205-15082-9*) Allyn.
— The Electronic Media: An Introduction to the Profession. 576p. (C). 1991. pap. text ed. 47.00 (*0-205-13032-1*) Allyn.
— Electronic Media Criticism: Applied Perspectives. (Illus.). 288p. 1994. pap. 34.95 (*0-240-80162-8*, Focal) Buttrwrth-Heinemann.
Orlikoff, James E. & Totten, Mary K. The Board's Role in Quality Care: A Practical Guide for Hospital Trustees. LC 90-14512. 157p. (Orig.). 1991. pap. 32.95 (*1-55648-061-X*, 196126) AHPI.
Orlikoff, James E. & Vanagunas, Audrone M. Malpractice Prevention & Liability Control for Hospitals. 2nd ed. LC 88-6158. 159p. 1988. pap. 35.00 (*1-55648-014-8*, 178156) AHPI.
Orlikoff, Robert F. & Baken, R. J. Clinical Speech & Voice Measurement: Laboratory Exercises. LC 93-14930. (Illus.). (Orig.). (C). 1993. pap. text ed. 45.95x (*1-879105-91-8*) Singular Publishing.
— Clinical Speech & Voice Measurement Laboratory Exercises: Instructor's Manual. (Illus.). 254p. (Orig.). (C). 1993. pap. text ed. write for info. (*1-56593-215-3*) Singular Publishing.
Orlin, Jay M. Training to Win: Strategies for Today's Industrial Challenges. 150p. 1989. 33.50 (*0-89397-323-8*) Nichols Pub.
***Orlin, Lena C.** Elizabethan Households: An Anthology. (Illus.). 176p. (C). 1995. pap. 24.95 (*0-295-97464-8*) U of Wash Pr.
— Private Matters & Public Culture in Post-Reformation England. (Illus.). 328p. 1994. 39.95 (*0-8014-2858-0*) Cornell U Pr.
Orlin, Louis L. Assyrian Colonies in Cappadocia. (Orig.). 1970. pap. text ed. 67.70 (*3-10-800110-8*) Mouton.
Orlin, Louis L., ed. Janus: Essays in Ancient & Modern Studies. LC 75-18943. 255p. (Orig.). 1975. pap. 10.00 (*0-915932-01-6*) Trillium Pr.
Orlinsky, H. M. Israel Exploration Journal Reader, 2 vols., Set. (Library of Biblical Studies). 1982. 99.50 (*0-87068-267-9*) Ktav.
Orlinsky, Harry M. Ancient Israel. 2nd ed. (Development of Western Civilization Ser.). (Illus.). 164p. 1960. 7.95 (*0-8014-9849-X*) Cornell U Pr.
— Essays in Biblical & Jewish Culture & Bible Translation. 1973. 25.00 (*0-87068-218-0*) Ktav.
— International Organization for Masoretic Studies, 1972 & 1973 Proceedings & Papers. LC 74-16568. (Society of Biblical Literature, Masoretic Studies). 175p. reprint ed. 49.90 (*0-8357-9573-X*, 2017535) Bks Demand.
— Understanding the Bible Through History & Archaeology. 1969. 17.50 (*0-87068-096-X*) Ktav.
Orlinsky, Harry M. & Bratcher, Robert G. A History of Bible Translation & the North American Contribution. 376p. 1991. 44.95 (*1-55540-571-1*); pap. 29.95 (*1-55540-572-X*) Scholars Pr GA.
Orloci, L. Conapack: Program for Canonical Analysis of Classification Tables. 126p. 1991. pap. 30.00 (*90-5103-063-0*, Pub. by SPB Acad Pub NE) Koeltz Sci Bks.
— Ecological Programs for Instructional Computing on the Macintosh. x, 131p. 1991. pap. 35.00 (*90-5103-060-6*, Pub. by SPB Acad Pub NE) Koeltz Sci Bks.
— Entropy & Information. xiv, 72p. 1991. pap. 29.00 (*90-5103-062-2*, Pub. by SPB Acad Pub NE) Koeltz Sci Bks.
Orloci, L., jt. ed. see Feoli, E.
Orloci, L., jt. auth. see Wildi, O.
Orloci, L., et al, eds. Multivariate Methods in Ecological Work. (Statistical Ecology Ser.: Vol. 7). 580p. 1980. 50. 00 (*0-89974-004-9*) Intl Co-Op.
Orlock, Carol. The Hedge, the Ribbon. LC 92-75709. 272p. (Orig.). 1993. pap. 13.95 (*0-913089-48-6*) Broken Moon.
— Inner Time: The Science of Body Clocks & What Makes Us Tick. 208p. 1993. 18.95 (*1-55972-194-4*, Birch Ln Pr) Carol Pub Group.
Orloff, Ann S. The Politics of Pensions: A Comparative Analysis of Britain, Canada, & the United States, 1880-1940. LC 92-50256. (Illus.). 398p. (Orig.). (C). 1993. lib. bdg. 60.00 (*0-299-13220-X*); pap. 19.95 (*0-299-13224-2*) U of Wis Pr.
Orloff, Chet, jt. auth. see Gleason, Norma C.
***Orloff, Gregg.** Biology 141 Instructor Notes. (Illus.). 113p. (C). 1995. 6.00 (*1-886855-02-1*) Tavenner Pub.
***Orloff, Gregg, ed.** Biology 143 Laboratory Exercises. (Illus.). 100p. (C). 1995. 5.50 (*1-886855-00-5*) Tavenner Pub.
Orloff, Jack & Berliner, Robert W., eds. Handbook of Physiology: Section 8, Renal Physiology. (American Physiological Society Book). (Illus.). 1090p. 1988. 130. 00 (*0-19-520683-5*) OUP.
Orloff, Nicholas, tr. see Orthodox Eastern Church.

O

An Asterisk (*) at the beginning of an entry indicates that the title is appearing in BIP for the first time.

Orloff, Nicolas, tr. Horologion: A Primer for Elementary Village Schools. Incl. Octoechos, or the Book of the Eight Tones. (*0-318-50614-9*); General Menaion, or the Book of Services Common to the Festivals of Our Lord Jesus Christ, of the Holy Virgin, & of the Different Orders of Saints. (*0-318-50615-7*); Ferial Menaion, or the Book of Services for the Twelve Great Festivals & the New Year's Day, 4 vols. (*0-318-50616-5*); Bk. 1. Ferial Menaion, or the Book of Services for the Twelve Great Festivals & the New Year's Day, 4 vols. 30.00 (*0-404-04851-X*); Bk. 2. Ferial Menaion, or the Book of Services for the Twelve Great Festivals & the New Year's Day, 4 vols. 30.00 (*0-404-04852-8*); Bk. 3. Ferial Menaion, or the Book of Services for the Twelve Great Festivals & the New Year's Day, 4 vols. 30.00 (*0-404-04853-6*); Bk. 4. Ferial Menaion, or the Book of Services for the Twelve Great Festivals & the New Year's Day, 4 vols. 30.00 (*0-404-04854-4*); Ferial Menaion, or the Book of Services for the Twelve Great Festivals & the New Year's Day, 4 vols. 30.00 (*0-404-04850-1*); reprint ed. write for info. (*0-318-50613-0*) AMS Pr.

***Orloff, Steve, ed.** Intermountain Alfalfa Production. LC 94-61790. 144p. 1995. pap. write for info. (*1-879906-24-4*, 3366) ANR Pubns CA.

***Orloff, Tracy M., et al.** Medicaid Cost-Based Reimbursement for State & Local Health Department Clinic Services. Glass, Karen, ed. 97p. (Orig.). 1993. pap. text ed. 15.00 (*1-55877-222-7*) Natl Governor.

Orlofsky, Myron, jt. auth. see Orlofsky, Patsy.

Orlofsky, Patsy & Orlofsky, Myron. Quilts in America. (Illus.). 368p. 1992. 55.00 (*1-55859-334-9*) Abbeville Pr.

Orlon, Peter Z., jt. auth. see Voeker, David H.

Orloski, Richard J. Criminal Law: An Indictment. LC 76-28995. 1977. 26.95 (*0-88229-211-0*) Nelson-Hall.

Orlosky, Donald, et al. Educational Administration Today. 368p. (C). 1984. write for info. (*0-675-20110-1*, Merrill Pub Co) Macmillan.

Orlosky, Donald E. Society, Schools & Teacher Preparation. LC 88-80932. 1988. pap. 6.25 (*0-89333-050-7*) Assn Tchr Ed.

Orlov, A. N., jt. ed. see Johnson, R. A.

***Orlov, D. S.** Humic Substances of Soils & General Theory of Humification. Kothekar, V. S., tr. (Russian Translations Ser. 109: No. 111). (Illus.). 266p. (C). 1995. text ed. 95.00 (*90-5410-249-7*, Pub. by A A Balkema NE) Ashgate Pub Co.

— Humus Acids of Soils. Kothekar, V., tr. 388p. (C). 1985. text ed. 85.00 (*90-6191-453-1*, Pub. by A A Balkema NE) Ashgate Pub Co.

— Soil Chemistry. Kothekar, V. S., ed. (Russian Translation Ser.: No. 92). (Illus.). 402p. (RUS.). (C). 1992. text ed. 95.00 (*90-6191-915-0*, Pub. by A A Balkema NE) Ashgate Pub Co.

Orlov, Georgi. The Black Knights Tango. Franett, Michael J., ed. (Illus.). 24p. (Orig.). 1991. pap. 5.95 (*1-879479-03-6*) ICE WA.

Orlov, Henry, ed. Vblizi Vestnikov: Near the Messengers - Baruzu Becthukob Russian. LC 88-91215. (Illus.). 325p. (Orig.). (RUS.). 1988. pap. 15.00 (*0-929647-00-9*) H A Frager & Co.

Orlov, V. Russian-English-German French Mathematics Dictionary. 300p. (C). 1987. 90.00 (*0-685-37161-1*, Pub. by Collets) St Mut.

Orlov, V. N. & Bulatova, N. Sh. Population Radiation Cytogenetics of Animals, Vol. 3. 50p. 1989. text ed. 36.00 (*3-7186-4882-2*) Gordon & Breach.

***Orlov, Vladimir N.** Letters from Russia. (Illus.). 48p. (Orig.). 1993. 5.95 (*1-878116-19-3*) JVC Bks.

Orlov, Yu I., jt. auth. see Kravtsov, Yu A.

Orlova, Aleksandra A. Musorgsky's Days & Works: A Biography in Documents. Guenther, Roy J., ed. & tr. by. LC 82-4826. (Russian Music Studies: No. 4). 719p. reprint ed. pap. 180.00 (*0-8357-1324-5*, 2070436) Bks Demand.

Orlova, Alexandra. Tchaikovsky: A Self-Portrait. Davison, R. M., tr. (Illus.). 476p. 1990. 55.00 (*0-19-315319-X*) OUP.

— Tchaikovsky Day by Day. Jonas, Florence, ed. & tr. by. LC 92-40183. (Russian Music Studies). 1993. 75.00 (*0-253-34265-1*) Ind U Pr.

Orlova, Alexandra, ed. Musorgsky Remembered. Zaytzeff, Veronique & Morrison, Frederick, trs. LC 90-25310. (Russian Music Studies). (Illus.). 212p. 1991. 27.50 (*0-253-34264-3*) Ind U Pr.

Orlova, Natalia, et al, illus. Hamlet. LC 92-14525. (Shakespeare: The Animated Tales Ser.). 48p. (J). (gr. 5 up). 1993. pap. 6.99 (*0-679-83871-6*) Knopf Bks Yng Read.

***Orlove, Ben.** In My Father's Study. LC 94-37406. (Singular Lives: The Iowa Series in North American Autobiography). (Illus.). 344p. 1995. text ed. 39.95x (*0-87745-490-6*); pap. 16.95 (*0-87745-491-4*) U of Iowa Pr.

Orlove, Benjamin S. & Custred, Glynn, eds. Land & Power in Latin America: Agrarian Economics & Social Process in the Andes. LC 79-26598. 258p. 1980. 39.50 (*0-8419-0476-6*) Holmes & Meier.

Orlovski, S. A., jt. ed. see Kacprzyk, Janusz.

Orlovski, Sergei A. Calculus of Properties, Fuzzy Sets, & Decisions. LC 94-2015. 1994. 75.00 (*0-89864-066-0*) Allerton Pr.

***Orlovsky, Daniel, ed.** Beyond Soviet Studies. 400p. (Orig.). 1995. pap. text ed. 24.95x (*0-943875-69-2*) Johns Hopkins.

Orlovsky, Daniel T. The Limits of Reform: The Ministry of Internal Affairs in Imperial Russia, 1802-1881. LC 80-18868. (Russian Research Center Studies: No. 81). 299p. reprint ed. pap. 85.30 (*0-7837-4708-X*, 2059060) Bks Demand.

Orlovsky, Daniel T., ed. Social & Economic History of Prerevolutionary Russia. LC 91-44282. (Articles on Russian & Soviet History, 1500-1991 Ser.: Vol. 4). 696p. 1992. 102.00 (*0-8153-0561-3*) Garland.

***Orlovsky, Peter.** Clean Asshole Poems & Smiling Vegetable Songs. LC 77-20019. Date not set. pap. 6.95 (*1-880811-08-1*) North Lights.

Orlovsky, Peter, ed. Francesco Clemente: Evening Raga 1992. LC 92-27818. (Illus.). 108p. 1993. pap. 35.00 (*0-8478-1669-9*) Rizzoli Intl.

Orlovsky, Peter, jt. auth. see Ginsberg, Allen.

Orlow, Dietrich. A History of Modern Germany: Eighteen Seventy-One to Present. 3rd ed. LC 94-14457. 400p. 1994. pap. text ed. write for info. (*0-13-104886-4*) P-H.

— The History of the Nazi Party, 1919-1933, Vol. 1. LC 69-20026. 352p. reprint ed. pap. 100.40 (*0-8357-4636-4*, 2037567) Bks Demand.

— Weimar Prussia, Nineteen Eighteen to Nineteen Twenty-Five: The Unlikely Rock of Democracy. LC 85-1187. (Illus.). 375p. 1985. 49.95 (*0-8229-3519-8*) U of Pittsburgh Pr.

— Weimar Prussia, 1925-33: The Illusion of Strength. LC 91-8117. 480p. 1991. 49.95 (*0-8229-3684-4*) U of Pittsburgh Pr.

Orlowek, Noach. My Child, My Disciple: A Practical, Torah-Based Guide to Effective Discipline in the Home. LC 93-46947. 1994. 15.95 (*0-87306-645-6*) Feldheim.

— My Disciple, My Child: A Practical, Torah-Based Guide to Effective Discipline in the Classroom. LC 93-46948. 1994. 16.95 (*0-87306-646-4*) Feldheim.

Orlowska, M. E. & Papazoglou, M. P. Advances in Database Research: Proceedings of the 4th Australian Database Conference. 388p. 1993. text ed. 116.00 (*981-02-1331-X*) World Scientific Pub.

Orlowski, S., jt. ed. see Simon, R.

***Orlowski, Thomas J.** Smart Selection & Management of Association Computer Systems. 87p. 1995. pap. 34.95 (*0-88034-098-3*) Am Soc Assn Execs.

Orlowsky, Dzvinia. A Handful of Bees. LC 93-73473. (Poetry Ser.). 64p. (Orig.). 1994. 17.95 (*0-88748-174-4*); pap. 10.95 (*0-88748-175-2*) Carnegie-Mellon.

Orman, John. Politics of Rock Music. LC 84-4846. (Illus.). 224p. 1984. pap. 19.95 (*0-8304-1119-4*) Nelson-Hall.

Orman, John M. Comparing Presidential Behavior: Carter, Reagan & the Macho Presidential Style. LC 86-19445. (Contributions in Political Science Ser.: No. 163). 200p. 1987. text ed. 49.95 (*0-313-25516-4*, OCP/, Greenwood Pr) Greenwood.

— Presidential Accountability: New & Recurring Problems. LC 89-26058. (Contributions in Political Science Ser.: No. 254). 184p. 1990. text ed. 45.00 (*0-313-27314-6*, OPA/, Greenwood Pr) Greenwood.

— Presidential Secrecy & Deception: Beyond the Power to Persuade. LC 79-8410. (Contributions in Political Science Ser.: No. 43). (Illus.). xv, 239p. 1980. text ed. 55.00 (*0-313-22036-0*, OPS/, Greenwood Pr) Greenwood.

***Orman, Kate.** Set Piece. (Dr. Who Ser.). (Illus.). Date not set. pap. 5.95 (*0-426-20436-0*, London Bridge) Genl Dist Srvs.

Orman, Larry & Sayer, Jim. Reviving the Sustainable Metropolis: Guiding Bay Area Conservation & Development into the 21st Century. (Illus.). 22p. (C). 1989. text ed. 5.00 (*0-685-45121-6*) Greenbelt.

Orman, Levent V. Elements of Information Systems: Components & Architecture. 272p. (C). 1991. Incl. transparency masters & instr's. manual. teacher ed, trans. write for info. (*0-02-389475-X*) Macmillan.

Orman, Mort. The Fourteen Day Stress Cure: A New Approach for Dealing with Stress That Can Change Your Life Forever. Reuter, Frank, ed. 275p. 1991. 21.95 (*0-685-40819-1*) Breakthru Pub.

Orman, Mort & Reuter, Frank. The Fourteen Day Stress Cure: A New Approach for Dealing with Stress That Can Change Your Life Forever. 350p. 1991. 22.95 (*0-685-50875-7*); pap. 13.95 (*0-942540-06-9*) Breakthru Pub.

Orman, Ray P. Repeal of the Missouri Compromise. (History - United States Ser.). 315p. 1992. reprint ed. lib. bdg. 89.00 (*0-7812-6150-3*) Rprt Serv.

Orman, Stanley. Faith in G.O.D.S. Stability in the Nuclear Age. (Illus.). 127p. 1991. 35.00 (*0-08-040979-2*, Pub. by Brasseys UK) Brasseys Inc.

***Orman, Suze.** You've Earned It, Don't Lose It: Mistakes You Can't Afford to Make When You Retire. LC 94-27895. 192p. 1994. 22.00 (*1-55704-212-8*) Newmarket.

Orman, Tony. 21 Great New Zealand Trout Waters. (Illus.). 136p. 1994. pap. 24.95 (*0-8117-2567-7*) Stackpole.

Ormandy, David, jt. ed. see Burridge, Roger.

Orme, A. R., et al, eds. Coasts under Stress. (Annals of Gemorphology Supplement Ser.: No. 34). (Illus.). 269p. (Orig.). 1980. pap. text ed. 98.50 (*3-443-21034-1*, Pub. by Gebruder Borntraeger GW) Lubrecht & Cramer.

Orme, Agnes, tr. see Wagner, Peter.

Orme, Alan D. Reviving Old Houses: Over Five Hundred Low-Cost Tips & Techniques. LC 93-46819. 1994. pap. 4.99 (*0-517-10105-X*, Pub. by Wings Bks) Random Hse Value.

— Reviving Old Houses: Over 500 Low-Cost Tips & Techniques. LC 89-45220. (Illus.). 180p. 1989. 16.95 (*0-88266-582-0*, Garden Way Pub); pap. 9.95 (*0-88266-563-4*, Garden Way Pub) Storey Comm Inc.

Orme, Antony, et al. Reusable Ada Components Sourcebook. (Ada Companion Ser.). (Illus.). 286p. (C). 1992. 59.95 (*0-521-40351-0*) Cambridge U Pr.

Orme, Bryony. Anthropology for Archaeologists. LC 80-69817. (Illus.). 293p. 1981. 45.00 (*0-8014-1398-2*) Cornell U Pr.

Orme, D. Creative Language: Photocopiable Resource. (C). 1990. 300.00 (*0-685-37717-2*, Pub. by S Thornes Pubs UK) St Mut.

Orme, D., jt. auth. see Andrew, M.

***Orme, Ian M.** Immunity to Mycobacteria. (Medical Intelligence Unit Ser.). 165p. 1995. write for info. (*1-57059-265-9*) R G Landes.

Orme, John D. Political Instability & American Foreign Policy: The Middle Options. 288p. 1989. text ed. 49.95 (*0-312-03212-9*); pap. 16.95 (*0-312-03213-7*) St Martin.

Orme, Nicholas. Education & Society in Medieval & Renaissance England. 304p. 1989. text ed. 55.00 (*1-85285-003-5*) Hambledon Press.

Orme, Robert. A History of the Military Transactions of the British Nation in Indostan from the Year MDCCXLV. (Illus.). 1160p. 1986. reprint ed. 100.00 (*0-88065-173-3*, Messers Today & Tomorrow) Scholarly Pubns.

Orme, William, ed. see Baxter, Richard.

Orme, William A., Jr. Continental Shift: Free Trade & the New North America. 235p. (C). 1993. pap. 49.95 (*0-9625971-2-0*) Washington Post.

Ormeling, F. J., Jr., comp. International Cartographic Association 1959-84: The First Twenty Years of the International Cartographic Association. 138p. 1988. pap. 69.00 (*90-70310-11-2*) Elsevier.

Ormeling, F. J., jt. ed. see Anson, R. W.

Ormeling, F. J., Jr.

Ormeling, Ferdinand J. The Timor Problem: A Geographical Interpretation of an Underdeveloped Island. LC 77-86997. (Illus.). 296p. reprint ed. 57.50 (*0-404-16769-1*) AMS Pr.

Ormell, Christopher. Behavioural Objectives in Education. 73p. (C). 1991. pap. 45.00x (*0-7300-1261-1*, ECT338, Pub. by Deakin Univ AT) St Mut.

— Introducing Modelled Variability. 58p. (C). 1991. pap. 38.00x (*0-7300-1303-0*, ECT408, Pub. by Deakin Univ AT) St Mut.

***Ormerod.** Midnight Pillow Fight. LC 92-53011. 1995. pap. text ed. 4.99 (*1-56402-520-9*) Candlewick Pr.

Ormerod, Allan. Modern Preparation & Weaving Machinery. 296p. 1983. text ed. 62.95 (*0-408-01212-9*) Buttrwrth-Heinemann.

Ormerod, D. A. & Wortham, C. J. Dr. Faustus: The A-Text. 159p. (C). 1985. pap. 14.95 (*0-85564-232-7*, Pub. by Univ of West Aust Pr AT) Intl Spec Bk.

Ormerod, Jan. Come Back, Kittens: A Hide & Seek Book with See-Through Pages. LC 91-30426. (Illus.). 32p. (J). (ps up). 1992. 13.00 (*0-688-09134-2*) Lothrop.

— Come Back, Puppies: A Hide & Seek Book with See-Through Pages. LC 91-30424. (Illus.). 32p. (J). (ps up). 1992. 13.00 (*0-688-09135-0*) Lothrop.

— Dad's Back. LC 84-12614. (Illus.). 24p. (J). (ps). 1985. 4.95 (*0-688-04126-4*) Lothrop.

— Jan Ormerod's To Baby with Love. LC 93-8093. (Illus.). (J). 1994. write for info. (*0-688-12558-1*); lib. bdg. write for info. (*0-688-12559-X*) Lothrop.

— Joe Can Count. LC 92-43781. (Illus.). 24p. (J). (ps up). 1993. pap. 3.95 (*0-688-04588-X*, Mulberry) Morrow.

— Kitten Day. LC 88-26687. (Illus.). 22p. (J). (ps-1). 1989. 13.95 (*0-688-08536-9*) Lothrop.

— Messy Baby. LC 84-12610. (Illus.). 24p. (J). (ps). 1985. 4.95 (*0-688-04128-0*) Lothrop.

— Midnight Pillow Fight. LC 92-53011. (Illus.). 32p. (J). (ps up). 1993. 14.95 (*1-56402-169-6*) Candlewick Pr.

— Mom's Home. LC 87-2712. (Illus.). 24p. (J). (ps). 1987. 5.95 (*0-688-07274-7*) Lothrop.

— Moonlight. LC 81-8290. (Illus.). 32p. (J). (ps-1). 1982. 14.95 (*0-688-00846-1*); lib. bdg. 14.88 (*0-688-00847-X*) Lothrop.

— One Hundred One Things to Do with a Baby. LC 84-4401. (Illus.). 32p. (J). (ps-2). 1984. lib. bdg. 13.88 (*0-688-03802-6*) Lothrop.

— One Hundred One Things to Do with a Baby. (Illus.). 32p. (J). (ps up). 1994. pap. 4.95 (*0-688-12770-3*, Mulberry) Morrow.

— Our Ollie. LC 85-17133. (Illus.). 24p. (J). (ps). 1986. 4.95 (*0-688-04208-2*) Lothrop.

— Reading. LC 84-12628. (Illus.). 24p. (J). (ps). 1985. 4.95 (*0-688-04127-2*) Lothrop.

— Silly Goose. LC 85-17131. (Illus.). 24p. (J). (ps). 1986. 4.95 (*0-688-04209-0*) Lothrop.

— The Story of Chicken Licken. LC 85-7911. (Illus.). 32p. (J). (ps-1). 1986. 13.00 (*0-688-06058-7*) Lothrop.

— Sunshine. (Picture Puffins Ser.). (Illus.). 32p. (J). (ps-00). 1984. pap. 3.50 (*0-14-050362-5*, Puffin) Puffin Bks.

— Sunshine. LC 80-84971. (Illus.). (J). (ps up). 1990. pap. 3.95 (*0-688-09353-1*, Mulberry) Morrow.

— This Little Nose. LC 87-2605. (Illus.). 24p. (J). (ps). 1987. 5.95 (*0-688-07276-3*) Lothrop.

— When We Went to the Zoo. (Illus.). (J). (ps-3). 1991. 13.95 (*0-688-09878-9*); 13.88 (*0-688-09879-7*) Lothrop.

— Young Joe. LC 85-17128. (Illus.). 24p. (J). (ps). 1985. 4.95 (*0-688-04210-4*) Lothrop.

Ormerod, Jan, illus. Sunflakes: Poems for Children. 96p. (J). (ps-3). 1992. 18.95 (*0-395-58833-2*, Clarion Bks) HM.

Ormerod, Jan & LLoyd, David. The Frog Prince. LC 89-12977. (Illus.). 32p. (J). (ps-3). 1990. 15.00 (*0-688-09568-2*); lib. bdg. 14.93 (*0-688-09569-0*) Lothrop.

Ormerod, M. G. Flow Cytometry. (Microscopy Handbooks Ser.). 144p. (Orig.). 1994. pap. 39.50x (*1-872748-39-2*, Pub. by Bios Scientific UK) Coronet Bks.

Ormerod, M. G., ed. Flow Cytometry: A Practical Approach. (Practical Approach Ser.: Vol. 142). (Illus.). 256p. 1994. pap. 48.00 (*0-19-963461-0*, IRL Pr) OUP.

— Flow Cytometry: A Practical Approach. 2nd ed. (Practical Approach Ser.: Vol. 142). (Illus.). 256p. 1994. 88.00 (*0-19-963462-9*, IRL Pr) OUP.

Ormerod, Neil. Introducing Contemporary Theologies. 1990. pap. 9.95 (*0-85574-268-2*, Pub. by E J Dwyer AT) Morehouse Pub.

***Ormerod, Neil & Ormerod, Thea.** When Ministers Sin: Sexual Abuse in the Churches. 178p. (Orig.). 1995. pap. 12.95 (*1-86429-011-0*, Pub. by Millennium Bks AT) Seven Hills Bk.

Ormerod, Oliver. The Picture of a Papist: Whereunto Is Annexed a Certain Treatise, Intituled Pagano-Papismus. LC 74-28878. (English Experience Ser.: No. 756). 1975. reprint ed. 35.00 (*90-221-0756-6*) Walter J Johnson.

— The Picture of a Puritane: Or, a Relation of the Opinions - of the Anabaptists in Germanie, & of the Puritanes in England. LC 74-28879. (English Experience Ser.: No. 757). 1975. reprint ed. 35.00 (*90-221-0757-4*) Walter J Johnson.

Ormerod, Paul. Economic Modelling. (C). 1979. text ed. 84.00 (*0-435-84585-3*) Ashgate Pub Co.

Ormerod, Roger. The Colour of Fear. large type ed. (Linford Mystery Library). 320p. 1994. pap. 14.95 (*0-7089-7487-2*, Linford) Ulverscroft.

— Double Take. large type ed. (Mystery Ser.). 320p. 1994. pap. 14.95 (*0-7089-7566-6*, Trailtree Bookshop) Ulverscroft.

— Full Fury. large type ed. (Linford Mystery Library). 368p. 1993. pap. 14.95 (*0-7089-7423-6*, Trailtree Bookshop) Ulverscroft.

— A Glimpse of Death. large type ed. (Linford Mystery Library). 304p. 1993. pap. 15.95 (*0-7089-7342-6*, Trailtree Bookshop) Ulverscroft.

— The Key to the Case. large type ed. LC 93-15032. 1993. 21.95 (*0-7927-1621-3*, Curley Lrg Print); pap. 19.95 (*0-7927-1620-5*, Curley Lrg Print) Chivers N Amer.

— One Deathless Hour. large type ed. (Mystery Library). 336p. 1995. pap. 14.95 (*0-7089-7650-6*, Linford) Ulverscroft.

— Sealed with a Loving Kill. large type ed. (Linford Mystery Library). 288p. 1994. pap. 14.95 (*0-7089-7480-5*, Linford) Ulverscroft.

— The Silence of the Night. (Black Dagger Crime Ser.). 200p. 1993. 16.50 (*0-7451-8613-0*, Black Dagger) Chivers N Amer.

— The Silence of the Night. large type ed. 1994. 18.95 (*0-7451-6457-9*, Scarlet Dagger Lrg Print) Chivers N Amer.

— A Spoonful of Luger. large type ed. (Linford Mystery Library). 288p. 1994. pap. 14.95 (*0-7089-7476-7*, Linford) Ulverscroft.

— Time To Kill. large type ed. (Linford Mystery Library). 320p. 1993. pap. 14.95 (*0-7089-7420-1*, Linford) Ulverscroft.

— The Weight of Evidence. large type ed. (Linford Mystery Large Pr. Ser.). 1994. pap. 14.95 (*0-7089-7634-4*) Ulverscroft.

Ormerod, Shirley D., jt. auth. see Woods, Donald R.

Ormerod, Stephen, jt. auth. see Tyler, Stephanie.

Ormerod, Thea, jt. auth. see Ormerod, Neil.

Ormerod, Thomas C., jt. auth. see Lansdale, Mark W.

Ormes, Robert M., jt. auth. see Colorado Mountain Club Staff.

Ormesher, Susan. Missouri Marriages Before 1840. LC 82-81219. 317p. 1986. 20.00 (*0-8063-0985-7*) Genealog Pub.

Ormesson, Linda. Jacobean Iron-on Transfer Patterns: Twenty-Four Authentic Embroidery Motifs. (Illus.). 1978. pap. 3.50 (*0-486-23639-0*) Dover.

Ormiston, Gayle & Sassower, Raphael. Narrative Experiments: The Discursive Authority of Science & Technology. 160p. 1989. text ed. 39.95 (*0-8166-1820-8*); pap. text ed. 14.95 (*0-8166-1821-6*) U of Minn Pr.

Ormiston, Gayle L., ed. From Artifact to Habitat: Studies in the Critical Engagement of Technology. LC 88-46174. (Research in Technology Studies: Vol. 3). 224p. 1990. 38.50 (*0-934223-09-2*) Lehigh Univ Pr.

Ormiston, Gayle L. & Sassower, Raphael, eds. Prescriptions: The Dissemination of Medical Authority. LC 89-17183. (Contributions in Medical Studies: No. 27). 210p. 1990. text ed. 49.95 (*0-313-26625-5*, OPR/, Greenwood Pr) Greenwood.

Ormiston, Gayle L. & Schrift, Alan D., eds. The Hermeneutic Tradition: From Ast to Ricoeur. LC 89-4173. (SUNY Series, Intersections: Philosophy & Critical Theory). 380p. 1989. 59.50 (*0-7914-0136-7*); pap. 19.95 (*0-7914-0137-5*) State U NY Pr.

— Transforming the Hermeneutic Context: From Nietzsche to Nancy. LC 89-4172. (SUNY Series, Intersections). 306p. 1989. 59.50 (*0-7914-0134-0*); pap. 19.95 (*0-7914-0135-9*) State U NY Pr.

Ormiston, Hugh & Ross, Donald M. New Patterns of Work. 144p. (C). 1992. pap. 40.00 (*0-86153-127-2*, Pub. by St Andrew UK) St Mut.

Ormiston, Michael B. Intermediate Microeconomics. 650p. (C). 1992. text ed. 60.25 (*0-15-541386-4*) Dryden Pr.

— Intermediate Microeconomics. 650p. (C). 1992. disk 14.50 (*0-15-500959-1*); disk 14.50 (*0-15-500960-5*) Dryden Pr.

Ormond, jt. auth. see Gwyn.

Ormond, George, jt. auth. see Ormond, Riette.

Ormond, John. Selected Poems. LC 87-60980. 142p. 1987. pap. 12.95 (*0-907476-73-2*, Pub. by Poetry Wales Pr UK) Dufour.

Ormond, John, ed. see Tripp, John.

Ormond, Leonee. Alfred Tennyson: A Literary Life. LC 93-2626. (Literary Lives Ser.). 240p. 1993. text ed. 35.00 (*0-312-09597-X*) St Martin.

Ormond, Leonee, ed. see Kipling, Rudyard.

Ormond, Mark. Craig Rubadoux: Works on Paper, 1962-1984. LC 85-80749. (Illus.). 48p. (Orig.). 1985. pap. 10.00 (*0-916758-20-6*) Ringling Mus Art.

— Joel Shapiro. LC 86-82010. (Illus.). 38p. 1986. pap. 10.00 (*0-916758-22-2*) Ringling Mus Art.

— Joel Shapiro: Selected Drawings, 1968-1990. LC 91-70757. (Illus.). 112p. 1992. pap. 29.95 (*0-295-97184-3*) U of Wash Pr.

O

An Asterisk (*) at the beginning of an entry indicates that the title is appearing in BIP for the first time.

— Robert Rauschenberg: Works from the Salvage Ser. LC 85-60057. (Illus.). 20p. 1985. pap. 3.00 (*0-916758-17-6*) Ringling Mus Art.

Ormond, Richard. Early Victorian Portraits, 2 Vol., Set. (Illus.). 900p. 1980. 160.00 (*0-312-22480-X*) St Martin.

Ormond, Richard & Blackett-Ord, Carol. Franz Xaver Winterhalter: And the Courts of Europe, 1830-70. (Illus.). 240p. 1992. 75.00 (*0-8109-3964-9*) Abrams.

Ormond, Riette & Ormond, George. Unique Program for Staying Healthy, Young, & Trim. 44p. (Orig.). 1982. pap. 6.95 (*0-9620518-0-2*) Ormond Assocs.

Ormond, Roger. A Dip Into Murder. large type ed. (Mystery Ser.). 304p. 1994. pap. 14.95 (*0-7089-7570-4*, Trailtree Bookshop) Ulverscroft.

Ormond, Rupert, jt. auth. see Bemert, Gunnar.

Ormond, Suzanne. Recipes from an Old New Orleans Kitchen. LC 88-12478. 1988. pap. 5.95 (*0-88289-699-7*) Pelican.

Ormond, Suzanne & Irvine, Mary. Louisiana's Art Nouveau: Pottery & Crafts of the Newcomb Style. (Illus.). 182p. 1976. 32.50 (*0-88289-112-X*) Pelican.

Ormond, Suzanne, et al. Favorite New Orleans Recipes. LC 78-18841. 120p. 1979. English Ed. spiral bd. 6.95 (*0-88289-198-7*); French Ed. spiral bd. 8.95 (*0-88289-199-5*); Spanish Ed. spiral bd. 8.95 (*0-88289-200-2*) Pelican.

Ormondroyd, Albert, III. Crazy Al's Cook Book & Party Book. LC 83-51789. (Illus.). 136p. 1984. pap. 8.95 (*0-915949-10-5*) Whitinsville Bk.

Ormont, Louis. The Group Therapy Experience: From Theory to Practice. 256p. 1991. 24.95 (*0-312-07036-5*) St Martin.

Ormont, Louis & Strean, Herbert S. The Practice of Conjoint Therapy: Combining Individual & Group Treatment. LC 77-17079. 231p. 1978. 35.95 (*0-87705-355-3*) Human Sci Pr.

Ormos, Maria. From Padua to Trianon, 1918-1920. 1991. text ed. 39.50 (*0-88033-195-X*) Col U Pr.

Ormrod. Human Learning: Principles, Theories & Educational Applications. 848p. (C). 1995. write for info. (*0-675-21044-5*, Merrill Pub Co) Macmillan.

Ormrod, Jeanne E. Educational Psychology: Principles & Applications. 848p. (C). 1994. pap. write for info. (*0-675-21086-0*, Merrill Pub Co) Macmillan.

— Human Learning. 2nd ed. LC 94-12863. 528p. (C). 1994. write for info. (*0-02-389482-2*, Merrill Pub Co) Macmillan.

— Using Your Head: An Owner's Manual. LC 89-30780. (Illus.). 224p. 1989. 19.95 (*0-87778-216-4*) Educ Tech Pubns.

Ormrod, John & Francis, Dennis, eds. Molecular & Cell Biology of the Plant Cell Cycle: Proceedings of a Meeting Held at Lancaster University, 9-10 April 1992. LC 92-36385. 236p. (C). 1993. lib. bdg. 118.00 (*0-7923-1767-X*) Kluwer Ac.

Ormrod, Mark. The Reign of Edward the Third: Crown & Political Society in England, 1327-1377. (Illus.). 352p. (C). 1991. text ed. 38.00 (*0-300-04875-0*) Yale U Pr.

Ormrod, Susan, jt. auth. see Cockburn, Cynthia.

***Ormrod, W. M.** Political Life in Medieval England, 1300-1450. LC 95-8258. (British History in Perspective Ser.). 1995. write for info. (*0-312-12722-7*) St Martin.

— The Reign of Edward the Third: Crown & Political Society in England, 1327-1377. (Illus.). 304p. (C). 1993. reprint ed. pap. text ed. 18.00 (*0-300-05506-4*) Yale U Pr.

Ormsbee, Helen. Backstage with Actors. LC 70-84522. (Illus.). 1972. 29.95 (*0-405-08830-2*) Ayer.

Ormsby, Eric. Bavarian Shrine & Other Poems. 62p. (C). 1990. pap. text ed. 12.00 (*1-55022-107-8*, Pub. by ECW Press CN) Genl Dist Srvs.

— Coastlines. 48p. (C). 1992. pap. 12.00 (*1-55022-176-0*, Pub. by ECW Press CN) Genl Dist Srvs.

— Theodicy in Islamic Thought. LC 84-3396. 320p. 1984. text ed. 49.50x (*0-691-07278-7*) Princeton U Pr.

Ormsby, Eric L., ed. Moses Maimonides & His Time. LC 88-18910. (Studies in Philosophy & the History of Philosophy: Vol. 19). 180p. 1989. 19.95 (*0-8132-0649-9*) Cath U Pr.

— Moses Maimonides & His Time. LC 88-18910. (Studies in Philosophy & the History of Philosophy: No. 19). reprint ed. pap. 53.60 (*0-7837-9105-4*, 2049907) Bks Demand.

Ormsby, Eric L., jt. auth. see Mach, Rudolph.

Ormsby, Frank. Poets from the North of Ireland. 312p. 1990. pap. 21.00 (*0-85640-444-6*, Pub. by Blackstaff Pr IE) Dufour.

Ormsby, Frank, ed. The Collected Poems of John Hewitt. 708p. 1991. 50.00 (*0-85640-459-4*, Pub. by Blackstaff Pr IE) Dufour.

— The Collected Poems of John Hewitt. 708p. 1993. pap. 35.00 (*0-85640-494-2*, Pub. by Blackstaff Pr IE) Dufour.

— Northern Windows: An Anthology of Ulster Autobiography. 256p. 1987. 22.00 (*0-85640-375-X*, Pub. by Blackstaff Pr IE) Dufour.

Ormsby, George S. & Young, Grant. Mud System Arrangements. (Mud Equipment Manual Ser.: No. 2). 44p. (Orig.). 1982. pap. 19.00 (*0-87201-614-5*) Gulf Pub.

Ormsby, Gregory & Cook, Wendy, eds. The Big Green Book: Northwest Music Industry Directory & Guide, 1993. 5th ed. (Illus.). 214p. 1993. pap. 19.95 (*0-9632474-5-X*) NW Intl Enter.

Ormsby, John R., Jr., jt. auth. see Johnson, James A.

Ormsby, Lawrence. Survivors in the Shadows: An Endangered Mammal Postcard Collection. (Illus.). 20p. (Orig.). 1994. pap. 7.95 (*0-87358-581-X*) Northland AZ.

Ormsby-Lennon, Hugh, jt. ed. see Roberts, Marie.

***Ormsby, Margaret A., ed.** A Pioneer Gentlewoman in British Columbia: The Recollections of Susan Allison. 196p. 1977. pap. 15.95 (*0-7748-0392-4*) U of Wash Pr.

***Ormsby, Michael.** Preparing Students for CLAS California Learning Assessment System: Reading & Writing-Elementary. 213p. 1994. pap. text ed. 18.95 (*0-9643281-0-0*) Catalysts for Lrning.

Ormsby, Ralph. A Man of Vision, Francis H. McLean, 1869-1945. LC 75-99972. 158p. reprint ed. pap. 45.10 (*0-685-24012-6*, 2031601) Bks Demand.

Ormsby, Waterman L. The Butterfield Overland Mail. Wright, Lyle H. & Bynum, Josephine M., eds. LC 91-22092. (Illus.). 182p. 1988. reprint ed. pap. 12.95 (*0-87328-095-4*) Huntington Lib.

Ormulum. The Ormulum, with the Notes & Glossary of Dr. Robert Meadows White, 2 vols. Holt, Robert, ed. reprint ed. write for info. (*0-318-50681-5*) AMS Pr.

— The Ormulum, with the Notes & Glossary of Dr. Robert Meadows White, 2 vols, Set. Holt, Robert, ed. LC 72-178548. reprint ed. 85.00 (*0-404-56654-5*) AMS Pr.

Orn, Michael K. Handbook of Engineering Control Methods for Occupational Radiation Protection. 240p. 1991. text ed. 69.00 (*0-13-173931-X*, 350702) P-H.

Orna, Elizabeth. Practical Information Policies: How to Manage Information Flow in Organizations. 263p. 1991. text ed. 69.95 (*0-566-03632-0*, Pub. by Gower UK) Ashgate Pub Co.

***Orna, Elizabeth & Pettitt, Charles.** Information Handling in Museums. fac. ed. LC 81-140240. 198p. 1980. reprint ed. pap. 56.50 (*0-7837-8201-2*, 2047959) Bks Demand.

***Orna, Elizabeth & Stevens, Graham.** Managing Information for Research. LC 95-13767. 1995. write for info. (*0-335-19398-6*, Open Univ Pr); pap. write for info. (*0-335-19397-8*, Open Univ Pr) Taylor & Francis.

***Orna, Mary V. & Goodstein, Madeline.** Chemistry & Artists' Colors. (Illus.). 426p. (C). 1993. pap. text ed. 22.00 (*0-9637747-0-0*) Chemsource.

***Orna, Mary V. & James, M. Lynn, eds.** Guidebook to Pre-Service Use of Chemsource. 95p. (Orig.). (C). 1994. pap. text ed. 15.00 (*0-9637747-7-8*) Chemsource.

Orna, Mary V., jt. ed. see Stock, John T.

***Orna, Mary V., et al, eds.** Sourcebook Vol. 1: Hard Copy Version. (Illus.). (Orig.). (C). 1994. pap. text ed. write for info. (*0-9637747-2-7*) Chemsource.

— Sourcebook Vol. 2: Hard Copy Version. (Illus.). (Orig.). (C). 1994. pap. text ed. write for info. (*0-9637747-3-5*) Chemsource.

— Sourcebook Vol. 3: Hard Copy Version. (Illus.). (Orig.). (C). 1994. pap. text ed. write for info. (*0-9637747-4-3*) Chemsource.

— Sourcebook Vol. 4: Hard Copy Version. (Illus.). (Orig.). (C). 1994. pap. text ed. write for info. (*0-9637747-5-1*) Chemsource.

— Sourcebook Vols. 1-4: Hardcopy Version Overall Bound Volumes, 4 Vols., Set. (Illus.). 2100p. (Orig.). (C). 1994. pap. text ed. 70.00 (*0-9637747-1-9*) Chemsource.

Ornas, Anders H. & Dahl, Gudrun. Responsible Man: The Atmaan Beja of Northeastern Sudan. (Stockholm Studies in Social Anthropology). 195p. (Orig.). 1991. pap. 61.00x (*91-7146-905-2*, Pub. by Almqv & Wiksell SW) Coronet Bks.

Ornato, Joseph P., ed. Cardiovascular Emergencies. LC 86-17130. (Clinics in Emergency Medicine Ser.: No. 9). (Illus.). 272p. reprint ed. pap. 77.60 (*0-7837-6250-X*, 2045962) Bks Demand.

— Field Drug Reference for Emergency Care Providers. (Illus.). viii, 237p. (Orig.). 1990. pap. text ed. 26.00 (*0-914768-47-6*) Drug Intell Pubns.

Ornato, Joseph P. & Gonzalez, Edgar R., eds. Drug Therapy in Emergency Medicine. (Illus.). 607p. 1990. pap. text ed. 63.00 (*0-443-08599-4*) Churchill.

Ornauer, H., ed. Images of the World in the Year Two Thousand: A Comparative Ten-Nation Study. (Publications of the European Coordination Centre for Research & Documentation). 719p. 1976. text ed. 89.35 (*90-279-7551-5*) Mouton.

Orndoff, Eleanor. Poetry Patterns. (Illus.). 48p. (J). (gr. 3-6). 1990. pap. 5.95 (*1-55799-176-6*, EMC245) Evan-Moor Corp.

Orndorff, Mary. Messages of Despair, Messages of Hope: A Guide to the Recovery from Eating Disorders. 70p. 1990. 8.95 (*0-9636536-0-1*) M Orndorff.

Ornduff, Donald R. The First Forty-Nine. LC 81-84498. (Illus.). 280p. 1981. 12.95 (*0-913504-73-4*) Lowell Pr.

Ornduff, Robert. Introduction to California Plant Life. (California Natural History Guides Ser.: No. 35). (Illus.). 1974. pap. 10.00 (*0-520-02735-3*) U CA Pr.

— Islands on Islands. LC 87-10941. (Harold L. Lyon Arboretum Lecture: No. 15). 32p. 1987. pap. text ed. 8.00 (*0-8248-1138-0*) UH Pr.

Orne, Martin T. On the Social Psychology of the Psychological Experiment: With Particular Reference to Demand Characteristics & Their Implications. (Irvington Reprint Series in Psychology). (C). 1991. reprint ed. pap. text ed. 1.30 (*0-8290-2624-X*, Y-678) Irvington.

Ornelas, Michael R. Beyond Eighteen Forty-Eight: Readings in the Modern Chicano Historical Experience. 336p. (C). 1993. per., pap. text ed. 28.95 (*0-8403-8818-7*) Kendall-Hunt.

Ornelas-Struve, Carole M. & Coulter, Fredrick L. Memphis, 1800-1900, 3 Bks. in slipcase, Set. Hassell, Joan, ed. LC 81-17920. (Illus.). 384p. 1982. pap. 24.95 (*0-941684-03-2*) Powers Pub.

— Memphis, 1800-1900, 3 Bks. in slipcase, Vol. I: Years of Challenge, 1800-1860. Hassell, Joan, ed. LC 81-17920. (Illus.). 384p. 1982. Vol. I-Years of Challenge, 1800-1860. pap. 9.95 (*0-941684-00-8*) Powers Pub.

— Memphis, 1800-1900, 3 Bks. in slipcase, Vol. II: Years of Crisis, 1860-1870. Hassell, Joan, ed. LC 81-17920. (Illus.). 384p. 1982. Vol. II-Years of Crisis, 1860-1870. pap. 9.95 (*0-941684-01-6*) Powers Pub.

— Memphis, 1800-1900, 3 Bks. in slipcase, Vol. III: Years of Courage, 1870-1900. Hassell, Joan, ed. LC 81-17920. (Illus.). 384p. 1982. Vol. III-Years of Courage, 1870-1900. pap. 9.95 (*0-941684-02-4*) Powers Pub.

Ornelles, Emory M. Both Wind & Tide. Dietrich, Helen R., ed. 623p. (Orig.). 1990. pap. 11.95 (*0-944784-04-6*) Habersham.

Orner, Christian K., jt. ed. see Chapin, F. Stuart, III.

Orner, Eric. The Mostly Unfabulous Social Life of Ethan Green. (Illus.). 128p. 1992. pap. 8.95 (*0-312-07635-5*) St Martin.

— The Seven Deadly Sins of Love: The Still Unfabulous Social Life of Ethan Green. 128p. 1994. pap. 8.95 (*0-312-10539-8*) St Martin.

Ornest, Noemi, ed. see Bonnick, Bertrand.

Ornig, Joseph. My Last Chance to Be a Boy: Theodore Roosevelt's South American Expedition of 1913-1914. (Illus.). 320p. 1994. 29.95 (*0-8117-1098-X*) Stackpole.

Ornish, Dean. Dr. Dean Ornish's Program for Reversing Heart Disease. (Illus.). 656p. 1990. 24.95 (*0-394-57565-2*) Random.

— Dr. Dean Ornish's Program for Reversing Heart Disease Without Drugs Or Surgery. (Illus.). 656p. 1992. pap. 15.00 (*0-345-37353-7*) Ballantine.

— Eat More, Weigh Less: Dr. Dean Ornish's Life Choice Program for Losing Weight Safely While Eating Abundantly. 320p. 1993. 25.00 (*0-06-016838-2*, HarpT) HarpC.

— Eat More Weigh Less: Dr. Dean Ornish's Life Choice Program for Losing Weight Safely While Eating Abundantly. 1994. pap. 14.00 (*0-06-092545-0*, PL) HarpC.

— Stress, Diet, & Your Heart. 384p. 1984. pap. 4.99 (*0-451-15853-9*, Sig) NAL-Dutton.

— Stress, Diet & Your Heart. 1984. 5.99 (*0-451-17113-6*, ROC) NAL-Dutton.

Ornish, Natalie. Pioneer Jewish Texans: Their Impact on Texas & American History for 400 Years, 1590-1990. (Illus.). 336p. 1989. 39.95 (*0-9620755-0-7*) TX Heritage Pr.

Ornitz, Laurel, ed. see Allen, Sam.

Ornitz, Samuel. Alrightniks Row: The Making of a Professional Jew, Haunch, Paunch & Jowl. LC 85-40730. (Masterworks of Modern Jewish Writing Ser.). 323p. 1986. reprint ed. 18.95 (*0-910129-49-5*); reprint ed. pap. 9.95 (*0-910129-46-0*) Wiener Pubs Inc.

Ornoy, A., et al, eds. Current Advances in Skeletogenesis: Induction, Biomineralization, Bone Seeking Hormones, Congenital & Metabolic Bone Diseases: Proceedings of the International Workshop on Calcified Tissue, 6th, Kiryat-Anavim, Israel, 18-23 March, 1984. (International Congress Ser.: No. 643). 500p. 1985. 168.75 (*0-444-80659-8*, Excerpta Medica) Elsevier.

***Ornoy, Asher.** Animal Models for Human Related Calcium Metabolic Disorders. 240p. 1995. 149.95 (*0-8493-6024-2*, 6024) CRC Pr.

Ornoy, Asher, et al, eds. Atlas of Fetal Skeletal Radiology & Morphology. (Illus.). 160p. 1988. 89.00 (*0-8151-6544-7*, ATF-1, Yr Bk Med Pubs) Mosby Yr Bk.

Ornstein. Roots of the Self. 1994. pap. 12.00 (*0-06-250789-3*, PL) HarpC.

Ornstein, Allan C. Secondary & Middle School Teaching. (C). 1991. text ed. 46.00 (*0-06-044928-4*) HarpCollege.

— Strategies for Effective Teaching. 508p. (C). 1990. text ed. 52.50 (*0-06-044927-6*) HarpCollege.

— Strategies for Effective Teaching. 2nd ed. 512p. (C). 1995. pap. text ed. write for info. (*0-697-24415-6*) Brown & Benchmark.

— Teaching in a New Era. 1976. pap. text ed. 6.80 (*0-87563-110-X*) Stipes.

Ornstein, Allan C. & Behar, Linda S., eds. Contemporary Issues in Curriculum. LC 94-7446. 1994. pap. text ed. write for info. (*0-205-15770-X*) Allyn.

Ornstein, Allan C. & Hunkins, Francis P. Curriculum: Foundations, Principles & Issues. (Illus.). 448p. (C). 1988. text ed. write for info. (*0-13-195777-5*) P-H.

— Curriculum - Foundations, Principles, & Issues. 2nd ed. LC 92-20517. 1993. text ed. write for info. (*0-205-14145-5*) Allyn.

Ornstein, Allan C., jt. auth. see Lunenburg, Fred C.

Ornstein, Allan C., et al. An Introduction to the Foundations of Education. 4th ed. 1988. teacher ed write for info. (*0-318-63327-2*); trans. write for info. (*0-318-63328-0*) HM.

— An Introduction to the Foundations of Education, 4 Vols. 4th ed. LC 88-81353. (C). 1988. text ed. 56.76 (*0-395-43228-6*) HM.

***Ornstein, Allyn C.** Teaching: Theory into Practice. LC 94-27202. 1994. pap. text ed. write for info. (*0-205-15778-5*) Allyn.

Ornstein, Beverly J., ed. Homeless: Portraits of Americans in Hard Times. LC 93-24683. 1993. 24.95 (*0-8118-0512-3*) Chronicle Bks.

Ornstein, Donald, et al. Equivalence of Measure Preserving Transformations. LC 82-4005. (Memoirs Ser.: No. 37/262). 120p. 1985. reprint ed. pap. 17.00 (*0-8218-2262-4*, MEMO 37/262) Am Math.

Ornstein-Galicia, Jacob, ed. Form & Function in Chicano English. LC 87-3379. 256p. (C). 1988. reprint ed. lib. bdg. 27.50 (*0-89464-233-2*) Krieger.

Ornstein-Galicia, Jacob, jt. auth. see Bixler-Marquez, Dennis J.

Ornstein-Galicia, Jacob L. Jewish Farmer in America: The Unknown Chronicle. LC 92-44246. (Illus.). 264p. 1993. text ed. 89.95 (*0-7734-9229-1*) E Mellen.

Ornstein, Jacob, ed. Three Essays on Linguistic Diversity in the Spanish-Speaking World: The U. S. Southwest & the River Plate Area. (Janua Linguarum, Ser Practica: No. 174). (Illus.). (Orig.). 1976. pap. text ed. 21.35 (*90-279-3167-4*) Mouton.

Ornstein, Jacob, jt. ed. see Gilbert, Glenn G.

Ornstein, Jacob, jt. ed. see Mackey, William F.

Ornstein, Judy, ed. see Peskoff, Joel.

Ornstein, Martha. The Role of Scientific Societies in the Seventeenth Century. LC 74-26282. (History, Philosophy & Sociology of Science Ser.). 1980. reprint ed. 25.95 (*0-405-06609-0*) Ayer.

Ornstein, Melvin, jt. auth. see Englebrecht, Ted. D., Jr.

Ornstein, Norman. Vital Statistics on Congress, 1989-1990. 275p. 1989. 44.95 (*0-87187-526-8*); pap. 30.95 (*0-87187-528-4*) Congr Quarterly.

— Vital Statistics on Congress 1990-1991. 1991. 44.95 (*0-87187-620-5*); pap. 28.95 (*0-87187-621-3*) Congr Quarterly.

— Vital Statistics on Congress, 1993-94. 275p. 1993. 44.95 (*0-87187-778-3*); pap. 30.95 (*0-87187-779-1*) Congr Quarterly.

Ornstein, Norman J. Debt & Taxes: How America Got into Its Budget Mess & What We Can Do to Get Out of It. 1994. 25.00 (*0-8129-2312-X*, Times Bks) Random.

— The Permanent Democratic Congress. (Essay Ser.: No. 3). 31p. (C). 1991. pap. text ed. 3.00 (*1-878802-02-X*) J M Ashbrook Ctr Pub Affairs.

Ornstein, Norman J. & Lambert, Richard D., eds. Changing Congress: The Committee System. LC 73-89780. (Annals Ser.: No. 411). 1974. pap. 18.00 (*0-87761-172-6*) Am Acad Pol Soc Sci.

Ornstein, Norman J., jt. auth. see Mann, Thomas E.

Ornstein, Norman J., jt. ed. see Mann, Thomas E.

Ornstein, Pamela O. Granny Poo's Restaurant Review. 60p. (Orig.). 1994. 19.95 (*0-944105-02-5*) Candico Prods.

Ornstein, Paul, ed. The Two Analyses of Mr. Z by Heinz Kohut. Date not set. 30.00 (*0-87668-552-1*) Aronson.

Ornstein, Paul H., ed. The Search for the Self: Selected Writings of Heinz Kohut, Vol. 3. 400p. 1991. 55.00 (*0-8236-6017-6*) Intl Univs Pr.

— The Search for the Self: Selected Writings of Heinz Kohut, Vol. 4. 500p. 1991. 60.00x (*0-8236-6018-4*) Intl Univs Pr.

— The Search for the Self: Selected Writings of Heinz Kohut 1950-1978, 2 vols., 1. LC 77-90229. 1978. text ed. 60.00 (*0-8236-6015-X*) Intl Univs Pr.

— The Search for the Self: Selected Writings of Heinz Kohut 1950-1978, 2 vols., 2. LC 77-90229. 1978. text ed. 60.00 (*0-8236-6016-8*) Intl Univs Pr.

Ornstein, Robert. A Kingdom for a Stage: The Achievement of Shakespeare's History Plays. LC 88-70855. 231p. (C). 1988. reprint ed. 20.75 (*0-9620257-0-4*) Arden Pr OH.

— Physiological Studies of Consciousness. 20p. 1973. pap. 6.00 (*0-904674-00-2*, Pub. by Octagon Pr UK) ISHK Bk Service.

Ornstein, Robert, et al. Psychology: The Study of Human Experience. 3rd ed. 850p. (C). 1990. text ed. 49.25 (*0-15-572685-4*) HB Coll Pubs.

Ornstein, Robert. Shakespeare's Comedies: From Roman Farce to Romantic Mystery. (Illus.). 272p. 1994. pap. 17.95 (*0-87413-541-9*) U Delaware Pr.

Ornstein, Robert E. The Evolution of Consciousness: The Origins of the Way We Think. (Illus.). 320p. 1992. pap. 14.00 (*0-671-79224-5*, Touchstone Bks) S&S Trade.

— Healthy Pleasures. 1989. 16.30 (*0-201-12669-9*) Addison-Wesley.

— Healthy Pleasures. 1990. pap. 10.58 (*0-201-52385-X*) Addison-Wesley.

— The Moral Vision of Jacobean Tragedy. LC 74-25893. 299p. 1975. reprint ed. text ed. 45.00 (*0-8371-7864-9*, ORJT, Greenwood Pr) Greenwood.

— Multimind: A New Way of Looking at Human Behavior. 1989. mass mkt. 9.95 (*0-385-26446-1*, Anchor NY) Doubleday.

— Psychology: The Study of Human Experience. 2nd ed. 766p. (C). 1988. Software, videotapes, slides & transparencies. disk, sl. write for info. (*0-318-62818-X*) HB Coll Pubs.

— Psychology Consciousness. rev. ed. 1986. pap. 9.95 (*0-14-022621-4*, Penguin Bks) Viking Penguin.

— The Psychology of Consciousness. (Orig.). 1975. mass mkt. 5.95 (*0-14-021679-0*, Penguin Bks) Viking Penguin.

— The Roots of the Self: Unraveling the Mystery of Who We Are. LC 92-56116. 240p. 1993. 25.00 (*0-06-250788-5*) Harper SF.

— Shakespeare's Comedies: From Roman Farce to Romantic Mystery. LC 85-40851. 272p. 1986. 42.50 (*0-87413-298-3*) U Delaware Pr.

Ornstein, Robert E. & Sobel, David. The Healing Brain: Breakthrough Medical Discoveries about How the Brain Manages Health. 1988. pap. 10.95 (*0-671-66236-8*, Touchstone Bks) S&S Trade.

Ornstein, Robert E. & Swencionis, Charles, eds. The Healing Brain: A Scientific Reader. LC 89-16968. 262p. 1990. lib. bdg. 45.00 (*0-89862-394-4*) Guilford Pr.

— The Healing Brain: A Scientific Reader. LC 89-16968. 262p. 1991. reprint ed. pap. text ed. 19.95 (*0-89862-463-0*) Guilford Pr.

Ornstein, Robert E. & Thompson, Richard F. The Amazing Brain. (Illus.). 224p. 1991. pap. 14.95 (*0-395-58572-4*) HM.

Ornstein, Yevrah. From the Hearts of Men. 352p. 1992. pap. 10.00 (*0-449-90775-9*, Columbine) Fawcett.

— From the Hearts of Men. LC 91-72316. 352p. 1991. pap. 16.95 (*0-9629211-5-7*) Harmonia.

Ornston, Darius G., Jr., ed. Translating Freud. LC 92-9151. 272p. (C). 1993. 32.00 (*0-300-05454-8*) Yale U Pr.

Ornston, L. N., et al, eds. Annual Review of Microbiology, Vol. 45. 1991. text ed. 41.00 (*0-8243-1145-0*) Annual Reviews.

***Ornston, L. Nicholas.** Annual Review of Microbiology, Vol. 49. 1995. lib. bdg. 48.00 (*0-8243-1149-3*) Annual Reviews.

Ornston, L. Nicholas, et al, eds. Annual Review of Microbiology, Vol. 37. LC 49-432. (Illus.). 1983. text ed. 41.00 (*0-8243-1137-X*) Annual Reviews.

— Annual Review of Microbiology, Vol. 38. LC 49-432. (Illus.). 1984. text ed. 41.00 (*0-8243-1138-8*) Annual Reviews.
— Annual Review of Microbiology, Vol. 39. LC 49-432. (Illus.). (C). 1985. text ed. 41.00 (*0-8243-1139-6*) Annual Reviews.
— Annual Review of Microbiology, Vol. 40. LC 49-432. (Illus.). 1986. text ed. 41.00 (*0-8243-1140-X*) Annual Reviews.
— Annual Review of Microbiology, Vol. 41. LC 49-432. (Illus.). 1987. text ed. 41.00 (*0-8243-1141-8*) Annual Reviews.
— Annual Review of Microbiology, Vol. 42. LC 49-432. (Illus.). 1988. text ed. 41.00 (*0-8243-1142-6*) Annual Reviews.
— Annual Review of Microbiology, Vol. 43. 1989. text ed. 41.00 (*0-8243-1143-4*) Annual Reviews.
— Annual Review of Microbiology, Vol. 44. 1990. 41.00 (*0-8243-1144-2*) Annual Reviews.
— Annual Review of Microbiology, Vol. 46. 1992. text ed. 45.00 (*0-8243-1146-9*) Annual Reviews.
— Annual Review of Microbiology, Vol. 47. (Illus.). 1993. text ed. 45.00 (*0-8243-1147-7*) Annual Reviews.
— Annual Review of Microbiology, Vol. 48. (Illus.). 1994. text ed. 60.00 (*0-8243-1148-5*) Annual Reviews.
Oro, J., ed. Life Sciences & Space Research (XXIII) (I) Exobiology Science & Primitive Solar System Bodies. (Advances in Space Research Ser.: Vol. 9). 1989. pap. 79.00 (*0-08-037381-X*, Pergamon Pr) Elsevier.
Oro, J., ed. see International Conference on the Origin of Life Staff, et al.
O'Roark, Ann M. & Exner, John E., Jr., eds. History & Directory: Society for Personality Assessment Fiftieth Anniversary. 192p. 1989. pap. 39.95 (*0-8058-0569-9*) L Erlbaum Assocs.
Orodenker, Sylvia Z. Family Caregiving in a Changing Society: The Effects of Employment on Caregiver Stress. LC 91-29925. (Studies on Elderly in America). 160p. 1991. 46.00 (*0-8153-0521-4*) Garland.
Orofino, James F., ed. Structural Materials. LC 89-6764. 592p. 1989. pap. text ed. 49.00 (*0-87262-699-7*, 699) Am Soc Civil Eng.
O'Rooney, Sean. The Flip Side of Webster or How to be a Wise Guy. LC 81-66616. 220p. 1982. pap. 7.95 (*0-933298-01-3*) Caspers Wine.
— Listen to the Flowers Grow. LC 78-74229. 180p. 1979. 4.95 (*0-933298-00-5*) Caspers Wine.
Oropesa, Jose D. Cosmologia: El Humanismo Cristiano. LC 90-82885. (Coleccion Polymita Ser.). 140p. (Orig.). 1990. pap. 9.95 (*0-89729-573-0*) Ediciones.
— Historiologia Cubana, 4 vols., II. LC 74-81336. (Coleccion Cuba y Sus Jueces Ser.). (Orig.). (SPA.). 1993. pap. 25.00 (*0-685-74171-0*) Ediciones.
— Historiologia Cubana, 4 vols., III. LC 74-81336. (Coleccion Cuba y Sus Jueces Ser.). (Orig.). (SPA.). 1993. pap. 25.00 (*84-399-2582-4*) Ediciones.
— Historiologia Cubana, 4 vols., Vol. I: Desde la Era Mesozoica Hasta 1898. LC 74-81336. (Coleccion Cuba y Sus Jueces Ser.). 430p. (Orig.). (SPA.). 1993. pap. 25.00 (*0-89729-490-4*) Ediciones.
— Historiologia Cubana, 4 vols., Vol. IV: Desde 1959 Hasta 1980. LC 74-81336. (Coleccion Cuba y Sus Jueces Ser.). 682p. (Orig.). (SPA.). 1993. pap. 39.00 (*0-89729-623-0*) Ediciones.
Oropeza, B. J. Ninety-Nine Reasons Why No One Knows When Christ Will Return. LC 94-3576. 180p. (Orig.). 1994. pap. 9.99 (*0-8308-1636-4*, 1636, Saltshaker Bk) InterVarsity.
Oropeza, Luis J. Tutelary Pluralism: A Critical Approach to Venezuelan Democracy. (Harvard Studies in International Affairs: No. 46). 144p. 1984. reprint ed. pap. text ed. 18.00 (*0-8191-4120-8*) U Pr of Amer.
***O'Rorke, Flannigan.** Massacre in Courtroom 425. 1995. 15. 95 (*0-944957-75-7*) Rivercross Pub.
Oros, John G., ed. see Masson, Dubos J. & Treasury Management Association Staff.
Orosius, Paulus. Historiarum Adversum Paganos Libri Septem. xxxix, 819p. (GER.). 1967. reprint ed. write for info. (*0-318-70524-9*, Pub. by Georg Olms GW) Lubrecht & Cramer.
— King Alfred's Orosius, Pt. 1. Sweet, H., ed. (EETS, OS Ser.: No. 79). 1969. 42.00 (*0-527-00079-5*) Periodicals Srv.
Orosz, Carmen. From the Ganges to the Indus: Religions, Shrines & Traveling. LC 93-72947. 1994. pap. 11.95 (*0-8158-0496-2*) Chris Mass.
Orosz, Joel J. Curators & Culture: The Museum Movement in America, 1740-1870. 320p. 1990. 36.50 (*0-8173-0475-4*) U of Ala Pr.
— The Eagle That Is Forgotten: Pierre Eugene Du Simitiere, Founding Father of American Numismatics. (Illus.). 76p. 1988. 19.95 (*0-943161-16-9*); pap. 9.95 (*0-943161-08-8*) Bowers & Merena.

***Orosz, Kathryn S. Miami Equals Oasis. (Illus.). 80p. 1995. 30.00 (*0-9644807-0-0*) Orosz FL.**
MIAMI = OASIS is a photojournalistic essay of striking color & images taken spontaneously all over Miami. Shots are engaging, rich with tropical blue waters, blue skies, a new style, character & a sense of humor that is Miami now. Piero Guerrini has been published in TIME, LIFE, NEWSWEEK, etc. & most recently was exhibited at the Guggenheim Museum in Venice, Italy. Writer, Kathryn Snyder Orosz has written for magazine & television concepts. This is her first book & the photographer's. Their work complements each other's in its freeform style. Written mostly in prose, this book dances in its light, lively & poetic style. MIAMI = OASIS lifts the spirit & gives insiders up close & personal perspective of a newly vibrant city that has found a way to become young again. Many cultures, new information shared have revitalized the picture in Miami. To order call (800) 664-4111. ***Publisher Provided Annotation.***

Orosz, Nicholas, jt. ed. see McCorquodale, Robert.
O'Rouke, T. D., ed. Guidelines for Tunnel Lining Design. 94p. 1984. 17.00 (*0-87262-402-1*) Am Soc Civil Eng.
***Orourke.** Bad Thing. 1995. mass mkt. 4.99 (*0-06-100720-X*, Harp PBks) HarpC.
O'Rourke, jt. auth. see Collins.
O'Rourke, ed. see Taine, Hippolyte A.
O'Rourke, A. Desmond. The World Apple Market. LC 93-7919. (Illus.). 238p. 1993. lib. bdg. 49.95 (*1-56022-041-4*) Haworth Pr.
O'Rourke, A. Desmond, ed. Understanding the Japanese Food & Agrimarket: A Multifaceted Opportunity. LC 92-20076. (Illus.). 212p. 1993. lib. bdg. 49.95 (*1-56022-029-5*) Haworth Jrnl Co-Edits.
O'Rourke, Betty. Mists of Remembrance. large type ed. (Linford Romance Library). 256p. 1992. pap. 14.95 (*0-7089-7135-0*, Linford) Ulverscroft.
O'Rourke, Brian. Blas Meala: Gaelic Folksongs with Translation. (Illus.). 128p. 1985. 25.00 (*0-7165-2358-2*, Pub. by Irish Acad Pr IE) Intl Spec Bk.
— Pale Rainbow: Gaelic Folksongs with English Translations. 96p. 1989. 25.00 (*0-7165-2425-2*, Pub. by Irish Acad Pr IE) Intl Spec Bk.
O'Rourke, Canon J. The Great Irish Famine. abr. ed. 300p. 1989. reprint ed. 49.95 (*1-85390-049-4*, Pub. by Veritas Pubns IE) Irish Bks Media.
O'Rourke, Dori. I Found the Golf God: Ten Secrets for Golfing Success. 99p. 1991. pap. 9.95 (*0-9628854-0-1*) On Target Enter.
***O'Rourke, Edward J.** Jesus, the Divine Teacher: Five New Decades of the Rosary. 32p. 1994. pap. 1.95 (*0-89243-680-8*) Liguori Pubns.
O'Rourke, Edward W. Roots of Human Rights. (Synthesis Ser.). 117p. 1981. 1.95 (*0-8199-0373-6*, Frncscn Herld) Franciscan Pr.
O'Rourke, Everett V. The Highest School in California: A Story of Bodie, California. (Illus.). 32p. (Orig.). (J). (gr. 1-4). 1978. 4.00 (*0-685-22567-4*) E ORourke.
— Sounds & Images of the Fabulous Fifties: History of the Tahoe Truckee Unified School District: 1949-1956. (Illus.). (Orig.). 1990. pap. text ed. 10.00 (*0-9621369-1-3*) E ORourke.
O'Rourke, Fran. Pseudo-Dionysius & the Metaphysics of Aquinas. LC 92-13959. (Studien und Texte zur Geistesgeschichte des Mittelalters Ser.: Vol. 32). xvi, 300p. 1992. 80.00 (*90-04-09466-0*) E J Brill.
O'Rourke, Fran, ed. At the Heart of the Real: Philosophical Essays in Honour of Archbishop Desmond Connell. 420p. 1992. text ed. 45.00 (*0-7165-2464-3*, Pub. by Irish Acad Pr IE) Intl Spec Bk.
O'Rourke, Frank. Burton & Stanley. (J). (gr. 4-7). 1993. 15. 95 (*0-87923-824-0*) Godine.
O'Rourke, J. Computer Technology & the Disabled. 1992. text ed. write for info. (*0-442-00507-5*) Van Nos Reinhold.
O'Rourke, J. Barry. Hot Shots: How to Photograph Beauty That Sells. (Illus.). 144p. 1992. 29.95 (*0-8174-3994-3*, Amphoto); pap. 22.50 (*0-8174-3995-1*, Amphoto) Watsn-Guptill.
— How to Photograph Women - Beautifully. (Illus.). 144p. 1986. pap. 18.95 (*0-8174-4004-6*, Amphoto) Watsn-Guptill.
O'Rourke, James. May Day - May Day. Van Treese, James B., ed. 414p. 1994. pap. 9.95 (*1-56901-063-3*) NW Pub.
O'Rourke, James J. The Problem of Freedom in Marxist Thought: An Analysis of the Treatment of Human Freedom by Marx, Engels, Lenin & Contemporary Soviet Philosophy. LC 73-86095. (Sovietica Ser.: No. 32). 240p. 1974. lib. bdg. 84.00 (*90-277-0383-3*) Kluwer Ac.
O'Rourke, James J., jt. auth. see Blakeley, Thomas J.
O'Rourke, Janet & Wallat, Lee. Peter Pirate's Hospital Coloring Book. 32p. (Orig.). 1982. pap. 2.95 (*0-89716-111-4*) P B Pubng.
O'Rourke, Joseph. Art Gallery Theorems & Algorithms. (International Series of Monographs on Computer Science: No. 3). (Illus.). 304p. 1987. 45.00 (*0-19-503965-3*) OUP.
— Computational Geometry in C. (Illus.). 320p. (C). 1994. 59.95 (*0-521-44034-3*); pap. 24.95 (*0-521-44592-2*) Cambridge U Pr.
O'Rourke, Joseph, jt. auth. see Dale, Edgar.
O'Rourke, Joseph P. Toward a Science of Vocabulary Development. LC 73-87530. (Janua Linguarum, Ser.: No. 183). (Illus.). 1974. pap. text ed. 44.65 (*90-279-2663-8*) Mouton.
O'Rourke, K. C. & Skuce, Anita. Everyone Wins! How We Can All Strike It Rich with Tax Reform. LC 85-70704. 132p. (Orig.). 1985. pap. text ed. 12.95 (*0-933815-00-X*) D C Marshall.
O'Rourke, K. J., jt. auth. see O'Grady, G. W.
O'Rourke, Kathy, jt. auth. see Worzbyt, John.
***O'Rourke, Kevin.** Currier & Ives: The Irish & America. LC 95-1154. 1995. write for info. (*0-8109-4036-1*) Abrams.
O'Rourke, Kevin, jt. auth. see Ashley, Benedict.
O'Rourke, Kevin D. Development of Church Teaching on Prolonging Life. 20p. 1988. pap. 3.00 (*0-87125-152-3*, 217) Cath Health.
— Reasons for Hope: Laity in Catholic Health Care Facilities. LC 83-7426. 60p. (Orig.). 1983. pap. 7.00 (*0-87125-084-5*) Cath Health.
O'Rourke, Kevin D. & Boyle, Philip, eds. Medical Ethics: Sources of Catholic Teaching. 2nd ed. LC 93-4895. 368p. (Orig.). 1993. pap. text ed. 35.00 (*0-87840-540-2*) Georgetown U Pr.
O'Rourke, Kevin D. & Brodeur, Dennis. Medical Ethics: Common Ground for Understanding, Vol. II. 180p. (Orig.). 1988. pap. 18.00 (*0-87125-145-0*, 410) Cath Health.
O'Rourke, Kevin D., jt. auth. see Ashley, Benedict.
O'Rourke, Lawrence M. Geno: The Life & Mission of Geno Baroni. 400p. 1991. pap. 11.95 (*0-8091-3274-5*) Paulist Pr.
***O'Rourke, Mary.** Your Will Be Done. 192p. 1994. per., pap. text ed. 14.95 (*0-7872-0191-X*) Kendall-Hunt.
O'Rourke, Mary-Jo. Nepali Phrasebook. 2nd ed. (Illus.). 144p. 1992. pap. 4.95 (*0-86442-145-1*) Lonely Planet.
O'Rourke, Mary K. No Sparrow Shall Fall: Leaving the Convent after Forty-Five Years Under Vows. (Illus.). 192p. 1988. 17.95 (*0-941974-10-3*) Baranski Pub Co.
O'Rourke, Michael. Darkling. 1994. mass mkt. 4.99 (*0-06-100719-6*, Harp PBks) HarpC.
— Principles of Three-Dimensional Computer Animation. (Illus.). 304p. 1995. 48.00 (*0-393-70202-2*) Norton.
O'Rourke, Michael, et al, eds. Arterial Vasodilation, Mechanisms & Therapy. LC 92-49292. (Illus.). 368p. 1992. text ed. 89.50 (*0-8121-1671-2*) Williams & Wilkins.
O'Rourke, Michael F., jt. auth. see Nichols, W. W.
O'Rourke, Michael G., jt. ed. see Emmett, Anthony J.
O'Rourke, Mike D. & Marich, Stephen, intros. International Heavy Haul Railway Conference, Fourth, 1989: Railways in Action. (Illus.). 682p. 1989. 115.25 (*0-85825-469-7*, Pub. by Inst Engrs Aust-EA Bks AT) Accents Pubns.
O'Rourke, P. J. All the Trouble in the World: The Lighter Side of Overpopulation, Famine, Plague, Ecological Disaster, Ethnic Hatred, & Poverty. 240p. 1994. 22.00 (*0-87113-580-9*) Grove-Atltic.
— Bachelor's Home Companion: A Practical Guide to Keeping House Like a Pig. LC 92-38785. 147p. 1993. 16.00 (*0-87113-489-6*) Grove-Atltic.
— Give War a Chance: Eyewitness Accounts of Mankind's Struggle Against Tyranny, Injustice, & Alcohol-Free Beer. LC 92-50591. 1993. pap. 12.00 (*0-679-74201-8*, Vin) Random.
— Holidays in Hell. 1989. pap. 12.00 (*0-679-72422-2*, Vin) Random.
— Holidays in Hell. 1992. pap. 12.00 (*0-394-23898-2*, Vin) Random.
— Parliament of Whores: A Lone Humorist Attempts to Explain the U. S. Government. 1992. pap. 12.00 (*0-679-73789-8*, Vin) Random.
— Republican Party Reptile. LC 86-26504. 220p. 1987. pap. 9.95 (*0-87113-145-5*) Grove-Atltic.
O'Rourke, Page, illus. Rub-a-Dub-Dub. (So Tall Board Bks.). 9p. (J). (ps-1). 1993. bds. 4.95 (*0-448-40521-0*, G&D) Putnam Pub Group.
O'Rourke, Page E., illus. See & Say: A Book of First Words. (Teddy Board Bks.). 12p. (J). (ps). 1993. bds. 4.95 (*0-448-40540-7*, G&D) Putnam Pub Group.
O'Rourke, Paul F., jt. auth. see Polakoff, Phillip L.
O'Rourke P.J. Modern Manners: An Etiquette Book for Rude People. LC 88-31834. 280p. 1990. pap. 9.95 (*0-87113-375-X*) Grove-Atltic.
***O'Rourke, Randy, photos.** John Hadamucin's Home for Christmas: Decorating, Cooking, Entertaining & Giving. LC 95-6992. (Illus.). 1995. write for info. (*0-517-70180-4*, Harmony) Crown Pub Group.
— John Hadamuscin's Simple Pleasures: One Hundred One Thoughts & Recipes for Savoring the Little Things in Life. LC 92-7506. 1992. 15.00 (*0-517-59081-6*, Harmony) Crown Pub Group.
O'Rourke, Rebecca. Reflecting on the Well of Loneliness: Stephen Gordon, A Lesbian's Heroine? (Heroines? Ser.). 96p. 1989. pap. 9.95 (*0-415-01841-2*) Routledge.
O'Rourke, Rebecca, jt. auth. see Milloy, Jean.
***O'Rourke, Richard J.** Anzio Annie, She Was No Lady. (Illus.). 256p. (Orig.). 1995. pap. text ed. 17.95 (*0-9645084-0-0*) ORourke Servs.
O'Rourke, Robert. What God Did for Zeke the Fuzzy Caterpillar. (Happy Day Bks.). (Illus.). 32p. (Orig.). (J). (gr. k-2). 1991. 2.50 (*0-87403-824-3*, 24-03924) Standard Pub.
O'Rourke, T. D. & Hobelman, A. G., eds. Excavation & Support for the Urban Infrastructure: Papers Presented for Sessions Sponsored by the Geotechnical Engineering Division of the American Society of Civil Engineers in Conjunction with the ASCE International Convention & Exposition, September 14 & 15, 1992 in New York, New York. LC 92-27782. (Geotechnical Special Publication Ser.: No. 33). 272p. 1992. 26.00 (*0-87262-906-6*) Am Soc Civil Eng.
O'Rourke, Terrence J. A Basic Course in Manual Communication. (Illus.). 1973. 11.95 (*0-913072-01-X*) Natl Assn Deaf.
— A Basic Vocabulary: American Sign Language for Parents & Children. 1978. pap. 8.95 (*0-932666-00-0*) T J Pubs.
O'Rourke, Thomas, jt. auth. see Collins, Denis.
O'Rourke, Thomas D., ed. The Loma Prieta, California, Earthquake of October 17, 1989 - Marina District. (Illus.). 215p. (Orig.). (C). 1993. pap. text ed. 45.00 (*0-7881-0175-7*) Diane Pub.
O'Rourke, Thomas P. The Franciscan Missions in Texas (1690-1793) LC 73-3559. (Catholic University of America. Studies in Romance Languages & Literatures: No. 5). reprint ed. 27.50 (*0-404-57755-5*) AMS Pr.
O'Rourke, Timothy. The Impact of Reapportionment. LC 78-62883. 325p. 1979. 32.95 (*0-87855-290-1*) Transaction Pubs.
O'Rourke, Vernon A. Juristic Status of Egypt & the Sudan. LC 75-138619. 184p. 1973. reprint ed. text ed. 49.75 (*0-8371-5731-5*, ORJS, Greenwood Pr) Greenwood.
O'Rourke, William. Signs of the Literary Times: Essays, Reviews, Profiles 1970-1992. LC 92-43027. (Margins of Literature Ser.). 250p. (C). 1993. 57.50 (*0-7914-1681-X*); pap. 18.95 (*0-7914-1682-8*) State U NY Pr.
Oroyan, Susanna. Fantastic Figures: Ideas & Techniques Using the New Clays. LC 94-4645. 1994. pap. 21.95 (*0-914881-00-0*) C & T Pub.
Oroyan, Susanna & Waugh, Carol-Lynn R. Contemporary Artist Dolls: A Collector's Guide. (Illus.). 224p. 1986. 19.95 (*0-87588-271-4*, 3259) Hobby Hse.
Orozco, C. R. Spanish-English, English-Spanish Commercial Dictionary. (ENG & SPA.). 1969. pap. 36.00 (*0-08-006380-2*, Pergamon Pr) Elsevier.
Orozco, David J., ed. see Imatani, Wendy J.
Orozco, David J., ed. see Twain, Mark, et al.
Orozco, E. C. Republican Protestantism in Aztlan. LC 80-82906. 261p. 1980. pap. 24.00 (*0-9606102-2-7*) Petereins Pr.
Orozco, Jose-Luis, tr. De Colores & Other Latin-American Folk Songs for Children. (Illus.). 56p. 1994. 16.99 (*0-525-45260-5*) Dutton Child Bks.
Orozco, Julio, tr. see Osborne, Cecil G.
Orozco, Samuel, jt. auth. see Street, Richard S.
Orpana, V. Production Research. 1993: Proceedings of the Twelfth International Conference on Production Research, Lappeenranta. Lukka, Orpena, ed. LC 93-25569. (Advances in Industrial Engineering Ser.: Vol. 17). 1993. write for info. (*0-444-89731-3*) Elsevier.
Orpen, Adela E. The Chronicles of the Sid, or, the Life & Travels of Adelia Gates. LC 72-5585. (Black Heritage Library Collection). 1977. reprint ed. 41.95 (*0-8369-9145-1*) Ayer.
Orpheus. Hymni. Quant, Wilhelm, ed. 93p. 1973. write for info. (*3-296-14800-0*, Pub. by Georg Olms GW) Lubrecht & Cramer.
Orpin, jt. ed. see Mountfort.
Orput, Fran, ed. see Bordenave, Eileen.
***Orr.** City of Salt. 1995. pap. text ed. (*0-8229-5557-1*) U of Pittsburgh Pr.
— Star Quality. 1993. pap. 6.00 (*1-85538-179-6*) Thorsons SF.
Orr, jt. auth. see Matteson.
Orr, jt. auth. see McCloskey.
Orr & Reno P. A. Staff. New Hampshire Environmental Practice: Regulation & Compliance. Platt, Thomas C. & Johnston, Cordell A., eds. LC 92-14890. 680p. 1994. ring bd. 95.00 (*1-56257-190-7*) Michie Butterworth.
Orr & Reno Staff. New Hampshire Environmental Practice: Regulation & Compliance. suppl. ed. Platt, Thomas C. & Johnston, Cordell A., eds. LC 92-14890. 1993. ring bd. 50.00 (*0-685-74438-8*) Butterworth Legal Pubs.
Orr, A., ed. see Shore, S. N., et al.
Orr, Akiva. Israel: Politics, Myths, & Identity Crises. LC 94-2269. (Middle Eastern Ser.). (C). 1994. text ed. 66.50 (*0-7453-0766-3*) Westview.
Orr, Alberta L. Vision & Aging: Crossroads for Service Delivery. LC 92-5088. 392p. 1992. 39.95 (*0-89128-216-5*) Am Foun Blind.
Orr, Alexandra L. Life & Letters of Robert Browning. (BCL1-PR English Literature Ser.). 431p. 1992. reprint ed. lib. bdg. 99.00 (*0-7812-7465-6*) Rprt Serv.
Orr, Alice. Camp Fear. (Intrigue Ser.). 1994. mass mkt. 2.99 (*0-373-22266-1*, 1-22266-0) Harlequin Bks.
— Key West Heat. (Intrigue Ser.). 1995. pap. 3.50 (*0-373-22324-2*, 1-22324-7) Harlequin Bks.
Orr, Alice H. Cold Summer. (Intrigue Ser.). 1993. pap. 2.89 (*0-373-22216-5*, 1-22216-5) Harlequin Bks.
***Orr, Aliva.** Israel: Politics, Myths, & Identity Crises. (C). 1994. pap. text ed. 18.95 (*0-7453-0767-1*) Westview.
Orr, Angus A. A Piece of Work. abr. ed. 260p. 1995. pap. 8.95 (*1-56901-320-9*) NW Pub.
Orr, Anne. Anne Orr's Afghans to Crochet & Knit. (Illus.). 32p. 1987. reprint ed. pap. 2.95 (*0-486-25440-2*) Dover.
— Anne Orr's Charted Designs. (Needlework Ser.). (Illus.). 1979. pap. 3.50 (*0-486-23704-4*) Dover.
— Anne Orr's Classic Tatting Patterns. LC 85-4523. 32p. 1985. reprint ed. pap. 2.95 (*0-486-24897-6*) Dover.
— Anne Orr's Filet Crochet Designs. 48p. (Orig.). 1986. pap. 2.95 (*0-486-25103-9*) Dover.
— Anne Orr's Treasury of Charted Designs, 3 bks. (Illus.). 112p. 1985. Set. pap. 11.50 (*0-486-25011-3*) Dover.
— Crochet Designs of Anne Orr. LC 77-92502. (Needlework Ser.). (Illus.). 1978. pap. 2.75 (*0-486-23621-8*) Dover.
— Crocheting with Anne Orr. (Illus.). 48p. (Orig.). 1988. pap. 3.50 (*0-486-25672-3*) Dover.
— Favorite Charted Designs. 40p. (Orig.). 1983. pap. 3.50 (*0-486-24484-9*) Dover.
— Quilting with Anne Orr. 1990. pap. 3.50 (*0-486-26325-8*) Dover.
— Tatting with Anne Orr. (J). 1989. pap. 2.50 (*0-486-25982-X*) Dover.
Orr, Ben, jt. ed. see Orr, Eliza C.
Orr, Bill. College Algebra. LC 91-55381. (Outline Ser.). (Illus.). 256p. (Orig.). (C). 1992. pap. 14.00 (*0-06-467140-2*, Harper Ref) HarpC.
— The Global Economy in the Nineties: A User's Guide. (Illus.). 330p. 1992. text ed. 75.00 (*0-8147-6176-3*) NYU Pr.

O

An Asterisk (*) at the beginning of an entry indicates that the title is appearing in BIP for the first time.

— The Global Economy in the 1990s: A User's Guide. (Illus.). 320p. (C). 1993. pap. text ed. 25.00 (0-8147-6181-X) NYU Pr.
Orr, Bud. Anthology of Mandolin Music. 1993. 15.00 (1-56222-009-8, 93952); audio 9.98 (1-56222-868-4, 93952) Mel Bay.
— Deluxe Country Mandolin Method. 1993. 8.95 (0-87166-962-5, 93719); audio 9.98 (0-87166-659-6, 93719) Mel Bay.
— Learn to Play Bluegrass Mandolin. 1993. 4.95 (0-87166-683-9, 93720) Mel Bay.
Orr, Bud, jt. auth. see Bay, William.
Orr, C. E. Food for Lambs. 168p. pap. 2.00 (0-686-29109-3) Faith Pub Hse.
— Heavenly Life for Earthly Living. 60p. pap. 0.75 (0-686-29111-5) Faith Pub Hse.
— Helps to Holy Living. 64p. pap. 0.40 (0-686-29112-3); pap. 1.00 (0-686-29113-1) Faith Pub Hse.
— The Hidden Life. 112p. pap. 1.00 (0-686-29149-2) Faith Pub Hse.
— How to Live a Holy Life. 112p. pap. 1.00 (0-686-29120-4) Faith Pub Hse.
— Odors from Golden Vials. 78p. pap. 1.00 (0-686-29131-X) Faith Pub Hse.
Orr, C. W. The Making of Northern Nigeria. 320p. 1986. 250.00 (1-85077-138-3, Darf Pubs Ltd) St Mut.
***Orr-Cahall, Christina.** Addison Mizner, Architect of Dreams & Realities, 1872-1933. 64p. 1977. 16.95 (0-615-00347-8) Norton Gal Art.
***Orr-Cahall, Christina, pref.** Man Ray's Man Rays. (Illus.). 76p. Date not set. 19.95 (0-89381-658-2) FS&G.
***Orr-Cahall, Christina & Tucker, Paul H.** Claude Monet: An Impression. 24p. 1993. 12.95 (0-943411-22-X) Norton Gal Art.
Orr, Carolyn & Kelley, Patricia. Sarayacu Quichua Pottery. (Museum of Anthropology Publications: No. 1). 37p. 1976. fiche 4.00 (0-88312-240-5) Summer Instit Ling.
Orr, Carolyn G. Scrimshaw. (Illus.). 48p. 1987. 24.00 (0-88014-069-0) Mosaic Pr OH.
Orr, Charles. History of the Pequot War: The Contemporary Accounts of Mason, Underhill, Vincent & Gardener. LC 76-43799. reprint ed. 37.50 (0-404-15655-X) AMS Pr.
Orr, Charles A. Stalin's Slave Camps. LC 74-22754. (Labor Movement in Fiction & Non-Fiction Ser.). reprint ed. 27.50 (0-404-58507-8) AMS Pr.
Orr, Chris, et al, illus. A First Poetry Book. 128p. (J). (gr. 1-3). 1987. pap. 6.95 (0-19-918112-8) OUP.
Orr, Chun-Hou, jt. ed. see Coulbeck, Bryan.
***Orr, Clarice C.** The Joy of Grandparenting: Grandparents Make a Difference. (Illus.). 224p. (Orig.). 1995. pap. 10.00 (1-886225-00-1) Dageforde Pub.
***Orr, Clarissa C., ed.** Women in the Victorian Art World. (Illus.). 256p. 1995. text ed. 69.95 (0-7190-4122-8, Pub. by Manchester Univ Pr UK); text ed. 19.95 (0-7190-4123-6, Pub. by Manchester Univ Pr UK) St Martin.
Orr, Clyde, ed. Filtration: Principles & Practices, Pt. 1. LC 75-18059. (Chemical Processing & Engineering Ser.: No. 10). (Illus.). 544p. reprint ed. pap. 155.10 (0-8357-6113-4, 2034559) Bks Demand.
— Filtration: Principles & Practices, Pt. 2. LC 75-18059. (Chemical Processing & Engineering Ser.: No. 10). 419p. pap. 119.50 (0-7837-0036-9, 2034559) Bks Demand.
Orr, D., ed. see Orr European Geophysical Symposium Staff.
Orr, David. Italian Renaissance Drama in England Before 1625. LC 77-17260. (University of North Carolina Studies in Comparative Literature: No. 49). 151p. reprint ed. 43.10 (0-8357-9704-X, 2017230) Bks Demand.
Orr, David B., ed. New Directions in Employability: Reducing Barriers to Full Employment. LC 73-6094. (Special Studies in U. S. Economic, Social & Political Issues). 1973. 39.50 (0-275-28838-2) Irvington.
Orr, David W. Earth in Mind: On Education, Environment, & the Human Prospect. LC 94-17546. 224p. 1994. text ed. 29.95 (1-55963-294-1); pap. 16.95 (1-55963-295-X) Island Pr.
— Ecological Literacy: Education & the Transition to a Postmodern World. LC 90-28767. (SUNY Series in Constructive Postmodern Thought). 210p. (C). 1991. 49.50 (0-7914-0873-6); pap. 16.95 (0-7914-0874-4) State U NY Pr.
Orr, David W. & Soroos, Marvin S., eds. The Global Predicament: Ecological Perspectives on World Order. LC 78-10207. 414p. reprint ed. pap. 118.00 (0-8357-4404-3, 2037224) Bks Demand.
Orr, David W., jt. ed. see Eagan, David J.
Orr, Dorothy B., jt. auth. see Orr, Robert T.
Orr, Ed. Enigmas: After de Chirico. 1986. pap. 5.00 (0-941240-06-1) Ommation Pr.
— Masking & Unmasking: Poems About Art. (Crow King Editions Ser.). 24p. (Orig.). 1981. pap. 1.00 (0-930600-16-9) Uzzano Pr.
Orr, Edwin. Hablando Con Franqueza Temas de Moral: Candid Questions about Morality. (SPA.). 4.95 (84-7228-506-5, 220437, Pub. by Edit Clie SP) TSELF.
Orr, Edwin J. Cien Preguntas Acerca De Dios: 100 Questions about God. (SPA.). 4.95 (84-7228-143-4, 220159, Pub. by Edit Clie SP) TSELF.
Orr, Elaine N. Tillie Olsen & a Feminist Spiritual Vision. LC 86-28925. (Illus.). 208p. 1987. 30.00 (0-87805-300-X) U Pr of Miss.
Orr, Eleanor W. Twice As Less: Black English & the Performance of Black Students in Mathematics & Science. LC 87-5758. 1987. 15.95 (0-393-02392-3) Norton.
— Twice As Less: Black English & the Performance of Black Students in Mathematics & Science. LC 87-5758. 1989. pap. 8.95 (0-393-30585-6) Norton.
***Orr, Eliza C. & Orr, Ben, eds.** Qanemcikarluni Tekitnarqelartuq: One Must Arrive with a Story to Tell : Traditional Narratives by the Elders of Tununak, Alaska. LC 95-2303. (ESK.). 1995. write for info. (1-55500-052-5) Alaska Native.
Orr, Elizabeth & Orr, William. Rivers of the West: A Guide to the Geology & History. LC 85-61228. (Illus.). 342p. (Orig.). 1985. 14.95 (0-9606502-1-0) W&E Orr.
Orr, Elizabeth, jt. auth. see Orr, William.
Orr, Elizabeth L., et al. Geology of Oregon. 272p. (C). 1992. pap. 24.95 (0-8403-8058-5) Kendall-Hunt.
Orr European Geophysical Symposium Staff. Geomagnetic Pulsations: Proceedings of the Orr European Geophysical Symposium, Budapest, August 1980. Orr, D., ed. 100p. 1983. pap. 30.00 (0-08-026508-1, Pergamon Pr) Elsevier.
Orr, F. William, et al. Microcirculation in Cancer Metastasis. 304p. 1991. 190.00 (0-8493-6154-0, RC269) CRC Pr.
Orr, Frank. Great Moments in Auto Racing. LC 73-18087. (Illus.). 160p. (J). 1974. lib. bdg. 3.69 (0-394-92763-X) Random Bks Yng Read.
Orr, Gregory. New & Selected Poems. LC 87-13681. (Wesleyan Poetry Ser.). 103p. 1988. 22.50 (0-8195-2140-X, Wesleyan Univ Pr); pap. 10.95 (0-8195-1141-2, Wesleyan Univ Pr) U Pr of New Eng.
— Richer Entanglements: Essays & Notes on Poetry & Poems. LC 93-10796. (Poets on Poetry Ser.). 190p. (C). 1993. text ed. 39.50 (0-472-09525-0); pap. 13.95 (0-472-06525-4) U of Mich Pr.
— Stanley Kunitz: An Introduction to the Poetry. LC 84-23213. (Columbia Introductions to Twentieth Century American Poetry Ser.). 296p. 1985. text ed. 35.00 (0-231-05234-0) Col U Pr.
Orr, H. Simon, jt. ed. see Harvey, Colin E.
Orr, H. Winnett. On the Contributions of Hugh Owen Thomas of Liverpool, Sir Robert Jones of Liverpool & London, John Ridlon, M. D. of New York & Chicago to Modern Orthopedic Surgery. Phillips, William R. & Rosenberg, Janet, eds. LC 79-6920. (Physically Handicapped in Society Ser.). 1980. reprint ed. lib. bdg. 26.95 (0-405-13129-1) Ayer.
Orr, J. B., jt. auth. see Beck, R. N.
Orr, J. B., et al. What Science Stands For. LC 72-134157. (Essay Index Reprint Ser.). 1977. 17.95 (0-8369-1938-6) Ayer.
Orr, J. Edwin. The Event of the Century: The 1857-1858 Awakening. Roberts, Richard O., ed. xviii, 384p. 1989. 27.50 (0-940033-39-9) R O Roberts.
— My All His All. Roberts, Richard O., ed. xiv, 170p. 1989. 14.95 (0-940033-40-2) R O Roberts.
Orr, J. M. Libraries as Communication Systems. LC 76-8739. (Contributions in Librarianship & Information Science Ser.: No. 17). 240p. 1977. text ed. 49.95 (0-8371-8936-5, ORL, Greenwood Pr) Greenwood.
Orr, Jack. Black Athlete: His Story in American History. (J). (gr. 6 up). 1969. lib. bdg. 14.95 (0-87460-104-5) Lion Bks.
Orr, James. Christian View of God & the World. LC 89-2580. 504p. 1989. pap. 15.99 (0-8254-3370-3) Kregel.
— Concepcion Cristiana de Dios y el Mundo (Christian View of God & the World) 598p. (SPA.). 1992. 16.95 (84-7645-550-X, 223486, Pub. by Edit Clie SP) TSELF.
— A Guide to Putting Yourself in the Movies. 246p. 1987. per. 9.95 (0-943629-01-2) Swan Pub.
— Progreso del Dogma: Progress of Dogma. (SPA.). 18.95 (84-7645-314-0, 223289, Pub. by Edit Clie SP) TSELF.
***Orr, James, ed.** International Standard Bible Encyclopedia (ISBE), 4 vols., Set. 1994. 179.95 (1-56563-026-2) Hendrickson MA.
Orr, James E. An Apprenticeship of Faith. LC 89-82774. Orig. Title: Can God. xvi, 144p. (Orig.). 1993. pap. 6.95 (0-926474-04-9) Intl Awakening Pr.
— Campus Aflame: A History of Evangelical Awakenings in Collegiate Communities. rev. ed. LC 93-78598. 286p. 1994. pap. text ed. 14.95 (0-926474-07-3) Intl Awakening Pr.
— The Event of the Century. 300p. 1989. lib. bdg. 27.50 (0-926474-01-4) Intl Awakening Pr.
— My All, His All. rev. ed. 215p. reprint ed. lib. bdg. 14.95 (0-926474-02-2) Intl Awakening Pr.
Orr, James R., et al. A Guide To...Putting Yourself in the Movies. Billac, Pete, ed. LC 87-91245. 246p. (gr. 12 up). 1987. pap. 9.95 (0-943629-26-8) Swan Pub.
Orr, James W., jt. auth. see Shingleton, Hugh M.
Orr, James W., Jr., et al. Complications in Gynecologic Surgery: Prevention, Recognition & Management. Sims, J. Marion, ed. LC 93-41475. (Illus.). 360p. 1994. pap. 69.50 (0-397-51269-4, Lippincott Medical) Lippincott.
Orr, Jean. Women's Health in the Community. (Illus.). 200p. 1987. pap. 17.00 (0-471-91105-4) Ishiyaku Euro.
Orr, Jean, jt. auth. see Luker, Karen A.
***Orr, Jerry.** Don't Kiss Your Turtle Goodbye: True Tales of a Hill Country Vet. (Illus.). 180p. (Orig.). 1995. pap. 13.95 (1-878086-45-6) Down Home NC.
Orr, Jessie F. Dare to Believe You Live after Death. 347p. (C). 1988. 40.00 (0-7212-0747-2, Pub. by Regency Press) St Mut.
Orr, Joel N., jt. auth. see Teicholz, Eric.
Orr, John. Cinema & Modernity. (Illus.). 232p. 1994. text ed. 49.95 (0-7456-0631-8); pap. text ed. 19.95 (0-7456-1186-9) Blackwell Pubs.
— The Making of the Twentieth-Century Novel: Lawrence, Joyce, Faulkner & Beyond. LC 86-20353. 232p. 1987. text ed. 35.00 (0-312-00220-3) St Martin.
Orr, John & Klaic, Dragan, eds. Terrorism & Modern Drama. 1991. text ed. 49.00 (0-7486-0173-2, Pub. by Edinburgh U Pr UK) Col U Pr.
— Terrorism & Modern Drama. 288p. 1992. pap. 24.95 (0-7486-0195-3, Pub. by Edinburgh U Pr UK) Col U Pr.
Orr, John, jt. auth. see Bartholomew.
Orr, John, tr. see Jordan, Jorgu.
Orr, John, jt. ed. see Nicholson, Colin.
***Orr, Julie.** Alphabet Fun. Hoffman, Joan, ed. (Jump Ahead Book Ser.). (Illus.). 32p. (J). (ps-k). 1994. student ed 1.99 (0-88743-115-1) Sch Zone Pub Co.
— Alphabet Seekers. Hoffman, Joan, ed. (Jump Ahead Book Ser.). (Illus.). 32p. (J). (ps-k). 1994. student ed 1.99 (0-88743-112-7) Sch Zone Pub Co.
— Animal Fun. Hoffman, Joan, ed. (Jump Ahead Book Ser.). (Illus.). 32p. (J). (ps-k). 1994. student ed 1.99 (0-88743-114-3) Sch Zone Pub Co.
— Finders Keepers. Hoffman, Joan, ed. (Jump Ahead Book Ser.). (Illus.). 32p. (J). (ps-k). 1994. student ed 1.99 (0-88743-111-9) Sch Zone Pub Co.
— Pathways to Fun. Hoffman, Joan, ed. (Jump Ahead Book Ser.). (Illus.). 32p. (J). (ps-k). 1994. student ed 1.99 (0-88743-113-5) Sch Zone Pub Co.
Orr, Katherine. The Coral Reef Coloring Book. (NaturEncyclopedia Library). (Illus.). 48p. (J). (gr. 2 up). 1988. pap. 5.95 (0-88045-090-8) Stemmer Hse.
— The Hawaiian Coral Reef Coloring Book. (NaturEncyclopedia Library). (Illus.). 48p. (Orig.). (J). (gr. 1-6). 1992. pap. 5.95 (0-88045-122-X) Stemmer Hse.
— My Grandpa & the Sea. LC 89-23876. (Illus.). 32p. (J). (ps-3). 1990. lib. bdg. 18.95 (0-87614-409-1, Carolrhoda) Lerner Group.
— My Grandpa & the Sea. (J). (ps-3). 1991. pap. 5.95 (0-87614-525-X, Carolrhoda) Lerner Group.
— Shells of North American Shores. (NaturEncyclopedia Library). (Illus.). 48p. 1989. pap. 5.95 (0-88045-097-5) Stemmer Hse.
— Story of a Dolphin. LC 92-28656. (Illus.). (J). (ps-3). 1993. 18.95 (0-87614-777-5, Carolrhoda) Lerner Group.
— Turtle Lore. (Illus.). 32p. 1989. pap. 6.95 (0-9613236-2-0) Florida Flair Bks.
Orr, Katherine S. & Berg, Carl J., Jr. The Queen Conch. (Illus.). 32p. 1987. pap. 2.95 (0-89317-038-0) Windward Pub.
Orr, Kathy, illus. A Christmas Garland. 40p. (J). 1991. lib. bdg. 8.95 (0-8378-2069-3) Gibson.
— Dearly Beloved Wedding Album. 64p. 1994. 20.00 (0-8378-2243-2) Gibson.
— Dearly Beloved Wedding Guest Book. 48p. 1994. 13.00 (0-614-04419-7) Gibson.
— Dearly Beloved Wedding Organizer. 1994. 20.00 (0-8378-2245-9) Gibson.
Orr, Ken. One Minute Methodology. LC 84-61222. 66p. 1990. pap. 12.00 (0-932633-17-X) Dorset Hse Pub Co.
Orr, Kenneth G. Field Notes on the Burmese Standard of Living. LC 77-87019. reprint ed. 21.75 (0-404-16848-5) AMS Pr.
Orr, Kenneth G., et al. The Zimmerman Site. Brown, James A., ed. (Reports of Investigations Ser.: No. 9). (Illus.). 86p. 1974. pap. 2.10 (0-89792-021-X) Ill St Museum.
Orr, Kenneth T. Structured Systems Development. LC 77-88593. (Illus.). 192p. (Orig.). 1986. pap. 19.95 (0-917072-06-5, Yourdon) P-H.
***Orr, Larry, et al, eds.** Impacts for Employment & Training Programs for the Disadvantaged: Evidence from the National JTPA Study. 375p. (C). 1995. lib. bdg. 69.50 (0-87766-646-6); pap. text ed. 34.50 (0-87766-647-4) Urban Inst.
***Orr, Leonard.** Babaji the Angel of the Lord. 1995. 20.00 (0-945793-18-9) Inspir Univ.
— Bhartriji - Immortal Yogi of Two Thousand Years. 1990. 12.00 (0-945793-05-7) Inspir Univ.
— A Catalogue Checklist of English Prose Fiction: 1750-1800. LC 79-64848. 204p. 1979. 13.50 (0-87875-171-8) Whitston Pub.
— The Common Sense of Physical Immortality. pap. 5.00 (0-318-23459-9) L Orr.
— Critical Essays on Coleridge. (Critical Essays on British Literature Ser.). 208p. 1994. text ed. 45.00 (0-8161-8867-X, Twayne) Macmillan.
— De-Structing the Novel: Essays in Postmodern Hermeneutics. LC 81-52811. 280p. (C). 1982. 22.50 (0-87875-223-4) Whitston Pub.
— The Death Urge. 1995. 20.00 (0-945793-15-4) Inspir Univ.
— A Dictionary of Critical Theory. LC 90-22816. 408p. 1991. text ed. 79.50 (0-313-23527-9, ODC, Greenwood Pr) Greenwood.
— The Energy of Success. 1990. 20.00 (0-945793-12-X) Inspir Univ.
— Existentialism & Phenomenology: A Guide for Research. LC 77-93782. 1978. 15.00 (0-87875-141-6) Whitston Pub.
— Government Without Taxes. 1991. 10.00 (0-945793-14-6) Inspir Univ.
— How to Be Successful in the Self Improvement Business. 1990. 10.00 (0-945793-07-3) Inspir Univ.
— How to Make Democracy Work. 1990. 10.00 (0-945793-06-5) Inspir Univ.
— How to Make Democracy Work. pap. 10.00 (0-318-23461-0) L Orr.
— The Money Seminar. 1990. 20.00 (0-945793-11-1) Inspir Univ.
— The Money System. 1990. 20.00 (0-945793-13-8) Inspir Univ.
— Physical Immortality & Transfiguration. pap. write for info. (0-318-62542-3) L Orr.
— Problems & Poetics of the Nonaristotelian Novel. LC 89-46139. 176p. 1991. 32.50 (0-8387-5182-2) Bucknell U Pr.
— Prosperity Consciousness Consultation. 1990. 20.00 (0-945793-10-3) Inspir Univ.
— Rebirthing in the New Age. pap. 9.95 (0-318-23462-9) L Orr.
— Secrets of Youthing. 1994. 22.00 (0-945793-16-2) Inspir Univ.
— Semiotic & Structuralist Analyses of Fiction: An Introduction & a Survey of Applications. LC 86-50685. 224p. 1986. 30.00 (0-87875-331-1) Whitston Pub.
— The Story of Rebirthing. 1990. 5.00 (0-945793-08-1) Inspir Univ.
— Turning Senility Misery into Victory. 1990. 10.00 (0-945793-17-0) Inspir Univ.
Orr, Leonard, comp. Research in Critical Theory since Nineteen Eighty-Five: A Classified Bibliography. LC 89-16863. (Bibliographies & Indexes in World Literature Ser.: No. 21). 480p. 1989. text ed. 85.00 (0-313-26388-4, ORC/, Greenwood Pr) Greenwood.
Orr, Leonard, ed. Yeats & Postmodernism. (Irish Studies). 192p. 1990. text ed. 29.95x (0-8156-2506-5) Syracuse U Pr.
Orr, Leonard & Ray, Sondra. Rebirthing in the New Age. LC 76-53337. 1978. pap. 12.95 (0-89087-134-5) Celestial Arts.
Orr, Leonard D. Common Sense of Physical Immortality. rev. ed. 1988. pap. 5.00 (0-945793-00-6) Inspir Univ.
— Physical Immortality. (YA). (gr. 7 up). 1988. pap. 10.00 (0-945793-01-4) Inspir Univ.
Orr, Leonard H., ed. see Herman, Stewart W., et al.
Orr, Lernard D. Breath Awareness: Breath Awareness for Public Schools, Medical Profession. (YA). (gr. 7 up). 1988. pap. 10.00 (0-945793-02-2) Inspir Univ.
Orr, Linda. Headless History: Nineteenth-Century French Historiography of the Revolution. LC 89-22140. (Illus.). 216p. 1990. 32.95 (0-8014-2379-1) Cornell U Pr.
— Jules Michelet: Nature, History, & Language. LC 76-13662. 256p. 1976. 33.95 (0-8014-0976-4) Cornell U Pr.
Orr, Lisa, ed. Censorship: Opposing Viewpoints. LC 90-42854. (Opposing Viewpoints Ser.). (Illus.). 240p. (YA). (gr. 10 up). 1990. lib. bdg. 19.95 (0-89908-479-6); pap. text ed. 11.55 (0-89908-454-0) Greenhaven.
— The Homeless: Opposing Viewpoints. LC 89-25734. (Opposing Viewpoints Ser.). (Illus.). 216p. (YA). (gr. 10 up). 1990. lib. bdg. 19.95 (0-89908-476-1); pap. text ed. 11.55 (0-89908-451-6) Greenhaven.
***Orr, Lynn F., et al.** Monet: Late Paintings of Giverny from the Musee Marmottan. 1994. pap. write for info. (0-8109-2610-5) Abrams.
Orr, Margaret T. Keeping Students in School: A Guide to Effective Dropout Prevention Programs & Services. LC 87-45502. (Education-Higher Education Ser.). 258p. 1987. 34.95x (1-55542-070-2) Jossey-Bass.
— What to do about Youth Dropouts? A Summary of Solutions. O'Connor, Mary L., ed. 32p. (Orig.). 1987. pap. 5.00 (0-943567-00-9) SEEDCO.
Orr, Marjorie. Lover's Guide: An Astrological Key to Relationships. (Illus.). 384p. 1994. pap. 8.00 (1-85538-315-2, Pub. by Aquarian Pr UK) Thorsons SF.
Orr, Marsha J., jt. auth. see Donovan, Ronald.
Orr, Mary. Claude Simon: The Interextual Dimension. 224p. 1993. 60.00 (0-85261-372-5, Pub. by Univ of Glasgow UK) St Mut.
— Grass Widows. 1976. pap. 4.75 (0-8222-0477-0) Dramatists Play.
— Roommates. 1989. pap. 2.75 (0-8222-0964-0) Dramatists Play.
— The Wisdom of Eve. Denham, Reginald, ed. 1964. pap. 4.75 (0-8222-1267-6) Dramatists Play.
— The Wisdom of Eve. rev. ed. 1994. pap. 4.75 (0-8222-1429-6) Dramatists Play.
— Women Must Weep. 1963. pap. 4.75 (0-8222-1273-0) Dramatists Play.
— Women Still Weep: A Sequel to Women Must Weep. 1980. pap. 4.75 (0-8222-1275-7) Dramatists Play.
Orr, Mary & Denham, Reginald. Be Your Age. 1953. pap. 13.00 (0-8222-1301-X) Dramatists Play.
— Dead Giveaway. 1982. pap. 4.75 (0-8222-0283-2) Dramatists Play.
— Minor Murder. 1967. pap. 13.00 (0-8222-0760-5) Dramatists Play.
Orr, N. Lee. Church Music Handbook: For Pastors & Musicians. 1991. 11.95 (0-687-07853-9) Abingdon.
Orr, N. Lee & Bertrand, Lynn W., eds. The Collected Works of John Hill Hewitt. LC 94-76. (Nineteenth-Century American Musical Theater Ser.: No. 6). 328p. 1994. reprint ed. 102.00 (0-8153-1370-5) Garland.
***Orr, Nancy & McKean, Kay.** The Disciple's Wedding: Planning a Wedding That Gives Glory to God. 80p. 1994. pap. 6.99 (1-884553-21-4) Discipleshp.
Orr, Oliver H., Jr. Saving American Birds: T. Gilbert Pearson & the Founding of the Audubon Movement. (Illus.). 272p. 1992. lib. bdg. 36.95 (0-8130-1129-9) U Press Fla.
Orr, Philip. Road to the Somme. 1987. pap. 22.00 (0-85640-390-3, Pub. by Blackstaff Pr IE) Dufour.
Orr, Robert. Religion in China. 144p. (Orig.). 1980. 4.95 (0-318-16788-3) US-China Peoples Friendship.
Orr, Robert M., Jr. The Emergence of Japan's Foreign Aid Power. 178p. (C). 1992. pap. 12.50 (0-231-07047-0) Col U Pr.
— Japan: Its Changing Foreign Aid Policy. 192p. 1990. text ed. 29.00 (0-231-07046-2) Col U Pr.
Orr, Robert M., jt. ed. see Koppel, Bruce, Jr.
Orr, Robert P. The Meaning of Transcendence. Dietrich, Wendell, ed. LC 80-12872. (American Academy of Religion, Dissertation Ser.). 172p. 1981. pap. 15.95 (0-89130-408-8, 01 01 35) Scholars Pr GA.
Orr, Robert T. Mammals of Lake Tahoe. (Illus.). 127p. 1949. 7.50 (0-940228-07-6) Calif Acad Sci.
— Vertebrate Biology. 5th ed. 568p. (C). 1982. text ed. 56.00 (0-03-057959-7) SCP.
Orr, Robert T. & Moffitt, James. Birds of the Lake Tahoe Region. (Illus.). 150p. 1971. 8.00 (0-940228-08-4) Calif Acad Sci.

O

An Asterisk (*) at the beginning of an entry indicates that the title is appearing in BIP for the first time.

Orr, Robert T. & Orr, Dorothy B. Mushrooms of Western North America. LC 77-93468. (California Natural History Guides Ser.: No.42). (Illus.). 1979. 35.00 (*0-520-03656-5*); pap. 11.00 (*0-520-03660-3*) U CA Pr.

Orr, Robert T., et al. Marine Mammals of California. LC 78-165233. (California Natural History Guides Ser.: No. 29). 88p. 1972. pap. 10.00 (*0-520-06515-8*) U CA Pr.

— Marine Mammals of California. rev. ed. (California Natural History Guides Ser.: No. 29). 1989. 40.00 (*0-520-06535-2*) U CA Pr.

Orr, Robin A., et al. Introduction to Consumer-based Nutrition. LC 89-84650. (Illus.). 160p. (C). 1989. spiral bd. 16.95 (*0-8138-0484-1*) Iowa St U Pr.

Orr, Sandra. Huron: Grand Bend to Southampton. Hudson, Noel, ed. (Illus.). 160p. 1993. 35.00 (*1-55046-059-5*, Pub. by Boston Mills Pr CN) Genl Dist Srvs.

***Orr, Susan.** Jerusalem & Athens: Reason & Revelation in the Works of Leo Strauss. 224p. 1995. lib. bdg. 56.50 (*0-8476-8010-X*); pap. text ed. 22.95 (*0-8476-8011-8*) Rowman.

***Orr, Tracy.** No Right Way. 1995. pap. 12.95 (*1-85727-087-8*) InBook.

***Orr, Walter.** Blood Water & Stone. LC 95-60834. 159p. 1996. pap. 8.95 (*1-55523-748-7*) Winston-Derek.

Orr, Wendy. Aa-Choo! (Illus.). 32p. (J). (ps-3). 1992. lib. bdg. 14.95 (*1-55037-209-2*, Pub. by Annick CN); pap. 4.95 (*1-55037-208-4*, Pub. by Annick CN) Firefly Bks Ltd.

— A Light in Space. (Illus.). 124p. (J). (gr. 4-6). 1994. lib. bdg. 14.95 (*1-55037-368-4*, Pub. by Annick CN) Firefly Bks Ltd.

— A Light in Space. (Illus.). 124p. (YA). 1994. pap. 4.95 (*1-55037-975-5*, Pub. by Annick CN) Firefly Bks Ltd.

— Pegasus & Ooloo-Moo-loo. (Illus.). 32p. (J). 1993. lib. bdg. 14.95 (*1-55037-278-5*, Pub. by Annick CN); pap. 4.95 (*1-55037-279-3*, Pub. by Annick CN) Firefly Bks Ltd.

Orr, William. Como Conocer la Voluntad De Dios: How to Know the Will of God. (SPA.). 2.95 (*84-7228-224-4*, 220165, Pub. by Edit Clie SP) TSELF.

— Como Hacer Feliz a la Esposa: How to Keep Your Wife Happy. (SPA.). 2.95 (*84-7228-668-1*, 220211, Pub. by Edit Clie SP) TSELF.

— Como Hacer Feliz Al Marido: How to Keep Your Husband Happy. (SPA.). 2.95 (*84-7228-669-X*, 220213, Pub. by Edit Clie SP) TSELF.

— Como Llevar Ninos a Cristo: How to Lead Young Kids to Christ. (SPA.). 3.25 (*84-7228-707-6*, 220218, Pub. by Edit Clie SP) TSELF.

— Como Orar y Obtener Respuesta: How to Pray & Get the Answer. (SPA.). 2.95 (*84-7228-711-4*, 220220, Pub. by Edit Clie SP) TSELF.

— Como Vencer las Preocupaciones: How to Win over Worry. (SPA.). 3.25 (*84-7645-307-8*, 223288, Pub. by Edit Clie SP) TSELF.

— Lo Que Toda Esposa Cristiana Debe Saber: What Every Christian Wife Should. (SPA.). 3.25 (*84-7228-227-9*, 220549, Pub. by Edit Clie SP) TSELF.

— Lo Que Toda Futura Madre Cristiana Debe Saber: What Every Christian Mother to Be. (SPA.). 2.95 (*84-7228-229-5*, 220546, Pub. by Edit Clie SP) TSELF.

— Lo Que Todo Esposo Cristiano Debe Saber: What Every Christian Husband. (SPA.). 3.25 (*84-7228-228-7*, 220550, Pub. by Edit Clie SP) TSELF.

Orr, William & Cowan, Stuart. The Truth about CB Antennas. (Illus.). 240p. pap. 11.95 (*0-8230-8708-5*, RAC Bks) Watsn-Guptill.

Orr, William & Cowan, Stuart D. All about Cubical Quad Antennas. (Illus.). 112p. pap. 11.95 (*0-8230-8703-4*, RAC Bks) Watsn-Guptill.

Orr, William & Guy, William. Living Hope: A Study of the New Testament Theme of Birth from Above. LC 88-34841. 208p. (Orig.). 1989. pap. 10.95 (*0-86534-132-X*) Sunstone Pr.

Orr, William & Orr, Elizabeth. Handbook of Oregon Plant & Animal Fossils. LC 81-90259. (Illus.). 285p. (Orig.). 1981. 10.95 (*0-9606502-0-2*) W&E Orr.

Orr, William, jt. auth. see Orr, Elizabeth.

Orr, William D. Conversational Computers. LC 68-30916. 261p. reprint ed. pap. 74.40 (*0-317-08453-4*, 2011954) Bks Demand.

— First Gentleman's Cookbook. Holloway-Eiche, Pamela, ed. (Illus.). 360p. (Orig.). 1989. pap. 12.50 (*0-9622297-7-6*) Gov Mansion Restor.

Orr, William F. Corinthians I. LC 75-42441. (Anchor Bible Ser.: Vol. 32). 1976. pap. 34.00 (*0-385-02853-9*) Doubleday.

Orr, William I. All about VHF Amateur Radio. 1991. pap. 11.95 (*0-933616-10-4*) Radio Pubns.

— All about VHF Amateur Radio. (Illus.). 172p. pap. 11.95 (*0-8230-8705-0*, RAC Bks) Watsn-Guptill.

— Radio Handbook. 23th ed. 672p. 1987. 39.95 (*0-672-22424-0*) Sams.

Orr, William I. & Cowan, S. D. Simple Low-Cost Wire Antennas for Radio Amateurs. 2nd ed. LC 76-190590. (Illus.). 192p. 1972. 11.95 (*0-933616-02-3*) Radio Pubns.

Orr, William I. & Cowan, Stuart D. All About Cubical Quad Antennas. 3rd ed. LC 82-80282. (Illus.). 112p. 1982. 9.95 (*0-933616-03-1*) Radio Pubns.

— All About Vertical Antennas. LC 86-61499. (Illus.). 192p. 1986. 10.95 (*0-933616-09-0*) Radio Pubns.

— All about Vertical Antennas. (Illus.). 192p. pap. 11.95 (*0-8230-8710-7*, RAC Bks) Watsn-Guptill.

— Beam Antenna Handbook. LC 83-61824. (Illus.). 271p. 1983. 11.95 (*0-933616-04-X*) Radio Pubns.

— Beam Antenna Handbook. (Illus.). 112p. pap. 11.95 (*0-8230-8704-2*, RAC Bks) Watsn-Guptill.

— Better Shortwave Reception. 5th ed. LC 57-14916. (Illus.). 160p. 1957. 9.95 (*0-933616-05-8*) Radio Pubns.

— The Radio Amateur Antenna Handbook. LC 78-53340. (Illus.). 191p. 1978. 11.95 (*0-933616-07-4*) Radio Pubns.

— The Radio Amateur Antenna Handbook. (Illus.). 192p. 1991. pap. 11.95 (*0-8230-8706-9*, RAC Bks) Watsn-Guptill.

— Simple, Low-Cost Wire Antennas for Radio Amateurs. (Illus.). 192p. pap. 11.95 (*0-8230-8707-7*, RAC Bks) Watsn-Guptill.

— The Truth about CB Antennas. 2nd ed. LC 70-164932. (Illus.). 240p. 1971. 11.95 (*0-933616-08-2*) Radio Pubns.

Orr, William I., ed. see Nelson, William.

Orr, William J., ed. see Zeh, Frederick.

Orr, William J., Jr.

Orr, William W. The Anguish of Earth's Tribulation. (Prophecy Ser.). 48p. reprint ed. pap. 3.50 (*0-944412-01-7*) Glad Tid.

— Believer's First Bible Course. (Basic Bible Ser.). 48p. reprint ed. pap. 3.50 (*0-944412-00-9*) Glad Tid.

— What Is Heaven Like? (Bible Answers Ser.). 48p. reprint ed. pap. 3.50 (*0-944412-02-5*) Glad Tid.

Orr, Willie. Discovering Argyll, Mull & Iona. 224p. (C). 1989. pap. text ed. 23.00 (*0-85976-269-6*, Pub. by J Donald) St Mut.

Orr, Wilson L. & White, Curt M., eds. Geochemistry of Sulfur in Fossil Fuels. LC 90-239. (ACS Symposium Ser.: No. 429). (Illus.). 693p. 1990. 109.95 (*0-8412-1804-8*) Am Chemical.

Orrego-Vicuna, Francisco. Antarctic Mineral Exploitation: The Emerging Legal Framework. LC 86-28392. (Studies in Polar Research). (Illus.). 450p. 1988. 125.00 (*0-521-32383-5*) Cambridge U Pr.

Orrego-Vicuna, Francisco, ed. Antarctic Resources Policy: Scientifc, Legal & Political Issues. LC 83-7871. (Studies in Polar Research). 300p. 1984. 105.00 (*0-521-25952-5*) Cambridge U Pr.

Orrell, John. The Quest for Shakespeare's Globe. LC 82-9445. (Illus.). 220p. 1983. 69.95 (*0-521-24751-9*) Cambridge U Pr.

— The Theatres of Inigo Jones & John Webb. (Illus.). 240p. 1985. 59.95 (*0-521-25546-5*) Cambridge U Pr.

Orrell, John, jt. auth. see Gurr, Andrew.

Orrelle, John. Fly Reels of the Past. (Illus.). 155p. 1987. pap. 14.95 (*0-936608-54-4*) F Amato Pubns.

Orren, Gary R., ed. Blurring the Lines: Candidates & Journalists in American Elections. 320p. 1992. 24.95 (*0-02-923476-X*) Free Pr.

Orren, Gary R. & Polsby, Nelson W., eds. Media & Momentum: The New Hampshire Primary & Nomination Politics. LC 87-13224. (Chatham House Series on Change in American Politics). 204p. 1987. pap. text ed. 14.95 (*0-934540-66-7*) Chatham Hse Pubs.

Orren, Gary R., jt. ed. see Mann, Thomas E.

Orren, Gary R., jt. auth. see Verba, Sidney.

Orren, Karen. Belated Feudalism: Labor, the Law & Liberal Development in the United States. 260p. (C). 1992. 59.95 (*0-521-41039-8*); pap. 17.95 (*0-521-42254-X*) Cambridge U Pr.

— Corporate Power & Social Change: The Politics of the Life Insurance Industry. LC 73-8118. (Illus.). 224p. reprint ed. pap. 63.90 (*0-317-41753-3*, 2025862) Bks Demand.

Orren, Karen & Skowronck, Stephen, eds. Studies in American Political Development, Vol. 4: An Annual. 320p. (C). 1990. pap. 19.00 (*0-300-04679-0*) Yale U Pr.

Orren, Karen & Skowronek, Stephen. Studies in American Political Development: An Annual, Vol. 3. 352p. (C). 1989. text ed. 38.00 (*0-300-04486-0*); pap. 16.00 (*0-300-04487-9*) Yale U Pr.

Orrey, Leslie. The Foundations of Harmony & Composition: Music Book Index. 137p. 1993. reprint ed. lib. bdg. 69.00 (*0-7812-9662-5*) Rprt Serv.

— Gluck. 1997. pap. 18.95 (*0-7145-3581-8*) Riverrun NY.

— Opera: A Concise History. LC 86-51512. (World of Art Ser.). (Illus.). 252p. 1987. pap. 14.95 (*0-500-20217-6*) Thames Hudson.

Orrick Herrington & Sutcliffe Staff. Arbitrage Rebate Manual. 300p. (Orig.). 1990. pap. text ed. 25.00 (*0-936093-41-2*) Packard Pr Fin.

Orrick, James. Matthew Arnold & Goethe. LC 70-179267. (Studies in Comparative Literature: No. 35). 1972. reprint ed. lib. bdg. 50.95 (*0-8383-1368-X*) M S G Haskell Hse.

Orridge, Dia. A Girl Called Judith. large type ed. (Linford Romance Library). 224p. 1988. pap. 11.95 (*0-7089-6587-3*, Linford) Ulverscroft.

— Through the Ivory Gate. large type ed. (Romance Ser.). 1989. 17.95 (*0-7089-2062-4*) Ulverscroft.

Orrin, Geoffrey R. Medieval Churches in the Vale of Glamorgan. 550p. (C). 1989. 175.00 (*0-905928-80-6*, Pub. by D Brown & Sons Ltd UK) St Mut.

— Medieval Churches in the Vale of Glamorgan. deluxe limited ed. 550p. (C). 1989. 350.00 (*0-905928-92-X*, Pub. by D Brown & Sons Ltd UK) St Mut.

Orringer, jt. auth. see Waldhausen.

Orringer, Carl, jt. auth. see Mercer, Nelda.

Orringer, Oscar, ed. Residual Stress in Rails, 2 vols., Set. (Engineering Application of Fracture Mechanics Ser.). 492p. (C). 1992. lib. bdg. 225.00 (*0-7923-1651-7*) Kluwer Ac.

Orringer, Oscar, jt. ed. see Tong, Pin.

***Orringer, Stephanie L.** Pedro Salinas' Theater of Self-Authentication. LC 94-28221. (AUS II: Vol. 199). 137p. (C). 1995. text ed. 39.95 (*0-8204-1994-X*) P Lang Pubs.

Orriols, Antoni L. Diccionari de la Ciencia i la Tecnologia Nuclears. 316p. (SPA.). 1979. pap. 29.95 (*0-7859-5876-2*, 8429714766) Fr & Eur.

Orrios, Angel G., ed. see Garcia Lorca, Federico.

Orrios, Angel G., tr. see Garcia Lorca, Federico.

Orrison, Katherine, jt. auth. see Wilcoxon, Henry.

Orrison, William. Introduction to Neuroimaging. (Illus.). 384p. 1988. 88.00 (*0-316-66492-8*, Little Med Div) Little.

***Orrison, William W.** Functional Atlas of Neuroanatomy & Neuroradiology. LC 94-46586. 1995. write for info. (*0-86577-528-1*) Thieme Med Pubs.

Orriss, N., tr. see Babin, Claude, ed.

Orrmont, Arthur & Rosenstiel, Leonie. Literary Agents of North America. 5th rev. ed. (Orig.). 1993. pap. 33.00 (*0-911085-12-2*) Author Aid.

Orrmont, Arthur & Rosenstiel, Leonie, eds. Literary Agents of North America. 3rd ed. 200p. (Orig.). 1988. pap. 19.95 (*0-911085-04-1*) Author Aid.

Orru, Marco. Anomie: History & Meanings. LC 86-32144. 288p. (C). 1987. text ed. 65.00 (*0-04-301267-1*) Routledge Chapman & Hall.

Orsag, Ann, jt. auth. see Fishman, Joel.

***Orsborn, Carol.** How Would Confucius Ask for a Raise? 336p. 1995. reprint ed. pap. 11.00 (*0-380-72250-X*) Avon.

— How Would Confucius Ask for a Raise? One Hundred Solutions for Tough Business Problems. LC 93-46306. 1994. 23.00 (*0-688-13074-7*) Morrow.

— Inner Excellence: Spiritual Principles of Life-Driven Business. LC 91-38491. 160p. 1993. reprint ed. pap. 11.95 (*1-880032-21-X*) New Wrld Lib.

***Orsborne.** Solved by Sunset. 1995. 20.00 (*0-517-70178-2*) Random Hse Value.

Orsburn, Douglas K. Spares Management: An Introduction. (Illus.). 250p. 1991. 49.95 (*0-8306-7626-0*, 3626) TAB Bks.

Orsburn, Jack D., et al. Self-Directed Work Teams: The New American Challenge. 353p. 1990. text ed. 40.00 (*1-55623-341-8*) Irwin Prof Pubng.

Orsden, Donald B. The Holy Bible - The Final Testament: What is the Significance of 666? (Illus.). 48p. (Orig.). (C). Date not set. pap. 9.99 (*1-881373-00-2*) Orsden Pr.

Orsenigo, Luigi. The Emergence of Biotechnology: Institutions & Markets in Industrial Innovation. LC 89-31999. 288p. 1989. text ed. 55.00 (*0-312-03197-1*) St Martin.

Orser, Charles E., Jr. The Material Basis of the Postbellum Tenant Plantation: Historical Archaeology in the South Carolina Piedmont. LC 87-12535. 320p. 1988. 35.00 (*0-8203-0986-9*) U of Ga Pr.

Orser, Charles E., Jr. & Fagan, Brian M. Historical Archaeology: A Brief Introduction. LC 94-18994. 291p. (C). 1994. 17.50 (*0-673-99094-X*) HarpCollege.

Orser, W. Edward. Blockbusting in Baltimore: The Edmondson Village Story. LC 94-8631. (Illus.). 256p. 1994. lib. bdg. 39.95x (*0-8131-1870-0*) U Pr of Ky.

Orsetti, Marion. The Computer Zone. LC 87-42912. 44p. (J). (ps-2). 1988. 8.95 (*1-55523-111-X*) Winston-Derek.

Orshalick, David W., jt. auth. see Dale, Nell B.

Orshan, G., ed. Plant Pheno. Morphological Studies in Mediterranean Type Ecosystems. (Geobotany Ser.). (C). 1988. lib. bdg. 234.00 (*90-6193-656-X*) Kluwer Ac.

Orsher. An Atlas of Diseases of the Ear in Dog & Cat. 1994. write for info. (*0-397-51199-X*) Lippincott.

Orsi-Battaglini, Andrea & Karpen, Ulrich, eds. Scientific Research in the Federal Republic of Germany: Essays on the Constitutional, Administrative & Financial Problems. 279p. 1990. 45.50 (*3-7890-1913-5*, Pub. by Nomos Verlags GW) Intl Bk Import.

Orsi, Maria. The Red Lion: The Elixir of Eternal Life. 364p. 1987. pap. 8.95 (*0-9632370-0-4*) Comput Composit.

Orsi, Pietro. Cavour & the Making of Modern Italy. LC 73-14461. (Heroes of the Nations Ser.). reprint ed. 30.00 (*0-404-58279-6*) AMS Pr.

Orsi, Richard J., et al, eds. Yosemite & Sequoia: A Century of California National Parks. LC 92-42370. 1993. 40.00 (*0-520-08160-9*); pap. 15.00 (*0-520-08161-7*) U CA Pr.

Orsi, Robert. The Madonna of One Hundred & Fifteenth Street: Faith & Community in Italian. LC 85-10799. 366p. (C). 1988. reprint ed. pap. 16.00 (*0-300-04264-7*) Yale U Pr.

***Orsini, Ann.** Can I Go Home Now? 237p. (Orig.). 1994. pap. 14.95 (*0-9642267-0-7*) Phoenix Sparks.

Orsini, D. L., et al. The Neuropsychology Casebook. (Illus.). 300p. 1988. 63.00 (*0-387-96681-1*) Spr-Verlag.

Orsini, Gian N. Organic Unity in Ancient & Later Poetics: The Philosophical Foundations of Literary Criticism. LC 75-17927. 131p. 1975. 8.95 (*0-8093-0728-6*) S Ill U Pr.

Orsini, Joseph. Father Orsini's Italian Kitchen. (Illus.). 288p. 1991. 19.95 (*0-312-06352-0*, Pub. by Thomas Dunne Bks) St Martin.

— Father Orsini's Italian Kitchen. (Illus.). 288p. 1993. pap. 10.95 (*0-312-09524-4*, Pub. by Thomas Dunne Bks) St Martin.

***Orsini, Joseph E.** Father Orsini's Pasta Perfetta. LC 94-22326. 1995. pap. text ed. 17.95 (*0-688-13520-X*) Hearst Bks.

Orsini, Joseph L., jt. ed. see Kassarjian, Harold H.

Orsini, Larry, et al. World Accounting Series, 3 vols. 1986. Looseleaf updates avail. write for info. (*0-8205-1835-2*) Bender.

Orsino, Joseph. Storage Battery Manufacturing Manual. 3rd ed. 1985. 35.00 (*0-685-12355-3*) IBMA Pubns.

Orsino, Philip, et al. Successful Business Expansion: Growing Without Going Under. LC 94-327. 1994. text ed. 34.95 (*0-471-59737-6*) Wiley.

***Orsino, Philip S.** Successful Business Expansion: Practical Strategies for Planning Profitable Growth. 1994. text ed. 17.95 (*0-471-08624-X*) Wiley.

Orska, Kr. Illustrated Poems for Children. (Illus.). (J). 1985. 12.95 (*0-02-689410-6*) Macmillan.

Orskov, Bob. The Feeding of Ruminants Principles & Practice. (Illus.). 94p. (Orig.). 1988. pap. text ed. 14.50 (*0-948617-09-8*) Scholium Intl.

Orskov, E. R. Protein Nutrition in Ruminants. 2nd ed. (Illus.). 175p. 1992. text ed. 55.00 (*0-12-528481-0*) Acad Pr.

Orskov, E. R. & Ryle, M. Energy Nutrition in Ruminants. 1990. 63.00 (*1-85166-439-4*) Elsevier.

Orskov, E. R., jt. auth. see Chesson, A.

Orso, Ethelyn. Modern Greek Humor: A Collection of Jokes & Ribald Tales. LC 78-24845. 288p. reprint ed. pap. 82.10 (*0-317-27841-X*, 2056049) Bks Demand.

— St. Joseph Altar Traditions of South Louisiana. LC 90-82375. (Louisiana Life Ser.: No. 4). 57p. 1990. pap. 5.00 (*0-940984-59-8*) U of SW LA Ctr LA Studies.

Orso, Ethelyn G. Louisiana Live Oak Lore. (Illus.). 117p. (C). 1992. text ed. 19.95 (*0-940984-74-1*) U of SW LA Ctr LA Studies.

— The Macha of Chira: Confessions of an Anthropologist. (Illus.). 177p. (Orig.). (C). 1991. pap. text ed. 10.00 (*0-9630475-0-7*) Lakeview LA.

***Orso, Mary E.** The Crab Lover's Book: Recipes & More. 256p. 1995. 40.00 (*0-87805-801-X*); pap. 14.95 (*0-87805-796-X*) U Pr of Miss.

Orso, Steven N. Art & Death at the Spanish Habsburg Court: The Royal Exequies for Philip IV. LC 89-4745. (Illus.). 192p. 1989. text ed. 32.00 (*0-8262-0710-3*) U of Mo Pr.

— Philip IV & the Decoration of the Alcazar of Madrid. LC 85-19442. (Illus.). 230p. 1986. text ed. 69.50x (*0-691-04036-2*) Princeton U Pr.

— Velazquez, "Los Borrachos," & Painting at the Court of Philip Fourth. LC 93-493. (Illus.). 264p. (C). 1994. 70.00 (*0-521-44452-7*) Cambridge U Pr.

Orsolini, Keith R. The Non-Intimidating Computer Book: The Absolute Bare Bones, Nuts & Bolts Couldn't Be Simpler, Guide to Understanding & Using Personal Computers. (Illus.). 84p. (Orig.). (C). 1989. pap. text ed. write for info. (*0-318-65725-2*) KRO Enterprises.

Orsolini, Margherita, jt. ed. see Pontecorvo, Clotilde.

Orstein, Norman J., jt. auth. see Mann, Thomas E.

Orsulak. Methods in Clinical Toxicology. 1995. write for info. (*0-8493-7883-4*) CRC Pr.

Orsund-Gassiot, Cindy A. & Lindsey, Sharon, eds. Handbook of Medical Staff Management. (Health Care Administration Ser.). 336p. 1990. 75.00 (*0-8342-0177-1*) Aspen Pub.

Orsy, Ladislas. The Lord of Confusion. 1969. 10.00 (*0-87193-064-1*) Dimension Bks.

— Marriage in Canon Law. LC 86-80421. 328p. (Orig.). 1986. pap. 16.95 (*0-8146-5651-X*) Liturgical Pr.

— The Profession of Faith & the Oath of Fidelity. 140p. (Orig.). 1990. pap. text ed. 5.95 (*0-8146-5798-2*) Liturgical Pr.

— Theology & Canon Law: New Horizons for Legislation & Interpretation. 200p. (Orig.). 1992. pap. text ed. 19.95 (*0-8146-5011-2*) Liturgical Pr.

Orsy, Ladislas M. From Vision to Legislation. From The Council to a Code of Laws. LC 85-60746. (Pere Marquette Lectures). 50p. 1985. 10.00 (*0-87462-540-8*) Marquette.

Orszag, S. A., ed. see Amini, S., et al.

Orszag, S. A., ed. see Bruch, E.

Orszag, S. A., ed. see Camp, C. V. & Gipson, G. S.

Orszag, S. A., ed. see Deconinck, J., et al.

Orszag, S. A., ed. see Hayami, K.

Orszag, S. A., jt. auth. see Mendez, Raul H.

Orszag, Steven A., jt. auth. see Bender, Carl M.

Orszag, Steven A., jt. ed. see Galperin, Boris.

Orszag, Steven A., jt. auth. see Gottlieb, David.

***Orszagh, L.** Comprehensive Hungarian-English Dictionary. 9th ed. 1991. 87.00 (*0-7859-8943-9*) Fr & Eur.

— English-Hungarian: Little. 17th ed. 608p. 1990. 16.00 (*963-05-5699-5*) IBD Ltd.

— English-Hungarian Comprehensive Dictionary, Vol. 1, A-M. (ENG & HUN.). 1992. write for info. (*0-7859-8856-4*) Fr & Eur.

— English-Hungarian Comprehensive Dictionary, Vol. 2, N-Z. (ENG & HUN.). 1992. Not sold separately (*0-615-00458-X*) Fr & Eur.

— English-Hungarian Comprehensive Dictionary: N-Z, 2 vols., Set. 11th ed. 2319p. (C). 1992. 150.00x (*963-05-6349-5*) IBD Ltd.

— English-Hungarian Deluxe Dictionary, 2 vols. 9th ed. 1992. reprint ed. 95.00 (*963-05-5797-5*, H331) Vanous.

— English-Hungarian Dictionary. (ENG & HUN.). 42.50 (*0-685-04465-3*, 043-7) Saphrograph.

— English-Hungarian Pocket Dictionary. 608p. (C). 1992. 21.00x (*963-05-6358-4*, Pub. by Akad Kiado HU) St Mut.

— English-Hungarian Pocket Dictionary. 18th ed. 1991. 15.00x (*963-05-5669-3*, H272) Vanous.

— Hungarian Deluxe Dictionary: Hungarian-English, Vol. 2. 8th ed. 1991. 95.00 (*963-05-0067-1*, H-330) Vanous.

— Hungarian-English: Comprehensive, 2 vols., Set. 9th ed. 1991. 87.00 (*963-05-5799-1*) IBD Ltd.

— Hungarian-English Comprehensive Dictionary Vol. 1: A-K; Vol. 2: L-ZS, 2 vols., Set. 2159p. (C). 1992. 141.00x (*963-05-6254-5*, Pub. by Akad Kiado HU) St Mut.

— Hungarian-English Dictionary, 2 vols. (ENG & HUN.). 49.50 (*0-685-04469-6*, 042-9) Saphrograph.

— Hungarian-English Dictionary (Little) 17th ed. 464p. (ENG & HUN.). 1990. 16.00 (*963-05-5700-2*, H273) IBD Ltd.

— Hungarian-English Pocket Dictionary. 464p. (C). 1992. 21.00x (*963-05-6359-2*, Pub. by Akad Kiado HU) St Mut.

Orszagh, L., ed. Magyar-Angol Szotar, Hungarian-English Dictionary, 2 vols. rev. ed. (ENG & HUN.). 49.00 (*0-685-04471-8*, 042-9) Saphrograph.

***Orszagh, L. & Magay, T.** A Concise English-Hungarian Dictionary. 1052p. (C). 1992. 54.00x (*963-05-6338-X*, Pub. by Akad Kiado HU) St Mut.

Orszagh, L., jt. auth. see Magay, T.

Orszagh, Laszlo. English-Hungarian Concise Dictionary. 12th rev. ed. 1052p. (ENG & HUN.). 1986. 59.95 (*0-8288-0511-3*, M8553) Fr & Eur.

An Asterisk (*) at the beginning of an entry indicates that the title is appearing in BIP for the first time.

— English-Hungarian Pocket Dictionary. 14th ed. 608p. (ENG & HUN.). 1984. pap. 19.95 (*0-8288-0512-1*, M8771) Fr & Eur.

— Hungarian-English Comprehensive Dictionary, 2 vols., Set. 8th rev. ed. 2319p. (ENG & HUN.). 1985. 150.00 (*0-8288-0513-X*, M8552) Fr & Eur.

— Hungarian-English Concise Dictionary. 10th ed. 1179p. (ENG & HUN.). 1985. 39.95 (*0-8288-0514-8*, M 8554) Fr & Eur.

— Hungarian-English Pocket Dictionary. 14th ed. 464p. (ENG & HUN.). 1984. 17.95 (*0-8288-0515-6*, M3168) Fr & Eur.

Orszagh, Laszlo, jt. ed. see Maqay, T.

Orszagh, V. A Concise English-Hungarian Dictionary. 1091p. (ENG & HUN.). 1981. 99.00 (*0-569-00407-1*, Pub. by Collets UK) St Mut.

— A Concise Hungarian-English Dictionary. 1180p. (ENG & HUN.). 1987. 95.00 (*0-569-00343-1*, Pub. by Collets) St Mut.

— English-Hungarian Dictionary, 2 vols. 2336p. (ENG & HUN.). 1988. 190.00 (*0-569-00359-8*, Pub. by Collets) St Mut.

— Hungarian-English Dictionary, 2 vols. 2160p. (ENG & HUN.). 1988. 190.00 (*0-569-00409-8*, Pub. by Collets) St Mut.

Orszagn, L. Angol-Magyar Szotar English-Hungarian Dictionary. 791p. (ENG & HUN.). 42.50 (*0-685-04460-2*, 043-7) Saphrograph.

Orszulik, S. T., jt. ed. see Mortier, K. M.

Ort, Daniel. My Mother Always Called Me by My Brother's Name. 128p. (Orig.). 1994. pap. 14.95 (*0-914061-45-3*) Orchises Pr.

— Ort Bran. LC 90-34158. 128p. (Orig.). 1990. pap. 14.95 (*0-914061-15-1*); boxed 20.00 (*0-914061-18-6*) Orchises Pr.

Ort, Harry H. Structured Data Processing Design. LC 84-14506. 224p. 1985. teacher ed write for info. (*0-201-05426-4*); pap. text ed. 17.56 (*0-201-05425-6*) Addison-Wesley.

Ort, Kathleen, ed. see Clarke, Herbert.

Ort, Kathleen, ed. see Constantz, George.

Ort, Kathleen, ed. see Gray, Mary T.

Ort, Kathleen, ed. see Harmon, David & Rubin, Amy S.

Ort, Kathleen, ed. see Horn, Elizabeth L.

Ort, Kathleen, ed. see Murphy, Alexandra L.

Ort, Kathleen, ed. see Rutter, Michael.

Ort, Kathleen, ed. see Taylor, Ronald J.

Ort, Kathleen, ed. see Taylor, Ronald J. & Douglas, George.

Ort, Kathleen, ed. see Wassink, Jan L.

Ort, Myron. Preserving Perishables with Vacuum Packing. 130p. (Orig.). 1981. pap. text ed. write for info. (*0-941446-00-X*) Tethys Pr.

Orta, G. D. Colloquies on the Simples & Drug of India. (C). 1988. 100.00 (*0-317-92358-7*, Scientific) St Mut.

— Colloquies on the Simples & Drugs of India. 509p. (C). 1985. text ed. 300.00 (*0-89771-616-7*, Pub. by Intl Bk Distr II) St Mut.

— Colloquies on the Simples & Drugs of India. 509p. (C). 1979. reprint ed. 300.00 (*0-685-21866-X*, Pub. by Intl Bk Distr II) St Mut.

Orta, John. Computer Applications in Nutrition & Dietetics: An Annotated Bibliography. LC 87-30450. (Reference Library of Social Science). 256p. 1988. lib. bdg. 43.00 (*0-8240-6621-9*) Garland.

Ortal, Yolanda. Balada Sonambula de los Desterrados Del Sueno. (Cine Ser.). 112p. (SPA.). 1989. pap. 10.00 (*0-945791-10-0*) Editorial Persona.

Ortalda, Robert A., Jr. How to Live Within Your Means & Stay Financially Secure. 1990. pap. 11.00 (*0-671-69607-6*, Fireside) S&S Trade.

Ortaldo, John, jt. ed. see Ransom, Janet H.

Ortberg, John, Jr., jt. auth. see Tan, Siang-Yang.

Ortega. Ortografia Programada. 3rd ed. 165p. 1982. text ed. 13.75 (*0-07-047711-6*) McGraw.

Ortega & Jose, Gasset. Notas, No. 45. 157p. (SPA.). 1967. write for info. (*0-8288-8550-8*) Fr & Eur.

Ortega, Adolfo. Calo Arbis: Semiotic Aspects of a Chicano Language Variety. LC 90-25441. (American University Studies: Linguistics: Ser. XIII, Vol. 21). 264p. (C). 1991. text ed. 45.95 (*0-8204-1542-1*) P Lang Pubs.

Ortega-Alcalde, D., jt. ed. see Candell-Riera, J.

Ortega Cavero, David. Diccionario Portugues-Espanol, Espanol-Portugues, 2 vols., Set. 1856p. (POR & SPA.). 1975. 175.00 (*0-8288-5832-2*, S12405) Fr & Eur.

Ortega, Claudia. Religious Clip Art Book. (Illus.). 64p. (Orig.). 1989. pap. 24.95 (*1-55612-311-6*) Sheed & Ward MO.

Ortega, Daniel & Sheehan, Daniel. Assault on Nicaragua: The Untold Story of the U. S. 'Secret War' Holt, Rod, ed. 115p. (Orig.). 1987. pap. write for info. (*0-929405-00-5*) Walnut Pub.

Ortega, Hernan & Vari, Richard P. Annotated Checklist of the Freshwater Fishes of Peru. LC 86-600237. (Smithsonian Contributions to Zoology Ser.: No. 437). 29p. reprint ed. pap. 25.00 (*0-8357-5612-2*, 2029554) Bks Demand.

Ortega, Idsa A., jt. ed. see Ortiz, Angel R.

Ortega, J. Numerical Analysis: A Second Course. (Classics in Applied Mathematics Ser.: No. 3). xiii, 201p. 1990. pap. 27.50 (*0-89871-250-5*) Soc Indus-Appl Math.

Ortega, James. An Introduction to FORTRAN for Scientific Computing. LC 93-39563. (C). 1994. text ed. 28.00 (*0-03-003128-1*) SCP.

— An Introduction to FORTRAN 90 for Scientific Computing. LC 94-15500. (C). 1994. text ed. 39.00 (*0-03-010198-0*) SCP.

Ortega, James M. Introduction to Parallel & Vector Solution of Linear Systems. LC 88-721. (Frontiers of Computer Science Ser.). (Illus.). 318p. 1988. 55.00 (*0-306-42862-8*, Plenum Pr) Plenum.

— Matrix Theory: A Second Course. LC 86-30312. (University Series in Mathematics). 274p. 1987. 39.50 (*0-306-42433-9*, Plenum Pr) Plenum.

Ortega, James M. & Rheinboldt, Werner C. Iterative Solution of Nonlinear Equations in Several Variables. (Computer Science & Applied Mathematics Ser.). 1970. text ed. 73.00 (*0-12-528550-7*) Acad Pr.

Ortega, James M. & Voigt, Robert G. Solution of Partial Differential Equations on Vector & Parallel Computers. (Miscellaneous Bks.: No. 13). iii, 96p. 1985. pap. 17.00 (*0-89871-055-3*) Soc Indus-Appl Math.

Ortega, James M., jt. auth. see Golub, Gene H.

Ortega, Jose. Alienacion y Agnesion En Juan Goytisolo En Senas De Identidad y Reivindicacion Del Conde Don Julian. 1973. 10.50 (*0-88303-012-8*); pap. 7.50 (*0-685-73216-9*) E Torres & Sons.

Ortega, Julio. Ayacucho, Goodbye; Moscow's Gold: Two Novellas on Peruvian Politics & Violence. Miller, Yvette E., ed. Grossman, Edith & Kelly, Alita, trs. LC 94-3634. (Discoveries Ser.). 104p. 1994. pap. 13.95 (*0-935480-66-8*) Lat Am Lit Rev Pr.

— Poetics of Change: The New Spanish-American Narrative. Greaser, Galen D., tr. (Texas Pan American Ser.). 200p. (C). 1984. reprint ed. text ed. 20.00 (*0-292-76488-X*); reprint ed. pap. 10.95 (*0-292-76508-8*) U of Tex Pr.

— Reapropiaciones: Cultura y Nueva Escritura en Puerto Rico. 264p. 1991. pap. 10.50 (*0-8477-3620-2*) U of PR Pr.

Ortega, Julio, ed. La Cervantiada. 1994. 12.95 (*0-8477-0182-4*) U of PR Pr.

— Gabriel Garcia Marquez & the Powers of Fiction. (Texas Pan American Ser.). 104p. 1988. 16.95 (*0-292-72740-2*) U of Tex Pr.

Ortega, Julio, ed. see Cortazar, Julio.

Ortega, Koryne. Proud Ones: Poems by Koryne Ortega. (Illus.). 46p. (Orig.). 1988. pap. 5.00 (*0-943557-00-3*) Esoterica Pr.

Ortega, M. Helen, et al. Learning Experience Guides for Nursing Students, 4 vols., Vol. 1. 5th ed. LC 93-351. 1993. pap. text ed. 34.95 (*0-8273-6046-0*) Delmar.

— Learning Experience Guides for Nursing Students, 4 vols., Vol. 2. 5th ed. LC 93-351. 1993. pap. text ed. 34.95 (*0-8273-6047-9*) Delmar.

— Learning Experience Guides for Nursing Students, 4 vols., Vol. 3. 5th ed. LC 93-351. 438p. 1993. pap. text ed. 34.95 (*0-8273-6062-2*) Delmar.

— Learning Experience Guides for Nursing Students, 4 vols., Vol. 4. 5th ed. LC 93-351. 320p. 1993. pap. text ed. 34.95 (*0-8273-6108-4*) Delmar.

Ortega, Marvin. Nicaraguan Repatriation to Mosquitia. (Illus.). 72p. (Orig.). 1991. pap. 7.50 (*0-924046-15-5*) Ctr EPRA.

Ortega, Mary, tr. see Telesis Corp. Staff.

Ortega, Mary H., et al. Learning Experience Guides for Nursing Students: Instructor's Guide. 5th ed. 65p. 1994. 15.00 (*0-8273-6172-6*) Delmar.

Ortega, Pedro R. Christmas in Old Santa Fe. LC 73-90581. (Illus.). 1982. pap. 8.95 (*0-913270-25-3*) Sunstone Pr.

Ortega, Pedro R., tr. see Dressman, John.

***Ortega, Rafael C.** Anthology of Mexican American Literature. LC 94-61116. 203p. (C). 1995. pap. 24.00 (*0-9643219-0-4*) Tara Pubng.

Ortega, Roberto. For Humanity: Teachings of Life & Truth. 325p. (Orig.). 1992. pap. write for info. (*0-9631824-0-4*) Three Eras.

Ortega Spottorno, Jose. Relatos en Espiral. (Nueva Austral Ser.: Vol. 143). (SPA.). 1991. pap. text ed. 24.95x (*84-239-1943-9*) Elliots Bks.

Ortega-Velez, Ruth. La Mujer en la Obra de Enrique Laguerre. LC 89-5382. 114p. (Orig.). 1989. pap. text ed. 8.95 (*0-8477-3636-9*) U of PR Pr.

***Ortega y Gasset, Jose.** The Dehumanization of Art; & Other Essays on Art, Culture, & Literature. LC 68-8963. (Princeton Paperbacks Ser.: Vol. 128). reprint ed. pap. 59.90 (*0-7837-9281-6*, 2060020) Bks Demand.

— La Deshumanizacion del Arte. (Nueva Austral Ser.: Vol. 13). (SPA.). 1991. pap. text ed. 24.95x (*84-239-1813-0*) Elliots Bks.

— Historical Reason. 1986. pap. 7.95 (*0-393-30287-3*) Norton.

— History As a System & Other Essays Toward a Philosophy of History. LC 81-13359. x, 269p. 1981. reprint ed. text ed. 59.75 (*0-313-23112-5*, ORHS, Greenwood Pr) Greenwood.

— An Interpretation of Universal History. Adams, Mildred, tr. 304p. 1984. reprint ed. pap. 7.95 (*0-393-00751-0*) Norton.

— Invertebrate Spain. Adams, Mildred, tr. LC 73-16212. 212p. 1995. reprint ed. lib. bdg. 35.00 (*0-86527-107-0*) Fertig.

— Meditations on Hunting. 144p. (Orig.). 1986. pap. 10.95 (*0-684-18630-6*, Scribners) S&S Trade.

— Mission of the University. 120p. (C). 1991. pap. text ed. 21.95 (*1-56000-560-2*) Transaction Pubs.

— Origin of Philosophy. (C). 1968. pap. text ed. 6.95 (*0-393-00128-8*) Norton.

— The Revolt of the Masses. Moore, Kenneth, ed. LC 81-40457. 240p. 1985. 28.95 (*0-268-01609-7*) U of Notre Dame Pr.

— The Revolt of the Masses. 192p. 1994. pap. 6.95 (*0-393-31095-7*) Norton.

— El Tema de Nuestro Tiempo. (Nueva Austral Ser.: Vol. 28). (SPA.). 1991. pap. text ed. 24.95x (*84-239-1828-9*) Elliots Bks.

Ortegel, Adelaide. Banners & Such. LC 86-62616. 128p. 1986. pap. 10.95 (*0-89390-092-3*) Resource Pubns.

Ortegel, Adelaide, jt. auth. see Schneider, Kent E.

Ortego, Hasa. Christmas Eve on the Big Bayou. 1974. 3.95 (*0-87511-091-6*) Claitors.

Ortego, Pedro R., tr. see LaFarge, Oliver.

Orteleva, Peter J. Nonlinear Chemical Waves. 302p. 1992. text ed. 195.00 (*0-471-93577-8*) Wiley.

***Ortelt, Ellen S.** Amazing Mazes. (Illus.). 40p. (J). 1995. pap. 7.95 (*0-8059-3736-6*) Dorrance.

Orten & McCracken. Small Animals Thoracic Surgery. 1994. 98.50 (*0-683-06670-6*) Williams & Wilkins.

Ortenberg, Veronica. The English Church & the Continent in the Tenth & Eleventh Centuries: Cultural, Spiritual, & Artistic Exchanges. (Illus.). 352p. 1992. 79.00 (*0-19-820159-1*) OUP.

Ortenburger, Rick. Black Forest Clocks. LC 90-63797. (Illus.). 300p. 1991. 79.95 (*0-88740-300-X*) Schiffer.

— Vienna Regulator Clocks. LC 89-64090. (Illus.). 180p. 1989. 39.95 (*0-88740-224-0*) Schiffer.

Ortese, Anna M. The Iguana. Martin, Henry, tr. LC 87-20258. 208p. 1988. 14.95 (*0-914232-87-8*); pap. 9.00 (*0-914232-95-9*) McPherson & Co.

— A Music Behind the Wall Vol. 1: Selected Stories. Martin, Henry, tr. & intro. by. 160p. 1994. 20.00 (*0-929701-39-9*) McPherson & Co.

Orteu, Henri, jt. auth. see Norman, Jill.

Orth. Handbook of Cosmetic Microbiology. (Cosmetic Science & Technology Ser.: Vol. 12). 608p. 1993. 199.00 (*0-8247-9012-X*) Dekker.

Orth, D. L. Calculus in a New Key. (Illus.). (Orig.). 1976. pap. text ed. 15.00 (*0-917326-05-9*) APL Pr.

Orth, Donald, ed. Place Names of America. (International Library of Names). 400p. (C). text ed. write for info. (*0-8290-1210-9*) Irvington.

Orth, Ghita. The Music of What Happens. LC 82-10280. (Eileen W. Barnes Award Ser.). (Illus.). 70p. (Orig.). 1982. pap. 5.50 (*0-938158-01-5*) Saturday Pr.

***Orth-Gomer, Kristina & Schneiderman, Neil, eds.** Behavioral Medicine Approaches to Coronary Heart Disease Prevention. LC 95-2986. 280p. 1995. text ed. 55.00 (*0-8058-1820-0*) L Erlbaum Assocs.

Orth, Hermann M. Model-Based Design of Water Distribution & Sewage Systems. LC 85-165361. 191p. 1986. text ed. 91.95 (*0-471-90877-0*) Wiley.

Orth, Jane, ed. see Maddox, Kathleen B.

Orth, John V. Combination & Conspiracy: A Legal History of Trade Unionism, 1721-1906. 224p. 1991. 79.00 (*0-19-825299-4*) OUP.

— The North Carolina State Constitution: A Reference Guide. LC 92-42676. (Reference Guides to the State Constitutions of the United States Ser.: No. 16). 216p. 1993. text ed. 65.00 (*0-313-27570-X*, ONC, Greenwood Pr) Greenwood.

— The North Carolina State Constitution: With History & Commentary. LC 95-14496. (Reference Guides to the State Constitutions of the United States Ser.: No. 16). 1995. pap. write for info. (*0-8078-4551-5*) U of NC Pr.

Orth, Marjorie H., jt. auth. see Voth, Harold M.

Orth, R. E., jt. auth. see Fisher, T. W.

Orth, Ralph H. & Johnson, Glen M., eds. The Topical Notebooks of Ralph Waldo Emerson, Vol. 3. (Illus.). 392p. 1994. text ed. 44.95 (*0-8262-0951-3*) U of Mo Pr.

Orth, Ralph H., jt. ed. see Bosco, Ronald A.

Orth, Ralph H., jt. ed. see Smith, Susan S.

Orth, Ralph H., et al, eds. The Poetry Notebooks of Ralph Waldo Emerson. LC 84-2184. 1024p. 1986. text ed. 70.00 (*0-8262-0444-9*) U of Mo Pr.

Orth, Samuel P. Centralization of Administration in Ohio. LC 68-56679. (Columbia University Studies in the Social Sciences Ser.: No. 43). reprint ed. 27.50 (*0-404-51043-4*) AMS Pr.

— Five American Politicians: Study in Evolution of American Politics. LC 73-19165. 448p. 1974. reprint ed. 34.95 (*0-405-05887-X*) Ayer.

Orth, Samuel P., ed. Readings on the Relation of Government to Property & Industry. LC 73-2527. (Big Business; Economic Power in a Free Society Ser.). 1973. reprint ed. 44.95 (*0-405-05106-9*) Ayer.

Orthmann, Rosemary. Out of Necessity: Women Working in Berlin at the Height of Industrialization, 1874-1913. LC 91-29385. (Modern European History Ser.: No. 2). (Illus.). 280p. 1991. 67.00 (*0-8153-0670-9*) Garland.

Orthner, Dennis K., jt. ed. see Bowen, Gary L.

Orthner, Donald P. Wellsprings of Life: Understanding Proverbs. (Illus.). xii, 228p. (Orig.). (YA). (gr. 9 up). 1989. pap. 7.95 (*0-317-93833-9*) Adon Bks.

Ortho Books Editorial Staff. All about Pruning. rev. ed. LC 88-63844. (Illus.). 112p. 1989. pap. 9.95 (*0-89721-198-7*) Ortho Info.

— The Birds Around Us. Mace, Alice E., ed. LC 85-72801. (Illus.). 352p. 1986. 24.95 (*0-89721-068-9*) Ortho Info.

— Gardening in Containers. Burke, Ken R., ed. LC 83-61314. (Illus.). 96p. (Orig.). 1983. pap. 9.95 (*0-89721-020-4*) Ortho Info.

Ortho Books Editorial Staff, ed. The World of Cactus & Succulents. LC 77-89689. (Illus.). 1978. pap. 9.95 (*0-917102-59-2*) Ortho Info.

Ortho Books Editorial Staff & Hildebrand, Ron. Wood Projects for the Home. LC 80-66343. (Illus.). 96p. (Orig.). 1981. pap. 9.95 (*0-917102-85-1*) Ortho Info.

Ortho Books Editorial Staff, ed. see Cotton, Lin & Williams, T. Jeff.

Ortho Books Editorial Staff, ed. see Horton, Alvin.

ORTHO Books Editorial Staff, ed. see Lammers, Susan.

Ortho Books Editorial Staff, jt. auth. see Williams, T. Jeff.

Ortho Books Editors & Fox, Jill. How to Install Ceramic Tile. Shakery, Karin, ed. LC 87-72099. (Illus.). 96p. (Orig.). 1989. pap. 9.95 (*0-89721-142-1*) Ortho Info.

Ortho Books-How to Staff, jt. auth. see Beckstrom, Robert J.

Ortho Books-Reference Staff. The Ortho Problem Solver. 4th rev. ed. Smith, Michael D., ed. LC 94-65696. (Illus.). 960p. 1994. pap. 180.00 (*0-89721-268-1*, UPC 06021) Ortho Info.

Ortho Books-Reference Staff, jt. auth. see Smith, Michael.

Ortho Books Staff. All about Perennials. rev. ed. Godwin, Sara, ed. LC 92-70588. (Illus.). 112p. 1992. pap. 9.95 (*0-89721-247-9*) Ortho Info.

— All about Trees. rev. ed. Arbuckle, Nancy & Crocker, Cederick, eds. LC 92-70589. (Illus.). 112p. 1992. pap. 9.95 (*0-89721-248-7*) Ortho Info.

ORTHO Books Staff. Protecting Your Garden from Animal Damage. Lipanovich, Marianne, ed. LC 94-65699. (Illus.). 96p. (Orig.). 1994. pap. 9.95 (*0-89721-267-3*, UPC 05425) Ortho Info.

Ortho Books Staff, ed. see Horton, Alvin.

ORTHO Books Staff, ed. see Sinnes, A. Cort & McKinley, Mike.

Ortho Staff. All about Growing Fruits, Berries, & Nuts. Ferguson, Barbara, ed. LC 87-70194. (Illus.). 112p. (Orig.). 1987. pap. 9.95 (*0-89721-096-4*) Ortho Info.

Orthodox Christian Educational Society, ed. see DeBallester, Archimandrite P.

Orthodox Christian Educational Society Staff, ed. see Agapius, et al.

Orthodox Christian Educational Society Staff, ed. see Holy Synod of the Ecumenical Patriarchate Staff & Anthimus.

Orthodox Christian Educational Society Staff, ed. see Livadeas, Themistocles & Charitos, Minas.

Orthodox Christian Educational Society Staff, ed. see Makrakis, Apostolos.

Orthodox Christian Educational Society Staff, ed. see Philaretos, S. D.

Orthodox Christian Educational Society Staff, ed. see Philaretos, Sotirios D.

Orthodox Christian Educational Society Staff, ed. see Photiou, Paul.

Orthodox Christian Educational Society Staff, ed. see Vassilakos, Aristarchus.

Orthodox Eastern Church. The General Menaion, or the Book of Services Common to the Festivals of Our Lord Jesus Christ, of the Holy Virgin, & of the Different Orders of Saints. Orloff, Nicholas, tr. pap. 15.00 (*0-89981-027-6*) Eastern Orthodox.

Orthodox Eastern Church Staff. Akathist to Great Martyr George. 1993. pap. 0.50 (*0-89981-142-6*) Eastern Orthodox.

— Divine Liturgy of St. John Chrysostom. large type ed. 1994. pap. 10.00 (*0-89981-306-2*) Eastern Orthodox.

— Liturgies of Saints Mark, James, Clement, Chrysostom, & the Church of Malabar. LC 76-83374. reprint ed. 42.00 (*0-404-04658-4*) AMS Pr.

— Liturgies of Saints Mark, James, Clement, Chrysostom, Basil. LC 79-80721. 1969. reprint ed. 42.00 (*0-404-04657-6*) AMS Pr.

— Offices of the Oriental Church. LC 73-79805. reprint ed. 34.50 (*0-404-00874-7*) AMS Pr.

— Prayer for the Dead. 1991. pap. 1.50 (*0-89981-045-4*) Eastern Orthodox.

— Prayers for the Sick. 1993. pap. 1.00 (*0-89981-114-0*) Eastern Orthodox.

— Service to a Fool for Christ Sake. pap. 0.75 (*0-89981-093-4*) Eastern Orthodox.

— Suffering of the Forty Holy Martyrs in Sebaste in Armenia. 1990. pap. 1.00 (*0-89981-122-1*) Eastern Orthodox.

— Synod of Sixteen Seventy-Two: Acts & Decrees of the Jerusalem Synod Held Under Dositheus, Containing the Confession Published Name of Cyril Lukaris. Robertson, J. N., tr. LC 78-81769. 1969. reprint ed. 41.50 (*0-404-03567-1*) AMS Pr.

Orthodox Eastern Church-Synod of Jerusalem Staff. Acts & Decrees of the Synod of Jerusalem, 1672. pap. 1.95 (*0-89981-001-2*) Eastern Orthodox.

Orthwein. Clutches & Brakes: Design & Selection. (Mechanical Engineering Ser.: Vol. 50). 368p. 1986. 125.00 (*0-8247-7393-4*) Dekker.

Orthwein, William C. Machine Component Design. Slaughter, Michael, ed. 999p. (C). 1990. text ed. 73.00 (*0-314-24257-0*) West Pub.

***Ortigao, J. A. R.** Soil Mechanics in the Light of Critical State Theories: An Introduction. (Illus.). 160p. (C). 1995. text ed. 65.00 (*90-5410-194-6*, Pub. by A A Balkema NE); pap. 35.00 (*90-5410-195-4*, Pub. by A A Balkema NE) Ashgate Pub Co.

Ortigoza, Brenda. How Institutions Voted on Social Policy Shareholder Resolutions in the 1993 Proxy Season. Mathiasen, Carolyn, ed. (Illus.). 137p. (Orig.). 1993. pap. text ed. 50.00 (*1-879775-13-1*) IRRC Inc DC.

Ortiz. People Shall Continue. (J). (gr. 4-7). 1994. pap. 6.95 (*0-89239-125-1*) Childrens Book Pr.

Ortiz, Adalberto. El Animal Herido; Antologia Poetica. (B. E. Ser.: No. 24). (SPA.). 1959. 20.00 (*0-8115-2975-4*) Periodicals Srv.

— Juyungo: Historia de un Negro, una Isla y Otros Negros. (B. E. Ser.: No. 23). (SPA.). 1943. 24.00 (*0-8115-2974-6*) Periodicals Srv.

— Juyungo: The First Black Ecuadorian Novel. Tittler, Jonathan & Hill, Susan, trs. LC 81-51674. x, 234p. (Orig.). 1993. reprint ed. pap. 12.00 (*0-89410-091-2*) Three Continents.

Ortiz, Alba A., jt. ed. see Ramirez, Bruce.

Ortiz, Alejandro & Zierer, Ernesto. Set Theory & Linguistics. (Janua Linguarum, Ser. Minor: No. 70). (Orig.). 1968. pap. text ed. 12.70 (*90-279-0597-5*) Mouton.

Ortiz, Alfonso. The Pueblo: Southwest. (Indians of North America Ser.). (Illus.). (J). (gr. 5 up). 1994. 18.95 (*1-55546-727-X*, Am Art Analog); pap. 7.95 (*0-7910-0396-5*, Am Art Analog) Chelsea Hse.

— Tewa World: Space, Time, Being, & Becoming in a Pueblo Society. LC 72-94079. 1972. pap. text ed. 10.95 (*0-226-63307-1*, P447) U Ch Pr.

O

An Asterisk (*) at the beginning of an entry indicates that the title is appearing in BIP for the first time.

Ortiz, Alfonso, ed. Southwest. LC 77-17162. (Handbook of North American Indians Ser.: Vol. 9). (Illus.). 700p. 1980. text ed. 23.00 (*0-87474-189-0*, ORV9) Smithsonian.

— Southwest: Handbook of North American Indians, Vol. 10. LC 77-17162. (Illus.). 868p. 1983. 25.00 (*0-87474-190-4*) Smithsonian.

Ortiz, Alfonso, jt. ed. see DeMallie, Raymond J.

Ortiz, Alfonso, jt. ed. see Erdoes, Richard.

Ortiz, Alfonso, jt. auth. see Sturtevant, William C.

Ortiz, Altagracia. Eighteenth Century Reforms in the Caribbean: Miguel De Muesas, Governor of Puerto Rico, 1769-76. LC 79-56408. (Illus.). 256p. 1983. 35.00 (*0-8386-3008-1*) Fairleigh Dickinson.

Ortiz, Angel R. & Ortega, Idsa A., eds. Puerto Rico en la Economia Politica del Caribe. LC 90-80515. 204p. 1990. pap. 11.95 (*0-929157-06-0*) Ediciones Huracan.

— Puerto Rico en las Relaciones Internacionales del Caribe. LC 90-80514. 197p. 1990. pap. 11.95 (*0-929157-05-2*) Ediciones Huracan.

Ortiz, Antonio D. Resplendence of the Spanish Monarchy: Renaissance Tapestries & Armor from the Patrimonio. 1991. 49.50 (*0-8109-6408-2*) Abrams.

Ortiz, Antonio D., et al. Resplendence of the Spanish Monarchy: Renaissance Tapestries & Armor from the Patrimonio. (Illus.). 172p. 1991. 19.95 (*0-87099-621-5*, Abrams) Metro Mus Art.

— Velazquez. 1989. 45.00 (*0-87099-554-5*, Abrams); pap. 19.95 (*0-87099-555-3*, Abrams) Metro Mus Art.

Ortiz-Aponte, Sally & Cabezas, Juan A. Las Mujeres De Clarin: Espermentos y Camafeos. Cabezas, Juan A., ed. 200p. (C). 1971. pap. 3.00 (*0-8477-3141-3*) U of PR Pr.

Ortiz, Bev. It Will Live Forever: Traditional Yosemite Indian Acorn Preparation. (Illus.). 160p. (Orig.). 1991. reprint ed. lib. bdg. 31.00x (*0-8095-4953-0*) Borgo Pr.

***Ortiz Blasco, M.** Tauromaquia A-Z: Diccionario Enciclopedico de la Historia la Tecnica y la Cultura Del Arte Del Toreo, 2 vols., Set. (Illus.). 1614p. (SPA.). 1993. 450.00x (*84-239-5888-4*) Elliots Bks.

Ortiz, Bobbye, tr. see Debray, Regis.

Ortiz-Buonafina, Marta. Profitable Export Marketing: A Strategy for U. S. Business. LC 92-15752. 1992. 24.00 (*0-8191-8733-X*) U Pr of Amer.

Ortiz-Buonafina, Marta, jt. auth. see Haar, Jerry.

Ortiz, C., jt. ed. see Poker, D.

Ortiz-Carboneres, Salvador, ed. Spanish History: Selected Texts from the Fall of Granada in 1492 to Modern Times. LC 89-31905. 221p. 1989. 44.95 (*0-85496-095-3*) Berg Pubs.

Ortiz-Carboneres, Salvador, jt. auth. see Leigh, Heather.

Ortiz, Darwin. Darwin Ortiz on Casino Gambling: The Complete Guide to Playing & Winning. (Illus.). 1990. reprint ed. pap. 8.95 (*0-8184-0525-2*, Citadel Pr) Carol Pub Group.

— Gambling Scams: How They Work - How to Detect Them - How to Protect Yourself. (Illus.). 262p. 1990. reprint ed. pap. 8.95 (*0-8184-0529-5*, Citadel Pr) Carol Pub Group.

Ortiz De Burgos, Jose. Diccionario Manual Italiano-Espanol, Spagnuolo-Italiano: Spanish & Italian. 16th ed. 960p. (ITA & SPA.). 1977. 14.95 (*0-8288-5354-1*, S50432) Fr & Eur.

Ortiz De Montellano, Bernard R. Aztec Medicine, Health, & Nutrition. LC 89-70142. (Illus.). 310p. (Orig.). (C). 1990. text ed. 40.00 (*0-8135-1562-9*); pap. text ed. 15.00 (*0-8135-1563-7*) Rutgers U Pr.

Ortiz De Montellano, Bernard R., tr. see Baudot, Georges.

Ortiz De Montellano, Bernard R., tr. see Lopez Austin, Alfredo L.

Ortiz De Montellano, Bernard R., tr. see Lopez Austin, Alfredo.

Ortiz De Montellano, Bernard R., tr. see Lujan, Leonardo L.

Ortiz De Montellano, Bernard R., tr. see Moctezuma, Eduardo M.

Ortiz de Montellano, Paul R., ed. Cytochrome P-450: Structure, Mechanism, & Biochemistry. LC 85-30103. 566p. 1986. 125.00 (*0-306-42147-X*, Plenum Pr) Plenum.

Ortiz De Montellano, Thelma, tr. see Baudot, Georges.

Ortiz De Montellano, Thelma, tr. see Lopez Austin, Alfredo L.

Ortiz De Montellano, Thelma, tr. see Lopez Austin, Alfredo.

Ortiz De Montellano, Thelma, tr. see Lujan, Leonardo L.

Ortiz De Montellano, Thelma, tr. see Moctezuma, Eduardo M.

Ortiz, E. L., ed. Numerical Approximation of Partial Differential Equations: Selected Papers Presented at the International Symposium of Numerical Analysis, Madrid, Spain, September 17-19, 1985. (North-Holland Mathematics Studies: No. 133). 440p. 1987. 95.00 (*0-444-70140-0*, North Holland) Elsevier.

Ortiz, Edgar, jt. ed. see Ghosh, Dilip K.

Ortiz, Elisabeth. Complete Book of Mexican Cooking. 1994. 9.98 (*0-88365-860-7*) Galahad Bks.

Ortiz, Elisabeth L. The Book of Latin American Cooking. LC 94-12452. 1994. 15.00 (*0-88001-382-6*) Ecco Pr.

— Clearly Delicious. LC 93-35418. (Illus.). 144p. 1994. 24.95 (*1-56458-513-1*) Dorling Kindersley.

— The Complete Book of Caribbean Cooking. 432p. 1986. mass mkt. 5.95 (*0-345-33256-3*) Ballantine.

— Complete Book of Japanese Cooking. 1994. 8.98 (*0-88365-854-2*) Galahad Bks.

— The Complete Book of Mexican Cooking. 304p. 1985. mass mkt. 5.99 (*0-345-32559-1*) Ballantine.

— The Complete Book of Mexican Cooking. LC 67-18534. (Illus.). 352p. 1967. 14.95 (*0-87131-074-0*); pap. 6.95 (*0-87131-333-2*) M Evans.

— The Festive Food of Mexico. (Illus.). 60p. 1994. 8.95 (*1-85626-060-7*) Trafalgar.

— The Food of Spain & Portugal. 320p. 1989. text ed. 22.50 (*0-689-12057-5*, Pub. by Ctrl Bur voor Schimmel NE) Macmillan.

— A Little Brazilian Cookbook. (Illus.). 60p. 1992. 7.95 (*0-8118-0110-1*) Chronicle Bks.

Ortiz, Elisabeth L. & Endo, Mitsuko. The Complete Book of Japanese Cooking. LC 76-16008. (Illus.). 264p. 1976. 12.50 (*0-87131-212-3*); pap. 6.95 (*0-87131-321-9*) M Evans.

Ortiz, Elisabeth L., ed. see Hazelton, Nika.

Ortiz, Elizabeth T. Your Complete Guide to Sexual Health. 1989. pap. 19.50 (*0-13-679572-2*) P-H.

Ortiz, Ernesto R., jt. auth. see De Lopez, Awilda P.

***Ortiz, Fernando.** Cuban Counterpoint: Tobacco & Sugar. De Onis, Harriet, tr. LC 94-38200. (Illus.). 408p. 1995. pap. text ed. 18.95 (*0-8223-1616-1*) Duke.

Ortiz, Fernando & Ortiz, Tatiana. Coral Peregrino: Del Caribe Mexicano a Biosfera-2. 88p. (SPA.). 1994. 8.95 (*1-882428-15-3*) Biosphere Pr.

Ortiz, Flora I. Career Patterns in Education: Men, Women & Minorities in Public School Administration. LC 80-29490. 192p. 1981. text ed. 38.50 (*0-275-90696-5*, C0696, Praeger Pubs) Greenwood.

— Career Patterns in Education: Women, Men & Minorities in Public School Education. (Illus.). 196p. 1982. 29.95 (*0-03-059223-2*, Bergin & Garvey) Greenwood.

— Schoolhousing: Planning & Designing Educational Facilities. LC 92-47103. 195p. (C). 1993. 59.50 (*0-7914-1727-1*); pap. 19.95 (*0-7914-1728-X*) State U NY Pr.

Ortiz, Flora I., jt. ed. see McKenna, Teresa.

Ortiz, Flora I., jt. auth. see Wissler, Dorothy F.

Ortiz Garcia, Angel L. La Ensenanza de los Estudios Sociales en la Escuela Elemental. 135p. 1990. 8.75 (*0-8477-2723-8*) U of PR Pr.

Ortiz, Gloria. The Dandy & the Senorito: Eros & Social Class in the Nineteenth-Century Novel. LC 91-31679. (Harvard Dissertations in the Romance Languages Ser.). 136p. 1991. 39.00 (*0-8153-0651-2*) Garland.

Ortiz-Griffin, Julia, jt. auth. see Sallese, Nicholas F.

Ortiz, Henry. Shop Math. LC 84-730297. (Series 950). (Orig.). 1984. student ed. pap. 7.00 (*0-8064-0435-3*); audio 219.00 (*0-8064-0436-1*) Bergwall.

Ortiz, Joe. Saved? What Do You Mean Saved? A Journalist's Report on Salvation. Feldstein, Mark D., ed. (Illus.). 95p. (Orig.). (C). 1983. pap. 4.95 (*0-912695-00-5*) GBM Bks.

— The Village Baker. 192p. 1993. 24.95 (*0-89815-489-8*) Ten Speed Pr.

Ortiz, Jose. Reflections of an Hispanic Mennonite. LC 89-11872. 96p. 1989. pap. 6.95 (*0-934672-78-4*) Good Bks PA.

Ortiz, Juan C. The Disciple. LC 74-29650. 144p. 1975. pap. 7.99 (*0-88419-145-1*, Creation Hse) Strang Comms Co.

— Discipulo. 192p. 1978. 3.95 (*0-88113-065-6*) Edit Betania.

— God Is Closer Than You Think: Taking the Distance Out of Your Relationship with the Lord. 174p. (Orig.). 1992. pap. 8.99 (*0-89283-799-3*, Vine Bks) Servant.

— Living with Jesus Today. LC 82-72240. 1982. 4.99 (*0-88419-187-7*, Creation Hse) Strang Comms Co.

Ortiz, Juan Carlos. Jesus en Nuestras Vidas - Hoy. Araujo, Juan S., tr. 160p. (SPA.). 1987. pap. 4.25 (*0-88113-157-1*) Edit Betania.

Ortiz, Juan Carlos & Buckingham, Jamie. Call to Discipleship. LC 75-7476. 136p. 1975. pap. 5.95 (*0-88270-122-3*) Bridge Pub.

Ortiz, Lucio. Sus Derechos de Credito en Estados Unidos. (Orig.). (SPA.). (YA). (gr. 9-12). 1989. pap. 6.00 (*0-685-28998-2*) Publicaciones Nuevos.

Ortiz, Manuel. The Hispanic Challenge: Opportunities Confronting the Church. LC 93-41900. 194p. (Orig.). 1993. pap. 14.99 (*0-8308-1773-5*, 1773) InterVarsity.

***Ortiz, Maria A.** El Discurso Afectuoso. 79p. (SPA.). 1994. lib. bdg. 10.00 (*1-881708-05-5*) Edcnes Mairena.

Ortiz-Monasterio, Fernando. Rhinoplasty. LC 93-33891. (Illus.). 304p. 1994. text ed. 132.50 (*0-7216-6786-4*) Saunders.

***Ortiz, Pamela D.** Running to Win. DHP, Inc. Staff, ed. (The Togetherness Ser.). (Illus.). 64p. (Orig.). 1994. pap. write for info. (*1-885531-07-9*) Doghouse Pubng.

Ortiz, Phil & Wakeman, Diana, illus. Walt Disney's Dumbo. (Little Nugget Bks.). 28p. (J). (ps). 1992. bds. write for info. (*0-307-12533-5*, 12533, Golden Pr) Western Pub.

Ortiz, Robert, et al. Management Audit of the Court Services Division of the Office of the Clerk of Court, Charlotte County, Florida. 138p. 1990. 8.50 (*0-685-38099-8*, SERO-062) Natl Ctr St Courts.

Ortiz, Simon. The People Shall Continue. LC 88-18929. (Illus.). 24p. (J). (gr. 2-7). 1988. 13.95 (*0-89239-041-7*) Childrens Book Pr.

Ortiz, Simon J. After & Before the Lightning. LC 94-5761. (Sun Tracks Ser.: Vol. 28). 160p. (Orig.). 1994. lib. bdg. 32.50 (*0-8165-1423-2*); pap. 15.95 (*0-8165-1448-8*) U of Ariz Pr.

— Earth Power Coming: Short Fiction in Native American Literature. 299p. 1983. pap. 16.00 (*0-912586-50-8*) Navajo Coll Pr.

— Woven Stone. LC 92-12507. (Sun Tracks Ser.: Vol. 21). 367p. 1992. lib. bdg. 45.00 (*0-8165-1294-9*); pap. 19.95 (*0-8165-1330-9*) U of Ariz Pr.

Ortiz, Sutti & Lees, Susan, eds. Understanding Economic Process. LC 92-24047. (Monographs in Economic Anthropology: No. 10). 220p. (Orig.). (C). 1992. lib. bdg. 51.00 (*0-8191-8827-1*, Soc Economic Anthropology); pap. text ed. 22.50 (*0-8191-8828-X*, Soc Economic Anthropology) U Pr of Amer.

Ortiz, Syliva P., jt. ed. see Matlon, Ronald J.

Ortiz, Tatiana, jt. auth. see Ortiz, Fernando.

Ortiz, Thomas, jt. auth. see Jahn, Dawn.

Ortiz, Victoria. The Legacy of Arthur Alfonso Schomburg: A Celebration of the Past, A Vision for the Future; with a Biographical Essay of Arthur A. Schomburg. Johnson, Glenderlyn, ed. (Illus.). 140p. (Orig.). (ENG & SPA.). 1986. pap. 10.00 (*0-87104-299-1*) NY Pub Lib.

— Sojourner Truth: A Self-Made Woman. LC 73-22290. (Illus.). 160p. (YA). (gr. 7 up). 1986. lib. bdg. 13.89 (*0-397-32134-1*, Lipp Jr Bks) HarpC Child Bks.

Ortiz, Victoria, tr. see De Chungara, Domitila B. & Viezzer, Moema.

Ortiz, Victoria, tr. see Froschel, Merle & Sprung, Barbara, eds.

Ortiz, Victoria, tr. see Guevarar, Ernesto.

Ortiz, Victoria, tr. see Soto, Pedro J.

Ortiz y Pino de Dinkel, Reynalda & Gonzales de Martinez, Dora, eds. Spanish Riddles & Colcha Designs. rev. ed. LC 94-17455. (ENG & SPA.). 1994. 10.95 (*0-86534-226-1*) Sunstone Pr.

Ortiz y Pino, Jose, III. Curandero. LC 82-19507. (Illus.). 111p. 1983. pap. 8.95 (*0-86534-020-X*) Sunstone Pr.

Ortiz y Pino, Jose. Don Jose: The Last Patron. LC 81-8817. 128p. 1981. 13.95 (*0-86534-006-4*); pap. 9.95 (*0-86534-007-2*) Sunstone Pr.

Ortiz y Pino, Yolanda. Original Native New Mexico Cooking. LC 93-29047. 32p. (Orig.). 1993. pap. 5.95 (*0-86534-210-5*) Sunstone Pr.

Ortiz, Yvonne. A Taste of Puerto Rico: Traditional & New Dishes from the Puerto Rican Community. LC 93-46165. 320p. 1994. 22.95 (*0-525-93812-5*) NAL-Dutton.

***Ortlund.** Disciplines of the Home. 1993. pap. text ed. (*0-8499-3518-0*) Word Inc.

Ortlund, Anne. Building a Great Marriage. LC 84-16078. 192p. 1984. pap. 8.99 (*0-8007-5234-1*) Revell.

— Children Are Wet Cement. 192p. (Orig.). 1995. mass mkt. 4.99 (*0-8007-8627-0*) Revell.

— The Disciplines of the Beautiful Woman. 1984. pap. write for info. (*0-8499-2983-0*) Word Inc.

— Disciplines of the Heart. 137p. 1987. write for info. (*0-318-61817-6*); pap. write for info. (*0-8499-3191-6*) Word Inc.

— Disciplining One Another. 185p. 1983. pap. write for info. (*0-8499-2960-1*) Word Inc.

— Fix Your Eyes on Jesus. 1991. 14.99 (*0-8499-0856-6*) Word Inc.

— Fix Your Eyes on Jesus. 1994. pap. 9.99 (*0-8499-3484-2*) Word Inc.

— My Sacrifice, His Fire: Weekday Readings for Christian Women. LC 93-17924. 1993. 15.99 (*0-8499-1070-6*) Word Pub.

— Up with Worship. rev. ed. LC 82-15063. (Orig.). 1982. pap. 6.99 (*0-8307-0867-7*, 5417706) Regal.

Ortlund, Anne, jt. auth. see Ortlund, Ray.

Ortlund, Ray. Loves of a Man. 1994. 15.99 (*0-8499-1069-2*) Word Inc.

— Three Priorities for a Strong Local Church. 126p. 1988. 8.99 (*0-8499-3101-0*) Word Inc.

***Ortlund, Ray & Ortlund, Anne.** In His Presence. 1995. 14.99 (*1-56507-282-0*) Harvest Hse.

Ortlund, Raymond. Senor: Haz de Mi Vida un Milagro! Lord: Make My Life a Miracle. (SPA.). 4.95 (*84-7228-277-5*, 220816, Pub. by Edit Clie SP) TSELF.

Ortlund, Raymond C., Jr. A Passion for God: A Book of Prayers & Devotions - Romans Newly Paraphrased. LC 93-38010. 224p. 1994. 15.99 (*0-89107-765-0*) Crossway Bks.

Ortman, Mark. Now That Makes Sense! Relating to People with Wit & Wisdom. rev. ed. 232p. 1993. pap. 11.95 (*0-9634699-9-1*) Wise Owl Bks & Mus.

— A Simple Guide to Self-Publishing: A Time & Money Saving Handbook to Printing, Distributing & Promoting Your Own Book. LC 93-61767. 64p. (Orig.). 1994. pap. 6.95 (*0-9634699-8-3*) Wise Owl Bks & Mus.

Ortman, Patricia E. Not for Teachers Only: Creating a Context of Joy for Learning & Growth. (Orig.). 1988. pap. 4.95 (*0-317-91345-X*) P E Ortman.

Ortman, Phyllis, ed. see Young, Michael B. & Lovil, Thomas M.

Ortmann, Otto. 'SPhysiological Mechanisms of Piano Technique. LC 80-26521. (Music Ser.). (Illus.). xvi, 396p. 1981. reprint ed. lib. bdg. 52.50 (*0-306-76058-4*) Da Capo.

Ortmayer, Louis, jt. auth. see Flinn, Joanna.

Ortmayer, Louis L. The U. S.-Japanese FSX Fighter Agreement. (Pew Case Studies in International Affairs). 50p. (C). 1992. pap. text ed. 2.50 (*1-56927-350-2*) Geo U Inst Dplmcy.

Ortmeyer, Charles P., jt. auth. see Rice, Denis T.

Ortner, Donald J., ed. How Humans Adapt: A Biocultural Odyssey. LC 82-600233. (International Symposia Ser.). (Illus.). 582p. 1983. pap. text ed. 17.95 (*0-87474-725-2*, ORHHP) Smithsonian.

Ortner, Donald J. & Aufderheide, Arthur C., eds. Human Paleopathology: Current Syntheses & Future Options. LC 90-10348. (Illus.). 320p. (C). 1991. 70.00 (*1-56098-039-7*) Smithsonian.

Ortner, Donald J. & Putschar, Walter G. Identification of Pathological Conditions in Human Skeletal Remains. LC 84-600075. (Illus.). 508p. 1985. text ed. 55.00 (*0-87474-728-7*, ORIP) Smithsonian.

Ortner, Gerard T., Jr., jt. auth. see Kennedy, Raymond P.

Ortner, Herbert E. Recycling of Papermaking Fibers: Flotation Deinking. Corwin, Harold E., ed. 38p. reprint ed. pap. 25.00 (*0-317-20560-9*, 2022814) Bks Demand.

Ortner, J. & Maseland, H., eds. Introduction to Solar-Terrestial Relations. 514p. 1965. text ed. 398.00 (*0-677-00650-0*) Gordon & Breach.

***Ortner, Jon, photos.** Manhattan Dawn & Dusk. (Illus.). 208p. 1995. 60.00 (*1-55670-426-7*) Stewart Tabori & Chang.

Ortner, Michael P. Legislative Modernization: A Choice for South Dakota Voters in 1974. 1974. 1.00 (*1-55614-060-6*) U of SD Gov Res Bur.

Ortner, S. B. High Religion: A Cultural & Political History of Sherpa Buddhism. 1992. 50.00 (*0-7855-0254-8*, Pub. by Ratna Pustak Bhandar) St Mut.

— High Religion - A Cultural & Political Historical History of Sherpa Buddhism. (C). 1991. text ed. 40.00 (*0-7855-0140-1*, Pub. by Ratna Pustak Bhandar) St Mut.

Ortner, Sherry & Whitehead, Harriet, eds. Sexual Meanings: The Cultural Construction of Gender & Sexuality. LC 80-26655. 448p. 1981. pap. 22.95 (*0-521-28375-2*) Cambridge U Pr.

Ortner, Sherry B. High Religion: A Cultural & Political History of Sherpa Buddhism. (Culture - Power - History Ser.). (Illus.). 265p. (C). 1989. 45.00 (*0-691-09439-X*); pap. 14.95 (*0-691-02843-5*) Princeton U Pr.

— Sherpas Through their Rituals. LC 76-62582. (Cambridge Studies in Cultural Systems). (Illus.). 196p. 1978. pap. 16.95 (*0-521-29216-6*) Cambridge U Pr.

Ortner, Toni. Requiem. LC 91-10019. (Illus.). 40p. (Orig.). 1991. pap. 6.95 (*0-941749-22-3*) Black Tie Pr.

***Ortner, Ulrich H.** World Anxiety & the End of the World. Stott, Douglas, tr. LC 95-5531. 1995. write for info. (*0-664-22062-2*) Westminster John Knox.

Ortner-Zimmerman, Toni. As If Anything Could Grow Back Perfect. 16p. (Orig.). 1979. pap. 5.00 (*0-932412-02-5*) Mayapple Pr.

Ortola, Marie-Sol. Un Estudio del Viaje de Turquia: Autobiografia o Ficcion. (Serie A: Monagrafias, LXXXVII). 160p. (SPA.). (C). 1983. 45.00 (*0-7293-0120-6*, Pub. by Tamesis Bks Ltd UK) Boydell & Brewer.

Ortolani, Al. The Last Hippie of Camp Fifty. DeGruson, Gene, ed. 64p. (Orig.). 1988. pap. 5.00 (*0-939391-10-4*) B Woodley Pr.

— Slow Stirring Spoon. 16p. 1981. pap. 2.00 (*0-913719-49-8*) High-Coo Pr.

***Ortolani, Benito.** The Japanese Theatre: From Shamanistic Ritual to Contemporary Pluralism. 1995. pap. write for info. (*0-691-04333-7*) Princeton U Pr.

Ortolani, Benito, ed. International Bibliography of Theatre: 1983. (International Bibliography of Theatre Ser.). 388p. 1986. lib. bdg. 90.00 (*0-89062-219-1*) Theatre Rsch Data Ctr.

— International Bibliography of Theatre, 1984. 852p. 1987. text ed. 120.00 (*0-89062-225-6*) Theatre Rsch Data Ctr.

— International Bibliography of Theatre, 1985. 1211p. (C). 1989. lib. bdg. 145.00 (*0-945419-00-7*) Theatre Rsch Data Ctr.

Ortolani, Benito, ed. & tr. Pirandello's Love Letters to Marta Abba. LC 93-38617. (ITA.). 1994. 35.00 (*0-691-03499-0*) Princeton U Pr.

Ortolani, Benito, et al, eds. International Bibliography of Theatre: 1982. 186p. 1985. 70.00 (*0-89062-207-8*) Theatre Rsch Data Ctr.

— International Bibliography of Theatre: 1987. 704p. 1992. lib. bdg. 175.00 (*0-945419-02-3*) Theatre Rsch Data Ctr.

— International Bibliography of Theatre: 1988-89. 951p. 1993. lib. bdg. 270.00 (*0-945419-03-1*) Theatre Rsch Data Ctr.

— International Bibliography of Theatre, 1986. 706p. 1991. lib. bdg. 145.00 (*0-945419-01-5*) Theatre Rsch Data Ctr.

— International Bibliography of Theatre, 1990-91. 970p. 1994. lib. bdg. 270.00 (*0-945419-04-X*) Theatre Rsch Data Ctr.

Ortolani, S. & Schnack, D. D. The Magnetohydrodynamics of Plasma Relaxation. 200p. 1993. text ed. 61.00 (*981-02-0860-X*) World Scientific Pub.

Ortolano, Leonard. Environmental Planning & Decision Making. LC 83-19820. 431p. (C). 1984. Net. text ed. write for info. (*0-471-87071-4*) Wiley.

Ortolano, Leonard, jt. auth. see Sinkule, Barbara J.

Ortoleva, Peter J. Geochemical Self-Organization. (Oxford Monographs on Geology & Geophysics: No. 23). (Illus.). 432p. 1994. 89.95 (*0-19-504476-2*) OUP.

***Ortoleva, Peter J., ed.** Basin Compartments & Seals. (AAPG Memoir Ser.: No. 61). (Illus.). xxxi, 477p. 1995. 149.00 (*0-89181-340-3*) AAPG.

Ortoleva, Peter J., jt. ed. see Meshri, Indu D.

Ortolo, F. Les Voceri de l'ile de Corse. LC 78-20119. (Collection de contes et de chansons populaires: Vol. 10). 1980. reprint ed. 21.50 (*0-404-60360-2*) AMS Pr.

Orton. Functional Appliances: Atlas of Clinical Prescription & Laboratory Construction. 1990. text ed. 68.00 (*0-86715-218-4*) Quint Pub Co.

Orton, Andrew. Structural Design of Masonry. 2nd ed. 159p. 1993. pap. text ed. 61.95 (*0-470-22048-1*) Halsted Pr.

— The Way We Build Now. (Illus.). 530p. 1988. pap. 80.95 (*0-7476-0011-2*) Chapman & Hall.

***Orton, Ann W.** Eternally Yours. 1994. pap. 1.95 (*0-88494-946-X*) Bookcraft Inc.

— Friend to Friend. 1994. pap. 1.95 (*0-88494-947-8*) Bookcraft Inc.

Orton, Anthony. Learning Mathematics. 2nd ed. 192p. 1992. text ed. 60.00 (*0-304-32553-8*); pap. text ed. 19.95 (*0-304-32555-4*) Cassell.

Orton, Chad M. More Faith Than Fear: The Los Angeles Stake Story. 12.95 (*0-88494-646-0*) Bookcraft Inc.

Orton, Christine. Sharing Your Home. (C). 1989. 20.00 (*0-86242-060-1*, Pub. by Age Concern Eng UK) St Mut.

Orton, Clive, jt. auth. see Hodder, Ian.

Orton, Clive, et al. Pottery in Archaeology. LC 92-25814. (Manuals in Archaeology Ser.). (Illus.). 288p. (C). 1993. 64.95 (*0-521-25715-8*); pap. 21.95 (*0-521-44597-3*) Cambridge U Pr.

Orton, Colin G., ed. Progress in Medical Radiation Physics, Vol. 1. 402p. 1982. 95.00 (*0-306-40713-2*, Plenum Pr) Plenum.

O

— Progress in Medical Radiation Physics, Vol. 2. 248p. 1985. 95.00 (*0-306-41789-8*, Plenum Pr) Plenum.

— Radiation Dosimetry: Physical & Biological Aspects. 340p. 1986. 89.50 (*0-306-42056-2*, Plenum Pr) Plenum.

Orton, D. E., jt. ed. see Gunn, D. M.

Orton, D. H., et al. The Solid State Master. LC 74-101374. (C). 1970. 126.00 (*0-08-006819-7*, Pub. by Pergamon Repr UK) Franklin.

Orton, David E., tr. see Raisenan, Heikki.

***Orton, Donald A. & Green, Thomas L.** Coincide: The Orton System of Pest Management. 189p. (Orig.). (C). Date not set. pap. text ed. 20.95 (*1-887619-03-8*) Plantsm ns Pubns.

Orton, Ed. A. & Wain, Geoffrey. Issues in Teaching Mathematics. (Education Ser.). (Illus.). 256p. 1994. 65.00 (*0-304-32678-X*); pap. 24.95 (*0-304-32680-1*) Cassell.

Orton, Fred. Figuring Jasper Johns. LC 94-12431. (Essays in Art & Culture Ser.). (Illus.). 248p. 1994. text ed. 39.95 (*0-674-30117-X*, ORTFIG) HUP.

Orton, Helen F. The Gold-Laced Coat. rev. ed. (Illus.). 226p. (J). (gr. 4-8). 1988. reprint ed. pap. 5.95 (*0-941967-07-7*) Old Fort Niagara Assn.

— The Treasure in the Little Trunk. (Illus.). 208p. (J). (gr. 4). 1989. reprint ed. pap. text ed. 5.95 (*0-685-29125-1*) Niagara Cnty Hist Soc.

***Orton, J. Robert, Jr.** Benevolence & Blasphemy: Memoirs of a Contemporary Art Collector. LC 95-60520. 288p. (Orig.). 1995. pap. 13.95 (*1-885983-05-0*) Turtle Point Pr.

Orton, J. W. Electron Paramagnetic Resonance. 240p. (C). 1969. 155.00 (*0-677-61900-6*) Gordon & Breach.

Orton, J. W. & Blood, Peter. The Electrical Characterisation of Semiconductors: Measurement of Minority Carrier Properties. (Techniques of Physics Ser.: Vol. 13). 291p. 1990. text ed. 88.00 (*0-12-528625-2*) Acad Pr.

Orton, J. W., jt. auth. see Blood, Peter.

Orton, Job. Discourses to the Aged. Stein, Leon, ed. LC 79-8697. (Growing Old Ser.). 1980. reprint ed. lib. bdg. 33.95 (*0-405-12795-2*) Ayer.

Orton, Joe. The Complete Plays. Incl. Entertaining Mr. Sloane. 1977. (*0-318-52761-8*); Erpingham Camp. 1977. (*0-318-52762-6*); Funeral Games. 1977. (*0-318-52763-4*); Good & Faithful Servant. 1977. (*0-318-52764-2*); Loot. 1977. (*0-318-52765-0*); Ruffian on the Stair. 1977. (*0-318-52766-9*); What the Butler Saw. 1977. (*0-318-52767-7*); 1977. Set pap. 6.95 (*0-394-17001-6*, B400) Grove-Atltic.

— Complete Plays. 448p. 1990. pap. 12.95 (*0-8021-3215-4*) Grove-Atltic.

Orton, Kay. Entree to Malta & Gozo. 1992. pap. 11.95 (*1-870948-61-0*, Pub. by Quiller Pr UK) St Mut.

Orton, Lawrence D. Polish Detroit & the Kolasinski Affair. LC 80-25290. (Illus.). 268p. 1981. 34.95 (*0-8143-1671-9*) Wayne St U Pr.

— The Prague Slav Congress of 1848. (East European Monographs: No. 46). 187p. 1978. text ed. 47.50 (*0-914710-39-7*) East Eur Quarterly.

Orton, Louis. Hypnotism Made Practical. 1976. pap. 5.00 (*0-87980-079-8*) Wilshire.

***Orton, Michael.** Once upon an Island: Images of Vancouver Island. 96p. 1992. 12.99 (*0-920501-82-6*) Orca Bk Pubs.

***Orton, Mildred E.** Cooking with Wholegrains. 72p. 1995. pap. 8.00 (*0-86547-485-0*, North Pt Pr) FS&G.

— Cooking with Wholegrains. rev. ed. LC 77-148706. (Illus.). 72p. 1971. pap. 6.95 (*0-374-50936-0*) FS&G.

Orton-Montanari, Ellen. One Hundred One Ways to Build Enrollment in Your Early Childhood Program. 135p. 1992. pap. text ed. 12.95 (*1-882149-39-4*) CPG Pub.

Orton, P. D., ed. see Watling, Roy & Gregory, Norma M.

Orton, Peter, jt. auth. see Fry, John.

Orton, Peter Z. Law School Admission Test Preparation Guide. 331p. (Orig.). (C). 1993. pap. text ed. 9.95 (*0-8220-2066-1*) Cliffs.

Orton, Peter Z., jt. auth. see Bobrow, Jerry.

Orton, Peter Z., jt. auth. see Covino, William A.

Orton, Peter Z., jt. auth. see Voelker, David H.

Orton, Samuel T. Reading, Writing, & Speech Problems in Children & Selected Papers. LC 88-30734. (PRO-ED Classics Ser.). (Illus.). 368p. (C). 1989. text ed. 37.00 (*0-89079-179-1*, 1468) PRO-ED.

Orton, Stephen A. Pan the Man. 36p. (Orig.). (YA). (gr. 7-12). 1991. pap. 3.00 (*0-88680-355-1*) I E Clark.

Orton, T. J., jt. ed. see Tanksley, S. D.

Orton, Terry C., jt. ed. see Tucker, Mary J.

Orton, V. Dreiserana: A Book about His Books. LC 72-6287. (American Literature Ser.: No. 49). 84p. (C). 1972. reprint ed. lib. bdg. 75.00 (*0-8383-1629-8*) M S G Haskell Hse.

***Orton, Vrest.** The American Cider Book. 136p. 1995. pap. text ed. 8.00 (*0-86547-484-2*, North Pt Pr) FS&G.

— Calvin Coolidge's Unique Vermont Inauguration. LC 81-66760. 96p. 1981. pap. 4.50 (*0-914960-31-8*) Academy Bks.

— The Forgotten Art of Building a Good Fireplace. LC 70-9285. (Forgotten Arts Ser.). (Illus.). 64p. (Orig.). 1969. pap. 6.95 (*0-911658-53-X*, 80-250-8) Yankee Bks.

— Vermont Afternoons with Robert Frost. LC 70-134029. 64p. 1981. pap. 4.50 (*0-914960-34-2*) Academy Bks.

Ortonne, Jean-Paul, et al. Vitiligo & Other Hypomelanoses of Hair & Skin. LC 82-16490. (Topics in Dermatology Ser.). 700p. 1983. 145.00 (*0-306-40974-7*, Plenum Med Bk) Plenum.

Ortony, Andrew, ed. Metaphor & Thought. 2nd ed. LC 92-37625. (Illus.). 768p. (C). 1993. pap. 29.95 (*0-521-40561-0*) Cambridge U Pr.

— Metaphor & Thought. 2nd ed. LC 92-37625. (Illus.). 768p. (C). 1994. 69.95 (*0-521-40547-5*) Cambridge U Pr.

Ortony, Andrew, et al. The Cognitive Structure of Emotions. (Illus.). 224p. (C). 1990. pap. 19.95 (*0-521-38664-0*) Cambridge U Pr.

Ortony, Andrew, et al, eds. Communication from an Artificial Intelligence Perspective: Theoretical & Applied Issues. LC 92-31538. xi, 260p. 1992. write for info. (*3-540-55881-0*); 77.00 (*0-387-55881-0*) Spr-Verlag.

Orts, J. C., et al. Breve Diccionario Espanol-Ruso: Ruso-Espanol de Terminos Cientificos & Tecnicos. deluxe ed. 438p. (RUS & SPA.). 1960. 35.00 (*0-8288-6832-8*, S-31835) Fr & Eur.

***Orttung, Robert W.** From Leningrad to St. Petersburg: Democratization in a Russian City. LC 94-40057. 1995. text ed. 49.95 (*0-312-12080-X*) St Martin.

Ortutay, G., jt. auth. see Balassa, I.

Ortuzar, Adolfo. Chile of Today: Its Commerce Production & Resources. 1976. lib. bdg. 69.95 (*0-8490-1605-3*) Gordon Pr.

Ortuzar, Juan D. & Willumen, Luis G. Modelling Transport. 2nd ed. LC 93-35746. 1994. text ed. 59.95 (*0-471-94193-X*) Wiley.

Ortuzar-Young, Ada. Tres Representaciones Literarias de la Vida Politica Cubana. LC 79-901197. (Senda de Estudios y Ensayos Ser.). (Orig.). (SPA.). 1979. pap. 10.95 (*0-918454-17-4*) Senda Nueva.

***Ortwein, Terrence.** Shel's Sister. 1994. 3.00 (*0-87129-476-1*, S32) Dramatic Pub.

Ortwerth, John & Nicks, Mel J. P. E. Curriculum Guide. (Illus.). 160p. (J). (gr. 1-6). 1984. student ed 12.95 (*0-86653-262-5*, GA 599) Good Apple.

Ortz, Jeff, et al, eds. IWW Songbook: To Fan the Flames of Discontent. 36th ed. 180p. 1993. pap. 8.00 (*0-917124-04-9*) Indus Workers World.

Ortzen, Tony. When Dead Kings Speak. 144p. (C). 1988. pap. 40.00 (*0-7212-0785-5*, Pub. by Regency Press) St Mut.

Oruka, H. Odera, ed. Sage Philosophy: Indigenous Thinkers & Modern Debate on African Philosophy. LC 90-45039. (Philosophy of History & Culture Ser.: Vol. 4). xxxi, 281p. 1990. 74.50 (*90-04-09283-8*) E J Brill.

***Orum, Anthony M.** City-Building in America. LC 94-38969. (C). 1995. text ed. 65.00 (*0-8133-0842-9*); pap. text ed. 19.95 (*0-8133-0843-7*) Westview.

***Orvell, Miles.** After the Machine: Visual Arts & the Erasing of Cultural Boundaries. (Illus.). 240p. 1995. text ed. 40.00 (*0-87805-754-4*); pap. 16.95 (*0-87805-755-2*) U Pr of Miss.

— Flannery O'Connor: An Introduction. LC 91-26494. 1991. 35.00 (*0-87805-534-7*); pap. 15.95 (*0-87805-542-8*) U Pr of Miss.

— The Real Thing: Imitation & Authenticity in American Culture, 1880-1940. LC 88-20886. (Cultural Studies of the United States). (Illus.). xxvi, 382p. (C). 1989. 45.00 (*0-8078-1837-2*); pap. 16.95 (*0-8078-4246-X*) U of NC Pr.

Orvig, S. Climates of the Polar Region. Lansberg, H. E., ed. (World Survey of Climatology Ser.: Vol. 14). 370p. 1971. 174.50 (*0-444-40828-2*) Elsevier.

Orvik, Nils. Decline of Neutrality, 1914-1941. 310p. 1971. 30.00 (*0-7146-2696-1*, Pub. by F Cass Pubs UK) Intl Spec Bk.

Orvik, Nils, ed. Semialignment & Western Security. LC 85-26274. 320p. 1986. text ed. 39.95 (*0-312-71274-X*) St Martin.

Orville-Thomas, W. J., et al, eds. Topics in Molecular Interactions. (Studies in Physical & Theoretical Chemistry: No. 37). 472p. 1985. 164.00 (*0-444-99556-0*) Elsevier.

Orville-Thomas, W. J & Redshaw, Mavis, eds. Internal Rotation in Molecules. LC 73-2791. (Wiley Monographs in Chemical Physics). (Illus.). 624p. reprint ed. pap. 177.90 (*0-685-20647-5*, 2030432) Bks Demand.

Orville-Thomas, W. J., jt. auth. see Hargittai, Istvan.

Orville-Thomas, W. J., jt. ed. see Jones, Hamlyn G.

***Orvin, George H.** Adolescents & Their Families. 224p. 1995. boxed 21.95 (*0-88048-651-1*, 8651) Am Psychiatric.

Orvis, jt. auth. see Harder, John.

Orvis, Bill. Visual BASIC for Applications by Example. 1993. pap. 29.99 (*1-56529-553-6*) Que.

***Orvis, William.** Develop a Professional Visual Basic Application in 14 Days. 1995. cd-rom, pap. 35.00 (*0-672-30596-8*) Sams.

— Do It Yourself Visual Basic for Windows. 2nd ed. 1992. pap. 24.95 (*0-672-30259-4*) Sams.

Orvis, William J. Do-It-Yourself Visual Basic. (First Book Ser.). (Illus.). 500p. (Orig.). 1992. pap. 19.95 (*0-672-27382-9*) Sams.

***Orwant, Jon.** 14 Days to Master Perl 5. 800p. 1995. cd-rom, pap. 39.95 (*1-57169-051-4*) Waite Group Pr.

Orwell, George. Animal Farm. LC 92-54299. 1993. 15.00 (*0-679-42039-8*, Everymans Lib) Knopf.

— Animal Farm. 15.95 (*0-8488-0120-2*) Amereon Ltd.

— Animal Farm. LC 54-11330. (Illus.). 160p. 1954. 12.95 (*0-15-107252-3*) HarBrace.

— Animal Farm. 132p. 1990. 15.95 (*0-15-107255-8*) HarBrace.

— Animal Farm. (Bridge Ser.). 122p. (YA). 1945. pap. text ed. 5.95 (*0-582-53008-3*) Longman.

— Animal Farm. 1983. mass mkt. 6.95 (*0-452-26277-1*, Plume); mass mkt. 8.95 (*0-452-26490-1*, Plume) NAL-Dutton.

— Animal Farm. 128p. (YA). (gr. 10). 1986. pap. 4.95 (*0-451-52466-7*, Sig Classics) NAL-Dutton.

— Animal Farm. large type ed. (Classics Ser.). 144p. 1984. 23.95 (*0-7089-8200-X*, Charnwood) Ulverscroft.

— Animal Farm. 1982. reprint ed. lib. bdg. 21.95 (*0-89966-369-9*) Buccaneer Bks.

— Burmese Days. 21.95 (*0-8488-0602-6*) Amereon Ltd.

— Burmese Days. LC 34-35694. 288p. 1950. 8.95 (*0-15-114975-5*) HarBrace.

— Burmese Days. LC 73-12947. 287p. 1974. reprint ed. pap. 8.95 (*0-15-614850-1*, Harvest Bks) HarBrace.

— Clergyman's Daughter. LC 60-10943. 320p. 1901. reprint ed. pap. 12.95 (*0-15-618065-0*, Harvest Bks) HarBrace.

— Collected Essays, Journalism & Letters, Vol. 1: An Age Like This, 1920-1940. Orwell, Sonia & Angus, Ian, eds. LC 68-12591. 574p. 1968. reprint ed. 17.95 (*0-15-118546-8*) HarBrace.

— Collected Essays, Journalism & Letters, Vol. 2: My Country Right or Left, 1940-1943. Orwell, Sonia & Angus, Ian, eds. LC 68-12591. 477p. 1968. reprint ed. 15.95 (*0-15-118547-6*) HarBrace.

— Collected Essays, Journalism & Letters, Vol. 3: As I Please, 1943-1945. Orwell, Sonia & Angus, Ian, eds. LC 68-12591. 1968. reprint ed. 15.95 (*0-15-118548-4*) HarBrace.

— Collection of Essays. LC 54-7594. 316p. 1970. reprint ed. pap. 9.95 (*0-15-618600-4*, Harvest Bks) HarBrace.

— Coming up for Air. LC 50-5002. 278p. 1969. reprint ed. pap. 8.95 (*0-15-619625-5*, HPL44, Harvest Bks) HarBrace.

— Dickens, Dali & Others. LC 63-22950. 243p. 1970. reprint ed. pap. 8.95 (*0-15-626053-0*, Harvest Bks) HarBrace.

— Down & Out in Paris & London. LC 65-67354. 213p. 1972. reprint ed. pap. 7.95 (*0-15-626224-X*, Harvest Bks) HarBrace.

— The English People. LC 74-7022. (British History Ser.: No. 30). 1974. lib. bdg. 75.00 (*0-8383-1897-5*) M S G Haskell Hse.

— La Ferme des Animaux. (FRE.). 1984. pap. 8.95 (*0-7859-4198-3*) Fr & Eur.

— Homage to Catalonia. LC 52-6442. 232p. 1969. reprint ed. pap. 7.95 (*0-15-642117-8*, Harvest Bks) HarBrace.

— Keep the Aspidistra Flying. 20.95 (*0-8488-0603-4*) Amereon Ltd.

— Keep the Aspidistra Flying. LC 56-5326. 250p. 1969. reprint ed. pap. 10.00 (*0-15-646899-9*, Harvest Bks) HarBrace.

— The Lion & the Unicorn: Socialism & the English Genius. LC 75-41205. reprint ed. 22.50 (*0-404-14691-0*) AMS Pr.

— Nineteen Eighty-Four. LC 92-52906. 384p. 1992. 17.00 (*0-679-41739-7*, Everymans Lib) Knopf.

— Nineteen Eighty-Four. LC 83-18442. 320p. 1983. 12.95 (*0-15-166038-7*) HarBrace.

— Nineteen Eighty-Four. 1983. pap. 9.95 (*0-452-26293-3*); mass mkt. 5.95 (*0-452-25426-4*, Plume) NAL-Dutton.

— Nineteen Eighty Four. 1950. pap. 4.95 (*0-451-52493-4*, Sig) NAL-Dutton.

— 1984. 1963. 5.00 (*0-87129-542-3*, N15) Dramatic Pub.

— Nineteen Eighty-Four. large type ed. (Classics Ser.). 428p. 1982. 23.95 (*0-7089-8027-9*, Charnwood) Ulverscroft.

— Nineteen Eighty-Four. 1982. reprint ed. lib. bdg. 21.95 (*0-89966-368-0*) Buccaneer Bks.

— Nineteen Eighty-Four: Commemorative Edition. 268p. 1950. pap. 3.95 (*0-451-52123-4*, Sig Classics) NAL-Dutton.

— Nineteen Eighty-Four: The Fascimile of the Extant Manuscript. Davison, Peter, ed. 406p. 1984. One of 55 copies. 525.00 (*0-685-09886-9*); One of 275 copies. bds. 275.00 (*0-87730-012-7*) M&S Pr.

— Nineteen Eighty-Four, the Facsimile. LC 81-3848. 416p. 1984. 75.00 (*0-15-166034-4*) HarBrace.

— Orwell: The Lost Writings. West, W. J., ed. 352p. 1988. mass mkt. 5.95 (*0-380-70118-9*) Avon.

— The Orwell Reader: Fiction, Essays, & Reportage. LC 61-1439. 456p. 1961. pap. 12.95 (*0-15-670176-6*, Harvest Bks) HarBrace.

— Orwell's Nineteen Eighty-Four: Text, Sources, Criticism. 2nd ed. Howe, Irving & Levin, David, eds. (Harbrace Sourcebooks Ser.). 450p. (C). 1982. pap. text ed. 18.75 (*0-15-565811-5*) HB Coll Pubs.

— The Road to Wigan Pier. LC 58-10888. 232p. 1972. reprint ed. pap. 8.95 (*0-15-676750-3*, Harvest Bks) HarBrace.

— Shooting an Elephant. LC 50-10343. 200p. 1950. 12.95 (*0-15-182043-0*) HarBrace.

Orwell, Sonia, ed. see Orwell, George.

Orwen, Gifford. Upgrade Your Italian: A Review Grammar. 1983. pap. 12.95 (*0-913298-12-3*) S F Vanni.

Orwicz, Michael R., ed. Art Criticism & Its Institutions in Nineteenth-Century France. LC 93-46023. 1994. text ed. 69.95 (*0-7190-3859-6*, Pub. by Manchester Univ Pr UK) St Martin.

Orwig, Gary. Creating Computer Programs for Learning: A Guide for Trainers, Parents & Teachers. 1983. pap. 16.95 (*0-8359-1168-3*, Reston) P-H.

Orwig, Gary W., jt. auth. see Barron, Ann E.

***Orwig, Sara.** Atlanta. 384p. (Orig.). 1995. mass mkt., pap. 4.99 (*0-451-40343-6*, Onyx) NAL-Dutton.

— Falcon's Lair. (Desire Ser.). 1995. mass mkt. 3.25 (*0-373-05938-8*, 1-05938-5) Silhouette.

— Hide in Plain Sight. 1995. pap. 3.75 (*0-373-07679-7*, 1-07679-3) Silhouette.

— Lightning Season. 320p. 1993. mass mkt. 3.99 (*0-8217-4052-0*) Zebra.

— The Mad, the Bad & the Dangerous. (Superromance Ser.). 1993. mass mkt. 3.50 (*0-373-70563-8*, 1-70563-1) Harlequin Bks.

— Memphis. 384p. (Orig.). 1994. pap. 4.99 (*0-451-40407-6*, Onyx) NAL-Dutton.

— New Orleans. 416p. (Orig.). 1993. pap. 4.99 (*0-451-40373-8*, Onyx) NAL-Dutton.

— Sweeter Than Sin. 368p. (Orig.). 1992. mass mkt. 4.99 (*0-446-36084-8*) Warner Bks.

— Texas Passion. 432p. 1994. mass mkt. 4.50 (*0-8217-4746-0*) Zebra.

— Warrior Moon. 384p. 1995. pap. 4.99 (*0-8217-5041-0*) Zebra.

Orwin, Clifford. The Humanity of Thucydides. LC 94-3111. 1994. 35.00 (*0-691-03449-4*) Princeton U Pr.

Orwin, Donna T. Tolstoy's Art & Thought, 1847-1880. LC 92-37860. 296p. (C). 1993. text ed. 35.00 (*0-691-06991-3*) Princeton U Pr.

***Orwin, Martin.** Colloquial Somali: A Complete Language Course. (Colloquial Ser.). 272p. (SOM.). 1995. pap. 18.95 (*0-415-10009-7*, B4032); audio, pap. 39.95 (*0-415-10011-9*, B4040); audio 24.95 (*0-415-10010-0*, B4036) Routledge.

***Ory.** Aging & Health Care: Social Science & Policy Perspectives. 284p. 1993. pap. 95.00 (*1-56593-576-4*, 0684) Singular Publishing.

Ory, Jean-Loys, jt. auth. see Salamolard, Michael.

Ory, John C. & Ryan, Katherine E. Testing & Grading: Tips for Classroom Practice. (Survival Skills for Scholars Ser.: Vol. 4). (Illus.). 128p. (C). 1993. text ed. 27.50 (*0-8039-4973-1*); pap. text ed. 12.95 (*0-8039-4974-X*) Sage.

Ory, John C., jt. auth. see Braskamp, Larry A.

Ory, Marcia G. & Bond, Kathleen, eds. Aging & Health Care: Social Science & Policy Perspectives. (Contemporary Issues in Health, Medicine, & Social Policy Ser.). 320p. 1989. 49.95 (*0-415-01716-5*); pap. 19.95 (*0-415-01717-3*) Routledge.

Ory, Marcia G. & Duncker, Alfred P., eds. In-Home Care for Older People: Health & Supportive Services. 224p. (C). 1991. text ed. 42.00 (*0-8039-4413-6*); pap. text ed. 18.95 (*0-8039-4414-4*) Sage.

Ory, Marcia G. & Warner, Huber R., eds. Gender, Health & Longevity: Multidisciplinary Perspectives. LC 90-35541. 208p. 1990. 34.95 (*0-8261-7140-0*) Springer Pub.

Ory, Marcia G., et al, eds. Aging, Health, & Behavior. 400p. (C). 1991. 58.00 (*0-8039-4342-3*); pap. 25.00 (*0-8039-4343-1*) Sage.

Ory, R. L. Antinutrients & Natural Toxicants in Foods. 378p. 1981. 74.00 (*0-917678-15-X*) Food & Nut Pr.

Ory, Robert L. Grandma Called It Roughage: Fiber Facts & Fallacies. LC 91-24259. (Illus.). 170p. 1991. 22.95 (*0-8412-1749-1*); pap. 12.95 (*0-8412-1764-5*) Am Chemical.

Ory, Robert L., ed. Plant Proteins: Applications, Biological Effects, & Chemistry. LC 86-10848. (ACS Symposium Ser.: No. 312). (Illus.). 296p. 1986. 65.95 (*0-8412-0976-6*) Am Chemical.

Ory, Robert L. & Rittig, Falk R. Bioregulators: Chemistry & Uses. LC 84-10987. (ACS Symposium Ser.: No. 257). 296p. 1984. 49.95 (*0-8412-0853-0*) Am Chemical.

Ory, Robert L. & St. Angelo, Allen J., eds. Enzymes in Food & Beverage Processing. LC 77-6645. (ACS Symposium Ser.: No. 47). 1977. 38.95 (*0-8412-0375-X*) Am Chemical.

Oryan, Baba T. The Rubaiyat of Baba Tahir Oryan of Hamadan. Nakosteen, Mehdi, tr. & intro. by. (Illus.). 60p. (PER.). (C). 1988. text ed. 20.00 (*0-936347-42-2*) Iran Bks.

O'Ryan, J. A. Pulmonary Rehabilitation: From Hospital to Home. 1991. 32.95 (*0-8151-6548-X*, Yr Bk Med Pubs) Mosby Yr Bk.

O'Ryan, S., jt. auth. see Foreman, C.

***Oryx Press Staff.** Directory of Biomedical & Health Care Grants 1996. 10th ed. Hannum, Millie & Woolum, Janet, eds. 664p. 1995. pap. 84.50 (*0-89774-878-6*, 2277) Oryx Pr.

— Directory of Grants in the Humanities 1994-95. 8th ed. 712p. 1994. pap. 84.50 (*0-89774-908-1*) Oryx Pr.

— Directory of Grants in the Humanities 1995-96. 9th ed. Hannum, Millie & Woolum, Janet, eds. 720p. 1995. pap. 84.50 (*0-89774-911-1*, 2333) Oryx Pr.

— Directory of Residential Centers for Adults with Mental Illnesses. 328p. 1990. pap. 68.50 (*0-89774-563-9*) Oryx Pr.

— Directory of Women's Health Care Centers: In Cooperation with the National Association of Women's Health Professionals. 160p. 1989. pap. 45.00 (*0-89774-525-6*) Oryx Pr.

— The Grants Subject Authority Guide. 88p. 1991. pap. 29.50 (*0-89774-720-8*) Oryx Pr.

— Substance Abuse & Kids: A Directory of Education, Information, Prevention, & Early Intervention Programs. 488p. 1989. pap. 65.00 (*0-89774-583-3*) Oryx Pr.

— Substance Abuse Residential Treatment Centers for Teens. 304p. 1990. pap. 55.00 (*0-89774-585-X*) Oryx Pr.

— Women's Recovery Programs: A Directory of Residential Addiction Treatment Centers. 360p. 1990. pap. 55.00 (*0-89774-584-1*) Oryx Pr.

Oryx Press Staff, ed. Bibliography of Agriculture Annual Cumulation, 1990, 2 vols. 1991. Pt. 1, 1920p. write for info. (*0-89774-634-1*); Pt. 2, 2128p. write for info. (*0-89774-635-X*) Oryx Pr.

— Current Index to Journals in Education: Semi-Annual Cumulations 1983, 2 vols. 1064p. 1980. Vol. 2, July to Dec. write for info. (*0-89774-120-X*) Oryx Pr.

— Current Index to Journals in Education Semi-Annual Cumulations 1986, 2 vols. 1987. Vol. 2, 1096p., July to Dec. write for info. (*0-318-68213-3*) Oryx Pr.

— Current Index to Journals in Education Semi-Annual Cumulations 1986, Jan. to June. 1248p. 1987. write for info. (*0-318-68212-5*) Oryx Pr.

— Current Index to Journals in Education Semi-Annual Cumulations 1986, 2 vols., Set. 1987. 181.00 (*0-685-72461-1*) Oryx Pr.

— Current Index to Journals in Education Semi-Annual Cumulations 1987, 2 vols., Set. 1988. 198.00 (*0-685-72460-3*) Oryx Pr.

— Current Index to Journals in Education Semi-Annual Cumulations 1987, Vol. 1, Jan. to June. 1168p. 1988. Vol. 1, 1168p., Jan. to June. write for info. (*0-318-68210-9*) Oryx Pr.

An Asterisk (*) at the beginning of an entry indicates that the title is appearing in BIP for the first time.

— Current Index to Journals in Education Semi-Annual Cumulations 1987, Vol. 2, July to Dec. 1120p. 1988. Vol. 2, 1120p., July to Dec. write for info. (0-318-68211-7) Oryx Pr.
— Current Index to Journals in Education Semi-Annual Cumulations 1989, 2 vols. 1990. Vol. 2, 1360p., July to Dec. write for info. (0-318-68207-9) Oryx Pr.
— Current Index to Journals in Education Semi-Annual Cumulations 1989, 2 vols., Set. 1990. 198.00 (0-685-38871-9) Oryx Pr.
— Current Index to Journals in Education Semi-Annual Cumulations 1989, Vol. 1, Jan. to June. 1256pp. 1990. Vol. 1, 1256p., Jan. to June. write for info. (0-318-68206-0) Oryx Pr.
— Current Index to Journals in Education Semi-Annual Cumulations 1990, Vol. 1, 1224p., Jan. to June. 1991. write for info. (0-318-68205-2) Oryx Pr.
— Current Index to Journals in Education Semi-Annual Cumulations 1990, Vol. 2, July to Dec. 1280p. 1991. Vol. 2, 1280p., July to Dec. write for info. (0-89774-677-5) Oryx Pr.
— Directory of Funding Sources for Community Development. 416p. 1995. pap. 47.50 (0-89774-947-2) Oryx Pr.
— Drugs, Alcohol, & Other Addictions: A Directory of Treatment Centers & Prevention Programs Nationwide. 2nd ed. 656p. 1993. pap. 195.00 (0-89774-623-6) Oryx Pr.
— Thesaurus of ERIC Descriptors, 1990. 12th ed. 656p. 1990. 69.50 (0-89774-561-2) Oryx Pr.

Orzalesi, N., jt. ed. see Bonomi, L.

Orzeanu, Irina. On the Wings of Emotions. LC 90-55257. 106p. (Orig.). 1991. pap. 6.00 (1-56002-066-0) Aegina Pr.

Orzech. Plane Algebraic Curves. (Pure & Applied Mathematics Ser.: Vol. 61). 240p. 1981. 110.00 (0-8247-1159-9) Dekker.

Orzechowski, Peter, jt. auth. see Slater, William.

Orzechowski, Z., jt. ed. see Bayvel, L. P.

Orzeck, Art, jt. auth. see Hendrickson, Al.

***Orzeck, Art Z.** Psychology in a Physical World: Forty Years of Just Thinking About Science. 108p. (Orig.). (C). 1995. pap. text ed. 17.50 (0-8191-9799-8) U Pr of Amer.

Orzeszkowa, Eliza. The Forsaken. Konigsberger, Edward, tr. 248p. (C). 1980. 50.00 (0-9508203-0-X, Pub. by Delamare UK) St Mut.

Os-Saltaneh, Taj. Khaterat-e Taj Os-Saltaneh: The Memoirs of Taj Os-Saltaneh. Sadounian, Cyrus, ed. 136p. (PER.). (C). 1991. reprint ed. pap. 15.00 (0-936347-22-8) Iran Bks.

***Osa, Osayimwense.** African Children's & Youth Literature. LC 94-44450. (Twayne's World Authors Ser.: Vol. 853). (YA). 1995. lib. bdg. 23.95x (0-8057-4524-6, Twayne) Macmillan.

***Osa, Osayimwense, ed.** The All White World of Children's Books & African American Children's Literature. 1995. pap. 14.95 (0-86543-477-8) Africa World.

Osa, T. & Atwood, Jerry L., eds. Inclusion Aspects of Membrane Chemistry. (C). 1991. lib. bdg. 109.50 (0-7923-1123-X) Kluwer Ac.

Osada & Nakagawa, eds. Membrane Science & Technology. 488p. 1992. 185.00 (0-8247-8694-7) Dekker.

Osada, Noriaki. Theory of International Physical Education & Sports Studies for the Achievement of Peace. 1991. 14.95 (0-533-09131-4) Vantage.

Osada, Takashi. The Five S's: Five Keys to a Total Quality Environment. 224p. 1991. text ed. 32.95 (92-833-1115-9, 311159, Pub. by APO JA); pap. text ed. 27.50 (92-833-1116-7, 311167, Pub. by APO JA) Qual Resc.

Osada, Takashi, jt. auth. see Takahasi, Yoshikazu.

Osadchy, Mykhaylo, ed. Kafedra, Issue 7. LC 89-80449. 224p. 1989. 10.00 (0-914834-61-4) Smoloskyp.
— Kafedra, Issue 8. LC 89-80449. 264p. 1989. 12.50 (0-914834-62-2) Smoloskyp.

Osadebay, Dennis C., jt. auth. see Dei-Anang, Michael F.

Osaigbovo, Rebecca F. Chosen Vessels: Women of Color, Keys to Change. LC 92-85567. (Illus.). 216p. (Orig.). 1993. pap. 9.95 (1-880560-57-7) DaBaR Srvs.

Osaki, S. Applied Stochastic System Modeling. (Illus.). 280p. 1992. 89.00 (0-387-54927-7) Spr-Verlag.
— Stochastic System Reliability Modeling. (Series in Modern Applied Mathematics: Vol. 5). 300p. 1985. text ed. 44.00 (9971-978-56-3) World Scientific Pub.

Osaki, S. & Murth, D. N. Stochastic Models in Engineering, Technology & Management: Proceeding of the 1st Australia-Japan Workshop. 500p. 1993. text ed. 121.00 (981-02-1452-9) World Scientific Pub.

Osaki, S. & Nishio, T. Reliability Evaluation of Some Fault-Tolerant Computer Architectures. (Lecture Notes in Computer Science Ser.: Vol. 97). 129p. 1980. pap. 21.00 (0-387-10274-4) Spr-Verlag.

Osaki, Shunji, jt. auth. see Mine, Hisashi.

Osaki, Yuji, et al, eds. Progress of Seismology of the Sun & Stars: Proceedings of the Oji International Seminar Held at Hakone, Japan, December 11-14, 1989. (Lecture Notes in Physics Ser.: Vol. 367). xiii, 467p. 1990. 57.00 (0-387-53091-6) Spr-Verlag.

Osako, Masako M., jt. ed. see Nusberg, Charlotte.

Osakwe, Christopher. Joint Ventures with the Soviet Republics: Law & Practice. 400p. 1993. ring bd. 125.00 (0-88063-374-3) Michie Butterworth.
— Joint Ventures with the Soviet Republics: Law & Practice. suppl. ed. 1993. ring bd. 55.00 (0-318-67229-4) Butterworth Legal Pubs.
— Soviet Business Law: Institutions, Principles & Processes. suppl. ed. 1992. ring bd. 90.00 (1-56257-194-X) Butterworth Legal Pubs.
— Soviet Business Law: Institutions, Principles & Processes. 2 vols., Set. 700p. 1992. ring bd. 180.00 (0-88063-338-7) Michie Butterworth.

Osakwe, Christopher, ed. see Glendon, Mary A.

Osama, Abdul R. The Dilemma of Development in the Arabian Peninsula. 208p. 1986. 59.50 (0-7099-4240-0, Pub. by Croom Helm UK) Routledge Chapman & Hall.

Osamu Sato. Art of Computer Designing. (Illus.). 128p. 1993. pap. 36.95 (4-7661-0736-5, Pub. by Graphic Sha JA) Bks Nippan.

Osamura. Composite Superconductors. (Applied Physics Ser.: Vol. 3). 440p. 1994. 175.00 (0-8247-9117-7) Dekker.

Osanka, Frank & Johann, Sara L. Sourcebook on Pornography. 576p. 1989. text ed. 99.95 (0-669-15858-5) Free Pr.

Osanka, Frank, jt. auth. see Johann, Sara L.

Osanka, Frank M., jt. auth. see Linedecker, Clifford L.

Osaragi, Jiro, pseud. Homecoming. Horwitz, Brewster, tr. LC 76-54833. 303p. 1977. reprint ed. text ed. 59.75 (0-8371-9369-9, OSHO, Greenwood Pr) Greenwood.

Osaragi, Jiro. The Journey. Morris, Ivan, tr. 350p. 1960. pap. 9.95 (0-8048-1377-9) C E Tuttle.

Osato, jt. auth. see Wilhelmus.

Osawa, Eiji & Yonemitsu, Osamu. Carbocyclic Cage Compounds: Chemistry & Applications. (Methods in Stereochemical Analysis Ser.). (Illus.). 409p. 1992. text ed. 95.00 (0-89573-728-0) VCH Pubs.

Osawa, S. & Honjo, T., eds. Evolution of Life: Fossils, Molecules, & Culture. xiii, 460p. 1991. 161.00 (0-387-70064-1) Spr-Verlag.

Osawa, S., et al, eds. Genetics & Evolution of RNA Polymerase & RNA Ribosomes. 670p. 1981. 137.50 (0-444-80288-6) Elsevier.

***Osawa, Syozo.** Evolution of the Genetic Code. (Illus.). 216p. 1995. 95.00 (0-19-854781-1) OUP.

Osawa, T. & Bonavida, B., eds. Tumor Necrosis Factor: Structure Function Relationship & Clinical Application. (Illus.). x, 292p. 1992. 223.25 (3-8055-5458-3) S Karger.

Osawa, Yasu, jt. auth. see Schatz, Dennis.

Osbakken, Mary, ed. NMR Techniques in the Study of Cardiovascular Structure & Functions. (Illus.). 368p. 1988. 62.00 (0-87993-315-1) Futura Pub.

Osband, Gillian. Boysie's First Birthday. (Boysie Bks.). (Illus.). 32p. (J). (ps-3). 1990. lib. bdg. 14.95 (0-87614-404-0, Carolrhoda) Lerner Group.
— Boysie's Kitten. (Boysie Bks.). (Illus.). 32p. (J). (ps-3). 1990. lib. bdg. 14.95 (0-87614-403-2, Carolrhoda) Lerner Group.
— Castles. LC 91-60082. (Illus.). 16p. (J). 1991. 17.95 (0-531-05949-9) Orchard Bks Watts.

Osband, Gillian, ed. The National Trust Family Handbook. (Illus.). 204p. Date not set. pap. 8.95 (0-7078-0171-0, Pub. by Natl Trust UK) Trafalgar.

Osband, Linda. Victorian House Style. (Illus.). 1992. 39.95 (0-7153-9841-5, Pub. by D & C Pub UK) Sterling.

Osband, Linda, comp. Famous Travellers of the Holy Land: Their Personal Impressions & Reflections. (Illus.). 159p. 1991. 19.95 (1-85375-031-X) Parkwest Pubns.

Osbeck, Kenneth W. Amazing Grace: 366 Hymn Stories for Personal Devotions. LC 90-37888. 418p. 1990. pap. 12.99 (0-8254-3425-4) Kregel.
— Devotional Warm-ups for Church Choirs. LC 85-17222. 96p. 1985. pap. 4.99 (0-8254-3421-1); pap. 54.00 (0-8254-3423-8) Kregel.
— Fifty-Two Hymn Stories Dramatized. LC 91-39320. 144p. 1992. pap. 9.99 (0-8254-3428-9) Kregel.
— Ministry of Music. LC 61-14865. 192p. 1975. pap. 8.99 (0-8254-3410-6) Kregel.
— My Music Workbook. 144p. 1982. pap. 7.99 (0-8254-3415-7) Kregel.
— One Hundred One Hymn Stories. LC 81-17165. 288p. (C). 1982. pap. 10.99 (0-8254-3416-5) Kregel.
— One Hundred One More Hymn Stories. LC 84-27847. 328p. (C). 1985. pap. 10.99 (0-8254-3420-3) Kregel.
— Pocket Guide for the Church Choir Member. 48p. 1984. pap. 1.99 (0-8254-3408-4); pap. 21.50 (0-8254-3417-3) Kregel.

Osberg, Lars, ed. Economic Inequality & Poverty: International Perspectives. LC 90-31795. 272p. 1991. 49.95 (0-87332-528-1); pap. text ed. 23.95 (0-87332-540-0) M E Sharpe.

Osberg, Richard H. Sir Gawain & the Green Knight. LC 89-13304. (American University Studies: English Language & Literature: Ser. IV, Vol. 112). 274p. 1990. text ed. 45.95 (0-8204-1160-4) P Lang Pubs.

Osberg, Susan, jt. auth. see Duden, Jane.

Osbey, Brenda M. Desperate Circumstances, Dangerous Woman. 103p. (Orig.). 1991. pap. 9.95 (0-934257-57-4) Story Line.
— In These Houses. LC 87-33297. (Wesleyan Poetry Ser.). 63p. 1988. 22.50 (0-8195-2146-9, Wesleyan Univ Pr); pap. 10.95 (0-8195-1147-1, Wesleyan Univ Pr) U Pr of New Eng.

Osbon, Diane, sel. A Joseph Campbell Companion: Reflections on the Art of Living. LC 90-56391. (Illus.). 320p. 1992. 22.50 (0-06-016718-1, HarpT) HarpC.

Osborn. Handbook in Radiology: Neuroradiology. 416p. 1991. pap. 36.95 (0-8151-6578-1, Yr Bk Med Pubs) Mosby Yr Bk.
— Mammals of Ancient Egypt. Date not set. pap. write for info. (0-85668-510-0, Pub. by Aris & Phillips UK) David Brown.
— Prospector's Field Book & Guide. 1987. pap. 9.95 (0-917914-57-0) Lindsay Pubns.

Osborn, jt. auth. see Hendrick.

Osborn, et al. Year Book of Neuroradiology: Head & Neck Radiology, 1992. 437p. 1992. 79.95 (0-8151-6588-9) Mosby Yr Bk.
— Year Book of Neuroradiology, 1993: Head & Neck Radiology. 350p. 1993. 79.95 (0-8151-6589-7, Yr Bk Med Pubs) Mosby Yr Bk.
— Year Book of Neuroradiology, 1994: Head & Neck Radiology. 800p. 1994. 79.95 (0-8151-6590-0, Yr Bk Med Pubs) Mosby Yr Bk.
— Year Book of Neuroradiology, 1995: Head & Neck Radiology. 350p. 1995. 79.95 (0-8151-6591-9, Yr Bk Med Pubs) Mosby Yr Bk.
— Year Book of Neuroradiology, 1996: Head & Neck Radiology. 350p. 1996. 79.95 (0-8151-6592-7, Yr Bk Med Pubs) Mosby Yr Bk.

Osborn, Albert S. The Mind of the Juror As Judge of the Facts or the Layman's View of the Law. xv, 239p. 1982. reprint ed. lib. bdg. 30.00 (0-8377-0926-1) Rothman.
— Problem of Proof: Especially As Exemplified in Disputed Documents Trials. LC 75-20212. 564p. 1975. reprint ed. 52.95 (0-88229-300-1) Nelson-Hall.
— Questioned Document Problems: The Discovery & Proof of the Facts. LC 84-14716. (Criminology, Law Enforcement, & Social Problems Ser.: No. 172). (Illus.). 570p. 1991. 45.00 (0-87585-172-X) Patterson Smith.
— Questioned Documents. 2nd ed. LC 74-78841. (Illus.). 1072p. 1974. reprint ed. 27.95 (0-88229-190-4) Nelson-Hall.
— Questioned Documents. 2nd rev. ed. LC 73-9875. (Criminology, Law Enforcement, & Social Problems Ser.: No. 207). (Illus.). 760p. 1973. lib. bdg. 27.50 (0-87585-207-6) Patterson Smith.

Osborn, Alex F. Applied Imagination. 3rd rev. ed. 1993. reprint ed. 25.95 (0-930222-73-3) Creative Ed.

Osborn, Anne G. Diagnostic Neuroradiology - a Text - Atlas. 800p. 1993. 185.00 (0-8016-7486-7) Mosby Yr Bk.
— An Introduction to Cerebral Angiography. (Illus.). 436p. 1980. text ed. 79.50 (0-06-141829-3, 14-18292) Lippincott.

Osborn, Arthur W. Cosmic Womb: An Interpretation of Man's Relationship to the Infinite. LC 69-17714. (Orig.). 1969. pap. 4.95 (0-8356-0001-7, Quest) Theos Pub Hse.

Osborn, Averil. Taking Part in Community Care Planning: The Involvement of User Groups, Career Groups & Voluntary Groups. (C). 1991. 60.00 (0-946505-84-5, Pub. by Age Concern Eng UK) St Mut.

Osborn, Barbara & Davis, J. Francis. Images of Conflict: Learning from Media Coverage of the Gulf War. Center for Media & Values Staff, ed. (Illus.). 60p. (C). 1992. teacher ed 34.95 (1-879419-04-1, W56WV) Ctr Media Values.

Osborn, Carolyn. The Fields of Memory. 288p. 1984. 14.95 (0-940672-23-5) Shearer Pub.
— Warriors & Maidens. LC 90-49280. 188p. 1991. 19.95 (0-87565-084-8) Tex Christian.

Osborn, Chase. The Soo-Scenes in & about Sault Ste. Marie Michigan in 1887. (Illus.). 46p. 1983. pap. 5.50 (0-912382-30-9) Black Letter.

Osborn, D. Keith. Early Childhood Education in Historical Perspective. rev. ed. LC 80-68813. 224p. (C). 1980. pap. 24.95 (0-685-01535-1) Daye Pr.
— Early Childhood Education in Historical Perspective. 3rd ed. LC 90-23294. 240p. 1991. pap. text ed. 24.95 (0-918772-22-2) Daye Pr.

Osborn, D. Keith & Osborn, Janie D. Discipline & Classroom Management. 3rd ed. (Illus.). 224p. 1989. lib. bdg. 17.95 (0-918772-18-4) Daye Pr.

Osborn, D. Keith, jt. auth. see Osborn, Janie D.

***Osborn, David.** Murder in the Napa Valley. 224p. 1995. mass mkt. 4.99 (0-8217-4844-0) Zebra.
— Murder in the Napa Valley: A Margaret Barlow Mystery. 224p. 1993. 19.00 (0-671-70487-7) S&S Trade.
— Murder on the Chesapeake: A Margaret Barlow Mystery. 304p. 1993. mass mkt. 3.99 (0-8217-4165-9) Zebra.

***Osborn, Diane K., ed.** A Joseph Campbell Companion. 1995. pap. 13.00 (0-06-092617-1, PL) HarpC.

Osborn, Donald E., ed. Selected Papers on Solar Radiation & Solar Thermal Systems. LC 92-19411. (Milestone Ser.: Vol. 54). 1992. write for info. (0-8194-0983-9); pap. write for info. (0-8194-0984-7) SPIE.

Osborn, Donald L. Joseph Brunner of Rothenstein, Schifferstadt, & Frederick. LC 91-60136. (Illus.). xiv, 586p. 1991. 150.00 (0-9629126-1-1) D L Osborn.
— Knowing the Bruners: Ancestry & Descendants of Samuel Bruner & His Wife, Catharine Briggs. LC 68-20641. (Illus.). xiv, 240p. 1958. 50.00 (0-9629126-0-3) D L Osborn.

Osborn, Donald W. & Dwyer, David J. A Fulfulde (Masina) -English-French Lexicon: A Root Based Compilation Drawn from Extant Sources Followed by English-Fulfulde & French-Fulfulde Listings. LC 92-35325. 1993. 69.95 (0-87013-326-8) Mich St U Pr.

Osborn, Duffield. Secret of the Crater. 1979. reprint ed. 8.50 (0-686-65259-2) Bookfinger.

Osborn, E. Heritage of Greece & Legacy of Rome. 1958. pap. 20.00 (0-87556-692-8) Saifer.

Osborn, E. F. The Philosophy of Clement of Alexandria. (Texts & Studies, New Ser.: Vol. 3). 1974. reprint ed. 28.00 (0-8115-1716-0) Periodicals Srv.

Osborn, Edward, jt. auth. see McManus, Judith A.

Osborn, Edward B. Literature & Life: Things Seen, Heard & Read. LC 68-16963. (Essay Index Reprint Ser.). 1977. reprint ed. 17.95 (0-8369-0755-8) Ayer.

***Osborn, Elane.** Shelter in His Arms. (Intimate Moments Ser.). 1995. mass mkt. 3.75 (0-373-07642-8, 1-07642-1) Silhouette.

Osborn, Elizabeth, jt. auth. see Sakheim, George S.

Osborn, Eric. The Emergence of Christian Theology. LC 92-11489. 356p. (C). 1993. 64.95 (0-521-43078-X) Cambridge U Pr.

Osborn, Eric F. Ethical Patterns in Early Christian Thought. LC 75-10040. 262p. reprint ed. pap. 74.70 (0-685-15653-2, 2026351) Bks Demand.

Osborn, Fairfield, ed. Our Crowded Planet: Essays on the Pressures of Population. LC 82-21145. 240p. 1983. reprint ed. text ed. 59.75 (0-313-22639-3, OSOC, Greenwood Pr) Greenwood.

Osborn, George. The R. L. Stevenson Trail Through the Cevennes. (C). 1989. pap. text ed. 40.00 (0-9515838-0-8, Pub. by GTBS Pubns UK) St Mut.

Osborn, George C. John James Tigert: American Educator. LC 74-6314. (Illus.). 560p. reprint ed. pap. 159.60 (0-7837-4947-3, 2044613) Bks Demand.
— Woodrow Wilson: The Early Years. LC 68-13451. 367p. 1968. pap. 104.60 (0-7837-8507-0, 2049315) Bks Demand.

Osborn, George K., et al, eds. Democracy, Strategy, & Vietnam: Assessing the Impact of the War on American Policymaking. 400p. 1987. text ed. 40.00 (0-669-16340-6); pap. 19.95 (0-669-16341-4) Free Pr.

Osborn, H. Cicadellidae of Hawaii. (BMB Ser.). 1972. reprint ed. pap. 15.00 (0-527-02240-3) Periodicals Srv.

Osborn, H., ed. Low-Dimensional Topology & Quantum Field Theory. (NATO ASI Series B, Physics: Vol. 315). (Illus.). 322p. (C). 1994. 105.00 (0-306-44578-6, Plenum Pr) Plenum.

Osborn, Hazel. Room for Loving, Room for Learning: Finding the Space You Need in Your Family Child Care Home. LC 94-2503. 1994. 11.50 (0-934140-98-7) Redleaf Pr.

Osborn, Henry. Men of the Old Stone Age, Their Environment, Life & Art. LC 78-72705. (Illus.). reprint ed. 47.00 (0-404-18276-3) AMS Pr.

Osborn, Henry F. Cope: Master Naturalist: Life & Letters of Edward Drinker Cope, with a Bibliography of His Writings. LC 77-81135. (Biologists & Their World Ser.). (Illus.). 1978. reprint ed. lib. bdg. 65.95 (0-405-10735-8) Ayer.
— From the Greeks to Darwin. LC 74-26283. (History, Philosophy & Sociology of Science Ser.). 1975. reprint ed. 34.95 (0-405-06610-4) Ayer.
— The Origin & Evolution of Life: On the Theory of Action, Reaction & Interaction of Energy. Gould, Stephen J., ed. LC 79-8340. (History of Paleontology Ser.). (Illus.). 1980. reprint ed. lib. bdg. 36.95 (0-405-12728-6) Ayer.

Osborn, Henry F., ed. Naturalist in the Bahamas: October 12, 1861 - June 25, 1891. LC 10-13587. 1910. 24.50 (0-404-04794-7) AMS Pr.

Osborn, Henry F., jt. auth. see Department of the Interior, U. S. Geological Survey, Monograph.

Osborn, Henry F., et al. Major Papers on Early Primates, Compiled from the Publications of the American Museum of Natural History: 1902 to 1940. LC 78-72712. 1980. 55.50 (0-404-18282-8) AMS Pr.

Osborn, Herbert. Bibliography of Ohio Zoology. (Bulletin Ser.: No. 23). 1930. 2.00 (0-86727-022-5) Ohio Bio Survey.
— The Fulgoridae of Ohio. 1938. 4.00 (0-86727-034-9) Ohio Bio Survey.
— The Leafhoppers of Ohio. (Bulletin Ser.: No. 14). 1928. 2.00 (0-86727-013-6) Ohio Bio Survey.
— The Membracidae of Ohio. (Bulletin Ser.: No. 37). 1940. 3.00 (0-86727-036-5) Ohio Bio Survey.

Osborn, Herbert, et al. Recent Insect Invasions in Ohio. 1948. 3.00 (0-86727-039-X) Ohio Bio Survey.

Osborn, Howard. Vector Bundles & Their Characteristic Classes: Vol. I, Vector Bundles & Stiefel-Whitney Classes. (Pure & Applied Mathematics Ser.). 1982. text ed. 106.00 (0-12-529301-1) Acad Pr.

Osborn, Irene, jt. auth. see Wild, Laura.

Osborn, J., jt. ed. see Benkart, G.

Osborn, J. A., ed. see Conference on Magnetism & Magnetic Materials.

Osborn, J. M., jt. ed. see Benkart, G.

Osborn, Jack L. Personal Information: Privacy at the Workplace. LC 78-18223. (AMA Management Briefing Ser.). 52p. reprint ed. pap. 25.00 (0-317-09614-1, 2050391) Bks Demand.

Osborn, Jack R. & Osborn, John C. Croquet, the Sport. (Illus.). 272p. 1989. 24.95 (0-9624568-0-2); pap. 15.95 (0-9624568-1-0) Farsight Comns.

Osborn, James. Area, Development Policy, & the Middle City in Malaysia. LC 73-92650. (Research Papers Ser.: No. 153). (Illus.). 291p. (C). 1974. pap. 12.00 (0-89065-060-8) U Chicago Comm Geo.
— Neo-Philobiblon: Ruminations on Manuscript Collecting. LC 72-619565. (Bibliographical Monograph: No. 7). (Illus.). 1973. 10.00 (0-87959-049-1) U of Tex H Ransom Ctr.

Osborn, James M. Young Philip Sidney, Fifteen Seventy-Two to Fifteen Seventy-Seven. LC 77-151584. (Elizabethan Club Ser.: No. 5). 591p. reprint ed. pap. 168.50 (0-317-29286-2, 2022026) Bks Demand.

Osborn, James M., jt. auth. see Neale, John.

Osborn, Janie D. & Osborn, D. Keith. Cognition in Early Childhood. LC 83-71727. (Illus.). 237p. (C). 1983. lib. bdg. 15.95 (0-918772-11-7); pap. text ed. 9.95 (0-918772-12-5) Daye Pr.

Osborn, Janie D., jt. auth. see Osborn, D. Keith.

Osborn, Jean, jt. ed. see Lehr, Fran.

Osborn, Jennifer L., ed. see Urquhart, Sharon C.

Osborn, Jennifer L., ed. see Yarnell, Mark B.

Osborn, John C., jt. auth. see Osborn, Jack R.

Osborn, John F., jt. auth. see Bulman, John S.

***Osborn, John J., Jr. & Robinette, Joseph.** The Paper Chase. 1981. 5.00 (0-87129-398-6, P54) Dramatic Pub.

Osborn, John M., ed. see McCoy, Betsy.

Osborn, June, ed. Influenza in America 1918-1976: History, Science, & Politics. LC 77-14344. 1977. lib. bdg. 12.00 (0-88202-176-1) Watson Pub Intl.

O

Osborn, June E., pref. AIDS Health Services at the Crossroads: Lessons for Community Care. LC 91-67786. 136p. (Orig.). 1991. pap. (*0-942054-04-0*) R W Johnson Found.

Osborn, Karen. Patchwork. 1991. 19.95 (*0-15-171292-1*) HarBrace.

— Patchwork. 1992. pap. 8.95 (*0-15-671365-9*, Harvest Bks) HarBrace.

Osborn, Kenton, jt. auth. see Jenkins, Wilmer.

Osborn, Kevin. A Day in the Life of a Seeing Eye Dog Trainer. LC 90-11076. (Day in the Life of...Ser.). (Illus.). 32p. (J). (gr. 4-8). 1991. lib. bdg. 11.79 (*0-8167-2218-8*); pap. text ed. 2.95 (*0-8167-2219-6*) Troll Assocs.

— Everything You Need to Know about Bias Incidents. (Need to Know Library). (YA). (gr. 7-12). 1993. lib. bdg. 15.95 (*0-8239-1530-1*) Rosen Group.

— The Peoples of the Arctic. (Peoples of North America Ser.). (Illus.). 112p. (YA). (gr. 5 up). 1990. 17.95 (*0-685-18912-0*) Chelsea Hse.

— Tolerance. rev. ed. (YA). (gr. 7-12). 1993. 13.95 (*0-8239-1508-5*) Rosen Group.

— The Ukrainian Americans. (Peoples of North America Ser.). (Illus.). 112p. (J). (gr. 5 up). 1989. lib. bdg. 17.95 (*1-55546-138-7*) Chelsea Hse.

Osborn, Leslie A. Living in a Changed World. 1994. 16.95 (*0-533-10724-5*) Vantage.

Osborn, Linda, jt. auth. see Odenbach, Ginny.

Osborn, Lisa G., jt. ed. see Johnson, Thomas D.

Osborn, Lucy M. & Whitman, Neal. Ward Attending: The Forty Day Month. 194p. 1991. text ed. 30.00 (*0-940193-09-4*) Univ UT Sch Med.

Osborn, M. & Weber, K., eds. Cytoskeletal Proteins in Tumor Diagnosis. (Current Communications in Molecular Biology Ser.). (Illus.). 244p. (C). 1989. pap. text ed. 24.00 (*0-87969-325-8*) Cold Spring Harbor.

Osborn, M. E., ed. On New Ground: Contemporary Hispanic-American Plays. LC 87-26734. 288p. (Orig.). 1987. pap. 13.95 (*0-930452-68-2*) Theatre Comm.

Osborn, M. Elizabeth & Richards, Gillian, eds. New Plays U. S. A. Two. 396p. 1984. 17.95 (*0-930452-35-6*); pap. 9.95 (*0-930452-36-4*) Theatre Comm.

Osborn, M. Elizabeth, ed. see Hoffman, William M., et al.

Osborn, M. Elizabeth, jt. ed. see Leverett, James.

Osborn, M. Livia, jt. auth. see Howells, John G.

Osborn, Marijane. Beowulf: A Verse Translation with Treasures of the Ancient North. LC 82-16135. (Illus.). 156p. reprint ed. pap. 44.50 (*0-7837-4677-6*, 2044424) Bks Demand.

Osborn, Marijane, jt. auth. see Overing, Gillian R.

Osborn, Marvin. Dynamic Devotions for Teens. Spear, Cindy G., ed. 108p. (Orig.). (YA). (gr. 7-12). 1993. spiral bd., pap. 9.95 (*0-941005-90-9*) Chrch Grwth VA.

Osborn, Marvin, jt. auth. see Copeland, James.

***Osborn, Marvin S. & Spear, Cindy G.** Super Saturday: An Evangelistic Event Full of Exciting Activities for Teens. 105p. 1995. audio, ring bd. 79.95 (*1-57052-016-X*) Chrch Grwth VA.

Osborn, Max. Die Teufelliteratur des 16 Jahrhunderts. vi, 236p. 1972. reprint ed. write for info. (*0-318-71850-2*, Pub. by Georg Olms GW) Lubrecht & Cramer.

Osborn, Michael & Osborn, Suzanne. Public Speaking. 2nd ed. (C). 1991. write for info. (*0-395-43257-X*) HM Soft Schl Col Div.

***Osborn, Nancy A.** Using Community Resources. Monroe, Martha C. & Cappaert, David, eds. (EEToolbox-Workshop Resource Manual Ser.). 44p. 1994. 8.00 (*1-884782-08-6*) Natl Consort EET.

Osborn, Nancy M., jt. auth. see Gradwohl, David M.

Osborn, Patricia. How Grammar Works: Self Teaching Guide. 207p. 1989. pap. text ed. 16.95 (*0-471-61297-9*) Wiley.

— Reading Smarter! More Than 200 Reproducible Activities to Build Reading Proficiency in Grades 7-12. LC 94-34552. 1995. spiral bd. 29.95 (*0-87628-850-6*) Ctr Appl Res.

Osborn, Peggy. G. B. Giraldi's "Altile" The Birth of a New Dramatic Genre in Renaissance Ferrara. LC 91-47936. (Studies in Renaissance Literature: Vol. 12). 260p. 1992. 89.95 (*0-7734-9445-6*) E Mellen.

Osborn, Peter. Engineer's Clean Air Handbook. 201p. 1990. text ed. 115.00 (*0-408-03393-2*) Buttrwrth-Heinemann.

Osborn, Peter D. Handbook of Energy Data & Calculations. 272p. (C). 1985. text ed. 95.00 (*0-408-01327-3*) Buttrwrth-Heinemann.

Osborn, R. Applied Quantum Mechanics. 196p. 1988. text ed. 48.00 (*9971-5-0294-1*); pap. text ed. 32.00 (*9971-5-0295-X*) World Scientific Pub.

Osborn, R. R., ed. Grounds of Hope: Essays in Faith & Freedom. 184p. 1968. 6.50 (*0-87921-055-9*) Attic Pr.

Osborn, Richard K. & Yip, S. Foundations of Neutron Transport Theory. (U. S. Atomic Energy Commission Monographs). 138p. 1966. text ed. 134.00 (*0-677-01170-9*) Gordon & Breach.

Osborn, Richard N., jt. auth. see Schermerhorn, John R.

Osborn, Richard N., et al. Organization Theory: An Integrated Approach. LC 83-27537. 632p. (C). 1984. reprint ed. lib. bdg. 44.00 (*0-89874-738-4*) Krieger.

Osborn, Richards C. Business Finance: The Management Approach. LC 65-15300. (Illus.). 1965. teacher ed write for info. (*0-89197-054-1*); text ed. 19.95 (*0-89197-053-3*) Irvington.

Osborn, Robert. Osborn Festival of Phobias. LC 78-162432. (Illus.). 1971. pap. 2.95 (*0-87140-250-5*) Liveright.

Osborn, Robert, ed. see Wordsworth, William.

Osborn, Robert T. The Barmen Declaration As a Paradigm for a Theology of the American Church. LC 91-44313. (Toronto Studies in Theology: Vol. 63). 168p. 1992. lib. bdg. 79.95 (*0-7734-9472-3*) E Mellen.

Osborn, Ronald E. Creative Disarray. 216p. (Orig.). 1992. pap. 18.99 (*0-8272-0462-0*) Chalice Pr.

— The Faith We Affirm. LC 79-21079. 1979. pap. 4.99 (*0-8272-1009-4*) Chalice Pr.

Osborn, Sannie K., ed. see Goldstein, Lynne G.

Osborn, Shars, jt. ed. see Kutler, Stanley.

Osborn, Sherard. Stray Leaves from an Arctic Journal: Or, Eighteen Months in the Polar Regions in Search of Sir John Franklin's Expedition in the Years 1850-1851. LC 74-5861. 1852. 12.50 (*0-404-11667-1*) AMS Pr.

Osborn, Sherard, ed. see McClure, Robert J.

Osborn, Susan. Free (& Almost Free) Things for Teachers. rev. ed. (Illus.). 128p. 1993. pap. 8.95 (*0-399-51795-2*, Perigree Bks) Berkley Pub.

***Osborn, Susan T., comp.** The Complete Guide to Christian Writing & Speaking. 320p. 1994. pap. 9.95 (*0-939497-35-2*) Promise Pub.

Osborn, Susan T. & Tangvald, Christine H. Children Around the World Celebrate Christmas! LC 93-6683. (Illus.). (J). (gr. 4 up). 1993. 10.99 (*0-87403-799-9*, 24-03664) Standard Pub.

Osborn, Susan T., jt. auth. see Weese, Wightman.

***Osborn, Susan Titus & Moses, Lucille.** Rest Stops for Single Mothers: Devotions to Encourage You on Your Journey. 1995. pap. 9.99 (*0-8054-5385-7*) Broadman.

Osborn, Suzanne, jt. auth. see Osborn, Michael.

Osborn, T. L. Healing the Sick. 420p. 1981. pap. 12.95 (*0-89274-187-2*, HH-187) Harrison Hse.

Osborn, Tap, ed. Large Print Crosswords Omnibus. large type ed. (Large Print Omnibus Ser.: No. 6). 240p. (Orig.). 1992. pap. 9.95 (*1-56138-138-1*) Running Pr.

— Large Print Crosswords Omnibus, No. 7. large type ed. 240p. (Orig.). 1993. spiral bd. 9.95 (*1-56138-205-1*) Running Pr.

— The Pen & Pencil Club Crosswords, No. 1. 96p. (Orig.). 1984. spiral bd. 5.95 (*0-89471-283-7*) Running Pr.

— The Pen & Pencil Club Crosswords, No. 2. 96p. (Orig.). 1985. spiral bd. 5.95 (*0-89471-325-6*) Running Pr.

— The Pen & Pencil Club Crosswords, No. 3. 96p. (Orig.). 1985. spiral bd. 5.95 (*0-89471-366-3*) Running Pr.

— Pen & Pencil Club Crosswords, No. 4. 96p. 1986. spiral bd. 5.95 (*0-89471-417-1*) Running Pr.

— The Pen & Pencil Club Crosswords, No. 5. 96p. (Orig.). 1986. spiral bd. 5.95 (*0-89471-458-9*) Running Pr.

— Pen & Pencil Club Crosswords, No. 6. 96p. 1987. spiral bd. 5.95 (*0-89471-505-4*) Running Pr.

— The Pen & Pencil Club Crosswords, No. 8. 96p. (Orig.). 1988. spiral bd. 5.95 (*0-89471-595-X*) Running Pr.

Osborn, Thomas C., jt. ed. see Beckmann, Jacques S.

Osborn, Thomas W. The Eleventh Corps Artillery at Gettysburg: The Papers of Major Thomas Ward Osborn. Crumb, Herb S., ed. LC 91-70764. (Illus.). vii, 90p. (Orig.). 1991. pap. 9.95 (*0-9622393-2-1*) Edmonston Pub.

— No Middle Ground: Thomas Ward Osborn's Letters from the Field (1862-1864) Crumb, Herb S. & Dhalle, Katherine, eds. LC 93-8590. (Illus.). 224p. 1993. 21.95 (*0-9622393-4-8*) Edmonston Pub.

Osborn, Tom & Gaye, Alphonse. Using Farmer Participatory Research to Improve Seed & Food Grain Production in Senegal. (Development Studies Paper). 25p. (Orig.). 1991. pap. 6.00 (*0-933595-57-3*) Winrock Intl.

Osborn, Tom, tr. see Wedekind, Frank.

Osborn, William. The Miami Jail: A Tree Party? 1994. 17.95 (*0-533-10946-9*) Vantage.

***Osborne.** Many Religions, One World. 16.99 (*0-679-93930-X*) Random.

— Promises to Keep. 1995. mass mkt. 4.50 (*0-06-108354-2*, Harp PBks) HarpC.

Osborne & Amann. Topical Drug Delivery Formulations. (Drugs & the Pharmaceutical Sciences Ser.: Vol. 42). 352p. 1990. 170.00 (*0-8247-8183-X*) Dekker.

Osborne, jt. auth. see Buriak.

Osborne, jt. auth. see Luinenberg.

Osborne, jt. auth. see Luinenburg.

Osborne, ed. see Thaxter.

Osborne, jt. auth. see Whiting.

Osborne, A. R., ed. Nonlinear Topics in Ocean Physics: Proceedings of the International School of Physics "Enrico Fermi," Course CIX, 26 July-Aug. 1988. (Enrico Fermi International Summer School of Physics Ser.: Vol. 109). 945p. 1991. 240.00 (*0-444-89017-3*, North Holland) Elsevier.

Osborne, Adam & Dvorak, John C. Hypergrowth: The Rise & Fall of the Osborne Computer Corporations. 224p. 1985. mass mkt. 5.95 (*0-380-69960-5*) Avon.

Osborne, Algernon A. Speculation on the New York Stock Exchange, September, 1904-March, 1907. (Columbia University. Studies in the Social Sciences: No. 137). reprint ed. 37.50 (*0-404-51137-6*) AMS Pr.

Osborne, Alice. Alice Osborne's Alaska. LC 84-50652. (Illus.). 92p. 1984. pap. 5.95 (*0-9610910-1-0*) Western Gull Pub.

Osborne, Allan G., et al. Effective Management of Special Education Programs: A Handbook for School Professionals. 160p. (C). 1993. text ed. 36.00 (*0-8077-3259-1*); pap. text ed. 16.95 (*0-8077-3258-3*) Tchrs Coll.

Osborne, Allen G., Jr. Complete Legal Guide to Special Education Services: A Handbook for Administrators, Counselors & Supervisors. 264p. 1988. text ed. 34.95 (*0-13-162025-8*) P-H.

***Osborne, Amy, ed.** Multables, Inc. (Illus.). 3p. (J). Date not set. 13.99 (*0-9645004-0-X*) Multables.

***Osborne, Andrew J.** J. Granville Doll & the Formative Years of Red Bluff. (ANCRR Occasional Publication Ser.: No. 11). 67p. 1985. 7.50 (*0-614-05681-0*) Assn NC Records.

Osborne, Angela. Abigail Adams. (American Women of Achievement Ser.). (Illus.). 112p. (YA). (gr. 5 up). 1989. 17.95 (*1-55546-635-4*); pap. 9.95 (*0-7910-0405-8*) Chelsea Hse.

— Miss America: The Dream Lives On. 240p. 1995. 39.95 (*0-87833-110-7*) Taylor Pub.

— Miss America: The Dream Lives On. limited ed. 1995. 75.00 (*0-87833-111-5*) Taylor Pub.

Osborne, Anne R. Reap the Whirlwind. 1990. 6.95 (*0-87844-087-9*) Sandlapper Pub Co.

— The South Carolina Story. (Illus.). 240p. 1988. 14.95 (*0-87844-083-6*) Sandlapper Pub Co.

Osborne, Arthur. For Those with Little Dust: Selected Writings of Arthur Osborne. (Insights on the Quest Ser.). 232p. 1990. pap. 12.95 (*1-878019-03-1*) Inner Drctns.

— The Incredible Sai Baba: The Life & Miracles of a Modern-Day Saint. 102p. 1985. pap. text ed. 4.95 (*0-86125-105-9*, Pub. by Orient Longman Ltd II) Apt Bks.

— Ramana Maharshi & the Path of Self-Knowledge. LC 76-18194. (Illus.). 219p. 1970. pap. 12.95 (*0-87728-071-1*) Weiser.

— The Teachings of Ramana Maharashi. 200p. 1962. pap. 9.95 (*0-87728-044-4*) Weiser.

Osborne, Avril, jt. ed. see Robertson, Alex.

Osborne, B. G., et al. Practical NIR Spectroscopy: With Applications in Food & Beverage Analysis. 2nd rev. ed. LC 92-36734. Orig. Title: Near Infrared Spectroscopy in Food Analysis. 1993. write for info. (*0-582-09946-3*) Longman.

Osborne, Brian, et al. Practical NIR Spectroscopy with Applications in Food & Beverage Analysis. 2nd ed. 227p. 1993. text ed. 155.00 (*0-470-22128-3*) Halsted Pr.

Osborne, Bruce A., jt. auth. see Geider, Richard J.

***Osborne, Carl A. & Finco, Delmar R., eds.** Canine & Feline Nephrology & Urology. LC 94-34694. 1995. write for info. (*0-683-06666-8*) Williams & Wilkins.

Osborne, Carol, et al. Museum Builders in the West: The Stanfords As Collectors & Patrons of Art, 1870-1906. LC 85-63383. (Illus.). 1986. pap. 9.95 (*0-685-70768-7*) Stanford Art.

Osborne, Carol L., jt. auth. see Morrissey, Muriel E.

Osborne, Carol M., jt. auth. see Steadman, David W.

Osborne, Carol M., et al. The Stanford Museum Centennial Handbook: One Hundred Works of Art. LC 90-72067. (Illus.). 128p. (Orig.). (C). 1991. 18.48 (*0-937031-00-3*); pap. 10.00 (*0-685-50060-8*) Stanford Art.

Osborne, Carolyn M., ed. see D'Harcourt, Raoul.

***Osborne, Catherine.** Eros Unveiled: Plato & the God of Love. 256p. 1995. text ed. 48.00 (*0-19-826761-4*) OUP.

— Rethinking Early Greek Philosophy: Hippolytus of Rome & the Presocratics. LC 87-47719. 400p. (C). 1987. 52.50 (*0-8014-2103-9*) Cornell U Pr.

Osborne, Cecil. Psicologia Del Matrimonio (Art of Understanding Your Mate) (SPA.). 1989. 4.99 (*0-945792-83-2*, 497704) Editorial Unilit.

Osborne, Cecil G. Amate Siquiera un Poco. Orozco, Julio, tr. LC 78-57808. 182p. (SPA.). 1978. pap. 5.75 (*0-89922-120-3*) Edit Caribe.

— The Art of Understanding Your Mate. 192p. 1988. pap. 8.99 (*0-310-30601-9*, 10481P, Pyranee) Zondervan.

***Osborne, Charles.** Bel Canto Operas: A Guide to the Operas of Rossini, Bellini, & Donizetti. 378p. 1994. pap. 19.95 (*0-931340-84-5*, Amadeus Pr) Timber.

— The Complete Operas of Mozart. LC 82-23639. (Quality Paperbacks Ser.). (Illus.). 349p. 1983. reprint ed. pap. 13.95 (*0-306-80190-6*) Da Capo.

— The Complete Operas of Puccini. LC 83-10142. (Quality Paperbacks Ser.). (Illus.). 282p. 1983. reprint ed. pap. 10.95 (*0-306-80200-7*) Da Capo.

— The Complete Operas of Richard Strauss. (Quality Paperbacks Ser.). (Illus.). 248p. 1991. reprint ed. pap. 13.95 (*0-306-80459-X*) Da Capo.

— The Complete Operas of Richard Wagner. LC 92-34417. (Illus.). 304p. 1992. pap. 13.95 (*0-306-80522-7*) Da Capo.

— The Complete Operas of Richard Wagner. (Illus.). 352p. 1991. 24.95 (*0-943955-33-5*, Trafalgar Sq Pub) Trafalgar.

— The Complete Operas of Verdi: An Interpretive Study of the Librettos & Music & Their Relation to the Composer's Life. LC 77-23409. (Quality Paperbacks Ser.). 1977. pap. 14.95 (*0-306-80072-1*) Da Capo.

— The Concert Song Companion. (Quality Paperbacks Ser.). 285p. 1985. reprint ed. pap. 8.95 (*0-306-80238-4*) Da Capo.

— Favourite Love Poems. (Illus.). 240p. 1988. 33.50 (*0-948397-08-X*, Pub. by M OMara Books UK) Trans-Atl Phila.

— Letter to W. H. Auden & Other Poems. (Orig.). 1985. pap. 8.95 (*0-7145-4036-6*) Riverrun NY.

— The Life & Crimes of Agatha Christie. large type ed. (Charnwood Library). (Orig.). 1991. 23.95 (*0-7089-8583-1*, Charnwood) Ulverscroft.

Osborne, Charles, comp. The Collins Book of Best-Loved Verse. large type ed. 288p. 1987. 16.95 (*0-7089-1696-1*) Ulverscroft.

Osborne, Charles, ed. Dictionary of Composers. LC 78-58291. (Illus.). 380p. 1981. pap. 17.95 (*0-8008-2195-5*) Taplinger.

Osborne, Charles, tr. see Leider, Frida.

Osborne, Charles, ed. see Wagner, Richard.

Osborne, Charles C. Jubal: The Life & Times of General Jubal A. Early, CSA Defender of the Lost Cause. LC 92-11982. xvi, 592p. 1994. pap. 16.95 (*0-8071-1913-X*) La State U Pr.

— Jubal Early: The Life & Times of General Jubal A. Early, CSA, Defender of the Lost Cause. LC 92-11982. 1992. 29.95 (*0-945575-35-1*) Algonquin Bks.

Osborne, Chris, ed. International Yearbook of Educational Training & Technology, 1992-1993: The Official Yearbook of the Association for Educational Training & Technology. rev. ed. 500p. (C). 1993. 99.00 (*0-89397-377-7*) Nichols Pub.

Osborne, Christine. Middle Eastern Cooking. 1994. 14.98 (*0-8317-1562-6*) Smithmark.

Osborne, Colin P., III. Day Dreaming-Night Thinking: Roaming in Two Worlds. LC 81-84497. (Illus.). 80p. 1982. 7.50 (*0-9607332-2-1*) Ololon Pubns.

***Osborne, Craig.** Civil Litigation: Legal Practice Course Guides. 424p. 1995. pap. 34.00 (*1-85431-367-3*, Pub. by Blackstone Pr UK) W W Gaunt.

Osborne, Craig & Tighe, Maria. Civil Litigation. 200p. 1993. 34.00 (*1-85431-292-8*, Pub. by Blackstone Pr UK) W W Gaunt.

— Criminal Litigation. 200p. 1993. 34.00 (*1-85431-294-4*, Pub. by Blackstone Pr UK) W W Gaunt.

Osborne, Cynthia M. Litigation Guide for Paralegals: Research & Drafting, Vol. 2. 2nd ed. LC 93-41880. 1994. text ed. 165.00 (*0-471-01644-6*) Wiley.

Osborne, D. G. Coal Preparation Technology, 2 vols., Set, Vols. 1 & 2. (C). 1988. Set. lib. bdg. 563.50 (*1-85333-092-2*, Pub. by Graham & Trotman UK) Kluwer Ac.

Osborne, D. R. Scatter Me: Poems - Nineteen Eighty to Nineteen Eighty-Nine. Duthie, P. E., ed. 95p. (Orig.). 1990. pap. 8.00 (*0-9626451-0-9*) Laughing Coyote.

Osborne, D. R. & Voogt, P. The Analysis of Nutrients in Foods. (Food Science & Technology Ser.). 1978. text ed. 121.00 (*0-12-529150-7*) Acad Pr.

Osborne, David. Economic Competitiveness: The States Take the Lead. LC 87-82983. 85p. (Orig.). 1987. per. 12.00 (*0-944826-00-8*) Economic Policy Inst.

— Laboratories of Democracy: A New Breed of Governor Creates Models for National Growth. 407p. 1988. pap. 16.95 (*0-87584-233-X*) Harvard Busn.

— Laboratories of Democracy: A New Breed of Governor Creates Models for National Growth. 1990. pap. text ed. 16.95 (*0-07-103260-6*) McGraw.

— State Technology Programs: A Preliminary Analysis of Lessons Learned. 75p. 1989. 10.00 (*0-934892-50-4*) CSPA.

Osborne, David & Gaebler, Ted. Reinventing Government. 1992. 23.99 (*0-201-52394-9*) Addison-Wesley.

— Reinventing Government: How the Entrepreneurial Spirit Is Transforming the Public Sector. 432p. 1993. pap. 13.95 (*0-452-26942-3*, Plume) NAL-Dutton.

***Osborne, David A.** Ergonomics at Work. 3rd ed. LC 94-28236. 1995. pap. text ed. 39.95 (*0-471-95235-4*) Wiley.

Osborne, David M. Robots, 2 Vols. Incl. Bk. 1. Robots, An Introduction to Basic Concepts & Applications. 1984. (*0-318-57976-6*); Bk. 2. Application of Robots to Practical Work. 1984. (*0-318-57977-4*); 1984. Set pap. 19.95 (*0-910853-03-7*) Midwest Sci-Tech.

— Robots, 2 Vols., Bk. 1. Incl. Bk. 1. Robots, An Introduction to Basic Concepts & Applications. 1984. (*0-318-57976-6*); Bk. 2. Application of Robots to Practical Work. 1984. (*0-318-57977-4*); 1984. 29.95 (*0-910853-00-2*) Midwest Sci-Tech.

— Robots, 2 Vols., Bk. 2. Incl. Bk. 1. Robots, An Introduction to Basic Concepts & Applications. 1984. (*0-318-57976-6*); Bk. 2. Application of Robots to Practical Work. 1984. (*0-318-57977-4*); 1984. 27.50 (*0-910853-02-9*) Midwest Sci-Tech.

***Osborne, Denise.** Cut to: Murder. LC 94-45808. (Mystery Ser.). 1995. 19.95 (*0-8050-3114-6*) H Holt & Co.

— Murder Offscreen. 1994. 19.95 (*0-8050-3113-8*) H Holt & Co.

Osborne, Dorothy. The Temple of Love. large type ed. (Linford Romance Library). 304p. 1987. pap. 8.95 (*0-7089-6379-X*, Linford) Ulverscroft.

***Osborne, Duncan E., ed.** Asset Protection: Domestic & International Law & Tactics. LC 95-8267. 1995. write for info. (*0-615-00663-9*) Clark Boardman Callaghan.

Osborne, Dwight. The Squiggly Wiggly Head Family. (Illus.). 16p. (J). 1992. pap. 5.95 (*0-9632817-0-4*) Osborne Bks.

Osborne, E., jt. auth. see Van Alstyne, Dorothy.

Osborne, E. F. Global Timing Systems of Nanosecond Accuracy Using Satellite References. LC 70-131393. 189p. 1969. 19.00 (*0-403-04526-6*) Scholarly.

Osborne, Eddie, ed. International Guide to Afrocentric Events & Merchandise, 1994. rev. ed. (Illus.). 200p. 1993. pap. 24.95 (*1-882272-01-3*) Osborne Comms.

— International Guide to Afrocentric Talent, 1992-93. (Illus.). 100p. (Orig.). 1992. pap. 10.95 (*1-882272-00-5*) Osborne Comms.

Osborne, Eddie, jt. auth. see Alphonse, Jocelyn.

Osborne, Eddie, jt. auth. see Gitonga, Jackson.

Osborne, Eddie, jt. auth. see Osborne, Sheila.

Osborne, Eddie, jt. auth. see Ouattara, Mouhamadou.

Osborne, Eddie, jt. auth. see Workinesh, Gulilat.

Osborne, Edward, jt. auth. see Phipps, Lloyd J.

Osborne, Edward H., jt. ed. see Houseknecht, David W.

***Osborne, Edward W.** Biological l Science Applications in Agriculture. (AgriScience & Technology Ser.). 467p. 1994. text ed. 43.95 (*0-8134-2957-9*); 9.95 (*0-8134-2958-7*) Interstate.

Osborne, Elsie, jt. ed. see Dowling, Emilia.

Osborne, Ernest L. & West, Victor. Men of Action: A History of the U. S. Life Saving Service on the Pacific Coast. LC 80-69563. (Illus.). 150p. (Orig.). 1981. pap. 10.00 (*0-932368-05-0*) Bandon Hist.

Osborne, Francis J. History of the Catholic Church in Jamaica. 1988. 15.95 (*0-8294-0544-5*) Loyola Univ Pr.

***Osborne, Frank.** Science & Technology. 80p. (C). 1994. pap. text ed., spiral bd. 17.00 (*0-8403-9569-8*) Kendall-Hunt.

Osborne, Frank H. Principles of Biology: Lecture Notes & Workbook. 172p. 1993. spiral bd. 21.95 (*0-8403-8376-2*) Kendall-Hunt.

— Principles of Microbiology. 136p. (C). 1993. spiral bd. 22.95 (*0-8403-8606-0*) Kendall-Hunt.

An Asterisk (*) at the beginning of an entry indicates that the title is appearing in BIP for the first time.

Osborne, George E. Cases & Materials on Secured Transactions. 559p. 1988. reprint ed. text ed. 37.00 (*0-314-28264-5*) West Pub.

Osborne, Gordon, ed. see Blewett, Mary H. & McKenna, Christine.

Osborne, Grant R. Hermeneutical Spiral: A Comprehensive Introduction to Biblical Interpretation. LC 91-31967. (Illus.). 392p. 1992. text ed. 27.99 (*0-8308-1272-5*, 1272) InterVarsity.

Osborne, Grant R. & Booher, Diana. They're Playing Our Secret. LC 87-28910. (Three Crucial Questions Ser.). 208p. (YA). 1995. pap. 13.99 (*0-8010-5273-4*) Baker Bk.

Osborne, Grant R., ed. see Belleville, Linda L.

Osborne, Grant R., ed. see Bock, Darrell L.

Osborne, Grant R., ed. see Marshall, I. Howard.

Osborne, Grant R., ed. see Stedman, Ray C.

Osborne, Grant R., ed. see Stulac, George M.

Osborne, Grant R., ed. see Towner, Philip H.

Osborne, Grant R., ed. see Wall, Robert W.

Osborne, Grant R., et al, eds. The IVP New Testament Commentary Series, 9 vols. 1992. 137.99 (*0-8308-1800-6*, 1800) InterVarsity.

Osborne, Harold. Aesthetics & Criticism. LC 73-3756. 341p. 1973. reprint ed. text ed. 65.00 (*0-8371-6847-3*, OSAC, Greenwood Pr) Greenwood.

— Bolivia: Land Divided. 1976. lib. bdg. 69.95 (*0-8490-1521-9*) Gordon Pr.

— Bolivia, a Land Divided. LC 85-24763. 193p. 1986. reprint ed. text ed. 49.75 (*0-313-24982-2*, OSBO, Greenwood Pr) Greenwood.

— Indians of the Andes: Incas, Aymaras, & Quechuas. 1977. lib. bdg. 59.95 (*0-8490-2054-9*) Gordon Pr.

Osborne, Harold, ed. Oxford Companion to Art. (Illus.). 1278p. 1970. 49.95 (*0-19-866107-X*) OUP.

— The Oxford Companion to Twentieth-Century Art. (Oxford Paperback Reference Ser.). (Illus.). 800p. 1988. pap. 22.50 (*0-19-282076-1*) OUP.

Osborne, Harold F. Little City by the Sea. (Illus.). 136p. (Orig.). 1990. pap. 10.95 (*0-9627567-0-9*) Apple Tree Pr.

Osborne, Hilary, ed. see Calvin, John.

***Osborne, Hilton.** Country Western Line Dancing: Run to the Floor For. (Illus.). 192p. (Orig.). 1994. pap. 19.95 (*1-882180-37-2*) Griffin CA.

Osborne, J. Grayson, jt. auth. see Martin, Garry L.

Osborne, J. L. & Wolfendale, Arnold W., eds. Origin of Cosmic Rays. LC 75-2436. (NATO Advanced Study Institutes Ser.: No. C14). x, 466p. 1975. lib. bdg. 117.00 (*90-277-0585-2*) Kluwer Ac.

Osborne, J. L., jt. auth. see Ginns, Patsy M.

Osborne, J. S. & Osborne, J. T. Social Credit for Beginners: An Armchair Guide. (Illus.). (Orig.). 1986. pap. 10.95 (*0-88978-175-3*) Left Bank.

Osborne, J. T., jt. auth. see Osborne, J. S.

Osborne, Jan, jt. ed. see Burns, Larry.

Osborne, Jane & Sugden, Chris. Luke. (Bible Study Commentaries Ser.). 1987. pap. 4.95 (*0-87508-168-1*) Chr Lit.

Osborne, Jean. Miracles with Love. 61p. (Orig.). 1982. write for info. (*0-915631-02-4*) Osborne Dr.

— Notes on Notes. 101p. (C). 1974. write for info. (*0-915631-01-6*) Osborne Dr.

Osborne, Jean, ed. Its Easier with Your Shoes Off. 50p. 1966. write for info. (*0-915631-00-8*) Osborne Dr.

Osborne, Jerry. Complete Library of American Phonograph Recordings, 1959. 256p. 1987. 24.95 (*0-932117-06-6*) Jellyroll Prodns.

— Complete Library of American Phonograph Recordings, 1960. 240p. 1987. 24.95 (*0-932117-05-8*) Jellyroll Prodns.

— Complete Library of American Phonograph Recordings, 1961. 249p. 1990. 24.95 (*0-932117-16-3*) Jellyroll Prodns.

— Country Music Buyers-Sellers Reference Book & Price Guide. (Illus.). 340p. 1984. pap. 14.95 (*0-932117-00-7*) Jellyroll Prodns.

— Elvis, Like Any Other Soldier. (Illus.). 160p. 1989. pap. 19.95 (*0-932117-11-2*) Jellyroll Prodns.

— The Official Price Guide to Compact Discs. 512p. 1994. pap. 15.00 (*0-87637-923-4*, House of Collect) Ballantine.

— The Official Price Guide to Elvis Presley Records & Memorabilia. (Illus.). 384p. 1994. pap. 14.00 (*0-87637-939-0*, House of Collect) Ballantine.

Osborne, Jerry, et al. The Official Price Guide to Memorabilia of Elvis Presley & the Beatles. 1988. pap. 12.00 (*0-87637-080-6*, House of Collect) Ballantine.

Osborne, Jerry. The Official Price Guide to Records. 10th ed. 800p. 1993. pap. 20.00 (*0-87637-905-6*, House of Collect) Ballantine.

— The Official Price Guide to Records. 11th ed. (Illus.). 992p. 1995. pap. 20.00 (*0-87637-963-3*, House of Collect) Ballantine.

***Osborne, Jerry, ed.** Jerry Osborne's Rockin' Records Buyers - Sellers Reference Book & Price Guide - 1995-1996. 17th ed. 632p. 1995. pap. 39.95 (*0-930625-33-1*) Antique Trader.

Osborne, Jill. Baby Animals Dot-To-Dot Activity Book. (J). 1989. pap. 1.25 (*0-89375-904-X*) Troll Assocs.

— Dinosaur Dot-To-Dot Activity Book. 32p. (J). 1989. pap. 1.25 (*0-89375-837-X*) Troll Assocs.

— Wild Animals Dot-To-Dot Activity Book. (J). 1989. pap. 1.25 (*0-89375-836-1*) Troll Assocs.

Osborne, Jill E. Make & Color Halloween Decoration. (J). (ps-3). 1989. pap. 1.95 (*0-89375-644-X*) Troll Assocs.

Osborne, Joan W. Gourmet Camping: A Menu Cookbook & Travel Guide for Campers, Canoeists, Cyclists, & Skiers. (Illus.). 224p. (Orig.). 1992. ring bd. 9.95 (*0-937552-45-3*) Quail Ridge.

Osborne, John. Almost a Gentleman, Vol. II: An Autobiography, 1955-1956. (Illus.). 304p. 1994. pap. 10.95 (*0-571-16635-0*) Faber & Faber.

— A Better Class of Person, Vol. I: John Osborne, an Autobiography, 1929-1956. 128p. 1994. pap. 10.95 (*0-571-16399-8*) Faber & Faber.

— Damn You England: Collected Prose. (Illus.). 268p. 1995. 22.95 (*0-571-16921-X*) Faber & Faber.

— Dejavu. (Orig.). 1994. 5.45 (*0-87129-237-8*, D56) Dramatic Pub.

— Dejavu. 160p. (Orig.). 1991. pap. 8.95 (*0-571-14345-8*) Faber & Faber.

— The Entertainer. LC 58-6810. 199p. 1994. 19.95 (*0-87599-082-7*) S G Phillips.

— Look Back in Anger. 1987. 5.45 (*0-87129-222-X*, L29) Dramatic Pub.

— Look Back in Anger. LC 57-9161. 199p. 1994. 19.95 (*0-87599-081-9*) S G Phillips.

— Look Back in Anger. 1982. pap. 7.95 (*0-14-048175-3*, Penguin Bks) Viking Penguin.

— Look Back in Anger & Other Plays: Collected Plays Vol. 1: Epitaph for George Dillon, the World of Paul Slickley & Dejavu. (Collected Plays Ser.). 384p. (Orig.). 1995. pap. 16.95 (*0-571-16908-2*) Faber & Faber.

— Luther. 1961. pap. 5.45 (*0-87129-208-4*, L37) Dramatic Pub.

— Luther. 1994. pap. 8.95 (*0-452-27355-2*, Plume) NAL-Dutton.

— The Meiningen Court Theatre, 1866-1890. (Illus.). 232p. 1988. 64.95 (*0-521-30394-X*) Cambridge U Pr.

— A Patriot for Me & a Sense of Detachment. 192p. (C). 1983. pap. 8.95 (*0-571-13041-0*) Faber & Faber.

Osborne, John, adapt. Strindberg's The Father & Ibsen's Hedda Gabler. 192p. 1989. pap. 10.95 (*0-571-14066-1*) Faber & Faber.

Osborne, John, tr. see Benjamin, Walter.

Osborne, John, et al. Global Studies: A Competency Review Text. 3rd ed. Gamsey, Wayne & Stich, Paul, eds. (Illus.). 384p. (YA). (gr. 7-12). 1992. pap. text ed. 8.33 (*0-935487-37-9*) N & N Pub Co.

— Global Studies: A Regents Review Text. 6th ed. Gamsey, Wayne & Stich, Paul, eds. (Illus.). 448p. (YA). (gr. 7-12). 1992. pap. text ed. 6.22 (*0-935487-35-2*) N & N Pub Co.

— Global Studies: Ten Day Competency Review. 2nd ed. Gamsey, Wayne & Stich, Paul, eds. (Illus.). 128p. (YA). (gr. 7-12). 1992. pap. text ed. 4.95 (*0-935487-53-0*) N & N Pub Co.

— Global Studies: Ten Day Regents Review. 2nd ed. Gamsey, Wayne & Stich, Paul, eds. (Illus.). 128p. (YA). (gr. 7-12). 1992. pap. text ed. 4.95 (*0-935487-48-4*) N & N Pub Co.

Osborne, John J., Jr. Paper Chase. 19.95 (*0-8488-0185-7*) Amereon Ltd.

Osborne, John T. Miracles. (Illus.). 90p. (J). 1988. pap. text ed. 5.75 (*0-929918-00-2*) Midstates Pub.

Osborne, John W. William Cobbett: His Thoughts & His Times. LC 81-13231. (Illus.). x, 272p. 1982. reprint ed. text ed. 52.50 (*0-313-23222-9*, OSWC, Greenwood Pr) Greenwood.

Osborne, John W. & Schweizer, Karl W. Cobbett & His Times. 192p. (C). 1990. text ed. 61.00 (*0-389-20932-5*) B&N Imports.

Osborne, Joseph & Parham, Bettie E. Washing the Elephant: An Authorized Biography of Bettie Esther Parham. (Illus.). 192p. 1994. text ed. 19.95 (*0-8059-3479-0*) Dorrance.

Osborne, Judy. My Teacher Said Goodbye Today: Planning for the End of the School Year. 2nd ed. (Illus.). 39p. (J). (ps-6). 1987. reprint ed. pap. text ed. 9.95 (*0-9618303-8-7*) Emijo Pubns.

— Stepfamilies: The Restructuring Process. 24p. (Orig.). 1983. pap. 5.00 (*0-9618303-3-6*) Emijo Pubns.

Osborne, Karen L. Carlyle Simpson. 255p. 1986. pap. 10.00 (*0-89733-204-0*) Academy Chi Pubs.

— Hawkwings. LC 91-11962. 224p. (Orig.). 1991. pap. 9.95 (*1-879427-00-1*) Third Side Pr.

Osborne, Karen L., ed. The Country of Herself: Short Fiction by Chicago Women. LC 93-28677. 240p. (Orig.). 1993. pap. 9.95 (*1-879427-14-1*) Third Side Pr.

Osborne, Kay. Do Cook for One. LC 84-90503. (Illus.). 216p. 1985. pap. 10.95 (*0-9613877-0-X*) K-D Enter.

Osborne, Kenan B. The Christian Sacraments of Initiation, Baptism, Confirmation, Eucharist. 256p. 1987. pap. 11.95 (*0-8091-2886-1*) Paulist Pr.

— Ministry: Lay Ministry in the Roman Catholic Church, Its History & Theology. LC 92-40299. 720p. 1993. pap. 29.95 (*0-8091-3371-7*) Paulist Pr.

— Reconciliation & Justification: The Sacrament & Its Theology. LC 89-48584. 320p. 1990. pap. 14.95 (*0-8091-3143-9*) Paulist Pr.

— Sacramental Guidelines: A Companion to the New Catechism for Religious Educators. LC 95-3249. 160p. (Orig.). 1995. pap. 12.95 (*0-8091-3565-5*) Paulist Pr.

— Sacramental Theology: A General Introduction. 160p. 1988. pap. 9.95 (*0-8091-2945-0*) Paulist Pr.

Osborne, Larry, jt. ed. see Goldman, Bert A.

Osborne, Larry N. & Nakamura, Margaret. Systems Analysis for Librarians & Information Professionals. 200p. 1994. lib. bdg. 42.00 (*1-56308-275-6*) Libs Unl.

Osborne, Laura, comp. The Rasta Cookbook: Vegetarian Cuisine - Eaten with the Salt of the Earth. LC 92-17760. (Illus.). 132p. (C). 1992. reprint ed. pap. 12.95 (*0-86543-133-7*) Africa World.

Osborne, Laurie E., ed. see Shakespeare, William.

Osborne, Lawrence. Paris Dreambook: An Unconventional Guide to the Splendor & Squalor of the City. 1992. pap. 11.00 (*0-679-73775-8*, Vin) Random.

— Poisoned Embrace: A Brief History of Sexual Pessimism. 1994. pap. 12.00 (*0-679-75414-8*, Vin) Random.

Osborne-LeBien, Lori, ed. see Smale, David.

***Osborne, Liz.** Resolving Patient Complaints: A Step-by-Step Guide to Effective Service Recovery. 256p. 1995. ring bd. 99.00 (*0-8342-0674-9*) Aspen Pub.

Osborne, M. R. Finite Algorithms in Optimization & Data Analysis. LC 84-11841. (Probability & Mathematical Statistics Ser.). 383p. 1985. text ed. 250.00 (*0-471-90539-9*, Wiley-Interscience) Wiley.

Osborne, M. Scott & Warner, G. The Selberg Trace Formula III: Inner Product Formulae (Initial Considerations) LC 83-3918. (Memoirs of the American Mathematical Society Ser.: No. 44/283). 209p. 1983. pap. 26.00 (*0-8218-2283-7*, MEMO 44/283) Am Math.

Osborne, Mabel. Meatless Dishes for Hay Dieters. 1974. lib. bdg. 69.95 (*0-685-51380-7*) Revisionist Pr.

***Osborne, Maggie.** The Brides of Chastity, Missouri. (Orig.). 1996. mass mkt. write for info. (*0-446-60324-4*) Warner Bks.

— The Seduction of Samantha Kincade. 384p. (Orig.). 1995. mass mkt. 5.99 (*0-446-60093-8*) Warner Bks.

— The Wives of Bowie Stone. 384p. (Orig.). 1994. mass mkt. 5.99 (*0-446-36533-5*) Warner Bks.

Osborne, Mark, jt. auth. see Johnston, Tom.

Osborne, Martha L. Genuine Risk: A Dialogue on Woman. LC 81-1987. (HPC Dialogues Ser.). 72p. (C). 1981. 21.50 (*0-915145-11-1*); pap. text ed. 3.95 (*0-915145-10-3*) Hackett Pub.

Osborne, Martha S. Wilcox - Wilcoxson Families of New England & Their Descendants: A Genealogical Dictionary, 3 vols., Set. rev. ed. xii, 1104p. 1993. pap. text ed. 61.00 (*1-55613-802-4*) Heritage Bk.

Osborne, Martin J. & Rubinstein, Ariel. Bargaining & Markets. (Economic Theory, Econometrics & Mathematical Economics Ser.). 216p. 1990. text ed. 53.00 (*0-12-528631-7*, AP Prof); pap. text ed. 21.00 (*0-12-528632-5*, AP Prof) Acad Pr.

— A Course in Game Theory. (Illus.). 420p. 1994. 40.00x (*0-262-15041-7*); pap. 18.95x (*0-262-65040-1*) MIT Pr.

Osborne, Martin R. & Crosby, Neil T. Benzopyrene. (Monographs on Cancer Research Ser.). 352p. 1987. 105.00 (*0-521-30122-X*) Cambridge U Pr.

***Osborne, Mary P.** Afternoon on the Amazon. LC 95-3237. (Magic Tree House Ser.: No. 6). (Illus.). 1995. 3.99 (*0-679-86372-9*); pap. 9.99 (*0-679-96372-3*) Random.

— American Tall Tales. LC 89-37235. (Illus.). 128p. (J). (gr. 1 up). 1991. 18.00 (*0-679-80089-1*); lib. bdg. 18.99 (*0-679-90089-6*) Knopf Bks Yng Read.

— Best Wishes, Joe Brady. (YA). 1994. pap. 4.99 (*0-679-84650-6*, Bullseye Bks) Random Bks Yng Read.

— Best Wishes, Joe Brady. 192p. (YA). (gr. 7 up). 1994. pap. 4.99 (*0-679-84560-7*, Bullseye Bks) Random Bks Yng Read.

— Christopher Columbus: Admiral of the Sea. (Yearling Biography Ser.: No. 2). (Orig.). (J). (gr. k-6). 1987. pap. 3.50 (*0-440-41275-7*, YB) Dell.

— Dinosaurs Before Dark. LC 91-51106. (First Stepping Stone Bks.). (Illus.). 80p. (Orig.). (J). (gr. 1-4). 1992. pap. 2.99 (*0-679-82411-6*) Random Bks Yng Read.

— Dinosaurs Before Dark. LC 91-51106. (First Stepping Stone Bks.). (Illus.). 80p. (Orig.). (J). (gr. 1-4). 1992. lib. bdg. 9.99 (*0-679-92411-0*) Random Bks Yng Read.

— Favorite Greek Myths. (Illus.). (J). (gr. 2-6). 1989. pap. 15.95 (*0-590-41338-4*) Scholastic Inc.

— George Washington: Leader of a New Nation. LC 90-42601. (Illus.). 96p. (J). (gr. 4-7). 1991. lib. bdg. 13.89 (*0-8037-0949-8*) Dial Bks Young.

— Haunted Waters. LC 93-47566. 160p. (J). (gr. 8-10). 1994. 14.95 (*1-56402-119-X*) Candlewick Pr.

— The Knight at Dawn. LC 92-13075. (Magic Tree House Ser.). (Illus.). 80p. (Orig.). (J). (gr. 1-4). 1993. lib. bdg. 9.99 (*0-679-92412-4*); pap. 2.99 (*0-679-82412-X*) Random Bks Yng Read.

— The Many Lives of Benjamin Franklin. (Illus.). (J). (gr. 5 up). 1990. 13.95 (*0-685-31008-6*) Dial Bks Young.

— Mo & His Friends. (J). (ps-3). 1991. pap. 3.95 (*0-8037-0924-2*, Dial Easy to Read) Puffin Bks.

— Molly & the Prince. LC 92-25305. (Illus.). 40p. (J). (ps-2). 1994. 15.00 (*0-679-81941-X*, Apple Soup Bks); lib. bdg. 15.99 (*0-679-91941-4*, Apple Soup Bks) Knopf.

— Moonhorse. LC 87-3818. (Illus.). 40p. (J). (ps-3). 1991. 14.95 (*0-394-88960-6*); lib. bdg. 15.99 (*0-394-98960-0*) Knopf Bks Yng Read.

— Moonhorse. (Dragonfly Bks.). (Illus.). 40p. (J). (ps-2). 1994. pap. 5.99 (*0-679-86709-0*) Knopf Bks Yng Read.

— Mummies in the Morning. (First Stepping Stone Bks.: Vol. 3). 80p. (J). (gr. 1-4). 1993. pap. 3.50 (*0-679-82424-3*) Random Bks Yng Read.

— Mummies in the Morning. (First Stepping Stone Bks.: Vol. 3). 80p. (J). (gr. 1-4). 1993. lib. bdg. 9.99 (*0-679-92424-8*) Random Bks Yng Read.

— Night of the Ninjas. LC 94-29142. (Magic Tree House Ser.: Vol. 5). (Illus.). (J). 1995. pap. 3.50 (*0-679-86371-0*) Random.

— Night of the Ninjas. LC 94-29142. (Magic Tree House Ser.: Vol. 5). (Illus.). (J). 1995. lib. bdg. 9.99 (*0-679-96371-5*) Random.

— Pirates Past Noon. LC 93-2039. (Magic Tree House Ser.: No. 4). (Illus.). 80p. (J). (gr. 1-4). 1994. pap. 2.99 (*0-679-82425-1*) Random.

— Pirates Past Noon. LC 93-2039. (Magic Tree House Ser.: No. 4). (Illus.). 80p. (J). (gr. 1-4). 1994. lib. bdg. 9.99 (*0-679-92425-6*) Random.

— Run, Run, As Fast As You Can. 1995. 17.50 (*0-8446-6829-X*) Peter Smith.

— Run, Run, As Fast As You Can. LC 81-68781. 156p. (J). (gr. 3-7). 1993. pap. 3.99 (*0-679-84649-2*, Bullseye Bks) Random Bks Yng Read.

— Spider Kane & the Mystery at Jumbo Nightcrawler's. LC 91-10983. (Illus.). 128p. (J). (gr. 1-5). 1993. 14.00 (*0-679-80856-6*) Knopf Bks Yng Read.

— Spider Kane & the Mystery at Jumbo Nightcrawler's. LC 91-10983. (Illus.). 128p. (J). (gr. 1-5). 1994. pap. 3.50 (*0-679-85393-6*) Random Bks Yng Read.

— Spider Kane & the Mystery under the May-Apple. LC 90-33524. (Illus.). 128p. (J). (gr. 1-7). 1992. 13.00 (*0-679-80855-8*) Knopf Bks Yng Read.

— Spider Kane & the Mystery under the May-Apple. LC 90-33524. (Illus.). 128p. (J). (gr. 1-7). 1993. pap. 3.50 (*0-679-84174-1*, Bullseye Bks) Knopf Bks Yng Read.

Osborne, Mary P., jt. auth. see Osborne, Will.

Osborne, Mary T., ed. The Great Torch Race: Essays in Honor of Reginald Harvey Griffith. LC 61-10425. (Illus.). 1961. 10.00 (*0-87959-063-7*) U of Tex H Ransom Ctr.

Osborne, Michael. Granite, Water & Light: Waterfalls of Yosemite Valley. Berrey, Henry, ed. (Illus.). 48p. (Orig.). 1983. pap. 5.95 (*0-939666-39-1*) Yosemite Assn.

Osborne, Michael A. Nature, the Exotic, & the Science of French Colonialism. LC 93-21489. (Science, Technology, & Society Ser.). 1994. 35.00 (*0-253-34266-X*) Ind U Pr.

Osborne, Michael J., et al, eds. A Lexicon of Greek Personal Names Vol. II: Attica. 516p. 1994. 95.00 (*0-19-814990-5*) OUP.

Osborne, Milton. Sihanouk: Prince of Light, Prince of Darkness. LC 93-48520. (C). 1994. 27.95 (*0-8248-1638-2*); pap. 17.95 (*0-8248-1639-0*) UH Pr.

— Southeast Asia: An Illustrated Introductory History. 4th ed. (Illus.). 264p. 1989. pap. text ed. 15.95 (*0-04-352238-6*) Routledge Chapman & Hall.

— Southeast Asia: An Illustrated Introductory History. 5th ed. (Illus.). 228p. 1994. pap. 19.95 (*0-04-442215-6*, Pub. by Allen Unwin AT) Broad St Bks.

— Southeast Asia: An Illustrated Introductory History. 6th ed. (Illus.). 272p. 1995. pap. 22.95 (*1-86373-823-1*) Paul & Co Pubs.

Osborne, Milton E. Singapore & Malaysia. LC 64-55818. (Cornell University, Southeast Asia Program, Data Paper Ser.: No. 53). 136p. reprint ed. pap. 38.80 (*0-8357-3535-4*, 2034586) Bks Demand.

— Strategic Hamlets in South Vietnam: A Survey & Comparison. LC 65-64732. (Cornell University, Southeast Asia Program, Data Paper Ser.: No. 55). 88p. reprint ed. pap. 25.10 (*0-8357-3668-7*, 2036394) Bks Demand.

Osborne, Mitchel L. Official World's Fair Pictorial Photography. 48p. 1984. 3.95 (*0-317-12231-2*) Picayune Pr.

Osborne, N., ed. Dale's Principle & Communication Between Neurons: Proceedings of a Colloquium of the Biochemical Society, University of Oxford, England, July 1982. 190p. 1983. 94.00 (*0-08-029789-7*, Pub. by Pergamon Repr UK) Franklin.

Osborne, Nalda. Separate Bedrooms. abr. ed. 140p. 1994. pap. 7.95 (*1-56901-429-9*) NW Pub.

Osborne, Neville N. Microchemical Analysis of Nervous Tissue. 1974. 104.00 (*0-08-018100-7*, Pub. by Pergamon Repr UK) Franklin.

Osborne, Neville N., ed. Biochemistry of Characterized Neurons. LC 76-55379. 1978. 139.00 (*0-08-021503-3*, Pub. by Pergamon Repr UK) Franklin.

— Biology of Serotonergic Transmission. LC 81-14671. (Illus.). 536p. reprint ed. pap. 152.80 (*0-8357-7242-X*, 2029646) Bks Demand.

— Progress in Retinal Research, Vol. 2. (Illus.). 330p. 1983. 91.00 (*0-08-030773-6*, 07, Pergamon Pr) Elsevier.

Osborne, Neville N. & Chader, G. J., eds. Progress in Retinal Research, Vol. 1. (Illus.). 245p. 1982. 105.00 (*0-08-028901-0*, Pergamon Pr) Elsevier.

— Progress in Retinal Research, Vol. 3. (Illus.). 366p. 1984. 81.00 (*0-08-031701-4*, Pergamon Pr) Elsevier.

— Progress in Retinal Research, Vol. 4. (Illus.). 330p. 1985. 120.00 (*0-08-031738-3*, Pergamon Pr) Elsevier.

Osborne, Neville N. & Hamon, M., eds. Neuronal Serotonin. LC 87-27933. 555p. 1988. text ed. 279.95 (*0-471-91154-2*) Wiley.

Osborne, Neville N., jt. ed. see Weiler, R.

***Osborne, Newton G.** Operation Medusa. 256p. 1995. text ed. 16.00 (*0-8059-3662-9*) Dorrance.

Osborne, Nigel, ed. see Clarke, Eric & Emmerson, Simon.

Osborne, Noel H. The Lytton Manuscripts. 79p. 1967. 45.00 (*0-900801-10-7*) St Mut.

Osborne, Ozzie, jt. auth. see Beagle, Ben.

Osborne, Peggy A. About Buttons: A Collector's Guide, A.D. 150 to the Present. (Illus.). 320p. 1993. 79.95 (*0-88740-555-X*) Schiffer.

— Button Button: Identification & Price Guide. LC 92-63104. (Illus.). 160p. (Orig.). 1993. pap. 16.95 (*0-88740-464-2*) Schiffer.

— Fun Buttons. LC 94-65981. (Illus.). 144p. 1994. 29.95 (*0-88740-691-2*) Schiffer.

***Osborne, Peter.** The Politics of Time. 224p. 1995. pap. text ed. 19.95 (*0-86091-652-9*, Viking) Viking Penguin.

Osborne, Peter, ed. Socialism & the Limits of Liberalism. 288p. 1991. 59.95 (*0-86091-326-0*, A5354, Pub. by Verso UK); pap. 18.95 (*0-86091-543-3*, A5358, Pub. by Verso UK) Routledge Chapman & Hall.

Osborne, Peter, jt. auth. see Benjamin, Andrew.

Osborne, Peter, jt. ed. see Benjamin, Andrew.

Osborne, Peter, jt. ed. see Sayers, Sean.

Osborne, Philip. Parenting for the '90s. LC 89-2009. 320p. 1989. pap. 9.95 (*0-934672-73-3*) Good Bks PA.

Osborne, Philip & Koppenhaver, Karen W., eds. Great Short Stories about Parenting. LC 90-71116. 288p. (Orig.). 1990. pap. 9.95 (*1-56148-008-8*) Good Bks PA.

Osborne, R., jt. ed. see Edgley, R.

Osborne, R. Travis. Twins: Black & White. LC 79-92757. (Illus.). 286p. (C). 1980. 20.00 (*0-936396-00-8*) Foun Human GA.

Osborne, Randall, jt. auth. see Weaver, Jeff.

***Osborne, Randall E.** Ring of Destiny, Ring of Fate. 270p. 1995. pap. 8.95 (*1-56901-632-1*) NW Pub.

Osborne, Richard. Demolition Man. 1993. pap. 4.50 (*0-451-18102-6*, Sig) NAL-Dutton.

O

An Asterisk (*) at the beginning of an entry indicates that the title is appearing in BIP for the first time.

— Freud for Beginners. 1993. pap. 9.95 (*0-86316-164-2*) Writers & Readers.

— Philosophy for Beginners. 2nd ed. (Orig.). 1992. pap. 9.95 (*0-86316-157-X*) Writers & Readers.

— Rossini. (Illus.). 345p. 1990. pap. 14.95 (*1-55553-088-5*) NE U Pr.

Osborne, Richard, et al. A Guide to Marine Mammals of Greater Puget Sound. LC 87-3414. (Illus.). 200p. (Orig.). 1988. pap. 14.95 (*0-9615580-1-6*) Island Pubs WA.

***Osborne, Richard E.** Tour Book for Antique Car Buffs. 2nd ed. LC 94-67962. (Illus.). 304p. (Orig.). 1994. per. 12.00 (*0-9628324-2-1*) Riebel Roque.

— Tour Guide of World War II Sites in the United States. LC 91-68129. (Illus.). (Orig.). 1995. pap. text ed. write for info. (*0-9628324-1-3*) Riebel Roque.

Osborne, Robert. Sixty-Five Years of the Oscar: The Official History of the Academy Awards. 1994. 59.95 (*1-55859-715-8*) Abbeville Pr.

Osborne, Robert A. Hardy Roses: An Organic Guide to Growing Frost- & Disease-Resistant Varieties. Art, Pam, ed. LC 91-55013. (Illus.). 144p. 1991. 24.95 (*0-88266-739-4*, Garden Way Pub) Storey Comm Inc.

Osborne, Robert D., jt. ed. see Cormack, Robert J.

Osborne, Robert H., ed. From Shoreline to Abyss: Contributions to Marine Geology in Honor of Francis Parker Shepard. (Special Publications Ser.: No. 46). (Illus.). 412p. 1991. 96.50 (*0-918985-92-7*) SEPM.

Osborne, Robin. Demos: The Discovery of Classical Attika. (Cambridge Classical Studies). (Illus.). 288p. 1985. 64.95 (*0-521-26776-5*) Cambridge U Pr.

Osborne, Robin & Alcock, Susan E., eds. Placing the Gods: Sanctuaries & Sacred Space in Ancient Greece. (Illus.). 288p. 1994. 55.00 (*0-19-814947-6*) OUP.

***Osborne, Robin & Hornblower, Simon, eds.** Ritual, Finance, Politics: Athenian Democratic Accounts Presented to David Lewis. (Illus.). 416p. 1995. text ed. 72.00 (*0-19-814992-1*) OUP.

Osborne, Robin, jt. ed. see Goldhill, Simon.

Osborne, Roger & Freyberg, Peter. Learning in Science: The Implications of Children's Science. LC 84-27915. 198p. (Orig.). (C). 1985. pap. text ed. 19.50 (*0-435-57260-1*) Heinemann.

Osborne, Roy. Designing with Color. (Illus.). 144p. 1991. 26.95 (*0-89134-404-7*, 30344) North Light Bks.

Osborne, Ruth F., jt. auth. see Kirkendall, Lester A.

***Osborne, Seward.** The Saga of the Mountain Legion (156th N. Y. Vols.) & the "Modest Hero Who Saved Our Flag" (Illus.). 40p. 1994. 6.00 (*0-944413-31-5*) Longstreet Hse.

Osborne, Seward R. Holding the Left at Gettysburg: The 20th New York State Militia on July 1, 1863. (Illus.). 36p. (Orig.). (C). 1990. pap. text ed. 6.00 (*0-944413-14-5*) Longstreet Hse.

Osborne, Seward R., ed. The Civil War Diaries of Col. Theodore B. Gates, Twentieth New York State Militia. (Illus.). 197p. (C). 1992. 25.00 (*0-944413-21-8*) Longstreet Hse.

Osborne, Sheila & Osborne, Eddie. Essential Jamaican Patwa: For English-Speaking Travelers. (Orig.). 1993. pap. 10.95 (*1-882272-08-0*) Osborne Comms.

Osborne, Sonny. Bluegrass Banjo Method. 1993. 4.95 (*0-87166-578-6*, 93243) Mel Bay.

Osborne, Super D. Super Dave: The Adventures of the World's Most Dangerous Man. LC 94-9309. 1994. 19.95 (*1-56530-125-0*) Summit TX.

Osborne, Thelma. The Adventures of Speedy. Caroland, Mary, ed. LC 90-71229. (Illus.). 44p. (J). (gr. k-3). 1991. 5.95 (*1-55523-383-X*) Winston-Derek.

Osborne, Theresa, jt. auth. see Haslam, Jonathan.

Osborne, Thomas J. Empire Can Wait: American Opposition to Hawaiian Annexation, 1893 - 1898. LC 81-8156. 197p. reprint ed. pap. 56.20 (*0-7837-0501-8*, 2040825) Bks Demand.

Osborne, Thomas L. Trial Handbook for Kentucky Lawyers. 2nd ed. 1992. 125.00 (*0-317-05373-6*) Lawyers Cooperative.

Osborne, Thomas M. Society & Prisons: With Intro. Added. LC 72-172587. (Criminology, Law Enforcement, & Social Problems Ser.: No. 177). 1975. 22.00 (*0-87585-177-0*) Patterson Smith.

— Within Prison Walls: A Week in Auburn Prison. 328p. 1991. reprint ed. pap. 9.95 (*0-9625714-3-1*) Spruce Gulch Pr.

— Within Prison Walls, Being a Narrative of Personal Experience During a Week of Voluntary Confinement in the State Prison at Auburn, New York. LC 69-14940. (Criminology, Law Enforcement, & Social Problems Ser.: No. 72). 1969. reprint ed. 16.00 (*0-87585-072-3*) Patterson Smith.

Osborne, Thomas R. A Grande Ecole for the Grands Corps: Brooklyn College Studies on Society in Change; Social Science Monographs. (East European Monographs). 168p. 1983. text ed. 38.50 (*0-88033-037-6*) East Eur Quarterly.

***Osborne, Victor.** How to Measure. LC 94-21039. (How Do We Know Ser.). 1995. lib. bdg. write for info. (*0-8114-3883-X*) Raintree Steck-V.

— Moondream. LC 88-13654. 128p. (J). (gr. 3-7). 1989. 11.95 (*0-688-08778-7*) Lothrop.

Osborne, W. C. Fans. 1977. 103.00 (*0-08-021725-7*, Pub. by Pergamon Repr UK) Franklin.

Osborne, Will. Joe Magarac. 1989. 9.95 (*0-943718-31-7*) Kipling Pr.

Osborne, Will & Osborne, Mary P. The Deadly Power of Medusa. 96p. (J). (gr. 3-7). 1992. pap. 2.75 (*0-590-45580-X*, Apple Paperbacks) Scholastic Inc.

***Osborne, William.** American Singing Societies & Their Partsongs: Ten Prominent American Composers of the Genre (1860-1940) & the Seminall Singing Societies That Performed the Repertory. (Monograph Ser.: No. 8). 112p. 1994. 15.00 (*0-614-05595-4*) Am Choral Dirs.

Osborne, William, ed. The Rape of the Powerless. 212p. 1971. text ed. 118.00 (*0-677-14720-1*); pap. 32.00 (*0-677-14725-2*) Gordon & Breach.

***Osborne, William L.** Foundations: Covering the Time Frame from Creation to 400 B. C. Winter, Ralph D., ed. LC 94-44909. (Global Civilization Ser.). 1994. write for info. (*0-87808-247-6*) William Carey Lib.

Osborne, William S., ed. see Kennedy, John P.

Osborne, William S., ed. see Kirkland, Caroline M.

Osbornova, J., et al, eds. Succession in Abandoned Fields: Studies in Central Bohemia, Czechoslovakia. (C). 1990. lib. bdg. 126.50 (*0-7923-0401-2*) Kluwer Ac.

Osborough, W. N., jt. ed. see Hogan, Daire.

Osbourn, Adeliese & Winter, Roger. Konversationen, Situationen. 1983. pap. text ed. 8.55 (*0-582-22310-5*, 70916) Longman.

Osbourn, R. A. Ashlawn. LC 83-15773. 1986. pap. 14.95 (*0-87949-240-6*) Ashley Bks.

Osbourne. O Paradisco. 1987. 22.95 (*0-399-13308-9*) Putnam Pub Group.

Osbourne, Alan. Modern Marine Engineer's Manual, 1. 2nd ed. Neild, A. Bayne, Jr., ed. LC 65-18208. (Illus.). 1176p. 1965. text ed. 55.00 (*0-87033-063-2*) Cornell Maritime.

***Osbourne, Cynthia D.** Between Heart & Mind. 12p. (Orig.). 1995. pap. write for info. (*1-885206-16-X*, Iliad Pr) Cader Pubng.

Osbourne, June. Stained Glass in England. 2nd rev. ed. LC 92-43356. (Illus.). 288p. 1993. 38.00 (*0-7509-0234-5*) A Sutton Pub.

Osbourne, Lloyd. Love, the Fiddler. LC 73-103526. (Short Story Index Reprint Ser.). 1977. 20.95 (*0-8369-3268-4*) Ayer.

— Motormaniacs. LC 70-85692. (Short Story Index Reprint Ser.). 1977. 19.95 (*0-8369-3035-5*) Ayer.

— Queen Versus Billy & Other Stories. LC 70-101286. (Short Story Index Reprint Ser.). 1977. 20.95 (*0-8369-3223-4*) Ayer.

Osbourne, Rick. Pull Your Own Weight: A to Z. 1992. 22.95 (*1-878602-60-8*) Sports Support.

Osbourne, Robert D., et al, eds. After the Reforms: Education & Policy in Northern Ireland. 304p. 1993. 59.95 (*1-85628-401-8*, Pub. by Avebury Pub UK) Ashgate Pub Co.

Osbourne, Thomas R. A Grand Ecole for the Grands Corps: The Recruitment & Training of the French Administration. No. 29a. 1983. write for info. (*0-318-60317-9*) Brooklyn Coll Pr.

Osbun, Lee A. The Problem of Participation: A Radical Critique of Contemporary Democratic Theory. LC 85-5308. 146p. (Orig.). 1985. lib. bdg. 41.50 (*0-8191-4640-4*) U Pr of Amer.

Osbun, Lee A. & Schmidt, Steffen W., eds. Issues in Iowa Politics. LC 90-4829. (Illus.). 276p. (C). 1990. text ed. 14.95 (*0-8138-0222-9*) Iowa St U Pr.

Osburn, A. E. Oklahoma Notes: Pediatrics. LC 92-49140. 280p. 1993. write for info. (*3-540-97955-7*) Spr-Verlag.

— Oklahoma Notes: Pediatrics. LC 92-49140. 280p. 1993. pap. 16.95 (*0-387-97955-7*) Spr-Verlag.

Osburn, Annie. Daryl Howard: The Source...the Image...the Journey. LC 90-83097. 144p. 1990. 75.00 (*0-9627207-0-4*) D Howard Art.

Osburn, Bernice B., jt. auth. see Osburn, Burl N.

Osburn, Burl N. & Osburn, Bernice B. Measured Drawings of Early American Furniture. LC 74-79936. (Illus.). 96p. 1975. reprint ed. pap. 5.95 (*0-486-23057-0*) Dover.

Osburn, Burl N. & Wilber, Gordon O. Pewter-Working: Instructions & Projects. LC 78-74121. (Illus.). 1979. reprint ed. pap. 6.95 (*0-486-23786-9*) Dover.

Osburn, Carroll D. The Peaceable Kingdom: Essays Favoring Non-Sectarian Christianity. 138p. 1993. pap. 8.95 (*0-9638994-0-6*) Restor Perspectives.

— Women in the Church: Refocusing the Discussion. 1994. pap. 7.95 (*0-9638994-1-4*) Restor Perspectives.

Osburn, Charles B. Academic Research & Library Resources: Changing Patterns in America. LC 78-20017. (New Directions in Librarianship Ser.: No. 3). (Illus.). 187p. 1979. text ed. 49.95 (*0-313-20722-4*, OAR/, Greenwood Pr) Greenwood.

— Present State of French Studies: A Collection of Research Reviews. LC 78-149990. 995p. 1971. 57.50 (*0-8108-0373-9*) Scarecrow.

— Research & Reference Guide to French Studies. 2nd ed. LC 81-5637. 570p. 1981. 42.50 (*0-8108-1440-4*) Scarecrow.

Osburn, Donald D., jt. auth. see Schneeberger, Kenneth C.

Osburn, Donald O. & Schneeberger, Kenneth C. Modern Agricultural Management. 2nd ed. 370p. (C). 1983. teacher ed write for info. (*0-8359-4551-0*, Reston) P-H.

Osburn, Jesse. The Last Lullaby. 160p. (Orig.). 1994. mass mkt. 3.99 (*0-380-77317-1*, Flare) Avon.

— Prom Night. 160p. (Orig.). 1995. mass mkt. 3.99 (*0-380-77318-X*, Flare) Avon.

Osburn, John D. Military Electromagnetic Compatibility Standards of the United States. LC 87-83430. (Electromagnetic Interference & Compatibility Ser.: Vol. 11). (Illus.). 340p. 1988. 75.00 (*0-944916-11-2*) D White Consult.

— Supporting & Unique Military Electromagnetic Compatibility Standards of the United States. LC 88-80526. (Electromagnetic Interference & Compatibility Ser.: Vol. 12). (Illus.). 276p. 1988. 65.00 (*0-944916-12-0*) D White Consult.

Osburn, Judy, jt. auth. see Osburn, Lynn.

Osburn, Lynn & Osburn, Judy. OroHemp: Economy & Ecology with Hemp. (Orig.). 1995. pap. 14.95 (*0-9629872-1-2*) Access Unlmtd.

***Oscard, Anne.** Ghosts of the Self. Woodyard, Chris & Rasmer, Raymond, eds. (Illus.). 128p. (Orig.). 1995. pap. 9.95 (*0-9645166-0-8*) Hermit Pubns.

Oschry, Leonard. The Story of the Vilna Gaon. 1.75 (*0-914131-62-1*, D520) Torah Umesorah.

Oschry, Leonard, tr. see Bachrach, Yehoshua.

Oschry, Leonard, tr. see Hayyim, Hafetz, pseud.

Oschry, Leonard, tr. see Kahana, Kalman.

Oschry, Leonard, tr. see Katz, Jacob.

Oschwald, W. R., ed. Crop Residue Management Systems. 248p. 1978. pap. 9.00 (*0-89118-050-8*) Am Soc Agron.

Oscilia, John. The Meat the Butcher Takes Home. 1989. 6.00 (*0-318-64606-4*) Giovanni Pub.

— The Meat the Butcher Takes Home: The Truth about Meat Cuts & The Way to Save Dollars. (Illus.). 108p. (Orig.). 1988. pap. 6.00 (*0-9620586-0-2*) Bacci Pub.

Osculati, Giorgio, jt. auth. see Bellabarba, Sergio.

O'Se, Diarmuid & Sheils, Joe. Teach Yourself Irish. (ENG & IRI.). 1993. pap. 18.95 (*0-7859-1059-X*, 0-340-564903); pap. 29.95 (*0-7859-1060-3*, 0-340-56492-X) Fr & Eur.

Oseghale, Braimoh D. Political Instability, Interstate Conflict Adverse Changes in Host Government Policies & Foreign Direct Investment: A Sensitivity Analysis. LC 92-40969. (Foreign Economic Policy of the United States Ser.). 192p. 1993. 47.00 (*0-8153-1254-7*) Garland.

***Osei, Akwasi O., comp.** Reflections: Verses from the Bahai Teachings. 128p. 1994. pap. 11.95 (*0-85398-386-0*) G Ronald Pub.

Osei, G. K. African: His Antecedents, His Genius, & His Destiny. 1971. 5.95 (*0-8216-0051-6*, Univ Bks) Carol Pub Group.

— The African Concept of Life & Death. Obaba, Al I., ed. (Illus.). 49p. (Orig.). (YA). 1991. pap. text ed. 3.00 (*0-916157-64-4*) African Islam Miss Pubns.

Osei-Hwedie, Bertha Z. & Osei-Hwedie, Kwaku. Tanzania-Zambia Railroad (TAZARA) An Analysis of Zambia's Decision-Making in Transportation. LC 90-80275. 166p. (Orig.). 1990. pap. text ed. 14.95 (*1-55618-081-0*) Brunswick Pub.

***Osei-Hwedie, Kwaku.** A Search for Legitimate Social Development Education & Practice Models for Africa. LC 95-9138. (Studies in African Economic & Social Development: Vol. 7). 288p. 1996. text ed. 89.95 (*0-7734-8887-1*) E Mellen.

Osei-Hwedie, Kwaku & Agyeman-Badu, Yaw. The Political Economy of Education in Ghana, 1920-1979: A Study of Education & National Development in Ghana. LC 84-61224. 189p. (Orig.). 1985. pap. 10.95 (*0-943324-13-0*) Omenana.

Osei-Hwedie, Kwaku & Ndulo, Muna, eds. Development at Crossroads: An African Experience. LC 90-83110. (Illus.). 412p. (Orig.). 1990. pap. text ed. 24.95 (*1-55618-085-3*) Brunswick Pub.

— The Development Puzzle: Some Insights from Africa. LC 90-83111. (Illus.). 520p. (Orig.). (C). 1990. pap. text ed. 24.95 (*1-55618-084-5*) Brunswick Pub.

— Issues in Zambian Development. 200p. (Orig.). 1985. pap. 12.95 (*0-943324-17-3*) Omenana.

Osei-Hwedie, Kwaku, jt. auth. see Boakye-Sarpong, Kwame.

Osei-Hwedie, Kwaku, jt. auth. see Osei-Hwedie, Bertha Z.

Oseid, Svein C. & Kai-Hakon, Carlsen, eds. Children & Exercise XIII. LC 88-26665. (International Series on Sport Sciences: Vol. 19). 464p. 1989. text ed. 52.00x (*0-87322-188-5*, BOSE0188) Human Kinetics.

***Oseman, Robert.** Conferences & Their Literature: A Question of Value. LC 90-121875. reprint ed. pap. 45.60 (*0-7837-9263-8*, 2060002) Bks Demand.

***Osen, Diane.** Royal Scandals: True Tales of Sex, Lust & Greed. LC 94-34641. 1995. write for info. (*1-56799-161-0*, MetroBooks) M Friedman Pub Grp Inc.

Osen, James L. Prophet & Peacemaker: The Life of Adolphe Monod. (Illus.). 420p. 1984. lib. bdg. 60.50 (*0-8191-3825-8*); pap. text ed. 31.00 (*0-8191-3826-6*) U Pr of Amer.

— Royalist Political Thought During the French Revolution. LC 94-25056. (Contributions to the Study of World History Ser.: Vol. 47). 168p. 1995. text ed. 55.00 (*0-313-29441-0*, Greenwood Pr) Greenwood.

Osen, Lynn M. Women in Mathematics. 224p. 1974. pap. 12.95 (*0-262-65009-6*) MIT Pr.

***Osen, Mary E.** I'll Be Seeing You: World War II Diary & Correspondence of Cpl. Mary E. Osen, February 1943 - September 1945. Nielsen, Lynn E. & Taylor, Mary T., eds. 143p. (Orig.). 1994. pap. 9.95 (*0-931209-54-4*) Mid Prairie Bks.

Osenbaugh, Scott E. Love--or Mush? Six Action-Packed Lessons on 1 Corinthians 13: 1-6 to Use with Junior Highers. LC 87-80603. (Illus.). 96p. (gr. 6-9). 1988. teacher ed, pap. 7.95 (*0-88243-745-3*, 02-0745) Gospel Pub.

Oseney Abbey Staff. The English Register of Oseney Abbey: Parts 1 & 2. (EETS, OS Ser.: No. 133, 144). 1972. reprint ed. 42.00 (*0-527-00130-9*) Periodicals Srv.

Osenton, J., jt. auth. see Dorian, A.

Oser, Fritz & Gmunder, Paul. Religious Judgement: A Developmental Perspective. Hahn, Norbert F., tr. Orig. Title: Der Mensch: Stufen Seiner Religiosen Entwicklung. 235p. (Orig.). 1991. pap. 18.95 (*0-89135-081-0*) Religious Educ.

Oser, Fritz, jt. ed. see Berkowitz, Marvin W.

Oser, Fritz K. & Scarlett, W. George, eds. Religious Development in Childhood & Adolescence. LC 85-644581. (New Directions for Child Development Ser.: No. CD 52). 1991. 17.95 (*1-55542-788-X*) Jossey-Bass.

Oser, Fritz K., et al, eds. Effective & Responsible Teaching: The New Synthesis. LC 92-11511. (Education-Higher Education Ser.). 480p. 1992. 45.00 (*1-55542-449-X*) Jossey-Bass.

Oser, H., et al, eds. Life Sciences & Space Research, No. XXIII: Gravitational Biology. (Advances in Space Research Ser.: No. 9). 294p. 1989. pap. 100.00 (*0-08-040154-6*, 1702; 0201; 0204; 0202; 0205; 0207, Pergamon Pr) Elsevier.

— Life Sciences & Space Research XXI (2) Proceedings of Workshops VII & XI & of the COSPAR Interdisciplinary Scientific Commission F (Meetings F1, F3, F5, F6, F7, & F9) of the COSPAR 25th Plenary Meeting Held in Graz, Austria, 25 June - 7 July 1984. (Illus.). 334p. 1985. pap. 54.00 (*0-08-032752-4*, Pub. by PPL UK) Elsevier.

Oser, Helen, jt. auth. see Stewart, Mary.

Oser, Jacob & Brue, Stanley L. The Evolution of Economic Thought. 4th ed. 527p. (C). 1988. text ed. 51.00 (*0-15-525003-5*) Dryden Pr.

***Oser, Marie.** Luscious Low-Fat Desserts. Joachim, David, ed. LC 94-26004. (Illus.). (Orig.). 1994. 11.95 (*0-9622565-7-9*) Chariot Pub PA.

Osers, Ewald, & tr. Contemporary Macedonian Poetry. (Illus.). 223p. (Orig.). 1992. pap. 21.00 (*0-948259-67-1*, Pub. by Forest Bks UK) Dufour.

Osers, Ewald, tr. Contemporary German Poetry. (Modern Poets Ser.: Vol. 5). 1976. pap. 4.95 (*0-902675-69-9*) Oleander Pr.

Osers, Ewald, tr. see Bernhard, Thomas.

Osers, Ewald, tr. see Capek, Karel.

Osers, Ewald, tr. see Cejka, Jaroslav, et al.

Osers, Ewald, tr. see Deist, Wilhelm, et al.

Osers, Ewald, tr. see Haffner, Sebastian.

Osers, Ewald, tr. see Hanzlik, Josef.

Osers, Ewald, tr. see Janovic, Vladimir.

Osers, Ewald, tr. see Klima, Ivan.

Osers, Ewald, tr. see Kruger, Michael.

Osers, Ewald, tr. see Maier, Klaus A., et al.

Osers, Ewald, tr. see Piontek, Heinz.

Osers, Ewald, tr. see Spindler, Konrad.

Oset, E., et al, eds. Pions in Nuclei: Proceedings of the International Workshop, Penyscola, Spain, 3-9 June 1991. 600p. (C). 1992. text ed. 130.00 (*981-02-0732-8*) World Scientific Pub.

Oseth, John M. Regulating U. S. Intelligence Operations: A Study in Definition of the National Interest. LC 84-22105. 254p. reprint ed. pap. 72.40 (*0-7837-2421-7*, 2042567) Bks Demand.

Osf Motif Series Staff. OSF-Motif Programmer's Guide. 1990. pap. text ed. 45.00 (*0-13-640525-8*) P-H.

— OSF-Motif Style Guide. 1990. pap. text ed. 30.00 (*0-13-640491-X*) P-H.

Osgood, C. E. Lectures on Language Performance. (Language & Communication Ser.: Vol. 7). (Illus.). 368p. 1980. 61.00 (*0-387-09901-8*) Spr-Verlag.

Osgood, C. G. The Classical Mythology of Milton's English Poems. (Reprints in History Ser.). reprint ed. lib. bdg. 36.00 (*0-697-00014-1*) Irvington.

Osgood, Carl C. Fatigue Design. 2nd ed. (International Series on the Strength & Fracture of Materials & Structures). 500p. 1982. text ed. 255.00 (*0-08-026167-1*, Pub. by Pergamon Repr UK) Franklin.

— The Travels of Frank Forrester. (Illus.). 198p. (Orig.). 1993. pap. 15.00 (*0-9638587-0-X*) Vista Hse.

Osgood, Charles E. & Sebeok, Thomas A., eds. Psycholinguistics. LC 76-2579. (Indiana Univ. Studies in the History & Theory of Linguistics). (Illus.). 307p. 1976. reprint ed. text ed. 55.00 (*0-8371-8730-3*, OSPS, Greenwood Pr) Greenwood.

Osgood, Charles E. & Tzeng, Oliver C., eds. Language, Meaning, & Culture: The Selected Papers of C. E. Osgood. LC 89-16055. (Centennial Psychology Ser.). 424p. 1990. text ed. 75.00 (*0-275-92521-8*, C2521, Praeger Pubs) Greenwood.

Osgood, Charles E., et al. Cross-Cultural Universals of Affective Meaning. LC 73-85570. (Illus.). 520p. 1975. 44.95 (*0-252-00426-4*); pap. 17.50 (*0-252-00550-3*) U of Ill Pr.

— The Measurement of Meaning. LC 56-5684. (Illus.). 356p. 1967. reprint ed. pap. 14.95 (*0-252-74539-6*) U of Ill Pr.

Osgood, Charles G. Classical Mythology of Milton's English Poems. LC 64-8180. 198p. 1964. reprint ed. 50.00 (*0-87752-080-1*) Gordian.

— Classical Mythology of Milton's English Poems. LC 65-15902. (Studies in Comparative Literature: No. 35). 1969. reprint ed. lib. bdg. 75.00 (*0-8383-0603-9*) M S G Haskell Hse.

— The Classical Mythology of Milton's English Poems. (BCL1-PR English Literature Ser.). 111p. 1992. reprint ed. lib. bdg. 69.00 (*0-7812-7387-0*) Rprt Serv.

— Concordance to the Poems of Edmund Spenser. 42.00 (*0-8446-1332-0*) Peter Smith.

— Poetry As a Means of Grace. LC 68-25106. 131p. 1965. reprint ed. 45.00 (*0-87752-081-X*) Gordian.

— Spenser's English Rivers. (Connecticut Academy of Arts & Sciences Ser., Trans.: Vol. 23). 1920. pap. 49.50 (*0-685-22835-5*) Elliots Bks.

Osgood, Charles G., Jr., ed. Pearl, a Middle English Poem. LC 78-144438. reprint ed. 30.00 (*0-404-53614-X*) AMS Pr.

Osgood, Charles G., tr. see Boccaccio, Giovanni.

Osgood, Cornelius. The Chinese: A Study of a Hong Kong Community, 3 vols., Set. LC 74-77207. 1264p. (C). 1975. 135.00 (*0-8165-0418-0*) U of Ariz Pr.

— Contributions to the Ethnography of the Kutchin. LC 73-118247. (Yale University Publications in Anthropology Reprints Ser.: No. 14). 190p. 1970. pap. 22.00x (*0-87536-522-1*) HRAFP.

— The Han Indians: A Compilation of Ethnographic & Historical Data on the Alaska-Yukon Boundary Area. LC 76-156892. (Publications in Anthropology: No. 74). 1971. pap. 7.50 (*0-913516-07-4*) Yale U Anthro.

— Ingalik Material Culture. LC 77-118248. (Yale University Publications in Anthropology Reprints Ser.: No. 22). 500p. 1970. pap. 30.00x (*0-87536-516-7*) HRAFP.

— The Koreans & Their Culture. LC 51-271. (Illus.). 435p. reprint ed. 124.00 (*0-8357-9523-3*, 2015843) Bks Demand.

O

An Asterisk (*) at the beginning of an entry indicates that the title is appearing in BIP for the first time.

— Village Life in Old China: A Community Study of Kao Yao Yhunnan. LC 63-19749. 415p. reprint ed. pap. 118. 30 (*0-317-11315-1*, 2012390) Bks Demand.

Osgood, D. Formas Efectivas De Vencer Tension (Surefire Ways to Beat Stress) (SPA.). Date not set. 2.49 (*0-685-74937-1*, 498058) Editorial Unilit.

Osgood, D. Wayne, jt. auth. see Gold, Martin.

***Osgood, Don.** Listening to God's Silent Language. 160p. 1995. pap. 8.99 (*1-55661-530-2*) Bethany Hse.

— Pressure Points: How To Deal with Stress. 1985. pap. 2.95 (*0-345-33064-1*) Ballantine.

Osgood, Ernest S., ed. see Clark, William.

Osgood Foster, Catharine. Building Healthy Gardens: A Safe & Natural Approach. rev. ed. Silva, Jeff, ed. LC 88-45486. Orig. Title: The Organic Gardener. (Illus.). 288p. 1989. reprint ed. pap. 11.95 (*0-88266-527-8*, Garden Way Pub) Storey Comm Inc.

Osgood, Henry O. So This Is Jazz. LC 77-17859. (Roots of Jazz Ser.). (Illus.). 1978. reprint ed. lib. bdg. 32.50 (*0-306-77540-9*) Da Capo.

Osgood, I. A Genealogy of the Descendants of John, Christopher & William Osgood Who Settled in New England Early in the Seventeenth Century. Putnam, Eben, ed. 491p. 1989. reprint ed. lib. bdg. 82.00 (*0-8328-0924-1*); reprint ed. pap. 74.00 (*0-8328-0925-X*) Higginson Bk Co.

Osgood, Joseph B. Notes of Travel: Recollections of Majunga, Zanzibar, Musca, Aden, Mocha, & Other Eastern Ports. LC 72-5546. (Black Heritage Library Collection). 1977. reprint ed. 28.95 (*0-8369-9146-X*) Ayer.

Osgood, Judy, ed. Meditations for Alcoholics & Their Families. LC 92-41267. (Gilgal Meditations Ser.). 72p. 1993. pap. 6.95 (*0-916895-04-1*) Gilgal Pubns.

— Meditations for Bereaved Parents. LC 86-15003. (Gilgal Meditations Ser.). 72p. (Orig.). 1984. pap. 6.95 (*0-916895-00-9*) Gilgal Pubns.

— Meditations for the Divorced. LC 87-17687. (Gilgal Meditations Ser.). 72p. (Orig.). 1987. pap. 5.95 (*0-916895-02-5*) Gilgal Pubns.

— Meditations for the Terminally Ill & Their Families. LC 88-36326. (Gilgal Meditations Ser.). 72p. 1989. pap. 5.95 (*0-916895-05-X*) Gilgal Pubns.

— Meditations for the Widowed. LC 86-15002. (Gilgal Meditations Ser.). 72p. (Orig.). 1985. pap. 6.95 (*0-916895-01-7*) Gilgal Pubns.

Osgood, K. M., jt. ed. see Ibbs, K. G.

Osgood, Nancy J. Suicide in Later Life: Recognizing the Warning Signs. 1992. text ed. 22.95 (*0-669-21214-8*) Free Pr.

Osgood, Nancy J., ed. Senior Settlers: Social Integration in Retirement Communities. LC 82-13352. 304p. 1982. text ed. 55.00 (*0-275-90873-9*, C0873, Praeger Pubs) Greenwood.

Osgood, Nancy J. & McIntosh, John L., comps. Suicide & the Elderly: An Annotated Bibliography & Review. LC 86-14935. (Bibliographies & Indexes in Gerontology Ser.: No. 3). 206p. 1986. text ed. 65.00 (*0-313-24786-2*, OSE/, Greenwood Pr) Greenwood.

Osgood, Nancy J. & Sontz, Ann H., eds. The Science & Practice of Gerontology: A Multidisciplinary Guide. LC 88-25100. 204p. 1989. text ed. 55.00 (*0-313-26161-X*, OSP/, Greenwood Pr) Greenwood.

Osgood, Nancy J., jt. auth. see Clark, Patricia A.

Osgood, Nancy J., et al. Suicide among the Elderly in Long-Term Care Facilities. LC 90-36738. (Contributions to the Study of Aging Ser.: No. 19). 216p. 1990. text ed. 49.95 (*0-313-26522-4*, ODD, Greenwood Pr) Greenwood.

***Osgood, Nancy J., et al, eds.** Alcoholism & Aging: An Annotated Bibliography & Review. LC 94-41371. (Bibliographies & Indexes in Gerontology Ser.: Vol. 24). 264p. 1995. text ed. 65.00 (*0-313-28398-2*, Greenwood Pr) Greenwood.

Osgood, Robert. The Weary & the Wary: U. S. & Japanese Security Policies in Transition. LC 71-186510. (Washington Center of Foreign Policy Research. Studies in International Affairs: No. 16). 106p. reprint ed. pap. 30.30 (*0-317-19919-6*, 2023132) Bks Demand.

Osgood, Robert, et al. Retreat from Empire? The First Nixon Administration. LC 72-12359. (America & the World Ser.: Vol. II). 360p. 1973. 52.00x (*0-8018-1493-6*); pap. 15.95 (*0-8018-1499-5*) Johns Hopkins.

Osgood, Robert E. Containment, Soviet Behavior, & Grand Strategy. LC 81-82418. (Policy Papers in International Affairs Ser.: No. 16). viii, 86p. 1981. pap. 5.50 (*0-87725-516-4*) U of Cal IAS.

— Ideals & Self-Interest in America's Foreign Relations. LC 53-10532. 1953. pap. 10.00 (*0-226-63778-6*) U Ch Pr.

— Limited War: The Challenge to American Strategy. LC 57-5275. 1957. lib. bdg. 19.00 (*0-226-63779-4*) U Ch Pr.

— NATO, the Entangling Alliance. LC 62-8348. 428p. reprint ed. pap. 122.00 (*0-317-08285-X*, 2007278) Bks Demand.

— The Successor Generation: Its Challenges & Responsibilities. 45p. (C). 1983. pap. 18.95x (*0-87855-874-8*) Transaction Pubs.

Osgood, Robert E., et al. Japan & the United States in Asia. LC 68-9699. (Washington Center of Foreign Policy Research. Studies in International Affairs: No. 8). 75p. reprint ed. pap. 25.00 (*0-317-19899-8*, 2023133) Bks Demand.

Osgood, Russell K. The Law of Pensions & Profit-Sharing. suppl. ed. LC 83-82690. 480p. 1984. 80.00 (*0-316-66614-9*) Little.

— Pensions - Profit. 1984. 125.00 (*0-316-66612-2*) Little.

— Supplement Pensions - Profit '87. 1987. 35.00 (*0-316-66616-5*) Little.

Osgood, Samuel. American Leaves: Familiar Notes of Thought & Life. LC 72-374. (Essay Index Reprint Ser.). 1977. reprint ed. 24.95 (*0-8369-2814-8*) Ayer.

Osgood, William F. Funktionentheorie, 2 Vols, 1. LC 63-11319. 24.95 (*0-8284-0193-4*) Chelsea Pub.

— Funktionentheorie, 2 Vols, 2. LC 63-11319. 24.95 (*0-8284-0182-9*) Chelsea Pub.

Osgood, William R. & Curtin, Dennis P. Preparing Your Business Plan with LOTUS 1-2-3. (Illus.). 176p. 1984. pap. 34.95 (*0-13-698424-X*); pap. 46.50 (*0-13-698432-0*); disk (*0-318-58084-5*) P-H.

— Preparing Your Business Plan with MULTIPLAN. 44.95 (*0-685-09440-5*) P-H.

— Preparing Your Business Plan with SYMPHONY. 27.95 (*0-685-09442-1*) P-H.

Osgood, William R., jt. auth. see Curtin, Dennis P.

Osguthorpe, Russel T. Manager's Guide to the Tutor-Notetaker. 122p. (C). 1980. pap. text ed. 9.50 (*0-88200-129-9*, N6796) Alexander Graham.

— Tutor-Notetaker. 98p. (Orig.). (C). 1980. pap. text ed. 9.50 (*0-88200-131-0*, N6680) Alexander Graham.

***Osguthorpe, Russell T., et al, eds.** Partner Schools: Centers for Educational Renewal. (Education Ser.). 352p. 1995. 32.95 (*0-7879-0065-6*) Jossey-Bass.

OSHA Staff. OSHA Regulated Hazardous Substances: Industrial Exposures & Control Technologies. 2400p. 1990. pap. text ed. 99.00 (*0-86587-795-5*, 795) Gov Insts.

Oshagan, Vahe, et al, eds. Armenia: Annual Volume Review of National Literatures. 260p. 1984. 43.00 (*0-685-06985-0*); pap. 23.00 (*0-918680-22-0*) Bagehot Council.

Oshagbemi, Titus. Leadership & Management in Universities: Britain & Nigeria. (Studies in Organization: No. 14). xx, 249p. (C). 1989. lib. bdg. 64.95 (*3-11-011514-X*) De Gruyter.

— Leadership & Management in Universities: Britain & Nigeria. (Studies in Organization: No. 14). xx, 249p. (C). 1989. 64.95 (*0-89925-426-8*) De Gruyter.

Oshana, Maryann. Women of Color: A Filmography of Minority & Third World Women. LC 82-49143. (Reference Library of Social Science). 350p. 1984. 40.00 (*0-8240-9140-X*) Garland.

O'Shanick, G. J., jt. ed. see Peterson, Linda G.

Oshanin, L. V. Anthropological Composition of the Population of Central Asia, the Ethnogenesis of Its Peoples, 1 Vol in 3 Nos, Set. Field, Henry, ed. Maurin, Vladimir M., tr. LC 65-112085. (Harvard University, Peabody Museum of Archaeology & Ethnology, Russian Translation Ser.: Vol. 2, Nos. 1-3). reprint ed. 124.50 (*0-404-52650-0*) AMS Pr.

***Oshaug, A., et al.** Educational Handbook for Nutrition Trainers: How to Increase Your Skills & Make It Easier for Students to Learn. 1993. 58.50 (*0-615-00200-5*) World Health.

***O'Shaughnessey, John.** Competitive Marketing. 3rd ed. 448p. 1995. 69.95 (*0-415-12786-6*, D1000); pap. 29.95 (*0-415-09317-1*, C0553) Routledge.

O'Shaughnessy & McKenna. Eenie, Meenie, Murphy, No! (J). 1992. pap. 3.25 (*0-590-42900-0*, Apple Paperbacks) Scholastic Inc.

O'Shaughnessy, Arthur. Poems. (BCL1-PR English Literature Ser.). 104p. 1992. reprint ed. lib. bdg. 69.00 (*0-7812-7611-X*) Rprt Serv.

O'Shaughnessy, Arthur E. Poems of Arthur O'Shaughnessy. Percy, William A., ed. LC 78-13947. 104p. 1979. reprint ed. text ed. 45.00 (*0-313-21101-9*, OSPO, Greenwood Pr) Greenwood.

O'Shaughnessy, Douglas. Speech Communications. (Electrical & Computer Engineering Ser.). (Illus.). 600p. (C). 1987. text ed. 64.95 (*0-201-16520-1*) Addison-Wesley.

O'Shaughnessy, Edith L. Diplomat's Wife in Mexico. LC 73-111727. (American Imperialism: Viewpoints of United States Foreign Policy, 1898-1941 Ser.). 1970. reprint ed. 34.95 (*0-405-02042-2*) Ayer.

— Diplomat's Wife in Mexico. (American Biography Ser.). 355p. 1991. reprint ed. lib. bdg. 79.00 (*0-7812-8303-5*) Rprt Serv.

— Married Life. LC 71-52952. (Short Story Index Reprint Ser.). 1977. reprint ed. 20.95 (*0-8369-3867-4*) Ayer.

— Other Ways & Other Flesh. LC 70-150482. (Short Story Index Reprint Ser.). 1977. reprint ed. 18.95 (*0-8369-3823-2*) Ayer.

O'Shaughnessy, Ellen. Somebody Called Me a Retard Today - & My Heart Felt Sad. LC 92-10812. (Illus.). 24p. (YA). 1992. 13.95 (*0-8027-8196-9*); lib. bdg. 14.85 (*0-8027-8197-7*) Walker & Co.

O'Shaughnessy, James C., ed. Environmental Engineering. 1084p. 1985. 103.00 (*0-87262-468-4*) Am Soc Civil Eng.

O'Shaughnessy, James P. Invest Like the Best: Using Your Computer to Unlock the Secrets of the Top Money Managers. 1993. text ed. 34.95 (*0-07-047984-4*) McGraw.

O'Shaughnessy, John. Competitive Marketing: A Strategic Approach. 2nd ed. (Illus.). 352p. 1988. pap. text ed. 27. 95 (*0-04-445117-2*) Routledge Chapman & Hall.

— Explaining Buyer Behavior: Central Concepts & Philosophy of Science Issues. 448p. 1992. 45.00 (*0-19-507108-5*) OUP.

— Why People Buy. (Illus.). 208p. (C). 1989. reprint ed. pap. text ed. 15.95 (*0-19-504087-2*) OUP.

O'Shaughnessy, Laura & Serra, Luis. The Church & Revolution in Nicaragua. LC 82-92625. (Monographs in International Studies, Latin America Ser.: No. 11). 118p. 1986. pap. 18.00 (*0-89680-126-8*, Ohio U Ctr Intl) Ohio U Pr.

O'Shaughnessy, Laura N., jt. auth. see Dodson, Michael.

O'Shaughnessy, Mary M. Feelings & Emotions in Christian Living. LC 87-21317. 152p. 1988. pap. 7.95 (*0-8189-0524-7*) Alba.

O'Shaughnessy, Michael, photos. A Kingdom of Saints: Early Bultos of New Mexico - A Postcard Collection. (Illus.). 22p. 1993. per. 8.95 (*1-878610-35-X*) Red Crane Bks.

— A Kingdom of Saints: Early Retablos of New Mexico - A Postcard Collection. (Illus.). 22p. 1993. per. 8.95 (*1-878610-36-8*) Red Crane Bks.

O'Shaughnessy, Michael J. Economic Democracy & Private Enterprise. LC 72-10848. (Essay Index Reprint Ser.). 1977. reprint ed. 18.95 (*0-8369-7235-X*) Ayer.

O'Shaughnessy, Nicholas J. The Phenomenon of Political Marketing. 262p. 1990. text ed. 45.00 (*0-312-03222-6*) St Martin.

O'Shaughnessy, Patrick, ed. Lincoln Fair & Other Poems by Bernard Gilbert. (Illus.). 72p. (C). 1989. text ed. 40.00 (*0-902662-34-1*, Pub. by R K Pubns UK); pap. text ed. 21.00 (*0-902662-35-X*, Pub. by R K Pubns UK) St Mut.

***O'Shaughnessy, Perri.** Motion to Suppress. LC 95-5615. 1995. 21.95 (*0-385-31410-8*) Delacorte.

O'Shaughnessy, Peter. Con's Fabulous Journey to the Land of Gobel O'Glug. rev. ed. (Illus.). 104p. (J). (gr. 6-10). 1992. reprint ed. pap. 5.95 (*0-947962-68-9*, Pub. by Anvil Bks Ltd IE) Irish Bks Media.

O'Shaughnessy, Tam, jt. auth. see Ride, Sally K.

***O'Shaughnessy, Teresa A.** The Snow Dome. LC 94-70626. (Illus.). 32p. (J). 1995. 17.95 (*0-9636274-4-9*) Coming Age Pr.

***O'Shaughnessy, Tim.** Adoption, Social Work & Social Theory: Making the Connections. 287p. 1994. 59.95 (*1-85628-883-8*, Pub. by Avebury Pub UK) Ashgate Pub Co.

O'Shay, Tracey A., jt. ed. see Hoddinott, Keith B.

O'Shea, ed. Design of Optical Systems Incorporating Low Power Lasers: Critical Review. 221p. 1987. 48.00 (*0-89252-776-5*, 741) SPIE.

— Selected Papers on Optomechanical Design. (Milestone Ser.). 1988. 79.00 (*0-89252-805-2*, 770) SPIE.

O'Shea & Fischer, eds. Simulation & Modeling of Optical Systems. 1988. 45.00 (*0-89252-927-X*, 892) SPIE.

O'Shea, Alan, jt. ed. see Nava, Mica.

O'Shea, B. P., jt. auth. see Taylor, R. B.

O'Shea, Brandy. The Black Cat Inn. LC 91-67920. (Illus.). (J). Date not set. pap. 8.00 (*1-56002-180-2*, Univ Edtns) Aegina Pr.

O'Shea, Catherine Q. & McIntosh, Crumbum. The Fifty Secrets of Highly Successful Cats. LC 94-4216. 1994. 7.95 (*0-440-50635-2*) Dell.

O'Shea, D., tr. see Arkhangel'skii, A. V., et al, eds.

O'Shea, D. C. Analysis of Optical Structures. 1992. 53.00 (*0-8194-0660-0*, 1532) SPIE.

O'Shea, Donagh. Go down to the Potter's House: A Journey into Meditation. 131p. 1988. pap. 7.95 (*0-8146-5638-2*) Liturgical Pr.

— Take Nothing for the Journey: Meditations on Time & Place. LC 90-70420. (Illus.). 136p. (Orig.). 1990. pap. 7.95 (*0-89622-444-9*) Twenty-Third.

O'Shea, Donald C. Elements of Modern Optical Design. LC 84-19708. (Pure & Applied Optics Ser.). 402p. 1985. text ed. 79.95 (*0-471-07796-8*) Wiley.

O'Shea, Donald C. & Peckham, Donald C., eds. Lasers. 144p. 1982. 18.00 (*0-318-41536-4*, RB36) Am Assn Physics.

O'Shea, Donald C., et al. Introduction to Lasers & Their Applications. (Physics Ser.). (C). 1977. text ed. 51.75 (*0-201-05509-0*) Addison-Wesley.

O'Shea, Francie J. Cooking at the Cafe: Lunch & Dinner Fare. (Illus.). 189p. (Orig.). 1992. pap. 14.95 (*0-9634342-0-9*, TXU 528 816) F OShea.

O'Shea, Gerald. Youth Soccer: Amateur Coach. 1986. 10.95 (*0-317-54063-7*) Viking Penguin.

O'Shea, Harriet E. A Study of the Effect of the Interest of a Passage of Learning Vocabulary. LC 71-177138. reprint ed. 37.50 (*0-404-55351-6*) AMS Pr.

O'Shea, J., ed. see IFAC Symposium, 3rd, Montreal, PQ, Canada, Aug. 1980.

O'Shea, John & Ludwickson, John. Archaeology & Ethnohistory of the Omaha Indians: The Big Village Site. LC 89-35986. (Studies in the Anthropology of North American Indians). (Illus.). xviii, 374p. 1992. 40. 00 (*0-8032-3556-9*) U of Nebr Pr.

O'Shea, John, jt. ed. see Halstead, Paul.

O'Shea, John, et al. Dyslexia: How Do We Learn? 108p. (Orig.). 1994. pap. 10.95 (*0-85572-236-3*, Pub. by Hill Content Pubng AT) Seven Hills Bk.

O'Shea, John J. Index to Richmond County History: 1969-1983, Vols. 1-15. LC 86-63441. 88p. (Orig.). 1987. pap. 7.00 (*0-937044-11-3*) Richmond Cty Hist Soc.

O'Shea, John M. Mortuary Variability: An Archaeological Investigation. (Studies in Archaeology). 1984. text ed. 54.00 (*0-12-528680-5*) Acad Pr.

O'Shea, John M. & Shott, Michael, eds. The Bridgeport Township Site: Archaeological Investigation at 20SA620, Saginaw County, Michigan. LC 89-48109. (Anthropological Papers: No. 81). (Illus.). xii, 304p. (Orig.). 1990. pap. 15.00 (*0-915703-19-X*) U Mich Mus Anthro.

***O'Shea, Kate S.** Finding Your Balance: Care of Mind, Body & Soul in Times of Discomfort, Instability and Surgery. (Illus.). 150p. (Orig.). 1995. pap. 13.95 (*0-9642676-9-1*) Inst Orthoped Psych.

O'Shea, M. V., ed. The Child: His Nature & His Needs. LC 74-21424. (Classics in Child Development Ser.). (Illus.). 576p. 1975. reprint ed. 56.95 (*0-405-06473-X*) Ayer.

O'Shea, Marie L., ed. see Field, Richard, et al.

***O'Shea, Mark.** Reptiles & Amphibians. (C). 1992. 21.00x (*0-907649-52-1*, Pub. by Expedit Advisory Centre UK) St Mut.

O'Shea, Maureen, jt. auth. see Gustafson, Helen.

O'Shea, Michael J. James Joyce & Heraldry. LC 85-26260. 196p. (C). 1986. 64.50 (*0-88706-269-5*); pap. 21.95 (*0-88706-270-9*) State U NY Pr.

O'Shea, Mortimer. Interior Furnishing, Vol. 11, No. 1. (C). 1981. pap. text ed. 120.00 (*0-900739-44-4*, Pub. by Textile Institue UK) St Mut.

O'Shea, Pat. The Hounds of the Morrigan. LC 85-16435. 469p. (J). (gr. 4 up). 1986. 15.95 (*0-8234-0595-8*) Holiday.

O'Shea, Peter. Guide to Adirondack Trails: Northern Region. 2nd rev. ed. Burdick, Neal, ed. LC 93-28566. (Forest Preserve Ser.: Vol. II). (Illus.). 256p. 1995. reprint ed. pap. 16.95 (*0-935272-63-1*) ADK Mtn Club.

O'Shea, Richard. American Heritage Battlemaps Civil War. 176p. 1994. 19.98 (*0-8317-1372-0*) Smithmark.

O'Shea-Roche, Annette & Malmberg, Sieglinde. Partners at Work & at Home: How Couples Can Build a Successful Business Together Without Killing Each Other. (Business Ser.). 200p. (Orig.). 1994. pap. 8.95 (*0-88908-521-8*) Self-Counsel Pr.

O'Shea, Shad. Beware...the Song Shark! (Illus.). 400p. (Orig.). 1990. pap. write for info. (*0-918243-01-7*) Positive Feedback Comns.

O'Shea, Tim & Self, John. Learning & Teaching with Computers: The Artificial Intelligence Revolution. 336p. 1983. pap. 12.95 (*0-13-527762-0*) P-H.

O'Shea, Tim & Sgurev, V., eds. Artificial Intelligence III - Mehtodology, Systems, Applications: Proc. of the 3rd Internat. Conf. (AIMSA '88), Varna, Bulgaria, 20-23 Sept., 1988. 444p. 1988. 92.50 (*0-444-70508-2*, North Holland) Elsevier.

O'Shea, Tim, jt. ed. see Scanlon, Eileen.

O'Shea, Tim, et al, eds. Intelligent Knowledge-Based Systems: An Introduction. 231p. 1988. pap. 42.00 (*0-89116-907-5*) Hemisp Pub.

O'Shea, Timothy J. The U. S.-Japanese Semiconductor Problem. (Pew Case Studies in International Affairs). 86p. (C). 1988. pap. text ed. 2.50 (*1-56927-139-9*) Geo U Inst Dplmcy.

Osher, Bill & Campbell, Sioux Henley. The Blue-Chip Graduate: A Four-Year College Plan for Career Success. 238p. 1987. pap. 14.95 (*0-934601-19-4*) Peachtree Pubs.

***Osher, Bill & Ward, Joann.** Engineering Success. 256p. (C). 1994. pap. text ed., spiral bd. 25.56 (*0-7872-0049-2*) Kendall-Hunt.

Osher, Carleen. Teaching Reflections. LC 91-44443. (Illus.). 100p. 1992. pap. 12.95 (*0-935834-80-X*) Rainbow Books.

Osher, S. J. Two Papers on Similarity of Certain Volterra Integral Operators. (Memoirs of the American Mathematical Society Ser.: Vol. 73). 47p. 1967. 16.00 (*0-8218-1273-4*, MEMO/1/73C) Am Math.

Osherenko, Gail & Young, Oran R. The Age of the Arctic: Hot Conflicts & Cold Realities. (Studies in Polar Research). (Illus.). (C). 1989. 79.95 (*0-521-36451-5*) Cambridge U Pr.

Osherenko, Gail, jt. ed. see Young, Oran R.

***Osheroff, Jerome A., ed.** Computers in Clinical Practice: Managing Patients, Information & Communication. LC 95-7875. (Information Technology Ser.). 1995. 46.00 (*0-943126-33-9*) Amer Coll Phys.

Osherov, V. I., jt. auth. see Medvedev, E. S.

Osherow, Jacqueline. Conversations with Survivors: Poems. LC 93-11652. 1993. pap. 9.95 (*0-8203-1612-1*) U of Ga Pr.

— Looking for Angels in New York. LC 88-4797. (Contemporary Poetry Ser.). 72p. 1988. 14.00 (*0-8203-1059-X*) U of Ga Pr.

***Osherson, Daniel N., ed.** An Invitation to Cognitive Science, 3 vols., Set. 2nd ed. (Illus.). 1300p. 1995. pap. 70.00x (*0-262-65045-2*, Bradford Bks) MIT Pr.

— An Invitation to Cognitive Science Vol. 1: Language. 2nd ed. (Illus.). 500p. 1995. 50.00x (*0-262-15044-1*, Bradford Bks); pap. 26.00x (*0-262-65044-4*, Bradford Bks) MIT Pr.

— An Invitation to Cognitive Science Vol. 2: Visual Cognition. 2nd ed. (Illus.). 400p. 1995. pap. 24.00x (*0-262-65042-8*, Bradford Bks) MIT Pr.

— An Invitation to Cognitive Science Vol. 2: Visual Cognition. 2nd ed. (Illus.). 400p. 1995. 45.00x (*0-262-15042-5*, Bradford Bks) MIT Pr.

— An Invitation to Cognitive Science Vol. 3: Thinking. 2nd ed. (Illus.). 400p. 1995. 45.00x (*0-262-15043-3*, Bradford Bks); pap. 24.00x (*0-262-65043-6*, Bradford Bks) MIT Pr.

Osherson, Daniel N. & Lasnik, Howard, eds. Language, Vol. 1: An Invitation to Cognitive Science. (Illus.). 296p. 1990. pap. 23.00 (*0-262-65033-9*) MIT Pr.

Osherson, Daniel N. & Smith, Edward E. Thinking, Vol. 3: An Invitation to Cognitive Science. (Illus.). 320p. (Orig.). 1990. 40.00 (*0-262-15037-9*); pap. 23.00 (*0-262-65035-5*) MIT Pr.

Osherson, Daniel N., et al. Systems That Learn: An Introduction to Learning Theory for Cognitive & Computer Scientist. (Learning, Development & Conceptual Change Ser.). 232p. 1986. pap. 12.95 (*0-262-65024-X*, Bradford Bks) MIT Pr.

Osherson, Daniel N., et al, eds. Visual Cognition & Action: An Invitation to Cognitive Science, Vol. II. 368p. (Orig.). 1990. pap. 23.00 (*0-262-65034-7*) MIT Pr.

Osherson, Samuel. Finding Our Fathers: How a Man's Life is Shaped by His Relationship with His Father. 1987. pap. 10.00 (*0-449-90247-1*, Columbine) Fawcett.

— Finding Our Fathers: The Unfinished Business of Manhood. 240p. 1986. text ed. 29.95 (*0-02-923690-8*) Free Pr.

— The Passions of Fatherhood. LC 94-25564. 304p. 1995. 23.00 (*0-449-90778-3*, Columbine) Fawcett.

— Wrestling with Love: How Men Struggle with Intimacy. 496p. 1993. pap. 10.00 (*0-449-90826-7*, Columbine) Fawcett.

O'Shiel, Eda, tr. see Buytendijk, Frederik J.

O

An Asterisk (*) at the beginning of an entry indicates that the title is appearing in BIP for the first time.

O'Shields, French. Slaying the Giant: Practical Help for Understanding Preventing & Overcoming Depression. 145p. (Orig.). 1994. pap. 7.99 (*0-9641901-0-9*) Hem Of His Garment.

Oshihara, Yuzuro. Children of the World: Malaysia. LC 86-42802. (Illus.). 64p. (J). (gr. 5-6). 1987. lib. bdg. 21.26 (*1-55532-160-7*) Gareth Stevens Inc.

Oshikoya, Temitope W. The Nigerian Economy: A Macroeconometric & Input-Output Model. LC 89-16352. 203p. 1990. text ed. 55.00 (*0-275-93417-9*, C317, Greenwood Pr) Greenwood.

Oshima, A. & Hogue, Oshimal A. Writing Academic English. 264p. (Orig.). (C). 1983. pap. text ed. 14.58 (*0-201-05479-5*) Addison-Wesley.

Oshima, E. & Van Rijn, C. F. Production Control in the Process Industry: Proceedings of the IFAC Workshop, Osaka, 29-31 October 1989 & Kariya, Japan, 1-2 November 1989. (IFAC Workshop Ser.: No. 9008). 260p. 1991. 155.00 (*0-08-036929-4*, Pergamon Pr) Elsevier.

Oshima, H., et al. Gastrokamera- und Roentgendiagnostik: Ein Atlas der kombinierten Magenuntersuchung mit histologischer Dokumentation. (Illus.). xii, 140p. (C). 1972. 226.95 (*3-11-001687-7*) De Gruyter.

Oshima, Harry T. Economic Growth in Monsoon Asia: A Comparative Study. 320p. 1987. 54.50 (*0-86008-402-7*, Pub. by U of Tokyo JA) Col U Pr.

— Strategic Processes in Monsoon Asia's Economic Development. LC 92-33545. (Studies in Development). 352p. (C). 1993. text ed. 55.00 (*0-8018-4479-7*) Johns Hopkins.

Oshima, Mark, tr. see Nakamura, Matazo.

Oshima, Nagisa. Cinema, Censorship, & the State: The Writings of Nagisa Oshima. Lawson, Dawn, tr. (October Bks.). (Illus.). 445p. 1992. pap. 37.50 (*0-262-15040-9*) MIT Pr.

— Cinema, Censorship, & the State: The Writings of Nagisa Oshima. 320p. 1993. pap. 15.95x (*0-262-65039-8*) MIT Pr.

Oshima, T., jt. ed. see Okamoto, Kiyosato.

Oshima, Y., ed. see IFAC International Symposium Staff.

Oshimata, Tana. Therapy of Mental Disorders: Medical Analysis Index with Research Bibliography. LC 85-47868. 150p. 1987. 37.50 (*0-88164-410-2*); pap. 34.50 (*0-88164-411-0*) ABBE Pubs Assn.

Oshinsky, David M. A Conspiracy So Immense: The World of Joe McCarthy. (Illus.). 1985. 24.95 (*0-02-923490-5*); pap. 16.95 (*0-02-923760-2*) Free Pr.

Oshinsky, David M., et al. The Case of the Nazi Professor. LC 88-16895. 220p. (C). 1989. text ed. 35.00 (*0-8135-1363-4*); pap. text ed. 15.00 (*0-8135-1427-4*) Rutgers U Pr.

Oshinsky, Jerold, et al. A Practitioner's Guide to Litigating Insurance Coverage Actions, 3 vols. 2300p. 1994. ring bd. 325.00 (*0-13-128166-6*) Aspen Law.

Oshiro, tr. see Ryokan.

Oshiro, Hide, tr. see Akiko, Yosano.

***Oshiro, T.** Laser Treatment for Naevi. text ed. 159.95 (*0-471-95243-5*) Wiley.

Oshiyama, O., jt. ed. see Kamimura, Hiroshi.

Osho. And the Flowers Showered: Discourses on Zen. Nirgun, Ma A., ed. (Zen Ser.). 256p. 1992. 14.95 (*81-7261-002-5*, Pub. by Rebel Hse GW) Osho Chidvilas.

— At the Feet of the Master. Sarito, Ma D., ed. (Initiation Talks Ser.). (Illus.). 404p. 1993. 28.95 (*3-89338-112-0*, Pub. by Rebel Hse GW) Osho Chidvilas.

— The Book of Wisdom: Discourses on Atisha's Seven Points of Mind Training. Prabhu, Swami K., ed. (Atisha Ser.). 545p. 1993. 24.95 (*3-89338-117-1*, Pub. by Rebel Hse GW) Osho Chidvilas.

— The Dhammapada: The Way of the Buddha, 12 vols. Swami Krishna Prabhu, ed. Incl. 1991. Vol. I, 253p. (*3-89338-091-4*); 1991. Vol. II, 258p. (*3-89338-092-2*); 1991. Vol. III, 258p. (*3-89338-093-0*); 1991. Vol. IV, 265p. (*3-89338-094-9*); 1991. Vol. V, 264p. (*3-89338-095-7*); 1991. Vol. VI, 281p. (*3-89338-096-5*); 1991. Vol. VII, 229p. (*3-89338-097-3*); 1991. Vol. VIII, 310p. (*3-89338-098-1*); 1991. Vol. IX, 232p. (*3-89338-099-X*); 1991. Vol. X, 313p. (*0-318-68806-9*); 1991. Vol. XI, 239p. (*3-89338-101-5*); 1991. Vol. XII, 247p. (*3-89338-102-3*); (Buddha Ser.). 3149p. 1991. Set boxed 166.00 (*0-685-50849-8*, Pub. by Rebel Hse GW) Osho Chidvilas.

— Dimensions Beyond the Known. 2nd ed. Prem, Ananda, ed. Chit, Sadhu A. & Arup, Prem, trs. (Early Talks Ser.). 200p. 1990. 14.95 (*3-89338-061-2*, Pub. by Rebel Hse GW) Osho Chidvilas.

— The Empty Boat: Talks on the Sayings of Chuang Tzu. Prabhu, Swami K., ed. (Tao Ser.). 326p. 1993. 18.95 (*3-89338-118-X*, Pub. by Rebel Hse GW) Osho Chidvilas.

— The Everyday Meditator. (Illus.). 216p. 1993. pap. 16.95 (*0-8048-1976-9*) C E Tuttle.

— Finger Pointing to the Moon. 1994. pap. 13.95 (*1-85230-598-3*) Element MA.

— From Bondage to Freedom: Answers to the Seekers of the Path. Devaraj, ed. (Talks in America Ser.). 512p. 1992. 24.95 (*3-89338-073-6*, Pub. by Rebel Hse GW) Osho Chidvilas.

— From Death to Deathlessness: Answers to the Seekers of the Path. Sambuddha Swami Devaraj, ed. (Talks in America Ser.). 520p. 1990. 24.95 (*3-89338-074-4*, Pub. by Rebel Hse GW) Osho Chidvilas.

— Glimpses of a Golden Childhood. Devaraj, ed. (Biography Ser.). 550p. 1991. 33.00 (*3-89338-012-4*, Pub. by Rebel Hse GW) Osho Chidvilas.

— God Is Dead: Now Zen Is the Only Living Truth. Robin, Anand, ed. (Zen Ser.). 320p. 1992. 18.95 (*3-89338-081-7*, Pub. by Rebel Hse GW) Osho Chidvilas.

— Gold Nuggets. Devaraj, Sw, ed. (Compilation Ser.). 184p. 1993. 12.95 (*0-685-75370-0*, Pub. by Rebel Hse GW) Osho Chidvilas.

— The Great Challenge. Robin, Swami A., ed. (Early Talks Ser.). 220p. 1993. 11.95 (*81-7261-007-6*, Pub. by Rebel Hse GW) Osho Chidvilas.

— Heart Sutra: Discourses on Prajnaparamita Hridayam Sutra of Gautama the Buddha. 1994. pap. 13.95 (*1-85230-477-4*) Element MA.

— Heartbeat of the Absolute. 1994. pap. 13.95 (*1-85230-476-6*) Element MA.

— The Hidden Harmony: Discourses on the Fragments of Heraclitus. Prabhu, Swami K., ed. 233p. 1991. 21.95 (*3-89338-110-4*, Pub. by Rebel Hse GW) Osho Chidvilas.

— I Am the Gate. Sagar, Ma D., ed. (Esoteric Ser.). 239p. 1991. 14.95 (*3-89338-088-4*, Pub. by Rebel Hse GW) Osho Chidvilas.

— I Celebrate Myself: God Is No Where: Life Is Now Here. Sagar, Dhyan, ed. (Zen Ser.). 304p. 1992. 18.95 (*3-89338-079-5*, Pub. by Rebel Hse GW) Osho Chidvilas.

— Impressions. Sarito, Ma D., ed. (Photo Compilation Ser.). (Illus.). 80p. 1993. 21.95 (*3-89338-114-7*, Pub. by Rebel Hse GW) Osho Chidvilas.

— In Search of the Miraculous, Vol. 2. Chinmaya, Swami Y., ed. (Meditation Ser.). 300p. 1992. 14.95 (*3-89338-601-7*, Pub. by Rebel Hse GW) Osho Chidvilas.

— Journey to the Heart. 1994. pap. 13.95 (*1-85230-595-9*) Element MA.

— Just Like That: Talks on Sufism. Prabhu, Sw K., ed. (Sufi Ser.). 455p. 1993. 24.95 (*3-89338-113-9*, Pub. by Rebel Hse GW) Osho Chidvilas.

— Kyozan: A True Man of Zen. Robin, Anand, ed. (Zen Ser.). 95p. 1992. 14.95 (*3-89338-080-9*, Pub. by Rebel Hse GW) Osho Chidvilas.

— Meditation: The Art & Ecstasy. Ma Prem Mangla, ed. 302p. 1992. 9.95 (*81-7261-000-9*, Pub. by Rebel Hse GW) Osho Chidvilas.

— Meditation: The First & Last Freedom: A Practical Guide to Meditation. Ranjana, Bodhisattva M. et al, eds. (Meditation Ser.). 280p. 1993. 16.95 (*3-89338-128-7*, Pub. by Rebel Hse GW) Osho Chidvilas.

— A Must for Contemplation Before Sleep. Robin, Swami A., ed. (Contemplation Ser.). 393p. 1991. 24.95 (*3-89338-105-8*, Pub. by Rebel Hse GW) Osho Chidvilas.

— A Must for Morning Contemplation. Robin, Swami A., ed. (Contemplation Ser.). 391p. 1991. 24.95 (*3-89338-104-X*, Pub. by Rebel Hse GW) Osho Chidvilas.

— Mustard Seed: Discourses on the Sayings of Jesus from the Gospel According to Thomas. 1994. pap. 14.95 (*1-85230-498-7*) Element MA.

— My Way, the Way of White Clouds. 1995. pap. 13.95 (*1-85230-699-8*) Element MA.

— No Water, No Moon: Talks on Zen Stories. 1994. pap. 13.95 (*1-85230-490-1*) Element MA.

— One Seed Makes the Whole Earth Green. Robin, Anand, ed. (Zen Ser.). 192p. 1992. 14.95 (*3-89338-077-9*, Pub. by Rebel Hse GW) Osho Chidvilas.

— The Psychology of the Esoteric. 3rd ed. Prem, Anand et al, eds. (Psychology Ser.). 184p. 1994. 12.95 (*3-89338-123-6*, Pub. by Rebel Hse GW) Osho Chidvilas.

— The Rebel. Mahasattva Swami Geet Govind, ed. (Questions & Answers Ser.). 358p. 1989. 21.95 (*3-89338-021-3*, Pub. by Rebel Hse GW) Osho Chidvilas.

— Returning to the Source. 1995. pap. 13.95 (*1-85230-700-5*) Element MA.

— The Search: Talks on the Ten Bulls of Zen. Anurag, Ma Y., ed. (Zen Ser.). 320p. 1993. 19.95 (*3-89338-116-3*, Pub. by Rebel Hse GW) Osho Chidvilas.

— Signatures on Water. Sarito, Ma D., ed. (Zen Ser.). 352p. 1992. 36.00 (*81-7261-005-X*, Pub. by Rebel Hse GW) Osho Chidvilas.

— Tantra: The Supreme Understanding Discourses of the Tantric Way of Tilopa's Song of Mahamudra. Maneesha, Ma P., ed. (Tantra Ser.). 263p. 1991. 17.95 (*3-89338-109-0*, Pub. by Rebel Hse GW) Osho Chidvilas.

— Tantra Experience. 1994. pap. 13.95 (*1-85230-597-5*) Element MA.

— Tantra Spirituality & Sex. Anutoshen, Swami D., ed. LC 94-7836. (Introduction to the Teachings of Osho Ser.). 160p. 1994. pap. 9.95 (*0-918963-03-6*) Osho Chidvilas.

— Tantric Transformation. 1994. pap. 13.95 (*1-85230-596-7*) Element MA.

— What Is Meditation? 1995. 10.95 (*1-85230-726-9*) Element MA.

— Yakusan: Straight to the Point of Enlightenment. Robin, Anand, ed. (Zen Ser.). 224p. 1992. 14.95 (*3-89338-084-1*, Pub. by Rebel Hse GW) Osho Chidvilas.

— Zarathustra, a God That Can Dance: Talks on Friedrich Nietzsche's Thus Spoke Zarathustra. Agama, P. & Nityo, P., eds. (Zarathustra Ser.). 570p. Date not set. pap. write for info. (*0-614-01947-8*, Pub. by Rebel Hse GW) Osho Chidvilas.

— Zarathustra, a God That Can Dance: Talks on Friedrich Nietzsche's Thus Spoke Zarathustra. Agama, Prem & Nityo, Prabodh, eds. (Zarathustra Ser.). 570p. Date not set. 24.95 (*3-89338-007-8*, Pub. by Rebel Hse GW) Osho Chidvilas.

— Zarathustra the Laughing Prophet: Talks on Friedrich Nietzsche's Thus Spoke Zarathustra. Suvarna, M. Shivam & Shanti, M. Anand, eds. (Zarathustra Ser.). 570p. Date not set. pap. write for info. (*0-614-01927-3*, Pub. by Rebel Hse GW) Osho Chidvilas.

— Zarathustra the Laughing Prophet: Talks on Friedrich Nietzsche's Thus Spoke Zarathustra. Suvarna, M. Shivam & Shanti, Ma Anand, eds. (Zarathustra Ser.). 570p. Date not set. 24.95 (*3-89338-008-6*, Pub. by Rebel Hse GW) Osho Chidvilas.

— Zen: The Mystery & the Poetry of the Beyond. Prabhu, Krishna, ed. (Zen Ser.). 176p. 1992. 14.95 (*3-89338-082-5*, Pub. by Rebel Hse GW) Osho Chidvilas.

— The Zen Manifesto: Freedom from Oneself. Sagar, Ma D., ed. (Zen Ser.). 1993. 18.95 (*3-89338-121-X*, Pub. by Rebel Hse GW) Osho Chidvilas.

***Osho International Foundation Staff.** Osho Zen Tarot: The Transcendental Game of Zen. (Illus.). 192p. (Orig.). 1995. pap. 19.95 (*0-312-11733-7*) St Martin.

Osho Rajneesh. Christianity the Deadliest Poison & Zen the Antidote to All Poisons. Swami Krishna Prabhu, ed. (Zen Ser.). 340p. 1990. 21.95 (*3-89338-071-X*, Pub. by Rebel Hse GW) Osho Chidvilas.

— Communism & Zen Fire, Zen Wind. Ma Deva Sarito & Ma Shivam Suvarna, eds. (Zen Ser.). 338p. 1990. 21.95 (*3-89338-072-8*, Pub. by Rebel Hse GW) Osho Chidvilas.

— Dogen, the Zen Master: A Search & a Fulfillment. Swami Anand Burt, ed. (Zen Ser.). 204p. 1989. 14.95 (*3-89338-063-9*, Pub. by Rebel Hse GW) Osho Chidvilas.

— From the False to the Truth: Answers to the Seekers of the Path. Sambodhi Ma Prem Maneesha & Ma Shivan Suvarna, eds. (Talks in America Ser.). 388p. 1988. 24.95 (*3-89338-022-1*, Pub. by Rebel Hse GW) Osho Chidvilas.

— The Golden Future. Bodhisattva Ma Nisango & Ma Prem Taranga, eds. (Mystery School Ser.). 414p. 1987. 24.95 (*3-89338-017-5*, Pub. by Rebel Hse GW) Osho Chidvilas.

— The Hidden Splendor. Ma Deva Sarito & Ma Prem Lisa, eds. (Mystery School Ser.). 332p. 1987. 21.95 (*3-89338-019-1*, Pub. by Rebel Hse GW) Osho Chidvilas.

— Hyakujo: The Everest of Zen: The Present Day Awakened One Speaks on the Ancient Masters of Zen. (Zen Ser.). 202p. 1989. 14.95 (*3-89338-066-3*, Pub. by Rebel Hse GW) Osho Chidvilas.

— Isan: No Footprints in the Blue Sky: The Present Day Awakened One Speaks on the Ancient Masters of Zen. Swami Krishna Prabhu, ed. (Zen Ser.). 202p. 1989. 14.95 (*3-89338-070-1*, Pub. by Rebel Hse GW) Osho Chidvilas.

— Joshu: The Lion's Roar: The Present Day Awakened One Speaks on the Ancient Masters of Zen. Ma Deva Sarito & Swami Prem Sushil, eds. (Zen Ser.). 198p. 1989. 14.95 (*3-89338-068-X*, Pub. by Rebel Hse GW) Osho Chidvilas.

— Ma Tzu: The Empty Mirror: The Present Day Awakened One Speaks on the Ancient Masters of Zen. Swami Deva Ashik, ed. (Zen Ser.). 202p. 1989. 14.95 (*3-89338-065-5*, Pub. by Rebel Hse GW) Osho Chidvilas.

— Nansen: The Point of Departure: The Present Day Awakened One Speaks on the Ancient Masters of Zen. Swami Anand Robin, ed. (Zen Ser.). 206p. 1989. 14.95 (*3-89338-067-1*, Pub. by Rebel Hse GW) Osho Chidvilas.

— The Razor's Edge. Bodhisattva Ma Deva Barkha, ed. (Mystery School Ser.). 374p. 1987. 21.95 (*3-89338-015-9*, Pub. by Rebel Hse GW) Osho Chidvilas.

— Rinzai: Master of the Irrational: The Present Day Awakened One Speaks on the Ancient Masters of Zen. Swami Krishna Prabhu, ed. (Zen Ser.). 202p. 1989. 14.95 (*3-89338-069-8*, Pub. by Rebel Hse GW) Osho Chidvilas.

— The Sword & the Lotus. Ma Dhyan Sagar, ed. (Talks in Himalayas Ser.). 338p. 1989. 21.95 (*3-89338-075-2*, Pub. by Rebel Hse GW) Osho Chidvilas.

Oshodi, John. Sex, Violence, Drugs & America: The Definition of A Culture. 114p. (Orig.). 1994. pap. 11.95 (*0-9644455-0-6*) Oshodi Fnd. This book is an indictment of the primitive marks of America's long-standing social & racial complications. A provocative overview of the history of psychology is offered. The book has been widely reviewed. Published by The Oshodi Foundation, 1994, 114 pages, paperback & softback. ISBN 0-9644455-0-6. Price $11.95 plus $2.00 shipping. Mail remittance by check or money order to: The Oshodi Foundation, 17325 N.W. 27th Avenue, Suite 209, Miami, FL 33056. Telephone: (305) 623-5979.** ***Publisher Provided Annotation.

Oshry, Barry. Controlling the Contexts of Consciousness: The I, the We, the All of Us. LC 75-9952. (Notes on Power Ser.). (Orig.). 1976. pap. 5.00 (*0-910411-02-6*) Power & Sys.

— Middle Power. (Notes on Power Ser.). (Orig.). 1980. pap. 8.50 (*0-910411-08-5*) Power & Sys.

— Middles of the World, Integrate! (Orig.). 1982. pap. 9.50 (*0-910411-09-3*) Power & Sys.

— Organic Power. LC 80-4780. (Notes on Power Ser.). (Orig.). 1976. pap. text ed. 5.50 (*0-910411-03-4*) Power & Sys.

— The Possibilities of Organization. 178p. (Orig.). (C). 1986. pap. text ed. 18.95 (*0-910411-10-7*) Power & Sys.

— Power & Position. LC 88-8848. (Notes on Power Ser.). (Orig.). 1977. pap. text ed. 11.50 (*0-910411-04-2*) Power & Sys.

— Seeing Systems: Unlocking the Mysteries of Organizational Life. (Illus.). 200p. 1995. 24.95 (*1-881052-73-7*) Berrett-Koehler.

— Success of a Business-Failure of Its Partners. (Notes on Power Ser.). (Orig.). 1980. pap. text ed. 6.00 (*0-910411-07-7*) Power & Sys.

— Take a Look at Yourself: Self-in-System Sensitizers. (Notes on Power Ser.). (Orig.). 1978. pap. text ed. 8.00 (*0-910411-05-0*) Power & Sys.

Oshry, Ephraim. Responsa from the Holocaust. Leiman, Y., tr. 260p. 1983. 14.95 (*0-910818-55-X*) Judaica Pr.

Osiadacz, A. J. Simulation & Analysis of Gas Networks. 274p. 1987. 49.00 (*0-87201-844-X*) Gulf Pub.

Osiadacz, Andrzej J. Transient Simulation Methods for Gas Networks. 300p. 1993. text ed. write for info. (*0-13-927963-6*) P-H.

Osiadacz, Andrzej J., ed. Simulation & Optimization of Large Systems. (Institute of Mathematics & Its Applications Conference Series, New Ser.: New Series 13). (Illus.). 352p. 1988. 75.00 (*0-19-853617-8*) OUP.

O'Siadhail, Michael. The Chosen Garden. (C). 1990. 23.00 (*0-948268-87-5*, Pub. by Dedalus Pr IE) St Mut.

— Hail! Madam Jazz: New & Selected Poems. 160p. 1993. 30.00 (*1-85224-225-6*, Pub. by Bloodaxe Bks UK); pap. 18.95 (*1-85224-208-6*, Pub. by Bloodaxe Bks UK) Dufour.

— Learning Irish. LC 87-51376. 320p. (C). 1988. 22.50 (*0-300-04224-8*) Yale U Pr.

O'Siadhail, Micheal. Modern Irish: Grammatical Structure & Dialectal Variation. (Cambridge Studies in Linguistics: Supplementary Volumes). (Illus.). (C). 1990. 74.95 (*0-521-37147-3*) Cambridge U Pr.

Osiander, Andreas. The States System of Europe, 1640-1990: Peacemaking & the Conditions of International Stability. 360p. 1994. 54.00 (*0-19-827887-X*) OUP.

Osiatynski, Jerzy. Michal Kalecki on Socialist Economy. Toporowski, Jan, tr. LC 87-33093. 200p. 1988. text ed. 49.95 (*0-312-01562-3*) St Martin.

Osiatynski, Jerzy, ed. Socialism - Economic Growth & Efficiency of Investment. Jung, Bohdan, tr. LC 92-26359. (ENG & POL.). 1993. 72.00 (*0-19-828666-X*, Clarendon Pr) OUP.

Osiatynski, Jerzy, ed. see Kalecki, Michal.

Osicka, V. & Poldauf, I. English-Czech Dictionary. 640p. (CZE & ENG.). 1980. 55.00 (*0-569-06529-1*, Pub. by Collets) St Mut.

O'Sickey, Ingeborg M. A Case of Betrayal? Women in Marguerite Yourcenar's Early Work. LC 93-36531. (American University Studies: Vol. 36). 1994. write for info. (*0-8204-1311-9*) P Lang Pubs.

Osiecki, Henry. Food of the Gods. 199p. (C). 1989. pap. 60.00 (*0-7316-5821-3*, Pub. by Bio Concepts AT) St Mut.

— Nutrients in Profile. 120p. (C). 1990. pap. 45.00 (*1-875239-04-9*, Pub. by Bio Concepts AT) St Mut.

— The Physicians Handbook of Clinical Nutrition. 252p. (C). 1990. pap. 50.00 (*1-875239-03-0*, Pub. by Bio Concepts AT) St Mut.

Osiek, Carolyn. Beyond Anger: On Being a Feminist in the Church. LC 85-62936. 96p. 1985. pap. 7.95 (*0-8091-2777-6*) Paulist Pr.

— Galatians. LC 80-66456. (New Testament Message Ser.: Vol. 12). 95p. 1980. pap. 6.95 (*0-8146-5135-6*) Liturgical Pr.

— Lesser Festivals Four. LC 84-18756. (Proclamation Ser.). 64p. 1987. pap. 4.50 (*0-8006-4136-1*, 1-4136, Fortress Pr) Augsburg Fortress.

— Rich & Poor in the Shepherd of Hermas: An Exegetical-Social Investigation. Vawter, Bruce, ed. LC 83-7385. (Catholic Biblical Quarterly Monographs: No. 15). xi, 184p. 1983. pap. 6.00 (*0-915170-14-0*) Catholic Bibl Assn.

— What Are They Saying about the Social Setting of the New Testament? enl. rev. ed. LC 92-16470. (What Are They Saying about...Ser.). 144p. (Orig.). 1992. pap. 7.95 (*0-8091-3339-3*) Paulist Pr.

Osiek, Carolyn, ed. see Leon, Harry J.

Osiek, Carolyn A. First Corinthians. (Read & Pray Ser.). 1980. 1.95 (*0-8199-0634-4*, Frncscn Herld) Franciscan Pr.

Osiek, O. Galatians. 1989. pap. 21.00 (*0-86217-030-3*, Pub. by Veritas IE) St Mut.

Osieke, E. Constitutional Law & Practice in the International Labour Organization. 1985. lib. bdg. 129.50 (*90-247-2985-8*) Kluwer Ac.

Osier. In the Eye of the Garden. 176p. 1993. 15.00 (*0-685-70479-3*) Macmillan.

— Ultra Marathoning. 1984. 14.95 (*0-02-499840-0*) Macmillan.

Osier, Jan, jt. auth. see Fox, Harold.

Osier, Jeffrey, jt. auth. see Ochoa, George.

***Osifchin, Gary & Trammell, Jeffrey, eds.** The International Washington Almanac, 1995. 1995. pap. 149.00 (*0-88622-013-0*) Almanac Pub.

Osifchin, Gary P., jt. auth. see Trammell, Jeffrey B.

Osigweh, Chimezie A., ed. Communicating Employee Responsibilities & Rights: A Modern Management Mandate. LC 86-25281. 268p. 1987. text ed. 59.95 (*0-89930-200-9*, OSC/, Quorum Bks) Greenwood.

— Managing Employee Rights & Responsibilities. LC 88-38310. 321p. 1989. text ed. 65.00 (*0-89930-336-6*, OME/, Quorum Bks) Greenwood.

Osigweh'g, C. A., ed. Organizational Science Abroad: Constraints & Perspectives. LC 88-28572. (Illus.). 364p. 1989. 47.50 (*0-306-42969-1*, Plenum Pr) Plenum.

O

An Asterisk (*) at the beginning of an entry indicates that the title is appearing in BIP for the first time.

Osiko, V. V., ed. Selective Laser Spectroscopy of Activated Crystals & Glasses. (Proceedings of the Institute of General Physics of the Academy of Sciences of the U. S. S. R. Ser.). 220p. (C). 1990. text ed. 115.00 (*0-941743-92-6*) Nova Sci Pubs.

— Selective Laser Spectroscopy of Activated Crystals & Glasses. (Proceedings of the Institute of General Physics of the Academy of Sciences of the U. S. S. R. Ser.: Vol. 9). 210p. (RUS.). 1990. text ed. 115.00 (*0-941743-31-4*) Nova Sci Pubs.

Osin, Luis, jt. auth. see Venezky, Richard.

Osing, Richard A. How to Love & Be Loved: Establishing & Maintaining Intimacy. 112p. (Orig.). 1992. pap. 11.95 (*0-945213-05-0*) Rudi Pub.

Osinski, A. Slownik Mitologiczny, 3 vols., Set. reprint ed. 280.00 (*0-318-23358-4*) Szwede Slavic.

Osinski, Alice. Andrew Jackson. LC 86-29983. (Encyclopedia of Presidents Ser.). (Illus.). 100p. (J). (gr. 3 up). 1987. lib. bdg. 14.40 (*0-516-01387-4*) Childrens.

— The Chippewa. LC 86-32687. (New True Bks.). (Illus.). 48p. (J). (gr. k-4). 1987. lib. bdg. 12.90 (*0-516-01230-4*); pap. 4.95 (*0-516-41230-2*) Childrens.

— The Eskimo: Inuit & Yupik. LC 85-9691. (New True Bks.). (Illus.). 45p. (J). (gr. 2-3). 1985. lib. bdg. 12.90 (*0-516-01267-3*); pap. 4.95 (*0-516-41267-1*) Childrens.

— Franklin D. Roosevelt. (Encyclopedia of Presidents Ser.). (Illus.). 100p. (J). (gr. 3 up). 1987. lib. bdg. 14.40 (*0-516-01395-5*) Childrens.

— The Navajo. (New True Bks.). (Illus.). (J). (gr. k-4). 1987. lib. bdg. 12.90 (*0-516-01236-3*); pap. 4.95 (*0-516-41236-1*) Childrens.

— The Nez Perce. LC 88-11822. (New True Bks.). (Illus.). 48p. (J). (gr. k-4). 1988. lib. bdg. 12.90 (*0-516-01154-5*); pap. 4.95 (*0-516-41154-3*) Childrens.

— The Sioux. LC 84-7629. (New True Bks.). (Illus.). 48p. (J). (gr. k-4). 1984. lib. bdg. 12.90 (*0-516-01929-5*); pap. 4.95 (*0-516-41929-3*) Childrens.

— The Tlingit. LC 89-25345. (New True Bks.). (Illus.). 48p. (J). (gr. k-4). 1990. lib. bdg. 12.90 (*0-516-01189-8*); pap. 4.95 (*0-516-41189-6*) Childrens.

— Woodrow Wilson. LC 88-8678. (Encyclopedia of Presidents Ser.). (Illus.). 100p. (J). (gr. 3 up). 1989. lib. bdg. 14.40 (*0-516-01367-X*) Childrens.

Osinski, F. W., et al, eds. Toward Gog & Magog Or? A Critical Review of the Literature of Adult Group Discussion. LC 72-6475. (Occasional Papers: No. 30). 80p. (Orig.). 1972. pap. 2.00 (*0-87060-053-2*, OCP 30) Syracuse U Cont Ed.

Osinski, Zbigniew. Grotowski & His Laboratory. Vallee, Lillian & Findlay, Robert, trs. (Illus.). 1986. 24.95 (*0-933826-89-3*) PAJ Pubns.

O'Siochain, Conchur. The Man from Cape Clear. Breatnach, Riobard B., tr. 28p. 1993. pap. 14.95 (*1-85635-014-2*, Pub. by Mercier Pr IE) Dufour.

O'Siochain, P. A. A Journey into Lost Time. 184p. 1985. 14. 95 (*0-685-09679-3*) Devin.

O'Siochfhradha, Padraig. Jimeen. 96p. 1984. 11.95 (*0-86278-059-4*, Pub. by OBrien Pr IE); pap. 7.95 (*0-86278-132-9*, Pub. by OBrien Pr IE) Dufour.

Osipov, K. A. Aspects of the Theory of Heat Resistance of Metals & Alloys. 256p. 1961. text ed. 67.00 (*0-7065-0165-9*, Pub. by Keter Pub IS) Coronet Bks.

Osipow, Samual H., jt. ed. see Walsh, W. Bruce.

Osipow, Samuel, jt. ed. see Walsh, W. Bruce.

Osipow, Samuel H. Theories of Career Development. 3rd ed. (Illus.). 320p. (C). 1982. text ed. write for info. (*0-13-913640-1*) P-H.

Osipow, Samuel H., jt. ed. see Walsh, W. Bruce.

Osis. Dosage Calculations in SI Units, No. 2. (Illus.). 192p. 1990. 15.95 (*0-8016-3753-8*) Mosby Yr Bk.

— Dosage Calculations in SI Units, No. 2. 176p. 1990. spiral bd. 15.95 (*0-8016-3721-X*) Mosby Yr Bk.

Osis, Karlis. Deathbed Observations by Physicians & Nurses. 4th ed. LC 61-18247. (Parapsychological Monograph Ser.: No. 3). 1961. pap. 7.00 (*0-912328-06-1*) Parapsych Foun.

Osis, Karlis & Haraldsson, Erlendur. At the Hour of Death. 2nd rev. ed. LC 86-82310. 272p. 1986. pap. 10.95 (*0-8038-9279-9*) Hastings.

— At the Hour of Death. LC 92-37016. (Collector's Library of the Unknown). 244p. 1993. reprint ed. write for info. (*0-8094-8125-1*) Time-Life.

Oskai, S. & Hatoyama, Y., eds. Stochastic Models in Reliability Theory. (Lecture Notes in Economics & Mathematical Systems Ser.: Vol. 235). vii, 212p. 1984. pap. 36.00 (*0-387-13888-9*) Spr-Verlag.

Oskam, Bob, jt. ed. see Choron, Sandra.

Oskam, H. J., ed. Plasma Processing of Materials. LC 84-14806. (Illus.). 268p. 1985. 36.00 (*0-8155-1003-9*) Noyes.

Oskam, H. J., jt. ed. see Hirsh, Merle N.

Oskamp, A., jt. ed. see Kaspersen, H. W.

Oskamp, Stuart. Applied Social Psychology. (Illus.). 464p. (C). 1984. text ed. write for info. (*0-13-043273-3*) P-H.

— Attitudes & Opinions. 2nd ed. 496p. (C). 1990. text ed. write for info. (*0-13-050592-7*) P-H.

Oskamp, Stuart, ed. People's Reactions to Technology: In Factories, Offices, & Aerospace. (Claremont Symposium on Applied Social Psychology Ser.). 296p. (C). 1990. text ed. 36.00 (*0-8039-3852-7*); pap. text ed. 16.95 (*0-8039-3853-5*) Sage.

Oskamp, Stuart & Costanzo, Mark, eds. Gender Issues in Social Psychology. (Claremont Symposium on Applied Social Psychology Ser.: Vol. 6). (Illus.). 164p. (C). 1993. text ed. 36.00 (*0-8039-5229-5*); pap. text ed. 16.95 (*0-8039-5230-9*) Sage.

Oskamp, Stuart, ed. see Claremont Graduate School, Symposium on Applied Social Psychology Staff.

Oskamp, Stuart, ed. see Claremont Symposium on Applied Social Psychology Staff.

Oskamp, Stuart, jt. auth. see Costanzo, Mark.

Oskamp, Stuart, jt. auth. see Spacapan, Shirlynn.

Oskamp, Stuart, jt. ed. see Spacapan, Shirlynn.

Oskarsson, A. Exposure of Infants & Children to Lead: Working Document for the 30th Meeting of the Joint FAO-WHO Expert Committee on Food Additives Held in Rome, 2-11 June 1986. (Food & Nutrition Paper Ser.: No. 45). (Illus.). 55p. 1989. pap. 9.00 (*92-5-102820-6*, F8206) UNIPUB.

Oski. Principles & Practice of Pediatrics. 2nd ed. (C). 1993. 99.50 (*0-397-51221-X*) Lippincott.

— Year Book of Pediatrics, 1991. 528p. 1991. 54.95 (*0-8151-6586-2*, Yr Bk Med Pubs) Mosby Yr Bk.

Oski, et al. Principles & Practice of Pediatrics. (Illus.). 2155p. 1989. text ed. 99.50 (*0-397-50707-0*) Lippincott.

Oski, Frank. Don't Drink Your Milk. 312p. pap. 4.95 (*0-671-22804-8*) Park City Pr.

Oski, Frank A. Don't Drink Your Milk. 9th rev. ed. LC 77-8102. 96p. 1994. per. 7.95 (*0-945383-34-7*, 945-5807) Teach Servs.

Oski, Frank A., ed. Year Book of Pediatrics, 1989. (Illus.). 694p. 1989. 54.95 (*0-8151-6561-7*, Yr Bk Med Pubs) Mosby Yr Bk.

Oski, Frank A., jt. auth. see Markel, Howard.

Osland, Birger. A Long Pull from Stavanger: The Reminiscences of a Norwegian Immigrant. 263p. 1945. 10.00 (*0-87732-027-6*) Norwegian-Am Hist Assn.

***Osland, Joyce S.** The Adventures of Working Abroad: Hero Tales from the Global Frontier. LC 95-8629. (Management Ser.). 1995. 25.00 (*0-7879-0108-3*) Jossey-Bass.

Oslear, Don & Mosey, Don. Wisden Book of Cricket Laws. (Illus.). 256p. 1994. 22.95 (*0-09-177345-8*, Pub. by S Paul UK) Trafalgar.

Osleeb, Jeffrey P., jt. auth. see ZumBrunnen, Craig.

Osler. Serious Runner's Handbook. 1978. pap. 5.95 (*0-02-499770-6*) Macmillan.

Osler, et al. Corporate Environmental Responsibilities. 256p. Date not set. 130.00 (*0-409-89718-3*) Butterworth Legal Pubs.

Osler, Audrey. Development Education: Global Perspectives in the Curriculum. (Council of Europe Ser.). 224p. 1994. text ed. 70.00 (*0-304-32567-8*); pap. text ed. 24.95 (*0-304-32565-1*) Cassell.

Osler, Jack. Fifty Great Mini-Trips for Indiana. (Illus.). 1978. pap. 2.95 (*0-89645-005-8*) Media Ventures.

Osler, Jack M. Fifty Great New Mini-Trips for Ohio. (Jack Osler's Mini-Trips Ser.). (Illus.). (Orig.). 1980. pap. 3.50 (*0-89645-013-9*) Media Ventures.

Osler, Margaret J. Divine Will & the Mechanical Philosophy: Gassendi & Descartes on Contingency & Necessity in the Created World. LC 93-37129. 256p. (C). 1994. 49.95 (*0-521-46104-9*) Cambridge U Pr.

Osler, Margaret J., ed. Atoms, Pneuma, & Tranquillity: Epicurean & Stoic Themes in European Thought. 288p. (C). 1991. 59.95 (*0-521-40048-1*) Cambridge U Pr.

Osler, Margaret J. & Farber, Paul L., eds. Religion, Science & Worldview: Essays in Honor of Richard S. Westfall. 320p. 1985. 64.95 (*0-521-30452-0*) Cambridge U Pr.

Osler, Mirabel. The Garden Bench. (Library of Garden Detail). (Illus.). 72p. 1992. 9.95 (*0-671-74403-8*) S&S Trade.

— The Garden Wall. LC 92-27716. (Library of Garden Detail). 1993. 9.95 (*0-671-79689-5*) S&S Trade.

— In the Eye of the Garden. LC 93-49784. 176p. 1994. reprint ed. text ed. 13.00 (*0-02-594065-1*) Macmillan.

— The Secret Gardens of France. 1993. 27.50 (*0-671-79889-8*, Horticulture Bk) P-H Gen Ref & Trav.

Osler, Sonia F. & Cooke, Robert E., eds. The Biosocial Basis of Mental Retardation. LC 65-17078. 168p. reprint ed. pap. 47.90 (*0-8357-7255-1*, 2020731) Bks Demand.

Osler, Tom. The Serious Runner's Handbook. LC 78-367. (Illus.). 187p. 1978. pap. 5.95 (*0-89037-126-1*) Anderson World.

Osler, Tom & Dodd, Ed. Ultramarathoning: The Next Challenge. LC 78-68612. (Illus.). 240p. 1980. 14.95 (*0-89037-169-5*) Anderson World.

Osler, William. Aequanimitas: With Other Addresses to Medical Students, Nurses & Practitioners of Medicine. 3rd ed. 421p. 1932. text ed. 50.00 (*0-07-047915-1*) Hlth Prof Div.

— The Cerebral Palsies of Children: A Clinical Study from the Infirmary for Nervous Diseases, Philadelphia. (Classics in Developmental Medicine Ser.: No. 1). (Illus.). 92p. (C). 1991. 15.95 (*0-521-41326-5*, Pub. by Mc Keith Pr UK) Cambridge U Pr.

— The Evolution of Modern Medicine: A Series of Lectures Delivered at Yale University on the Silliman Foundation in April, 1913. LC 77-140610. (Medicine & Society in America Ser.). (Illus.). 264p. 1980. reprint ed. 24.95 (*0-405-02805-9*) Ayer.

— Science & Immortality. Kastenbaum, Robert, ed. LC 76-19586. (Death & Dying Ser.). 1977. reprint ed. lib. bdg. 17.95 (*0-405-09581-3*) Ayer.

— Student Life, & Other Essays. LC 67-23256. (Essay Index Reprint Ser.). 1977. 18.95 (*0-8369-0756-6*) Ayer.

— A Way of Life. 1937. text ed. 11.95 (*0-06-141860-9*) Lippincott.

— A Way of Life: An Address Delivered to Yale Students Sunday Evening, April 20, 1913. (Illus.). 56p. 1969. 18. 95 (*0-398-01433-7*) C C Thomas.

Osler, William, jt. auth. see McKusick, Victor A.

Osley, A. S. Calligraphy & Palaeography. (Illus.). 1966. 25. 00 (*0-8079-0020-6*) October.

Osley, Carol A. Beyond the Storm. (Orig.). 1985. write for info. (*0-910119-13-9*) SOCO Pubns.

— Computing to Success. (Orig.). 1985. write for info. (*0-910119-14-7*) SOCO Pubns.

— Creative Writing Workbook: Instructor's Manual. 180p. (Orig.). (C). 1983. 15.00 (*0-910119-10-4*) SOCO Pubns.

— Creative Writing Workbook: Student's Manual. 180p. (Orig.). (C). 1983. 15.00 (*0-910119-09-0*) SOCO Pubns.

— Getting Around Writer's Block. 1982. pap. 2.50 (*0-686-39243-4*) SOCO Pubns.

— Helpful Hints for Writers. (Orig.). (C). 1983. pap. 3.00 (*0-910119-06-6*) SOCO Pubns.

— How Not to Get Published. (Orig.). (C). 1983. pap. 2.75 (*0-910119-08-2*) SOCO Pubns.

— How to Properly Prepare Poems. (Orig.). 1983. 4.25 (*0-910119-11-2*) SOCO Pubns.

— How to Set up Secretarial Inservice Classes. (Illus.). 1982. pap. 4.25 (*0-686-39240-X*) SOCO Pubns.

— My Personal Tribute to President Ronald Reagan: The President in Verse. (Orig.). (C). 1983. pap. 4.00 (*0-910119-07-4*) SOCO Pubns.

— Reflections of Love. 42p. (Orig.). 1982. pap. 4.25 (*0-910119-01-5*) SOCO Pubns.

— The Soldier, America & Me. 1982. pap. 4.50 (*0-910119-00-7*) SOCO Pubns.

— The Tender Beguilement. (Orig.). 1985. write for info. (*0-910119-12-0*) SOCO Pubns.

— Writer's Do's & Don'ts. (Orig.). (C). 1982. pap. 2.00 (*0-910119-03-1*) SOCO Pubns.

Oslie, Pamala. Life Colors. LC 91-40295. 380p. 1991. pap. 14.95 (*0-931432-81-2*) New Wrld Lib.

Oslin, George P. The Story of Telecommunications. LC 92-38503. (C). 1992. 35.00 (*0-86554-418-2*) Mercer Univ Pr.

Oslow, Darlene & Shilling, Dana, eds. Hiring Handbook. 400p. 1991. reprint ed. text ed. 96.00 (*1-878375-85-7*) Panel Pubs.

***Osman.** Janani. (Asian Writers Ser.). 213p. 1994. pap. 9.95 (*0-435-95083-5*) Heinemann.

Osman, A. E., et al, eds. The Role of Legumes in the Farming Systems of the Mediterranean Areas. (C). 1990. lib. bdg. 109.50 (*0-7923-0419-5*) Kluwer Ac.

Osman, Ahmed. The House of the Messiah: A Brilliant New Solution to the Enduring Mystery of the Historical Jesus. (Illus.). 243p. (Orig.). 1994. pap. 11.00 (*0-586-21685-5*, IntlDept) HarpC.

— Idegen a Kiralyok Volgyeben: Egy Mumia Titka. Gaal, Violetta, tr. 160p. (HUN.). 1993. 18.48 (*0-9637584-0-3*) Violetta Gaal.

— Moses: Pharoah of Egypt: The Mystery of Akhenaten Resolved. (Illus.). 262p. (Orig.). 1994. pap. 11.00 (*0-586-09034-7*, IntlDept) HarpC.

— Stranger in the Valley of Kings: The Idenfification of Yuya As the Patriarch Joseph. (Illus.). 190p. (Orig.). 1994. pap. 11.00 (*0-586-08784-2*, IntlDept) HarpC.

Osman, Alice H. & McConochie, Jean. If You Feel Like Singing: American Folksongs & Activities for Students of English. (English As a Second Language Bk.). (Illus.). 1979. pap. text ed. 10.95 (*0-582-79724-1*, 74985) Longman.

Osman, Beshir M. Regionalisation in the Sudan. (C). 1986. 29.00 (*0-685-30259-8*, Pub. by Oxford Polytechnic UK) St Mut.

Osman, Betty B. No One to Play With. 1989. pap. 10.00 (*0-87879-687-8*) Acad Therapy.

Osman, Betty B., jt. auth. see Greenhill, Laurence L.

Osman, Christopher, ed. Butterworths Employment Law Guide. 1990. U.K. pap. 84.00 (*0-406-13579-7*) Butterworth Legal Pubs.

Osman, Fathi. Jihad: A Legitimate Struggle for Human Rights. 60p. 1991. pap. text ed. 3.00 (*1-881504-05-0*) Minaret Pubns.

— Muslim Women: In the Family & the Society. 60p. 1991. pap. text ed. 3.00 (*1-881504-02-6*) Minaret Pubns.

— Muslim World Issues & Challenges. 510p. 1989. pap. text ed. 10.00 (*1-881504-06-9*) Minaret Pubns.

Osman, Jack D. Fat Fat Fat: A Threefold Look at Fat Control. LC 84-81813. (Illus.). 134p. (Orig.). 1985. 14. 95 (*0-685-09743-9*); pap. 7.95 (*0-918275-00-8*) Fat Control.

Osman, Jena. Amblyopia. 48p. (Orig.). (C). 1993. pap. text ed. 8.00 (*0-939691-09-4*) Avenue B.

— Amblyopia. deluxe ed. 48p. (Orig.). (C). 1993. pap. text ed. 18.00 (*0-685-66301-9*) Avenue B.

— Twelve Parts of Her. (Burning Deck Poetry Chapbooks Ser.). 24p. 1989. pap. 4.00 (*0-930901-63-0*) Burning Deck.

— Underwater Dive, Version One. (Illus.). 24p. (Orig.). 1990. pap. 4.00 (*0-945926-22-7*) Paradigm RI.

Osman, Jena & Spahr, Juliana, eds. Gender & Editorial Practice. 288p. (C). 1994. pap. 7.95 (*0-922668-12-4*) SUNYB Poetry Rare Bks.

Osman, Karen. Gangs. LC 92-28009. (Overview Ser.). (Illus.). 112p. (J). (gr. 5-8). 1992. lib. bdg. 16.95 (*1-56006-131-6*) Lucent Bks.

Osman, Loren H. W. D. Hoard: A Man for His Time. LC 84-62450. (Illus.). 451p. 1985. 14.95 (*0-932147-00-3*) Hoard & Sons Co.

Osman, Madina & Zorc, R. David. Somali Handbook. LC 92-84028. 84p. (Orig.). 1993. pap. 5.00 (*0-931745-96-9*); audio 5.00 (*0-931745-95-0*) Dunwoody Pr.

Osman, Marilyn & Ruben, Doug. Seducing Spirits. Van Treese, James B., ed. 18p. 1994. pap. 7.95 (*1-56901-021-8*) NW Pub.

Osman, Taib, ed. Malaysian World-View. 294p. 1986. pap. text ed. 14.75 (*9971-988-12-7*, Pub. by Inst SE Asian Studies SI) Ashgate Pub Co.

Osmanczyk, Edmund J., ed. Encyclopedia of the United Nations & International Agreements. 2nd rev. ed. 1059p. 1990. 295.00 (*0-85066-833-6*, Pub. by Tay Francis Ltd UK) Taylor & Francis.

Osmani, S. R., ed. Nutrition & Poverty. (WIDER Studies in Development Economics). (Illus.). 384p. 1993. 65.00 (*0-19-828396-2*) OUP.

Osmania University, Dept. of English Staff. Critical Responses Vol. II: British & American Literature. (C). 1993. 29.50x (*81-207-1636-1*, Pub. by Sterling Plns Pvt II) S Asia.

Osmanov, M. Persian-Russian Dictionary, 2 vols., Set. 1600p. (PER & RUS.). 1983. 95.00 (*0-8288-0800-7*, F46360) Fr & Eur.

Osmaston, A. E. Forest Flora for Kumaon. 605p. (C). 1976. 250.00 (*0-685-21865-1*, Pub. by Intl Bk Distr II) St Mut.

Osmaston, F. B., tr. see Hegel, Georg W.

Osmaston, F. C. Management of Forest. 384p. (C). 1985. reprint ed. 220.00 (*81-7089-031-4*, Pub. by Intl Bk Distr II) St Mut.

Osmer-Newhouse, Carol, jt. auth. see Kaufer, Nelly.

Osmer, Patrick, et al, eds. Proceedings of a Workshop on Optical Surveys for Quasars. LC 88-71919. (Astronomical Society of the Pacific Conference Ser.: Vol. 2). (Illus.). 394p. 1988. 25.00 (*0-937707-19-8*) Astron Soc Pacific.

Osmer, Richard R. A Teachable Spirit: Recovering the Teaching Office in the Church. 340p. (Orig.). 1990. pap. 15.99 (*0-664-25079-3*) Westminster John Knox.

— Teaching for Faith: A Guide for Teachers of Adult Classes. 224p. (Orig.). 1992. pap. 13.99 (*0-664-25217-6*) Westminster John Knox.

***Osmers, R. & Kurjak, A.** Ultrasound & the Uterus. (Progress in Obstetric & Gynecological Sonography Ser.). (Illus.). 150p. (C). 1995. text ed. 78.00 (*1-85070-613-1*) Prthnon Pub.

Osmon, Humphry, jt. auth. see Hoffer, Abram.

Osmond & Hoffer. New Hope for Alcoholics. 7.50 (*0-8216-0007-9*, Univ Bks) Carol Pub Group.

Osmond, C. B., et al, eds. Plant Biology of the Basin & Range. (Ecological Studies: Vol. 80). 384p. 1990. 83.00 (*0-387-51219-5*) Spr-Verlag.

Osmond, D., tr. see Steiner, Rudolf.

Osmond, D. S., tr. see Steiner, Rudolf.

Osmond, Dorothy, tr. see Steiner, Rudolf.

Osmond, Dorothy S., tr. see Steiner, Rudolf.

Osmond, J. K. & Cowart, J. B. Natural Uranium & Thorium Series Disequilibrium: New Approaches to Geochemical Problems. (Nuclear Science Applications Ser.: Section B). 50p. 1982. pap. text ed. 61.00 (*3-7186-0131-1*) Gordon & Breach.

***Osmond, John.** Changing Wales Vol. III: The Democratic Challenge. 1993. pap. 21.00 (*0-86383-927-4*, Pub. by Gomer Pr UK) St Mut.

— The Reality of Dyslexia. 1995. pap. text ed. 14.95 (*0-614-05646-2*) Brookline Bks.

— The Reality of Dyslexia. (Education Ser.). (Illus.). 160p. 1993. 60.00 (*0-304-32762-X*); pap. 22.50 (*0-304-32763-8*) Weidner & Sons.

Osmond, John, ed. The National Question Again. 323p. (C). 1985. pap. 20.00x (*0-86383-132-X*, Pub. by Gomer Pr UK) St Mut.

Osmond, Nick, ed. see Rimbaud, Arthur.

Osmond, Olive D. Let's Be Organized: How to Organize Your Entire Life with 5 x 8 Cards. (Illus.). (Orig.). 1990. pap. text ed. 5.95 (*0-929786-00-9*) Know Unltd UT.

— Mother Osmond's Favorite Recipes, Vol. I. 150p. 1990. pap. text ed. write for info. (*0-929786-01-7*) Know Unltd UT.

Osmond, P. The Mystical Poets of the English Church. 1972. 59.95 (*0-8490-0696-1*) Gordon Pr.

Osmond, Rosalie. Mutual Accusation: Seventeenth-Century Body & Soul Dialogues in Their Literary & Theological Context. 272p. 1990. 50.00 (*0-8020-5843-4*) U of Toronto Pr.

Osmond-Smith, David. Berio. (Oxford Studies of Composers: No. 20). (Illus.). 176p. 1991. 49.95 (*0-19-315478-1*); pap. 21.00 (*0-19-315455-2*) OUP.

Osmond-Smith, David, ed. see Berio, Luciano, et al.

Osmond, Tony, jt. auth. see Lambert, David.

Osmont, Kelly. More Than Surviving: Caring for Yourself While You Grieve. (Illus.). 52p. (Orig.). 1990. pap. 3.75 (*1-56123-004-9*) Centering Corp.

— What Can I Say? How to Help Someone Who Is Grieving: A Guide. McFarlane, Marilyn, ed. 36p. 1988. pap. 3.95 (*0-941211-02-9*) Nobility Pr.

Osmont, Kelly & McFarlane, Marilyn. Parting Is Not Goodbye. LC 86-63796. 144p. (Orig.). 1987. 19.95 (*0-941211-00-2*); pap. 17.95 (*0-941211-01-0*) Nobility Pr.

Osmont, Marie L. Normandy Diary of Marie Louise Osmot. 1994. 17.00 (*0-679-43438-0*) Random.

Osmowej, M. N. Polish-Russian Dictionary of Economics. deluxe ed. 494p. (POL & RUS.). 1977. 35.00 (*0-8288-5511-0*, M9121) Fr & Eur.

Osmun, et al. Discoveries in Earth Science: Testing Program Master Sheets. 56p. (Orig.). 1990. 49.95 (*0-937323-10-1*) United Pub Co.

Osmun, Richard, et al. Discoveries in Earth Science. (Upco's Science Ser.). (Illus.). (Orig.). 1987. teacher ed 9.95 (*0-937323-07-1*); student ed 5.95 (*0-937323-06-3*) United Pub Co.

Osmundson, T. Roof Garden Design & Implementation. 1985. text ed. write for info. (*0-442-27297-9*) Van Nos Reinhold.

Osmus, Kathy, ed. see Echaore-Yoon, Susan.

Osmus, Mary R. Machine Embroidery: Stitches & Techniques Instruction Workbook. 130p. 1990. Spiral bdg., wkbk. student ed, spiral bd. 22.95 (*1-883118-01-8*) MRayOs Fiberwrks.

— Machine Embroidery, Vol. I: Beginning & Intermediate Patterns. 64p. 1992. student ed 15.95 (*1-883118-02-6*) MRayOs Fiberwrks.

— Machine Embroidery, Vol. II: Intermediate & Advanced Patterns. 106p. 1992. student ed 19.95 (*1-883118-03-4*) MRayOs Fiberwrks.

Osnato, John, Jr. Lawyer in the House. 1994. 16.95 (*0-533-10811-X*) Vantage.

Osnes, E., jt. auth. see Kuo, T. T.

Osnos, Peter, ed. see Birnbaum, Jeffrey H. & Murray, Alan S.

Osoba, David. Effect of Cancer on Quality of Life. 1991. 115.00 (0-8493-6977-0, SB324) CRC Pr.

Osoba, Segun, jt. ed. see Ikime, Obaro.

***Osofisan, Femi.** The Oriki of a Grasshopper, & Other Plays. LC 95-6636. 1995. write for info. (0-88258-181-3) Howard U Pr.

Osofsky, Audrey. Dreamcatcher. LC 91-20029. (Illus.). 32p. (J). (ps-2). 1992. 15.95 (0-531-05988-X); lib. bdg. 15.99 (0-531-08588-0) Orchard Bks Watts.

— My Buddy. LC 92-3028. (Illus.). 32p. (J). (gr. k-3). 1992. 14.95 (0-8050-1747-X, Bks Young Read) H Holt & Co.

— My Buddy. (Illus.). (J). (PS-3). 1994. pap. 5.95 (0-8050-3546-X) H Holt & Co.

Osofsky, Barbara L. Homological Dimensions of Modules. LC 72-6826. (CBMS Regional Conference Series in Mathematics: No. 12). 89p. 1979. reprint ed. pap. 17.00 (0-8218-1662-4, CBMS-12) Am Math.

Osofsky, Howard J. & Blumenthal, Susan J. Premenstrual Syndrome: Current Findings & Future Directions. LC 85-6100. (Progress in Psychiatry Ser.). 112p. 1985. text ed. 21.00 (0-88048-071-8, 48-071-8) Am Psychiatric.

Osofsky, Joy D., ed. Handbook of Infant Development. 2nd ed. LC 86-28906. (Personality Processes Ser.). 1424p. 1987. text ed. 162.50 (0-471-88565-7) Wiley.

Osorio, Fernando C., jt. auth. see Glorioso, Robert M.

Osorio Lizarazа, J. A. The Illuminated Island. Nolan, James I., tr. 1976. lib. bdg. 59.95 (0-8490-2034-4) Gordon Pr.

Osoro, R. The African Identity in Crisis. (African Identity, Negation Freedom Ser.). (C). 1993. pap. text ed. 17.95 (0-9636956-0-6) Bayana Pubs.

Osostowicz, Krysia, tr. see Eigeldinger, Jean-Jacques.

O'Souza, Philip. Of Human Phenomena. 136p. 1985. 13.95 (0-318-37151-0) Asia Bk Corp.

Ospina, Clara, jt. auth. see Dorland, Gil.

Ospina, Enrique & Sims, Cami S., eds. The Role of State Government in Agriculture. 153p. 1988. per. 16.00 (0-933595-16-6) Winrock Intl.

Ospina, Enrique, jt. auth. see Gunderson, Ralph O.

***Ospina, Hernando C.** Salsa! (Illus.). 180p. 1995. pap. 14.00 (0-85345-956-8, PB9568) Monthly Rev.

Ospital, John. We Wore Jump Boots & Baggy Pants. (Illus.). 118p. (Orig.). 1977. pap. 8.75 (0-89839-047-8) Battery Pr.

Ospovat, Dov. The Development of Darwin's Theory: Natural History, Natural Theology, & Natural Selection, 1838-1859. LC 81-4077. (Illus.). 228p. 1994. 52.50 (0-521-23818-8) Cambridge U Pr.

— The Development of Darwin's Theory: Natural History, Natural Theology, & Natural Selection, 1838-1859. (Illus.). 320p. (C). 1995. pap. 22.95 (0-521-46940-6) Cambridge U Pr.

Osprey. Airfreighters. 1990. 12.99 (0-517-01220-0) Random Hse Value.

Oss, Kathleen A., jt. auth. see Bean, Barton A.

Oss, O. T. & Oeric, O. N. Psilocybin: Magic Mushroom Growers Guide. (Illus.). 100p. (Orig.). reprint ed. pap. 16.95 (0-932551-06-8) Quick Am Pub.

Ossa, Mikka. The Serpentine Rouletted Stamps of Finland: Issues of 1860 & 1866, Vol. 2. Koplowitz, G. B., ed. Aro, Kauko I., tr. (Illus.). 116p. (Orig.). 1985. pap. text ed. 18.50 (0-936493-08-9) Scand Philatelic.

Ossana, Diana, jt. auth. see McMurtry, Larry.

Osselton, John W., et al. Manual of Clinical Neurophysiology, Vol. 1. (Illus.). 448p. 1994. 125.00 (0-7506-1183-9) Buttrwrth-Heinemann.

Ossenbruggen, Paul J. Fundamental Principles of Systems Analysis & Decision-Making. LC 93-35998. 1994. pap. text ed. write for info. (0-471-52156-6) Wiley.

— Systems Analysis for Civil Engineers. LC 83-14595. 571p. 1984. Net. text ed. write for info. (0-471-09889-2); teacher ed 20.00 (0-471-89118-5) Wiley.

Ossendowski, Ferdinand. Beasts, Men & Gods. 1991. lib. bdg. 79.95 (0-8490-5030-8) Gordon Pr.

Osseo-Asare, Fran. Good Soup Attracts Chairs: A First African Cookbook for American Kids. LC 92-42982. (Illus.). 160p. 1993. 18.95 (0-88289-816-7) Pelican.

Osseo-Asare, K., ed. see International Symposium on Hydrometallurgy Staff.

Osserman, R., jt. auth. see Hoffman, D. A.

Osserman, R., ed. see Pure Mathematics Symposium Staff.

Osserman, Richard A., jt. auth. see Ruskay, Joseph A.

***Osserman, Robert.** Poetry of the Universe: A Mathematical Exploration of the Cosmos. LC 94-27971. (Illus.). 210p. 1995. 18.95 (0-385-47340-0, Anchor NY) Doubleday.

— A Survey of Minimal Surfaces. 192p. 1986. reprint ed. pap. 8.95 (0-486-64998-9) Dover.

Osserman, Robert & Weinstein, Alan, eds. Geometry of the LaPlace Operator. LC 79-26934. (Proceedings of Symposia in Pure Mathematics Ser., Humboldt State University, Arcata, CA, July 29-August 16, 1974: Vol. 36). 323p. 1982. reprint ed. pap. 42.00 (0-8218-1439-7, PSPUM-36) Am Math.

Ossian. Poems of Ossian. 492p. reprint ed. lib. bdg. 79.00 (0-7812-0259-0) Rprt Serv.

— Poems of Ossian. Macpherson, James, ed. LC 76-107180. 1970. reprint ed. 49.00 (0-403-00036-X) Scholarly.

Ossianic Society of Dublin Staff. Transactions, 6 Vols, Set. LC 78-144462. reprint ed. 72.50 (0-404-09070-2) AMS Pr.

Ossiannilsson, F. The Auchenorrhyncha (Homoptera) of Fennoscandia & Denmark, Pt. 1: Introduction, Infraorder Fulgoromorpha. (Fauna Entomologica Scandinavica Ser.: No. 7-1). (Illus.). 222p. 1978. text ed. 42.00 (87-87491-24-9) Lubrecht & Cramer.

— The Auchenorrhyncha (Hompotera) of Fennoscandia & Denmark, Pt. 2: The Families Cicadidae, Cercopidae, Membracidae, & Cicadellidae (Excluding Deltocephalinae) (Fauna Entomologica Scandinavica Ser.: No. 7-2). (Illus.). 408p. 1981. text ed. 53.00 (87-87491-36-2) Lubrecht & Cramer.

— The Psylloidea (Homoptera) of Fennoscandia & Demark. LC 92-16949. (Fauna Entomologica Scandinavica Ser.: Vol. 26). (Illus.). 347p. 1992. 103.00 (90-04-09610-8) E J Brill.

Ossif & Karlan. Laser Surgery in Otolaryngology. 1991. 42.95 (0-8151-6574-9, Yr Bk Med Pubs) Mosby Yr Bk.

Ossin, Archie & Ossin, Myrna. How to Start & Run a Profitable Craft Business. LC 77-88745. (Illus.). (C). 1977. pap. 7.95 (0-930912-00-4) Ossi Pubns.

Ossin, Myrna, ed. Culinary Arts & Crafts, a Cookbook for Moms, Dads & Kids. (Illus.). 1984. pap. 12.00 (0-9613532-0-1) Park Maitland.

Ossin, Myrna, jt. auth. see Ossin, Archie.

Ossip, Kathleen. Living English for Spanish Speakers. (Complete Living Language Course Ser.). (ENG & SPA.). 1993. 20.00 (0-517-59045-X, Living Language) Crown Pub Group.

— Living English for Spanish Speakers: Conversational Manual. rev. ed. (Complete Living Language Course Ser.). (ENG & SPA.). 1993. pap. 6.00 (0-517-59046-8, Living Language) Crown Pub Group.

— Living English for the Spanish Speaker: Dictionary. rev. ed. (Complete Living Language Course Ser.). (ENG & SPA.). 1993. pap. 5.00 (0-517-59047-6, Living Language) Crown Pub Group.

Ossipov, Dimitri, tr. see Zigel, Felix Y.

***Ossipova, Victoria.** Introduction to Discrete Mathematics. LC 94-44215. 1994. write for info. (1-885978-00-6); pap. write for info. (1-885978-01-4) Wrld Fed Pubs.

Ossman, David. Hopi Set. 12p. 1985. pap. 12.00 (0-918824-52-4) Turkey Pr.

— The Moon Sign Book: A Book of Poetry. 24p. 1984. pap. text ed. 12.00 (0-918824-44-3) Turkey Pr.

— The Rainbow Cafe. limited ed. (Illus.). 20p. 1982. 12.00 (0-918824-37-0) Turkey Pr.

Ossman, Susan. Setting Sights: Pictures, People & Power in Casablanca. LC 93-36561. 1994. 40.00x (0-520-08402-0); pap. 15.00 (0-520-08403-9) U CA Pr.

Ossoff & Duncavage. Lasers in Otolaryngology: Head & Neck Surgery. (Illus.). 400p. 1991. 92.50 (0-8016-3749-X) Mosby Yr Bk.

Ossoff, Robert H., jt. auth. see Krespi, Yosef P.

Ossoinig, K. C., ed. Ophthalmic Echography. (Documenta Ophthalmologica Proceedings Ser.). (C). 1987. lib. bdg. 257.50 (0-89838-873-2) Kluwer Ac.

Ossoli, Margaret F. Summer on the Lakes. LC 68-24991. (Concordance Ser.: No. 37). 1969. reprint ed. lib. bdg. 75.00 (0-8383-0225-4) M S G Haskell Hse.

— Woman in the Nineteenth Century: And Kindred Papers Relating to the Sphere, Condition & Duties, of Woman. Fuller, Arthur B., ed. LC 72-312. (Essay Index Reprint Ser.). 1977. reprint ed. 26.95 (0-8369-2815-6) Ayer.

— Woman in the Nineteenth Century & Kindred Papers. 1972. 59.95 (0-8490-1315-1) Gordon Pr.

Ossoli, Margaret S. Love Letters of Margaret Fuller 1845-1846. LC 72-122592. reprint ed. 41.50 (0-404-04835-8) AMS Pr.

— Papers on Literature & Art, 2 pts. in 1. LC 76-144668. reprint ed. 49.50 (0-404-04836-6) AMS Pr.

Ossoli, Sarah. Writings of Margaret Fuller. (BCL1-PS American Literature Ser.). 608p. 1993. reprint ed. lib. bdg. 109.00 (0-7812-6996-2) Rprt Serv.

Ossoli, Sarah M. Love-Letters of Margaret Fuller, 1845-1846. (BCL1-PS American Literature Ser.). 228p. 1992. reprint ed. lib. bdg. 79.00 (0-7812-6817-6) Rprt Serv.

— Marchesa D'. Summer on the Lakes in 1843. (BCL1 - United States Local History Ser.). 256p. 1991. reprint ed. lib. bdg. 79.00 (0-7812-6320-4) Rprt Serv.

— Papers on Literature & Art, 2 vols. in 1, Set. (BCL1-PS American Literature Ser.). 1992. reprint ed. lib. bdg. 99.00 (0-7812-6816-8) Rprt Serv.

— Writings of Margaret Fuller. Wade, Mason, ed. LC 72-122079. 1973. reprint ed. lib. bdg. 49.50 (0-678-03177-0) Kelley.

Ossorio, Joseph D. & Salvadeo, Michele B. How Did Cats Get Their Tails. (Under Twenty Writing Society Ser.). (Illus.). 48p. (J). (gr. 2-4). 1994. pap. 6.95 (1-56721-055-4) Twnty-Fifth Cent Pr.

— Mikey's Walk in Space. (Under Twenty Writing Society Ser.). (Illus.). 60p. (J). (gr. 4-6). 1994. pap. 6.95 (1-56721-053-8) Twnty-Fifth Cent Pr.

— Misadventures of the Friendly Shark. (Under Twenty Writing Society Ser.). (Illus.). 60p. (J). (gr. 3-5). 1994. pap. 6.95 (1-56721-054-6) Twnty-Fifth Cent Pr.

Ossorio, Joseph D., jt. auth. see Salvadeo, Michele B.

Ossorio, Joseph D., et al. The Court of the Lost Woods. (Under Twenty Writing Society Ser.). (Illus.). 48p. (J). (gr. 3-5). 1994. pap. 6.95 (1-56721-052-X) Twnty-Fifth Cent Pr.

— Drums. (Under Twenty Writing Society Ser.). (Illus.). 48p. (J). (gr. 3-5). 1994. pap. 6.95 (1-56721-078-3) Twnty-Fifth Cent Pr.

— Kid's Writing Society Membership Manual. (Under Twenty Writing Society Ser.). (Illus.). 60p. (J). (gr. 4-7). 1994. pap. 6.95 (1-56721-071-6) Twnty-Fifth Cent Pr.

— The Little Duke. (Under Twenty Writing Society Ser.). (Illus.). 48p. (J). (gr. 3-5). 1994. pap. 6.95 (1-56721-049-X) Twnty-Fifth Cent Pr.

— Poor, Rich & Happy. (Life's Roadmap Ser.). (Illus.). 60p. (J). (gr. 4-6). 1994. pap. 6.95 (1-56721-043-0) Twnty-Fifth Cent Pr.

— Truth about the Chase. (Life's Roadmap Ser.). (Illus.). 60p. (J). (gr. 4-6). 1994. pap. 6.95 (1-56721-044-9) Twnty-Fifth Cent Pr.

— Under Twenty Writing Society Membership Manual. (Under Twenty Writing Society Ser.). (Illus.). 72p. (YA). (gr. 8-12). 1994. pap. 8.95 (1-56721-072-4) Twnty-Fifth Cent Pr.

***Ossorio, Manuel.** Spanish Dictionary of Law & Political & Social Science. 21th rev. ed. 1030p. 1994. 60.00x (950-885-005-1) IBD Ltd.

***Ossorio, Nelson A.** Danger in the Land of Mavericks. (Orig.). 1995. pap. 11.95 (1-56721-124-0) Twnty-Fifth Cent Pr.

— Dignity: The Key to Giving. (Orig.). 1995. pap. 10.95 (1-56721-099-6) Twnty-Fifth Cent Pr.

— Insights from the Other Side of Life. (Orig.). 1995. pap. 10.95 (1-56721-123-2) Twnty-Fifth Cent Pr.

— Journeys Through Time. (Orig.). 1995. pap. 8.95 (1-56721-113-5) Twnty-Fifth Cent Pr.

— The Myth of Teaching. (Orig.). 1995. pap. 8.95 (1-56721-122-4) Twnty-Fifth Cent Pr.

— Power of the Shadow. (Orig.). 1995. pap. 11.95 (1-56721-119-4) Twnty-Fifth Cent Pr.

— Reflections on Being. (Orig.). 1995. pap. 10.95 (1-56721-112-7) Twnty-Fifth Cent Pr.

— Selections from the Journeys - Selecciones de las Jornadas. 3rd ed. (Illus.). 140p. (Orig.). (ENG & SPA.). 1994. 14.95 (1-56721-088-0) Twnty-Fifth Cent Pr.

— Something to Lose. (Orig.). 1995. pap. 12.95 (1-56721-091-0) Twnty-Fifth Cent Pr.

— A Stroll Through Life. (Orig.). 1995. pap. 11.95 (1-56721-111-9) Twnty-Fifth Cent Pr.

***Ossorio, Nelson A. & Eisberg, George.** The Mountains of Glemts. (Orig.). 1995. pap. 12.95 (1-56721-121-6) Twnty-Fifth Cent Pr.

***Ossorio, Nelson A. & Eisberg, George L.** The Book of Forgiveness. (Orig.). 1995. pap. 8.95 (1-56721-095-3) Twnty-Fifth Cent Pr.

— The Caves of Amanao. (Orig.). 1995. pap. 12.95 (1-56721-120-8) Twnty-Fifth Cent Pr.

— Flowers on the Road. (Orig.). 1995. pap. 8.95 (1-56721-105-4) Twnty-Fifth Cent Pr.

— For Children over Fifty. (Orig.). 1995. pap. 10.95 (1-56721-129-1) Twnty-Fifth Cent Pr.

— The Helpful Hand. (Orig.). 1995. pap. 6.95 (1-56721-094-5) Twnty-Fifth Cent Pr.

— The Road Taken. (Orig.). 1995. pap. 11.95 (1-56721-107-0) Twnty-Fifth Cent Pr.

— To Tread Gently. (Orig.). 1995. pap. 8.95 (1-56721-098-8) Twnty-Fifth Cent Pr.

— To Walk in Silence. (Orig.). 1995. pap. 9.95 (1-56721-131-3) Twnty-Fifth Cent Pr.

Ossorio, Nelson A. & Salvadeo, Michele B. Boy of la Mancha. (Spark of Life Ser.). (Illus.). 60p. (J). (gr. 4-6). 1994. pap. 6.95 (1-56721-068-6) Twnty-Fifth Cent Pr.

— Castles & Other Dreams. (Life's Roadmap Ser.). (Illus.). 60p. (J). (gr. 4-6). 1994. pap. 6.95 (1-56721-065-1) Twnty-Fifth Cent Pr.

— Horse in the Bleachers. (Illus.). 60p. (J). (gr. 4-6). 1994. pap. 6.95 (1-56721-058-9) Twnty-Fifth Cent Pr.

— Puppy & the Parrot. (Illus.). 60p. (J). (gr. 4-6). 1994. pap. 6.95 (1-56721-059-7) Twnty-Fifth Cent Pr.

— The Song No One Liked. (To Be Your Own Ser.). (Illus.). 48p. (J). (gr. 3-5). 1994. pap. 6.95 (1-56721-050-3) Twnty-Fifth Cent Pr.

— To Be Beautiful: or The Story of the Butterfly. (To Be Your Own Ser.). (Illus.). 48p. (J). (gr. 3-5). 1994. pap. 6.95 (1-56721-046-5) Twnty-Fifth Cent Pr.

Ossorio, Nelson A., jt. ed. see Bolinger, Loren.

Ossorio, Nelson A., jt. auth. see Eisberg, George L.

Ossorio, Nelson A., jt. auth. see Rotton, Peter J.

Ossorio, Nelson A., jt. auth. see Rotton, Wendy.

Ossorio, Nelson A., et al. Through Grandpa's Eyes. (We Are All Whole Ser.). (Illus.). 60p. (J). (gr. 4-6). 1994. pap. 6.95 (1-56721-051-1) Twnty-Fifth Cent Pr.

— Tiger's New Prey. (Wildlife among Us Ser.). (Illus.). 48p. (J). (gr. 4-6). 1994. pap. 6.95 (1-56721-074-0) Twnty-Fifth Cent Pr.

— To Run Like the Wind: or The Wisdom of the Cheetah. (To Be Your Own Ser.). (Illus.). 48p. (J). (gr. 4-6). 1994. pap. 6.95 (1-56721-047-3) Twnty-Fifth Cent Pr.

Ossowski, Leonie. Star Without a Sky. LC 84-21834. Orig. Title: Stern Ohne Himmel. 216p. (J). (gr. 3-6). 1985. 19.95 (0-8225-0771-4, Lerner Publctns) Lerner Group.

Osswald, W., ed. Problems of Adrenergic Mechanisms in Blood Vessel. (Journal: Blood Vessels: Vol. 21, No. 3, 1984). (Illus.). 44p. 1984. pap. 32.00 (3-8055-3927-4) S Karger.

Ost, B. W., jt. auth. see Burg, R. G.

Ost, David. Solidarity & the Politics of Anti-Politics: Opposition & Reform in Poland since 1968. (Labor & Social Change Ser.). 272p. (C). 1990. 39.95 (0-87722-655-5); pap. 18.95 (0-87722-900-7) Temple U Pr.

Ost, David, ed. see Michnik, Adam.

Ost, Francois & Van de Kerchove, Michel. The Legal System: Between Order & Disorder. Stewart, Iain, tr. 224p. 1994. 45.00 (0-19-825692-2) OUP.

Ost, Hans. Leonardo-Studien. (Beitraege zur Kunstgeschichte Ser.: Vol. 11). (Illus.). xii, 750p. (GER.). (C). 1975. 165.40 (3-11-005727-1) De Gruyter.

Ostacher, Joan, ed. see Rothstein, Evelyn, et al.

Ostacher, Joan, ed. see Waters, Michelle & Mehlmann, Marybeth.

Ostacher, Joan, ed. see Waters, Michelle & Mehlmann, Marybeth A.

Ostadal, Bohuslav & Dhalla, Naranjan S., eds. Heart Function in Health & Disease: Proceedings of the Cardiovascular Program Sponsored by the Council of Cardiac Metabolism of the International Society & Federation of Cardiology During the Regional Meeting of the International Union of Physiological Sciences, Prague, Czechoslovakia, June 30 - July 5, 1991. LC 92-48911. (Developments in Cardiovascular Medicine Ser.: Vol. DICM 140). 352p. (C). 1993. lib. bdg. 115.00 (0-7923-2052-2) Kluwer Ac.

Ostapenko, N. I., et al. Spectroscopy of Defects in Organic Crystals. Onipko, Alexander I., tr. LC 93-3224. 272p. (C). 1993. Acid-free paper. lib. bdg. 123.00 (0-7923-2230-4) Kluwer Ac.

Ostar, Allan W., jt. auth. see Harcleroad, Fred F.

***Ostarch, Valerie, et al.** S.A.T. - P.S.A.T. The Betz Guide. (Betz Guide Ser.: 8). (Illus.). 128p. (Orig.). (YA). (gr. 7-12). 1995. pap. 12.95 (0-941406-50-4) Betz Pub Co Inc.

Ostaszewski, A. Advanced Mathematical Methods. (London School of Economics Mathematics Ser.). (Illus.). 400p. (C). 1991. 125.00 (0-521-24788-8); pap. 42.95 (0-521-28964-5) Cambridge U Pr.

Ostaszewski, Adam. Mathematics in Economics: Models & Methods. LC 92-32454. 1993. 54.95 (0-631-18055-9); pap. 29.95 (0-631-18056-7) Blackwell Pubs.

Ostaszewski, K. Henstock Integration in the Plane. LC 86-17399. (Memoirs of the American Mathematical Society Ser.: No. 63/353). 106p. 1986. pap. text ed. 21.00 (0-8218-2416-3, MEMO 63/353) Am Math.

Ostaszewski, Krzysztof. An Investigation into Possible Applications of Fuzzy Set Methods in Actuarial Science. 1993. text ed. 20.00 (0-938959-27-1) Soc Actuaries.

Ostberg, Donald E., jt. auth. see Finney, Ross L.

Ostberg, Donald R., jt. auth. see Lynch, Ransom V.

Ostberg, Kay. If You Want to Sue a Lawyer: A Directory of Legal Malpractice Attorneys. (Random House Practical Law Manual Ser.). 127p. 1991. pap. 10.00 (0-679-73870-3) HALT DC.

— Probate - Settling an Estate: A Step-by-Step Guide. (Random House Practical Law Manual Ser.). 162p. 1990. pap. write for info. (0-679-72960-7) HALT DC.

— Using a Lawyer. (Random House Practical Law Manual Ser.). 146p. 1990. pap. write for info. (0-679-72970-4) HALT DC.

Ostblom, Svante, jt. auth. see Karlof, Bengt.

Ostby, C. Kittelsen, Theodore: Drawings & Water Colors. 1978. 85.00 (82-09-01227-4, N-534) Vanous.

Ostby, Marnald. Matching Up: Winning with Team Defense. 57p. (Orig.). 1985. pap. 8.95 (0-932741-03-7) Championship Bks & Vid Prodns.

Ostdiek, Gilbert. Catechesis for Liturgy. 1986. 10.95 (0-912405-23-6) Pastoral Pr.

Ostdiek, Vern J. & Bord, Donald J. Inquiry into Physics. 2nd ed. Westby, ed. 572p. (C). 1991. text ed. 59.75 (0-314-79885-4) West Pub.

— Inquiry into Physics. 3rd ed. LC 94-33566. 575p. 1994. pap. text ed. 54.75 (0-314-04354-3) West Pub.

Osteaux, M. & Meirleir, K., eds. Magnetic Resonance Imaging & Spectroscopy in Sports Medicine. (Illus.). 216p. 1991. 109.00 (0-387-52548-3) Spr-Verlag.

Osteaux, M., et al, eds. Hospital Integrated Picture Archiving & Communication Systems: A Second Generation PACS Concept. (Illus.). 384p. 1992. 198.00 (0-387-54592-1) Spr-Verlag.

Osteen, jt. auth. see Steele.

O'Steen, Darlene, jt. auth. see Needle's Prayse Staff.

Osteen, Ike. A Place Called Baca. LC 79-51775. 1979. lib. bdg. 10.75 (0-9602724-0-2) I Osteen.

Osteen, John. Reigning in Life As a King. 140p. (Orig.). 1984. pap. 4.95 (0-912631-01-5) J O Pubns.

— There Is a Miracle in Your Mouth. pap. 1.99 (0-912631-14-7) J O Pubns.

***Osteen, Mark.** The Economy of Ulysses: Making Both Ends Meet. (Irish Studies). 416p. 1995. text ed. 49.95x (0-8156-2653-3); pap. text ed. 17.95x (0-8156-2661-4) Syracuse U Pr.

O'Steen, Neal. Making Heroes of Scholars: The Honor Society of Phi Kappa Phi, 1971-1983. (Illus.). 142p. 1985. 10.00 (0-9614651-0-7); pap. 6.00 (0-9614651-1-5) Honor Soc P K P.

Osten, James, ed. see Siembieda, Kevin & Bartold, Thomas.

Osten-Sacken, C. R. & Smith, K. G. Record of My Life-Work in Entomology. 1978. 50.00 (0-317-07172-6) St Mut.

Osten, Wolfgang, et al, eds. Fringe, '89: Automatic Processing of Fringe Patterns. (Chemical Research Ser.: Vol. 10). 168p. 1989. pap. text ed. 27.00 (3-05-500682-8) VCH Pubs.

Ostendarp, Carol, jt. auth. see Hekelman, Francine.

Ostendorf, Lloyd. Photographs of Mary Todd Lincoln. 64p. 1989. reprint ed. pap. text ed. 5.00 (0-942579-05-4) IHPA.

Ostendorf, Lloyd, jt. auth. see Hamilton, Charles.

Ostendorf, Virginia A., jt. ed. see Roybal, Mary A.

Ostenfeld, E. Forms Matter & Mind. 1982. lib. bdg. 94.00 (90-247-3051-1) Kluwer Ac.

Ostenfeld, Erik. Ancient Greek Psychology and the Modern Mind-Body Debate. 109p. (Orig.). 1986. pap. 20.00 (87-7288-010-4) Coronet Bks.

Oster. Assessing Adolescents. (C). 1988. pap. 19.95 (0-205-14444-6, H4444) Allyn.

Oster, Andrew G., tr. see Burghardt, Erich.

Oster, Clinton V., Jr., jt. auth. see Meyer, John R.

Oster, Clinton V., Jr., et al. Why Airplanes Crash: Aviation Safety in a Changing World. 192p. 1992. 29.95 (0-19-507223-5) OUP.

Oster, Don. Largemouth Bass. LC 83-166989. (Hunting & Fishing Library). (Illus.). 160p. 1983. 19.95 (0-86573-005-9) Cy De Cosse.

Oster, Ernst, tr. see Schenker, Heinrich.

Oster, G. F., et al, eds. Irreversible Thermodynamics & the Origin of Life. 80p. 1974. text ed. 114.00 (0-677-14270-6) Gordon & Breach.

Oster, George F. & Wilson, Edward O. Caste & Ecology in the Social Insects. LC 78-51185. (Monographs in Population Biology: Vol. 12). (Illus.). 1978. pap. 19.95 (0-691-02361-1) Princeton U Pr.

Oster, Gerald D. & Caro, Janice E. Understanding & Treating Depressed Adolescents & Their Families. LC 08-937665. (Personality Processes Ser.). 228p. 1990. text ed. 52.50 (0-471-60897-1) Wiley.

Oster, Gerald D. & Gould, Patricia. Using Drawings in Assessment & Therapy: A Guide for Mental Health Professionals. LC 86-30958. (Illus.). 208p. 1987. pap. 21.95 (0-87630-478-1) Brunner-Mazel.

Oster, Gerald D. & Montgomery, Sarah. Helping Your Depressed Teenager: A Guide for Parents & Caregivers. LC 94-16197. 1994. pap. text ed. 16.95 (0-471-62184-6) Wiley.

Oster, Judith. Toward Robert Frost: The Reader & the Poet. LC 90-11277. 352p. 1991. 45.00 (0-8203-1322-X) U of Ga Pr.

— Toward Robert Frost: The Reader & the Poet. LC 90-11277. 352p. 1994. pap. 20.00 (0-8203-1621-0) U of Ga Pr.

Oster, Kurt A., et al. Homogenized Milk May Cause Your Heart Attack: The XO Factor. (Advances in Preventive Health Ser.). (Illus.). 312p. (Orig.). 1983. 14.95 (0-943550-01-7); pap. 10.95 (0-943550-02-5) Park City Pr.

***Oster, Maggie.** Bamboo Baskets: Japanese Art & Culture Interwoven with the Beauty of Ikebana. (Illus.). 144p. 1995. 34.95 (0-670-86187-1, Viking Studio); pap. 22.95 (0-14-024341-0, Viking Studio) Studio Bks.

— Flowering Herbs Postcard Book. 48p. 1992. 6.95 (0-681-41661-0) Longmeadow Pr.

— Gift & Crafts from the Garden. LC 88-14845. 192p. 1988. 19.95 (0-87857-775-0, 01-144-0) Rodale Pr Inc.

— Gifts & Crafts from the Garden: Over 100 Easy-to-Make Projects. LC 93-3939. 1993. reprint ed. 11.99 (0-517-09363-4, Pub. by Wings Bks) Random Hse Value.

— Herbal Vinegar. Steege, Gwen, ed. LC 93-20858. (Illus.). 176p. 1994. 18.95 (0-88266-876-5, Storey Pub); pap. text ed. 12.95 (0-88266-843-9) Storey Comm Inc.

— The Potato Garden: A Grower's Guide. LC 92-31649. (Illus.). 128p. 1993. 17.00 (0-517-59117-0, Harmony) Crown Pub Group.

— Recipes from an American Herb Garden. LC 92-31370. 160p. 1993. text ed. 30.00 (0-02-594025-2) Macmillan.

— Reflections of the Spirit: Japanese Gardens in America. (Illus.). 240p. 1993. 40.00 (0-525-93566-5, Dutton Studio) Studio Bks.

— Reflections of the Spirit: Japanese Gardens in America. (Illus.). 240p. 1994. 25.00 (0-525-48618-6, Viking Studio) Studio Bks.

— The Rose Book: How to Grow Roses Organically & Use Them in over 50 Beautiful Crafts. (Illus.). 288p. 1994. 24.95 (0-87596-607-1) Rodale Pr Inc.

Oster, Merrill J. Commodity Futures for Profit. LC 77-92119. 1983. 30.00 (0-914230-04-2) Investor Pubns.

— How to Multiply Your Money. LC 78-14888. 1985. 14.95 (0-914230-03-4) Investor Pubns.

Oster, Merrill J., et al. Multiply Your Money Trading Soybeans: A Beginner's Guide to Speculating in Soybean Futures. 198p. 1981. 14.95 (0-914230-10-7) Investor Pubns.

Oster, Patrick. The Mexicans: A Personal Portrait of a People. LC 89-45843. 352p. 1990. reprint ed. pap. 12.00 (0-06-097310-2, PL) HarpC.

Oster, Richard. The Acts of the Apostles, Pt. 2. LC 79-63269. 180p. 1984. 12.95 (0-915547-25-2) Abilene Christ U.

Oster, Richard E. A Bibliography of Ancient Ephesus. LC 87-12617. (American Theological Library Association Monograph: No. 19). 181p. 1987. 25.00 (0-8108-1996-1) Scarecrow.

Oster, Sharon M. Modern Competitive Analysis. 2nd ed. LC 93-9826. (Illus.). 424p. 1994. 35.00 (0-19-507579-X) OUP.

— Strategic Management for Nonprofit Organizations: Theory & Cases. (Illus.). 288p. 1995. 35.00 (0-19-508503-5) OUP.

Oster, Sharon M., ed. Management of Non-Profit Organizations. (International Library of Management). 544p. 1994. 157.95 (1-85521-465-2, Pub. by Dartmth Pub UK) Ashgate Pub Co.

Oster Soussouev, Pierre. Robert Dictionnaire des Citations Francaises. 934p. (FRE.). 1992. 95.00 (0-8288-9467-1) Fr & Eur.

Osterberg, Arvid, et al, eds. Design Research Interactions. (EDRA Proceedings Ser.). 600p. 1981. pap. text ed. 30. 00 (0-939922-03-7) EDRA.

Osterberg, E. & Saila, S. -L. Natural Experiments with Decreased Availability of Alcoholic Beverages: Finnish Alcohol Strikes in 1972 & 1985. (Finnish Foundation for Alcohol Studies: Vol. 40). 1991. pap. 35.00 (951-9192-49-2) Rutgers Ctr Alcohol.

Osterberg, Eva & Linstrom, Dag. Crime & Social Control in Medieval & Early Modern Swedish Towns. (Studia Historica Upsaliensia: No. 152). 170p. (Orig.). 1988. pap. 37.50x (91-554-2246-2, Pub. by Uppsala Univ Acta Univ Uppsaliensis SW) Coronet Bks.

Osterberg, Jan. Self & Others. (C). 1988. lib. bdg. 97.50 (90-277-2648-5) Kluwer Ac.

Osterberg, Richard. Sterling Silver Flatware for Dining Elegance. LC 94-65622. (Illus.). 256p. (Orig.). 1994. pap. 39.95 (0-88740-630-0) Schiffer.

Osterberg, Rolf. Corporate Renaissance: Business As an Adventure in Human Development. 196p. 1993. 18.95 (1-882591-12-7) Nataraj Pub.

Osterberg, Susan S. & Jackson, R. Eugene. Bumper Snickers. 30p. (Orig.). (J). (gr. 6-12). 1978. pap. 2.50 (0-88680-015-3) I E Clark.

Osterbind, Carter C. & O'Rand, Angela M., eds. Older People in Florida: A Statistical Abstract 1978. 2nd ed. 277p. reprint ed. pap. 79.00 (0-7837-0597-2, 2040945) Bks Demand.

— Older People in Florida: A Statistical Abstract 1978. LC 82-1284. reprint ed. pap. 74.80 (0-7837-5827-8, 2045499) Bks Demand.

Osterbind, Carter C., jt. ed. see Kraft, John.

Osterbind, Carter C., ed. see Southern Conference on Gerontology Staff.

Osterbrock, Donald E. Astrophysics of Gaseous Nebulae & Active Galactic Nuclei. (Illus.). 325p. (C). 1989. text ed. 36.00 (0-935702-22-9) Univ Sci Bks.

— Pauper & Prince: Ritchey, Hale, & Big American Telescopes. LC 92-42704. (Illus.). 375p. 1993. 45.00 (0-8165-1199-3) U of Ariz Pr.

— Stars & Galaxies (SAR) Citizens of the Universe. LC 89-48325. (Readings from Scientific American Ser.). (Illus.). 184p. (C). 1995. text ed. write for info. (0-7167-2069-8) W H Freeman.

Osterbrock, Donald E. & Miller, Joseph S., eds. Active Galactic Nuclei. (C). 1989. lib. bdg. 175.50 (0-7923-0256-7); pap. text ed. 77.50 (0-7923-0257-5) Kluwer Ac.

Osterbrock, Donald E. & Raven, Peter H. Origins & Extinctions. LC 88-1396. (C). 1988. 22.00 (0-300-04260-4) Yale U Pr.

— Origins & Extinctions. (Illus.). (C). 1992. reprint ed. pap. text ed. 11.00 (0-300-05471-8) Yale U Pr.

Osterburg, J., jt. ed. see Haile, D.

Osterburg, James W. The Crime Laboratory: Case Studies of Scientific Investigation. 2nd ed. LC 81-7694. 1982. pap. 19.95 (0-87632-364-6) Clark Boardman Callaghan.

Osterburg, James W. & Ward, Richard H. Criminal Investigation: A Method for Reconstructing the Past. LC 90-84735. (Illus.). 875p. (C). 1992. text ed. 44.95 (0-87084-671-X) Anderson Pub Co.

Ostereng, Willy, jt. ed. see Andresen, Steinar.

Osterfeld, David. Prosperity Versus Planning: How Government Stifles Economic Growth. (Illus.). 416p. (C). 1992. pap. text ed. 19.95 (0-19-507614-1) OUP.

Osterfelt, Susan, jt. auth. see Inmon, W. H.

Osterfelt, Susan, jt. auth. see Inmon, William H.

Ostergaard, D. Eugene. Advanced Diemaking. (Diemaking Ser.). 166p. 43.95 (0-07-046093-0) McGraw.

— Basic Diemaking. (Diemaking Ser.). 208p. (Orig.). 1982. pap. 37.95 (0-910399-34-4) McGraw.

Ostergaard, J. M. Fossil Marine Mollusks of Oahu. (BMB Ser.: No. 51). 1969. reprint ed. pap. 15.00 (0-527-02157-1) Periodicals Srv.

— Recent & Fossil Marine Molluska of Tongatabu. (BMB Ser.). 1974. reprint ed. pap. 15.00 (0-527-02237-3) Periodicals Srv.

Ostergaard, Lise, ed. Gender & Development: A Practical Guide. LC 91-16824. 224p. 1992. 57.50 (0-415-07131-3, A6685); pap. 15.95 (0-415-07132-1, A6689) Routledge.

Ostergaard, Tom. SADCC - Beyond Transportation: The Challenge of Industrial Cooperation in Southern Africa. (Scandinavian Institute of African Studies). 136p. (Orig.). 1989. pap. 48.00x (91-7106-294-7, Pub. by Umea U Bibl SW) Coronet Bks.

***Ostergard, Carey.** A Trunk Full of Adventure. 24p. (J). (gr. 4-12). 1992. pap. 5.00 (1-886210-08-X) Tyketoon Yng Author.

***Ostergard, Derek E. & Hoff, Marlise.** Along the Royal Road: Berlin & Potsdam in KPM Porcelain. (Illus.). 251p. Date not set. pap. 45.00 (0-614-07358-8) Bard Grad Ctr.

Ostergard, Derek E., jt. auth. see Schmuttermeier, Elisabeth.

***Ostergard, Derek E., et al.** Along the Royal Road: Berlin & Potsdam in KPM Porcelain & Painting 1815-1848. 251p. 1993. pap. text ed. write for info. (1-887506-00-4) Bard Grad Ctr.

— Cast Iron from Central Europe 1800-1850. 351p. 1994. pap. text ed. write for info. (1-887506-01-2) Bard Grad Ctr.

Ostergard, Donald R. & Bent, Alfred E. Urogynecology & Urodynamics. 3rd ed. (Illus.). 692p. 1991. 98.00 (0-683-06647-1) Williams & Wilkins.

Ostergard, Donald R., jt. auth. see Sand, Peter K.

Ostergren, Robert C. A Community Transplanted: The Trans-Atlantic Experience of a Swedish Immigrant Settlement in the Upper Middle West, 1835-1915. LC 88-211. (Illus.). 416p. (Orig.). (C). 1988. text ed. 45.00 (0-299-11320-5); pap. text ed. 19.95 (0-299-11324-8) U of Wis Pr.

Osterhang, Kathryn L., et al. Preparing, Cooking Various Seafoods: Salmon, Halibut, Shrimp, Oysters, Clams. (Shorey Lost Arts Ser.). (Illus.). 90p. reprint ed. pap. 4.95 (0-8466-6053-9) Shorey.

***Osterhaus, A. D., ed.** Virus Infections of Rodents & Lagomorphs. LC 94-21040. (Virus Infections of Vertebrates Ser.: Vol. 5). 1994. write for info. (0-444-81909-6) Elsevier.

Osterhaus, A. D. & Uytedehaag, F. G., eds. Idiotype Networks in Biology & Medicine: Proceedings of the International Congress on Idiotype Networks in Biology & Medicine, 17-20 April, 1989. (International Congress Ser.: No. 862). 310p. 1990. 92.50 (0-685-45393-6) Elsevier.

Osterhaus, James. Bonds of Iron: Forging Lasting Male Relationships. 1994. 16.99 (0-8024-7129-3) Moody.

— Building Strong Male Relationships. 1993. pap. 2.99 (0-8024-3710-9) Moody.

***Osterhaus, Rick & Dallmann-Jones, Anthony.** Is Education Having a Heart Attack? Eight Symptoms & a Plan for Rehabilitation. 68p. (Orig.). 1994. pap. 7.95 (1-881952-20-7) Three Blue Herons.

Osterhaven, M. Eugene, jt. tr. see Miller, Allen O.

Osterhoff, Robert & Weaver, Alan T. Greenberg's Guide to Lionel Prewar Parts & Instruction Sheets. 2nd ed. 352p. (Orig.). Date not set. pap. text ed. write for info. (0-89778-340-9, 10-7835) Greenberg Bks.

Osterhoff, Robert J. Greenberg's Guide to Lionel Paper & Collectibles. Floyd, Cindy L. & Norbeck, Carole A., eds. (Illus.). 184p. 1990. 40.00 (0-89778-152-X, 10-6735HB); pap. 29.95 (0-89778-077-9, 10-6735) Greenberg Bks.

***Osterholm, J. Roger.** Bing Crosby: A Bio-Bibliography. LC 94-28690. (Bio-Bibliographies in the Performing Arts Ser.: Vol. 58). 504p. 1994. text ed. 65.00 (0-313-27726-5, Greenwood Pr) Greenwood.

Osterholm, Michael, et al, eds. Infectious Diseases in Child Day Care: Management & Protection. viii, 176p. 1987. lib. bdg. 30.00 (0-226-63947-9) U Ch Pr.

Osterhoudt, Robert G. The Philosophy of Sport: An Overview. 518p. (C). 1991. text ed. 31.80x (0-87563-370-6) Stipes.

Osteria, Trinidad S., comp. The Poor in ASEAN Cities. 187p. 1991. text ed. 42.00 (981-3035-84-6, Pub. by Inst SE Asian Studies SI) Ashgate Pub Co.

Osteria, Trinidad S., ed. Women in Health Development: Case Studies of Selected Ethnic Groups in Rural Asia-Pa. 132p. 1991. pap. 22.00 (981-3035-88-9, Pub. by Inst SE Asian Studies SI) Ashgate Pub Co.

Osterink, Carol. My Sticker Dictionary. (Illus.). 64p. (J). (ps-2). 1992. pap. 5.95 (1-56293-250-0) McClanahan Bk.

— Search for Delicious. Friedland, J. & Kessler, R., eds. (Novel-Ties Ser.). (J). (gr. 3-5). 1994. student ed, pap. text ed. 15.95 (1-56982-061-9) Lrn Links.

***Osterink, Carole & Spencer, Beth.** Sounds in Stories - Long Vowel Sounds. Friedland, J. & Kessler, R., eds. (Novel-Ties Ser.). (J). (gr. k-2). 1993. student ed, pap. text ed. 20.95 (1-56982-031-7) Lrn Links.

— Sounds in Stories - Short Vowel Sounds. Friedland, J. & Kessler, R., eds. (Novel-Ties Ser.). (J). (gr. k-2). 1993. student ed, pap. text ed. 20.95 (1-56982-033-3) Lrn Links.

Osterkamp, Ernst. Lucifer Stationen eines Motivs. (Komparatistische Studien: Vol. 9). (C). 1979. 104.60 (3-11-007804-X) De Gruyter.

Osterkamp, Lynn & Press, Allan N. Stress? Find Your Balance. rev. ed. 160p. 1988. reprint ed. pap. 5.95 (0-9620725-0-8) Preventive Measures.

Osterkamp, Peggy. How to Wind a Warp & Use a Paddle. (Peggy Osterkamp's New Guide to Weaving Ser.: No. 1). (Illus.). 102p. 1992. pap. 14.95 (0-9637793-0-3) Lease Sticks.

— Making Your Loom Ready & Tying on New Warps. (Peggy Osterkamp's New Guide to Weaving Ser.: No. 2). 1995. pap. write for info. (0-9637793-1-1) Lease Sticks.

Osterle, Hubert, et al. Total Information Systems Management: Guidelines & Examples on How to Get More Value Out of Your Information System. LC 93-12283. (Series in Information Systems). 400p. 1993. text ed. 51.95 (0-471-93932-3) Wiley.

Osterlind, Steven J. Test Item Bias. (Quantitative Applications in the Social Sciences Ser.: Vol. 30). 88p. 1983. pap. 9.95 (0-8039-1989-1) Sage.

Osterling, Jorge P. Democracy in Colombia: Clientelistic Politics & Guerrilla Warfare. 350p. 1989. 39.95 (0-88738-229-0) Transaction Pubs.

Osterloh, jt. auth. see Cohen.

Osterloh, Karl-Heinz, jt. auth. see Cohen, Ulrike.

Osterman & Terrill. Wrist Arthroscopy. 275p. 1991. 139.00 (0-8151-6510-2, Yr Bk Med Pubs) Mosby Yr Bk.

***Osterman, Bernt.** Value & Requirements: An Inquiry Concerning the Origin of Value. 202p. 1995. boxed, pap. 59.95 (1-85972-028-5, Pub. by Avebury Pub UK) Ashgate Pub Co.

Osterman, Fred, jt. auth. see Gorka, Gary.

Osterman, Fred J. Shortwave Receivers Past & Present. (Illus.). 104p. 1987. pap. 6.95 (1-882123-05-0) Universal Radio Rsch.

Osterman, H., ed. see Rasmussen, Knud J.

Osterman, Joe. Fifty Years in "Old" El Toro: A Family, a Time, a Place. 3rd ed. LC 81-85994. (Illus.). 290p. 1992. reprint ed. 14.95 (1-881129-00-4) Old El Toro Pr.

— The Old El Toro Reader: A Guide to the Past. Walker, Doris & Osterman, Tim, eds. LC 92-96902. (Illus.). 112p. (J). 1992. pap. 9.95 (1-881129-02-0) Old El Toro Pr.

— Stories of Saddleback Valley. LC 85-63697. (Illus.). 160p. (Orig.). 1992. pap. 9.00 (1-881129-01-2) Old El Toro Pr.

Osterman, Karen F. & Kottkamp, Robert B. Reflective Practice for Educators: Improving Schooling Through Professional Development. 228p. 1993. 40.00 (0-8039-6046-8); pap. 20.00 (0-8039-6047-6) Corwin Pr.

Osterman, L. A. Methods of Protein & Nucleic Acid Research: Electrophoresis, Isoelectric Focusing, Ultracentrifugation, Vol. 1. (Illus.). 370p. 1985. 177.00 (0-387-12735-6) Spr-Verlag.

— Methods of Protein & Nucleic Acid Research: Immunoelectrophoresis - Application of Radioisotopes. (Illus.). 220p. 1988. 122.00 (0-387-13094-2) Spr-Verlag.

— Methods of Protein & Nucleic Acid Research Vol. 3: Chromatography. (Illus.). 520p. 1986. 225.00 (0-387-16855-9) Spr-Verlag.

***Osterman, Marilyn & Kluge, Marilyn.** The Dancing Spider. 1979. write for info. (0-87129-238-6, D29) Dramatic Pub.

Osterman, Mark. Justifiable Homicide. LC 93-11988. 288p. (Orig.). 1993. pap. 5.95 (1-877633-17-8) Luthers.

Osterman, Paul. Employment Futures: Reorganization, Dislocation & Public Policy. (Illus.). 224p. 1988. 35.00 (0-19-505279-X) OUP.

Osterman, Paul, jt. auth. see Kochan, Thomas A.

Osterman, Paul, jt. auth. see Marshall, Ray.

Osterman, Susan. Strip Mining. (Cambric Poetry Ser.). 72p. (Orig.). 1987. pap. 7.00 (0-918342-26-0) Cambric.

Osterman, Tim, ed. see Osterman, Joe.

Ostermann, R., jt. ed. see Dirschedl, P.

Ostermiller, L. Barnese Mountain Dogs. (Illus.). 192p. 1993. 11.95 (0-86622-572-2, KW202) TFH Pubns.

Ostermiller, R. Kenneth. Talking with Your Child about Sexuality. LC 90-21702. (Growing Together Ser.). (Orig.). 1991. pap. 1.95 (0-8298-0863-9) Pilgrim OH.

Ostermiller, R. Kenneth, jt. auth. see Monkres, Peter R.

Ostermoller, Wolfgang. Aquariums. (Illus.). 80p. 1984. pap. 5.95 (0-86622-144-1, PB-101) TFH Pubns.

Osterreich, Shelley A., comp. The American Indian Ghost Dance, 1870 & 1890: An Annotated Bibliography. LC 91-7957. (Bibliographies & Indexes in American History Ser.: No. 19). 296p. 1991. text ed. 42.95 (0-313-27469-X, OGD, Greenwood Pr) Greenwood.

Osterreicher, John M. The Unfinished Dialogue: Martin Buber & the Christian Way. 136p. 1987. reprint ed. pap. 5.95 (0-8065-1050-1, Citadel Pr) Carol Pub Group.

Osterrieth, P., et al. Improving Education for Disadvantaged Children: Some Belgian Studies. LC 79-4086. 1979. 91.00 (0-08-024265-0, Pub. by Pergamon Repr UK) Franklin.

Osterritter, John F., jt. auth. see Elgin, Kathleen.

Ostertag, George, jt. auth. see Ostertag, Rhonda.

Ostertag, J. Keith & De La Pena McCook, Kathleen, eds. Library Support Staff: Challengers for the Nineties. LC 92-46388. 1992. write for info. (0-8389-7638-7) ALA.

Ostertag, Rhonda. Fifty Hikes in Oregon's Coast Range & Siskiyous. LC 89-3150. (Illus.). 224p. (Orig.). 1989. pap. 10.95 (0-89886-200-0) Mountaineers.

***Ostertag, Rhonda & Ostertag, George.** California State Parks: A Complete Recreation Guide. (Illus.). 400p. 1995. pap. 16.95 (0-89886-419-4) Mountaineers.

— Day Hikes from Oregon Campgrounds. LC 91-22622. (Illus.). 256p. 1991. pap. 12.95 (0-89886-310-4) Mountaineers.

— One Hundred Hikes in Oregon. LC 92-18750. (One Hundred Hikes Ser.). (Illus.). (Orig.). 1992. pap. 14.95 (0-89886-298-1) Mountaineers.

Osterud, Nancy G. Bonds of Community: The Lives of Farm Women in Nineteenth-Century New York. LC 90-41814. (Illus.). 320p. 1991. 45.00 (0-8014-2510-7); pap. 14.95 (0-8014-9798-1) Cornell U Pr.

***Osterwald, Doris B.** Beyond the Third Rail with Monte Ballough & His Camera. (Illus.). 216p. 1994. 44.95 (0-931788-40-4) Western Guideways.

— Cinders & Smoke: A Mile by Mile Guide for the Durango & Silverton Narrow Gauge Railroad. 7th rev. ed. LC 68-4969. (Illus.). 168p. (YA). 1995. pap. 7.95 (0-931788-95-1) Western Guideways.

— High Line to Leadville: A Mile by Mile Guide for the Leadville, Colorado & Southern Railroad. (Illus.). 160p. (Orig.). 1991. pap. 9.95 (0-931788-70-6) Western Guideways.

— Rocky Mountain Splendor: A Mile by Mile Guide for Rocky Mountain National Park. (Illus.). 272p. (Orig.). (YA). 1989. pap. 13.95 (0-931788-89-7) Western Guideways.

— Ticket to Toltec: A Mile by Mile Guide for the Cumbres & Toltec Scenic Railroad. LC 78-102355. (Illus.). 1976. pap. 5.50 (0-931788-25-0) Western Guideways.

— Ticket to Toltec: A Mile by Mile Guide for the Cumbres & Toltec Scenic Railroad. (Illus.). 128p. 1992. pap. 9.95 (0-931788-26-9) Western Guideways.

Osterwalder, K. & Stora, R., eds. Critical Phenomena, Random Systems, Gauge Theories, 2 Vols., 1. 1240p. 1986. 195.00 (0-444-87006-7, North Holland) Elsevier.

— Critical Phenomena, Random Systems, Gauge Theories, 2 Vols., 2. 1240p. 1986. 231.00 (0-444-87007-5, North Holland) Elsevier.

— Critical Phenomena, Random Systems, Gauge Theories, 2 Vols., Set. 1240p. 1986. 364.00 (0-444-86980-8, North Holland) Elsevier.

***Osterwalder, Marcus.** Dictionnaire Des Illustrateurs: 1890-1945, No. 2. 1384p. (FRE.). 1989. text ed. 325.00 (0-7859-8038-5, 2825800392) Fr & Eur.

— Dictionnaire des Illustrateurs Vol. 1: 1800-1914. 1223p. (FRE.). 1989. 325.00 (0-7859-8037-7, 2825800309) Fr & Eur.

Osterweis, Marian & Garfinkel, Stephen, eds. The Roles of Physician Assistants & Nurse Practitioners in Primary Care. (Orig.). 1993. pap. write for info. (1-879694-07-7) AAH Ctrs.

Osterweis, Marian, ed. see Institute of Medicine Staff.

Osterweis, Rollin G. The Sesquicentennial History of the Connecticut Academy of Arts & Sciences. (Connecticut Academy of Arts & Sciences Ser., Trans.: Vol. 38, Pt. 2). 1949. pap. 29.50 (0-685-22901-7) Elliots Bks.

— Three Centuries of New Haven, 1638-1938. LC 52-12064. (Illus.). 559p. reprint ed. pap. 159.40 (0-8357-8351-0, 2033849) Bks Demand.

Osterwold, Tilman, text. Mark di Suvero. (Illus.). 224p. 1988. pap. 65.00 (0-9624258-7-7) Flynn Gallery.

Osterwold, Tilman, jt. auth. see Felix, Zdenek.

Osteryoung, Jerome & Lamothe, Richard. Spreadsheet Applications in Financial Analysis: Includes Super Calc3 Educational Version. 294p. (C). 1985. reprint ed. pap. 31.50 (0-471-82498-4) Krieger.

Osteryoung, Jerome S., jt. auth. see McCarty, Daniel E.

Osteyee, Carol H., jt. auth. see Hoffman, Preston.

Ostfeld, Adrian M., et al. Stress, Crowding & Blood Pressure in Prison. (Health Environment Ser.). 256p. 1987. text ed. 49.95 (0-89859-574-6) L Erlbaum Assocs.

Ostfeld, F. J. Under the Golden Roof: A Swedish Intermezzo. (Illus.). 80p. (Orig.). 1989. pap. 9.95 (0-9620757-0-1) Belvedere WA.

Osthaus, Carl R. Freedmen, Philanthropy & Fraud: A History of the Freedman's Savings Bank. LC 75-23214. (Blacks in the New World Ser.). 276p. 1976. 29.95 (0-252-00305-5) U of Ill Pr.

— Partisans of the Southern Press: Editorial Spokesman of the Nineteenth Century. LC 94-16880. 288p. 1994. lib. bdg. 39.95x (0-8131-1875-1) U Pr of Ky.

Ostheeren, Ingrid. I'm the Real Santa Claus! Lanning, Rosemary, tr. LC 94-10275. 1994. 14.95 (1-55858-318-1); lib. bdg. 14.88 (1-55858-319-X) North-South Bks NYC.

— Martin & the Pumpkin Ghost. adapted ed. James, J. Alison, ed. & tr. by. LC 93-42051. (Illus.). 32p. (J). (gr. k-3). 1994. 14.95 (1-55858-267-3); lib. bdg. 14.88 (1-55858-268-1) North-South Bks NYC.

O

Ostheeren, Ingrid & Corderoc'h, Jean-Pierre. The New Dog. James, J. Alison, tr. LC 93-10100. (Illus.). 32p. (J). (gr. k-3). 1993. 14.95 (*1-55858-218-5*); lib. bdg. 14.88 (*1-55858-219-3*) North-South Bks NYC.

Ostheimer, Gerard W. Manual of Obstetric Anesthesia. 2nd ed. (Illus.). 468p. (Orig.). 1992. 57.00 (*0-443-08743-1*) Churchill.

Ostheimer, Gerard W., jt. ed. see Datta, Sanjay.

Osthoff, Hermann & Brugman, Karl. Morphologische Untersuchungen Auf Dem Gebiete der Indogermanischen Sprachen, 3 vols., Set. (Documenta Semiotica, Series Linguistica). lxxx, 1810p. 1974. reprint ed. write for info. (*3-487-05079-X*, Pub. by Georg Olms GW) Lubrecht & Cramer.

Ostianu, N. M. & Pontryagin, L. S., eds. Geometry I: Basic Ideas & Concepts of Differential Geometry. (Encyclopaedia of Mathematical Sciences Ser.: Vol. 28). (Illus.). viii, 256p. 1991. 65.00 (*0-387-51999-8*) Spr-Verlag.

Ostino, G., et al, eds. Progress in Clinical Pharmacy IV: Proceedings of the European Symposium, Tenth, Stresa, Italy, October 14-17, 1981. (Progress in Clinical Pharmacy Ser.: No. IV). 274p. 1982. 83.00 (*0-444-80437-4*) Elsevier.

Ostle, ed. Studies in Modern Arabic Literature. 1975. 35.00 (*0-85668-030-3*, Pub. by Aris & Phillips UK); pap. write for info. (*0-85668-044-3*, Pub. by Aris & Phillips UK) David Brown.

Ostle, Bernard & Malone, Linda C. Statistics in Research: Basic Concepts & Techniques for Research Workers. 4th ed. (Illus.). 682p. 1988. text ed. 51.95 (*0-8138-1569-X*) Iowa St U Pr.

Ostle, Robin. Modern Literature in the Near & Middle East. 256p. (C). 1991. text ed. 74.50 (*0-415-05822-8*, A5644) Routledge.

Ostler, Barbara, jt. auth. see Featherston, Phyllis.

Ostler, Barbara, jt. auth. see Featherstun, Phyllis.

Ostler, Barbara F., jt. auth. see Featherston, Phyllis.

Ostler, H. Bruce. Diseases of the External Eye & Adnexa: A Text & Atlas. (Illus.). 864p. 1993. 250.00 (*0-683-06651-X*) Williams & Wilkins.

Ostler, H. Bruce, et al. Color Atlas of Infectious & Inflammatory Diseases of the External Eye. LC 86-15941. (Illus.). 166p. 1987. 145.00 (*0-683-06650-1*) Williams & Wilkins.

Ostler, James, jt. auth. see Rodee, Marian.

Ostler, Jeffrey. Prairie Populism: The Fate of Agrarian Radicalism in Kansas, Nebraska, & Iowa, 1880-1892. LC 93-14828. (Rural America Ser.). 272p. 1993. 29.95 (*0-7006-0606-8*) U Pr of KS.

Ostler, Jim, jt. auth. see Rodee, Marian.

Ostler, Jolene N., jt. auth. see Hare, Patrick H.

***Ostler, Larry J., et al.** The Closing of American Library Schools: Problems & Opportunities. LC 94-46942. (Contributions in Librarianship & Information Science Ser.: No. 85). 176p. 1995. text ed. 49.95 (*0-313-28461-X*, Greenwood Pr) Greenwood.

Ostler, Rosemarie. Theoretical Syntax 1980-1990: An Annotated & Classified Bibliography. LC 91-42086. (Library & Information Sources in Linguistics: No. 21). viii, 192p. 1992. 53.00x (*1-55619-251-7*) Benjamins North Am.

Ostler, Scott, jt. auth. see Haywood, Spencer.

Ostlie, Dale A., jt. auth. see Carroll, Bradley W.

Ostling, Joan K., jt. auth. see Christopher, Joe R.

Ostling, Richard N., jt. auth. see Nathanson, Bernard N.

Ostlund, Neil S., jt. auth. see Szabo, Attila.

Ostlund, S., jt. ed. see Steinhardt, P.

Ostman, Ellen. Dear Client: A Complete Handbook for Divorce Litigation. Jacob, Karen L., ed. (Illus.). 560p. 1995. pap. 24.95 (*0-936417-44-7*) Axelrod Pub.

Ostman, Ellen D. Open Secret: A Divorce Litigation Guide. 90p. Date not set. student ed 10.30 (*0-9638633-7-1*) Hearsay Pr FL.

Ostman, Hans. Swedish Non-Academic Criticism in the Era of Freedom, 1718-1772. (Stockholm Studies in the History of Literature: No. 32). 106p. (Orig.). 1993. pap. 36.50x (*91-22-01563-9*, Pub. by Almqv & Wiksell SW) Coronet Bks.

Ostman, Jan-Ola. You Know: A Discourse-Functional Study. (Pragmatics & Beyond Ser.: II: 7). ix, 91p. (Orig.). 1981. pap. 29.00x (*90-272-2516-8*) Benjamins North Am.

Ostman, Lars, jt. auth. see Johansson, Sven-Erik.

Ostman, Ronald E., ed. Communication & Indian Agriculture. 320p. (C). 1989. text ed. 25.00 (*0-8039-9599-7*) Sage.

Ostmeyer, J., tr. see Svrcek, Mirko.

Ostoia, Vera K., tr. see D'Allemagne, Henry R.

***Ostoja-Starzewski, Martin & Jasiuk, Iwona, eds.** Micromechanics of Random Media: Selected & Revised Proceedings of the Symposium on Micromechanics of Random Media, MEET'N '93. 240p. 1994. pap. 170.00 (*0-615-00328-1*) ASME.

Ostolaza, Margarita. Politica Sexual en Puerto Rico. LC 88-83952. 204p. 1989. pap. 11.95 (*0-929157-00-1*) Ediciones Huracan.

Ostor, Akos. Vessels of Time: An Essay on Temporal Change & Social Transformation. 116p. 1994. 13.95 (*0-19-563285-0*) OUP.

Ostor, Akos, et al. Concepts of Person: Kinship, Caste, & Marriage in India. (Harvard Studies in Cultural Anthropology: Vol. 5). (Illus.). 288p. 1982. 45.50 (*0-674-15765-6*) HUP.

Ostor, Akos, et al, eds. Concepts of Person: Kinship, Caste, & Marriage in India. (Oxford India Paperbacks Ser.). (Illus.). 312p. 1993. pap. 10.95 (*0-19-563033-5*) OUP.

Ostosky-Solis, Peggy, jt. auth. see Ardila, Alfredo.

Ostovar, Pat. Great Danes in Canada. LC 82-9737. (Breed Bks.). (Illus.). 96p. 1982. 29.95 (*0-87714-080-4*); pap. 19.95 (*0-685-42104-X*) Denlingers.

Ostovic, V. Dynamics of Saturated Electric Machines. (Illus.). xiii, 445p. 1989. 73.00 (*0-387-97079-7*, 3103) Spr-Verlag.

Ostovic, Vlado. Computer-aided Analysis of Electric Machines: A Mathematical Approach. LC 93-23664. 400p. 1994. pap. text ed. 73.00 (*0-13-068859-2*, P-H Intl) P-H.

Ostovich, Steve. Reason in History. 289p. 1990. 22.95 (*1-55540-424-3*); pap. 14.95 (*1-55540-425-1*) Scholars Pr GA.

Ostow, Miriam, jt. auth. see Ginzberg, Eli.

Ostow, Mortimer. Psychoanalysis & Judaism. 1982. pap. 14.95 (*0-87068-713-1*) Ktav.

Ostow, Mortimer & Scharfstein, Ben-Ami. The Need to Believe: The Psychology of Religion. 1969. reprint ed. pap. text ed. 24.95 (*0-8236-8159-9*, 23520) Intl Univs Pr.

Ostow, Robin. Jews in Contemporary East Germany: The Children of Moses in the Land of Marx. LC 89-30606. 190p. 1989. text ed. 45.00 (*0-312-03118-1*) St Martin.

Ostrach, S. & Scanlan, R. Developments in Mechanics, Vol. 2, Pt. 2: Solid Mechanics. LC 61-17719. 1965. 239.00 (*0-08-011844-5*, Pub. by Pergamon Repr UK) Franklin.

Ostrach, S., jt. auth. see Eaton, J. Robert.

Ostrager, Barry R. & Newman, Thomas. Handbook on Insurance Coverage Disputes. 1989. write for info. (*0-318-66843-2*) P-H.

Ostrager, Barry R. & Newman, Thomas R. Handbook on Insurance Coverage Disputes. 6th ed. LC 93-35775. 1028p. 1993. 150.00 (*0-13-109141-7*) Aspen Law.

Ostram, Vincent. The Political Theory of a Compound Republic: Designing the American Experiment. LC 86-7063. 270p. reprint ed. pap. 77.00 (*0-7837-6012-4*, 2045823) Bks Demand.

Ostrand, Kenneth. As I Recall: Sources in Western Civilization (Renaissance to the Present) 2nd ed. 284p. (C). 1992. pap. text ed. 32.00 (*0-9627173-5-5*) Intl Horizons.

— As I Recall: Sources in Western Civilization (to the Renaissance) 2nd ed. 300p. (C). 1992. pap. text ed. 32.00 (*0-9627173-4-7*) Intl Horizons.

— Dinner Lectures. 21p. 9.95 (*0-914951-16-5*) LERN.

— Trips & Tours Manual. 147p. 29.95 (*0-914951-04-1*) LERN.

Ostrand, Kenneth D. As I Recall...Sources in Western Civilization: Ancient Times to the Renaissance, Vol. 1. 212p. (C). 1989. pap. text ed. 18.00 (*0-318-41279-9*) Le Storti Graphics.

— As I Recall...Sources in Western Civilization, Vol. 2: Renaissance to Napoleon. 164p. 1989. pap. text ed. 18.00 (*0-317-01806-X*) Le Storti Graphics.

***Ostrand, Kenneth P.** Egypt: Beneath the Surface. 2nd ed. 234p. (C). 1993. pap. text ed. 35.00 (*0-9627173-3-9*) Intl Horizons.

Ostrander, Arthur E. & Wilson, Dana. Contemporary Choral Arranging. 256p. (C). 1986. text ed. 59.33 (*0-13-169756-0*) P-H.

Ostrander, Betty. Woman's Guide to Autos. 2nd ed. (Illus.). 85p. 1993. 59.00x (*1-56216-153-9*); pap. 29.00x (*1-56216-154-7*) Systems Co.

— A Woman's Guide to Autos: Basics, Operation, Safety & Maintenance. (Illus.). 60p. 1991. 48.00x (*1-56216-015-X*); pap. 28.00x (*1-56216-016-8*) Systems Co.

Ostrander, Curtis & Schwartz, Joseph. Crime at College: The Student Guide to Personal Safety. 200p. 1994. 24.95 (*0-9628092-5-X*); pap. 14.95 (*0-9628092-6-8*) New Strategist.

Ostrander, Edgar A. Evidence That Ancient Mayan Cosmology Incorporated the Internal Functioning of the Human Brain. LC 83-72070. (Illus.). 56p. 1983. 10.00 (*0-9611638-0-1*) Bks of New Univ.

Ostrander, Gary K., jt. ed. see Malins, Donald C.

Ostrander, Gilman H. Early Colonial Thought. 1970. pap. text ed. write for info. (*0-88273-221-8*) Forum Pr IL.

Ostrander, John. Penguin Triumphant. O'Neil, Dennis, ed. 48p. 1992. pap. 4.95 (*1-56389-030-5*) DC Comics.

— The Spectre: Crimes & Punishments. Kahan, Bob, ed. (Illus.). 104p. (YA). 1993. pap. 9.95 (*1-56389-127-1*) DC Comics.

Ostrander, John & Wein, Len. Legends. Kahan, Bob, ed. (Illus.). 160p. (YA). 1993. pap. 9.95 (*1-56389-095-X*) DC Comics.

Ostrander, John, jt. auth. see Shooter, Jim.

Ostrander, Kate. Love's Tender Tears. (Orig.). 1979. pap. 1.95 (*0-89083-504-7*) Zebra.

Ostrander, Kenneth H. The Legal Structure of Collective Bargaining in Education. LC 87-8470. (Contributions to the Study of Education Ser.). 164p. 1987. text ed. 45.00 (*0-313-24474-X*, OLS/, Greenwood Pr) Greenwood.

Ostrander, Norma. Ivanhoe Notes. 1967. pap. 3.75 (*0-8220-0663-4*) Cliffs.

— Passage to India Notes. 1967. pap. 3.75 (*0-8220-0985-4*) Cliffs.

Ostrander, Sheila & Schroeder, Lynn. Superlearning Two Thousand. LC 94-6402. 1994. 21.95 (*0-385-31274-1*) Delacorte.

— Supermemory: The Revolution. 384p. 1991. 21.95 (*0-88184-691-0*) Carroll & Graf.

Ostrander, Sheila, et al. Superlearning. 360p. 1982. mass mkt. 5.99 (*0-440-38424-9*, LE) Dell.

***Ostrander, Stephen.** Natural Acts Ohio. LC 94-66496. (Illus.). 264p. (Orig.). 1994. pap. 16.95 (*1-882203-02-X*) Orange Frazer.

***Ostrander, Stephen J.** 75 Great Natural Areas in Eastern Pennsylvania. (Illus.). 382p. 1996. pap. 19.95 (*0-8117-2574-X*) Stackpole.

***Ostrander, Susan A.** Money for Change: Social Movement Philanthropy at Haymarket People's Fund. LC 95-12095. 256p. (C). 1995. lib. bdg. 34.95 (*1-56639-363-9*); pap. text ed. 19.95 (*1-56639-364-7*) Temple U Pr.

— Women of the Upper Class. LC 83-18214. (Women in the Political Economy Ser.). 256p. 1984. pap. 16.95 (*0-87722-475-7*) Temple U Pr.

Ostransky, Leroy. The Anatomy of Jazz. LC 73-11857. (Illus.). xiii, 362p. 1973. reprint ed. text ed. 35.00 (*0-8371-7092-3*, OSAJ, Greenwood Pr) Greenwood.

— Sharkey's Kid: A Memoir. LC 90-13558. 288p. 1991. 23.00 (*0-688-10325-1*) Morrow.

Ostreiko, V. N. Calculation of Electromagnetic Fields in Multilayer Media. xiv, 156p. 1989. text ed. 135.00 (*2-88124-674-5*) Gordon & Breach.

Ostreng, Willy. The Soviet Union in Arctic Waters. (Law of the Sea Occasional Papers: No. 36). 87p. (Orig.). 1987. pap. 10.00 (*0-911189-15-7*) Law Sea Inst.

Ostreng, Willy, jt. ed. see Andresen, S.

Ostreng, Willy, jt. ed. see Jorgensen-Dahl, Arnfinn.

Ostria Gutierrez, Alberto. The Tragedy of Bolivia: A People Crucified. Golden, Eithne, tr. LC 81-2424. Orig. Title: Un Pueblo en la Cruz. 224p. 1981. reprint ed. text ed. 35.00 (*0-313-22935-X*, GUTB, Greenwood Pr) Greenwood.

Ostriker, Alicia. A Dream of Springtime. LC 78-59769. 62p. (Orig.). 1979. pap. 6.00 (*0-912292-53-9*) The Smith.

— The Imaginary Lover. LC 86-7005. (Poetry Ser.). 110p. 1986. 19.95 (*0-8229-3543-0*); pap. 10.95 (*0-8229-5385-4*) U of Pittsburgh Pr.

— The Nakedness of the Fathers: Biblical Visions & Revisions. LC 94-14616. 225p. (C). 1994. 22.00 (*0-8135-2125-4*) Rutgers U Pr.

— Once More Out of Darkness. 32p. 1974. pap. 5.95 (*0-917658-00-0*) BPW & P.

— A Woman under the Surface: Poems & Prose Poems. LC 81-47938. (Contemporary Poets Ser.). 77p. 1982. 21.95 (*0-691-06512-8*); pap. 10.95 (*0-691-01390-X*) Princeton U Pr.

— Writing Like a Woman. (Poets on Poetry Ser.). 200p. 1983. pap. 13.95 (*0-472-06347-2*) U of Mich Pr.

Ostriker, Alicia, ed. Blake: Complete Poems. 1978. pap. 12.95 (*0-14-042215-3*, Penguin Classics) Viking Penguin.

Ostriker, Alicia S. Feminist Revision & the Bible. LC 92-25489. (Bucknell Lectures in Literary Theory). 160p. 1993. 29.95 (*0-631-18797-9*); pap. 15.95 (*0-631-18798-7*) Blackwell Pubs.

— Green Age. LC 89-32020. (Poetry Ser.). 72p. 1989. 19.95 (*0-8229-3624-0*); pap. 10.95 (*0-8229-5421-4*) U of Pittsburgh Pr.

— Stealing the Language: The Emergence of Women's Poetry in America. LC 85-73368. 336p. 1987. pap. 16.00x (*0-8070-6303-7*, BP 763) Beacon Pr.

— Unwritten Volume: Rethinking the Bible. Payne, Michael & Schweizer, Harold, eds. 1993. text ed. write for info. (*0-318-71692-5*) Blackwell Pubs.

Ostriker, J. P., ed. Selected Works of Yakow Borisovich Zeldovich, Vol. II: Particles, Nuclei, & the Universe. Granik, A. & Jackson, E., trs. 644p. 1993. text ed. 69.50 (*0-691-08742-3*) Princeton U Pr.

Ostriker, Jeremiah P. Development of Large Scale Structure in the Universe. (Lezione Fermiane Ser.). (Illus.). 120p. (C). 1992. pap. 22.95 (*0-521-42361-9*) Cambridge U Pr.

Ostrikova, O., jt. auth. see Bezborodova, V.

Ostrikova, O., jt. ed. see Bezborodova, V.

Ostrin, S. L., jt. ed. see Ring, A. M.

Ostrin, Samuel L. Powderburns: Munitions & Medicine. LC 93-93760. 200p. 1994. pap. 12.00 (*1-56002-325-2*, Univ Edtns) Aegina Pr.

Ostro. Liposomes: From Biophysics to Therapeutics. 418p. 1987. 175.00 (*0-8247-7762-X*) Dekker.

Ostroff, Anthony & Van Loen, Alfred. The Endless Line. 64p. 1985. pap. 7.00 (*0-913057-05-3*) L I U Press.

— The Endless Line. deluxe limited ed. 64p. 1985. 20.00 (*0-913057-06-1*) L I U Press.

Ostroff, E. D., et al. Solid-State Radar Transmitters. 272p. (C). 1985. text ed. 29.00 (*0-89006-169-6*) Artech Hse.

Ostroff, Harriet & Nichols, Tom. Specialty Cookbooks: A Bibliography. LC 91-37398. 672p. 1992. 90.00 (*0-8240-6947-1*, H1297) Garland.

Ostroff, Jeffrey M. Successful Marketing to the Fifty Plus Consumer. 352p. 1989. text ed. 59.95 (*0-13-860271-9*) P-H.

— Successful Marketing to the 50 Plus Consumer. 1990. pap. 19.95 (*0-13-860297-2*) P-H.

Ostroff, Jonathan S. Temporal Logic for Real Time Systems. 209p. 1989. text ed. 118.95 (*0-471-92402-4*) Wiley.

Ostrogorski, Moisei. Democracy & the Organization of Political Parties, 2 vols. abr. ed. LC 81-2862. (Social Science Classics Ser.). 350p. (C). 1982. reprint ed. Vol. 1: England, 350p. pap. 29.95 (*0-87855-877-2*); reprint ed. Vol. 2: United States, 418p. pap. 29.95 (*0-87855-878-0*) Transaction Pubs.

— Democracy & the Organization of Political Parties, 2 Vols. LC 72-122620. (World History Ser.: No. 48). 1970. reprint ed. lib. bdg. 150.00 (*0-8383-1003-6*) M S G Haskell Hse.

— Democracy & the Organization of Political Parties, 2 vols., Set. abr. ed. LC 81-2862. (Social Science Classics Ser.). (C). 1982. reprint ed. pap. 39.95 (*0-87855-921-3*) Transaction Pubs.

— Democracy & the Party System in the United States: A Study in Extra Constitutional Government. LC 73-19166. (Politics & People Ser.). 480p. 1974. reprint ed. 35.95 (*0-405-05888-8*) Ayer.

Ostrogorskii, Moisei A. The Rights of Women: A Comparative Study in History & Legislation. LC 80-21262. xv, 232p. 1981. reprint ed. lib. bdg. 35.00 (*0-87991-960-4*) Porcupine Pr.

Ostrogorsky, George. History of the Byzantine State. 624p. 1986. pap. text ed. 22.95 (*0-8135-1198-4*) Rutgers U Pr.

***Ostrom.** Paragraph Writing Simplified. 1994. pap. text ed. (*0-8230-4971-X*) Watsn-Guptill.

Ostrom, Bob, illus. The Masked Motorcyclist: Biker Mice from Mars. (Picturebacks Ser.). 24p. (Orig.). (J). (ps-3). 1994. pap. 2.50 (*0-679-86652-3*) Random Bks Yng Read.

Ostrom, Brian & Hairston, Steve. State Court Caseload Statistics: Annual Report, 1990. 316p. (Orig.). 1992. pap. text ed. 6.95 (*0-89656-111-9*, R132) Natl Ctr St Courts.

Ostrom, Carl. Video Compression. 1992. text ed. write for info. (*0-442-01422-8*) Van Nos Reinhold.

Ostrom, Charles W., Jr. Time Series Analysis: Regression Techniques. 2nd ed. (Quantitative Applications in the Social Sciences Ser.: Vol. 9). (Illus.). 96p. (C). 1990. pap. 9.50 (*0-8039-3135-2*) Sage.

Ostrom, Elinor. Crafting Institutions for Self-Governing Irrigation Systems. 1992. pap. 9.95 (*1-55815-168-0*) ICS Pr.

— Decision-Related Research on the Organization of Service Delivery Systems in Metropolitan Areas: Police Protection. LC 79-83821. 1979. write for info. (*0-89138-983-0*) ICPSR.

— Governing the Commons: The Evolution of Institutions for Collective Action. (Political Economy of Institutions & Decisions Ser.). (Illus.). 300p. (C). 1990. 59.95 (*0-521-37101-5*); pap. 16.95 (*0-521-40599-8*) Cambridge U Pr.

Ostrom, Elinor, jt. auth. see Keohane, Robert O.

Ostrom, Elinor, et al. Institutional Incentives & Sustainable Development: Infrastructure Policies in Perspective. (Theoretical Lenses on Public Policy Ser.). 266p. (C). 1993. text ed. 55.50 (*0-8133-1618-9*); pap. text ed. 22.50 (*0-8133-1619-7*) Westview.

— Rules, Games, & Common-Pool Resources. LC 93-44406. 370p. (C). 1994. text ed. 55.00 (*0-472-09546-3*); pap. text ed. 18.95 (*0-472-06546-7*) U of Mich Pr.

***Ostrom, Gladys S.** Creative Artistic Training. 1995. pap. 14.95 (*0-533-11235-4*) Vantage.

Ostrom, Hans. Langston Hughes. (Twayne's Studies in Short Fiction). 170p. 1993. text ed. 23.95 (*0-8057-8343-1*, Pub. by Royal Botanic Garden UK) Macmillan.

— Lives & Moments: An Introduction to Short Fiction. 900p. (C). 1991. pap. text ed. 25.50 (*0-03-030374-5*); pap. text ed. 28.50 (*0-03-030377-X*) HB Coll Pubs.

— Three to Get Ready. Chirich, Nancy, ed. LC 89-942. 199p. 1991. pap. 9.95 (*0-912761-30-X*) Cliffhanger Pr.

Ostrom, Hans, jt. ed. see Bishop, Wendy.

Ostrom, Hans, jt. auth. see Lulofs, Timothy J.

Ostrom, Hans A., et al. Spectrum: A Reader. 552p. (C). 1987. teacher ed write for info. (*0-15-583187-9*); pap. text ed. 18.75 (*0-15-583186-0*) HB Coll Pubs.

Ostrom, John. Dinosaurs. 2nd ed. Head, J. J., ed. LC 84-71139. (Carolina Biology Readers Ser.: No. 98). (Illus.). 32p. (J). (gr. 10 up). 1984. pap. 3.00 (*0-89278-201-3*, 45-9698) Carolina Biological.

Ostrom, John & Cook, William. Better Paragraphs, Plus. 6th ed. 208p. (C). 1990. pap. text ed. 14.50 (*0-06-044973-X*) HarpCollege.

— Paragraph Writing Simplified. LC 92-17962. (Simplified Ser.). (C). 1992. 8.50 (*0-06-501150-3*, HarpT) HarpC.

Ostrom, John, ed. see Poe, Edgar Allan.

Ostrom, Joseph. You & Your Aura. (Illus.). 124p. (Orig.). 1989. pap. 9.95 (*0-85030-549-7*, Pub. by Aquarian Pr UK); pap. 10.00 (*1-85538-292-X*, Pub. by Aquarian Pr UK) Thorsons SF.

Ostrom, Kjell, jt. ed. see Seers, Dudley.

Ostrom, Lee T. Creating the Ergonomically Sound Workplace. LC 93-41614. (The Management Ser.). 1994. 37.95 (*1-55542-621-2*); pap. 25.95 (*0-685-71220-6*) Jossey-Bass.

Ostrom, Neenyah. America's Biggest Cover-Up: Fifty More Things Everyone Should Know about the Chronic Fatigue Syndrome Epidemic & Its Link to AIDS. 100p. 1993. 14.95 (*0-9624142-3-9*) That New Mag.

— The Chronic Fatigue Story: Medical Cover-Up of the Century. 60p. (Orig.). 1989. pap. 6.95 (*0-685-29178-2*) That New Mag.

— Fifty Things You Should Know about Chronic Fatigue Syndrome. 1992. pap. 6.95 (*0-9624142-2-0*) That New Mag.

— What Really Killed Gilda Radner? Frontline Reports on the Chronic Fatigue Syndrome Epidemic. 400p. 1991. pap. 14.95 (*0-9624142-1-2*) That New Mag.

Ostrom, Neeyah. Fifty Things You Should Know about the Chronic Fatigue Symdrome Epidemic. 1993. mass mkt. 3.99 (*0-312-95043-8*) St Martin.

Ostrom, T. G., ed. see International Conference on Projective Planes Staff.

Ostrom, Vincent. The Intellectual Crisis in American Public Administration. 2nd ed. LC 88-15677. 232p. (C). 1989. pap. 14.50 (*0-8173-0418-5*) U of Ala Pr.

— The Meaning of American Federalism: Constituting a Self-Governing Society. 301p. 1991. 24.95 (*1-55815-076-5*) ICS Pr.

— The Meaning of American Federalism: Constituting a Self-Governing Society. 301p. 1991. pap. 14.95 (*1-55815-393-4*) ICS Pr.

— Political Theory of a Compound Republic. 240p. 1971. 25.00 (*0-685-70222-7*); pap. 8.95 (*0-685-70223-5*) ICS Pr.

Ostrom, Vincent, et al. Local Government in the United States. LC 88-23003. 250p. (C). 1988. 29.95 (*1-55815-030-7*); pap. 12.95 (*1-55815-029-3*) ICS Pr.

Ostrom, Vincent, et al, eds. Rethinking Institutional Analysis & Development: Issues, Alternatives & Choices. LC 88-28421. 480p. 1988. text ed. 34.95 (*1-55815-024-2*) ICS Pr.

— Rethinking Institutional Analysis & Development: Issues, Alternatives, & Choices. rev. ed. LC 93-16940. 1993. pap. 18.95 (*1-55815-264-4*) ICS Pr.

Ostrom, William. In God We Live. LC 86-61674. (Orig.). 1986. pap. 3.00 (*0-87574-268-8*) Pendle Hill.

O

An Asterisk (*) at the beginning of an entry indicates that the title is appearing in BIP for the first time.

Ostroske, Walter & Devaney, John. Break One Hundred in Twenty-One Days: A How-To Guide for the Weekend Golfer. (Illus.). 128p. 1990. pap. 8.95 (*0-399-51600-X*, Perigree Bks) Berkley Pub.
— Correct the Ten Most Common Golf Problems in Ten Days. (Illus.). 128p. 1991. pap. 8.95 (*0-399-51656-5*, Perigree Bks) Berkley Pub.
— Master Your Short Game in Sixteen Days: A How-to Guide for the Weekend Golfer. LC 93-36213. (Illus.). 128p. (Orig.). 1994. pap. 9.95 (*0-399-51861-4*, Perigree Bks) Berkley Pub.
— Power Swing in Fifteen Days: A How-to Guide for the Weekend Golfer. LC 92-35956. (Illus.). 128p. (Orig.). 1993. pap. 8.95 (*0-399-51797-9*) Putnam Pub Group.
— Two-Putt Greens in Eighteen Days: A How-to Guide for the Weekend Golfer. (Illus.). 128p. (Orig.). 1992. pap. 8.95 (*0-399-51747-2*, Perigree Bks) Berkley Pub.

Ostrosky-Solis, P., jt. ed. see Ardila, A.

Ostroumoff, Ivan N. The History of the Council of Florence. 189p. 1972. pap. 6.00 (*0-913026-03-4*) St Nectarios.

Ostroumov, S. A., jt. auth. see Yablokov, A. V.

Ostrov, Benjamin C. Conquering Resources: The Growth & Decline of the PLA's Science & Technology Commission for National Defense. LC 90-26809. (Studies on Contemporary China). 176p. (C). 1991. 57.95 (*0-87332-654-7*) M E Sharpe.

Ostrov, Rick. Power Reading. (Orig.). 1978. pap. write for info. (*0-9601706-2-6*) Educ Pr CA.

Ostrove, Karen, jt. auth. see Miller, Deborah.

Ostrove, S., jt. ed. see Henon, B. K.

Ostrovskii, Aleksandr N. Easy Money, & Two Other Plays: Even a Wise Man Stumbles, & Wolves & Sheep. Magarshack, David, tr. LC 78-110861. 296p. 1970. reprint ed. text ed. 67.50 (*0-8371-4532-5*, OSEM) Greenwood.

Ostrovskii, B. I. Physics Reviews: X-Ray Diffraction Study of Nematic, Smectic A & C Liquid Crystals, Vol. 12. Gol'danskii, V. I. et al, eds. (Soviet Scientific Reviews Ser.: Vol. 12, Pt. 2). ii, 68p. 1989. pap. text ed. 45.00 (*3-7186-4907-1*) Gordon & Breach.

Ostrovskii, I. A., jt. ed. see Shapiro, Leonid B.

Ostrovskii, I. V., ed. see Govorov, N. V.

Ostrovskii, Iosif V., jt. auth. see Linnik, Jurii V.

Ostrovskii, Nikolai A. Born of the Storm. Hiler, Louise L., tr. LC 74-10089. (Soviet Literature in English Translation Ser.). 251p. 1975. reprint ed. 20.00 (*0-88355-175-6*) Hyperion Conn.

Ostrovskii, V. N., jt. auth. see Demkov, Yu. N.

Ostrovsky. Mathematical Modeling of Chemical Processes. 1991. 98.95 (*0-8493-7132-5*, TP155) CRC Pr.

Ostrovsky, Alexander. Plays. Noyes, George R., ed. LC 70-98632. reprint ed. 24.00 (*0-404-04837-4*) AMS Pr.
— The Storm. Magarshack, David, tr. 120p. 1988. pap. 5.00 (*0-88233-551-0*) Ardis Pubs.
— Too Clever by Half or The Diary of a Scoundrel. Ackland, Rodney & Gerould, Daniel, trs. (Old Vic Theatre Collection Ser.: Vol. 3). 120p. (Orig.). 1988. pap. 7.95 (*1-55783-023-1*) Applause Theatre Bk Pubs.
— Without a Dowry & Other Plays. Henley, Norman, ed. & tr. by. 1995. 37.95 (*0-88233-933-8*) Ardis Pubs.

Ostrovsky, Alexandr. Besely Clon (Merry Elephant) (Illus.). 32p. (Orig.) (RUS.). (J). 1991. pap. 14.95 (*0-934393-22-2*) Rector Pr.
— Birthday (Den Rosdenia) (Childrens Ser.). (Illus.). 16p. (Orig.). (RUS.). (J). 1982. pap. 14.95 (*0-934393-17-6*) Rector Pr.
— Clouds (Oblaka) (Childrens Ser.). (Illus.). 16p. (Orig.). (RUS.). (J). 1984. pap. 14.95 (*0-934393-20-6*) Rector Pr.
— Graphics (Graphika) (Art Ser.). (Illus.). 10p. (Orig.). (RUS.). 1989. pap. 24.95 (*0-934393-19-2*) Rector Pr.
— Paper Kite (Bumazhni Emei) (Childrens Ser.). (Illus.). 30p. (Orig.). (RUS.). (J). 1987. pap. 14.95 (*0-934393-18-4*) Rector Pr.

Ostrovsky, Erika. A Constant Journey: The Fiction of Monique Wittig. LC 89-49482. 208p. (C). 1991. 24.95 (*0-8093-1642-0*) S Ill U Pr.
— Eye of Dawn: The Rise & Fall of Mata Hari. (Reprints Ser.). (Illus.). 271p. 1990. reprint ed. 17.95 (*0-88029-389-6*) Dorset Pr.

Ostrovsky, L. A., jt. auth. see Naugolnykh, K. A.

Ostrovsky, Victor. By Way of Deception. 1991. mass mkt. 5.99 (*0-312-92614-6*) St Martin.
— Lion of Judah. 320p. 1993. 21.95 (*0-312-10016-7*) St Martin.
— The Other Side of Depression: A Rogue Agent Exposes the Mossad's Secret Agenda. LC 94-30942. 1994. 24.00 (*0-06-017635-0*) HarpC.

Ostrovsky, Yu I., et al. Holographic Interferometry in Experimental Mechanics. (Optical Sciences Ser.: Vol. 60). (Illus.). 272p. 1991. text ed. 77.00 (*0-387-52604-8*) Spr-Verlag.
— Interferometry by Holography. (Optical Sciences Ser.: Vol. 20). (Illus.). 280p. 1980. 54.00 (*0-387-09886-0*) Spr-Verlag.

Ostrow. Bile Pigments & Jaundice: Molecular, Metabolic & Medical Aspects. (Liver: Normal Function & Disease Ser.: Vol. 4). 744p. 1986. 215.00 (*0-8247-7428-0*) Dekker.

Ostrow, Andrew C. Physical Activity & the Older Adult: Psychological Perspectives. LC 83-63191. (Illus.). 192p. 1984. pap. text ed. 14.95 (*0-916622-28-2*) Princeton Bk Co.

Ostrow, Andrew C., ed. Directory of Psychological Tests in the Sport & Exercise Sciences. LC 90-84378. (Illus.). 291p. (C). 1990. text ed. 36.00 (*0-9627926-0-8*) Fit Info Tech.

***Ostrow, David.** Mental Health Aspects of HIV-AIDS. (Second Decade of AIDS Ser.). (Illus.). 400p. (Orig.). (C). 1995. pap. text ed. 49.95x (*1-886330-06-9*) Hatherleigh.

Ostrow, David G., ed. Behavioral Aspects of AIDS. LC 90-7242. (Illus.). 430p. 1990. 59.50 (*0-306-43452-0*, Plenum Pr) Plenum.
— Biobehavioral Control of AIDS. (Illus.). 250p. (C). 1987. text ed. 29.50 (*0-8290-2354-2*) Irvington.

Ostrow, David G. & Kessler, R. C., eds. Methodological Issues in AIDS Behavioral Research. (AIDS Prevention & Mental Health Ser.). (Illus.). 335p. (C). 1993. 49.50 (*0-306-44439-9*, Plenum Pr) Plenum.

Ostrow, David G., jt. ed. see Nichols, Stuart E.

Ostrow, David G., et al, eds. Sexually Transmitted Diseases in Homosexual Men: Diagnosis, Treatment, & Research. LC 83-10957. (Illus.). 292p. 1983. 65.00 (*0-306-41337-X*, Plenum Pr) Plenum.

Ostrow, Eileen J., ed. Center Stage: An Anthology of Twenty-One Contemporary Black-American Plays. LC 80-53143. (Illus.). 328p. (Orig.). 1981. pap. 29.95 (*0-9605208-0-5*) Sea Urchin.
— Center Stage: An Anthology of Twenty-One Contemporary Black-American Plays. (Illus.). 328p. (Orig.). 1991. pap. 19.95 (*0-252-06178-0*) U of Ill Pr.

Ostrow, James M. Social Sensitivity: A Study of Habit & Experience. LC 89-35027. (SUNY Series in Philosophy of the Social Sciences). 137p. 1990. 59.50 (*0-7914-0215-0*); pap. 19.95 (*0-7914-0216-9*) State U NY Pr.

Ostrow, Lauren S., jt. auth. see Carter, Lanie.

Ostrow, M. A Complete Introduction to Gerbils. (Complete Introduction to...Ser.). (Illus.). 128p. (Orig.). 1987. pap. 5.95 (*0-86622-299-5*, CO-018S) TFH Pubns.

Ostrow, Marshall. Bettas. (Illus.). 96p. 1980. 9.95 (*0-86622-745-8*, KW-052) TFH Pubns.
— Goldfish: A Complete Pet Owner's Manual. (Pet Care Ser.). 80p. (Orig.). 1985. pap. 5.95 (*0-8120-2975-5*) Barron.

Ostrow, Marshall E. Breeding Hamsters. (Illus.). 96p. 1989. 9.95 (*0-86622-564-1*, KW-134) TFH Pubns.

Ostrow, Patricia C., et al, eds. Cost-Effectiveness of Rehabilitation: A Guide to Research Relevant to Occupational Therapy. 284p. 1987. pap. 32.50 (*0-910317-43-7*) Am Occup Therapy.

Ostrow, Rona & Smith, Sweetman R. The Dictionary of Marketing. (Illus.). 250p. 1987. text ed. 26.50 (*0-87005-573-9*) Fairchild.
— Fairchild's Dictionary of Retailing. (Illus.). 220p. (C). 1984. lib. bdg. 26.50 (*0-87005-437-6*) Fairchild.

Ostrow, Stephen E., ed. Visions & Revisions. LC 66-29132. (Illus.). 1968. 2.00 (*0-911517-42-1*) Mus of Art RI.

Ostrow, Vivian, jt. auth. see Ostrow, William.

Ostrow, William & Ostrow, Vivian. All about Asthma. Levine, Abby, ed. LC 89-5254. (Illus.). 32p. (J). (gr. 2-6). 1989. lib. bdg. 11.95 (*0-8075-0276-6*); pap. 4.95 (*0-8075-0275-8*) A Whitman.

***Ostrower, Francie.** Why the Wealthy Give: The Culture of Elite Philanthropy. LC 95-2854. 1995. write for info. (*0-691-04434-1*) Princeton U Pr.

Ostrower, Francie, jt. auth. see DiMaggio, Paul.

Ostrower, Gary B. Collective Insecurity: The United States and the League of Nations During the Early Thirties. LC 76-754. 287p. 1979. 37.50 (*0-8387-1799-3*) Bucknell U Pr.
— The League of Nations, 1919-1929. LC 94-8337. 1994. write for info. (*0-89529-636-5*) Avery Pub.

Ostrowky, Nicole, jt. ed. see Stanley, H. Eugene.

Ostrowski, Alexander. Aufgabensammlung zur Infinitesimalrechnung. Incl. Vol. 1. Funktionen Einer Variablen. 341p. 1980. 68.00 (*0-8176-0290-9*); Vol. 2A. Differentialrechnung auf dem Gebiete Mehrerer Varibalen. Aufgaben und Hinweise. 300p. 1980. 67.00 (*0-8176-0534-7*); Vol. 2B. Differentialrechnung auf dem Gebiete Mehrerer Variablen, Losungen. 233p. 1980. 50.00 (*0-8176-0572-X*); Vol. 3. Integralrechnung auf dem Gebiete Mehrerer Variablen: Differentialrechnung auf dem Gebiete Mehrerer Variablen, Losungen. 398p. 1977. 53.95 (*0-685-00763-4*); (Mathematische Reihe Ser.: Vols. 28, 38, 47 & 56). (GER.). write for info. (*0-318-51085-5*) Birkhauser.
— Collected Papers, 6 vols., Set, Vol. 4, X-XII. 600p. (ENG, FRE & GER.). 1983. Six-vol. set. 530.00 (*0-8176-1512-1*) Birkhauser.
— Collected Papers, Vol. 4, X-XII. 600p. (ENG, FRE & GER.). 1984. 77.00 (*0-8176-1509-1*) Birkhauser.
— Collected Papers, Vol. 5. (Contemporary Mathematicians Ser.). 560p. 1985. text ed. 72.00 (*0-8176-1510-5*) Birkhauser.
— Collected Papers: Alexander Ostrowski, Vol. 6. (Contemporary Mathematicians Ser.). 720p. 1985. pap. 93.00 (*0-8176-1511-3*) Birkhauser.

Ostrowski, John W., jt. auth. see Sacco, John F.

Ostrowsky & Puech, eds. Advanced Optoelectronic Technology. 1987. 45.00 (*0-89252-899-0*, 864) SPIE.

Ostrowsky, Daniel B. & Reinisch, Raymond, eds. Guided Wave Nonlinear Optics: Proceedings of the NATO Advanced Study Institute, Cargese, France, August 12-24, 1991. LC 92-10359. (NATO Advanced Science Institutes Series C: Mathematical & Physical Sciences: Vol. 214). 672p. (C). 1992. lib. bdg. 191.00 (*0-7923-1727-0*) Kluwer Ac.

Ostrowsky, Daniel B. & Spitz, E., eds. New Directions in Guided Wave & Coherent Optics, 2 Vols., Set. 1984. lib. bdg. 212.50 (*90-247-2938-6*) Kluwer Ac.

Ostrowsky, Nicole, jt. ed. see Stanley, H. Eugene.

Ostrum, Meg, ed. Deer Camp: Last Light in the Northeast Kingdom. 129p. 1992. 29.95x (*0-262-13283-4*) MIT Pr.

Ostry, Jonathan D., jt. auth. see Krueger, Thomas H.

Ostry, Sylvia. Authority & Academic Scribblers: The Role of Research in East Asian Policy Reform. 181p. 1991. pap. 12.95 (*1-55815-132-X*); 2.00 (*1-55815-141-9*) ICS Pr.
— Governments & Corporations in a Shrinking World: Trade & Innovation Policy in the United States, Europe & Japan. LC 89-20978. 148p. 1990. pap. 14.95 (*0-87609-079-X*) Coun Foreign.
— The Threat of Managed Trade to Transforming Economics. (Orig.). 1993. pap. text ed. write for info. (*1-56708-088-X*) Grp of Thirty.

***Ostry, Sylvia & Nelson, Richard R.** High-Tech Industrial Policies: Conflict & Cooperation. (Integrating National Economies Ser.). 160p. (C). 1995. 28.95x (*0-8157-6674-2*); pap. 10.95x (*0-8157-6673-4*) Brookings.

Ostrye, Anne T. Foreign Investment in the American & Canadian West, Eighteen Seventy-Nineteen Forteen: An Annotated Bibliography. LC 85-27657. 200p. 1986. 27.50 (*0-8108-1866-3*) Scarecrow.

***Ostrzenski, Adam.** Laproscopic Panhysterectomy with Reconstructive Posterior Culdeplasty & Vaginal Vault Suspension. (Illus.). 109p. (C). (gr. 12 up). 1994. 78.00 (*0-9638210-0-8*) Med Sci Pub.

Ostuni, Elizabeth & Santo Pietro, Mary Jo. Getting Through: Communicating When Someone You Care for Has Alzheimer's Disease. rev. ed. LC 86-61472. (Illus.). 100p. (Orig.). 1991. pap. 18.95 (*0-937857-01-7*, 1331) Speech Bin.

Ostuni, Elizabeth E. & Silver, Elaine N. I'm Good at Speech: Music & Activities to Teach Children Good Communication Skills. (Illus.). 112p. (Orig.). 1990. pap. text ed. 14.95 (*1-879267-00-4*); audio 9.95 (*1-879267-01-2*) Accent Pub NJ.

Ostwald, Martin. Anarke in Thucydides. LC 88-32781. (American Philological Association, American Classical Studies). 92p. 1989. 18.95 (*1-55540-279-8*, 40 04 18); pap. 12.95 (*1-55540-280-1*) Scholars Pr GA.
— Autonomia: Its Genesis & Early History. (American Classical Studies). 82p. 1982. pap. 15.95 (*0-89130-572-6*, 40 04 11) Scholars Pr GA.
— From Popular Sovereignty to the Sovereignty of Law: Law, Society, & Politics in Fifth Century Athens. LC 85-690. 500p. 1986. 90.00 (*0-520-05426-1*); pap. 19.00 (*0-520-06798-3*) U CA Pr.
— Nicomachean Ethics: Aristotle. 352p. (C). 1962. pap. write for info. (*0-02-389530-6*) Macmillan.

Ostwald, Martin, ed. see Plato.

Ostwald, Peter. Schumann: The Inner Voices of a Musical Genius. (Illus.). 390p. 1987. reprint ed. pap. text ed. 15.95 (*1-55553-014-1*) NE U Pr.
— Vaslav Nijinsky: The Leap into Madness. 1990. 19.95 (*0-8184-0535-X*) Carol Pub Group.

Ostwald, Peter & Zegans, Leonard S., eds. The Pleasures & Perils of Genius: Mostly Mozart. LC 93-24461. (Mental Health Library: Monograph 2). 228p. (C). 1993. 32.00 (*0-8236-4162-7*) Intl Univs Pr.

Ostwald, Peter, tr. see Nauhaus, Gerd.

Ostwald, Phillip F. A M Cost Estimator. (Illus.). 560p. 1989. reprint ed. 102.50 (*0-932905-06-4*) Penton Pub.
— Engineering Cost Estimating. 3rd ed. 576p. 1991. text ed. 79.00 (*0-13-276627-2*) P-H.

Ostwald, Phillip F., ed. Manufacturing Cost Estimating. LC 79-67648. 266p. reprint ed. pap. 75.90 (*0-317-28115-1*, 2055738) Bks Demand.

Ostwalt, Conrad E., Jr. After Eden: The Secularization of American Space in the Fiction of Willa Cather & Theodore Dreiser. LC 89-42505. 160p. 1990. 32.50 (*0-8387-5168-7*) Bucknell U Pr.

Ostwalt, Conrad E., Jr., jt. ed. see Martin, Joel W.

OSU Dept. of Linguistics Staff. Language Files: Materials for an Introduction to Language & Linguistics. 5th ed. 464p. (C). 1991. pap. text ed. 30.95 (*0-8142-0525-9*) Ohio St U Pr.

O'Suilleabhain, Sean. Handbook of Irish Folklore. 1995. reprint ed. 58.00 (*1-55888-835-7*) Omnigraphics Inc.

O'Sullivan. Gasmakers. 1989. pap. 18.95 (*0-86278-143-4*, Pub. by OBrien Pr IE) Dufour.

O'Sullivan, A. W., tr. see Hurgronje, Christian Snouck.

O'Sullivan, Anna-Margaret. The Green Bank Year. LC 88-62114. 255p. (J). 1989. pap. 6.95 (*1-55523-183-7*) Winston-Derek.

O'Sullivan, Arthur, et al. Property Taxes & Tax Revolts: The Legacy of Proposition 13. (Illus.). 262p. (C). 1995. 39.95 (*0-521-46159-6*) Cambridge U Pr.

O'Sullivan, Arthur M. Essentials of Urban Economics. LC 92-24424. 512p. (C). 1992. text ed. 56.95 (*0-256-12330-6*) Irwin.
— Urban Economics. 2nd ed. LC 92-17150. 768p. (C). 1992. text ed. 61.95 (*0-256-09617-1*) Irwin.

O'Sullivan, Barbara. Staff Orientation in Early Childhood Programs. (Illus.). 172p. (Orig.). 1987. pap. 14.95 (*0-934140-42-1*) Redleaf Pr.

O'Sullivan, Bill. Precious Blood. LC 91-47500. 202p. 1992. 18.95 (*0-939149-67-2*) Soho Press.

O'Sullivan, Carol. Alcohol: Understanding Words in Context. LC 89-11712. (Opposing Viewpoints Juniors Ser.). (Illus.). 32p. (J). (gr. 3-6). 1990. lib. bdg. 11.95 (*0-89908-634-9*) Greenhaven.
— Death Penalty: Identifying Propaganda Techniques. LC 89-11033. (Opposing Viewpoints Juniors Ser.). (Illus.). 32p. (J). (gr. 3-6). 1990. lib. bdg. 11.95 (*0-89908-636-5*) Greenhaven.
— Drugs & Sports: Locating the Author's Main Idea. LC 89-36322. (Opposing Viewpoints Juniors Ser.). (Illus.). 32p. (J). (gr. 3-6). 1990. lib. bdg. 11.95 (*0-89908-637-3*) Greenhaven.
— Gun Control: Distinguishing Between Fact & Opinion. LC 89-2226. (Opposing Viewpoints Juniors Ser.). (Illus.). 32p. (J). (gr. 3-6). 1990. lib. bdg. 10.95 (*0-89908-638-1*) Greenhaven.
— Poverty: Locating the Authors Main Idea. LC 89-17069. (Opposing Viewpoints Juniors Ser.). (Illus.). 32p. (J). (gr. 3-6). 1990. lib. bdg. 11.95 (*0-89908-641-1*) Greenhaven.
— Television: Identifying Propaganda Techniques. LC 90-3785. (Opposing Viewpoints Juniors Ser.). (Illus.). 32p. 1990. lib. bdg. 11.95 (*0-89908-606-3*) Greenhaven.

***O'Sullivan, D. & Ramadurai, S., eds.** Charge Composition of Ultra Heavy Nuclei. 88p. 1995. pap. 94.00 (*0-08-042556-9*, Pergamon Pr) Elsevier.

O'Sullivan, Dan, jt. auth. see Lockyer, Roger.

O'Sullivan, David. Manufacturing Systems Design Roadmap. 224p. 1994. text ed. 45.00 (*0-13-072786-5*) P-H.

O'Sullivan, Deirdre & Young, Robert. The English Heritage Book of Lindisfarne: Holy Island. (Illus.). 136p. 1994. pap. 34.95 (*0-7134-7229-4*, Pub. by Batsford UK) Trafalgar.

O'Sullivan, Denis. Commitment, Educative Action & Adults: Learning Programmes with a Social Purpose. 215p. 1993. 59.95 (*1-85628-292-9*, Pub. by Avebury Pub UK) Ashgate Pub Co.

O'Sullivan, Denis, jt. ed. see Peache, Robert J.

O'Sullivan, Donal. The Irish Free State & Its Senate: A Study in Contemporary Politics. LC 72-4286. (World Affairs Ser.: National & International Viewpoints). 696p. 1972. reprint ed. 44.95 (*0-405-04579-4*) Ayer.

O'Sullivan, Donal, ed. Songs of the Irish. 1981. pap. 16.95 (*0-85342-653-8*) Dufour.

***O'Sullivan, Elizabethann & Rassel, Gary R.** Research Methods for Public Administrators. 2nd ed. 576p. (C). 1995. text ed. 47.95 (*0-8013-1172-1*) Longman.

O'Sullivan, Ellen L. Marketing for Parks, Recreation, & Leisure. LC 91-65916. 275p. 1991. 24.95 (*0-910251-43-6*) Venture Pub PA.

O'Sullivan, George, jt. auth. see Bancroft, Gordon.

O'Sullivan, Helene, jt. ed. see Jenkinson, William.

O'Sullivan, Humphrey. The Diary of An Irish Countryman 1827-1835. De Bhaldraithe, Tomas, tr. 140p. 1993. pap. 11.95 (*1-85635-042-8*, Pub. by Mercier Pr IE) Dufour.

O'Sullivan, Ivo, tr. see Giles.

***O'Sullivan, James N.** Xenophon of Ephesus: His Compositional Technique & the Birth of the Novel. (Untersuchungen zur Antiken Literatur und Geschichte Ser.: Vol. 44). 227p. (C). 1994. lib. bdg. 107.70 (*3-11-014310-0*) De Gruyter.

O'Sullivan, James N., ed. Lexicon to Achilles Tatius. (Untersuchungen zur Antiken Literatur und Geschichte Ser.: Vol. 18). 442p. (GER.). (C). 1980. text ed. 176.95 (*3-11-007844-9*) De Gruyter.

O'Sullivan, Jan. Journeys Through Microsoft Excel 4.0. LC 92-43204. (Macintosh Guide Ser.). 1993. write for info. (*0-201-63157-1*) Addison-Wesley.

O'Sullivan, Jeremiah F. Cistercian Settlements in Wales & Monmouthshire, 1140-1540. LC 48-6318. (Fordham University Studies. History Ser.: No. 2). 151p. reprint ed. pap. 43.10 (*0-7837-5577-5*, 2045359) Bks Demand.

O'Sullivan, Jeremiah F., tr. see Idung Of Prufening.

O'Sullivan, Jeremiah F., tr. see Lackner, Bede K., ed.

O'Sullivan, John. Law for Nurses. 3rd ed. xi, 282p. 1983. pap. 44.00 (*0-455-20495-0*, Pub. by Law Bk Co) W W Gaunt.

O'Sullivan, John & Keuchel, Edward F. American Economic History: From Abundance to Constraint. 2nd ed. LC 80-25339. (History Texts Ser.). 300p. (Orig.). (C). 1989. reprint ed. 29.95 (*1-55876-009-1*); reprint ed. pap. text ed. 16.95 (*1-55876-010-5*) Wiener Pubs Inc.

O'Sullivan, John, et al, eds. The Draft & Its Enemies: A Documentary History. LC 74-10979. 309p. reprint ed. pap. 88.10 (*0-317-08169-1*, 2022262) Bks Demand.

O'Sullivan, John C. Joyce's Use of Colors: Finnegans Wake & the Earlier Works. LC 87-13741. (Studies in Modern Literature: No. 75). 216p. reprint ed. pap. 61.60 (*0-8357-1816-6*, 2070647) Bks Demand.

O'Sullivan, John L. Report in Favor of the Abolition of the Punishment of Death by Law, Made to Legislature of the State of New York April 14, 1841. LC 74-3846. (Criminal Justice in America Ser.). 1974. reprint ed. 20.95 (*0-405-06162-5*) Ayer.

O'Sullivan, Judy. The Pasadena Playhouse: A Celebration of One of the Oldest Theatrical Organizations in America. (Orig.). 1992. 89.95 (*0-9633603-0-2*); pap. 39.95 (*0-9633603-1-0*) Theatre Corp Am.

O'Sullivan, Kathleen. A Way of Life: A Human-Spiritual Growth Series for Lay Groups. 126p. 1989. pap. 22.00 (*0-86217-203-9*, Pub. by Veritas IE) St Mut.

O'Sullivan, Kathleen F. One Impulsive Black Rose. Danbury, Richard S., III, ed. 160p. (Orig.). 1994. pap. 8.95 (*0-89754-089-1*) Dan River Pr.

O'Sullivan, Kevin. Living Parables. 120p. 1979. 7.50 (*0-8199-0780-4*, Frncscn Herld) Franciscan Pr.

***O'Sullivan, Mark.** Melody for Nora. 1995. pap. 8.95 (*0-86327-425-0*) Dufour.

O'Sullivan, Maureen & Kaplan, Harvey, eds. Immigration Litigation: Winning in Federal & Immigration Courts. 254p. (Orig.). (C). 1993. pap. text ed. 45.00 (*1-878677-50-0*) Amer Immi Law Assn.

***O'Sullivan, Maurice & Jones, Jane A., eds.** Florida in Poetry: A History of the Imagination. 260p. 1995. 24.95 (*1-56164-083-2*) Pineapple Pr.

***O'Sullivan, Maurice & Lane, Jack.** Florida Reader. LC 84-4272. 274p. 1991. pap. 16.95 (*1-56164-062-X*) Pineapple Pr.

O'Sullivan, Maurice & Lane, Jack, eds. The Florida Reader: Visions of Paradise. LC 90-39065. 270p. 1991. 18.95 (*0-910923-71-X*) Pineapple Pr.

O'Sullivan, Maurice J. Shakespeare's Other Lives. LC 91-3473. 1995. text ed. 35.00 (*0-89341-680-0*, Longwood Academic) Hollowbrook.

***O'Sullivan, Michael.** Boiling Water: The World's Best Vegetarian Recipes from America's Premier Vegetarian Chef - Fast, Simple, Filling. 114p. 1995. pap. 10.95 (*0-9636867-0-4*) Leichman Assocs.
— The Physics of Parting. 66p. (Orig.). 1992. pap. 14.95 (*1-55605-226-X*) Wyndhall Pr.

O'Sullivan, Nadine. Dysphagia Care: Team Approach. (Team Approach with Acute & Long Term Patients). (Illus.). 112p. (Orig.). (C). 1990. pap. 29.95 (*0-9633234-0-7*) Cottage Sq Pr.

— Dysphagia Care Team Approach with Acute & Long Term Patients. 2nd ed. Turner, Arthur C., ed. (Illus.). 212p. (C). 1995. pap. 20.97 (*0-9633234-1-5*) Cottage Sq Pr.

O'Sullivan, Neal. Santayana. 112p. 1993. 19.95 (*1-870626-33-8*, Pub. by Claridge Pr UK); pap. 12.95 (*1-870626-38-9*, Pub. by Claridge Pr UK) Paul & Co Pubs.

O'Sullivan, Neil. Alcidamas, Aristophanes & the Beginnings of Greek Stylistic Theory. 176p. (Orig.). 1992. pap. 54.00 (*3-515-05420-0*) Coronet Bks.

O'Sullivan, Noel. The Structure of Modern Ideology: Critical Perspectives on Social & Political Theory. 208p. 1989. text ed. 69.95 (*1-85278-036-3*, Pub. by E Elgar Pub UK) Ashgate Pub Co.

O'Sullivan, Owen. A Basic Catholic Dictionary. (C). 1988. 50.00 (*0-685-22279-9*, Pub. by St Paul Pubns UK) St Mut.

O'Sullivan, P., ed. Passive Solar Energy in Buildings: Report Number 17. 70p. 1989. 61.25 (*1-85166-280-4*) Elsevier.

O'Sullivan, Paddy, jt. ed. see Coleman, Stephen.

O'Sullivan, Patrick. A Country Diary: The Year in Kerry. (Illus.). 160p. (Orig.). 1993. pap. 13.95 (*0-947962-76-X*, Pub. by Anvil Bks Ltd IE) Irish Bks Media.

— Geopolitics. LC 86-1269. 192p. 1986. text ed. 35.00 (*0-312-32381-6*) St Martin.

— I Heard the Wild Birds Sing: A Kerry Childhood. (Illus.). 208p. (Orig.). 1991. pap. 9.95 (*0-947962-55-7*, Pub. by Anvil Bks Ltd IE) Irish Bks Media.

— Irish Women & Irish Migration. LC 94-24613. (Irish World Wide Ser.: Vol. 4). 1995. write for info. (*0-7185-1425-4*, Pub. by Leicester Univ Pr) St Martin.

— Terrain & Tactics. LC 91-12223. (Contributions in Military Studies: No. 115). 192p. 1991. text ed. 49.95 (*0-313-27923-3*, OTT, Greenwood Pr) Greenwood.

O'Sullivan, Patrick, ed. The Creative Migrant. (Irish World Wide Ser.). 256p. 1994. text ed. 69.00 (*0-7185-1423-8*, Pub. by Pinter Pubs UK) St Martin.

— The Irish in the New Communities. (Irish World Wide Ser.). 256p. (C). 1992. text ed. 59.00 (*0-7185-1427-0*, Pub. by Pinter Pubs UK) St Martin.

— Patterns of Migration. (Irish World Wide Ser.). 240p. (C). 1992. text ed. 59.00 (*0-7185-1422-X*, Pub. by Pinter Pubs UK) St Martin.

O'Sullivan, Patrick V. Irish Superstitions & Legends of Animals & Birds. 1991. pap. 11.95 (*0-85342-957-X*) Dufour.

O'Sullivan, Paul. All About the Angels. LC 90-70122. 148p. 1990. reprint ed. pap. 5.00 (*0-89555-388-0*) TAN Bks Pubs.

— An Easy Way to Become a Saint. LC 90-70237. 105p. 1990. reprint ed. pap. 5.00 (*0-89555-398-8*) TAN Bks Pubs.

— The Holy Ghost, Our Greatest Friend - He Who Loves Us Best. LC 91-75171. 72p. 1991. reprint ed. pap. 1.50 (*0-89555-448-8*) TAN Bks Pubs.

— How to Avoid Purgatory. LC 92-64438. 39p. 1992. pap. 1.00 (*0-89555-477-1*) TAN Bks Pubs.

— How to Be Happy, How to Be Holy. LC 89-51901. 234p. 1989. reprint ed. pap. 7.00 (*0-89555-386-4*) TAN Bks Pubs.

— Read Me or Rue It. LC 92-61256. 48p. 1992. pap. 1.25 (*0-89555-458-5*) TAN Bks Pubs.

— The Secret of Confession Including the Wonders of Confession. LC 92-61255. 96p. 1992. reprint ed. pap. 4.50 (*0-89555-459-3*) TAN Bks Pubs.

— St. Philomena, the Wonder-Worker. LC 93-61563. 155p. 1927. text ed. 6.00 (*0-89555-501-8*) TAN Bks Pubs.

— The Wonders of the Holy Name. LC 93-60345. 45p. 1993. pap. 1.50 (*0-89555-490-9*) TAN Bks Pubs.

— The Wonders of the Mass. LC 93-60344. 42p. 1993. pap. 1.00 (*0-89555-491-7*) TAN Bks Pubs.

O'Sullivan, Paul, ed. Field & Shore. 83p. 1987. reprint ed. pap. 8.95 (*0-905140-13-3*, Pub. by OBrien Pr IE) Dufour.

— World of Stone: Life, Folklore & Legends of the Aran Islands. 80p. 1988. pap. 8.95 (*0-905140-12-5*, Pub. by OBrien Pr IE) Dufour.

***O'Sullivan, Philip, et al.** Irish Planning Law & Practice, 2 binders, Set. 1991. ring bd. 311.00 (*1-85475-004-6*, IE) Butterworth Legal Pubs.

O'Sullivan, Richard. Fifty-Fifth Virginia Infantry. (Virginia Regimental Histories Ser.). (Illus.). 160p. 1989. 19.95 (*0-930919-73-4*) H E Howard.

O'Sullivan, Richard, tr. see Maritain, Jacques.

O'Sullivan, Rita G. & Tennant, Cheryl V. Programs for At-Risk Students: A Guide to Evaluation. (Essential Tools for Educators Ser.). 92p. 1993. pap. 16.95 (*0-8039-6043-3*) Corwin Pr.

O'Sullivan, Sean. Island Stories: Tales & Legends from the West. 80p. 1986. reprint ed. pap. 7.95 (*0-905140-22-2*, Pub. by OBrien Pr IE) Dufour.

O'Sullivan, Sean, tr. Folktales of Ireland. LC 66-11885. (Folktales of the World Ser.). 1968. pap. text ed. 14.95 (*0-226-64000-0*, FW4) U Ch Pr.

O'Sullivan, Sue & Parmar, Pratibha. Lesbians Talk (Safer) Sex. 64p. (Orig.). 1992. pap. 8.50 (*1-85727-020-7*, Pub. by Scarlet Pr UK) InBook.

O'Sullivan, Susan B. Physical Rehabilitation: Assessment & Treatment. 3rd ed. LC 94-955. 748p. 1994. 55.00 (*0-8036-6699-3*) Davis Co.

O'Sullivan, Thomas. North Star Statehouse: An Armchair Guide to the Minnesota State Capitol. LC 94-66863. (Illus.). 124p. (Orig.). 1995. pap. 16.95 (*1-880654-07-5*) Pogo Pr.

O'Sullivan, Thomas, ed. The Prints of Adolf Dehn: A Catalogue Raisonne. LC 87-7776. (Illus.). 268p. 1987. 75.00 (*0-87351-203-0*) Minn Hist.

O'Sullivan, Thomas J. Pioneer Airplane Mails of the United States. 346p. 25.00 (*0-939429-13-6*) Am Air Mail.

O'Sullivan, Tim. Expose: The Art of Tattoo. (Illus.). 112p. 1993. pap. 19.95 (*0-8065-1430-2*, Citadel Pr) Carol Pub Group.

O'Sullivan, Tim, ed. see Hartley, John, et al.

O'Sullivan, Tim, et al. Key Concepts in Communication & Cultural Studies. 2nd ed. LC 93-7405. (Studies in Culture & Communication). 1993. write for info. (*0-415-01411-5*); pap. write for info. (*0-415-06173-3*) Routledge.

— Studying the Media: An Introduction. LC 94-14195. 256p. 1994. pap. 15.95 (*0-340-59828-X*, Pub. by E Arnold UK) Routledge Chapman & Hall.

O'Sullivan, Vincent. Aspects of Wilde. 1976. lib. bdg. 59.95 (*0-8490-1460-3*) Gordon Pr.

— The Houses of Sin, 1897: With Poems, 1896. LC 93-41352. (Decadents, Symbolists, Anti-Decadents Ser.). 1994. 49.50 (*1-85477-153-1*, Pub. by Woodstock Bks UK) Cassell.

— Opinions. LC 79-8072. reprint ed. 23.50 (*0-404-18382-4*) AMS Pr.

O'Sullivan, Vincent, ed. An Anthology of Twentieth Century New Zealand Poetry. 3rd ed. (Illus.). 460p. 1987. pap. 22.95 (*0-19-558163-6*) OUP.

O'Sullivan, Vincent, sel. The Oxford Book of New Zealand Short Stories. 464p. 1994. pap. 16.95 (*0-19-558291-8*) OUP.

O'Sullivan, Vincent, ed. see Bethell, Ursula.

O'Sullivan, Vincent, ed. see Mansfield, Katherine.

Osumi, Midori. Tinrin Grammar. (Oceanic Linguistics Special Publication Ser.: No. 25). 340p. (C). 1994. pap. text ed. 35.00 (*0-8248-1629-3*) UH Pr.

Osuna, Juan J. A History of Education in Puerto Rico. 2nd ed. 12.50 (*0-685-26799-7*) Univ Place.

— A History of Education in Puerto Rico. LC 74-14239. (Puerto Rican Experience Ser.). (Illus.). 686p. 1975. reprint ed. 56.95 (*0-405-06227-3*) Ayer.

Osundare, Niyi. Selected Poems. (African Writers Ser.). 116p. 1992. pap. 8.95 (*0-435-91195-3*, 91195) Heinemann.

Osuntogun, Adeniyi & Adewunmi, Wole, eds. Rural Banking in Nigeria. LC 82-176. (Illus.). 144p. reprint ed. pap. 41.10 (*0-8357-2964-8*, 2039226) Bks Demand.

Osuntoki, Chief. The Book of African Names. LC 90-82690. 32p. 1991. reprint ed. pap. 5.95 (*0-933121-24-5*) Black Classic.

Osuntokun, Akinjide. Chief S. Ladoke Akintola: His Life & Times. (Illus.). 212p. 1984. text ed. 29.50 (*0-7146-3219-8*, BHA-00169, Pub. by F Cass Pubs UK) Intl Spec Bk.

Osur, Alan M. Blacks in the Army Air Forces During World War II. (Illus.). 227p. 1986. reprint ed. pap. write for info. (*0-912799-23-4*) Off Air Force.

— Blacks in the Army Air Forces During World War II: The Problem of Race Relations. Gilbert, James B., ed. LC 79-7291. (Flight: Its First Seventy-Five Years Ser.). (Illus.). 1980. reprint ed. lib. bdg. 30.95 (*0-405-12199-7*) Ayer.

Oswald, A. J. & Mascarenhas, S. J. New Product Development: Its Marketing Research & Management. (C). 1987. 17.50 (*81-204-0231-6*, Pub. by Oxford IBH II) S Asia.

Oswald, Allan. History & Practice of Falconry. (Illus.). 129p. 1984. 15.00 (*0-87556-661-8*) Saifer.

Oswald, Andrew J., ed. Surveys in Economics, Vol. 1. 256p. (C). 1991. 59.95 (*0-631-17972-0*); pap. 24.95 (*0-631-17973-9*) Blackwell Pubs.

Oswald, Andrew J., jt. auth. see Blanchflower, David G.

Oswald, Andrew J., jt. auth. see Carruth, Alan A.

Oswald, Andrew T., ed. Surveys in Economics, Vol. 2. 312p. (C). 1991. 59.95 (*0-631-17974-7*); pap. 24.95 (*0-631-17975-5*) Blackwell Pubs.

Oswald, David, tr. see Rilke, Maria R.

Oswald, Debra. Dags. 57p. 1990. pap. 4.25 (*0-87129-012-X*, D48) Dramatic Pub.

***Oswald, Gert.** Lexikon der Heraldik. 478p. (GER.). 1985. 79.95 (*0-7859-8349-X*, 3411021497) Fr & Eur.

Oswald, Gregory J., tr. see Carlton, Robert G., ed.

Oswald, H., ed. Luther's Works: Lectures on the Minor Prophets, 2: Jonah & Habakkuk, Vol. 19. LC 55-9893. 1974. 19.95 (*0-570-06419-8*, 15-1761) Concordia.

Oswald, Hilton, ed. Luther's Works, Vol. 11. Bowman, Herbert J., tr. LC 55-9893. 560p. 1976. 19.95 (*0-570-06411-2*, 15-1753) Concordia.

Oswald, Hilton C., tr. see Hans-Joachim, Kraus.

Oswald, I., ed. see International Congress of Pharmacology Staff.

Oswald, J. Gregory, tr. see Krueger, Rudolph.

Oswald, J. W., jt. auth. see Krar, S. F.

Oswald, Jacques R. Diacritical Analysis of Systems. (Ellis Horwood Series in Science & Technology). 488p. 99.00 (*0-13-208752-9*, 270612) P-H.

Oswald, James L. Wiros & Deiwos; He Who Would be God: The Story of the Indo-Europeans. (Illus.). 210p. (Orig.). 1986. pap. 11.11 (*0-9613882-0-X*) G J Ludwig.

Oswald, James L., jt. auth. see Ballantine, Frederick W.

Oswald, James W., jt. auth. see Krar, Stephen F.

Oswald, Jean A. Yours for Health: The Life & Times of Herbert M. Shelton. (Illus.). 168p. (Orig.). 1989. pap. 9.95 (*0-9620490-0-X*) Franklin Bks.

Oswald, Laura. Jean Genet & the Semiotics of Performance. LC 88-45447. (Advances in Semiotics Ser.). 188p. 1989. 34.95 (*0-253-33152-8*) Ind U Pr.

Oswald, Martin, jt. auth. see Jowett, Benjamin E.

***Oswald, R. M., et al.** Married to the Minister. Date not set. pap. 8.75 (*1-56699-077-7*, OD28) Alban Inst.

Oswald, Roy M. Clergy Self-Care: Finding a Balance for Effective Ministry. LC 90-86201. 234p. (Orig.). 1991. pap. 17.95 (*1-56699-044-0*, AL125) Alban Inst.

— Ending Well, Starting Strong: Your Personal Pastorate Start-up Workshop. Date not set. audio 89.95 (*1-56699-143-9*, AL157) Alban Inst.

— Finding Leaders for Tomorrow's Churches: The Growing Crisis in Clergy Recruitment. LC 93-73156. 132p. (Orig.). 1993. pap. 13.95 (*1-56699-116-1*, AL145) Alban Inst.

— How to Build a Support System for Your Ministry. LC 90-86200. 109p. (Orig.). 1991. pap. 10.25 (*1-56699-043-2*, AL124) Alban Inst.

— How to Minister Effectively in Family, Pastoral, Program, Or Corporate Size Churches. Date not set. pap. 7.50 (*1-56699-111-0*, OD96) Alban Inst.

— Making Your Church More Inviting: A Step-by-Step Guide for In-Church Training. LC 92-72456. (Orig.). 1992. pap. 14.95 (*1-56699-055-6*, AL134) Alban Inst.

— New Beginnings: A Pastorate Start up Workbook. rev. ed. 90p. 1989. pap. 12.95 (*1-56699-032-7*, AL111) Alban Inst.

Oswald, Roy M. & Kroeger, Otto. Personality Type & Religious Leadership. LC 88-70758. 183p. (Orig.). 1988. pap. 17.95 (*1-56699-025-4*, AL103) Alban Inst.

— Who Ministers to Ministers? A Study of Support Systems for Clergy & Spouses. LC 87-72687. 104p. (Orig.). 1987. pap. 10.95 (*1-56699-022-X*, AL101) Alban Inst.

Oswald, Roy M. & Leas, Speed B. The Inviting Church. LC 87-71965. 119p. (Orig.). 1987. pap. 11.95 (*1-56699-020-3*, AL99) Alban Inst.

***Oswald, Roy M. & Saarinen, Martin.** Why Some Churches Don't Grow: Factors That Might Motivate Those Not Interested in Growth. Date not set. pap. 9.50 (*1-56699-127-7*, OD103) Alban Inst.

Oswald, Roy M., et al. New Visions for the Long Pastorate. LC 83-73205. 111p. (Orig.). 1983. pap. 10.95 (*1-56699-010-6*, AL73) Alban Inst.

***Oswalt.** New International Commentary on the Old Testament Isaiah 1-39. 1994. (*0-8028-2529-X*) Eerdmans.

Oswalt, Jerry E. Proclaiming the Whole Counsel of God: Suggestions for Planning & Preparing Doctrinal Sermons. 66p. (Orig.). (C). 1993. pap. text ed. 14.50 (*0-8191-9011-X*) U Pr of Amer.

Oswalt, John N. The Book of Isaiah, Chapters 1-39. (New International Commentary on the Old Testament Ser.). 672p. 1986. 34.99 (*0-8028-2368-8*) Eerdmans.

Oswalt, Wendell H. Bashful No Longer: An Alaskan Eskimo Ethnohistory, 1778-1988. LC 89-37036. (Civilization of the American Indian Ser.: No. 199). (Illus.). 288p. 1990. 24.95 (*0-8061-2256-0*) U of Okla Pr.

— This Land Was Theirs: A Study of North American Indians. 4th ed. 467p. (C). 1987. pap. text ed. 35.95 (*0-87484-815-6*) Mayfield Pub.

Oswatitsch, K. & Rues, D., eds. Symposium Transsonicum 2. (International Union of Theoretical & Applied Mechanics Symposia Ser.). 1976. 73.00 (*0-387-07526-7*) Spr-Verlag.

Oswatitsch, Ruthild W., jt. auth. see Eigen, Manfred.

***Osweiler, Gary D.** Toxicology. LC 94-49123. (National Veterinary Medical Series for Independent Study). 1995. write for info. (*0-683-06664-1*) Williams & Wilkins.

***Oswin, Maureen.** Am I Allowed to Cry? 1995. pap. 10.95 (*0-285-65096-3*, Pub. by Souvenir UK) Atrium Pubs.

Oszuscik, Philippe. Louisiana's Gothic Revival Architecture. 1973. 8.95 (*0-87511-093-2*) Claitors.

***Oszustowicz, Kathy, ed.** Eye-D Picture Challenges: 125 Famous Pictures & 625 Challenging Questions about Them. (Illus.). 125p. (J). (gr. 1-2). 1994. pap. 12.95 (*1-56530-154-4*) Summit TX.

— Eye-D Picture Challenges: 125 Famous Pictures & 625 Challenging Questions about Them. (Illus.). 125p. (J). (gr. 3-4). 1994. pap. 12.95 (*1-56530-155-2*) Summit TX.

— Eye-D Picture Challenges: 125 Famous Pictures & 625 Challenging Questions about Them. (Illus.). 125p. (J). (gr. 5-6). 1994. pap. 12.95 (*1-56530-156-0*) Summit TX.

***Oszustowicz, Len.** Death at Sea: A Murder Mystery in 3-D. Towle, Mike, ed. (Illus.). 80p. (YA). (gr. 6 up). 1994. 12.95 (*1-56530-165-X*) Summit TX.

Oszustowicz, Len, jt. auth. see Colf, Mary K.

Oszustowicz, Len, et al. Barney Fife's Guide to Life, Love & Self-Defense. LC 93-42332. (Illus.). 167p. 1993. 12.95 (*1-56530-103-X*) Summit TX.

Ota, Inazo N., see Inazo Nitobe, pseud..

Ota, K., et al, eds. Current Concepts in Peritoneal Dialysis: Proceedings of the Fifth Congress of the International Society for Peritoneal Dialysis, Kyoto, July 21-24, 1990. LC 92-14693. (International Congress Ser.: No. 947). 1992. 295.75 (*0-444-81389-6*, Excerpta Medica) Elsevier.

Ota, Mitchell. Pinshooting: A Complete Guide. 1991. 14.95 (*1-879356-04-X*) Wolfe Pub Co.

OTA Staff. Protecting the Nation's Ground Water from Contamination. (C). 1987. text ed. 125.00 (*81-85046-52-2*, Pub. by Scientific Pubs II) St Mut.

Ota, Yasuto, et al. Setsuko Migishi: A Retrospective. LC 91-7707. (Illus.). 136p. 1991. pap. 21.95 (*0-940979-16-0*, NE U Pr) Natl Museum Women.

***Otabil, Kwesi.** Agonistic Imperative: The Rational Burden of Africa-Centeredness. 250p. (Orig.). (C). Date not set. pap. text ed. 24.95 (*1-55605-244-8*) Wyndhall Pr.

— Agonistic Imperative: The Rational Burden of Africa-Centeredness. 250p. (Orig.). (C). Date not set. text ed. 34.95x (*1-55605-245-6*) Wyndhall Pr.

Otaguro, Deborah, et al, eds. Technical, Trade & Business School Data Handbook, 1991-93. 4th ed. 1700p. (Orig.). 1991. pap. 55.00 (*1-878172-04-2*); pap. 55.00 (*1-878172-03-4*) Wintergrn-Orchard Hse.

— Technical, Trade & Business School Data Handbook, 1991-93, 2 vols., Set. 4th ed. 1700p. (Orig.). 1991. ring bd. 95.00 (*1-878172-05-0*) Wintergrn-Orchard Hse.

Otaka, Terumi. Lovable Mini Dolls. (Illus.). 96p. 1982. pap. 14.95 (*0-87040-518-7*) Japan Pubns USA.

Otaki, Tadao, jt. auth. see Draeger, Donn F.

Otanes, Fe T., jt. auth. see Schachter, Paul.

Otani, Kosho K. The Successor: My Life. LC 84-23016. (Illus.). 114p. 1985. 18.95 (*0-914910-50-7*) Buddhist Bks.

Otani, Ryuji. Ready-to-Use Gourmet Food Illustrations. (Clip Art Ser.). (Illus.). 64p. (Orig.). 1991. pap. 4.50 (*0-486-26652-4*) Dover.

Otani, Takeshi. The Honeybee. Pohl, Kathy, ed. LC 85-28230. (Nature Close-Ups Ser.). (Illus.). 32p. (J). (gr. 3-7). 1986. text ed. 10.95 (*0-8172-2537-4*) Raintree Steck-V.

Otani, Y. & El-Hodiri, M. A. Microeconomic Theory. (Illus.). 310p. 1987. pap. 45.00 (*0-387-17994-1*) Spr-Verlag.

Otar, Jim C. CHEMCALC (TM) 5: Heat Exchanger Network Optimization. LC 85-16856. (CHEMCALC (TM) Software for Chemical Engineers Ser.). 80p. 1986. disk 295.00 (*0-87201-089-9*) Gulf Pub.

Otawa, Toru, et al. Indiana Wind Energy: A Guide to Harnessing Hoosier Wind Power. (Illus.). 108p. (Orig.). 1982. pap. 7.00 (*0-912431-00-8*) Ctr Env Des Res.

Otchere, Freda E. African Studies Thesaurus: Subject Headings for Library Users. LC 92-12523. (Bibliographies & Indexes in Afro-American & African Studies: No. 29). 480p. 1992. text ed. 79.50 (*0-313-27437-1*, OAB/, Greenwood Pr) Greenwood.

***O'Teaberry, Thomas.** Kids. 300p. 1995. pap. 9.95 (*1-56901-915-0*) NW Pub.

Otebele, David O. Altruism. 1994. 16.95 (*0-533-10768-7*) Vantage.

Otega, Jose, jt. auth. see Ferres, Antonio.

Otegui, Miguel, et al. Diccionario Espanol de la Lengua China: Spanish Dictionary of the Chinese Language. 2nd ed. 1381p. (CHI & SPA.). 1979. 350.00 (*0-8288-5339-8*, S31804) Fr & Eur.

Otenasek, Mildred B. Alexander Hamilton's Financial Policies. Bruchey, Stuart, ed. LC 76-39837. (Nineteen Seventy-Seven Dissertations Ser.). 1977. lib. bdg. 20.95 (*0-405-09917-7*) Ayer.

Otensmann, John R. & Neuenschwander, Jan. Working with Lotus Agenda. 1989. pap. 24.95 (*0-07-156244-3*) McGraw.

Oteri, Laura, ed. see International Conference, Geneva Staff.

Otero, Carlos P. Letras, I. (Serie A: Monagrafias, VIII). 202p. (Orig.). (SPA.). (C). 1966. pap. 35.00 (*0-900411-47-3*, Pub. by Tamesis Bks Ltd UK) Boydell & Brewer.

Otero, Carlos P., ed. Noam Chomsky: Critical Assessments, 4 vols., Set. LC 92-47084. 2000p. 1993. 595.00 (*0-415-01005-5*, B2431, Routledge NY) Routledge.

Otero, Corazon. Manuel Ponce & the Guitar. Roberts, J. D., tr. (Guitar Study Ser.). (Illus.). 90p. 1993. 23.95 (*0-685-70189-1*); pap. 15.95 (*0-933224-85-0*) Bold Strummer Ltd.

Otero, Elizabeth, tr. see Catala, Rafael.

Otero, Francisco M. Cinquenta Anos de Periodismo. 108p. (Orig.). (SPA.). 1985. pap. 6.00 (*0-89729-376-2*) Ediciones.

Otero, George & Smith, Gary. Teaching about Food & Hunger. 2nd ed. (Illus.). 124p. (Orig.). 1989. pap. 24.95 (*0-943804-67-1*) U of Denver Teach.

Otero, George G. Teaching about Population Growth. (Illus.). (gr. 6-12). 1983. pap. 7.50 (*0-943804-01-9*) U of Denver Teach.

— Teaching about Population Issues. (Illus.). 81p. (gr. 6-12). 1983. pap. 7.50 (*0-943804-02-7*) U of Denver Teach.

Otero, George G. & Harris, Zoanne. Death: A Part of Life. rev. ed. (Illus.). 147p. (gr. 4-12). 1981. pap. 12.00 (*0-943804-10-8*) U of Denver Teach.

Otero, George G., Jr. & Moeller, Carol. Teaching Reading: A Global Approach. rev. ed. (Illus.). 191p. (Orig.). (gr. 6-12). 1994. pap. 26.95 (*0-943804-30-2*) U of Denver Teach.

Otero, George G. & Smith, Gary R. Teaching about Cultural Awareness with Student Handouts in Spanish. Espinosa, Ann L. & Espinosa, Ismael E., trs. (Illus.). 235p. (gr. 4-12). 1982. pap. 8.50 (*0-943804-26-4*) U of Denver Teach.

— Teaching about Ethnic Heritage. rev. ed. (Illus.). 147p. (Orig.). (gr. k-12). 1977. pap. 15.95 (*0-943804-06-X*) U of Denver Teach.

Otero, George G., jt. auth. see Smith, Gary R.

Otero, George G., jt. auth. see West, Patricia M.

***Otero, Jesus.** Schoolmaster's Son. (American Autobiography Ser.). 130p. 1995. reprint ed. lib. bdg. 69.00 (*0-7812-8605-0*) Rprt Serv.

Otero, Manuel R. Invitacion al Polvo. (Biblioteca de Autores de Puerto Rico Ser.). 74p. (Orig.). (SPA.). 1991. pap. text ed. 5.00 (*1-56328-005-1*) Edit Plaza Mayor.

Otero, Maria & Rhyne, Elisabeth, eds. The New World of Microenterprise Finance: Building Healthy Financial Institutions for the Poor. LC 93-47513. (Library of Management for Development). (Illus.). 304p. 1994. 42.00 (*1-56549-031-2*); pap. 26.95 (*1-56549-030-4*) Kumarian Pr.

Otero, Miguel A. Otero, 3 vols. in 1. LC 73-14420. (Mexican American Ser.). 1036p. 1977. reprint ed. 75.95 (*0-405-05685-0*) Ayer.

Otero, Raymond B. Laboratory Exercises in Microbiology. 4th ed. 264p. 1993. spiral bd. 23.95 (*0-8403-8563-3*) Kendall-Hunt.

Otero, Rosalie. Guide to American Drama Explication. 1995. 40.00 (*0-8161-7351-6*) G K Hall.

Otey, Don, jt. auth. see Sehlinger, Bob.

An Asterisk (*) at the beginning of an entry indicates that the title is appearing in BIP for the first time.

Otey, Elizabeth L. The Beginnings of Child Labor Legislation in Certain States: A Comparative Study. Bremner, Robert H., ed. LC 74-1697. (Children & Youth Ser.). 230p. 1974. reprint ed. 23.95 (*0-405-05974-4*) Ayer.

Otey, Frank M. & Grant, Alice M. Eatonville, Florida: A Brief History of One of America's First Freedmen's Towns. 92p. (Orig.). 1991. pap. 8.95 (*0-9625423-0-X*) Four-G Pubs.

Otey, Michael, ed. Application Developer's Handbook for the AS-400. 832p. (Orig.). 1993. pap. 129.00 (*0-9628743-3-7*) Duke Commns Intl.

***Otey, Mike.** How to Build Client Server Applications for the AS-400. 1995. pap. 89.00 (*1-882419-21-9*) Duke Commns Intl.

Otey, Mimi. Blue Moon Soup Spoon. (J). (ps-3). 1993. 15.00 (*0-374-30851-9*) FS&G.

— Daddy Has a Pair of Striped Shorts. LC 90-55289. (Illus.). 32p. (J). (ps-3). 1990. 13.95 (*0-374-31675-9*) FS&G.

Otfinoski, Stephen. Nineteenth Century Writers. (America Profiles Ser.). (Illus.). 128p. (YA). (gr. 7-12). 1991. 16.95 (*0-8160-2486-3*) Facts on File.

Otfinoski, Steve. Gun Control: Is It a Right or a Danger to Bear Arms? (Issues of Our Time Ser.). (Illus.). 64p. (J). (gr. 5-8). 1993. lib. bdg. 15.98 (*0-8050-2570-7*) TFC Bks NY.

— Marian Wright Edelman: Defender of Children's Rights. (Library of Famous Women). (Illus.). 64p. (J). (gr. 3-7). 1992. lib. bdg. 14.95 (*1-56711-029-0*) Blackbirch.

— Marion Wright Edelman: Defender of Children's Rights. (Library of Famous Women). (Illus.). 64p. (J). (gr. 3-7). 1991. pap. 7.95 (*1-56711-060-6*) Blackbirch.

— Oprah. (Library of Famous Women). (Illus.). 64p. (J). (gr. 3-7). 1993. pap. 7.95 (*1-56711-061-4*) Blackbirch.

— Oprah Winfrey: Television Star. (Library of Famous Women). (Illus.). 64p. (J). (gr. 3-7). 1993. lib. bdg. 14.95 (*1-56711-015-0*) Blackbirch.

— Putting It in Writing. (YA). (gr. 4-7). 1994. pap. 4.95 (*0-590-49459-7*) Scholastic Inc.

— The Scholastic Guide to Putting It In Writing. LC 92-47492. (J). 1993. 10.95 (*0-590-49458-9*) Scholastic Inc.

Otfinoski, Steven. Alexander Fleming: Conquering Disease with Penicillin. LC 92-9910. (Makers of Modern Science Ser.). (Illus.). 128p. (J). (gr. 5 up). 1993. lib. bdg. 16.95 (*0-8160-2752-8*) Facts on File.

— Bill Gaines. LC 93-16177. (Made in America Ser.). (J). 1993. write for info. (*0-86592-080-X*) Rourke Enter.

— Blizzards. (When Disaster Strikes Ser.). (Illus.). 64p. (J). (gr. 5-8). 1994. lib. bdg. 15.98 (*0-8050-3093-X*) TFC Bks NY.

— Boris Yeltsin & the Rebirth of Russia. LC 94-20296. (Illus.). 112p. (YA). (gr. 7 up). 1994. 15.90 (*1-56294-478-9*) Millbrook Pr.

— Great Black Writers. LC 93-39871. (American Profiles Ser.). (Illus.). 128p. (YA). (gr. 4-11). 1994. 16.95 (*0-8160-2906-7*) Facts on File.

— Joseph Stalin: Russia's Last Czar. LC 92-41143. (Illus.). 128p. (J). (gr. 2-4). 1992. 15.90 (*1-56294-240-9*) Millbrook Pr.

— Mikhail Gorbachev: The Soviet Innovator. (Great Lives Ser.). (Illus.). 128p. 1989. pap. 3.95 (*0-449-90400-8*, Columbine) Fawcett.

— Nelson Mandela: The Fight Against Apartheid. LC 91-35031. (Illus.). 128p. (YA). (gr. 7 up). 1992. lib. bdg. 15.90 (*1-56294-067-8*) Millbrook Pr.

— Scott Joplin: A Life in Ragtime. LC 95-8526. (Impact Biographies Ser.). (Illus.). (YA). (gr. 7-12). 1995. lib. bdg. 15.47 (*0-531-11244-6*) Watts.

— The Stolen Signs. (Southside Sluggers Ser.). (Illus.). 112p. (J). (gr. 2-6). 1992. pap. 2.95 (*0-671-72930-6*, S&S Bks Young Read) S&S Childrens.

— Triumph & Terror: The French Revolution. LC 92-37131. (World History Library). (Illus.). 128p. (YA). (gr. 6-9). 1993. 16.95 (*0-8160-2762-5*) Facts on File.

— The Truth about Three Billy Goats Gruff. LC 93-42391. (Illus.). 32p. (J). (gr. k-3). 1994. pap. text ed. 2.95 (*0-8167-3013-X*) Troll Assocs.

— Truth about Three Billy Goats Gruff. LC 93-42391. (Illus.). 32p. (J). (gr. k-3). 1994. lib. bdg. 11.59 (*0-8167-3012-1*) Troll Assocs.

— Who Stole Home Plate? (Southside Sluggers Ser.). (Illus.). 112p. (J). (gr. 2-6). 1992. pap. 2.95 (*0-671-72932-2*, S&S Bks Young Read) S&S Childrens.

— Whodunit? Science Solves the Crime. LC 95-11961. (Mysteries of Science Ser.). (Illus.). (J). 1995. text ed. write for info. (*0-7167-6515-2*, Sci Am Yng Rdrs); pap. text ed. write for info. (*0-7167-6559-4*, Sci Am Yng Rdrs) W H Freeman.

Otfinski, Steven. Igor Sikorsky. LC 93-2822. (Masters of Invention Ser.). (J). 1993. 15.93 (*0-86592-100-8*); 11.95 (*0-685-66610-7*) Rourke Enter.

***Otger, Neufang.** Elektronik-Woerterbuch: English-German. 4th ed. 369p. (ENG & GER.). 1993. 75.00 (*0-7859-8553-0*, 3922410294) Fr & Eur.

***Otha L. Co. Staff.** FCC Radar Endorsement Examination Study Guide. (FCC Radio Operators Examination Study Guide Ser.). 60p. (C). 1994. pap. text ed. write for info. (*0-9642235-1-1*) OC Communs.

Otheguy, Ricardo, jt. auth. see Garcia, Ofelia.

Othersen. The Pediatric Airway. (Illus.). 256p. 1991. text ed. 91.95 (*0-7216-2778-1*) Saunders.

Othman, Abdul H. & Awang, Amir, eds. Counseling in the Asia-Pacific Region. LC 92-45074. (Contributions in Psychology Ser.: No. 20). 168p. 1993. text ed. 55.00 (*0-313-28799-6*, GM8799, Greenwood Pr) Greenwood.

Othman, Haroub, jt. ed. see Oden, Bertil.

***Othman, Zaharah & Atmosumarto, Sutanto.** Colloquial Malay: A Complete Language Course. (Colloquial Ser.). 1995. 39.95 (*0-415-11014-9*, B4024); pap. 18.95 (*0-415-11012-2*, B4538) Routledge.

***Othmer, Ekkehard & Othmer, Seiglinde C.** The Clinical Interview Using DSM-IV Vol. 2: The Difficult Patient. 576p. 1994. boxed 45.00 (*0-88048-520-5*, 8520) Am Psychiatric.

Othmer, Ekkehard & Othmer, Sieglinde C. The Clinical Interview Using DSM-IV, Vol. 1: Fundamentals. 1994. text ed. 45.00 (*0-88048-541-8*) Am Psychiatric.

— Life on a Roller Coaster: Coping with the Ups & Downs of Mood Disorders. 160p. (Orig.). 1989. pap. 7.95 (*0-929162-13-7*) PIA Pr.

Othmer, H., ed. Some Mathematical Questions in Biology: The Dynamics of Excitable Media. LC 89-17794. 181p. 1989. pap. 37.00 (*0-8218-1171-1*, LLSCI-21) Am Math.

Othmer, H. G., ed. Nonlinear Oscillations in Biology & Chemistry. (Lecture Notes in Biomathematics Ser.: Vol. 66). vi, 289p. 1986. pap. 42.00 (*0-387-16481-2*) Spr-Verlag.

Othmer, H. G., et al, eds. Experimental & Theoretical Advances in Biological Pattern Formation. (NATO ASI Series A, Life Sciences: Vol. 259). (Illus.). 388p. (C). 1994. 115.00 (*0-306-44661-8*, Plenum Pr) Plenum.

Othmer, Konstantin. Debugging MacIntosh Software & MacsBug Includes MacsBug 6.2 with Disk. 1991. pap. 34.95 (*0-201-57049-1*) Addison-Wesley.

Othmer, Seiglinde C., jt. auth. see Othmer, Ekkehard.

Otiri, Godfrey. Femini Island. 1993. 16.95 (*0-533-10642-7*) Vantage.

***Otis.** Upside Your Head! Rhythm & Blues on Central Avenue. 1995. pap. text ed. (*0-8195-6287-4*, Wesleyan Univ Pr) U Pr of New Eng.

Otis, Alicia. The First Koshare. Smith, James C., Jr., ed. LC 90-35788. (Illus.). 128p. (Orig.). 1991. pap. 8.95 (*0-86534-144-3*) Sunstone Pr.

— Spiderwoman's Dream. LC 87-1944. 64p. (Orig.). 1987. pap. 7.95 (*0-86534-099-4*) Sunstone Pr.

Otis, Carol L. & Goldingay, Roger. Campus Health Guide: The College Student's Handbook for Healthy Living. 460p. 1989. pap. 14.95 (*0-87447-317-9*) College Bd.

Otis, Caroline, ed. see Brown, Christopher.

Otis, Caroline H. The Cone with the Curl on Top: The "Dairy Queen" Story. Mundale, Susan et al, eds. 160p. (Orig.). 1990. pap. 29.95 (*0-9629040-0-7*) Intl Dairy Queen.

Otis, Charles E. Aircraft Gas Turbine Powerplants. 2nd ed. LC 91-14478. (Aviation Maintenance Training Course Ser.). (Illus.). 468p. 1989. reprint ed. pap. 17.95 (*0-89100-255-3*, EA-TEP-2) IAP.

— Aircraft Gas Turbine Powerplants Workbook. IAP Staff, ed. (Illus.). 188p. (Orig.). (C). 1989. pap. 9.95 (*0-89100-342-8*, EA-TEP-2W) IAP.

Otis, Charles E. & Vosbury, Peter A. Aircraft Gas Turbine Engines of the World & Dictionary of the Gas Turbine. LC 91-28478. (Illus.). 455p. 1991. pap. text ed. 22.95 (*0-89100-390-8*, EA-390) IAP.

Otis, Clyman. Adventures in Yap. 1994. 13.95 (*0-533-10762-8*) Vantage.

Otis, Delos S. The Dawes Act & the Allotment of Indian Lands. LC 72-3597. (Civilization of the American Indian Ser.: No. 123). 226p. reprint ed. pap. 64.50 (*0-8357-8088-0*, 2033965) Bks Demand.

Otis, Denise, jt. auth. see Maia, Ronaldo.

Otis, Denise, ed. see Maia, Ronaldo.

Otis, F. N. Illustrated History of the Panama Railroad. LC 77-184965. 150p. 19.95 (*0-87026-045-6*) Westernlore.

Otis, Fessenden N. Illustrated History of the Panama Railroad. enl. rev. ed. LC 72-128415. reprint ed. write for info. (*0-404-04838-2*) AMS Pr.

Otis, George. Hielo y Fuego: Eldridge Cleaver: Ice & Fire. (SPA.). 2.95 (*84-7228-446-8*, 220346, Pub. by Edit Clie SP) TSELF.

Otis, George, Jr. The Last of the Giants: Lifting the Veil on Islam & the End Times. LC 91-21233. 224p. (Orig.). 1991. pap. 10.99 (*0-8007-9192-4*) Chosen Bks.

Otis, George. Terror en Tenerife: Terror in Tenerife. (SPA.). 4.95 (*84-7228-415-8*, 360800, Pub. by Edit Clie SP) TSELF.

***Otis, George H.** Second Wisconsin Infantry. Gaff, Alan D., ed. (Illus.). 372p. 1984. 30.00 (*0-89029-082-2*) Morningside Bkshop.

Otis, Harry B., ed. The Best of the Cockle Bur: A Collection of Wit, Wisdom, Humor & Beauty. (Illus.). 241p. 1987. pap. 11.95 (*0-9619994-0-3*) Bur Inc.

Otis, James. Some Political Writings of James Otis, 2 vols. in 1. LC 75-31099. reprint ed. 16.50 (*0-404-13516-1*) AMS Pr.

— Toby Tyler. 152p. (J). 1981. reprint ed. lib. bdg. 21.95 (*0-89966-363-X*) Buccaneer Bks.

— Toby Tyler. 188p. (J). 1981. reprint ed. lib. bdg. 19.95 (*0-89967-037-7*) Harmony Raine.

Otis, John W. Your International Business Plan. (Network Workbooks Ser.). 54p. (C). 1990. student ed 14.95 (*1-878475-02-9*) Oregon Small Busn Dev Ctr.

Otis, Johnny. Upside Your Head! Rhythm & Blues on Central Avenue. LC 93-13611. (Music - Culture Ser.). (Illus.). 212p. 1993. 25.00 (*0-8195-5263-1*, Wesleyan Univ Pr) U Pr of New Eng.

Otis, Laura. Organic Memory: History & the Body in the Late Nineteenth & Early Twentieth Centuries. LC 93-47280. (Texts & Contexts Ser.: No. 11). 304p. 1994. text ed. 37.50 (*0-8032-3561-5*) U of Nebr Pr.

Otis, Margaret R. Relics Recycled on Cloud Nine. LC 81-18286. (Illus.). 96p. 1981. pap. 4.95 (*0-915010-30-5*) Sutter House.

Otis, Pauletta J. & Kaplan, Steven A., eds. Between the Lines: International Short Stories of War. LC 94-650. 384p. (C). 1994. 26.95 (*0-87081-328-5*); pap. 14.95 (*0-87081-329-3*) Univ Pr Colo.

Otis, Philo A. The Chicago Symphony Orchestra. LC 79-37904. (Select Bibliographies Reprint Ser.). 1977. reprint ed. 35.95 (*0-8369-6742-9*) Ayer.

Otis Public Library Staff. Washington County, Colorado. (Illus.). 323p. 1989. 50.00 (*0-88107-140-4*) Curtis Media.

Otis, Rose, ed. Among Friends. LC 92-21792. 1992. pap. 14.95 (*0-8280-0692-X*) Review & Herald.

— A Gift of Love: A Daily Devotional for Women. LC 94-32834. 1994. write for info. (*0-8280-0889-2*) Review & Herald.

Otis, S. U. S. vs. Steven F. Soliah. (Monograph Ser.: No. CR-6). 1975. 4.00 (*1-55524-006-2*) Ctr Respon Psych.

Otis, Sharon. My Kid Won't Eat Cookbook. (Orig.). 1986. pap. 5.00 (*0-9617737-1-5*) Total Lrn.

Otis, Sharon & Walker, Lois. Jeffrey's Laugh. (Illus.). (Orig.). (J). (ps-6). 1987. student ed 6.50 (*0-9617737-2-3*) Total Lrn.

— Tammy's Smile. (Illus.). (Orig.). (J). (ps-7). 1985. student ed 6.00 (*0-9617737-0-7*) Total Lrn.

Otis, William B. American Verse, Sixteen Twenty-Five to Eighteen Hundred Seven: A History. 303p. (C). 1966. lib. bdg. 75.00 (*0-8383-0605-5*) M S G Haskell Hse.

Otken, Charles H. The Ills of the South. LC 72-11345. (American South Ser.). 1973. reprint ed. 28.95 (*0-405-05061-5*) Ayer.

Otlewis, Julie. Hooked on Golf. (Illus.). 168p. (Orig.). 1994. pap. 5.95 (*1-56245-082-4*) Great Quotations.

— A Lifetime of Love. 168p. (Orig.). 1994. pap. 5.95 (*1-56245-087-5*) Great Quotations.

— Love, Honor, Cherish. (Orig.). 1994. pap. 7.95 (*1-56245-081-6*) Great Quotations.

— Simply the Best Mom. 366p. 1993. spiral bd., pap. 8.95 (*1-56245-076-X*) Great Quotations.

— Thank You. 78p. (Orig.). 1994. pap. 7.95 (*1-56245-037-9*) Great Quotations.

Otness, Harold M. Index to Early Twentieth Century City Plans Appearing in Guidebooks: Baedeker, Muirhead-Blue Guides, Murray, I. J. G. R., Etc., Plus Selected Other Works to Provide Worldwide Coverage of Over 2,000 Plans to Over 1,200 Communities, Found in 74 Guidebooks. LC 78-15094. (Occasional Papers: No. 4). (Illus.). 124p. (Orig.). 1978. pap. 6.00 (*0-939112-05-1*) Western Assn Map.

— Index to Nineteenth Century City Plans Appearing in Guidebooks: Baedeker, Murray, Joanne, Black, Appleton, Meyer, Plus Selected Other Works to Provide Coverage of Over 1,800 Plans to Nearly 600 Communities Found in 164 Guidebooks. LC 80-24483. (Occasional Papers: No. 7). (Illus.). 108p. (Orig.). 1980. pap. 6.00 (*0-939112-08-6*) Western Assn Map.

Otness, Harold M., comp. The Shakespeare Folio Handbook & Census: Bibliographies & Indexes in World Literature, No. 25. LC 89-28650. 146p. 1990. text ed. 49.95 (*0-313-27257-3*, OSA/, Greenwood Pr) Greenwood.

Otobe, S. Oral Implantology. 1990. text ed. 80.00 (*1-57235-013-X*) Piccin NY.

Otomo & Duffy, Jo. Akira, No. 1. 64p. 1988. 3.95 (*0-87135-584-1*) Marvel Entmnt.

— Akira, No. 2. 64p. 1988. 3.95 (*0-87135-585-X*) Marvel Entmnt.

— Akira, No. 11. 64p. 1989. 3.50 (*0-87135-586-8*) Marvel Entmnt.

— Akira, No. 12. 64p. 1989. 3.50 (*0-87135-587-6*) Marvel Entmnt.

— Akira, No. 13. 64p. 1989. 3.50 (*0-87135-588-4*) Marvel Entmnt.

— Akira, No. 14. 64p. 1989. 3.50 (*0-87135-589-2*) Marvel Entmnt.

— Akira, No. 15. 64p. 1989. 3.50 (*0-87135-590-6*) Marvel Entmnt.

— Akira, No. 16. 64p. 1989. 3.95 (*0-87135-591-4*) Marvel Entmnt.

— Akira, No. 17. 64p. 1990. 3.95 (*0-87135-618-X*) Marvel Entmnt.

— Akira, No. 18. 64p. 1990. 3.95 (*0-87135-619-8*) Marvel Entmnt.

— Akira, No. 19. 64p. 1990. 3.95 (*0-87135-620-1*) Marvel Entmnt.

— Akira, No. 20. 64p. 1990. 3.95 (*0-87135-621-X*) Marvel Entmnt.

— Akira, No. 21. 64p. 1990. 3.95 (*0-87135-622-8*) Marvel Entmnt.

— Akira, No. 22. 64p. 1990. 3.95 (*0-87135-623-6*) Marvel Entmnt.

— Akira, No. 23. 64p. 1990. 3.95 (*0-87135-624-4*) Marvel Entmnt.

— Akira, No. 24. 64p. 1990. 3.95 (*0-87135-683-X*) Marvel Entmnt.

— Akira, No. 25. 64p. 1990. 3.95 (*0-87135-684-8*) Marvel Entmnt.

— Akira, No. 26. 64p. 1990. 3.95 (*0-87135-685-6*) Marvel Entmnt.

— Akira, No. 27. 64p. 1991. 3.95 (*0-87135-686-4*) Marvel Entmnt.

— Akira, No. 28. 64p. 1991. 3.95 (*0-87135-687-2*) Marvel Entmnt.

— Akira, No. 29. 64p. 1991. 3.95 (*0-87135-688-0*) Marvel Entmnt.

— Akira, No. 30. 64p. 1991. 3.95 (*0-87135-689-9*) Marvel Entmnt.

— Akira, No. 31. 64p. 1991. 3.95 (*0-87135-690-2*) Marvel Entmnt.

— Akira, No. 32. 64p. 1991. 3.95 (*0-87135-793-3*) Marvel Entmnt.

— Akira, No. 33. 1993. 3.95 (*0-87135-794-1*) Marvel Entmnt.

— Akira, No. 34. 64p. Date not set. 3.95 (*0-87135-795-X*) Marvel Entmnt.

— Akira, No. 35. 64p. Date not set. 3.50 (*0-87135-796-8*) Marvel Entmnt.

— Akira, No. 36. 64p. Date not set. 4.50 (*0-87135-797-6*) Marvel Entmnt.

— Akira, No. 37. 64p. Date not set. 4.50 (*0-87135-910-3*) Marvel Entmnt.

— Akira, Vol. 2. 192p. 1991. pap. 14.95 (*0-87135-782-8*) Marvel Entmnt.

— Akira, Vol. 3. 192p. 1991. pap. 14.95 (*0-87135-831-X*) Marvel Entmnt.

— Akira, Vol. 4. 192p. 1992. pap. 14.95 (*0-87135-832-8*) Marvel Entmnt.

— Akira, Vol. 5. 192p. 1992. pap. 14.95 (*0-87135-900-6*) Marvel Entmnt.

— Akira, Vol. 6. 192p. 1992. pap. 14.95 (*0-87135-901-4*) Marvel Entmnt.

Otomo, Katsuhiro. Art of Otomo. 1991. 35.00 (*0-685-59751-2*) Marvel Entmnt.

Oton, Jose M. Smart Cards. LC 94-7671. 1994. 63.00 (*0-89006-687-6*) Artech Hse.

O'Toole, Anita W. & Welt, Sheila R. Interpersonal Theory in Nursing Practice: Selected Works of Hildegard E. Peplau. 400p. 1989. 42.95 (*0-8261-6060-3*) Springer Pub.

***O'Toole, Barry & Jordan, A. Grant, eds.** Next Steps: Improving Management in Government. 160p. 1995. 59.95 (*1-85521-491-1*) Ashgate Pub Co.

O'Toole, C. P., jt. ed. see O'Mongain, Eon.

O'Toole, Christopher. The Dragonfly over the Water. LC 87-42613. (Animal Habitats Ser.). (Illus.). 32p. (J). (gr. 4-6). 1988. lib. bdg. 17.27 (*1-55532-306-5*) Gareth Stevens Inc.

— The Honeybee in the Meadow. LC 89-33935. (Animal Habitats Ser.). (Illus.). 32p. (J). (gr. 4-6). 1989. lib. bdg. 17.27 (*0-8368-0117-2*) Gareth Stevens Inc.

— Insects in Camera. (Illus.). 1985. 29.95 (*0-19-217694-3*) OUP.

O'Toole, Christopher, ed. The Encyclopedia of Insects. (Illus.). 160p. 1986. 24.95 (*0-8160-1358-6*) Facts on File.

O'Toole, Christopher & Raw, Anthony. Bees of the World. (Of the World Ser.). (Illus.). 192p. 1992. lib. bdg. 25.95 (*0-8160-1992-4*) Facts on File.

O'Toole, Christopher & Stidworthy, John. Mammals: The Hunters. (Encyclopedia of the Animal World Ser.). (Illus.). 96p. (YA). 1988. 17.95 (*0-8160-1959-2*) Facts on File.

O'Toole, Coleen. The Search for Purity: A Retrospective Policy Analysis of Decision to Chlorinate Cincinnati's Public Water Supply, 1890-1920. LC 90-13865. (Environment: Problems & Solutions Ser.: Vol. 26). 184p. 1990. 48.00 (*0-8240-9792-0*) Garland.

O'Toole, Donna. Aarvy Aardvark Finds Hope: A Read-Aloud Story for People of All Ages. (Illus.). 80p. (Orig.). (J). (ps up). 1989. audio 10.95 (*0-685-20985-7*, Mntn Rainbow) Rainbow NC.

— Aarvy Aardvark Finds Hope: A Read-Aloud Story for People of All Ages. (Illus.). 80p. (Orig.). (J). (ps up). 1989. teacher ed 6.95 (*1-878321-26-9*, Mntn Rainbow); pap. 11.95 (*1-878321-25-0*, Mntn Rainbow) Rainbow NC.

— Healing & Growing Through Grief. (Illus.). 20p. (J). 1986. pap. 3.25 (*0-685-31273-9*, HG-02-4) Rainbow NC.

O'Toole, Donna R. Bridging the Bereavement Gap: A Comprehensive Manual for the Preparation & Programming of Hospice Bereavement Services. 2nd ed. 291p. (C). 1988. reprint ed. pap. 49.00 (*0-685-44864-9*); reprint ed. ring bd. 49.00 (*1-878321-01-3*) Rainbow NC.

— Growing Through Grief: A K-Twelve Curriculum to Help Young People Through All Kinds of Loss. rev. ed. (Illus.). 392p. (J). (gr. k-12). 1989. ring bd. 59.95 (*1-878321-00-5*, Mntn Rainbow) Rainbow NC.

O'Toole, Eamonn. Decorations & Medals of the Republic of Ireland. enl. rev. ed. (Illus.). 1990. pap. 13.95 (*0-685-54342-0*) Medallic Pub.

— Medals of the Republic of Ireland. (Illus.). 86p. 1990. pap. 14.00 (*0-9624663-5-2*) Medallic Pub.

O'Toole, Edward. Opportunities in Securities Industry. (Illus.). 160p. 1981. 13.95 (*0-8442-6641-8*, VGM Career Bks); pap. 10.95 (*0-8442-6642-6*, VGM Career Bks) NTC Pub Grp.

O'Toole, G. J. The Encyclopedia of American Intelligence & Espionage: From the Revolutionary War to the Present. (Illus.). 560p. 1988. 50.00 (*0-8160-1011-0*) Facts on File.

— Honorable Treachery. LC 91-13203. 591p. 1993. pap. 15.00 (*0-87113-492-6*) Grove-Atltic.

— The Spanish War: An American Epic, 1898. (Illus.). 448p. 1986. reprint ed. pap. 14.95 (*0-393-30304-7*) Norton.

O'Toole, James. The Executive's Compass: Business & the Good Society. LC 92-32157. 176p. (C). 1993. 19.95 (*0-19-508119-6*) OUP.

— The Executive's Compass: Business & the Good Society. (Illus.). 176p. 1995. pap. 9.95 (*0-19-509644-4*) OUP.

— Leading Change: Overcoming the Ideology of Comfort & the Tyranny of Custom. LC 94-39421. (Management Ser.). 304p. 1995. 25.00 (*1-55542-608-5*) Jossey-Bass.

— Work, Learning & the American Future. LC 76-50726. 256p. reprint ed. pap. 73.00 (*0-8357-4956-8*, 2037888) Bks Demand.

O'Toole, James, ed. Work & the Quality of Life. LC 74-548. 360p. (C). 1974. pap. 8.95 (*0-262-65010-X*) MIT Pr.

O'Toole, James, et al. Three Views: Tenure. 56p. 1979. pap. text ed. 12.95 (*0-915390-21-3*) Transaction Pubs.

O'Toole, James, et al, eds. Working: Changes & Choices. LC 81-6773. 525p. (C). 1981. Reader, 525p. pap. 24.95 (*0-89885-111-4*); Study guide, 54p. student ed, pap. 18.95 (*0-89885-112-2*); pap. 18.95 (*0-89885-113-0*) Human Sci Pr.

O'Toole, James M. Militant & Triumphant: William Henry O'Connell & the Catholic Church in Boston, 1859-1944. LC 91-50570. (C). 1992. text ed. 28.95 (*0-268-01393-4*) U of Notre Dame Pr.

— Militant & Triumphant: William Henry O'Connell & the Catholic Church in Boston, 1859-1944. LC 91-50570. (C). 1993. pap. text ed. 14.95 (*0-268-01403-5*) U of Notre Dame Pr.

— Understanding Archives & Manuscripts. (Archival Fundamentals Ser.). 76p. 1990. pap. 25.00 (*0-931828-77-5*) Soc Am Archivists.

O

O'Toole, James M., jt. ed. see Sullivan, Robert E.
O'Toole, John. The Process of Drama. LC 92-7785. (Illus.). 224p. 1992. 69.95 (0-415-08243-9, A9660); pap. 15.95 (0-415-08244-7, A9664) Routledge.
O'Toole, John & Richmond, Marvin. Tornado! Eighty-Four Minutes Ninety-Four Lives. LC 93-70976. (Illus.). 320p. (Orig.). 1993. pap. 16.95 (0-9636277-0-8); audio 34.95 (0-9636277-2-4); vhs 19.95 (0-9636277-1-6) Databks.
O'Toole, John, jt. auth. see Haseman, Brad.
***O'Toole, Judith H.** George Luks: Expressionist Master of Color - the Watercolors Rediscovered. 2nd ed. LC 94-69203. (Illus.). 65p. 1994. pap. write for info. (0-9644071-0-8) Canton Art Inst.
— Severin Roesen. LC 89-45930. (Illus.). 176p. 1992. 55.00 (0-8387-5184-9) Bucknell U Pr.
O'Toole, Judith H., et al. Scavnicky: Portrait of an Anthracite Family Nelson Morris, Photographer. (Illus.). 47p. (Orig.). (C). 1992. pap. 5.00 (0-942945-02-6) Sordoni Gal.
O'Toole, L. M. Structure, Style & Interpretation in the Russian Short Story. LC 81-11650. 288p. 1982. 37.00 (0-300-02730-3) Yale U Pr.
O'Toole, Larry. Street Rods in Color. (Illus.). 112p. 1990. pap. 15.95 (0-949398-72-1, Pub. by Graffiti AT) Motorbooks Intl.
O'Toole, Laurence. The Cornish Captain's Tale. (C). 1989. 50.00 (1-85022-011-5, Pub. by Dyllansow Truran UK) St Mut.
O'Toole, Laurence J., Jr., ed. American Intergovernmental Relations: Foundations, Perspectives, & Issues. 2nd ed. LC 92-30912. 311p. 1992. 25.95 (0-87187-718-X) Congr Quarterly.
O'Toole, Laurence J. & Montjoy, Robert S. Regulatory Decision Making: The Virginia State Corporation Commission. LC 84-5146. 405p. reprint ed. pap. 115.50 (0-8357-2715-7, 2039829) Bks Demand.
O'Toole, Lawrence G. Introduction to Supernatural. 252p. (Orig.). 1991. pap. 55.00 (1-878960-05-9) WH&O Intl.
O'Toole, Lela, ed. The International Heritage of Home Economics in the United States. 1988. write for info. (0-318-62843-0) Am Home Eco.
O'Toole, Lulu. Narrow Passages. LC 88-71827. 200p. (Orig.). 1989. pap. 6.95 (0-918897-03-3) Devonshire Pub.
O'Toole, Margarette. Jesus, the Word of God. 96p. (Orig.). 1993. pap. text ed. 9.95 (0-8146-2235-6) Liturgical Pr.
O'Toole, Maureen A. Ama & the White Crane. (Orig.). (J). 1991. Playscript. pap. 6.00 (0-87602-295-6) Anchorage.
O'Toole, Michael. The Language of Displayed Art. (Illus.). 300p. 1994. 38.50 (0-8386-3604-7) Fairleigh Dickinson.
— More Kicks Than Pence. 1992. pap. 15.95 (1-85371-143-8, Pub. by Poolbeg Pr IE) Dufour.
Otoole, Patricia. The Five of Hearts: An Intimate Portrait of Henry Adams & His Friends (1880-1918) 1990. 25.00 (0-517-56350-9, C P Pubs) Crown Pub Group.
O'Toole, Randal. Reforming the Forest Service. (Illus.). 248p. (Orig.). 1988. 34.95 (0-933280-49-1); pap. 19.95 (0-933280-45-9) Island Pr.
O'Toole, Richard, jt. auth. see Trela, James E.
O'Toole, Robert F. Who Is a Christian? A Study in Pauline Ethics. (Zacchaeus Studies: New Testament). 167p. (C). 1990. pap. 10.95 (0-8146-5678-1) Liturgical Pr.
O'Toole, Roger, ed. Sociological Studies in Roman Catholic Religion: Historical & Contemporary Perspectives. LC 89-37719. (Studies in Religion & Society: Vol. 24). 192p. 1989. lib. bdg. 79.95 (0-88946-850-8) E Mellen.
O'Toole, Shirley, ed. see Topeka Genealogical Society Staff.
O'Toole, Simon. Confessions of an American Scholar. LC 71-123152. 117p. reprint ed. pap. 33.40 (0-317-29453-9, 2055895) Bks Demand.
O'Toole, Thomas. Economic History of the United States. (Economics for Today Ser.). (Illus.). 88p. (J). (gr. 5 up). 1990. 21.50 (0-8225-1776-0, Lerner Publctns) Lerner Group.
— Global Economics. (Economics for Today Ser.). (Illus.). 80p. (J). (gr. 5 up). 1991. lib. bdg. 21.50 (0-8225-1782-5, Lerner Publctns) Lerner Group.
O'Toole, Thomas, tr. see Kalck, Pierre.
O'Toole, Thomas E. Historical Dictionary of Guinea: Republic of Guinea - Conakry. 2nd ed. LC 87-9830. (African Historical Dictionaries Ser.: No. 16). (Illus.). 232p. 1987. 25.00 (0-8108-2000-5) Scarecrow.
***Otooni, Monde A., ed.** Science & Technology of Rapid Solidification & Processing: Proceedings of the NATO Advanced Research Workshop, West Point Military Academy, New York, NY, U. S. A., June 21-24, 1994. (NATO Advanced Science Institutes: Series E). 392p. (C). 1994. lib. bdg. 176.00 (0-7923-3203-2) Kluwer Ac.
Ototani, T. Calcium Clean Steel. (Materials Research & Engineering Ser.). (Illus.). 160p. 1986. 104.00 (0-387-16346-8) Spr-Verlag.
Otrakul, Ampha. Thai-German Dictionary: Thai-Deutsches Woerterbuch. 779p. (GER & THA.). 1986. write for info. (0-8288-1722-7, F65790) Fr & Eur.
Otrio, jt. ed. see Lutz.
Otrio, G., ed. Optical Space Communication. 261p. 1989. 53.00 (0-8194-0167-6, 1131) SPIE.
Ots, Peter. Learn Ami Pro in a Day: Version 2.0 & 3.0. (Popular Applications Ser.). (Illus.). 144p. (Orig.). 1993. disk 15.95 (1-55622-301-3) Wordware Pub.
Otstot, Charles M. The Descendants & Antecedents of Alfred & Catherine (Dawley) Fellows. LC 87-80062. 140p. (Orig.). 1987. pap. 15.00 (0-9603808-1-7) C M Otstot.
Otstot, Charles Mathieson. A History of the Otstot Family in America: Also Being a Guide to the Descendents of Jost & Katherine Otstadt. LC 72-97229. (Illus.). 1459p. 1973. 35.00 (0-9603808-0-9) C M Otstot.
Otsu, Syoichi, jt. ed. see Oota, Kunio.
Otsuka, Akira & Nakajima, Akihiko. MIDI Basics. (Illus.). 64p. 1987. pap. 12.95 (0-7119-0952-0, AM63447) Music Sales.
Otsuka, K. Multilayer Ceramic Substrate-Technology for VLSI Package - Multichip Module: Ceramic Research & Development in Japan. xii, 244p. 1993. 144.00 (1-85166-579-X, Pub. by Elsevier Applied Sci UK) Elsevier.
Otsuka, K. & Shimizu, K., eds. Shape Memory Materials: Materials Research Society International Symposium Proceedings-IMAM, No. 9. 641p. 1989. text ed. 85.00 (1-55899-038-0) Materials Res.
Otsuka, Katsuo, jt. auth. see Kazushi, Ohkawa.
Otsuka, Keijiro, jt. ed. see David, Christina C.
Otsuka, Keijiro, jt. auth. see Hayami, Yujiro.
Otsuka, Masanori & Hall, Z. W., eds. Neurobiology of Chemical Transmission. LC 78-24602. 336p. reprint ed. 95.80 (0-8357-9940-9, 2015711) Bks Demand.
Otsuka, Ronald Y., jt. auth. see White, Julia M.
Otsuka, S. & Yamanaka, T., eds. Metalloproteins: Chemical Properties & Biological Effects. (Bioactive Molecules Ser.: No. 8). 572p. 1989. 231.00 (0-444-98887-4) Elsevier.
Otsuka, Sei, jt. ed. see Eliel, Ernest L.
Otsuka, T., jt. ed. see Gruber, B.
Otsuki, S., jt. ed. see Lewis, Res.
Ott & Bezella. Nuclear Reactor Statics. rev. ed. 1989. 47.00 (0-89448-033-2, 350013) Am Nuclear Soc.
Ott & Neuhold. Introductory Nuclear Reactor Dynamics. 376p. 1985. 43.00 (0-89448-029-4, 350011) Am Nuclear Soc.
Ott, jt. auth. see Barker.
***Ott, Anneliese.** The Art of Dried & Scented Flowers. (Illus.). 160p. 1995. 14.95 (0-304-34661-6, Pub. by Cassell UK) Sterling.
Ott, Attiat F. Public Sector Budgets: A Comparative Study. (Illus.). 304p. 1993. 59.95 (1-85278-618-3, Pub. by E Elgar Pub UK) Ashgate Pub Co.
Ott, Attiat F. & Gray, Wayne B. The Massachusetts Health Plan: The Right Prescription? LC 88-62773. (Pioneer Paper Ser.: No. 1). 123p. (Orig.). 1988. pap. 10.00 (0-929930-00-2) Pioneer Inst.
Ott, Attiat F. & Hartley, Keith. Privatization & Economic Efficiency: A Comparative Analysis of Developed & Developing Countries. 288p. 1991. text ed. 69.95 (1-85278-414-8, Pub. by E Elgar Pub UK) Ashgate Pub Co.
Ott, Attiat F., jt. auth. see Ott, David J.
Ott, B., jt. auth. see Philpott, Brian.
Ott, Bertrand. Lisztian Keyboard Energy - Liszt et la Pedagogie Du Piano: An Essay on the Pianism of Franz Liszt. Windham, Donald H., tr. LC 92-25796. (Illus.). 308p. (FRE.). 1992. reprint ed. text ed. 99.95 (0-7734-9589-4) E Mellen.
Ott, Bill, ed. see American Library Associations Booklist Magazine Staff.
Ott, David H. Palestine in Perspective: Politics, Human Rights & the West Bank. 14.95 (0-7043-2263-3, Pub. by Quartet UK) Charles River Bks.
Ott, David J. & Fayez, Jamil A. Hysterosalpingography: A Text & Atlas. (Illus.). 144p. 1991. text ed. 78.00 (0-683-06658-7) Williams & Wilkins.
Ott, David J. & Meltzer, Allan H. Federal Tax Treatment of State & Local Securities. LC 79-27915. (Brookings Institution, National Committee on Government Finance, Studies of Government Finance). (Illus.). xiv, 146p. 1980. reprint ed. text ed. 52.50 (0-313-22306-8, OTFT) Greenwood.
Ott, David J. & Ott, Attiat F. Federal Budget Policy. 3rd ed. LC 77-24198. (Studies of Government Finance). 178p. 1977. 26.95 (0-8157-6710-2); pap. 9.95 (0-8157-6709-9) Brookings.
Ott, David J., jt. auth. see Meschan, Isadore.
Ott, Douglas E. & Wilderotter, Thomas J. A Designer's Guide to VHDL Synthesis. LC 94-20003. 336p. (C). 1994. lib. bdg. 84.00 (0-7923-9472-0) Kluwer Ac.
Ott, E. Revision der Sektion Chronopus Bge. der Gattung Astragalus. L. (Phanerogamarum Monographiae: No. 9). (Illus.). 1979. lib. bdg. 30.00 (3-7682-1187-8) Lubrecht & Cramer.
Ott, Edward. Chaos in Dynamical Systems. LC 93-9344. (Illus.). 425p. (C). 1993. 74.95 (0-521-43215-4); pap. 32.95 (0-521-43799-7) Cambridge U Pr.
Ott, Edward, et al, eds. Coping with Chaos: Analysis of Chaotic Data & the Exploitation of Chaotic Systems. LC 93-49071. 418p. 1994. text ed. 49.95 (0-471-02556-9) Wiley.
Ott, Ellis R. Process Quality Control. 2nd ed. 496p. 1990. text ed. 54.00 (0-07-047924-0) McGraw.
Ott, Franklyn D. Agardh's Eighteen Twenty-Four Systema Algarum: A Bibliographical Source & Index with a Brief Historical Account of the Early Development of Phycology, 2 vols. 1200p. 1990. lib. bdg. 546.00 (3-443-50012-9, Pub. by Gebruder Borntraeger GW) Lubrecht & Cramer.
Ott, Franziska C. Cincinnati German Imprints: A Checklist. LC 92-15690. (New German-American Studies: Vol. 7). 378p. 1992. 58.95 (0-8204-1900-1) P Lang Pubs.
Ott, Frederick W. The Films of Carole Lombard. (Illus.). 256p. 1974. reprint ed. pap. 14.95 (0-8065-0449-8, Citadel Pr) Carol Pub Group.
— The Films of Fritz Lang. 1979. 17.95 (0-8065-0435-8, Citadel Pr) Carol Pub Group.
— The Great German Films. LC 85-29068. (Illus.). 304p. (C). 1986. 24.94 (0-8065-0961-9, Citadel Pr) Carol Pub Group.
— Great German Films. 1991. pap. 15.95 (0-8065-1218-0, Citadel Pr) Carol Pub Group.
Ott, Gil. Public Domain. 84p. (Orig.). 1989. pap. 8.50 (0-937013-29-3) Potes Poets.
— Traffic. 24p. (Orig.). 1985. pap. 2.50 (0-935162-06-2) Singing Horse.
— Within Range. (Poetry Chapbooks Ser.). 28p. (Orig.). 1986. pap. 4.00 (0-930901-38-X) Burning Deck.
— The Yellow Floor: Poems 1978-1983. 75p. 1987. 6.95 (0-940650-89-4) Sun & Moon CA.
Ott, Gil, ed. see Brutus, Dennis.
Ott, H., jt. ed. see L'Hermite, P. L.
Ott, H., jt. ed. see Versino, B.
Ott, H. R., ed. Ten Years of Superconductivity, 1980-1990. LC 92-38477. (Perspectives in Condensed Matter Physics Ser.: Vol. 7). 328p. (C). 1993. lib. bdg. 127.00 (0-7923-2067-0) Kluwer Ac.
Ott, Helmut. Perfect in Christ. Wheeler, Gerald, ed. 160p. 1987. 16.95 (0-8280-0396-3) Review & Herald.
Ott, Henry. Noise Reduction Techniques in Electronic Systems. 2nd ed. 426p. 1988. text ed. 69.95 (0-471-85068-3) Wiley.
Ott, Hugo. Martin Heidegger: An Intellectual & Political Portrait. Blunden, Allan, tr. LC 91-59018. 352p. 1993. 30.00 (0-465-02898-5) Basic.
Ott, J., ed. Models & Methods for the Genetic Analysis of Pedigree Data. (Journal: Reprint from Human Heredity Ser.: Vol. 42, No. 1, 1992). (Illus.). 92p. 1992. 36.00 (3-8055-5762-0) S Karger.
— Models & Methods for the Genetic Analysis of Pedigree Data: Journal: Human Heredity, Vol. 42, No. 1, 1992. (Illus.). 92p. 1992. pap. 30.50 (3-8055-5583-0) S Karger.
Ott, J. Steven. Classic Readings in Organizational Behavior. 638p. (C). 1989. pap. 24.95 (0-534-11073-8) Intl Thomson.
— The Organizational Culture Perspective. 231p. 1989. pap. 24.95 (0-534-10918-7) Intl Thomson.
Ott, J. Steven, jt. auth. see Shafritz, Jay M.
Ott, Jack. Digital Mathematics, Infinity & Revival. (Illus.). 130p. (Orig.). 1988. pap. 7.95 (0-9621493-0-6) J Appleseed Pr.
Ott, James & Gesar, Aram. Jets: Airliners of the Golden Age. Fotos, Christopher, ed. (Illus.). 160p. 1993. 29.95 (0-87938-806-4) Motorbooks Intl.
***Ott, James D. & Neidl, Raymond E.** Airline Odyssey: The World's Airline Turbulent Flight into the Future. 1995. text ed. 22.95 (0-07-048030-3) McGraw.
Ott, Jeff. Ten Minute Guide to Lotus 1-2-3, Release 3.4. 1993. pap. 10.95 (1-56761-172-9) Alpha Bks IN.
— Ten Minute Guide to Paradox 4.0. 1992. pap. 10.95 (1-56761-027-7) Alpha Bks IN.
Ott, John. Health & Light. 220p. 1990. pap. 10.95 (0-89804-098-1) Ariel GA.
Ott, John N. Health & Light. (Illus.). 225p. 1988. 10.95 (0-8159-5703-3) Devin.
— Light, Radiation & You: How to Stay Healthy. LC 81-69951. (Illus.). 175p. 1990. pap. 11.95 (0-8159-6121-9) Devin.
— My Ivory Cellar. (Illus.). 10.50 (0-8159-6217-7) Devin.
Ott, John S. & Malloy, Dick. The Tacoma Public Utilities Story: The First 100 Years. LC 93-60904. (Illus.). 300p. 1993. 30.00 (0-9637684-0-9); pap. 20.00 (0-9637684-1-7) Tacoma Pub Util.
***Ott, Jonathan.** Ayahuasca Analogues - Pangaean Entheogens. 128p. 1994. 30.00 (0-9614234-4-7); pap. 15.00 (0-9614234-5-5) Natural Prod.
— Ayahuasca Analogues - Pangaean Entheogens. deluxe limited ed. 128p. 1994. boxed 60.00 (0-614-00875-1) Natural Prod.
— The Cacahuatl Eater: Ruminations of an Unabashed Chocolate Addict. (Illus.). 128p. (Orig.). 1985. 15.00 (0-9614234-0-4); pap. 7.50 (0-9614234-1-2) Natural Prod.
— Pharmacotheon - Entheogenic Drugs, Their Plant Sources & History. 640p. Date not set. 70.00 (0-9614234-2-0); pap. 40.00 (0-9614234-3-9) Natural Prod.
Ott, Jurg. Analysis of Human Genetic Linkage. 2nd rev. ed. LC 91-7048. (Series in Contemporary Medicine & Public Health). (Illus.). 320p. 1991. text ed. 47.50 (0-8018-4257-3) Johns Hopkins.
Ott, Jurg, jt. auth. see Terwilliger, Joseph D.
Ott, K. O. & Spnrad, Bernard I., eds. Nuclear Energy: A Sensible Alternative. 408p. 1985. 39.50 (0-306-41441-4, Plenum Pr) Plenum.
Ott, L., jt. auth. see Lewis, C. L.
Ott, Linda M., jt. auth. see Rauscher, Tomlinson G.
Ott, Ludwig. Fundamentals of Catholic Dogma. Bastible, James C., ed. Lynch, Patrick, tr. Orig. Title: Grundriss der Katholischen Dogmatik. 1974. reprint ed. pap. 20.00 (0-89555-009-1) TAN Bks Pubs.
Ott, Lyman, jt. auth. see Hildebrand, David K.
Ott, Margaret V., jt. auth. see Swanson, Gloria M.
***Ott, Martin.** Misery Loves. 32p. (Orig.). 1994. pap. 4.00 (1-881168-49-2) Red Danceflr.
Ott, N. Intrafamily Bargaining & Household Decisions. Guth, W. et al, eds. (Microeconomic Studies). (Illus.). viii, 242p. 1992. 69.00 (0-387-55061-5) Spr-Verlag.
Ott, R. Lyman. An Introduction to Statistical Methods & Data Analysis. 4th ed. LC 92-31934. 1051p. 1993. text ed. 57.95 (0-534-93150-2) Intl Thomson.
Ott, R. Lyman & Mendenhall, William. Understanding Statistics. 5th ed. (C). 1990. text ed. 52.95 (0-534-92154-X) Intl Thomson.
— Understanding Statistics. 6th ed. 598p. 1994. text ed. 56.95 (0-534-20922-X) Intl Thomson.
Ott, R. Lyman, et al. Statistics: A Tool for the Social Sciences. 5th ed. 634p. (C). 1992. text ed. 49.95 (0-534-92931-1) Intl Thomson.
Ott, Richard. Creating Demand: Powerful Tips & Tactics for Marketing Your Product or Service. 250p. 1991. 30.00 (1-55623-560-7) Irwin Prof Pubng.
— Oriental Design Stained Glass Pattern Book. 48p. 1986. pap. 3.95 (0-486-25229-9) Dover.
Ott, Richard & Snead, Martin. Unleashing Productivity! Your Guide to Unlocking the Secrets of Super Performance. LC 93-11585. 264p. 1993. text ed. 23.00 (1-55623-931-9) Irwin Prof Pubng.
***Ott, Richard, et al, eds.** Managed Care & the Cardiac Patient. LC 94-40714. (Illus.). 400p. 1995. text ed. 48.00 (1-56053-122-3) Hanley & Belfus.
Ott, Robert W. & Hurwitz, Al, eds. Art in Education: An International Perspective. LC 83-43226. (Illus.). 336p. 1984. 35.00 (0-271-00372-3) Pa St U Pr.
Ott, Sandra. The Circle of Mountains: A Basque Shepherding Community. LC 93-13842. (Basque Ser.). (Illus.). 272p. 1993. pap. 12.95 (0-87417-224-1) U of Nev Pr.
Ott, Thomas O. The Haitian Revolution, 1789-1804. LC 72-85085. (Illus.). 246p. 1973. pap. 15.95x (0-87049-545-3) U of Tenn Pr.
Ott, Ulrich. Die Kunst Des Gegensatzes in Theokrits Hirtengedichten. Bd. XXII. x, 231p. 1969. write for info. (0-318-70993-7, Pub. by Georg Olms GW) Lubrecht & Cramer.
Ott, W. E., jt. auth. see Wong, Y. J.
Ott, Wayne R. Environmental Statistics & Data Analysis. 300p. 1994. 69.95 (0-87371-848-8, L848) Lewis Pubs.
Ott, Wendell L., frwd. Director's Invitational, September 16-November 6, 1988. (Illus.). 14p. (Orig.). 1988. pap. 2.00 (0-924335-06-8) Tacoma Art Mus.
Ott, William. California College Review. 80p. (C). 1994. 7.16 (0-8403-9217-6) Kendall-Hunt.
Ott-Worrow, Karen. Caring for Children with Special Needs. (BNA Special Report Series on Work & Family: No. 43). 32p. 1991. 35.00 (1-55871-230-5, BSP221) BNA.
Ottanelli, Fraser M. The Communist Party of the United States from the Depression to World War II. LC 90-34391. 300p. (C). 1991. text ed. 45.00 (0-8135-1612-9); pap. text ed. 15.00 (0-8135-1613-7) Rutgers U Pr.
Ottar, Brynjulf, jt. ed. see Pacyna, Jozef M.
***Ottati, Douglas F.** Reforming Protestantism: Christian Commitment in Today's World. LC 95-10454. 1995. write for info. (0-664-25604-X) Westminster John Knox.
Ottaviani, Alfredo C. Duties of the Catholic State in Regard to Religion. Fahey, Denis, tr. & frwd. by. 26p. 1993. reprint ed. pap. 3.50 (0-935952-89-6) Angelus Pr.
Ottaviani, Alfredo C. & Bacci, Antonio C. The Ottaviani Intervention: Short Critical Study of the New Order of Mass. Cekada, Anthony, tr. LC 92-60956. 63p. (Orig.). 1992. pap. 5.00 (0-89555-470-4) TAN Bks Pubs.
***Ottaviani, G., ed.** Financial Risk in Insurance. LC 94-46824. 1995. 89.00 (0-387-57054-3) Spr-Verlag.
Ottaviano, E., et al, eds. Angiosperm Pollen & Ovules. LC 92-1605. (Illus.). xxvi, 465p. 1992. 87.00 (0-387-97888-7) Spr-Verlag.
Ottaviano, Juan, jt. auth. see De Ottaviano, Aida B.
Ottaviano, Veniero A. The Pianist. 1993. 13.95 (0-533-10542-0) Vantage.
Ottaviano, Victor B. National Mechanical Estimator. 3rd ed. (C). 1993. pap. text ed. 90.00 (0-13-748583-2) P-H.
— National Mechanical Estimator. 23th ed. LC 93-17560. 1993. write for info. (0-88173-186-2) Fairmont Pr.
— National Mechanical Estimator. 23th ed. 1993. pap. 85.00 (1-878656-04-X) Ottaviano Tech Serv.
— National Mechanical Estimator. 24th ed. 1995. pap. 95.00 (1-878656-05-8) Ottaviano Tech Serv.
— National Plumbing Estimator. 8th ed. (Illus.). 792p. 1992. pap. 85.00 (1-878656-01-5) Ottaviano Tech Serv.
Ottaway. Technology of Vitamins in Food. 1994. text ed. 99.95 (0-442-30864-7) Van Nos Reinhold.
Ottaway, C. W., ed. see Stubbs, George.
Ottaway, David, jt. auth. see Ottaway, Marina.
Ottaway, David B. Chained Together: Mandela, De Klerk, & the Struggle to Remake South Africa. 1993. 25.00 (0-8129-2014-7, Times Bks) Random.
Ottaway, Hugh. Mozart. LC 79-91954. (Illus.). 208p. reprint ed. pap. 59.30 (0-7837-3642-8, 2043510) Bks Demand.
Ottaway, J. H. Regulation of Enzyme Activity: In Focus. (In Focus Ser.). (Illus.). 100p. 1988. pap. 13.95 (1-85221-072-9, IRL Pr) OUP.
Ottaway, John R., jt. auth. see Baer, Charles J.
***Ottaway, Marina.** Democratization & Ethnic Nationalism: African & Eastern European Experiences. LC 94-36131. (Policy Essay Ser.: Vol. 14). 1994. pap. 9.95 (1-56517-019-9) Overseas Dev Council.
— South Africa: The Struggle for a New Order. 1993. 34.95 (0-8157-6716-1); pap. 14.95 (0-8157-6715-3) Brookings.
Ottaway, Marina, ed. The Political Economy of Ethiopia. LC 89-77108. (SAIS Studies of Africa). 264p. 1990. text ed. 55.00 (0-275-93472-1, C3472, Greenwood Pr) Greenwood.
Ottaway, Marina & Ottaway, David. Afrocommunism. 2nd ed. (Illus.). 280p. (C). 1986. text ed. 39.50 (0-8419-1034-0); pap. text ed. 18.95 (0-8419-1035-9) Holmes & Meier.
— Ethiopia: Empire in Revolution. LC 77-28370. (Illus.). 250p. 1978. 35.00 (0-8419-0362-X, Africana) Holmes & Meier.
Ottaway, Patrick. The English Heritage Book of Roman York. (Illus.). 152p. 1993. pap. 34.95 (0-7134-7083-6, Pub. by Batsford UK) Trafalgar.
— A Traveller's Guide to Roman Britain. 1986. 14.95 (0-918678-19-6) Natl Hist Soc.
Ottaway, Richard N. Change Agents at Work. LC 79-24. (Contributions in Economics & Economic History Ser.: No. 27). 169p. 1979. text ed. 49.95 (0-313-21252-X, OCA/, Greenwood Pr) Greenwood.
Ottchen, Cynthia J., jt. auth. see Hill, Wayne F.
Otte, Alfred. The HG Panzer Division. LC 89-63360. (Illus.). 176p. 1989. 24.95 (0-88740-206-2) Schiffer.
Otte, Carel, jt. ed. see Kruger, Paul.

O

An Asterisk (*) at the beginning of an entry indicates that the title is appearing in BIP for the first time.

***Otte, Daniel.** The Crickets of Hawaii: Origin, Systematics & Evolution. (Publications on Orthopteran Diversity). (Illus.). 396p. (Orig.). 1994. pap. text ed. 75.00 (*0-9640101-0-0*) Orthopterists.

— The North American Grasshoppers: Acrididae - Gomphocerinae & Acridinae, Vol. 1. (Illus.). 304p. (C). 1981. 72.00 (*0-674-62660-5*) HUP.

— The North American Grasshoppers: Acrididae, Oedipodinae, Vol. 2. (Illus.). 352p. 1985. 82.00 (*0-674-62661-3*) HUP.

— Orthoptera Species File, No. 1: Crickets (Grylloidea) (Illus.). 120p. (Orig.). 1994. pap. text ed. 50.00 (*0-9640101-2-7*) Orthopterists.

— Orthoptera Species File Series. (Illus.). (Orig.). 1994. pap. text ed. write for info. (*0-9640101-1-9*) Orthopterists.

Otte, Daniel & Alexander, Richard D. The Australian Crickets (Orthoptera: Gryllidae) (Monograph: No. 22). (Illus.). 477p. 1983. lib. bdg. 20.00 (*0-685-08425-6*); pap. 15.00 (*0-910006-30-X*) Acad Nat Sci Phila.

Otte, Daniel & Endler, John A., eds. Speciation & Its Consequences. LC 89-5867. (Illus.). 679p. 1989. pap. text ed. 35.95 (*0-87893-658-0*) Sinauer Assocs.

Otte, E., jt. auth. see Lockhart, James.

Otte, E. C., tr. see Von Humboldt, Alexander.

Otte, Elmer. Engaging the Aging in Ministry. 1981. pap. 7.95 (*0-9602938-5-X*) Retirement Res.

— Inherit Your Own Money. LC 78-13201. 169p. 1979. 9.95 (*0-685-04337-1*); pap. 6.95 (*0-9602938-4-1*) Retirement Res.

— Rehearse Before You Retire. 3rd rev. ed. LC 77-79286. 208p. 1977. pap. 5.50 (*0-9602938-1-7*) Retirement Res.

— Retirement Planning Kit, 1984. 2nd ed. LC 84-4530. 1984. teacher ed, audio 47.50 (*0-9602938-0-9*) Retirement Res.

— Retirement Rehearsal Guidebook. 5th rev. ed. LC 84-453. 1984. pap. 9.95 (*0-9602938-2-5*) Retirement Res.

— Welcome Retirement. LC 73-11880. 1974. pap. 3.50 (*0-9602938-3-3*) Retirement Res.

Otte, Fred L. & Hutchinson, Peggy G. Helping Employees Manage Careers. 208p. 1991. pap. text ed. write for info. (*0-13-385287-3*) P-H.

Otte, George & Palumbo, Linda J. Casts of Thought. 695p. (C). 1990. pap. write for info. (*0-02-389961-1*) Macmillan.

Otte, George, jt. auth. see Mason, Nondita.

Otte, Heinrich. Archaologisches Worterbuch Zur Erklarung der in Den Schriften Uber Christliche Kunstalterthumer Vorkommenden Kunstausdrucke. viii, 488p. 1978. reprint ed. write for info. (*3-487-06455-3*, Pub. by Georg Olms GW) Lubrecht & Cramer.

Otte, Linda, ed. see King, Robert L.

***Otte, Peter.** Lode Runner: The Official Strategy. 1994. pap. 19.95 (*1-55958-779-2*) Prima Pub.

Otte, Thomas G., jt. auth. see Dorman, Andrew M.

Otten, jt. ed. see Lane.

Otten, C. Michael. Power, Values & Society: An Introduction to Sociology. LC 80-29411. (C). 1981. pap. text ed. write for info. (*0-394-33295-4*) Random.

Otten, Catherine. The Corner Grocery Store. (Illus.). 148p. (Orig.). 1980. pap. 4.95 (*0-937816-02-7*) Tech Data.

***Otten, Charlotte.** The Book of Birth Poetry. LC 94-27156. 1995. pap. 10.95 (*0-553-37449-4*) Bantam.

Otten, Charlotte, ed. A Lycanthropy Reader: Werewolves in Western Culture. (Illus.). 352p. 1986. pap. text ed. 15.95 (*0-8156-2384-4*) Syracuse U Pr.

Otten, Charlotte F. Environ'd with Eternity: God, Poems, & Plants in Sixteenth & Seventeenth Century England. (Illus.). 200p. 1984. 19.95 (*0-87291-168-3*) Coronado Pr.

Otten, Charlotte F., ed. English Women's Voices, 1540-1700. 448p. (C). 1991. lib. bdg. 49.95 (*0-8130-1083-7*); pap. text ed. 24.95 (*0-8130-1099-3*) U Press Fla.

— A Lycanthropy Reader: Werewolves in Western Culture. (Reprints Ser.). (Illus.). 337p. 1990. reprint ed. 19.95 (*0-88029-400-0*) Dorset Pr.

Otten, Charlotte F. & Schmidt, Gary D., eds. The Voice of the Narrator in Children's Literature: Insights from Writers & Critics. LC 88-7709. (Contributions to the Study of World Literature Ser.). 432p. 1989. text ed. 59.95 (*0-313-26370-1*, OVN) Greenwood.

Otten, Charlotte M., ed. Anthropology & Art: Readings in Cross-Cultural Aesthetics. LC 75-43853. (Sourcebooks in Anthropology: No. 10). 456p. 1976. pap. 19.95 (*0-292-70313-9*) U of Tex Pr.

Otten, D., jt. auth. see Karpe, H. J.

Otten, E. W. Investigation of Short-Lived Isotopes by Laser Spectroscopy. Letokhov, V. S., ed. (Laser Science & Technology Ser.: Vol. 5). viii, 76p. 1989. pap. text ed. 53.00 (*3-7186-4892-X*) Gordon & Breach.

Otten, G., jt. ed. see Lane, R. W.

Otten, Gerard A., jt. auth. see Cannan, Stephen J.

Otten, Klaus. Integrated Document & Image Management. 66p. (Orig.). 1987. pap. text ed. 29.00 (*0-89258-104-2*, RO25) Assn Inform & Image Mgmt.

Otten, Lambert, jt. ed. see Fayed, M. E.

Otten, Laura A. Women's Rights & the Law. LC 93-20127. 264p. 1993. text ed. 59.95 (*0-275-93184-6*, C3184, Praeger Pubs); pap. text ed. 18.95 (*0-275-93185-4*, B3185, Praeger Pubs) Greenwood.

Otten, Leaun G. & Caldwell, C. Max. Sacred Truths of the Doctrine & Covenants, Vol. 1. LC 82-71971. xi, 355p. 1983. 14.95 (*0-87579-783-0*) Deseret Bk.

— Sacred Truths of the Doctrine & Covenants, Vol. 2. LC 82-71791. xii, 412p. 1993. 14.95 (*0-87579-784-9*) Deseret Bk.

Otten, Mariel. Transmigrasi - Indonesian Resettlement Policy, 1965-1985: Myths & Realities. (IWGIA Document Ser.: No. 57). (Illus.). 254p. (Orig.). 1986. pap. text ed. 49.00x (*0-317-65617-1*) Coronet Bks.

Otten, R. H. & Van Ginneken, L. P. The Annealing Algorithm. (International Series in Engineering & Computer Science, VLSI, Computer Architecture, & Digital Screen Processing). 224p. (C). 1989. lib. bdg. 81.00 (*0-7923-9022-9*) Kluwer Ac.

Otten, Terry. The Crime of Innocence in the Fiction of Toni Morrison. LC 89-4851. 104p. 1991. pap. 9.95 (*0-8262-0711-1*) U of Mo Pr.

Otten, Willemien. The Anthropology of Johannes Scottus Eriugena. LC 90-42391. (Brill's Studies in Intellectual History: Vol. 20). viii, 242p. 1990. 51.50 (*90-04-09302-8*) E J Brill.

Otten, Willemien, jt. ed. see McGinn, Bernard.

Ottenbacher, Kenneth, jt. ed. see Short-DeGraff, Margaret A.

Ottenbacher, Kenneth J. & Short, Margaret A., eds. Vestibular Processing Dysfunction in Children. LC 85-8636. (Physical & Occupational Therapy in Pediatrics Ser.: Vol. 5, Nos. 2 & 3). 152p. 1985. text ed. 49.95 (*0-86656-431-4*); pap. text ed. 14.95 (*0-86656-432-2*) Haworth Pr.

Ottenberg, Hans-Gunter. C. P. E. Bach. Whitmore, Philip J., tr. (Illus.). 296p. 1988. 75.00 (*0-19-315246-0*) OUP.

— C. P. E. Bach. Whitmore, Philip J., tr. (Illus.). 304p. 1991. reprint ed. pap. 29.95 (*0-19-816245-6*) OUP.

Ottenberg, June C. Opera Odyssey: Toward History of Opera in Nineteenth Century America. LC 93-35861. (Contributions to the Study of Music & Dance Ser.: No. 32). 224p. 1994. text ed. 49.95 (*0-313-27841-5*, Greenwood Pr) Greenwood.

Ottenberg, Simon. Double Descent in an African Society. LC 84-45540. (American Ethnological Society Monographs: No. 47). 1988. reprint ed. 36.00 (*0-404-62945-8*) AMS Pr.

Ottenberite & Butler. Anticancer & Interferon Inducing Agents: Synthesis and Properties. (Drugs & Pharmaceutical Science Ser.: Vol. 24). 344p. 1984. 140.00 (*0-8247-7189-3*) Dekker.

Ottenbreit, Gerald E., Jr. A State of the Society Address: Selected Writings, Musings & Poetry of a Curmudgeon (Including Armenia & Kuwait) 113p. 1992. pap. 12.00 (*0-9634509-0-5*) Bookshelf Pubs.

Ottenbrite, Raphael & Chiellini, Emo, eds. Polymers in Medicine: Biomedical & Pharmaceutical Applications. LC 92-60021. 265p. 1992. text ed. 59.00 (*0-87762-929-3*) Technomic.

Ottenbrite, Raphael M., ed. Polymeric Drugs & Drug Administration. LC 93-48086. (ACS Symposium Ser.: No. 545). 278p. 1994. 69.95 (*0-8412-2744-6*) Am Chemical.

Ottenbrite, Raphael M., jt. ed. see Dunn, Richard L.

Ottenbrite, Raphael M., et al. Current Topics in Polymer Science, Vol. 1: Polymer Chemistry & Polymer Physics. 343p. (C). 1987. text ed. 119.50 (*1-56990-070-1*) Hanser-Gardner.

— Current Topics in Polymer Science, Vol. 2: Rheology & Polymer Processing - Multiphase Systems. 376p. (C). 1987. text ed. 119.50 (*1-56990-071-X*) Hanser-Gardner.

Ottenheimer. Dreams: Hidden Meanings & Secrets. 1983. pap. 9.00 (*0-671-76268-0*, Fireside) S&S Trade.

— Martin Luther King, Jr. (Great Americans Ser.). (J). (gr. 2-5). 1987. pap. 2.50 (*0-671-63632-4*, Litl Simon S&S) S&S Childrens.

Ottenheimer, Harriet, jt. auth. see Ottenheimer, Martin.

Ottenheimer, Harriet J., jt. auth. see Joseph, Pleasant.

Ottenheimer, Laurence. Japan: Land of Samurai & Robots. LC 87-34524. (Illus.). 38p. (J). (gr. k-5). 1988. 5.95 (*0-944589-11-1*, 111) Young Discovery Lib.

— Livre de l'Automne. (Gallimard - Decouverte Cadet Ser.: No. 6). (Illus.). 90p. (FRE.). (J). (gr. 4-9). 1983. 8.95 (*2-07-039506-5*) Schoenhof.

— Livre de l'Ete. (Gallimard - Decouverte Cadet Ser.: No. 8). (Illus.). 88p. (FRE.). (J). (gr. 4-9). 1983. 15.95 (*2-07-039508-1*) Schoenhof.

— Livre de L'Hiver. (Gallimard - Decouverte Cadet Ser.: No. 5). (Illus.). 93p. (FRE.). (J). (gr. 4-9). 1983. 15.95 (*2-07-039505-7*) Schoenhof.

— Livre du Printemps. (Gallimard - Decouverte Cadet Ser.: No. 7). 96p. (FRE.). (J). (gr. 4-9). 1983. 15.95 (*2-07-039507-3*) Schoenhof.

***Ottenheimer, Martin.** Marriage in Domoni: Husbands & Wives in an Indian Ocean Community. 106p. (Orig.). (C). 1994. reprint ed. pap. text ed. 8.95 (*1-879215-23-3*) Sheffield WI.

Ottenheimer, Martin & Ottenheimer, Harriet. Historical Dictionary of Comoro Islands. LC 93-42244. (African Historical Dictionaries Ser.). 1994. 25.00 (*0-8108-2819-7*) Scarecrow.

***Ottenheimer, Peter.** Toy Autos: 1890-1939. Levy, Allen, ed. (Illus.). 168p. Date not set. pap. 25.00 (*1-872727-61-1*, Pub. by New Cavendish UK) Pincushion Pr.

Ottenhoff, Tom & De Vries, Rene. Recognition of M. Leprae Antigens. (Development in Hematology & Immunology Ser.). (C). 1987. lib. bdg. 54.00 (*0-317-59613-6*) Kluwer Ac.

Ottenjann & Classen. Atlas of Gastrointestinal Endoscopy. (Illus.). 550p. (C). 1990. 165.00 (*1-55664-203-2*) Mosby Yr Bk.

Ottenjann, R., jt. ed. see Maratka, Zdenek.

Ottens, Allen & Myer, Rick. Coping with Satanism. Rosen, Ruth, ed. (Coping Ser.). (YA). (gr. 7-12). 1994. 15.95 (*0-8239-1423-2*) Rosen Group.

Ottens, Allen J. Coping with Academic Anxiety. rev. ed. (Coping Ser.). 140p. 1991. lib. bdg. 15.95 (*0-8239-1337-6*) Rosen Group.

— Coping with Romantic Breakup. (Coping Ser.). 147p. (YA). (gr. 7-12). 1987. lib. bdg. 15.95 (*0-8239-0649-3*) Rosen Group.

Ottensmann, John R. & Neuenschwander, Jan. Working with Lotus Agenda. (Illus.). 256p. 1989. pap. 24.95 (*0-8306-3161-5*, 3161) TAB Bks.

— Working with Lotus Agenda 2.0. (Illus.). 384p. 1991. pap. 24.95 (*0-8306-3703-6*, 3703, Windcrest) TAB Bks.

Ottensmeyer, Ed, jt. ed. see McGowan, Robert.

Ottensmeyer, Edward, jt. ed. see McGowan, Robert.

Ottensmeyer, Edward J., jt. ed. see McGowan, Robert P.

Ottensoser, Max & Roberg, Alex, eds. Israelitische Lehrerbildungsanstalt Wurzburg. LC 81-81930. (Illus.). 256p. 1982. 12.95 (*0-8187-0046-7*) Harlo Press.

Ottenstein, Claire. Catch a Whiffle-Poofle! (Illus.). 64p. (Orig.). (J). 1991. lib. bdg. 8.95 (*1-878149-03-2*) Counterpoint Pub.

— The Healing Touch of Poetry. (Illus.). 52p. (Orig.). 1990. lib. bdg. 6.95 (*1-878149-07-5*) Counterpoint Pub.

— In the Shadow of His Wings. (Illus.). 28p. (Orig.). 1995. pap. 5.00 (*1-878149-32-6*) Counterpoint Pub.

— The Poetry Fun Book. (Illus.). 40p. (Orig.). (J). 1992. pap. 7.95 (*1-878149-20-2*) Counterpoint Pub.

— Seven Steps to Getting Published. LC 92-73827. 56p. (Orig.). 1992. pap. 6.00 (*1-878149-14-8*) Counterpoint Pub.

***Ottenstein, Claire, ed. & intro.** Anthology of Children's Poetry. (Illus.). 36p. (Orig.). (J). (gr. 1-5). 1993. pap. 4.00 (*1-878149-23-7*) Counterpoint Pub.

Ottenstein, Claire, ed. Anthology of Children's Poetry, 1992. (Illus.). 36p. (Orig.). 1992. pap. 4.00 (*1-878149-15-6*) Counterpoint Pub.

— Anthology of Children's Poetry, 1994. (Illus.). 36p. (Orig.). (J). (gr. 1-5). 1994. pap. 4.00 (*1-878149-30-X*) Counterpoint Pub.

— Texas Rib-Ticklers! (Illus.). 84p. 1990. lib. bdg. 7.95 (*1-878149-00-8*) Counterpoint Pub.

***Ottenstein, Claire & Newton, Violette.** Because We Dream. LC 94-70819. (Illus.). 68p. 1994. lib. bdg. 8.00 (*1-878149-25-3*) Counterpoint Pub.

Otter, Floyd L. Men of Mammoth Forest. (Illus.). 169p. 1973. reprint ed. 19.95 (*0-9614459-1-2*) Otter Veterinary.

Otter, P. W. Dynamic Feature Space Modelling, Filtering & Self-Tuning Control of Stochastic Systems. (Lecture Notes in Economics & Mathematical Systems Ser.: Vol. 246). xiv, 177p. 1985. pap. 31.00 (*0-387-15654-2*) Spr-Verlag.

Otter, R. A., ed. Civil Engineering Heritage: Southern England. 304p. 1994. 24.00 (*0-685-75140-6*, 1971-8) Am Soc Civil Eng.

***Otter, William.** History of My Own Times: Or, the Life & Adventures of William Otter, Sr., Comprising a Series of Events, & Musical Incidents Altogether Original. Stott, Richard B., ed. (Documents in American Social History Ser.). (Illus.). 256p. 1995. 39.95x (*0-8014-2667-7*); pap. 14.95 (*0-8014-9961-5*) Cornell U Pr.

Otterbein College Dept. Foreign Languages Staff, ed. see Galin, Muge.

Otterbein College Staff. Russian Listening Comprehension II, Pt. B: "An Office Affair" (RUS.). (C). 1992. student ed, pap. 8.00 (*0-87415-186-4*, 74); teacher ed, audio 60.00 (*0-87415-187-2*, 74A); pap. 5.00 (*0-87415-173-2*, 74C) OSU Foreign Lang.

— Russian Listening Comprehension II, Pt. B: "An Office Affair", 2 cass., Set. (RUS.). (C). 1992. audio 10.00 (*0-87415-188-0*, 74B) OSU Foreign Lang.

Otterbein College Staff, ed. see Gilson, Erika H.

Otterbein College Staff, ed. see Humesky, Assya, et al.

Otterbein, Keith F. Evolution of War: A Cross-Cultural Study. 3rd ed. LC 79-87852. (Comparative Studies). 184p. 1989. pap. 20.00 (*0-87536-324-5*) HRAFP.

— The Ultimate Coercive Sanction: A Cross-Cultural Study of Capital Punishment. LC 86-80163. 164p. (C). 1987. pap. 16.00 (*0-87536-346-6*) HRAFP.

Otterbein, Keith F., ed. Feuding & Warfare: Selected Works of Keith F. Otterbein. LC 93-11752. 1993. text ed. 45.00 (*2-88124-620-6*); pap. text ed. 22.00 (*2-88124-621-4*) Gordon & Breach.

***Otterbourg, Robert J.** Kiplinger's Retire & Thrive! 1995. pap. 15.00 (*0-8129-2646-3*, Times Bks) Random.

Otterbourg, Robert K. It's Never Too Late: One Hundred-Fifty Men & Women Who Changed Their Careers. 240p. 1993. pap. 9.95 (*0-8120-1464-2*) Barron.

— You Don't Have to Retire. 1995. 12.95 (*0-938721-39-9*) Kiplinger Bks.

Otterbourg, Susan D. School Partnerships Handbook: How to Set up & Administer Programs with Business, Government & Your Community. 336p. 1986. 29.95 (*0-13-793852-7*) P-H.

Otterbrandt, T. & Lodhi, A. Kortfattad Swahili-Svensk. (SWA & SWE.). 1980. 59.95 (*0-8288-1101-6*, M 2174) Fr & Eur.

Otterholt, Howard V. How to Be Your Own Good Samaritan. LC 81-3465. 1982. 22.95 (*0-87949-195-7*) Ashley Bks.

Otterloo, Van. A Contour-Oriented Approach to Digital Shape. 380p. 1991. text ed. 54.00 (*0-13-173840-2*) P-H.

Otterman, George R., jt. ed. see Lima, Joseph A.

Otterman, J., jt. ed. see Godby, E. A.

Otterman, Ken. Cash Flow: The First Step to Wealth Through Real Estate. 256p. 1986. 16.95 (*0-910019-32-0*) United Support.

Otterman, Lillian. Clinker Islands: A Complete History of the Galapagos Archipelago. LC 92-62391. 276p. 1993. pap. 16.95 (*1-881117-03-0*) McGuinn & McGuire.

Otterness, Ivan, et al, eds. Therapeutic Control of Inflammatory Diseases. (Advances in Inflammation Research Ser.: Vol. 7). 326p. 1984. text ed. 104.50 (*0-89004-983-1*) Raven.

— Therapeutic Control of Inflammatory Diseases: New Approaches to Antirheumatic Drugs. (Advances in Inflammation Research Ser.: Vol. 11). (Illus.). 352p. 1986. text ed. 126.00 (*0-88167-133-9*) Raven.

Ottersen, Ole P. & Storm-Mathisen, Jon, eds. Glycine Neurotransmission. 508p. 1990. text ed. 229.95 (*0-471-92717-1*) Wiley.

Ottersen, Ole P., ed. see Storm-Mathisen, Jon, et al.

Ottersen, Signe R., ed. see International Institute for Environment & Development (I.I.E.D.) Staff.

Otterson, Dorothy, jt. auth. see Stephenson, Harriet.

Otterson, Lynn, ed. see Cottingham, Carl D., et al.

Otterspeer, Willem, ed. Leiden Oriental Connections, Eighteen Fifty to Nineteen Forty. (Studies in the History of Leiden University: Vol. 5). (Illus.). vii, 391p. 1989. pap. 80.00 (*90-04-09022-3*) E J Brill.

Otterstrom, Thorvald. A Theory of Modulation. LC 74-34379. (Music Reprint Ser.). (Illus.). viii, 162p. (ENG & GER.). 1975. reprint ed. lib. bdg. 29.50 (*0-306-70721-7*) Da Capo.

Ottery, Rudi, jt. auth. see Ottery, Will.

***Ottery, Will & Ottery, Rudi.** A Man Called Sampson, 1580-1989: The Ancestry & Progeny of Sampson, a Mashantucket Pequot Indian. 432p. 1989. 85.00 (*0-929539-51-6*) Picton Pr.

Ottesen, Carol C. L.A. Stories: The Voices of Cultural Diversity. LC 93-36926. 180p. 1993. pap. 12.95 (*1-877864-26-9*) Intercult Pr.

Ottesen, Carole. The Native Plant Primer. LC 94-19383. 1995. 50.00 (*0-517-59215-0*, Harmony) Crown Pub Group.

— Ornamental Grasses: The Amber Wave. 2nd ed. 1995. pap. text ed. 24.95 (*0-07-048021-4*) McGraw.

Ottesen, Frances. Speak Like Rain. 50p. (Orig.). 1986. pap. 6.00 (*0-9605220-1-8*) Otafra.

— Sun-Spaces. (Illus.). 76p. 1981. 7.95 (*0-9605220-0-X*) Otafra.

***Ottesen, Johnny T.** Infinite Dimensional Groups & Algebras in Quantum Physics. LC 95-7866. (Lecture Notes in Physics: New Series M; Monographs: Vol. 27). 227p. 1995. 49.00 (*3-540-58914-7*) Spr-Verlag.

Ottesen, M., jt. auth. see Magnusson, S.

Otteson, Orlo J., jt. auth. see Pattee, James J.

Otteson, Orlo J., jt. auth. see Seifert, Milton H., Jr.

Ottestad, P. Statistical Models & Their Experimental Applications. (Griffin's Statistical Monographs: No. 25). 88p. 1970. pap. text ed. 17.95 (*0-85264-166-4*) Lubrecht & Cramer.

***Ottewell, Guy.** Astronomical Calendar 1995. 1994. pap. 16.00 (*0-934546-30-4*) Astron Wkshp.

— Astronomical Companion. (Illus.). (C). 1979. pap. 12.00 (*0-934546-01-0*) Astron Wkshp.

— Language. 1987. 9.00 (*0-934546-17-7*) Astron Wkshp.

— To Know the Stars. (Illus.). 41p. (J). (gr. 3 up). 1983. pap. 7.00 (*0-934546-12-6*) Astron Wkshp.

— The Under-Standing of Eclipses. (Illus.). 93p. (Orig.). 1991. pap. 12.95 (*0-934546-24-X*) Astron Wkshp.

Ottewell, Guy & Schaaf, Fred. Mankind's Comet: Halley's Comet in the Past, the Future, & Especially the Present. (Illus.). 1985. pap. 11.00 (*0-934546-15-0*) Astron Wkshp.

Ottewell, O. Wildlife Walks in the North Cotswolds. (C). 1988. pap. 29.00 (*0-946328-00-5*, Pub. by Thornhill Pr UK) St Mut.

Ottewill, David. The Edwardian Garden. LC 88-50427. 240p. (C). 1989. pap. text ed. 50.00 (*0-300-04338-4*) Yale U Pr.

***Ottewill, R. H. & Rennie, A R., eds.** Trends in Colloid & Interface Science VIII. (Progress in Colloid & Polymer Science Ser.: Vol. 97). 340p. 1995. 139.00 (*3-7985-0984-0*) Spr-Verlag.

Ottewill, R. H., ed. see International Union of Pure & Applied Chemistry.

Ottewill, Ronald H., jt. ed. see Candau, Francoise.

***Ottewitte, Eric & Weiss, Alex, eds.** Slow Positron Beam Techniques for Solids & Surfaces. LC 94-71036. (AIP Conference Proceedings Ser.: No. 303). 640p. 1994. pap. text ed. 623.00x (*1-56396-267-5*) Am Inst Physics.

Otting, Rae. When Jesus Was a Lad. (Illus.). (J). (gr. 1-2). 1978. pap. 1.25 (*0-89508-055-9*) Rainbow Bks.

Ottinger, Cecelia, ed. Community, Technical & Junior College Fact Book. 1988. write for info. (*0-318-63184-9*, 2004) Macmillan.

Ottinger, Cecilia, ed. Fact Book on Higher Education, 1986-1987. 224p. 1986. text ed. write for info. (*0-318-62001-4*, ACE) Macmillan.

Ottinger, R. L., jt. ed. see Hohmeyer, O.

Ottinger, Richard L., jt. ed. see Hohmeyer, Olav.

Ottinger, Richard L., jt. auth. see Pace University, Center for Environmental Legal Studies Staff.

Ottino, J. M. The Kinetics of Mixing: Stretching, Chaos & Transport. (Cambridge Texts in Applied Mathematics Ser.: No. 4). (Illus.). 375p. 1989. 99.95 (*0-521-36335-7*); pap. 42.95 (*0-521-36878-2*) Cambridge U Pr.

Ottino, P. L' Etrangere Intime. (Ordres Sociaux Ser.). 1986. text ed. 153.00 (*2-88124-088-7*) Gordon & Breach.

— L' Etrangere Intime, 2 vols., Set. 607p. (FRE.). 1986. pap. text ed. 50.00 (*2-88124-095-X*) Gordon & Breach.

Ottis, Kenneth, et al. Experimental Animal Physiology: A Contemporary Systems Approach. 4th ed. 240p. (Orig.). (C). 1991. spiral bd. 21.95 (*0-8403-7127-6*) Kendall-Hunt.

Ottley, Allan R., ed. John A. Sutter's Last Days: The Bidwell Letters. LC 86-61877. (Illus.). 72p. 1986. lib. bdg. 37.50 (*0-9617334-0-3*) Sacto Bk Collectors.

Ottley, Bruce L., jt. auth. see Polelle, Michael J.

***Ottley, Darron L.** Inversions. 400p. (Orig.). 1995. pap. 14.95 (*0-9643967-5-0*) Taurian Pubng.

Ottley, Roi. New World A-Coming: Inside Black America. LC 68-29014. (American Negro: His History & Literature, Ser. No. 1). 1969. reprint ed. 17.95 (*0-405-01833-9*) Ayer.

Ottlik, Geza & Kelsey, Hugh. Adventures in Card Play. (Master Bridge Ser.). (Illus.). 288p. 1983. pap. 19.95 (*0-575-03365-7*, Pub. by V Gollancz UK) Trafalgar.

O

Ottman, Jacquelyn. Green Marketing: Responding to Environmental Consumer Demands. 1993. 24.95 (*0-8442-3250-5*, NTC Busn Bks) NTC Pub Grp.
Ottman, Jacquelyn A. Green Marketing: Challenges & Opportunities for the New Marketing Age. 1994. pap. 14.95 (*0-8442-3290-4*) NTC Pub Grp.
Ottman, Robert W. Advanced Harmony. 3rd ed. (Illus.). 416p. 1984. pap. text ed. 57.33 (*0-13-011370-0*) P-H.
— Advanced Harmony, Theory & Practice. 4th ed. 384p. 1992. pap. text ed. 52.00 (*0-13-006016-X*) P-H.
— Elementary Harmony. 4th ed. 464p. (C). 1989. pap. text ed. write for info. (*0-13-257288-5*) P-H.
— Music for Sight Singing. 3rd ed. 304p. 1986. pap. text ed. write for info. (*0-13-607532-0*) P-H.
Ottman, Robert W. & Dworak, Paul. Basic Ear Training Skills. 1991. pap. text ed. 23.00 (*0-13-058926-8*, 650202) P-H.
Ottman, Robert W. & Mainous, Frank D. Programmed Rudiments of Music. 1979. pap. text ed. 56.67 (*0-13-729962-1*) P-H.
— Programmed Rudiments of Music. 2nd ed. LC 92-46702. 1993. pap. text ed. 45.33 (*0-13-138042-7*) P-H.
— Rudiments of Music. 2nd ed. (Illus.). 320p. (C). 1987. write for info. (*0-318-61355-7*) P-H.
— Rudiments of Music. 3rd ed. LC 94-41687. 326p. 1995. pap. text ed. 37.33 (*0-13-706740-2*) P-H.
Ottmann, Henning. Individuum und Gemeinschaft bei Hegel: Hegel im Spiegel der Interpretationen, Vol. 1. (Quellen und Studien zur Philosophie Ser.). (C). 1977. 106.95 (*3-11-007134-7*) De Gruyter.
Ottmann, Klaus. Astrid Klein. (Illus.). 12p. 1991. pap. 6.00 (*0-929687-08-6*) E & C Zilkha Gal.
— Mary Kelly: Gloria Patri. (Illus.). 38p. (Orig.). (C). 1992. 12.00 (*0-929687-11-6*) E & C Zilkha Gal.
— Otto Kunzli: Oh, Say. (Illus.). 32p. (C). 1992. 10.00 (*0-929687-10-8*) E & C Zilkha Gal.
— Rotraut Uecker Klein. (Illus.). 32p. (Orig.). (C). 1989. pap. 12.00 (*0-929687-02-7*) E & C Zilkha Gal.
Ottmann, Klaus, ed. Jessica Stockholder, Pt. 3: The Broken Mirror. (Illus.). 4p. (C). 1991. 5.00 (*0-929687-07-8*) E & C Zilkha Gal.
Ottmann, Klaus & Bleckner, Ross. David Deutsch. Cunnick, Elizabeth, ed. (Illus.). 36p. (Orig.). 1989. pap. 10.00 (*0-924008-02-4*) Blum Helman.
Ottmann, Klaus & Lowe, Celia. Exotism: Art of Incorporation. (Illus.). 20p. (Orig.). (C). 1990. pap. text ed. 8.00 (*0-929687-03-5*) E & C Zilkha Gal.
Ottmann, Klaus, ed. see Laramee, Eve A.
Ottmann, Klaus, ed. see Restany, Pierre.
Ottmann, T., ed. Automata, Languages & Programming. (Lecture Notes in Computer Science Ser.: Vol. 267). (Illus.). x, 565p. 1987. pap. text ed. 57.00 (*0-387-18088-5*) Spr-Verlag.
Ottmar, Jerome, jt. auth. see Hart, James A.
Otto. Camouflage. (J). Date not set. 14.00 (*0-06-023342-7*, Festival); lib. bdg. 13.89 (*0-06-023343-5*, Festival) HarpC Child Bks.
— Chemotherapy Quick Reference. 64p. 1994. pap. 8.95 (*0-8016-7815-3*) Mosby Yr Bk.
— Oncology Nursing. (Illus.). 592p. 1991. pap. 43.95 (*0-8016-5875-6*) Mosby Yr Bk.
Otto & Blitt. Percutaneous Invasive Hemodynamic Monitoring. 1991. 59.95 (*0-8151-6577-3*, Yr Bk Med Pubs) Mosby Yr Bk.
Otto, A. S., ed. Chairman's Chat-Life Lines. 120p. 1981. vinyl bd. 24.95 (*0-912132-11-6*) Dominion Pr.
— Comprehensive Immortalist Primer. 1975. 24.95 (*0-912132-06-X*) Dominion Pr.
— Invisible Ministry Annual Reports. 120p. 1989. vinyl bd. 19.95 (*0-912132-12-4*) Dominion Pr.
— Theologia Twenty-One, 3 vols., Set. 150p. 1991. vinyl bd. 69.95 (*0-912132-08-6*) Dominion Pr.
— The Theologia Twenty-One Encyclopedia, 3 vols., Set. 700p. 1991. vinyl bd. 54.95 (*0-912132-16-7*) Dominion Pr.
Otto, August. Die Sprichworter und Sprichwortlichen Redensarten der Romer. xlv, 436p. 1988. reprint ed. write for info. (*3-487-00240-X*, Pub. by Georg Olms GW) Lubrecht & Cramer.
Otto, Bridget, ed. see PGE Chef's Night Out Committee.
Otto, Carolyn. First Church. (J). 1997. 15.95 (*0-8050-2554-5*) H Holt & Co.
— I Can Tell by Touching. LC 93-18630. (Let's-Read-&-Find-Out Science Bk.). (Illus.). 32p. (J). (ps-1). 1994. 15.00 (*0-06-023324-9*); lib. bdg. 14.89 (*0-06-023325-7*); pap. 4.95 (*0-06-445125-9*, Trophy) HarpC Child Bks.
— One Dog Twenty Stars. (J). 1997. write for info. (*0-8050-2369-0*) H Holt & Co.
Otto, Carolyn B. Dinosaur Chase. LC 90-2021. (Illus.). 32p. (J). (ps-1). 1991. lib. bdg. 14.89 (*0-06-021614-X*) HarpC Child Bks.
— Raccoon at Clear Creek Road. (Smithsonian's Backyard Ser.). (Illus.). 32p. (J). (ps-3). 1995. 15.95 (*1-56899-175-4*); 4.95 (*1-56899-176-2*); 12.95 (*1-56899-178-9*); audio 19.95 (*1-56899-179-7*); 29.95 (*1-56899-181-9*) Soundprints.
— That Sky, That Rain. LC 89-36582. (Trophy Picture Bk.). (Illus.). 32p. (J). (ps-3). 1992. pap. 4.95 (*0-06-443290-4*, Trophy) HarpC Child Bks.
Otto, Catherine M. & Pearlman, Alan S. Textbook of Clinical Echocardiography. LC 94-6846. (Illus.). 416p. 1994. text ed. 95.00 (*0-7216-6634-5*) Saunders.
Otto, Christian F., ed. see Klingensmith, Samuel J.
Otto, Christian F., jt. auth. see Pommer, Richard.
Otto, Daniel & Johnson, Tom, eds. Microcomputer Based Input-Output Modeling: Applications to Economic Development. 228p. (C). 1993. pap. text ed. 40.00 (*0-8133-1046-6*) Westview.
Otto, David, jt. auth. see Knops, Robert D.
Otto, Dixon P. On Orbit: The First Space Shuttle Era. (Illus.). 112p. (Orig.). Date not set. pap. text ed. 9.95 (*0-936447-00-1*) Main Stage.
***Otto, Don H.** Finding Your Church. 116p. (Orig.). 1994. pap. 4.95 (*1-886349-00-2*) D H Otto.
***Otto, Donna.** Between Women of God: Passing on the Convictions of Our Hearts, the Passion of Our Lives. (Orig.). 1995. pap. 8.99 (*1-56507-365-7*) Harvest Hse.
— Get More Done in Less Time - And Get on with the Good Stuff! (Orig.). 1994. pap. 8.99 (*1-56507-253-7*) Harvest Hse.
— The Stay-at-Home Mom: For Women at Home & Those Who Want to Be. 224p. (Orig.). 1991. pap. 7.99 (*0-89081-877-0*) Harvest Hse.
Otto-Dorn, Katerina. The Art & Architecture of the Islamic World. Date not set. 65.00 (*0-520-04325-1*) U CA Pr.
Otto, E. & Smolska, J. Nomography. LC 63-10028. (International Series of Monographs on Pure & Applied Mathematics: Vol. 42). 1963. 130.00 (*0-08-010164-X*, Pub. by Pergamon Repr UK) Franklin.
Otto, Eberhard, jt. auth. see Helck, Wolfgang.
Otto, Ernst. Zur Grundlegung der Sprachwissenschaft. vi, 39p. reprint ed. write for info. (*0-318-71464-7*, Pub. by Georg Olms GW) Lubrecht & Cramer.
Otto, Friedrich, jt. auth. see Book, Ronald V.
Otto, Gilbert, ed. Proceedings of the Heartworm Symposium, '89. 1990. text ed. 43.00 (*0-940275-01-5*) Am Heartworm Soc.
Otto, Gordon H. & Soules, James G. Statistical Tools for Total Quality Management: Using Lotus 1-2-3, Version D-1.0. LC 94-60523. (Illus.). 140p. (Orig.). 1994. pap. 29.00 (*0-9639553-2-2*) Verenikia Pr.
Otto, Gottlieb F. Lexicon der Seit Dem 15: Jahrhundert Verstorbenen und Jetzt Lebenden Oberlausitzischen Schriftsteller und Kunstler, 3 vols., Set. 1983. fiche write for info. (*0-318-71937-1*, Pub. by Georg Olms GW) Lubrecht & Cramer.
Otto, Hans-Uwe & Flosser, Gaby, eds. How to Organize Prevention: Political, Organizational & Professional Challenges to Social Services. (Prevention & Intervention in Childhood & Adolescence Ser.: No. 12). xvi, 424p. (C). 1992. lib. bdg. 84.95 (*3-11-013536-1*, 45-92) De Gruyter.
Otto, Hans-Uwe, jt. ed. see Albrecht, Gunter.
Otto, Helen T. Our Revelationary Age. Myers, Gene & Meyers, Jim, eds. 576p. 1993. text ed. 39.95 (*1-884332-08-0*); pap. text ed. 29.95 (*1-884332-09-9*) Netwrk Pr TX.
— Our Revolutionary Age: The Prophecies for WWIII & the Year 2000. LC 94-60322. 526p. (Orig.). 1994. 34.00 (*0-9639553-0-6*); pap. 20.00 (*0-9639553-1-4*) Verenikia Pr.
Otto, Herbert & Tuedio, James, eds. Perspectives on Mind. (C). 1987. lib. bdg. 117.00 (*90-277-2640-X*) Kluwer Ac.
Otto, Herbert A. New Orgasm Options: Expanding Sexual Pleasure. 289p. 1995. 22.95 (*0-8290-2408-5*) Irvington.
Otto, Herbert A., ed. Human Potentialities: The Challenge & the Promise. LC 67-26016. 231p. reprint ed. pap. 65.90 (*0-317-10387-3*, 2012193) Bks Demand.
Otto, Herbert A. & Knight, James W., eds. Dimensions in Wholistic Healing: New Frontiers in the Treatment of the Whole Person. LC 78-27071. 568p. 1979. 39.95 (*0-88229-513-6*) Nelson-Hall.
Otto, Jacob A. Treatise of the Structure & Preservation of the Violin. 1976. lib. bdg. 45.00 (*0-403-03760-3*) Scholarly.
— Treatise of the Structure & Preservation of the Violin. 1988. reprint ed. lib. bdg. 59.00 (*0-7812-0345-7*) Rprt Serv.
Otto, John, tr. see Oury, Guy.
Otto, John S. Cannon's Point Plantation, 1794-1860: Living Conditions & Status Patterns in the Old South. LC 83-15784. (Studies in Historical Archaeology). 1984. text ed. 47.00 (*0-12-531060-9*) Acad Pr.
— Southern Agriculture During the Civil War Era, 1860-1880. LC 93-32981. (Contributions in American History Ser.: No. 153). 184p. 1994. text ed. 49.95 (*0-313-26714-6*, Greenwood Pr) Greenwood.
— The Southern Frontiers, 1607-1860: The Agricultural Frontiers of the Colonial & Antebellum South. LC 88-32793. (Contributions in American History Ser.: No. 133). 190p. 1989. text ed. 49.95 (*0-313-26092-3*, OSF, Greenwood Pr) Greenwood.
Otto, Jonathan. NGOs in the Sahel: Issues in Cooperation for Natural Resources Management. (Occasional Paper Ser.). 1991. 3.00 (*0-932288-86-3*) Ctr Intl Ed U of MA.
Otto, Joseph, jt. auth. see Nordenstam, Garry.
Otto, Joseph C. Spreadsheet Applications: Job-Based Tasks. 160p. (C). 1993. teacher ed, disk 69.00 (*1-56118-388-1*); teacher ed, disk 69.00 (*1-56118-389-X*); disk 11.95 (*1-56118-447-0*); disk 11.95 (*1-56118-448-9*) Paradigm MN.
Otto, Julie H., illus. Ancestors of American Presidents. rev. ed. LC 89-83321. 350p. 1989. 30.00 (*0-936124-15-6*) C Boyer.
Otto, Lon. Cover Me. LC 88-11817. 142p. (Orig.). 1988. pap. 9.95 (*0-918273-40-4*) Coffee Hse.
— A Nest of Hooks: The 1978 Iowa Short Fiction Award. LC 78-16507. (Iowa Short Fiction Award Ser.). 152p. 1978. 19.95 (*0-87745-089-7*); pap. 12.95 (*0-87745-090-0*) U of Iowa Pr.
Otto, Luther B. Helping Your Child Choose a Career. 240p. (Orig.). 1995. pap. 14.95 (*1-56370-184-7*, J1847) JIST Works.
Otto, Nancy. Almanac of America Cook Book. LC 86-90559. (Illus.). 263p. 1986. 16.95 (*0-9617435-0-6*) N L Otto.
Otto, Paul B. Physical Science for the Elementary Teacher. LC 90-24212. (American University Studies: Education: Ser. XIV, Vol. 31). (Illus.). 280p. (Orig.). (C). 1991. pap. text ed. 44.95 (*0-8204-1455-7*) P Lang Pubs.
Otto, Peter, jt. ed. see Coleman, Deirdre.
Otto, Randall E. Coming in the Clouds: An Evangelical Case for the Invisibility of Christ at His Second Coming. LC 93-49434. 308p. (Orig.). (C). Date not set. lib. bdg. 55.00 (*0-8191-9442-5*); pap. text ed. 26.50 (*0-8191-9443-3*) U Pr of Amer.
— The God of Hope: The Trinitarian Vision of Jurgen Moltman. 260p. (C). 1992. lib. bdg. 43.00 (*0-8191-8290-7*) U Pr of Amer.
Otto, Robert C. Publishing for the People: The Firm Posrednik, 1885-1905. LC 87-240. (Modern European History Ser.). 264p. 1987. 15.00 (*0-8240-8060-2*) Garland.
Otto, Rudolf. Idea of the Holy. 2nd ed. Harvey, John W., tr. 1958. pap. 9.95 (*0-19-500210-5*) OUP.
Otto, Shirley & Orford, Jim. Not Quite Like Home: Small Hostels for Alcoholics & Others. LC 77-12664. 234p. reprint ed. pap. 66.70 (*0-317-28157-7*, 2024282) Bks Demand.
***Otto, Shirley E.** Pocket Guide to Oncology Nursing. 1994. pap. 19.95 (*0-8151-6547-1*) Mosby Yr Bk.
Otto, Shirley E., ed. Oncology Nursing. 2nd ed. LC 93-28963. 700p. 1993. 49.95 (*0-8016-7816-1*) Mosby Yr Bk.
***Otto, Simon.** Grandmother Moon Speaks. (Illus.). 1995. pap. 12.95 (*1-882376-10-2*) Thunder Bay Pr.
— Walk in Peace: Legends & Stories of the Michigan Indians. 2nd ed. Bussey, M. T., ed. (Illus.). 50p. (J). (gr. 3-4). 1992. pap. 9.95 (*0-9617707-5-9*) Grnd Rpds Intertribal.
***Otto, Stella.** The Backyard Berry Book: A Hands-on Guide to Growing Berries, Brambles, & Vine Fruit in the Home. (Illus.). 288p. (Orig.). 1995. pap. 15.95 (*0-9634520-6-1*) OttoGraphics.
— The Backyard Orchardist: A Complete Guide to Growing Fruit Trees in the Home Garden. 2nd rev. ed. (Illus.). 264p. (Orig.). 1995. pap. 14.95 (*0-9634520-3-7*) OttoGraphics.
Otto, Walter F. Dionysus: Myth & Cult. Palmer, Robert B., tr. LC 86-13742. (Dunquin Ser.: No. 14). xxi, 243p. (C). 1965. reprint ed. pap. 15.00 (*0-88214-214-3*) Spring Pubns.
— Gestez Urbild & Mythos. Bolle, Kees W., ed. LC 77-82281. (Mythology Ser.). (GER.). 1978. reprint ed. lib. bdg. 19.95 (*0-405-10572-X*) Ayer.
— The Homeric Gods: The Spiritual Significance of Greek Religion. Bolle, Kees W., ed. LC 77-79149. (Mythology Ser.). 1978. reprint ed. lib. bdg. 24.95 (*0-405-10558-4*) Ayer.
Otto, Walter G. Priester und Tempel Im Hellenistischen Agypten: Ein Beitrag Zur Kulturgeschichte Des Hellenismus, 2 vols. in 1. LC 75-10645. (Ancient Religion & Mythology Ser.). (GER.). 1976. reprint ed. 68.95 (*0-405-07278-3*) Ayer.
Otto, Wayne, et al. Focused Reading Instruction. (C). 1974. text ed. write for info. (*0-201-05511-2*) Addison-Wesley.
Otto, Whitney. How to Make an American Quilt. large type ed. 294p. 1992. text ed. 19.95 (*0-8161-5338-8*) G K Hall.
— How to Make an American Quilt. large type ed. 294p. 1992. pap. 16.95 (*0-8161-5365-5*, Large Print Bks) Hall.
— How to Make an American Quilt. 1992. reprint ed. mass mkt. 5.99 (*0-345-37080-5*) Ballantine.
— How to Make an American Quilt: A Novel. 192p. 1994. pap. 10.00 (*0-345-38896-8*, Ballantine Trade) Ballantine.
— Make an American Quilt. 1991. 18.00 (*0-679-40070-2*, Villard Bks) Random.
— Now You See Her. 320p. 1995. pap. 12.00 (*0-345-37826-1*) Ballantine.
— Now You See Her. LC 93-6321. 1994. 20.00 (*0-679-41583-1*, Villard Bks) Random.
— Now You See Her. large type ed. LC 94-18646. 388p. 1994. lib. bdg. 21.95 (*0-8161-7407-5*) G K Hall.
Ottoboni, Alice. The Dose Makes the Poison: A Plain Language Guide to Toxicology. 2nd enl. ed. 272p. 1991. text ed. 24.95 (*0-442-00660-8*) Van Nos Reinhold.
Ottobre, Frances M., ed. see International Association for Educational Assessment Staff.
Ottokar, Peter. Diccionario Rioduero: Quimica. 3rd ed. 272p. (SPA.). 1982. write for info. (*0-7859-5071-0*) Fr & Eur.
Ottomanelli, Gennaro. HIV Infection & Intravenous Drug Use. LC 92-3260. 160p. 1992. text ed. 45.00 (*0-275-94301-1*, C4301, Praeger Pubs) Greenwood.
Ottosen, Garry K. Making American Government Work: A Proposal to Reinvigorate Federalism. 191p. (Orig.). (C). 1992. lib. bdg. 39.50 (*0-8191-8792-5*); pap. text ed. 22.50 (*0-8191-8793-3*) U Pr of Amer.
— Monopoly Power: How It Is Measured & How It Has Changed. LC 89-81840. 125p. 1990. pap. 9.95 (*0-9624038-1-4*) Crossroads Rsch.
Ottosen, Joleen. The Blood Conspiracy: How to Avoid Getting AIDS & Hepatitis in a Transfusion. Ross, Marilyn, ed. LC 92-71818. 326p. 1993. 24.95 (*0-9632963-3-7*) Aspen Leaf Pr.
Ottosen, Knud. The Responsories & Versicles of the Latin Office of the Dead. (Illus.). 501p. 1993. 87.50 (*87-7288-315-4*, Pub. by Aarhus Univ Pr DK) Coronet Bks.
Ottosen, Niels S. & Petersson, Hans. Introduction to the Finite Element Methods. 430p. 1992. pap. text ed. 44.00 (*0-13-473877-2*) P-H.
Ottoson, D., ed. Duality & Unity of the Brain: Unified Functioning & Specialisation of the Hemispheres. LC 87-42720. (Wenner-Gren International Symposia Ser.: Vol. 47). 516p. 1987. 125.00 (*0-306-42720-6*, Plenum Pr) Plenum.
Ottoson, D., et al, eds. Progress in Sensory Physiology: Ionic & Volume Changes in the Microenvironment of Nerve & Receptor Cells, Vol. 13. (Illus.). 176p. 1992. 100.00 (*0-387-54553-0*) Spr-Verlag.
Ottoson, David, jt. ed. see Bartfai, Tamas.
Ottoson, H. W., et al. Land & People in the Northern Plains Transition Area. Bruchey, Stuart, ed. LC 78-56708. (Management of Public Lands in the U. S. Ser.). (Illus.). 1979. reprint ed. lib. bdg. 31.95 (*0-405-11349-8*) Ayer.
Ottoson, Howard W., ed. see Homestead Centennial Symposium Staff.
Ottoson, O. O. Animal Physiology: Index of New Information with Authors, Subjects & Bibliography. rev. ed. 1994. 49.50 (*0-7883-0166-7*); pap. 45.50 (*0-7883-0167-5*) ABBE Pubs Assn.
Ottova, A., jt. ed. see Blazej, Anton.
Ottow, E., et al, eds. Stereoselective Synthesis: Lectures Honouring Rudolf Wiechert. LC 93-34943. 160p. 1994. 89.00 (*0-387-57202-3*) Spr-Verlag.
Ottow, Harriett. Ruth's Adventures in Israel. LC 87-51493. 44p. (J). (gr. k-2). 1988. 5.95 (*1-55523-133-0*) Winston-Derek.
Ottoway, Patrick. Archaeology in British Towns. LC 91-41071. (Illus.). 208p. 1992. 69.95 (*0-415-00068-8*, A7637) Routledge.
Otts, Lee M., jt. auth. see Egger, Bruce E.
***Ottum, Bob, ed.** A Day in the Life of the Amish. 100p. Date not set. 14.98 (*0-89821-126-3*) Reiman Pubns.
Ottum, Bob & Wood, JoAnne. Santa's Beard Is Soft & Warm. (Golden Touch & Feel Bks.). (Illus.). (J). (ps). 1974. write for info. (*0-307-12148-8*, Golden Bks) Western Pub.
Otubusin, Paul O. Exploitation, Unequal Exchange & Dependency: A Dialectical Development. LC 90-6019. (American University Studies: Philosophy: Ser. V, Vol. 88). 165p. (C). 1992. text ed. 23.95 (*0-8204-1234-1*) P Lang Pubs.
Otugen, M. V., jt. ed. see Huang, T. T.
Otumokala, Jean, et al. Black-American Women African Men: Myths Misconceptions & Misunderstandings. Ettah, Geneieve, ed. 197p. (Orig.). 1994. pap. 19.95 (*0-9629214-4-0*) Intl Spectrum.
Otway, Graham. Wisden Book of Heroic Performances. 1992. pap. 15.95 (*0-09-174410-5*, Pub. by Hutchinson UK) Trafalgar.
Otway, H., jt. ed. see Gow, H. B.
Otway, Harry J. & Peltu, Malcolm. New Office Technology. LC 82-24473. 248p. 1983. text ed. 55.00 (*0-89391-198-4*) Ablex Pub.
Otway, John. John Otway: Cor Baby, That's Really Me! (Illus.). 200p. 1990. pap. 11.95 (*0-7119-2148-2*, OP45855) Omnibus NY.
Otway, Thomas. Complete Works, 3 Vols, Set. Summers, Montague, ed. LC 27-20965. (Chertsey Worthies' Library). reprint ed. 210.00 (*0-404-04860-9*) AMS Pr.
— The Orphan. Taylor, Aline M., ed. LC 75-13067. (Regents Restoration Drama Ser.). 148p. 1976. reprint ed. pap. 72.20 (*0-7837-8910-6*, 2049621) Bks Demand.
***Otway, Thomas, et al.** Four Restoration Marriage Plays. Cordner, Michael, ed. (World's Classics Ser.). 512p. 1995. pap. 12.95 (*0-19-282570-4*) OUP.
Otwell. Seafood Product Safety. 1994. write for info. (*0-8493-4296-1*) CRC Pr.
Otwell, Steven & Rodrick, Gary E. Molluscan Shellfish Depuration. (Illus.). 380p. 1991. 125.00 (*0-8493-4295-3*, SH) CRC Pr.
Ou, S. H. Rice Diseases. 2nd ed. 380p. 1985. text ed. 83.50 (*0-85198-545-9*) CAB Intl.
Oualline, Steve. C Elements of Style: The Programming Guide to Developing Well-Written C & C Plus Plus Programs. LC 92-33734. 200p. (Orig.). 1992. pap. 26.95 (*1-55851-291-8*) M&T Bks.
— Handbook for Practical C Plus Plus. 450p. 1995. 24.95 (*1-56592-116-X*) OReilly & Assocs.
Ouasha, George, ed. see Jabes, Edmond.
Ouattara, Mouhamadou & Osborne, Eddie. Essential Bambara: For English-Speaking Travelers. 80p. (Orig.). 1992. pap. 10.95 (*1-882272-03-X*) Osborne Comms.
— Essential Fulani: For English-Speaking Travelers. 80p. (Orig.). 1992. pap. 10.95 (*1-882272-04-8*) Osborne Comms.
— Essential Wolof: For English-Speaking Travelers. 80p. (Orig.). 1992. pap. 10.95 (*1-882272-02-1*) Osborne Comms.
Ouazar, D. & Brebbia, C. A., eds. Computational Transport Phenomena. (Computer Methods & Water Resources Ser.: Vol. 5). 270p. 1988. 66.00 (*0-387-18857-6*) Spr-Verlag.
— Computer Methods & Water Resources, Vol. 1: Groundwater & Aquifer Modelling. LC 87-73387. 210p. 1988. 51.00 (*0-931215-89-7*) Computational Mech MA.
— Computer Methods & Water Resources, Vol. 4: Computer Aided Engineering in Water Resources. LC 87-73387. 500p. 1988. 108.00 (*0-931215-92-7*) Computational Mech MA.
— Computer Methods & Water Resources, Vol. 5: Computational Transport Phenomena. LC 87-73387. 250p. 1988. 60.00 (*0-931215-93-5*) Computational Mech MA.
— Groundwater & Aquifer Modeling. (Computer Methods & Water Resources Ser.: Vol. 1). 210p. 1988. 57.00 (*0-387-18852-5*) Spr-Verlag.
Ouazar, D., jt. ed. see Blain, W. R.
Ouazar, D., et al, eds. Computational Hydraulics. (Computer Methods & Water Resources Ser.: Vol. 2). 470p. 1988. 119.00 (*0-387-18854-1*) Spr-Verlag.
— Computer Methods & Water Resources, Vol. 2: Computational Hydraulics. LC 87-73387. 500p. 1988. 108.00 (*0-931215-90-0*) Computational Mech MA.
— Computer Methods & Water Resources, Vol. 3: Computational Hydrology. LC 87-73387. 300p. 1988. 71.50 (*0-931215-91-9*) Computational Mech MA.
— Computer Methods & Water Resources, Vol. 6: Water Quality, Planning Management. LC 87-73387. 300p. 1988. 71.50 (*0-931215-94-3*) Computational Mech MA.

O

An Asterisk (*) at the beginning of an entry indicates that the title is appearing in BIP for the first time.

— Water Quality, Planning & Management. (Computer Methods & Water Resources Ser.: Vol. 6). 310p. 1988. 87.00 (*0-387-18858-4*) Spr-Verlag.

Ouboter, Paul E., ed. The Freshwater Ecosystems of Suriname. LC 93-5180. (Monographiae Biologicae Ser.: Vol. 70). 292p. (C). 1993. lib. bdg. 142.00 (*0-7923-2408-0*) Kluwer Ac.

Oubre, Elton J. Vacherie, St. James Parish, Louisiana: History & Genealogy. LC 86-62380. (Illus.). 576p. 1986. 30.00 (*0-9617559-0-3*) Oubres Bks.

Ouby, Ian. Literary Britain & Ireland. 2nd ed. (Blue Guides Ser.). 1990. pap. 19.95 (*0-393-30490-6*) Norton.

Ouchi, Glenn I. Lotus in the Lab: Spreadsheet Applications for Scientists & Engineers. 196p. (C). 1988. pap. 24.95 (*0-201-14307-0*, Adv Bk Prog) Addison-Wesley.

— Personal Computers for Scientists. LC 86-24846. (Illus.). x, 250p. 1986. 34.95 (*0-8412-1000-4*); pap. 22.95 (*0-8412-1001-2*) Am Chemical.

Ouchi, Hajime. Japanese Optical & Geometrical Art. LC 77-82360. (Orig.). 1977. pap. 8.95 (*0-486-23553-X*) Dover.

Ouchi, K., jt. ed. see Gorbaty, Martin L.

Ouchi, William G. M-Form Society. 352p. 1986. mass mkt. 4.95 (*0-380-69914-1*) Avon.

— Theory Z: How American Business Can Meet the Japanese Challenge. 1982. mass mkt. 5.99 (*0-380-59451-X*) Avon.

— Theory Z: How American Business Can Meet the Japanese Challenge. 256p. 1993. pap. 10.00 (*0-380-71944-4*) Avon.

Ouchi, William G., jt. ed. see Barney, Jay B.

Ouchterlony, O., ed. see WHO, 43rd Nobel Symposium, Stockholm, August 1978.

Oudar, jt. ed. see Marcus.

Oudar, Jacques, jt. ed. see Wise, Henry.

Oudega, Martin, et al. Development of the Rat Spinal Cord: Immuno- & Enzyme Histochemical Approaches. LC 93-44601. 1994. write for info. (*3-540-57173-6*); 99.00 (*0-387-57173-6*) Spr-Verlag.

Oudel, Solomon & Barfield, Owen. Reminiscences & ... 1986. pap. 3.95 (*0-916786-89-7*, Saint George Pubns) R Steiner Col Pubns.

Oudemans, T. C. & Lardinois, A. P. Tragic Ambiguity: Anthropology, Philosophy & Sophocles' Antigone. (Brill's Studies in Intellectual History: Vol. 4). 280p. 1987. 71.50 (*90-04-08417-7*) E J Brill.

Ouden, Den C. & Nicolay, D., eds. First E. C. Conference on Solar Heating. 1984. lib. bdg. 241.50 (*90-277-1875-X*) Kluwer Ac.

Ouderkirk, H. John, ed. The Ouderkerk Family Genealogy from 1660. LC 85-71712. 154p. reprint ed. 40.00 (*0-916497-65-8*); reprint ed. fiche 6.00 (*0-916497-64-X*) Burnett Micro.

Oudheusden, Susan. Go for It! A Student's Guide to Independent Projects. 75p. (J). (gr. 3-9). pap. 14.95 (*0-936386-51-7*) Creative Learning.

Oudijk, G. & Mujica, K. Handbook for the Identification, Location & Investigation of Pollution Sources Affecting Ground Water. 185p. 1989. 22.50 (*1-56034-062-2*, T502) Natl Water Well.

***Oudin, Bernard.** Dictionnaire des Architectes de l'Antiquite a nos Jours. 568p. (FRE.). 1983. pap. 34.95 (*0-7859-7796-1*, 2221010906) Fr & Eur.

Oudin, Cesar. Refranes O Proverbios Castellanos Traduzidos En Lingua Francesca. 256p. reprint ed. write for info. (*0-318-71627-5*, Pub. by Georg Olms GW) Lubrecht & Cramer.

Ouditt, Sharon. Fighting Forces, Writing Women: Identity & Ideology in the First World War. LC 93-15511. 192p. 1993. 59.95 (*0-415-04704-8*, A7955) Routledge.

Oudot, J. S. Guide to Correspondence in French. (C). 1984. 60.00 (*0-8442-1501-5*, Pub. by S Thornes Pubs UK) St Mut.

Oudot, S. French Verbs & Essentials of Grammar. (C). 1984. 50.00 (*0-8442-1500-7*, Pub. by S Thornes Pubs UK) St Mut.

Oudot, Simone, ed. Guide to Correspondence in French. 144p. (C). 1987. 65.00 (*0-85950-232-5*, Pub. by S Thornes Pubs UK) St Mut.

Oudot, Simone & Gobert, David. Conversational French. 320p. 1988. pap. 20.95 (*0-8442-1505-8*, Passport Bks) NTC Pub Grp.

Oudot, Simone & Gobert, David L. La France, Culture, Economie, Commerce: An Introduction to Business French. (Illus.). 193p. (FRE.). (C). 1992. reprint ed. pap. text ed. 14.95 (*0-88133-692-0*) Waveland Pr.

Oudshoorn, Nelly. Beyond the Natural Body: An Archaeology of Sex Hormones. LC 94-4945. 240p. 1994. 55.00x (*0-415-09190-X*, A9978); pap. 16.95 (*0-415-09191-8*, A9982) Routledge.

Ouellet, F. L' Etude des Religions dans les Ecoles: L'Experience Americaine, Anglaise et Canadienne. (SR Editions Ser.: No. 7). 666p. (FRE.). (C). 1985. pap. 19.95 (*0-88920-183-8*, Pub. by Wilfrid Laurier CN) Humanities.

Ouellet, Fernand, et al. Constitutionalism & Nationalism in Lower Canada: Essays. LC 75-431747. (Canadian Historical Readings Ser.: No. 5). 106p. reprint ed. pap. 30.30 (*0-8357-6377-3*, 2035731) Bks Demand.

Ouellet, Jo. The Collected Wonderword, Vol. 3. 104p. 1982. pap. 4.95 (*0-8362-2501-5*) Andrews & McMeel.

Ouellet, Lawrence J. Pedal to the Metal: The Work Life of Truckers. 336p. (C). 1994. text ed. 49.95 (*1-56639-175-X*); pap. 16.95 (*1-56639-176-8*) Temple U Pr.

Ouellette, et al. Macross II: Deck Plans, Vol. 1. Siembieda, Kevin et al, eds. (Macross II RPG Ser.). (Illus.). 64p. (Orig.). (YA). (gr. 8 up). 1994. pap. 9.95 (*0-916211-66-5*, 592) Palladium Bks.

***Ouellette, Daniel.** The PEN Connection: A Guide to Pen Connection. 1995. pap. text ed. 32.00 (*0-07-048011-7*) McGraw.

Ouellette, Dean C., ed. see Rockman, Richard G., Jr.

Ouellette, Deborah. Getting Started in the Modeling-Talent Industry. Neumann, Sarah, ed. LC 90-80008. (Illus.). 200p. (Orig.). 1990. pap. 24.95 (*0-9625405-0-1*) Aries MI.

Ouellette, F., ed. International Workshop on Photoinduced Self-Organization Effects in Optical Fiber: May 1991, Quebec. 1991. write for info. (*0-8194-0643-0*, VOL. 1516) SPIE.

Ouellette, Frances, jt. auth. see Redmond, Gertrude T.

Ouellette, Guillemond B., jt. ed. see Petrini, Orlando.

Ouellette, Helen T., ed. William of Malmesbury: Polyhistor: A Critical Edition. LC 81-18918. (Medieval & Renaissance Texts & Studies: Vol. 10). 176p. 1982. 25.00 (*0-86698-017-2*) MRTS.

***Ouellette-Howitz, Jeannine.** Mama Moon. LC 95-732. (Illus.). 32p. (J). (ps-1). 1995. 14.95 (*0-531-09472-3*); lib. bdg. 14.99 (*0-531-08772-7*) Orchard Bks Watts.

Ouellette, L. Paul. How to Market the IS Department Internally: Getting the Recognition & Strategic Position You Merit. 224p. 1992. 28.95 (*0-8144-5997-8*) AMACOM.

— I. S. at Your Service: Knowing & Keeping Your Clients. 176p. 1993. boxed 29.95 (*0-8403-8765-2*) Kendall-Hunt.

Ouellette, Pierre. The Deus Machine: A Novel. LC 93-18767. 1994. 22.50 (*0-679-42407-5*, Villard Bks) Random.

Ouellette, Raymond. Holistic Healing & the Edgar Cayce Readings. LC 80-80446. 384p. 1980. 11.95 (*0-936450-07-X*); pap. 7.75 (*0-685-00141-5*) Aero Pr.

— Life & Death & the Edgar Cayce Readings. LC 82-70682. 256p. 1982. 8.95 (*0-936450-09-6*) Aero Pr.

— Nineteen Ninety-Eight: The Year of Destiny, 2 bks., Bk. 1. LC 77-89344. (Illus.). 1978. 9.95 (*0-936450-27-4*) Aero Pr.

— Nineteen Ninety-Eight: The Year of Destiny, 2 bks., Bk. 2. LC 77-89344. (Illus.). 1978. 8.95 (*0-936450-29-0*) Aero Pr.

— Nineteen Ninety-Eight: The Year of Destiny, 2 bks., Set. LC 77-89344. (Illus.). 1978. write for info. (*0-936450-28-2*) Aero Pr.

— Psychic Magic. LC 74-78491. (Illus.). 343p. 1974. 12.95 (*0-936450-00-2*) Aero Pr.

Ouellette, Robert J. Introduction to General Organic & Biological Chemistry. 3rd rev. ed. (Illus.). 768p. (C). 1991. text ed. write for info. (*0-02-390245-0*); student ed, pap. write for info. (*0-02-389934-4*) Macmillan.

— Introduction to General Organic & Biological Chemistry. 3rd rev. ed. (Illus.). 768p. (C). 1992. student ed, pap. write for info. (*0-02-389933-6*) Macmillan.

— Organic Chemistry: A Brief Introduction. LC 93-16739. (Illus.). 624p. (C). 1993. text ed. write for info. (*0-02-389591-8*) Macmillan.

— Organic Chemistry: A Brief Introduction. LC 93-16739. (Illus.). 624p. (C). 1994. student ed, pap. write for info. (*0-02-389592-6*); write for info. (*0-318-69913-3*) Macmillan.

— Student Solutions Manual to Accompany Understanding Chemistry. 144p. (C). 1987. pap. write for info. (*0-02-389640-X*) Macmillan.

— Understanding Chemistry. 826p. (C). 1987. write for info. (*0-02-389750-3*) Macmillan.

Ouellette, Robert J. & Manchester, Jason H. Understanding Chemistry. 194p. (C). 1987. Lab manual. pap. write for info. (*0-02-389720-1*) Macmillan.

— Understanding Chemistry. 194p. (C). 1987. Study guide. student ed, pap. write for info. (*0-02-389740-6*) Macmillan.

Ouellette, Robert P., jt. auth. see Cheremisinoff, Paul N.

Ouellette, Roland. Management of Aggressive Behavior: A Comprehensive Guide to Learning How to Recognize, Reduce, Manage, & Control Aggressive Behavior. LC 92-44600. 1993. 14.95 (*1-879411-22-9*) Perf Dimensions Pub.

Ouennell, C. H., jt. auth. see Ouennell, Marjorie.

Ouennell, Marjorie & Ouennell, C. H. Everyday Life in Roman & Anglo-Saxon Times. 1987. 17.95 (*0-88029-125-7*) Dorset Pr.

Ough, C. S. & Amerine, Maynard A. Methods Analysis of Musts & Wines. 2nd ed. LC 87-28004. 377p. 1988. text ed. 139.00 (*0-471-62757-7*) Wiley.

Ough, Cornelius S. Winemaking Basics. LC 91-2253. (Illus.). 340p. 1992. lib. bdg. 49.95 (*1-56022-005-8*); pap. 24.95 (*1-56022-006-6*) Haworth Pr.

Ough, Richard & Adams, John N. Ough: The Mareva Injunction & Anton Piller Order. 2nd ed. 200p. 1992. U.K. pap. 80.00 (*0-406-11647-4*) Butterworth Legal Pubs.

Oughourlian, Jean-Michel. The Puppet of Desire: The Psychology of Hysteria, Possession & Hypnosis. Webb, Eugene, tr. LC 90-42448. 289p. 1991. 35.00 (*0-8047-1823-7*) Stanford U Pr.

***Oughstun, K. E., et al.** Electromagnetic Pulse Propagation in Causal Dielectrics. 16. Brekhovskikh, L. M. & Felsen, L. B., eds. (Wave Phenomena Ser.). 479p. 1994. 198.00 (*0-387-57892-7*) Spr-Verlag.

Oughten, Jerrie. The Magic Weaver of Rugs. LC 93-4850. (Illus.). (J). 1994. 14.95 (*0-395-66140-4*) HM.

Oughton, D. R., jt. auth. see Martin, P. L.

Oughton, D. R., jt. rev. see Martin, P. L.

Oughton, D. W., jt. auth. see Cooke, P. J.

***Oughton, David & Lowry, John.** Q & A Law of Torts. (Questions & Answers Ser.). 201p. 1994. pap. 20.00 (*1-85431-308-8*) W W Gaunt.

Oughton, David W. Consumer Law: Text, Cases & Materials. xxxii, 436p. (C). 1991. pap. 54.00 (*1-85431-173-5*, Pub. by Blackstone Pr UK) W W Gaunt.

Oughton, Jerrie. How the Stars Fell into the Sky. (Illus.). 32p. (J). (gr. k-3). 1992. 14.95 (*0-395-58798-0*) HM.

— Music from a Place Called Half Moon. LC 94-25368. (J). 1995. 13.95 (*0-395-70737-4*) HM.

Oughton, Marguerita & Pinchemel, Philippe. Geographers, Vol. 1: Biobibliographical Studies. Freeman, T. W. et al, eds. (Illus.). 138p. 1977. pap. text ed. 70.00 (*0-7201-0637-0*, Mansell Pub) Cassell.

Oughton, R. D. & Tyler, E. L. Tyler's Family Provision. 2nd ed. 1984. 90.00 (*0-86205-075-8*) Butterworth Legal Pubs.

Oughton, R. D., jt. auth. see Tyler, E. L.

Ouhalla, Jamal. Functional Categories & Parametric Variation. (Theoretical Linguistics Ser.). 224p. 1991. 74.50 (*0-415-05641-1*, A6155) Routledge.

— Introducing Transformational Grammar: From Rules to Principles Parameters. 384p. 1994. pap. 18.95 (*0-340-55630-7*, Pub. by E Arnld UK) St Martin.

***Ouhgton, John.** The Gearing of Love. 64p. 1995. lib. bdg. 20.00 (*0-8095-4547-0*) Borgo Pr.

Ouida, pseud. A Dog of Flanders. (Illus.). 80p. (J). 1992. reprint ed. pap. 1.00 (*0-486-27087-4*) Dover.

— The Massarenes. LC 79-8186. reprint ed. 44.50 (*0-404-62087-6*) AMS Pr.

***Ouida.** Under Two Flags. Sutherland, John, ed. (Oxford Popular Fiction Ser.). 560p. 1995. pap. 12.95 (*0-19-282328-0*) OUP.

Ouida, pseud. Under Two Flags, 3 vols. in 2, Set. LC 79-8187. reprint ed. 84.50 (*0-404-62088-4*) AMS Pr.

Ouimet, Donald P. Woodcraft Gift Projects. LC 79-15909. (Illus.). 1979. 12.50 (*0-8246-0243-9*) Jonathan David.

Ouimette, Helen E. Country Catalog of Memories: A Childhood on a German-American Farm in the Late 1920s & Early 1930s. rev. ed. (Illus.). 204p. (Orig.). 1987. pap. 14.95 (*0-9617116-1-2*) H Ouimette.

Ouimette, Janice. Perinatal Nursing: Care of the High Risk Infant. 461p. (C). 1986. boxed 52.50 (*0-86720-356-0*) Jones & Bartlett.

Ouimette, Victor. Reason Aflame: Unamuno & the Heroic Will. (Romantic Studies, Second Ser.: No. 24). 1974. 35.00 (*0-300-01666-2*) Yale U Pr.

Oulanoff, Hongor. The Prose Fiction of Veniamin A. Kaverin. v, 203p. 1976. pap. 17.95 (*0-89357-032-X*) Slavica.

***Ould, Martyn A.** Business Processes: Modelling & Analysis for Re-Engineering & Improvement. LC 95-3608. 1995. text ed. 45.00 (*0-471-95352-0*) Wiley.

— Strategies for Software Engineer: The Management of Risk & Quality. 243p. 1990. text ed. 48.95 (*0-471-92628-0*) Wiley.

Ould, Martyn A. & Unwin, Charles, eds. Testing in Software Development. (British Computer Society Monographs in Informatics). 130p. 1987. pap. 27.95 (*0-521-33786-0*) Cambridge U Pr.

Ould, Martyn A., jt. auth. see Birrell, N. D.

***Oulette, et al.** Macross II: Deck Plans. Siembieda, K. et al, eds. (Macross II RPG Sourcebook Ser.: Vol. 3). (Illus.). 64p. (Orig.). (YA). (gr. 8 up). 1994. pap. 9.95 (*0-916211-75-4*, 594) Palladium Bks.

— Macross II: Deck Plans, Vol. 2. Siembieda, K. et al, eds. (Macross II RPG Sourcebook Ser.). (Illus.). 64p. (Orig.). (YA). (gr. 8 up). 1994. pap. 9.95 (*0-916211-74-6*, 593) Palladium Bks.

Oulman, Charles S. & Lee, Motoko. Macro Programming Using 1-2-3 for Engineers. Slaughter, Michael, ed. 156p. (C). 1990. pap. text ed. 39.00 (*0-314-68317-8*) West Pub.

Oulton, Derek, ed. see Lewis, David.

Oulton, Nicholas & O'Mahony, Mary. Productivity & Growth. (National Institute of Economic & Social Research Occasional Papers: No. 46). (Illus.). 344p. (C). 1994. 59.95 (*0-521-45345-3*) Cambridge U Pr.

***Oulton, W. E.** Technocrat: Biography of a Boffin. 1995. 15.95 (*0-533-11221-4*) Vantage.

Oumano, Elena. Marianne Williamson: Her Life, Her Message, Her Miracles. 1992. mass mkt. 4.99 (*0-312-95041-1*) St Martin.

— Paul Newman. large type ed. 332p. 1990. 11.47 (*1-85089-476-0*, Pub. by ISIS UK) Transaction Pubs.

Oumano, Elena, jt. auth. see Lubetkin, Barry.

Oumet, Ronald P. Eighty Woodcraft Projects. 320p. 1980. 17.95 (*0-8246-0260-9*) Jonathan David.

Oung, Kin. Who Kolled Aung San? 101p. (C). 1993. 17.50 (*1-879155-12-5*); pap. 10.00 (*1-879155-13-3*) Lotus WA.

Ounn, Troy. Industry Secrets: Inside Techniques That Will Save You Thousands. Klunder, Virgil, ed. LC 91-70193. (Illus.). 60p. (Orig.). 1990. pap. 19.95 (*1-879499-23-1*) Caradium Pub.

Ounsted, Christopher, et al. Temporal Lobe Epilepsy, 1948 to 1986. (Clinics in Developmental Medicine Ser.: No. 103). 1991. 49.95 (*0-521-41220-X*) Cambridge U Pr.

— Temporal Lobe Epilepsy 1948-1986. (Clinics in Developmental Medicine Ser.: No. 103). (Illus.). 129p. (C). 1987. text ed. 49.50 (*0-685-41924-X*, Pub. by Mc Keith Pr UK) Cambridge U Pr.

Ouologuem, Yambo. Bound to Violence. (African Writers Ser.). 182p. 1971. pap. 9.95 (*0-435-90099-4*) Heinemann.

Our Lady of Perpetual Help Church Women's Guild Staff. Simple Elegance: A Culinary Collection of Simple to Elegant Recipes. 288p. 1992. 16.95 (*0-9633165-0-8*) Our Lady Perpet HCWG.

Our Town Revision Committee Staff. Our Town, Mesa, Arizona: The Story of Mesa. 6th rev. ed. (Illus.). 208p. 1991. 24.95 (*0-9629563-0-9*) Mesa Pub Schl.

Oura, jt. auth. see Chiogioji.

Ourada, Patricia K. The Menominee. (Indians of North America Ser.). (Illus.). 112p. (J). (gr. 5 up). 1990. 17.95 (*1-55546-715-6*) Chelsea Hse.

Ourdan, J. P. The Art of Retouching by Burrows & Colton. LC 72-9187. (Literature of Photography Ser.). 1973. reprint ed. 17.95 (*0-405-04898-X*) Ayer.

Ouren, Dallas L. A Reexamination of Sir William Hamilton's Philosophy: Mill on Hamilton. LC 91-44634. (Illus.). 216p. 1992. lib. bdg. 89.95 (*0-7734-9940-7*) E Mellen.

***Ouriel, Kenneth, ed.** Lower Extremity Vascular Disease. LC 95-6842. 1995. text ed. 135.00 (*0-7216-4749-9*) Saunders.

Ouriou, Susan, tr. see Marineau, Michele.

Ourisson, G., jt. auth. see Mathieu, Jean P.

Ours, Robert. College Football Encyclopedia: The Authoritative Guide to 124 Years of College Football. (Illus.). 500p. 1993. 29.95 (*1-55958-411-4*); pap. 19.95 (*1-55958-217-0*) Prima Pub.

Ours, Robert M. Journalism at West Virginia University. LC 77-84188. (Illus.). 1977. pap. 3.00 (*0-930362-01-2*) Sch Journal WVU.

Oursler, Fulton. The Greatest Book Ever Written. LC 91-13856. 412p. 1991. reprint ed. pap. 9.95 (*0-89243-499-6*, Triumph Books) Liguori Pubns.

— The Greatest Story Ever Told. 1994. reprint ed. lib. bdg. 21.95x (*1-56849-555-2*) Buccaneer Bks.

— The Greatest Story Ever Told. 1989. reprint ed. mass mkt. 10.95 (*0-385-08028-X*, D121, Image Bks) Doubleday.

— The Greatest Story Ever Told: The Timeless Bestselling Life of Jesus Christ. large type ed. LC 94-33202. 416p. 1994. pap. 14.95 (*0-8027-2683-6*) Walker & Co.

Ourth, John & Tamarri, Kathie T. Career Caravan. 64p. (J). (gr. 4-8). 1979. 7.95 (*0-916456-52-8*, GA121) Good Apple.

Ourusoff de Fernandez-Gimenez, Elizabeth, jt. auth. see Mundy, E. James.

Oury, Guy. The Mass: Spirituality, History, Practice. Otto, John, tr. 126p. 1988. pap. 4.50 (*0-89942-126-1*, 126-04) Catholic Bk Pub.

***Oury, Guy-Marie.** Dictionnaire de la Foi Catholique. 267p. (FRE.). 1986. 59.95 (*0-7859-8088-1*, 2854432169) Fr & Eur.

— Dictionnaire de la Priere. 236p. (FRE.). 1990. 75.00 (*0-7859-8091-1*, 2854432169) Fr & Eur.

Ousby, Ian. Blue Guide: Burgundy. (Illus.). 212p. 1992. pap. 19.95 (*0-393-30886-3*) Norton.

— England. 10th ed. (Blue Guides Ser.). (Illus.). 1989. pap. 22.50 (*0-393-30608-9*) Norton.

— The Englishman's England: Taste, Travel, & the Rise of Tourism. (Illus.). 240p. (C). 1990. 54.95 (*0-521-37374-3*) Cambridge U Pr.

Ousby, Ian, ed. The Cambridge Guide to Literature in English. 2nd ed. (Illus.). 1061p. (C). 1994. 49.95 (*0-521-44086-6*) Cambridge U Pr.

Ousby, Ian, jt. ed. see Bradley, John F.

***Ousby, Jan.** England. 11th ed. (Blue Guide Ser.). (Illus.). 784p. 1995. pap. 24.00 (*0-393-31340-9*, Norton Paperbks) Norton.

Ousby, William J. Theory & Practice of Hypnotism: How to Liberate & Use the Full Potential of the Unconscious Mind. 1991. pap. 6.95 (*0-7225-2388-2*) Thorsons SF.

Ouseley, S. G. Colour Meditations. 90p. 1967. reprint ed. spiral bd. 4.40 (*0-7873-1175-8*) Mokelumne.

— The Power of the Rays. 99p. 1976. reprint ed. spiral bd. 5.50 (*0-7873-0648-7*) Mokelumne.

Ouseley, William, tr. see Hawqal, Ibn.

Ouseley, William G. Remarks on the Statistics & Political Institutions of the United States. LC 70-117887. (Select Bibliographies Reprint Ser.). 1977. reprint ed. 21.95 (*0-8369-5340-1*) Ayer.

Ouslander, Joseph G., et al. Medical Care in the Nursing Home. 461p. 1991. text ed. 54.00 (*0-07-047949-6*) Hlth Prof Div.

Ousler, Will. The Healing Power of Faith. 366p. 1989. reprint ed. pap. 8.95 (*0-930298-14-4*) Westwood Pub Co.

Ousley, Pamela D. The Law & Mercury-Free Dentistry. 260p. (Orig.). 1994. pap. 19.65 (*0-941011-11-9*) Bio-Probe.

Ousley-Robles, David A. The Burden of Love. (Burden Fovres Ser.: No. 1). 195p. 1984. 15.95 (*0-932167-00-4*) Taven-Lourveney.

Ousmane, Sembene. The Black Docker. Schwartz, Ros, tr. (African Writers Ser.). Orig. Title: Le Docker Noir. 128p. (Orig.). (C). 1987. pap. 8.95 (*0-435-90896-0*) Heinemann.

— God's Bits of Wood. Price, Francis, tr. (African Writers Ser.). 245p. 1987. reprint ed. pap. 10.95 (*0-435-90892-8*) Heinemann.

— The Last of the Empire. Adams, Adrian, tr. (African Writers Ser.). Orig. Title: Le Dernier de L'Empire. 238p. (Orig.). (C). 1983. pap. 11.95 (*0-435-90250-4*) Heinemann.

— The Money-Order with White Genesis. Wake, Clive, tr. (African Writers Ser.). 138p. (C). 1987. pap. 9.95 (*0-435-90894-4*) Heinemann.

— Niiwam & Taaw. 110p. 1992. pap. 8.95 (*0-435-90671-2*) Heinemann.

— Tribal Scars & Other Stories. LC 87-25035. (African Writers Ser.). 117p. 1987. pap. 8.95 (*0-435-90142-7*) Heinemann.

— Xala. Wake, Clive, tr. LC 75-41811. (Illus.). 112p. 1983. pap. 8.95 (*1-55652-070-0*) L Hill Bks.

Ouspensky, Leonid. Theology of the Icon, 2 vols., 1. Gythiel, Anthony & Meyendorff, Elizabeth, trs. LC 92-12323. (Illus.). 728p. (C). 1992. 12.95 (*0-88141-122-1*) St Vladimirs.

— Theology of the Icon, 2 vols., 2. Gythiel, Anthony & Meyendorff, Elizabeth, trs. LC 92-12323. (Illus.). 728p. (C). 1992. 14.95 (*0-88141-123-X*) St Vladimirs.

— Theology of the Icon, 2 vols., Set, Vols. 1 & 2. Gythiel, Anthony & Meyendorff, Elizabeth, trs. LC 92-12323. (Illus.). 728p. (C). 1992. Set. 25.95 (*0-88141-124-8*) St Vladimirs.

Ouspensky, Leonid, jt. auth. see Lossky, Vladimir.

O

Ouspensky, P. D. Conscience the Search for Truth. 160p. 1989. pap. 10.00 (0-14-019011-2, Arkana) Viking Penguin.
— Fourth Way. 1971. pap. 13.00 (0-394-71672-8, Vin) Random.
— In Search of the Miraculous: Fragments of an Unknown Teaching. 399p. 1965. pap. 9.95 (0-15-644508-5, Harvest Bks) HarBrace.
— Letters from Russia 1919. (Illus.). 80p. 1992. pap. 7.00 (0-14-019293-X, Arkana) Viking Penguin.
— New Horizons: Explorations in Science. LC 90-82356. (Illus.). 222p. 1990. reprint ed. pap. 14.95 (0-936385-21-9) J Friedlander.
— New Model of the Universe: Principles of the Psychological Method in Its Application to Problems of Science, Religion & Art. LC 35-8632. 1971. pap. 16.00 (0-394-71524-1, Vin) Random.
— Psychology of Man's Possible Evolution. 1973. pap. 8.00 (0-394-71943-3, Vin) Random.
— A Record of Meetings. 672p. 1993. pap. 17.00 (0-14-019307-3, Arkana) Viking Penguin.
— Strange Life of Ivan Osokin. 1988. pap. 8.95 (0-14-019058-9, Penguin Bks) Viking Penguin.
— The Symbolism of the Tarot. Pogossky, A. L., tr. (Illus.). 64p. 1976. reprint ed. pap. 2.50 (0-486-23291-3) Dover.
— Tertium Organum: A Key to the Enigmas of the World. Kadloubovsky, E., tr. LC 81-52264. 320p. 1982. pap. 15.00 (0-394-75168-X, Vin) Random.
Oussaid, Brick. The Mountains Forgotten by God. Woollcombe, Ann, tr. 170p. 1989. 18.00 (0-89410-481-0); pap. 10.00 (0-89410-482-9) Three Continents.
***Oussiemi, Maria & Abuhaidar, Lamia.** Caught in the Crossfire: Young Victims of War Speak Out. (YA). 1995. 19.95 (0-8027-8363-5); lib. bdg. 20.85 (0-8027-8364-3) Walker & Co.
Ousterhou. Aesthetic Contouring of the Craniofacial Skeleton. 1991. 340.00 (0-316-67410-9) Little.
Ousterhout, Anne M. A State Divided: Opposition in Pennsylvania to the American Revolution. LC 86-29573. (Contributions in American History Ser.: No. 123). 358p. 1987. text ed. 59.95 (0-313-25728-0, OUS/, Greenwood Pr) Greenwood.
Ousterhout, John K. TCL & the TK Toolkit. 1994. pap. 35.95 (0-201-63337-X) Addison-Wesley.
***Ousterhout, Robert & Basgelen, Nezih.** Monuments of Unaging Intellect: Historic Postcards of Byzantine Istanbul. (Illus.). 136p. (C). 1995. pap. 29.95 (0-252-06473-9) U of Ill Pr.
Ousterhout, Robert & Brubaker, Leslie, eds. The Sacred Image East & West. LC 93-43343. (Illinois Byzantine Studies: Vol. 4). 320p. 1994. 29.95 (0-252-02096-0) U of Ill Pr.
Ousterhout, Robert G. Architecture of the Kariye Camii in Istanbul. LC 87-22279. (Dumbarton Oaks Studies: Vol. 25). (Illus.). 292p. 1988. 45.00 (0-88402-165-3) Dumbarton Oaks.
***Ouston, Rick.** Finding Family. 214p. (Orig.). 1994. pap. 11.00 (0-921586-31-0, Pub. by New Star Bks CN) InBook.
Out el Kouloub. Ramza. Atiya, Nayra, tr. (Contemporary Issues in the Middle East Ser.). (Illus.). 128p. 1994. text ed. 30.00 (0-8156-2618-5); pap. 14.50 (0-8156-0280-4) Syracuse U Pr.
Out Magazine Editors. Out in America: A Portrait of Gay & Lesbian Life. (Illus.). 256p. 1994. 34.95 (0-670-85850-1, Viking Studio) Studio Bks.
***Out Magazine Editors Staff.** The Gay & Lesbian Address Book. LC 94-44475. 288p. 1995. pap. 13.00 (0-399-51933-5, Perigee Bks) Berkley Pub.
Outaiba Elhuwaib, tr. see Abdulhamid Jodah Al Sahhar.
Outcault, R. F. Yellow Kid. (Illus.). 1990. 49.95 (1-56060-059-4) Eclipse Bks.
Outcault, Richard F. Buster Brown. (Illus.). 32p. (Orig.). 1974. reprint ed. pap. 4.95 (0-486-23006-6) Dover.
— Buster Brown: An Original Compilation, First Collection in Full Continuity of a Complete Year from the Sunday Strip (1906). Blackbeard, Bill, ed. LC 76-53053. (Classic American Comic Strips Ser.). (Illus.). 1977. 16.50 (0-88355-661-8); pap. 10.00 (0-88355-660-X) Hyperion Conn.
Outdoor Action Communications & Sparano, Vin. The Northeast Guide to Saltwater Fishing & Boating. 1993. pap. 24.95 (0-07-158023-9) McGraw.
Outdoor Action Communications Staff. The Northeast Guide to Saltwater Fishing & Boating - Outdoor Communications. (Illus.). 448p. 1993. pap. 24.95 (0-87742-317-2, 60291) Intl Marine.
— The Southeast Guide to Saltwater Fishing & Boating. 1993. pap. text ed. 24.95 (0-07-047979-8) McGraw.
Outdoor Action, Inc. Staff. Southeast Guide to Saltwater Fishing & Boating. (Illus.). 448p. 1993. pap. 24.95 (0-87742-322-9, 60299) Intl Marine.
Outdoor Life Staff. Deer Hunter's Yearbook 1987. 1987. 19.95 (0-943822-77-7) Times Mir Mag Bk Div.
— Guns & Shooting Yearbook, 1987. 1987. 19.95 (0-943822-84-X) Times Mir Mag Bk Div.
Outdoor Writers Association of America Staff. Campsite to Kit: Tastes & Traditions from America's Great Outdoors. Boker, Carol & Goldsworthy, Sharon, eds. (Illus.). 224p. 1994. 15.95 (1-879958-24-4) Tradery Hse.
— Outdoor Writers Association of America Outdoor Style Manual. Kersavage, Carol J. et al, eds. LC 91-61065. 88p. (Orig.). 1991. pap. 10.00 (0-944973-00-0) Outdoor Writ.
Outhwaite, Barbara. Using Word Processing Effectively. LC 92-12940. 1992. write for info. (0-07-707269-3) McGraw.
***Outhwaite, Lucille C.** Flowers in the Wind. LC 94-92291. (Illus.). 88p. (Orig.). 1994. pap. 19.95 (0-9631722-3-9) Hamilton Print.
***Outhwaite, R. B.** Clandestine Marriage in England, 1500-1850. LC 95-13102. 1995. write for info. (1-85285-130-9) Hambledon Press.
Outhwaite, R. B., jt. ed. see McKendrick, Neil.
***Outhwaite, William.** Habermas: A Critical Introduction. (Key Contemporary Thinkers Ser.). 165p. (C). 1995. 35.00x (0-8047-2478-4); pap. 12.95 (0-8047-2479-2) Stanford U Pr.
— New Philosophies of Social Science: Realism, Hermeneutics & Critical Theory. LC 87-10083. 160p. 1988. text ed. 39.95 (0-312-00395-1) St Martin.
— New Philosophies of Social Science: Realism, Hermeneutics & Critical Theory. LC 87-10083. (Theoretical Traditions in the Social Sciences Ser.). 145p. 1991. pap. 16.95 (0-312-06047-5) St Martin.
Outhwaite, William & Bottomore, Tom, eds. The Blackwell Dictionary of Twentieth-Century Social Thought. LC 92-20837. 1993. 59.95 (0-631-15262-8) Blackwell Pubs.
— The Blackwell Dictionary of Twentieth-Century Social Thought. 880p. (C). 1994. pap. text ed. 27.95 (0-631-19575-0) Blackwell Pubs.
Outhwaite, William & Mulkay, Michael, eds. Social Theory & Social Criticism: Essay for Tom Bottomore. (Modern Revivals in Sociology Ser.). 273p. 1992. 59.95 (0-7512-0073-5, Pub. by Gregg Revivals UK) Ashgate Pub Co.
Outing Club of Virginia Tech Staff. Trails in Southwest Virginia: James River to New River. 64p. (Orig.). 1993. pap. 6.95 (0-936015-41-1) Pocahontas Pr.
Outka, Gene. Agape: An Ethical Analysis. LC 78-88070. (Publications in Religion Ser.: No. 17). 336p. 1977. pap. 15.00 (0-300-02122-4) Yale U Pr.
***Outland, Barbara.** Reading! 320p. (C). 1994. per., pap. text ed. 29.95 (0-7872-0409-9) Kendall-Hunt.
Outland, Charles F. Mines, Murders, & Grizzlies: Tales of California's Ventura Back Country. rev. ed. LC 69-19561. (Illus.). 151p. 1986. 25.00 (0-87062-172-6); pap. 10.95 (0-87062-173-4) A H Clark.
Outland, Wendy, ed. see Duval, Cynthia.
Outlaw, et al. A Survey of the New Testament. Harrison, Harrold D., ed. (Orig.). 1984. pap. 9.95 (0-89265-090-7) Randall Hse.
— A Survey of the Old Testament. Harrison, Harrold D., ed. (Orig.). 1984. pap. 9.95 (0-89265-089-3) Randall Hse.
Outlaw, Alain C. Governor's Land: Archaeology of Early Seventeenth-Century Virginia Settlements. LC 80-20340. (Illus.). 205p. 1990. text ed. 30.00 (0-8139-0875-2) U Pr of Va.
Outlaw, Larry A., jt. auth. see Hetrick, Patrick K.
Outlaw, Lena D. Dickinson Genealogy. LC 81-670103. 336p. reprint ed. 40.00 (0-916497-05-4); reprint ed. fiche 6.00 (0-916497-02-X) Burnett Micro.
Outlaw, Stanley. Questions from Text of Old Testament. 1977. pap. 4.95 (0-89265-049-4) Randall Hse.
— Questions from the Text of the New Testament. 36p. 1977. pap. 4.95 (0-89265-050-8) Randall Hse.
Outlaw, Stanley & O'Donnell, J. D. A Survey of the Pentateuch. 93p. 1975. pap. 3.95 (0-89265-027-3) Randall Hse.
Outlaw, Stanley, et al. A Survey of the General Epistles & Revelation. 1976. pap. 3.95 (0-89265-036-2) Randall Hse.
Outler, Albert, ed. John Wesley. 1980. pap. 15.95 (0-19-502810-4) OUP.
Outlet Book Co Staff. All New Borden Pies: American Favorites Kit. 1992. pap. 6.99 (0-517-06674-2) Random Hse Value.
Outlet Book Co. Staff. Cars of the Fifties & Sixties. 1990. 19.99 (0-517-37557-5) Random Hse Value.
— Grandma Moses. (American Art Ser.). 1991. 15.99 (0-517-05237-7) Random Hse Value.
— Grandmother's Household Hints. 1991. 4.99 (0-517-03742-4) Random Hse Value.
— Grandmother's Pies & Cakes. 1991. 4.99 (0-517-03739-4) Random Hse Value.
— Grandmother's Treats. 1991. 4.99 (0-517-03740-8) Random Hse Value.
— Hot & Spicy Cooking. Date not set. 9.99 (0-685-65127-4) Random Hse Value.
— Instant Guide to Reptiles & Amphibians. 1988. 4.99 (0-517-61800-1) Random Hse Value.
— Jane's Fighting Ships of World War One. 1990. 14.99 (0-517-03375-5) Random Hse Value.
— Maine. (Picture Memory Ser.). (Illus.). 1992. 7.99 (0-517-07269-6) Random Hse Value.
— Native American Art & Folklore. Campbell, David, ed. (Illus.). 224p. 1993. 19.99 (0-517-06975-X) Random Hse Value.
— Santa Fe Art. (American Art Ser.). (Illus.). 1993. 15.99 (0-517-08659-X) Random Hse Value.
Outlet Book Company Staff. Alaska. (Picture Memory Ser.). (Illus.). 1992. 7.99 (0-517-07270-X) Random Hse Value.
— America's National Parks: Photographic Journey. (Illus.). 1993. 14.99 (0-517-07257-2) Random Hse Value.
— Chesapeake Bay: Photographic Journey. (Illus.). 1993. 14.99 (0-517-07252-1) Random Hse Value.
— Everglades: Photographic Journey. (Illus.). 1992. 14.99 (0-517-07254-8) Random Hse Value.
— Friendship Is Forever: Keepsake Collection. 1992. 5.99 (0-517-08142-3) Random Hse Value.
— Garden of Inspiration: Keepsake Collection. 1992. 5.99 (0-517-08141-5) Random Hse Value.
— Great Lakes: Photographic Journey. (Illus.). 1993. 14.99 (0-517-07255-6) Random Hse Value.
— Greece: A Photographic Journey. (Illus.). 1992. 14.99 (0-517-07350-1) Random Hse Value.
— Host of Angels: Keepsake Collection. 1992. 5.99 (0-517-08140-7) Random Hse Value.
— International Great Meals in Minutes. 1992. 17.99 (0-517-07775-2) Random Hse Value.
— Massachusetts: Photographic Journey. (Illus.). 1992. 14.99 (0-517-07256-4) Random Hse Value.
— Microwave Craft Magic. 1992. 12.99 (0-517-07318-8) Random Hse Value.
— Russia: Photographic Journey. (Illus.). 1992. 14.99 (0-517-07678-0) Random Hse Value.
— Southern Cooking: Regional & Ethnic Cooking. 1992. 10.99 (0-517-06604-1) Random Hse Value.
— Southwestern Cooking: Regional & Ethnic Cooking. 1992. 10.99 (0-517-06605-X) Random Hse Value.
— Spain: Photographic Journey. (Illus.). 1992. 14.99 (0-517-07679-9) Random Hse Value.
— Yellowstone. (Picture Memory Ser.). (Illus.). 1992. 7.99 (0-517-07268-8) Random Hse Value.
Outlet Staff. Albert Bierstadt. (American Art Ser.). 1993. 15.99 (0-517-08658-1) Random Hse Value.
— America's National Parks. 1993. 14.99 (0-517-06044-2) Random Hse Value.
— At the Farm. (Learn-a-Word Board Bks.). (J). 1991. bds. 3.99 (0-517-05401-9) Random Hse Value.
— At the Zoo. (Learn-a-Word Board Bks.). (J). 1991. bds. 3.99 (0-517-05402-7) Random Hse Value.
— BB-Style Anything Bk. No. 1. (BB-Style Ser.). 1994. 3.99 (0-517-11945-5) Random Hse Value.
— BB-Style Anything Bk. No. 2. (BB-Style Ser.). 1994. 3.99 (0-517-11946-3) Random Hse Value.
— BB-Style Anything Bk. No. 3. (BB-Style Ser.). 1994. 3.99 (0-517-11947-1) Random Hse Value.
— BB-Style Anything Bk. No. 4. (BB-Style Ser.). 1994. 3.99 (0-517-11948-X) Random Hse Value.
— Black Beauty. (J). 1993. 6.99 (0-517-08777-4) Random Hse Value.
— Botticelli. 1994. 8.99 (0-517-10100-9) Random Hse Value.
— Cinderella. (J). 1993. 12.99 (0-517-03707-6) Random Hse Value.
— Complete Book of Dogs. 1993. 14.99 (0-517-06594-0) Random Hse Value.
— The Complete Book of Home Details. 1993. 29.99 (0-517-06113-9) Random Hse Value.
— Country Music Stars of Today. Date not set. 9.99 (0-517-08930-0) Random Hse Value.
— Don't Be Scared Little Lamb. 1991. 3.99 (0-517-05685-2) Random Hse Value.
— Dreams of Childhood. 1994. pap. 12.99 (0-517-11934-X) Random Hse Value.
— Ferrari. 1993. 12.99 (0-517-07295-5) Random Hse Value.
— Floral Garden. 1994. pap. 12.99 (0-517-11933-1) Random Hse Value.
— Frederic Remington Paintings & Sculpture. (Illus.). 1993. 4.99 (0-517-09354-5) Random Hse Value.
— Fruits of the Earth. 1994. pap. 12.99 (0-517-11935-8) Random Hse Value.
— Gifts from the Kitchen. 1993. 5.99 (0-517-08772-3) Random Hse Value.
— Glory of Angels. 1994. pap. 12.99 (0-517-11936-6) Random Hse Value.
— Great Photographers of World War II. 1993. 15.99 (0-517-08660-3) Random Hse Value.
— Guide to North America's Breweries & Microbreweries. 1994. 12.99 (0-517-10232-3) Random Hse Value.
— Holiday Cookies. 1993. 5.99 (0-517-08773-1) Random Hse Value.
— Instant Business Forms. Date not set. pap. 7.99 (0-517-10348-6) Random Hse Value.
— Ireland: A Book to Remember Her By. 1993. 6.99 (0-517-24616-3) Random Hse Value.
— Irish Country Cooking. 1993. 17.99 (0-517-08663-8) Random Hse Value.
— Journeys Through Oz. 1985. 7.99 (0-517-29490-7) Random Hse Value.
— The Kids' Cookbook. (J). 1993. 7.99 (0-517-05589-9) Random Hse Value.
— Kitchen Companion. 1993. 12.99 (0-517-08771-5) Random Hse Value.
— Klee. 1994. 8.99 (0-517-10095-9) Random Hse Value.
— Klimt. 1994. 8.99 (0-517-10096-7) Random Hse Value.
— The Language of Flowers. 1994. 9.99 (0-517-11944-7) Random Hse Value.
— Legendary Native American Indians. 1993. 15.99 (0-517-07344-7) Random Hse Value.
— Little Red Riding Hood. (J). 1992. 3.99 (0-517-08664-6) Random Hse Value.
— London. 1993. 14.99 (0-517-08622-0) Random Hse Value.
— Lost in the Haunted Mansion. (J). 1991. pap. 3.99 (0-517-06138-4) Random Hse Value.
— Maui. (Picture Memory Ser.). 1992. 7.99 (0-517-07267-X) Random Hse Value.
— Maxfield Parrish. (American Art Ser.). 1993. 16.99 (0-517-06714-5) Random Hse Value.
— Mexico: Photographic Journey. 1993. 14.99 (0-517-07016-2) Random Hse Value.
— Mexico: Picture Memory. Date not set. 7.99 (0-517-07690-X) Random Hse Value.
— Missing Snowman: Look & Look Again. (J). 1991. 3.99 (0-517-06142-2) Random Hse Value.
— Modigliani. 1994. 8.99 (0-517-10099-1) Random Hse Value.
— More Five Minute Bunny Tales for Bedtime. (J). 1993. 7.99 (0-517-08769-3) Random Hse Value.
— Native American Indians. (Pocket Guides Ser.). 1993. 5.99 (0-517-08653-0) Random Hse Value.
— New Orleans Cooking. 1993. 10.99 (0-517-07298-X) Random Hse Value.
— On the Wings of Angels. 1993. 8.99 (0-517-08137-7) Random Hse Value.
— Picture Framing. Date not set. 5.99 (0-517-08778-2) Random Hse Value.
— Pissaro. 1994. 8.99 (0-517-10092-4) Random Hse Value.
— The Plains Indians. 1994. pap. 24.99 (0-517-10280-3) Random Hse Value.
— Porsche. 1993. 12.99 (0-517-07294-7) Random Hse Value.
— Rembrandt. 1994. 8.99 (0-517-10090-8) Random Hse Value.
— Renoir. 1994. 8.99 (0-517-10091-6) Random Hse Value.
— Schiele. 1994. 8.99 (0-517-10103-3) Random Hse Value.
— Soup & Sandwiches Cookbook. 1992. 12.99 (0-517-06955-5) Random Hse Value.
— Staining & Varnishing. Date not set. 5.99 (0-517-08779-0) Random Hse Value.
— Step by Step Table Decorating. 1993. 15.99 (0-517-08662-X) Random Hse Value.
— That's My Hat: Dial the Answer. (J). 1992. 3.99 (0-517-06617-3) Random Hse Value.
— Tilling. Date not set. 5.99 (0-517-08780-4) Random Hse Value.
— Undersea Warriors of the World. 1991. 19.99 (0-517-03585-5) Random Hse Value.
— Van Gogh. 1994. 8.99 (0-517-10089-4) Random Hse Value.
— Vegetables. (Food Essentials Ser.). 1993. 15.99 (0-517-06118-X) Random Hse Value.
— Victorian Jewelry. (Illus.). 304p. 1991. 12.99 (0-517-05395-0) Random Hse Value.
— Visit to Sesame Street Zoo. (J). Date not set. pap. 3.99 (0-517-11124-1) Random Hse Value.
— Wallpapering. Date not set. 5.99 (0-517-08781-2) Random Hse Value.
— Warbirds: Airpower. 1990. 19.99 (0-517-01218-9) Random Hse Value.
— Wisconsin: A Picture Memory. (Illus.). 1991. 7.99 (0-517-06026-4) Random Hse Value.
— Wreaths. 1993. 5.99 (0-517-08775-8) Random Hse Value.
Outlka, Gene & Reeder, John P., Jr., eds. Prospects for a Common Morality. LC 92-5681. 296p. 1992. text ed. 55.00 (0-691-07418-6); pap. text ed. 16.95 (0-691-02093-0) Princeton U Pr.
Outram, Dorinda. The Body & the French Revolution: Sex, Class & Political Culture. LC 89-31406. (C). 1989. text ed. 35.00 (0-300-04436-4) Yale U Pr.
Outram, Dorinda, jt. ed. see Abir-Am, Pnina G.
Outside Magazine Editing Staff. Parting Shots. 1993. pap. 9.95 (0-671-75465-3, Fireside) S&S Trade.
Outside Magazine Editors Staff. Exposure. (Illus.). 144p. 1992. 45.00 (0-671-75464-5) S&S Trade.
Outslay, Edmund, jt. auth. see Moore, Michael L.
Outten, Wayne N., et al. The Rights of Employees & Union Members: The Basic ACLU Guide to the Rights of Employees & Union Members. rev. ed. LC 93-16895. (American Civil Liberties Union Handbook Ser.). 604p. (C). 1994. pap. 14.95 (0-8093-1914-4) S Ill U Pr.
— The Rights of Employees & Union Members: The Basic ACLU Guide to the Rights of Employees & Union Members. 2nd rev. ed. LC 93-16895. (American Civil Liberties Union Handbook Ser.). 604p. (C). 1994. 39.95 (0-8093-1913-6) S Ill U Pr.
Outteridge, P. M., jt. ed. see Dineen, J. K.
Outteridge, Peter M. Veterinary Immunology. (Monograph). 1985. text ed. 124.00 (0-12-531130-3) Acad Pr.
— Veterinary Immunology. 280p. 1986. pap. text ed. 42.00 (0-12-531131-1) Acad Pr.
***Outtz, Janice H.** Demographics of American Families. 24p. 1993. 12.00 (0-937846-54-6) Inst Educ Lead.
— Shattering Stereotypes: A Demographic Look at the Facts about Children in the United States. 52p. 1994. 12.00 (0-937846-45-7) Inst Educ Lead.
Outtz, Janice H., jt. auth. see Hodgkinson, Harold L.
***Outward Bound, Inc. Staff.** Field Work: Expeditionary. 176p. 1994. per., pap. text ed. 14.50 (0-7872-0229-0) Kendall-Hunt.
Outwater. Sludge & Minor Wastewater Residuals Reuse. 1994. write for info. (0-87371-677-9) Lewis Pubs.
Ouvaroff, M. The Mysteries of Eleusis. Price, J. D., tr. 1992. reprint ed. pap. 35.00 (1-55818-195-4) Holmes Pub.
Ouverson, Marlin. Dr. Dobb's Journal Bound, Vol. 4. 467p. 1987. 30.75 (0-934375-14-3) M&T Bks.
— Dr. Dobb's Journal Bound, Vol. 8. 798p. 1985. pap. 35.75 (0-934375-00-3) M&T Bks.
Ouverson, Marlin, ed. Dr. Dobb's Journal Bound, Vol. 9. 982p. 1986. pap. 35.75 (0-934375-08-9) M&T Bks.
Ouverson, Martin. Macintosh for Kids. write for info. (0-318-58226-0) P-H.
Ouvray, H. A., tr. see Nasse, Erwin.
Ouvrier, John. Master. abr. ed. 140p. 1995. pap. 7.95 (1-56901-526-0) NW Pub.
Ouvrier, Robert A., et al. Peripheral Neuropathy in Childhood. (International Review of Child Neurology Ser.). 256p. 1990. 98.50 (0-88167-690-X) Raven.
Ouvry, Philip, jt. auth. see Langley-Price, Pat.
Ouvry, Philip, jt. auth. see Price, Pat L.
Ouwehand, Terre. The Debris of the Encounter: A Recovery of Self. LC 89-38700. 88p. (Orig.). (C). 1990. pap. 7.95 (0-89390-137-7) Resource Pubns.
— Voices from the Well. (Illus.). 1986. pap. 8.95 (0-914598-44-9) Pr MacDonald & Reinecke.
— Voices from the Well. deluxe ed. (Illus.). 1986. 12.95 (0-914598-41-4) Pr MacDonald & Reinecke.
— Writing Your Way to Wholeness: Creative Exercises for Personal Growth. LC 94-24332. 240p. (Orig.). (C). 1994. pap. 17.95 (0-89390-312-4) Resource Pubns.
Ouweneel, Arij, jt. auth. see Pansters, Wil.
Ouweneel, W. J. Creation or Evolution-What Is the Truth? 58p. pap. 3.95 (0-88172-145-X) Believers Bkshelf.
— What Is Election? pap. 2.25 (0-88172-162-X) Believers Bkshelf.
— What Is Eternal Life? pap. 2.50 (0-88172-149-2) Believers Bkshelf.
— What Is the Christian's Hope? 53p. pap. 2.95 (0-88172-116-6) Believers Bkshelf.

O

An Asterisk (*) at the beginning of an entry indicates that the title is appearing in BIP for the first time.

— What Is the Sonship of Christ? pap. 2.25 (*0-88172-167-0*) Believers Bkshelf.

Ouweneel, Willen. Biologia y Origenes: Biology & Origins. (SPA.). 4.95 (*84-7645-002-8*, 223063, Pub. by Edit Clie SP) TSELF.

Ouwerkerk, C. Theory of Macroscopic Systems. (Illus.). 288p. 1991. pap. 34.00 (*0-387-51575-5*) Spr-Verlag.

Ouwerkerk, C. van, jt. ed. see Soane, B. D.

***Ouwerkerk, Louise.** No Elephants for the Maharaja: Social & Political Change in Travancore 1921-1947. (C). 1994. text ed. 27.50 (*81-7304-068-0*, Pub. by Manohar II) S Asia.

***Ovadi, Judit.** Cell Architecture & Metabolite Channelling. (Molecular Biology Intelligence Unit Ser.). 191p. 1995. write for info. (*1-57059-270-5*) R G Landes.

Ovando, Carlos & Collier, Virginia. Bilingual & ESL Classrooms: Teaching in Multicultural Contexts. 1985. text ed. 25.95 (*0-07-047951-8*) McGraw.

Ovando, J. El Mejor Regalo Para un Soltero (The Best Gift for a Single) (SPA.). 1993. 3.99 (*1-56063-107-4*, 498539) Editorial Unilit.

Ovando, J. A. Seras Tu el Lider Que Dios Necesita? (Are You the Leader God Needs?) (SPA.). Date not set. 2.49 (*1-56063-017-5*, 498054) Editorial Unilit.

Ovando, Natascha M., jt. auth. see Edwards, Charles J.

Ovard, Glen F. Administration of the Changing Secondary School. 1966. text ed. write for info. (*0-685-14568-9*) Macmillan.

Ovard, Glen F., jt. auth. see Kapfer, Philip G.

Ovaris, Wendy. After the Nightmare: The Treatment of Non-Offending Mothers of Sexually Abused Children. 1991. pap. 16.95 (*1-55691-041-X*) Learning Pubns.

Ovassapian, Andranik. Fiberoptic Airway Endoscopy in Anesthesia & Critical Care. 192p. 1990. 110.50 (*0-88167-591-1*) Raven.

Ovcharenko, F. D., et al. Investigations of the Physiochemical Mechanics of Clay-Mineral Dispersions. 160p. 1964. text ed. 44.00 (*0-7065-0540-9*, Pub. by Keter Pub IS) Coronet Bks.

Ovchinnikov, A. A. & Timashev, S. F., eds. Kinetics of Diffusion Controlled Chemical Processes. 227p. (C). 1989. text ed. 110.00 (*0-941743-52-7*) Nova Sci Pubs.

Ovchinnikov, A. A. & Ukrainskii, I. I., eds. Low-Dimensional Conductors & Superconductors: Electron-Electron Correlation Effects In. (Research Reports in Physics). (Illus.). ix, 161p. 1991. pap. 69.00 (*0-387-54248-5*) Spr-Verlag.

Ovchinnikov, V. I., ed. The Method of Orbits in Interpolation Theory. (Mathematical Reports Ser.: Vol. 1, Pt. 2). 170p. 1984. text ed. 76.00 (*3-7186-0259-8*) Gordon & Breach.

Ovchinnikov, Y. A. & Hucho, F. Receptors & Ion Channels: Proceedings of the Symposium on Receptors & Ion Channels, Tashkent, U. S. S. R., October 2-5, 1986. xi, 351p. (Orig.). 1987. lib. bdg. 169.25 (*0-89925-375-X*) De Gruyter.

Ovchinnikov, Y. A., jt. ed. see Hucho, F.

Ovchinnikov, Yu. A., ed. FEBS: Proceedings of the 16th Congress, Moscow, 1986, 3 vols., Set. (Illus.). 1589p. 1985. lib. bdg. 395.00 (*90-6764-044-1*, Pub. by VSP NE) Coronet Bks.

— Retinal Proteins. 590p. 1987. lib. bdg. 179.00 (*90-6764-102-2*, Pub. by VSP NE) Coronet Bks.

Ovchinnko, Yu A. & Ivanov, V. T. Conformational States & Biological Activity of Cyclic Peptides. Barton, Derek H., ed. 1976. pap. 15.50 (*0-08-020426-0*, Pergamon Pr) Elsevier.

Ove Arup & Partners Consultant Engineers Staff. Ove Arup & Partners. (Academy Bks.). (Illus.). 216p. 1987. 49.50 (*0-312-00094-4*) St Martin.

Ove Arup & Partners Staff, et al. Compas Project - Stress Analysis of HLW Containers Intermediate Testwork, No. EUR 12593. 55p. 1990. pap. 6.00 (*92-826-1157-4*, CD-NA-12593-EN-C) UNIPUB.

Ove Arup Partnership Committee, jt. auth. see Whittle, Robin.

Ovechka, G. Hamsters As a Hobby. (Illus.). 96p. 1993. 7.95 (*0-86622-412-2*, TT006) TFH Pubns.

Ovechka, Greg. Ferrets As a New Pet. (Illus.). 64p. 1991. pap. 5.95 (*0-86622-622-2*, TU-014) TFH Pubns.

***Ovecka, Janice.** Captive of Pittsford Ridge. LC 94-24533. 128p. (Orig.). (YA). 1994. pap. 10.95 (*1-881535-11-8*) New Eng Pr VT.

— Cave of Falling Water. LC 92-56713. (Illus.). (J). 1992. 9.95 (*0-933050-98-4*) New Eng Pr VT.

Oved, Yaacov. Two Hundred Years of American Communes. Lash, Hannah, tr. 419p. 1988. 44.95 (*0-88738-113-8*) Transaction Pubs.

— Two Hundred Years of American Communes. 516p. (C). 1992. pap. 24.95 (*1-56000-647-1*) Transaction Pubs.

Ovello, A. C. Building Blocks of Nuclear Structure: The Fourth International Spring Seminar on Nuclear Physics. 648p. 1993. text ed. 135.00 (*981-02-1069-8*) World Scientific Pub.

Ovelmen-Levitt, Janice. Deafferentation Pain Syndromes: Pathophysiology & Treatment. Nashold, Blaine S., Jr., ed. (Advances in Pain Research & Therapy Ser.: Vol. 19). 368p. 1991. 108.50 (*0-88167-823-6*) Raven.

Ovendale, Ritchie. Appeasement & the English Speaking World. v, 353p. 1975. 25.00 (*0-7083-0589-X*, Pub. by U of Wales UK) Bks Intl VA.

— Britain, the United States & the End of the Palestine Mandate 1942-1948. (Studies in Celtic History: No. 57). 344p. (C). 1989. 71.00 (*0-86193-214-5*) Boydell & Brewer.

— British Defence Policy since 1945. LC 94-12637. (Documents in Contemporary History Ser.). 1994. text ed. 49.95 (*0-7190-4014-0*, Pub. by Manchester Univ Pr UK); text ed. 24.95 (*0-7190-4015-9*, Pub. by Manchester Univ Pr UK) St Martin.

— The English Speaking Alliance: Britain, the United States, the Dominions & Cold War, 1945-1951. LC 85-11075. 280p. 1985. text ed. 60.00 (*0-04-327078-6*) Routledge Chapman & Hall.

— Longman Companion to the Middle East since 1914. 392p. (C). 1992. pap. text ed. 23.95 (*0-582-06305-1*, 79367) Longman.

— The Origins of the Arab-Israeli Wars. 2nd ed. (Origins of Modern War Ser.). (Illus.). 264p. (C). 1992. pap. text ed. 25.50 (*0-582-06369-8*) Longman.

Ovenden, Graham, ed. A Victorian Album: Julia Margaret Cameron & Her Circle. LC 75-18728. (Photography Ser.). (Illus.). 119p. 1975. lib. bdg. 45.00 (*0-306-70749-7*) Da Capo.

Ovens, Carrie, jt. auth. see Carre, Clive.

Ovens, E. Albert. Transportation & Traffic Management, 4 vols., Set. 16th ed. Butler, Robert M. et al, eds. LC 74-19874. (Illus.). 1191p. 1981. pap. text ed. 85.00 (*0-87408-012-6*) Intl Thom Trans Pr.

— Transportation & Traffic Management, 4 vols., Vol. I. 16th ed. Butler, Robert M. et al, eds. LC 74-19874. (Illus.). 273p. 1981. pap. text ed. 23.00 (*0-87408-029-0*) Intl Thom Trans Pr.

— Transportation & Traffic Management, 4 vols., Vol. II. 16th ed. Butler, Robert M. et al, eds. LC 74-19874. (Illus.). 262p. 1981. pap. text ed. 23.00 (*0-87408-030-4*) Intl Thom Trans Pr.

— Transportation & Traffic Management, 4 vols., Vol. III. 16th ed. Butler, Robert M. et al, eds. LC 74-19874. (Illus.). 310p. 1981. pap. text ed. 23.00 (*0-87408-031-2*) Intl Thom Trans Pr.

— Transportation & Traffic Management, 4 vols., Vol. IV. 16th ed. Butler, Robert M. et al, eds. LC 74-19874. (Illus.). 346p. 1981. pap. text ed. 23.00 (*0-87408-032-0*) Intl Thom Trans Pr.

Ovens, William G. Design Manual for Water Wheels. 77p. 1988. 7.25 (*0-86619-045-7*) Vols Tech Asst.

***Ovensen, Geir.** Responding to Change: Trends in Palestinian Household Economy. 223p. 1994. pap. 20.00 (*82-7422-121-4*) Inst Palestine.

Ovensen, Geir, jt. auth. see Heiberg, Marianne.

Over, D. E., jt. auth. see Manktelow, K. I.

Over, D. E., jt. ed. see Manktelow, K. I.

Over, Mead. Economics for Health Sector Analysis: Concepts & Cases. (EDI Seminar Ser.). 224p. 1991. 11.95 (*0-8213-1335-5*, 11335) World Bank.

Over, Naomi L. Ruby Glass of the Twentieth Century. (Illus.). 128p. (Orig.). 1990. 29.95 (*0-915410-67-2*, 3085HB); pap. 21.95 (*0-915410-68-0*, 3084SB) Antique Pubns.

Overacker, Louise. Money in Elections. LC 73-19167. (Politics & People Ser.). (Illus.). 490p. 1974. reprint ed. 36.95 (*0-405-05889-6*) Ayer.

— Presidential Campaign Funds. LC 76-29407. reprint ed. 29.50 (*0-404-15341-0*) AMS Pr.

— The Presidential Primary. LC 73-19168. (Politics & People Ser.). (Illus.). 318p. 1974. reprint ed. 26.95 (*0-405-05890-X*) Ayer.

Overall. Clinical Small Animal Behavior. 350p. 1994. pap. 39.00 (*0-8016-6820-4*) Mosby Yr Bk.

Overall, Christine. Ethics & Human Reproduction: A Feminist Analysis. 256p. 1987. text ed. 39.95 (*0-04-497009-9*); pap. text ed. 19.95 (*0-04-497010-2*) Routledge Chapman & Hall.

— Human Reproduction: Principles, Practices, Policies. 184p. 1993. pap. 22.00 (*0-19-540961-2*) OUP.

Overall, Christine & Zion, William P., eds. Perspectives on AIDS: Ethical & Social Issues. 192p. 1991. 24.95 (*0-19-540749-0*) OUP.

Overall, John. Convocation Book of Sixteen Six. LC 77-173482. (Library of Anglo-Catholic Theology: No. 15). reprint ed. 27.50 (*0-404-52107-X*) AMS Pr.

Overall, John E. & Klett, C. James. Applied Multivariate Analysis. LC 81-20944. 522p. (C). 1983. reprint ed. lib. bdg. 48.50 (*0-89874-325-7*) Krieger.

Overall, Kitty, ed. see Van Duyne, Marie A.

Overbeck, Bernhard H., jt. auth. see Burns, Thomas S.

Overbeck, Buz. Introduction to the New Astrology. LC 81-66053. (Matrix Seminar Ser.). 64p. 1981. 10.00 (*0-86690-130-2*, 01329-014) Am Fed Astrologers.

Overbeck, Cynthia. Ants. LC 81-17216. (Natural Science Bks.). (Illus.). 48p. (J). (gr. 4 up). 1982. lib. bdg. 19.95 (*0-8225-1468-0*, Lerner Publctns); pap. 5.95 (*0-8225-9525-7*, Lerner Publctns) Lerner Group.

— Cactus. LC 82-211. (Natural Science Bks.). (Illus.). 48p. (J). (gr. 4 up). 1982. lib. bdg. 19.95 (*0-8225-1469-9*, Lerner Publctns); pap. 5.95 (*0-8225-9556-7*, Lerner Publctns) Lerner Group.

— Carnivorous Plants. LC 81-17234. (Natural Science Bks.). (Illus.). 48p. (J). (gr. 4 up). 1982. lib. bdg. 19.95 (*0-8225-1470-2*, Lerner Publctns); pap. 5.95 (*0-8225-9535-4*, Lerner Publctns) Lerner Group.

— Cats. LC 83-17530. (Lerner Natural Science Bks.). (Illus.). 48p. (J). (gr. 4 up). 1983. lib. bdg. 19.95 (*0-8225-1480-X*, Lerner Publctns) Lerner Group.

— Elephants. LC 80-27550. (Lerner Natural Science Bks.). (Illus.). 48p. (J). (gr. 4 up). 1981. lib. bdg. 19.95 (*0-8225-1452-4*, Lerner Publctns) Lerner Group.

— How Seeds Travel. LC 81-17217. (Lerner Natural Science Bks.). (Illus.). 48p. (J). (gr. 4 up). 1982. lib. bdg. 19.95 (*0-8225-1474-5*, Lerner Publctns) Lerner Group.

— How Seeds Travel. (Illus.). 48p. (J). (gr. 4 up). reprint ed. 5.95 (*0-8225-9569-9*, Lerner Publctns) Lerner Group.

— Monkeys. LC 81-1961. (Lerner Natural Science Bks.). (Illus.). 48p. (J). (gr. 4 up). 1981. lib. bdg. 19.95 (*0-8225-1464-8*, Lerner Publctns) Lerner Group.

Overbeck, Cynthia, jt. auth. see Thompson, Brenda.

Overbeck, J., et al, eds. The Second Workshop on Measurement of Microbial Activity in the Carbon Cycle of Aquatic Ecosystems: Proceedings. (Advances in Limnology Ser.: No. 19). (Illus.). 328p. 1984. pap. text ed. 110.00 (*3-510-47017-6*, Pub. by Schweitzerbart'sche GW) Lubrecht & Cramer.

Overbeck, Joy, jt. auth. see Pogzeba, Wolfgang.

Overbeck, Jurgen & Chrost, Ryszard J., eds. Microbial Ecology of Lake Plusssee. LC 93-5258. (Ecological Studies: Vol. 105). 1993. 89.00 (*0-387-94120-7*) Spr-Verlag.

Overbeck, Jurgen, et al, eds. Aquatic Microbial Ecology: Biochemical & Molecular Approaches. (Contemporary Bioscience Ser.). 224p. 1990. 49.00 (*0-387-97222-6*) Spr-Verlag.

Overbeck, Wayne & Pullen, Rick. Major Principles of Media Law, 1991. rev. ed. 336p. (C). 1991. pap. text ed. 26.75 (*0-03-074222-6*) HB Coll Pubs.

Overbeck, Werner & Bohm, Dieter, eds. Body Composition - Research Techniques & Nutritional Assessment. (Internationale Zeitschrift fuer Infusionstherapie, Klinische Ernahrung und Transfusionsmedizin Ser.: Supplement 3 zu Band 17, April 1990). 1990. 17.00 (*3-8055-5228-9*) S Karger.

Overbeek, Henk. Global Capitalism & National Decline: The Thatcher Decade in Perspective. 272p. 1990. text ed. 60.00 (*0-04-445413-9*); pap. text ed. 18.95 (*0-04-445639-5*) Routledge Chapman & Hall.

Overbeek, Henk, ed. Restructuring Hegemony in the Global Political Economy. LC 92-35537. 272p. 1993. 74.50 (*0-415-05595-4*, A5933) Routledge.

Overbeek, Johannes. The Modern World Economy: Theories & Policies. 480p. (Orig.). (C). 1993. lib. bdg. 56.50 (*0-8191-9131-0*); pap. text ed. 44.50 (*0-8191-9132-9*) U Pr of Amer.

— The Population Challenge: A Handbook for Non-Specialists. LC 76-5328. (Contributions in Sociology Ser.: No. 19). (Illus.). 224p. 1976. text ed. 55.00 (*0-8371-8896-2*, OPC/, Greenwood Pr) Greenwood.

Overbeek, Johannes, ed. The Evolution of Population Theory: A Documentary Sourcebook. LC 76-43138. (Contributions in Sociology Ser.: No. 23). 277p. 1977. text ed. 47.95 (*0-8371-9313-3*, OVP/, Greenwood Pr) Greenwood.

Overbeek, Johannes, intro. Two Essays by Wilhelm Roepke: The Problem of Economic Order, Welfare, Freedom & Inflation. LC 86-33982. 114p. (Orig.). (C). 1987. lib. bdg. 34.50 (*0-8191-6125-X*); pap. text ed. 14.00 (*0-8191-6126-8*) U Pr of Amer.

Overbeek, R., jt. ed. see Lusk, Ewing L.

Overbeek, Ross A. Assembler Language with Assist & Assist I. 4th ed. 572p. (C). 1990. write for info. (*0-02-390005-9*) Macmillan.

Overbeek, Ross A. & Singletary, Wilson E. Introduction to COBOL. 400p. (C). 1986. pap. text ed. write for info. (*0-318-59748-9*); 8.00 (*0-201-16316-0*) Addison-Wesley.

— Introduction to COBOL: A Primer & a Programmer's Guide. LC 84-14491. 408p. 1985. pap. write for info. (*0-201-16310-1*); 5.50 (*0-685-10456-7*) Addison-Wesley.

Overbeek, Ross A., jt. ed. see Lusk, Ewing L.

Overbeeke, J. L. Application of Welded Botled & Riveted Connections in HSLA Steel in Structures, No. EUR 13626. 174p. 1991. pap. 19.00 (*92-826-2819-1*, CD-NA-13626-EN-C) UNIPUB.

Overberg, Ken R. Roots & Branches: Grounding Religion in Human Experience. rev. ed. LC 91-61103. 160p. (C). 1991. pap. 10.95 (*1-55612-457-0*, LL1457) Sheed & Ward MO.

Overberg, Kenneth. Journey to Jerusalem. (Illus.). (Orig.). 1991. pap. text ed. 6.95 (*0-932506-76-3*, 6763) St Bedes Pubns.

Overberg, Kenneth R. Conscience in Conflict: How to Make Moral Choices. 162p. 1991. 6.95 (*0-86716-124-8*) St Anthony Mess Pr.

— To Comfort & Confront. 78p. (Orig.). 1983. pap. 4.95 (*0-914544-49-7*) Living Flame Pr.

Overberg, Kenneth R., ed. AIDS, Ethics & Religion: Embracing a World of Suffering. LC 93-42176. 256p. (Orig.). 1994. pap. 18.95 (*0-88344-949-8*) Orbis Bks.

— Mercy or Murder? Euthanasia, Morality & Public Policy. 280p. (Orig.). 1993. pap. 15.95 (*1-55612-609-3*) Sheed & Ward MO.

Overbey, Daniel L. Railroads: The Free Enterprise Alternative. LC 82-7503. (Illus.). 296p. 1982. text ed. 49.95 (*0-89930-031-6*, OVR/, Quorum Bks) Greenwood.

***Overbey, Scot.** Vladimir Zhirinovsky: The Man Who Would Be God. (Illus.). 150p. (Orig.). 1994. pap. 9.95 (*1-879366-74-6*) Hearthstone OK.

Overbury, Thomas. Conceited News of Sir Thomas Overbury & His Friends: With Sir Thomas Overbury His Wife. Savage, James E., ed. LC 68-29084. 1968. 60.00 (*0-8201-1039-6*) Schol Facsimiles.

— The Overburian Characters, to Which Is Added, a Wife. Paylor, W. J., ed. LC 75-41207. reprint ed. 15.75 (*0-686-77165-6*) AMS Pr.

— The Overburian Characters, to Which Is Added, a Wife. Paylor, W. J., ed. LC 75-41207. Date not set. reprint ed. write for info. (*0-404-14580-9*) AMS Pr.

— Sir T. Overbury His Observations in His Travailes. LC 70-26399. (English Experience Ser.: No. 154). 28p. 1969. reprint ed. 25.00 (*90-221-0154-1*) Walter J Johnson.

Overby, A. J., jt. ed. see Cross, H. R.

Overby, L. Marvin, jt. auth. see Burns, James M.

Overby, Lacy R., ed. see International Max von Pettenkofer Symposium Ser.

Overby, Lynette Y. & Humphrey, James H., eds. Dance, Vol. 3. LC 87-47814. (Illus.). 310p. 1992. 37.50 (*0-404-63853-8*) AMS Pr.

— Dance: Current Selected Research, 4 vols., Vols. 1-4. LC 87-47814. 1993. 37.50 (*0-404-63850-3*) AMS Pr.

Overby, Lynnette Y., ed. Early Childhood Creative Arts. (Illus.). 265p. (Orig.). 1991. pap. text ed. 22.00 (*0-88314-522-7*) AAHPERD.

Overby, Osmund & Larson, Sidney. Fred Shane Paintings, 1923-1979. 48p. (Orig.). 1982. pap. 7.50 (*0-910501-00-9*) U of Missouri Mus Art Arch.

Overby, Paul. Holy Blood: An Inside View of the Afghan War. LC 93-20126. 248p. 1993. Alk. paper. text ed. 55.00 (*0-275-94622-3*, C4622, Praeger Pubs) Greenwood.

Overbye, Dennis. Lonely Hearts of the Cosmos: The Story of the Scientific Quest for the Secret of the Universe. LC 89-45700. (Illus.). 416p. 1992. reprint ed. pap. 13.00 (*0-06-092271-0*, PL) HarpC.

Overcash, Michael. Techniques for Industrial Pollution Prevention. (Illus.). 200p. 1986. 64.95 (*0-87371-071-1*, TD897, CRC Reprint) Franklin.

Overcash, Michael R., et al. Livestock Waste Management, 2 vols., I. 512p. 1983. 144.00 (*0-8493-5595-8*, TD930) CRC Pr.

— Livestock Waste Management, 2 vols., II. 512p. 1983. 137.00 (*0-8493-5596-6*, TD930) CRC Pr.

— Livestock Waste Management, 2 vols., Set. 512p. 1983. write for info. (*0-318-57538-8*, TD930) CRC Pr.

Overcash, Michael R. Techniques for Industrial Pollution Prevention. 203p. 1986. 10.00 (*0-317-05673-5*, P89004HAZ); 10.00 (*0-317-05691-3*, P93002WAT) Assn Bay Area.

Overcast, Thomas, jt. auth. see Edelhertz, Herbert.

Overdieck, D., jt. auth. see Esser, D. G.

***Overduin, Nick.** Job: Challenging a Silent God : a Study Guide. 1994. 4.05 (*1-56212-065-4*) CRC Pubns.

***Overeaters Anonymous, Inc. Staff.** Abstinence: Members of Overeaters Anonymous Share Their Experience, Strength, & Hope. LC 94-67576. 1994. pap. 6.99 (*0-9609898-7-0*) Overeaters Anym.

— The Twelve-Step Workbook of Overeaters Anonymous. LC 93-83640. 1993. pap. 6.99 (*0-9609898-5-4*) Overeaters Anym.

— The Twelve Steps & Twelve Traditions of Overeaters Anonymous. LC 93-85052. 1993. 9.99 (*0-9609898-6-2*) Overeaters Anym.

Overend, R. P., jt. ed. see Hall, D. O.

Overend, R. P., jt. ed. see Hall, David O.

Overend, R. P., et al, eds. Fundamentals of Thermochemical Biomass Conversion: Based on the Edited & Refereed Papers from the International Conference Held in Estes Park, Colorado, 18-22 October 1982. (Illus.). xxix, 1192p. 1985. 264.75 (*0-85334-306-3*, Pub. by Elsevier Applied Sci UK) Elsevier.

Overfelt, Kathy & Overfelt, Tony. No Thanks - I'll Sell It Myself. 128p. 1991. pap. 3.95 (*0-380-76186-6*) Avon.

Overfelt, Robert C. The Val Verde Winery. (Southwestern Studies: No. 75). 76p. 1985. pap. 10.00 (*0-87404-151-1*) Tex Western.

Overfelt, Tony, jt. auth. see Overfelt, Kathy.

Overfield, James H. Humanism & Scholasticism in Late Medieval Germany. LC 84-42568. (Illus.). 368p. 1984. text ed. 55.00 (*0-691-07292-2*) Princeton U Pr.

— Humanism & Scholasticism in Late Medieval Germany. LC 84-42568. Date not set. reprint ed. pap. 103.50 (*0-7837-9410-X*, 2060155) Bks Demand.

Overfield, James H., jt. auth. see Andrea, Alfred J.

Overfield, Joan. Belle of the Ball. 224p. (Orig.). 1993. mass mkt. 3.99 (*0-380-76923-9*) Avon.

— Bride's Leap. 224p. (Orig.). 1991. pap. 3.95 (*0-449-21933-X*, Crest) Fawcett.

— The Dutiful Duke. 224p. (Orig.). 1994. mass mkt. 3.99 (*0-380-77400-3*) Avon.

— Hearts Disguise. 1991. pap. 3.95 (*0-8217-3546-2*) Zebra.

— A Matchmaking Miss. 288p. 1992. mass mkt. 3.99 (*0-8217-3944-1*) Zebra.

— A Proper Taming. 224p. (Orig.). 1994. mass mkt. 3.99 (*0-380-77401-1*) Avon.

— A Spirited Bluestocking. 1992. pap. 3.50 (*0-8217-3727-9*) Zebra.

— The Traitor's Daughter. 320p. 1994. mass mkt. 3.99 (*0-8217-4633-2*) Zebra.

— The Viscount's Vixen. 224p. (Orig.). 1992. mass mkt. 3.99 (*0-380-76922-0*) Avon.

Overfield, Loyd J., II, ed. The Little Big Horn, 1876: The Official Communications, Documents & Reports. LC 90-12353. (Illus.). 203p. 1990. reprint ed. pap. 10.95 (*0-8032-8601-5*, Bison Books) U of Nebr Pr.

Overfield, Richard A. Science with Practice: Charles E. Bessey & the Maturing of American Botany. LC 91-16180. (History of Science & Technology Reprint Ser.). (Illus.). 276p. 1993. 37.95 (*0-8138-1822-2*) Iowa St U Pr.

***Overfield, Theresa.** Biological Variation in Health & Illness: Race, Age, & Sex Differences. 2nd ed. LC 94-42293. 240p. 1995. 139.95 (*0-8493-4577-4*, 4577) CRC Pr.

Overgaard, B., ed. see Hermodsson, Ivan.

Overgaard, Jens, ed. Hyperthermic Oncology: Proceedings of the Fourth International Conference on Hyperthermic Oncology, 1984, 2 vols., Set. 1270p. 1984. 209.00 (*0-8002-3824-9*) Taylor & Francis.

— Hyperthermic Oncology, Vol. 1: Summary Papers. 870p. 1984. 154.00 (*0-85066-273-7*) Taylor & Francis.

— Hyperthermic Oncology, Vol. 2: Review Lectures, Symposium Summaries & Workshop Summaries. 400p. 1984. 88.00 (*0-85066-281-8*) Taylor & Francis.

Overgard, Zeta, ed. The Best of Quick 'n Easy Cookin', 1986-87. 82p. 1987. pap. 6.95 (*0-9618379-0-X*) Parkside Pubns.

— The Best of Quick 'n Easy Cookin', 1988-89. 124p. 1989. pap. 6.95 (*0-9618379-1-8*) Parkside Pubns.

Overhage, Carl. Six One-Day Walks in the Pecos Wilderness. rev. ed. LC 80-20061. 60p. 1984. pap. 4.95 (*0-86534-044-7*) Sunstone Pr.

Overhauser, David, jt. auth. see Kong, Jeong-Taek.

O

An Asterisk (*) at the beginning of an entry indicates that the title is appearing in BIP for the first time.

Overheim, R. Daniel & Wagner, David L. Light & Color. LC 81-21955. 269p. (C). 1982. Net. text ed. write for info. (*0-471-08348-8*) Wiley.

Overhof, H. & Thomas, P. Electronic Transport in Hydrogenated Amorphous Semiconductors. (Tracts in Modern Physics Ser.: Vol. 114). (Illus.). 190p. 1989. 83.00 (*0-387-50186-X*) Spr-Verlag.

Overholdt, William H. The Rise of China: How Economic Reform Is Creating a New Superpower. 1994. pap. 14.00 (*0-393-31245-3*) Norton.

Overholser, Lee, jt. auth. see Pelton, Ross.

***Overholser, Lee C.** Ericksonian Hypnosis. LC 82-6627. 1982. pap. 32.95 (*0-8290-0738-5*) Irvington.

— Ericksonian Hypnosis: A Handbook of Clinical Practice. rev. ed. 324p. 1994. reprint ed. pap. 29.95 (*0-8290-2635-5*) Irvington.

Overholser, Marguariete. A Man Is a Man: Hooker Family Saga. LC 93-70835. (Illus.). 344p. 1993. pap. 19.95 (*0-8323-0500-6*) Binford Mort.

Overholser, Wayne. Land of Promises. 176p. 1989. pap. 2.75 (*0-380-70679-2*) Avon.

— Proud Journey. 176p. 1989. pap. 2.75 (*0-380-70678-4*) Avon.

— Red Is the Valley. 160p. 1988. pap. 2.75 (*0-380-70680-6*) Avon.

Overholser, Wayne D. The Best Western Stories of Wayne D. Overholser. Pronzini, Bill & Greenberg, Martin H., eds. LC 83-20111. (Best Western Stories Ser.). 220p. 1989. reprint ed. pap. 12.95 (*0-8040-0913-9*) Swallow.

— The Bitter Night. large type ed. LC 93-5485. 1993. pap. 17.95 (*0-7927-1786-4*, Curley Lrg Print) Chivers N Amer.

— Buckaroo's Code. (Orig.). 1994. 14.95 (*0-7451-4594-9*, Gunsmoke) Chivers N Amer.

— Buckaroo's Code. 192p. (Orig.). 1992. reprint ed. pap. 3.50 (*0-8439-3290-2*) Dorchester Pub Co.

— Desperate Man. 192p. 1992. pap. 3.50 (*0-8439-3175-2*) Dorchester Pub Co.

— Draw or Drag. 1994. lib. bdg. 15.95 (*0-7451-4606-6*, Gunsmoke) Chivers N Amer.

— Gunlock. 192p. 1992. reprint ed. pap. 3.50 (*0-8439-3302-X*) Dorchester Pub Co.

— Hearn's Valley. 192p. 1992. reprint ed. pap. 3.50 (*0-8439-3261-9*) Dorchester Pub Co.

— Hearn's Valley - Tough Hand. 384p. 1995. mass mkt. 4.99 (*0-8439-3831-5*) Dorchester Pub Co.

— Judas Gun. 192p. 1992. reprint ed. pap. 3.50 (*0-8439-3251-1*) Dorchester Pub Co.

— The Lone Deputy. large type ed. LC 94-13808. 1994. 19.95 (*0-7927-2119-5*, Curley Lrg Print); pap. 18.95 (*0-7927-2118-7*, Curley Lrg Print) Chivers N Amer.

— The Lone Deputy. 192p. 1991. reprint ed. pap. 3.50 (*0-8439-3193-0*) Dorchester Pub Co.

— The Lone Deputy-Desperate Man. 384p. 1995. mass mkt., pap. text ed. 4.99 (*0-8439-3782-3*) Dorchester Pub Co.

— Steel to the South - Fabulous Gunman. 416p. 1994. mass mkt. 4.99 (*0-8439-3700-9*) Dorchester Pub Co.

— Sun on the Wall. 1981. pap. 1.75 (*0-345-29493-9*) Ballantine.

— Tough Hand. 192p. 1992. reprint ed. pap. 3.50 (*0-8439-3279-1*) Dorchester Pub Co.

— The Trial of Billy Peale. large type ed. LC 93-40605. 1994. 18.95 (*0-7927-1938-7*, Curley Lrg Print); pap. 17.95 (*0-7927-1937-9*, Curley Lrg Print) Chivers N Amer.

— Valley of Guns - Cast a Long Shadow, 2 vols. in 1. 384p. 1994. mass mkt., pap. text ed. 4.99 (*0-8439-3655-X*) Dorchester Pub Co.

— The Violent Land. 192p. 1992. reprint ed. pap. 3.50 (*0-8439-3233-3*) Dorchester Pub Co.

— The Violent Land-the Judas Gun. 400p. 1995. mass mkt., pap. text ed. 4.99 (*0-8439-3802-1*) Dorchester Pub Co.

— West of Rimrock - Draw or Drag, 2 vols. in 1. 384p. 1994. mass mkt., pap. text ed. 4.99 (*0-8439-3635-5*) Dorchester Pub Co.

— West of the Rimrock. 1995. 15.95 (*0-7451-4625-2*) Chivers N Amer.

Overholt, Bergin F. & Chobanian, Sarkis J. Office Endoscopy. 216p. 1990. 49.00 (*0-683-06660-9*) Williams & Wilkins.

***Overholt, Catherine & Sauders, Margaret K., eds.** Policy Choices & Practical Problems in Health Economics: Cases from Latin America & the Caribbean. LC 94-29559. (EDI Development Policy Case Ser., Teaching Cases: Vol. 3). 1994. write for info. (*0-8213-3012-8*) World Bank.

***Overholt, Catherine, et al, eds.** Gender Roles in Development Projects: A Case Book. fac. ed. LC 84-23325. (Kumarian Press Case Studies Ser.). (Illus.). 340p. 1994. pap. 96.90 (*0-7837-7574-1*, 2047327) Bks Demand.

Overholt, Dorothy. Exchanging Real Estate Made Simple. 112p. (Orig.). 1992. pap. 24.95 (*0-9631409-0-6*) Invest Realty.

Overholt, James. Anderson County Tennessee: A Pictorial History. (Illus.). 1989. 29.95 (*0-89865-770-9*) Donning Co.

Overholt, James L. Math Wise: Hands-on Activities & Worksheets for Elementary Students. 288p. 1993. spiral bd. 27.95 (*0-87628-555-8*) Ctr Appl Res.

Overholt, James L., jt. auth. see Foster, David R.

Overholt, James L., jt. auth. see Foster, David.

Overholt, James L., et al. Math Problem Solving for Grades 4 Through 8. 428p. (gr. 4-8). 1983. pap. text ed. 36.00 (*0-205-08024-3*, H80245) Allyn.

— Math Stories for Problem Solving Success: Ready-to-Use Activities for Grades 7-12. 256p. 1989. spiral bd. 27.95 (*0-87628-570-1*) Ctr Appl Res.

Overholt, Jim, ed. These Are Our Voices: The Story of Oak Ridge, 1942-1970. (Illus.). 535p. 1987. 19.95 (*0-9606832-4-0*) Chldrns Mus.

Overholt, Mary K., ed. American Cooperation, 1984. LC 26-276. (Illus.). 375p. 1984. write for info. (*0-938868-07-1*); pap. 12.00 (*0-938868-06-3*) Am Inst Cooperation.

Overholt, Thomas W. Channels of Prophecy: The Social Dynamics of Prophetic Activity. LC 89-39172. 208p. 1989. 25.00 (*0-8006-2411-4*, 1-2411) Augsburg Fortress.

— Prophecy in Cross Cultural Perspective: A Sourcebook for Biblical Researchers. (Society of Biblical Literature Ser.). (C). 1985. pap. 31.95 (*0-89130-901-2*, 06-03-17) Scholars Pr GA.

Overholt, Thomas W. & Callicott, J. Baird. Clothed-in-Fur & Other Tales: An Introduction to an Ojibwa World View. LC 81-43673. 198p. (Orig.). 1982. lib. bdg. 57.00 (*0-8191-2364-1*); pap. text ed. 22.50 (*0-8191-2365-X*) U Pr of Amer.

Overholt, Thomas W., jt. ed. see Culley, Robert C.

Overholt, Thomas W., jt. ed. see Merrill, Arthur L.

Overholt, William H. The Rise of China: How Economic Reform Is Creating a New Superpower. LC 93-4634. 1993. 25.00 (*0-393-03533-6*) Norton.

Overholtzer, Ruth. Elijah. (Illus.). 36p. (J). (gr. k-6). 1967. pap. text ed. 9.45 (*1-55976-009-5*) CEF Press.

— Elisha. (Illus.). 33p. (J). (gr. k-6). 1967. pap. text ed. 9.45 (*1-55976-010-9*) CEF Press.

— From Then Till Now. 155p. 1990. 5.99 (*1-55976-122-9*) CEF Press.

— Joshua. (Illus.). 62p. (J). (gr. k-6). 1987. pap. text ed. 9.45 (*1-55976-012-5*) CEF Press.

— Moses, Vol. I. (Illus.). 50p. (J). (gr. k-6). 1957. pap. text ed. 9.45 (*1-55976-007-9*) CEF Press.

— Moses, Vol. II. (Illus.). 50p. (J). (gr. k-6). 1967. pap. text ed. 9.45 (*1-55976-008-7*) CEF Press.

— Salvation Songs, Vol. I. 100p. (J). (gr. k-6). 1975. pap. text ed. 2.99 (*3-901171-00-2*) CEF Press.

— Salvation Songs, Vol. II. 105p. (J). (gr. k-4). 1979. pap. text ed. 2.99 (*1-55976-201-2*) CEF Press.

— Salvation Songs, Vol. III. 100p. (J). (gr. k-6). 1975. pap. text ed. 2.99 (*1-55976-202-0*) CEF Press.

— Salvation Songs, Vol. IV. (Illus.). 96p. (J). (gr. k-6). 1979. pap. text ed. 2.99 (*1-55976-203-9*) CEF Press.

— Wordless Book Visualized. (Illus.). 54p. (J). (gr. k-6). 1979. pap. text ed. 8.99 (*1-55976-027-3*) CEF Press.

Overholtzer, Ruth P. Life of Peter. (Illus.). 21p. (J). (gr. k-6). 1964. pap. text ed. 9.45 (*1-55976-013-3*) CEF Press.

Overing, Gillian R. Language, Sign, & Gender in Beowulf. LC 89-5922. 160p. (C). 1990. 24.50 (*0-8093-1563-7*) S Ill U Pr.

Overing, Gillian R. & Osborn, Marijane. Landscape of Desire: Partial Stories of the Northern Medieval World. LC 93-32773. 1994. text ed. 39.95 (*0-8166-2374-0*); pap. text ed. 16.95 (*0-8166-2375-9*) U of Minn Pr.

Overing, Gillian R., jt. ed. see Caywood, Cynthia.

Overing, Gillian R., jt. ed. see Harwood, Britton J.

Overing, Joanna, ed. Reason & Morality. (ASA Monographs). 240p. 1985. pap. 15.95 (*0-422-79810-X*, 9605, Pub. by Tavistock UK) Routledge Chapman & Hall.

Overington, I. Computer Vision: A Unified, Biologically-Inspired Approach. 350p. 1991. 95.00 (*0-444-88972-8*, North Holland) Elsevier.

Overington, Michael A., jt. auth. see Mangham, Iain L.

Overkleeft, D. & Groosman, L. E., eds. The Dekker Perspective. (C). 1988. lib. bdg. 34.00 (*1-85333-108-2*, Pub. by Graham & Trotman UK) Kluwer Ac.

Overlach, Theodore W. Foreign Financial Control in China. Bruchey, Stuart & Bruchey, Eleanor, eds. LC 76-5027. (American Business Abroad Ser.). 1976. reprint ed. 30.95 (*0-405-09293-8*) Ayer.

Overlake School Staff. The Overlake School Cookbook. 3rd ed. Mickelson, Bonnie S., ed. LC 89-63118. (Illus.). 190p. 1984. 11.95 (*0-9612946-0-4*) Overlake Schl.

***Overland, Brian.** C in Plain English. LC 95-18697. 1995. pap. 19.95 (*1-55828-430-3*) H Holt & Co.

Overland, Carlton, jt. auth. see Cox, Richard.

Overland, Larry. Early Settlement of Lake Cushman. 2nd ed. (Illus.). 46p. (Orig.). 1981. reprint ed. pap. 3.75 (*0-935693-02-5*) Mason Cty Hist.

Overland, Orm, ed. & tr. Johan Schroder's Travels in Canada, 1863. (McGill-Queen's Studies in Ethnic History). (Illus.). 160p. (C). 1989. text ed. 39.95 (*0-7735-0718-3*, Pub. by McGill CN) U of Toronto Pr.

***Overlee, Vern.** The Great Beyond. 224p. 1995. 19.95 (*0-9645230-2-7*) Mora Pr.

— The Psychic. 204p. 1983. 11.95 (*0-9645230-1-9*) Mora Pr.

Overlie, George, illus. The Adventure of Black Peter & The 'Gloria Scott, Vol. I. (Match Wits with Sherlock Holmes Ser.). (J). (gr. 4-7). 1990. lib. bdg. 17.50 (*0-87614-385-0*, Carolrhoda) Lerner Group.

— The Adventure of the Cardboard Box & Scandal in Bohemia, Vol. II. (Match Wits with Sherlock Holmes Ser.). (J). (gr. 4-6). 1990. lib. bdg. 14.95 (*0-87614-386-9*, Carolrhoda) Lerner Group.

— The Adventure of the Copper Beeches & The Redheaded League, Vol. IV. (Match Wits with Sherlock Holmes Ser.). (J). (gr. 4-7). 1990. lib. bdg. 17.50 (*0-87614-388-5*, Carolrhoda) Lerner Group.

— The Adventure of the Dancing Men: The Three Garridebs. LC 92-21787. (Match Wits with Sherlock Holmes Ser.: Vol. 7). (J). 1993. pap. 4.95 (*0-87614-555-1*, Carolrhoda) Lerner Group.

— The Adventure of the Dancing Men: The Three Garridebs. LC 92-21787. (Match Wits with Sherlock Holmes Ser.: Vol. 7). (J). (gr. 4-7). 1993. lib. bdg. 17.50 (*0-87614-716-3*, Carolrhoda) Lerner Group.

— The Adventure of the Six Napoleons & the Blue Carbuncle, Vol. III. (Match Wits with Sherlock Holmes Ser.). (J). (gr. 4-7). 1990. lib. bdg. 17.50 (*0-87614-387-7*, Carolrhoda) Lerner Group.

— Match Wits with Sherlock Holmes, Vol. V: "The Adventure of the Speckled Bird" & "The Sussex Vampire" 64p. (J). (gr. 4-7). 1991. lib. bdg. 17.50 (*0-87614-665-5*, Carolrhoda) Lerner Group.

— Match Wits with Sherlock Holmes, Vol. VI: "The Adventure of Abbey Grange" & "The Boscombe Valley Mystery" 64p. (J). (gr. 4-7). 1991. lib. bdg. 17.50 (*0-87614-666-3*, Carolrhoda) Lerner Group.

Overlock, Leland. Windships of Warren, Maine, Seventeen Seventy to Eighteen Sixty-Seven. LC 88-90850. (Illus.). 306p. 1988. lib. bdg. 30.00 (*0-941216-42-X*); pap. 18.00 (*0-941216-41-1*) Cay-Bel.

Overlook Hospital Auxilary Staff. Cooking Is Our Bag. Lamberto, Charlanne & Morrow, Nancy, eds. (Illus.). 250p. 1980. 9.95 (*0-9604560-0-7*) Overlook Hosp.

Overly, Norman V., ed. Lifelong Learning: A Human Agenda. LC 78-78229. (Nineteen Seventy-Nine Yearbook). (Illus.). 200p. (Orig.). 1979. pap. text ed. 9.75 (*0-87120-093-7*, 610-79160) Assn Supervision.

Overman, Andrew, ed. see Sloyan, Gerard S.

Overman, E. Samuel, ed. see Campbell, Donald T.

Overman, E. Samuel, jt. auth. see Garson, G. David.

***Overman, J. Andrew.** Church & Community in Crisis: The Gospel According to Matthew. (New Testament in Context Ser.). 1995. pap. 24.00 (*1-56338-101-X*) TPI PA.

— Matthew's Gospel & Formative Judaism: The Social World of the Matthean Community. LC 90-43336. 176p. (Orig.). 1990. pap. 14.00 (*0-8006-2451-3*, 1-2451, Fortress Pr) Augsburg Fortress.

Overman, J. Andrew & MacLennan, Robert. Diaspora Jews & Judaism: Essays in Honor of & in Dialogue with A. Thomas Kraabel. (USF Studies in the History of Judaism). 388p. (C). 1992. 74.95 (*1-55540-696-3*, 240041) Scholars Pr GA.

Overman, Larry. Organic Syntheses, Vol. 71. 320p. 1993. text ed. 42.95 (*0-471-30531-6*) Wiley.

Overman, Marjorie. The Edge of Forever. (Illus.). 80p. (Orig.). pap. 8.95 (*0-9614853-0-2*) Overman Pub.

Overman, Marvin, jt. auth. see Henderson, R. Winn.

Overmars, M. H. The Design of Dynamic Data Structures. (Lecture Notes in Computer Science Ser.: Vol. 156). 181p. 1987. pap. 30.00 (*0-387-12330-X*) Spr-Verlag.

Overmeyer, Allen, jt. auth. see Shook, Hal.

Overmier, Bruce J., jt. auth. see Brush, Robert.

Overmier, J. Bruce & Burke, Patricia D., eds. Animal Models of Human Pathology: A Bibliography of a Quarter Century of Behavioral Research, 1967-1992. 336p. 1992. pap. 27.50 (*1-55798-184-1*) Am Psychol.

Overmier, Judith A. & Senior, John E. Books & Manuscripts of the Bakken. LC 92-8512. (Illus.). 525p. 1992. 79.50 (*0-8108-2570-8*) Scarecrow.

Overmyer, Daniel. The Religions of China. LC 85-42789. 128p. (Orig.). 1986. pap. text ed. 10.00 (*0-06-066401-0*) Harper SF.

Overmyer, Daniel L. Folk Buddhist Religion: Dissenting Sects in Late Traditional China. LC 75-23467. (Harvard East Asian Ser.: No. 83). 311p. reprint ed. pap. 88.70 (*0-317-55369-0*, 2029172) Bks Demand.

Overmyer, Daniel L., jt. auth. see Jordan, David K.

Overmyer, Eric. Eric Overmyer: Collected Plays. (Plays for Actors Ser.). 336p. 1993. 23.95 (*1-880399-40-7*); pap. 14.95 (*1-880399-33-4*) Smith & Kraus.

— Native Speech. 96p. 1984. pap. 4.95 (*0-88145-017-0*) Broadway Play.

— On the Verge. 76p. (Orig.). 1986. pap. 4.95 (*0-88145-046-4*) Broadway Play.

Overmyer, Grace. America's First Hamlet. LC 75-31964. (Illus.). 439p. 1976. reprint ed. text ed. 49.75 (*0-8371-8446-0*, OVAH, Greenwood Pr) Greenwood.

Overmyer, James. Effa Manley & the Newark Eagles. LC 93-5377. (American Sports History Ser.: No. 1). (Illus.). 324p. 1993. 29.50 (*0-8108-2703-4*) Scarecrow.

Overs, Susan R., ed. see Indiana Donors Alliance Staff.

Oversby, V. M. & Brown, P. W., eds. Scientific Basis for Nuclear Waste Management XIII: Materials Research Society Symposium Proceedings, Vol. 176. 1990. text ed. 55.00 (*1-55899-064-X*) Materials Res.

Overseas Development Council Staff & McLaughlin, Martin M. The United States & World Development: Agenda 1979. LC 78-71589. 348p. 1979. text ed. 59.95 (*0-275-90392-3*, C0392, Praeger Pubs) Greenwood.

Overshiner, Elwyn E. Course 095 to Eternity. 2nd ed. LC 80-82005. (Illus.). 256p. 1989. 10.95 (*0-936940-07-7*) Helm Pub.

Overson, David. Perspectives from the Passenger Seat. Jones, M. L., ed. 105p. (Orig.). (YA). 1993. pap. text ed. 6.95 (*1-882270-09-6*) Old Rugged Cross.

Overstone, Samuel J. Evidence Given by Lord Overstone on Bank Acts. LC 68-30538. (Library of Money & Banking History). 1973. reprint ed. 39.50 (*0-678-00955-4*) Kelley.

— Tracts & Other Publications on Metallic & Paper Currency: With Further Reflections on the State of the Currency (1837), 2 vols. in 1. LC 67-20089. (Library of Money & Banking History). 1972. reprint ed. 49.50 (*0-678-00902-3*) Kelley.

***Overstreet, Alfred T.** Are Men Born Sinners? The Myth of Original Sin. 275p. (Orig.). 1995. pap. 19.95 (*0-9644832-0-3*) Evangel Bks Pub.

Overstreet, Bonaro W. Signature: New & Selected Poems. 1978. pap. 3.95 (*0-393-04511-0*) Norton.

Overstreet, Bonaro W., jt. auth. see Overstreet, Harry A.

Overstreet, Charles W. Plains Indian & Mountain Man Arts & Crafts: An Illustrated Guide. Smith, Monte & Knight, Denise, eds. LC 93-74239. (Illus.). 160p. (Orig.). (YA). 1994. per. 13.95 (*0-943604-41-9*) Eagles View.

Overstreet, Daphne. Arizona Territory Cookbook. 1995. pap. 5.95 (*0-914846-75-2*) Golden West Pub.

— Unclaimed Money, Lost & Found: With Billions Waiting to Be Claimed, Chances Are Good Some Is Yours. LC 90-83754. 235p. (Orig.). 1991. pap. 10.95 (*0-9627416-0-4*) J Alexander Bks.

Overstreet, David F. Chesrow: A Paleoindian Complex in the Southern Lake Michigan Basin. (Case Studies in Great Lakes Archaeology). (Illus.). 183p. (C). 1993. pap. 15.00 (*1-881354-02-4*) Gt Lks Archaeol.

Overstreet, David F., et al. Archaeological Studies on the Southeast Wisconsin Uplands, Kenosha County. (Case Studies in Great Lakes Archaeology). 143p. (C). 1992. pap. 15.00 (*1-881354-00-8*) Gt Lks Archaeol.

Overstreet, George A., Jr. & Rubin, Geoffrey M. Blurred Vision: Challenges in Credit Union Research & Modeling. 45p. 1991. pap. 50.00 (*1-880572-00-1*) Filene Res.

Overstreet, Harry A. Guide to Civilized Leisure. LC 73-84357. (Essay Index Reprint Ser.). 1977. 20.95 (*0-8369-1151-2*) Ayer.

Overstreet, Harry A. & Overstreet, Bonaro W. Communism. 1958. 6.50 (*0-393-05277-X*) Norton.

— Iron Curtain. 1963. 4.50 (*0-393-05303-2*) Norton.

— Strange Tactics of Extremism. 1964. 5.95 (*0-393-05268-0*) Norton.

— Strange Tactics of Extremism. (C). 1965. pap. text ed. 4.95 (*0-393-09749-8*) Norton.

— War Called Peace: Khrushchev's Communism. 1961. 4.95 (*0-393-05286-9*) Norton.

Overstreet, Larry C. Morale in Health, Life & Work: Index of Modern Authors & Subjects with Guide for Rapid Research. LC 90-56276. 160p. 1991. 44.50 (*1-55914-334-7*); pap. 39.50 (*1-55914-335-5*) ABBE Pubs Assn.

— Morals & Issues: Index of Modern Information. rev. ed. 145p. 1994. 44.50 (*0-7883-0466-6*); pap. 39.50 (*0-7883-0467-4*) ABBE Pubs Assn.

***Overstreet, Lee.** Golden Sun - from the Journal of William Henry. 190p. (Orig.). 1995. pap. 7.95 (*0-7610-0052-6*) NW Pub.

Overstreet, Paul. Paul Overstreet - Heroes. Okun, Milton, ed. pap. 14.95 (*0-89524-626-0*) Cherry Lane.

— Paul Overstreet - Sowin' Love. Okun, Milton, ed. pap. 12.95 (*0-89524-485-3*) Cherry Lane.

Overstreet, Robert. The Overstreet Comic Price Guide. 24th ed. 1994. pap. 15.00 (*0-380-77854-8*) Avon.

Overstreet, Robert M. The Official Overstreet Comic Book Price Guide. 18th ed. (Illus.). 740p. pap. 12.95 (*0-685-07938-4*) Overstreet.

— The Official Overstreet Guide to Indian Arrowheads. 2nd ed. (Illus.). 768p. pap. 19.00 (*0-685-60183-8*) Overstreet.

— The Overstreet Comic Book Companion: Identification & Price Guide. 6th ed. (Confident Collector Ser.). (Illus.). 608p. 1992. mass mkt. 6.00 (*0-380-76911-5*, Confident Collect) Avon.

— The Overstreet Comic Book Price Guide. 22th ed. 544p. (Orig.). 1992. pap. 15.00 (*0-380-76912-3*, Confident Collect) Avon.

— The Overstreet Comic Book Price Guide. 23th ed. 760p. (Orig.). 1993. pap. 15.00 (*0-380-77220-5*, Confident Collect) Avon.

— The Overstreet Comic Book Price Guide. 25th ed. (Illus.). 816p. (Orig.). 1995. pap. 17.00 (*0-380-78210-3*, Confident Collect) Avon.

— The Overstreet Comics & Cards Price Guide. 464p. (Orig.). 1993. mass mkt. 6.00 (*0-380-77310-4*, Confident Collect) Avon.

— Overstreet Premium Ring Price Guide. (Illus.). 336p. 1994. pap. 14.95 (*0-930625-45-5*) Antique Trader.

Overstreet, Robert M. & Carter, Gary. The Overstreet Comic Book Grading Guide. 320p. (Orig.). 1992. pap. 12.00 (*0-380-76910-7*, Confident Collect) Avon.

Overstreet, Robert M. & Peake, Howard. The Overstreet Indian Arrowheads: Identification & Price Guide. 3rd ed. xvi, 784p. (Orig.). 1993. pap. 20.00 (*0-380-77186-1*, Confident Collect) Avon.

— The Overstreet Indian Arrowheads: Identification & Price Guide. 4th ed. (Illus.). 816p. (Orig.). 1995. pap. 20.00 (*0-380-78211-1*, Confident Collect) Avon.

Overstreet, Thomas R., Jr., jt. auth. see Ippolito, Pauline M.

***Overstreet, William C. & Blakely, Jeffrey A., eds.** Environmental Research in Support of Archaeological Investigations in the Yemen Arab Republic, 1982-1987. (Wadi Al-Jubah Archaeological Project Ser.: Vol. 5). Date not set. write for info. (*0-614-01752-1*, Am Foun Study) Eisenbrauns.

Overstreet, William C., et al, eds. Geological & Archaeological Reconnaissance in the Yemen Arab Republic. (Wadi al-Jubah Archaeological Project Ser.: Vol. 4). 1989. text ed. 55.00 (*0-685-46081-9*, Am Foun Study) Eisenbrauns.

Overton, Barbara, jt. auth. see Carroll, James.

Overton, Basil. Gems from Greek. 1991. 10.95 (*0-89137-125-7*); pap. 8.50 (*0-685-51733-0*) Quality Pubns.

— Highest Peak of Human Performance. 1990. pap. 6.25 (*0-89137-118-4*) Quality Pubns.

— Mule Musings. 1983. 7.95 (*0-89137-106-0*); pap. 5.50 (*0-89137-105-2*) Quality Pubns.

— When Christ Was Preached to Christ. 1983. pap. 6.95 (*0-89137-545-7*) Quality Pubns.

Overton, Charles E. Studies of Narcosis. Lipnick, Robert L., ed. xi, 203p. (C). 1990. 65.00 (*0-412-35240-0*) Wood Lib-Mus.

Overton, David. Common Market Digest: An Information Guide to the European Communities. LC 83-14172. (Illus.). 435p. reprint ed. pap. 124.00 (*0-7837-5294-6*, 2031557) Bks Demand.

An Asterisk (*) at the beginning of an entry indicates that the title is appearing in BIP for the first time.

Overton, Grant M. Authors of the Day: Studies in Contemporary Literature. LC 75-156700. (Essay Index Reprint Ser.). 1977. reprint ed. 28.95 (*0-8369-2289-1*) Ayer.

— Cargoes for Crusoes. LC 72-1316. (Essay Index Reprint Ser.). 1977. reprint ed. 30.95 (*0-8369-2851-2*) Ayer.

— When Winter Comes to Main Street. LC 72-37798. (Essay Index Reprint Ser.). 1977. reprint ed. 26.95 (*0-8369-2616-1*) Ayer.

— Why Authors Go Wrong, & Other Explanations. LC 68-22936. (Essay Index Reprint Ser.). 1977. 19.95 (*0-8369-0757-4*) Ayer.

— Women Who Make Our Novels. rev. ed. LC 67-23257. (Essay Index Reprint Ser.). 1977. 23.95 (*0-8369-0758-2*) Ayer.

Overton, Gwedolen. The Heritage of Unrest. LC 68-57544. 329p. reprint ed. lib. bdg. 27.00 (*0-8398-1454-2*) Irvington.

Overton, James B. Rolling Thunder: January, 1967-November, 1968. 53p. 1993. reprint ed. pap. 9.00 (*0-923135-71-5*) Dalley Bk Service.

Overton, Jane T. The Potter's Clay. LC 84-51432. 68p. 1984. 5.95 (*0-938232-52-5*) Winston-Derek.

Overton, Jenny. The Ship from Simnel Street. LC 85-21965. 224p. (J). (gr. 5 up). 1986. 10.25 (*0-688-06182-6*) Greenwillow.

Overton, John. Colonial Green Revolution? Food, Irrigation & the State in Colonial Malaya. 250p. 1994. 54.00x (*0-85198-912-8*) CAB Intl.

Overton, John H. & Relton, Frederic. English Church from the Accession of George First to the End of the Eighteenth Century, 1714-1800. (History of the English Church Ser.: No. 7). reprint ed. 62.50 (*0-404-50757-3*) AMS Pr.

Overton, John R., ed. see Ettinger, Karl E.

Overton, Meredith H. & Lukert, Barbara P. Clinical Nutrition: A Physiologic Approach. (Illus.). 1977. pap. 26.50 (*0-8151-5648-0*, Yr Bk Med Pubs) Mosby Yr Bk.

— Clinical Nutrition: A Physiologic Approach. LC 77-81527. (Illus.). 182p. reprint ed. pap. 51.90 (*0-8357-7626-3*, 2056949) Bks Demand.

***Overton, Mike & Shier, Amy, illus.** Coding Illustrated Eye Muscle & Adnexa. (Coding Illustrated Ser.). (Orig.). 1995. pap. 39.95 (*1-56337-142-1*) Medicode Pubns.

— Coding Illustrated The Breast. (Coding Illustrated Ser.). 133p. 1993. 39.95 (*1-56337-097-2*) Medicode Pubns.

Overton, Mike, jt. illus. see Shier, Amy.

Overton, Patrick, intro. Grassroots & Mountain Wings: The Arts in Rural & Small Communities. 135p. reprint ed. pap. write for info. (*0-9639060-1-1*) CC CC&CS.

Overton, Richard C. Perkins-Budd: Railway Statesmen of the Burlington. LC 81-6961. (Contributions in Economics & Economic History Ser.: No. 45.). (Illus.). xxiv, 271p. 1982. text ed. 59.95 (*0-313-23173-7*, OPB/, Greenwood Pr) Greenwood.

Overton, Ron. Hotel Me. 1994. pap. 10.00 (*1-882413-08-3*); boxed 18.00 (*1-882413-09-1*) Hanging Loose.

— Love on the Alexander Hamilton. 88p. 1985. pap. 6.00 (*0-914610-39-2*) Hanging Loose.

Overton, Ted. Sports after Fifty: Fit Yourself into Fun Sports. LC 88-70544. (Illus.). 224p. 1988. 17.95 (*0-913179-20-5*) Azimuth Pr.

Overton, Valerie, jt. auth. see Applegate, April.

Overton, W. F., ed. Reasoning, Necessity & Logic: Developmental Perspectives. (Jean Piaget Symposium Ser.). 344p. (C). 1990. text ed. 69.95 (*0-8058-0090-5*) L Erlbaum Assocs.

Overton, William C., Jr., jt. ed. see Weinstock, Harold.

Overton, Willis F., ed. The Relationship Between Social & Cognitive Development. (Jean Piaget Society Ser.). 272p. (C). 1983. text ed. 49.95 (*0-89859-249-6*) L Erlbaum Assocs.

Overton, Willis F. & Palermo, David S., eds. The Nature & Ontogenesis of Meaning. (Jean Piaget Symposia Ser.). 320p. 1994. text ed. 69.95 (*0-8058-1211-3*) L Erlbaum Assocs.

***Overton, Yvonne.** Romantic Applique. (Illus.). 96p. 1995. pap. 12.95 (*0-614-07136-4*, Pub. by S Milner AT); pap. 14.95 (*1-86351-140-7*, Pub. by S Milner AT) Sterling.

Overturf, Stephen F. The Economic Principles of European Integration. LC 86-21271. 196p. 1986. pap. text ed. 15. 95 (*0-275-92277-4*, B2277, Praeger Pubs) Greenwood.

— The Economic Principles of European Integration. LC 86-21271. 196p. 1986. text ed. 55.00 (*0-275-92276-6*, C2276, Praeger Pubs) Greenwood.

Overy, jt. ed. see Allen.

Overy, Angela. The Foliage Garden: Creating Beauty Beyond Bloom. LC 92-26930. (Illus.). 1993. 35.00 (*0-517-59173-1*, Harmony) Crown Pub Group.

O'Very, David P. Controlling the Atom in the Twenty-First Century. 397p. (C). 1993. text ed. 59.85 (*0-8133-8816-3*) Westview.

Overy, Paul. DeStijl. LC 90-72120. (World of Art Ser.). (Illus.). 216p. (Orig.). 1991. pap. 12.95 (*0-500-20240-0*) Thames Hudson.

Overy, R. J. The Air War, Nineteen Thirty-Nine to Nineteen Forty-Five. LC 80-6200. (Illus.). 288p. 1981. pap. 12.95 (*0-8128-6156-6*, Scrbrough Hse) Madison Bks UPA.

— The Inter-War Crisis, 1919-1939. LC 94-359. (Seminar Studies in History). (C). 1995. pap. text ed. 11.95 (*0-582-35379-3*, Pub. by Longman UK) Longman.

— War & Economy in the Third Reich. (Illus.). 420p. 1994. 55.00 (*0-19-820290-3*) OUP.

— War & Economy in the Third Reich. (Illus.). 410p. 1995. pap. 24.95 (*0-19-820599-6*) OUP.

Overy, Richard. The Road to War: Origins of World War II. 416p. 1990. 24.95 (*0-394-58260-8*) Random.

Overzee, Anne H. The Body Divine: The Symbol of the Body in the Works of Teilhard de Chardin & Ramanuja. (Studies in Religious Traditions: No. 2). 224p. (C). 1992. 64.95 (*0-521-38516-4*) Cambridge U Pr.

Ovesen, Ellis. Memories of South Dakota. Leih, Janet, ed. LC 93-60173. 60p. (Orig.). 1993. 14.00 (*1-877649-19-8*); 5.00 (*1-877649-18-X*) Tesseract SD.

Oviatt, Edwin. Beginnings of Yale, Seventeen Hundred One to Seventeen Twenty-Six. LC 70-89214. (American Education: Its Men, Institutions & Ideas, Ser. 1). 1978. reprint ed. 23.95 (*0-405-01453-8*) Ayer.

***Oviatt, Joan.** Amazing but True Mormon Stories. 144p. 1994. 10.98 (*0-88290-507-4*, 1050) Horizon Utah.

Oviatt, Mark D. & Miller, Richard K. Industrial Pneumatic Systems: Noise Control & Energy Conservation. 39.00 (*0-915586-19-3*) Fairmont Pr.

Ovid. Amores. Kenney, Edwin J., ed. Incl. Medicamina Faciei Femineae. 1961. (*0-318-54803-8*); Ars Amatoria. 1961. (*0-318-54804-6*); Remedia Amoria. 1961. (*0-318-54805-4*); (Oxford Classical Texts Ser.). 1961. 21. 00 (*0-19-814642-6*) OUP.

— Amores II. Booth, ed. (Classical Texts Ser.). 49.85 (*0-85668-174-1*, Pub. by Aris & Phillips UK); pap. 24.95 (*0-85668-175-X*, Pub. by Aris & Phillips UK) David Brown.

— Amores, Medicamina Faciei Femineae, Ars Amatoria, Remedia Amoris. 2nd ed. Kenney, E. J., ed. (Classical Texts). (Illus.). 280p. 1994. 17.50 (*0-19-814969-7*) OUP.

— Ars Amatoria, Bk. 1. (Illus.). 196p. 1989. reprint ed. pap. 24.95 (*0-19-814736-8*) OUP.

— The Art of Beauty - De Medicamine Faciei Femihae. limited ed. (Illus.). 18p. 1990. 350.00 (*0-923980-28-8*) Arundel Pr.

— The Art of Love. Humphries, Rolfe, tr. LC 57-7706. (Greek & Latin Classics Ser.). 208p. 1957. 25.00 (*0-253-10391-6*); pap. 7.95 (*0-253-20002-4*, MB-2) Ind U Pr.

— Art of Love & Other Poems. (Loeb Classical Library: No. 232). 396p. 1979. text ed. 18.95 (*0-674-99255-5*) HUP.

— A Choice of Ovid: Selections from Metamorphoses, Fasti & Tristia. Kennedy, E. C., ed. (College Classical Ser.). (LAT.). (C). 1984. pap. text ed. 16.00 (*0-89241-472-3*) Caratzas.

— De Arte Amatoria Libri Tres. Brandt, Paul, ed. xxiii, 255p. 1991. reprint ed. write for info. (*3-487-05033-1*, Pub. by Georg Olms GW) Lubrecht & Cramer.

— The Erotic Poems. Green, Peter, tr. 1983. pap. 9.95 (*0-14-044360-6*, Penguin Classics) Viking Penguin.

— Fasti. (Loeb Classical Library: No. 253). 494p. 1931. text ed. 18.95 (*0-674-99279-2*) HUP.

— Fastorum Libri Sex. Merkelio, R., ed. ccxciv, 320p. 1971. reprint ed. write for info. (*3-487-04087-5*, Pub. by Georg Olms GW) Lubrecht & Cramer.

— Fastorum Libri Sex, 5 vols., Set. Frazer, James G., tr. & comment by. xlii, 1855p. 1973. reprint ed. write for info. (*3-487-04612-1*, Pub. by Georg Olms GW) Lubrecht & Cramer.

— Heroides. 288p. 1990. pap. 8.95 (*0-14-042355-9*, Penguin Classics) Viking Penguin.

— Heroides: Select Epistles. Knox, Peter E., ed. (Cambridge Greek & Latin Classics Ser.). 328p. (C). 1995. pap. write for info. (*0-521-36834-0*) Cambridge U Pr.

— Heroides: Select Epistles. Knox, Peter E., ed. (Cambridge Greek & Latin Classics Ser.). 328p. (C). 1995. write for info. (*0-521-36279-2*) Cambridge U Pr.

— Heroides & Amores. (Loeb Classical Library: No. 41). 536p. 1977. text ed. 18.95 (*0-674-99045-5*) HUP.

— Love Poems. 1990. pap. 8.95 (*0-19-282194-6*) OUP.

— Metamorphosen, Bd. I, Buch 1-7. Haupt, Moritz et al, eds. viii, 502p. 1966. write for info. (*3-296-14811-6*, Pub. by Georg Olms GW) Lubrecht & Cramer.

— Metamorphosen, Bd. I, Buch 8-15. Haupt, Moritz et al, eds. viii, 559p. 1975. write for info. (*3-296-14812-4*, Pub. by Georg Olms GW) Lubrecht & Cramer.

— Metamorphoses. Humphries, Rolfe, tr. LC 55-6269. (Greek & Latin Classics Ser.). 416p. (C). 1955. 20.00 (*0-253-33755-0*); pap. 6.95 (*0-253-20001-6*, MB-1) Ind U Pr.

— Metamorphoses. Gregory, Horace, tr. 1960. pap. 5.99 (*0-451-62622-2*, Ment) NAL-Dutton.

— Metamorphoses. Melville, A. D., tr. (World's Classics Ser.). 528p. 1987. pap. 5.95 (*0-19-281691-8*) OUP.

— Metamorphoses. Innes, Mary, tr. (Classics Ser.). 1955. mass mkt. 7.95 (*0-14-044058-5*, Penguin Classics) Viking Penguin.

— Metamorphoses, Bk. VIII. Hollis, Adrian S., ed. 1984. reprint ed. pap. 26.00 (*0-19-814460-1*) OUP.

— Metamorphoses, Bks. 1-8. (Loeb Classical Library: No. 42-43). 484p. 1916. text ed. 18.95 (*0-674-99046-3*) HUP.

— Metamorphoses, Bks. 9-15. (Loeb Classical Library: No. 42-43). 510p. 1916. text ed. 18.95 (*0-674-99047-1*) HUP.

— Metamorphoses, Vol. I-IV. Hill, ed. (Classical Texts Ser.). 1985. 49.95 (*0-85668-256-X*, Pub. by Aris & Phillips UK); pap. 24.95 (*0-85668-257-8*, Pub. by Aris & Phillips UK) David Brown.

— Metamorphoses, Vol. V-VIII. Hill, ed. (Classical Texts Ser.). 1992. write for info. (*0-85668-394-9*, Pub. by Aris & Phillips UK); pap. write for info. (*0-85668-395-7*, Pub. by Aris & Phillips UK) David Brown.

— Ovid: The Art of Love & Remedies for Love. Shapiro, Jack, tr. LC 66-22893. (Orig.). 1967. pap. 6.95 (*0-685-02945-X*) Laurida.

— Ovid: The Art of Love & Remedies for Love. Shapiro, Jack, tr. (Orig.). 1967. pap. 6.95 (*0-934810-09-5*) Laurida.

— Ovid in Sicily. Mandelbaum, Allen, tr. & intro. by. (Illus.). 76p. 1987. 35.00 (*0-935296-64-6*) Sheep Meadow.

— Ovid's Art of Love, 3 Vols. Dryden, John et al, trs. LC 73-161789. (Augustan Translators Ser.). reprint ed. 49. 50 (*0-404-54127-5*) AMS Pr.

— Ovid's Metamorphoses in Fifteen Books. Dryden, Joan et al, trs. LC 70-158323. (Augustan Translators Ser.). reprint ed. 105.00 (*0-404-54128-3*) AMS Pr.

— P. Ovidi Nasonis Metamorphoseon: Ovid's Metamorphoses, 15 bks., Set. lib. bdg. write for info. (*0-318-50866-4*) Ayer.

— P. Ovidi Nasonis Metamorphoseon liber I. Lee, A. G., ed. LC 78-67140. 170p. reprint ed. pap. 48.50 (*0-317-27536-4*, 2024505) Bks Demand.

— The Poems of Exile. Green, Peter, tr. & intro. by. 560p. 1994. 10.95 (*0-14-044407-6*, Penguin Classics) Viking Penguin.

— Roman Holidays: Ovid's Fasti. Nagle, Betty R., tr. & notes by. LC 94-21660. Orig. Title: Fasti. (ENG.). 1995. 25.00 (*0-253-33967-7*); pap. 8.95 (*0-253-20933-1*) Ind U Pr.

— Sorrows of an Exile: Tristia. Melville, A. D., tr. LC 92-5682. (Illus.). 206p. (ENG & LAT.). 1992. 55.00 (*0-19-814792-9*, Old Oregon Bk Store) OUP.

— Sorrows of an Exile (Tristia) Melville, A. D., tr. (The World's Classics Ser.). (Illus.). 208p. 1995. pap. 10.95 (*0-19-282452-X*) OUP.

— Tristia, & Ex Ponto. (Loeb Classical Library: No. 151). 556p. 1931. text ed. 18.95 (*0-674-99167-2*) HUP.

— Tristia, Ibis, Ex Ponto, Halieutica, Fragmenta. Owen, S. G., ed. (Oxford Classical Texts Ser.). 1922. 23.00 (*0-19-814626-4*) OUP.

Ovide. L' Art de l'Aimer, Les Remedes a l'Amour, Les Produits de Beaute. (FRE.). 1974. pap. 10.95 (*0-7859-4024-3*) Fr & Eur.

Ovidius Naso, Publius. The XV Bookes Entytuled Metamorphosis. Golding, Arthur, tr. LC 77-7418. (English Experience Ser.: No. 881). 1977. reprint ed. lib. bdg. 40.00 (*90-221-0881-3*) Walter J Johnson.

Ovilo y Otero, Manuel. Manual De Biografia y De Bibliografia De los Escritores Espanoles Del Siglo, No. XIX. vii, 540p. 1976. reprint ed. write for info. (*3-487-05861-8*, Pub. by Georg Olms GW) Lubrecht & Cramer.

Oving, Maud & Joiner, Tricia. Hindeloopen: A Traditional Dutch Folk Painting, Vol. 1. (Illus.). 56p. 1986. pap. 10. 95 (*0-941284-34-4*) J Shaw Studio.

Ovington, J. D., ed. Temperate Broad-Leaved Evergreen Forests. (Ecosystems of the World Ser.: Vol. 10). 242p. 1984. 113.00 (*0-444-42091-6*, I-399-83) Elsevier.

Ovington, Mary W. The Awakening. LC 70-39096. (Black Heritage Library Collection). 1977. reprint ed. 15.95 (*0-8369-9034-X*) Ayer.

— Black & White Sat Down Together: Reminiscences of an NAACP Founder. Luker, Ralph E., ed. 200p. 1995. 19. 95 (*1-55861-099-5*) Feminist Pr.

— Half a Man: The Status of the Negro in New York. LC 79-84692. 236p. 1970. reprint ed. text ed. 45.00 (*0-8371-1263-X*, OVH&, Negro U Pr) Greenwood.

— Hazel. LC 72-4639. (Black Heritage Library Collection). (Illus.). 1977. reprint ed. 23.95 (*0-8369-9117-6*) Ayer.

— The Shadow. LC 72-4736. (Black Heritage Library Collection). 1977. reprint ed. 31.95 (*0-8369-9118-4*) Ayer.

— Walls Came Tumbling Down. LC 69-18543. (American Negro: His History & Literature, Ser. No. 2). 1969. reprint ed. 29.95 (*0-405-01884-3*) Ayer.

***Ovington, Ray.** Birds of Prey in Florida. 2nd ed. 1995. pap. 3.95 (*0-8200-0908-3*) Great Outdoors.

— Commonsense Fly Fishing. LC 82-17029. (Illus.). 192p. 1983. pap. 10.95 (*0-8117-2167-1*) Stackpole.

— How to Take Trout on Wet Flies & Nymphs. 1974. 9.95 (*0-88395-020-0*) Freshet Pr.

— Pelican. LC 76-3763. (Illus.). 1977. pap. 2.95 (*0-8200-0905-9*) Great Outdoors.

— Tactics on Trout. (Illus.). 135p. 1983. pap. 14.95 (*0-684-17861-3*, Scribners) S&S Trade.

Ovitt, George, Jr. The Restoration of Perfection: Labor & Technology in Medieval Culture. 276p. 1987. text ed. 40.00 (*0-8135-1235-2*) Rutgers U Pr.

***Ovnick, Merry.** Los Angeles: The End of the Rainbow. LC 94-7219. (Illus.). 384p. (Orig.). 1994. pap. 34.95 (*0-9643119-0-9*) Balcony Pr.

***Ovretvelt, John.** Measuring Service Quality: Practical Guidelines. (C). 1994. 150.00x (*0-946655-75-8*, Pub. by S Thornes Pubs UK) St Mut.

Ovsenbury, M. Descendants of Thomas Carhart. (Illus.). 142p. 1989. reprint ed. lib. bdg. 35.00 (*0-8328-1310-9*); reprint ed. pap. 25.00 (*0-8328-1311-7*) Higginson Bk Co.

Ovshinsky, Stanford R. Disordered Materials: Science & Technology. (Institute for Amorphous Studies Ser.). (Illus.). 336p. 1991. 79.50 (*0-306-43385-0*, Plenum Pr) Plenum.

Ovsianikov, Yuri. Invitation to Russia. LC 89-61939. (Illus.). 192p. 1990. 37.50 (*0-8478-1160-3*) Rizzoli Intl.

Ovsiannikov, L. V. Group Analysis by Differential Equations. Ames, William F., tr. 1982. text ed. 121.00 (*0-12-531680-1*) Acad Pr.

Ovsienko, D. E. Growth & Imperfections of Metallic Crystals. LC 68-13058. (Illus.). 278p. reprint ed. pap. 79. 30 (*0-317-09379-7*, 2020677) Bks Demand.

Ovsiyenko, Y. G. Russian for Beginners. 448p. (C). 1992. 17. 95 (*0-8285-4999-0*) Firebird NY.

Ovsychuk, Volodimir, jt. auth. see Ripko, Olena.

***Ovunc, B. A., et al, eds.** Structural Dynamics & Vibration: The Energy & Environmental Expo '95 - The Energy-Sources Technology Conference & Exhibition, Houston, Texas - January 29-February 1, 1995. (PD Ser.: Vol. 70). 252p. 1995. 94.00 (*0-7918-1293-6*, H00925) ASME.

— Structural Dynamics & Vibration 1994, Vol. 63. LC 93-74684. 168p. 1994. pap. 42.50 (*0-7918-1191-3*) ASME.

***Ow, Francis M.** Origami Hearts. (Illus.). 112p. (Orig.). 1996. pap. 15.00 (*0-87040-957-3*) Japan Pubns USA.

***Ow-Taylor, Chwee-Huay.** Sales Success in Asia: Dealing with Customers in Singapore. 150p. 1995. pap. 19.95 (*1-884015-66-2*) St Lucie Pr.

Owa, S., jt. auth. see Srivastava, H. M.

Owago, Naohiro, jt. ed. see Ermisch, John F.

Owaida, Mohammad T. Glimpses of Islam. Obaba, Al I., ed. 49p. (Orig.). 1977. pap. text ed. 1.50 (*0-916157-70-9*) African Islam Miss Pubns.

Owan-McMenamin, Jan, jt. auth. see Spaude, Pam.

Oweida, A. M. The New Medical-Pharmaceutical Dictionary. 2404p. (ARA & ENG.). 1970. 150.00 (*0-8288-6550-7*, M-9766) Fr & Eur.

Oweiss, Ibrahim, jt. auth. see Al-Qazzaz, Ayad.

Oweiss, Ibrahim M., ed. The Political Economy of Contemporary Egypt. 330p. (Orig.). 1990. text ed. 34.95 (*0-932568-20-3*); pap. text ed. 16.95 (*0-932568-21-1*) GU Ctr CAS.

Oweiss, Ibrahim M., jt. ed. see Atiyeh, George N.

***Owen.** Actor's Scenebook: Scenes for Beginning Actors to Create. 1994. pap. text ed. (*0-8230-4951-5*) Watsn-Guptill.

— Beating Your Competition Through Quality. 144p. 1989. 39.75 (*0-8247-8065-5*) Dekker.

— Stages of Acting. 1994. pap. text ed. (*0-8230-4952-3*) Watsn-Guptill.

Owen & Donohoe. Clinical Atlas of Auditory Evoked Potentials. 1987. text ed. 66.00 (*0-8089-1896-6*, Grune) Saunders.

Owen, jt. auth. see Odeh.

Owen, jt. auth. see Oden.

Owen, A. E. Flexible Assembly Systems: Assembly by Robots & Computerized Integrated Systems. LC 84-4852. 242p. 1984. 75.00 (*0-306-41527-5*, Plenum Pr) Plenum.

Owen, A. J., tr. see De Aldama, A. M.

Owen, A. L. Conservation under FDR. LC 83-3966. 288p. 1983. text ed. 49.95 (*0-275-91055-5*, C1055, Praeger Pubs) Greenwood.

— The Famous Druids: A Survey of Three Centuries of English Literature in the Druids. LC 78-13614. (Illus.). 264p. 1979. reprint ed. text ed. 35.00 (*0-313-20629-5*, OWFD, Greenwood Pr) Greenwood.

Owen, A. S. Euripides: Ion. 240p. 1987. reprint ed. 21.95 (*0-86292-039-6*, Pub. by Brstl Class Pr UK) Focus Info Gr.

Owen, Albert K. Integral Cooperation: Its Practical Application. LC 74-32103. (American Utopian Adventure Ser.). (Illus.). 208p. 1975. reprint ed. lib. bdg. 35.00 (*0-87991-019-4*) Porcupine Pr.

Owen, Aloysius, tr. see Alessio, Luis & Munoz, Hector.

Owen, Aloysius, tr. see Bojorge, Horacio.

Owen, Aloysius, tr. see Philipon, M. M.

Owen, Alun. A Hard Day's Night: A Screen Adaptation from an Original Screenplay, Directed by Richard Lester. Garrett, George P. et al, eds. LC 71-135273. (Film Scripts Ser.). pap. text ed. 19.95 (*0-89197-782-1*) Irvington.

Owen, Amy E., ed. see LaVigne, Michelle.

Owen, Anita Y. & Frankle, Reva T. Nutrition in the Community: The Art of Delivering Services. 3rd ed. LC 92-30864. 567p. 1992. 46.95 (*0-8016-6637-6*) Mosby Yr Bk.

Owen, Anna. Pocket Guide to Critical Care Monitoring. 206p. 1992. spiral bd. 19.95 (*0-8016-3728-7*) Mosby Yr Bk.

Owen, Annie. Goodnight Bear! LC 93-79577. (Animal Friends Board Bks.). (Illus.). 14p. (J). (ps). 1994. bds. 4.95 (*1-85697-945-8*, Kingfisher LKC) LKC.

— Hungry Panda. LC 93-79580. (Animal Friends Board Bks.). (Illus.). 14p. (J). (ps). 1994. bds. 4.95 (*1-85697-946-6*, Kingfisher LKC) LKC.

— Playtime Duck. LC 93-79579. (Animal Friends Board Bks.). (Illus.). 14p. (J). (ps). 1994. bds. 4.95 (*1-85697-947-4*, Kingfisher LKC) LKC.

— Pumpkins & Pajamas: A Calendar of Words & Pictures. LC 95-10535. (Illus.). (J). 1995. lib. bdg. write for info. (*1-56294-086-4*) Millbrook Pr.

— Wake up Frog! LC 93-79578. (Animal Friends Board Bks.). (Illus.). 14p. (J). (ps). 1994. bds. 4.95 (*1-85697-948-2*, Kingfisher LKC) LKC.

Owen, Anthony D. Economics of Uranium. LC 85-3583. 240p. 1985. text ed. 59.95 (*0-275-90151-3*, C0151, Praeger Pubs) Greenwood.

Owen, Ashford, pseud. A Lost Love. LC 79-8188. reprint ed. 44.50 (*0-404-62092-2*) AMS Pr.

Owen, Barbara. By Myself But Not Alone: A Prayer Journal for Divorced Moms. LC 93-42901. 1994. pap. 10.00 (*0-8170-1201-X*) Judson.

— God Hears Me. LC 94-71288. (J). (ps-3). 1994. pap. 4.99 (*0-8066-2696-8*, 9-2696, Augsburg) Augsburg Fortress.

— Look, I'm Cooking! Simple Recipes for Preschoolers. Gross, Karen, ed. 64p. (Orig.). (J). (ps). 1993. pap. text ed. 5.95 (*1-56309-079-1*, New Hope) Womans Mission Union.

Owen, Barbara, comp. Charles Brenton Fisk: Organ Builder, Vol. II: His Work. 198p. 1986. write for info. (*0-9616755-2-7*) Westfield Ctr.

Owen, Barbara, intro. The American Musical Directory. LC 80-16490. (Music Reprint Ser.). (Illus.). 260p. 1980. reprint ed. lib. bdg. 35.00 (*0-306-76037-1*) Da Capo.

Owen, Barbara, jt. auth. see Williams, Peter.

Owen, Barbara A. The Reproduction of Social Control: A Study of Prison Workers at San Quentin. LC 87-36113. 168p. 1988. text ed. 49.95 (*0-275-92818-7*, C2818, Praeger Pubs) Greenwood.

Owen, Ben. With Popski's Private Army. 1993. 21.95 (*1-85756-037-X*, Pub. by Janus Pub UK) Intl Spec Bk.

Owen, Betty. Typing for Beginners. rev. ed. (Practical Handbook Ser.). 80p. 1985. pap. 7.95 (*0-399-51147-4*, Perigree Bks) Berkley Pub.

O

Owen, Bishop. Exploring Forth. 178p. 1985. 10.95 (0-13-296534-8) P-H.
Owen, Bob, ed. see Waldman, David.
Owen, Bobbi. Costume Design on Broadway: Designers & Their Credits, 1915-1985. LC 87-7515. (Bibliographies & Indexes in the Performing Arts Ser.: No. 5). (Illus.). 269p. 1987. text ed. 79.50 (0-313-25524-5, OCD/, Greenwood Pr) Greenwood.
— Lighting Design on Broadway: Designers & Their Credits, 1915-1990. LC 91-24007. (Bibliographies & Indexes in the Performing Arts Ser.: No. 11). 176p. 1991. text ed. 45.00 (0-313-26533-X, OLD, Greenwood Pr) Greenwood.
— Scenic Design on Broadway: Designers & Their Credits, 1915-1990. LC 91-25254. (Bibliographies & Indexes in the Performing Arts Ser.: No. 10). 320p. 1991. text ed. 65.00 (0-313-26534-8, OSN, Greenwood Pr) Greenwood.
Owen, Brooks. How to Make PVC Furniture for Profits. (Illus.). 151p. (Orig.). 1994. pap. text ed. 19.00 (0-939349-00-0) Owen Pub.
Owen, Bruce M. & Wildman, Steven S. Video Economics. (Illus.). 364p. (C). 1992. 39.95 (0-674-93716-3) HUP.
Owen, Bruce M., jt. auth. see Frankena, Mark W.
Owen, Bruce M., jt. auth. see Noll, Roger G.
***Owen, Bruce M., et al.** The Economics of a Disaster: The Exxon Valdez Oil Spill. LC 95-3782. 1995. text ed. write for info. (0-89930-987-9, Quorum Bks) Greenwood.
Owen, Bryn, et al. Achieving ISO Registration. 416p. 1994. text ed. 75.00 (0-945320-41-8) SPC Pr.
Owen, C. James & Willburn, York. Governing Metropolitan Indianapolis: The Politics of Unigov. LC 85-2776. 239p. 1985. 19.95 (0-87772-348-6) UCB IGS.
Owen, Carole. Bellefontaine: A Historical Narrative. (Illus.). 70p. (Orig.). 1989. pap. write for info. (0-9624102-1-7) Canyon Ranch.
— Bellefontaine: An Historical Narrative. (Illus.). 120p. (Orig.). 1989. 14.95 (0-685-28881-1) Canyon Ranch.
Owen, Charles A., Jr. Biochemical Aspects of Copper: Copper Proteins, Ceruloplasmin, & Copper Protein Binding. LC 81-18988. (Copper in Biology & Medicine Ser.). 205p. 1982. 28.00 (0-8155-0891-3) Noyes.
— Biological Aspects of Copper: Occurrence, Assay & Interrelationships. LC 82-7931. (Copper in Biology & Medicine Ser.). 156p. 1983. 28.00 (0-8155-0918-9) Noyes.
— Copper Deficiency & Toxicity: Acquired & Inherited, in Plants, Animals, & Man. LC 81-11061. (Copper in Biology & Medicine Ser.). 189p. 1982. 28.00 (0-8155-0868-9) Noyes.
— The Manuscripts of the Canterbury Tales. (Chaucer Studies: No. XVI). 160p. (C). 1991. text ed. 71.00 (0-85991-334-1) Boydell & Brewer.
— Physiological Aspects of Copper: Copper in Organs & Systems. LC 82-3421. (Copper in Biology & Medicine Ser.). 286p. 1982. 28.00 (0-8155-0904-9) Noyes.
— Wilson's Disease. LC 81-16805. (Copper in Biology & Medicine Ser.). 215p. 1982. 28.00 (0-8155-0879-4) Noyes.
Owen, Charles A., ed. Discussions of the Canterbury Tales. LC 77-20278. (Illus.). 110p. 1978. reprint ed. text ed. 35.00 (0-313-20012-2, OWDC, Greenwood Pr) Greenwood.
Owen, Cheryl. Art of Paper Crafts. 1994. 14.98 (0-8317-0435-7) Smithmark.
— Dough Folk Art: How to Make Beautiful & Lasting Objects from Flour, Salt & Water. LC 94-48296. (Illus.). 160p. 1995. 24.95 (0-8069-0850-5) Sterling.
— My Naturecrafts Book. LC 92-10187. (Illus.). (J). 1993. 14.95 (0-316-67715-9) Little.
— Step By Step Art of Floral Paper Crafts. 1994. 12.98 (0-7858-0073-5) Bk Sales Inc.
— Step By Step Art of Making Soft Toys. 1994. 14.98 (0-7858-0075-1) Bk Sales Inc.
— Step by Step Art of Papercrafts. 1993. 12.98 (1-55521-884-9) Bk Sales Inc.
***Owen, Cheryl & Elliot, Marion.** My Party Book. (Illus.). (J). (gr. 2-6). 1995. 14.95 (0-316-77114-7) Little.
Owen, D., ed. Green Reporting: Accountancy & the Challenge of the 90s. 256p. 1991. 75.00 (0-412-40130-4, A5789) Chapman & Hall.
Owen, D. B., jt. auth. see Odeh, Robert E.
Owen, D. D. Eleanor of Aquitaine: Queen & Legend. LC 92-28890. 224p. 1993. 21.95 (0-631-17072-3) Blackwell Pubs.
Owen, D. D., intro. The Song of Roland. (Illus.). 160p. (C). 1990. 28.00 (0-85115-537-5) Boydell & Brewer.
Owen, D. D., ed. see De Troyes, Chretien.
Owen, D. D., tr. see Le Clerc, Guillaume.
Owen, D. D. R., jt. ed. see Monks, Peter R.
Owen, D. Huw, ed. Settlement & Society in Wales. (Illus.). 315p. (C). 1989. text ed. 61.25 (0-7083-0985-2, Pub. by U of Wales UK) Bks Intl VA.
Owen, D. I. & Morrison, M. A., eds. Studies on the Civilization & Culture of Nuzi & the Hurrians, Vol. 2: General Studies & Excavations at Nuzi 9-1. LC 81-15123. (Illus.). ix, 723p. 1987. text ed. 65.00 (0-931464-37-4) Eisenbrauns.
Owen, D. I., jt. ed. see Morrison, M. A.
Owen, D. R. A First Course in the Mathematical Foundations of Thermodynamics. (Undergraduate Texts in Mathematics Ser.). (Illus.). 190p. 1983. 45.00 (0-387-90897-8) Spr-Verlag.
Owen, D. R., jt. auth. see Hinton, E.
Owen, D. R., jt. ed. see Wilshire, B.
Owen, D. W., jt. auth. see Green, A. E.
Owen, Dan R. That You May Believe. 1993. pap. 7.50 (0-89137-337-3) Quality Pubns.
Owen, David. Alfa Romeo: Ninety Years of Success on Road & Track. (Illus.). 160p. 1993. 39.95 (1-85260-446-8, Pub. by J H Haynes & Co UK) Motorbooks Intl.
— The Complete Home Video Director: Produce Better Videos Immediately. (Illus.). 192p. (Orig.). 1994. pap. 14.95 (0-572-01784-7, Pub. by W Foulsham UK) Trans-Atl Phila.
— The Complete Wedding Video Organiser. 192p. (Orig.). 1993. pap. 19.95 (0-572-01817-7, Pub. by W Foulsham UK) Trans-Atl Phila.
— Face the Future. LC 81-83484. 352p. 1981. text ed. 59.95 (0-275-91700-2, C1700, Praeger Pubs) Greenwood.
— Facilities Planning & Relocation, 2 vols., Set. 1993. 99.95 (0-87629-281-3, 67301) R S Means.
— The Government of Victorian London, 1855-1889: The Metropolitan Board of Works, the Vestries, & the City Corporation. LC 81-7173. (Illus.). 480p. 1990. 39.95 (0-674-35885-6) Belknap Pr.
— JVC Make Your Home Video More Professional. 144p. 1995. 17.95 (0-572-01151-2, Pub. by Foulsham UK) Atrium Pubs.
— Make Better Home Videos. 192p. (Orig.). 1993. pap. 12.95 (0-572-01933-5, Pub. by W Foulsham UK) Trans-Atl Phila.
— Maturity & Modernity: Nietzsche, Weber, Foucault, & the Ambivalence of Reason. LC 93-38534. 1994. 65.00 (0-415-05398-6) Routledge.
— My Usual Game: Adventures in Golf. 1995. 23.00 (0-679-41487-8, Villard Bks) Random.
— The Walls Around Us: The Thinking Person's Guide to How a House Works. LC 91-50064. 308p. 1991. 20.50 (0-394-57824-4, Villard Bks) Random.
— The Walls Around Us: The Thinking Person's Guide to How a House Works. LC 92-50070. 1992. pap. 12.00 (0-679-74144-5, Vin) Random.
Owen, David, jt. auth. see Cummins, Robert.
Owen, David, jt. auth. see Green, Anne.
Owen, David, et al. Democracy Must Work: A Trilateral Agenda for the Decade. (Triangle Papers). 1984. 6.00 (0-685-70506-4) Trilateral Comm.
Owen, David A. & Kelly, James K. Atlas of Gastrointestinal Pathology. LC 94-989. 1994. text ed. 185.00 (0-7216-6730-9) Saunders.
Owen, David I. Neo-Sumerian Archival Texts Primarily from Nippur in the University Museum, the Oriental Institute & the Iraq Museum. LC 82-1358. (Illus.). xiii, 85p. 1982. text ed. 40.00 (0-931464-09-9) Eisenbrauns.
Owen, David I. & Lacheman, E. R., eds. General Studies & Excavations at Nuzi, Vol. 9, Pt. 3. (Studies on the Civilization & Culture of Nuzi & the Hurrians: Bk. 5). xii, 420p. 1995. text ed. 65.00 (0-931464-67-6) Eisenbrauns.
***Owen, David I. & Wilhelm, Gernot, eds.** Edith Porada Memorial Volume. LC 95-35. (Studies on the Civilization & Culture of Nuzi & the Hurrians: Vol. 7). x, 159p. (C). 1995. 50.00 (1-883053-07-2) CDL Pr.
Owen, David I., ed. see Rabinowitz, Isaac.
Owen, David I., jt. auth. see Stone, Elizabeth C.
Owen, David M. Something of a Saint. 1991. pap. 5.95 (0-687-86239-6) Abingdon.
***Owen, David R. & Tolley, Michael C.** Courts of Admiralty in Colonial America: The Maryland Experience, 1634-1776. LC 95-68702. (Illus.). 446p. (C). 1995. 45.00 (0-89089-856-1) Carolina Acad Pr.
Owen, Dean. The Gunpointer. large type ed. (Linford Western Library). 302p. 1989. pap. 11.95 (0-7089-6674-8, Linford) Ulverscroft.
— Guns of Spring. 1993. 14.95 (0-7451-4559-0, Gunsmoke) Chivers N Amer.
— Guns of Spring. large type ed. (Linford Western Library). 1989. pap. 11.95 (0-7089-6771-X, Trailtree Bookshop) Ulverscroft.
— A Killer's Bargain. 1993. 14.95 (0-7451-4576-0, Gunsmoke) Chivers N Amer.
— A Killer's Bargain. large type ed. (Linford Western Library). 1989. pap. 11.95 (0-7089-6681-0, Trailtree Bookshop) Ulverscroft.
— Last-Chance Range. large type ed. (Linford Western Library). 1989. pap. 11.95 (0-7089-6723-X, Linford) Ulverscroft.
— The Outlaws. 1992. 13.95 (0-7451-4527-2, Gunsmoke) Chivers N Amer.
Owen, Denis. Camouflage & Mimicry. LC 82-2566. (Phoenix Ser.). (Illus.). 160p. (C). 1982. pap. text ed. 12.50 (0-226-64188-0) U Ch Pr.
— What Is Ecology? 2nd ed. (Illus.). 1980. pap. 14.95 (0-19-289140-5) OUP.
Owen, Denis F. Animal Ecology in Tropical Africa. 2nd ed. LC 75-46586. (Tropical Ecology Ser.). (Illus.). 140p. reprint ed. pap. 39.90 (0-8357-6016-2, 2034502) Bks Demand.
Owen, Diana. Media Messages in American Presidential Elections. LC 90-43384. (Contributions to the Study of Mass Media & Communications Ser.: No. 25). 216p. 1991. text ed. 49.95 (0-313-26362-0, OMD/, Greenwood Pr) Greenwood.
Owen, Dolores B. Abstracts & Indexes in Science & Technology: A Descriptive Guide. 2nd ed. LC 84-10902. 252p. 1984. 22.50 (0-8108-1712-8) Scarecrow.
— Directory of Associations in Louisiana. 303p. 1991. spiral bd. 22.50 (0-9630719-0-4) Owen Hse.
— Guide to Genealogical Resources in the British Isles. LC 88-22574. (Illus.). 409p. 1989. 39.50 (0-8108-2153-2) Scarecrow.
Owen, Donald B., ed. On the History of Statistics & Probability. (Statistics: Vol. 17). 484p. 1976. 115.00 (0-8247-6390-4) Dekker.
— The Search for Oil: Some Statistical Methods & Techniques. LC 75-25162. (Statistics, Textbooks & Monographs: No. 13). (Illus.). 208p. reprint ed. pap. 59.30 (0-7837-0975-7, 2041281) Bks Demand.
Owen, Donald B., jt. auth. see Lieberman, Gerald J.
Owen, Dorian. Money, Wealth & Expenditure: Integrated Modelling of Consumption & Portfolio Behaviour. (Illus.). 200p. 1986. 59.95 (0-521-26761-7) Cambridge U Pr.
Owen, Dorothy, ed. A History of Lincoln Minster. (Illus.). 300p. (C). 1994. 69.95 (0-521-25429-9) Cambridge U Pr.
Owen, Dwayne G., jt. auth. see Ruhl, Roland A.
Owen, E., jt. auth. see Sundstol, F.
Owen, E. D. Degradation & Stabilisation of PVC. (Illus.). 314p. 1984. 90.00 (0-85334-265-2, I-219-84, Pub. by Elsevier Applied Sci UK) Elsevier.
Owen, E. T. The Story of the Iliad. Betts, John H., ed. 248p. (C). 1989. reprint ed. pap. 14.00 (0-86516-235-2) Bolchazy-Carducci.
Owen, Ed. Playing & Coaching Wheelchair Basketball. LC 81-10456. (Illus.). 320p. 1982. pap. 18.95 (0-252-00867-7) U of Ill Pr.
Owen, Eileen, ed. see Steves, Rick.
Owen, Eleanor. Connections. rev. ed. 250p. (C). 1989. pap. text ed. 18.00 (0-926980-00-9) WA Advocates.
— Connections: A Self-Help & Resource Guide for the Mentally Ill, Their Families, & Social Service Professionals. rev. ed. Fallow, Jean, ed. 198p. reprint ed. 9.25 (0-317-93431-7) WA Advocates.
Owen, Elias. Welsh Folk-Lore: A Collection of Folk-Tales & Legends of North Wales. 1977. reprint ed. 29.00 (0-7158-1179-7) Charles River Bks.
Owen, F., ed. The Molecular Biology of Neuropsychiatric Disease. (Molecular & Cell Biology of Human Diseases Ser.). (Illus.). 220p. 1993. text ed. 79.95 (0-412-47800-5) Chapman & Hall.
Owen, Felicity & Brown, David. Sir George Beaumont: A Collector of Genius. LC 87-26114. 248p. (C). 1988. text ed. 45.00 (0-300-04183-7) Yale U Pr.
Owen, Felicity, et al. Noble & Patriotic: The Beaumont Gift, 1828. (Illus.). 64p. 1988. pap. 14.95 (0-295-96898-2) U of Wash Pr.
Owen, Frank. Campaign in Burma. 192p. (C). 1989. 60.00 (81-7002-052-2, Pub. by Himalayan Bks II) St Mut.
— The Purple Sea: More Splashes of Chinese Color. Reginald, R. & Melville, Douglas, eds. LC 77-84262. (Lost Race & Adult Fantasy Ser.). 1978. reprint ed. lib. bdg. 19.95 (0-405-11003-0) Ayer.
— The Wind That Tramps the World: Splashes of Chinese Color, Vol. 1. LC 72-4426. (Short Story Index Reprint Ser.). 1977. reprint ed. 18.95 (0-8369-4186-1) Ayer.
Owen, Frank & Jones, Ron. Statistics. 4th ed. 512p. (Orig.). 1994. pap. 47.50 (0-273-60320-5, Pub. by Pitman Pub Ltd UK) Trans-Atl Phila.
Owen, G., jt. ed. see Grofman, B.
Owen, G. Dyfnallt. Wales in the Reign of James I. (Royal Historical Society: Studies in History: No. 53). 1988. 63.00 (0-86193-210-2) Boydell & Brewer.
Owen, G. Dyfnallt, ed. Manuscripts of the Marquess of Salisbury, Addenda 1562-1605. (Reports & Calendars, Series 9: Vol. 23). 294p. 1973. 7.00 (0-11-440042-3, HM00423, Pub. by HMSO UK) UNIPUB.
Owen, G. Dynfallt, ed. Manuscripts of the Marquess of Bath: Talbot, Dudley & Devereux Papers, 1533-1659. (Reports & Calendars, Series 58: Vol. 5). 376p. 1980. 19.00 (0-11-440092-X, HM092X, Pub. by HMSO UK) UNIPUB.
— Manuscripts of the Marquess of Salisbury, Addenda 1605-1668. (Reports & Calendars, Series 9: Vol. 24). 417p. 1976. 19.00 (0-11-440062-8, HM00628, Pub. by HMSO UK) UNIPUB.
— Manuscripts of the Marquess of Salisbury, 1612-1668. (Reports & Calendars, Series 9: Vol. 22). 607p. 1971. 12.00 (0-11-440019-9, HM00199, Pub. by HMSO UK) UNIPUB.
Owen, G. Dynnfallt, ed. Manuscripts of the Marquess of Downshire, Papers of William Trumbull the Elder, September 1614 - August 1616. (Reports & Calendars, Series 75: Vol. 5). 682p. 1988. 115.00 (0-11-440217-5, HM2175, Pub. by HMSO UK) UNIPUB.
Owen, G. Dynnfallt & Anderson, Sonia P., eds. Manuscripts of the Marquess of Downshire, Papers of William Trumbull the Elder, September 1616 - December 1618. (Reports & Calendars, Series 75: Vol. 6). 1994. 230.00 (0-11-440230-2, HM402302, Pub. by HMSO UK) UNIPUB.
Owen, G. E. Logic, Science, & Dialectic: Collected Papers in Greek Philosophy. LC 85-17479. 394p. 52.50 (0-8014-9359-5); pap. 22.95 (0-685-67649-8) Cornell U Pr.
Owen, G. Frederick. Abraham Lincoln: The Man & His Faith. 232p. 1981. pap. 9.99 (0-8423-0000-7) Tyndale.
Owen, Gareth. Accounting for Hospitality, Tourism & Leisure. 352p. (Orig.). 1994. pap. 49.50 (0-273-60263-2, Pub. by Pitman Pub Ltd UK) Trans-Atl Phila.
Owen, George E. Fundamentals of Scientific Mathematics. LC 61-12287. 286p. reprint ed. pap. 81.60 (0-317-20656-7, 2024140) Bks Demand.
— The Universe of the Mind. LC 76-125674. (Seminars in the History of Ideas Ser.: No. 4). (Illus.). 368p. 1971. 54.00x (0-8018-1131-7); pap. 14.95 (0-8018-1179-1) Johns Hopkins.
Owen, Goodwin & Bickersteth, Warfield. Classics on the Trinity. abr. rev. ed. Green, Jay P., Sr., ed. (Fifty Greatest Christian Classics Ser.). 672p. 1991. 29.95 (1-878442-61-9) Sovereign Grace Trust Fund.
Owen, Grace M. Health Visiting. 2nd ed. 352p. 1983. pap. text ed. 21.95 (0-7020-0981-4, Bailliere-Tindall) Saunders.
Owen, Guillermo. Game Theory. 2nd ed. 1982. text ed. 66.00 (0-12-531150-8) Acad Pr.
***Owen, Guillermo.** Game Theory. 3rd ed. LC 95-12397. 1995. text ed. write for info. (0-12-531151-6) Acad Pr.
Owen, Guy. The Ballad of the Flim-Flam Man. LC 84-45411. reprint ed. 29.50 (0-404-19939-9) AMS Pr.
— Flim-Flam Man & the Apprentice Grifter. LC 84-45575. reprint ed. 28.00 (0-404-19940-2) AMS Pr.
Owen, Guy & Williams, Mary C., eds. Contemporary Poetry of North Carolina. LC 77-20809. 171p. 1977. 12.95 (0-910244-98-7) Blair.
Owen, H. Goddard. A Recollection of Marcella Sembrich. LC 81-22197. (Music Reprint Ser.). (Illus.). 80p. 1982. reprint ed. lib. bdg. 21.50 (0-306-76141-6) Da Capo.
Owen, Harold. Modal & Tonal Counterpoint. 400p. (C). 1992. pap. 33.00 (0-02-872145-4) Schirmer Bks.
Owen, Harrison. Leadership Is. LC 87-70469. (Illus.). 164p. (Orig.). (C). 1990. pap. 20.00 (0-9618205-1-9) Abbott Pub.
— The Millennium Organization. LC 94-94260. (Illus.). 174p. (Orig.). 1994. pap. 20.00 (0-9618205-4-3) Abbott Pub.
— Open Space Technology: A User's Guide. LC 92-75371. (Illus.). 145p. (Orig.). 1993. pap. 20.00 (0-9618205-3-5) Abbott Pub.
— Riding the Tiger: Doing Business in a Transforming World. LC 91-76873. 216p. (Orig.). (C). 1992. pap. 20.00 (0-9618205-2-7) Abbott Pub.
— Spirit - Transformation & Development in Organizations. LC 87-70469. 248p. (Orig.). (C). 1987. pap. text ed. 20.00 (0-9618205-0-0) Abbott Pub.
***Owen, Harrison, ed.** Tales from Open Space. 1995. pap. write for info. (0-9618205-5-1) Abbott Pub.
Owen, Henry, ed. The Next Phase in Foreign Policy. LC 73-1077. 357p. reprint ed. pap. 101.80 (0-317-26338-2, 2025397) Bks Demand.
Owen, Henry & Smith, John T., II, eds. Gerard C. Smith: A Career in Progress. LC 89-5774. (Illus.). 152p. (C). 1989. lib. bdg. 42.50 (0-8191-7444-0) U Pr of Amer.
Owen, Henry D., jt. ed. see Fried, Edward R.
***Owen, Henry W.** The Edward Clarence Plummer History of Bath. (Illus.). 575p. 1995. reprint ed. lib. bdg. 61.00 (0-8328-4687-2) Higginson Bk Co.
Owen, Herb. The Complete Guide to Starting or Evaluating a Children's Ministry. Spear, Cindy G., ed. 156p. 1993. How to Shepherd Children in a World Full of Wolves. pap. text ed. 8.95 (0-941005-66-6); Resource pkt. incl. text, planning & teaching instructions & audiotapes. ring bd. 69.95 (0-941005-67-4) Chrch Grwth VA.
Owen, Hilary & Pritchard, Jacki, eds. Good Practice in Child Protection: A Training Manual for Professionals. 240p. 1993. pap. 36.00 (1-85302-205-5, Pub. by J Kingsley Pubs UK) Taylor & Francis.
Owen, Howard. Fat Lightning. LC 93-6339. 220p. 1994. 22.00 (1-877946-41-9) Permanent Pr.
— Littlejohn. LC 93-10068. 1993. 18.00 (0-679-42769-4, Villard Bks) Random.
— Littlejohn. 1994. pap. 10.00 (0-679-75001-0, Vin) Random.
— Littlejohn. large type ed. LC 92-45722. (Americana Ser.). 306p. 1993. reprint ed. bds. 19.95 (1-56054-658-1) Thorndike Pr.
Owen, Hugh. The Indian Nationalist Movement c. 1912-22: Leadership, Organisation & Philosophy. 276p. 1990. text ed. 35.00 (81-207-1209-9, Pub. by Sterling Pubs II) Apt Bks.
Owen, Huw P. Christian Theism: A Study in Its Basic Principles. 184p. 1984. 29.95 (0-567-09336-0, Pub. by T & T Clark UK) Bks Intl VA.
Owen, Hylda. Bloodhounds. (Illus.). 160p. 1989. 11.95 (0-86622-675-3, KW-166) TFH Pubns.
Owen, J. Getting the Most from Your Computer. 1985. pap. text ed. 10.95 (0-07-047953-4, BYTE Bks) McGraw.
Owen, J., ed. see Brambilla, R. & Crotti, A.
Owen, J. A., jt. ed. see Truswell, E.
Owen, J. B. & Axford, R. F., eds. Breeding for Disease Resistance in Farm Animals. 500p. 1991. text ed. 104.50 (0-85198-710-9) CAB Intl.
Owen, J Bradley. Dead Season. 368p. (Orig.). 1988. pap. 3.95 (0-8439-2593-0) Dorchester Pub Co.
Owen, J. G. The Management of Curriculum Development. LC 72-97876. 186p. reprint ed. pap. 53.10 (0-317-27540-2, 2024506) Bks Demand.
Owen, J. Glyn. From Simon to Peter. 1985. pap. 12.99 (0-85234-195-4, Pub. by Evangel Pr UK) Presby & Reformed.
Owen, J. H., jt. ed. see Barnes, G. R.
Owen, J. I., ed. Brassey's Infantry Weapons of the World. 2nd ed. 488p. 1979. 170.00 (0-08-027013-1, Pergamon Pr) Elsevier.
— Infantry Weapons of the Armies of Africa, the Orient & Latin America. 196p. 1980. pap. 35.95 (0-08-027017-4, Pergamon Pr) Elsevier.
— Infantry Weapons of the NATO Armies. 2nd ed. 192p. 1979. pap. 35.95 (0-08-027015-8, Pergamon Pr) Elsevier.
— Infantry Weapons of the Warsaw Pact Armies. 2nd ed. 160p. 1979. pap. 35.95 (0-08-027016-6, Pergamon Pr) Elsevier.
Owen, J. M. & Rogers, R. H. Flow & Heat Transfer in Rotating-Disc Systems Vol. 1: Rotor-Stator Systems. (Mechanical Engineering Dynamics Ser.). 278p. 1989. text ed. 130.00 (0-471-92474-1) Wiley.
Owen, Jack. Mystery in the High Cascades. abr. ed. 160p. 1995. pap. 7.95 (1-56901-458-2) NW Pub.
— Palm Beach - An Irreverent Guide. (Illus.). 52p. (Orig.). 1986. pap. 5.95 (0-938673-00-9) Old Bk Shop Pubn.
— Palm Beach Scandals: An Intimate Guide. LC 92-26781. (First One Hundred Years Ser.: Vol. 1). 224p. 1992. pap. 15.95 (0-935834-90-7) Rainbow Books.
Owen, Jackie. Early Settlers on the Poor Fork of the Cumberland River, Harlan County, Kentucky & Adjoining Counties. LC 89-69853. (Illus.). 176p. 1990. 32.00 (0-9625700-0-1) J Owen.
Owen, Jackie, jt. auth. see Laemmlen, Ann.

O

An Asterisk (*) at the beginning of an entry indicates that the title is appearing in BIP for the first time.

Owen, James D. Christian Psychology's War on God's Word: The Victimization of the Believer. LC 93-70361. 218p. (Orig.). 1993. pap. 9.95 (*0-941717-08-9*) EastGate Pubs.

Owen, James P. The Prudent Investor: The Definitive Guide to Professional Investment Management. 200p. 1993. reprint ed. pap. 21.95 (*1-55738-490-8*) Probus Pub Co.

Owen, Jan. Guidebook to Adventure, Vol. II. 2nd ed. (Illus.). 112p. 1985. pap. 16.95 (*0-13-368846-1*) P-H.

— Guidebook to Adventure, Volume 2. write for info. (*0-318-59626-1*) S&S Trade.

Owen, Jane. Eccentric Gardens. (Illus.). 160p. 1990. 24.95 (*0-394-58447-3*, Villard Bks) Random.

Owen, Jeffrey H. & Davis, Hallowell, eds. Evoked Potential Testing: Clinical Applications. 272p. 1985. text ed. 50.95 (*0-8089-1707-2*, 793225, Grune) Saunders.

Owen, Jennie S. The Annals of Kansas, 1886-1925, 2 vols., Set. Mechem, Kirke, ed. Incl. Vol. 1. LC 55-62029. 526p. 1954. 4.00 (*0-87726-009-5*); Vol. 2. LC 55-62029. 551p. 1956. 7.00 (*0-87726-010-9*); LC 55-62029. (Illus.). 12.50 (*0-87726-008-7*) Kansas St Hist.

Owen, Jennifer. The Ecology of a Garden: The First Fifteen Years. (Illus.). 368p. (C). 1991. 115.00 (*0-521-34335-6*) Cambridge U Pr.

— Feeding Strategy. LC 82-2569. (Phoenix Ser.). (Illus.). 160p. (C). 1982. pap. text ed. 12.50 (*0-226-64186-4*) U Ch Pr.

— Insect Life. (Mysteries & Marvels Ser.). (Illus.). 32p. (J). (gr. 4-7). 1985. lib. bdg. 13.96 (*0-88110-173-7*, Usborne); pap. 5.95 (*0-86020-843-5*, Usborne) EDC.

Owen, John. Apostasy from the Gospel. 184p. 1992. reprint ed. pap. 6.95 (*0-85151-609-2*) Banner of Truth.

— Biblical Theology. Kistler, Don, ed. Westcott, Stephen, tr. 931p. 1994. 50.00 (*1-877611-83-2*) Soli Deo Gloria.

— Cattle Feeding. (Illus.). 182p. 24.95 (*0-85236-134-3*, Pub. by Farming Pr UK) Diamond Farm Bk.

— Communion with God. Law, R. J., ed. 224p. 1991. pap. text ed. 6.95 (*0-85151-607-6*) Banner of Truth.

— The Correspondence: With an Account of His Life & Work. Toon, Peter, ed. 215p. 1970. 14.00 (*0-227-67746-3*) Attic Pr.

— Death of Death. 1983. pap. 13.95 (*0-85151-382-4*) Banner of Truth.

— Evenings with the Skeptics, 2 vols. 1973. 200.00 (*0-8490-0139-0*) Gordon Pr.

— The Five Great Skeptical Dramas of History. LC 72-295. (Essay Index Reprint Ser.). 1977. reprint ed. 24.95 (*0-8369-2816-4*) Ayer.

— Glory of Christ. 1987. pap. 3.99 (*0-946462-13-5*, Pub. by Evangel Pr UK) Presby & Reformed.

— The Glory of Christ. abr. ed. 168p. Date not set. pap. 6.95 (*0-85151-661-0*) Banner of Truth.

— Gourmand Gutbusters. (Illus.). 152p. (Orig.). 1980. pap. 4.50 (*0-914687-02-6*) Intermed Eater.

— Hebrews: The Epistle of Warning. LC 68-57719. 288p. 1973. pap. 10.99 (*0-8254-3407-6*) Kregel.

— The Intermediate Eater's Great Grub Hunt. (Illus.). 172p. (Orig.). 1989. pap. 7.95 (*0-914687-03-4*) Intermed Eater.

— The Intermediate Eater's Seattle Cookbook. (Illus.). 110p. (Orig.). 1983. pap. 7.95 (*0-914687-01-8*) Intermed Eater.

— Life by His Death. 1992. pap. 4.99 (*0-85234-763-4*, Pub. by Evangel Pr UK) Presby & Reformed.

— Press Pass. 231p. 1994. pap. 14.95 (*0-9624559-2-X*) Seattle Post.

— Seattle Cookbook. (Illus.). 105p. 1993. pap. 14.95 (*0-9624559-1-1*) Seattle Post.

— Sin & Temptation: The Challenge to Personal Godliness. Houston, James H., ed. (Classics of Faith & Devotion Ser.). 204p. 1994. reprint ed. spiral bd., pap. 12.95 (*1-57383-033-X*) Regent College.

— The Skeptics of the French Renaissance. 1972. 59.95 (*0-8490-1058-6*) Gordon Pr.

— The Skeptics of the Italian Renaissance. 1972. 59.95 (*0-8490-1059-4*) Gordon Pr.

— Works of John Owen, 16 vols., Set. 1980. 399.95 (*0-85151-392-1*) Banner of Truth.

— Works of John Owen, Vol. I. 1980. 27.95 (*0-85151-123-6*) Banner of Truth.

— Works of John Owen, Vol. II. 1980. 27.95 (*0-85151-124-4*) Banner of Truth.

— Works of John Owen, Vol. III. 1980. 27.95 (*0-85151-125-2*) Banner of Truth.

— Works of John Owen, Vol. IV. 1980. 27.95 (*0-85151-068-X*) Banner of Truth.

— Works of John Owen, Vol. V. 1980. 27.95 (*0-85151-067-1*) Banner of Truth.

— Works of John Owen, Vol. VI. 1980. 27.95 (*0-85151-126-0*) Banner of Truth.

— Works of John Owen, Vol. VII. 1980. 27.95 (*0-85151-127-9*) Banner of Truth.

— Works of John Owen, Vol. VIII. 1980. 27.95 (*0-85151-066-3*) Banner of Truth.

— Works of John Owen, Vol. IX. 1980. 27.95 (*0-85151-065-5*) Banner of Truth.

— Works of John Owen, Vol. X. 1980. 27.95 (*0-85151-064-7*) Banner of Truth.

— Works of John Owen, Vol. XI. 1980. 27.95 (*0-85151-128-7*) Banner of Truth.

— Works of John Owen, Vol. XII. 1980. 27.95 (*0-85151-129-5*) Banner of Truth.

— Works of John Owen, Vol. XIII. 1980. 27.95 (*0-85151-063-9*) Banner of Truth.

— Works of John Owen, Vol. XIV. 1980. 27.95 (*0-85151-062-0*) Banner of Truth.

— Works of John Owen, Vol. XV. 1980. 27.95 (*0-85151-130-9*) Banner of Truth.

— Works of John Owen, Vol. XVI. 1980. 27.95 (*0-85151-061-2*) Banner of Truth.

Owen, John, tr. see Calvin, John.

Owen, John, tr. see John, Calvin.

*__Owen, John C.__ Budapest 1896 International Chess Tournament: The First Great Chess Tournament in Hungary. (Great Tournament Ser.). (Illus.). 205p. 1994. 36.00 (*0-939433-20-6*) Caissa Edit.

— The Match Tournament at St. Petersburg, 1895-6. (World's Greatest Chess Tournaments Ser.). (Illus.). 118p. 1989. 22.00 (*0-939433-10-9*) Caissa Edit.

Owen, John D. Reduced Working Hours: Cure for Unemployment Or Economic Burden? LC 88-30352. 192p. 1989. text ed. 34.50 (*0-8018-3784-7*) Johns Hopkins.

— School Inequality & the Welfare State. LC 74-6834. 222p. reprint ed. pap. 63.30 (*0-685-23647-1*, 2027901) Bks Demand.

— Why Our Kids Don't Study: An Economic Analysis of Causes & Proposed Remedies. 136p. 1995. text ed. 29.95 (*0-8018-4925-X*) Johns Hopkins.

Owen, John M. Program Evaluation: Forms & Approaches. 176p. 1994. pap. 22.95 (*1-86373-462-7*, Pub. by Allen Unwin AT) Paul & Co Pubs.

Owen, Jon, jt. auth. see Bloor, Susan.

Owen, Keith & Coley, Trevor. Automotive Fuels Handbook. 704p. 1990. 125.00 (*1-56091-064-X*, R-105) Soc Auto Engineers.

— Automotive Fuels Handbook. 2nd ed. 800p. 1995. 129.00 (*1-56091-589-7*, R151) Soc Auto Engineers.

Owen, Kenneth, jt. auth. see Oakley, Brian.

Owen, L. A., jt. ed. see Derbyshire, E.

Owen, Lewis. The Running Register: Recording the State of the English Colledges in All Forraine Parts. LC 68-54654. (English Experience Ser.: No. 19). 118p. 1968. reprint ed. 13.00 (*90-221-0019-7*) Walter J Johnson.

Owen, Lewis A., jt. auth. see Pickering, Kevin T.

Owen, Lewis J. & Owen, Nancy H., eds. Middle English Poetry: An Anthology. LC 76-138662. (Library of Literature). 1971. pap. 7.50 (*0-672-60984-3*, LL-12, Bobbs) Macmillan.

Owen, Lonny. What's Wrong with Me? Breaking the Chain of Adolescent Codependency. LC 91-70383. (Illus.). 128p. 1991. 8.95 (*0-925190-14-4*) Fairview Press.

Owen, Lyla H. & Murphy, Owen. Creoles of New Orleans: People of Color. 102p. (Orig.). 1987. pap. 15.95 (*0-940835-00-2*) First Quarter Pub.

*__Owen, Lynette.__ Selling Rights. 2nd ed. 244p. 1994. 39.95 (*1-85713-007-3*) Chapman & Hall.

Owen, M. Herbs, Greens, & Aromatics. 1991. pap. 14.95 (*1-55821-110-1*) Lyons & Burford.

Owen, M. C. Sewell. The Sewells of the Isle of Wight, England, with an Account of Some of the Families Connected by Marriage. 204p. 1993. reprint ed. lib. bdg. 42.00 (*0-8328-3748-2*); reprint ed. pap. 32.00 (*0-8328-3749-0*) Higginson Bk Co.

Owen, M. J. & Lamb, J. R. Immune Recognition: In Focus. (In Focus Ser.). 84p. 1988. pap. 13.95 (*1-85221-062-1*, IRL Pr) OUP.

Owen, M. J., jt. ed. see Bodmer, W. F.

Owen, Mack. The Actor's Scenebook. (C). 1992. 21.00 (*0-06-500145-1*) HarpCollege.

— The Stages of Acting: A Practical Approach for Beginning Actors. LC 92-20698. (C). 1992. text ed. 37.50 (*0-06-500632-1*) HarpCollege.

Owen, Marion. Apologies & Remedial Interchanges: A Study of Language Use in Social Interaction. LC 83-13375. (Linguistic Supplementary Studies). x, 192p. 1983. 70.00 (*90-279-3360-X*); pap. 21.55 (*90-279-3370-7*) Mouton.

*__Owen, Marna.__ Animal Rights: Yes or No? (YA). (gr. 6 up). 1994. 17.50 (*0-8225-2603-4*, Lerner Publctns) Lerner Group.

***Owen-Martin, Lydi. Don't Take My Baby Away! The Unexplored Cause Of Child Abuse in America. 295p. (Orig.). 1995. 23.95 (*0-9646739-1-6*) Home Birthing Serv.**

Immediate separation of mother & infant after birth leads to an aberration of maternal attachment & the bonding process, often unleashing in the mother aggressive behavior towards her child/children later. As a society, we do gross injustice to the significance of the birthing experience & it's potential impact on our society by not daring to admit that we are perhaps governed by laws other than those of our own making. We imagine that we are immune to the laws of nature that govern all other animals, laws that when broken result in death & abandonment... yet, when our human children are abandoned, abused, & killed in record numbers, we just scratch our heads in bewilderment & wonder what happened. The number of abusive deaths of children in America is estimated to be six per day! This book tells the story of one woman's birth experiences & feelings that led her to become a midwife & author & lecturer with the hope of changing present maternity care policies & procedures in the immediate post-partum period...the only period in which the vital imprinting process occurs. This imprint is vital to preventing maternal attachment disorders so rampant in America today! To order call 702-454-2233 or write, Home Birthing Service, c/o Lydi Owen-Martin, P.O. Box 50334, Henderson, NV 89016. Hardcover, $23.95, plus shipping. Softcover, $14.95, plus shipping. ***Publisher Provided Annotation.***

— Don't Take My Baby Away! The Unexplored Cause Of Child Abuse in America. 295p. (Orig.). 1995. pap. 14.95 (*0-9646739-0-8*) Home Birthing Serv.

Owen, Mary A. Voodoo Tales As Told among the Negroes of the Southwest. LC 70-149874. (Black Heritage Library Collection). (Illus.). 1977. 30.95 (*0-8369-8754-3*) Ayer.

Owen, Maureen. Hearts in Space. (Illus.). 7.00 (*0-686-73477-7*); pap. 3.50 (*0-686-73478-5*) Kulchur Foun.

— Imaginary Income. 1992. pap. 9.00 (*0-914610-97-X*); boxed 16.00 (*0-914610-98-8*) Hanging Loose.

— Untapped Maps. 96p. (Orig.). 1993. pap. 9.50 (*0-937013-44-7*) Potes Poets.

Owen, Maureen, ed. see Bennett, Will.

Owen, Maureen, ed. see Cataldo, Susan.

Owen, Maureen, ed. see Dawson, Fielding.

Owen, Maureen, ed. see Friedman, Ed.

Owen, Maureen, ed. see Gontarek, Leonard.

Owen, Maureen, ed. see Hamill, Janet.

Owen, Maureen, ed. see Hartman, Yuki.

Owen, Maureen, ed. see Howe, Fanny.

Owen, Maureen, ed. see Vega, Janine P.

Owen, Maureen, ed. see Weigel, Tom.

Owen, Maureen, ed. see Wright, Rebecca.

Owen, Max. In the Minds of Men. 256p. 1989. 21.95 (*0-8027-1071-9*) Walker & Co.

Owen, May A. Folk-Lore of the Musquakie Indians of North America & Catalogue of Musquakie Beadwork & Other Objects in the Collection of the Folk-Lore Society. (Folk-Lore Society, London, Monographs: Vol. 51). 1972. reprint ed. pap. 15.00 (*0-8115-0523-5*) Periodicals Srv.

Owen, Michael S., jt. auth. see Newman, Sandra J.

Owen, Morag. Social Justice & Children in Care. 165p. 1992. 55.95 (*1-85628-372-0*, Pub. by Avebury Pub UK) Ashgate Pub Co.

Owen, Morag, jt. auth. see Farmer, Elaine.

Owen, Morfydd E., jt. ed. see Jenkins, Dafydd.

Owen, Myrfyn. The Barnacle Goose. 1989. pap. 25.00 (*0-7478-0053-7*, Pub. by Shire UK) St Mut.

Owen, Myrfyn & Black, Jeffrey M. Waterfowl Ecology. (Tertiary Level Biology Ser.). (Illus.). 200p. 1990. text ed. 69.95 (*0-412-02191-9*, A3617, Chap & Hall NY); pap. text ed. 35.00 (*0-412-02201-X*, A3621, Chap & Hall NY) Chapman & Hall.

Owen, Nancy H., jt. ed. see Owen, Lewis J.

Owen, Nancy R., jt. auth. see Combs, Richard E.

Owen, Natasha, tr. see Kokoshvili, Simon, et al.

Owen, Norman G., ed. Death & Disease in Southeast Asia: Explorations in Social, Medical & Demographic History. (Illus.). 297p. 1987. pap. 25.00 (*0-19-588853-7*) OUP.

— The Philippine Economy & the United States: Studies in Past & Present Interactions. LC 82-74314. (Michigan Papers on South & Southeast Asia: No. 22). xvi, 208p. (Orig.). 1984. text ed. 16.95 (*0-89148-024-2*); pap. 16.95 (*0-89148-025-0*) Ctr S&SE Asian.

Owen, Oliver S. Acorn to Oak Tree. LC 94-6302. (J). 1994. lib. bdg. 14.96 (*1-56239-289-1*) Abdo & Dghtrs.

— Bulb to Tulip. (Lifewatch Ser.). (J). 1995. write for info. (*1-56239-488-6*) Abdo & Dghtrs.

— Calf to Dolphin. LC 94-19967. (Lifewatch Ser.). (Illus.). (J). 1994. lib. bdg. 14.96 (*1-56239-292-1*) Abdo & Dghtrs.

— Caterpillar to Butterfly. LC 94-14306. (Lifewatch Ser.). (J). 1994. lib. bdg. 14.96 (*1-56239-290-5*) Abdo & Dghtrs.

— Doctors, Dollars & Death: Bad Medicine in America. 115p. (Orig.). (C). 1994. pap. text ed. 17.50 (*0-87527-508-7*) Green.

— Eco-Solutions: It's in Your Hands. LC 93-19132. (Target Earth Ser.). (J). 1993. lib. bdg. 14.96 (*1-56239-203-4*) Abdo & Dghtrs.

— Eco-Solutions: It's in Your Hands. LC 93-19132. (Target Earth Ser.). (J). 1993. pap. 7.49 (*1-56239-426-6*) Abdo & Dghtrs.

— Egg to Snake. LC 94-12943. (Lifewatch Ser.). (J). 1994. lib. bdg. 14.96 (*1-56239-294-8*) Abdo & Dghtrs.

— From Egg to Robin. LC 94-10523. (Life Watch Ser.). (J). 1994. lib. bdg. 14.96 (*1-56239-293-X*) Abdo & Dghtrs.

— Intro to Your Environment. Italia, Bob, ed. LC 93-7746. (Target Earth Ser.). (J). 1993. lib. bdg. 14.96 (*1-56239-204-2*) Abdo & Dghtrs.

— Intro to Your Environment. Italia, Bob, ed. LC 93-7746. (Target Earth Ser.). (J). 1993. pap. 7.49 (*1-56239-418-5*) Abdo & Dghtrs.

— Pup to Grizzly Bear. LC 95-3317. (Lifewatch Ser.). (J). 1995. lib. bdg. 14.96 (*1-56239-486-X*) Abdo & Dghtrs.

— Pup to Timber Wolf. LC 95-1172. (Lifewatch Ser.). (J). 1995. lib. bdg. 14.96 (*1-56239-487-8*) Abdo & Dghtrs.

— Seed to Peanut. LC 95-10523. (Lifewatch Ser.). (J). 1995. write for info. (*1-56239-489-4*) Abdo & Dghtrs.

— Tadpole to Frog. LC 94-11370. (Lifewatch Ser.). (J). 1994. lib. bdg. 14.96 (*1-56239-291-3*) Abdo & Dghtrs.

Owen, Oliver S. & Chiras, Daniel D. Natural Resource Conservation: An Ecological Approach. 5th ed. 1064p. (C). 1990. text ed. write for info. (*0-02-390111-X*) Macmillan.

— Natural Resource Conservation: Management for a Sustainable Future. 6th ed. LC 94-17797. 1995. text ed. 61.00 (*0-02-390121-7*) P-H.

Owen, P. & Foster, T., eds. Immunochemical & Molecular Genetic Analysis of Bacterial Pathogens. 320p. 1989. 128.25 (*0-444-81000-5*) Elsevier.

*__Owen, Pamela & Pumfrey, Peter, eds.__ Children Learning to Read - International Concerns: Curriculum & Assesment Issues, 2 Vols., Vol. 2. LC 49-37967. 210p. 1995. pap. 24.95 (*0-7507-0366-0*, Falmer Pr) Taylor & Francis.

— Children Learning to Read - International Concerns: Curriculum & Assesment Issues, 2 Vol., Vol. 2. LC 49-37967. 210p. 1995. 75.00 (*0-7507-0365-2*, Falmer Pr) Taylor & Francis.

— Children Learning to Read - International Concerns: Emergent & Developing Reading, 2 Vols., Vol. 1. LC 94-37967. 210p. 1995. pap. 24.95 (*0-7507-0364-4*, Falmer Pr) Taylor & Francis.

— Children Learning to Read - International Concerns: Emergent & Developing Reading, 2 Vols., Vol. 1. LC 94-37967. 210p. 1995. 75.00 (*0-7507-0363-6*, Falmer Pr) Taylor & Francis.

Owen, Pat. Bing & Grondahl Christmas Plates: The First Hundred Years. (Illus.). 256p. 1995. 35.00 (*0-913428-76-0*) Landfall Pr.

— Story of Bing & Grondahl Christmas Plates. (Illus.). 1995. ring bd. 25.00 (*0-911576-02-9*) Viking Import.

— Story of Royal Copenhagen Christmas Plates. (Illus.). 1995. ring bd. 25.00 (*0-911576-01-0*) Viking Import.

Owen, Patricia M. Sudden Cardiac Death: Theory & Practice. LC 90-14506. 272p. 1991. text ed. 55.00 (*0-8342-0200-X*) Aspen Pub.

Owen, Peter. The Book of Decorative Knots. (Illus.). 144p. 1994. pap. 12.95 (*1-55821-304-X*) Lyons & Burford.

— The Book of Outdoor Knots. (Illus.). 144p. 1993. pap. 12.95 (*1-55821-225-6*) Lyons & Burford.

— The Craft & Hobby Airbrush Book. (Illus.). 96p. 1995. pap. 17.95 (*1-55821-333-3*) Lyons & Burford.

— The Juggling Book. (Illus.). 96p. 1996. pap. 12.95 (*1-55821-326-0*) Lyons & Burford.

— Printing Terms. (On the Spot Guide Ser.). (Illus.). 96p. 1994. 7.95 (*1-56970-507-0*, Nippan Pubns) Bks Nippan.

Owen, Peter, ed. & intro. Publishing - The Future. LC 88-61919. 128p. 1988. 21.00 (*0-7206-0720-5*, Pub. by P Owen Ltd UK); pap. 14.95 (*0-7206-0721-3*) Dufour.

Owen, Peter, ed. Publishing Now. 176p. (Orig.). 1993. pap. 22.95 (*0-7206-0887-2*, Pub. by Peter Owen Ltd UK) Paul & Co Pubs.

Owen, Peter, intro. The Peter Owen Anthology: Forty Years of Independent Publishing. 231p. 1991. 35.00 (*0-7206-0810-4*, Pub. by P Owen Ltd UK) Dufour.

Owen, Peter & Rollason, Jane. The Complete Manual of Airbrushing. LC 87-46100. (Illus.). 256p. 1988. 34.50 (*0-394-56852-4*) Knopf.

Owen, Peter & Sutcliffe, John. Airbrush Maintenance. (On the Spot Guides Ser.). (Illus.). 96p. 1994. 7.95 (*1-56970-500-3*, Nippan Pubns) Bks Nippan.

— The Complete Airbrush & Photo-Retouching Manual. (Illus.). 160p. 1985. 24.95 (*0-89134-170-6*, 7326) North Light Bks.

Owen, R., jt. auth. see Findlay, G. F.

Owen, Raymond S. Fred K. Owen, Newspaper Man. LC 83-50687. (Illus.). 128p. (Orig.). 1984. pap. 7.95 (*0-931474-27-2*) TBW Bks.

Owen, Richard. A History of British Fossil Mammals & Birds. LC 72-1705. (Illus.). reprint ed. 52.50 (*0-404-07991-1*) AMS Pr.

— The Hunterian Lectures in Comparative Anatomy. Sloan, Phillip R., ed. (Illus.). 362p. 1992. pap. text ed. 18.95 (*0-226-64190-2*) U Ch Pr.

— The Hunterian Lectures in Comparative Anatomy. Sloan, Phillip R., ed. (Illus.). 362p. 1992. lib. bdg. 42.00 (*0-226-64189-9*) U Ch Pr.

— Letters from Moscow. 263p. 1988. 29.95 (*0-575-03766-0*, Pub. by V Gollancz UK) Trafalgar.

— Memoir on the Pearly Nautilus. LC 72-1700. (Illus.). reprint ed. 12.50 (*0-404-07978-4*) AMS Pr.

— On the Anatomy of Vertebrates, 3 Vols, Set. LC 72-1701. (Illus.). reprint ed. 225.00 (*0-404-08300-5*) AMS Pr.

— Paleontology: Or, a Systematic Summary of Extinct Animals & Their Geological Relations. Gould, Stephen J., ed. LC 79-8342. (History of Paleontology Ser.). (Illus.). 1980. reprint ed. lib. bdg. 40.95 (*0-405-12732-4*) Ayer.

Owen, Richard S. The Life of Richard Owen, 2 vols. LC 72-1697. (Illus.). reprint ed. 124.50 (*0-404-07995-4*) AMS Pr.

Owen, Robert. A Development of the Principles & Plans on Which to Establish Self-Supporting Home Colonies. LC 72-2941. reprint ed. 34.50 (*0-404-10707-9*) AMS Pr.

— The Life & Ideas of Robert Owen. 256p. 1969. pap. 1.95 (*0-7178-0115-2*) Intl Pubs Co.

— Life of Robert Owen: With Selections from His Writings & Correspondence, 2 vols. in 1, Vols. 1-1A. LC 66-21690. 1858. 65.00 (*0-678-00271-1*) Kelley.

— Life of Robert Owen, Written by Himself, 2 vols. 1973. 200.00 (*0-8490-0536-1*) Gordon Pr.

— New View of Society. LC 70-134407. reprint ed. 36.00 (*0-404-08453-2*) AMS Pr.

— A New View of Society. LC 91-31814. 194p. 1991. reprint ed. 48.00 (*1-85477-077-2*, Pub. by Woodstock Bks UK) Cassell.

— A New View of Society & Other Writings. 416p. 1991. pap. 11.95 (*0-14-043348-1*, Penguin Classics) Viking Penguin.

— Report of the County of Lanark of a Plan for Relieving Public Distress & Removing Discontent by Giving Permanent, Productive Employment to the Poor & Working Classes. LC 72-2942. reprint ed. 34.50 (*0-404-10708-7*) AMS Pr.

— Robert Owen's Millennial Gazette, Set, Nos. 1-16. LC 74-134408. reprint ed. Set. 49.50 (*0-404-08454-0*) AMS Pr.

O

An Asterisk (*) at the beginning of an entry indicates that the title is appearing in BIP for the first time.

— Selected Works of Robert Owen, Vol. 4. Claeys, Gregory, ed. 1577p. 1993. 395.00 (1-85196-088-0, Pub. by Pickering & Chatto UK) Ashgate Pub Co.

Owen, Robert & Dale, David. The Story of New Lanark. (C). 1989. 35.00 (0-948473-02-9) St Mut.

***Owen, Robert C.** The Modern Gaelic-English Dictionary. 139p. 1993. pap. 29.95 (1-871901-29-4) Colton Bk.

Owen, Robert D. Footfalls on the Boundary of Another World. 529p. 1972. reprint ed. spiral bd. 19.25 (0-7873-0649-5) Mokelumne.

— Hints on Public Architecture. LC 77-17509. (Architecture & Decorative Art Ser.). (Illus.). 1978. reprint ed. lib. bdg. 85.00 (0-306-77545-X) Da Capo.

— Hints on Public Architecture. LC 77-17509. (Illus.). 120p. 1978. reprint ed. 55.00 (0-87474-736-8, OWHP) Smithsonian.

— Threading My Way: Twenty-Seven Years of Autobiography. LC 67-18582. 1967. reprint ed. 45.00 (0-678-00261-4) Kelley.

— To Holland & to New Harmony: Robert Dale Owen's Travel Journal, 1825-1826. Elliott, Josephine M., ed. 122p. 1969. pap. 6.95 (0-87195-040-5) Ind Hist Soc.

Owen, Robert D. & Schnell, Gary D. Oklahoma Mammalogy: An Annotated Bibliography & Checklist. LC 88-27959. (Oklahoma Museum of Natural History Publication Ser.). 240p. 1989. 26.95 (0-8061-2185-8) U of Okla Pr.

***Owen, Robert L.** Dr. Anne's Cancer Journal. LC 90-81824. 414p. 1990. pap. 14.00 (1-882657-06-3) Health Hope.

***Owen, Rodrick.** Braids: 250 Patterns from Japan, Peru & Beyond. 160p. 1995. 24.95 (1-883010-06-3) Interweave.

Owen, Roger. Middle East in the World Economy, 1800-1914. 400p. 1987. pap. 25.00 (0-416-03272-9) Routledge Chapman & Hall.

— The Middle East in the World Economy 1800-1914. 378p. 1993. text ed. 19.95 (1-85043-658-4, Pub. by I B Tauris UK) St Martin.

— State, Power & Politics in the Making of the Modern Middle East. (Illus.). 288p. 1992. 55.00 (0-415-07590-4, A7076); pap. 18.95 (0-415-07591-2, A7080) Routledge.

Owen, Roger, ed. Studies in the Economic & Social History of Palestine in the 19th & 20th Centuries. LC 82-80662. 271p. 1982. 29.95 (0-8093-1089-5) S Ill U Pr.

Owen, Roger, jt. ed. see Asad, Talal.

Owen, Roger, jt. ed. see Louis, William R.

Owen, Roger, jt. ed. see Tripp, Charles R.

Owen, Rosamund. The Art of Side Saddle: History, Etiquette, Showing. 176p. 1989. 90.00 (0-9509663-0-4) St Mut.

Owen, Rosemary C. Smashing Times: The History of the Irish Suffrage Movement 1876-1922. (Illus.). 160p. (C). 1995. pap. 17.99 (0-946211-08-6, Pub. by Attic IE) InBook.

Owen, Roy. The Ibis & the Egret. LC 92-26220. (Illus.). 32p. (J). (ps-3). 1993. 14.95 (0-399-22504-8, Philomel Bks) Putnam Pub Group.

— My Night Forest. LC 93-45666. (Illus.). 32p. (J). (ps-2). 1994. text ed. 14.95 (0-02-769005-9, Four Winds Pr) S&S Childrens.

Owen, Roy, ed. & tr. The Romance of Reynard the Fox. (World's Classics Ser.). 304p. 1994. pap. 9.95 (0-19-282801-0) OUP.

***Owen, Ruth.** Sorcerer. (Loveswept Ser.: No. 714). 1994. pap. 3.50 (0-553-44428-X, Loveswept) Bantam.

— Taming the Pirate. (Loveswept: No. 705). 1994. pap. 3.50 (0-553-44427-1) Bantam.

Owen, S. G. Electrocardiography: A Programmed Text. rev. ed. 180p. 1973. pap. 18.00 (0-316-67724-8) Little.

Owen, S. G., ed. see Ovid.

***Owen, Sally.** The Story of Christmas. (Illus.). 12p. (J). (gr. 1 up). 1994. pap. 12.99 (0-8423-6027-1) Tyndale.

Owen, Samuel A., Jr. Letting God Plan Your Family. LC 90-80626. 160p. (Orig.). 1990. pap. 7.95 (0-89107-585-2) Crossway Bks.

Owen, Sandy & McNeil, Dani. Divorce Can Be Fun. 128p. (Orig.). pap. 7.00 (0-317-57794-8) Triumph Pr.

Owen-Smith, Eric. The German Economy. LC 93-34911. 624p. 1994. 89.95x (0-415-06288-8, B3916); pap. 29.95 (0-415-06289-6, B3920) Routledge.

Owen-Smith, R. Norman. Megaherbivores: The Influence of Very Large Body Size on Ecology. (Cambridge Studies in Ecology). (Illus.). 360p. (C). 1989. 89.95 (0-521-36020-X) Cambridge U Pr.

— Megaherbivores: The Influence of Very Large Body Size on Ecology. (Studies in Ecology). (Illus.). 384p. (C). 1992. pap. 37.95 (0-521-42637-5) Cambridge U Pr.

Owen, Sri. Exotic Feasts: Sri Owen's Book of Seasonal Menus. (Illus.). 224p. 1994. pap. 16.95 (1-85626-100-X) Trafalgar.

— Indonesian Regional Cooking. 1995. 18.95 (0-312-11832-5) St Martin.

— The Rice Book: The Definitive Book on the Magic of Rice, with Hundreds of Exotic Recipes from Around the World. (Illus.). 416p. 1994. 24.95 (0-312-10532-0) St Martin.

Owen, Stephen. Analogy for Automated Reasoning. (Perspectives in Artificial Intelligence Ser.: Vol. 9). (Illus.). 234p. 1990. text ed. 53.00 (0-12-531715-8) Acad Pr.

— Mi-Lou: Poetry & the Labyrinth of Desire. LC 88-28393. (Studies in Comparative Literature: No. 39). 240p. 1989. 35.00 (0-674-57275-0) HUP.

— Planning Settlements Naturally. (Illus.). 154p. (C). 1994. text ed. 175.00 (1-85341-029-2, Pub. by Surrey Beatty & Sons AT) St Mut.

— The Poetry of Meng Chiao & Han Yu. LC 74-29732. 304p. reprint ed. pap. 86.70 (0-8357-8273-5, 2033850) Bks Demand.

— Readings in Chinese Literary Thought. (Harvard-Yenching Institute Monograph Ser.: No. 30). 600p. 1992. 55.00 (0-674-74920-0) Harvard E Asian.

— Remembrances: The Experience of the Past in Classical Chinese Literature. 159p. 1986. 24.50 (0-674-76015-8) HUP.

— Traditional Chinese Poetry & Poetics: Omen of the World. LC 83-40269. 320p. 1985. text ed. 27.50 (0-299-09420-0) U of Wis Pr.

***Owen, Stephen, ed. & tr.** An Anthology of Chinese Literature: Beginnings to 1911. LC 95-11409. 1996. write for info. (0-393-03823-8) Norton.

Owen, Stephen, jt. auth. see Lin, Shuen-Fu.

Owen, Steven M. & Brooker, Alan T. A Guide to Modern Inorganic Chemistry. 328p. 1991. pap. text ed. 34.95 (0-470-21694-8) Wiley.

Owen, Sue. The Book of Winter. (Journal Award in Poetry). 60p. 1988. 18.95 (0-8142-0474-0); pap. 12.95 (0-8142-0475-9) Ohio St U Pr.

— Nursery Rhymes for the Dead. LC 80-18778. 61p. 1980. pap. 4.00 (0-87886-112-2, Greenfld Rev Pr) Greenfld Rev Lit.

Owen, Susan & Haine, Angela. Discovering Country Walks in South London. 1989. pap. 25.00 (0-7478-0114-2, Pub. by Shire UK) St Mut.

Owen, Susan, jt. auth. see Haine, Angela.

Owen, Susanne, et al. Biofeedback in Neuromuscular Re-Education: History, Uses, Procedures. LC 27-954. (Illus.). 1975. pap. 5.50 (0-685-64751-X) Biofeedback Research.

Owen, Suzanne, ed. see Alpert, Gerri.

Owen, T. C. Characterization of Organic Compounds by Chemical Methods: An Introductory Laboratory Textbook. 256p. 1969. 50.00 (0-8247-1510-1) Dekker.

Owen, Terry, jt. auth. see Chall, Miriam.

Owen, Thomas C. Capitalism & Politics in Russia: A Social History of the Moscow Merchants, 1855 to 1905. LC 80-11279. (Illus.). 352p. 1981. 44.50 (0-521-23173-6) Cambridge U Pr.

— The Corporation under Russian Law, 1800-1917: A Study in Tsarist Economic Policy. 240p. (C). 1991. 59.95 (0-521-39126-1) Cambridge U Pr.

— Russian Corporate Capitalism from Peter the Great to Perestroika. (Illus.). 288p. 1995. 49.95 (0-19-509677-0) OUP.

Owen, Thomas M. Revolutionary Soldiers in Alabama. 131p. 1990. reprint ed. 14.00 (0-685-60352-0, 4350) Clearfield Co.

Owen, Tim & Livingstone, Stephen. Prison Law: Text & Materials. 584p. 1994. 69.00 (0-19-876265-8); pap. 35.00 (0-19-876264-X) OUP.

Owen, Tobias & Morrison, David. The Planetary System. (Physics Ser.). 600p. (C). 1988. text ed. 49.50 (0-201-10487-3) Addison-Wesley.

Owen, Tobias, jt. auth. see Goldsmith, Donald.

Owen-Towle, Tom. Brother-Spirit: Men Joining Together in the Quest for Intimacy & Ultimacy. 180p. 1991. pap. 11.95 (0-9630636-0-X) Bald Eagle Mtn.

— Generation to Generation: A Father Writes His Kids about Choosing the Good Life. LC 86-61696. (Illus.). 112p. (Orig.). 1986. pap. 7.95 (0-931104-19-X) Sunflower Ink.

— The Gospel of Universalism: Hope, Courage, & the Love of God. LC 93-8307. 1993. 10.00 (1-55896-315-4, Skinner Hse Bks) Unitarian Univ.

— New Men - Deeper Hungers. LC 88-63742. (Illus.). 146p. (Orig.). (C). 1988. pap. 7.95 (0-931104-25-4) Sunflower Ink.

— Spiritual Fitness. LC 89-63710. 394p. (Orig.). 1989. pap. 12.00 (0-931104-27-0) Sunflower Ink.

— Staying Together: Forty Ways to Make your Marriage Work. LC 87-62585. (Illus.). 108p. (Orig.). 1987. pap. 7.95 (0-931104-21-1) Sunflower Ink.

Owen-Towle, Tom, jt. auth. see Hassett, Chris.

Owen, Trefor M. The Customs & Traditions of Wales. (Pocket Guides Ser.). 104p. 1991. pap. 9.95 (0-7083-1118-0, Pub. by U of Wales UK) Bks Intl VA.

— Welsh Folk Customs. 197p. 1987. pap. 20.00 (0-85088-347-4, Pub. by Gomer Pr UK) St Mut.

— Welsh for Customs. 197p. (C). 1987. pap. 50.00 (0-685-60036-X, Pub. by Gomer Pr UK) St Mut.

Owen, Trevor. Making Organizations Work. (International Series on the Quality of Working Life: Vol. 7). 1978. pap. text ed. 33.00 (90-207-0779-5) Kluwer Ac.

— The Manager & Industrial Relations. 1979. 80.00 (0-08-022471-7, Pub. by Pergamon Repr UK) Franklin.

Owen, Valarie. Christ, Resurrection Life. 268p. (Orig.). 1985. pap. text ed. 7.95 (0-914307-32-0) R Tilton Ministries.

— In the Beginning God. 224p. (Orig.). (C). 1983. pap. text ed. 6.95 (0-914307-00-2) R Tilton Ministries.

— Let My People Go. 395p. (Orig.). 1983. pap. text ed. 9.95 (0-914307-10-X, Harrison Hse) R Tilton Ministries.

— Possess the Land. 193p. (Orig.). (ps-1). 1984. pap. text ed. 6.95 (0-914307-17-7, Harrison Hse) R Tilton Ministries.

— Wonderful Wisdom. 137p. (Orig.). 1984. pap. text ed. 4.95 (0-914307-24-X) R Tilton Ministries.

Owen, W. G., jt. ed. see Machovich, R.

Owen, W. J., ed. see Wordsworth, William.

Owen, W. J., ed. see Wordsworth, William & Coleridge, Samuel Taylor.

Owen, W. J., ed. see Wordsworth, William.

Owen, W. M. Camp & Battle with Washington Artillery. 36.50 (0-8488-1120-8) Amereon Ltd.

Owen, Walton H., II, jt. auth. see Cooling, Benjamin F., III.

Owen, Wanda. The Captain's Vixen. 400p. (Orig.). 1981. pap. 2.50 (0-89083-709-0) Zebra.

— Deceptive Desires. 1990. mass mkt. 4.50 (0-8217-2887-3) Zebra.

— Golden Desire. 480p. 1994. mass mkt. 4.50 (0-8217-4559-X) Zebra.

— Golden Gypsy. (Orig.). 1983. pap. 3.75 (0-8217-1188-1) Zebra.

— Kiss of Fire. 1990. mass mkt. 4.50 (0-8217-3091-6) Zebra.

— Louisiana Lovesong. 480p. 1993. mass mkt. 4.50 (0-8217-4287-6) Zebra.

— Moonlit Splendor. 496p. 1987. pap. 3.95 (0-8217-2008-2) Zebra.

— Rapture's Bounty. 1982. pap. 3.50 (0-8217-1002-8) Zebra.

— Reckless Ecstasy. pap. 3.95 (0-317-43144-7) Zebra.

— Savage Fury. 448p. 1989. pap. 3.95 (0-8217-2676-5) Zebra.

— Savage Passion. 448p. 1993. mass mkt. 4.50 (0-8217-4089-X) Zebra.

— Sea Princess. 400p. 1995. pap. 4.99 (0-8217-5084-4) Zebra.

— Summer Splendor. 512p. 1988. pap. 3.95 (0-8217-2424-X) Zebra.

— Tempting Texas Treasures. 448p. 1991. mass mkt. 4.50 (0-8217-3312-5) Zebra.

— Texas Captive. 512p. 1988. pap. 3.95 (0-8217-2251-4) Zebra.

— Texas Magic. 432p. 1992. mass mkt. 4.50 (0-8217-3898-4) Zebra.

— Wild Magnolia. 1992. mass mkt. 4.50 (0-8217-3657-4) Zebra.

Owen, Warwick J. Wordsworth As Critic. LC 73-398699. 254p. reprint ed. pap. 72.40 (0-8357-8381-2, 2034009) Bks Demand.

Owen, Wendy. Cat Lover & Other Stories. 128p. 1976. 24.00 (0-7206-0104-5, Pub. by P Owen Ltd UK) Dufour.

Owen, Wilfred. Collected Poems. rev. ed. Lewis, C. Day, ed. LC 64-10290. 1964. pap. 8.95 (0-8112-0132-5, NDP210) New Directions.

— The Metropolitan Transportation Problem. rev. ed. LC 66-21151. 280p. reprint ed. pap. 79.80 (0-317-26343-9, 2025398) Bks Demand.

— Poetry of the First World War. Hudson, Edward, ed. (J). (gr. 3-6). 1990. 22.95 (0-685-45375-8, Lerner Publctns) Lerner Group.

— Strategy for Mobility. LC 78-17067. 249p. 1978. reprint ed. text ed. 59.75 (0-313-20571-X, OWSM, Greenwood Pr) Greenwood.

— Transportation & World Development. LC 87-4154. 176p. 1987. text ed. 28.50x (0-8018-3495-3) Johns Hopkins.

— Transportation for Cities: The Role of Federal Policy. LC 75-44508. 70p. 1976. pap. 8.95 (0-8157-6773-0) Brookings.

— Wilfred Owen. Breen, Jennifer, ed. (English Texts Ser.). 244p. (Orig.). 1988. pap. text ed. 12.95 (0-415-00733-X) Routledge.

Owen, Wilfred, Jr., ed. see Carpenter, Allan.

Owen, William. Diary: From November 10, 1824 to April 20, 1825. (American Biography Ser.). 134p. 1991. reprint ed. lib. bdg. 59.00 (0-7812-8304-3) Rprt Serv.

— Diary of William Owen from Nov. 10, 1824 to April 20, 1825. Hiatt, Joel W., ed. LC 72-77057. 1973. reprint ed. lib. bdg. 27.50 (0-678-00918-X) Kelley.

— Modern Magazine Design. LC 91-2257. (Illus.). 240p. 1991. 50.00 (0-8478-1385-1) Rizzoli Intl.

Owen, William, jt. auth. see Brown, Tom, Jr.

Owen, William B. & Cutlip, W. Frederick. Finite Mathematics. 678p. (C). 1991. text ed. 50.75 (0-15-527546-1) SCP.

Owen, William B. & Goodspeed, Edgar J. Homeric Vocabularies: Greek & English Word-Lists for the Study of Homer. LC 68-31669. (ENG & GRE.). (YA). (gr. 9 up). 1969. pap. 10.95 (0-8061-0828-2) U of Okla Pr.

Owen, William C. Economics of Herbert Spencer. 1977. lib. bdg. 59.95 (0-8490-1747-5) Gordon Pr.

— Selected Writings of William C. Owen. 1977. lib. bdg. 69.95 (0-8490-2591-5) Gordon Pr.

Owen, William M. Autopsy of a Merger: Trans Union: The Deal That Rocked the Corporate World, Vol. 1. LC 83-91307. 341p. 1986. 19.95 (0-9613247-0-8) W M Owen.

— In Camp & Battle with the Washingtons Artillery of New Orleans. 467p. 1983. reprint ed. 32.50 (0-942211-86-3) Olde Soldier Bks.

Owen, William P., jt. auth. see Culp, Wesner, Clup, Inc.

Owen, Wyn F. & Ruby, Douglas A. Guide to Graduate Study in Economics, Agricultural Economics, & Doctoral Programs in Business & Administration in the United States & Canada. 8th ed. 503p. (C). 1989. pap. text ed. write for info. (0-88036-016-X) Econ Inst.

Owens, jt. auth. see Kozacari.

Owens, jt. auth. see Lappas.

Owens, Anthony. Assessment in Specific Circumstances. (C). 1991. pap. 45.00x (0-7300-1336-7, ECT338, Pub. by Deakin Univ AT) St Mut.

Owens, Bill. How to Build a Small Brewery: Draught Beer in Ten Days. (Illus.). 50p. (Orig.). 1994. pap. 10.95 (0-9619072-7-4) G W Kent.

Owens, Bill, intro. California Brew: A Guide to Brewpubs & Microbreweries in the Golden State. (Illus.). (Orig.). 1991. pap. 9.95 (0-9627649-2-2) Trumpetvine.

Owens, Bobby. The Command Sergeant Major's Interventions. LC 93-73657. (Illus.). 1995. 40.00 (1-884308-07-4); pap. text ed. 25.95 (1-884308-08-2) Enlisted Ldrship.

— The Diamond. LC 93-90791. 217p. 1993. 34.00 (1-884308-01-5); pap. text ed. 10.95 (1-884308-02-3) Enlisted Ldrship.

— The Military Years. LC 93-90793. 80p. 1994. 25.00 (1-884308-09-0); pap. text ed. 15.00 (1-884308-10-4) Enlisted Ldrship.

— Platoon Sergeant. LC 93-90792. (Illus.). 224p. 1994. 25.00 (1-884308-03-1); pap. text ed. 14.95 (1-884308-04-X) Enlisted Ldrship.

— Squad Leader. LC 93-93623. 147p. 1993. pap. text ed. 25.00 (1-884308-05-8); pap. text ed. 14.95 (1-884308-06-6) Enlisted Ldrship.

— The Star & the Wreath. 227p. (Orig.). 1993. 33.95 (1-884308-00-7) Enlisted Ldrship.

***Owens, Bobby & Wright, David B.** First Sergeant Spouse's Notes. (Illus.). (Orig.). 1995. pap. text ed. 8.95 (1-884308-27-9) Enlisted Ldrship.

— First Sergeant Spouse's Notes. (Illus.). (Orig.). 1995. 16.95 (1-884308-26-0) Enlisted Ldrship.

Owens, Boone B., ed. Batteries for Implantable Biomedical Devices. LC 86-582. 380p. 1986. 89.50 (0-306-42148-8, Plenum Pr) Plenum.

Owens, Boone B., ed. see Symposium on Power Sources for Biomedical Implantable Applications Staff.

Owens, Carole. The Berkshire Cottages: A Vanishing Era. (Illus.). 240p. (Orig.). 1984. pap. 27.95 (0-918343-00-3) Cottage Pr.

— The Lost Days. 1995. write for info. (0-918343-03-8) Cottage Pr.

Owens, Carole, ed. see Kerness, Elton J.

Owens, Carolyn. Color Me...Cuddly! (Illus.). 32p. (J). (ps-4). 1982. pap. 1.19 (0-87123-695-8) Bethany Hse.

Owens, Carolyn & Roggow, Linda M. Pregnant & Single: Help for the Tough Choices. 144p. 1990. pap. 7.95 (0-685-33050-8) Zondervan.

Owens, Claire M. The Unpredictable Adventure: A Comedy of Women's Independence. (Utopianism & Communitarianism Ser.). (Illus.). 1992. reprint ed. pap. 16.95 (0-8156-2583-9) Syracuse U Pr.

Owens, Coilin D. & Radner, Joan N., eds. Irish Drama, 1900-1980. LC 89-727. 754p. 1989. pap. 24.95 (0-8132-0705-3) Cath U Pr.

***Owens-Couture, Janet.** Hula Dancing. (You Can Do It! Ser.). (Illus.). 80p. (Orig.). (J). (ps up). Date not set. pap. 12.95 (1-56530-078-5) Summit TX.

— Lasso Roping. (You Can Do It! Ser.). (Illus.). 64p. (Orig.). (J). (ps up). Date not set. pap. 12.95 (1-56530-075-0) Summit TX.

Owens, Craig. Beyond Recognition: Representation, Power, & Culture. 1992. 30.00 (0-520-07739-3) U CA Pr.

— Beyond Recognition: Representation, Power, & Culture. LC 92-5314. 1994. pap. 15.00 (0-520-07740-7) U CA Pr.

Owens, D. Alfred & Wagner, Mark, eds. Progress in Modern Psychology: The Legacy of American Functionalism. LC 92-15990. 352p. 1992. text ed. 65.00 (0-275-93055-6, C3055, Praeger Pubs) Greenwood.

Owens, D. H., jt. auth. see Edwards, J. B.

Owens, D. H., jt. ed. see Nichols, N. K.

Owens, D. H., jt. auth. see Rogers, E. T.

Owens, D. R. Human Insulin. 1986. lib. bdg. 136.00 (0-85200-951-8) Kluwer Ac.

***Owens, D. W.** The Gods of Man. 60p. 1994. pap. 5.00 (1-57353-103-0) Eschaton Prods.

Owens, Dan & Platt, John. Kids Study Groups: From Classroom Meetings to Peer Counseling. LC 81-67380. 112p. (Orig.). (C). 1981. pap. text ed. 6.00 (0-918560-26-8) Adler Sch Prof Psy.

Owens, David. Causes & Coincidences. (Studies in Philosophy). (Illus.). 200p. (C). 1992. 47.95 (0-521-41650-7) Cambridge U Pr.

— Multivariable & Optimal Systems. LC 81-67886. 1981. text ed. 112.00 (0-12-531720-4); pap. text ed. 49.00 (0-12-531722-0) Acad Pr.

— A Tribute to Toshiro Mifune. (Illus.). 32p. 1984. pap. 3.50 (0-317-65759-3) Japan Soc.

Owens, David W. Conflicts of Interest in Land Use Management Decisions. 105p. (Orig.). (C). 1991. pap. text ed. 9.00 (1-56011-175-5) Institute Government.

— An Introduction to Zoning. (Orig.). (C). 1995. pap. text ed. write for info. (1-56011-275-1, 95.18) Institute Government.

— Legislative Zoning Decisions in North Carolina. 294p. (Orig.). (C). 1993. text ed. 21.00 (1-56011-256-5, 93-05); pap. text ed. 18.00 (1-56011-217-4, 93-05) Institute Government.

— Public Rights in Shoreline Recreation Areas: A Selectively Annotated Bibliography, No. 894. 1975. 5.00 (0-686-20369-0) CPL Biblios.

Owens, David W., comp. Planning Legislation in North Carolina. 17th ed. 440p. (C). 1992. pap. text ed. 20.00 (1-56011-181-X) Institute Government.

Owens, Dean L. Practical Principles of Ion-Exchange Water Treatment. LC 85-51869. 320p. 1985. 45.00 (0-927188-00-7) Tall Oaks Pub.

Owens, DeDe & Bunker, Linda K. Advanced Golf. LC 92-5940. (Illus.). 176p. 1992. pap. 15.95 (0-88011-464-9, POWE0464) Human Kinetics.

— Coaching Golf Effectively. LC 88-13843. (Coaching Effectively Ser.). (Illus.). 200p. 1989. pap. text ed. 18.00 (0-88011-345-6, POWE0345) Human Kinetics.

— Golf: Steps to Success. LC 88-2459. (Steps to Success Activity Ser.). (Illus.). 224p. (C). 1989. pap. text ed. 14.95x (0-88011-321-9, POWE0321) Human Kinetics.

— Golf: Steps to Success. 2nd ed. LC 95-1518. (Steps to Success Activity Ser.). (Illus.). 168p. 1995. pap. 14.95 (0-87322-578-3, POWE0578) Human Kinetics.

— Teaching Golf: Steps to Success. LC 88-648. (Steps to Success Activity Ser.). (Illus.). 208p. (Orig.). (C). 1989. pap. text ed. 19.95 (0-88011-322-7, POWE0322) Human Kinetics.

Owens, DeDe, jt. auth. see Bunker, Linda K.

Owens, Delia. Eye of the Elephant: An Epic Adventure in the African Wilderness. 1993. pap. 12.95 (0-395-68090-5) HM.

Owens, Delia, jt. auth. see Owens, Mark.

Owens, Derek. Resisting Writings (& the Boundaries of Composition) LC 93-18752. (SMU Studies in Composition & Rhetoric). 212p. 1994. text ed. 24.95 (0-87074-343-0) SMU Press.

***Owens, Dorothy V.** Command Sergeants Major Spouse's Notes. (Illus.). 190p. (Orig.). 1995. pap. text ed. 6.95 (1-884308-25-2) Enlisted Ldrship.

O

An Asterisk (*) at the beginning of an entry indicates that the title is appearing in BIP for the first time.

— Command Sergeants Major Spouse's Notes. (Illus.). 190p. (Orig.). 1995. 15.95 (1-884308-24-4) Enlisted Ldrship.
— D. V. O. Models. LC 93-90794. (Illus.). 100p. 1993. write for info. (1-884308-11-2); pap. write for info. (1-884308-12-0) Enlisted Ldrship.
Owens, E. J. The City in the Greek & Roman World. (Illus.). 224p. 1992. pap. 15.95 (0-415-08224-2, A7630) Routledge.
Owens, Edgar. The Future of Freedom in the Developing World: Economic Development As Political Reform. LC 86-25568. 1987. 32.00 (0-08-034697-9, Pergamon Pr); pap. 17.95 (0-08-034696-0, Pergamon Pr) Elsevier.
Owens, Eleanor, et al. Tennis: Easy on-Easy Off. 70p. 1975. 3.95 (0-938822-10-1) USTA.
Owens, Elisabeth A. Bibliography on Taxation of Foreign Operations & Foreigners. LC 68-23792. 112p. (Orig.). 1968. pap. 5.00 (0-915506-09-2) Harvard Law Intl Tax.
— International Aspects of U. S. Income Taxation: Cases & Materials, Vol. III, Parts 4 & 5. LC 80-18605. 512p. (C). 1980. pap. text ed. 12.50 (0-915506-24-6) Harvard Law Intl Tax.
Owens, Elisabeth A. & Ball, Gerald T. Indirect Credit: A Study of Various Foreign Tax Credits Granted to Domestic Shareholders Under U. S. Income Tax Law, Vol. 1. LC 75-14037. (Illus.). 497p. 1975. 50.00 (0-915506-17-3) Harvard Law Intl Tax.
— Indirect Credit: A Study of Various Foreign Tax Credits Granted to Domestic Shareholders Under U. S. Income Tax Law, Vol. 2. LC 75-14037. (Illus.). 404p. 1979. 50.00 (0-915506-18-1) Harvard Law Intl Tax.
Owens, Elisabeth A. & Hovemeyer, Gretchen A. Bibliography on Taxation of Foreign Operations & Foreigners, 1968-1975. LC 76-14456. 122p. (Orig.). 1976. pap. 7.50 (0-915506-21-1) Harvard Law Intl Tax.
— Bibliography on Taxation of Foreign Operations & Foreigners, 1976-1982. LC 83-18402. 206p. (Orig.). 1983. pap. text ed. 12.50 (0-915506-27-0) Harvard Law Intl Tax.
Owens, Emiel. Financial Markets & Institutions. 736p. (C). 1995. text ed. write for info. (0-02-390281-7) Macmillan.
Owens, F. J. Signal Processing of Speech. 1993. text ed. 30.00 (0-07-047955-0) McGraw.
Owens, Frank, jt. auth. see Iqbal, Zafar.
Owens, Garland C., jt. auth. see Cashin, James A.
Owens, Gene, ed. see Elliott, Ryan.
Owens, George. The Judas Pool. LC 93-31260. 240p. 1994. 21.95 (0-399-13925-7, Putnam) Putnam Pub Group.
Owens, Graham W. & Cheal, Brian. Structural Steelwork Connections. (Illus.). 330p. 1989. text ed. 119.00 (0-408-01214-5, Butterwrth Archit) Buttrwrth-Heinemann.
***Owens, Greg & Staples, David.** The Giant Mine Massacre: The Shocking True Story of a Bitter Labor Struggle & the Cold-Blooded Murder of Nine Yellowknife Miners. (Illus.). 272p. 1995. pap. write for info. (0-88995-131-4, Pub. by Red Deer CN) BookWorld Dist.
— The Third Suspect. 1995. pap. write for info. (0-614-07032-5, Pub. by Red Deer CN) BookWorld Dist.
Owens, Gwendolyn. Nature Transcribed: The Landscapes & Still Lifes of David Johnson, 1827-1908. LC 88-82997. (Illus.). 87p. 1989. pap. 16.95 (0-87451-487-8) U Pr of New Eng.
Owens, Gwendolyn, jt. auth. see Milroy, Elizabeth.
Owens, Harry P. Steamboats & the Cotton Economy: River Trade in the Yazoo-Mississippi Delta. LC 90-33067. 250p. 1990. 35.00 (0-87805-436-7) U Pr of Miss.
***Owens, Hilda F., et al.** College Student Personnel Administration: An Anthology. (Illus.). 416p. 1982. pap. 29.95 (0-398-06310-9) C C Thomas.
— College Student Personnel Administration: An Anthology. (Illus.). 416p. (C). 1982. 45.95 (0-398-04643-3) C C Thomas.
Owens, J. E. The City in the Greek & Roman World: Ancient Town Planning. 224p. 1990. 52.50 (0-415-01896-X, A4870) Routledge.
— Revolutionary Soul. 51p. 1994. pap. text ed. 11.95 (0-9642191-0-7) Promiseland.
Owens, J. F., jt. ed. see Duke, D. W.
Owens, J. J., jt. auth. see Yates, Kyle M.
Owens, Jesse & Neimark, Paul. Jesse: The Man Who Outran Hitler. (Black History Titles Ser.). 1985. mass mkt. 4.95 (0-449-13056-8, GM) Fawcett.
Owens, Jessie A. Claudio Merulo Il Primo Libro de Madrigali a Cinque Voci (Venice, 1566) LC 93-33356. (Sixteenth Century Madrigal Ser.: Vol. 18). 232p. 1994. 78.00 (0-8240-5518-7) Garland.
Owens, Jessie A., ed. Alfonso Dalla Viola: Il Secondo Libro Di Madrigali (4) (Ferrara, 1540) LC 90-754166. (Sixteenth Century Madrigal Ser.: Vol. 6). 240p. 1991. 86.00 (0-8240-5506-3) Garland.
— Alfonso Dalla Viola: Primo Libro Di Madrigali (4) (Ferrara, 1539) LC 90-754039. (Sixteenth Century Madrigal Ser.: Vol. 5). 275p. 1990. 86.00 (0-8240-5505-5) Garland.
— Baldissare Donato: Il Primo Libro Di Madrigali a Cinque & a Sei Voici (Venice, 1560) LC 90-755248. (Sixteenth Century Madrigal Ser.: Vol. 10). 328p. 1991. 86.00 (0-8240-5510-1) Garland.
— Briulio Fiesco. (Sixteenth Century Madrigal Ser.: Vol. 15). 1995. 86.00 (0-8240-5512-8) Garland.
— Claudio Merulo: Il Secondo Libro de Madrigali a Cinque Voci (Venice, 1604) LC 93-49757. (Sixteenth-Century Madrigal Ser.: Vol. 19). 208p. 1994. 71.00 (0-8240-5519-5) Garland.
— Claudio Veggio: Madrigali a Guattro Voci (Venice, 1540) LC 92-772058. (Sixteenth Century Madrigal Ser.: Vol. 4). (Illus.). 216p. 1992. 69.00 (0-8240-5504-7) Garland.
— Domenico Ferrabosco: Il primo llibro de madrigali a quatro voci (Venice, 1542) LC 94-41447. (Sixteenth Century Madrigal Ser.: Vol. 11). 248p. 1995. 84.00 (0-8240-5511-X) Garland.
— Francesco Dalla Viola (d. 1568) Il Primo Libro di Madrigali a Quatro Voci (Venice: Antonio Gardene, 1550), Vol. 7. LC 88-751231. (Italian Madrigal in the Sixteenth Century Ser.). 1988. lib. bdg. 81.00 (0-8240-5507-1) Garland.
— Francesco Manara: Il Primo Libro di Madrigali a Quattro Voci (Venice, 1555) LC 94-295. (Sixteenth Century Madrigal Ser.: Vol. 17). (Illus.). 176p. 1994. 67.00 (0-8240-5517-9) Garland.
— Giachet de Berchem: Madrigali a Cinque Voci. . . Libro Primo (Venice, 1546) LC 93-9142. (Sixteenth Century Madrigal Ser.: Vol. 1). 280p. 1993. 85.00 (0-8240-5501-2) Garland.
— Giacomo Fogliano: Madrigali a Cinque Voci il Primo Libro (Padua, 1547) LC 94-294. (Sixteenth Century Madrigal Ser.: Vol. 13). 268p. 1994. 89.00 (0-8240-5513-6) Garland.
— The Italian Madrigal in the Sixteenth Century: Primo libro de madrigali quatro voci (Venice: Antonio Garane, 1547) - The Italian Madrigal in the Sixteenth Century, Vol. 8. LC 87-733554. 188p. 1988. lib. bdg. 81.00 (0-8240-5508-X) Garland.
— Jan Nasco: Il Primo Libro de Madrigali a Quatro Voci (Venice, 1554) LC 91-755866. (Sixteenth Century Madrigal Ser.: Vol. 20). 176p. 1992. 70.00 (0-8240-5520-9) Garland.
— Jan Nasco: Il Secondo Libro D'i Madrigali a Cinque Voci (Venice, 1557) LC 92-755826. (Sixteenth Century Madrigal Ser.: Vol. 21). 272p. 1992. 80.00 (0-8240-5521-7) Garland.
— Marc'Antonio Ingegneri: Il Secondo Libro de Madrigali a Quattro Voci (Venice, 1579) LC 93-18257. (Sixteenth Century Madrigal Ser.: Vol. 16). 104p. 1993. 48.00 (0-8240-5516-0) Garland.
— Perissone Cambio. LC 89-753449. (Sixteenth Century Madrigal Ser.). 143p. 1989. reprint ed. 76.00 (0-8240-5503-9) Garland.
— Perissone Cambio. LC 90-751362. (Sixteenth Century Madrigal Ser.). 232p. 1990. reprint ed. 86.00 (0-8240-5502-0) Garland.
— Philippe Verdelot, Vol. 1: Madrigals for Four & Five Voices. LC 88-32982. 152p. 1989. 76.00 (0-8240-5530-6) Garland.
— Pietro Taglia: Il Primo Libro De Madrigali a Quattro Voci (Milan, 1555) LC 95-3164. (Sixteenth-Century Madrigal Ser.: Vol. 27). 160p. 1995. 70.00 (0-8240-5529-2) Garland.
— Vincenzo Ruffo (c. 1508-1587) Madrigali a sei, sette e otto voci--Venice: Girolamo Scotto, 1554, Vol. 26. (Italian Madrigal in the Sixteenth Century Ser.). 1988. lib. bdg. 92.00 (0-8240-5528-4) Garland.
— Vincenzo Ruffo (c. 1508-1587) Primo Libro di madrigali a cinque voci--Venice: Girolamo Scotto 1533, Vol. 25. (Italian Madrigal in the Sixteenth Century Ser.). 1989. lib. bdg. 97.00 (0-8240-5527-6) Garland.
***Owens, Jessie A. & Nagaoka, Megumi, eds.** Guglielmo Gonzaga: Madrigali a Cinque Voci (Venice, 1583) LC 95-700102. (Sixteenth-Century Madrigal Ser.: Vol. 14). (Illus.). 320p. 1995. 95.00 (0-8240-5514-4) Garland.
Owens, Jimmy, jt. auth. see Skillings, Otis.
Owens, Joanne. The Official Sunday School Teacher's Handbook. LC 87-43102. (Illus.). 240p. (Orig.). 1987. pap. 9.95 (0-916260-42-9, B-152) Meriwether Pub.
Owens, John, tr. see Calvin, John.
Owens, John, jt. auth. see Smith, Reid.
Owens, John D., III, ed. see Tarry, Tarnie G.
Owens, John G., jt. auth. see Fewkes, Jesse W.
Owens, John J. Analytical Key to the Old Testament, 4 vols. LC 89-437. Set. 189.95 (0-8010-6754-5) Baker Bk.
— Analytical Key to the Old Testament, Vol. 2: Judges - 2 Chronicles. LC 89-437. 960p. 1992. 49.99 (0-8010-6753-7) Baker Bk.
— Analytical Key to the Old Testament, Vol. 3: Ezra-Song of Solomon. LC 89-437. 656p. 1991. text ed. 49.99 (0-8010-6715-4) Baker Bk.
— Analytical Key to the Old Testament, Vol. 4: Isaiah-Malachi. LC 89-437. 960p. 1989. 49.99 (0-8010-6713-8) Baker Bk.
Owens, John J., ed. Analytical Key to the Old Testament, Vol. 1: Genesis-Joshua. LC 89-437. 1032p. 1990. text ed. 49.99 (0-8010-6714-6) Baker Bk.
Owens, John M., jt. auth. see Bennett, Gary W.
Owens, John R., Jr., jt. auth. see McCarthy, Margaret E.
Owens, Jonathan. Early Arabic Grammatical Theory: Heterogeneity & Standardization. LC 90-57. (Studies in the History of the Language Sciences: Vol. 53). xvi, 294p. 1990. 65.00 (90-272-4538-X) Benjamins North Am.
— The Foundations of Grammar: An Introduction to Medieval Arabic Grammatical Theory. LC 87-897. (Studies in the History of the Language Sciences: No. 45). xii, 371p. (C). 1988. 71.00x (90-272-4528-2) Benjamins North Am.
Owens, Joseph. Aristotle: The Collected Papers of Joseph Owens. Catan, John R., ed. LC 81-7602. 264p. 1981. 59.50 (0-87395-534-X); pap. 19.95 (0-87395-535-8) State U NY Pr.
— Cognition: An Epistemological Inquiry. LC 92-70254. (C). 1992. text ed. 29.95 (0-268-00792-6); pap. text ed. 14.95 (0-268-00791-8) U of Notre Dame Pr.
— An Elementary Christian Metaphysics. 399p. 1985. pap. 12.95 (0-685-31938-5) Ctr Thomistic.
— An Elementary Christian Metaphysics. LC 84-23888. 399p. (C). 1985. reprint ed. pap. text ed. 12.95 (0-268-00916-3) U of Notre Dame Pr.
— History of Ancient Western Philosophy. 1959. text ed. write for info. (0-13-389098-8) P-H.
— An Interpretation of Existence. LC 84-23805. 153p. 1987. pap. 7.95 (0-685-31941-5) Ctr Thomistic.
— An Interpretation of Existence. LC 84-23805. 162p. (C). 1987. reprint ed. pap. text ed. 7.95 (0-268-01157-5) U of Notre Dame Pr.
— Saint Thomas Aquinas on the Existence of God: The Collected Papers of Joseph Owens. Catan, John R., ed. LC 79-13885. 291p. 1980. 59.50 (0-87395-401-7); pap. 19.95 (0-87395-446-7) State U NY Pr.
— Towards a Christian Philosophy. LC 89-10008. 332p. 1990. 44.95 (0-8132-0714-2) Cath U Pr.
Owens, Joseph, jt. auth. see Anderson, C. Anthony.
Owens, Joseph C. St. Thomas & the Future of Metaphysics. LC 57-7374. (Aquinas Lectures). 1957. 10.00 (0-87462-122-4) Marquette.
***Owens, Karen.** Parenting. 456p. (C). 1995. text ed. write for info. (0-89876-215-4) Gardner Pr.
— Raising Your Child's Inner Self-Esteem: The Authoritative Guide from Infancy Through the Teen Years. (Illus.). 375p. 1995. 24.95 (0-306-45084-4, Plenum Pr) Plenum.
— The World of the Child. 640p. (C). 1987. text ed. 44.00 (0-03-069853-7) HB Coll Pubs.
— The World of the Child. LC 92-9837. 752p. (C). 1992. write for info. (0-675-21336-3, Merrill Pub Co) Macmillan.
***Owens, Kenneth.** Perilous Passage: Ed Purple's Narrative of the Montana Gold Rush, 1862-1863. (Illus.). 1995. write for info. (0-917298-35-7) MT Hist Soc.
Owens, Kenneth N., ed. John Sutter & a Wider West. LC 93-36522. (Illus.). x, 138p. (C). 1994. text ed. 22.50 (0-8032-3560-7) U of Nebr Pr.
Owens, L., ed. Black Beauty & Other Horse Stories. (Illus.). 1983. 7.98 (0-685-07113-8) Random Hse Value.
Owens, Larry. How to Keep Your Subaru Alive: A Manual of Step-by-Step Procedures for the Compleat Idiot. 2nd ed. 480p. 1989. pap. 21.95 (0-945465-11-4) John Muir.
— How to Keep Your Toyota Pick-Up Alive: A Manual of Step by Step Procedures for the Compleat Idiot. (Illus.). 392p. (Orig.). 1988. pap. 21.95 (0-912528-89-3) John Muir.
Owens, Laurella, ed. see Brown, Virginia P.
Owens, Laurella, jt. auth. see Brown, Virginia P.
Owens, Laurella, jt. ed. see Brown, Virginia P.
Owens, Lee & Barnes, Jenny. Learning Preference Skills. (C). 1992. 90.00 (0-86431-113-3, Pub. by Aust Council Educ Res AT) St Mut.
Owens, Leslie H. This Species of Property: Slave Life & Culture in the Old South. LC 75-38110. 1977. pap. 10.95 (0-19-502245-9) OUP.
Owens, Lillian. Through the Valley. 96p. 1986. pap. 3.50 (0-89114-159-6) Baptist Pub Hse.
Owens, Louis. Bone Game: A Novel. LC 94-13882. (American Indian Literature & Critical Studies: Vol. 10). 1994. 19.95 (0-8061-2664-7) U of Okla Pr.
— Other Destinies: Understanding the American Indian Novel. LC 92-3507. (American Indian Literature & Critical Studies: Vol. 3). 304p. (Orig.). 1994. pap. 12.95 (0-8061-2673-6) U of Okla Pr.
— The Sharpest Sight: A Novel. LC 91-33072. (American Indian Literature & Critical Studies: Vol. 1). 272p. 1992. 19.95 (0-8061-2404-0) U of Okla Pr.
— Wolfsong: A Novel. LC 94-36435. (American Indian Literature & Critical Studies Ser.: Vol. 17). 256p. 1995. pap. 12.95 (0-8061-2737-6) U of Okla Pr.
Owens, Louis, ed. American Literary Scholarship: An Annual, 1990. 545p. 1992. lib. bdg. 50.00 (0-8223-1234-4) Duke.
Owens, Louis D. The Grapes of Wrath: Trouble in the Promised Land. (Masterwork Studies). 128p. (C). 1989. text ed. 21.95 (0-8057-7998-1, Pub. by Royal Botanic Garden UK) Macmillan.
— The Grapes of Wrath: Trouble in the Promised Land. (Twayne's Masterwork Studies: No. 27). 144p. 1989. pap. 12.95 (0-8057-8047-5, Pub. by Royal Botanic Garden UK) Macmillan.
Owens, Loulie L. Dramatizing Your Church's History. Deweese, charles W., ed. (Resource Kit for Your Church's History Ser.). 8p. 1984. pap. 0.60 (0-939804-21-2) Hist Comm S Baptist.
Owens, M., ed. see Wu, Tai T., et al.
Owens, Maire. The Acquisition of Irish: A Case Study. (Multilingual Matters Ser.: No. 72). 300p. 1992. 99.00 (1-85359-114-9, Pub. by Multilingual Matters UK); pap. 39.95 (1-85359-113-0, Pub. by Multilingual Matters UK) Taylor & Francis.
***Owens, Marilyn A. & Loken, Michael R.** Flow Cytometry Principles for Clinical Laboratory Practice: Quality Assurance for Quantitative Immunophenotyping. LC 94-35038. 1994. write for info. (0-471-02176-8) Wiley-Liss.
Owens, Mark & Owens, Delia. Cry of the Kalahari. (Illus.). 352p. 1992. pap. 12.95 (0-395-64780-0) HM.
Owens, Martin. Legal Eagles. (Illus.). 192p. (Orig.). 1986. pap. 7.95 (0-918432-74-X) Baseline Bks.
Owens, Mary B. A Caribou Alphabet. (Illus.). 40p. (J). (ps-3). 1990. pap. 4.95 (0-374-41043-7, Sunburst Bks) FS&G.
— A Caribou Alphabet. (Illus.). 40p. (J). (gr. k-6). 1988. 16.95 (0-937966-25-8) Tilbury Hse.
— Counting Cranes. (J). (ps-3). 1993. 14.95 (0-316-67719-1) Little.
Owens, Mary F. Layman's Bible Book Commentary: Ezra, Nehemiah, Esther, Job, Vol. 7. 1991. 8.99 (0-8054-1177-1) Broadman.
Owens, Middleton U. A Poem for You. 1992. 9.95 (0-533-09671-5) Vantage.
Owens, Milton E., Jr., ed. Outstanding Black Sermons, Vol. 3. 80p. 1982. pap. 9.00 (0-8170-0973-6) Judson.
Owens, N. P., jt. auth. see Castle, E. F.
Owens, Ned & Haynes, J. H. Haynes Honda CB900 C (Custom) DOHC Four Owners Workshop Manual, No. M728: '80-'81. pap. 16.95 (0-85696-728-9) Haynes Pubns.
Owens, Owen. Living Waters: How to Save Your Local Stream. LC 93-7641. (Illus.). 220p. (C). 1993. text ed. 35.00 (0-8135-1997-7); pap. 14.95 (0-8135-1998-5) Rutgers U Pr.
Owens, P. J. & Rae, Alexander C. Bluff Your Way in the Occult. (Bluffers Ser.). 77p. (Orig.). 1993. pap. 3.95 (1-57143-009-1) RDR Bks.
Owens, Peter L., jt. auth. see Owens, Susan.
Owens, Philip. Look, Christ. (C). 1979. pap. 23.00 (0-85088-601-5, Pub. by Gomer Pr UK) St Mut.
Owens, R., jt. auth. see Gabby, D.
Owens, R. Glynn, jt. auth. see Ashcroft, Jennifer J.
Owens, Richard. Peaceful Warrior: A Biography of Horace Porter, 1837-1921. LC 90-48478. (Dissertations in Nineteenth-Century American Political & Social History: Vol. 1). 300p. 1990. 20.00 (0-8240-8195-1) Garland.
— The Professional Singer's Guide to New York. Stallings, Connie, ed. LC 84-70649. 120p. 1983. lib. bdg. 9.95 (0-915357-05-4) AIMS.
— Towards a Career in Europe. 5th ed. LC 84-120169. 90p. (C). 1983. 15.00 (0-915357-00-3) AIMS.
Owens, Richard, ed. see International Joint Conference on Artificial Intelligence.
Owens, Robert. Fillers: All the News That Fits. 150p. (Orig.). 1987. pap. 9.95 (0-918343-02-X) Cottage Pr.
Owens, Robert E., Jr. Language Development: An Introduction. 3rd ed. (Illus.). 576p. (C). 1992. pap. write for info. (0-02-390181-0) Macmillan.
— Language Disorders: A Functional Approach to Assessment & Intervention. 2nd ed. LC 94-17792. 1994. pap. text ed. 44.00 (0-02-390271-X) Allyn.
— Language Disorders: Functional Approach to Assessment & Intervention. 464p. (C). 1990. pap. write for info. (0-675-20773-8, Merrill Pub Co) Macmillan.
Owens, Robert G. Organizational Behavior in Education. 5th ed. LC 94-14853. 1994. text ed. write for info. (0-205-15416-6) Allyn.
Owens, Rochelle. Futz & Who Do You Want, Peire Vidal. 50p. (Orig.). 1986. pap. 4.95 (0-88145-040-5) Broadway Play.
— I Am the Babe of Joseph Stalin's Daughter. pap. 3.50 (0-686-09754-8) Kulchur Foun.
— The Joe Chronicles, Pt. 2. LC 78-11387. 180p. (Orig.). 1979. pap. 5.00 (0-87685-296-7) Black Sparrow.
— The Joe Eighty-Two Creation Poems. LC 74-20591. 136p. (Orig.). 1974. pap. 4.00 (0-87685-216-9) Black Sparrow.
— Paysanne: New & Selected Poems, 1960-1990. (Illus.). 200p. (Orig.). (C). 1991. pap. text ed. 10.00 (0-936556-23-4) Contact Two.
— Rubbed Stones: Collected Poems, 1960-1990. 108p. (Orig.). 1994. pap. 8.00 (0-9641837-0-6) Texture Pr.
— W. C. Fields in French Light. Gosciak, Josh & Kenny, Maurice, eds. LC 86-16843. 60p. (Orig.). 1986. pap. 4.50 (0-936556-14-5) Contact Two.
— The Widow & the Colonel. 1977. pap. 2.75 (0-8222-1252-8) Dramatists Play.
Owens, Rochelle, tr. see Atlan, Liliane.
***Owens, Ron, frwd.** Finding What's Missing: Keys to Full-Color Living in a Spiritually Colorless World. Date not set. pap. 7.99 (1-886797-20-X) Fresh Springs.
***Owens, Rosemary C.** Smashing Times: The History of the Irish Suffrage Movement 1876-1922. (Illus.). 160p. 1995. write for info. (0-614-05165-7, Pub. by Attic IE) InBook.
Owens, S. P., ed. see De Larkin, E. Martin, Jr.
Owens, Sally, ed. see Therrell, Jim.
Owens, Sally L. Compact Dish: The Bread & Breakfast Cookbook. LC 93-71980. (Compact Dish Cookbooks Ser.). 60p. (Orig.). 1993. spiral bd. write for info. (1-883810-06-X) Compact Ckbk.
— Compact Dish: The Casual Chic Cookbook. LC 93-71980. (Compact Dish Cookbooks Ser.). 60p. (Orig.). 1993. spiral bd. write for info. (1-883810-02-7) Compact Ckbk.
— Compact Dish: The Cuisine with Kids Cookbook. LC 93-71980. (Compact Dish Cookbooks Ser.). 60p. (Orig.). 1993. spiral bd. write for info. (1-883810-04-3) Compact Ckbk.
— Compact Dish: The Double Income, No Kids Cookbook. LC 93-71980. (Compact Dish Cookbooks Ser.). 60p. (Orig.). 1993. spiral bd. write for info. (1-883810-03-5) Compact Ckbk.
— Compact Dish: The Rush Hour Cookbook. LC 93-71980. (Compact Dish Cookbooks Ser.). 60p. (Orig.). 1993. spiral bd. write for info. (1-883810-01-9) Compact Ckbk.
— Compact Dish Cookbook Series, 6 vols., Set. LC 93-71980. 360p. (Orig.). 1993. spiral bd. write for info. (1-883810-00-0) Compact Ckbk.
Owens, Sally L., jt. auth. see Atkins, Cary C.
Owens, Scott. The Persistence of Faith. 40p. (Orig.). 1993. pap. 5.95 (0-9635391-2-4) Sandstone NC.
Owens, Shelby. About That Hair. LC 89-91010. (Illus.). 144p. (Orig.). 1989. pap. 8.95 (0-9622542-0-7) S Owens.
***Owens, Sherman.** Why Don't They Teach This in Bible School? 31 Master Secrets Rarely Discovered. LC 94-96199. 78p. (Orig.). 1994. pap. 5.95 (0-9642305-0-X) Ldrship Pubng.
Owens, Susan & Owens, Peter L. Environment, Resources & Conservation. (Topics in Geography Ser.: No. 2). (Illus.). 96p. (C). 1991. pap. 15.50 (0-521-31378-3) Cambridge U Pr.
Owens, Thomas. Bebop: The Music & Its Players. LC 93-32504. (Illus.). 336p. 1995. 25.00 (0-19-505287-0) OUP.
Owens, Thomas S. Collecting Baseball Cards. LC 92-18166. (Illus.). 80p. (J). (gr. 4 up). 1993. lib. bdg. 15.40 (1-56294-254-9); pap. 8.95 (1-56294-713-3) Millbrook Pr.

O

— Collecting Comic Books: A Young Person's Guide. LC 94-48117. (Illus.). 80p. (YA). (gr. 4 up). 1995. lib. bdg. 18.90 (*1-56294-580-7*) Millbrook Pr.

— Collecting Comic Books: A Young Person's Guide. LC 94-48117. (Illus.). 80p. (J). (gr. 4 up). 1995. pap. 8.95 (*1-56294-904-7*) Millbrook Pr.

Owens, Tom. Collecting Sports Autographs: Fun & Profit from This Easy-to-Learn Hobby. 131p. (Orig.). (YA). (gr. 7 up). 1989. pap. 6.95 (*0-933893-79-5*) Bonus Books.

Owens, Tom & Browning, Rod. Lying Eyes: The Shocking Truth Behind the Corruption & Brutality of the LAPD & the Beating of Rodney King. 304p. 1994. 22.95 (*1-56025-074-7*) Thunders Mouth.

Owens, Tom, jt. auth. see Craft, David.

Owens, Tom, ed. see Dixon, Sheila A. & Crowell, Richard D.

***Owens, Tuppy.** High Teas: Twelve Easy to Feed Each Other Recipes. (Illus.). 28p. 1993. 8.00 (*1-872819-01-X*, Pub. by Tuppy Owens UK) AK Pr Dist.

— Safer Planet Sex: The Handbook. (Illus.). 270p. (Orig.). 1994. pap. 14.95 (*1-872819-11-7*, Pub. by Tuppy Owens UK) AK Pr Dist.

— Sensations. (Orig.). 1993. pap. 6.95 (*1-56333-081-4*) Masquerade.

— Shaggy Birthday. (Illus.). 28p. 1993. 5.00 (*1-872819-02-8*, Pub. by Tuppy Owens UK) AK Pr Dist.

Owens, Valerie. The Holy Spirit of God. 168p. (Orig.). 1985. pap. text ed. 6.50 (*0-914307-39-8*) R Tilton Ministries.

***Owens, Virginia S.** Assault on Eden. LC 95-3452. 176p. 1995. reprint ed. pap. 15.99 (*0-8010-5241-6*) Baker Bk.

— At Point Blank: A Suspense Novel. LC 92-11716. 240p. 1992. 14.99 (*0-8010-6724-3*); pap. 9.99 (*0-8010-6752-9*) Baker Bk.

— Congregation: A Suspense Novel. LC 92-38643. 224p. 1992. 14.99 (*0-8010-6750-2*); pap. 9.99 (*0-8010-6751-0*) Baker Bk.

— Daughters of Eve: Women of the Bible Speak to Women of Today. 200p. 1995. pap. text ed., pap. 10.00 (*0-89109-824-0*, NavPr); student ed, per. 5.00 (*0-89109-825-9*, NavPr) NavPress.

— Generations of Women: A Novel. 252p. 1995. 14.00 (*0-89109-821-6*); pap. 10.00 (*0-89109-819-4*) Pinon Press.

— If You Do Love Old Men. LC 90-31158. 217p. reprint ed. pap. 61.90 (*0-7837-6566-5*, 2046131) Bks Demand.

— A Multitude of Sins: A Suspence Novel. LC 39-8971. 272p. 1993. 16.99 (*0-8010-6758-8*); pap. 11.99 (*0-8010-6756-1*) Baker Bk.

Owens, Vivian W. Create a Math Environment: Arithmetic Made Touchable. (Illus.). 192p. (Orig.). 1992. pap. 13.95 (*0-9623839-1-0*) Eschar Pubns.

— Nadanda, the Wordmaker: Hide the Doll. Maxwell, Carolyn, ed. LC 93-74671. (Illus.). 248p. (YA). 1994. 16.95 (*0-9623839-3-7*) Eschar Pubns.

— Parenting for Education. LC 89-80830. 112p. (Orig.). 1989. pap. 6.00 (*0-9623839-0-2*) Eschar Pubns.

Owens, Vivian W., ed. see Tarry, Tarnie G.

Owens, W. A. Martin Fierro. 1974. 200.00 (*0-8490-0586-8*) Gordon Pr.

Owens, W. R., ed. see Bunyan, John.

Owens, W. R., jt. auth. see Furbank, P. N.

Owens, William A. Eye-Deep in Hell: A Memoir of the Liberation of the Philippines, 1944-45. LC 88-42637. (Illus.). 260p. 1989. 24.95 (*0-87074-279-5*) SMU Press.

— Fever in the Earth. 384p. 1984. reprint ed. pap. 9.95 (*0-940672-20-0*) Shearer Pub.

— High Seas: The Naval Passage to an Uncharted World. LC 94-38465. (Illus.). 200p. 1995. 27.95 (*1-55750-661-2*) Naval Inst Pr.

— Look to the River. LC 87-40267. (Texas Tradition Ser.: No. 8). 134p. 1988. reprint ed. pap. 11.95 (*0-87565-026-0*) Tex Christian.

— Tell Me a Story, Sing Me a Song: A Texas Chronicle. 336p. 1983. 25.00 (*0-292-75523-6*); pap. 17.95 (*0-292-78056-7*) U of Tex Pr.

— Texas Folk Songs. rev. ed. LC 76-43005. (Texas Folklore Society Publications: No. 23). (Illus.). 212p. 1976. reprint ed. 15.00 (*0-87074-157-8*) UNTX Pr.

— This Stubborn Soil. 312p. 1992. 19.95 (*0-941130-19-3*) Lyons & Burford.

— This Stubborn Soil. 1989. pap. 8.95 (*0-679-72227-0*, Vin) Random.

— Three Friends: Bedichek, Dobie, Webb. A Personal History. LC 70-82957. 335p. 1975. pap. 7.95 (*0-292-78012-5*) U of Tex Pr.

— Walking on Borrowed Land. LC 87-40266. (Texas Tradition Ser.: No. 9). 320p. 1988. reprint ed. pap. 11.95 (*0-87565-028-7*) Tex Christian.

Owens, William A. & Grant, Lyman, eds. Letters of Roy Bedichek. 600p. 1985. 24.95 (*0-292-70742-8*) U of Tex Pr.

Owens, William A., jt. auth. see Frary, Michael.

Owens, William F. Doctor Shakspear. (Illus.). 215p. 1987. 20.00 (*0-9619127-0-7*) King Wales.

Owens, William L., ed. see American Society of Mechanical Engineers, Meeting Staff.

Owensby, Clenton E. Kansas Prairie Wildflowers. LC 80-17791. (Illus.). 124p. 1980. pap. text ed. 13.95 (*0-8138-1160-0*) Iowa St U Pr.

Owensby, Craig, ed. see Grant, Lee.

Owensby, Craig, ed. see Kramer, Phil & Patrick, Randal.

Owensby, Craig, ed. see Nickell, Lawrence.

Owensby, Craig, ed. see Patrick, Randal.

Owensby, Everett V., Jr. Basic Rules of Capitalism. 1992. 12.95 (*0-533-10196-4*) Vantage.

Owensby, Jacob. Dilthey & the Narrative of History. 208p. 1994. 29.95 (*0-8014-3011-9*) Cornell U Pr.

***Owensby, Jean, et al.** Apple Pie: Delta's Beginning ESL Program, Bk. 1A. rev. ed. Iwataki, Adae, ed. (Illus.). 222p. 1995. student ed, pap. text ed. 7.95 (*0-937354-56-2*); teacher ed, pap. text ed. 12.95 (*0-937354-60-0*); audio 10.95 (*0-937354-99-6*) Delta Systems.

— Apple Pie: Delta's Beginning ESL Program, Bk. 1A Visuals. rev. ed. Iwataki, Adae, ed. (Illus.). 123p. 1995. pap. text ed. 24.95 (*0-937354-64-3*) Delta Systems.

— Apple Pie: Delta's Beginning ESL Program, Bk. 1B. rev. ed. Iwataki, Sadae, ed. (Illus.). 238p. 1995. student ed, pap. text ed. 7.95 (*0-937354-57-0*); teacher ed, pap. text ed. 12.95 (*0-937354-61-9*); audio 10.95 (*0-937354-50-3*) Delta Systems.

— Apple Pie: Delta's Beginning ESL Program, Bk. 1B Visuals. rev. ed. Iwataki, Sadae, ed. (Illus.). 133p. 1995. pap. text ed. 24.95 (*0-937354-65-1*) Delta Systems.

— Apple Pie: Delta's Beginning ESL Program, Bk. 2A. rev. ed. Iwataki, Sadae, ed. (Illus.). 248p. 1995. student ed, pap. text ed. 7.95 (*0-937354-58-9*) Delta Systems.

— Apple Pie: Delta's Beginning ESL Program, Bk. 2A. rev. ed. Iwataki, Sadae, ed. (Illus.). 120p. 1995. teacher ed, pap. text ed. 12.95 (*0-937354-62-7*) Delta Systems.

— Apple Pie: Delta's Beginning ESL Program, Bk. 2A. rev. ed. Iwataki, Sadae, ed. (Illus.). 1995. audio 10.95 (*0-937354-51-1*) Delta Systems.

— Apple Pie: Delta's Beginning ESL Program, Bk. 2A Visuals. rev. ed. Iwataki, Sadae, ed. (Illus.). 187p. 1995. pap. text ed. 24.95 (*0-937354-66-X*) Delta Systems.

— Apple Pie: Delta's Beginning ESL Program, Bk. 2B. rev. ed. Iwataki, Sadae, ed. (Illus.). 240p. 1995. student ed, pap. text ed. 7.95 (*0-937354-59-7*) Delta Systems.

— Apple Pie: Delta's Beginning ESL Program, Bk. 2B. rev. ed. Iwataki, Sadae, ed. (Illus.). 136p. 1995. teacher ed, pap. text ed. 12.95 (*0-937354-63-5*) Delta Systems.

— Apple Pie: Delta's Beginning ESL Program, Bk. 2B. rev. ed. Iwataki, Sadae, ed. (Illus.). 1995. audio 10.95 (*0-937354-52-X*) Delta Systems.

— Apple Pie: Delta's Beginning ESL Program, Bk. 2B Visuals. rev. ed. Iwataki, Sadae, ed. (Illus.). 141p. 1995. pap. text ed. 24.95 (*0-937354-67-8*) Delta Systems.

***Owensby, Phil.** Sun 'n' Soak: Clothing Optional Naturally. (Illus.). 144p. 1994. 21.95 (*0-9643762-0-2*) Solavescence.

Owensby, Walter L. Economics for Prophets: A Primer on Concepts, Realities, & Values in our Economic System. 216p. 1988. pap. 9.99 (*0-8028-0357-1*) Eerdmans.

— Economics for Prophets: A Primer on Concepts, Realities, & Values in Our Economic System. fac. ed. LC 88-1402. (Illus.). 219p. 1988. reprint ed. pap. 62.50 (*0-7837-7969-0*, 2047725) Bks Demand.

***Owenson, Sidney.** The Wild Irish Girl. LC 94-44534. (Revolution & the Age of Romanticism, 1789-1834, Ser.). 1995. 85.00 (*1-85477-189-2*, Pub. by Woodstock Bks UK) Cassell.

Ower, Ernest & Pankhurst, F. C. Measurement of Air Flow: In SI-Metric Units. 5th ed. 1977. 156.00 (*0-08-021282-4*, Pub. by Pergamon Repr UK) Franklin.

Owings. LIKE. 1988. 175.00 (*0-295-77020-1*) U of Wash Pr.

Owings, Alison. Frauen: German Women Recall the Third Reich. LC 92-42097. 550p. (C). 1993. 27.95 (*0-8135-1992-6*) Rutgers U Pr.

— Frauen: German Women Recall the Third Reich. 494p. 1995. pap. text ed. 16.95 (*0-8135-2200-5*) Rutgers U Pr.

Owings, Chloe. Women Police, a Study of the Development & Status of the Women Police Movement. LC 69-14941. (Criminology, Law Enforcement, & Social Problems Ser.: No. 28). 1969. reprint ed. 24.00 (*0-87585-028-6*) Patterson Smith.

Owings, Richard. Non-Operative Aspects of Pediatric Surgery. LC 72-176176. 160p. 1973. 8.50 (*0-87527-118-9*) Green.

Owl Magazine Editors. Amazing but True. (Illus.). 96p. (J). (gr. 3 up). 1992. pap. 3.95 (*0-920775-69-1*, Pub. by Greey dePencier CN) Firefly Bks Ltd.

— Bee Hives & Bat Caves: Amazing Animal Homes. (Illus.). 48p. (J). (gr. 1 up). 1992. pap. 6.95 (*0-920775-46-2*, Pub. by Greey dePencier CN) Firefly Bks Ltd.

— Jokes & Riddles. (Illus.). 96p. (J). (gr. 3 up). 1992. pap. 3.95 (*0-919872-85-9*, Pub. by Greey dePencier CN) Firefly Bks Ltd.

OWL Magazine Editors. The Kids' Question & Answer Book. (Illus.). 80p. (J). (gr. 3-7). 1988. 11.95 (*0-448-19221-7*, G&D) Putnam Pub Group.

Owl Magazine Editors. My Summer Book. (Illus.). 64p. (J). (gr. 3 up). 1992. pap. 8.95 (*0-920775-36-5*, Pub. by Greey dePencier CN) Firefly Bks Ltd.

— Nature What's It? Creatures, Plants, Nature's Oddities & More. (Illus.). 32p. (J). (gr. 4 up). 1992. pap. 4.95 (*0-920775-38-1*, Pub. by Greey dePencier CN) Firefly Bks Ltd.

— Puzzles & Puzzlers. (Illus.). 96p. (J). (gr. 3 up). 1992. pap. 3.95 (*0-920775-67-5*, Pub. by Greey dePencier CN) Firefly Bks Ltd.

— Singing Fish & Flying Rhinos: Amazing Animal Habits. (Illus.). 48p. (J). (gr. 2 up). 1992. pap. 6.95 (*0-920775-45-4*, Pub. by Greey dePencier CN) Firefly Bks Ltd.

— Summer Fun. (Illus.). 128p. (J). (gr. 4 up). 1992. pap. 8.95 (*0-919872-87-5*, Pub. by Greey dePencier CN) Firefly Bks Ltd.

— Weird & Wonderful. (Illus.). 96p. (J). (gr. 3 up). 1992. pap. 3.95 (*0-919872-81-6*, Pub. by Greey dePencier CN) Firefly Bks Ltd.

— What's It? Gadgets, Objects, Machines & More. (Illus.). 32p. (J). (gr. 3 up). 1992. pap. 4.95 (*0-920775-30-6*, Pub. by Greey dePencier CN) Firefly Bks Ltd.

Owl Magazine Editors, ed. The Kids' Cat Book. (Illus.). 96p. (J). (gr. 3 up). 1992. pap. 9.95 (*0-920775-51-9*, Pub. by Greey dePencier CN) Firefly Bks Ltd.

— The Kids' Dog Book. (Illus.). 96p. (J). (gr. 3 up). 1992. pap. 9.95 (*0-920775-50-0*, Pub. by Greey dePencier CN) Firefly Bks Ltd.

Owl Magazine Editors & Chickadee Magazine Editors. Magic Fun: Mystery Potions, Card Magic, Vanishing Tricks Plus Puzzles, Treats, & Much More. (Illus.). 32p. (J). (gr. 1-5). 1992. 14.95 (*0-316-67741-8*, Joy St Bks) Little.

— Party Fun. (Illus.). 32p. (J). (gr. 3 up). 1992. pap. 7.95 (*0-920775-41-1*, Pub. by Greey dePencier CN) Firefly Bks Ltd.

OWL Magazine Editors Staff. The Kids' Question & Answer Book Two. (Illus.). 80p. (J). (gr. 3-7). 1988. 11.95 (*0-448-09276-X*, G&D) Putnam Pub Group.

Owl Magazine Staff. Dinosaur Question & Answer Book: Everything Kids Want to Know about Dinosaurs, Fossils, And... (J). (gr. 4-7). 1992. 16.95 (*0-316-67736-1*, Joy St Bks) Little.

— Winter Fun: A Book Full of Things to Do in Cold Weather. (Illus.). 128p. (J). (gr. 3 up). 1992. pap. 9.95 (*0-919872-86-7*, Pub. by Greey dePencier CN) Firefly Bks Ltd.

Owl Magazine Staff, ed. see Funston, Sylvia.

***Owl, Michael W.** Flat Peyote Stitch. Aberbach, Jason & McCluhan, Michael, eds. (Illus.). 70p. (Orig.). 1993. 19.95 (*0-9643662-0-7*) White Owl Pubns.

Owler, L. W. & Brown, J. L. Wheldon's Cost Accounting. 15th ed. (Illus.). 706p. 1984. 37.50 (*0-7121-2327-X*) Trans-Atl Phila.

— Wheldon's Costing Simplified. 5th ed. (Illus.). 336p. (C). 1978. pap. text ed. 23.50 (*0-7121-2309-1*, Pub. by MacDonald & Evans UK) Trans-Atl Phila.

Owles, Clementina. Growing up Yesterday. 130p. (C). 1988. 35.00 (*0-7212-0692-1*, Pub. by Regency Press) St Mut.

— Salad Days in Baghdad. 130p. 1986. 45.00 (*0-7212-0712-X*, Pub. by Regency Press) St Mut.

Owles, Derrick. Avoiding Liability for Defective Products. (C). 1987. 155.00 (*0-685-33792-8*, Pub. by Witherby & Co UK) St Mut.

Owles, Derrick & Owles, Margot. Independent Taxation of the Husband & Wife. (C). 1991. lib. bdg. 52.00 (*1-85333-384-0*, Pub. by Graham & Trotman UK) Kluwer Ac.

Owles, Lois. Single Serving Recipes: For Special Diets. Ingram, tr. 180p. 1991. pap. text ed. 12.95 (*1-880416-03-4*) NW Pub.

Owles, Margot, jt. auth. see Owles, Derrick.

Owlett, Steven E. Seasons along the Tiadaghton: An Environmental History of the Pine Creek Gorge. 104p. 1993. 39.95 (*0-9635905-0-2*); pap. 23.95 (*0-9635905-1-0*) S E Owlett.

Owman, Christer & Edvinsson, Lars, eds. Neurogenic Control of the Brain Circulation. LC 77-30303. 1977. 216.00 (*0-08-021553-X*, Pub. by Pergamon Repr UK) Franklin.

Owman, Christer & Hardebo, J. E., eds. Neural Regulation of Brain Circulation. (Fernstrom Foundation Ser.: No. 8). 648p. 1987. 249.75 (*0-444-80777-2*) Elsevier.

Ownbey, Gerald B. & Morley, Thomas. Vascular Plants of Minnesota: A Checklist & Atlas. (Illus.). 317p. (C). 1991. pap. text ed. 29.95x (*0-8166-1915-8*) U of Minn Pr.

Ownby, C. L. & Odell, G. V., eds. Natural Toxins: Characterization, Pharmacology & Therapeutics - Proceedings of the 9th World Congress on Animal, Plant & Microbial Toxins, Stillwater, Oklahoma, August 1988. LC 89-3848. (Illus.). 224p. 1989. 80.00 (*0-08-036139-0*, Pub. by Aberdeen U Pr) Macmillan.

Ownby, David & Heidhues, Mary S., eds. Secret Societies Reconsidered: Perspectives on the Social History of Early Modern South China & Southeast Asia. (Studies on Modern China). (Illus.). 272p. (C). 1993. text ed. 62.95 (*1-56324-198-6*, East Gate Bk); pap. text ed. 23.95 (*1-56324-199-4*, East Gate Bk) M E Sharpe.

Ownby, Miriam L. Explore the Everglades. (Illus.). 144p. 1992. pap. 9.95 (*0-937281-06-9*) Geotravel Res Ctr.

Ownby, Raymond L. Psychological Reports: A Guide to Report Writing in Professional Psychology. 2nd rev. ed. LC 91-70437. (Illus.). 198p. (C). 1991. pap. text ed. 21.95 (*0-88422-019-2*) Clinical Psych.

Ownby, Ted. Subduing Satan: Religion, Recreation, & Manhood in the Rural South, 1865-1920. LC 89-48578. (Fred W. Morrison Series in Southern Studies). (Illus.). xiv, 286p. (C). 1990. 32.50 (*0-8078-1913-1*) U of NC Pr.

— Subduing Satan: Religion, Recreation, & Manhood in the Rural South, 1865-1920. LC 89-48578. (Fred W. Morrison Series in Southern Studies). (Illus.). xxii, 286p. 1993. reprint ed. pap. 12.95 (*0-8078-4429-2*) U of NC Pr.

Ownby, Ted, ed. Black & White: Cultural Interaction in the Antebellum South. LC 92-45586. (Chancellor's Symposium on Southern History Ser.). 264p. 1993. text ed. 42.00 (*0-87805-620-3*); pap. text ed. 18.95 (*0-87805-621-1*) U Pr of Miss.

Owne, Trefor M. Welsh Folk Customs. 197p. (C). 1987. text ed. 40.00 (*0-685-50525-1*, Pub. by Gomer Pr UK) St Mut.

Owner Builder Center Staff, jt. auth. see Roskind, Robert.

Ownsbey, Betty J. Alias "Paine" Lewis Thornton Powell, the Mystery Man of the Lincoln Conspiracy. LC 92-56677. (Illus.). 247p. 1993. lib. bdg. 29.95 (*0-89950-874-X*) McFarland & Co.

Owoeye, Jide. Japan's Policy in Africa. LC 92-41579. 200p. 1993. text ed. 79.95 (*0-7734-9236-4*) E Mellen.

Owomoyela, Oyekan. A Ki I: Yoruba Proscriptive & Prescriptive Proverbs. (Yoruba Proverbs: A Comprehensive Standard Source Ser.). 398p. (C). 1988. lib. bdg. 53.00 (*0-8191-6502-6*) U Pr of Amer.

— Visions & Revisions: Essays on African Literature & Criticism. LC 91-6763. (American University Studies: African Literature: Ser. XVIII, Vol. 3). 239p. (C). 1991. text ed. 41.95 (*0-8204-1471-9*) P Lang Pubs.

Owomoyela, Oyekan, ed. A History of Twentieth-Century African Literatures. LC 92-37874. x, 411p. (C). 1993. 55.00 (*0-8032-3552-6*); pap. 25.00 (*0-8032-8604-X*) U of Nebr Pr.

Owram, Doug. The Government Generation: Canadian Intellectuals & the State, 1900-1945. 402p. 1986. text ed. 45.00 (*0-8020-2581-1*) U of Toronto Pr.

— Promise of Eden: The Canadian Expansionist Movement & the Idea of the West, 1856-1900. LC 80-491231. 276p. reprint ed. pap. 78.70 (*0-317-27003-6*, 2023658) Bks Demand.

— Promise of Eden: The Canadian Expansionist Movement & the Idea of the West, 1856-1900. (Reprints in Canadian History Ser.). 288p. 1992. reprint ed. pap. 22.95 (*0-8020-7390-5*) U of Toronto Pr.

Owram, Doug, jt. auth. see Moyles, R. G.

Owram, Doug, jt. ed. see Taylor, M. Brook.

Owre, J. R., ed. see Miami University, Hispanic American Institute Staff.

Owre, J. Riis, ed. see Casona, Alejandro.

Owre, Oscar T. Adaptations for Locomotion & Feeding in the Anhinga & the Double-Crested Cormorant. 138p. 1967. 6.00 (*0-943610-06-0*) Am Ornithologists.

Owsia, Parviz. Formation of Contract: A Comparative Study under English, French, Islamic, & Iranian Law. LC 93-19096. 640p. (C). 1994. lib. bdg. 275.00 (*1-85333-263-1*, Pub. by Graham & Trotman UK) Kluwer Ac.

Owsley, jt. auth. see Gayle.

Owsley, Beatrice R. Hispanic Americans: An Oral History of the American Dream. (Twayne's Oral History Ser.). 200p. 1992. pap. 14.95 (*0-8057-9115-9*, Pub. by Royal Botanic Garden UK) Macmillan.

— Hispanic Americans: An Oral History of the American Dream. (Twayne's Oral History Ser.). 200p. 1993. text ed. 26.95 (*0-8057-9107-8*, Pub. by Royal Botanic Garden UK) Macmillan.

Owsley, Douglas W. & Jantz, Richard L., eds. Skeletal Biology in the Great Plains: Migration, Warfare, Health, & Substinence. LC 91-14388. (Illus.). 408p. (C). 1994. text ed. 45.00 (*1-56098-093-1*) Smithsonian.

Owsley, Frank L., Jr. The C.S.S. Florida: Her Building & Operations. LC 86-19362. 224p. 1987. 19.50 (*0-8173-0336-7*) U of Ala Pr.

Owsley, Frank L. King Cotton Diplomacy: Foreign Relations of the Confederate States of America. LC 58-11952. 637p. reprint ed. pap. 180.00 (*0-8357-8931-4*, 2056767) Bks Demand.

— Plain Folk of the Old South. LC 82-9903. (Walter Lynwood Fleming Lectures in Southern History). 234p. (C). 1982. text ed. 30.00 (*0-8071-1062-0*); pap. text ed. 9.95 (*0-8071-1063-9*) La State U Pr.

— State Rights in the Confederacy. 11.75 (*0-8446-1337-1*) Peter Smith.

Owsley, Frank L., Jr. The Struggle for the Gulf Borderlands: The Creek War & the Battle of New Orleans, 1812-1815. LC 80-11109. (Illus.). vii, 255p. 1981. 32.95 (*0-8130-0662-7*) U Press Fla.

Owsley, Frank L., Jr., ed. see Halbert, H. S. & Ball, T. H.

Owsley, Frank L., Jr., ed. see Reid, John & Eaton, John.

Owsley, Harriet C. Frank Lawrence Owsley: Historian of the Old South. LC 90-46836. (Illus.). xvi, 242p. (Orig.). (C). 1990. 29.95 (*0-8265-1242-9*); pap. 14.95 (*0-8265-1243-7*) Vanderbilt U Pr.

Owsley, Harriet C., jt. ed. see Smith, Sam B.

Owsley, Jim, et al. Wolverine vs. Spider-Man. 64p. 1990. 5.95 (*0-87135-645-7*) Marvel Entmnt.

Owsley, John Q. Aesthetic Facial Surgery. LC 93-2826. (Illus.). 416p. 1993. text ed. 165.00 (*0-7216-3364-1*) Saunders.

Owst, Ken. Laurel & Hardy in Hull. (C). 1989. text ed. 35.00 (*0-948929-34-0*) St Mut.

Owuso, Maxwell, ed. Colonialism & Change: Essays Presented to Lucy Mair. LC 74-83128. (Studies in Anthropology: No. 4). (Illus.). 264p. 1975. pap. text ed. 44.65 (*90-279-3187-9*) Mouton.

Owusu-Ansah, David. Islamic Talismanic Tradition in Nineteenth Century Asante. LC 91-27337. (African Studies: Vol. 21). (Illus.). 268p. 1991. lib. bdg. 89.95 (*0-7734-9726-9*) E Mellen.

Owusu-Ansah, David & McFarland, Daniel M. Historical Dictionary of Ghana. 2nd ed. LC 94-18978. (African Historical Dictionaries Ser.: No. 63). 1994. 52.50 (*0-8108-2919-3*) Scarecrow.

Owusu-Bampah, jt. auth. see Howitt.

Owusu-Bempah, J., jt. auth. see Howitt, Dennis.

Owusu, Martin. Drama of the Gods: A Study of Seven African Plays. 175p. (Orig.). 1983. pap. 8.95 (*0-685-06783-1*) Omenana.

Owyang, G. H. Foundations for Microwave Circuits. (Illus.). 904p. 1989. 79.50 (*0-387-96989-6*) Spr-Verlag.

— Foundations of Optical Waveguides. 246p. 1981. 80.25 (*0-444-00560-9*) Elsevier.

Owyang, Gregory R. Taking a Stand for God. 226p. (Orig.). 1987. pap. 3.50 (*0-945304-00-5*) FCBC.

Owyong & Chan, Laurence. Handbook of Singapore Tax Statutes. 1989. pap. 162.00 (*0-409-99571-1*) Butterworth Legal Pubs.

Oxaal, Ivar. Black Intellectuals & the Dilemmas of Race & Class in Trinidad. LC 72-170653. 334p. 1982. pap. text ed. 22.95 (*0-87073-417-2*) Schenkman Bks Inc.

— Race & Revolutionary Consciousness: A Documentary Interpretation of the 1970 Black Revolt in Trinidad. 96p. 1971. boxed 28.95 (*0-87073-066-5*) Transaction Pubs.

Oxaal, Ivar, et al, eds. Jews, Antisemitism & Culture in Vienna. 280p. 1987. lib. bdg. 55.00 (*0-7102-0899-5*, RKP) Routledge.

An Asterisk (*) at the beginning of an entry indicates that the title is appearing in BIP for the first time.

Oxborrow, Mike. A Practical Reference to SNA. LC 92-43138. 1993. 24.95 (*0-07-707791-1*) McGraw.
Oxbury, John, jt. ed. see Swash, Michael.
Oxelheim, Lars. International Financial Integration. xviii, 389p. 1990. 83.00 (*0-387-52629-3*) Spr-Verlag.
Oxelheim, Lars, ed. The Global Race for Foreign Direct Investment: Prospects for the Future. LC 93-5807. (Illus.). xiv, 273p. 1993. 98.00 (*0-387-56846-8*) Spr-Verlag.
Oxelheim, Lars & Wihlborg, Clas. Macroeconomic Uncertainty: International Risks & Opportunities for the Corporation. LC 87-8333. 320p. 1987. text ed. 76.95 (*0-471-91480-0*) Wiley.
— Macroeconomic Uncertainty: International Risks & Opportunities for the Corporation. LC 87-8333. 251p. 1988. pap. text ed. 49.95 (*0-471-92013-4*) Wiley.
Oxenberg, Christina. Taxi. (Illus.). 208p. 1988. 14.95 (*0-7043-2517-9*, Pub. by Quartet UK) Interlink Pub.
Oxenburgh. Increasing Productivity & Profit Through Health & Safety. 320p. 1992. 90.00 (*0-685-67176-3*, 4703) Commerce.
***Oxenbury.** Animal Scrables. LC 94-68897. 1995. pap. text ed. 4.99 (*1-56402-571-3*) Candlewick Pr.
— People. LC 94-68898. 1995. pap. text ed. 4.99 (*1-56402-572-1*) Candlewick Pr.
Oxenbury, Helen. All Fall Down. (Macmillan Big Board Bks.). (Illus.). 10p. (J). (ps-00). 1987. pap. 6.95 (*0-02-769040-7*, Aladdin Paperbacks) S&S Childrens.
— Beach Day. LC 81-69273. (Illus.). 14p. (J). (ps-00). 1991. bds. 3.95 (*0-8037-0992-7*) Dial Bks Young.
— The Birthday Party. (Illus.). 24p. (J). (ps-1). 1993. pap. 3.99 (*0-14-054947-1*, Puff Pied Piper) Puffin Bks.
— The Car Trip. (Out & about Bk.). (Illus.). 24p. (J). (ps-1). 1983. 3.95 (*0-8037-0009-1*, 0383-120) Dial Bks Young.
— The Car Trip. (Out & about Bks.). (Illus.). 24p. (J). (ps-1). 1994. pap. 3.99 (*0-14-050377-3*, Puff Pied Piper) Puffin Bks.
— The Checkup. (Out & about Bks.). (Illus.). 24p. (J). (ps-1). 1994. pap. 3.99 (*0-14-055275-8*, Puff Pied Piper) Puffin Bks.
— Clap Hands. (Macmillan Big Board Bks.). (Illus.). 10p. (J). (ps). 1987. pap. 6.95 (*0-02-769030-X*, Aladdin Paperbacks) S&S Childrens.
— The Dancing Class. (Illus.). 24p. (J). (ps-1). 1993. pap. 3.99 (*0-14-054934-X*, Puff Pied Piper) Puffin Bks.
— Dressing. (Oxenbury Board Bks.). (Illus.). 14p. (J). (ps-00). 1981. 3.95 (*0-671-42113-1*, Litl Simon S&S) S&S Childrens.
— Eating Out. (Out & about Bks.). (Illus.). 24p. (J). (ps-1). 1994. pap. 3.99 (*0-14-054948-X*, Puff Pied Piper) Puffin Bks.
— Family. (Oxenbury Board Bks.). (Illus.). 14p. (J). (ps-00). 1981. 3.95 (*0-671-42110-7*, Litl Simon S&S) S&S Childrens.
— Favorite Nursery Stories. 1994. pap. text ed. 3.95 (*0-689-71879-9*, Aladdin Paperbacks) S&S Childrens.
— First Day of School. (Illus.). 24p. (J). (ps-1). 1993. pap. 3.99 (*0-14-054977-3*, Puff Pied Piper) Puffin Bks.
— Friends. (Oxenbury Board Bks.). (Illus.). 14p. (J). (ps-00). 1981. 3.95 (*0-671-42111-5*, Litl Simon S&S) S&S Childrens.
— Good Night, Good Morning. LC 81-69272. (Illus.). 14p. (J). (ps-00). 1991. bds. 3.95 (*0-8037-0993-5*) Dial Bks Young.
— Grandma & Grandpa. (Illus.). 24p. (J). (ps-1). 1993. pap. 3.99 (*0-14-054978-1*, Puff Pied Piper) Puffin Bks.
— Helen Oxenbury Favorite Nursery. (J). 1994. pap. 47.40 (*0-689-71882-9*, Aladdin Paperbacks) S&S Childrens.
— The Helen Oxenbury Nursery. Date not set. pap. 7.99 (*0-517-13398-9*) Random.
— Helen Oxenbury's ABC of Things. (Illus.). 28p. (J). (ps). 1993. bds. 3.95 (*0-689-71761-X*, Aladdin Paperbacks) S&S Childrens.
— Helen Oxenbury's First Nursery Stories. (Illus.). 32p. (J). (ps-00). 1994. pap. 3.95 (*0-689-71825-X*, Aladdin Paperbacks) S&S Childrens.
— I Can. (Baby Beginner Board Bks.). (J). 1995. write for info. (*1-56402-547-0*) Candlewick Pr.
— I Hear. (Baby Beginner Board Bks.). (J). 1995. 4.95 (*1-56402-548-9*) Candlewick Pr.
— I See. 2nd ed. (Baby Beginner Board Bks.). (J). 1995. 4.95 (*1-56402-549-7*) Candlewick Pr.
— I Touch. 2nd ed. (Baby Beginner Board Bks.). (J). 1995. 4.95 (*1-56402-550-0*) Candlewick Pr.
— The Important Visitor. (Out & about Bks.). (Illus.). 24p. (J). (ps-1). 1994. pap. 3.99 (*0-14-050379-X*, Puff Pied Piper) Puffin Bks.
— It's My Birthday. LC 93-39667. (Illus.). 24p. (J). (ps up). 1994. 9.95 (*1-56402-412-1*) Candlewick Pr.
— Monkey See, Monkey Do. LC 81-69271. (Illus.). 14p. (J). (ps-00). 1991. bds. 3.95 (*0-8037-0994-3*) Dial Bks Young.
— Mother's Helper. LC 81-68773. (Illus.). 14p. (J). (ps-00). 1991. bds. 3.95 (*0-8037-0995-1*) Dial Bks Young.
— Our Dog. (Out & about Bks.). (Illus.). 24p. (J). (ps-1). 1994. pap. 3.99 (*0-14-050392-7*, Puff Pied Piper) Puffin Bks.
— Pippo Gets Lost. LC 89-340. (Tom & Pippo Bks.). (Illus.). 14p. (J). (ps-00). 1989. bds. 5.95 (*0-689-71336-3*, Aladdin Paperbacks) S&S Childrens.
— Playing. (Oxenbury Board Bks.). (Illus.). 14p. (J). (ps-00). 1981. 3.95 (*0-671-42109-3*, Litl Simon S&S) S&S Childrens.
— Say Goodnight. (Macmillan Big Board Bks.). 10p. (J). (ps). 1987. pap. 6.95 (*0-02-769010-5*, Aladdin Paperbacks) S&S Childrens.
— Shopping Trip. LC 81-69274. (Very First Bks.). 14p. (J). (ps-00). 1982. bds. 3.50 (*0-8037-7939-9*) Dial Bks Young.
— Shopping Trip. LC 81-69274. (Illus.). 14p. (J). (ps-00). 1991. bds. 3.95 (*0-8037-0997-8*) Dial Bks Young.
— Tickle, Tickle. (Macmillan Big Board Bks.). (Illus.). 10p. (J). (ps). 1987. pap. 6.95 (*0-02-769020-2*, Aladdin Paperbacks) S&S Childrens.
— Tom & Pippo & the Dog. LC 89-341. (Tom & Pippo Bks.). (Illus.). 14p. (J). (ps-00). 1989. bds. 5.95 (*0-689-71338-X*, Aladdin Paperbacks) S&S Childrens.
— Tom & Pippo & the Washing Machine. LC 89-37431. (Tom & Pippo Bks.). (Illus.). 14p. (J). (ps-00). 1988. pap. 5.95 (*0-689-71255-3*, Aladdin Paperbacks) S&S Childrens.
— Tom & Pippo Go for a Walk. LC 87-37432. (Tom & Pippo Bks.). (Illus.). 14p. (J). (ps-00). 1988. pap. 5.95 (*0-689-71254-5*, Aladdin Paperbacks) S&S Childrens.
— Tom & Pippo Go Shopping. LC 88-10497. (Tom & Pippo Bks.). (Illus.). 14p. (J). (ps-1). 1989. reprint ed. pap. 5.95 (*0-689-71278-2*, Aladdin Paperbacks) S&S Childrens.
— Tom & Pippo in the Garden. LC 88-9145. (Tom & Pippo Bks.). (Illus.). 14p. (J). (ps-1). 1989. reprint ed. pap. 5.95 (*0-689-71275-8*, Aladdin Paperbacks) S&S Childrens.
— Tom & Pippo in the Snow. LC 89-336. (Tom & Pippo Bks.). (Illus.). 14p. (J). (ps-00). 1989. bds. 5.95 (*0-689-71337-1*, Aladdin Paperbacks) S&S Childrens.
— Tom & Pippo Make a Friend. LC 89-337. (Tom & Pippo Bks.). (Illus.). 14p. (J). (ps-00). 1989. bds. 5.95 (*0-689-71339-8*, Aladdin Paperbacks) S&S Childrens.
— Tom & Pippo Make a Mess. LC 87-37437. (Tom & Pippo Bks.). (Illus.). 14p. (J). (ps-00). 1988. pap. 5.95 (*0-689-71253-7*, Aladdin Paperbacks) S&S Childrens.
— Tom & Pippo on the Beach. LC 92-53130. (Illus.). 24p. (J). (ps). 1993. 5.95 (*1-56402-181-5*) Candlewick Pr.
— Tom & Pippo Read a Story. LC 87-37438. (Tom & Pippo Bks.). (Illus.). 14p. (J). (ps-00). 1988. pap. 5.95 (*0-689-71252-9*, Aladdin Paperbacks) S&S Childrens.
— Tom & Pippo See the Moon. (Tom & Pippo Bks.). (Illus.). 14p. (J). (ps-1). 1989. reprint ed. pap. 5.95 (*0-689-71277-4*, Aladdin Paperbacks) S&S Childrens.
— Tom & Pippo's Day. (Tom & Pippo Bks.). (Illus.). 14p. (J). (ps-1). 1989. reprint ed. pap. 5.95 (*0-689-71276-6*, Mac Bks Young Read) S&S Childrens.
— Working. (Oxenbury Board Bks.). (Illus.). 7p. (J). (ps). 1981. 3.95 (*0-671-42112-3*, Litl Simon S&S) S&S Childrens.
Oxender, Dale L. & Fox, C. Fred, eds. Protein Engineering. 392p. 1987. text ed. 89.95 (*0-471-63066-7*) Wiley.
Oxender, Jean J. Kinder-Fun More Insects Series, 6 bks., Set. (Kinder-Fun Ser.). (Illus.). 96p. (Orig.). (gr. k-3). pap. text ed. 15.00 (*0-87879-691-6*, Ann Arbor Div) Acad Therapy.
Oxendine, Bess H. Miriam. LC 93-61292. (Illus.). 44p. (J). (gr. 2-6). 1994. 6.95 (*1-55523-665-0*) Winston-Derek.
***Oxendine, Joseph.** American Indian Sports Heritage. (Illus.). 480p. 1995. pap. 16.95 (*0-8032-8609-0*, Bison Books) U of Nebr Pr.
Oxendine, Joseph B. American Indian Sports Heritage. LC 87-2860. (Illus.). 352p. 1988. text ed. 39.00x (*0-87322-120-6*, BOXE0120) Human Kinetics.
Oxendine, Reginald. An Educational American Indian Coloring Book. (Illus.). 31p. 1994. pap. text ed. 5.95 (*0-944049-05-2*) Arrow Pub NC.
— An Educational American Leaders Coloring Book. (Illus.). 39p. 1994. pap. text ed. 5.95 (*0-944049-04-4*) Arrow Pub NC.
— Great African American Leaders. (Illus.). 34p. (Orig.). 1994. pap. text ed. 5.95 (*0-944049-03-6*) Arrow Pub NC.
— Our Family Can Read, 2 bks. (Illus.). 76p. (Orig.). (J). (gr. k up). 1992. 29.95 (*0-944049-01-X*); 29.95 (*0-944049-02-8*) Arrow Pub NC.
— Our Family Can Read, 2 bks., Set. (Illus.). 76p. (Orig.). (J). (gr. k up). 1992. audio 29.95 (*0-944049-00-1*) Arrow Pub NC.
Oxendorf, Eric, photos. Domes of America. LC 94-7930. (Illus.). 108p. 1994. 22.95 (*0-87654-070-1*) Pomegranate Calif.
Oxenfeldt, A. R., jt. auth. see Brown, F. E.
Oxenfeldt, Alfred R. Cost-Benefit Analysis for Executive Decision Making: The Danger of Plain Common Sense. LC 79-14617. 442p. reprint ed. pap. 126.00 (*0-317-28147-X*, 2055748) Bks Demand.
— Pricing Strategies. LC 74-78207. 267p. reprint ed. pap. 76.10 (*0-317-27307-8*, 2023527) Bks Demand.
Oxenfeldt, Alfred R. & Schwartz, Jonathan E. Competitive Analysis. (Special Study-Presidents Association Ser.: No. 75). 96p. reprint ed. pap. 27.40 (*0-317-28694-3*, 2051610) Bks Demand.
Oxenford, Lyn. Design for Movement. 1951. pap. 9.95 (*0-87830-561-0*, Theatre Arts Bks) Routledge Chapman & Hall.
— Playing Period Plays. (Illus.). 1984. 12.95 (*0-85343-549-9*, P66); pap. 9.95 (*0-685-57688-4*) Dramatic Pub.
Oxenham, J., jt. ed. see Watson, K.
Oxenham, John. Selected Poems of John Oxenham. Wallis, Charles L., ed. LC 71-179735. (Biography Index Reprint Ser.). 1977. reprint ed. 18.95 (*0-8369-8103-0*) Ayer.
Oxenham, Larry. The Million Dollar Book Writing Formula: It Can Make You Rich (Even if You Can't Write!) (Illus.). 156p. (Orig.). 1988. 14.95 (*0-943813-02-6*) Page One Pub.
— What You Must Know about Home Lenders: Seventeen Answers - the Answer Book, Vol. I. (Illus.). 40p. (Orig.). 1987. pap. 4.75 (*0-943813-00-X*) Page One Pub.
— You Should Not Get a Home Equity Line of Credit: Thirteen Reasons - the Answer Book. (Answer Book Ser.: Vol. II). (Illus.). 40p. 1987. 4.75 (*0-943813-01-8*) Page One Pub.
***Oxenhandler, Neal.** Looking for Heroes in Postwar France: Albert Camus, Max Jacob, Simone Weil. (Illus.). 224p. (C). 1995. 24.95 (*0-87451-731-1*) U Pr of New Eng.
Oxenhandler, Neal, jt. ed. see Nelson, Robert J.
Oxenhorn, Douglas. Money for Film & Video Artists: A Comprehensive Resource Guide. LC 93-38044. 1993. pap. 14.95 (*1-879903-09-1*) Am Council Arts.
— Money for Visual Artists: A Comprehensive Resource Guide. LC 93-25366. 1993. pap. 14.95 (*1-879903-05-9*) Am Council Arts.
Oxenhorn, Harvey. Elemental Things: The Poetry of Hugh MacDiarmid. 215p. 1984. 24.00 (*0-85224-475-4*, Pub. by Edinburgh U Pr UK) Col U Pr.
Oxenius, J. Kinetic Theory of Particles & Photons. (Electrophysics Ser.: Vol. 20). (Illus.). 370p. 1986. 89.00 (*0-387-15809-X*) Spr-Verlag.
Oxenstierna, Susanne. From Labour Shortage to Unemployment? The Soviet Labour Movement in the 1980s. (Swedish Institute for Social Research Ser.: No. 12). 311p. (Orig.). 1990. pap. 59.50x (*91-7604-033-X*, Pub. by Almqv & Wiksell SW) Coronet Bks.
Oxfam Images Working Party Staff. How Does the World Look to You? (C). 1992. pap. text ed. 24.00 (*0-85598-156-3*, Pub. by Oxfam Pubns UK) St Mut.
Oxfam Publications Staff. Art for a Fairer World. (C). 1992. pap. text ed. 21.00 (*0-85598-208-X*, Pub. by Oxfam Pubns UK) St Mut.
— The Kei Road Eviction. (C). 1990. pap. text ed. 24.00 (*0-85598-167-9*, Pub. by Oxfam Pubns UK) St Mut.
— Oxfam Emergency Water Supply Manuals Pack. (C). 1992. text ed. 80.00 (*0-85598-239-X*, Pub. by Oxfam Pubns UK) St Mut.
— Oxfam Peters Projection World Map. (C). 1990. 20.00 (*0-85598-129-6*, Pub. by Oxfam Pubns UK); 30.00 (*0-85598-141-5*, Pub. by Oxfam Pubns UK) St Mut.
— The Oxfam Report: It's Time for a Fairer World. (C). 1991. pap. text ed. 35.00 (*0-85598-181-4*, Pub. by Oxfam Pubns UK) St Mut.
— Oxfam Well Digging Manuals Pack. (C). 1992. text ed. 80.00 (*0-85598-238-1*, Pub. by Oxfam Pubns UK) St Mut.
Oxfeld, Ellen. Blood, Sweat, & Mahjong: Family & Enterprise in an Overseas Chinese Community. LC 92-56779. (Anthropology of Contemporary Issues Ser.). (Illus.). 320p. 1993. 42.50 (*0-8014-2593-X*); pap. 16.95 (*0-8014-9908-9*) Cornell U Pr.
***Oxford.** Patterns of Cultural Identity: Advanced Culture-Tapestry. (College ESL Ser.). 1995. pap. 18.95 (*0-8384-4123-8*) Heinle & Heinle.
Oxford & Scarcella. The Tapestry of Language Learning. 1992. pap. 22.95 (*0-8384-2359-0*) Heinle & Heinle.
Oxford, jt. auth. see Crookall.
Oxford Analytica Staff. Latin America in Perspective. (C). 1991. write for info. (*0-395-52583-7*) HM Soft Schl Col Div.
Oxford Center for Tourism & Leisure Studies, Oxford Brooks University Staff. Cassell Directory of U. K. Visitor Attractions. (Illus.). 256p. 1994. pap. text ed. 250.00 (*0-304-32694-1*) Cassell.
Oxford Conference on Microscopy of Semiconducting Materials Staff. Microscopy of Semiconducting Materials, 1981: Proceedings of the Royal Microscopical Society Conference Held in St. Catherine's College, Oxford, 6-10 April 1981. Cullis, A. G. & Joy, D. C., eds. (Conference Ser.: No. 60). 476p. reprint ed. pap. 135.70 (*0-7837-3255-4*, 2043274) Bks Demand.
Oxford, Earl. Electricity & Magnetism: Physics Laboratory Manual. 128p. (C). 1991. spiral bd. 8.45 (*0-8403-6958-1*) Kendall-Hunt.
— Heat, Sound & Light: Physics Laboratory Manual. 112p. (C). 1990. spiral bd. 8.45 (*0-8403-7475-5*) Kendall-Hunt.
Oxford, Geoffrey S. Protein Polymorphism. Rollinson, David, ed. (Systematics Association Special Ser.: Vol. 24). 1984. text ed. 148.00 (*0-12-531780-8*) Acad Pr.
Oxford, Gerry S. & Armstrong, Clay, eds. Secretion & Its Control. 347p. 1989. 50.00 (*0-87470-045-0*) Rockefeller.
Oxford, Gerry S. & Armstrong, Clay M. Secretion & Its Control. 354p. 1990. 50.00 (*0-685-54188-6*) Rockefeller.
Oxford, J., ed. Chemoprophylaxis & Virus Infections of the Respiratory Tract, 1. (Uniscience Ser.). 1977. 84.00 (*0-8493-5136-7*, RC732, CRC Reprint) Franklin.
— Chemoprophylaxis & Virus Infections of the Respiratory Tract, 2. (Uniscience Ser.). 1977. 84.00 (*0-8493-5137-5*, RC732, CRC Reprint) Franklin.
Oxford, John S. & Oberg, B. Conquest of Viral Diseases: Perspectives in Medical Virology, Vol. 1. 740p. 1985. 260.50 (*0-444-80566-4*) Elsevier.
Oxford, John S., ed. see Collier, Leslie.
Oxford, John S., jt. ed. see Stuart-Harris, Charles.
Oxford, John S., et al, eds. Drug Resistance in Viruses, Other Microbes & Eukaryotes. 232p. 1987. pap. text ed. 64.00 (*0-12-531765-4*) Acad Pr.
Oxford, Mariesa. Going to Grandma's. (Publish-a-Book Contest Ser.). (Illus.). (J). (gr. 2-6). 1992. lib. bdg. 19.97 (*0-8114-3575-X*) Raintree Steck-V.
Oxford Polytechnic Staff. The Socio-Economic Effects of Power Stations on Their Localities. (C). 1989. write for info. (*0-318-66594-8*, Pub. by Oxford Polytechnic UK) St Mut.
Oxford, Rebecca. Language Learning Strategies. 1990. pap. 22.95 (*0-8384-2862-2*, Newbury) Heinle & Heinle.
Oxford Staff & Asquith, Herbert H. Studies & Sketches. LC 68-54366. (Essay Index Reprint Ser.). 1977. 18.95 (*0-8369-0759-0*) Ayer.
Oxford University, British Commonwealth Group Staff. Germany's Colonial Demands. Bullock, Alan L., ed. LC 75-8482. (Illus.). 274p. 1975. reprint ed. text ed. 49.75 (*0-8371-8154-2*, BUGC, Greenwood Pr) Greenwood.
Oxford University Press, English Language Teaching Development Unit Staff, jt. auth. see Donovan, Peter.
Oxford University Press Staff. Business Map of the Arab World. 1980. pap. text ed. 17.00 (*0-86010-211-4*) G & T Inc.
— The Original Oxford English Dictionary on Compact Disc - Single Disc Version. rev. ed. (C). 1988. Incl. instruction book. cd-rom 950.00 (*0-944674-01-1*) Tri Star Pub.
— Oxford-Duden Pictorial Italian & English Dictionary. (Illus.). 880p. (ENG & ITA.). 1995. pap. 39.95 (*0-19-864516-3*) OUP.
***Oxford University Press Staff, ed.** The Oxford Children's Science Library, 3 vols., Set. (Illus.). 160p. (J). (gr. 3-9). 1995. 90.00 (*0-19-521142-1*) OUP.
Oxford University Press Staff & Graham & Trotman Ltd. Staff. Business Map of Nigeria. 1980. pap. text ed. 17.00 (*0-86010-194-0*) G & T Inc.
Oxford University Socialist Discussion Group Staff, ed. Out of Apathy: Voices of the New Left 30 Years On. 160p. 1989. 45.00 (*0-86091-232-9*, A2778, Pub. by Verso UK); pap. 15.95 (*0-86091-945-5*, A2782, Pub. by Verso UK) Routledge Chapman & Hall.
Oxford University. Taylor Institution Staff. Studies in European Literature, Being the Taylorian Lectures 1920-1930. LC 76-90673. (Essay Index Reprint Ser.). 1977. 26.95 (*0-8369-1232-2*) Ayer.
Oxford, William. The Ferry Steamers. (Illus.). 128p. (Orig.). pap. 14.95 (*1-55046-078-1*, Pub. by Boston Mills Pr CN) Genl Dist Srvs.
Oxhandler, Richard. Parents Carry a Full Credit Load Too. 208p. 1989. per. 22.95 (*0-8403-5429-0*) Kendall-Hunt.
***Oxhorn, Philip.** Organizing Civil Society: The Popular Sectors & the Struggle for Democracy. LC 94-34682. 448p. 1995. 55.00 (*0-271-01435-0*); pap. 18.95 (*0-271-01436-9*) Pa St U Pr.
Oxlade, C. & Stockley, C. The World of the Microscope. (Science & Experiments Ser.). (Illus.). 48p. (YA). 1989. lib. bdg. 13.96 (*0-88110-364-0*); pap. 7.95 (*0-7460-0289-0*) EDC.
Oxlade, C., jt. auth. see Wertheim, J.
Oxlade, Chris. Air. LC 94-5547. (Science Magic Ser.). (Illus.). 30p. (J). (gr. 2-5). 1994. 12.95 (*0-8120-6444-5*); pap. 4.95 (*0-8120-1983-0*) Barron.
— Canals & Waterways. LC 93-49749. (Technology Craft Topics Ser.). (Illus.). (J). 1994. 12.60 (*0-531-14331-7*) Watts.
— Fantastic Transport Machines. LC 94-30820. (X-Ray Picture Bks.). (Illus.). 48p. (J). (gr. 5-8). 1995. lib. bdg. 14.98 (*0-531-14351-1*) Watts.
— Fantastic Transport Machines. (X-Ray Picture Bks.). (Illus.). 48p. (J). (ps-3). 1995. pap. 8.95 (*0-531-15733-4*) Orchard Bks Watts.
— Flags. LC 95-11604. (Craft Topics Ser.). (J). 1995. write for info. (*0-531-14386-4*) Watts.
— Houses & Homes. LC 94-15514. (Technology Craft Topics Ser.). (Illus.). 32p. (J). (gr. 5-7). 1994. lib. bdg. 12.60 (*0-531-14330-9*) Watts.
— Light. LC 94-5549. (Science Magic Ser.). (Illus.). 30p. (J). (gr. 2-5). 1994. 12.95 (*0-8120-6445-3*); pap. 4.95 (*0-8120-1984-9*) Barron.
— Science Magic with Forces. LC 94-32052. (Science Magic Ser.). 1994. pap. write for info. (*0-8120-9191-4*) Barron.
— Science Magic with Forces. LC 94-32052. (Science Magic Ser.). (J). 1994. write for info. (*0-8120-6502-6*) Barron.
— Science Magic with Machines. LC 94-40702. (Science Magic Ser.). (J). 1995. write for info. (*0-8120-6517-4*); pap. write for info. (*0-8120-9368-2*) Barron.
— Science Magic with Magnets. LC 94-32055. (Science Magic Ser.). (J). 1994. pap. write for info. (*0-8120-9190-6*) Barron.
— Science Magic with Magnets. LC 94-32055. (Science Magic Ser.). (J). 1994. write for info. (*0-8120-6501-8*) Barron.
— Science Magic with Shapes & Materials. LC 94-40701. (Science Magic Ser.). (J). 1995. write for info. (*0-8120-6518-2*); pap. write for info. (*0-8120-9369-0*) Barron.
— Science Magic with Sound. LC 94-5550. (Science Magic Ser.). (Illus.). 30p. (J). (gr. 2-5). 1994. 12.95 (*0-8120-6446-1*); pap. 4.95 (*0-8120-1985-7*) Barron.
— Water. LC 94-5548. (Science Magic Ser.). (Illus.). 30p. (J). (gr. 2-5). 1994. 12.95 (*0-8120-6448-8*); pap. 4.95 (*0-8120-1986-5*) Barron.
— Writing & Printing. LC 94-37191. (Craft Topics Ser.). (J). 1995. lib. bdg. 12.95 (*0-531-14371-6*) Watts.
Oxlade, Chris & Ganeri, Anita. Everyday Things. LC 94-14376. (Technology Craft Topics Ser.). (Illus.). 32p. (J). (gr. 5-7). 1994. lib. bdg. 12.60 (*0-531-14329-5*) Watts.
Oxlafe, Chris. Bridges & Tunnels. LC 93-41962. (Technology Craft Topics Ser.). (Illus.). (J). 1994. lib. bdg. 12.60 (*0-531-14328-7*) Watts.
Oxlee, G. Air Reconnaissance. (Air Power: Aircraft Weapons Systems & Technology Ser.). (Illus.). 200p. 1994. 40.00 (*0-08-036272-9*); 25.00 (*0-08-036271-0*) Elsevier.
Oxley, Alan. The Challenge of Free Trade: Report to the Eminent Persons Group on World Trade. LC 90-9109. 262p. 1990. text ed. 39.95 (*0-312-05675-3*) St Martin.
Oxley, Beverly, jt. auth. see Duewel, Wesley L.
Oxley, Connie, ed. see Barrett, Patricia R.
Oxley, Connie, ed. see Hart, Rhonda M.
Oxley, Connie, ed. see Hobson, Phyllis.
Oxley, Constance, ed. see Bennett, Bob.
Oxley, Constance, ed. see Dooley, Beth.
Oxley, Constance, ed. see Garden Way Publishing Editors.
Oxley, Constance, ed. see Harrington, Geri.
Oxley, Constance, ed. see Hendrickson, Audra & Hendrickson, Jack.
Oxley, Constance, ed. see Johnson, Pam.
Oxley, Constance, ed. see O'Keefe, John M.
Oxley, Constance, tr. see Reavis, Charles.
Oxley, Constance, ed. see Stovel, Edith.
Oxley, Debra F. Glass Elegance. (Illus.). 40p. 1989. pap. 14.95 (*0-935133-27-5*) CKE Pubns.
— Glass Elegance, No. 2. 40p. 1992. pap. 14.95 (*0-935133-42-9*) CKE Pubns.
Oxley, Debra F. & Dobbins, Norman. Glass Etching 2 - Carving Techniques & Designs. 72p. 1994. pap. text ed. 19.95 (*0-935133-47-X*) CKE Pubns.

O

An Asterisk (*) at the beginning of an entry indicates that the title is appearing in BIP for the first time.

Oxley, Debra F., jt. auth. see Dobbins, Norman.
Oxley, J. Handbook of Logistic & Distribution Management. 339p. (C). 1989. 320.00 (0-685-39896-X, Inst Pur & Supply) St Mut.
Oxley, J., jt. auth. see Rushton, A.
Oxley, James G. Matroid Theory. LC 92-20802. (Illus.). 544p. (C). 1993. 79.00 (0-19-853563-5) OUP.
Oxley, Jane. A Taste of Lemon. 1994. 8.95 (0-533-10874-8) Vantage.
Oxley, John, ed. Excavations at Southampton Castle. (Illus.). 124p. 1993. pap. text ed. 22.00 (0-901723-10-X) A Sutton Pub.
Oxley, Jolyon, et al, eds. Chronic Toxicity of Antiepileptic Drugs. 318p. 1983. text ed. 76.00 (0-89004-947-5) Raven.
Oxley, L., et al, eds. Surveys in Econometrics. (Illus.). 400p. (C). 1994. pap. 29.95 (0-631-19065-1) Blackwell Pubs.
Oxley-Oxland, J. Federal Constitutional Law. 2nd ed. (LBC Nutshell Ser.). xi, 100p. 1989. pap. 11.95 (0-455-20905-7, Pub. by Law Bk Co) W W Gaunt.
— New South Wales Police Law Handbook. 1988. Australia. pap. 33.00 (0-409-49319-8) Butterworth Legal Pubs.
— Principles of Criminal Law in New South Wales. 1985. Australia. pap. 54.00 (0-409-49135-7) Butterworth Legal Pubs.
Oxley-Oxland, J. & Freilich, A. Y. Butterworths Student Companions: Commercial Law, 2 vols., Set. (Student Companion Ser.). 90p. 1986. pap. 14.00 (0-409-49095-4, Austral) Butterworth Legal Pubs.
Oxley-Oxland, J. & Stein, R. T. Understanding Land Law. xx, 171p. 1985. 39.50 (0-455-20303-2, Pub. by Law Bk Co); pap. 22.00 (0-455-20304-0, Pub. by Law Bk Co) W W Gaunt.
Oxley, R. & Poskitt, J. Management Techniques Applied to the Construction Industry. 2nd ed. 1971. pap. 28.00 (0-8464-0593-8) Beekman Pubs.
Oxley, T. & Gobert, E. Dampness in Buildings: Diagnosis, Treatment, Instruments. (Illus.). 132p. 1983. text ed. 16.95 (0-408-01463-6) Buttrwrth-Heinemann.
Oxley, T. A. & Gobert, E. G. Dampness in Buildings: The Professional's & Home Owner's Guide. 2nd ed. LC 94-7413. (Illus.). 136p. 1994. pap. 19.95 (0-7506-2059-5) Buttrwrth-Heinemann.
Oxman, Bernard, ed. The Law of the Sea: U. S. Policy Dilemma. LC 83-107880. 184p. (C). 1983. text ed. 39.95 (0-917616-59-6); pap. 18.95 (0-917616-53-7) Transaction Pubs.
Oxman, Fannie-Rose, jt. auth. see Harnett, Juli O.
Oxman, Michael, ed. see Shrayer, Daivd.
Oxman, Thomas E., jt. ed. see Emery, V. Olga.
Oxmoor House Editors. Best Selling Bazaar Patchwork. 160p. 1992. 24.99 (0-8487-1092-4) Oxmoor Hse.
— Christmas Is Coming, Vol. 2. 144p. 1992. pap. 9.99 (0-8487-1110-6) Oxmoor Hse.
— Christmas with Southern Living, 1992. 160p. 1992. 24.99 (0-8487-1091-6) Oxmoor Hse.
— Cooking Light Cookbook, 1993. 272p. 1993. 24.99 (0-8487-1104-1) Oxmoor Hse.
— Great American Quilts, 1993. 144p. 1993. 24.99 (0-8487-1098-3) Oxmoor Hse.
— Quilter's Complete Guide. 256p. 1993. 29.99 (0-8487-1099-1) Oxmoor Hse.
— Vanessa-Ann's Holidays in Cross-Stitch, 1993. 144p. 1993. 24.99 (0-8487-1086-X) Oxmoor Hse.
***Oxmoor House Staff.** Bubba Gump Shrimp Co. Cookbook: Recipes & Reflections from Forrest Gump. 1994. 14.95 (0-8487-1479-2) Oxmoor Hse.
— Complete Step-by-Step Diabetic Cookbook. 1995. 17.95 (0-8487-1431-8) Oxmoor Hse.
— Cook Healthy Cook Quick. 1995. 29.95 (0-8487-1424-5) Oxmoor Hse.
— Cooking Light Cookbook, 1995. 1995. 24.95 (0-8487-1408-3) Oxmoor Hse.
— Crochet Collection. 1995. pap. 14.95 (0-942237-55-2) Leisure AR.
— Essential Guide to Six Flags Theme Parks. 1995. pap. 12.95 (0-8487-1247-1) Oxmoor Hse.
— McCalls Needlework: 150 Best Loved Christmas Ornaments. 1995. pap. 14.95 (0-8487-1466-0) Oxmoor Hse.
— Quick & Cozy Afghans. 1995. pap. 14.95 (0-942237-48-X) Leisure AR.
— Quick Method Quilts. 1994. pap. 19.95 (0-942237-54-4) Leisure AR.
— Quick Rotary Cutter Quilts. 1994. pap. 19.95 (0-8487-1412-1) Oxmoor Hse.
— Scrap Savers One Hundred One Great Little Gifts. 1994. pap. 14.95 (0-8487-1419-9) Oxmoor Hse.
— Sewing Express. 1994. pap. 14.95 (0-8487-1413-X) Oxmoor Hse.
— Stocking Stuffers. 1994. pap. 14.95 (0-8487-1420-2) Oxmoor Hse.
— Vanessa Anns Holidays in Cross Stitch Vol. 1. 1995. pap. 14.95 (0-8487-1406-7) Oxmoor Hse.
Oxmoor House Staff, ed. The Best of Vanessa-Ann's Cross-Stitch Collection: Cross-Stitch Collection. (Illus.). 160p. 1992. 24.99 (0-8487-1112-2) Oxmoor Hse.
Oxmoor House Staff, ed. see Zieman, Nancy.
Oxmoor Staff. Amer Best Recipes - 94. 1994. 17.95 (0-8487-1163-7) Oxmoor Hse.
— American Country Christmas Bk. 2. 1994. pap. 14.95 (0-8487-1186-6) Oxmoor Hse.
— Best of Just Cross Stitch. 1994. pap. 14.95 (0-8487-1421-0) Oxmoor Hse.
— The Best of Paula Vaughan. 1994. 29.95 (0-942237-49-8) Leisure AR.
— Biltmore Estate Specialities of the House. 1994. 22.95 (0-8487-1246-3) Oxmoor Hse.
— Christmas Is Coming, 1994 Vol. 4: Holiday Projects for Children & Parents. 1994. pap. 14.95 (0-8487-1414-8) Oxmoor Hse.
— Great American Quilts - 95. 1994. 24.95 (0-8487-1401-6) Oxmoor Hse.
— Historic Charleston. Date not set. 13.95 (0-8487-1108-4) Oxmoor Hse.
— Low-Fat Way to Cook Chicken. (Illus.). 144p. 1995. 18.95 (0-8487-2200-0) Oxmoor Hse.
— Low-Fat Way to Cook Pasta. (Illus.). 144p. 1995. 18.95 (0-8487-2201-9) Oxmoor Hse.
— Southern Living Annual Recipes - 94. 1994. 29.95 (0-8487-1403-2) Oxmoor Hse.
— Spirit of Christmas, Bk. 7. LC 93-78118. 1993. 24.95 (0-942237-22-6) Leisure AR.
Oxnam, Garfield B. Preaching in a Revolutionary Age. LC 75-142687. (Essay Index Reprint Ser.). 1977. reprint ed. 20.95 (0-8369-2421-5) Ayer.
Oxnam, Robert B. The Ch'ing Game: History & Simulation. (Foreign Area Materials Center Ser.). 80p. 1972. pap. 2.00 (0-89192-138-9) Interbk Inc.
— Ming: A Novel of Seventeenth Century China. 1994. 21.95 (0-312-11315-3) St Martin.
Oxnard, Charles. The Order of Man: A Biomathematical Anatomy of the Primates. LC 83-50630. 396p. 1984. 47.00 (0-300-03073-8) Yale U Pr.
Oxnard, Charles E. Form & Pattern in Human Evolution. 256p. 1973. lib. bdg. 17.00 (0-226-64251-8) U Ch Pr.
— Fossils, Teeth & Sex: New Perspectives on Human Evolution. LC 86-1328. (Illus.). 310p. 1986. 35.00 (0-295-96389-1) U of Wash Pr.
— Humans, Apes & Chinese Fossils: New Implications for Human Evolution. (C). 1985. pap. text ed. 35.00 (962-209-073-7, Pub. by Hong Kong U Pr HK) St Mut.
— Uniqueness & Diversity in Human Evolution: Morphometric Studies of Australopithecines. LC 74-16689. viii, 134p. 1975. lib. bdg. 17.50 (0-226-64253-4) U Ch Pr.
Oxnard, Charles E., et al. Animal Lifestyles & Anatomies: The Case of the Prosimian Primates. (Illus.). 184p. 1989. 50.00 (0-295-96839-7) U of Wash Pr.
Oxner. FET Technology & Application. (Electrical Engineering & Electronics Ser.: Vol. 54). 288p. 1989. 99.75 (0-8247-8050-7) Dekker.
Oxner, Edward, ed. see Siliconix, Inc. Staff.
Oxner, T. H., et al. The Internal Auditor Job Market, 1992. Campbell, Lee A., ed. 287p. 1992. pap. text ed. 30.00 (0-89413-275-X) Inst Inter Aud.
Oxner, Thomas J., jt. auth. see Kusel, Jimie.
***Oxorn, Harry.** The First Fifty Years, 1944-1994, Society of Obstetricians & Gynaecologists of Canada. 1994. 58.00 (1-85070-562-3) Prthnon Pub.
— Oxorn-Foote Human Labor & Birth. 5th ed. (Illus.). 918p. 1986. pap. text ed. 45.00 (0-8385-7665-6, A7665-1) Appleton & Lange.
Oxrieder, C. A. Your Number's Up: A Calculus Approach to Successful Math Study. 1982. teacher ed 1.50 (0-201-05527-9); text ed. write for info. (0-201-05526-0) Addison-Wesley.
Oxtoby, David W. & Nachtrieb, Norman H. Principles of Modern Chemistry. 2nd ed. 928p. (C). 1991. text ed. 71.00 (0-03-047422-1) SCP.
Oxtoby, David W., et al. Chemistry: Science of Change. 848p. (C). 1990. text ed. 69.25 (0-03-004814-1) SCP.
Oxtoby, J. C. Measure & Category: A Survey of the Analogies Between Topological & Measure Spaces. 2nd rev. ed. LC 73-149248. (Graduate Texts in Mathematics Ser.: Vol. 2). (C). 1987. 39.00 (0-387-90508-1) Spr-Verlag.
Oxtoby, J. C., et al, eds. John Von Neumann, 1903-1957 - JVNM. (Bulletin Ser.: Vol. 64, No. 3). 129p. 1988. reprint ed. pap. 38.00 (0-8218-0021-3, JVN) Am Math.
Oxtoby, L., tr. see Denecke, H. J. & Meyer, R.
Oxtoby, M., ed. Children in Care: The Medical Contribution. (C). 1989. 50.00 (0-903534-81-9, Pub. by Brit Ag for Adopt & Fost UK) St Mut.
— Genetics in Adoption & Fostering: Guidelines & Resources. (C). 1989. 39.00 (0-903534-41-X, Pub. by Brit Ag for Adopt & Fost UK) St Mut.
Oxtoby, Willard G., jt. ed. see Ching, Julia.
Oxton, John R., jt. auth. see Collins, D. Ray.
Oxtopcu, Kurtulus, jt. auth. see Abouv, Zhoumagaly.
Oya, H., jt. ed. see Tsurutani, B. T.
Oyama, Mas. Mas Oyama's Essential Karate. LC 77-79509. (Illus.). 256p. 1979. reprint ed. pap. 14.95 (0-8069-8844-4) Sterling.
Oyama, S. Ted & Hightower, Joe W., eds. Catalytic Selective Oxidation: Developed from a Symposium. LC 92-45894. (ACS Symposium Ser.: No. 523). (Illus.). 466p. 1993. 109.95 (0-8412-2637-7) Am Chemical.
Oyama, T., ed. Endocrinology & the Anaesthetist. (Monographs in Anaesthesiology: Vol. 11). 272p. 1984. 121.75 (0-444-80450-1) Elsevier.
Oyama, T. & Smith, G., eds. Pain & Kampo: The Use of Japanese Herbal Medicine in Management of Pain. LC 93-47603. 1994. write for info. (4-431-70135-4); write for info. (3-540-70135-4); write for info. (0-387-70135-4) Spr-Verlag.
Oyama, Toshikazu, et al, eds. Shakespeare Translation: Annual Publication, 13 vols. 1980. write for info. (0-404-19572-5) AMS Pr.
***Oyamo.** I Am a Man. (Orig.). 1995. pap. 6.95 (1-55783-211-0) Applause Theatre Bk Pubs.
Oyatieva, E. The Dawn of Art: Palaeolithic, Neolithic, Bronze Age & Iron Age Remains Found in the Territory of the Soviet Union. (Hermitage Collection Ser.). 196p. 1974. 35.00 (0-317-14229-1, Pub. by Collets UK) St Mut.
Oye, Kenneth A. Economic Discrimination & Political Exchange: World Political Economy in the 1930s & 1980s. (Studies in International History & Politics). 244p. 1993. text ed. 39.50 (0-691-07849-1); pap. text ed. 16.95 (0-691-00083-2) Princeton U Pr.
Oye, Kenneth A., ed. Cooperation under Anarchy. LC 85-42936. 330p. 1985. 42.50 (0-691-07695-2); pap. 13.95 (0-691-02240-2) Princeton U Pr.
Oye, Kenneth A., et al. Eagle in a New World. (C). 1991. text ed. 31.50 (0-06-500143-5) HarpCollege.
— Eagle Resurgent: The Reagan Era in American Foreign Policy. (C). 1987. pap. text ed. 14.50 (0-673-39469-7) HarpCollege.
Oyediran, Oyeleye, ed. Nigerian Government & Politics under Military Rule 1966-1979. LC 79-15018. 1980. text ed. 32.50 (0-312-57272-7) St Martin.
Oyen, Duane B. Business Fluctuations & Forecasting. LC 85-183986. 600p. 1991. text ed. 46.75 (0-88462-922-8, 4106-35) Dearborn Finan.
Oyen, Else. Comparative Methodology: Theory & Practice in International Social Research. (Studies in International Sociology). (Illus.). 224p. (C). 1990. 45.00 (0-8039-8325-5); pap. 18.95 (0-8039-8326-3) Sage.
Oyen, Else, ed. Comparing Welfare States & Their Futures. 252p. 1986. text ed. 59.95 (0-566-00910-2) Ashgate Pub Co.
Oyer, Herbert J., et al. Speech, Language, & Hearing Disorders: A Guide for the Teacher. 2nd ed. LC 93-22943. 256p. 1993. pap. 31.95 (0-205-14908-1) Allyn.
Oyer, John S. & Kreider, Robert S. Mirror of the Martyrs. LC 90-71117. (Illus.). 96p. (Orig.). 1990. pap. 9.95 (1-56148-003-7) Good Bks PA.
Oyer, Phyllis S. Oyer & Allied Families: Their History & Genealogy, Supplement I. (Illus.). 100p. 1988. pap. 10.00 (0-9620297-0-X) P S Oyer.
Oyewole, A. Historical Dictionary of Nigeria. LC 85-1792. (African Historical Dictionaries Ser.: No. 40). 411p. 1987. 42.50 (0-8108-1787-X) Scarecrow.
***Oyhamburu, Philippe.** Dictionnaire des Patronymes Basques: Euskal Deiruren Hiztegia, Vol. 1. 788p. (BAQ & FRE.). 1991. 75.00 (0-7859-8242-6, 2908132028) Fr & Eur.
Oyibo, G. A. New Group Theory for Mathematical Physics Gas Dynamics & Turbulence. 187p. 1993. lib. bdg. 85.00 (1-56072-123-5) Nova Sci Pubs.
Oyle, Irving. The Healing Mind. LC 74-10069. (Illus.). 128p. 1974. pap. 7.95 (0-912310-80-4) Celestial Arts.
— The New American Medicine Show. LC 78-31345. 176p. (Orig.). (C). 1981. pap. 5.95 (0-913300-18-7) Celestial Arts.
— Time, Space & Mind. LC 76-11339. 168p. (Orig.). 1976. pap. 6.95 (0-89087-122-1) Celestial Arts.
Oyle, Irving & Jean, Susan. The Wizdom Within: On Daydreams, Realities, & Revelations. LC 92-53162. 228p. 1992. pap. 12.95 (0-915811-42-1) H J Kramer Inc.
Oyler, Phyllis. Sandyvale Cemetery, Johnstown, PA: A Recreation of Burials, 1850-1906. 363p. 1989. pap. text ed. 30.00 (0-933227-72-8) Closson Pr.
Oyola, Eliezer, tr. see Dobbins, Richard D.
Oyola, Eliezer, tr. see Hayford, Jack W.
Oyono, Eric. Gollo & the Lion. LC 94-7276. (Illus.). 32p. (J). (ps-3). 1995. 14.95 (0-7868-0041-0); lib. bdg. 14.89 (0-7868-2034-9) Hyprn Child.
Oyono, Ferdinand. Chemin d'Europe. (FRE.). 1973. pap. 14.95 (0-7859-3183-X, 2264004304) Fr & Eur.
— Houseboy. Reed, John, tr. (African Writers Ser.). 122p. (Orig.). (C). 1991. pap. 9.95 (0-435-90532-5) Heinemann.
— The Old Man & the Medal. Reed, John, tr. (African Writers Ser.). 167p. (Orig.). 1969. reprint ed. pap. 8.95 (0-435-90039-0) Heinemann.
— Road to Europe. Bjornson, Richard, tr. LC 86-51301. 120p. (Orig.). 1989. 24.00 (0-89410-590-6); pap. 10.00 (0-89410-591-4) Three Continents.
— Une Vie de Boy. (FRE.). 1970. pap. 9.95 (0-7859-3430-8) Fr & Eur.
— Le Vieux Negre et la Medaille. (FRE.). 1972. pap. 14.95 (0-7859-3195-3, 2264009624) Fr & Eur.
Oyono-Mbia, Guillaume, et al. Faces of African Independence: Three Plays. Arnold, A. J. & Drame, K., eds. Blair, Dorothy & Wake, Clive, trs. LC 88-6976. (CARAF Bks.). 127p. (Orig.). 1988. 25.00 (0-8139-1186-9); pap. 12.95 (0-8139-1187-7) U Pr of Va.
Oyos, Lynwood. Over a Century of Leadership: South Dakota Territorial & State Governors. LC 87-71833. (Illus.). 250p. 1987. 17.95 (0-931170-34-6) Ctr Western Studies.
— Over a Century of Leadership: South Dakota Territorial & State Governors. deluxe ed. LC 87-71833. (Illus.). 250p. 1987. 75.00 (0-931170-35-4) Ctr Western Studies.
Oyos, Lynwood E. A Noble Calling: Teacher Education at Lutheran Normal School & Augustana College, 1889-1989. LC 90-30516. 100p. (Orig.). 1990. pap. 4.00 (0-931170-45-1) Ctr Western Studies.
O'Young, Bryan, jt. ed. see Young, Mark.
Oystaeyen, F. M., ed. Ring Theory. (Lecture Notes in Mathematics Ser.: Vol. 1197). v, 231p. 1986. pap. 29.30 (0-387-16496-0) Spr-Verlag.
Oyster, et al. Introduction to Research: A Guide for the Health Science Professional. LC 64-4347. 1987. text ed. 21.50 (0-397-54626-2, Lippincott Medical) Lippincott.
***Oyster Books Staff.** My Ballet Collection: Sleeping Beauty. (Illus.). 32p. (J). 1995. 4.95 (0-8362-0769-6) Andrews & McMeel.
— My Ballet Collection: Swan Lake. (Illus.). 32p. (J). 1995. 4.95 (0-8362-0771-8) Andrews & McMeel.
— My Ballet Collection: The Nutcracker. (Illus.). 32p. (J). 1995. 4.95 (0-614-06516-X) Andrews & McMeel.
Oyster, Esther M., jt. auth. see Moench, John O.
Oyston, Mildred V. Joseph's Sojourn in Egypt. 60p. 4.95 (0-89036-153-3) Hawkes Pub Inc.
Oyuela-Caycedo, Augusto. History of Latin American Archaeology. LC 94-4854. (Worldwide Archaeology Ser.: Vol. 15). 1994. 71.95 (1-85628-714-9, Pub. by Avebury Pub UK) Ashgate Pub Co.
Oyugi, Walter, et al. Democratic Theory & Practice in Africa. LC 88-21101. 237p. (Orig.). (C). 1988. pap. text ed. 18.50 (0-435-08026-1, 08026) Heinemann.
Oz, Amos. Black Box. De Lange, Nicholas, tr. (Vintage International Ser.). 1989. pap. 11.00 (0-679-72185-1, Vin) Random.
— Elsewhere, Perhaps. De Lange, Nicholas, tr. LC 73-8628. (Helen & Kurt Wolff Bk.). 324p. 1985. pap. 9.95 (0-15-628475-8, Harvest Bks) HarBrace.
— Fima. 1994. pap. 11.95 (0-15-600143-8) HarBrace.
— The Hill of Evil Counsel. 1991. pap. 7.95 (0-15-640275-0, Harvest Bks) HarBrace.
— In the Land of Israel. 1993. pap. 11.95 (0-15-648114-6) HarBrace.
— Israel, Palestine, & Peace. 1995. pap. 13.00 (0-15-600192-6) HarBrace.
— My Michael. 1992. pap. 11.00 (0-679-72804-X, Vin) Random.
— A Perfect Peace. Halkin, Hillel, tr. LC 84-25171. (Helen & Kurt Wolff Bk.). 400p. 1985. 16.95 (0-15-171696-X) HarBrace.
— Perfect Peace. 1993. pap. 11.95 (0-15-671683-6) HarBrace.
— The Slopes of Lebanon. Goldberg-Bartura, Maurie, tr. 1989. 18.95 (0-15-183090-8) HarBrace.
— Slopes of Lebanon. 1992. pap. 11.00 (0-679-73144-X, Vin) Random.
— Soumchi. Farmer, Penelope, tr. LC 94-45033. (Illus.). 96p. (J). (gr. 4 up). 1995. pap. 10.00 (0-15-600193-4, Harvest Bks) HarBrace.
— The Third State. De Lange, Nicholas, tr. LC 92-44200. 1993. 22.95 (0-15-189851-0) HarBrace.
— To Know a Woman. 1991. 19.95 (0-15-190499-5) HarBrace.
— To Know a Woman. 1992. pap. 8.95 (0-15-690680-5, Harvest Bks) HarBrace.
— Touch the Water, Touch the Wind. 1991. pap. 7.95 (0-15-690772-0, Harvest Bks) HarBrace.
— Under This Blazing Light. De Lange, Nicholas, tr. 224p. (C). 1995. 19.95 (0-521-44367-9) Cambridge U Pr.
— Unto Death. LC 77-15963. (Illus.). 168p. 1978. pap. 3.95 (0-15-693170-2, Harvest Bks) HarBrace.
Oz, Avraham. The Yoke of Love: Prophetic Riddles in The Merchant of Venice. LC 93-31278. 264p. 1995. 39.50 (0-87413-490-0) U Delaware Pr.
Oz, Effy. Ethics for an Information Age. 336p. 1994. pap. write for info. (0-697-20462-6); Casebook. write for info. (0-697-20463-4) Bus & Educ Tech.
***Oz, Robin, illus.** Peanut Butter. 2nd ed. (Let Me Read, Level 2, Ser.). (J). 1995. bds. 2.95 (0-673-36271-X) GdYrBks.
***Oz-Salzberger, Fania.** Translating the Enlightenment: Scottish Civic Discourse in Eighteenth-Century Germany. (Oxford Historical Monographs). 360p. 1995. 55.00 (0-19-820519-8) OUP.
Oza, S. S. & Bhatt, R. G. Modern Combined Dictionary: English - Gujarti & Gujarti - English. 103p. 1992. reprint ed. 29.95 (0-8288-8471-4) Fr & Eur.
Ozaeta, Pablo. Mis Primeros Cuentos. Frank, Marjorie & Lono, Luz P., eds. LC 75-16546. (Illus.). (J). (gr. 4-8). 1985. teacher ed 10.60 (0-8325-9641-8, Natl Textbk); 76.60 (0-8325-9640-X, Natl Textbk); student ed, pap. 6.60 (0-8325-9642-6, Natl Textbk) NTC Pub Grp.
Ozaga, John. Whitetail Country. 1993. pap. 19.95 (1-55971-207-4) NorthWord.
Ozak, Muzaffer. Love Is the Wine: Talks of a Sufi Master in America. LC 87-51082. 108p. (Orig.). 1987. pap. 9.00 (0-939660-22-9) Threshold VT.
Ozaki, Hosai. Right under the Big Sky, I Don't Wear a Hat: The Haiku & Prose of Hosai Ozaki. Sato, Hiroaki, tr. LC 93-3814. 144p. (Orig.). 1993. pap. 12.00 (1-880656-05-1) Stone Bridge Pr.
Ozaki, M., jt. ed. see Gladstone, A.
Ozaki, Muneto, et al. Labour Relations in the Public Service: Developing Countries. xv, 205p. (Orig.). 1988. pap. 22.00 (92-2-106394-1) Intl Labour Office.
— Technological Change & Labour Relations. xiv, 205p. 1992. pap. 24.00 (92-2-107753-5) Intl Labour Office.
Ozaki, Robert. Human Capitalism: The Japanese Enterprise System As World Model. LC 91-8095. 224p. 1991. 19.95 (4-7700-1549-6) Kodansha.
— Human Capitalism: The Japanese Enterprise System as World Model. 224p. 1992. pap. 10.00 (0-14-016933-4, Penguin Bks) Viking Penguin.
Ozaki, Robert S. Japanese: A Cultural Portrait. 328p. 1991. pap. 8.95 (0-8048-1670-0) C E Tuttle.
Ozaki, Y. T., ed. Japanese Fairy Tales. 1977. lib. bdg. 250.00 (0-8490-2091-3) Gordon Pr.
Ozaki, Yei T. Japanese Fairy Book. 1992. 15.00 (0-8446-2690-2) Peter Smith.
Ozaki, Yei T., comp. The Japanese Fairy Book. LC 70-109415. (Illus.). 320p. (J). (gr. 3-8). 1970. pap. 12.95 (0-8048-0885-6) C E Tuttle.
Ozan, Turgut M. Applied Mathematical Programming for Production & Engineering Management. 656p. 1986. teacher ed write for info. (0-8359-0028-2, Reston); text ed. 63.00 (0-8359-0026-6, Reston) P-H.
***Ozaniec, Naomi.** Chakras for Beginners. (For Beginners Ser.). (Illus.). 112p. 1995. pap. 9.95 (0-340-62082-X, Pub. by Headway UK) Trafalgar.
— Daughter of the Goddess: The Sacred Priestess. (Illus.). 1993. pap. 14.00 (1-85538-280-6, Pub. by Aquarian Pr UK) Thorsons SF.
— Dowsing. (For Beginners Ser.). (Illus.). 112p. 1995. pap. 9.95 (0-340-60882-X, Pub. by Hodder & Stoughton Ltd UK) Trafalgar.
— Element Tarot Handbook: Initiation into the Key Elements of the Tarot. 1994. pap. 14.95 (1-85230-488-X) Element MA.
— Elements of Egyptian Wisdom. 1994. pap. 9.95 (1-85230-497-9) Element MA.

An Asterisk (*) at the beginning of an entry indicates that the title is appearing in BIP for the first time.

— Elements of the Chakras. 1990. pap. 9.95 (*1-85230-174-0*) Element MA.

Ozanne, Adam. Perverse Supply Response in Agriculture: The Importance of Produced Means of Production & Uncertainty. 188p. 1992. 68.95 (*1-85628-375-5*, Pub. by Avebury Pub UK) Ashgate Pub Co.

***Ozanne, Charles.** Life & Soul of Mortal Man. 32p. 1995. pap. 2.50 (*1-880573-21-0*) Grace WI.

— The Pastorals in Perspective. 40p. (Orig.). 1993. pap. 1.25 (*1-880573-10-5*) Grace WI.

***Ozanne-Rivierre, Francoise.** Dictionnaire Iaai. 1984. write for info. (*0-7859-8078-4*, 2-85297-126-7) Fr & Eur.

Ozanne, Robert W. Wages in Practice & Theory: McCormick & International Harvester, 1860-1960. LC 68-19572. (Illus.). 195p. reprint ed. pap. 55.60 (*0-8357-6778-7*, 2035454) Bks Demand.

Ozanne, Roy, jt. auth. see Halfpenny, James.

Ozar. Dental Ethics at Chairside: Professional Principles. 250p. 1993. pap. 29.00 (*0-8016-7400-X*) Mosby Yr Bk.

***Ozar, Lorraine, ed.** By Their Fruits You Shall Know Them. 27p. (Orig.). 1995. pap. 10.60 (*1-55833-145-X*) Natl Cath Educ.

***Ozar, Lorraine A.** Creating a Curriculum That Works. (Illus.). 172p. (Orig.). 1994. pap. 16.60 (*1-55833-143-3*) Natl Cath Educ.

***Ozarowski, Joseph S.** To Walk in God's Ways: Jewish Pastoral Perspectives on Illness & Bereavement. LC 94-40782. 232p. 1995. text ed. 30.00 (*1-56821-388-3*) Aronson.

Ozawa. Analog Methods for Computer-Aided Circuit Analysis & Diagnosis. (Electrical Engineering & Electronics Ser.: No. 48). 440p. 1988. 135.00 (*0-8247-7843-X*) Dekker.

Ozawa, E., jt. ed. see Ebashi, Setsuro.

Ozawa, E., et al, eds. Frontiers in Muscle Research: Myogenesis, Muscle Contraction & Muscle Dystrophy. (International Congress Ser.: No. 942). 448p. 1991. 217.50 (*0-444-81390-X*, Excerpta Medica) Elsevier.

Ozawa, Ichiro. Blueprint for a New Japan: The Rethinking of a Nation. Rubinfein, Louisa, tr. 224p. 1994. 25.00 (*4-7700-1871-1*) Kodansha.

— Blueprint for a New Japan: The Rethinking of a Nation. Rubenfein, Louisa, tr. 208p. Date not set. 10.00 (*4-7700-2034-1*) FS&G.

Ozawa, K. Liver Surgery Approached Through the Mitochondria. (Illus.). 222p. 1993. 121.75 (*3-8055-5716-7*) S Karger.

— Living Related Donor Liver Transplantation: Assessment of Graft Viability Based on the Redox Theory. (Illus.). xii, 212p. 1994. 179.25 (*3-8055-5800-7*) S Karger.

Ozawa, K. A. High Density Magnetic Recording for Home Vtr. (Japanese Tecnology Reviews, Section A). 1993. pap. text ed. 45.00 (*2-88124-887-X*) Gordon & Breach.

Ozawa, Lyuji. Cathodo-luminescence: Theory & Applications. 308p. 1990. lib. bdg. 155.00 (*0-89573-936-4*) VCH Pubs.

Ozawa, Martha N., ed. Women's Life Cycle & Economic Insecurity: Problems & Proposals. LC 89-7505. (Contributions in Women's Studies: No. 108). 248p. 1989. text ed. 55.00 (*0-313-26753-7*, OWC/, Praeger Pubs); pap. text ed. 17.95 (*0-275-93348-2*, B3348, Praeger Pubs) Greenwood.

Ozawa, T., ed. New Trends in Biological Chemistry. (Illus.). 440p. 1991. 124.00 (*0-387-53935-2*) Spr-Verlag.

Ozawa, T., jt. ed. see Kim, C. H.

Ozawa, T., et al, eds. Prostglandins & Cardiovascular Disease. 220p. 1986. 95.00 (*0-85066-357-1*) Taylor & Francis.

Ozawa, Terutomo. Multinationalism, Japanese Style: The Political Economy of Outward Dependency. LC 79-84007. 320p. (Orig.). 1982. reprint ed. pap. 15.95 (*0-691-00367-X*) Princeton U Pr.

— People & Productivity in Japan. (Studies in Productivity: Vol. 25). 42p. 1982. pap. 55.00 (*0-08-029506-1*) Work in Amer.

***Ozbalkan, N.** English-Turkish Dictionary of Technical Terms. 7th ed. (ENG & TUR.). 1989. 117.00 (*0-7859-8973-0*) Fr & Eur.

— English-Turkish Dictionary of Technical Terms. 7th ed. 960p. 1989. 117.00 (*975-7609-02-1*) IBD Ltd.

— Textile Dictionary in Four Languages. 1053p. (ENG, FRE, GER & TUR.). 94.00 (*0-88431-308-5*) IBD Ltd.

— Turkish-English Dictionary of Technical Terms. 2nd rev. ed. 1152p. 1989. 117.00 (*975-7368-19-9*) IBD Ltd.

***Ozbalkan, Nuri.** Ingilizce-Turkce Teknik Terimler Sozlugu. 7th ed. 976p. (ENG & TUR.). 1989. write for info. (*0-7859-6786-9*) Fr & Eur.

— Turkish-English Dictionary of Technical Terminology. 1152p. (ENG & TUR.). 1984. 150.00 (*0-8288-0672-1*, M1980) Fr & Eur.

Ozbudum, Ergun, jt. auth. see Weiner, Myron.

Ozbudun, Ergun. Social Change & Political Participation in Turkey. LC 76-3013. (Center for International Affairs at Harvard University Ser.). 1976. 42.50x (*0-691-07580-8*) Princeton U Pr.

Ozbudun, Ergun & Ulusan, Aydin, eds. The Political Economy of Income Distribution in Turkey. LC 79-2781. (Political Economy of Income Distribution in Developing Countries Ser.: Vol. III). 1980. 85.00 (*0-8419-0563-0*) Holmes & Meier.

***Ozcan, Gul B.** Small Firms & Local Economic Developments: Entrepreneurship in Southern Europe & Turkey. 240p. 1995. boxed, pap. 63.95 (*1-85972-117-6*, Pub. by Avebury Pub UK) Ashgate Pub Co.

Ozeki, Kazuo, jt. ed. see Asaka, Tetsuichi.

Ozeki, Yuzuru, jt. auth. see Tavlas, George S.

Ozekici, S., ed. Queueing Theory & Applications. (Proceedings of the Arab School of Science & Technology Ser.). 210p. 1990. 83.00 (*0-89116-995-4*) Hemisp Pub.

Ozelton, E. C., jt. auth. see Baird, J. A.

***Ozenbaugh.** EMI Filter Design. (Electrical Engineering & Electronics Ser.). 524p. 1995. write for info. (*0-8247-9631-4*) Dekker.

Ozenda, P. Lichens. (Encyclopedia of Plant Anatomy Ser.: Vol. VI, 9). (Illus.). 200p. (FRE.). 1963. lib. bdg. 66.00 (*3-443-39010-2*) Lubrecht & Cramer.

Ozenfant, Amadee & Le Corbusier, eds. L' Esprit Nouveau, 8 Vols, Set. LC 68-26816. (Illus.). (FRE.). 1968. reprint ed. lib. bdg. 450.00 (*0-306-71149-4*) Da Capo.

Ozer. Management of Persons with Stroke. 502p. 1993. 39.95 (*0-8016-6801-8*) Mosby Yr Bk.

Ozer, D. J. Consistency in Personality. (Recent Research in Psychology Ser.). (Illus.). 82p. 1986. pap. 42.00 (*0-387-96299-9*) Spr-Verlag.

Ozer, Elizabeth M. & Toure, Nkenge. Staying Safe: How to Protect Yourself Against Sexual Assault. (Illus.). 23p. (Orig.). (J). (gr. 2-6). 1984. pap. text ed. 3.00 (*0-318-04650-4*) Rape Crisis Ctr.

Ozer, Jan. Video Compression for Multimedia. 387p. 1994. cd-rom, pap. 39.95 (*0-12-531940-1*, AP Prof) Acad Pr.

Ozer, Jerome S., ed. Film Review Annual, 1981. xiii, 1153p. 1982. lib. bdg. 125.00 (*0-89198-125-X*) Ozer.

— Film Review Annual, 1982. 1362p. 1983. 125.00 (*0-89198-126-8*) Ozer.

— Film Review Annual, 1983. 1538p. 1984. lib. bdg. 125.00 (*0-89198-131-4*) Ozer.

— Film Review Annual, 1984. (Film Review Annual Ser.). 1548p. 1985. 125.00 (*0-89198-133-0*) Ozer.

— Film Review Annual, 1985. 1554p. 1986. 125.00 (*0-89198-134-9*) Ozer.

— Film Review Annual, 1986. 6th ed. 1650p. 1987. 125.00 (*0-89198-135-7*) Ozer.

— Film Review Annual, 1987. 1672p. 1988. 125.00 (*0-89198-136-5*) Ozer.

— Film Review Annual, 1988. xiii, 1773p. 1989. 125.00 (*0-89198-138-1*) Ozer.

— Film Review Annual, 1989. xiii, 1792p. 1991. 125.00 (*0-89198-139-X*) Ozer.

— Film Review Annual, 1990. xiv, 1658p. 1991. 125.00 (*0-89198-142-X*) Ozer.

— Film Review Annual, 1991. xvi, 1726p. 1992. lib. bdg. 125.00 (*0-89198-144-6*) Ozer.

— Film Review Annual, 1992, Vol. 12. xiv, 1714p. 1993. 125.00 (*0-89198-145-4*) Ozer.

— Film Review Annual, 1993, Vol. 13. 1738p. 1994. 125.00 (*0-89198-146-2*, Film Review Pubns) Ozer.

— Film Review Annual, 1994 Vol. 14. xiv, 1746p. 1995. 125.00 (*0-89198-147-0*, Film Review Pubns) Ozer.

— Opera Annual: U. S., 1984-1985. (Opera Annual Ser.). (Illus.). 1988. lib. bdg. 48.00 (*0-89198-132-2*) Ozer.

— Women's Rights & Liberation, 13 vols., Set. 1969. reprint ed. 321.50 (*0-405-00101-0*) Ayer.

Ozer, Jerome S., ed. see Carpenter, Niles.

Ozer, Kemal. Like a Flame. Barkan, Stanley H., ed. Halman, Talat S., tr. (Review Turkish Writers Chapbook Ser.: No. 4). 48p. (ENG & TUR.). 1991. 15.00 (*0-89304-280-3*); 15.00 (*0-89304-282-X*); pap. 5.00 (*0-89304-281-1*); pap. 5.00 (*0-89304-283-8*) Cross-Cultrl NY.

Ozer, Mark N. The Management of Persons with Spinal Cord Injury. LC 88-70004. 125p. (Orig.). 1988. pap. 24.95 (*0-939957-10-8*) Demos Vermande.

— Solving Learning & Behavior Problems of Children: A Planning System Integrating Assessment & Treatment. LC 79-28316. (Jossey-Bass Social & Behavioral Science Ser.). 272p. reprint ed. pap. 77.60 (*0-8357-6882-1*, 2037934) Bks Demand.

Ozer, Steven. Netherlands. (Let's Visit Places & Peoples of the World Ser.). (Illus.). 104p. (J). (gr. 5 up). 1990. 14.95 (*0-7910-1107-0*) Chelsea Hse.

Ozergene, Nil. Lessons of the Pipeline Negotiations. (CISA Working Paper Ser.: No. 40). 45p. (Orig.). Date not set. pap. 10.00 (*0-86682-052-3*) Ctr Intl Relations.

Ozersky, Josh, ed. Readings for the 21st Century: Tomorrow's Issues for Today's Students. 2nd ed. LC 93-33503. 1993. write for info. (*0-205-15874-9*); pap. text ed. 18.00 (*0-205-15536-7*) Allyn.

Ozete, Ocsar & Guillen, Sergio D. Contigo: Essentials of Spanish. 2nd ed. (Illus.). 368p. (C). 1991. pap. text ed. write for info. (*0-03-029979-9*) HB Coll Pubs.

— Instructors Edition Contigo: Essentials of Spanish. 2nd ed. (Illus.). 368p. (C). 1991. teacher ed. pap. text ed. write for info. (*0-318-67327-4*) HB Coll Pubs.

Ozete, Oscar & Guillen, Sergio D. Contigo: Essentials of Spanish. 384p. (C). 1987. pap. text ed. 40.00 (*0-03-001828-5*) HB Coll Pubs.

Ozga, Jenny, ed. Schoolwork: Approaches to the Labor of Teaching. Vol. 1. 224p. 1987. 90.00 (*0-335-15554-5*, Open Univ Pr) Taylor & Francis.

— Women in Educational Management. LC 92-17389. (Gender & Education Ser.). 1993. 27.00 (*0-335-09340-X*, Open Univ Pr) Taylor & Francis.

Ozga, Jenny, jt. ed. see Moore, Rob.

Ozgediz, Selcuk. Governance & Management of CGIAR Centers. (CGIAR Study Paper Ser.: No. 27). 200p. 1991. 11.95 (*0-8213-1848-9*, 11848) World Bank.

Ozguler, A. Linear Multichannel Control. 224p. 1994. text ed. 70.00 (*0-13-155558-8*) P-H.

Ozguner, Fusun & Ercal, Fikret, eds. Parallel Computing on Distributed Memory Multiprocessors. LC 92-43569. (NATO ASI Series F: Computer & Systems Sciences, Special Programme AET: Vol. 103). 1993. 89.00 (*0-387-56295-8*) Spr-Verlag.

Ozgur, Ozdemir A. Apartheid: The United Nations & Peaceful Change in South Africa. LC 83-23972. 240p. (Orig.). 1982. lib. bdg. 35.00 (*0-941320-01-4*) Transnatl Pubs.

Ozhegov, S. I. Dictionary of the Russian Language. 798p. (C). 1988. 135.00 (*0-569-07728-1*, Pub. by Collets) St Mut.

***Ozick, Cynthia.** Bloodshed & Three Novellas. (Library of Modern Jewish Literature). 192p. 1995. pap. 14.95 (*0-8156-0352-5*) Syracuse U Pr.

— The Cannibal Galaxy. 1984. pap. 7.95 (*0-525-48133-8*, Obelisk) NAL-Dutton.

— The Cannibal Galaxy. (Library of Modern Jewish Literature). 162p. 1995. pap. 14.95 (*0-8156-0354-1*) Syracuse U Pr.

— Levitations: Five Fictions. (Library of Modern Jewish Literature). 158p. 1995. pap. 14.95 (*0-8156-0353-3*) Syracuse U Pr.

— The Messiah of Stockholm. 1987. 15.95 (*0-394-54701-2*) Knopf.

— The Messiah of Stockholm. LC 87-45911. 160p. 1988. reprint ed. pap. 11.00 (*0-394-75694-0*, Vin) Random.

— Metaphor & Memory. LC 92-50093. (Vintage International Ser.). 304p. 1991. pap. 13.00 (*0-679-73425-2*, Vin) Random.

— The Pagan Rabbi & Other Stories. (Library of Modern Jewish Literature). 228p. 1995. pap. 14.95 (*0-8156-0351-7*) Syracuse U Pr.

— The Pagan Rabbi & Other Stories. 288p. 1991. pap. 11.00 (*0-14-015343-8*, Penguin Bks) Viking Penguin.

— Shawl. 1989. 12.95 (*0-394-57976-3*) Knopf.

— The Shawl. LC 89-40638. 74p. 1990. pap. 7.95 (*0-679-72926-7*, Vin) Random.

— What Henry James Knew. (Chapbooks in Literature Ser.). (Illus.). 40p. (Orig.). 1993. pap. text ed. 5.00 (*1-878603-05-1*) Bennington Coll.

***Oziedzinski, Stanislaw.** Life & Times of a Polish Coal Miners Son. 230p. (YA). 1995. pap. 8.95 (*1-56901-686-0*) NW Pub.

Ozieva, Albina, et al. Collins Russian-English, English-Russian Dictionary. LC 94-13824. (ENG & RUS.). 1994. pap. 20.00 (*0-06-276528-0*) HarpC.

Ozima, Minoru. Geohistory: Global Evolution of the Earth. Wakabayashi, J. F., tr. 170p. (C). 1987. pap. text ed. 38.00 (*0-387-16595-9*) Spr-Verlag.

Ozimek, John. Targeting for Success: A Guide to New Techniques for Measurement & Analysis in Database & Direct Marketing. LC 93-10242. (Marketing for Professionals Ser.). 1993. write for info. (*0-07-707766-0*) McGraw.

Ozinga, James. Communism: The Story of the Idea & Its Implementation. 2nd ed. 272p. (C). 1990. pap. text ed. write for info. (*0-13-171125-3*) P-H.

Ozio, David & Herbst, Dan. Bowl Like a Pro: Winning Techniques That Will Raise Your Average. LC 92-11488. (Illus.). 224p. 1992. pap. 11.95 (*0-8092-4039-4*) Contemp Bks.

Ozisik. Boundary Value Problems of Heat Conduction. 1989. pap. 11.95 (*0-486-65990-9*) Dover.

Ozisik, M. N., jt. auth. see Mikhailov, M. D.

Ozisik, M. Necati. Basic Heat Transfer. LC 85-23213. 590p. 1987. reprint ed. text ed. 49.50 (*0-89874-942-5*) Krieger.

— Finite Difference Methods in Heat Transfer. LC 94-3162. 1994. write for info. (*0-8493-2491-2*) CRC Pr.

— Heat Conduction. 2nd ed. 712p. 1993. text ed. 89.95 (*0-471-53256-8*) Wiley.

— Heat Transfer: A Basic Approach. (Illus.). 800p. (C). 1985. text ed. write for info. (*0-07-047982-8*) McGraw.

Ozisik, M. Necati, jt. auth. see Bayazitoglu, Yildiz.

Ozisik, M. Necati, jt. auth. see Mikhailov, M. D.

Ozkan, jt. auth. see Raghavan.

***Ozkan, Umit S., et al, eds.** Reduction of Nitrogen Oxide Emissions. LC 95-2400. (ACS Symposium Ser.: No. 587). 1995. write for info. (*0-8412-3150-8*) Am Chemical.

Ozkaya, Nihat & Nordin, Margareta. Fundamentals of Biomechanics. (Illus.). 416p. 1991. text ed. 69.95 (*0-442-00313-7*) Van Nos Reinhold.

Ozken, Doreen. An Early Woodland Community at the Schultz Site 20SA2 in the Saginaw Valley. (Anthropological Papers: No. 70). 1982. pap. 5.00 (*0-932206-92-1*) U Mich Mus Anthro.

Ozman. Jennifer's Birthday Present. LC 73-87798. (Illus.). 32p. (J). (gr. k-3). 1974. lib. bdg. 9.95 (*0-87783-125-4*) Oddo.

— Jennifer's Birthday Present. deluxe ed. LC 73-87798. (Illus.). 32p. (J). (gr. k-3). 1974. pap. 3.94 (*0-87783-126-2*) Oddo.

Ozment, James L., et al. Dreams, Visions & Visionaries. (Colorado Rail Annual Ser.: No. 20). (Illus.). 240p. 1993. 42.95 (*0-918654-20-3*) CO RR Mus.

Ozment, Stephen. The Age of Reform Twelve Fifty to Fifteen Fifty: An Intellectual & Religious History of Late Medieval & Reformation Europe. LC 79-24162. (Illus.). 1981. pap. 18.00 (*0-300-02760-5*) Yale U Pr.

Ozment, Steven. Magdalena & Balthasar: An Intimate Portrait of Life in Sixteenth-Century Europe Revealed in the Letters of a Nuremberg Husband & Wife. LC 86-15545. (Illus.). 192p. (C). 1989. pap. 12.00 (*0-300-04378-3*) Yale U Pr.

— Protestants: Birth of a Revolution. LC 93-16872. 1993. 12.95 (*0-385-47101-7*) Doubleday.

— Three Behaim Boys: Growing Up in Early Modern Germany - A Chronicle of Their Lives. LC 89-27312. 312p. (C). 1990. 32.00 (*0-300-04670-7*) Yale U Pr.

— When Fathers Ruled: Family Life in Reformation Europe. LC 83-6098. (Illus.). 256p. (C). 1983. 29.95 (*0-674-95120-4*) HUP.

— When Fathers Ruled: Family Life in Reformation Europe. (Studies in Cultural History). 256p. 1985. pap. 13.95 (*0-674-95121-2*) HUP.

Ozment, Steven, ed. Three Behaim Boys: Growing up in Early Modern Germany. (Illus.). 312p. (C). 1991. reprint ed. pap. text ed. 16.00 (*0-300-05133-6*) Yale U Pr.

— Three Behaim Boys: Growing Up in Early Modern Germany: A Chronicle of Their Lives. braille ed. 662p. 1993. text ed. 52.96 (*1-56956-401-9*, BR9066) W A T Braille.

Ozment, Steven, jt. auth. see Kagan, Donald.

Ozment, Steven E. The Reformation in the Cities: The Appeal of Protestantism to Sixteenth-Century Germany & Switzerland. LC 75-8444. 248p. 1980. pap. 13.00 (*0-300-02496-7*) Yale U Pr.

Ozment, Steven E., ed. Reformation Europe: A Guide to Research. 390p. 1982. 18.50 (*0-910345-01-5*); pap. 13.50 (*0-686-82436-9*) Center Reform.

Ozmidov, R. V. Diffusion of Contaminants in the Ocean. (C). 1990. lib. bdg. 164.00 (*0-7923-0611-2*) Kluwer Ac.

Ozmidov, R. V., jt. auth. see Monin, A. S.

Ozmon, H. Twelve Great Western Philosophers. LC 68-16403. (Illus.). 48p. (J). (gr. 4 up). 1967. lib. bdg. 9.95 (*0-87783-046-0*) Oddo.

— Twelve Great Western Philosophers. deluxe ed. LC 68-16403. (Illus.). 48p. (J). (gr. 4 up). 1967. pap. 3.94 (*0-87783-115-7*) Oddo.

Ozmon, Howard & Craver, Samuel. Philosophical Foundations of Education. 4th ed. 432p. (C). 1990. pap. write for info. (*0-675-21133-6*, Merrill Pub Co) Macmillan.

***Ozmon, Howard A. & Craver, Samuel M.** Introduction to Philosophical Foundations of Education. 5th ed. 1994. write for info. (*0-02-390311-2*) Merrill.

Ozmun, John, jt. auth. see Gallahue, David L.

Oznakawanie, Malowanie, jt. auth. see Wrobel, Jaroslaw.

Oznobishev, M. A. Russko-Ispanskii Aviatsionno-Kosmicheskii Slovar: Russian-Spanish Aviation & Aerospace Dictionary. 920p. (RUS & SPA.). 1980. write for info. (*0-8288-0755-8*, M6131) Fr & Eur.

Ozog, A. Conrad, jt. ed. see Jones, Gary M.

***Ozoga, John.** Whitetail Winter. (Seasons of the Whitetail Ser.). (Illus.). 160p. 1995. 29.50 (*1-57223-027-4*, WCP) Outlook Pubng.

Ozoga, John J. Whitetail Autumn. LC 94-32654. (Seasons of the Whitetail Ser.). (Illus.). 160p. 1994. 29.50 (*1-57223-007-X*) Outlook Pubng.

— Whitetail Country. Petrie, Chuck, ed. & frwd. by. (Illus.). 144p. 1988. 39.00 (*0-932558-43-7*) Willow Creek Pr.

Ozolins, Uldis. The Politics of Language in Australia. LC 92-30377. (Illus.). 304p. (C). 1993. 64.95 (*0-521-41794-5*) Cambridge U Pr.

Ozols, Robert F., ed. Drug Resistance in Cancer Therapy. (C). 1989. lib. bdg. 112.50 (*0-7923-0244-3*) Kluwer Ac.

— Molecular & Clinical Advances in Anticancer Drug Resistance. (Cancer Treatment & Research Ser.). 320p. (C). 1991. lib. bdg. 137.00 (*0-7923-1212-0*) Kluwer Ac.

Ozols, Robert F., jt. ed. see Goldstein, Lori T.

Ozols, Violet, tr. see Lorber, Jakob.

Ozorio de Almeida, Anna L. The Colonization of the Amazon. LC 92-5938. (Translations from Latin America Ser.). (Illus.). 389p. (C). 1992. text ed. 30.00 (*0-292-71146-8*) U of Tex Pr.

Ozouf, Mona. Festivals & the French Revolution. Sheridan, Alan, tr. LC 87-14958. (Illus.). 398p. 1988. 48.00 (*0-674-29883-7*) HUP.

— Festivals & the French Revolution. 398p. (C). 1991. pap. 18.95 (*0-674-29884-5*) HUP.

— Fete Revolutionnaire, 1789-1799. (Folio-Histoire Ser.: No. 22). (FRE.). pap. 18.95 (*2-07-032496-6*) Schoenhof.

Ozouf, Mona, jt. auth. see Furet, Francois.

Ozouf, Mona, jt. ed. see Furet, Francois.

Ozsu, M. Tamer & Valduriez, Patrick. Principles of Distributed Database Systems. 528p. 1990. text ed. 64.00 (*0-13-691643-0*) P-H.

Ozsu, M. Tamer, et al. Distributed Object Management. LC 93-31654. 500p. 1993. pap. 49.95 (*1-55860-256-9*) Morgan Kaufmann.

Ozsvath, Zsuzsanna & Turner, Frederick, trs. Foamy Sky: The Major Poems of Miklos Radnoti. (Lockert Library of Poetry in Translation). 160p. 1992. text ed. 24.95 (*0-691-06954-9*); pap. text ed. 9.95 (*0-691-01530-9*) Princeton U Pr.

Oztopcu, Kurtulus. Azerbaijani, Colloquial. 66p. 1994. 9.95 (*0-88432-789-2*); audio 75.00 (*0-88432-788-4*) Audio-Forum.

— Uzbek, Colloquial. 54p. 1994. 5.95 (*0-88432-744-2*, AFUZ91); 75.00 (*0-88432-743-4*, AFUZ10) Audio-Forum.

Ozturk, Aydin, et al, eds. The Frontiers of Statistical Scientific Theory & Industrial Applications, Vol. 2: Proceedings of the ICOSCO-I Conference (First International Conference on Statistical Computing, Cesme, Izmir, Turkey, March-April 1987) LC 90-85327. (Series in Mathematical & Management Sciences: Vol. 26). 450p. 1991. 110.00 (*0-935950-28-1*) Am Sciences Pr.

P

P-51 Mustang Pilots Assoc. Staff. The P-51 Mustang. LC 87-51161. 144p. 1987. 48.00 (*0-938021-56-7*) Turner Pub KY.

P. A. R., jt. auth. see Smith, Barry.

P. E. Lewis & Ward Staff. The Finite Element Method: Principles & Applications. (Illus.). 421p. (C). 1991. text ed. 41.95 (*0-201-54415-6*) Addison-Wesley.

P. F. Collier Staff. Collier's Encyclopedia, 1995 Edition, 24 vols., Set. LC 94-70743. (Illus.). 19900p. 1995. write for info. (*1-57161-003-0*) P F Collier.

— Collier's Encyclopedia, 1995 Edition, Vol. 1. LC 94-70743. (Illus.). 628p. 1995. 35.00 (*1-57161-004-9*) P F Collier.

— Collier's Encyclopedia, 1995 Edition, Vol. 2. LC 94-70743. (Illus.). 780p. 1995. 35.00 (*1-57161-005-7*) P F Collier.

— Collier's Encyclopedia, 1995 Edition, Vol. 3. LC 94-70743. (Illus.). 783p. 1995. 35.00 (1-57161-006-5) P F Collier.
— Collier's Encyclopedia, 1995 Edition, Vol. 4. LC 94-70743. (Illus.). 764p. 1995. 35.00 (1-57161-007-3) P F Collier.
— Collier's Encyclopedia, 1995 Edition, Vol. 5. LC 94-70743. (Illus.). 726p. 1995. 35.00 (1-57161-008-1) P F Collier.
— Collier's Encyclopedia, 1995 Edition, Vol. 6. LC 94-70743. (Illus.). 762p. 1995. 35.00 (1-57161-009-X) P F Collier.
— Collier's Encyclopedia, 1995 Edition, Vol. 7. LC 94-70743. (Illus.). 772p. 1995. 35.00 (1-57161-010-3) P F Collier.
— Collier's Encyclopedia, 1995 Edition, Vol. 8. LC 94-70743. (Illus.). 788p. 1995. 35.00 (1-57161-011-1) P F Collier.
— Collier's Encyclopedia, 1995 Edition, Vol. 9. LC 94-70743. (Illus.). 760p. 1995. 35.00 (1-57161-012-X) P F Collier.
— Collier's Encyclopedia, 1995 Edition, Vol. 10. LC 94-70743. (Illus.). 740p. 1995. 35.00 (1-57161-013-8) P F Collier.
— Collier's Encyclopedia, 1995 Edition, Vol. 11. LC 94-70743. (Illus.). 761p. 1995. 35.00 (1-57161-014-6) P F Collier.
— Collier's Encyclopedia, 1995 Edition, Vol. 12. LC 94-70743. (Illus.). 793p. 1995. 35.00 (1-57161-015-4) P F Collier.
— Collier's Encyclopedia, 1995 Edition, Vol. 13. LC 94-70743. (Illus.). 766p. 1995. 35.00 (1-57161-016-2) P F Collier.
— Collier's Encyclopedia, 1995 Edition, Vol. 14. LC 94-70743. (Illus.). 766p. 1995. 35.00 (1-57161-017-0) P F Collier.
— Collier's Encyclopedia, 1995 Edition, Vol. 15. LC 94-70743. (Illus.). 760p. 1995. 35.00 (1-57161-018-9) P F Collier.
— Collier's Encyclopedia, 1995 Edition, Vol. 16. LC 94-70743. (Illus.). 754p. 1995. 35.00 (1-57161-019-7) P F Collier.
— Collier's Encyclopedia, 1995 Edition, Vol. 17. LC 94-70743. (Illus.). 774p. 1995. 35.00 (1-57161-020-0) P F Collier.
— Collier's Encyclopedia, 1995 Edition, Vol. 18. LC 94-70743. (Illus.). 776p. 1995. 35.00 (1-57161-021-9) P F Collier.
— Collier's Encyclopedia, 1995 Edition, Vol. 19. LC 94-70743. (Illus.). 760p. 1995. 35.00 (1-57161-022-7) P F Collier.
— Collier's Encyclopedia, 1995 Edition, Vol. 20. LC 94-70743. (Illus.). 716p. 1995. 35.00 (1-57161-023-5) P F Collier.
— Collier's Encyclopedia, 1995 Edition, Vol. 21. LC 94-70743. (Illus.). 721p. 1995. 35.00 (1-57161-024-3) P F Collier.
— Collier's Encyclopedia, 1995 Edition, Vol. 22. LC 94-70743. (Illus.). 763p. 1995. 35.00 (1-57161-025-1) P F Collier.
— Collier's Encyclopedia, 1995 Edition, Vol. 23. LC 94-70743. (Illus.). 800p. 1995. 35.00 (1-57161-026-X) P F Collier.
— Collier's Encyclopedia, 1995 Edition, Vol. 24. LC 94-70743. (Illus.). 1049p. 1995. 35.00 (1-57161-027-8) P F Collier.

P-H Learning Systems Staff. Mathematics Resource Center: Level A, Boxed Kit. 1976. 84.00 (0-685-03880-7) P-H.
— Mathematics Resource Center: Level A, Boxed Kit, Set. 1976. 120.00 (0-13-565291-X) P-H.
— Mathematics Resource Center: Level B, Boxed Kit, Set. 1976. 120.00 (0-685-03881-5) P-H.

P. I. E. Books Editors. Business Card Graphics Two. (Illus.). 224p. 1993. 79.95 (4-938586-31-2, Pub. by PIE Bks JA) Bks Nippan.
— Diagram Graphics. (Illus.). 224p. 1993. 79.95 (4-938586-34-7) Bks Nippan.
— Special Event Graphics. (Illus.). 224p. 1993. 79.95 (4-938586-35-5, Pub. by PIE Bks JA) Bks Nippan.

P. I. E. Books Staff. Advertising Greeting Cards, No. 3. (Illus.). 224p. 1993. 79.95 (4-938586-41-X, Pub. by PIE Bks JA) Bks Nippan.
— Brochure Design Forum, No. 2. (Illus.). 224p. 1993. 79.95 (4-938586-38-X, Pub. by PIE Bks JA) Bks Nippan.
— New Typo Graphics. (Illus.). 224p. 1993. 79.95 (4-938586-43-6, Pub. by PIE Bks JA) Bks Nippan.
— One & Two Color Graphics. (Illus.). 224p. 1993. 79.95 (4-938586-46-0, Pub. by PIE Bks JA) Bks Nippan.
— Retail Identity Graphics. (Illus.). 224p. 1993. 84.95 (4-938586-37-1, Pub. by PIE Bks JA) Bks Nippan.

P. L. A. Staff. All India Banking Law Judgments 1940-1988. (C). 1989. 1,400.00 (0-685-46467-9) St Mut.
— Supreme Court & Full Bench Election Cases (1950-1989), 2 vols., Set. (C). 1989. 440.00 (0-685-46479-2) St Mut.

***P., Lerat.** Law Dictionary of Contract Terminology with Equivalents in English & German. (ENG & GER.). 1994. 95.00 (0-7859-8892-0) Fr & Eur.

P-M in Defense Technology Seminar Staff. Powder Metallurgy in Defense Technology: Proceedings of the P-M in Defense Technology Seminar, Held at Yuma, AZ, November 13 & 14, 1979, Vol. 5. (Illus.). 128p. reprint ed. pap. 36.50 (0-7837-1561-7, 2041853) Bks Demand.

P, Pevet, ed. Adaptations to Climatic Changes. (Limited Volume Series: Comparative Physiology of Environmental Adaptations: Vol. 3). (Illus.). vii, 188p. 1987. 142.50 (3-8055-4472-3) S Karger.

Pa Chin. Family. 332p. (C). 1988. reprint ed. text ed. 6.50 (0-88133-373-5) Waveland Pr.

Pa, Chin, ed. see Li, Fei-Kan.

Pa, G. Am. The Jewel Ornament of Liberation. Guenther, Herbert V., tr. LC 86-11839. 333p. 1986. reprint ed. pap. 20.00 (0-87773-378-3) Shambhala Pubns.

Pa Kin. Le Jardin de Repos. (FRE.). 1981. pap. 10.95 (0-7859-4147-9) Fr & Eur.
— Nuit Glacee. (FRE.). 1983. pap. 15.95 (0-7859-4195-9) Fr & Eur.

Paahana, Nikki, ed. see Boone, Louis E. & Kurtz, David L.

Paal & Menon. Hydrogen Effects in Catalysis: Fundamentals & Practical Applications. (Chemical Industries Ser.: Vol. 31). 784p. 1988. 235.00 (0-8247-7774-3) Dekker.

Paalman, Anthony. Training Showjumpers. 352p. 1990. 62.00 (0-85131-260-8, Pub. by J A Allen & Co UK) St Mut.

Paalman, M., ed. Promoting Safer Sex. 240p. 1990. 42.00 (90-265-1012-8, Pub. by Swets Pub Serv NE) Taylor & Francis.

Paamoni, Zev. Aaron, the High Priest. (Shulsinger Biblical Ser.). (Illus.). (J). (gr. 5-10). 1970. 3.00 (0-914080-27-X) Shulsinger Sales.
— The Adventures of Jacob. (Shulsinger Biblical Ser.). (Illus.). (J). (gr. 5-10). 1970. 3.00 (0-914080-26-1) Shulsinger Sales.
— Benjamin, the Littlest Brother. (Shulsinger Biblical Ser.). (Illus.). (J). (gr. 5-10). 1970. 3.00 (0-914080-28-8) Shulsinger Sales.
— Yitzchak, Son of Abraham. (Shulsinger Biblical Ser.). (Illus.). (J). (gr. 5-10). 1970. 4.00 (0-914080-25-3) Shulsinger Sales.

***Paananen.** William Blake. rev. ed. 1995. 22.95 (0-8057-7053-4, Twayne) Macmillan.

Paananen, Donna, ed. see Rey, Anthony M. & Wieland, Ferdinand.

Paananen, Eloise. The Military. LC 92-29008. (Good Citizenship Ser.). (Illus.). 48p. (J). (gr. 5-6). 1992. lib. bdg. 22.13 (0-8114-7353-8) Raintree Steck-V.

Paananen, Lauri, jt. auth. see Engle, Eloise.

Paananen, Victor. William Blake. (English Authors Ser.: No. 202). 176p. 1977. text ed. 21.95 (0-8057-6672-3, Pub. by Royal Botanic Garden UK) Macmillan.

Paans, R. A Close Look at MVS Systems: Mechanisms, Performance & Security. 572p. 1986. 123.00 (0-444-70008-0, North Holland) Elsevier.

***Paap, David A.** Biblical Equipping: A New Way of Exploring & Applying the Bible for an Active Life of Christian Discipleship. 50p. (Orig.). Date not set. pap. text ed. 3.95 (0-9633831-2-4) Stephen Minist.

Paar, H. P., jt. auth. see Caldwell, D. O.

Paar, Vladimir, jt. auth. see Meyer, Richard A.

Paardecamp, Karen M. How the Bond Market Works. 2nd ed. 1994. pap. 15.95 (0-13-124306-3) P-H.

Paarlberg, Don. An Analysis & History of Inflation. LC 92-17815. 208p. 1992. text ed. 49.95 (0-275-94416-6, C4416, Praeger Pubs) Greenwood.
— Farm & Food Policy: Issues of the 1980s. LC 79-17496. x, 338p. 1980. 25.00 (0-8032-3656-5) U of Nebr Pr.
— Farmers of Five Continents. LC 83-17090. 124p. reprint ed. pap. 35.40 (0-7837-1825-X, 2042025) Bks Demand.

***Paarlberg, Robert & Breth, Steven, eds.** Assisting Sustainable Food Production: Action or Apathy? 92p. (Orig.). (C). 1994. pap. text ed. 9.95x (0-933595-95-6) Winrock Intl.

Paarlberg, Robert, jt. auth. see Lipton, Michael.

***Paarlberg, Robert L.** Countrysides at Risk: The Political Geography of Sustainable Agriculture. LC 94-43973. (Policy Essay Ser.: Vol. 16). 1994. pap. 9.95 (1-56517-021-0) Overseas Dev Council.
— Food Trade & Foreign Policy: India, the Soviet Union, & the United States. LC 84-29335. 272p. (C). 1985. 39.95 (0-8014-1772-4); pap. 17.95 (0-8014-9345-5) Cornell U Pr.
— Leadership Abroad Begins at Home: U.S. Foreign Economic Policy after the Cold War. (Integrating National Economies Ser.). 144p. (C). 1995. 28.95x (0-8157-6804-4); pap. 10.95x (0-8157-6803-6) Brookings.

Paarlberg, Robert L., et al, eds. Diplomatic Dispute: U. S. Conflict with Iran, Japan & Mexico. (Harvard Studies in International Affairs: No. 39). 174p. 1984. reprint ed. pap. text ed. 24.00 (0-8191-4063-5) U Pr of Amer.

***Paas, John R.** Hollstein's German Engravings, Etchings & Woodcuts 1400-1700 Vol. XXXVIII: Jacob Von Sandrart. 251p. 1994. 335.00 (90-72658-42-6) IBD Ltd.

Paas, Martha W. Population Change, Labor Supply, & Agriculture in Ausburg, 1480-1618: A Study of Early Demographic-Economic Interactions. Bruchey, Stuart, ed. LC 80-2821. (Dissertations in European Economic History Ser.). (Illus.). 1981. lib. bdg. 29.95 (0-405-14005-3) Ayer.

Paasch, Henri. Dictionnaire Anglais-Francais et Francais-Anglais des Termes et Locutions Maritimes. 2nd ed. 320p. (ENG & FRE.). 1974. pap. 23.50 (0-7859-0749-1, M-6437) Fr & Eur.

Paasche, Carol L. Children with Special Needs in Early Childhood Settings: Identification, Intervention. 1990. text ed. 22.00 (0-201-23139-5) Addison-Wesley.

***Paasilinna, Arto.** The Year of the Hare. Lomas, Herbert, tr. 135p. 1995. 29.00 (0-7206-0949-6, Pub. by P Owen Ltd UK) Dufour.

Paasivirta, Esa. Participation of States in International Contracts & Arbitral Settlement of Disputes. 346p. (Orig.). 1990. pap. 147.50x (951-640-519-3, Pub. by Almqv & Wiksell SW) Coronet Bks.

Paasivirta, Jaakko. Chemical Ecotoxicology. 155p. 1991. 64.95 (0-87371-366-4, TD193) Lewis Pubs.

Paasivirta, Juhani. Finland & Europe: International Crises in the Period of Autonomy, 1808-1914. Kirby, D. G., ed. Upton, Anthony F. & Upton, Sirkka R., trs. LC 82-133218. (Nordic Ser.: No. 7). 282p. reprint ed. pap. 80.40 (0-7837-2931-6, 2057523) Bks Demand.

Paasonen, M., jt. auth. see Tuomisto, J.

Paaswell, Robert E. & Recker, Wilfred W. Problems of the Carless. LC 77-13730. (Praeger Special Studies). 208p. 1978. text ed. 45.00 (0-275-90308-7, C0308, Praeger Pubs) Greenwood.

Paaswell, Robert E., et al, eds. Site Impact Traffic Assessment: Problems & Solutions, Proceedings of the Conference Sponsored by the Urban Transportation Division of the American Society of Civil Engineers in Cooperation with Institute of Transportation Engineers, Urban Land Institute, National Association of Regional Councils. LC 92-13902. 256p. 1992. pap. text ed. 29.00 (0-87262-870-1) Am Soc Civil Eng.

Paat, Jude B. Stardust to Twilight: A Collection of Poems. (Illus.). 75p. (Orig.). 1992. pap. 6.25 (971-10-0495-X, Pub. by New Day Pub PH) Cellar.

Paatalo, Kalle. Storm over the Land: A Novel about War. Impola, Richard A., tr. & frwd. by. 579p. (Orig.). 1993. pap. 15.00 (1-880474-06-9) FATA.

Paauw, Douglas S. & Fei, John C. The Transition in Open Dualistic Economies: Theory & Southeast Asian Experience. LC 73-77163. (Illus.). 312p. 1973. 45.00 (0-300-01641-7) Yale U Pr.

Paauwe, Jac, jt. auth. see Spain, Ian L.

***Paavilainen, E. & Paivanen, J.** Peatland Forestry: Ecology & Principles. LC 95-2115. (Ecological Studies: Vol. 111). (GER.). 1995. write for info. (3-540-58252-5); write for info. (0-387-58252-5) Spr-Verlag.

Paavo Nurmi Symposium Staff. Early Diagnosis of Coronary Heart Disease: Proceedings of the Paavo Nurmi Symposium, 2nd, Porvoo, September 1971. Halonen, P. & Louhija, A., eds. (Advances in Cardiology Ser.: Vol. 8). 1973. 62.50 (3-8055-1352-6) S Karger.
— Physical Activity & Coronary Heart Disease: Proceedings of the Paavo Nurmi Symposium, 2nd, Helsinki, 1975. Manninen, V., ed. (Advances in Cardiology Ser.: Vol. 18). (Illus.). 240p. 1976. 96.00 (3-8055-2356-4) S Karger.
— Sudden Coronary Death: Proceedings of the Paavo Nurmi Symposium, 4th, Helsinki, September 15-17, 1977. Manninen, V., ed. (Advances in Cardiology Ser.: Vol. 25). (Illus.). 1978. 94.50 (3-8055-2881-7) S Karger.
— Thrombosis & Coronary Heart Disease: Proceedings of the Paavo Nurmi Symposium, 1st, Finland, 1969. Halonen, P. I. & Louhija, A., eds. (Advances in Cardiology Ser.: Vol. 4). 1970. 72.00 (3-8055-0727-5) S Karger.

Pabalan, R. T., jt. ed. see Interrante, C. G.

Pabbisetty, Seshu V., jt. ed. see Lee, Thomas W.

Paber, Stanley W., ed. Callville: Head of Navigation, Arizona Territory. (Illus.). 40p. 1981. pap. 4.95 (0-913814-39-3) Nevada Pubns.

Pabian, James A. Immigrant's Son. LC 91-67914. 300p. 1993. pap. 12.00 (1-56002-181-0, Univ Edtns) Aegina Pr.

Pabich, Jill, tr. see Ross, Steven.

Pabisch, Peter, ed. From Wilson to Waldheim: Proceedings of a Workshop on Austrian-American Relations, 1917-1987. (Studies in Austrian Literature, Culture, & Thought). (Illus.). 354p. 1989. 37.50 (0-929497-04-X); pap. 25.00 (0-929497-09-0) Ariadne CA.

Pabla, B. S., jt. auth. see Adithan, M.

Pable, Martin. Catholics & Fundamentalists: What's the Difference? LC 91-70460. 64p. (Orig.). 1991. pap. 4.95 (0-937997-18-8) Hi-Time Pub.

Pabon, Jose M. Vox-Diccionario Manual Griego-Espanol: Greek-Spanish. 11th ed. 724p. (GRE & SPA.). 1979. 39.95 (0-8288-4854-8, S12136) Fr & Eur.

Pabrai, Uday O. UNIX Internetworking. LC 93-7164. 1993. text ed. 65.00 (0-89006-685-X) Artech Hse.

Pabrai, Uday O. & Shah, Hemant. X Window System User's Guide. LC 93-39579. 236p. 1994. 49.00 (0-89006-740-6) Artech Hse.

Pabst, G. W. & Vajda, Ladislaus. Pandora's Box (Lulu) (Illus.). 136p. (Orig.). 1988. pap. 9.95 (0-571-12615-4) Faber & Faber.

Pabst, Janet, jt. ed. see Henke, Russell.

Pabst, Martin. Technologisches Woerterbuch Franzoisisch. 550p. (FRE & GER.). 1971. 175.00 (0-8288-6482-9, M-7662) Fr & Eur.

Pabst, Mary S., jt. auth. see Greif, Geoffrey L.

Pabst, W. R., Jr. Butter & Oleomargarine. LC 70-76644. (Columbia University. Studies in the Social Sciences: No. 427). reprint ed. 20.00 (0-404-51427-8) AMS Pr.

Pabst, William R. Jury Manual: A Guide for Prospective Jurors. Carson, Christopher et al, eds. (Illus.). 108p. (Orig.). 1985. 19.95 (0-933745-00-1); pap. 9.65 (0-933745-01-X) Metro Pub.

Pabtonsky, Samuel. Rose Hill. 420p. 1994. pap. 12.95 (1-56901-151-6) NW Pub.

Pacault, A., jt. ed. see Vidal, C.

Pacaut, Marcel. Doctrines Politiques et Structures Ecclesiastiques dans l'Occident Medieval. (Collected Studies: No. CS 223). 304p. (FRE.). (C). 1985. reprint ed. lib. bdg. 89.95 (0-86078-171-2, Pub. by Variorum UK) Ashgate Pub Co.

Paccaud, F., et al, eds. Assessing AIDS Prevention: Selected Papers Presented at the International Conference Held in Montreux (Switzerland), October 29-November 1, 1990. x, 305p. 1992. 147.50 (0-8176-2722-7) Birkhauser.

Pacchioni, G., et al, eds. Cluster Models for Surface & Bulk Phenomena. (NATO ASI Series B, Physics: Vol. 283). (Illus.). 678p. 1992. 149.50 (0-306-44102-0, Plenum Pr) Plenum.

Paccia-Cooper, Jeanne, jt. auth. see Cooper, William E.

Pace. Family Papers: A Reader for Writers. (C). 1993. text ed. 26.00 (0-06-501222-4) HarpCollege.

Pace, et al. Human Resource Development: The Field. 272p. 1991. pap. text ed. 31.40 (0-13-446394-3, 140108) P-H.

PACE - Grace Lutheran School Staff. Seasoned with Sunshine. Sizemore, Deborah & Coleman, Linda, eds. (Illus.). 350p. 1982. reprint ed. 9.95 (0-9612728-0-5) PACE Grace.

***Pace, Adele & Jones, Maria.** The Busy Executive's Guide to Total Fitness. 1995. pap. text ed. 14.95 (0-13-310855-4) P-H.

Pace, Anita, et al. Write from the Heart - Lesbians Healing from Heartache: An Anthology. 226p. 1992. pap. 10.95 (0-9631666-0-3) Baby Steps Pr.

Pace, Anita L. If You Want to Soar You've Got to Learn How to Fly. (Illus.). 256p. (Orig.). 1993. pap. 10.95 (0-9631666-1-1) Baby Steps Pr.

***Pace, Anita L., et al.** Life Isn't Just a Panic: Stories of Hope by Recovering Agoraphobics. 240p. (Orig.). 1995. pap. text ed. 10.95 (0-9631666-3-8) Baby Steps Pr.

Pace, Antonio, ed. & intro. Luigi Castiglioni's "Viaggio" Travels in the United States of America, 1785-1787. (Illus.). 496p. 1983. text ed. 45.00x (0-8156-2264-3) Syracuse U Pr.

Pace-Asciak, C. & Granstrom, E., eds. Prostaglandins & Related Substances. (New Comprehensive Biochemistry Ser.: Vol. 5). 255p. 1983. 82.75 (0-444-80517-6, I-380-83) Elsevier.

Pace-Asciak, C. R., jt. ed. see Schror, K.

Pace-Asciak, Cecil R. Mass Spectra of Prostaglandins & Related Products. (Advances in Prostaglandin, Thromboxane, & Leukotriene Research Ser.: Vol. 18). 592p. 1989. 127.50 (0-88167-474-5) Raven.

Pace, Brian P., jt. ed. see Zipperer, Lorri A.

Pace, Charles R. Measuring Outcomes of College: Fifty Years of Findings & Recommendations for the Future. LC 79-88774. (Jossey-Bass Series in Higher Education). 200p. reprint ed. pap. 57.00 (0-8357-4957-6, 2037889) Bks Demand.

Pace, Claire. Felibien's Life of Poussin. (Illus.). 160p. pap. 29.95 (0-302-00542-0, Pub. by Zwemmer Bks UK) Sothebys Pubns.

Pace, Dale, ed. Summer Computer Simulation Conference Proceedings: Baltimore, MD, 1991. 1256p. 1991. 150.00 (0-911801-91-X, SCSC91) Soc Computer Sim.

***Pace, David.** Shouting Sharon: A Riotous Counting Rhyme. LC 94-76897. (Illus.). 32p. (J). (ps). 1995. 12.95 (0-307-17518-9, Artsts Writrs) Western Pub.

Pace, David, illus. The Princess & the Pea. (Fairy Tale Pop-ups Ser.). 16p. (J). 1994. 3.95 (0-7214-9421-8) Ladybird Bks.
— Three Billy Goats Gruff. (Fairy Tale Pop-ups Ser.). 16p. (J). 1994. 3.95 (0-7214-9418-8) Ladybird Bks.
— The Three Little Pigs. (Fairy Tale Pop-ups Ser.). 16p. (J). 1994. 3.95 (0-7214-9419-6) Ladybird Bks.
— The Ugly Duckling. (Fairy Tale Pop-ups Ser.). 16p. (J). 1994. 3.95 (0-7214-9420-X) Ladybird Bks.

***Pace, David & Pugh, Sharon L.** Studying for History. LC 95-12331. (C). 1995. 13.50 (0-06-500649-6) HarpCollege.

Pace, David P. & Barksdale, E. C. As Dreams Are Made On: Previews of the Human Mind. LC 87-91102. 1988. 18.95 (0-87212-209-3) Libra.

Pace, De Wanna. Surrender Sweet Stranger. 1988. 3.95 (0-517-00652-9) Random Hse Value.

Pace, Denny F. Concepts of Vice, Narcotics & Organized Crime. 3rd ed. 320p. (C). 1990. pap. text ed. write for info. (0-13-173691-4) P-H.

***Pace, Denny F. & Nicholson, Cyn.** The Latchkey Man. 270p. 1996. pap. 8.95 (0-7610-0522-6) NW Pub.

Pace, Edgardo, ed. Edgardo Coghlan: Retrospectiva 1952-1992. New York Spanish Institute Staff, tr. (Illus.). 184p. (ENG & SPA.). 1993. 100.00 (0-9636207-0-3) S Pace.

Pace, Edmond E., et al. Developing a Basic Loan Training Program. 2nd ed. LC 87-7936. 108p. 1987. pap. 37.00 (0-936742-41-0) Robt Morris Assocs.

Pace, Frank J., jt. auth. see Mosier, Alice.

Pace, George B., ed. see Chaucer, Geoffrey.

***Pace, George R.** Cracking the SAT II: Spanish Subject Test, 1996 Edition. (Princeton Review Ser.). 1995. student ed, pap. 17.00 (0-679-75920-4) Random.
— Princeton Review Cracking the SAT II: Spanish 1995 Edition. 1994. pap. 16.00 (0-679-75359-1, Villard Bks) Random.

Pace, George W. Our Search to Know the Lord. LC 88-18862. v, 229p. 1988. 10.95 (0-87579-136-0) Deseret Bk.

Pace, Glenn L. Spiritual Plateaus. LC 90-22973. 160p. 1991. 10.95 (0-87579-337-1) Deseret Bk.
— Spiritual Plateaus. LC 90-22973. xv, 160p. 1995. pap. 6.95 (0-87579-962-0) Deseret Bk.
— Spiritual Revival. LC 93-9902. viii, 198p. 1993. 12.95 (0-87579-733-4) Deseret Bk.

***Pace, Glennellen, ed.** Whole Learning in the Middle School: Evolution & Transition. 320p. (J). (gr. 5-9). 1995. pap. text ed. 27.95 (0-926842-44-7) CG Pubs Inc.

Pace International Research, Inc. Staff. ABC (Active Basic Communication), Program 1. (ABC Video Ser.). (Illus.). 157p. 1984. text ed. 8.95 (0-89209-215-7); pap. text ed. 4.25 (0-89209-326-9); audio 4.00 (0-89209-327-7); vhs 115.00 (0-89209-178-9) Pace Intl Res.
— ABC (Active Basic Communication), Program 10. (ABC Video Ser.). (Illus.). 171p. 1984. text ed. 8.95 (0-89209-224-6); pap. text ed. 4.25 (0-89209-344-7); audio 4.00 (0-89209-345-5); vhs 115.00 (0-89209-187-8) Pace Intl Res.
— ABC (Active Basic Communication), Program 11. (ABC Video Ser.). (Illus.). 151p. 1984. text ed. 8.95 (0-89209-225-4); pap. text ed. 4.25 (0-89209-346-3); audio 4.00 (0-89209-347-1); vhs 115.00 (0-89209-188-6) Pace Intl Res.

P
Q

An Asterisk (*) at the beginning of an entry indicates that the title is appearing in BIP for the first time.

— ABC (Active Basic Communication), Program 12. (ABC Video Ser.). (Illus.). 173p. 1984. text ed. 8.95 (0-89209-226-2); pap. text ed. 4.25 (0-89209-348-X); audio 4.00 (0-89209-349-8); vhs 115.00 (0-89209-189-4) Pace Intl Res.

— ABC (Active Basic Communication), Program 13. (ABC Video Ser.). (Illus.). 153p. 1984. text ed. 8.95 (0-89209-227-0); pap. text ed. 4.25 (0-89209-375-7); audio 4.00 (0-89209-376-5); vhs 115.00 (0-89209-190-8) Pace Intl Res.

— ABC (Active Basic Communication), Program 14. (ABC Video Ser.). (Illus.). 153p. 1984. text ed. 8.95 (0-89209-228-9); pap. text ed. 4.25 (0-89209-377-3); audio 4.00 (0-89209-378-1); vhs 115.00 (0-89209-191-6) Pace Intl Res.

— ABC (Active Basic Communication), Program 15. (ABC Video Ser.). (Illus.). 177p. 1984. text ed. 8.95 (0-89209-229-7); pap. text ed. 4.25 (0-89209-379-X); audio 4.00 (0-89209-380-3); vhs 115.00 (0-89209-192-4) Pace Intl Res.

— ABC (Active Basic Communication), Program 16. (ABC Video Ser.). (Illus.). 145p. 1984. text ed. 8.95 (0-89209-230-0); pap. text ed. 4.25 (0-89209-381-1); audio 4.00 (0-89209-382-X); vhs 115.00 (0-89209-193-2) Pace Intl Res.

— ABC (Active Basic Communication), Program 2. (ABC Video Ser.). (Illus.). 177p. 1984. text ed. 8.95 (0-89209-216-5); pap. text ed. 4.25 (0-89209-328-5); audio 4.00 (0-89209-329-3); vhs 115.00 (0-89209-179-7) Pace Intl Res.

— ABC (Active Basic Communication), Program 3. (ABC Video Ser.). (Illus.). 149p. 1984. text ed. 8.95 (0-89209-217-3); pap. text ed. 4.25 (0-89209-330-7); audio 4.00 (0-89209-331-5); vhs 115.00 (0-89209-180-0) Pace Intl Res.

— ABC (Active Basic Communication), Program 4. (ABC Video Ser.). (Illus.). 167p. 1984. text ed. 8.95 (0-89209-218-1); pap. text ed. 4.25 (0-89209-332-3); audio 4.00 (0-89209-333-1); vhs 115.00 (0-89209-181-9) Pace Intl Res.

— ABC (Active Basic Communication), Program 5. (ABC Video Ser.). (Illus.). 147p. 1984. text ed. 8.95 (0-89209-219-X); pap. text ed. 4.25 (0-89209-334-X); audio 4.00 (0-89209-335-8); vhs 115.00 (0-89209-182-7) Pace Intl Res.

— ABC (Active Basic Communication), Program 6. (ABC Video Ser.). (Illus.). 167p. 1984. text ed. 8.95 (0-89209-220-3); pap. text ed. 4.25 (0-89209-336-6); audio 4.00 (0-89209-337-4); vhs 115.00 (0-89209-183-5) Pace Intl Res.

— ABC (Active Basic Communication), Program 8. (ABC Video Ser.). (Illus.). 195p. 1984. text ed. 8.95 (0-89209-222-X); pap. text ed. 4.25 (0-89209-340-4); audio 4.00 (0-89209-341-2); vhs 115.00 (0-89209-185-1) Pace Intl Res.

— ABC (Active Basic Communication), Program 9. (ABC Video Ser.). (Illus.). 157p. 1984. text ed. 8.95 (0-89209-223-8); pap. text ed. 4.25 (0-89209-342-0); audio 4.00 (0-89209-343-9); vhs 115.00 (0-89209-186-X) Pace Intl Res.

— E-2, 3. (E-2 Video Ser.). (Illus.). 103p. 1984. write for info. (0-89209-255-6) Pace Intl Res.

— E-2, 4. (E-2 Video Ser.). (Illus.). 103p. 1984. write for info. (0-89209-256-4) Pace Intl Res.

— E-2, 5. (E-2 Video Ser.). (Illus.). 110p. 1984. write for info. (0-89209-258-0) Pace Intl Res.

— E-2, 6. (E-2 Video Ser.). (Illus.). 110p. 1984. write for info. (0-89209-257-2) Pace Intl Res.

— E-2, 11. (E-2 Video Ser.). (Illus.). 102p. 1984. write for info. (0-89209-259-9) Pace Intl Res.

— E-2, 12. (E-2 Video Ser.). (Illus.). 102p. 1984. write for info. (0-89209-260-2) Pace Intl Res.

— E-2, 13. (E-2 Video Ser.). (Illus.). 108p. 1984. write for info. (0-89209-261-0) Pace Intl Res.

— E-2, 14. (E-2 Video Ser.). (Illus.). 108p. 1984. write for info. (0-89209-262-9) Pace Intl Res.

— E-2, 17. (E-2 Video Ser.). (Illus.). 113p. 1984. write for info. (0-89209-263-7) Pace Intl Res.

— E-2, 18. (E-2 Video Ser.). (Illus.). 113p. 1984. write for info. (0-89209-264-5) Pace Intl Res.

— E-2, Vol. 1. (E-2 Video Ser.). (Illus.). 103p. 1984. text ed. 8.95 (0-89209-250-5); pap. text ed. 4.25 (0-89209-295-5) Pace Intl Res.

— E-2, Vol. 2. (E-2 Video Ser.). (Illus.). 110p. 1984. text ed. 8.95 (0-89209-251-3); pap. text ed. 4.25 (0-89209-296-3) Pace Intl Res.

— E-2, 2 vols., Vol. 7. (E-2 Video Ser.). (Illus.). 103p. 1984. audio 8.00 (0-89209-265-3) Pace Intl Res.

— E-2, Vol. 8. (E-2 Video Ser.). (Illus.). 110p. 1984. audio 8.00 (0-89209-266-1) Pace Intl Res.

— E-2, Vol. 9. (E-2 Video Ser.). (Illus.). 102p. 1984. text ed. 8.95 (0-89209-252-1); pap. text ed. 4.25 (0-89209-297-1) Pace Intl Res.

— E-2, Vol. 10. (E-2 Video Ser.). (Illus.). 108p. 1984. text ed. 8.95 (0-89209-253-X); pap. text ed. 4.25 (0-89209-298-X) Pace Intl Res.

— E-2, 2 vols., Vol. 15. (E-2 Video Ser.). (Illus.). 108p. 1984. audio 8.00 (0-89209-267-X); audio 8.00 (0-685-55708-1) Pace Intl Res.

— E-2, Vol. 16. (E-2 Video Ser.). (Illus.). 113p. 1984. text ed. 8.95 (0-89209-254-8); pap. text ed. 4.25 (0-89209-299-8) Pace Intl Res.

— E-2, 2 vols., Vol. 19. (E-2 Video Ser.). (Illus.). 113p. 1984. audio 8.00 (0-89209-268-8) Pace Intl Res.

— E-2, 2 vols., Vols. 3 & 4. (E-2 Video Ser.). (Illus.). 103p. 1984. vhs 230.00 (0-89209-280-7) Pace Intl Res.

— E-2, 2 vols., Vols. 5 & 6. (E-2 Video Ser.). (Illus.). 110p. 1984. vhs 230.00 (0-89209-281-5) Pace Intl Res.

— E-2, 2 vols., Vols. 11 & 12. (E-2 Video Ser.). (Illus.). 102p. 1984. vhs 230.00 (0-89209-284-X) Pace Intl Res.

— E-2, 2 vols., Vols. 13 & 14. (E-2 Video Ser.). (Illus.). 108p. 1984. vhs 230.00 (0-89209-285-8) Pace Intl Res.

— E-2, 2 vols., Vols. 17 & 18. (E-2 Video Ser.). (Illus.). 113p. 1984. vhs 230.00 (0-685-09187-2) Pace Intl Res.

— Life in Western America. (AAA Video Ser.). (Illus.). 132p. 1984. text ed. 8.95 (0-89209-049-9); pap. text ed. 4.25 (0-89209-080-4); digital audio 3.25 (0-89209-081-2); vhs 60.00 (0-89209-046-4) Pace Intl Res.

— San Francisco--I Love It! (AAA Video Ser.). (Illus.). 144p. 1984. text ed. 8.95 (0-89209-047-2); pap. text ed. 4.25 (0-89209-076-6); audio 3.25 (0-89209-077-4); vhs 60.00 (0-89209-044-8) Pace Intl Res.

— Seattle & Its People. (AAA Video Ser.). (Illus.). 135p. 1984. text ed. 8.95 (0-89209-048-0); pap. text ed. 4.25 (0-89209-078-2); audio 3.25 (0-89209-079-0); vhs 60.00 (0-89209-045-6) Pace Intl Res.

Pace International Research, Inc. Staff & Cornelius, Edwin T., Jr. Encounters, Bk. 1, Tasks 1-24. (Encounters Video Ser.). (Illus.). 150p. 1988. student ed 6.95 (0-89209-656-X); pap. text ed. 7.95 (0-89209-650-0); vhs 59.95 (0-89209-675-6); vhs 59.95 (0-89209-676-4) Pace Intl Res.

— Encounters, Bk. 2, Tasks 24-48. (Encounters Video Ser.). (Illus.). 155p. 1988. student ed 6.95 (0-89209-657-8); pap. text ed. 7.95 (0-89209-651-9); vhs 59.95 (0-89209-677-2); vhs 59.95 (0-89209-678-0) Pace Intl Res.

— Encounters, Bk. 3, Tasks 49-72. (Encounters Video Ser.). (Illus.). 171p. 1988. student ed 6.95 (0-89209-658-6); pap. text ed. 7.95 (0-89209-652-7); vhs 59.95 (0-89209-679-9); vhs 59.95 (0-89209-680-2) Pace Intl Res.

— Encounters, Bk. 4, Tasks 73-96. (Encounters Video Ser.). (Illus.). 181p. 1988. student ed 6.95 (0-89209-659-4); pap. text ed. 7.95 (0-89209-653-5); vhs 59.95 (0-89209-681-0); vhs 59.95 (0-89209-682-9) Pace Intl Res.

Pace, James O. Amendment to the Constitution: Averting the Decline & Fall of America. 179p. (Orig.). 1985. pap. text ed. 10.00 (0-9615268-0-7) JP SF.

Pace Jeansonne, Sharon. The Old Greek Translation of Daniel 7-12. Karris, Robert J., ed. LC 87-15865. (Catholic Biblical Quarterly Monographs: No. 19). x, 147p. 1988. pap. 5.00 (0-915170-18-3) Catholic Bibl Assn.

Pace, Jill H., jt. auth. see Teich, Albert H.

Pace, Joseph M. Passing Through. 144p. 1993. 11.95 (0-8059-3320-4) Dorrance.

Pace, Kathy. The Best from Gooseberry Hill: Patterns for Stuffed Animals & Dolls. Townsend, Louise O. & Lytle, Joyce E., eds. LC 93-24448. (Illus.). 80p. (Orig.). 1993. pap. 16.95 (0-914881-69-8) C & T Pub.

Pace, Larry, jt. auth. see Pace, Philip.

Pace, Larry A., jt. auth. see Smits, Stanley.

Pace, Laurel. Blood Ties. (Intrigue Ser.). 1993. mass mkt. 2.99 (0-373-22247-5, 1-22247-0) Harlequin Bks.

— Destiny's Promise. (Historical Ser.). 1993. mass mkt. 3.99 (0-373-28772-0, 1-28772-1) Harlequin Bks.

— Winds of Destiny. 1994. mass mkt. 3.99 (0-373-28842-5, 1-28842-2) Harlequin Bks.

Pace, M. O., jt. ed. see Christophorou, Loucas G.

***Pace, Mildred M.** Friend of Animals: The Story of Henry Bergh. 2nd ed. Miller, Danny L., ed. & intro. by. LC 94-2193. (Illus.). (J). (gr. 4 up). 1995. reprint ed. 12.00 (0-945084-47-1) J Stuart Found.

— Kentucky Derby Champion. rev. ed. Gifford, James M. et al, eds. LC 93-18595. (Illus.). 144p. (J). (gr. 3 up). 1993. reprint ed. 12.00 (0-945084-36-6) J Stuart Found.

Pace, Miriam. Delta Desire: New Orleans II. (New Orleans Ser.). 1982. pap. 3.50 (0-8217-1021-4) Zebra.

— New Orleans. (Orig.). 1981. pap. 3.50 (0-89083-826-7) Zebra.

Pace, N. Proceedings of the International Meeting of the IUPS Commission on Gravitational Physiology. (Illus.). 266p. (Orig.). (C). 1994. pap. text ed. 95.00 (1-56806-264-8) Diane Pub.

Pace, Nicholas M., jt. auth. see Kakalik, James S.

Pace, P. J., jt. auth. see Sim, R. S.

Pace, Peter. The Architecture of George Pace. (Illus.). 288p. 1991. 60.00 (0-7134-6273-6, Pub. by Batsford UK) Trafalgar.

Pace, Philip & Pace, Larry. Logic Tools for Programming. 320p. (C). 1987. teacher ed 10.00 (0-8273-2583-5); pap. text ed. 31.95 (0-8273-2582-7) Delmar.

Pace, R. Wayne & Faules, Don F. Organizational Communication. 3rd ed. LC 93-31436. 1993. text ed. write for info. (0-13-643800-8) P-H.

Pace, Rich. Talos: Crossroads of the Galaxy. 371p. 1992. pap. 5.95 (0-9632819-0-9) RASP Pubns.

Pace, Richard. De Fructu Qui Ex Doctrina Percipitur (The Benefit of a Liberal Education, 1517) Manley, Francis & Sylvester, Richard S., eds. LC 66-21029. (Renaissance Text Ser.: No. 2). xxvi, 190p. 1967. 8.50 (0-9602696-1-4) Renaiss Society Am.

Pace, Robert. Piano for Classroom Music. 2nd ed. LC 71-98966. (Music Ser.). (Illus.). 1970. pap. text ed. write for info. (0-13-674994-1) P-H.

Pace, Rosella. Portugal: The Villages. 1977. 2.00 (0-88031-039-1) Invisible-Red Hill.

Pace, Ruth & McGee, Mary P. The Life & Times of Ridgeway, Virginia 1728-1990. LC 90-37899. (Illus.). x, 282p. 1990. 42.00 (0-936015-25-X) Pocahontas Pr.

Pace, S. & Acquarone, M., eds. Superconductivity - Prog in Hts, Vol. 27: Proceedings of the Twenty-Fourth Italian National School on Condensed Matter. 550p. (C). 1991. text ed. 129.00 (981-02-0328-4) World Scientific Pub.

Pace, Steve. B-25 Mitchell. 128p. 1994. pap. 19.95 (0-87938-939-7) Motorbooks Intl.

— Edward's AFB: Experimental Flights Test Center. (Illus.). 192p. 1994. pap. 24.95 (0-87938-869-2) Motorbooks Intl.

— F-117A Stealth Fighter. (Aero Ser.). 80p. 1992. pap. 10.95 (0-8306-2795-2, 3962, TAB-Aero) TAB Bks.

— The F-117A Stealth Fighter. (Illus.). 1992. pap. 10.95 (0-07-048055-9) McGraw.

— The Grumman X-29. (Aero Ser.: Vol. 4). (Illus.). 96p. 1990. pap. 10.95 (0-8306-3498-3, 3498) TAB Bks.

— Lockheed F-104 Starfighter. (Warbird Color History Ser.). (Illus.). 144p. 1992. pap. 9.98 (0-87938-608-8) Motorbooks Intl.

— Lockheed Skunk Works. LC 92-28518. (Illus.). 192p. 1992. pap. 24.95 (0-87938-632-0) Motorbooks Intl.

— North American XB-70 Valkyrie, Vol. 30. 2nd ed. (Aero Ser.). (Illus.). 96p. 1989. pap. 11.95 (0-8306-8620-7, TAB-Aero) TAB Bks.

— Valkyrie North American X-B 70 A. Gentle, Ernest J., ed. (Aero Ser.: Vol. 30). (Illus.). 104p. (Orig.). 1984. pap. 10.95 (0-8168-0610-1, 20610, TAB-Aero) TAB Bks.

— Voughts F-8 Crusader, Pt. 1: Development & Testing Foreign Users & F8U-3. (Naval Fighters Ser.: No. 16). 114p. 1988. pap. 16.95 (0-942612-16-7) Naval Fighters.

— X-Fighters. (Illus.). 224p. 1991. pap. 7.98 (0-87938-540-5) Motorbooks Intl.

— X-Planes at Edwards. (Enthusiast Color Ser.). (Illus.). 96p. 1995. pap. 12.95 (0-87938-985-0) Motorbooks Intl.

Pace University, Center for Environmental Legal Studies Staff & Ottinger, Richard L. Environmental Costs of Electricity. 769p. 1990. lib. bdg. 75.00 (0-379-11179-9) Oceana.

Pacejka, Hans B., ed. Tyre Models for Vehicle Dynamic Analysis: Proceedings of the First International Colloquium on Tyre Models for Vehicle Dynamics Analysis, Held in Delft, The Netherlands, Oct. 21-22, 1991. LC 92-46188. 1993. 145.00 (90-265-1332-1, Pub. by Swets Pub Serv NE) Taylor & Francis.

Pacejka, Hans B., jt. auth. see De Pater, A. D.

Pacela, A. F., ed. Bioengineering Education Directory. (Official Directory of the Alliance for Engineering in Medicine & Biology Ser.). (Orig.). 1990. pap. 39.00 (0-930844-24-6) Quest Pub.

— Journal of Clinical Engineering Reprint Series Publication No. 4: Cost-Effective Financial Management of Clinical Engineering Departments. 32p. 1991. pap. 20.00 (0-930844-32-7) Quest Pub.

Pacela, Allan F. Survey of Biomedical & Clinical Engineering Department in U. S. Hospitals, 1985. 27p. (Orig.). 1985. pap. text ed. 40.00 (0-930844-18-1) Quest Pub.

— Survey of Salaries & Responsibilities for Hospital Biomedical - Clinical Engineering & Technology Personnel, 1992. (Illus.). 24p. (Orig.). 1992. pap. 80.00 (0-930844-36-X) Quest Pub.

Pacela, Allan F., ed. Biomedical Careers Book. (Illus.). 93p. (Orig.). 1992. pap. 40.00 (0-930844-37-8) Quest Pub.

— Clinical Engineering & Hospital Technology Management. (Journal of Clinical Engineering Reprint Ser.: No. 1). 56p. (Orig.). 1991. pap. 28.00 (0-930844-29-7) Quest Pub.

— Cost-Effective Financial Management of CE Departments. (Journal of Clinical Engineering Reprint Ser.: No. 4). 32p. (Orig.). 1991. pap. 20.00 (0-685-62309-2) Quest Pub.

— Evolution of the Clinical Engineering Profession. (Journal of Clinical Engineering Reprint Ser.: No. 5). 52p. (Orig.). 1991. pap. 26.00 (0-930844-33-5) Quest Pub.

— Productivity of Clinical Engineering Departments: Definitions, Techniques & Management. (Journal of Clinical Engineering Reprint Ser.: No. 3). 64p. (Orig.). 1991. pap. 32.00 (0-930844-31-9) Quest Pub.

— Safety Hazards & Ethics in Clinical Engineering. (Journal of Clinical Engineering Reprint Ser.: No. 2). 56p. (Orig.). 1991. pap. 28.00 (0-930844-30-0) Quest Pub.

Pacela, Allan F., ed. see Shepherd, Marvin.

Pacella, Mark, jt. auth. see Wachowski, Larry.

Pacelle, Richard L., Jr. The Transformation of the Supreme Court's Agenda: From the New Deal to the Reagan Administration. 264p. 1991. text ed. 55.50 (0-8133-8376-5) Westview.

Pacelli, Albert P. The Speculator's Edge: Strategies for Profit in the Futures Market. 304p. 1989. text ed. 29.95 (0-471-50360-6) Wiley.

Pacelli, Joseph G. Building Your High School Football Program: In Pursuit of Excellence. LC 86-27706. (Illus.). 160p. 1987. text ed. 19.95 (0-88011-286-7, PPAC0286) Human Kinetics.

Pacelli, Joseph G., jt. auth. see Allen, George H.

Pacelli, William M. Radio Advertising Sales Success--The Game Plan. 176p. 1988. 19.95 (0-945664-00-1) Cambridge Hse Assocs.

Pacepa, Ion M. Red Horizons: Chronicles of a Communist Spy Chief. LC 87-26378. (Illus.). 396p. 1987. lib. bdg. 19.95 (0-89526-570-2) Regnery Pub.

— Red Horizons: The True Story of Nicolae & Elena Ceausescus' Crimes, Lifestyle, & Corruption. LC 87-26378. (Illus.). 456p. 1990. pap. 12.95 (0-89526-746-2) Regnery Pub.

Pacer, Leonard A., jt. auth. see Pfeister, Joseph L.

Pacernick, Gary. The Jewish Poems. 70p. (Orig.). 1985. pap. 6.50 (0-932429-00-9) Univ Monographs.

— Memory & Fire: Ten American Jewish Poets. (Twentieth Century American Jewish Writers Ser.). 259p. (C). 1989. text ed. 45.70 (0-8204-0419-5) P Lang Pubs.

— Something Is Happening: Poems. LC 91-48235. 60p. 1992. pap. 12.95 (0-7734-9439-1, Mellen Poetry Pr) E Mellen.

— Talking Together: Letters of David Ignatow, 1946-1990. LC 91-41087. (Illus.). 280p. (C). 1992. text ed. 29.95 (0-8173-0584-X) U of Ala Pr.

Pacetta, Frank. Don't Fire Them, Fire Them Up. 1994. 23.00 (0-671-86949-3) S&S Trade.

— Don't Fire Them, Fire Them Up. 1995. pap. 12.00 (0-684-80050-0, Fireside) S&S Trade.

Pacetti, David. Sozo What It Means to Be Saved. 62p. 1985. pap. 2.95 (0-88144-041-8) Christian Pub.

Pacey, Arnold. The Culture of Technology. (Illus.). 224p. 1983. pap. 12.95 (0-262-66056-3) MIT Pr.

— The Maze of Ingenuity: Ideas & Idealism in the Development of Technology. LC 74-18380. 337p. 1975. 34.95 (0-8419-0181-3) Holmes & Meier.

— The Maze of Ingenuity: Ideas & Idealism in the Development of Technology. 2nd ed. (Illus.). 320p. 1992. 27.50 (0-262-16128-1); pap. 14.50 (0-262-66075-X) MIT Pr.

— Technology in World Civilization: A Thousand-Year History. (Illus.). 200p. 1990. 27.50 (0-262-16117-6) MIT Pr.

— Technology in World Civilization: A Thousand-Year History. (Illus.). 256p. 1991. pap. 13.50 (0-262-66072-5) MIT Pr.

Pacey, Arnold, ed. Sanitation in Developing Countries. LC 78-4215. 252p. reprint ed. pap. 71.90 (0-8357-6942-9, 2039001) Bks Demand.

— Water for the Thousand Millions, Vol. 4. LC 77-23127. 1977. pap. 8.00 (0-08-021805-9, Pergamon Pr) Elsevier.

Pacey, Arnold & Thrupp, Lori A. Farmer First: Farmer Innovation & Agricultural Research. Chambers, Robert, ed. (Illus.). 192p. 1989. pap. 13.50 (0-942850-20-3) Bootstrap Pr.

Pacey, G. E., jt. auth. see Karlberg, B.

Pacey, Lorene M., ed. Readings in the Development of Settlement Work. LC 79-142688. (Essay Index Reprint Ser.). 1977. 23.95 (0-8369-2198-4) Ayer.

Pacey, Philip. David Jones & Other Wonder Voyagers: Essays. 134p. 1982. 35.00 (0-907476-14-7) Dufour.

— Family Art. (Illus.). 120p. 1989. 24.95 (0-7456-0664-4) Blackwell Pubs.

Pach, Andrzej, tr. see Dziech, Andrzej.

Pach, Chester J., Jr. Arming the Free World: The Origins of the United States Military Assistance Program, 1945-1950. LC 90-41120. x, 322p. 1991. pap. text ed. 14.95x (0-8078-1943-3) U of NC Pr.

Pach, Chester J., Jr. & Richardson, Elmo. The Presidency of Dwight D. Eisenhower. rev. ed. LC 90-45952. (American Presidency Ser.). xiv, 290p. 1991. 25.00 (0-7006-0436-7); pap. 12.95 (0-7006-0437-5) U Pr of KS.

Pach, Janos, ed. New Trends in Discrete & Computational Geometry. LC 92-23684. (Algorithms & Combinatorics Ser.: Vol. 10). 1993. 89.00 (0-387-55713-X) Spr-Verlag.

***Pach, Janos & Agarwal, Pankaj.** Combinatorial Geometry. LC 94-48203. (Discrete Mathematics & Optimization Ser.). 1995. write for info. (0-471-58890-3) Wiley-Interscience.

***Pach, P. Z.** Eighth International Economic History Congress, Budapest 1982. International Economic History Assoc. Staff, ed. 1909p. (C). 1982. pap. 36.00x (963-05-3104-6, Pub. by Akad Kiado HU) St Mut.

Pach, Paul S. Studies on the Hungarian Economy in Early Modern Times. (Collected Studies Ser.: CS 469). 320p. 1994. 95.00 (0-86078-462-2) Ashgate Pub Co.

Pach, Walter. Ingres. LC 83-45830. (Illus.). reprint ed. 84.50 (0-404-20195-4) AMS Pr.

— Masters of Modern Art. LC 72-5633. (Essay Index Reprint Ser.). 1977. reprint ed. 27.95 (0-8369-7295-3) Ayer.

— Queer Thing, Painting: Forty Years in the World of Art. LC 79-156701. (Essay Index Reprint Ser.). 1977. reprint ed. 27.95 (0-8369-2328-6) Ayer.

— Renoir. (Masters of Art Ser.). 1983. 22.95 (0-8109-1593-6) Abrams.

— Vincent Van Gogh, Eighteen Fifty-Three to Eighteen Ninety. LC 78-99666. (Select Bibliographies Reprint Ser.). 1977. 21.95 (0-8369-5095-X) Ayer.

Pacha, Sergio, jt. ed. see Williams, Frederick G.

Pachai, Bridglal. Malawi: The History of the Nation. LC 73-173415. (Illus.). 336p. reprint ed. pap. 95.80 (0-8357-6200-9, 2034472) Bks Demand.

Pachard, jt. auth. see Nichols.

Pachauri, R. K. Contemporary India. 192p. 1992. 27.50 (0-7069-6078-5, Pub. by Vikas II) S Asia.

Pachauri, R. K., ed. Global Energy Interactions: Proceedings of the Fifth Annual Conference of the International Association of Energy Economists New Delhi, 1984. LC 85-61079. 1272p. (C). 1987. 69.00 (0-913215-04-X) Riverdale Co.

Pachauri, Rajendra K. Political Economy of Global Energy. LC 84-21825. 208p. (C). 1985. pap. text ed. 13.95x (0-8018-2501-6) Johns Hopkins.

Pachauri, Saroj, ed. Reaching India's Poor: Non-Governmental Approaches to Community Health. LC 94-4731. 420p. 1994. 29.95 (0-8039-9172-X) Sage.

Pache, Rene. The Inspiration & Authority of Scripture. 349p. (C). 1992. reprint ed. pap. text ed. 15.95 (1-879215-11-X) Sheffield WI.

— Person & Work of the Holy Spirit. (C). 1960. pap. 10.99 (0-8024-6471-8) Moody.

— Persona & Obra del Espiritu Santo: Person & Work of the Holy Spirit. (SPA.). 5.95 (84-7228-665-7, 220690, Pub. by Edit Clie SP) TSELF.

Pacheco, jt. auth. see Teixeira.

Pacheco, Anne M. My Other Dad. LC 90-7170. 138p. (YA). 1991. pap. 6.95 (1-55523-404-6) Winston-Derek.

Pacheco, Beth. Academic Reading & Studying Skills. 320p. (C). 1985. pap. text ed. 21.50 (0-03-062034-1) HB Coll Pubs.

Pacheco, Beth M. Academic Reading & Study Skills: A Theme-Centered Approach. 2nd ed. 332p. (C). 1992. pap. text ed. 22.00 (0-03-055533-7); teacher ed, pap. text ed. write for info. (0-03-055867-0) HB Coll Pubs.

P Q

An Asterisk (*) at the beginning of an entry indicates that the title is appearing in BIP for the first time.

Pacheco, Beth M., jt. auth. see Gregg, Joan Y.

***Pacheco, Christine.** The Rogue & the Rich Girl. 1995. mass mkt. 3.25 (*0-373-05960-4*, 1-05960-9) Silhouette.

Pacheco, David & Clay, Jesse, illus. Walt Disney's Bambi. LC 92-54876. (Illustrated Classics Ser.). 96p. (J). 1993. 14.95 (*1-56282-442-2*); lib. bdg. 14.89 (*1-56282-443-0*) Disney Pr.

Pacheco, F. H., ed. see Menendez Pidal, Ramon.

Pacheco, Ferdie. Muhammad Ali: A View from the Corner. (Illus.). 256p. 1992. 21.95 (*1-55972-100-6*, Birch Ln Pr) Carol Pub Group.

— Ybor City Chronicles: A Memoir. LC 94-822. (Illus.). 320p. 1994. 24.95 (*0-8130-1296-1*) U Press Fla.

Pacheco, Ferdie, jt. auth. see Gonzmart, Adela H.

Pacheco, Gilda. Nicaraguan Refugees in Costa Rica: Adjustment to Camp Life. 80p. (Orig.). 1989. pap. text ed. 7.50 (*0-924046-10-4*) Ctr EPRA.

Pacheco, Jose E. An Ark for the Next Millennium: Poems. LC 92-41086. (Texas Pan American Ser.). (Illus.). 152p. (SPA.). (C). 1993. text ed. 19.95 (*0-292-76547-9*); pap. 9.95 (*0-292-76548-7*) U of Tex Pr.

— Battles in the Desert & Other Stories. Silver, Katherine, tr. LC 86-28596. 128p. 1987. 19.95 (*0-8112-1019-7*); pap. 8.95 (*0-8112-1020-0*, NDP637) New Directions.

— A Distant Death. Scheer, Linda, tr. (Sun & Moon Classics Ser.: No. 41). 186p. (Orig.). 1995. text ed. 21.95 (*1-55713-155-4*) Sun & Moon CA.

— Don't Ask Me How the Time Goes By: Poems. Reid, Alastair, tr. LC 77-10530. 1978. text ed. 42.00 (*0-231-04284-1*); pap. text ed. 17.00 (*0-231-04285-X*) Col U Pr.

— Selected Poems. McWhirter, George, ed. Hoeksema, Thomas et al, trs. LC 86-31075. 224p. 1987. 23.95 (*0-8112-1021-9*); pap. 11.95 (*0-8112-1022-7*, NDP638) New Directions.

Pacheco, Josephine F., ed. Antifederalism: The Legacy of George Mason. LC 92-9206. (George Mason Lectures). 144p. (C). 1992. 42.50 (*0-913969-47-8*, G Mason Univ Pr) Univ Pub Assocs.

— To Secure the Blessings of Liberty: Rights in American History. 204p. 1993. lib. bdg. 42.50 (*0-913969-61-3*) U Pr of Amer.

Pacheco, Josephine F., jt. auth. see Foner, Philip S.

Pacheco, Larry & Post, Alan, eds. Nashville Red Book: The Complete Directory of Nashville's Music & Entertainment Industry 1988-89. 108p. 1989. write for info. (*0-318-64828-8*) Nashvll Red Bk.

Pacheco, M. Economic Terminology English-Spanish. 480p. (ENG & SPA.). 1967. 19.95 (*0-7859-0832-3*, M-7354) Fr & Eur.

Pacheco, M. A., jt. auth. see Sanchez, J. L.

Pacheco, Nelson S. Once a Panther. (Illus.). 184p. (Orig.). 1994. pap. text ed. 10.00 (*1-885152-02-7*) Bendan Pr.

Pacheco, Nelson S. & Blann, Tommy R. Unmasking the Enemy. (Illus.). 406p. (Orig.). 1994. pap. 14.95 (*1-885152-01-9*) Bendan Pr.

***Pacheco, Peter.** Programming Parallel Processors Using MPI. 1995. 29.95 (*1-55860-339-5*) Morgan Kaufmann.

Pacheco, Richard, et al. Winning Career Strategies: Teaching - K-12. Parkerson, Janet, ed. (C). 1989. pap. text ed. write for info. (*0-935423-07-9*) Educ Pubns.

***Pacheco, Victor, et al.** Lista Anotada de los Mamiferos Peruanos. 32p. (SPA.). 1994. pap. 7.00 (*1-881173-06-2*) Conser Intl.

Pacheko, Pedro. The Correspondence of Pedro Pacheko. 160p. 1992. pap. write for info. (*0-9634659-0-2*) Av-Garde Bks.

Pachelbel, Johann. Magnificat in C. Score for Orchestral Accompaniment. Woodward, Henry, ed. 148p. reprint ed. pap. 42.20 (*0-317-09818-7*, 2003450) Bks Demand.

Pacheleke, Calisto, jt. auth. see Darch, Colin.

Pachell, Michael, jt. auth. see Sabella, Tom.

Pacher, Sara, jt. auth. see Davis-March, Linda.

Pachman, Ludek. Decisive Games in Chess History. viii, 258p. 1987. reprint ed. pap. 7.95 (*0-486-25323-6*) Dover.

— Modern Chess Strategy. Russell, Allen S., tr. (Illus.). 1971. reprint ed. pap. 6.95 (*0-486-20290-9*) Dover.

Pachman, Stuart L. & Conover, John L. New Jersey Corporate Forms, 2 vols. suppl. ed. 1993. ring bd. 75.00 (*0-685-74626-7*) Butterworth Legal Pubs.

— New Jersey Corporate Forms, Set. 1990. disk 75.00 (*0-685-74627-5*) Butterworth Legal Pubs.

— New Jersey Corporate Forms, 2 vols., Set. 1260p. 1990. disk, ring bd. 239.00 (*0-8342-0155-0*) Michie Butterworth.

Pachmuss, Temira. D. S. Merezhkovsky in Exile: The Master of the Genre of Biographie Romancee. LC 89-13253. (American University Studies: Slavic Languages & Literature: Ser. XII, Vol. 12). 338p. (C). 1990. text ed. 64.00 (*0-8204-1254-6*) P Lang Pubs.

— A Moving River of Tears: Russia's Experience in Finland. LC 92-25217. (American University Studies: Slavic Languages & Literature: Ser. XII, Vol. 15). 289p. (C). 1993. text ed. 49.95 (*0-8204-1956-7*) P Lang Pubs.

— Russian Literature in the Baltic Between the World Wars. 448p. 1988. 24.95 (*0-89357-181-4*) Slavica.

Pachmuss, Temira, ed. & tr. A Russian Cultural Revival: A Critical Anthology of Russian Emigre Literature Before 1939. LC 80-20670. 476p. 1981. 45.00x (*0-87049-296-9*); pap. 21.00x (*0-87049-306-X*) U of Tenn Pr.

Pachmuss, Temira, ed. see Hippius, Zinaida N.

Pachmuss, Temira, ed. see Hippius, Zinaida.

Pachner, Edmond. Architectural Contract Administration. 248p. 1992. pap. text ed. 64.95 (*0-471-55004-3*) Wiley.

Pachnicke, Peter, et al, contribs. John Heartfield. LC 92-19588. (Illus.). 352p. 1993. 95.00 (*0-8109-3413-2*) Abrams.

Pacholczyk, A. G. The Catastrophic Universe: An Essay in the Philosophy of Cosmology. LC 83-62523. (Philosophy in Science Library: Vol. 2). (Illus.). 128p. 1984. pap. 9.95 (*0-88126-702-3*) Pachart Pub Hse.

— Central Lithuania: Specialized Stamp Catalogue. LC 90-70422. (Illus.). 208p. 1990. pap. 67.50 (*1-878543-01-6*) Stochastic Pr.

— Handbook of Radio Sources, Part II. Vol. 13. write for info. (*0-318-60788-3*) Pachart Pub Hse.

— Radio Galaxies: Radiation Transfer, Dynamics, Stability & Evolution of a Synchroton Plasmon. LC 76-27283. 1977. 124.00 (*0-08-021031-7*, Pub. by Pergamon Repr UK) Franklin.

Pacholczyk, A. G., jt. ed. see Ferrari, Attilio.

Pacholski, Richard, jt. auth. see Corr, Charles A.

Pacholski, Richard A., ed. Re-Searching Death: Selected Essays in Death Education & Counseling. (Illus.). vii, 241p. (Orig.). 1986. pap. 15.00 (*0-9607394-3-2*) Assn Death Educ.

Pacholski, Richard A. & Corr, Charles A., eds. New Directions in Death Education & Counseling. xvi, 346p. 1981. pap. 12.95 (*0-9607394-0-8*) Assn Death Educ.

— Priorities in Death Education & Counseling. viii, 282p. 1982. pap. 12.95 (*0-9607394-1-6*) Assn Death Educ.

Pachomius. History of the Monks at Tabenna. pap. 2.95 (*0-89981-029-2*) Eastern Orthodox.

— Instructions of St. Pachomius. Budge, E. Wallis, tr. pap. text ed. 2.95 (*0-89981-036-5*) Eastern Orthodox.

— Rule of St. Pachomius. Budge, E. A., tr. 1975. reprint ed. pap. 2.95 (*0-89981-078-0*) Eastern Orthodox.

Pachon, Harry, jt. auth. see Moore, Joan W.

Pachon, Harry P. & Desipio, Louis. New Americans by Choice: Political Perspectives of Latino Immigrants. 224p. (C). 1994. pap. text ed. 35.00 (*0-8133-8794-9*) Westview.

Pachonski, Jan & Wilson, Reuel K. Poland's Caribbean Tragedy: A Study of Polish Legions in the Haitian War of Independence 1802-1803. (East European Monographs). (Illus.). 386p. 1986. text ed. 47.50 (*0-88033-093-7*) Col U Pr.

Pachori, L. N. The Erotic Sculpture of Khajuraho. (C). 1989. 27.00 (*81-85109-79-6*, Pub. by Naya Prokash IA) S Asia.

Pachori, Satya S., ed. see Jones, William.

Pachovsky, Vasyl. Collected Poems, Vol. 1. 420p. 1984. 12.00 (*0-930013-00-X*) Assn Ukrainian Writers.

Pacht, Judith. Lean or Lavish: Two Tempting Versions of Each Dish. 1991. pap. 12.95 (*0-446-39221-9*) Warner Bks.

Pachter, Barbara. Prentice Hall Complete Business Etiquette Handbook. 1994. text ed. 29.95 (*0-13-156951-1*) P-H.

Pachter, Barbara, jt. auth. see Brody, Marjorie.

Pachter, Henry. Socialism & History: The Political Essays of Henry Pachter. Bronner, Stephen E., ed. LC 83-18904. (Illus.). 300p. 1984. text ed. 49.00 (*0-231-05660-5*) Col U Pr.

— The Weimar Etudes. Bronner, Stephen E., ed. LC 82-1122. (Illus.). 360p. 1982. text ed. 39.50 (*0-231-05360-6*) Col U Pr.

Pachter, Josh, tr. see Luitjters, Guus & Timmer, Gerard.

Pachter, L. M. Latino Folk Illness. 1993. pap. text ed. 61.00 (*2-88124-636-2*) Gordon & Breach.

Pachter, M., jt. ed. see Yavin, Y.

Pachulski, Roman. Psychiatry Notes. 150p. 1990. pap. text ed. 18.95 (*0-8385-6246-9*, A6246-1) Appleton & Lange.

Pachuta, Kate, ed. see Marion, James B. & Heald, Mark A.

Paci, Enzo. The Function of the Sciences & the Meaning of Man. Piccone, Paul & Hansen, James, trs. (Studies in Phenomenology & Existential Philosophy). 475p. 1972. pap. 17.95 (*0-8101-0618-3*) Northwestern U Pr.

Paciesas, W. & Fishman, G. Gamma-Ray Bursts. (Conference Proceeding Ser.: No. 265). 500p. 1992. 115.00 (*1-56396-018-4*) Am Inst Physics.

Pacific-10 Conference Staff. PAC-Ten Football Yearbook, 1993: Official Guide of the Pacific-10 Conference. 250p. 1993. pap. 8.95 (*1-880141-47-7*) Triumph Bks.

Pacific Asia Resource Center Staff. The People vs. Global Capital - the G-7, TNCs, SAPs, & Human Rights: Report of the International Peoples Tribunal to Judge the G-7, Tokyo, July 1993. 184p. (Orig.). 1995. pap. 14.95x (*0-945257-23-6*) Apex Pr.

***Pacific Economic Cooperation Council Staff.** Pacific Economic Development Report, 1995. Borthwick, E. Mark, ed. (Illus.). 192p. (Orig.). 1994. pap. text ed. write for info. (*1-886418-00-4*) US Natl Committee.

Pacific Entomological Survey Publications Staff. Society Islands Insects. (BMB Ser.). 1935. 21.00 (*0-527-02219-5*) Periodicals Srv.

Pacific Fast Mail Staff, ed. see Asay, Jeff.

Pacific Fast Mail Staff, ed. see Austin, Ed & Dill, Tom.

Pacific Fast Mail Staff, ed. see Beckstrom, Paul & Braun, David W.

Pacific Fast Mail Staff, ed. see Dill, Tom & Grande, Walter R.

Pacific Fast Mail Staff, ed. see Farrell, Jack W.

Pacific Fast Mail Staff, ed. see Ferrell, Mallory H.

Pacific Fast Mail Staff, ed. see Garmany, John B.

Pacific Fast Mail Staff, ed. see Jones, Robert.

Pacific Fast Mail Staff, ed. see King, Frank A.

Pacific Fast Mail Staff, ed. see Kohl, Phil & Kohl, Ruth.

Pacific Fast Mail Staff, ed. see Pfeifer, Jack A.

Pacific Fast Mail Staff, ed. see Riegger, Hal.

Pacific Fast Mail Staff, ed. see Wing, Warren W.

Pacific Fast Mail Staff, ed. see Wood, Charles & Wood, Dorothy.

Pacific Fast Mail Staff, et al, eds. Southern Pacific in Oregon. 2nd ed. (Illus.). 320p. 1994. 54.50 (*0-685-72111-6*) Pac Fast Mail.

Pacific Forum Staff, et al. Summaries of Three Bilateral Conferences: Held in Beijing & Shanghai, the People's Republic of China, October 15-30, 1986. 88p. 1988. pap. text ed. 9.95 (*0-8248-1175-5*, Pacific Forum) UH Pr.

Pacific Historian Staff, ed. John Muir: Life & Legacy. (Illus.). 192p. 1986. pap. 10.00 (*0-317-46609-7*) Holt-Atherton.

Pacific Information Management, Inc. Staff. Information Engineering Management Guide. LC 89-64246. (Illus.). 280p. 1989. 95.00 (*0-9624554-0-7*) Pac Info Mgmt.

Pacific Northwest National Parks & Forests Association Staff, jt. auth. see Gibson, William.

Pacific School of Religion Staff. Religious Progress on the Pacific Slope: Addresses & Papers at the Celebration of the Semi-Centennial Anniversary of Pacific School of Religion, Berkeley, California. LC 68-22941. (Essay Index Reprint Ser.). 1977. reprint ed. 21.95 (*0-8369-0820-1*) Ayer.

Pacific Science Congress Staff. Ryukyuan Culture & Society: Proceedings of the Pacific Science Congress, 10th, Honolulu, 1961. LC 63-19525. 121p. reprint ed. pap. 34.50 (*0-317-08484-4*, 2000073) Bks Demand.

— Society & Non-Timber Products in Tropical Asia. Fox, Jefferson, ed. LC 94-48590. (Occasional Papers: Environment Ser.: No. 19). 1995. write for info. (*0-86638-169-4*) EW Ctr HI.

Pacific Telecommunications Council Staff. PTC '84 Proceedings. Wedemeyer, Dan J. & Harms, L. S., eds. 236p. 1984. pap. text ed. 12.50 (*0-8248-0958-0*) Pac Telecom.

Pacific Trade & Development Conference Staff. Trade & Employment in Asia & the Pacific: Proceedings of the Eighth Pacific Trade & Development Conference, Pattaya, Thailand, July 10-14, 1976. Akrasanee, Narongchai et al, eds. 469p. reprint ed. pap. 133.70 (*0-7837-1304-5*, 2041452) Bks Demand.

Pacific War Research Society Staff. The Day Man Lost: Hiroshima, 6 August 1945. LC 80-85386. (Illus.). 312p. 1981. reprint ed. pap. 7.95 (*0-87011-471-9*) Kodansha.

Pacific War Research Society Staff, ed. Japan's Longest Day: Surrender - The Last Twenty-Four Hours Through Japanese Eyes. LC 68-17573. (Illus.). 340p. 1980. pap. 10.00 (*0-87011-422-0*) Kodansha.

Pacifici, Sergio. From Verismo to Experimentalism: Essays on the Modern Italian Novel. LC 74-98980. (Midland Book Ser.: MB 134). 316p. reprint ed. pap. 90.10 (*0-317-28582-3*, 2055204) Bks Demand.

— A Guide to Contemporary Italian Literature: From Futurism to Neorealism. LC 73-8698. (Arcturus Books Paperbacks). 352p. 1972. pap. 9.95 (*0-8093-0593-3*) S Ill U Pr.

— The Modern Italian Novel: From Pea to Moravia. LC 67-13047. (Crosscurrents Modern Critiques Ser.). 288p. 1979. 16.95 (*0-8093-0873-8*) S Ill U Pr.

Pacifico, A. D., jt. ed. see Stark, J.

Pacifico, Albert D., jt. auth. see Soto, Benigno.

Pacifico, Carl. Think Better, Feel Better. LC 89-91280. 1990. 20.00 (*0-87212-224-7*) Libra.

Pacifico, James J. The Synermergency: A Clarion Call to Anything But Arms. rev. ed. LC 91-92488. 184p. 1992. 8.95 (*0-9632022-4-3*); lib. bdg. 24.95 (*0-9632022-1-9*); pap. 8.95 (*0-9632022-2-7*); 13.00 (*0-9632022-3-5*) Holy Grail.

— The Synermergency: A Clarion Call to Anything But Arms. 2nd rev. ed. LC 91-92488. 184p. 1992. 24.95 (*0-9632022-0-0*) Holy Grail.

Pacilio, Nicola. Reactor-Noise Analysis in the Time Domain. LC 79-600321. (AEC Critical Review Ser.). 102p. 1969. pap. 10.50 (*0-87079-335-7*, TID-24512); fiche 9.00 (*0-87079-336-5*, TID-24512) DOE.

Pacinelli, Donna, illus. Heidi. (Gateway Classic Ser.). 48p. (J). (gr. 2-5). 1991. 6.95 (*0-88101-112-6*) Unicorn Pub.

Pacini, Deborah & Franquemont, Christine, eds. Coca & Cocaine: Effects on People & Policy in Latin America. (Cultural Survival Reports: No. 23). 170p. 1986. pap. 8.00 (*0-939521-24-5*) Cultural Survival.

Pacini, F., ed. High Energy Phenomena Around Collapsed Stars. 1987. lib. bdg. 117.00 (*90-277-2453-9*) Kluwer Ac.

Pacini, Giovanni. Il Barone Di Dolsheim: Libretto by Felice Romani, Music by Giovanni Pacini First Performance Milan, Teatro Alla Scala, 23 September 1818. LC 89-38889. (Italian Opera 1810-1840 Ser.: Vol. 29). 328p. 1990. 119.00 (*0-8240-6578-6*) Garland.

— Il Corsaro. Gossett, Philip, ed. (Italian Opera 1810-1840 Ser.: Vol. 34). 330p. 1985. 108.00 (*0-8240-6583-2*) Garland.

— Saffo & Excerpts from Furio Cammila. (Italian Opera 1810-1840 Ser.). 330p. 1986. lib. bdg. 108.00 (*0-8240-6585-9*) Garland.

— L' Ultimo Giorno di Pomoei & Excerpts from Niobe, Vol. 32. (Italian Opera II Ser.). 315p. 1985. lib. bdg. 108.00 (*0-8240-6581-6*) Garland.

***Pacini-Hernandez, Deborah.** Bachata: Social History of a Dominican Popular Music. 1995. text ed. 49.95 (*0-615-00084-3*) Temple U Pr.

— Bachata: Social History of a Dominican Popular Music. (Illus.). (Orig.). (C). 1995. text ed. 49.95 (*1-56639-299-3*); pap. text ed. 18.95 (*1-56639-300-0*) Temple U Pr.

Pacini, Kathy, ed. see Nixon, Joan L.

Pacioli, Luca. The Divine Proportion. (Janus Ser.). (C). Date not set. 25.00 (*0-89835-065-4*) Abaris Bks.

***Pacione, Michael.** Glasgow: The Socio-Spatial Development of the City. LC 94-46872. (Belhaven World Cities Ser.). 1995. text ed. 54.95 (*0-471-94947-7*) Wiley.

— Urban Problems & Planning in the Developed World. 1981. text ed. 39.95 (*0-312-83465-9*) St Martin.

Pacione, Michael, ed. The Geography of the Third World: Progress & Prospect. 416p. 1988. lib. bdg. 62.50 (*0-415-00467-5*) Routledge.

— Historical Geography: Progress & Prospect. LC 86-24301. (Progress in Geography Ser.). 320p. (C). 1987. 59.95 (*0-7099-4046-7*, Pub. by Croom Helm UK) Routledge Chapman & Hall.

— Population Geography: Progress & Prospects. (Progress in Geography Ser.). 336p. 1987. 49.95 (*0-7099-4045-9*, Pub. by Croom Helm UK) Routledge Chapman & Hall.

— Problems & Planning in Third World Cities. 1981. text ed. 35.00 (*0-312-64737-9*) St Martin.

— Progress in Agricultural Geography. (Progress in Geography Ser.). 288p. 1986. 55.00 (*0-7099-2095-4*, Pub. by Croom Helm UK) Routledge Chapman & Hall.

— Progress in Rural Geography. LC 82-22756. (Illus.). 268p. (C). 1983. text ed. 41.50 (*0-389-20358-0*, N7218) B&N Imports.

— Progress in Urban Geography. LC 82-22757. (Illus.). 296p. (C). 1983. text ed. 46.00 (*0-389-20357-2*, N7217) B&N Imports.

— Social Geography: Progress & Prospect. LC 87-506. 328p. 1987. 57.50 (*0-7099-4026-2*, Pub. by Croom Helm UK) Routledge Chapman & Hall.

***Paciorek, Karen M. & Munro, Joyce H., eds.** Annual Editions: Early Childhood Edition, 95-96. 16th rev. ed. (Illus.). 256p. (C). 1995. pap. text ed. 12.95x (*1-56134-351-X*) Dushkin Pub.

Paciorek, Michael & Jones, Jeffery. Sports & Recreation for the Disabled. 2nd ed. (Illus.). 550p. (C). 1994. pap. write for info. (*1-884125-04-2*) Cooper Pubng.

Paciorek, Michael J. & Jones, Jeffery A. Sports & Recreation for the Disabled. LC 94-16013. (Illus.). 468p. 1994. reprint ed. pap. 19.95 (*1-57028-012-6*) Masters Pr IN.

Pacis, Vicente A., jt. auth. see Aguinaldo, Emilio.

Pacius, Julius. In Porphyrii Isagogen et Aristotelis Organum, Commentarius Analyticus. xii, 536p. 1966. reprint ed. write for info. (*0-318-71270-9*, Pub. by Georg Olms GW) Lubrecht & Cramer.

Pack & Henrichsen. Sentence Combination. 2nd ed. 1992. teacher ed, pap. 7.95 (*0-8384-3018-X*) Heinle & Heinle.

— Sentence Construction. 2nd ed. 1992. teacher ed 5.00 (*0-8384-3016-3*) Heinle & Heinle.

Pack, A. J. The Man Who Burned the White House: The Story of Admiral of the Fleet Sir George Cockburn (1772-1853) (Maritime) 288p. 1987. 65.00 (*0-85937-332-0*, Pub. by K Mason Pubns Ltd UK) St Mut.

— Nelson's Blood. 160p. 1987. 45.00 (*0-85937-279-0*, Pub. by K Mason Pubns Ltd UK) St Mut.

Pack, Alice C. & Henrichsen, Lynn. Sentence Combination: Writing & Combining Standard English Sentences, Bk. II. 2nd ed. 160p. (Orig.). (C). 1992. pap. 17.95 (*0-8384-3017-1*) Heinle & Heinle.

Pack, Alice C. & Henrichsen, Lynn E. Sentence Construction: Writing & Combining Standard English Sentence, Bk. I. 2nd ed. 176p. 1992. pap. 17.95 (*0-8384-3015-5*) Heinle & Heinle.

Pack, Allan I., jt. ed. see Dempsey, Jerome A.

Pack, C. D., jt. ed. see Cohen, J. W.

Pack, Frank. The Gospel According to John, Pt. 1. LC 79-632639. 1984. 12.95 (*0-915547-22-8*) Abilene Christ U.

— The Gospel According to John, Pt. 2. LC 79-63269. 1984. 12.95 (*0-915547-23-6*) Abilene Christ U.

— Message of the New Testament: Revelations, 2 vols., 176. (Way of Life Ser.: Nos. 176 & 177). 1984. pap. 6.95 (*0-89112-176-5*) Abilene Christ U.

— Message of the New Testament: Revelations, 2 vols., 177. (Way of Life Ser.: Nos. 176 & 177). 1984. pap. 6.95 (*0-89112-177-3*) Abilene Christ U.

Pack, Greta, jt. auth. see Davis, Mary L.

Pack, Howard, jt. ed. see Heston, Alan W.

Pack, Janet. Fueling the Future. LC 91-34602. (Saving Planet Earth Ser.). 128p. (J). (gr. 4-8). 1992. lib. bdg. 20.55 (*0-516-05512-7*) Childrens.

Pack, Janet R. Urban Models. (Monograph Ser.: No. 7). 1978. 27.50 (*1-55869-129-4*) Regional Sci Res Inst.

Pack, Jay J., jt. auth. see Dunnan, Nancy.

Pack, Nancy C., jt. ed. see Foos, Donald D.

Pack, Phillip. AP Biology. (Illus.). 555p. 1994. pap. 14.95 (*0-8220-2301-6*) Cliffs.

Pack, Robert. Affirming Limits: Essays on Mortality, Choice, & Poetic Form. LC 85-2768. 272p. (Orig.). 1985. 30.00 (*0-87023-483-8*); pap. 16.95 (*0-87023-653-9*) U of Mass Pr.

— Before It Vanishes. 85p. 1989. pap. 9.95 (*0-87923-813-5*) Godine.

— Clayfeld Rejoices, Clayfeld Laments: A Sequence of Poems. LC 87-7414. 112p. 1987. 14.95 (*0-87923-695-7*); pap. 9.95 (*0-87923-696-5*) Godine.

— Edward Bennett Williams for the Defense. 2nd ed. 465p. 1988. reprint ed. pap. 12.95 (*0-915765-47-0*, Zenith Edit) Natl Pr Bks.

— Faces in a Single Tree. LC 83-49005. 96p. 1984. 13.95 (*0-87923-521-7*); pap. 8.95 (*0-87923-525-X*) Godine.

— Fathering the Map: New & Selected Later Poems. LC 93-3689. 248p. 1993. Acid-free paper. 24.95 (*0-226-64405-7*) U Ch Pr.

— The Long View: Essays on the Discipline of Hope & Poetic Craft. LC 91-13598. 296p. (C). 1992. lib. bdg. 32.50x (*0-87023-761-6*) U of Mass Pr.

— The Octopus Who Wanted to Juggle. (Illus.). (Orig.). (J). (ps-7). 1990. text ed. 13.95 (*0-913123-26-9*) Galileo.

— Waking to My Name: New & Selected Poems. LC 79-3651. 272p. 1980. 25.00 (*0-8018-2357-9*) Johns Hopkins.

— Wallace Stevens: An Approach to His Poetry & Thought. LC 68-24044. 203p. 1967. reprint ed. 45.00 (*0-87752-082-8*) Gordian.

Pack, Robert & Parini, Jay, eds. American Identities: Contemporary Multicultural Voices. LC 94-8809. (Bread Loaf Anthology Ser.). 1994. 29.95 (*0-87451-641-2*) U Pr of New Eng.

PQ

An Asterisk (*) at the beginning of an entry indicates that the title is appearing in BIP for the first time.

— The Bread Loaf Anthology of Contemporary American Essays. LC 88-40352. (Bread Loaf Anthology Ser.). 389p. 1989. 35.00 (*0-87451-476-2*); pap. 15.95 (*0-87451-475-4*) U Pr of New Eng.

— The Bread Loaf Anthology of Contemporary American Short Stories. LC 86-40387. (Bread Loaf Anthology Ser.). 341p. (C). 1987. 40.00 (*0-87451-392-8*); pap. 16.95 (*0-87451-401-0*) U Pr of New Eng.

— Poems for a Small Planet: Contemporary American Nature Poetry. LC 92-56909. (Bread Loaf Anthology Ser.). 320p. (C). 1993. 35.00 (*0-87451-620-X*); pap. 16. 95 (*0-87451-621-8*) U Pr of New Eng.

— Touchstones: American Poets on a Favorite Poem. (Bread Loaf Anthology Ser.). 1996. pap. 17.95 (*0-87451-723-0*) U Pr of New Eng.

— Touchstones: American Poets on a Favorite Poem. (Bread Loaf Anthology Ser.). 352p. (C). 1996. 39.95 (*0-87451-722-2*) U Pr of New Eng.

— Writers on Writing. LC 91-50372. (Bread Loaf Anthology Ser.). 306p. 1991. 35.00 (*0-87451-559-9*); pap. 16.95 (*0-87451-560-2*) U Pr of New Eng.

Pack, Robert, jt. auth. see Byron, John.

Pack, Robert, jt. auth. see Pankau, Ed.

Pack, Robert, jt. auth. see Speakes, Larry.

Pack, Robert, et al, eds. The Bread Loaf Anthology of Contemporary American Poetry. LC 85-40489. (Bread Loaf Anthology Ser.). 367p. 1985. pap. 17.95 (*0-87451-350-2*) U Pr of New Eng.

Pack, S. W. Invasion North Africa, Nineteen Forty-Two. (Illus.). 1981. 4.95 (*0-684-15921-X*, Scribners) S&S Trade.

Pack, Spencer J. Capitalism As a Moral System: Adam Smith's Critique of the Free Market Economy. 320p. 1991. text ed. 59.95 (*1-85278-442-3*, Pub. by E Elgar Pub UK) Ashgate Pub Co.

Pack, Spencer L. Reconstructing Marxian Economics: Marx Based Upon a Sraffian Commodity Theory of Value. LC 84-26279. 174p. 1985. text ed. 49.95 (*0-275-90152-1*, C0152, Praeger Pubs) Greenwood.

Packan, N. H., et al, eds. Effects of Radiation on Materials: 14th International Symposium, Vol. I. LC 89-18449. (Special Technical Publication Ser.: No. 1046). (Illus.). 700p. 1990. text ed. 127.00 (*0-685-33032-X*, 04-01046-35) ASTM.

***Packard.** The Computer Takeover. (Choose Your Own Adventure Ser.: No. 160). (J). 1995. mass mkt. 3.50 (*0-553-56402-1*) Bantam.

— Typhoon. (Choose Your Own Adventure Ser.: No. 162). (J). 1995. mass mkt. 3.50 (*0-553-56624-5*) Bantam.

Packard & Axelrod. Instructor's Guide to Concepts & Cases in Fashion Buying & Merchandising. 1977. 2.50 (*0-87005-197-0*) Fairchild.

Packard, Alpheus S. The Cave Fauna of North America: Remarks on the Anatomy of the Brain & Origin of the Blind Species. Egerton, Frank N., 3rd, ed. LC 77-74244. (History of Ecology Ser.). (Illus.). 1978. reprint ed. lib. bdg. 18.95 (*0-405-10413-8*) Ayer.

— The Labrador Coast: A Journal of Two Summer Cruises to That Region. LC 74-5862. reprint ed. 65.00 (*0-404-11668-X*) AMS Pr.

— Lamarck: The Founder of Evolution; His Life & Work; with Translations of His Writings on Organic Evolution. Cohen, I. Bernard, ed. LC 79-7980. (Three Centuries of Science in America Ser.). (Illus.). 1980. reprint ed. lib. bdg. 42.95 (*0-405-12562-3*) Ayer.

Packard, Ann & Stafford, Shirley. Holidays. (Learning Experiences for Young Children Ser.). 116p. (J). 1983. write for info. (*0-9607580-4-6*) S Stafford.

— Space. (Learning Experiences for Young Children Ser.). 58p. (J). (ps-3). 1981. write for info. (*0-9607580-2-X*) S Stafford.

— Time of the Dinosaurs. (Learning Experiences for Young Children Ser.). 92p. (J). (ps-3). 1981. write for info. (*0-9607580-1-1*) S Stafford.

Packard, Bob. The Pro. 1979. pap. 2.25 (*0-8439-0647-2*) Dorchester Pub Co.

Packard, Dane. The Church Becoming Christ's Body: The Small Church's Manual of Dances for Holy Seasons. Adams, Doug, ed. 110p. (Orig.). 1985. pap. 7.95 (*0-941500-35-7*) Sharing Co.

***Packard, Dave.** Grow Your Own Crystals. (J). (gr. 4-7). 1995. pap. 6.95 (*0-8167-3525-5*) Troll Assocs.

— The HP Way: How Bill Hewlett & I Built Our Company. 1995. 17.00 (*0-88730-747-7*) Harper Busn.

Packard, David. The Ball Game. LC 92-36008. (Illus.). (J). 1993. 3.95 (*0-590-46193-1*) Scholastic Inc.

Packard, David W. Concordance to Livy, 4 Vols, Set. LC 68-29181. 5395p. 1968. 340.00 (*0-674-15890-3*) HUP.

Packard, Dennis J. & Faulconer, James E. Introduction to Logic. LC 79-64449. 436p. 1980. 14.50 (*0-442-25781-3*) Van Nos Reinhold.

***Packard, E. P. W.** Marital Powers Exemplified in Mrs. Packard's Trial & Self-Defence from the Charge of Insanity; or Three Years' Imprisonment for Religious Belief... (Women & the Law Reprint Ser.). xxiv, 137p. 1994. reprint ed. lib. bdg. 37.50x (*0-8377-2552-6*) Rothman.

Packard, Edward. The Cave of Time. (Choose Your Own Adventure Ser.: No. 1). (J). (gr. 4-8). 1982. pap. 3.50 (*0-553-26965-8*) Bantam.

— The Cave of Time. large type ed. (Choose Your Own Adventure Ser.). (Illus.). 115p. (J). (gr. 3-7). 1987. 8.95 (*0-942545-01-X*); lib. bdg. 9.95 (*0-942545-07-9*) Grey Castle.

— Comet Crash. (Choose Your Own Adventure Ser.: No. 144). (J). (gr. 4-7). 1994. pap. 3.50 (*0-553-56009-3*) Bantam.

— The Curse of the Haunted Mansion. (Choose Your Own Adventure Ser.: No. 5). (J). 1982. pap. 3.50 (*0-553-27419-8*) Bantam.

— Cyberspace Warrior. (Choose Your Own Adventure Ser.: No. 154). (J). (gr. 4-7). 1994. pap. 3.50 (*0-553-56400-5*) Bantam.

— A Day with the Dinosaurs, No. 46. (Skylark Choose Your Own Adventure Ser.). 64p. (Orig.). (J). 1988. pap. 2.99 (*0-553-15612-8*, Skylark) Bantam.

— Dinosaur Island. (Choose Your Own Adventure Ser.: No. 138). (J). (gr. 4-7). 1993. pap. 3.50 (*0-553-56007-7*) Bantam.

— Dinosaur Island. large type ed. LC 94-24103. (ChooseYour own Adventure Ser.: No. 138). (Illus.). 128p. (J). 1995. lib. bdg. 15.93 (*0-8368-1306-5*) Gareth Stevens Inc.

— Ghost Hunter. (Choose Your Own Adventure Ser.: No. 52). 128p. (Orig.). (J). (gr. 4). 1986. pap. 3.50 (*0-553-26983-6*) Bantam.

— Horror House. (Choose Your Own Adventure Ser.: No. 143). (YA). 1993. pap. 3.25 (*0-553-56008-5*) Bantam.

— Imagining the Universe: A Visual Journey. LC 94-17980. 160p. (Orig.). 1994. pap. 15.00 (*0-399-52124-0*) Berkley Pub.

— Journey to the Year Three Thousand: Cyoa Superadventure. (Choose Your Own Super Adventure Ser.: No. 1). (Orig.). (J). (gr. 4). 1987. pap. 3.50 (*0-553-26157-6*) Bantam.

— Kidnapped. (Choose Your Own Adventure Ser.: No. 116). (YA). 1991. pap. 3.50 (*0-553-29143-2*) Bantam.

— The Luckiest Day of Your Life. (Choose Your Own Adventure Ser.: No. 132). (J). (gr. 4-7). 1993. pap. 3.25 (*0-553-29304-4*) Bantam.

— Magic Master. (Choose Your Own Adventure Ser.: No. 122). (J). 1992. pap. 3.50 (*0-553-29606-X*) Bantam.

— Magic Master. large type ed. LC 94-44196. (Choose Your Own Adventure Ser.: No. 122). (Illus.). 128p. (J). 1995. lib. bdg. 15.93 (*0-8368-1308-1*) Gareth Stevens Inc.

— Night of the Werewolf. (Choose Your Own Nightmare Ser.: No. 1). (J). (gr. 4-7). 1995. pap. 3.50 (*0-553-48229-7*) Bantam.

— Reality Machine. (Choose Your Own Adventure Ser.: No. 142). (YA). 1993. pap. 3.50 (*0-553-56401-3*) Bantam.

— Roller Star. (Choose Your Own Adventure Ser.: No. 136). (J). (gr. 4-7). 1993. pap. 3.25 (*0-553-56006-9*) Bantam.

— Secret of the Dolphins. (Choose Your Own Adventure Ser.: No. 134). (J). (gr. 4-7). 1993. pap. 3.50 (*0-553-29300-1*) Bantam.

— Skateboard Champion. (Choose Your Own Adventure Ser.: No. 112). (YA). 1991. pap. 3.50 (*0-553-28898-9*) Bantam.

— Sky-Jam! (Choose Your Own Adventure Ser.: No. 158). (YA). 1995. pap. 3.50 (*0-553-56623-7*) Bantam.

— Soccer Star. (Young Readers Ser.: No. 146). (J). 1994. pap. 3.50 (*0-553-56011-5*) Bantam.

— Superbike. (Choose Your Own Adventure Ser.: No. 124). (J). (gr. 4-7). 1992. pap. 3.50 (*0-553-29294-3*) Bantam.

— Through the Black Hole. (Choose Your Own Adventure Ser.: No. 97). (J). 1990. pap. 3.50 (*0-553-28440-1*) Bantam.

— Vampire Invaders. (Choose Your Adventure Ser.: No. 118). (J). (gr. 4-7). 1991. pap. 3.50 (*0-553-29212-9*) Bantam.

— Viking Raiders. (Choose Your Own Adventure Ser.: No. 128). (J). (gr. 4-7). 1992. pap. 3.25 (*0-553-29302-8*) Bantam.

— War with Mutant Spider Ants. (Choose Your Own Adventure Ser.: No. 152). (YA). 1994. pap. 3.50 (*0-553-56399-8*) Bantam.

— Who Are You? (Choose Your Own Adventure Ser.: No. 150). (J). (gr. 4-7). 1994. pap. 3.50 (*0-553-56398-X*) Bantam.

— Who Killed Harlowe Thrombey?, No. 9. large type ed. (Choose Your Own Adventure Ser.). 121p. (J). (gr. 3-7). 1987. reprint ed. 8.95 (*0-942545-13-3*); reprint ed. lib. bdg. 9.95 (*0-942545-18-4*) Grey Castle.

— Worst Day of Your Life. (Choose Your Own Adventure Ser.: No. 100). (J). 1990. pap. 3.50 (*0-553-28316-2*) Bantam.

— The Worst Day of Your Life. large type ed. (Choose Your Own Adventure Ser.: No. 100). (Illus.). 128p. (J). 1995. lib. bdg. 15.93 (*0-8368-1312-X*) Gareth Stevens Inc.

— You Are an Alien. (Choose Your Own Adventure Ser.: No. 156). (YA). 1995. pap. 3.50 (*0-553-56010-7*) Bantam.

— You Are Microscopic. (Choose Your Own Adventure Ser.: No. 130). (J). (gr. 4-7). 1992. pap. 3.50 (*0-553-29298-6*) Bantam.

— Your Code Name Is Jonah. large type ed. (Choose Your Own Adventure Ser.). 114p. (J). (gr. 3-7). 1987. reprint ed. 8.95 (*0-942545-15-X*); reprint ed. lib. bdg. 9.95 (*0-942545-20-6*) Grey Castle.

Packard, Elisabeth, jt. auth. see Zeri, Federico.

Packard, Elizabeth P. Great Disclosure of Spiritual Wickedness in High Places: With Appeal to the Government to Protect the Inalienable Rights of Married Women. LC 74-3965. (Women in America Ser.). (Illus.). 162p. 1974. reprint ed. 18.95 (*0-405-06114-5*) Ayer.

— Modern Persecution; or, Insane Asylums Unveiled, As Demonstrated by the Report of the Investigating Committee of the Legislature of Illinois, 2 vols. in 1. LC 73-2410. (Mental Illness & Social Policy; the American Experience Ser.). 1973. reprint ed. 57.95 (*0-405-05220-0*) Ayer.

Packard, Francis R. Guy Patin & the Medical Profession in Paris in the XVIIth Century. LC 78-95624. (Illus.). 1968. reprint ed. 39.50 (*0-678-03759-0*) Kelley.

Packard, Francis R., ed. see Pare, Ambroise.

Packard, Frank L. Jimmie Dale & the Blue Envelope Murder. reprint ed. lib. bdg. 21.95 (*0-88411-582-8*, Aeonian Pr) Amereon Ltd.

— Tiger Claws. reprint ed. lib. bdg. 22.95 (*0-88411-581-X*, Aeonian Pr) Amereon Ltd.

Packard, Frederic A. Daily Public School in the United States. LC 73-89215. (American Education: Its Men, Institutions & Ideas, Ser. 1). 1974. reprint ed. 16.95 (*0-405-01454-6*) Ayer.

Packard, George R., jt. auth. see Johnson, U. Alexis.

Packard, Gwen K. Coping in an Interfaith Family. LC 92-39454. (J). 1993. 15.95 (*0-8239-1452-6*) Rosen Group.

— Coping When a Parent Goes Back to Work. LC 94-13198. (J). 1994. 15.95 (*0-8239-1698-7*) Rosen Group.

Packard, Hewlett, Staff, jt. auth. see Gunn, Cathy.

Packard, Jasper. History of La Porte County, Indiana. 467p. 1993. reprint ed. lib. bdg. 47.50 (*0-8328-3452-1*) Higginson Bk Co.

Packard, Jerome L. A Linguistic Investigation of Aphasic Chinese Speech. LC 93-28051. (Studies in Theoretical Psycholinguistics: Vol. 18). 344p. (C). 1993. lib. bdg. 124.00 (*0-7923-2466-8*) Kluwer Ac.

***Packard, Jerrold M.** Farewell in Splendor: The Passing of Queen Victoria & Her Age. LC 94-30225. 1995. 22.95 (*0-525-93730-7*, Dutton) NAL-Dutton.

— Neither Friend Nor Foe: The European Neutrals. 544p. 1992. text ed. 30.00 (*0-684-19248-9*, Scribners) S&S Trade.

***Packard, Joan.** Natural Breast Enlargement Through Effective Relaxation Techniques. 1981. pap. 6.95 (*0-915190-30-3*) Jalmar Pr.

Packard, John H. A Manual of Minor Surgery. LC 88-60670. (American Civil War Surgery Ser.: No. 10). 288p. 1989. reprint ed. 45.00 (*0-930405-08-0*) Norman SF.

Packard, Kathleen W. La Guardia's Fire Chief. rev. ed. (Illus.). 206p. reprint ed. pap. 9.95 (*0-925165-11-5*) Fire Buff Hse.

Packard, Laurence B. The Age of Louis the Fourteenth. rev. ed. (Illus.). 64p. (C). 1991. pap. text ed. 2.25 (*1-877891-04-5*) Paperbook Pr Inc.

Packard, M. The Kite. (My First Reader Ser.). (Illus.). 28p. (J). (ps-2). 1990. lib. bdg. 10.50 (*0-516-05355-8*); pap. 3.95 (*0-516-45355-6*) Childrens.

— Surprise! (My First Reader Ser.). (Illus.). 28p. (J). (ps-2). 1990. lib. bdg. 10.50 (*0-516-05360-4*); pap. 3.95 (*0-516-45360-2*) Childrens.

— Where Is Jake? (My First Reader Ser.). (Illus.). 28p. (J). (ps-2). 1990. lib. bdg. 10.50 (*0-516-05361-2*); pap. 3.95 (*0-516-45361-0*) Childrens.

Packard, Mary. Bubble Trouble. LC 94-16975. (My First Hello Reader! Ser.). (Illus.). (J). 1995. 3.95 (*0-590-48513-X*) Scholastic Inc.

— Christmas Kitten. (J). (ps-1). 1994. pap. 3.95 (*0-516-45364-5*) Childrens.

— Christmas Kitten. LC 94-12301. (My First Reader Ser.). (Illus.). 28p. (J). (ps-1). 1994. lib. bdg. 10.50 (*0-516-05364-7*) Childrens.

— Dinosaurs. (Illus.). 48p. (J). (ps-3). 1981. pap. 9.95 (*0-671-43040-8*, S&S Bks Young Read) S&S Childrens.

— Disney's Two-Minute Good Night Stories. (J). 1994. write for info. (*0-318-72883-4*, Golden Bks) Western Pub.

— Fairest of All. LC 93-11056. (Better World Ser.). (Illus.). 40p. (J). (ps-4). 1993. lib. bdg. 11.85 (*0-516-00826-9*) Childrens.

— I Am King! LC 94-12245. (My First Reader Ser.). (Illus.). 28p. (J). (ps-1). 1994. lib. bdg. 10.50 (*0-516-05365-5*); pap. 3.95 (*0-516-45365-3*) Childrens.

— The Lion King: Best Friends. (Golden Sturdy Shape Bks.). (Illus.). 14p. (J). 1994. write for info. (*0-307-12499-1*, Golden Bks) Western Pub.

— My First Answer Book. (Illus.). (J). (ps-5). 1984. pap. 7.95 (*0-671-49312-4*, Litl Simon S&S) S&S Childrens.

— My Messy Room. LC 92-36009. (Illus.). (J). 1993. 3.95 (*0-590-46192-3*) Scholastic Inc.

— The Pet That I Want. LC 94-16976. (My First Hello Reader! Ser.). (J). 1995. 3.95 (*0-590-48512-1*) Scholastic Inc.

— Playing by the Rules. LC 93-4423. (Better World Ser.). (Illus.). 40p. (J). (ps-4). 1993. lib. bdg. 11.85 (*0-516-00827-7*) Childrens.

— Rocks & Minerals. (J). (gr. 4-7). 1995. pap. 6.95 (*0-8167-3527-1*) Troll Assocs.

— Safe & Sound. LC 93-11058. (Better World Ser.). (Illus.). 40p. (J). (ps-4). 1993. lib. bdg. 11.85 (*0-516-00828-5*) Childrens.

— Save the Swamp. LC 93-11059. (Better World Ser.). (Illus.). 40p. (J). (ps-4). 1993. lib. bdg. 11.85 (*0-516-00829-3*) Childrens.

— Scaredy Ghost. LC 93-24845. (Illus.). 24p. (J). (gr. k-2). 1993. pap. text ed. 1.50 (*0-8167-3246-9*) Troll Assocs.

— Sleep-over Mouse. (My First Reader Ser.). (Illus.). 28p. (J). (ps-2). 1994. lib. bdg. 10.50 (*0-516-05367-1*); pap. 3.95 (*0-516-45367-X*) Childrens.

— Spike & Mike & the Treasure Hunt. LC 92-50295. (Pictureback Ser.). (J). 1993. write for info. (*0-679-93936-9*); lib. bdg. write for info. (*0-679-83936-4*) Random Bks Yng Read.

— Stars & Planets. (J). (ps-3). 1995. pap. 6.95 (*0-8167-3563-8*) Troll Assocs.

— Starting Over. LC 93-11060. (Better World Ser.). (Illus.). 40p. (J). (ps-4). 1993. lib. bdg. 11.85 (*0-516-00831-5*) Childrens.

— World up Close. (J). (gr. 4-7). 1994. pap. 6.95 (*0-8167-3524-7*) Troll Assocs.

Packard, Mary, jt. auth. see Hall, N.

Packard, Mary, jt. auth. see Hall, Nancy.

Packard, Mary E. The Witch Who Couldn't Fly. LC 93-2212. (Glow-in-the-Dark Book Ser.). (Illus.). (J). (gr. k-3). 1993. pap. 2.95 (*0-8167-3256-6*) Troll Assocs.

***Packard, Michael E.** Choosing a Management Company No. 8: Choosing a Management Company. 3rd rev. ed. (GAP Ser.: No. 8). 16p. (C). 1994. pap. 14.50 (*0-944715-33-8*) CAI.

Packard, Peter, jt. auth. see Slater, John.

Packard, Philip C. Critical Path Analysis for Development Administration. LC 72-85842. (Institute of Social Studies Publications: No. 7). (Illus.). 84p. (Orig.). 1972. pap. text ed. 12.35 (*90-279-2174-1*) Mouton.

— Project Appraisal for Development Administration. LC 74-75576. (Publications of the Institute of Social Studies: No. 12). 158p. 1974. pap. text ed. 21.35 (*90-279-3452-5*) Mouton.

Packard, Randall M. Chiefship & Cosmology: An Historical Study of Political Competition. LC 81-47013. (African Systems of Thought Ser.). (Illus.). 256p. 1981. 25.00 (*0-253-30831-3*) Ind U Pr.

— White Plague, Black Labor: Tuberculosis & the Political Economy of Health & Disease in South Africa. 1989. 52. 00 (*0-520-06574-3*); pap. 17.00 (*0-520-06575-1*) U CA Pr.

Packard, Richard B. & Kinnear, Fiona C. Manual of Cataract & Intraocular Lens Surgery. (Illus.). 127p. 1991. text ed. 82.00 (*0-443-04091-5*) Churchill.

Packard, Robert T. & Korab, Balthazar. Encyclopedia of American Architecture. 2nd ed. 1994. text ed. 89.50 (*0-07-048010-9*) McGraw.

Packard, Robert T., jt. ed. see Wilkes, Joseph A.

Packard, Rosa C. The Hidden Hinge. LC 74-188958. 1977. pap. 10.00 (*0-8190-0074-4*) R C Packard.

Packard, Sidney. The Fashion Business: Dynamics & Careers. 294p. (C). 1983. text ed. 36.75 (*0-03-054026-7*) HB Coll Pubs.

— Strategies & Tactics in Fashion Marketing: Selected Readings. LC 82-70063. (Illus.). 143p. reprint ed. pap. 40.80 (*0-8357-3714-4*, 2036436) Bks Demand.

Packard, Sidney & Axelrod, Nathan. Concepts & Cases in Fashion Buying & Merchandising. LC 76-50439. (C). 1977. text ed. 16.50 (*0-87005-182-2*) Fairchild.

Packard, Sidney & Guerreiro, Miriam. The Buying Game: Fashion Buying & Merchandising. (Illus.). (C). 1979. student ed 17.50 (*0-87005-315-9*); teacher ed 2.50 (*0-87005-331-0*) Fairchild.

Packard, Sidney, et al. Fashion Buying & Merchandising. 2nd ed. (Illus.). 400p. (C). 1983. teacher ed 2.50 (*0-87005-446-5*); text ed. 24.00 (*0-87005-445-7*) Fairchild.

Packard, Vance. The Ultra Rich: How Much Is too Much? 1989. 22.95 (*0-316-68752-9*) Little.

***Packard, Vance & Horowitz, Daniel, eds.** The Status Seekers. 224p. 1995. pap. text ed. 8.65 (*0-312-11180-0*) St Martin.

Packard, Vernal S. Processed Foods & the Consumer: Additives, Labeling, Standards, & Nutrition. LC 75-32670. 367p. reprint ed. pap. 104.60 (*0-7837-2930-8*, 2057524) Bks Demand.

Packard, Wellman. Early Emigration to California. 32p. 1971. reprint ed. pap. 2.00 (*0-87770-068-0*) Ye Galleon.

Packard, William. The Art of Poetry Writing: A Guide for Poets, Students, & Readers. 240p. 1992. 18.95 (*0-312-07641-X*) St Martin.

— The Poet's Dictionary: A Handbook of Prosody & Poetic Devices. 240p. 1994. reprint ed. pap. 12.00 (*0-06-272045-7*, Harper Ref) HarpC.

— Shipping Pools. 1989. 85.00 (*1-85044-239-8*) Lloyds London Pr.

Packard, William & Mitchell, John D. Women - Men (Femmes - Hommes) The Erotic Poetry of Paul Verlaine. LC 77-23853. (Illus.). 150p. (Orig.). (ENG & FRE.). (C). 1991. reprint ed. pap. 24.95 (*1-882763-01-7*) IASTA.

Packard, William, et al, eds. Facts on File Dictionary of the Theatre. 1989. 35.00 (*0-8160-1841-3*) Facts on File.

***Packard, Wyman H.** A Century of U. S. Naval Intelligence. LC 94-35197. 1995. text ed. write for info. (*0-945274-25-4*) Naval Hist Ctr.

Packe, Michael. King Edward III. Seaman, L. C., ed. 336p. 1984. 27.95 (*0-685-10058-8*); pap. 8.95 (*0-7448-0023-4*) Routledge Chapman & Hall.

Packel, E. W. The Mathematics of Games & Gambling. LC 80-85037. (New Mathematical Library: No. 28). 151p. 1981. pap. 17.50 (*0-88385-628-X*) Math Assn.

Packel, Ed & Wagon, Stan. Animating Calculus: Mathematica Notebooks for the Laboratory. LC 93-21054. (C). 1995. pap. text ed. write for info. (*0-7167-2428-6*) W H Freeman.

Packel, Edward W. Functional Analysis: A Short Course. Anderson, Richard D. & Rosenberg, Alex, eds. LC 79-21888. 192p. 1980. reprint ed. lib. bdg. 16.00 (*0-89874-019-3*) Krieger.

Packel, Leonard & Spina, Dolores B. Trial Advocacy: A Systematic Approach. LC 84-70166. 206p. 1984. 76.00 (*0-8318-0453-X*, B548) Am Law Inst.

Packel, Leonard, et al, eds. Trial Practice for the General Practitioner. 114p. 1980. pap. 5.00 (*0-686-32427-7*, B190) Am Law Inst.

Packenham, Robert A. The Dependency Movement: Scholarship & Politics in Development Studies. 362p. (C). 1992. 47.50 (*0-674-19810-7*) HUP.

— Liberal America & the Third World: Political Development Ideas in Foreign Aid & Social Science. LC 72-1987. 376p. 1973. pap. 17.95 (*0-691-02176-7*) Princeton U Pr.

***Packer & Cadenas, eds.** Biothiols in Health & Disease. (Antioxidants in Health & Disease Ser.). 721p. 1995. write for info. (*0-8247-9654-3*) Dekker.

Packer, jt. ed. see Fuchs.

Packer, jt. auth. see Livrea.

Packer, Alex J. Bringing up Parents: The Teenager's Handbook. Espeland, Pamela, ed. LC 92-36625. (Illus.). 272p. (YA). (gr. 7 up). 1993. reprint ed. pap. 12.95 (*0-915793-48-2*) Free Spirit Pub.

— 365 Ways to Love Your Child. LC 94-48755. 1995. write for info. (*0-440-50590-9*) Dell.

Packer, Andrew J., ed. Manual of Retinal Surgery. (Illus.). 128p. 1989. pap. text ed. 52.00 (*0-443-08605-2*) Churchill.

Packer, Ann. Mendocino & Other Stories. LC 93-36315. 192p. 1994. pap. 9.95 (*0-8118-0629-4*) Chronicle Bks.

Packer, Arnold E., jt. auth. see Johnston, William B.

Packer, Bernard. Flags of Convenience. 1992. 21.95 (*0-395-58680-1*) Ticknor & Fields.

Packer, Bill & Kronbergs, Z. Butterworths Personal Tax Service. 1991. 280.00 (*0-406-00186-3*, U.K.) Butterworth Legal Pubs.

Packer, Boyd K. A Christmas Parable. 1993. 9.95 (*0-88494-901-X*) Bookcraft Inc.

— The Holy Temple. 10.95 (*0-88494-411-5*) Bookcraft Inc.

— Let Not Your Heart Be Troubled. 1991. 12.95 (*0-88494-787-4*) Bookcraft Inc.

— Our Father's Plan. rev. ed. LC 84-72516. 62p. 1994. 12.95 (*0-87579-820-9*) Deseret Bk.

— Teach Ye Diligently. rev. ed. LC 75-22704. x, 388p. 1991. reprint ed. pap. 9.95 (*0-87579-476-9*) Deseret Bk.

— That All May Be Edified. 10.95 (*0-88494-473-5*) Bookcraft Inc.

Packer, Cathy. Freedom of Expression in the American Military: A Communication Modeling Analysis. LC 88-27508. (Illus.). 279p. 1989. text ed. 65.00 (*0-275-93028-9*, C3028, Greenwood Pr) Greenwood.

Packer, Craig. Into Africa. LC 94-8428. 1994. 24.95 (*0-226-64429-4*) U Ch Pr.

Packer, Donna S. On Footings from the Past. 19.95 (*0-88494-681-9*) Bookcraft Inc.

Packer, Duane, jt. auth. see Roman, Sanaya.

Packer-Fletcher, Dorothy G. Basic Code Enforcement. 289p. write for info. (*0-318-61820-6*) Bldg Code Admins.

Packer, George. The Half Man: A Novel. LC 90-52895. 320p. 1991. 19.50 (*0-394-58192-X*) Random.

— The Village of Waiting. LC 87-45912. (Departures Ser.). 352p. (Orig.). 1988. pap. 12.00 (*0-394-75754-8*, Vin) Random.

Packer, Herbert L. Ex-Communist Witnesses: Four Studies in Fact Finding. viii, 279p. 1962. 37.50 (*0-8047-0121-0*) Stanford U Pr.

— The Limits of the Criminal Sanction. LC 68-26780. xi, 385p. 1968. reprint ed. 47.50 (*0-8047-0656-5*); reprint ed. pap. 15.95 (*0-8047-0899-1*) Stanford U Pr.

Packer, J. I. Bondage of the Will. LC 58-8662. 1990. pap. 12.99 (*0-8007-5342-9*) Revell.

— Concise Theology: A Guide to Historic Christian Beliefs. LC 92-37771. 1993. 16.99 (*0-8423-1111-4*) Tyndale.

— Conociendo a Dios: Knowing God. (SPA.). 6.95 (*84-7645-014-1*, 223083, Pub. by Edit Clie SP) TSELF.

— Dios, Yo Quiero Ser Cristiano: God: I Want to Be a Christian. (SPA.). 7.95 (*84-7228-775-0*, 220309, Pub. by Edit Clie SP) TSELF.

— Evangelism & the Sovereignty of God. LC 67-28875. 1961. pap. 8.99 (*0-8309-1339-4*, 1339) InterVarsity.

— Everyday Life in the Bible: The Old & New Testament. 1989. 7.99 (*0-517-67885-3*) Random Hse Value.

— God Has Spoken. 176p. 1988. pap. 6.99 (*0-8010-7107-0*) Baker Bk.

— God Has Spoken: Revelation & the Bible. 176p. (Orig.). 1994. pap. 7.99 (*0-8010-7128-3*) Baker Bk.

— God's Words: Studies of Key Bible Themes. 223p. 1988. pap. 9.99 (*0-8010-7105-4*) Baker Bk.

— Growing in Christ. LC 93-50566. 1994. pap. 11.99 (*0-89107-794-4*) Crossway Bks.

— Hot Tub Religion. 246p. Date not set. pap. 4.99 (*0-8423-1381-8*) Tyndale.

— Keep in the Step with the Spirit. LC 84-1304. 1987. pap. 8.99 (*0-8007-5235-X*) Revell.

— Knowing Christianity. 220p. 1995. 15.99 (*0-87788-058-1*) Shaw Pubs.

— Knowing God: Twentieth Anniversary Edition. rev. ed. LC 73-81573. 288p. 1993. reprint ed. pap. 10.99 (*0-8308-1650-X*, 1650) InterVarsity.

— Knowing God: Twentieth Anniversary Edition. rev. ed. LC 73-81573. 312p. 1993. 19.99 (*0-8308-1651-8*, 1651) InterVarsity.

— Knowing Man. LC 79-52495. 1979. pap. 5.99 (*0-89107-175-X*) Crossway Bks.

— Meeting God. (LifeGuide Bible Studies). 64p. (Orig.). 1986. pap. 4.99 (*0-8308-1057-9*, 1057) InterVarsity.

— A Quest for Godliness: The Puritan Vision of the Christian Life. LC 94-10535. 368p. 1994. pap. 14.99 (*0-89107-819-3*) Crossway Bks.

— Rediscovering Holiness. 260p. 1992. 16.99 (*0-89283-734-9*, Vine Bks) Servant.

— Rediscovering Holiness. 278p. 1994. pap. 9.99 (*0-89283-860-4*, Vine Bks) Servant.

— Thy Will Be Done: Daily Devotions on Knowing & Doing God's Will. 370p. 1995. 13.99 (*0-89283-927-9*, Vine Bks) Servant.

Packer, J. I. & Wilkinson, Loren, eds. Alive to God: Studies in Spirituality Presented to James M. Houston. LC 92-31340. 314p. 1992. pap. 19.99 (*0-8308-1767-0*) InterVarsity.

***Packer, J. I., et al.** Knowing God. aniversary ed. (Orig.). 1993. student ed. pap. 4.99 (*0-8308-1649-6*, 1649) InterVarsity.

— O Mundo Do Novo Testamento. 192p. (POR.). 1990. 8.95 (*0-8297-1590-8*) Life Pubs Intl.

***Packer, James I.** Freedom & Authority. (ICBA Foundation Ser.). 32p. 1992. reprint ed. pap. 2.99 (*1-57383-035-6*) Regent College.

— Fundamentalism & the Word of God. 1958. pap. 7.99 (*0-8028-1147-7*) Eerdmans.

— A Passion for Faithfulness: Wisdom from the Book of Nehemiah. LC 94-24366. (Living Insights Ser.). 224p. 1995. 14.99 (*0-89107-731-2*) Crossway Bks.

— Your Father Loves You: Daily Insights for Knowing God. Watson, Jean, ed. & comp. by. LC 86-1770. 392p. 1986. 14.99 (*0-87788-875-2*) Shaw Pubs.

***Packer, Jane.** The Complete Guide to Flower Arranging: A Practical Illustrated Guide to Choosing, Arranging, & Displaying Fresh Dried Flowers. LC 94-31858. (Illus.). 192p. 1995. 29.95 (*1-56458-868-8*) Dorling Kindersley.

— Flowers for All Seasons: Fall. (Illus.). 120p. 1989. 17.95 (*0-449-90413-X*, Columbine) Fawcett.

— Flowers for All Seasons: Summer. LC 88-26833. 1989. 17.95 (*0-449-90412-1*, Columbine) Fawcett.

— Flowers for All Seasons: Winter. LC 88-92871. 120p. 1989. 17.95 (*0-449-90414-8*, Columbine) Fawcett.

— Jane Packer's New Flower Arranging. (Illus.). 128p. 1994. 24.95 (*0-943955-90-4*, Trafalgar Sq Pub) Trafalgar.

Packer, Joan G. Rebecca West: An Annotated Bibliography. LC 91-11183. 164p. 1991. 20.00 (*0-8240-5692-2*, H1158) Garland.

Packer, John G., jt. auth. see Moss, Ezra H.

Packer, John W. Acts of the Apostles. (Cambridge Bible Commentary on the New English Bible, New Testament Ser.). (Orig.). (C). 1966. pap. 19.95 (*0-521-09383-X*) Cambridge U Pr.

Packer, Kenneth J., jt. auth. see McBrierty, Vincent J.

Packer, Kenneth L. Puberty: The Story of Growth & Change. LC 89-5665. (Venture Bks.). (Illus.). 109p. (J). (gr. 6-9). 1989. lib. bdg. 14.28 (*0-531-10810-4*) Watts.

Packer, L., jt. ed. see Ong, A. S.

Packer, L., et al, eds. Free Radicals in the Brain: Aging, Neurological, & Mental Disorders. LC 92-49895. (Illus.). xi, 181p. 1992. 89.00 (*3-540-55619-2*) Spr-Verlag.

Packer, Leslie, jt. ed. see Colowick, Sidney P.

Packer, Lester, ed. Methods in Enzymology, Vol. 234: Oxygen Radicals in Biological Systems, Pt. D. 704p. 1994. text ed. 99.00 (*0-12-182135-8*) Acad Pr.

Packer, Lester & Fuchs, Jurgen, eds. Vitamin E in Health & Disease: Biochemistry & Clinical Applications. LC 92-49976. 1024p. 1992. 210.00 (*0-8247-8692-0*) Dekker.

***Packer, Lester & Wirtz, Karel W., eds.** Signalling Mechanisms: From Transcription Factors to Oxidative Stress. LC 95-10171. (NATO ASI Ser.: Series H, Cell Biology: Vol. 92). 1995. write for info. (*3-540-59127-3*) Spr-Verlag.

Packer, Lester, jt. ed. see Colowick, Sidney P.

Packer, Lester, jt. ed. see Rajamanickam, C.

Packer, Lester, et al, eds. Methods in Enzymology: Oxygen Radicals in Biological Systems: Oxygen Radicals & Antioxidants, Vol. 186, Part B. 855p. 1990. text ed. 127.00 (*0-12-182087-4*) Acad Pr.

— Methods in Enzymology Vol. 251: Biothiols, Pt. A: Monothiols & Dithiols, Protein Thiols & Thiyl Radicals. (Illus.). 543p. 1995. text ed. 85.00 (*0-12-182152-8*) Acad Pr.

— Methods in Enzymology Vol. 252: Biothiols: Glutathione & Thioredoxin: Thiols in Signal Transduction & Gene Regulation. (Illus.). 432p. 1995. boxed write for info. (*0-12-182153-6*) Acad Pr.

— Methods in Enzymology, Vol. 167: Cyanobacteria. 750p. 1988. text ed. 149.00 (*0-12-182068-8*) Acad Pr.

— Methods in Enzymology, Vol. 189: Retinoids, Pt. A: Molecular & Metabolic Aspects. 583p. 1990. text ed. 105.00 (*0-12-182090-4*) Acad Pr.

— Methods in Enzymology, Vol. 190: Retinoids, Pt. B: Cell Differentiation & Clinical Applications. 488p. 1990. text ed. 92.00 (*0-12-182091-2*) Acad Pr.

— Methods in Enzymology, Vol. 233: Oxygen Radicals in Biological Systems, Pt. C. (Illus.). 711p. 1994. text ed. 99.00 (*0-12-182134-X*) Acad Pr.

Packer, M. J. The Structure of Moral Action: A Hermeneutic Study of Moral Conflict. (Contributions to Human Development Ser.: Vol. 13). (Illus.). xii, 164p. 1985. 77.75 (*3-8055-3999-1*) S Karger.

Packer, Martin J. & Addison, Richard B., eds. Entering the Circle: Hermeneutic Investigation in Psychology. LC 88-24908. 329p. 1989. 74.50 (*0-7914-0014-X*); pap. 24.95 (*0-7914-0015-8*) State U NY Pr.

Packer, Martin J., jt. ed. see Tappan, Mark B.

Packer, Miriam. Take Me to Coney Island. (Prose Ser.: No. 25). 185p. 1993. pap. 13.00 (*0-920717-92-6*) Guernica Editions.

Packer, Nancy E. White Gloves & Red Bricks: APVA 1889-1989. (Illus.). 87p. 1989. pap. 9.95 (*0-917565-02-9*) Assn Preserv VA.

Packer, Nancy H. Women Who Walk. Stories. LC 88-28617. x, 184p. 1989. 17.95 (*0-8071-1458-8*) La State U Pr.

Packer, Nancy H. & Timpane, John. Writing Worth Reading: A Practical Guide. 2nd ed. LC 92-75239. 504p. (C). 1993. pap. text ed. 9.50 (*0-312-09206-7*, Bedford Bks) St Martin.

— Writing Worth Reading: A Practical Guide with Handbook. 2nd ed. LC 88-70424. 572p. (C). 1989. pap. text ed. 0.18 (*0-312-01258-6*, Bedford Bks) St Martin.

Packer, Nancy H., jt. auth. see Stone, Wilfred.

Packer, Paul C. Housing of High School Programs. LC 70-177140. (Columbia University. Teachers College. Contributions to Education Ser.: No. 159). reprint ed. 37.50 (*0-404-55159-9*) AMS Pr.

Packer, Roger J., et al, eds. Pediatric Neuro-Oncology: New Trends in Clinical Research. LC 90-4990. (Monographs in Clinical Pediatrics: Vol. 3). 320p. 1991. text ed. 88.00 (*3-7186-0524-4*) Gordon & Breach.

Packer, Steve, jt. auth. see Bray, Mark.

***Packer, Toni.** The Work of This Moment. 128p. (Orig.). 1995. pap. 12.95 (*0-8048-3062-2*) C E Tuttle.

Packer, W. Art of Vogue Covers. 256p. 1984. 9.98 (*0-517-44647-2*) Random Hse Value.

Packer, William. The Art of Vogue Covers: 1909 to 1940. (Illus.). 256p. 1980. 10.98 (*0-517-53838-5*) Random Hse Value.

Packer, William A., tr. see Medvedev, Roy A.

Packer, William A., tr. see Zevi, Bruno.

***Packham.** Freedom & Anarchy. 187p. 1995. lib. bdg. 57.00 (*1-56072-232-0*) Nova Sci Pubs.

***Packham, Chris.** Wild Shots: A New Look at Photographing the Wildlife. (Illus.). 160p. 1994. 39.95 (*1-85585-189-X*) Trafalgar.

Packham, D. E., ed. Handbook of Adhesion. LC 92-15139. (Polymer Science & Technology Ser.). 1993. text ed. 250.00 (*0-470-21870-3*) Halsted Pr.

***Packham, Jo.** Glue Crafts: More Things to Do with Glue Than You Ever Imagined. LC 95-11240. (Illus.). 144p. 1995. 24.95 (*0-8069-3187-6*, Chapelle) Sterling.

— Making Fabulous Pincushions: 93 Designs for Spectacular & Unusual Projects. LC 94-23821. (Illus.). 144p. 1995. 24.95 (*0-8069-0994-3*, Chapelle) Sterling.

— Wedding Attendants: Selecting & Directing Your Supporting Cast. LC 93-14159. (Wedding Ser.). 96p. 1993. pap. 5.95 (*0-8069-8829-0*) Sterling.

— Wedding Ceremonies: Planning Your Special Day. LC 92-44207. (Illus.). 112p. 1993. pap. 5.95 (*0-8069-8834-7*, Chapelle) Sterling.

— Wedding Flowers: Choosing & Making Beautiful Bouquets & Arrangements. LC 92-43728. (Illus.). 96p. 1993. pap. 5.95 (*0-8069-8830-4*, Chapelle) Sterling.

— Wedding Gowns & Other Bridal Apparel: Looking Beautiful on Your Special Day. LC 93-43684. 96p. 1994. pap. 5.95 (*0-8069-0588-3*, Chapelle) Sterling.

— Wedding Parties & Showers: Planning Memorable Celebrations. LC 92-41335. 96p. 1993. 5.95 (*0-8069-8828-2*, Chapelle) Sterling.

— Wedding Photography: Getting the Perfect Pictures. LC 93-46749. 96p. 1994. pap. 5.95 (*0-8069-0586-7*, Chapelle) Sterling.

— Wedding Proposals & Engagement: A Guide to Happy Beginnings. LC 93-21518. (Wedding Ser.). 112p. 1993. pap. 5.95 (*0-8069-8835-5*) Sterling.

— Wedding Receptions: Arranging a Joyous Celebration. LC 93-25930. (Wedding Ser.). 112p. 1993. pap. 5.95 (*0-8069-8833-9*, Chapelle) Sterling.

— Wedding Stationery: Perfect Invitations, Enclosures, Thank You's & More. LC 93-25090. (Wedding Ser.). 96p. 1993. pap. 5.95 (*0-8069-8831-2*, Chapelle) Sterling.

— Wedding Toasts & Speeches: Finding the Perfect Words. LC 92-41319. (Illus.). 96p. 1993. pap. 5.95 (*0-8069-8832-0*, Chapelle) Sterling.

Packham, John R., et al. Functional Ecology of Woodlands. (Illus.). 384p. (C). 1992. text ed. 85.00 (*0-412-44390-2*, A7417); pap. text ed. 35.00 (*0-412-43950-6*, A7204) Chapman & Hall.

Packo, John E. Coping with Cancer: Twelve Creative Choices. LC 90-62157. 225p. 1991. 7.99 (*0-87509-438-4*) Chr Pubns.

***Packull, Werner O.** Hutterite Beginnings: Communitarian Experiments During the Reformation. (Illus.). 488p. 1995. text ed. 59.95x (*0-8018-5048-7*) Johns Hopkins.

— Mysticism & the Early South German-Austrian Anabaptist 1525-1531. LC 76-46557. (Studies in Anabaptist & Mennonite History: No. 19). 296p. 1977. 19.95 (*0-8361-1130-3*) Herald Pr.

Packwood, Bob. Senator Bob Packwood's Secret Diary. 1994. pap. 4.99 (*1-56171-315-5*, S P I Bks) Sure Sellers.

Packwood, Burley. Bird Turd Peppers & Other Delights. (Illus.). 313p. (Orig.). 1993. pap. 7.95 (*0-9624358-1-3*) Quantum Pr AZ.

— Quail in my Bed. LC 89-92060. (Illus.). 195p. (Orig.). 1989. pap. 6.95 (*0-9624358-0-5*) Quantum Pr AZ.

Packwood, T., et al. Hospitals in Transition: The Resource Management Experiment. (State of Health Ser.). 160p. 1991. 90.00 (*0-335-09951-3*, Open Univ Pr); pap. 32.00 (*0-335-09950-5*, Open Univ Pr) Taylor & Francis.

Paclisanu, Zenobius. Hungary's Struggle to Annihilate Its National Minorities: Based on Secret Hungarian Documents. 182p. 1985. write for info. (*0-937019-00-3*); pap. 18.00 (*0-937019-01-1*) Romanian Hist.

Paco, Mariano, ed. see Buero Vallejo, Antonio.

Paco, Mariano D., ed. see Benavente, Jacinto.

Paco, Mariano D., ed. see Buero Vallejo, Antonio.

Pacolet, Jozef & Wilderom, Celeste. Economics of Care of the Elderly. 335p. 1991. 63.95 (*1-85628-196-5*, Pub. by Avebury Pub UK) Ashgate Pub Co.

Pacosz, Christina. This Is Not a Place to Sing. 48p. (Orig.). (C). 1987. pap. 4.95 (*0-931122-47-3*) West End.

Pacosz, Christina V. Some Winded, Wild Beast. 1985. pap. 2.50 (*0-934868-28-X*) Black & Red.

Pacotti, Pamela. Legacy of Secrets. 1988. 3.95 (*0-517-00036-9*) Random Hse Value.

— The Lost Heiress of Merriott Manor. (Orig.). 1982. pap. 2.25 (*0-89083-919-0*) Zebra.

***Pacovska, Kveta.** Flying. LC 95-8327. (J). 1995. write for info. (*1-55858-496-X*) North-South Bks NYC.

— The Little Flower King. Bell, Anthea, tr. LC 92-6046. (Illus.). 36p. (J). 1992. pap. 15.95 (*0-88708-221-1*, Picture Book Studio) S&S Childrens.

— The Midnight Play. LC 93-16258. (Illus.). (J). (ps-8). 1993. 15.95 (*0-88708-317-X*, Picture Book Studio) S&S Childrens.

— Midnight Play. LC 94-26546. (Illus.). 48p. (J). 1994. 28.00 (*1-55858-341-6*) North-South Bks NYC.

— Midnight Play. Clements, Andrew, tr. LC 94-26546. (Illus.). (J). 1994. 28.00 (*1-55858-252-5*) North-South Bks NYC.

— One Five Many. (J). (ps-3). 1990. 16.95 (*0-685-54064-2*, Clarion Bks) HM.

***Pacovska, Kveta, illus.** Art of Kveta Pacovska. 112p. (YA). 1994. 39.95 (*1-55858-233-9*) North-South Bks NYC.

Pacsy, V. A. & Bennet, J. V. Cost-Managerial Accounting: Robotor Inc. Job Order System & Cost Control. 96p. 1986. 10.05 (*0-07-004702-2*) McGraw.

Pacsy, V. A. & Bennett, J. V. Cost-Managerial Accounting: Comptech Manufacturer Standard Costs & Budgeting. 64p. 1986. 10.05 (*0-07-004704-9*) McGraw.

Pact, Virginia, et al. The Muscle Testing Handbook. 194p. 1984. 36.95 (*0-316-68768-5*) Little.

Pacteau, Francette. The Symptom of Beauty. LC 93-38507. (Essays in Art & Culture Ser.). 232p. 1994. 35.00 (*0-674-85987-1*) HUP.

— The Symptom of Beauty: Essays in Art & Culture. (Illus.). 232p. (Orig.). (C). 1995. pap. text ed. 19.95 (*0-674-85988-X*) HUP.

Pacter, Paul. Reporting Disaggregated Information. LC 93-70113. (Financial Accounting Standards Board Research Report Ser.). 423p. 1993. pap. 25.00 (*0-910065-54-3*) Finan Acct Found.

Pacter, Trudi. The Sleeping Partner. 1992. mass mkt. 4.99 (*0-06-100515-0*, Harp PBks) HarpC.

Pacter, Trudy. Kiss & Tell. 1990. mass mkt. 4.95 (*0-06-100022-1*, Harp PBks) HarpC.

Pactor, Howard S., comp. Colonial British Caribbean Newspapers: A Bibliography & Directory. LC 90-35630. (Bibliographies & Indexes in World History Ser.: No. 19). 160p. 1990. text ed. 65.00 (*0-313-27232-8*, PBC/, Greenwood Pr) Greenwood.

Pactor, Peter A. The Day the Pig Got Loose in School (& Other Strange Stories) 139p. 1993. pap. 10.95 (*0-9638569-0-1*) P A Pactor.

— Thoughts to Hold Onto: Just for Teenagers. 48p. (Orig.). (YA). 1995. pap. 5.95 (*0-9638569-1-X*) P A Pactor.

Paculla, Nicholas. Artificer Asylum. 260p. 1993. pap. 7.95 (*0-9638757-0-1*) Asylum Pubns.

Pacwa, Mitch. Catholics & the New Age: How Good People Are Being Drawn into Jungian Psychology, the Enneagram, & the Age of Aquarius. 235p. (Orig.). 1992. pap. 8.99 (*0-89283-756-X*) Servant.

— Father Forgive Me for I Am Frustrated: Growing in Your Faith - Even When It Isn't Easy Being Catholic. 220p. 1996. pap. 8.99 (*0-89283-840-X*, Charis) Servant.

Pacy, James S. & Wertheimer, Alan P., eds. Perspectives on the Holocaust: Essays in Honor of Raul Hilberg. 1994. text ed. 49.95 (*0-8133-2034-8*) Westview.

Pacyga, Dominic. Polish Immigrants & Industrial Chicago: Workers on the South Side, 1880-1922. (Urban Life & Urban Landscape Ser.). 298p. 1991. lib. bdg. 42.50 (*0-8142-0541-0*) Ohio St U Pr.

Pacyga, Dominic A., et al. Chicago: City of Neighborhoods. 600p. (Orig.). 1986. pap. 22.95 (*0-8294-0497-X*) Loyola Univ Pr.

Pacyna, Jozef M. & Ottar, Brynjulf, eds. Control & Fate of Atmospheric Trace Metals. (C). 1989. lib. bdg. 130.00 (*0-7923-0152-8*) Kluwer Ac.

Paczolay, Gy. Comparative Dictionary of Proverbs. 300p. (C). 1987. 99.00 (*0-685-54133-9*, Pub. by Collets) St Mut.

Paczuska, Anna & Grillet, Sophie. Socialism for Beginners. (Writers & Readers Documentary Comic Bks.). (Illus.). (C). 1986. pap. 6.95 (*0-906495-92-X*) Writers & Readers.

Padadoyannis. HPLC in Clinical Chemistry. (Chromatographic Science Ser.: Vol. 54). 504p. 1990. 165.00 (*0-8247-8139-2*) Dekker.

Padak, Nancy, jt. ed. see Rasinski, Tim.

***Padaki, Vijay.** Development Intervention & Programme Evaluation: Concepts & Cases. LC 95-8277. 216p. (C). 1995. 29.95 (*0-8039-9240-8*); pap. 14.95 (*0-8039-9241-6*) Sage.

Padam, Sundarsanam. Bus Transport in India: The Structure, Management & Performance of Road Transport Corporation. 1990. 32.50 (*81-202-0222-8*, Pub. by Ajanta II) S Asia.

Padamsee, Sultan. Poems. (Redbird Ser.). 1976. 9.00 (*0-89253-123-1*); 6.75 (*0-89253-138-X*) Ind-US Inc.

Padawer, Patricia, jt. auth. see Goldstein, Joan.

Padawitz, P. Computing in Horn Clause Theories. (EATCS Monographs on Theoretical Computer Science). (Illus.). xi, 322p. 1988. 53.00 (*0-387-19427-4*) Spr-Verlag.

— Deductive & Declarative Programming. (Tracts in Theoretical Computer Science Ser.: No. 28). (Illus.). 250p. (C). 1992. 47.95 (*0-521-41723-6*) Cambridge U Pr.

Padberg, John W. Colleges in Controversy: The Jesuit Schools in France from Revival to Suppression, 1815-1880. LC 75-78523. (Historical Studies: No. 83). 347p. 1969. 25.00 (*0-674-14160-1*) HUP.

— Together As a Companionship: A History of the Thirty-First, Thirty-Second, & Thirty-Third General Congregations of the Society of Jesus. (Series IV: No. 15). viii, 145p. (Orig.). Date not set. 14.95 (*1-880810-08-5*) Inst Jesuit.

Padberg, John W., ed. Documents of the Thirty-First & Thirty-Second General Congregations of the Society of Jesus: An English Translation of the Official Latin Texts of the General Congregations & of the Accompanying Papal Documents. LC 77-70881. (Jesuit Primary Sources in English Translation Series I: No. 2). x, 598p. 1977. pap. 6.00 (*0-912422-26-2*) Inst Jesuit.

Padberg, John W., jt. auth. see O'Malley, John W.

***Padberg, Manfred.** Linear Optimization & Extensions. LC 94-47365. (Algorithms & Combinatorics Ser.: Vol. 12). 1995. write for info. (*3-540-58734-9*) Spr-Verlag.

Padbury, Andy, ed. My War: Or How I Survived in the Royal Air Force Without Being a Hero. (C). 1989. 45.00 (*0-685-52931-2*) St Mut.

Padda, Darshan S. Selected Essays on Food & Agriculture in the Virgin Islands. (Illus.). 700p. (Orig.). 1991. pap. text ed. write for info. (*0-9628909-0-1*) U VI CES.

Padden, Carol, jt. auth. see Baker, Charlotte.

An Asterisk (*) at the beginning of an entry indicates that the title is appearing in BIP for the first time.

Padden, Carol A. & Humphries, Tom L. Deaf in America: Voices from a Culture. LC 88-11769. (Illus.). 160p. 1988. 24.00 (*0-674-19423-3*) HUP.
— Deaf in America: Voices from a Culture. (Illus.). 144p. 1990. pap. text ed. 9.95 (*0-674-19424-1*) HUP.
Padden, Carol A., jt. auth. see Humphries, Tom L.
Padden, Patti, ed. see Crumble, Mortimer.
Padden, R. C. Hummingbird & the Hawk: Conquest & Sovereignty in the Valley of Mexico, 1503-1541. (C). 1975. pap. text ed. 14.00 (*0-06-131898-1*, TB1898, Torch) HarpC.
Padden, R. C., ed. see Arzans de Orsua y Vela, Bartolome.
***Paddie, Dennis.** Morning Wounds in the Warehouse. (Illus.). 64p. (Orig.). 1993. pap. 12.00 (*0-9631569-1-8*) Backyard Pr.
Paddington Bear. Childhood Memories. large type ed. 194p. (J). 1991. 21.95 (*1-85089-456-6*, Pub. by ISIS UK) Transaction Pubs.
Paddio-Johnson, Eunice. Pat's First Book of Thoughts in Poetry & Prose. 1991. write for info. (*1-880143-00-3*) Paddio-Johnson.
Paddison, Max. Adorno's Aesthetics of Music. LC 92-46202. (Illus.). 350p. (C). 1993. 64.95 (*0-521-43321-5*) Cambridge U Pr.
Paddison, Patricia L., ed. Treatment of Adult Survivors of Incest. LC 92-17653. (Clinical Practice Ser.: No. 27). 160p. 1993. 25.00 (*0-88048-469-1*) Am Psychiatric.
Paddison, R. & Bailey, S. J., eds. Local Government Finance: An International Comparison. 208p. 1988. lib. bdg. 59.50 (*0-415-00529-9*) Routledge.
Paddison, R., jt. auth. see Bailey, S. J.
Paddison, Ronan, jt. auth. see Muir, Richard.
Paddison, Ronan, et al, eds. International Perspectives in Urban Studies. 163p. 1993. pap. 42.00 (*1-85302-163-6*, Pub. by J Kingsley Pubs UK) Taylor & Francis.
— International Perspectives in Urban Studies 2. 328p. 1994. pap. 39.95 (*1-85302-216-0*, Pub. by J Kingsley Pubs UK) Taylor & Francis.
Paddison, Sara. The Hidden Power of the Heart: Achieving Balance & Fulfillment in a Stressful World. 280p. 1995. 11.95 (*1-879052-35-0*) Planetary Pubns.
— The Hidden Power of the Heart: Achieving Balance & Fulfillment in a Stressful World. 288p. (C). 1992. reprint ed. lib. bdg. 31.00x (*0-8095-5809-2*) Borgo Pr.
Paddison, Sara & Rozman, Deborah. Just Love the People: The Family Frequency. 208p. (Orig.). 1991. reprint ed. lib. bdg. 31.00x (*0-8095-5800-9*) Borgo Pr.
***Paddock, Bruce.** Victorian Christmas. LC 94-78179. (Traditional Country Life Recipe Ser.). (Illus.). 96p. 1994. pap. 9.95 (*1-883283-06-X*) Brick Tower.
Paddock, C. L. Life's Detours. large type ed. 32p. 1952. pap. 3.95 (*0-8163-0074-7*, 12225-9) Pacific Pr Pub Assn.
Paddock, Charles E. Structured FORTRAN for Business. LC 84-18377. (Illus.). 272p. (C). 1985. pap. text ed. 32.00 (*0-13-854233-3*) P-H.
Paddock, G. J. The Sectional Title Handbook. 2nd ed. 216p. 1990. pap. write for info. (*0-7021-2346-3*, Pub. by Juta SA) W W Gaunt.
Paddock, Harold. A Dialect Survey of Carbonear, Newfoundland. (Publication of American Dialect Society Bks.: No. 68). (Illus.). 85p. 1908. pap. 8.50 (*0-8173-0093-7*) U of Ala Pr.
Paddock, Joe. Boars' Dance. LC 92-54183. 80p. (Orig.). 1993. pap. 8.95 (*0-930100-51-4*) Holy Cow.
— Earth Tongues: Poems. LC 85-61268. (Lakes & Prairies Ser.). 72p. (Orig.). 1985. pap. 6.00 (*0-915943-07-7*) Milkweed Ed.
Paddock, John. Lord Five Flower's Family: Rulers of Zaachila & Cuilapan. (Publications in Anthropology: No. 29). (Illus.). 124p. 1983. pap. 12.90 (*0-935462-20-1*) Vanderbilt Pubns.
— Oaxacans in Mesoamerica. (Illus.). 200p. Date not set. 24.95 (*0-939923-22-X*); pap. 14.95 (*0-939923-23-8*) M & W Pub Co.
Paddock, John, ed. Ancient Oaxaca: Discoveries in Mexican Archeology & History. (Illus.). xvi, 416p. 1966. 42.50 (*0-8047-0170-9*) Stanford U Pr.
Paddock, Lowell C., jt. auth. see Friedman, Dave.
Paddock, T. B. Plagiotropis Pfitzer & Tropodoneis Cleve, a Summary Account. (Bibliotheca Diatomologica Ser.: Vol. 16). (Illus.). 190p. 1988. pap. 76.00 (*3-443-57007-0*) Lubrecht & Cramer.
Paddock, Todd & Patrick, Ruth, eds. Proceedings of the Fourth National Conference: Solid Waste Management. LC 90-82564. (Illus.). 355p. (Orig.). 1990. pap. 15.00 (*0-910006-50-4*) Acad Nat Sci Phila.
Paddon, D. J., ed. Supercomputers & Parallel Computations. (Institute of Mathematics & Its Applications Conference Series, New Ser.). (Illus.). 1984. 70.00 (*0-19-853601-1*) OUP.
Paddon, D. J. & Holstein, H., eds. Multigrid Methods for Integral & Differential Equations. (Institute of Mathematics & Its Applications Conference Series, New Ser.). 1985. 60.00 (*0-19-853606-2*) OUP.
Paddon, Derek, jt. auth. see Willis, Claire.
Paddon, Michael, jt. auth. see Busfield, Joan.
***Pade, Victoria.** Baby My Baby: (A Ranching Family) (Special Edition Ser.). 1995. pap. 3.75 (*0-373-09946-0*, 1-09946-4) Silhouette.
— The Case of the Accidental Heiress. (American Romance Ser.). 1995. mass mkt. 3.50 (*0-373-16594-3*, 1-16594-3) Harlequin Bks.
— The Case of the Borrowed Bride. (American Romance Ser.). 1995. mass mkt. 3.50 (*0-373-16588-9*, 1-16588-5) Harlequin Bks.
— The Case of the Maybe Babies. (American Romance Ser.). 1995. mass mkt. 3.50 (*0-373-16590-0*, 1-16590-1) Harlequin Bks.
— Cowboy's Kin: A Ranching Family. 1994. mass mkt. 3.50 (*0-373-09923-1*, 1-09923-3) Harlequin Bks.
— Cowboy's Kiss. (Special Edition Ser.). 1995. mass mkt. 3.75 (*0-373-09970-3*, 1-09970-4) Silhouette.
— Ladylight. 368p. (Orig.). 1987. pap. 3.95 (*0-380-75320-0*) Avon.
— Unmarried with Children. (Silhouette Special Edition Ser.). 1993. mass mkt. 3.50 (*0-373-09852-9*, 5-09852-0) Silhouette.
Padel, Ruth. Angel. 80p. 1994. pap. 14.95 (*1-85224-278-7*, Pub. by Bloodaxe Bks UK) Dufour.
— In & Out of the Mind: Greek Images of the Tragic Self. 215p. 1991. text ed. 29.95 (*0-691-07379-1*) Princeton U Pr.
— In & Out of the Mind: Greek Images of the Tragic Self. 215p. 1994. pap. 12.95 (*0-691-03766-3*) Princeton U Pr.
— Whom God Destroys: Elements of Greek & Tragic Madness. LC 94-25529. 1994. 29.95 (*0-691-03360-9*) Princeton U Pr.
Padel, S., jt. ed. see Lampkin, N. H.
Padelford, Frederick M. Early Sixteenth-Century Lyrics. LC 70-144436. (Belles Lettres Series, Section 2: No. 3). reprint ed. 30.00 (*0-404-53613-1*) AMS Pr.
— Political & Ecclesiastical Allegory of the First Book of the Fairie Queen. LC 70-111785. reprint ed. 20.00 (*0-404-04856-0*) AMS Pr.
Padelford, Philip, ed. see Honyman, Robert.
Paden, Ann, jt. ed. see Carter, Gwendolen M.
Paden, Donald W. An Introduction to Economic Analysis. LC 74-28440. 470p. reprint ed. pap. 134.00 (*0-317-20530-7*, 2022844) Bks Demand.
Paden, Elaine P. Exercises in Phonetic Transcription: A Programmed Workbook. 2nd ed. 33p. (C). 1989. pap. text ed. 13.00 (*0-8134-2825-4*, 3441) Buttrwrth-Heinemann.
Paden, Elaine P., jt. auth. see Hodson, Barbara W.
Paden, Irene, jt. auth. see Schlichtmann, Margaret.
Paden, Irene D. Prairie Schooner Detours. 2nd ed. (Illus.). 310p. 1990. reprint ed. pap. 12.95 (*0-935284-77-X*) Patrice Pr.
Paden, John N., ed. Ahmadu Bello: Sardauna of Sokoto Values & Leadership in Nigeria. xvi, 800p. 1986. pap. 13.50 (*0-340-38967-2*, 00589) Heinemann.
Paden, John N. & Soja, Edward W., eds. The African Experience, Vol. 3-A, Bibliography. LC 70-98466. reprint ed. pap. 120.00 (*0-8357-5233-X*, 2016720) Bks Demand.
— The African Experience, Vol. 3-B, Guide to Resources. LC 70-98466. 149p. reprint ed. pap. 42.50 (*0-8357-5234-8*) Bks Demand.
— The African Experience: Volume 3B, Guide to Resources. 141p. 1970. 35.00 (*0-89771-005-3*) St Mut.
Paden, Joseph. Sarcosomataceae (Pezizales Sarcosyphgineae) LC 83-8056. (Flora Neotropica Monograph Ser.: No. 37). (Illus.). 16p. (Orig.). 1983. pap. 5.50 (*0-89327-250-7*) NY Botanical.
Paden, Margaret S., tr. see Rulfo, Juan.
Paden, Mary, ed. see Snyder, Sarah A.
***Paden, Ross.** The Cottonwood Stage. (Black Horse Westerns Ser.). 159p. 1995. 14.95 (*0-7090-5227-8*) Parkwest Pubns.
Paden, W. D., tr. see Dinesen, Isak.
Paden, William D., ed. The Future of the Middle Ages: Medieval Literature in the 1990s. (Illus.). 200p. (C). 1994. lib. bdg. 37.95 (*0-8130-1278-3*); pap. text ed. 17.95 (*0-8130-1279-1*) U Press Fla.
— The Voice of the Trobairitz: Perspectives on the Women Troubadours. LC 89-4920. (Middle Ages Ser.). (Illus.). 274p. (C). 1989. text ed. 34.95x (*0-8122-8167-5*) U of Pa Pr.
Paden, William E. Interpreting the Sacred: Ways of Viewing Religion. LC 91-12152. 176p. 1992. pap. 14.00 (*0-8070-7707-0*) Beacon Pr.
— Religious Worlds: The Comparative Study of Religion. LC 88-47658. 240p. 1988. 22.00 (*0-8070-1210-6*); pap. 13.00 (*0-8070-1211-4*, BP 806) Beacon Pr.
— Religious Worlds: The Comparative Study of Religion. 2nd ed. LC 93-43025. 208p. 1994. 13.00 (*0-8070-1229-7*) Beacon Pr.
Pader. Oral Hygiene: Products & Practice. (Cosmetic Science & Technology Ser.: Vol. 6). 552p. 1988. 199.00 (*0-8247-7701-8*) Dekker.
Pader, Olga F. A Guide & Handbook for Parents of Mentally Retarded Children. (Illus.). 268p. 1981. 38.95 (*0-398-04566-6*) C C Thomas.
— A Guide & Handbook for Parents of Mentally Retarded Children. (Illus.). 268p. 1981. pap. 24.95 (*0-398-06311-7*) C C Thomas.
Paderewski, Ignacy J., ed. see Chopin, Frederic.
Paderewski, Jan I. & Lawton, Mary. The Paderewski Memoirs. LC 80-21323. (Music Ser.). 1980. reprint ed. 45.00 (*0-306-76046-0*) Da Capo.
Padesky, Christine A., jt. auth. see Dattilio, Frank M.
Padesky, Christine A., jt. auth. see Greenberger, Dennis.
Padfield, Harland & Martin, William E. Farmers, Workers & Machines: Technological & Social Change in Farm Industries of Arizona. LC 65-25018. 341p. reprint ed. pap. 97.20 (*0-317-51987-5*, 2027385) Bks Demand.
Padfield, K. Randall. Flying in Adverse Conditions. 1994. text ed. 29.95 (*0-07-048139-3*); pap. text ed. 18.95 (*0-07-048140-7*) McGraw.
Padfield, Paul L., jt. ed. see Baylis, Peter H.
Padfield, Peter. Armada. LC 87-63369. (Illus.). 192p. 1988. 28.95 (*0-87021-006-8*) Naval Inst Pr.
— Himmler: Reichsfuhrer-SS. 672p. 1993. pap. 19.95 (*0-8050-2699-1*) H Holt & Co.
Padfield, R. Randall. Cross Country Flying. 1991. pap. 19.95 (*0-07-048126-1*) McGraw.
— Cross-Country Flying. 3rd ed. (Practical Flying Ser.). (Illus.). 320p. 1991. 29.95 (*0-8306-7640-6*, 3640, TAB-Aero); pap. 19.95 (*0-8306-3640-4*, TAB-Aero) TAB Bks.
— Cross Country Flying. 3rd ed. 1991. 29.95 (*0-07-048127-X*) McGraw.
— Learning to Fly Helicopoters. 1992. text ed. 29.95 (*0-07-157725-4*); pap. text ed. 19.95 (*0-07-157724-6*) McGraw.
— Learning to Fly Helicopters. 368p. 1992. 29.95 (*0-8306-2113-X*); pap. 19.95 (*0-8306-2092-3*) TAB Bks.
***Padgaonkar, Dileep, ed.** When Bombay Burned: Reportage & Comments on the Riots & Blasts from the Times of India. (C). 1993. 22.50 (*81-85944-55-5*, Pub. by UBS Pubs Dist II) S Asia.
Padgaonkar, Latika, tr. see Vincent, Rose, ed.
Padgen, Anthony. The Uncertainties of Empire: Essays in Iberian & Ibero-American Intellectual History. (Collected Studies Ser.: CS 468). 320p. 1994. 87.50 (*0-86078-461-4*, Pub. by Variorum UK) Ashgate Pub Co.
Padgett, ed. Proceedings of the Third Workshop on Neural Networks. 662p. 1993. pap. 90.00 (*1-56555-007-2*, WNN92-1) Soc Computer Sim.
Padgett, et al. Windmore Writers Anthology. 1993. pap. 8.50 (*0-9636786-0-4*) Blue Rdge Mntns.
Padgett, Abigail. Child of Silence. 208p. 1993. 17.95 (*0-89296-488-X*) Mysterious Pr.
— Child of Silence. 208p. 1994. mass mkt. 4.99 (*0-446-40184-6*, Mysterious Paperbk) Warner Bks.
— Moonbird Boy. 1996. write for info. (*0-89296-613-0*) Mysterious Pr.
— Strawgirl. 256p. 1994. 18.95 (*0-89296-489-8*) Mysterious Pr.
— Strawgirl. 240p. 1995. mass mkt. 5.50 (*0-446-40199-4*, Mysterious Paperbk) Warner Bks.
— Turtle Baby. 288p. 1995. 19.95 (*0-89296-580-0*) Mysterious Pr.
— Turtle Baby. 256p. 1996. mass mkt. 5.99 (*0-446-40478-0*, Mysterious Paperbk) Warner Bks.
Padgett, Alan G., ed. The Mission of the Church in Methodist Perspective: The World Is My Parish. LC 92-34032. (Studies in the History of Missions: Vol. 10). 196p. 1992. text ed. 79.95 (*0-7734-9157-0*) E Mellen.
— Reason & the Christian Religion: Essays in Honour of Richard Swinburne. 378p. 1995. text ed. 65.00 (*0-19-824042-2*) OUP.
Padgett, Allen & Smith, Bruce. On Rope. (Illus.). 340p. 1987. 25.00 (*0-9615093-2-5*) Natl Speleological.
Padgett, Barbara, jt. auth. see Denver Parent, Inc. Staff.
Padgett, Bill. Dragons. (Illus.). 174p. 1984. 17.95 (*0-934073-00-7*) Rountree Pub NC.
— In Search of the Big Cookie. 1986. 9.50 (*0-934073-02-3*) Rountree Pub NC.
— Juliet. (Illus.). 52p. 1986. write for info. (*0-934073-03-1*) Rountree Pub NC.
— Sippin' (Illus.). 52p. 1988. 12.95 (*0-934073-04-X*) Rountree Pub NC.
— Snowflakes & Flowers. 52p. 1995. 12.95 (*0-614-06924-6*) Rountree Pub NC.
Padgett, Deborah. Settlers & Sojourners: A Study of Serbian Adaptation in Milwaukee, Wisconsin. LC 88-46193. (Immigrant Communities & Ethnic Minorities in the U. S. & Canada Ser.: No. 39). 1989. 57.50 (*0-404-19449-4*) AMS Pr.
Padgett, Deborah K., ed. Handbook on Ethnicity, Aging & Mental Health. LC 94-11220. 376p. 1995. text ed. 95.00 (*0-313-28204-8*, Greenwood Pr) Greenwood.
Padgett, Hilda. The Erwin Nine. (Illus.). 154p. 1993. pap. 9.95 (*0-932807-97-6*) Overmountain Pr.
Padgett, James E. True Gospel (of Salvation) Revealed Anew by Jesus, 3 Vols., Vols. III & IV. 1940. write for info. (*0-686-37147-X*) Found Ch Divine Truth.
Padgett, James E. & Samuels, Daniel G. Angelic Revelations of Divine Truth, 2 vols., Set. 437p. 1992. Vol. I, 437p. pap. 17.00 (*0-317-04950-X*); pap. 17.00 (*0-317-05505-4*) Found Ch Divine Truth.
Padgett, James R. Paper Mansions. LC 86-13628. (Illus.). 264p. 1986. 14.95 (*0-917485-12-4*) Bright Mtn Bks.
Padgett, Jim. Read 'n Grow Picture Bible. (Illus.). 1991. 14.99 (*0-8499-0813-2*) Word Inc.
Padgett, JoAnn, ed. Start Your Own: One Hundred One Extra Income Ideas. LC 94-6928. 144p. 1994. pap. 12.95 (*0-89384-265-6*) Pfeiffer & Co.
— Start Your Own Coffee & Tea Store. LC 94-8601. (Start Your Own Ser.). 272p. 1994. pap. 12.95 (*0-89384-262-1*) Pfeiffer & Co.
— Start Your Own Gift Basket Business. LC 94-4935. (Start Your Own Ser.). 256p. 1994. pap. 12.95 (*0-89384-261-3*) Pfeiffer & Co.
— Start Your Own Temporary Help Agency. LC 94-4494. (Start Your Own Ser.). 224p. 1994. pap. 12.95 (*0-89384-264-8*) Pfeiffer & Co.
Padgett, JoAnn, ed. see Cohen, William A.
Padgett, JoAnn, ed. see Cragg, Claudia.
Padgett, JoAnn, ed. see Drummond, Mary-Ellen.
Padgett, JoAnn, ed. see Hopson, Barrie & Scally, Mike.
Padgett, JoAnn, ed. see Hopson, Barrie, et al.
Padgett, JoAnn, ed. see Larsen, Earnie & Goodstein, Jeanette.
Padgett, JoAnn, ed. see Lundy, James L.
Padgett, JoAnn, ed. see Macdonald, John & Piggot, John.
Padgett, JoAnn, ed. see Nolan, Timothy M., et al.
Padgett, JoAnn, ed. see Prince, Frank A.
Padgett, JoAnn, ed. see Prokop, Marian K.
Padgett, JoAnn, ed. see Tagliere, Daniel.
Padgett, JoAnn, ed. see Wainwright, Gordon.
Padgett, Julianna D., jt. auth. see Graubarth-Szyller, Bobbie R.
Padgett, Larry R., jt. auth. see Sinha, Mihir K.
Padgett, Mark E. Milady's a Contemporary Approach to Permanent Waving. LC 93-28020. 142p. 1994. pap. text ed. 13.95 (*1-56253-101-8*) Milady Pub.
Padgett, Mary L., ed. International Simulation Technology Conference, 1991. 632p. 1991. 80.00 (*0-911801-98-7*, SIMTEC 91) Soc Computer Sim.
— Proceedings of the First Workshop on Neural Networks, 1990: Academic-Industrial-NASA-Defense. 516p. 1990. pap. 80.00 (*0-911801-66-9*, WNN90-1) Soc Computer Sim.
— Proceedings of the Second Workshop on Neural Networks, 1991: Academic-Industrial-NASA-Defense. 816p. 1991. pap. 100.00 (*0-911801-77-4*, WNN91-1) Soc Computer Sim.
***Padgett, Michael.** A Goodly Heritage: A History of the Church of Mountain Assembly, Inc. 180p. 1995. pap. 10.00 (*0-9646344-0-6*) M Padgett.
***Padgett, Michael J., et al.** Vase Painting in Italy: Red-Figure & Related Works in the Museum of Arts, Boston. (Illus.). 275p. 1993. pap. 30.00 (*0-87846-406-9*) Mus Fine Arts Boston.
Padgett, Ron. The Big Something. 64p. 1990. per. 7.50 (*0-935724-38-9*) Figures.
— Blood Work. 104p. 1993. pap. 12.00 (*0-917453-26-3*) Bamberger.
— Blood Work. 104p. 1994. lib. bdg. 31.00 (*0-8095-6512-9*) Borgo Pr.
— Crazy Compositions. (Orig.). 1974. 2.50 (*0-929844-01-7*) Big Sky Bolinas.
— Great Balls of Fire. rev. ed. LC 90-2457. 92p. 1990. reprint ed. pap. 8.95 (*0-918273-80-3*) Coffee Hse.
— New & Selected Poems. LC 95-15239. 1995. write for info. (*1-56792-038-1*) Godine.
— Poetic Forms. 1988. student ed, audio 47.95 (*0-915925-25-7*) Tchrs & Writers Coll.
— Ted. 1993. pap. 10.00 (*0-935724-60-5*) Figures.
— Tulsa Kid. Elmslie, Kenward, ed. (Illus.). (Orig.). 1980. 10.00 (*0-915990-16-4*); pap. 5.00 (*0-915990-17-2*) Z Pr.
— The Writing Book. 12p. (gr. 3-6). 1986. teacher ed, pap. 5.95 (*0-915924-70-6*) Tchrs & Writers Coll.
Padgett, Ron, ed. The Teachers & Writers Guide to Walt Whitman. (Illus.). 224p. (Orig.). 1991. pap. 13.95 (*0-915924-36-6*) Tchrs & Writers Coll.
— The Teachers & Writers Handbook of Poetic Forms. 230p. (J). 1987. 22.95 (*0-915924-24-2*); pap. 13.95 (*0-915924-23-4*) Tchrs & Writers Coll.
— White Dove Review, Nos. 1-5. (Avant-Garde Magazines Ser.). 1974. reprint ed. 18.95 (*0-405-01757-X*) Ayer.
Padgett, Ron & Coolidge, Clark. Supernatural Overtones. 1990. pap. 7.50 (*0-935724-40-0*) Figures.
Padgett, Ron & Roussel, Raymond. Among the Blacks. LC 88-70205. 64p. (Orig.). 1988. pap. 7.50 (*0-939691-02-7*); 18.00 (*0-685-18885-X*) Avenue B.
Padgett, Ron, tr. see Cendrars, Blaise.
Padgett, Ron, ed. see Ceravolo, Joseph.
Padgett, Ron, jt. ed. see Edgar, Christopher.
Padgett, Ron, jt. ed. see Shapiro, Nancy Larson.
Padgett, Ron, jt. ed. see Zavatsky, Bill.
Padgett, Ron, et al. Pantoum. 1989. student ed, disk 34.95 (*0-915924-89-7*) Tchrs & Writers Coll.
Padgett, Stephen. Parties & Party Systems in the New Germany. LC 93-2710. 230p. 1993. 57.95 (*1-85521-237-4*, Pub. by Dartmth Pub UK) Ashgate Pub Co.
Padgett, Stephen & Burkett, Tony. Political Parties & Elections in West Germany: The Search for a New Stability. LC 86-20436. 320p. 1987. pap. 14.95 (*0-312-00100-2*) St Martin.
Padgett, Stephen, ed. see Abromeit, Heidrun, et al.
Padgett, Stephen, jt. auth. see Paterson, William.
Padgett, Tricia. The Tempting of Audra Grey. (Destiny Ser.). 159p. 1992. pap. 8.95 (*0-8163-1069-6*) Pacific Pr Pub Assn.
Padgitt, Donald L. A Short History of the Early American Microscopes, Vol. 12. LC 74-30750. (Illus.). 1975. 30.00 (*0-904962-04-0*) Microscope Pubns.
Padhi, B. C. Socioeconomic Conditions of the Tribal under British Rule (1803-1936) (C). 1992. 30.00 (*0-685-61701-7*, Pub. by Punthi Pus II) S Asia.
Padhi, Bibhu. D. H. Lawrence: Modes of Fictional Style. LC 87-50832. Orig. Title: Modes of Style in Lawrence's Fiction. 225p. 1989. 22.50 (*0-87875-354-0*) Whitston Pub.
Padhi, Bibhu & Padhi, Minakshi. Indian Philosophy & Religion: A Reader's Guide. LC 89-42745. 423p. 1990. lib. bdg. 49.95x (*0-89950-446-9*) McFarland & Co.
Padhi, G. S., ed. Forestry in India, a Critical Study. 170p. (C). 1982. 125.00 (*81-7089-008-X*, Pub. by Intl Bk Distr II) St Mut.
Padhi, Minakshi, jt. auth. see Padhi, Bibhu.
***Padhy, Drushna S.** Indian Press Role & Responsibility. (C). 1994. text ed. 27.50 (*81-7024-636-9*, Pub. by Ashish II) S Asia.
Padhy, K. S. & Mahapatra, Jayashree. Reservation Policy in India. (C). 1988. 27.00 (*81-7024-195-2*, Pub. by Ashish II) S Asia.
Padhy, K. S. & Muni, P. K. Corruption in Indian Politics. 221p. 1987. 37.97 (*0-318-37295-9*) Asia Bk Corp.
Padhy, K. S. & Satapathy, P. C. Tribal India. (C). 1988. 18.00 (*81-7024-225-8*, Pub. by Ashish II) S Asia.
Padhye, A. M. The Framework of Nagarjuna's Philosophy. (Bibliotheca Indo-Buddhica Ser.: No. 35). 1988. text ed. 15.00 (*81-7030-124-6*) S Asia.
PADI Staff, ed. see Tackett, Eric.
Padian, Kevin. Beginning of the Age of Dinosaurs. 1988. pap. 44.95 (*0-521-36779-4*) Cambridge U Pr.
Padian, Kevin, ed. The Origin of Birds & the Evolution of Flight. (Memoirs of the California Academy of Sciences Ser.: No. 8). 98p. 1986. pap. text ed. 13.00 (*0-940228-14-9*) Calif Acad Sci.
***Padilla.** Nuevas Alternatives. 1987. pap. text ed. (*0-8028-0904-9*) Eerdmans.
Padilla, Amado M. Public Library Services for Immigrant Populations in California. (Partnerships for Change Ser.: No. 4). 48p. 1992. pap. text ed. 8.50 (*0-929722-49-3*) CA State Library Fndtn.

P Q

***Padilla, Amado M., ed.** Hispanic Psychology: Critical Issues in Theory & Research. 336p. 1994. 52.00 (0-8039-5552-9) Sage.

— Hispanic Psychology: Critical Issues in Theory & Research. 336p. 1994. pap. 24.95 (0-8039-5553-7) Sage.

Padilla, Amado M., jt. auth. see Keefe, Susan F.

Padilla, Amado M., et al, eds. Bilingual Education: Issues & Strategies. (Focus Editions Ser.: Vol. 112). (Illus.). 272p. (C). 1990. 46.00 (0-8039-3638-9, D1478); pap. 23.95 (0-8039-3639-7, D1478) Corwin Pr.

— Foreign Language Education: Issues & Strategies. 264p. 1990. 42.95 (0-8039-3640-0, D1478); pap. text ed. 21.95 (0-8039-3641-9, D1478) Corwin Pr.

Padilla, B., ed. see Cuza-Male, Belkis.

Padilla, C. Rene, ed. see Foulkes, Ricardo.

Padilla, C. Rene, tr. see Marcel, Pierre C.

Padilla, C. Rene, ed. see Marshall, I. Howard.

Padilla, C. Rene, tr. see Stott, John R.

Padilla, C. Rene, ed. see Tutu, Desmond M.

***Padilla, Christina.** Why Wait? Graduate! 80p. (Orig.). (YA). 1995. pap. 6.95 (0-7610-0051-8) NW Pub.

Padilla, Elena. Up from Puerto Rico. LC 58-7171. 317p. 1958. text ed. 43.00 (0-231-02213-1) Col U Pr.

Padilla, Ezequiel. Free Men of America. LC 72-4624. (Essay Index Reprint Ser.). 1977. reprint ed. 19.95 (0-8369-2965-9) Ayer.

***Padilla, Felix, ed.** Handbook of Hispanic Cultures in U. S. Sociology. LC 93-13348. 350p. 1994. 60.00 (1-55885-101-1) Arte Publico.

Padilla, Felix M. The Gang as an American Enterprise. LC 91-36793. 212p. (C). 1992. text ed. 40.00 (0-8135-1805-9); pap. text ed. 15.00 (0-8135-1806-7) Rutgers U Pr.

— Latino Ethnic Consciousness: The Case of Mexican Americans & Puerto Ricans in Chicago. LC 85-8576. 196p. 1986. 24.95 (0-268-01274-1); pap. 11.95 (0-268-01275-X) U of Notre Dame Pr.

Padilla, Felix M & Santiago, Lourdes. Outside the Wall: The Life of a Prisoner's Wife. LC 92-41731. 250p. 1993. text ed. 40.00 (0-8135-1986-1); pap. 14.95 (0-8135-1987-X) Rutgers U Pr.

Padilla, Genaro, jt. ed. see Gutierrez, Ramon.

Padilla, Genaro M. My History, Not Yours: The Formation of Mexican American Autobiography. LC 93-3457. (Studies in American Autobiography). (Illus.). 224p. (Orig.). (C). 1993. lib. bdg. 40.00 (0-299-13970-0); pap. 17.95 (0-299-13974-3) U of Wis Pr.

Padilla, Genaro M., ed. The Short Stories of Fray Angelico Chavez. LC 87-5992. (Illus.). 159p. 1987. pap. 11.95 (0-8263-0950-X) U of NM Pr.

Padilla, George, jt. ed. see Rauckman, E. J.

Padilla, Geraldine V., et al. Interacting with Dying Patients: An Inter-Hospital Nursing Research & Nursing Education Project. 219p. (Orig.). 1975. pap. text ed. 7.00 (0-940876-00-0) City Hope.

Padilla, Gilbert. Refreshment in the Desert: Spiritual Connections in Daily Life. LC 85-50663. 128p. (Orig.). 1992. pap. 7.95 (0-89622-228-4) Twenty-Third.

Padilla, Heberto. Fountain, a House of Stone. Reid, Alastair & Coleman, Alexander, trs. 1992. pap. 10.00 (0-374-52364-9, Noonday) FS&G.

— A Fountain, a House of Stone: Poems. Reid, Alastair & Coleman, Alexander, trs. 128p. (ENG & SPA.). 1991. 19.95 (0-374-15781-2) FS&G.

— Legacies: Selected Poems. Reid, Alastair & Hurley, Andrew, trs. 192p. 1984. pap. 9.95 (0-374-51736-3) FS&G.

— Self-Portrait of the Other: A Memoir. Coleman, Alexander, tr. 220p. 1990. 19.95 (0-374-26086-9) FS&G.

Padilla, Jaime & Taylor, Maurie. Easy Spanish Word Games. (Illus.). 64p. (SPA.). (J). (gr. 4 up). 1985. pap. 4.95 (0-8442-7242-6, Natl Textbk) NTC Pub Grp.

Padilla, Jose A. On the Definition of Binding Domains in Spanish: Evidence from Child Language. (C). 1990. lib. bdg. 82.00 (0-7923-0744-5) Kluwer Ac.

Padilla, Mario R. Reaching Back for the Neverendings. 100p. 1993. 8.95 (1-881168-32-8) Red Danceflr.

Padilla, Napoleon S. Memorias de un Cubano Sin Importancia. 328p. 1988. pap. 10.00 (0-9620495-0-6) N S Padilla.

Padilla, Raymond V., ed. Ethnoperspectives in Bilingual Education Research, Vol. I: Bilingual Education & Public Policy in the United States. LC 79-9265. 507p. 1979. pap. 19.00 (0-916950-43-3) Biling Rev-Pr.

— Ethnoperspectives in Bilingual Education Research, Vol. II: Theory in Bilingual Education. LC 80-68525. 430p. 1980. pap. 19.00 (0-916950-44-1) Biling Rev-Pr.

— Ethnoperspectives in Bilingual Education Research, Vol. III: Bilingual Education Technology. LC 81-68614. 482p. 1981. pap. 19.00 (0-916950-45-X) Biling Rev-Pr.

— Theory, Technology & Public Policy on Bilingual Education. LC 83-60508. 425p. (Orig.). 1983. pap. 10.00 (0-89763-066-1) Natl Clearinghse Bilingual Ed.

Padilla, Raymond V. & Benavides, Alfredo H., eds. Critical Perspectives on Bilingual Education Research. LC 91-21873. 432p. 1992. pap. 22.00 (0-927534-20-7) Biling Rev-Pr.

Padilla, Raymond V. & Chavez, Chavez, eds. The Leaning Ivory Tower: Latino Professors in American Universities. (SUNY Series, United States Hispanic Studies). 224p. (C). 1995. 54.50 (0-7914-2427-8); pap. 17.95 (0-7914-2428-6) State U NY Pr.

Padilla, Raymond V., jt. ed. see Garcia, Eugene E.

Padilla, Salvador M., ed. see Tugwell, Rexford G.

Padilla, Stan. A Natural Education. rev. ed. LC 94-5479. (Illus.). 80p. (YA). (gr. 7-12). 1994. pap. text ed. 8.95 (0-913990-14-0) Book Pub Co.

Padilla, Stan, ed. A Natural Education. LC 92-1315. (Illus.). 80p. 1994. pap. 8.95 (0-913990-90-6) Book Pub Co.

***Padilla, Victoria.** Southern California Gardens: An Illustrated History. LC 94-77674. (Illus.). 376p. 1994. 39.95 (0-9627297-1-X) A A Knoll Pubs.

Padilla, Washington. Amos - Abdias: Comentario Biblico Hispanoamericano. 244p. 1991. 18.95 (0-89922-375-3) Edit Caribe.

Padip, Sinha, ed. The Urban Experience: Calcutta: Essays in Honour of Professor Nisith Ranjan Ray. 186p. (C). 1987. 17.50 (0-685-19667-4, Pub. by KP Bagchi IA) S Asia.

Padisak, J., et al, eds. Intermediate Disturbance Hypothesis in Phytoplankton Ecology: Proceedings of the 8th Workshop of the International Association of Phytoplankton Taxonomy & Ecology Held in Baja (Hungary), 5-15 July 1992. LC 92-41133. (Developments in Hydrobiology Ser.: Vol. 81). 208p. (C). 1993. lib. bdg. 122.00 (0-7923-2097-2) Kluwer Ac.

Padiyar, K. R. HVDC Power Transmission Systems: Technology & System Interaction. 289p. 1991. text ed. 55.95 (0-470-21706-5) Halsted Pr.

Padiyar, Sunil. Netware 4.0: Planning & Implementation. 1993. pap. 27.95 (1-56205-159-8) New Riders Pub.

***Padlan, E. A.** Antigen-Antibody Complexes. (Molecular Biology Intelligence Unit Ser.). 100p. 1994. 89.95 (1-57059-181-4) R G Landes.

***Padlan, Eduardo.** Antibody-Antigen Complexes. LC 94-36304. (Molecular Biology Intelligence Unit Ser.). 1994. 89.95 (1-57059-918-1) R G Landes.

Padley, F. B. & Podmore, J. The Role of Fats in Human Nutrition. LC 85-5491. 210p. 1985. lib. bdg. 65.00 (0-89573-398-6) VCH Pubs.

Padley, Fred B., ed. Advances in Applied Lipid Research, Vol. 1. 1991. 90.25 (1-55938-317-8) Jai Pr.

Padley, G. A. Grammatical Theory in Western Europe 1500-1700: Trends in Vernacular Grammar II. 560p. 1988. 94.95 (0-521-33514-0) Cambridge U Pr.

Padlipsky, Michael A. Elements of Networking Style: Essays & Animadversions on the Art of Intercomputer Networking. (Illus.). 236p. (C). 1984. pap. 32.95 (0-13-268111-0) P-H.

Padma, B. Costumes, Coiffure & Ornaments in the Temple Sculpture of Northern Andhra. (C). 1991. 56.00 (0-8364-2640-1, Pub. by Agam Kala Prakashan) S Asia.

Padmakara Translation Group, tr. see Rinpoche, Dilgo K.

Padmakara Translation Group Staff, tr. see Dalai Lama.

Padmanab, S. Ages of Birds. (Writers Workshop Redbird Ser.). 54p. 1976. 10.00 (0-86578-244-X); 6.00 (0-86578-245-8) Ind-US Inc.

Padmanab, S. A Separate Life. 9.00 (0-89253-712-4); 4.80 (0-89253-713-2) Ind-US Inc.

Padmanabha, K. Hosala Sculptures: A Cultural Study. (C). 1989. 96.00 (81-85067-17-1, Pub. by Sundeep II) S Asia.

Padmanabha, K. P. History of Kerala, 4 vols., Set, Vols. 1-4. Menon, T. K., ed. (C). 1982. reprint ed. Set. 130.00 (0-8364-2401-8, Pub. by Asian Educ Servs II) S Asia.

Padmanabhan, Chandra. Dakshin: Vegetarian Dishes from South India. (Illus.). 1994. 26.00 (0-207-18477-1) Thorsons SF.

Padmanabhan, K. P. Rural Credit: Lessons for Rural Bankers & Policy Makers. 160p. 1989. text ed. 45.00 (0-312-03175-0) St Martin.

Padmanabhan, Neela. The Generations. Subramanyam, Ka N., tr. (Orient Paperbacks Ser.). 192p. 1972. pap. 2.50 (0-88253-110-7) Ind-US Inc.

Padmanabhan, S. Y., jt. auth. see Gangopadhyay, S.

Padmanabhan, T. Structure Formation in the Universe. (Illus.). 400p. (C). 1993. 94.95 (0-521-41448-2); pap. 37.95 (0-521-42486-0) Cambridge U Pr.

Padmarajiah, Y. J. A Comparative Study of the Jaina Theories of Reality & Knowledge. 432p. 1986. reprint ed. 22.00 (81-208-0036-2, Pub. by Motilal Banarsidass II) S Asia.

Padmasambhava. Dakini Teachings: Padmasambhava's Oral Instructions to Lady Tsogyal. Kunsang, Erik P., tr. LC 89-43403. (Dragon Editions Ser.). 200p. (Orig.). 1990. pap. 18.00 (0-87773-546-8, Sham Dragon Edits) Shambhala Pubns.

— Self-Liberation Through Seeing with Naked Awareness: An introduction to the Nature of One's Own Mind in the Tibetan Dzogchen Tradition. Quasha, George, ed. Reynolds, John M., tr. (Illus.). 240p. (C). 1989. 14.95 (0-88268-050-1) Station Hill Pr.

Padmasambhava, Guru. The Legend of the Great Stupa. LC 73-79059. (Tibetan Translation Ser.: Vol. 2). (Illus.). 144p. 1973. pap. 10.95 (0-913546-03-8) Dharma Pub.

Padmore, George. Africa & World Peace. 285p. 1972. reprint ed. 35.00 (0-7146-1764-4, BHA-01764, Pub. by F Cass Pubs UK) Intl Spec Bk.

— The Life & Struggles of Negro Toilers. LC 85-4221. (Sidewinder Studies in History & Sociology: No. 2). 126p. 1985. lib. bdg. 25.00x (0-89370-721-X, Sidewinder Press) Borgo Pr.

Padoa-Schioppa, Tommaso. Europe after 1992: Three Essays. Riccardi, Margaret B., ed. LC 91-18803. (Essays in International Finance Ser.: No. 182). 1991. pap. text ed. 8.00 (0-88165-089-7) Princeton U Int Finan Econ.

— The Road to Monetary Union in Europe. 280p. 1995. 49.95 (0-19-828843-3) OUP.

— Tripolarism: Regional & Global Economic Cooperation. (Orig.). 1993. pap. write for info. (1-56708-089-8) Grp of Thirty.

Padoa-Schioppa, Tommaso, et al. Efficiency, Stability, & Equity: A Strategy for the Evolution of the Economic System of the European Community. (Illus.). 208p. 1988. 45.00 (0-19-828630-9); pap. 16.95 (0-19-828629-5) OUP.

Padoan, Gianni. Danger Kid. LC 90-48381. (J). 1989. 11.95 (0-85953-312-3) Childs Play.

— Remembering Grandad. (J). 1989. 11.95 (0-85953-311-5) Childs Play.

Padoan, Gianni & Collini, Emanuela. Follow My Leader. (J). (gr. 4 up). 1989. 11.95 (0-85953-313-1) Childs Play.

Padoan, P. C., jt. auth. see Gandolfo, Giancarlo.

Padoan, Pier C. The Political Economy of International Financial Instability. 240p. 1986. 45.00 (0-7099-4003-3, Pub. by Croom Helm UK) Routledge Chapman & Hall.

Padoan, Pier C., ed. The International Impact of 1992: Toward Regionalisation in the International Economy. 200p. 1992. 69.95 (0-7103-0431-5, A7588, Pub. by Kegan Paul Intl UK) Routledge Chapman & Hall.

Padoan, Pier C., jt. ed. see Guerrieri, Palo.

Padoan, Pier C., jt. ed. see Guerrieri, Paolo.

Padoan, Pier C., jt. ed. see Lombardini, Siro.

Padoch, C., jt. ed. see Denevan, W. M.

Padoch, Christine, jt. ed. see Denslow, Julie S.

Padoch, Christine, jt. ed. see Redford, Kent H.

***Padol, Brian.** The A-Z Crossword Puzzle Solver. 1408p. (Orig.). 1995. mass mkt. 7.99 (0-380-77518-2) Avon.

Padoux, Andre. Vac: The Concept of the Word in Selected Hindu Tantras. Gontier, Jacques, tr. LC 89-11436. (SUNY Series in the Shaiva Traditions of Kashmir). 460p. 1990. 59.50 (0-7914-0257-6); pap. 19.95 (0-7914-0258-4) State U NY Pr.

***Padovani, Giuseppe.** Dictionnaire Bilingue: French-Italian, Italian-French. 536p. (FRE & ITA.). 1987. pap. 14.95 (0-7859-7846-1, 2253002798) Fr & Eur.

Padovani, Martin H. Healing Wounded Emotions: Overcoming Life's Hurts. LC 86-51614. 128p. (Orig.). 1987. 12.95 (0-89622-346-9); pap. 6.95 (0-89622-333-7) Twenty-Third.

Padovano, Anthony. The Process of Sculpture. 352p. 1986. pap. 16.95 (0-306-80273-2) Da Capo.

Padovano, Anthony T. A Celebration of Life: Catholic Spirituality Today. LC 90-61563. 112p. (Orig.). 1990. pap. text ed. 7.95 (0-9623410-9-6) Resurrection.

— The Church Today: Belonging & Believing. (Catholic Home Library). (Illus.). 128p. 1989. 4.95 (1-55944-001-5) Franciscan Comns.

— Conscience & Conflict: A Trilogy of One-Actor Plays: Thomas Merton, Pope John XXIII, Martin Luther. 128p. 1988. pap. 7.95 (0-8091-3001-7) Paulist Pr.

— Love & Destiny. 96p. 1987. pap. 3.95 (0-8091-2895-0) Paulist Pr.

— Reform & Renewal: Essays on Authority, Ministry & Social Justice in the American Church. LC 89-63119. 152p. (Orig.). (C). 1990. pap. 9.95 (1-55612-266-7) Sheed & Ward MO.

— Scripture in the Streets: Reflections on Holy Week, Contemporary Spirituality. LC 92-20687. 88p. 1992. pap. 5.95 (0-8091-3335-0) Paulist Pr.

Padovano, Michael. Networking Applications on UNIX System V Release 4.0. LC 93-22196. 1993. Casebound. text ed. 53.00 (0-13-613555-2) P-H.

Padover, Saul, ed. see Jefferson, Thomas.

Padover, Saul K. Jefferson. 1952. pap. 3.50 (0-451-62516-1, Ment) NAL-Dutton.

— Jefferson. 1989. pap. 4.50 (0-451-62647-8) NAL-Dutton.

— Jefferson: A Great American's Life & Ideas. 192p. 1952. pap. 4.99 (0-451-62797-0, Ment) NAL-Dutton.

— The Living U. S. Constitution. 3rd rev. ed. 416p. 1995. pap. 14.95 (0-452-01147-7, Mer) NAL-Dutton.

Padover, Saul K., ed. Confessions & Self-Portraits. LC 68-58807. (Essay Index Reprint Ser.). 1977. 23.95 (0-8369-1048-6) Ayer.

Padover, Saul K., ed. see Jefferson, Thomas.

Padover, Saul K., ed. see U. S. Constitutional Convention Staff.

Padrick, Kevin, jt. ed. see Perris, Liz.

Padron, C. E. Flora y Vegetacion Liquenica Epifita de los Sabinares Herrenos. (Bibliotheca Lichenologica Ser.: Vol. 27). (Illus.). 342p. (SPA.). 1987. pap. 104.00 (3-443-58006-8) Lubrecht & Cramer.

Padron, Francisco M., ed. The Journal of Don Francisco de Saavedra, 1780-1783. Topping, Aileen M., tr. LC 88-14260. 424p. (Orig.). 1989. 34.95 (0-8130-0877-8) U Press Fla.

Padron, Justo J. On the Cutting Edge: Selected Poems. Bourne, Louis, tr. & intro. by. LC 87-82774. 156p. (Orig.). 1988. pap. 19.95 (0-948259-42-6, Pub. by Forest Bks UK) Dufour.

— Solo Muere la Mano Que Te Escribe. (Nueva Austral Ser.: Vol. 98). (SPA.). 1991. pap. text ed. 24.95x (84-239-1898-X) Elliots Bks.

Padrow, Ben, jt. auth. see Cogan, Elaine.

Padua, David, et al, eds. Languages & Compilers for Parallel Computing: (Papers Presented at a Workshop Held at the University of Illinois at Urbana-Champaign) 560p. (C). 1990. pap. text ed. 260.00 (0-273-08820-3, Pub. by Pitman Pubng UK) St Mut.

Paduano, Joseph. Art of Infrared Photography: A Comprehensive Guide to the Use of Black & White Infrared Film. (Illus.). 1995. pap. 17.95 (0-936262-32-X) Amherst Media.

— Infrared Nude Photography. (Illus.). 80p. 1991. pap. 18.95 (0-936262-10-9) Amherst Media.

— Seascapes: A Collection of Photographs of the Jersey Shore. LC 83-91284. (Illus.). 48p. (Orig.). 1983. pap. 9.95 (0-9612590-0-0, TR 24.N5) J Paduano.

Paduda, Joe. Art of Sculling. 1992. pap. 14.95 (0-87742-308-3) Intl Marine.

Paduda, Joe, ed. The Art of Sculling. (Illus.). 1991. pap. text ed. 14.95 (0-07-158010-7) McGraw.

Padula, Alfred, jt. auth. see Smith, Lois M.

Padula, Helen. Developing Adult Day Care: An Approach to Maintaining Independence for Impaired Older Persons. 192p. 1982. 15.00 (0-910883-61-0, 270) Natl Coun Aging.

Padula, Robert. Arco Building Custodian, Building Engineer, Building Superintendent. 8th ed. 1992. pap. 14.00 (0-671-86851-9, Arco Test) P-H Gen Ref & Trav.

Padula, William V. A Behavioral Vision Approach for Persons with Physical Disabilities. Corngold, Sally M., ed. (Illus.). 208p. (C). 1988. 49.50 (0-943599-04-0) OEPF.

— Neuro-Optometric Rehabilitation. 2nd rev. ed. Corngold, Sally M., ed. 240p. 1993. reprint ed. lib. bdg. 29.50 (0-943599-65-2) OEPF.

Padus, Emrika, ed. The Complete Guide to Your Emotions & Your Health: Hundreds of Proven Techniques to Harmonize Mind & Body for Happy, Healthy Living. 656p. 1992. 26.95 (0-87596-144-4, 05-713-2) Rodale Pr Inc.

Padwa. Organic Photochemistry, Vol. 4. 360p. 1979. 190.00 (0-8247-6908-2) Dekker.

— Organic Photochemistry, Vol. 5. 512p. 1981. 190.00 (0-8247-1343-5) Dekker.

— Organic Photochemistry, Vol. 6. 464p. 1983. 190.00 (0-8247-7003-X) Dekker.

— Organic Photochemistry, Vol. 7. 512p. 1985. 190.00 (0-8247-7421-3) Dekker.

— Organic Photochemistry, Vol. 8. 392p. 1987. 190.00 (0-8247-7702-6) Dekker.

— Organic Photochemistry, Vol. 9. 368p. 1987. 190.00 (0-8247-7775-1) Dekker.

— Organic Photochemistry, Vol. 10. 512p. 1989. 190.00 (0-8247-7920-7) Dekker.

— Organic Photochemistry, Vol. 11. 456p. 1991. 199.00 (0-8247-8561-4) Dekker.

Padwa, Albert. One, Three-Dipolar Cycloaddition Chemistry, 2 vols., Set. (General Heterocyclic Chemistry Ser.: No. 1-128). 1521p. 1984. text ed. 599.00 (0-471-08364-X, Wiley-Interscience) Wiley.

***Padwa, Lynette.** The Impostor's Handbook: Everything You Pretend to Know & Are Afraid Someone Will Ask You. LC 95-15763. 1995. pap. write for info. (0-14-051322-1, Penguin Bks) Viking Penguin.

Padwe, Gerald W., et al, intros. Obtaining IRS Private Letter Rulings: A Manual of Forms & Procedures from Touche Ross & Company. LC 82-22311. 1983. ring bd. 150.00 (0-379-20826-1) Oceana.

Padwick, Gordon. CorelDraw 4 Instance Reference. LC 93-85060. 471p. 1993. pap. 12.99 (0-7821-1307-9) Sybex.

— HP Guide to Color Printing Techniques: How to Get the Most out of Your Black & Color HP DeskJet Printer. 340p. 1995. pap. 30.00 (0-679-75323-0) Random.

— Paradox for Windows Acceso Facil. 337p. 1993. pap. text ed. 16.95 (968-6346-69-4, Pub. by Ventura Ediciones MX) Computer & Tech.

Padzik, Alicja, ed. At Babci's Knee. Zurawiecka, Aska, tr. LC 85-51371. (Little La Ser.). (Illus.). 165p. (Orig.). (ENG & POL.). (J). (ps). 1985. pap. 25.00 (0-935003-01-0); audio (0-935003-00-2) Talent-Ed.

Pae, K. D., ed. U. S. - Japan Seminar of Piezoelectric Polymers, Proceedings: Honolulu, Hawaii, July 1983: Special Issue of Journal Ferroelectrics. (Ferroelectricity & Related Materials Ser.). 354p. 1984. text ed. 149.00 (0-677-16555-2) Gordon & Breach.

Pae, Sung M. Korea Leading Developing Nations: Economy, Democracy & Welfare. LC 92-16787. 536p. (Orig.). (C). 1992. lib. bdg. 52.00 (0-8191-8742-9); pap. text ed. 34.00 (0-8191-8743-7) U Pr of Amer.

Paefeny, Starets. Spiritual Counsels of Starets Parfeny. 1991. pap. 1.00 (0-89981-135-3) Eastern Orthodox.

P'aegwan Chapki of O Sukkwon Staff. A Korean Storyteller's Miscellany. Lee, Peter H., tr. (Library of Asian Translations). 280p. (C). 1989. text ed. 45.00 (0-691-06771-6) Princeton U Pr.

Paehlke, Robert. Environmentalism & the Future of Progressive Politics. LC 88-27529. 320p. (C). 1989. 35.00 (0-300-04021-0) Yale U Pr.

***Paehlke, Robert, ed.** Conservation & Environmentalism: An Encyclopedia. LC 94-49708. (Reference Library of Social Science: Vol. 645). (Illus.). 768p. 1995. 95.00 (0-8240-6101-2) Garland.

Paehlke, Robert & Torgerson, Douglas, eds. Managing Leviathan: Environmental Politics & the Administrative State. 310p. 1990. pap. 22.95 (0-921149-54-9) Broadview Pr.

Paehlke, Robert C. Environmentalism & the Future of Progressive Politics. 320p. (C). 1991. reprint ed. pap. text ed. 16.00 (0-300-04826-2) Yale U Pr.

Paek, Min. Aekyung's Dream. LC 88-18928. (Illus.). 24p. (ENG & KOR.). (J). (gr. 2-7). 1988. 13.95 (0-89239-042-5) Childrens Book Pr.

***Paelet, Lawrence D., et al.** A Legal Guide for Connecticut Entrepreneurs. 104p. 1994. pap. text ed. 9.95 (1-886277-00-1) CT Small Busn.

Paelian, Frances. The Mystical Marriage of Science & Spirit. LC 81-70272. (Illus.). 200p. 1981. pap. 11.95 (0-918936-11-X) Astara.

Paelian, G. Nicholas Roerich. LC 74-11757. 1974. 10.00 (0-911794-34-4) Aqua Educ.

Paelinck & Vossen, P. H. Axiomatics & Pragmatics of Conflict Analysis. (Interdisciplinary Studies: Vol. 3). 350p. 1987. text ed. 79.95 (0-566-05207-5, Pub. by Avebury Pub UK) Ashgate Pub Co.

Paelinck, J. H. Qualitative & Quantitative Mathematical Economics. 1982. lib. bdg. 74.50 (90-247-2623-9) Kluwer Ac.

Paelinck, J. H., jt. auth. see Duru, G.

Paen, Alex. Love from America. LC 87-62008. 216p. 1989. 17.95 (0-915677-33-4) Roundtable Pub.

Paenson, Isaac. Abridged Economics Glossary. (ENG, FRE, RUS & SPA.). 1983. write for info. (0-8288-0152-5, M 15495) Fr & Eur.

— Environment in Key Words: A Multilingual Handbook of the Environment. rev. ed. (Illus.). 935p. 1990. 450.00 (0-08-024524-2, Pergamon Pr) Elsevier.

P Q

— Handbuch der Terminologie des Volkerrechts: Friedensrecht; Recht der Bewaffneten Konfilkte, 2 vols., Bd. 1. (GER.). 1993. Bd.1, 12/1990. lib. bdg. write for info. (3-598-10917-2) K G Saur.

— Handbuch der Terminologie des Volkerrechts: Friedensrecht; Recht der Bewaffneten Konfilkte, 2 vols., Bd. 2. (GER.). 1992. Bd.2, 12/1992. lib. bdg. write for info. (3-598-10918-0) K G Saur.

— Handbuch der Terminologie des Volkerrechts: Friedensrecht; Recht der Bewaffneten Konfilkte, 2 vols., Set. (GER.). lib. bdg. write for info. (3-598-10916-4) K G Saur.

— Manual of the Terminology of Public International Law & International Organizations. 1983. text ed. 301.00 (90-6544-052-6) Kluwer Law Tax Pubs.

— Manual of the Terminology of Public International Law & Organizations. 846p. (ENG, FRE, RUS & SPA.). 1983. 295.00 (0-8288-0413-3, M6435) Fr & Eur.

— Manual of the Terminology of the Law of Armed Conflicts & of International Humanitarian Organizations. 864p. (ENG, FRE, RUS & SPA.). 1989. lib. bdg. 334.00 (90-247-3466-5) Kluwer Ac.

— Systematic Glossary of Selected Economics & Social Terms. 450p. (ENG, FRE, RUS & SPA.). 1982. 175.00 (0-8288-0153-3, M 8172) Fr & Eur.

— Systematic Glossary of the Terminology of Statistical Methods. 544p. (ENG, FRE, RUS & SPA.). 1982. 295.00 (0-8288-2354-5, M8173) Fr & Eur.

Paepcke, Andreas, ed. Object-Oriented Programming: The CLOS Perspective. LC 92-41474. 350p. 1993. 42.50 (0-262-16136-2) MIT Pr.

Paepe, Roland, et al, eds. Greenhouse Effect, Sea Level & Drought. (NATO Advanced Science Institutes Series C: Mathematical & Physical Sciences). 736p. (C). 1990. lib. bdg. 218.50 (0-7923-1017-9) Kluwer Ac.

Paepke, Andreas, jt. auth. see Kiczales, Gregor.

Paeth, Alan W., ed. Graphics Gems V, For IBM. (Illus.). 600p. 1995. text ed. 49.95 (0-12-543455-3); text ed. 49.95 (0-12-543457-X) Acad Pr.

Paetkau, Paul, et al. God-Man-Land. LC 78-55244. 1978. 5.25 (0-87303-008-7) Faith & Life.

Paetow, Louis J. Guide to the Study of Medieval History. rev. ed. LC 80-81364. 1969. reprint ed. 65.00 (0-527-69101-1) Periodicals Srv.

Paetow, Louis J., ed. Crusades & Other Historical Essays, Presented to Dana C. Munro by His Former Students. LC 68-14902. (Essay Index Reprint Ser.). 1977. 23.95 (0-8369-0354-4) Ayer.

Paetro, Maxine. How to Put Your Book Together & Get a Job in Advertising. rev. ed. Bendinger, Bruce, ed. (Illus.). 211p. (C). 1991. pap. 18.95 (0-9621415-1-8) Copy Wrkshp.

Paetro, Maxine, jt. auth. see Darin, Dodd.

Paetsch, Michael. Mobile Communications in the U. S. & Europe: Regulation, Technology, & Markets. LC 93-12354. 417p. 1993. 89.00 (0-89006-688-4) Artech Hse.

***Paetzold, Ramona L. & Willborn, Steven L.** The Statistics of Discrimination: Using Statistical Evidence in Discrimination Cases. LC 94-26042. (Individual Rights Ser.). 1994. write for info. (0-07-172474-5) Shepards-McGraw.

Paevsky, L. Basis for the Veneration of Saints. 1993. pap. 0.25 (0-89981-143-4) Eastern Orthodox.

Paffen, K. A. Deutsch-Russisches Satzlexikon: German-Russian Syntax Lexicon, 2 vols., Set. 1680p. (GER & RUS.). 1980. 110.00 (0-8288-1240-3, F19660) Fr & Eur.

Pafford, F. William. Handbook of Survey Note Keeping. LC 83-12004. 152p. (C). 1983. reprint ed. pap. 19.95 (0-89874-645-0) Krieger.

Pafford, J. H., ed. see Shakespeare, William.

Pafford, John M. The Critical Years: Relations Between Elizabeth & the Papacy 1558-1572. LC 88-71468. 196p. (Orig.). (C). 1987. pap. 5.95 (0-9620878-0-7) Anglican Heritage Pubns.

Pafford, Ward. Obligations. 100p. (Orig.). 1994. per., pap. 10.00 (1-883199-03-4) W GA College.

Paffrath, Christine, ed. see Paffrath, James D.

Paffrath, Christine, ed. see Paffrath, Jim & Cangialosi, Karen.

Paffrath, James D. How Do You Think Japan? Photographs of a Foreign Resident. Paffrath, Christine, ed. LC 82-90777. (Illus.). 96p. (Orig.). 1982. pap. 8.95 (0-910703-01-9) JP Pubns CA.

Paffrath, Jim & Cangialosi, Karen. L.I.S.T. A Listing of International Schools Today. Gilbride, Colleen & Paffrath, Christine, eds. (Orig.). 1984. pap. 3.95 (0-910703-09-4) JP Pubns CA.

Pafik, Marie-Reine A. Sheet Music Reference & Price Guide. 1992. pap. 18.95 (0-89145-492-6) Collector Bks.

Pafik, Marie-Reine A., jt. auth. see Guiheen, Anna M.

Pagan. GED in Espanol. 4th ed. (SPA.). 1994. pap. 15.00 (0-671-88506-5, Arco Test) P-H Gen Ref & Trav.

Pagan, A. R., jt. auth. see Preston, A. J.

Pagan, Frank G. A Practical Guide to Algol 68. LC 75-6925. (Wiley Series in Computing). 223p. reprint ed. pap. 63.60 (0-7837-4388-2, 2044128) Bks Demand.

Pagan, Jill C. Taxation Aspects of Currency Fluctuations. 2nd ed. 1991. 150.00 (0-406-50886-0, U.K.) Butterworth Legal Pubs.

Pagan, Juan A. Lorca En la Lirica Puertorriquena. LC 80-17628. (Mente y Palabra Ser.). (Illus.). 359p. 1981. 12.00 (0-8477-0574-9); pap. 9.60 (0-8477-0575-7) U of PR Pr.

***Pagan, Kevin & Fuller, Scott.** Learn CompuServe for Windows in a Day. (Popular Applications Ser.). 160p. (Orig.). 1995. pap. 15.95 (1-55622-442-7) Wordware Pub.

Pagan, Kevin D., jt. auth. see Fuller, Scott M.

Pagan, Margarita, tr. see Mozeleski, Peter A.

Pagan, Nicholas. Rethinking Literary Biography: A Postmodern Approach to Tennessee Williams. LC 92-55117. 1993. 29.50 (0-8386-3516-4) Fairleigh Dickinson.

Pagan, Samuel. Pulpito, Teologia y Esperanza. 146p. 1988. pap. 4.25 (0-89922-239-0) Edit Caribe.

Pagana. Diagnostic Testing & Nursing Implications: A Case Study Approach. (Illus.). 528p. 1990. pap. 25.95 (0-8016-5841-1) Mosby Yr Bk.

— Mosby's Diagnostic & Laboratory Test Reference. 752p. 1991. 23.95 (0-8016-3756-2) Mosby Yr Bk.

Pagana, Kathleen D. & Pagana, Timothy J. Diagnostic Testing & Nursing Implications: A Case Study Approach. 4th ed. LC 93-5961. 540p. 1993. pap. 24.95 (0-8016-6779-8) Mosby Yr Bk.

— Mosby's Diagnostic & Laboratory Test Reference. 2nd ed. LC 94-29518. 1994. write for info. (0-8151-6628-1) Mosby Yr Bk.

Pagana, Timothy J., jt. auth. see Pagana, Kathleen D.

Paganelli, C. V. & Farhi, Leon E., eds. Physiological Function in Special Environments. (Illus.). 240p. 1989. 96.00 (0-387-96833-4) Spr-Verlag.

Paganetti, J. & Seklemian, M. The Best in Retail Ads. (Illus.). 424p. 1982. 19.95 (0-934590-09-5) Retail Report.

Paganetti, JoAn, ed. The Best in Sale Ads, Vol. I. (Illus.). 300p. 1984. 19.95 (0-934590-13-3) Retail Report.

***Pagani, Mark, et al.** The Sea Around Us. 144p. (C). 1994. pap. text ed., spiral bd. 19.50 (0-7872-0063-8) Kendall-Hunt.

Paganini, Emil P., ed. Acute Continuous Renal Replacement Therapy. (Developments in Nephrology Ser.). (C). 1986. lib. bdg. 80.50 (0-89838-793-0) Kluwer Ac.

Paganini, Maria. Reading Proust: In Search of the Wolf-Fish. Litherland, Caren, tr. LC 93-27830. (Theory & History of Literature Ser.: Vol. 84). 1994. text ed. 49.95 (0-8166-2039-3); pap. 19.95 (0-8166-2040-7) U of Minn Pr.

Paganini, N. Moto Perpetuo for Violin & Piano, Op. 11. Mittell, P., ed. (Carl Fischer Music Library: No. 88). 1968. pap. 6.00 (0-8258-0014-5, L88) Fischer Inc NY.

Pagano, Christian, jt. auth. see Fages, Jean-Baptiste.

Pagano, Jo. Golden Wedding. LC 74-17941. (Italian American Experience Ser.). 308p. 1975. reprint ed. 21.95 (0-405-06412-8) Ayer.

Pagano, Jo Anne. Exiles & Communities: Teaching in the Patriarchal Wilderness. LC 89-29352. (SUNY Series, Feminist Theory in Education). 165p. 1990. 59.50 (0-7914-0273-8); pap. 19.95 (0-7914-0274-6) State U NY Pr.

Pagano, John O. Healing Psoriasis: The Natural Alternative. (Illus.). (Orig.). 1991. pap. 24.95 (0-9628847-0-7) Pagano Organization.

Pagano, Jules, jt. auth. see Hoffman, Hy.

Pagano, Marcello & Gauvreau, Kimberlee. Principles of Biostatistics. LC 92-32841. 524p. 1993. text ed. 52.95 (0-534-14064-5) Intl Thomson.

***Pagano, Michael A. & Bowman, Ann O.** Cityscapes & Capital: The Politics of Urban Development. (Illus.). 224p. 1994. text ed. 32.50x (0-8018-5034-7) Johns Hopkins.

Pagano, Michael A. & Moore, Richard. Cities & Fiscal Choices: A New Model of Urban Public Investment. LC 85-16211. (Duke Press Policy Studies). xii, 166p. 1985. 39.50 (0-8223-0653-0) Duke.

Pagano, Michael P. Communicating Effectively in Medical Records: A Guide for Physician-Authors. 128p. (C). 1992. 34.00 (0-8039-4316-4); pap. 15.95 (0-8039-4317-2) Sage.

Pagano, Michael P. & Ragan, Sandra L. Communication Skills for Professional Nurses. 160p. (C). 1992. 34.00 (0-8039-4556-6); pap. 15.95 (0-8039-4557-4) Sage.

***Pagano, Michele, ed.** Cell Cycle: Materials & Methods. LC 95-3810. (Laboratory Ser.). 1995. 79.00 (3-540-58066-2) Spr-Verlag.

Pagano, N. J., ed. Interlaminar Response of Composite Materials. (Composite Materials Ser.: No. 5). 272p. 1989. 102.75 (0-444-87285-X) Elsevier.

Pagano, N. J., jt. auth. see Wright-Patterson Air Force Base, Air Force Materials Lab Staff.

Pagano, Nicholas J., jt. auth. see Pei Chi Chou.

Pagano, Robert R. Understanding Statistics in the Behavioral Sciences. 3rd ed. Perlee, Clyde, ed. 542p. (C). 1990. text ed. 54.75 (0-314-66792-X) West Pub.

— Understanding Statistics in the Behavioral Sciences. 4th ed. Perlee, ed. LC 93-41157. 550p. (C). 1994. text ed. 57.50 (0-314-02691-6) West Pub.

Pagano, Ugo. Work, Welfare & Economic Theory. 264p. 1985. 64.95 (0-631-13728-9) Blackwell Pubs.

Paganuzzi, P. N. Visoko-Dechanskaja Lavra na Kosovje Polje (v Serbii) 1976. pap. 1.00 (0-317-30331-7) Holy Trinity.

Pagden, Anthony. European Encounter with the New World: From Renaissance to Romanticism. (Illus.). 256p. (C). 1993. text ed. 27.50 (0-300-05285-5); pap. 12.00 (0-300-05950-7) Yale U Pr.

— The Fall of Natural Man: The American Indian & the Origins of Comparative Ethnology. LC 82-1137. (Cambridge Iberian & Latin American Studies). 272p. 1987. pap. 19.95 (0-521-33704-6) Cambridge U Pr.

— Lords of All the Worlds: Ideologies of Empire in Spain, Britain & France c.1500-c.1850. LC 95-13867. 1995. write for info. (0-300-06415-2) Yale U Pr.

— Spanish Imperialism & the Political Imagination. LC 89-22644. 196p. (C). 1990. text ed. 26.00 (0-300-04676-6) Yale U Pr.

Pagden, Anthony, ed. The Languages of Political Theory in Early Modern Europe. (Ideas in Context Ser.). 280p. 1990. pap. 22.95 (0-521-38666-7) Cambridge U Pr.

Pagden, Anthony, jt. ed. see Canny, Nicholas.

Pagden, Anthony, ed. see Cortes, Hernan.

Pagden, Anthony, ed. see Vitoria, Francisco.

Pagden, Tim. VLSI Design: From System to Silicon. 400p. 1992. pap. text ed. 42.00 (0-13-950940-2) P-H.

Page. Ancient Egyptian Figured Ostraca. (Petrie Collection Ser.). 1983. pap. 32.00 (0-85668-216-0, Pub. by Aris & Phillips UK) David Brown.

— Checkpoints. 2nd ed. (C). 1993. text ed. 32.50 (0-06-501366-2); teacher ed, pap. text ed. 10.00 (0-06-501367-0) HarpCollege.

— Effective Company Command for Company Officers in the Professional Fire Service. 1973. 12.95 (0-87505-121-9) Borden.

— File on Pinter. (Methuen Writer-Files Ser.). (C). 1993. pap. 14.95 (0-413-53620-3, A0677, Pub. by Methuen UK) Heinemann.

— Ion Coupled Sugar Transport in Microorganisms. 1995. write for info. (0-8493-6529-5) CRC Pr.

— Jonah & the Big Fish & Other Favorite Bible Stories. 1995. pap. 4.99 (0-679-87222-1) Random.

— Platelet in Health-Disease. 290p. 1991. 135.00 (0-632-02714-2) Blackwell Sci.

Page, jt. auth. see Greenberg.

***Page, A. C. & Ferguson, R. B.** Investor Protection. (Law in Context Ser.). 384p. (C). 1994. text ed. 70.00 (0-297-82131-8, Trans); pap. text ed. 37.95 (0-297-82132-6, Trans) Northwestern U Pr.

Page, A. J. Relational Databases: Concepts, Selection & Implementation. 240p. (Orig.). 1990. pap. 37.50 (1-85058-140-1, Pub. by Sigma Press UK) Coronet Bks.

Page, A. L., jt. ed. see Klute, A.

Page, A. L., et al, eds. Land Application of Sludge. (Illus.). 168p. 1987. 59.95 (0-87371-083-5, S657, CRC Reprint) Franklin.

Page, Adrian & Bloom, Clive, eds. The Death of the Playwright? Modern British Drama & Literary Theory. (Insights Ser.). 192p. 1992. text ed. 49.95 (0-312-06537-X) St Martin.

Page, Alex, tr. see Buber, Martin.

Page, Alison. Road Trip. (Spring Break Ser.: No. 1). (YA). 1994. pap. 1.99 (0-06-106224-3, Pub. by Haags Gemeentemuseum) HarpC.

Page, Allison. Spring Break, No. 1: Road Trip. 1991. mass mkt. 3.50 (0-06-106050-X, Harp PBks) HarpC.

— Spring Break, No. 2: Beach Boys. 1991. mass mkt. 3.50 (0-06-106051-8, Harp PBks) HarpC.

— Spring Break, No. 3: Last Fling. 1991. mass mkt. 3.50 (0-06-106119-0, Harp PBks) HarpC.

Page, Andre. Photographic Interpretation. (Illus.). 128p. 1973. 12.00 (0-7207-0633-5) Transatl Arts.

Page, B. & Conacher, H. Survey of Analytical Methods Available for Estimation: Artificial Sweeteners in Food. (International Union of Pure & Applied Chemistry Ser.). 1978. 8.00 (0-08-022342-7, Pub. by Pergamon Repr UK) Franklin.

Page, B. M., ed. see Zonenshain, L. P., et al.

Page, Benjamin B., ed. Marxism & Spirituality: An International Anthology. LC 92-18499. 248p. 1993. text ed. 52.95 (0-89789-291-7, H291, Bergin & Garvey) Greenwood.

Page, Benjamin I. Who Gets What from Government. LC 82-13454. 264p. 1983. pap. 14.00 (0-520-04703-6) U CA Pr.

Page, Benjamin I. & Shapiro, Robert Y. The Rational Public: Fifty Years of Trends in Americans' Policy Preferences. (Illus.). 488p. 1992. pap. text ed. 19.95 (0-226-64478-2) U Ch Pr.

Page, Benjamin I., jt. auth. see Greenberg, Edward S.

Page, Benjamin I., jt. auth. see Resnick.

Page, Bernd, jt. ed. see Guariso, Giorgio.

Page, Beverly. Cartoon Art: An Adventure in Creativity. Smith, Linda H., ed. 1980. pap. 5.95 (0-936386-10-X) Creative Learning.

Page, Bill, jt. auth. see Pierce, Carol.

Page, Brian, jt. auth. see Beeching, Kate.

Page, Brian, tr. see Bidault, Francis.

***Page, Brian T.** Assessment Center Handbook. 1995. pap. 17.95 (0-87526-429-8) Gould.

— Getting Ready for That Assessment Center. (Illus.). 120p. (Orig.). 1983. pap. 8.95 (0-9611284-0-2) Sweets Corners.

Page, Burdys. Learning to Color with Rhymes. (Illus.). 32p. (Orig.). (J). 1990. pap. 6.95 (0-86534-146-X) Sunstone Pr.

Page, C., ed. see Harper, Linda L.

Page, C. E. How to Feed the Baby to Make It Healthy & Happy. 1991. lib. bdg. 66.95 (0-8490-4521-5) Gordon Pr.

— How to Feed the Baby to Make It Healthy & Happy. 162p. 1967. reprint ed. spiral bd. 6.05 (0-7873-0650-9) Mokelumne.

Page, C. H., jt. auth. see Stacey, T. R.

Page, C. L., et al, eds. Corrosion of Reinforcement in Concrete. 614p. 1990. 126.00 (1-85166-487-4) Elsevier.

Page, C. P. & Gardiner, P. J. Airways Hyperresponsiveness, Is It Really Important for Asthma? (Illus.). 384p. 1993. 135.00 (0-632-03061-5) Blackwell Sci.

Page, C. P., et al, eds. Pharmacology of Asthma. (Handbook of Experimental Pharmacology Ser.: No. 98). (Illus.). 352p. 1991. 246.00 (0-387-52839-3) Spr-Verlag.

Page, Camille. American Knives & Weapons to 1900. (Illus.). 60p. (FRE.). 1993. reprint ed. 25.00 (0-87556-181-0) Saifer.

Page, Carey P. & Hardin, Thomas C. Nutritional Assessment & Support: A Primer. (Illus.). 196p. (Orig.). 1994. pap. 19.00 (0-683-06705-2) Williams & Wilkins.

***Page, Carl.** Philosophical Historicism & the Betrayal of First Philosophy. 256p. 1995. 35.00 (0-271-01330-3) Pa St U Pr.

Page, Carol G., jt. auth. see Dickinson, Richard W.

Page, Carol G., jt. auth. see Dickinson, Richards W.

Page, Carole G. Bouquet of Good-Byes. (Kasey Carlone Ser.). (YA). 1992. pap. 4.99 (0-8024-8180-9) Moody.

— Carrie: Springsong. (YA). 1994. pap. 3.99 (1-55661-523-X) Bethany Hse.

— Change of Plans. (Kasey Carlone Ser.). (YA). 1992. pap. 4.99 (0-8024-8179-5) Moody.

— Hallie's Secret. (Sensitive Issues Ser.). 144p. (J). 1987. pap. text ed. 4.99 (0-8024-3476-2) Moody.

— Heather's Choice. LC 82-3417. (Sensitive Issues Ser.). 128p. (J). (gr. 7 up). 1982. pap. 4.99 (0-8024-8453-0) Moody.

— Kara. (Springsong Ser.). (Orig.). (YA). 1994. pap. 3.99 (1-55661-448-9) Bethany Hse.

— Maria's Search: A Story of Loneliness. (Sensitive Issues Ser.). 1985. pap. text ed. 4.99 (0-8024-8452-2) Moody.

— Neeley Never Said Good-By. (Sensitive Issues Ser.). (Orig.). (J). (gr. 7 up). 1984. pap. 4.99 (0-8024-8454-9) Moody.

— Petals in the Storm: A Collection of Short Stories about Women Making Life-Changing Decisions. Fell, Doris E., ed. LC 91-13343. 225p. 1991. pap. 9.99 (0-8307-1483-9, 5422507) Regal.

— A Song for Kasey. (Kasey Carlone Ser.). (J). 1992. pap. 4.99 (0-8024-8176-0) Moody.

— Summer of a Stranger. (Kasey Carlone Ser.). (J). 1992. pap. 4.99 (0-8024-8177-9) Moody.

— Taste of Fame. (Kasey Carlone Ser.). (J). (gr. 2-6). 1992. pap. 4.99 (0-8024-8178-7) Moody.

Page, Carolyn. Troy Corner Poems. Zarucchi, Roy, ed. & illus. by. (Chapbook Ser.). 24p. (Orig.). 1994. pap. 5.00 (1-879205-46-7) Nightshade Pr.

Page, Carolyn, ed. see Allen, M. Ray.

Page, Carolyn, ed. see Barnes, Jack.

Page, Carolyn, ed. see Blomain, Karen.

Page, Carolyn, ed. see Chitwood, Michael.

Page, Carolyn, ed. see Chute, Robert M.

Page, Carolyn, ed. see Cirino, Leonard.

Page, Carolyn, ed. see Coulehan, Jack.

Page, Carolyn, ed. see Deisroth, Nancy.

Page, Carolyn, ed. see Doreski, William.

Page, Carolyn, ed. see Franklin, Walt.

Page, Carolyn, ed. see Goodrich, Patricia.

Page, Carolyn, ed. see Holmes, Edward M.

Page, Carolyn, ed. see Kaufman, Debra.

Page, Carolyn, ed. see Little, Carl.

Page, Carolyn, ed. see Longley, Judy.

Page, Carolyn, ed. see Maginnes, Al.

Page, Carolyn, ed. see Mandel, Peter.

Page, Carolyn, ed. see McKee, Glenn.

Page, Carolyn, ed. see McKee, Louis.

Page, Carolyn, ed. see Merrick, Beverly.

Page, Carolyn, ed. see Murphy, Carole.

Page, Carolyn, ed. see New, Joan C.

Page, Carolyn, ed. see Persun, Terry.

Page, Carolyn, ed. see Peterson, Walt.

Page, Carolyn, ed. see Pies, Ronald M.

Page, Carolyn, ed. see Pobo, Ken.

Page, Carolyn, ed. see Raby, Elizabeth.

Page, Carolyn, ed. see Robinson, Diane.

Page, Carolyn, ed. see Rossel, Muriel.

Page, Carolyn, ed. see Rule, Rebecca.

Page, Carolyn, ed. see Smith, R. T.

Page, Carolyn, ed. see Stanko, Mary R.

Page, Carolyn, ed. see Stephenson, Shelby.

Page, Carolyn, ed. see Tiger, Madeline.

Page, Carolyn, ed. see Towle, Parker.

Page, Carolyn, ed. see Watson, Ron.

Page, Carolyn, ed. see Wood, Bill.

Page, Carolyn, jt. ed. see Zarucchi, Roy.

Page, Charles H. Fifty Years in the Sociological Enterprise: A Lucky Journey. LC 82-7046. 288p. 1985. lib. bdg. 30.00 (0-87023-373-4); pap. 16.95 (0-87023-490-0) U of Mass Pr.

***Page, Charles R., 3rd.** Jesus & the Land. LC 95-7415. 224p. (Orig.). 1995. pap. text ed. 14.95 (0-687-00544-2) Abingdon.

Page, Charles R. & Volz, Carl. The Land & the Book. LC 92-43245. 288p. (Orig.). 1993. pap. 15.95 (0-687-46289-4) Abingdon.

Page, Cheryl A., jt. auth. see Cook, Sybilla A.

Page, Christine R. Frontiers of Health: From Healing to Wholeness. 1995. pap. 19.95 (0-85207-256-2, Pub. by C W Daniel UK) Atrium Pubs.

— Frontiers of Health from Healing to Wholeness. 256p. (Orig.). Date not set. pap. 29.95 (0-8464-4180-2) Beekman Pubs.

Page, Christopher. Discarding Images: Reflections on Music & Culture in Medieval France. (Illus.). 256p. 1993. 42.00 (0-19-816346-0) OUP.

— The Owl & the Nightingale: Musical Life & Ideas in France, 1100-1300. (Illus.). 291p. 1990. 40.00 (0-520-06944-7) U CA Pr.

Page, Christopher, ed. Summa Musice: A Thirteenth-Century Manual for Singers. (Musical Texts & Monographs). (Illus.). 250p. (C). 1991. 74.95 (0-521-40420-7) Cambridge U Pr.

Page, Clarence, ed. see McClain, Leanita.

Page, Clarence, jt. auth. see McClain, Leanita.

Page, Cleveland. The Laboratory Piano Course: For Laboratory or Conventional Class Instruction, Bk. 1. (Illus.). 131p. (C). 1990. 35.50 (0-06-045006-1) HarpCollege.

Page, Clint & Cuff, Penelope. Negotiating for Amenities: Zoning & Management Tools That Build Livable Cities, Pt. II: Models & Resources. (Illus.). 80p. (Orig.). 1982. pap. 12.50 (0-941182-06-1) Partners Livable.

— The Public Sector Designs. LC 83-82147. (Illus.). 64p. (Orig.). 1984. pap. 12.00 (0-941182-12-6) Partners Livable.

Page, Clint & Cuff, Penelope, eds. Negotiating for Amenities: Zoning & Management Tools That Build Livable Cities, Pt. I, Models & Resources. (Illus.). 165p. (Orig.). 1982. pap. 12.50 (0-941182-07-X) Partners Livable.

Page, Clive. The Professional Programmers Guide to Fortran 77. 180p. (C). 1988. pap. text ed. 110.00 (0-273-02856-1, Pub. by Pitman Pubng UK) St Mut.

Page, Clive & Black, Judith, eds. Airways & Vascular Remodelling in Asthma & Cardiovascular Disease: Implications for Therapeutic Intervention. (Illus.). 189p. 1994. boxed 82.50 (0-12-543540-1) Acad Pr.

Page, Clive P. & Metzger, W. James, eds. Drugs & the Lung. (Advances in Clinical Pharmacology Ser.: Vol. 1). 624p. 1994. 125.00 (0-7817-0135-X) Raven.

Page, Collin F. & Kitching, John. Technical Aids to Teaching Higher Education. 3rd ed. 92p. 1981. pap. 32.00 (0-900868-49-X, Open Univ Pr) Taylor & Francis.

Page, Curtis H., tr. see De Ronsard, Pierre.

Page, Curtis W. & Selden, Charles J. Asking "Just Right" Business Questions: A Proven Process for Developing Leaders & Organizations. rev. ed. LC 94-76163. 200p. 1994. 21.95 (1-885207-00-X); pap. 14.95 (1-885207-01-8) Graham Page.

Page, Curtis W., jt. auth. see Ends, Earl J.

Page, D. E. Observations of the Outer Heliosphere. (Advances in Space Research Ser.: Vol. 13). 312p. 1993. pap. 195.00 (0-08-042208-X, Pergamon Pr) Elsevier.

Page, D. E., ed. see ESLAB-ESRIN Symposium Staff.

Page, D. E., jt. ed. see Grzedzielski, S.

Page, Daniel E., jt. auth. see Jahera, John S., Jr.

Page, Dave. Marianne Moore. LC 93-3375. (Voices in Poetry Ser.). 1994. lib. bdg. 16.95 (0-88682-615-2) Creative Ed.

— Ship Versus Shore: Civil War Engagements Between Land & Sea. (Illus.). 320p. (J). 1994. 22.95 (1-55853-267-6) Rutledge Hill Pr.

Page, David, ed. see Boyle, H. B.

***Page, David A. & Chval, Kathryn.** Maneuvers with Number Patterns. (Maneuvers with Math Ser.). (Illus.). 118p. (Orig.). 1994. teacher ed 15.95 (0-86651-935-1) Seymour Pubns.

— Maneuvers with Number Patterns. (Maneuvers with Math Ser.). (Illus.). 116p. (Orig.). (J). (gr. 5-8). 1994. student ed 5.50 (0-86651-934-3) Seymour Pubns.

Page, David E. The Lemonade War. (Illus.). 64p. (J). (gr. 1-3). 1993. pap. 2.50 (0-87406-648-4) Willowisp Pr.

— Valerie & the Jelly Bean Trail. (Illus.). 24p. (J). (gr. k-3). 1995. pap. 2.99 (0-87406-732-4) Willowisp Pr.

Page, David L. & Anderson, Thomas J. Diagnostic Histopathology of the Breast. (Illus.). 362p. 1987. text ed. 149.95 (0-443-02240-2) Churchill.

Page, David L., et al. Atlas of Tumor Pathology: Tumors of the Adrenal. rev. ed. (Second Ser.: Fascicle 23). (Illus.). 279p. 1990. per., pap. 20.00 (0-16-001862-5, S/N 008-023-001) USGPO.

Page, David P. Theory & Practice of Teaching. LC 77-89216. (American Education: Its Men, Institutions & Ideas, Ser. 1). 1970. reprint ed. 18.95 (0-405-01455-4) Ayer.

Page, Denys L. Folktales in Homer's Odyssey. LC 73-75056. (Carl Newell Jackson Lectures: 1972). 152p. reprint ed. pap. 43.40 (0-317-09805-5, 2017684) Bks Demand.

— The Homeric Odyssey. LC 76-39798. (Mary Flexner Lectures Ser., 1954). 186p. 1982. reprint ed. text ed. 71.50 (0-8371-9308-7, PAHO, Greenwood Pr) Greenwood.

Page, Denys L., ed. Epigrammata Graeca: From the Beginning to the Garland of Phillip. (Oxford Classical Texts Ser.). 1976. 35.00 (0-19-814581-0) OUP.

— Further Greek Epigrams: Epigrams Before A. D. 50 from the Greek Anthology & Other Sources. LC 79-42646. (Illus.). 700p. 1982. 215.00 (0-521-22903-0) Cambridge U Pr.

— Lyrica Graece Selecta. (Oxford Classical Texts Ser.). 1968. 19.95 (0-19-814567-5) OUP.

Page, Denys L., ed. see Aeschylus.

Page, Don. The Answers for Mail Order Riches! 24p. 1986. pap. text ed. 6.00 (0-937514-50-0) Prime Pubs.

— Universal Guide to Success in Any Endeavor. (Illus.). 106p. (Orig.). 1986. pap. text ed. 12.00 (0-937514-49-7) Prime Pubs.

Page, Donald, jt. ed. see Hillmer, Norman.

Page, Dorothy & Wiedman, Katie. Building Profitable Nutrition Practices. (Illus.). 350p. 1992. text ed. 49.95 (0-442-00914-3) Van Nos Reinhold.

Page, E. S. & Wilson, Leslie B. An Introduction to Computational Combinatorics. LC 78-54722. (Cambridge Computer Science Texts Ser.: No. 9). (Illus.). 1979. 59.95 (0-521-22427-6) Cambridge U Pr.

Page, Earle C. Looking at Type. LC 83-2028. (Illus.). 44p. 1983. pap. 3.00 (0-935652-09-4) Ctr Applications Psych.

— Una Mirada a los Tipos Psichologicos: Una Descripcion de las Preferencias Dadas Por el Indicador de Tipos Psicologicos Myers-Briggs (MBTI) Moody, Raymond A., tr. LC 93-40958. (Illus.). 41p. (SPA.). 1993. pap. 5.50x (0-935652-18-3) Ctr Applications Psych.

Page, Edward. Liberty & Jobs for All. Van Treese, James B., ed. 220p. 1994. pap. 7.95 (1-56901-079-X) NW Pub.

— One Hundred One Timex-Sinclair 1000 ZX-81 Programming Tips & Tricks. 128p. (Orig.). (gr. 7-12). 1982. pap. 7.95 (0-86668-020-9) ARCsoft.

— Practical Timex-Sinclair Computer Programs for Beginners. 96p. 1983. 7.95 (0-86668-027-6) ARCsoft.

— Thirty-Seven Timex-Sinclair 1000 ZX-81 Computer Programs for Home, School & Office. (Illus.). 96p. (Orig.). 1982. pap. 8.95 (0-86668-021-7) ARCsoft.

— Timex-Sinclair Computer Games Programs. 96p. 1983. 7.95 (0-86668-026-8) ARCsoft.

Page, Edward C. Localism & Centralism in Europe: The Political & Legal Bases of Local Self-Government. (Comparative European Politics Ser.). 200p. 1992. 55.00 (0-19-827727-X) OUP.

— Political Authority & Bureaucratic Power: A Comparative Analysis. LC 84-21895. 202p. (C). 1985. text ed. 26.00x (0-87049-454-6) U of Tenn Pr.

Page, Edward C. & Goldsmith, Michael J., eds. Central & Local Government Relations: A Comparative Analysis of West European Unitary States. (Modern Politics Ser.: Vol. 13). 184p. (C). 1987. text ed. 45.00 (0-8039-8071-X) Sage.

Page, Elizabeth. The Tree of Liberty. 1000p. 1990. reprint ed. lib. bdg. 57.95 (0-89966-658-2) Buccaneer Bks.

Page, Elwin L. George Washington in New Hampshire. (Portsmouth Marine Society Ser.). (Illus.). 95p. 1990. reprint ed. 25.00 (0-915819-15-5, 16) Portsmouth Marine Soc.

Page, Emma. Every Second Thursday. large type ed. (Mystery Ser.). 304p. 1983. 21.95 (0-7089-0922-1) Ulverscroft.

— Scent of Death. large type ed. (Mystery Ser.). 352p. 1987. 16.95 (0-7089-1579-5) Ulverscroft.

Page, Eugene R. George Colman, the Elder. LC 74-181965. reprint ed. 21.50 (0-404-04857-9) AMS Pr.

Page, Evelyn & Page, Tim. Party Punches. LC 86-202652. (Illus.). 190p. (Orig.). 1986. pap. 14.95 (0-942557-00-X) Page Pr & Assocs.

Page, Frederick, ed. see Byron, George G.

Page, Frederick, ed. see Meynell, Alice C.

Page, G. F., et al, eds. Application of Neural Networks to Modelling & Control. LC 93-14878. 1993. Alk. paper. write for info. (0-412-54760-X) Chapman & Hall.

Page, G. Terry, jt. auth. see Johannsen, Hano.

Page, G. William, ed. Planning for Groundwater Protection. 387p. 1987. text ed. 69.00 (0-12-543615-7) Acad Pr.

Page, G. William & Patton, Carl V. Quick Answers to Quantitative Problems: A Pocket Primer. (Illus.). 277p. 1991. pap. text ed. 29.95 (0-12-543570-3) Acad Pr.

Page, Geoff. Winter Vision. 200p. (Orig.). 1989. pap. 14.95 (0-7022-2239-9, Pub. by Univ Queensland Pr AT) Intl Spec Bk.

***Page, George C.** In My Own Words George C. Page. (Illus.). 160p. (Orig.). 1995. pap. text ed. 10.95 (1-882180-12-7) Griffin CA.

Page, Gerald W., ed. Nameless Places. LC 75-2525. 1975. 10.00 (0-87054-073-4) Arkham.

Page, Glen B. A Book of Hard Criticisms: Watching the America Show (versus) A Revisioning for an Alternative America in the Twenty-First Century. LC 90-85738. 368p. 1991. 22.00 (0-9628845-0-2) Canopus Pub.

Page, Gordon T. Deals on Wheels: How to Buy, Care for & Sell a Car: Complete Buyer's Guide & Expose of the Automotive Jungle. (Illus.). 304p. (Orig.). 1984. pap. 9.95 (0-9607804-0-8) Page Pub WI.

Page, H. Thoreau: His Life & Aims. 1972. 59.95 (0-8490-1205-8) Gordon Pr.

— Thoreau: His Life & Aims. LC 72-3653. (American Literature Ser.: No. 49). 1972. reprint ed. lib. bdg. 59.95 (0-8383-1585-2) M S G Haskell Hse.

Page, Harry R. Public Purchasing & Materials Management. LC 79-2039. 528p. 1983. pap. 26.00 (0-685-03027-X) Free Pr.

Page, Hilary. Color Right from the Start: Progressive Lessons in Seeing & Understanding Color. LC 93-48927. (Illus.). 144p. 1994. 29.95 (0-8230-0751-0, Watson-Guptill) Watson-Guptill.

— Watercolor Right from the Start. LC 92-17440. (Illus.). 144p. 1992. 29.95 (0-8230-5688-0, Watson-Guptill) Watson-Guptill.

Page, Hilary & Lesthaeghe, Ron J., eds. Child-Spacing in Tropical Africa: Traditions & Change. (Studies in Population). 1981. text ed. 112.00 (0-12-543620-3) Acad Pr.

Page, Hiram. The Ramtha-Joseph Smith Dialogues. Senestraro, A., ed. (Illus.). 85p. (Orig.). 1993. pap. 14.00 (0-931553-14-8) Oneiric Pr.

— The Sprague River Scrolls: The Dialogues of Joseph Smith & Ramtha, Vol. I. Senestraro, Alwyn, ed. (Illus.). 85p. (Orig.). 1993. pap. 14.00 (0-685-64804-4) Oneiric Pr.

— The Sprague River Scrolls: Writings of an Early Mormon Heretic. 120p. (Orig.). 1991. pap. 9.00 (0-931553-10-5) Oneiric Pr.

Page, Ian, ed. Parallel Architectures & Computer Vision. (Illus.). 348p. 1988. 55.00 (0-19-853740-9) OUP.

Page, Ian & Dever, Joe. World of Lone Wolf No. 1: Grey Star the Wizard. 240p. 1987. pap. 4.50 (0-425-09590-8, Berkley-Pacer) Berkley Pub.

— World of Lone Wolf No. 2: The Forbidden City. 1987. pap. 3.50 (0-425-09710-2, Berkley-Pacer) Berkley Pub.

Page, Ian, jt. auth. see Dever, Joe.

Page, Irvine. Hypertension Mechanisms. 992p. 1987. text ed. 110.00 (0-8089-1768-4, 793228, Grune) Saunders.

Page, J. A. A Guide to the Qutb. Delhi. 1986. reprint ed. 85.00 (81-85046-33-6, Scientific) St Mut.

Page, J. K. Advances in European Solar Radiation Climatology. (C). 1986. 100.00 (0-685-33086-9, Pub. by Interntl Solar Energy Soc UK) St Mut.

Page, J. K., ed. Prediction of Solar Radiation on Inclined Surfaces. 1986. lib. bdg. 139.00 (90-277-2260-9) Kluwer Ac.

Page, Jake. The Deadly Canyon. LC 93-22130. 240p. 1994. 20.00 (0-345-37930-6, Ballantine Trade) Ballantine.

— The Deadly Canyon. 1995. mass mkt., pap. 4.99 (0-345-37931-4, House of Collect) Ballantine.

— The Knotted Strings. LC 94-25940. 1995. 20.00 (0-345-38782-1) Ballantine.

— Smithsonian Guide: Southwest. Date not set. 30.00 (0-679-44152-2) Random.

— The Smithsonian Guide to Natural America: The Southwest. 1995. 19.95 (0-679-76154-3) Random.

— Smithsonian's New Zoo. LC 89-29626. (Illus.). 224p. 1990. 29.95 (0-87474-734-1) Smithsonian.

— Songs to Birds. 144p. 1993. 18.95 (0-87923-957-3) Godine.

— The Stolen Gods. LC 92-53457. 256p. 1993. 19.00 (0-345-37928-4, Ballantine Trade) Ballantine.

— The Stolen Gods. (Southwest Mysteries Ser.). 1994. mass mkt. 4.99 (0-345-37929-2) Ballantine.

— Zoo: The Modern Ark. (Illus.). 192p. 1990. 35.00 (0-8160-2345-X) Facts on File.

***Page, Jake & Morton, Eugene S.** Lords of the Air: The Smithsonian Book of Birds. LC 95-8553. (Illus.). 1995. reprint ed. 24.99 (0-517-14749-1, Pub. by Wings Bks) Random.

Page, Jake, jt. auth. see Leeming, David.

Page, Jake, jt. auth. see Officer, Charles.

Page, Jake, jt. auth. see Page, Susanne.

Page, James A. Black Olympian Medalists. 190p. 1991. pap. 27.50 (0-87287-618-7) Libs Unl.

Page, James D., jt. auth. see Landis, Carney.

Page, James L. Applied Visualization: A Mind-Body Program. LC 90-27419. 144p. 1991. reprint ed. pap. 9.95 (0-87542-597-6) Llewellyn Pubns.

— Love Spells: Creative Techniques for Magical Relationships. LC 91-28524. 160p. 1991. pap. 9.95 (0-87542-598-4) Llewellyn Pubns.

— Love Spells for More Fulfilling & Intimate Relationships. 144p. (Orig.). 1992. pap. 27.50 (0-572-01621-2, Pub. by W Foulsham UK) Trans-Atl Phila.

Page, James O. The EMS Legal Primer. 20p. 1985. 3.00 (0-317-47413-8) Jems Comm.

— The Magic of Three A.M. Griffiths, Keith, ed. LC 86-82551. 177p. 1986. text ed. 14.95 (0-936174-02-1) Jems Comm.

Page, Jean R. From Hoof to Wheel. (Illus.). 75p. (Orig.). (YA). (gr. 7-12). 1992. pap. 7.95 (0-9632755-0-X) Jean Page.

***Page, Jeanette, ed.** A Country Diary. (Illus.). 160p. 1995. 19.95 (1-85702-254-8, Pub. by Fourth Estate UK) Trafalgar.

Page, Jesse. The Black Bishop: Samuel Adjai Crowther. LC 75-106783. (Illus.). 440p. 1979. reprint ed. text ed. 59.75 (0-8371-4610-0, PBB&, Negro U Pr) Greenwood.

— David Brainerd, Vol. 2. 1979. pap. 4.99 (0-88019-015-9) Schmul Pub Co.

Page, John. Cost Estimating Man-Hour Manual for Pipelines & Marine Structures. LC 76-40868. 336p. 1977. 49.00 (0-87201-157-7) Gulf Pub.

— Masonry Arch Bridges. (TRL State of the Art Reviews Ser.). 134p. 1994. 79.95 (0-11-551190-3, HM11903, Pub. by HMSO UK) UNIPUB.

Page, John & Hooper, Paul. Accounting & Information Systems. 4th ed. 864p. (C). 1992. text ed. write for info. (0-13-006040-2) P-H.

Page, John R. What Will Dr. Newman Do? John Henry Newman & Papal Infallibility, 1865-1875. LC 94-5538. (John Henry Newman & Papal Infallibility Ser.). 472p. 1994. 24.95 (0-8146-5027-9) Liturgical Pr.

Page, John R. & Hooper, H. Paul. Microcomputer Accounting & Information Systems. (C). 1985. teacher ed write for info. (0-8359-9122-9, Reston) P-H.

Page, John R., jt. auth. see Stillman, Richard J.

Page, John S. Conceptual Cost Estimating Manual. LC 83-22601. 332p. 1984. spiral bd. 55.00 (0-87201-134-8) Gulf Pub.

— Estimator's Electrical Man-Hour Manual. 2nd ed. LC 78-73000. (Estimator's Man-Hour Library). 428p. 1979. 49.00 (0-87201-252-2) Gulf Pub.

— Estimator's Equipment Installation Man-Hour Manual. 2nd ed. LC 78-53193. (Estimator's Man-Hour Library). 254p. 1978. 49.00 (0-87201-276-X) Gulf Pub.

— Estimator's General Construction Man-Hour Manual. 2nd ed. LC 60-1386. (Estimator's Man-Hour Library). 274p. 1977. 49.00 (0-87201-320-0) Gulf Pub.

— Estimator's Man-Hour Manual on Heating, Air Conditioning, Ventilating & Plumbing. 2nd ed. LC 61-10176. (Estimator's Man-Hour Library). 218p. 1978. 49.00 (0-87201-364-2) Gulf Pub.

— Estimator's Piping Man-Hour Manual. 4th ed. 240p. 1987. 49.00 (0-87201-708-7) Gulf Pub.

Page-Jones, Meilir. Practical Guide to Structured Systems Design. 2nd ed. (Illus.). 384p. 1988. pap. text ed. 53.33 (0-13-690769-5) P-H.

— Practical Project Management: Restoring Quality to DP Projects & Systems. LC 85-71101. (Illus.). 248p. (Orig.). 1985. pap. 30.00 (0-932633-00-5) Dorset Hse Pub Co.

***Page, Joseph A.** The Brazilians. 560p. 1995. 26.50 (0-201-40913-5) Addison-Wesley.

— The Law of Premises Liability. LC 76-11993. 325p. 1976. text ed. 49.75 (0-87084-683-3) Anderson Pub Co.

— The Law of Premises Liability. suppl. ed. LC 76-11993. 325p. 1986. Suppl. 1985-86. 24.75 (0-685-41980-0) Anderson Pub Co.

— The Law of Premises Liability. 2nd ed. 413p. 1988. 75.00 (0-87084-684-1) Anderson Pub Co.

— The Law of Premises Liability. 2nd suppl. ed. 413p. 1988. 25.00 (0-685-54372-2) Anderson Pub Co.

***Page, Judith.** Maybe Grace. 66p. (Orig.). 1994. pap. 8.95 (0-9635391-6-7) Sandstone NC.

Page, Judith W. Wordsworth & the Cultivation of Women. LC 93-34121. (C). 1994. 35.00 (0-520-08493-4) U CA Pr.

Page, Julia V. Intelligence Officer in the Peninsula: Letters & Diaries of Major the Hon. Edward Charles Cocks 1786-1812. 256p. (C). 1991. 95.00 (0-946771-71-5, Pub. by Spellmount UK) St Mut.

Page, Kagan. Trade Contacts in China. 357p. 1987. pap. 110.00 (1-85091-340-4, 073029-M99348) Gale.

***Page, Katherine H.** The Body in the Basement. (Faith Fairchild Mystery Ser.). 304p. 1995. reprint ed. mass mkt. 4.99 (0-380-72339-5) Avon.

— The Body in the Belfry. 256p. 1991. reprint ed. mass mkt. 4.99 (0-380-71328-4) Avon.

— The Body in the Bouillon. 224p. 1992. mass mkt. 4.50 (0-380-71896-0) Avon.

— The Body in the Bouillon. 224p. 1991. 17.95 (0-312-06309-1, Pub. by Thomas Dunne Bks) St Martin.

— The Body in the Cast. 272p. 1994. mass mkt. 4.99 (0-380-72338-7) Avon.

— The Body in the Cast. 224p. 1993. 19.95 (0-312-09755-7, Pub. by Thomas Dunne Bks) St Martin.

— The Body in the Kelp. 1990. 16.95 (0-312-05392-4) St Martin.

— Body in the Kelp. 1992. mass mkt. 4.99 (0-380-71329-2) Avon.

— The Body in the Vestibule. 224p. 1993. mass mkt. 4.99 (0-380-72079-5) Avon.

— The Body in the Vestibule. 234p. 1992. 17.95 (0-312-08148-0, Pub. by Thomas Dunne Bks) St Martin.

— The Ghost of Winthrop: A Mystery Jigsaw Puzzle. (BePuzzled Ser.). (Orig.). (C). 1993. 20.00 (0-922242-55-0) Lombard Mktg.

— Magic in the Attic: Adventure Mystery for Kids Ages 8-12. (Spider Tales Ser.). (Orig.). (J). (gr. 3-7). 1995. 14.00 (0-922242-78-X) Bepuzzled.

Page, Kathryn, ed. Union List of Telephone Directories, 1985. 244p. (Orig.). 1985. pap. 16.95 (0-685-22535-6) BAL & Info Sys.

Page, Kenneth R. The Physiology of the Human Placenta. 192p. 1993. 75.00 (1-85728-065-2, Pub. by UCL Pr UK); pap. 29.50 (1-85728-066-0, Pub. by UCL Pr UK) Taylor & Francis.

Page, Kirby, jt. auth. see Eddy, George S.

Page, Kogan. Strategies of Human Resource Management. 224p. 1995. write for info. (0-88415-820-9) Gulf Pub.

Page, Lavon B. Probability for Engineering with Applications to Reliability. 233p. (C). 1995. text ed. 35.95 (0-7167-8187-5, Computer Sci Pr) W H Freeman.

Page, Lawrence M. The Genera & Subgenera of Darters: (Percidae, Etheostomatini) (Occasional Papers: No. 90). 69p. 1981. 1.00 (0-317-04830-9) U of KS Mus Nat Hist.

— Redescription of Etheostoma Australe & a Key for the Identification of Mexican Etheostoma (Percidae) (Occasional Papers: No. 89). 10p. 1981. 1.00 (0-317-04828-7) U of KS Mus Nat Hist.

Page, Lawrence M. & Braasch, Marvin E. Systematic Studies of Darters of the Subgenus Catonotus (Percidae), with the Description of a New Species from the Lower Cumberland & Tennessee River Systems. (Occasional Papers: No. 60). 18p. 1976. pap. 1.00 (0-686-79828-7) U of KS Mus Nat Hist.

— Systematic Studies of Darters of the Subgenus Catonotus with the Description of a New Species from the Duck River System. (Occasional Papers: No. 63). 18p. 1977. pap. 1.00 (0-686-79827-9) U of KS Mus Nat Hist.

Page, Lawrence M. & Burr, Brooks. A Field Guide to Freshwater Fishes: North America North of Mexico. (Peterson Field Guide Ser.). (Illus.). 544p. 1991. 24.95 (0-395-35307-6); pap. 16.95 (0-395-53933-1) HM.

Page, Lawrence M. & Burr, Brooks M. Three New Species of Darters (Percidae, Etheostoma) of the Subgenus Nanostoma from Kentucky & Tennessee. (Occasional Papers: No. 101). (Illus.). 20p. 1982. 1.00 (0-317-04835-X) U of KS Mus Nat Hist.

Page, Lawrence M., jt. auth. see Braasch, Marvin E.

Page, Lawrence M., jt. ed. see Lingquist, David G.

Page, Leigh. The Emission Theory of Electromagnetism. (Connecticut Academy of Arts & Sciences Ser., Trans.: Vol. 26). 1924. pap. 79.50 (0-685-22821-5) Elliots Bks.

— The Principle of General Relativity & Einstein's Theory of Gravitation. (Connecticut Academy of Arts & Sciences Ser., Trans.: Vol. 23). 1920. pap. 49.50 (0-685-22830-4) Elliots Bks.

***Page, Lesley, ed.** Effective Group Practice in Midwifery. (Illus.). 224p. 1994. pap. 24.95 (0-632-03825-X, Pub. by Blckwell Sci Pubns UK) Blackwell Sci.

Page, Lincoln R., ed. Contributions to the Stratigraphy of New England. LC 76-9220. (Memoir Ser.: No. 148). (Illus.). 451p. 1976. 7.50 (0-8137-1148-7) Geol Soc.

Page, Linda G. Healthy Healing. 9th rev. ed. 376p. 1994. pap. text ed. 26.95 (1-884334-50-4) Hlthy Healing.

— Menopause & Osteoporosis. (Healthy Healing Library Ser.). 32p. 1994. 2.95 (1-884334-26-1) Hlthy Healing.

Page, Linda G. & Smith, Hilton, eds. The Foxfire Book of Appalachian Toys & Games. LC 93-9660. (Illus.). xx, 204p. 1993. reprint ed. pap. 16.95 (0-8078-4425-X) U of NC Pr.

Page, Linda G. & Wigginton, Eliot, eds. Aunt Arie: A Foxfire Portrait. LC 91-50882. (Illus.). xxxii, 196p. (C). 1992. reprint ed. 14.95 (0-8078-4377-6) U of NC Pr.

— The Foxfire Book of Appalachian Cookery. LC 92-53627. xxii, 330p. 1992. reprint ed. pap. 17.95 (0-8078-4395-4) U of NC Pr.

Page, Linda M. & Johnsey, Betty Z., eds. Frantic Elegance: Recipes from Clock Conscious Cooks. (Illus.). 283p. (Orig.). 1989. pap. 13.50 (0-9623309-0-6) Arendell Parrott.

***Page, Linda R.** Colds & Flu & You. rev. ed. (Healthy Healing Library Ser.). (Illus.). 32p. 1994. pap. 2.95 (1-884334-28-8) Hlthy Healing.

— Fighting Infections with Herbs. rev. ed. (Healthy Healing Library Ser.). (Illus.). 32p. 1994. pap. 2.95 (1-884334-29-6) Hlthy Healing.

— How to Be Your Own Herbal Pharmacist. 208p. 1994. reprint ed. pap. 15.95 (1-884334-52-0) Hlthy Healing.

— Renewing Male Health & Energy. rev. ed. (Healthy Healing Library Ser.). (Illus.). 32p. 1994. pap. 2.95 (1-884334-30-X) Hlthy Healing.

P Q

An Asterisk (*) at the beginning of an entry indicates that the title is appearing in BIP for the first time.

— Stress & Tension Relief. rev. ed. (Healthy Healing Library Ser.). (Illus.). 32p. 1994. pap. 2.95 (*1-884334-33-4*) Hlthy Healing.

Page, Lot B., jt. ed. see Horan, Michael J.

Page, Louise. Diplomatic Wives. (Methuen Modern Plays Ser.). 90p. (Orig.). 1989. pap. 9.95 (*0-413-61430-1*, Pub. by Methuen UK) Heinemann.

— Page: Plays One. (Methuen World Dramatists Ser.). 324p. (Orig.). 1990. pap. 13.95 (*0-413-64500-2*, A0498, Pub. by Methuen UK) Heinemann.

— Real Estate. (Methuen New Theatrescripts Ser.). 39p. (Orig.). 1988. pap. 7.95 (*0-413-57950-6*, A0233, Pub. by Methuen UK) Heinemann.

— Salonika. (Methuen New Theatrescripts Ser.). 35p. 1988. pap. 6.95 (*0-413-52180-X*, A0252, Pub. by Methuen UK) Heinemann.

Page, Lucius R. The History of Hardwick, Mass., with a Genealogical Register. 555p. 1989. reprint ed. lib. bdg. 55.75 (*0-8328-0830-X*, MA0187) Higginson Bk Co.

Page, Luke J. Page: Genealogical Registers of Ancestors & Descendants of Lemuel Page & Polly Paige, Peter Joslin & Sarah Kidder, with Brief Accounts of Them & Their Ancestors. (Illus.). 155p. 1994. reprint ed. lib. bdg. 35.00 (*0-685-75321-2*); reprint ed. pap. 25.00 (*0-685-75322-0*) Higginson Bk Co.

Page, M. I., ed. The Chemistry of B-Lactams. 320p. 1992. 159.95 (*0-7514-0061-0*, A6875, Pub. by Blackie Acad & Prof UK) Routledge Chapman & Hall.

— The Chemistry of Enzyme Action. (New Comprehensive Biochemistry Ser.: Vol. 6). 568p. 1984. 106.75 (*0-444-80504-4*, I-017-84) Elsevier.

***Page, Malcolm.** All Time Favorite Recipes. 1994. 16.99 (*0-376-02158-6*) Sunset Menlo Pk.

— File on Frayn. 96p. 1994. pap. 13.95 (*0-413-65310-2*, Pub. by Methuen UK) Heinemann.

Page, Malcolm, comp. Arden on File. (Methuen Writer-Files Ser.). 96p. 1988. pap. 10.95 (*0-413-56280-8*, A0011, Pub. by Methuen UK) Heinemann.

Page, Malcolm, ed. File on Osborne. (Methuen Writer-Files Ser.). 96p. 1988. pap. 9.95 (*0-413-14460-7*, A0098, Pub. by Methuen UK) Heinemann.

Page, Malcolm & Morgan, Margery, eds. File on Shaw. (Methuen Writer-Files Ser.). 124p. (Orig.). 1989. pap. 9.95 (*0-413-15280-4*, A0102, Pub. by Methuen UK) Heinemann.

Page, Malcolm & Trussler, Simon. File on Edgar. (Methuen Writer-Files Ser.). 95p. (C). 1991. pap. 9.95 (*0-685-62987-2*, A0552) Heinemann.

— File on Hare. (Methuen Writer-Files Ser.). 87p. (C). 1988. pap. 9.95 (*0-413-15620-6*, A0095, Pub. by Methuen UK) Heinemann.

Page, Malcolm & Trussler, Simon, eds. File on Stoppard. (Methuen Writer-Files Ser.). 96p. 1988. pap. 9.95 (*0-413-57280-3*, A0103, Pub. by Methuen UK) Heinemann.

Page, Malcolm, jt. ed. see Trussler, Simon.

***Page, Margot.** Little Rivers: Tales of a Woman Angler. (Illus.). 144p. Date not set. 16.95 (*1-55821-367-8*) Lyons & Burford.

Page, Marian. Furniture Designed by Architects. (Illus.). 224p. 1983. pap. 24.95 (*0-8230-7181-2*, Whitney Lib) Watsn-Guptill.

Page, Marion R. & Symonds, David. Ancestors of Charles A. Stymus & His Wife Ella C. Smith: Orleans County New York, Back to New Jersey, New England, 1620-1989. LC 89-61922. (Illus.). 104p. 1989. 20.00 (*0-9623355-0-9*) M R Page.

Page, Martyn, jt. auth. see Bailey, John.

Page, Mary & Stearn, William T. Culinary Herbs. (Wisley Handbooks: The Royal Horticultural Society Ser.). (Illus.). 64p. 1992. pap. 5.95 (*0-304-32031-5*, Pub. by Cassell UK) Sterling.

Page, Melvin. Your Body Is Your Best Doctor. Orig. Title: Health Versus Disease. 236p. 1991. reprint ed. pap. 5.95 (*0-87983-540-0*) Keats.

Page, Melvin E. Chiwaya War. (History & Warfare Ser.). 1929. text ed. 39.95 (*0-8133-0735-X*) Westview.

Page, Melvin E., ed. Africa & the First World War. LC 86-29831. 270p. 1987. text ed. 45.00 (*0-312-00411-7*) St Martin.

Page, Michael. The Power of Ch'i: An Introduction to Chinese Mysticism & Philosophy. 1994. reprint ed. pap. 10.00 (*1-85538-363-2*, Pub. by Aquarian Pr UK) Thorsons SF.

Page, Michael & Ingpen, Robert. Encyclopedia of Things That Never Were. 240p. 1987. pap. 25.00 (*0-670-81607-8*, Viking Studio) Studio Bks.

— Worldly Dogs. 1988. 16.95 (*0-85091-324-1*, Pub. by Lothian Pub AT) Intl Spec Bk.

Page, Monte M., ed. see Nebraska Symposium on Motivation Staff.

Page, Myra. Daughter of the Hills: A Woman's Part in the Coal Miners' Struggles. LC 86-9866. (Novels of the Thirties Ser.). 304p. 1983. reprint ed. pap. 8.95 (*0-935312-59-5*) Feminist Pr.

— Moscow Yankee. LC 95-2992. (Radical Novel Reconsidered Ser.). 1995. pap. write for info. (*0-252-06499-2*) U of Ill Pr.

Page, N. S., jt. auth. see Webster, G. C.

Page, Neil, intro. & pref. Dynamic Loading in Manufacturing & Service. (National Conference Publication Ser.: No. 93-1). (Illus.). 254p. (Orig.). 1993. pap. 96.00 (*0-85825-571-5*, Pub. by Inst Engrs Aust-EA Bks AT) Accents Pubns.

***Page, Nick.** Sing & Shine On! The Classroom Teacher's Guide to Multicultural Song Leading. LC 95-12279. (Illus.). 1995. pap. 19.95 (*0-435-08673-1*) Heinemann.

Page, Norman. Bleak House: A Novel of Connections. Lecker, Robert, ed. (Twayne's Masterwork Studies: No. 42). 1990. text ed. 21.95 (*0-8057-8082-3*, 455, Twayne); pap. 12.95 (*0-8057-8128-5*, Twayne) Macmillan.

— A Byron Chronology. 144p. 1988. text ed. 38.50 (*0-8161-8952-8*, Hall Reference) Macmillan.

— A Dickens Chronology. 144p. 1988. text ed. 38.50 (*0-8161-8949-8*, Hall Reference) Macmillan.

— A Dr. Johnson Chronology. 140p. 1990. text ed. 38.50 (*0-8161-9091-7*, Hall Reference) Macmillan.

— E. M. Forster. (Modern Novelists Ser.). 143p. 1993. text ed. 12.95 (*0-333-40695-8*, Pub. by Macm UK) St Martin.

— Muriel Spark. LC 89-36704. (Modern Novelists Ser.). 140p. 1990. text ed. 29.95 (*0-312-04039-3*) St Martin.

— An Oscar Wilde Chronology. (Author Chronologies Ser.). 128p. 1991. text ed. 39.95 (*0-8161-7298-6*, Hall Reference) Macmillan.

— Speech in the English Novel. rev. ed. LC 87-19718. 208p. (C). 1988. pap. 17.50 (*0-391-03563-0*) Humanities.

— Tennyson: An Illustrated Life. (Illus.). 192p. 1993. 30.00 (*1-56131-060-3*) New Amsterdam Bks.

Page, Norman, ed. Dr. Johnson: Interviews & Recollections. 256p. 1986. 53.00 (*0-389-20628-8*, N8186) B&N Imports.

— Henry James: Interviews & Recollections. LC 83-16111. 240p. 1984. text ed. 29.95 (*0-312-36899-2*) St Martin.

— Nabokov: The Critical Heritage. (Critical Heritage Ser.). 400p. 1982. 69.50 (*0-7100-9223-7*, RKP) Routledge.

— Tennyson: Interviews & Recollections. (Interviews & Recollections Ser.). 218p. 1983. 44.00 (*0-389-20066-2*, N6836) B&N Imports.

— Wilkie Collins: The Critical Heritage. (Critical Heritage Ser.). 1974. 69.50 (*0-7100-7843-9*, RKP) Routledge.

Page, Norman, ed. see Bishop, Edward L.

Page, Norman, ed. see Brown, Richard.

Page, Norman, ed. see Collins, Wilkie.

Page, Norman, ed. see Dickens, Charles.

Page, Norman, ed. see Hardy, Thomas.

Page, Norman, ed. see McEwan, Neil.

Page, Norman, ed. see Tennyson, Alfred Lord.

***Page, P., ed.** Organosulphur Chemistry: Synthetic Aspects. (Illus.). 288p. 1995. boxed 82.50 (*0-12-543560-6*) Acad Pr.

Page, P. K. A Flask of Sea Water. (Illus.). 34p. (J). (gr. 2 up). 1989. bds. 17.00 (*0-19-540704-0*) OUP.

Page, Parker. Getting Along: A Set of Fun-Filled Stories, Songs, & Activities to Help Children Work & Play Together. LC 88-71899. (Illus.). 64p. (Orig.). (J). (ps-5). 1989. 13.95 (*0-929831-00-4*) Childrens TV Resource.

Page, Parker, et al. Getting Along Complete Kit. (J). (gr. k-4). 1991. 114.95 (*0-88671-407-9*, 4670) Am Guidance.

— Getting Along Student Activities: Level 1. (Orig.). (J). (gr. k-1). 1991. pap. 2.70 (*0-88671-409-5*, 4672) Am Guidance.

— Getting Along Student Activities: Level 2. (Orig.). (J). (gr. 2-4). 1991. pap. 2.95 (*0-88671-410-9*, 4676) Am Guidance.

— Getting Along Teachers Guide. (Orig.). 1991. pap. 10.95 (*0-88671-408-7*, 4671) Am Guidance.

Page, Patricia N. All God's People Are Ministers: Equipping Church Members for Ministry. LC 93-19835. 112p. 1993. pap. 9.99 (*0-8066-2643-7*, 9-2643) Augsburg Fortress.

Page, Patrick & Goshman, Albert. Magic by Gosh: The Life Times of Albert Goshman. Diamond, Kathy, ed. LC 85-90956. 160p. 1985. 49.95 (*0-318-19317-5*) Magic By Gosh.

Page, Penny B. Children of Alcoholics: A Sourcebook. LC 91-19611. 270p. 1991. 35.00 (*0-8240-3045-1*, 461) Garland.

Page, Priscilla. A Mallorcan Affair. large type ed. (Linford Romance Library). 256p. 1993. pap. 14.95 (*0-7089-7472-4*, Linford) Ulverscroft.

Page, R. Good News for Landlords & Tenants. (Illus.). 184p. (Orig.). 1982. pap. 12.95 (*0-9609672-0-6*) Jeanies Classics.

— Man & Machines. 1975. pap. 3.55 (*0-08-016889-2*, Pergamon Pr) Elsevier.

Page, R. C. & Schroeder, H. E. Periodontitis in Man & Other Animals. (Illus.). x, 330p. 1982. 119.25 (*3-8055-2479-X*) S Karger.

Page, R. I. Matthew Parker & His Books: Sandars Lectures in Bibliography Delivered on 14, 16, & 18 May 1990 at the University of Cambridge. LC 93-1097. (C). 1993. 40.00 (*1-879288-20-6*) Medieval Inst.

— Norse Myths. (Legendary Past Ser.). (Illus.). 80p. 1991. pap. 9.95 (*0-292-75546-5*) U of Tex Pr.

— Runes & Runic Inscriptions: Collected Essays on Anglo-Saxon & Viking Runes. (Illus.). 352p. 1995. text ed. 71.00 (*0-85115-387-9*) Boydell & Brewer.

Page, Ralph. An Elegant Collection of Contras & Squares. LC 84-10687. (Orig.). 1984. pap. 5.00 (*0-915213-00-1*) L Shaw Found.

— Heritage Dances of Early America. 64p. 1976. pap. 6.00 (*0-915213-02-8*) L Shaw Found.

Page, Randy & Page, Tana. Fostering Emotional Well-Being in The Classroom. (Health Science Ser.). 350p. (C). 1993. pap. text ed. 31.25 (*0-86720-753-1*) Jones & Bartlett.

Page, Randy, et al. Basic Epidemilgcl Method & Biostat. (Life Science Ser.). 350p. (C). 1994. pap. text ed. 35.00 (*0-86720-869-4*) Jones & Bartlett.

Page, Reba. Lower-Track Classrooms: A Curricular & Cultural Perspective. 288p. (C). 1991. text ed. 47.95 (*0-8077-3093-9*); pap. text ed. 22.95 (*0-8077-3092-0*) Tchrs Coll.

Page, Reba & Valli, Linda, eds. Curriculum Differentiation: Interpretive Studies in U. S. Secondary Schools. LC 90-31585. (SUNY Series, Frontiers in Education). 261p. (C). 1990. text ed. 64.50 (*0-7914-0469-2*); pap. 21.95 (*0-7914-0470-6*) State U NY Pr.

Page, Rex L., jt. auth. see Mueller, Robert A.

Page, Rex L., et al. FORTRAN '77 for Humans. 3rd ed. LC 85-20318. (Illus.). 462p. (C). 1986. pap. text ed. 48.00 (*0-314-93404-9*) West Pub.

Page, Richard C. Page: Genealogy of the Page Family in Virginia, Also a Condensed Account of the Nelson, Walker, Pendleton & Randolph Families with References to Other Distinguished Families in Virginia. 2nd ed. (Illus.). 275p. 1993. reprint ed. lib. bdg. 55.00 (*0-8328-3092-5*); reprint ed. pap. 45.00 (*0-8328-3093-3*) Higginson Bk Co.

Page, Richard C. & Berkow, Daniel N. Creating Contact, Choosing Relationship: The Dynamics of Unstructured Group Therapy. LC 93-48625. (Social & Behavioral Science Ser.). 360p. 1994. 34.95 (*1-55542-654-9*) Jossey-Bass.

Page, Robert, jt. auth. see Deakin, Nicholas.

Page, Robert, jt. ed. see Ferris, John.

Page, Robert E., III. Page, Carolina Pages: A Compilation of Genealogical Information on Page Families in the Carolinas Beginning in 1521 to Present Time. (Illus.). 293p. 1992. lib. bdg. 55.00 (*0-8328-2700-2*); pap. 45.00 (*0-8328-2701-0*) Higginson Bk Co.

Page, Robert G., ed. see Conference on the Optimal Preparation for the Study of Medicine, (1967: University of Chicago).

Page, Robert M. The Origin of Radar. LC 78-25844. (Illus.). 196p. 1979. reprint ed. text ed. 38.50 (*0-313-20781-X*, PAOR, Greenwood Pr) Greenwood.

Page, Roberta. Horace Morris. (J). (gr. 4 up). 1992. 7.95 (*0-533-09733-9*) Vantage.

Page, Robin. Cooking the Country Way. 1993. pap. 21.00 (*1-85183-061-8*, Silent Bks) St Mut.

— Gardening the Country Way. (Illus.). 64p. (C). 1989. 65.00 (*1-85183-030-8*, Silent Bks) St Mut.

— Mother Goose Sticker Book. (Illus.). 28p. (J). (ps-3). 1995. 12.95 (*0-395-71542-3*) Ticknor & Flds Bks Yng Read.

Page, Roland. How to Be Prepared for Any Crisis. 69p. 1974. pap. 3.95 (*0-89036-033-2*) Hawkes Pub Inc.

Page, Rosewell. Thomas Nelson Page: A Memoir of a Virginia Gentleman, by His Brother. (BCL1-PS American Literature Ser.). 210p. 1992. reprint ed. lib. bdg. 79.00 (*0-7812-6916-4*) Rprt Serv.

Page, Russell. The Education of a Gardener. (Illus.). 384p. 1994. pap. 15.00 (*0-00-271374-8*, Pub. by HarpC UK) HarpC.

Page, Ruth. Ambiguity & the Presence of God. 240p. (C). 1985. pap. text ed. 19.95 (*0-334-00022-X*, SCM Pr) TPI PA.

— Incarnation of Freedom & Love. LC 92-40520. 224p. (C). 1993. reprint ed. pap. 15.95 (*0-8298-0949-X*) Pilgrim OH.

***Page, Sheila.** How Developing Countries Trade: The Institutional Constraints. 288p. (Orig.). 1994. 69.95 (*0-415-11777-1*, B4572); pap. 22.95 (*0-415-11778-X*, B4576) Routledge.

— Trade, Finance & Developing Countries: Strategies & Constraints in the 1990s. 426p. (C). 1989. lib. bdg. 76.50 (*0-389-20890-6*, N 8446) B&N Imports.

Page, Sheila, ed. Monetary Policy in Developing Countries. LC 92-24740. (Illus.). 368p. 1992. 59.95 (*0-415-08822-4*, A9938) Routledge.

Page, Sheila, jt. auth. see Davenport, Michael.

Page, Stanley, jt. auth. see Faith, Carl.

Page, Stanley W. The Geopolitics of Leninism. (East European Monographs: No. 97). 238p. 1982. text ed. 42.00 (*0-914710-91-5*) East Eur Quarterly.

— Lenin: Dedicated Marxist or Revolutionary Pragmatist. LC 77-76608. (Problems in Civilization Ser.). 1977. pap. text ed. write for info. (*0-88273-402-4*) Forum Pr IL.

Page, Stephanie. Trying Drug Cases in Massachusetts. LC 92-62586. 610p. 1992. ring bd. 75.00 (*0-944490-43-3*) Mass CLE.

***Page, Stephen.** Introductory Marketing. 288p. (C). 1994. 75.00x (*0-7487-1783-8*, Pub. by S Thornes Pubs UK) St Mut.

— The Soviet Union & the Yemens. LC 84-512. 254p. 1985. text ed. 55.00 (*0-275-90153-X*, C0153, Praeger Pubs) Greenwood.

— Urban Tourism. LC 94-28174. (Topics in Tourism Ser.). 224p. 1995. pap. 15.95 (*0-415-11218-4*, B4858) Routledge.

Page, Stephen J. Transport for Tourism. LC 93-39536. (Topics in Tourism Ser.). 176p. (Orig.). 1994. pap. 15.95 (*0-415-10238-3*, B4436, Routledge NY) Routledge.

***Page, Steve & Smillie, Joseph.** Orchard Almanac: A Seasonal Guide to Healthy Fruit Trees. 3rd ed. (Illus.). 158p. (Orig.). 1995. pap. 16.95 (*0-932857-15-9*) Ag Access.

Page, Steve & Wosket, Val. Supervising the Counsellor: A Cyclical Model. LC 94-8492. (Illus.). 256p. 1995. 59.95x (*0-415-10212-X*, B4074); pap. 19.95 (*0-415-10213-8*, B4078) Routledge.

Page, Susan. If Im So Wonderful Why Am I Still Single? 1990. mass mkt. 5.99 (*0-553-28299-9*) Bantam.

— If I'm So Wonderful, Why Am I Still Single? Ten Strategies That Will Change Your Love Life Forever. braille ed. 539p. 1992. Braille. vinyl bd. 43.12 (*1-56956-263-6*, BR7460) W A T Braille.

— Now That I'm Married, Why Isn't Everthing Perfect? The Eight Essential Traits of Couples Who Thrive. 1994. 19.95 (*0-316-68837-1*) Little.

— Now That I'm Married, Why Isn't Everything Perfect? 1995. pap. 5.99 (*0-440-22071-8*) Dell.

Page, Susanne & Page, Jake. Hopi. LC 94-4489. 1994. reprint ed. write for info. (*0-8109-8127-0*) Abrams.

— Navajo. LC 95-5579. 1995. write for info. (*0-8109-3679-8*) Abrams.

***Page, Sydney H.** Powers of Evil: A Biblical Study of Satan & Demons. 304p. (Orig.). 1995. pap. 19.99 (*0-8010-7137-2*) Baker Bk.

Page, Talbot. Conservation & Economic Efficiency: An Approach to Materials Policy. LC 76-22846. 266p. 1977. pap. 14.95 (*0-8018-1951-2*) Resources Future.

Page, Tana, jt. auth. see Page, Randy.

Page, Terry, ed. Business & Technology. 154p. (C). 1987. 75.00 (*1-85184-027-3*) St Mut.

Page, Thomas. Sigmet Active: A Novel. LC 78-53307. 1978. write for info. (*0-8129-0774-3*, Times Bks) Random.

Page, Thomas N. Bred in the Bone. LC 77-86151. (Short Story Index Reprint Ser.). 1977. 20.95 (*0-8369-3057-6*) Ayer.

— The Burial of the Guns. 1972. reprint ed. 24.25 (*0-8422-8103-7*) Irvington.

— Burial of the Guns. (C). 1986. reprint ed. pap. text ed. 7.95 (*0-8290-1905-7*) Irvington.

— Elsket, & Other Stories. LC 73-85693. (Short Story Index Reprint Ser.). 1977. 19.95 (*0-8369-3036-3*) Ayer.

— In Ole Virginia: Or, Marse Chan & Other Stories. LC 68-23723. (Americans in Fiction Ser.). 230p. reprint ed. lib. bdg. 19.00 (*0-8398-1550-6*) Irvington.

— In Ole Virginia: Or, Marse Chan & Other Stories. (Americans in Fiction Ser.). 230p. (C). 1986. reprint ed. pap. text ed. 7.95 (*0-8290-1864-6*) Irvington.

— In Ole Virginia: Or, Marse Chan & Other Stories. (Southern Classics Ser.). 250p. (C). 1991. reprint ed. pap. 8.95 (*1-879941-04-X*) J S Sanders.

— The Novels, Stories, Sketches & Poems of Thomas Nelson Page, 18 vols., Set. (BCL1-PS American Literature Ser.). 1992. reprint ed. lib. bdg. 1,350.00 (*0-7812-6821-4*); reprint ed. pap. text ed. 990.00 (*0-685-51403-X*) Rprt Serv.

— Old South: Essays Social & Political. LC 69-14026. (Illus.). 269p. 1970. reprint ed. text ed. 38.50 (*0-8371-1977-4*, PAO&, Negro U Pr) Greenwood.

— Old South: Essays Social & Political. LC 68-24992. (American History & Americana Ser.: No. 47). 1969. reprint ed. lib. bdg. 49.95 (*0-8383-0226-2*) M S G Haskell Hse.

— The Old South: Essays Social & Political. (BCL1 - United States Local History Ser.). 344p. 1991. reprint ed. text ed. 89.00 (*0-7812-6284-4*) Rprt Serv.

— On Newfound River. LC 78-110427. reprint ed. 39.50 (*0-404-04858-7*) AMS Pr.

— On Newfound River. (BCL1-PS American Literature Ser.). 240p. 1992. reprint ed. lib. bdg. 79.00 (*0-7812-6823-0*) Rprt Serv.

— Pastime Stories. LC 76-75784. (Short Story Index Reprint Ser.). (Illus.). 1977. 19.95 (*0-8369-3009-6*) Ayer.

— Red Rock. Carpenter, Lucas, ed. 1991. 16.95 (*0-8084-0439-3*) NCUP.

— Red Rock, a Chronicle of Reconstruction. LC 67-29275. (Americans in Fiction Ser.). (Illus.). 599p. reprint ed. lib. bdg. 22.00 (*0-8398-1551-4*) Irvington.

— Red Rock, a Chronicle of Reconstruction. (Americans in Fiction Ser.). (Illus.). 599p. 1986. reprint ed. pap. text ed. 9.95 (*0-8290-1920-0*) Irvington.

— Social Life in Old Virginia Before the War. (Illus.). 80p. 1994. pap. 9.95 (*0-939218-02-X*) Chapman Billies.

— Social Life in Old Virginia Before the War. LC 73-130560. (Select Bibliographies Reprint Ser.). (Illus.). 1977. reprint ed. 13.95 (*0-8369-5533-1*) Ayer.

Page, Thomas N., jt. auth. see Gordon, A. C.

Page, Thomas N., et al. Stories of the South. LC 74-110217. (Short Story Index Reprint Ser.). 1977. 24.95 (*0-8369-3369-9*) Ayer.

Page, Thomas Nelson. In Ole Virginia: or Marse Chan & Other Stories. (BCL1-PS American Literature Ser.). 230p. 1992. reprint ed. lib. bdg. 79.00 (*0-7812-6822-2*) Rprt Serv.

Page, Thomas W. Making Tariff in the United States. (Brookings Institution Reprint Ser.). reprint ed. lib. bdg. 37.50 (*0-685-70237-5*) Irvington.

***Page, Tim.** Mid-Term Report. LC 94-60653. (Illus.). 112p. 1995. pap. 29.95 (*0-500-27795-8*) Thames Hudson.

— Music from the Road: Views & Reviews, 1978-1992. 256p. 1992. 24.95 (*0-19-507315-0*) OUP.

— Tim Page's Nam. LC 94-61398. (Illus.). 120p. 1995. pap. 19.95 (*0-500-27280-8*) Thames Hudson.

Page, Tim, ed. Glenn Gould Reader. LC 90-50141. 496p. 1990. pap. 15.95 (*0-679-73135-0*, Vin) Random.

Page, Tim, jt. auth. see Page, Evelyn.

Page, Tim, ed. see Powell, Dawn.

Page, Vicki. Jo Lane: Store Nurse. large type ed. LC 93-9367. 1993. 18.95 (*0-7927-1548-9*, Curley Lrg Print) Chivers N Amer.

— Love & Nurse Jeni. large type ed. 1992. pap. 16.95 (*0-7927-1159-9*, Atlantic Lrg Print) Chivers N Amer.

Page, Victor W. Chevy Six, the Early Years: Construction, Operation, Service for the Restorer. LC 76-26324. (Illus.). 912p. 1979. reprint ed. 28.95 (*0-911160-40-X*) Post Group.

Page, Virginia, ed. see Garnsey, Wayne H.

Page, W. R. Government & Politics at Work in Britain. LC 73-92007. (Illus.). 219p. reprint ed. pap. 62.50 (*0-317-08740-1*, 2010164) Bks Demand.

Page, Walter H. Rebuilding of Old Commonwealths. LC 79-125175. reprint ed. 34.50 (*0-404-04859-5*) AMS Pr.

— The Rebuilding of Old Commonwealths: Being Essays Towards the Training of the Forgotten Man in the Southern States. (BCL1 - United States Local History Ser.). 153p. 1991. reprint ed. text ed. 69.00 (*0-7812-6293-3*) Rprt Serv.

Page, Warren, ed. American Perspectives on the Fifth International Congress on Mathematical Education. 134p. 1984. pap. 5.00 (*0-88385-055-9*, NTE-05) Math Assn.

— Two-Year College Mathematics Readings. LC 80-81044. 312p. (C). 1980. pap. 15.00 (*0-88385-435-X*) Math Assn.

Page, Wayne E. Ten Steps to Dynamic Presentations. 256p. (C). 1991. spiral bd. 12.95 (*0-8403-6629-9*) Kendall-Hunt.

Page, Wayne E., jt. auth. see Levin, Alan M.

Page, William. Play Is Work. 40p. (Orig.). 1992. pap. text ed. 6.00 (0-935493-94-8) Programs Educ.

Page, William, ed. Commerce & Industry: A Historical View of the Economic Conditions of the British Empire 1815-1914, 2 Vols in One. LC 67-19709. (Reprints of Economic Classics Ser.). 1968. reprint ed. 65.00 (0-678-00404-8) Kelley.

— The Future of Politics. LC 82-25183. 229p. 1983. text ed. 29.95 (0-312-31481-7) St Martin.

— Letters of Denization & Acts of Naturalization for Aliens in England, 1509-1603. Bd. with Pt. 1. Registers of the French Church. (Huguenot Society of London Publications Ser.: Vols. 8 & 9). 1969. reprint ed. (0-8115-1646-6) Periodicals Srv.

Page, William F. The Health of Former Prisoners of War: Results from the Medical Examination Survey of Former POWs of World War II & the Korean Conflict. 176p. (C). 1992. pap. text ed. 31.00 (0-309-04791-9) Natl Acad Pr.

Page, William F., ed. Epidemiology in Military & Veteran Populations: Proceedings of the Second Biennial Conference. 112p. 1991. 19.00 (0-309-04548-7) Natl Acad Pr.

Page, Winni R. Panning for Pleasure: An Alaska Cookbook. Andrews et al, eds. (Illus.). 262p. 1991. reprint ed. write for info. (0-9621777-0-9) W R Page.

Page-Wood, Ann & Davies, Jill. Irritable Bowel Syndrome Special Diet Cookbook. (Illus.). 1992. pap. 10.95 (0-7225-2344-0) Thorsons SF.

Page Works Staff, ed. see Fowler, Jack.

***Pagel, B. G. & Thomson, W. T.** Insecticide, Herbicide, Fungicide Quick Guide, 1995. rev. ed. 198p. 1994. pap. 18.50 (0-614-07075-9) Thomson Pubns.

Pagel, David. Los Angeles: Not Paintings? 41p. (Orig.). 1993. write for info. (0-318-71699-2) San Barb CAF.

Pagel, Horst, et al, eds. Pathophysiology & Pharmacology of Erythropoietin. LC 92-2312. (Illus.). xv, 328p. 1992. 79.00 (0-387-54777-0) Spr-Verlag.

Pagel, J. L. Biographisches Lexikon hervorragender Aerzte des 19, Jahrhunderts: Mit einer historischen Einleitung. (Illus.). xxxii, 998p. 1989. reprint ed. 233.75 (3-8055-4817-6) S Karger.

Pagel, Mark D., jt. auth. see Harvey, Paul H.

Pagel, Mary E. Computer Tutor 1.0: Your Complete Guide to Self Computer Training. (Illus.). 106p. (Orig.). (C). 1989. teacher ed write for info. (0-318-64482-7); pap. text ed. 14.95 (0-9621823-0-3) Comput Tutor.

Pagel, Maurice & Leroy, Jacques L., eds. Source, Transport & Deposition of Metals: Proceedings of the 25 Years SGA Anniversary Meeting, Nancy, 30 August-3 September 1991. (Illus.). 850p. 1991. text ed. 140.00 (90-5410-020-6, Pub. by A A Balkema NE) Ashgate Pub Co.

Pagel, Ulrich, jt. ed. see Skorpski, Tadeusz.

Pagel, Ulrich, jt. ed. see Skorupski, Tadeusz.

Pagel, W. New Light on William Harvey. (Illus.). 200p. 1975. 72.00 (3-8055-2209-6) S Karger.

— Paracelsus. 2nd ed. (Illus.). xii, 400p. 1982. 111.25 (3-8055-3518-X) S Karger.

— The Smiling Spleen. (Illus.). x, 214p. 1984. 122.50 (3-8055-3707-7) S Karger.

Pagel, Walter. From Paracelsus to Van Helmont: Studies in Renaissance Medicine & Science. Winder, Marianne, ed. (Collected Studies: No. CS235). (Illus.). 350p. (C). 1986. reprint ed. text ed. 95.00 (0-86078-183-6, Pub. by Variorum UK) Ashgate Pub Co.

— Joan Baptista Van Helmont: Reformer of Science & Medicine. LC 81-24193. (Cambridge Monographs on the History of Medicine). (Illus.). 192p. 1982. 64.95 (0-521-24807-8) Cambridge U Pr.

— Religion & Neoplatonism in Renaissance Medicine. Winder, Marianne, ed. (Collected Studies: No. CS226). (Illus.). 346p. (C). 1985. reprint ed. text ed. 95.00 (0-86078-174-7, Pub. by Variorum UK) Ashgate Pub Co.

Pagel, Walter, jt. ed. see Needham, Joseph.

Pageler, Elaine. Numero Uno Gang Mysteries, 5 novels, Set. (Illus.). 240p. (Orig.). (J). (gr. 3-9). 1988. pap. 17.00 (0-87879-550-2) High Noon Bks.

— The Riddle Street Mystery Series: Wrong Robber Mystery, Market Stake-Out Mystery, Haunted Apartment House Mystery, Book Party Mystery, Radio Station Mystery, 5 bks., Set. Kratoville, B. L., ed. (Illus.). 48p. (J). (gr. 1 up). 1994. pap. text ed. 17.00 (0-87879-983-4) Acad Therapy.

— Runaway Magic. Kratoville, Betty L., ed. (Meridian Bks.). (Illus.). 64p. (J). (gr. 3-9). 1989. lib. bdg. 4.95 (0-87879-652-5) High Noon Bks.

Pagell, Ruth A. & Halperin, Michael. International Business Information: How to Find It, How to Use It. (Illus.). 384p. 1994. 74.95 (0-89774-736-4) Oryx Pr.

Pagelow, Mildred D. Family Violence. LC 84-8244. 608p. 1984. text ed. 69.50 (0-275-91239-6, C1239, Praeger Pubs); pap. text ed. 22.95 (0-275-91623-5, B1623, Praeger Pubs) Greenwood.

Pagels, Elaine. Adam, Eve & the Serpent. LC 87-43227. 224p. 1988. 17.95 (0-394-52140-4) Random.

— Adam, Eve & the Serpent. 1989. pap. 9.00 (0-679-72232-7, Vin) Random.

— The Gnostic Gospels. LC 89-40159. 224p. 1989. pap. 9.00 (0-679-72453-2, Vin) Random.

— Gnostic Gospels. 1980. pap. 5.95 (0-394-74043-2) Random.

— Origins of Satan: The New Testament Origins of Christianity's Demonization of Jews, Pagans & Heretics. 1995. pap. 23.00 (0-679-40140-7) Random.

Pagels, Elaine H. The Gnostic Paul: Gnostic Exegesis of the Pauline Letters. LC 92-7932. 192p. 1992. pap. 14.95 (1-56338-039-0) TPI PA.

— The Johannine Gospel in Gnostic Exegesis: Heracleon's Commentary on John. 128p. 1972. pap. 15.95 (1-55540-334-4, 06-00-17) Scholars Pr GA.

Pagels, Heinz R. Cosmic Code. 1984. mass mkt. 5.95 (0-553-24625-9) Bantam.

Pagels, Heinz R., pref. Computer Culture: The Scientific, Intellectual, & Social Impact of the Computer. (Annals Ser.: Vol. 426). 228p. 1984. lib. bdg. 66.00 (0-89766-244-X); pap. 66.00 (0-89766-245-8) NY Acad Sci.

Pagels, Jurgen. Character Dance. LC 82-49013. (Illus.). 208p. 1984. 25.00 (0-253-31337-6) Ind U Pr.

Pagen, Dennis. Hang Gliding Flying Skills. (Illus.). 173p. (Orig.). 1989. pap. 9.95 (0-936310-01-4, Sport Aviation Pubns) Black Mntn.

— Hang Gliding Training Manual: Learning Hang Gliding Skills for Beginner to Intermediate Pilots. (Illus.). 370p. 1995. pap. 29.95 (0-936310-12-X, Sport Aviation Pubns) Black Mntn.

— Paragliding Flight: Walking on Air. (Illus.). 200p. 1990. 19.95 (0-936310-09-X, Sport Aviation Pubns) Black Mntn.

— Performance Flying: Hang Gliding Techniques for Intermediate & Advanced Pilots. (Illus.). 350p. (Orig.). 1993. pap. 29.95 (0-936310-11-1, Sport Aviation Pubns) Black Mntn.

— Powered Ultralight Flying. (Illus.). 190p. (Orig.). 1983. pap. 11.95 (0-936310-06-5, Sport Aviation Pubns) Black Mntn.

— Powered Ultralight Training Course. rev. ed. (Illus.). 110p. 1991. pap. 9.95 (0-936310-04-9, Sport Aviation Pubns) Black Mntn.

— Understanding the Sky. (Illus.). 290p. 1992. 19.95 (0-936310-10-3, Sport Aviation Pubns) Black Mntn.

Pagen, Frank G. Formal Specifications of Programming Language: A Panoramic Primer. (Illus.). 256p. 1981. text ed. 57.00 (0-13-329052-2) P-H.

Pagenkopf, Gordon K. Introduction to Natural Water Chemistry. LC 78-16089. (Environmental Science & Technology Ser.: No. 3). 286p. reprint ed. pap. 81.60 (0-7837-0105-5, 2040383) Bks Demand.

***Pager, Sean.** Hawaii: Off the Beaten Path: A Guide to Unique Places. 2nd ed. LC 94-37560. (Illus.). 288p. 1995. 11.95 (1-56440-503-6) Globe Pequot.

Pages, Alain, jt. ed. see Thomson, Clive.

***Pages, Beatriz.** Can Cuba Survive? An Interview with Fidel Castro. 105p. 1993. pap. 9.95 (1-875284-58-3, Pub. by Ocean Pr AT) Talman.

Pages, J. C., et al, eds. Meeting the Challenge: Informatics & Medical Education. 366p. 1983. 61.75 (0-444-86728-7, I-411-83, North Holland) Elsevier.

Paget, Becky. The Belle of Nauvoo. Date not set. pap. 8.95 (1-55503-690-2, 01111698) Covenant Comms.

— Romancing the Nephites. LC 92-70860. 1993. pap. 7.95 (1-55503-552-3, 29004780) Covenant Comms.

Paget, Derek. True Stories? Documentary Drama on Radio, Screen & Stage. (Cultural Politics Ser.). 208p. 1990. text ed. 49.95 (0-7190-2962-7, Pub. by Manchester Univ Pr UK); text ed. 16.95 (0-7190-2963-5, Pub. by Manchester Univ Pr UK) St Martin.

Paget, Francis E. St. Antholin's; or, Old Churches & New: A Tale for the Times, 1841. Wolff, Robert L., ed. Bd. with Milford Malvoisin; or, Pews & Pew-Holders, 1842. LC 75-469. LC 75-469. (Victorian Fiction Ser.). 1975. Set lib. bdg. 73.00 (0-8240-1547-9) Garland.

Paget, George. The Light Cavalry Brigade in the Crimea. 1977. reprint ed. 21.00 (0-7158-1046-4) Charles River Bks.

***Paget, James C.** The Epistle of Barnabas. Outlook & Background. (WissUNT Zum Neuen Testament Ser.). 340p. (Orig.). 1994. pap. text ed. 51.50 (3-16-146161-4, Pub. by J C B Mohr GW) Coronet Bks.

Paget, John. An Answer to the Unjust Complaints of W. Best: Also an Answer to Mr. John Davenport. LC 76-57403. (English Experience Ser.: No. 819). 1977. reprint ed. lib. bdg. 20.00 (90-221-0819-8) Walter J Johnson.

— Hungary & Transylvania: With Remarks on Their Social, Political & Economical Condition. LC 79-135827. (Eastern Europe Collection Ser.). 1971. reprint ed. 65.95 (0-405-02769-9) Ayer.

— Judicial Puzzles, Gathered from the State Trials. (Legal Recreations Ser.: Vol. 3). 155p. 1979. reprint ed. lib. bdg. 15.00 (0-8377-1003-0) Rothman.

— Paradoxes & Puzzles, Historical, Judicial & Literary. LC 75-30035. reprint ed. 57.50 (0-404-14037-8) AMS Pr.

Paget, Julian. Discovering London Ceremonial & Traditions. 1989. pap. 25.00 (0-85263-994-5, Pub. by Shire UK) St Mut.

Paget, Marianne A. A Complex Sorrow: Reflections on Cancer & an Abbreviated Life. DeVault, Marjorie L., ed. LC 92-49403. (Illus.). 176p. 1993. 29.95 (1-56639-041-9) Temple U Pr.

— Complex Sorrow: Reflections on Cancer & an Abbreviated Life. DeVault, Marjorie L., ed. LC 92-49403. (Illus.). 176p. (C). 1994. pap. 16.95 (1-56639-192-X) Temple U Pr.

— The Unity of Mistakes: A Phenomenological Interpretation of Medical Work. LC 87-26716. 224p. (C). 1988. 32.95 (0-87722-533-8) Temple U Pr.

Paget, R. L. Cap & Gown: Third Series. LC 78-74825. (Granger Poetry Library). 1979. reprint ed. 24.50 (0-89609-144-9) Roth Pub Inc.

Paget, Richard. Beyond Death's Door. LC 78-14485. 1979. 22.95 (0-87949-113-2) Ashley Bks.

Paget, Richard A. Human Speech: Some Observations, Experiments, & Conclusions As to the Origin, Purpose, & Possible Improvement of Human Speech. LC 75-41208. reprint ed. 27.50 (0-404-14692-9) AMS Pr.

Paget, Stephen. I Have Reason to Believe. LC 68-16964. (Essay Index Reprint Ser.). 1977. reprint ed. 14.95 (0-8369-0763-9) Ayer.

— I Sometimes Think. LC 67-26769. (Essay Index Reprint Ser.). 1977. 18.95 (0-8369-0764-7) Ayer.

— I Wonder: Essays for the Young People. LC 68-54365. (Essay Index Reprint Ser.). (YA). (gr. 7 up). 1977. reprint ed. 17.95 (0-8369-0765-5) Ayer.

Paget, Stephen & Fields, Theodore. Rheumatic Disorders. 372p. 1992. text ed. 45.00 (0-9626521-4-8, Andover Med Pubs) Buttrwrth-Heinemann.

Paget, Stephen, ed. see Cornell University Medical College Staff.

Paget-Thomlinson, Edward. The Illustrated History of Canal & River Navigations. (Illus.). 450p. 1993. 35.00 (1-85075-276-1, Pub. by Sheffield Acad UK); pap. 19.95 (1-85075-277-X, Pub. by Sheffield Acad UK) CUP Services.

Paget-Tomlinson, Edward. The Railway Carriers. 192p. (C). 1989. 60.00 (0-86138-082-7, Pub. by T Dalton UK) St Mut.

Paget, Violet. Baldwin: Being Dialogues on Views & Aspirations. LC 72-291. (Essay Index Reprint Ser.). 1977. reprint ed. 23.95 (0-8369-2817-2) Ayer.

— For Maurice: Five Unlikely Stories. Reginald, R. & Menville, Douglas, eds. LC 76-1462. 1976. reprint ed. lib. bdg. 23.95 (0-405-08423-4) Ayer.

— Hauntings: Fantastic Stories. LC 75-37280. (Short Story Index Reprint Ser.). 1977. reprint ed. 19.95 (0-8369-4093-8) Ayer.

Paget-Wilkes, M. Poverty, Revolution & the Church. 142p. (Orig.). 1982. pap. text ed. 13.50 (0-85364-285-0) Attic Pr.

Pagis, Dan. Hebrew Poetry of the Middle Ages & the Renaissance. LC 90-23508. (Taubman Lectures in Jewish Studies: No. 2). 100p. 1991. 25.00 (0-520-06547-6) U CA Pr.

— Last Poems. Keller, tr. (QRL Poetry Book Ser.: Vol. XXXI). 20.00 (0-614-06444-9) Quarterly Rev.

— Last Poems. Keller, tr. (QRL Poetry Book Ser.: Vol. XXXI). pap. 10.00 (0-614-06445-7) Quarterly Rev.

Paglia, et al. Textbook of Medical Pathology. 692p. 1979. 60.00 (1-55664-193-1) Mosby Yr Bk.

Paglia, Camille. Sex, Art, & American Culture. LC 91-50933. 1992. pap. 13.00 (0-679-74101-1, Vin) Random.

— Sexual Personae: Art & Decadence from Nefertiti to Emily Dickinson. LC 91-50024. 736p. 1991. pap. 16.00 (0-679-73579-8, Vin) Random.

— Sexual Personae: Art & Decadence from Nefertiti to Emily Dickinson. LC 89-31659. 712p. (C). 1990. 40.00 (0-300-04396-1) Yale U Pr.

— Vamps & Tramps: New Essays. 1994. pap. 15.00 (0-679-75120-3, Vin) Random.

***Pagliari, Joseph L., Jr.** Handbook of Real Estate Portfolio Management. 1995. write for info. (1-55623-539-9) Irwin Prof Pubng.

Pagliari, Robert. Fourteen Steps to Dynamic Preaching. 96p. (Orig.). 1993. pap. 9.95 (0-89243-525-9) Liguori Pubns.

— Fourteen Steps to Dynamic Preaching Workbook. 62p. (Orig.). 1993. pap. text ed. 4.95 (0-89243-626-3) Liguori Pubns.

Pagliaro, Ann M., jt. ed. see Pagliaro, Louis A.

Pagliaro, Harold. Selfhood & Redemption in Blakes's Songs. LC 86-43162. (Illus.). 176p. 1987. 27.50 (0-271-00603-X) Pa St U Pr.

Pagliaro, James D. Mr. Pizza's Secrets of Homemade Pizza: A Complete Guide for Those Wishing to Make Their Own Pizza from Scratch. (Illus.). 30p. 1987. pap. 4.95 (0-9619740-0-1) Alligator Pr.

***Pagliaro, Louis A. & Pagliaro, Ann M., eds.** Problems in Pediatric Drug Therapy. 3rd ed. LC 94-37762. 1100p. 1995. text ed. 69.50 (0-914768-53-0) Drug Intell Pubns.

Pagliaro, Michael J. Everything You Should Know about Musical Instruments but Didn't Have Time to Learn. (Illus.). 134p. (Orig.). (C). 1992. pap. text ed. 17.95 (0-945864-49-3) Columbia Pacific U Pr.

— The Violin. (How Musical Instruments Work Ser.: Vol. I). (Illus.). 60p. (J). (gr. 4-8). 1993. student ed 6.95 (1-884417-00-0) Ardsley Pr.

Pagliaro, Penny, ed. I Like Poems & Poems Like Me. LC 76-50343. (Illus.). (J). (gr. 1-6). 1977. lib. bdg. 8.95 (0-916630-03-X) Pr Pacifica.

***Pagliassoti, Edward J., et al.** White Papers on Facility Topics Vol. I. (Illus.). 78p. (Orig.). 1994. pap. 25.00 (1-883176-01-8) Intl Facility Mgmt Assn.

Paglin, Max D., ed. A Legislative History of the Communications Act of 1934. (Illus.). 1008p. 1990. 98.00 (0-19-504915-2) OUP.

Paglin, Morton. Poverty & Transfers In-Kind: A Re-Evaluation of Poverty in the United States. LC 79-88586. (Publication Ser.: No. 219). 108p. 1980. pap. 2.78 (0-8179-7192-0) Hoover Inst Pr.

Paglino, Joseph R., jt. auth. see Corvasce, Mauro V.

Pagliore, Virginia. Oracles of Light. LC 84-61992. 96p. 1986. pap. 8.00 (0-918618-26-6) Pella Pub.

Pagliuca, William, ed. Perspectives on Grammaricalization. LC 94-14551. (Current Issues in Linguistic Theory Ser.: No. 109). 1994. lib. bdg. 79.00 (1-55619-563-X) Benjamins North Am.

Pagna, Tom & Best, Bob. Notre Dame's Era of Ara. (Illus.). 310p. 1994. reprint ed. pap. 12.95 (0-912083-74-3) Diamond Communications.

Pagni, Carlo A., jt. auth. see Cassinari, Valentino.

Pagni, Patrick J. & Grant, Cecile E., eds. Fire Safety Science: Proceedings of the August International Symposium. 1226p. 1986. 184.00 (0-89116-456-1) Hemisp Pub.

Pagni, Patrick J., jt. auth. see Levine, Robert S.

Pagnol, Marcel. Angele. pap. 9.95 (0-685-23894-6, F117230) Fr & Eur.

— Angele. 216p. (FRE.). 1976. pap. 10.95 (0-8288-9889-8, F117420) Fr & Eur.

— Cesar. 1956. 11.50 (0-685-23892-X) Fr & Eur.

— Cesar. 292p. (FRE.). 1976. 13.95 (0-8288-9890-1, F117430) Fr & Eur.

— Le Chateau de Ma Mere. 280p. (FRE.). 13.95 (0-8288-9897-9, F117481) Fr & Eur.

— Cigalon. 180p. 1978. 9.95 (0-686-54820-5) Fr & Eur.

— Confidences. (FRE.). 1990. pap. 13.95 (0-7859-3329-8, 2877060691) Fr & Eur.

— Critique des Critiques. (Coll. Litterature). 168p. (FRE.). 1987. pap. 19.95 (0-7859-1548-6, 2826308173) Fr & Eur.

— Discours sous la Coupole. 76p. (FRE.). 1961. pap. 10.95 (0-7859-5389-2) Fr & Eur.

— L' Eau des Collines, 2 tomes. Incl. Tome I. Jean de Florette. 19.95 (0-685-73273-8); Tome II. Manon des Sources. 19.95 (0-685-73274-6); write for info. (0-318-51988-7) Fr & Eur.

— Fabien: Theatre. 331p. (FRE.). 1976. 27.95 (0-7859-5559-3) Fr & Eur.

— Fanny. 283p. (FRE.). 1970. 13.95 (0-8288-9891-X, F117440) Fr & Eur.

— La Femme du Boulanger. 279p. (FRE.). 1974. 13.95 (0-8288-9892-8, F117450); pap. 4.95 (0-685-23893-8) Fr & Eur.

— La Fille du Puisatier. pap. 9.95 (0-685-37002-X) Fr & Eur.

— La Fille du Puisatier. (Illus.). 304p. (FRE.). 1975. pap. 13.95 (0-7859-0112-4, M3832) Fr & Eur.

— La Gloire de Mon Pere. (FRE.). 13.95 (0-8288-9896-0, F117480) Fr & Eur.

— Jazz. (Illus.). 296p. (FRE.). 1976. 10.95 (0-7859-0113-2, M3834) Fr & Eur.

— Jazz: Comedie Dramatique en 4 Actes. pap. 4.95 (0-685-37003-8) Fr & Eur.

— Jean de Florette. 320p. (FRE.). 1976. 13.95 (0-8288-9893-6, F117460) Fr & Eur.

— Jean de Florette. 318p. (FRE.). 1988. pap. 13.95 (0-7859-1668-7, 2877060543) Fr & Eur.

— Jofroi. 160p. (FRE.). 1990. pap. 13.95 (0-7859-1562-1, 2877060675) Fr & Eur.

— Judas. (Illus.). 258p. (FRE.). 1975. pap. 11.95 (0-7859-0114-0, M3836) Fr & Eur.

— Manon des Sources. 320p. (FRE.). 1976. 13.95 (0-8288-9894-4, F117461) Fr & Eur.

— Manon des Sources. 318p. (FRE.). 1988. pap. 13.95 (0-7859-1657-1, 2877060551) Fr & Eur.

— Marius. (Illus.). 297p. (FRE.). 1973. 13.95 (0-8288-9895-2, F117470) Fr & Eur.

— Le Masque de Fer. pap. 9.50 (0-685-37005-4) Fr & Eur.

— Les Merchands de Gloire: Piece en Cinq Actes. 291p. (FRE.). 1976. write for info. (0-7859-4879-1) Fr & Eur.

— Merlusse-Cigalon. (FRE.). 1974. 19.95 (0-7859-0115-9, M3838) Fr & Eur.

— Nais: Theatre. 160p. (FRE.). 1990. pap. 13.95 (0-7859-1561-3, 2877060659) Fr & Eur.

— Notes sur le Rire. 127p. (FRE.). 1987. pap. 13.95 (0-7859-1549-4, 2826308203) Fr & Eur.

— La Petite Fille aux Yeux Sombres. (FRE.). 1991. pap. 13.95 (0-7859-3330-1, 2877060713) Fr & Eur.

— Pirouettes. pap. 9.95 (0-685-37007-0) Fr & Eur.

— Pirouettes. (FRE.). 1991. pap. 13.95 (0-7859-3440-5) Fr & Eur.

— Le Premier Amour. 298p. (FRE.). 1978. write for info. (0-7859-4776-0) Fr & Eur.

— Priere aux Etoiles. 386p. (FRE.). 1978. 39.95 (0-7859-4775-2) Fr & Eur.

— Regain. 254p. (FRE.). 1973. 11.95 (0-8288-9750-6, 2877060632) Fr & Eur.

— Le Schpountz. pap. 9.95 (0-685-37008-9) Fr & Eur.

— Le Schprountz. (Illus.). 288p. (FRE.). 1976. 10.95 (0-7859-0119-1, M3842) Fr & Eur.

— Le Secret du Masque de Fer. (Illus.). 416p. (FRE.). 1978. 27.95 (0-7859-4880-5) Fr & Eur.

— Les Sermons de Marcel Pagnol. Calmels, ed. 12.50 (0-685-37009-7) Fr & Eur.

— Souvenirs d'Enfance, 3 tomes. Incl. Tome I. Gloire de Mon Pere. 14.95 (0-685-37010-0); Tome II. Chateau de Ma Mere. 15.50 (0-685-37011-9); Tome III. Temps des Secrets. 15.95 (0-685-37012-7); write for info. (0-318-52267-5) Fr & Eur.

— Souvenirs d'Enfance: Le Temps des Amours, Vol. 4. 290p. (FRE.). 1979. 21.95 (0-7859-4730-2) Fr & Eur.

— Le Temps de Amours. (Souvenirs d'Enfance Ser.: No. 4). (FRE.). 1988. pap. 13.95 (0-7859-3334-4, 2877060535) Fr & Eur.

— Le Temps des Secrets. (Souvenirs d'Enfance Ser.: No. 3). (FRE.). 1988. pap. 13.95 (0-7859-3327-1, 2877060527) Fr & Eur.

— Topaze. (FRE.). 1988. pap. 13.95 (0-7859-3328-X, 2877060594) Fr & Eur.

— Topaze: Comedie en 4 Actes. pap. 9.95 (0-685-37013-5) Fr & Eur.

Pagnoni, A. Project Engineering: Computer-Oriented Planning & Operational Decision Making. 256p. 1990. text ed. 32.00 (0-387-52475-4) Spr-Verlag.

***Pagnoni, Mario.** The Joy of Bocce. (Illus.). (Orig.). 1995. pap. 12.95 (1-57028-044-4) Masters Pr IN.

***Pagnoni, Mario & Robinson, Gerald.** Softball: Fast & Slow Pitch. LC 95-5365. (Spalding Sports Library). (Illus.). 156p. (Orig.). 1995. pap. 12.95 (1-57028-025-8) Masters Pr IN.

Pagnoulle, Christine. David Jones: A Commentary on Some Poetic Fragments. viii, 162p. 1989. 35.00 (0-7083-0962-3, Pub. by U of Wales UK) Bks Intl VA.

Pagnucci, Franco. I Never Had a Pet. Pagnucci, Gian, ed. (Illus.). 32p. (Orig.). (J). (gr. 1-5). 1992. pap. 5.95 (0-929326-09-1) Bur Oak Pr Inc.

Pagnucci, Franco & Pagnucci, Susan. Paul Revere & Other Story Hours. (Illus.). 72p. (Orig.). (J). (gr. k-6). 1988. pap. 8.95 (0-929326-00-8) Bur Oak Pr Inc.

— Story - Start Dinosaurs. 1991. 8.99 (0-86653-998-0) Fearon Teach Aids.

An Asterisk (*) at the beginning of an entry indicates that the title is appearing in BIP for the first time.

— Story - Start Monsters. 1991. 8.99 (*0-86653-999-9*) Fearon Teach Aids.

Pagnucci, Franco, jt. auth. see Pagnucci, Susan.

Pagnucci, Franco & Susan. Story Start Animals. (J). (gr. 2-5). 1990. pap. 8.99 (*0-8224-6398-9*) Fearon Teach Aids.

Pagnucci, Gian, ed. see Pagnucci, Franco.

Pagnucci, Gianfranco. Out Harmsen's Way. 62p. (Orig.). 1991. pap. 7.00 (*1-878660-10-1*) Fireweed WI.

Pagnucci, Gianfranco, ed. Face the Poem. (Illus.). 32p. (Orig.). (J). (gr. 2-8). 1979. Incl. animal poems with animal face masks for choral readings. 3.95 (*0-929326-02-4*) Bur Oak Pr Inc.

Pagnucci, Susan. Games to Cut. (Illus.). 20p. (Orig.). (J). (gr. k-3). 1978. Incl. 5 reading & math games to make & use. 4.95 (*0-929326-03-2*) Bur Oak Pr Inc.

— Number Chomp. (Illus.). 48p. (Orig.). (J). (gr. 1-2). 1984. Incl. reproducible math sheets with numbers 0-9 addition & subtraction. 4.50 (*0-929326-04-0*) Bur Oak Pr Inc.

— Shortcuts for Librarians & Teachers. (Illus.). 64p. (Orig.). 1993. pap. 8.95 (*0-929326-05-9*) Bur Oak Pr Inc.

Pagnucci, Susan & Pagnucci, Franco. Do Me! Stories. (Illus.). 64p. (Orig.). (J). (ps-3). 1993. pap. 8.95 (*0-929326-07-5*) Bur Oak Pr Inc.

— I Can! Folktales: Stories from Around the World for Young Children. (Illus.). 64p. (Orig.). (J). (ps-3). 1995. pap. 8.95 (*0-929326-10-5*) Bur Oak Pr Inc.

— The 3 Bears: And Other Great Stories with Hats. (Illus.). 64p. (Orig.). (J). (ps-3). 1995. pap. 8.95 (*0-929326-12-1*) Bur Oak Pr Inc.

— The 3 Little Pigs: And Other Great Stories with Masks. (Illus.). 64p. (Orig.). (J). (ps-3). 1994. pap. 8.95 (*0-929326-11-3*) Bur Oak Pr Inc.

Pagnucci, Susan, jt. auth. see Pagnucci, Franco.

Pagoan, Gianni. Break-Up. LC 90-46156. (J). 1989. 10.95 (*0-85953-310-7*) Childs Play.

Pagoldh, Susanne. Nordic Knitting. Rhoades, Carol, tr. LC 91-28263. (Illus.). 120p. 1991. 21.95 (*0-934026-68-8*) Interweave.

Pagone, Tony, jt. auth. see Wallace, Jude.

Pagonis, William G. Moving Mountains: Lessons in Leadership & Logistics from the Gulf War. 1994. pap. 14.95 (*0-87584-508-8*) Harvard Busn.

Pagonis, William G. & Cruikshank, Jeffrey L. Moving Mountains: Lessons in Leadership & Logistics from the Gulf War. LC 92-15641. 272p. 1992. 29.95 (*0-87584-360-3*) Harvard Busn.

— Moving Mountains: Lessons in Leadership & Logistics from the Gulf War. 1992. text ed. 24.95 (*0-07-103388-2*) McGraw.

— Moving Mountains: Lessons in Leadership & Logistics from the Gulf War. 1994. pap. text ed. 14.95 (*0-07-103587-7*) McGraw.

Pagoota, Terry. The Angel Drank Diet Soda: Eleven Plays & Sketches for Performance & Praise. 1989. 8.50 (*0-8341-9049-4*, BCMP-654) Lillenas.

Pagoulatos, Angelos. Major Determinants Affecting the Demand & Supply of Energy Resources: An Analysis of the Petroleum Market. Bruchey, Stuart, ed. LC 78-22704. (Energy in the American Economy Ser.). (Illus.). 1979. lib. bdg. 23.95 (*0-405-12006-0*) Ayer.

Pagoulatou, Regina. The Ambassadors. LC 85-73011. 112p. (GRE.). 1985. pap. 8.00 (*0-918618-31-2*) Pella Pub.

— From the U. S. A. LC 84-72488. 151p. (GRE.). 1984. pap. 8.00 (*0-317-39603-X*) Pella Pub.

— The Magic World & Ninety-One Other Stories. LC 83-72497. 275p. 1983. 10.00 (*0-317-39604-8*) Pella Pub.

— Motherhood. LC 85-62595. 80p. 1985. pap. 10.00 (*0-918618-25-8*) Pella Pub.

Pagter, Carl, jt. auth. see Dundes, Alan.

Pagter, Carl R., jt. auth. see Dundes, Alan.

Pagurek, Joyce. Writing Workshop: Paragraph & Sentence Practice. 1984. pap. 17.95 (*0-8384-2998-X*, Newbury) Heinle & Heinle.

Pahari, S. Physical Chemistry, Vol. 1. (C). 1989. 150.00 (*0-89771-408-3*, Current Dist) St Mut.

Pahek, Zelijko. Once upon a Time in the Future. (Illus.). 46p. 1991. pap. 9.95 (*1-56398-023-1*) Malibu Graphics.

Paher, Stanley, ed. see Fey, Marshall.

Paher, Stanley W. Colorado River Ghost Towns. (Illus.). 80p. 1976. pap. 14.95 (*0-913814-08-3*) Nevada Pubns.

— Death Valley Ghost Towns. LC 72-97900. (Illus.). 48p. 1973. 14.95 (*0-913814-03-2*) Nevada Pubns.

— Death Valley Ghost Towns, Vol. 1. LC 82-97900. (Illus.). 32p. 1981. pap. 4.95 (*0-913814-35-0*) Nevada Pubns.

— Death Valley Ghost Towns, Vol. 2. (Illus.). 32p. 1982. 4.95 (*0-913814-36-9*) Nevada Pubns.

— Death Valley's Scotty's Castle. LC 82-84292. (Story Behind the Scenery Ser.). (Illus.). 48p. (Orig.). 1985. pap. 6.95 (*0-916122-87-5*) KC Pubns.

— Death Valley's Scotty's Castle. (Story Behind the Scenery Ser.). (Illus.). 48p. (Orig.). 1986. 6.95 (*0-913814-81-4*) Nevada Pubns.

— Goldfield: Boom Town of Nevada. (Illus.). 17p. 1977. 2.95 (*0-913814-14-8*) Nevada Pubns.

— If Thou Hadst Known. (Illus.). 1978. 9.95 (*0-913814-21-0*) Nevada Pubns.

— Lake Tahoe: The Story Behind the Scenery. LC 94-78129. (Illus.). 48p. 1994. pap. 6.95 (*0-88714-088-2*) KC Pubns.

— Las Vegas, As It Began, As It Grew. LC 70-175144. (Illus.). 1971. 35.00 (*0-913814-01-6*); pap. 19.95 (*0-913814-74-1*) Nevada Pubns.

— Nevada: An Annotated Bibliography. (Illus.). 585p. 1980. 95.00 (*0-913814-26-1*) Nevada Pubns.

— Nevada Ghost Towns & Mining Camps. (Illus.). 492p. 1970. 44.95 (*0-913814-04-0*) Nevada Pubns.

— Nevada Ghost Towns & Mining Camps, Vols. 1-2: An Illustrated Atlas, 2 vols. (Illus.). 1993. write for info. (*0-913814-09-1*) Nevada Pubns.

— Nevada Ghost Towns & Mining Camps, Vols. 1-2: An Illustrated Atlas, 2 vols., Set. (Illus.). 1993. 29.95 (*0-913814-11-3*) Nevada Pubns.

— Nevada Ghost Towns & Mining Camps, Vols. 1-2: An Illustrated Atlas, 2 vols., Vol. 1. (Illus.). 104p. 1993. 14.95 (*0-685-74591-0*) Nevada Pubns.

— Nevada Ghost Towns & Mining Camps, Vols. 1-2: An Illustrated Atlas, 2 vols., Vol. 2. (Illus.). 104p. 1993. 14.95 (*0-685-74592-9*) Nevada Pubns.

— Ponderosa Country: A Scenic & Historic Guide to Reno & Vicinity. LC 72-87135. (Illus.). 1972. 11.95 (*0-913814-02-4*) Nevada Pubns.

— Tonopah Nevada Silver Camp. (Illus.). 1978. pap. 2.95 (*0-913814-18-0*) Nevada Pubns.

— Western Arizona Ghost Towns. (Illus.). 64p. 6.95 (*0-913814-89-X*) Nevada Pubns.

Paher, Stanley W., ed. Chloride Mines & Murals. (Illus.). 1978. pap. 3.95 (*0-913814-15-6*) Nevada Pubns.

— Fort Churchill: Nevada Military Outpost of the 1860's. (Illus.). 48p. 1981. pap. 4.50 (*0-913814-38-5*) Nevada Pubns.

— Nevada Towns & Tales: North, Vol. 1. (Illus.). 1981. 14.95 (*0-913814-41-5*) Nevada Pubns.

— Nevada Towns & Tales: South, Vol. 2. (Illus.). 1982. 14.95 (*0-913814-45-8*) Nevada Pubns.

Paher, Stanley W., ed. see Curran, Harold.

Paher, Stanley W., jt. auth. see Gamett, James.

Paher, Stanley W., jt. auth. see Spude, Robert L.

Pahissa, Jaime. Manuel De Falla, His Life & Works. Wagstaff, Jean, tr. LC 78-66917. (Encore Music Editions Ser.). 1986. reprint ed. 21.50 (*0-88355-756-8*) Hyperion Conn.

Pahkinen, Erkki J., jt. auth. see Lehtonen, Risto.

Pahl, David. West Point. 1987. 7.98 (*0-671-08917-X*) S&S Trade.

Pahl, G. & Beitz, W. Engineering Design. Wallace, K., ed. (Illus.). 460p. 1984. 78.40 (*0-387-13601-0*) Spr-Verlag.

— Engineering Design. (Illus.). 420p. 1993. pap. 39.00 (*0-387-50442-7*) Spr-Verlag.

— Engineering Design: A Systematic Approach. Wallace, Ken, ed. & tr. by. Pomerans, Arnold J., tr. (Illus.). 400p. (C). 1988. pap. 34.95x (*0-85072-239-X*, Pub. by Design Council Bks UK) Ashgate Pub Co.

Pahl, Gary W., ed. Periphery of the Southeastern Classic Maya Realm. LC 86-7502. (Latin American Indians Ser.). 304p. (Orig.). 1986. pap. 48.50 (*0-87903-061-5*) UCLA Lat Am Ctr.

***Pahl, Gerald & Beitz, Wolfgang.** Engineering Design: A Systematic Approach. Wallace, Ken, ed. & tr. by. Blessing, Lucienne et al, trs. LC 95-10248. 1995. write for info. (*3-540-19917-9*) Spr-Verlag.

Pahl, Jan, ed. Private Violence & Public Policy: The Needs of Battered Women & the Response of the Public. 208p. (Orig.). 1985. pap. 13.95 (*0-7100-9992-4*, RKP) Routledge.

Pahl, John. Ghost Towns & Ghosts. (Illus.). 40p. 1992. pap. 6.00 (*0-9626408-5-9*) Priscilla Pr.

Pahl, Jon. Hopes & Dreams of All: The International Walther League. 360p. 1993. write for info. (*0-9636446-0-2*); pap. 15.00 (*0-9636446-1-0*) Wheat Rdge Minist.

— Paradox Lost: Free Will & Political Liberty in American Culture, 1637-1760. (New Studies in American Intellectual & Cultural History). 224p. 1992. text ed. 37.50x (*0-8018-4334-0*) Johns Hopkins.

Pahl, Paul D., tr. Luther's Works, Vol. 6. LC 55-9893. 1969. 19.95 (*0-570-06406-6*, 15-1748) Concordia.

— Luther's Works, Vol. 7. LC 55-9893. 1964. 19.95 (*0-570-06407-4*, 15-1749) Concordia.

— Luther's Works: Genesis Chapters 45-50, Vol. 8. LC 55-9893. 1965. 19.95 (*0-570-06408-2*, 15-1750) Concordia.

Pahl, R. E. Divisions of Labour. 376p. 1984. pap. 21.95 (*0-631-13274-0*) Blackwell Pubs.

Pahl, R. E., ed. On Work: Historical, Comparative & Theoretical Approaches. (Illus.). 320p. 1988. pap. text ed. 24.95 (*0-631-15762-X*) Blackwell Pubs.

Pahl, Raymond E., et al. Structures & Processes of Urban Life. 2nd ed. LC 82-13093. (Aspects of Modern Sociology: the Social Structure of Modern Britain Ser.). 170p. reprint ed. pap. 48.50 (*0-7837-1581-1*, 2041873) Bks Demand.

Pahl, Teresa, jt. auth. see Dickinson, Karen.

***Pahl-Wostl, Claudia.** The Dynamic Nature of Ecosystems: Chaos & Order Entwined. LC 94-39319. 1995. text ed. 79.95 (*0-471-95570-1*) Wiley.

***Pahlavan, Kaveh & Levesque, Allen H.** Wireless Information Networks. LC 94-22900. (Telecommunications & Signal Processing Ser.). 1995. text ed. 74.95 (*0-471-10607-0*) Wiley.

***Pahlavi, Asaraf.** Time for Truth. Keitlen, Tomi, ed. (Illus.). 224p. 1995. pap. 14.95 (*1-886966-00-1*) In Print.

Pahlen, Kurt & Dox, Thurston J. World of the Oratorio. Schaeffer, Judith, tr. LC 89-17757. (Illus.). 397p. 1990. 39.95 (*0-931340-11-X*, Amadeus Pr) Timber.

Pahler, Arnold J. Study Guide to Accompany Advanced Accounting: Concepts & Practice. 7th ed. 265p. (C). 1994. pap. text ed. 21.00 (*0-03-098067-4*) Dryden Pr.

Pahler, Arnold J. & Mori, Joseph E. Advanced Accounting: Concepts & Practice. 4th ed. 1310p. (C). 1990. text ed. 61.75 (*0-15-501204-5*) Dryden Pr.

— Advanced Accounting: Concepts & Practice. 5th ed. LC 93-71908. 1325p. (C). 1993. text ed. 68.00 (*0-03-098697-4*) Dryden Pr.

— Advanced Accounting: Concepts & Practice. 5th ed. LC 93-71908. 1325p. (C). 1994. 207.50 (*0-03-006818-5*); 207.50 (*0-03-006817-7*) Dryden Pr.

— Advanced Accounting: Concepts & Practice: Instructor's Resource Manual & Testbook to Accompany. 5th ed. 500p. (C). 1994. pap. text ed. 41.75 (*0-03-003589-9*) Dryden Pr.

Pahlitzsch, G. Dictionary of Production Engineering: Electroerosive & Electrochemical Removal, Vol. 9. 170p. (ENG, FRE & GER.). 1984. 75.00 (*0-8288-0606-3*, M 4000) Fr & Eur.

***Pahlka, William H.** Saint Augustine's Meter & George Herbert's Will. fac. ed. LC 87-4252. 263p. 1994. pap. 75.00 (*0-7837-7629-2*, 2047381) Bks Demand.

Pahlow, Mannfried. The Healing Plants. (Illus.). 224p. 1993. pap. 16.95 (*0-8120-1498-7*) Barron.

Pahomov, George S. In Earthbound Flight: Romanticism in Turgenev. 234p. 1985. 21.00 (*0-685-28454-9*) Kingston Pr.

Pahor, Boris. Pilgrim among the Shadows. Biggins, Michael, tr. LC 94-20605. 1995. 20.00 (*0-15-171958-6*) HarBrace.

Pahre, Robert, jt. auth. see Dogan, Mattei.

Pahud, P., jt. auth. see Del Pedro, M.

Pahwa, Ash. The CD-Recordable Bible: An Essential Guide for Any Business. 185p. 1994. pap. 24.95 (*0-910965-11-0*) Online.

Pahz, Cheryl, jt. auth. see Pahz, James.

Pahz, James & Pahz, Cheryl. Robin Sees a Song. 1977. pap. 3.75 (*0-913072-27-3*) Natl Assn Deaf.

Pai, Anna C. Foundations of Genetics. 2nd ed. 480p. 1985. text ed. write for info. (*0-07-048094-X*) McGraw.

Pai, E., jt. auth. see Farkas-Janke, M.

Pai, K. M., tr. see Dubinin, G. N.

Pai, K. M., tr. see Samsonov, G. V., ed.

Pai, M. A. Energy Function Analysis for Power System Stability. (C). 1989. lib. bdg. 91.00 (*0-7923-9035-0*) Kluwer Ac.

Pai, Margaret K. The Dreams of Two Yi-Min. LC 88-29539. (Illus.). 216p. 1989. 22.95 (*0-8248-1179-8*, Kolowalu Bk) UH Pr.

Pai, S. I., jt. ed. see Diaz, J. G.

Pai, S. T. & Zhang, Qi. Introduction to High Power Pulse Technology. (Series in Electrical & Computer Engineering). 500p. 1995. text ed. 90.00 (*981-02-1714-5*) World Scientific Pub.

Pai, Seong-Tong, jt. auth. see Kim, Chong-Lim.

Pai Shih-I. Magnetogasdynamics & Plasma Dynamics. (Illus.). 1962. 33.00 (*0-387-80608-3*) Spr-Verlag.

Pai, Shih-I. Two-Phase Flows. (Vieweg Tracts in Pure & Applied Physics Ser.: Vol. 3). xii, 360p. 1977. 70.00 (*3-528-08340-9*, Pub. by Vieweg & Sohn GW) Ballen Bkslr.

Pai, Shih-I & Luo, Shijun. Theoretical & Computational Dynamics of a Compressible Flow. (Illus.). 740p. 1991. text ed. 110.00 (*0-442-30310-6*) Chapman & Hall.

Pai, Sudha. Uttar Pradesh Agrarian Change & Electoral Politics. (Illus.). 183p. 1993. 18.00 (*81-85402-21-3*, Pub. by Shipra Pubns II) Nataraj Bks.

Pai, Young. Cultural Foundations of Education. 272p. (C). 1990. pap. write for info. (*0-675-20934-X*, Merrill Pub Co) Macmillan.

Pai, Young, jt. auth. see Morris, Van Cleave.

Paic, Guy, ed. Ionizing Radiation: Protection & Dosimetry. (Health Physicists Ser.). 272p. 1988. 191.00 (*0-8493-6713-1*, QC795) CRC Pr.

Paic, Guy & Slaus, Ivo, eds. Few Body Problems, Light Nuclei & Nuclear Interactions, 2 vols., Vol. 1. 444p. 1968. text ed. 342.00 (*0-677-12760-X*) Gordon & Breach.

— Few Body Problems, Light Nuclei & Nuclear Interactions, 2 vols., Vol. 2. 1968. Set. text ed. 571.00 (*0-677-13440-1*); text ed. 406.00 (*0-677-13020-1*) Gordon & Breach.

Paice, Chris, jt. ed. see McEnery, Tony.

***Paice, Edward.** Bradt Guide to Eritrea. LC 95-6908. (Bradt Guides Ser.). (Illus.). 204p. (Orig.). 1995. pap. 16.95 (*1-56440-696-2*, Pub. by Bradt Pubns UK) Globe Pequot.

Paice, Michael G., jt. ed. see Lewis, Norman G.

Paidar, Meridith. Merchandising Mathematics: High Margin Returns for Retailers & Vendors. LC 93-25984. 405p. 1994. pap. text ed. 33.50 (*0-8273-5703-6*) Delmar.

— Merchandising Mathematics: High Margin Returns for Retailers & Vendors. 71p. 1994. teacher ed 14.00 (*0-8273-5704-4*) Delmar.

***Paidar, Parvin.** Women & the Political Process in Twentieth-Century Iran. (Cambridge Middle East Studies: No. 1). 392p. (C). 1995. 59.95 (*0-521-47340-3*) Cambridge U Pr.

Paidoussis, M. P. & Au-Yang, M. K., eds. Third International Symposium on Flow-Induced Vibration & Noise, Vol. 5: Axial & Annular Flow-Induced Vibrations & Instabilities. (PVP Ser.: Vol. 244). 232p. 1992. 57.50 (*0-7918-1082-8*, G00726) ASME.

Paidoussis, M. P. & Namachchivaya, N. S., eds. Third International Symposium on Flow-Induced Vibration & Noise, Vol. 8: Stability & Control of Pipes Conveying Fluid. (AMD Ser.: Vol. 152). 140p. 1992. 45.00 (*0-7918-1085-2*, G00729) ASME.

Paidoussis, M. P. & Sandifer, J. B., eds. Third International Symposium on Flow-Induced Vibration & Noise, Vol. 4: Acoustical Effects in FSI. (PVP Ser.: Vol. 243). 164p. 1992. 45.00 (*0-7918-1081-X*, G00725) ASME.

Paidoussis, M. P., jt. ed. see Farabee, T. M.

Paidoussis, M. P., et al, eds. Third International Symposium on Flow-Induced Vibration & Noise, Vol. 1: FSI - FIV in Cylinder Arrays in Cross-Flow. (HTD Series, Vol. 230: NE: Vol. 9). 284p. 1992. 62.50 (*0-7918-1078-X*, G00722) ASME.

— Third International Symposium on Flow-Induced Vibration & Noise, Vol. 2: Cross-Flow Induced Vibration of Cylinder Arrays. (PVP Ser.: Vol. 242). 356p. 1992. 65.00 (*0-7918-1079-8*, G00723) ASME.

— Third International Symposium on Flow-Induced Vibration & Noise, Vol. 6: Bluff-Body - Fluid & Hydraulic Machine Interactions. (FED Ser.: Vol. 138). 264p. 1992. 62.50 (*0-7918-1083-6*, G00727) ASME.

— Third International Symposium on Flow-Induced Vibration & Noise, Vol. 7: Fundamental Aspects of Fluid-Structure Interactions. (AMD Series, Vol. 151: PVP: Vol. 247). 232p. 1992. 57.50 (*0-7918-1084-4*, G00728) ASME.

Paietta, Ann C. Access Services: A Handbook. LC 90-53601. 220p. 1991. lib. bdg. 24.95x (*0-89950-599-6*) McFarland & Co.

***Paietta, Ann C. & Kauppila, Jean L.** Animals on Screen & Radio: An Annotated Sourcebook. LC 94-29182. 1994. 42.50 (*0-8108-2939-8*) Scarecrow.

Paiewonsky, Michael. Conquest of Eden: 1493-1515: Other Voyages of Columbus. (Illus.). 176p. 1990. 34.95 (*0-926330-03-9*) Mapes Monde.

— Conquest of Eden: 1493-1515: 1493-1515 Other Voyages of Columbus. (Illus.). 176p. 1993. reprint ed. pap. 23.95 (*0-926330-04-7*) Mapes Monde.

Paige. Clinical Nutrition. 2nd ed. (Illus.). 960p. 1988. 59.00 (*0-8016-3873-9*) Mosby Yr Bk.

Paige, Andrew. Coming Apart, Coming Together: One Man's Journey Out of Depression. 96p. (Orig.). 1994. pap. 5.95 (*0-89243-540-2*) Liguori Pubns.

Paige, D. D., tr. see Pavese, Cesare.

Paige, D. D., ed. see Pound, Ezra.

Paige, David. A Day in the Life of a Forest Ranger. LC 78-68809. (Illus.). 32p. (J). (gr. 4-8). 1980. lib. bdg. 11.79 (*0-89375-227-4*); pap. 2.95 (*0-89375-231-2*) Troll Assocs.

— A Day in the Life of a Librarian. LC 84-8552. (Day in the Life of...Ser.). (Illus.). 32p. (J). (gr. 4-8). 1985. lib. bdg. 11.79 (*0-8167-0101-6*); pap. text ed. 2.95 (*0-8167-0102-4*) Troll Assocs.

— A Day in the Life of a Marine Biologist. LC 80-54097. (Illus.). 32p. (J). (gr. 4-8). 1981. lib. bdg. 11.79 (*0-89375-446-3*); pap. 2.95 (*0-89375-447-1*) Troll Assocs.

— A Day in the Life of a Police Detective. LC 80-54102. (Illus.). 32p. (J). (gr. 4-8). 1981. lib. bdg. 11.79 (*0-89375-442-0*) Troll Assocs.

— A Day in the Life of a Rock Musician. LC 78-68808. (Illus.). 32p. (J). (gr. 4-8). 1980. lib. bdg. 11.79 (*0-89375-225-8*); pap. 2.95 (*0-89375-229-0*) Troll Assocs.

— A Day in the Life of a School Basketball Coach. LC 80-54101. (Illus.). 32p. (J). (gr. 4-8). 1981. lib. bdg. 11.79 (*0-89375-452-8*) Troll Assocs.

— A Day in the Life of a Sports Therapist. LC 84-2433. (Day in the Life of...Ser.). (Illus.). 32p. (J). (gr. 4-8). 1985. lib. bdg. 11.79 (*0-8167-0099-0*); pap. text ed. 2.95 (*0-8167-0100-8*) Troll Assocs.

— A Day in the Life of a Zoo Veterinarian. LC 84-6538. (Day in the Life of...Ser.). (Illus.). 32p. (J). (gr. 4-8). 1985. lib. bdg. 11.79 (*0-8167-0095-8*); pap. text ed. 2.95 (*0-8167-0096-6*) Troll Assocs.

Paige, E. G., jt. auth. see Ash, E. A.

Paige, Frances. The Distaff Side. large type ed. 1989. 23.95 (*0-7089-8531-9*, Trail West Pubs) Ulverscroft.

— Men Who March Away. large type ed. (General Fiction Ser.). 1993. 23.95 (*0-7089-8591-2*, Charnwood) Ulverscroft.

— The Sholtie Flyer. large type ed. 1991. 23.95 (*0-7089-8597-1*, Trail West Pubs) Ulverscroft.

Paige, Glen D., jt. ed. see Gilliatt, Sarah.

Paige, Glenn D. To Nonviolent Political Science: From Seasons of Violence. LC 93-31768. 1993. 5.00 (*1-880309-07-6*) S M Matsunaga.

Paige, Glenn D. & Gilliatt, Sarah, eds. Nonviolence in Hawaii's Spiritual Traditions. LC 91-36117. 112p. 1991. 5.00 (*1-880309-00-9*) S M Matsunaga.

Paige, Glenn D., ed. see Governor's Conference on the Year 2000.

Paige, Glenn D., jt. auth. see Snyder, Richard C.

Paige, Harry W. The Eye of the Heart: Portraits of Passionate Spirituality. LC 89-40243. 128p. (Orig.). 1990. 8.95 (*0-940989-58-1*) Meyer Stone Bks.

— Land of the Spotted Eagle: Portrait of the Reservation Sioux. LC 87-26252. (Illus.). 96p. (C). 1988. 19.95 (*0-8294-0581-X*, Campion Bks) Loyola Univ Pr.

— Songs of the Teton Sioux. (Great West & Indian Ser.: Vol. 39). (Illus.). 1969. 9.50 (*0-87026-019-7*) Westernlore.

Paige, Irene, ed. Antiques: A Buyer's Guide to London. 3rd ed. (Illus.). 160p. 1989. pap. 7.95 (*0-938699-03-2*) Paige Pubns.

Paige, Irene E. Antiques: A Buyers' Guide to London. rev. ed. (Illus.). 160p. 1987. pap. 6.95 (*0-938699-01-6*) Paige Pubns.

Paige, Jeffery M. Agrarian Revolution: Social Movements & Export Agriculture in the Underdeveloped World. LC 74-25601. 1978. pap. 14.95 (*0-02-923550-2*) Free Pr.

Paige, Jeffrey, jt. auth. see Haller, James.

Paige, Jeffrey M., jt. auth. see Paige, Karen E.

Paige, Jeffrey S. The Shaker Kitchen: Shaker-inspired Cooking from the Canterbury Village. LC 93-2360. 1994. 22.00 (*0-517-58838-2*, C P Pubs) Crown Pub Group.

Paige, Judith & Gordon, Pamela. Choice Years: Health, Happiness & Beauty Through Menopause & Beyond. 1992. mass mkt. 5.99 (*0-449-22190-3*, Crest) Fawcett.

Paige, Karen E. & Paige, Jeffrey M. The Politics of Reproductive Ritual. 392p. 1981. pap. 14.00 (*0-520-04782-6*) U CA Pr.

Paige, Laurie. Caleb's Son. (Silhouette Romance Ser.). 1994. pap. 2.75 (*0-373-08994-5*, 5-08994-1) Silhouette.

— Cara's Beloved. (Silhouette Romance Ser.). 1993. pap. 2.69 (*0-373-08917-1*, 5-08917-2) Silhouette.

— Christmas Kisses for a Dollar. 1995. pap. 3.50 (*0-373-52009-3*, 1-52009-7) Silhouette.

— Father Found. (Montana Mavericks Ser.). 1995. mass mkt. 3.99 (*0-373-50173-0*, 1-50173-1) Harlequin Bks.

P
Q

— Home for a Wild Heart. (Silhouette Special Edition Ser.). 1993. mass mkt. 3.50 (*0-373-09828-6*, 5-09828-0) Silhouette.

— The Once & Future Wife. 1994. mass mkt. 3.99 (*0-373-50168-4*, 1-50168-3) Harlequin Bks.

— A Place for Eagles. (Wild River Trilogy Ser.). 1993. mass mkt. 3.50 (*0-373-09839-1*, 5-09839-7) Silhouette.

— A River to Cross. (Special Edition Ser.). 1994. mass mkt. 3.50 (*0-373-09910-X*, 1-09910-0) Harlequin Bks.

— A Rogue's Heart. (Silhouette Romance Ser.). 1994. pap. 2.75 (*0-373-19013-1*, 5-19013-7) Harlequin Bks.

— A Rougue's Heart. 1994. pap. 2.75 (*0-373-91013-4*, 5-91013-8) Harlequin Bks.

— Sally's Beau. large type ed. LC 93-21001. 1993. 13.95 (*0-7862-0059-6*) Thorndike Pr.

— Victoria's Conquest. (Silhouette Romance Ser.). 1993. pap. 2.69 (*0-373-08933-3*, 5-08933-9) Silhouette.

— The Way of a Man: Wild River Trilogy. (Silhouette Special Edition Ser.). 1993. mass mkt. 3.50 (*0-373-09849-9*, 5-09849-6) Silhouette.

— Wild Is the Wind. 1994. 3.50 (*0-373-09887-1*) Silhouette.

Paige, LeRoy, pseud. Maybe I'll Pitch Forever. LC 92-35221. xiv, 298p. 1993. 35.00 (*0-8032-3702-2*); pap. 10.95 (*0-8032-8732-1*) U of Nebr Pr.

***Paige, LeRoy.** Pitchin' Man. (American Autobiography Ser.). 96p. 1995. reprint ed. lib. bdg. 69.00 (*0-7812-8606-9*) Rprt Serv.

Paige, Leroy S. Pitchin' Man: Satchel Paige's Own Story. (Baseball & American Society Ser.: No. 20). (Illus.). 130p. 1992. lib. bdg. 29.50 (*0-88736-836-0*) Mecklermedia.

Paige, Leslie Zeldin. The Identification & Treatment of School Phobia. 1993. pap. text ed. 19.00 (*0-932955-08-8*) Natl Assn Psych.

Paige, Lori A. Passion's Legacy. 256p. (Orig.). 1991. pap. 8.95 (*0-941483-81-9*) Naiad Pr.

Paige, Lowell J., et al. Elements of Linear Algebra. 2nd ed. LC 83-14891. 298p. 1983. reprint ed. lib. bdg. 29.50 (*0-89874-668-X*) Krieger.

Paige, Lucius R. History of Cambridge, Massachusetts, 1630-1877. 732p. 1986. reprint ed. 50.00 (*1-55613-011-2*) Heritage Bk.

— History of Hardwick MA: With a Genealogical Register. 571p. (Orig.). 1994. pap. text ed. 35.00 (*0-7884-0021-5*) Heritage Bk.

— List of Freemen of Massachusetts, 1630-1691. LC 78-50979. 60p. 1988. reprint ed. pap. 5.00 (*0-8063-0806-0*) Genealog Pub.

Paige, Marvin, jt. auth. see Logan, Tom.

Paige, Mary, jt. auth. see Guthrie, Peter.

Paige, Michele A. After the SATs: An Insider's Guide to Freshman Year. 240p. 1991. pap. 9.95 (*0-8120-4477-0*) Barron.

Paige, Morton L. Things Your Family Should Know. 88p. 1992. student ed 14.95 (*0-9635236-0-0*) Paige Pub CA.

Paige, Nigel, jt. auth. see George, Susan.

Paige, Pat. Cowbells & Courage. Johnson, Joy, ed. (Illus.). 24p. 1993. pap. 3.00 (*1-56123-067-7*) Centering Corp.

Paige, R. Michael, ed. Cross Cultural Orientation: New Conceptualizations & Applications. LC 86-15999. (Orig.). (C). 1986. pap. 31.00 (*0-8191-5608-6*, CIEE) U Pr of Amer.

— Education for the Intercultural Experience. LC 93-31313. 336p. (Orig.). 1993. pap. text ed. 25.95 (*1-877864-25-0*) Intercult Pr.

Paige, Richard. The Door to December. 408p. 1985. pap. 4.99 (*0-451-13605-5*, Sig) NAL-Dutton.

— Door to December. 1990. pap. 4.95 (*0-451-16667-1*) NAL-Dutton.

***Paige, Richard E.** Little Inventions That Made Big Money. (Illus.). 155p. (Orig.). 1983. pap. text ed. write for info. (*1-877782-11-4*) M&M Assocs.

— The Science of Creating Ideas for Industry. 113p. (Orig.). 1980. pap. text ed. write for info. (*1-877782-12-2*) M&M Assocs.

Paige, Robert, et al, eds. Parallel Algorithm Derivation & Program Transformation. LC 93-1687. (International Series in Engineering & Computer Science, VLSI, Computer Architecture, & Digital Screen Processing). 248p. (C). 1993. lib. bdg. 77.50 (*0-7923-9362-7*) Kluwer Ac.

Paige, Robert A. Formal Differentiation: A Program Synthesis Technique. LC 81-7632. (Computer Science: Artificial Intelligence Ser.: No. 6). 289p. reprint ed. pap. 82.40 (*0-685-20829-X*, 2070045) Bks Demand.

Paige, Robin. Death at Bishop's Keep. 272p. (Orig.). 1994. mass mkt. 4.99 (*0-380-77498-4*) Avon.

— Death at Gallows Green. (Victorian Mystery Ser.). 272p. (Orig.). 1995. mass mkt. 4.99 (*0-380-77499-2*) Avon.

Paige, Roger. Dealing with Divorce. 1979. pap. 6.50 (*0-8309-0240-6*) Herald Hse.

Paige, S., et al. Reconnaissance of the Point Barrow Region, Alaska. (Shorey Historical Ser.). (Illus.). 56p. reprint ed. pap. 4.95 (*0-8466-8004-1*, G4) Shorey.

Paige, T., jt. ed. see Wilkins, M.

Paige, Vernon, jt. auth. see Lamit, Louis G.

Paik, Hae J., jt. auth. see Comstock, George.

Paik, Woon K. & Kim, Sangduk, eds. Protein Methylation. 432p. 1989. 240.00 (*0-8493-6818-9*, QP551) CRC Pr.

Paikeday, Thomas M. The Native Speaker Is Dead! An Informal Discussion of a Linguistic Myth. 120p. (Orig.). (C). 1985. pap. 16.00 (*0-920865-00-3*) Paikeday Pub.

— The Native Speaker Is Dead! An Informal Discussion of a Linguistic Myth, with Noam Chomsky & Other Linguists, Philosophers, Lexicographers & Psychologists. 128p. 1985. pap. 15.00 (*0-318-41767-7*) Paikeday Pub.

Paikoff, Roberta L., ed. Shared Views in the Family During Adolescence. LC 85-644581. (New Directions for Child Development Ser.: No. CD 51). 1991. 17.95 (*1-55542-787-1*) Jossey-Bass.

Pailet, Joshua M. The World's Fair, New Orleans. LC 85-81259. (Illus.). 120p. 1987. 39.95 (*0-9615647-0-9*) Gallery Fine.

***Pailin.** Probing the Foundations: A Study in Theistic Foundations. 1993. pap. text ed. (*0-8028-6172-5*) Eerdmans.

Pailin, David A. The Anthropological Character of Theology: Conditioning Theological Understanding. 300p. (C). 1990. 69.95 (*0-521-39069-9*) Cambridge U Pr.

— God & the Processes of Reality: Foundations of a Credible Theism. 256p. 1989. 42.50 (*0-415-02106-5*) Routledge.

Pailin, David A., jt. ed. see Coakley, Sarah.

Paillard, Jacques, ed. Brain & Space. (Illus.). 520p. 1991. 90.00 (*0-19-854284-4*) OUP.

***Paillard, Philippe.** Dictionnaire des Communes Savoyardes. 450p. (FRE.). 1981. 150.00 (*0-7859-7949-2*, 2717102299) Fr & Eur.

Paillat, P. M. & Bunch, M. E., eds. Age, Work & Automation. (Interdisciplinary Topics in Gerontology Ser.: Vol. 6). 1970. 24.00 (*3-8055-0507-8*) S Karger.

***Paillere, A. M.** Application of Admixtures in Concrete. (Rilem Report Ser.: No. 10). 131p. 1994. 67.00 (*0-419-19960-8*, E & FN Spon) Routledge Chapman & Hall.

Paillet, Frederick & Cheng, C. H., eds. Acoustic Waves in Boreholes. (Illus.). 176p. 1991. 98.95 (*0-8493-8890-2*, TN871) CRC Pr.

Paillet, Frederick L. & Saunders, Wayne R., eds. Geophysical Applications for Geotechnical Investigations. LC 90-40924. (Special Technical Publication (STP) Ser.: STP 1101). (Illus.). 118p. 1990. text ed. 40.00 (*0-8031-1403-6*, 04-01101-38) ASTM.

Paillet, Jean-Pierre & Dugas, Andre. Approaches to Syntax. (Lingvisticae Investigationes Supplementa Ser.: 5). viii, 282p. 1982. 71.00x (*90-272-3115-X*) Benjamins North Am.

Paillotin, Guy, ed. The Living Cell in Four Dimensions. LC 91-55209. (AIP Conference Proceedings Ser.: No. 226). 608p. 1991. 105.00 (*0-88318-794-9*) Am Inst Physics.

***Pailloz, Valerie & Kennedy, Dorothy.** Southern Legacy. 1995. 11.95 (*0-8062-5208-1*) Carlton.

Paimquist, Peter, jt. auth. see Cranston, Jerneral W.

Pain, Andrew J. Adverse Possession: A Conveyancer's Guide. 224p. 1992. 84.00 (*1-85190-183-3*, Pub. by Tolley Pubng UK) St Mut.

Pain, Andrew J., jt. auth. see Convey, Stephen R.

Pain, Barry E. Humorous Stories. LC 79-37281. (Short Story Index Reprint Ser.). 1977. reprint ed. 39.95 (*0-8369-4091-1*) Ayer.

Pain, Deborah & Dixon, James, eds. Bird Conservation & Farming Policy in the European Community. (Illus.). 400p. 1996. boxed write for info. (*0-12-544280-7*) Acad Pr.

Pain, H. J. Physics of Vibrations & Waves. 3rd ed. LC 83-5880. 416p. 1983. text ed. 84.95 (*0-471-90181-4*) Wiley.

— The Physics of Vibrations & Waves. 4th ed. 479p. 1993. text ed. 89.95 (*0-471-93619-7*); pap. text ed. 34.95 (*0-471-93742-8*) Wiley.

Pain, Herbert J. The Physics of Vibrations & Waves. 3rd ed. LC 86-1597. (Illus.). 432p. reprint ed. pap. 123.20 (*0-7837-1876-4*, 2042077) Bks Demand.

Pain, Kenneth W. Licensing Practice & Procedure. 202p. 1986. 125.00 (*1-85190-009-8*, Pub. by Fourmat Pub UK) St Mut.

— Licensing Practice & Procedure. 250p. 1990. 69.00 (*1-85190-102-7*, Pub. by Tolley Pubng UK) St Mut.

— Licensing Practice & Procedure. 3rd ed. 228p. (C). 1988. 90.00 (*1-85190-059-4*, Pub. by Fourmat Pub UK) St Mut.

— Minors - The Law & Practice: The Juvenile Courts - The Offences - The Role of the Local Authorities. 293p. 1987. 136.00 (*1-85190-030-6*, Pub. by Fourmat Pub UK) St Mut.

Pain, Kenneth W. & Whale, Stephen J. Emergency Applications to Magistrates. 179p. 1986. 104.00 (*1-85190-001-2*, Pub. by Fourmat Pub UK) St Mut.

Pain, P. Where to Join. 1990. pap. 24.00 (*0-7463-0378-5*, Pub. by Northcote UK) St Mut.

Pain, R. H. & Smith, B. J., eds. New Techniques in Biophysics & Cell Biology Vol. 1. LC 72-8611. 259p. 1974. reprint ed. pap. 73.90 (*0-317-29873-9*, 2016156) Bks Demand.

— New Techniques in Biophysics & Cell Biology Vol. 2 - 1975. LC 72-8611. 407p. 1975. reprint ed. pap. 116.00 (*0-7837-8634-4*, 2016156) Bks Demand.

— New Techniques in Biophysics & Cell Biology Vol. 3 - 1976. fac. ed. LC 72-8611. 253p. 1976. pap. 72.20 (*0-7837-8635-2*, 2016156) Bks Demand.

Pain, Roger H., ed. Mechanisms of Protein Folding. LC 93-47574. (Illus.). 288p. (C). 1994. 68.00 (*0-19-963396-7*, IRL Pr); pap. 43.00 (*0-19-963397-5*, IRL Pr) OUP.

Pain, Timmothy, jt. auth. see Bickersteth, John.

Paine. Rights of Man. 1994. pap. 17.00 (*0-679-43314-7*) Random.

Paine, ed. see Stryker & Bingham.

Paine, A. J., jt. ed. see Dayan, A. D.

Paine, Alan. Ode to Madonna & Other Poems. (Illus.). 160p. (Orig.). (YA). (gr. 4 up). 1992. pap. 12.95 (*0-9632582-1-4*) Diogenes Pr.

Paine, Albert. The Hollow Tree & Deep Woods Book. 272p. 1993. 20.95 (*0-89190-368-2*, Am Repr) Amereon Ltd.

Paine, Albert B. The Arkansas Bear: A Tale of Fanciful Adventure Told in Song & Story. 20.95 (*0-89190-367-4*, Am Repr) Amereon Ltd.

— Captain Bill McDonald Texas Ranger. LC 86-61298. (Illus.). 454p. 1986. reprint ed. pap. 14.95 (*0-938349-03-1*) State House Pr.

— The Great White Way: An Unusual Voyage of Discovery, & Some Romantic Love Affairs Amid Strange Surroundings. LC 74-16514. (Science Fiction Ser.). (Illus.). 330p. 1975. reprint ed. 26.95 (*0-405-06309-1*) Ayer.

— Hollow Tree Snowed-in Book. 21.95 (*0-8488-1121-6*) Amereon Ltd.

— Mark Twain, a Biography, 3 vols. 1992. reprint ed. lib. bdg. 225.00 (*0-7812-5072-2*) Rprt Serv.

— The Mystery of Evelin Delorme: A Hypnotic Story. Reginald, R. & Menville, Douglas, eds. LC 75-46299. (Supernatural & Occult Fiction Ser.). 1976. reprint ed. lib. bdg. 17.95 (*0-405-08159-6*) Ayer.

— Thomas Nast: His Period & His Pictures. LC 78-177504. (Illus.). 1972. reprint ed. 30.95 (*0-405-08831-0*) Ayer.

Paine, Charles. The Art of Railroading. 143p. 1987. pap. 6.95 (*0-933905-03-3*) Claycomb Pr.

Paine, Crispin, jt. auth. see Ambrose, Tim.

Paine, D. C., jt. ed. see Bravman, J. C.

Paine, David P. Aerial Photography & Image Interpretation for Resource Management. LC 81-4287. 571p. 1981. Net. text ed. write for info. (*0-471-01857-0*) Wiley.

Paine, F. Modern Processing, Packaging & Distribution Systems for Food. 1987. text ed. 61.95 (*0-442-20510-4*) Van Nos Reinhold.

— Packaging User's Handbook. 1991. text ed. 139.95 (*0-442-30283-5*) Chapman & Hall.

Paine, Francis F. Diego Rivera. LC 74-169310. (Museum of Modern Art Publications in Reprint). (Illus.). 128p. 1979. reprint ed. 25.95 (*0-405-01569-0*) Ayer.

Paine, Fred K. & Paine, Nancy E. Magazines: A Bibliography for Their Analysis with Annotations & Study Guide. LC 86-29825. 698p. 1987. 62.50 (*0-8108-1975-9*) Scarecrow.

Paine-Gernee, Karen & Rothstein, Larry. Secrets to Tell, Secrets to Keep: How to Best Handle Your Hidden Thoughts & Feelings & Move Beyond Therapy to a Truly Joyous, Creative & Fulfilling Life. 240p. (Orig.). 1994. pap. 10.99 (*0-446-39479-3*) Warner Bks.

***Paine, Gordon.** The Choral Journal: An Index to Volumes 1-18. (Monograph Ser.: No. 3). 170p. 1978. 7.50 (*0-614-05590-3*) Am Choral Dirs.

Paine, Gordon, ed. Five Centuries of Choral Music: Essays in Honor of Howard Swan. LC 87-32816. (Festschrift Ser.: No. 6). 250p. 1989. lib. bdg. 48.00 (*0-918728-84-3*) Pendragon NY.

Paine, Gregory. Southern Prose Writers: Representative Selections. (BCL1-PS American Literature Ser.). 392p. 1993. reprint ed. lib. bdg. 89.00 (*0-7812-6930-X*) Rprt Serv.

Paine, Gregory L., ed. Southern Prose Writers. LC 79-101832. (Biography Index Reprint Ser.). 1977. 39.95 (*0-8369-8006-9*) Ayer.

Paine, H. O., ed. Paine Family Records: A Journal of Genealogical & Biographical Information Respecting the American Family of Payne, Paine, Payn, Etc., 2 vols. in 1. (Illus.). 522p. 1989. reprint ed. lib. bdg. 86.00 (*0-8328-0928-4*); reprint ed. pap. 78.00 (*0-8328-0929-2*) Higginson Bk Co.

Paine, J. G. & Morton, R. A. Shoreline & Vegetation-Line Movement, Texas Gulf Coast, 1987 to 1982. (Geological Circular Ser.: GC 89-1). (Illus.). 50p. 1974. 3.00 (*0-317-03108-2*) Bur Econ Geology.

***Paine, J. G., et al.** Geophysical & Geochemical Delineation of Sites of Saline-Water Inflow to the Canadian River, New Mexico & Texas. (Report of Investigations Ser.: No. RI 225). (Illus.). Date not set. 4.50 (*0-614-06196-2*) Bur Econ Geology.

Paine, J. R. Smart Homeseller's Sale by Owner Kit. 1986. 19.95 (*0-8187-0065-3*) Harlo Press.

Paine, James R., ed. IUCN Directory of Protected Areas in Oceania. 472p. 1991. 40.00 (*2-8317-0069-8*, B710, Pub. by IUCN SZ) Island Pr.

Paine, Jeffery M. The Simplication of American Life: Hollywood's Films of the 1930's. 1977. 29.95 (*0-405-09893-6*, 11489) Ayer.

Paine, Jim, ed. see Brown, Charlene.

Paine, Jocelyn. The Logic Programming Tutor. 320p. 1992. lib. bdg. 62.50 (*0-7923-1448-4*) Kluwer Ac.

Paine, Joclyn. The Logic Programming Tutor. 366p. 1992. pap. text ed. 37.95 (*1-871516-09-9*, Pub. by Intellect Bks UK) Cromland.

Paine, John K. Complete Piano Music. LC 83-18890. (Earlier American Music Ser.: No. 27). 100p. 1984. reprint ed. lib. bdg. 25.00 (*0-306-77323-6*) Da Capo.

— The History of Music to the Death of Schubert. LC 78-127280. (Music Ser.). (Illus.). 1971. reprint ed. lib. bdg. 37.50 (*0-306-70038-7*) Da Capo.

— Symphony No. One: Opus 23. LC 73-171077. (Earlier American Music Ser.: No. 1). 180p. 1972. reprint ed. lib. bdg. 32.50 (*0-306-77301-5*) Da Capo.

Paine, Lauran. Adobe Empire. large type ed. LC 93-13365. 1993. 18.95 (*0-7927-1701-5*, Roundup Lrg Print Westerns); pap. 16.95 (*0-7927-1700-7*, Roundup Lrg Print Westerns) Chivers N Amer.

— The Blue Basin Country. 1987. 15.95 (*0-8027-4070-7*) Walker & Co.

— Custer Meadow. 1988. 16.95 (*0-8027-4072-3*) Walker & Co.

— The Devil on Horseback. 224p. 1995. 19.95 (*0-8027-4148-7*) Walker & Co.

— The Fifth Horseman. large type ed. LC 93-30321. 1994. 18.95 (*0-7927-1857-7*, Roundup Lrg Print Westerns); pap. 16.95 (*0-7927-1856-9*, Roundup Lrg Print Westerns) Chivers N Amer.

— Greed at Gold River. large type ed. LC 94-11176. (Western Ser.). 175p. 1994. 17.95 (*0-7862-0257-2*) Thorndike Pr.

— The Homesteaders. 192p. 1987. pap. 2.75 (*0-380-70185-5*) Avon.

— The Horseman. 192p. 1986. 15.95 (*0-8027-4063-4*) Walker & Co.

— Kiowa Apache. 1994. 14.95 (*0-7451-4595-7*, Gunsmoke) Chivers N Amer.

— The Manhunter. large type ed. LC 94-45644. 214p. 1995. 18.95 (*0-7862-0397-8*) Thorndike Pr.

— The Marshal. 154p. 1985. 14.95 (*0-8027-4053-7*) Walker & Co.

— The Marshall. 176p. 1987. pap. 2.50 (*0-380-70187-1*) Avon.

— Moon Prairie. large type ed. LC 94-11175. 233p. Date not set. bds. 17.95 (*0-7862-0256-4*) Thorndike Pr.

— New Mexico Heritage. 208p. 1987. 15.95 (*0-8027-0940-0*) Walker & Co.

— Nightrider's Moon. 160p. 1988. 16.95 (*0-8027-4083-9*) Walker & Co.

— The Open Range Men. 206p. 1990. 19.95 (*0-8027-4105-3*) Walker & Co.

— The Open Range Men. large type ed. LC 90-40665. 304p. 1990. reprint ed. lib. bdg. 16.95 (*1-56054-041-9*) Thorndike Pr.

— Outpost. large type ed. LC 93-4530. 1993. 18.95 (*0-7927-1717-1*, Roundup Lrg Print Westerns); pap. 16.95 (*0-7927-1716-3*, Roundup Lrg Print Westerns) Chivers N Amer.

— The Prairieton Raid. 192p. 1994. 19.95 (*0-8027-4139-8*) Walker & Co.

— The Prairieton Raid. large type ed. LC 94-32216. 245p. 1995. lib. bdg. 18.95 (*0-7862-0328-5*) Thorndike Pr.

— The Renegade. large type ed. LC 94-45643. 219p. 1995. 18.95 (*0-7862-0396-X*) Thorndike Pr.

— Riders of the Trojan Horse. 192p. 1991. 19.95 (*0-8027-4116-9*) Walker & Co.

— Riders of the Trojan Horse. large type ed. 302p. 1991. reprint ed. lib. bdg. 16.95 (*1-56054-241-1*) Thorndike Pr.

— Skye. 192p. 1987. pap. 2.75 (*0-380-70186-3*) Avon.

— Spirit Meadow. 192p. 1987. 15.95 (*0-8027-0970-2*) Walker & Co.

— The Squaw Men. 192p. 1992. 19.95 (*0-8027-4126-6*) Walker & Co.

— The Squaw Men. large type ed. 290p. 1992. reprint ed. lib. bdg. 17.95 (*1-56054-507-0*) Thorndike Pr.

— The Taurus Gun. 192p. 1989. 18.95 (*0-8027-4086-3*) Walker & Co.

— Thunder Valley. 198p. 1993. 19.95 (*0-8027-1235-5*) Walker & Co.

— Thunder Valley. large type ed. LC 93-1385. 1993. 17.95 (*1-56054-720-0*) Thorndike Pr.

— Timberline. large type ed. LC 94-45642. 1995. write for info. (*0-7862-0398-6*) Thorndike Pr.

— The Undertaker. large type ed. 384p. 1992. reprint ed. lib. bdg. 17.95 (*1-56054-401-5*) Thorndike Pr.

— Vengeance Trail. large type ed. LC 93-50790. 1994. 18.95 (*0-7927-2009-1*, Roundup Lrg Print Westerns); pap. 16.95 (*0-7927-2008-3*, Roundup Lrg Print Westerns) Chivers N Amer.

Paine, Melanie. Fabric Magic. LC 87-43004. 216p. 1989. pap. 24.00 (*0-679-72598-9*) McKay.

— Fabric Magic. LC 87-43004. 1992. pap. 24.00 (*0-394-24138-X*) Pantheon.

— The New Fabric Magic. (Illus.). 216p. 1995. pap. 25.00 (*0-679-75840-2*) Pantheon.

Paine, Melanie, jt. auth. see Clifton-Mogg, Caroline.

Paine, Michael. Harrap's Spanish Commercial Correspondence. 1994. pap. 12.00 (*0-671-89991-0*) P-H.

Paine, Nancy E., jt. auth. see Paine, Fred K.

Paine, Orphelia. Look & See the Town: Historic Sites of Nashville & Davidson County. 68p. 1989. pap. write for info. (*0-9630176-0-8*) Metro Hist Comm.

Paine, Penelope, ed. see Rosentheil, Agnes.

Paine, Penelope, tr. see Rosentheil, Agnes.

Paine, Penelope C. Molly's Magic. (Key Concepts in Personal Development Ser.). (Illus.). 32p. (J). (gr. 1-4). 1995. 16.95 (*1-55942-068-5*, 7660) Marshfilm.

— Time for Horatio. Stryker, Sandy, ed. LC 89-18304. (Illus.). 48p. (J). (ps-6). 1990. 14.95 (*0-911655-33-6*) Advocacy Pr.

Paine, Penelope C. & Bingham, Mindy. My Way Sally. LC 88-2653. (Illus.). 48p. (J). (ps-6). 1988. 14.95 (*0-911655-27-1*) Advocacy Pr.

Paine, Penelope C., ed. see Bingham, Mindy & Stryker, Sandy.

Paine, Ralph D. The Book of Pirate Treasures: Being a True History of the Gold, Jewels, & Plate of Pirates, Galleons, Etc., Which Are Sought for to This Day. (Illus.). 472p. 1992. pap. 15.00 (*0-87380-177-6*) Rio Grande.

— Joshua Barney: A Forgotten Hero of Blue Water. LC 79-124249. (Select Bibliographies Reprint Ser.). 1977. reprint ed. 29.95 (*0-8369-5437-8*) Ayer.

Paine, Richard. Hispanic Traditions in Twentieth-Century Catalan Music: With Particular Reference to Gerhard, Mompou, & Montsalvatge. (Outstanding Dissertations in Music from British Universities Ser.). 328p. 1989. 25.00 (*0-8240-2019-7*) Garland.

Paine, Richmond, et al. Dyslexia & Reading Disabilities. 224p. 1972. text ed. 29.50 (*0-8422-7005-1*) Irvington.

Paine, Richmond S., jt. auth. see Crothers, Bronson.

Paine, Robert. Herds of the Tundra: A Portrait of Saami Reindeer Pastoralism. LC 93-38390. (Ethnographic Inquiry Ser.). (Illus.). 272p. (C). 1994. text ed. 59.00 (*1-56098-271-3*) Smithsonian.

Paine, Robert, et al. Generation & Interpretation of the Electrocardiogram. LC 87-25996. 291p. (Orig.). reprint ed. pap. 83.00 (*0-7837-2736-4*, 2043116) Bks Demand.

Paine, Robert T. & Soper, Alexander. The Art & Architecture of Japan. 3rd ed. (Pelican History of Art Ser.). (Illus.). 521p. (C). 1974. reprint ed. text ed. 55.00 (*0-300-05332-0*) Yale U Pr.

An Asterisk (*) at the beginning of an entry indicates that the title is appearing in BIP for the first time.

— The Art & Architecture of Japan. 3rd ed. (Pelican History of Art Ser.). (Illus.). 521p. (C). 1981. reprint ed. pap. text ed. 26.50 (*0-300-05333-9*) Yale U Pr.

Paine, Ruth B. Thematic Analysis of Francois Mauriac's "Genitrix, le Desert De L'amour, & le Noeud De Viperes" LC 76-8024. (Romance Monographs: No. 20). 1976. 26.00 (*84-399-4950-2*) Romance.

Paine, S., ed. Six Children Draw. LC 81-69580. 1982. text ed. 35.00 (*0-12-543950-4*) Acad Pr.

Paine, S. C. Paine Ancestry: The Family of Robert Treat Paine, Signer of the Declaration of Independence, Including Maternal Lines. Pope, C. H., ed. 336p. 1989. reprint ed. lib. bdg. 58.50 (*0-8328-0926-8*); reprint ed. pap. 50.50 (*0-8328-0927-6*) Higginson Bk Co.

Paine, Sheila. The Afghan Amulet: Travels from the Hindu Kush to Razgad. 304p. 1994. 21.95 (*0-312-11236-X*) St Martin.

— Chikan Embroidery: The Floral Whitework of India. (Shire Ethnography Ser.). (Illus.). 60p. 1989. pap. 10.50 (*0-7478-0009-X*, Pub. by Shire Pubns UK) Lubrecht & Cramer.

— Embroidered Textiles: Traditional Patterns from Five Continents. LC 90-52601. (Illus.). 192p. 1990. 35.00 (*0-8478-1231-6*) Rizzoli Intl.

Paine, Shepard. Building & Painting Scale Figures. Emmerich, Michael, ed. (Illus.). (Orig.). 1993. pap. 17.95 (*0-89024-069-8*) Kalmbach.

Paine, Sheperd. How to Build Dioramas. Hayden, Bob, ed. LC 80-82164. (Illus.). 104p. (Orig.). 1980. pap. 14.95 (*0-89024-551-7*) Kalmbach.

— Modeling Tanks & Military Vehicles. Angle, Burr, ed. (Illus.). 76p. (Orig.). 1982. pap. 11.95 (*0-89024-045-0*) Kalmbach.

Paine, Stan C., et al. Structuring Your Classroom for Academic Success. LC 83-61812. (Illus.). 176p. 1983. pap. 13.95 (*0-87822-228-6*, 2286) Res Press.

***Paine, Stefani.** The World of the Arctic Whales: Belugas, Bowheads & Narwhals. LC 95-1168. (Illus.). 128p. 1995. 26.00 (*0-87156-378-9*) Sierra.

— The World of the Sea Otter. LC 93-2820. (Illus.). 144p. 1993. 25.00 (*0-87156-546-3*) Sierra.

Paine, Stephen W. Beginning Greek: A Functional Approach. (YA). (gr. 9 up). 1961. 24.95 (*0-19-501013-2*) OUP.

Paine, Suzanne, jt. ed. see Nolan, Peter.

Paine, Thomas. Age of Reason. 18.95 (*0-8488-0604-2*) Amereon Ltd.

— Age of Reason. 192p. 1995. pap. 8.95 (*0-8065-0549-4*, Citadel Pr) Carol Pub Group.

— The Age of Reason. LC 84-62825. (Great Books in Philosophy). 190p. 1985. pap. 13.95 (*0-87975-273-4*) Prometheus Bks.

— The Age of Reason. LC 92-35924. (Library of America). 1993. 6.99 (*0-517-09118-6*, Pub. by Gramercy) Random Hse Value.

— Age of Reason. 1986. reprint ed. lib. bdg. 18.95 (*0-89966-543-8*) Buccaneer Bks.

— The Age of Reason. 194p. 1974. reprint ed. spiral bd. 8.25 (*0-7873-0651-7*) Mokelumne.

— Age of Reason: Special Two Hundreth Anniversary Edition. LC 92-64310. 155p. 1992. reprint ed. pap. 5.00 (*0-9632612-2-3*) Wet Water.

— The Age of Reason, Pt. 3: Examination of the Prophecies. Zindler, Frank, ed. LC 92-45546. 95p. 1993. pap. 12.00 (*0-910309-70-1*, 5575) Am Atheist.

— Common Sense. 16.95 (*0-8488-1088-0*) Amereon Ltd.

— Common Sense. (American Library). 1982. pap. 6.95 (*0-14-039016-2*, Penguin Classics) Viking Penguin.

— Common Sense. (Great Books in Philosophy Ser.). 67p. (C). 1994. pap. text ed. 5.95 (*0-87975-918-6*) Prometheus Bks.

— Common Sense. 1986. reprint ed. lib. bdg. 17.95 (*0-89966-542-X*) Buccaneer Bks.

— Common Sense & the Rights of Man. 1984. mass mkt. 4.95 (*0-452-00712-7*, Plume) NAL-Dutton.

— Common Sense, the Rights of Man, & Other Essential Writings of Thomas Paine. 288p. 1984. pap. 10.95 (*0-452-00921-9*, Mer) NAL-Dutton.

— The Crisis Essays. Norman, Charles J., ed. 1991. 11.95 (*0-8084-0434-2*) NCUP.

— Political Writings. Kuklick, Bruce, ed. (Cambridge Texts in the History of Political Thought Ser.). (C). 1989. 39. 95 (*0-521-36665-8*); pap. 7.95 (*0-521-36678-X*) Cambridge U Pr.

— Public Good. 41p. 1989. reprint ed. 5.00 (*0-935680-24-1*) Kentucke Imprints.

— Rights of Man. 17.95 (*0-8488-1443-6*) Amereon Ltd.

— Rights of Man. 1976. pap. 3.95 (*0-8065-0548-6*, Citadel Pr) Carol Pub Group.

— Rights of Man. LC 92-20305. 226p. (C). 1992. lib. bdg. 27.50 (*0-87220-148-1*); pap. text ed. 4.50 (*0-87220-147-3*) Hackett Pub.

— The Rights of Man. 288p. 1993. pap. 6.95 (*0-460-87140-4*, Everyman's Classic Lib) C E Tuttle.

— The Rights of Man. LC 86-64007. (Great Books in Philosophy). 188p. pap. 7.95 (*0-87975-379-X*) Prometheus Bks.

— The Rights of Man. (Pelican Classics Ser.). 1984. mass mkt. 8.95 (*0-14-039015-4*, Penguin Classics) Viking Penguin.

— The Rights of Man. 1989. reprint ed. lib. bdg. 18.95 (*0-89966-626-4*) Buccaneer Bks.

— The Rights of Man, Pt. I. LC 92-25538. 174p. 1992. reprint ed. 48.00 (*1-85477-109-4*, Pub. by Woodstock Bks UK) Cassell.

— Rights of Man, Common Sense, & Other Writings. Philp, Mark, ed. & intro. by. (The World's Classics Ser.). 544p. 1995. pap. 9.95 (*0-19-282865-7*) OUP.

— Writings, Vol. 76. Foner, Eric, ed. LC 94-25756. 906p. 1995. 35.00 (*1-883011-03-5*) Library of America.

— The Writings of Thomas Paine: The Standard Edition, 4 vols. Conway, Moncure D., ed. reprint ed. write for info. (*0-318-50759-5*) AMS Pr.

— The Writings of Thomas Paine: The Standard Edition, 4 vols, 1. Conway, Moncure D., ed. LC 78-181966. reprint ed. 43.75 (*0-404-04871-4*) AMS Pr.

— The Writings of Thomas Paine: The Standard Edition, 4 vols, 2. Conway, Moncure D., ed. LC 78-181966. reprint ed. 43.75 (*0-404-04872-2*) AMS Pr.

— The Writings of Thomas Paine: The Standard Edition, 4 vols, 3. Conway, Moncure D., ed. LC 78-181966. reprint ed. 43.75 (*0-404-04873-0*) AMS Pr.

— The Writings of Thomas Paine: The Standard Edition, 4 vols, 4. Conway, Moncure D., ed. LC 78-181966. reprint ed. 43.75 (*0-404-04874-9*) AMS Pr.

— The Writings of Thomas Paine: The Standard Edition, 4 vols, Set. Conway, Moncure D., ed. LC 78-181966. reprint ed. 175.00 (*0-404-04870-6*) AMS Pr.

Paine, Thomas, jt. auth. see Burke, Edmund E.

Paine, Thomas O., ed. Leaving the Cradle: Human Exploration of Space in the 21st Century - 28th Goddard Memorial Symposium. LC 57-43769. (Science & Technology Ser.: Vol. 78). (Illus.). 348p. 1991. lib. bdg. 70.00 (*0-87703-336-6*, Pub. by Am Astro Soc); pap. 55.00 (*0-87703-337-4*, Pub. by Am Astro Soc) Univelt Inc.

Paine, Wingate. Tilling the Soul. 215p. 1984. pap. 10.95 (*0-943358-20-5*) Aurora Press.

Paineau, Georges. Bouquet de Bretagne: Seasonal Recipes from Le Bretagne, Questembert. (Illus.). 96p. 1993. 17. 95 (*1-85145-788-7*, Pub. by Pavilion UK) Trafalgar.

Paino, Frankie. The Rapture of Matter. (Cleveland Poets Ser.: No. 47). 61p. (Orig.). 1991. pap. 8.00 (*0-914946-91-9*) Cleveland St Univ Poetry Ctr.

Paino, Jon, jt. auth. see Messinger, Lisa.

Paino, Paul E. Is the Holy Spirit Real? 80p. 1992. pap. 7.95 (*1-882357-01-9*) P E Paino Minist.

— The Ministry: What's Right? What's Wrong? 48p. 1992. pap. 4.95 (*1-882357-02-7*) P E Paino Minist.

— The Missing Element in Church Development. 224p. 1992. pap. 12.95 (*1-882357-03-5*) P E Paino Minist.

— Our Father's Promises ... to Us! 64p. 1992. pap. 6.95 (*1-882357-00-0*) P E Paino Minist.

Paint, Box Books. Make Believe Monsters. 1989. pap. 0.71 (*0-394-82278-1*) Random.

Painter. Close Corp, 2 vols., 1. 3rd ed. 1991. 175.00 (*0-316-68874-6*) Little.

— Close Corp, 2 vols., 2. 3rd ed. 1991. 175.00 (*0-316-68879-7*) Little.

— Close Corp, 2 vols., Set. 3rd ed. 1991. 325.00 (*0-316-68880-0*) Little.

— Early Language Development. 1992. text ed. 49.00 (*0-86187-463-3*, Pub. by Pinter Pubs UK) St Martin.

Painter, Ann F., ed. Reader in Classification & Descriptive Cataloging. LC 72-78204. 320p. 1983. text ed. 55.00 (*0-313-24035-3*, ZRC/, Praeger Pubs) Greenwood.

Painter, Anthony. Butterworths Food Law. 618p. 1992. U.K. pap. 75.00 (*0-406-00642-3*) Butterworth Legal Pubs.

Painter, Anthony A. & Harvey, Brian W., eds. O'Keefe: The Law of Weights & Measures, 2 vols., Set. 2nd ed. ring bd. 390.00 (*0-406-32645-2*) Butterworth Legal Pubs.

Painter, Anthony A., et al, eds. Butterworths Law of Food & Drugs, 6 vols. 1991. Set, U.K. ring bd. 1,190.00 (*0-406-11610-5*) Butterworth Legal Pubs.

Painter, Carol. Friends Helping Friends: A Manual for Peer Counselors. Sorenson, Don L., ed. 224p. (Orig.). (YA). (gr. 9-12). 1989. pap. text ed. 9.95 (*0-932796-28-1*) Ed Media Corp.

— Leading a Friends Helping Friends Program. Sorenson, Don L., ed. 160p. (Orig.). (YA). (gr. 9-12). 1989. pap. text ed. 8.95 (*0-932796-29-X*) Ed Media Corp.

— Workshop Winners: Developing Creative & Dynamic Workshops. LC 93-70535. 184p. (Orig.). (C). 1993. pap. text ed. 12.95 (*0-932796-57-5*) Ed Media Corp.

Painter, Charles C. The Condition of Affairs in Indian Territory & California. LC 74-15121. reprint ed. 29.50 (*0-404-11981-6*) AMS Pr.

Painter, Charlotte. Gifts of Age: Portraits & Essays of 32 Remarkable Women. LC 85-13267. 1985. pap. 16.95 (*0-87701-368-3*) Chronicle Bks.

— Who Made the Lamb. LC 88-72025. 224p. (Orig.). 1988. reprint ed. pap. 8.95 (*0-88739-063-3*) Creat Arts Bk.

Painter, Charlotte, jt. ed. see Moffat, Mary J.

Painter, Clare. Learning the Mother Tongue. (Language Education Ser.). 68p. 1989. pap. text ed. 8.75 (*0-19-437159-X*) OUP.

— Learning the Mother Tongue. 2nd ed. 93p. (C). 1991. pap. 48.00x (*0-7300-1249-2*, ECS805, Pub. by Deakin Univ AT) St Mut.

Painter, Colin. Gonja: A Phonological & Grammatical Study. (African Ser.: Vol. 1). (Illus.). 1970. pap. text ed. 20.00 (*0-87750-139-4*) Res Inst Inner Asian Studies.

Painter, David S. Allied Relations in Iran, 1941-1945. (Pew Case Studies in International Affairs). 50p. (C). 1986. pap. text ed. 2.50 (*1-56927-425-8*) Geo U Inst Dplmcy.

— The Baruch Plan & the International Control of Atomic Energy. (Pew Case Studies in International Affairs). 50p. (C). 1990. pap. text ed. 2.50 (*1-56927-324-3*) Geo U Inst Dplmcy.

— Deciding Germany's Future, 1943-1945. (Pew Case Studies in International Affairs). 50p. (C). 1992. pap. text ed. 2.50 (*1-56927-323-5*) Geo U Inst Dplmcy.

— The German Question & the Cold War. (Pew Case Studies in International Affairs). 50p. (C). 1994. pap. text ed. 2.50 (*1-56927-415-0*) Geo U Inst Dplmcy.

— Oil & the American Century: The Political Economy of U. S. Foreign Oil Policy, 1941-1954. LC 85-24216. (Studies in Historical & Political Science: No. 1). 336p. 1986. text ed. 47.00 (*0-8018-2693-4*) Johns Hopkins.

— The United States, Great Britain & Mossadegh. (Pew Case Studies in International Affairs). 50p. (C). 1993. pap. text ed. 2.50 (*1-56927-332-4*) Geo U Inst Dplmcy.

Painter, David S., jt. auth. see Fain, William T.

Painter, David S., jt. auth. see Howard, James R.

Painter, David S., jt. auth. see Irvine, Sally G.

Painter, David S., jt. ed. see Leffler, Melvyn P.

Painter, Desmond. Columbus. Yapp, Malcolm et al, eds. (World History Ser.). (Illus.). 32p. (YA). (gr. 6-11). 1980. reprint ed. pap. text ed. 4.35 (*0-89908-017-0*) Greenhaven.

— Mao Tse-Tung. Yapp, Malcolm et al, eds. (World History Ser.). (Illus.). (YA). (gr. 6-11). 1980. reprint ed. pap. 4.35 (*0-89908-102-9*) Greenhaven.

Painter, Desmond, et al. Religion. Yapp, Malcolm et al, eds. (World History Ser.). (Illus.). 32p. (YA). (gr. 6-11). 1980. reprint ed. pap. text ed. 4.35 (*0-89908-120-7*) Greenhaven.

Painter, Floyd, jt. auth. see Hranicky, W. Jack.

Painter, Floyd, jt. auth. see Hranicky, Wm. Jack.

Painter, Francis O., jt. auth. see Gherman, Paul M.

Painter, Franklin V. History of Education. enl. rev. ed. LC 73-137265. reprint ed. 29.50 (*0-404-04866-8*) AMS Pr.

— Poets of the South. LC 68-57064. (Granger Index Reprint Ser.). 1977. 17.95 (*0-8369-6037-8*) Ayer.

Painter, Franklin V., ed. Great Pedagogical Essays: Plato to Spencer. LC 77-137266. reprint ed. 47.50 (*0-404-04865-X*) AMS Pr.

Painter, Genevieve & Corsini, Ray. Effective Discipline in the Home & School. LC 89-84337. 468p. 1990. pap. text ed. 26.95 (*0-915202-89-1*) Accel Devel.

Painter, Genevieve, et al, eds. Alfred Adler: As We Remember Him. 2nd ed. (Illus.). 122p. 1988. pap. write for info. (*0-926164-00-7*) N Am Soc Adlerian.

Painter, George D. Marcel Proust. 1989. 39.95 (*0-394-57669-1*) Random.

— Marcel Proust: A Biography, 2 vols. 1978. pap. 4.95 (*0-685-04271-5*, Vin) Random.

Painter, Hal. The Captain Nemo Cookbook Papers. (Illus.). 144p. 1986. 10.95 (*0-87742-206-0*) Intl Marine.

Painter, Jack W. Deep Bodywork & Personal Development: Harmonizing Our Bodies, Emotions, & Thoughts. 1987. 19.00 (*0-938405-01-2*) Bodymind Bks.

— Technical Manual of Deep Wholistic Bodywork: Postural Integration. 203p. 1987. pap. 22.00 (*0-938405-05-5*) Bodymind Bks.

Painter, Jacqueline B. The German Invasion of Western North Carolina: A Pictorial History. LC 92-93524. (Illus.). 128p. (YA). (gr. 8 up). 1992. 28.00 (*0-9634256-0-9*) J B Painter.

Painter, James. Bolivia & Coca: A Study in Dependency. LC 93-32723. (Studies on the Impact of the Illegal Drug Trade: Vol. 1). 194p. 1994. lib. bdg. 36.50 (*1-55587-490-8*) Lynne Rienner.

— Guatemala: False Hope, False Freedom. rev. ed. (Latin America Bureau Ser.). 135p. (C). 1989. text ed. 22.00 (*0-906156-32-7*); pap. text ed. 8.95 (*0-906156-41-6*) Monthly Rev.

— Guatemala: False Hope, False Freedom. rev. ed. (Illus.). 160p. 1989. pap. 8.95 (*0-85345-732-8*, Pub. by Lat Am Bur UK) Monthly Rev.

— Guatemala: False Hope, False Freedom. 2nd rev. ed. (Illus.). 160p. 1989. 24.00 (*0-85345-748-4*, Pub. by Lat Am Bur UK) Monthly Rev.

Painter, James, ed. The Dance of the Millions: Latin America & the Debt Crisis. 272p. 1988. pap. 11.00 (*0-85345-742-5*, Pub. by Lat Am Bur UK) Monthly Rev.

Painter, James & CIIR & Latin America Bureau, eds. Guatemala: False Hope, False Freedom. 144p. (C). 1987. 90.00 (*0-685-44907-6*); pap. 40.00 (*0-685-29894-9*) St Mut.

Painter, Jeff. Laser Locator: Reference Manual & Workbook. Blinn, William, ed. 1992. 50.00 (*1-880933-01-2*) Mgmt Comp Srvs.

***Painter, Jerry.** Great Trails for Family Hiking: The Tetons. (Illus.). 164p. (Orig.). 1995. pap. 15.00 (*0-87108-857-6*) Pruett.

Painter, John. The Quest for the Messiah: The History, Literature & Theology of the Johannine. LC 93-31675. 466p. (C). 1994. pap. text ed. 24.95 (*0-687-35153-7*) Abingdon.

— The Quest for the Messiah: The History, Literature & Theology of the Johannine. 2nd ed. 429p. 1991. text ed. 39.95 (*0-567-09592-4*, Pub. by T & T Clark UK) Bks Intl VA.

***Painter, Julie.** The King Maker. 280p. 1995. pap. 8.95 (*1-56901-536-8*) NW Pub.

Painter, Lee J. If Forever Came Tomorrow: These Are the Things I'd Like to Do Today. LC 93-79665. 64p. 1993. 8.95 (*1-56352-108-3*) Longstreet Pr Inc.

***Painter, Louis W.** Israel Is Real. LC 94-71504. 1995. 21.95 (*0-8158-0502-0*) Chris Mass.

***Painter, Mark P. & Looker, James M.** Ohio Driving under the Influence Law. 3rd ed. 524p. pap. text ed. 55.00 (*0-8322-0507-9*) Banks-Baldwin.

Painter, Michael & Durham, William H., eds. The Social Causes of Environmental Destruction in Latin America. (Linking Levels of Analysis Ser.). (Illus.). 350p. 1994. text ed. 59.50 (*0-472-09560-9*); pap. text ed. 23.95 (*0-472-06560-2*) U of Mich Pr.

Painter, Mirra, ed. see Shakked, Shlomit, et al.

Painter, Muriel T. With Good Heart: Yaqui Beliefs & Ceremonies in Pascua, Village. Spicer, Edward H. & Kaemlein, Wilma, eds. LC 86-893. (Illus.). 533p. 1986. 45.00 (*0-8165-0875-5*) U of Ariz Pr.

— A Yaqui Easter. LC 74-153706. 40p. 1971. pap. 7.50 (*0-8165-0168-8*) U of Ariz Pr.

Painter, Neil S. Diverticular Disease of the Colon. LC 76-58771. (Illus.). 320p. 1977. 12.95 (*0-87983-144-8*) Keats.

Painter, Nell I. Exodusters: Black Migration to Kansas After Reconstruction. (Illus.). 1992. reprint ed. pap. 10. 95 (*0-393-00951-3*) Norton.

— The Narrative of Hosea Hudson. (Illus.). 424p. 1993. pap. 12.95 (*0-393-31015-9*) Norton.

— The Narrative of Hosea Hudson, His Life As a Negro Communist in the South. LC 79-4589. 413p. reprint ed. pap. 118.60 (*0-7837-2308-3*, 2057396) Bks Demand.

— Standing at Armageddon: The United States, 1877-1919. LC 86-33111. 1989. pap. 12.95 (*0-393-30588-0*) Norton.

Painter, Nell I., ed. see Harris, Robert L., Jr.

Painter, Nell I., ed. see Wilson, Terry P.

Painter, P., jt. auth. see Homes, H.

Painter, Pamela, jt. auth. see Bernays, Anne.

Painter, Paul, jt. auth. see Coleman, Michael.

Painter, R., jt. auth. see Holmes, A.

Painter, R. W., jt. auth. see Holmes, A. E.

Painter, Richard, jt. auth. see Holmes, Ann.

Painter, Richard W. & Puttick, Keith. Employment Rights: A Reference Handbook. LC 93-15994. 450p. (C). 1993. text ed. 90.00 (*0-7453-0584-9*); pap. text ed. 40.00 (*0-7453-0589-X*) Westview.

Painter, Richard W., et al. Cases & Materials on Employment Law. 672p. 1995. pap. 54.00 (*1-85431-197-2*, Pub. by Blackstone Pr UK) W W Gaunt.

Painter, Robert B., jt. auth. see Gatti, Richard A.

Painter, Robert B., jt. ed. see Gatti, Richard A.

Painter, Sandra J. Orthopaedic Patient Education Resource Manual. LC 94-1342. 1994. 179.00 (*0-8342-0545-9*, S126) Aspen Pub.

Painter, Sandra J., ed. see Aspen Reference Group Staff.

Painter, Sandra J., jt. ed. see Lawrence, Kenneth E.

Painter, Sidney. French Chivalry: Chivalric Ideas & Practices in Medieval France. 188p. 1957. pap. 9.95 (*0-8014-9061-8*) Cornell U Pr.

— Mediaeval Society. 107p. 1951. 8.95 (*0-8014-9850-3*) Cornell U Pr.

— Medieval Society: Everyday Life in the Middle Ages. rev. ed. (Illus.). 64p. (C). 1991. pap. text ed. 2.25 (*1-877891-06-1*) Paperbook Pr Inc.

— The Reign of King John. 1979. 33.95 (*0-405-10619-X*) Ayer.

— Rise of the Feudal Monarchies. 147p. 1951. 8.95 (*0-8014-9851-1*) Cornell U Pr.

— Studies in the History of the English Feudal Barony. LC 78-64191. (Johns Hopkins University. Studies in the Social Sciences. Thirtieth Ser. 1912: 3). reprint ed. 20.00 (*0-404-61298-9*) AMS Pr.

— William Marshall: Knight-Errant, Baron, & Regent of England. (Medieval Academy Reprints for Teaching Ser.). 318p. 1982. pap. 14.95 (*0-8020-6498-1*) U of Toronto Pr.

Painter, Sidney, jt. auth. see Tierney, Brian.

Painter, Sigrid D. Aussprache des Fruehneuhochdeutschen nach Lesemeistern des 16. Jahrhunderts. (Berkeley Insights in Linguistics & Semiotics Ser.: Vol. 1). 200p. 1989. text ed. 39.95 (*0-8204-0498-5*) P Lang Pubs.

Painter, Suzanne, jt. ed. see Wetzel, Keith.

Painter, William. The Palace of Pleasure, 3 vols. 4th ed. No. 3. cvii, 1224p. 1968. reprint ed. Set. write for info. (*0-318-71604-6*, Pub. by Georg Olms GW) Lubrecht & Cramer.

— The Palace of Pleasure: Elizabethan Versions of Italian & French Novels from Boccaccio, Bandello, Cinthio, Straparola, Queen Margaret of Navarre & Others, 3 vols., Set. 4th ed. (Anglistica & Americana Ser.: No. 3). 1968. reprint ed. 219.70 (*0-685-66499-6*, 05101931, Pub. by Georg Olms GW) Lubrecht & Cramer.

Painter, William H. Business Planning: Problems & Materials. 2nd ed. LC 84-2186. (American Casebook Ser.). 1008p. (C). 1989. reprint ed. text ed. 47.00 (*0-314-80258-4*) West Pub.

— Business Planning, Teacher's Manual to Accompany. 3rd ed. (American Casebook Ser.). 137p. 1994. pap. text ed. write for info. (*0-314-04066-8*) West Pub.

— Business Planning, 1990 Supplement: Problems & Materials In. 2nd ed. (American Casebook Ser.). 256p. 1990. pap. text ed. 15.50 (*0-314-72204-1*) West Pub.

— Corporate & Tax Aspects of Closely Held Corporations. 2nd ed. 670p. 1981. 80.00 (*0-316-68854-1*) Little.

— Problems & Materials in Business Planning. 3rd ed. (American Casebook Ser.). 1107p. 1994. text ed. 52.00 (*0-314-03451-X*) West Pub.

Painter, William M. Musical Story Hours: Using Music with Storytelling & Puppetry. LC 88-31446. 172p. (C). 1989. lib. bdg. 29.50 (*0-208-02205-8*, Lib Prof Pubns) Shoe String.

— Palace of Pleasure, 4 Vols, 1. Miles, Hamish, ed. LC 30-20341. reprint ed. write for info. (*0-404-04881-1*) AMS Pr.

— Palace of Pleasure, 4 Vols, 2. Miles, Hamish, ed. LC 30-20341. reprint ed. write for info. (*0-404-04882-X*) AMS Pr.

— Palace of Pleasure, 4 Vols, 3. Miles, Hamish, ed. LC 30-20341. reprint ed. write for info. (*0-404-04883-8*) AMS Pr.

— Palace of Pleasure, 4 Vols, 4. Miles, Hamish, ed. LC 30-20341. reprint ed. write for info. (*0-404-04884-6*) AMS Pr.

— Palace of Pleasure, 4 Vols, Set. Miles, Hamish, ed. LC 30-20341. reprint ed. 240.00 (*0-404-04880-3*) AMS Pr.

— Storyhours with Puppets & Other Props. LC 90-6554. vi, 187p. 1990. lib. bdg. 29.50 (*0-208-02284-8*, Lib Prof Pubns) Shoe String.

— Storytelling with Music, Puppets, & Arts for Libraries & Classrooms. LC 94-20096. (Illus.). 164p. (C). 1994. pap. text ed. 27.50 (*0-208-02372-0*, Lib Prof Pubns) Shoe String.

Painting Department Staff. The Museum of Fine Arts Postcard Book: Thirty-Two American Impressionist Paintings in Color. (Illus.). 32p. (Orig.). 1985. pap. 7.95 (*0-87846-257-0*) Mus Fine Arts Boston.

Paipetis, S. A. & Holister, G. S., eds. Photoelasticity in Engineering Practice. LC 85-6914. 244p. 1985. 68.50 (*0-85334-363-2*, Pub. by Elsevier Applied Sci UK) Elsevier.

Pair, Joyce, ed. Women & the Constitution: Symposium Papers Collection. 169p. (C). 1990. pap. text ed. 14.95 (*1-879413-01-9*) Emory U Carter Ctr.

Pairaudeau, Natasha, tr. see Couture, Pascale.

Pairo, Preston. Beach Money. 208p. 1991. 18.95 (*0-8027-5786-3*) Walker & Co.

— Breach of Trust. LC 95-14712. 1995. write for info. (*0-312-13034-1*) St Martin.

— One Dead Judge. 204p. 1993. 19.95 (*0-8027-1250-9*) Walker & Co.

Pairo, Preston A., III. The Captain Drowns. (Ocean City Mysteries Ser.). 177p. (Orig.). 1986. pap. 2.95 (*0-9616584-0-1*) Maryland Locale.

Pais, Abraham. Einstein Lived Here: Essays for the Layman. LC 93-32095. (Illus.). 224p. 1994. 25.00 (*0-19-853994-0*, Clarendon Pr) OUP.

— Inward Bound: Of Matter & Forces in the Physical World. 700p. 1988. pap. 22.50 (*0-19-851997-4*) OUP.

— Niels Bohr's Times: In Physics, Philosophy, & Polity. 604p. 1991. 35.00 (*0-19-852049-2*) OUP.

— Niels Bohr's Times: In Physics, Philosophy, & Polity. (Illus.). 604p. 1994. reprint ed. pap. 17.95 (*0-19-852048-4*) OUP.

— Subtle Is the Lord: The Science & Life of Albert Einstein. LC 82-2273. (Illus.). 1982. 35.00 (*0-19-853907-X*) OUP.

— Subtle Is the Lord: The Science & Life of Albert Einstein. LC 82-2273. (Illus.). 1983. pap. 16.95 (*0-19-520438-7*) OUP.

Pais, Arthur J., jt. auth. see DeWitt, Dave.

Pais, Ettore. Ancient Legends of Roman History. Cosenza, Mario E., tr. LC 74-179532. (Select Bibliographies Reprint Ser.). 1977. reprint ed. 35.95 (*0-8369-6661-9*) Ayer.

Pais, Janet. Suffer the Children. 1991. pap. 9.95 (*0-8091-3226-5*) Paulist Pr.

***Paisey, David, comp.** Catalogue of Books Printed in the German-Speaking Countries & of German Books Printed in Other Countries from 1601 to 1700 Now in the British Library, 5 vols., Set. (Catalogues of the British Library Collections). 3024p. 1994. 590.00 (*0-7123-0351-0*, Pub. by Brit Library UK) U of Toronto Pr.

Paish, F. W. & Schwartz, G. L. Insurance Funds & Their Investment. (London School of Economic & Political Science Studies in Economics & Commerce: Vol. 2). 1969. reprint ed. pap. 35.00 (*0-8115-3299-2*) Periodicals Srv.

Paish, Frank W. Long-Term & Short-Term Interest Rates in the United Kingdom. LC 67-4633. 1967. 12.50 (*0-678-06764-3*) Kelley.

Paish, Wilf. Introduction to Athletics. (Illus.). 1974. 9.50 (*0-571-10191-7*) Transatl Arts.

— Nutrition for Sport. (Illus.). 128p. 1991. pap. 22.95 (*1-85223-380-X*, Pub. by Crowood Pr UK) Trafalgar.

— Training for Peak Performance. (Illus.). 160p. 1991. pap. 24.95 (*0-7136-3404-9*, Pub. by A&C Black UK) Talman.

Paisley Abbey Staff. Registrum Monasterii De Passelet. Innes, Cosmo, ed. LC 75-174311. (Maitland Club, Glasgow. Publications: No. 17). reprint ed. 52.50 (*0-404-52954-2*) AMS Pr.

Paisley, Clifton. From Cotton to Quail: An Agricultural Chronicle of Leon County, Florida, 1860-1967. LC 68-9708. (Illus.). xi, 162p. 1981. reprint ed. pap. 18.95 (*0-8130-0718-6*) U Press Fla.

Paisley, Clifton L. The Red Hills of Florida, 1528-1865. LC 88-5767. 304p. (C). 1989. pap. 27.95 (*0-8173-0412-6*) U of Ala Pr.

Paisley, Clyde A. Wouldn't You Rather Be Rich? How to Achieve Financial Independence Soundly & Surely. Selph, Alexa, ed. LC 88-9188. 320p. 1990. pap. 13.95 (*0-87797-163-3*) Cherokee.

***Paisley, Dennis, ed.** Selected Papers on Scientific & Engineering High-Speed Photography: Technology, Systems, & Applications. LC 95-1595. (Milestone Ser.: Vol. MS 109). 1995. text ed. write for info. (*0-8194-1854-4*) SPIE.

Paisley, Ian, Jr. Reasonable Doubt: The Case for the UDR Four. (Illus.). 156p. 1991. 30.00 (*0-85342-962-6*, Pub. by Mercier Pr IE) Dufour.

Paisley, Melvyn & Paisley, Vicki. Ace! Autobiography of a Fighter Pilot World War II. 350p. 1992. 22.95 (*0-8283-1943-X*) Branden Pub Co.

Paisley, Pam, ed. see Petersen, Phil.

Paisley, Pamela O. & Hubbard, Glenda T. Developmental School Counseling Programs: From Theory to Practice. LC 94-850. 240p. 1994. 23.95 (*1-55620-139-7*) Am Coun Assn.

Paisley, Rebeca. Diamonds & Dreams. 432p. (Orig.). 1991. mass mkt. 4.50 (*0-380-76564-0*) Avon.

Paisley, Rebecca. The Barefoot Bride. 400p. 1990. pap. 3.95 (*0-380-76019-3*) Avon.

— Heartstrings. 1994. mass mkt. 4.99 (*0-440-21650-8*) Dell.

— Midnight & Magnolias. 416p. (Orig.). 1992. mass mkt. 4.50 (*0-380-76566-7*) Avon.

— Moonlight & Magic. 1990. pap. 3.95 (*0-380-76020-7*) Avon.

— Rainbows & Rapture. 400p. (Orig.). 1992. mass mkt. 4.50 (*0-380-76565-9*) Avon.

***Paisley, Rebecca, et al.** Love Potion. 272p. (Orig.). 1995. pap. text ed. 4.99 (*0-515-11549-5*) Jove Pubns.

Paisley, Vicki, jt. auth. see Paisley, Melvyn.

Paisley, William, jt. ed. see Butler, Matilda.

Paisley, William, jt. ed. see Chen, Milton.

Paisley, William J., jt. ed. see Rice, Ronald E.

Paisner, Daniel. Horizontal Hold: The Making & Breaking of a Network Pilot. (Illus.). 256p. 1992. 18.95 (*1-55972-148-0*, Birch Ln Pr) Carol Pub Group.

Paitnaik, Prabhat. Economics & Egalitarianism. (Oxford India Paperbacks Ser.). 46p. (C). 1991. 4.95 (*0-19-562496-3*) OUP.

Paitson, Hupi. Maui Booklet. (Illus.). 1970. pap. 0.50 (*0-941200-00-0*) Aquarius.

Paitson, Hupi & Paitson, Lloyd. Maui: Notes from a Private Guidebook. (Illus.). (Orig.). 1970. pap. 1.50 (*0-941200-01-9*) Aquarius.

Paitson, Lloyd, jt. auth. see Paitson, Hupi.

Paiva, jt. auth. see Chang.

Paiva, Bob. The Program Director's Handbook. (Orig.). 1983. pap. 16.95 (*0-07-155791-1*) McGraw.

— The Program Director's Handbook. (Illus.). 168p. (Orig.). 1983. pap. 16.95 (*0-8306-1363-3*, 1363) TAB Bks.

***Paiva, Bonnie S.** My Best to You: A Collection of Choice Recipes for the New Cook. (Orig.). 1994. pap. 12.50 (*0-9639227-1-8*) B S Paiva.

Paiva, Judith L., jt. auth. see O'Donnell, Teresa D.

Paiva, M. M., jt. auth. see Engel, L. A.

Paiva, Marcelo R. Happy Old Year. George, David, tr. LC 90-26921. 232p. 1991. pap. 15.95 (*0-935480-53-6*) Lat Am Lit Rev Pr.

Paiva, Ricardo M. & Tolman, Jon M. Travessia Manual de Laboratorio. (Travessia, Portuguese Language Textbook Program Ser.). 248p. (Orig.). (C). 1991. teacher ed 13.00 (*0-87840-235-7*) Georgetown U Pr.

Paivanen, J., jt. auth. see Paavilainen, E.

Paivarinta, L. J. & Somersalo, E., eds. Inverse Problems in Mathematical Physics: Proceedings of the Lapland Conference on Inverse Problems Held at Saariselka, Finland, 14-20 June 1992. LC 93-29276. (Lecture Notes in Physics Ser.: Vol. 422). 256p. 1993. 59.00 (*0-387-57195-7*) Spr-Verlag.

Paivio, Allan. Imagery & Verbal Processes. LC 73-150787. 608p. 1971. text ed. 99.95 (*0-89859-069-8*) L Erlbaum Assocs.

— Mental Representations: A Dual Coding Approach. (Oxford Psychology Ser.: No. 9). (Illus.). 336p. 1990. reprint ed. pap. 25.95 (*0-19-506666-9*) OUP.

Paizis, Suzanne. Getting Her Elected: A Political Woman's Handbook. 1977. pap. 5.95 (*0-917982-03-7*) Cougar Bks.

Pajaczkowska, Claire, tr. see Blandonu, Gerard.

Pajak, Edward. Approaches to Clinical Supervision: Alternatives for Improving Instruction. 352p. (C). 1993. text ed. 42.95 (*0-926842-27-7*) CG Pubs Inc.

Pajares, C. Multiparticle Dynamics, 1992: Twenty-Second International Symposium. 700p. 1993. text ed. 178.00 (*981-02-1239-9*) World Scientific Pub.

Pajares, J. M., et al, eds. Helicobacter Pylori & Gastroduodenal Pathology. LC 92-30270. 1993. 198.00 (*0-387-55432-7*) Spr-Verlag.

Pajares, Maria T., jt. auth. see Callejo, Alfonso.

Pajari, George. Writing UNIX Device Drivers. 1991. pap. 34.95 (*0-201-52374-4*) Addison-Wesley.

Pajaujis-Javis, Joseph. Soviet Genocide in Lithuania. 1980. 10.95 (*0-87141-060-5*) Manyland.

Pajeon, Kala & Pajeon, Ketz. The Candle Magick Workbook. (Illus.). 256p. 1991. pap. 9.95 (*0-8065-1268-7*, Citadel Pr) Carol Pub Group.

— The Talisman Magick Workbook: Master Your Destiny Through the Use of Talismans. LC 92-28896. (Illus.). 256p. 1992. pap. 9.95 (*0-8065-1366-7*, Citadel Pr) Carol Pub Group.

Pajeon, Ketz, jt. auth. see Pajeon, Kala.

Pajer, Beverly A., jt. auth. see Milstead, Jessica L.

Pajestka, Josef & Feinstein, Charles H. The Relevance of Economic Theories. 1980. text ed. 39.95 (*0-312-67054-0*) St Martin.

Pajgrt, O., et al, eds. Processing of Polyester Fibres. (Textile Science & Technology Ser.: Vol. 2). 550p. 1980. 154.00 (*0-444-99860-8*) Elsevier.

Pajonk, G. M., et al, eds. Spillover of Adsorbed Species. (Studies in Surface Science & Catalysis: Vol. 17). 320p. 1983. 100.00 (*0-444-42224-2*, I-271-83) Elsevier.

Pajot-Smith, Jean. Li'l Tuffy & His ABC's. (Ebony Jr. Bks.). (Illus.). 64p. (J). (ps-4). pap. 5.00 (*0-87485-063-0*) Johnson Chi.

— Li'l Tuffy & His Friends. (ENG & SPA.). 1976. 5.00 (*0-87485-077-0*) Johnson Chi.

Pajpai, U. S. & Viswam, S., eds. UNESCO: In Retrospect & Prospect. 197p. 1986. 25.00 (*81-7062-000-7*, Pub. by Lancer II) S Asia.

Pak, C. Y., ed. Pharmacological Treatment of Endocrinopathies. (Progress in Basic & Clinical Pharmacology Ser.: Vol. 5). (Illus.). x, 142p. 1991. 116.00 (*3-8055-5214-9*) S Karger.

Pak, Charles Y., ed. Renal Stone Disease: Pathogenesis, Prevention, & Treatment. (Topics in Renal Medicine Ser.). (C). 1987. lib. bdg. 108.50 (*0-89838-886-4*) Kluwer Ac.

Pak, Charles Y., jt. auth. see Resnick, Donald.

Pak, Charles Y. C. & Adams, Perrie M., eds. Techniques of Patient-Oriented Research. LC 93-4602. 224p. 1994. 49.50 (*0-7817-0107-4*) Raven.

Pak, Chi-Young. Political Opposition in Korea, 1945-1960. (Institute of Social Sciences Korean Studies: No. 2). 251p. 1980. text ed. 18.00 (*0-8248-0932-7*) UH Pr.

Pak, Gary. The Watcher of Waipuna & Other Stories. LC 92-426. (Bamboo Ridge Ser.: Nos. 55-56). 1992. pap. 8.00 (*0-910043-28-0*) Bamboo Ridge Pr.

Pak, Mog-wol. Selected Poems of Pak Mogwol. Kim, Uchang, tr. & intro. by. LC 90-39264. 214p. reprint ed. pap. 61.00 (*0-7837-5212-1*, 2044943) Bks Demand.

Pak, Pyfong-ho. Modernization & Its Impact upon Korean Law. LC 80-84987. (California University Center for Korean Studies.-Korea Research Monograph: No. 3). 163p. pap. 46.50 (*0-317-09997-3*, 2019469) Bks Demand.

Pak, Ty. An Axiomatic Theory of Language with Applications to English. LC 80-12010. (Edward Sapir Monograph Ser. in Language, Culture & Cognition: No. 6). vi, 129p. (Orig.). (C). 1979. pap. 10.00 (*0-933104-08-1*) Jupiter Pr.

— Guilt Payment. LC 83-71242. 196p. (Orig.). 1983. pap. 6.00 (*0-910043-01-9*) Bamboo Ridge Pr.

Pakaluk, Michael, ed. Other Selves: Philosophers on Friendship. 288p. (C). 1991. lib. bdg. 32.50 (*0-87220-114-7*); pap. text ed. 7.95 (*0-87220-113-9*) Hackett Pub.

Pakan, William A., ed. see Stevenson, George A.

Pakarinan, U., jt. auth. see Hukki, P.

Pake, George E., jt. auth. see Feenberg, Eugene.

Pakenham, Frank. Peace by Ordeal: The Negotiation of the Anglo-Irish Treaty, 1921. (Illus.). 318p. 1993. pap. 19.95 (*0-7126-9835-3*, Pub. by Pimlico) Trafalgar.

Pakenham, Kenneth J. Expectations: Language & Reading Skills for Students of ESL. (Illus.). 400p. (C). 1985. pap. text ed. 18.00 (*0-13-294414-6*) P-H.

— Making Connections: An Interactive Approach to. 352p. 1993. pap. text ed. 15.00 (*0-312-06515-9*) St Martin.

Pakenham, Thomas. The Boer War. LC 79-4779. 1979. 29.95 (*0-394-42742-4*) Random.

— The Boer War. LC 93-26234. (Illus.). 1994. 40.00 (*0-679-43047-4*) Random.

— The Boer War. 784p. 1992. reprint ed. pap. 15.00 (*0-380-72001-9*) Avon.

— The Scramble for Africa: The White Man's Conquest of the Dark Continent from 1876 to 1912. LC 91-52681. (Illus.). 784p. 1991. 31.50 (*0-394-51576-5*) Random.

— The Scramble for Africa: The White Man's Conquest of the Dark Continent from 1876 to 1912. 800p. 1992. reprint ed. pap. 16.00 (*0-380-71999-1*) Avon.

— The Year of Liberty: The History of the Great Irish Rebellion of 1798. 1993. pap. 12.00 (*0-679-74802-4*) Random.

Pakenham, Thomas & Pakenham, Valerie. Dublin: A Traveller's Companion. 1988. write for info. (*0-318-62730-2*) Macmillan.

Pakenham, Thomas C., jt. auth. see Abdullah, Achmed.

Pakenham, Valerie, jt. auth. see Pakenham, Thomas.

Pakenham, W. T. Naval Command & Control. (Naval Weapons Systems and Technology Ser.: No. 8). 147p. (Orig.). 1989. 40.00 (*0-08-034750-9*, Pub. by Brasseys UK); 25.00 (*0-08-036254-0*, Pub. by Brasseys UK) Brasseys Inc.

Paker, Josephine. Beating the Drum. LC 92-5164. (Millbrook Arts Library). (Illus.). 48p. (J). (gr. 2-6). 1992. lib. bdg. 14.40 (*1-56294-093-7*) Millbrook Pr.

— I Wonder Why Flutes Have Holes: And Other Questions about Music. LC 94-45002. (I Wonder Why Ser.). (J). 1995. write for info. (*1-85697-583-5*, Kingfisher LKC) LKC.

— Music from Strings. LC 92-5162. (Millbrook Arts Library Ser.). (Illus.). 48p. (J). (gr. 2-6). 1992. lib. bdg. 14.40 (*1-56294-283-2*) Millbrook Pr.

Paker, Saliha, tr. see Tekin, Latife.

Paker, Y. Minicomputers: A Reference Book for Engineers, Scientists & Managers. (Abacus Bks.). 505p. 1981. text ed. 154.00 (*0-85626-188-2*) Gordon & Breach.

Paker, Yacup. Multi-Microprocessor Systems. (APIC Studies in Data Processing: No. 18). 1983. text ed. 66.00 (*0-12-543980-6*) Acad Pr.

Paker, Yacup, et al, eds. Distributing Operating System. (NATO Asi Series F: Vol. 28). x, 379p. 1987. 91.00 (*0-387-17699-3*) Spr-Verlag.

Paker, Yacup, ed. see Verjus, J. P.

***Paker, Yakup & Wilbur, Sylvia, eds.** Image Processing for Broadcast & Video Production: Proceedings of the European Workshop on Combined Real & Synthetic Image Processing for Broadcast & Video Production, Hamburg, 23-24 November 1994. LC 94-49416. (Workshops in Computing Ser.). 1995. write for info. (*3-540-19947-0*) Spr-Verlag.

Pakes, Anthony G. & Maller, R. A. Mathematical Ecology of Plant Species Competition. (Cambridge Studies in Mathematical Biology). (Illus.). 302p. (C). 1990. 59.95 (*0-521-37388-3*) Cambridge U Pr.

Pakesch, G., jt. ed. see Lenz, G.

Pakin, Sandra & Computer Innovations Staff. APL: A Short Course. (Illus.). 176p. 1973. pap. text ed. 25.00 (*0-13-038877-7*) P-H.

Pakin, Sandra, & Associates, Inc. Staff. DDM: The Documentation Development Methodology. LC 82-90102. (Illus.). 230p. (C). 1986. pap. write for info. (*0-9608178-1-6*); ring bd. 95.00 (*0-9608178-0-8*) Pakin Assocs.

Pakiser, L. C. & Mooney, W. D., eds. Geophysical Framework of the Continental United States. (Memoir Ser.: No. 172). (Illus.). 840p. 1990. 92.50 (*0-8137-1172-X*) Geol Soc.

Pakistani. English-Urdu Dictionary. (ENG & URD.). 65.00 (*0-935782-96-6*) Kazi Pubns.

Pakizer, Debi & Sears, Mary A. Vaulting: The Art of Gymnastics on Horseback. Anderson, Julia & Barnette, Jackie, eds. (Illus.). 24p. (Orig.). (J). (gr. k-6). Date not set. pap. 5.00 (*0-9639785-6-X*) M A Sears.

Pakrasi, Himadri, jt. ed. see Ho, Tuan-Hua D.

Pakravan, Karim. Oil Supply Disruptions in the Nineteen Eighties: An Economic Analysis. (Publication Ser.: No. 290). (Illus.). 100p. 1984. pap. text ed. 9.95 (*0-8179-7902-6*) Hoover Inst Pr.

Paksoy, H. B., ed. Central Asia Reader: The Rediscovery of History. 216p. (C). 1994. text ed. 60.00 (*1-56324-201-X*); pap. text ed. 21.95 (*1-56324-202-8*) M E Sharpe.

Pakuda, Bahya I. The Book of Direction to the Duties of the Heart: Hovot Ha-Levavot. Mansoor, Menahem, ed. & tr. by. Dannhauser, Shoshana et al, trs. (Littman Library of Jewish Civilization). 480p. 1973. 19.50 (*0-19-710020-1*, Pub. by Littman Lib Jew UK) Bnai Brith Bk.

Pakvasa, S. & Tuan, S. F., eds. Hawaii Topical Conferences in Particle Physics: Selected Lectures, 2 vols., 1. 1006p. 1983. text ed. write for info. (*9971-950-16-2*); pap. text ed. write for info. (*9971-950-17-0*) World Scientific Pub.

— Hawaii Topical Conferences in Particle Physics: Selected Lectures, 2 vols., 2. 1006p. 1983. text ed. 130.00 (*9971-950-36-7*); pap. text ed. 63.00 (*9971-950-37-5*) World Scientific Pub.

Pal, Aswwini. Wheat Revolution in India: Constraints & Prospects. 1990. 58.00 (*81-7099-198-6*, Pub. by Mittal II) S Asia.

Pal, G. & Macskasy, H. Plastics: Their Behaviour in Fires. (Studies in Polymer Science: No. 6). 436p. 1991. 234.50 (*0-444-98766-5*) Elsevier.

Pal, H. Bhisham. Handicrafts of Rajasthan. (Illus.). 71p. 1984. 14.95 (*0-318-36263-5*) Asia Bk Corp.

— The Plunder of Art. (C). 1992. 72.00 (*81-7017-285-3*, Pub. by Abhinav II) S Asia.

Pal, J. C., ed. Current Trends in Surgery, Vol. I. (C). 1989. 75.00 (*0-89771-368-0*, Current Dist) St Mut.

— Current Trends in Surgery, Vol. II. (C). 1989. 150.00 (*0-89771-369-9*, Current Dist) St Mut.

Pal, J. K., jt. ed. see Tzafestas, Spyros G.

Pal, L., jt. auth. see Donner, R. O.

Pal, Leslie, jt. auth. see Campbell, Robert.

Pal, Leslie A. Interests of State: The Politics of Language, Multiculturalism, & Feminism in Canada. 344p. 1993. 39.95 (*0-7735-0974-7*, Pub. by McGill CN) U of Toronto Pr.

— State, Class, & Bureaucracy: Canadian Unemployment Insurance & Public Policy. 365p. 1987. 44.95 (*0-7735-0623-3*, Pub. by McGill CN) U of Toronto Pr.

Pal, M. K., et al. Medium & High Energy Nuclear Physics: Proceedings of the Conference. 240p. 1992. text ed. 95.00 (*981-02-1095-7*) World Scientific Pub.

Pal, Mahesh. Population & Rural Poor in India. (C). 1991. 21.00 (*0-8364-2762-9*, Pub. by Chugh Pubns II) S Asia.

Pal, Palash B., jt. auth. see Mohapatra, R. N.

Pal, Pratapaditya. Art of Nepal: A Catalogue of the Los Angeles County Museum of Art Collection. 1985. pap. 38.00 (*0-520-05407-5*) U CA Pr.

— Art of Tibet: A Catalogue of the Los Angeles County Museum of Art Collection. (Illus.). 328p. 1990. 60.00 (*0-8109-1899-4*) Abrams.

— Court Paintings of India. (Illus.). 344p. 1983. 140.00 (*0-9611400-0-3*) N Kumar.

— Hindu Religion & Iconology According to the Tantrasara. LC 81-52893. (Tantric Tradition Ser.). Orig. Title: Tantrasara. (Illus.). 172p. 1982. pap. 10.95 (*0-941582-00-0*) Vichitra Pr.

— The Ideal Image: The Gupta Sculptural Tradition & Its Influence. LC 78-14901. (Illus.). 1978. 19.95 (*0-87848-052-8*) Asia Soc.

— Indian Painting: A Catalogue of the Los Angeles County Museum of Art Collection. LC 93-317. 1993. 65.00 (*0-8109-3465-5*) Abrams.

— Indian Sculpture, Vol. 1. 1987. pap. 38.00 (*0-520-05992-1*) U CA Pr.

— Indian Sculpture, Vol. 2 (700-1800) A Catalog of the Los Angeles County Museum of Art Collection. 300p. 1989. 90.00 (*0-520-06477-1*); pap. 45.00 (*0-520-06479-8*) U CA Pr.

— Non-Western Art: The Classical Tradition in Rajput Painting. LC 78-66424. (Illus.). 210p. 1978. 29.00 (*0-934483-01-9*) Gal Assn NY.

Pal, Pratapaditya & Dehejia, Vidya. From Merchants to Emperors: British Artist in India, 1757-1930. LC 85-48273. (Illus.). 264p. 1986. 78.50 (*0-8014-1907-7*); pap. 32.50 (*0-8014-9386-2*) Cornell U Pr.

Pal, Pratapaditya & Meech-Pekarik, Julia. Buddhist Book Illuminations. LC 87-92183. (Illus.). 339p. 1988. lib. bdg. 225.00 (*0-318-40043-X*) Hacker.

Pal, Pratapaditya & Reynolds, Valrae, contribs. Art of the Himalayas: Treasures from Nepal & Tibet. LC 91-71551. (Illus.). 208p. 1991. 50.00 (*1-55595-066-3*) Hudson Hills.

***Pal, Pratapaditya, et al.** The Peaceful Liberators: Jain Art from India. LC 94-61006. (Illus.). 280p. 1994. 65.00 (*0-500-01650-X*) Thames Hudson.

— Pleasure Gardens of the Mind: Indian Painting from the Jane Greenough Green Collections. LC 92-38050. (Illus.). 160p. (C). 1995. 50.00 (*0-295-97255-6*, Pub. by Grantha India) U of Wash Pr.

Pal, R., jt. auth. see Brown, A. W.

Pal, R., ed. see Kanda.

Pal, S. B., ed. Handbook of Laboratory Health & Safety Measurement. 2nd rev. ed. 600p. 1991. lib. bdg. 177.00 (*0-7462-0077-3*) Kluwer Ac.

— Handbook of Laboratory Health & Safety Measures. 1985. lib. bdg. 195.50 (*0-85200-766-3*) Kluwer Ac.

— Immunoassay Technology. (Illus.). x, 247p. 1986. pap. 119.25 (*3-11-010948-4*) De Gruyter.

— Immunoassay Technology, Vol. 1. viii, 192p. 1985. pap. 106.95 (*0-89925-082-3*) De Gruyter.

— Immunoassay Technology, Vol. 2. (Illus.). x, 247p. 1986. pap. 119.25 (*0-89925-195-1*) De Gruyter.

— Immunoassay Technology, Vol. 1. viii, 192p. 1985. pap. 106.95 (*3-11-010062-2*) De Gruyter.

— Reviews of Immunoassay, 2 vols. 1988. lib. bdg. write for info. (*0-318-63139-3*) Routledge Chapman & Hall.

— Reviews of Immunoassay, 2 vols., Vol. 1. 200p. 1988. lib. bdg. 89.95 (*0-412-01841-1*) Routledge Chapman & Hall.

— Reviews of Immunoassay, 2 vols., Vol. 2. 208p. 1988. lib. bdg. 89.95 (*0-412-01851-9*) Routledge Chapman & Hall.

Pal, S. B., jt. ed. see Fotherby, K.

Pal, Sankar K., jt. ed. see Bezdek, James C.

P Q

An Asterisk (*) at the beginning of an entry indicates that the title is appearing in BIP for the first time.

Pal, Yash, ed. Space & Development: Proceedings of Vikram Sarabhi Symposium of the Twenty-Second Plenary Meeting of the Committee on Space Research, Bangalore, India, 29 May -9 June 1979. LC 79-41358. (Illus.). 100p. 1980. 25.00 (0-08-024441-6, Pergamon Pr) Elsevier.

***Pal, Yash, et al, eds.** Science & Society: Some Perspectives. (C). Date not set. 32.00 (81-212-0458-5, Pub. by Gian Publng Hse II) S Asia.

Pala, Dolores. Trumpet for a Walled City. 1979. pap. 1.75 (0-449-23913-6, Crest) Fawcett.

***Palacas, James G., ed.** Petroleum Geochemistry & Source Rock Potential of Carbonate Rocks. (AAPG Studies in Geology: No. 18). (Illus.). viii, 208p. 1984. pap. 30.00 (0-89181-024-2) AAPG.

***Palacci, Patrick.** Optional Implant Positioning & Soft Tissue Management for the Branemark System. LC 95-15503. (Illus.). 1995. write for info. (0-86715-308-3) Quint Pub Co.

Palace, Jon, ed. see Kibel, Harvey R.

Palache, John. Four Novelists of the Old Regime: Crebillon, Laclos, Diderot, Restif de la Bretonne. LC 73-132443. (Studies in French Literature: No. 45). 1970. reprint ed. lib. bdg. 53.95 (0-8383-1193-8) M S G Haskell Hse.

Palache, John G. Gautier & the Romantics. 1972. 35.00 (0-8490-0212-5) Gordon Pr.

Palacio Atard, Vicente. Juan Carlos I y el Advenimiento de la Democracia. (Nueva Austral Ser.: Vol. 87). (SPA.). 1991. pap. text ed. 24.95x (84-239-1887-4) Elliots Bks.

— Manual de Historia de Espana Vol. 4: Edad Contemporanea, I (1808-1898) 644p. (SPA.). 1991. 125. 00x (84-239-5094-8) Elliots Bks.

Palacio Valdes, Armando. La Aldea Perdida. Ruiz de la Pena, Alvaro, ed. (Nueva Austral Ser.: Vol. 180). (SPA.). 1991. pap. text ed. 24.95x (84-239-1980-3) Elliots Bks.

Palacios, Argentina. Christmas for Chabelita. LC 94-9833. (Illus.). 32p. (J). (gr. k-4). 1994. lib. bdg. 14.95 (0-8167-3545-X) BrdgeWater.

— Christmas for Chabelita. LC 94-9833. (Illus.). 32p. (J). (gr. k-4). 1994. pap. 3.95 (0-8167-3541-7) BrdgeWater.

— A Christmas Surprise for Chabelita. LC 93-22336. (Illus.). 32p. (J). (gr. k-4). 1993. pap. 3.95 (0-8167-3132-2) BrdgeWater.

— The Hummingbird King: A Guatemalan Legend. LC 92-21437. (Legends of the World Ser.). (Illus.). 32p. (J). (gr. 2-5). 1993. lib. bdg. 11.89 (0-8167-3051-2); pap. text ed. 3.95 (0-8167-3052-0) Troll Assocs.

— Llama's Secret: A Peruvian Legend. LC 92-21436. (Legends of the World Ser.). (Illus.). 32p. (J). (gr. 2-5). 1993. lib. bdg. 11.89 (0-8167-3049-0); pap. text ed. 3.95 (0-8167-3050-4) Troll Assocs.

— Peanut Butter, Apple Butter, Cinnamon Toast: Food Riddles for You to Guess. (Ready-Set-Read Ser.). (Illus.). 24p. (J). (ps-2). 1990. lib. bdg. 17.84 (0-8172-3584-1); lib. bdg. 10.95 (0-685-58553-0) Raintree Steck-V.

— El Rey Colibri - the Hummingbird King: Una Leyenda Guatemalteca. LC 92-21437. (J). (gr. 4-7). 1993. lib. bdg. 11.89 (0-8167-3122-5); pap. 3.95 (0-8167-3071-7) Troll Assocs.

— El Secreto de la Llama - the Llama's Secret: Una Leyenda Peruana. LC 93-21436. (J). (gr. 4-7). 1993. lib. bdg. 11. 89 (0-8167-3123-3); pap. 3.95 (0-8167-3072-5) Troll Assocs.

— Sorpresa de Navidad para Chabilita. (Illus.). 32p. (J). (gr. k-4). 1994. lib. bdg. 14.95 (0-615-00369-9); pap. 3.95 (0-615-00370-2) BrdgeWater.

— Standing Tall: The Stories of Ten Hispanic Americans. (J). (gr. 4-7). 1994. pap. 3.50 (0-590-47140-6) Scholastic Inc.

Palacios, Argentina, tr. see Bargar, Sherie & Johnson, Linda.

Palacios, Argentina, tr. see Bridwell, Norman.

Palacios, Argentina, tr. see Bright, Robert.

Palacios, Argentina, tr. see Lindsay, Jeanne W. & Brunelli, Jean.

Palacios, Argentina, tr. see Lindsay, Jeanne W.

Palacios, Argentina, tr. see Pico, Fernando.

Palacios, Argentina, tr. see Rowe, Erna.

Palacios, Argentina, tr. see Selsam, Millicent E.

Palacios, Argentina, jt. auth. see Sorensen, Lynda.

Palacios, Carl, ed. English-Spanish Cross-World Puzzles: Bilingual Crossword Puzzles, No. 1. 96p. (ENG & SPA.). 1982. pap. 3.95 (0-940038-00-5) Andante Pub.

Palacios, E., et al. Magnetic Resonance of the Temporomandibular Joint. (Illus.). 135p. 1990. text ed. 73.00 (0-86577-363-7) Thieme Med Pubs.

Palacios, E. J. The Stone of the Sun & the First Chapter of the History of Mexico. 1977. lib. bdg. 59.95 (0-8490-2670-9) Gordon Pr.

Palacios, Esteban J. Yo Vengo de los Arabos. LC 86-82605. (Coleccion Caniqui Ser.). 131p. (Orig.). 1987. pap. 9.95 (0-89729-420-3) Ediciones.

Palacios, Fernando A., ed. see Sanchez, Francisco.

Palacios, Rafael. New Horizons in Nitrogen Fixation: Proceedings of the 9th International Congress on Nitrogen Fixation, Cancun, Mexico, December 6-12, 1992. (Current Plant Science & Biotechnology in Agriculture Ser.). 808p. (C). 1993. lib. bdg. 189.50 (0-7923-2207-X) Kluwer Ac.

Palacios, Rafael & Verma, Desh P., eds. Molecular Genetics of Plant Microbe Interactions - 1988. LC 88-82736. (Illus.). 401p. 1988. 25.00 (0-89054-096-9) Am Phytopathol Soc.

Palacioso, Argentina. A Christmas Surprise for Chabelita. LC 93-22336. (Illus.). 32p. (J). (gr. k-4). 1994. 14.95 (0-8167-3131-4) BrdgeWater.

***Palacious.** Peanut Butter, Apple Butter, Cinnamon Toast: Food Riddles for You to Guess. (J). 1995. pap. text ed. (0-8114-6745-7) Raintree Steck-V.

Palade, George E., et al, eds. Annual Review of Cell Biology, Vol. 1. (Illus.). (C). 1985. text ed. 41.00 (0-8243-3101-X) Annual Reviews.

— Annual Review of Cell Biology, Vol. 2. (Illus.). 1986. text ed. 41.00 (0-8243-3102-8) Annual Reviews.

— Annual Review of Cell Biology, Vol. 3. (Illus.). 1987. text ed. 41.00 (0-8243-3103-6) Annual Reviews.

— Annual Review of Cell Biology, Vol. 4. (Illus.). 1988. text ed. 41.00 (0-8243-3104-4) Annual Reviews.

— Annual Review of Cell Biology, Vol. 5. 1989. text ed. 41. 00 (0-8243-3105-2) Annual Reviews.

— Annual Review of Cell Biology, Vol. 6. 1990. 41.00 (0-8243-3106-0) Annual Reviews.

— Annual Review of Cell Biology, Vol. 7. 1991. text ed. 41. 00 (0-8243-3107-9) Annual Reviews.

— Annual Review of Cell Biology, Vol. 8. 1992. text ed. 46. 00 (0-8243-3108-7) Annual Reviews.

— Annual Review of Cell Biology, Vol. 9. (Illus.). 1993. text ed. 46.00 (0-8243-3109-5) Annual Reviews.

Paladin, David C. Painting the Dream: The Visionary Art of Navajo Painter David Chethlahe Paladin. (Illus.). 96p. (Orig.). 1992. pap. 24.95 (0-89281-440-3, Park St Pr) Inner Tradit.

Paladin, Vivian A., ed. C. M. Russell: The Mackay Collection. 28p. 1979. pap. 3.50 (0-917298-08-X) MT Hist Soc.

Paladino, Catherine. Land, Sea, & Sky: Poems to Celebrate the Earth. (J). (ps-3). 1993. 15.95 (0-316-68892-4) Little.

— Our Vanishing Farm Animals: Saving America's Rare Breeds. (J). (ps-3). 1991. 15.95 (0-316-68891-6) Little.

— Pomona: The Birth of a Penguin. (New England Aquarium Book Ser.). (Illus.). (J). (gr. 2-4). 1991. lib. bdg. 13.72 (0-531-10988-7) Watts.

— Spring Fleece: A Day of Sheepshearing. (J). (ps-3). 1990. 14.95 (0-316-68890-8, Joy St Bks) Little.

Paladino, Enzo. Novo Dicionario Tecnico de Informatica Ingles - Portuguese. (ENG & POR.). 1986. pap. 75.00 (0-8288-3965-4, F119705) Fr & Eur.

Palagia, Olga. The Pediments of the Parthenon. LC 92-23466. (Monumenta Graeca et Romana Ser.: Vol. 7). (Illus.). 74p. 1993. 91.50 (90-04-09683-3) E J Brill.

Palaia, Franc. Great Walls of China. (Illus.). 72p. (Orig.). (CHI & ENG.). 1984. pap. 14.95 (0-89860-125-8) Eastview.

Palairet, Michael, tr. see Emmerich, Anne C.

Palais, James B. Politics & Policy in Traditional Korea. (East Asian Monographs: No. 159). (Illus.). 390p. (C). 1992. pap. text ed. 16.00 (0-674-68771-X) HUP.

— Politics & Policy in Traditional Korea, 1864-1876. (East Asian Monographs). 288p. 1990. 24.50 (0-674-19058-0) HUP.

Palais, Joseph C. Fiber Optics Communications. 3rd ed. 352p. 1992. text ed. 66.00 (0-13-473554-4) P-H.

Palais, Richard S. The Classification of G-Spaces. 4th ed. LC 52-42839. (Memoirs Ser.: No. 1/36). 72p. 1987. reprint ed. pap. 17.00 (0-8218-1236-X, MEMO 1/36) Am Math.

— A Global Formulation of the Lie Theory of Transformation Groups. LC 52-42839. (Memoirs Ser.: No. 1/22). 123p. 1991. reprint ed. pap. 17.00 (0-8218-1222-X, MEMO 1/22) Am Math.

Palaliko, Lee & DeFries, Eleanora, eds. Light upon the Mist: A Reflection of Wisdom for the Future Generations of Native Hawaiians. 125p. Date not set. reprint ed. pap. text ed. 12.95 (0-9635173-0-9) Mahina Prods.

Palamas, Gregory. The Decalogue. 1988. pap. 0.50 (0-89981-202-3) Eastern Orthodox.

Palamas, Keostees. The Twelve Words of the Gypsy. Will, Frederic, tr. & intro. by. LC 64-17223. 229p. reprint ed. pap. 65.30 (0-7837-6175-9, 2045897) Bks Demand.

Palamas, Kostis. The Twelve Lays of the Gypsy. 146p. 1971. 28.00 (0-8464-0939-9) Beekman Pubs.

Palamidese, Patrizia, ed. Scientific Visualization: Advanced Software Techniques. LC 93-19127. (Ellis Horwood Workshop Ser.). 1993. 59.50 (0-13-710337-9, Tavistock-E Horwood) Routledge Chapman & Hall.

Palamodov, V. P. Linear Differential Operators with Constant Coefficients. Brown, A. A., tr. LC 79-104712. (Grundlehren der Mathematischen Wissenschaften Ser.: Vol. 168). 1970. 89.00 (0-387-04838-3) Spr-Verlag.

Palan, Ronen P. & Gills, Barry, eds. Transcending the State-Global Divide: A Neostructuralist Agenda in International Relations. LC 93-8935. (Critical Perspectives on World Politics Ser.). 286p. 1994. lib. bdg. 44.00 (1-55587-395-2) Lynne Rienner.

Palandri, Angela, ed. Modern Verse from Taiwan. LC 79-161994. 225p. reprint ed. pap. 64.20 (0-318-34903-5, 2031311) Bks Demand.

Palandri, Enrico. Way Back. 1994. pap. 14.99 (1-85242-246-7) Serpents Tail.

Palandro, Michael & Lestarjette, Steve. The Essentials of Christian Relationship. 56p. 1987. pap. text ed. 2.95 (0-939079-00-3) ChristLife Pubs.

Palange, Ralph C. & Zavala, Alfonso. Control de la Contaminacion del Agua: Guias para la Planificacion Y Financiamiento de Proyectos. (Technical Paper Ser.: No. 735). 252p. (SPA.). 1989. Spanish edition. 12.95 (0-685-58464-X, 11273); write for info. (0-8213-1273-1) World Bank.

Palangi, Paula. Last Straw. LC 91-44346. (J). (ps-3). 1992. pap. 9.99 (0-7814-0562-9, Chariot Bks) Chariot Family.

Palani, Satya. Ominous Evenings: Memories of Madness by Satya Palani. LC 94-67019. 72p. 1994. pap. 7.00 (0-9641928-0-2) Ominous Whispers.

Palaniappan, S. P. Cropping Systems in the Tropics: Principles & Management. (C). 1986. pap. 11.50 (0-85226-712-6, Pub. by Wiley Eastern II) S Asia.

Palanithurai, G. Dynamics of Tamil Nadu Politics in Sri Lankan Ethnicity. 1993. 14.00 (81-7211-040-5, National Bk Ctr) S Asia.

— Management of Ethnic Conflict in India & Canada: A Comparative Analysis. (C). 1993. 16.00x (81-85475-74-1, Pub. by Kanishka) S Asia.

Palanithurai, G., ed. Perspectives on Indian Regionalism. (C). 1992. 16.00 (81-85475-58-X, Pub. by Kanishka) S Asia.

Palankai, Tibor. The European Community & Central European Integration: The Hungarian Case. 79p. (C). 1991. pap. text ed. 14.85 (0-8133-8280-7) Westview.

Palant, C. E., jt. ed. see Yanagawa, N.

Palao, George. The Guns & Towers of Gibraltar. (C). 1988. text ed. 25.00 (0-948466-01-4, Pub. by Gibraltar Bks UK) St Mut.

Palardy, Jean, jt. auth. see Wilson, P. Roy.

***Palarine, John.** Creating the Vision: Developing Youth Ministry. rev. ed. 96p. 1996. pap. 8.95 (0-8192-1641-0) Morehouse Pub.

Palas, Lisa, ed. Many Thanks: Loving Thoughts for All Occasions. LC 89-63923. (Illus.). 64p. 1990. 7.99 (0-88088-426-6) Peter Pauper.

Palasota, Venie, ed. The American Psychiatric Association Auxiliary Cookbook: One Hundred Fifty Years of Cooking & Caring. LC 94-11008. 1994. write for info. (0-89042-249-4) Am Psychiatric.

Palassis, Neketas S. The Life of Our Father among the Saints: Moses the Ethiopian. (Orig.). 1992. pap. 2.00 (0-913026-30-1) St Nectarios.

Palassis, Neketas S., ed. A Lenten Cookbook for Orthodox Christians. 260p. 1982. pap. 8.50 (0-913026-13-1) St Nectarios.

— St. Nectarios Orthodox Conference. LC 80-53258. 176p. (Orig.). 1981. pap. 15.00 (0-913026-14-X) St Nectarios.

Palastanga. Anatomy & Human Movement. (Illus.). 891p. 1989. pap. 60.00 (0-7506-0134-5) Buttrwrth-Heinemann.

Palastanga, jt. auth. see Forster.

Palastanga, Nigel, jt. ed. see Boyling, Jeffrey D.

***Palastanga, Nigel, et al.** Anatomy & Human Movement: Structure & Function. 2nd ed. LC 94-24695. 1994. write for info. (0-7506-0970-2) Buttrwrth-Heinemann.

Palat, Ravi A., ed. Pacific-Asia & the Future of the World-System. LC 92-18384. (Contributions in Economics & Economic History Ser.: No. 142). 224p. 1993. text ed. 55.00 (0-313-28401-6, PPG, Greenwood Pr) Greenwood.

***Palatini, Margie.** Piggie Pie. LC 94-19726. (Illus.). 1995. 13.95 (0-395-71691-8) HM.

Palatnik, Lori. Friday Night & Beyond: The Shabbat Experience - Step-by-Step. LC 93-26264. 200p. 1994. pap. 25.00 (1-56821-035-3) Aronson.

Palau. A Cara Descubierta (Time to Stop Pretending) (SPA.). Date not set. write for info. (1-56063-116-3, 498016) Editorial Unilit.

— A Favor o En Contra De Dios? (For Against God?) (SPA.). Date not set. write for info. (0-8423-6519-2, 498008) Editorial Unilit.

Palau & Dobson. Una Mirada Biblica a la Familia (A Biblical Look at the Family) (SPA.). Date not set. 1.79 (1-56063-348-4, 497440) Editorial Unilit.

Palau, Gabriel. The Active Catholic. LC 84-50405. 224p. 1984. reprint ed. pap. 6.00 (0-89555-238-8) TAN Bks Pubs.

Palau, I. Amor y Pasion (Love & Passion) (SPA.). Date not set. 1.79 (1-56063-180-5, 498014) Editorial Unilit.

— A Su Manera (Scheamer & the Dreamer) (SPA.). Date not set. 4.25 (0-8423-6483-8, 498022) Editorial Unilit.

Palau i Fabre, Josep. Picasso: The Early Years, 1881-1907. (Illus.). 560p. 1985. boxed 300.00 (1-55660-166-2) A Wofsy Fine Arts.

Palau, Joseph, ed. Europe at Peace: VIII Convention for European Nuclear Disarmament. (Orig.). 1990. 75.00 (0-85124-518-8, Pub. by Spkesman UK); pap. 32.00 (0-85124-519-6, Pub. by Spkesman UK) Dufour.

Palau, L. Com. Bib. Continente Nuevo (New Continent Com) Juan (John), Vol. I. (SPA.). Date not set. 12.99 (1-56063-089-2, 498631); pap. 8.99 (0-685-74915-0, 498632) Editorial Unilit.

— Com. Bib. Continente Nuevo (New Continent Com) Juan (John), Vol. II. (SPA.). Date not set. 12.99 (1-56063-115-5, 498633); pap. 8.99 (0-685-74916-9, 498634) Editorial Unilit.

— Con Quien Me Casare? (Whom Shall I Marry?) (SPA.). 1976. 3.99 (0-8423-6451-X, 498017) Editorial Unilit.

— Una Conciencia Transparente (A Clear Conscious) (SPA.). Date not set. 1.79 (0-8423-6338-6, 498004) Editorial Unilit.

— Crecimiento Dinamico (Three Stages of the Christian Life) (SPA.). Date not set. 1.79 (1-56063-007-8, 498009) Editorial Unilit.

— Cristo a las Naciones (Christ to the Nations) (SPA.). Date not set. 5.99 (0-945792-22-0, 498023) Editorial Unilit.

— Decisiones a la Sombra De la Cruz (Decisions in Shadow-Cross) (SPA.). Date not set. 1.79 (0-8423-6477-3, 498005) Editorial Unilit.

— Decisiones Equivocadas (Wrong Decisions) Caida Sin Retorno? (Falling Off Without Return?) (SPA.). Date not set. 1.79 (1-56063-540-1, 498027) Editorial Unilit.

— Disciplinas Libertadoras (Liberating Disciplines) (SPA.). Date not set. 2.50 (0-8423-6484-6, 498021) Editorial Unilit.

— Eres Cristiano, Si O No? (Are You Christian Yes-No?) (SPA.). Date not set. 1.79 (0-8423-6336-X, 498003) Editorial Unilit.

— Me Quiere Mucho-Poquito-Nada (He Love's Me a Lot-Little-Not at All) (SPA.). Date not set. 1.79 (1-56063-541-X, 498028) Editorial Unilit.

— Ocultismo y Brujeria Frente a Dios (Witchcraft & Occult Before God) (SPA.). Date not set. 1.79 (0-8423-6518-4, 498007) Editorial Unilit.

— Por la Senda Del Perdon (The Walk of Forgiveness) (SPA.). Date not set. 1.79 (1-56063-117-1, 498011) Editorial Unilit.

— Que Quieres Que Haga Por Ti? (What Do You Want Me to Do?) (SPA.). Date not set. 1.79 (0-8423-6337-8, 498002) Editorial Unilit.

— Quieres un Hogar Feliz? (Want a Happy Home?) (SPA.). Date not set. 1.79 (1-56063-322-0, 498001) Editorial Unilit.

— Renovacion Interior (Interior Renewal) Moda Pasajera (Transient Fashion) (SPA.). Date not set. 1.79 (0-685-74979-7, 498012) Editorial Unilit.

— Sexo y Juventud (Sex & Youth) (SPA.). Date not set. 3.99 (0-8423-6522-2, 498019) Editorial Unilit.

— Suena Grandes Suenos (Dream Great Dreams) (SPA.). Date not set. 1.79 (0-8423-6479-X, 498006) Editorial Unilit.

— Tengo Todo...Casi Todo (I Have It All...Almost All) (SPA.). Date not set. 1.79 (1-56063-118-X, 498013) Editorial Unilit.

Palau, L. P. Papa, Mama, Quiero Ir al Cielo (Mom, Dad, I Want to Go to Heaven) (SPA.). Date not set. 1.79 (1-56063-181-3, 498015) Editorial Unilit.

Palau, Luis. Anda Sobre las Aguas Pedro: Walk on Water Peter. (SPA.). 3.25 (84-7228-160-4, 220032, Pub. by Edit Clie SP) TSELF.

— Armagedon (Armageddon) El Climax de la Historia (The Climax of History) (SPA.). 1992. 3.50 (0-8423-6476-5, 498020) Editorial Unilit.

— Cuando la Soledad Duele. (SPA.). Date not set. pap. 1.89 (0-88113-119-9) Edit Betania.

— De la Mano De Jesus (So You Want to Grow?) (SPA.). 1990. 4.99 (1-56063-006-X, 498024) Editorial Unilit.

— Dios Esta a Mi Lado. (SPA.). Date not set. pap. 1.89 (0-88113-113-X) Edit Betania.

— Grito de Victoria! Calcada, Leticia, tr. 144p. (SPA.). 1986. pap. 4.95 (0-311-46106-9) Casa Bautista.

— Healthy Habits for Spiritual Growth: Fifty-Two Principles for Personal Change. 1994. pap. 8.99 (0-929239-87-3) Discovery Hse Pubs.

— Mi Respuesta (My Response) (SPA.). 1987. 3.79 (0-8423-6485-4, 498018) Editorial Unilit.

— Quien Ganara Esta Guerra? (Say Yes! How to Renew Your Spiritual Passion) (SPA.). 1992. 4.50 (1-56063-179-1, 498499) Editorial Unilit.

— Say Yes! How to Renew Your Spiritual Passion. 172p. (Orig.). 1991. pap. 8.99 (0-88070-412-8, Multnomah Bks) Questar Pubs.

***Palau, Silvio M.** The English-Only Restaurant. (Illus.). (Orig.). Date not set. pap. write for info. (0-9627499-0-7) Ediciones Pirata.

***Palau, Susan M. & Melzer, Marilyn.** Learning Strategies for Allied Health Students. LC 95-901. (Illus.). 368p. 1995. pap. text ed. 24.95 (0-7216-5603-X) Saunders.

Palau, Susan M., jt. auth. see Meltzer, Marilyn.

Palay, Andrew J. Searching with Probabilities. (Research Notes in Artificial Intelligence Ser.). 1985. 29.95 (0-273-08664-2) Morgan Kaufmann.

Palay, David A., jt. auth. see Krachmer, Jay H.

Palay, Simin. Dictionnaire du Bearnais et du Gascon Modernes. 1072p. (FRE.). 1991. 95.00 (0-8288-6022-X, M6645) Fr & Eur.

Palay, Thomas, jt. auth. see Galanter, Marc.

Palaz, I. & Sengupta, S., eds. Automated Pattern Analysis in Petroleum Exploration. (Illus.). 304p. 1991. 99.00 (0-387-97468-7) Spr-Verlag.

Palazotto, Anthony N. & Dennis, Scott T. Nonlinear Analysis of Shell Structures. (Educ Ser.). 245p. (C). 1992. text ed. 61.95 (1-56347-033-0) AIAA.

Palazuelos. Mexico Beautiful Cookbook Engagement Calendar. (Arab Translation Ser.). 1992. 17.95 (0-00-255054-7, HarpT) HarpC.

Palazuelos, Susanna. Mexican Favorites. Wertz, Laurie, ed. LC 93-28229. (Williams-Sonoma Kitchen Library). (Illus.). 108p. 1994. 17.95 (0-7835-0270-2); lib. bdg. write for info. (0-7835-0271-0) Time-Life.

— Mexico the Beautiful Cookbook. (Beautiful Cookbook Ser.). 256p. 1991. 45.00 (0-00-215949-X) Collins SF.

Palazzeschi, Aldo. Man of Smoke. Perella, Nicholas J. & Stefanini, Ruggero, trs. LC 92-1240. 272p. (Orig.). 1992. pap. 14.95 (0-934977-26-7) Italica Pr.

Palazzi, Antonella. The Great Book of Vegetables. LC 92-20963. (Illus.). 320p. 1993. 40.00 (0-671-79664-X) S&S Trade.

Palazzi, F. New Dictionary of the Italian Language: Novissimo Dizionario della Lingua Italiana. Folena, G., ed. 1624p. (ITA.). 1981. 150.00 (0-8288-4673-1, M9363) Fr & Eur.

Palazzi, Tonya, ed. see Brylske, Alex.

Palazzi, Tonya, ed. see Brylske, Alex, et al.

Palazzini, Fiora S. Coca-Cola Superstar. 144p. 1989. 11.95 (0-8120-5998-0) Barron.

Palazzo-Craig, Janet. Case of the Missing Cat. LC 81-7635. (Easy-to-Read Mystery Ser.). (Illus.). 48p. (J). (gr. 2-4). 1982. lib. bdg. 10.89 (0-89375-594-X); pap. text ed. 3.50 (0-89375-595-8) Troll Assocs.

— Mystery of the Missing Wigs. LC 81-7615. (Easy-to-Read Mystery Ser.). (Illus.). 48p. (J). (gr. 2-4). 1982. lib. bdg. 10.89 (0-89375-592-3); pap. text ed. 3.50 (0-89375-593-1) Troll Assocs.

— The Upside-Down Boy. LC 85-14067. (Illus.). 48p. (Orig.). (J). (gr. 1-3). 1986. lib. bdg. 10.59 (0-8167-0604-2); pap. text ed. 3.50 (0-8167-0605-0) Troll Assocs.

— Who's Who at the Zoo! LC 85-14123. (Illus.). 48p. (Orig.). (J). (gr. 1-3). 1986. lib. bdg. 10.59 (0-8167-0658-1); pap. text ed. 3.50 (0-8167-0659-X) Troll Assocs.

P Q

Palazzo, Janet. Our Friend the Sun. LC 81-11460. (Now I Know Ser.). (Illus.). 32p. (J). (gr. k-2). 1982. lib. bdg. 11.59 (*0-89375-650-4*); pap. 2.95 (*0-89375-651-2*) Troll Assocs.

— Rainy Day Fun. LC 87-10842. (Illus.). 32p. (J). (gr. k-2). 1988. lib. bdg. 11.59 (*0-8167-1095-3*); pap. text ed. 2.95 (*0-8167-1096-1*) Troll Assocs.

— What Makes the Weather. LC 81-11383. (Now I Know Ser.). (Illus.). 32p. (J). (gr. k-2). 1982. lib. bdg. 11.59 (*0-89375-654-7*); pap. 2.95 (*0-89375-655-5*) Troll Assocs.

Palazzo, Tony. The Biggest & the Littlest Animals. LC 77-112374. (Illus.). 40p. (J). (gr. k-3). 1973. lib. bdg. 13.95 (*0-87460-225-4*) Lion Bks.

— Magic Crayon. (Illus.). (J). (gr. k-2). 1967. lib. bdg. 12.95 (*0-87460-089-8*) Lion Bks.

Palazzoli, Mara S. Self-Starvation: From Individual to Family Therapy in the Treatment of Anorexia Nervosa. LC 78-60671. 320p. 1985. 40.00 (*0-87668-757-5*) Aronson.

Palazzoli, Mara S., et al. Family Games. Kleiber, Veronica, tr. 1989. 27.95 (*0-393-70070-4*) Norton.

— The Hidden Games of Organizations. LC 86-5079. 212p. 1987. 23.95 (*0-87630-619-9*) Brunner-Mazel.

— Paradox & Counterparadox. Burt, Elisabeth V., tr. LC 84-45862. 208p. 1990. reprint ed. 30.00 (*0-87668-764-8*) Aronson.

— Paradox & Counterparadox: A New Model in the Therapy of the Family in Schizophrenic Transaction. LC 84-45862. 202p. 1994. pap. 22.00 (*1-56821-305-0*) Aronson.

***Palazzolo, Carl R.** The Texas Job Line Directory. Melby, Michelle, ed. 192p. 1994. 29.95 (*0-9642464-2-2*) Inside Line.

— The Texas Job Line Directory. Melby, Michelle & Michaud, Kathryn, eds. 192p. 1994. 21.95 (*0-9642464-1-4*) Inside Line.

Palazzolo, Daniel J. The Speaker & the Budget: Leadership in the Post-Reform House of Representatives. LC 92-11903. (Series in Policy & Institutional Studies). 272p. (C). 1992. text ed. 49.95 (*0-8229-3715-8*) U of Pittsburgh Pr.

Palca, Julia. Employment Law Checklists, 1993. (Blackstone's Employment Law Library). 1992. pap. 58.00 (*1-85431-212-X*, Pub. by Blackstone Pr UK) W W Gaunt.

Palchik, M. Ya, jt. auth. see Fradkin, E. S.

***Palchikov, V. G. & Shevelko, V. P.** Reference Data on Multicharged Ions. LC 94-29200. (Series on Atoms & Plasmas: Vol. 16). 1994. 139.00 (*0-387-58259-2*) Spr-Verlag.

Palciauskas, Victor, jt. auth. see Gueguen, Yves.

Palda, Filip. How Much Is Your Vote Worth? 1993. pap. 11.95 (*1-55815-284-9*) ICS Pr.

Paldan, Leena, jt. ed. see Hanninen, Sakari.

***Palder, Edward L.** The Catalog of Catalogs IV: The Complete Mail-Order Directory. 550p. (Orig.). (C). 1995. pap. 22.95 (*0-933149-75-1*) Woodbine House.

Paldiel, Mordecai. The Path of the Righteous: Gentile Rescuers of Jews During the Holocaust. write for info. (*0-88125-376-6*) Ktav.

***Paldy, Lester G.** For an Okay Free Woman. LC 92-80282. 58p. 1992. pap. 9.95 (*0-9632277-0-X*) Night Heron.

— Wildflowers at Babi Yar. LC 94-67429. 40p. (Orig.). 1994. pap. 6.95 (*0-9632277-1-8*) Night Heron.

Palecek, F., jt. auth. see Aviado, D. M.

***Palecek, Libuse.** Brave As a Tiger. LC 94-40904. (Illus.). 32p. (J). (gr. k-2). 1995. 14.95 (*1-55858-395-5*); lib. bdg. 14.88 (*1-55858-396-3*) North-South Bks NYC.

Palek, Jiri. Erythrocytes. (Current Opinion in Hematology Ser.). (Illus.). 176p. (Orig.). 1994. pap. text ed. 39.95 (*1-85922-655-8*) Current Science.

Palen, Adeline. Death among the Lilacs. 218p. (Orig.). 1987. pap. 5.95 (*0-9619488-0-9*) Blue Spruce Pr.

Palen, J. John. Suburbs. 1994. pap. text ed. write for info. (*0-07-048128-8*) McGraw.

— The Urban World. 3rd ed. 504p. 1987. text ed. write for info. (*0-07-048111-3*) McGraw.

Palen, J. John & London, Bruce, eds. Gentrification, Displacement & Neighborhood Revitalization. LC 83-5038. (SUNY Series in Urban Public Policy). 271p. 1985. 59.50 (*0-87395-784-9*); pap. 19.95 (*0-87395-785-7*) State U NY Pr.

Palen, J. W., ed. Heat Exchanger Sourcebook. 805p. 1986. 81.00 (*0-89116-451-0*) Hemisp Pub.

Palen, Jerry. Stampede, the First Really Big Book. (Illus.). 54p. (Orig.). 1986. pap. 6.95 (*0-941803-00-7*) Stampede Cartoons.

Palen, John J. The Urban World. 4th ed. 1992. text ed. write for info. (*0-07-048120-2*) McGraw.

***Palen, Margaret K.** German Settlers of Iowa: Their Descendants & European Ancestors. 360p. (Orig.). 1994. pap. text ed. 29.50 (*1-55613-981-0*) Heritage Bk.

Palencia, E. Sanchez, jt. auth. see Hubert, J. Sanchez.

Palencia, Elaine F. Small Caucasian Woman. 176p. 1993. pap. 10.95 (*0-8262-0943-2*) U of Mo Pr.

Palenick, Joe. Writer's Resource Guide to Seattle: A Directory, 1987-88. Griffin, William R., ed. & intro. by. (Illus.). 65p. (Orig.). (C). 1987. pap. text ed. 3.00 (*0-910303-06-1*) Writers Pub Serv.

Palenik, jt. auth. see Miller.

Palenski, Joseph. Kids Who Run Away. LC 83-62298. 160p. (Orig.). (C). 1984. pap. text ed. 15.95 (*0-88247-727-7*) R & E Pubs.

Palenski, Joseph E., jt. ed. see Launer, Harold M.

Palenski, Ronald J. ADAPSO Sales & Use Tax Survey. rev. ed. write for info. (*0-318-62080-4*) ITAA.

Paleo, Lyn, jt. ed. see Garber, Eric.

Paleoloque, Maurice. Cavour. Morrow, Ian F. & Morrow, Muriel M., trs. LC 77-130561. (Select Bibliographies Reprint Ser.). 1977. reprint ed. 23.95 (*0-8369-5534-X*) Ayer.

Paleos, Constantinos M. Polymerization in Organized Media. 454p. 1992. text ed. 110.00 (*2-88124-538-2*) Gordon & Breach.

Palerm, Angel, jt. auth. see Kelly, Isabel T.

Palerm, Juan-Vicente. Chicano & Mexican Communities in Rural California. (Conflict & Social Change Ser.). 180p. (C). 1929. pap. text ed. 29.95 (*0-8133-8399-4*) Westview.

Palermo, Blinky. Palermo. Greenidge, Delano & Maas, Erich, eds. LC 88-51594. 160p. (ENG & GER.). 1989. 45.00 (*0-929445-01-5*) D Greenidge Editions.

Palermo, David S., ed. Coping with Uncertainty: Behavioral & Developmental Perspectives. (Penn State Series on Child & Adolescent Development). 224p. 1989. 45.00 (*0-8058-0157-X*) L Erlbaum Assocs.

Palermo, David S., jt. ed. see Overton, Willis F.

Palermo, David S., jt. ed. see Weimer, Walter B.

***Palermo, George B.** The Faces of Violence. LC 94-31664. (American Series in Behavioral Science & Law). 300p. (C). 1994. text ed. 68.95x (*0-398-05934-9*); pap. 37.95x (*0-398-05952-7*) C C Thomas.

Palermo, Phil, jt. auth. see Mackie, Hank.

Palermo, Richard C. & Watson, Gregory H., eds. A World of Quality: The Timeless Passport. LC 93-35607. 212p. 1993. 29.95 (*0-87389-290-9*) ASQC Qual Pr.

Pales Matos, Luis. Obras: Luis Pales Matos, Nineteen Fourteen to Nineteen Fifty-Nine, 2 vols., Set. Arce de Vazquez, Margot, ed. LC 79-16469. 609p. (SPA.). 1984. 25.00 (*0-8477-3219-3*) U of PR Pr.

— Obras: Luis Pales Matos, Nineteen Fourteen to Nineteen Fifty-Nine, 2 vols., Vol. I: Poetry. Arce de Vazquez, Margot, ed. LC 79-16469. 609p. (SPA.). 1984. 15.00 (*0-8477-3220-7*) U of PR Pr.

— Obras: Luis Pales Matos, Nineteen Fourteen to Nineteen Fifty-Nine, 2 vols., Vol. II: Prose. Arce de Vazquez, Margot, ed. LC 79-16469. 609p. (SPA.). 1984. 10.00 (*0-8477-3221-5*) U of PR Pr.

— Poesia: 1915-1956. 5th rev. ed. 304p. (SPA.). 1974. 5.00 (*0-88473-212-6*) U of PR Pr.

Palese, P. Genetics of Influenza Viruses. (Illus.). 340p. 1983. 94.00 (*0-387-81743-3*) Spr-Verlag.

Palese, Peter, ed. see New York Academy of Sciences Staff.

Palestine, jt. auth. see Nussenblatt.

Palestine Economic Society Bulletin Staff. Palestine Economic Society Bulletin: Proceedings of the Bulletin of the Palestine Economic Society, Tel Aviv, Aug. 21 - Feb., 1934, 6 vols. in 5, Set. reprint ed. write for info. (*0-404-56240-X*) AMS Pr.

Palestine Pilgrims' Text Society Staff. The Library of the Palestine Pilgrims' Text Society: Circa 1480-1483 A.D., 11 vols., Set. Stewart, Aubrey, tr. LC 74-141802. (Palestine Pilgrims' Text Society Ser.: Nos. 7-10). reprint ed. 124.50 (*0-404-09140-7*) AMS Pr.

Palestrant, Ellen. Have You Ever Had a Hunch? Getting Your Inner Critics Out of the Way. Westheimer, Mary, ed. (Illus.). 192p. (Orig.). (C). 1994. pap. 12.95 (*1-885001-01-0*) Via Press.

Palestrina, Giovanni P. Ten Four-Part Motets for the Church's Year. Harman, Alec, tr. (ENG & LAT.). 1985. 24.95 (*0-19-353332-4*) OUP.

Palestrini, Giovanni P. Pope Marcellus Mass. rev. ed. Lockwood, Lewis, ed. (Critical Scores Ser.). (C). 1975. pap. text ed. 6.95 (*0-393-09242-9*) Norton.

Paletta, LuAnn & Worth, Fred. World Almanac of Presidential Facts. rev. ed. LC 92-38611. 1993. 21.95 (*0-88687-714-8*); pap. 10.95 (*0-88687-713-X*) Wrld Almnc.

Paletz, David. Political Communication Research: Approaches, Studies, Assessments. Voigt, Melvin J., ed. LC 86-17475. (Communication & Information Science Ser.). 288p. (C). 1987. text ed. 49.50 (*0-89391-329-4*) Ablex Pub.

***Paletz, David L., ed. & tr.** Political Communication in Action: States, Institutions, Movements, Audiences. (Communication Series). 384p. (C). 1995. text ed. 72.50 (*1-57273-000-5*) Hampton Pr NJ.

— Political Communication in Action: States, Institutions, Movements, Audiences. (Communication Series). 384p. (C). 1995. pap. text ed. 26.50 (*1-57273-001-3*) Hampton Pr NJ.

Paletz, David L. & Entman, Robert M. Media Power Politics. 304p. 1981. 19.95 (*0-02-923650-9*); pap. 13.95 (*0-685-03271-X*) Macmillan.

— Media, Power, Politics. LC 80-1642. 1982. pap. 16.95 (*0-02-923660-6*) Free Pr.

Paletz, David L. & Schmid, Alex P., eds. Terrorism & the Media. (Illus.). 320p. (C). 1992. 42.00 (*0-8039-4482-9*); pap. 18.95 (*0-8039-4483-7*) Sage.

Paletz, David L., jt. ed. see Bennett, W. Lance.

Paletz, David L., ed. see Semetko, Holli & Schoenbach, Klaus.

Paletz, David L., ed. see Steinman, Clay, et al.

***Paletz, David L., et al.** Glasnost & After: Media & Change in Central & Eastern Europe. (Communication Series). 256p. 1995. text ed. 49.50 (*1-881303-86-1*) Hampton Pr NJ.

— Glasnost & After: Media & Change in Central & Eastern Europe. (Communication Series). 256p. 1995. pap. text ed. 19.95 (*1-881303-87-X*) Hampton Pr NJ.

Palev, T. D., jt. ed. see Doebner, H. D.

Paleveda, Carl A. Is the U. S. Constitution Unconstitutional? (Illus.). 136p. (C). 1991. text ed. 19.95 (*0-9626760-1-2*) Paleveda Pres.

Paleveda, Gloria S. The Best of Times. (Illus.). 139p. 1986. pap. 8.95 (*0-936676-83-3*) Better Baby.

Palevsky, Nicholas, jt. auth. see Kinoshita, June.

Paley. Ilizarov Technique. 1993. write for info. (*0-397-51086-1*) Lippincott.

Paley, Aaron, ed. see Fringe Festival-Los Angeles Staff & Community Arts Resources, Inc. Staff.

Paley, Alan. Karl Marx: Philosophical Father of Communism. Rahmas, D. Steve, ed. (Outstanding Personalities Ser.: No. 79). 32p. 1975. lib. bdg. 4.95 (*0-87157-579-5*) SamHar Pr.

— The Spanish Civil War. Rahmas, Sigurd C., ed. (Events of Our Times Ser.: No. 23). 32p. (Orig.). 1982. 4.95 (*0-87157-724-0*) SamHar Pr.

Paley, Alan L. Andrew Johnson: The President Impeached. Rahmas, D. Steve, ed. LC 74-190248. (Outstanding Personalities Ser.: No. 31). 32p. (J). (gr. 7-12). 1972. lib. bdg. 4.95 (*0-87157-531-0*) SamHar Pr.

— Edgar Allan Poe: American Poet & Mystery Writer. Rahmas, D. Steve, ed. (Outstanding Personalities Ser.: No. 84). 32p. (YA). (gr. 7-12). 1975. lib. bdg. 4.95 (*0-87157-584-1*) SamHar Pr.

— The Establishment of Communism in China. (Events of Our Times Ser.: No. 16). 32p. (Orig.). (gr. 7-12). lib. bdg. 4.95 (*0-87157-717-8*) SamHar Pr.

— H. G. Wells: Author of Famous Science Fiction Stories. Rahmas, D. Steve, ed. (Outstanding Personalities Ser.: No. 51). 32p. (Orig.). (YA). (gr. 7-12). 1972. lib. bdg. 4.95 (*0-87157-554-X*) SamHar Pr.

— Munich & the Sudeten Crisis. Rahmas, D. Steve, ed. LC 72-89217. (Events of Our Times Ser.: No. 8). 32p. 1973. lib. bdg. 4.95 (*0-87157-703-8*) SamHar Pr.

— Russo-Finnish War. Rahmas, D. Steve, ed. LC 72-89216. (Events of Our Times Ser.: No. 5). 32p. 1973. lib. bdg. 4.95 (*0-87157-705-4*) SamHar Pr.

— Sigmund Freud: Father of Psychoanalysis. Rahmas, D. Steve, ed. LC 74-14694. (Outstanding Personalities Ser.: No. 73). 32p. 1974. lib. bdg. 4.95 (*0-87157-573-6*) SamHar Pr.

— Sinclair Lewis: Twentieth Century American Author & Nobel Prize Winner. Rahmas, D. Steve, ed. LC 73-87626. (Outstanding Personalities Ser.: No. 67). 32p. (Orig.). (YA). (gr. 7-12). 1974. lib. bdg. 4.95 (*0-87157-567-1*) SamHar Pr.

— Soren Kierkegaard: Modern Philosopher & Existentialist. LC 72-81903. (Outstanding Personalities Ser.: No. 40). 32p. 1972. lib. bdg. 4.95 (*0-87157-550-7*) SamHar Pr.

— Stalin: The Iron Fisted Dictator of Russia. Rahmas, D. Steve, ed. LC 76-185663. (Outstanding Personalities Ser.: No. 7). 32p. 1972. lib. bdg. 4.95 (*0-87157-507-8*) SamHar Pr.

— Theodore Dreiser: American Editor & Novelist. Rahmas, D. Steve, ed. (Outstanding Personalities Ser.: No. 55). 32p. 1973. lib. bdg. 4.95 (*0-87157-557-4*) SamHar Pr.

***Paley, Albert.** The Metalwork of Albert Paley. (Illus.). 56p. 1980. pap. 8.50 (*0-932718-06-X*) Kohler Arts.

Paley, F. A., comment. Euripides, 3 vols. 2nd rev. ed. cxxxiv, 1829p. (ENG & GER.). write for info. (*0-318-70528-1*, Pub. by Georg Olms GW) Lubrecht & Cramer.

Paley, Grace. The Collected Stories. LC 93-42230. 1994. 27.50 (*0-374-12636-4*) FS&G.

— The Collected Stories. 386p. 1995. pap. 14.00 (*0-374-52431-9*, Noonday) FS&G.

— Enormous Changes at the Last Minute. 208p. 1985. pap. 10.00 (*0-374-51524-7*) FS&G.

— Enormous Changes Last Minute. 1980. 5.99 (*0-86068-108-4*, Pub. by Virago Pr UK) Random.

— Later the Same Day. (Contemporary American Fiction Ser.). 224p. 1986. pap. 11.00 (*0-14-008641-2*, Penguin Bks) Viking Penguin.

— The Little Disturbances of Man. (Fiction Ser.). 192p. 1985. pap. 9.95 (*0-14-007557-7*, Penguin Bks) Viking Penguin.

— Long Walks & Intimate Talks. (Illus.). 80p. 1991. 29.95 (*1-55861-043-X*); pap. 12.95 (*1-55861-044-8*) Feminist Pr.

— New & Collected Poems. 160p. 1992. 19.95 (*0-88448-098-4*); pap. 12.95 (*0-88448-099-2*) Tilbury Hse.

Paley, Grace, pref. A Dream Compels Us: Voices of Salvadoran Women. LC 89-11598. (Illus.). 248p. 1989. 25.00 (*0-89608-369-1*); pap. 11.00 (*0-89608-368-3*) South End Pr.

Paley, Grace, et al. Ergo! The Bumbershoot Literary Magazine, Vol. 7, No. 1. 144p. 1992. pap. 8.00 (*0-929696-04-2*) Bumbershoot.

Paley, Guillermo. Las Epistolas De Pablo: Paul's Epistles. (SPA.). 6.95 (*84-7228-920-6*, 223000, Pub. by Edit Clie SP) TSELF.

Paley, Helen N., ed. see Abrams, Michael J., et al.

Paley, Karl & Mendoza, Carlos. Values for Tomorrow: Educating Citizens for the 21st Century. 212p. 1991. 35.95 (*1-880294-01-X*); pap. 16.95 (*1-880294-02-8*) Panacea Pr.

Paley, Morton D. The Apocalyptic Sublime. LC 86-1706. 208p. 1986. 42.00 (*0-300-03674-4*) Yale U Pr.

Paley, Morton D., ed. see Blake, William, et al.

Paley, Morton D., jt. auth. see Essick, Robert.

Paley, Morton D., jt. ed. see Fulford, Tim.

***Paley, Nicholas.** Finding Art's Place: Experiments in Contemporary Education & Culture. 1994. 49.95 (*0-415-90606-7*, A7344); pap. 19.95 (*0-415-90607-5*, A7348) Routledge.

Paley, Nina. Nina's Adventures. (Illus.). 96p. 1993. pap. 7.95 (*0-9637283-1-8*) Pentshack Pr.

Paley, Nina, illus. Inside-Out Feelings. LC 93-8953. (Contemporary Health Ser.). (J). 1993. write for info. (*1-56071-315-1*) ETR Assocs.

— What about Me? LC 93-8955. (Contemporary Health Ser.). (J). 1993. write for info. (*1-56071-314-3*) ETR Assocs.

Paley, Norton. The Manager's Guide to Competitive Marketing Strategies. rev. ed. LC 88-47708. 390p. 1990. pap. 24.95 (*0-8144-7748-8*) AMACOM.

— The Strategic Marketing Planner. LC 90-53216. 304p. 1991. ring bd. 75.00 (*0-8144-1149-5*) AMACOM.

Paley, Norton, jt. auth. see Elam, Houston G.

Paley, Raymond & Wiener, Norbert. Fourier Transforms in the Complex Domain. LC 35-3273. (Colloquium Publications: Vol. 19). 183p. 1987. reprint ed. pap. 45.00 (*0-8218-1019-7*, COLL-19) Am Math.

***Paley, S. M.** Robotics Illustrated Dictionary. (Illus.). (ENG, FRE, GER & RUS.). 1993. 85.00 (*0-7859-8827-0*) Fr & Eur.

— Robotics Illustrated Dictionary French-English-German-Russian. (Illus.). 347p. (ENG, FRE & GER.). 1993. 85.00x (*2-85608-052-9*, Pub. by La Maison Du Dict FR) IBD Ltd.

Paley, Vivian G. Bad Guys Don't Have Birthdays: Fantasy Play at Four. LC 87-21748. x, 118p. 1991. pap. 9.95 (*0-226-64496-0*) U Ch Pr.

— The Boy Who Would Be a Helicopter. 163p. 1990. 26.50 (*0-674-08030-0*) HUP.

— The Boy Who Would Be a Helicopter. 163p. 1991. pap. text ed. 9.95 (*0-674-08031-9*) HUP.

— Boys & Girls: Superheroes in the Doll Corner. LC 84-93. xii, 116p. (C). 1986. pap. 8.95 (*0-226-64492-8*) U Ch Pr.

— Kwanzaa & Me: A Teacher's Story. LC 94-25002. 148p. 1995. text ed. 18.95 (*0-674-50585-9*, PALKWA) HUP.

— Mollie Is Three: Growing up in School. xvi, 144p. 1988. pap. 9.95 (*0-226-64494-4*) U Ch Pr.

— Molly Is Three: Growing up in School. LC 85-24589. xvi, 144p. (C). 1986. 15.95 (*0-226-64493-6*) U Ch Pr.

— Wally's Stories: Conversations in the Kindergarten. LC 80-21882. 223p. 1987. pap. text ed. 10.95 (*0-674-94593-X*) HUP.

— White Teacher. 156p. 1989. reprint ed. pap. text ed. 9.95 (*0-674-95186-7*) HUP.

— You Can't Say You Can't Play. (Illus.). 134p. 1992. text ed. 19.95 (*0-674-96589-2*) HUP.

— You Can't Say You Can't Play. 134p. 1993. pap. text ed. 10.00 (*0-674-96590-6*) HUP.

Paley, William. Natural Theology. (C). 1986. reprint ed. lib. bdg. 24.95 (*0-935005-61-7*); reprint ed. pap. 15.95 (*0-935005-62-5*) Lincoln-Rembrandt.

— A Treatise on the Law of Principal & Agent, Chiefly with Reference to Mercantile Transactions. 2nd ed. xvi, 202p. 1982. reprint ed. lib. bdg. 25.00 (*0-8377-1010-3*) Rothman.

Palfai, Tibor & Jankiewicz, Henry. Drugs & Human Behavior. 544p. (C). 1991. pap. write for info. (*0-697-06431-X*) Brown & Benchmark.

Palfey, Colin. The Scottish Trip. 1986. 30.00 (*0-86243-041-0*, Pub. by Y Lolfa UK) St Mut.

Palffy-Muhoray, P., jt. auth. see Cladis, P. E.

***Palfin, Richard A. & Danninger, Brent B.** Hedonic Damages: Proving Damages for Lost Enjoyment of Living. 491p. 1990. 80.00 (*0-87473-647-1*) Michie Butterworth.

Palfreeman, Anthony C., jt. auth. see Mediansky, Fedor.

Palfreman, David, jt. auth. see Beardshaw, John.

Palfreman, Jon. Dream Machine: Exploring the Computer Age. 1993. pap. 22.95 (*0-563-36992-2*, Pub. by BBC UK) Parkwest Pubns.

Palfreman, Jon, jt. auth. see Langston, J. William.

Palfreman, P. Business Law. (C). 1990. 130.00 (*0-7487-0406-X*, Pub. by S Thornes Pubs UK) St Mut.

Palfrey, Colin, et al. Policy Evaluation in the Public Sector: Approaches & Methods. 182p. 1992. 59.95 (*1-85628-393-3*, Pub. by Avebury Pub UK) Ashgate Pub Co.

Palfrey, John G. History of New England, 5 Vols. reprint ed. write for info. (*0-318-50605-X*) AMS Pr.

— History of New England, 5 Vols, 1. LC 01-7587. reprint ed. 39.50 (*0-404-04911-7*) AMS Pr.

— History of New England, 5 Vols, 2. LC 01-7587. reprint ed. 39.50 (*0-404-04912-5*) AMS Pr.

— History of New England, 5 Vols, 3. LC 01-7587. reprint ed. 39.50 (*0-404-04913-3*) AMS Pr.

— History of New England, 5 Vols, 4. LC 01-7587. reprint ed. 39.50 (*0-404-04914-1*) AMS Pr.

— History of New England, 5 Vols, 5. LC 01-7587. reprint ed. 39.50 (*0-404-04915-X*) AMS Pr.

— History of New England, 5 Vols, Set. LC 01-7587. reprint ed. 345.00 (*0-404-04910-9*) AMS Pr.

Palfrey, Judith S. Community Child Health: An Action Plan for Today. LC 94-8641. 328p. 1994. text ed. 55.00 (*0-275-94696-7*, Praeger Pubs) Greenwood.

Palfrey, Thomas R. Panorama Litteraire de l'Europe 1833-1834. LC 73-128990. (Northwestern Humanities Ser.: No. 22). (FRE.). reprint ed. 22.00 (*0-404-50722-0*) AMS Pr.

Palfrey, Thomas R., ed. Laboratory Research in Political Economy. 300p. (C). 1991. text ed. 52.50 (*0-472-10203-6*) U of Mich Pr.

Palfrey, Thomas R. & Kinder, Donald R., eds. Experimental Foundations of Political Science. (Michigan Studies in Political Analysis). (Illus.). 376p. (C). 1992. text ed. 59.50 (*0-472-10273-7*); pap. text ed. 22.95 (*0-472-08181-0*) U of Mich Pr.

Palfrey, Thomas R. & Srivastava, Sanjay. Bayesian Implementation. Postlewaite, A., ed. LC 92-32494. (Fundamentals of Pure & Applied Economics Ser.: Vol. 53). 1993. pap. text ed. 22.00 (*3-7186-5314-1*) Gordon & Breach.

Palfrey, Thomas R. & Will, Samuel F., eds. Petite Anthologie: Poesies Francaises. (Orig.). (FRE.). 1961. pap. text ed. 7.95 (*0-89197-337-0*) Irvington.

Palfreyman, Michael G., et al, eds. Direct & Allosteric Control of Glutamate Receptors. LC 94-7075. (Series on Pharmacology & Toxicology). 1994. 129.95 (*0-8493-8307-2*, 8307) CRC Pr.

An Asterisk (*) at the beginning of an entry indicates that the title is appearing in BIP for the first time.

— Enzymes As Targets for Drug Design. 267p. 1989. text ed. 68.00 (*0-12-544030-8*) Acad Pr.

Palgrave, Derek A., ed. Fluid Fertilizer Science & Technology. (Fertilizer Science & Technology Ser.: Vol. 7). 648p. 1991. 215.00 (*0-8247-7703-4*) Dekker.

Palgrave, F. M., ed. A List of Words & Phrases in Every-Day Use by the Natives of Hetton-Le-Hole. (English Dialect Society Publications Ser.: No. 74). 1969. reprint ed. pap. 15.00 (*0-8115-0492-1*) Periodicals Srv.

***Palgrave, Frances.** Astrology & Alchemy. 1994. pap. 6.95 (*1-55818-295-0*) Holmes Pub.

Palgrave, Francis. The History of Normandy & England, 4 vols. LC 80-2218. reprint ed. 345.00 (*0-404-18770-6*) AMS Pr.

Palgrave, Francis T. Francis Turner Palgrave: His Journals & Memories of His Life. Palgrave, Gwenllian F., ed. LC 73-148283. reprint ed. 45.00 (*0-404-04867-6*) AMS Pr.

— The Golden Treasury. 483p. 1990. reprint ed. lib. bdg. 27.95 (*0-89966-721-X*) Buccaneer Bks.

— Landscape in Poetry from Homer to Tennyson. 1972. 59.95 (*0-8490-0484-5*) Gordon Pr.

Palgrave, Francis T., comp. & notes. The Golden Treasury. 528p. 1992. reprint ed. pap. 11.95 (*0-14-042364-8*, Penguin Classics) Viking Penguin.

Palgrave, Francis T., ed. The Golden Treasury of English Songs & Lyrics. rev. ed. 496p. 1991. pap. 9.95 (*0-460-87029-7*, Everyman's Classic Lib) C E Tuttle.

— The Golden Treasury of the Best Songs & Lyrical Poems in the English Language. 672p. 1994. 30.00 (*0-19-254202-8*) OUP.

***Palgrave, Francis T., sel.** The Golden Treasury of the Best Songs & Lyrical Poems in the English Language. 6th ed. (Oxford Standard Authors Ser.). 720p. 1996. pap. 15.95 (*0-19-282315-9*) OUP.

Palgrave, Francis T. & Press, John, eds. Golden Treasury of the Best Songs & Lyrical Poems in the English Language: From Shakespeare to Larkin. 5th ed. (Oxford Standard Authors Ser.). (J). (gr. 5-9). 1987. pap. 10.95 (*0-19-282035-4*) OUP.

Palgrave, Gwenllian F., ed. see Palgrave, Francis T.

Palgrave, W. Central & Eastern Arabia. 448p. 1985. 370.00 (*1-85077-039-5*, Darf Pubs Ltd) St Mut.

Palgrave, William G. Narrative of a Year's Journey Through Central & Eastern Arabia, 1862-63, 2 vols. (Illus.). xii, 864p. reprint ed. write for info. (*0-318-71549-X*, Pub. by Georg Olms GW) Lubrecht & Cramer.

— Reise In Arabien, 2 vols. in 1. xii, 646p. reprint ed. write for info. (*0-318-71548-1*, Pub. by Georg Olms GW) Lubrecht & Cramer.

Palia, Kyamas A., et al. Grand Corporate Strategy & Critical Functions: Interactive Effects of Organizational Dimensions. LC 82-430. 236p. 1982. text ed. 49.95 (*0-275-90876-3*, C0876, Praeger Pubs) Greenwood.

Palic, Vladimir M. Government Publications, Vol. 1. 1977. 228.00 (*0-08-021457-6*, Pub. by Pergamon Repr UK) Franklin.

Palich, E. Hungarian-Serbocroatian Concise Dictionary. 3rd ed. 944p. (HUN & SER.). 1982. 49.95 (*0-8288-1669-7*, M8579) Fr & Eur.

***Palics, E.** Hungarian-Serbo Croatian Concise Dictionary. 944p. 1988. 36.00x (*963-205-217-X*, Pub. by Akad Kiado HU) St Mut.

Palidan, Vivian, ed. see Callaway, Lew L.

Palihawadana, Mahinda, jt. tr. see Carter, John R.

Palik, Edward D., ed. Handbook of Optical Constants of Solids. 1985. text ed. 169.00 (*0-12-544420-6*) Acad Pr.

— Handbook of Optical Constants of Solids II. 1096p. 1991. text ed. 182.00 (*0-12-544422-2*) Acad Pr.

***Palika, Liz.** The Australian Shepherd Dog: Champion of Versatility. LC 95-3753. 1995. 29.95 (*0-87605-039-9*) Howell Bk.

— Fido, Come: Training Your Dog With Love & Understanding. Luther, Luana, ed. LC 93-71334. (Illus.). 256p. 1994. 24.95 (*0-944875-29-7*) Doral Pub.

— The German Shepherd Dog. (Owner's Guide to a Happy, Healthy Pet Ser.). 160p. Date not set. 12.95 (*0-87605-382-7*) Howell Bk.

Palin, David. Groundwork of Philosophy of Religion. (Groundwork Ser.). 272p. (C). 1986. pap. text ed. 18.95 (*0-7162-0418-5*, Epworth Pr) TPI PA.

Palin, G. Plastics for Engineers: An Introductory Course. LC 66-28420. 1967. 74.00 (*0-08-012130-6*, Pub. by Pergamon Repr UK) Franklin.

Palin, G. R. Electrochemistry for Technologists. 1969. 100.00 (*0-08-013434-3*, Pub. by Pergamon Repr UK) Franklin.

***Palin, Michael.** Around the World in Eighty Days. LC 94-41914. (Illus.). 288p. 1995. pap. 17.95 (*0-912333-39-1*) KQED.

— Around the World in Eighty Days. large type ed. 1991. 23.95 (*0-7089-8573-4*, Charnwood) Ulverscroft.

— Pole to Pole: North to South by Camel, River Raft, & Balloon. (Illus.). 336p. 1992. pap. 17.95 (*0-912333-41-3*) KQED.

— Pole to Pole: With Michael Palin. (Illus.). 320p. 1993. 29.95 (*0-563-36283-9*, BBC-Parkwest) Parkwest Pubns.

— Ripping Yarns. 1991. pap. 17.95 (*0-413-63980-0*) Routledge Chapman & Hall.

***Palin, Roger H.** Multinational Military Forces: Problems & Prospects: A European Perspective. (Adelphi Papers). 1995. pap. text ed. 23.00 (*0-19-828025-4*) OUP.

***Paling, John & Paling, Sean.** Up to Your Armpits in Alligators? How to Sort Out What Risks Are Worth Worrying About! (Illus.). 155p. (Orig.). 1994. pap. 15.00 (*0-9642236-0-0*) J Paling & Co.

Paling, Sean, jt. auth. see Paling, John.

Palingenius, Marcellus. The Zodiake of Life. Googe, Barnabe, tr. LC 48-275. 1977. reprint ed. 60.00 (*0-8201-1214-3*) Schol Facsimiles.

Palinkas, Lawrence A. Methods in Medical Anthropology. 1929. text ed. 29.95 (*0-8133-0691-4*) Westview.

Paliouras, John D. & Meadows, Douglas S. Complex Variables for Scientists & Engineers. 2nd ed. (Illus.). 805p. (C). 1990. pap. write for info. (*0-02-390561-1*) Macmillan.

Palis, J., Jr., ed. Geometric Dynamics. (Lecture Notes in Mathematics Ser.: Vol. 1007). 827p. 1983. pap. 65.90 (*0-387-12336-9*) Spr-Verlag.

Palis, Jacob & Takens, Floris. Hyperbolicity, Stability & Chaos at Homoclinic Bifurcations: Fractal Dimensions & Infinitely Many Attractors in Dynamics. (Studies in Advanced Mathematics: No. 35). (Illus.). 250p. (C). 1993. 59.95 (*0-521-39064-8*) Cambridge U Pr.

Palisca, Claude V. Baroque Music. 2nd ed. (History of Music Ser.). (Illus.). 1981. text ed. 19.95 (*0-13-055954-7*) P-H.

— Baroque Music. 3rd ed. 1990. pap. text ed. 35.00 (*0-13-058496-7*, 650102) P-H.

— Humanism in Italian Renaissance Musical Thought. 484p. (C). 1990. reprint ed. 22.00 (*0-300-04962-5*) Yale U Pr.

— The Norton Anthology of Western Music. (Orig.). (C). 1980. pap. text ed. 19.95 (*0-393-95155-3*) Norton.

— Studies in the History of Italian Music & Music Theory. (Illus.). 528p. 1994. 55.00 (*0-19-816167-0*) OUP.

— Study Guide for Norton Anthology of Western Music, Second Edition, & History of Western Music, Fourth Edition. (Illus.). (C). 1992. pap. text ed. write for info. (*0-393-96231-8*) Norton.

***Palisca, Claude V., ed.** Musica Enchiriadis: And Scolica Enchiriadis. Erickson, Raymond, tr. & intro. by. LC 94-34601. (Music Theory Translation Ser.). 1995. 27.50 (*0-300-05818-7*) Yale U Pr.

— The Norton Anthology of Western Music, 2 vols. (Orig.). (C). 1988. lp 45.00 (*0-393-99138-5*) Norton.

— The Norton Anthology of Western Music, 2 vols. 2nd ed. (Orig.). (C). 1988. Album II. lp 32.95 (*0-393-99144-X*) Norton.

— The Norton Anthology of Western Music, 2 vols., II. (Orig.). (C). 1988. pap. text ed. 27.95 (*0-393-95644-X*) Norton.

— The Norton Anthology of Western Music, 2 vols., Vol. I. 2nd ed. 500p. (Orig.). (C). 1988. pap. text ed. 27.95 (*0-393-95642-3*) Norton.

— The Norton Anthology of Western Music Vol. I: Ancient to Baroque. 3rd ed. 600p. 1996. pap. 29.95 (*0-393-96906-1*) Norton.

— The Norton Anthology of Western Music Vol. II: Classic to Modern. 3rd ed. 800p. 1996. pap. 29.95 (*0-393-96907-X*) Norton.

Palisca, Claude V., ed. see Burmeister, Joachim.

Palisca, Claude V., ed. see Gaffurio, Franchino.

Palisca, Claude V., jt. auth. see Grout, Donald J.

Palisca, Claude V., jt. ed. see Holoman, D. Kern.

Palisca, Claude V., tr. see Zarlino, Gioseffo.

Palisono, Robert, ed. see Campbell, Suzann K.

Palit, D. K. War in High Himalaya: The Indian Army in Crisis, 1962. (C). 1991. 30.00 (*81-7062-138-0*, Pub. by Lancer International II) S Asia.

Palit, P., jt. ed. see Sen, S. P.

Paliwal, B. B. The Poetic Revolution of the Nineteen Twenties. 232p. 1974. text ed. 20.00 (*0-685-13728-7*) Coronet Bks.

Paliwal, Bhudatt R., et al, eds. Biological, Physical & Clinical Aspects of Hyperthermia: Proceedings of the 1987 AAPM - NAHG Hyperthermia School Held at the Sheraton University Center, Durham, North Carolina, April 27-May 1, 1987. (American Association of Physicists in Medicine Symposium Ser.: No. 16). 483p. 1988. 75.00 (*0-88318-558-X*) Am Inst Physics.

— Optimization of Cancer Radiotherapy: Proceedings of the Second International Conference on Dose, Time Fractionation in Radiation Oncology Held at the University of Wisconsin, Madison, Wisconsin, September 12-14, 1984. (American Association of Physicists in Medicine Symposium Ser.: No. 5). 560p. 1985. 45.00 (*0-88318-483-4*) Am Inst Physics.

— Prediction of Response in Radiation Therapy, Pts. 1 & 2: Proceedings of the Third International Conference on Dose, Time & Fractionation Held at the University of Wisconsin, Madison, Wisconsin, September 14-17, 1988, Pt. 1. (American Association of Physicists in Medicine Symposium Ser.: No. 7). 770p. 1989. 60.00 (*0-685-72476-X*) Am Inst Physics.

— Prediction of Response in Radiation Therapy, Pts. 1 & 2: Proceedings of the Third International Conference on Dose, Time & Fractionation Held at the University of Wisconsin, Madison, Wisconsin, September 14-17, 1988, Pt. 2. 770p. 1989. text ed. write for info. (*0-318-68430-6*) Am Inst Physics.

Paliwal, G. S. The Vegetational Wealth of Himalaya. (C). 1988. 40.00 (*0-317-92315-3*, Scientific) St Mut.

***Paliwal, K. V., ed.** Pesticidal Pollution of Environment & Control: An Annotated Bibliography. 589p. 1994. 180.00x (*81-85880-23-9*, Pub. by Print Hse II) St Mut.

Paliwal, M. R. Social Change & Education. 1985. 30.00 (*0-8364-1255-9*, Pub. by Uppal Pub Hse II) S Asia.

Paliwal, Rajesh K. Janata Phase in Indian Politics. 200p. 1986. 31.00 (*81-7032-026-7*, Pub. by Manohar II) S Asia.

Paliwala, A. H., jt. auth. see Chalmers, D. R.

Paliwala, Abdul, jt. ed. see Adelman, Sammy.

Paliwoda, Stanley J. Essence of International Marketing. 192p. 1993. pap. 19.95 (*0-13-284803-1*) P-H.

— Investing in Eastern Europe: Opportunities Explored. (C). 1993. text ed. 27.95 (*0-201-59373-4*) Addison-Wesley.

Paliwoda, Stanley J., ed. New Perspectives on International Marketing. 272p. (C). 1991. text ed. 74.00 (*0-415-05344-7*, A5117) Routledge.

***Paliwoda, Stanley J. & Ryans, John K., Jr., eds.** International Marketing Reader. LC 94-43146. 288p. 1995. 65.00x (*0-415-11400-4*, C0417); pap. 19.95 (*0-415-10039-9*, C0481) Routledge.

Paliwoda, Stanley J., jt. ed. see Turnbull, Peter W.

Paliwodac, Stanley. International Marketing. 2nd ed. 540p. 1992. pap. 39.95 (*0-7506-0424-7*) Buttrwrth-Heinemann.

Palka, B. P. An Introduction to Complex Function Theory. Ewing, J. H. 117 et al et al, eds. (Undergraduate Texts in Mathematics Ser.). (Illus.). 560p. 1990. 39.00 (*0-387-97427-X*) Spr-Verlag.

Palkes, Helen, jt. auth. see Prensky, Arthur L.

Palkhivala, B. A., jt. auth. see Palkhivala, N. A.

Palkhivala, N. A. & Palkhivala, B. A. Tax Audit Manual. 2nd ed. (C). 1989. 440.00 (*0-685-36450-X*) St Mut.

***Palkhivala, Nani A.** We, the Nation: The Lost Decades. (C). 1994. 9.50x (*81-85944-90-3*, Pub. by UBS Pubs Dist II) S Asia.

Palkhivala, P., jt. auth. see Kanga, K.

Palko. Appleton & Lange's Review for the Medical Assistant. 4th ed. (C). 1994. pap. text ed. 24.95 (*0-8385-0197-4*) Appleton & Lange.

Palko, Hilda, jt. auth. see Palko, Tom.

***Palko, Tom & Palko, Hilda.** Laboratory Procedures for the Medical Office. LC 94-22538. (Illus.). 1994. 27.00 (*0-02-800065-X*) Glencoe.

Palkovic, M. Hormones, Lipoproteins & Atherosclerosis: Proceedings of a Satellite Symposium of the 28th International Congress of Physiological Sciences, Bratislava, Czechoslovakia, 1980. LC 80-41926. (Advances in Physiological Sciences Ser.: Vol. 35). (Illus.). 300p. 1981. 230.00 (*0-08-027357-2*, Pub. by Pergamon Repr UK) Franklin.

Palkovic, Mark. Musical Boxes. LC 82-91144. (Illus.). 64p. 1983. 28.00 (*0-88014-056-9*) Mosaic Pr OH.

***Palkovic, Mark, comp.** Harp Music Bibliography: Compositions for Solo Harp & Harp Ensemble. LC 94-44094. 1995. write for info. (*0-253-32887-X*) Ind U Pr.

Palkovic, Mark, ed. see Zingel, Hans J.

Palkovich, Ann M. Pueblo Population & Society: The Arroyo Hondo Skeletal & Mortuary Remains. LC 80-51310. (Arroyo Hondo Archaeological Ser.: Vol. 3). (Illus.). 222p. 1981. pap. 12.00 (*0-933452-03-9*) Schol Am Res.

Palkovits. Topographical Anatomy of Neuropeptides in the Rat Brain. 1992. write for info. (*0-8493-6270-9*, CRC Reprint) Franklin.

Palkovits, M., jt. auth. see Mitro, A.

Palkovitz, Robin J. & Sussman, Marvin B., eds. Transitions to Parenthood. LC 88-853. (Marriage & Family Review Ser.: Vol. 12, Nos. 3-4). (Illus.). 396p. 1988. text ed. 49.95 (*0-86656-787-9*) Haworth Pr.

Pall, A., jt. auth. see Inczedy, J.

Pall, Gabriel A. Quality Management. (Illus.). 256p. (C). 1987. text ed. 54.00 (*0-13-745027-3*) P-H.

Pall, Michael L. & Streit, Lois B. Let's Talk about It: The Book for Children about Child Abuse. LC 82-60527. 125p. (Orig.). (gr. 6-12). 1983. pap. 6.95 (*0-88247-682-3*) R & E Pubs.

Palladin, A. & Freusinger, F. Problems of Biochemistry of the Nervous System. LC 63-10030. 1964. 144.00 (*0-08-010165-8*, Pub. by Pergamon Repr UK) Franklin.

Palladini, David. Aquarian Tarot. 16p. 1970. 12.95 (*0-913866-69-5*) US Games Syst.

Palladini, David & Junjulas, Craig. Aquarian Tarot Deck-Book Set. (Illus.). 126p. 1985. 23.95 (*0-88079-592-1*) US Games Syst.

Palladino, Connie. Developing Self-Esteem. rev. ed. Gerould, W. Philip, ed. LC 93-74716. (Illus.). 114p. (Orig.). 1994. pap. 9.95 (*1-56052-261-5*) Crisp Pubns.

— Developing Self-Esteem for Students. Gerould, W. Philip, ed. LC 93-74716. (Illus.). (Orig.). 1994. pap. 9.95 (*1-56052-289-5*) Crisp Pubns.

Palladino, Grace. Another Civil War: Labor, Capital, & the State in Anthracite Regions of Pennsylvania, 1840 to 1868. (Working Class in America History Ser.). 216p. 1990. 26.50 (*0-252-01671-8*) U of Ill Pr.

Palladino, Joseph J., jt. auth. see Davis, Stephen F.

Palladino, L. & Perry, J. Hairdressing Management. (C). 1982. 65.00 (*0-85950-338-0*, Pub. by S Thornes Pubs UK) St Mut.

Palladino, Leo & Hunt, June. The Nail File. (Illus.). 154p. 1992. pap. text ed. 22.95 (*0-333-52584-1*, Pub. by Macmill Press UK) Scholium Intl.

Palladio, Andrea. Four Books of Architecture. Ware, Isaac, ed. 1738. pap. text ed. 14.95 (*0-486-21308-0*) Dover.

— The Four Books of Architecture. 24.25 (*0-8446-5464-7*) Peter Smith.

— I'Quattro Libri dell'Architettura. (Illus.). iv, 312p. 1979. reprint ed. write for info. (*3-487-06824-9*, Pub. by Georg Olms GW) Lubrecht & Cramer.

Palladius. The Lausiac History. (Ancient Christian Writers Ser.: No. 34). 1985. 18.95 (*0-8091-0083-5*) Paulist Pr.

— Life of St. Moses the Black. 1990. pap. 1.00 (*0-89981-113-2*) Eastern Orthodox.

— Spiritual Struggles of the Early Ascetics. 1991. pap. 2.95 (*0-89981-115-9*) Eastern Orthodox.

Palladius, Rutilius T. Palladius on Husbondrie. Lodge, Barton & Herrtage, S. J., eds. (EETS, OS Ser.: No. 52, 72). 1974. reprint ed. 52.00 (*0-527-00047-7*) Periodicals Srv.

Pallady, Stephen. Irony in the Poetry of Jose de Espronceda, 1834-1842. LC 90-44200. (Hispanic Literature Ser.: Vol. 8). 184p. 1991. lib. bdg. 79.95 (*0-88946-227-5*) E Mellen.

Pallai, K. Your Guide to Budapest: Budapest Teka, 1988. (Illus.). 182p. (C). 1988. 75.00 (*0-685-32398-6*, Pub. by Collets UK) Pro-Am Music.

Pallain, G., ed. Ambassade de Talleyrand a Londres: 1830-1831. LC 72-12238. (Europe 1815-1945 Ser.). 464p. 1973. reprint ed. lib. bdg. 59.50 (*0-306-70575-3*) Da Capo.

Pallain, Georges M. The Correspondence of Prince Tallyrand & King Louis XVIII During the Congress of Vienna. LC 70-126616. (Europe 1815-1945 Ser.). 654p. 1973. reprint ed. lib. bdg. 69.50 (*0-306-70047-6*) Da Capo.

Pallais, Don, et al. Guide to Forecasts & Projections, 3 vols. 1994. ring bd. 125.00 (*1-56433-434-1*) Prctnrs Pub Co.

— Guide to Forecasts & Projections, 2 vols., 1. 1993. write for info. (*1-56433-295-0*) Prctnrs Pub Co.

— Guide to Forecasts & Projections, 2 vols., 2. 1993. write for info. (*1-56433-296-9*) Prctnrs Pub Co.

— Guide to Forecasts & Projections, 3 vols., Set. Date not set. ring bd. 130.00 (*1-56433-600-X*) Prctnrs Pub Co.

— Guide to Forecasts & Projections, 2 vols., Set. 1993. ring bd. 115.00 (*1-56433-294-2*) Prctnrs Pub Co.

— Guide to Forecasts & Projections, 2 vols., Set. rev. ed. 830p. 1991. ring bd. 115.00 (*1-56433-013-3*) Prctnrs Pub Co.

— Guide to Forecasts & Projections, Vol. 1. Date not set. ring bd. write for info. (*1-56433-601-8*) Prctnrs Pub Co.

— Guide to Forecasts & Projections, Vol. 1. 1994. ring bd. write for info. (*1-56433-435-X*) Prctnrs Pub Co.

— Guide to Forecasts & Projections, Vol. 1. rev. ed. 450p. 1991. write for info. (*1-56433-014-1*) Prctnrs Pub Co.

— Guide to Forecasts & Projections, Vol. 2. Date not set. ring bd. write for info. (*1-56433-602-6*) Prctnrs Pub Co.

— Guide to Forecasts & Projections, Vol. 2. 1994. ring bd. write for info. (*1-56433-436-8*) Prctnrs Pub Co.

— Guide to Forecasts & Projections, Vol. 2. rev. ed. 380p. 1991. write for info. (*1-56433-015-X*) Prctnrs Pub Co.

— Guide to Forecasts & Projections, Vol. 3. Date not set. ring bd. write for info. (*1-56433-603-4*) Prctnrs Pub Co.

— Guide to Forecasts & Projections, Vol. 3. 1993. ring bd. 120.00 (*1-56433-389-2*) Prctnrs Pub Co.

— Guide to Forecasts & Projections, Vol. 3. 1994. ring bd. write for info. (*1-56433-437-6*) Prctnrs Pub Co.

***Pallais, Don M., et al.** Guide to Nontraditional Engagements, 2 vols., Set. 1994. ring bd. 125.00 (*1-56433-579-8*) Prctnrs Pub Co.

— Guide to Nontraditional Engagements, Vol. 1. 1994. ring bd. write for info. (*1-56433-580-1*) Prctnrs Pub Co.

— Guide to Nontraditional Engagements, Vol. 2. 1994. ring bd. write for info. (*1-56433-581-X*) Prctnrs Pub Co.

Pallak, Michael S. & Perloff, Robert, eds. Psychology & Work: Productivity, Change, & Employment. LC 86-7952. (Master Lecture Ser.: Vol. 5). 220p. (Orig.). 1986. pap. 24.95 (*0-912704-48-9*) Am Psychol.

Pallamary, Matthew J. The Small Dark Room of the Soul: And Other Stories. 150p. (Orig.). 1994. pap. 14.95 (*1-885516-00-2*) SD Writs Mnthly.

***Pallangyo, E. P.** Environmental Concern & the Sustainability of Africa's Agriculture in the 1990's & Beyond. 1994. 12.95 (*0-533-10682-6*) Vantage.

Pallant, N. Holding the Line. (Preserving the Kent & East Sussex Railway Ser.). (Illus.). 1994. 32.00 (*0-7509-0548-4*) A Sutton Pub.

Pallanti, Giuseppe. La Maremma Senese Nella Crisi Del Seicento. Bruchey, Stuart, ed. LC 80-2820. (Dissertations in European Economic History Ser.). (Illus.). 1981. lib. bdg. 23.95 (*0-405-14004-5*) Ayer.

Pallares, D. Sodi. My Heart's Health: A New Revolutionary View. 198p. 1989. pap. text ed. 15.00 (*1-57235-064-4*) Piccin NY.

Pallares, Eduardo. Diccionario de Derecho Procesal Civil. 877p. (SPA.). 37.50 (*0-7859-0710-6*, S-12340) Fr & Eur.

— Diccionario Teorico y Practico del Juicio de Amparo. 321p. (SPA.). 24.95 (*0-7859-0717-3*, S-21916) Fr & Eur.

Pallares, Jose C. A Poor Man Called Jesus: Reflections on the Gospel of Mark. Barr, Robert R., tr. LC 85-15339. 144p. reprint ed. pap. 41.10 (*0-7837-6974-1*, 2046785) Bks Demand.

Pallas-Avery, Ramon, et al. Sensors & Signal Conditioning. 416p. 1993. text ed. 74.95 (*0-471-54565-1*) Wiley.

Pallas, Norvin. Calculator Puzzles, Tricks & Games. 1991. pap. 3.95 (*0-486-26670-2*) Dover.

— Games with Codes & Ciphers. LC 94-12569. (Illus.). 112p. (J). (gr. 4-7). 1994. pap. text ed. 3.95 (*0-486-28209-0*) Dover.

Pallas, P. S. Travels Through the Southern Provinces of the Russian Empire Performed in the Years 1793 & 1794, 2 Vols, 1. LC 72-115573. (Russia Observed, Series I). 1970. reprint ed. 35.95 (*0-405-03238-2*) Ayer.

— Travels Through the Southern Provinces of the Russian Empire Performed in the Years 1793 & 1794, 2 Vols, 2. LC 72-115573. (Russia Observed, Series I). 1970. reprint ed. 35.95 (*0-405-03239-0*) Ayer.

— Travels Through the Southern Provinces of the Russian Empire Performed in the Years 1793 & 1794, 2 Vols, Set. LC 72-115573. (Russia Observed, Series I). 1971. reprint ed. 66.95 (*0-405-03055-X*) Ayer.

Pallasch, Thomas J. & Oksas, Richard M. Synopsis of Pharmacology for Students in Dentistry. LC 74-8951. 152p. reprint ed. 43.40 (*0-8357-9422-9*, 2014571) Bks Demand.

Pallaschke, D., jt. ed. see Neumann, K.

Pallaschke, D., jt. ed. see Oettli, W.

Pallavicini, R., ed. Hot Thin Plasmas in Astrophysics. (C). 1988. lib. bdg. 144.00 (*90-277-2812-7*) Kluwer Ac.

Pallavicino, Ferrante. Whore's Rhetorick. 1961. 10.95 (*0-8392-1132-5*) Astor-Honor.

Pallay, Steven G., comp. Cross Index Title Guide to Classical Music. LC 86-25723. (Music Reference Collection Ser.: No. 12). 215p. 1987. text ed. 59.95 (*0-313-25531-8*, PCR/, Greenwood Pr) Greenwood.

Pallay, Steven G., ed. Cross Index Title Guide to Opera & Operetta. LC 89-2131. (Music Reference Collection Ser.: No. 19). 222p. 1989. text ed. 49.95 (*0-313-25622-5*, PCX, Greenwood Pr) Greenwood.

Pallen, Conde B. Meaning of the Idylls of the King. LC 65-26453. (Studies in Tennyson: No. 27). (C). 1969. reprint ed. lib. bdg. 75.00 (*0-8383-0607-1*) M S G Haskell Hse.

P
Q

Pallen, Conde B., tr. see Salvany, Feliz S.

Pallen, Conde B., tr. see Sarda y Salvany, Felix.

Pallen, Conte B. Crucible Island. 1972. 59.95 (*0-87968-971-4*) Gordon Pr.

Paller, Alan & Laska, Richard. The EIS Book: Building Information Systems for Top Managers. 344p. 1990. text ed. 35.00 (*1-55623-244-6*) Irwin Prof Pubng.

Palleschi. Chemical Sensors for IN Vivo Monitoring. 1992. write for info. (*0-8493-6139-7*) CRC Pr.

Pallett, E. H. Automatic Flight Control. 4th ed. LC 93-25282. 1993. pap. text ed. 45.00x (*0-632-03495-5*) Blackwell Pubs.

Palley, Howard A. & Oktay, Julianne S., eds. The Chronically Limited Elderly: The Case for a National Policy for In-Home & Supportive Community-Based Services. LC 83-10686. (Home Health Care Services Quarterly Ser.: Vol. 4, No. 2). 142p. 1983. text ed. 37.95 (*0-86656-236-2*, B236) Haworth Pr.

Palley, Howard A., jt. auth. see Palley, Marian L.

Palley, Julian. Pictures at an Exhibition: Poems. 88p. (Orig.). 1989. pap. 6.00 (*0-9624205-0-6*) Inevitable Pr.

Palley, Julian, ed. Best New Chicano Literature 1986. 84p. 1986. pap. 8.00 (*0-916950-66-2*) Biling Rev-Pr.

— Best New Chicano Literature, 1989. 126p. 1989. pap. 9.00 (*0-927534-01-0*) Biling Rev-Pr.

Palley, Julian, tr. see Castellanos, Rosario.

Palley, Marian & Preston, Michael, eds. Minorities & Policy Studies. (C). 1978. pap. 12.00 (*0-918592-29-1*) Pol Studies.

Palley, Marian L. & Palley, Howard A. Urban America & Public Policies. 2nd ed. 336p. 1981. pap. text ed. 17.50 (*0-669-04004-5*) Heath.

Palley, Marian L., jt. ed. see Galb, Joyce.

Palley, Marian L., jt. auth. see Gelb, Joyce.

Palli, K. Your Guide to Budapest. (Illus.). 172p. (C). 1988. 75.00 (*0-685-37546-3*, Pub. by Collets) St Mut.

Palli, Vanamali T. Dieter's Quote Book. (Illus.). 80p. 1995. 7.00 (*0-87573-059-0*) Jain Pub Co.

Palliere, Aime. The Unknown Sanctuary. Wise, Louise W., tr. LC 79-150294. 243p. 1985. pap. 8.95 (*0-8197-0498-9*) Bloch.

Pallin, Paddy. Never Truly Lost: The Recollections of Paddy Pallin. 1987. pap. 19.95 (*0-86840-194-3*, Pub. by New South Wales Univ Pr AT) Intl Spec Bk.

Palling, Bruce. India: A Literary Companion. (Illus.). 272p. 1993. pap. 24.95 (*0-7195-5183-8*, Pub. by John Murray UK) Trafalgar.

Palling, S. J., ed. Developments in Food Packaging, Vol. 1. (Illus.). 192p. 1980. 66.75 (*0-85334-917-7*, Pub. by Elsevier Applied Sci UK) Elsevier.

Pallis, M., tr. see Minces, Juliet.

Pallis, M., tr. see Schuon, Frithjof.

Pallis, Marco. Peaks & Lamas. 1975. lib. bdg. 300.00 (*0-87968-327-9*) Gordon Pr.

— Way & the Mountain. 1991. pap. 22.00 (*0-7206-0841-4*) Dufour.

Pallis, Michael, tr. see Ghassemlou, A. R., et al.

Pallis, Svend A. The Antiquity of Iraq. LC 78-72755. (Ancient Mesopotamian Texts & Studies). reprint ed. 37.50 (*0-404-18199-6*) AMS Pr.

— The Babylonian Akitu Festival. LC 78-72756. (Ancient Mesopotamian Texts & Studies). reprint ed. 42.50 (*0-404-18203-8*) AMS Pr.

Palliser. Palliser's New Cottage Homes & Details. LC 75-4887. (Architecture & Decorative Art Ser.). (Illus.). 180p. 1975. reprint ed. lib. bdg. 55.00 (*0-306-70744-6*) Da Capo.

Palliser, Bury. History of Lace. enl. rev. ed. 672p. 1984. reprint ed. pap. 14.95 (*0-486-24742-2*) Dover.

— History of Lace. (Illus.). 1977. reprint ed. 49.00 (*0-685-01033-3*) Charles River Bks.

***Palliser, Charles.** Betrayals. LC 94-22769. 1995. 23.00 (*0-345-36959-9*) Ballantine.

— Quincunx. braille ed. 2288p. 1991. Braille. vinyl bd. 183.04 (*1-56956-306-3*, BR8076) W A T Braille.

— The Quincunx. 800p. 1990. reprint ed. pap. 14.00 (*0-345-37113-5*, Ballantine Trade) Ballantine.

Palliser, D. M. The Age of Elizabeth: England under the Later Tudors, 1547-1603. 2nd ed. 516p. (C). 1992. pap. text ed. 32.50 (*0-582-01322-4*, 79279) Longman.

Palliser, David. York Company of Merchant Adventurers. (C). 1990. 30.00 (*0-685-37378-9*, Pub. by W Sessions UK) St Mut.

Palliser, David & Palliser, Mary. York As They Saw It From Alcuin to Lord Esher. (C). 1988. 60.00 (*0-900657-45-6*, Pub. by W Sessions UK) St Mut.

Palliser, David, jt. auth. see Rees, Yvonne.

Palliser, David M., ed. The Royal Historical Society Annual Bibliography of British & Irish History: Publications of 1986. LC 81-641280. 175p. 1987. text ed. 35.00 (*0-312-01587-9*) St Martin.

Palliser, Margaret A. Christ, Our Mother of Mercy: Divine Mercy & Compassion in the Theology of the Shewings of Julian of Norwich. LC 92-24301. xiv, 262p. (C). 1992. lib. bdg. 129.25 (*3-11-013558-2*) De Gruyter.

Palliser, Mary, jt. auth. see Palliser, David.

Palliser Palliser & Co Staff. American Victorian Cottage Homes. 1990. pap. 6.95 (*0-486-26506-4*) Dover.

Pallister, Christopher J. Self-Assessment in Hematology. (Illus.). 192p. 1991. pap. 40.00 (*0-7506-1216-9*) Buttrwrth-Heinemann.

Pallister, Jan. Confrontations. Westburg, John E., ed. LC 76-29602. (Illus.). 1976. pap. 6.00 (*0-87423-022-5*) Westburg.

Pallister, Jan, tr. see Mansour, Joyce.

Pallister, Janis L. Aime Cesaire. (Twayne's World Authors Ser.: No. 821). 130p. 1992. text ed. 24.95 (*0-8057-8266-4*, Twayne) Macmillan.

— The Cinema of Quebec: Masters in their Own House. LC 94-43507. 1995. write for info. (*0-8386-3562-8*) Fairleigh Dickinson.

Pallister, Janis L., tr. see Pare, Ambroise.

Pallister, John C. In the Steps of the Great American Entomologist, Frank Eugene Lutz. Forbes, John R., ed. (In the Steps of the Great American Naturalists Ser.). (Illus.). 127p. 1976. reprint ed. 3.95 (*0-916544-10-9*) Natural Sci Youth.

Pallister, John S., jt. auth. see Du Bray, Edward A.

Pallmann, Ludwig F. & Stevens, Wendelle C. UFO Contact from ITIBI-RA: The Cancer Planet Mission. (Factbooks Ser.). (Illus.). 286p. 1986. lib. bdg. 14.95 (*0-934269-04-1*) UFO Photo.

Pallone, Dave & Steinberg, Alan. Behind the Mask. (Illus.). 352p. 1991. pap. 5.99 (*0-451-17029-6*, Sig) NAL-Dutton.

Pallone, Nathaniel J. Mental Disorder among Prisoners: Toward an Epidemiologic Inventory. 186p. (C). 1990. 32.95 (*0-88738-383-1*) Transaction Pubs.

— On the Social Utility of Psychopathology: A Deviant Majority & Its Keepers. 110p. 1985. 29.95 (*0-88738-048-4*) Transaction Pubs.

— Rehabilitating Criminal Sexual Psychopaths: Legislative Mandates, Clinical Quandries. 140p. 1990. 29.95 (*0-88738-340-8*) Transaction Pubs.

***Pallone, Nathaniel J., ed.** Young Victims, Young Offenders. LC 94-31967. (Journal of Offender Rehabilitation Ser.). (Illus.). 252p. 1994. lib. bdg. 39.95 (*1-56024-703-7*) Haworth Pr.

Pallone, Nathaniel J. & Hennessy, James J. Criminal Behavior: A Process Psychology Analysis. 436p. (C). 1992. 34.95 (*1-56000-044-9*) Transaction Pubs.

— Criminal Behavior: A Process Psychology Analysis. 436p. (C). 1994. pap. 24.95 (*1-56000-729-X*) Transaction Pubs.

***Pallone, Nathaniel J. & Hennessy, James J., eds.** Fraud & Fallible Judgment: Varieties of Deception in the Social & Behavioral Sciences. LC 94-46395. 1995. write for info. (*1-56000-210-7*) Transaction Pubs.

Pallone, Nathaniel J., jt. ed. see Chaneles, Sol.

Pallone, Nathaniel J., jt. ed. see Hillbrand, Marc.

***Pallot, James, ed.** The Motion Picture Guide Annual 1995: The Films of 1994. 600p. 1995. 164.95 (*0-933997-35-3*) Bowker.

— The Motion Picture Guide 1993 Annual: The Films of 1992. 635p. 1993. 148.50 (*0-918432-95-2*) Baseline Two.

***Pallot, James & Cinebooks Editors.** The Movie Guide. 1088p. (Orig.). 1995. pap. 25.00 (*0-399-51914-9*, Perigree Bks) Berkley Pub.

Pallot, Judith & Shaw, Denis J. Landscape & Settlement in Romanov Russia, 1613 to 1917. (Illus.). 336p. 1990. 69.00 (*0-19-823246-2*) OUP.

Pallot, William, jt. auth. see Callard, Lloyd.

Pallotta, Jerry. The Bird Alphabet Book. (Jerry Pallotta's Alphabet Bks.). (Illus.). 32p. (J). (ps-3). 1989. 14.95 (*0-88106-457-2*); pap. 6.95 (*0-88106-451-3*) Charlesbridge Pub.

— The Bird Alphabet Book. (Jerry Pallotta's Alphabet Bks.). (Illus.). 32p. (J). (ps-3). 1989. lib. bdg. 15.88 (*0-88106-677-X*) Charlesbridge Pub.

— Cuenta los Insectos (The Icky Bug Counting Book) (Illus.). 32p. (J). (ps-3). 1993. lib. bdg. 15.88 (*0-88106-639-7*); pap. 6.95 (*0-88106-419-X*) Charlesbridge Pub.

— The Desert Alphabet Book. LC 93-42651. (Illus.). 32p. (Orig.). (J). (ps-4). 1994. 14.95 (*0-88106-473-4*); lib. bdg. 15.88 (*0-88106-687-7*); pap. 6.95 (*0-88106-472-6*) Charlesbridge Pub.

— The Dinosaur Alphabet Book. (Jerry Pallotta's Alphabet Bks.). (Illus.). 32p. (Orig.). (J). (ps-4). 1990. 14.95 (*0-88106-467-X*); lib. bdg. 15.88 (*0-88106-683-4*); pap. 6.95 (*0-88106-466-1*) Charlesbridge Pub.

— The Extinct Alphabet Book. LC 93-1512. (Jerry Pallotta's Alphabet Bks.). (Illus.). (J). 1993. 14.95 (*0-88106-471-8*); lib. bdg. 15.88 (*0-88106-686-9*); pap. 6.95 (*0-88106-470-X*) Charlesbridge Pub.

— The Flower Alphabet Book. (Jerry Pallotta's Alphabet Bks.). (Illus.). 32p. (J). (ps-3). 1989. 14.95 (*0-88106-459-9*); pap. 6.95 (*0-88106-453-X*) Charlesbridge Pub.

— The Flower Alphabet Book. (Jerry Pallotta's Alphabet Bks.). (Illus.). 32p. (J). (ps-3). 1989. lib. bdg. 15.88 (*0-88106-679-6*) Charlesbridge Pub.

— The Frog Alphabet Book. (Jerry Pallotta's Alphabet Bks.). (Illus.). 32p. (Orig.). (J). (ps-4). 1990. 14.95 (*0-88106-463-7*); lib. bdg. 15.88 (*0-88106-681-8*); pap. 6.95 (*0-88106-462-9*) Charlesbridge Pub.

— The Furry Alphabet Book. (Jerry Pallotta's Alphabet Bks.). (Illus.). 32p. (Orig.). (J). (ps-4). 1990. 14.95 (*0-88106-465-3*); lib. bdg. 15.88 (*0-88106-682-6*); pap. 6.95 (*0-88106-464-5*) Charlesbridge Pub.

— Going Lobstering. (Illus.). 32p. (Orig.). (J). (ps-4). 1990. 15.95 (*0-88106-475-0*); pap. 7.95 (*0-88106-474-2*) Charlesbridge Pub.

— Going Lobstering. (Illus.). 32p. (Orig.). (J). (ps-8). 1990. lib. bdg. 16.88 (*0-88106-689-3*) Charlesbridge Pub.

— The Icky Bug Counting Book. (Illus.). 32p. (J). (ps-8). 1991. 14.95 (*0-88106-497-1*); pap. 6.95 (*0-88106-496-3*) Charlesbridge Pub.

— The Icky Bug Counting Book. (Illus.). 32p. (J). (ps-8). 1991. lib. bdg. 15.88 (*0-88106-690-7*) Charlesbridge Pub.

— The Ocean Alphabet Book. (Jerry Pallotta's Alphabet Bks.). (Illus.). 32p. (J). (ps-3). 1989. 14.95 (*0-88106-458-0*); lib. bdg. 15.88 (*0-88106-678-8*); pap. 6.95 (*0-88106-452-1*) Charlesbridge Pub.

— The Spice Alphabet Book: Herbs, Spices, & Other Natural Flavors. (Jerry Pallotta Alphabet Bks.). (Illus.). 32p. (Orig.). (J). (ps-4). 1994. 14.95 (*0-88106-898-5*); lib. bdg. 15.88 (*0-88106-899-3*); pap. 6.95 (*0-88106-897-7*) Charlesbridge Pub.

— The Underwater Alphabet Book. (Jerry Pallotta's Alphabet Bks.). (Illus.). 32p. (J). (ps-8). 1991. 14.95 (*0-88106-461-0*); lib. bdg. 15.88 (*0-88106-684-2*); pap. 6.95 (*0-88106-455-6*) Charlesbridge Pub.

— Yucky Reptile Alphabet Book. (Jerry Pallotta Alphabet Bks.). (J). (ps-3). 1990. 14.95 (*0-88106-460-2*); lib. bdg. 15.88 (*0-88106-680-X*); pap. 6.95 (*0-88106-454-8*) Charlesbridge Pub.

Pallotta, Jerry & Thomson, Bob. The Victory Garden Vegetable Alphabet Book. (Alphabet Book Ser.). (Illus.). 32p. (J). (gr. 3-8). 1992. 14.95 (*0-88106-469-6*); lib. bdg. 15.88 (*0-88106-685-0*); pap. 6.95 (*0-88106-468-8*) Charlesbridge Pub.

Pallotta, Jerry, jt. auth. see Cassie, Brian.

Pallotta, Joseph. Union Station Remembered. 2nd ed. (Illus.). 173p. 1985. pap. 19.95 (*0-9616091-0-9*) J & C Bks.

Pallottino, Massimo. A History of Earliest Italy. Ryle, Martin & Soper, Kate, trs. 190p. (C). 1990. reprint ed. text ed. 37.50 (*0-472-10097-1*) U of Mich Pr.

Pallozzi, Dennis. Helping Your Gifted Child: A Home Study Course. (Home Study Ser.). 39p. 1984. student ed 30.00 (*0-939926-22-9*); audio write for info. (*0-939926-21-0*) Fruition Pubns.

Pallud, Jean-Paul. Ardennes 1944: Peiper & Skorzeny. (Elite Ser.: No. 11). (Illus.). 64p. pap. 12.95 (*0-85045-740-8*, 9410, Pub. by Osprey UK) Stackpole.

Palluth, William. Composition Made Easy. (How to Draw & Paint Ser.). (Illus.). 32p. (Orig.). 1989. pap. 5.95 (*0-929261-43-7*, HT194) W Foster Pub.

— Landscapes You Can Paint. (How to Draw & Paint Ser.). (Illus.). 32p. (Orig.). 1989. pap. 5.95 (*1-56010-038-9*, HT172) W Foster Pub.

— Painting in Four Mediums: Oil, Watercolor, Acrylic, Pastel. (How to Draw & Paint Ser.). (Illus.). 32p. (Orig.). 1990. pap. 5.95 (*1-56010-055-9*, HT226) W Foster Pub.

— Painting in Oils. (Artist's Library). (Illus.). 64p. (Orig.). 1989. pap. 6.95 (*0-929261-01-1*, AL01) W Foster Pub.

Palluzi, Richard P. Pilot Plant and Laboratory Safety. LC 93-23629. 1994. text ed. 50.00 (*0-07-048181-4*) McGraw.

— Pilot Plant Design, Construction & Operation. 256p. 1992. text ed. 52.00i (*0-07-048180-6*) McGraw.

Pally, Marcia. Sex & Sensibility: The Vanity of Bonfires. LC 93-40142. 1994. 13.00 (*0-88001-364-8*) Ecco Pr.

Palm, C., ed. Intensity Variations in Telephone Traffic. 210p. 1988. 77.00 (*0-444-70472-8*, North Holland) Elsevier.

Palm, Charlene F. Driving in Britain: What the Guide Books Don't Tell You. LC 83-72089. (Illus.). 168p. (Orig.). 1984. pap. 10.00 (*0-9611962-0-3*) Bittersweet Evanston.

Palm, Charles G. & Reed, Dale, comps. Guide to the Hoover Institution Archives. (Bibliographical Ser.: No. 59). 430p. 1980. 50.00 (*0-8179-2591-0*) Hoover Inst Pr.

Palm, E., ed. see Ophthalmic Microsurgery Study Group Staff.

Palm, Franklin C. Calvinism & the Religious Wars. LC 83-45628. reprint ed. 22.50 (*0-404-19880-5*) AMS Pr.

Palm, Franz C. & Smit, Hidde P. Economic Modelling & Policy Analysis. 402p. 1991. text ed. 84.95 (*1-85628-076-4*, Pub. by Avebury Pub UK) Ashgate Pub Co.

Palm, G., jt. ed. see Shaw, G.

Palm, Gordon F. Advances in Phosphate Fertilizer Technology. Atwood, Wes et al, eds. LC 93-12275. (Symposium Ser.: No. 292, Vol. 89). 1993. 75.00 (*0-8169-0593-2*) Am Inst Chem Eng.

Palm, James E. & Poethig, Eunice B. Acting in Faith: A Study Guide on the Philippines. 48p. (Orig.). 1989. pap. 4.95 (*0-377-00193-7*) Friendship Pr.

***Palm, L. C., ed.** The Collected Letters of Antoni van Leeuwenhoek Pt. XIII. 444p. 1994. 265.00 (*90-265-1239-2*, Pub. by Swets Pub Serv NE) Taylor & Francis.

Palm, Mary E., et al, eds. Mycologia Index, 1967-1988, Vols. 59-80. LC 57-51730. vii, 491p. 1991. lib. bdg. 79.00 (*0-89327-357-0*) NY Botanical.

Palm, Miriam, et al, eds. If We Build It: Scholarly Communications & Networking Technologies: Proceedings of the North American Serials Interest Group, Inc., 7th Annual Conference June 18-21, 1992, the University of Illinois at Chicago. LC 93-19928. (Serials Librarian Ser.: Vol. 23, Nos. 3-4). (Illus.). 328p. 1993. lib. bdg. 24.95 (*1-56024-450-X*) Haworth Pr.

***Palm, Risa.** Earthquake Insurance: A Longitudinal Study of California Homeowners. LC 94-38714. (C). 1994. pap. text ed. 39.95 (*0-8133-8898-8*) Westview.

Palm, Risa, jt. auth. see Grow, Claudia.

Palm, Risa I. Natural Hazards: An Integrative Framework for Research & Planning. LC 89-45490. 224p. 1990. text ed. 35.00 (*0-8018-3866-5*) Johns Hopkins.

— Real Estate Agents & Special Studies Zones Disclosure: The Response of California Home Buyers to Earthquake Hazards Information. (Program on Environment & Behavior Monograph Ser.: No. 32). 147p. (Orig.). (C). 1981. pap. 8.00 (*0-685-28106-X*) Natural Hazards.

Palm, Risa I. & Hodgson, Michael E. After a California Earthquake: Attitude & Behavior Change. LC 91-857. (Illus.). 144p. 1992. pap. text ed. 15.00 (*0-226-64499-5*) U Ch Pr.

— Earthquake & Hurricane Hazard in Puerto Rico: A Survey of Attitudes & Behavior. LC 92-44744. (Program on Environment & Behavior Monograph Ser.: No. 55). 1993. 10.00 (*1-877943-09-6*) Natural Hazards.

Palm, Risa I., jt. auth. see Lanegran, David.

Palm, Risa I., et al. Home Mortgage Lenders, Real Property Appraisers & Earthquake Hazards. (Program on Environment & Behavior Monograph Ser.: No. 38). 152p. (Orig.). (C). 1984. pap. 8.00 (*0-685-28112-4*) Natural Hazards.

Palm, William J. Control Systems Engineering. LC 85-26590. 695p. (C). 1986. Net. text ed. write for info. (*0-471-81086-X*) Wiley.

— Modeling, Analysis & Control of Dynamic Systems. LC 82-8530. 740p. (C). 1983. Net. text ed. write for info. (*0-471-05800-9*); write for info. (*0-471-88581-9*) Wiley.

Palma, Anthony D. Truth-Antidote for Error. LC 76-52177. (Radiant Life Ser.). 128p. 1977. teacher ed 4.50 (*0-88243-174-9*, 32-0174); pap. 2.95 (*0-88243-904-9*, 02-0904) Gospel Pub.

Palma, Clemente. Malignant Tales. Castillo-Feliu, Guillermo I., tr. LC 87-35997. (C). 1988. lib. bdg. 25.50 (*0-8191-6879-3*) U Pr of Amer.

Palma De Villarreal, M. L., jt. auth. see Hoyos de Martens, Veronica.

Palma, Gloria M., see Marigloria Palma, pseud..

Palma, Gregory J. Chaff & Wheat: Poems: Nineteen Twenty-Nine, to Seventy-Nine. LC 79-56716. 203p. (Orig.). 1979. 14.00 (*0-933402-08-2*); pap. 9.00 (*0-933402-01-5*) Charisma Pr.

Palma, Marigloria. Cuentos De la Abeja Encinta. LC 76-6153. (UPREX, Ficcion Ser.: No. 48). (Orig.). (SPA.). 1976. pap. 1.50 (*0-8477-0048-8*) U of PR Pr.

Palma, Marigloria, pseud. Versos de Cada Dia: Estampas Numeradas. LC 79-10463. (UPREX, Poesia Ser.: No. 58). 228p. (Orig.). 1980. pap. 1.50 (*0-8477-0058-5*) U of PR Pr.

Palma, Michael, tr. The Man I Pretend to Be: The Colloquies & Selected Poems of Guido Gozzano. LC 80-8551. (Lockert Library of Poetry in Translation). 264p. 1981. pap. 10.95 (*0-691-01378-0*) Princeton U Pr.

— My Name on the Wind: Selected Poems of Diego Valeri. 168p. 1989. text ed. 29.95 (*0-691-06776-7*); pap. 12.95 (*0-691-01462-0*) Princeton U Pr.

Palma, Michael, jt. ed. see Gioia, Dana.

Palma, Michael, tr. see Herder, Johann G.

Palma, Robert J. Karl Barth's Theology of Culture. LC 83-2371. (Pittsburgh Theological Monographs, New Ser.: No. 2). 122p. 1983. pap. 10.00 (*0-915138-54-9*) Pickwick.

***Palma, Robert J., Sr. & Espenscheid, Mark.** The Complete Guide to Household Chemicals. 300p. 1995. 24.95 (*0-87975-983-6*) Prometheus Bks.

— The Consumer's Guide to Household Chemicals. 175p. (C). 1992. 22.95 (*0-87975-794-9*) Prometheus Bks.

Palmadesco, Peter J. & Papadopoulos, K., eds. Wave Instabilities in Space Plasmas. (Astrophysics & Space Science Library: No. 74). 1979. lib. bdg. 84.00 (*90-277-1028-7*) Kluwer Ac.

Palmaitis, Letas, jt. auth. see Gudjedjiani, Chato.

Palman, Joel & Spencer, John P. A Sight So Nobly Grand: Joel Palmen on Mt. Hovel in 1845. (Illus.). 72p. 1994. pap. 7.95 (*0-87595-252-6*) Oregon Hist.

Palmanteer & Rogers. Man Spirit. 1979. 4.00 (*0-912678-38-0*, Greenfld Rev Pr) Greenfld Rev Lit.

Palmarini, Terra, jt. auth. see Baldwin, Rahima.

Palmason, G., ed. Continental & Ocean Rifts. (Geodynamics Ser.: Vol. 8). 309p. 1982. 26.00 (*0-87590-504-8*) Am Geophysical.

Palmatier, George E. & Shull, Joseph E. The Marketing Edge: The New Leadership Role of Sales & Marketing in Manufacturing. LC 88-51917. 183p. 1988. 40.00 (*0-939246-08-2*) Oliver Wight.

***Palmatier, Robert A.** Speaking of Animals: A Dictionary of Animal Metaphors. LC 94-29273. 496p. 1995. text ed. 69.50 (*0-313-29490-9*, Greenwood Pr) Greenwood.

Palmatier, Robert A. & Ray, Harold L. Sports Talk: A Dictionary of Sports Metaphors. LC 88-24646. 245p. 1989. text ed. 45.00 (*0-313-26426-0*, PSK, Greenwood Pr) Greenwood.

Palmatier, Robert S. & Ray, Harold L. Dictionary of Sports Idioms. 228p. 1993. pap. 14.95 (*0-8442-9123-4*, Natl Textbk) NTC Pub Grp.

Palmatier, Susan M., jt. auth. see Bremer, Suzanne W.

Palmberg, jt. auth. see Roguski.

Palmberg, Mai, jt. ed. see Hallencreutz, Carl F.

Palmblad, Harry V. Strindberg's Conception of History. 1972. 250.00 (*0-8490-1144-2*) Gordon Pr.

Palme, Cole, ed. see Dee, Denise.

***Palme, Jacob.** Electronic Mail. LC 94-23898. 1995. write for info. (*0-89006-802-X*) Artech Hse.

Palme, Joakim. Pension Rights in Welfare Capitalism: The Development of Old-Age Pensions in 18 OECD Countries 1930-1985. (Swedish Institute for Social Research Ser.: No. 14). 196p. (Orig.). 1990. pap. 70.00x (*91-7604-039-9*, Pub. by Almqv & Wiksell SW) Coronet Bks.

***Palme, Klaus, ed.** Signals & Signal Transduction Pathways in Plants. LC 94-48295. 452p. (C). 1995. lib. bdg. 165.00 (*0-7923-3364-0*) Kluwer Ac.

Palmedo, Philip & Beltrami, Edward. The Wines of Long Island: Birth of a Region. (Illus.). 160p. (Orig.). 1993. pap. 16.95 (*0-9628492-1-9*) Waterline Bks.

Palmegiani, Francesco. Matta Battistini: Il Re Dei Baritoni. Farkas, Andrew, ed. LC 76-29960. (Opera Biographies Ser.). (Illus.). (ITA.). 1977. reprint ed. lib. bdg. 23.95 (*0-405-09700-X*) Ayer.

Palmegiano, E. M., comp. Crime in Victorian Britain: An Annotated Bibliography from Nineteenth-Century British Magazines. LC 92-44640. (Bibliographies & Indexes in World History Ser.: No. 31). 192p. 1993. text ed. 59.95 (*0-313-26523-2*, PCM, Greenwood Pr) Greenwood.

Palmeirim, Jorge M. Bats of Portugal: Zoogeography & Systematics. (Miscellaneous Publications: No. 82). (Illus.). 53p. (C). 1990. pap. text ed. 3.25 (*0-89338-034-2*) U of KS Mus Nat Hist.

Palmen, Connie. The Laws: A Novel. Huijing, Richard, tr. LC 93-3796. 208p. 1993. 18.50 (*0-8076-1329-0*) Braziller.

Palmen, Pauline K., jt. auth. see Giordano, Albert G.

Palmen, Ralph. Principles & Success Strategies for Everyday Living. (Orig.). 1991. pap. 7.95 (*1-56233-010-1*) Star Song TN.

Palmen, Ralph H. Principles & Success Strategies for Everyday Living. (Orig.). 1986. pap. 6.95 (*0-9617213-0-8*) Palmen Inst.

An Asterisk (*) at the beginning of an entry indicates that the title is appearing in BIP for the first time.

Palmer. ABC Chart Erection. 224p. 1971. 11.00 (*0-86690-137-X*, P1364-014) Am Fed Astrologers.
— Brain Train. 1995. pap. (*0-419-19830-X*) Routledge Chapman & Hall.
— Cattleman's Choice. 1995. mass mkt. 4.99 (*1-55166-056-3*, Mira Bks) Harlequin Bks.
— Collective Agreement Arbitration in Canada. 3rd ed. 904p. 1991. 145.00 (*0-409-89647-0*) Butterworth Legal Pubs.
— Identifying Guide to Dog Breeds. 1995. (*0-7858-0326-2*) Bk Sales Inc.
— MRI of Musculoskeletal System. 1994. vdisk 700.00 (*1-56815-021-0*) Image Premast.
— My Adam & Eve Book of Opposites. (J). 1995. pap. 4.99 (*0-570-04780-3*) Concordia.
— My Baby Jesus Book of Numbers. (J). 1995. pap. 4.99 (*0-570-04782-X*) Concordia.
— My Bible Story Book of ABCs. (J). 1995. pap. 4.99 (*0-570-04783-8*) Concordia.
— My Noah's Ark Book of Colors. (Illus.). (J). 1995. pap. 4.99 (*0-570-04781-1*) Concordia.
— Perspectives on Film Noir. 1995. text ed. 50.00 (*0-8161-1601-6*) G K Hall.
— Sweet William. 1995. mass mkt. 5.50 (*0-671-88017-9*) PB.
Palmer & Rains. Local Area Networking with Novell Software. 320p. 1991. 22.00 (*0-87835-497-2*) Boyd & Fraser.
Palmer & Short. Health Care & Public Policy: An Australian Analysis. 2nd ed. 350p. 1994. 69.95 (*0-7329-2008-6*, Pub. by Macmill Educ AT); pap. 34.95 (*0-7329-2007-8*, Pub. by Macmill Educ AT) Paul & Co Pubs.
Palmer & Welling. Canadian Company Law: Cases, Notes & Materials. 3rd ed. 592p. 1986. pap. 65.00 (*0-409-80510-6*) Butterworth Legal Pubs.
Palmer, A. R., ed. Perspectives in Regional Geological Synthesis: Planning for the Geology of North America. LC 82-9331. (DNAG Special Pub. Ser.: No. 1). (Illus.). 180p. 1982. pap. 2.00 (*0-8137-5201-9*) Geol Soc.
Palmer, A. R., jt. ed. see Bally, A. W.
Palmer, A. Smythe. The Samson Saga & Its Place in Comparative Religion. 1977. lib. bdg. 59.95 (*0-8490-2565-6*) Gordon Pr.
Palmer, Abram. Folk-Etymology: A Dictionary of Verbal Corruptions or Words Perverted in Form. LC 68-26365. (Studies in Language: No. 41). 1969. reprint ed. lib. bdg. 59.95 (*0-8383-0279-3*) M S G Haskell Hse.
Palmer, Abram S. Folk-Etymology, a Dictionary of Verbal Corruptions or Words Perverted in Form or Meaning, by False Derivation or Mistaken Analogy. LC 68-57636. (Illus.). 664p. 1970. reprint ed. text ed. 85.00 (*0-8371-1153-6*, PAFE) Greenwood.
— Samson-Saga & Its Place in Comparative Religion. Dorson, Richard M., ed. LC 77-70613. (International Folklore Ser.). 1977. reprint ed. lib. bdg. 25.95 (*0-405-10112-0*) Ayer.
Palmer, Adele R. & Larson, Eric V. Cost Factors in the Army, Vol. 2: Factors, Methods, & Models. LC 92-15576. 1992. write for info. (*0-8330-1241-X*, R-4078/2-PA&E) Rand Corp.
Palmer, Adele R., jt. auth. see Larson, Eric V.
Palmer, Adell. Butterfly Children. 1974. pap. 3.95 (*0-89036-050-2*) Hawkes Pub Inc.
Palmer, Adrian. Principles of Services Marketing. LC 94-4289. 1994. 18.95 (*0-07-707746-6*) McGraw.
***Palmer, Adrian & Cole, Catherine.** Services Marketing: Principles & Practice. LC 94-36242. 389p. 1995. text ed. 67.00 (*0-02-390563-8*) P-H.
Palmer, Adrian S., jt. auth. see Brown, J. Marvin.
Palmer, Agnes M. To God Be All Glory. (Illus.). (Orig.). 1988. write for info. (*0-318-68750-X*) Forest Hills.
— To God Be All Glory: Mini-Biography (Authentic Excerpts) (Illus.). 149p. (Orig.). 1987. 12.00 (*0-9617983-1-9*) Forest Hills.
Palmer, Alan. Crimean War. 1992. 24.95 (*0-88029-776-X*) Marboro Bks.
— The Decline & Fall of the Ottoman Empire. LC 93-24525. 1994. 22.50 (*0-87131-754-0*) M Evans.
— Twilight of the Hapsburgs: The Life & Times of Emperor Franz Josef. 384p. 1995. 27.50 (*0-8021-1560-8*) Grove-Atltic.
Palmer, Alan & Palmer, Veronica. Who's Who in Bloomsbury. LC 87-28467. 225p. 1988. text ed. 35.00 (*0-312-01630-1*) St Martin.
— Who's Who in Shakespeare's England. (Illus.). 350p. 1981. 32.50 (*0-312-87096-5*) St Martin.
Palmer, Alex. Figments, Perverse Urges & Mr. Plerp: A Story about What Could Happen a Zillion Years from Now. (Illus.). 80p. (Orig.). 1993. pap. 7.95 (*0-9638437-0-2*) Inspired Whimsy.
Palmer, Alfred B. & Curtis, Mary E. The Pirate of Tobruk: A Sailor's Life on the Seven Seas, 1916-1948. LC 94-10450. (Illus.). 224p. 1994. 26.95 (*1-55750-667-1*) Naval Inst Pr.
Palmer, Alice E. Chicago Child. (Illus.). 276p. Date not set. text ed. write for info. (*0-9638309-0-2*) A E Palmer.
Palmer, Andrew, et al, trs. The Seventh Century in the West-Syrian Chronicles. (Translated Texts for Historians Ser.). 272p. (Orig.). 1993. pap. text ed. 18.95 (*0-85323-238-5*, Pub. by Liverpool Univ Pr UK) U of Pa Pr.
Palmer, Andrew N. Monk & Mason on the Tigris Frontier. (University of Cambridge Oriental Publications). (Illus.). 280p. (C). 1990. 74.95 (*0-521-36026-9*) Cambridge U Pr.
Palmer, Ann. Busted in Mexico. 48p. 1978. pap. 3.50 (*0-89540-044-8*, SB-044) Sun Pub.
Palmer, Anne, jt. auth. see Morton-Cooper, Alison.
Palmer, Anne R., jt. auth. see Candoy-Sekse, Rebecca.
Palmer, Anthony. Concept & Object: The Unity of the Proposition in Logic & Psychology. (Studies in Philosophical Psychology). 176p. 1988. text ed. 32.50 (*0-415-00172-2*) Routledge.
Palmer, Anthony M., et al, eds. Reflective Practice in Nursing: The Growth of the Professional Practitioner. LC 93-38307. (Illus.). 176p. 1994. pap. 24.95 (*0-632-03597-8*) Blackwell Sci.
Palmer, Arlene. Glass in Early America: Selections from the Henry Francis DuPont Winterthur Museum. LC 93-32489. 426p. 1993. write for info. (*0-393-03660-X*) Winterthur.
Palmer, Arnold & Guest, Larry. Arnie: Inside the Legend. 1993. 19.99 (*0-941263-92-4*, Tribune) Contemp Bks.
Palmer, Arnold, jt. auth. see Hauser, Thomas.
Palmer, Arthur N. A Geological Guide to Mammoth Cave National Park. LC 79-5041. (Illus.). 210p. (Orig.). 1981. 11.95 (*0-914264-27-3*); pap. 6.95 (*0-914264-28-1*) Cave Bks MO.
***Palmer, Arthur N. & Lavoie, Kathleen H.** Introduction to Speleology. (Illus.). 176p. (Orig.). 1996. 35.00 (*0-939748-42-8*) Cave Bks MO.
— Introduction to Speleology. (Illus.). 176p. (Orig.). (C). 1996. pap. 12.95 (*0-939748-18-5*) Cave Bks MO.
Palmer, Arthur N., jt. ed. see Palmer, Margaret V.
***Palmer, B. M.** The Broken Home: Lessons in Sorrow. Duncan, J. Ligon, 3rd, ed. 112p. (C). 1995. reprint ed. pap. text ed. 6.95 (*1-884416-07-1*) A Press.
— Life & Letters of James Henley Thornwell. 610p. 1986. reprint ed. 32.95 (*0-85151-195-3*) Banner of Truth.
Palmer, Barbara. Early Art of the West Riding of Yorkshire: A Subject List of Extant & Lost Art Including Items Relevant to Early Drama. (Early Drama, Art & Music Reference Ser.: No. 6). 1990. 37.95 (*0-918720-32-X*); pap. 17.95 (*0-918720-33-8*) Medieval Inst.
Palmer, Barbara C. Figurative Language Interpretation Test. 1991. teacher ed 5.00 (*0-685-47777-0*); teacher ed 8.00 (*0-685-47778-9*); teacher ed, pap. text ed. 15.00 (*0-87879-895-1*, 895-1A_______6); student ed, pap. text ed. 15.00 (*0-685-47779-7*); teacher ed, ring bd. 45.00 (*0-685-39287-2*, 895-1-A) Acad Therapy.
— Figurative Language Interpretation Test, Forms A & B. 1991. teacher ed 22.00 (*0-87879-896-X*) Acad Therapy.
Palmer, Barbara C., et al. Developing Cultural Literacy Through the Writing Process: Empowering Learners across all Grades. LC 93-23699. 480p. 1995. pap. 36.95 (*0-205-13989-2*, Longwood Div) Allyn.
Palmer, Barry, jt. auth. see McCaughan, Nano.
Palmer, Barton, ed. The Cinematic Text: Methods & Approaches. LC 87-45796. (Georgia State Literary Studies: No. 3). 1988. 45.00 (*0-404-63203-3*) AMS Pr.
Palmer, Benjamin M. Life & Letters of James Henry Thornwell. LC 78-83432. (Religion in America, Ser. 1). 1970. reprint ed. 43.95 (*0-405-00257-2*) Ayer.
Palmer-Bermudez, Neyssa A. Las Mujeres en los Cuentos de Rene Marquez. LC 85-26384. 103p. 1988. pap. 7.50 (*0-8477-3803-5*) U of PR Pr.
Palmer, Bernard. Hijo Mio, Hijo Mio: My Son, My Son. (SPA.). 6.00 (*84-7228-272-4*, 220454, Pub. by Edit Clie SP) TSELF.
— My Son, My Son. (Living Bks.). 288p. (Orig.). 1987. pap. 4.99 (*0-8423-4639-2*) Tyndale.
— What Are They Trying to Do to Us? The Truth about the Animal Rights Movement & the New Age. 207p. (Orig.). (C). 1994. pap. 9.95 (*0-9636072-1-9*) J Honea Pubs.
Palmer, Bernard, ed. Medicine & the Bible. 272p. 1992. pap. 17.95 (*0-85364-423-3*, Pub. by Paternoster UK) Attic Pr.
Palmer, Bernard & Palmer, Marjorie. Light a Small Candle. LC 82-84439. 1982. pap. 8.95 (*0-685-42641-6*) Free Church Pubns.
— Who Helps. (Illus.). 32p. (Orig.). (J). (ps-00). 1982. pap. 3.99 (*0-934998-08-6*) Bethel Pub.
— Who Shows. (Illus.). 32p. (Orig.). (J). (ps-00). 1982. pap. 3.99 (*0-934998-09-4*) Bethel Pub.
Palmer, Bernard, jt. auth. see Dunn, Jerry G.
Palmer, Bernard, jt. auth. see Palmer, Marjorie.
Palmer, Betty. Travelling the Miracle Road. LC 88-90635. (Orig.). 1988. pap. 5.95 (*0-910487-16-2*) Royalty Pub.
— Travelling the Miracle Road. Scoggan, Nita, ed. LC 88-90635. (Illus.). 224p. (Orig.). 1988. 10.00 (*0-910487-17-0*) Royalty Pub.
Palmer, Beverly W. The Selected Letters of Charles Sumner, Set, Vols. 1 & 2. (Illus.). 1504p. 1990. Set. text ed. 170.00 (*1-55553-078-8*) NE U Pr.
Palmer, Beverly W. & Ochoa, Holly B., eds. The Thaddeus Stevens Papers: Guide & Index to the Microfilm Edition. LC 94-2585. 184p. 1994. pap. 40.00 (*0-8420-4146-X*) Scholarly Res Inc.
Palmer, Bill, tr. see Lesley, Ted.
***Palmer, Bill, et al.** The Encyclopedia of Martial Arts Movies. (Illus.). 492p. 1995. 69.50 (*0-8108-3027-2*) Scarecrow.
Palmer, Bob, jt. auth. see Stone, Bob.
Palmer, Bruce, III. How to Restore Your Harley-Davidson Motorcycle. (Illus.). 480p. 1994. pap. 26.95 (*0-87938-934-6*) Motorbooks Intl.
Palmer, Bruce, Jr. Intervention in the Caribbean: The Dominican Crises of 1965. LC 89-16761. 256p. 1989. 28.00 (*0-8131-1691-0*) U Pr of Ky.
Palmer, Bruce. The Karma Charmer. LC 94-8. 1994. 20.00 (*0-517-59919-8*, Harmony) Crown Pub Group.
— Man over Money: The Southern Populist Critique of American Capitalism. LC 79-24698. (Fred W. Morrison Series in Southern Studies). xviii, 311p. 1980. 34.95 (*0-8078-1427-X*) U of NC Pr.
Palmer, Bruce, Jr. The Twenty-Five-Year War: America's Military Role in Vietnam. LC 84-5091. (Illus.). 248p. 1984. 27.00 (*0-8131-1513-2*) U Pr of Ky.
— The Twenty-Five Year War: America's Military Role in Vietnam. (Quality Paperbacks Ser.). (Illus.). 264p. 1990. pap. 12.95 (*0-306-80383-6*) Da Capo.
Palmer, Bruce R., ed. see Western Regional Conference on Gold, Silver, Uranium, & Coal Staff.
***Palmer, Bryan.** Objections & Oppositions: The Histories & Politics of E. P. Thompson. 1994. 59.95 (*1-85984-975-X*, B4642, Pub. by Verso UK); pap. 18.95 (*1-85984-070-1*, B4545, Pub. by Verso UK) Routledge Chapman & Hall.
Palmer, Bryan D. A Culture in Conflict: Skilled Workers & Industrial Capitalism in Hamilton, Ontario 1860-1914. LC 80-481234. 361p. reprint ed. pap. 102.90 (*0-7837-1024-0*, 2041335) Bks Demand.
— Descent into Discourse. 312p. 1990. 34.95 (*0-87722-678-4*); pap. 18.95 (*0-87722-720-9*) Temple U Pr.
— Goodyear Invades the Backcountry: The Corporate Takeover of a Rural Town. (Illus.). 176p. (C). 1994. text ed. 38.00 (*0-85345-909-6*, Pub. by Lat Am Bur UK) Monthly Rev.
— Goodyear Invades the Backcountry: The Corporate Takeover of a Rural Town. (Illus.). (Orig.). (C). 1994. pap. text ed. 15.00 (*0-85345-910-X*) Monthly Rev.
Palmer, C. Harvey. Optics: Experiments & Demonstrations. 340p. 1962. 49.50x (*0-8018-0518-X*) Johns Hopkins.
Palmer, Carl. Chemistry of Ground Water. (Illus.). 300p. 1995. 49.95 (*0-87371-077-0*) Lewis Pubs.
Palmer, Carleton H. Report of the Ellis Island Committee. LC 78-145478. (American Immigration Library). 149p. 1971. reprint ed. lib. bdg. 22.95 (*0-89198-021-0*) Ozer.
Palmer, Carolann M. Nifty Ninepatches. McGehee, Liz, ed. LC 91-36166. (Illus.). 72p. 1992. pap. 17.95 (*0-943574-95-1*) That Patchwork.
— Quilts for Kids. Weiland, Barbara, ed. LC 93-15933. (Illus.). 80p. (Orig.). 1993. pap. 16.95 (*1-56477-036-2*, B159) That Patchwork.
Palmer, Carole, jt. auth. see Arvetis, Chris.
Palmer, Carole, et al. Nutrition, Diet & Dental Health: Concepts & Methods. 78p. 1981. 32.00 (*0-318-17799-4*) Am Dental Hygienists.
Palmer, Carole L., jt. auth. see McCombs, Judith.
Palmer, Caroline, ed. Arthurian Bibliography Three, 1978-1992. (Arthurian Studies: Vol. 31). 694p. (C). 1995. text ed. 108.00 (*0-85991-399-6*) Boydell & Brewer.
Palmer, Caroline, tr. see Pinet, Helene.
Palmer, Carolyn, jt. auth. see Harnisch, Delwyn.
***Palmer, Carolyn J.** Tracks of Eternity: Birthday Date Book. 192p. 1994. 12.95 (*0-9643952-0-7*) Eternity MI.
— Violent Crimes & Other Forms of Victimization in Residence Halls. LC 93-18795. (Higher Education Administration Ser.). 128p. 1994. pap. 16.95 (*0-912557-15-X*) Coll Admin Pubns.
Palmer, Carolyn J. & Gehring, Donald D., eds. A Handbook for Complying with the Program & Review Requirements of the 1989 Amendments to the Drug-Free Schools & Communities Act. LC 92-23726. 1992. ring bd. 33.00 (*0-685-60785-2*) Coll Admin Pubns.
— A Handbook for Complying with the Program & Review Requirements of the 1989 Amendments to the Drug-Free Schools & Communities Act. LC 92-23726. 224p. 1994. pap. 22.95 (*0-912557-14-1*) Coll Admin Pubns.
— A Handbook for Complying with the Program & Review Requirements of the 1989 Amendments to the Drug-Free Schools & Communities Act. 224p. 1994. 33.00 (*0-614-05282-3*) Coll Admin Pubns.
***Palmer, Catherine.** Falcon Moon. 352p. (Orig.). 1994. pap. 4.99 (*0-7865-0045-X*) Diamond.
— For the Love of a Child. (Silhouette Intimate Moments Ser.). 1994. mass mkt. 3.50 (*0-373-07551-0*, 5-07551-0) Silhouette.
— Gunman's Lady. 336p. (Orig.). 1993. mass mkt. 4.99 (*1-55773-893-9*) Diamond.
— His Best Friend's Wife. (Intimate Moments Ser.). 1995. pap. 3.75 (*0-373-07627-4*, 1-07627-2) Silhouette.
— Outlaw Heart. (Wildflower Ser.). 352p. (Orig.). 1992. mass mkt. 4.99 (*1-55773-735-5*) Diamond.
— Renegade Flame. 1993. mass mkt. 4.99 (*1-55773-952-8*) Diamond.
Palmer, Cecil, jt. ed. see Saintsbury, Harry A.
Palmer, Charles E., jt. auth. see Brock, Horace R.
Palmer, Charles F. Inebriety: Its Source, Prevention, & Cure. Grob, Gerald N., ed. LC 80-1242. (Addiction in America Ser.). 1981. reprint ed. lib. bdg. 15.95 (*0-405-13612-9*) Ayer.
***Palmer, Charles J. & Palmer, Jacqueline.** Chasing Rainbows & Ribbons. LC 94-62143. (Illus.). 1994. 49.00 (*1-881808-16-5*) Creat Arts & Sci.
— Fire from Within. LC 94-94136. (Illus.). 248p. 1994. 49.95 (*1-881808-09-2*) Creat Arts & Sci.
— Garden of Thoughts. (Illus.). 300p. (Orig.). 1993. 49.00 (*1-881808-02-5*) Creat Arts & Sci.
— Inspirations in Ink. LC 94-94487. (Illus.). 260p. 1994. 49.95 (*1-881808-10-6*) Creat Arts & Sci.
— International Directory of Authors & Artists, 1994. 138p. 1994. pap. 15.00 (*1-881808-13-0*) Creat Arts & Sci.
— Pen Etched Memories. LC 94-68657. (Illus.). 230p. 1994. 49.95 (*1-881808-12-2*) Creat Arts & Sci.
— Starburst. (Quarterly Journal of the International Society of Authors & Artists Ser.: Vol. I, No. 1). (Illus.). 25p. 1993. pap. 6.00 (*1-881808-03-3*) Creat Arts & Sci.
— Starburst: Quarterly Journal of the International Society of Authors & Artists, Vol. 1, No. 3. (Illus.). 30p. 1993. pap. write for info. (*1-881808-06-8*) Creat Arts & Sci.
— Starburst: Quarterly Journal of the International Society of Authors & Artists, Vol. 1, No. 4. (Illus.). 30p. Date not set. pap. 6.00 (*1-881808-07-6*) Creat Arts & Sci.
— Starburst: Quarterly Journal of the International Society of Authors & Artists, Vol. 2, No. 2. (Illus.). 30p. Date not set. pap. 6.00 (*1-881808-11-4*) Creat Arts & Sci.
— Starburst: Quarterly Journal of the International Society of Authors & Artists, Vol. 2, Number 3. (Illus.). 30p. 1994. pap. 6.00 (*1-881808-14-9*) Creat Arts & Sci.
— Starburst Vol. 2, No. 4: Quarterly Journal of the International Society of Authors & Artists. (Illus.). 30p. 1994. pap. 6.00 (*1-881808-15-7*) Creat Arts & Sci.
— Starburst, Vol. 1, No. 2: Quarterly Journal of the International Society of Authors & Artists. (Illus.). 30p. 1993. pap. 6.00 (*1-881808-05-X*) Creat Arts & Sci.
— Starburst, Vol. 2, No. 1: Journal for the International Society of Authors & Artists. (Illus.). 30p. 1994. pap. 6.00 (*1-881808-08-4*) Creat Arts & Sci.
— Tapestry of Words. LC 93-73453. (Illus.). 240p. 1993. 49.00 (*1-881808-04-1*) Creat Arts & Sci.
— Visions & Beyond. LC 92-73144. (Illus.). 300p. 1992. 48.00 (*1-881808-00-9*) Creat Arts & Sci.
Palmer, Charles J., ed. see Manship, Henry.
Palmer, Chris. Dynamics of Natal Astrology. LC 83-71153. 152p. 1984. 15.00 (*0-86690-244-9*, P2297-014) Am Fed Astrologers.
Palmer, Christopher. The Composer in Hollywood. (Illus.). 320p. 1990. 35.00 (*0-7145-2885-4*) M Boyars Pubs.
— The Composer in Hollywood. 1992. 19.95 (*0-7145-2950-8*) M Boyars Pubs.
— Delius: Portrait of a Cosmopolitan. LC 76-8893. (Illus.). 199p. 1976. 34.50 (*0-8419-0274-7*) Holmes & Meier.
— Dimitri Tiomkin: A Portrait. (Illus.). 144p. 1985. 22.00 (*0-9509439-0-8*, Pub. by Scolar Pr UK) Ashgate Pub Co.
Palmer, Christopher, tr. see Milhaud, Darius.
Palmer, Christopher, ed. see Prokofiev, Sergei.
Palmer, Christopher M., et al. Principles of Contaminant Hydrogeology. 170p. 1991. 54.95 (*0-87371-280-3*, TD426) Lewis Pubs.
Palmer, Clara. You Can Be Healed. 1937. 6.95 (*0-87159-181-2*) Unity Bks.
Palmer, Claude I. & Mrachek, L. A. Practical Mathematics. 7th ed. 560p. 1985. text ed. 33.95 (*0-07-048254-3*) McGraw.
***Palmer, Colin.** The First Passage: Blacks in the Americas, 1501-1617. (The Young Oxford History of African Americans Ser.: No. 1). (Illus.). 128p. (J). 1995. 17.95 (*0-19-509905-2*); lib. bdg. 21.00 (*0-19-508699-6*) OUP.
***Palmer, Colin A.** Human Cargoes: The British Slave Trade to Spanish America, 1700-1739. LC 81-3326. (Blacks in the New World Ser.). 200p. 1981. reprint ed. pap. 57.00 (*0-7837-8082-6*, 2047835) Bks Demand.
— Slaves of the White God: Blacks in Mexico, 1570-1650. LC 75-34054. 246p. reprint ed. pap. 70.20 (*0-8357-8324-3*, 2033938) Bks Demand.
Palmer, Colin A., jt. ed. see Knight, Franklin W.
Palmer, D., et al. Atomic Collision Phenomena in Solids. 1970. 82.00 (*0-444-10021-0*) Elsevier.
Palmer, D. D. The Chiropractor. 115p. 1970. reprint ed. spiral bd. 7.70 (*0-7873-0652-5*) Mokelumne.
Palmer, D. G., jt. auth. see Weston, W. J.
Palmer, Darwin, et al. The Infection Control Book. 400p. (C). 1994. ring bd. 59.95 (*0-944132-95-2*) Skidmore Roth Pub.
Palmer, Daryl W. Hospitable Performances: Dramatic Genre & Cultural Practices in Early Modern England. LC 91-16223. 240p. 1992. 28.50 (*1-55753-014-9*) Purdue U Pr.
Palmer, Dave R. Seventeen Ninety Four: America, Its Army, & the Birth of the Nation. LC 93-45935. 1994. 24.95 (*0-89141-523-8*) Presidio Pr.
— 1794: America, Its Army, & the Birth of the Nation. 304p. 1995. pap. 14.95 (*0-89141-560-2*) Presidio Pr.
— Summons of the Trumpet: U. S.-Vietnam in Perspective. 304p. 1995. pap. 14.95 (*0-89141-550-5*) Presidio Pr.
— The Way of the Fox: American Strategy in the War for America, 1775-1783. LC 74-5992. (Contributions to Military History Ser.: No. 8). 229p. 1975. text ed. 37.50 (*0-8371-7531-3*, PAF/, Greenwood Pr) Greenwood.
Palmer, David, jt. ed. see Bradbury, Malcolm.
Palmer, David A. Handbook of Applied Thermodynamics. 2nd ed. 1994. 207.00 (*0-8493-4484-0*, TJ265) CRC Pr.
— In Search of Cumorah: New Evidences for the Book of Mormon from Ancient Mexico. LC 80-83866. (Illus.). 300p. 1981. 17.98 (*0-88290-169-9*, 1063) Horizon Utah.
Palmer, David A., ed. Handbook of Applied Thermodynamics. 304p. 1987. 216.95 (*0-8493-3271-0*, TJ265) CRC Pr.
Palmer, David C., jt. auth. see Donahoe, John W.
Palmer, David J., jt. ed. see Chaker, Victor.
Palmer, David R. Summons of the Trumpet. 384p. 1984. pap. 3.95 (*0-345-31583-9*) Ballantine.
Palmer, David R., jt. auth. see Hassel, Patricia L.
Palmer, David S. Peru: The Authoritarian Tradition. LC 80-12176. 156p. 1980. text ed. 29.95 (*0-275-90531-4*, C0531, Praeger Pubs) Greenwood.
— Shining Path of Peru. 2nd ed. 1994. text ed. 17.95 (*0-312-10619-X*) St Martin.
Palmer de Dueno, Rosa M. Sentido, Forma y Estilo de "Redentores" de Manuel Zeno Gandia. (UPREX, Estudios Literarios Ser.: No. 34). 124p. (C). 1974. pap. 1.50 (*0-8477-0034-8*) U of PR Pr.
Palmer, Derecke. The Generalized Reciprocal Method of Seismic Refraction Interpretation. Burke, Kenneth B., ed. LC 80-52549. (Illus.). 104p. 1980. 25.00 (*0-931830-14-1*, 511) Soc Expl Geophys.
Palmer, Derek. Surrey Rambles. 64p. 1987. 35.00 (*0-905392-77-9*) St Mut.
Palmer, Diana. Amelia. (Orig.). 1993. mass mkt. 5.99 (*0-8041-0974-5*) Ivy Books.
— The Australian. 1993. mass mkt. 4.50 (*0-373-48269-8*, 5-48269-0) Silhouette.
— The Best Is Yet to Come. large type ed. (Silhouette Desire Ser.). 1994. 17.95 (*0-373-58853-4*, Silhouette Lrg Print); pap. 16.95 (*0-373-59075-X*, Silhouette Lrg Print) Chivers N Amer.

— Betrayed by Love. (Western Lovers Ser.). 1995. mass mkt. 3.99 (*0-373-88501-6*, 1-88501-1) Harlequin Bks.

— Brianna et le Roi. (Azur Ser.). (FRE.). 1994. pap. 3.50 (*0-373-34436-8*, 1-34436-5) Harlequin Bks.

— Calamity Mom. (To Mother with Love Ser.). 1993. mass mkt. 4.99 (*0-373-48254-X*, 5-48254-2) Silhouette.

— Emmett. (Silhouette Romance Ser.). 1993. pap. 2.69 (*0-373-08910-4*, 5-08910-7) Silhouette.

— Enamored. 1994. mass mkt. 4.50 (*0-373-48305-8*, 5-48305-2) Silhouette.

— Fire & Ice. 1993. mass mkt. 4.50 (*0-373-48268-X*, 5-48268-2) Silhouette.

— Friends & Lovers. 1995. pap. 4.99 (*1-55166-076-8*, 1-66076-0, Mira Bks) Harlequin Bks.

— Heart of Ice. (Western Lovers Ser.). 1996. mass mkt. 3.99 (*0-373-88524-5*, 1-88524-3) Harlequin Bks.

— Heather's Song. 1993. mass mkt. 4.50 (*0-373-48267-1*, 5-48267-4) Silhouette.

— If Winter Comes & Now & Forever. (Diana Palmer Duets Ser.: No. 3). 1990. mass mkt. 3.25 (*0-373-48224-8*) Harlequin Bks.

— King's Ransom. (Silhouette Romance Ser.). 1993. pap. 2.75 (*0-373-08971-6*, 5-08971-9) Silhouette.

— Lacy. (Orig.). 1991. mass mkt. 5.99 (*0-8041-0790-4*) Ivy Books.

— Lady Love. 1995. mass mkt. 4.99 (*1-55166-031-8*, 1-66031-5, Mira Bks) Harlequin Bks.

— Maggie's Dad (1,000 Book Celebration) 1995. mass mkt. 3.75 (*0-373-09991-6*, 1-09991-0) Silhouette.

— Night of Love: Man of the Month. (Silhouette Desire Ser.). 1993. mass mkt. 2.99 (*0-373-05799-7*, 5-05799-7) Silhouette.

— Noelle. 1995. pap. 5.99 (*0-8041-1281-9*) Ivy Books.

— Nora. 1994. mass mkt. 5.99 (*0-8041-0975-3*) Ivy Books.

— The Rawhide Man. 1994. pap. 4.99 (*1-55166-009-1*, 1-66009-1, Mira Bks) Harlequin Bks.

— The Rawhide Man. 1994. mass mkt. 4.50 (*0-373-48315-5*, 5-48315-1) Silhouette.

— Regan's Pride. (Silhouette Romance Ser.). 1994. pap. 2.75 (*0-373-19000-X*, 5-19000-4) Harlequin Bks.

— Regan's Pride. (Silhouette Romance Ser.). 1994. pap. 2.75 (*0-373-91000-2*, 5-91000-5) Silhouette.

— Secret Agent Man: (Man of the Month) (Silhouette Desire Ser.). 1994. mass mkt. 2.99 (*0-373-05829-2*, 5-05829-2) Silhouette.

— Soldier of Fortune. 1994. mass mkt. 4.50 (*0-373-48292-2*, 5-48292-2) Silhouette.

— Soldier of Fortune. 1995. pap. 4.99 (*1-55166-047-4*, 1-66047-1, Mira Bks) Harlequin Bks.

— That Burke Man: (Man of the Month) (Desire Ser.). 1995. pap. 3.25 (*0-373-05913-2*, 1-05913-8) Silhouette.

— Trilby. (Orig.). 1993. mass mkt. 4.99 (*0-8041-1011-5*) Ivy Books.

Palmer, Diana, jt. auth. see Pappano, Marilyn.

Palmer, Donald. Does the Center Hold? An Introduction to Western Philosophy. 529p. 1991. pap. text ed. 22.95 (*0-87484-911-X*) Mayfield Pub.

— Looking at Philosophy: The Unbearable Heaviness of Philosophy Made Lighter. 2nd ed. LC 93-4006. (Illus.). 412p. (C). 1994. pap. text ed. 18.95 (*1-55934-230-7*) Mayfield Pub.

— Sartre for Beginners. (Illus.). 176p. 1995. pap. 11.00 (*0-86316-177-4*) Writers & Readers.

Palmer, Donald C. Managing Conflict Creatively: A Guide for Missionaries & Christian Workers. (Illus.). 116p. (Orig.). (C). 1991. 7.95 (*0-87808-231-X*, WCL231-X) William Carey Lib.

Palmer, Dorothy A., jt. auth. see Lee, Raymond L.

Palmer, Doug. In Quire. 1973. pap. 2.50 (*0-685-29876-0*) Oyez.

Palmer, Douglas & Rickards, Barrie, eds. Graptolites: Writing in the Rocks. (Fossil Ser.). (Illus.). 256p. 1991. 79.00 (*0-85115-262-7*) Boydell & Brewer.

Palmer, Douglas, ed. see Whittington, H. B.

Palmer, Douglas J. Hy-Teck the Alien & Friends, Vol. 1. (Illus.). 150p. (Orig.). 1983. pap. 2.95 (*0-916511-00-6*) Hy-Teck Prods.

Palmer, E. H. Haroun Al-Raschid: Caliph of Bagdad. 1976. lib. bdg. 59.95 (*0-8490-1934-6*) Gordon Pr.

— Oriental Mysticism: A Treatise on Sufistic & Unitarian Theosophy of the Persians. 84p. 1974. 10.00 (*0-900860-33-2*) ISHK Bk Service.

Palmer, E. H., ed. see Conder, Claude R.

Palmer, E. Laurence. Fossils. (Illus.). 136p. 2.50 (*0-87710-376-3*) Paleo Res.

Palmer, E. Lawrence. Fieldbook of Natural History. 2nd ed. (Illus.). (J). 1975. 42.95 (*0-07-048196-2*) McGraw.

Palmer, E. R., jt. auth. see Burley, J.

Palmer, Earl. CC, NT, Vol. 12: First, Second, Third John & Revelation. 259p. 1982. write for info. (*0-8499-0165-0*) Word Inc.

— Communicator's Commentary, Vol. 12: 1, 2, 3 John & Revelations. 259p. 1991. reprint ed. pap. text ed. 10.99 (*0-8499-3285-8*) Word Inc.

Palmer, Earl F. Prayer - Between Friends: Cultivating Our Friendship with God. LC 91-21869. 224p. 1991. 14.99 (*0-8007-1655-8*) Revell.

Palmer, Ed, jt. ed. see Huber, Brigitte T.

Palmer, Edgar M. Graphical Evolution: An Introduction to the Theory of Random Graphs. 200p. (C). 1989. lib. bdg. 41.95 (*0-471-81577-2*) Krieger.

Palmer, Edgar M., jt. auth. see Harary, Frank.

*__Palmer, Edward.__ Pumpkin Carving. LC 95-11549. 96p. 1995. pap. 10.95 (*0-8069-1388-6*, Chapelle) Sterling.

Palmer, Edward H. The Desert of the Exodus: Journeys on Foot in the Wilderness of the Forty Years Wanderings, 2 vols. in one. Davis, Moshe, ed. (America & the Holy Land Ser.). (Illus.). 1977. lib. bdg. 56.95 (*0-405-10276-3*) Ayer.

Palmer, Edward L. Barron's How to Prepare for the Graduate Record Examination - GRE: The Psychology Test. 3rd ed. 272p. 1989. pap. 11.95 (*0-8120-4192-5*) Barron.

— Children & the Faces of Television: Teaching, Violence, Selling. 1980. text ed. 63.00 (*0-12-544480-X*) Acad Pr.

— Television & America's Children: A Crisis of Neglect. (Communication & Society Ser.). 224p. 1990. reprint ed. pap. 8.95 (*0-19-506321-X*) OUP.

Palmer, Edwin H. Doctrinas Claves. 187p. 1976. 2.95 (*0-85151-407-3*) Banner of Truth.

— Five Points of Calvinism: A Study Guide. LC 72-85671. 1972. pap. 5.99 (*0-8010-6926-2*) Baker Bk.

Palmer, Edwin L., et al. Practical Nuclear Medicine. (Illus.). 409p. 1992. text ed. 81.50 (*0-7216-7030-X*) Saunders.

Palmer, Elihu. Principles of Nature. LC 75-3301. reprint ed. 16.50 (*0-404-59286-4*) AMS Pr.

Palmer, Elizabeth. Ikebana. 1989. 10.98 (*1-55521-415-0*) Bk Sales Inc.

— Plucking the Apple. 272p. 1994. 20.95 (*0-312-11326-9*, Pub. by Thomas Dunne Bks) St Martin.

— Scarlet Angel. 1993. 19.95 (*0-312-09917-7*, Pub. by Thomas Dunne Bks) St Martin.

Palmer, Elsie & Oeltjen, Jody. Eating the Oregon Way. LC 82-73683. (Illus.). 180p. (Orig.). 1982. pap. 11.95 (*0-9609912-0-4*) Berry Patch.

Palmer, Erskine L. & Martin, Mary L. An Atlas of Mammalian Viruses. 163p. 1982. 79.00 (*0-8493-6628-3*, QR363, CRC Reprint) Franklin.

— Electron Microscopy in Viral Diagnosis. 208p. 1988. 168.00 (*0-8493-4747-5*, QR387) CRC Pr.

Palmer, Eustace, jt. ed. see Jones, Eldred D.

Palmer, Eve. The Plains of Camdeboo. large type ed. 560p. 1985. 15.95 (*0-7089-1242-7*) Ulverscroft.

Palmer, Evie, ed. see Roberts, Howard & Hagberg, Garry.

Palmer, F. Photoplay Plot Encyclopedia. 1976. lib. bdg. 59.95 (*0-8490-2437-4*) Gordon Pr.

Palmer, F. R. The English Verb. 2nd ed. (Linguistics Library). 288p. (C). 1988. text ed. 35.95 (*0-582-01470-0*); pap. text ed. 18.95 (*0-582-29714-1*) Longman.

— Grammatical Roles & Relations. (Cambridge Textbooks in Linguistics Ser.). 262p. (C). 1994. 59.95 (*0-521-45204-X*); pap. 18.95 (*0-521-45836-6*) Cambridge U Pr.

— Modality & the English Modals. 2nd ed. (Linguistics Library). 224p. (C). 1989. pap. text ed. 16.95 (*0-582-03486-8*, 78294) Longman.

— Mood & Modality. (Cambridge Textbooks in Linguistics Ser.). (Illus.). 225p. 1986. 49.95 (*0-521-26516-9*); pap. 19.95 (*0-521-31930-7*) Cambridge U Pr.

*__Palmer, F. R., ed.__ Grammar & Meaning: Essays in Honour of Sir John Lyons. (Illus.). 280p. (C). 1995. write for info. (*0-521-46221-5*) Cambridge U Pr.

*__Palmer-Fernandez, Gabriel.__ Waging Modern War: An Analysis of the Moral Literature on the Nuclear Arms Debate. LC 94-33707. (San Francisco State University Series in Philosophy: Vol. 8). 1995. write for info. (*0-8204-2621-0*) P Lang Pubs.

Palmer, Francis A. History of the Town of Grafton, VT. 120p. 1993. reprint ed. lib. bdg. 21.00 (*0-8328-3176-X*) Higginson Bk Co.

Palmer, Francis H. Russian Life in Town & Country. LC 76-115574. (Russia Observed Ser., No. 1). 1970. reprint ed. 19.95 (*0-405-03056-8*) Ayer.

*__Palmer, Frank.__ Bent Grasses: An Inspector "Jacko" Jackson Mystery. 1994. 18.95 (*0-312-11752-3*) St Martin.

— Grammar. 2nd ed. 208p. 1989. pap. 7.95 (*0-14-022507-2*, Penguin Bks) Viking Penguin.

— Literature & Moral Understanding: A Philosophical Essay on Ethics, Aesthetics, Education, & Culture. LC 92-9977. 272p. 1992. 65.00 (*0-19-824232-8*) OUP.

— Testimony. LC 92-37741. 208p. 1993. 17.95 (*0-312-09064-1*) St Martin.

— Unfit to Plead: A Detective Inspector Jacko Jackson Mystery. 224p. 1994. 19.95 (*0-312-10569-X*) St Martin.

Palmer, Frank, jt. auth. see Fowell, Frank.

Palmer, Frank R., et al. Tool Steel Simplified. 4th ed. LC 78-7181. 555p. reprint ed. pap. 158.20 (*0-317-55805-6*, 2029387) Bks Demand.

Palmer, Frank S., ed. see St. Joseph Church Committee Staff.

Palmer, Frederick. America in France. LC 74-12754. (Illus.). 479p. 1975. reprint ed. text ed. 65.00 (*0-8371-7752-9*, PAAF, Greenwood Pr) Greenwood.

— Bliss, Peacemaker: The Life & Letters of General Tasker Howard Bliss. LC 70-130562. (Select Bibliographies Reprint Ser.). 1977. reprint ed. 28.95 (*0-8369-5535-8*) Ayer.

— Central America & Its Problems. (Central America Ser.). 1979. lib. bdg. 69.95 (*0-8490-2882-5*) Gordon Pr.

— Clark of the Ohio. 1993. reprint ed. lib. bdg. 89.00 (*0-7812-5395-0*) Rprt Serv.

— John J. Pershing, General of the Armies, a Biography. (History - United States Ser.). 380p. 1993. reprint ed. lib. bdg. 89.00 (*0-7812-4839-6*) Rprt Serv.

— Practical Upholstering: And the Cutting of Slip Covers. LC 80-51766. (Illus.). 288p. 1982. pap. 11.95 (*0-8128-6170-1*, Scrbrough Hse) Madison Bks UPA.

— Ways of the Service. LC 70-100290. (Short Story Index Reprint Ser.). 1977. 21.95 (*0-8369-3326-5*) Ayer.

Palmer, G. Structure & Bonding, Vol. 75: Long-Range Electron Transfer in Biology. (Illus.). 240p. 1991. 98.00 (*0-387-53260-9*) Spr-Verlag.

*__Palmer, G. E.__ Philokalia Vol. 2: The Complete Text. 1990. pap. 16.95 (*0-571-15466-2*) Faber & Faber.

Palmer, G. E. & Sherrard, Philip, eds. Philokalia, Vol. III. Ware, Kalistos, tr. 432p. 1984. reprint ed. 29.95 (*0-571-11726-0*); reprint ed. pap. 16.95 (*0-571-12549-2*) Faber & Faber.

Palmer, G. E., tr. see Lossky, Vladimir & Ouspensky, Leonid.

Palmer, G. E., tr. see Schuon, Frithjof.

Palmer, G. E., et al, eds. Philokalia, Vol. II. 408p. 1981. reprint ed. 30.00 (*0-571-11725-2*); reprint ed. pap. 16.95 (*0-571-12548-4*) Faber & Faber.

*__Palmer, G. E., et al, trs.__ The Philokalia: The Complete Text, Vol. IV. (Philokalia Ser.: Vol. IV). 340p. 1995. 29.95 (*0-571-11727-9*) Faber & Faber.

— The Philokalia, Vol. I: The Complete Text Compiled By St. Nikodimos of the Holy Mountain & St. Markarios of Corinth, Vol. 1. 384p. (C). 1983. pap. 14.95 (*0-571-13013-5*) Faber & Faber.

Palmer, Gabriella G., comp. El Camino Real de Tierra Adentro. (Cultural Resources Ser.: No. 11). (Illus.). 200p. (Orig.). 1992. 8.00 (*1-878178-12-1*) Bureau of Land Mgmt NM.

Palmer, Gabrielle. The Politics of Breastfeeding. (Illus.). 309p. 1989. pap. 15.00 (*0-04-440877-3*, Pub. by Pandora UK) Thorsons SF.

Palmer, Gail. Candy Goes to Hollywood: The Gail Palmer Story. (Illus.). 272p. 1995. 22.95 (*1-55970-245-1*) Arcade Pub Inc.

*__Palmer, Gayle, ed.__ The River Remembers: A History of Tumwater, 1845-1995. LC 95-2619. 1995. pap. write for info. (*0-89865-930-2*) Donning Co.

Palmer, Geoffrey, ed. see Guruswamy, Lakshman D.

Palmer, George & Stuckey, Martha. Western Tree Book. Bierly, Ken, ed. (Illus.). 144p. 1987. reprint ed. pap. 8.95 (*0-911518-75-4*) Touchstone Oregon.

Palmer, George E. Law of Restitution, 4 vols., Set. LC 77-71510. 1978. 425.00 (*0-316-69005-8*) Little.

Palmer, George E., et al. Palmer's Cases & Materials on Trusts & Succession. 4th ed. LC 83-8853. (University Casebook Ser.). 894p. 1989. reprint ed. 30.00 (*0-88277-115-9*) Foundation Pr.

Palmer, George H. Autobiography of a Philosopher. (American Biography Ser.). 137p. 1991. reprint ed. lib. bdg. 59.00 (*0-7812-8305-1*) Rprt Serv.

— Formative Types in English Poetry. Earl Lectures of 1917. LC 68-20328. (Essay Index Reprint Ser.). 1977. 20.95 (*0-8369-0766-3*) Ayer.

Palmer, George H., jt. auth. see Markus, Richard M.

Palmer, George W., ed. see Kuhn, Glenda P.

Palmer, Gerald E., et al, eds. Prayer of the Heart: Writings from the Philokalia. Sherrard, Philip et al, trs. LC 92-56453. (Centaur Editions Ser.). (Illus.). 160p. (Orig.). 1993. pap. 9.00 (*0-87773-890-4*) Shambhala Pubns.

Palmer, Gill, jt. auth. see Gospel, Howard F.

Palmer, Gladys L. Union Tactics & Economic Change: A Case Study of Three Philadelphia Textile Unions. LC 71-156438. (American Labor Ser., No. 2). 1978. reprint ed. 19.95 (*0-405-02936-5*) Ayer.

Palmer, Gladys L. & Wood, Katherine D. Urban Workers on Relief, 2 Vols. in 1, Set. LC 75-165688. (Research Monograph Ser.: Vol. 4). 1971. reprint ed. lib. bdg. 59.50 (*0-306-70336-X*) Da Capo.

Palmer, Gladys L., jt. ed. see Hourwich, Andrea T.

Palmer, Glenda. Blue Galoshes in Spring: God's Wonderful World of Seasons. LC 92-34716. (Almost on My Own Ser.). (Illus.). (J). 1993. pap. 4.99 (*0-7814-0710-9*, Chariot Bks) Chariot Family.

— My Birthday Book of Opposites Board Book. Date not set. pap. 3.99 (*0-8423-3981-7*) Tyndale.

— My Thanksgiving Book of Senses. (J). (ps). 1993. 3.99 (*0-8423-3983-3*) Tyndale.

— P Is for Pink Polliwogs: God's Wonderful World of Letters. LC 92-34715. (Almost on My Own Ser.). (Illus.). (J). 1993. pap. 4.99 (*0-7814-0708-7*, Chariot Bks) Chariot Family.

— Sidewalk Squares & Triangle Birds: God's Wonderful World of Shapes. LC 92-34717. (Almost on My Own Ser.). (Illus.). (J). 1993. pap. 4.99 (*0-7814-0711-7*, Chariot Bks) Chariot Family.

— Two Enormous Elephants: God's Wonderful World of Numbers. LC 92-34714. (Almost on My Own Ser.). (Illus.). (J). 1993. pap. 4.99 (*0-7814-0709-5*, Chariot Bks) Chariot Family.

Palmer, Glenn R., jt. auth. see Lyman, Jane W.

Palmer, Gordon. By Freedom's Holy Light. 1964. 9.95 (*0-8159-5110-8*) Devin.

Palmer, Gorham. Pirates. Ruemmler, John D., ed. (Rolemaster Ser.). (Illus.). 160p. (Orig.). (C). 1990. pap. 15.00 (*1-55806-085-5*, 1040) Iron Crown Ent Inc.

Palmer, Greg. Death: The Trip of a Lifetime. LC 92-56122. 224p. 1993. 15.00 (*0-06-250802-4*) Harper SF.

— Death: The Trip of a Lifetime. 1995. pap. 12.00 (*0-06-250803-2*, PL) HarpC.

— The Falcon. (Orig.). (J). 1993. pap. 5.00 (*0-87602-319-7*) Anchorage.

Palmer, Gregory. Biographical Sketches of Loyalists of the American Revolution. LC 83-12137. 1200p. 1984. text ed. 395.00 (*0-313-28102-5*, PBL/, Greenwood Pr) Greenwood.

— A Guide to Americana: The American Collections of the British Library. (Great Collections & Collectors Ser.: Vol. 1). 250p. 1988. lib. bdg. 60.00 (*0-86291-475-2*) Bowker-Saur.

— The McNamara Strategy & the Vietnam War: Program Budgeting in the Pentagon, 1960-1968. LC 77-94744. (Contributions in Political Science Ser.: No. 13). 169p. 1978. text ed. 55.00 (*0-313-20313-X*, PMS/, Greenwood Pr) Greenwood.

Palmer, Gregory, ed. A Bibliography of Loyalist Source Material in the United States, Canada & Great Britain. LC 80-19682. 1073p. 1982. text ed. 195.00 (*0-313-28103-3*, PBE/, Greenwood Pr) Greenwood.

Palmer, H. Enneagram in Love & Work. Date not set. pap. 14.00 (*0-06-250721-4*, PL) HarpC.

Palmer, Hap. Hap Palmer: Songs to Enhance the Movement Vocabulary of Young Children. Schiff, Ronny, ed. 1987. pap. text ed. 18.95 (*0-88284-357-5*, 2072) Alfred Pub.

Palmer, Harold S. Geology of Kaula, Nihoa, Necker & Gardner Islands & French Frigates Shoal. (BMB Ser.: No. 35). 1969. reprint ed. pap. 15.00 (*0-527-02138-5*) Periodicals Srv.

*__Palmer, Harry.__ Living Deliberately: The Discovery & Development of Avatar. (Illus.). 127p. 1994. text ed. 15.00 (*0-9626874-3-X*) Stars Edge.

— ReSurfacing: Techniques for Exploring Consciousness. 128p. (Orig.). 1994. student ed 15.00 (*0-9626874-4-8*) Stars Edge.

*__Palmer, Helen.__ African Fables. 1995. 10.95 (*0-8062-5074-7*) Carlton.

— El Eneagrama - The Enneagram: Understanding Yourself & Others in Your Life. 416p. 1994. 12.00 (*0-06-633700-3*) HarpC.

— The Enneagram: Understanding Yourself & the Others in Your Life. LC 87-45716. (Illus.). 416p. 1991. pap. 13.00 (*0-06-250683-8*) Harper SF.

— The Enneagram in Love & Work: Understanding Your Intimate & Business Relationships. LC 92-56417. 320p. 1994. 22.00 (*0-06-250679-X*) Harper SF.

— A Fish Out of Water. LC 61-9579. (Illus.). 72p. (J). (ps-3). 1961. 7.99 (*0-394-80023-0*); lib. bdg. 7.99 (*0-394-90023-5*) Beginner.

— A Fish Out of Water in English & Spanish. Rivera, Carlos, tr. (Spanish Beginner Bks.). (Illus.). (J). (gr. k-3). 1967. lib. bdg. 5.99 (*0-394-91598-4*) Random Bks Yng Read.

— The Pocket Enneagram: Understanding the 9 Types of People. LC 95-14044. 1995. pap. 7.50 (*0-06-251327-3*) Harper SF.

Palmer, Helen & Dyson, Anne J. English Novel Explication: Criticisms to 1972. (Novel Explication Ser.). vi, 329p. (Orig.). 1973. 37.50 (*0-208-01322-9*) Shoe String.

Palmer, Helen M., ed. see Smith, George.

Palmer, Henrietta R., ed. In Dixie Land: Stories of the Reconstruction Era, by Southern Writers. LC 73-267. (Short Story Index Reprint Ser.). (Illus.). 1977. reprint ed. 22.95 (*0-8369-4250-7*) Ayer.

Palmer, Hugh. Circumnavigating Father. 176p. 1990. pap. 12.95 (*0-88839-235-4*) Hancock House.

Palmer, Humphrey, ed. see Evans, Donald.

Palmer, Humphrey, tr. see Kant, Immanuel.

Palmer, Ian. Computer Security Risk Management. 1990. text ed. 72.95 (*0-442-30290-8*) Van Nos Reinhold.

Palmer, Inez S. Fortune Or Fantasy: Wilson Stricklands 1476 Acres. (Illus.). (C). 1993. write for info. (*1-881321-00-2*) LBCo Pub.

Palmer, Ingrid. Gender & Population in the Adjustment of African Economics: Planning for Change. (Women, Work & Development Ser.: No.19). vi, 187p. (Orig.). 1991. pap. 22.00 (*92-2-107739-X*) Intl Labour Office.

— The Impact of Agrarian Reform on Women. LC 85-5250. (Kumarian Press Case Studies on Women's Roles & Gender Differences in Development: No.6). 55p. (Orig.). 1985. pap. 8.95 (*0-931816-21-1*) Kumarian Pr.

— Impact of Male Out-Migration on Women in Farming. LC 85-5240. (Kumarian Press Case Studies on Women's Roles & Gender Differences in Development: No. 7). 78p. (Orig.). 1985. pap. 8.95 (*0-931816-22-X*) Kumarian Pr.

— Indonesian Economy since Nineteen Sixty-Six. 196p. 1978. 37.50 (*0-7146-3088-8*, Pub. by F Cass Pubs UK) Intl Spec Bk.

— The Nemow Case. LC 84-28893. (Kumarian Press Case Studies on Women's Roles & Gender Differences in Development: No.1). 53p. 1985. pap. 8.95 (*0-931816-16-5*) Kumarian Pr.

Palmer, J. Rudyard Kipling. LC 73-21706. (English Literature Ser.: No. 33). 1974. lib. bdg. 49.95 (*0-8383-1830-4*) M S G Haskell Hse.

— The Vinson Court Era: The Supreme Court's Conference Votes: Data & Analysis. LC 89-45875. (Studies in Social History: No. 9). 1990. 57.50 (*0-404-61609-7*) AMS Pr.

Palmer, J. D. Biological Rhythms & Living Clocks. 2nd ed. Head, J. J., ed. LC 84-70786. (Carolina Biology Readers Ser.: No. 92). (Illus.). 16p. (J). (gr. 10 up). 1984. pap. 2.75 (*0-89278-192-0*, 45-9692) Carolina Biological.

— Human Biological Rhythms. Head, J. J., ed. LC 81-67983. (Carolina Biology Readers Ser.: No. 104). (Illus.). 16p. (J). (gr. 10 up). 1983. pap. 2.75 (*0-89278-304-4*, 45-9704) Carolina Biological.

Palmer, J. D. & Saeks, R. The World of Large Scale Systems. LC 82-6169. 360p. 1982. 49.95 (*0-87942-161-4*, PC01560); pap. 39.95 (*0-87942-162-2*, PP01578) Inst Electrical.

Palmer, J. J. Froissart, Historian. 216p. 1981. 71.00 (*0-85115-146-9*) Boydell & Brewer.

Palmer, J. J., jt. ed. see English, Barbara B.

Palmer, J. J., jt. ed. see English, Barbara.

Palmer, J. M., et al. CIE Guides to Insects of Importance to Man, No. 2: Thysanoptera. 73p. (Orig.). 1989. pap. text ed. 24.00 (*0-85198-634-X*) CAB Intl.

Palmer, Jacqueline, jt. auth. see Palmer, Charles J.

Palmer, Jacqueline S., jt. auth. see Killingsworth, M. Jimmie.

*__Palmer, James.__ The Governor's Wife: A Novel of the Civil War in New Mexico. 166p. (Orig.). 1995. pap. write for info. (*1-885591-62-4*) Morris Pubng.

Palmer, James & Riley, Michael. The Films of Joseph Losey. LC 92-37480. (Cambridge Film Classics Ser.). (Illus.). 192p. (C). 1993. 47.95 (*0-521-38386-2*); pap. 13.95 (*0-521-38780-9*) Cambridge U Pr.

An Asterisk (*) at the beginning of an entry indicates that the title is appearing in BIP for the first time.

Palmer, James, et al. Compressible Flow Tables for Engineers: With Appropriate Computer Programs for Estimating Property Changes Caused by Friction, Heat Transfer &, or Shock Waves. (Illus.). 95p. (Orig.). (C). 1987. pap. text ed. 21.50 (*0-333-44764-6*, Pub. by Macmill Press UK) Scholium Intl.

Palmer, James D., jt. auth. see Sage, Andrew P.

Palmer, James E. Schaum's Outline of Introduction to Digital Systems: Including 183 Solved Problems. 1992. pap. text ed. 12.95 (*0-07-048439-2*) McGraw.

Palmer, James M., ed. Optical Radiation Measurement. 285p. 1989. 53.00 (*0-8194-0145-5*, VOL. 1109) SPIE.

Palmer, James O. The Experience of Anxiety: A Casebook. 2nd ed. Goldstein, Michael J., ed. (C). 1975. pap. text ed. 16.95 (*0-19-501921-0*) OUP.

Palmer, Jane. The Watcher. 178p. 1993. pap. 3.95 (*0-685-66673-5*, Pub. by Womens Pr UK) Interlink Pub.

Palmer, Jane, jt. auth. see Snyder, Thomas.

Palmer, Jane, jt. auth. see Snyder, Tom.

Palmer, Janet L. From the Greenroom to the Boardroom: Performance Studies as Management Training. 20p. (Orig.). (C). 1988. pap. text ed. 4.00 (*0-317-91220-8*) Comn Excellence.

Palmer, Janet L., ed. Communication As Performance. (Illus.). 171p. (Orig.). (C). 1986. pap. text ed. 25.00 (*0-9620922-0-7*) Comn Excellence.

Palmer, Janice B., ed. Spanish Plat Book of Land Records: District of Pensacola in West Florida: British & Spanish Land Grants - 1763-1820. Moreno, Fernando J., tr. (Illus.). 600p. (C). 1995. pap. text ed. 40.00 (*1-885787-01-4*) Antiq Complng.

Palmer, Jannine. The Star Caster: Cast the Stars & Read Your Future. 2nd ed. 72p. 1993. pap. text ed. 30.00 (*0-9636085-0-9*) Jasmine Prods.

Palmer, Jean B. KLIATT Audiobook Guide. (Illus.). 250p. 1994. lib. bdg. 34.00 (*1-56308-123-7*) Libs Unl.

Palmer, Jeanne, jt. auth. see Leontos, Carolyn.

Palmer, Jed. Everything You Need to Know When You Are the Victim of a Violent Crime. LC 94-6042. (J). 1994. write for info. (*0-8239-1693-6*) Rosen Pub.

Palmer, Jerry. The Logic of the Absurd: On Film & TV Comedy. 232p. 1987. 35.00 (*0-85170-204-X*, Pub. by British Film Inst UK); pap. 15.95 (*0-85170-205-8*, Pub. by British Film Inst UK) Ind U Pr.

— Potboilers: Methods, Concepts & Case Studies in Popular Fiction. (Communication & Society Ser.). 240p. (Orig.). 1992. 69.50 (*0-415-00977-4*, A6779); pap. 16.95 (*0-415-00978-2*, A6783) Routledge.

— Taking Humour Seriously. LC 93-15323. 1993. write for info. (*0-415-10266-9*); pap. write for info. (*0-415-10267-7*) Routledge.

***Palmer, Jerry & Dodson, Mo, eds.** Design & Aesthetics: A Reader. LC 95-8710. 1995. write for info. (*0-415-07232-8*); write for info. (*0-415-07233-6*) Routledge.

Palmer, Jessica. Cradlesong. Todd, Rebecca, ed. 320p. (Orig.). 1993. mass mkt. 4.99 (*0-671-73421-0*) PB.

— Dark Lullaby. Peters, Sally, ed. 352p. (Orig.). 1991. mass mkt. 4.95 (*0-671-70309-9*) PB.

— Shadow Dance. Todd, Rebecca, ed. 304p. (Orig.). 1994. mass mkt. 5.50 (*0-671-78715-2*) PB.

Palmer, Jim. Accountability Through Student Tracking. 1990. pap. 18.50 (*0-87117-219-4*) Am Assn Comm Coll.

— Game Wardens vs. Poachers: Tickets Still Available. LC 92-74795. 160p. 1993. pap. 12.95 (*0-87341-218-4*) Krause Pubns.

— Palmer: Editorial Cartoons from the Montgomery Advertiser. 160p. 1992. 9.95 (*1-882616-00-6*) Advertiser.

***Palmer, Jim & Dale, Jim.** Together We Were Eleven Foot Nine: The Twenty-Year Friendship of Hall of Fame Pitcher Jim Palmer & Orioles Manager Earl Weaver. (Illus.). 1996. 19.95 (*0-8362-0781-5*) Andrews & McMeel.

Palmer, Jim & Vaughan, George, eds. Fostering a Climate for Faculty Scholarship at Community, Technical & Junior Colleges. 98p. (Orig.). (C). 1992. pap. text ed. 20.00 (*0-87117-238-0*) Am Assn Comm Coll.

Palmer, Joan. A Dog Owner's Guide to Training Your Dog. (Illus.). 118p. 10.95 (*3-923880-76-6*, 16033) Tetra Pr.

— Illustrated Encyclopedia of Dog Breeds. 1994. 19.98 (*0-7858-0030-1*) Bk Sales Inc.

— A Practical Guide to Selecting a Large Dog. (Illus.). 119p. 10.95 (*3-923880-78-2*, 16018) Tetra Pr.

— A Practical Guide to Selecting a Small Dog. (Illus.). 119p. 10.95 (*3-923880-79-0*, 16019) Tetra Pr.

Palmer, Joan A. Memories of a Riverina Childhood. (Illus.). 200p. Date not set. pap. 19.95 (*0-86840-341-5*, Pub. by New South Wales Univ Pr AT) Intl Spec Bk.

Palmer, Joe E. Love Me, Love My Bookie: Petting & Betting. 200p. (Orig.). 1989. pap. 9.95 (*0-9622549-1-6*, TXU 161-521) Remlap Pub.

— Old Baseball Scout & His Players: Horsehide & Hollywood. 171p. 1987. pap. 9.95 (*0-9622549-0-8*, TXU 251-619) Remlap Pub.

— Slide, Bloomer, Slide. 170p. (Orig.). 1990. pap. write for info. (*0-9622549-2-4*, TXU 228 191) Remlap Pub.

Palmer, Joel. Journal of Travels. 187p. 1984. reprint ed. 14.95 (*0-87770-299-3*) Ye Galleon.

***Palmer, John.** Drawing & Sketching. (Ron Ranson's Painting School Ser.). (Illus.). 120p. 1995. 22.95 (*1-85470-061-8*, Pub. by Anaya Pubs UK) Trafalgar.

Palmer, John, jt. auth. see Menhennet, David.

Palmer, John A. A Walk to Somewhere: On the Road During the Great Depression. Stasa, Suzanne, ed. (Illus.). 88p. (Orig.). Date not set. pap. 8.95 (*1-56550-015-6*) Vis Bks Intl.

Palmer, John C. The Morgan Affair & Anti-Masonry. 117p. 1992. reprint ed. pap. 12.95 (*1-56459-052-6*) Kessinger Pub.

Palmer, John D. The Biological Rhythms & Clocks of Intertidal Animals. (Illus.). 224p. 1995. 65.00 (*0-19-509435-2*) OUP.

Palmer, John F., jt. auth. see McMenamin, Stephen M.

Palmer, John J. In Pictures Sequoia-Kings Canyon: The Continuing Story. LC 90-60039. (Illus.). 48p. 1990. pap. 6.95 (*0-88714-049-1*) KC Pubns.

Palmer, John J. & Flanagan, Stephen. Comparative Negligence Manual. LC 85-21297. 1986. ring bd. 135.00 (*0-685-59925-6*) Clark Boardman Callaghan.

Palmer, John L. Income Security in America: The Record & the Prospects. LC 88-17102. (Report Ser.: No. 88-3). (Illus.). 44p. (Orig.). (C). 1988. pap. text ed. 11.50 (*0-87766-418-8*) Urban Inst.

— Studies in the Contemporary Theatre. LC 70-97716. (Essay Index Reprint Ser.). 1977. 20.95 (*0-8369-1369-8*) Ayer.

Palmer, John L., ed. Creating Jobs: Public Employment Programs & Wage Subsidies. LC 78-12241. (Studies in Social Economics). 379p. 1978. pap. 14.95 (*0-8157-6891-5*) Brookings.

— Perspectives on the Reagan Years. LC 86-13160. (Illus.). 215p. (Orig.). 1986. lib. bdg. 27.50 (*0-87766-403-X*); pap. text ed. 12.95 (*0-87766-402-1*) Urban Inst.

Palmer, John L. & Pechman, Joseph A., eds. Welfare in Rural Areas: The North Carolina-Iowa Income Maintenance Experiment. LC 77-91826. (Studies in Social Economics). 273p. 1978. 34.95 (*0-8157-6896-6*); pap. 14.95 (*0-8157-6895-8*) Brookings.

Palmer, John L. & Sawhill, Isabel V., eds. The Reagan Experiment: An Examination of Economic & Social Policies under the Reagan Administration. (Illus.). 530p. (Orig.). 1982. lib. bdg. 71.00 (*0-87766-315-7*); pap. text ed. 24.00 (*0-87766-316-5*) Urban Inst.

Palmer, John L., jt. ed. see Haveman, Robert H.

Palmer, John L., jt. ed. see Mills, Gregory B.

Palmer, John L., et al, eds. The Vulnerable. LC 88-17397. (Changing Domestic Priorities Ser.). (Illus.). 458p. (Orig.). (C). 1988. pap. text ed. 28.50 (*0-87766-419-6*) Urban Inst.

Palmer, John M. America in Arms. Kohn, Richard H., ed. LC 78-22392. (American Military Experience Ser.). 1980. reprint ed. lib. bdg. 18.95 (*0-405-11868-6*) Ayer.

— Anatomy for Speech & Hearing. 4th ed. (Illus.). 304p. 1993. pap. 29.00 (*0-683-06737-0*) Williams & Wilkins.

— Survey of Communication Disorders. (Illus.). 288p. 1990. 39.00 (*0-683-06743-5*) Williams & Wilkins.

Palmer, John M., jt. ed. see De Vere White, Ralph.

Palmer, John T. Career Education For Physically Disabled Students: Development As A Lifetime Activity. LC 80-82642. 64p. 1980. 2.00 (*0-686-38799-6*) Human Res Ctr.

Palmer, John W. Constitutional Rights of Prisoners. 4th rev. ed. LC 90-82311. 874p. (C). 1990. text ed. 37.95 (*0-87084-692-2*) Anderson Pub Co.

— Ohio Courtroom Evidence. suppl. ed. 1994. ring bd. 37.00 (*0-614-03765-4*) Butterworth Legal Pubs.

— Ohio Courtroom Evidence. 2nd ed. 500p. 1988. ring bd. 115.00 (*1-55943-132-6*) Michie Butterworth.

— Pioneer Days in San Francisco. Jones, William R., ed. (Illus.). 24p. 1977. reprint ed. pap. 3.95 (*0-89646-015-0*) Vistabooks.

Palmer, Jon. Wineries of the Mid-Atlantic. 220p. (Orig.). (C). 1988. text ed. 35.00 (*0-8135-1346-4*); pap. 12.95 (*0-8135-1351-0*) Rutgers U Pr.

Palmer, Jonathan, jt. auth. see Camden, Thomas M.

Palmer, Joseph W. Cataloging & the Small Special Library. 49p. 1992. 28.00 (*0-87111-370-8*) SLA.

Palmer, Joy. Deserts. LC 92-12406. (First Starts Ser.). (Illus.). 32p. (J). (gr. 2-3). 1992. lib. bdg. 19.97 (*0-8114-3402-8*) Raintree Steck-V.

— Deserts. (First Starts Ser.). (J). (ps-3). 1993. pap. 4.95 (*0-8114-4912-2*) Raintree Steck-V.

— Geography in the Early Years. LC 93-41050. (Teaching & Learning in the First Three Years of School Ser.). (Illus.). 224p. (Orig.). 1994. pap. 16.95x (*0-415-09830-0*, B4170, Routledge NY) Routledge.

— Oceans. LC 92-12409. (First Starts Ser.). (Illus.). 32p. (J). (gr. 2-3). 1992. lib. bdg. 19.97 (*0-8114-3401-X*) Raintree Steck-V.

— Oceans. (J). (ps-3). 1993. pap. 4.95 (*0-8114-4915-7*) Raintree Steck-V.

— Polar Lands. LC 92-12405. (First Starts Ser.). (Illus.). 32p. (J). (gr. 2-3). 1992. lib. bdg. 19.97 (*0-8114-3403-6*) Raintree Steck-V.

— Polar Lands. (J). (ps-3). 1993. pap. 4.95 (*0-8114-4916-5*) Raintree Steck-V.

— Rain. LC 92-38554. (First Starts Ser.). (Illus.). 32p. (J). (gr. 2-3). 1992. lib. bdg. 19.97 (*0-8114-3413-3*) Raintree Steck-V.

— Rain. (J). (ps-3). 1994. 4.95 (*0-8114-7774-6*) Raintree Steck-V.

— Rain Forests. LC 92-10634. (First Starts Ser.). (Illus.). 32p. (J). (gr. 2-3). 1992. lib. bdg. 19.97 (*0-8114-3400-1*) Raintree Steck-V.

— Rain Forests. (J). (ps-3). 1993. pap. 4.95 (*0-8114-4911-4*) Raintree Steck-V.

— Snow & Ice. LC 92-38438. (First Starts Ser.). (Illus.). 32p. (J). (gr. 2-3). 1992. lib. bdg. 19.97 (*0-8114-3414-1*) Raintree Steck-V.

— Snow & Ice. (J). (ps-3). 1994. 4.95 (*0-8114-7775-4*) Raintree Steck-V.

— Sunshine. LC 92-38437. (First Starts Ser.). (Illus.). 32p. (J). (gr. 2-3). 1992. lib. bdg. 19.97 (*0-8114-3416-8*) Raintree Steck-V.

— Sunshine. (J). (ps-3). 1994. 4.95 (*0-8114-6440-7*) Raintree Steck-V.

— Waste & Recycling. (Conservation 2000 Ser.). 64p. (J). (gr. 6-9). 1995. 24.95 (*0-7134-7201-4*, Pub. by A Deutsch UK) Trafalgar.

— Wind. LC 92-38439. (First Starts Ser.). (Illus.). 32p. (J). (gr. 2-3). 1992. lib. bdg. 19.97 (*0-8114-3415-X*) Raintree Steck-V.

Palmer, Joy & Neal, Philip. The Handbook of Environmental Education. LC 93-37815. 288p. 1994. 59.95x (*0-415-09313-9*, B3708); pap. 19.95 (*0-415-09314-7*, B3712) Routledge.

Palmer, Joy, jt. auth. see Stevenson, Rosemary.

***Palmer, Joy A. & Cooper, David E.** Just Environments: Intergenerational, International, & Inter-Species Issues. LC 94-23953. 208p. 1995. 59.95x (*0-415-10335-5*, C0016); pap. 16.95 (*0-415-10336-3*, C0017) Routledge.

Palmer, Joy A. & Pettitt, Deirdre. Topic Work in the Early Years: Organising the Curriculum for Four to Eight-Year-Olds. LC 92-47344. 192p. 1993. pap. 18.95 (*0-415-08041-X*, B2550) Routledge.

Palmer, Joy A., jt. ed. see Cooper, David E.

Palmer, Julia R. Read for Your Life: Two Successful Efforts to Help People Read & an Annotated List of Books That Made Them Want To. LC 73-14695. 508p. 1974. 37.50 (*0-8108-0654-1*) Scarecrow.

Palmer, K. & Brann, D. Illustrations of Fossils of the Ithaca Area. (Illus.). 1966. 2.00 (*0-87710-377-1*) Paleo Res.

Palmer, K. A. Local Government Law in New Zealand. 2nd ed. 1993. write for info. (*0-455-21180-9*, Pub. by Law Bk Co); pap. write for info. (*0-455-21181-7*, Pub. by Law Bk Co) W W Gaunt.

Palmer, K. J., jt. auth. see Kirchgraber, U.

Palmer, K. T. Notes for the MRCGP. 2nd ed. (Illus.). 336p. 1992. pap. 39.95 (*0-632-02909-9*) Blackwell Sci.

Palmer, Karen, et al. Power Plant Fuel Supply Contracts: The Changing Nature of Long-Term Relationships. 120p. 1992. pap. 35.00 (*0-910325-43-X*) Public Util.

Palmer, Katherine V. The Unpublished Velins of Lamarck, 1802 to 1809: Illustrations of Fossils of the Paris Basin Eocene. (Illus.). 67p. 1977. 15.00 (*0-87710-373-9*) Paleo Res.

Palmer, Kathleen, ed. see Basler, Lucille.

Palmer, Kenneth, ed. see Shakespeare, William.

Palmer, Kenneth J., jt. ed. see Kloeden, Peter E.

Palmer, Kenneth T., et al. Maine Politics & Government. LC 92-6080. (Politics & Governments of the American States Ser.). (Illus.). xxviii, 240p. 1992. 40.00 (*0-8032-3680-8*); pap. 14.95 (*0-8032-8718-6*) U of Nebr Pr.

Palmer, King C. Teach Yourself Piano. (Teach Yourself Ser.). 1974. pap. 7.95 (*0-679-10256-6*) McKay.

Palmer, L. A Genealogical Record of the Descendants of John & Mary Palmer of Concord, Chester (Now Delaware County), Pennsylvania, Especially Through Their Son, John, Jr. & Sons-in-Law, William & James Trimble. (Illus.). 474p. 1989. reprint ed. lib. bdg. 84.00 (*0-8328-0930-6*); reprint ed. pap. 74.00 (*0-8328-0931-4*) Higginson Bk Co.

— Palmer (& Trimble) Genealogical Record of the Descendants of John & Mary Palmer of Concord, PA. Also Includes Surnames Almond, Arment, Baker, & Others. (Illus.). 725p. 1990. reprint ed. lib. bdg. 115.00 (*0-8328-1526-8*); reprint ed. pap. 107.00 (*0-8328-1527-6*) Higginson Bk Co.

— Trimble (& Palmer) A Genealogical Record of Descendants of William & Ann Trimble of Concord Co., PA & James & Mary Trimble of Chester Co., PA & Others. (Illus.). 398p. 1990. reprint ed. lib. bdg. 67.50 (*0-8328-1528-4*); reprint ed. pap. 59.50 (*0-8328-1529-2*) Higginson Bk Co.

Palmer, L. M., ed. see Croce, Benedetto.

Palmer, L. R. The Latin Language. LC 87-40564. 384p. 1988. pap. 19.95 (*0-8061-2136-X*) U of Okla Pr.

Palmer, Larry. Harpsichord in America: A Twentieth-Century Revival. LC 88-45446. (Illus.). 218p. 1989. 25.00 (*0-253-32710-5*); pap. 12.95 (*0-253-20840-8*) Ind U Pr.

Palmer, Laura. Shrapnel in the Heart: Letters & Remembrances from the Vietnam Veterans Memorial. 1988. pap. 9.00 (*0-394-75988-5*, Vin) Random.

— Shrapnel in the Heart: Letters & Remembrances from the Vietnam Memorial. LC 87-42652. (Illus.). 272p. 1987. 17.95 (*0-394-56027-2*) Random.

Palmer, Laura & Willison, Marilyn. Touched by Magic. 238p. (Orig.). 1992. pap. 19.95 (*0-9631899-0-5*) Angel Ink.

Palmer, Laura, jt. auth. see Berendzen, Richard.

Palmer, Laura K. Osgood & Anthony Perkins: A Comprehensive History of Their Work in Theatre, Film & Other Media, with Credits & an Annotated Bibliography. LC 90-53518. (Illus.). 423p. 1991. lib. bdg. 49.95x (*0-89950-577-5*) McFarland & Co.

Palmer, Leon. The Trained Eye: An Introduction to Astronomical Observing. (Illus.). 274p. (C). 1991. pap. text ed. 9.50 (*0-03-047363-2*) SCP.

***Palmer, Leonard.** The Sherman Letter. 200p. 1995. 18.95 (*1-885173-08-3*) Write Way.

Palmer, Leonard R. Mycenaeans & Minoans: Aegean Prehistory in the Light of the Linear B Tablets. 2nd ed. LC 79-22315. (Illus.). 368p. 1980. reprint ed. text ed. 37.50 (*0-313-22160-X*, PAMY, Greenwood Pr) Greenwood.

Palmer, Les. Bowling. (Illus.). 54p. 1981. pap. text ed. 5.95x (*0-89641-063-3*) American Pr.

Palmer, Les & Johnson, Dewayne J. Softball. (Illus.). 54p. 1980. pap. text ed. 5.95x (*0-89641-044-7*) American Pr.

Palmer, Leslie & King, Coretta Scott. Lena Horne. (Black Americans of Achievement Ser.). (Illus.). 112p. (J). (gr. 5 up). 1989. lib. bdg. 17.95 (*1-55546-594-3*) Chelsea Hse.

Palmer, Lloyd. Steam Towards the Sunset: The Railroads of Lincoln County. LC 82-84454. (Lincoln County Historical Society Ser.: No. 23). (Illus.). 192p. (Orig.). 1982. pap. 19.95 (*0-911443-00-2*) Lincoln Coun Hist.

Palmer, Louis. Adventures in Afghanistan. 239p. 1990. 24.00 (*0-86304-053-5*, Pub. by Octagon Pr UK); pap. 11.00 (*0-86304-057-8*, Pub. by Octagon Pr UK) ISHK Bk Service.

Palmer, Louis, jt. auth. see Cleckley, Franklin.

Palmer, Lynn M. & Toms, Janice E. Manual for Functional Training. 3rd ed. LC 91-34541. (Illus.). 351p. 1992. pap. text ed. 25.95 (*0-8036-6759-0*) Davis Co.

Palmer, Lynne. ABC Basic Chart Reading. 76p. 1974. 10.00 (*0-86690-136-1*, P1363-014) Am Fed Astrologers.

— Astro-Guide to Nutrition. 1993. 12.00 (*0-86690-438-7*) Am Fed Astrologers.

— Astrological Almanac for 1995. 134p. 1994. 12.00 (*0-86690-443-3*) Am Fed Astrologers.

— Astrological Compatibility. LC 76-25674. 352p. 1976. 14.00 (*0-86690-139-6*, P1366-014) Am Fed Astrologers.

— Do-It-Yourself Publicity Directory. LC 84-70907. 184p. 1984. 17.00 (*0-86690-274-0*, P2532-014) Am Fed Astrologers.

— Gambling to Win. 118p. 1994. 12.95 (*0-86690-444-1*, P3503-014) Am Fed Astrologers.

— Nixon's Horoscope. 176p. 1975. 7.00 (*0-86690-140-X*, P1367-014) Am Fed Astrologers.

— Pluto Ephemeris: 1900-2000. LC 74-181511. 316p. 1974. 14.00 (*0-86690-200-7*, P1680-004) Am Fed Astrologers.

— Use Astrology & Change Your Name. LC 83-72652. 296p. 1983. 17.00 (*0-86690-262-7*, P2428-014) Am Fed Astrologers.

Palmer, M. Mapping of Bermuda: Bibiliography 1548-1907. (Illus.). 37.50 (*0-87556-682-0*) Saifer.

— The Onset of Industrialisation. (C). 1976. text ed. 45.00 (*0-685-22171-7*, Pub. by Univ Nottingham UK) St Mut.

— Practical Wave Flying. 2nd ed. (Illus.). 112p. (Orig.). 1989. pap. 12.95 (*0-9624979-0-8*) Lenticular Pub.

Palmer, M., et al. Religion for a Change, Bk. 2. (C). 1991. text ed. 45.00 (*0-7487-0474-4*, Pub. by S Thornes Pubs UK) St Mut.

— Religion for a Change, Bk. 3. (C). 1991. text ed. 45.00 (*0-7487-0475-2*, Pub. by S Thornes Pubs UK) St Mut.

— Religion for a Change Teacher's Book for Books 1 & 2. (C). 1991. text ed. 50.00 (*0-7487-0476-0*, Pub. by S Thornes Pubs UK) St Mut.

Palmer, M. D. Henry VIII. 2nd ed. (Seminar Studies in History). (Illus.). (C). 1983. pap. text ed. 11.95 (*0-582-35437-4*, 72225) Longman.

***Palmer, M. Dale.** True Esoteric Traditions: A Search for Western Cultural Values. LC 94-66752. (Illus.). 350p. (C). 1994. 29.00 (*0-9642633-0-0*) Noetics Inst.

Palmer, Margaret & Browman, Ethel. The Bride's Book of Ideas. rev. ed. 192p. 1970. 12.99 (*0-8423-0180-1*) Tyndale.

Palmer, Margaret V., ed. Cave Research Foundation Annual Report, 1980. (Illus.). 51p. (Orig.). 1981. pap. 5.00 (*0-939748-03-7*) Cave Bks MO.

Palmer, Margaret V. & Palmer, Arthur N., eds. Cave Research Foundation Annual Report, 1982. (Illus.). 45p. (Orig.). 1983. pap. 5.00 (*0-939748-06-1*) Cave Bks MO.

Palmer, Marilyn. Framework Knitting. 1989. pap. 30.00 (*0-85263-668-7*, Pub. by Shire UK) St Mut.

Palmer, Marilyn & Neaverson, Peter. Industry in the Landscape. LC 93-49805. 1994. write for info. (*0-415-11206-0*) Routledge.

Palmer, Marilyn, jt. auth. see Evans, A. J.

Palmer, Marion, ed. see Harris, Joel C.

Palmer, Marjorie & Palmer, Bernard. While the Sun is High. LC 83-83388. (Heritage Ser.: Vol. 7). 1984. 10.95 (*0-911802-60-6*) Free Church Pubns.

Palmer, Marjorie, jt. auth. see Palmer, Bernard.

Palmer, Marlene. Expert Systems & Related Topics: A Selected Bibliography & Guide to Information Sources. LC 89-81134. 250p. 1990. pap. 32.95 (*1-878289-03-9*) Idea Group Pub.

Palmer, Martha. Advanced Multiplication & Division. Hoffman, Joan, ed. (I Know It! Bks.). (Illus.). 32p. (J). (gr. 5-6). 1980. student ed 1.99 (*0-938256-36-X*) Sch Zone Pub Co.

— Beginning Addition & Subtraction. Hoffman, Joan, ed. (I Know It! Bks.). (Illus.). 32p. (J). (gr. 1). 1980. student ed 1.99 (*0-938256-29-7*) Sch Zone Pub Co.

— Beginning Multiplication & Division. Hoffman, Joan, ed. (I Know It! Bks.). (Illus.). 32p. (J). (gr. 3-4). 1980. student ed 1.99 (*0-938256-34-3*) Sch Zone Pub Co.

— Fractions. Hoffman, Joan, ed. (I Know It! Bks.). (Illus.). 32p. (J). (gr. 5-6). 1981. student ed 1.99 (*0-938256-43-2*) Sch Zone Pub Co.

— Transition Math. Hoffman, Joan, ed. (I Know It! Bks.). (Illus.). 32p. (J). (gr. k-1). 1979. student ed 1.99 (*0-938256-27-0*) Sch Zone Pub Co.

Palmer, Martha S. Semantic Processing for Finite Domains. (Studies in Natural Language Processing). 248p. (C). 1990. 64.95 (*0-521-36226-1*) Cambridge U Pr.

— A Sower Went Forth. 1978. 7.75 (*0-686-24055-3*) Rod & Staff.

Palmer, Martin. Elements of Taoism. 1991. pap. 9.95 (*1-85230-231-3*) Element MA.

— Living Christianity. 1993. pap. 11.95 (*1-85230-327-1*) Element MA.

***Palmer, Martin, et al.** Religion for a Change: An Integrated Course in Religious & Personal Education, Bk. 2. 80p. (Orig.). (C). 1991. pap. text ed. 35.00x (*0-7478-0474-5*, Pub. by S Thornes Pubs UK) St Mut.

***Palmer, Martin & Ramsay, Jay.** I Ching: The Shamanic Oracle of Change. (Illus.). 1995. pap. 16.00 (*1-85538-416-7*) Thorsons SF.

Palmer, Martin, et al. The Fortune Teller's I Ching. 1987. text ed. 9.95 (*0-345-34539-8*, Ballantine Trade) Ballantine.

— Religion for a Change: An Integrated Course in Religious & Personal Education. 96p. (Orig.). (C). 1991. pap. 35.00x (*0-7478-0475-3*, Pub. by S Thornes Pubs UK) St Mut.

— Religion for a Change: An Integrated Course in Religious & Personal Education, 3 vols. (Illus.). 272p. (Orig.). (YA). (gr. 7-10). 1991. pap. 42.50 (0-7487-0473-6, Pub. by Stanley Thornes UK) Trans-Atl Phila.
— Religion for a Change: An Integrated Course in Religious & Personal Education, Bk. 1. 96p. (Orig.). (C). 1991. pap. 35.00x (0-7478-0473-7, Pub. by S Thornes Pubs UK) St Mut.
— Religion for a Change: An Integrated Course in Religious & Personal Education Teacher's Book. (C). 1991. pap. 35.00x (0-7478-0476-1, Pub. by S Thornes Pubs UK) St Mut.
Palmer, Mary, jt. ed. see Paterson, David.
Palmer, Mary, ed. see Stevens, C. A.
Palmer, Mary E. A Rating Scale to Be Used As a Guide in Grade Determination for Clinical Practice in the Medical & Surgical Nursing Course of a Specific Basic Collegiate Program. LC 60-12193. 99p. reprint ed. pap. 28.30 (0-317-30004-0, 2051860) Bks Demand.
Palmer, Mary R. As Clean As a Whistle. LC 90-70148. 48p. (J). (ps-4). 1990. pap. 5.95 (0-932433-66-9) Windswept Hse.
— Poems Downeast. Whitaker, Kate, ed. (Illus.). 96p. 1994. pap. 8.95 (1-883650-10-0) Windswept Hse.
— Sharing Secrets. LC 91-65294. (Illus.). 60p. (J). (ps-4). 1991. pap. 6.95 (0-932433-82-0) Windswept Hse.
Palmer, Mary S. & Coffman, Elizabeth T. MemoraMOBILEia: Alabama Gulf Coast Potpourri. 195p. Date not set. pap. 11.95 (0-9639773-0-X) Mobile & Bayside.
Palmer, Melvyn D., jt. ed. see Zepp, Ira G., Jr.
Palmer Memorial Episcopal Churchwomen, Houston, Texas Staff. Not by Bread Alone: Recipes of the Women of Palmer Church. Roberts, Michele S., ed. (Illus.). 288p. (Orig.). pap. text ed. 12.95 (0-318-20648-X) D Armstrong.
***Palmer, Michael.** At Passages. LC 94-43613. 128p. (Orig.). 1995. pap. 11.95 (0-8112-1294-7) New Directions.
— The European Parliament: What It Is-What It Does-How It Works. 128p. 1981. text ed. 102.00 (0-08-024536-6, Pub. by Pergamon Repr UK) Franklin.
— Exact Change Yearbook, No. 1. 1994. 35.00 (1-878972-17-0) Exact Change.
— Extreme Measures. 1992. mass mkt. 5.99 (0-553-29577-2) Bantam.
— Flashback. (Orig.). 1991. mass mkt. 5.99 (0-553-27329-9) Bantam.
— Love of Glory & the Common Good: Aspects of the Political Thought of Thucydides. 188p. (C). 1992. text ed. 48.50 (0-8476-7731-1); pap. text ed. 17.95 (0-8476-7732-X) Rowman.
— Moral Problems: A Coursebook. 232p. (C). 1995. pap. 17.95 (0-8020-7661-0) U of Toronto Pr.
— Natural Causes. LC 93-26832. 1994. 21.95 (0-553-09553-6) Bantam.
— Natural Causes. 1995. mass mkt. 5.99 (0-553-56876-0) Bantam.
— Origins of the Maritime Strategy: American Naval Strategy in the First Postwar Decade. (Contributions to Naval History Ser.: No. 1). (Illus.). 129p. (C). 1988. pap. 7.50 (0-945274-01-7) Naval Hist Ctr.
— Paul Tillich's Philosophy of Art. LC 83-15056. (Theologische Bibliothek Toepelmann Ser.: Vol. 41). xxii, 217p. 1983. 76.15 (3-11-009681-1) De Gruyter.
— Side Effects. 1991. mass mkt. 5.99 (0-553-27618-2) Bantam.
— Silent Treatment. 1995. 21.95 (0-553-09516-1) Bantam.
— Sisterhood. 1991. mass mkt. 5.99 (0-553-27570-4) Bantam.
***Palmer, Michael, ed.** Chinese Law & Legal Theory. (International Library of Essays in Law & Legal Theory). 500p. 1996. 150.00x (0-8147-6617-X) NYU Pr.
Palmer, Michael, intro. Code of Signals: Recent Writings in Poetics. 275p. (Orig.). 1983. 25.00 (0-938190-26-1); pap. 12.95 (0-938190-22-9) North Atlantic.
***Palmer, Michael & Pangle, Thomas L., eds.** Political Philosophy & the Human Soul: Essays in Memory of Allan Bloom. 320p. (C). 1995. text ed. 34.95 (0-8476-8059-2) Rowman.
Palmer, Michael, tr. see Aragon, Louis, et al, eds.
Palmer, Michael, tr. see Berger, John & Tanner, Alain.
Palmer, Michael, tr. see Hocquard, Emmanuel.
Palmer, Michael, tr. see Parshchikov, Alexei.
Palmer, Michael, ed. see Tillich, Paul.
Palmer, Michael, jt. auth. see Tunstall, Jeremy.
Palmer, Michael A. Guardians of the Gulf: A History of America's Expanding Role in the Persian Gulf, 1883-1991. 1992. text ed. 27.95 (0-02-923843-9) Free Pr.
— On Course to Desert Storm: The United States Navy & the Persian Gulf. (Illus.). 201p. (Orig.). (C). 1993. pap. text ed. 34.95 (1-56806-556-6) Diane Pub.
— On Course to Desert Storm: The United States Navy & the Persian Gulf. (Contributions to Naval History Ser.: No. 5). (Illus.). 201p. (Orig.). (C). 1992. pap. 11.00 (0-945274-08-4) Naval Hist Ctr.
— Origins of the Maritime Strategy: American Naval Strategy in the First Postwar Decade. (Illus.). 151p. 1989. per. 7.50 (0-16-002056-5) USGPO.
— Origins of the Maritime Strategy: The Development of American Naval Strategy, 1945-1955. LC 90-30117. (Illus.). 192p. 1990. 21.95 (0-87021-667-8) Naval Inst Pr.
— The War That Never Was. (Illus.). 368p. 1994. 19.95 (0-918339-28-6) Vandamere.
Palmer, Michael J., jt. auth. see Rains, Alvin L.
Palmer, Michael W. Levels of Constituent Structure in New Testament Greek. LC 93-30457. (Studies in Biblical Greek: Vol. 4). 160p. (C). 1995. pap. text ed. 24.95 (0-8204-2115-4) P Lang Pubs.
Palmer, Michele. Zoup Soup. LC 78-66342. (Illus.). (J). (ps-1). 1978. pap. 1.95 (0-932306-00-4) Rocking Horse.
Palmer, Michele, ed. A Mother Goose Feast: Rhymes & Recipes. LC 79-65819. (Illus.). (J). (ps-12). 1979. pap. 1.95 (0-932306-01-2) Rocking Horse.
— Rainy Day Rhymes: A Collection of Chants, Forecasts & Tales. LC 84-60412. (Illus.). 24p. (Orig.). (J). (gr. k up). 1984. pap. 2.95 (0-932306-02-0) Rocking Horse.
***Palmer, Mike.** Better Golf: The Systematic Way. LC 94-25147. Orig. Title: Advanced Systematic Golf. (Illus.). 160p. 1995. pap. 14.95 (0-8069-0980-3) Sterling.
— Systematic Golf: A Complete Golf Instruction Course. LC 92-38184. (Illus.). 160p. 1993. pap. 14.95 (0-8069-0329-5) Sterling.
Palmer, Millie. Conversations with the Soul. (Illus.). 44p. (Orig.). 1992. pap. text ed. 6.95 (1-56315-063-8) Sterling Hse.
Palmer, Monica B. Infection Control: A Policy & Procedure Manual. (Blue Book Ser.). (Illus.). 359p. 1984. pap. text ed. 35.95 (0-7216-7054-7) Saunders.
Palmer, Monte. Dilemmas of Political Development. 4th ed. LC 88-60934. 403p. 1989. pap. 29.00 (0-87581-331-3) Peacock Pubs.
Palmer, Monte, et al. The Egyptian Bureaucracy. 200p. 1988. 34.95x (0-8156-2455-7) Syracuse U Pr.
Palmer, Myles. New Wave Explosion. (Illus.). 128p. 1981. pap. 11.95 (0-906071-49-6, PR10987, Pub. by Proteus UK) Music Sales.
— Small Talk, Big Names: Forty Years of Rock Quotes 1953-1993. 192p. 1994. pap. 11.95 (1-85158-573-7, Pub. by Mnstream UK) Trafalgar.
Palmer, N. E. Bailment. cvi, 1056p. 1979. 148.50 (0-455-19610-9, Pub. by Law Bk Co) W W Gaunt.
***Palmer, Nancy S. & Tangel-Rodriguez, Ana.** When Your Ex Won't Pay: Getting Your Kids the Financial Support They Deserve. 176p. (Orig.). 1995. pap. 12.00 (0-89109-879-8) Pinon Press.
Palmer, Nettie. Nettie Palmer. Smith, Vivian, ed. LC 88-17606. (UQP Australian Authors Ser.). 548p. (Orig.). 1989. pap. text ed. 20.95 (0-7022-2130-9, Pub. by Univ Queensland Pr AT) Intl Spec Bk.
Palmer, Noel. Daily Notes to God. 112p. 1991. 7.00 (0-9631717-0-4) N Palmer.
***Palmer, Norma E.** San Luis Obispo County. rev. ed. Van Wingerden, Judy, ed. 144p. 1994. pap. 7.95 (1-56413-185-8) Auto Club.
— Santa Barbara & Ventura Counties. rev. ed. Van Wingerden, Judy, ed. 239p. 1994. pap. 7.95 (1-56413-186-6) Auto Club.
Palmer, Norman D. Elections & Political Development: The South Asian Experience. LC 75-4032. 350p. reprint ed. pap. 99.80 (0-317-42140-9, 2026212) Bks Demand.
— The New Regionalism in Asia & the Pacific. 228p. 1990. 39.95 (0-669-20971-6); pap. text ed. 19.95 (0-669-20972-4) Heath.
— The United States & India: The Dimensions of Influence. LC 84-8272. (Studies of Influence in International Relations). 316p. 1984. text ed. 49.95 (0-275-91240-X, C1240, Praeger Pubs); pap. text ed. 18.95 (0-275-91624-3, B1624, Praeger Pubs) Greenwood.
Palmer, Otto. Rudolf Steiner on His Book, The Philosophy of Freedom. Spock, Marjorie, tr. 1975. 6.95 (0-910142-68-8) Anthroposophic.
Palmer, P., tr. see Bloch, Ernst.
Palmer, P. E. Manual of Darkroom Technique: WHO Basic Radiological System. 25p. 1985. pap. 4.80 (92-4-154178-4) World Health.
Palmer, P. E., et al. Manual of Radiographic Interpretation for General Practitioners: WHO Basic Radiological System. (Illus.). 216p. 1985. pap. 13.80 (92-4-154177-6) World Health.
***Palmer, P. L.** Stability of Collisionless Stellar Systems: Mechanisms for the Dynamical Structure of Galaxies. LC 94-32551. (Astrophysics & Space Science Library: Vol. 185). 360p. (C). 1994. lib. bdg. 138.00 (0-7923-2455-2) Kluwer Ac.
Palmer, Paige. Alaska on Your Own - By Car! rev. ed. LC 88-31807. (Illus.). 64p. 1992. pap. 5.95 (0-87576-157-7) Pilot Bks.
— The Best of India. LC 86-25304. 196p. 1987. pap. 7.95 (0-87576-128-3) Pilot Bks.
— Budget Traveler's Guide to Great Off-Beat Vacations in the United States & Canada. LC 90-48747. 64p. (Orig.). 1991. pap. 4.95 (0-87576-149-6) Pilot Bks.
— Senior Citizen's Guide to Budget Travel in Europe. rev. ed. LC 82-441. 62p. 1993. pap. 5.95 (0-87576-173-9) Pilot Bks.
— Senior Citizen's Guide to Budget Travel in the United States & Canada. rev. ed. LC 83-3949. 61p. 1994. pap. 5.95 (0-87576-184-4) Pilot Bks.
— Senior Citizen's Ten Minutes a Day Fitness Plan. LC 83-17331. 40p. 1986. pap. 3.50 (0-87576-107-0) Pilot Bks.
— The Travel & Vacation Discount Guide. LC 86-30514. 64p. 1994. pap. 5.95 (0-87576-189-5) Pilot Bks.
Palmer, Pamela, jt. auth. see Dameron, J. Lasley.
Palmer, Parker J. The Active Life: A Spirituality of Work, Creativity, & Caring. LC 89-45932. 160p. 1992. pap. 5.00 (0-06-066459-2) Harper SF.
— The Active Life: Wisdom for Work, Creativity, & Caring. LC 91-55088. 160p. 1991. reprint ed. pap. 11.00 (0-06-066458-4) Harper SF.
— The Company of Strangers: Christians & the Renewal of America's Public Life. 169p. 1981. reprint ed. pap. 9.95 (0-8245-0601-4) Crossroad NY.
— In the Belly of a Paradox: The Thought of Thomas Merton. LC 78-71769. 1979. pap. 3.00 (0-87574-224-6) Pendle Hill.
— A Place Called Community. LC 77-75909. (Orig.). 1977. pap. 3.00 (0-87574-212-2) Pendle Hill.
— To Know As We Are Known: A Spirituality of Education. 144p. 1993. reprint ed. pap. 10.00 (0-06-066451-7) Harper SF.
Palmer, Parker J., et al, eds. Caring for the Commonweal: Education for Religious & Public Life. LC 89-78103. 272p. (C). 1990. 30.00 (0-86554-358-5, MUP-H286) Mercer Univ Pr.
Palmer, Pat. I Wish I Could Hold Your Hand: A Child's Guide to Grief & Loss. (Illus.). 32p. (J). (ps-6). 1994. pap. 6.95 (0-915166-82-8) Impact Pubs CA.
Palmer, Pat & Froehner, Melissa A. Teen Esteem: A Self-Direction Manual for Young Adults. LC 89-39305. 128p. (Orig.). 1989. pap. 7.95 (0-915166-66-6) Impact Pubs CA.
Palmer, Pati. Book of American Clocks. 19.95 (0-02-594590-4) Macmillan.
— Restitution, 4 vols., 1. 1978. 165.00 (0-316-69000-7) Little.
— Restitution, 4 vols., 2. 1978. 165.00 (0-316-69001-5) Little.
— Restitution, 4 vols., 3. 1978. 165.00 (0-316-69002-3) Little.
— Restitution, 4 vols., 4. 1978. 165.00 (0-316-69003-1) Little.
— Treasury of American Clocks. 21.95 (0-02-594580-7) Macmillan.
Palmer, Pati & Epler. Clinical Assessment Procedures in Physical Therapy. (Illus.). 390p. 1989. text ed. 42.95 (0-397-54807-9) Lippincott.
Palmer, Pati & Pletsch, Susan. Easy, Easier, Easiest Tailoring. rev. ed. LC 83-61672. 1983. pap. 8.95 (0-935278-09-5) Palmer-Pletsch.
— Mother Pletsch's Painless Sewing with Pretty Pati's Perfect Pattern Primer. (C). 1979. pap. 8.95 (0-935278-00-1) Palmer-Pletsch.
— Pants for Any Body. rev. ed. LC 82-61290. 128p. (Orig.). 1982. pap. 8.95 (0-935278-08-7) Palmer-Pletsch.
Palmer, Pati, jt. auth. see Brown, Gail.
Palmer, Pati, ed. see Cherry, Winky.
Palmer, Pati, jt. auth. see Price, Ann.
***Palmer, Pati, et al.** Creative Serging. 1995. pap. 8.95 (0-935278-12-5) Palmer-Pletsch.
— New Creative Serging Illustrated: The Complete Guide to Decorative Overlock Sewing. rev. ed. LC 93-38107. (Creative Machine Arts Ser.). (Illus.). 144p. 1993. pap. 18.95 (0-8019-8382-7) Chilton.
Palmer, Patricia. Liking Myself. LC 77-88185. (Illus.). 80p. (J). (gr. k-4). 1977. pap. 7.95 (0-915166-41-0) Impact Pubs CA.
— The Mouse, the Monster & Me. LC 77-88186. (Illus.). 80p. (Orig.). (J). (gr. 3-6). 1977. pap. 6.95 (0-915166-43-7) Impact Pubs CA.
Palmer, Patricia G. & Gerbeth-Jones, Susan. A Scanning Electron Microscope Survey of the Epidermis of East African Grasses, Vol. 4. LC 80-19201. (Smithsonian Contributions to Botany Ser.: No. 62). 124p. reprint ed. pap. 35.40 (0-317-55524-3, 2029551) Bks Demand.
Palmer, Patricia G., et al. A Scanning Electron Microscope Survey of the Epidermis of East African Grasses, Pt. 3. LC 80-19201. (Smithsonian Contributions to Botany Ser.: No. 55). 142p. reprint ed. pap. 40.50 (0-317-42001-1, 2025684) Bks Demand.
Palmer, Paul, jt. auth. see Wellman, Frank.
Palmer, Paul C., jt. auth. see O'Neil, A. W.
Palmer, Paul M. One Hundred Twenty-One Real Estate T. I. P. S. Techniques & Ideas on Purchasing & Selling. Lipstein, Sherman & Cockhill, Pat B., eds. 272p. (Orig.). 1985. pap. 12.95 (0-935679-01-4) Applied Pub MN.
Palmer, Paulina. Contemporary Women's Fiction: Narrative Practice & Feminist Theory. 232p. 1989. 32.50 (0-87805-396-4) U Pr of Miss.
Palmer, Pauline. Contemporary Lesbian Writing: Dreams, Desire, Difference. LC 93-2467. (Gender in Writing Ser.). 160p. 1994. 90.00 (0-335-09039-7, Open Univ Pr); pap. 27.50 (0-335-09038-9, Open Univ Pr) Taylor & Francis.
Palmer, Pete & Thom, John, eds. The Baseball Record Book. (Official Major League Baseball Bks.). (Illus.). 96p. (J). (gr. 3 up). 1991. pap. 5.95 (0-671-70444-3, Litl Simon S&S) S&S Childrens.
Palmer, Pete, jt. auth. see Clifton, Merritt.
Palmer, Pete, jt. auth. see Thorn, John.
Palmer, Pete, jt. ed. see Thorn, John.
Palmer, Peter, tr. see Brinkmann, Reinhold.
Palmer, Peter, tr. see Kropfinger, Klaus.
Palmer, Peter, tr. see Lukacs, Georg.
Palmer, Philip M. & More, Robert P. Sources of the Faust Tradition. LC 65-29231. (Studies in Comparative Literature: No. 35). 1969. reprint ed. lib. bdg. 75.00 (0-8383-0608-X) M S G Haskell Hse.
Palmer, Phobe. Entire Devotion to God. 1979. 3.99 (0-88019-021-3) Schmul Pub Co.
— Full Salvation. 1979. pap. 5.99 (0-88019-028-0) Schmul Pub Co.
Palmer, Phoebe. The Promise of the Father. pap. 12.99 (0-88019-099-X) Schmul Pub Co.
— The Way of Holines. 1988. pap. 9.99 (0-88019-233-X) Schmul Pub Co.
Palmer, Phyllis. Domesticity & Dirt: Housewives & Domestic Servants in the United States, 1920-1945. (Women in the Political Economy Ser.). 248p. 1990. 34.95 (0-87722-585-0); pap. 18.95 (0-87722-901-5) Temple U Pr.
Palmer, Princess, ed. see Beery, R., et al.
Palmer, Prudence T. & Palmer, T. J. St. Clements: The Chronicle of a Connecticut River Castle. (Illus.). 208p. (Orig.). 1992. pap. 25.00 (0-9634150-0-X) Paper Rock Pub.
Palmer Publications Staff, ed. see Faythines.
Palmer Publications Staff, ed. see Thompson, Walter C.
Palmer, R. A., jt. auth. see Ladd, M. F.
Palmer, R. A., jt. ed. see Ladd, M. F.
Palmer, R. B., ed. Chaucer's French Contemporaries: The Poetry - Poetics of Self & Tradition. LC 91-58148. (Georgia State Literary Studies: No. 10). 1992. 45.00 (0-404-63210-6) AMS Pr.
Palmer, R. Barton. Hollywood's Dark Cinema: The American Film Noir. (Twayne's Filmmakers Ser.). (Illus.). 200p. 1994. text ed. 26.95 (0-8057-9324-0, Pub. by Royal Botanic Garden UK); pap. 15.95 (0-8057-9335-6, Pub. by Royal Botanic Garden UK) Macmillan.
Palmer, R. Barton, ed. Guillaume de Machaut: Fonteinne Amoureuse. LC 93-1095. (Library of Medieval Literature). 360p. 1993. lib. bdg. 52.00 (0-8240-8781-X) Garland.
— Guillaume de Machaut: The Judgement of the King of Navarre (Le Jugement Dou Roy de Navarre) LC 88-3786. (Library of Medieval Literature). 284p. 1988. lib. bdg. 20.00 (0-8240-8638-4) Garland.
Palmer, R. Barton, ed. & tr. Guillaume de Machaut: Le Confort D'ami (Comfort for a Friend) LC 91-39839. (Library of Medieval Literature: Vol. 67A). 314p. 1992. 42.00 (0-8240-4032-5) Garland.
Palmer, R. E., jt. ed. see Beecroft, K. A.
Palmer, R. E., ed. see Library Association, Conference Staff.
Palmer, R. H. Foundry Techniques for the Do It Your Selfer. (Illus.). 389p. 1991. reprint ed. 29.00 (1-877767-40-9); reprint ed. pap. 19.00 (1-877767-39-5) Univ Publng Hse.
Palmer, R. Heather, et al. Striving for Quality in Health Care: An Inquiry into Policy & Practice. LC 91-7024. 177p. 1991. pap. 30.00 (0-910701-69-5, 0904) Health Admin Pr.
Palmer, R. L. Anorexia Nervosa. 160p. 1981. mass mkt. 4.95 (0-14-022065-8, Penguin Bks) Viking Penguin.
— Anorexia Nervosa: A Guide for Sufferers & Their Families. 144p. 1989. pap. 11.95 (0-14-010034-2, Penguin Bks) Viking Penguin.
Palmer, R. R. The Improvement of Humanity: Education & the French Revolution. LC 84-15048. 360p. 1985. 49.50 (0-691-05434-7) Princeton U Pr.
— The School of the French Revolution: A Documentary History of the College of Louis-le-Grand & Its Director, Jean-Francois Champagne, 1762-1814. 1975. 49.50 (0-691-05229-8) Princeton U Pr.
Palmer, R. R., ed. The Two Tocquevilles, Father & Son: Herve & Alexis de Tocqueville on the Coming of the French Revolution. (Illus.). 264p. 1987. text ed. 39.50 (0-691-05495-9) Princeton U Pr.
***Palmer, R. R., tr.** The School of the French Revolution: A Documentary History of the College of Louis-le-Grand & Its Director, Jean-Francois Champagne, 1762-1814. LC 74-25625. Date not set. reprint ed. pap. 88.70 (0-7837-9412-6, 2060157) Bks Demand.
***Palmer, R. R. & Colton, Joel.** A History of the Modern World Vol. 1: To 1815. 8th ed. LC 94-26364. 1994. 25.00 (0-07-040829-7) McGraw.
— A History of the Modern World Vol. 1: To 1815, Vol. 2. 7th ed. 1992. pap. text ed. write for info. (0-07-048564-X) McGraw.
— A History of the Modern World Vol. 2: Since 1815. 8th ed. LC 94-26364. 1994. 25.00 (0-07-040830-0) McGraw.
— A History of the Modern World Vol. 2: Since 1815, Vol. 3. 7th ed. 1992. pap. text ed. write for info. (0-07-048565-8) McGraw.
Palmer, R. R. & Colton, Joel, eds. A History of the Modern World. 7th ed. 1991. 54.50 (0-679-41014-7) Knopf.
Palmer, R. R., tr. see Bergeron, Louis.
Palmer, R. R., tr. see Bertaud, Jean-Paul.
Palmer, Rachel. Love Beyond Desire. large type ed. (Romance Ser.). 496p. 1983. 15.95 (0-7089-0962-0) Ulverscroft.
***Palmer, Ralph.** Real Estate Principles & Practices. rev. ed. 375p. Date not set. pap. text ed. 28.00 (0-89787-928-7) Gorsuch Scarisbrick.
***Palmer, Ralph A. & Bailey, Joanne T.** Maryland Real Estate Principles. (Illus.). 480p. (C). 1995. pap. text ed. write for info. (0-89787-944-9) Gorsuch Scarisbrick.
***Palmer, Ralph A. & Fraser, Margaret.** Michigan Real Estate: Principles & Practices. (Illus.). 456p. (C). 1995. pap. text ed. write for info. (0-89787-943-0) Gorsuch Scarisbrick.
***Palmer, Ralph A. & Joseph, Joan.** Illinois Real Estate: Principles & Practices. 441p. 1993. pap. write for info. (0-89787-929-5) Gorsuch Scarisbrick.
Palmer, Ralph A., jt. auth. see Hagen, David A.
***Palmer, Ralph A., et al.** Maine Real Estate: Principles & Practices. 3rd ed. 340p. 1994. pap. 31.00 (0-89787-933-3) Gorsuch Scarisbrick.
Palmer, Ralph S. Handbook of North American Birds: Condors & Raptors, Vol. 4, Pt. 1. LC 62-8259. 448p. (C). 1988. 45.00 (0-300-04059-8) Yale U Pr.
— Handbook of North American Birds: Condors & Raptors, Vol. 5, Pt. 2. LC 62-8259. (C). 1988. 45.00 (0-300-04060-1) Yale U Pr.
Palmer, Ransford W. Caribbean Dependence on the United States Economy. LC 78-19770. (Praeger Special Studies). 192p. 1979. text ed. 38.95 (0-275-90406-7, C0406, Praeger Pubs) Greenwood.
— Contemporary Caribbean Migration to the U. S. LC 94-36254. (Immigrant Heritage of America Ser.). 1995. pap. 15.95 (0-8057-4546-7, Twayne) Macmillan.
— Contemporary Caribbean Migration to the U. S. The Economics of West Indian Migration to America. LC 94-36254. (Immigrant Heritage of America Ser.). 1995. lib. bdg. 26.95x (0-8057-8431-4, Twayne) Macmillan.
Palmer, Ransford W., ed. In Search of a Better Life: Perspectives on Migration from the Caribbean. LC 89-29658. (Illus.). 200p. 1990. text ed. 45.00 (0-275-93409-8, C3409, Greenwood Pr) Greenwood.

An Asterisk (*) at the beginning of an entry indicates that the title is appearing in BIP for the first time.

Palmer, Raymond M. Wolf Road. LC 90-71989. 73p. (Orig.). 1992. pap. 4.50 (*1-56002-049-0*) Aegina Pr.

Palmer, Richard. English for Students. 250p. 1991. pap. 11.95 (*0-419-14640-7*, A5606, E & FN Spon) Routledge Chapman & Hall.

Palmer, Richard & Pope, Chris. Brain Train: Studying for Success. 230p. 1984. pap. 12.95 (*0-419-13110-8*, NO. 9185, E & FN Spon) Routledge Chapman & Hall.

Palmer, Richard E. Hermeneutics: Interpretation Theory in Schleiermacher, Dilthey, Heidegger, & Gadamer. LC 68-54885. (Studies in Phenomenology & Existential Philosophy). 283p. 1969. pap. 14.95 (*0-8101-0459-8*) Northwestern U Pr.

Palmer, Richard E., jt. ed. see Michelfelder, Diane P.

Palmer, Richard F. & Butler, Karl D. Brigham Young: The New York Years. Alexander, Thomas G. & Christy, Howard A., eds. (Charles Redd Monographs in Western History: No. 14). (Illus.). 106p. 1982. 9.95 (*0-941214-07-9*, Signature Bks) C Redd Ctr.

Palmer, Richard F. & Roehl, Harvey N. Railroads in Early Postcards, Vol. 1: Upstate New York. LC 89-70721. (Illus.). 112p. (Orig.). 1990. pap. 11.95 (*0-911572-87-2*) Vestal.

Palmer, Richard H. The Critics' Canon: Standards of Theatrical Reviewing in America. LC 88-5671. (Contributions in Drama & Theatre Studies: No. 26). 195p. 1988. text ed. 49.95 (*0-313-26211-X*, PAO/, Greenwood Pr) Greenwood.

— The Lighting Art: The Aesthetics of Stage Lighting Design. 2nd ed. LC 93-225. 1993. text ed. 50.00 (*0-13-501081-0*) P-H.

— Tragedy & Tragic Theory: An Analytical Guide. LC 91-46861. 252p. 1992. text ed. 59.95 (*0-313-28203-X*, PTT, Greenwood Pr) Greenwood.

Palmer, Richard P. Case Studies in Library Computer Systems. LC 73-17008. (Bowker Series in Problem-Centered Approaches to Librianship). 230p. reprint ed. pap. 65.60 (*0-317-42309-6*, 2023052) Bks Demand.

Palmer, Richard P. & Varnet, Harvey. How to Manage Information: A Systems Approach. (Illus.). 152p. 1990. pap. 29.50 (*0-89774-603-1*) Oryx Pr.

Palmer, Rob. Baja Mar; the Shallow Seas: A Diver's Guide to the Underwater World of the Bahamas. 160p. (C). 1990. 125.00 (*0-907151-82-5*, Pub. by IMMEL Pubng UK) St Mut.

— Undersea Britain. 160p. (C). 1990. 125.00 (*0-907151-52-3*, Pub. by IMMEL Pubng UK) St Mut.

Palmer, Robert. Deep Blues. 1982. pap. 11.95 (*0-14-006223-8*, Penguin Bks) Viking Penguin.

— Rock & Roll: An Unruly History. LC 95-13367. 1995. 40.00 (*0-517-70050-6*, Harmony) Crown Pub Group.

— A Tale of Two Cities: Memphis Rock, New Orleans Roll. (I.S.A.M. Monographs: No. 12). (Illus.). 38p. 1979. pap. 8.00 (*0-914678-12-4*) Inst Am Music.

— Which Father Are You Following? 64p. 1987. pap. text ed. 1.95 (*0-937580-11-2*) LeSEA Pub Co.

***Palmer, Robert, ed.** Underwater Expeditions. (C). 1990. 30.00x (*0-907649-31-9*, Pub. by Expedit Advisory Centre UK) St Mut.

Palmer, Robert, ed. see Smith, Clyde L.

Palmer, Robert B., tr. see Otto, Walter F.

Palmer, Robert C. The County Courts of Medieval England, 1150-1350. LC 81-47939. 379p. reprint ed. pap. 108.10 (*0-7837-0094-6*, 2040371) Bks Demand.

— English Law in the Age of the Black Death, 1348-1381: A Transformation of Governance & Law. LC 93-592. (Studies in Legal History). xvi, 452p. 1993. 49.95 (*0-8078-2099-7*) U of NC Pr.

— The Whilton Dispute, 1264-1380. LC 83-13858. 1984. 47.50x (*0-691-05404-5*) Princeton U Pr.

— The Whilton Dispute, 1264-1380: A Social-Legal Study of Dispute Settlement in Medieval England. LC 83-13858. 318p. reprint ed. pap. 90.70 (*0-8357-7073-7*, 2033377) Bks Demand.

Palmer, Robert E. King & the Comitium: A Study of Rome's Oldest Public Document. 63p. (Orig.). 1969. pap. text ed. 42.50 (*3-515-00260-X*) Coronet Bks.

— Roman Religion & Roman Empire: Five Essays. LC 73-89289. (Haney Foundation Ser.: No. 15). 303p. reprint ed. 86.40 (*0-685-07759-4*, 2055281) Bks Demand.

— Studies of the Northern Campus Martius in Ancient Rome. LC 90-55217. (Transactions Ser.: Vol. 80, Pt. 2). (Illus.). 64p. (C). 1990. pap. 12.00 (*0-87169-802-1*, T802-PAR) Am Philos.

***Palmer, Robert G. & Troeh, Frederick R.** Introductory Soil Science Laboratory Manual. 3rd ed. 112p. (C). 1995. pap. text ed. 21.95 (*0-19-509436-0*) OUP.

Palmer, Robert R. Age of the Democratic Revolution: A Political History of Europe & America, 1760-1800. Incl. Vol. I. Challenge. 1959. pap. 19.95 (*0-691-00569-9*); Vol II. Struggle. 1964. pap. 19.95 (*0-691-00570-2*, 192); write for info. (*0-318-55348-1*) Princeton U Pr.

— Historical Atlas of the World. 1994. pap. 8.95 (*0-528-17756-7*) Rand McNally.

— History of the Modern World. 8th ed. 1995. 65.00 (*0-679-43253-1*) Knopf.

— The Improvement of Humanity: Education & the French. LC 84-15048. Date not set. reprint ed. pap. 101.50 (*0-7837-9411-8*, 2060156) Bks Demand.

— Twelve Who Ruled. 1941. 65.00x (*0-691-05119-4*); pap. 16.95x (*0-691-00761-6*) Princeton U Pr.

Palmer, Robert R., ed. & tr. From Jacobin to Liberal: Marc-Antoine Jullien, 1775-1848. LC 92-46872. 272p. 1993. text ed. 39.50 (*0-691-03299-8*) Princeton U Pr.

Palmer, Robert R., tr. see Lefebvre, Georges.

Palmer, Robert S. Courts Without Justice: How a Conspiracy to Fabricate a Million Dollar Bankruptcy Was Aided by the Chief Justice, U. S. Attorney General, & the California State Bar. LC 92-13044. (Illus.). 1992. 24.95 (*0-9632867-0-6*) Focus Bk CA.

Palmer, Robin. Dictionary of Mythical Places. 15.95 (*0-8488-1122-4*) Amereon Ltd.

Palmer, Robin & Birch, Isobel. Zimbabwe: A Land Divided. (C). 1992. pap. text ed. 50.00 (*0-85598-178-4*, Pub. by Oxfam Pubns UK) St Mut.

Palmer, Rodney, jt. auth. see Belford, Ros.

Palmer, Roger C. The Bar Code Book: Reading, Printing & Specification of Bar Code Symbols. 253p. 1990. 35.00 (*0-685-45326-X*); pap. 24.95 (*0-685-45327-8*) Helmers Pub.

— The Bar Code Book: Reading, Printing, & Specification of Bar Code Symbols. 2nd ed. (Illus.). 320p. 1991. pap. 29.95 (*0-911261-06-0*) Helmers Pub.

— Online Reference & Information Retrieval. 2nd ed. 250p. 1987. lib. bdg. 26.50 (*0-87287-536-9*) Libs Unl.

Palmer, Roger F., ed. see Clinical Pharmacology Symposium Staff.

Palmer, Ronald D. & Reckford, Thomas J. Building ASEAN: Twenty Years of Southeast Asian Cooperation. LC 87-14609. (Washington Papers: No. 127). 162p. 1987. text ed. 45.00 (*0-275-92815-2*, C2815, Praeger Pubs); pap. text ed. 14.95 (*0-275-92816-0*, B2816, Praeger Pubs) Greenwood.

Palmer, Rose, jt. auth. see Rosen, Steve.

Palmer, Ross, jt. auth. see Schlichter, Carol.

Palmer, Roy. The Sound of History: Songs & Social Comment. (Illus.). 384p. 1988. 55.00 (*0-19-215890-2*) OUP.

— Strike the Bell. LC 78-1282. (Resources of Music Ser.: No. 18). (Illus.). 1978. pap. 9.95 (*0-521-21921-3*) Cambridge U Pr.

Palmer, Roy, ed. The English Country Songbook. (Illus.). 256p. 1986. pap. 12.95 (*0-7119-0968-7*, AM) Omnibus NY.

Palmer, S. Blue Whales. (Whale Discovery Library). (Illus.). 24p. (J). (gr. k-5). 1988. lib. bdg. 11.94 (*0-86592-480-5*) Rourke Corp.

— Delfines (Dolphins) (Spanish Language Books, Set 4: Mamifero Marino (Sea Mammals)). (J). 1991. 8.95 (*0-86592-849-5*) Rourke Enter.

— Dolphins. (Sea Mammal Discovery Library). (Illus.). (J). (gr. k-5). 1989. 8.95 (*0-685-58619-7*); lib. bdg. 11.94 (*0-86592-363-9*) Rourke Corp.

— Fin Whales. (Whale Discovery Library). (Illus.). 24p. (J). (gr. k-5). 1988. 8.95 (*0-685-58331-7*); lib. bdg. 11.94 (*0-86592-479-1*) Rourke Corp.

— Gray Whales. (Whale Discovery Library). (Illus.). 24p. (J). (gr. k-5). 1988. 8.95 (*0-685-58327-9*); lib. bdg. 11.94 (*0-86592-477-5*) Rourke Corp.

— Great White Sharks. (Shark Discovery Library). (Illus.). 24p. (J). (gr. k-5). 1988. 8.95 (*0-685-58314-7*); lib. bdg. 11.94 (*0-86592-462-7*) Rourke Corp.

— Hammerhead Sharks. (Shark Discovery Library). (Illus.). 24p. (J). (gr. k-5). 1988. 8.95 (*0-685-67680-3*); lib. bdg. 11.94 (*0-86592-461-9*) Rourke Corp.

— Humpback Whales. (Whale Discovery Library). (Illus.). 24p. (J). (gr. k-5). 1988. 8.95 (*0-685-58329-5*); lib. bdg. 11.94 (*0-86592-478-3*) Rourke Corp.

— Killer Whales. (Whale Discovery Library). (Illus.). 24p. (J). (gr. k-5). 1988. 8.95 (*0-685-58330-9*); lib. bdg. 11.94 (*0-86592-481-3*) Rourke Corp.

— Leones Marinos (Sea Lions) (Spanish Language Books, Set 4: Mamifero Marino (Sea Mammals)). (J). 1991. 8.95 (*0-86592-674-3*) Rourke Enter.

— Mako Sharks. (Shark Discovery Library). (Illus.). 24p. (J). (gr. k-5). 1989. 8.95 (*0-685-58310-4*); lib. bdg. 11.94 (*0-86592-458-9*) Rourke Corp.

— Manatees. (Sea Mammal Discovery Library). (Illus.). 24p. (J). (gr. k-5). 1989. 8.95 (*0-685-58620-0*); lib. bdg. 11.94 (*0-86592-359-0*) Rourke Corp.

— Manaties (Manatees) (Spanish Language Books, Set 4: Mamifero Marino (Sea Mammals)). (J). 1991. 8.95 (*0-86592-672-7*) Rourke Enter.

— Morsas (Walruses) (Spanish Language Books, Set 4: Mamifero Marino (Sea Mammals)). (J). 1991. 8.95 (*0-86592-689-1*) Rourke Enter.

— Narwhals. (Whale Discovery Library). (Illus.). 24p. (J). (gr. k-5). 1988. 8.95 (*0-685-58328-7*); lib. bdg. 11.94 (*0-86592-476-7*) Rourke Corp.

— Nurse Sharks. (Shark Discovery Library). (Illus.). 24p. (J). (gr. k-5). 1988. 8.95 (*0-685-58311-2*); lib. bdg. 11.94 (*0-86592-459-7*) Rourke Corp.

— Nutrias de Mar (Sea Otters) (Spanish Language Books, Set 4: Mamifero Marino (Sea Mammals)). (J). 1991. 8.95 (*0-86592-681-6*) Rourke Enter.

— Osos Polares (Polar Bears) (Spanish Language Books, Set 4: Mamifero Marino (Sea Mammals)). (J). 1991. 8.95 (*0-86592-673-5*) Rourke Enter.

— Polar Bears. (Sea Mammal Discovery Library). (Illus.). 24p. (J). (gr. k-5). 1989. lib. bdg. 11.94 (*0-86592-360-4*) Rourke Corp.

— Sea Lions. (Sea Mammal Discovery Library). (Illus.). 24p. (J). (gr. k-5). 1989. lib. bdg. 11.94 (*0-86592-362-0*); lib. bdg. 8.95 (*0-685-58622-7*) Rourke Corp.

— Sea Otters. (Sea Mammal Discovery Library). (Illus.). 24p. (J). (gr. k-5). 1989. lib. bdg. 11.94 (*0-86592-361-2*) Rourke Corp.

— Spanish Language Books, Set 4: Mamifero Marino (Sea Mammals), 6 bks. (J). 1991. 53.70 (*0-86592-835-5*) Rourke Enter.

— Thresher Sharks. (Shark Discovery Library). (Illus.). 24p. (J). (gr. k-5). 1988. lib. bdg. 11.94 (*0-86592-460-0*); lib. bdg. 8.95 (*0-685-58313-9*) Rourke Corp.

— Walruses. (Sea Mammal Discovery Library). (Illus.). 24p. (J). (gr. k-5). 1989. lib. bdg. 11.94 (*0-86592-358-2*); lib. bdg. 8.95 (*0-685-58621-9*) Rourke Corp.

— Whale Sharks. (Shark Discovery Library). (Illus.). 24p. (J). (gr. k-5). 1988. lib. bdg. 11.94 (*0-86592-463-5*); lib. bdg. 8.95 (*0-685-58309-0*) Rourke Corp.

Palmer, S. & Humphrey, J. A. Deviant Behavior: Patterns, Sources, & Control. LC 88-23264. (Illus.). 312p. 1990. 45.00 (*0-306-43285-4*, Plenum Pr) Plenum.

Palmer, S. A., et al. Metal-Cyanide Containing Wastes: Treatment Technologies. LC 88-17878. (Pollution Technology Review Ser.: No. 158). (Illus.). 721p. 1989. 74.00 (*0-8155-1179-5*) Noyes.

Palmer, Sarah. Sea Mammal Discovery Library, 6 bks., Reading Level 2. (Illus.). 144p. (J). (gr. k-5). 1989. lib. bdg. 53.70 (*0-685-58759-2*) Rourke Corp.

— Sea Mammal Discovery Library, 6 bks., Set, Reading Level 2. (Illus.). 144p. (J). (gr. k-5). 1989. Set. lib. bdg. 71.60 (*0-86592-357-4*) Rourke Corp.

— World of Sharks, 6 vols. (J). 1990. 7.99 (*0-517-02747-X*) Random Hse Value.

— World of Whales, 6 vols. (J). 1990. 7.99 (*0-517-02746-1*) Random Hse Value.

Palmer, Scott. Access 2 for Dummies. 1994. pap. 19.95 (*1-56884-090-X*) IDG Bks.

— British Film Actors' Credits, 1895-1987. LC 87-31098. 935p. 1988. lib. bdg. 82.00x (*0-89950-316-0*) McFarland & Co.

— DBase for DOS for Dummies. 1994. pap. 19.95 (*1-56884-188-4*) IDG Bks.

— DBase for Windows for Dummies. 1994. pap. 19.95 (*1-56884-179-5*) IDG Bks.

— The Films of Agatha Christie. (Illus.). 192p. 1994. 29.95 (*0-7134-7205-7*, Pub. by Batsford UK) Trafalgar.

— Jack the Ripper: A Reference Guide. LC 95-1498. 1995. write for info. (*0-8108-2996-7*) Scarecrow.

— A Who's Who of Australian & New Zealand Film Actors: The Sound Era. LC 87-32215. 179p. 1988. 22.50 (*0-8108-2090-0*) Scarecrow.

— Windows Programming with MicroSoft Visual C Plus Plus. 1994. pap. 35.00 (*0-679-79136-1*) Random.

Palmer, Scott & Rock. Teach Yourself Paradox for Windows in Twenty-One Days. 800p. 1993. 24.95 (*0-672-30351-5*) Sams.

Palmer, Scott, jt. auth. see Kaufeld, John.

Palmer, Scott D. Domine Turbo Pascal 6. 597p. 1992. pap. text ed. write for info. (*968-6346-38-4*, Pub. by Ventura Ediciones MX) Computer & Tech.

— Mastering Turbo Pascal 6. LC 90-71957. 712p. 1991. 27.95 (*0-89588-675-8*) Sybex.

— Programming in Borland Pascal. LC 92-63264. 922p. 1993. 34.95 (*0-7821-1151-3*) Sybex.

Palmer, Scott D., jt. auth. see Tigner, Mike.

Palmer, Shirley, jt. auth. see Palmer, Stuart.

Palmer, Spencer J. Confucian Rituals in Korea. LC 84-256844. (Religions of Asia Ser.: No. 3). 274p. pap. 78.10 (*0-8357-4423-X*, 2037253) Bks Demand.

Palmer, Spencer J., ed. Mormons & Muslims. 11.95 (*0-88494-483-2*) Bookcraft Inc.

Palmer, Stan. Skiing Fit: The Fitness Guide Specifically Designed for Skiers. (Illus.). 96p. 1991. pap. 19.95 (*1-85223-126-2*, Pub. by Crowood Pr UK) Trafalgar.

Palmer, Stanley. Police & Protest in England & Ireland, 1780-1850. 736p. 1988. 79.95 (*0-521-30216-1*) Cambridge U Pr.

Palmer, Stanley & Reinhartz, Dennis, eds. Essays on the History of North American Discovery & Exploration. LC 87-10166. (Walter Prescott Webb Memorial Lectures: No. 21). (Illus.). 160p. 1988. 17.50 (*0-89096-373-8*) Tex A&M Univ Pr.

Palmer, Stanley, jt. ed. see Wolfskill, George.

Palmer, Stephen. Human Ontology & Rationality. (Series in Philosophy). 236p. 1992. 63.95 (*1-85628-235-X*, Pub. by Avebury Pub UK) Ashgate Pub Co.

***Palmer, Stephen & Dryden, Windy.** Counselling for Stress Problems. (Counselling in Practice Ser.). 240p. 1995. text ed. 44.00 (*0-8039-8862-1*); pap. text ed. 19.95 (*0-8039-8863-X*) Sage.

Palmer, Stephen & Wilkinson, Theon, eds. Pensions - Involving the Members: A Review & Assessment of Current Practice. (C). 1983. 39.00 (*0-85292-324-4*) St Mut.

Palmer, Stephen E., Jr. & King, Robert. Yugoslav Communism & the Macedonian Question. 247p. 1971. 69.50 (*0-208-00821-7*) Elliots Bks.

Palmer, Stephen P. & Lingley, William S., Jr. An Assessment of the Oil & Gas Potential of the Washington Outer Continental Shelf. (Washington State & Offshore Oil & Gas Ser.). (Illus.). 83p. (Orig.). 1989. pap. 45.00 (*0-934539-09-X*, WSG89-2) Wash Sea Grant.

Palmer, Steve & Birkett, Ken, eds. The Change Agent: Pay's New Role. 150p. (C). 1989. 65.00 (*0-85292-416-X*) St Mut.

Palmer, Stuart. Deviance & Conformity. 1969. 21.95 (*0-317-18409-1*) NCUP.

— The Green Ace. (Black Dagger Crime Ser.). 176p. 1989. reprint ed. text ed. 16.50 (*0-86220-758-4*, Black Dagger) Chivers N Amer.

— Murder on the Blackboard. LC 92-70420. 185p. 1992. reprint ed. pap. 5.95 (*1-55882-124-4*, Lib Crime Classics) Intl Polygonics.

— Murder on Wheels. 307p. pap. 6.95 (*1-55882-113-9*) Intl Polygonics.

— The Penguin Pool Murder. LC 90-84274. 182p. 1990. reprint ed. pap. 7.95 (*1-55882-076-0*) Intl Polygonics.

— Puzzle of the Pepper Tree. Date not set. pap. 6.95 (*1-55882-137-6*) Intl Polygonics.

— Understanding Other People. 208p. 1977. pap. 1.75 (*0-449-30815-4*, Prem) Fawcett.

— The Violent Society. 1972. pap. 21.95 (*0-8084-0353-2*) NCUP.

Palmer, Stuart & Palmer, Shirley. Glass Engraving: Drill Techniques. (Illus.). 192p. 1990. 65.00 (*0-7134-6008-3*, Pub. by Batsford UK) Trafalgar.

Palmer, Stuart & Rice, Craig. People vs Withers & Malone. LC 90-84275. 254p. 1990. reprint ed. pap. 7.95 (*1-55882-077-9*) Intl Polygonics.

Palmer, Susan J. Moon Sisters, Krishna Mothers, Rajneesh Lovers: Women's Roles in New Religions. LC 94-17364. (Women & Gender in North American Religion Ser.). (Illus.). 208p. 1994. 24.95 (*0-8156-0297-9*) Syracuse U Pr.

— Rajneesh Papers: Studies in a New Religious Movement. (C). 1993. text ed. 24.00 (*81-208-1080-5*, Pub. by Motilal Banarsidass II) S Asia.

Palmer, T. J., jt. auth. see Palmer, Prudence T.

Palmer, T. Norman, ed. Alcoholism: A Molecular Perspective. (NATO ASI Series A, Life Sciences: Vol. 206). (Illus.). 358p. 1991. 95.00 (*0-306-43926-3*, Plenum Pr) Plenum.

— The Molecular Pathology of Alcoholism. (Molecular Medicine Ser.). (Illus.). 312p. 1991. pap. 39.95 (*0-19-261903-9*) OUP.

Palmer, T. S. Chronology of the Death Valley Region in California, 1849-1949, & Place Names of the Death Valley Region in California & Nevada, 1845-1947. LC 88-34098. (West Coast Studies: No. 3). 102p. (C). 1989. reprint ed. lib. bdg. 25.00x (*0-89370-837-2*); reprint ed. pap. 15.00x (*0-89370-937-9*) Borgo Pr.

— Index Generum Mammalium: A List of the Genera & Families of Mammals. 1968. reprint ed. 120.00 (*3-7682-0535-5*) Lubrecht & Cramer.

Palmer, Ted. A Profile of Correctional Effectiveness & New Directions for Research. LC 93-24925. (New Directions in Crime & Justice Studies). 339p. 1994. 59.50 (*0-7914-1909-6*); pap. 19.95 (*0-7914-1910-X*) State U NY Pr.

— The Re-Emergence of Correctional Intervention: Developments Through the 1980s & Prospects for the Future. 200p. (C). 1992. 44.00 (*0-8039-4537-X*); pap. 19.95 (*0-8039-4538-8*) Sage.

Palmer, Thelma. The Sacred Round. LC 85-18006. (Illus.). 68p. (Orig.). 1985. pap. 7.95 (*0-9615580-0-8*) Island Pubs WA.

— The Sacred Round. 2nd ed. (Illus.). 68p. (Orig.). 1988. pap. 7.95 (*0-9615580-3-2*) Island Pubs WA.

Palmer, Thelma, jt. auth. see Moss, Peter.

Palmer, Thelma, jt. auth. see Tursi, John.

Palmer, Theodore W. Banach Albegras & the General Theory of Algebras, Vol. 1: Algebras & Banach Algebras. (Encyclopedia of Mathematics & Its Applications Ser.: No. 49). 800p. (C). 1994. 94.95 (*0-521-36637-2*) Cambridge U Pr.

Palmer, Thomas. An Essay of the Meanes How to Make Our Travailes More Profitable. LC 72-6020. (English Experience Ser.: No. 546). 140p. 1973. reprint ed. 30.00 (*90-221-0546-6*) Walter J Johnson.

— Reflections. 1986. pap. 7.50 (*0-317-60613-1*) Latitudes Pr.

— The Transfer. 448p. 1984. pap. 3.50 (*0-345-30996-0*) Ballantine.

Palmer, Tim. Lifelines: The Case for River Conservation. LC 94-8951. 200p. 1994. text ed. 35.00 (*1-55963-219-4*); pap. 16.95 (*1-55963-220-8*) Island Pr.

— Rivers of Pennsylvania. LC 79-15378. (Keystone Bks.). (Illus.). 208p. 1980. pap. 14.50 (*0-271-00246-8*) Pa St U Pr.

— The Sierra Nevada: A Mountain Journey. LC 88-13019. (Illus.). 334p. 1988. 31.95 (*0-933280-54-8*); pap. 15.95 (*0-933280-53-X*) Island Pr.

— The Snake River: Window to the West. LC 91-8585. (Illus.). 320p. (Orig.). 1991. 34.95 (*0-933280-59-9*); pap. 17.95 (*0-933280-60-2*) Island Pr.

— Stanislaus, the Struggle for a River. LC 81-43692. (Illus.). 311p. reprint ed. pap. 88.70 (*0-7837-4696-2*, 2044443) Bks Demand.

— The Wild & Scenic Rivers of America. LC 92-32660. (Illus.). 339p. 1993. text ed. 45.00 (*1-55963-145-7*); pap. 22.95 (*1-55963-144-9*) Island Pr.

— Yosemite: The Promise of Wildness. LC 94-21789. (Illus.). 120p. 1994. 29.95 (*0-939666-77-4*) Yosemite Assn.

— Youghiogheny: Appalachian River. LC 84-2301. (Illus.). 350p. 1984. 35.00 (*0-8229-3495-7*); pap. 19.95 (*0-8229-5361-7*) U of Pittsburgh Pr.

Palmer, Tim, ed. California's Threatened Environment: Restoring the Dream. LC 92-30944. (Illus.). 306p. 1992. 29.95 (*1-55963-173-2*); pap. 16.95 (*1-55963-172-4*) Island Pr.

***Palmer, Tobias.** Angel in My House. 1994. 12.00 (*0-06-251194-7*) Harper SF.

Palmer, Todd S. Rhino & Mouse. LC 93-33299. 40p. (J). (ps-3). 1994. 12.99 (*0-8037-1322-3*); lib. bdg. 12.89 (*0-8037-1323-1*) Dial Bks Young.

Palmer, Tom. La Grande Compagnie de Colonisation: Documents of a New Plan. 10.00 (*0-914206-20-6*) Clark U Pr.

— Helena: The Town & the People. (Illus.). 96p. (Orig.). 1987. 14.95 (*0-938314-41-6*); pap. 9.95 (*0-938314-32-7*) Am Wrld Geog.

Palmer, Tom G. Philanthropy in Central & Eastern Europe: A Resource Book for Foundations, Corporations, & Individuals. 114p. (Orig.). 1991. pap. 6.95 (*0-89617-300-3*) Instit Humane.

Palmer, Tony. Menuhin: A Family Portrait. 1992. 19.95 (*0-571-16582-6*) Faber & Faber.

Palmer, Vance. Legend of the Nineties. 2nd ed. 1966. pap. 14.95 (*0-522-83690-9*) Intl Spec Bk.

Palmer, Vernon V. The Paths to Privity: The History of Third Party Beneficiary Contracts at English Law. LC 92-29490. 250p. 1993. 69.95 (*1-880921-16-2*); pap. 44.95 (*1-880921-15-4*) Austin & Winfield.

Palmer, Veronica, jt. auth. see Palmer, Alan.

Palmer, Virginia A., jt. auth. see Buck, Diane M.

Palmer, W. John, ed. see Onishi, Katsuhito.

Palmer, W. Robert. How to Understand the Bible. 2nd ed. 118p. (C). 1980. reprint ed. pap. 6.99 (*0-89900-140-8*) College Pr Pub.

Palmer, W. S., tr. see Bergson, Henri.

P Q

An Asterisk (*) at the beginning of an entry indicates that the title is appearing in BIP for the first time.

Palmer, Walter L., ed. Gastric Irradiation in Peptic Ulcer. LC 73-87306. 173p. reprint ed. pap. 49.40 (0-317-07775-9, 2019981) Bks Demand.

Palmer, Wendy. Intuitive Body: Aikido As a Clairsentient Practice. LC 94-6799. (Illus.). 152p. (Orig.). 1994. pap. 12.95 (1-55643-171-6) North Atlantic.

Palmer, Willard A., ed. J. S. Bach: An Introduction to His Keyboard Music. (Alfred Masterwork Editions Ser.). 64p. (Orig.). 1991. pap. text ed. 7.95 (0-88284-253-6, 638) Alfred Pub.

— J. S. Bach: Inventions & Sinfonias. (Alfred Masterwork Editions Ser.). 114p. (Orig.). (C). 1991. pap. text ed. 13. 95 (0-88284-626-4, 606C) Alfred Pub.

— J. S. Bach: Selections from Anna Magdalena's Notebook. (Alfred Masterwork Editions Ser.). 48p. (Orig.). 1992. pap. text ed. 5.95 (0-88284-262-5, 605) Alfred Pub.

— J. S. Bach: The Well-Tempered Clavier. (Alfred Masterwork Editions Ser.). 220p. (Orig.). 1981. pap. text ed. 22.00 (0-88284-120-3, 2098) Alfred Pub.

— W.A. Mozart: An Introduction to His Keyboard Works. (Alfred Masterwork Editions Ser.). 64p. (Orig.). 1992. pap. text ed. 7.95 (0-88284-254-4, 664) Alfred Pub.

Palmer, Willard A., ed. see Bach, J. S.

Palmer, Willard A., et al. Alfred's Basic Adult Piano Course: Lesson Book, Level One. (Alfred's Basic Piano Library). 96p. (Orig.). 1983. pap. text ed. 8.50 (0-88284-616-7, 2236) Alfred Pub.

— Lesson Book: Level One. (Basic Adult Piano Library). 64p. (Orig.). 1984. pap. text ed. 7.95 (0-88284-635-3, 2462) Alfred Pub.

— Lesson Book: Level Three. (Basic Adult Piano Library). 96p. (Orig.). 1987. pap. text ed. 8.95 (0-88284-636-1, 2263) Alfred Pub.

— Lesson Book: Level Two. (Basic Adult Piano Library). 96p. (Orig.). 1984. pap. text ed. 8.50 (0-88284-634-5, 2461) Alfred Pub.

— Theory Piano Book: Level Two. (Basic Adult Piano Library). 48p. (Orig.). 1985. pap. text ed. 6.95 (0-88284-637-X, 2118) Alfred Pub.

Palmer, William. The Political Career of Oliver St. John, 1637-1649. LC 91-51138. 160p. (C). 1992. 32.50 (0-87413-453-6) U Delaware Pr.

— The Problem of Ireland in Tudor Foreign Policy, 1485-1603. 192p. (C). 1995. text ed. 53.00 (0-85115-562-6) Boydell & Brewer.

Palmer, William G. Experimental Inorganic Chemistry. 612p. reprint ed. pap. 174.50 (0-317-27574-7, 2024514) Bks Demand.

— Experimental Physical Chemistry. 2nd ed. LC 42-10734. 333p. reprint ed. pap. 95.00 (0-317-08952-8, 2050760) Bks Demand.

Palmer, William J. The Detective & Mr. Dickens. 1992. reprint ed. mass mkt. 3.99 (0-345-37471-1) Ballantine.

— The Films of the Eighties: A Social History. LC 92-33720. (Illus.). 376p. (C). 1995. reprint ed. pap. 18.95x (0-8093-1837-7) S Ill U Pr.

— The Highwayman & Mr. Dickens. 1993. reprint ed. mass mkt. 4.99 (0-345-38252-8) Ballantine.

Palmer, William J., ed. The Highwayman & Mr. Dickens: A Secret Victorian Journal, Attributed to Wilkie Collins. 288p. 1992. text ed. 18.95 (0-312-08207-X) St Martin.

Palmer, William J. & Selvin, Paul P. The Development of Law in California. 1983. write for info. (0-318-58310-0) West Pub.

Palmer, William J., jt. auth. see Coombs, William E.

Palmer, William M. Cambridge Castle. rev. ed. (Cambridge Town, Gown & County Ser.: Vol. 5). (Illus.). 1976. pap. 4.95 (0-902675-67-2) Oleander Pr.

— Poisonous Snakes of North Carolina. (Illus.). 22p. (YA). (gr. 6-12). 1974. pap. 2.00 (0-917134-00-1) NC Natl Sci.

Palmer, William M. & Braswell, Alvin L. Reptiles of North Carolina. LC 94-5711. (Illus.). Date not set. write for info. (0-8078-2158-6) U of NC Pr.

Palmer, William R. Why the North Star Stands Still. LC 57-11627. (Illus.). 118p. 1978. pap. 2.95 (0-915630-12-5) Zion.

Palmer, Winthrop. Like a Passing Shadow. (Poetry Edition Ser.: No. 1). 1968. pap. 3.95 (0-911660-09-7) Yankee Peddler.

Palmeri & Milligan. French for Reading Knowledge. 1969. 33.95 (0-442-24121-6) Heinle & Heinle.

Palmeri, Frank. Critical Essays on Jonathan Swift. (Critical Essays on British Literature Ser.). 200p. 1993. lib. bdg. 40.00 (0-685-60864-6, Twayne) Macmillan.

— Satire in Narrative: Petronius, Swift, Gibbon, Melville, & Pynchon. 195p. 1990. text ed. 30.00x (0-292-77631-4) U of Tex Pr.

Palmeri, Frank, ed. Critical Essays on Jonathan Swift. LC 92-42993. (Critical Essays on British Literature Ser.). 288p. 1993. text ed. 45.00 (0-7838-0003-7) G K Hall.

Palmerio, Giovanni. Perspectives on Economic Thought. (Luiss Ser.). 222p. 1991. 55.95 (1-85521-189-0, Pub. by Dartmth Pub UK) Ashgate Pub Co.

***Palmerson, James N.** Population - Control, Density, Dynamics, Growth, & Surveillance: Index of New Information with Authors, Subjects & Bibliography. rev. ed. LC 94-34027. 136p. 1994. 49.50 (0-7883-0382-1); pap. 44.50 (0-7883-0383-X) ABBE Pubs Assn.

Palmerston, H. J. New Whig Guide. 1974. reprint ed. 20.00 (0-527-69350-2) Periodicals Srv.

— Opinions & Policy. 1974. reprint ed. 39.00 (0-527-69360-X) Periodicals Srv.

Palmerston, Henry T. The Palmerston Papers, Gladstone & Palmerston. Guedalla, Philip, ed. LC 73-157351. (Select Bibliographies Reprint Ser.). 1977. reprint ed. 28.95 (0-8369-5812-8) Ayer.

Palmes, J. C. Architectural Drawing in the R. I. B. A. pap. 7.95 (0-685-20562-2) Transatl Arts.

Palmes, J. C., ed. see Fletcher, Banister.

Palmes, James, tr. see Breton, Genevieve.

Palmes, James, tr. see Burckhardt, Jacob.

Palmetto Cabinet Staff. A Taste of South Carolina. (Illus.). 345p. 1985. reprint ed. spiral bd. 14.95 (0-87844-064-X) Sandlapper Pub Co.

Palmgen, V. & Hartmann, E. Svensk-Dansk Ordbog: Swedish-Danish Dictionary. 251p. (DAN & SWE.). 1978. 39.95 (0-8288-5273-1, M1287) Fr & Eur.

Palmier, L. H. Social Status & Power in Java. (London School of Economics Monographs on Social Anthropology: No. 20). 174p. (C). 1969. pap. 16.95 (0-485-19620-4, Pub. by Athlone Pr UK) Humanities.

Palmier, Leslie. The Control of Bureaucratic Corruption: Case Studies in Asia. 292p. 1985. 37.95 (0-317-38650-6, Pub. by Allied Pubs II) Asia Bk Corp.

Palmier, Leslie, ed. Understanding Indonesia. LC 84-21133. 128p. 1985. text ed. 46.95 (0-566-00784-3) Ashgate Pub Co.

Palmieri, Anthony F. Elmer Rice: A Playwright's Vision of America. LC 78-75182. 248p. 1970. 33.50 (0-8386-2333-6) Fairleigh Dickinson.

Palmieri, Deborah A. Russia & the NIS in the World Economy: East-West Investment, Financing & Trade. LC 93-48213. 200p. 1994. text ed. 55.00 (0-275-94531-6, Praeger Pubs) Greenwood.

Palmieri, Deborah A., ed. The U. S. S. R. & the World Economy: Challenges for the Global Integration of Soviet Markets under Perestroika. LC 91-44452. 208p. 1992. text ed. 55.00 (0-275-94015-2, C4015, Praeger Pubs) Greenwood.

Palmieri, Deborah A., jt. auth. see Adelman, Jonathan R.

Palmieri, Dennis. Counselor. LC 93-87613. 416p. (Orig.). 1994. pap. 28.00 (0-9646354-1-0) Epiphany CA.

Palmieri, F. & Quagliariello, E., eds. Molecular Basis of Biomembrane Transport: Proceedings of the International Symposium on Molecular Basis of Biomembrane Transport, Bari, Italy, 30 May to 2 June. (Developments in Bioenergetics & Biomembranes Ser.: No. 7). 284p. 1988. 92.50 (0-444-81028-5, Excerpta Medica) Elsevier.

Palmieri, F., jt. ed. see Quagliariello, E.

Palmieri, F., et al, eds. Vectoral Reactions in Electron & Ion Transport in Michondria & Bacteria. (Developments in Bioenergetics & Biomembranes Ser.: Vol. 5). 430p. 1981. 121.75 (0-444-80372-6) Elsevier.

Palmieri, Francesco. Lab Manual EE266. 83p. (C). 1993. student ed 14.69 (1-56870-045-8) RonJon Pub.

Palmieri, Frank, jt. auth. see Thurman, John.

Palmieri, John, et al. Pennsylvania Juvenile Delinquency & Deprivation. 340p. 1994. text ed. 42.50 (0-317-03823-0) Bisel Co.

Palmieri, Margaret W., jt. ed. see Palmieri, Robert.

Palmieri, Marina. Daydreams. 224p. (Orig.). 1991. pap. 2.95 (1-878702-53-X, Kismet) Meteor Pub.

***Palmieri, Patricia A.** In Adamless Eden: The Community of Women Faculty at Wellesley. LC 94-31662. 1995. 35. 00 (0-300-05529-3) Yale U Pr.

Palmieri, Robert. Piano Information Guide: An Aid to Research. (Music Research & Information Guides Ser.). (Illus.). 329p. 1989. 51.00 (0-8240-7778-4) Garland.

Palmieri, Robert & Palmieri, Margaret W., eds. Encyclopedia of Keyboard Instruments, Vol. 1: The Piano. LC 93-4742. 536p. 1993. 95.00 (0-8240-5685-X, H1131) Garland.

Pal'mina, N. P., jt. ed. see Kurganov, B. I.

Palmiotto, Michael J. Criminal Investigation. LC 92-14264. 425p. 1994. 38.95 (0-8304-1180-1); teacher ed write for info. (0-8304-1404-5); write for info. (0-8304-1399-5) Nelson-Hall.

— Critical Issues in Criminal Investigation. 130p. 1984. pap. 9.95 (0-932930-64-6) Pilgrimage Inc.

— Critical Issues in Criminal Investigation. 2nd ed. 280p. 1988. pap. 19.95 (0-932930-81-6) Anderson Pub Co.

Palmisano, Donald J. & Mang, Herbert J., Jr. Informed Consent: A Survival Guide. 47p. (C). Date not set. Generic version. 15.00 (0-940019-00-0); South Carolina Version. 15.00 (0-940019-01-9) Invictus LA.

Palmisano, Joseph M., jt. ed. see Morgan, Bradley J.

Palmisano, Tony. Restoration to Fellowship. 32p. 1988. pap. 0.75 (0-88144-126-0) Christian Pub.

Palmiter, Larry & Wheeling, Terry. SUNCODE Documentation & User's Manual. 235p. 1981. ring bd. 35.00 (0-934478-29-5) Ecotope.

Palmiter, Larry, ed. see Straub, Davis.

Palmo, Artis, ed. Career Development: Contemporary Readings. LC 77-2721. (Illus.). 367p. (C). 1977. text ed. 36.50 (0-8422-5270-3) Irvington.

Palmo, Artis J. & Weikel, William J., eds. Foundations of Mental Health Counseling. (Illus.). 414p. (C). 1986. 67. 95 (0-398-05234-4) C C Thomas.

— Foundations of Mental Health Counseling. (Illus.). 414p. 1986. pap. 37.95 (0-398-06312-5) C C Thomas.

Palmonari, Augusto, jt. auth. see Doise, Willem.

Palmonari, C., jt. ed. see Meriani, S.

Palmore, Erdman. Ageism: Negative & Positive. LC 90-9775. (Adulthood & Aging Ser.: Vol. 25). 232p. 1990. 29.95 (0-8261-7000-5) Springer Pub.

— Facts on Aging Quiz. (Adulthood & Aging Ser.). 176p. (C). 1988. 25.95 (0-8261-5770-X) Springer Pub.

— The Honorable Elders: A Cross-Cultural Analysis of Aging in Japan. LC 75-13808. xii, 148p. 1975. pap. 13. 95 (0-8223-0453-8) Duke.

— Retirement: Causes & Consequences. LC 84-16057. 375p. 1985. 28.95 (0-8261-4720-8) Springer Pub.

— Social Patterns in Normal Aging: Findings from the Duke Longitudinal Studies. LC 81-9800. xii, 135p. 1981. 26.95 (0-8223-0458-9) Duke.

Palmore, Erdman, ed. Normal Aging 1: Reports from the Duke Longitudinal Study, 1955-1969. LC 74-132028. xxiv, 431p. 1970. 41.95 (0-8223-0238-1) Duke.

— Normal Aging 2: Reports from the Duke Longitudinal Study, 1970-1973. LC 74-132028. xix, 316p. 1974. 41.95 (0-8223-0311-6) Duke.

Palmore, Erdman & Maeda, Daisaku. Honorable Elders Revisited. LC 85-16138. (Illus.). xix, 136p. 1985. 27.00 (0-8223-0261-6); pap. 14.95 (0-8223-0263-2) Duke.

Palmore, Erdman, et al, eds. Normal Aging 3: Reports from the Duke Longitudinal Studies, 1975-84. LC 85-1598. (Illus.). xx, 468p. (C). 1985. 41.95 (0-8223-0624-7) Duke.

Palmore, Erdman B., ed. Developments & Research on Aging. LC 92-25737. 456p. 1993. text ed. 85.00 (0-313-27785-0, PDV, Greenwood Pr) Greenwood.

— Handbook on the Aged in the United States. LC 84-4463. (Illus.). xxix, 458p. 1984. text ed. 105.00 (0-313-23721-2, PHA/, Greenwood Pr) Greenwood.

— International Handbook on Aging: Contemporary Developments & Research. LC 78-73802. (Illus.). xviii, 529p. 1980. text ed. 59.95 (0-313-20890-5, PIH/, Greenwood Pr) Greenwood.

Palmore, James A. & Gardner, Robert W. Measuring Mortality, Fertility, & Natural Increase: A Self-Teaching Guide to Elementary Measures. LC 82-24171. xi, 140p. (Orig.). 1983. pap. text ed. 6.00 (0-86638-004-3) EW Ctr HI.

— Measuring Mortality, Fertility, & Natural Increase: A Self-Teaching Guide to Elementary Measures. rev. ed. 1994. pap. 15.00 (0-86638-165-1) EW Ctr HI.

Palmore, James A., et al. Family Planning Accessibility & Adoption: The Korean Population Policy & Program Evaluation Study. LC 88-3761. (Papers of the East-West Population Institute: No. 108). xii, 125p. 1987. 3.00 (0-86638-106-6) EW Ctr HI.

Palmore, John S. & Eades, Ronald W. Kentucky Instructions to Juries, Vol. 2. rev. ed. Booth, Robert A., ed. 400p. 1989. text ed. 85.00 (0-87084-510-1) Anderson Pub Co.

Palmore, Phyllis & Andre, Nevin. Small Appliance Repair. Schuler, Charles A., ed. LC 79-19186. (Basic Skills in Electricity & Electronics Ser.). (Illus.). 192p. (gr. 9-12). 1980. text ed. 26.96 (0-07-048361-2) McGraw.

Palmos, Frank, ed. see Ninh, Bao.

Palmour, Hayne, III, jt. ed. see Kriegel, W. W., III.

Palmour, Hayne, III, ed. see Research Conference on Structure & Property of Engineering Materials Staff.

Palmour, Jody. On Moral Character: A Practical Guide to Aristotle's Virtues & Vices. 350p. (Orig.). 1987. 24.95 (0-9616203-1-5); pap. 13.95 (0-9616203-0-7) Archon Inst Leader Dev.

Palmour, Vernon E., et al, comps. A Study of the Characteristics, Costs & Magnitude of Interlibrary Loans in Academic Libraries. LC 70-39344. 127p. 1972. text ed. 42.95 (0-8371-6340-4, PIL/); pap. 8.50 (0-685-02011-8) Greenwood.

Palmquist, Bradley, ed. see Volunteers in Asia Staff.

Palmquist, Joe, ed. see Odell, Michael E.

Palmquist, John. Minnesota Connection. (SPA.). 3.95 (84-7228-495-6, 360430, Pub. by Edit Clie SP) TSELF.

Palmquist, John C., ed. Wisconsin's Door Peninsula: A Natural History. (Illus.). 196p. (Orig.). 1989. pap. 10.95 (0-929682-00-9) Perin Pr.

Palmquist, M. K., tr. see Maffesoli, Michel.

Palmquist, Peter, ed. The Daguerreian Annual, 1992. 264p. 1992. pap. 30.00 (1-881186-92-X) Daguerreian.

— Photography in the West II. (Illus.). 132p. 1989. pap. 15. 00 (0-318-41434-1) Sunflower U Pr.

Palmquist, Peter, ed. see Rudisill, Richard.

Palmquist, Peter, et al. Silver Shadows: A Directory & History of Early Photography in Chico & the Twelve Counties of Northern California. LC 92-73662. 84p. 1993. pap. 24.95 (0-9634512-0-0) Chico Mus Assn.

***Palmquist, Peter E.** A Bibliography of Writings by & about Women in Photography, 1850-1990. 2nd ed. 332p. 1995. reprint ed. lib. bdg. 57.00x (0-8095-5956-0) Borgo Pr.

— Shadowcatchers: A Directory of Women in California Photography, 2 vols., Vol. 1, Before 1901. 1991. reprint ed. lib. bdg. 67.00 (0-8095-5950-1) Borgo Pr.

— Shadowcatchers: A Directory of Women in California Photography, 2 vols., Vol. 2, 1901-1920. 1991. reprint ed. 77.00 (0-8095-5951-X) Borgo Pr.

— With Nature's Children: Emma B. Freeman, (1880-1928) 134p. 1991. reprint ed. lib. bdg. 37.00x (0-8095-5955-2) Borgo Pr.

Palmquist, Peter E., ed. Camera Fiends & Kodak Girls I - Fifty Selections by & about Women in Photography. LC 89-61496. (Illus.). 272p. (Orig.). 1989. pap. text ed. 14. 90 (1-877675-00-8) Midmarch Arts-WAN.

— Camera Fiends & Kodak Girls II - Sixty Selections by & about Women in Photography 1855-1965. LC 93-81153. 362p. (Orig.). 1995. pap. 18.00 (1-877675-15-6) Midmarch Arts-WAN.

— The Daguerreian Annual, 1991. 264p. 1991. pap. 30.00 (1-881186-91-1) Daguerreian.

— The Daguerreian Annual 1993. (Illus.). 288p. (Orig.). 1993. pap. 30.00 (1-881186-93-8) Daguerreian.

— The Danguerreian Annual, 1990. 202p. 1990. pap. 30.00 (1-881186-90-3) Daguerreian.

— Photography in the West. (Illus.). 116p. 1987. pap. 15.00 (0-89745-102-3) Sunflower U Pr.

Palmquist, Peter E. & Irvine, Jack, intros. In the Redwoods' Realm: Humboldt County, California. viii, 120p. 1991. reprint ed. lib. bdg. 47.00x (0-8095-5952-8) Borgo Pr.

Palmquist, Roland E. Electrical Course for Apprentices & Journeymen. 3rd ed. 480p. 1988. text ed. 22.00 (0-02-594550-5) Macmillan.

— Guide to the Nineteen Ninety National Electrical Code. 664p. 1990. text ed. 24.95 (0-02-594565-3, Audel) Macmillan.

— Guide to the 1993 National Electrical Code. 609p. 1993. pap. 25.00 (0-02-077761-2) Macmillan.

— House Wiring. 7th ed. 272p. 1991. text ed. 22.95 (0-02-594692-7) Macmillan.

— Questions & Answers for Electricians Examinations. 8th ed. 1984. 12.95 (0-672-23399-1, Audel) Macmillan.

Palmquist, Stephen R. Kant's System of Perspectives & Architectonic Interpretation of the Critical Philosophy. LC 92-33937. 490p. (C). 1992. lib. bdg. 57.50 (0-8191-8927-8) U Pr of Amer.

Palmquist, Vicki L. Grandma's Better Than Gourmet Cooking. (Illus.). 54p. (Orig.). 1989. pap. 3.95 (0-9623686-0-1) Castalia MN.

Palmrich, Adolf, jt. auth. see Gitsch, Eduard.

***Palms, Roger.** Celebrate Life after 50. 1995. pap. 9.99 (1-56476-453-2, 6-3453, Victor Books) SP Pubns.

Palms, Roger C. Bible Readings on Hope. LC 87-17565. (Bible Readings Ser.). 112p. (Orig.). 1987. pap. 5.99 (0-8066-2275-X, 10-0694, Augsburg) Augsburg Fortress.

— Enjoying the Closeness of God. 1989. 14.95 (0-89066-171-5) World Wide Pubs.

Palo Alto Historical Association Staff & Winslow, Ward. Palo Alto: A Centennial History. LC 93-85698. (Illus.). 352p. 1993. write for info. (0-9638098-3-0) Palo Alto Hist.

Palo Alto Pre-School Staff, jt. auth. see Jackins, Tim.

Palo Pinto County Historical Commission. History of Palo Pinto County Texas. (Illus.). 698p. 1986. 57.50 (0-88107-070-X) Curtis Media.

Palo, R. Thomas & Robbins, Charles T. Plant Defenses Against Mammalian Herbivory. 192p. 1991. 115.00 (0-8493-6550-3, SB292) CRC Pr.

***Paloczi, Katalin.** Clinical Applications of Immunophenotypic Analysis. LC 94-32881. (Medical Intelligence Unit). 1994. 89.95 (1-57059-194-6) R G Landes.

Paloian, Ranata, tr. see Wadham, Mary M.

Palomar, Joyce D. Title Insurance Law. LC 93-50657. (Real Property-Zoning Ser.). 1994. ring bd. 135.00 (0-87632-989-X) Clark Boardman Callaghan.

***Palomares, Susanna & Schilling, Dianne.** Life Skills for Teens. (Illus.). 91p. (Orig.). (YA). (gr. 7-12). Date not set. pap. text ed. 24.95 (1-56499-024-9) Innerchoice Pub.

Palomares, Susanna, jt. auth. see Schuster, Sandy.

Palomba, Rossella, jt. ed. see Morrs, Hein.

***Palombo, Bernadette J.** Academic Professionalism in Law Enforcement. LC 94-47477. (Current Issues in Criminal Justice Ser.: Vol. 11). 296p. 1995. 44.00 (0-8153-1863-4, SS998) Garland.

Palombo, Ruth D., ed. see Massachusetts General Hospital Department of Dietetics Staff.

Palomo, Jose. Recollection of Olden Days. (Educational Ser.: No. 13). (Illus.). 175p. (C). 1992. 9.95 (1-878453-11-4) Univ Guam MAR Ctr.

Palonsky, Stuart B. Nine Hundred Shows a Year. 288p. 1986. pap. text ed. write for info. (0-07-554645-0) McGraw.

Palos, Monika, tr. see Lendvai, Erno.

Palossy, L., et al. Earth Walls. 336p. 1993. text ed. 105.00 (0-13-223876-4) P-H.

***Palotas, Emil.** Machtpolitik & Wirtschaftsinteressen: Der Balkan & Rubland in der Osterreichischungarischen Aubenpolitik, 1878-1895. 400p. (GER.). 1995. 60.00 (963-05-6817-9, Pub. by A K HU) Intl Spec Bk.

Palotta, Jerry. The Icky Bug Alphabet Book. (Jerry Pallotta's Alphabet Bks.). (Illus.). 32p. (J). (ps-3). 1989. 14.95 (0-88106-456-4); lib. bdg. 15.88 (0-88106-676-1); pap. 6.95 (0-88106-450-5) Charlesbridge Pub.

Palotta, Joseph L. The Robot Psychiatrist. 603p. 1981. pap. 29.95 (0-9604852-0-1) Revelation Hse.

— Success over Stress. 184p. 1990. pap. 6.95 (0-9604852-3-6) Revelation Hse.

— That Your Joy Might Be Full. 247p. 1981. pap. 6.95 (0-9604852-1-X) Revelation Hse.

— True Riches. 319p. (Orig.). 1985. pap. 8.95 (0-9604852-2-8) Revelation Hse.

Palou, Francisco. Historical Memoirs of New California, 4 vols., Set. (BCL1 - United States Local History Ser.). 1991. reprint ed. lib. bdg. 300.00 (0-7812-6340-9) Rprt Serv.

— Life & Apostolic Labors of the Venerable Father Junipero Serra, Founder of the Franciscan Missions of California. 1992. reprint ed. lib. bdg. 75.00 (0-7812-5073-0) Rprt Serv.

Palou, Pedro A., tr. see Watt, Donley.

Palous, J., et al, eds. Evolution of Interstellar Matter & Dynamics of Galaxies. (Illus.). 450p. (C). 1992. 69.95 (0-521-41984-0) Cambridge U Pr.

Palow, jt. auth. see Jordan.

Palrewala, Rajni, jt. ed. see Dube, Leela.

Pals, Daniel L. The Victorian "Lives" of Jesus. Hayes, John H., ed. LC 82-81018. (Monograph Series in Religion: Vol. VII). 223p. 1982. write for info. (0-911536-95-7) Trinity U Pr.

Pals, Ellen. Create a Celebration. (Illus.). 368p. (J). (gr. 4-12). Date not set. pap. 22.95 (0-9627721-0-0) Aladdin CO.

***Pals, Jean K., et al, eds.** Basic Cardiac Life Support (BCLS) "Quick Reference Guide" in Algorithm Format. 2nd ed. 36p. 1994. pap. text ed. 3.50 (1-887272-03-8) Amer Med Pub.

Palsberg, Jens & Schwartzbach, Michael J. Object-Oriented Type Systems. LC 93-29412. 1994. text ed. 49.95 (0-471-94128-X) Wiley.

Palsson, Erik K. Niels Stensen: Scientist & Saint. De Murville, M. Couve, tr. 76p. (Orig.). 1988. pap. text ed. 7.95 (1-85390-077-X, Pub. by Veritas Pubns IE) Irish Bks Media.

— Niels Stensen: Scientist & Saint. 75p. (Orig.). 1989. pap. 22.00 (0-685-65148-7, Pub. by Veritas IE) St Mut.

Palsson, Gisli. Coastal Economies, Cultural Accounts: Human Ecology & Icelandic Discourse. LC 90-29067. 224p. 1991. text ed. 69.95 (0-7190-3543-0, Pub. by Manchester Univ Pr UK) St Martin.

An Asterisk (*) at the beginning of an entry indicates that the title is appearing in BIP for the first time.

P Q

— Coastal Economies, Cultural Accounts: Human Ecology & Icelandic Discourse. (Themes in Social Anthropology Ser.). 224p. 1994. text ed. 29.95 (*0-7190-4386-7*, Pub. by Manchester Univ Pr UK) St Martin.

***Palsson, Gisli & Durrenberger, E. Paul, eds.** Images of Contemporary Iceland: Everyday Lives & Global Contexts. (Illus.). 272p. 1996. text ed. 29.95x (*0-87745-528-7*) U of Iowa Pr.

Palsson, Gisli, jt. ed. see Durrenberger, E. P.

Palsson, Gisli, et al, eds. Beyond Boundaries: Understanding, Translation & Anthropological Discourse. LC 92-10102. (Explorations in Anthropology Ser.). (Illus.). 272p. 1993. 54.95 (*0-85496-813-X*) Berg Pubs.

P'alsson, Herman & Edwards, Paul. Knytlinga Saga: History of the Kings of Denmark. 198p. (Orig.). 1986. pap. text ed. 34.50 (*91-7492-571-7*) Coronet Bks.

Palsson, Hermann. Eyrbyggja Saga. Edwards, Paul, tr. LC 72-97525. (Unesco Collection of Representative Works, Series of Translations from the Literature of the Union of Soviet Socialist Republics). (Illus.). 198p. reprint ed. pap. 56.50 (*0-8357-8128-3*, 2034055) Bks Demand.

— Gautrek's Saga, & Other Medieval Tales. LC 68-16829. 156p. reprint ed. pap. 44.50 (*0-317-08221-3*, 2050246) Bks Demand.

— Gongu-Hrolfs Saga. (UNESCO Collection of Representative Works. Icelandic Ser.). 128p. reprint ed. pap. 36.50 (*0-8357-6364-1*, 2035718) Bks Demand.

— Hrolf Gautreksson, a Viking Romance. LC 73-185728. 149p. reprint ed. pap. 42.50 (*0-8357-4163-X*, 2036937) Bks Demand.

Palsson, Hermann, tr. Hrafnkel's Saga. (Classics Ser.). 1971. mass mkt. 9.95 (*0-14-044238-3*, Penguin Classics) Viking Penguin.

Palsson, Hermann & Edwards, Paul, trs. Egil's Saga. 1977. mass mkt. 10.95 (*0-14-044321-5*, Penguin Classics) Viking Penguin.

— Eyrbyggja Saga. 192p. 1989. pap. 8.95 (*0-14-044530-7*, Penguin Classics) Viking Penguin.

— The Orkneyinga Saga. (Classics Ser.). 256p. 1981. mass mkt. 8.95 (*0-14-044383-5*, Penguin Classics) Viking Penguin.

— Seven Viking Romances. (Classics Ser.). 304p. 1986. pap. 8.95 (*0-14-044474-2*, Penguin Classics) Viking Penguin.

Palsson, Hermann, jt. tr. see Fox, Denton.

Palsson, Hermann, jt. tr. see Magnusson, Magnus.

Palsson, Lennart. Marriage in Comparative Conflict of Laws. 464p. 1981. lib. bdg. 186.50 (*90-247-2548-8*) Kluwer Ac.

Palsson, S. H., jt. ed. see Edwards, Paul.

Palsson, S. H., tr. see Edwards, Paul & Palsson, S. H., eds.

Palstra. Telex English. 64p. (C). 1990. pap. text ed. 10.00 (*0-13-902826-9*) P-H.

Paltauf, F., jt. ed. see Ceve, G.

***Palter, D. C. & Kaoro Horiuchi.** Kinki Japanese: A Guide to the Kansai Region-Its Culture & Dialects. (Illus.). 152p. (Orig.). (ENG & JPN.). 1995. pap. 9.95 (*0-8048-2017-1*) C E Tuttle.

Palter, Robert, jt. auth. see Basalla, George.

Palti, Yoram, jt. ed. see Rosen, Michael R.

Paltin, D. M. The Parents' Hyperactivity Handbook: Helping the Fidgety Child. LC 92-44171. (Illus.). 305p. (C). 1993. 27.50 (*0-306-44465-8*, Plenum Insight) Plenum.

Paltock, Robert. Life & Adventures of Peter Wilkins. LC 73-13261. (Classics of Science Fiction Ser.). (Illus.). 370p. 1974. reprint ed. 15.25 (*0-88355-115-2*) Hyperion Conn.

— Peter Wilkins. Bentley, Christopher, ed. (World's Classics Ser.). (Illus.). 430p. 1990. pap. 8.95 (*0-19-282704-9*) OUP.

Paltro, Piera. Angel of God. Daughters of St. Paul Staff, tr. (Illus.). 14p. (Orig.). (J). (ps-1). 1981. pap. 2.50 (*0-8198-0739-7*, CH0031P) Pauline Bks.

— Eternal Rest: A Prayer for People Who Have Died. Daughters of St. Paul Staff, tr. (Illus.). 15p. (Orig.). (J). (gr. k-3). 1992. pap. 2.50 (*0-8198-2332-5*) Pauline Bks.

— Glory to the Father. Daughters of St. Paul Staff, tr. (Illus.). 24p. (Orig.). (J). (ps up). 1987. pap. 2.50 (*0-8198-3043-7*, CH0227) Pauline Bks.

— Hail, Holy Queen. Daughters of St. Paul Staff, tr. (Illus.). 16p. (Orig.). (J). (gr. k-3). 1992. pap. 2.50 (*0-8198-3365-7*) Pauline Bks.

— Hail Mary. Daughters of St. Paul Staff, tr. (Illus.). 24p. (J). (gr. k-3). 1992. pap. 2.50 (*0-8198-3316-9*) Pauline Bks.

— I Believe: The Profession of Faith or Creed. Daughters of St. Paul Staff, tr. (Illus.). 29p. (Orig.). (J). (gr. k-3). 1992. pap. 2.50 (*0-8198-3664-8*) Pauline Bks.

— My Mass. Daughters of St. Paul Staff, tr. (Illus.). 31p. (Orig.). (J). (gr. k-3). 1992. pap. 2.50 (*0-8198-4765-8*) Pauline Bks.

— Our Father. Daughters of St. Paul Staff, tr. (Illus.). 24p. (Orig.). (J). (ps-1). 1991. pap. 2.50 (*0-8198-5416-6*, CH0416P) Pauline Bks.

Paltrowitz, Donna, jt. auth. see Paltrowitz, Stuart.

Paltrowitz, Stuart & Paltrowitz, Donna. Content Area Reading Skills-Competency Canada: Main Idea. (Illus.). (J). (gr. 4). 1987. pap. text ed. 3.25 (*0-89525-853-6*) Ed Activities.

— Content Area Reading Skills-Competency Mexico: Locating Details. (Illus.). (J). (gr. 4). 1987. pap. text ed. 3.25 (*0-89525-854-4*) Ed Activities.

— Content Area Reading Skills-Competency U. S. History: Detecting Sequence. (Illus.). (J). (gr. 4). 1987. pap. text ed. 3.25 (*0-89525-856-0*) Ed Activities.

— Content Area Reading Skills U. S. Geography: Cause & Effect. (Illus.). (J). (gr. 4). 1987. pap. text ed. 3.25 (*0-89525-855-2*) Ed Activities.

Pal'tsev, A. A., jt. auth. see Krylov, V. I.

Paltsits, Victor H., ed. Minutes of the Commissioners for Detecting & Defeating Conspiracies in the State of New York, 3 vols. in 2, Set. LC 72-8752. (American Revolutionary Ser.). 1972. reprint ed. lib. bdg. 110.00 (*0-8398-1574-3*) Irvington.

— Washington's Farewell Address. LC 74-137706. (New York Public Library Publications in Reprint). (Illus.). 1971. reprint ed. 31.95 (*0-405-01742-1*) Ayer.

Paltsits, Victor H., ed. see Albany County Sessions Staff.

Paltsits, Victor H., ed. see Melville, Herman.

Paltz, Johannes von. Werke, Vol. 2. (Illus.). 504p. 1983. 176.95 (*3-11-004955-4*) De Gruyter.

Palubniak, Nancy, jt. auth. see Gross, Gay M.

Palucki, Michael. Chicago Bicycle Guidebook: Great Bicycle Riding Through Chicago's Lakefront Neighborhoods. LC 92-85158. (Illus.). (Orig.). 1993. pap. 9.95 (*0-9634829-7-1*) Pastime.

Paludan, Ann. The Chinese Spirit Road: The Classical Tradition of Stone Tomb Statuary. (Illus.). 256p. (C). 1991. text ed. 45.00 (*0-300-04597-2*) Yale U Pr.

— Chinese Tomb Figurines. (Images of Asia Ser.). (Illus.). 96p. 1994. 16.95 (*0-19-585817-4*) OUP.

— The Imperial Ming Tombs. LC 80-23829. (Illus.). 272p. (C). 1981. 48.00 (*0-300-02511-4*) Yale U Pr.

— The Ming Tombs. (Images of Asia Ser.). (Illus.). 94p. 1991. 13.95 (*0-19-585003-3*) OUP.

Paludan, Eve. The Romance Writer's Pink Pages: The Insider's Guide to Getting Your Romance Novel Published. 250p. (Orig.). 1993. pap. 12.95 (*1-55958-349-5*) Prima Pub.

— Romance Writer's Pink Pages, 1995-1996: The Insider's Guide to Getting Your Romance Novel. 1994. pap. 12.95 (*1-55958-581-1*) Prima Pub.

Paludan, Jacob. Jorgen Stein. Malmberg, Carl, tr. (Nordic Translation Ser.). 744p. 1977. pap. 6.00 (*0-299-04174-3*) U of Wis Pr.

***Paludan, Lis.** Crochet: History & Technique. Olsen, Jean & Fredricksson, Kristine, trs. 320p. 1995. 35.00 (*1-883010-09-8*) Interweave.

Paludan-Muller, Frederik. Adam Homo. Klass, Stephen, tr. LC 81-58568. (Illus.). 543p. (Orig.). (C). 1981. pap. 26.95 (*0-936726-02-4*) Twickenham Pr.

***Paludan, Phillip S.** A Covenant with Death: The Constitution, Law, & Equality in the Civil War Era. LC 74-34324. 325p. 1975. reprint ed. pap. 92.70 (*0-7837-8083-4*, 2047836) Bks Demand.

— The Presidency of Abraham Lincoln. LC 93-46830. (American Presidency Ser.). 408p. (Orig.). (C). 1995. 29.95 (*0-7006-0671-8*) U Pr of KS.

— The Presidency of Abraham Lincoln. LC 93-46830. (Orig.). (C). 1995. pap. 15.95 (*0-7006-0745-5*) U Pr of KS.

— Victims: A True Story of the Civil War. LC 81-2578. 160p. 1981. 21.00x (*0-87049-316-7*); pap. 11.00x (*0-87049-442-2*) U of Tenn Pr.

***Paludi, Michele A.** Exploring - Teaching the Psychology of Women: A Manual of Resources. 2nd ed. (Psychology of Women Ser.). 160p. (C). 1996. text ed. 59.50x (*0-7914-2771-4*); pap. 19.95x (*0-7914-2772-2*) State U NY Pr.

— Exploring--Teaching the Psychology of Women: A Manual of Resources. LC 88-6412. (SUNY Series, The Psychology of Women). 256p. (C). 1990. 64.50 (*0-7914-0515-X*); pap. 21.95 (*0-88706-872-3*) State U NY Pr.

— The Psychology of Women. 416p. (C). 1992. pap. text ed. write for info. (*0-697-11499-6*) Brown & Benchmark.

Paludi, Michele A., ed. Ivory Power: Sexual Harassment on Campus. LC 90-9478. (SUNY Series, the Psychology of Women). 335p. 1991. 69.50 (*0-7914-0457-9*); pap. 24.95 (*0-7914-0458-7*) State U NY Pr.

— Sexual Harassment on College Campuses: Abusing the Ivory Power. LC 95-15813. (Psychology of Women Ser.). 1996. write for info. (*0-7914-2801-X*); pap. write for info. (*0-7914-2802-8*) State U NY Pr.

Paludi, Michele A. & Barickman, Richard B. Academic & Workplace Sexual Harassment: A Resource Manual. LC 90-24364. (Psychology of Women Ser.). 235p. 1991. 59.50 (*0-7914-0829-9*); pap. 19.95 (*0-7914-0830-2*) State U NY Pr.

Paludi, Michele A. & Steuernagel, Gertrude A., eds. Foundations for a Feminist Restructuring of the Academic Disciplines. LC 89-15529. (Haworth Series on Women: No. 3). 276p. 1990. text ed. 39.95 (*0-86656-878-6*) Haworth Pr.

Paludi, Michele A., jt. ed. see Denmark, Florence L.

Paludi, Michele A., jt. auth. see Doyle, James A.

Paludi, Michele A., jt. auth. see Tedisco, James N.

Palumbo, Dennis, ed. Evaluating & Optimizing Public Policy. (C). 1980. pap. 12.00 (*0-918592-38-0*) Pol Studies.

Palumbo, Dennis & Calista, Donald, eds. Implementation: What We Have Learned & Still Need to Know. (Orig.). 1987. pap. 12.00 (*0-918592-96-8*) Pol Studies.

Palumbo, Dennis, jt. ed. see Nagel, Stuart.

Palumbo, Dennis G. Secret Nidan Techniques of Hakkoryu Jujutsu. (Illus.). 136p. 1988. pap. 14.00 (*0-87364-455-7*) Paladin Pr.

— The Secrets of Hakkoryu Jujutsu: Shodan Tactics. (Illus.). 144p. 1987. pap. 12.50 (*0-87364-422-0*) Paladin Pr.

Palumbo, Dennis J. Public Policy in America: Government in Action. 385p. (C). 1988. text ed. 32.00 (*0-15-573811-9*) HB Coll Pubs.

— Statistics in Political & Behavioral Science. 2nd ed. LC 76-15572. 469p. 1977. text ed. 51.50 (*0-231-04010-5*) Col U Pr.

Palumbo, Dennis J., ed. The Politics of Program Evaluation. 304p. (C). 1987. text ed. 44.00 (*0-8039-2736-3*); pap. text ed. 21.95 (*0-8039-2737-1*) Sage.

Palumbo, Dennis J. & Calista, Donald J., eds. Implementation & the Policy Process: Opening up the Black Box. LC 89-23640. (Contributions in Political Science Ser.: No. 252). 298p. 1990. text ed. 49.95 (*0-313-27283-2*, PIP/, Greenwood Pr) Greenwood.

Palumbo, Dennis J. & Maynard-Moody, Steven W. Contemporary Public Administration. 385p. (C). 1991. text ed. 47.95 (*0-8013-0033-9*, 75698) Longman.

Palumbo, Dennis J., jt. auth. see Hallett, Michael A.

Palumbo, Donald, ed. Eros in the Mind's Eye: Sexuality & the Fantastic in Art & Film. LC 85-24777. (Contributions to the Study of Science Fiction & Fantasy Ser.: No. 21). (Illus.). 318p. 1986. text ed. 59.95 (*0-313-24102-3*, PER/) Greenwood.

— Erotic Universe: Sexuality & Fantastic Literature. LC 85-14696. (Contributions to the Study of Science Fiction & Fantasy Ser.: No. 18). 323p. 1986. text ed. 49.95 (*0-313-24101-5*, PAE/, Greenwood Pr) Greenwood.

— Spectrum of the Fantastic: Selected Essays from the Sixth International Conference on the Fantastic in the Arts. LC 87-25216. (Contributions to the Study of Science Fiction & Fantasy Ser.: No. 31). (Illus.). 288p. 1988. text ed. 59.95 (*0-313-25502-4*, PPF/) Greenwood.

Palumbo, E. The Literary Use of Formulas in Guthlac II & Their Relation to Felix's Vita Sancti Guthlaci. (De Proprietatibus Litterarum, Ser. Practica: No. 37). 1977. 23.00 (*90-279-7695-3*) Mouton.

Palumbo, Eugene, tr. see Lopez Vigil, Maria.

Palumbo, Frank A. Major General George Henry Thomas: The Dependable General. LC 83-17261. (Illus.). 496p. 1983. 35.00 (*0-89029-311-2*) Morningside Bkshop.

Palumbo, Giorgio G. Catalogue of Radial Velocities of Galaxies. 596p. 1983. text ed. 207.00 (*0-677-06090-4*) Gordon & Breach.

Palumbo, Hayat. A Passion for Needlepoint. LC 91-52860. (Illus.). 160p. 1991. 37.50 (*0-8478-1425-4*) Rizzoli Intl.

Palumbo, Linda J. & Gaik, Frank J. Vocabulary for a New World. (Illus.). 384p. (Orig.). (C). 1992. pap. write for info. (*0-02-390567-0*) Macmillan.

Palumbo, Linda J., jt. auth. see Otte, George.

***Palumbo-Liu, David.** The Ethnic Canon: Histories, Institutions, & Interventions. 1995. text ed. 49.95 (*0-8166-2556-5*); pap. text ed. 19.95 (*0-8166-2557-3*) U of Minn Pr.

— The Poetics of Appropriation: The Literary Theory & Practice of Huang Tingjian. LC 92-22990. 280p. 1993. 39.50 (*0-8047-2126-2*) Stanford U Pr.

Palumbo, Michael. Human Rights: Meaning & History. Snyder, Louis, ed. LC 81-18592. (Anvil Ser.). 208p. (Orig.). (C). 1982. pap. text ed. 10.50 (*0-89874-259-5*) Krieger.

— The Palestinian Catastrophe. pap. 11.95 (*0-7043-0099-0*, Pub. by Quartet UK) Interlink Pub.

Palumbo, Michael & Shanahan, William O., eds. Nationalism: Essays in Honor of Louis L. Snyder. LC 81-6501. (Contributions in Political Science Ser.: No. 65). 232p. 1981. text ed. 55.00 (*0-313-23176-1*, PNA/, Greenwood Pr) Greenwood.

Palumbo, Nancy. A Birthday Present for Ree-Ree: Un Cadeau d'Anniversaire Pour Ree-Ree. (Illus.). 32p. (Orig.). (J). (ps-6). 1989. student ed 5.95 (*0-927024-15-2*) Crayons Pubns.

— A Birthday Present for Ree-Ree: Un Regalo Cumpleanos Para Ree-Ree. (Illus.). 32p. (Orig.). (J). (gr. k-6). 1989. student ed 5.95 (*0-927024-14-4*) Crayons Pubns.

— Early Learning Shape Book: El Libro de Figuras Geometricas. (Illus.). 32p. (J). (gr. k-6). 1989. student ed 5.95 (*0-927024-06-3*) Crayons Pubns.

— Early Learning Shape Book: Le Livre Des Formes. (Illus.). 32p. (J). (gr. k-6). 1989. student ed 5.95 (*0-927024-07-1*) Crayons Pubns.

— J.J. Goes to School: J.J. Va a L E'cole. (Illus.). 32p. (J). (gr. k-6). 1989. student ed 5.95 (*0-927024-13-6*) Crayons Pubns.

— J.J. Goes to School: J.J. Va a la Escuela. (Illus.). 32p. (J). (gr. k-6). 1989. student ed 5.95 (*0-927024-12-8*) Crayons Pubns.

— Lets Color & Count: Colorions et Comptons. (Illus.). 32p. (J). (gr. k-6). 1989. student ed 5.95 (*0-927024-09-8*) Crayons Pubns.

— Meet Penelope P'Nutt: Conoza Penelope P'Nutt. (Illus.). 32p. (J). (gr. k-6). 1989. student ed 5.95 (*0-927024-04-7*) Crayons Pubns.

— Meet Penelope P'Nutt: Viens Recontrer Penelope P'Nutt. (Illus.). 32p. (J). (gr. k-6). 1989. student ed 5.95 (*0-927024-05-5*) Crayons Pubns.

— Penelope P'Nutt & the Spirit of Christmas: Penelope P'Nutt et L'Ambiance De Noel. (Illus.). 16p. (J). (gr. k-6). 1989. student ed 5.95 (*0-927024-03-9*) Crayons Pubns.

— Penelope P'Nutt & the Spirit of Christmas: Penelope P'Nutt y el Espiritu de la Navidad. (Illus.). 16p. (J). (gr. k-6). 1989. student ed 5.95 (*0-927024-02-0*) Crayons Pubns.

— Penelope P'Nutt at Play: Los Juegos de Penelope P'Nutt. (Illus.). 32p. (J). (gr. k-6). 1989. student ed 5.95 (*0-927024-16-0*) Crayons Pubns.

— Penelope P'Nutt at Play: Penelope P'Nutt au Jeu. (Illus.). 32p. (Orig.). (J). (gr. k-6). 1989. student ed 5.95 (*0-927024-17-9*) Crayons Pubns.

— Rainy Days Are for Baking: Les Recettes Preferee de Penelope P'Nutt. (Illus.). 32p. (J). (gr. k-6). 1989. student ed 5.95 (*0-927024-01-2*) Crayons Pubns.

— Rainy Days Are for Baking: Penelope P'Nutt los Dias Lluviosos Son Para Cocinar. (Illus.). 1988. 5.95 (*0-927024-00-4*) Crayons Pubns.

Palumbo, P. J. & Margic, Joyce D. The All-in-One Diabetic Cookbook. 1989. pap. 12.95 (*0-452-26467-7*, Plume) NAL-Dutton.

Palumbo, Thomas. Language Arts Thinking Motivators. 96p. (J). (gr. 2-7). 1988. student ed 9.95 (*0-86653-432-6*, GA1050) Good Apple.

Palumbo, Thomas J. Creative Writing Motivators. (Illus.). 144p. (J). (gr. 2-7). 1994. 12.95 (*0-86653-819-4*, GA1511) Good Apple.

— Integrating the Literature of John Bellairs in the Classroom. (Illus.). 176p. (J). (gr. 3-7). 1994. 13.95 (*0-86653-808-9*, GA1500) Good Apple.

— Thursday Think Time. (Illus.). 64p. (J). (gr. 3-8). 1985. student ed 8.95 (*0-86653-311-7*, GA 650) Good Apple.

— Tuesday Timely Teasers. (Illus.). 64p. (J). (gr. 3-8). 1985. student ed 8.95 (*0-86653-309-5*, GA 648) Good Apple.

— Wednesday Midweek Winners. (Illus.). 64p. (J). (gr. 3-8). 1985. student ed 8.95 (*0-86653-310-9*, GA 649) Good Apple.

Palumbo, Tom. Integrating the Literature of Beverly Cleary in the Classroom. 176p. 1991. 13.95 (*0-86653-610-8*, GA1329) Good Apple.

— Integrating the Literature of Chris Van Allsburg in the Classroom. (Illus.). 176p. 1992. 13.95 (*0-86653-658-2*, GA1390) Good Apple.

— Integrating the Literature of Judy Blume in the Classroom. 176p. 1990. 13.95 (*0-86653-558-6*, GA1152) Good Apple.

— Measurement Motivators. 96p. (J). (gr. 3-7). 1989. 10.95 (*0-86653-500-4*, GA1095) Good Apple.

Palus, Charles J., jt. auth. see Drath, Wilfred H.

Palus, Charles J., et al. Understanding Executive Performance: A Life-Story Perspective. (Report Ser.: No. 148G). 48p. 1991. pap. 15.00 (*0-912879-45-9*, 148) Ctr Creat Leader.

Palusamy, S. S., ed. see Pressure Vessels & Piping Conference Staff.

Paluska, Lynn M. Instructor's Manual to Accompany Kochanek - Hillman - Norgaard's Financial Accounting. 2nd ed. 456p. (C). 1992. pap. text ed. 8.75 (*0-15-500349-6*) Dryden Pr.

Paluszek, John L. Business & Society: 1976-2000. LC 75-44485. (AMA Survey Report Ser.). 46p. reprint ed. pap. 25.00 (*0-8357-7485-6*, 2050198) Bks Demand.

Palvia, Prashant, et al, eds. The Global Issues of Information Technology Management. LC 90-82964. 688p. (C). 1992. text ed. 84.95 (*1-878289-10-1*) Idea Group Pub.

Palvino, Nancy M. Bibliography on Autism. (Bibliographies Ser.: No. 4). 9p. (C). 1992. 3.50 (*1-883215-03-X*) Ramdil.

Palwick, Susan. Flying in Place. 224p. 1993. mass mkt. 4.99 (*0-8125-1334-7*) Tor Bks.

Paly, M., jt. auth. see Goldstein, E.

Palya, V. Manual for Production of Marek's Disease, Gumboro Disease & Inactivated Newcastle Disease. (Animal Production & Health Papers: No. 89). 98p. 1991. pap. 9.00 (*92-5-102919-9*, F9199) UNIPUB.

Palyi, Melchior. The Chicago Credit Market: Organization & Institutional Structure. LC 75-2659. (Wall Street & the Security Market Ser.). 1975. reprint ed. 40.95 (*0-405-06983-9*) Ayer.

— Hauptprobleme der Soziologie: Erinnerungsgabe Fuer Max Weber: Major Problems in Socology, 2 vols. in one. LC 74-25773. (European Sociology Ser.). 741p. 1975. reprint ed. 53.95 (*0-405-06527-2*) Ayer.

— Managed Money at the Crossroads: The European Experience. LC 57-11375. 206p. reprint ed. pap. 58.80 (*0-317-42114-X*, 2025945) Bks Demand.

Palyutin, E., jt. auth. see Ershov, Yu.

Palz, W., jt. ed. see Luque, A.

Palz, Wolfgang. Photovoltaic Power Generation. 1982. lib. bdg. 112.50 (*90-277-1386-3*) Kluwer Ac.

— Third E. C. Photovoltaic Solar Energy Conference. 1981. lib. bdg. 145.50 (*90-277-1230-1*) Kluwer Ac.

Palz, Wolfgang, ed. Photovoltaic Power Generation. 1984. lib. bdg. 94.00 (*90-277-1725-7*) Kluwer Ac.

— Solar Energy Data. 1983. lib. bdg. 99.00 (*90-277-1566-1*) Kluwer Ac.

— Solar Radiation Data. 1982. lib. bdg. 56.50 (*90-277-1387-1*) Kluwer Ac.

Palz, Wolfgang & Chartier, P., eds. Energy from Biomass in Europe. (Illus.). 248p. 1980. 63.00 (*0-85334-934-7*, Pub. by Elsevier Applied Sci UK) Elsevier.

Palz, Wolfgang & Fittipaldi, F., eds. Photovoltaic Solar Energy Conference, Fifth E. C. 1984. lib. bdg. 281.50 (*90-277-1724-9*) Kluwer Ac.

Palz, Wolfgang & Pirrwitz, D. Energy from Biomass. 1983. lib. bdg. 136.50 (*90-277-1700-1*) Kluwer Ac.

Palz, Wolfgang & Schnell, W. Wind Energy. 1983. lib. bdg. 70.00 (*90-277-1603-X*) Kluwer Ac.

Palz, Wolfgang & Steemers, Theo C., eds. Solar Energy Applications to Dwellings. 1982. lib. bdg. 70.00 (*90-277-1372-3*) Kluwer Ac.

— Solar Houses in Europe: How They Have Worked. LC 80-49715. (Illus.). 320p. 1981. text ed. 134.00 (*0-08-026743-2*, Pub. by Pergamon Repr UK) Franklin.

Palz, Wolfgang & Treble, F. C., eds. Sixth E. C. Photovoltaic Solar Energy Conference. 1985. lib. bdg. 266.00 (*90-277-2104-1*) Kluwer Ac.

Palz, Wolfgang, jt. ed. see Chartier, P.

Palz, Wolfgang, jt. ed. see Grassi, G.

Palz, Wolfgang, jt. ed. see Hall, D. O.

Palz, Wolfgang, ed. see International Conference on Biomass Staff.

Palz, Wolfgang, jt. auth. see Schmid, J.

Palz, Wolfgang, jt. auth. see Starr, Michael R.

Palz, Wolfgang, jt. ed. see Steemers, Theo C.

Palz, Wolfgang, jt. ed. see Van OverStraeten, R. J.

Palz, Wolfgang, et al, eds. Energy from Biomass - Third E. C. Conference: Proceedings of the Third International Conference on Biomass, Venice, Italy, 25-29 March, 1985. xxv, 1211p. 1985. 182.00 (*0-85334-396-9*, Pub. by Elsevier Applied Sci UK) Elsevier.

P
Q

An Asterisk (*) at the beginning of an entry indicates that the title is appearing in BIP for the first time.

— Solar Collectors in Architecture: Integration of Photovoltaic & Thermal Collectors in New & Old Building Structures. 320p. 1984. lib. bdg. 98.00 (*90-277-1784-2*) Kluwer Ac.

Palzer, Bob & Palzer, Jody. Whitewater, Quietwater. LC 83-80899. (Illus.). 160p. 1983. pap. 12.95 (*0-89732-086-7*) Menasha Ridge.

— Whitewater; Quietwater: A Guide to the Wild Rivers of Wisconsin, Upper Michigan, & Northeast Minnesota. 5th ed. LC 83-80899. (Illus.). 160p. 1983. pap. 9.95 (*0-916166-04-X*) Evergreen WI.

— Whitewater; Quietwater: A Guide to the Wild Rivers of Wisconsin, Upper Michigan, & Northeast Minnesota. 5th suppl. ed. (Illus.). 160p. 1985. (*0-318-51868-6*) Evergreen WI.

Palzer, Jody, jt. auth. see Palzer, Bob.

Pam, Martin D., jt. ed. see Meisel, Juergen M.

Pama, R. P., jt. auth. see Cusens, Anthony R.

Pama, R. P., et al, eds. Low Income Housing: Technology & Policy: Proceedings of the International Conference, Bangkok, June 1977, 3 vols. 1978. 627.00 (*0-08-023241-8*, Pub. by Pergamon Repr UK) Franklin.

Paman, Jose G. & Goodwin, Rod. Comprehensive Self-Defense. LC 93-70988. (Illus.). (Orig.). 1993. pap. 14.00 (*0-9636286-8-2*) Eghty-Three Brixton.

Pamel, Gregory J., jt. ed. see Arca, Emil.

***Pamensky, Robin.** Mitzvah Car. (J). 1995. text ed. 12.95 (*965-229-138-2*, Pub. by Gefen Pub Hse IS) Gefen Bks.

Pamental, George L. Ethics in the Business Curriculum: A Preliminary Survey of Undergraduate Business Programs. LC 87-37193. 210p. (Orig.). (C). 1988. pap. text ed. 22.50 (*0-8191-6871-8*) U Pr of Amer.

Pamepinto, Sharon. Can States Stop Corporate Takeovers? 51p. 1987. pap. 25.00 (*0-931035-20-1*) IRRC Inc DC.

Pamepinto, Sharon & Sander, Bill. A Shareholders' Guide to ESOPs. 100p. 1991. pap. 75.00 (*0-931035-78-3*) IRRC Inc DC.

Pamer, Nan M. Modesty. LC 90-30491. (Illus.). 50p. (Orig.). (YA). 1990. pap. 2.99 (*0-932581-62-5*) Word Aflame.

***Pamintuan, Ana M.** The Face of the Enemy. 1994. 19.95 (*0-533-11026-2*) Vantage.

Pammel, L. H. A Manual of Poisonous Plants: Chiefly of Eastern North America, with Brief Notes on Economic & Medicinal Plants. (Illus.). 977p. 1992. reprint ed. lib. bdg. 75.00 (*0-945345-43-7*) Lubrecht & Cramer.

Pammer, William J., Jr. Managing Fiscal Strain in Major American Cities: Understanding Retrenchment in the Public Sector. LC 89-17073. (Contributions in Political Science Ser.: No. 247). 151p. 1990. text ed. 47.95 (*0-313-26656-5*, PMF/, Greenwood Pr) Greenwood.

Pampallis, John. Foundations of the New South Africa. LC 90-26476. 336p. (C). 1991. text ed. 49.95 (*1-85649-004-1*, Pub. by Zed Books UK); pap. 15.00 (*1-85649-005-X*, Pub. by Zed Books UK) Humanities.

Pampaloni, P. Microwave Radiometry & Remote Sensing Applications. (Illus.). 167p. 1989. 135.00 (*90-6764-108-1*, Pub. by VSP NE) Coronet Bks.

***Pampaloni, P., ed.** Passive Microwave Remote Sensing of Land-Atmosphere Interactions. 680p. 1994. 245.00 (*90-6764-186-3*, Pub. by VSP NE) Coronet Bks.

— Passive Microwave Remote Sensing of Land-Atmosphere Interactions. 680p. 1994. pap. 99.50 (*90-6764-188-X*, Pub. by VSP NE) Coronet Bks.

Pampatti. Dance, Snake! Dance! Buck, David C., tr. 12.00 (*0-89253-797-3*); 8.00 (*0-89253-798-1*) Ind-US Inc.

Pampel, Fred C. & Williamson, John B. Age, Class, Politics, & the Welfare State. (ASA Rose Monograph Ser.). (Illus.). 240p. (C). 1992. pap. 17.95 (*0-521-43791-1*) Cambridge U Pr.

Pampel, Fred C., jt. ed. see Tracy, Martin B.

Pampel, Fred C., jt. auth. see Williamson, John B.

Pampero Foundation Staff, ed. see De Valencia, Ruby & Volsky, Jeannine S.

Pamphilon. Modern Transfusion Medicine: A Practical Approach. 1994. write for info. (*0-8493-8922-4*) CRC Pr.

Pampillo, C. A., ed. see American Society for Metals Staff.

Pampillo, C. A., ed. see Symposium Aluminum Transformation Technology & Its Applications (1978).

***Pamplin.** Heritage: The Making of an American Family. 1995. pap. text ed. 12.95 (*0-942691-96-2*) Beta Bks.

Pamplin, Brian R. Crystal Growth. 2nd ed. 1980. 248.00 (*0-08-026489-1*, Pub. by Pergamon Repr UK) Franklin.

— Crystal Growth. 2nd ed. LC 79-42662. (International Series of Monographs on the Strength & Fracture of Materials & Structures: Vol. 16). 1980. 248.00 (*0-08-025043-2*, Pub. by Pergamon Repr UK) Franklin.

— Molecular Beam Epitaxy. (Illus.). 178p. 1980. 48.00 (*0-08-025050-5*, Pergamon Pr) Elsevier.

Pamplin, Brian R., ed. Inorganic Biological Crystal Growth. (Illus.). 284p. 1981. 73.00 (*0-08-028420-5*, C999, H210, H999, Pergamon Pr) Elsevier.

— Progress in Crystal Growth, Vol. 2, Complete. (Illus.). 404p. 1981. 140.00 (*0-08-026040-3*, Pergamon Pr) Elsevier.

— Progress in Crystal Growth & Characterization, Pt. 2. 1978. pap. 28.00 (*0-08-023050-4*, Pub. by Pergamon Repr UK) Franklin.

— Progress in Crystal Growth & Characterization, Pt. 3. 1978. pap. 28.00 (*0-08-023051-2*, Pub. by Pergamon Repr UK) Franklin.

— Progress in Crystal Growth & Characterization, Pt. 4. 1979. pap. 21.00 (*0-08-023083-0*, Pub. by Pergamon Repr UK) Franklin.

— Progress in Crystal Growth & Characterization, Vol. 1. (Illus.). 248p. 1980. 140.00 (*0-08-026013-6*, Pergamon Pr) Elsevier.

— Progress in Crystal Growth & Characterization, Vol. 3 Complete. (Illus.). 390p. 1981. 171.00 (*0-08-028405-1*, Pub. by Pergamon Repr UK) Franklin.

— Progress in Crystal Growth & Characterization, Vol. 3, No. 2-3. (Illus.). 166p. 1981. pap. 72.00 (*0-08-027149-9*, Pergamon Pr) Elsevier.

— Progress in Crystal Growth & Characterization, Vol. 5. (Illus.). 425p. 1983. 155.00 (*0-08-031011-7*, Pergamon Pr) Elsevier.

— Progress in Crystal Growth & Characterization, Vol. 6. (Illus.). 424p. 1984. 155.00 (*0-08-030997-6*, Pergamon Pr) Elsevier.

— Progress in Crystal Growth & Characterization, Vol. 8. (Illus.). 475p. 1985. 180.00 (*0-08-032736-2*, Pub. by PPL UK) Elsevier.

— Progress in Crystal Growth & Characterization, Vol. 9. (Illus.). 385p. 1985. 180.00 (*0-08-032737-0*, Pub. by PPL UK) Elsevier.

— Progress in Crystal Growth & Characterization, Vol. 4. (Illus.). 345p. 1982. 160.00 (*0-08-029681-5*, Pergamon Pr) Elsevier.

Pamplin, Brian R., et al, eds. Progress in Crystal Growth & Characterization, Vol. 10: Proceedings of the 6th International Conference on Ternary & Multinary Compounds, Car acas, Venezuela, 15-17 August 1984. (Illus.). 430p. 1985. 180.00 (*0-08-032344-8*, Pergamon Pr) Elsevier.

Pamplin, Jean, jt. ed. see Thompson, Larry.

Pamplin, Laurel J. Masquerade on the Western Trail. Roberts, M., ed. (Illus.). 112p. (J). (gr. 4-8). 1991. 9.95 (*0-89015-755-3*) Sunbelt Media.

***Pamplin, Robert, Jr., et al.** Heritage: The Making of an American Family. 510p. 1995. pap. 12.95 (*1-57101-041-6*) MasterMedia Ltd.

— Prelude to Surrender: The Pamplin Family & the Siege of Petersburg. 64p. 1995. 10.95 (*1-57101-049-1*) MasterMedia Ltd.

Pamplin, Robert B. Heritage: The Making of an American Family. 1994. 24.95 (*0-942361-96-2*) MasterMedia Ltd.

***Pamplin, Robert B., Jr. & Eisler, Gary K. American Heroes: Their Lives, Their Values, Their Beliefs. LC 95-76884. 256p. 1995. 18.95 (*1-57101-010-6*) MasterMedia Ltd.**
WHAT DOES IT TAKE TO BE AN AMERICAN HERO? "It can be done! Check small things. Share credit. Have a vision. Be demanding. Perpetual optimism is a force multiplier."--General Colin Powell. "My faith means a lot to me. I can face challenging situations & feel that it's not all just on my shoulders."--Elizabeth Dole. In a world of turmoil, what qualities do our inspirational leaders & heroes of the twentieth century possess? Author & businessman Dr. Robert B. Pamplin, Jr., profiles American men & women of outstanding achievement. They share their stories of courage, integrity & compassion. Billy Graham, Colin Powell, Elie Wiesel, Oprah Winfrey, Johnny Cash, Jackie Joyner-Kersee, Chris Burke, Elizabeth Dole, Bill Cosby & others discuss the inner values that guide their lives & make possible their incredible achievements. ABOUT THE AUTHORS: Dr. Robert B. Pamplin, Jr, has experienced incredible financial success. As an undergraduate in the 1960s, he caught the rise of the stock market, making his first million. He later invested those profits in timber & farmlands just before they shot up in value. And his $30,000 investment in an unproven "cutting" horse led to $2million in stud fees, & the horse's eventual sale for $850,000. Dr. Pamplin & his father R.B. Pamplin, run a corporation that owns 19 textile facilities & a concrete & asphalt company, with annual revenues of approximately $800 million. He has written 12 books & been awarded many honorary degrees. Gary K. Eisler is a writer, published in The Wall Street Journal & Forbes. *Publisher Provided Annotation.*

Pamplin, Timothy R., ed. The Illinois Register of Expert Witnesses. 297p. 1991. pap. 55.00 (*1-880554-00-3*) Wmster Legal.

— The Wisconsin-Illinois Register of Expert Witnesses. 55.00 (*1-880554-01-1*) Wmster Legal.

Pampreen, Ronald C. Compressor Surge & Stall. LC 92-70348. 600p. 1993. text ed. 125.00 (*0-933283-05-9*) Concepts ETI.

Pampuch, R. Constitution & Properties of Ceramic Materials. (Materials Science Monographs: No. 58). 460p. 1990. 151.25 (*0-444-98794-0*) Elsevier.

Pamuk, Orhan. The Black Book. Gun, Guneli, tr. LC 94-4791. 1994. 25.00 (*0-374-11394-7*) FS&G.

— The White Castle. Holbrook, Victoria, tr. 162p. 1991. 17.50 (*0-8076-1264-2*) Braziller.

Pamukcu, Sibel. Second International Symposium on Environmental Geotechnology (May 15-18, 1989). Vol. 2: Proceedings: 15-18, 1989. Hsai-Yang Fang, ed. LC 89-80286. 375p. 1991. pap. 55.00 (*0-932871-18-6*) Envo Pub Co.

Pamukcu, Sibel, jt. ed. see Hsai-Yang Fang.

Pan-Am Editors. Artists of the Southwest. (Illus.). 105p. 1988. pap. 14.95 (*0-932906-22-2*) Pan-Am Publishing Co.

Pan-Am Editors, ed. Artists of New Mexico. LC 86-8172. (Illus.). 105p. (Orig.). 1986. pap. 14.95 (*0-932906-15-X*) Pan-Am Publishing Co.

Pan American Union Staff, ed. Mexico. 1976. lib. bdg. 34.95 (*0-8490-0622-8*) Gordon Pr.

Pan American University Press, ed. see Green, Shirley B.

Pan, B. W., tr. see Rusthoi, Ralph W.

Pan, C. H., jt. ed. see Ling, Frederick F.

***Pan, Erica Y.** The Impact of the 1906 Earthquake on San Francisco's Chinatown. LC 94-25600. 1995. write for info. (*0-8204-2607-5*) P Lang Pubs.

***Pan, Lawrence S., ed.** Diamond: Electronic Properties & Applications. (International Series in Engineering & Computer Science, Natural Language Processing & Machine Translation). 488p. (C). 1994. lib. bdg. 145.00 (*0-7923-9524-7*) Kluwer Ac.

Pan, Loretta. Character Text for Speak Chinese. 1964. 9.95 (*0-88710-009-0*) Yale Far Eastern Pubns.

Pan, Lynn. Alcohol in Colonial Africa. (Finnish Foundation for Alcohol Studies: Vol. 22). 1975. 6.50 (*951-9191-20-8*) Rutgers Ctr Alcohol.

— Shanghai: The Paris of the Orient. 2nd ed. 1993. pap. 14.95 (*0-8442-9686-4*, Passport Bks) NTC Pub Grp.

— Sons of the Yellow Emperor: A History of the Chinese Diaspora. De Angelis, Paul, ed. (Illus.). 448p. 1994. pap. 15.00 (*1-56836-032-0*) Kodansha.

— Tracing It Home: A Chinese Journey. De Angelis, Paul, ed. LC 93-20563. 256p. 1993. 22.00 (*1-56836-009-6*) Kodansha.

— Tracing It Home: A Chinese Journey. 240p. 1994. reprint ed. pap. 12.00 (*1-56836-043-6*) Kodansha.

***Pan, Lynn & Wiltshire, Trea.** Saturday's Child: Hong Kong in the Sixties. (Illus.). 88p. 1995. 40.00 (*962-7283-10-X*, Pub. by FormAsia HK) Weatherhill.

Pan, Lynn, jt. auth. see Holledge, Simon.

Pan, Tianmin, et al, eds. Unsteady Aerodynamics & Aeroelasticity of Turbomachines & Propellers: Proceedings of the Fifth International Symposium, Beijing, China, 18-21 September, 1989. (International Academic Publishers Ser.). 528p. 1990. 135.00 (*0-08-040187-2*, Pub. by IAP UK) Elsevier.

Pan, Victor, jt. auth. see Bini, Dario.

P'an Wei-Tung. The Chinese Constitution: A Study of Forty Years of Constitution-Making in China. LC 79-1639. 1985. reprint ed. 27.00 (*0-88355-942-0*) Hyperion Conn.

Pan, Winston, jt. auth. see Min Chen.

***Pan, Zhongdang, et al.** To See Ourselves: Comparing Traditional Chinese & American Cultural Values. LC 94-33499. 1994. text ed. 49.95 (*0-8133-2075-5*) Westview.

Pana, Irina G., jt. tr. see Sorkin, Adam J.

Panabaker, John H., jt. auth. see Blain, Brad.

Panaf Books Editors. Forward Ever: The Life of Kwame Nkrumah. 78p. (C). 1977. pap. 3.95 (*0-901787-42-6*, Pub. by Panaf Bks UK) Humanities.

— Some Essential Features of Nkrumaism. 167p. (C). 1975. pap. 5.95 (*0-901787-15-9*, Pub. by Panaf Bks UK) Humanities.

Panaf Staff. Eduardo Mondlane. (Panaf Great Lives Ser.). 174p. (C). 1972. pap. 7.95 (*0-901787-24-8*, Pub. by Panaf Bks UK) Humanities.

— Frantz Fanon. (Panaf Great Lives Ser.). 200p. (C). 1975. pap. 8.95 (*0-901787-30-2*, Pub. by Panaf Bks UK) Humanities.

— Kanyama Chiume. (Panaf Great Lives Ser.). 252p. (C). 1982. pap. 9.95 (*0-901787-18-3*, Pub. by Panaf Bks UK) Humanities.

— Nelson Mandela. (Panaf Great Lives Ser.). 192p. (C). 1980. pap. 7.95 (*0-901787-17-5*, Pub. by Panaf Bks UK) Humanities.

— Patrice Lumumba. (Panaf Great Lives Ser.). 215p. (C). 1973. pap. 9.95 (*0-901787-31-0*, Pub. by Panaf Bks UK) Humanities.

— Sekou Toure. (Panaf Great Lives Ser.). 208p. (C). 1978. pap. 8.95 (*0-901787-43-4*, Pub. by Panaf Bks UK) Humanities.

Panagariya, Arvind, jt. auth. see De Melo, Jaime.

Panagariya, Arvind, jt. ed. see De Melo, Jaime.

***Panaggio, Leonard J.** Portrait of Newport II. (Illus.). 160p. (Orig.). 1994. pap. text ed. 9.95 (*0-9642783-0-8*) Bank of Newport.

Panagiotopoulos. Computational Modelling - Frictional Contact - Solid Mechanics. 1995. write for info. (*0-8493-8334-X*) CRC Pr.

Panagiotopoulos, P. D. Hemivariational Inequalities: Applications in Mechanics & Engineering. (Illus.). 465p. 1993. write for info. (*3-540-54963-5*); 119.00 (*0-387-54963-5*) Spr-Verlag.

Panagiotopoulos, P. D., jt. auth. see Antes, H.

Panagiotopoulos, P. D., jt. ed. see Moreau, J. J.

Panagiotopoulos, P. D., jt. auth. see Naniewicz, Z.

Panagopoulos, Epaminodes P. New Smyrna: An Eighteenth Century Greek Odyssey. 2nd ed. LC 77-16303. (Illus.). 207p. 1978. reprint ed. 10.00 (*0-916586-13-8*); reprint ed. pap. 4.50 (*0-916586-14-6*) Holy Cross Orthodox.

***Panagopoulos, Janie L.** Erie Trail West: A Dream-Quest Adventure. 184p. (J). (gr. 3-7). 1995. 13.95 (*0-938682-35-0*) River Rd Pubns.

— Journey Back to Lumberjack Camp: A Dream-Quest Adventure. 176p. (J). (gr. 3-6). 1993. 13.95 (*0-938682-26-1*) River Rd Pubns.

— Traders in Time: A Dream-Quest Adventure. 200p. (J). (gr. 3-6). 1993. 13.95 (*0-938682-24-5*) River Rd Pubns.

— Traders in Time: A Dream-Quest Adventure. (J). (gr. 3-6). 1994. pap. 6.95 (*0-938682-27-X*) River Rd Pubns.

Panak, Michele J., jt. auth. see Horovitz, Jacques.

Panak, Michele Jurgens, jt. auth. see Horovitz, Jacques.

Panamanian Business Law Staff. Panamanian Business Law. 308p. reprint ed. pap. 87.80 (*0-7837-2409-8*, 2040094) Bks Demand.

***Panamarioff, Rob & Pikok, Bob.** King Horse & the Totem Bird. Manring, Rob, ed. (Illus.). 111p. (Orig.). 1995. pap. 9.95 (*0-944193-04-8*) Rainbow Family Productions.

Panandiker, D. H. Pollution Control in Indian Industry. (C). 1991. 14.50 (*81-7018-633-1*, Pub. by BR Pub II) S Asia.

Panandiker, D. H., jt. auth. see Economic.

Panandiker, V. A., jt. auth. see Malgavkar, P. D.

Panandiker, Vapai & Mehra, A. K. People's Participation in Family Planning. 1987. 29.00 (*81-85024-10-3*, Pub. by Uppal Pub Hse II) S Asia.

Panarese, W. C., et al. Concrete Masonry Handbook for Architects, Engineers, Builders. 5th rev. ed. LC 90-6460. (Illus.). 264p. (C). 1991. pap. 33.00 (*0-89312-093-6*, EB008M) Portland Cement.

Panaro. Employment Law Manual, No. 2195: Recruitment, Selection, Termination. 608p. 1990. boxed 115.00 (*0-7913-0375-6*) Warren Gorham & Lamont.

— Employment Law Manual, No. 2195: Recruitment, Selection, Termination. suppl. ed. 608p. 1990. Supplemented annually, write for info. 60.00 (*0-685-56161-5*) Warren Gorham & Lamont.

Panaro, Gerard P. Pregnancy & Childcare Issues in the Workplace. 1987. pap. 39.95 (*0-88057-775-4*) Exec Ent Pubns.

Panaro, Gerard P., ed. Personnel Practice Ideas. 115.00 (*0-685-69668-5*, PPI) Warren Gorham & Lamont.

Panas, Epaminondas E. Almost Homogeneous Functions: A Theoretical & Empirical Analysis with Special Emphasis on Labour Input-The Case of Swedish Manufacturing Industries. (Studia Oeconomica Upsaliensia: No. 11). 130p. (Orig.). 1987. pap. text ed. 35.50x (*91-554-1972-0*, Pub. by Uppsala Univ Acta Univ Upsaliensis SW) Coronet Bks.

Panas, Jerold. Boardroom Verities. LC 91-66145. 238p. 1991. 40.00 (*0-944496-26-1*) Precept Pr.

— Born to Raise: What Makes a Great Fundraiser, What Makes a Fundraiser Great. LC 88-61232. 228p. 1988. 40.00 (*0-944496-02-4*) Precept Pr.

— Mega Gifts. LC 83-62498. (Who Gives Them, Who Gets Them Ser.). 224p. 1984. text ed. 40.00 (*0-931028-39-6*) Precept Pr.

— Official Fundraising Almanac. LC 89-61428. 410p. 1989. 50.00 (*0-944496-07-5*) Precept Pr.

Panas, Peter, illus. The Shalom Sesame Players Present: The Story of Passover. (Sharing Passover Ser.). 32p. (J). 1994. pap. 5.95 (*1-884857-02-7*) Comet Intl.

Panasenko, G., jt. auth. see Bakhvalov, N.

Panassie, Hughes. Hot Jazz: The Guide to Swing Music. LC 74-135606. 363p. 1970. reprint ed. text ed. 35.00 (*0-8371-5181-3*, PAJ&, Negro U Pr) Greenwood.

— The Real Jazz. LC 73-13328. 284p. 1973. reprint ed. text ed. 59.75 (*0-8371-7123-7*, PARJ, Greenwood Pr) Greenwood.

Panassie, Hughes & Gautier, M. Dictionnaire du Jazz. rev. ed. 384p. (FRE.). 1987. pap. 49.95 (*0-8288-2170-4*, M6648) Fr & Eur.

Panassie, Hugues. Louis Armstrong. LC 79-20828. (Roots of Jazz Ser.). (Illus.). 148p. 1979. reprint ed. lib. bdg. 25.00 (*0-306-79611-2*); reprint ed. pap. 7.95 (*0-306-80116-7*) Da Capo.

Panasyuk, V. V. Limiting Equilibrium of Brittle Solids with Fractures. LC 75-135093. 325p. 1969. 39.00 (*0-403-04527-4*) Scholarly.

***Panasyuk, V. V., ed.** Advances in Fracture Resistance & Structural Integrity: Selected Papers from the Eighth International Conference on Fractures (ICF8), Kyiv, Ukraine, 8-14 June 1993. LC 94-34031. (International Series on the Strength & Fracture of Materials & Structure). 1994. 210.00 (*0-08-042256-X*, Pergamon Pr) Elsevier.

Panati, Charles. Panati's Extraordinary Endings of Practically Everything & Everybody. LC 89-45111. (Illus.). 464p. 1989. pap. 10.95 (*0-06-096279-8*, PL 6279, PL) HarpC.

— Panati's Extraordinary Origins. 1989. pap. 15.00 (*0-06-096419-7*, PL) HarpC.

— Panati's Parade of Fads, Follies, & Manias: The Origins of Our Most Cherished Obsessions. LC 90-56433. 480p. (Orig.). 1991. pap. 13.00 (*0-06-096477-4*, PL) HarpC.

Panati, Charles & Hudson, Michael. The Silent Intruder: Surviving the Radiation Age. 224p. 1981. 9.95 (*0-685-02309-5*) HM.

Panayi, G. S., ed. Immunology of Connective Tissue Diseases. LC 93-39860. (Immunology & Medicine Ser.: Vol. 22). 416p. (C). 1994. lib. bdg. 114.00 (*0-7923-8988-3*) Kluwer Ac.

Panayi, Panikos. The Enemy in Our Midst: Germans in Britain During the First World War. LC 89-18464. 324p. 1991. 66.50 (*0-85496-308-1*) Berg Pubs.

— German Immigrants in Britain during the 19th Century, 1830-1914. 352p. 1995. 52.95 (*1-85973-092-2*) Berg Pubs.

— Immigration, Ethnicity, & Racism in Britain, 1815-1945. LC 93-49041. (New Frontiers in History Ser.). 1994. text ed. 59.95 (*0-7190-3697-6*, Pub. by Manchester Univ Pr UK); text ed. 14.95 (*0-7190-3698-4*, Pub. by Manchester Univ Pr UK) St Martin.

Panayi, Panikos, ed. Minorities in Wartime: National & Racial Groupings in Europe, North America, & Australia During the Two World Wars. LC 92-15669. 280p. 1993. 59.95 (*0-85496-339-1*) Berg Pubs.

Panayiotis, jt. auth. see Nellas.

An Asterisk (*) at the beginning of an entry indicates that the title is appearing in BIP for the first time.

*Panayotakis, Costas. Theatrum Arbitri: Theatrical Elements in the Satyrica of Petronius. LC 94-40910. (Mnemosyne, Bibliotheca Classica Batava Thesis). 1995. write for info. (90-04-10229-9) E J Brill.

Panayotou, T. & Jetanavanich, S. The Economics & Management of Thai Fisheries. (ICLARM Studies & Reviews: No. 14). 1987. pap. 9.00 (971-10-2225-7, Pub. by ICLARM PH) Intl Spec Bk.

Panayotou, Theodore. Green Markets: The Economics of Sustainable Development. LC 92-38901. (Sector Studies: No. 7). 192p. 1993. 29.95 (1-55815-244-X); pap. 14.95 (1-55815-222-9) ICS Pr.

Panayotou, Theodore & Ashton, Peter S. Not by Timber Alone: Economics & Ecology for Sustaining Tropical Forests. LC 92-10222. 280p. 1992. 40.00 (1-55963-195-3); pap. 22.00 (1-55963-196-1) Island Pr.

Panayotou, Theodore, et al. The Economics of Catfish Farming in Central Thailand. (ICLARM Technical Reports: No. 4). (Illus.). 60p. (Orig.). 1983. pap. 10.00 (971-02-0338-X, Pub. by ICLARM PH) Intl Spec Bk.

Panayotov, Ivan, jt. ed. see Bailey, Douglass W.

Panayotova, Dora. Bulgarian Mural Paintings of the 14th Century. Alexieva, Marguerite & Athanassova, Theodora, trs. (Illus.). 37.50 (0-8057-5003-7) Irvington.

Panaza, Henry G. Handbook for Construction Accounting & Auditing. 2nd ed. 330p. 1988. text ed. 52.95 (0-13-372616-9, Busn) P-H.

Panbratz, Roger, jt. ed. see Houston, W. Robert.

Panc, V. Theories of Elastic Plates. (Mechanics of Surface Structures Ser.: No. 2). 736p. 1975. lib. bdg. 164.50 (90-286-0104-X) Kluwer Ac.

*Pancak, Katherine A. Connecticut Supplement for Modern Real Estate Practice. 6th ed. LC 94-46598. 1995. pap. 12.95 (0-7931-1327-X) Dearborn Finan.

Pancake, Breece D'J. The Stories of Breece D'J Pancake. LC 83-22530. 192p. 1984. pap. 9.95 (0-8050-0720-2, Owl) H Holt & Co.

Pancake, John S. Seventeen Seventy-Seven: The Year of the Hangman. LC 76-30797. 280p. 1992. pap. 15.95 (0-8173-0687-0) U of Ala Pr.

— This Destructive War: The British Campaign in the Carolinas, 1780-1782. LC 83-5025. 320p. 1992. pap. 15.95 (0-8173-0688-9) U of Ala Pr.

Pancaldi, Giuliano. Darwin in Italy: Science Across Cultural Frontiers. Morelli, Ruey B., tr. LC 90-25528. (Illus.). 246p. 1991. 35.00 (0-253-34287-2) Ind U Pr.

Pancaratra, Narada-Pancaratra. Sri Narada Pancharatnam, the Jnanamrita Sara Samhita. Swami Vijnanananda, tr. LC 73-3816. (Sacred Books of the Hindus: No. 23). reprint ed. 32.50 (0-404-57823-3) AMS Pr.

Pancel, Laslo, ed. Tropical Forestry Handbook, 2 vols., Set. LC 93-34006. (Illus.). 1900p. 1993. 498.00 (0-387-56420-9) Spr-Verlag.

*Pancer, Nancy W. Locks, Crocs, & Skeeters: The Story of the Panama Canal. (Illus.). 32p. (J). 1996. 15.00 (0-688-12241-8); lib. bdg. 14.93 (0-688-12242-6) Greenwillow.

*Pancero, Jim. Leading Your Sales Team: How to Manage a Winning Sales Team. 241p. 1995. 29.95 (0-614-07233-6) Dartnell Corp.

— Leading Your Sales Team: How to Manage a Winning Sales Team. 275p. 1995. 29.95 (0-85013-200-2) Dartnell Corp.

Panchadasi, Swami. Astral World. pap. 3.00 (0-911662-36-7) Yoga.

— Clairvoyance & Occult Powers. 12.00 (0-911662-35-9) Yoga.

— A Course of Advanced Lessons in Clairvoyance & Occult Powers. 319p. 1976. reprint ed. spiral bd. 11.00 (0-7873-0653-3) Mokelumne.

— Human Aura. pap. 3.00 (0-911662-37-5) Yoga.

Panchal. Yeast Strain Selection. (Bioprocess Technology Ser.: Vol. 8). 368p. 1990. 160.00 (0-8247-8276-3) Dekker.

Pancham Sinh, tr. see Svatmarama, S.

Panchamukhi, V. R. Planning, Development & the World Economic Order. 452p. 1987. text ed. 50.00 (81-7027-109-6, Pub. by Radiant Pubs II) S Asia.

*Panchamukhi, V. R., et al. Complementarity in Trade & Production: Intra-South Potentials. LC 94-23401. (Indo-Dutch Studies on Development Alternatives: Vol. 15). 1994. 25.00 (0-8039-9206-8) Sage.

Panchani, Chander S. Arunachal Pradesh: Religion, Culture & Society. vi, 347p. 1989. text ed. 35.00 (0-685-32870-8, Pub. by Konark Pubs Pvt Ltd II) Advent Bks Div.

Panchartek, J., jt. auth. see Sterba, V.

Panchen, A. L. Batrachosauria (Anthrosauria) (Encyclopedia of Paleoherpetology Ser.: Pt. 5-A). (Illus.). 1970. pap. text ed. 46.80 (3-437-30111-X) Lubrecht & Cramer.

Panchen, Alec L. Classification, Evolution, & the Nature of Biology. (Illus.). 350p. (C). 1992. pap. 34.95 (0-521-31578-6) Cambridge U Pr.

— Evolution. LC 93-18377. (Mind Matters Ser.). 182p. 1993. text ed. 24.95 (0-312-09697-6) St Martin.

Pancheri, Francesco S. The Universal Primacy of Christ. Carol, Juniper B., tr. Orig. Title: Il Primato universale de Christo. 144p. (Orig.). (C). 1984. pap. 6.95 (0-931888-16-6) Christendom Pr.

Pancheri, Paolo & Zichella, Lucio, eds. Biorhythms & Stress in the Physiopathology of Reproduction. (Series in Health Psychology & Behavioral Medicine). 580p. 1988. 110.00 (0-89116-567-3) Hemisp Pub.

Panchev, S. Dynamic Meteorology. 1985. lib. bdg. 162.50 (90-277-1744-3) Kluwer Ac.

Panchishkin, A. A., et al. Non-Archimedean L-Functions: Of Siegel & Hilbert Modular Forms. Dold, A. et al, eds. (Lecture Notes in Mathematics Ser.: Vol. 1471). vii, 157p. 1991. pap. 27.00 (0-387-54137-3) Spr-Verlag.

Panchyk, Katherine & Panchyk, Richard. The CADD Department. (Illus.). 200p. 1991. pap. 32.95 (0-442-00509-1) Chapman & Hall.

Panchyk, Richard. Birth Index for Buda Jewry: Covering the Years 1820-49 for Neolog Jews in Buda (Budapest), Hungary. 56p. (Orig.). 1993. pap. text ed. 3.75 (0-9622473-6-7) No Ink.

— Streetlamps & Distant Stars: A Collection of Poems (1986-89) 36p. (Orig.). 1989. pap. 2.25 (0-9622473-0-8) No Ink.

Panchyk, Richard, jt. auth. see Panchyk, Katherine.

Pancner, jt. auth. see Mosillo.

Pancoast, Chalmers L. Trail Blazers of Advertising: Stories of the Romance & Adventure of the Old-Time Advertising Game. LC 75-39264. (Getting & Spending: the Consumer's Dilemma Ser.). (Illus.). 1976. reprint ed. 26.95 (0-405-08037-9) Ayer.

Pancoast, Diane, jt. auth. see Garland, Diana.

Pancoast, Diane L., jt. auth. see Collins, Alice H.

Pancoast, Diane L., et al, eds. Rediscovering Self-Help: Its Role in Social Care. LC 83-3126. (Social Service Delivery Systems Ser.: No. 6). 295p. reprint ed. pap. 84.10 (0-8357-8503-3, 2034782) Bks Demand.

Pancoast, Henry S., ed. Standard English Poems. LC 72-149107. (Granger Index Reprint Ser.). 1977. 42.95 (0-8369-6232-X) Ayer.

— Vista of English Verse. LC 76-149108. (Granger Index Reprint Ser.). 1977. 40.95 (0-8369-6233-8) Ayer.

Pancoast, S. The Kabbala: Or True Science of Light: An Introduction to the Philosophy & Theosophy of the Ancient Sages Together with a Chapter on Light in the Vegetable Kingdom. 312p. 1992. pap. 24.95 (1-56459-167-0) Kessinger Pub.

Pancoast, Scott R. & White, Lance M. Business Grammar Handbook. LC 85-20248. (Illus.). 210p. 1992. pap. 9.95 (0-87131-709-5) M Evans.

Pancoast, William T. Crashing. 187p. 1983. 7.95 (0-9610562-0-7) Blazing Flowers.

*Pancoe, Joan. Openings: A Guide to Psychic Living in the Real World. LC 95-3846. 352p. (Orig.). 1995. pap. 18.95 (0-9644936-0-8) Modern Myst.

Pancol, Katherine. Call Me Scarlett. 416p. 1986. 18.95 (0-930267-20-6) Bergh Pub.

Panconcelli-Calzia, Giulio. Geschichtszahlen der Phonetik: Quellenatlas der Phonetic. LC 93-37819. (Studies in the History of the Language Sciences: No. 16). 250p. 1993. reprint ed. 65.00 (90-272-0957-X) Benjamins North Am.

Pancsofar, Ernest & Blackwell, Robert. A User's Guide to Community Entry for the Severely Handicapped. LC 84-24139. (SUNY Series in Special Education). 182p. 1985. 64.50 (0-88706-034-X); pap. 21.95 (0-88706-035-8) State U NY Pr.

Panczenko, Russell, ed. Patrick Ireland: Labyrinths, Language, Pyramids, & Related Acts. (Illus.). 112p. 1994. pap. 24.95 (0-932900-33-X) Elvejhem Mus.

Panczenko, Russell, jt. ed. see Golay, Jean-Pierre.

Panczner, Bill, jt. auth. see Panczner, Sharon.

Panczner, Sharon & Panczner, Bill. Arizona Traveler: Gems & Minerals of Arizona--A Guide to Arizona's Native Gemstones. (American Traveler Ser.). (Illus.). 48p. (Orig.). 1988. pap. 4.95 (1-55838-097-3) R H Pub.

Panczner, W. D. Rocky Mountain Traveler: A Travelers Guide to Tracking Dinosaurs in the Western U. S. 1994. pap. 4.95 (1-55838-149-X) R H Pub.

Panczner, William D. Minerals of Mexico. (Illus.). 352p. 1986. text ed. 65.00 (0-442-27285-5) Chapman & Hall.

Panda, Bishnupada, ed. Palas of Sri Kavi Karna, 3. (C). 1982. 40.00 (81-208-0961-0, Pub. by Motilal Banarsidass II) S Asia.

— Palas of Sri Kavi Karna, 4. (C). 1982. 40.00 (81-208-0962-9, Pub. by Motilal Banarsidass II) S Asia.

Panda, N. Principles of Host-Plant Resistance to Insect Pests. LC 78-59169. (Illus.). 406p. 1980. text ed. 54.00 (0-916672-93-X) Rowman.

*Panda, N. & Kush, G. S. Host Plant Resistance to Insects. 450p. 1995. 99.00 (0-85198-963-2) CAB Intl.

Panda, N. C. Maya in Physics. (C). 1991. 32.00 (81-208-0698-0, Pub. by Motilal Banarsidass II) S Asia.

Panda, R. K. Agricultural Indebtedness & Institutional Finance, India. 1985. 24.00 (0-8364-1385-7, Pub. by Ashish II) S Asia.

— Industrial Sickness: A Study of Small Scale Industries. (C). 1992. 18.00 (81-7024-452-8, Pub. by Ashish II) S Asia.

*Panda, Rajaram. Japan & the Third World: Political & Economic Inter-actions, 1980's-1990's. (C). 1995. 28.00x (81-7095-046-5, Pub. by Lancers Bks II) S Asia.

Panda, Snehalata. Determinants of Political Participation: Women & Public Activity. 1990. 20.00 (0-685-34755-9, Pub. by Ajanta II) S Asia.

— Women & Social Change in India. viii, 124p. 1992. 12.95 (1-881338-14-2) Nataraj Bks.

— Women & Social Change in India. (C). 1991. 17.50 (81-7024-423-4, Pub. by Ashish II) S Asia.

Panday, Daulat. The Tales of India, Vol. 1. 114p. (J). (gr. 3-8). 1985. pap. 5.95 (0-89071-330-8, Pub. by SAA II) Aurobindo Assn.

— The Tales of India, Vol. 2. 126p. (J). (gr. 3-8). 1985. pap. 5.95 (0-89071-331-6, Pub. by SAA II) Aurobindo Assn.

Panday, S. R., ed. see Borre, Ole, et al.

Pande, A. Handbook of Moisture Determination & Control: Principles, Techniques, Applications, 4 vols., Vol. 1. LC 73-86820. (Illus.). 280p. reprint ed. pap. 75.60 (0-7837-0654-5, 2040993) Bks Demand.

— Handbook of Moisture Determination & Control: Principles, Techniques, Applications, 4 vols., Vol. 2. LC 73-86820. (Illus.). 335p. reprint ed. pap. 95.50 (0-7837-0655-3) Bks Demand.

— Handbook of Moisture Determination & Control: Principles, Techniques, Applications, 4 vols., Vol. 3. LC 73-86820. (Illus.). 302p. reprint ed. pap. 86.10 (0-7837-0656-1) Bks Demand.

— Handbook of Moisture Determination & Control: Principles, Techniques, Applications, 4 vols., Vol. 4. LC 73-86820. (Illus.). 327p. reprint ed. pap. 93.20 (0-7837-0657-X) Bks Demand.

Pande, B. N. Centenary History of Indian National Congress. (Illus.). 1986. Vol. I: 1885-1919; 645p. write for info. (0-7069-3012-6, Pub. by Vikas II); Vol. II: 1919-1935; 672 pgs. write for info. (0-7069-3013-4, Pub. by Vikas II); Vol. III: 1935-1947; 886 pgs. write for info. (0-7069-3014-2, Pub. by Vikas II) S Asia.

— Centenary History of Indian National Congress, Set. (Illus.). 1986. text ed. 150.00 (0-317-46164-8, Pub. by Vikas II) S Asia.

Pande, B. N., ed. A Centenary History of Indian National Congress, Vol. IV. 1990. text ed. 60.00 (0-7069-4986-2, Pub. by Vikas II) S Asia.

Pande, Badri D. Development of Higher Education in Nepal, 1918-1976. 230p. pap. 18.00 (0-317-04778-7) Am-Nepal Ed.

Pande, C. S. & Marsh, S. P., eds. Modeling of Coarsening & Grain Growth. 1993. 66.00 (0-87339-210-8, 468) Minerals Metals.

Pande, C. S., ed. see American Society for Metals Staff.

Pande, G. C. Foundations of Indian Culture, Vol. II: Dimensions of Ancient Indian Social History. 1990. 47.50 (81-208-0711-1, Pub. by Motilal Banarsidass II) S Asia.

— Foundations of Indian Culture Vol. 1: Spiritual Vision & Symbolic Forms in Ancient India. 1990. 44.00 (81-208-0710-3, Pub. by Motilal Banarsidass II) S Asia.

— Indian Tribes: Habitat, Society, Economy & Change. (C). 1991. 46.00 (0-685-59771-7, Pub. by Anmol II) S Asia.

Pande, G. N. & Middleton, J., eds. Numerical Methods in Engineering (NUMETA 90) Theory & Applications, 2 vols., Set. 1990. 300.00 (1-85166-462-9) Elsevier.

— Numerical Methods in Engineering (NUMETA 90) Theory & Applications, Vol. 1. 672p. 1990. 131.00 (1-85166-463-7) Elsevier.

— Numerical Methods in Engineering (NUMETA 90) Theory & Applications, Vol. 2. 521p. 1990. 102.50 (1-85166-464-5) Elsevier.

— Numerical Techniques for Engineering Analysis & Design, Set. (C). 1987. lib. bdg. 240.00 (0-685-19351-9) Kluwer Ac.

— Numerical Techniques for Engineering Analysis & Design, Vol. 1. (C). 1987. Vol. 2, Transient-Dynamic Analysis & Constitutive Laws for Engineering Materials. lib. bdg. 209.50 (90-247-3565-3) Kluwer Ac.

— Numerical Techniques for Engineering Analysis & Design, Vol 1: Engineering. (C). 1987. Vol. 1, Engineering. lib. bdg. 194.50 (90-247-3564-5) Kluwer Ac.

Pande, G. N. & Pietruszczak, S., eds. Numerical Models in Geomechanics: Proceedings of the Fourth International Symposium - NUMOG IV - Swansea, U. K. 24-27 August 1992, 2 vols., Set. (Illus.). (C). 1992. text ed. 185.00 (90-5410-088-5, Pub. by A A Balkema NE) Ashgate Pub Co.

Pande, G. N. & Zienkiewicz, O. C., eds. Soil Mechanics, Transient & Cyclic Loads: Constitutive Relations & Numerical Treatment. LC 81-16485. (Wiley Series in Numerical Methods in Engineering). (Illus.). 639p. reprint ed. pap. 180.00 (0-318-39649-1, 2033053) Bks Demand.

— Soils under Cyclic & Transient Loading: Proceedings from the International Symposium, Swansea, 7-11th January 1980, 2 vols., Set. 894p. (C). 1980. text ed. 240.00 (90-6191-076-5, Pub. by A A Balkema NE) Ashgate Pub Co.

Pande, G. N., jt. ed. see Middleton, J.

Pande, G. N., et al. Numerical Methods in Rock Mechanics. (Numerical Methods in Engineering Ser.). 327p. 1990. text ed. 110.95 (0-471-92021-5) Wiley.

Pande, J. N., ed. Respiratory Medicine in the Tropics. (Illus.). 500p. 1995. 39.95 (0-19-563311-3) OUP.

Pande, Janak N. Mental Retardation in Nepal. 65p. 1983. pap. 10.00 (0-318-03449-2) Am-Nepal Ed.

Pande, P. N. Self-Employment Programme in India. (C). 1988. 17.50 (81-7024-213-4, Pub. by Ashish II) S Asia.

Pande, P. N., ed. Wage Equality among Sexes - a Study of Equal Remuneration Act. 275p. (C). 1992. 150.00 (81-85009-39-2, Pub. by Print Hse II) St Mut.

Pande, Rekha. Succession in the Dehli Sultante. 1990. 29.00 (81-7169-069-6, Commonwealth) S Asia.

Pande, Savita. Pakistan's Nuclear Policy. (C). 1991. 14.00 (81-7018-657-9, Pub. by BR Pub II) S Asia.

Pande, Sunanda. Trends of Occupational Mobility among Migrants. 232p. (C). 1986. 31.00 (81-7033-023-8, Pub. by Rawat II) S Asia.

Pandeez. Pre-Historic Archaelogy of Madhya Pradesh. (C). 1987. 62.50 (81-85067-04-X, Pub. by Sundeep II) S Asia.

Pandell, Karen. By Day & by Night. Kramer, Linda, ed. LC 90-52635. (Illus.). 32p. (J). (ps-2). 1991. 14.95 (0-915811-26-X) H J Kramer Inc.

— I Love You, Sun I Love You, Moon. (Illus.). 18p. (J). (ps). 1994. bds. 5.95 (0-399-22628-1) Putnam Pub Group.

— Land of Dark, Land of Light: The Arctic National Wildlife Refuge. LC 92-40405. (Illus.). 32p. (J). (ps-3). 1993. 14.99 (0-525-45094-7, DCB) Dutton Child Bks.

*Pandell, Karen & Bryant, Barry. Learning from the Dalai Lama: Secrets of the Wheel of Time. (Illus.). 40p. (J). (gr. 3-7). 1995. 14.99 (0-525-45063-7) Dutton Child Bks.

Pandell, Karen & Stall, Chris. Animal Tracks of the Pacific Northwest. LC 81-2041. (Illus.). 120p. (Orig.). 1981. pap. 5.95 (0-89886-012-1) Mountaineers.

Pandey, A. K. Kinship & Tribal Polity. (C). 1989. 37.50 (81-7033-077-7, Pub. by Rawat II) S Asia.

Pandey, B. N. Role of Science & Technology in Rural & Economic Development of India. 220p. 1983. 27.95 (0-318-37334-3) Asia Bk Corp.

Pandey, B. N., ed. Role of Science & Technology in Rural & Economic Development in India. 1983. text ed. 26.50 (0-685-14096-2) Coronet Bks.

Pandey, B. P. Gandhi Sarvodaya & Organizations. (C). 1988. 26.00 (81-85076-55-3, Pub. by Chugh Pubns II) S Asia.

Pandey, B. P., ed. Gandhi & Economic Development. 233p. 1991. text ed. 35.00 (0-685-40677-6, Pub. by Radiant Pubs II) S Asia.

Pandey, Chandra B. Risis in Ancient India. 265p. 1987. 26.00 (0-8364-2022-5, Pub. by Sundeep II) S Asia.

Pandey, D. & Wadhawan, V. K., eds. Modulated Structures, Polytypes & Quasicrystals: Proceedings of the International Conference in India, December 1988: A Special Issue of the Journal Phase Transitions. xii, 636p. 1989. pap. text ed. 867.00 (0-677-25810-0) Gordon & Breach.

*Pandey, D. P. & Sharma, V. P. Collins Gem English-Hindi Dictionary. 755p. (ENG & HIN.). 1993. write for info. (0-7859-7416-4, 0004589645) Fr & Eur.

Pandey, D. P., jt. auth. see Murthy, Anjneya N.

Pandey, D. P., jt. auth. see Murthy, N. A.

Pandey, Gaya, jt. auth. see Saran, A. B.

Pandey, Gaya, jt. auth. see Upadhyay, V. S.

Pandey, Geetanjali. Between Two Worlds an Intellectual Biography of Premchand. (C). 1989. 25.00 (81-85054-59-2, Pub. by Manohar II) S Asia.

Pandey, Gyanendra. The Construction of Communalism in Colonial North India. (Oxford India Paperbacks Ser.). 320p. 1992. pap. 8.95 (0-19-563010-6) OUP.

— Medicinal Flowers: Puspayurveda Medicinal Flowers of India & Adjacent Regions. (Indian Medical Science Ser.: No. 14). (C). 1992. 18.00 (81-7030-351-6) S Asia.

— Uncommon Plant Drugs of Ayurveda. (C). 1995. 34.00x (81-7030-404-0, Pub. by Sri Satguru Pubns II) S Asia.

Pandey, Gyanendra, ed. The Indian Nation in Nineteen Forty-Two. (C). 1988. 22.50 (81-7074-024-X) S Asia.

Pandey, Gyanendra, jt. ed. see Chatterjee, Partha.

Pandey, I. C. Tectonic & Metamorphic Investigations of Kumaon-Garhwal Himachal Lesser Himalaya. Saklani, P. S., ed. (Current Trends in Geology Ser.: Vol. 13). (Illus.). 179p. 1991. 65.00 (1-55528-240-7, Messers Today & Tomorrow) Scholarly Pubns.

Pandey, Indu P. Romantic Feminism in Hindi Novels Written by Women. 1989. 21.50 (81-85313-00-8, Pub. by Usha II) S Asia.

Pandey, Janak, ed. Psychology in India: The State-of-the-Art, Vol. 1: Personality & Mental Process. 336p. (C). 1989. text ed. 35.00 (0-8039-9552-0) Sage.

— Psychology in India: The State-of-the-Art, Vol. 2: Basic & Applied Social Psychology. 356p. (C). 1989. text ed. 35.00 (0-8039-9553-9) Sage.

— Psychology in India: The State-of-the-Art, Vol. 3: Organizational Behavior & Mental Health. 342p. (C). 1989. text ed. 35.00 (0-8039-9554-7) Sage.

— Social Reality: Perspectives & Understanding. (C). 1988. 19.00 (81-7022-199-4, Pub. by Concept II) S Asia.

Pandey, Jitendra. Civil Liberty under Indian Constitution. (C). 1992. 28.00 (81-7100-383-4, Pub. by Deep) S Asia.

Pandey, K. & Shukla, J. P. Elements of Toxicology. (C). 1991. 24.00 (81-85484-26-0, Pub. by Classical Pub II) S Asia.

Pandey, Kanti C. An Outline of History of Saiva Philosophy. Dwivedi, R. C., ed. 300p. 1986. reprint ed. 15.00 (81-208-0091-5, Pub. by Motilal Banarsidass II) S Asia.

*Pandey, Manaj & Kedia, Onkar. Fundamentals of Indian Constitution. (C). 1995. 16.00x (0-7069-8380-7, Pub. by Vikas II) S Asia.

Pandey, Manoj, jt. auth. see Gusain, P. P.

Pandey, N. P. Geography of Transportation: A Case Study of Western Madhya Pradesh. 1990. 48.50 (81-210-0252-4, Pub. by Inter-India Pubns) S Asia.

Pandey, Pradyumana, ed. Modern Geographical Trends Felicitation: Volume in Honour of Professor Enayat Ahmad. xxxvi, 616p. 1984. 89.00 (1-55528-068-4, Pub. by Today & Tomorrows P & P II) Scholarly Pubns.

Pandey, R., ed. Biotechnology & Comparative Medicine. (Progress in Veterinary Microbiology & Immunology Ser.: Vol. 3). (Illus.). xvi, 268p. 1987. 168.00 (3-8055-4399-9) S Karger.

— Infection & Immunity in Farm Animals. (Progress in Veterinary Microbiology & Immunology Ser.: Vol. 1). (Illus.). xiv, 258p. 1984. 131.25 (3-8055-3925-8) S Karger.

— Moving Frontiers in Veterinary Immunology. (Progress in Veterinary Microbiology & Immunology Ser.: Vol. 4). (Illus.). xii, 252p. 1987. 168.00 (3-8055-4632-7) S Karger.

— Nononcogenic Avian Viruses. (Progress in Veterinary Microbiology & Immunology Ser.: Vol. 5). (Illus.). viii, 136p. 1989. 92.00 (3-8055-4827-3) S Karger.

— Veterinary Microbiology. (Progress in Veterinary Microbiology & Immunology Ser.: Vol. 2). (Illus.). x, 222p. 1985. 118.50 (3-8055-4067-1) S Karger.

Pandey, R., et al, eds. Veterinary Vaccines. (Progress in Vaccinology Ser.: Vol. 4). (Illus.). 376p. 1992. 164.00 (0-387-97819-4) Spr-Verlag.

Pandey, R. C. & Bhatt, S. R., eds. Knowledge Culture & Value: Papers Presented at the World Conference New Delhi at the Time of Golden Jubilee Session of the Indian Philosophical Congress 1975-76. 215p. 1977. 19.00 (0-88065-175-X, Messers Today & Tomorrow) Scholarly Pubns.

Pandey, R. K. A Farmer's Primer on Growing Cowpea on Riceland. (Illus.). 224p. (Orig.). 1987. pap. 14.95 (0-8138-1498-7) Iowa St U Pr.

P
Q

— A Farmer's Primer on Growing Soybean on Riceland. (Illus.). 222p. (Orig.). 1987. pap. 14.95 (*0-8138-1476-6*) Iowa St U Pr.

Pandey, R. N. Commercial Banks & Rural Development. (C). 1989. 250.00 (*0-685-46468-7*) St Mut.

Pandey, R. P., jt. auth. see Shetty, B. V.

Pandey, Rajbali. Hindu Samskaras: Socio-Religious Study of the Hindu Sacraments. (C). 1987. 22.00 (*81-208-0396-5*, Pub. by Motilal Banarsidass II); pap. 15.50 (*81-208-0434-1*, Pub. by Motilal Banarsidass II) S Asia.

Pandey, Rajendra. Breast Feeding & the Working Women of India. 1990. 40.00 (*81-85076-92-8*, Pub. by Chugh Pubns II) S Asia.

— The Caste System in India: Myth & Reality. 241p. 1986. 25.00 (*0-8364-1861-1*, Pub. by Minerva II) S Asia.

— Social Problems of Contemporary India. (Illus.). vi, 373p. 1994. 43.00x (*81-7024-604-0*, Pub. by Ashish Pub Hse II) Nataraj Bks.

— Street Children of India. (C). 1991. 42.50 (*81-85613-37-0*, Pub. by Chugh Pubns II) S Asia.

Pandey, Rama S., jt. auth. see Jones, John T.

Pandey, Rehka & Upadnyay, Neelam U. Women in India Past & Present. (C). 1991. pap. 11.00 (*0-685-49090-4*, Pub. by Chugh Pubns II) S Asia.

Pandey, Rekha. Women from Subjection to Liberation. (C). 1989. 34.00 (*81-7099-085-8*, Pub. by Mittal II) S Asia.

Pandey, S. K. Indian Rock Art. (C). 1993. 82.00 (*81-7305-032-5*, Pub. by Aryan Bks Intl IA) S Asia.

Pandey, S. N. & Sinha, B. K. Plant Physiology. rev. ed. 594p. (C). 1986. text ed. 45.00 (*0-7069-4763-0*, Pub. by Vikas II) S Asia.

Pandey, S. N., jt. auth. see Tripathi, A. K.

Pandey, Sachchidanand. Naxal Violence. 1985. 18.00 (*81-7001-003-9*, Pub. by Chanakya II) S Asia.

Pandey, Shashi. Community Action for Social Justice: Grassroots Organizations in India. 258p. 1991. text ed. 32.00 (*0-8039-9674-8*) Sage.

Pandey, Shashi R., jt. auth. see Tantiwiramanond, Darunee.

Pandey, Sheojee. Sri Aurobindo & Vedanta Philosophy. (C). 1987. 21.00 (*81-7100-028-2*, Pub. by Deep) S Asia.

Pandey, Suchakar, ed. Contemporary Indian Drama. 120p. 1990. text ed. 15.95 (*0-685-56101-1*, Pub. by Prestige II) Advent Bks Div.

Pandey, Sudhakar, ed. George Bernard Shaw - A Critical Response. 150p. 1991. text ed. 22.95 (*81-85218-36-6*) Advent Bks Div.

— Glimpses of Ancient Indian Poetics: (From Bharata to Jagannatha) (Sri Garib Dass Oriental Ser.: No. 166). (C). 1993. 21.00 (*81-7030-360-5*) S Asia.

Pandey, Sumana. Women in Politics. 1990. 26.50 (*81-7033-088-2*, Pub. by Rawat II) S Asia.

Pandey, V. N. Textbook of Labour & Industrial Laws. 416p. 1980. 90.00 (*0-317-54680-5*) St Mut.

Pandeya, R. C., ed. Pramanavarttika of Dharmakirti (with Dharmakirti's Own Commentary on the Third Chapter & Manorathanandin's Commentary on the Entire Text. (C). 1989. 42.00 (*81-208-0546-1*, Pub. by Motilal Banarsidass II) S Asia.

Pandeya, Raghunath. The Madhyamakasastram of Nagarjuna, Vol. 1. (C). 1988. 58.00 (*81-208-0554-2*, Pub. by Motilal Banarsidass II) S Asia.

Pandeya, Raghunath, ed. The Madhyamakasastram of Nagarjuna, Vol. 2. (C). 1989. 48.50 (*81-208-0555-0*, Pub. by Motilal Banarsidass II) S Asia.

Pandeya, Ram C. Nagarjuna's Philosophy of No-Identity: With Philosophical Translations of the Madhyamaka-Karika, Sunyata-Saptati & Vigrahavyavartani. (C). 1991. 20.00 (*0-685-63332-2*, Pub. by Eastern Bk Linkers II) S Asia.

Pandeya, Ram C. & Manju. Nagarjuna's Philosophy of No-Identity: With Philosophical Translations of the Madhyamaka-Karika, Sunyata-Saptati & Vigrahavyavartani. xxvi, 165p. 1991. 18.00 (*0-685-62634-2*, Estrn Bk Linkers) Nataraj Bks.

Pandeya, S. C. & Lieth, Helmut, eds. Ecology of Cenchrus Grass Complex: Environmental Conditions & Population Differences in Western India. LC 92-18658. (Tasks for Vegetation Science Ser.: Vol. 23). 248p. (C). 1993. lib. bdg. 156.00 (*0-7923-0768-2*) Kluwer Ac.

***Pandher, Nick.** Chicago Quick Reference. 1994. pap. 9.99 (*1-56529-931-0*) Que.

Pandian, J. Nationalism & Ethnicity: An Interpretation of Tamil Cultural History & Social Order. 1987. 27.00 (*0-86132-136-7*, Pub. by Popular Prakashan II) S Asia.

Pandian, Jacob. Anthropology & the Western Tradition: Toward An Authentic Anthropology. 135p. (Orig.). 1985. pap. text ed. 9.50 (*0-88133-127-9*) Waveland Pr.

— Culture, Religion, & the Sacred Self: A Critical Introduction to the Anthropological Study of Religion. 352p. (C). 1990. pap. text ed. write for info. (*0-13-194226-3*) P-H.

— The Making of India & Indian Traditions. LC 94-16912. 304p. 1994. pap. text ed. write for info. (*0-13-124421-3*) P-H.

Pandian, M. S. The Image Trap: M. G. Ramachandran in Film & Politics. (Illus.). 164p. (C). 1992. text ed. 28.00 (*0-8039-9403-6*) Sage.

— The Political Economy of Agrarian Change: Nanchilnadu, 1880-1939. (Illus.). 196p. (C). 1990. 25.00 (*0-8039-9642-X*) Sage.

Pandian, Natasa & Sanders, Stephen P. Textbook of Echocardiography. 750p. 1994. write for info. (*0-683-06744-3*) Williams & Wilkins.

Pandian, P. S. Indian Philosophy - Study of Hindutva. 126p. (C). 1991. text ed. 18.95 (*81-207-1376-1*, Pub. by Sterling Pubs II) Apt Bks.

Pandian, S. K. The Hidden Heritage. 125p. 1987. text ed. 18.95 (*81-207-0661-7*, Pub. by Sterling Pubs II) Apt Bks.

Pandian, T. J. & Vernberg, F. John, eds. Animal Energetics, Vol. 1: Protozoa Through Insects. 523p. 1987. text ed. 178.00 (*0-12-544791-4*) Acad Pr.

— Animal Energetics, Vol. 2: Bivalvia Through Reptilia. 631p. 1987. text ed. 174.00 (*0-12-544792-2*) Acad Pr.

Pandiscia, Anthony. For God & Neighbour: The Life & Work of Padre Pio. (C). 1990. 45.00 (*0-85439-373-0*, Pub. by St Paul Pubns UK) St Mut.

Pandit, B. N. Mirror of Self-Supremacy or Svatantrya-Darpana. (C). Date not set. 12.50 (*81-215-0559-3*, Pub. by Munshiram Manoharial II) S Asia.

Pandit, B. N., tr. Essence of the Exact Reality or Parmathasara of Abhinavagupta. (C). 1991. 10.00 (*0-685-54511-3*, Pub. by Munshiram Manoharial II) S Asia.

Pandit, Bansi. The Hindu Mind: Fundamentals of Hindu Religion & Philosophy For All Ages. 2nd ed. LC 93-72469. 432p. 1993. pap. 14.95 (*0-9634798-1-4*) B&V Ent.

— Hindu Mind: Fundamentals of Hindu Religion & Philosophy for All Ages. 2nd ed. LC 93-72469. 432p. 1997. 19.95 (*0-9634798-2-2*) B&V Ent.

Pandit, G. L. Methodological Variance: Essays in Epistemological Ontology & the Methodology of Science. (Boston Studies in the Philosophy of Science). 440p. (C). 1991. lib. bdg. 142.00 (*0-7923-1263-5*) Kluwer Ac.

Pandit, H. N. Fragments of History: India's Freedom Movement & After. 299p. 1982. 35.95 (*0-940500-55-8*, Pub. by Sterling II) Asia Bk Corp.

— Subhas Chandra Bose: From Kabul to Battle of Imphal. 360p. 1988. text ed. 40.00 (*0-685-19794-8*, Pub. by Sterling Pubs II) Apt Bks.

Pandit, Lalita, jt. ed. see Hogan, Patrick C.

Pandit, M. D. Mathematics As Known to the Vedic Samhitas. (Sri Garib Dass Oriental Ser.: No. 169). (C). 1993. text ed. 22.00 (*81-7030-368-0*) S Asia.

Pandit, M. P. Aditi & Other Deities in the Veda. 1979. 6.95 (*0-941524-01-9*) Lotus Light.

— Dhyana. 60p. 1990. reprint ed. pap. 1.95 (*0-941524-03-5*) Lotus Light.

— Dynamics of Yoga, Vol. I. 182p. 1979. 9.95 (*0-941524-05-1*) Lotus Light.

— Dynamics of Yoga, Vol. II. 183p. 1979. 9.95 (*0-941524-06-X*) Lotus Light.

— Kundalini Yoga: A Brief Study of Sir John Woodroffe's "The Serpent Power" 2nd ed. LC 79-88734. 74p. 1993. pap. 4.95 (*0-941524-50-7*) Lotus Light.

— Legends in the Life Divine. 284p. 1988. 16.00 (*0-941524-34-5*) Lotus Light.

— More on Tantras. 152p. 1986. text ed. 22.50 (*81-207-0122-4*, Pub. by Sterling Pubs II) Apt Bks.

— Occult Lines Behind Life. 100p. (Orig.). 1992. reprint ed. pap. 7.95 (*0-941524-35-3*) Lotus Light.

— Satsang, Vol I. Golikhere, Vasanti R., ed. 298p. (Orig.). 1979. pap. 11.00 (*0-941524-10-8*) Lotus Light.

— Sri Aurobindo & His Yoga. LC 87-80572. 196p. (Orig.). 1987. pap. 6.95 (*0-941524-25-6*) Lotus Light.

— Studies in the Tantras & the Veda. 176p. 1988. text ed. 25.00 (*81-207-0883-0*, Pub. by Sterling Pubs II) Apt Bks.

— Traditions in Mysticism. 1987. text ed. 45.00 (*81-207-0669-2*, Pub. by Sterling Pubs II) Apt Bks.

— Upanishads: Gateways of Knowledge. LC 88-83077. 270p. (Orig.). 1988. pap. 9.95 (*0-941524-44-2*) Lotus Light.

— Vedic Deities. LC 89-84765. 129p. (Orig.). 1989. pap. 7.95 (*0-941524-45-0*) Lotus Light.

— Wisdom of the Gita: First Series. 144p. 1992. pap. 9.95 (*0-941524-72-8*) Lotus Light.

— Wisdom of the Veda. LC 89-84764. 112p. (Orig.). 1990. pap. 7.95 (*0-941524-55-8*) Lotus Light.

— Yoga for the Modern Man. 128p. 1988. text ed. 12.95 (*81-207-0759-1*, Pub. by Sterling Pubs II) Apt Bks.

— Yoga for the Modern Man. 115p. 1979. 4.00 (*0-941524-13-2*) Lotus Light.

— Yoga in Sri Aurobindo's Epic Savitri. 236p. 1979. 10.95 (*0-941524-15-9*) Lotus Light.

— The Yoga of Knowledge: Talks at Centre, Vol. II. LC 86-80692. 282p. (Orig.). 1986. pap. 7.95 (*0-941524-23-X*) Lotus Light.

— The Yoga of Love. LC 81-86373. (Talks at Center Ser.: Vol. III). 112p. (Orig.). 1982. pap. 3.95 (*0-941524-16-7*) Lotus Light.

— Yoga of Self-Perfection. LC 83-81299. (Talks at Center Ser.: Vol. IV). 312p. (Orig.). 1983. pap. 7.95 (*0-941524-20-5*) Lotus Light.

— The Yoga of Works: Talks at Centre I. LC 85-50695. 192p. (C). 1985. pap. 7.95 (*0-941524-21-3*) Lotus Light.

Pandit, M. P., ed. see Aurobindo, Sri.

Pandit, M. P., tr. see Parasurama.

Pandit, Milind S. How Computers Really Work: A Guide for the Excessively Obsessively Insanely Curious. (Illus.). 1993. pap. text ed. 21.95 (*0-07-881936-9*) McGraw.

Pandit, N. P. Traditions in Occultism. 108p. 1987. text ed. 15.95 (*81-207-0660-9*, Pub. by Sterling Pubs II) Apt Bks.

Pandit, P. N. The Novels of Graham Greene: Impact of Childhood on Adult Life. 208p. 1990. text ed. 27.50 (*81-85218-17-X*, Pub. by Prestige II) Advent Bks Div.

Pandit, Ranjit S., tr. Kahlanas' Rajatarangini: The Saga of the Kings of Kashmir. (C). 1991. 25.00 (*0-8364-2629-0*, Pub. by National Sahitya Akademi) S Asia.

Pandit, S. M. & Wu, S. M. Time Series & System Analysis with Applications. 606p. 1993. 79.50 (*0-89464-844-6*) Krieger.

Pandit, Sakya, jt. auth. see Nagarjuna.

Pandit, Sri M. Japa. 41p. 1991. reprint ed. 2.50 (*0-941524-09-4*) Lotus Light.

Pandit, Sudhakar M. Modal & Spectrum Analysis: Data Dependent Systems in State Space. 415p. 1991. text ed. 89.95 (*0-471-63705-X*) Wiley.

Pandit, U. K. & Alderweireldt, F. C., eds. Bioorganic Chemistry in Healthcare & Technology. (NATO ASI Series A, Life Sciences: Vol. 207). (Illus.). 326p. 1991. 95.00 (*0-306-44007-5*, Plenum Pr) Plenum.

***Pandit, V., ed.** Coastal Fishery Projects: Construction, Maintenance & Development. Tankha, Brij, tr. (Illus.). 482p. (ENG.). (C). 1994. text ed. 85.00 (*90-5410-229-2*, Pub. by A A Balkema NE) Ashgate Pub Co.

Pandit, Yeshwant S. India's Balance of Indebtedness: Eighteen Ninety-Eight to Nineteen Thirteen. Wilkins, Mira, ed. LC 78-3944. (International Finance Ser.). 1979. reprint ed. lib. bdg. 21.95 (*0-405-11244-0*) Ayer.

Pandita, Sayadaw U. In This Very Life: The Liberation Teachings of the Buddha. Wheeler, Kate, ed. LC 92-42813. 300p. 1992. pap. 16.00 (*0-86171-094-0*) Wisdom MA.

Panditrao, Y. A. Gandhian Approach to Economic Development. 1992. 27.50 (*81-7040-438-X*, Pub. by Himalaya II) Apt Bks.

Pandley, B. N., ed. see De Silva, Chandra R.

Pando, Magdalen M. Cuba's Freedom Fighter, Antonio Maceo: Eighteen Forty-Five to Eighteen Ninety-Six. LC 79-93001. (Illus.). 144p. (Orig.). (gr. 10-12). 1980. pap. 9.95 (*0-9603846-0-X*) Felicity.

Pando, Miguel, ed. see Huidobro, Matias M., et al.

Pando, Patricia N., jt. auth. see Gould, Florence C.

Pando y Villaroya, Jose L. Diccionario de Marina. 2nd ed. 252p. 1985. pap. 39.95 (*0-7859-6031-7*, 8439847068) Fr & Eur.

Pandolf. Exercise & Sports Sciences Review, Vol. 14. 1986. text ed. 53.95 (*0-07-105347-6*) McGraw.

— Exercise & Sports Sciences Review, Vol. 15. 1991. text ed. 59.95 (*0-07-105348-4*) McGraw.

Pandolf, Kent, et al, eds. Human Performance Physiology & Environmental Medicine at Terrestrial Extremes. (Illus.). 637p. (C). reprint ed. text ed. 48.00 (*1-884125-02-6*) Cooper Pubng.

Pandolf, Kent B. Exercise & Sports Sciences Review, Vol. 18. (Illus.). 480p. 1990. 46.95 (*0-683-00047-0*) Williams & Wilkins.

Pandolf, Kent B., ed. Exercise & Sports Sciences Review, Vol. 17. (American College of Sports Medicine Ser.). (Illus.). 584p. 1989. pap. 46.95 (*0-683-00046-2*) Williams & Wilkins.

Pandolf, Kent B., et al. Human Performance Physiology & Environmental Medicine at Terrestrial Extremes. (Illus.). 637p. 1988. boxed write for info. (*0-697-14823-8*) Brown & Benchmark.

Pandolfini, Bruce. The ABCs of Chess. 1986. pap. 10.00 (*0-671-61982-9*, Fireside) S&S Trade.

— Beginning Chess: Over Three Hundred Elementary Problems for Players New to the Game. LC 93-9693. (Illus.). 256p. (Orig.). 1993. pap. 12.00 (*0-671-79501-5*, Fireside) S&S Trade.

— Bobby Fischer's Outrageous Chess Moves. 1993. pap. 10.00 (*0-671-87432-2*, Fireside) S&S Trade.

— Chess Openings: Traps & Zaps. 1989. pap. 11.00 (*0-671-65690-2*, Fireside) S&S Trade.

— Chess Target Practice. 1994. pap. 12.00 (*0-671-79500-7*, Fireside) S&S Trade.

— Chess Thinking. 1995. pap. 15.00 (*0-671-79502-3*, Fireside) S&S Trade.

— Chessercizes: New Winning Techniques for Players of All Levels. (Illus.). 224p. (Orig.). 1991. pap. 10.00 (*0-671-70184-3*, Fireside) S&S Trade.

— Let's Play Chess: A Step-By-Step Guide for All First-Time Players. 1986. pap. 9.00 (*0-671-61983-7*, Fireside) S&S Trade.

— More Chess Openings. 1993. pap. 11.00 (*0-671-79499-X*, Fireside) S&S Trade.

— More Chessercizes: Checkmate! Three Hundred Winning Stratagems for Players of All Levels. (Illus.). 208p. 1991. pap. 10.00 (*0-671-70185-1*, Fireside) S&S Trade.

— One-Move Chess Problems by the Champions. write for info. (*0-318-59565-6*) S&S Trade.

— Pandolfini's Complete Chess: The Most Comprehensive Guide to the Game, from History to Strategy. LC 92-16152. 1992. pap. 15.00 (*0-671-70186-X*, Fireside) S&S Trade.

— Pandolfini's Endgame Course. (Illus.). 288p. 1988. pap. 11.00 (*0-671-65688-0*, Fireside) S&S Trade.

— The Principles of the New Chess: Make the Last International Training Secrets Work for You. 188p. 1986. pap. 10.00 (*0-671-60719-7*, Fireside) S&S Trade.

— Square One: The Best Chess Drill Book for Beginners of All Ages. LC 94-17956. 1994. write for info. (*0-671-88424-7*, Fireside) S&S Trade.

— Weapons of Chess: An Omnibus of Chess Strategy. 1989. pap. 11.00 (*0-671-65972-3*, Fireside) S&S Trade.

Pandosy, Marie C. Grammar & Dictionary of the Yakama Language. LC 10-30204. (Library of American Linguistics: Vol. 6). reprint ed. 42.75 (*0-404-50986-X*) AMS Pr.

Pandozzi, Frank W. Medigap Insurance: A License to Steal. 61p. (Orig.). 1990. pap. 9.95 (*0-9628734-0-3*) Aa Zz Pub.

Pandratz, Ronald, jt. auth. see Preston, Seaton T., Jr.

Pandrich, Bruce, jt. ed. see Spear, Hilda D.

Pandurangarao, Malyala. Consecration of Idols. (Illus.). 32p. (Orig.). 1984. pap. 4.00 (*0-938924-21-4*) Sri Shirdi Sai.

— Hanumaan Chaaleesa. (Illus.). 16p. (Orig.). 1984. pap. 2.00 (*0-317-07665-5*) Sri Shirdi Sai.

Pandurangarao Malyaya. Model Building of Solar Systems. (Worship Technology Around the World Ser.: No. 1). Orig. Title: Sri Satyanarayana Katha. (Illus.). 100p. (Orig.). 1981. 9.99 (*0-938924-00-1*) Sri Shirdi Sai.

Pandy, A. K. Local Level Planning & Rural Development: An Analytical Study. 1990. 21.50 (*81-7099-189-7*, Pub. by Mittal II) S Asia.

Pandya, et al, eds. Energy: A Classified Bibliography (1970-1985) (C). 1991. 28.00 (*81-85119-99-6*, Pub. by Northern Bk Ctr II) S Asia.

***Pandya, Abhijit S. & Macy, Robert B.** Pattern Recognition with Neural Networks in C Plus Plus. 464p. 1995. 69.95 (*0-8493-9462-7*, 9462) CRC Pr.

Pandya, Basudev. Indian Bureaucracy. 213p. 1978. 19.95 (*0-318-36585-5*) Asia Bk Corp.

Pandya, C. G. Hazards in Chemical Units. 1988. 20.00 (*81-204-0242-1*, Pub. by Oxford IBH II) S Asia.

***Pandya, Meenal.** Here Comes Diwali. (Illus.). 16p. (J). 1994. pap. text ed. 6.95 (*0-9635539-1-7*) Meera Pubns.

Pandya, Michael. Indian Vegetarian Cooking. 1989. pap. 10.95 (*0-89281-342-3*) Inner Tradit.

Pandya, Vishwajit. Above the Forest: A Study of Andamanese Ethnoanemology, Cosmology, & the Power of Ritual. 356p. 1993. 24.00 (*0-19-562971-X*) OUP.

Pane, Armijn. Shackles: A Novel. McGlynn, John H., tr. LC 84-18930. (Monographs in International Studies, Southeast Asia Ser.: No. 67). 136p. reprint ed. pap. 38.80 (*0-7837-6478-2*, 2046483) Bks Demand.

Panek, Julian, ed. Building Seals & Sealants-STP 606. 356p. 1976. 36.00 (*0-8031-0608-4*, 04-606000-10) ASTM.

Panek, Julian R. & Cook, John P. Construction Sealants & Adhesives. 3rd ed. (Series of Practical Construction Guides: No. 1344). 400p. 1991. text ed. 74.95 (*0-471-53474-9*) Wiley.

Panek, LeRoy L. An Introduction to the Detective Story. LC 87-70502. 214p. 1987. 23.95 (*0-87972-377-7*); pap. 12.95 (*0-87972-378-5*) Bowling Green Univ.

— Probable Cause: Crime Fiction in America. LC 89-81987. 167p. (C). 1990. lib. bdg. 34.95 (*0-87972-485-4*); pap. 16.95 (*0-87972-486-2*) Bowling Green Univ.

Panek, Paul E., jt. auth. see Hayslip, Bert, Jr.

***Panek, Richard.** Waterloo Diamonds. 304p. 1995. 21.95 (*0-312-13209-3*) St Martin.

Panel of Bioethical Concerns of the National Council of Churches of Christ-U. S. A. Genetic Engineering. 5.95 (*0-685-16485-3*, CS1011) General Board.

Panel on Child Care Policy, National Research Council, et al. Who Cares for America's Children? Hayes, C. O. et al, eds. 388p. 1990. 29.95 (*0-309-04032-9*) Natl Acad Pr.

Panel on Foreign Trade Statistics Staff & National Research Council Staff. Behind the Numbers: U. S. Trade in the World Economy. Kester, Anne Y., ed. 312p. 1992. 29.95 (*0-309-04590-8*) Natl Acad Pr.

Panel on Indonesia, Committee on Population & Demography, et al. Recent Trends in Fertility & Mortality in Indonesia. LC 87-11178. (Papers of the East-West Population Institute: No. 105). (Illus.). xvi, 96p. (Orig.). 1987. pap. text ed. 3.00 (*0-86638-092-2*) EW Ctr HI.

Panel on the Applications of Biotechnology to Traditional Fermented Foods. Applications of Biotechnology in Traditional Fermented Foods. 208p. (C). 1992. pap. text ed. 19.00 (*0-309-04685-8*) Natl Acad Pr.

Panel on the Assessment of Wind Engineering Issues in the United States Staff, et al. Wind & the Built Environment: U. S. Needs in Wind Engineering & Hazard Mitigation. 144p. (Orig.). (C). 1993. pap. text ed. 35.00 (*0-309-04449-9*) Natl Acad Pr.

Panel on the Future Design & Implementation of U. S. National Security Export Controls Staff, et al. Finding Common Ground: U. S. Export Controls in a Changed Global Environment. 412p. 1991. 34.95 (*0-309-04392-1*) Natl Acad Pr.

Panel on the Government Role in Civilian Technology Staff. The Government Role in Civilian Technology: Building a New Alliance. 240p. 1992. pap. text ed. 22.95 (*0-309-04630-0*) Natl Acad Pr.

Panel Publishers, Inc. Staff. Multistate Corporate Tax Almanac, 2 Vol. Set, 1. write for info. (*1-878375-05-9*) Panel Pubs.

— Multistate Corporate Tax Almanac, 2 Vol. Set, 2. write for info. (*1-878375-06-7*) Panel Pubs.

— Multistate Corporate Tax Almanac, 2 Vol. Set, Set. pap. 185.00 (*1-878375-23-7*) Panel Pubs.

Panella, Deborah S. Basics of Law Librarianship. (Haworth Series in Special Librarianship). 136p. (C). 1991. text ed. 32.95 (*0-86656-989-8*); pap. text ed. 14.95 (*0-86656-990-1*) Haworth Pr.

Panella, John, Jr. Day Care Programs for Alzheimer's Disease & Related Disorders. LC 87-71317. 160p. 1987. text ed. 39.95 (*0-939957-05-1*) Demos Vermande.

Panem, Sandra. The Interferon Crusade. LC 84-17629. 109p. 1984. 22.95 (*0-8157-6900-8*); pap. 8.95 (*0-8157-6899-0*) Brookings.

Panem, Sandra, ed. Biotechnology: Implications for Public Policy. LC 85-48176. (Dialogues on Public Policy Ser.). 99p. 1986. pap. 10.95 (*0-8157-6903-2*) Brookings.

— Public Policy, Science, & Environmental Risk. LC 83-73029. 65p. 1983. pap. 10.95 (*0-8157-6901-6*) Brookings.

Panem, Sandra & Thier, Samuel. The AIDS Bureaucracy. LC 87-22972. 208p. 1988. 32.00 (*0-674-01270-4*); pap. text ed. 11.95 (*0-674-01271-2*) HUP.

Panepinto. Miniature Swine in Biomedical Research: Symposium. 1994. write for info. (*0-8493-0189-0*) CRC Pr.

Panepinto, Roshlind. Monarch Notes: Isak Dinesen's Out of Africa. 128p. 1988. pap. 4.50 (*0-671-67127-8*, Arco Test) P-H Gen Ref & Trav.

Panero, Jose L. Systematics of Pappobolus (Asteraceae-Heliantheae) Anderson, Christiane, ed. (Systematic Botany Monographs: Vol. 36). (Illus.). 195p. 1993. pap. 25.00 (*0-685-68876-3*) Am Soc Plant.

Panero, Julius & Zelnik, Martin. Human Dimension & Interior Space. (Illus.). 352p. 1979. 39.95 (*0-8230-7271-1*, Whitney Lib) Watsn-Guptill.

Panet, J. P. & Hart, Leah. Honduras & the Bay Islands. LC 90-61338. (Illus.). 246p. (Orig.). 1990. pap. 12.95 (*0-930016-14-9*) Passport Pr.

Panet, Jean-Pierre. Latin America on Bicycle. Lewis, Zack, ed. LC 87-62242. 160p. (Orig.). 1987. pap. 12.95 (*0-930016-07-6*) Passport Pr.

An Asterisk (*) at the beginning of an entry indicates that the title is appearing in BIP for the first time.

Paneth, Nigel, et al. Brain Damage in the Preterm Infant. (Clinics in Developmental Medicine Ser.: No. 131). (Illus.). 300p. (C). 1995. 69.95 (*0-521-68300-9*) Cambridge U Pr.

Panetta, Vincent J., ed. & tr. Treatise on Harpsichord Tuning by Jean Denis. (Cambridge Musical Texts & Monographs). 120p. 1987. pap. 18.95 (*0-521-31402-X*) Cambridge U Pr.

Panetto, C., jt. auth. see Heudin, J. C.

Panferov, Fedor I. Brusski: A Story of Peasant Life in Soviet Russia. LC 75-37341. (Early Soviet Literature Ser.). (Orig.). 1977. lib. bdg. 21.45 (*0-88355-414-3*) Hyperion Conn.

Panfili, Peach. Lavish Flowers. (Illus.). 176p. 1995. 32.00 (*0-207-17298-6*, IntlDept) HarpC.

Panfilov, V. Z. Grammar & Logic. LC 68-15535. (Janua Linguarum, Ser. Minor: No. 63). (Orig.). 1968. pap. text ed. 18.70 (*90-279-0591-6*) Mouton.

Pang, Catherine C.Y. The Effects of Drugs in the Venous System. LC 94-3530. (Medical Intelligence Unit Ser.). 130p. 1994. 89.95 (*1-57059-138-5*, LN9138) R G Landes.

Pang, Chia S. & Hock, Goh E. T'ai Chi: Ten Minutes to Health. LC 85-22388. (Illus.). 131p. (Orig.). 1986. pap. 16.95 (*0-916360-30-X*) CRCS Pubns CA.

Pang, Chien-Kuo. The State & Economic Transformation: The Taiwan Case. LC 91-41620. (Developing Economies of the Third World Ser.). 336p. 1992. 71.00 (*0-8153-0635-0*) Garland.

Pang, Dachling, ed. Disorders of the Pediatric Spine. LC 94-9398. 694p. 1995. 185.00 (*0-7817-0158-9*) Raven.

Pang Eng Fong. Regionalisation & Labour Flows in Pacific Asia. 92p. (Orig.). 1993. pap. text ed. 18.00 (*92-64-14008-5*, 41-93-16-1) OECD.

Pang, Eul-Soo. Bahia in the First Brazilian Republic: Coronelismo & Oligarchies, 1889-1934. LC 78-2682. (Latin American Monographs: Ser. 2, No. 23). (Illus.). 294p. reprint ed. pap. 83.80 (*0-7837-4942-2*, 2044608) Bks Demand.

— In Pursuit of Honor & Glory: Noblemen of the Southern Cross in Nineteenth-Century Brazil. LC 86-7081. (Illus.). 360p. 1988. 41.95 (*0-8173-0317-0*) U of Ala Pr.

Pang, G. K. & McFarlane, A. G. An Expert Systems Approach to Computer-Aided Design of Multivariable Systems. (Lecture Notes in Control & Information Sciences Ser.: Vol. 89). (Illus.). xiii, 325p. 1988. pap. 41.00 (*0-387-17356-0*) Spr-Verlag.

Pang Guek Cheng. Canada. LC 93-11018. (Cultures of the World Ser.). (J). (gr. 5 up). 1993. 21.95 (*1-85435-579-1*) Marshall Cavendish.

Pang Guek Cheng-Chen & Barlas, Robert. Culture Shock! Canada. (Illus.). 256p. 1992. 10.95 (*1-55868-087-X*) Gr Arts Ctr Pub.

Pang, Hilda D. Pre-Columbian Art: Investigations & Insights. LC 91-23661. (Illus.). 352p. (C). 1992. 65.00 (*0-8061-2379-6*) U of Okla Pr.

Pang Jeng Lo, Benjamin, tr. see Chen Wei-Ming.

Pang Jeng Lo, Benjamin, et al. The Essence of T'ai Chi Ch'uan: The Literary Tradition. Inn, Martin et al, eds. (Illus.). 104p. 1979. 20.00 (*0-913028-67-3*); pap. 8.95 (*0-913028-63-0*) North Atlantic.

Pang, Keum-Young C. Everyday Life, Health, Illness of Elderly Korean Immigrants: Cultural Construction of Illness. (Immigrant Communities & Ethnic Minorities in the U. S. & Canada Ser.: No. 69). 1991. 59.50 (*0-404-19479-6*) AMS Pr.

Pang, Lucy F., jt. auth. see Fang, Percy J.

Pang, Mary. Wok with Mary Pang. 1991. pap. 12.95 (*0-89716-371-0*) P B Pubng.

Pang, May. John Lennon: The Lost Weekend - a Year & a Half of Living, Loving & Rock & Roll. 1992. pap. 5.99 (*1-56171-176-4*) Sure Sellers.

Pang, P. K., ed. see Epple, A.

Pang Pang. The Death of Hu Yaobang. Si Ren, tr. (Illus.). 84p. (Orig.). 1990. pap. text ed. 9.95 (*0-8248-1331-6*) UH Pr.

Pang, Peter K. & Schreibman, Martin P., eds. Vertebrate Endocrinology: Fundamentals & Biomedical Implications, Vol. 3: Regulation of Calcium & Phosphate. 365p. 1989. text ed. 176.00 (*0-12-544903-8*) Acad Pr.

— Vertebrate Endocrinology, Vol. 4, Pt. A: Fundamentals & Biomedical Implications. 396p. 1991. text ed. 204.00 (*0-12-544904-6*) Acad Pr.

— Vertebrate Endocrinology, Vol. 4, Pt. B: Fundamentals & Biomedical Implications. 350p. 1991. text ed. 204.00 (*0-12-544905-4*) Acad Pr.

Pang, Peter K. & Screibman, Martin P. Vertebrate Endocrinology: Fundamentals & Biomedical Implications, Vol. 1. 1986. text ed. 176.00 (*0-12-544901-1*) Acad Pr.

Pang, Peter T., et al, eds. Vertebrate Endocrinology, Fundamentals & Biomedical Implications, Vol. 2: Regulation of Water & Electrolytes. 321p. 1987. text ed. 151.00 (*0-12-544902-X*) Acad Pr.

Pang, Peter Y., jt. auth. see Agarwal, Ravi P.

Pang, S. F. & Tang, F., eds. Special Neuroendocrine Systems: Journal: Neuroendocrinology, Vol. 53, Suppl. 1, 1991. (Illus.). iv, 84p. 1991. pap. 49.75 (*3-8055-5357-9*) S Karger.

Pang, S. F., et al, eds. Putative Melatonin Receptors in Peripheral Tissues. (Journal: Biological Signals: Vol. 2, No. 4, 1993). (Illus.). 64p. 1994. pap. 26.50 (*3-8055-5947-X*) S Karger.

Pang, Shin Hak. Acupuncture Treatment. LC 73-92157. (Illus.). 1973. 6.95 (*0-914524-00-3*) Dong Nam P & C.

Pang, T. Typhoid Fever: Strategies for the Nineties. 300p. 1992. text ed. 95.00 (*981-02-0953-3*) World Scientific Pub.

Pang, T. Y. On Tai Chi Chuan. (Illus.). 325p. (Orig.). 1988. 50.00 (*0-9612070-1-9*); pap. 35.00 (*0-685-44394-9*) Tai Chi Schl Philos.

Pang, Trude & Shinoki, Amy. Keyboarding with Computer Applications. 176p. 1992. pap. text ed. 24.95 (*0-89863-145-9*) Star Pub CA.

Pang-Yuan, Chi, et al. An Anthology of Contemporary Chinese Literature, 2 vols., Set. 1976. 50.00 (*0-295-95504-X*) U of Wash Pr.

Pangaea Pr. Staff, ed. see Wing, Ralph.

Pangaea Press Staff, ed. see Wing, Ralph.

Pangalis, Celia S., jt. auth. see Galaydh, Ali K.

Pangalis, Gerassimos A. & Polliack, Aaron, eds. Benign & Malignant Lymphadenopathies: A Guide to Clinical & Laboratory Diagnosis. LC 92-49470. 1993. text ed. 95.00 (*3-7186-5232-3*) Gordon & Breach.

Pangallo, Karen L. George Eliot: A Reference Guide, 1972-1987. (Reference Guides to Literature Ser.). 335p. 1989. text ed. 45.00 (*0-8161-8973-0*, Hall Reference) Macmillan.

Pangallo, Karen L., ed. The Critical Response to George Eliot. LC 93-41224. (Critical Responses in Arts & Letters Ser.: No. 11). 256p. 1994. text ed. 55.00 (*0-313-28773-2*, Greenwood Pr) Greenwood.

Pangallo, Michelle. North American Forts & Fortifications. (Illus.). 48p. (J). (gr. 4 up). 1986. 13.95 (*0-521-26642-4*); pap. 7.95 (*0-521-31982-X*) Cambridge U Pr.

Panganiban, J. Villa. Concise English-Tagalog Dictionary. LC 69-13501. 170p. (ENG & TAG.). 1969. bds. 14.95 (*0-8048-0119-3*) C E Tuttle.

Pangborn, Brenda J., ed. Culinary Counterpoint: Detroit Symphony Orchestra Cookbook. LC 83-71434. (Illus.). 432p. (Orig.). 1983. pap. 12.00 (*0-9611348-0-1*) Detroit Symphony.

Pangborn, Cyrus R. Zoroastrianism. 178p. 1982. text ed. 25.00 (*0-89891-006-4*) Advent Bks Div.

Pangborn, Edgar. Davy. 288p. 1982. pap. 2.75 (*0-345-30702-X*) Ballantine.

— A Mirror for Observers. 1993. reprint ed. lib. bdg. 18.95 (*0-89968-358-4*, Lghtyr Pr) Buccaneer Bks.

Pangborn, Georgia W. The Wind at Midnight. 1989. lib. bdg. 25.00 (*0-910489-19-X*) Scream Pr.

Pangburn, Robert P. No Better Place: Than in the Center of His Presence. 308p. 1993. pap. write for info. (*0-9638693-0-2*) Pearl Pubng.

Pangburn, Thelma I. Raoul Wallenberg: Hero of the Holocaust. Buchanan, John G., ed. (Outstanding Personalities Ser.: No. 97). (YA). (gr. 7-12). 1987. lib. bdg. 4.95 (*0-87157-597-3*) SamHar Pr.

Panger, Daniel. The Dance of the Wild Mouse. LC 79-51409. 240p. (C). 1979. 9.95 (*0-9601428-4-3*); pap. 7.95 (*0-9601428-5-1*) Entwhistle Bks.

— Soldier Boys. LC 87-62533. 240p. (Orig.). (C). 1988. pap. 16.95 (*0-89390-102-4*) Resource Pubns.

Panger, Janet S., ed. see Frye, Nora.

Pangestu, Mari, jt. auth. see Bhattacharya, Amarendra.

Pangestu, Mari, jt. ed. see Soesastro, Hadi.

***Pangle, Lorraine S. & Pangle, Thomas L.** The Learning of Liberty: The Educational Ideas of the American Founders. LC 92-29956. (American Political Thought Ser.). (Orig.). (C). 1995. pap. 19.95x (*0-7006-0746-3*) U Pr of KS.

— The Learning of Liberty: The Educational Ideas of the American Founders. LC 92-29956. (American Political Thought Ser.). 370p. (Orig.). (C). 1995. reprint ed. 35.00x (*0-7006-0581-9*) U Pr of KS.

Pangle, Mary Ann, jt. auth. see Forte, Imogene.

Pangle, Thomas L. The Ennobling of Democracy: The Challenge of the Postmodern Age. LC 91-20720. (Series in Constitutional Thought). 288p. 1991. 35.00 (*0-8018-4262-X*) Johns Hopkins.

— The Ennobling of Democracy: The Challenge of the Postmodern Age. (Series in Constitutional Thought). 288p. 1993. reprint ed. pap. 13.95 (*0-8018-4635-8*) Johns Hopkins.

— Montesquieu's Philosophy of Liberalism: A Commentary on the Spirit of the Laws. LC 73-77139. (Illus.). x, 342p. 1989. pap. text ed. 14.95 (*0-226-64545-2*) U Ch Pr.

— The Spirit of Modern Republicanism: The Moral Vision of the American Founders & the Philosophy of Locke. LC 87-30885. (Exxon Lecture Ser.). x, 334p. 1990. pap. 15.95 (*0-226-64547-9*) U Ch Pr.

Pangle, Thomas L., ed. The Roots of Political Philosophy: Ten Forgotten Socratic Dialogues. LC 87-47550. 424p. (C). 1987. 49.95 (*0-8014-1986-7*); pap. 16.95 (*0-8014-9465-6*) Cornell U Pr.

Pangle, Thomas L., jt. ed. see Palmer, Michael.

Pangle, Thomas L., jt. auth. see Pangle, Lorraine S.

Pangle, Thomas L., tr. see Plato.

Pangle, Thomas L., ed. see Strauss, Leo, et al.

***Pangman, Julie K., ed.** Guide to Environmental Issues. (Illus.). 84p. (Orig.). (C). 1994. pap. text ed. 35.00x (*0-7881-1415-8*) Diane Pub.

Pangonis, William J. Tables of Light Scattering Functions for Spherical Particles. LC 56-12604. 123p. reprint ed. pap. 35.10 (*0-7837-3790-4*, 2043610) Bks Demand.

Pangonis, William J. & Heller, Wilfried. Angular Scattering Functions for Spherical Particles. LC 60-8930. 227p. reprint ed. pap. 64.70 (*0-7837-3828-5*, 2043649) Bks Demand.

Pangotra, Prem, jt. ed. see Huddleston, Jack.

Pangrazi, Robert P. & Darst, Paul W. Dynamic Physical Education for Secondary School Students. 2nd ed. 480p. (C). 1990. write for info. (*0-02-390674-X*) Macmillan.

Pangrazi, Robert P. & Dauer, Victor P. Dynamic Physical Education for Elementary School Children. 10th ed. (Illus.). 752p. (C). 1991. text ed. write for info. (*0-02-327821-8*) Macmillan.

— Dynamic Physical Education for Elementary School Children. 11th ed. LC 94-316. 800p. (C). 1994. write for info. (*0-02-390691-X*, Maxwell Macmillan) Macmillan.

Pangrazi, Robert P., jt. auth. see Corbin, Charles B.

Pangrazzi, Arnaldo. Your Words in Prayer in Time of Illness. 72p. (Orig.). 1982. pap. 1.95 (*0-8189-0417-8*) Alba.

Panholzer, Rudolf, ed. Proceedings of the Fourth International Symposium on Integrated Ferroelectrics. (Illus.). (Orig.). (C). 1992. pap. 55.00 (*0-9634605-0-1*) ISOI Ferroelect.

***Panhorst, Don.** How Ordinary People Can Become Extraordinary Leaders: Empowerment Principles for Leadership Success. 213p. 1993. 24.95 (*0-9634723-4-8*) Baton Pub.

Panhuis, Dirk G. The Communicative Perspective in the Sentence: A Study of Latin Word Order. (Studies in Language Companion: No. 11). viii, 172p. 1982. 52.00x (*90-272-3010-2*) Benjamins North Am.

Panhuys. Yearbook of the AAA, 1974: 1974. (Association of Attenders & Alumni of the Hague Academy of International Law Ser.: No. 44). 1977. pap. text ed. 70.00 (*90-247-1945-3*) Kluwer Ac.

Pani, A. Hygiene in Mexico. 1976. lib. bdg. 59.95 (*0-8490-2029-8*) Gordon Pr.

***Pani, Binita.** Indian Scriptures & the Life Divine. (C). 1993. 32.00x (*81-7024-592-3*, Pub. by Ashish II) S Asia.

Pani, Jiwan. Sonal Mansingh: Contribution to Odissi Dance. (C). 1992. 5.00 (*81-7304-002-8*, Pub. by Manohar II) S Asia.

Pani, Narendar. Redefining Conservatism: An Essay on the Bias of India's Economic Reform. LC 93-48277. 1994. 28.50 (*0-8039-9164-9*) Sage.

Paniagua, Freddy A. Assessing & Treating Culturally Diverse Clients: A Practical Guide. LC 94-17662. (Multicultural Aspects of Counseling Ser.: Vol. 4). 136p. 1994. 36.00 (*0-8039-5495-6*); pap. 16.95 (*0-8039-5496-4*) Sage.

Paniague, Blanca L., tr. see Cripps, Louise.

Panic, M. National Management of the International Economy. LC 87-18764. 450p. 1988. text ed. 59.95 (*0-312-01294-2*) St Martin.

Panicello, Joseph F. Vindicated. 260p. 1994. pap. 9.95 (*0-9640677-0-6*) Nth Hills Pubs.

Panichas, George A. The Burden of Vision: Dostoevsky's Spiritual Art. LC 84-25925. 216p. 1985. pap. 8.95 (*0-89526-821-3*) Regnery Pub.

— The Critic As Conservator: Essays in Literature, Society, & Culture. LC 91-32217. 262p. 1992. text ed. 49.95 (*0-8132-0762-2*) Cath U Pr.

— The Reverent Discipline: Essays in Literary Criticism & Culture. LC 73-15749. 488p. 1974. 45.00x (*0-87049-149-0*) U of Tenn Pr.

— The Reverent Discipline: Essays in Literary Criticism & Culture. LC 73-15749. Date not set. reprint ed. pap. 139.10 (*0-7837-9507-6*, 2060257) Bks Demand.

Panichas, George A., ed. Simone Weil Reader. 529p. 1985. pap. 10.95 (*0-918825-01-6*) Moyer Bell.

Panichas, George A., intro. Modern Age: The First Twenty-Five Years: A Selection. LC 88-8600. 914p. (C). 1988. text ed. 17.50 (*0-86597-061-0*); pap. 8.50 (*0-86597-062-9*) Liberty Fund.

Panichas, George A. & Ryn, Claes G., eds. Irving Babbitt in Our Time. LC 85-21260. 256p. 1986. 27.95 (*0-8132-0625-1*) Cath U Pr.

Panichas, George A. & Warren, Austin. The Courage of Judgment: Essays in Criticism, Culture & Society. LC 81-4050. 318p. 1982. text ed. 36.00x (*0-87049-325-6*) U of Tenn Pr.

Panichas, George A., ed. see Babbitt, Irving.

Panici, William F., ed. Three French Short Verse Satirists. LC 90-3800. (Studies in Comparative Literature). 152p. 1990. reprint ed. 15.00 (*0-8240-0010-2*) Garland.

Panico, Carlo. Interest & Profit in the Theories of Value & Distribution. LC 86-17699. 250p. 1988. text ed. 49.95 (*0-312-41910-4*) St Martin.

Panico, Carlo & Salvadori, Neri, eds. Post-Keynesian Theory of Growth & Distribution. (International Library of Critical Writings in Business History). 464p. 1992. 139.95 (*1-85278-613-2*, Pub. by E Elgar Pub UK) Ashgate Pub Co.

Panico, Marie J., jt. auth. see Bejel, Emilio.

Panidis, John P. Cardiac Ultrasound. 354p. 1994. pap. write for info. (*0-86542-275-3*) Blackwell Sci.

Panigrahi, Lalita. British Social Policy & Female Infanticide in India. 1972. 16.00 (*0-8364-2617-7*, Pub. by Munshiram Manoharial II) S Asia.

Panigrahi, Sarat C. Testing, Evaluation & Measurements in Metal Casting. 304p. (C). 1987. 15.00 (*81-204-0171-9*, Pub. by Oxford IBH II) S Asia.

***Panigraphy, Didakar.** New Dimensions in Modern Management. 130p. (C). 1994. 45.00x (*81-85880-24-7*, Pub. by Print Hse II) St Mut.

Panik, Michael J. Fundamentals of Convex Analysis: Duality, Separation, Representation, & Resolution. LC 93-17082. (Theory & Decision Library, Series B, Mathematical & Statistical Methods: Vol. 24). 320p. (C). 1993. lib. bdg. 108.00 (*0-7923-2279-7*) Kluwer Ac.

Panik, Sharon, jt. auth. see Parke, Marilyn.

Panikar, K. A., ed. Malayalam Short Stories. 152p. 1981. 16.95 (*0-318-36917-6*) Asia Bk Corp.

Paniker. International Cooperation in the Higher Education of Science & Technology. (C). 1985. 32.50 (*81-204-0067-4*, Pub. by Oxford IBH II) S Asia.

Paniker, Ayyappa, ed. Making of Indian Literature: A Consolidated Report of Workshops on Literary Translation, 1986-88. (C). 1991. 17.50 (*81-7201-115-6*, Pub. by Sahitya Akademi II) S Asia.

Paniker, Ayyappa, jt. ed. see Singh, Amritjit.

Paniker, Jayaram, jt. auth. see Ananthanarayan, R.

Paniker, K. Ayyappa, ed. Indian English Literature since Independence. 220p. 1991. text ed. 25.00 (*81-85218-34-X*, Pub. by Prestige II) Advent Bks Div.

Paniker, K. Ayyappa, jt. ed. see Nair, D. Appukuttan.

Panikkar, K. Madhu. Revolution in Africa. LC 74-27428. 202p. 1975. reprint ed. text ed. 55.00 (*0-8371-7901-7*, PARA, Greenwood Pr) Greenwood.

Panikkar, K. N. Against Lord & State: Religion & Peasant Uprisings in Malabar (1836-1921) (Illus.). 248p. 1989. 28.00 (*0-19-562139-5*) OUP.

— Communalism in India: History, Politics & Culture. (C). 1991. 21.50 (*81-85425-51-5*, Pub. by Manohar II) S Asia.

Panikkar, Kavalam N. Karimkutty & the Lone Tusker. (C). 1992. pap. text ed. 5.00 (*81-7046-092-1*, Pub. by Seagull Bks II) S Asia.

— Right to Rule & the Domain of the Sun. (C). 1989. pap. 10.00 (*81-7046-071-9*, Pub. by Seagull Bks II) S Asia.

Panikkar, Kavilam M. In Two Chinas: Memoirs of a Diplomat. LC 79-2836. 183p. 1985. reprint ed. 19.00 (*0-8305-0013-8*) Hyperion Conn.

Panikkar, M. V., jt. auth. see Devi, K. Usha.

Panikkar, Raimon. The Cosmotheandric Experience: Emerging Religious Consciousness. LC 92-46195. 150p. 1993. 24.95 (*0-88344-862-9*) Orbis Bks.

— A Dwelling Place for Wisdom. Kidder, Annemarie S., tr. LC 92-19450. 176p. (Orig.). 1993. pap. 12.99 (*0-664-25362-8*) Westminster John Knox.

— Invisible Harmony: Essays on Contemplation & Responsibility. Cargas, Harry J., ed. LC 95-10456. 1995. write for info. (*0-8006-2609-5*, Fortress Pr) Augsburg Fortress.

Panikkar, Raimundo. Intrareligious Dialogue. LC 78-58962. 136p. 1978. pap. 6.95 (*0-8091-2728-8*) Paulist Pr.

— The Silence of God: The Answer of the Buddha. Barr, Robert R., tr. LC 89-2950. (Faith Meets Faith Series in Interreligious Dialogue). 400p. 1989. 39.95 (*0-88344-445-3*); pap. 16.95 (*0-88344-446-1*) Orbis Bks.

— The Trinity & the Religious Experience of Man: Icon, Person, Mystery. LC 73-77329. 98p. reprint ed. pap. 28.00 (*0-317-26668-3*, 2025122) Bks Demand.

— The Unknown Christ of Hinduism. LC 81-2886. 208p. (Orig.). 1981. reprint ed. pap. 16.95 (*0-88344-523-9*) Orbis Bks.

— Worship & Secular Man: An Essay on the Liturgical Nature of Man. LC 72-93339. 119p. reprint ed. pap. 34.00 (*0-317-26670-5*, 2025123) Bks Demand.

Panikkar, T. K. Malabar & Its Folk. 288p. 1986. reprint ed. 12.00 (*0-8364-1730-5*, Pub. by Manohar II) S Asia.

Panimolle, Salvatore. Like the Deer That Yearns. 128p. (C). 1990. 39.00 (*0-85439-319-6*, Pub. by St Paul Pubns UK) St Mut.

Panin, George, ed. see Zetlin, Mikhail O.

Panini. Astadhyayi of Panini. Katre, Sumitra M., tr. (Texas Linguistics Ser.). 1376p. 1987. text ed. 100.00 (*0-292-70394-5*) U of Tex Pr.

Panini, M. N. From the Female Eye: Account of Women Field Workers Studying Their Own Communities. (C). 1991. 12.50 (*81-7075-020-2*, Pub. by Hindustan IA) S Asia.

Panish, M. B. & Temkin, H. Gas Source Molecular Beam Epitaxu: Growth & Properties of Phosphorus Containing III-V Heterostructures. (Materials Science Ser.: Vol. 26). (Illus.). 450p. 1993. write for info. (*3-540-56540-X*) Spr-Verlag.

— Gas Source Molecular Beam Epitaxy: Growth & Properties Containing III-Vheterostructures. LC 93-7842. (Materials Science Ser.: Vol. 26). 1993. 69.00 (*0-387-56540-X*) Spr-Verlag.

Panisha. The New Astrology. 1990. pap. 28.95 (*0-86690-346-1*, 2813-014) Am Fed Astrologers.

Panisset, Maurice, jt. auth. see Sonea, Sorin.

Panitch, Leo. Working Class Politics in Crisis: Essays on Labour & the State. 264p. (C). 1988. text ed. 44.95 (*0-86091-142-X*, A1106, Pub. by Verso UK); pap. text ed. 14.95 (*0-86091-849-1*, A1905, Pub. by Verso UK) Routledge Chapman & Hall.

Panitch, Leo, ed. The Canadian State: Political Economy & Political Power. 1977. pap. 18.95 (*0-8020-6322-5*) U of Toronto Pr.

***Panitch, Leo & Wood, Ellen, eds.** The Socialist Register, 1995: Why Not Capitalism? 256p. 1995. 60.00 (*0-85036-449-3*, Pub. by Merlin Pr UK) Humanities.

— The Socialist Register 1995: Why Not Capitalism? 256p. 1995. 60.00 (*0-614-07248-4*) Humanities.

Panitch, Leo, jt. ed. see Miliband, Ralph.

Panitz, Esther L. Simon Wolf: Private Conscience & Public Image. LC 86-45378. (Illus.). 224p. 1987. 35.00 (*0-8386-3293-9*) Lubrecht & Cramer.

Panizzon, R. G., jt. auth. see Goldschmidt, H. L.

Panja, Ranjit K. MCQ 1001 Dermatology Venereology Leprology. 1985. 79.00 (*0-317-38787-1*, Current Dist) St Mut.

Panjabi, jt. auth. see White.

***Panjabi, Camellia.** The Great Curries of India. LC 94-44460. 1995. 30.00 (*0-684-80383-6*) S&S Trade.

Panjani, Shakuntala. Pancadasi: A Critical Study. 1985. 29.95 (*0-318-37028-X*) Asia Bk Corp.

Panje, William R. Practical Endoscopic Sinus Surgery. Anand, Vijay K., ed. LC 92-49884. (Illus.). 186p. 1993. text ed. 129.00 (*0-07-105419-7*) Hlth Prof Div.

Panje, William R. & Moran, William J. Free Flap Reconstruction of the Head & Neck. (American Academy of Facial Plastic & Reconstructive Surgery Monograph). (Illus.). 112p. 1989. text ed. 65.00 (*0-86577-303-3*) Thieme Med Pubs.

Panje, William R., et al. Musculocutaneous Flap Reconstruction of the Head & Neck. 254p. 1989. 127.50 (*0-88167-494-X*, 1974) Raven.

Panjer, H., ed. Actuarial Mathematics. LC 86-3306. (Proceedings of Symposia in Applied Mathematics Ser.: Vol. 35). 127p. 1990. reprint ed. pap. 29.00 (*0-8218-0096-5*, PSAPM-35) Am Math.

PQ

An Asterisk (*) at the beginning of an entry indicates that the title is appearing in BIP for the first time.

Panjer, H. H. & Willmot, G. E. Insurance Risk Models. (Orig.). 1992. text ed. 35.00 (*0-938959-25-5*) Soc Actuaries.

Panjwani, H. Ergonomics: Practical Guide. (General Engineering Ser.). 1993. text ed. write for info. (*0-442-00742-6*) Van Nos Reinhold.

***Pank, Rachel.** Leo & the Wallpaper Jungle. LC 94-28714. (J). 1995. write for info. (*0-8120-9167-1*); write for info. (*0-8120-6493-3*) Barron.

— Sonia & Barnie & the Noise in the Night. (J). 1991. pap. 13.95 (*0-590-44657-6*) Scholastic Inc.

— Under the Blackberries. (J). 1992. 13.95 (*0-590-45481-1*, Scholastic Hardcover) Scholastic Inc.

Pankaja, Ma P., ed. see Rajneesh, Osho.

Pankake, Anita M., Jr. & Burnett, I. Emett. The Effective Elementary School Principal. (Effective School Administration Ser.: No. 3). (Illus.). 128p. 1990. 19.95 (*0-88280-094-9*) ETC Pubns.

Pankake, Jon, jt. auth. see Pankake, Marcia.

Pankake, Marcia & Pankake, Jon. A Prairie Home Companion Folk Song Book. LC 87-40660. 288p. 1988. 22.95 (*0-670-82159-4*) Viking Penguin.

Pankau, Ed & Pack, Robert. Presumed Quilty. Date not set. pap. write for info. (*0-688-12482-8*) Morrow.

Pankau, Ed. J., jt. auth. see Thomas, Ralph D.

Pankau, Edmund J. Check It Out: A Top Investigator Tells You How to Use Publicly Available Sources. 1992. pap. 10.95 (*0-8092-3945-0*) Contemp Bks.

— Check It Out: Everyone's Guide to Investigation. 146p. (Orig.). 1991. pap. 19.95 (*0-89896-444-X*) Larksdale.

— How to Make One Hundred Thousand Dollars a Year As a Private Investigator. (Illus.). 112p. 1993. pap. 19.95 (*0-87364-720-3*) Paladin Pr.

Panken, Peter M., ed. Resource Materials: Labor & Employment Law, 2 vols. 5th ed. 1650p. 1990. pap. text ed. 50.00 (*0-8318-0170-0*, R170) Am Law Inst.

— Resource Materials: Labor & Employment Law, 2 vols., Set. 6th ed. 1812p. 1992. pap. text ed. 150.00 (*0-8318-0176-X*, R176) Am Law Inst.

Panken, Shirley. The Joy of Suffering: Psychoanalytic Theory & Therapy of Masochism. LC 83-15841. 264p. 1993. 30.00 (*1-56821-120-1*) Aronson.

— Virginia Woolf & the "Lust of Creation" A Psychoanalytic Exploration. LC 86-29991. 336p. 1987. 64.50 (*0-88706-200-8*); pap. 24.95 (*0-88706-201-6*) State U NY Pr.

Pankey, Eric. Apocrypha. 1993. pap. 12.00 (*0-679-74732-X*) Knopf.

Pankey, Lindsey D. & Davis, William J. A Philosophy of the Practice of Dentistry. Sanitate, Veronica, ed. (Illus.). 323p. 1987. text ed. 69.50 (*0-944742-01-7*); audio 127. 50 (*0-944742-02-5*) Med Coll of OH Pr.

Pankey, Robert. To Fall from Athletics Gracefully. 156p. 1993. per. 10.95 (*0-8403-8962-0*) Kendall-Hunt.

Pankhania, Josna. Liberating the National History Curriculum. 192p. 1994. 75.00 (*0-7507-0208-7*, Falmer Pr); pap. 27.00 (*0-7507-0209-5*, Falmer Pr) Taylor & Francis.

Pankhurst, Alula. Settlement & Famine in Ethiopia: The Villagers' Experience. LC 91-18748. (Themes in Social Anthropology Ser.). 224p. 1992. text ed. 69.95 (*0-7190-3537-6*, Pub. by Manchester Univ Pr UK) St Martin.

Pankhurst, Emmeline. My Own Story. LC 85-952. (Illus.). xviii, 364p. 1985. reprint ed. text ed. 59.75 (*0-313-24926-1*, PMOS, Greenwood Pr) Greenwood.

Pankhurst, Estelle S. Ex-Italian Somaliland. LC 79-97317. 460p. 1970. reprint ed. text ed. 65.00 (*0-8371-2556-1*, PAEI, Greenwood Pr) Greenwood.

Pankhurst, F. C., jt. auth. see Ower, Ernest.

Pankhurst, Helen. Gender, Development & Identity: An Ethiopian Study. LC 92-35076. 192p. (C). 1992. text ed. 49.95 (*1-85649-157-9*, Pub. by Zed Books UK); pap. 19. 95 (*1-85649-158-7*, Pub. by Zed Books UK) Humanities.

Pankhurst, James, et al, eds. Learnability & Second Languages: A Book of Readings. vi, 208p. 1989. pap. 42. 90 (*90-6765-389-6*) Mouton.

Pankhurst, Jerry G. & Sacks, Michael P., eds. Contemporary Soviet Society: Sociological Perspectives. LC 80-22324. 296p. 1980. text ed. 49.95 (*0-275-90532-2*, C0532, Praeger Pubs) Greenwood.

Pankhurst, Jerry G., jt. ed. see Sacks, Michael P.

Pankhurst, R. J. Designs for a Global Plant Species Information System. Bisby, F. A. & Russell, G. F., eds. (Systematics Association Special Volume Ser.: Vol. 48). (Illus.). 368p. 1994. 90.00 (*0-19-857760-5*) OUP.

Pankhurst, R. J., tr. see Weberling, F.

Pankhurst, Richard. History of Ethiopian Towns, Set. 734p. text ed. 250.00x (*0-317-63022-9*) Coronet Bks.

— History of Ethiopian Towns, Vol. 1: From the Middle Ages to Early 19th Century. 734p. Vol. 1: From the Middle Ages to Early Nineteenth Century. write for info. (*3-515-03204-5*) Coronet Bks.

— History of Ethiopian Towns, Vol. 2: From the Mid-Nineteenth Century to 1935. 734p. Vol. 2: From the Mid-Noneteenth Century to 1935. write for info. (*3-515-03963-5*) Coronet Bks.

— An Introduction to the Medical History of Ethiopia. LC 90-50990. 340p. (C). 1990. 45.00 (*0-932415-44-X*); pap. 14.95 (*0-932415-45-8*) Red Sea Pr.

— A Social History of Ethiopia. LC 92-14746. (Illus.). 385p. 1992. 49.95 (*0-932415-85-7*); pap. 16.95 (*0-932415-86-5*) Red Sea Pr.

Pankhurst, Richard, jt. ed. see Bullock, Ian.

***Pankhurst, Richard J.** A Concise Dictionary of Plant Names. 512p. 1995. 25.00 (*0-19-866189-4*) OUP.

— Practical Taxonomic Computing. (Illus.). 160p. 1991. 45.00 (*0-340-55149-6*, A5557, Pub. by E Arnold UK) Routledge Chapman & Hall.

— Practical Taxonomic Computing. (Illus.). 160p. (C). 1992. 54.95 (*0-521-41760-0*) Cambridge U Pr.

Pankhurst, Richard K. The Ethiopian Royal Chronicles: Extracts. LC 68-81028. (Illus.). 240p. reprint ed. pap. 68. 40 (*0-317-11021-7*, 2002314) Bks Demand.

Pankhurst, Richard K. & Ingrams, Leila. Ethiopia Engraved. (Illus.). 140p. 1987. lib. bdg. 59.95 (*0-7103-0241-X*, Pub. by Kegan Paul Intl UK) Routledge Chapman & Hall.

Pankhurst, Richard K., ed. see Huntingford, G. W.

Pankhurst, Sylvia. The Suffragette Movement. 631p. 1990. pap. 24.95 (*0-86068-026-6*, Pub. by Virago Pr UK) Trafalgar.

Pankin, Boris. Demanding Literature: Soviet Literature of the 70s & Early 80s. 340p. 1984. 30.00 (*0-317-56655-5*, Pub. by Collets UK) Pro-Am Music.

Pankin, Robert M., ed. Social Approaches to Sport. LC 81-65466. (Illus.). 360p. 1982. 39.50 (*0-8386-3015-4*) Fairleigh Dickinson.

***Panko, Bill & Panko, Margaret.** Groaning for Miracles. 250p. 1994. per. 14.95 (*1-885342-02-0*) Creative Ways.

— The Miracle of Marriage. 48p. 1994. per. 3.95 (*1-885342-00-4*) Creative Ways.

— The Supernatural Weapon of Love. 112p. 1995. per., pap. 7.95 (*1-885342-01-2*) Creative Ways.

Panko, Margaret, jt. auth. see Panko, Bill.

Panko, Raymond R. End User Computing: Management Applications & Technology. LC 88-10706. 753p. 1988. Net. text ed. write for info. (*0-471-01102-9*) Wiley.

Pankoch, Leanne, ed. see Fanning, Larry A.

Pankov, A. A. Bounded & Almost Periodic Solutions of Nonlinear Operator Differential Equations. (C). 1990. lib. bdg. 115.50 (*0-7923-0585-X*) Kluwer Ac.

Pankove, J. I., ed. Display Devices. (Topics in Applied Physics Ser.: Vol. 40). (Illus.). 300p. 1980. 60.00 (*0-387-09868-2*) Spr-Verlag.

Pankove, Jacques I. Optical Processes in Semiconductors. 2nd ed. LC 75-16756. (Illus.). 448p. 1976. reprint ed. pap. text ed. 10.95 (*0-486-60275-3*) Dover.

Pankow, Eleanor. Let's Talk about Jesus. (Illus.). (J). (gr. k-6). 1963. 3.99 (*3-901170-15-4*) CEF Press.

Pankow, H., et al. Die Algenflora in der Schirmacheroase: Ostantarktika. (Nova Hedwigia Beiheft Ser.: No. 103). (Illus.). 198p. (GER.). 1991. pap. text ed. 105.00 (*3-443-51025-6*, Pub. by Gebrueder Borntraeger GW) Lubrecht & Cramer.

Pankow, James F. Aquatic Chemistry Concepts. 1000p. 1991. 69.95 (*0-87371-150-5*, GB855) Lewis Pubs.

— Aquatic Chemistry Problems. (Illus.). 500p. (Orig.). 1992. pap. 34.95 (*0-9627452-3-5*) Titan Pr OR.

Pankow, James F., tr. see Schwille, Friedrich.

Pankratz, Alan. Forecasting with Dynamic Regression Models. (Probability & Mathematical Statistics: Applied Probability & Statistics Section Ser.: No. 1346). 400p. 1991. text ed. 94.95 (*0-471-61528-5*) Wiley.

— Forecasting with Univariate Box-Jenkins Models: Concepts & Cases. LC 83-1404. (Probability & Mathematical Statistics: Applied Probability & Statistics Section Ser.). 562p. 1983. text ed. 107.00 (*0-471-09023-9*, 1-346, Wiley-Interscience) Wiley.

Pankratz, Carol, jt. ed. see Mayers, Marlene G.

Pankratz, David B. Multiculturalism & Public Arts Policy. LC 93-25008. 248p. 1993. text ed. 49.95 (*0-89789-361-1*, H361, Bergin & Garvey) Greenwood.

Pankratz, David B. & Morris, Valerie B., eds. The Future of the Arts: Public Policy & Arts Research. LC 90-32098. 336p. 1990. text ed. 49.95 (*0-275-93377-6*, C3377, Greenwood Pr) Greenwood.

Pankratz, David B. & Mulcahy, Kevin V., eds. The Challenge to Reform Arts Education: What Role Can Research Play? LC 88-34274. (ACA Arts Research Seminar Series Paper). 98p. (Orig.). 1989. pap. 9.95 (*0-915400-73-1*, ACA Bks) Am Council Arts.

Pankratz, Elsie P. Through the Years: Memoirs of Elsie Penner Pankratz. LC 93-61427. (Illus.). xiv, 149p. (Orig.). 1993. pap. 12.00 (*0-945530-10-2*) Wordsworth KS.

Pankratz, Judy. Pin Ups: Bulletin Board Games for Speech & Language Learning. (Illus.). 128p. (gr. k-8). 1991. 16. 95 (*0-937857-21-1*, 1585) Speech Bin.

Pankratz, Ronald, jt. auth. see Preston, Seaton T., Jr.

Pankratz, Ronald E., jt. auth. see Preston, Seaton T., Jr.

***Pankratz, Tom.** Screening Equipment Handbook. LC 94-62045. 300p. 1995. text ed. 45.00 (*1-56676-256-1*) Technomic.

— Wastewater Treatment, an Environmental Primer. LC 93-91544. (Illus.). 72p. (C). 1993. pap. 12.95 (*0-929244-00-1*) Lone Oak Pub Co.

Pankratz, Tom M. Dictionary of Water & Wastewater Treatment Trademarks & Brand Names. 160p. 1991. 49. 95 (*0-87371-673-6*, HD0971) Lewis Pubs.

— Screening Equipment Handbook: For Industrial & Municipal Water & Wastewater Treatment. LC 88-50738. 272p. 1988. 39.95 (*0-87762-630-8*) Technomic.

Panksepp, jt. auth. see Morgane.

Panksepp, J., jt. ed. see Clynes, Manfred.

Panksepp, J., jt. ed. see Morgane, P.

Panlwala, H. A. Study of the Concept of Transfer & Closure under Industrial Disputes Act, 1947. (C). 1990. 30.00 (*0-89771-306-0*) St Mut.

Panman, Richard, jt. auth. see Panman, Sandra.

Panman, Sandra & Panman, Richard. The Active Reader for Writers. 288p. (Orig.). 1991. pap. text ed. 12.95 (*0-912813-16-4*) Active Lrn.

— Essays - Letters - Reports. rev. ed. Gluck, Linda, ed. (Illus.). 128p. 1990. pap. text ed. 5.95 (*0-912813-15-6*) Active Lrn.

— Writing Basics. rev. ed. Gluck, Linda, ed. (Illus.). 128p. 1991. pap. text ed. 5.95 (*0-912813-20-2*) Active Lrn.

— Writing Guides. 2nd ed. 1990. teacher ed write for info. (*0-912813-08-3*); pap. text ed. 13.50 (*0-912813-14-8*); pap. text ed. 12.95 (*0-912813-13-X*); 1.95 (*0-912813-11-3*) Active Lrn.

— Writing Paragraphs. Gluck, Linda, ed. (Illus.). 96p. (Orig.). 1988. pap. text ed. 4.95 (*0-912813-09-1*) Active Lrn.

Pannain, Guido. Modern Composers. LC 76-99644. (Essay Index Reprint Ser.). 1977. 23.95 (*0-8369-1715-4*) Ayer.

Pannam, C. L. The Horse & the Law. 2nd ed. xv, 327p. 1986. 48.50 (*0-455-20646-5*, Pub. by Law Bk Co) W W Gaunt.

Pannbacker, Mary & Middleton, Grace. Introduction to Clinical Research in Communication Disorders. (Illus.). 224p. (Orig.). (C). 1994. pap. text ed. 34.95 (*1-56593-219-6*, 0579) Singular Publishing.

Pannekoek, A. History of Astronomy. 1989. pap. 11.95 (*0-486-65994-1*) Dover.

Pannell, Alastair D., tr. see Beller, Ilex.

Pannell, Clifton. East Asia: Geographical & Historical Approaches to Foreign Area Studies. 272p. 1983. per. 21.95 (*0-8403-2875-3*) Kendall-Hunt.

Pannell, Clifton W. T'ai-Chung, T'ai-Wan: Structure & Function. LC 72-91223. (Research Papers Ser.: No. 144). (Illus.). (Orig.). 1973. pap. 12.00 (*0-89065-051-9*, 144) U Chicago Comm Geo.

Pannell, David J. Introduction to Practical Linear Programming. 1994. write for info. (*0-471-51789-5*) Wiley.

Pannell, Dorothy V. School Foodservice Handbook. 96p. (Orig.). 1987. pap. text ed. 13.00 (*0-910170-48-7*) Assn Sch Busn.

Pannell, Gerard. MMXXVI - The Vision. LC 93-84363. (Illus.). 12p. (Orig.). (YA). 1993. pap. 9.50 (*1-883588-00-6*) PAAS Pr.

Pannell, Henry C. The Preparation & Work of Alabama High School Teachers. LC 77-177142. (Columbia University. Teachers College. Contributions to Education Ser.: No. 551). reprint ed. 37.50 (*0-404-55551-9*) AMS Pr.

Pannell, Ian. Shoot Pool. 1989. 12.98 (*1-55521-413-4*) Bk Sales Inc.

***Pannell, Maggie.** Recipes for Health: High Blood Pressure. 1995. pap. 9.00 (*0-7225-3144-3*) Thorsons SF.

Pannell, Marjorie, ed. see Kelly, Robert E.

Pannell, Nancy. Being a Minister's Wife...& Being Yourself. (Orig.). 1993. pap. 8.99 (*0-8054-5359-8*) Broadman.

Pannell, William. The Coming Race Wars? A Cry for Reconciliation. LC 92-41877. 144p. 1993. pap. 9.99 (*0-310-38181-9*) Zondervan.

— Evangelism from the Bottom Up. 128p. 1992. pap. 10.99 (*0-310-52221-8*) Zondervan.

Pannenberg, Wolfhart. Christianity in a Secularized World. 96p. 1989. pap. 8.95 (*0-8245-0936-6*) Crossroad NY.

— Ethics. Crim, Keith, tr. LC 81-13051. Orig. Title: Ethik und Ekklesiologie. 222p. 1981. pap. 14.99 (*0-664-24392-4*, Westminster) Westminster John Knox.

— Human Nature, Election, & History. LC 77-22026. 116p. reprint ed. pap. 33.10 (*0-7837-2628-7*, 2042978) Bks Demand.

— The Idea of God & Human Freedom. LC 73-3165. 224p. 1973. 10.00 (*0-664-20971-8*, Westminster) Westminster John Knox.

— Introduction to Systematic Theology. (Orig.). 1991. pap. 8.99 (*0-8028-0546-9*) Eerdmans.

— Jesus: God & Man. 2nd ed. Wilkins, Lewis L. & Priebe, Duane A., trs. LC 76-26478. 428p. (C). 1982. reprint ed. pap. 22.99 (*0-664-24468-8*, Westminster) Westminster John Knox.

— Metaphysics & the Idea of God. 1990. 19.99 (*0-8028-3681-X*) Eerdmans.

— Systematic Theology, Vol. 1. Bromiley, Geoffrey W., tr. xiv, 460p. (C). 1991. 39.99 (*0-8028-3656-9*) Eerdmans.

— Systematic Theology, Vol. 2. Bromiley, Geoffrey W., tr. 480p. (C). 1994. text ed. 39.99 (*0-8028-3707-7*) Eerdmans.

— Toward a Theology of Nature: Essays on Science & Faith. Peters, Ted, ed. LC 93-19480. 208p. (Orig.). 1993. pap. 19.99 (*0-664-25384-9*) Westminster John Knox.

Pannenborg, Charles O. A New International Health Order. 476p. 1980. lib. bdg. 67.00 (*90-286-0239-9*) Kluwer Ac.

Pannes, Ernestine D. Waters of the Lonely Way: A Chronicle of Weston, Vermont from 1761-1978. LC 82-13314. (Illus.). 352p. 1982. 22.00 (*0-914016-89-X*) Phoenix Pub.

Pannese, E. The Satellite Cells of the Sensory Ganglia. (Advances in Anatomy, Embryology & Cell Biology Ser.: Vol. 65). (Illus.). 98p. 1981. pap. 44.00 (*0-387-10219-1*) Spr-Verlag.

Pannesse, Ennio. Neurocytology: Fine Structure of Neurons, Nerve Processes, & Neuroglial Cells. LC 93-18191. 1994. 89.00 (*0-86577-456-0*) Thieme Med Pubs.

***Pannet, Robert, et al.** Dictionnaire Marial. 1991. write for info. (*0-7859-8092-X*, 2-85443-217-7) Fr & Eur.

Pannett, Alan. Managing the Law Firm. 174p. (C). 1992. 24. 00 (*1-85431-168-9*, Pub. by Blackstone Pr UK) W W Gaunt.

— Managing the Law Firm: Legal Practice Handbook. 2nd ed. 184p. 1995. pap. 26.00 (*1-85431-457-2*, Pub. by Blackstone Pr UK) W W Gaunt.

— Principles of Hotel & Catering Law. 3rd ed. LC 92-34125. 384p. 1992. text ed. 60.00 (*0-304-32609-7*); pap. 30.00 (*0-304-32466-3*) Cassell.

— Recruitment & Training in the Solicitors' Practice. 1989. U.K. pap. 62.00 (*0-406-12750-6*) Butterworth Legal Pubs.

Pannett, Alan, jt. auth. see Johnson, Nick.

Pannick, David. Advocates. 320p. 1993. reprint ed. pap. 12. 95 (*0-19-285289-2*) OUP.

Panniker, Raimundo. The Vedic Experience. 937p. 1983. 15. 00 (*0-89744-011-0*) Auromere.

Panning, Anne. The Price of Eggs. LC 92-817. (Orig.). 1992. pap. 11.95 (*0-918273-95-1*) Coffee Hse.

Panning, Armin J. The Life of Christ. 1971. pap. 3.95 (*0-8100-0018-0*, 09-0932) Northwest Pub.

Pannonius, Ionnas S. Grammatica Hungaro-Latina. LC 68-65313. (Uralic & Altaic Ser.: Vol. 55). 78p. 1968. pap. text ed. 8.00 (*0-87750-019-3*) Res Inst Inner Asian Studies.

Pannor, Reuben, jt. auth. see Baran, Annette.

Pannuti, F., ed. Anti-Oestrogens in Oncology, Past, Present, & Prospects: Proceedings of the International Symposium on Hormonotherapy, Bologna, 6-8 June 1985. (Current Clinical Practice Ser.: Vol. 31). 312p. 1987. 132.50 (*0-444-90444-1*) Elsevier.

Panny, Judith D. I Have What I Gave: The Fiction of Janet Frame. 194p. 1993. 20.00 (*0-8076-1308-8*); pap. 10.95 (*0-8076-1309-6*) Braziller.

Pano, Nicholas C. Albania. (Marxist Regimes Ser.). 220p. 1989. 47.50 (*0-86187-392-0*, Pub. by Pinter Pubs UK); pap. 17.50 (*0-86187-393-9*, Pub. by Pinter Pubs UK) St Martin.

Panoff, Renee, jt. auth. see Neuman, Susan B.

Panoff, Renee, jt. auth. see Neuman, Susan.

Panofsky, Dora & Panofsky, Erwin. Pandora's Box: The Changing Aspects of a Mythical Symbol. (Bollingen Ser.: Vol. 52). (Illus.). 170p. 1991. pap. text ed. 15.95 (*0-691-01824-3*) Princeton U Pr.

Panofsky, Erwin. Codex Huygens & Leonardo Da Vinci's Art Theory. LC 79-109814. (Illus.). 1971. reprint ed. lib. bdg. 26.00 (*0-8371-4306-3*, PACH, Greenwood Pr) Greenwood.

— Gothic Architecture & Scholasticism. (Illus.). (C). 1974. pap. 12.00 (*0-452-00995-2*, Mer) NAL-Dutton.

— Life & Art of Albrecht Durer. (Illus.). 1955. pap. 29.95 (*0-691-00303-3*) Princeton U Pr.

— Meaning in the Visual Arts. LC 82-13600. (Right Brain - Whole Brain Learning Ser.). (Illus.). xx, 364p. (C). 1983. pap. text ed. 16.95 (*0-226-64551-7*) U Ch Pr.

— Meaning in the Visual Arts: Views from the Outside: A Centennial Commemoration of Edwin Panofsky (1892-1968) Lavin, Irving, ed. LC 95-10534. 1995. write for info. (*0-691-00630-X*) Princeton U Pr.

— Perspective As Symbolic Form. Wood, Christopher S., tr. LC 91-10716. (Illus.). 196p. 1991. 24.95 (*0-942299-52-3*) Zone Bks.

— Renaissance & Renascences in Western Art. (Icon Editions Ser.). (Illus.). 380p. 1972. pap. text ed. 21.00 (*0-06-430026-9*, IN-26, Icon Edns) HarpC.

— Studies in Iconology: Humanistic Themes in the Art of the Renaissance. 1992. 30.50 (*0-8446-6619-X*) Peter Smith.

— Studies in Iconology: Humanistic Themes in the Art of the Renaissance. (Icon Editions Ser.). (Illus.). 306p. 1972. reprint ed. pap. text ed. 21.00 (*0-06-430025-0*, IN-25, Icon Edns) HarpC.

— Three Essays on Style. Lavin, Irving, ed. (Illus.). 132p. 1995. 35.00 (*0-262-16151-6*) MIT Pr.

— Tomb Sculpture: Its Changing Aspects from Ancient Egypt to Bernini. (Illus.). 320p. 1992. 75.00 (*0-8109-3870-7*) Abrams.

Panofsky, Erwin, jt. auth. see Panofsky, Dora.

Panofsky, Hans E. A Bibliography of Africana. LC 72-823. (Contributions in Librarianship & Information Science Ser.: No. 11). 350p. 1975. text ed. 59.95 (*0-8371-6391-9*, PAA/, Greenwood Pr) Greenwood.

Panofsky, Margaret. Bass Viol Technique. (Educational Ser.: No. 1). (Illus.). xiv, 336p. (Orig.). 1991. pap. text ed. 40. 00 (*1-56571-042-8*) PRB Prods.

Panofsky, Ruth. Adele Wiseman: An Annotated Bibliography. 150p. (C). 1992. text ed. 30.00 (*1-55022-103-5*, Pub. by ECW Press CN) Genl Dist Srvs.

Panofsky, Wolfgang K. Particles & Policy. LC 93-14011. (Masters of Modern Physics Ser.: Vol. 8). 232p. 1994. 29.95 (*1-56396-060-5*) Am Inst Physics.

Panofsky, Wolfgang K. & Phillips, Melba. Classical Electricity & Magnetism. 2nd ed. (C). 1962. text ed. 55. 95 (*0-201-05702-6*) Addison-Wesley.

Panogopoulos, Andreas. Captives & Hostages in the Peloponnesian War. 296p. 1989. pap. 42.00 (*90-256-0935-X*, Pub. by A M Hakkert NE) Benjamins North Am.

Panola Genealogical & Historical Society. History of Panola County. (Illus.). 558p. 1987. 60.00 (*0-88107-074-2*) Curtis Media.

Panopolitanus, Nonnus. Dionysiaca, Vol. I. Keydell, Rudolf, ed. lxxxiv, 500p. 1959. write for info. (*3-296-14701-2*, Pub. by Georg Olms GW) Lubrecht & Cramer.

— Dionysiaca, Vol. II. Keydell, Rudolf, ed. iv, 555p. 1959. write for info. (*3-296-14702-0*, Pub. by Georg Olms GW) Lubrecht & Cramer.

Panopolos, Gersten G. Religion with Medical, Psychological & Philosophical Aspects: Index of New Information & Bible of Progress. 160p. Date not set. 44.50 (*0-7883-0226-4*); pap. 39.50 (*0-7883-0227-2*) ABBE Pubs Assn.

Panopoulos, Nickolas J. Genetic Engineering in the Plant Sciences. LC 81-10564. 288p. 1981. text ed. 65.00 (*0-275-90698-1*, C0698, Praeger Pubs) Greenwood.

Panos Institute Staff & Sabatier, Renee. AIDS & the Third World. (Illus.). 192p. (Orig.). 1988. 39.95 (*0-86571-143-7*); pap. 16.95 (*0-86571-144-5*) New Soc Pubs.

Panos, Maesimund B. & Heimlich, Jane. Homeopathic Medicine at Home. LC 79-63802. 288p. 1981. pap. 10. 95 (*0-87477-195-1*) J P Tarcher.

Panou, Stavros, et al, eds. Contemporary Conceptions of Social Philosophy: Proceedings of the 12th World Congress on Philosophy of Law. 237p. (Orig.). 1988. pap. 67.50 (*3-515-04983-5*) Coronet Bks.

— Human Being & the Cultural Values: Proceedings of the 12th World Congress on Philosophy of Law. 240p. (Orig.). 1988. pap. 67.50 (*3-515-04982-7*) Coronet Bks.

P Q

An Asterisk (*) at the beginning of an entry indicates that the title is appearing in BIP for the first time.

— Philosophy of Law in the History of Human Thought: Proceedings of the 12th World Congress on Philosophy of Law. 260p. (Orig.). 1988. pap. 67.50 (*3-515-04980-0*) Coronet Bks.

— Theory & Systems of Legal Philosophy: Proceedings of the 12th World Congress on Philosophy of Law. 272p. (Orig.). 1988. pap. 67.50 (*3-515-04981-9*) Coronet Bks.

***Panourgia, Neni.** Fragments of Death, Fables of Identity: An Athenian Anthropography. LC 95-6196. (New Directions in Anthropological Writing Ser.). 1995. write for info. (*0-299-14560-3*); pap. write for info. (*0-299-14564-6*) U of Wis Pr.

Panov, E. N. Population Ethology, Vol. 3. 92p. 1989. text ed. 46.00 (*3-7186-4881-4*) Gordon & Breach.

***Panov, Kathleen & Salomon, Larry.** The Art of OS-2 Version 3-C Programming. 2nd ed. Date not set. text ed. 44.95 (*0-471-08633-9*) Wiley.

Panov, Kathleen, et al. The Art of OS-2 2.1 C Programming. 320p. 1993. disk, pap. 39.95 (*0-471-58802-4*) Wiley.

— The Art of OS-2 2.1 C Programming. 1993. pap. 39.95 (*0-89435-446-9*) Wiley.

Panov, V. N., jt. auth. see Estrin, Yakov B.

Panova, V. On Faraway Street. Gabel, Rya, tr. LC 68-12891. (Illus.). 129p. (J). (gr. 3-7). 1968. 3.95 (*0-8076-0445-3*) Braziller.

Panova, V. F. Serezha. 230p. (C). 1984. 30.00 (*0-317-92435-4*, Pub. by Collets UK) Pro-Am Music.

Panova, Vera. Seryozha: Several Stories From the Life of a Very Small Boy. Bierkoff, Nicholas & Krooth, Ann, trs. (Illus.). 110p. 1995. 10.95 (*0-939074-10-9*) Harvest Pubns.

Panova, Vera F. Span of the Year. Traill, Vera, tr. LC 75-39007. (Soviet Literature in English Translation Ser.). 282p. 1994. reprint ed. 36.00 (*0-88355-410-0*) Hyperion Conn.

Panovski, Naum. Directing Poiesis. LC 92-43331. (American University Studies: Fine Arts: Ser. XX, Vol. 18). 235p. (C). 1994. text ed. 49.95 (*0-8204-2074-3*) P Lang Pubs.

Panozzo, Joseph G. An American in Jeopardy. LC 85-90478. 215p. (Orig.). 1986. text ed. 14.95 (*0-9615974-0-2*); pap. text ed. 9.95 (*0-9615974-1-0*) J G Panozzo.

Panozzo, Michael E., jt. auth. see Mizerak, Steve.

Panozzo, Patricia. Breakfast at Panozzo's: A Cookbook by Patricia Panozzo. 192p. (Orig.). 1989. pap. 9.95 (*0-685-27009-2*) PRP Pub.

Panshin, A. J. & De Zeeuw, Carl. Textbook of Wood Technology, Vol. 1. 4th ed. 1980. text ed. write for info. (*0-07-048441-4*) McGraw.

Panshin, Alexei. Heinlein in Dimension. rev. ed. LC 68-2797. 1968. reprint ed. 14.00 (*0-911682-01-5*); reprint ed. pap. 7.00 (*0-911682-12-0*) Advent.

Panshin, Alexei & Panshin, Cory. SF in Dimension: A Book of Explorations. 2nd ed. LC 80-68572. 1980. pap. 8.00 (*0-911682-24-4*) Advent.

Panshin, Cory, jt. auth. see Panshin, Alexei.

Pansini, A. & Conti, P. Median Longitudinal Cervical Somatotomy. 158p. 1986. text ed. 64.00 (*1-57235-044-X*) Piccin NY.

Pansini, A. J. & Smalling, K. D. Guide to Electric Power Generation. LC 93-35833. 1994. 95.00 (*0-88173-174-9*) Fairmont Pr.

Pansini, Anna, ed. Best Jokes & Riddles. LC 89-20324. (Illus.). 48p. (J). (gr. 2-6). 1990. lib. bdg. 8.59 (*0-8167-1917-9*); pap. text ed. 2.50 (*0-8167-1918-7*) Troll Assocs.

— Great Answer Book. LC 90-44452. (Illus.). 48p. (J). (gr. 3-6). 1991. lib. bdg. 10.89 (*0-8167-2308-7*); pap. text ed. 2.95 (*0-8167-2309-5*) Troll Assocs.

— Great Riddles, Giggles & Jokes. LC 89-5200. (Illus.). 48p. (J). (gr. 2-6). 1990. lib. bdg. 8.59 (*0-8167-1915-2*); pap. text ed. 2.50 (*0-8167-1916-0*) Troll Assocs.

— I Wonder Why. LC 90-44455. (Illus.). 48p. (J). (gr. k-2). 1991. lib. bdg. 10.89 (*0-8167-2304-4*); pap. text ed. 2.95 (*0-8167-2305-2*) Troll Assocs.

— Kids' Question & Answer Book. LC 90-43969. (Illus.). 48p. (J). (gr. 2-4). 1991. lib. bdg. 10.89 (*0-8167-2306-0*); pap. text ed. 2.95 (*0-8167-2307-9*) Troll Assocs.

Pansini, Anthony, et al. Guid eto Electric Power Generation. 230p. 1994. text ed. 95.00 (*0-13-300021-4*) P-H.

Pansini, Anthony J. Basic of Electric Motors. 224p. 1989. text ed. 53.00 (*0-13-060070-9*) P-H.

— Electrical Distribution Engineering. 2nd ed. (Illus.). 437p. 1991. 74.95 (*0-88173-121-8*) Fairmont Pr.

— Electrical Transformers & Power Equipment. (Illus.). 400p. (C). 1988. text ed. 65.00 (*0-13-247602-9*) P-H.

— Guide to Electrical Power Distribution Systems. 256p. 1992. text ed. 54.00 (*0-13-059460-1*) P-H.

— Machiavelli & the United States: 500th Anniversary Edition, 6 vols. in 1. LC 70-108252. 1371p. 1969. 20.00 (*0-911876-02-2*) Greenvale.

— Maximizing Management Effectiveness. LC 77-85653. (Illus.). 1977. pap. 15.00 (*0-911876-04-9*, 0-911876-04) Greenvale.

— The Northeast Be Dammed! rev. ed. LC 77-140933. 1971. pap. 50.00 (*0-911876-01-4*) Greenvale.

— Power Systems Stability Handbook. LC 92-27249. 259p. 1992. 67.00 (*0-88173-130-7*) Fairmont Pr.

— Power Transmission & Distribution. 1991. 74.00 (*0-88173-112-9*) Fairmont Pr.

— Power Transmission & Distribution. 419p. 1991. text ed. 79.00 (*0-13-680737-2*, 410501) P-H.

***Pansini, Anthony J. & Smalling, Kenneth D.** High Voltage Power Equipment Engineering. LC 94-27238. 1994. write for info. (*0-88173-175-7*) Fairmont Pr.

— Undergrounding Electric Lines. 2nd ed. LC 92-41799. 1993. write for info. (*0-88173-162-5*) Fairmont Pr.

Pansini, Anthony J., jt. auth. see Fairmont Press Staff.

Pansini, Anthony J., tr. see Levi-Malvano, E.

Pansini, Anthony J., et al. Undergrounding Electric Lines. 2nd ed. 224p. (C). 1993. text ed. 74.00 (*0-13-066929-6*) P-H.

Pansini La Haye, Mary E. It Started with a Nickel. LC 88-90548. (Illus.). 107p. 1988. 12.95 (*0-9620345-0-9*) Nickel Pubns.

Pansius, David K., jt. auth. see Nanda, Ved P.

Pansky, Ben. Review of Gross Anatomy. 5th ed. 527p. 1984. pap. text ed. 36.95 (*0-07-105339-5*) Hlth Prof Div.

— Review of Gross Anatomy. 6th ed. (Illus.). 527p. 1995. pap. text ed. 32.00 (*0-07-105446-4*) Hlth Prof Div.

— Review of Neuroscience. 2nd ed. 576p. 1988. pap. text ed. 37.00 (*0-07-105304-2*) Hlth Prof Div.

***Pansters, Wil.** Politics & Power in Puebla: The Political History of a Mexican State, 1937-1987. (CEDLA Latin America Studies (CLAS): No. 57). 240p. 1990. pap. 28.50 (*90-70280-03-5*, Pub. by Thesis Pubs NE) IBD Ltd.

***Pansters, Wil & Ouweneel, Arij.** Region, State & Capitalism in Mexico: Nineteenth & Twentieth Centuries. (CEDLA Latin America Studies (CLAS): No. 54). 232p. 1989. pap. 27.00 (*90-70280-61-2*, Pub. by Thesis Pubs NE) IBD Ltd.

Pansy, jt. auth. see Betty.

Pansy, Michael D. A Guide to Planning Your Wedding Reception. (Illus.). 1978. ring bd. 6.95 (*0-9602460-1-0*) P D Michael.

Pant, Apa. The Survival of the Individual. 176p. 1983. text ed. 20.00 (*0-86131-400-X*, Pub. by Orient Longman Ltd II) Apt Bks.

Pant, Apa B. Undiplomatic Incidents. 1987. text ed. 12.50 (*0-86131-690-8*, Pub. by Orient Longman Ltd II) Apt Bks.

Pant, G. N. Indian Archery. (C). 1993. reprint ed. 110.00 (*0-8364-2873-0*, Pub. by Agam II) S Asia.

— Mughal Weapons in the Babur Nama. (C). 1989. 125.00 (*0-8364-2473-5*, Pub. by Agam II) S Asia.

Pant, Gauri. Staircase Seventeen. (Writers Workshop Redbird Ser.). 1975. 8.00 (*0-88253-644-3*); pap. text ed. 4.00 (*0-88253-643-5*) Ind-US Inc.

— Weeping Season. (Redbird Ser.). 36p. 1975. 4.80 (*0-88253-717-2*); pap. 4.00 (*0-88253-847-0*) Ind-US Inc.

Pant, Girish. Foreign Aid, Economic Growth & Social Cost-Benefit Analysis: Some Experiences from Nepal. 427p. 1991. text ed. 85.95 (*1-85628-222-8*, Pub. by Avebury Pub UK) Ashgate Pub Co.

Pant, Govind B. Selected Works of Govind Ballabh Pant, Vol. I. Nanda, B. R., ed. (Illus.). 356p. 1994. 24.95 (*0-19-563150-1*) OUP.

— Selected Works of Govind Ballabh Pant, Vol. 4. Nanda, B. R., ed. (Illus.). 422p. 1995. 24.95 (*0-19-563674-0*) OUP.

— Selected Works of Govind Ballabh Pant, Vol. 5. Nanda, B. R., ed. (Illus.). 520p. 1995. 35.00 (*0-19-563675-9*) OUP.

Pant, Kusum. The Kashmiri Pandit: Story of a Community in Exile in the 19th & 20th Centuries. 1987. 17.50 (*0-8364-2279-1*, Pub. by Allied II) S Asia.

Pant, Niranjan. New Trend in Indian Irrigation: Commercialisation of Ground Water. (C). 1992. 14.50 (*81-7024-467-6*, Pub. by Ashish II) S Asia.

Pant, Niranjan & Rai, R. P. Community Tubewell & Agricultural Development. 1985. 15.00 (*0-8364-1380-6*, Pub. by Ashish II) S Asia.

Pant, S. D. Social Economy of the Himalayas. (C). 1988. 31.50 (*0-8364-2431-X*, Pub. by Mittal II) S Asia.

Pant, Y. P. Population Growth & Employment Opportunities in Nepal. 1985. 12.50 (*0-8364-1277-X*, Pub. by Oxford IBH II) S Asia.

— Trade & Cooperation in South Asia: A Nepalese Perspective. (C). 1992. 15.95 (*0-7069-5694-X*, Pub. by Vikas II) S Asia.

Pantaleoni, Hewitt. On the Nature of Music. LC 85-50599. (Illus.). 464p. (C). 1985. 36.00 (*0-9614873-0-5*) Welkin Bks.

Pantaleoni, Hewitt, ed. see Serwadda, W. Moses.

Pantaleoni, Maffeo. Pure Economics. 1957. reprint ed. 37.50 (*0-678-00674-1*) Kelley.

Pantalone, Gerald M., ed. Personnel Management in the Travel Industry. 361p. (Orig.). 1989. pap. 35.00 (*0-931202-17-5*) Inst Cert Trav Agts.

***Pantalone, John & Bodah, Paula.** Rhode Island: Off the Beaten Path: A Guide to Unique Places. (Off the Beaten Path Ser.). (Illus.). 160p. (Orig.). 1995. pap. text ed. 9.95 (*1-56440-651-2*) Globe Pequot.

Pantano, C. G. & Chen, E. J., eds. Interfaces in Composites: Materials Research Society Symposium Proceedings, Vol. 170. 1990. text ed. 46.00 (*1-55899-058-5*) Materials Res.

Pantazis, Andreas. Epsilon of Aurigae. 1990. pap. 9.95 (*0-948259-87-6*) Dufour.

Pantazopol, D. French-Rumanian Dictionary of Aeronautics: Dictionar de Aeronautica Francez-Roman. (FRE & RUM.). 1984. write for info. (*0-8288-1171-7*, M15834) Fr & Eur.

Pantazopoulos, N. J. Church & Law in the Balkan Peninsula during the Ottoman Rule. (Illus.). 125p. 1983. reprint ed. pap. text ed. 24.00 (*0-317-54442-X*, Pub. by A M Hakkert SP) Coronet Bks.

Pantel, Pauline S., jt. auth. see Zaidman, Louise B.

Pantel, Pauline Schmidt, et al, eds. History of Women in the West, Vol. 1: From Ancient Goddesses to Christian Saints. Goldhammer, Arthur, tr. 572p. (C). 1994. pap. text ed. 15.95 (*0-674-40369-X*) Belknap Pr.

Pantel, Pauline Schmidt & Duby, Georges, eds. A History of Women in the West, Vol. I: From Ancient Goddesses to Christian Saints. Goldhammer, Arthur, tr. (Illus.). 572p. (C). 1992. text ed. 29.95 (*0-674-40370-3*) Belknap Pr.

Panteli, Stravros. Historical Dictionary of Cyprus. LC 94-18869. (European Historical Dictionaries Ser.: No. 6). 1995. write for info. (*0-8108-2912-6*) Scarecrow.

Pantelides, S. T., jt. ed. see Lucovsky, G.

Pantelides, Sokrates T. Deep Centers in Semiconductors: A State-of-the-Art Approach. 783p. 1986. text ed. 179.00 (*2-88124-109-3*) Gordon & Breach.

Pantelides, Sokrates T., ed. Deep Centers in Semiconductors: A State of the Art Approach. 2nd ed. LC 92-18744. 1992. text ed. 140.00 (*2-88124-562-5*) Gordon & Breach.

Pantelidis, Veronica S. The Arab World: Libraries & Librarianship 1960-1976; a Bibliography. 116p. 1979. pap. 70.00 (*0-7201-0821-7*, Mansell Pub) Cassell.

— Robotics in Education: An Information Guide. LC 91-24541. 449p. 1991. 47.50 (*0-8108-2466-3*) Scarecrow.

Pantell, Richard H. Techniques of Environmental Systems Analysis. LC 76-98. (Illus.). 195p. reprint ed. pap. 55.60 (*0-7837-3524-3*, 2057859) Bks Demand.

Pantell, Robert H., et al. Taking Care of Your Child. rev. ed. 1990. pap. 15.95 (*0-201-08278-0*) Addison-Wesley.

— Taking Care of Your Child: A Parent's Guide to Complete Medical Care. 4th ed. (Illus.). 608p. 1993. pap. 17.26 (*0-201-63293-4*) Addison-Wesley.

Pantelouris, E. & Kerkut, G. A. Common Liver Fluke: Fasciola Hepatica L. LC 63-21135. (International Series Mono in Pure & Applied Biology: Vol. 21). 1965. 109.00 (*0-08-010482-7*, Pub. by Pergamon Repr UK) Franklin.

***Panter, Barry M., et al.** Creativity & Madness: Psychological Studies of Art & Artists, Vol. I. LC 94-94521. (Illus.). 320p. 1995. 24.95 (*0-9641185-1-3*) AIMED.

Panter-Brick, Keith, ed. Soldiers & Oil: The Transformation of Nigeria. (Studies in Commonwealth Politics & History: No. 5). 375p. 1978. 37.50 (*0-7146-3098-5*, Pub. by F Cass Pubs UK) Intl Spec Bk.

***Panter, Nicole.** Mr. Right On & Other Stories. 110p. (Orig.). 1994. pap. 10.00 (*0-9627013-8-6*, Incommunicado) Rockpress Pub.

***Pantev, Christo, et al, eds.** Oscillatory Event-Related Brain Dynamics: Proceedings of a NATO ARW Held in Tecklenburg, Germany, September 1-5, 1993. LC 94-48769. (NATO ASI Series A, Life Sciences: Vol. 271). 460p. 1995. 120.00 (*0-306-44894-7*, Plenum Pr) Plenum.

***Pantham, Thomas.** Political Theories & Social Reconstruction: A Critical Survey of the Literature on India. LC 94-45237. 1995. pap. 25.00 (*0-8039-9217-5*) Sage.

— Political Theories & Social Reconstruction: A Critical Survey of the Literature on India. LC 94-45237. 200p. 1995. 24.00 (*0-8039-9216-5*) Sage.

Panthel, Hans W., tr. see Dewran, Hasan.

Pantheon Photo Library. American Photographers of the Depression. Incl. Eugene Atget. 1985. (*0-318-59515-X*); Henri Cartier-Bresson. 1985. (*0-318-59516-8*); Robert Frank. 1985. (*0-318-59517-6*); 1985. (*0-318-59518-4*); 1985. Set pap. 7.95 (*0-394-74086-6*) Pantheon.

Panther, Abraham. A Very Surprising Narrative of a Young Woman Discovered in a Rocky Cave after Having Been Taken by the Savage Indians of the Wilderness in the Year 1777. 1972. reprint ed. 6.95 (*0-87770-121-0*); reprint ed. pap. 4.95 (*0-87770-095-8*) Ye Galleon.

Panthey, Saroj. Iconography of Siva in Pahari Paintings. (C). 1987. 78.00 (*81-7099-016-5*, Pub. by Motilal Banarsidass II) S Asia.

Pantic, Vladmir, jt. ed. see McKerns, Kenneth W.

Pantiel, Mindy & Petersen, Becky. Kids, Teachers, & Computers: A Guide to Computers in the Elementary School. (Illus.). 176p. (J). 1984. pap. text ed. 25.00 (*0-13-515420-0*); pap. text ed. 16.95 (*0-13-515396-4*) P-H.

— The Senior High Computer Connection. LC 85-3660. (Illus.). 272p. 1985. pap. 22.95 (*0-13-806530-6*) P-H.

Pantin, W. A. The English Church in the Fourteenth Century. (Medieval Academy Reprints for Teaching Ser.). 1980. pap. 7.50 (*0-8020-6411-6*) U of Toronto Pr.

Panting, Gerald E., jt. auth. see Sager, Eric W.

Pantke, Mechthild. Der Arabische Bahram-Roman: Untersuchungen zur Quellen- und Stoffgeschichte. (Studien zur Sprache, Geschichte und Kultur des Islamischen Orients: Vol. 6). 230p. (C). 1973. 115.40 (*3-11-003990-7*) De Gruyter.

Pantle, Mark L., jt. auth. see Pantle, Tonya T.

Pantle, Tonya T. & Pantle, Mark L. Seeing Red, Feeling Blue, or In the Pink. 224p. 1993. pap. 9.99 (*0-310-48251-8*) Zondervan.

Pantoja-Hidalgo, Cristina. I Remember...Travel Essays. 122p. (Orig.). 1993. pap. 7.25 (*971-10-0522-0*, Pub. by New Day Pub PH) Cellar.

Pantoja-Hidalgo, Cristina & Patajo-Legasto, Priscelina, eds. Philippine Post-Colonial Studies: Essays on Language & Literature. 140p. 1993. pap. text ed. 12.00 (*971-542-021-4*, Pub. by U of Philippines Pr) UH Pr.

Pantojas-Garcia, Emilio. Development Strategies as Ideologies: Puerto Rico's Export-Led Industrialization Experience. LC 90-33397. 208p. 1990. lib. bdg. 37.00 (*1-55587-198-4*) Lynne Rienner.

— Development Strategies As Ideology. LC 90-33397. 205p. 1990. 18.50 (*0-8477-0175-1*) U of PR Pr.

Panton, G. A., jt. ed. see Donaldson, D.

Panton, Ronald L. Incompressible Flow. LC 83-23342. 780p. 1984. text ed. 94.95 (*0-471-89765-5*) Wiley.

— Incompressible Flow. 2nd ed. LC 95-10084. 1996. write for info. (*0-471-59358-3*) Wiley-Interscience.

Pantos, Spiros. Catalyses Catacoustical. 1979. 9.95 (*0-87881-074-9*) Mojave Bks.

***Pantry, S.** Occupational Health. 336p. 1995. pap. 39.95 (*1-56593-415-6*, 1081) Singular Publishing.

Pantsios, Joan L., jt. ed. see Hartman, Marshall J.

Panttaja, Dawn. Play Guide One: Building Adventures. (Illus.). 1989. teacher ed 10.00 (*1-879616-00-9*, 34891) Brio Scanditoy.

Pantulu, G. R. Folk-Lore of the Telugus. (C). 1991. text ed. 14.00 (*81-206-0691-4*, Pub. by Asian Educ Servs II) S Asia.

Pantumsinchai, Pricha, et al. BASIC Programs for Production & Operations Management. (Illus.). 448p. (C). 1983. pap. 23.33 (*0-685-55652-2*) P-H.

***Pantuso, Joe.** Doom Game Editor. 1995. disk, pap. 24.95 (*0-471-12128-2*) Wiley.

Pantuso, John C., ed. see Graham, Robert A. & Lichten, Joseph L.

Panum, Hortense. The Stringed Instruments of the Middle Ages. LC 73-127279. (Music Ser.). (Illus.). 1971. reprint ed. lib. bdg. 55.00 (*0-306-70039-5*) Da Capo.

Panunzi, Paul. Love As Strong As Death. LC 66-30822. (Encounter Ser.). (J). (gr. 3-7). 1966. 3.00 (*0-8198-0239-5*) Pauline Bks.

Panunzio, Constantine. Immigration Crossroads. LC 79-145489. (American Immigration Library). xii, 308p. 1971. reprint ed. lib. bdg. 34.95 (*0-89198-022-9*) Ozer.

Panunzio, Constantine M. Deportation Cases of Nineteen-Nineteen to Nineteen-Twenty. LC 77-109547. (Civil Liberties in American History Ser.). 1970. reprint ed. lib. bdg. 18.50 (*0-306-71901-0*) Da Capo.

— Soul of an Immigrant. LC 69-18787. (American Immigration Collection Ser., No. 1). 1969. reprint ed. 16.95 (*0-405-00535-0*) Ayer.

Panuthos, Claudia. Transformation Through Birth: A Woman's Guide. LC 83-15559. (Illus.). 208p. 1984. pap. text ed. 14.95 (*0-89789-038-8*, Bergin & Garvey) Greenwood.

Panuthos, Claudia & Romeo, Catherine. Ended Beginnings: Healing Childbearing Losses. LC 84-12284. (Illus.). 224p. 1984. text ed. 29.95 (*0-89789-053-1*, Bergin & Garvey); pap. text ed. 14.95 (*0-89789-054-X*, Bergin & Garvey) Greenwood.

Panvini, R. S., ed. Particle Searches & Discoveries: Proceedings, International Conference, Vanderbilt University, 1-3 March 1976. LC 76-19949. (AIP Conference Proceedings Ser.: No. 30). 1976. 18.50 (*0-88318-129-0*) Am Inst Physics.

Panvini, R. S. & Csorna, S. E., eds. High Energy E Plus E Minus Interactions Vanderbilt 1980. LC 80-53377. (AIP Conference Proceedings Ser.: No. 62). 405p. 1980. lib. bdg. 23.00 (*0-88318-161-4*) Am Inst Physics.

— New Results in High Energy Physics 1978: Proceedings of the 3rd International Conference, Vanderbilt Univ., Mar. 1978. LC 78-67196. (AIP Conference Proceedings Ser.: No. 45). (Illus.). 1978. lib. bdg. 20.25 (*0-88318-144-4*) Am Inst Physics.

Panvini, R. S. & Weiler, T., eds. Quarks, Strings, Dark Matter & All the Rest: Proceedings of the Vanderbilt High Energy Physics Conference, 7th, Nashville, Tennessee, May 15-17, 1987. 344p. 1987. pap. 40.00 (*9971-5-0278-X*) World Scientific Pub.

Panvini, R. S. & Word, G. B., eds. High Energy & Interactions: Vanderbilt 1984. LC 84-72632. (AIP Conference Proceedings Ser.: No. 121). 429p. 1984. lib. bdg. 43.75 (*0-88318-320-X*) Am Inst Physics.

Panvini, R. S., ed. see American Institute of Physics.

Panvini, R. S., et al, eds. Novel Results in Particle Physics. LC 82-73954. (AIP Conference Proceedings Ser.: No. 93). 384p. 1982. lib. bdg. 35.00 (*0-88318-192-4*) Am Inst Physics.

***Pany, Kurt & Whittington, O. Ray.** Auditing. 232p. (C). 1993. student ed, text ed. 25.50 (*0-256-11642-3*) Irwin.

Pany, Kurt, jt. auth. see Whittington, O. Ray.

Pany, Kurt J. & Whittington, O. Ray. Auditing. LC 93-4070. 752p. (C). 1993. Alk. paper. text ed. 68.95 (*0-256-11637-7*) Irwin.

Panyan, Marion V. How to Use Shaping. (How to Teach Ser.). 30p. 1980. pap. 8.00 (*0-89079-050-7*, 1006) PRO-ED.

Panych. Other Schools of Thought: Three Dramatic Pieces. (NFS Canada Ser.). 1994. pap. 12.95 (*0-88922-346-7*, Pub. by Talonbooks CN) InBook.

Panych, Morris. The Ends of the Earth. 144p. 1994. pap. 10.95 (*0-88922-334-3*, Pub. by Talonbooks CN) InBook.

Panza-Ella, Tracy, jt. auth. see Nielsen, Greg.

Panzano, Phyllis, jt. auth. see Campbell, Paul B.

Panzardi, Anthony. Pyxis: Among Lost Children & Grizzled Dogs. LC 93-13585. 64p. 1993. pap. 12.95 (*0-7734-2774-0*, Mellen Poetry Pr) E Mellen.

Panzarino, Connie. The Me in the Mirror. LC 93-41623. 272p. (Orig.). 1994. pap. 12.95 (*1-878067-45-1*) Seal Pr Feminist.

Panzarino, Gale G. The Naked Truth. 1994. 7.95 (*0-8062-4978-1*) Carlton.

Panzer, B. I., jt. auth. see Grove, David J.

Panzer, Georg W. Annalen der Alteren Deutschen Literatur, 3 vols., Set. 1961. reprint ed. write for info. (*0-318-71851-0*, Pub. by Georg Olms GW) Lubrecht & Cramer.

— Annales Typographici, 11 vols., Set. 1964. reprint ed. write for info. (*0-318-71852-9*, Pub. by Georg Olms GW) Lubrecht & Cramer.

Panzer, Martin. How to Develop a Winning Personality. 1975. pap. 7.00 (*0-87980-057-7*) Wilshire.

Panzer, Mary. In My Studio: Rudolf Eickemeyer,Jr., & the Art of the Camera, 1885-1930. (Illus.). 112p. (Orig.). (C). 1987. pap. 21.95 (*0-87474-739-2*) Smithsonian.

— In My Studio: Rudolf Eickemeyer, Jr. & the Art of the Camera, 1885-1930. LC 87-401421. (Illus.). 106p. (Orig.). 1986. pap. 9.50 (*0-943651-01-8*) Hudson Riv.

Panzer, Nora, ed. Celebrate America: In Poetry & Art. LC 93-32336. (Illus.). 96p. (YA). (gr. 5 up). 1995. 18.95 (*1-56282-664-6*); lib. bdg. 18.89 (*1-56282-665-4*) Hyprn Child.

Panzer, Robert J., et al, eds. Diagnostic Strategies for Common Medical Problems. 550p. 1991. pap. 38.00 (*0-943126-20-7*, DIS91) Amer Coll Phys.

Panzer, Ursula, ed. see Husserl, Edmund.

P Q

Panzieri, Peter. Little Big Horn 1876. (Campaign Ser.). (Illus.). 96p. 1995. pap. 14.95 (*1-85532-458-X*, 9535, Pub. by Osprey UK) Stackpole.

Pao, C. V. Nonlinear Parabolic & Elliptic Equations. LC 92-30342. (Illus.). 780p. (C). 1993. 125.00 (*0-306-44343-0*, Plenum Pr) Plenum.

*__Pao, John, ed.__ The CRM Study Bible: New Testament. 848p. (CHI.). 1992. 20.00 (*1-56582-000-2*) Christ Renew Min.

— The CRM Study Bible (Simplified Script) New Testament. deluxe ed. 712p. (CHI.). 1994. 16.00 (*1-56582-050-9*) Christ Renew Min.

Pao-min Chang. Beijing, Hanoi & the Overseas Chinese. LC 82-2641. (China Research Monographs: No. 24). 1982. pap. 3.50 (*0-912966-50-5*) IEAS.

Pao, Miranda L. Concepts in Information Retrieval. 285p. 1989. lib. bdg. 35.00 (*0-87287-405-2*) Libs Unl.

Pao, Ping-Nie. Schizophrenic Disorders: Theory & Treatment from a Psychodynamic Point of View. LC 77-92180. 456p. 1979. text ed. 65.00x (*0-8236-5990-9*) Intl Univs Pr.

Pao, Y. C. & Foltz, Michael E. Engineering Drafting & Solid Modeling with SilverScreen. 1992. 45.00 (*0-8493-4471-9*, T353) CRC Pr.

Pao, Y. C., jt. auth. see Smith, T. C.

Pao, Yih-Ho & Goldburg, Arnold, eds. Clear Air Turbulence & Its Detection: Proceedings of a Symposium. LC 73-76507. 556p. reprint ed. pap. 158.50 (*0-685-15683-4*, 2026290) Bks Demand.

Paola, Angelo S., jt. auth. see Lamm, Donald L.

Paola, C., jt. ed. see Kleinspehn, K.

*__Paola, Suzanne.__ Glass. (QRL Poetry Book Ser.: Vol. XXXIV). 20.00 (*0-614-06456-2*) Quarterly Rev.

— Glass. (QRL Poetry Book Ser.: Vol. XXXIV). pap. 10.00 (*0-614-06457-0*) Quarterly Rev.

— Petitioner. (Poetry Chapbook Ser.). 46p. (Orig.). 1985. pap. 7.00 (*0-937669-17-2*) Owl Creek Pr.

Paolantonio, S. A. Frank Rizzo: The Last Big Man in Big City America. LC 93-12076. (Illus.). 412p. 1993. 22.00 (*0-940159-18-X*) Camino Bks.

*__Paolella, Michael A.__ Auditing Health Care Benefits: How to Effectively Manage Costs & Minimize Risk. LC 95-12461. 1995. text ed. 105.00 (*0-471-11918-0*) Wiley.

*__Paolella, Peter.__ Introduction to Molecular Genetics. 352p. (C). 1995. pap. write for info. (*0-697-20939-3*) Wm C Brown Pubs.

Paoletti, A., ed. Physics of Magnetic Garnets. (Enrico Fermi International Summer School of Physics Ser.: Vol. 70). 546p. 1979. 156.50 (*0-444-85200-X*, North Holland) Elsevier.

Paoletti, John T. The Critical Eye I. LC 83-51290. (Illus.). 87p. 1984. 12.95 (*0-930606-46-9*) Yale Ctr Brit Art.

— From Minimal to Conceptual Art: Works from the Dorothy & Herbert Vogel Collection. LC 94-11322. 141p. 1994. pap. 25.00 (*0-89468-206-7*) Natl Gallery Art.

Paoletti, M. G., et al, eds. Agricultural Ecology & Environment: Proceedings of an International Symposium, Padova, Italy, 5-7 April, 1988. 644p. 1990. reprint ed. 143.75 (*0-444-88610-9*) Elsevier.

Paoletti, P. & Walker, Barbara G., eds. Multidisciplinary Aspects of Brain Tumor Therapy. (Neurooncology Ser.: Vol. 1). 404p. 1979. 97.50 (*0-444-80170-7*, North Holland) Elsevier.

Paoletti, P., et al, eds. Neuro-Oncology. (Developments in Oncology Ser.). (C). 1991. lib. bdg. 161.50 (*0-7923-1215-5*) Kluwer Ac.

Paoletti, Rodolfo. Exercise Bioenergetic & Gas Exchange. write for info. (*0-318-56695-8*) Elsevier.

*__Paoletti, Rodolfo, ed.__ Oxidative Processes & Antioxidants. LC 94-36148. 248p. 1995. 99.00 (*0-7817-0248-8*) Raven.

Paoletti, Rodolfo & Kritchevsky, David, eds. Advances in Lipid Research, Vol. 22. (Serial Publication Ser.). 199p. 1988. text ed. 85.00 (*0-12-024922-7*) Acad Pr.

— Advances in Lipid Research, Vol. 23. (Serial Publication Ser.). 305p. 1989. text ed. 104.00 (*0-12-024923-5*) Acad Pr.

Paoletti, Rodolfo, ed. see Atherosclerosis Reviews Staff.

Paoletti, Rodolfo, jt. auth. see Gotto, Antonio M., Jr.

Paoletti, Rodolfo, jt. ed. see Gotto, Antonio M., Jr.

Paoletti, Rodolfo, ed. see International Congress for Fat Research Staff.

Paoletti, Rodolfo, ed. see International Symposium on Atherosclerosis & the Reticuloendothelial System (1966: Como, Italy).

Paoletti, Rodolfo, jt. ed. see Kritchevsky, David.

Paoletti, Rodolfo, jt. ed. see Samuelsson, Bengt.

Paoletti, Rodolfo, jt. auth. see Trabucchi, E.

Paoletti, Rodolfo, jt. ed. see Vanhoutte, Paul M.

Paoletti, Rudolfo, ed. see Atherosclerosis Reviews Staff.

Paoli, Arturo. Meditations on Saint Luke. McWilliams, Bernard F., tr. LC 76-58539. 204p. reprint ed. pap. 58.20 (*0-8357-8949-7*, 2033514) Bks Demand.

*__Paoli, Francisco M.__ El Cerco de Dios. (Illus.). 157p. (SPA.). 1995. lib. bdg. 10.00 (*1-881708-09-8*) Edcnes Mairena.

Paoli, Francisco Matos. Song of Madness & Other Poems. Miller, Yvette E., ed. Aparicio, Frances, tr. LC 85-11. 160p. (ENG & SPA.). 1985. pap. 12.95 (*0-935480-18-8*) Lat Am Lit Rev Pr.

Paoli Memorial Hospital Auxiliary Staff. Quilted Quisine. LC 92-11047. 1992. write for info. (*0-87197-337-5*) Favorite Recipes.

Paoli, Shirley B. Poetry: A Legacy of Love. 55p. (Orig.). 1989. pap. 5.95 (*0-685-50285-6*) S B Paoli.

— Poetry - A Legacy of Love: Featuring an Era of Poetry Then & Now. 62p. (Orig.). 1989. pap. 5.95 (*0-685-44869-X*) S B Paoli.

Paolieri, Annarita. Paolo Uccello, Domenico Veneziano, Andrea del Castagno. Pelletti, Lisa, tr. (Library of Great Masters). (Illus.). 80p. (Orig.). 1991. pap. 12.99 (*1-878351-20-6*) Riverside NY.

*__Paolini & Meisner.__ Teach Yourself ObjectPAL Programming in 21 Days. (Illus.). 750p. (Orig.). 1995. pap. 29.99 (*0-672-30698-0*) Sams.

Paolini, Gilbert, ed. LA CHISPA '81: Selected Proceedings. LC 81-52692. 360p. (POR & SPA.). 1981. pap. 30.00 (*0-9607798-0-9*) Tulane U Conf Hispanic Lit.

— LA CHISPA '83: Selected Proceedings. LC 83-81630. 336p. (Orig.). 1983. pap. 30.00 (*0-9607798-1-7*) Tulane U Conf Hispanic Lit.

— LA CHISPA '85: Selected Proceedings. LC 85-51632. 400p. 1985. pap. 30.00 (*0-9607798-2-5*) Tulane U Conf Hispanic Lit.

— LA CHISPA '87: Selected Proceedings. LC 87-51270. 352p. 1987. pap. 30.00 (*0-9607798-3-3*) Tulane U Conf Hispanic Lit.

— La Chispa, '93: Selected Proceedings. 334p. (SPA.). 1993. pap. 50.00 (*0-9607798-5-X*) Tulane U Conf Hispanic Lit.

Paolini, Gilbert, intro. La Chispa, '89: Selected Proceedings. LC 89-51388. 424p. (Orig.). (ENG & SPA.). 1989. pap. 50.00 (*0-9607798-4-1*) Tulane U Conf Hispanic Lit.

Paolini, Mary. Moments with God. 1986. 5.95 (*0-88271-028-1*) Regina Pr.

Paolini, Shirley J. Creativity, Culture, & Values: Comparative Essays in Literary Aesthetics. LC 90-5873. (New Studies in Aesthetics: Vol. 5). 239p. (C). 1991. text ed. 47.95 (*0-8204-1341-0*) P Lang Pubs.

Paolino, Adele. Agoraphobia: Fear of Fear. 256p. 1985. pap. text ed. 8.95 (*0-9611448-1-5*) A Paolino.

— Agoraphobia: How I Overcame This Crippling Disease. 80p. 1983. pap. 5.95 (*0-9611448-0-7*) A Paolino.

Paolino, Andrea R., ed. see Krill, Mary A.

Paolino, Thomas J. & McCrady, Barbara S., eds. Marriage & Marital Therapy: Psychoanalytic, Behavioral & Systems Theory Perspectives. LC 78-17398. 612p. 1978. 48.95 (*0-87630-171-5*) Brunner-Mazel.

Paolino, Thomas J., Jr., jt. ed. see Nichols, Michael P.

Paolo, Frank. How to Make a Great Presentation in Two Hours. 1993. pap. 12.95 (*0-8119-0827-5*) LIFETIME.

Paolozzi, Gabriel & Sedwick, Frank. Conversation in Italian: Points of Departure. 3rd ed. 120p. (C). 1985. pap. 26.95 (*0-8384-1276-9*) Heinle & Heinle.

Paolucci, Anne. The Actor in Search of His Mask: A One-Act Play. 1987. 11.50 (*0-685-17466-2*); pap. 8.95 (*0-918680-26-3*) Bagehot Council.

— The Armenian Literary Legacy: A Bridge Among the Nations. pap. 2.00 (*0-918680-30-1*) Bagehot Council.

— CIPANGO! A One Act Play in Three Scenes about Christopher Columbus. LC 85-14731. 1985. 11.50 (*0-918680-29-8*) Bagehot Council.

— Eight Short Stories. 1977. pap. 9.95 (*0-918680-04-2*) Bagehot Council.

— Gorbachev in Concert (& Other Poems) 60p. 1991. 19.95 (*0-918680-47-6*); pap. 9.95 (*0-685-47784-3*) Bagehot Council.

— Poems Written for Sbek's Mummies, Marie Menken & Other Important Persons, Places & Things. pap. 9.95 (*0-918680-03-4*) Bagehot Council.

— Riding the Mast Where It Swings. 2nd ed. 1981. pap. 10.95 (*0-918680-10-7*) Bagehot Council.

Paolucci, Anne, ed. Comparative Literary Theory: An Overview: Annual Volume Review of National Literatures. 148p. 1987. 23.00 (*0-918680-24-7*) Bagehot Council.

Paolucci, Anne & Paolucci, Henry. Dante & the "Quest for Eloquence" in India's Vernacular Languages. 78p. 1984. pap. 10.45 (*0-918680-28-X*) Bagehot Council.

— Mandragola: Machiavelli. 80p. (C). 1957. pap. write for info. (*0-02-391350-9*) Macmillan.

Paolucci, Anne & Paolucci, Henry, eds. Columbus, America, & the World. 1991. 23.00 (*0-918680-33-6*) Bagehot Council.

Paolucci, Anne & Puchala, Donald, eds. Problems in National Literary Identity & the Writer As Social Critic: Selected Papers of the Fourth Annual NDEA Seminar on Foreign Area Studies, Columbia University, February 28-29, 1980. 72p. pap. 6.95 (*0-918680-11-5*) Bagehot Council.

Paolucci, Anne & Warwick, Ronald, eds. India: Review of National Literatures. LC 77-126039. 240p. 1979. 23.00 (*0-918680-20-4*) Bagehot Council.

Paolucci, Anne, ed. see Hegel, Georg W.

Paolucci, Anne, jt. auth. see Paolucci, Nishan.

Paolucci, Antonio. Luca Signorelli. Pelletti, Lisa, tr. (Library of Great Masters). (Illus.). 80p. (Orig.). 1990. pap. 12.99 (*1-878351-12-5*) Riverside NY.

Paolucci, Antonio, et al. Michelangelo: The Medici Chapel. LC 94-60290. (Illus.). 216p. 1994. 65.00 (*0-500-23690-9*) Thames Hudson.

Paolucci, Beatrice, jt. auth. see Brown, Marjorie.

Paolucci, Beatrice, et al. Personal Perspectives. 2nd ed. (Illus.). (gr. 9-12). 1978. text ed. 32.80 (*0-07-048438-4*) McGraw.

Paolucci, Bridget. Beverly Sills: Opera Singer. LC 89-17324. (American Women of Achievement Ser.). (Illus.). 112p. (YA). (gr. 5 up). 1990. 17.95 (*1-55546-677-X*) Chelsea Hse.

Paolucci, Henry. A Brief History of Political Thought & Statecraft. 9.95 (*0-918680-08-5*) Bagehot Council.

— Iran, Israel, & the United States: An American Foreign Policy Background Study. xii, 404p. 1991. 39.95 (*0-918680-44-1*); pap. 29.95 (*0-685-30655-0*) Bagehot Council.

— Kissinger's War: 1957-1980. 1980. pap. 10.95 (*0-918680-14-X*) Bagehot Council.

— The Political Thought of G. W. Hegel. 1978. pap. 3.00 (*0-918680-06-9*) Bagehot Council.

— A Separate & Equal Station: Hegel, America & the Nation-State System. 1978. pap. 3.00 (*0-918680-05-0*) Bagehot Council.

— The South & the Presidency: From Reconstruction to Carter. 1978. pap. 3.00 (*0-918680-07-7*) Bagehot Council.

— War, Peace & the Presidency. LC 68-8774. 20.00 (*0-685-06495-6*) Bagehot Council.

— Who Is Kissinger? 1980. pap. 4.00 (*0-918680-13-1*) Bagehot Council.

— Zionism, the Superpowers, & the P. L. O. LC 82-15728. 80p. 1982. pap. 9.95 (*0-918680-18-2*, GHGP 708) Bagehot Council.

Paolucci, Henry, tr. see Beccaria, Cesare.

Paolucci, Henry, ed. see Hegel, Georg W.

Paolucci, Henry, jt. auth. see Paolucci, Anne.

Paolucci, Henry, jt. ed. see Paolucci, Anne.

Paolucci, Henry, ed. see St. Augustine.

Paolucci, Nishan & Paolucci, Anne. Grandma, Pray for Me. 68p. 1990. pap. 10.00 (*0-918680-43-3*) Bagehot Council.

Paolucci, Robert, tr. see Forte, Bruno.

Paone, Rocco M. Strategic Nonfuel Minerals & Western Security. 242p. (C). 1992. lib. bdg. 39.50 (*0-8191-8469-1*) U Pr of Amer.

*__Paonessa, Pamela N.__ Public & Social Policy: Subject Analysis with Reference Bibliography. rev. ed. LC 94-3138. 1994. 39.50 (*0-7883-0346-5*); pap. 34.50 (*0-7883-0347-3*) ABBE Pubs Assn.

Paoni, Frank. Strategies & Techniques for Successful Teaching. 148p. (C). 1994. per. 24.95 (*0-8403-9276-1*) Kendall-Hunt.

Paorici, C., jt. ed. see Rodriguez-Clemente, R.

Paounova, E., jt. auth. see Alexieva, M.

Pap, Arthur, jt. ed. see Edwards, Paul.

Pap, Arthur, tr. see Kraft, Viktor.

Pap, J. M., et al, eds. The Sun As a Variable Star. (Illus.). 380p. (C). 1994. 59.95 (*0-521-42006-7*) Cambridge U Pr.

*__Pap, Judit M., ed.__ The Sea As a Variable Star: Solar & Stellar Irradiance Variations: Proceedings of the 143rd Colloquim of the International Astronomical Union Held in Clarion Harvest House, Boulder, California, June 20-25, 1993. 328p. (C). 1994. lib. bdg. 132.00 (*0-7923-3040-4*) Kluwer Ac.

*__Pap, Judit M., et al, eds.__ The Sun As a Variable Star: Solar & Stellar Irradiance Variations, Proceedings of the 143rd IAU Colloquium, Boulder, CO, 1993. 312p. 1994. 132.00 (*0-615-00322-2*) Kluwer Ac.

Pap, Leo. The Portuguese in the United States: A Bibliography. LC 76-9270. (Bibliographies & Documentation Ser.). 1976. pap. 9.95 (*0-913256-21-8*) Ctr Migration.

Papa, jt. ed. see Kuryla.

*__Papa-Adams, Theo.__ The Unification. 290p. 1995. pap. 8.95 (*1-56901-829-4*) NW Pub.

Papa, Costas. Fuzzy Sets, Uncertainty, & Information. 1987. text ed. 77.00 (*0-13-345984-5*) P-H.

Papa, Ethyl & Papa, Randal. A Very Special Family: Behavior Management System. (Illus.). 32p. (Orig.). 1987. 5.95 (*0-915925-02-8*) Innovative Educ Pub.

— A Very Special Family: The Parts of Speech Family. (Illus.). 128p. (Orig.). 1987. teacher ed 34.95 (*0-915925-01-X*) Innovative Educ Pub.

Papa, Ethyl R. A Very Special Family: A Story Book to Color & Teach Your Child to Read. (Illus.). 32p. (J). (ps-2). 1983. 9.95 (*0-915925-00-1*) Innovative Educ Pub.

Papa, Iantorno. Turning Points Four. (Turning Points Ser.). 128p. (YA). (gr. 7-12). 1989. pap. text ed. 11.32 (*0-201-06324-7*) Addison-Wesley.

— Turning Points Four: Teachers Edition. (Secondary ESOL Ser.). 208p. 1987. teacher ed 12.60 (*0-201-06326-3*) Addison-Wesley.

Papa Jim, pseud. Book of Shadows: Personal Use. Ayala, Leticia M., ed. (Illus.). 60p. 1990. pap. 3.95 (*1-878575-05-8*) El Rey Pub.

— Papa Jim Magical Herb Book: How to Use Herbs for Magical Purposes. Ayala, Leticia M., ed. (Papa Jim Bks.: No. 1). (Illus.). 63p. 1985. pap. 3.95 (*1-878575-00-7*) El Rey Pub.

— Papa Jim Magical Oil Book: How to Use Oils for Magical Purposes. Ayala, Leticia M., ed. (Papa Jim Bks.: No. 2). (Illus.). 55p. 1989. pap. 3.95 (*1-878575-01-5*) El Rey Pub.

— Papa Jim Medicinal Herbs: Commonly Used Herbs. Ayala, Leticia M., ed. (Papa Jim Bks.: No. 4). (Illus.). 106p. 1990. pap. 3.95 (*1-878575-03-1*) El Rey Pub.

— Papa Jim's Herbs for Illnesses: Herbs & Herbal Combinations. Ayala, Leticia M., ed. (Papa Jim Bks.: No. 5). (Illus.). 78p. 1990. pap. 3.95 (*1-878575-02-3*) El Rey Pub.

— Papa Jim's Spell Book: Rituals & Spells for Voodoo. Ayala, Leticia M., ed. (Papa Jim Bks.: No. 3). (Illus.). 69p. 1989. pap. 3.95 (*1-878575-04-X*) El Rey Pub.

Papa, John. Fragments of Hawaiian History. rev. ed. Barrere, Dorothy B., ed. Pukui, Mary K., tr. (Special Publication Ser.: No. 70). (Illus.). 212p. 1983. pap. 19.95 (*0-910240-31-0*) Bishop Mus.

*__Papa, Juliet.__ Ladykiller. 1995. mass mkt. 5.50 (*0-312-95467-0*) St Martin.

Papa, Kondaveeti. Women in Rural Areas. (C). 1992. 16.00 (*81-85613-60-5*, Pub. by Chugh Pubns II) S Asia.

*__Papa, Mario.__ Turning Points Placement Tests. 80p. 1995. pap. write for info. (*0-201-53804-0*) Addison-Wesley.

Papa, Mario & Iantorno, Giuliano. Turning Points. (ESL Ser.). (Illus.). (C). pap. text ed. write for info. (*0-201-53814-8*); write for info. (*0-201-53815-6*) Addison-Wesley.

— Turning Points: Book 4. (Illus.). 1987. audio 78.60 (*0-201-06364-6*) Addison-Wesley.

Papa, Mario, jt. auth. see Iantorno, Giuliano.

*__Papa, Michael J.__ Your Practical Guide to Love. Ingram, tr. 100p. 1996. pap. 7.95 (*0-7610-0439-4*) NW Pub.

Papa, Mike, Jr. The Papa Gambit vs. the French Defense: Beating the French. (Illus.). 50p. (Orig.). 1991. pap. text ed. 10.00 (*0-9628959-0-3*) Mich Pubns.

Papa, O. A., jt. auth. see Boelhouwer, P.

Papa, Randal, jt. auth. see Papa, Ethyl.

Papa, Robert D. Let the Seasons Change: Four Introspections on God's Providence. 100p. (Orig.). 1993. pap. 5.95 (*0-9638855-0-2*) Prisoners Web.

*__Papa, S. & Tager, J. M., eds.__ Biochemistry of Cell Membranes. LC 95-10623. (Molecular & Cell Biology Updates Ser.). 1995. pap. write for info. (*0-8176-5056-3*) Birkhauser.

Papa, S., et al, eds. Adenine Nucleotides in Cellular Energy Transfer & Signal Transduction. LC 92-17729. (Molecular & Cell Biology Updates Ser.). ix, 476p. 1992. 116.00 (*0-8176-2673-5*, Pub. by Birkhauser Vlg SZ) Birkhauser.

— Cytochrome Systems: Molecular Biology & Bioenergetics. LC 87-25766. 822p. 1988. 135.00 (*0-306-42693-5*, Plenum Pr) Plenum.

Papaconstantinou, Helen. Free Trade & Competition in the EEC: Law, Policy & Practice. 256p. 1988. lib. bdg. 57.50 (*0-415-00110-2*) Routledge.

Papacosma, S. Victor. The Military in Greek Politics: The 1909 Coup D'Etat. LC 77-22391. 266p. reprint ed. pap. 75.90 (*0-7837-0505-0*, 2040829) Bks Demand.

Papacosma, S. Victor, ed. see Gazdag, Ferenc, et al.

Papacosma, Victor S. & Rubin, Mark R., eds. Europe's Neutral & Nonaligned States Between Nato & the Warsaw Pact. LC 87-33545. 246p. 1989. 40.00 (*0-8420-2269-4*) Scholarly Res Inc.

Papacostas, C. S. Regional Energy Self-Sufficiency: Some Public Policy Implications. (Working Papers Ser.: No. 83-3). 22p. 1983. pap. text ed. 5.00 (*0-686-88340-3*, CRD157) UNIPUB.

Papacostas, C. S., ed. Energy Systems for the Twenty-First Century. LC 86-25916. 112p. 1986. 15.00 (*0-87262-571-0*) Am Soc Civil Eng.

Papacostas, C. S. & Prevedouros, P. D. Transportation Engineering & Planning. 2nd ed. 656p. 1992. text ed. 77.00 (*0-13-958075-1*) P-H.

Papadakis, Andreas, ed. Art Meets Science & Spirituality. (Academy Editions Ser.). (Illus.). 96p. (Orig.). 1991. pap. 21.95 (*0-312-06172-2*) St Martin.

— Free Space Architecture: Architectural Design. (Illus.). 96p. (Orig.). 1992. pap. 26.95 (*0-312-07897-8*, Academy Edits) St Martin.

— Modern Pluralism: Just Exactly What Is Going On? (Illus.). 96p. (Orig.). 1992. pap. 21.95 (*0-312-07539-1*, Academy Edits) St Martin.

— New Art International. (Academy Editions Ser.). (Illus.). 88p. (Orig.). 1990. pap. 21.95 (*0-312-03983-2*) St Martin.

— A New Spirit in Architecture. (Academy Editions Ser.). (Illus.). 96p. (Orig.). 1991. pap. 21.95 (*0-312-06502-7*) St Martin.

— Patrick Caulfield. (Art & Design Monographs: No. 27). (Illus.). 96p. (Orig.). 1993. pap. 26.95 (*1-85490-180-X*, Academy Edits) St Martin.

Papadakis, Andreas & Farrow, Clare, eds. New Art: An International Perspective. LC 90-52752. (Illus.). 360p. 1991. 75.00 (*0-8478-1282-0*) Rizzoli Intl.

Papadakis, Andreas, et al, eds. Deconstruction: The Omnibus Volume. (Illus.). 264p. 1989. pap. 45.00 (*0-8478-1066-6*) Rizzoli Intl.

— A Free Spirit in Architecture: Omnibus Volume. 264p. (Orig.). 1992. 80.00 (*1-85490-129-X*, Academy Edits); pap. 50.00 (*1-85490-130-3*, Academy Edits) St Martin.

Papadakis, Aristeides. The Christian East & the Rise of the Papacy: The Church 1071-1453 A.D. LC 94-16429. 434p. 1994. 29.95 (*0-88141-057-8*); pap. 16.95 (*0-88141-058-6*) St Vladimirs.

— Crisis in Byzantium: The Filioque Controversy in the Patriarchate of Gregory II of Cyprus (1283-1289) LC 82-70444. (Illus.). x, 190p. 1986. 50.00 (*0-8232-1088-X*) Fordham.

Papadakis, C., jt. ed. see Webb, D.

Papadakis, C. N., ed. see American Society of Mechanical Engineers Staff.

Papadakis, Constantine & Scarton, Henry, eds. Fluid Transients & Acoustics in the Power Industry: Presented at the Winter Annual Meeting of the American Society of Mechanical Engineers, San Francisco, California, December 10-15, 1978. LC 78-60044. (Illus.). 366p. reprint ed. pap. 104.40 (*0-317-11149-3*, 2013875) Bks Demand.

Papadakis, Elim. Politics & the Environment. 240p. (Orig.). 1993. pap. text ed. 22.95 (*1-86373-363-9*, Pub. by Allen Unwin AT) Paul & Co Pubs.

Papadakis, Elim & Taylor-Gooby, Peter. The Private Provision of Public Welfare: Market, State & Family. LC 87-9425. 240p. 1988. text ed. 39.95 (*0-312-00950-X*) St Martin.

Papadakis, Myron P., jt. auth. see McCormick, Barnes W.

Papadatos, Costa & Papadatou, Danai, eds. Children & Death. (Death Education, Aging & Health Care Ser.). 280p. 1991. 63.00 (*1-56032-046-X*) Hemisp Pub.

Papadatou, Danai, jt. ed. see Papadatos, Costa.

Papademetriou, Demetr. At the Precipice? Europe & Migration. 1993. pap. 9.95 (*0-87003-038-8*) Carnegie Endow.

Papademetriou, Demetrios. New Immigrants to Brooklyn & Queens: Policy Implications, Especially with Regard to Housing. LC 83-14400. (CMS Occasional Papers & Documentation Ser.). (Illus.). 165p. (C). 1986. pap. text ed. 35.00 (*0-913256-63-3*) Ctr Migration.

Papademetriou, Demetrios, jt. ed. see Lowell, Lindsay.

Papademetriou, Demetrios G. & DiMarzio, Nicholas. Undocumented Aliens in the New York Metropolitan Area. LC 85-23385. (C). 1986. pap. 14.95 (*0-913256-99-4*) Ctr Migration.

P
Q

An Asterisk (*) at the beginning of an entry indicates that the title is appearing in BIP for the first time.

Papademetriou, Demetrious G. & Martin, Philip L., eds. The Unsettled Relationship: Labor Migration & Economic Development. LC 90-45603. (Contributions in Labor Studies: No. 33). 336p. 1991. text ed. 65.00 (0-313-25463-X, PDA, Greenwood Pr) Greenwood.

Papademetriou, George. The Cults. 20p. 1985. pap. 1.00 (0-917651-20-0) Holy Cross Orthodox.

— An Introduction to Orthodox Spirituality. 24p. (Orig.). 1988. pap. 1.50 (0-917651-53-7) Holy Cross Orthodox.

Papademetriou, George C. Essays on Orthodox Christian-Jewish Relations. LC 90-50392. 135p. (C). 1990. text ed. 24.95 (1-55605-165-4); pap. text ed. 14.95 (1-55605-164-6) Wyndhall Pr.

Papademetriou, Theresa. A Comparative Survey of the Laws on Abortion of Selected Countries. 181p. (Orig.). (C). 1993. pap. text ed. 29.95 (1-56806-214-1) Diane Pub.

Papadiamantis, Alexandros. The Murderess. Levi, Peter, tr. 127p. 1983. 13.95 (0-904613-94-1); pap. 5.95 (0-906495-72-5) Writers & Readers.

— Tales from a Greek Island. Constantinides, Elizabeth, tr. LC 86-20957. 192p. 1987. 29.95x (0-8018-3333-7) Johns Hopkins.

— Tales from a Greek Island. 200p. (C). 1994. reprint ed. pap. text ed. 12.95 (0-8018-4846-6) Johns Hopkins.

Papadimitrakopoulos, Elias. Toothpaste with Chlorophyll & Maritime Hot Baths. Taylor, John, tr. & intro. by. LC 91-76941. (Illus.). 104p. (Orig.). 1992. 17.95 (1-878580-42-6); pap. 8.95 (1-878580-43-4) Asylum Arts.

Papadimitriou, Christos H. Computational Complexity. LC 93-5662. 1993. write for info. (0-02-015308-2) Addison-Wesley.

— Computational Complexity. (Illus.). 528p. (C). 1994. text ed. 45.25 (0-201-53082-1) Addison-Wesley.

Papadimitriou, Christos H., jt. auth. see Lewis, Harry R.

Papadimitriou, Dimitri, et al. An Alternative in Small Business Finance. (Public Policy Brief Ser.: No. 12). (Illus.). 48p. (Orig.). 1994. pap. write for info. (0-941276-00-7, Edith C Blum Inst) Bard Coll Pubns.

Papadimitriou, Dimitri B., ed. Aspects of Distribution of Wealth & Income. LC 93-40402. 1994. text ed. 65.00 (0-312-12101-6) St Martin.

— Profits, Deficits & Instability. LC 91-17892. 480p. 1992. text ed. 75.00 (0-312-06721-6) St Martin.

***Papadimitriou, Dimitri B. & Wray, L. Randall.** Monetary Policy Uncovered: Flying Blind: The Federal Reserve's Experiment with Unobservables. (Public Policy Brief Ser.). (Illus.). 60p. (Orig.). 1994. pap. write for info. (0-941276-03-1, J Levy Econ Inst) Bard Coll Pubns.

Papadimitriou, Dimitri B., jt. ed. see Fazzari, Steven.

Papadimitrou, John M., et al, eds. Diagnostic Ultrastructure of Non-Neoplastic Diseases. (Illus.). 728p. 1992. text ed. 375.00 (0-443-03464-8) Churchill.

Papadin, Valentin. Teach Yourself to Be a Madman: Memories of a Young Russian Soldier. LC 93-70077. (Illus.). 108p. (Orig.). 1993. pap. 12.95 (1-883014-22-0) Brning Bush.

Papadopoullos, Theodore H. Greek Church & People under Turkish Domination. 2nd ed. 580p. 1990. text ed. 109.95 (0-86078-278-6, Pub. by Variorum UK) Ashgate Pub Co.

— Studies & Documents Relating to the History of the Greek Church & People Under Turkish Domination. LC 78-38759. reprint ed. 27.50 (0-404-56314-7) AMS Pr.

Papadopoulo, Alexandre. Islam & Muslim Art. Wolf, Robert E., tr. (Illus.). 1994. 175.00 (0-8109-0641-4) Abrams.

Papadopoulos & Lizardos, trs. The Miracles of Our Holy Father Spyridon of Tremithus. 20p. (Orig.). 1985. pap. 2.00 (0-912927-54-2, Y003) St John Kronstadt.

Papadopoulos, Athanase. Multilateral Diplomacy Within the Commonwealth. 1982. lib. bdg. 89.00 (90-247-2568-2) Kluwer Ac.

Papadopoulos, Athanase, jt. auth. see Coornaert, Michel.

Papadopoulos, C. True Visual Magnitude Photographic Star Atlas: Southern Stars & Equatorial Stars. 1979. 865.00 (0-08-021622-6, Pergamon Pr) Elsevier.

Papadopoulos, Chris. Sexual Aspects of Cardiovascular Disease. LC 89-3973. (Sexual Medicine Ser.: No. 10). 136p. 1989. text ed. 55.00 (0-275-92523-4, C2523, Praeger Pubs) Greenwood.

Papadopoulos, George A. Fracture Mechanics: The Experimental Method of Caustics & the Det. - Criterion of Fracture. LC 92-27308. 1992. write for info. (0-387-19768-0) Spr-Verlag.

Papadopoulos, Gerasimos. Orthodoxy, Faith & Life: Christ & the Church, Vol. 2. 151p. (C). 1981. 10.95 (0-916586-48-0); pap. 5.95 (0-916586-47-2) Holy Cross Orthodox.

— Orthodoxy, Faith & Life: Christ in the Gospels, Vol. 1. 164p. 1980. 9.50 (0-916586-38-3); pap. 4.95 (0-916586-37-5) Holy Cross Orthodox.

Papadopoulos, Gregory M. Implementation of a General Purpose Dataflow Multiprocessor. (Pitman Ser.). 175p. 1990. 27.95x (0-262-66069-5) MIT Pr.

Papadopoulos, H. T., et al. Queueing Theory in Manufacturing Systems Analysis & Design. LC 93-34100. 393p. 1993. 84.95 (0-412-38720-4, Chap & Hall NY) Chapman & Hall.

Papadopoulos, K., jt. ed. see Palmadesco, Peter J.

Papadopoulos, Nicolas & Heslop, Louise A. Product-Country Images: Impact & Role in International Marketing. LC 91-35947. (Illus.). 480p. 1993. lib. bdg. 59.95 (1-56024-236-1) Haworth Pr.

Papadopoulos, Renos, ed. Carl Gustav Jung: Critical Assessments, 4 vol. set. LC 92-1044. 1650p. 1993. 499.00 (0-415-04830-3, A7769) Routledge.

Papadopoulou, T. Elementary Particle Physics: Proceedings of the First Hellenic School held in Corfu, Greece, Sept. 12-30, 1982. 700p. (C). 1984. 108.00 (9971-950-99-5) World Scientific Pub.

Papadopulos, Leo, jt. auth. see Holy Apostles Convent Staff.

Papadopulos, Leonidas, tr. see St. Nectarios Press Staff, ed.

Papadopulos, Leonidas J. & Lizardos, Georgia, trs. The Life & Sufferings of Saint Catherine the Great Martyr. (Illus.). 1986. pap. 2.00 (0-913026-63-8) St Nectarios.

Papadrakakis, Manolis, ed. Solving Large-Scale Problems in Mechanics: The Development & Application of Computational Solution Methods. LC 92-43970. 472p. 1993. text ed. 115.00 (0-471-93809-2) Wiley.

***Papaellinas.** Republica. 1995. pap. 12.00 (0-207-18406-2) HarpC.

Papaevangelou, G. & Hennessen, W., eds. Viral Hepatitis: Standardization in Immunoprophylaxis of Infections by Hepatitis Viruses. (Developments in Biological Standardization Ser.: Vol. 54). (Illus.). xviii, 590p. 1983. pap. 108.00 (3-8055-3826-X) S Karger.

Papagapitos, Karen. Gemini Code II. Kleinman, Estelle, ed. (JB Ser.). (Illus.). 96p. (Orig.). (J). (gr. 5-8). 1994. 7.95 (0-9637328-2-X) Kapa Hse Pr.

— Jose's Basket. (JB Ser.). (J). 1993. 6.95 (0-9637328-1-1) Kapa Hse Pr.

— Socorro, Daughter of the Desert. Kleinman, Estelle, ed. (JB Ser.). (Illus.). 64p. (J). (gr. 1-4). 1993. 6.95 (0-9637328-0-3) Kapa Hse Pr.

Papageorgiou, Demetrios, ed. Liberalizing Foreign Trade Vol. 1: The Experience of Argentina, Chile & Uruguay. (Illus.). 500p. 1991. text ed. 75.00 (0-631-16666-1) Blackwell Pubs.

Papageorgiou, Demetrios & Michaely, Michael. Liberalizing Foreign Trade Vol. 2: The Experience of Korea, the Philippines & Singapore. Choksi, Armeane, ed. (Illus.). 1991. text ed. 75.00 (0-631-16667-X) Blackwell Pubs.

Papageorgiou, Demetrios, et al, eds. Liberalizing Foreign Trade: The Experience of Israel & Yugoslavia, Vol. 3. 1991. text ed. 75.00 (0-631-16668-8) Blackwell Pubs.

Papageorgiou, Demetris, ed. Liberalizing Foreign Trade Vol. 4: The Experience of Brazil, Colombia, & Peru. (Illus.). 500p. 1989. text ed. 75.00 (0-631-16669-6) Blackwell Pubs.

— Liberalizing Foreign Trade Vol. 5: The Experience of Indonesia, Pakistan, & Sri Lanka. (Illus.). 500p. 1988. text ed. 75.00 (0-631-16671-8) Blackwell Pubs.

— Liberalizing Foreign Trade Vol. 7: Lessons of Experience in the Developing World. (Illus.). 448p. 1991. text ed. 75.00 (0-631-16673-4) Blackwell Pubs.

Papageorgiou, Demetros, ed. Liberalizing Foreign Trade Vol. 6: The Experience of Spain, New Zealand, & Turkey. 500p. 1990. text ed. 75.00 (0-631-16672-6) Blackwell Pubs.

Papageorgiou, G. C., et al, eds. Ion Interactions in Energy Transfer Biomembranes. LC 85-31707. 344p. 1986. 79.50 (0-306-42220-4, Plenum Pr) Plenum.

Papageorgiou, M. Concise Encyclopedia of Traffic & Transportation Systems. (Advances in Systems Control & Information Engineering Ser.: No. 6). (Illus.). 700p. 1991. 425.00 (0-08-036203-6, Pergamon Pr) Elsevier.

Papageorgiou, Vasilis. Euripides' Medea & Cosmetics. 112p. (Orig.). 1986. pap. text ed. 37.50x (91-22-00797-0, Pub. by Almqv & Wiksell SW) Coronet Bks.

Papageorgiou, Y. Y. The Isolated City State: An Economic Geography of Urban-Spatial Structure. 512p. 1989. 139.50 (0-415-03032-3) Routledge.

Papagiannis, George, jt. ed. see Bock, John.

Papagiannis, George J., jt. auth. see Bock, John C.

Papagiannis, Michael, ed. The Search for Extraterrestrial Life: Recent Developments. 1985. lib. bdg. 145.50 (90-277-2113-0) Kluwer Ac.

Papagiannis, Michael D. Space Physics & Space Astronomy. LC 72-179021. (Illus.). 308p. (C). 1972. text ed. 135.00 (0-677-04000-8) Gordon & Breach.

Papagiannis, Michael D., ed. Relativistic Astrophysics Eighth Symposium, Texas, Vol. 302. (Annals Ser.). 689p. 1977. 47.00 (0-89072-048-7) NY Acad Sci.

Papagno, Noella C. Desairology: Hairstyling of the Deceased. 4th rev. ed. LC 91-90370. (Illus.). 105p. 1991. pap. 16.95 (0-9604610-5-1) JJ Pub FL.

Papahadjopoulos, Demetrios, ed. Liposomes & Their Uses in Biology & Medicine. (Annals Ser.: Vol. 308). 462p. 1978. 59.00 (0-89072-064-9) NY Acad Sci.

Papahristodoulou, Christos. Inventions, Innovations, & Economic Growth in Sweden: An Appraisal of the Schumpeterian Theory. (Studia Oeconomica Upsaliensia: No. 12). 152p. (Orig.). 1987. pap. 37.50x (91-554-1983-6) Coronet Bks.

Papai, Franki B. Cat Lover's Cookbook. 1993. pap. 6.95 (0-312-08904-X) St Martin.

Papai, George B. Fight for Survival in World War Two: Ten Year Saga of Emigration. 1994. 21.95 (0-533-10789-X) Vantage.

Papaioannou, G. From Mars Hill to Manhattan. 1976. pap. 7.95 (0-937032-08-5) Light&Life Pub Co MN.

Papaioannou, George, ed. see Rouvelas, Marilyn.

Papaioannou, George J., jt. ed. see Fischer, Klaus P.

Papaj, Daniel R. & Lewis, Alcinda C., eds. Insect Learning: Ecological & Evolutionary Perspectives. (Illus.). 448p. 1992. 55.00 (0-412-02561-2, A4259, Chapman & Hall) Chapman & Hall.

Papajani, Janet. Museums. LC 82-23621. (New True Bks.). (Illus.). 48p. (J). (gr. k-4). 1983. pap. 4.95 (0-516-41682-0) Childrens.

Papajohn. Intensive Behavior Therapy. (C). 1982. 32.95 (0-205-14448-9, H4448) Allyn.

Papajohn, John & Spiegel, John. Transactions in Families. LC 74-6740. (Jossey-Bass Behavioral Science Ser.). 335p. reprint ed. pap. 95.50 (0-685-16151-X, 2027764) Bks Demand.

Papalambros, Panos Y. & Wilde, Douglass J. Principles of Optimal Design: Modeling & Computation. (Illus.). 450p. 1991. pap. 37.95 (0-521-42362-7) Cambridge U Pr.

Papalas, Anthony. Ancient Icaria. 1991. 39.00 (0-86516-243-3); pap. 24.00 (0-86516-244-1) Bolchazy-Carducci.

***Papalia, Diane E. & Olds, Sally W.** A Child's World: Infancy Through Adolescence. LC 95-10671. 1996. write for info. (0-07-048765-0) McGraw.

— A Child's World: Infancy Through Adolescence. 6th ed. LC 92-11246. 1993. text ed. write for info. (0-07-048749-9) McGraw.

— Human Development. 5th ed. 1992. text ed. write for info. (0-07-048557-7) McGraw.

— Human Development. 5th ed. 1992. pap. text ed. write for info. (0-07-048559-3) McGraw.

— Human Development. 6th ed. LC 94-7636. 1994. text ed. write for info. (0-07-048760-X) McGraw.

— Psychology. 2nd ed. 816p. 1988. text ed. write for info. (0-07-048534-8) McGraw.

Papaloizos, Theodore C. A Grammar of Modern Greek in English. 76p. (Orig.). Date not set. student ed 2.50 (0-932416-05-5, 05); pap. 3.50 (0-932416-04-7, 04) Papaloizos.

— Modern Greek for Adults, Pt. I. (Illus.). 173p. 1978. pap. 5.00 (0-932416-01-2, 01) Papaloizos.

— Modern Greek for Adults, Pt. II. (Illus.). 300p. 1978. student ed 3.00 (0-932416-03-9, 03); pap. 6.00 (0-932416-02-0, 02) Papaloizos.

— Workbook for My Greek Reader. (Illus.). 88p. (Orig.). (GRE.). 1986. pap. 4.50 (0-932416-47-0) Papaloizos.

***Papamichalis, Panos & Kerwin, Robert, eds.** Digital Signal Processing Technology: Proceedings of a Conference Held 17-18 April, 1995, Orlando, Florida. LC 95-131. (Critical Reviews of Optical Science & Technology Ser.: Vol. 57). 1995. write for info. (0-8194-1847-1) SPIE.

Papamichalis, Panos, jt. auth. see Texas Instruments, Inc. Staff.

Papanastasiou, Tasos C. Applied Fluid Mechanics. 500p. 1994. text ed. 74.00 (0-13-060799-1) P-H.

Papanastasis, V., ed. Fodder Trees & Shrubs in the Mediterranean Production Systems: Objecties & Agrimed Research Programme, No. EUR 14459. 210p. 1993. pap. 35.00 (92-826-5150-9, CH-NA-14459-EN-C, Pub. by Europ Com) UNIPUB.

Papandreou, Andreas. Externality & Institutions. LC 93-48886. (Illus.). 288p. 1994. 55.00 (0-19-828775-5) OUP.

Papandreou, Andreas G. Paternalistic Capitalism. LC 79-187169. 198p. reprint ed. pap. 56.50 (0-7837-2929-4, 2057525) Bks Demand.

Papandreou, V., jt. auth. see Christophersen, H.

Papanek, Ernest. The Austrian School Reform: Its Bases, Principles & Development--The Twenty Years Between the Two World Wars. LC 78-866. 130p. 1978. reprint ed. text ed. 45.00 (0-313-20292-3, PAAS, Greenwood Pr) Greenwood.

Papanek, Gustav F. A Plan for Planning: The Need for a Better Method of Assisting Underdeveloped Countries on Their Economic Policies. LC 78-38759. (Harvard University. Center for International Affairs. Occasional Papers in International Affairs: No. 1). reprint ed. 27.50 (0-404-54601-3) AMS Pr.

Papanek, Gustav F., ed. The Indonesian Economy. LC 80-18752. 460p. 1981. text ed. 75.00 (0-275-90699-X, C0699, Praeger Pubs) Greenwood.

Papanek, Gustav F., jt. ed. see Falcon, Walter P.

Papanek, Victor. Design for the Real World: Human Ecology & Social Change. 2nd rev. ed. (Illus.). 405p. (C). 1992. reprint ed. pap. 17.00 (0-89733-153-2) Academy Chi Pubs.

— The Green Imperative: Natural Design for the Real World. LC 95-60281. (Illus.). 256p. (Orig.). Date not set. pap. 19.95 (0-500-27846-6) Thames Hudson.

Papanicolaou & Tung. Genitourinary Radiology: The Requisites. 384p. 1994. 65.00 (0-8016-7482-4) Mosby Yr Bk.

Papanicolaou, A. C. Emotion: A Reconsideration of the Somatic Theory. 156p. 1988. text ed. 38.00 (2-88124-274-X); pap. text ed. 21.00 (2-88124-283-9) Gordon & Breach.

Papanicolaou, Andrew C. & Gunter, Pete A., eds. Bergson & Modern Thought Towards a Unified Science. (Models of Scientific Thought Ser.: Vol. 3). 376p. 1987. text ed. 86.00 (3-7186-0380-2) Gordon & Breach.

Papanicolaou, G., ed. Hydrodynamic Behavior & Interacting Particle System. (IMA Ser.: Vol. 9). 215p. 1987. 31.00 (0-387-96584-X) Spr-Verlag.

Papanicolaou, George, ed. & intro. Advances in Multiphase Flow & Related Problems. LC 87-60050. (Proceedings in Applied Mathematics Ser.: No. 26). (Illus.). x, 295p. 1987. text ed. 29.50 (0-89871-212-2) Soc Indus-Appl Math.

Papanicolaou, George C., jt. ed. see Caflisch, Russel E.

Papanicolaou, N. I., et al. Handbook of Calculated Electron Momentum Distributions, Compton Profiles, & X-Ray Form Factors of Elemental Solids. (Illus.). 144p. 1991. 99.95 (0-8493-0538-1, QC176) CRC Pr.

Papanicolas, C. N., et al, eds. Electron Scattering in Nuclear & Particle Science. LC 87-72403. (Conference Proceeding Ser.: No. 161). 256p. 1987. lib. bdg. 60.00 (0-88318-361-7) Am Inst Physics.

Papanikola-Bakirtzis, Demetra, et al. Ceramic Art from Byzantine Serres. LC 92-21776. (Illinois Byzantine Studies: Vol. 3). (Illus.). 88p. (C). 1992. pap. 27.95 (0-252-06303-1) U of Ill Pr.

Papanikolas, Helen. Small Bird, Tell Me. LC 93-8426. 208p. 1993. 24.95 (0-8040-0974-0) Swallow.

— Small Bird, Tell Me: Stories of Greek Immigrants in Utah. LC 93-8426. 208p. 1994. reprint ed. pap. 15.95 (0-8040-0982-1, Swallow) Ohio U Pr.

***Papanikolas, Helen Z.** Aimilia-Georgios - Emily-George. LC 86-28266. (Utah Centennial Ser.: No. 3). 341p. (ENG & GRE.). 1987. pap. 97.20 (0-7837-8552-6, 2049367) Bks Demand.

Papanikolas, Zeese. Buried Unsung: Louis Tikas & the Ludlow Massacre. LC 82-13475. (University of Utah Publications in the American West: No. 14). (Illus.). 351p. reprint ed. pap. 100.10 (0-8357-8821-0, 2033358) Bks Demand.

— Buried Unsung: Louis Tikas & the Ludlow Massacre. LC 90-49908. (Illus.). xx, 331p. 1991. reprint ed. pap. 11.95 (0-8032-8727-5, Bison Books) U of Nebr Pr.

— Trickster in Land of Dreams. (C). 1995. 22.50 (0-8032-3703-0) U of Nebr Pr.

***Papanikolau.** Technical Greek-English & English-Greek Dictionary. 684p. (ENG & GRE.). 1990. 150.00 (0-7859-9052-6) Fr & Eur.

Papantchev, George D. Colloquial Bulgarian. LC 93-26730. 1994. write for info. (0-415-07963-2, Routledge NY); audio write for info. (0-415-07965-9, Routledge NY); write for info. (0-415-07964-0, Routledge NY) Routledge.

Papantoni-Kazakos, P. & Kazakos, Dimitri, eds. Nonparametric Methods in Communications. LC 77-14049. (Electrical Engineering & Electronics Ser.: No. 2). 303p. reprint ed. pap. 86.40 (0-7837-3347-X, 2043305) Bks Demand.

Papantoniou, D. The Greek Children. (Illus.). (GRE.). (J). (gr. 2-3). student ed 2.50 (0-686-79629-2); text ed. 4.00 (0-686-79628-4) Divry.

— Greek Letters. 158p. (GRE.). (J). (gr. 4-5). 4.00 (0-686-79634-9) Divry.

— Greek Stories. (GRE.). (J). (gr. 3-4). 4.00 (0-686-79633-0) Divry.

***Papantoniou, Pando C.** Marketing the Complete Awakening. (C). 1990. 79.00x (1-872684-30-0, Pub. by P A S S Pubns UK); pap. 60.00x (1-872684-18-1, Pub. by P A S S Pubns UK) St Mut.

Papapetrou, A. Lectures on General Relativity. LC 74-81943. 203p. 1974. lib. bdg. 84.00 (90-277-0514-3); pap. text ed. 45.50 (90-277-0540-2) Kluwer Ac.

Paparella. Yearbook of Otolaryngology: Head & Neck Surgery, 1991. 297p. 1991. 57.95 (0-8151-0535-5) Mosby Yr Bk.

Paparella, Emanuel L. Hermeneutics in the Philosophy of Giambattista Vico: A Revolutionary Humanistic Vision for the New Age. LC 93-13091. 220p. 1993. pap. 29.95 (0-7734-1939-X) E Mellen.

Paparella, Michael M. & Shumrick, Donald A. Otolaryngology, 4 vols., 1. 3rd ed. Meyerhoff, William L., ed. LC 77-25566. (Illus.). 3536p. 1990. text ed. 169.00 (0-7216-1505-8) Saunders.

— Otolaryngology, 4 vols., 2. 3rd ed. Meyerhoff, William L., ed. LC 77-25566. (Illus.). 3536p. 1990. text ed. 169.00 (0-7216-1506-6) Saunders.

— Otolaryngology, 4 vols., 3. 3rd ed. Meyerhoff, William L., ed. LC 77-25566. (Illus.). 3536p. 1990. text ed. 169.00 (0-7216-1507-4) Saunders.

— Otolaryngology, 4 vols., 4. 3rd ed. Meyerhoff, William L., ed. LC 77-25566. (Illus.). 3536p. 1990. text ed. 169.00 (0-7216-3446-X) Saunders.

— Otolaryngology, 4 vols., Set. 3rd ed. Meyerhoff, William L., ed. LC 77-25566. (Illus.). 3536p. 1990. text ed. 525.00 (0-7216-1504-X) Saunders.

Paparian, Michael, ed. California Energy Directory: A Guide to Organizations & Information Resources. LC 78-78313. (California Information Guides Ser.). (Illus.). 98p. (Orig.). 1980. pap. 16.50 (0-912102-51-9) Cal Inst Public.

Paparone, Pam. Who Built the Ark? LC 93-31383. (J). 1994. 15.00 (0-671-87129-3, S&S Bks Young Read) S&S Childrens.

***Paparone, Pamela, illus.** Five Little Ducks: An Old Rhyme. LC 95-13136. (J). 1995. write for info. (1-55858-473-0) North-South Bks NYC.

— Five Little Ducks: An Old Rhyme. LC 95-13136. (J). 1995. lib. bdg. write for info. (1-55858-474-9) North-South Bks NYC.

Papas, jt. auth. see Nizel.

Papas, et al. Geriatric Dentistry: Aging & Oral Health. 352p. 1991. 35.95 (0-8016-5790-3) Mosby Yr Bk.

Papas, A., jt. auth. see Raizis, M. Byron.

Papas, Al, Jr. Gopher Sketch Book: Drawing Sketches & Thumbnail Sketches from the "U" of Minnesota's Earliest Football Days to Now. (Illus.). 1990. 2.98 (0-931714-41-9) Nodin Pr.

Papas, Anthony A. Greece. (European Financial Reporting Ser.). 240p. 1992. 89.95 (0-415-06196-2, A9717) Routledge.

Papas, Bill, jt. auth. see Papas, Tessa.

Papas, Charles H. Theory of Electromagnetic Wave Propagation. 257p. 1988. reprint ed. pap. 6.95 (0-486-65678-0) Dover.

Papas, Meryl, jt. auth. see Vyse, Maureen.

Papas, T. S. & Vande Woude, George F., eds. Oncogenes: Gene Amplification & Analysis, Vol. 4. 310p. 1986. 77.00 (0-444-01116-1) Elsevier.

Papas, T. S., jt. ed. see Chirikjian, J. C.

Papas, Takis S., ed. Gene Regulation & AIDS: Transcriptional Activation, Retroviruses, & Pathogenesis. (Advances in Applied Biotechnology Ser.: Vol. 7). (Illus.). 400p. (C). 1990. 55.00 (0-943255-11-2) Portfolio Pub.

***Papas, Tessa & Papas, Bill.** Papas' Portland. (Illus.). 96p. (Orig.). 1994. pap. 24.95 (0-9644651-0-8) Chetwynd Stapylton.

Papas, Tony & Keith, Hamash. Bayswater Brasserie Book of Food. (Illus.). 192p. 1990. reprint ed. 24.95 (0-89815-367-0) Ten Speed Pr.

Papasaki, Andreas. Andreas Papadakis Presents Theory & Experimantation: An Intellectual Extravaganza. 1993. 95.00 (0-312-08935-X, Academy Edits) St Martin.

Papasian, Gerald E. Anoush: An Opera by Armen Tigranian. 59p. 1982. pap. 5.95 (0-8143-1708-1) Wayne St U Pr.

PQ

An Asterisk (*) at the beginning of an entry indicates that the title is appearing in BIP for the first time.

Papasogil, Giorgio. St. Teresa of Avila. rev. ed. Anzilotti, Gloria I., tr. LC 58-12223. 1988. reprint ed. pap. 9.95 (*0-8198-6880-9*) Pauline Bks.

Papasogli, Benedetta. Wisdom of the Heart. LC 93-78050. 1993. 11.95 (*0-910984-57-3*) Montfort Pubns.

Papastavridis, Stavros G., jt. ed. see Godole, Anant P.

Papastavrov, Vasilli. Whale. (Eyewitness Bks.). (Illus.). 64p. (J). (gr. 5 up). 1993. 16.00 (*0-679-83884-8*) Knopf Bks Yng Read.

— Whale. (Eyewitness Bks.). (Illus.). 64p. (J). (gr. 5 up). 1993. lib. bdg. 16.99 (*0-679-93884-2*) Knopf Bks Yng Read.

Papastergiadis, Nikos. Modernity As Exile: The Stranger in John Berger's Writing. LC 92-2492. 256p. 1993. text ed. 69.95 (*0-7190-3876-6*, Pub. by Manchester Univ Pr UK) St Martin.

***Papastvro, Tellis S.** Gnosis & the Law. (Illus.). 504p. 1972. 25.00 (*0-614-06564-X*) Grp Avatar.

Papatassos, jt. auth. see Winterer, Mary.

Papataxiarchis, Evthymios, jt. ed. see Loizos, Peter.

Papathanassopoulos, S., jt. auth. see Hills, Jill.

Papatheofanis, F. J. Bioelectromagnetics: Biophysical Principles in Medicine & Biology. (Experimental Biology & Medicine Ser.: Vol. 12). (Illus.). x, 98p. 1987. 78.50 (*3-8055-4587-8*) S Karger.

Papathomas, Thomas V., et al, eds. Early Vision & Beyond. LC 94-3117. 384p. 1995. 60.00x (*0-262-16146-X*, Bradford Bks) MIT Pr.

***Papatola, Kathleen J.** Balancing Your Work/Family Responsibilities: A Guide for Employees. 1993. pap. 3.95 (*1-56246-083-8*, P316) Johnsn Inst.

— How to Help Your Employees Balance Work & Family Responsibilities: A Guide for Managers. 56p. 1993. pap. 6.95 (*1-56246-082-X*, P287) Johnsn Inst.

Papatsonis, Takis. Ursa Minor & Other Poems. Friar, Kimon & Myrsiades, Kostas, trs. (Modern Greek History & Culture Ser.). 103p. 1988. 25.00 (*0-932963-05-6*) Nostos Bks.

Papavero, N. The World Oestridae (Diptera), Mammals & Continental Drift. (Series Entomologica: No. 14). 1977. lib. bdg. 94.00 (*90-6193-124-X*) Kluwer Ac.

Papavizas, George C., ed. Biological Control in Crop Production. LC 81-65017. (Beltsville Symposia in Agricultural Research Ser.: No. 5). 474p. 1982. text ed. 64.50 (*0-86598-037-3*) Rowman.

Papayanis, Nicholas. Coachmen of Nineteenth-Century Paris: Service Workers & Class Consciousness. LC 93-834. 269p. (C). 1993. text ed. 45.00 (*0-8071-1814-1*) La State U Pr.

Papazian, Charlie. The Complete Joy of Home Brewing. (Illus.). 352p. (Orig.). 1984. pap. 8.95 (*0-380-88369-4*) Avon.

— The Homebrewer's Companion. LC 94-1647. 320p. (Orig.). 1994. pap. 11.00 (*0-380-77287-6*) Avon.

— The New Complete Joy of Home Brewing. 416p. 1991. pap. 11.00 (*0-380-76366-4*) Avon.

Papazian, Charlie, jt. auth. see Gayre, Robert.

Papazian, Ed. Medium Rare: The Evolution, Workings & Impact of Commercial Television. LC 89-60516. 680p. (Orig.). 1989. pap. 35.00 (*0-9621947-0-0*) Media Dynamics.

— Medium Rare: The Evolution, Workings & Impact of Commercial Television. rev. ed. LC 90-64055. 578p. (Orig.). (C). 1991. pap. 35.00 (*0-9621947-1-9*) Media Dynamics.

Papazian, K. S. Merchants from Ararat. Manuelian, P. M., ed. LC 79-63061. 1979. pap. 3.50 (*0-933706-04-9*) Ararat Pr.

Papazoglou, J. P., jt. ed. see Schemel, J. H.

Papazoglou, M. P. & Valder, W. Relational Database Management: A Systems Programming Approach. 400p. 1989. text ed. 80.00 (*0-13-771866-7*) P-H.

Papazoglou, M. P., jt. auth. see Orlowska, M. E.

Papazoglou, M. P., et al, eds. The Next Generation of Information Systems: From Data to Knowledge - A Selection of Papers Presented at Two IJCAI-91 Workshops, Sydney, Australia, August 26, 1991. LC 92-21889. (Lecture Notes in Artificial Intelligence Ser.: Vol. 611). viii, 310p. 1992. write for info. (*3-540-55616-8*); pap. 52.00 (*0-387-55616-8*) Spr-Verlag.

Papazoglou, Orania. Charisma. 384p. 1993. mass mkt. 5.99 (*0-8217-4119-5*) Zebra.

Papazoglu, Fanula. The Central Balkan Tribes in Pre-Roman Times: Triballi, Autariatae, Dardanians, Scordisci, & Moesians. Stansfield-Popovic, Mary, tr. xii, 664p. 1978. pap. 140.00 (*90-256-0793-4*, Pub. by A M Hakkert NE) Benjamins North Am.

Papconstantopoulos, D. A. Handbook of the Band Structure of Elemental Solids. LC 86-22667. 422p. 1986. 105.00 (*0-306-42338-3*, Plenum Pr) Plenum.

Papcun, Ron. A Scentimental Journey: Reflections on Life. 128p. (Orig.). 1994. pap. 7.95 (*0-9641644-0-X*) Regenerat Concepts.

Pape, ed. Advances in Optical Information Processing, No. III. 1988. 51.00 (*0-89252-971-7*, 936) SPIE.

Pape, et al. Oddo Sound Series: 1968, 1974, 1978, 10 vols., Set. (Illus.). (J). (gr. 2-5). 1978. lib. bdg. 109.50 (*0-87783-165-3*) Oddo.

Pape, D. L. King Robert, the Resting Ruler. LC 68-56823. (Sound Ser.). (Illus.). 48p. (J). (gr. 2-5). 1968. lib. bdg. 10.95 (*0-87783-021-5*) Oddo.

— Liz Dearly's Silly Glasses. LC 68-56824. (Sound Ser.). (Illus.). 48p. (J). (gr. 2-5). 1968. lib. bdg. 10.95 (*0-87783-023-1*) Oddo.

— Professor Fred & the Fid Fuddlephone. LC 68-56825. (Sound Ser.). (Illus.). 48p. (J). (gr. 2-5). 1968. lib. bdg. 10.95 (*0-87783-032-0*) Oddo.

— Scientist Sam. LC 68-56826. (Sound Ser.). (Illus.). 48p. (J). (gr. 2-5). 1968. lib. bdg. 10.95 (*0-87783-034-7*) Oddo.

— Shoemaker Fooze. LC 68-56827. (Sound Ser.). (Illus.). 48p. (J). (gr. 2-5). 1969. lib. bdg. 10.95 (*0-87783-036-3*) Oddo.

— Three Thinkers of Thay-Lee. LC 68-56828. (Sound Ser.). (Illus.). 48p. (J). (gr. 2-5). 1968. lib. bdg. 10.95 (*0-87783-040-1*) Oddo.

Pape, D. R., ed. Advances in Optical Information Processing IV. 1990. 70.00 (*0-8194-0347-4*, VOL. 1296) SPIE.

Pape, Dan. Astrology Test. (Illus.). 32p. (Orig.). (C). 1993. pap. text ed. write for info. (*1-882330-17-X*) Magni Co.

— The Cambridge Love & Relationships Test. 33p. (Orig.). (C). 1995. write for info. (*1-882330-41-2*) Magni Co.

— Childrens Self Scoring I. Q. Test. (Illus.). 40p. (Orig.). (C). Date not set. pap. text ed. write for info. (*1-882330-14-5*) Magni Co.

— Personality Test: See Yourself As Others See You. (Illus.). 32p. (Orig.). (C). 1993. pap. text ed. write for info. (*1-882330-16-1*) Magni Co.

— Self Scoring I. Q. Test. (Illus.). 32p. (Orig.). (C). 1993. pap. text ed. write for info. (*1-882330-13-7*) Magni Co.

Pape, David S., ed. The Story Hour, Vol. 1. (Illus.). 166p. (J). (gr. 3-8). 1994. 11.95 (*0-922613-64-8*) Hachai Pubns.

— The Story Hour Vol. 2: A Collection for Young Readers. (Illus.). 160p. (J). (gr. 3-9). 1995. write for info. (*0-922613-65-6*) Hachai Pubns.

Pape, David S., ed. see Rosenfeld, Dina.

Pape, Donna L. The Children's Arkansas Puzzle Book. (Illus.). 28p. (J). (gr. k up). 1984. pap. 2.00 (*0-914546-55-4*) Rose Pub.

Pape, Donna L., et al. Country Music Puzzle Book. (Illus.). 159p. (Orig.). 1985. pap. 3.95 (*0-938232-54-1*) Winston-Derek.

— The Tennessee Puzzle Book. 71p. 1984. pap. 3.95 (*0-938232-55-X*) Winston-Derek.

***Pape, Garry, et al.** Flying Wings of Jack Northrop: A Photo Chronicle. (Illus.). 80p. (Orig.). 1994. pap. 9.95 (*0-88740-597-5*) Schiffer.

Pape, Garry R. & Harrison, Ronald C. Queen of the Midnight Skies. LC 92-60359. (Illus.). 320p. 1992. text ed. 45.00 (*0-88740-415-4*) Schiffer.

***Pape, Garry R., et al.** Northrop P-61 Black Widow: The Complete History & Combat Record. (Illus.). 128p. 1995. pap. 24.95 (*0-88740-738-2*) Schiffer.

Pape, Greg. Black Branches. LC 83-12520. (Poetry Ser.). 81p. 1984. 19.95 (*0-8229-3489-2*); pap. 10.95 (*0-8229-5357-9*) U of Pittsburgh Pr.

— Storm Pattern. LC 91-50873. (Poetry Ser.). 81p. 1992. 19.95 (*0-8229-3708-5*); pap. 10.95 (*0-8229-5472-9*) U of Pittsburgh Pr.

— Sunflower Facing the Sun. LC 92-5881. 96p. 1992. pap. 10.95 (*0-87745-382-9*) U of Iowa Pr.

Pape, H. D., et al, eds. Carcinoma of the Oral Cavity & Oropharynx. LC 93-30355. (Recent Results in Cancer Research Ser.: Vol. 134). 1994. 98.00 (*0-387-56819-0*) Spr-Verlag.

Pape, Ian. Designer's Mix & Match Type. 1992. 39.95 (*0-07-048758-8*) McGraw.

— Designer's Mix & Match Type. 224p. 1992. 39.95 (*0-8306-4269-2*, 4303, Design Pr) TAB Bks.

Pape, John. Hill Country Chronicles: Sophisticated Tales of Life in the Texas Hill Country. LC 92-16978. (Illus.). 1992. pap. text ed. 10.95 (*1-877740-18-7*) Nel-Mar Pub.

Pape, Larry, ed. see Stuckey, M. M.

Pape, Marieanna. Composition Companion. 2nd ed. 80p. (Orig.). 1993. pap. text ed. 13.95 (*0-940139-28-6*) Consortium RI.

Pape, Mark, jt. auth. see Brockett, Oscar G.

Pape, Moritz E. The Lost Gospel Also Depth of Soul & Quest of Man. (Illus.). 24p. 1992. lib. bdg. 2.50 (*0-9630599-0-4*) Ltd Ex Pr.

— Poetic Variables & Other Thoughts. (Illus.). 50p. (Orig.). 1990. text ed. 4.50 (*0-9630599-1-2*, TXU432-733) Ltd Ex Pr.

— Schemers. 1993. 8.75 (*0-8062-4904-8*) Carlton.

Pape, Ralph. Beyond Your Command. 1988. pap. 4.75 (*0-8222-0113-5*) Dramatists Play.

— Girls We Have Known & Other One Act Plays. 1983. pap. 4.75 (*0-8222-0449-5*) Dramatists Play.

— Say Goodnight, Gracie. 1979. pap. 4.75 (*0-8222-0993-4*) Dramatists Play.

***Pape, Robert A.** Bombing to Win: Air Power & Coercion in War. (Studies in Security Affairs). (Illus.). 408p. 1996. 49.95x (*0-8014-3134-4*); pap. 19.95 (*0-8014-8311-5*) Cornell U Pr.

Pape, Sharon. The Portal. 1994. mass mkt. 3.50 (*0-373-27033-X*, 5-27033-5) Harlequin Bks.

Pape, Thomas. The Sarcophagidae (Diptera) of Fennoscandia & Denmark. (Fauna Entomologica Scandinavica Ser.: No. 19). (Illus.). 203p. 1987. text ed. 51.00 (*90-04-08184-4*) Lubrecht & Cramer.

Pape, Walter. Joachim Ringelnatz: Parodie und Selbstparodie in Leben und Werk. LC 73-88303. (Quellen und Forschungen zur Sprach und Kulturgeschichte der Germanischen Voelker Ser.: NF 62). 457p. (GER.). (C). 1974. 106.95 (*3-11-004483-8*) De Gruyter.

Pape, Walter, ed. German Unifications & the Change of Literary Discourse, 1870-71 - 1989-1990: European Cultures - Studies in Literature & the Arts. LC 93-35566. (European Cultures Ser.: Vol. 1). vi, 382p. 1993. lib. bdg. 49.95 (*3-11-013878-6*) De Gruyter.

***Pape, Walter & Burwick, Frederick, eds.** Reflecting Senses: Perception & Appearance in Literature, Culture & the Arts. LC 94-37129. 375p. (C). 1995. lib. bdg. 190.00 (*3-11-014580-4*) De Gruyter.

Pape, Walter, jt. ed. see Burwick, Frederick.

Papegaaij, B. C. Word Expert Semantics: An Interlingual Knowledge-Based Approach. (Distributed Language Translation Ser.). x, 254p. 1986. 73.85 (*3-11-013331-8*) Mouton.

Papegaaij, Bart & Schubert, Klaus. Text Coherence in Translation. (Distributed Language Translation Ser.). 180p. (Orig.). (C). 1988. pap. 52.35 (*3-11-013107-2*) Mouton.

Papegaay, B. C. Word Expert Semantics: An Interlingual Knowledge-Based Approach. (Distributed Language Translation Ser.). x, 254p. 1986. pap. 60.75 (*90-6765-261-X*) Mouton.

Papel, Ira D. & Nachlas. Facial Plastic & Reconstructive Surgery. 592p. 1991. 125.00 (*0-8016-3696-5*) Mosby Yr Bk.

Papell, Ben, jt. ed. see Lowe, James L.

Papell, Catherine P. & Rothman, Beulah, eds. Co-Leadership in Social Work with Groups. LC 80-28698. (Social Work with Groups Ser.: Vol. 3, No. 4). 81p. (Orig.). 1981. pap. text ed. 14.95 (*0-917724-90-9*) Haworth Pr.

Papendick, R. I., et al, eds. Multiple Cropping. (Illus.). 378p. 1976. pap. 9.00 (*0-89118-045-1*) Am Soc Agron.

Papendieck, Henner. Britische Managing Agencies in Indischen Kohlenbergrau, 1893-1918. Bruchey, Stuart, ed. LC 80-2822. (Dissertations in European Economic History Ser.). (Illus.). 1981. lib. bdg. 42.95 (*0-405-14006-1*) Ayer.

Papenfuse, Edward C. In Pursuit of Profit: The Annapolis Merchants in the Era of the American Revolution, 1763-1805. LC 74-6835. (Maryland Bicentennial Ser.). (Illus.). 320p. 1975. 47.50x (*0-8018-1573-8*) Johns Hopkins.

Papenfuse, Edward C., intro. An Historical List of Public Officials of Maryland: Governors, Legislators & Other Prin. Officers of Government, 1632 to 1990. (Archives of Maryland New Ser.: Vol. 1). 542p. 1990. 30.00 (*0-942370-26-0*, 575) MD St Archives.

Papenfuse, Edward C. & Stiverson, Gregory A., illus. The Decisive Blow Is Struck. (Orig.). 1977. pap. 2.00 (*0-942370-00-7*) MD St Archives.

Papenfuse, Edward C., et al. Guide to Government Records at the Maryland State Archives. rev. ed. Swanson, Kevin et al, eds. (Comprehensive List by Agency & Record Ser.). 235p. 1992. pap. 25.00 (*0-942370-35-X*) MD St Archives.

— Maryland: A New Guide to the Old Line State. LC 76-17224. (Illus.). 488p. 1976. 29.50 (*0-8018-1874-5*) Johns Hopkins.

Papenfuse, Edward C., et al, eds. An Inventory of Maryland State Papers: The Revolutionary War Era 1775-1789, Pt. 1. 1977. 16.00 (*0-942370-04-X*) MD St Archives.

***Paper Bag Players Staff.** Out of the Bag. LC 94-46006. (Illus.). (J). 1996. write for info. (*0-7868-0176-X*); lib. bdg. write for info. (*0-7868-2148-5*); pap. write for info. (*0-7868-1061-0*) Hyprn Child.

Paper, Herbert H., ed. Language & Texts: The Nature of Linguistic Evidence. LC 75-36885. 204p. (Orig.). 1975. pap. 10.00 (*0-915932-02-4*) Trillium Pr.

— The Musa-Nama of R. Shim'on Hakham. (Judeo-Iranian Text Ser.: No. 1). 518p. 1986. pap. 40.00 (*0-87820-550-0*) Hebrew Union Coll Pr.

Paper, Herbert H., ed. & tr. A Short Sketch of Tajik Grammar. LC 64-63907. (General Publications). 1993. reprint ed. 19.90 (*0-685-62480-3*) Res Inst Inner Asian Studies.

***Paper, Herbert H. & Jazayery, Mohammad A.** English for Iranians. (English for Foreigners Ser.). xiv, 318p. (ENG & PER.). 1980. student ed. pap. 20.00x (*0-87950-304-1*) Spoken Lang Serv.

— English for Iranians. (English for Foreigners Ser.). xiv, 318p. (ENG & PER.). 1980. reprint ed. audio 100.00 (*0-87950-619-9*) Spoken Lang Serv.

— The Writing System of Modern Persian. LC 76-40543. 40p. (C). 1976. reprint ed. pap. 5.00 (*0-87950-284-3*) Spoken Lang Serv.

Paper, Jordan. Offering Smoke: The Sacred Pipe & Native American Religion. LC 88-28378. (Illus.). 192p. 1989. pap. 22.95 (*0-89301-126-6*) U of Idaho Pr.

— The Spirits Are Drunk: Comparative Approaches to Chinese Religion. LC 94-9954. (Chinese Philosophy & Culture Ser.). (Illus.). 315p. 1994. pap. 17.95 (*0-7914-2316-6*) State U NY Pr.

— The Spirits Are Drunk: Comparative Approaches to Chinese Religion. LC 94-9954. (Chinese Philosophy & Culture Ser.). (Illus.). 315p. 1995. 54.50 (*0-7914-2315-8*) State U NY Pr.

Paper, Lewis J. Brandeis: An Intimate Biography. reprint ed. pap. 9.95 (*0-8065-0966-X*, Citadel Pr) Carol Pub Group.

— John F. Kennedy: The Promise & the Performance. xi, 408p. 1980. reprint ed. pap. 9.95 (*0-306-80114-0*) Da Capo.

***Paper Machine Dynamic - Foundation Design Comt. Staff.** Paper Machine Dynamic - Foundation Design. 82p. 1994. 45.00 (*0-89852-284-6*, 0101R239) TAPPI.

Paper Tiger Television Collective Staff. The Paper Tiger Guide to TV Repair. 32p. (Orig.). 1992. pap. 5.00 (*0-930495-19-5*) San Fran Art Inst.

— Roar! The Paper Tiger Television Guide to Media Activism. Marcus, Daniel, ed. (Illus.). 67p. (Orig.). (C). 1991. pap. 10.00 (*0-9630999-3-0*) Paper Tiger TV.

Papera, Susan, jt. auth. see Lichtman, Ronnie.

Paperno, Irina. Chernyshevsky & the Age of Realism: A Study in the Semiotics of Behavior. LC 88-2311. (Illus.). 320p. 1988. 37.50 (*0-8047-1453-3*) Stanford U Pr.

Paperno, Irina & Grossman, Joan D., eds. Creating Life: The Aesthetic Utopia of Russian Modernism. LC 93-27948. 1994. write for info. (*0-8047-2288-9*) Stanford U Pr.

Paperno, Irina, jt. ed. see Hughes, Robert P.

Paperno, Lora. Getting Around Town in Russian: Situational Dialogs. Sylvester, Richard D., tr. (Illus.). 123p. (Orig.). (C). 1987. pap. text ed. 9.95 (*0-89357-171-7*) Slavica.

Paperno, Lora, ed. see Baranskaya, Natalya.

Paperno, Slava, jt. auth. see Leed, Richard L.

Paperno, Slava, ed. see Zoshchenko, Mikhail.

Paperno, Slava, et al. Intermediate Russian: The Twelve Chairs. (Illus.). 326p. (Orig.). (C). 1985. pap. text ed. 19.95 (*0-89357-144-X*) Slavica.

Papernow, Patricia L. Becoming a Stepfamily: Patterns of Development in Remarried Families. LC 93-21716. (Social & Behavioral Science Ser.). 448p. 1993. 30.95 (*1-55542-551-8*) Jossey-Bass.

Papert, Seymour. The Children's Machine: Rethinking School in the Age of the Computer. 256p. 1994. reprint ed. pap. 12.00 (*0-465-01063-6*) Basic.

Papert, Seymour, jt. ed. see Harel, Idit.

Papert, Seymour A. Mindstorms: Children, Computers & Powerful Ideas. 2nd ed. LC 92-53249. 256p. 1993. pap. 14.00 (*0-465-04674-6*) Basic.

Papert, Seymour A., jt. auth. see Minsky, Marvin L.

Papert, Seymour A., jt. auth. see Taylor, James G.

***Papesca, John P.** Fetch. 32p. 1994. pap. 5.95 (*0-9643082-0-7*) White Knuckle.

***Papgapitos, Karen.** Genesis Code II. Kleinman, Estelle & Nicholson, David, eds. (JB Ser.). (Illus.). 96p. (Orig.). (J). (gr. 5-9). 1994. pap. 4.95 (*0-9637328-3-8*) Kapa Hse Pr.

Papi, Floriano, ed. Animal Homing. (Animal Behaviour Ser.). (Illus.). 336p. 1993. 79.95 (*0-412-36390-9*, A9442) Chapman & Hall.

Papi, Liza. Carnavalia! African-Brazilian Folklore & Crafts. LC 93-38451. (Illus.). 48p. (J). 1994. 16.95 (*0-8478-1779-2*) Rizzoli Intl.

Papia, Dan, tr. see Kawakami, Kenji.

Papierski, Betty P. Flat Tires & Coffe Fires: Being Tales from the TIL Ranch. (Illus.). 160p. 1993. 22.50 (*0-914224-25-5*) Tales Mojave Rd.

Papilion, Andrea, ed. see Gerich, Michael D., et al.

Papillon, J. B. Traite Historique et Pratique de la Gravure en Bois, 2 vols. 1125p. 1985. pap. text ed. 268.00 (*2-903928-30-4*) Gordon & Breach.

Papillon, Marie. A Million & One Love Strategies: How to Meet, Intrigue & Keep a Lover. (Orig.). 1993. pap. 8.99 (*1-56171-231-0*, S P I Bks) Sure Sellers.

Papin, Liliane. L' Autre Scene: Le Theatre de Marguerite Duras. (Stanford French & Italian Studies: No. 54). 176p. (FRE.). 1988. pap. 46.50 (*0-915838-70-2*) Anma Libri.

Papinchak, Robert A. Sherwood Anderson: A Study of the Short Fiction. (Twayne's Studies in Short Fiction: No. 33). 200p. 1992. text ed. 22.95 (*0-8057-8339-3*, 33, Pub. by Royal Botanic Garden UK) Macmillan.

Papineau, Andre. Biblical Blues: Growing Through Setups & Letdowns. LC 89-37532. (Illus.). 240p. (C). 1989. pap. 7.95 (*0-89390-157-1*) Resource Pubns.

— Breakthrough: Stories of Conversion. (Illus.). 152p. (C). 1988. pap. 7.95 (*0-89390-128-8*) Resource Pubns.

— Jesus on the Mend: Healing Stories for Ordinary People. LC 88-35660. (Illus.). 168p. (C). 1989. pap. 7.95 (*0-89390-140-7*) Resource Pubns.

— Let Your Light Shine: Scripture Stories for Self-Esteem. LC 90-70561. 144p. (Orig.). 1990. pap. 7.95 (*0-89622-438-4*) Twenty-Third.

— Lightly Goes the Good News: Making the Gospel Your Own Story. LC 88-51814. 144p. (Orig.). 1989. pap. 7.95 (*0-89622-376-0*) Twenty-Third.

— Sermons for Sermon Haters. LC 91-48019. 184p. (Orig.). 1992. pap. 10.95 (*0-89390-229-2*) Resource Pubns.

Papineau, David. Philosophical Naturalism. LC 93-3214. 240p. 1993. 44.95 (*0-631-18902-5*); pap. 19.95 (*0-631-18903-3*) Blackwell Pubs.

— Reality & Representation. 304p. (C). 1987. pap. 24.95 (*0-631-17552-0*) Blackwell Pubs.

Papini, Giovanni. The Failure. Pope, Virginia, tr. LC 76-137070. 326p. 1972. reprint ed. text ed. 35.00 (*0-8371-5533-9*, PAFA, Greenwood Pr) Greenwood.

— Four & Twenty Minds. LC 78-121496. (Essay Index Reprint Ser.). 1977. 21.95 (*0-8369-1770-7*) Ayer.

— Four & Twenty Minds. LC 76-174357. 1972. reprint ed. 26.95 (*0-405-08832-9*, Pub. by Blom Pubns UK) Ayer.

Papini, M., et al, eds. Development, Handicap, Rehabilitation: Practice & Theory: Proceedings of the International Congress, along the Way of Adriano Comparetti's Experience & Philosophy, Florence, Italy, 9-11 November, 1989. (International Congress Ser.: No. 902). 290p. 1990. 92.50 (*0-444-81178-8*, Excerpta Medica) Elsevier.

Papirmeister, Bruno, et al. Medical Defense Against Mustard Gas: Toxic Mechanisms & Pharmacological Implications. (Illus.). 360p. 1991. 110.00 (*0-8493-4257-0*, RA1247) CRC Pr.

Papirno, Ralph, jt. ed. see Richard, Chait.

Papirno, Ralph, et al, eds. Factors That Affect the Precision of Mechanical Tests. LC 89-34779. (Special Technical Publication Ser.: No. STP 1025). (Illus.). 250p. 1989. text ed. 59.00 (*0-8031-1251-3*, 04-010250-23) ASTM.

***Papka, Raymond E., ed. & contrib.** Anatomy: Embryology, Gross Anatomy, Neuroanatomy, Microanatomy. LC 94-45449. (Oklahoma Notes Ser.). 1995. write for info. (*0-387-94395-1*) Spr-Verlag.

Papke, Mary E. Susan Glaspell: A Research & Production Sourcebook. LC 92-42696. (Modern Dramatists Research & Production Sourcebooks Ser.: No. 4). 320p. 1993. text ed. 69.50 (*0-313-27383-9*, PSA, Greenwood Pr) Greenwood.

— Verging on the Abyss: The Social Fiction of Kate Chopin & Edith Wharton. LC 90-38412. (Contributions in Women's Studies: No. 119). 208p. 1990. text ed. 49.95 (*0-313-26877-0*, PAJ, Greenwood Pr) Greenwood.

Papke, William L. The Living Trust: A Private Will That Does Not Have to Be Probated. (Illus.). 144p. (Orig.). 1987. pap. 14.95 (*0-9619568-0-1*) Wm L Papke.

***Papma, Frans.** Contesting the Household Estate: Southern Brazilian Peasant & Modern Agriculture. (CEDLA Latin America Studies (CLAS): No. 67). 286p. 1992. pap. 27.00 (*90-70280-84-1*, Pub. by Thesis Pubs NE) IBD Ltd.

An Asterisk (*) at the beginning of an entry indicates that the title is appearing in BIP for the first time.

PQ

Papo, Eliezer. The Essential Pele Yoetz: An Encyclopedia of Ethical Jewish Living. Angel, Marc D., tr. & intro. by. 320p. 1991. 25.00 (*0-87203-137-3*) Hermon.

Papolos, Demitri & Papolos, Janice. Overcoming Depression: The Respected Reference for the Millions Who Suffer Depression & Manic Depression & for Their Families. rev. ed. LC 91-58472. (Illus.). 400p. 1992. pap. 14.00 (*0-06-096594-0*, HarpT) HarpC.

Papolos, Demitri F. & Lachman, Herbert M., eds. Genetic Studies in Affective Disorders: Overview of Basic Methods, Current Directions, & Critical Research Issues. LC 93-6161. (Publication Series of the Department of Psychiatry Albert Einstein College of Medicine of Yeshiva University: Vol. 8). 1994. text ed. 49.95 (*0-471-00075-2*) Wiley.

Papolos, Janice, jt. auth. see Papolos, Demitri.

Papoulias, F., jt. ed. see Falzarano, J. M.

Papoulis, Athanasios. Circuits & Systems: A Modern Approach. 435p. (C). 1981. text ed. 62.75 (*0-03-056097-7*); Solutions manual. write for info. (*0-03-057693-8*) SCP.

— The Fourier Integral & Its Applications. (Classic Textbook Reissue Ser.). 1962. text ed. write for info. (*0-07-048447-3*) McGraw.

— Probability & Statistics. 512p. 1989. boxed 46.00 (*0-685-27164-1*) P-H.

— Probability, Random Variances & Stochastic Processes. 3rd ed. 1991. text ed. write for info. (*0-07-048477-5*) McGraw.

— Signal Analysis. (C). 1977. text ed. write for info. (*0-07-048460-0*) McGraw.

— Systems & Transforms with Applications in Optics. LC 81-5995. 484p. (C). 1981. reprint ed. lib. bdg. 48.50 (*0-89874-358-3*) Krieger.

Papousek, D. & Aliev, M. R. Molecular Vibrational-Rotational Spectra. (Studies in Physical & Theoretical Chemistry: Vol. 17). 324p. 1982. 113.00 (*0-444-99737-7*) Elsevier.

Papousek, H., et al, eds. Nonverbal Vocal Communication: Comparative & Developmental Approaches. (Studies in Emotion & Social Interaction). (Illus.). 288p. (C). 1992. 59.95 (*0-521-41265-X*) Cambridge U Pr.

Papp, Daniel S. Contemporary International Relations: Frameworks for Understanding. 4th ed. 637p. (C). 1994. pap. write for info. (*0-02-390881-5*) Macmillan.

Papp, Daniel S. & Diehl, John, eds. The United Nations: Issues of Peace & Conflict, 1989: The Study & Background Guide, Set. LC 89-64408. 1990. 60.00 (*0-935082-15-8*) Southern Ctr Intl Stud.

Papp, Daniel S. & McIntyre, John R., eds. International Space Policy: Legal, Economic, & Strategic Options for the Twentieth Century & Beyond. LC 87-2519. 360p. 1987. text ed. 79.50 (*0-89930-215-7*, PPS/, Quorum Bks) Greenwood.

Papp, Daniel S., jt. ed. see McIntyre, John R.

Papp, Daniel S., ed. see Rusk, Dean & Rusk, Richard.

Papp, Ferenc. Contrastive Studies. 168p. 1984. 35.00 (*0-569-08800-3*, Pub. by Collets) St Mut.

— Mathematical Linguistics in the Soviet Union. (Janua Linguarum, Ser. Minor: No. 40). (Orig.). 1966. pap. text ed. 20.80 (*0-686-22446-9*) Mouton.

Papp, Ferenc & Szepe, Gyorgy, eds. Papers in Computational Linguistics. (Janua Linguarum, Ser. Major: No. 91). 585p. 1977. text ed. 147.70 (*90-279-3285-9*) Mouton.

***Papp, I.** Finnish-Hungarian Concise Dictionary. 1120p. (C). 1993. 54.00x (*963-05-6498-X*, Pub. by Akad Kiado HU) St Mut.

***Papp, I. & Jakab, L.** Hungarian-Finnish Concise Dictionary. 855p. (C). 1993. 54.00x (*963-05-6594-3*, Pub. by Akad Kiado HU) St Mut.

— Hungarian-Finnish Dictionary: Magyar-Finn Szotar. 855p. (FIN & HUN.). 1985. 49.95 (*0-8288-1657-3*, M4580) Fr & Eur.

***Papp, J. Gy.** Cardiovascular Pharmacology '87. 649p. (C). 1986. 210.00x (*963-05-4651-5*) St Mut.

Papp, J. Gy., jt. auth. see Szekeres, L.

***Papp, Jeffrey.** Lecture Notes on Radiographic Equipment, Exposure, & Radiation Protection. (Illus.). 204p. (Orig.). (C). 1995. pap. text ed. 14.80 (*0-87563-539-3*) Stipes.

Papp, John P., ed. Endoscopic Control of Gastrointestinal Hemorrhage. 200p. 1981. 134.00 (*0-8493-6295-4*, RC802, CRC Reprint) Franklin.

Papp, Joseph & Kirkland, Elizabeth, eds. Shakespeare Alive! 1988. mass mkt. 4.95 (*0-553-27081-8*) Bantam.

Papp, Julius Gy. & Szekeres, Laszlo, eds. Pharmacology of Smooth Muscle. LC 94-17635. (Handbook of Experimental Pharmacology Ser.: Vol. 111). 1994. write for info. (*0-387-57888-9*) Spr-Verlag.

Papp, L., jt. auth. see Soos, A.

Papp, L., jt. ed. see Soos, A.

Papp, Laszlo. Emefesz, az Amerikai Magyar Egyetemistak Mozgalma az 1956 os Forradalon Utan. (Tanuk Korukrol Ser.). (Illus.). 96p. 1988. pap. 7.00 (*0-910539-04-9*) Hungarian Alumni.

Papp, Laszlo, jt. auth. see Soos, Arpad.

Papp, M., ed. European Pancreatic Club EPC, 20th Meeting, Budapest, August 1988, Abstracts. (Journal: Digestion: Vol. 40, No. 2, 1988). 68p. 1988. pap. 46.50 (*3-8055-4902-4*) S Karger.

Papp, Peggy. Family Therapy: Full Length Case Studies. LC 77-16641. 1977. text ed. 24.95 (*0-89876-019-4*) Gardner Pr.

— The Process of Change. LC 83-12814. (Guilford Family Therapy Ser.). 248p. 1983. lib. bdg. 30.00 (*0-89862-052-X*) Guilford Pr.

— The Process of Change. 248p. 1994. pap. text ed. 18.95 (*0-89862-501-7*) Guilford Pr.

Papp, Z. Obstetric Genetics. 627p. (C). 1990. text ed. 69.00 (*963-05-5689-8*, Pub. by A K HU) Intl Spec Bk.

Papp, Zoltan, ed. Atlas of Fetal Diagnosis. LC 92-14609. 1992. 249.75 (*0-444-98675-8*) Elsevier.

Pappageotes, George. Say It in Modern Greek. 1956. pap. 2.95 (*0-486-20813-3*) Dover.

Pappageotes, George C., tr. see Kazantzakis, Nikos.

Pappalardo, Carlos, jt. auth. see Monafo, William W.

Pappalardo, Ed. Tales of Terror for the Pleasure Boater. LC 94-96101. 235p. (Orig.). 1994. pap. 16.95 (*0-9641978-0-4*) Hickory NY.

Pappani, Debra A. Just Look into My Eyes. (Illus.). 106p. (Orig.). 1981. pap. 4.95 (*0-9606062-0-3*) Pappani.

Pappanikou, A. J. & Paul, James L., eds. Mainstreaming Emotionally Disturbed Children. (Special Education & Rehabilitation Monograph Ser.: No. 10). (C). 1981. pap. 16.95x (*0-8156-2246-5*) Syracuse U Pr.

Pappano, Marilyn. Finally a Father: (Romantic Traditions) (Silhouette Intimate Moments Ser.). 1994. mass mkt. 3.50 (*0-373-07542-1*, 5-07542-9) Silhouette.

— Guilt by Association. large type ed. (Silhouette Sensation Ser.). 1994. 17.95 (*0-373-58855-0*, Silhouette Lrg Print) Chivers N Amer.

— In Sinful Harmony. 416p. (Orig.). 1995. mass mkt. 5.99 (*0-446-60116-0*) Warner Bks.

— A Man Like Smith: (Southern Knights) (Intimate Moments Ser.). 1995. pap. 3.75 (*0-373-07626-6*, 1-07626-4) Silhouette.

— Memories of Laura. (Silhouette Intimate Moments Ser.). 1993. mass mkt. 3.39 (*0-373-07486-7*, 5-07486-9) Silhouette.

— Michael's Gift: (American Hero, New Orleans Knights) (Intimate Moments Ser.). 1994. mass mkt. 3.50 (*0-373-07583-9*, 1-07583-7) Harlequin Bks.

— Passion. 416p. (Orig.). 1996. mass mkt. 5.99 (*0-446-60117-9*) Warner Bks.

— Regarding Remy: Southern Knights. (Intimate Moments Ser.). 1994. mass mkt. 3.50 (*0-373-07609-6*, 1-07609-0) Silhouette.

— Something in Heaven. large type ed. (Sensation Ser.). 1994. 17.95 (*0-373-58861-5*, Silhouette Lrg Print) Chivers N Amer.

— Sweet Annie's Pass. (Silhouette Intimate Moments Ser.). 1993. mass mkt. 3.50 (*0-373-07512-X*, 5-07512-2) Silhouette.

— Within Reach. (Men Made in America Ser.). 1995. mass mkt. 3.59 (*0-373-45181-4*, 1-45181-4) Silhouette.

Pappano, Marilyn & Palmer, Diana. Christmas Memories: Room at the Inn; Woman Hater. (Harlequin Reprint Ser.). 1994. mass mkt. 4.99 (*0-373-15186-1*, 1-15186-9) Harlequin Bks.

Papparella, jt. auth. see Holt.

***Pappas.** Greek Cooking. 1995. 7.98 (*0-88365-893-3*) Galahad Bks.

Pappas, Anthony, Jr. The Complete Telemarketing Handbook for Recruiting & Retaining Students. 125p. 1988. pap. 89.00 (*0-912150-16-5*) Magna Pubns.

Pappas, Anthony. Money, Motivation, & Mission in the Small Church. Walrath, Douglas A., ed. (Small Church in Action Ser.). 128p. (Orig.). 1989. pap. 10.00 (*0-8170-1146-3*) Judson.

Pappas, Anthony & Planting, Scott. Mission: The Small Church Reaches Out. LC 93-1337. (Small Church in Action Ser.). 128p. 1993. pap. 10.00 (*0-8170-1174-9*) Judson.

Pappas, Anthony G. Entering the World of the Small Church: A Guide for Leaders. LC 88-71623. 97p. (Orig.). 1988. pap. 10.25 (*1-56699-030-0*, AL109) Alban Inst.

— Pastoral Stress: Sources of Tension, Resources for Transformation. 1995. 14.95 (*1-56699-150-1*, AL160) Alban Inst.

Pappas, Arthur M. & Vitolo, John, eds. Upper Extremity Injuries of the Athlete. (Illus.). 700p. 1994. text ed. 149.95 (*0-443-08836-5*) Churchill.

Pappas, Barbara. Are You Saved? The Orthodox Christian Process of Salvation. 2nd ed. (Illus.). 52p. 1987. reprint ed. write for info. (*0-318-65528-4*) Amnos Pubns.

— The Christian Life in the Early Church & Today: According to St. Paul's First Epistle to the Corinthians. xvi, 172p. (Orig.). 1989. pap. write for info. (*0-9623721-3-7*) Amnos Pubns.

Pappas, Charles. Momentary Regards. 80p. 1991. pap. 9.95 (*0-916147-16-9*) Regent Pr.

Pappas, Charles N. The Life & Times of G. V. Black. (Illus.). 128p. (Orig.). 1983. pap. text ed. 38.00 (*0-931386-55-1*) Quint Pub Co.

Pappas, Chris. C Plus Plus Visual Handbook. 1994. pap. text ed. 29.95 (*0-07-882056-1*) Osborne-McGraw.

Pappas, Chris H., jt. auth. see Murray, William H.

Pappas, Chris H., jt. auth. see Murray, William H., III.

Pappas, Christine C., et al. An Integrated Language Perspective in the Elementary School: Theory & Action. 2nd ed. (Illus.). 368p. (C). 1995. pap. text ed. 42.00 (*0-8013-1181-0*) Longman.

— An Integrated Language Perspective in the Elementary School: Theory into Action. 384p. (Orig.). (C). 1990. pap. text ed. 38.95 (*0-8013-0175-0*, 75834) Longman.

Pappas, Debra S., ed. see Goudeaux, Phillip G.

Pappas, Debra S., ed. see Larson, Verna.

Pappas, Edward H. & Steiger, Jon R. Michigan Business Torts. LC 91-73439. 332p. 1991. 115.00 (*0-685-51910-4*, 91-009) U MI Law CLE.

Pappas, Evangeline, ed. see Utility Data Institute Staff.

Pappas, George, ed. Justification & Knowledge: New Studies in Epistemology. (Philosophical Studies in Philosophy Ser.: No. 17). 1979. lib. bdg. 64.00 (*90-277-1023-6*); pap. text ed. 26.50 (*90-277-1024-4*) Kluwer Ac.

Pappas, George S. Laboratory Manual of Histology. 176p. (C). 1989. spiral bd. write for info. (*0-697-09715-3*) Wm C Brown Pubs.

— Laboratory Manual of Histology. 2nd ed. 176p. (C). 1993. spiral bd. write for info. (*0-697-12244-1*) Wm C Brown Pubs.

— To the Point: The United States Military Academy, 1802-1902. LC 92-36632. 528p. 1993. text ed. 55.00 (*0-275-94329-1*, C4329, Praeger Pubs) Greenwood.

Pappas, Gregory. The Magic City: Unemployment in a Working-Class Community. LC 88-47935. (Anthropology of Contemporary Issues Ser.). (Illus.). 232p. 1989. 35.00 (*0-8014-2277-9*); pap. 14.95 (*0-8014-9548-2*) Cornell U Pr.

Pappas, Ioannis A. & Tatsiopoulos, Ilias P., eds. Advances in Production Management Systems: Proceedings of the IFIP TC5 - WG5.7 Fifth International Conference on Advances in Production Management Systems, APMS '93, Athens, Greece, 28-30 September 1993. LC 93-27019. (IFIP Transactions B: Applications in Technology Ser.: Vol. B-13). 1993. write for info. (*0-444-81598-8*, North Holland) Elsevier.

Pappas, Irene, ed. see Quinby, Marge M.

Pappas, James G., jt. auth. see Lulat, Y. G-M.

Pappas, James L., jt. auth. see Hirschey, Mark.

Pappas, John J., intro. Annual Review of Communications: National Engineering Consortium, Vol. XXXXVI. (Illus.). 1108p. 1992. 139.00 (*0-933217-08-0*) Prof Educ Intl.

Pappas, Joseph, ed. see Gonzalez, Steve.

Pappas, Joseph, ed. see Hunter, Diana.

Pappas, Lou S. Biscotti. (Illus.). 72p. 1992. 9.95 (*0-8118-0095-4*) Chronicle Bks.

— Bread Baking. rev. ed. 176p. (Orig.). 1992. pap. 8.95 (*1-55867-042-4*, Nitty Gritty Ckbks) Bristol Pub Ent CA.

— Cheesecakes. LC 92-47463. 1993. 9.95 (*0-8118-0322-8*) Chronicle Bks.

— Chutneys & Relishes. LC 94-43153. (Illus.). 1995. 9.95 (*0-8118-0840-8*) Chronicle Bks.

— Cinnamon. LC 93-42979. (Illus.). 72p. 1994. 9.95 (*0-8118-0344-9*) Chronicle Bks.

— Extra-Special Crockery Pot Recipes. rev. ed. (Illus.). 160p. 1995. pap. 8.95 (*1-55867-107-2*, Nitty Gritty Ckbks) Bristol Pub Ent CA.

— Favorite Cookie Recipes. Reynolds, Maureen, ed. LC 80-81247. (Illus.). 192p. 1980. pap. 6.95 (*0-911954-57-0*) Bristol Pub Ent CA.

— Favorite Cookie Recipes. rev. ed. (Illus.). 176p. 1994. pap. 8.95 (*1-55867-090-4*, Nitty Gritty Ckbks) Bristol Pub Ent CA.

— Ginger. LC 95-12943. (Illus.). 1996. write for info. (*0-8118-0579-4*) Chronicle Bks.

— Holiday Feasts: Festive Cooking for Family & Friends. LeBlond, Bill, ed. LC 92-41106. (Illus.). 72p. 1993. 9.95 (*0-8118-0264-7*) Chronicle Bks.

— Pesto: Fresh Herb Sauces & Spreads. LeBlond, Bill, ed. (Illus.). 72p. 1994. 9.95 (*0-8118-9175-5*) Chronicle Bks.

Pappas, Lou S. & Salerno, Steven, illus. Pesto: Fresh Herb Sauces & Spreads. LC 93-24860. 72p. 1994. 9.95 (*0-8118-0426-7*) Chronicle Bks.

***Pappas, Michael G.** The BioBusiness Handbook: How to Organize & Operate a Biotechnology Business. LC 93-1612. (Including the Most Promising Applications for the 1990s Ser.). (Illus.). 480p. 1994. ring bd. 189.50 (*0-89603-218-3*) Humana.

— The Biotech Business Handbook: How to Organize & Operate a Biotechnology Business. (Including the Most Promising Applications for the 1990s Ser.). (Illus.). 480p. 1994. ring bd. 189.50 (*0-89603-320-1*) Humana.

— Sweet Dreams for Little Ones. (Illus.). 64p. (Orig.). (J). 1985. pap. 10.00 (*0-86683-641-1*, AY8156) Harper SF.

Pappas, Nicholas L. Digital Design. Gordon, ed. LC 93-9764. 600p. (C). 1994. text ed. 70.25 (*0-314-01230-3*) West Pub.

***Pappas, Nickolas.** Plato & the Republic. LC 94-33894. (Philosophy Guidebooks Ser.). 208p. 1995. 45.00 (*0-415-09531-X*, C0409); pap. 9.95 (*0-415-09532-8*, C0410) Routledge.

Pappas, Paul. The United States & the Greek War for Independence 1821-1828. 1985. text ed. 36.00 (*0-88033-065-1*, 173) Col U Pr.

Pappas, Peter. A Biology of the Eucestoda, Vol. 1. Arme, Christopher, ed. 1984. text ed. 139.00 (*0-12-062101-0*) Acad Pr.

Pappas, Peter, jt. ed. see Arme, Christopher.

Pappas, S. Peter, ed. UV Curing: Science & Technology. LC 78-56293. (Illus.). 1978. per. 95.00 (*0-936840-04-8*) Tech Marketing.

— UV Curing, Vol. 2: Science & Technology. 360p. 1985. text ed. 99.00 (*0-936840-08-0*) Tech Marketing.

Pappas, S. Peter & Winslow, F. H., eds. Photodegradation & Photostabilization of Coatings. LC 81-467. (ACS Symposium Ser.: No. 151). 1981. 43.95 (*0-8412-0611-2*) Am Chemical.

Pappas, Stephen G. Church Development & Operating Process. (Illus.). 72p. 1987. student ed 8.00 (*0-9619920-0-X*) HOME Inc.

— Property Manager's Handbook: Business Planning for the Professional. 304p. 1991. 32.95 (*0-7931-0214-6*, 4105-10) Dearborn Finan.

Pappas, Steven. Managing Mobile Home Parks. (IREM Monograph). (Illus.). 194p. (Orig.). (C). 1991. pap. text ed. 34.95 (*0-944298-57-5*) Inst Real Estate.

Pappas, Theoni. Fractals, Googols, & Other Mathematical Tales. LC 92-41343. (Illus.). 72p. (Orig.). (J). (gr. 4 up). 1993. pap. 9.95 (*0-933174-89-6*) Wide World-Tetra.

— The Joy of Mathematics. 2nd rev. ed. (Illus.). 256p. (Orig.). 1989. pap. 10.95 (*0-933174-65-9*) Wide World-Tetra.

— Let's Dance: The Greek Way. (Illus.). 1977. pap. 2.95 (*0-933174-07-1*) Wide World-Tetra.

— Magic of Mathematics: Discovering the Spell of Mathematics. 1994. pap. 10.95 (*0-933174-99-3*) Wide World-Tetra.

— Math Talk. LC 90-25380. (Illus.). 72p. (Orig.). 1991. pap. 8.95 (*0-933174-74-8*) Wide World-Tetra.

— Mathematics Appreciation. 154p. 1987. pap. 10.95 (*0-933174-28-4*) Wide World-Tetra.

— Mathematics Quotations. (Illus.). (Orig.). 1995. pap. 9.95 (*1-884550-04-5*) Wide World-Tetra.

— More Joy of Mathematics. LC 91-11295. (Illus.). 304p. (Orig.). 1991. pap. 10.95 (*0-933174-73-X*) Wide World-Tetra.

— What Do You See? An Optical Illusion Slide Show. rev. ed. 32p. 1988. sl. 29.95 (*0-933174-78-0*) Wide World-Tetra.

Pappas, Theoni & Monroe, Elvira. Greek Cooking for Everyone. 2nd ed. (Orig.). 1989. pap. 8.95 (*0-933174-61-6*) Wide World-Tetra.

Pappas, Theresa. Flash Paper. 1985. pap. 4.50 (*0-89823-074-8*) New Rivers Pr.

Pappas, William. Many Streams: A Stream of Hope. 1993. 8.95 (*0-533-10344-4*) Vantage.

Pappe, Ilan. Britain & the Arab-Israeli Conflict, 1948-51. LC 87-22509. 320p. 1988. text ed. 55.00 (*0-312-01573-9*) St Martin.

— The Making of the Arab-Israeli Conflict, 1947-1951. 320p. 1992. text ed. 69.50 (*1-85043-357-7*, Pub. by I B Tauris UK) St Martin.

— The Making of the Arab-Israeli Conflict, 1947-1951. 336p. 1994. text ed. 24.95 (*1-85043-819-6*, Pub. by I B Tauris UK) St Martin.

Pappe, Ilan, jt. ed. see Nevo, Joseph.

***Papper, E. M.** Romance, Poetry & Surgical Sleep: Literature Influences Medicine. LC 94-24189. (Contributions in Medical Studies: Vol. 42). 176p. 1995. text ed. 55.00 (*0-313-29405-4*, Greenwood Pr) Greenwood.

***Papper, Robert A.** Broadcast News Writing Stylebook. LC 94-25081. 1994. pap. text ed. write for info. (*0-205-14693-7*) Allyn.

Papper, Solomon. Doing Right: Everyday Medical Ethics. 148p. 1983. 30.95 (*0-316-69044-9*) Little.

— Sodium: Its Biological Significance. (CRC Uniscience Ser. on Cations of Biological Significance). 304p. 1981. 113.95 (*0-8493-5873-6*, RC632) CRC Pr.

Papper, Solomon, jt. auth. see Kaufman, Christian E., Jr.

Papper, Solomon, et al. Manual of Medical Care of the Surgical Patient. 3rd ed. 304p. 1985. 24.50 (*0-316-69058-9*, Little Med Div) Little.

Pappi, Franz Urban, jt. auth. see Klingemann, Hans D.

***Pappillion, Marie.** Million & One Love Strategies. 1995. mass mkt. 5.99 (*0-312-95466-2*) St Martin.

Pappin, Joseph, III. The Metaphysics of Edmund Burke. LC 92-41383. 188p. 1993. 30.00 (*0-8232-1365-X*); pap. 19.95 (*0-8232-1366-8*) Fordham.

Pappo, M., jt. ed. see Marty, M.

Pappoutsakis, James, ed. see Brooke, A.

Pappu, S. S. & Rao, R., eds. The Dimensions of Karma. 450p. (C). 1987. 42.95 (*0-685-43948-8*) Asia Bk Corp.

***Pappu, S. S. Rama Rao, ed.** Dimension of Karma. (C). 1994. 34.00x (*81-7001-101-9*, Pub. by Chanakya II) S Asia.

Pappworth, M. Primer of Medicine. 5th ed. 384p. 1984. pap. text ed. 75.00 (*0-407-62605-0*) Buttrwrth-Heinemann.

Paprocki, Steven L. & Bothwell, Robert O. Corporate Grantmaking: Giving to Racial - Ethnic Populations. LC 94-20702. (Illus.). 643p. (C). reprint ed. pap. text ed. 55.00 (*0-8191-9573-1*) U Pr of Amer.

Papson, Stephen. In a World Not of His Own Making. 195p. (Orig.). 1993. pap. 7.95 (*0-9635722-0-2*) Blue Canary.

Papson, Thomas C. & Young, Charlotte D. Business Uses of the Freedom of Information Act, No. 14. 2nd ed. (Corporate Practice Ser.). 1991. ring bd. 95.00 (*1-55871-231-3*) BNA.

***Papstein, Robert.** Eritrea: A Tourist Guide. 1995. pap. 12.95 (*1-56902-011-6*) InBook.

— Eritrea: Revolution at Dusk: A Pictorial Rendering. LC 90-81661. (Illus.). 200p. (C). 1991. 49.95 (*0-932415-63-6*); pap. 18.95 (*0-932415-64-4*) Red Sea Pr.

Papuchon, Michel R., et al, eds. ECIO '89: Fifth European Conference on Integrated Optics. 264p. 1989. 70.00 (*0-8194-0177-3*, VOL. 1141) SPIE.

***Papurt, David M.** Inside the Object Model: The Sensible Use of C Plus Plus. LC 94-39287. (Advances in Object Technology Ser.: Vol. 4). (Illus.). 550p. (Orig.). (C). 1995. pap. 39.00 (*1-884842-05-4*) SIGS Bks.

Papus, pseud. Reincarnation. Vallior, Marguerite, tr. (Illus.). 132p. (Orig.). 1991. pap. 6.95 (*0-922802-10-6*) Kessinger Pub.

Papus. Tarot of the Bohemians. 1978. pap. 7.00 (*0-87980-158-1*) Wilshire.

— What Is Occultism? 104p. 1981. pap. 10.00 (*0-89540-073-1*, SB-073) Sun Pub.

Papus & Vallior, Marguerite, trs. Reincarnation: Physical, Astral & Spiritual Evolution. 142p. 1967. reprint ed. spiral bd. 6.60 (*0-7873-0654-1*) Mokelumne.

Papworth, David. Concise Encyclopedia of Garden Flowers. 1987. 12.99 (*0-517-63953-X*) Random Hse Value.

Papworth, N., jt. auth. see Ratcliff, J.

Papy, C. I., ed. see Papy, Frank M.

Papy, Frank. Cruising Guide to the Florida Keys. 6th ed. Methven, Barbara, ed. LC 81-176805. (Illus.). 240p. 1988. pap. 14.95 (*0-9619838-0-9*) F Papy Cruising Guide.

Papy, Frank M. Cruising Guide to the Florida Keys. 8th ed. Gregg, R. L., ed. (Illus.). 260p. 1992. pap. 18.95 (*0-9619838-2-5*) F Papy Cruising Guide.

PQ

— Cruising Guide to the Florida Keys. 9th ed. Gregg, R. L., ed. (Illus.). 256p. 1995. pap. text ed. 19.95 (*0-9619838-3-3*) F Papy Cruising Guide.

— Cruisins Guide to the Florida Keys. 7th ed. Papy, C. I., ed. (Illus.). 256p. 1989. pap. 16.95 (*0-9619838-1-7*) F Papy Cruising Guide.

Paq, Stephen & Smillie, Joseph. Orchard Almanac. 3rd ed. LC 86-60398. (Illus.). 10.00 (*0-9616523-2-2*) Spraysaver Pubns.

Paquet, jt. auth. see Carr.

Paquet, J., jt. auth. see Dercourt, J.

Paquet, J. G. & Le Maitre, J. F. Methodes Pratiques d'Etude des Oscillations Non Lineaires: Theorie Des Systemes. 172p. 1970. text ed. 169.00 (*0-677-50200-1*) Gordon & Breach.

Paquet, Jacques, jt. auth. see Dercourt, Jean.

Paquet, K. J. & Schoelmerich, J., eds. Pfortaderhochdruck. (Illus.). x, 702p. (GER.). 1992. 167.25 (*3-8055-5659-4*) S Karger.

Paquet, K. J., jt. ed. see Kozuschek, W.

Paquet, K. J., jt. ed. see Nilius, R.

Paquet, K. J., et al. Portale Hypertension. Denck, H. & Berchtold, R., eds. x, 282p. 1982. pap. 52.00 (*3-8055-3480-9*) S Karger.

Paquette. Psychiatric Nursing Diagnosis Care Plans. 1991. pap. text ed. 36.25 (*0-86720-310-2*) Jones & Bartlett.

Paquette, jt. auth. see Davies.

Paquette, Gerard A. Structured COBOL. 2nd ed. 848p. (C). 1991. pap. write for info. (*0-697-07763-2*) Bus & Educ Tech.

— Structured COBOL. 3rd ed. 864p. 1994. pap. write for info. (*0-697-12394-4*) Bus & Educ Tech.

Paquette, Gerard A., et al. Advanced Structured COBOL. 2nd ed. 608p. (C). 1991. student ed. write for info. (*0-697-07773-X*); pap. write for info. (*0-697-07771-3*) Bus & Educ Tech.

Paquette, Jean C. The Wizard. 1992. 15.95 (*0-533-10220-0*) Vantage.

Paquette, Jerry. Social Purpose & Schooling: Alternatives, Agendas & Issues. 204p. 1991. 60.00 (*1-85000-920-1*, Falmer Pr); pap. 29.00 (*1-85000-921-X*, Falmer Pr) Taylor & Francis.

Paquette, Lee. Only More So: The History of East Hartford, 1783-1976. LC 92-61362. 372p. 1992. reprint ed. 30.00 (*0-89725-076-1*) Picton Pr.

Paquette, Leo A. Organic Reactions, Vol. 41. 672p. 1992. text ed. 98.00 (*0-471-54409-4*) Wiley.

— Organic Reactions, Vol. 42. 696p. 1992. text ed. 107.00 (*0-471-54410-8*) Wiley.

— Organic Reactions, Vol. 43. 823p. 1993. text ed. 98.00 (*0-471-58479-7*) Wiley.

— Organic Reactions, Vol. 45. 1994. text ed. 95.00 (*0-471-03161-5*) Wiley.

— Organic Syntheses, Vol. 69. 328p. 1991. text ed. 52.95 (*0-471-54560-0*) Wiley.

— The Renaissance in Cyclooctatetraene Chemistry. Barton et al, eds. 1976. pap. 15.50 (*0-08-020479-1*, Pergamon Pr) Elsevier.

***Paquette, Leo A., ed.** Encyclopedia of Reagents for Organic Synthesis, Vol. 8. Date not set. text ed. 2,250.00 (*0-471-93623-5*) Wiley.

— Organic Reactions, Vol. 40. 528p. 1991. text ed. 105.00 (*0-471-53841-8*) Wiley.

— Organic Reactions, Vol. 44. 624p. 1993. text ed. 98.00 (*0-471-30302-X*) Wiley.

— Organic Reactions, Vol. 47. 1995. text ed. 89.95 (*0-471-11737-4*) Wiley.

Paquette, Leo A. & Doherty, A. M. Polyquinane Chemistry Synthesis & Reactions. (Reactivity & Structure Ser.: Vol. 26). (Illus.). 250p. 1987. 115.00 (*0-387-17703-5*) Spr-Verlag.

***Paquette, Leo A., et al, eds.** Organic Reactions Vol. 46, Vol. 46. 393p. 1994. text ed. 89.95 (*0-471-08619-3*) Wiley.

Paquette, Mary, ed. see NANDA Staff.

Paquette, Mary G. Basques to Bakersfield. (Illus.). 138p. 1982. 15.00 (*0-943500-00-1*) Kern Historical.

Paquette, Mary G., ed. see De Rutte, Theophile.

Paquette, Penny, jt. auth. see Tuttle, Cheryl G.

Paquette, Randor J., jt. auth. see Wright, Paul H.

Paquette, Robert L. Sugar Is Made with Blood: The Conspiracy of la Escalera & the Conflict Between Empires over Slavery in Cuba. LC 87-34503. (Illus.). 365p. 1990. text ed. 40.00 (*0-8195-5192-9*, Wesleyan Univ Pr); pap. 16.95 (*0-8195-6233-5*, Wesleyan Univ Pr) U Pr of New Eng.

Paquette, Yvan, tr. see Dexter, Gerry L., ed.

Paquin, J. R. & Crowley, R. E. Die Design Fundamentals. 2nd ed. LC 86-19132. (Illus.). 256p. 1987. 26.95 (*0-8311-1172-0*) Indus Pr.

Paquin, Larue. Frontiering at Fifty. Downeast Graphics & Printing Inc. Staff, ed. (Illus.). 71p. (Orig.). (C). 1985. write for info. (*0-318-60174-5*) L Paquin Pub.

Paquin, Laurent. English - French Vocabulary of Road Transport Vehicles. 167p. (ENG & FRE.). 1991. pap. 49.95 (*0-8288-9416-7*) Fr & Eur.

Paquin, R. A. Dimensional Stability, Vol. 1335. 1990. 53.00 (*0-8194-0396-2*) SPIE.

Paquot, Annette, jt. ed. see Maniet, Albert.

Paquot, Annette, ed. see Plautus.

Para, Gladys C., ed. see Gotchy, Joe.

Paracelsus. Alchemical Medicine. 1986. pap. 4.95 (*0-916411-30-3*) Holmes Pub.

— Alchemy: The Third Column of Medicine. Waite, A. E., tr. 1989. pap. 3.95 (*1-55818-120-2*) Holmes Pub.

— The Aurora of the Philosophers. Waite, A. E., tr. 1985. reprint ed. pap. 3.95 (*0-916411-50-8*) Holmes Pub.

— Coelum Philosophorum: Or the Book of Vexations. Waite, A. E., tr. reprint ed. pap. 3.95 (*0-916411-13-3*) Holmes Pub.

— Coelum Philosophorum: The Seven Canons of the Metals. Waite, Arthur E., tr. 1982. reprint ed. pap. 4.50 (*0-945303-08-4*) Evanescent Pr.

— Concerning the Degrees, Grades & Compositions of Alchemy. 1990. reprint ed. pap. 4.95 (*1-55818-126-1*) Holmes Pub.

— Concerning the Spirits of the Planets. 1983. 3.95 (*0-916411-14-1*, Sure Fire) Holmes Pub.

— Hermetic Astronomy. Waite, A. E., tr. 1983. reprint ed. pap. 4.95 (*0-916411-09-5*, Sure Fire) Holmes Pub.

— Paracelsus: Selected Writings. 2nd ed. Jacobi, J., ed. Gutterman, Norman, tr. (Bollingen Ser.: Vol. 28). (Illus.). 1958. 55.00 (*0-691-09810-7*); pap. 15.95 (*0-691-01876-6*) Princeton U Pr.

— The Prophecies of Paracelsus. Kohn, J., tr. 1992. reprint ed. pap. 8.95 (*1-55818-188-1*) Holmes Pub.

— The Revelation of Hermes. 1984. reprint ed. pap. 3.95 (*0-916411-81-8*) Holmes Pub.

— Seven Defenses Against Those Who Would Seek to Defame Me. (Orig.). 1994. pap. 6.95 (*1-55818-280-2*) Holmes Pub.

— The Tincture of the Philosophers. Waite, A. E., tr. 1984. reprint ed. pap. 3.95 (*0-916411-45-1*) Holmes Pub.

— A Treatise Concerning the Medicinal Philosophic Stone. 1989. pap. 3.95 (*1-55818-161-X*) Holmes Pub.

— Werke, 5 vols., Set. (GER.). reprint ed. 369.60 (*3-7965-0471-X*) Adlers Foreign Bks.

Paracelsus College Staff, ed. see Schmidt, Felix.

Paracelsus, Theophrastus. The Archidoxes of Magic: Of the Supreme Mysteries of Nature, of the Spirits of Planets, Secrets of Alchemy, Occult Philosophy, Signs of the Zodiac, Magical Cure of Diseases, & Celestial Medicines. 160p. 1992. pap. 17.95 (*1-56459-171-9*) Kessinger Pub.

Paracer, Surindar, jt. auth. see Ahmadjian, Vernon.

***Parachin, Victor M.** Daily Strength: One Year of Experiencing the Psalms. 384p. 1995. pap. 12.95 (*0-89243-677-8*) Liguori Pubns.

— Grief Relief. 128p. (Orig.). 1991. pap. 9.99 (*0-8272-1236-4*) Chalice Pr.

— How to Bring Help & Hope to the Grieving. 1992. pap. 2.50 (*1-877871-30-3*, 9260) Ed Ministries.

— The Lord Is My Shepherd: A Psalm for the Grieving. LC 91-76660. 64p. (Orig.). 1992. pap. 2.95 (*0-89243-415-5*) Liguori Pubns.

— Our Father: A Prayer for the Grieving. 64p. (Orig.). 1993. pap. text ed. 2.95 (*0-89243-521-6*) Liguori Pubns.

— Scripture Pathways to Inner Healing. LC 94-75227. 144p. (Orig.). 1994. pap. 6.95 (*0-89243-591-7*) Liguori Pubns.

— Ties That Bind: Remaining Happy As a Couple after the Wedding. LC 92-32942. 80p. (Orig.). 1993. pap. 7.99 (*0-8272-3630-1*) Chalice Pr.

***Parachute.** Piggies Piggies Piggies. (J). Date not set. lib. bdg. 16.98 (*0-671-75241-3*, S&S Bks Young Read) S&S Childrens.

Parachute Press Staff. The Story of Davey Crockett. (Illus.). (J). 1993. pap. 3.50 (*0-440-40881-4*) Dell.

— The Twelve Days of Christmas. (Sing-a-Story Ser.). 24p. (J). 1988. pap. 2.50 (*0-553-15638-1*, Bantam Aud Pub) Bantam.

Parad, Howard J., ed. Crisis Intervention: Selected Readings. LC 65-20273. 384p. reprint ed. pap. 109.50 (*0-7837-1630-3*, 2041923) Bks Demand.

Parad, Howard J. & Parad, Libbie G., eds. Crisis Intervention, Bk. 2: The Practitioner's Sourcebook for Brief Therapy. LC 89-17151. x, 402p. 1990. pap. 27.95 (*0-87304-237-9*) Families Intl.

Parad, Libbie G., jt. ed. see Parad, Howard J.

Parada, Carlos. Genealogical Guide to Greek Mythology. 262p. 1993. 137.50x (*91-7081-062-1*, Pub. by Almqv & Wiksell SW) Coronet Bks.

Paradaens, J., ed. Databases. (International Lecture Series in Computer Mathematics). 261p. 1987. text ed. 70.00 (*0-12-544962-3*) Acad Pr.

Parade Magazine Staff, jt. auth. see Eastman Kodak Company Staff.

Paradeise, Catherine, jt. auth. see Laufer, Romain.

Paradellis, T., jt. auth. see Vourvopoulos, G.

Paradice, David B., jt. auth. see Courtney, James F.

Paradice, Sam. How To Be A Business Tycoon. 48p. 1987. pap. 15.00 (*0-915665-16-6*) Premier Publishers.

Paradigm Publishing Staff. Fast File. 112p. (C). 1991. teacher ed 5.80 (*1-56118-298-2*); pap. text ed. 14.50 (*1-56118-295-8*) Paradigm MN.

Paradin, Claude. Devises Heroiques. (Illus.). 304p. 1989. text ed. 48.95 (*0-85967-771-0*, Pub. by Scolar Pr UK) Ashgate Pub Co.

— Heroical Devises of M. Claudius Paradin. LC 84-1402. 1984. reprint ed. 50.00 (*0-8201-1391-3*) Schol Facsimiles.

Paradis, Adrian. Opportunities in Cleaning Service Careers. (Opportunities in...Ser.). (Illus.). 160p. 1992. 13.95 (*0-8442-4016-8*, VGM Career Bks); pap. 10.95 (*0-8442-4017-6*, VGM Career Bks) NTC Pub Grp.

— Opportunities in Military Careers. 1989. 13.95 (*0-8442-8648-6*, VGM Career Bks); pap. 10.95 (*0-8442-8649-4*, VGM Career Bks) NTC Pub Grp.

— Opportunities in Vocational & Technical Careers. 2nd ed. (Opportunities in...Ser.). (Illus.). 160p. 1992. 13.95 (*0-8442-4007-9*, VGM Career Bks); pap. 10.95 (*0-8442-4008-7*, VGM Career Bks) NTC Pub Grp.

— Planning Your Career of Tomorrow. (Illus.). 160p. 1986. pap. 6.95 (*0-8442-6678-7*, Passport Bks) NTC Pub Grp.

Paradis, Adrian A. Opportunities in Airline Careers. (Illus.). 160p. 1987. 13.95 (*0-8442-6028-2*, VGM Career Bks); pap. 10.95 (*0-8442-6029-0*, VGM Career Bks) NTC Pub Grp.

— Opportunities in Banking. (Illus.). 160p. 1986. 13.95 (*0-8442-6213-7*, VGM Career Bks); pap. 10.95 (*0-8442-6214-5*, VGM Career Bks) NTC Pub Grp.

— Opportunities in Nonprofit Organization Careers. LC 93-4667. (Opportunities in...Ser.). 1994. 13.95 (*0-8442-4088-5*, VGM Career Bks); pap. 10.95 (*0-8442-4089-3*, VGM Career Bks) NTC Pub Grp.

— Opportunities in Part Time & Summer Jobs. 160p. 1987. text ed. 13.95 (*0-8442-6300-1*, VGM Career Bks); pap. 10.95 (*0-8442-6302-8*, VGM Career Bks) NTC Pub Grp.

— Opportunities in Transportation Careers. (Illus.). 160p. 1988. 13.95 (*0-8442-6567-5*, VGM Career Bks); pap. 10.95 (*0-8442-6568-3*, VGM Career Bks) NTC Pub Grp.

— Opportunities in Vocational & Technical Careers. 160p. 1987. text ed. 13.95 (*0-8442-6018-5*, VGM Career Bks); pap. 10.95 (*0-8442-6019-3*, VGM Career Bks) NTC Pub Grp.

— The Small Business Information Source Book. 136p. (Orig.). 1987. pap. 7.95 (*0-932620-81-7*) Betterway Bks.

Paradis, Adrian A., jt. auth. see Mills, Jason.

Paradis, Carole. Lexical Phonology & Morphology: The Nominal Classes in Fula. LC 92-10160. (Outstanding Dissertations in Linguistics Ser.). 336p. 1992. 78.00 (*0-8153-0697-0*) Garland.

Paradis, Carole & Prunet, Jean-Francois, eds. The Special Status of Cornals: Internal & External Evidence. (Phonetics & Phonology Ser.: Vol. 2). 231p. 1991. text ed. 88.00 (*0-12-544966-6*); pap. text ed. 50.00 (*0-12-544967-4*) Acad Pr.

Paradis, James & Postlewait, Thomas, eds. Victorian Science & Victorian Values: Literary Perspectives. LC 80-29513. 362p. 1981. pap. 72.00 (*0-89766-110-9*) NY Acad Sci.

— Victorian Science & Victorian Values: Literary Perspectives. 375p. (C). 1985. pap. text ed. 15.00 (*0-8135-1107-0*) Rutgers U Pr.

Paradis, James & Williams, George C. Evolution & Ethics: T. H. Huxley's "Evolution & Ethics" with New Essays on Its Victorian & Sociobiological Context. (Illus.). 242p. (C). 1989. text ed. 45.00 (*0-691-08535-8*); pap. text ed. 17.95 (*0-691-02423-5*) Princeton U Pr.

Paradis, James, jt. ed. see Bazerman, Charles.

***Paradis, James G.** T. H. Huxley: Man's Place in Nature. LC 78-5492. 240p. 1978. reprint ed. pap. 68.40 (*0-7837-8911-4*, 2049622) Bks Demand.

Paradis, Jean. Lord, Teach Me to Pray! (C). 1988. 39.00 (*0-85439-256-4*, Pub. by St Paul Pubns UK) St Mut.

Paradis, Jean-Guy. Lord, Teach Me to Pray. LC 87-50003. 240p. (C). 1985. reprint ed. pap. 9.95 (*0-89622-335-3*) Twenty-Third.

Paradis, Jean P. Dear Old Kennebago. (Illus.). 110p. 1992. pap. 20.00 (*0-9610570-1-7*) Bks by Village.

***Paradis, Line.** Graphics Art Vocabulary. (Terminology Bulletin Ser.: No. 210). (Illus.). 573p. (Orig.). 1993. pap. 48.05x (*0-660-58025-X*, Pub. by Canada Commun Grp CN) Accents Pubns.

Paradis, M. Bilingual Aphasia Test, Nineteen Ninety-One. Single language stimulus book. 34.50 (*1-56321-087-8*) LEA S&AM.

Paradis, M. & Lebrun, Y., eds. Early Bilingualism & Child Development. (Neurolinguistics Ser.: Vol. 13). 236p. 1984. 40.00 (*90-265-0463-2*, Pub. by Swets Pub Serv NE) Taylor & Francis.

***Paradis, Michael, ed.** Aspects of Bilingual Aphasia. LC 95-13571. 1995. text ed. 96.00 (*0-08-042570-4*, Pergamon Pr) Elsevier.

Paradis, Michel. The Assessment of Bilingual Aphasia. 1987. 17.50 (*0-8058-0849-3*); 19.95 (*0-8058-0848-5*) L Erlbaum Assocs.

— The Assessment of Bilingual Aphasia. 1987. 34.50 (*0-8058-0850-7*) L Erlbaum Assocs.

— Foundations of Aphasia Rehabilitation. LC 93-1040. 1993. text ed. 125.00 (*0-08-041940-2*, Pergamon Pr) Elsevier.

Paradis, Michel & Hildebrandt, Nancy. Neurolinguistic Aspects of the Japanese Writing System. (Perspectives in Neurolinguistics, Neuropsychology & Psycholinguistics Ser.). 1985. text ed. 75.00 (*0-12-544965-8*) Acad Pr.

Paradis, Michel & Libben, G. The Assessment of Bilingual Aphasia. 264p. 1987. text ed. 45.00 (*0-89859-650-5*) L Erlbaum Assocs.

***Paradis, Norman A., et al, eds.** Cardiac Arrest: The Pathophysiology & Therapy of Sudden Death. LC 95-14196. (Illus.). 1995. write for info. (*0-683-06765-6*) Williams & Wilkins.

Paradis, Phillip. From Gobbler's Knob. LC 89-38963. v, 30p. 1989. pap. 5.00 (*0-926487-02-7*) Rowan Mtn Pr.

***Paradis, Roger L.** Creating Your Personal Journey: A Primer: To Discover Who You Are & to Uncover Your True Desires. White, Carol, ed. LC 94-69155. 200p. 1995. 9.95 (*0-9643604-0-3*) Concord Pr MA.

Paradise, Lee. Readings in English, Bk. 4: The Arts. (Readings in English Ser.). 118p. (gr. 9-12). 1987. pap. text ed. write for info. (*0-13-756040-0*, 18885) Prentice ESL.

Paradise, Louis V., jt. auth. see VanHoose, William.

***Paradise, Mark.** Chicago Entertainment Guide. 62p. 1993. pap. text ed. 4.95 (*0-9642574-0-8*) Backstage Promot.

— Chicago Entertainment Guide. (Illus.). 70p. 1995. pap. text ed. 4.95 (*0-9642574-1-6*) Backstage Promot.

Paradise, Nathaniel B., jt. ed. see Brooke, C. F.

Paradise, Paul R. African Grey Parrots. (Illus.). 1979. 9.95 (*0-86622-721-0*, KW-018) TFH Pubns.

— Amazon Parrots. (Illus.). 1989. 9.95 (*0-87666-985-2*, KW-012) TFH Pubns.

— Canaries. (Illus.). 1979. 9.95 (*0-86622-725-3*, KW-004) TFH Pubns.

— Gerbils. (Illus.). 96p. 1980. 9.95 (*0-87666-927-5*, KW-037) TFH Pubns.

— Rabbits. (Illus.). 1979. 9.95 (*0-86622-832-2*, KW-021) TFH Pubns.

Paradise, Paul R., ed. Goldfish. (Illus.). 1979. 9.95 (*0-86622-726-1*, KW-014) TFH Pubns.

***Paradise, Winston J.** Pathway to Paradise. LC 93-84542. (Illus.). 113p. 1993. per. 9.95 (*1-883122-02-3*) Pearce Pub.

***Paradiso, Catherine, ed.** Fluids & Electrolytes. LC 94-23575. (Review Ser.). 1995. write for info. (*0-397-55083-9*) Lippincott.

— Pathophysiology. LC 94-40504. (Review Ser.). 1995. pap. write for info. (*0-397-55100-2*) Lippincott.

Paradiso, Dorene. Strawberry Verses. 160p. 1992. 14.95 (*0-9632050-0-5*) Paradise CA.

Paradissis. Greek Cookery. 5th ed. (Illus.). 1985. pap. 18.00 (*0-88431-756-0*) IBD Ltd.

Paraf, A. & Peltre, G. Immunoassays in Food & Agriculture. (C). 1991. lib. bdg. 127.00 (*0-7462-0123-0*) Kluwer Ac.

Paraf, A., jt. ed. see Nicolau, C.

Paragon House Staff. Paragon House Spelling Dictionary. 1994. pap. 12.95 (*1-56924-866-4*) Marlowe & Co.

Paragon Project Staff. Scandal Annual, 1993. 1992. pap. 6.99 (*0-312-92936-6*) St Martin.

Paraicz, E., ed. ICP in Infancy & Childhood. (Monographs in Pediatrics: Vol. 15). (Illus.). viii, 148p. 1982. pap. 78.50 (*3-8055-3475-2*) S Karger.

Parain, Brice. Histoire de la Philosophie: Orient-Antiquite Moyen Age, Vol. 1. (Historique Ser.). 1760p. 63.50 (*0-686-56454-5*) Fr & Eur.

— Histoire de la Philosophie, Vol. 1: Orient-Antiquite Moyan Age. 1752p. 1969. 135.00 (*0-7859-4551-2*) Fr & Eur.

Paraire, Philippe. Fifty Years of Rock Music. (Compact Reference Ser.). (Illus.). 256p. (Orig.). 1992. pap. 9.95 (*0-550-17011-1*, Chambers LKC) LKC.

Parajuli, Chandra R. Education of the Blind in Nepal. 77p. 1984. 8.00 (*0-8135-04169-3*) Am-Nepal Ed.

Parakilas, James. Ballads Without Words: Chopin & the Tradition of the Instrumental Ballade. LC 91-30216. (Illus.). 358p. 1992. 34.95 (*0-931340-47-0*, Amadeus Pr) Timber.

Parakkal, P. F., jt. auth. see Montagna, William.

***Parakrama, Arjuna.** De-Hegemonizing Language Standards: Learning from (Post) Colonial Englishes about "English" LC 94-25478. 1994. write for info. (*0-312-12316-7*) St Martin.

Paral, Vladimir. Catapult. LC 88-34053. 240p. 1989. 15.95 (*0-945774-04-4*, PG 5039.26.A7K313) Catbird Pr.

— Catapult. Harkins, William, tr. LC 88-34053. 224p. 1993. reprint ed. pap. 10.95 (*0-945774-17-6*, PG5039-26-A7K313) Catbird Pr.

— The Four Sonyas. Harkins, William, tr. LC 92-30413. 400p. 1993. 22.95 (*0-945774-15-X*, PG5039.26A7P713) Catbird Pr.

***Param, S.** The Eternal Journey: A Guide to Enlightenment. 192p. (Orig.). 1995. 24.95 (*0-9637659-1-4*) Dawn Pubns MD.

Param, Swami. The American Dream: Waking Up. LC 93-91691. 182p. (Orig.). 1994. pap. 14.95 (*0-9637659-0-6*) Dawn Pubns MD.

***Paramahamsa, Muktananda.** From the Finite to the Infinite. LC 94-43555. 1994. write for info. (*0-911307-31-1*) SYDA Found.

***Paramahansa Yogananda.** Autobiography of a Yogi. LC 78-151319. (HIN.). 1971. pap. 4.00x (*0-87612-077-X*) Self Realization.

— The Divine Romance. LC 86-63172. (Illus.). 496p. 1986. 12.00 (*0-87612-240-3*); pap. 6.50 (*0-87612-241-1*) Self Realization.

Paramananda. Problem of Life & Death. pap. 1.95 (*0-87481-543-6*, Pub. by Ramakrishna Math II) Vedanta Pr.

Paramananda, Swami. Book of Daily Thoughts & Prayers. 1977. 7.95 (*0-911564-32-2*) Vedanta Ctr.

— Christ & Oriental Ideals. 5th ed. 1989. pap. 5.95 (*0-911564-14-4*) Vedanta Ctr.

— Concentration & Meditation. 8th ed. 1974. pap. 3.95 (*0-911564-07-1*) Vedanta Ctr.

— Emerson & Vedanta. 2nd ed. 1985. reprint ed. pap. 3.95 (*0-911564-13-6*) Vedanta Ctr.

— Faith Is Power. 2nd ed. Orig. Title: Faith as Constructive Force. 1961. 4.50 (*0-911564-09-8*); pap. 3.95 (*0-685-05238-9*) Vedanta Ctr.

— Healing Meditations. 3rd ed. 1980. pap. 1.95 (*0-911564-28-4*) Vedanta Ctr.

— Path of Devotion. 8th ed. 1940. 3.95 (*0-911564-00-4*) Vedanta Ctr.

— Principles & Purposes of Vedanta. 8th ed. 1937. pap. 1.95 (*0-911564-30-6*) Vedanta Ctr.

— Right Resolutions. 2nd ed. 1981. pap. 1.95 (*0-911564-29-2*) Vedanta Ctr.

— Science & Practice of Yoga. 1918. pap. 0.75 (*0-911564-31-4*) Vedanta Ctr.

— Secret of Right Activity. 4th ed. 1964. 4.95 (*0-911564-12-8*) Vedanta Ctr.

— Self Mastery. 5th ed. 1961. pap. 3.95 (*0-911564-08-X*) Vedanta Ctr.

— Silence As Yoga. 4th ed. 1974. pap. 3.95 (*0-911564-11-X*) Vedanta Ctr.

— Spiritual Healing. 4th ed. 1975. pap. 3.95 (*0-911564-10-1*) Vedanta Ctr.

— Srimad-Bhagavad-Gita. 7th ed. Orig. Title: Bhagavad-Gita, Srimad. 1981. 5.95 (*0-911564-03-9*); 3.95 (*0-685-05240-0*) Vedanta Ctr.

— Upanishads. 4th ed. 1981. 6.95 (*0-911564-02-0*); 5.95 (*0-685-05242-7*) Vedanta Ctr.

— Vedanta in Practice. 3rd ed. 1985. pap. 3.95 (*0-911564-04-7*) Vedanta Ctr.

— Way of Peace & Blessedness. 4th ed. 1961. 6.95 (*0-911564-06-3*) Vedanta Ctr.

***Paramesaran, Uma.** The Door I Shut Behind Me. 1990. pap. 13.00 (*81-85336-34-2*) Three Continents.

Parameshwaran, K. Power of Taxation under the Constitution. (C). 1987. 65.00 (*0-685-38629-5*) St Mut.

Parameswara Ram, jt. auth. see Krishnamurthy, V.

P Q

An Asterisk (*) at the beginning of an entry indicates that the title is appearing in BIP for the first time.

Parameswara, S. Development & Backwardness: Coexistence or Confrontation? (Sociological Publications in Honour of Dr. K. Ishwaran: No. 6). 1990. text ed. 30.00 (81-85047-62-6, Pub. by Reliance Pub Hse II) Apt Bks.

Parameswaran, P. Marx & Vivekananda. 144p. (C). 1988. text ed. 20.00 (81-207-0701-X, Pub. by Sterling Pubs II) Apt Bks.

Parameswaran, Uma. Cyclic Hope, Cyclic Pain. (Writers Workshop Redbird Ser.). 23p. 1975. 8.00 (0-88253-520-X); pap. text ed. 4.00 (0-88253-519-6) Ind-US Inc.

— Trishanku. 1988. 9.50 (0-920661-04-1) S Asia.

Parameswaran, V. S., ed. see Mikhailov, K. V., et al.

Paramo, Constanza G., jt. auth. see Davis, Scott E.

Paramo, Constanza G., tr. see Davis, Scott E. & Paramo, Constanza G.

Paramo, Constanza G., ed. see Davis, Scott E.

Paramonov, A. A. Plant-Parasitic Nematodes, 2 vols., Set, Vols. 1 & 3. 408p. 1972. Set, vol. 1, vol. 3. text ed. 111.00 (0-7065-1250-2, Pub. by Keter Pub IS) Coronet Bks.

Paramoo, R. Studies in Modern Indian Art. (Illus.). 246p. 1975. pap. 16.95 (0-318-36267-8) Asia Bk Corp.

Paranikas, Matthaios K., jt. auth. see Von Christ, Wilhelm.

Paranjape, Makarand. Decolonization & Development: Hind Svaraj Revisioned. LC 93-7496. (Illus.). 300p. (C). 1993. 28.50 (0-8039-9116-9) Sage.

— This Time I Promise It'll Be: Different Short Stories. (C). 1994. 7.50x (81-85944-46-6, Pub. by UBS Pubs Dist II) S Asia.

Paranjpe, Anand C. Theoretical Psychology: The Meeting of East & West. (PATH in Pathology Ser.). 344p. 1984. 70.00 (0-306-41400-7, Plenum Pr) Plenum.

Paranjpe, Anand C., et al, eds. Asian Contributions to Psychology. LC 88-2334. 307p. 1988. text ed. 69.50 (0-275-92524-2, C2524, Praeger Pubs) Greenwood.

Paranjpe, Shrikant. India & South Asia since 1971. xi, 107p. 1986. text ed. 15.95 (81-7027-083-9, Pub. by Radiant Pubs II) S Asia.

— U. S. Nonproliferation Policy in Action: South Asia. LC 87-80662. 192p. 1988. text ed. 22.50 (0-938719-18-1, Envoy Pr) Apt Bks.

Paranjpe, Vasant V. Homa Therapy: Our Last Chance. rev. ed. 79p. 1989. pap. text ed. write for info. (0-944909-01-9) Fivefold Path.

Paransky, Leah. Climbing the Third Stair. 64p. (Orig.). 1981. pap. 3.95 (0-931642-09-4) Lintel.

— Flowers & Other Flagrancies. 64p. (Orig.). 1979. pap. 3.95 (0-931642-05-1) Lintel.

— A Gentle Echo. 64p. (Orig.). 1984. pap. text ed. 3.95 (0-931642-14-0) Lintel.

— Paper Napkin Poems. 62p. (Orig.). 1980. pap. 3.95 (0-931642-07-8) Lintel.

— Ticker Tapes. 64p. 1978. pap. 3.95 (0-931642-01-9) Lintel.

Paraoptometric Section of the American Optometric Association Staff. Home Study Course for Optometric Assisting. (Illus.). 450p. 1987. text ed. 170.00 (0-87873-079-6, Prof Pr Bks NYC) Buttrwrth-Heinemann.

Parapsychological Association Staff. Research in Parapsychology 1972: Abstracts & Papers from the 15th Annual Convention of the Parapsychological Association, 1972. Roll, William G. et al, eds. LC 66-28580. 249p. 1973. 20.00 (0-8108-0666-5) Scarecrow.

— Research in Parapsychology 1977: Abstracts & Papers from the 20th Annual Convention of the Parapsychological Association, 1977. Roll, William G., ed. LC 66-28580. 279p. 1978. lib. bdg. 20.00 (0-8108-1131-6) Scarecrow.

— Research in Parapsychology 1978. Roll, William G., ed. LC 66-28580. 238p. 1979. 20.00 (0-8108-1195-2) Scarecrow.

— Research in Parapsychology 1979: Abstracts & Papers from the 22nd Annual Convention of the Parapsychological Association. Roll, William G., ed. LC 66-2858. 238p. 1980. 20.00 (0-8108-1327-0) Scarecrow.

— Research In Parapsychology 1981: Abstracts & Papers from the Twenty-Fourth Annual Convention of the Parapsychological Association, 1981. LC 66-28580. 252p. 1982. 20.00 (0-8108-1550-8) Scarecrow.

— Research in Parapsychology, 1983: Abstracts & Papers from the Twenty-Sixth Annual Convention of the Parapsychological Association, 1983. LC 66-28580. 196p. 1984. 20.00 (0-8108-1695-4) Scarecrow.

— Research in Parapsychology 1984: Abstracts & Papers from the Twenty-Seventh Annual Convention of the Parapsychological Association, 1984. LC 66-28580. 215p. 1985. 20.00 (0-8108-1812-4) Scarecrow.

— Research in Parapsychology 1985: Abstracts & Papers from the Twenty-Eighth Annual Convention of the Parapsychological Association, 1985. LC 66-28580. (Illus.). 256p. 1987. 25.00 (0-8108-1936-8) Scarecrow.

— Research in Parapsychology 1986: Abstracts & Papers from the Annual Convention of the Parapsychological Association 1986 29th. LC 66-28580. 256p. 1987. 27.50 (0-8108-2068-4) Scarecrow.

— Research in Parapsychology, 1987: Abstracts & Papers from the Thirtieth Annual Convention of the Parapsychological Association, 1987. LC 66-28580. 229p. 1988. 25.00 (0-8108-2128-1) Scarecrow.

— Research in Parapsychology, 1988: Abstracts & Papers from the Thirty-First Annual Convention of the Parapsychological Association, 1988. LC 66-28580. (Illus.). 200p. 1989. 25.00 (0-8108-2214-8) Scarecrow.

— Research in Parapsychology 1989: Abstracts & Papers from the Thirty-Second Annual Convention of the Parapsychological Association, 1989. LC 66-28580. (Illus.). 186p. 1990. 25.00 (0-8108-2339-X) Scarecrow.

Parapsychological Association Staff, et al, eds. Research in Parapsychology 1980: Abstracts & Papers from the Twenty-Third Annual Convention of the Parapsychological Association, 1980. LC 66-28580. 173p. 1981. 20.00 (0-8108-1425-0) Scarecrow.

— Research in Parapsychology 1982: Jubilee Centenary Issue: Abstracts & Papers from the Twenty-Fifth Annual Convention of the Parapsychological Association, 1982. LC 66-28580. 382p. 1983. 27.50 (0-8108-1627-X) Scarecrow.

Paraquin, Charles. Optical Illusion Puzzles. Kuttner, Paul, tr. LC 83-18198. (Illus.). 96p. (Orig.). (J). (gr. 7 up). 1984. 12.95 (0-8069-6868-0) Sterling.

Paraquin, Charles H. Eye Teasers: Optical Illusion Puzzles. Kuttner, Paul, tr. LC 76-21844. (Illus.). (J). (gr. 3 up). 1976. 7.95 (0-8069-4538-9); lib. bdg. 9.99 (0-8069-4539-7) Sterling.

— World's Best Optical Illusions. Kuttner, Paul, tr. LC 87-13885. (Illus.). 96p. (Orig.). (YA). (gr. 4-12). 1987. pap. 4.95 (0-8069-6644-0) Sterling.

Paras, Jason. The Music for Viola Bastarda. Houle, George & Houle, Glenna, eds. LC 84-43068. (Music: Scholarship & Performance Ser.). (Illus.). 252p. 1986. spiral bd., pap. 29.95 (0-253-38824-4) Ind U Pr.

Paras, Peter, ed. see DOE Technical Information Center Staff.

Parasara, S. Maharishi. Brihat Parasara Hora Sastra: Guide to Hindu Astrology, 2 vols., Set. Santhanam, R., tr. (C). 1989. 58.50 (0-8364-2545-6, Pub. by Ranjan Pubs II) S Asia.

Parascandola, John. The Development of American Pharmacology: John J. Abel & the Shaping of a Discipline. (Illus.). 224p. 1992. text ed. 33.50x (0-8018-4416-9) Johns Hopkins.

Parascandola, John, ed. The History of Antibiotics: A Symposium. (Illus.). 137p. (Orig.). 1980. pap. 8.00 (0-931292-08-5) Am Inst Hist Pharm.

Parascandola, John & Keeney, Elizabeth. Sources in the History of American Pharmacology. 1983. pap. 5.60 (0-931292-12-3) Am Inst Hist Pharm.

Parascandola, John & Whorton, James C., eds. Chemistry & Modern Society. LC 83-11740. (ACS Symposium Ser.: No. 228). 203p. 1983. lib. bdg. 27.95 (0-8412-0795-X); pap. 16.95 (0-8412-0803-4) Am Chemical.

Parascenzo, Marino. Eighty-Fifth U. S. Open Presented by Rolex. Norwood, Bev, ed. (Illus.). 64p. 1985. 15.00 (0-9615344-0-0) Intl Merc OH.

— Eighty-Sixth U. S. Open Presented by Rolex. Norwood, Bev, ed. (Illus.). 64p. 1986. 15.00 (0-9615344-1-9) Intl Merc OH.

Paraschos, Manny E., jt. auth. see Zaharopoulos, Thimios.

Parashar, Archana. Women & Family Law Reform in India: Uniform Civil Code & Gender Equality. 348p. (C). 1992. 38.00 (0-8039-9423-0) Sage.

Parashar, Rajan, jt. auth. see Murthi, R. K.

Parasher, Aloka. Mlecchas in Early India. (C). 1991. 29.50 (0-685-59768-7, Pub. by Munshiram Manoharial II) S Asia.

Parasher-Sen, Aloka, ed. Social & Economic History of Early Deccan: Some Interpretations. (C). 1993. 29.50 (81-7304-053-2, Pub. by Manohar II) S Asia.

Parashuram. Anandibai & Other Stories. Dutta, Swapna, tr. (C). 1992. pap. text ed. 6.00 (81-7201-263-2, Pub. by National Sahitya Akademi) S Asia.

***Paraskevas, Betty.** The Ferocious Beast. LC 95-1847. (Illus.). (J). 1996. write for info. (0-15-200838-1) HarBrace.

— Gracie Graves & the Kids from Room 402. LC 94-32661. (Illus.). (J). 1995. write for info. (0-15-200321-5) HarBrace.

— Junior Kroll. LC 92-14207. (Illus.). (J). (gr. k up). 1993. 13.95 (0-15-241497-5) HarBrace.

— Junior Kroll & Company. LC 93-9138. (Illus.). (J). (ps-6). 1994. 13.95 (0-15-292855-3) HarBrace.

— Junior Kroll, Esquire. 1993. pap. 7.95 (0-15-646572-8) HarBrace.

— Monster Beach. LC 93-46927. (J). 1995. 15.00 (0-15-292882-0) HarBrace.

— On the Edge of the Sea. LC 91-31489. (Illus.). 32p. (J). 1992. lib. bdg. 13.89 (0-8037-1263-4) Dial Bks Young.

— Shamlanders. LC 92-32980. (J). 1993. 13.95 (0-15-292854-5) HarBrace.

— The Strawberry Dog. LC 92-18216. (Illus.). (J). (ps-3). 1993. 13.99 (0-8037-1367-3) Dial Bks Young.

— A Very Kroll Christmas. LC 93-41624. (Illus.). (J). 1994. 14.95 (0-15-292883-9) HarBrace.

Paraskevas, Frixos, jt. ed. see Froese, Arnold.

Paraskevopoulos, John N., jt. auth. see Kirk, Samuel A.

Paraskos, P. Introducing Economics. 1990. pap. 21.00 (0-7463-0578-8, Pub. by Northcote UK) St Mut.

Paraskos, P., ed. Introducing the European Community: A Young Persons Guide to European Union. 1990. pap. 27.00 (0-7463-0034-4, Pub. by Northcote UK) St Mut.

Paraskou, Gregory, ed. Erisman's Reversible Errors in California Criminal Cases. 1993. ring bd. 150.00 (1-878337-35-1) Knowles Law.

Parasnis, Arawind S. Modern Optics for Researchers. LC 93-3140. 400p. 0995. text ed. 39.95 (0-470-22133-X) Halsted Pr.

Parasnis, D. S. Mining Geophysics. 2nd ed. (Methods in Geochemistry & Geophysics Ser.: Vol. 3). 395p. 1975. pap. 69.25 (0-444-41324-3) Elsevier.

— Principles of Applied Geophysics. 450p. 1986. text ed. 75.00 (0-412-28320-4, 9937); pap. text ed. 19.95 (0-412-28330-1, 9947) Chapman & Hall.

Parasuram, T. V. India's Jewish Heritage. 136p. 1982. 15.95 (0-318-37144-8) Asia Bk Corp.

Parasurama. Bases of Tantra Sadhana. Pandit, M. P., tr. 52p. (SAN.). 1991. reprint ed. 2.00 (0-941524-02-7) Lotus Light.

Parasuraman, A. Marketing Research. (C). 1986. Instr's. manual, test bank & transparency masters. teacher ed, trans. write for info. (0-201-06052-3); text ed. 39.96 (0-201-06051-5, 85-1354) Addison-Wesley.

Parasuraman, A., ed. AMA Educators' Proceedings Enhancing Knowledge Development in Marketing, 1990. LC 86-643031. 506p. (Orig.). 1990. pap. text ed. 50.00 (0-685-47693-6) Am Mktg.

Parasuraman, A., jt. auth. see Berry, Leonard L.

Parasuraman, R., jt. auth. see Davies, D. R.

Parasuraman, Raja & Davies, D. R. Varieties of Attention. (Cognition & Perception Ser.). 1984. text ed. 91.00 (0-12-544970-4) Acad Pr.

Parasuraman, Robert A. Marketing Research. 2nd ed. (Illus.). 800p. (C). 1991. text ed. 61.25 (0-201-50282-8) Addison-Wesley.

Paratore, Coleen M. Remembering. (Books Worth Writing). 128p. 1992. 24.95 (0-9630250-0-7) Bks Worth Writing.

Paravisini-Gebert, Lizabeth & Esteves, Carmen, eds. Green Cane & Juicy Flotsam: Short Stories by Caribbean Women. 220p. (C). 1991. text ed. 35.00 (0-8135-1737-0); pap. 11.95 (0-8135-1738-9) Rutgers U Pr.

Paravisini-Gebert, Lizabeth, jt. ed. see Olmos, Margarite F.

Parazzoli, Ferruccio. Informal Meditations for Informal People, Cycle C: The Sunday Gospel for the Rest of the Week, Cycle C. O'Connell, Matthew, tr. 120p. 1990. pap. text ed. 7.95 (0-8146-1843-X) Liturgical Pr.

Parberry, Ian. Circuit Complexity & Neural Networks. (Foundations of Contemporary Interpretation Ser.). (Illus.). 296p. 1994. 37.50x (0-262-16148-6) MIT Pr.

— Problems on Algorithms. LC 94-48519. 1995. pap. text ed. 21.00 (0-13-433558-9) P-H.

Parberry, Ian, ed. Parallel Complexity Theory. 216p. (C). 1987. pap. text ed. 180.00 (0-273-08783-5, Pub. by Pitman Pubng UK) St Mut.

Parbetsi, Ghazar. Patmut'iwn Hayots: History of the Armenians. Kouymjian, Dickran, ed. LC 85-11340. 1986. reprint ed. 50.00 (0-88206-031-7) Caravan Bks.

Parbhoo, Santilal, jt. ed. see Stoll, Basil A.

Parboni, Ricardo. The Dollar & Its Rivals: Recession, Inflation & International Finance. Rothschild, Jon, tr. 207p. 1985. pap. text ed. 15.95 (0-86091-744-4) Routledge Chapman & Hall.

Parbrook. Basic Physics & Measurement in Anesthesia. 3rd ed. 1991. pap. 60.00 (0-7506-0047-0) Buttrwrth-Heinemann.

Parbury, Kathleen. Women of Grace: A Biographical Dictionary of British Women Saints, Martyrs & Reformers. 224p. 1984. 25.00 (0-85362-213-2) Routledge.

Parca, M. G., ed. Ptocheia or Odysseus in Disguise at Troy: P. Koln VI 245. 156p. 1991. 54.95 (1-55540-570-3) Scholars Pr GA.

Parcel. Basic Emergency Care. 4th ed. (Illus.). 368p. (C). 1989. pap. 21.95 (0-8016-4267-1) Mosby Yr Bk.

Parcel, John & Moorman, Robert B. Analysis of Statically Indeterminate Structures. LC 55-6908. 597p. reprint ed. pap. 170.20 (0-8357-5432-4, 2055946) Bks Demand.

Parcel, Toby L. & Menaghan, Elizabeth G. Parents' Jobs & Children's Lives. (Sociology & Economics Ser.). 232p. 1994. lib. bdg. 39.95 (0-202-30483-3); pap. 18.95 (0-202-30484-1) Aldine de Gruyter.

Parcell, Lillian. Horn of the Unicorn. (Destiny Ser). 7.50 (0-686-00947-9) Wagon & Star.

Parcell, Stephen, jt. ed. see Perez-Gomez, Alberto.

Parcher, James V. A History of the Oklahoma State University College of Engineering, Architecture & Technology. Carlson, Ann, ed. LC 87-34987. (Centennial Histories Ser.). (Illus.). 304p. 1988. 14.95 (0-914956-32-9) Okla State Univ Pr.

Parcher, Jean, ed. see Bianchi, Susan & Butler, Jan.

Parchert, Gloryl. Jimtown Mystery. LC 90-70569. 187p. 1990. 8.95 (1-55523-351-1) Winston-Derek.

Parchment, S. R. Ancient Operative Masonry. 209p. 1975. reprint ed. spiral bd. 8.25 (0-7873-1114-6) Mokelumne.

— Astrology: Mundane & Spiritual, 2 vols., Set. 1968. reprint ed. spiral bd. 30.25 (0-7873-0657-6) Mokelumne.

— The Just Law of Compensation. 126p. 1967. reprint ed. spiral bd. 3.30 (0-7873-0656-8) Mokelumne.

— The Middle Path - the Safest: The Religion of "Head & Heart" 119p. 1967. reprint ed. spiral bd. 6.60 (0-7873-0655-X) Mokelumne.

— Steps to Self-Mastery. 3rd ed. 242p. 1974. reprint ed. spiral bd. 8.80 (0-7873-1095-6) Mokelumne.

Parchomenko, Walter. Soviet Images of Dissidents & Nonconformists. LC 86-3178. 266p. 1986. text ed. 49.95 (0-275-92021-6, C2021, Praeger Pubs) Greenwood.

Parco, Vincent. Researching Public Records: How to Get Anything on Anybody. LC 93-44224. 1994. 8.95 (0-8065-1522-8, Citadel Pr) Carol Pub Group.

Pardailhe-Galabrun, Annik. The Birth of Intimacy: Privacy & Domestic Life in Early Modern Paris. Phelps, Jocelyn, tr. LC 91-50607. 256p. (C). 1992. text ed. 41.95 (0-8122-3124-4) U of Pa Pr.

Pardal, J. Elephant Hunting in Portuguese East Africa. deluxe limited ed. (Illus.). 288p. 1990. boxed 65.00 (0-940143-50-X) Safari Pr.

Pardalos, P. M., et al. Topics in Parallel Computing in Mathematical Programming. Du Dingzhu, ed. (Applied Discrete Mathematics & Theoretical Computer Science Ser.: Vol. 2). 124p. 1993. 32.95 (1-880132-11-7) Sci Pr NY.

Pardalos, Panos M. Complexity in Numerical Optimization. LC 93-4827. 400p. 1993. text ed. 121.00 (981-02-1415-4) World Scientific Pub.

Pardalos, Panos M., jt. auth. see Du, D. Z.

Pardalos, Panos M., jt. auth. see Floudas, C. A.

Pardalos, Panos M., jt. ed. see Floudas, Christodoulos A.

Pardalos, Panos M., jt. ed. see Horst, Reiner.

***Pardalos, Panos M., et al, eds.** Parallel Processing of Discrete Optimization Problems: DIMACS Workshop, April 28-29, 1994. LC 95-10880. (DIMACS Series in Discrete Mathematics & Theoretical Computer Science: Vol. 22). 1995. write for info. (0-8218-0240-2) Am Math.

Pardech, J. T. & Murphy, J. W., eds. Computers in Human Services: An Overview for Clinical & Welfare Services. x, 150p. 1990. text ed. 52.00 (3-7186-5009-6); pap. text ed. 26.00 (3-7186-5005-3) Gordon & Breach.

Pardeck, J. T., ed. Child Abuse & Neglect: Theory, Research & Practice. x, 194p. 1989. text ed. 42.00 (0-677-25860-7) Gordon & Breach.

Pardeck, J. T. & Murphy, J. W. Microcomputers in Early Childhood Education. 157p. 1989. text ed. 59.00 (0-677-21900-8) Gordon & Breach.

Pardeck, Jean A. & Pardeck, John T. Young People with Problems: A Guide to Bibliotherapy. LC 83-18601. xv, 176p. 1984. text ed. 47.95 (0-313-23836-7, PYP/, Greenwood Pr) Greenwood.

Pardeck, Jean A., ed. see Pardeck, John T.

Pardeck, Jean A., jt. ed. see Pardeck, John T.

Pardeck, John T. Bibliotherapy: A Guide to Using Books in Clinical Practice. Pardeck, Jean A., ed. LC 92-49235. 168p. 1992. pap. text ed. 59.95 (0-7734-1954-3) E Mellen.

— The Forgotten Children: A Study of the Stability & Continuity of Foster Care. LC 82-20007. (Illus.). 116p. (Orig.). (C). 1983. pap. text ed. 18.00 (0-8191-2845-7) U Pr of Amer.

— Using Bibliotherapy in Clinical Practice: A Guide to Self-Help Books. LC 93-20499. (Contributions in Psychology Ser.: No. 22). 160p. 1993. text ed. 49.95 (0-313-27991-8, PUB/, Greenwood Pr) Greenwood.

Pardeck, John T., ed. Books for Early Childhood: A Developmental Perspective. LC 86-14989. (Bibliographies & Indexes in Psychology Ser.: No. 3). 182p. 1986. text ed. 49.95 (0-313-24576-2, PBK/, Greenwood Pr) Greenwood.

— Technology & Human Service Delivery: Challenges & a Critical Perspective. LC 88-2794. (Computers in Human Services Ser.: Vol. 3, Nos. 1-2). (Illus.). 161p. 1988. text ed. 39.95 (0-86656-731-3) Haworth Pr.

Pardeck, John T. & Pardeck, Jean A., eds. Bibliotherapy: A Clinical Approach for Helping Children. LC 92-49528. (Special Aspects of Education Ser.: Vol. 16). 1993. pap. text ed. 24.00 (3-7186-5347-8) Gordon & Breach.

Pardeck, John T., jt. auth. see Murphy, John W.

Pardeck, John T., jt. ed. see Murphy, John W.

Pardeck, John T., jt. auth. see Pardeck, Jean A.

Pardee, et al. Essentials of Cell Biology. 250p. write for info. (1-55664-228-8) Mosby Yr Bk.

Pardee, Arthur B. & Veer Reddy, G. P. Cancer: Fundamental Ideas. 2nd ed. Head, J. J., ed. LC 86-72193. (Carolina Biology Readers Ser.: No. 128). (Illus.). 32p. (YA). (gr. 10 up). 1986. pap. 3.00 (0-89278-128-9, 45-9728) Carolina Biological.

Pardee, Bettie B. Great Entertaining. LC 90-41753. 128p. 1990. pap. 11.95 (1-56145-001-4) Peachtree Pubs.

— Great Weekend Entertaining. 128p. 1991. pap. 9.95 (1-56145-022-7) Peachtree Pubs.

***Pardee, Blaine.** Star Trek Starfleet Academy, the Official Strategy Guide. (Illus.). 208p. (Orig.). 1995. pap. text ed. 14.99 (1-56686-233-7) Brady Compu Bks.

Pardee, Caroline J., jt. auth. see Jones, Robert H.

Pardee, Peter W. Scales & Arpeggios for Five String Banjo. 2nd ed. (Illus.). 180p. (Orig.). 1985. pap. 25.00 (0-933611-00-5) Harbinger Pubns.

Pardee, W. D., jt. ed. see McDonald, M. B., Jr.

Pardeiro, Nancy, ed. see Finley, Ernestine & Finley, Mark.

Pardeiro, Nancy, ed. see Thompson, Walter C.

Pardella, Edward R. Shirley Temple Dolls & Fashions: A Collector's Guide to the World's Darling. LC 92-60624. (Illus.). 176p. 1992. pap. 29.95 (0-88740-420-0) Schiffer.

Pardes, Herbert, jt. ed. see Pincus, Harold A.

Pardes, Ilana. Countertraditions in the Bible: A Feminist Approach. 1992. 32.00 (0-674-17542-5) HUP.

— Countertraditions in the Bible: A Feminist Approach. 194p. 1993. pap. 13.95 (0-674-17545-X) HUP.

— The Shulamite's Song: A Feminist Approach to the Bible. (Illus.). 240p. (C). 1992. text ed. 29.95 (0-674-80733-2) HUP.

Pardey, David. Marketing for Schools. (Kogan Page Educational Management Ser.). 238p. 1991. pap. 34.00 (0-7494-0464-7, Pub. by Kogan Page Educ UK) Taylor & Francis.

Pardey, Larry. Details of Classic Boat Construction. (Illus.). 1991. 75.00 (0-393-03323-6) Norton.

Pardey, Larry & Pardey, Lin. The Self-Sufficient Sailor. (Illus.). 1982. 30.00 (0-393-03269-8) Norton.

— Storm Tactic Handbook: Modern Methods of Heaving-to in Extreme Conditions. (Illus.). 156p. (Orig.). 1995. pap. 19.95 (0-9646036-6-7) Pardey Prods.

Pardey, Larry, jt. auth. see Pardey, Lin.

***Pardey, Lin & Pardey, Larry.** The Capable Cruiser. (Illus.). 400p. 1987. 32.00 (0-9646036-2-4) Pardey Prods.

— Cruising in Seraffyn. LC 76-19358. (Illus.). 192p. 1976. 16.95 (0-915160-19-6) Seven Seas.

— Cruising in Seraffyn. (Illus.). 192p. 1987. text ed. 16.60 (0-915160-87-0, 60333) Seven Seas.

— Cruising in Seraffyn. (Illus.). 192p. 1992. pap. 14.95 (0-924486-36-8) Sheridan.

— Seraffyn's Mediterranean Adventure. (Illus.). 256p. 1991. pap. 14.95 (0-924486-15-5) Sheridan.

Pardey, Lin, jt. auth. see Pardey, Larry.

Pardey, Lin, et al. The Care & Feeding of Sailing Crew. 2nd ed. (Illus.). 500p. 1995. 35.00 (0-393-03726-6) Norton.

PQ

An Asterisk (*) at the beginning of an entry indicates that the title is appearing in BIP for the first time.

Pardey, Philip G. & Roseboom, Johannes, eds. ISNAR Agricultural Research Indicator Series: A Global Database on National Agricultural Research Systems. (Illus.). (C). 1989. 89.95 (0-521-37368-9) Cambridge U Pr.

Pardey, Philip G., jt. auth. see Alston, Julian M.

Pardey, Philip G., et al, eds. Agricultural Research Policy: International Quantitative Perspectives. (Illus.). 484p. (C). 1991. 47.95 (0-521-40009-0) Cambridge U Pr.

Pardington, G. P. Studies in Christian Doctrine, 4 Vols. Schroeder, E. H., ed. 312p. 1964. pap. 3.99 (0-685-06470-0) Chr Pubns.

— Studies in Christian Doctrine, 4 Vols., 1. Schroeder, E. H., ed. 312p. 1964. write for info. (0-87509-135-0) Chr Pubns.

— Studies in Christian Doctrine, 4 Vols., 2. Schroeder, E. H., ed. 312p. 1964. write for info. (0-87509-136-9) Chr Pubns.

— Studies in Christian Doctrine, 4 Vols., 3. Schroeder, E. H., ed. 312p. 1964. write for info. (0-87509-137-7) Chr Pubns.

— Studies in Christian Doctrine, 4 Vols., 4. Schroeder, E. H., ed. 312p. 1964. write for info. (0-87509-138-5) Chr Pubns.

Pardington, George. La Crisis De la Vida Espiritual: The Crisis in the Spiritual Life. (SPA.). 4.25 (84-7228-960-5, 223027, Pub. by Edit Clie SP) TSELF.

— Estudios de Doctrina Cristiana: Lectures on Christian Doctrine. (SPA.). 6.95 (84-7228-982-6, 223049, Pub. by Edit Clie SP) TSELF.

Pardington, George P. The Crisis of the Deeper Life. LC 91-70910. 176p. 1991. 7.99 (0-87509-454-6) Chr Pubns.

— Outline Studies in Christian Doctrine. 370p. 1988. pap. 7.99 (0-87509-116-4) Chr Pubns.

Pardini, Alan & Lerner, Deborah. Health Promotion for Older Persons: A Selected Annotated Bibliography. 41p. 1986. write for info. (0-318-61575-4) US HHS.

Pardini, Alan & Mahoney, Connie. A Resource Guide for Fitness Programs for Older Persons. 115p. 1986. write for info. (0-318-61580-0) US HHS.

***Pardini, Jane C.** The Baby-Sitter Book: All the Information Your Baby-Sitter Must Have Before You Close the Door. (Illus.). 100p. (Orig.). Date not set. pap. write for info. (0-9642238-9-9) Partners Pub.

Pardo, Angel. Neomambi. LC 89-83445. (Coleccion Espejo de Paciencia Ser.). (Illus.). 94p. (Orig.). (SPA.). 1989. pap. 9.95 (0-89729-530-7) Ediciones.

Pardo, Antonio. Lecciones Basicus para la Formacion de Nuevos Creyentes (Basic Lessons for New Believers) 192p. (Orig.). (SPA.). 1992. pap. 5.95 (84-7645-556-9, Pub. by Edit Clie SP) TSELF.

Pardo Bazan, Emilia. The House of Ulloa: A Novel by Emilia Pardo Bazan. Caminals-Heath, Roser, tr. LC 91-12757. 352p. 1992. 35.00 (0-8203-1372-6) U of Ga Pr.

— Insolacion. (Nueva Austral Ser.: Vol. 25). (SPA.). 1991. pap. text ed. 24.95x (84-239-1825-4) Elliots Bks.

— Los Pazos de Ulloa. (SPA.). 1989. 9.95 (0-8288-2571-8) Fr & Eur.

— Pazos de Ulloa. 317p. (SPA.). 1984. 10.00 (0-8288-8586-9) Fr & Eur.

***Pardo, Bonnye G.** Intimate Encounters: Creating Healthy Relationships. 107p. (Orig.). 1991. pap. 10.00 (0-9645437-2-9) B G Pardo.

Pardo, Edmund. The Golden Years. 1980. 2.95 (0-935210-02-4) Dundee Pub.

Pardo, J. Joaquin. Catalogo de los Manuscritos Existentes en la Coleccion Latino Americana de la Biblioteca de la Universidad de Texas Relativos a la History de Centro America. 45p. 1988. reprint ed. pap. 6.50 (0-913129-19-4) La Tienda.

Pardo, Jose C., ed. Economic Effects of the European Expansion, 1492-1824. 512p. (Orig.). 1993. pap. 117.50 (3-515-06240-8) Coronet Bks.

***Pardo, Jose C. & Schneider, Friedrich, eds.** Current Issues in Public Choice. 1996. write for info. (1-85898-134-4, Pub. by E Elgar Pub UK) Ashgate Pub Co.

Pardo-Llada, Jose. Yo Me Acuerdo: Diccionario de Nostalgias Cubanas. LC 93-72254. (Coleccion Diccionarios Ser.). (Illus.). 256p. (SPA.). 1993. pap. 19.00 (0-89729-701-6) Ediciones.

Pardo-Maurer, R. The Contras, 1980-1989: A Special Kind of Politics. LC 90-44608. (Washington Papers: No. 147). 288p. 1990. text ed. 49.95 (0-275-93817-4, B3818, Praeger Pubs); pap. text ed. 12.95 (0-275-93818-2, C3817, Praeger Pubs) Greenwood.

Pardo-Maurer, R & Rodriguez, Judith. Access Mexico: Emerging Market Handbook & Directory. (Emerging Market Access Ser.). (Illus.). 650p. 1992. 239.00 (1-881765-00-8) Cambridge Data & Dev.

Pardo, Robert. Design, Testing, & Optimization of Trading Systems. LC 92-372. (Traders Library). 176p. 1992. text ed. 34.95 (0-471-55446-4) Wiley.

Pardo, William B. & Robertson, Harry S., eds. Plasma Instabilities & Anomalous Transport. LC 66-25666. (Illus.). 1966. pap. 5.95 (0-87024-064-1) U of Miami Pr.

Pardoe, Alan. A Practical Guide for Employer & Employee to the Industrial Relations Act, 1971. xx, 319p. 1972. pap. text ed. 6.50 (0-85308-024-0) Rothman.

***Pardoe, Blain & Bradygames Staff.** Official Veteran Pilots' Guide to Wing Commander 3. (Illus.). 208p. (Orig.). 1995. pap. text ed. 19.99 (1-56686-238-8) Brady Compu Bks.

***Pardoe, Blaine.** The Lemmings Chronicles: Official Strategy Guide. (Illus.). 228p. (Orig.). 1995. pap. text ed. 19.99 (1-56686-245-0) Brady Compu Bks.

***Pardoe, Blaine L.** Highlander Gambit. (Battletech Ser.: No. 18). 288p. (Orig.). 1995. mass mkt. 4.99 (0-451-45381-6, ROC) NAL-Dutton.

Pardoe, E. F. Communication in Writing. 1965. 44.00 (0-08-011136-X, Pub. by Pergamon Repr UK) Franklin.

Pardoe, G., et al. Technology & the Future of Europe. 162p. 1993. pap. 25.00 (92-826-4626-2, CD-NA-14456-EN-, Pub. by Europ Com) UNIPUB.

Pardoe, G. K., ed. Remote Sensing: Proceedings of an EARSEL-ESA Symposium, Guildford, U. K., April 8-11. (Illus.). 64p. 1985. pap. 39.00 (0-08-032538-6, Pub. by PPL UK) Elsevier.

Pardoe, Geoffrey K., ed. Space Industry International. 353p. 1987. 155.00 (0-582-00314-8, 071053-99584) Longman.

Pardoe, Jenifer. How Many Times Can You Say Goodbye? 112p. (Orig.). 1992. pap. text ed. 6.95 (0-8146-2109-0) Liturgical Pr.

Pardoe, Julia. The City of the Sultan: And Domestic Manners of the Turks in 1836, 2 vols., Set. LC 77-87633. reprint ed. 45.00 (0-404-16540-0) AMS Pr.

Pardoe, T. D. & Wenig, R. P. Data Communications & Networking Dictionary. LC 91-38380. 155p. 1992. pap. 12.00 (1-878956-06-X) CBM Bks.

Pardoe, T. Earl. Pantomimes for Stage & Study. LC 73-173118. 1972. reprint ed. 29.95 (0-405-08833-7, Pub. by Blom Pubns UK) Ayer.

Pardoen, Alan, ed. see Boyle, Patrick G.

Pardoen, Gerald C., ed. Recent Advances in Structural Dynamics. (Sessions Proceedings Ser.). 53p. 1986. 12.00 (0-87262-530-3) Am Soc Civil Eng.

Pardon, William. Local Surgery & the Exact Sequence of a Localization for Wall Groups. LC 77-11963. (Memoirs Ser.: No. 12/196). 171p. 1977. pap. 22.00 (0-8218-2196-2, MEMO 12/196) Am Math.

Pardoux, E., jt. ed. see Metivier, Michel.

Pardridge, William M. Peptide Drug Delivery to the Brain. 368p. 1991. 138.50 (0-88167-793-0) Raven.

Pardridge, William M., ed. The Blood-Brain Barrier: Cellular & Molecular Biology. LC 92-48543. 496p. 1993. 95.00 (0-7817-0015-9) Raven.

Pardthaisong, Tieng. Factors in the Achievement of Below Replacement Fertility in Chiang Mai, Thailand. LC 86-4584. (Papers of the East-West Population Institute: No. 96). (Illus.). viii, 46p. (Orig.). 1986. pap. 3.00 (0-86638-074-4) EW Ctr HI.

***Parducci, Allen.** Happiness, Pleasure, & Judgment: The Contextual Theory & Its Applications. 232p. 1995. text ed. 45.00 (0-8058-1891-X) L Erlbaum Assocs.

Parducci, Allen, jt. ed. see Sarris, Viktor.

Pardue, Diana. Chispas!: Cultural Warriors of New Mexico, February 15, 1992-April 25, 1993: Eppie Archuleta, Teresa Archuleta-Sagel, Charles Carrillo, Marie Romero Cash, Juanita Jaramillo-Lavadie, Felix Lopez et al. Brennan, Mary, ed. (Illus.). 34p. (Orig.). 1992. pap. 6.95 (0-934351-34-1) Heard Mus.

Pardue, Harry L., jt. auth. see Bodner, George M.

***Pardue, Lisa D.** Let's Take a Wingwalk. (Illus.). 48p. (Orig.). 1994. pap. 8.99 (1-877633-25-9) Luthers.

Pardun, Robert. The Steel Fabricator's Handbook. (Illus.). 99p. (Orig.). 1991. student ed, spiral bd. 9.50 (0-9630780-0-3) Pardun Pub.

Pare, jt. auth. see Makkai.

Pare, Ambroise. An Explanation of the Fashion & Use of Instruments of Chirurgery. Crooke, H., tr. LC 75-26045. (English Experience Ser.: No. 141). 64p. 1969. reprint ed. 35.00 (90-221-0141-X) Walter J Johnson.

— Life & Time of Ambroise Pare. Packard, Francis R., ed. LC 79-160607. (Illus.). 1972. reprint ed. 23.95 (0-405-08834-5, Pub. by Blom Pubns UK) Ayer.

— On Monsters & Marvels. Pallister, Janis L., tr. LC 81-16297. (Illus.). 280p. (C). 1983. pap. 14.95 (0-226-64563-0) U Ch Pr.

Pare, C., jt. auth. see Marks, J.

Pare, Eugene G. & Shook, Micheal. Computer Graphics Project for Design & Descriptive Geometry. 149p. (C). 1986. pap. write for info. (0-02-390980-3) Macmillan.

Pare, Eugene G., et al. Descriptive Geometry. 8th ed. 1991. Workshop with Comp Graph, Ser. B. write for info. (0-318-68104-8); Workshop with Comp Graph, Ser. A. write for info. (0-318-68105-6) Macmillan.

— Descriptive Geometry. 8th ed. 464p. (C). 1991. write for info. (0-02-391331-2) Macmillan.

— Descriptive Geometry: Worksheets with Computer Graphics. 8th ed. 160p. (C). 1991. Series A. pap. write for info. (0-02-390951-X); Series B. pap. write for info. (0-02-391301-0) Macmillan.

Pare, George. The Catholic Church in Detroit, 1701-1888. LC 83-67420. 733p. 1983. pap. 24.95 (0-8143-1758-8) Wayne St U Pr.

Pare, J. A. & Fraser, Robert G. Synopsis of Diseases of the Chest. 2nd rev. ed. LC 93-25873. (Illus.). 732p. 1993. reprint ed. text ed. 92.50 (0-7216-3669-1) Saunders.

Pare, J. A., jt. auth. see Fraser, Robert G.

Pare, J A., jt. auth. see Zagelbaum, Gary L.

***Pare, Michael A.** Sports Stars. LC 94-21835. (J). 1994. 38.00 (0-8103-9859-1) Gale.

— Sports Stars, Vol. 1. LC 94-21835. 1994. write for info. (0-8103-9860-5, UXL) Gale.

— Sports Stars, Vol. 2. LC 94-21835. 1994. write for info. (0-8103-9861-3, UXL) Gale.

Pare, Paul, jt. auth. see Kasenow, Michael.

Pare, R. Circus Days. (Illus.). 24p. (J). (ps-8). 1988. lib. bdg. 14.95 (1-55037-021-9, Pub. by Annick CN); pap. 4.95 (1-55037-020-0, Pub. by Annick CN) Firefly Bks Ltd.

— A Friend Like You. (Illus.). 24p. (J). (ps-8). 1984. 12.95 (0-920303-04-8, Pub. by Annick CN); pap. 4.95 (0-920303-05-6, Pub. by Annick CN) Firefly Bks Ltd.

— Play Time. (Illus.). 24p. (J). (ps-8). 1988. 12.95 (1-55037-087-1, Pub. by Annick CN); pap. 4.95 (1-55037-086-3, Pub. by Annick CN) Firefly Bks Ltd.

— Summer Days. (Illus.). 24p. (J). (ps-8). 1988. 12.95 (1-55037-043-X, Pub. by Annick CN); pap. 4.95 (1-55037-044-8, Pub. by Annick CN) Firefly Bks Ltd.

Pare, Richard. Photography & Architecture: Eighteen Thirty-Nine to Nineteen Thirty-Nine. (Illus.). 282p. 1985. reprint ed. 75.00 (0-262-16101-X) MIT Pr.

Pare, Richard, pref. Roger Fenton. (Masters of Photography Ser.: Vol. 4). (Illus.). 96p. 1988. 19.95 (0-89381-270-6); pap. 12.95 (0-89381-271-4) Aperture.

Pare, Roger. L' Alphabet: A Child's Introduction to the Letters & Sounds of French. (Illus.). 32p. (J). 1991. 7.95 (0-8442-1395-0, Natl Textbk) NTC Pub Grp.

— Animal Capers. (Illus.). 24p. (J). 1992. lib. bdg. 14.95 (1-55037-243-2, Pub. by Annick CN); pap. 4.95 (1-55037-244-0, Pub. by Annick CN) Firefly Bks Ltd.

— The Annick ABC. (Annick Press Ser.: Series 6). (Illus.). 24p. (J). (ps-2). 1989. pap. 0.99 (0-920303-78-1, Pub. by Annick CN) Firefly Bks Ltd.

— A Friend Like You. (Annick Press Ser.: Series 6). (Illus.). 24p. (J). (ps-2). 1989. pap. 0.99 (0-920303-80-3, Pub. by Annick CN) Firefly Bks Ltd.

— Winter Games. (Illus.). 24p. (J). 1991. lib. bdg. 14.95 (1-55037-187-8, Pub. by Annick CN); pap. 4.95 (1-55037-184-3, Pub. by Annick CN) Firefly Bks Ltd.

Pare, William. Co-Operative Agriculture. LC 76-47884. reprint ed. 29.00 (0-685-00375-2) AMS Pr.

***Paredaens, J. & Tenenbaum, L., eds.** Advances in Database Systems. (CISM International Centre for Mechanical Sciences Ser.: Vol. 347). 377p. 1994. pap. 85.00 (3-211-82614-9) Spr-Verlag.

Paredes, Alfonso, et al, eds. Cocaine: Physiological & Physiopathological Effects. LC 92-19390. (Journal of Addictive Diseases: Vol. 11, No. 4). (Illus.). 120p. 1993. 29.95 (1-56024-311-2) Haworth Pr.

Paredes, Americo. Between Two Worlds. LC 90-38832. 144p. (Orig.). 1991. pap. 7.00 (1-55885-022-8) Arte Publico.

— Folklore & Culture on the Texas-Mexican Border. Bauman, Richard, ed. 288p. 1993. 34.95 (0-292-72472-1, Ctr Mex Am Stud) U of Tex Pr.

— Folklore & Culture on the Texas-Mexican Border. Bauman, Richard, ed. (Illus.). 317p. 1995. pap. 18.95 (0-292-76564-9) U of Tex Pr.

— George Washington Gomez. LC 89-48145. 302p. (Orig.). 1990. text ed. 9.50 (1-55885-012-0) Arte Publico.

— The Hammon & the Beans. LC 93-45644. 1994. 9.95 (0-685-72613-4) Arte Publico.

— The Hammon & the Beans & Other Stories. LC 93-45644. 220p. 1994. pap. 9.95 (1-55885-071-6) Arte Publico.

— Mexican-American Authors. Adams, William, ed. (Multi-Ethnic Literature Ser.). (gr. 9-12). 1976. pap. 18.32 (0-395-24041-7); teacher ed 8.24 (0-685-02295-1) HM.

— A Texas-Mexican Cancionero: Folksongs of the Lower Border. (Illus.). 218p. (SPA.). 1995. pap. 10.95 (0-292-76558-4) U of Tex Pr.

— With His Pistol in His Hand: A Border Ballad & Its Hero. (Illus.). 275p. 1958. pap. 9.95 (0-292-70128-4) U of Tex Pr.

Paredes, Americo, comp. Uncle Remus Con Chile. LC 92-14986. 200p. 1992. 12.00 (1-55885-053-8) Arte Publico.

Paredes, Americo, ed. Humanidad: Essays in Honor of George I. Sanchez. (Monograph: No. 6). 144p. 1977. pap. 5.95 (0-89551-007-3) UCLA Chicano Studies.

Paredes, Carlos & Sachs, Jeffrey D., eds. Peru's Path to Recovery: A Plan for Economic Stabilization & Growth. 336p. 1991. 39.95 (0-8157-6914-8); pap. 19.95 (0-8157-6913-X) Brookings.

Paredes, J. Anthony, ed. Indians of the Southeastern United States in the Late Twentieth Century. 256p. (C). 1992. pap. 21.95 (0-8173-0534-3) U of Ala Pr.

Paredes, Joseph. Mary & the Kingdom of God: A Synthesis of Mariology. (C). 1990. 49.00 (0-85439-379-X, Pub. by St Paul Pubns UK) St Mut.

Paredes, Laura E., tr. see Grant, Wilson.

Paredes-Lopez, Octavio, ed. Amaranth: Biology, Chemistry, & Technology. LC 93-36812. 1994. write for info. (0-8493-5374-2) CRC Pr.

Paredes, Raymund, jt. ed. see Romo, Ricardo.

***Paredes, Ricardo & Riveros, Luis A., eds.** Human Resources & the Adjustment Process. (Inter-American Development Bank Ser.). 204p. (Orig.). 1994. 18.50x (0-940602-90-3) IADB.

Paredes, Ruby R., ed. Philippine Colonial Democracy. LC 87-51575. (Monograph Ser.: No. 32). (Illus.). 166p. 1989. pap. 15.00 (0-938692-34-8) Yale U SE Asia.

Paredi, Angela. St. Ambrose: His Life & Times. LC 63-19325. 495p. reprint ed. pap. 141.10 (0-317-26143-6, 2024372) Bks Demand.

***Pareek, Udai.** Beyond Management: Essays on Institution Building & Related Topics. 2nd ed. 446p. 1994. text ed. 34.50 (81-204-0902-7, Pub. by Oxford & IBH Pubng II) Science Pubs.

Pareek, Udai, jt. auth. see Lynton, Rolf P.

Pareek, Udai, jt. ed. see Lynton, Rolf P.

Parekh. Reverse Osmosis Technology: Applications of High-Purity-Water Production. (Chemical Industries Ser.: Vol. 35). 536p. 1988. 175.00 (0-8247-7985-1) Dekker.

Parekh, B. C., jt. ed. see King, Preston T.

Parekh, B. K. & Groppo, J. G., eds. Processing of Utilization of High-Sulfur Coals 5. (Coal Science & Technology Ser.: Vol. 21). 638p. 1993. 388.50 (0-444-81476-0) Elsevier.

Parekh, Bhikhu. Colonialism, Tradition & Reform: An Analysis of Gandhi's Political Discourse. 288p. (C). 1989. text ed. 24.00 (0-8039-9605-5) Sage.

— Marx's Theory of Ideology. LC 81-48079. 256p. 1982. text ed. 36.50 (0-8018-2771-X) Johns Hopkins.

Parekh, Bhikhu, ed. Jeremy Bentham: Critical Assessments, 2 vols., Set. LC 92-21151. (Critical Assessments of Leading Political Philosophers Ser.). 2672p. 1993. 530.00 (0-415-04654-8, B2382, Routledge NY) Routledge.

Parekh, Bhikhu, jt. auth. see Baxi Upendra.

Parekh, Bhikhu, jt. ed. see Pieterse, Jan N.

Parekh, Bhikhu, jt. ed. see Pieterse, Jan.

Parekh, Bhikhu C., ed. Jeremy Bentham: Ten Critical Essays. 204p. 1974. 32.00 (0-7146-2959-6, Pub. by F Cass Pubs UK) Intl Spec Bk.

***Parekh, D. E., ed.** Turbulence Control. LC 94-71667. (Fluid Engineering Division Conference Ser.: Vol. 193). 63p. 1994. pap. 25.00 (0-7918-1376-2) ASME.

Parekh, D. E. & Morris, M. J., eds. Turbulent Mixing 1993. LC 93-73259. 77p. Date not set. pap. 35.00 (0-7918-1023-2) ASME.

Parekh, M. P., et al, eds. Nehru & India's Labour Movement. (C). 1991. text ed. 16.00 (81-204-0581-1, Pub. by Oxford IBH II) S Asia.

Parekh, R., jt. auth. see Fowler, M.

Parekh, S. I., jt. auth. see Barton, Derek H.

Parel, A. J. & Keith, R. C. Comparative Political Philosophy: Studies under the Upas Tree. 260p. (C). 1992. 29.95 (0-8039-9412-5); pap. 14.95 (0-8039-9413-3) Sage.

Parel, Anthony, ed. The Political Calculus: Essays on Machiavelli's Philosophy. LC 77-185729. 232p. reprint ed. pap. 66.20 (0-317-07879-8, 2014330) Bks Demand.

Parel, Anthony J. The Machiavellian Cosmos. 216p. (C). 1992. text ed. 32.50 (0-300-05169-7) Yale U Pr.

Parel, J., ed. Ophthalmic Technologies II. 1992. 77.00 (0-8194-0790-9, 1644) SPIE.

Pareles, Jon, ed. see Rolling Stone Press Staff.

Parella, Frederick J., jt. ed. see Bulman, Raymond F.

Parella, Robert E. & Miller, Joel E. Modern Trust Forms & Checklists. 1990. Supplemented semi-annually. 170.00 (0-88262-275-7) Warren Gorham & Lamont.

— Modern Trust Forms & Checklists, No. 1. suppl. ed. 1992. 93.00 (0-7913-1182-1) Warren Gorham & Lamont.

— Modern Trust Forms & Checklists, No. 2. suppl. ed. 1992. 97.00 (0-685-32294-7) Warren Gorham & Lamont.

Parelli, Pat & Kadash, Kathy. Natural Horsemanship. (Illus.). 223p. (Orig.). 1993. pap. 14.95 (0-911647-27-9) Western Horseman.

Parelli, Robert. Medicolegal Issues for Radiographers. 2nd ed. 188p. (C). 1994. pap. text ed. 23.95 (1-881795-07-1) Eastwind Pub.

Parelli, Robert J. An Analysis of Fluoroscopic Principles, Image Intensification, & Television Systems: Workbook & Laboratory Manual. 115p. (C). 1991. text ed. 35.00 (1-880359-00-6) Par Rad.

— Basic Principles of Fluoroscopic Image Intensifier & Television Systems, Set, Vols. I & II. 175p. 1993. pap. text ed. 35.00 (1-880359-07-3) Par Rad.

— Medicolegal Issues for Radiographers. 115p. (C). 1991. pap. text ed. 23.95 (0-9628440-2-0) Eastwind Pub.

— Radiographic Technique: Laboratory Manual. 79p. (C). 1990. text ed. 18.95 (1-880359-01-4) Par Rad.

— Radiologic Technology Clinical Manual. 282p. (C). 1991. text ed. 52.95 (1-880359-04-9) Par Rad.

— Radiology Physics - Electronics: Student Workbook. 101p. (C). 1992. pap. text ed. 15.95 (1-880359-06-5) Par Rad.

— Radiology Technology Clinical Manual. 325p. (C). 1993. pap. text ed. write for info. (1-881795-01-2) Eastwind Pub.

Parelli, Robert J., jt. auth. see Ross, Lynn.

Parello, Anthony. The Ultimate Guide to Scales. 2nd ed. LC 92-93279. 96p. (Orig.). 1992. 14.95 (0-9632995-0-6); text ed. 12.95 (0-9632995-2-2); lib. bdg. 13.95 (0-9632995-1-4); pap. 9.95 (0-9632995-3-0); pap. text ed. 10.95 (0-9632995-4-9) Theory Guides.

Parelskin, Debra M., jt. auth. see Silber, Kathleen.

Parens, Henri. Aggression in Our Children: Coping with It Constructively. LC 87-19547. 224p. 1993. pap. 25.00x (1-56821-076-0) Aronson.

— The Development of Aggression in Early Childhood. LC 94-41957. 426p. 1995. pap. 35.00 (1-56821-441-3) Aronson.

Parens, Henri & Kramer, Selma, eds. Prevention in Mental Health. LC 93-19429. 232p. 1993. pap. 27.50 (1-56821-027-2) Aronson.

Parens, Henri, jt. ed. see Akhtar, Salman.

***Parens, Joshua.** Metaphysics As Rhetoric: Alfarabi's Summary of Plato's "Laws" (Middle Eastern Studies). 224p. 1995. text ed. 54.50x (0-7914-2573-8); pap. 17.95x (0-7914-2574-6) State U NY Pr.

Parent. Comparative Biology of the Normal Lung. 1992. 163.95 (0-8493-8839-2, RC732) CRC Pr.

— Texas. 1995. 39.95 (1-55868-202-3) Gr Arts Ctr Pub.

***Parent, Andre.** Human Neuroanatomy. 9th ed. LC 94-40506. 1995. write for info. (0-683-06752-4) Williams & Wilkins.

Parent-Child Nursing Department. Empty Arms & Aching Hearts. Laprise, Susan et al, eds. (Illus.). 16p. (Orig.). 1987. reprint ed. pap. 2.50 (0-9615491-6-5) Loma Linda U.

Parent, D. P. Exercises in Number Theory. Cole, M., tr. (Problem Books in Mathematics). x, 542p. 1984. 56.00 (0-387-96063-5) Spr-Verlag.

Parent, David J., tr. see Landauer, Gustav.

Parent, David J., ed. see Landmann, Michael.

Parent, David J., tr. see Landmann, Michael.

Parent, David J., tr. see Neumayr, Anton.

Parent, David J., tr. see Schutz, Alfred & Luckmann, Thomas.

Parent-Duchatelet, Alexandre J. Prostitution in Paris, Considered Morally, Politically, & Medically: Prepared for Philanthropists & Legislators from Statistical Documents. LC 72-9671. reprint ed. 37.50 (0-404-57488-2) AMS Pr.

Parent, Edward A., jt. auth. see Gaunt, Larene.

Parent, Frederick, jt. auth. see Rundquist, Thomas J.

Parent, Gail, et al. What's Stopped Happening to Me? 1990. 12.00 (0-8184-0522-8, L Stuart) Carol Pub Group.

An Asterisk (*) at the beginning of an entry indicates that the title is appearing in BIP for the first time.

Parent, J. D. Storage of Natural Gas As Hydrate. (Research Bulletin Ser.: No. 1). iv, 40p. 1948. 2.50 (0-317-56708-X) Inst Gas Tech.

Parent, J. D. & Katz, S. Equilibrium Compositions & Enthalpy Changes for the Reactions of Carbon, Oxygen & Steam. (Research Bulletin Ser.: No. 2). vi, 110p. 1948. 10.00 (0-317-56764-0) Inst Gas Tech.

Parent, J. D., jt. auth. see Bloomer, O. T.

Parent, Joseph D. A Survey of United States & Total World Production, Proved Reserves, & Remaining Recoverable Resources of Fossil Fuels & Uranium, as of December 31, 1982. xviii, 250p. 1984. 30.00 (0-910091-52-8) Inst Gas Tech.

Parent, Laurence. The Hiker's Guide to New Mexico. (Falcon Guide Ser.). (Illus.). 200p. 1991. pap. 12.95 (1-56044-064-3) Falcon Pr MT.

— The Hiker's Guide to Texas. Bates, Malcolm, ed. (Falcon Guide Ser.). (Illus.). 200p. (Orig.). 1992. pap. 12.95 (1-56044-102-X) Falcon Pr MT.

— New Mexico Scenic Drives. LC 94-1355. (FalconGuide Ser.). 160p. (Orig.). 1994. pap. 12.95 (1-56044-259-X) Falcon Pr MT.

— Sights & Scenes of Texas: Austin. 64p. 1995. 7.95 (0-88719-260-2) Gulf Pub.

— Sights & Scenes of Texas: Hill Country. 64p. 1995. 7.95 (0-88719-262-9) Gulf Pub.

— The Texas Hill Country: A Postcard Book. (Illus.). 48p. (Orig.). 1992. pap. 8.95 (0-9634758-0-0) L Parent Photo.

— Texas Scenic Drives. (Illus.). 184p. (Orig.). 1995. pap. 14. 95 (1-56044-339-1) Falcon Pr MT.

***Parent, Laurence, photos & text.** Austin. LC 94-43909. (Texas Monthly Sights & Scenes Ser.). 64p. 1995. pap. 7.95 (0-87719-260-X, 9260) Gulf Pub.

— The Hill Country. LC 94-43862. (Texas Monthly Sights & Scenes Ser.). (Illus.). 1995. write for info. (0-87719-262-6, 9262) Gulf Pub.

Parent, Laurence E. Big Thicket National Preserve. Priehs, T. J. & Foreman, Ronald J., eds. LC 92-62154. 16p. (Orig.). 1993. pap. 2.95 (1-877856-21-5) SW Pks Mnmts.

— Capulin Volcano National Monument. Priehs, T. J. & Jorgen, Randolph, eds. LC 91-60463. (Illus.). 16p. (Orig.). (YA). 1991. pap. 2.95 (0-911408-94-0) SW Pks Mnmts.

— Chickasaw National Recreation Area. Foreman, Ronald J. & Scott, Sandra, eds. LC 92-62474. (Illus.). 16p. (Orig.). 1993. pap. 2.95 (1-877856-28-2) SW Pks Mnmts.

— Chiricahua National Monument. Scott, Sandra & Priehs, T. J., eds. LC 93-86935. (Illus.). 16p. (Orig.). (YA). 1994. pap. 2.95 (1-877856-41-X) SW Pks Mnmts.

— Gila Cliff Dwellings National Monument. Jorgen, Randolph & Foreman, Ronald J., eds. LC 91-60461. (Illus.). 16p. (Orig.). (YA). 1992. pap. 2.95 (0-911408-96-7) SW Pks Mnmts.

— Lake Meredith National Recreation Area. Foreman, Ronald J. & Scott, Sandra, eds. LC 92-62160. (Illus.). 16p. (Orig.). (YA). 1993. pap. 2.95 (1-877856-16-9) SW Pks Mnmts.

Parent, Len, jt. auth. see Williams, Anna F.

Parent, Michel & Laurgeau, Claude. Robot Technology: Logic & Programming, Vol. 5. (Illus.). 192p. (C). 1985. text ed. 66.00 (0-13-782178-6) P-H.

Parent, Neil A., ed. Serving Life & Faith: Adult Religious Education & the American Catholic Community. 72p. 1986. pap. 6.95 (1-55586-982-3) US Catholic.

Parent, Phil, frwd. Public Works Guide to Automated Mapping & Facilities Management. (Special Report Ser.: No. 64). (Illus.). 167p. (Orig.). 1992. pap. text ed. 75.00 (0-917084-40-3) Am Public Works.

Parent, Remi. A Church of the Baptized: Overcoming Tension Between the Clergy & the Laity. Andt, Stephen W., tr. 1989. pap. 12.95 (0-8091-3076-9) Paulist Pr.

Parent, Richard. In Heavenly Places. LC 93-61524. 64p. (Orig.). pap. 5.95 (0-945383-48-7) Teach Servs.

Parent, Shaun. North of Superior Orient Bay Ice Climber's Guide. Hynek, Don, ed. (Illus.). 104p. (Orig.). 1993. pap. write for info. (0-9619571-3-1) Granite WI.

***Parent, Sylvain.** Dictionnaire des Science de l'Environnement Terminologie. 748p. (ENG & FRE.). 1991. 95.00 (0-7859-7911-5, 2700211065) Fr & Eur.

Parent, Wayne, jt. ed. see Perry, Huey L.

Parent, Wendy S., et al. Vocational Integration Index. 112p. 1992. pap. 48.00 (0-9626521-9-9) PRO-ED.

— Vocational Integration Index: Measuring Integration of Workers with Disabilities. LC 94-40055. 1995. write for info. (0-89079-659-9) PRO-ED.

Parent, William, ed. see Thomson, Judith J.

Parent, William A., jt. ed. see Meyer, Michael J.

Parente, Audrey. Pulp Man's Odyssey: The Hugh B. Cave Story. LC 87-26706. (Starmont Popular Culture Studies: Vol. 6). xiv, 146p. 1988. 27.00x (1-55742-039-4); pap. 17.00x (1-55742-038-6) Borgo Pr.

— Pulpmaster: The Theodore Roscoe Story. (Starmont Popular Culture Studies: No. 13). xvi, 173p. 1992. 29. 00x (1-55742-170-6); pap. 19.00x (1-55742-169-2) Borgo Pr.

Parente Cunha, Helena. Woman Between Mirrors. Ellison, Fred P. & Lindstrom, Naomi, trs. LC 89-14613. (Texas Pan American Ser.). 144p. 1989. pap. 10.95 (0-292-79052-X) U of Tex Pr.

***Parente, Diane & Petersen, Stephanie.** Mastering Your Professional Image: Dressing to Enhance Your Credibility. Johnson, Karen, ed. (Illus.). 160p. (Orig.). 1995. pap. write for info. (0-9646688-0-7) Image Dev & Mgt.

Parente, Diane, jt. auth. see Parsons, Alyce.

Parente, Fausto, ed. see Smith, Morton.

Parente, James A. & Schade, Richard E., eds. Studies in German & Scandinavian Literature after 1500: A Festschrift in Honor of George C. Schoolfield. (Studies in German Literature, Linguistics & Culture). 500p. 1993. 65.00 (1-879751-23-2) Camden Hse.

Parente, James A., Jr., et al. Literary Culture in the Holy Roman Empire, 1555-1720. LC 90-12891. (Germanic Languages & Literatures Ser.: No. 113). (Illus.). xiv, 292p. (C). 1991. 37.50 (0-8078-8113-9) U of NC Pr.

Parente, Pascal P. Beyond Space. 1977. reprint ed. pap. 7.00 (0-89555-053-9) TAN Bks Pubs.

— City on a Mountain - Padre Pio. Orig. Title: Padre Pio. 154p. 1968. pap. 4.95 (0-911988-35-1) AMI Pr.

Parente, Rick & Anderson-Parente, Janet K. Retraining Memory Techniques & Applications. (Illus.). (C). 1991. 49.95 (0-945541-02-3) CSY Pub Inc.

Parenteau, John. Prisoner for Peace: Aang San Suu Kyi & Burma's Struggle for Democracy. LC 94-4100. (Champions of Freedom Ser.). (Illus.). 160p. (YA). (gr. 6 up). 1994. 18.95 (1-883846-05-6) M Reynolds.

Parenteral Drug Association Incorporated Staff. PDA International Conference on Liquid Borne Particle Inspection & Metrology: Conference Proceedings. Feldman, Marcy, ed. (Illus.). 662p. 1987. pap. text ed. 95.00 (0-939459-12-4) PDA.

Parenti, F., jt. auth. see Lancini, G.

Parenti, Marino, jt. auth. see Frati, Carlo.

***Parenti, Michael.** Against Empire. 256p. (Orig.). 1995. pap. text ed. 12.95 (0-87286-298-4) City Lights.

— Democracy for the Few. 384p. 1994. pap. text ed. 14.00 (0-312-05233-2) St Martin.

— Land of Idols: Political Mythology in America. 224p. 1993. pap. text ed. 14.00 (0-312-09497-3) St Martin.

— Power & Pluralism: A View from the Bottom. (Reprint Series in Social Sciences). (C). 1993. reprint ed. pap. text ed. 2.30 (0-8290-3569-9, PS-528) Irvington.

Parenti, Michael J. Ethnic & Political Attitudes. LC 74-17942. (Italian American Experience Ser.). 354p. 1979. 30.95 (0-405-06413-6) Ayer.

— Inventing Reality: Politics & the Mass Media. LC 85-61250. 320p. (Orig.). 1985. 16.95 (0-312-43473-1) St Martin.

— Land of Idols: Political Mythology in America. 304p. 1993. 22.95 (0-312-09841-3) St Martin.

— Make-Believe Media: Politics of Film & Television. 1991. 19.95 (0-312-05894-2) St Martin.

— Make-Believe Media: The Politics of Entertainment. LC 90-63541. 304p. (Orig.). (C). 1991. pap. text ed. 14.00 (0-312-05603-6) St Martin.

— The Sword & the Dollar. 240p. 1988. 16.95 (0-312-02295-6) St Martin.

— The Sword & the Dollar: Imperialism, Revolution & the Arms Race. LC 88-60536. 206p. (Orig.). (C). 1988. pap. text ed. 14.00 (0-312-01167-9) St Martin.

Parenti, Umberto. Diccionario de Zoologia. 3rd ed. 244p. (SPA.). 1982. 29.95 (0-8288-2390-1, S50257) Fr & Eur.

Parents Magazine Editors. Parents Book for Raising a Healthy Child. (Orig.). 1987. pap. 3.95 (0-345-31430-1) Ballantine.

— Parents Book of Pregnancy & Birth. 352p. (Orig.). 1984. mass mkt. 4.99 (0-345-30446-2) Ballantine.

Parents Magazine Editors, jt. auth. see Kelly, Martin.

Parer, Julian T. Handbook of Fetal Heart Rate Monitoring. (Illus.). 240p. 1983. pap. text ed. 47.95 (0-7216-7071-7) Saunders.

Parer, Julian T., jt. ed. see Nathanielsz, Peter W.

Pares, Bearnard. History of Russia. 1992. 24.95 (0-88029-665-8) Marboro Bks.

Pares, Bernard. The Fall of the Russian Monarchy: A Study of Evidence. LC 83-45831. reprint ed. 47.50 (0-404-20196-2) AMS Pr.

— A History of Russia. LC 77-78308. (Illus.). 688p. reprint ed. write for info. (0-404-15122-1) AMS Pr.

— My Russian Memoirs. LC 78-96471. reprint ed. write for info. (0-404-04878-1) AMS Pr.

— Russia & Reform. LC 73-849. (Russian Studies: Perspectives on the Revolution). 576p. 1981. reprint ed. 41.25 (0-88355-046-6) Hyperion Conn.

Pares, Bernard, tr. see Krylov, Ivan A.

Pares, Richard. Colonial Blockade & Neutral Rights 1739-1763. LC 75-25796. (Perspectives in European History Ser.: No. 10). vii, 323p. 1975. reprint ed. lib. bdg. 37.50 (0-87991-616-8) Porcupine Pr.

Pares, Richard & Taylor, Alan J., eds. Essays Presented to Sir Lewis Namier. LC 70-134124. (Essay Index Reprint Ser.). 1977. 36.95 (0-8369-2010-4) Ayer.

Pares, Susan, jt. auth. see Hoare, James.

Pareschi, Remo, jt. ed. see Tokor, Mario.

Paret, P. Lautrec: Women. (Rhythem & Color Two Ser.). 1970. 9.95 (0-8288-9520-1) Fr & Eur.

Paret, Peter. Art as History: Episodes in the Culture & Politics of Nineteenth-Century Germany. 240p. 1989. text ed. 37.50 (0-691-05541-6) Princeton U Pr.

— The Berlin Secession: Modernism & Its Enemies in Imperial Germany. (Illus.). 279p. 1989. pap. text ed. 15. 95 (0-674-06774-6) Belknap Pr.

— Clausewitz & the State: The Man, His Theories, & His Times. LC 85-6570. 480p. 1985. pap. text ed. 18.95x (0-691-00806-X) Princeton U Pr.

— On Clausewitz & the History of War: Essays. 224p. 1992. text ed. 35.00 (0-691-03199-1) Princeton U Pr.

— Understanding War: Essays on Clausewitz & the History of Military Power. 239p. 1993. pap. text ed. 15.95 (0-691-00090-5) Princeton U Pr.

Paret, Peter, et al, eds. Makers of Modern Strategy from Machiavelli to the Nuclear Age. LC 85-17029. (Illus.). 944p. 1986. text ed. 79.50 (0-691-09235-4); pap. 19.95 (0-691-02764-1) Princeton U Pr.

Paret, Peter & Moran, Daniel, eds. Carl Von Clausewitz: Historical & Political Writings. Moran, Daniel, tr. (Illus.). 422p. 1992. text ed. 35.00 (0-691-03192-4) Princeton U Pr.

Paret, Peter, ed. see Clausewitz, Carl Von.

Paret, Peter, tr. see Meinecke, Friedrich.

Paret, Peter, tr. see Ritter, Gerhard.

Paret, Peter, ed. see Von Clausewitz, Claude.

Paret, Peter, tr. see Von Clausewitz, Claude.

Paret, Peter, et al. Persuasive Images: Posters of War & Revolution from the Archives of the Hoover Institution. (Illus.). 280p. 1992. 45.00 (0-691-03204-1) Princeton U Pr.

Pareto, Vilfredo. Compendium of General Sociology: Abridged in Italian with Approval of the Author by Giulio Farina from Pareto's Trattato di Sociologia Generale. Abbott, Elisabeth, ed. LC 79-24899. 517p. reprint ed. pap. 147.40 (0-7837-2928-6, 2057526) Bks Demand.

— Manuel D'Economie Politique. Bonnet, Alfred, tr. LC 79-108770. reprint ed. 55.00 (0-404-04879-X) AMS Pr.

— The Mind & Society, 4 vols., Set. Livingston, Arthur, ed. Bongiorno, Andrew, tr. LC 78-63704. (Studies in Fascism: Ideology & Practice). reprint ed. 300.00 (0-404-16990-2) AMS Pr.

— The Rise & Fall of Elites: An Application of Theoretical Sociology. 120p. (C). 1991. pap. 14.95 (0-88738-872-8) Transaction Pubs.

— The Rise & Fall of the Elites: An Application of Theoretical Sociology. Coser, Lewis A. & Powell, Walter W., eds. LC 79-7011. (Perennial Works in Sociology Ser.). 1980. reprint ed. lib. bdg. 19.95 (0-405-12110-5) Ayer.

— The Ruling Class in Italy Before 1900. LC 73-20130. 143p. 1975. reprint ed. 30.00 (0-86527-176-3) Fertig.

— The Transformation of Democracy. Powers, Charles, ed. Girola, Renata, tr. 128p. (Orig.). 1984. pap. 14.95 (0-87855-949-3) Transaction Pubs.

Paretsky, Sara. Bitter Medicine. 272p. 1988. mass mkt. 5.95 (0-345-34722-6) Ballantine.

— Blood Shot. 1989. mass mkt. 5.99 (0-440-20420-8) Dell.

— Blood Shot. large type ed. (General Ser.). 1989. 20.95 (0-8161-4775-2, Large Print Bks) Hall.

— Burn Marks. 1991. mass mkt. 5.99 (0-440-20845-9) Dell.

— Burn Marks. large type ed. (Large Print Books General Ser.). 533p. 1990. lib. bdg. 19.95 (0-8161-5004-4) G K Hall.

— Deadlock. 1992. mass mkt. 5.99 (0-440-21332-0) Dell.

— Deadlock: A V.I. Warshawski Mystery. large type ed. LC 92-38595. (General Ser.). 271p. 1993. 20.95 (0-8161-5561-5); pap. 17.95 (0-8161-5562-3) G K Hall.

— Guardian Angel. 1992. 20.00 (0-385-29931-1) Delacorte.

— Guardian Angel. 1993. mass mkt. 5.99 (0-440-21399-1) Dell.

— Guardian Angel. large type ed. LC 92-17881. (General Ser.). 544p. 1992. lib. bdg. 21.95 (0-8161-5541-0); pap. 16.95 (0-8161-5542-9) G K Hall.

— Indemnity Only. 1991. mass mkt. 5.99 (0-440-21069-0) Dell.

— Indemnity Only. large type ed. (General Ser.). 381p. 1992. 20.95 (0-8161-5455-4, Large Print Bks); pap. 16. 95 (0-8161-5456-2, Large Print Bks) Hall.

— Killing Orders. 1993. mass mkt. 5.99 (0-440-21528-5, Dell Trade Pbks) Dell.

— Killing Orders. large type ed. LC 93-13221. 1993. 21.95 (0-8161-5598-4); pap. 16.95 (0-8161-5599-2) Thorndike Pr.

— Three Complete Novels: Indemnity Only; Blood Shot; Burn Marks. LC 95-10833. 1995. 13.99 (0-517-14801-3, Pub. by Wings Bks) Random.

— Tunnel Vision. large type ed. LC 94-40740. (Large Print Book Ser.). 1994. pap. text ed. 22.95 (1-56895-084-5) Wheeler Pub.

— Tunnel Vision: A V. I. Warshawski Novel. 1995. mass mkt. (0-440-21752-0) Dell.

— Tunnell Vision. 1994. 21.95 (0-385-29932-X) Delacorte.

— Windy City Blues. LC 95-8302. 1995. write for info. (0-385-31502-3) Delacorte.

Paretsky, Sara, intro. A Woman's Eye: A Large Print Anthology. large type ed. (General Ser.). 569p. 1992. lib. bdg. 21.95 (0-8161-5457-0, Large Print Bks) Hall.

— A Woman's Eye: Twenty-One Stories. 1992. reprint ed. mass mkt. 5.99 (0-440-21335-5) Dell.

Paretsky, Zev. The Last Wagon Out. 1990. 10.95 (1-56062-052-8); pap. 7.95 (0-00-002845-2) CIS Comm.

Paretta, Joseph, ed. see Vollaro, Joseph.

Paretzky, Yvonne R. Guide to the London Insurance Market. LC 88-7344. 246p. reprint ed. pap. 70.20 (0-7837-4594-X, 2044313) Bks Demand.

Parezo, Nancy J. Navajo Sandpainting: From Religious Act to Commercial Art. LC 91-16956. (Illus.). 274p. 1991. reprint ed. pap. 19.95 (0-8263-1296-9) U of NM Pr.

Parezo, Nancy J., ed. Hidden Scholars: Women Anthropologists & the Native American Southwest. LC 93-9994. 451p. 1993. 47.50x (0-8263-1428-7) U of NM Pr.

Parezo, Nancy J., et al. Southwest Native American Visual Arts, Crafts & Material Culture: A Resource Guide, Set. LC 90-21395. (Studies in Ethnic Art: Vols. 1 & 2). 1520p. 1991. 165.00 (0-8240-7093-3) Garland.

Parfaict, Claude, jt. auth. see Parfaict, Francois.

Parfaict, Francois & Parfaict, Claude. Histoire de l'Ancien Theatre Italien: Depuis son Origine en France Jusqu'a sa Suppression en l'Annee 1697. LC 76-43932. (Music & Theatre in France in the 17th & 18th Centuries Ser.). reprint ed. 62.50 (0-404-60178-2) AMS Pr.

— Memoires pour Servir a l'Histoire des Spectacles de la Foire, 2 vols. in 1. LC 76-43933. (Music & Theatre in France in the 17th & 18th Centuries Ser.). reprint ed. 72.50 (0-404-60179-0) AMS Pr.

Parfenov, B. G., et al. Corrosion of Zirconium & Zirconium Alloys. 188p. 1969. text ed. 49.00 (0-685-13634-5, Pub. by Keter Pub IS) Coronet Bks.

Parfionovitch, Yuri, et al, eds. Tibetan Medical Paintings: Illustrations of the Blue Beryl Treatise of Sangye Gyamtso (1653-1705), Set, Vols. I & II. (Illus.). 1992. Set. boxed 195.00 (0-8109-3861-8) Mosby Yr Bk.

Parfit, Derek. Reasons & Persons. (Illus.). 543p. 1986. pap. text ed. 26.00 (0-19-824908-X) OUP.

Parfit, Michael. South Light. large type ed. 400p. 1992. 23. 95 (0-7089-8627-7, Trail West Pubs) Ulverscroft.

***Parfitt.** New Living Qabalah. 1995. pap. text ed. 15.95 (1-85230-682-3) Element MA.

Parfitt & Patsis. Organic Coatings: Science & Technology, Vol. 7. 432p. 1984. 185.00 (0-8247-7242-3) Dekker.

— Organic Coatings, Science & Technology, Vol. 8. 552p. 1986. 190.00 (0-8247-7486-8) Dekker.

Parfitt, jt. auth. see Eicke.

Parfitt, Clara M. In Love to Him: Reaching out in Love to Them. 149p. 1985. pap. 4.95 (0-88144-050-7) Christian Pub.

Parfitt, Geoffrey D. & Rochester, Colin H., eds. Absorption from Solution at the Solid Liquid Interface. 1983. text ed. 180.00 (0-12-544980-1) Acad Pr.

Parfitt, Geoffrey D., jt. auth. see Trotman-Dickenson, A. F.

Parfitt, George. English Poetry of the First World War: Context & Themes. 192p. 1990. 69.00 (0-389-20940-6) B&N Imports.

— English Poetry of the Seventeenth Century. 2nd ed. 288p. (C). 1993. pap. text ed. 24.95 (0-582-08437-7, 79369) Longman.

Parfitt, George & Houlbrooke, Ralph, eds. The Courtship Narrative of Leonard Wheatcroft: Derbyshire Yeoman. 96p. 1986. 23.00 (0-7049-0111-0, WK2, Whiteknights) MRTS.

Parfitt, George & Shepherd, Simon, eds. Thomas of Woodstock: An English History Play of Shakespeare's Time. (C). 1989. 35.00 (0-907839-36-3, Pub. by Brynmill Pr Ltd UK) St Mut.

Parfitt, George, ed. see Jonson, Ben.

Parfitt, Patsis. Advances in Organic Coatings, Vol. 5. 384p. 1983. 190.00 (0-8247-1905-0) Dekker.

— Advances in Organic Coatings, Vol. 6. LC 83-10379. 544p. 1983. 190.00 (0-8247-7044-7) Dekker.

Parfitt, Phillip. Racing at Crystal Palace. (Illus.). 128p. 1991. 27.95 (0-947981-38-1, Pub. by Motor Racing UK) Motorbooks Intl.

Parfitt, Robert T., jt. auth. see Casy, Alan F.

Parfitt, Trevor & Riley, Stephen. The African Debt Crisis. 256p. 1989. 49.95 (0-415-00441-1) Routledge.

Parfitt, Tudor. The Jews in Palestine, Eighteen Hundred to Eighteen Eighty-Two. (Royal Historical Society: Studies in History). 1988. 63.00 (0-86193-209-9) Boydell & Brewer.

Parfitt, Tudor, jt. ed. see Abramson, Glenda.

Parfitt, Will. Elements of Psychosynthesis. 1990. pap. 9.95 (1-85230-156-2) Element MA.

— The Elements of the Qabalah. (Illus.). 144p. 1991. pap. 9.95 (1-85230-230-5) Element MA.

— Walking Through Walls: Practical Esoteric Psychology. 1990. pap. 14.95 (1-85230-115-5) Element MA.

Parfrey, Adam. Apocalypse Culture. rev. ed. (Illus.). 360p. (Orig.). 1990. pap. 12.95 (0-922915-05-9) Feral Hse.

— Cult Rapture: Revelations of the Apocalyptic Mind. 1994. pap. 14.95 (0-922915-22-9) Feral Hse.

Parfrey, Patrick S. & Harnett, John D., eds. Cardiac Dysfunction in Chronic Uremia. (Topics in Renal Medicine Ser.). (C). 1991. lib. bdg. 158.50 (0-7923-1351-8) Kluwer Ac.

Pargament, Kenneth I., et al. Religion & Prevention in Mental Health: Research, Vision & Action. LC 92-5887. (Prevention in Human Services Ser.: Vol. 9, No.2). (Illus.). 232p. 1992. text ed. 59.95 (1-56024-225-6); pap. text ed. 24.95 (1-56024-226-4) Haworth Pr.

Pargeter, Edith. Afterglow & Nightfall: The Brothers of Gwynedd IV. 342p. 1991. pap. 10.95 (0-7472-3030-7, Pub. by Headline UK) Trafalgar.

— A Bloody Field by Shrewsbury. 378p. 1991. pap. 11.95 (0-7472-3366-7, Pub. by Headline UK) Trafalgar.

— The Brothers of Gwynedd Quartet. 822p. 1990. pap. 15. 95 (0-7472-3267-9, Pub. by Headline UK) Trafalgar.

— Dragon at Noonday: The Brothers of Gwynedd II. 342p. 1991. pap. 11.95 (0-7472-3071-X, Pub. by Headline UK) Trafalgar.

— The Eighth Champion of Christendom. 286p. 1991. pap. 13.95 (0-7472-3290-3, Pub. by Headline UK) Trafalgar.

— The Heaven Tree Trilogy. 912p. 1993. 24.95 (0-446-51708-9) Warner Bks.

— The Hounds of Sunset: The Brothers of Gwynedd III. 340p. 1991. pap. 11.95 (0-7472-3029-3, Pub. by Headline UK) Trafalgar.

— Reluctant Odyssey. 295p. 1991. pap. 13.95 (0-7472-3336-5, Pub. by Headline UK) Trafalgar.

— She Goes to War. 313p. 1991. pap. 9.95 (0-7472-3277-6, Pub. by Headline UK) Trafalgar.

— She Goes to War. large type ed. (General Ser.). 512p. 1993. 21.95 (0-7089-2717-3, Trail West Pubs) Ulverscroft.

— Sunrise in the West: The Brothers of Gwynedd I. 342p. 1991. pap. 11.95 (0-7472-3003-X, Pub. by Headline UK) Trafalgar.

— Warfare Accomplished. 362p. 1991. pap. 13.95 (0-7472-3399-3, Pub. by Headline UK) Trafalgar.

Pargeter, Edith, tr. see Hrabal, Bohumil.

Pargeter, Edith, tr. see Nemcova, Bozena.

Pargeter, Edith, tr. see Neruda, Jan.

Pargeter, R. J. Quantifying Weldability. (Illus.). 76p. (Orig.). (C). 1988. pap. 63.00 (0-85300-222-3, Pub. by Welding Inst UK) Air Sci Co.

Pargeter, R. J., jt. auth. see Bailey, N.

Pargeter, William. Observations on Maniacal Disorders: (1792) Jackson, Stanley, ed. (Tavistock Classic Reprints in the History of Psychiatry Ser.). 208p. 1989. 37.50 (0-415-00638-4) Routledge.

Pargetter, Robert, jt. auth. see Bigelow, John.

Pargman, David. Stress & Motor Performance: Understanding & Coping. (Illus.). 204p. 1986. pap. 15.95 (0-685-17375-5) Mouvement Pubns.

Pargman, David, ed. Psychological Bases of Sport Injuries. 315p. 1993. 38.00 (0-9627926-3-2) Fit Info Tech.

Pargman, David, jt. auth. see Greenberg, Jerrold S.

Parham. Play in Occupational Therapy. 350p. 1995. pap. 38.95 (0-8016-7838-2) Mosby Yr Bk.

Parham, A. Philip. Letting God. LC 86-45835. (Illus.). 384p. 1987. pap. 11.00 (0-06-250669-2) Harper SF.

Parham, Bettie E., jt. auth. see Osborne, Joseph.

Parham, Ellen. Baby. 150p. (Orig.). 1992. pap. 12.95 (0-9630835-1-1) Whitefield Bks.

Parham, H. B. Fiji Native Plants, with Their Medicinal & Other Uses. LC 75-35146. reprint ed. 16.50 (0-404-14162-5) AMS Pr.

Parham, H. J. & Belfield, E. M. Unarmed into Battle: The Story of the Air Observation Post. 1987. reprint ed. 91.00 (0-317-90385-3, Pub. by Picton UK) St Mut.

Parham, Iris A., ed. Gerontological Social Work: An Annotated Bibliography. LC 92-21543. (Bibliographies & Indexes in Gerontology Ser.: No. 19). 224p. 1993. text ed. 55.00 (0-313-28538-1, PHG, Greenwood Pr) Greenwood.

Parham, Iris A., jt. comp. see Teitelman, Jodi L.

Parham, Jim. Forty-Nine Fun & Inexpensive Things to Do in the Smokies with Children. (Illus.). 72p. (Orig.). 1993. pap. 5.95 (0-9631861-2-4) WMC Pubng.

— Off the Beaten Track Vol. I: A Guide to Mountain Biking in Western North Carolina - The Smokies. rev. ed. (Off the Beaten Track Mountain Bike Guide Ser.). (Illus.). 75p. 1994. pap. 12.95 (0-9631861-4-0) WMC Pubng.

— Off the Beaten Track Vol. II: A Guide to Mountain Biking in Western North Carolina - Pisgag National Forest. rev. ed. (Off the Beaten Track Mountain Bike Guide Ser.). (Illus.). 88p. 1995. pap. 12.95 (0-9631861-6-7) WMC Pubng.

— Off the Beaten Track Vol. IV: A Guide to Mountain Biking in East Tennessee. (Off the Beaten Track Mountain Bike Guide Ser.). (Illus.). 69p. (Orig.). 1994. pap. 12.95 (0-9631861-5-9) WMC Pubng.

— Off the Beaten Track Vol. V: A Guide to Mountain Biking in Northern Virginia. (Off the Beaten Track Mountain Bike Guide Ser.). (Illus.). 83p. (Orig.). 1995. pap. 12.95 (0-9631861-7-5) WMC Pubng.

— Off the Beaten Track Vol. VI: A Guide to Mountain Biking in West Virginia. (Off the Beaten Track Mountain Bike Guide Ser.). (Illus.). 83p. (Orig.). 1995. pap. 12.95 (0-9631861-8-3) WMC Pubng.

— Off the Beaten Track, Vol. III: A Guide to Mountain Biking in North Georgia. (Illus.). 74p. (Orig.). 1993. pap. 12.95 (0-9631861-3-2) WMC Pubng.

Parham, Robert. Loving Neighbors Across Time: A Christian Guide to Protecting the Earth. Nelson, Becky, ed. 114p. (Orig.). 1991. pap. text ed. 6.95 (1-56309-042-2, New Hope) Womans Mission Union.

Parham, Russell A. & Gray, Richard L. The Practical Identification of Wood Pulp Fibers. LC 82-50114. 220p. 1982. 118.00 (0-89852-400-8, 0101R100) TAPPI.

— The Practical Identification of Wood Pulp Fibers. LC 82-50114. reprint ed. pap. 55.00 (0-317-20555-2, 2022820) Bks Demand.

***Parham, Sydney F., Jr.** Title Examination in Virginia. 207p. 1965. 17.50 (0-614-05983-6) Michie Butterworth.

Parham, Sydney F. A Virginia Title Examiners' Manual. rev. ed. 517p. 1973. Incl. 1977 cumulative suppl. 35.00 (0-87215-151-4) Michie Butterworth.

— A Virginia Title Examiners' Manual. suppl. ed. 517p. 1977. Nineteen Seventy-Seven suppl. only. 15.00 (0-87215-290-1) Michie Butterworth.

Parham, Vanessa R. The African-American Child's Heritage Cookbook. Rolle-Whatley, R., ed. LC 92-60006. (Illus.). 296p. (Orig.). (J). 1992. pap. 19.95 (0-9627756-2-2) Sandcastle Pub.

Parham, Vistara. What's Wrong with Eating Meat? LC 79-52319. (Illus.). (Orig.). 1979. pap. 3.50 (0-88476-009-X) Ananda Marga.

Parham, Will E. Blount County, Tennessee, Marriages, 1795-1865. iv, 422p. 1982. 25.00 (0-89308-240-6, TN 52) Southern Hist Pr.

Parhi, Keshab K., jt. auth. see Hartley, Richard.

Parhi, Keshab K., jt. auth. see Shanbhag, Naresh R.

Paribatra, Sukhumbhand, jt. ed. see Snitwongse, Kusuma.

Paribeni, Roberto. Optimus Princeps: Saggio Sulla Storia & Sui Tempi Dell' Imperatore Traiano. LC 75-7334. (Roman History Ser.). (Illus.). (ITA.). 1975. reprint ed. 58.95 (0-405-07051-9) Ayer.

Paridis, Lenora F., ed. & intro. Stress & Burnout among Providers Caring for the Terminally Ill & Their Families. LC 87-25949. (Hospice Journal Ser.: Vol. 3, Nos. 2-3). 276p. 1988. text ed. 32.95 (0-86656-674-0) Haworth Pr.

Pariente, Vita, jt. ed. see Rowe, Gilbert T.

***Paries, Ralph E.** When Midnight Turns to Dawn. 308p. (Orig.). 1994. pap. 9.99 (1-56043-822-3) Destiny Image.

Parietti, Jeff. The Greatest Sports Excuses, Alibis, & Explanations. (Illus.). 224p. (Orig.). 1990. pap. 9.95 (0-8092-4088-2) Contemp Bks.

Parigi, Sam F. A Case Study of Latin American Unionization in Austin, Texas. Cortes, Carlos E., ed. LC 76-1265. (Chicano Heritage Ser.). 1977. 28.95 (0-405-09518-X) Ayer.

Parikh, Ajay M. Magnetic Resonance Image Techniques. (Illus.). 349p. 1991. text ed. 56.00 (0-8385-6084-9, A6084-6) Appleton & Lange.

Parikh, Anoop. Making the Most of Small Spaces. 80p. 1994. 18.95 (0-8478-1801-2) Rizzoli Intl.

Parikh, Ashok. The Economics of Fertiliser Use in Developing Countries. 208p. 1990. text ed. 59.95 (0-566-05607-0, Pub. by Avebury Pub UK) Ashgate Pub Co.

Parikh, Bharati A. Feminine Sensibility: A Study of Black American & Indian Women Novelists. 200p. 1993. text ed. 35.00 (81-85218-37-4, Pub. by Prestige II) Advent Bks Div.

Parikh, Carol A. The Unreal Life of Oscar Zariski. (Illus.). 264p. 1990. text ed. 49.95 (0-12-545030-3) Acad Pr.

Parikh, Girish. How to Measure Programmer Productivity. LC 81-9046. (Illus.). 95p. 1981. pap. 20.00 (0-685-04593-5) Shetal Ent.

— The One Minute Organizing Secret: Finding Electronic Files, Papers, Books & Almost Everything Fast! LC 85-62926. 64p. (Orig.). 1985. pap. 11.00 (0-932888-37-2, POT) Shetal Ent.

— Techniques of Program System Maintenance. 2nd ed. LC 87-36023. 483p. reprint ed. pap. 137.70 (0-7837-4065-4, 2044015) Bks Demand.

— There Is a Fortune to be Made in Software Maintenance: Opportunities in the 30 Billion Dollar Software AfterMarket. LC 84-51942. (Illus.). 402p. (Orig.). 1985. pap. 500.00 (0-932888-00-3, TFSM) Shetal Ent.

Parikh, Indira J. Women Weavers. (C). 1991. 12.50 (81-204-0597-8, Pub. by Oxford IBH II) S Asia.

Parikh, Indira J. & Garg, Pulin K. Indian Women: An Inner Dialogue. 224p. (C). 1989. text ed. 25.00 (0-8039-9597-0); pap. text ed. 12.50 (0-8039-9598-9) Sage.

Parikh, Indira J., jt. auth. see Garg, Pulin K.

Parikh, Jagdish. Managing Your Self: Management by Detached Involvement. (Developmental Management Ser.). 1994. pap. 19.95 (0-631-19307-3) Blackwell Pubs.

Parikh, Jagdish, et al. Intuition: The New Frontier of Management. (Developmental Management Ser.). (Illus.). 320p. 1994. 34.95 (0-631-19225-5) Blackwell Pubs.

Parikh, Jyoti. Superconductors in Power Systems. (C). 1990. text ed. 21.00 (81-7023-295-3, Pub. by Allied II) S Asia.

Parikh, Jyoti K., ed. Sustainable Development of Agriculture. (C). 1988. lib. bdg. 144.00 (90-247-3642-0) Kluwer Ac.

Parikh, Kirit S. Towards Free Trade in Agriculture. (C). 1988. lib. bdg. 93.00 (90-247-3632-3) Kluwer Ac.

Parikh, N. D., ed. see Desai, Mahadev.

Parikh, Narahari D., ed. see Gandhi, Mohandas K.

Parikh, R., ed. Logics of Programs. (Lecture Notes in Computer Science Ser.: Vol. 193). vi, 424p. 1985. pap. 42.00 (0-387-15648-8) Spr-Verlag.

Parikh, R., ed. see Logic Symposium Staff.

Parikh, R. D. The Press & Society. 154p. 1965. 9.95 (0-318-37280-0) Asia Bk Corp.

Parikh, Rohit, ed. Theoretical Aspects of Reasoning about Knowledge: Proceedings of the Third Conference, Tark 1990. 1990. 39.95 (1-55860-105-8) Morgan Kaufmann.

Parilla, Catherine A. A Theory for Reading Dramatic Texts: Selected Plays by Pirandello & Garcia Lorca. (Currents in Comparative Romance Languages & Literatures Ser.: Vol. 24). 200p. (C). 1995. text ed. 44.95 (0-8204-2368-8) P Lang Pubs.

Parillo, John. John Parillo's Fifty Workout Secrets. Greenwood-Robinson, Maggie, ed. (Illus.). 192p. (Orig.). 1994. pap. 16.00 (0-399-51862-2, Perigee Bks) Berkley Pub.

Parillo, Mark P. The Japanese Merchant Marine in World War II. LC 92-33299. (Illus.). 308p. 1993. 28.95 (1-55750-677-9) Naval Inst Pr.

Parilov & Ushakov. Testing Adjustment of Steam Boilers. 1990. 131.00 (1-56032-094-X) Hemisp Pub.

Parimoo, B. N. The Ascent of Self: A Reinterpretation of the Mystical Poetry of Lalla-Ded. 2nd rev. ed. (C). 1987. 15.00 (81-208-0305-1, Pub. by Motilal Banarsidass II) S Asia.

Parimoo, Ratan, et al, eds. Ellora Caves: Sculptures & Architecture. (C). 1988. 95.00 (81-85016-23-2, Pub. by Bks & Bks IA) S Asia.

Parin, Edgar P., jt. auth. see D'Aulaire, Ingri.

Parin, Paul, et al. Fear Thy Neighbor As Thyself: Psychoanalysis & Society Among the Anyi of West Africa. Klamerth, Patricia, tr. LC 79-24360. 416p. 1980. lib. bdg. 31.00 (0-226-64583-5) U Ch Pr.

Parinder, Patrick, ed. see Gissing, George R.

Parinello, Anthony. Selling to Vito: The Very Important Top Officer. 1994. pap. 10.95 (1-55850-386-2) Adams Pubng.

Paringaux, Philippe. Love Shots. Metz, Bernd, ed. Bell, Elizabeth, tr. (Illus.). 64p. (Orig.). 1989. pap. 11.95 (0-87416-059-6) Catalan Communs.

— New York - Miami. Metz, Bernd, ed. Bell, Elizabeth, tr. (Illus.). 64p. (Orig.). 1990. pap. 11.95 (0-87416-073-1) Catalan Communs.

Paringer, William A. John Dewey & the Paradox of Liberal Reform. LC 89-77669. (SUNY Series, Global Conflict & Peace Education). 215p. 1990. 59.50 (0-7914-0253-3); pap. 19.95 (0-7914-0254-1) State U NY Pr.

Paringnaux, Philippe. Hearts of Sand. Metz, Bernd, ed. Bell, Elizabeth, tr. (Illus.). 72p. (Orig.). 1991. pap. 13.95 (0-87416-134-7) Catalan Communs.

Parini. John Steinbeck: A Biography. 1995. 30.00 (0-8050-1673-2) H Holt & Co.

Parini, Jay. Benjamin's Crossing. 1995. 23.00 (0-8050-3180-4) H Holt & Co.

— An Invitation to Poetry. 416p. (C). 1986. pap. text ed. write for info. (0-13-505546-6) P-H.

— The Love Run. (Orig.). 1989. pap. 4.95 (0-929654-22-6, 66) Blue Moon Bks.

— The Patch Boys. LC 86-4823. 1988. pap. 8.95 (0-8050-0770-9, Owl) H Holt & Co.

— Robert Frost: A Biography. 1996. 28.95 (0-8050-3181-2) H Holt & Co.

— Theodore Roethke: An American Romantic. LC 79-4022. 216p. 1979. lib. bdg. 27.50x (0-87023-270-3) U of Mass Pr.

***Parini, Jay, ed.** The Columbia Book of American Poetry. LC 94-32423. 1995. write for info. (0-231-08122-7) Col U Pr.

— The Columbia History of American Poetry. LC 92-29399. 1993. 59.95 (0-231-07836-6) Col U Pr.

— Gore Vidal: Writer Against the Grain. 389p. (C). 1993. text ed. 20.00 (0-231-07208-2); pap. 16.95 (0-231-07209-0) Col U Pr.

Parini, Jay, jt. ed. see Pack, Robert.

Parins, James W. John Rollin Ridge: His Life & Works. LC 90-40464. (American Indian Lives Ser.). (Illus.). x, 260p. 1991. 30.00 (0-8032-3683-2) U of Nebr Pr.

Parins, James W. & Littlefield, Daniel F., Jr., eds. Ke-Ma-Ha: The Omaha Stories of Francis la Flesche. LC 94-9362. 1995. text ed. 25.00 (0-8032-2910-0) U of Nebr Pr.

Parins, James W., jt. auth. see Littlefield, Daniel F., Jr.

Parins, James W., jt. ed. see Littlefield, Daniel F., Jr.

Parins, Marylyn. Malory. (Critical Heritage Ser.). 420p. 1988. text ed. 75.00 (0-415-00223-0) Routledge.

Parionovich, Y., ed. see Roerich, Y. N.

Paris. Foundation Stories: The Stories on Which Literature Is Built. 176p. (C). 1992. pap. text ed. 18.95 (0-8403-8245-6) Kendall-Hunt.

Paris, Alain. Dictionnaire General de la Technique Industrielle: Francais - Allemand. 3rd ed. 1110p. 1990. pap. 49.95 (0-7859-4740-X) Fr & Eur.

Paris, Alexander P. A Complete Guide to Trading Profits. LC 75-84640. 196p. 1981. reprint ed. 24.95 (0-934380-05-8) Traders Pr.

Paris, Arthur E. Black Pentecostalism: Southern Religion in an Urban World. LC 81-16169. 192p. 1982. lib. bdg. 25.00 (0-87023-353-X) U of Mass Pr.

Paris Assemblee Electorale Staff. Assemblee Electorale de Paris, 18 Novembre 1790-15, Juin 1791: Collection de Documents Relatifs a l'Histoire de Paris Pendant la Revolution Francaise. LC 79-173488. reprint ed. 96.50 (0-404-52614-4) AMS Pr.

— Assemblee Electorale de Paris, 2 Septembre 1792. LC 75-38036. reprint ed. 96.50 (0-404-52616-0) AMS Pr.

— Assemblee Electorale de Paris, 26 Aout 1791-12 Aout 1792: Collection de Documents Relatifs a l'Histoire de Paris Pendant la Revolution Francaise. LC 71-38035. reprint ed. 96.50 (0-404-52615-2) AMS Pr.

Paris, B. J. Bargains with Fate: Psychological Crises & Conflicts in Shakespeare & His Plays. LC 90-28612. (Illus.). 280p. 1991. 24.95 (0-306-43760-0, Plenum Insight) Plenum.

Paris, Barry. Garbo: A Biography. LC 93-12088. 1995. 35.00 (0-394-58020-6) Knopf.

Paris, Beltran. Beltran: Basque Sheepman of the American West. LC 79-20311. (Basque Ser.). (Illus.). 208p. 1988. reprint ed. pap. 16.95 (0-87417-144-X) U of Nev Pr.

Paris, Bernard J. Character As a Subversive Force in Shakespeare: The History & Roman Plays. LC 90-55839. 224p. 1991. 39.50 (0-8386-3429-X) Fairleigh Dickinson.

— Experiments in Life: George Eliot's Quest for Values. LC 65-13719. 296p. reprint ed. pap. 84.40 (0-7837-3613-4, 2043479) Bks Demand.

— Karen Horney: A Psychoanalyst's Search for Self-Understanding. (Illus.). 288p. 1994. 30.00 (0-300-05956-6) Yale U Pr.

Paris, Bernard J., ed. Third Force Psychology & the Study of Literature. LC 85-47629. 344p. 1986. 45.00 (0-8386-3263-7) Fairleigh Dickinson.

Paris, Bernard J., ed. see Holland, Norman N.

Paris. Bibliotheque Nationale Staff. Cinquantenaire du symbolisme: Exposition de manuscrits autographes, estamps, peintures, sculptures, editions rares, portraits, objets d'art. LC 77-11471. (Symbolists Ser.). (Illus.). (FRE.). reprint ed. 54.00 (0-404-16333-5) AMS Pr.

Paris, Bob. Beyond Built: Bob Paris' Guide to Achieving the Ultimate Look. 1991. pap. 14.99 (0-446-39146-8) Warner Bks.

— Flawless: The Ten-Week, Total-Image Method for Transforming Your Physique. (Illus.). 304p. (Orig.). 1993. pap. 14.99 (0-446-39406-8) Warner Bks.

— Natural Fitness. 304p. (Orig.). 1996. pap. 13.99 (0-446-67029-4) Warner Bks.

Paris, C., ed. Critical Readings in Planning Theory. (Urban & Regional Planning Ser.: Vol. 27). (Illus.). 260p. 1982. text ed. 140.00 (0-08-024681-8, Pub. by Pergamon Repr UK) Franklin.

***Paris, Catherine & Batouka, Niaz.** Dictionnaire Abkhaz. 1992. write for info. (0-7859-8185-3, 2-87723-044-9) Fr & Eur.

Paris, Cecile. User Modeling in Text Generation. (Communication in Artificial Intelligence Ser.). 240p. 1993. text ed. 79.00 (0-86187-809-4, Pub. by Pinter Pubs UK) St Martin.

Paris Commune, 1789-1794 Staff. Actes de la Commune de Paris Pendant la Revolution, 9 vols., Set. LC 73-15863. (Second Ser.). reprint ed. 868.00 (0-404-52630-6) AMS Pr.

— Actes de la Commune de Paris Pendant la Revolution, 10 vols., Set. LC 72-173489. (First Ser.). 1994. reprint ed. 965.00 (0-404-52620-9) AMS Pr.

Paris, Cynthia L. Teacher Agency & Curriculum Making in the Classroom. LC 92-34554. 176p. (C). 1993. pap. text ed. 18.95 (0-8077-3225-7) Tchrs Coll.

Paris-Dauphine Conference on Money & International Monetary Problems Staff. Recent Issues in the Theory of Flexible Exchange Rates: Proceedings of the Paris-Dauphine Conference on Money & International Monetary Problems, 5th, 1981. Claassen, E. M. & Sali, P., eds. (Studies in Monetary Economics: Vol. 8). 274p. 1983. 64.00 (0-444-86389-3, North Holland) Elsevier.

***Paris, David C.** Ideology & Educational Reform: Themes & Theories in Public Education. (C). 1995. pap. text ed. 18.95 (0-8133-2340-1) Westview.

— Ideology & Educational Reform: Themes & Theories in Public Education. (C). 1995. text ed. 49.95 (0-8133-2341-X) Westview.

Paris, Don. Regaining Wholeness Through the Subtle Dimensions: Where Science Meets Magic. (Illus.). 160p. (Orig.). 1993. pap. 12.95 (1-884246-00-1) Liv from Vis.

Paris, Don Q. Craniographic Positioning with Comparison Studies. LC 82-14074. (Illus.). 162p. 1983. 25.00 (0-8036-6768-X) Davis Co.

Paris, Edmond. The Secret History of the Jesuits. rev. ed. 208p. 1982. reprint ed. pap. 7.50 (0-937958-10-7) Chick Pubns.

Paris, Eileen, jt. auth. see Paris, Thomas.

***Paris, Emilie.** Valentine. (Orig.). 1994. pap. 5.95 (1-56201-072-7) Blue Moon Bks.

Paris, Erna. The Garden & the Gun. 292p. 1991. 24.95 (1-879601-00-1); pap. 16.95 (1-879601-01-X) Semaphore Bks.

Paris, G. & Langlois, E. Chrestomathie du Moyen Age. 366p. 1970. 18.95 (0-8288-7440-9) Fr & Eur.

Paris, Gaston. Mediaeval French Literature. LC 78-154160. (Select Bibliographies Reprint Ser.). 1977. reprint ed. 19.95 (0-8369-5776-8) Ayer.

Paris, Gaston B. Francois Villon. LC 70-178550. reprint ed. 37.50 (0-404-56657-X) AMS Pr.

— La Litterature Francaise au Moyen Age (Eleventh to Fourteenth Centuries) LC 73-178583. reprint ed. 62.50 (0-404-56658-8) AMS Pr.

Paris, Ginette. Pagan Grace: Dionysos, Hermes & Goddess Memory in Daily Life. Mott, Joanna, tr. LC 89-26330. 152p. (Orig.). 1990. pap. 16.00 (0-88214-342-5) Spring Pubns.

— Pagan Meditations: The Worlds of Aphrodite, Artemis, & Hestia. Moore, Gwendolyn, tr. LC 86-6675. 204p. (Orig.). (C). 1986. pap. 16.00 (0-88214-330-1) Spring Pubns.

— The Sacrament of Abortion. Mott, Joanna, tr. LC 91-46372. 113p. (Orig.). 1992. pap. 12.00 (0-88214-352-2) Spring Pubns.

Paris, H. & Hunt, W. H., eds. Advances in Magnesium Alloys & Composites. LC 88-60116. (Illus.). 152p. 1989. 65.00 (0-87339-038-5, 324) Minerals Metals.

Paris, Henry G., ed. see Minerals, Metals, & Materials Society Staff.

Paris, Howard. Clip-Art Activity Features for Children. (REPRObooks Ser.). (Illus.). 104p. (Orig.). 1992. pap. 5.99 (0-8010-7119-4) Baker Bk.

— Clip-Art Panel Cartoons for Churches, 2. 96p. 1987. pap. 4.99 (0-8010-7098-8) Baker Bk.

Paris, Howard, comp. Clip-Art Panel Cartoons for Churches, 3. 80p. (Orig.). 1989. pap. 4.99 (0-8010-7110-0) Baker Bk.

Paris, Howard, illus. Clip-Art Features for Church Newsletters, No. 4. 96p. 1988. pap. 6.99 (0-8010-5490-7) Baker Bk.

— Clip-Art Features for Church Newsletters, No. 5. 96p. 1989. pap. 6.99 (0-8010-5281-5) Baker Bk.

— Clip-Art Sentence Sermons for Church Publications, No. 1. 96p. 1986. pap. 4.99 (0-8010-5475-3) Baker Bk.

— Clip-Art Sentence Sermons for Church Publications, No. 2. 1988. pap. 4.99 (0-8010-5495-8) Baker Bk.

Paris, Howard, tr. Clip-Art Features for Church Newsletters, No. 7. (REPRObooks Ser.). (Illus.). 104p. 1992. pap. 6.99 (0-8010-5254-8) Baker Bk.

Paris, I. Mark, tr. The Splendor of Ethnic Jewelry: From the Colette & Jean-Pierre Ghysels Collection. LC 94-8417. 1994. write for info. (0-8109-4453-7) Abrams.

Paris, I. Mark, tr. see Anthonioz, Michel.

Paris, I. Mark, tr. see Erlande-Brandenburg, Alain.

Paris, I. Mark, tr. see Loyrette, Henri.

Paris, I. Mark, tr. see Maury, Jean-Pierre.

Paris, I. Mark, tr. see Thuan, Trinh X.

Paris, J. B. The Uncertain Reasoner's Companion: A Mathematical Perspective. (Tracts in Theoretical Computer Science Ser.: No. 39). 180p. (C). 1995. 39.95 (0-521-46089-1) Cambridge U Pr.

Paris, J. B., et al, eds. Logic Colloquium '84: Proceedings of the Colloquium, Manchester, U. K., July 1984. (Studies in Logic & the Foundations of Mathematics: Vol. 120). 400p. 1986. 97.50 (0-444-87999-4) Elsevier.

Paris, James & Dicks, J. W. Financial CPR. LC 93-71206. 192p. (Orig.). 1993. pap. 9.99 (0-88419-335-7, Creation Hse) Strang Comms Co.

***Paris, James L.** Living Financially Free. 1995. pap. 15.99 (1-56507-331-2) Harvest Hse.

Paris, James L., jt. auth. see Dicks, J. W.

Paris, James R. Classic Foreign Films: From Nineteen Sixty to Today. (Illus.). 256p. 1993. pap. 17.95 (0-8065-1442-6, Citadel Pr) Carol Pub Group.

— The Great French Films. (Illus.). 288p. 1983. 18.95 (0-8065-0806-X, Citadel Pr) Carol Pub Group.

— The Great French Films. 256p. 1986. reprint ed. pap. 16.95 (0-8065-1003-X, Citadel Pr) Carol Pub Group.

Paris, Janelle A. Planning Bulletin Boards for Church & Synagogue Libraries. LC 83-7331. (Guide Ser.: No. 11). 48p. (Orig.). 1984. pap. 8.25 (0-915324-20-2); pap. 6.50 (0-685-07181-2) CSLA.

Paris, Jim. Financial Boot Camp. LC 92-72774. 236p. (Orig.). 1992. pap. 9.99 (0-88419-325-X, Creation Hse) Strang Comms Co.

Paris, Joel. Borderline Personality Disorder: A Multidimensional Approach. 1994. boxed 29.95 (0-88048-655-4) Am Psychiatric.

Paris, Joel, ed. Borderline Personality Disorder: Etiology & Treatment. LC 92-7020. 400p. 1992. text ed. 46.50 (0-88048-408-X) Am Psychiatric.

An Asterisk (*) at the beginning of an entry indicates that the title is appearing in BIP for the first time.

Paris, John. Computer Projections of National Skier Population & Colorado Lift Ticket Sales: 1980-1998. 55p. 1985. pap. 25.00 (*0-89478-090-5*) U CO Busn Res Div.

Paris, Katherine W., ed. Gloria Dell' Arte: A Renaissance Perspective. LC 79-89876. (Illus.). 88p. (Orig.). 1979. pap. 6.00 (*0-86659-000-5*) Philbrook Mus Art.

Paris Logic Group Staff. Logic Colloquium, 1985: Proceedings of the Colloquium, Orsay, France, July 1985. (Studies in Logic & the Foundations of Mathematics: No. 122). 308p. 1987. 97.50 (*0-444-70211-3*, North Holland) Elsevier.

Paris, Marion. Library School Closings: Four Case Studies. LC 88-7276. 176p. 1988. 20.00 (*0-8108-2130-3*) Scarecrow.

Paris, Matthew. English History, from the Year Twelve Hundred Thirty-Five to Twelve Hundred Seventy-Three, 3 Vols, Set. Giles, J. A., tr. LC 68-55554. (Bohn's Antiquarian Library). reprint ed. 150.00 (*0-404-50050-1*) AMS Pr.

***Paris, Michael.** From the Wright Brothers to Top Gun: Aviation & Popular Cinema. LC 94-29774. 1995. text ed. write for info. (*0-7190-4074-4*, Pub. by Manchester Univ Pr UK); text ed. write for info. (*0-7190-4073-6*, Pub. by Manchester Univ Pr UK) St Martin.

— The Novels of World War Two: An Annotated Bibliography of World War Two Fiction. LC 90-176799. reprint ed. pap. 55.90 (*0-7837-9271-9*, 2060009) Bks Demand.

— Silvertown 1917. 1993. pap. 8.00 (*0-86025-401-1*, Pub. by Ian Henry Pubns UK) Empire Pub Srvs.

Paris, Mike & Comber, Chris. Jimmie the Kid: The Life of Jimmie Rodgers. LC 80-29198. (Quality Paperbacks Ser.). (Illus.). 211p. 1981. reprint ed. pap. 8.95 (*0-306-80133-7*) Da Capo.

Paris, Nancy M. My Brother Is Different. (Illus.). (J). (gr. 1-4). 1992. 6.95 (*1-55523-512-3*) Winston-Derek.

Paris, P. C., ed. Fracture Mechanics: 12th Conference - STP 700. 587p. 1980. 53.25 (*0-8031-0363-8*, 04-700000-30) ASTM.

Paris, Pat. Old MacDonald Had a Farm. (Illus.). 12p. (J). (ps-1). 1989. text ed. 11.95 (*0-8120-6107-1*) Barron.

— On a Rainy Day: A Playtime Pop-Up. (Illus.). 10p. (J). (ps). 1992. boxed, pap. 4.95 (*0-671-74175-6*, Litl Simon S&S) S&S Childrens.

— On a Windy Day: A Playtime Pop-Up. (Illus.). 10p. (J). (ps). 1992. boxed, pap. 4.95 (*0-671-74174-8*, Litl Simon S&S) S&S Childrens.

— On Christmas Day. (Illus.). 10p. (J). (ps). 1991. boxed, pap. 4.95 (*0-671-74173-X*, Litl Simon S&S) S&S Childrens.

— Pop up Frog. (J). 1989. 4.95 (*0-671-67554-0*) S&S Trade.

— This Old Man. (Illus.). 12p. (J). (ps-1). 1989. text ed. 9.95 (*0-8120-6109-8*) Barron.

Paris, Pat, illus. Bear Cubs. (Baby Animal Pop-Up Bks.). 10p. (J). (ps). 1989. 4.95 (*0-8120-5987-5*) Barron.

— Bunnies. (Baby Animal Pop-Up Bks.). 10p. (J). (ps). 1989. 4.95 (*0-8120-5990-5*) Barron.

— Kittens. (Baby Animal Pop-Up Bks.). 10p. (J). (ps). 1989. 4.95 (*0-8120-5989-1*) Barron.

— Puppies. (Baby Animal Pop-Up Bks.). 10p. (J). (ps). 1989. 4.95 (*0-8120-5988-3*) Barron.

— Who's in the Box, Bobby? 22p. (J). (ps). 1991. 12.95 (*0-8431-1906-3*) Price Stern.

Paris, Paul M. & Stewart, Ronald D. Pain Management in Emergency Medicine. (Illus.). 526p. (C). 1988. boxed 85.00 (*0-8385-7695-8*, A7695-8) Appleton & Lange.

Paris, Paul M., jt. auth. see Dunmire, Susan M.

Paris, Peter J. Black Religious Leaders: Conflict in Unity: Insights from Martin Luther King, Jr., Malcolm X, Joseph H. Jackson, & Adam Clayton Powell, Jr. (Illus.). 272p. (Orig.). 1991. pap. 15.99 (*0-664-25145-5*) Westminster John Knox.

— The Social Teaching of the Black Churches. LC 84-47930. 176p. 1985. pap. 13.00 (*0-8006-1805-X*, 1-1805, Fortress Pr) Augsburg Fortress.

— The Spirituality of African Peoples: The Search for a Common Moral Discourse. LC 94-32866. 1995. pap. 13.00 (*0-8006-2854-3*, Fortress Pr) Augsburg Fortress.

Paris, Pierre. Lexique Des Antiquites Grecques. (FRE.). 1909. pap. 39.95 (*0-8288-6890-5*, M-6438) Fr & Eur.

— Manual of Ancient Sculpture. Harrison, Jane E., tr. (Illus.). 1984. lib. bdg. 55.00 (*0-89241-373-5*) Caratzas.

Paris, Quirino. An Economic Interpretation of Linear Programming. LC 90-31285. (Illus.). 352p. (C). 1991. text ed. 41.95 (*0-8138-0469-8*) Iowa St U Pr.

Paris, Reine-Marie. Camille Claudel. LC 88-1759. (Illus.). 114p. 1988. Dist. by NE U Pr. pap. 24.95 (*0-940979-04-7*) Natl Museum Women.

Paris, Scott, et al, eds. Learning & Motivation in the Classroom. LC 83-3962. 347p. reprint ed. pap. 98.90 (*0-7837-2424-1*, 2042571) Bks Demand.

Paris, Scott G. Propositional Logical Thinking & Comprehension of Language Connectives: A Developmental Analysis. LC 74-75824. (Janua Linguarum, Series Minor: No. 216). (Illus.). 101p. 1975. pap. text ed. 23.10 (*90-279-3197-6*) Mouton.

Paris, Scott G. & Ayres, Linda R. Becoming Reflective Students & Teachers with Portfolios & Authentic Assessment. (Psychology in the Classroom Ser.). (Illus.). 178p. (Orig.). 1994. pap. text ed. 17.95 (*1-55798-252-X*) Am Psychol.

Paris, Susan. Mommy & Daddy Are Fighting: A Book for Children about Family Violence. LC 85-22193. (New Leaf Ser.). (Illus.). 24p. (Orig.). (J). (ps-4). 1986. pap. 8.95 (*0-931188-33-4*) Seal Pr Feminist.

Paris, Thomas & Paris, Eileen. I'll Never Do to My Kids What My Parents Did to Me! 176p. 1994. pap. 8.99 (*0-446-39546-3*) Warner Bks.

— I'll Never Do to My Kids What My Parents Did to Me: A Guide to Conscious Parenting. 168p. 1992. 18.95 (*0-929923-58-8*) Lowell Hse.

— I'll Never Do to My Kids What My Parents Did to Me! A Guide to Conscious Parenting. 168p. 1993. pap. 9.95 (*1-56565-031-X*) Lowell Hse.

Paris, Twila & Webber, Robert. In This Sanctuary. 158p. pap. 10.99 (*1-56233-109-4*) Star Song TN.

Paris, William F. Personalities in American Art. LC 72-107731. (Essay Index Reprint Ser.). 1977. 17.95 (*0-8369-1582-8*) Ayer.

Paris, Yvette. Queen of Burlesque: The Autobiography of Yvette Paris. (Sexual Autobiographies Ser.). (Illus.). 188p. (C). 1990. 22.95 (*0-87975-639-X*) Prometheus Bks.

Parise, Charles J., ed. Science & Technology of Building Seals, Sealants, Glazing & Waterproofing. LC 92-23699. (Special Technical Publication Ser.: No. STP 1168). (Illus.). 180p. 1992. text ed. 61.00 (*0-685-63257-1*, 04-011680-10) ASTM.

— Science & Technology of Building Seals, Sealants, Glazing & Waterproofing, No. STP 1168. LC 92-23699. 169p. 1992. 61.00 (*0-8031-1482-6*) ASTM.

— Science & Technology of Glazing Systems. LC 89-28496. (Special Technical Publication Ser.: No. 1054). (Illus.). 150p. 1990. text ed. 29.00 (*0-8031-1286-6*, 04-010540-10) ASTM.

Parise, Dick. Save Your Business! 1991. pap. 8.95 (*1-878901-24-9*) Hampton Roads Pub Co.

Parise, Frank, jt. auth. see Marum, Andrew.

Parise, Goffredo. Abecedary. Marcus, James, tr. LC 90-60881. 147p. 1990. pap. 10.95 (*0-910395-61-6*) Marlboro Pr.

— Abecedary. Marcus, James, tr. LC 90-60881. 147p. 1990. 17.95 (*0-910395-60-8*) Marlboro Pr.

Pariseau, Earl J., ed. Handbook of Latin American Studies, Vol. 24: 1962. LC 36-32633. 1962. 44.95 (*0-8130-0178-1*) U Press Fla.

Pariseau, Earl J. & Adams, Henry E., eds. Handbook of Latin American Studies, Vol. 28: Humanities 1962-64. LC 36-32633. 1966. 44.95 (*0-8130-0181-1*) U Press Fla.

Parisen, Maria, comp. Angels & Mortals: Their Co-Creative Power. LC 90-50205. (Illus.). 307p. (Orig.). 1990. pap. 14.95 (*0-8356-0665-1*, Quest) Theos Pub Hse.

Pariser, David M., jt. auth. see Eaglstein, William H.

Pariser, E. R. & Lombardi, Donald P. Chitin Sourcebook. 688p. 1989. text ed. 265.00 (*0-471-62423-3*) Wiley.

Pariser, H. Adventure Guide to Barbados. (Illus.). 256p. (Orig.). 1990. pap. 16.95 (*1-55650-277-X*) Hunter NJ.

Pariser, Harry. Jamaica: A Visitor's Guide. 2nd ed. (Caribbean Guides Ser.). (Illus.). 256p. (Orig.). 1992. pap. 15.95 (*1-55650-536-1*) Hunter NJ.

Pariser, Harry S. Adventure Guide to Belize. 3rd ed. (Adventure Guides Ser.). (Illus.). 288p. 1994. pap. 14.95 (*1-55650-647-3*) Hunter NJ.

— The Adventure Guide to Puerto Rico. 2nd ed. (Where to Stay Ser.). (Illus.). 300p. 1994. pap. 14.95 (*1-55650-628-7*) Hunter NJ.

— Dominican Republic "Adventure Guide" 2nd ed. (Illus.). 288p. 1994. pap. 14.95 (*1-55650-629-5*) Hunter NJ.

Pariser, Michael. Elie Wiesel: Bearing Witness. LC 93-37126. (Gateway Biography Ser.). (Illus.). 48p. (J). (gr. 2-4). 1994. 13.40 (*1-56294-419-3*); pap. 6.95 (*1-56294-743-5*) Millbrook Pr.

Pariser, Stephen F. & Levine, Stephen B., eds. Clinical Sexuality. LC 83-2096. (Reproductive Medicine Ser.: No. 3). (Illus.). 232p. reprint ed. pap. 66.20 (*0-7837-0936-6*, 2041241) Bks Demand.

***Parish.** Teach Us, Amelia Bedelia. 1995. pap. (*0-590-53773-3*) Scholastic Inc.

Parish, Charles. Tristram Shandy Notes. 1968. pap. 4.50 (*0-8220-1311-8*) Cliffs.

Parish, Charles C. Queen of the Mist. Percy, John W., ed. (Illus.). 152p. (Orig.). 1987. pap. 9.95 (*0-932334-89-X*, NY32025) Hrt of the Lakes.

Parish, D. H. Possibilities for the Improvement of Nitrogen Fertilizer Efficiency in Rice Production. (Paper Ser.: No. P-1). 1980. pap. text ed. 4.00 (*0-88090-061-X*) Intl Fertilizer.

Parish, D. H., et al. Research on Modified Fertilizer Materials for Use in Developing-Country Agriculture. (Paper Ser.: No. P-2). 1980. pap. text ed. 4.00 (*0-88090-062-8*) Intl Fertilizer.

Parish, David. Successful Rifle Shooting. (Illus.). 144p. 1989. 34.95 (*1-85223-013-4*, Pub. by Crowood Pr UK) Trafalgar.

Parish, David W. Changes in American Society, Nineteen Sixty to Nineteen Seventy-Eight: An Annotated Bibliography of Official Government Publications. LC 80-12561. 478p. 1980. 35.00 (*0-8108-1309-2*) Scarecrow.

Parish, Dennis H. Agricultural Productivity, Sustainability, & Fertilizer Use. LC 93-16931. (Paper Ser.: No. P-18). (Illus.). 21p. (Orig.). 1993. pap. text ed. 4.00 (*0-88090-102-0*) Intl Fertilizer.

Parish, Dennis L., jt. auth. see Tolson, David A.

Parish, Edward J., jt. ed. see Nes, David W.

Parish, Elijah, jt. auth. see M'Clure, David.

Parish, Helen R. Bartolome de las Casas: The Only Way. Sullivan, Francis P., tr. LC 91-32835. (Sources of American Spirituality Ser.). 288p. 1992. 22.95 (*0-8091-0367-2*) Paulist Pr.

Parish, Herman. Good Driving, Amelia Bedelia. LC 94-4112. (Illus.). 40p. (J). (gr. 1 up). 1995. 15.00 (*0-688-13358-4*); lib. bdg. 14.93 (*0-688-13359-2*) Greenwillow.

Parish, J. H., ed. Developmental Biology of Prokaryotes. LC 79-10275. (Studies in Microbiology: Vol. 1). 1979. 85.00 (*0-520-04016-3*) U CA Pr.

Parish, James R. Film Actors Guide: Western Europe. LC 77-22485. 621p. 1977. 45.00 (*0-8108-1044-1*) Scarecrow.

— Gays & Lesbians in Mainstream Cinema: Plots, Critiques, Casts & Credits for 272 Theatrical & Made-for-Television Hollywood Releases. LC 92-56678. (Illus.). 520p. 1993. lib. bdg. 49.95 (*0-89950-791-3*) McFarland & Co.

— Ghosts & Angels in Hollywood Films: Plots, Critiques, Casts & Credits for 264 Theatrical & Made-for-Television Releases. LC 93-41192. 431p. 1994. lib. bdg. 49.95 (*0-89950-676-3*) McFarland & Co.

— The Great Combat Pictures: Twentieth-Century Warfare on the Screen. LC 90-8457. (Illus.). 486p. 1990. 47.50 (*0-8108-2315-2*) Scarecrow.

— The Great Cop Pictures. LC 90-39259. (Illus.). 693p. 1990. 62.50 (*0-8108-2316-0*) Scarecrow.

— Hollywood Celebrity Death Book. 2nd ed. 1993. pap. 16.95 (*1-55698-369-7*) Movie Pubs Servs.

— Hollywood Death Book: The Amazing Finales of Hollywood's Well Known Players over the Last... 1992. pap. 14.95 (*1-55698-307-7*) Movie Pubs Servs.

— Marriage & Divorce - Hollywood Style. 1994. pap. 16.95 (*1-55698-333-6*) Movie Pubs Servs.

— New Country Music Stars. 1993. pap. 16.95 (*1-55698-374-3*) Movie Pubs Servs.

— New Country Music Superstakes. 1994. pap. 16.95 (*1-55698-337-9*) Movie Pubs Servs.

— Pirates & Seafaring Swashbucklers on the Hollywood Screen: Plots, Critiques, Casts & Credits for 137 Theatrical & Made-for-Television Releases. 356p. 1995. lib. bdg. 39.95x (*0-89950-935-5*) McFarland & Co.

— Prison Pictures from Hollywood: Plots, Critiques, Casts & Credits for 293 Theatrical & Made-for-Television Releases. LC 90-53519. (Illus.). 544p. 1991. lib. bdg. 55.00x (*0-89950-563-5*) McFarland & Co.

— Prostitution in Hollywood Films: Plots, Critiques, Casts & Credits for 389 Theatrical & Made-for-Television Releases. LC 91-51213. 616p. 1992. lib. bdg. 55.00x (*0-89950-677-1*) McFarland & Co.

— Today's Black Hollywood. 1995. pap. 4.99 (*0-7860-0104-6*, Pinnacle NY) Windsor NY.

— Unofficial Murder She Wrote Casebook. 1994. pap. 14.95 (*1-55698-346-8*) Movie Pubs Servs.

Parish, James R. & Hill, George H. Black Action Films: Plots, Critiques, Cast & Credits for 235 Theatrical & Made-for-TV Releases. LC 89-42871. 399p. 1989. lib. bdg. 49.95x (*0-89950-456-6*) McFarland & Co.

Parish, James R. & Pitts, Michael R. The Great Detective Pictures. LC 90-8551. (Illus.). 630p. 1990. 59.50 (*0-8108-2286-5*) Scarecrow.

— Great Gangster Pictures. LC 75-32402. (Illus.). 439p. 1976. 37.50 (*0-8108-0881-1*) Scarecrow.

— The Great Gangster Pictures II. LC 86-28002. (Illus.). 407p. 1987. 37.50 (*0-8108-1961-9*) Scarecrow.

— The Great Hollywood Musical Pictures. LC 92-7483. (Illus.). 816p. 1992. 79.50 (*0-8108-2529-5*) Scarecrow.

— The Great Science Fiction Pictures II. 2nd ed. LC 89-24058. (Illus.). 499p. 1990. 49.50 (*0-8108-2247-4*) Scarecrow.

— The Great Spy Pictures. LC 73-19509. (Illus.). 585p. 1974. 39.50 (*0-8108-0655-X*) Scarecrow.

— The Great Spy Pictures II. LC 86-11900. (Illus.). 444p. 1986. 39.50 (*0-8108-1913-9*) Scarecrow.

— The Great Western Pictures. LC 76-28224. (Illus.). 477p. 1976. 35.00 (*0-8108-0980-X*) Scarecrow.

— The Great Western Pictures II. LC 88-6528. (Illus.). 438p. 1988. 45.00 (*0-8108-2106-0*) Scarecrow.

— Hollywood Songsters: A Biographical Dictionary. LC 90-41110. (Reference Library of the Humanities: Vol. 1164). (Illus.). 840p. 1990. 75.00 (*0-8240-3444-9*, H1164) Garland.

Parish, James R. & Stanke, Don. Hollywood Baby Boomers: A Biographical Dictionary. LC 91-38768. (Illus.). 686p. 1992. 75.00 (*0-8240-6104-7*, H1295) Garland.

Parish, James R. & Stanke, Don E. The All-Americans. (Illus.). 1978. pap. 12.95 (*0-89508-011-7*) Rainbow Bks.

Parish, James R. & Terrace, Vincent. The Complete Actors' Television Credits, 1948- 1988, Vol. 1: Actors. 2nd ed. LC 89-10607. (Illus.). 560p. 1989. 62.50 (*0-8108-2204-0*) Scarecrow.

— Complete Actors' Television Credits, 1948-1988, Vol. 2: Actresses. 2nd ed. LC 89-10607. (Illus.). 447p. 1990. 49.50 (*0-8108-2258-X*) Scarecrow.

Parish, James R., et al. Film Directors Guide: Western Europe. LC 76-1891. (Illus.). 300p. 1976. 26.00 (*0-8108-0908-7*) Scarecrow.

Parish, John C. Persistence of the Westward Movement, & Other Essays. LC 68-14909. (Essay Index Reprint Ser.). 1977. 19.95 (*0-8369-0767-1*) Ayer.

Parish, L. C. & Gschnait, F., eds. Sexually Transmitted Diseases: A Guide for Clinicians. (Illus.). xiv, 388p. 1988. 121.00 (*0-387-96776-1*) Spr-Verlag.

Parish, Lawrence, et al. Color Atlas of Sexually Transmitted Diseases. LC 90-5080. (Illus.). 184p. 1991. 110.00 (*0-89640-192-8*) Igaku-Shoin.

Parish, Lawrence C. Aesthetic Dermatology. 400p. 1991. text ed. 115.00 (*0-07-048476-7*) Hlth Prof Div.

Parish, Lawrence C. & Millikan, Larry E., eds. Global Dermatology: Diagnosis & Management According to Geography, Climate, & Culture. LC 93-26905. 1994. 150.00 (*0-387-94140-1*) Spr-Verlag.

Parish, Lawrence C., jt. auth. see Crissey, John T.

Parish, Lawrence C., et al. Color Atlas of Difficult Diagnoses in Dermatology. LC 92-1573. (Illus.). 184p. 1993. 135.00 (*0-89640-226-6*) Igaku-Shoin.

Parish, Lawrence C., et al, eds. Cutaneous Infestations of Man & Animal. LC 82-18946. 408p. 1983. text ed. 75.00 (*0-275-91407-0*, C1407, Praeger Pubs) Greenwood.

— Textbook of Pediatric Dermatology. (Illus.). 880p. 1989. text ed. 220.00 (*0-8089-1863-X*, 793249, Grune) Saunders.

***Parish, Lawrence Charles, et al.** Color Atlas of Cutaneous Infections. 1995. write for info. (*0-86542-435-7*) Blackwell Sci.

Parish of St. Mary Labeth Staff. The London County Council, Pt. 2. LC 74-6546. (London County Council. Survey of London Ser.: No. 26). reprint ed. 74.50 (*0-404-51676-9*) AMS Pr.

Parish, Peggy. Amelia Bedelia. LC 91-10163. (I Can Read Bk.). (Illus.). 64p. (J). (gr. k-3). 1992. 14.95 (*0-06-020186-X*); lib. bdg. 14.89 (*0-06-020187-8*); pap. 3.50 (*0-06-444155-5*, Trophy) HarpC Child Bks.

— Amelia Bedelia & the Baby. (Snuggle & Read Story Bks.). (Illus.). 64p. (J). (gr. k-3). 1982. pap. 3.99 (*0-380-57067-X*, Camelot) Avon.

— Amelia Bedelia & the Baby. LC 80-22263. (Greenwillow Read-Alone Bks.). (Illus.). 64p. (J). (gr. 1-3). 1981. 14.00 (*0-688-00316-8*); lib. bdg. 13.93 (*0-688-00321-4*) Greenwillow.

— Amelia Bedelia & the Surprise Shower. LC 66-18655. (Harper I Can Read Bk.). (Illus.). 64p. (J). (gr. k-3). 1966. 13.95 (*0-06-024642-1*); lib. bdg. 13.89 (*0-06-024643-X*) HarpC Child Bks.

— Amelia Bedelia & the Surprise Shower. LC 66-18655. (Trophy I Can Read Bk.). (Illus.). 64p. (J). (ps-3). 1979. pap. 3.50 (*0-06-444019-2*, Trophy) HarpC Child Bks.

— Amelia Bedelia & the Surprise Shower. unabridged ed. (I Can Read Book Ser.). (Illus.). (J). (ps-3). 1990. audio, pap. 6.95 (*1-55994-216-9*, Caedmon) HarperAudio.

— Amelia Bedelia Goes Camping. 1986. pap. 3.99 (*0-380-70067-0*, Camelot) Avon.

— Amelia Bedelia Goes Camping. LC 84-7979. (Greenwillow Read-Alone Bks.). (Illus.). 56p. (J). (gr. 1-3). 1985. 14.00 (*0-688-04058-6*); lib. bdg. 13.93 (*0-688-04057-8*) Greenwillow.

— Amelia Bedelia Helps Out. (Snuggle & Read Story Bks.). (Illus.). 64p. (J). (gr. k-3). 1981. pap. 3.99 (*0-380-53405-3*, Camelot) Avon.

— Amelia Bedelia Helps Out. LC 79-11729. (Greenwillow Read-Alone Bks.). (Illus.). 64p. (J). (gr. 1-3). 1979. 15.00 (*0-688-80231-1*); lib. bdg. 13.93 (*0-688-84231-3*) Greenwillow.

— Amelia Bedelia's Family Album. 48p. (J). 1989. mass mkt. 5.95 (*0-380-70760-8*, Camelot) Avon.

— Amelia Bedelia's Family Album. 48p. (J). 1991. pap. 3.99 (*0-380-71698-4*, Camelot) Avon.

— Amelia Bedelia's Family Album. LC 87-15641. (Illus.). 48p. (J). (gr. 3-9). 1988. 13.95 (*0-688-07676-9*); lib. bdg. 11.88 (*0-688-07677-7*) Greenwillow.

— The Cats' Burglar. LC 82-11751. (Greenwillow Read-Alone Bks.). (Illus.). 64p. (J). (gr. 1-3). 1983. 12.95 (*0-688-01825-4*); lib. bdg. 13.93 (*0-688-01826-2*) Greenwillow.

— Clues in the Woods. 160p. (J). (gr. k-6). 1980. pap. 3.50 (*0-440-41461-X*, YB) Dell.

— Come Back, Amelia Bedelia. LC 73-121799. (Harper I Can Read Bk.). (Illus.). 64p. (J). (ps-3). 1971. 14.95 (*0-06-024667-7*); lib. bdg. 14.89 (*0-06-024668-5*) HarpC Child Bks.

— Come Back, Amelia Bedelia. LC 73-121799. (Trophy I Can Read Book & Cassette Set). (Illus.). 64p. (J). (gr. k-3). 1978. pap. 3.50 (*0-06-444016-8*, Trophy) HarpC Child Bks.

— Come Back, Amelia Bedelia. LC 94-29904. (I Can Read Ser.). (Illus.). 64p. (J). (gr. k-3). 1995. 14.95 (*0-06-026688-0*); lib. bdg. 14.89 (*0-06-026691-0*) HarpC Child Bks.

— Come Back, Amelia Bedelia. unabridged ed. (I Can Read Book Ser.). (Illus.). (J). (ps-3). 1990. audio, pap. 6.95 (*1-55994-225-8*, Caedmon) HarperAudio.

— Dinosaur Time. LC 73-14331. (Early I Can Read Bk.). (Illus.). 32p. (J). (gr. k-3). 1974. 14.95 (*0-06-024653-7*); lib. bdg. 14.89 (*0-06-024654-5*) HarpC Child Bks.

— Dinosaur Time. LC 73-14331. (Trophy Early I Can Read Bk.). (Illus.). 32p. (J). (ps-2). 1983. pap. 3.50 (*0-06-444037-0*, Trophy) HarpC Child Bks.

— The Ghosts of Cougar Island. (Orig.). (J). (gr. 2-4). 1986. pap. 3.50 (*0-440-42872-6*, YB) Dell.

— Good Hunting, Blue Sky. LC 84-43143. (Harper I Can Read Bk.). (Illus.). 64p. (J). (gr. k-3). 1988. lib. bdg. 14.89 (*0-06-024662-6*) HarpC Child Bks.

— Good Hunting, Blue Sky. LC 84-43143. (Trophy I Can Read Bk.). (Illus.). 64p. (J). (gr. k-3). 1991. pap. 3.50 (*0-06-444148-2*, Trophy) HarpC Child Bks.

— Good Work, Amelia Bedelia. (Illus.). 164p. (J). (gr. k-5). 1980. pap. 3.99 (*0-380-49171-0*, Camelot) Avon.

— Good Work, Amelia Bedelia. LC 75-20360. (Greenwillow Read-Alone Bks.). (Illus.). 56p. (J). (gr. 1-4). 1976. 14.00 (*0-688-80022-X*); lib. bdg. 13.93 (*0-688-84022-1*) Greenwillow.

— Haunted House. 160p. (J). (gr. k-6). 1981. pap. 3.50 (*0-440-43459-9*, YB) Dell.

— Haunted House. (J). (gr. 4-6). 1991. 17.00 (*0-8446-6391-3*) Peter Smith.

— Key to the Treasure. 160p. (J). (gr. k-6). 1980. pap. 3.50 (*0-440-44438-1*, YB) Dell.

— Let's Be Early Settlers with Daniel Boone. LC 67-14068. (Illus.). 96p. (J). (gr. 3-5). 1967. lib. bdg. 14.89 (*0-06-024648-0*) HarpC Child Bks.

— Merry Christmas, Amelia Bedelia. LC 85-24919. (Greenwillow Read-Alone Bks.). (Illus.). 64p. (J). (gr. 1-4). 1986. 13.00 (*0-688-06101-X*); lib. bdg. 14.93 (*0-688-06102-8*) Greenwillow.

— Merry Christmas, Amelia Bedelia. (Illus.). 64p. (J). 1987. reprint ed. pap. 3.99 (*0-380-70325-4*, Camelot) Avon.

— Mind Your Manners. LC 77-19096. (Greenwillow Read-Alone Bks.). (Illus.). 56p. (J). (gr. 1-3). 1978. lib. bdg. 13.88 (*0-688-84157-0*) Greenwillow.

— Mind Your Manners. LC 93-11732. (Illus.). 56p. (J). (gr. 1 up). 1994. reprint ed. pap. 4.95 (*0-688-13109-3*, Mulberry) Morrow.

P
Q

— No More Monsters for Me. LC 81-47111. (Harper I Can Read Bk.). (Illus.). 64p. (J). (gr. k-3). 1981. lib. bdg. 14. 89 (*0-06-024658-8*) HarpC Child Bks.

— No More Monsters for Me! LC 81-47111. (Trophy I Can Read Bk.). (Illus.). 64p. (J). (gr. k-3). 1987. pap. 3.50 (*0-06-444109-1*, Trophy) HarpC Child Bks.

— Pirate Island Adventure. 176p. (J). (gr. k-6). 1981. pap. 3.50 (*0-440-47394-2*, YB) Dell.

— Pirate Island Adventure. (J). (gr. 3-6). 1991. 17.00 (*0-8446-6453-7*) Peter Smith.

— Play Ball, Amelia Bedelia. LC 71-85028. (Harper I Can Read Bk.). (Illus.). 64p. (J). (gr. k-3). 1972. 14.95 (*0-06-024655-3*); lib. bdg. 14.89 (*0-06-024656-1*) HarpC Child Bks.

— Play Ball, Amelia Bedelia. LC 71-85028. (Trophy I Can Read Book & Cassette Set). (Illus.). 64p. (J). (ps-3). 1978. pap. 3.50 (*0-06-444005-2*, Trophy) HarpC Child Bks.

— Play Ball, Amelia Bedelia. (Illus.). 64p. (J). (gr. k-3). pap. 1.95 (*0-590-06203-4*) Scholastic Inc.

— Play Ball, Amelia Bedelia. unabridged ed. (I Can Read Book Ser.). (Illus.). (J). (ps-3). 1990. audio 6.95 (*1-55994-241-X*, Caedmon) HarperAudio.

— Scruffy. LC 87-45564. (Harper Early I Can Read Bk.). (Illus.). 64p. (J). (gr. k-3). 1988. lib. bdg. 14.89 (*0-06-024660-X*) HarpC Child Bks.

— Scruffy. LC 87-45564. (Trophy I Can Read Bk.). (Illus.). 64p. (J). (gr. k-3). 1990. pap. 3.50 (*0-06-444137-7*, Trophy) HarpC Child Bks.

— Teach Us, Amelia Bedelia. LC 76-22663. (Greenwillow Read-Alone Bks.). (Illus.). 56p. (J). (gr. 1-4). 1977. 12.95 (*0-688-80069-6*); lib. bdg. 12.88 (*0-688-84069-8*) Greenwillow.

— Teach Us, Amelia Bedelia. (Illus.). 64p. (J). (gr. k-3). 1987. pap. 2.95 (*0-590-43345-8*) Scholastic Inc.

— Thank You, Amelia Bedelia. LC 92-5746. (I Can Read Bk.). (Illus.). 64p. (J). (gr. k-3). 1993. 14.95 (*0-06-022979-9*); lib. bdg. 14.89 (*0-06-022980-2*) HarpC Child Bks.

— Thank You, Amelia Bedelia. (Illus.). (J). (ps-3). 1995. audio, pap. 6.95 (*0-694-70002-9*) HarperAudio.

— Thank You, Amelia Bedelia: Newly Illustrated Edition. LC 92-5746. (Trophy I Can Read Bk.). (Illus.). 64p. (J). (ps-3). 1993. pap. 3.50 (*0-06-444171-7*, Trophy) HarpC Child Bks.

— Too Many Rabbits. (J). (ps-3). 1992. pap. 3.50 (*0-440-40591-2*) Dell.

Parish, Peggy & Lobel, Arnold. Dinosaur Time. (I Can Read Bk. & Cassette). 32p. (J). (ps-2). 1990. pap. 6.95 (*1-55994-262-2*, Caedmon) HarperAudio.

Parish, Peter. The American Civil War. LC 74-84660. 728p. 1975. reprint ed. 55.00 (*0-8419-0176-7*) Holmes & Meier.

Parish, Peter J. Slavery: History & Historians. 1990. pap. 11.00 (*0-06-430182-6*, Icon Edns) HarpC.

Parish, Robert. Alaska Where Only the Tough Survive. (Illus.). 1987. 6.95 (*0-9607358-7-9*) Fathom Pub.

Parish, Steven. Moral Knowing in a Hindu Sacred City: An Exploration of Mind, Emotion, & Self. LC 94-366. 1994. 49.50 (*0-231-08438-2*); pap. write for info. (*0-231-08439-0*) Col U Pr.

Parish, W. Alton & Kindsfather, William. Essentials of Business Mathematics. 4th ed. 368p. (C). 1988. pap. text ed. 32.95 (*0-89863-120-3*) Star Pub CA.

Parish, W. D. & Shaw, W. F. A Dictionary of the Kentish Dialect & Provicialisms in Use in the County of Kent. (English Dialect Society Publications Ser.: No. 54). 1972. reprint ed. pap. 20.00 (*0-8115-0476-X*) Periodicals Srv.

Parish, William J. Charles Ilfeld Company: A Study in the Rise & Decline of Mercantile Capitalism in New Mexico. LC 61-9687. (Studies in Business History: No. 20). (Illus.). 452p. 1961. 29.95 (*0-674-11075-7*) HUP.

Parish, William L., ed. Chinese Rural Development: The Great Transformation. LC 84-22193. 286p. 1985. pap. text ed. 25.95 (*0-87332-344-0*) M E Sharpe.

Parish, William L. & Whyte, Martin K. Village & Family in Contemporary China. LC 78-3411. (Illus.). 1980. pap. text ed. 16.00 (*0-226-64591-6*, P899) U Ch Pr.

Parish, William L., jt. auth. see Whyte, Martin K.

***Parisher, Roy A. & Rhea, Robert A.** Pipe Drafting & Design: Using Manual, AutoCAD, & PRO-PIPE Applications. LC 95-13984. 1995. write for info. (*0-88415-657-5*) Gulf Pub.

***Parisi, Barbara & Pasternack, Barbara.** Empowerment Through Communication. 256p. (C). 1994. per., pap. text ed. 26.95 (*0-8403-9821-2*) Kendall-Hunt.

Parisi, Francesco. Liability for Negligence & Judicial Discretion. 2nd ed. LC 92-13434. (Research Ser.: No. 82). 1992. 18.50 (*0-87725-702-7*) U of Cal IAS.

Parisi, G. Field Theory, Disorder & Stimulations. (Lecture Notes in Physics Ser.). 512p. 1992. pap. text ed. 46.00 (*981-02-1356-5*) World Scientific Pub.

Parisi, Gino. Design for Grammar: A New Focus for Intermediate Spanish. 225p. (ENG & SPA.). (C). 1983. pap. text ed. 18.00 (*0-669-02632-8*) Heath.

Parisi, Giorgio. Field Theory, Disorder & Simulations. 500p. 1992. text ed. 86.00 (*981-02-0964-9*) World Scientific Pub.

— Statistical Field Theory. (C). 1988. text ed. 48.50 (*0-317-69757-9*) Addison-Wesley.

Parisi, Helen. Introduction to Telecommunications. Doyle, Maureen et al, eds. (Illus.). 196p. (Orig.). (C). 1990. reprint ed. pap. 32.00 (*0-9625818-0-1*, 103-1) A G Comns Systs.

— Telecommunications Applications: An Introduction to Designing Solutions to Meet Telecommunication Needs. Doyle, Maureen et al, eds. (Illus.). 182p. (Orig.). (C). 1989. pap. text ed. 32.00 (*0-9625818-1-X*, 105-1) A G Comns Systs.

Parisi, J., jt. ed. see Kapusta, F.

Parisi, Joseph, ed. Marianne Moore: The Art of a Modernist. LC 89-20476. (Studies in Modern Literature: No. 109). 202p. (C). reprint ed. 57.60 (*0-8357-2031-4*, 2070665) Bks Demand.

Parisi, Joseph, jt. ed. see Hine, Daryl.

Parisi, L. The World: Lands & Peoples: Copy Masters. (Illus.). 236p. 1992. 105.00 (*0-87746-361-1*) Graphic Learning.

Parisi, Lynn, ed. see Rocky Mountain Region Japan Project Model District Teams Staff.

Parisi, Lynn, jt. auth. see Turner, Mary J.

Parisi, Lynn S., ed. Hot Rods: Storage of Spent Nuclear Fuel. 2nd ed. (Creative Role-Playing Exercises in Science & Technology Ser.). 60p. 1989. pap. 9.95 (*0-89994-343-8*) Soc Sci Ed.

Parisi, Paul, jt. auth. see Merrill-Oldham, Jan.

Parisi, Peter, ed. Artist of the Actual: Essays on Paul Goodman. LC 85-19583. 204p. 1986. 22.50 (*0-8108-1843-4*) Scarecrow.

Parisi, Philip. Your Own Risk. 28p. (Orig.). 1981. pap. 2.50 (*0-914278-34-7*) Copper Beech.

Parisien, J. Serge. Arthroscopic Surgery. (Illus.). 400p. 1988. text ed. 165.00 (*0-07-048474-0*) Hlth Prof Div.

— Current Techniques in Arthroscopy. (Illus.). 256p. 1994. text ed. 149.95 (*1-878132-04-0*) Current Med.

— Current Techniques in Arthroscopy. 2nd ed. (Illus.). 240p. 1995. text ed. 149.95 (*1-878132-63-6*) Current Med.

— Techniques in Therapeutic Arthroscopy. 392p. 1993. 152. 50 (*0-7817-0054-X*) Raven.

— Techniques in Therapeutic Arthroscopy. 392p. 1994. sl. 500.00 (*0-7817-0055-8*) Raven.

Parisot, Christian. Modigliani's Complete Paintings, Drawings & Watercolors: Catalogue Raisonne I & II, 2 vols. (Illus.). (FRE.). 1990. Vol. I, 368p. write for info. (*0-318-68556-6*); Vol. II, 384p. write for info. (*0-318-68557-4*) A Wofsy Fine Arts.

— Modigliani's Complete Paintings, Drawings & Watercolors: Catalogue Raisonne I & II, 2 vols., Set. (Illus.). (FRE.). 1990. 950.00 (*1-55660-149-2*) A Wofsy Fine Arts.

— Modigliani's Drawings & Watercolors: Catalogue Raisonne I. (Illus.). 368p. (FRE.). 1990. 500.00 (*1-55660-147-6*) A Wofsy Fine Arts.

— Modigliani's Paintings, Drawings & Watercolors: Catalogue Raisonne II. (Illus.). 384p. (FRE.). 1990. 500. 00 (*1-55660-148-4*) A Wofsy Fine Arts.

Parisot, Jean, jt. auth. see Leroy-Terquem, Gerald.

Parisotto, G. Learning Portuguese Without a Teacher. 60p. 1991. Includes tape. audio write for info. (*0-9629515-9-5*); pap. write for info. (*0-9629515-3-6*) Sunrising Pub.

***Parissakis, George, ed.** Science Policy & Research Management in the Balkan Countries: Proceedings of the NATO Advanced Research Workshop, Athens, Greece, November 23-25, 1994. (NATO Advanced Science Institutes - Partnership Sub Series 3). 248p. (C). 1995. lib. bdg. 157.00 (*0-7923-3599-6*) Kluwer Ac.

Parisse, Alan, jt. auth. see Wollack, Richard.

Parisse, Rita, ed. see Joseph, Oreste.

Parisse, Rita, jt. auth. see Joseph, Oreste.

Parisse, Rita, ed. see Joseph, Oroste.

***Parissien, Steven.** Adam Style. (Illus.). 240p. 1995. pap. 35. 00 (*0-7148-3453-X*, Pub. by Phaidon Press UK) Chronicle Bks.

— Adam Style. (Illus.). 240p. 1992. 60.00 (*0-89133-197-2*) Preservation Pr.

— The Georgian House in Britain & America. LC 95-1233. (Illus.). 240p. 1995. 60.00 (*0-8478-1911-6*) Rizzoli Intl.

— Palladian Style. (Illus.). 240p. (C). 1994. 49.95 (*0-7148-2921-8*, Pub. by Phaidon Press UK) Chronicle Bks.

— Regency Style. (Illus.). 240p. 1995. pap. 35.00 (*0-7148-3454-8*, Pub. by Phaidon Press UK) Chronicle Bks.

— Regency Style. (Illus.). 240p. 1992. 60.00 (*0-89133-172-7*) Preservation Pr.

Paritsis, N. C. & Stewart, D. J. A Cybernetic Approach to Colour Perception. LC 81-1624. (Studies in Cybernetics: Vol. 2). (Illus.). 182p. 1983. text ed. 74.00 (*0-677-05620-6*) Gordon & Breach.

Paritzky-Joshua, Karin, tr. see Hirsch, Sampson R.

Paritzky, Karen, tr. see Ehrmann, Naftali H.

Paritzky, Karen, tr. see Hirsch, Samson R.

Parium, Marmor. Chronicum Parium. Jacoby, F., ed. 219p. 1980. pap. 20.00 (*0-89005-362-6*) Ares.

Pariza, Michael W., et al, eds. Mutagens & Carcinogens in the Diet. (Progress in Clinical & Biological Research Ser.). 348p. 1990. text ed. 159.95 (*0-471-56813-9*) Wiley.

Parizeau, Alice & Szabo, Denis. Le Traitement De la Criminalite Au Canada. LC 77-479632. 436p. (FRE.). reprint ed. pap. 124.00 (*0-7837-6948-2*, 2046777) Bks Demand.

Parizkova, Jane, jt. ed. see Shephard, R. J.

***Park.** Anesthesia & Intensive Care for the Patient with Liver Disease. 1995. 75.00 (*0-7506-1249-5*, Focal) Buttrwrth-Heinemann.

— Handbook of Practical Pediatric Cardiology. 296p. 1991. pap. 24.95 (*0-8151-6612-5*, Yr Bk Med Pubs) Mosby Yr Bk.

***Park, Alison.** Textured Canvas Work. (Milner Craft Ser.). (Illus.). 128p. 1995. pap. 14.95 (*1-86351-132-6*, Pub. by S Milner AT) Sterling.

Park, Andrew S. The Wounded Heart of God. 224p. (Orig.). 1993. pap. 16.95 (*0-687-38536-9*) Abingdon.

Park, Barbara. Beanpole. 160p. (J). (gr. 5 up). 1984. pap. 2.95 (*0-380-69840-4*, Flare) Avon.

— Buddies. (YA). (gr. 7 up). 1986. pap. 2.95 (*0-380-69992-3*, Flare) Avon.

— Dear God, Help! Love, Earl. LC 92-20909. 108p. (J). (gr. 3-7). 1994. pap. 3.99 (*0-679-85395-2*) Random Bks Yng Read.

— Don't Make Me Smile. 132p. (J). (gr. 4-7). 1983. pap. 2.95 (*0-380-61994-6*, Camelot) Avon.

— Don't Make Me Smile. LC 81-4880. 128p. (J). (gr. 3-7). 1990. reprint ed. pap. 4.50 (*0-394-84745-8*) Random Bks Yng Read.

— Junie B. Jones & a Little Monkey Business. LC 92-56706. (First Stepping Stone Bks.). (Illus.). 80p. (Orig.). (J). (gr. 1-4). 1993. lib. bdg. 9.99 (*0-679-93886-9*); pap. 2.99 (*0-679-83886-4*) Random Bks Yng Read.

— Junie B. Jones & Her Big Fat Mouth. LC 92-50957. (First Stepping Stone Bks.). (Illus.). 80p. (Orig.). (J). (gr. 1-4). 1993. pap. 2.99 (*0-679-84407-4*) Random Bks Yng Read.

— Junie B. Jones & Her Big Fat Mouth. LC 92-50957. (First Stepping Stone Bks.). (Illus.). 80p. (Orig.). (J). (gr. 1-4). 1993. lib. bdg. 9.99 (*0-679-94407-9*) Random Bks Yng Read.

— Junie B. Jones & Some Sneaky Peeky Spying. LC 93-5557. (First Stepping Stone Bks.). (Illus.). 80p. (Orig.). (J). (gr. 1-4). 1994. pap. 2.99 (*0-679-85101-1*) Random Bks Yng Read.

— Junie B. Jones & Some Sneaky Peeky Spying. LC 93-5557. (First Stepping Stone Bks.). (Illus.). 80p. (Orig.). (J). (gr. 1-4). 1994. lib. bdg. 9.99 (*0-679-95101-6*) Random Bks Yng Read.

— Junie B. Jones & the Stupid Smelly Bus. LC 91-51104. (First Stepping Stone Bks.). (Illus.). 80p. (Orig.). (J). (gr. 1-4). 1992. lib. bdg. 9.99 (*0-679-92642-9*) Random Bks Yng Read.

— Junie B. Jones & the Stupid Smelly Bus. LC 91-51104. (First Stepping Stone Bks.). (Illus.). 80p. (Orig.). (J). (gr. 1-4). 1992. pap. 2.99 (*0-679-82642-4*) Random Bks Yng Read.

— Junie B. Jones & the Yucky Blucky Fruitcake. LC 94-40891. (First Stepping Stone Bks.). (Illus.). (J). 1996. 3.99 (*0-679-86694-9*); lib. bdg. 9.99 (*0-679-96694-3*) Random Bks Yng Read.

— The Kid in the Red Jacket. LC 86-20113. 128p. (J). (gr. 3-7). 1988. reprint ed. 3.99 (*0-394-80571-2*) Knopf Bks Yng Read.

— Maxie, Rosie, & Earl...Partners in Grime. LC 89-28027. 128p. (J). (gr. 3-7). 1990. 13.00 (*0-679-80212-6*) Random Bks Yng Read.

— Mick Harte Was Here. LC 94-27272. (J). 1995. 15.00 (*0-679-87088-1*); 16.99 (*0-679-97088-6*) Knopf.

— My Mother Got Married: (And Other Disasters) LC 88-27257. 128p. (J). (gr. 3-7). 1989. lib. bdg. 13.99 (*0-394-92149-6*) Knopf Bks Yng Read.

— Operation: Dump the Chump. LC 81-8147. 128p. (J). 1989. reprint ed. pap. 4.50 (*0-394-82592-6*) Knopf Bks Yng Read.

— Operation: Dump the Chump. 112p. (J). (gr. 3-7). 1983. pap. 2.75 (*0-380-63974-2*, Camelot) Avon.

— Rosie Swanson: Fourth-Grade Geek for President. LC 91-8616. 114p. (J). (gr. 3-6). 1991. 14.00 (*0-679-82094-9*) Knopf Bks Yng Read.

— Skinnybones. LC 81-20791. 128p. (J). (gr. 3-6). 1982. lib. bdg. 10.99 (*0-394-94988-9*) Knopf Bks Yng Read.

— Skinnybones. LC 81-20791. 112p. (J). (gr. 3-6). 1989. reprint ed. pap. 3.99 (*0-394-82596-9*) Knopf Bks Yng Read.

Park, Bert E. Ailing, Aging, & Addicted Leaders: Studies of Compromised Leadership. LC 93-19550. 288p. 1993. 29. 00 (*0-8131-1853-0*) U Pr of Ky.

— Catastrophic Illness & the Family. LC 91-70967. 1992. 19.95 (*0-8158-0471-7*) Chris Mass.

— The Impact of Illness on World Leaders. LC 86-16136. 396p. 1986. 36.95 (*0-8122-8005-9*) U of Pa Pr.

Park, Byung H. & Good, Robert A. Principles of Modern Immunobiology: Basic & Clinical. LC 73-13831. (Illus.). 627p. reprint ed. 178.70 (*0-8357-9416-4*, 2014573) Bks Demand.

Park, C. Taxonomy of Polygonum Section Echinocaulon (Polygonaceae) LC 88-5361. (Memoirs Ser.: Vol. 47). (Illus.). 82p. (C). 1988. pap. text ed. 19.00 (*0-89327-329-5*) NY Botanical.

Park, C., jt. ed. see Lanzerotti, L. J.

Park, C. H., ed. Law of the Sea in the Nineteen Eighties, 14th Annual Conference Proceeding. 636p. 1983. 18.00 (*0-911189-05-X*) Law Sea Inst.

Park, C. H., jt. ed. see Nordquist, M.

Park, Carol M., jt. auth. see Reid, Philip E.

Park, Chan S. Contemporary Engineering Economics. (Illus.). 850p. (C). 1993. text ed. write for info. (*0-201-14508-1*); pap. text ed. 22.75 (*0-201-53277-8*) Addison-Wesley.

— Interactive Microcomputer Graphics. 1985. text ed. 54.95 (*0-201-05541-4*) Addison-Wesley.

Park, Chan S. & Sharp-Bette, Gunther. Advanced Engineering Economics. 740p. 1990. Net. text ed. write for info. (*0-471-79989-0*) Wiley.

Park, Charles F., Jr. & Freeman, Margaret C. Earthbound: Minerals, Energy & Man's Future (With Prologue) LC 73-87688. (Illus.). 1975. pap. text ed. 33.75 (*0-87735-318-2*) Jones & Bartlett.

Park, Charles F., jt. auth. see Guilbert, John M.

***Park, Charles L., Jr.** True Grits...What Else?!? 190p. (Orig.). Date not set. pap. 12.95 (*0-9645040-0-6*) Chaka Pub.

Park, Charles S. Conflict at the Border: True Tales of a U. S. Customs Border Officer. LC 89-1923. (Illus.). 160p. (Orig.). 1989. pap. 5.00 (*0-914846-41-8*) Golden West Pub.

Park, Chong Kee. Social Security in Korea: An Approach to Socio-Economic Development. 1975. text ed. 10.00 (*0-8248-0537-2*) UH Pr.

Park, Chong Kee, ed. Essays on the Korean Economy: Vol. IV--Human Resources & Social Development in Korea. 383p. 1981. text ed. 15.00 (*0-8248-0755-3*) UH Pr.

Park, Choon-ho. East Asia & the Law of the Sea. (Institute of Social Sciences International Studies: No. 5). 458p. 1983. text ed. 25.00 (*0-8248-1001-5*) UH Pr.

Park, Choon-Ho, et al. Korean International Law. (Korea Research Monographs: No. 4). 53p. 1982. pap. 4.00 (*0-912966-40-8*) IEAS.

Park, Choon-ho & Jae Kyu Park, eds. The Law of the Sea: Problems from the East Asian Perspective. (Law of the Sea Workshop Ser.: No. 8). 620p. 1987. 42.00 (*0-911189-14-9*) Law Sea Inst.

Park, Chris. Sacred Worlds: An Introduction to Geography & Religion. LC 93-36709. (Illus.). 352p. 1994. 79.95x (*0-415-09012-1*, A9824); pap. 25.00 (*0-415-09013-X*, A9828) Routledge.

Park, Chris C. Acid Rain: Rhetoric & Reality. LC 87-20398. 1989. pap. 25.00 (*0-416-92200-7*) Routledge Chapman & Hall.

— Acid Rain: Rhetoric & Reality. (Illus.). 272p. 1990. pap. 25.00 (*0-685-26313-4*) Routledge Chapman & Hall.

— Caring for Creation. 192p. 1992. pap. 12.99 (*0-551-02275-2*) HarpC.

— Chernobyl: The Long Shadow. 192p. 1989. 39.95 (*0-415-03553-8*, A3394) Routledge.

— Tropical Rainforests. LC 92-5659. (Illus.). 208p. 1992. 59. 95 (*0-415-06238-1*, A7390); pap. 15.95 (*0-415-06239-X*, A7416) Routledge.

Park, Chris C., ed. Environmental Policies: An International Review. LC 85-22370. 336p. 1985. 45.00 (*0-7099-2062-8*, Pub. by Croom Helm UK) Routledge Chapman & Hall.

Park, Chris C., ed. see Jones, G. E.

Park, Chul. Nonequilibrium Hypersonic Aerothermodynamics. LC 08-914775. 358p. 1990. text ed. 89.95 (*0-471-51093-9*) Wiley.

Park, Chung I. Advertisement Digest: Library & Information Services, 1978. 89p. 1979. pap. 5.00 (*0-939670-06-2*) Info Digest.

— Best Books by Consensus, 1983-1984. (Orig.). 1984. pap. 3.25 (*0-939670-05-4*) Info Digest.

— Best Books by Consensus, 1984-1985. LC 84-648497. 48p. 1985. pap. 4.25 (*0-939670-08-9*) Info Digest.

— Best Sellers & Best Choices, 1980. x, 95p. 1981. pap. 4.00 (*0-939670-00-3*) Info Digest.

— Best Sellers & Best Choices, 1981. LC 81-640911. x, 112p. (Orig.). 1982. pap. 4.00 (*0-939670-01-1*) Info Digest.

— Best Sellers & Best Choices, 1982. LC 81-640911. 146p. (Orig.). pap. 4.95 (*0-939670-02-X*) Info Digest.

Park, Chung I., ed. Best Books by Consensus, 1985-1986. 50p. (Orig.). 1986. pap. 4.25 (*0-939670-14-3*) Info Digest.

— Best Books by Consensus, 1986-87. 1987. pap. 4.25 (*0-939670-19-4*) Info Digest.

— Best Books by Consensus, 1987-1988. 1988. pap. 4.25 (*0-939670-21-6*) Info Digest.

— Communications & Information Handling Equipment & Services, 1979. 244p. 1979. pap. 5.00 (*0-939670-07-0*) Info Digest.

Park, Clara C. & Shapiro, Leon N. You Are Not Alone: Understanding & Dealing with Mental Illness. 1979. 17. 50 (*0-316-69073-2*) Little.

Park, Colin. Management Training: Starting up Training & Development Programs in Medium-Sized Corporations. (Illus.). 180p. pap. 15.00 (*0-318-13279-6*, PAMPB) Am Soc Train & Devel.

Park, D. Classical Dynamics & Its Quantum Analogues. 2nd enl. ed. (Illus.). 352p. 1990. reprint ed. 51.00 (*0-387-51398-1*) Spr-Verlag.

Park, Dabney G., Jr. Strategic Planning & the Nonprofit Board. (Nonprofit Governance Ser.: No. 06). 12p. (Orig.). (C). 1992. reprint ed. pap. text ed. 10.00 (*0-925299-06-5*) Natl Ctr Nonprofit.

Park, Dave, jt. auth. see Anderson, Neil T.

Park, Dave, jt. auth. see Anderson, Neil.

Park, David. The How & the Why: An Essay on the Origins & Development of Physical Theory. (Illus.). 488p. (C). 1990. text ed. 59.50 (*0-691-08492-0*); pap. text ed. 16.95 (*0-691-02508-8*) Princeton U Pr.

— The Image of Eternity: Roots of Time in the Physical World. LC 79-22984. 160p. 1980. lib. bdg. 22.50 (*0-87023-286-X*) U of Mass Pr.

— Oranges from Spain: Short Stories. 200p. 1992. pap. 13.95 (*0-224-03156-2*, Pub. by Jonathan Cape UK) Trafalgar.

Park, David, ed. The Conservation of Wall Paintings. LC 91-19192. 130p. 1991. pap. 42.50 (*0-89236-162-X*) J P Getty Trust.

Park, David, jt. ed. see Davis, Philip J.

Park, David A. Introduction to the Quantum Theory. 3rd ed. 1992. text ed. write for info. (*0-07-048554-2*) McGraw.

Park, David A., jt. ed. see Norton, Christopher.

Park-Davis & Company Staff. Medical Word Building. 125p. 1970. pap. 21.50 (*0-87489-043-8*) Med Economics.

Park, Dorcas D., jt. auth. see Park, Maurice E.

Park, E. K., ed. Computer Applications in Design, Simulation & Analysis: Proceedings of ISMM Symposium, New Orleans, U. S. A., March 5-7, 1990. 323p. 1990. 95.00 (*0-88986-140-4*) Acta Pr.

Park, E. K. & Chae, K., eds. Computer Communications & Networks (IC3N) (Conference Proceedings Ser.). 327p. 1992. write for info. (*1-880843-01-3*) Int Soc Comp App.

Park, E. K., jt. ed. see Hudson, D.

Park, E. K., jt. ed. see Suda, T.

Park, Ed, jt. auth. see Park, Lue.

Park, Edwards. Fighters: The World's Great Aces & Their Planes. LC 90-11093. (Illus.). 228p. 1990. 19.98 (*0-934738-65-3*) Thomasson-Grant.

— Nanette: Her Pilot's Love Story. (Illus.). 1989. pap. 12.95 (*0-87474-737-6*) Smithsonian.

— Treasures of the Smithsonian. LC 83-40203. (Illus.). 496p. 1983. 42.96 (*0-89599-012-1*) Smithsonian Bks.

An Asterisk (*) at the beginning of an entry indicates that the title is appearing in BIP for the first time.

— Treasures of the Smithsonian. LC 94-19263. (Illus.). 1994. reprint ed. 39.99 (*0-517-11955-2*, Pub. by Wings Bks) Random Hse Value.

*Park, Edwards, text. The Art of William S. Phillips: The Glory of Flight. (Illus.). 160p. 1994. 60.00 (*0-86713-022-9*) Greenw Pr Ltd.

Park, Edwards & Carlhian, Jean P. A New View from the Castle: The Smithsonian's Museum & Garden Complex on the National Mall. LC 87-42555. (Illus.). 160p. (C). 1987. pap. 11.95 (*0-87474-749-X*) Smithsonian.

Park, Francis Y. Speaking Korean, Bk. I. rev. ed. LC 84-80023. 484p. (ENG & KOR.). 1994. pap. text ed. 29.50x (*1-56591-101-6*); audio 125.00 (*0-930878-77-9*) Hollym Intl.

— Speaking Korean, Bk. II. LC 84-80023. 493p. 1994. pap. 33.50x (*1-56591-103-2*) Hollym Intl.

— Speaking Korean, Bk. III: A Guide to Chinese Characters. LC 89-83652. 401p. 1989. 44.50 (*0-930878-81-7*) Hollym Intl.

Park, Gilbert & Fulton, Barbara. The Management of Acute Pain. (Illus.). 176p. 1991. 59.95 (*0-19-263016-4*); pap. 32.50 (*0-19-263003-2*) OUP.

Park, Gilbert R. & Gang, Yoo Goo, eds. Anesthesia & Intensive Care for Patients with Liver Disease. LC 94-11812. 1994. write for info. (*0-7506-9554-4*) Buttrwrth-Heinemann.

Park, Han S. Human Needs & Political Development: Dissent to Utopian Solutions. 280p. 1984. 29.95 (*0-87073-997-2*); pap. 22.95 (*0-87073-998-0*) Schenkman Bks Inc.

***Park, Han S., ed.** North Korea: Ideology, Politics, & Economy. LC 94-48394. 1995. pap. text ed. 24.00 (*0-13-102161-3*) P-H.

Park, Heon-Joo. Housing Land in Government Intervention: With Special Reference to Land Readjustment in Seoul, Korea, & Municipal Site-Leasehold in Stockholm. (University of Stockholm Human Geography Ser.: No. B76). 306p. (Orig.). 1991. pap. 109.00x (*91-7146-924-9*, Pub. by Almqv & Wiksell SW) Coronet Bks.

Park, Heung S., jt. auth. see Larson, James F.

Park, Hongsuk H. American Politics & Foreign Economic Challenge. LC 90-41583. (Foreign Economic Policy of the United States Ser.). 283p. 1990. reprint ed. 25.00 (*0-8240-7434-3*) Garland.

***Park, Innwon.** Regional Integration Among the Asian Nations: A Computable General Equilibrium Model Study. LC 94-37884. 176p. 1995. text ed. 55.00 (*0-275-94981-8*, Praeger Pubs) Greenwood.

Park, Insook H., et al. Korean Immigrants & U. S. Immigration Policy: A Predeparture Perspective. (Papers of the East-West Population Institute: No. 114). xi, 119p. (Orig.). 1990. 3.00 (*0-86638-123-6*) EW Ctr HI.

Park, Irene. Witch That Switched. 96p. 1992. pap. 1.99 (*0-88368-254-0*) Whitaker Hse.

Park, J. B. Biomaterials Science & Engineering. LC 84-16016. 474p. 1984. 55.00 (*0-306-41689-1*, Plenum Pr) Plenum.

Park, J. B. & Lakes, R. S. Biomaterials: An Introduction. 2nd ed. (Illus.). 395p. (C). 1992. 55.00 (*0-306-43992-1*, Plenum Pr) Plenum.

Park, J. F. & Pelroy, R. A., eds. Multilevel Health Effects Research: From Molecules to Man: From Molecules to Man. LC 89-18083. (Proceedings of the 27th Hanford Symposium on Health & the Environment (Oct. 1988) Ser.). 492p. 1990. pap. text ed. 57.50 (*0-935470-55-7*) Battelle.

Park, J. R., ed. Environmental Management in Agriculture: European Perspectives. (Belhaven Press Bk.). (Illus.). 224p. 1992. 67.95 (*1-85293-036-5*, Pub. by Pinter Pubs Ltd UK) CRC Pr.

— Environmental Management in Agriculture: European Perspectives. LC 08-735133. 1994. text ed. 59.95 (*0-471-94742-3*) Wiley.

Park, Jack. MVP-FORTH Expert System Toolkit. Haydon, Glen B., ed. (MVP-Forth Bks.: Vol. 4). 80p. (Orig.). 1984. pap. 22.00 (*0-317-56526-5*) Mntn View Pr.

Park, Jack L. Ohio State Football . . . The Great Tradition. Stephenson, Dave, ed. LC 92-90355. (Illus.). 248p. 1992. 19.95 (*1-881462-45-5*) Lexington OH.

Park, Jacquelyn H. A Stone Gone Mad. LC 91-52674. 336p. 1991. 19.50 (*0-394-55861-8*) Random.

Park, James. Becoming More Authentic: The Positive Side of Existentialism. LC 83-8851. 96p. 1983. pap. 4.00 (*0-89231-100-2*) Existential Bks.

— Becoming More Authentic: The Positive Side of Existentialism. 2nd rev. ed. 96p. (C). 1990. pap. text ed. 14.00 (*0-89231-101-0*) Existential Bks.

— Capacities of the Human Spirit: Spirituality for Humanists. 1983. pap. 1.00 (*0-89231-021-9*) Existential Bks.

— Icons: An A-Z Guide to the People Who Shaped Our Time. 508p. 1992. pap. 12.00 (*0-02-047100-9*, Pub. by Gebrueder Borntraeger GW) Macmillan.

— Romans: An Existential Interpretation. 2nd ed. LC 83-8852. 75p. 1991. pap. text ed. 9.00 (*0-89231-200-9*) Existential Bks.

— Shrinks: The Analysts Analyzed. 224p. 1993. 34.95 (*0-7475-0794-5*, Pub. by Bloomsbury Pub Ltd UK) Trafalgar.

***Park, James W.** Latin American Underdevelopment: A History of Perspectives in the United States, 1870-1965. LC 94-37209. (Illus.). 312p. 1995. text ed. 37.50 (*0-8071-1969-5*) La State U Pr.

— Rafael Nunez & the Politics of Colombian Regionalism, 1863-1886. LC 85-5256. xii, 304p. 1985. text ed. 40.00 (*0-8071-1235-6*) La State U Pr.

Park, Jeff, jt. auth. see Powell, Betty B.

***Park, Jennifer, et al.** Creative Aerobic Fitness. 144p. (C). 1994. per., pap. text ed. 16.95 (*0-8403-9884-0*) Kendall-Hunt.

Park, Jihang. Profit-Sharing & Industrial Co-Partnership in British Industry, 1880-1920: Class Conflict or Class Collaboration. (Modern European History Ser.). 512p. 1987. lib. bdg. 15.00 (*0-8240-7827-6*) Garland.

Park, Jong C. Paul Tillich's Categories for the Interpretation of History: An Application to the Encounter of Eastern & Western Cultures. LC 93-11395. (American University Studies: Vol. 165). 1994. write for info. (*0-8204-2281-9*) P Lang Pubs.

Park, Joseph H. British Prime Ministers of the Nineteenth Century. LC 76-111855. (Essay Index Reprint Ser.). 1977. 28.95 (*0-8369-1892-4*) Ayer.

— British Prime Ministers of the Nineteenth Century: Policies & Speeches. (Essay Index Reprint Ser.). 390p. 1982. reprint ed. lib. bdg. 22.00 (*0-8290-0788-1*) Irvington.

— English Reform Bill of Eighteen Sixty-Seven. LC 76-78002. (Columbia University. Studies in the Social Sciences: No.210). reprint ed. 22.50 (*0-404-51210-0*) AMS Pr.

***Park, Joseph S.** AS-400 Security in a Client-Server Environment. (Wiley Technical Communication Library). Date not set. pap. text ed. 39.95 (*0-471-11683-1*) Wiley.

Park, Julian, ed. see Balmain, Aleksandr.

Park, Jung S. Contractarian Liberal Ethics & the Theory of Rational Choice. LC 91-18282. (American University Studies: Philosophy: Ser. V, Vol. 122). 291p. (C). 1992. text ed. 49.95 (*0-8204-1566-9*) P Lang Pubs.

Park, K. C., ed. see American Society of Mechanical Engineers Staff.

Park, Karin R. & Luey, Beth, eds. Publication Grants for Writers & Publishers: How to Find Them, Win Them, & Manage Them! 112p. 1991. pap. 29.50 (*0-89774-557-4*) Oryx Pr.

Park, Katharine. Doctors & Medicine in Early Renaissance Florence. LC 84-42898. (Illus.). 1985. text ed. 49.50x (*0-691-08373-8*) Princeton U Pr.

Park, Keith, jt. auth. see Grove, Nicola.

Park, Keith, jt. ed. see Lederman, Jess.

Park, Keith K. & Van Agtmael, Antoine W., eds. The World's Emerging Stock Markets: Structure, Development, Regulations & Opportunities. (Guide to World Markets Ser.). 375p. 1992. 55.00 (*1-55738-240-9*) Probus Pub Co.

Park, Kinam, et al. Biodegradable Hydrogels for Drug Delivery. LC 93-60193. 250p. 1993. text ed. 85.00 (*1-56676-004-6*) Technomic.

Park, Kyong, ed. Storefront for Art & Architecture. (Illus.). 268p. (Orig.). Date not set. pap. 29.95 (*1-56898-016-7*) Princeton Arch.

Park, Leslie D. How to Be a Friend to the Handicapped. 1986. 13.95 (*0-533-06864-9*) Vantage.

Park, Leslie D., jt. ed. see Warms, Dorothy.

Park, Lue & Park, Ed. The Smoked-Foods Cookbook: How to Flavor, Cure, & Prepare Savory Meats, Game, Fish, Nuts, & Cheese. LC 92-7047. 224p. 1992. 16.95 (*0-8117-0116-6*) Stackpole.

Park, M. E. & Maxey, M. Two Studies on the Roman Lower Classes: An Original Anthology. LC 75-7347. (Roman History Ser.). 1977. reprint ed. 33.95 (*0-405-07069-1*) Ayer.

Park, Margaret. Crab-Bags & Other Bean-Beings. (Illus.). (J). (gr. 5 up). 1979. pap. 2.95 (*0-915556-05-7*) Great Ocean.

***Park, Marian F.** In Retrospect. 42p. (Orig.). 1994. 5.95 (*1-878116-30-4*) JVC Bks.

— Reflections. 35p. (Orig.). 1991. pap. 6.00 (*1-879533-01-4*) Poetic Page.

— A Season of Pause. (Illus.). 44p. (Orig.). 1994. 5.95 (*1-878116-46-0*) JVC Bks.

Park, Marlene & Markowitz, Gerald E. New Deal for Art: The Government Art Projects of the 1930s with Examples from New York City & State. (Illus.). 172p. 1977. 30.00 (*0-934483-00-0*) Gal Assn NY.

Park, Maurice E. & Park, Dorcas D. Real Estate Law, with Forms: 85 Pocket Parts, 2 vols. 2nd ed. LC 80-54847. (Massachusetts Practice Ser.). 1981. 106.00 (*0-685-42577-0*) West Pub.

Park, Maxwell G. Training in Objective Educational Measurements for Elementary School Teachers. LC 70-177143. (Columbia University. Teachers College. Contributions to Education Ser.: No. 520). (C). reprint ed. 37.50 (*0-404-55520-9*) AMS Pr.

Park, Michael A., jt. auth. see Feder, Kenneth L.

Park, Mungo & Rennell, James. Travels in the Interior Districts of Africa. 1977. 18.95 (*0-405-18974-5*, 16889) Ayer.

Park, Myosik. Jungsoon. LC 84-90581. (Illus.). 304p. 1984. 15.95 (*0-932187-00-5*) M P Pubns.

Park, Myung K. & Guntheroth. How to Read Pediatric ECGS. 3rd ed. 248p. 1992. pap. 39.95 (*0-8016-6834-4*) Mosby Yr Bk.

Park, O. Pselaphidae of Oceania, with Special Reference to the Fiji Islands. (BMB Ser.). 1974. reprint ed. pap. 15.00 (*0-527-02315-9*) Periodicals Srv.

Park, P., ed. Prevention & Social Medicine. 12th ed. (C). 1989. 110.00 (*0-685-36223-X*, Current Dist) St Mut.

Park, P. K., jt. auth. see Champ, Michael A.

***Park, Paul.** Coelestis: Man into Beast. 288p. 1995. 21.95 (*0-8125-85899-X*) Tor Bks.

— The Cult of Loving Kindness. 320p. 1992. mass mkt. 4.50 (*0-380-71819-7*, AvoNova) Avon.

— The Cult of Loving Kindness. (Starbridge Chronicles Ser.). 1991. 20.00 (*0-688-10574-2*) Morrow.

— Soldiers of Paradise. 288p. 1990. pap. 3.95 (*0-380-70581-8*) Avon.

— Sugar Rain. 384p. 1990. reprint ed. pap. 3.95 (*0-380-71179-6*) Avon.

Park, Peter. Sociology Tomorrow: An Evaluation of Sociological Theories in Terms of Science. LC 68-27989. 1968. reprint ed. pap. 9.95 (*0-672-63596-8*) Irvington.

Park, Peter, jt. auth. see Moses, James.

Park, Peter, et al, eds. Voices of Change: Participatory Research in the United States & Canada. LC 92-42898. 232p. 1993. text ed. 49.95 (*0-89789-334-4*, H334, Bergin & Garvey) Greenwood.

Park, Polly, ed. To Save Their Heathen Souls: Voyage to & Life in Foochow, China, Based on Wentworth Diaries & Letters, 1854-1858. LC 84-4247. (Pittsburgh Theological Monographs, New Ser.: No. 9). (Illus.). (Orig.). 1984. pap. 6.00 (*0-915138-66-2*) Pickwick.

Park, R. E. Sketch of Twelfth Alabama Infantry. 24.95 (*0-8488-0218-7*, J M C & Co) Amereon Ltd.

Park, R. W., jt. auth. see Harrigan, W. F.

Park, Rebecca, tr. see Mamonova, Tatyana, ed.

Park, Richard L. & Lambert, Richard D., eds. The American Revolution Abroad. LC 76-19935. (Annals Ser.: No. 428). 200p. 1976. 27.00 (*0-87761-206-4*); pap. 18.00 (*0-87761-207-2*) Am Acad Pol Soc Sci.

Park, Richard L., jt. auth. see Bueno De Mesquita, Bruce.

Park, Richard L., ed. see Newell, Richard S.

Park, Richard W., jt. auth. see Koff, Theodore H.

Park, Robert. The Inventor's Handbook: How to Develop, Protect, & Market Your Invention. 2nd ed. (Illus.). 232p. (Orig.). 1990. pap. 14.95 (*1-55870-149-4*) Betterway Bks.

Park, Robert & Gamble, W. L. Reinforced Concrete Structures. LC 80-10229. 618p. 1981. text ed. 75.95 (*0-471-65915-0*, Wiley-Interscience) Wiley.

Park, Robert & Paulay, Thomas. Reinforced Concrete Structures. LC 74-28156. 769p. 1975. text ed. 94.95 (*0-471-65917-7*, Wiley-Interscience) Wiley.

Park, Robert E. & Burgess, Ernest W. Introduction to the Science of Sociology. 3rd ed. Janowitz, Morris B., ed. LC 69-15366. (Heritage of Sociology Ser.). 1969. lib. bdg. 40.00 (*0-226-64604-1*) U Ch Pr.

Park, Robert E. & Miller, Herbert A. Old World Traits Transplanted. LC 69-18788. (American Immigration Collection Ser., No. 1). (Illus.). 1969. reprint ed. 16.95 (*0-405-00536-9*) Ayer.

Park, Robert E., et al. The City. LC 66-23694. (Heritage of Sociology Ser.). 1984. reprint ed. pap. text ed. 15.95 (*0-226-64611-4*) U Ch Pr.

Park, Roberta J. & Eckert, Helen M., eds. New Possibilities, New Paradigms? LC 90-23215. (American Academy of Physical Education Papers). 176p. 1991. pap. text ed. 20.00x (*0-87322-313-6*, BPAR0313) Human Kinetics.

Park, Roberta J., jt. ed. see Berryman, Jack W.

Park, Roberta J., jt. ed. see Harris, Janet C.

Park, Roberta J., jt. ed. see Mangan, J. A.

Park, Roger & McFarland, Douglas D. Computer-Aided Exercises on Civil Procedure. 3rd ed. 210p. 1993. reprint ed. pap. text ed. 19.50 (*0-314-86711-2*) West Pub.

***Park, Roger C. & McFarland, Douglas D.** Computer-Aided Exercises on Civil Procedure. 4th ed. LC 95-16454. 239p. (C). 1995. pap. text ed. 21.00 (*0-314-06194-0*) West Pub.

Park, Roger C., jt. auth. see Waltz, Jon R.

Park, Rolla E. Incremental Costs & Efficient Prices with Lumpy Capacity: The Two Product Case. LC 94-9620. 1994. write for info. (*0-8330-1523-0*, MR-427-ICTF) Rand Corp.

Park, Rosemarie, et al. Reading: Skill Enhancement. 200p. 1993. disk 20.00 (*1-56118-203-6*); disk 20.00 (*1-56118-202-8*) Paradigm MN.

— Reading: Skill Enhancement. 200p. 1994. 8.00 (*0-318-70382-3*); pap. text ed. 9.95 (*1-56118-204-4*) Paradigm MN.

— Reading for Workplace Success. 351p. (C). 1991. pap. text ed. 15.95 (*1-56118-200-1*); teacher ed. pap. text ed. 8.00 (*1-56118-201-X*) Paradigm MN.

Park, Ruth. Playing Beatie Bow. (Storybooks Ser.). 200p. (J). (gr. 5-9). 1984. pap. 3.99 (*0-14-031460-1*, Puffin) Puffin Bks.

— Things in Corners. 208p. (J). (gr. 5 up). 1993. pap. 3.99 (*0-14-032713-4*, Puffin) Puffin Bks.

***Park, Sam O. & LeHeron, Richard, eds.** The Asian Pacific Rim & Globalization. 202p. 1995. boxed, pap. 55.95 (*1-85628-894-3*, Pub. by Avebury Pub UK) Ashgate Pub Co.

Park, Severna. Speaking Dreams. LC 92-5384. 256p. (Orig.). 1992. lib. bdg. 20.95 (*1-56341-015-X*); pap. 9.95 (*1-56341-014-1*) Firebrand Bks.

Park, Sung-Bae. Buddhist Faith & Sudden Enlightenment. LC 82-10459. 211p. 1983. 59.50 (*0-87395-673-7*); pap. 19.95 (*0-87395-674-5*) State U NY Pr.

Park, Sung-Bong. An Aesthetics of the Popular Arts. (Aesthetica Upsaliensia Ser.: No. 5). 188p. (Orig.). 1993. pap. 47.50x (*91-554-3047-3*, Pub. by Uppsala Universitet SW) Coronet Bks.

Park, Sung H. Bridge Inspection & Structural Analysis: Handbook of Bridge Inspection. LC 80-81421. (Illus.). 312p. (Orig.). 1980. pap. text ed. 20.00 (*0-9604440-0-9*) S H Park.

— Bridge Rehabilitation & Replacement (Bridge Repair Practice) LC 82-90094. (Illus.). 818p. (C). 1984. text ed. 70.00 (*0-9604440-1-7*) S H Park.

Park, Sung-Jo, ed. East Asia International Review, Vol. 6: Global Competition & Human Resources. (C). 1993. text ed. 57.50 (*0-8133-1975-7*) Westview.

— Managerial Efficiency in Competition & Cooperation: Japanese, West- & East-European Strategies & Perspectives. LC 92-24385. 361p. (C). 1992. pap. text ed. 59.50 (*0-8133-1676-6*) Westview.

Park, Susan, jt. ed. see Starr, Mildred.

Park, T. S. Spinal Dysraphism. (Contemporary Issues in Neurological Surgery Ser.). (Illus.). 208p. 1992. 80.00 (*0-86542-105-6*) Blackwell Sci.

***Park, Taisoo, ed.** Taxonomy & Distribution of the Marine Calanoid Copepod Family Euchaetidae. LC 94-28941. 1995. pap. text ed. 26.00 (*0-520-09802-1*) U CA Pr.

Park, Thelma. The House of Neh. (Illus.). 178p. (Orig.). 1986. pap. 9.95 (*1-55630-023-9*) Brentwood Comm.

Park, Thomas, ed. Harleian Miscellany, 10 Vols, Set. LC 02-21219. reprint ed. 950.00 (*0-404-03140-4*) AMS Pr.

Park, Thomas, ed. see Harington, John.

Park, Thomas K., ed. Risk & Tenure in Arid Lands: The Political Ecology of Development in the Senegal River Basin. LC 93-9691. (Monographs on Arid Lands Development). 383p. 1993. 29.95 (*0-8165-1374-0*) U of Ariz Pr.

Park, Thomas K., et al. Conflicts over Land & the Crisis of Nationalism in Mauritania. (LTC Research Paper Ser.: No. 142). 55p. 1991. pap. 7.00 (*0-685-49240-0*) U of Wis Land.

***Park, Vicki.** Live! Don't Diet! The Low-Fat Cookbook That Can Change Your Life. LC 94-68759. 242p. (Orig.). 1995. pap. 16.95 (*0-9642733-0-6*) Pepper Tree Pr.

Park, W. H. & Enos, J. L. The Adoption & Diffusion of Imported Technology: The Case of Korea. 224p. 1985. 55.00 (*0-7099-2030-X*, Pub. by Croom Helm UK) Routledge Chapman & Hall.

Park, W. R. & Maillie, J. B. Strategic Analysis for Venture Evaluation: The Safe Approach to Business Decisions. 224p. 1982. text ed. 33.95 (*0-442-24507-6*) Van Nos Reinhold.

Park, W. W. & Corkhill, J. W. The Histology of Borderline Cancer. LC 79-26151. (Illus.). 480p. 1980. 93.00 (*3-540-09792-9*) Spr-Verlag.

Park, William. The Idea of Rococo. LC 90-51017. (Illus.). 144p. (C). 1993. 55.00 (*0-87413-434-X*) U Delaware Pr.

Park, William D., jt. auth. see Cromie, Stephen.

Park, William R. & Chapin-Park, Sue. How to Succeed in Your Own Business. LC 77-28955. (Wiley-Interscience Publication Ser.). 362p. reprint ed. pap. 103.20 (*0-317-26295-5*, 2025179) Bks Demand.

Park, William R. & Chapin, Wayne B., Jr. Construction Bidding: Strategic Pricing for Profit. 2nd ed. (Practical Construction Guides Ser.). 328p. 1992. text ed. 69.95 (*0-471-54763-8*) Wiley.

***Park, William W.** International Forum Selection. LC 94-47495. 1995. write for info. (*90-6544-883-7*) Kluwer Law Tax Pubs.

Park, Won C., ed. see International Congress on Applied Mineralogy in the Minerals Industry Staff.

Park, Won C., ed. see Metallurgical Society of AIME Staff.

Park, Y. H. & Leibowitz, Jeff. Fighting Back: Taekwondo for Women. (Illus.). 160p. (Orig.). 1994. pap. 14.95 (*0-9637151-1-9*) YH Pk Taekwondo.

— Tae Kwon Do Dinosaurs: How Dinosaurs Train to Get Their Black Belts. (Illus.). 32p. (Orig.). (J). 1994. pap. 5.95 (*0-9637151-2-7*) YH Pk Taekwondo.

— Taekwondo for Children: The Ultimate Reference Guide for Children Interested in the World's Most Popular Martial Art. (Illus.). 128p. (Orig.). (J). (gr. 4-8). 1994. pap. 9.95 (*0-9637151-0-0*) YH Pk Taekwondo.

Park, Yoon S., ed. International Banking & Financial Centers. (C). 1989. lib. bdg. 67.00 (*0-7923-9016-4*) Kluwer Ac.

Park, Yung C., jt. auth. see Cole, David C.

Park, Yung C., jt. ed. see Patrick, Hugh T.

Park, Yung H. Bureaucrats & Ministers in Contemporary Japanese Government. LC 85-82273. (Japan Research Monograph: No. 8). 192p. 1986. pap. 7.50 (*0-912966-84-X*) IEAS.

Parkash, I. Desert Ecology. (C). 1988. text ed. 125.00 (*81-85046-75-1*, Pub. by Scientific Pubs II) St Mut.

Parkash, Ram. Advances in Forestry Research in India, Vols. 1-6. 265p. 1990. 148.00 (*0-685-49623-6*, Pub. by Intl Bk Distr II) St Mut.

— Advances in Forestry Research in India, Vols. 1-10. 265p. 1993. 198.00 (*81-7089-901-X*, Pub. by Intl Bk Distr II) St Mut.

— Forest Management. 256p. 1986. 125.00 (*81-7089-082-9*, Pub. by Intl Bk Distr II) St Mut.

— Forest Management. 256p. (C). 1986. 295.00 (*0-685-61462-X*, Pub. by Intl Bk Distr II); text ed. 150.00 (*0-685-52005-6*, Pub. by Intl Bk Distr II) St Mut.

— Propagation & Practice of Important Indian Trees. 460p. (C). 1991. text ed. 400.00 (*81-7089-112-4*, Pub. by Intl Bk Distr II) St Mut.

— Silviculture & Propagation of Indian Forest Trees. 400p. 1990. 210.00 (*81-7089-113-2*, Pub. by Intl Bk Distr II) St Mut.

— Theory & Practice of Silvicultural Systems. 256p. (C). 1983. text ed. 150.00 (*0-685-52006-4*, Pub. by Intl Bk Distr II) St Mut.

— Theory & Practice of Silvicultural Systems. 256p. 1991. 175.00 (*81-7089-062-4*, Pub. by Intl Bk Distr II) St Mut.

— Theory & Practice of Silvicultural Systems. 256p. (C). 1991. 260.00 (*0-685-61461-1*, Pub. by Intl Bk Distr II) St Mut.

Parkay, Forrest, jt. auth. see Greenwood, Gordon.

Parkay, Forrest W., ed. Curriculum Planning: A New Approach. 6th ed. LC 92-26341. 1992. pap. text ed. write for info. (*0-205-14620-1*) Allyn.

Parkay, Forrest W. & Hall, Gene E. Becoming a Principal: The Challenges of Beginning Leadership. 432p. (C). 1991. text ed. 63.00 (*0-205-13180-8*) Allyn.

Parkay, Forrest W. & Hardcastle, Beverly. Becoming a Teacher: Accepting the Challenge of a Profession. 560p. 1990. text ed. 47.00 (*0-205-11910-7*, H19102); teacher ed, trans. write for info. (*0-318-66360-0*, H19110) Allyn.

Parkay, Forrest W. & Stanford, Beverly H. Becoming a Teacher: Accepting the Challenge of a Profession. 2nd ed. 576p. (C). 1993. text ed. 47.00 (*0-205-13327-4*) Allyn.

P Q

An Asterisk (*) at the beginning of an entry indicates that the title is appearing in BIP for the first time.

— Becoming a Teacher: Accepting the Challenge of a Profession. 3rd ed. LC 94-28853. 1994. text ed. write for info. (*0-205-16293-2*) Allyn.

Parkay, Forrest W., jt. auth. see Greenwood, Gordon E.

Parkay, Forrest W., et al, eds. Quest for Quality: Improving Basic Skills Instruction in the 1980s. 136p. (Orig.). (C). 1984. pap. text ed. 14.50 (*0-8191-3783-9*) U Pr of Amer.

***Parke.** Biography. 1995. text ed. 22.95 (*0-8057-0965-7*) Macmillan.

Parke, jt. auth. see Floyd.

***Parke, Barbara.** Toni Morrison: A Guide to Her Novels. 32p. 1994. pap. text ed. 4.50 (*0-9644061-0-1*) Angell Pubns.

Parke, Caroline, ed. see Lodo, Venerable L.

Parke, Caroline, ed. see Lodo, Venerable Larma.

Parke, Caroline M., ed. see Rinpoche, Kalu.

Parke, Catherine N. Other People's Lives. LC 93-48034. 64p. (Orig.). 1994. pap. 9.00 (*0-933532-97-0*) BkMk.

— Samuel Johnson & Biographical Thinking. 200p. 1991. text ed. 34.95 (*0-8262-0789-8*) U of Mo Pr.

Parke, Catherine N., ed. & intro. In the Shadow of Parnassus: Zoe Akin's Essays on American Poetry. LC 94-6472. 1995. write for info. (*0-945636-60-1*) Susquehanna U Pr.

Parke, Charles R. Dreams to Dust: A Diary of the California Gold Rush, 1849-1850. Davis, James E., ed. LC 88-27763. (Illus.). xxxiv, 280p. 1989. 35.00 (*0-8032-3674-3*) U of Nebr Pr.

Parke County Hist. Society Staff & Turner Publishing Co., Staff. History & Families Parke County, Indiana. LC 88-51840. 392p. 1989. 49.95 (*0-938021-33-8*) Turner Pub KY.

Parke, D. V. The Biochemistry of Foreign Compounds. 1968. 120.00 (*0-08-012202-7*, Pub. by Pergamon Repr UK) Franklin.

Parke, David. The Epic of Unitarianism. 1992. pap. 16.00 (*0-933840-05-5*, Skinner Hse Bks) Unitarian Univ.

***Parke, Diana.** North Cyprus. (Bradt Country Guides Ser.). (Illus.). 214p. (Orig.). 1994. pap. 13.95 (*1-56440-544-3*, Pub. by Bradt Pubns UK) Globe Pequot.

Parke, Frederick I. & Waters, Keith. Computer Facial Animation. (Illus.). 450p. (C). 1995. text ed. 59.95 (*1-56881-014-8*) AK Peters.

***Parke, Gertrude.** Big Chocolate Cookbook. 1994. pap. 8.98 (*0-88365-609-4*) Galahad Bks.

Parke, H. W. Festivals of the Athenians. LC 76-12819. (Aspects of Greek & Roman Life Ser.). (Illus.). 208p. 1977. pap. 14.95 (*0-8014-9440-0*) Cornell U Pr.

— Greek Mercenary Soldiers. 250p. Date not set. pap. 20.00 (*0-89005-386-3*) Ares.

— The Oracles of Apollo in Asia Minor. LC 85-24260. (Illus.). 312p. 1993. pap. 19.95 (*0-415-09571-9*, B0419) Routledge.

— Sibyls & Sibylline Prophecy in Classical Antiquity. McGing, Brian C., ed. 256p. 1988. lib. bdg. 42.50 (*0-415-00343-1*) Routledge.

— Sibyls & Sibylline Prophecy in Classical Antiquity. 1992. pap. 16.95 (*0-415-07638-2*, Pub. by Tavistock UK) Routledge Chapman & Hall.

Parke, J. P. & Ward, T. Lloyd: Genealogical Notes Relating to the Families of Lloyd, Pemberton, Hutchinson, Hudson & Parke. Glenn, T. A., ed. 89p. 1992. reprint ed. lib. bdg. 28.00 (*0-8328-2678-2*); reprint ed. pap. 18.00 (*0-8328-2679-0*) Higginson Bk Co.

Parke, Lawrence. Acting Truths & Fictions. (Orig.). 1995. write for info. (*0-318-70265-7*) Acting World Bks.

— Acting Truths & Fictions. LC 95-75729. 448p. (Orig.). 1995. pap. 22.50 (*0-9615288-7-7*) Acting World Bks.

— The Film Actor's Complete Career Guide. LC 91-73555. (Illus.). 394p. (Orig.). (C). 1992. pap. 24.95 (*0-9615288-9-3*) Acting World Bks.

— How to Start Acting in Film & Television Wherever You Are in America. LC 93-70044. (Illus.). 144p. (Orig.). 1993. pap. 19.95 (*0-9615288-4-2*) Acting World Bks.

— Since Stanislavski & Vakhtangov: The Method As a System for Today's Actor. 272p. (Orig.). 1986. pap. 12.95 (*0-9615288-8-5*) Acting World Bks.

Parke, Margaret. A Garden for Cutting: Gardening for Flower Arrangements. LC 93-10806. 224p. 1993. 35.00 (*1-55670-250-7*) Stewart Tabori & Chang.

***Parke, Marilyn & Panik, Sharon.** A Quetzalcoatl Tale of Chocolate: Legends from Mexico & Central America. (Illus.). 48p. (J). 1994. 8.95 (*0-86653-959-X*) Good Apple.

— A Quetzalcoatl Tale of Colored Cotton: Legends from Mexico & Central America. (Illus.). 48p. (J). 1995. 8.95 (*0-614-05247-5*) Good Apple.

— A Quetzalcoatl Tale of Corn. (SPA.). 1992. pap. 8.99 (*0-86653-964-6*) Fearon Teach Aids.

— A Quetzalcoatl Tale of Corn. (Illus.). 48p. (J). 1992. 8.95 (*0-86653-965-4*) Good Apple.

— A Quetzalcoatl Tale of the Ball Game. (SPA.). 1992. pap. 8.99 (*0-86653-961-1*) Fearon Teach Aids.

— A Quetzalcoatl Tale of the Ball Game. (Illus.). 48p. (J). 1992. 8.95 (*0-86653-962-X*) Good Apple.

— A Quetzalcoatl Tale of the Ball Game - Teachers Guide. 1992. pap. 8.99 (*0-86653-960-3*) Fearon Teach Aids.

— A Teacher's Guide to a Quetzalcoatl Tale of Chocolate. 48p. 1994. teacher ed 8.95 (*0-614-05246-7*) Good Apple.

— A Teacher's Guide to a Quetzalcoatl Tale of Colored Cotton. 48p. 1995. teacher ed 8.95 (*0-614-05248-3*) Good Apple.

— Teacher's Guide to a Quetzalcoatl Tale of Corn. 48p. 1992. teacher ed 8.95 (*0-86653-963-8*) Good Apple.

Parke, Peter S., comp. Satellite Imagery Interpretation for Forecasters, 3 vols., Set. (Monograph Ser.: No. 2-86). (C). 1993. reprint ed. pap. text ed. 51.00 (*1-883563-04-6*) Natl Weather.

— Satellite Imagery Interpretation for Forecasters, Vol. 1. (Monograph Ser.: No. 2-86). 240p. (C). 1993. reprint ed. pap. text ed. 20.00 (*1-883563-01-1*) Natl Weather.

— Satellite Imagery Interpretation for Forecasters, Vol. 2. (Monograph Ser.: No. 2-86). 248p. (C). 1993. reprint ed. pap. text ed. 20.00 (*1-883563-02-X*) Natl Weather.

— Satellite Imagery Interpretation for Forecasters, Vol. 3. (Monograph Ser.: No. 2-86). (C). 1993. reprint ed. pap. text ed. 20.00 (*1-883563-03-8*) Natl Weather.

Parke, Preston G. Biorhythms, Biological Clocks & Periodicity: Index of New Information with Authors & Subjects. 180p. 1993. 49.50 (*1-55914-900-0*); pap. 39.50 (*1-55914-901-9*) ABBE Pubs Assn.

Parke, Ross D. Fathers. LC 80-29079. (Developing Child Ser.). (Illus.). 144p. (C). 1981. pap. text ed. 6.95 (*0-674-29516-1*) HUP.

Parke, Ross D., ed. Review of Child Development Research, Vol. 7. LC 64-20472. (Review of Child Development Research Ser.). x, 470p. 1985. lib. bdg. 30.00 (*0-226-64666-1*) U Ch Pr.

Parke, Ross D. & Kellam, Sheppard G., eds. Exploring Family Relationships with Other Social Contexts. (Advances in Family Research Ser.). 248p. 1993. text ed. 59.95 (*0-8058-1073-0*) L Erlbaum Assocs.

Parke, Ross D. & Ladd, Gary W., eds. Family-Peer Relationships: Modes of Linkage. 424p. 1992. text ed. 89.95 (*0-8058-0600-8*); pap. 36.00 (*0-8058-0601-6*) L Erlbaum Assocs.

Parke, Ross D., jt. auth. see Hetherington, E. Mavis.

Parke, Ross D., et al, eds. A Century of Developmental Psychology. 695p. 1994. text ed. 49.95 (*1-55798-233-7*); pap. text ed. 29.95 (*1-55798-238-4*, 431-6411) Am Psychol.

Parke, Sara. No Fair Peeking. LC 90-85436. (Minnie 'n Me Ser.). (Illus.). 32p. (J). (gr. k-3). 1991. 5.95 (*1-56282-037-0*) Disney Pr.

Parke, Solitaire. Beyond the Astral Planes. (Larger World Trilogy Ser.). (Illus.). 245p. (C). 1994. text ed. 21.95 (*1-885431-00-7*) Gray Wolf Prods.

Parke, William T. Musical Memoirs, Comprising an Account of the General State of Music in England. 2 Vols. in 1. LC 77-125058. (Music Ser.). 1970. reprint ed. lib. bdg. 85.00 (*0-306-70023-9*) Da Capo.

Parkel, Paula. Raven Cloud's Poems to Her Father: A Healing Journey. Rhiannon, Thea, ed. 26p. (Orig.). 1991. pap. text ed. 5.95 (*0-9629349-0-9*) Raven Cloud.

Parkenham, Bette M. Menstruation Disorders: Medical Subject Analysis with Research Bibliography. LC 84-45648. 150p. 1987. 44.50 (*0-88164-234-7*); pap. 39.50 (*0-88164-235-5*) ABBE Pubs Assn.

***Parker.** Alarming Animals. (Illus.). (J). 1995. pap. text ed. (*0-8114-6332-X*) Raintree Steck-V.

— Algorithms & Data Structures in C Plus Plus. 1993. 49.95 (*0-8493-7171-6*, QA) CRC Pr.

— Alone in the Dark. (Baby-Sitter's Nightmares Ser.: No. 1). 1995. mass mkt. 3.50 (*0-06-106302-9*, Harp PBks) HarpC.

— Awesome Amphibians. (Illus.). (J). 1995. pap. text ed. (*0-8114-6334-6*) Raintree Steck-V.

— Battle of the Strong: A Romance of Two Kingdoms. (Jersey Heritage Editions Ser.). 1991. write for info. (*0-86120-020-9*, Pub. by Aris & Phillips UK) David Brown.

— Beastly Bugs. (Illus.). (J). 1995. pap. text ed. (*0-8114-6333-8*) Raintree Steck-V.

— Cumulative Trauma Disorders: Current Issues & Ergonomic. 1992. 62.95 (*0-87371-322-2*, RD97) Lewis Pubs.

— Deterministic Scheduling Theory. 1995. (*0-412-05051-X*) Chapman & Hall.

— Graphite. 1990. pap. 2.00 (*0-916562-08-5*) Truck Pr.

— How Do You Know Who You Are? 1980. 14.95 (*0-02-594720-6*) Macmillan.

— I Love Spiders. (J). 1989. pap. 19.95 (*0-590-50153-4*) Scholastic Inc.

— Image Reconstruction in Radiology. 1990. 130.95 (*0-8493-0150-5*, RC78) CRC Pr.

— Modern Chinchilla Fur Farming. 1975. 32.00 (*0-87505-126-X*) Borden.

— The Norfin Trolls from A to Z. (J). 1993. pap. 2.50 (*0-590-46957-6*) Scholastic Inc.

— Perchance to Dream. 1994. pap. 5.99 (*0-517-13004-1*) Random.

— Revolting Reptiles. (Illus.). (J). 1995. pap. text ed. (*0-8114-6335-4*) Raintree Steck-V.

— Russia Reborn? The Labor Pains of the New Russia. 1996. 25.00 (*0-02-874078-5*) Free Pr.

— Topley & Wilson's Principles of Bacteriology, Virology & Immunity, 5 vols., Set. 2456p. 1990. 395.00 (*1-55664-288-1*) Mosby Yr Bk.

Parker, jt. auth. see Agre.

Parker, jt. auth. see Ensminger.

Parker, jt. auth. see Murphy.

Parker, et al. The Skin: Cutaneous Medicine & Surgery. 2000p. Date not set. 350.00 (*0-8016-6417-9*) Mosby Yr Bk.

Parker, A. Parker in America, Sixteen Thirty to Nineteen Ten, Genealogy, Biography, & History. (Illus.). 608p. 1989. reprint ed. lib. bdg. 99.00 (*0-8328-0936-5*); reprint ed. pap. 91.00 (*0-8328-0937-3*) Higginson Bk Co.

Parker, A. & Sellwood, B. W., eds. Sediment Diagenesis. 1983. pap. text ed. 55.50 (*90-277-1874-1*) Kluwer Ac.

Parker, A. A. The Philosophy of Love in Spanish Literature. 245p. 1985. 15.00 (*0-85224-491-6*, Pub. by Edinburgh U Pr UK) Col U Pr.

Parker, A. C. Archeological History of New York, 2 vols., Set. 1993. reprint ed. lib. bdg. 150.00 (*0-7812-5163-X*) Rprt Serv.

— Constitution of the Five Nations. 158p. 1993. reprint ed. lib. bdg. 69.00 (*0-7812-5161-3*) Rprt Serv.

— Seneca Myths & Folktales. 465p. 1993. reprint ed. lib. bdg. 99.00 (*0-7812-5162-1*) Rprt Serv.

Parker, A. E. Booby Trapped. (Clue Ser.: No. 6). (J). (gr. 4-7). 1994. pap. 3.25 (*0-590-47805-2*) Scholastic Inc.

— The Case of the Invisible Cat. (Clue Ser.: No. 3). (J). (gr. 4-7). 1992. pap. 2.95 (*0-590-45632-6*) Scholastic Inc.

— The Clue in the Shadows. (Clue Ser.: No. 08). (J). (gr. 4-7). 1995. pap. 3.25 (*0-590-48934-8*) Scholastic Inc.

— Midnight Phone Calls. (Clue Ser.: No. 5). (J). (gr. 4-7). 1994. pap. 3.25 (*0-590-47804-4*) Scholastic Inc.

— Mystery at the Masked Ball. (Clue Ser.: No. 4). (J). (gr. 4-7). 1993. pap. 2.95 (*0-590-45633-4*) Scholastic Inc.

— Mystery in the Moonlight. (Clue Bks.: No. 9). (J). (gr. 4-9). 1995. pap. 3.25 (*0-590-48935-6*) Scholastic Inc.

— The Picture-Perfect Crime. (Clue Ser.: No. 07). (J). (gr. 4-7). 1994. pap. 3.25 (*0-590-48735-3*) Scholastic Inc.

Parker, A. E., creator. Who Killed Mr. Boddy? (Clue Ser.: No. 1). 160p. (J). (gr. 4 up). 1992. pap. 2.95 (*0-590-46110-9*, Apple Paperbacks) Scholastic Inc.

Parker, A. H., tr. see Steiner, Rudolf.

Parker, A. J., jt. auth. see Carter, R. W.

Parker, A. J., jt. ed. see Carter, R. W.

Parker, A. J., et al, eds. Mafic Dykes & Emplacement Mechanisms: Proceedings of the Second International Conference, Adelaide, South Australia, 12 - 15 September 1990. (Illus.). 560p. (C). 1990. text ed. 95.00 (*90-6191-158-3*, Pub. by A A Balkema NE) Ashgate Pub Co.

Parker, A. Morgan. Psalms from the Sea. 56p. 1982. pap. 2.50 (*0-8341-0745-7*) Beacon Hill.

***Parker, Addison.** How to Obtain Business Loans: An Insider's Guide. Date not set. 17.95 (*0-945456-16-6*) PT Pubns.

— How to Obtain Business Loans: Your Insider's Guide. LC 94-32763. 350p. 1995. 17.95 (*0-945456-14-X*) PT Pubns.

Parker, Alan, jt. auth. see Bateson, Keith.

Parker, Alan J. BASIC for Business for the VAX & PDP-11. 2nd ed. (C). 1983. text ed. 30.00 (*0-8359-0358-3*, Reston); pap. text ed. 28.00 (*0-8359-0357-5*, Reston) P-H.

— TRS-80 Disk BASIC for Business for the Model II & Model III. 1982. pap. 14.95 (*0-8359-7872-9*, Reston) P-H.

Parker, Alan J. & Stewart, John F. Accountant's BASIC Programming for the Apple II. 1983. 18.95 (*0-8359-0047-9*, Reston) P-H.

— Apple BASIC Business: For the Apple II. 1984. text ed. 19.95 (*0-8359-0228-5*, Reston) P-H.

— Applesoft BASIC for the Business Executive. 1984. pap. text ed. write for info. (*0-8359-0075-4*, Reston) P-H.

— The Executive Guide to the Apple Computer, BASIC: Programming & VisiCalc. 1984. disk 59.95 (*0-8359-1808-4*, Reston) P-H.

Parker, Albert. Survey Methodology & Uses. Bryant, Laurie, ed. 15p. (Orig.). 1979. pap. 9.00 (*0-317-04922-4*) Natl Coun Econ Dev.

Parker, Alexander A. The Mind & Art of Calderon: Essays on the Comedias. (Illus.). 416p. (C). 1989. 89.95 (*0-521-32334-7*) Cambridge U Pr.

Parker, Alice. Melodious Accord: Good Singing in Church. (Illus.). 100p. (Orig.). 1991. pap. 5.95 (*0-929650-43-3*) Liturgy Tr Pubns.

Parker, Alice, jt. ed. see Meese, Elizabeth.

Parker, Alice A. Understand Your Dreams: 1001 Basic Dream Images & How to Interpret Them. Carleton, Nancy, ed. LC 90-50862. 216p. 1991. pap. 9.95 (*0-915811-32-4*) H J Kramer Inc.

— Understand Your Dreams: 1500 Basic Dream Images & How to Interpret Them. 2nd ed. Carleton, Nancy, ed. LC 94-36260. 228p. 1995. pap. 10.95 (*0-915811-59-6*) H J Kramer Inc.

Parker, Alice A. & Meese, Elizabeth A., eds. Feminist Critical Negotiations. LC 91-46958. (Critical Theory Ser.: No. 9). xiv, 172p. 1992. 56.00x (*1-55619-175-8*); pap. 27.95 (*1-55619-176-6*) Benjamins North Am.

Parker, Alice C. The Exploration of the Secret Smile: The Language of Art & of Homosexuality in Frank O'Hara's Poetry. (American University Studies: American Literature: Ser. XXIV, Vol. 25). 164p. (C). 1989. text ed. 38.95 (*0-8204-0958-8*) P Lang Pubs.

Parker, Amasa J. Landmarks of Albany County, New York, Part II: Biography. (Illus.). 1992. reprint ed. lib. bdg. 58.50 (*0-8328-2891-2*) Higginson Bk Co.

Parker, Amasa J., ed. Landmarks of Albany County, New York, Pt. I: History. (Illus.). 1992. reprint ed. lib. bdg. 58.50 (*0-8328-2890-4*) Higginson Bk Co.

Parker, Amos A. Trip to the West & Texas: Far Western Frontier. LC 72-9463. (Illus.). 1973. reprint ed. 28.95 (*0-405-04991-9*) Ayer.

***Parker, Andrew & Sellwood, Bruce W., eds.** Quantitative Diagenesis: Recent Developments & Applications to Reservoir Geology. LC 94-39299. (NATO ASI Series, Series C, Mathematical & Physical Sciences: Vol. 453). 1995. lib. bdg. 119.00 (*0-7923-3261-X*) Kluwer Ac.

Parker, Andrew, jt. ed. see Sedgwick, Eve K.

Parker, Andrew, et al, eds. Nationalisms & Sexualities. (Illus.). 384p. 1991. 49.95 (*0-415-90432-3*, A5727, Routledge NY); pap. 15.95 (*0-415-90433-1*, A5731, Routledge NY) Routledge.

Parker, Andrew D. Keeping the Promise: A Guide for Mentors & Confirmands. 48p. 1994. pap. 6.95 (*0-8192-4113-X*); pap. 5.95 (*0-8192-4114-8*) Morehouse Pub.

***Parker, Ann, photos.** Hajj Paintings: Folk Art of the Great Pilgrimage. LC 95-14994. (Illus.). 176p. 1995. 50.00 (*1-56098-546-1*) Smithsonian.

Parker, Ann, jt. auth. see Berberich, Ralph.

Parker, Ann N. A Christmas Trilogy. (Sandman Ser.: Pt. II). (Illus.). (J). (gr. k-4). 1988. pap. 3.95 (*0-943487-14-5*) Sevgo Pr.

— Home Is Where the Shade Tree Is. (Sandman Ser.). (Illus.). 18p. (J). (gr. k-4). 1988. pap. 3.95 (*0-943487-13-7*) Sevgo Pr.

Parker, Arthur C. The Archaeological History of New York, 2 vols. in 1. LC 76-43800. (New York State Museum Bulletin Ser.: Nos. 235, 236, 237, 238). reprint ed. 53.50 (*0-404-15656-8*) AMS Pr.

— The Indian How Book. LC 74-18592. (Illus.). 335p. 1975. reprint ed. pap. 5.95 (*0-486-21767-1*) Dover.

— The Life of General Ely S. Parker: Last Grand Sachem of the Iroquois & General Grant's Military Secretary. LC 83-19752. (Buffalo Historical Society, Publication Ser.: 23). (Illus.). 408p. reprint ed. 52.50 (*0-404-15658-4*) AMS Pr.

— Manual for History Museums. LC 36-985. reprint ed. 20.00 (*0-404-04887-0*) AMS Pr.

— Seneca Myths & Folk Tales. LC 89-4869. (Illus.). xxxiv, 483p. 1989. pap. 13.95 (*0-8032-8723-2*, Bison Books) U of Nebr Pr.

— Seneca Myths & Folk Tales. LC 76-43803. (Buffalo Historical Society, Publication Ser.: Vol. 27). reprint ed. 74.50 (*0-404-15659-2*) AMS Pr.

— Skunny Wundy: Seneca Indian Tales. (Iroquois & Their Neighbors Ser.). (Illus.). 224p. (C). 1994. reprint ed. pap. 12.95 (*0-8156-0292-8*) Syracuse U Pr.

Parker, B. Invisible Matter & the Fate of the Universe. (Illus.). 290p. 1989. 23.50 (*0-306-43294-3*, Plenum Pr) Plenum.

— Let There Be Reign. 1977. pap. 2.95 (*0-449-12744-3*) Fawcett.

— Long Live the King. 1977. pap. 1.95 (*0-449-12613-7*) Fawcett.

— Peasants Are Revolting. 1985. pap. 2.95 (*0-449-12403-7*) Fawcett.

— Stairway to the Stars: The Story of the World's Largest Observatory. (Illus.). 315p. 1994. 27.95 (*0-306-44763-0*, Plenum Pr) Plenum.

— There's a Fly in My Swill. 1985. pap. 1.95 (*0-449-12740-0*) Fawcett.

— The Vindication of the Big Bang: Breakthroughs & Barriers. (Illus.). 300p. (C). 1993. 24.95 (*0-306-44469-0*, Plenum Pr) Plenum.

Parker, B., ed. Terrestrial Biology II. (Antarctic Research Ser.: Vol. 37). 170p. 37.00 (*0-87590-185-9*) Am Geophysical.

— Terrestrial Biology Three, 9 papers, Set 30-9. (Antarctic Research Ser.: Vol. 30). (Illus.). 155p. 1979. 42.00 (*0-685-55232-2*); Paper 1: Identification of Some Fungi from Soil & Air of Antarctica, 26p. write for info. (*0-87590-145-X*); Papers 2 & 3: Ecological Investigations of Yeasts in Antarctic Soils & Taxonomy of Antarctic Bacteri. write for info. (*0-87590-146-8*); Paper 4: Crustacean Branchiopid Distribution & Speciation in Mesozoic Lakes of the Southern Continen. write for info. (*0-87590-147-6*); Paper 5: Taxonomy of Some Antarctic Bacillus & Corynebacterium Species, 2p. write for info. (*0-87590-148-4*); Papers 6-9: Feeding Chases in the Adelie Penguin; The Mummified Seals of Southern Victoria Land, Ant. write for info. (*0-87590-175-1*) Am Geophysical.

Parker, B. & Hart, Johnny. Every Man Is Innocent Until. 1983. pap. 1.75 (*0-449-13650-7*) Fawcett.

Parker, B., jt. auth. see Hart, Johnny.

Parker, B. F. History of Wolfeboro. (Illus.). 557p. 1989. reprint ed. lib. bdg. 57.50 (*0-8328-0569-6*) Higginson Bk Co.

Parker, B. F., ed. Solar Energy in Agriculture, Vol. 4. (Energy in World Agriculture Ser.). 462p. 1991. 200.00 (*0-444-88622-2*) Elsevier.

***Parker, Barbara.** Suspicion of Guilt. 400p. 1995. 22.95 (*0-525-93769-2*, Dutton) NAL-Dutton.

— Suspicion of Guilt. large type ed. 1995. 25.95 (*1-56895-232-5*) Wheeler Pub.

— Suspicion of Innocence. 1994. 20.95 (*0-525-93747-1*, Dutton) NAL-Dutton.

— Suspicion of Innocence. 432p. 1994. pap. 5.99 (*0-451-17340-6*, Sig) NAL-Dutton.

— Suspicion of Innocence. large type ed. LC 94-6064. 602p. 1994. reprint ed. lib. bdg. 21.95 (*0-7862-0212-2*) Thorndike Pr.

Parker, Barbara, jt. auth. see George, Ted.

Parker, Barbara, jt. auth. see McFarlane, Judith.

Parker, Barbara J. Suspicion of Innocence. LC 93-17971. 352p. 1994. 20.95 (*0-525-93744-7*, Dutton) NAL-Dutton.

Parker, Barbara N., jt. ed. see Phillips, John M.

Parker, Barry. Colliding Galaxies: The Universe in Turmoil. LC 90-40651. (Illus.). 310p. 1990. 23.95 (*0-306-43566-7*, Plenum Pr) Plenum.

— Cosmic Time Travel: A Scientific Odyssey. (Illus.). 320p. 1991. 24.50 (*0-306-43966-2*, Plenum Pr) Plenum.

— Creation: The Story of the Origin & Evolution of the Universe. LC 88-17893. (Illus.). 312p. 1988. 22.95 (*0-306-42952-7*, Plenum Pr) Plenum.

— Einstein's Dream: The Search for a Unified Theory of the Universe. LC 86-15139. 298p. 1986. 19.95 (*0-306-42343-X*, Plenum Pr) Plenum.

— For the People: The Commitment Continues. 160p. 1993. 25.00 (*0-9637427-0-1*) Univ Hosp GA.

— Search for a Supertheory: From Atoms to Superstrings. (Illus.). 302p. 1987. 21.95 (*0-306-42702-8*, Plenum Pr) Plenum.

Parker, Barry M. The Folger Shakespeare Filmography: A Directory of Feature Films Based on the Works of Shakespeare. LC 79-3141. (Folger Guides to the Age of Shakespeare Ser.). 1979. pap. 7.95 (*0-918016-19-3*) Folger Bks.

Parker, Bart. A Close Brush with Reality: Photographs & Writings, 1970-1981. LC 81-51478. (Artist's Bks.). (Illus.). 56p. (Orig.). 1981. pap. 12.95 (*0-89822-018-1*) Visual Studies.

Parker, Ben H., Jr. Colorado Placers & Placering. Carson, Mary, ed. (Illus.). 112p. 1994. reprint ed. pap. 10.95 (*0-941620-61-1*) Carson Ent.

P Q

An Asterisk (*) at the beginning of an entry indicates that the title is appearing in BIP for the first time.

— Gold Panning & Placering in Colorado: How & Where. (Information Ser.: No. 33). (Illus.). 83p. (Orig.). 1992. pap. 12.00 (*1-884216-23-4*) Colo Geol Survey.

Parker, Bess. The Herbalist Guide to Supersex. write for info. (*0-318-58992-3*) World Pr Ltd.

Parker, Beth. Thomas Knew There Were Pirates Living in the Bathroom. (Illus.). 28p. (J). (ps-3). 1990. 12.95 (*0-88753-224-1*, Pub. by Black Moss Pr CN); pap. 4.95 (*0-88753-201-2*, Pub. by Black Moss Pr CN) Firefly Bks Ltd.

Parker, Betty J. Women's Education, 2 vols., Set. 1981. text ed. 125.00 (*0-313-23205-9*, PEV/, Greenwood Pr) Greenwood.

Parker, Betty J., ed. Women's Education, A World View: Annotated Bibliography of Doctoral Dissertations, Vol. 1. LC 78-73791. xii, 470p. 1979. text ed. 75.00 (*0-313-20891-3*, PEW/, Greenwood Pr) Greenwood.

Parker, Betty J. & Parker, Franklin. American Dissertations on Foreign Education: A Bibliography with Abstracts: Central America. LC 73-155724. (American Dissertations on Foreign Education Ser.: Vol. 10). 1979. 38.50 (*0-87875-133-5*) Whitston Pub.

Parker, Betty J., jt. auth. see Parker, Francis.

Parker, Betty J., jt. auth. see Parker, Franklin.

Parker, Betty J., jt. ed. see Parker, Franklin.

Parker, Betty June, jt. auth. see Parker, Franklin.

Parker, Beulah. The Evolution of a Psychiatrist: Memoirs of a Woman Doctor. LC 86-28069. 237p. reprint ed. pap. 67.60 (*0-7837-4531-1*, 2080212) Bks Demand.

— A Mingled Yarn: Chronicle of a Troubled Family. LC 72-75206. 320p. 1978. pap. 17.00 (*0-300-02292-1*) Yale U Pr.

— My Language Is Me. (Psychoanalysis: Examined & Re-Examined Ser.). 397p. 1986. reprint ed. lib. bdg. 39.50 (*0-306-76295-1*) Da Capo.

Parker, Bill. Building a Classical Music Library: Makes Music Appreciation Approachable. 3rd rev. ed. Caravella, Jack, ed. (Illus.). 300p. 1995. pap. 14.95 (*0-9641332-0-2*) Jormax Pubng.

***Parker, Bob.** The Complete Book of Hot Wheels. (Illus.). 160p. (Orig.). 1995. pap. 19.95 (*0-88740-827-3*) Schiffer.

— Hot Wheels: A Collectors Guide. LC 92-63206. (Illus.). 160p. (Orig.). 1993. pap. 16.95 (*0-88740-488-X*) Schiffer.

Parker, Brad. Oh Boy! Sex Comics by Brad Parker. (Illus.). 96p. (Orig.). 1988. pap. 10.95 (*0-943595-11-8*) Leyland Pubns.

Parker, Brant & Hart, Johnny. I Dig Freedom. 1985. pap. 2.95 (*0-449-12646-3*, GM) Fawcett.

Parker, Brant, jt. auth. see Hart, Johnny.

Parker, Brant, et al. Crock, No. 4. 128p. (Orig.). 1979. pap. 1.25 (*0-449-13868-2*, GM) Fawcett.

Parker, Brenda. Arresting Love. large type ed. (Linford Romance Library). 1991. pap. 13.95 (*0-7089-7063-X*, Linford) Ulverscroft.

— Safe Harbour. large type ed. (Linford Romance Library). 288p. 1993. pap. 14.95 (*0-7089-7321-3*, Linford) Ulverscroft.

Parker, Brian, ed. see Shakespeare, William.

Parker, Bruce B., ed. Tidal Hydrodynamics. 912p. 1991. text ed. 135.00 (*0-471-51498-5*) Wiley.

Parker, Bruce C., ed. Conservation Problems in Antarctica. LC 72-85836. (Illus.). 356p. 1972. 30.00 (*0-8139-0840-X*) U Pr of Va.

— Environmental Impact in Antarctica. (Illus.). 390p. 1978. 19.95 (*0-8139-0847-7*) U Pr of Va.

Parker, Bruce C. & Brown, R. Malcolm. Contributions in Phycology. LC 72-170365. (Illus.). 196p. 1971. 25.00 (*0-8139-0841-8*) U Pr of Va.

***Parker, Bruce L., et al, eds.** Thrips Biology & Management: Proceedings of a NATO ARW on Thysanoptera: Toward Understanding Thrips Management Held at the University of Vermont, Burlington, September 28-30, 1993. (NATO ASI Series A, Life Sciences: Vol. 276). 630p. 1995. 145.00 (*0-306-45013-5*) Plenum.

Parker, C. & Riches, C. Parasitic Weeds of the World. 300p. 1993. text ed. 85.50 (*0-85198-873-3*) CAB Intl.

Parker, C. A., et al, eds. Ecology & Management of Soilborne Plant Pathogens. 358p. 1985. text ed. 35.00 (*0-89054-066-7*) Am Phytopathol Soc.

Parker, C. E. Gunfire at Timberline. 208p. 1983. pap. 2.25 (*0-8439-2037-8*) Dorchester Pub Co.

Parker, Cam. Camp Off-the-Wall. 128p. (J). (gr. 3-7). 1987. pap. 2.50 (*0-380-75196-8*, Camelot) Avon.

— A Horse in New York. 144p. (Orig.). (J). (gr. 5 up). 1989. pap. 2.75 (*0-380-75704-4*, Camelot) Avon.

Parker, Canaan. The Color of Trees. LC 92-30486. 221p. (Orig.). 1992. pap. 8.95 (*1-55583-207-5*) Alyson Pubns.

Parker, Carleton H. The Casual Laborer & Other Essays. LC 76-172904. (Americana Library Ser.: No. 25). 227p. 1972. reprint ed. 25.00 (*0-295-95184-2*) U of Wash Pr.

Parker, Carol. Why Do You Call Me Chocolate Boy? LC 93-79098. (Illus.). 28p. (Orig.). (J). (gr. 2-6). 1993. pap. 7.95 (*0-9637267-0-6*) Gull Crest.

Parker, Carole, ed. see Marney-Petix, V. C.

Parker, Carolyn. The Friends in Action Manual: A Model for Establishing a Volunteer Program to Build Caring & Supportive Relationships with Poor & Homeless Families. (Illus.). 200p. (Orig.). (C). 1993. pap. text ed. 19.95 (*0-9631995-0-1*) Comm Minist Mont Cty.

***Parker, Carolyn, photos & sel.** The Poetry of Roses. LC 94-42121. (Illus.). 1995. write for info. (*0-8109-3736-0*) Abrams.

Parker, Carolyn & Arnold, Stephen, eds. When the Drumbeat Changes. 293p. (Orig.). 1981. 22.00 (*0-89410-262-1*); pap. 14.00 (*0-89410-263-X*) Three Continents.

Parker, Charles. Going for Growth: Technological Innovation in Manufacturing Industries. LC 84-21902. 251p. 1985. text ed. 53.95 (*0-471-90633-6*) Wiley.

— Management Information Systems. 2nd ed. 1993. text ed. write for info. (*0-07-048573-9*) McGraw.

— Understanding Computers & Information Processing with Basic. 3rd ed. 768p. (C). 1990. text ed. 45.00 (*0-03-030909-3*) Dryden Pr.

Parker, Charles S. Computers & Their Applications. 3rd ed. 406p. (C). 1992. teacher ed, 3.5 hd 14.75 (*0-03-096887-9*) Dryden Pr.

— Computers & Their Applications. 3rd ed. 406p. (C). 1992. teacher ed, mac hd 14.75 (*0-03-097781-9*) Dryden Pr.

— Computers & Their Applications. 3rd ed. 473p. (C). 1993. pap. text ed. 37.25 (*0-03-096821-6*); teacher ed, pap. text ed. 9.50 (*0-03-096886-0*) Dryden Pr.

— Computers & Their Applications with Productivity Software Guide. 3rd ed. LC 92-82774. 950p. (C). 1993. pap. text ed. 44.00 (*0-03-096883-6*) Dryden Pr.

— Computers & Their Applications with Productivity Software Tools. 2nd ed. 792p. (C). 1991. pap. text ed. 47.00 (*0-03-053353-8*) Dryden Pr.

— Database Management with dBASE IV: Productivity Software Guide Module. 4th ed. 95p. (C). 1993. pap. text ed. 9.75 (*0-03-097120-9*) Dryden Pr.

— Disk Operating System - DOS Module from Productivity Software Guide. 4th ed. 64p. (C). 1993. pap. text ed. 9.75 (*0-03-097121-7*) Dryden Pr.

— Instructor's Manual & Transparency Masters to Accompany "Computers & Their Applications," Third Edition. 3rd ed. 292p. (C). 1993. pap. text ed. 7.75 (*0-03-096884-4*) Dryden Pr.

— Microcomputers: Concepts & Applications. (Illus.). 608p. (C). 1991. pap. text ed. 43.00 (*0-03-047432-9*) Dryden Pr.

— Productivity Software Guide. 3rd ed. (C). 1991. pap. text ed. 23.50 (*0-03-054993-0*); disk 40.00 (*0-03-054994-9*); disk 39.00 (*0-03-054997-3*) Dryden Pr.

— Productivity Software Guide. 4th ed. LC 92-72677. 440p. (C). 1993. pap. text ed. 28.00 (*0-03-096591-8*) Dryden Pr.

— Productivity Software Guide. 4th ed. LC 92-72677. 440p. (C). 1993. disk 14.75 (*0-03-098700-8*); disk 14.75 (*0-03-098699-0*); disk 14.75 (*0-03-098698-2*) Dryden Pr.

— Spreadsheets with Lotus 1-2-3: Productivity Software Guide Module. 4th ed. 96p. (C). 1993. pap. text ed. 9.75 (*0-03-097122-5*) Dryden Pr.

— Spreadsheets with Lotus 1-2-3 & Joe Spreadsheet. 80p. (C). 1991. pap. text ed. 9.50 (*0-03-072287-X*) Dryden Pr.

— Test Bank to Accompany Understanding Computers & Information Processing: Today & Tomorrow. 5th ed. 435p. (C). 1994. pap. text ed. 28.50 (*0-03-098350-9*) Dryden Pr.

— Understanding Computers & Information Processing. 4th ed. 770p. (C). 1992. pap. text ed. 41.75 (*0-03-055753-4*) Dryden Pr.

— Understanding Computers & Information Processing: Today & Tomorrow with Basic. 5th ed. 650p. (C). 1994. text ed. 44.00 (*0-03-097905-6*); disk 21.50 (*0-03-098353-3*); disk 21.50 (*0-03-098352-5*); disk 21.50 (*0-03-098351-7*) Dryden Pr.

— Understanding Computers & Information Processing with BASIC. 4th ed. 770p. (C). 1992. text ed. 44.25 (*0-03-055754-2*) Dryden Pr.

— Word Processing with WordPerfect 4.2, 5.0, & 5.1. 80p. (C). 1991. pap. text ed. 9.50 (*0-03-072288-8*) Dryden Pr.

— Word Processing with WordPerfect 5.1: Productivity Software Guide Module. 4th ed. 72p. (C). 1993. pap. text ed. 9.75 (*0-03-097123-3*) Dryden Pr.

Parker, Charles S. & Ralya, Jerry. Study Guide to Accompany Understanding Computers & Information Processing: Today & Tomorrow. 5th ed. 550p. (C). 1994. pap. text ed. 20.50 (*0-03-097907-2*) Dryden Pr.

Parker, Charles S., jt. auth. see Martin, Edward B.

Parker, Charles S., jt. auth. see Martin, Edward G.

Parker, Christopher. The English Historical Tradition since 1850. 256p. (C). 1990. text ed. 85.00 (*0-85976-293-9*) Humanities.

Parker, Christopher, ed. The English Historical Tradition since Eighteen Fifty. 260p. (C). 1989. text ed. 75.00 (*0-685-65184-3*, Pub. by J Donald) St Mut.

— Gender Roles & Sexuality in Victorian Literature. LC 94-42738. 160p. 1995. 59.95 (*1-85928-146-X*, Pub. by Scolar Pr UK) Ashgate Pub Co.

Parker, Christopher, jt. auth. see Kakabadse, Andrew.

Parker, Clayton A. My Will Be Done. 201p. 1982. pap. 3.00 (*0-686-86578-2*, 0-9606438) C A Parker Pubns.

Parker, Clyde A., jt. auth. see Davis, Gordon B.

Parker, Colin & Roberts, Tim, eds. Energy from Waste: An Evaluation of Conversion Technologies. (Illus.). xi, 217p. 1985. 66.75 (*0-85334-352-7*, Pub. by Elsevier Applied Sci UK) Elsevier.

Parker, Constance-Anne. George Stubbs: Art, Animals & Anatomy. (Illus.). 64p. 1990. pap. 24.00 (*0-85131-398-1*, Pub. by J A Allen & Co UK) St Mut.

— A Picture of the Royal Academy. 80p. (C). 1989. 110.00 (*0-903696-33-9*, Pub. by Hurtwood Pr Ltd); pap. 70.00 (*0-903696-34-7*, Pub. by Hurtwood Pr Ltd) St Mut.

Parker, Cordell, jt. auth. see Hamilton, Cheryl.

Parker, Courtney. How to Eat Like a Southerner & Live to Tell the Tale. 1992. 20.00 (*0-517-57683-X*, C P Pubs) Crown Pub Group.

Parker, Craig, ed. see Cristall, Robert.

Parker, D. & Turk, J. L., eds. Contact Hypersensitivity in Experimental Animals. (Monographs in Allergy: Vol. 8). (Illus.). 182p. 1974. 67.25 (*3-8055-1666-5*) S Karger.

Parker, D., ed. see Bettencourt, K. C.

Parker, D., ed. see Collegium Internationale Allergologicum Staff.

Parker, D. C. Codex Bezae: An Early Christian Manuscript & Its Text. 384p. (C). 1992. 99.95 (*0-521-40037-6*) Cambridge U Pr.

— Some Aspects of Gipsy Music. 61p. 1991. reprint ed. 59.00 (*0-7812-9317-0*) Rprt Serv.

Parker, D. M. & Deregowski, J. B. Perception & Artistic Style. (Advances in Psychology Ser.: No. 73). 292p. 1991. 108.75 (*0-444-88702-4*, North Holland) Elsevier.

Parker, D. M., jt. ed. see Crawford, J. R.

Parker, D. R. Polymer Chemistry. (Illus.). 251p. 1971. 54.00 (*0-85334-571-6*, Pub. by Elsevier Applied Sci UK) Elsevier.

Parker, D. W. Calendar of Papers in Washington Archives Relating to the Territories of the United States, to 1873. (Carnegie Institute Ser.: Vol. 4). 1911. 36.00 (*0-527-00684-X*) Periodicals Srv.

— Guide to the Materials for United States History in Canadian Archives. (Carnegie Institute Ser.: Vol. 9). 1913. 35.00 (*0-527-00689-0*) Periodicals Srv.

Parker, D. Young, ed. see Pavela, Gary.

Parker, Dana. New Rider's Guide to CD-ROM. 2nd ed. (Orig.). 1994. Incl. CD-ROM. cd-rom 35.00 (*1-56205-308-6*) New Riders Pub.

***Parker, Dana & Starrett, Robert.** CD-ROM Professional's CD-Recordable Handbook. 256p. 1995. cd-rom, pap. 34.95 (*0-910965-18-8*, Pembrtn Pr Bks) Online.

Parker, Dana J., jt. auth. see Starrett, Bob.

Parker, Dana T. Square Riggers in the United States & Canada: A Current Directory of Sailing Ships. Harris, Marion, ed. LC 94-4536. (Illus.). 72p. 1994. pap. 9.50 (*0-933449-19-4*) Transport Trails.

Parker, Danny S. The Battle of the Bulge: Hitler's Ardennes Offensive 1944-1945. (Illus.). 320p. 1991. 34.95 (*0-938289-04-7*) Combined Bks.

— To Win the Winter Sky: Air War over the Ardennes, 1944-1945. (Illus.). 320p. 1994. 29.95 (*0-938289-35-7*, 7344) Combined Bks.

Parker, David. Essence of the Economy. 1991. pap. 53.33 (*0-13-284696-9*) P-H.

— Ethics, Theory, & the Novel. LC 93-43929. 250p. (C). 1995. 54.95 (*0-521-45283-X*) Cambridge U Pr.

— The Making of French Absolutism. LC 83-16123. 200p. 1983. text ed. 29.95 (*0-312-50730-5*) St Martin.

***Parker, David, ed.** Through Different Eyes: The Cultural Identity of Young Chinese in Britain. (Research in Ethnic Relations Ser.). 285p. 1995. 59.95 (*1-85628-923-0*, Pub. by Avebury Pub UK) Ashgate Pub Co.

Parker, David & Stead, Richard, eds. Profit & Enterprise: The Political Economy of Profit. LC 90-48084. 224p. 1991. 49.95 (*0-312-05684-2*) St Martin.

Parker, David, jt. auth. see Clark, Charles.

Parker, David, jt. auth. see Nellis, Joseph G.

Parker, David, jt. auth. see Oldcorn, Roger.

***Parker, David A. & De Cecco, John P., eds.** Sex, Cells, & Same-Sex Desire: The Biology of Sexual Preference. LC 95-6140. 1995. write for info. (*1-56024-700-2*) Haworth Pr.

Parker, David B. Alias Bill Arp: Charles Henry Smith & the South's "Goodly Heritage" LC 90-45162. 224p. 1991. 30.00 (*0-8203-1310-6*) U of Ga Pr.

Parker, David E., jt. auth. see Luxon, James T.

Parker, De Witt. The Analysis of Art. LC 75-3304. reprint ed. 39.50 (*0-404-59289-9*) AMS Pr.

— Human Values: An Interpretation of Ethics Based on a Study of Values. LC 75-3305. reprint ed. 55.00 (*0-404-59290-2*) AMS Pr.

— The Self & Nature. LC 75-3306. reprint ed. 22.50 (*0-404-59291-0*) AMS Pr.

Parker, Deborah. Commentary & Ideology: Dante in the Renaissance. LC 92-12651. (Illus.). 264p. 1992. text ed. 32.95 (*0-8223-1281-6*) Duke.

Parker, Dee, jt. auth. see Parker, Weldon.

Parker, Denise M., jt. auth. see Damsey, Joan.

Parker, Dennis. Parrots As a Hobby. (Illus.). 96p. 1994. pap. 7.95 (*0-7938-0094-3*, TT037) TFH Pubns.

Parker, Dennis & Handmer, John, eds. Hazard Management & Emergency Planning: Perspectives on Britain. (Illus.). 286p. (Orig.). (C). 1991. 60.00 (*1-873936-06-0*, Pub. by J & J Sci Pubs UK) Bks Intl VA.

Parker, Dennis, et al. Urban Flood Protection Benefits: A Project Appraisal Guide. Orig. Title: The Indirect Benefits of Urban Flood Alleviation. 1987. text ed. 159.95 (*0-291-39707-7*, Pub. by Gower UK) Ashgate Pub Co.

***Parker, Derek.** Dreaming. 1989. pap. 16.00 (*0-671-76630-9*, Fireside) S&S Trade.

— New Compleat Astrologer. 1990. 15.99 (*0-517-69700-9*) Random Hse Value.

Parker, Derek & Chandler, John. Wiltshire Churches: An Illustrated History. LC 93-5449. 196p. 1993. pap. 30.00 (*0-7509-0152-7*) A Sutton Pub.

Parker, Derek & Parker, Julia. Aquarius. LC 92-52794. (Sun & Moon Signs Library). (Illus.). 64p. 1992. 8.95 (*1-56458-094-6*) Dorling Kindersley.

— Aries. LC 92-52784. (Sun & Moon Signs Library). (Illus.). 64p. (Orig.). 1992. 8.95 (*1-56458-084-9*) Dorling Kindersley.

— Cancer. LC 92-52787. (Sun & Moon Signs Library). (Illus.). 64p. 1992. 8.95 (*1-56458-087-3*) Dorling Kindersley.

— Capricorn. LC 92-52793. (Sun & Moon Signs Library). (Illus.). 64p. 1992. 8.95 (*1-56458-093-8*) Dorling Kindersley.

— Gemini. LC 92-52786. (Sun & Moon Signs Library). (Illus.). 64p. 1992. 8.95 (*1-56458-086-5*) Dorling Kindersley.

— Leo. LC 92-52788. (Sun & Moon Signs Library). (Illus.). 64p. 1992. 8.95 (*1-56458-088-1*) Dorling Kindersley.

— Libra. LC 92-52790. (Sun & Moon Signs Library). (Illus.). 64p. 1992. 8.95 (*1-56458-090-3*) Dorling Kindersley.

— Parkers' Astrology. LC 91-60388. (Illus.). 416p. 1991. pap. 19.95 (*1-56458-710-X*) Dorling Kindersley.

— Parkers' Astrology. LC 91-60388. (Illus.). 416p. 1991. 29.95 (*1-879431-00-9*) Dorling Kindersley.

— Pisces. LC 92-52795. (Sun & Moon Signs Library). (Illus.). 64p. 1992. 8.95 (*1-56458-095-4*) Dorling Kindersley.

— The Power of Magic: Ancient Secrets & Modern Mysteries. LC 92-12175. 1993. 20.00 (*0-671-76921-9*) S&S Trade.

— Sagittarius. LC 92-52792. (Sun & Moon Signs Library). (Illus.). 64p. 1992. 8.95 (*1-56458-092-X*) Dorling Kindersley.

— Scorpio. LC 92-52791. (Sun & Moon Signs Library). (Illus.). 64p. 1992. 8.95 (*1-56458-091-1*) Dorling Kindersley.

— Taurus. LC 92-52785. (Sun & Moon Signs Library). (Illus.). 64p. 1992. 8.95 (*1-56458-085-7*) Dorling Kindersley.

— Virgo. LC 92-52789. (Sun & Moon Signs Library). (Illus.). 64p. 1992. 8.95 (*1-56458-089-X*) Dorling Kindersley.

Parker, Derek, jt. auth. see Parker, Julia.

Parker, Diane, ed. see Anderberg, Nadine.

Parker, Diane, ed. see Annigian, Victor.

Parker, Diane, ed. see Antonuccio, David O.

Parker, Diane, ed. see Barbour, James R.

Parker, Diane, ed. see Beck, Terry.

Parker, Diane, ed. see Brinegar, Mark.

Parker, Diane, ed. see Brineger, Russell.

Parker, Diane, ed. see Cain, Terry.

Parker, Diane, ed. see Carrington-Musci, John.

Parker, Diane, ed. see Chamberlain, Robert.

Parker, Diane, ed. see Cheney, Margaret.

Parker, Diane, ed. see Contos, Steve G.

Parker, Diane, ed. see Courtney, William A.

Parker, Diane, ed. see Decker, Scott H.

Parker, Diane, ed. see DeYoung, Howard.

Parker, Diane, ed. see Dixon, Daniel J. & Dalben, Antonio F.

Parker, Diane, ed. see Engelmann, Larry.

Parker, Diane, ed. see Fikes, Robert, Jr.

Parker, Diane, ed. see Flemming, Gerhard.

Parker, Diane, ed. see Freese, Joyce.

Parker, Diane, ed. see Fung, John.

Parker, Diane, ed. see Gosse, Richard.

Parker, Diane, ed. see Grimsley, Kent.

Parker, Diane, ed. see Gustafson, Mardel E.

Parker, Diane, ed. see Haan, Nicholas V.

Parker, Diane, ed. see Hains, Shaun.

Parker, Diane, ed. see Herron, Rita B.

Parker, Diane, ed. see Herron, Rita.

Parker, Diane, ed. see Hertz, Andrew.

Parker, Diane, ed. see Heuser, John.

Parker, Diane, ed. see Hillman, Rich & Mickle, Steven M.

Parker, Diane, ed. see Hipschman, Don C. & Waltz, James R.

Parker, Diane, ed. see Irick, Susan.

Parker, Diane, ed. see Jensen, R. M.

Parker, Diane, ed. see Katz, Judith H.

Parker, Diane, ed. see Kearns, John & Schulman, Garry.

Parker, Diane, ed. see Kearton, Fran.

Parker, Diane, ed. see Knight, Judy W.

Parker, Diane, ed. see Kremm, Andrian.

Parker, Diane, ed. see Kuhry, Robert.

Parker, Diane, ed. see Lansing, Jewel.

Parker, Diane, ed. see Levy, Danielle.

Parker, Diane, ed. see Marsh, Henri C.

Parker, Diane, ed. see Mayer, Michael J.

Parker, Diane, ed. see McEachern, Robert.

Parker, Diane, ed. see McLaughlin, Dan J.

Parker, Diane, ed. see McWilliams, Phil.

Parker, Diane, ed. see Meinberg, Sherry L.

Parker, Diane, ed. see Mock, Esther.

Parker, Diane, ed. see Nelson, Robert E., Jr.

Parker, Diane, ed. see Nigro, Susan L.

Parker, Diane, ed. see Oglesbee, Maggie.

Parker, Diane, ed. see Payne, Arlie J.

Parker, Diane, ed. see Peterson, Craig.

Parker, Diane, ed. see Petrini, Frank.

Parker, Diane, ed. see Piret, John A.

Parker, Diane, ed. see Radcliffe, Evelyn.

Parker, Diane, ed. see Reed, Robert D. & Kaus, Danek S.

Parker, Diane, ed. see Reed, Robert D. & Kaus, Danek.

Parker, Diane, ed. see Satchwell, Karla.

Parker, Diane, ed. see Shadzi, Judith.

Parker, Diane, ed. see Silverman, Arthur.

Parker, Diane, ed. see Simmermacher, Don G.

Parker, Diane, ed. see Smith, Donald M.

Parker, Diane, ed. see Smith, Ronald R.

Parker, Diane, ed. see Smith, Siddy.

Parker, Diane, ed. see Spencer, M. M.

Parker, Diane, ed. see Taylor, John F. & Latta, R. Sharon.

Parker, Diane, ed. see Trotter, Tamera & Allen, Joycelyn.

Parker, Diane, ed. see Walsh, Robin.

Parker, Diane, ed. see Ward, M. R.

Parker, Diane, ed. see Weeks, Drew W.

Parker, Diane, ed. see Wells, Jan-Marie.

Parker, Diane, ed. see Woodlock, Rosemary.

Parker, Diane, ed. see Yoke, James H.

Parker, Diane, ed. see Zeavin, Edna A.

Parker, Don. Officer Needs Assistance...Again! 256p. 1990. 15.95 (*0-9620073-2-3*) Caroldon Bks.

— You're under Arrest, I'm Not Kidding: The Trials & Tribulations of a Reluctant Cop. 243p. 1990. reprint ed. pap. 9.95 (*0-9620073-1-5*) Caroldon Bks.

Parker, Don, jt. auth. see Alexander, Tom.

Parker, Don, ed. see Alexander, Tom.

Parker, Don H., et al. The Metric System: Syllabus. 1974. pap. text ed. 16.50 (*0-89420-052-6*, 280222); audio 18.15 (*0-89420-163-8*, 280000) Natl Book.

Parker, Donald & Hewitt, David. Table Tennis. (Play the Game Ser.). (Illus.). 80p. (YA). (gr. 10-12). 1993. pap. 7.95 (*0-7137-2412-9*, Pub. by Blandford Pr UK) Sterling.
— Table Tennis. rev. ed. (Illus.). 80p. (YA). (gr. 10-12). 1993. pap. 7.95 (*0-7063-7159-3*, Pub. by Ward Lock UK) Sterling.
Parker, Donald D. Local History: How to Gather It, Write It, & Publish It. LC 78-11873. 186p. 1979. reprint ed. text ed. 52.50 (*0-313-21100-0*, PLAH, Greenwood Pr) Greenwood.
— Local History; How to Gather It, Write It, & Publish It. (History - United States Ser.). 186p. 1993. reprint ed. lib. bdg. 69.00 (*0-7812-4842-6*) Rprt Serv.
Parker, Donald E. Management Application of Value Engineering: For Business & Government. LC 94-76015. (Illus.). 204p. (C). 1994. text ed. 44.95 (*0-9641052-0-9*) L D Miles.
Parker, Donald E. & Dell'Isola, Alphonse. Project Budgeting for Buildings. (Illus.). 256p. 1991. text ed. 49.95 (*0-442-00483-4*) Chapman & Hall.
Parker, Donald L., jt. auth. see Busby, Linda J.
Parker, Donn B. A Manager's Guide to Computer Security. 1983. 19.50 (*0-8359-4232-5*, Reston) P-H.
Parker, Donn B. & Anderson, James, eds. Information Systems Security. 137.00 (*0-685-69693-6*, ZISS) Warren Gorham & Lamont.
Parker, Donn B., et al. Ethical Conflicts in Information & Computer Science, Technology, & Business. 245p. 1989. pap. 34.95 (*0-471-58803-2*) Wiley.
Parker, Doraetta H. How to Kill Cockroaches & Never Again Be Reinfested & Other Good News. (Illus.). 80p. (Orig.). 1986. 14.95 (*0-937305-00-6*); pap. 12.95 (*0-937305-01-4*); audio 19.00 (*0-937305-02-2*) ABC Inst.
Parker, Dorian L. Doughnuts: Over 45 Crullers, Fritters, & Other Homemade Treats. LC 93-8739. 1994. 11.00 (*0-517-59439-0*, C P Pubs) Crown Pub Group.
— Pancakes: From Flapjacks to Crepes. 128p. 1987. 12.00 (*0-517-56136-0*, C P Pubs) Crown Pub Group.
***Parker, Dorothy.** Collected Stories. Breese, Mikki, ed. LC 95-15524. 1995. pap. write for info. (*0-14-018939-4*, Penguin Bks) Viking Penguin.
— Cooking with Potatoes. 1990. pap. 2.95 (*0-88266-601-0*, Garden Way Pub) Storey Comm Inc.
— Dorothy Parker at Her Best. 24.95 (*0-8488-0117-2*, Amereon Hse) Amereon Ltd.
— Dorothy Parker Stories. 1992. 11.99 (*0-517-08466-X*) Random Hse Value.
— Dorothy Parker's Favorites. 18.95 (*0-8488-0095-8*, Amereon Hse) Amereon Ltd.
— Poetry & Short Stories of Dorothy Parker. 1994. 15.50 (*0-679-60132-5*, Modern Lib) Random.
Parker, Dorothy, ed. Modern American Drama: Williams, Miller, Albee, & Shepard. pap. 17.95 (*0-8020-3434-9*) U of Toronto Pr.
Parker, Dorothy & Evans, Ross. The Coast of Illyria: A Play in Three Acts. LC 89-20251. (Illus.). 232p. (Orig.). 1990. 29.95x (*0-87745-273-3*); pap. 15.95 (*0-87745-288-1*) U of Iowa Pr.
Parker, Dorothy M., ed. see Lee, Cazenove G.
Parker, Dorothy R. The Portable Dorothy Parker. rev. ed. (Portable Library: No. 74). 1976. pap. 13.95 (*0-14-015074-9*, Penguin Bks) Viking Penguin.
— Singing an Indian Song: A Biography of D'Arcy McNickle. LC 92-7616. (American Indian Lives Ser.). (Illus.). x, 317p. 1992. 35.00x (*0-8032-3687-5*) U of Nebr Pr.
— Singing an Indian Song: A Biography of D'Arcy McNickle. LC 92-7616. (American Indian Lives Ser.). (Illus.). x, 317p. 1992. pap. 13.00 (*0-8032-8730-5*) U of Nebr Pr.
Parker, Dorothy R., ed. see Brown, George D.
Parker, Douglas C. George Bizet: His Life & Works. 278p. 1990. reprint ed. lib. bdg. 69.00 (*0-7812-9050-3*) Rprt Serv.
— Georges Bizet, His Life & Works. LC 73-94280. (Select Bibliographies Reprint Ser.). 1977. 23.95 (*0-8369-5054-2*) Ayer.
***Parker, Douglas H., ed.** A Proper Dyaloge Betwene a Gentillman & an Husbandman. 300p. (C). 1995. 50.00 (*0-8020-0735-X*) U of Toronto Pr.
Parker, Douglas H., ed. see Barlowe, Jerome & Roye, William.
Parker, Douglas H., jt. auth. see Bowe, William J.
Parker, Douglass, ed. & tr. Lysistrata. 128p. 1988. pap. 2.95 (*0-318-41484-8*, Ment) NAL-Dutton.
Parker, E. & Goedhart, Coba, trs. Astrology & Its Practical Application. 202p. 1970. reprint ed. spiral bd. 9.35 (*0-7873-0658-4*) Mokelumne.
Parker, E. H. Thousand Years of the Tartars. 247p. 1988. 19.95 (*0-88029-136-2*) Dorset Pr.
Parker, E. H., jt. auth. see Croydon, W. F.
Parker, E. H., jt. ed. see Dowsett, M. G.
Parker, E. J. The Doctor's Guide to Partnership Accounts. 76p. 1984. 25.00 (*0-7212-0698-0*, Pub. by Regency Press) St Mut.
Parker, E. M., jt. ed. see Kasper, E.
Parker, Earl R. & Colombo, Umberto, eds. The Science of Materials Used in Advanced Technology. LC 73-1065. 572p. reprint ed. pap. 163.10 (*0-317-08187-X*, 2015173) Bks Demand.
***Parker, Earle W.** Kangaroos, Characters & Bunyips. 88p. 1994. pap. 7.95 (*1-57087-088-8*) Prof Pr NC.
Parker, Ed, illus. Jack & the Beanstalk. LC 78-18072. 32p. (J). (gr. k-4). 1979. lib. bdg. 9.79 (*0-89375-125-1*); pap. 2.50 (*0-89375-103-0*) Troll Assocs.
— Three Billy Goats Gruff. LC 78-18068. 32p. (J). (gr. k-3). 1979. lib. bdg. 9.79 (*0-89375-121-9*); pap. 2.50 (*0-89375-099-9*); audio 9.95 (*0-685-04953-1*) Troll Assocs.

Parker, Edward. Manual of British Standards in Engineering Drawing & Design. 2nd ed. (C). 1989. 160.00 (*0-09-172938-6*, Pub. by S Thornes Pubs UK) St Mut.
Parker, Edward, jt. auth. see Lewington, Anna.
Parker, Edward A., tr. see Declareuil, Joseph.
Parker, Edward E. History of Brookline, New Hampshire, Formerly Raby, with Tables of Family Records & Genealogies. (Illus.). 664p. 1988. reprint ed. lib. bdg. 71.00 (*0-8328-0043-0*, NH0051) Higginson Bk Co.
Parker, Edward G. Reminiscences of Rufus Choate, the Great American Advocate. Mersky, Roy M. & Jacobstein, J. Myron, eds. (Classics in Legal History Reprint Ser.: Vol. 16). 524p. 1972. reprint ed. lib. bdg. 45.00 (*0-89941-015-4*, 301130) W S Hein.
Parker, Edward L. History of Londonderry, New Hampshire, Comprising the Towns of Derry & Londonderry. (Illus.). 418p. 1988. reprint ed. lib. bdg. 43.00 (*0-8328-0062-7*, NH0054) Higginson Bk Co.
Parker, Edwin B., jt. ed. see Greenberg, Bradley S.
Parker, Edwin B., et al. Rural America in the Information Age: Telecommunications Policy for Rural Development. 186p. (Orig.). (C). 1989. lib. bdg. 38.50 (*0-8191-7493-9*, Aspen Inst for Humanistic Studies); pap. text ed. 19.50 (*0-8191-7494-7*, Aspen Inst for Humanistic Studies) U Pr of Amer.
Parker, Eleanor. Dad's Doodle-Bug. (Stories We Tell Ser.). 27p. 1993. pap. 4.00 (*1-884983-05-7*) Homegrown Bks.
Parker, Eleanor, ed. see Brummell, George B.
Parker, Elinor, ed. Inkle Weaving. (Illus.). 214p. 1991. reprint ed. pap. 19.95 (*0-9620543-1-3*) Flower Valley Pr.
Parker, Elisabeth, jt. auth. see Sosinsky, Barrie.
Parker, Elizabeth. Gilded Splendor. 400p. (Orig.). 1993. pap. 4.99 (*0-505-51914-3*, Love Spell) Dorchester Pub Co.
— The Seven Ages of Woman. Breck, Evelyn, ed. LC 60-8739. 621p. reprint ed. pap. 177.00 (*0-317-07935-2*, 2014853) Bks Demand.
Parker, Elizabeth C. Cloisters: Papers in Honor of the Fiftieth Anniversary. 1994. 50.00 (*0-8109-6453-8*) Abrams.
— Cloisters Cross: Its Art & Meaning. 1994. 60.00 (*0-8109-6434-1*) Abrams.
Parker, Elizabeth C. & Little, Charles T. The Cloisters Cross: Its Art & Meaning. LC 93-8585. (Illus.). 336p. 1993. 60.00 (*0-87099-682-7*, Abrams) Metro Mus Art.
Parker, Elizabeth L., ed. Cobb County, Georgia Cemeteries, Vol. II. LC 81-45599. (Illus.). 756p. 1991. lib. bdg. 65.00 (*1-879768-00-3*) Cobb Cnty Geneal.
Parker, Elizabeth S., jt. ed. see Weingartner, Herbert.
Parker, Elmer O., jt. auth. see Holcomb, Brent H.
Parker, Elsa. Astrology & Its Practical Application. (Arcana Ser.). 1977. pap. 5.95 (*0-87877-039-9*) Newcastle Pub.
Parker, Emmett. Albert Camus: The Artist in the Arena. 262p. 1966. pap. 9.95 (*0-299-03554-9*) U of Wis Pr.
Parker, Eric. Colonel Hawker's Shooting Diaries. 2nd ed. (Fifty Greatest Bks.). (Illus.). 300p. 1990. reprint ed. 35.00 (*1-56416-000-9*) Derrydale Pr.
Parker, Eugene N. Interplanetary Dynamical Processes. LC 63-13630. (Interscience Monographs & Texts in Physics & Astronomy: No. 8). (Illus.). 272p. reprint ed. pap. 79.60 (*0-7837-3461-1*, 2057789) Bks Demand.
— Spontaneous Current Sheets in Magnetic Fields: With Applications to Stellar X-Rays. (International Series in Astronomy & Astrophysics). (Illus.). 400p. 1994. 85.00 (*0-19-507371-1*) OUP.
Parker, F. Calvin. Jonathan Goble of Japan: Marine, Missionary, Maverick. LC 89-27253. (Illus.). 356p. (C). 1990. lib. bdg. 53.00 (*0-8191-7639-7*) U Pr of Amer.
— The Southern Baptist Mission in Japan, 1889-1989. (Illus.). 362p. (Orig.). (C). 1991. lib. bdg. 51.00 (*0-8191-8107-2*); pap. text ed. 31.50 (*0-8191-8108-0*) U Pr of Amer.
Parker, F. Charles, IV. Vietnam: Strategy for a Stalemate. LC 88-25482. 268p. 1988. text ed. 19.95 (*0-88702-041-0*) Washington Inst Pr.
Parker, F. M. The Assassins. large type ed. (General Ser.). 350p. 1990. 18.95 (*0-8161-4999-2*, Large Print Bks) Hall.
— The Highbinders. 192p. 1988. pap. 2.75 (*0-451-14942-4*, Sig) NAL-Dutton.
— The Predators. large type ed. (General Ser.). 413p. 1991. text ed. 19.95 (*0-8161-5240-3*, Large Print Bks) Hall.
— Shadow of the Wolf. 192p. 1988. pap. 2.75 (*0-317-66101-9*, Sig) NAL-Dutton.
— The Slavers. large type ed. LC 92-14128. (General Ser.). 352p. 1992. text ed. 19.95 (*0-8161-5482-1*, Large Print Bks) Hall.
***Parker-Fairbanks, Dixie, et al.** Richard Fairbanks 1929-1989: A Retrospective. Nix, Neeleke, ed. Goebel, Robert & Alport, Rita, trs. (Illus.). 50p. 1995. pap. 8.95 (*1-881067-05-X*) N Nelleke Studio.
Parker, Fan & Parker, Stephen J. Russia on Canvas: Ilya Repin. LC 79-20577. (Illus.). 196p. 1980. 35.00 (*0-271-00252-2*) Pa St U Pr.
Parker, Farris, jt. auth. see Miller, Judy.
Parker, Faye W. Mental, Physical, Spiritual Health. LC 79-56170. 80p. 1980. pap. 2.95 (*0-87516-397-1*) DeVorss.
Parker, Florence E. & Stewart, Estelle M. Care of the Aged Persons in the United States. LC 75-17235. (Social Problems & Social Policy Ser.). 1976. reprint ed. 25.95 (*0-405-07504-9*) Ayer.
Parker, Fran. Listen. 50p. 1983. pap. 8.00 (*0-686-40982-5*) TarPar.
— Mushrooms, Turnip Greens & Pickled Eggs. 2nd ed. 288p. 1975. 5.25 (*0-686-11664-X*) TarPar.
— Ponderings. 50p. 1976. pap. 3.50 (*0-686-40981-7*) TarPar.
Parker, Fran, jt. auth. see Tartan, Beth.
Parker, Francis & Parker, Betty J. American Dissertations on Foreign Education: Israel, Vol. XIII. LC 73-155724. 464p. 1980. 32.00 (*0-87875-152-1*) Whitston Pub.

Parker, Francis H. Reason & Faith Revisited. LC 79-154285. (Aquinas Lectures). 10.00 (*0-87462-136-4*) Marquette.
— The Story of Western Philosophy. LC 67-13033. 352p. reprint ed. pap. 100.40 (*0-317-08916-1*, 2050087) Bks Demand.
***Parker, Francis J.** Civil War Infantry, the Story of the 32nd Massachusetts Infantry, Whence It Came, Where It Went, What It Saw & What It Did. (Illus.). 260p. 1995. reprint ed. lib. bdg. 35.00 (*0-8328-4632-5*) Higginson Bk Co.
— Genealogy of Ainsworth Families in America. 212p. 1988. reprint ed. lib. bdg. 40.00 (*0-8328-0094-5*); reprint ed. pap. 32.00 (*0-8328-0095-3*) Higginson Bk Co.
Parker, Francis W. Talks on Pedagogics: An Outline of the Theory of Concentration. LC 70-89217. (American Education: Its Men, Institutions & Ideas, Ser. 1). 1978. reprint ed. 23.95 (*0-405-01456-2*) Ayer.
Parker, Frank. Togo. (World Bibliographical Ser.). 1993. lib. bdg. 54.00 (*1-85109-160-2*) ABC-CLIO.
Parker, Frank, ed. Institutional Real Estate Strategies. 96p. 1988. pap. 40.95 (*0-87420-674-X*) Urban Land.
Parker, Frank & Riley, Kathryn. Linguistics for Non-Linguistics: A Primer with Exercises. 2nd ed. LC 93-17981. 1994. pap. text ed. 40.00 (*0-205-15083-7*) Allyn.
— Writing for Academic Publication: A Guide to Getting Started. 150p. 1995. pap. text ed. write for info. (*0-9644636-1-X*) Parlay Enter.
Parker, Frank J. Caryl Chessman: The Red Light Bandit. LC 75-8760. (Illus.). 243p. 1975. 28.95 (*0-88229-188-2*) Nelson-Hall.
— The Law & the Poor. LC 72-97696. 230p. reprint ed. pap. 65.60 (*0-8357-8937-3*, 2033512) Bks Demand.
Parker, Frank R. Black Votes Count: Political Empowerment in Mississippi after 1965. LC 89-39074. (Illus.). xviii, 254p. (C). 1990. 34.95 (*0-8078-1901-8*); pap. 14.95 (*0-8078-4274-5*) U of NC Pr.
Parker, Frank S. Applications of Infrared, Raman, & Resonance Raman Spectroscopy in Biochemistry. 516p. 1983. 120.00 (*0-306-41206-3*, Plenum Pr) Plenum.
Parker, Franklin. George Peabody: A Biography. rev. ed. LC 94-24306. 250p. (C). 1994. 29.95 (*0-8265-1255-0*); pap. 16.95 (*0-8265-1256-9*) Vanderbilt U Pr.
Parker, Franklin & Parker, Betty J. American Dissertations on Foreign Education: A Bibliography with Abstracts: South America. LC 73-155724. (American Dissertations on Foreign Education Ser.: Vol. 9). 1977. 30.00 (*0-87875-101-7*) Whitston Pub.
— Education in the People's Republic of China Past & Present: A Bibliography. LC 84-48394. (Books in International Education). 896p. 1986. lib. bdg. 105.00 (*0-8240-8797-6*) Garland.
Parker, Franklin & Parker, Betty J., eds. American Dissertations on Foreign Education: A Bibliography with Abstracts, Australia-New Zealand, Vol. XIX, No. 19. LC 73-155724. xxv, 300p. 1988. 38.50 (*0-87875-341-9*) Whitston Pub.
— American Dissertations on Foreign Education: A Bibliography with Abstracts: Britain, Vol. XX. LC 73-155724. 460p. 1990. 55.00 (*0-87875-368-0*) Whitston Pub.
— American Dissertations on Foreign Education: A Bibliography with Abstracts, Pacific, Vol. XVII. LC 73-155724. xiii, 208p. 1986. 25.00 (*0-87875-327-3*) Whitston Pub.
— American Dissertations on Foreign Education: A Bibliography with Abstracts, Philippines, 2 vols., Set. LC 73-155724. xxv, 1062p. 1986. 80.00 (*0-87875-333-8*) Whitston Pub.
— American Dissertations on Foreign Education: Asia. (American Dissertations of Foreign Education Ser.: Vol. XVI). 877p. 1986. 58.00 (*0-87875-284-6*) Whitston Pub.
— American Dissertations on Foreign Education: Mexico. LC 73-155724. (American Dissertations on Foreign Education Ser.: Vol. 8). xiv, 456p. 1976. 16.00 (*0-87875-086-X*) Whitston Pub.
— Women's Education, A World View: Vol. 2-Annotated Bibliography of Books & Reports, Vol. 2. LC 78-73791. xv, 689p. 1981. text ed. 85.00 (*0-313-23206-7*, PEY/, Greenwood Pr) Greenwood.
Parker, Franklin & Parker, Betty June. Education in Puerto Rico: Abstracts of American Doctoral Dissertations. LC 77-87895. 1977. 27.00 (*0-913480-36-3*) Inter Am U Pr.
Parker, Franklin, jt. auth. see Parker, Betty J.
Parker, Franklin D. The Central American Republics. LC 81-5272. (Illus.). x, 348p. 1981. reprint ed. text ed. 59.75 (*0-313-22991-0*, PACA, Greenwood Pr) Greenwood.
— Troubled Earth Acquires Lunar Perspective: A World History, 1961-1970. LC 82-45052. 922p. (Orig.). (C). 1982. pap. text ed. 64.00 (*0-8191-2478-8*) U Pr of Amer.
Parker, Freda. Victorian Embroidery. 1991. 14.99 (*0-517-06588-6*) Random Hse Value.
— Victorian Patchwork. (Illus.). 112p. 1992. 29.95 (*0-943955-56-4*, Trafalgar Sq Pub) Trafalgar.
Parker, Freddie L. Running for Freedom: Slave Runaways in North Carolina, 1775 to 1840. LC 92-38603. (Studies in African American History & Culture). 264p. 1993. 61.00 (*0-8153-1005-6*) Garland.
Parker, Freddie L., ed. Stealing a Little Freedom: Advertisements for Slave Runaways in North Carolina, 1791-1840. LC 93-36958. 912p. 1994. 95.00 (*0-8153-1532-5*, H1812) Garland.
Parker, G. A., ed. River Meandering. (Water Resources Monograph Ser.: Vol. 12). 496p. 1989. pap. 26.00 (*0-87590-316-9*) Am Geophysical.
Parker, G. J. Introductory Semiconductor Device Physics. LC 93-24965. 304p. 1994. pap. text ed. 40.00 (*0-13-143777-1*) P-H.
Parker, Gail R. The Bed 'N Breakfast Directory, 1984-1985. 3rd ed. 56p. 1984. pap. 3.95 (*0-910115-01-X*) PS Pubns.

— Holidays for One: Vacations for the Solo Traveler. (Illus.). 64p. (Orig.). 1981. pap. 5.50 (*0-910115-00-1*) PS Pubns.
— Recipes & Rendezvous. (Illus.). 108p. (Orig.). 1984. pap. 5.95 (*0-910115-02-8*) PS Pubns.
Parker, Gail T. Mind Cure in New England: From the Civil War to World War I. LC 72-92704. 209p. reprint ed. pap. 59.60 (*0-317-55651-7*, 2029254) Bks Demand.
Parker, Garda. Arizona Temptation. 1992. mass mkt. 4.25 (*0-8217-3763-5*) Zebra.
— Blue Mountain Magic. 416p. 1994. mass mkt. 4.50 (*0-8217-4603-0*) Zebra.
— Consenting Hearts. 512p. 1994. mass mkt. 4.99 (*0-8217-4690-1*) Zebra.
— Love at Last. 544p. 1993. mass mkt. 4.50 (*0-8217-4158-6*) Zebra.
— Out of the Blue. 512p. 1992. mass mkt. 4.50 (*0-8217-3798-8*) Zebra.
— Scarlet Lady. 416p. 1993. mass mkt. 4.50 (*0-8217-4416-X*) Zebra.
— Temptation's Flame. 384p. 1993. mass mkt. 4.25 (*0-8217-4047-4*) Zebra.
***Parker, Gary.** Desert Water. 312p. 1995. pap. 9.99 (*1-56476-450-8*, 6-3450, Victor Books) SP Pubns.
— Dry Bones & Other Fossils. LC 79-51174. (Illus.). (J). (gr. 2-4). 1979. pap. 5.95 (*0-89051-118-7*) Master Bks.
— Life Before Birth. (Orig.). (J). (gr. 1-8). 1987. 10.95 (*0-89051-117-9*) Master Bks.
Parker, Gary E. Guilt Trip: Getting Off a Dead-End Street. LC 93-78996. 220p. 1993. 17.95 (*1-56977-600-8*) McCracken Pr.
— Principles Worth Protecting. LC 93-14911. 96p. 1993. pap. 9.95 (*1-880837-18-8*) Smyth & Helwys.
Parker, Gary E., jt. auth. see Bliss, Richard B.
Parker, Genevieve. The Afterglow. LC 93-86984. 248p. 1994. 22.95 (*0-9638987-0-1*) Parker Homestead.
Parker, Geoffrey. Army of Flanders & the Spanish Road: 1567-1659. LC 76-180021. (Cambridge Studies in Early Modern History). (Illus.). 288p. 1975. pap. 24.95 (*0-521-09907-2*) Cambridge U Pr.
— The Countries of Community Europe: A Geographical Survey of Contemporary Issues. LC 78-23239. 1979. text ed. 29.95 (*0-312-17037-8*) St Martin.
— The Dutch Revolt. rev. ed. 336p. 1989. pap. 8.95 (*0-14-055233-2*, Penguin Bks) Viking Penguin.
— The Geopolitics of Domination: Territorial Supremacy in Europe & the Mediterranean from the Ottoman Empire to the Soviet Union. 240p. 1988. lib. bdg. 55.00 (*0-415-00483-7*) Routledge.
— The Military Revolution: Military Innovation & the Rise of the West, 1500-1800. (Illus.). 251p. (C). 1989. pap. 19.95 (*0-521-37680-7*) Cambridge U Pr.
— Philip II. 3rd ed. 260p. 1995. pap. text ed. 14.95 (*0-8126-9279-9*) Open Court.
— The Thirty Years War. (Illus.). 320p. 1985. 47.50 (*0-7100-9788-3*, RKP) Routledge.
— Thirty Years' War. 1988. pap. 16.95 (*0-415-02534-6*) Routledge.
***Parker, Geoffrey, ed.** The Cambridge Illustrated History of Warfare. (Cambridge Illustrated Histories Ser.). (Illus.). 416p. (C). 1995. 39.95 (*0-521-44073-4*) Cambridge U Pr.
— The Thirty Years' War. 384p. (C). 1988. pap. text ed. 15.95 (*0-7102-1181-3*, RKP) Routledge.
— Thirty Years War. (Reprints Ser.). 416p. 1989. 24.95 (*0-88029-296-2*) Dorset Pr.
Parker, Geoffrey & Smith, Lesley M., eds. The General Crisis of the Seventeenth Century. 296p. 1985. pap. 12.95 (*0-7102-0545-7*, RKP) Routledge.
Parker, Geoffrey, jt. ed. see Kagan, Richard L.
Parker, Geoffrey, jt. auth. see Martin, Colin.
Parker, George. Lexico-Concordancia del Nuevo Testamento en Griego y Espanol. 1000p. (SPA.). 1991. pap. 25.95 (*0-311-42065-6*) Casa Bautista.
— Physics 205 & 208 Test Book. 128p. (C). 1994. pap. text ed., spiral bd. 5.00 (*0-8403-9883-2*) Kendall-Hunt.
Parker, George D., jt. auth. see Millman, R. S.
Parker, George D., jt. auth. see Millman, Richard S.
Parker, George F. Recollections of Grover Cleveland. LC 70-165649. (Select Bibliographies Reprint Ser.). 1977. reprint ed. 36.95 (*0-8369-5958-2*) Ayer.
Parker, George G. & Beals, Terrence. The Stanford Bank Game, Version 10. 124p. (C). 1988. pap. text ed. 23.50 (*0-89426-129-0*); Teaching notes. write for info. (*0-89426-130-4*) Boyd & Fraser.
***Parker, George G. & Beals, Terry.** The Stanford Bank Game: Version 11. LC 94-43533. 1995. write for info. (*0-87709-876-X*) Boyd & Fraser.
Parker, George L. The Beginnings of the Book Trade in Canada. 376p. 1985. 50.00 (*0-8020-2547-1*) U of Toronto Pr.
Parker, George W. Children of the Sun. 31p. 1981. reprint ed. pap. 2.00 (*0-933121-10-5*) Black Classic.
— How to Win an Impossible Election: The Authentic Campaign of One Who Did. rev. ed. LC 87-83521. (Illus.). 125p. 1988. pap. 15.95 (*0-944950-00-0*) Civic Enterprises.
Parker, Gerald. How to Play: The Theatre of James Reaney. 260p. (C). 1991. pap. text ed. 25.00 (*1-55022-119-1*, Pub. by ECW Press CN) Genl Dist Srvs.
***Parker, Gerry.** Eastern Coyote: The Soty of Its Success. (Illus.). 208p. 1995. pap. 17.95 (*1-55109-111-9*, Pub. by Nimbus Publishing Ltd CN) Chelsea Green Pub.
Parker, Gertrude M. Little Drops of Water Little Grains of Sand. 32p. (Orig.). 1983. pap. write for info. (*0-89279-055-5*) G M Parker.
Parker, Gilbert. Adventurer of the North. LC 74-98589. (Short Story Index Reprint Ser.). 1977. 19.95 (*0-8369-3163-7*) Ayer.
— Battle of the Strong. 1976. lib. bdg. 18.50 (*0-89968-078-X*, Lghtyr Pr) Buccaneer Bks.
— Born with a Golden Spoon. 1976. lib. bdg. 13.85 (*0-89968-081-X*, Lghtyr Pr) Buccaneer Bks.

An Asterisk (*) at the beginning of an entry indicates that the title is appearing in BIP for the first time.

— The Hill of Pains. 1976. lib. bdg. 9.95 (*0-89968-082-8*, Lghtyr Pr) Buccaneer Bks.
— The Judgement House. 1976. lib. bdg. 19.50 (*0-89968-080-1*, Lghtyr Pr) Buccaneer Bks.
— Pierre & His People. LC 74-101287. (Short Story Index Reprint Ser.). 1977. 21.95 (*0-8369-3224-2*) Ayer.
— The Right of Way. 1976. lib. bdg. 16.25 (*0-89968-079-8*, Lghtyr Pr) Buccaneer Bks.
— Romany of the Snows. LC 79-94741. (Short Story Index Reprint Ser.). 1977. 19.95 (*0-8369-3121-1*) Ayer.
— Seats of the Mighty. 1976. lib. bdg. 16.75 (*0-89968-077-1*, Lghtyr Pr) Buccaneer Bks.
— The Trespasser. 1976. lib. bdg. 13.85 (*0-89968-083-6*, Lghtyr Pr) Buccaneer Bks.

Parker, Gilbert & Bryan, Claude G. Old Quebec, the Fortress of New France. (Illus.). 486p. 1992. reprint ed. pap. 30.00 (*1-55613-594-7*) Heritage Bk.

Parker, Gillian. Getting & Spending: Credit & Debt in Britain. 246p. 1990. text ed. 68.95 (*1-85628-053-5*, Pub. by Avebury Pub UK) Ashgate Pub Co.
— With This Body: Caring & Disability in Marriage. LC 92-18284. 1993. 90.00 (*0-335-09947-5*, Open Univ Pr); pap. 32.50 (*0-335-09946-7*, Open Univ Pr) Taylor & Francis.

Parker, Gillian, jt. ed. see Walker, Robert.

Parker, Glenn M. Cross-Functional Teams: Working with Allies, Enemies, & Other Strangers. LC 93-48674. (Business-Management Ser.). 225p. 1994. 24.00 (*1-55542-609-3*) Jossey-Bass.
— Team Players & Teamwork: The New Competitive Business Strategy. LC 90-53093. (Management Ser.). 202p. 1990. 26.00 (*1-55542-257-8*) Jossey-Bass.

***Parker, Glenn M. & Kropp, Richard P., Jr.** Fifty Activities for Self-Directed Teams. 250p. 1994. ring bd. 139.95 (*0-87425-969-X*) Human Res Dev Pr.

Parker, Glenn R. Homeward Bound: Explaining Changes in Congressional Behavior. LC 86-4098. (Series in Policy & Institutional Studies). 230p. 1986. 49.95 (*0-8229-3536-8*) U of Pittsburgh Pr.
— Institutional Change, Discretion, & the Making of Modern Congress: An Economic Interpretation. 186p. (C). 1992. text ed. 34.50 (*0-472-10329-6*) U of Mich Pr.

Parker, Glenn R., ed. Studies of Congress. LC 84-16993. (Illus.). 586p. reprint ed. pap. 167.10 (*0-8357-8536-X*, 2034839) Bks Demand.

Parker, Glenn R. & Parker, Suzanne L. Factions in House Committees. LC 83-3150. 336p. 1985. text ed. 37.00x (*0-87049-467-8*) U of Tenn Pr.

***Parker, Graham W.** Achieving Cost-Efficient Quality: A PARSEC Guide. 128p. 1994. pap. 71.95 (*0-566-07582-2*, Pub. by Gower UK) Ashgate Pub Co.
— The Internal Audit. LC 95-1063. (PRASEC Guide Ser.). 1995. write for info. (*0-566-07584-9*, Pub. by Gower UK) Ashgate Pub Co.

Parker, Grant. Mayday: The History of a Village Holocaust. 260p. 1992. reprint ed. pap. 8.95 (*0-9604958-0-0*) Parker Pr MI.

Parker, Gwendolyn M. These Same Long Bones. 1994. 21.95 (*0-395-67172-8*) HM.
— These Same Long Bones. LC 95-740. 1995. 10.95 (*0-452-27428-1*, Plume) NAL-Dutton.

Parker, H. Ancient Ceylon. (Illus.). 696p. 1986. reprint ed. 32.00 (*0-8364-1742-9*, Pub. by Manohar II) S Asia.

Parker, H. & Pitt, G. D. Pollution Control Instrumentation for Oil & Effluents. (C). 1987. lib. bdg. 70.00 (*0-317-58402-2*, Pub. by Graham & Trotman UK) Kluwer Ac.
— Pollution Control Instrumentation for Oil & Effluents. 272p. 1987. reprint ed. lib. bdg. 96.00 (*0-86010-368-4*) G & T Inc.

***Parker, H. Dennison, ed.** GIS Applications in Natural Resources 2. (Illus.). 600p. 1995. pap. text ed. 34.95 (*1-882610-17-2*) GIS World Bks.

Parker, H. M. The Roman Legions. 286p. 1980. reprint ed. 20.00 (*0-89005-356-1*) Ares.

Parker, Hankins. Memory Loss - Changing Tracks - Glowing Older: Don't Act Your Age. (Illus.). (Orig.). 1994. pap. 5.00 (*0-85132-200-X*) Park Hurst Pubs.
— Micajah's White Horse & Red Wagon. (Illus.). 189p. (Orig.). 1995. pap. 12.50 (*1-885132-02-6*) Park Hurst Pubs.

Parker Hanni Law Corporation Staff. Industrial Pneumatic Technology. Schrader, Lawrence F, Jr., ed. (Illus.). 150p. (Orig.). 1980. teacher ed 24.45 (*1-55769-016-2*, 0275-B2); 2.10 (*0-685-35409-1*); pap. text ed. 19.30 (*1-55769-015-4*, 0275-B1); trans. 456.75 (*1-55769-017-0*, 0275-B3) Parker Hannifin.

Parker Hannifin Corp. Staff. Industrial Hydraulic Technology Lab Manual Servo-Valve Supplement. Schrader, L. F., Jr., ed. (Illus.). 20p. 1987. student ed 22.50 (*1-55769-005-7*, 0229-S) Parker Hannifin.

Parker Hannifin Corporation Staff. Analyzing Hydraulic Systems. Schrader, L. F., Jr., ed. (Illus.). 244p. (Orig.). (C). 1977. teacher ed 31.20 (*1-55769-007-3*, 0222-B2); pap. text ed. 19.30 (*1-55769-006-5*, 02229-B1); trans. 448.35 (*1-55769-008-1*, 0222-B3) Parker Hannifin.
— Design Engineers Handbook. Schrader, Lawrence F., Jr., ed. (Illus.). 304p. (Orig.). (C). 1979. pap. text ed. 19.30 (*1-55769-018-9*, 0224-B1) Parker Hannifin.
— Fluid Power, No. 1. Schrader, Lawrence F., Jr., ed. (Illus.). 174p. (Orig.). (C). 1984. teacher ed 23.65 (*1-55769-010-3*, 0225-B2); pap. text ed. 19.30 (*1-55769-009-X*, 0225-B1); trans. 368.55 (*1-55769-011-1*, 0225-B3) Parker Hannifin.
— Hydraulic Maintenance Technology. Cohn, Joseph, Jr., ed. (Illus.). 148p. (Orig.). 1989. teacher ed 27.50 (*1-55769-024-3*, 0240-B2); pap. text ed. 19.30 (*1-55769-019-7*, 0240-B1); trans. 464.00 (*1-55769-020-0*, 0240-B3) Parker Hannifin.
— Industrial Hydraulic Technology. Schrader, Lawrence F., Jr., ed. (Illus.). 229p. (Orig.). (C). 1973. teacher ed 29.65 (*1-55769-001-4*, 0221-B2); student ed 28.90 (*0-685-18894-9*, 0229) Parker Hannifin.
— Industrial Hydraulic Technology. rev. ed. Schrader, Lawrence F., Jr., ed. (Illus.). 229p. (Orig.). (C). 1973. student ed 30.00 (*1-55769-021-9*, 0231); 2.10 (*1-55769-022-7*, 0221-B7); pap. text ed. 19.30 (*1-55769-000-6*, 0221-B1); trans. 456.75 (*1-55769-002-2*, 0221-B3) Parker Hannifin.
— Industrial Hydraulic Technology. 2nd ed. Schrader, Lawrence F., ed. (Illus.). 331p. (Orig.). 1991. pap. text ed. write for info. (*1-55769-025-1*, BUL. 0232-B1) Parker Hannifin.

Parker, Harold M., Jr. The United Synod: The Southern New School Presbyterian Church. LC 87-37564. (Contributions to the Study of Religion Ser.: No. 20). 363p. 1988. text ed. 55.00 (*0-313-26289-6*, PSY/, Greenwood Pr) Greenwood.

Parker, Harold M., Jr., comp. Bibliography of Published Articles on American Presbyterianism, 1901-1980. LC 85-7987. (Bibliographies & Indexes in Religious Studies: No. 4). xv, 261p. 1985. text ed. 55.00 (*0-313-24544-4*, PBP/, Greenwood Pr) Greenwood.

Parker, Harold T. An Administrative Bureau During the Old Regime: The Bureau of Commerce & Its Relations to French Industry from May 1781 to November 1783. LC 92-50634. 160p. 1993. Alk. paper. 29.50 (*0-87413-467-6*) U Delaware Pr.
— Three Napoleonic Battles. LC 82-21082. (Illus.). xxiii, 235p. 1983. reprint ed. pap. text ed. 15.95 (*0-8223-0547-X*) Duke.

Parker, Harold T. & Herr, Richard, eds. Ideas in History: Essays Presented to Louis Gottschalk by His Former Students. LC 65-14546. 400p. reprint ed. 114.00 (*0-8357-9107-6*, 2017918) Bks Demand.

Parker, Harold T., jt. ed. see Iggers, Georg G.

Parker, Harriet F., jt. auth. see Marsh, Lucius B.

Parker, Harriette. Alaska's Mushrooms: A Practical Guide. LC 94-6298. (Illus.). 96p. (Orig.). 1994. pap. 12.95 (*0-88240-453-9*) Alaska Northwest.

Parker, Harrison. Hawley, Massachusetts: The First Fifty Years: 1770-1820. LC 92-28144. 1992. 35.00 (*0-9633340-1-8*) Sara Pub MA.

Parker, Harry. Simplified Design of Structural Wood. 4th ed. LC 88-154. 305p. 1988. text ed. 49.95 (*0-471-85134-5*) Wiley.
— Simplified Design of Wood Structures. 5th ed. LC 93-35635. 1994. text ed. 54.95 (*0-471-30366-6*) Wiley.
— Simplified Mechanics & Strength of Materials. 5th ed. (Parker Series of Simplified Design Guides: No. 1879). 408p. 1992. text ed. 54.95 (*0-471-54170-2*) Wiley.

Parker, Harry & Ambrose, James E. Simplified Design of Steel Structures. 6th ed. 437p. 1990. text ed. 54.95 (*0-471-50539-0*) Wiley.

Parker, Harry, jt. auth. see Ambrose, James E.

Parker, Harry L. Clinical Studies in Neurology. 384p. 1969. 48.95 (*0-398-01449-3*) C C Thomas.
— Clinical Studies in Neurology. 384p. 1969. pap. 29.95 (*0-398-06313-3*) C C Thomas.

Parker, Harry W. Iron John Reflections, No. 1: Choose - One Precious Thing. (Orig.). 1992. pap. 5.95 (*0-89672-311-9*) Tex Tech Univ Pr.

Parker, Harvey C. The ADD Hyperactivity Handbook for Schools: Effective Strategies for Identifying & Teaching ADD Students in Elementary & Secondary Schools. (Illus.). 330p. (Orig.). 1992. pap. 27.00 (*0-9621629-2-2*) Spec Pr FL.
— The ADD Hyperactivity Workbook for Parents, Teachers & Kids. (Illus.). 108p. (Orig.). 1988. 12.95 (*0-685-23302-2*) Spec Pr FL.
— Cuaderno Do Trabajo Para Padres, Maestros y Ninos Sobre el Trasterno de Bajo Nivel de Atencion (ADD) O Hiperactividad. (Illus.). 142p. 1994. student ed, pap. 16.00 (*0-9621629-5-7*) Spec Pr FL.

Parker, Harvey C., jt. auth. see Parker, Roberta N.

Parker, Helen N. Biological Themes in Modern Science Fiction. LC 84-8768. (Studies in Speculative Fiction: No. 6). 115p. reprint ed. pap. 32.80 (*0-8357-1577-9*, 2070516) Bks Demand.

Parker, Henry. The Case of Shipmony Briefly Discoursed, According to the Grounds of Law, Policy & Conscience. LC 76-57404. (English Experience Ser.: No. 820). 1977. reprint ed. lib. bdg. 7.00 (*90-221-0820-1*) Walter J Johnson.
— The Rich & the Poor. LC 77-7419. (English Experience Ser.: No. 882). 1977. reprint ed. lib. bdg. 69.00 (*90-221-0882-1*) Walter J Johnson.
— Village Folk-Tales of Ceylon, 3 vols., 1. Dorson, Richard M., ed. LC 77-70614. (International Folklore Ser.). 1977. reprint ed. lib. bdg. 36.95 (*0-405-10114-7*) Ayer.
— Village Folk-Tales of Ceylon, 3 vols., 2. Dorson, Richard M., ed. LC 77-70614. (International Folklore Ser.). 1977. reprint ed. lib. bdg. 36.95 (*0-405-10115-5*) Ayer.
— Village Folk-Tales of Ceylon, 3 vols., 3. Dorson, Richard M., ed. LC 77-70614. (International Folklore Ser.). 1977. reprint ed. lib. bdg. 36.95 (*0-405-10116-3*) Ayer.
— Village Folk-Tales of Ceylon, 3 vols, Set. Dorson, Richard M., ed. LC 77-70614. (International Folklore Ser.). 1977. reprint ed. lib. bdg. 108.95 (*0-405-10113-9*) Ayer.

Parker, Henry T. Eighth Notes: Voices & Figures of Music & the Dance. LC 68-29236. (Essay Index Reprint Ser.). 1977. 19.95 (*0-8369-0768-X*) Ayer.

Parker, Herbert M. The Squares of the Natural Numbers in Radiation Protection. (Taylor Lecture Ser.: No. 1). 1977. 15.00 (*0-913392-39-1*) NCRP Pubns.

Parker, Hermione, ed. see Williams, Brandon R.

Parker, Herschell. Discovering Dinosaurs. (Illus.). 16p. (Orig.). (J). (gr. 1-5). 1994. pap. 7.95 (*1-57102-000-4*, Ideals Child) Hambleton-Hill.

Parker, Hershel. Flawed Texts & Verbal Icons: Literary Authority in American Fiction. LC 84-613439. 249p. 1984. 36.95 (*0-8101-0666-3*); pap. 12.95 (*0-8101-0667-1*) Northwestern U Pr.
— Reading Billy Budd. 190p. (Orig.). 1990. 29.95 (*0-8101-0961-1*); pap. 12.95 (*0-8101-0962-X*) Northwestern U Pr.

***Parker, Hershel, ed.** Pierre or the Ambiguities. (Illus.). 1995. 25.00 (*0-06-118009-2*, HarpT) HarpC.

Parker, Hershel & Hayes, Kevin, eds. Checklist of Melville Reviews. 157p. 1992. 34.95 (*0-8101-1028-8*) Northwestern U Pr.

Parker, Hershel, jt. ed. see Higgins, Brian.

Parker, Hershel, ed. see Melville, Herman.

Parker, Hilary. Flight to Enchantment. large type ed. (Linford Romance Library). 1989. pap. 11.95 (*0-7089-6788-4*, Trailtree Bookshop) Ulverscroft.

Parker Historical Society of Clay County Staff, ed. The History of Clay County, Iowa, Vol. I. (Illus.). 536p. 1984. 60.00 (*0-88107-022-X*) Curtis Media.

Parker, Hohn & Bryan, Peter. Landscape Management & Maintenance: A Guide to Its Costing & Organization. (Illus.). 176p. 1989. text ed. 49.95 (*0-566-09018-X*) Ashgate Pub Co.

***Parker, Holiday, contrib.** The Jazz Source Book. 1994. 14.95 (*0-8256-1408-2*, AM91543) Music Sales.

Parker, Homer W., Sr. Evolution of Man Since the Earth Was Created: Mankind's Roots. LC 89-91069. 144p. (Orig.). 1989. pap. 12.95 (*0-922958-06-8*) H W Parker.

Parker, Homer W., Sr., ed. Software Handbook for DOS for IBM PC, XT, AT, PS2 & Compatibles. LC 88-92322. 240p. (Orig.). 1989. pap. 12.95 (*0-922958-00-9*) H W Parker.

Parker, Horatio. Hora Novissima (Opus 30) LC 75-169652. (Earlier American Music Ser.: No. 2). 167p. 1972. reprint ed. lib. bdg. 32.50 (*0-306-77302-3*) Da Capo.

Parker, Horatio W., ed. Music & Public Entertainment. LC 74-24180. (Illus.). reprint ed. 49.50 (*0-404-13082-8*) AMS Pr.

Parker, Howard. View from the Boys: Sociology of Down-Town Adolescents. (Modern Revivals in Sociology Ser.). 238p. 1992. 49.95 (*0-7512-0046-8*, Pub. by Gregg Revivals UK) Ashgate Pub Co.

Parker, Howard & Jarvis, Graham. Unmasking the Magistrates: The "Custody-or-Not" Decision in Sentencing Young Offenders. 176p. 1989. 90.00 (*0-335-09936-X*, Open Univ Pr); pap. 32.00 (*0-335-09935-1*, Open Univ Pr) Taylor & Francis.

Parker, Howard, et al. Living with Heroin: The Impact of a Drugs 'Epidemic" on an English Community. 192p. 1988. 90.00 (*0-335-15565-0*, Open Univ Pr); pap. 34.00 (*0-335-15564-2*, Open Univ Pr) Taylor & Francis.

Parker, Ian. The Crisis in Modern Social Psychology: How to End It. 176p. 1989. 45.00 (*0-685-26090-9*, A1668); pap. 12.95 (*0-415-01494-8*, A3373) Routledge Chapman & Hall.
— Discourse Dynamics: Critical Analysis for Social & Individual Psychology. 144p. 1991. 59.95 (*0-415-05017-0*, A5958); pap. 16.95 (*0-415-05018-9*, A6654) Routledge.

Parker, Ian & Shotter, John, eds. Deconstructing Social Psychology. 224p. 1990. 49.95 (*0-415-01077-2*, A4030); pap. 14.95 (*0-415-01074-8*, A4034) Routledge.

Parker, Ian, jt. ed. see Burman, Erica.

Parker, Idella & Keating, Mary. Idella: Marjorie Rawlings' "Perfect Maid" (Illus.). 156p. 1992. 23.95 (*0-8130-1143-4*); pap. 13.95 (*0-8130-1144-2*) U Press Fla.

Parker, J. Anthony, jt. auth. see Holman, B. Leonard.

Parker, J. Carlyle. City, County, Town & Township Index to the 1850 Federal Census Schedules. (Gale Genealogy & Local History Ser.: Vol. 6). 215p. 1990. reprint ed. fiche 9.95 (*0-934153-06-X*, OCLZ 27863673) Marietta Pub.
— Going to Salt Lake City to Do Family History Research. 2nd rev. ed. LC 92-29080. 200p. (Orig.). 1993. pap. 12.95 (*0-934153-10-8*, OCLC 26398866) Marietta Pub.
— Music Directors' & Accompanists' Index to "Hymns" (1985) & "Simplified Accompaniments" (1986) LC 88-21565. 66p. (Orig.). pap. 3.95 (*0-934153-04-3*, OCLC 18163152) Marietta Pub.
— Pennsylvania & Middle Atlantic States Genealogical Manuscripts: A User's Guide to the Manuscript Collections of the Genealogical Society of Pennsylvania as Indexed in Its Manuscript Materials Index. LC 86-2504. 1986. pap. 14.95 (*0-934153-01-9*, OCLC 13214741) Marietta Pub.

Parker, J. Carlyle, comp. Rhode Island Biographical & Genealogical Sketch Index. LC 90-25871. 1991. 29.95 (*0-934153-08-6*, OCLC 22859101) Marietta Pub.

Parker, J. Carlyle & Parker, Janet G. Nevada Biographical & Genealogical Sketch Index. 1986. 23.95 (*0-934153-02-7*, OCLC 13642809) Marietta Pub.

Parker, J. D., ed. Energy Conservation Measures: Proceedings of the International Symposium, Kuwait, 6-8 February 1983. LC 83-25137. 332p. 1984. 132.00 (*0-08-031141-5*, Pub. by Pergamon Repr UK) Franklin.
— The Sheet-Forming Process. LC 72-75337. 104p. 1972. pap. 33.00 (*0-685-45540-8*, 0102BS09) TAPPI.

Parker, J. D., et al. Introduction to Fluid Mechanics & Heat Transfer. (Engineering Ser.). (C). 1969. text ed. write for info. (*0-201-05710-7*) Addison-Wesley.

***Parker, J. Harold, ed.** Environmental Handbook for Fertilizer & Agrichemical Dealers. 250p. (Orig.). (C). 1994. pap. text ed. 75.00x (*0-7881-1223-6*) Diane Pub.

Parker, J. Harold, ed. see Nelson, Lewis B.

Parker, J. M., jt. ed. see Cable, M.

Parker, J. R. Practical Computer Vision Using C. LC 93-549. 476p. 1993. disk 69.95 (*0-471-59262-5*); disk 32.00 (*0-471-59411-3*) Wiley.

Parker, J. R., ed. Petroleum Geology of Northwest Europe: Proceedings of the 4th Conference. (Illus.). 1600p. (C). 1993. 250.00 (*0-903317-85-0*, Pub. by Geol Soc Pub Hse UK) AAPG.

Parker, J. S. Asking the Right Questions: Case Studies in Library Development Consultancy. 248p. 1988. text ed. 80.00 (*0-7201-1898-0*, Mansell Pub) Cassell.

Parker, J. S., ed. Information Consultants in Action. 272p. 1986. text ed. 90.00 (*0-7201-1753-4*, Mansell Pub) Cassell.

Parker, Jack. Shipwrecks of Lake Huron: The Great Sweet Water Sea. 4th ed. LC 86-70155. (Illus.). 175p. (Orig.). 1986. pap. 11.95 (*0-932212-45-X*) Avery Color.

Parker, Jack H. Gil Vicente. LC 67-25183. (Twayne's World Authors Ser.). 1967. lib. bdg. 17.95 (*0-8057-2956-9*) Irvington.

Parker, James. The Concept of Apokatastasis in Acts: A Study in Primitive Christian Theology. 140p. 1981. pap. text ed. 5.95 (*0-931016-01-0*) Schola Pr TX.

***Parker, James & Stallman, James.** Managerial Accounting Microcomputer Exercises for the IBM PC. 5th ed. 296p. (C). 1988. text ed., disk 22.95 (*0-256-06543-8*) Irwin.

Parker, James, jt. auth. see Endler, Norman.

***Parker, James E., Jr.** Codename: Mule: Fighting the Secret War in Laos for the C.I.A. Gatlin, Mark, ed. LC 94-48538. (Naval Institute Special Warfare Ser.). (Illus.). 232p. 1995. 27.95 (*1-55750-668-X*) Naval Inst Pr.

Parker, James E. The Journey. Van Treese, James B., ed. 320p. 1994. pap. 8.95 (*1-56901-060-9*) NW Pub.

Parker, James E., jt. auth. see Raabe, William A.

Parker, James G. Lord Curzon, 1859-1925: A Bibliography. LC 91-9473. (Bibliographies of British Statesmen Ser.: No. 5). 136p. 1991. text ed. 55.00 (*0-313-28122-X*, PLZ, Greenwood Pr) Greenwood.

Parker, James H. Health Care & Freedom: An American Dilemma. 88p. (Orig.). (C). 1993. lib. bdg. 28.50 (*0-8191-9302-X*); pap. text ed. 12.50 (*0-8191-9303-8*) U Pr of Amer.
— Logics, No. Two: A Sociobiological Approach to Social & Other Logics. LC 92-23596. 104p. (Orig.). (C). 1993. lib. bdg. 34.50 (*0-8191-8881-6*); pap. text ed. 16.50 (*0-8191-8882-4*) U Pr of Amer.
— The New England Book of the Dead. LC 95-4058. 1995. write for info. (*0-8191-9902-8*); pap. write for info. (*0-8191-9903-6*) U Pr of Amer.
— Social History & the Dynamics of Belief. LC 94-9254. (Illus.). 130p. (Orig.). (C). 1994. pap. text ed. 24.50 (*0-8191-9518-9*) U Pr of Amer.

Parker, James R. Practical Computer Vision Using C. 1993. pap. text ed. 37.95 (*0-471-59259-5*) Wiley.

Parker, James W. & Dublin, Wayne. First Aid to Dating. 1989. write for info. (*0-9625950-0-4*) Entrprse NY.

Parker, Jane, jt. auth. see Symons, Allene.

Parker, Janet, jt. auth. see Nicholson, Peter.

Parker, Janet G., jt. auth. see Parker, J. Carlyle.

Parker, Jay, jt. auth. see Wooden, Wayne S.

Parker, Jeanine F. Starmakers, All: How to Find & Use Your Personal Power. (Illus.). 155p. 1992. pap. 9.95 (*0-9629300-0-8*) Poco Pr.

Parker, Jeffery G., jt. ed. see Gottman, John M.

***Parker, Jennifer.** An Artist's Resource Book. 197p. (Orig.). (C). 1993. pap. text ed. 12.00 (*0-9644338-0-X*) Go Far Press.

Parker, Jerald D., jt. auth. see McQuiston, Faye C.

Parker, Jerry. Dissolving the Reins of Mental Control & Physical Domination. 120p. Date not set. pap. 15.00 (*0-9637021-0-6*, 055795981) Gldn Obelisk.
— Off the Beaten Track: The Odyssey of a Naturalist. LC 85-6079. (Illus.). 1985. pap. 9.75 (*0-916955-01-X*) Arcus Pub.

Parker, Joan H., jt. auth. see Parker, Robert B.

Parker, John. At the Heart of Darkness: Witchcraft, Black Magic & Satanism Today. (Illus.). 332p. 1993. pap. 12.95 (*0-8065-1428-0*, Citadel Pr) Carol Pub Group.
— Discovery: Developing Views of the Earth from Ancient Times to Captain Cook. (Illus.). 216p. 1990. 17.95 (*0-88029-460-4*) Dorset Pr.
— Five for Hollywood: Their Friendship, Their Fame, Their Tragedies. 1991. 19.95 (*0-8184-0539-2*) Carol Pub Group.
— King of Fools. (Illus.). 320p. 1990. mass mkt. 5.95 (*0-312-92091-1*) St Martin.
— Kremlin in Transition: From Brezhnev to Gorbachev, 1978-1989, Vol. 2. 368p. (C). 1990. text ed. 65.00 (*0-04-445890-8*) Routledge Chapman & Hall.
— Kremlin in Transition: From Brezhnev to Gorbachev 1978-1989, Vol.1. 480p. (C). 1990. text ed. 75.00 (*0-685-46016-9*) Routledge Chapman & Hall.
— Polanski. (Illus.). 288p. 1995. 29.95 (*0-575-05615-0*, Pub. by V Gollancz UK) Trafalgar.
— Prince Philip. large type ed. (Non-Fiction Ser.). 528p. 1992. 23.95 (*0-7089-8642-0*) Ulverscroft.
— The Queen: The New Biography. large type ed. (Charnwood Library). (Illus.). 736p. 1993. 23.95 (*0-7089-8713-3*, Trail West Pubs) Ulverscroft.
— Sean Connery. 228p. 1993. 17.95 (*0-8092-3668-0*) Contemp Bks.
— The Twelfth Man. (Illus.). 208p. 1992. 23.95 (*0-233-98769-X*, Pub. by A Deutsch UK) Trafalgar.
— Windows into China. 1978. 3.00 (*0-89073-050-4*) Boston Public Lib.
— The World for a Marketplace: Episodes in the History of European Expansion. LC 78-71068. (Illus.). 1978. 15.00 (*0-9601798-0-1*) Assocs James Bell.

Parker, John & Urness, Carol, eds. The American Revolution: A Heritage of Change. LC 75-24503. 1975. 10.00 (*0-685-00552-6*) Assocs James Bell.
— The American Revolution: A Heritage of Change. 1975. 10.00 (*0-87018-078-9*) Ross.

Parker, John, jt. ed. see DeVorsey, Louis, Jr.

Parker, John, jt. ed. see Duffy, John.

P Q

Parker, John, ed. see Raleigh, Walter.
Parker, John, tr. see Torres, Antonio.
Parker, John A., jt. ed. see D'Alelio, Gaetano F.
***Parker, John D.** Humphrey the Odd Looking Camel. (Illus.). 24p. (J). (gr. k-3). 1995. pap. 6.00 (*0-8059-3758-7*) Dorrance.
Parker, John E. The Economics of Innovation: The National & Multinational Enterprise in Technological Change. 2nd ed. LC 77-14535. 406p. reprint ed. pap. 115.80 (*0-7837-1606-0*, 2041898) Bks Demand.
Parker, John F. The Independent Writer. 782p. (C). 1986. pap. text ed. 22.75 (*0-15-541340-6*); pap. text ed. 2.25 (*0-15-541341-4*) HB Coll Pubs.
— Twenty-Minute Workshops. rev. ed. (Illus.). (Orig.). 1992. pap. 150.00 (*0-9694762-1-3*); disk write for info. (*0-9694762-2-1*) JFP Prodns.
— Workshops for Active Learning. (Illus.). 194p. (Orig.). 1990. student ed, pap. 19.95 (*0-9694762-0-5*) JFP Prodns.
Parker, John H. Concise Glossary of Architectural Terms. 1989. 6.99 (*0-517-68134-X*) Random Hse Value.
— We Remember Cuba. Gianelloni, Giles S., ed. (Illus.). 233p. (Orig.). 1993. pap. 21.95 (*0-9635705-0-1*) Gldn Quill FL.
Parker, John L. Aerobic Chic & Other Delusions. (Orig.). 1983. pap. 3.95 (*0-915297-03-5*) Cedarwinds.
— Living off the Country: For Fun & Profit. Lever, B., ed. (Fun & Profit Ser.). (Illus.). 1978. 7.95 (*0-916302-23-7*); pap. 4.95 (*0-916302-24-5*) Bookworm Pub.
Parker, John L., Jr. Once a Runner. rev. ed. LC 78-59993. 194p. (Orig.). 1990. pap. 9.95 (*0-915297-01-9*, OAR) Cedarwinds.
— Runners & Other Dreamers. 208p. (Orig.). 1988. pap. 9.95 (*0-915297-05-1*) Cedarwinds.
Parker, John L., jt. ed. see Gunn, Robert.
Parker, John L., ed. see Shapiro, James E., et al.
Parker, John M., tr. see Dourado, Autran.
Parker, John M., tr. see Garrett, Almeida.
Parker, John R. BURP: A Journal about Food & How to Enjoy It. (Illus.). 190p. (Orig.). 1986. pap. 8.95 (*0-912095-01-6*) Johmax Bks Inc.
— How to Sink a Sub: A Substitute Teacher's Rather Strange Appraisal of the American Educational System. (Illus.). 175p. (Orig.). 1990. pap. 8.95 (*0-912095-02-4*) Johmax Bks Inc.
— No Butts about It: How to Want to Stop Smoking. 3rd ed. (Illus.). 88p. (Orig.). 1989. pap. 6.95 (*0-912095-00-8*) Johmax Bks Inc.
Parker, John R., ed. The Euterpeiad or Musical Intelligencer, 3 Vols, Set. LC 65-23389. (Music Ser.). 1977. reprint ed. lib. bdg. 110.00 (*0-306-70920-1*) Da Capo.
Parker, John W., ed. see International Leucocyte Culture Conference, 15th: 1982: Asilomar, Pacific Grove, CA.
Parker, Joni M. & Maurer, Ruth A. An Economic Feasibility Study for a Geothermal-Coal Hybrid Power Plant in Chaffee County, Colorado. Raese, Jon W. & Goldberg, J. H., eds. LC 83-1922. (Colorado School of Mines Quarterly Ser.: Vol. 78, No. 1). (Illus.). 34p. 1983. pap. 12.00 (*0-686-45174-0*) Colo Sch Mines.
Parker, Joseph. From Outhouse to In-House & Much More. 1994. 7.95 (*0-8062-4831-9*) Carlton.
— Preaching Through the Bible, 14 vols. 1987. reprint ed. 295.00 (*0-8010-7032-5*) Baker Bk.
— Studies in Texts. 1250p. 1990. reprint ed. pap. 49.95 (*0-8010-6932-7*) Baker Bk.
Parker, Joseph A. Essentials of Microeconomics. (Illus.). 221p. (C). 1990. pap. text ed. 24.00 (*0-936285-05-2*) U New Haven Pr.
Parker, Joseph B. Morrison Era: Reform Politics in New Orleans. LC 74-7142. 16.95 (*0-88289-009-3*) Pelican.
— Politics in Mississippi. 308p. (Orig.). (C). 1993. pap. text ed. 15.50 (*1-879251-15-9*) Sheffield WI.
Parker, Joy. Scarlet Christmas: Abortion: The Grandparent Connection. 32p. (Orig.). 1991. pap. 2.95 (*0-9628088-1-4*) Laser Pr Pubs.
Parker, Joy, ed. see Spraguer, Hart.
Parker, Judith R. The House Sitter. 320p. 1994. mass mkt. 4.50 (*0-8217-4594-8*) Zebra.
Parker, Julia. The Zodiac Family. 1989. 18.95 (*0-87951-374-8*) Overlook Pr.
— Zodiac Family: How Astrology Can Help You Understand & Raise Your Child. (Illus.). 1992. pap. 10.95 (*0-87951-378-0*) Overlook Pr.
***Parker, Julia & Parker, Derek.** Parkers' Complete Book of Dreams. LC 94-27918. (Illus.). 208p. 1995. 24.95 (*1-56458-855-6*) Dorling Kindersley.
— The Secret World of Your Dreams. 240p. 1991. reprint ed. pap. 11.00 (*0-399-51700-6*, Perigree Bks) Berkley Pub.
Parker, Julia, jt. auth. see Parker, Derek.
Parker, Julie. All about Cotton: A Fabric Dictionary & Swatchbook. LC 93-148962. (Fabric Reference Ser.). 120p. 1993. pap. 29.95 (*0-9637612-1-8*) Rain City.
— All about Silk: A Fabric Dictionary & Swatchbook. LC 93-117999. (Fabric Reference Ser.). 92p. 1992. pap. 29.95 (*0-9637612-0-X*) Rain City.
— All about Wool: A Fabric Dictionary & Swatchbook. (Fabric Reference Ser.). Date not set. pap. write for info. (*0-9637612-2-6*) Rain City.
— The Astrologer's Handbook. (Illus.). 256p. (Orig.). 1995. pap. 10.95 (*0-916360-59-8*) CRCS Pubns CA.
— Everything You Need to Know about Living in a Shelter. LC 94-21280. (Need to Know Library). (Illus.). 64p. (YA). (gr. 7-12). 1995. 15.95 (*0-8239-1874-2*) Rosen Group.
Parker, Julie F. Careers for Women As Clergy. Rosen, Ruth, ed. (Careers in Depth Ser.). (YA). (gr. 7-12). 1993. lib. bdg. 14.95 (*0-8239-1424-0*); pap. 9.95 (*0-8239-1727-4*) Rosen Group.
Parker, Julien, jt. auth. see Haysom, David.
Parker, Julius. Grab Life & Hang On: Insights into the Art of Everyday Living. 249p. 1990. 21.95 (*0-9627915-0-4*) Harvest Hill Pr.
Parker, K. J., jt. ed. see Birch, Gordon G.
Parker, K. Langloh, comp. Wise Women of the Dreamtime: Aboriginal Tales of the Ancestral Powers. (Illus.). 124p. (Orig.). 1993. pap. 12.95 (*0-89281-477-2*) Inner Tradit.
Parker, K. Michael, jt. ed. see Hicks, Jocelyn M.
Parker, K. T. Drawings of Antoine Watteau. LC 77-116345. (Illus.). 1970. reprint ed. 50.00 (*0-87817-050-2*) Hacker.
Parker, Katharine O., ed. see Carpenter, Charles H., Jr. & Zapata, Jane.
Parker, Kathleen M., jt. intro. see Green, John.
Parker, Kathleene. The Only True People: A History of the Native Americans of the Colorado Plateau. (Illus.). 84p. (Orig.). 1991. pap. 10.95 (*0-9625717-0-9*) Thunder Mesa.
Parker, Kathryn E. Talking with Your Child about Feelings. LC 90-33014. (Growing Together Ser.). (Orig.). 1990. pap. 1.95 (*0-8298-0861-2*) Pilgrim OH.
Parker, Kathryn E., ed. see Ebbers, Bert C.
***Parker, KayLee.** Grocery List--Alphabetical Check Off. rev. ed. (Illus.). 50p. 1995. pap. 3.95 (*1-883924-08-1*, 220) Your Moms Organizers.
— Grocery List--Category Write in. rev. ed. (Illus.). 50p. 1995. pap. 3.95 (*1-883924-07-3*, 210) Your Moms Organizers.
— Grocery Lists--Category Check Off. rev. ed. (Illus.). 50p. 1995. pap. 3.95 (*1-883924-09-X*, 230) Your Moms Organizers.
— Mom, Help! It's the Holidays: Holiday Planning Book. rev. ed. (Illus.). 68p. 1995. pap. 4.95 (*1-883924-12-X*, 430) Your Moms Organizers.
— Mom, How Do You Get a Meal on the Table? rev. ed. (Illus.). 106p. 1995. pap. 8.95 (*1-883924-04-9*, 200) Your Moms Organizers.
— Mom, How Do You Get Organized? rev. ed. (Illus.). 110p. 1995. pap. 8.95 (*1-883924-02-2*, 400) Your Moms Organizers.
— Mom, How Do You Plan a Camping Trip? rev. ed. (Illus.). 114p. 1995. pap. 8.95 (*1-883924-11-1*, 330) Your Moms Organizers.
— Mom's Packing Lists. rev. ed. (Illus.). 52p. 1995. pap. 4.95 (*1-883924-10-3*, 310) Your Moms Organizers.
— Permanent Menu Planning List: Mom's Meal Planners. rev. ed. (Illus.). 52p. 1995. pap. 3.95 (*1-883924-06-5*, 250) Your Moms Organizers.
— Weekly Menu Planning List: Mom's Meal Planners. rev. ed. 52p. 1995. pap. 3.95 (*1-883924-05-7*, 240) Your Moms Organizers.
Parker, Ken. No Longer Lonely. 21p. 1982. 0.50 (*0-89814-056-0*) Grace Publns.
— Purposeful Prayer. 20p. 1980. 0.50 (*0-89814-051-X*) Grace Publns.
— What Happens When a Christian Sins. 18p. 1980. 0.50 (*0-89814-050-1*) Grace Publns.
Parker, Kenneth, ed. The South African Novel in English: Essays in Criticism & Society. LC 78-18343. 202p. 1979. 39.50 (*0-8419-0425-1*, Africana) Holmes & Meier.
Parker, Kenneth L. The English Sabbath, 1558-1660: A Study of Doctrine & Discipline from the Reformation to the Civil War. (Illus.). 224p. 1988. 74.95 (*0-521-30535-7*) Cambridge U Pr.
Parker, Kenneth P. The Boundary-Scan Handbook. LC 92-27976. 288p. (C). 1992. lib. bdg. 93.50 (*0-7923-9270-1*) Kluwer Ac.
— Integrating Design & Test - Using CAE Tools for ATE Programming. LC 87-70816. 144p. 1987. 10.95 (*0-8186-8788-6*, 788) IEEE Comp Soc.
Parker, Kim, jt. auth. see Gulley, Greg.
Parker, Kim I. Wisdom & Law in the Reign of Solomon. LC 92-45201. 136p. 1993. text ed. 69.95 (*0-7734-2356-7*) E Mellen.
Parker, Kim I., ed. Liberal Democracy & the Bible. LC 92-23478. 196p. 1992. text ed. 79.95 (*0-7734-9154-6*) E Mellen.
Parker, Kimberly C. Is Clinton's Health Care Plan Socialized Medicine? What You're Not Being Told. LC 94-76322. 112p. 1994. 4.99 (*1-56384-070-7*) Huntington Hse.
Parker, Kittie F. An Illustrated Guide to Arizona Weeds. LC 72-75471. 338p. 1972. pap. 19.95 (*0-8165-0288-9*) U of Ariz Pr.
Parker, Kristy. My Dad the Magnificent. LC 86-24077. (Illus.). 32p. (J). (ps-2). 1987. 10.95 (*0-525-44314-2*, DCB) Dutton Child Bks.
— My Dad the Magnificent. LC 86-24077. (Unicorn Paperbacks Ser.). (Illus.). 32p. (J). (ps-2). 1990. pap. 3.95 (*0-525-44607-9*, DCB) Dutton Child Bks.
Parker, L. Craig, Jr. The Japanese Police System Today: An American Perspective. LC 83-48877. (Illus.). 216p. 1988. pap. 5.95 (*0-87011-853-6*) Kodansha.
— Parole & the Community-Based Treatment of Offenders in Japan & the United States. LC 86-50431. (Illus.). 200p. (Orig.). 1986. pap. text ed. 10.95 (*0-936285-03-6*) U New Haven Pr.
Parker, L. H. Barry Family Records Vol. I: Capt. Charles Barry & His Descendants. (Illus.). 148p. 1991. reprint ed. pap. 25.00 (*0-685-50980-X*) Higginson Bk Co.
Parker, L. N. History & Genealogy of the Ancestors & Descendants of Captain Israel Jones Who Removed from Enfield to Barkhamstead, Conn. in 1759. (Illus.). 303p. reprint ed. lib. bdg. 53.50 (*0-8328-0721-4*); reprint ed. pap. 45.50 (*0-8328-0722-2*) Higginson Bk Co.
Parker, L. Stevenson, jt. auth. see Rosenbaum, Robert D.
Parker, Larry. Principles of Electronic Devices & Circuits - Ross & LaLond: Flashcards. 128p. 1994. 14.95 (*0-8273-6420-2*) Delmar.
Parker, Laura. Beguiled. 1993. mass mkt. 4.99 (*0-440-21240-5*) Dell.
— Caprice. 1994. mass mkt. 4.99 (*0-440-21238-3*) Dell.
— Impetuous. 1995. pap. 4.99 (*0-440-21527-7*) Dell.
— Indiscreet. (Intrigue Ser.). 1995. mass mkt. 3.50 (*0-373-22327-7*, 1-22327-0) Harlequin Bks.
— Stranger in Town. (Silhouette Intimate Moments Ser.). 1994. mass mkt. 3.50 (*0-373-07562-6*, 5-07562-7) Silhouette.
— Together Again. 1995. pap. 3.75 (*0-373-07682-7*, 1-07682-7) Silhouette.
Parker, Laurie, ed. see Catala, Rafael.
Parker, Leonard & Christensen, Steven M. Math Tensor: A System for Doing Tensor Analysis by Computer. 1994. write for info. (*0-318-72530-4*) Addison-Wesley.
— MathTensor: A System for Doing Tensor Analysis by Computer. (C). 1994. text ed. 49.50 (*0-201-56990-6*) Addison-Wesley.
Parker, Lewis. Dropping in on Mexico. LC 93-42777. (J). 1994. write for info. (*1-55916-001-2*) Rourke Bk Co.
Parker, Lewis C. What Squashes Your Spirit. 1992. pap. 7.95 (*1-55673-493-X*, 7943) CSS OH.
Parker, Lewis K. Australia. LC 94-4249. (Dropping in On Ser.). (J). 1994. write for info. (*1-55916-007-1*) Rourke Bk Co.
— Canada. LC 93-42778. (Dropping in On Ser.). (J). 1994. write for info. (*1-55916-002-0*) Rourke Bk Co.
— Dropping in on Egypt. LC 93-47098. (Dropping in On Ser.). (J). 1994. write for info. (*1-55916-004-7*) Rourke Bk Co.
— England. LC 94-5471. (Dropping in On Ser.). (J). 1994. write for info. (*1-55916-006-3*) Rourke Corp.
— India. LC 94-614. (Dropping in On Ser.). (J). 1994. write for info. (*1-55916-005-5*) Rourke Bk Co.
— Japan. LC 93-47097. (Dropping in On Ser.). 1994. write for info. (*1-55916-003-9*) Rourke Bk Co.
— Vietnam. LC 94-7558. (Dropping in On Ser.). (J). 1994. write for info. (*1-55916-008-X*) Rourke Bk Co.
Parker, Linda S. Native American Estate: The Struggle over Indian & Hawaiian Lands. LC 89-4892. 256p. 1989. text ed. 24.00 (*0-8248-1119-4*) UH Pr.
Parker, Lisa A. Larry the Lobster: Everyday Songs from Everywhere. Bennett, Michael D., ed. 40p. (Orig.). 1993. pap. 10.95 (*0-934017-19-0*) Memphis Musicraft.
Parker, Liz, ed. see Bankier, William.
Parker, Liz, ed. see Bricker, Sandra D.
Parker, Liz, ed. see Brin, Susannah.
Parker, Liz, ed. see Buchanan, Paul.
Parker, Liz, ed. see Cruise, Robin.
Parker, Liz, ed. see Horton, Randy.
Parker, Liz, ed. see Kim, Kenneth H.
Parker, Liz, ed. see Press, Skip.
Parker, Liz, ed. see Schraff, Anne.
Parker, Liz, ed. see Steel, Richard.
Parker, Liz, ed. see Welch, Irene.
Parker, Liz, ed. see Wells, Colin.
Parker, Liz, ed. see Woodson, Farnk.
Parker, Liz, ed. see Woodson, Frank.
Parker, Lois & McConnell, David. A Little Peoples' Beginning on Michigan. (Illus.). 32p. (Orig.). (J). (gr. 1-2). 1981. pap. 5.50 (*0-910726-06-X*) Hillsdale Educ.
Parker, Lorne A. & Monson, Mavis K. Teletechniques: An Instructional Model for Interactive Teleconferencing. Langdon, Danny G., ed. LC 79-24442. (Instructional Design Library). 108p. 1980. 23.95 (*0-87778-158-3*) Educ Tech Pubns.
Parker, Lucile. Mississippi Wildflowers. LC 80-20433. (Illus.). 144p. 1981. 34.95 (*0-88289-165-0*) Pelican.
Parker, Lucinda M. The Little Falls & Dolgeville Railroad. 70p. (Orig.). 1986. pap. text ed. 7.95 (*0-914821-25-3*) Worden Pr.
Parker, Lucy. How to Open & Operate a Home-Based Writing Business: An Unabridged Guide. unabridged ed. LC 93-48966. 224p. 1994. pap. 14.95 (*1-56440-396-3*) Globe Pequot.
Parker, Lula J. Parker's History of Bedford County, Virginia. rev. ed. Viemeister, Peter, ed. & pref. by. LC 88-82103. (Indexed Edition Ser.). 160p. 1988. reprint ed. pap. 17.95 (*0-9608598-4-5*) Hamiltons.
Parker, Lynn, jt. auth. see Olkowski, Thomas T.
Parker, M. Socrates & Athens. 88p. 1986. reprint ed. 10.75 (*0-86292-185-6*, Pub. by Brstl Class Pr UK) Focus Info Gr.
Parker, M., ed. Growth Regulation by Nuclear Hormone Receptors. (Cancer Surveys Ser.: Vol. 14). (Illus.). 256p. (C). 1992. text ed. 66.00 (*0-87969-371-1*) Cold Spring Harbor.
***Parker, M. & Tyrrell, R.** Rumrunner: The Life & Times of Johnny Schnaw. 224p. (Orig.). 1993. pap. 10.95 (*0-920501-94-X*) Orca Bk Pubs.
Parker, M., et al, eds. Polycrystalline Thin Films - Structure, Texture, Properties & Applications: Materials Research Society Symposium Proceedings, Vol. 343. 1994. text ed. 57.00 (*1-55899-243-X*) Materials Res.
Parker, M. A. & Dennis, L. J. Engineering Drawing Fundamentals. (Illus.). 160p. (Orig.). 1992. pap. 36.00x (*0-7487-1559-2*, Pub. by S Thornes Pubs UK) St Mut.
***Parker, M. A. & Pickup, F.** Engineering Drawing with Worked Examples, Bk. 1. 232p. (C). 1976. pap. 27.00x (*0-7487-0311-X*, Pub. by S Thornes Pubs UK) St Mut.
— Engineering Drawing with Worked Examples, Bk. 2. 272p. (C). 1981. pap. 27.00x (*0-7487-1014-0*, Pub. by S Thornes Pubs UK) St Mut.
Parker, M. B. Scribes, Scripts & Readers. 304p. 1991. boxed 65.00 (*1-85285-050-7*) Hambledon Press.
Parker, M. Yvonne. Pioneers' Pathway to the Future: The History of the Mt. Adams School District. LC 93-26898. 1993. 24.95 (*0-87770-521-6*) Ye Galleon.
***Parker, Madison.** Sabotage. 350p. (Orig.). Date not set. pap. 9.95 (*0-7610-0192-1*) NW Pub.
Parker, Malcolm G., ed. Nuclear Hormone Receptors: Molecular Mechanisms, Cellular Functions Clinical Abnormalities. 404p. 1991. text ed. 110.00 (*0-12-545072-9*) Acad Pr.
— Steroid Hormone Action. LC 93-1165. 1993. 68.00 (*0-19-963393-2*, IRL Pr); pap. 42.00 (*0-19-963392-4*, IRL Pr) OUP.
Parker, Margaret. The Didactic Structure & Content of el Libro de Calila e Digna. LC 76-51194. (Coleccion de Estudios Hispanicos - Hispanic Studies Collection). 1978. pap. 10.00 (*0-89729-188-3*) Ediciones.
— How to Hear the Living Word. LC 93-4252. 144p. (Orig.). 1994. pap. 5.99 (*1-56476-270-X*, Victor Books) SP Pubns.
Parker, Margot. What Is Martin Luther King, Jr. Day? LC 89-29254. (Understanding Holidays Ser.). (Illus.). 48p. (J). (ps-3). 1990. 11.85 (*0-516-03784-6*); pap. 4.95 (*0-516-43784-4*) Childrens.
— What Is Thanksgiving Day? LC 88-11112. (Understanding Holidays Ser.). (Illus.). 48p. (J). (ps-3). 1988. pap. 4.95 (*0-516-43783-6*) Childrens.
Parker, Maria G., jt. auth. see Imber, Brenda P.
Parker, Marilyn, ed. Nursing Theories in Practice. 320p. 1991. 25.95 (*0-88737-497-2*) Natl League Nurse.
Parker, Marilyn E., ed. Patterns of Nursing Theories in Practice. LC 93-3402. 1993. 29.95 (*0-88737-600-2*, 15-2548) Natl League Nurse.
Parker, Marilyn M. Information Economics: Linking Business Performance to Information Technology. 1988. text ed. 75.00 (*0-13-464595-2*) P-H.
— Information Strategy & Economics. 1989. pap. text ed. 55.00 (*0-13-464901-X*) P-H.
Parker, Marjorie. Bread from My Oven. (Quiet Time Books for Women). 128p. 1972. pap. 3.99 (*0-8024-0910-5*) Moody.
— Creating Shared Vision: The Story of a Pioneering Approach to Organizational Revitalization. (Illus.). (Orig.). 1991. pap. 14.95 (*0-9630000-0-4*) Dialog Intl.
Parker, Marjorie, et al. Quiet Time Books for Women, 14 Bks., Set. pap. 55.86 (*0-8024-6870-5*) Moody.
Parker, Marjorie H. Jellyfish Can't Swim, & Other Secrets from the Animal World. LC 91-3236. (J). (gr. 4-7). 1991. pap. 4.99 (*1-55513-393-2*, Chariot Bks) Chariot Family.
Parker, Mark, jt. auth. see McKnew, Ed.
Parker, Mark, jt. auth. see McNew, Ed.
***Parker, Mark M.** Fat Free Jokes for Fun-Loving Folks: Lighten up America. (Illus.). 155p. (Orig.). 1994. pap. 7.95 (*0-9644629-0-7*) Laugh Out Loud.
Parker, Mark R., jt. auth. see Scanlon, Leo J.
Parker, Marshall E. & Peattie, Edward G. Pipe Line Corrosion & Cathodic Protection. 3rd ed. LC 83-22630. 166p. 1984. 29.00 (*0-87201-149-6*) Gulf Pub.
Parker, Martha. Mother Goose: Designs for Applique & Embroidery Based on Traditional Nursery Rhymes. (Illus.). 48p. (Orig.). 1983. pap. 8.00 (*0-932946-10-0*) Burdett CA.
— Washington & Oregon, A Map History of the Oregon Country. 1988. 25.00 (*0-685-19905-3*) Ye Galleon.
Parker, Martha B. Kin-i-wak, Kenewick, Tehe, Kennewick. 414p. 1987. 22.95 (*0-87770-397-3*) Ye Galleon.
— Tales of Richland, White Bluffs & Hanford 1805-1943. (Illus.). 407p. 1987. 22.95 (*0-87770-223-3*) Ye Galleon.
Parker, Martin, jt. auth. see Hassard, John.
Parker, Martin, jt. ed. see Hassard, John.
Parker, Martyn J. & Pryor, Glyn. Hip Fracture Management. LC 92-49128. 1993. 140.00 (*0-632-03263-4*) Blackwell Sci.
***Parker, Mary Ann.** Eighteenth-Century Music in Theory & Practice: Essays in Honor of Alfred Mann. LC 94-34216. (Festschrift Ser.: No. 13). 1994. 48.00 (*0-945193-11-4*) Pendragon NY.
Parker, Mary C. Kids T. A. L. K! Teach Articulation & Language to Kids: A Communication Development Program for K-6th Grades Regular-Special-Bilingual Education. (Illus.). 535p. 1988. 195.00 (*0-9621178-0-3*) Kids TALK.
Parker, Matilda M. Real Estate Questions & Answers: Passing the North Carolina Real Estate Licensing Exam. 168p. (Orig.). 1992. pap. text ed. 24.95 (*0-9627684-0-5*) Urban NC.
Parker, Matthew & June, Lee N., comps. The Black Family: Past, Present, & Future. 240p. 1991. pap. 14.99 (*0-310-45591-X*) Zondervan.
***Parker, Maurice.** Manual of British Standards in Engineering Drawing & Design. 264p. (C). 1988. 54.00x (*0-7487-1031-0*, Pub. by S Thornes Pubs UK) St Mut.
Parker, Meg, ed. Socrates: The Wisest & Most Just. LC 79-11761. (Translations from Greek & Roman Authors Ser.). (Illus.). 1980. pap. 10.50 (*0-521-22813-1*) Cambridge U Pr.
Parker, Michael. The Geographical Cure: Novellas & Stories. LC 93-40188. 288p. 1994. text ed. 20.00 (*0-684-19682-4*, Scribners) S&S Trade.
— The Geographical Cure: Novellas & Stories. 304p. 1995. pap. 10.95 (*0-14-024390-9*, Penguin Bks) Viking Penguin.
— Hello down There. (Contemporary American Fiction Ser.). 288p. 1994. pap. 9.95 (*0-14-023424-1*, Penguin Bks) Viking Penguin.
— Hello Down There. large type ed. LC 92-47099. (General Ser.). 432p. 1993. reprint ed. lib. bdg. 18.95 (*1-56054-671-9*) Thorndike Pr.
— Hello Down There: A Novel. LC 92-17627. 288p. 1993. text ed. 20.00 (*0-684-19424-4*, Scribners) S&S Trade.
— Seamus Heaney: The Making of the Poet. LC 92-61949. (Illus.). 306p. 1993. text ed. 27.95 (*0-87745-398-5*) U of Iowa Pr.
***Parker, Michael & Starkey, Roger, eds.** Postcolonial Literatures: Achebe, Ngugi, Desai, Walcott. LC 95-9734. (New Casebooks Ser.). 1995. write for info. (*0-312-12664-6*) St Martin.

An Asterisk (*) at the beginning of an entry indicates that the title is appearing in BIP for the first time.

Parker, Michael A. War of Tomorrow: Arctic Strike, A Visual Novel of Michael A. Parker. (Illustrated History of Near Future Warfare Ser.: No. 2). (Illus.). 224p. (Orig.). 1991. mass mkt. 6.95 (*0-380-75844-X*) Avon.

Parker, Mike. Inside the Circle: A Union Guide to Quality of Work Life. LC 85-50600. (Illus.). 153p. 1985. pap. 10.00 (*0-685-11936-X*) Labor Notes.

— Inside the Circle: A Union Guide to Quality of Work Life. LC 85-50600. (Illus.). 153p. 1985. pap. 15.00 (*0-89608-302-0*) Labor Notes.

— Prospects for Hard Coal in Europe. 75p. (C). Date not set. pap. 14.95x (*0-905031-79-2*) Brookings.

Parker, Mike & Slaughter, Jane. Choosing Sides: Unions & the Team Concept. LC 88-80585. (Illus.). 240p. 1988. pap. 16.00 (*0-685-20979-2*) Labor Notes.

— Choosing Sides: Unions & the Team Concept. LC 88-80585. (Illus.). 240p. 1988. pap. 16.00 (*0-89608-347-0*) Labor Notes.

— Wording Smart: A Union Guide to Participation Programs & Reeingineering. LC 94-73182. (Illus.). 317p. (Orig.). 1994. pap. 20.00 (*0-914093-08-8*) Labor Notes.

Parker, Mike & Whitfield, Paul. The Rough Guide to Wales. (Rough Guides Ser.). (Illus.). 288p. (Orig.). 1994. pap. 14.95 (*1-85828-096-6*, Penguin Bks) Viking Penguin.

Parker, Monique, jt. auth. see Cahen, Michel.

***Parker, Morris B.** Mules, Mines & Me in Mexico, 1895-1932. Day, James M, ed. LC 79-15206. (Illus.). 248p. Date not set. reprint ed. pap. 70.70 (*0-7837-9235-2*, 2049986) Bks Demand.

Parker, Muriel. Illuminated Letter Designs in the Historiated Style of the 13th to 15th Centuries. (International Design Library). (Illus.). 48p. 1986. pap. 5.95 (*0-88045-082-7*) Stemmer Hse.

Parker, Muriel M. Calligraphy: A Practical Handbook for the Beginner. 1982. 6.98 (*0-517-38135-4*) Random Hse Value.

Parker, N. C., et al. Fish-Marking Techniques. LC 90-84827. (Symposium Ser.: No. 7). 879p. (C). 1990. text ed. 78.50 (*0-913235-59-8*) Am Fisheries Soc.

***Parker, Nancy.** The Omega Transmissions. 404p. 1994. pap. 12.95 (*0-9642272-0-7*) Ashland Hills.

Parker, Nancy W. Frogs, Toads, Lizards & Salamanders. (Illus.). (J). (gr. 1 up). 1990. 15.00 (*0-688-08680-2*); lib. bdg. 14.93 (*0-688-08681-0*) Greenwillow.

— Money, Money, Money: The Meaning of the Art & Symbols on United States Paper Currency. LC 93-43534. (Illus.). 32p. (J). (gr. 2-7). 1995. 14.95 (*0-06-023411-3*) HarpC Child Bks.

— Money, Money, Money: The Meaning of the Art & Symbols on United States Paper Currency. LC 93-43534. (Illus.). 32p. (J). (gr. 2-7). 1995. lib. bdg. 14.89 (*0-06-023412-1*) HarpC Child Bks.

— The President's Cabinet & How It Grew. LC 89-70851. (Illus.). 40p. (J). (gr. 3-5). 1991. lib. bdg. 14.89 (*0-06-021618-2*) HarpC Child Bks.

— Working Frog. LC 90-24173. 40p. (J). (gr. k up). 1992. 14.00 (*0-688-09918-1*); lib. bdg. 13.93 (*0-688-09919-X*) Greenwillow.

Parker, Nancy W. & Wright, Joan R. Bugs. LC 86-29387. (Illus.). 40p. (J). (gr. 1-4). 1987. 15.00 (*0-688-06623-2*); lib. bdg. 14.93 (*0-688-06624-0*) Greenwillow.

— Bugs. LC 86-29387. (Illus.). 40p. (J). (gr. k up). 1988. pap. 4.95 (*0-688-08296-3*, Mulberry) Morrow.

Parker, Nathan H. The Minnesota Handbook for 1856-7. LC 75-114. (Mid-American Frontier Ser.). 1975. reprint ed. 16.95 (*0-405-06880-8*) Ayer.

Parker, Noel. Portrayals of Revolution: Images, Debates, & Patterns of Thought on the French Revolution. LC 89-26365. (Illus.). 256p. (C). 1990. 30.00 (*0-8093-1684-6*) S Ill U Pr.

Parker, Norton & Norton, Kallie. Time of Fury. 1980. pap. 2.25 (*0-8439-0791-6*) Dorchester Pub Co.

Parker, Norton S. Audiovisual Script Writing. 1974. reprint ed. pap. 15.00 (*0-8135-0797-9*) Rutgers U Pr.

Parker, Oliver. Cover Your Own Boat or Start Your Own Marine Canvas Business. (Illus.). 1982. pap. 24.95 (*0-937155-00-4*) O Parker Pub.

Parker, Ophelia S. Forgive Me My Debts: Credit Repair Guide. LC 93-91060. 528p. (Orig.). 1994. ring bd. 64.95 (*0-937895-03-2*) By Faith Direct.

— In the Black Plus...Call Us. 324p. 1990. pap. 40.00 (*0-937895-02-4*) By Faith Direct.

— Thoughts - Shackles of the Mind. (Illus.). (Orig.). 1986. 14.95 (*0-937895-01-6*); pap. 12.95 (*0-937895-00-8*) By Faith Direct.

Parker, Owen. Tack Now, Skipper. 1979. 29.95 (*0-8464-0065-0*) Beekman Pubs.

Parker, P. & Dennis, D., eds. Mechanical Engineering Design No. One: Organization & Control. (C). 1989. 90.00 (*0-09-175676-6*, Pub. by S Thornes Pubs UK) St Mut.

Parker, P., jt. auth. see Carlisel, C.

Parker, P., ed. see Pickup, P.

Parker, Pat. Jonestown & Other Madness. LC 85-1679. 80p. 1985. lib. bdg. 16.95 (*0-932379-01-X*); pap. 7.95 (*0-932379-00-1*) Firebrand Bks.

— Movement in Black. LC 90-80060. 160p. 1990. reprint ed. lib. bdg. 18.95 (*0-932379-75-3*); reprint ed. pap. 8.95 (*0-932379-74-5*) Firebrand Bks.

Parker, Patricia. Literary Fat Ladies: Rhetoric, Gender, Property. 320p. 1988. text ed. 47.50 (*0-416-91600-7*); pap. text ed. 15.95 (*0-416-91610-4*) Routledge Chapman & Hall.

Parker, Patricia & Hartman, Geoffrey, eds. Shakespeare & the Question of Theory. 300p. 1986. 27.00 (*0-416-36920-0*, 9479); pap. 19.95 (*0-416-36930-8*, 9480) Routledge Chapman & Hall.

Parker, Patricia & Quint, David, eds. Literary Theory-Renaissance Texts. LC 85-23799. 384p. 1986. text ed. 59.50x (*0-8018-3294-2*); pap. text ed. 16.95x (*0-8018-3295-0*) Johns Hopkins.

Parker, Patricia, jt. ed. see Hendricks, Margo.

Parker, Patricia, jt. ed. see Hosek, Chaviva.

Parker, Patricia A. Inescapable Romance: Studies in the Poetics of a Mode. LC 78-70312. 300p. reprint ed. pap. 85.50 (*0-8357-3693-8*, 2036417) Bks Demand.

Parker, Patricia L., jt. auth. see King, Thomas F.

Parker, Patrick J., jt. ed. see Dailey, Brian D.

Parker, Patty, jt. ed. see Fara, Frank.

***Parker, Paul.** Free-Heel Skiing: Telemark & Parallel Techniques for All Conditions. LC 95-12628. (Illus.). 1995. write for info. (*0-89886-412-7*) Mountaineers.

Parker, Paul O. Dust & Pneumoconiosis: Medical Subject Analysis & Research Guidebook with Bibliography. LC 84-45868. 150p. 1987. 39.50 (*0-88164-284-3*); pap. 34.50 (*0-88164-285-1*) ABBE Pubs Assn.

— Industry & Health Affairs: Index of Modern Authors & Subjects with Guide for Rapid Research. LC 90-56270. 200p. 1991. 44.50 (*1-55914-308-8*); pap. 39.50 (*1-55914-309-6*) ABBE Pubs Assn.

— Peripheral Nerve Injuries: Medical Subject Analysis with Reference Bibliography. LC 85-48078. 1987. 44.50 (*0-88164-426-9*); pap. 39.50 (*0-88164-427-7*) ABBE Pubs Assn.

Parker, Paul P., ed. Standing with the Poor: Theological Reflections on Economic Reality. LC 92-36254. (Illus.). 160p. (Orig.). 1992. pap. 12.95 (*0-8298-0926-0*) Pilgrim OH.

Parker-Pearson, Michael. English Heritage Book of Bronze Age Britain. (Illus.). 152p. 1993. 55.00 (*0-7134-6801-7*, Pub. by Batsford UK); pap. 34.95 (*0-7134-6856-4*, Pub. by Batsford UK) Trafalgar.

Parker, Peter. Ackerley: The Life of J. R. Ackerley. 1989. 27.95 (*0-374-10050-0*) FS&G.

— Ackerley: The Life of J. R. Ackerley. (Illus.). 288p. 1991. pap. 15.00 (*0-374-52279-0*, Noonday) FS&G.

***Parker, Peter & Kermode, Frank.** A Reader's Guide to the Twentieth-Century Novel. 784p. 1995. 35.00 (*0-19-521153-7*) OUP.

Parker, Peter D., ed. Chloride Electrometallurgy: Proceedings of a Symposium. LC 82-63095. (Conference Proceedings Ser.). (Illus.). 243p. reprint ed. pap. 69.30 (*0-685-23389-8*, 2032593) Bks Demand.

Parker, Peter J. & Katan, Matilda. Molecular Biology of Oncogenes & Cell Control Mechanisms. 200p. 1990. text ed. write for info. (*0-13-599499-3*) P-H.

***Parker, Philip.** Global Cities. LC 94-22445. (Project Eco-City Ser.). (Illus.). 48p. (J). (gr. 4-6). 1995. 15.95 (*1-56847-286-2*) Thomson Lrning.

— Town Life. LC 94-22443. (Project Eco-City Ser.). (Illus.). 48p. (J). (gr. 4-6). 1995. 15.95 (*1-56847-287-0*) Thomson Lrning.

— Your Living Home. (Project Eco-City Ser.). (Illus.). 48p. (J). (gr. 4-6). 1994. 15.95 (*1-56847-246-3*) Thomson Lrning.

— Your Wild Neighborhood. (Project Eco-City Ser.). (Illus.). 48p. (J). (gr. 4-6). 1994. 15.95 (*1-56847-247-1*) Thomson Lrning.

***Parker, Philip M.** Climatic Effects on Individual, Social & Economic Behavior: A Physioeconomic Review of Research Across Disciplines. LC 94-41521. (Bibliographies & Indexes in Geography Ser.: Vol. 2). 304p. 1995. text ed. 79.50 (*0-313-29400-3*, Greenwood Pr) Greenwood.

Parker, Phyllis R. Brazil & the Quiet Intervention, 1964. (Texas Pan American Ser.). 161p. 1979. text ed. 14.50 (*0-292-78507-0*) U of Tex Pr.

***Parker, Pierce.** The Netherworld of New England: A Chronicle of Life in New England. 2nd ed. (Illus.). 253p. 1994. pap. 19.95 (*0-9645099-0-3*) Transcont Pr.

Parker, R. The Study of Benthic Communities. LC 73-20941. (Oceanography Ser.: Vol. 9). 279p. 1975. 102.75 (*0-444-41203-4*) Elsevier.

Parker, R., tr. see Gladkov, Fedor V.

Parker, R. A. Coke of Norfolk: A Financial & Agricultural Study, 1707-1842. (Illus.). 1975. 39.00 (*0-19-822403-6*) OUP.

— Struggle for Survival: The History of the Second World War. (Illus.). 370p. 1990. 24.95 (*0-19-219126-8*) OUP.

— Struggle for Survival: The History of the Second World War. (Illus.). 370p. 1991. pap. 11.95 (*0-19-289112-X*) OUP.

Parker, R. A., jt. auth. see Neugebauer, O.

***Parker, R. A. C.** Chamberlain & Appeasement: British Policy & the Coming of the Second World War. 384p. 1993. pap. text ed. 14.50 (*0-312-09969-X*) St Martin.

Parker, R. Charles. Going for Growth: Technological Innovation in Manufacturing Industries. LC 84-21902. 273p. reprint ed. pap. 77.90 (*0-8357-6943-7*, 2039002) Bks Demand.

— The Management of Innovation. LC 82-2737. (Illus.). 239p. reprint ed. pap. 68.20 (*0-8357-4321-7*, 2037120) Bks Demand.

Parker, R. E. Introductory Statistics for Biology. 2nd ed. (Studies in Biology: No. 43). 128p. 1979. pap. 14.95 (*0-521-42778-9*) Cambridge U Pr.

Parker, R. E., ed. The Middle English Stanzaic Versions of the Life of Saint Anne. (EETS, OS Ser.: No. 174). 1974. reprint ed. 32.00 (*0-527-00171-6*) Periodicals Srv.

***Parker, R. Gary.** Deterministic Scheduling Theory. LC 95-15181. 1995. write for info. (*0-412-99681-2*) Chapman & Hall.

Parker, R. Gary & Rardin, Ronald L., eds. Discrete Optimization. (Computer Science & Scientific Computing Ser.). 472p. 1988. text ed. 99.00 (*0-12-545075-3*) Acad Pr.

Parker, R. H. Bibliographies for Accounting Historians. Brief, Richard P., ed. LC 80-1462. (Dimensions of Accounting Theory & Practice Ser.). 1980. lib. bdg. 37.95 (*0-405-13484-3*) Ayer.

— British Accountants: A Biographical Sourcebook. Brief, Richard P., ed. LC 80-1463. (Dimensions of Accounting Theory & Practice Ser.). 1980. lib. bdg. 31.95 (*0-405-13485-1*) Ayer.

— The Development of the Accountancy Profession in Britain to the Early Twentieth Century. (Monograph Series of the Academy of Accounting Historians: Monograph 5). 74p. 1986. pap. 10.00 (*1-879750-03-1*) Acad Acct Hist.

— An Introduction to Chemical Metallurgy: In SI-Metric Units. 2nd ed. 1978. 151.00 (*0-08-022125-4*, Pub. by Pergamon Repr UK) Franklin.

Parker, R. H. & Nobes, C. W., eds. An International View of True & Fair Accounting. LC 94-6174. (Series on International Accounting & Finance). (Illus.). 128p. 1994. 55.00 (*0-415-11463-2*, B4184) Routledge.

Parker, R. H. & Yamey, B. S., eds. Accounting History: Some British Contributions. 672p. 1994. 72.00 (*0-19-828886-7*) OUP.

Parker, R. H., jt. auth. see Kitchen, J.

Parker, R. H., jt. ed. see Nobes, Christopher W.

Parker, R. K., jt. ed. see Fliflet, A. W.

Parker, R. L., et al, eds. Crystal Growth 1977. 1978. 179.50 (*0-444-85088-0*, North Holland) Elsevier.

Parker, R. N. Forest Flora for the Punjab with Hazara & Delhi. 577p. (C). 1973. reprint ed. 250.00 (*0-685-21864-3*, Pub. by Intl Bk Distr II) St Mut.

Parker, R. N., ed. Forest Flora for the Punjab with Hazara & Delhi. 591p. (C). 1984. text ed. 375.00 (*0-89771-618-3*, Pub. by Intl Bk Distr II) St Mut.

Parker, R. S. Traumatic Brain Injury & Neuropsychological Impairment. xii, 452p. 1990. 72.00 (*0-387-97239-0*) Spr-Verlag.

Parker, R. Wayne. The Computer Buyer's Handbook: How to Select & Buy Personal Computers for Your Home or Business. LC 90-83233. (Illus.). 240p. (Orig.). 1991. pap. 16.95 (*0-9627370-6-2*) Fast Forward Pub.

Parker, Randall & Szymanski, Edna, eds. Rehabilitation Counseling: Basics & Beyond. 2nd ed. LC 91-29220. 444p. (Orig.). 1992. pap. text ed. 34.00 (*0-89079-518-5*, 1409) PRO-ED.

Parker, Randy S., jt. ed. see McElmurry, Beverly J.

Parker, Ray. RV Having Fun Yet? Comic Adventures on the Road. LC 94-65905. (Illus.). 151p. (Orig.). 1995. 12.95 (*0-9640924-0-9*) Oldfield Pub. Written by a veteran Hollywood comedy writer, this funny & often hilarious book is a vivid account of what life aboard an RV can be like for full-time travelers. After a career writing for Linkletter, Bob Hope & other TV stars, Parker tells how he & his wife Ethel bought a motorhome -- & found themselves on the zaniest adventure of their lives. You don't have to be an RVer to enjoy the laughs in Parker's book. Besides being fun to read, it's quite revealing in a light-hearted way about both the pleasures & pitfalls of the RV lifestyle. RV HAVING FUN YET? would make a good gift for RVers & humor lovers in general, as well as for people nearing retirement who dream of traveling America in an RV themselves some day. For orders, call (800) 879-4214 or Bookworld or write Oldfield Publishing, P.O. Box 1264, Thousand Oaks, CA 91358-0264. ***Publisher Provided Annotation.***

Parker, Reese, jt. auth. see McFarland, Thomas D.

Parker, Reeve. Coleridge's Meditative Art. LC 74-25367. 270p. 1975. 36.50 (*0-8290-0340-1*) Irvington.

Parker, Reuel. The New Cold-Molded Boatbuilding: From Lofting to Launching. 1992. pap. text ed. 21.95 (*0-07-048578-X*) McGraw.

— Sharpie Book. 1993. pap. text ed. 19.95 (*0-87742-304-0*) Intl Marine.

Parker, Reuel B. The New Cold-Molded Boatbuilding: From Lofting to Launching. (Illus.). 336p. 1992. pap. 19.95 (*0-87742-358-X*, 60115) Intl Marine.

— The Sharpie Book. 1994. pap. text ed. 19.95 (*0-07-158013-1*) McGraw.

Parker, Rey. Safeguarding Standards. (C). 1990. 45.00 (*0-902789-68-6*, Pub. by Natl Inst Soc Work) St Mut.

Parker-Rhodes, A. F. The Theory of Indistinguishables: A Search for Explanatory Principles Below the Level of Physics. 248p. 1981. lib. bdg. 84.00 (*90-277-1214-X*) Kluwer Ac.

Parker-Rhodes, Frederick. Wholesight. LC 77-95406. 30p. (Orig.). 1978. pap. 3.00 (*0-87574-217-3*) Pendle Hill.

Parker, Rich. The Power of Serius. 1992. pap. write for info. (*0-318-69258-9*) Reader Netwk.

Parker, Richard. Bodies, Pleasures, & Passions: Sexual Culture in Contemporary Brazil. 224p. 1993. pap. 15.00 (*0-8070-4103-3*) Beacon Pr.

— Easy Object Programming for Windows Using Visual C. 1994. pap. 34.95 (*0-13-291337-2*) P-H.

— The Official Book of Space Trivia. pap. 2.95 (*0-932298-43-5*) Tri-State Pr Corp.

— The Old Powder Line. (J). (gr. 4-7). 19.75 (*0-8446-6432-4*) Peter Smith.

— Troubleshooting DC-AC Circuits with Electronics Workbench. 52p. 1994. pap. text ed. 24.95 (*0-8273-6721-X*) Delmar.

— Wildflowers. LC 81-51068. (Illus.). 128p. (Orig.). 1986. pap. 7.95 (*0-89317-034-8*) Windward Pub.

Parker, Richard & Daniel, Herbert. Sexuality, Politics & AIDS in Brazil: In Another World? (Social Aspects of AIDS Ser.). 196p. 1993. 75.00 (*0-7507-0135-8*, Falmer Pr); pap. 25.00 (*0-7507-0136-6*, Falmer Pr) Taylor & Francis.

Parker, Richard & Gagnon, John, eds. Conceiving Sexuality: Approaches to Sex Research in a Postmodern World. LC 94-17761. 320p. 1994. 59.95 (*0-415-90927-9*, B3844, Routledge NY) Routledge.

Parker, Richard & Gagnon, John H., eds. Conceiving Sexuality: Approaches to Sex Research in a Postmodern World. LC 94-17761. 320p. 1994. pap. 18.95 (*0-415-90928-7*, B3848, Routledge NY) Routledge.

Parker, Richard, jt. auth. see Cordesman, Anthony H.

Parker, Richard, jt. auth. see Ensminger, M. E.

Parker, Richard, jt. auth. see Moore, Brooke N.

Parker, Richard A. Demotic Mathematical Papyri. LC 77-177501. (Brown Egyptological Studies: No. 7). 142p. reprint ed. pap. 40.50 (*0-8357-5549-5*, 2035168) Bks Demand.

— Troubleshooting Electronic Devices with Electronics Workbench. 57p. 1994. pap. text ed. 24.95 (*0-8273-6760-0*) Delmar.

Parker, Richard A., ed. A Vienna Demotic Papyrus on Eclipes & Lunar-Omina. (Brown Egyptological Studies: No. 2). 76p. reprint ed. pap. 25.00 (*0-317-09427-0*, 2022398) Bks Demand.

Parker, Richard A., jt. auth. see Rea, Louis M.

Parker, Richard B. North Africa: Regional Tensions & Strategic Concerns. LC 87-6954. 226p. 1987. text ed. 55.00 (*0-275-92773-3*, C2773, Praeger Pubs); pap. text ed. 16.95 (*0-275-92774-1*, B2774, Praeger Pubs) Greenwood.

— The Politics of Miscalculation in the Middle East. LC 92-23947. (Indiana Series in Arab & Islamic Studies). 320p. (C). 1993. 45.00 (*0-253-34298-8*); pap. 17.95 (*0-253-20781-9*, MB-781) Ind U Pr.

Parker, Richard B., et al. Islamic Monuments in Cairo: A Practical Guide. (Illus.). 352p. (C). 1993. 34.95 (*977-424-290-4*, Pub. by Am Univ Cairo Pr UA) Col U Pr.

Parker, Richard D. Here, the People Rule: A Constitutional Populist Manifesto. LC 94-2387. 142p. 1994. text ed. 29.95 (*0-674-38925-5*, PARHER); pap. text ed. 14.95 (*0-674-38926-3*, PARHEX) HUP.

Parker, Richard O. Easy Object Programming for Macintosh Using AppMaker & THINK C. 1993. pap. 35.95 (*0-13-092966-2*) P-H.

— Easy Object Programming for the Macintosh Using AppMaker & THINK Pascal. LC 92-42971. 1993. pap. 35.95 (*0-13-092974-3*) P-H.

***Parker, Rick.** Aquaculture Science. LC 94-34435. 672p. 1995. 33.95 (*0-8273-6454-7*) Delmar.

Parker, Robert. Paper Doll. 288p. 1994. pap. text ed. 5.99 (*0-425-14155-1*) Berkley Pub.

— Perchance to Dream. 288p. (Orig.). 1993. mass mkt. 5.99 (*0-425-13131-9*) Berkley Pub.

Parker, Robert, ed. Adam Rener, Collected Works. (Gesamtausgaben - Collected Works Ser.: Vol. II, Pt. 2). 160p. 1975. lib. bdg. 7.00 (*0-912024-43-7*) Inst Mediaeval Mus.

— A Dictionary of Business Quotations. 240p. 1990. 30.00 (*0-685-35584-5*) S&S Trade.

Parker, Robert, jt. auth. see Chandler, Raymond.

Parker, Robert, jt. auth. see Medinnis, Bernice.

Parker, Robert, jt. ed. see Nobes, Christopher.

Parker, Robert A. Yankee Saint: John Humphrey Noyes & the Oneida Community. 322p. 1993. reprint ed. lib. bdg. 89.00 (*0-7812-5314-4*) Rprt Serv.

Parker, Robert A., illus. The Woman Who Fell from the Sky: The Iroquois Story of Creation. LC 92-5591. 32p. (J). (gr. k up). 1993. 15.00 (*0-688-10680-3*); lib. bdg. 14.93 (*0-688-10681-1*) Morrow Jr Bks.

Parker, Robert B. All Our Yesterdays. LC 94-2583. 1994. 22.95 (*0-385-30437-4*) Delacorte.

— All Our Yesterdays. 1994. 27.95 (*0-385-31374-8*) Delacorte.

Parker, Robert B., Jr. A Catskill Eagle. 1986. mass mkt. 4.99 (*0-440-11132-3*) Dell.

— Ceremony. 1992. mass mkt. 4.99 (*0-440-10993-0*) Dell.

— Crimson Joy. 1989. mass mkt. 4.99 (*0-440-20343-0*) Dell.

Parker, Robert B. Double Deuce. 256p. 1993. mass mkt. 5.99 (*0-425-13793-7*) Berkley Pub.

— Double Deuce: A Spenser Thriller. 224p. 1992. 100.00 (*0-399-13754-8*, Putnam) Putnam Pub Group.

Parker, Robert B., Jr. Double Deuce. large type ed. LC 92-38590. (General Ser.). 233p. 1993. 20.95 (*0-8161-5596-8*); pap. 16.95 (*0-8161-5597-6*) G K Hall.

Parker, Robert B. Early Autumn. large type ed. LC 91-37915. 285p. 1992. reprint ed. lib. bdg. 20.95 (*1-56054-286-1*) Thorndike Pr.

Parker, Robert B., Jr. Early Autumn. 1992. mass mkt. 5.99 (*0-440-12214-7*) Dell.

— The Early Spenser: Three Complete Novels: The Godwulf Manuscript, God Save the Child, Mortal Stakes. 1989. 13.95 (*0-385-29728-9*) Delacorte.

— God Save the Child. 1987. mass mkt. 5.99 (*0-440-12899-4*) Dell.

Parker, Robert B. The Godwulf Manuscript. large type ed. LC 93-33303. 1994. 19.95 (*0-7927-1884-4*, Eagle Lrg Print) Chivers N Amer.

— The Godwulf Manuscript. large type ed. 1994. pap. 18.95 (*0-7927-1883-6*, Paragon Lrg Print) Chivers N Amer.

— The Godwulf Manuscript. 1994. reprint ed. lib. bdg. 32.95 (*1-56849-317-7*) Buccaneer Bks.

Parker, Robert B., Jr. The Godwulf Manuscript. 208p. 1993. mass mkt. 4.99 (*0-440-12961-3*) Dell.

Parker, Robert B. The Judas Goat. 18.95 (*0-89190-371-2*, Am Repr) Amereon Ltd.

An Asterisk (*) at the beginning of an entry indicates that the title is appearing in BIP for the first time.

— The Judas Goat. large type ed. LC 95-14360. 1995. write for info. (*0-7862-0389-7*) Thorndike Pr.

Parker, Robert B., Jr. The Judas Goat. 1987. mass mkt. 4.99 (*0-440-14196-6*) Dell.

Parker, Robert B. Looking for Rachel Wallace. large type ed. 288p. 1992. reprint ed. bds. 20.95 (*1-56054-312-4*) Thorndike Pr.

Parker, Robert B., Jr. Looking for Rachel Wallace. 224p. 1987. mass mkt. 4.99 (*0-440-15316-6*) Dell.

— Love & Glory. 224p. 1984. mass mkt. 4.99 (*0-440-14629-1*) Dell.

Parker, Robert B. Mortal Stakes. 1994. reprint ed. lib. bdg. 32.95 (*1-56849-316-9*) Buccaneer Bks.

— Mortal Stakes: A Spenser Novel. large type ed. LC 92-23911. 290p. 1992. reprint ed. bds. 20.95 (*1-56054-314-0*) Thorndike Pr.

Parker, Robert B., Jr. Mortal Stakes. 1987. mass mkt. 4.99 (*0-440-15758-7*) Dell.

— Pale Kings & Princes. 1988. 14.95 (*0-671-66073-X*) S&S Trade.

— Pale Kings & Princes. 1988. reprint ed. mass mkt. 5.99 (*0-440-20004-0*) Dell.

— Pale Kings & Princes: A Spenser Novel. limited ed. LC 86-29195. 288p. 1987. 75.00 (*0-385-29568-5*) Delacorte.

Parker, Robert B. Paper Doll. LC 92-30528. 224p. 1993. 19.95 (*0-399-13818-8*, Putnam) Putnam Pub Group.

— Paper Doll. large type ed. LC 93-22854. 1993. write for info. (*0-7862-0003-0*); pap. 13.95 (*0-7862-0004-9*) Thorndike Pr.

— Paper Doll. limited ed. LC 92-30528. 224p. 1993. 100.00 (*0-399-19195-X*, Putnam) Putnam Pub Group.

— Pastime. 1992. reprint ed. mass mkt. 5.99 (*0-425-13293-5*) Berkley Pub.

Parker, Robert B., Jr. Pastime. large type ed. (General Ser.). 269p. 1992. text ed. 20.95 (*0-8161-5347-7*, Large Print Bks); pap. 15.95 (*0-8161-5348-5*, Large Print Bks) Hall.

***Parker, Robert B.** Perchance to Dream. 192p. 1991. 4.99 (*1-56865-105-8*, GuildAmerica) Dbldy Bk Music.

— Perchance to Dream. large type ed. LC 91-3776. 304p. 1991. reprint ed. lib. bdg. 20.95 (*1-56054-186-5*) Thorndike Pr.

— Perchance to Dream. large type ed. LC 91-3776. 304p. 1992. reprint ed. pap. 13.95 (*1-56054-977-7*) Thorndike Pr.

— Playmates. 1990. mass mkt. 5.99 (*0-425-12001-5*) Berkley Pub.

— Playmates. large type ed. LC 89-20218. 268p. 1990. pap. 11.95 (*0-89621-947-X*) Thorndike Pr.

— Promised Land. large type ed. LC 92-14247. 299p. 1992. reprint ed. lib. bdg. 20.95 (*1-56054-313-2*) Thorndike Pr.

Parker, Robert B., Jr. Promised Land. 224p. 1993. mass mkt. 4.99 (*0-440-17197-0*) Dell.

— A Savage Place. 1992. mass mkt. 5.99 (*0-440-18095-3*) Dell.

Parker, Robert B. Spenser's Boston. 208p. 1994. 22.50 (*1-883402-50-6*) S&S Trade.

— Sports Illustrated Training with Weights. (Orig.). 1990. pap. 8.95 (*1-56800-032-4*, Pub. by Sports Illus Bks) Natl Bk Netwk.

— Stardust. 1991. mass mkt. 5.99 (*0-425-12723-0*) Berkley Pub.

— Stardust. 224p. 1990. 18.95 (*0-399-13537-5*, Putnam); audio 14.95 (*0-685-58515-8*, Putnam) Putnam Pub Group.

— Stardust. large type ed. LC 90-11276. 306p. 1990. reprint ed. lib. bdg. 20.95 (*1-56054-068-0*) Thorndike Pr.

— Stardust. large type ed. LC 90-11276. 306p. 1991. pap. 13.95 (*1-56054-996-3*) Thorndike Pr.

Parker, Robert B., Jr. Taming a Sea-Horse. 250p. 1987. mass mkt. 4.99 (*0-440-18841-5*, Sey Lawr) Dell.

***Parker, Robert B.** Thin Air. 1995. 21.95 (*0-399-14020-4*, Putnam) Putnam Pub Group.

— Thin Air. limited ed. 1995. 21.95 (*0-399-14063-8*) Putnam Pub Group.

— Thin Air: A Spenser Novel. large type ed. LC 95-15712. 1995. 26.95 (*1-56895-212-0*) Wheeler Pub.

— Three Complete Novels, 3 vols. Incl. Godwulf Manuscript. LC 95-15248. 1995. Not sold separately (*0-615-00743-0*, Pub. by Wings Bks); God Save the Child. LC 95-15248. 1995. Not sold separately (*0-615-00744-9*, Pub. by Wings Bks); Mortal Stakes. LC 95-15248. 1995. Not sold separately (*0-615-00745-7*, Pub. by Wings Bks); LC 95-15248. write for info. (*0-517-14802-1*, Pub. by Wings Bks) Random.

Parker, Robert B., Jr. Valediction. 1992. mass mkt. 5.99 (*0-440-19246-3*) Dell.

***Parker, Robert B.** Walking Shadow. 304p. 1995. pap. text ed. 5.99 (*0-425-14774-6*) Berkley Pub.

— Walking Shadow. 224p. 1994. 19.95 (*0-399-13920-6*, Putnam) Putnam Pub Group.

— Walking Shadow. large type ed. LC 94-19124. 1994. 25.95 (*1-56895-106-X*) Wheeler Pub.

— Walking Shadow. limited ed. 224p. 1994. 100.00 (*0-399-13961-3*, Putnam) Putnam Pub Group.

Parker, Robert B., Jr. The Widening Gyre. 1984. mass mkt. 4.99 (*0-440-19535-7*) Dell.

Parker, Robert B. Wilderness. large type ed. 1994. 19.95 (*0-7927-1726-0*, Paragon Lrg Print); pap. 18.95 (*0-7927-1725-2*, Paragon Lrg Print) Chivers N Amer.

Parker, Robert B., Jr. Wilderness. 256p. 1980. mass mkt. 4.99 (*0-440-19328-1*) Dell.

Parker, Robert B. & Parker, Joan H. Year At the Races. LC 89-40797. 120p. 1991. 35.00 (*0-670-82678-2*, Viking Studio) Studio Bks.

Parker, Robert B., jt. auth. see Chandler, Raymond.

Parker, Robert C., jt. auth. see Carlisle, John A.

Parker, Robert D. Absalom, Absalom! The Questioning of Fictions. (Twayne's Masterwork Studies: No. 76). 184p. (C). 1991. text ed. 21.95 (*0-8057-8071-8*, Twayne); pap. 12.95 (*0-8057-8116-1*, Twayne) Macmillan.

— Faulkner & the Novelistic Imagination. LC 84-2519. 176p. 1985. 19.95 (*0-252-01155-4*) U of Ill Pr.

— The Unbeliever: The Poetry of Elizabeth Bishop. LC 87-34285. 184p. 1988. 24.95 (*0-252-01509-6*) U of Ill Pr.

Parker, Robert E. Flesh Peddlers & Warm Bodies: The Temporary Help Industry & Its Workers. LC 93-24222. (Arnold & Caroline Rose Monograph Series of the American Sociological Association). 187p. (C). 1994. text ed. 40.00 (*0-8135-2036-3*); pap. text ed. 14.00 (*0-8135-2089-4*) Rutgers U Pr.

Parker, Robert H. Wines of Burgundy. 1990. 39.95 (*0-671-63378-3*) S&S Trade.

Parker, Robert H., ed. Accounting in Australia: Historical Essays. (Accounting History & Thought Ser.). 500p. 1990. reprint ed. 50.00 (*0-8240-3324-8*) Garland.

Parker, Robert H. & Harcourt, G. C., eds. Readings in the Concept & Measurement of Income. LC 75-87137. 410p. reprint ed. pap. 116.90 (*0-317-27570-4*, 2024513) Bks Demand.

Parker, Robert H., jt. auth. see Cooke, Terence E.

Parker, Robert H., ed. see Haverstock, Henry.

Parker, Robert L. Geophysical Inverse Theory. LC 93-44915. 1994. text ed. 39.50 (*0-691-03634-9*) Princeton U Pr.

Parker, Robert L., ed. see American Gas Association Operating Section Compressor Committee.

Parker, Robert L., ed. see American Gas Association Operating Section Corrosion Control & System Protection Committee.

Parker, Robert L., tr. see Niggli, Paul.

Parker, Robert M., Jr. Bordeaux: A Comprehensive Guide to the Wines Produced from 1961-1990. rev. ed. (Illus.). 700p. 1991. 35.00 (*0-671-67460-9*) S&S Trade.

— Burgundy. write for info. (*0-318-69054-3*) S&S Trade.

— Parker's Wine Buyer's Guide. 3rd ed. (Illus.). 960p. 1993. pap. 21.00 (*0-671-79914-2*, Fireside) S&S Trade.

— The Wines of the Rhone Valley & Provence: The Definitive Guide. (Illus.). 480p. 1987. 22.45 (*0-671-63379-1*) S&S Trade.

Parker, Robert N. & Rebhun, Linda-Anne. Alcohol & Homicide: A Deadly Combination of Two American Traditions. (Violence Ser.). 160p. (C). 1995. text ed. 49.50 (*0-7914-2463-4*); pap. 16.95 (*0-7914-2464-2*) State U NY Pr.

Parker, Robert P. & Collins, Gerarda M. Shih Tzu. (Illus.). 1990. 11.95 (*0-685-62703-9*, KW-084) TFH Pubns.

Parker, Robert P. & Davis, Frances A., eds. Developing Literacy: Young Children's Use of Language. LC 82-20329. 195p. reprint ed. pap. 55.60 (*0-8357-8650-1*, 2035094) Bks Demand.

Parker, Robert P. & Goodkin, Vera. The Consequences of Writing: Enhancing Learning in the Disciplines. LC 86-14712. 183p. (Orig.). (C). 1987. pap. text ed. 17.50 (*0-86709-117-7*) Boynton Cook Pubs.

***Parker, Roberta N. & Parker, Harvey C.** Como Pasar de Grado: La Lucha de un Adolescente Con ADD. (Illus.). 48p. (Orig.). 1994. pap. 11.00 (*0-9621629-7-3*) Spec Pr FL.

— Making the Grade: An Adolescent's Struggle with ADD. DiMatteo, Richard, tr. (Illus.). 48p. (Orig.). (J). (gr. 5-10). 1992. pap. 12.00 (*0-9621629-1-4*) Spec Pr FL.

— Slam Dunk: A Young Boy's Struggle with Attention Deficit Disorder. (Illus.). 55p. (Orig.). (J). (gr. 3-8). 1993. pap. 11.00 (*0-9621629-4-9*) Spec Pr FL.

Parker, Rodger D. Wellsprings of a Nation: America Before 1801. LC 77-72082. (Illus.). 1977. pap. 10.00 (*0-912296-13-5*, U Pr of Va) Am Antiquarian.

***Parker, Roger.** Freelance Graphics X for Windows for Dummies. 1995. pap. 19.99 (*1-56884-236-8*) IDG Bks.

— Mastering the Power of Persuasion. 300p. 1990. pap. 28.00 (*1-55623-243-8*) Irwin Prof Pubng.

— MS Office 95 for Dummies. 1995. pap. 19.99 (*1-56884-917-6*) IDG Bks.

— Roger Parker's One Minute Designer. (Illus.). 256p. (Orig.). 1993. pap. 19.95 (*1-56529-216-2*) Que.

Parker, Roger, ed. The Oxford Illustrated History of Opera. (Illus.). 400p. 1995. 39.95 (*0-19-816282-0*) OUP.

Parker, Roger, jt. ed. see Abbate, Carolyn.

Parker, Roger, tr. see Baldini, Gabriele.

Parker, Roger, jt. auth. see Barry, Malcolm.

Parker, Roger, jt. ed. see Groos, Arthur.

Parker, Roger, tr. see Petrobelli, Pierluigi.

Parker, Roger, ed. see Verdi, Giuseppe.

***Parker, Roger C.** Desktop Publishing & Design for Dummies. 1995. pap. 19.99 (*1-56884-234-1*) IDG Bks.

— Desktop Publishing with WordPerfect: For 5.0 & 5.1. 2nd ed. LC 90-34751. (Illus.). 350p. 1990. 21.95 (*0-940087-47-2*) Ventana Pr.

— From Writer to Designer: Twenty Steps from Word Processing to Mastering the Basics of Desktop Publishing. Benst, Jesse, ed. (Illus.). 196p. 1992. pap. 24.95 (*1-878567-05-5*) Serif Pub.

— Harvard Graphics 2 for Windows for Dummies. 1994. pap. 19.95 (*1-56884-092-6*) IDG Bks.

— Looking Good in Print. 3rd ed. 1993. pap. 24.95 (*1-56604-047-7*) Ventana Pr.

— The Makeover Book. LC 89-5780. (Illus.). 275p. (Orig.). 1989. pap. 17.95 (*0-940087-20-0*) Ventana Pr.

— Mastering the Printed Page: Electronic Publishing with Quark XPress. (Illus.). 224p. 1988. 29.95 (*0-8306-0223-2*, 3023); pap. 19.95 (*0-8306-9323-8*) TAB Bks.

— Microsoft Office 4 for Windows for Dummies. 1994. pap. 19.95 (*1-56884-183-3*) IDG Bks.

— The Ventana Looking Good Library. (Illus.). 959p. 1992. pap. 52.95 (*1-56604-001-9*) Ventana Pr.

Parker, Roger C. & Holzgang, David. WordPerfect 6 Secrets. 672p. 1993. pap. 39.95 (*1-56884-040-3*) IDG Bks.

Parker, Roger C. & Tyson, ERic. Personal Finance for Dummies. 1994. pap. 16.95 (*1-56884-150-7*) IDG Bks.

Parker, Rolland S. Effective Decisions & Emotional Fulfillment. LC 76-54652. 308p. 1977. 29.95 (*0-88229-303-6*) Nelson-Hall.

Parker, Rollin J. Advances in Permanent Magnetism. 1990. text ed. 114.00 (*0-471-82293-0*) Wiley.

Parker, Ron. Under the Influence. (Illus.). 42p. (Orig.). 1993. pap. 4.00 (*0-88680-378-0*); 40.00 (*0-685-66608-5*) I E Clark.

***Parker, Ron, et al.** Small Enterprises Adjusting to Liberalization in Five African Contries. LC 95-191. (Discussion Papers: Africa Technical Department Ser.: Vol. 271). 1995. write for info. (*0-8213-3154-X*) World Bank.

Parker, Ronald, et al. Administrative Law. (Illus.). 245p. 1990. pap. 35.00 (*0-685-14620-0*) NJ Inst CLE.

Parker, Rosetta E. Housing for the Elderly: The Handbook for Managers. Moore, Betty T., ed. LC 83-81942. (Series on Specific Property Types). (Illus.). 153p. (Orig.). 1984. pap. 34.95 (*0-912104-68-6*, 840) Inst Real Estate.

Parker, Rowland. The Common Stream: Two Thousand Years of the English Village. 252p. 1994. reprint ed. pap. 12.00 (*0-89733-391-8*) Academy Chi Pubs.

— Men of Dunwich: The Story of a Vanished Town. (Illus.). 272p. 1981. pap. 9.00 (*0-586-08330-8*, Pub. by Granada UK) Academy Chi Pubs.

Parker, Rowland & Rubinstein, Michael. Malta's Ancient Temples & Ruts. (Institute for Cultural Research Monograph: No. 26). (Illus.). 70p. (Orig.). 1988. pap. 10.00 (*0-904674-14-2*, Pub. by Octagon Pr UK) ISHK Bk Service.

Parker, Roy, Jr. Cumberland County: A Brief History. (Illus.). xi, 158p. (Orig.). 1990. pap. 8.00 (*0-86526-243-8*) NC Archives.

Parker, Roy. Safeguarding Standards. (C). 1990. 45.00 (*0-7855-0066-9*, Pub. by Natl Inst Soc Work) St Mut.

Parker, Roy H. The Final Four. LC 81-69265. 259p. 1981. 14.95 (*0-941974-00-6*) Baranski Pub Co.

— The Final Four. rev. ed. 1988. pap. 3.95 (*0-944003-00-1*) Faction Pub.

Parker, Rozsika. The Subversive Stitch: Embroidery & the Making of the Feminine. (Illus.). 246p. 1987. pap. 14.95 (*0-7043-3883-1*, Pub. by Womens Pr UK) Interlink Pub.

— The Subversive Stitch: Embroidery & the Making of the Feminine. 247p. 1989. pap. 15.95 (*0-415-90206-1*, A3787, Routledge NY) Routledge.

Parker, Ruth E. Mathematical Power: Lessons from a Classroom. LC 92-46283. 48p. 1993. pap. text ed. 18.50 (*0-435-08339-2*, 08339) Heinemann.

Parker, S., jt. auth. see Lewes, F.

Parker, S. R. & Brown, R. K. The Sociology of Industry. 4th ed. 208p. 1983. pap. text ed. 16.95 (*0-04-301129-2*) Routledge Chapman & Hall.

Parker, S. Thomas. Romans & Saracens: A History of the Arabian Frontier. LC 85-25217. (American Schools of Oriental Research Dissertations Ser.: Vol. 6). (Illus.). xiii, 238p. 1986. pap. text ed. 35.50x (*0-89757-106-1*) Am Sch Orient Res.

Parker, Samanthe. Star Vision. (Illus.). 64p. (Orig.). 1992. pap. 4.95 (*0-910241-00-7*) ShaunTar Ent.

Parker, Samuel. A Free & Impartial Censure of the Platonick Philosophie: Being a Letter Written to His Much Honoured Friend Mr. N. B. rev. ed. LC 83-46032. (Scientific Awakening in the Restoration Ser.: No. 3). 144p. 1985. reprint ed. 45.00 (*0-404-63303-X*) AMS Pr.

— Journal of an Exploring Tour Beyond the Rocky Mountains. LC 90-46021. (Idaho Yesterdays Ser.). (Illus.). 392p. (C). 1990. reprint ed. pap. 14.95 (*0-89301-140-1*) U of Idaho Pr.

— Journal of Exploring Tour Etc. 1976. reprint ed. 15.00 (*0-87018-046-0*) Ross.

Parker, Sandra & Will, Carol. Activities for the Elderly, Vol. 2: A Guide to Working with Residents with Significant Physical & Cognitive Disabilities. (Activities Ser.). 170p. 1993. pap. 30.00 (*1-882883-01-2*) Idyll Arbor.

Parker, Sandra D., et al. Activities for the Elderly, Vol. 1: A Guide to Quality Programming. (Activities Ser.). 171p. 1993. reprint ed. pap. 30.00 (*1-882883-00-4*) Idyll Arbor.

Parker, Sandra V. Richmond's Civil War Prisons. (Virginia Civil War Battles & Leaders Ser.). (Illus.). 101p. 1990. 19.95 (*0-930919-97-1*) H E Howard.

Parker, Sara, jt. auth. see Smith, Jewell.

Parker School of Foreign & Comparative Law, Columbia University Staff. International Commercial Arbitration & the Courts: A Source Guide. 472p. (C). 1989. lib. bdg. 95.00 (*0-929179-12-9*) Transnatl Juris Pubns.

Parker School of Foreign & Comparative Law, Columbia University Staff, ed. Guide to International Arbitration & Arbitrators, 1992, 2 vols., Set. 1992. lib. bdg. 245.00 (*0-929179-61-7*) Transnatl Juris Pubns.

Parker, Simon. The Pre-Biblical Narrative Tradition. (Society of Biblical Literature Resources for Biblical Study). 1989. 31.95 (*1-55540-300-X*, 06 03 24); pap. 20.95 (*1-55540-301-8*) Scholars Pr GA.

Parker, Stan, jt. auth. see Aungles, Stan.

Parker, Stephen. The Craft of Writing. 245p. 1993. pap. 29.00 (*1-85396-200-7*, Pub. by Paul Chapman UK) Taylor & Francis.

Parker, Stephen, jt. auth. see Hayhoe, Mike.

Parker, Stephen, jt. ed. see Hayhoe, Mike.

***Parker, Stephen, et al.** Australian Family Law in Context: Commentary & Materials. 938p. 1994. pap. 95.00 (*0-455-21222-8*, Pub. by Law Bk Co) W W Gaunt.

Parker, Stephen G., jt. auth. see Irving, Gary.

Parker, Stephen J. The Achievements of Vladimir Nabokov: Essays, Studies, Reminiscences & Stories. Gibian, George, ed. 256p. (Orig.). (C). 1984. pap. text ed. 6.95 (*0-86731-079-0*) Cornell CIS RDC.

— Understanding Vladimir Nabokov. (Understanding Contemporary American Literature Ser.). 170p. 1987. 34.95 (*0-87249-494-2*); pap. 14.95 (*0-87249-495-0*) U of SC Pr.

Parker, Stephen J., jt. auth. see Parker, Fan.

Parker, Steve. Alarming Animals. LC 93-6651. (Creepy Creatures Ser.). (Illus.). 38p. (J). (gr. 3-6). 1993. lib. bdg. 21.36 (*0-8114-0658-X*) Raintree Steck-V.

— Albert Einstein & the Laws of Relativity. LC 94-43924. (Science Discoveries Ser.). (Illus.). 32p. (J). (gr. 3 up). 1995. lib. bdg. 13.95 (*0-7910-3003-2*) Chelsea Hse.

— Animal Babies: A Habitat-by-Habitat Guide to How Young Animals Grow. LC 93-28287. (Illus.). 176p. 1994. 30.00 (*0-87596-595-4*) Rodale Pr Inc.

— Animals Can Think? LC 94-19405. (How Do We Know Ser.). (J). (gr. k up). 1995. lib. bdg. write for info. (*0-8114-3882-1*) Raintree Steck-V.

— Aristotle & Scientific Thought. LC 94-8263. (Science Discoveries Ser.). (Illus.). 32p. (YA). (gr. 3 up). 1995. lib. bdg. 13.95 (*0-7910-3004-0*) Chelsea Hse.

— Aristotle & Scientific Thought. (Science Discoveries Ser.). (Illus.). 32p. (J). (gr. 3 up). 1995. lib. bdg. 13.95 (*0-7910-3005-9*) Chelsea Hse.

— Awesome Amphibians. LC 92-43196. (Creepy Creatures Ser.). (Illus.). 38p. (J). (gr. 3-6). 1993. lib. bdg. 21.36 (*0-8114-0661-X*) Raintree Steck-V.

— Be an Animal Detective. (Be a Nature Detective Ser.). 40p. (J). (gr. 2 up). 1989. 3.99 (*0-517-68023-8*) Random Hse Value.

— Beastly Bugs. LC 92-43197. (Creepy Creatures Ser.). (Illus.). 38p. (J). (gr. 3-6). 1993. lib. bdg. 21.36 (*0-8114-0689-X*) Raintree Steck-V.

— Benjamin Franklin. LC 94-25255. (Science Discoveries Ser.). (Illus.). 32p. (J). (gr. 3 up). 1995. lib. bdg. 13.95 (*0-7910-3006-7*) Chelsea Hse.

— The Body & How It Works. LC 91-58203. (See & Explore Library). (Illus.). 64p. (J). (gr. 3 up). 1992. 11.95 (*1-879431-95-5*); lib. bdg. 12.99 (*1-879431-96-3*) Dorling Kindersley.

— The Body Atlas. LC 92-54307. (Illus.). 64p. (J). (gr. 3 up). 1993. 19.95 (*1-56458-224-8*) Dorling Kindersley.

— Brain & Nervous System. rev. ed. (Human Body Ser.). (J). (gr. 5-7). 1990. lib. bdg. 13.93 (*0-531-14026-1*) Watts.

— The Brain & Nervous System. rev. ed. (Human Body Ser.). (Illus.). 48p. (J). (gr. 5-8). 1991. pap. 6.95 (*0-531-24600-0*) Watts.

— Catching a Cold: How You Get Ill, Suffer & Recover. (Body in Action Ser.). (Illus.). 32p. (J). (gr. k-4). 1992. lib. bdg. 12.25 (*0-531-14146-2*) Watts.

— Charles Darwin & Evolution. LC 94-20656. (Science Discoveries Ser.). (Illus.). 32p. (YA). (gr. 3 up). 1995. lib. bdg. 13.95 (*0-7910-3007-5*) Chelsea Hse.

— Creepy Creatures, 8 vols. (J). (gr. 4-7). 1994. lib. bdg. 111.84 (*0-8114-0711-X*) Raintree Steck-V.

— Cunning Carnivores. LC 93-27256. (Creepy Creatures Ser.). (Illus.). (J). 1993. 21.36 (*0-8114-2347-6*) Raintree Steck-V.

— Dime Como Funciona (How Things Work) (Illus.). 164p. (SPA.). (J). (gr. 4 up). 1992. lib. bdg. 19.90 (*1-56294-179-8*) Millbrook Pr.

— Dinosaurs! A Sport-the-Difference Puzzle Book. LC 94-34687. (Illus.). (J). 1995. 12.00 (*0-679-86715-5*) Random Bks Yng Read.

— Dinosaurs & How They Lived. LC 91-60143. (See & Explore Library). (Illus.). 64p. (J). (gr. 3 up). 1991. 11.95 (*1-879431-13-0*); lib. bdg. 12.99 (*1-879431-28-9*) Dorling Kindersley.

— The Ear & Hearing. rev. ed. LC 88-51611. (Human Body Ser.). (Illus.). 48p. (J). (gr. 5-6). 1989. lib. bdg. 13.93 (*0-531-10712-4*) Watts.

— The Ear & Hearing. rev. ed. (Human Body Ser.). (Illus.). 48p. (J). (gr. 5 up). 1991. pap. 5.95 (*0-531-24601-9*) Watts.

— The Earth & How It Works. LC 92-54317. (See & Explore Library). (Illus.). 64p. (YA). (gr. 3 up). 1993. 12.95 (*1-56458-235-3*) Dorling Kindersley.

— Eating a Meal: How You Eat, Drink & Digest. LC 90-77856. (Body in Action Ser.). (Illus.). 32p. (J). (gr. k-4). 1991. lib. bdg. 12.25 (*0-531-14086-5*) Watts.

— Electricity. LC 92-6926. (Eyewitness Science Ser.). (Illus.). 64p. 1992. 15.95 (*1-879431-82-3*) Dorling Kindersley.

— Everyday Things & How They Work. LC 91-213. (Tell Me about Bks.). (Illus.). 40p. (Orig.). (J). (gr. 2-5). 1991. pap. 4.99 (*0-679-80866-3*) Random Bks Yng Read.

— Eye & Seeing. LC 88-51606. (Human Body Ser.). (J). 1989. lib. bdg. 13.93 (*0-531-10654-3*) Watts.

— The Eye & Seeing. rev. ed. (Human Body Ser.). (Illus.). 48p. (J). (gr. 5 up). 1991. pap. 6.95 (*0-531-24602-7*) Watts.

— Fearsome Fish. LC 93-28905. (Creepy Creatures Ser.). (Illus.). (J). 1993. 21.36 (*0-8114-2346-8*) Raintree Steck-V.

— Fish. LC 89-36445. (Eyewitness Bks.). (Illus.). 64p. (J). (gr. 5 up). 1990. 15.00 (*0-679-80439-0*) Random Bks Yng Read.

— Fish. LC 89-36445. (Eyewitness Bks.). (Illus.). 64p. (J). (gr. 5 up). 1990. lib. bdg. 18.99 (*0-679-90439-5*) Random Bks Yng Read.

— Flight & Flying Machines. LC 92-54316. (See & Explore Library). (Illus.). 64p. (J). (gr. 3-7). 1993. 12.95 (*1-56458-236-1*) Dorling Kindersley.

— The Flying Bedstead & Other Ingenious Inventions. LC 95-6107. (J). 1995. pap. write for info. (*1-85697-574-6*, Kingfisher LKC) LKC.

— Food & Digestion. LC 89-36399. (Human Body Ser.). 1990. lib. bdg. 13.93 (*0-531-14027-X*) Watts.

— Food & Digestion. rev. ed. (Human Body Ser.). (Illus.). 48p. (J). (gr. 5 up). 1991. pap. 6.95 (*0-531-24603-5*) Watts.

P
Q

An Asterisk (*) at the beginning of an entry indicates that the title is appearing in BIP for the first time.

— Frogs & Toads. LC 93-38519. (Look into Nature Ser.). (Illus.). 60p. (J). (gr. 3-6). 1994. 16.95 (*0-87156-466-1*) Sierra.
— Galileo & the Universe. LC 94-20659. (Science Discoveries Ser.). (Illus.). 32p. (YA). (gr. 3 up). 1995. lib. bdg. 13.95 (*0-7910-3008-3*) Chelsea Hse.
— Guglielmo Marconi & Radio. LC 94-8253. (Science Discoveries Ser.). (Illus.). (YA). (gr. 3 up). 1995. lib. bdg. 13.95 (*0-7910-3009-1*) Chelsea Hse.
— The Heart & Blood. rev. ed. LC 88-51610. (Human Body Ser.). (Illus.). 48p. (J). (gr. 5-6). 1989. lib. bdg. 13.23 (*0-531-10711-6*) Watts.
— The Heart & Blood. rev. ed. (Human Body Ser.). (Illus.). 48p. (J). (gr. 5 up). 1991. pap. 6.95 (*0-531-24604-3*) Watts.
— How It Works. (FunFax Ser.). (Illus.). 48p. (J). (gr. 3-6). 1992. pap. 2.95 (*1-56680-010-2*) Mad Hatter Pub.
— How the Body Works. LC 93-31689. (Illus.). 192p. 1994. 24.00 (*0-89577-575-1*) RD Assn.
— The Human Body. LC 93-7752. (Eyewitness Science Ser.). (Illus.). 64p. (J). (gr. 3-6). 1993. 15.95 (*1-56458-325-2*) Dorling Kindersley.
— Human Body. LC 93-31076. (Eyewitness Explorers Ser.). (Illus.). 64p. (J). (gr. 3 up). 1994. 9.95 (*1-56458-322-8*) Dorling Kindersley.
— I Wonder Why Tunnels Are Round: And Other Questions about Building. LC 94-45113. (I Wonder Why Ser.). (J). 1995. 8.95 (*1-85697-580-0*) LKC.
— Inside Dinosaurs & Other Prehistoric Creatures. LC 93-10045. (J). (gr. 1-8). 1994. 16.95 (*0-385-31143-5*) Delacorte.
— Inside Dinosaurs & Other Prehistoric Creatures. LC 93-10045. (J). (gr. 1-8). 1995. pap. 10.95 (*0-385-31189-3*) Delacorte.
— Isaac Newton & Gravity. LC 94-8260. (Science Discoveries Ser.). (Illus.). 32p. (YA). (gr. 3 up). 1995. lib. bdg. 13.95 (*0-7910-3010-5*) Chelsea Hse.
— Japan. Kossmann, Walter & Fink, Joanne, eds. (Countries Ser.). (Illus.). 48p. (J). (gr. 5 up). 1991. lib. bdg. 14.95 (*0-382-24246-7*) Silver Burdett Pr.
— Keeping Cool: How You Sweat, Shiver & Keep Warm. LC 91-42675. (Body in Action Ser.). (Illus.). 32p. (J). (gr. k-4). 1992. lib. bdg. 12.25 (*0-531-14147-0*) Watts.
— Learning a Lesson: How You See, Think & Remember. LC 89-77860. (Body in Action Ser.). (Illus.). 32p. (J). (gr. k-4). 1991. lib. bdg. 12.25 (*0-531-14087-3*) Watts.
— Living with Blindness. LC 89-9091. (Living with Ser.). (Illus.). 32p. (J). (gr. 5-8). 1989. lib. bdg. 13.23 (*0-531-10843-0*) Watts.
— Living with Heart Disease. LC 89-8979. (Illus.). 32p. (J). (gr. 5-8). 1989. lib. bdg. 13.23 (*0-531-10845-7*) Watts.
— The Living World. (FunFax Ser.). (Illus.). 48p. (J). (gr. 3-6). 1992. pap. 2.95 (*1-56680-011-0*) Mad Hatter Pub.
— Louis Pasteur & Germs. LC 94-8262. (Science Discoveries Ser.). (Illus.). 32p. (YA). (gr. 3 up). 1995. lib. bdg. 13.95 (*0-7910-3002-4*) Chelsea Hse.
— The Lungs & Breathing. rev. ed. (Human Body Ser.). (Illus.). 48p. (J). (gr. 5 up). 1991. pap. 6.95 (*0-531-24605-1*) Watts.
— Mammal. LC 88-22656. (Eyewitness Bks.). (Illus.). 64p. (J). (gr. 5 up). 1989. 16.00 (*0-394-82258-7*) Knopf Bks Yng Read.
— Mammal. LC 88-22656. (Eyewitness Bks.). (Illus.). 64p. (YA). (gr. 5 up). 1989. lib. bdg. 16.99 (*0-394-92258-1*) Knopf Bks Yng Read.
— Mammals. LC 94-1595. (Inside-Outside Ser.). (J). 1995. 16.00 (*0-679-84919-X*) Random.
— Marie Curie & Radium. LC 94-20657. (Science Discoveries Ser.). (Illus.). 32p. (YA). (gr. 3 up). 1995. lib. bdg. 13.95 (*0-7910-3011-3*) Chelsea Hse.
— Medicine. LC 94-34860. (Eyewitness Science Ser.). (Illus.). 64p. (J). (gr. 4-7). 1995. 15.95 (*1-56458-882-3*) Dorling Kindersley.
— Mysterious Microbes. LC 93-36476. (Creepy Creatures Ser.). (Illus.). (J). 1994. 21.36 (*0-8114-2344-1*) Raintree Steck-V.
— Our Planet Earth. LC 94-16302. (One Hundred One Questions & Answers Ser.). (J). 1994. write for info. (*0-8160-3216-5*) Facts on File.
— Pond & River. LC 88-1575. (Eyewitness Bks.). (Illus.). 64p. (J). (gr. 5 up). 1988. 16.00 (*0-394-89615-7*) Knopf Bks Yng Read.
— Pond & River. LC 88-1575. (Eyewitness Bks.). (Illus.). 64p. (J). (gr. 5 up). 1988. lib. bdg. 16.99 (*0-394-99615-1*) Knopf Bks Yng Read.
— Practical Paleontologist. 1991. pap. 14.95 (*0-671-69307-7*, Fireside) S&S Trade.
— Prehistoric Life. LC 92-54452. (See & Explore Library). (Illus.). 64p. (J). (gr. 3-7). 1993. 12.95 (*1-56458-238-8*) Dorling Kindersley.
— The Random House Book of How Nature Works. LC 92-14566. (How Things Work! Ser.). (Illus.). 128p. (J). (gr. 3-7). 1993. lib. bdg. 19.99 (*0-679-93700-5*); pap. 15.00 (*0-679-83700-0*) Random Bks Yng Read.
— The Random House Book of How Things Work. LC 90-9137. (Illus.). 160p. (Orig.). (J). (gr. 3-7). 1991. lib. bdg. 19.99 (*0-679-90908-7*); pap. 16.00 (*0-679-80908-2*) Random Bks Yng Read.
— Revolting Reptiles. LC 92-43725. (Creepy Creatures Ser.). (Illus.). 38p. (J). (gr. 3-6). 1992. lib. bdg. 21.36 (*0-8114-0692-X*) Raintree Steck-V.
— Rock & Minerals. LC 93-12643. (Eyewitness Explorers Ser.). (Illus.). 64p. (J). (gr. 3 up). 1993. 9.95 (*1-56458-394-5*) Dorling Kindersley.
— Running a Race: How You Walk, Run & Jump. LC 90-31110. (Body in Action Ser.). (Illus.). 32p. (J). (gr. k-4). 1991. lib. bdg. 12.25 (*0-531-14096-2*) Watts.
— Scary Spiders. LC 93-27876. (Creepy Creatures Ser.). (Illus.). (J). 1993. 21.36 (*0-8114-2345-X*) Raintree Steck-V.
— Science Discoveries, 12 bks., Set. (Illus.). 32p. (YA). (gr. 3 up). 1995. lib. bdg. 13.95 (*0-7910-3001-6*) Chelsea Hse.
— Seashore. LC 88-27173. (Eyewitness Bks.). (Illus.). 64p. (J). (gr. 5 up). 1989. 16.00 (*0-394-82254-4*) Knopf Bks Yng Read.
— Seashore. LC 88-27173. (Eyewitness Bks.). (Illus.). 64p. (J). (gr. 5 up). 1989. lib. bdg. 18.99 (*0-394-92254-9*) Knopf Bks Yng Read.
— Seashore. (Illus.). 48p. (J). (gr. 7-9). 1992. 13.95 (*0-563-34410-5*, BBC-Parkwest); pap. 6.95 (*0-563-34411-3*, BBC-Parkwest) Parkwest Pubns.
— Singing a Song: How You Sing, Speak & Make Sounds. Kline, Marjory, ed. LC 91-17018. (Body in Action Ser.). (Illus.). 32p. (J). (gr. k-4). 1992. lib. bdg. 12.25 (*0-531-14212-4*) Watts.
— Skeleton. LC 87-26314. (Eyewitness Bks.). (Illus.). 64p. (J). (gr. 5 up). 1988. 16.00 (*0-394-89620-3*); lib. bdg. 16.99 (*0-394-99620-8*) Knopf Bks Yng Read.
— The Skeleton & Movement. rev. ed. LC 88-51608. (Human Body Ser.). (Illus.). 48p. (J). (gr. 4-7). 1989. lib. bdg. 13.93 (*0-531-10709-4*) Watts.
— The Skeleton & Movement. rev. ed. (Human Body Ser.). (Illus.). 48p. (J). (gr. 5 up). 1991. pap. 6.95 (*0-531-24606-X*) Watts.
— The Story of Dinosaurs. LC 91-39007. (Story of Ser.). (Illus.). 32p. (J). (gr. 1-4). 1993. lib. bdg. 11.89 (*0-8167-2707-4*); pap. text ed. 3.95 (*0-8167-2708-2*) Troll Assocs.
— Thomas Edison & Electricity. LC 92-6805. (Science Discoveries Ser.). (Illus.). 32p. (J). (gr. 3-7). 1992. 14.00 (*0-06-020859-7*) HarpC Child Bks.
— Thomas Edison & Electricity. LC 94-20658. (Science Discoveries Ser.). (Illus.). 32p. (YA). (gr. 3 up). 1995. lib. bdg. 13.95 (*0-7910-3012-1*) Chelsea Hse.
— Touch, Taste & Smell. rev. ed. LC 88-51607. (Human Body Ser.). (Illus.). 48p. (J). (gr. 5-6). 1989. lib. bdg. 13.93 (*0-531-10655-1*) Watts.
— Touch, Taste & Smell. rev. ed. (Human Body Ser.). (Illus.). 48p. (J). (gr. 5 up). 1991. pap. 6.95 (*0-531-24607-8*) Watts.
— Touching a Nerve: How You Touch, Sense & Feel. (Body in Action Ser.). (Illus.). 32p. (J). (gr. k-4). 1992. lib. bdg. 112.25 (*0-531-14215-9*) Watts.
— Whales & Dolphins. LC 93-38518. (Look into Nature Ser.). (Illus.). 60p. (J). (gr. 3-6). 1994. 16.95 (*0-87156-465-3*) Sierra.
— What's Inside Airplanes? LC 94-48544. (What's Inside? Ser.). (Illus.). 44p. (J). (gr. 3 up). 1995. 16.95 (*0-87226-394-0*) P Bedrick Bks.
— What's Inside Buildings? LC 94-48543. (What's Inside? Ser.). (Illus.). 44p. (J). (gr. 3 up). 1995. 16.95 (*0-87226-395-9*) P Bedrick Bks.
— The Wright Brothers. LC 94-25254. (Science Discoveries Ser.). (Illus.). 32p. (J). (gr. 3 up). 1995. lib. bdg. 13.95 (*0-7910-3013-X*) Chelsea Hse.
Parker, Steve, ed. Eyewitness Natural World. LC 94-18467. (Illus.). 192p. (J). (gr. 7 up). 1995. 29.95 (*1-56458-719-3*) Dorling Kindersley.
***Parker, Steve & West, David.** Brain Surgery for Beginners & Other Major Operations for Minors. (Illus.). 64p. (J). (gr. 4-12). 1995. lib. bdg. 15.90 (*1-56294-604-8*) Millbrook Pr.
— Fifty Three & a Half Things That Changed the World & Some That Didn't. LC 94-36649. (Illus.). 64p. (J). (gr. 4-12). 1995. 15.90 (*1-56294-603-X*) Millbrook Pr.
— Fifty Three & a Half Things That Changed the World & Some That Didn't. LC 94-36649. (Illus.). 64p. (J). (gr. 4-12). 1995. pap. 6.95 (*1-56294-894-6*) Millbrook Pr.
Parker, Steve, tr. see Nusom, Lynn.
Parker, Steven & Zuckerman, Barry, eds. Behavioral & Developmental Pediatrics: A Handbook for Primary Care. LC 94-17875. 1994. 39.95 (*0-316-69090-2*) Little.
Parker, Steven H. & Jobe, William E., eds. Percutaneous Breast Biopsy. LC 93-14055. 192p. 1993. 85.00 (*0-7817-0010-8*) Raven.
***Parker, Steven W., ed.** CorpTech Directory of Technology Companies: 1995 Edition, 4 vols., Set. 1995. 575.00 (*1-57114-008-5*) CorpTech.
Parker, Sue & Nix, Rebekah. Sounding the Silence: Why People Sing in the Shower. (Illus.). 172p. (Orig.). 1994. pap. 12.99 (*0-9641407-0-5*) RNIX.
Parker, Sue T. & Gibson, Kathleen, eds. Language & Intelligence in Monkeys & Apes: Comparative Developmental Perspectives. (Illus.). 608p. (C). 1994. pap. 24.95 (*0-521-45969-9*) Cambridge U Pr.
Parker, Sue T. & Gibson, Kathleen R., eds. Language & Intelligence in Monkeys & Apes: Comparative Developmental Perspectives. (Illus.). 576p. (C). 1990. 74.95 (*0-521-38028-6*) Cambridge U Pr.
Parker, Sue T., jt. auth. see Meikle, W. Eric.
Parker, Sue T., et al, eds. Self-Awareness in Animals & Humans: Developmental Perspectives. (Illus.). 450p. (C). 1994. 59.95 (*0-521-44108-0*) Cambridge U Pr.
Parker, Susan D. Second Stitches: Recycle As You Sew. (Illus.). 144p. 1993. pap. 18.95 (*0-8019-8476-9*) Chilton.
***Parker, Susan J.** Napa Valley Mustard Celebration Cookbook. 152p. 1995. pap. text ed. 11.95 (*1-887534-02-4*) NVMC.
Parker, Suzanne & Burke, Claire. German for Business Studies. 192p. (Orig.). 1994. pap. 43.50 (*0-273-60459-7*, Pub. by Pitman Pub Ltd UK) Trans-Atl Phila.
Parker, Suzanne L., jt. auth. see Parker, Glenn R.
Parker, Sybil P. McGraw-Hill Concise Encyclopedia of Science & Technology. 3rd ed. 1994. text ed. 115.50 (*0-07-045560-0*) McGraw.
— McGraw-Hill Dictionary of Scientific & Technical Terms. 5th ed. 1994. text ed. 110.50 (*0-07-042333-4*) McGraw.
— McGraw-Hill Encyclopedia of Chemistry. 2nd ed. 1993. text ed. 95.50 (*0-07-045455-8*) McGraw.
— McGraw-Hill Encyclopedia of Environmental Science & Engineering. 3rd ed. 1993. text ed. 85.50 (*0-07-051396-1*) McGraw.
— McGraw-Hill Encyclopedia of Physics. 2nd ed. 1993. text ed. 95.50 (*0-07-051400-3*) McGraw.
— McGraw-Hill Encyclopedia of Science & Technology, 20 vols., Set. 7th ed. 1992. text ed. 1,900.00 (*0-07-909206-3*) McGraw.
Parker, Sybil P., ed. Diccionario McGraw-Hill de Biologia. 1992. text ed. 32.95 (*0-07-104155-9*) McGraw.
— Diccionario McGraw-Hill de Computacion. 1992. text ed. 32.95 (*0-07-104152-4*) McGraw.
— Diccionario McGraw-Hill de Fisica. 1992. text ed. 32.95 (*0-07-104157-5*) McGraw.
— Diccionario McGraw-Hill de Ingenieria Electrica y Electronica. 1992. text ed. 32.95 (*0-07-104153-2*) McGraw.
— Diccionario McGraw-Hill de Ingenieria Mecanica. 1992. text ed. 32.95 (*0-07-104154-0*) McGraw.
— Diccionario McGraw-Hill de Quimica. 1992. text ed. 32.95 (*0-07-104156-7*) McGraw.
— McGraw-Hill Encyclopedia of Engineering. 2nd ed. (Illus.). 1414p. 1993. text ed. 105.00 (*0-07-051392-9*, 6397U) McGraw.
— World Geographical Encyclopedia. LC 94-29086. Orig. Title: Enciclopedia Geografica Universale. (Illus.). 1995. Set. text ed. 500.00 (*0-07-911496-2*) McGraw.
Parker, Sybil P. & Pasachoff, Jay M., eds. McGraw-Hill Encyclopedia of Astronomy. 2nd ed. LC 92-40523. 1993. text ed. 75.50 (*0-07-045314-4*) McGraw.
Parker, Sybil P., ed. see McGraw-Hill Editors.
Parker, T., jt. auth. see Haynes, J. H.
***Parker, T. H.** Calvin. LC 95-1055. 1995. pap. write for info. (*0-664-25602-3*) Westminster John Knox.
— Calvin's New Testament Commentaries. 2nd rev. ed. LC 93-2043. 256p. 1993. pap. 16.99 (*0-664-25489-6*) Westminster John Knox.
— Calvin's Old Testament Commentaries. 248p. 1986. 33.95 (*0-567-09365-4*, Pub. by T & T Clark UK) Bks Intl VA.
— Calvin's Preaching. 240p. (Orig.). 1992. pap. 22.99 (*0-664-25309-1*) Westminster John Knox.
— Commentaries on Romans Fifteen Thirty-Two to Fifteen Forty-Two. 240p. 1986. 37.95 (*0-567-09366-2*, Pub. by T & T Clark UK) Bks Intl VA.
Parker, T. H., tr. Daniel. 1993. write for info. (*0-318-70136-7*) Eerdmans.
Parker, T. Jefferson. Laguna Heat-MTV. 1993. mass mkt. 4.99 (*0-312-95205-8*) St Martin.
— Little Saigon. 1989. mass mkt. 4.95 (*0-312-91593-4*) St Martin.
— Pacific Beat. 1992. mass mkt. 5.99 (*0-312-92792-4*) St Martin.
— Summer of Fear. 384p. 1993. 19.95 (*0-312-09396-9*) St Martin.
— Summer of Fear. 1994. mass mkt. 5.99 (*0-312-95237-6*, Pub. by Thomas Dunne Bks) St Martin.
— Summer of Fear. large type ed. LC 94-6445. 1994. 23.95 (*0-7927-2060-1*, Eagle Lrg Print) Chivers N Amer.
— Summer of Fear. large type ed. LC 94-6445. 1995. pap. 22.95 (*0-7927-2059-8*, Paragon Lrg Print) Chivers N Amer.
Parker, T. S. & Chua, L. O. Practical Numerical Algorithms for Chaotic Systems. (Illus.). xiv, 348p. 1991. reprint ed. 49.50 (*0-387-96689-7*) Spr-Verlag.
Parker, Terrence C. Country Cop. 138p. (Orig.). 1989. pap. 8.95 (*0-685-30391-8*) Tihtiyas Pub.
Parker, Theodore. Boston Kidnapping: A Discourse to Commemorate the Rendition of Thomas Simms. LC 70-82208. (Anti-Slavery Crusade in America Ser.). 1969. reprint ed. 7.50 (*0-405-00646-2*) Ayer.
— A Discourse of Matters Pertaining to Religion. LC 72-4968. (Romantic Tradition in American Literature Ser.). 510p. 1972. reprint ed. 38.95 (*0-405-04639-1*) Ayer.
— A Letter to the People of the U. S. Touching the Matter of Slavery. LC 76-92450. 120p. 1972. reprint ed. 13.00 (*0-403-00180-3*) Scholarly.
— Letter to the People of the United States: Touching the Matter of Slavery. LC 76-154086. (Black Heritage Library Collection). 1977. 17.95 (*0-8369-8797-7*) Ayer.
— A Letter to the People of the United States Touching the Matter of Slavery. rev. ed. 122p. 1991. pap. text ed. 34.95 (*0-9627882-5-2*) Bradley Mann.
— The Nebraska Question: Some Thoughts on the New Assault upon Freedom in America & the General State of the Country in Relation Thereunto. 1977. 12.95 (*0-8369-9191-5*, 9060) Ayer.
— Slave Power. LC 74-82209. (Anti-Slavery Crusade in America Ser.). 1970. reprint ed. 27.95 (*0-405-00647-0*) Ayer.
— Trial of Theodore Parker: For the Misdemeanor of a Speech in Fanenil Hall Against Kidnapping. LC 70-154087. (Black Heritage Library Collection). 1977. 28.95 (*0-8369-8798-5*) Ayer.
— The Trial of Theodore Parker, with the Defence by Theodore Parker. (American Biography Ser.). 221p. 1991. reprint ed. lib. bdg. 69.00 (*0-7812-8306-X*) Rprt Serv.
— Works: Centenary Edition, 15 vols., Set. LC 75-3307. reprint ed. 595.00 (*0-404-59300-3*) AMS Pr.
***Parker, Theodore A., 3rd & Bailey, Brent, eds.** A Biological Assessment of the Alto Madidi Region & Adjacent Areas of Northwest Bolivia, May 18 - June 15, 1990. LC 91-78133. 108p. 1991. pap. 7.00 (*1-881173-05-4*) Conser Intl.
***Parker, Theodore A., 3rd & Carr, John L., eds.** Status of Forest Remnants in the Cordillera de la Costa & Adjacent Areas of Southwestern Ecuador. LC 92-73741. 172p. 1992. pap. 10.00 (*1-881173-06-6*) Conser Intl.
Parker, Theodore A., III, et al. An Annotated Checklist of Peruvian Birds. LC 81-60046. (Illus.). 104p. (Orig.). 1982. pap. 20.00 (*0-931130-07-7*) Harrell Bks.
***Parker, Theodore A., 3rd, et al.** A Biological Assessment of the Columbia River Forest Reserve, Toledo District, Belize. LC 93-71145. 81p. 1993. pap. 7.00 (*1-881173-03-8*) Conser Intl.
— The Lowland Dry Forests of Santa Cruz, Bolivia: A Global Conservation Priority. LC 93-72263. 104p. 1993. pap. 7.00 (*1-881173-02-X*) Conser Intl.
Parker, Thomas. America's Foreign Policy, Nineteen Forty-Five to Nineteen Seventy-Six: Its Creators & Critics. LC 80-21192. 272p. reprint ed. pap. 77.60 (*0-8357-4249-0*, 2037038) Bks Demand.
— The Road to Camp David: U. S. Negotiating Strategy Towards the Arab-Israeli Conflict. (American University Studies: Political Science: Ser. X, Vol. 9). 175p. (C). 1989. text ed. 39.00 (*0-8204-0495-0*) P Lang Pubs.
Parker, Thomas & Nelson, Douglas. Day by Day: The Sixties, 2 vols., Set. 1136p. 1983. 195.00 (*0-87196-648-4*) Facts on File.
Parker, Thomas H. Calvin's Old Testament Commentaries. LC 93-23798. 248p. 1993. pap. 16.99 (*0-664-25490-X*) Westminster John Knox.
Parker, Thomas M. Postural Relations to the Autonomic Nervous System. 32p. 1963. reprint ed. spiral bd. 8.80 (*0-7873-1264-9*) Mokelumne.
Parker, Thomas R. Flying in Northern California. 106p. (Orig.). 1987. pap. 65.00 (*0-9618154-0-X*) T R Parker.
Parker, Thomas T. Anna, Ann, Annie. LC 93-49586. 336p. 1994. pap. 10.95 (*0-452-27225-4*, Plume) NAL-Dutton.
Parker, Thomas W. The Knights Templars in England. LC 63-11983. 207p. reprint ed. pap. 59.00 (*0-317-08903-X*, 2055370) Bks Demand.
Parker, Tim. UNIX Survival Guide. 1990. pap. 24.95 (*0-201-57078-5*) Addison-Wesley.
— UNIX User's Handbook. Leventhal, Lance A., ed. LC 91-53067. (Lance A. Leventhal Microtrend Ser.). 600p. (Orig.). 1992. pap. 29.95 (*0-915391-47-3*, Microtrend) Slawson Comm.
***Parker, Timothy.** Teach Yourself TCP-IP in 14 Days. 464p. 1994. 29.99 (*0-672-30549-6*) Sams.
Parker, Tom. Rules of Thumb, Vol. 1. 1983. pap. 8.95 (*0-395-34642-8*) HM.
Parker, Tom, jt. auth. see Kurtzig, Sandra L.
Parker, Tom, jt. auth. see Winfield, Dave.
Parker, Tony. Bird, Kansas. 1989. 19.95 (*0-394-57794-9*) Knopf.
— Bird, Kansas. 352p. 1990. pap. 8.95 (*0-380-71137-0*) Avon.
— May the Lord in His Mercy Be Kind to Belfast. LC 93-40754. 1994. 25.00 (*0-8050-3053-0*) H Holt & Co.
— May the Lord in His Mercy Be Kind to Belfast. 368p. 1995. pap. 13.95 (*0-8050-3806-X*, Owl) H Holt & Co.
— Violence of Our Lives. 384p. 1995. 22.50 (*0-8050-3058-1*) H Holt & Co.
Parker, Tony, jt. auth. see Hills, Andrew.
Parker, Trillis. Horses Talk: It Pays to Listen. rev. ed. LC 88-93037. (Illus.). 205p. 1989. pap. 19.95 (*0-915700-07-7*) Jacada Pubns.
***Parker, V.** Test Your Spelling. (Test Your Self Ser.). (Illus.). 32p. (J). (gr. 4 up). 1995. lib. bdg. 12.96 (*0-88110-754-9*, Usborne); pap. 5.95 (*0-7460-1735-9*, Usborne) EDC.
Parker, V. & Kape, W. Costing in the Furniture Industry. LC 65-14786. (Pergamon Series of Monographs on Furniture & Timber: Vol. 2). 1965. 71.00 (*0-08-013776-8*, Pub. by Pergamon Repr UK) Franklin.
Parker, V. D., jt. auth. see Hammerich, O.
Parker, Valerie. A Lowfat Lifeline for the 1990s: How to Survive in a Fat-Filled World. LC 90-61458. 288p. (Orig.). 1990. pap. 12.95 (*0-9626398-0-X*) Lowfat Pubns.
Parker, Valerie, jt. auth. see Gates, Ronda.
***Parker, Vaughn.** Aquaculture Science. 2nd abr. rev. ed. 384p. 1995. text ed. 62.50 (*0-8273-6976-X*) Delmar.
***Parker, Victoria.** Test Your Punctuation. (Test Yourself Ser.). (Illus.). 32p. (J). (gr. 4 up). 1995. lib. bdg. 12.96 (*0-88110-766-2*, Usborne); pap. 5.95 (*0-7460-1749-9*, Usborne) EDC.
Parker, Violette & Mammen, Lori. TAAS Quick Review Reading: Grade 4. (Illus.). 96p. 1992. pap. text ed. 12.95 (*0-944459-36-6*) ECS Lrn Systs.
Parker, Virgil & Howard, Frank. Howard: The Clemson Legend. (Illus.). 240p. (Orig.). 1990. pap. write for info. (*0-934904-22-7*) J & L Lee.
Parker, W., ed. Alicyclic Chemistry, Vols. 2-6. Incl. 1972 LiteratureLC 72-83459. 1974. Vol. 2, 1974. 47.00 (*0-85186-522-4*); Vol. 3. 1973 Literature. LC 72-82047. 1973. 61.00 (*0-85186-552-6*); 1974 LiteratureLC 72-83459. 1976. 70.00 (*0-85186-582-8*); 1975 LiteratureLC 72-83459. 1977. 72.00 (*0-85186-612-3*); 1976 LiteratureLC 72-23822. 1978. 73.00 (*0-85186-632-8*); LC 72-82047. write for info. (*0-318-50459-6*) Am Chemical.
Parker, W. B. Argentines of Today, 2 vols, Set. 1971. 400.00 (*0-87968-658-8*) Gordon Pr.
— Through Unexplored Texas. LC 84-80800. 242p. 1990. reprint ed. 21.95 (*0-87611-064-2*); reprint ed. pap. 12.95 (*0-87611-065-0*) Tex St Hist Assn.
Parker, W. H. Health & Disease in Farm Animals. 3rd ed. 1980. text ed. 86.00 (*0-08-025900-6*, Pergamon Pr); pap. text ed. 21.00 (*0-08-025899-9*, Pergamon Pr) Elsevier.
Parker, W. H., tr. Priapea: Poems for a Phallic God. 240p. 1988. 27.00 (*0-7099-4099-8*, Pub. by Croom Helm UK) Routledge Chapman & Hall.
Parker, W. J. The Great Coal Schooners of New England, 1870-1909. LC 49-3820. (Marine Historical Association, Publication Ser.: Vol. 2, No. 6). 139p. reprint ed. pap. 39.70 (*0-8357-2789-0*, 2039915) Bks Demand.
Parker, W. M., ed. see Scott, Walter.
Parker, W. Oren. Sceno Graphic Techniques. 92p. 1969. spiral bd. 7.95 (*0-685-83021-7*) Scenographic.
— Sceno-Graphic Techniques. 3rd ed. LC 86-17859. (Illus.). 158p. (C). 1987. pap. 15.95 (*0-8093-1350-2*) S Ill U Pr.

P Q

— Stage Lighting: Practice & Design. 256p. (C). 1987. text ed. 37.25 (*0-03-011912-X*) HB Coll Pubs.

Parker, W. Oren & Wolf, R. Craig. Scene Design & Stage Lighting. 6th ed. (Illus.). 624p. (C). 1990. text ed. 41.25 (*0-03-028777-4*) HB Coll Pubs.

Parker, W. R. Developments in Coastal & Estuarine Pollution: Proceedings of an IAWPRC Conference Held in Fukuoka, Japan, 18-21 October, 1987. LC 82-645900. (Water Science & Technology Ser.: No. 20). (Illus.). 300p. 1988. pap. 155.00 (*0-08-036885-9*, Pergamon Pr) Elsevier.

Parker, W. S. & Nelson, A. M. Public & Community Health. (Illus.). 176p. 1971. pap. text ed. 24.95 (*0-8464-1269-1*) Beekman Pubs.

Parker, Walter. Renewing the Social Studies Curriculum. 1991. pap. 13.95 (*0-87120-177-1*, 611-91022) Assn Supervision.

Parker, Walter & Jarolimek, John. Citizenship & the Critical Role of the Social Studies. LC 84-60983. (Bulletin Ser.: No. 72). 64p. (Orig.). 1984. pap. text ed. 7.95 (*0-89994-287-3*, 498-15316) Nat Coun Soc Studies.

***Parker, Walter C., ed.** Educating the Democratic Mind. (SUNY Series, Democracy & Education). 256p. 1995. text ed. 59.50 (*0-7914-2707-2*) State U NY Pr.

— Educating the Democratic Mind. (SUNY Series, Democracy & Education). 256p. 1995. pap. 18.95x (*0-7914-2708-0*) State U NY Pr.

Parker, Walter C., jt. auth. see Jarolimek, John.

Parker, Watson. Deadwood: The Golden Years. LC 80-24100. (Illus.). xiv, 334p. 1981. pap. 12.95 (*0-8032-8702-X*) U of Nebr Pr.

Parker, Watson & Lambert, Hugh K. Black Hills Ghost Towns. (Illus.). 215p. 1993. reprint ed. pap. 24.95 (*0-8040-0638-5*, Swallow) Swallow.

Parker, Wayne, tr. see Baumann, Bommi.

Parker, Wayne R. The Computer Buyer's Handbook: How to Select & Buy Personal Computers for Your Home or Business. 2nd braille ed. 652p. (Orig.). 1993. vinyl bd. 52.16 (*1-56956-410-8*, BR9070) W A T Braille.

Parker, Weldon & Parker, Dee. Down the Magical Mississippi. (Illus.). (Orig.). 1985. pap. 6.95 (*0-9614662-0-0*) Sun Seeker Bks.

Parker, William. Homosexuality Bibliography: Second Supplement, 1976-1982. LC 84-20299. 401p. 1985. 35.00 (*0-8108-1753-5*) Scarecrow.

— Homosexuality Bibliography: Supplement, 1970-1975. LC 77-1114. 343p. 1977. 29.50 (*0-8108-1050-6*) Scarecrow.

— Paris Bourse & French Finance with Reference to Organized Speculation in New York. LC 20-18734. (Columbia University. Studies in the Social Sciences: No. 204). reprint ed. 20.00 (*0-404-51204-6*) AMS Pr.

Parker, William B. Life & Public Services of Justin Smith Morrill. LC 79-87371. (American Scene Ser.). (Illus.). 1971. reprint ed. lib. bdg. 49.50 (*0-306-71595-3*) Da Capo.

Parker, William C., ed. The Fabric of Friendship. LC 74-22705. (Illus.). 224p. 1975. pap. 5.95 (*0-915102-00-5*) Eastham Edns.

Parker, William D. A Concise History of the United States Marine Corps, 1775 to 1969. LC 80-29554. (Illus.). x, 143p. 1981. reprint ed. text ed. 35.00 (*0-313-22854-X*, PACO, Greenwood Pr) Greenwood.

Parker, William E., ed. see Schwarz, Heinrich.

Parker, William H. Navy. Evans, Clement A., ed. (Confederate Military History Extended Edition Ser.: Vol. XVII). (Illus.). 512p. 1989. reprint ed. 50.00 (*1-56837-036-9*) Broadfoot.

— Recollections of a Naval Officer, 1841-1865. LC 84-22788. (Classics of Naval Literature Ser.). 403p. 1985. reprint ed. 32.95 (*0-87021-533-7*) Naval Inst Pr.

Parker, William L. General James Dearing. (Virginia Civil War Battles & Leaders Ser.). (Illus.). 112p. 1990. 19.95 (*1-56190-001-X*) H E Howard.

Parker, William M. Modern Scottish Writers. LC 68-26463. (Essay Index Reprint Ser.). 1977. reprint ed. 20.95 (*0-8369-0769-8*) Ayer.

Parker, William N. Essays on the Economic History of Western Capitalism, Vol. 1: Europe & the World Economy. LC 84-3161. (Studies in Economic History & Policy: The United States in the Twentieth Century). (Illus.). 272p. 1984. pap. 17.95 (*0-521-27480-X*) Cambridge U Pr.

— Essays on the Economic History of Western Capitalism, Vol. 2: America & the Wider World. (Studies in Economic History & Policy: The United States in the Twentieth Century). (Illus.). 350p. (C). 1991. 69.95 (*0-521-25466-3*); pap. 19.95 (*0-521-27479-6*) Cambridge U Pr.

Parker, William N., jt. ed. see Maczak, Antoni.

***Parker, William R.** Milton: A Biographical Commentary. 2nd ed. (Illus.). 832p. 1995. 72.00 (*0-19-812900-9*) OUP.

— Milton: A Biography. (Illus.). 704p. 1995. 55.00 (*0-19-812889-4*) OUP.

— Milton's Contemporary Reputation. LC 70-122996. (Studies in Milton: No. 22). 1970. reprint ed. lib. bdg. 75.00 (*0-8383-1129-6*) M S G Haskell Hse.

Parker, William T. Parker: Gleanings from Colonial & American Records of Parker & Morse Families, 1585-1915. (Illus.). 62p. 1993. reprint ed. pap. 13.00 (*0-8328-3377-0*) Higginson Bk Co.

Parker, Willie J. Game Warden: Chesapeake Assignment. LC 82-74134. (Illus.). 288p. 1983. 18.95 (*0-87033-302-X*, Tidewtr Pubs) Cornell Maritime.

Parker, Woodrow, et al. Multicultural Relations on Campus: A Personal Growth Approach. LC 92-52504. xii, 156p. (Orig.). (C). 1992. pap. text ed. 15.95 (*1-55959-033-5*) Accel Devel.

***Parker, Woodrow M.** Consciousness-Raising: A Primer for Multicultural Counseling. 170p. 1988. pap. 19.95 (*0-398-06314-1*) C C Thomas.

— Consciousness-Raising: A Primer for Multicultural Counseling. 170p. (C). 1988. text ed. 35.95x (*0-398-05416-9*) C C Thomas.

***Parker, Yana.** Blue Collar and Beyond. 128p. (Orig.). 1995. pap. 8.95 (*0-89815-689-0*) Ten Speed Pr.

— Damn Good Resume Guide. rev. ed. 1989. pap. 6.95 (*0-89815-348-4*) Ten Speed Pr.

— Ready to Go Resumes. 208p. (Orig.). 1995. pap. 29.95 (*0-89815-683-1*) Ten Speed Pr.

— Ready-to-Go Resumes. LC 95-1099. 1995. pap. write for info. (*0-89815-733-1*) Ten Speed Pr.

— The Resume Catalog: 200 Damn Good Examples. LC 87-7057. 320p. (Orig.). 1988. pap. 15.95 (*0-89815-219-4*) Ten Speed Pr.

— The Resume Pro: The Professional's Guide. (Illus.). 416p. (Orig.). 1992. pap. 24.95 (*0-89815-466-9*) Ten Speed Pr.

Parkerson, Codman. A Brief History of Bullet Moulds. 1974. 1.75 (*0-913150-26-6*) Pioneer Pr.

— Those Strange Louisiana Names. 1969. pap. 1.50 (*0-685-08223-7*) Claitors.

***Parkerson, Donald H.** The Agricultural Transition in New York State: Markets & Migration in Mid-Nineteenth Century America. LC 95-16272. (Henry A. Wallace Series on Agricultural History & Rural Life). 1995. write for info. (*0-8138-2492-3*) Iowa St U Pr.

Parkerson, Janet, ed. see Knoll, Judy.

Parkerson, Janet, ed. see Lizon, Lulu.

Parkerson, Janet, ed. see Meyers, Reva.

Parkerson, Janet, ed. see Pacheco, Richard, et al.

Parkerson, Janet, ed. see Witzman, Joseph E. & Block, Jack.

***Parkes, Adam.** Modernism & the Theater of Censorship. (Illus.). 256p. 1995. 45.00 (*0-19-509702-5*) OUP.

Parkes, Andrew M., ed. Driving Future Vehicles. 386p. 1993. 85.00 (*0-7484-0042-7*) Taylor & Francis.

Parkes, Brenda. Farmer Schnuck. LC 92-31078. (Voyages Ser.). (Illus.). (J). 1993. 4.25 (*0-383-03568-6*) SRA Schl Grp.

— One Foggy Night. LC 92-32514. (Voyages Ser.). (Illus.). (J). 1993. 4.25 (*0-383-03588-0*) SRA Schl Grp.

Parkes, Carl. Southeast Asia Handbook. 2nd ed. LC 93-30740. (Illus.). 875p. (Orig.). 1994. pap. 21.95 (*1-56691-002-1*) Moon Pubns CA.

— Thailand Handbook. (Illus.). 600p. (Orig.). 1992. pap. 16.95 (*0-918373-82-4*) Moon Pubns CA.

Parkes, Colin M. Bereavement. 2nd ed. 1987. text ed. 37.50x (*0-8236-0481-0*) Intl Univs Pr.

***Parkes, Colin M. & Weiss, Robert S.** Recovery from Bereavement. LC 94-77919. 344p. 1995. pap. text ed. 35.00 (*1-56821-361-1*) Aronson.

Parkes, Colin M., et al, eds. Attachment Across the Life Cycle. (Illus.). 336p. 1991. 99.95 (*0-415-05650-0*, A5199, Tavistock) Routledge.

— Attachment Across the Life Cycle. 336p. 1993. pap. 25.00 (*0-415-05651-9*, B0621) Routledge.

Parkes, Don & Thrift, Nigel. Times, Spaces & Places: A Chronogeographic Perspective. LC 79-40523. 543p. reprint ed. pap. 154.80 (*0-318-34960-4*, 2030757) Bks Demand.

Parkes, E. W. Braced Frameworks: An Introduction to the Theory of Structures. 2nd ed. LC 74-10556. 1974. 92.00 (*0-08-018078-7*, Pub. by Pergamon Repr UK) Franklin.

Parkes, Geoffrey, jt. auth. see Cornell, Alan.

Parkes, Graham. Composing the Soul: The Reaches of Nietzsche's Philosophy. 440p. 1994. 37.95 (*0-226-64686-6*) U Ch Pr.

Parkes, Graham, ed. Heidegger & Asian Thought. LC 87-19073. 292p. 1990. reprint ed. pap. text ed. 12.95 (*0-8248-1312-X*) UH Pr.

— Nietzsche & Asian Thought. 200p. 1991. 27.50 (*0-226-64683-1*) U Ch Pr.

Parkes, Graham, tr. see Keiji Nishitani.

Parkes, Henry B. The American Experience: An Interpretation of the History & Civilization of the American People. LC 82-15518. xii, 355p. 1982. text ed. 65.00 (*0-313-22574-5*, PAAE, Greenwood Pr) Greenwood.

— Fifty Years in the Making of Australian History, 2 vols, Set. LC 74-150195. (Select Bibliographies Reprint Ser.). 1977. reprint ed. 54.95 (*0-8369-5708-3*) Ayer.

— History of Mexico. (American Heritage Library). (Illus.). 1972. pap. 12.95 (*0-395-08410-5*, 61, SenEd) HM.

— Jonathan Edwards, the Fiery Puritan. LC 75-3135. reprint ed. 37.50 (*0-404-59144-2*) AMS Pr.

Parkes, J. D. Sleep & Its Disorders. (Major Problems in Neurology Ser.). (Illus.). 430p. 1986. text ed. 83.95 (*0-7216-1858-8*) Saunders.

Parkes, J. D., et al, eds. Neurological Disorders. (Treatment in Clinical Medicine Ser.). 235p. 1988. pap. 90.00 (*0-387-17013-8*) Spr-Verlag.

Parkes, James W. The Jew in the Medieval Community. (Judaic Studies Library: No. SHP3). 456p. 1976. pap. 16.00 (*0-87203-060-1*) Hermon.

Parkes, Joan. Travel in England in the Seventeenth Century. LC 70-109817. 354p. 1970. reprint ed. text ed. 59.75 (*0-8371-4308-X*, PATE, Greenwood Pr) Greenwood.

Parkes, K. Stuart. Writers & Politics in West Germany. LC 86-13900. 256p. 1986. text ed. 35.00 (*0-312-89347-7*) St Martin.

Parkes, M. B. Pause & Effect: An Introduction to the History of Punctuation in the West. 400p. 1993. 60.00 (*0-520-07941-8*) U CA Pr.

Parkes, M. B., ed. The Medieval Manuscripts of Kebel College, Oxford. 1979. 189.95 (*0-85967-504-1*, Pub. by Scolar Pr UK) Ashgate Pub Co.

Parkes, Oscar. British Battleships, Eighteen Sixty to Nineteen Fifty. LC 90-61164. (Illus.). 701p. 1990. 59.95 (*1-55750-075-4*) Naval Inst Pr.

***Parkes, Thomas K.** American Short Story: A Collection of the Best-Known & Most Memorable Stories by the Great. 1994. 15.98 (*0-88365-873-9*) Galahad Bks.

Parkes, W. B. Clay Bonded Foundry Sand. (Illus.). vii, 367p. 1971. 63.00 (*0-85334-833-2*, Pub. by Elsevier Applied Sci UK) Elsevier.

Parkes, W. Raymond. Occupational Lung Disorders. 3rd ed. (Illus.). 912p. 1994. 195.00 (*0-7506-1403-X*) Buttrwrth-Heinemann.

Parkes, William. The Curtaine-Drawer of the World: Or, Chamberlaine of That Inne of Iniquity. LC 79-84130. (English Experience Ser.: No. 948). 76p. 1979. reprint ed. lib. bdg. 9.00 (*90-221-0948-8*) Walter J Johnson.

Parkhill, D. F. & Emslow, P. H., Jr., eds. So This Is Nineteen Eighty-Four: Some Personal Views by Governors of the International Council for Computer Communication. 76p. 1984. 46.25 (*0-444-87638-3*, North Holland) Elsevier.

Parkhill, Joe M. God Did Not Create Sickness or Disease. 160p. (Orig.). 1983. pap. text ed. 6.95 (*0-936744-05-7*) Country Bazaar.

— Here's to You Honey: The Book That up Takes Where the World of Honey Leaves off, Vol. 2. 160p. 1992. spiral bd. 7.95 (*0-936744-03-0*) Country Bazaar.

— Honey God's Gift for Health & Beauty. 7.95 (*0-686-87212-6*, 259) Country Bazaar.

— Honey-God's Gift-for Health & Beauty: Cooking & Canning with Honey, Food Value Versus Sugar. 158p. 1989. spiral bd. 7.95 (*0-936744-02-2*) Country Bazaar.

— The Wonderful World of Honey: The Only Nutrition-Wise Sugarless Cookbook, Beauty Aids & Preventive Medicine. 160p. 1994. spiral bd. 7.95 (*0-936744-01-4*) Country Bazaar.

— The Wonderful World of Pollen. 160p. (Orig.). 1982. pap. text ed. 7.95 (*0-936744-06-5*) Country Bazaar.

Parkhill, Joe M. & Perry, Theodore. Countdown. (Orig.). 1983. spiral bd. 4.95 (*0-936744-09-X*) Country Bazaar.

***Parkhill, Matthew.** And I Loved Them Madly. 296p. Date not set. pap. 9.95 (*0-7490-0261-1*, London Bridge) Genl Dist Srvs.

Parkhill, Rick. The Power of Nine Hundred: A Guidebook to Caller-Paid Services. 162p. (Orig.). 1991. pap. 45.00 (*0-929870-23-9*) Advanstar Commns.

***Parkhill, Stephen C.** Answer Cancer, Answers for Living: A Mind Model for Healing. LC 94-49127. 200p. (Orig.). 1995. pap. 9.95 (*1-55874-333-2*, 332) Health Comm.

Parkhill, Thomas. The Forest Setting in Hindu Epics. 1994. write for info. (*0-318-72416-2*, Mellen Univ Pr) E Mellen.

— The Forest Setting in Hindu Epics: Princes, Sages, Demons. LC 93-23732. 238p. 1994. text ed. 89.95 (*0-7734-2213-7*) E Mellen.

Parkhouse. The Management of Sport: Its Foundation & Applications. (Illus.). 480p. (C). 1990. 39.95 (*0-8016-3812-7*) Mosby Yr Bk.

Parkhouse & Ridgeway. Doctor Who: Voyager. (Illus.). 100p. 1989. 8.95 (*1-85400-045-4*) Marvel Entmnt.

Parkhouse, James. Doctors' Careers: Aims & Experiences of Medical Graduates. 256p. (C). 1991. text ed. 65.00 (*0-415-04649-1*, A5069) Routledge.

Parkhouse, Steve, jt. auth. see Moore, Alan.

Parkhurst, Bond. At Speed. (Illus.). 158p. write for info. (*0-87880-013-1*) At Speed Pr.

Parkhurst, C. R. & Mountney, G. J. Poultry Egg & Meat Production. (Illus.). 300p. (C). 1987. text ed. 54.95 (*0-442-27497-1*) Chapman & Hall.

Parkhurst, Carol A., ed. Library Perspectives on NREN: The National Research & Education Network. 75p. 1990. pap. 10.95 (*0-8389-7477-5*) ALA.

Parkhurst, Carole. Visiting Tacoma. (Color-A-Story Ser.). (Illus.). 24p. (Orig.). (J). (gr. 1-4). 1983. pap. 2.75 (*0-933992-38-6*) Coffee Break.

Parkhurst, Charles H. Our Fight with Tammany. 1970. 25.95 (*0-405-02470-3*, 18944) Ayer.

— Our Fight with Tammany. LC 70-119941. (Select Bibliographies Reprint Ser.). reprint ed. 16.50 (*0-8369-5384-3*) Ayer.

Parkhurst, Christine & Fellows, Marian. Script Ease: A Step-by-Step Guide from Manuscript to Calligraphy. (Illus.). 64p. (gr. 1-12). 1982. 6.95 (*0-9607366-5-4*) Kino Pubns.

Parkhurst, Christine, jt. auth. see Fellows, Marian.

***Parkhurst, David L., et al.** National Water-Quality Assessment--Central Oklahoma Aquifer. LC 94-31134. (Water Supply Papers: Vol. 2357). 1995. write for info. (*0-615-00381-8*) US Geol Survey.

Parkhurst, G., ed. see Finney, Charles G.

Parkhurst, Genevieve. Glorious Victory Thru Healing Memories. 4.95 (*0-910924-55-4*) Macalester.

Parkhurst, L. B., jt. auth. see Finney, Charles G.

Parkhurst, L. G., ed. see Finney, Charles G.

Parkhurst, L. G., Jr.

Parkhurst, L. G., Jr., ed. see Finney, Charles J.

Parkhurst, L. G., ed. see Finney, Charles.

Parkhurst, L. G., Jr.

Parkhurst, L. G., ed. see Murray, Andrew & Finney, Charles G.

Parkhurst, L. G., ed. see Murray, Andrew & Spurgeon, Charles.

Parkhurst, L. G., Jr., ed. see Murray, Andrew & Edwards, Jonathan.

Parkhurst, Louis, jt. auth. see Finney, Charles.

Parkhurst, Louis, ed. see Finney, Charles.

Parkhurst, Louis G., Jr., ed. see Finney, Charles G.

Parkhurst, Louis G.

Parkhurst, Sue, ed. see Nation, Nyle N.

Parkhurst, Violet. Ocean Sunsets. (How to Draw & Paint Ser.). (Illus.). 32p. (Orig.). 1989. pap. 5.95 (*0-929261-63-1*, HT101) W Foster Pub.

Parkhurst, William. The Eloquent Executive. 144p. 1990. mass mkt. 6.95 (*0-380-70759-4*) Avon.

— True Detectives: The Real World of Today's Private Investigators. 1988. 18.95 (*0-517-56554-4*); 4.99 (*0-517-05608-9*) Random Hse Value.

Parkin. Differential Diagnosis in AIDS. 159p. 1991. pap. 19.95 (*0-8151-6634-6*) Mosby Yr Bk.

Parkin, jt. auth. see Shefler.

Parkin, A., et al. COBOL for Students. 3rd ed. 288p. 1990. pap. text ed. 16.95 (*0-340-51798-0*, A4401, Pub. by E Arnold UK) Routledge Chapman & Hall.

Parkin, Alan J. Memory: Phenomena, Experiment, & Theory. LC 92-35260. 1993. 39.95 (*0-631-15711-5*); pap. 17.95 (*0-631-15712-3*) Blackwell Pubs.

— Memory & Amnesia: An Introduction. 240p. 1987. pap. text ed. 22.95 (*0-631-14869-8*) Blackwell Pubs.

Parkin, Andrew. File on Nichols. 96p. 1993. pap. 15.95 (*0-413-65600-4*, Pub. by Methuen UK) Heinemann.

Parkin, Andrew, ed. see Boucicault, Dion.

Parkin, Andrew, ed. see Yeats, William Butler.

Parkin, Beverley. Flowers with Love. (Illus.). 40p. 1986. 8.99 (*0-85648-905-0*) Lion USA.

Parkin, Beverly. Flowers of the Wayside. (Illus.). 48p. 1989. text ed. 8.99 (*0-7459-1603-1*) Lion USA.

— Flowers with Love. 1994. 12.95 (*0-7459-2908-7*) Lion USA.

— Inspired by Flowers. 1994. 12.95 (*0-7459-2911-7*) Lion USA.

Parkin, Blaine R., ed. see Fluids Engineering Conference Symposium on Cavity Flows Staff.

Parkin, Blaine R., ed. see International Symposium on Cavitation Inception Staff.

Parkin, Bond L. Finding a Job in Florida. LC 92-33933. 1993. pap. 14.95 (*1-56164-027-1*) Pineapple Pr.

— The Florida Entrepreneur. 344p. 1994. pap. 18.95 (*1-56164-041-7*) Pineapple Pr.

Parkin, D. M. Cancer Occurrence in Developing Countries. (IARC Scientific Publications: No. 75). (Illus.). 200p. 1986. 40.00 (*92-832-1175-8*) OUP.

Parkin, D. M., ed. see International Agency for Research on Cancer Staff.

Parkin, D. M., et al, eds. Cancer Incidence in Five Continents, Vol. 6. (IARC Scientific Publications: No. 120). (Illus.). 1076p. 1993. 185.00 (*92-832-2120-6*) OUP.

— International Incidence of Childhood Cancer. (IARC Scientific Publications: No. 87). (Illus.). 432p. 1988. 75.00 (*92-832-1187-1*) OUP.

— The Role of the Registry in Cancer Control. (IARC Scientific Publications: No. 66). (Illus.). 1986. 20.00 (*0-19-723066-0*) OUP.

Parkin, D. T. Molecular Methods in Ecology. 1994. pap. write for info. (*0-632-03437-8*) Blackwell Sci.

Parkin, David. The Sacred Void: Spatial Images of Work & Ritual among the Giriama of Kenya. (Cambridge Studies in Social & Cultural Anthropology: No. 80). (Illus.). 280p. (C). 1991. 64.95 (*0-521-40466-5*) Cambridge U Pr.

— Speaking of Arts: A Giriama Impression. LC 82-70267. (First Annual Alan P. Merriam Lecture). 1982. pap. text ed. 5.00 (*0-941934-37-3*) Indiana Africa.

Parkin, David, ed. The Anthropology of Evil. 288p. 1987. pap. 21.95 (*0-631-15432-9*) Blackwell Pubs.

Parkin, David & Nyamwaya, David, eds. Transformations of African Marriage. (International African Seminars Ser.). 384p. 1988. text ed. 65.00 (*0-7190-2325-4*, Pub. by Manchester Univ Pr UK) St Martin.

— Transformations of African Marriage. (International African Seminars Ser.). 384p. 1989. text ed. 22.95 (*0-7190-2326-2*, Pub. by Manchester Univ Pr UK) St Martin.

Parkin, David, jt. ed. see Croll, Elisabeth.

Parkin, David, ed. see International African Seminar Staff.

***Parkin, David J.** Palms, Wine & Witnesses: Public Spirit & Private Gain in an African Farming Community. (Illus.). 113p. (C). 1994. pap. text ed. 8.50x (*0-88133-802-8*) Waveland Pr.

Parkin, Dorothy, tr. see Merle, Marcel.

Parkin, Frank. Durkheim. (Past Masters). 112p. 1993. pap. 7.95 (*0-19-287672-4*) OUP.

— Marxism & Class Theory: A Bourgeois Critique. LC 79-14222. 1983. pap. text ed. 17.00 (*0-231-04881-5*) Col U Pr.

— Max Weber. (Key Sociologists Ser.). 123p. 1982. pap. 8.95 (*0-85312-409-4*, NO. 3676, Tavistock-E Horwood) Routledge Chapman & Hall.

Parkin, J. M., jt. auth. see Nye, K. E.

Parkin, James. Judging Plans & Projects: Analysis & Public Participation in the Evaluation Process. (Studies in Green Research). 224p. 1993. 59.95 (*1-85628-434-4*, Pub. by Avebury Technical UK) Ashgate Pub Co.

— Public Management: Technocracy, Democracy, & Organizational Reform. 153p. (C). 1993. text ed. 51.95 (*1-85628-685-1*, Pub. by Avebury Pub UK) Ashgate Pub Co.

Parkin, Jane, jt. ed. see Dowrick, Stephanie.

Parkin, John. Henry Miller: The Modern Rabelais. LC 90-6091. (Studies in Comparative Literature: Vol. 10). 292p. 1990. lib. bdg. 89.95 (*0-88946-628-9*) E Mellen.

— Interpreting Rabelais: An Open Text Reading of an Open Text. LC 93-32357. 232p. 1993. text ed. 89.95 (*0-7734-9388-3*) E Mellen.

Parkin, John H. Bell & Baldwin, Their Development of Aerodomes & Hydrodomes at Baddeck, Nova Scotia. LC 65-1207. 619p. reprint ed. pap. 176.50 (*0-8357-7122-9*, 2014333) Bks Demand.

Parkin, Michael. Economics. (Illus.). (C). 1990. text ed. 54.95 (*0-201-05931-2*); Macroeconomics. pap. text ed. 38.75 (*0-201-09444-4*); Macroeconomics. pap. text ed. 38.75 (*0-201-09445-2*); student ed. pap. text ed. 17.25 (*0-201-05932-0*) Addison-Wesley.

— Economics. 2nd ed. LC 92-15707. 1120p. (C). 1993. text ed. 56.95 (*0-201-54697-3*) Addison-Wesley.

— Economics. 2nd ed. LC 93-46051. (C). 1994. text ed. 52.95 (*0-201-50031-0*) Addison-Wesley.

— Economics. 3rd ed. 1024p. (C). 1996. text ed. write for info. (*0-201-53762-1*) Addison-Wesley.

An Asterisk (*) at the beginning of an entry indicates that the title is appearing in BIP for the first time.

— Macroeconomics. 2nd ed. LC 92-15486. 624p. (C). 1993. pap. text ed. 40.95 (*0-201-54699-X*) Addison-Wesley.

— Macroeconomics. 2nd ed. LC 93-46052. 598p. (C). 1994. text ed. 37.95 (*0-201-50033-7*) Addison-Wesley.

— Macroeconomics. 3rd ed. 576p. (C). 1996. pap. text ed. write for info. (*0-201-60982-7*) Addison-Wesley.

— Microeconomics. 2nd ed. LC 92-15487. (Illus.). 688p. (C). 1993. pap. text ed. 40.95 (*0-201-54698-1*) Addison-Wesley.

— Microeconomics. 2nd ed. LC 93-45830. (C). 1994. text ed. 37.95 (*0-201-50032-9*) Addison-Wesley.

— Microeconomics. 3rd ed. 624p. (C). 1996. pap. text ed. write for info. (*0-201-60981-9*) Addison-Wesley.

Parkin, Michael, ed. The Theory of Inflation. LC 94-13969. (International Library of Critical Writings in Business History: Vol. 41). 680p. 1994. 187.95 (*1-85278-299-4*, Pub. by E Elgar Pub UK) Ashgate Pub Co.

Parkin, Michael & Bade, Robin. Macroeconomics. 2nd ed. 800p. (C). 1991. text ed. write for info. (*0-13-544255-9*) P-H.

Parkin, Michael & Sumner, Michael T., eds. Incomes Policy & Inflation. (Studies in Inflation: No. I). 296p. (C). 1993. reprint ed. text ed. 68.95 (*0-7512-0206-1*, Pub. by Gregg Revivals UK) Ashgate Pub Co.

— Inflation in the United Kingdom. (Studies in Inflation: No. VI). 192p. (C). 1993. reprint ed. text ed. 54.95 (*0-7512-0208-8*, Pub. by Gregg Revivals UK) Ashgate Pub Co.

Parkin, Michael & Zis, George, eds. Inflation in Open Economics. (Studies in Inflation: No. V). 312p. (C). 1993. reprint ed. text ed. 61.95 (*0-7512-0207-X*, Pub. by Gregg Revivals UK) Ashgate Pub Co.

— Inflation in the World Ecomony. (Studies in Inflation: No. IV). 352p. (C). 1993. reprint ed. text ed. 65.95 (*0-7512-0205-3*, Pub. by Gregg Revivals UK) Ashgate Pub Co.

Parkin, Rex. The Red Carpet. LC 92-19912. (Illus.). 48p. (J). (gr. k-3). 1993. reprint ed. pap. 4.95 (*0-689-71678-8*, Aladdin Paperbacks) S&S Childrens.

Parkin, Robert. Applied Robotic Analysis. 448p. 1991. text ed. 91.00 (*0-13-773391-7*) P-H.

— A Guide to Austroasiatic Speakers & Their Languages. LC 90-15572. (Oceanic Linguistics Special Publications: No. 23). 1991. pap. text ed. 21.00 (*0-8248-1377-4*) UH Pr.

***Parkin, Robert S.** Blood on the Sea: American Destroyers Lost in WWII. (Illus.). 304p. 1995. 24.95 (*1-885119-17-8*) Sarpedon.

Parkin, S. S., ed. Magnetic Surfaces, Thin Films & Multilayers: Materials Research Society Symposium Proceedings, Vol. 231. 1992. text ed. 72.00 (*1-55899-125-5*) Materials Res.

***Parkin, Sara.** Life & Death of Petra Kelly. 1995. 22.00 (*0-04-440896-X*) Routledge Chapman & Hall.

Parkin, Stanley F. Notes on Pediatric Dentistry. 200p. 1991. pap. text ed. 37.50 (*0-7236-1643-4*) Buttrwrth-Heinemann.

Parkin, T., jt. auth. see Horwood, D.

Parkin, Tim G. Demography & Roman Society. (Ancient Society & History Ser.). 240p. 1992. text ed. 32.50x (*0-8018-4377-4*) Johns Hopkins.

Parkin, Tom. Green Giants: Rainforests of the Pacific Northwest. (Earthcare Bks.). (Illus.). 48p. (Orig.). (YA). (gr. 8-12). 1992. pap. 7.95 (*1-895565-07-3*) Firefly Bks Ltd.

Parkin, Vincent. Chronic Inflation in an Industrializing Economy: The Brazilian Experience. (Illus.). 275p. (C). 1991. 59.95 (*0-521-37540-1*) Cambridge U Pr.

Parkington, J., jt. ed. see Bailey, G. N.

Parkington, M., jt. auth. see McGillivray, E. J.

Parkins, A. W. & Poller, R. C. An Introduction to Organometallic Chemistry. (Illus.). 264p. 1986. pap. 18.95 (*0-19-505061-4*) OUP.

Parkins, Almon E. South, Its Economic-Geographic Development. LC 70-98865. 528p. 1970. reprint ed. text ed. 85.00 (*0-8371-2904-4*, PATS, Greenwood Pr) Greenwood.

Parkins, Charles W. & Anderson, Samuel W., eds. Cochlear Prostheses: An International Symposium. 1983. 100.00 (*0-89766-202-4*); pap. 100.00 (*0-89766-203-2*, VOL. 405) NY Acad Sci.

Parkins, E. J. Equilibration, Mind & Brain: Toward an Integrated Psychology. LC 90-32179. 224p. 1990. text ed. 55.00 (*0-275-93609-0*, C3609, Praeger Pubs) Greenwood.

Parkins, R. N., ed. Corrosion Processes. (Illus.). 317p. 1982. 93.75 (*0-85334-147-8*, I-356-82, Pub. by Elsevier Applied Sci UK) Elsevier.

— Electrochemical Test Methods for Stress Corrosion Cracking: Selected Papers from the Conference on Electrochemical Test Methods for Stress Corrosion Cracking, Firminy, France, Sept. 1980. (Illus.). 160p. 1981. pap. 18.75 (*0-08-026140-X*, Pergamon Pr) Elsevier.

— Engineering Solutions for Corrosion in Oil & Gas Applications. (Illus.). 448p. 1991. 10.00 (*1-877914-28-2*) NACE Intl.

— Life Prediction of Corrodible Structures. (Illus.). 1670p. 1994. 200.00 (*1-877914-60-6*) NACE Intl.

Parkins, R. N., jt. auth. see Arup, H.

Parkinson, Benson Y. S. Dilworth Young: A Scouting Life. LC 94-5519. 1994. write for info. (*1-55503-660-0*) Covenant Comms.

— Set Apart: A Novel. LC 94-28269. 1994. pap. 11.00 (*1-55503-710-0*) Covenant Comms.

***Parkinson, Bradford W. & Spilker, James J., Jr., eds.** The Global Positioning System: Theory & Application, 2 vols., Vol. 1. LC 94-44737. 1995. write for info. (*1-56347-106-X*) AIAA.

— The Global Positioning System: Theory & Application, 2 vols., Vol. 2. LC 94-44737. 1995. write for info. (*1-56347-107-8*) AIAA.

***Parkinson, Brian.** Ideas & Realities of Emotion. LC 95-1096. (International Library of Psychology). 1995. write for info. (*0-415-02858-2*); pap. write for info. (*0-415-02859-0*) Routledge.

Parkinson, C. E. A Forest Flora of the Anadaman Islands. 326p. (C). 1984. 90.00 (*81-7089-012-8*, Pub. by Intl Bk Distr II) St Mut.

Parkinson, C. Northcote. Brittania Rules. 144p. 1992. reprint ed. pap. text ed. 12.00 (*0-86299-468-3*) A Sutton Pub.

— In-Laws & Outlaws. 1993. reprint ed. lib. bdg. 18.95 (*1-56849-102-6*) Buccaneer Bks.

— The Law & the Profits. 1993. reprint ed. lib. bdg. 18.95 (*1-56849-101-8*) Buccaneer Bks.

— The Life & Times of Horatio Hornblower. 1994. reprint ed. lib. bdg. 32.95 (*1-56849-318-5*) Buccaneer Bks.

— Parkinson: The Law Complete, Pt. II. 224p. 1983. pap. 3.50 (*0-345-30064-5*) Ballantine.

— Parkinson's Law. 1993. reprint ed. lib. bdg. 18.95 (*1-56849-015-1*) Buccaneer Bks.

— Portsmouth Point: British Navy in Fiction, 1793-1815. 15.00 (*0-87556-509-3*) Saifer.

— Trade in the Eastern Seas, 1793-1813. (Illus.). 437p. 1966. 35.00 (*0-7146-1348-7*, Pub. by F Cass Pubs UK) Intl Spec Bk.

Parkinson, Carolyn S. My Mommy Has Cancer. (Illus.). 20p. (J). (ps-4). 1991. pap. 8.95 (*0-9630287-0-7*) Solace Pub.

Parkinson, Cecil. Right of the Centre: An Autobiography of Cecil Parkinson. (Illus.). 312p. 1993. 39.95 (*0-297-81262-9*) Trafalgar.

Parkinson, Charles P. Slow to Learn. Kinsey, Bernard B., ed. 363p. (Orig.). 1989. pap. 14.95 (*0-9621383-0-4*) Topline Pubs.

Parkinson, Claire L. Breakthroughs: A Chronology of Great Achievements in Science & Mathematics, 1200-1930. (Reference Books - Science). (Illus.). 624p. 1985. text ed. 40.00 (*0-8161-8706-1*, Hall Reference) Macmillan.

— Gospel Cryptograms. (Quiz & Puzzle Bks.). (Illus.). 64p. 1994. pap. 4.99 (*0-8010-7127-5*) Baker Bk.

Parkinson, Claire L., jt. auth. see Washington, Warren M.

Parkinson, Connie, jt. ed. see Foster, Kim.

Parkinson, Connie, ed. see Hopley, Claire.

Parkinson, Connie, ed. see Karoff, Barbara.

Parkinson, Connie, ed. see Lilie, Tish.

Parkinson, Connie, ed. see Peddie, Mary, et al.

Parkinson, Connie, ed. see Siegler, Madeleine H.

Parkinson, Cornelia M. Alex Livingston, the Tomato Man. (Illus.). 20p. (J). (gr. 4 up). 1985. pap. 1.50 (*0-938404-05-9*, AWL) Hist Tales.

— Historical Tales of Old Reynoldsburg: Selections from the First Five Years of the Courier. (Illus.). 152p. (Orig.). 1980. pap. 5.00 (*0-938404-00-8*) Hist Tales.

— History of Reynoldsburg & Truro Township, Ohio. (Illus.). 200p. 1981. 32.00 (*0-938404-02-4*) Hist Tales.

— More Historical Tales of Old Reynoldsburg, Vol. II. (Illus.). 168p. (Orig.). 1985. pap. 5.00 (*0-938404-04-0*, MORE HT) Hist Tales.

Parkinson, Curtis. Tom Foolery. LC 92-7852. (Illus.). 32p. (J). (ps-2). 1993. lib. bdg. 13.95 (*0-02-770025-9*, Bradbury S&S) S&S Childrens.

Parkinson, Cyril N. East & West. LC 81-1195. (Illus.). xxii, 330p. 1981. reprint ed. text ed. 59.75 (*0-313-22955-4*, PAEW, Greenwood Pr) Greenwood.

Parkinson, D. A. Value-Added Tax in the EEC. 260p. 1980. lib. bdg. 48.50 (*0-86010-190-8*) G & T Inc.

Parkinson, D. R., ed. see European School of Oncology Staff.

Parkinson, Dan. The Covenant of the Forge. (Dwarven Nations Trilogy Ser.). 320p. (Orig.). 1993. 4.95 (*1-56076-558-5*) TSR Inc.

— Drifter's Luck. 288p. 1991. pap. 3.95 (*0-8217-3396-6*) Zebra.

— Dust on the Wind. 1992. mass mkt. 3.99 (*0-8217-3635-3*) Zebra.

— Fox & the Faith. 1989. pap. 3.95 (*1-55817-204-1*, Pinnacle NY) Windsor NY.

— Fox & the Flag. 1990. pap. 3.95 (*1-55817-349-8*, Pinnacle NY) Windsor NY.

— The Fox & the Fortune. 1992. mass mkt. 3.99 (*1-55817-600-4*, Pinnacle NY) Windsor NY.

— Fox & the Fury. 1989. pap. 3.95 (*1-55817-291-2*, Pinnacle NY) Windsor NY.

— The Gates of Thorbardin. LC 89-51892. (Dragonlance Heroes II Trilogy Ser.: Vol. 2). (Illus.). 320p. (Orig.). 1990. pap. 4.95 (*0-88038-912-5*) TSR Inc.

— The Guns of No Man's Land. 320p. 1992. mass mkt. 3.99 (*0-8217-3960-3*) Zebra.

— Hammer & Axe. (Dwarven Nations Trilogy Ser.: No. 2). 320p. (Orig.). 1993. 4.95 (*1-56076-627-1*) TSR Inc.

— Jubilation Gap. 1987. pap. 3.95 (*0-8217-2209-3*) Zebra.

— Man Called Wolf. 1989. pap. 3.95 (*0-8217-2794-X*) Zebra.

— Ride the Devil's Trail. 1990. pap. 3.95 (*0-8217-2894-6*) Zebra.

— Shadow of the Hawk. 432p. 1988. pap. 3.95 (*0-8217-2259-X*) Zebra.

— The Slanted Colt. 224p. 1984. pap. 2.25 (*0-8217-1413-9*) Zebra.

— Starsong. LC 87-51261. 352p. (Orig.). 1988. pap. 3.95 (*0-318-32501-2*) TSR Inc.

— Summer Land. 352p. 1989. pap. 3.95 (*0-8217-2683-8*) Zebra.

— Sundown Breed. 240p. 1986. pap. 2.50 (*0-8217-1860-6*) Zebra.

— The Swordsheath Scroll. (Dwarven Nations Trilogy Ser.: No. 3). 320p. (Orig.). 1994. pap. 4.95 (*1-56076-686-7*) TSR Inc.

— Thunderland. 368p. 1987. pap. 3.50 (*0-8217-1991-2*) Zebra.

— The Way to Wyoming. 432p. 1988. pap. 3.95 (*0-8217-2411-8*) Zebra.

— The Westering. 352p. 1989. pap. 3.95 (*0-8217-2559-9*) Zebra.

Parkinson, Dan & Hicks, David. Gunpowder Wind. 400p. 1988. pap. 3.95 (*0-8217-2456-8*) Zebra.

— Texians. 1990. pap. 3.95 (*0-8217-3097-5*) Zebra.

Parkinson, David. The History of Film. LC 94-60287. (World of Art Ser.). (Illus.). 217p. 1995. pap. 14.95 (*0-500-20277-X*) Thames Hudson.

***Parkinson, David, ed.** The Graham Greene Film Reader: Reviews, Essays, Interviews & Film Stories. LC 94-33547. (Film Reader Ser.). 776p. 1994. 35.00 (*1-55783-188-2*) Applause Theatre Bk Pubs.

Parkinson, David, ed. see Douglas, Gavin.

Parkinson, David H. & Mulhall, Brian E. The Generation of High Magnetic Fields. LC 67-13568. (International Cryogenics Monograph Ser.). 179p. reprint ed. pap. 51.10 (*0-317-27895-9*, 2055789) Bks Demand.

Parkinson, Dennis, ed. Massively Parallel: Computing with the DAP. 320p. (C). 1990. pap. text ed. 200.00 (*0-273-08809-2*, Pub. by Pitman Pubng UK) St Mut.

— Massively Parallel Computing with the DAP. (Research Monographs in Parallel & Distributed Computing). 320p. 1989. 29.95x (*0-262-66065-2*) MIT Pr.

Parkinson, Dilworth B. Constructing the Social Context of Communication: Terms of Address in Egyptian Arabic. (Contributions to the Sociology of Language Ser.: Vol. 41). x, 239p. 1985. 75.40 (*0-89925-148-X*) Mouton.

***Parkinson, Eric.** Clixi Technology. Stillman, Meg, ed. (Illus.). 25p. (J). (gr. 3-9). 1994. 9.95 (*1-884461-10-7*) NES Arnold.

— Teaching Techniques. rev. ed. Doyle, Connie, ed. (Design & Make Ser.). (Illus.). 45p. (J). (gr. 3-6). reprint ed. 12.95 (*1-884461-05-0*) NES Arnold.

Parkinson, Eric, jt. auth. see Carlton, Kevin.

Parkinson, F. Conquering the Past: Austrian Nazism Yesterday & Today. LC 88-31328. 348p. 1989. 39.95 (*0-8143-2054-6*); pap. 18.95 (*0-8143-2055-4*) Wayne St U Pr.

Parkinson, Frank. Post-Trauma Stress. LC 93-37229. 192p. 1993. pap. 12.95 (*1-55561-058-7*) Fisher Bks.

Parkinson, G. H. Handbook of Western Philosophy. 1988. text ed. 100.00 (*0-02-949593-8*) Macmillan.

— Spinoza's Theory of Knowledge. (Modern Revivals in Philosophy Ser.). 198p. 1993. 59.95 (*0-7512-0159-6*, Pub. by Gregg Pub UK) Ashgate Pub Co.

Parkinson, G. H., ed. Routledge History of Philosophy, Vol. 4: The Renaissance & Seventeenth Century Rationalism. LC 92-37350. 480p. 1993. 75.00 (*0-415-05378-1*, B0731, Routledge NY) Routledge.

Parkinson, G. H., tr. see Leibniz, Gottfried W.

Parkinson, G. H., ed. see Leibniz, Gottfried W.

Parkinson, George. Guide to Coal Mining Collections in the United States. 182p. 1978. pap. 22.00 (*0-318-36154-X*) West Va U Pr.

Parkinson, George H. Leibniz on Human Freedom. (Studia Leibnitiana: No. 2). 73p. (Orig.). 1970. pap. text ed. 47.50 (*3-515-00272-3*) Coronet Bks.

Parkinson, George H., ed. Truth, Knowledge, & Reality: Inquiries into the Foundations of 17th Century Rationalism. (Studia Leibnitiana: No. 9). 167p. (Orig.). 1981. pap. 48.50 (*3-515-03350-5*) Coronet Bks.

***Parkinson-Hardman, Joanna.** Heart of Gold: Poems by Joanna Parkinson - Hardman & Some Celebrity Friends. (Illus.). 64p. (J). (gr. 5-7). 1995. 8.95 (*0-563-36798-9*) Parkwest Pubns.

***Parkinson, Henry J.** How Things Got Better: Speech, Writing, Printing & Cultural Change. LC 94-38492. 192p. 1995. text ed. 49.95 (*0-89789-431-6*, Bergin & Garvey) Greenwood.

***Parkinson, J. E.** Corporate Power & Responsibility: Issues in the Theory of Company Law. 496p. 1995. pap. 32.00 (*0-19-825989-1*) OUP.

Parkinson, J. R., jt. auth. see Faaland, J.

Parkinson, J. R., jt. auth. see Faaland, Just.

***Parkinson, J. Robert.** Get Working. 96p. (C). 1995. per., pap. text ed. 16.95 (*0-7872-1111-7*) Kendall-Hunt.

— How to Get People to Do Things Your Way. (Illus.). 160p. 1989. pap. 4.95 (*0-8442-6676-0*, Crain Bks) NTC Pub Grp.

— How to Get Things Your Way. 2nd ed. (Orig.). 1995. 12.95 (*0-8442-4488-0*, VGM Career Bks) NTC Pub Grp.

— Planning Your Young Child's Education. 1986. pap. 6.95 (*0-8442-6683-3*, Passport Bks) NTC Pub Grp.

Parkinson, James. Organic Remains of a Former World, 3 vols. Albritton, Claude C., Jr., ed. LC 77-6534. (History of Geology Ser.). (Illus.). 1978. lib. bdg. 108.95 (*0-405-10454-5*) Ayer.

Parkinson, James W. Focus on Your Language. LC 75-17952. 279p. 1976. teacher ed 6.67 (*0-672-61363-8*, Bobbs); pap. 9.50 (*0-672-61358-1*, Bobbs) Macmillan.

Parkinson, Jane, ed. see Hargrave, Harriet.

Parkinson, Jane P., ed. see Hargrave, Harriet.

Parkinson, Jerry, jt. auth. see Rossow, Lawrence.

Parkinson, John. The Diplomatic Sailor. 1981. 23.00 (*0-7223-1360-8*, Pub. by A H S Ltd UK) St Mut.

— Garden of Pleasant Flowers. 1991. pap. 19.95 (*0-486-26758-X*) Dover.

— Paradisi in Sole, Paradisus Terrestris, or a Garden of All Sorts of Pleasant Flowers Which Our English Ayre Will Permit. LC 74-28880. (English Experience Ser.: No. 758). 1975. reprint ed. 145.00 (*90-221-0758-2*) Walter J Johnson.

Parkinson, John A. Victorian Music Publishers: An Annotated List. LC 90-4831. (Detroit Studies in Music Bibliography: No. 64). 315p. 1990. 40.00 (*0-89990-051-8*) Info Coord.

Parkinson, John E. Corporate Power & Social Responsibility: Issues in the Theory of Company Law. (Clarendon Press Ser.). 540p. 1994. 75.00 (*0-19-825288-9*) OUP.

Parkinson, Joy E. A Manual of English for the Overseas Doctor. 4th ed. (Illus.). 286p. 1991. pap. text ed. 29.00 (*0-443-04188-1*) Churchill.

Parkinson, Kathy, illus. The Enormous Turnip. LC 85-14432. 32p. (J). (ps-1). 1985. 13.95 (*0-8075-2062-4*) A Whitman.

— The Farmer in the Dell. LC 87-25322. 32p. (J). (ps-2). 1988. lib. bdg. 13.95 (*0-8075-2271-6*) A Whitman.

Parkinson, Kenneth L. & Kallberg, Jarl G. Corporate Liquidity: A Guide to Managing Working Capital. LC 93-21755. 500p. 1993. text ed. 55.00 (*1-55623-864-9*) Irwin Prof Pubng.

Parkinson, Kenneth L. & Stanley, Linda. Cash Management Templates: Basic Models in Banking, Forecasting, Investment & Currency Management. 1993. disk 159.00 (*0-685-69583-2*, CMSM) Warren Gorham & Lamont.

— Cash Management Templatis: Basic Models in Banking, Forecasting, Investment & Currency Management. 256p. 1992. 175.00 (*0-7913-1820-6*) Warren Gorham & Lamont.

Parkinson, Kenneth L., jt. auth. see Kallberg, Jarl G.

***Parkinson, Kent, et al.** Sunsoft Solaris 2.X for Managers & Administrators. 1995. disk 29.95 (*0-934605-87-4*, OnWord Pr) High Mtn.

— Sunsoft Solaris 2.X for Managers & Administrators. (Illus.). 550p. 1995. pap. 34.95 (*0-934605-75-0*, 5084, OnWord Pr) High Mtn.

Parkinson, M., ed. see Kayat, Claude.

Parkinson, Marie & Zervas, Naoni. The Total Drill Team Dimension: A Textbook for Student & Adult Leaders. (Illus.). 541p. (C). 1985. pap. text ed. 29.95 (*0-89641-153-2*) American Pr.

Parkinson, Michael, ed. Reshaping Local Government, Vol. III. (Reshaping the Public Sector Ser.). 256p. 1988. 29.95 (*0-946967-19-9*); pap. 18.95 (*0-946967-31-8*) Transaction Pubs.

Parkinson, Michael, jt. ed. see Bianchini, Franco.

Parkinson, Michael, et al, eds. European Cities Towards Two Thousand: Profiles, Policies, & Prospects. LC 93-27981. 1994. text ed. 69.95 (*0-7190-4166-X*, Pub. by Manchester Univ Pr UK) St Martin.

Parkinson, Norman & Ackerley, Lisa. Your Food. (C). 1989. 30.00 (*0-86242-099-7*, Pub. by Age Concern Eng UK) St Mut.

Parkinson, P. G., jt. auth. see Chapman, V. J.

***Parkinson, Patrick.** Tradition & Change in Australian Law. 280p. 1995. pap. 39.00 (*0-455-21292-9*, Pub. by Law Bk Co) W W Gaunt.

Parkinson, R. B. Voices from Ancient Egypt: An Anthology of Middle Kingdom Writings. LC 91-7250. (Oklahoma Series in Classical Culture: Vol. 9). (Illus.). 160p. (Orig.). 1991. pap. 21.95 (*0-8061-2362-1*) U of Okla Pr.

Parkinson, Richard. A Tour in America in Seventeen Ninety-Eight, Seventeen Ninety-Nine, & 1800..., 2 vols., Set. (BCL1 - U. S. History Ser.). 1991. reprint ed. lib. bdg. 150.00 (*0-7812-6014-0*) Rprt Serv.

***Parkinson, Richard & Quirke, Stephen.** Papyrus. (Egyptian Bookshelf Ser.). (Illus.). 100p. (Orig.). 1995. pap. 19.95 (*0-292-76563-0*) U of Tex Pr.

Parkinson, Richard N. Edward Gibbon. LC 72-13382. (Twayne's English Authors Ser.). 158p. (C). 1973. lib. bdg. 15.95 (*0-8057-1218-6*) Irvington.

Parkinson, Robert W. Growing up on Purpose. LC 84-63042. (Illus.). 75p. 1985. pap. 7.95 (*0-87822-239-1*, 2391) Res Press.

— Growing up on Purpose, Set. braille ed. 73p. (J). 1989. Braille. vinyl bd. 5.84 (*1-56956-248-2*, BR7839) W A T Braille.

Parkinson, Roger. Clausewitz. LC 79-150602. (Illus.). 1979. reprint ed. pap. 12.95 (*0-8128-6021-7*, Scrbrough Hse) Madison Bks UPA.

Parkinson, Ronald, jt. auth. see Casteras, Susan P.

Parkinson, Stanley, jt. auth. see Levine, Gustav.

Parkinson, T., jt. auth. see Fox, C.

Parkinson, T. J., jt. ed. see Raw, M. E.

Parkinson, T. J., jt. ed. see Raw, Mary E.

Parkinson, T. J., jt. auth. see Raw, Mary-Elizabeth.

Parkinson, Thomas. Hart Crane & Yvor Winters: Their Literary Correspondence. LC 77-80475. 1978. pap. 10.00 (*0-520-04642-0*) U CA Pr.

— Poems: New & Selected. 140p. 1988. 20.00 (*0-915032-98-8*); pap. 12.95 (*0-915032-96-1*) Natl Poet Foun.

— Poets, Poems, Movements. Litz, A. Walton, ed. LC 86-30910. (Studies in Modern Literature: No. 64). 340p. reprint ed. pap. 96.90 (*0-8357-1783-6*, 2070748) Bks Demand.

— Thanatos: Earth Poems. 1976. pap. 2.00 (*0-685-79271-4*) Oyez.

— Yorkshire Legends & Traditions. Dorson, Richard M., ed. LC 77-70615. (International Folklore Ser.). 1977. reprint ed. lib. bdg. 21.95 (*0-405-10117-1*) Ayer.

Parkinson, Thomas, ed. see Yeats, William Butler.

Parkinson, Thomas F. Hart Crane & Yvor Winters: Their Literary Correspondence. LC 77-80475. 198p. reprint ed. pap. 56.50 (*0-685-23563-7*, 2029055) Bks Demand.

— W. B. Yeats, Self-Critic: A Study of His Early Verse, & the Later Poetry, 2 vols. in one. LC 75-160480. 484p. reprint ed. pap. 138.00 (*0-685-23980-2*, 2031544) Bks Demand.

Parkinson, Wenda. This Gilded African: Toussaint L'Ouverture. 12.95 (*0-7043-2187-4*, Pub. by Quartet UK) Charles River Bks.

Parkis, Michael. Everything You Always Wanted to Know about Arithmetic. (J). (gr. 4-8). 1987. 6.50 (*0-87879-804-8*, Ann Arbor Div) Acad Therapy.

PQ

Parkison, Jami. Pequena the Burro. LC 93-30377. (Key Concepts in Personal Development Ser.). (Illus.). 32p. (J). (gr. 1-4). 1994. 16.95 (*1-55942-055-3*, 7657); teacher ed, vhs 79.95 (*1-55942-058-8*, 9376) Marshfilm.

Parkison, Ralph F. Big Red & the Fence Post. Withrow, Marion O., ed. (Illus.). 53p. (Orig.). (J). (gr. 2-8). 1988. pap. write for info. (*0-318-63993-9*) Little Wood Bks.

— Days. Withrow, Marion O., ed. (Illus.). 60p. (Orig.). (J). (gr. 2-8). 1988. pap. write for info. (*0-318-64003-1*) Little Wood Bks.

— Eovl. Withrow, Marion O., ed. (Illus.). 36p. (Orig.). (J). (gr. 2-8). 1988. pap. write for info. (*0-318-63994-7*) Little Wood Bks.

— In the Middle of the Corn Patch. Withrow, Marion O., ed. (Illus.). 55p. (Orig.). (J). (gr. 2-8). 1988. pap. write for info. (*0-318-64002-3*) Little Wood Bks.

— The Little Flea. Withrow, Marion O., ed. (Illus.). 21p. (Orig.). (J). (gr. 2-8). 1988. pap. write for info. (*0-318-63995-5*) Little Wood Bks.

— The Little Girl & the Inchworm. Withrow, Marion O., ed. (Illus.). 75p. (Orig.). (J). (gr. 2-8). 1988. pap. write for info. (*0-318-63996-3*) Little Wood Bks.

— The Little Girl, the Lillipop, & the Green Bird, Bk. 1. Withrow, Marion O., ed. (Illus.). 31p. (Orig.). (J). (gr. 2-6). 1988. pap. 4.25 (*0-929949-00-5*) Little Wood Bks.

— The Old Goat. Withrow, Marion O., ed. (Illus.). 112p. (Orig.). (J). (gr. 2-8). 1988. pap. write for info. (*0-318-64004-X*) Little Wood Bks.

— The Pea in the Pod, Bk. 3. Withrow, Marion O., ed. (Illus.). 10p. (Orig.). (J). (gr. 2-6). 1988. pap. text ed. 3.00 (*0-929949-02-1*) Little Wood Bks.

— The Pencil. Withrow, Marion O., ed. (Illus.). 47p. (Orig.). (J). (gr. 2-8). 1988. pap. write for info. (*0-318-64000-7*) Little Wood Bks.

— Santa's Wheat Kernels. Withrow, Marion O., ed. (Illus.). 60p. (Orig.). (J). (gr. 2-8). 1988. pap. write for info. (*0-318-64005-8*) Little Wood Bks.

— Seeds & Seeds & Seeds. Withrow, Marion O., ed. (Illus.). 65p. (Orig.). (J). (gr. 2-8). 1988. pap. write for info. (*0-318-64001-5*) Little Wood Bks.

— The Soda Pop Can & the Road Sign, Bk. 4. Withrow, Marion O., ed. (Illus.). 13p. (Orig.). (J). (gr. 2-6). 1988. pap. text ed. 3.73 (*0-929949-03-X*) Little Wood Bks.

— The Spot on the Ground. Withrow, Marion O., ed. (Illus.). 83p. (Orig.). (J). (gr. 2-8). 1988. pap. write for info. (*0-318-63997-1*) Little Wood Bks.

— A This or a That. Withrow, Marion O., ed. (Illus.). 53p. (Orig.). (J). (gr. 2-8). 1988. pap. write for info. (*0-318-63999-8*) Little Wood Bks.

— The Twig & the Mouse, Bk. 2. Withrow, Marion O., ed. (Illus.). 17p. (Orig.). (J). (gr. 2-6). 1988. pap. 4.25 (*0-929949-01-3*) Little Wood Bks.

— Yodeling. Withrow, Marion O., ed. (Illus.). 71p. (Orig.). (J). (gr. 2-8). 1988. pap. write for info. (*0-318-63998-X*) Little Wood Bks.

Parkman, Allen M. No-Fault Divorce: What Went Wrong? 167p. 1992. text ed. 33.00 (*0-8133-1433-X*) Westview.

Parkman, Anna W., jt. auth. see Surkin, Howard B.

Parkman, Aubrey L. David Jayne Hill & the Problem of World Peace. LC 72-3530. 293p. 1975. 39.50 (*0-8387-1259-2*) Bucknell U Pr.

Parkman, C., jt. ed. see Eck, C.

Parkman, Elmerina L. & Leone, Norma L. From Nonnie's Italian Kitchen: The Recipes of Mary Baldini Leonardi. LC 88-13414. 160p. (Orig.). 1988. pap. 8.95 (*0-936635-25-8*) Lion Pr & Vid.

Parkman, Francis. The Conspiracy of Pontiac: From the Spring of 1763 to the Death of Pontiac, Vol. 2. 1994. pap. 12.50 (*0-8032-8737-2*, Bison Books) U of Nebr Pr.

— The Conspiracy of Pontiac: To the Massacre at Michillimackinac, Vol. 1. (Illus.). 387p. 1994. pap. 12.50 (*0-8032-8733-X*, Bison Books) U of Nebr Pr.

Parkman, Francis, Jr. Discovery of the Great West: La Salle. Taylor, William R., ed. LC 86-22763. 377p. 1986. reprint ed. text ed. 89.50 (*0-313-24223-2*, PDGW, Greenwood Pr) Greenwood.

Parkman, Francis. France & England in North America, 2 vols. Levin, David, ed. Incl. Vol. I. Pioneers of France in the New World; The Jesuits in North America in the 17th Century; La Salle & the Discovery of the Great West, the Old Regime in Canada. LC 82-18658. 1504p. 1983. 32.50 (*0-940450-10-0*); Vol. II. Count Frontenac & New France under Louis XIV. LC 82-18658. 1620p. 1983. 37.50 (*0-940450-11-9*); Montcalm & Wolfe. LC 82-18658. 1983. (*0-318-63076-1*); LC 82-18658. 1983. write for info. (*0-318-63074-5*) Library of America.

— Half-Century of Conflict, 2 vols., Set. 1993. reprint ed. lib. bdg. 150.00 (*0-7812-5194-X*) Rprt Serv.

— The Jesuits in North America. 586p. 1970. reprint ed. 25.00 (*0-87928-016-6*) Corner Hse.

— La Salle & the Discovery of the Great West. 560p. 1968. reprint ed. 25.00 (*0-87928-004-2*) Corner Hse.

— La Salle & the Discovery of the Great West. 1993. reprint ed. lib. bdg. 75.00 (*0-7812-5892-8*) Rprt Serv.

— Letters of Francis Parkman, 2 Vols, 1. Jacobs, Wilbur R., ed. LC 60-8754. (Illus.). reprint ed. 54.00 (*0-8357-9730-9*, 2010100) Bks Demand.

— Letters of Francis Parkman, 2 Vols, 2. Jacobs, Wilbur R., ed. LC 60-8754. (Illus.). reprint ed. 65.00 (*0-685-07758-6*) Bks Demand.

— Montcalm & Wolfe: The French & Indian War. (Illus.). 674p. 1995. reprint ed. pap. 18.95 (*0-306-80621-5*) Da Capo.

— Oregon Trail. (Airmont Classics Ser.). (J). (gr. 6 up). 1964. pap. 1.50 (*0-8049-0037-X*, CL-37) Airmont.

— The Oregon Trail. Feltskog, E. N., ed. (Illus.). 874p. 1994. pap. 22.50 (*0-8032-8739-9*, Bison Books) U of Nebr Pr.

— The Oregon Trail. Feltskog, E. N., ed. LC 68-9017. 854p. reprint ed. pap. 180.00 (*0-317-42104-2*, 2025948) Bks Demand.

— Oregon Trail: The Sketches of Prairie & Rocky-Mountain Life. 479p. 1980. reprint ed. 25.00 (*0-87928-103-0*) Corner Hse.

Parkman, Francis, Jr. Oregon Trail. 288p. (J). 1950. pap. 4.95 (*0-451-52513-2*, Sig Classics) NAL-Dutton.

— The Oregon Trail. Levin, David, ed. (American Library). 1982. mass mkt. 9.95 (*0-14-039042-1*, Penguin Classics) Viking Penguin.

Parkman, Francis. The Oregon Trail & The Conspiracy of Pontiac. Taylor, William R., ed. 951p. 1991. 35.00 (*0-940450-54-2*) Library of America.

— Pioneers of France in the New World. 493p. 1970. reprint ed. 25.00 (*0-87928-017-4*) Corner Hse.

— Representative Selections. (BCL1-PS American Literature Ser.). 1993. reprint ed. lib. bdg. write for info. (*0-7812-6997-0*) Rprt Serv.

Parkman, Francis, Jr. La Salle & Discovery of Great West. 1990. pap. 9.50 (*0-679-72615-2*, Vin) Random.

Parkman, Francis. Some Reasons Against Woman Suffrage. Tanis, Norman E., ed. (Northridge Facsimile Ser.: Pt. VIII). 1977. pap. 10.00 (*0-937048-07-0*) CSUN.

— Works, 20 vols, Set. LC 69-19160. (Illus.). reprint ed. 1, 395.00 (*0-404-04920-6*) AMS Pr.

— Works, 12 vols., Set. (BCL1 - History - Canada Ser.). 1991. reprint ed. lib. bdg. 1,060.00 (*0-7812-6353-0*) Rprt Serv.

Parkman, Francis, intro. Historical Account of Bouquet's Expedition Against the Ohio Indians in 1764. (Illus.). 162p. 1993. reprint ed. lib. bdg. 25.00 (*0-8328-3000-3*) Higginson Bk Co.

Parkman, Mary R. Fighters for Peace. LC 73-167399. (Essay Index Reprint Ser.). 1977. reprint ed. 23.95 (*0-8369-2439-8*) Ayer.

— Heroines of Service. LC 68-58808. (Essay Index Reprint Ser.). 1977. 23.95 (*0-8369-1152-0*) Ayer.

— High Adventurers. LC 67-26770. (Essay Index Reprint Ser.). 1977. 20.95 (*0-8369-0770-1*) Ayer.

Parkman, Patricia. Insurrectionary Civic Strikes in Latin America: 1931-1961. (Monograph Ser.). 55p. 1990. 3.00 (*1-880813-00-9*) A Einstein Inst.

— Nonviolent Insurrection in El Salvador: The Fall of Maximiliano Hernandez Martinez. LC 88-9432. 165p. 1988. 28.95 (*0-8165-1062-8*) U of Ariz Pr.

Parkman, R. The Cybernetic Society. 402p. (C). 1973. 167.00 (*0-08-016949-X*, Pub. by Pergamon Repr UK) Franklin.

Parkoff, Eliezer. Fine Lines of Faith. LC 93-48518. 1994. 18.95 (*0-87306-669-3*) Feldheim.

Parkosewich, Paul R. A Mid-Level Practitioner's Guide to Correctional Medicine. LC 83-61416. 80p. (Orig.). 1983. spiral bd., pap. 3.50 (*0-9611870-0-X*) Neo Med Pub.

Parks. Pastors As Artists. Date not set. 18.00 (*0-06-066447-9*, HarpT) HarpC.

Parks & Wiseman. Maryland: Unity in Diversity - Essays on Maryland Life & Culture. 224p. 1989. per., pap. text ed. 16.95 (*0-8403-5674-9*) Kendall-Hunt.

Parks, A. Marine Insurance & Average: The Law & Practice, 2 Vols. (C). 1988. 1,145.00 (*0-685-45042-2*, Pub. by Witherby & Co UK) St Mut.

Parks, A. Franklin, et al. Structuring Paragraphs: A Guide to Effective Writing. 3rd ed. LC 89-63925. 256p. (C). 1991. pap. text ed. 21.00 (*0-312-03506-3*); pap. text ed. 0.40 (*0-312-05586-2*) St Martin.

Parks, Aileen W. Davy Crockett: Young Rifleman. LC 86-10781. (Childhood of Famous Americans Ser.). (Illus.). 192p. (J). (gr. 2-6). 1986. reprint ed. pap. 3.95 (*0-02-041840-X*, Aladdin Paperbacks) S&S Childrens.

Parks, Alex L. The Law & Practice of Marine Insurance & Average, 2 vols. LC 87-13667. 1700p. 1987. text ed. 190.00 (*0-87033-368-2*) Cornell Maritime.

Parks, Alex L. & Cattell, Edward V., Jr. Law of Tug, Tow & Pilotage. 3rd ed. 1410p. 1994. text ed. 175.00x (*0-87033-448-4*) Cornell Maritime.

Parks, Annette W. Qhawalali: Water Coming down Place; a History of Gualala, Mendocino County; California. LC 80-82462. (Illus.). 150p. 1981. 24.95 (*0-9605550-0-5*) FreshCut.

Parks, Anthony D. I Poet: Stories That Rhyme. McDonald, W. W., ed. 160p. 1992. text ed. 11.95 (*0-9635350-0-5*) Joy Voyage.

Parks, Arnold G. Black Elderly in Rural America: A Comprehensive Study. LC 88-40246. (Illus.). 345p. (C). 1988. text ed. 39.95 (*0-685-29607-5*); pap. text ed. 29.95 (*1-55605-054-2*) Wyndhall Pr.

Parks, Arva M. Harry Truman & the Little White House in Key West. LC 93-144349. (Illus.). 63p. 1991. pap. 4.95 (*0-9629402-0-8*) Centennial Pr.

— Miami: The Magic City. 2nd ed. LC 91-75436. (Illus.). 256p. 1991. 39.95 (*0-9629402-2-4*) Centennial Pr.

— Miami: Then & Now. LC 92-85502. (Illus.). 64p. 1992. pap. 4.95 (*0-9629402-1-6*) Centennial Pr.

Parks, B. J. Frogs, Hogs, & Memories. LC 90-71952. 222p. 1991. pap. 7.95 (*1-55523-414-3*) Winston-Derek.

***Parks, Barbara.** Barbara Parks Series. Date not set. 24.98 (*0-679-87019-9*) Random.

Parks, Barbara, jt. auth. see Catron, Carol.

Parks, Barbara A., jt. auth. see Johnson, Dewayne J.

Parks, Betsy M. The Dictionary of Initials. 1981. 12.95 (*0-8065-0750-0*, Citadel Pr) Carol Pub Group.

Parks, Brenda, ed. see Smith, Doris M.

Parks, Carol. Complete Book of Window Treatments & Curtains: Traditional & Innovative Ways to Dress Up Your Windows. LC 93-39113. 143p. 1990. 24.95 (*0-8069-0612-X*) Sterling.

— Complete Book of Window Treatments & Curtains: Traditional & Innovative Ways to Dress up Your Windows. (Illus.). 144p. 1995. pap. 14.95 (*0-8069-0613-8*) Sterling.

— Home Decorating with Fabric: More Than Eighty Projects from Cushions to Comforters. LC 95-4590. (Illus.). 144p. 1995. 27.95 (*0-8069-3158-2*, Lark Bks) Sterling.

— Make Your Own Great Vests: 90 Ways to Jazz up Your Wardrobe. LC 94-35537. (Illus.). 160p. 1995. 24.95 (*0-8069-0972-2*) Sterling.

— Sewing the New Classics: Clothes with Easy Style. LC 95-20037. (Illus.). 160p. 1995. 27.95 (*0-8069-3193-0*, Lark Bks) Sterling.

Parks, Clark. Traveling I-80 with Otto: Travel Guide. 3rd ed. 384p. 1993. pap. text ed. 12.95 (*1-878959-01-8*) Trav Guide Pubns.

Parks, Clark K. Traveling I-80 with Otto. 2nd ed. 288p. 1992. pap. 9.95 (*0-685-59727-X*) Trav Guide Pubns.

Parks, Craig, jt. auth. see Komorita, Samuel S.

Parks, David. GI Diary. (Howard University Press Library of Contemporary Literature). 133p. 1984. pap. 9.95 (*0-88258-113-9*) Howard U Pr.

Parks, David C. Environmental Management for Real Estate Professionals. LC 91-45631. (Illus.). 225p. 1992. text ed. 44.95 (*0-944298-69-9*, 763) Inst Real Estate.

— A Guide to CFC Reclamation & Retrofit. 15p. 1992. pap. 24.95 (*0-685-71670-8*, 887) Inst Real Estate.

***Parks, Deborah.** Climb Away: Chasing the Dream. LC 95-8684. 1995. write for info. (*0-382-39093-8*); pap. write for info. (*0-382-39094-6*) Silver Burdett Pr.

Parks, Don & Dyer, William. Jo. 1964. pap. 4.75 (*0-8222-0592-0*) Dramatists Play.

Parks, Douglas R. Traditional Narratives of the Arikara Indians, 2 vols. (Studies in the Anthropology of North American Indians). 1991. audio 20.00 (*0-8032-3697-2*) U of Nebr Pr.

— Traditional Narratives of the Arikara Indians, 2 vols., Set. (Studies in the Anthropology of North American Indians). 1991. 125.00 (*0-8032-3693-X*) U of Nebr Pr.

— Traditional Narratives of the Arikara Indians, 2 vols., Set. LC 90-12889. (Studies in the Anthropology of North American Indians). (Illus.). 1991. 75.00 (*0-8032-3696-4*) U of Nebr Pr.

— Traditional Narratives of the Arikara Indians, 2 vols., Vol. 1: Stories of Alfred Morsette. (Studies in the Anthropology of North American Indians). xxiv, 684p. 1991. 70.00 (*0-8032-3691-3*) U of Nebr Pr.

— Traditional Narratives of the Arikara Indians, 2 vols., Vol. 2: Stories of Other Narrators. (Studies in the Anthropology of North American Indians). xiv, 659p. 1991. 70.00 (*0-8032-3692-1*) U of Nebr Pr.

— Traditional Narratives of the Arikara Indians, 2 vols., Vol. 3: Stories of Alfred Morsette. LC 90-12889. (Studies in the Anthropology of North American Indians). (Illus.). 468p. 1991. 40.00 (*0-8032-3694-8*) U of Nebr Pr.

— Traditional Narratives of the Arikara Indians, 2 vols., Vol. 4: Stories of Other Narrators. LC 90-12889. (Studies in the Anthropology of North American Indians). (Illus.). xvii, 431p. 1991. 40.00 (*0-8032-3695-6*) U of Nebr Pr.

Parks, Douglas R., jt. ed. see DeMallie, Raymond J.

Parks, Douglas R., ed. see Murie, James R.

Parks-Doyle, Jodi, jt. ed. see Bayles, Patricia.

Parks, E. Taylor. Colombia & the United States. LC 77-111728. (American Imperialism: Viewpoints of United States Foreign Policy, 1898-1941 Ser.). 1970. reprint ed. 34.95 (*0-405-02043-0*) Ayer.

— Colombia & the United States, 1765-1934. (History - United States Ser.). 554p. 1993. reprint ed. lib. bdg. 99.00 (*0-7812-4865-5*) Rprt Serv.

Parks, E. Taylor, ed. see Anderson, Richard C.

Parks, Edd W. Henry Timrod. (Twayne's United States Authors Ser.). 1964. pap. 13.95 (*0-8084-0154-8*, T53) NCUP.

— Southern Poets. LC 74-93251. 567p. (C). 1970. reprint ed. 75.00 (*0-87753-032-7*) Phaeton.

— Teddy Roosevelt: Young Rough Rider. LC 89-37819. (Childhood of Famous Americans Ser.). (Illus.). 192p. (J). (gr. 2-6). 1989. reprint ed. pap. 3.95 (*0-689-71349-5*, Aladdin Paperbacks) S&S Childrens.

Parks, Edilbert P. The Roman Rhetorical Schools As Preparation for the Courts Under the Early Empire. LC 78-64198. (Johns Hopkins University. Studies in the Social Sciences. Thirtieth Ser. 1912: 2). reprint ed. 16.00 (*0-404-61304-7*) AMS Pr.

***Parks, Edward.** The Apartment Hunter's Guide: Boston: How to Find Your Perfect Apartment for No Money. LC 95-60224. (Illus.). 96p. (Orig.). 1995. pap. 7.95 (*0-9645575-0-9*) Tri Light Pub Grp.

Parks, Edwin. Diex Aix: God Help Us: The Guernseymen Who Marched Away 1914-1918. 188p. 1993. pap. text ed. 15.00 (*1-871560-85-3*) A Sutton Pub.

***Parks, F. Newton.** Happiness Is Shooting Your Age. 1994. pap. 11.95 (*0-89876-213-8*) Gardner Pr.

Parks, F. S. Genealogy of the Parke Family of Connecticut; Including Robert of New London, Edward of Guilford & Others: Also a List of Parke, Park, Parks, Etc. Who Fought in the Revolution. (Illus.). 333p. 1989. reprint ed. lib. bdg. 58.00 (*0-8328-0932-2*); reprint ed. pap. 50.00 (*0-8328-0933-0*) Higginson Bk Co.

***Parks-Flack, Carla.** Tarot 2000: Lifting the Veil of Illusion, Incls. 72 cards. (Illus.). 201p. 1995. text ed. 24.95 (*1-885499-52-3*) Angelight.

Parks, Fred. Fred Parks Guide to Gaming & Fun. 127p. (Orig.). 1988. pap. 9.95 (*0-9620980-0-0*) Parks Pub.

Parks, Frederick J. The Celebrated Oyster House Cookbook. LC 85-221680. (Illus.). 65p. (Orig.). 1985. pap. 9.95 (*0-911403-28-0*, F J Parks) Seven Hills Bk.

Parks, George B., ed. see Thomas, William.

Parks, George K. Physics of Space Plasmas. (Illus.). 538p. (C). 1991. 47.95 (*0-201-50821-4*, Adv Bk Prog) Addison-Wesley.

Parks, Gordon. Arias in Silence. LC 93-47352. (Illus.). 128p. 1994. 40.00 (*0-8212-2120-5*) Bulfinch Pr.

— A Choice of Weapons. LC 86-17993. xiv, 274p. 1986. reprint ed. pap. 10.95 (*0-87351-202-2*, Borealis Book) Minn Hist.

— The Learning Tree. 1987. mass mkt. 4.95 (*0-449-21504-0*, Crest) Fawcett.

— Voices in the Mirror: An Autobiography. 368p. 1992. pap. 12.95 (*0-385-26699-5*, Anchor NY) Doubleday.

Parks, Greg. Freedom, Justice, & Equality: The Teachings of the Nation of Islam. 48p. (Orig.). 1992. pap. 4.95 (*1-56411-023-0*) Untd Bros & Sis.

Parks, H. R. Explicit Determination of Area Minimizing Hypersurfaces, II. LC 86-1039. (Memoirs of the AMS Ser.: No. 60/342). 90p. 1986. pap. text ed. 18.00 (*0-8218-2339-6*, MEMO 60/342) Am Math.

Parks, Harold R., jt. auth. see Krantz, Steven G.

Parks, J. E., jt. ed. see Miller, C.

Parks, J. S., jt. ed. see Laron, Z.

Parks, James D. Robert S. Duncanson: Nineteenth Century Black Romantic Painter. (YA). 1990. 12.95 (*0-87498-011-9*) Assoc Pubs DC.

Parks, Janet, ed. Contemporary Architectural Drawings: Donations to the Avery Library Centennial Drawings Archive. LC 91-4216. (Illus.). 143p. 1991. 35.00 (*0-87654-767-6*); pap. 24.95 (*0-87654-766-8*) Pomegranate Calif.

Parks, Janet, jt. ed. see Wright, Gwendolyn.

Parks, Janet B. & Zanger, Beverly R., eds. Sport & Fitness Management: Career Strategies & Professional Skills. LC 89-71722. (Illus.). 288p. (C). 1990. text ed. 40.00 (*0-87322-269-5*, BPAR0269) Human Kinetics.

Parks, Jerald. False Security: Has the New Age Given Us a False Hope? LC 92-73708. 208p. 1992. pap. 9.99 (*1-56384-012-X*) Huntington Hse.

Parks, Joe E. Christmas Around the World. (J). 1981. 4.95 (*0-685-68526-8*, MC-45); audio 10.98 (*0-685-68527-6*, TA-9034C) Lillenas.

— Rejoice, O Earth. 1974. 5.25 (*0-685-68501-2*, MC-29) Lillenas.

Parks, John. Breeding Better Beagles. (Illus.). 96p. 1990. pap. 6.95 (*0-936369-49-3*) Son Rise Pubns.

Parks, John G. E. L. Doctorow. (Literature & Life Ser.). 192p. 1990. 19.95 (*0-8264-0488-X*, F Ungar Bks) Continuum.

Parks, Joseph H. General Edmund Kirby Smith, C.S.A. (Southern Biography Ser.). (Illus.). 537p. 1992. pap. 16.95 (*0-8071-1800-1*) La State U Pr.

— General Leonidas Polk, C.S.A. The Fighting Bishop. LC 62-15028. (Southern Biography Ser.). (Illus.). 408p. 1992. pap. 16.95 (*0-8071-1801-X*) La State U Pr.

Parks, Joyce. Single, but Not Sorry. 2nd rev. ed. 235p. 1986. pap. 6.95 (*0-89084-307-4*) Bob Jones Univ Pr.

Parks, Judith A. Biology Laboratory Manual for Majors. 184p. 1992. spiral bd. 16.95 (*0-8403-8072-0*) Kendall-Hunt.

Parks, K. S. Human Reliability: Analysis, Prediction, & Prevention of Human Errors. (Advances in Human Factors-Ergonomics Ser.: No. 7). 340p. 1987. 110.25 (*0-444-42727-9*) Elsevier.

Parks, Kathy, jt. auth. see Lichty, Tom.

Parks, Lloyd C., tr. see Stendhal.

Parks, Lois F., ed. see Chivers, Thomas Holley.

Parks, M. G., ed. see Howe, Joseph.

Parks, Marjorie M., jt. ed. see Harvey, John H.

Parks, Marty. All Hail King Jesus. 1991. 5.25 (*0-8341-9205-5*, ME-41); audio 10.98 (*0-685-68615-9*, TA-9138C) Lillenas.

Parks, Mercer H. The Task Worthy of Travail. LC 74-11835. 527p. 1975. 19.00 (*0-87201-784-2*) Gulf Pub.

Parks, Michael E. The Art Teacher's Desktop Reference. LC 93-8104. 272p. 1994. pap. text ed. 44.00 (*0-13-052234-1*) P-H.

Parks, Pat. The Railroad That Died at Sea: The Florida East Coast's Key West Extension. LC 68-54448. (Illus.). 48p. 1986. reprint ed. pap. 6.95 (*0-911607-05-6*) Langley Pr Inc.

Parks, Patrick & Hahn, Volker. Stability Theory. LC 92-18501. (International Systems & Control Engineering Ser.). 1993. text ed. 50.00 (*0-13-834045-5*) P-H.

***Parks, Penny.** Counsellor's Guide to Parks Inner Child Therapy. 1995. pap. 14.95 (*0-285-63172-1*, Pub. by Souvenir UK) Atrium Pubs.

Parks, R. E. Large Optics II. 1992. 42.00 (*0-8194-0755-0*) SPIE.

Parks, R. E., jt. ed. see Arnold, J. B.

Parks, Randolph W., et al, eds. Neuropsychology of Alzheimer's Disease & Other Dementias. LC 92-49274. (Illus.). 698p. 1993. 75.00 (*0-19-506612-X*) OUP.

Parks, Richard M., ed. Manual on the Use of Thermocouples in Temperature Measurement. LC 92-47237. (Manual Ser.: No. MNL 12). (Illus.). 311p. 1993. text ed. 49.00 (*0-8031-1466-4*, 28-012093-40) ASTM.

Parks, Richard S. The Music of Claude Debussy. 360p. (C). 1990. text ed. 42.00 (*0-300-04439-9*) Yale U Pr.

Parks, Rick. The Classical Organist, Vol. 2. 1987. 8.95 (*0-685-71345-8*, MB-583) Lillenas.

Parks, Rick, contrib. The Classical Organist, Vol. 3. 1989. 8.95 (*0-8341-9132-6*, MB-607) Lillenas.

— The Classical Organist, Vol.1. 1985. 8.95 (*0-8341-9236-5*, MB-550) Lillenas.

— Organ Exaltation. 1982. 7.95 (*0-8341-9234-9*, MB-503) Lillenas.

— Organ Praises. 1983. 7.95 (*0-685-68342-7*, MB-524) Lillenas.

Parks, Rick, des. The Classical Organist, Vol. 4. 1994. 8.95 (*0-8341-9029-X*, MB-675) Lillenas.

Parks, Rita. The Western Hero in Film & Television: Mass Media Mythology. LC 81-21826. (Studies in Cinema: No. 10). 198p. reprint ed. pap. 56.50 (*0-8357-1287-7*, 2070675) Bks Demand.

P Q

An Asterisk (*) at the beginning of an entry indicates that the title is appearing in BIP for the first time.

*Parks, Robert, et al. From Jackson to Lincoln: Democracy & Dissent. (Illus.). 80p. (Orig.). 1995. pap. text ed. 25.95 (0-8122-1577-X) U of Pa Pr.

*Parks, Robert H. The Witch Doctor of Wall Street: A Noted Financial Expert Guides You Through Today's Voodoo Economics. 335p. 1996. 25.95 (1-57392-018-5) Prometheus Bks.

Parks, Robert J. European Origins of the Economic Ideas of Alexander Hamilton. Bruchey, Stuart, ed. LC 76-39838. (Nineteen Seventy-Seven Dissertations Ser.). 1977. lib. bdg. 23.95 (0-405-09918-5) Ayer.

*Parks, Roger, ed. Bibliographies of New England History No. 9: Additions to 1994. (Bibliographies of New England History Ser.). 324p. 1995. text ed. 40.00 (0-87451-714-1) U Pr of New Eng.

— Connecticut: A Bibliography of Its History. LC 85-40931. (Bibliographies of New England History Ser.: No. 6). 635p. 1986. text ed. 70.00 (0-87451-361-8) U Pr of New Eng.

— New England: A Bibliography of Its History. LC 89-40231. (Bibliographies of New England History Ser.: Vol. 7). 317p. 1989. text ed. 40.00 (0-87451-496-7) U Pr of New Eng.

— New England: Additions to the Six State Bibliographies. LC 89-40232. (Bibliographies of New England History Ser.: Vol. 8). 800p. 1989. text ed. 80.00 (0-87451-497-5) U Pr of New Eng.

— Rhode Island: A Bibliography of Its History. LC 83-50139. (Bibliographies of New England History Ser.: No. 5). 263p. 1983. text ed. 40.00 (0-87451-284-0) U Pr of New Eng.

Parks, Roger N., jt. ed. see Conrad, Dennis M.

Parks, Rosa. Rosa Parks: My Story. Haskins, Jim. LC 89-1124. (Illus.). 200p. (J). 1992. 17.00 (0-8037-0673-1) Dial Bks Young.

*Parks, Rosa & Reed, Gregory J. Quiet Strength: The Faith, the Hope, & the Heart of a Woman Who Changed a Nation. LC 94-46141. 1995. 12.99 (0-310-50150-4) Zondervan.

Parks, Roy, jt. auth. see Wireman, Terry.

Parks, Ruth. Playing Beatie Bow. LC 81-8097. 208p. (J). (gr. 5-9). 1982. text ed. 14.95 (0-689-30889-2, Atheneum Bks Young) S&S Childrens.

Parks, Ruth M. Treacle on the Tongue. Egan, Roger E., Sr., ed. (Illus.). 80p. (Orig.). 1994. pap. 12.00 (0-9632687-3-2) PenRose Pub.

Parks, Sandy, jt. auth. see Miller, Ruth.

*Parks, Sarah T. APlus Certification Success Guide: For Computer Technicians. 1995. pap. text ed. 29.95 (0-07-048596-8) McGraw.

Parks, Sharon, jt. ed. see Dykstra, Craig.

*Parks, Stephanie, ed. Help: When the Parent is Handicapped. braille ed. 1481p. 1991. text ed. 118.48 (1-56956-501-5, BR8362) W A T Braille.

Parks, Stephen. The Elizabethan Club of Yale University & Its Library. LC 86-7789. 280p. 1986. text ed. 42.00 (0-300-03669-8) Yale U Pr.

Parks, Stephen M. Jim Wagner, Taos: An American Artist. LC 93-5732. (Illus.). 264p. 1993. 87.50 (0-9636890-0-2) Rancho Milagro. LIBRARY JOURNAL: "One of the finest contemporary interpreters of the region's ethos, Wagner was influenced by the multicultural roots--European, Native American, & Hispanic--of New Mexican arts...his art conveys a range of emotions from whimsy to satire. A subjective study of the artist & his more than 40-year career...richly evocative, telling the reader a great deal more than factual studies...this book is a fascinating, well-illustrated story of a man who knows how to live an artist's life to its fullest extent & celebrate his environment in the bargain. A worthwhile acquisition for public & academic libraries of the Southwest." THE SANTA FE NEW MEXICAN: "Whether people like art or not, they're relating to this book." NEW MEXICO MAGAZINE: "thorough & enchanting..." JIM WAGNER, TAOS contains 230 color plates, 48 black & white photographs, a chronology, bibliography, & registry of 2,343 pieces of Wagner's art. Its pages measure 12" by 10" & are acid free, stitched & hardcover bound. Shipping is via UPS @ $5.50 per book. To order by telephone (MasterCard & Visa only) please call (505) 776-1651. Please send mail orders (prepaid) to Rancho Milagro Productions, P.O. Box 767, Taos, NM 87571. *Publisher Provided Annotation.*

Parks, Susan H., jt. auth. see Pilisuk, Marc.

Parks, Suzan-Lori. The America Play. 1995. pap. 4.75 (0-8222-1423-7) Dramatists Play.

— The American Play & Other Works. 208p. 1995. pap. 14.95 (1-55936-092-5) Theatre Comm.

Parks, Taylor E. Colombia & the United States. 1976. lib. bdg. 59.95 (0-8490-1644-4) Gordon Pr.

Parks, Thomas W., jt. auth. see Burrus, C. S.

Parks, Tim. Family Planning. 288p. 1991. pap. 11.95 (0-8021-3243-X) Grove-Atltic.

— Goodness: A Novel. 1993. pap. 9.95 (0-8021-3304-5) Grove-Atltic.

— An Italian Education: The Further Adventures of an Expatriate in Verona. 352p. 1994. 22.00 (0-8021-1508-X, Grove) Grove-Atltic.

— Italian Neighbors: Or, a Lapsed Anglo-Saxon in Verona. 288p. 1993. pap. 10.00 (0-449-90818-6, Columbine) Fawcett.

— Juggling the Stars. large type ed. LC 93-13512. 1993. 21.95 (0-7927-1642-6, Curley Lrg Print); pap. 19.95 (0-7927-1641-8, Curley Lrg Print) Chivers N Amer.

— Shear. 224p. 1994. 21.00 (0-8021-1552-7) Grove-Atltic.

Parks, Tim, tr. see Calvino, Italo.

Parks, Tim, tr. see Jaeggy, Fleur.

Parks, Tim, tr. see Moravia, Alberto.

Parks, Tim, tr. see Tabucchi, Antonio.

Parks, Tom. The Promise of the Faraway Flower. 96p. (C). 1993. boxed 9.95 (0-8403-8780-6) Kendall-Hunt.

Parks, Virginia. Pensacola: Spaniards to Space Age. (Illus.). 128p. 1986. 9.95 (0-939566-04-4) Pensacola Hist.

Parks, Virginia & Bense, Judith A. Underground Pensacola. (Illus.). 96p. (C). 1989. lib. bdg. write for info. (0-318-65197-1) Pensacola Archaeol.

Parks, Virginia & Bowden, Jesse E. Siege. (Society Quarterly Ser.: Vol. II, Nos. 2 & 3). (Illus.). 92p. (Orig.). 1981. pap. 5.00 (0-939566-00-1) Pensacola Hist.

*Parks, W. Crime & the Law. 1994. pap. 42.00 (0-409-30518-9, Austral) Butterworth Legal Pubs.

Parks, W., jt. auth. see Boulle, L.

*Parks, Walter P. The Miracle of Mata Ortiz: Juan Quezada & the Potters of Northern Chihuahua. 142p. 1994. pap. 19.95 (0-9637655-0-7) Coulter Pr.

Parks, Ward. Verbal Dueling in Heroic Narrative: The Homeric & Old English Traditions. 232p. 1990. text ed. 35.00 (0-691-06780-5) Princeton U Pr.

Parkside Publication Inc. Staff. Quick 'N Easy Country Cookin' Best of 1992-1993. Schrag, Pam, ed. 106p. 1994. pap. 6.95 (0-9618379-7-7) Parkside Pubns.

Parkus, H. Thermoelasticity. 2nd enl. rev. ed. 1976. pap. 36.00 (0-387-81375-6) Spr-Verlag.

Parkus, H., ed. Electromagnetic Interactions in Elastic Solids. (CISM Courses & Lectures Ser.: Vol. 257). (Illus.). 425p. 1979. pap. 51.00 (0-387-81509-0) Spr-Verlag.

Parkus, H., ed. see CISM (International Center for Mechanical Sciences).

Parkyn, Herbert A. Auto-Suggestion. 190p. 1993. pap. 15.00 (0-89540-199-1, SB-199) Sun Pub.

Parkyns, Mansfield. Life in Abyssinia: Being Notes Collected During Three Years' Residence & Travels in That Country. (Illus.). 446p. 1966. 45.00 (0-7146-1844-6, Pub. by F Cass Pubs UK) Intl Spec Bk.

Parlagreco, C. Dizionario Portoghese-Italiano, Italiano-Portoghese: Portuguese-Italian, Italian-Portuguese Dictionary. 1138p. (ITA & POR.). 1979. 49.95 (0-8288-4736-3, M9183) Fr & Eur.

Parlakian, Nishan, tr. see Asadour, Zabel.

Parlakian, Nishan, tr. see Shirvanzade, Alexandre.

Parland, Oscar. The Enchanted Way. Tate, Joan, tr. 202p. 1991. 32.00 (0-7206-0829-5, Pub. by P Owen Ltd UK) Dufour.

— The Year of the Bull. Tate, Joan, ed. 198p. 1991. 31.00 (0-7206-0807-4, Pub. by P Owen Ltd UK) Dufour.

Parlar, H., jt. auth. see Scheunert, I.

Parlato, Salvatore. America from A to Z. Freifeld, Art, ed. (Illus.). 161p. (C). 1989. student ed, pap. text ed. 14.95 (0-916177-67-X) Am Eng Pubns.

Parlato, Salvatore J., Jr. Superfilms: An International Guide to Award Winning Educational Films. LC 76-10801. 365p. 1976. 26.00 (0-8108-0953-2) Scarecrow.

Parlatore, Anselm. The Circa Poems. 1975. pap. 5.00 (0-685-56281-6) Stone-Marrow Pr.

— Hybrid Inoculum. LC 75-302485. 66p. 1974. 3.45 (0-87886-049-5, Greenfld Rev Pr) Greenfld Rev Lit.

— Provisions. 1971. pap. 5.00 (0-685-90032-0) Stone-Marrow Pr.

Parle, G. J. Two Were Prisoners. 493p. 1986. 35.00 (0-7223-1941-X, Pub. by A H S Ltd UK) St Mut.

Parlett, David. A Dictionary of Card Games. (Oxford Paperback Reference). (Illus.). 400p. 1992. pap. 12.95 (0-19-869173-4) OUP.

— Oxford Guide to Card Games. (Illus.). 382p. 1990. 35.00 (0-19-214165-1) OUP.

— The Oxford Guide to Card Games. (Illus.). 384p. 1991. reprint ed. pap. 13.95 (0-19-282905-X) OUP.

— Patience Games: Card Games. (Know the Game Ser.). (Illus.). 1976. pap. 2.50 (0-7158-0501-0) Charles River Bks.

Parlett, David, tr. & intro. Selections from the "Carmina Burana" A Verse Translation. 336p. 1986. pap. 8.95 (0-14-044440-8, Penguin Classics) Viking Penguin.

Parlett, David, tr. see Bachmann, MArie L.

*Parlett, Isabel. Cracking the SAT II: French Subject Test, 1996 Edition. (Princeton Review Ser.). 1995. student ed, pap. 17.00 (0-679-75916-6) Random.

— Princeton Review Cracking the SAT II: French 1995 Edition. 1994. pap. 16.00 (0-679-75358-3, Villard Bks) Random.

Parlett, K. Teach Yourself Card Games for Two. (Teach Yourself Ser.). 1980. pap. 7.95 (0-679-12054-8) McKay.

Parlett, Malcolm & Dearden, Garry, eds. Introduction to Illuminative Evaluation: Studies in Higher Education. 1977. pap. text ed. 7.95 (0-937012-10-6) Coun Indep Colleges.

Parlette, Ralph. The University of Hard Knocks. 1966. 8.99 (0-915720-05-1); 8.99 (0-915720-03-5) Brownlow Pub Co.

Parlevliet, J. E., jt. ed. see Jacobs, Thomas.

Parley, Peter, pseud. Recollections of a Lifetime: or, Men & Things I Have Seen, 2 vols., Set. (American Biography Ser.). 1991. reprint ed. lib. bdg. 148.00 (0-7812-8149-0) Rprt Serv.

Parliamentary Debates, Great Britain Staff. Report from the Select Committee on the High Price of Gold Bullion. Wilkins, Mira, ed. LC 78-3915. (International Finance Ser.). 1979. reprint ed. lib. bdg. 33.95 (0-405-11219-X) Ayer.

*Parlier, Jaki. Poking Holes in the Darkness. 192p. 1994. pap. 8.95 (0-939497-34-4) Promise Pub.

Parliment, Thomas H. & Croteau, Rodney, eds. Biogeneration of Aromas. LC 86-3534. (ACS Symposium Ser.: No. 317). (Illus.). ix, 399p. 1986. 82.95 (0-8412-0987-1) Am Chemical.

Parliment, Thomas H., et al, eds. Thermally Generated Flavors: Maillard, Microwave, & Extrusion Processes. LC 93-36609. (ACS Symposium Ser.: No. 543). (Illus.). 492p. 1994. 109.95 (0-8412-2742-X) Am Chemical.

Parlin, Andrew, jt. auth. see Harper, John L.

Parlin, Andrew, jt. auth. see Harper, John.

Parlin, John. Amelia Earhart. (Illus.). 80p. 1991. pap. 3.50 (0-440-40117-8) Dell.

— Amelia Earhart: Pioneer in the Sky. (Discovery Biographies Ser.). (Illus.). 80p. (J). (gr. 2-6). 1992. reprint ed. lib. bdg. 12.95 (0-7910-1437-1) Chelsea Hse.

— Andrew Jackson: Pioneer & President. (Discovery Biographies Ser.). (Illus.). 80p. (J). (gr. 2-6). 1991. reprint ed. lib. bdg. 12.95 (0-7910-1442-8) Chelsea Hse.

Parloff, Morris B., ed. see Conference on Research in Psychotherapy Staff.

Parlor, Randy E. Common Sense: Receiving God's Financial Promises. LC 93-90574. 120p. (Orig.). 1993. student ed 10.00 (0-9637561-1-7); pap. 10.00 (0-9637561-0-9) Com Sense Christian.

Parlour, Margaret, illus. Vermont Kitchens Revisited. 288p. (Orig.). 1990. pap. 14.95 (0-9627253-0-7) VT Kitchen.

*Parlour, Richard. Butterworths Guide to International Money Laundering Laws. 223p. 1994. pap. text ed. 176.00 (0-406-03494-X, UK) Butterworth Legal Pubs.

Parlour, Richard R., jt. ed. see Jones, L. Ralph.

*Parma, Art. Biennial Flight Review. (Illus.). 62p. (Orig.). 1994. pap. 7.95 (0-9631973-0-4) Flight Time.

— Instrument Flight Refresher. (Flight Bay Ser.). (Illus.). 64p. (Orig.). 1995. pap. 8.95 (0-9631973-1-2) Flight Time.

— Student Pilot Handbook. (Illus.). 84p. (Orig.). 1992. reprint ed. pap. 9.95 (0-9631973-3-9) Flight Time.

Parma, S., jt. auth. see Gulati, Ramesh D.

Parma, Terra. Christmas Traditions in Glass. (Illus.). 52p. 1994. 10.95 (0-936459-25-5) Stained Glass.

— Floral Images by Terra. Stained Glass Images Inc. Staff, ed. (Illus.). 64p. 1987. 10.95 (0-936459-02-6) Stained Glass.

— Holiday Images. (Illus.). 52p. 1993. 10.95 (0-936459-19-0) Stained Glass.

— Images by Terra. Stained Glass Images, Inc. Staff, ed. (Illus.). 76p. 1986. pap. 10.95 (0-936459-00-X) Stained Glass.

— Images of Elegance. Stained Glass Images Inc. Staff, ed. (Illus.). 64p. 1988. 10.95 (0-936459-06-9) Stained Glass.

— Images of Nature. Stained Glass Images Inc. Staff, ed. (Illus.). 64p. 1988. 10.95 (0-936459-05-0) Stained Glass.

— Potpourri in Glass. Stained Glass Images Staff, ed. (Illus.). 52p. 1991. 10.95 (0-936459-16-6) Stained Glass.

— Stained Glass Bouquet. Stained Glass Images Inc. Staff, ed. (Illus.). 64p. 1989. text ed. 10.95 (0-936459-12-3) Stained Glass.

— The Stained Glass Gift Shoppe. Stained Glass Images Inc. Staff, ed. (Illus.). 1988. 10.95 (0-936459-08-5) Stained Glass.

— Ultimate Images. (Illus.). 52p. 1995. 10.95 (0-936459-28-X) Stained Glass.

Parmadale Christmas Committee. Beyond the Village Gate: Cookbook. (Illus.). 320p. 1985. 11.95 (0-9615123-0-X) Parmadale.

*Parmahans, Yogeshwaranand. First Steps to Higher Yoga: An Exposition of First Five Constituents of Yoga. Brahmachari, Bala & Shastri, Ram P., trs. xxxiv, 384p. 1985. 20.00 (0-614-06350-7, Pub. by Yoga Niketan II) Nataraj Bks.

— Himalaya Ka Yogi, 2 vols., Set. 1991. 30.00 (0-614-06356-6, Pub. by Yoga Niketan II) Nataraj Bks.

— Science of Divine Lights: A Latest Research on Self & God-Realization the of 154 Divine Lights. Kapoor, Devendra K., tr. xviii, 262p. 1991. 12.00 (0-614-06355-8, Pub. by Yoga Niketan II) Nataraj Bks.

— Science of Divinity. 480p. 1992. 20.00 (0-614-06351-5, Pub. by Yoga Niketan II) Nataraj Bks.

Parmakian, John. Waterhammer Analysis. 1955. pap. 6.95 (0-486-61061-6) Dover.

Parmalee, Patty L. Brecht's America. LC 80-25857. 317p. 1981. 39.50 (0-8142-0307-8) Ohio St U Pr.

Parmalee, Paul W. Amphibians of Illinois. (Story of Illinois Ser.: No. 10). (Illus.). 38p. 1954. pap. 1.00 (0-89792-011-2) Ill St Museum.

Parmalee, Paul W. & Oesch, Ronald D. Pleistocene & Recent Faunas from the Brynjulfson Caves, Missouri. (Reports of Investigations Ser.: No. 25). (Illus.). 52p. 1972. pap. 2.00 (0-89792-049-X) Ill St Museum.

Parmalee, Paul W., jt. auth. see Paul, John R.

Parmalee, Paul W., et al. Animals Utilized by Woodland Peoples Occupying the Apple Creek Site, Illinois. (Reports of Investigations Ser.: No. 23). (Illus.). 62p. 1972. pap. 3.00 (0-89792-048-1) Ill St Museum.

— Pleistocene & Recent Vertebrate Faunas from Crankshaft Cave, Missouri. (Reports of Investigations Ser.: No.14). (Illus.). 37p. 1969. pap. 1.00 (0-89792-036-8) Ill St Museum.

Parman, Donald L. Indians & the American West in the Twentieth Century. LC 93-48060. (American West in the Twentieth Century Ser.). 1994. 29.95 (0-253-34289-9); pap. 12.92 (0-253-20892-0) Ind U Pr.

Parman, Ray, Jr. & Brown, Donald N. Rare & Unusual Artifacts of the First Americans. (Illus.). 296p. (Orig.). 1989. pap. 24.95 (0-9623868-0-4) F Pruett.

Parman, Susan. Dream & Culture: An Anthropological Study of the Western Intellectual Tradition. LC 90-7459. 144p. 1990. text ed. 39.95 (0-275-93230-3, C3230, Praeger Pubs) Greenwood.

— Scottish Crofters: A Historical Ethnography of a Celtic Village. Youngblood, Dawn, ed. LC 89-15392. (George & Louise Spindler Series in Anthropology). 160p. (C). 1990. pap. text ed. 13.50 (0-03-030754-6) HB Coll Pubs.

Parman, Susan, jt. ed. see Norbeck, Edward.

Parmann, Georg, jt. ed. see Bergesen, Helge O.

Parmann, Georg, jt. ed. see Bergesen, Helge O.

Parmar, H. A., jt. auth. see Taylor, S. E.

*Parmar, Inderjeet. Special Interests, the State & the Anglo-American Alliance, 1939-1945. LC 95-14432. 1995. write for info. (0-7146-4569-9, Pub. by F Cass Pubs UK) Intl Spec Bk.

*Parmar, Leena. Society, Culture & Military System. (C). 1995. 22.00x (81-7033-264-8, Pub. by Rawat II) S Asia.

Parmar, Mary. Development Planning in India. 1993. 30.00 (0-685-65106-1, Pub. by Reliance Pub Hse II) Apt Bks.

*Parmar, Pramila. Mithai: Collection of Traditional Indian Sweets. (C). 1994. 14.00 (81-85944-88-1, Pub. by UBS Pubs Dist II) S Asia.

Parmar, Pratibha, jt. auth. see O'Sullivan, Sue.

Parmar, Shyam. Folklore of Madhya Pradesh. 204p. 1972. 8.95 (0-318-36318-6) Asia Bk Corp.

Parmar, Y. A. The Mahyavanshi: The Success Story of a Scheduled Caste. 248p. (C). 1987. 27.00 (0-317-89483-8, Pub. by Mittal II) S Asia.

Parmasto, Erast & Parmesto, Ilmi. Variation of Basidiospores in the Hymenomycetes & Its Significance to Their Taxonomy. (Bibliotheca Mycologica Ser.: Vol. 115). (Illus.). 168p. 1987. pap. 56.00 (3-443-59016-0) Lubrecht & Cramer.

Parmee, D., ed. see Baudelaire, Charles P.

Parmee, Douglas, tr. see De Laclos, Choderlos.

Parmee, Douglas, tr. see De Maupassant, Guy.

Parmee, Douglas, ed. see Flaubert, Gustave.

Parmee, Douglas, tr. see Fontane, Theodor.

Parmee, Douglas, ed. see Zola, Emile.

Parmee, Douglas, tr. see Zola, Emile.

Parmee, Douglas, ed. see Zola, Emile.

Parmeggiani, Lougi, ed. Encyclopedia of Occupational Health & Safety 1983, 2 vols., Set. 3rd rev. ed. 1983. 240.00 (92-2-103289-2) Intl Labour Office.

Parmelee, Alice. All the Birds of the Bible. 1988. pap. 9.95 (0-87983-468-4) Keats.

— Guide to the New Testament. LC 79-87617. (All About the Bible Ser.: Bk. 3). (Illus.). 144p. 1980. pap. 4.00 (0-8192-1255-5) Morehouse Pub.

— Guide to the Old Testament & Apocrypha. LC 79-87618. (All About the Bible Ser.: Bk. 2). (Illus.). 150p. 1980. pap. 4.00 (0-8192-1254-7) Morehouse Pub.

Parmelee, Cullen W. & Harman, Cameron G. Ceramic Glazes. 3rd ed. LC 70-183371. (Illus.). 624p. reprint ed. text ed. 50.00 (1-878907-05-0, RAN) TechBooks.

Parmelee, David F. Antarctic Birds: An Ecological & Behavioral Approach (Exploration of Palmer Archipelago by an Artist-Ornithologist. (Illus.). 221p. (C). 1992. 39.95 (0-8166-2000-8) U of Minn Pr.

Parmelee, Deolece, jt. auth. see Henson, Margaret S.

Parmelee, Maurice. The Principles of Anthropology & Sociology in Their Relations to Criminal Procedure. viii, 410p. 1980. reprint ed. 30.00 (0-8377-1004-9) Rothman.

Parmenides of Elea. Parmenides of Elea: Fragments: A Text & Translation with an Introduction. Gallop, David, ed. (Phoenix Supplementary Volumes Ser.: Vol. XVIII; Pre-Socratics I). 160p. 1991. pap. 17.95 (0-8020-6908-8) U of Toronto Pr.

Parmenter, Barbara, tr. see Abouzeid, Leila.

Parmenter, Barbara M. Giving Voice to Stones: Place & Identity in Palestinian Literature. LC 94-8643. (Illus.). 128p. (C). 1994. text ed. 25.00 (0-292-72751-8); pap. 9.95 (0-292-76555-X) U of Tex Pr.

Parmenter, Barbara M., tr. see Al-Amir, Daisy.

Parmenter, Barbara M., jt. auth. see Doughty, Robin W.

Parmenter, C. O. History of Pelham, MA, from Seventeen Thirty-Eight to Eighteen Ninety-Eight, Including the Early History of Prescott. (Illus.). 531p. 1990. reprint ed. lib. bdg. 54.00 (0-8328-1638-8) Higginson Bk Co.

Parmenter, Fisher & Mallette Staff. Fisher: The Life of George Fisher (1795-1873) & the History of the Fisher Family in Mississippi. (Illus.). 299p. 1991. reprint ed. lib. bdg. 57.00 (0-8328-1905-0); reprint ed. pap. 47.00 (0-8328-1906-9) Higginson Bk Co.

Parmenter, Mary F. The Life of George Fisher. 1959. 10.00 (0-686-61037-7) Ragusan Pr.

Parmenter, Michael M. Theory of Interest & Life Contingencies, with Pension Applications: A Problem-Solving Approach. LC 88-38947. (Illus.). 246p. (Orig.). 1988. pap. text ed. 40.00 (0-936031-04-2) Actex Pubns.

Parmenter, Ross. D. H. Lawrence in Oaxaca: A Quest for the Novelist in Mexico. (Illus.). 384p. 1984. 22.95 (0-318-35420-9) Hawkshead Bk.

— Explorer, Linguist & Ethnologist: A Descriptive Bibliography of the Published Works of Alphonse Louis Pinart, with Notes on His Life. LC 66-24190. (Frederick Webb Hodge Publications: No. 9). (Illus.). 1966. 12.50 (0-916561-20-8) Southwest Mus.

— Four Lienzos of the Coixtlahuaca Valley. LC 82-4967. (Studies in Pre-Columbian Art & Archaeology: No. 26). (Illus.). 88p. 1982. pap. 15.00 (0-88402-109-2) Dumbarton Oaks.

— House for Buddha: A Memoir with Drawings. (Illus.). 540p. 1995. text ed. 35.00 (*1-885241-00-3*) Woodstock Pr.

— The Lienzo of Tulancingo: An Introductory Study of a Ninth Painted Sheet from the Coixtlahuaca Valley. LC 93-73287. (Transactions Ser.: Vol. 83, Pt. 7). (Illus.). 86p. (C). 1994. pap. 15.00 (*0-87169-837-4*, T827-PAR) Am Philos.

Parmenter, Ross, jt. ed. see Smith, Mary E.

Parmenter, Trevor. Bridges from School to Working Life for Handicapped Youth: The View from Australia. (Monograph Ser.: No. 33). 76p. 1986. pap. text ed. 2.00 (*0-939986-47-7*) World Rehab Fund.

Parmentier, L., jt. ed. see Bidez, J.

Parmentier, Michel A. Mise Au Point. 486p. (FRE.). (C). 1989. pap. text ed. 26.75 (*0-03-922556-9*); pap. text ed. 22.75 (*0-03-922572-0*) HB Coll Pubs.

***Parmentier, R. D. & Pedersen, N. F.** Nonlinear Superconducting Devices & High-Tc Materials: Proceedings of the International Conference. 492p. 1995. text ed. 150.00 (*981-02-2091-X*) World Scientific Pub.

Parmentier, R. D., jt. ed. see Christiansen, Peter L.

Parmentier, Richard A., jt. ed. see Mertz, Elizabeth.

Parmentier, Richard J. The Sacred Remains: Myth, History, & Polity in Belau. LC 87-6051. (Illus.). 368p. (Orig.). 1987. lib. bdg. 49.95 (*0-226-64695-5*) U Ch Pr.

— The Sacred Remains: Myth, History, & Polity in Belau. LC 87-6051. (Illus.). 368p. (Orig.). 1988. pap. text ed. 15.95 (*0-226-64696-3*) U Ch Pr.

— Signs in Society: Studies in Semiotic Anthropology. LC 93-27758. 1994. 35.00 (*0-253-32757-1*) Ind U Pr.

Parmer, H. A., jt. auth. see Taylor, S. E.

Parmer, J. Norman. Colonial Labor Policy & Administration 1910-1941. 6.00 (*0-685-71735-6*) J J Augustin.

Parmer, Jean M. & Parmer, Jerome F. Maritime Bibliography & Price Guide. 312p. (Orig.). 1994. pap. text ed. 49.95 (*0-685-58855-6*) Parmer Bks.

Parmer, Jerome F., jt. auth. see Parmer, Jean M.

Parmesto, Ilmi, jt. auth. see Parmasto, Erast.

Parmet, Robert D. Labor & Immigration in Industrial America. LC 86-15193. 268p. (C). 1987. reprint ed. pap. text ed. 15.50 (*0-89874-968-9*) Krieger.

Parmet, Robert D., jt. auth. see Leonard, Ira M.

Parmeter, J. R., ed. Rhizoctonia Solani: Biology & Pathology. LC 69-16510. (Illus.). (C). 1970. 52.50 (*0-520-01497-9*) U CA Pr.

Parmett, Doris. Risk. 336p. (Orig.). 1994. mass mkt. 4.99 (*0-515-11333-6*) Jove Pubns.

Parmigiani, Stefano & Von Saal, Frederick S., eds. Infanticide & Parental Care. LC 93-41749. (Ettore Majorana International Life Sciences Ser.: Vol. 13). 1994. text ed. 86.00 (*3-7186-5505-5*) Gordon & Breach.

Parmisano, Stan. Testament. LC 91-72452. 184p. (Orig.). 1991. pap. 6.95 (*0-87793-458-4*) Ave Maria.

***Parmley, Robert O.** Field Engineer's Manual. 2nd ed. 1995. pap. text ed. 44.50 (*0-07-048579-8*) McGraw.

— HVAC Design Data Sourcebook. 1994. text ed. 49.50 (*0-07-048572-0*) McGraw.

— HVAC Field Manual. 608p. 1988. text ed. 45.50 (*0-07-048524-0*) McGraw.

— Hydraulics Field Manual. LC 92-12036. 1992. text ed. 44.50 (*0-07-048556-9*) McGraw.

— Standard Handbook of Fastening & Joining. 2nd ed. 704p. 1989. text ed. 79.50 (*0-07-048522-4*) McGraw.

Parmley, William W., et al, eds. Cardiology, 2 vols. (Illus.). 2500p. Date not set. Set, Annual new page service. ring bd. 225.00 (*0-685-61017-9*, H3192S1) Lippincott.

Parnall, Peter. Apple Tree. LC 86-23730. (Illus.). 32p. (J). (gr. k-3). 1988. lib. bdg. 14.95 (*0-02-770160-3*, Mac Bks Young Read) S&S Childrens.

— Feet! LC 88-5272. (Illus.). 32p. (J). (ps-1). 1988. text ed. 14.95 (*0-02-770110-7*, Mac Bks Young Read) S&S Childrens.

— Marsh Cat. LC 90-25733. (Illus.). 128p. (J). (gr. 3 up). 1991. text ed. 13.95 (*0-02-770120-4*, Mac Bks Young Read) S&S Childrens.

— Quiet. LC 89-2847. (Illus.). 32p. (J). 1989. 13.95 (*0-688-08204-1*); lib. bdg. 13.88 (*0-688-08205-X*) Morrow Jr Bks.

— Spaces. LC 92-1712. (Illus.). 32p. (J). (gr. k-3). 1993. lib. bdg. 15.40 (*1-56294-336-7*) Millbrook Pr.

— Water Pup. LC 92-40850. (Illus.). 144p. (J). (gr. 3 up). 1993. text ed. 13.95 (*0-02-770151-4*, Mac Bks Young Read) S&S Childrens.

Parnaso. Diccionario Sopena De Literatura, 3 vols., Set. 1820p. (SPA.). 150.00 (*0-7859-0886-2*, S-50140) Fr & Eur.

Parnass, Barbara, ed. see Caldwell, Mark.

Parnau, Jeffery. The Handbook of Magazine Production. 1985. 59.95 (*0-918110-11-4*) Hanson Pub Grp.

Parnau, Jeffery R. Desktop Publishing: The Awful Truth. Lefevre, Ken, ed. 128p. 1989. pap. 19.95 (*0-9623020-0-7*) Parnau Graphics.

Parnavelas, John G., et al, eds. The Making of the Nervous System. (Illus.). 528p. 1988. 99.00 (*0-19-854224-0*) OUP.

Parncutt, R. Harmony: A Psychoacoustical Approach. (Information Sciences Ser.: Vol. 19). (Illus.). 225p. 1989. 69.00 (*0-387-51279-9*) Spr-Verlag.

Parnegg, Janee, jt. auth. see Larsen, Earnie.

Parnell, Allan M., jt. auth. see Kasarda, John D.

Parnell, Andrea. Devil Moon. 448p. 1994. mass mkt. 4.50 (*0-8217-4747-9*) Zebra.

— My Only Desire. 416p. 1993. mass mkt. 4.50 (*0-8217-4383-X*) Zebra.

— Small Town Secrets. 320p. 1993. mass mkt. 4.50 (*0-8217-4264-7*) Zebra.

***Parnell, Anthony D. In Search of Soul: A Collection of Poems. LC 94-74124. 57p. (Orig.). 1995. pap. 7.95 (*0-9644205-0-3*) Dreams & Visions.**

IN SEARCH OF SOUL is a collection of poems offering a unique perspective on male-female relationships. As presented through the eyes of a young African-American male, IN SEARCH OF SOUL provokes thought concerning aspirations to find a life companion - a soul mate, & simultaneously, to discover the beauty & depth of one's own soul. Part One, Looking For Love, includes poems that speak directly to everyday challenges experienced in maintaining romantic relationships: communication, understanding & acceptance. Part Two, In Search of Soul, includes poems concerning being at peace with one's ideas & beliefs about life while learning to love others. IN SEARCH OF SOUL appeals to adults of all ages who are romantic, tender-hearted & lovers of love. To order IN SEARCH OF SOUL, mail check or money order to Dreams & Visions Publishing, P.O. Box 6767, Altadena, CA 91003. Please enclose $2.00 to cover shipping & handling for the first book & $.50 for each additional book. Call Anthony Parnell (818) 973-3159 for credit card orders & Quantity Discount Information. ***Publisher Provided Annotation.***

Parnell, Ben. Carpetbaggers: America's Secret War in Europe. rev. ed. Roberts, Melissa, ed. (Illus.). 224p. 1993. 24.95 (*0-89015-592-5*) Sunbelt Media.

Parnell, Dale. Dateline 2000: The New Higher Education Agenda. 300p. 1990. pap. 27.50 (*0-87117-198-8*, 1210) Am Assn Comm Coll.

— LogoLearning: Searching for Meaning in Education. (Illus.). 1994. 26.50 (*1-55502-519-6*) CORD Commns.

— The Neglected Majority. 1985. pap. 27.50 (*0-87117-154-6*, 1068) Am Assn Comm Coll.

Parnell, Dale, ed. Associate Degree Preferred. 88p. (Orig.). reprint ed. pap. 25.10 (*0-7837-2484-5*, 2042641) Bks Demand.

Parnell, Dale, jt. auth. see Hull, Dan.

Parnell, Frances B. Skills for Living. LC 93-3891. (Illus.). 632p. 1994. text ed. 43.00 (*0-87006-060-0*) Goodheart.

Parnell, Geoffrey. The English Heritage Book of the Tower of London. (Illus.). 136p. 1994. pap. 29.95 (*0-7134-6864-5*, Pub. by Batsford UK) Trafalgar.

Parnell, Helga. Cooking the German Way. (Easy Menu Ethnic Cookbooks Ser.). (Illus.). 48p. (J). (gr. 5 up). 1988. lib. bdg. 14.95 (*0-8225-0918-0*, Lerner Publctns) Lerner Group.

— Cooking the South American Way. (Easy Menu Ethnic Cookbooks Ser.). (Illus.). 48p. (J). (gr. 5 up). 1991. lib. bdg. 14.95 (*0-8225-0925-3*, Lerner Publctns) Lerner Group.

Parnell, J., ed. Basins on the Atlantic Seaboard: Petroleum Geology, Sedimentology & Basin Evolution. (Geological Society Special Publications: No. 62). (Illus.). x, 470p. (C). 1992. 120.00 (*0-903317-76-1*, Pub. by Geol Soc Pub Hse UK) AAPG.

— Geofluids: Origin, Migration & Evolution of Fluids in Sedimentary Basins. (Geological Society Special Publication Ser.: No. 78). (Illus.). 374p. 1994. 108.00 (*1-897799-05-5*, Pub. by Geol Soc Pub Hse UK) AAPG.

Parnell, J., et al. Bitumens in Ore Deposits. LC 92-36492. (Society for Geology Applied to Mineral Deposits Special Publication Ser.: No. 9). 1993. 179.00 (*0-387-55621-4*) Spr-Verlag.

Parnell, James F., jt. auth. see Biggs, Walter C., Jr.

Parnell, James F., jt. auth. see Lee, David S.

***Parnell, Joan W. & Kendrick, Kevin.** Study Skills for Nursing: A Practical Guide. LC 94-26096. 1994. write for info. (*0-443-04686-7*) Churchill.

Parnell, John. Original Mini Coop: The Restorer's Guide to All MKI, MKII, MKIII Models. (Bayview Ser.). (Illus.). 128p. 1993. 34.95 (*1-870979-32-X*) Motorbooks Intl.

Parnell, Martha A. Bye-Bye Poverty! Ole Mexico! LC 90-91761. 192p. (Orig.). 1990. pap. 8.95 (*0-9626982-0-2*) M Parnell.

Parnell, Martin F. The German Tradition of Organized Capitalism: Self-Government in the Coal Industry. (Government-Industry Relations Ser.: No. 7). 280p. 1994. 55.00 (*0-19-827761-X*) OUP.

Parnell, Mary D. Block Salt & Candles: A Rhondda Childhood. (Illus.). 192p. 1991. 27.50 (*1-85411-056-X*, Pub. by Seren Bks UK) Dufour.

— Block Salt & Candles: A Rhondda Childhood. (Illus.). 200p. 1994. pap. 16.95 (*1-85411-103-5*, Pub. by Seren Bks UK) Dufour.

— Snobs & Sardines: Rhondda Schooldays. (Illus.). 192p. 1994. 24.00 (*1-85411-095-0*, Pub. by Poetry Wales Pr UK) Dufour.

Parnell, Michael, ed. see Thomas, Gwyn.

Parnell, Peter. Flaubert's Latest. 1993. 4.75 (*0-8222-1328-1*) Dramatists Play.

— An Imaginary Life. 1994. pap. 4.75 (*0-8222-1394-X*) Dramatists Play.

— The Rise & Rise of Daniel Rocket. 1984. pap. 4.75 (*0-8222-0956-X*) Dramatists Play.

— Scooter Thomas Makes It to the Top of the World. 1982. pap. 2.75 (*0-8222-1000-2*) Dramatists Play.

Parnell, Philip C. Escalating Disputes: Social Participation & Change in the Oaxacan Highlands. LC 88-17114. (PROFMEX Ser.). 175p. 1988. 28.95 (*0-8165-1053-9*) U of Ariz Pr.

Parnell, Thomas. Poetical Works. LC 70-39664. (Select Bibliographies Reprint Ser.). 1977. reprint ed. 19.95 (*0-8369-9942-8*) Ayer.

— The Poetical Works. Mitford, John, ed. (Anglistica & Americana Ser.: No. 158). xxxii, 185p. 1976. reprint ed. 37.70 (*3-487-05844-8*, Pub. by Georg Olms GW) Lubrecht & Cramer.

Parnes, Beatrice & Murto, Nancy. S.O.I. Success Oriented Instruction for Special Education. (Illus.). 88p. 1981. pap. text ed. 6.00 (*0-914634-86-0*, 8105) DOK Pubs.

Parnes, Beatrice, jt. auth. see Potter, Tom.

Parnes, Herbert S. Developing Human Capital. 46p. 1986. 5.50 (*0-318-22075-X*, IN 306) Ctr Educ Trng Employ.

— Policy Issues in Work & Retirement. LC 83-4950. 288p. 1983. pap. text ed. 14.00 (*0-88099-010-4*) W E Upjohn.

Parnes, Herbert S., et al. Retirement Among American Men. LC 85-6876. (Illus.). 256p. 1985. text ed. 35.00 (*0-669-10334-9*) Free Pr.

— Work & Retirement: A Longitudinal Study of Men. (Illus.). 320p. 1981. 45.00 (*0-262-16079-X*) MIT Pr.

Parnes, Irwin & Parnes, Joy. Bull by the Horns. LC 88-50419. 1988. pap. 10.50 (*0-685-45839-3*) World Univ AZ.

Parnes, Joy, jt. auth. see Parnes, Irwin.

Parnes, Marvin, ed. Innovations in Social Group Work: Feedback from Practice to Theory. LC 85-30222. (Social Work with Groups Supplement Ser.: No. 1). 203p. 1986. 39.95 (*0-86656-564-7*) Haworth Pr.

Parnes, Robert. Canoeing the Jersey Pine Barrens. 4th ed. (East Woods Book Ser.). (Illus.). 256p. 1994. pap. 11.95 (*1-56440-373-4*) Globe Pequot.

— Fertile Soil: A Grower's Guide to Organic & Inorganic Fertilizers. 190p. (Orig.). (C). 1990. pap. text ed. 39.95 (*0-932857-03-5*) Ag Access.

— Organic & Inorganic Fertilizers. 167p. (Orig.). pap. text ed. 39.95 (*0-9603554-3-X*) Woods End.

Parnes, S. E. The Personnel Manager's Handbook of Performance Evaluation Programs. 1982. pap. 24.95 (*1-55645-117-2*) Busn Legal Reports.

Parnes, Sidney J. A Facilitating Style of Leadership. (Illus.). 56p. (Orig.). 1985. pap. 8.50 (*0-943456-08-8*) Bearly Ltd.

— Visionizing. 1992. reprint ed. 22.95 (*0-930222-88-1*) Creat Educ Found.

Parnes, Sidney J., ed. Source Book for Creative Problem Solving: A Fifty Year Digest of Proven Innovation Processes. (Orig.). 1992. pap. 34.95 (*0-930222-92-X*) Creat Educ Found.

Parnes, Stephan. Art of the Passover. 1994. 35.00 (*0-88363-494-5*) H L Levin.

Parnes, Steven. Productivity & the Quality of Working Life. (Studies in Productivity: Highlights of the Literature Ser.: Vol. 2). 43p. 1978. pap. 55.00 (*0-89361-014-3*) Work in Amer.

Parness, Jeffrey M. The Complete Guide to Washington Internships, Vol. 1. LC 88-83185. 144p. (Orig.). (C). 1989. pap. text ed. 16.95 (*0-9621953-0-8*) JMP Enter.

Parnet, Claire, jt. auth. see Deleuze, Gilles.

Parneti, Michael. Inventing Reality: The Politics of News Media. 2nd ed. LC 92-50023. 274p. (C). 1992. 19.95 (*0-312-08629-6*) St Martin.

— Inventing Reality: The Politics of News Media. 2nd ed. LC 92-50023. 274p. (C). 1992. pap. text ed. 14.00 (*0-312-02013-9*) St Martin.

Parnham, M. J. & Bruinvels, J., eds. Haemodynamic, Hormones & Inflammation. (Discoveries in Pharmacology Ser.: Vol. 2). 1985. 224.75 (*0-444-80578-8*) Elsevier.

— Pharmacological Methods, Receptors & Chemotherapy. (Monographs in Primatology: Vol. 5). 404p. 1986. 206.25 (*0-444-80752-7*) Elsevier.

— Psycho & Neuro-Pharmacology. (Discoveries in Pharmacology Ser.: Vol. 1). 507p. 1984. 216.00 (*0-444-80493-5*) Elsevier.

— Selections from Discoveries in Pharmacology. 240p. 1987. pap. 37.00 (*0-444-80922-8*) Elsevier.

Parnham, M. J. & Van Den Berg, W. B., eds. Drugs in Inflammation. (Agents & Actions Supplements Ser.: Vol. 32). 264p. 1991. 124.00 (*0-8176-2504-6*) Spr-Verlag.

Parnham, Michael J. Cologne Atherosclerosis Conference No. 2: Lipids. (Agents & Actions Supplements Ser.: No. 16). 1984. text ed. 57.50 (*0-8176-1645-4*) Birkhauser.

Parnham, Michael J. & Niemann. Fourth Atherosclerosis Conference: Cholesterol Homeostasis. (Agents & Actions Supplements Ser.: No. 26). 425p. 1988. 74.00 (*0-8176-2247-0*) Birkhauser.

Parnham, Michael J. & Prop, G., eds. Cologne Atherosclerosis Conference Three: Platelets. (Agents & Actions Supplements Ser.: No. 20). 278p. 1986. 65.00 (*0-8176-1805-8*) Birkhauser.

Parnov, E. I. At the Crossroads of Infinities. Talmy, Vladimir, tr. 397p. 1971. 19.95 (*0-8464-0159-2*) Beekman Pubs.

Parnwell, E. C. New Oxford Picture Dictionary. LC 87-23950. 1988. pap. 9.25 (*0-19-434199-2*) OUP.

— Oxford Picture Dictionary of American English. (Illus.). 1978. Monolingual ed. pap. 8.25 (*0-19-502332-3*); English-Spanish ed. pap. 8.25 (*0-19-502333-1*); Monolingual ed. with French index. pap. 8.25 (*0-19-502334-X*) OUP.

— Oxford Picture Dictionary of American English. (Illus.). 1980. audio 21.95 (*0-19-502750-7*); 44.95 (*0-19-502730-2*) OUP.

— Oxford Picture Dictionary of American English. (Illus.). 1988. pap. write for info. (*0-318-54877-1*) OUP.

Parnwell, E. C., ed. New Oxford Picture Dictionary: American English - Spanish. 1989. pap. 9.25 (*0-19-434355-3*) OUP.

Parnwell, Michael J., jt. ed. see King, Victor J.

Parnwell, Mike. Population Movements & the Third World. LC 92-13687. (Introductions to Development Ser.). (Illus.). 176p. 1993. pap. 14.95 (*0-415-06953-X*, A4477) Routledge.

Parod, Ted W. Oh, Oh ... Daddy's Cooking! LC 91-75372. (Illus.). 128p. 1994. spiral bd. 9.95 (*0-9627432-4-0*) Echo Lake Pr.

— Old Indian Recipes (Not Really) A Father's Method of Feeding His "Tribe" (Illus.). 118p. 1990. spiral bd. 9.95 (*0-9627432-3-2*) Echo Lake Pr.

Paroda, R. S., jt. auth. see Chopra, V. L.

Parodi, R., ed. Computer Communications: Towards a New World. 750p. 1992. 140.00 (*90-5199-110-X*, Pub. by IOS Pr NE) IOS Press.

Paroissien, David. The Companion to Oliver Twist. (Illus.). 400p. 1991. text ed. 69.00 (*0-7486-0272-0*, Pub. by Edinburgh U Pr UK) Col U Pr.

Parole Commission, Commonwealth of Pennsylvania. The Report of the Pennsylvania State Parole Commission to the Legislature, 1927 Part I, & Part Ii. LC 74-3849. (Criminal Justice in America Ser.). 1974. reprint ed. 28.95 (*0-405-06163-3*) Ayer.

Parolini, Cindy, ed. Group's Best Jr. High Meetings, Vol. 1. 323p. (Orig.). 1987. pap. 19.99 (*0-931529-58-1*) Group Pub.

Parolini-Ruffini, Elvira. Charted Swiss Folk Designs. LC 77-87356. (Illus.). 1978. reprint ed. pap. 2.50 (*0-486-23574-2*) Dover.

***Parolini, Stephen.** Acting Out Jesus' Parables. Keffer, Lois & Schultz, Joani, eds. (Projects with a Purpose for Youth Ministry Ser.). 38p. 1994. pap. 9.99 (*1-55945-147-5*) Group Pub.

— Celebrating Christ with Youth-Led Worship. Warden, Michael, ed. (Projects with a Purpose for Youth Ministry Ser.). 37p. 1994. pap. 9.99 (*1-55945-410-5*) Group Pub.

— Controversial Discussion Starters for Youth Ministry. 108p. 1992. pap. 12.99 (*1-55945-156-4*, Group Bks) Group Pub.

— Sermon on the Mount. (Active Bible Curriculum Ser.). (Illus.). 48p. 1992. pap. 9.99 (*1-55945-129-7*) Group Pub.

— Sharing Your Faith Without Fear. Warden, Michael, ed. (Projects with a Purpose for Youth Ministry Ser.). 44p. 1994. pap. 9.99 (*1-55945-409-1*) Group Pub.

— Today's Music: Good or Bad? (Active Bible Curriculum Ser.). 48p. (Orig.). 1990. pap. 9.99 (*1-55945-101-7*) Group Pub.

Parolini, Stephen, ed. Peer Pressure. (Active Bible Curriculum Ser.). 48p. (Orig.). 1990. pap. 9.99 (*1-55945-103-3*) Group Pub.

***Parolini, Stephen & Lauffer, Lisa B.** Fun Bible-Learning Projects for Young Teenagers. LC 95-7800. 1995. 13.99 (*1-55945-796-1*) Group Pub.

Parolini, Stephen, ed. see Duckworth, John.

Parolini, Stephen, ed. see McGill, Dan.

Parolini, Stephen, ed. see Roehlkepartain, Jolene.

Parolini, Stephen, ed. see Rydberg, Denny.

Parolini, Stephen, ed. see Warden, Michael.

Parolini, Stephen, ed. see Wilger, Jennifer.

Parolini, Stephen, ed. see Woods, Paul.

Parot, Joseph J. Polish Catholics in Chicago, 1850-1920: A Religious History. LC 81-11297. 298p. 1982. 25.00 (*0-87580-081-5*); pap. 12.50 (*0-87580-527-2*) N Ill U Pr.

Parotti, Phillip. The Greek Generals Talk: Memoirs of the Trojan War. Stories. LC 85-27516. (Illinois Short Fiction Ser.). 190p. 1986. 14.95 (*0-252-01304-2*) U of Ill Pr.

— The Trojan Generals Talk: Memoirs of the Greek War. Stories. LC 87-34282. (Illinois Short Fiction Ser.). 184p. 1988. 14.95 (*0-252-01510-X*) U of Ill Pr.

Paroubkova. Czech-English, English-Czech Medical Dictionary. (CZE & ENG.). 1991. 95.00 (*0-8288-7198-1*, F26310) Fr & Eur.

Paroush, Jacob, jt. auth. see Nitzan, Shmuel.

***Paroutaud, Margaret.** Lilac & Roses. 100p. 1995. pap. 7.95 (*0-614-03590-2*) NW Pub.

Parouty, Michel. Mozart: From Child Prodigy to Tragic Hero. Skrine, Celia, tr. (Discoveries Ser.). (Illus.). 192p. 1993. pap. 12.95 (*0-8109-2846-9*) Abrams.

Parparov, L. F. German-Russian Dictionary of Military Abbreviations: Deutsch-Russisches Woerterbuch der Militaerischen Abkuerzungen. 320p. (GER & RUS.). 1983. 29.95 (*0-8288-1165-2*, M15317) Fr & Eur.

Parpart, Jane L., ed. Women & Development in Africa: Comparative Perspectives. LC 88-36271. (Dalhousie African Studies: No. 7). (Illus.). 354p. (Orig.). (C). 1989. lib. bdg. 57.00 (*0-8191-7378-9*, Dalhousie Univ Pr); pap. text ed. 35.50 (*0-8191-7379-7*, Dalhousie Univ Pr) U Pr of Amer.

Parpart, Jane L. & Staudt, Kathleen A., eds. Women & the State in Africa. LC 88-23974. 225p. 1987. pap. text ed. 16.95 (*1-55587-223-9*) Lynne Rienner.

Parpart, Jane L., jt. ed. see Marchand, Marianne H.

Parpart, Jane L., jt. ed. see Stichter, Sharon.

Parpart, Paulette K. Index to the Death & Burial Records of Missoula County, Montana, Vol. 1: Burials: Missoula City Cemetery. 212p. (Orig.). 1989. pap. 17.00 (*0-9624566-1-6*) Western MT Geneal.

— Index to the Death & Burial Records of Missoula County, Montana, Vol. 2: Burials: Carlton, Fort Missoula, Frenchtown, St. Mary's, St. Mary's Annex, Sunset Memorial Park, Sunset Crematorium Records, & Other Small Private Cemeteries or Burials. LC 89-51676. 142p. (Orig.). 1989. write for info. (*0-9624566-0-8*); pap. 13.00 (*0-9624566-2-4*) Western MT Geneal.

An Asterisk (*) at the beginning of an entry indicates that the title is appearing in BIP for the first time.

Parpola, Asko. Deciphering the Indus Script. LC 92-37773. (Illus.). 400p. (C). 1994. 95.00 (*0-521-43079-8*) Cambridge U Pr.

Parpola, Asko & Hansen, Bent S., eds. South Asian Religion & Society. (Studies on Asian Topics (Scandinavian Institute of Asian Studies): No. 11). 262p. (C). 1986. pap. 25.00 (*0-913215-16-3*) Riverdale Co.

Parpola, Simo. Collations to Neo-Assyrian Legal Texts from Nineveh. LC 82-151156. (Assur Ser.: Vol. 2, Pt. 5). 89p. 1979. pap. 18.00 (*0-89003-004-9*) Undena Pubns.

Parpola, Simo, ed. The Correspondence of Sargon Second, Pt. 1: Letters from Assyria & the West. (State Archives of Assyria Ser.: Vol. 1). (Illus.). xxvi, 262p. 1987. text ed. 55.00 (*951-570-004-3*, Pub. by Helsinki Univ Pr FI); pap. 45.00 (*951-570-003-5*, Pub. by Helsinki Univ Pr FI) Eisenbrauns.

Parpola, Simo & Watanabe, Kazuko, eds. Neo-Assyrian Treaties & Loyalty Oaths. (State Archives of Assyria Ser.: Vol. 2). (Illus.). lxii, 124p. 1988. text ed. 45.00 (*951-570-034-5*, Pub. by Helsinki Univ Pr FI); pap. 29. 50 (*951-570-033-7*, Pub. by Helsinki Univ Pr FI) Eisenbrauns.

Parpola, Simo, jt. ed. see Lanfranchi, Giovanni B.

Parque, Richard. A Distant Thunder. 352p. 1989. pap. 3.95 (*0-8217-2557-2*) Zebra.

— Firefight. 352p. 1986. pap. 3.95 (*0-8217-1876-2*) Zebra.

— Hellbound. 1985. pap. 3.50 (*0-8217-1591-7*) Zebra.

— Sweet Vietnam. 288p. 1984. pap. 3.50 (*0-8217-1423-6*) Zebra.

Parr & Rudnitsky. The Superstar Workout. Date not set. pap. write for info. (*0-671-89675-X*) PB.

Parr, A. N., ed. see Jonson, Ben.

Parr, Alan, jt. auth. see Cornelius, Michael.

Parr, Andrew. Hydraulics & Pneumatics: A Technician's & Engineer's Guide. (Illus.). 234p. 1992. pap. 37.95 (*0-7506-0793-9*) Buttrwrth-Heinemann.

Parr, Andrew, ed. Hydraulics & Pneumatics. 223p. 1991. text ed. 59.95 (*0-7506-0015-2*) Buttrwrth-Heinemann.

Parr, Barry. Compass American Guide: San Francisco. 3rd ed. (Compass American Guides Ser.). 1994. pap. 16.95 (*1-878867-70-9*, Compass Amrcn) Fodors Travel.

— Guangzhou; Canton: Where China Meets the 21st Century. 1993. pap. 14.95 (*0-8442-9954-5*, Passport Bks) NTC Pub Grp.

— San Francisco & the Bay Area. Castleman, Deke, ed. (Discover America Ser.). (Illus.). 396p. 1992. 22.95 (*1-878867-02-4*, Compass Amrcn); pap. 12.95 (*1-878867-00-8*, Compass Amrcn) Fodors Travel.

— San Francisco & the Bay Area. 2nd ed. Castleman, Deke, ed. (Discover America Ser.). (Illus.). 396p. 1992. pap. 14.95 (*1-878867-16-4*, Compass Amrcn) Fodors Travel.

Parr, Barry, ed. see Burt, Nathaniel.

Parr, Barry, ed. see Castleman, Deke.

Parr, Barry, ed. see Cheek, Lawrence W.

Parr, Barry, ed. see Tirrel, Norma.

Parr, Barry, ed. see Wharton, Tom & Wharton, Gayen.

Parr, Benard F. Sports: Index of Modern Developments for Prompt Applications. LC 90-56308. 160p. 1991. 44.50 (*1-55914-390-8*); pap. 39.50 (*1-55914-391-6*) ABBE Pubs Assn.

Parr, C. Marcus. The Devil Visits Confidence. (Petites Major Ser.). 40p. 1993. pap. 4.00 (*1-884754-00-7*) Potpourri Pubns.

Parr, Catharine. Prayers or Meditations, Where the Mind Is Stirred Patiently to Suffer All Afflictions Here. LC 76-57370. (English Experience Ser.: No. 788). 1977. reprint ed. lib. bdg. 20.00 (*90-221-0788-4*) Walter J Johnson.

Parr, Charles H. Preliminary List of Early Alaska Imprints, Eighteen Sixty-Nine Through Nineteen Thirteen. LC 76-623405. (Elmer E. Rasmuson Library Occasional Papers: No. 3). 66p. 1974. pap. 2.00 (*0-937592-04-8*) U Alaska Rasmuson Lib.

Parr, Charles M. So Noble a Captain: The Life & Times of Ferdinand Magellan. LC 75-31439. (Illus.). 423p. 1975. reprint ed. text ed. 49.75 (*0-8371-8521-1*, PASN, Greenwood Pr) Greenwood.

Parr, Daniel, jt. auth. see Rockford, T. Jay.

***Parr, Delia.** Evergreen Vol. 1. 1995. mass mkt. 4.99 (*0-312-95376-3*) St Martin.

Parr, E. A. Industrial Control Handbook, Vol. 1: Tranducers. LC 87-3675. (Illus.). 304p. 1987. 34.95 (*0-8311-1175-5*) Indus Pr.

— Industrial Control Handbook, Vol. 2: Techniques. LC 87-3675. (Illus.). 453p. 1987. 34.95 (*0-8311-1178-X*) Indus Pr.

— Industrial Control Handbook, Vol. 3: Theory & Applications. (Illus.). 397p. 1989. 34.95 (*0-8311-1179-8*) Indus Pr.

— The Logic Designer's Guidebook. 480p. 1984. text ed. 65. 00 (*0-07-048492-9*) McGraw.

— Logic Designer's Handbook. 2nd ed. LC 92-31023. 488p. 1993. pap. 39.95 (*0-7506-0535-9*) Buttrwrth-Heinemann.

— Programmable Controllers. LC 92-30189. 1993. 52.95 (*0-7506-0498-0*) Buttrwrth-Heinemann.

***Parr, E.A.** A Handbook of Industrial Control. 2nd ed. LC 94-26857. (Illus.). 896p. 1995. 120.00 (*0-7506-2000-5*) Buttrwrth-Heinemann.

Parr, Elizabeth, jt. auth. see Poole, Catherine.

Parr, Frederique, ed. see Waggoner, Carmen.

Parr, Henry H. Bubi. 190p. 1995. pap. 7.95 (*1-56901-249-0*) NW Pub.

Parr, J. F., et al, eds. Water Potential Relations in Soil Microbiology. 151p. 1981. pap. 6.25 (*0-89118-767-7*) Soil Sci Soc Am.

Parr, J. G., et al. Stainless Steel. (Illus.). 173p. 1985. 79.00 (*0-87170-208-8*, 6230U) ASM.

Parr, Jack E., jt. ed. see Horowitz, Emanual.

Parr, James. Don Quixote: Anatomy of a Subversive Discourse. Lathrop, Thomas et al, eds. (Documentacion Cervantina Ser.: No. 8). 193p. 1988. pap. 14.00 (*0-936388-40-4*) Juan de la Cuesta.

Parr, James, et al. On Cervantes: Essays for L. A. Murillo. Lathrop, Thomas et al, eds. (Documentacion Cervantina Ser.: No. 11). 305p. 1991. 22.00 (*0-936388-49-8*) Juan de la Cuesta.

Parr, James A., ed. see De Molina, Tirso.

Parr, James G. Man, Metals, & Modern Magic. LC 77-25186. 238p. 1978. reprint ed. text ed. 59.75 (*0-313-20122-6*, PAMM, Greenwood Pr) Greenwood.

Parr, James G. & Hanson, Albert. An Introduction to Stainless Steel. LC 65-27458. 157p. reprint ed. pap. 44. 80 (*0-317-08561-1*, 2050985) Bks Demand.

Parr, John. Baby Animals. LC 79-62943. (Cloth Bks.). (Illus.). (J). (ps). 1979. 3.50 (*0-394-84244-8*) Random Bks Yng Read.

— Introduction to Ophthalmology. 3rd ed. (Illus.). 244p. 1989. pap. 35.00 (*0-19-261743-5*) OUP.

Parr, John M., jt. auth. see Phillips, Charles L.

Parr, Joy. The Gender of Breadwinners: Women, Men & Change in Two Industrial Towns, 1880-1950. 320p. 1990. text ed. 45.00 (*0-8020-5853-1*); pap. text ed. 20.95 (*0-8020-6760-3*) U of Toronto Pr.

— Labouring Children: British Immigrant Apprentices to Canada, 1869-1924. (Reprints in Canadian History Ser.). 224p. 1993. pap. 19.95 (*0-8020-7443-X*) U of Toronto Pr.

***Parr, Joy, ed.** A Diversity of Women: Women in Ontario since 1945. (Illus.). 392p. 1995. 65.00 (*0-8020-2615-X*) U of Toronto Pr.

— A Diversity of Women: Women in Ontario since 1945. (Illus.). 392p. 1995. pap. 24.95 (*0-8020-7695-5*) U of Toronto Pr.

Parr, Judith D. I Talk with the Trees. Rome, Dorothy, ed. (Illus.). 21p. 1991. pap. 2.50 (*0-941971-09-0*) Peacock CO.

— Many Avenues of Healing. Rome, Dorothy, ed. (Illus.). 169p. 1989. pap. 8.95 (*0-941971-06-6*) Peacock CO.

— Meditations from My Garden. Gay, Marie, ed. (Illus.). 126p. 1987. spiral bd. 7.95 (*0-941971-00-7*) Peacock CO.

— The Upward Climb: An Epic Poem. 55p. 1994. pap. 4.50 (*0-941971-10-4*) Peacock CO.

— Wise Woman: Whisperings of the Angels. Rome, Dorothy, ed. (Illus.). 52p. 1990. write for info. (*0-941971-08-2*); audio, pap. 15.95 (*0-941971-07-4*) Peacock CO.

Parr, Lance. Police Report Writing Essentials. LC 91-70495. (Orig.). 1991. 9.95 (*0-942728-47-5*) Copperhouse.

Parr, Larry. Springwood. 170p. 1981. 11.95 (*0-940812-00-2*) Plantagenet Hse.

— Viktors Pupols, American Master. Long, Robert B., ed. (Illus.). 78p. (Orig.). 1983. pap. 8.50 (*0-938650-31-9*) Thinkers Pr.

Parr, Larry, ed. see Pelts, Roman & Alburt, Lev.

Parr, Leland W. Introduction to the Anthropology of the Near East in Ancient & Recent Times, with a Chapter on Near Eastern Bloodgroups. 1980. lib. bdg. 59.95 (*0-8490-3164-8*) Gordon Pr.

Parr, Letitia. When Sea & Sky Are Blue. LC 78-151272. (Illus.). 32p. (J). (ps-3). 7.95 (*0-87592-059-4*) Scroll Pr.

***Parr, M. J. & Craft, T. M.** Resuscitation: Key Data. 2nd ed. 112p. 1995. pap. 29.50 (*1-85996-060-X*, Pub. by Bios Scientific UK) Coronet Bks.

— Resuscitation: Key Data: Treatment Protocols for Trauma, Burns, Cardiac Arrhythmias, Drug Overdose, Etc. 96p. (Orig.). 1994. pap. 29.50 (*1-872748-53-8*, Pub. by Bios Scientific UK) Coronet Bks.

Parr, Marilyn K., ed. The Presidents of the United States: The First Twenty Years. LC 92-18145. 1992. 5.50 (*0-8444-0698-8*) Lib Congress.

***Parr, Martin.** Home & Abroad. (Illus.). 60p. 1995. 45.00 (*0-224-03132-5*, Pub. by Jonathan Cape UK) Trafalgar.

— Home & Abroad. (Illus.). 60p. 1995. pap. 29.95 (*0-224-03876-1*, Pub. by Jonathan Cape UK) Trafalgar.

Parr, Peggy. Mountain High-Mountain Rescue. LC 86-25773. (Illus.). 192p. 1986. 15.95 (*1-55591-005-X*) Fulcrum Pub.

***Parr, Randy E.** A Heart Beat in Time. 300p. Date not set. pap. 9.95 (*0-7610-0299-5*) NW Pub.

Parr, Raymond. Process, Person, Presence. (Orig.). 1990. pap. 12.95 (*0-88347-263-5*) Thomas More.

Parr, Robert, ed. see International Congress of Quantum Chemistry Staff.

Parr, Robert E. Cobra for Insurance Agents. 1992. 29.50 (*1-56461-110-8*, 46190) Rough Notes.

— Principles of Mechanical Design. (Illus.). (C). 1969. text ed. 45.95 (*0-07-048512-7*) McGraw.

Parr, Robert G. & Weitao, Yang. Density-Functional Theory of Atoms & Molecules. (International Series of Monographs on Chemistry: Vol. 16). (Illus.). 352p. 1994. reprint ed. pap. 35.00 (*0-19-509276-7*) OUP.

Parr, Roger P. Matthieu de Vendome, ars Versificatoria. Robb, James, ed. LC 80-84768. 1981. pap. 15.00 (*0-87462-222-0*) Marquette.

Parr, Roger P., tr. Geoffery of Vinsauf: Instruction in the Method & Art of Speaking & Versifying. (Medieval Philosophical Texts in Translation Ser.). 1968. pap. 15. 00 (*0-87462-217-4*) Marquette.

Parr, Russell L. Intellectual Property Infringement Damages: A Litigation Support Handbook. 352p. 1993. text ed. 115.00 (*0-471-58979-9*) Wiley.

— Investing in Intangible Assets: Finding & Profiting from Hidden Corporate Value. 237p. 1991. text ed. 34.95 (*0-471-53038-7*) Wiley.

Parr, Russell L., jt. auth. see Smith, Gordon V.

Parr, Samuel, ed. Metaphysical Tracts by English Philosophers of the 18th Century. 351p. reprint ed. lib. bdg. 63.70 (*3-487-05311-X*, Pub. by Georg Olms GW) Lubrecht & Cramer.

Parr, Susan. The Moral of the Story: Literature, Values & American Education. (C). 1982. pap. text ed. 17.95 (*0-8077-2716-4*) Tchrs Coll.

Parr, Susan R. & Savery, Pancho, eds. Approaches to Teaching Ellison's Invisible Man. LC 88-13786. (Approaches to Teaching World Literature Ser.: No. 24). xi, 154p. 1989. text ed. 37.50 (*0-87352-505-1*, AP24C); pap. 18.00x (*0-87352-506-X*, AP24P) Modern Lang.

Parr, Timothy P., jt. ed. see Kuo, Kenneth K.

Parra-Elliott, Ligia, jt. ed. see Ramirez, Bernardo.

Parra, Fernando. Dictionary of Ecology & the Environment: Diccionario de Ecologia, Ecologismo y Medio Ambiente. 288p. (SPA.). 1984. pap. 19.95 (*0-8288-1404-X*, S60012) Fr & Eur.

Parra Murga, Eduardo. Diccionario de Publicidad y Marketing. 238p. 1990. 75.00 (*0-7859-6348-0*, 8485783069) Fr & Eur.

Parra, Nicanor. Antipoems: New & Selected. Unger, David, ed. Ferlinghetti, Lawrence et al, trs. LC 85-11507. 224p. 1985. 19.95 (*0-8112-0959-8*); pap. 8.95 (*0-8112-0960-1*, NDP603) New Directions.

— Emergency Poems. Williams, Miller, ed. & tr. by. LC 71-181896. 160p. 1972. 8.75 (*0-8112-0340-9*) New Directions.

— Sermons & Homilies of the Christ of Elqui by Nicanor Parra. Reyes, Sandra, tr. LC 84-2187. 120p. 1984. 13.50 (*0-8262-0451-1*) U of Mo Pr.

Parra, Raul. Laparoscopic Urologic Surgery. 250p. 1995. text ed. 135.00 (*0-07-048580-1*) Hlth Prof Div.

Parra, Yazmin J. El ABC de dBase IV 1.5. 358p. 1992. pap. text ed. 24.95 (*968-6346-59-7*, Pub. by Ventura Ediciones MX) Computer & Tech.

***Parramon Ediciones Editorial Team.** The Basics of Oil Painting. LC 95-12037. (Complete Course on Painting & Drawing Ser.). Orig. Title: Bases de la Pintura Al Oleo. (Illus.). 1995. write for info. (*0-8120-9403-4*) Barron.

***Parramon Ediciones Editorial Team, ed.** Painting Flowers with Watercolors. Barron's Educational Series, Inc. Staff, tr. LC 94-46433. (Easy Painting & Drawing Ser.). (Illus.). (ENG & SPA.). 1995. write for info. (*0-8120-9292-9*) Barron.

— Painting Pets with Watercolors. Barron's Educational Series, Inc. Staff, tr. LC 94-46432. (Easy Painting & Drawing Ser.). (Illus.). (ENG & SPA.). 1995. write for info. (*0-8120-9293-7*) Barron.

***Parramon Ediciones Staff, ed.** Drawing Basic Subjects. LC 95-2347. (Easy Painting & Drawing Ser.). Orig. Title: Temas Basicos de Dibujo. 1995. write for info. (*0-8120-9290-2*) Barron.

— Painting Landscapes in Oil. LC 94-49011. (Easy Painting & Drawing Ser.). (Illus.). 1995. write for info. (*0-8120-9291-0*) Barron.

Parramon Editorial Team Staff. Los Elementos. (Discover My World Ser.). (Illus.). 96p. (J). (ps-1). 1994. 16.95 (*0-8120-6441-0*) Barron.

— The Elements. (Discover My World Ser.). (Illus.). 96p. (J). (ps-1). 1994. 16.95 (*0-8120-6440-2*) Barron.

— The Senses. (Discover My World Ser.). (Illus.). 96p. (J). (ps-1). 1994. 16.95 (*0-8120-6442-9*) Barron.

— Los Sentidos. (Discover My World Ser.). (Illus.). 96p. (J). (ps-1). 1994. 16.95 (*0-8120-6443-7*) Barron.

Parramon, J. M. Los Arboles Frutales. (J). (ps-3). 1991. pap. 6.95 (*0-8120-4714-1*) Barron.

— El Bosque. (J). (ps-3). 1991. pap. 6.95 (*0-8120-4712-5*) Barron.

— The Fascinating World of Ants. (Fascinating World of... Ser.). (Illus.). 48p. (J). (gr. 3-7). 1991. pap. 7.95 (*0-8120-4721-4*) Barron.

— The Fascinating World of Bees. (Fascinating World of... Ser.). (Illus.). 48p. (J). (gr. 3-7). 1991. pap. 6.95 (*0-8120-4720-6*) Barron.

— The Fascinating World of Butterflies. (Fascinating World of...Ser.). (Illus.). 48p. (J). (gr. 3-7). 1991. pap. 7.95 (*0-8120-4722-2*) Barron.

Parramon, J. M., et al. El Fuego. (Four Elements Ser.). 32p. (SPA.). (J). (ps). 1985. pap. 6.95 (*0-8120-3619-0*) Barron.

Parramon, J. M. El Huerto. (J). (ps-3). 1991. pap. 6.95 (*0-8120-4716-8*) Barron.

— El Jardin. (J). (ps-3). 1991. pap. 6.95 (*0-8120-4713-3*) Barron.

— Mi primera Visita a La Granja. (J). 1990. pap. 5.95 (*0-8120-4400-2*) Barron.

— Mi Primera Visita al Zoo. (J). 1990. pap. 5.95 (*0-8120-4402-9*) Barron.

— Mi Primera Vista al Aviario. (J). 1990. pap. 5.95 (*0-8120-4403-7*) Barron.

— Mi Primeros Colores. (SPA.). (J). (ps-3). 1991. pap. 6.95 (*0-8120-4726-5*) Barron.

— Mi Primeros Formas. (SPA.). (J). (ps-3). 1991. pap. 6.95 (*0-8120-4728-1*) Barron.

— Mi Primeros Numeros. (SPA.). (J). (ps-3). 1991. pap. 6.95 (*0-8120-4727-3*) Barron.

— My First Colors. (My First Ser.). (Illus.). 32p. (J). (ps). 1991. pap. 5.95 (*0-8120-4725-7*) Barron.

— My First Numbers. (My First Ser.). (Illus.). 32p. (J). (ps). 1991. pap. 5.95 (*0-8120-4723-0*) Barron.

— My First Series, 3 vols., Set. (J). (ps). 1991. Boxed set. boxed 17.95 (*0-8120-7791-1*) Barron.

— My First Shapes. (My First Ser.). (Illus.). 32p. (J). (ps). 1991. pap. 5.95 (*0-8120-4724-9*) Barron.

— My First Visit to a Farm. (J). 1990. pap. 5.95 (*0-8120-4305-7*) Barron.

— My First Visit to the Aquarium. (My First Visit Ser.). 32p. (J). (ps). 1990. pap. 6.95 (*0-8120-4304-9*) Barron.

— My First Visit to the Aviary. (My First Visit Ser.). 32p. (J). (ps). 1990. pap. 4.95 (*0-8120-4303-0*) Barron.

— My First Visit to the Zoo. (My First Visit Ser.). 32p. (J). (ps). 1990. pap. 6.95 (*0-8120-4302-2*) Barron.

— Plants & Trees, 4 vols., Set. (J). (ps-3). 1991. Boxed set. boxed, pap. 23.95 (*0-8120-7771-7*) Barron.

— Primera Vista al Acuaria. 1990. pap. 5.95 (*0-8120-4401-0*) Barron.

Parramon, J. M. & Puig, J. J. Hearing. (Child's Guide to the Five Senses Ser.). (Illus.). 32p. (Orig.). (J). (ps). 1985. pap. 6.95 (*0-8120-3563-1*); Span. ed. pap. 6.95 (*0-8120-3606-9*) Barron.

— Sight. (Child's Guide to the Five Senses Ser.). (Illus.). 32p. (Orig.). (J). (ps). 1985. pap. 6.95 (*0-8120-3564-X*); pap. 6.95 (*0-8120-3605-0*) Barron.

— Smell. (Child's Guide to the Five Senses Ser.). (Illus.). 32p. (J). (ps). 1985. pap. 6.95 (*0-8120-3565-8*); pap. 6.95 (*0-8120-3607-7*) Barron.

— Taste. (Child's Guide to the Five Senses Ser.). (Illus.). 32p. (J). (ps). 1985. pap. 6.95 (*0-8120-3566-6*); Span. ed. pap. 6.95 (*0-8120-3608-5*) Barron.

— Touch. (Child's Guide to the Five Senses Ser.). (Illus.). 32p. (Orig.). (J). (ps). 1985. pap. 6.95 (*0-8120-3567-4*); Span. ed. pap. 6.95 (*0-8120-3609-3*) Barron.

Parramon, J. M. & Rius, Maria. Life in the Air. (Habitats Ser.). 32p. (J). (gr. 3-5). 1987. Eng. ed. pap. 5.95 (*0-8120-3863-0*); Span. ed.: La Vida en el Aire. pap. 6.95 (*0-8120-3867-3*) Barron.

— Life in the Sea. (Habitats Ser.). 32p. (J). (gr. 3-5). 1987. Eng. ed. pap. 6.95 (*0-8120-3865-7*); Span. ed.: La Vida en el Mar. pap. 6.95 (*0-8120-3869-X*) Barron.

— Life on the Land. (Habitats Ser.). 32p. (J). (gr. 3-5). 1987. Eng. ed. pap. 5.95 (*0-8120-3864-9*); Span. ed.: La Vida Sobre la Tierra. pap. 6.95 (*0-8120-3868-1*) Barron.

— Life Underground. (Habitats Ser.). 32p. (J). (gr. 3-5). 1987. Eng. ed. pap. 5.95 (*0-8120-3862-2*); Span. ed.: La Vida Bajo la Tierra. pap. 6.95 (*0-8120-3866-5*) Barron.

Parramon, J. M., jt. auth. see Rius, Maria.

Parramon, J. M., et al. El Agua. (Four Elements Ser.). 32p. (SPA.). (J). (ps). 1985. pap. 6.95 (*0-8120-3621-2*) Barron.

— Air. (Four Elements Ser.). 32p. (J). (ps). 1985. pap. 6.95 (*0-8120-3597-6*) Barron.

— El Aire. (Four Elements Ser.). 32p. (SPA.). (J). (ps). 1985. pap. 5.95 (*0-8120-3620-4*) Barron.

— Children. (Barron's Family Ser.). 32p. (J). (gr. 3-5). 1987. pap. 6.95 (*0-685-73872-8*); Eng. ed. pap. 6.95 (*0-8120-3850-9*); Span. ed.: Los Ninos. pap. 6.95 (*0-8120-3854-1*) Barron.

— Earth. (Four Elements Ser.). 32p. (J). (ps). 1985. pap. 6.95 (*0-8120-3596-8*) Barron.

— Fire. LC 85-6106. (Four Elements Ser.). 32p. 1985. pap. 6.95 (*0-8120-3598-4*) Barron.

— Five Senses, 5 bks., Set. (J). (ps). 1985. boxed 32.95 (*0-8120-7365-7*) Barron.

— The Four Elements, 4 Bks. (J). (ps). 1985. boxed 23.95 (*0-8120-7367-3*) Barron.

— Grandparents. (Barron's Family Ser.). 32p. (J). (gr. 3-5). 1987. Eng. ed. pap. 6.95 (*0-8120-3853-3*); Span. ed.: Los Abuelos. pap. 6.95 (*0-8120-3857-6*) Barron.

— El Invierno. (Four Seasons Ser.). 32p. (SPA.). 1987. pap. 6.95 (*0-8120-3647-6*) Barron.

— El Otono. (Four Seasons Ser.). 32p. (SPA.). 1987. pap. 6.95 (*0-8120-3646-8*) Barron.

— Parents. 32p. (J). (gr. 3-5). 1987. Eng. ed. pap. 6.95 (*0-8120-3852-5*); Span. ed.: Los Padres. pap. 6.95 (*0-8120-3856-8*) Barron.

— La Primavera. (Four Seasons Ser.). (SPA.). (J). (ps). 1986. pap. 6.95 (*0-8120-3648-4*) Barron.

— Teenagers. (Barron's Family Ser.). 32p. (J). (gr. 3-5). 1987. Eng. ed. pap. 3.95 (*0-8120-3851-7*); Span. ed.: Los Jovenes. pap. 6.95 (*0-8120-3855-X*) Barron.

— La Tierra. (Four Elements Ser.). 32p. (SPA.). (J). (ps). 1985. pap. 6.95 (*0-8120-3618-2*) Barron.

— El Verano. (Four Seasons Ser.). (SPA.). (J). (ps). 1986. pap. 6.95 (*0-8120-3645-X*) Barron.

— Water. (Four Elements Ser.). 32p. (J). (ps). 1985. pap. 6.95 (*0-8120-3599-2*) Barron.

Parramon, Jose M. The Basics of Artistic Drawing. (Complete Course on Painting & Drawing Ser.). (Illus.). 128p. 1994. pap. 16.95 (*0-8120-1929-6*) Barron.

— The Basics of Artistic Painting. (Complete Course on Painting & Drawing Ser.). (Illus.). 128p. 1994. pap. 16. 95 (*0-8120-1928-8*) Barron.

— The Big Book of Drawing. (Illus.). 192p. 1993. pap. 27.50 (*0-8230-0492-9*, Watsn-Guptill) Watsn-Guptill.

— The Big Book of Oil Painting. (Illus.). 192p. 1990. pap. 27.50 (*0-8230-0498-8*, Watsn-Guptill) Watsn-Guptill.

— The Big Book of Watercolor. (Illus.). 192p. 1984. 32.50 (*0-8230-0496-1*, Watsn-Guptill) Watsn-Guptill.

— The Book of Color. LC 92-38381. (Illus.). 160p. 1993. pap. 27.50 (*0-8230-0516-X*, Watsn-Guptill) Watsn-Guptill.

— Color Theory. (Artist's Library). (Illus.). 112p. 1989. pap. 14.95 (*0-8230-0755-3*, Watsn-Guptill) Watsn-Guptill.

— Creative Watercolor. LC 92-34437. (Artist's Library). (Illus.). 112p. 1993. pap. 14.95 (*0-8230-5683-X*, Watsn-Guptill) Watsn-Guptill.

— Drawing with Crayons, Pastels, Sanguine, & Chalks. (Complete Course on Painting & Drawing Ser.). (Illus.). 128p. 1994. pap. 16.95 (*0-8120-1931-8*) Barron.

— First Steps in Painting. (Artist's Library). (Illus.). 112p. 1991. pap. 12.95 (*0-8230-1826-1*, Watsn-Guptill) Watsn-Guptill.

— How to Draw Heads & Portraits. (Artist's Library). (Illus.). 112p. 1989. pap. 14.95 (*0-8230-2357-5*, Watsn-Guptill) Watsn-Guptill.

— How to Draw the Human Figure. (Artist's Library). (Illus.). 112p. 1990. pap. 14.95 (*0-8230-2358-3*, Watsn-Guptill) Watsn-Guptill.

— How to Paint in Oil. LC 92-18142. (Artist's Library). (Illus.). 112p. 1993. pap. 14.95 (*0-8230-3277-9*, Watsn-Guptill) Watsn-Guptill.

— How to Paint with Colored Pencils. (Artist's Library). (Illus.). 112p. 1989. pap. 14.95 (*0-8230-2463-6*, Watsn-Guptill) Watsn-Guptill.

— How to Paint with Pastels. (Artist's Library). (Illus.). 112p. 1991. pap. 14.95 (*0-8230-2464-4*, Watsn-Guptill) Watsn-Guptill.

P Q

An Asterisk (*) at the beginning of an entry indicates that the title is appearing in BIP for the first time.

— Human Anatomy. (Illus.). 96p. 1991. pap. 12.95 (0-8230-2499-7, Watsn-Guptill) Watsn-Guptill.
— Painting Flowers in Watercolor. (Painting Library). (Illus.). 64p. 1990. pap. 8.95 (0-8230-1852-0, Watsn-Guptill) Watsn-Guptill.
— Painting in Watercolors, Markers, Acrylics, & Gouache. LC 93-6203. (Complete Course on Painting & Drawing Ser.). (Illus.). 128p. 1994. pap. 16.95 (0-8120-1926-1) Barron.
Parramon, Jose M. & Ferron, Miquel. The Big Book of Airbrush. (Illus.). 144p. 1990. pap. 24.95 (0-8230-0164-4, Watsn-Guptill) Watsn-Guptill.
Parramon, Josep M., jt. auth. see Rius, Maria.
Parramon, Merce. The Digestive System. (Invisible World Ser.). (Illus.). 32p. (J). (gr. 4 up). 1994. lib. bdg. 14.95 (0-7910-2126-2, Am Art Analog) Chelsea Hse.
— How Our Blood Circulates. (Invisible World Ser.). (Illus.). 32p. (J). (gr. 4 up). 1994. lib. bdg. 14.95 (0-7910-2127-0, Am Art Analog) Chelsea Hse.
— The Miracle of Life. (Invisible World Ser.). (Illus.). 32p. (J). (gr. 4 up). 1994. lib. bdg. 14.95 (0-7910-2130-0, Am Art Analog) Chelsea Hse.
Parramon Staff. Electromagnets in Action. (Super-Charged Science Projects Ser.). (Illus.). 48p. (J). (gr. 5 up). 1994. 12.95 (0-8120-6437-2) Barron.
— Magnets & Electric Current. (Super-Charged Science Projects Ser.). (Illus.). 48p. (J). (gr. 5 up). 1994. 12.95 (0-8120-6436-4) Barron.
Parramona, Joan B. New Dictionary of the Catalan Dictionary: Nou Diccionari de la Llengua Catalana. 11th ed. 832p. (CAT.). 1990. 26.95 (0-7859-4961-5) Fr & Eur.
Parramore, Barbara & Hopke, Bill. Activities for the Children's Dictionary of Occupations. (Illus.). 20p. (J). (gr. 3-4). 1992. student ed 12.95 (1-56191-191-7) Meridian Educ.
— Activities for the Children's Dictionary of Occupations. (Illus.). 20p. (J). (gr. 5-6). 1992. student ed 12.95 (1-56191-192-5) Meridian Educ.
— The Children's Dictionary of Occupations. rev. ed. (Illus.). 130p. (J). (gr. 3-6). 1992. pap. text ed. 12.95 (1-56191-190-9) Meridian Educ.
Parramore, Barbara & Hopke, William E. Career Exploration Activities Booklet: 25 Activities to Help Explore Occupations. 48p. (Orig.). (J). (gr. 6 up). 1989. pap. text ed. 17.75 (0-685-31414-6) Careers Inc.
Parramore, Barbara, jt. auth. see Parramore, Tom.
Parramore, Barbara M. & Hopke, William E. Early Occupational Awareness Program for Kindergarten & Grades One & Two. LC 93-50858. (Illus.). 105p. (Orig.). 1994. pap. 17.95 (1-880774-06-2) Garrett Pk.
Parramore, Thomas C. Carolina Quest. (gr. 7-8). 1978. text ed. 22.80 (0-13-114900-8) P-H.
— Triumph at Kitty Hawk: The Wright Brothers & Powered Flight. (Illus.). ix, 124p. (Orig.). (YA). (gr. 8-12). 1993. pap. 8.00 (0-86526-259-4) NC Archives.
Parramore, Thomas C., et al. Norfolk: The First Four Centuries. LC 94-9457. 480p. (C). 1994. 20.00 (0-8139-1557-0) U Pr of Va.
Parramore, Tom & Parramore, Barbara. Looking for the "Lost Colony" (Illus.). 32p. 1984. pap. 3.00 (0-318-03650-9) Tanglewood Press.
Parratore, Phil M. Wacky Science: A Cookbook for Elementary Teachers. 152p. 1993. per. 24.90 (0-8403-9013-0) Kendall-Hunt.
Parratt, David. Radioimmunoassay of Antibody & Its Clinical Applications. LC 81-12939. 174p. reprint ed. pap. 49.60 (0-318-34726-1, 2031940) Bks Demand.
***Parratt, James R., ed.** Control & Manipulation of Calcium Movement: A Biological Council Symposium. fac. ed. LC 84-42718. (Illus.). 408p. Date not set. pap. 116.30 (0-7837-7219-X, 2047079) Bks Demand.
Parravicini, G. Pastori, jt. auth. see Bassani, F.
Parrell, Mary Agnes, Sr. Profiles of Dobbs Ferry. LC 76-21031. (Illus.). 118p. 1976. lib. bdg. 15.00 (0-379-01100-X) Oceana.
***Parrella, Deborah.** Project Seasons. 2nd ed. (Illus.). 336p. 1995. pap. write for info. (0-9642163-0-2) Shelburne Farms.
Parrenas, Celine, intro. Smell This, Vol. 2. (Illus.). 142p. (Orig.). (C). 1991. pap. 9.95 (0-9627988-1-9) Ctr Rac Ed.
Parreno, R. J., ed. Abstracts, Sixth World Congress of the International Rehabilitation Medicine Association, Madrid, 17-22 June, 1990. (International Congress Ser.: No. 927). 348p. 1990. 80.00 (0-444-81132-X, Excerpta Medica) Elsevier.
Parrent, George B., jt. auth. see Beran, Mark J.
Parrent, George B., Jr., ed. see Reynolds, George O., et al.
Parret, H. H. & Bouveresse, Jacques, eds. Meaning & Understanding. 442p. (C). 1981. 106.15 (3-11-008116-4) De Gruyter.
Parret, Herman. The Aesthetics of Communication: Pramatics & Beyond. (Library of Rhetorics Ser.). 184p. (C). 1993. lib. bdg. 79.50 (0-7923-2198-7) Kluwer Ac.
— Contexts of Understanding, Vol 1. (Pragmatics & Beyond Ser.: Vol. 1, No. 6). viii, 109p. 1980. pap. 29.00x (90-272-2509-5) Benjamins North Am.
— Discussing Language: Dialogues with N. Chomsky, A. J. Greimas, M. A. K. Holiday, et al. 1974. pap. text ed. 50.00 (90-279-2705-7) Mouton.
— Language & Discourse. LC 73-170002. (Janua Linguarum, Ser. Minor: No. 119). (Illus.). 292p. (Orig.). 1971. pap. text ed. 49.25 (90-279-1854-6) Mouton.
— Semiotics & Pragmatics: An Evaluative Comparison of Conceptual Frameworks. (Pragmatics & Beyond Ser.: Vol. IV, No. 7). xii, 136p. (Orig.). 1983. pap. 44.00x (90-272-2532-X) Benjamins North Am.
— Le Sublime du Quotidien. (AS-6 Ser.). 286p. (Orig.). (FRE.). 1988. pap. 65.00x (90-272-2266-5) Benjamins North Am.
Parret, Herman, ed. History of Linguistic Thought & Contemporary Linguistics: Foundations of Communication. 816p. (C). 1975. 188.50 (3-11-005818-9) De Gruyter.
— On Believing-De La Croyance: Epistemological & Semetic Approaches. LC 83-15232. (Foundations of Communication & Cognition Ser.). viii, 359p. 1983. 113.10 (3-11-008884-3) De Gruyter.
— Peirce & Value Theory: On Peircian Ethics & Aesthetics. LC 93-39339. (Semiotic Crossroads (SC) Ser.: No. 6). xv, 371p. 1993. 95.00 (1-55619-340-8) Benjamins North Am.
— Pretending to Communicate. LC 93-46021. 1993. 136.95 (3-11-011832-7) De Gruyter.
Parret, Herman & Ruprecht, H., eds. Aims & Prospects of Semiotics: To Honor A. J. Greimas, 2 Vols., 1. LC 85-11049. lxxxv, 550p. 1985. write for info. (90-272-2020-4) Benjamins North Am.
— Aims & Prospects of Semiotics: To Honor A. J. Greimas, 2 Vols., 2. LC 85-11049. lxxxv, 550p. 1985. write for info. (90-272-2021-2) Benjamins North Am.
— Aims & Prospects of Semiotics: To Honor A. J. Greimas, 2 Vols., Set. LC 85-11049. lxxxv, 550p. 1985. 260.00 (90-272-2019-0) Benjamins North Am.
Parret, Herman, jt. auth. see Alexandrescu, Sorin.
Parret, Herman, et al. Le Langage en Contexte: Etudes Philosophiques et Linguistiques de Pragmatique. (Linguisticae Investigationes Supplementa Ser.: Vol. 3). iv, 790p. 1980. 143.00x (90-272-3112-5, 3) Benjamins North Am.
Parret, Herman, et al, eds. Possibilities & Limitations of Pragmatics: Proceedings of the Conference on Pragmatics, Urbino, Italy, July 8-14, 1979. (Studies in Language Companion: No. 7). x, 854p. 1981. 177.00 (90-272-3006-4) Benjamins North Am.
Parrett, Richard. DC - AC Circuits: Concepts & Applications. 600p. 1991. boxed, text ed. 44.00 (0-13-200858-0, 420102) P-H.
— DC - AC Circuits: Concepts & Applications. 480p. (C). 1992. pap. text ed. write for info. (0-13-042615-6) P-H.
Parrett, Sherii & Brown, Sylvia. Slippy Cleans Up. (Tub Tales of Slippy Jr. Ser.). (Illus.). 24p. (Orig.). (J). (ps-6). 1992. pap. 5.99 (1-56722-002-9) Word Aflame.
Parrett, William H., jt. auth. see Barr, Robert D.
Parrette, James. Gallows Gold. (Orig.). 1980. pap. 1.95 (0-89083-687-6) Zebra.
Parrette, William A. Motif Programming in the X Window Environment. 608p. 1993. text ed. 45.00 (0-07-031722-4) McGraw.
— Motif Programming in the X Window Environment. 608p. 1993. pap. text ed. 34.95 (0-07-031723-2) McGraw.
— Unix for Application Developers. 352p. 1991. pap. text ed. 27.95 (0-07-031697-X) McGraw.
Parriaud, Cosabeth, jt. auth. see Flocard, Marie-Christine.
Parrill, William. The Long Haul: Conversations with Southern Novelists. 194p. (Orig.). (C). Date not set. lib. bdg. 46.50 (0-8191-9077-2); pap. text ed. 18.50 (0-8191-9078-0) U Pr of Amer.
Parrillo, John & Greenwood-Robinson, Maggie. High-Performance Bodybuilding. LC 92-15571. (Illus.). 192p. (Orig.). 1993. pap. 16.00 (0-399-51771-5, Perigree Bks) Berkley Pub.
Parrillo, Joseph & Bone, Roger C. Critical Care Medicine: Principles & Management. 1800p. 1994. 159.00 (0-8016-7005-5) Mosby Yr Bk.
Parrillo, Joseph E. Current Therapy in Critical Care Medicine. 2nd ed. 368p. (C). 1990. 92.00 (1-55664-268-7) Mosby Yr Bk.
Parrillo, Richard. Blackjack by the Numbers. 628p. (Orig.). 1992. pap. 22.95 (0-9631961-0-3) Sibylline Bks.
— Blackjack by the Numbers. rev. ed. (By the Numbers Ser.). (Illus.). 186p. (Orig.). 1994. pap. 14.95 (0-9631961-4-6) Sibylline Bks.
Parrillo, Rosemary. Welcome to Exit Four: Enter at Own Risk. LC 93-72527. 224p. (Orig.). 1994. pap. 12.00 (0-9635720-1-6) August Pr.
Parrillo, Vincent, jt. auth. see Stimson, Ardyth.
Parrillo, Vincent N. Strangers to These Shores: Race & Ethnic Relations in the United States. 4th ed. LC 93-12047. 656p. (C). 1994. write for info. (0-02-391752-0) Macmillan.
Parrillo, Vincent N., ed. Rethinking Today's Minorities. LC 90-40733. (Contributions in Sociology Ser.: No. 93). 224p. 1991. text ed. 49.95 (0-313-27537-8, PRT, Greenwood Pr) Greenwood.
Parrillo, Vincent N., et al. Contemporary Social Problems. 2nd ed. 660p. (C). 1989. write for info. (0-02-391731-8) Macmillan.
Parrinder, E. G. A Book of World Religions. (C). 1965. text ed. 70.00 (0-7175-0443-3, Pub. by S Thornes Pubs UK) St Mut.
— A Dictionary of Non-Christian Religions. (C). 1981. text ed. 90.00 (0-7175-0972-9, Pub. by S Thornes Pubs UK) St Mut.
Parrinder, Edward G. West African Psychology. LC 74-15076. reprint ed. 27.50 (0-404-12125-X) AMS Pr.
***Parrinder, G.** Mysticism in the World's Religions. 220p. 1995. pap. 16.99 (1-85168-101-9) Onewrld Pubns.
— Sexual Morality in the World's Religions. 290p. 1995. pap. 14.95 (1-85168-108-6) Onewrld Pubns.
Parrinder, Geoffrey. African Traditional Religion. 3rd ed. LC 76-22490. (Illus.). 156p. 1970. reprint ed. text ed. 48.50 (0-8371-3401-3, PAF&, Greenwood Pr) Greenwood.
— Comparative Religion. LC 73-19116. 130p. 1975. reprint ed. text ed. 55.00 (0-8371-7301-9, PACR, Greenwood Pr) Greenwood.
— Encountering World Religions. 224p. 1987. 15.95 (0-8245-0826-2) Crossroad NY.
— Jesus in the Qur'an. 1995. pap. 13.95 (1-85168-094-2) Onewrld Pubns.
— Religion in an African City. LC 74-142921. (Illus.). 211p. 1973. reprint ed. text ed. 45.00 (0-8371-5947-4, PAC&, Negro U Pr) Greenwood.
— Sex in the World's Religions. 1980. pap. 14.95 (0-19-520202-3) OUP.
— Son of Joseph: The Parentage of Jesus. 132p. 1992. pap. text ed. 17.95 (0-567-29213-4, Pub. by T & T Clark UK) Bks Intl VA.
— Worship in the World's Religions. 2nd ed. (Quality Paperback Ser.: No. 316). 239p. 1976. reprint ed. pap. 16.00 (0-8226-0316-0) Littlefield.
Parrinder, Geoffrey, ed. World Religions: From Ancient History to the Present. (Illus.). 528p. 1984. 35.00 (0-87196-129-6); pap. 16.95 (0-8160-1289-X) Facts on File.
Parrinder, Patrick. Authors & Authenticity. 400p. 1991. text ed. 79.00 (0-231-07646-0); pap. text ed. 25.00 (0-231-07647-9) Col U Pr.
— James Joyce. 272p. 1984. 59.95 (0-521-24014-X); pap. 16.95 (0-521-28398-1) Cambridge U Pr.
Parrinder, Patrick, ed. H. G. Wells: The Critical Heritage. (Critical Heritage Ser.). 1972. 69.50 (0-7100-7387-9, RKP) Routledge.
— Science Fiction: A Critical Guide. LC 78-40686. 252p. reprint ed. pap. 71.90 (0-8357-3528-1, 2034476) Bks Demand.
Parrinder, Patrick & Rolfe, Christopher, eds. H. G. Wells under Revision: Proceedings of the International H. G. Wells Symposium, London, July 1986. LC 88-43425. 264p. 1990. 40.00 (0-945636-05-9) Susquehanna U Pr.
Parrinder, Patrick, et al. H. G. Wells: Reality & Beyond. LC 86-62053. (Illus.). 91p. 1986. pap. 5.00 (0-9617184-0-4) Champaign Pub Lib.
Parrington. Whillian's Tax Tables 1993-94. 1993. pap. 6.00 (0-406-01615-1, UK) Butterworth Legal Pubs.
***Parrington, Sheila, ed.** Whillan's Tax Tables 1994-95. 47th ed. 1994. pap. 3.50 (0-406-03644-6) Butterworth Legal Pubs.
— Whillans's Tax Tables 1992-1993. 45th ed. 1992. pap. 6.00 (0-406-00850-7) Butterworth Legal Pubs.
— Whillans's Tax Tables 1994-1995. 48th ed. 1994. pap. write for info. (0-406-04979-3) Butterworth Legal Pubs.
Parrington, V. L. Main Currents in American Thought, 3 vols., Set. 1993. reprint ed. lib. bdg. 225.00 (0-7812-5283-0) Rprt Serv.
Parrington, Vernon L. Sinclair Lewis: Our Own Diogenes. LC 73-11205. (American Literature Ser.: No. 49). 1974. lib. bdg. 75.00 (0-8383-1720-0) M S G Haskell Hse.
Parrini, Paolo, ed. Kant & Contemporary Epistemology. LC 93-48849. (University of Western Ontario Series in Philosophy of Science). 384p. (C). 1994. lib. bdg. 120.00 (0-7923-2681-4) Kluwer Ac.
Parrino, Janice. Welcome to Good Cooking. LC 87-90514. (Illus.). (Orig.). pap. write for info. (0-9618347-0-6) N A & J Parrino.
Parrino, Maria, jt. ed. see Albright, Carol B.
Parriott, Donald, ed. A Practical Guide to HPLC Detection. LC 92-13082. (Illus.). 293p. 1992. text ed. 59.95 (0-12-545680-8) Acad Pr.
Parris, C. Mastering Executive Arts & Skills. 14.95 (0-13-560086-3, Parker Publishing Co) P-H.
Parris, Judith H. The Convention Problem: Issues in Reform of Presidential Nominating Procedures. LC 72-143. (Brookings Institution Studies in Presidential Selection). 208p. reprint ed. pap. 59.30 (0-317-26344-7, 2025399) Bks Demand.
Parris, Judith H., jt. auth. see Bain, Richard C.
Parris, Judith H., jt. auth. see Sayre, Wallace S.
Parris, L. Eileen, ed. Guide to the Manuscript Collections of the Colonial Williamsburg Foundation. LC 93-8035. 1993. 16.00 (0-87935-096-2) Colonial Williamsburg.
Parris, Leslie. Constable. 1993. 95.00 (1-55859-636-4) Abbeville Pr.
***Parris, Leslie, ed.** The Pre-Raphaelites. (Illus.). 312p. 1995. pap. 60.00 (1-85437-144-4) U of Wash Pr.
Parris, Leslie, jt. auth. see Shields, Conal.
Parris, Lorri A., tr. see Lispector, Clarice.
Parris, Matthew. Inca-Kola: A Traveller's Tale of Peru. large type ed. (Non-Fiction Ser.). 576p. 1992. 21.95 (0-7089-2630-4) Ulverscroft.
Parris, Preston. Treasure in the Sand: How & Where to Find Hundreds of Gold & Silver Rings, Hundreds of Silver Coins & Hundreds of Dollars. LC 89-80193. 225p. 1992. pap. 19.95 (0-9631917-0-5) The Hunter Pub.
Parris, Ronald G. Rendille. LC 94-7246. (Heritage Library of African Peoples). (J). 1994. 15.95 (0-8239-1763-0) Rosen Group.
Parris, Winston C., ed. Contemporary Issues in Chronic Pain Management. (Current Management of Pain Ser.). 311p. (C). 1991. lib. bdg. 126.00 (0-7923-1182-5) Kluwer Ac.
***Parrish.** Maxfield Parrish: Postcard Book. (Illus.). 1992. pap. text ed. 8.95 (0-87654-942-3) Pomegranate Calif.
— Scanning Technique for Magnetic Resonance Imaging. 250p. 1994. pap. 50.00 (0-8016-6324-5) Mosby Yr Bk.
Parrish, A., ed. Mechanical Engineer's Reference Book. 12th ed. 752p. 1994. 175.00 (0-7506-1195-2) Buttrwrth-Heinemann.
***Parrish, Alfredo.** Know Your Rights: A Guide Through Iowa's Criminal Justice System. (Orig.). Date not set. pap. 12.00 (0-9645860-0-2) A Parrish.
Parrish, Anne. All Kneeling. 1976. lib. bdg. 13.95 (0-89968-154-9, Lghtyr Pr) Buccaneer Bks.
— The Perennial Bachelor. 1976. lib. bdg. 13.95 (0-89968-153-0, Lghtyr Pr) Buccaneer Bks.
Parrish, Annette, ed. see Finley, Tom.
Parrish, Annette, ed. see Myers, Bill.
Parrish, Carl. The Notation of Medieval Music. LC 78-11831. 230p. 1978. lib. bdg. 30.00 (0-918728-08-8) Pendragon NY.
— Treasury of Early Music. (Illus.). 1964. lp write for info. (0-318-54701-5) Norton.
Parrish, Carl & Ohl, John F. Masterpieces of Music Before 1750. (Illus.). (C). 1950. text ed. 14.95 (0-393-09739-0) Norton.
Parrish, Carl, tr. see Tinctoris, Johannes.
Parrish, Clarence R. Expressions of Faith. (Illus.). Date not set. 15.00 (0-9638379-1-5) P & P Pubng.
— Images of Democracy: (I Can't Go Home) Date not set. 10.00 (0-9638379-0-7) P & P Pubng.
Parrish, Darrell. The Car Buyer's Art: How to Beat the Salesman at His Own Game. 4th rev. ed. (Illus.). 296p. 1994. mass mkt. 6.95 (0-9612322-7-7) Bk Express.
— Lease Cars: How to Get One. (Illus.). 294p. 1995. mass mkt., pap. text ed. 6.95 (0-9612322-8-5) Bk Express.
— Used Cars...How to Buy One. (Illus.). 235p. 1995. 5.95 (0-9612322-3-4) Bk Express.
Parrish, Darrell B. Lease Cars: How to Get One. (Illus.). 246p. 1992. pap. text ed. 6.95 (0-9612322-4-2) Bk Express.
Parrish, David. Flexible Manufacturing. LC 90-2181. (Illus.). 147p. 1993. pap. 29.95 (0-7506-1657-1) Buttrwrth-Heinemann.
Parrish, Dee A. Abused: A Handbook for Adult Survivors of Child Abuse. 1990. pap. 8.95 (0-88268-089-7) Station Hill Pr.
— How to Break the Vicious Circles in Your Relationships: A Guide for Couples. LC 93-4794. 1993. 8.95 (0-88268-144-3) Station Hill Pr.
Parrish, Duane. A Postcard to Heaven. LC 93-84140. 150p. (Orig.). 1994. pap. 8.95 (0-89221-235-7) New Leaf.
Parrish, Edwin. Children of the Mist. 328p. (Orig.). 1992. pap. 13.95 (1-56672-008-7) Seabar Pub.
Parrish, Frank. Fire in the Barley. large type ed. (Mystery Ser.). 267p. 1980. 15.95 (0-7089-0450-5) Ulverscroft.
— Snare in the Dark. large type ed. (Mystery Ser.). 320p. 1983. 15.95 (0-7089-1007-6) Ulverscroft.
— Sparks from His Heart. 110p. 1992. pap. text ed. 9.00 (1-881068-00-5) Oaktree Bks.
— Sting of the Honeybee. large type ed. 339p. 1980. 12.00 (0-7089-0520-X) Ulverscroft.
***Parrish, Fred.** Photojournalism: An Introduction. 420p. 1995. pap. text ed. write for info. (0-314-04564-3) West Pub.
Parrish, Fred L. A Yank in the British YMCA. 183p. 1975. pap. text ed. 25.00 (0-89126-009-9) MA-AH Pub.
Parrish, Fredrick, Jr. Introductory Meats. 1993. spiral bd. 18.50 (0-88252-161-6) Paladin Hse.
Parrish, G. & Harper, G. S. Production Gas Carburizing. (Materials Engineering Practice Ser.). (Illus.). 250p. 1985. 132.00 (0-08-027312-2, Pub. by Pergamon Repr UK) Franklin.
Parrish, Geoffrey. The Influence of Microstructure on the Properties of Case-Carburized Components. LC 80-10679. (Illus.). 248p. reprint ed. pap. 70.70 (0-8357-6156-8, 2034309) Bks Demand.
Parrish-Harra, Carol. The Book of Rituals: Personal & Planetary Transformation. (Orig.). 1990. 14.95 (0-945027-10-9) Sparrow Hawk Pr.
— The Book of Rituals: Personal & Planetary Transformation. 400p. (Orig.). (C). 1990. reprint ed. lib. bdg. 47.00x (0-8095-6567-6) Borgo Pr.
— Messengers of Hope. 1983. 7.95 (0-945027-03-6) Sparrow Hawk Pr.
— The New Age Handbook on Death & Dying. 1982. 9.95 (0-945027-09-5) Sparrow Hawk Pr.
Parrish-Harra, Carol W. The Aquarian Rosary: Reviving the Art of Mantra Yoga. LC 87-63437. (Illus.). 136p. 1988. pap. 8.95 (0-945027-01-X) Sparrow Hawk Pr.
— Messengers of Hope. (Illus.). 244p. 1983. pap. 7.95 (0-87613-079-1) Sparrow Hawk Pr.
Parrish, J. Totman, jt. ed. see McCabe, P. J.
Parrish, James. Mobsters on the Screen. 1992. pap. 14.95 (1-55698-352-2) Movie Pubs Servs.
Parrish, James R. Let's Talk: America's Favorite Talk Show Hosts. 1993. pap. 14.95 (1-55698-364-6) Movie Pubs Servs.
— Today's Black Hollywood. 480p. 1995. pap. 4.99 (0-8217-0104-5) Zebra.
Parrish, John A., et al. UV-A: Biological Effects of Ultraviolet Radiation with Emphasis on Human Responses to Longwave Ultraviolet. LC 78-14968. 272p. reprint ed. pap. 77.60 (0-317-26187-8, 2052076) Bks Demand.
Parrish, John A., et al, eds. Photoimmunology. LC 83-4216. 320p. 1983. 85.00 (0-306-41280-2, Plenum Pr) Plenum.
Parrish, Joseph. Alcoholic Inebriety from a Medical Standpoint. Grob, Gerald N., ed. LC 80-1243. (Addiction in America Ser.). 1981. reprint ed. lib. bdg. 18.95 (0-405-13613-7) Ayer.
Parrish, Judith T. & Barron, Eric J. Paleoclimates & Economic Geology. (Short Course Notes Ser.: No. 18). 162p. 1986. pap. 17.00 (0-918985-60-9) SEPM.
Parrish, Karen, jt. auth. see Schaum, Melita.
Parrish, Katherine. Dustmop Devotionals. (Orig.). 1990. pap. 4.99 (0-529-06785-4) World Bible.
— Dustmop Devotionals. large type ed. 83p. 1990. pap. 3.99 (0-529-07127-4, Meridian IA) World Bible.
Parrish Kvaltine & Associates, Inc. Staff. Lightning Protection Manual for Rural Electric Systems. 1993. pap. text ed. write for info. (0-917599-12-8) Natl Rural.
Parrish, Lila S. A History of Searles Castle in Great Barrington, Massachusetts. 32p. 1985. pap. text ed. 5.00 (0-941583-08-2) Attic Rev Pr.
Parrish, Lydia. Slave Songs of the Georgia Sea Islands. LC 91-22948. (Brown Thrasher Bks.). (Illus.). 312p. 1992. reprint ed. 45.00 (0-8203-1397-1); reprint ed. pap. 19.95 (0-8203-1389-0) U of Ga Pr.
Parrish, M. Battle for Moscow: The 1942 Soviet General Staff Study. (Illus.). 226p. 1989. 45.00 (0-08-035977-9) Brasseys Inc.

An Asterisk (*) at the beginning of an entry indicates that the title is appearing in BIP for the first time.

Parrish, Mary E. Events of the Tulsa Disaster. 1992. pap. 8.95 (*0-88378-000-3*) Third World.

Parrish, Maxfield. Knave of Hearts. 1993. 12.95 (*0-89815-552-5*) Ten Speed Pr.

Parrish, Michael. Careers in Business & the Public Sector: An Annotated Bibliography. 34p. 1986. pap. text ed. 8.00 (*0-9617990-0-5*) Ars Biblio.

— The Lesser Terror: Soviet State Security 1939-1953. LC 94-38565. 1995. text ed. write for info. (*0-275-95113-8*, Praeger Pubs) Greenwood.

— Soviet Security & Intelligence Organizations 1917-1990: A Biographical Dictionary & Review of Literature in English. LC 91-34996. 704p. 1992. text ed. 79.50 (*0-313-28305-2*, PSV/, Greenwood Pr) Greenwood.

Parrish, Michael, jt. ed. see Hopkins, Jack.

Parrish, Michael E. The Anxious Decades: America in Prosperity & Depression 1920-1941. (Illus.). 560p. 1992. 29.95 (*0-393-03394-5*) Norton.

— Anxious Decades: America in Prosperity & Depression 1920-1941. 1994. pap. 12.95 (*0-393-31134-1*) Norton.

— Felix Frankfurter & His Times: The Reform Years, Vol.1. (Illus.). 332p. 1982. text ed. 22.95 (*0-02-923740-8*, 92374) Free Pr.

— Securities Regulation & the New Deal. LC 70-118735. (Yale Historical Publications: Miscellany: No. 93). 282p. reprint ed. pap. 80.40 (*0-317-09459-9*, 2022027) Bks Demand.

Parrish, Noel F. Behind the Sheltering Bomb. Kohn, Richard H., ed. LC 78-22415. (American Military Experience Ser.). 1980. lib. bdg. 24.95 (*0-405-11889-9*) Ayer.

Parrish, Phyllis W. & Parrish, Stephen R. House Management: A Guide for Greek Chapter Houses: How to Successfully Operate a Fraternity or Sorority House, Vol. 1. (Illus.). 496p. 1989. pap. 75.00 (*0-9623776-0-0*) P Parrish.

Parrish, Preston. The Lions' Den: Facing Yours. 88p. 1992. pap. text ed. 4.95 (*0-9633470-8-X*) Awakenings.

Parrish, R. G., jt. auth. see Bell, K. W.

Parrish, Randall. Bob Hampton of Placer. 1976. lib. bdg. 16.70 (*0-89968-084-4*, Lghtyr Pr) Buccaneer Bks.

— Contraband, A Romance of the North Atlantic. 1976. lib. bdg. 18.25 (*0-89968-085-2*, Lghtyr Pr) Buccaneer Bks.

— My Lady of the North. 1976. lib. bdg. 16.30 (*0-89968-086-0*, Lghtyr Pr) Buccaneer Bks.

— My Lady of the South. 1976. lib. bdg. 16.30 (*0-89968-087-9*, Lghtyr Pr) Buccaneer Bks.

Parrish, Rhett. Puppy Dogs Polka at the Kitty Cat Carnival: A Music Gift Set with a Fun Approach to Learning. 48p. (J). (ps-2). 1991. audio 14.95 (*0-9632433-0-6*) RPM Record.

Parrish, Richard. The Dividing Line. 1994. 5.99 (*0-451-40430-0*, Onyx) NAL-Dutton.

— Nothing but the Truth. 304p. 1995. 20.95 (*0-525-93852-4*, Dutton) NAL-Dutton.

— Our Choice of Gods. Richardson, Stewart, ed. 464p. 1989. 19.95 (*1-55972-002-6*, Birch Ln Pr) Carol Pub Group.

— Versions of the Truth. LC 93-4885. 320p. 1994. 19.95 (*0-525-93652-1*, Dutton) NAL-Dutton.

— Versions of the Truth. 416p. 1994. pap. 5.99 (*0-451-40523-4*, Onyx) NAL-Dutton.

Parrish, Richard M., jt. auth. see Kells, H. R.

***Parrish, Robert.** Great Tricks Revisited: New Approaches, Applications, Routines & Patter for Classic Magic Tricks. Willmarth, Phil, ed. & pref. by. (Illus.). 136p. 1995. 25.00 (*0-916638-80-4*) Meyerbooks.

— Growing up in Hollywood. (Illus.). 236p. 1988. 17.95 (*0-316-69256-5*); pap. 9.95 (*0-316-69257-3*) Little.

— Hollywood Doesn't Live Here Anymore. (Illus.). 240p. 1989. reprint ed. pap. 9.95 (*0-316-69258-1*) Little.

— Words about Wizards: Recollections of Magicians & Their Magic, 1930-1950. (Illus.). 72p. 1994. 25.00 (*0-916638-79-0*) Meyerbooks.

Parrish, Robert D. Combat Recon. 1992. mass mkt. 5.99 (*0-312-92713-4*) St Martin.

Parrish, Ruth G. Eugenics: Index of Modern Information with Bibliography. LC 88-47789. 150p. (Orig.). 1988. 39.50 (*0-88164-898-1*); pap. 34.50 (*0-88164-899-X*) ABBE Pubs Assn.

Parrish, Stephen, ed. see Yeats, William Butler.

Parrish, Stephen E., jt. auth. see Beckwith, Francis J.

Parrish, Stephen M., ed. see Austen, Jane.

Parrish, Stephen M., ed. see Coleridge, Samuel Taylor.

Parrish, Stephen M., ed. see De la Fontaine, Jean.

Parrish, Stephen M., ed. see Wordsworth, William.

Parrish, Stephen R., jt. auth. see Parrish, Phyllis W.

Parrish, T. Michael. Richard Taylor: Soldier Prince of Dixie. LC 91-46467. (Illus.). xvi, 554p. (C). 1992. 34.95 (*0-8078-2032-6*) U of NC Pr.

Parrish, T. Michael & Willingham, Robert M. Confederate Imprints: A Bibliography of Southern Publications from Secession to Surrender. (Illus.). 1133p. 1987. 95.00 (*0-318-37956-2*, PA-999-2) Jenkins.

Parrish, Thomas. The Cold War Encyclopedia. 544p. 1996. pap. 60.00 (*0-8050-2778-5*) H Holt & Co.

— Roosevelt & Marshall. 1989. 24.95 (*0-07-040585-9*) McGraw.

— Roosevelt & Marshall: The War They Fought, the Change They Wrought. Lee, Bruce, ed. LC 89-30489. (Illus.). 600p. 1991. pap. 15.00 (*0-688-10740-0*, Quill) Morrow.

Parrish, Vernon. Earning Megabucks the Video Way in the 90's. LC 91-91353. 179p. (Orig.). 1992. pap. 19.95 (*0-9615774-1-X*) V Parrish.

Parrish, W. D. A Dictionary of the Sussex Dialect & Collection of Provincialisms in Use in the County of Sussex. (English Dialect Society Publications Ser.: No. 6). 1972. reprint ed. pap. 16.00 (*0-8115-0440-9*) Periodicals Srv.

Parrish, Wayland M. & Hochmuth, Marie, eds. American Speeches. LC 69-14028. 518p. 1969. reprint ed. text ed. 35.00 (*0-8371-1962-6*, PAAM, Greenwood Pr) Greenwood.

Parrish, Wendy. Blenheim Palace. 48p. 1983. pap. 3.00 (*0-89823-046-2*) New Rivers Pr.

— Conversations in the Gallery. (Illus.). 1977. per. 3.00 (*0-912284-92-7*) New Rivers Pr.

Parrish, William, et al. Missouri: The Heart of the Nation. 2nd ed. (Illus.). 423p. 1992. text ed. write for info. (*0-88295-888-7*); pap. text ed. write for info. (*0-88295-887-9*) Harlan Davidson.

Parrish, William E. A History of Missouri, Volume III: 1860 to 1875. LC 76-155844. (Missouri Sesquicentennial History Ser.). (Illus.). 344p. 1973. 27.50 (*0-8262-0148-2*) U of Mo Pr.

Parrish, William E., ed. The Civil War: A Second American Revolution? LC 77-15658. (American Problem Studies). 158p. (gr. 11-12). 1978. reprint ed. pap. text ed. 9.50 (*0-88275-637-0*) Krieger.

***Parrot.** Career Counselor. 1995. pap. text ed. (*0-8499-3677-2*) Word Inc.

Parrot, Andre. The Temple of Jerusalem. Hooke, Beatrice E., tr. LC 85-8037. (Studies in Biblical Archaeology: No. 5). (Illus.). 112p. 1985. reprint ed. text ed. 38.50 (*0-313-24224-0*, PATJ, Greenwood Pr) Greenwood.

Parrot, Andrea. Acquaintance Rape & Sexual Assault Prevention Training Manual. 5th ed. 1991. 19.95 (*1-55691-076-2*, 762) Learning Pubns.

— Coping with Date Rape & Acquaintance Rape. rev. ed. Rosen, Roger, ed. (Coping Ser.). (YA). (gr. 7 up). 1993. lib. bdg. 15.95 (*0-8239-1649-9*) Rosen Group.

— Rape 101. Date not set. write for info. (*1-55691-099-1*) Learning Pubns.

Parrot, Andrea & Bechhofer, Laurie, eds. Acquaintance Rape: The Hidden Crime. (Personality Processes Ser.). 401p. 1991. text ed. 52.50 (*0-471-51023-8*) Wiley.

Parrot, Andrea, jt. auth. see Bohmer, Carol.

Parrot, Andrea, jt. ed. see Feldman, Harold.

Parrot, Edward, ed. see Borelli, Antonio A., et al.

Parrot, Edward, ed. see De Oliveira, Plinio C.

Parrot, Friedrich. Journey to Ararat. LC 73-115576. (Russia Observed, Series I). 1970. reprint ed. 23.95 (*0-405-03057-6*) Ayer.

Parrot, J. Edward, ed. see Marin, Antonio R.

Parrot, Jasper, jt. auth. see Ashkenazi, Vladimir.

Parrot, Roxanne L., jt. auth. see Maibach, Edward.

***Parrott.** Two for Your Money. 1994. 19.95 (*1-56477-737-5*) That Patchwork.

Parrott, Allen, jt. auth. see Flude, Ray.

Parrott, Andrew, ed. see Keyte, Hugh.

Parrott, Bruce, ed. The Dynamics of Soviet Defense Policy. 400p. 1990. text ed. 25.25 (*0-943875-25-0*, Johns Hopkins) W Wilson Ctr Pr.

— Trade, Technology & Soviet-American Relations. LC 84-48549. (CSIS Publication Series on the Soviet Union in the 1980's; Midland Bks.). (Illus.). 414p. 1985. 35.00 (*0-253-36025-0*); pap. 17.95 (*0-253-20351-1*, MB 351) Ind U Pr.

Parrott, Bruce & Dawisha, Karen, eds. State Building & Military Power in Russia & the New States of Eurasia. (International Politics of Eurasia Ser.: Vol. 5). (Illus.). 300p. 1995. 49.95 (*1-56324-360-1*); pap. 19.95 (*1-56324-361-X*) M E Sharpe.

Parrott, Bruce, jt. auth. see Dawisha, Karen.

Parrott, Bruce, jt. ed. see Dawisha, Karen.

Parrott, Bruce, jt. ed. see Starr, S. Frederick.

Parrott, Carol L., tr. see Beverly, Cal, ed.

Parrott, Cecil, tr. see Hasek, Jaroslav.

Parrott, David. The Deception of the Thrush. 1986. 50.00 (*0-7223-2049-3*, Pub. by A H S Ltd UK) St Mut.

Parrott, Douglas M., ed. Nag Hammadi: Codices III, 3-4 & V, 1: Eugnostos & the Sophia of Jesus Christ. LC 91-19243. (Nag Hammadi Studies: Vol. 27). xxii, 216p. 1991. 83.00 (*90-04-08366-9*) E J Brill.

Parrott, E. O., comp. The Penguin Book of Limericks. (Illus.). 304p. 1987. pap. 11.00 (*0-14-007669-7*, Penguin Bks) Viking Penguin.

Parrott, E. O., ed. How to Be Well-Versed in Poetry. 288p. 1992. pap. 10.00 (*0-14-011275-8*, Penguin Bks) Viking Penguin.

***Parrott, Ian.** The Spiritual Pilgrims. fac. ed. LC 72-466773. (Illus.). 228p. 1969. pap. 65.00 (*0-7837-7302-1*, AU00451) Bks Demand.

***Parrott III, Les & Parrott, Leslie.** Saving Your Marriage Before It Starts: Seven Questions to Ask Before (& After) You Marry. 2nd ed. 1995. audio 12.99 (*0-310-49248-3*) Zondervan.

— Saving Your Marriage Before It Starts-Workbook for Women: Seven Questions to Ask Before (& After) You Marry. 2nd ed. 64p. 1995. 4.99 (*0-310-48741-2*) Zondervan.

Parrott, Iva J. Not Just Quilts. Weiland, Barbara, ed. LC 91-46223. (Quilt Shop Ser.). (Illus.). 72p. (Orig.). 1992. pap. 19.95 (*1-56477-006-0*) That Patchwork.

— Template-Free Stars. Reikes, Ursula, ed. LC 92-21194. (Illus.). 64p. (Orig.). 1993. pap. 14.95 (*1-56477-024-9*, B151) That Patchwork.

Parrott, Jo. Two for Your Money. Reinstatler, Laura, ed. LC 94-20459. (Illus.). 82p. (Orig.). 1994. pap. 19.95 (*1-56477-073-7*) That Patchwork.

Parrott, John L., jt. auth. see Parrott, William W.

Parrott, Les, III. Love's Unseen Enemy: How to Overcome Guilt to Build Healthy Relationships. 208p. 1994. 15.99 (*0-310-40150-X*) Zondervan.

***Parrott, Les, 3rd.** 7 Secrets of a Healthy Dating Relationship. 104p. (YA). Date not set. per., pap. 7.95 (*0-8341-1554-9*) Beacon Hill.

***Parrott, Les & Parrott, Leslie.** Becoming Soul Mates: Cultivating Spiritual Intimacy in the Early Years of Marriage. 160p. 1995. 14.99 (*0-310-20014-8*) Zondervan.

***Parrott, Les, 3rd & Parrott, Leslie.** The Marriage Mentor Manual: How You Can Help the Newlywed Couple Stay Married. 80p. 1995. pap. 5.99 (*0-310-50131-8*) Zondervan.

***Parrott, Les, III & Parrott, Leslie.** Saving Your Marriage Before It Starts: Seven Questions to Ask Before (& After) You Marry. 2nd ed. 208p. 1995. 15.99 (*0-310-49240-8*) Zondervan.

***Parrott, Les, 3rd & Parrott, Leslie.** Saving Your Marriage Before It Starts: A Marriage Curriculum for Engaged, About-to-Be-Engaged, & the Very Newly Married. 48p. 1995. write for info. (*0-310-20448-8*); teacher ed, vdisk 149.99 (*0-310-20451-8*) Zondervan.

— Saving Your Marriage Before It Starts Vol. 1: A Marriage Curriculum for Engaged, About-to-Be-Engaged, & the Very Newly Married. 1995. vdisk write for info. (*0-310-20447-X*) Zondervan.

— Saving Your Marriage Before It Starts Vol. 2: A Marriage Curriculum for Engaged, About-to-Be-Engaged, & the Very Newly Married. 1995. vdisk write for info. (*0-310-20449-6*) Zondervan.

***Parrott, Les, III & Parrott, Leslie.** Saving Your Marriage Before It Starts-Workbook for Men: Seven Questions to Ask Before (& After) You Marry. 2nd ed. 64p. 1995. 4.99 (*0-310-48731-5*) Zondervan.

Parrott, Les, III, jt. auth. see Parrott, Leslie.

Parrott, Leslie. Battle for Your Mind. 199p. 1986. pap. 6.95 (*0-8341-1124-1*) Beacon Hill.

— The Bible Speaks to Me about My Church. 111p. (Orig.). 1987. pap. 5.95 (*0-8341-1213-2*) Beacon Hill.

— Future Church. 179p. (Orig.). 1988. pap. 8.95 (*0-8341-1261-2*) Beacon Hill.

Parrott, Leslie, Jr. The Greeter's Manual: A Guide to Warm-Hearted Churches. 48p. 1993. Saddle stitch. pap. 4.99 (*0-310-37481-2*) Zondervan.

Parrott, Leslie, III. Helping the Struggling Adolescent: A Counseling Guide. 144p. 1993. pap. 12.99 (*0-310-61511-9*) Zondervan.

— Helping the Struggling Adolescent: A Guide for Parents, Counselors & Youth Workers. 272p. 1993. pap. 12.99 (*0-310-57821-3*) Zondervan.

— How to Write Psychology Papers. LC 93-3171. (C). 1993. text ed. 4.50 (*0-06-501798-6*) HarpCollege.

Parrott, Leslie. Keeping Love in the Family. 189p. 1987. pap. 8.95 (*0-8341-1195-0*) Beacon Hill.

— Motivating Volunteers in the Local Church. 141p. 1991. pap. 8.95 (*0-8341-1415-1*) Beacon Hill.

— Softly & Tenderly: The Altar: A Place for Meeting God. 240p. 1989. 14.95 (*0-8341-1304-X*) Beacon Hill.

Parrott, Leslie, III. Usher's Manual. 1970. pap. 4.99 (*0-310-30651-5*, 10513P) Zondervan.

***Parrott, Leslie & Parrott, Les, III.** The Career Counselor: Guidance for Planning Careers & Managing Career Crises. LC 95-3274. (Contemporary Christian Counseling Ser.: Vol. 11). 1995. 16.99 (*0-8499-1074-9*); pap. 10.99 (*0-614-03764-6*) Word Inc.

Parrott, Leslie, jt. auth. see Parrott III, Les.

Parrott, Leslie, jt. auth. see Parrott, Les, III.

Parrott, Leslie, jt. auth. see Parrott, Les.

Parrott, Leslie, jt. auth. see Parrott, Les, 3rd.

Parrott, Leslie, jt. auth. see Schmelzenbach, Elmer.

Parrott, Linda J., jt. ed. see Reese, Hayne W.

Parrott, Martin. Tasks for Language Teachers: A Resource Book for Training & Development. LC 92-34467. (Teacher Training & Development Ser.). 256p. (C). 1993. 49.95 (*0-521-41648-5*); pap. 24.95 (*0-521-42666-9*) Cambridge U Pr.

***Parrott, Robert H. & Rathlev, Mary.** Access to Primary Health Care for Children with HIV: A Guide for Pediatricians, Family Physicians & Nurse Practitioners. 1993. pap. 9.95 (*0-9634295-1-5*) Childs Hosp.

Parrott, S. Relativistic Electrodynamics & Differential Geometry. (Illus.). 320p. 1986. 64.00 (*0-387-96435-5*) Spr-Verlag.

Parrott, Thomas M. A Companion to Victorian Literature. 1988. reprint ed. lib. bdg. 59.00 (*0-7812-0070-9*) Rprt Serv.

— Studies of a Booklover. LC 67-28763. (Essay Index Reprint Ser.). 1977. 20.95 (*0-8369-0771-X*) Ayer.

Parrott, Thomas M. & Craig, Hardin, eds. The Tragedy of Hamlet: A Critical Edition of the Second Quarto. LC 75-42328. 256p. 1976. reprint ed. 50.00 (*0-87752-172-7*) Gordian.

Parrott, Thomas M. & Long, Augustus W. English Poems from Chaucer to Kipling. LC 75-108587. (Granger Index Reprint Ser.). 1977. 20.95 (*0-8369-6115-3*) Ayer.

Parrott, Thomas M. & Robert, Martin. A Companion to Victorian Literature. 1981. reprint ed. lib. bdg. 59.00 (*0-403-01495-6*) Scholarly.

Parrott, Thomas M. & Thorp, Willard, eds. Poetry of the Transition, 1850-1914. LC 72-5594. (Granger Index Reprint Ser.). 1977. reprint ed. 44.95 (*0-8369-6384-9*) Ayer.

Parrott, William W. & Parrott, John L. You Can Afford to Retire! The No-Nonsense Guide to Pre-Financial Planning. 1992. pap. 14.95 (*0-13-980160-X*, Busn) P-H.

Parrow, Kathleen. From Defense to Resistance: Justification of Violence During the French Wars of Religion. LC 93-72130. (Transactions Ser.: Vol. 83, Pt. 6). 80p. 1993. pap. 15.00 (*0-87169-836-6*, T836-PAK) Am Philos.

***Parry.** Monster Man. Date not set. pap. write for info. (*0-449-70444-0*) Fawcett.

— William Morris Textiles. 1995. (*0-517-12055-0*) Random Hse Value.

Parry & Watt. A Handbook of Skills & Methods in Mental Health Research. 336p. 1989. 69.95 (*0-86377-115-7*); pap. text ed. 34.50 (*0-86377-121-1*) L Erlbaum Assocs.

Parry, jt. auth. see McConkie.

Parry, jt. auth. see Morcom.

Parry, Adam M. The Language of Achilles & Other Papers. (Illus.). 352p. 1989. 89.00 (*0-19-814892-5*) OUP.

— Logos & Ergon in Thucydides. rev. ed. Connor, W. R., ed. LC 80-2660. (Monographs in Classical Studies). 1981. lib. bdg. 29.95 (*0-405-14045-2*) Ayer.

Parry, Adam M. & Dorson, Richard M., eds. The Making of Homeric Verse: The Collected Papers of Milman Parry. LC 80-747. (Folklore of the World Ser.). (Illus.). 1981. reprint ed. lib. bdg. 63.95 (*0-405-13321-9*) Ayer.

Parry, Adam M., ed. see Parry, Milman.

***Parry, Alan.** Follow the Star: All the Way to Bethlehem. (J). (ps-8). 1994. 12.99 (*0-8499-1144-3*) Word Inc.

— The Lost Coin. (Illus.). 24p. (J). (ps-00). 1994. 3.99 (*0-8499-1088-9*) Word Inc.

— The Lost Pearl. (Illus.). 24p. (J). (ps-00). 1994. 3.99 (*0-8499-1087-0*) Word Inc.

— The Lost Sheep. (Illus.). 24p. (J). (ps-5). 1994. 3.99 (*0-8499-1089-7*) Word Inc.

— The Lost Son. (Illus.). 24p. (J). (ps-00). 1994. 3.99 (*0-8499-1086-2*) Word Inc.

Parry, Alan & Doan, Robert E. Story Re-Visions: Narrative Therapy in the Postmodern World. LC 94-18296. 200p. 1994. lib. bdg. 35.00 (*0-89862-213-1*, 2213) Guilford Pr.

— Story Revisions: Narrative Therapy in the Postmodern World. LC 94-18296. 1994. pap. text ed. 15.95 (*0-89862-570-X*) Guilford Pubns.

Parry, Alan & Parry, Linda. Bruno Helps Out. LC 91-70401. (Bruno Bks.). (Illus.). 16p. (J). (ps-00). 1991. bds. 1.49 (*0-8066-2528-7*, 9-2528, Augsburg) Augsburg Fortress.

— Bruno Is Sorry. LC 91-70402. (Bruno Bks.). (Illus.). 16p. (J). (ps-00). 1991. bds. 1.49 (*0-8066-2529-5*, 9-2529, Augsburg) Augsburg Fortress.

— Bruno Says Thanks. LC 91-70404. (Bruno Bks.). (Illus.). 16p. (J). (ps-00). 1991. bds. 1.49 (*0-8066-2531-7*, 9-2531, Augsburg) Augsburg Fortress.

— Caleb & Katie's Big Book of Bible Adventures. (Illus.). 64p. (J). (gr. k-5). 1993. 12.99 (*0-8499-0982-1*) Word Inc.

— Noah & the Ark. (Little Bible Story Bks.). (Illus.). 24p. (J). (ps). 1990. pap. 0.99 (*0-8066-2475-2*, 9-2475) Augsburg Fortress.

— Paul Meets Jesus. (Little Bible Story Bks.). (Illus.). 24p. (J). (ps). 1990. pap. 0.99 (*0-8066-2480-9*, 9-2480) Augsburg Fortress.

Parry, Alan, jt. auth. see Parry, Linda.

Parry, Albert. America Learns Russian: A History of the Teaching of the Russian Language in the United States. LC 67-27162. 217p. reprint ed. pap. 61.90 (*0-8357-5351-4*, 2027399) Bks Demand.

— Terrorism. 1980. 24.50 (*0-8149-0746-6*) Random.

Parry, Albert, jt. auth. see Moore, Harry T.

Parry, Albert W. Education in England in the Middle Ages. LC 77-178584. reprint ed. 24.50 (*0-404-56659-6*) AMS Pr.

Parry, Ann. The Poetry of Rudyard Kipling: Rousing the Nation. 160p. 1992. 90.00 (*0-335-09495-3*, Open Univ Pr); pap. 27.50 (*0-335-09494-5*, Open Univ Pr) Taylor & Francis.

Parry, Anne. Physiotherapy Assessment. 2nd ed. LC 85-4615. 168p. (Orig.). 1985. pap. 17.95 (*0-7099-4009-2*, Pub. by Croom Helm UK) Routledge Chapman & Hall.

Parry, Anne, et al. Choosing Nonviolence: The Rainbow House Handbook to a Violence-Free Future for Young Children. LC 90-62582. (Illus.). (Orig.). 1990. pap. 25.45 (*0-9627528-9-4*) Rainbow Hse.

***Parry, Anne S.** Below the Surface. 1994. 10.00 (*0-207-18043-1*, Pub. by Angus & Robertson AT) HarpC.

Parry, Betty. Shake the Parrot Cage. 112p. 1994. 10.00 (*0-932616-47-X*) New Poets Chestnut Hills.

Parry, Betty, ed. The Unicorn & the Garden. LC 78-64531. (Illus.). 1978. per. 15.00 (*0-915380-04-8*) Word Works.

Parry, Charles. Johann Sebastian Bach: The Story of the Development of a Great Personality. 1988. reprint ed. lib. bdg. 59.00 (*0-7812-0778-9*) Rprt Serv.

— Style in Musical Art. lib. bdg. 25.00 (*0-403-01752-1*) Scholarly.

Parry, Charles H. The Evolution of the Music. 483p. 1990. reprint ed. lib. bdg. 89.00 (*0-7812-9024-4*) Rprt Serv.

— Johann Sebastian Bach. LC 73-109818. 584p. 1970. reprint ed. text ed. 65.00 (*0-8371-4309-8*, PAJB, Greenwood Pr) Greenwood.

— Style in Musical Art. LC 78-13864. (Encore Music Editions Ser.). 1979. reprint ed. 32.45 (*0-88355-807-6*) Hyperion Conn.

— Style in Musical Art. 438p. 1990. reprint ed. lib. bdg. 89.00 (*0-7812-9128-3*) Rprt Serv.

Parry, Christopher. English Through Drama: A Way of Teaching. LC 72-184902. 243p. reprint ed. pap. 69.30 (*0-685-43695-0*, 2026352) Bks Demand.

Parry, Cindy. Activities That Build Young Women, Vol. 2. 48p. (YA). 1993. pap. 6.98 (*0-88290-457-4*) Horizon Utah.

— Activities That Inspire Young Women, Vol. 1. 48p. 1994. 6.98 (*0-88290-489-2*, 2063) Horizon Utah.

— Activities That Inspire Young Women, Vol. 2. 48p. (YA). 1994. pap. 6.98 (*0-88290-490-6*, 2064) Horizon Utah.

— Young Women Activities: Activities That Build Young Women, Activities That Build Young Women, Set Vols. 1 & 2. 1994. pap. 13.98 (*0-88290-472-8*) Horizon Utah.

— Young Women Inspirational Activities: Activities That Inspire Young Women, Activities That Inspire Young Women, Set, Vols. 1 & 2. 1994. pap. 13.98 (*0-88290-518-X*) Horizon Utah.

Parry, Clive. The Sources & Evidences of International Law. LC 65-17525. (Melland Schill Lectures). 130p. reprint ed. pap. 37.10 (*0-317-30008-3*, 2051868) Bks Demand.

PQ

Parry, Clive M., ed. Consolidated Treaty Series, 1648-1920, 243 vols., Set. annot. ed. LC 70-76750. 1977. write for info. (*0-379-13000-9*) Oceana.

— Index-Guide to Treaties Based on the Consolidated Treaty Series & All Other Series Therein Utilized, 12 vols., Set, Vols. 1-5. LC 79-91238. (Consolidated Treaty Ser.). 1986. Vols. 1-5: General Chronology & Vols. 1 & 2: Special Chronology. Vols. 1-5: Party Index A-Z. 1, 500.00 (*0-379-13002-5*) Oceana.

— Law Officers' Opinions to the Foreign Office, 1793-1860: A Reproduction of the Manuscript Series with Index & Commentary, 97 vols., Set. (Manuscript Ser.). 1975. reprint ed. 2,500.00 (*0-379-13400-4*) Oceana.

Parry, Clive M. & Hopkins, J. A., eds. Commonwealth International Law Cases, 17 vols., Set. LC 73-20151. 1974. lib. bdg. 1,054.00 (*0-379-00950-1*) Oceana.

Parry, Clive M., et al, eds. Encyclopaedic Dictionary of International Law. LC 85-21496. 564p. 1986. 65.00 (*0-379-20828-8*) Oceana.

***Parry, Colin & Parry, Wendy.** Tim: An Ordinary Boy. (Illus.). 240p. 1995. 29.95 (*0-340-61789-6*, Pub. by H & S UK) Trafalgar.

***Parry, Danaan.** Essene Book of Days 1995. rev. ed. (Illus.). 416p. 1994. pap. 12.95 (*0-913319-24-4*) Sunstone Pubns.

— Essene Book of Days 1996. rev. ed. (Illus.). 416p. 1995. pap. 14.95 (*0-913319-12-0*) Sunstone Pubns.

— Essene Book of Meditations & Blessings. 128p. (Orig.). 1991. pap. 4.95 (*0-913319-17-1*) Sunstone Pubns.

— Essene Engagement Book of 1996, Set. rev. ed. (Illus.). 144p. 1995. pap. 9.95 (*0-913319-22-8*) Sunstone Pubns.

— Warriors of the Heart. LC 90-70815. (Illus.). 224p. (Orig.). 1991. pap. 9.95 (*0-913319-09-0*) Sunstone Pubns.

Parry, Danaan & Forest, Lila. Earthsteward's Handbook. rev. ed. LC 88-134579. (Illus.). 160p. (Orig.). 1991. pap. 6.95 (*0-913319-19-8*) Sunstone Pubns.

Parry, David. Households of God. (Cistercian Studies: No. 39). (Orig.). 1980. pap. 7.95 (*0-87907-939-8*) Cistercian Pubns.

Parry, David, ed. Fibrous Proteins: Scientific, Industrial & Medical Aspects, Vol. 1. LC 79-41004. 1980. text ed. 143.00 (*0-12-545701-4*) Acad Pr.

— Fibrous Proteins: Scientific, Industrial & Medical Aspects, Vol. 2. 1980. text ed. 139.00 (*0-12-545702-2*) Acad Pr.

Parry, David A. & Steinert, Peter M. Intermediate Filament Structure. (Molecular Biology Intelligence Unit Ser.). 186p. 1995. 69.00 (*1-57059-120-2*, LN9120) R G Landes.

Parry, David H. The Sanctity of Contracts in English Law. (Hamlyn Lectures Legal Reprint Ser.). viii, 72p. 1986. reprint ed. lib. bdg. 20.00 (*0-8377-2509-7*) Rothman.

Parry, David M. Hegel's Phenomenology of the "We" (American University Studies: Philosophy: Ser. V, Vol. 57). 272p. (C). 1988. text ed. 39.80 (*0-8204-0733-X*) P Lang Pubs.

— Scarlet Empire. LC 77-154456. (Utopian Literature Ser.). (Illus.). 1976. reprint ed. 33.95 (*0-405-03538-1*) Ayer.

Parry, David W. Plant Pathology in Agriculture. (Illus.). 300p. (C). 1990. 105.00 (*0-521-36351-9*); pap. 37.95 (*0-521-36890-1*) Cambridge U Pr.

Parry, Deborah L. Butterworths Trading & Consumer Law: The Law Relating to Trade Descriptions, 2 vols., Set. 1990. ring bd. 390.00 (*0-406-32634-7*, UK) Butterworth Legal Pubs.

Parry, Deborah L., jt. auth. see Harvey, Brian W.

Parry, Donald A., jt. ed. see Hinde, Robert A.

Parry, Donald W., ed. Temples of the Ancient World: Ritual & Symbolism. LC 93-36629. xxiv, 805p. 1994. 29.95 (*0-87579-811-X*) Deseret Bk.

Parry, Donald W. & Ricks, Stephen D. A Bibliography on Temples of the Ancient Near East & Mediterranean World: Arranged by Subject & by Author. Welch, John W., ed. LC 91-516. (Ancient Near Eastern Texts & Studies: Vol. 9). 324p. 1991. lib. bdg. 99.95 (*0-7734-9775-7*) E Mellen.

Parry, E. J. Encyclopedia of Perfumery, 2 vols., Set. 1992. lib. bdg. 1,500.75 (*0-8490-5418-4*) Gordon Pr.

Parry, Edward A. The Overbury Mystery: A Chronicle of Fact & Drama of the Law. LC 71-174850. 1972. reprint ed. 22.95 (*0-405-08835-3*) Ayer.

— Seven Lamps of Advocacy. LC 68-16965. (Essay Index Reprint Ser.). 1977. reprint ed. 17.95 (*0-8369-0773-6*) Ayer.

— Vagabonds All. LC 73-93370. (Essay Index Reprint Ser.). 1977. 23.95 (*0-8369-1425-2*) Ayer.

— What the Judge Thought. LC 68-29237. (Essay Index Reprint Ser.). 1977. 20.95 (*0-8369-0772-8*) Ayer.

Parry, Ellwood C. Friedrich Schiller in America. 1976. lib. bdg. 59.95 (*0-8490-1866-8*) Gordon Pr.

Parry, Elwood C., III. The Art of Thomas Cole: Ambition & Imagination. LC 85-40511. (Illus.). 424p. 1989. 95.00 (*0-87413-214-2*) U Delaware Pr.

Parry, Evelyn P. On the Yaquina & Big Elk. (Illus.). (Orig.). 1985. pap. text ed. 8.50 (*0-911443-07-X*) Lincoln Coun Hist.

— Pictorial Toledo, Ore. Then & Now. LC 83-81298. (Illus.). 97p. (Orig.). 1983. pap. 7.50 (*0-911443-01-0*) Lincoln Coun Hist.

Parry, G. Trilingual Cotton Terminology: Terminologie Cotonniere Trilingue. 87p. (ENG, FRE & SPA.). 1986. pap. 34.95 (*0-8288-0039-1*, M15818) Fr & Eur.

Parry, G., jt. auth. see Potts, W.

Parry, G. J. A Protestant Vision: William Harrison & the Reformation of Elizabethan England. LC 86-17091. (Camnbridge Studies in the History & Theory of Politics). 360p. 1987. 74.95 (*0-521-32997-3*) Cambridge U Pr.

Parry, G. J., et al. Political Participation & Democracy in Britain. (Illus.). 504p. (C). 1992. 89.95 (*0-521-33298-2*); pap. 39.95 (*0-521-33602-3*) Cambridge U Pr.

Parry, Gareth J. Guillain-Barre Syndrome. LC 92-49287. 208p. 1992. 57.00 (*0-86577-444-7*) Thieme Med Pubs.

Parry, Geraint. Political Elites. (Studies in Political Science). 1969. pap. text ed. 15.95 (*0-04-320059-1*) Routledge Chapman & Hall.

Parry, Geraint, ed. Politics in an Interdependent World: Essays Presented to Ghita Ionescu. 224p. Date not set. text ed. 67.95 (*1-85278-737-6*, Pub. by E Elgar Pub UK) Ashgate Pub Co.

Parry, Geraint & Moran, Michael, eds. Democracy & Democratization. LC 93-725. 256p. 1993. 62.50 (*0-415-09049-0*, B2437, Routledge NY); pap. 17.95 (*0-415-09050-4*, B2441, Routledge NY) Routledge.

Parry, Glenys. Coping with Crises. (Problems in Practice Ser.). (Illus.). 276p. 1990. pap. 18.95 (*0-415-03546-5*, A4925) Routledge.

Parry, Graham. The Golden Age Restor'd: The Culture of the Stuart Court, 1603-42. LC 81-32544. 276p. 1986. text ed. 18.95 (*0-312-33195-9*) St Martin.

— The Seventeenth Century, the Intellectual & Cultural Context of English Literature, 1603-1700. (Literature in English Ser.). 336p. (Orig.). (C). 1989. pap. text ed. 22. 95 (*0-582-49376-5*, 73590) Longman.

— The Trophies of Time: English Antiquarians of the Seventeenth Century. (Illus.). 320p. 1995. 56.00 (*0-19-812962-9*) OUP.

Parry, Gwyn. The Hurricane. (Poetry Wales Poets Ser.: Vol. 9). 48p. 1988. pap. 9.95 (*0-907476-80-5*, Pub. by Poetry Wales Pr UK) Dufour.

— Parys Mountain. (Illus.). 48p. (Orig.). 1990. pap. 13.95 (*1-85411-038-1*, Pub. by Poetry Wales Pr UK) Dufour.

Parry, Herbert B. Scrapie Disease in Sheep: Historical, Clinical, Epidemiological, Pathological & Practical Aspects of the Natural Disease. 1984. text ed. 95.00 (*0-12-545750-2*) Acad Pr.

Parry, Hildegarde W., tr. see Leipp, Emile.

Parry, Hugh. Thelxis: Magic & Imagination in Greek Myth & Poetry. 344p. (C). 1992. lib. bdg. 46.00 (*0-8191-8657-0*) U Pr of Amer.

Parry, J., jt. auth. see Arlidge, A.

Parry, J. H. The Age of Reconnaissance: Discovery, Exploration, & Settlement, 1450-1650. LC 81-51175. (Illus.). 400p. 1982. pap. 14.00 (*0-520-04235-2*) U CA Pr.

Parry, J. H., pseud. The Audiencia of New Galicia in the Sixteenth Century: A Study in Spanish Colonial Government. LC 85-10039. (Illus.). xii, 207p. 1985. reprint ed. text ed. 59.75 (*0-313-24957-1*, PANG, Greenwood Pr) Greenwood.

Parry, J. H. The Discovery of the Sea. LC 81-51174. 350p. 1981. pap. 14.00 (*0-520-04237-9*) U CA Pr.

— Offences Against Property. (Criminal Law Library: Vol. 7). 464p. 1989. 100.00 (*0-08-033070-3*, Waterlow) Macmillan.

— The Spanish Seaborne Empire. 417p. 1990. pap. 14.00 (*0-520-07140-9*) U CA Pr.

Parry, J. T., jt. ed. see Eden, M. J.

***Parry, James K.** USENET According to Kibo, Premier Edition. (Illus.). 500p. (Orig.). 1995. pap. 29.99 (*0-672-30622-0*) Sams.

Parry, Jay, jt. auth. see Hanks, Kurt.

Parry, Jay A. The Burning. LC 91-11107. 208p. (Orig.). 1991. pap. 8.95 (*0-87579-521-8*) Deseret Bk.

— Soldiers, Statesman & Heroes: America's Founding Presidents. LC 88-21146. (Illus.). 250p. 1990. 15.95 (*0-88080-027-5*) Natl Ctr Constitutional.

— Traveling with Kids - One Hundred One Tips for a Great Trip. (Illus.). 193p. (Orig.). 1989. pap. text ed. 7.95 (*0-944803-69-5*) Brite Music.

Parry, Jay A. & Allison, Andrew M. The Real George Washington. LC 90-5607. (American Classic Ser.). (Illus.). 928p. 1990. 24.95 (*0-88080-013-5*); pap. 19.95 (*0-88080-014-3*) Natl Ctr Constitutional.

Parry, Jay A., jt. auth. see Price, Alvin.

Parry, Jo-Ann & Hornsby, David. Write On: A Conference Approach to Writing. LC 87-22929. vi, 92p. (Orig.). 1988. pap. text ed. 16.50 (*0-435-08460-7*) Heinemann.

Parry, Joan & Freudenberg, Marie. Creativity Doesn't Die. Costa, Gwen, ed. 1990. pap. 13.95 (*0-87949-337-2*) Ashley Bks.

Parry, Joan K. Social Work Theory & Practice with the Terminally Ill. LC 88-29623. (Social Work Practice Ser.: No. 3). (Illus.). 137p. 1989. text ed. 29.95 (*0-86656-750-X*) Haworth Pr.

Parry, Joan K., ed. Social Work Practice with the Terminally Ill: A Transcultural Perspective. 250p. (C). 1990. text ed. 51.95x (*0-398-05697-8*) C C Thomas.

— Social Work Practice with the Terminally Ill: A Transcultural Perspective. 250p. 1990. pap. 30.95 (*0-398-06315-X*) C C Thomas.

***Parry, Joan K. & Ryan, Angela S., eds.** A Cross-Cultural Look at Death, Dying, & Religion. LC 94-42941. (Social Work Ser). 1995. write for info. (*0-8304-1333-2*) Nelson-Hall.

Parry, John. The Americans with Disabilities Act Manual State & Local Government Services, Employment, & Public Accommodations. 111p. (Orig.). (C). 1992. pap. 13.95 (*0-89707-801-2*) ABA Prof Educ Pubns.

Parry, John & Keith, Robert G., eds. New Iberian World: A Documentary History of the Discovery & Settlement of Latin America to the Early 17th. Century, 5 vols., Set. LC 82-19664. (New Iberian World Ser.). 1988. 250.00 (*0-8240-4839-3*) Garland.

Parry, John H., ed. Establishment of the European Hegemony: 1415-1715: Trade & Exploration in the Age of the Renaissance. 1961. pap. text ed. 12.00 (*0-06-131045-X*, TB1045, Torch) HarpC.

Parry, Jonathan. The Rise Fall of Liberal Government in Victorian Britain. LC 93-5937. 392p. 1994. 40.00 (*0-300-05779-2*) Yale U Pr.

Parry, Jonathan & Bloch, Maurice, eds. Money & the Morality of Exchange. (C). 1989. 59.95 (*0-521-36597-X*); pap. 17.95 (*0-521-36774-3*) Cambridge U Pr.

Parry, Jonathan, jt. ed. see Bloch, Maurice.

Parry, Jonathan P. Death in Banaras. LC 93-31990. (Lewis Henry Morgan Lectures: No. 1990). (Illus.). 352p. (C). 1994. 69.95 (*0-521-46074-3*) Cambridge U Pr.

— Death in Banaras. LC 93-31990. (Lewis Henry Morgan Lectures: No. 1990). (Illus.). 352p. (C). 1995. pap. 24.95 (*0-521-46625-3*) Cambridge U Pr.

Parry-Jones, D. Welsh Legends & Folklore. 1972. 59.95 (*0-8490-1282-1*) Gordon Pr.

Parry-Jones, Jemima. Amazing Birds of Prey. LC 92-909. (Eyewitness Juniors Ser.). (Illus.). 32p. (Orig.). (J). (gr. 1-5). 1992. lib. bdg. 9.99 (*0-679-92771-9*); pap. 7.99 (*0-679-82771-4*) Knopf Bks Yng Read.

— Jemima Parry-Jones' Falconry: Care by Captive Breeding & Conservation. 1994. 29.95 (*0-7153-0105-5*, Pub. by D & C Pub UK) Sterling.

— Training Birds of Prey. (Illus.). 160p. 1994. 29.95 (*0-7153-0142-X*, Pub. by D & C Pub UK) Sterling.

Parry, Julie. Induction: Library Training Guide. 64p. 1993. pap. 35.00 (*1-85604-078-X*, LAP078X, Pub. by Lib Assn Pub UK) UNIPUB.

Parry, Kate. Reading for a Purpose. LC 91-68108. 400p. (Orig.). (C). 1992. pap. text ed. 18.50 (*0-312-03627-2*); pap. text ed. 0.56 (*0-312-03628-0*) St Martin.

Parry, Kate, jt. ed. see Hill, Clifford.

***Parry, Ken.** The American Winemakers Cookbook. (Illus.). 200p. (Orig.). 1995. pap. 13.95 (*1-886026-03-3*) Wine Grape.

***Parry, Ken, ed.** The California Winemaker's Cook Book. 180p. 1994. pap. text ed. 13.95 (*1-886026-00-9*) Wine Grape.

— The Italian Winemaker's Cook Book. 180p. 1996. pap. text ed. 13.95 (*1-886026-02-5*) Wine Grape.

— The Winemaker's Cook Book. 125p. 1993. pap. text ed. 9.95 (*1-886026-01-7*) Wine Grape.

Parry, Leonard A. History of Torture in England: With Intro. & Index Added. LC 74-172590. (Criminology, Law Enforcement, & Social Problems Ser.: No. 180). 1975. 30.00 (*0-87585-180-0*) Patterson Smith.

— Some Famous Medical Trials. LC 74-95631. 1974. reprint ed. 39.50 (*0-678-03754-X*) Kelley.

Parry, Linda. Textiles of the Arts & Crafts Movement. LC 87-51290. (Illus.). 200p. 1988. pap. 22.50 (*0-500-27497-5*) Thames Hudson.

***Parry, Linda, ed.** Mealtime Prayers. LC 94-5435. (Little Prayers Ser.). (Illus.). (J). 1995. 3.99 (*0-8499-1149-4*) Word Pub.

***Parry, Linda, ed. & comp.** Morning Prayers. LC 94-28656. (My Family & Friends Prayers Ser.). (Illus.). (J). 1995. 3.99 (*0-8499-1160-5*) Word Pub.

***Parry, Linda, ed.** Prayers of Praise: Thank You Prayers. LC 94-3641. (Little Prayers Ser.). (Illus.). (J). 1995. 3.99 (*0-8499-1159-1*) Word Pub.

Parry, Linda & Parry, Alan. Jesus & You. LC 91-71033. (Mix-&-Match Bks.). (Illus.). 10p. (J). (ps-00). 1991. 3.99 (*0-8066-2557-0*, 9-2557, Augsburg) Augsburg Fortress.

— Jesus Loves You. LC 91-71034. (Mix-&-Match Bks.). 10p. (J). 1991. 3.99 (*0-8066-2558-9*, 9-2558, Augsburg) Augsburg Fortress.

— Wonderful Jesus! A Pop-up Activity Book. (Illus.). 12p. (J). 1993. 15.99 (*0-7847-0045-1*, 24-03643) Standard Pub.

Parry, Linda, jt. auth. see Parry, Alan.

Parry, M. L., et al. The Impact of Climatic Variations on Agriculture, Vol. 1: Assessments in Cool Temperate & Cold Regions. (C). 1988. lib. bdg. 157.50 (*90-277-2700-7*) Kluwer Ac.

— The Impact of Climatic Variations on Agriculture, Vol. 2: Assessments in Semi-Arid Regions. (C). 1988. lib. bdg. 144.00 (*90-277-2719-8*) Kluwer Ac.

Parry, Marian, illus. City Mouse - Country Mouse & Two More Mouse Tales from Aesop. (J). (gr. 2-3). 1989. 28. 67 (*0-590-65228-1*) Scholastic Inc.

***Parry, Martin.** Climate Change World Economy. Date not set. 24.95 (*1-85383-109-3*, Pub. by Erthscan Pubns UK) Island Pr.

***Parry, Martin & Duncan, R.** Economic Implications Climate Change Brit. 1995. 24.95 (*1-85383-240-5*, Pub. by Erthscan Pubns UK) Island Pr.

Parry, Michael. Harrap's Arabic Phrase Book. 1993. pap. 4.00 (*0-671-84765-1*, Harraps) P-H Gen Ref & Trav.

Parry, Millman. Serbocroation Heroic Songs, Vol. III: Wedding of Smailagic Meho. Lord, Albert B. & Bynum, David E., eds. Bynum, David E., tr. 338p. 1974. 22.50 (*0-674-80163-6*) HUP.

Parry, Milman. The Making of Homeric Verse: The Collected Papers of Milman Parry. Parry, Adam M., ed. 528p. 1987. pap. 26.00 (*0-19-520560-X*) OUP.

— Serbocroatian Heroic Songs: Bihacka Krajina: Epics from Bihac, Cazin, & Kulen Vakuf, Vol. 4. Bynum, David E., ed. (Milman Parry Collection, Texts & Translation Ser.). (Illus.). 529p. (C). 1980. 22.50 (*0-674-80165-2*) HUP.

Parry, P. & Pawsey, P. Principles of Microbiology. (C). 1984. 110.00 (*0-7487-0320-9*, Pub. by S Thornes Pubs UK) St Mut.

Parry, Pamela J., comp. Contemporary Art & Artists: An Index to Reproductions. LC 78-57763. 327p. 1978. text ed. 59.95 (*0-313-20544-2*, PCO/, Greenwood Pr) Greenwood.

— Photography Index: A Guide to Reproductions. LC 78-20013. 372p. 1979. text ed. 42.95 (*0-313-20700-3*, PPI/, Greenwood Pr) Greenwood.

Parry, Pamela J. & Chipman, Kathe, comps. Print Index: A Guide to Reproductions. LC 83-12824. (Art Reference Collection Ser.: No. 4). xxiv, 310p. 1983. text ed. 59.95 (*0-313-22063-8*, PPR/, Greenwood Pr) Greenwood.

Parry, R. B. & Perkins, C. R. World Mapping Today. (Illus.). 608p. 1987. text ed. 220.00 (*0-408-02850-5*) Buttrwrth-Heinemann.

Parry, R. B., jt. ed. see Perkins, C. R.

Parry, R. H., ed. The English Civil War & After, 1642-1658. LC 74-111423. (C). 1970. pap. 13.00 (*0-520-01783-8*) U CA Pr.

Parry, R. H., jt. auth. see Fookes, P. G.

Parry, R. T., jt. auth. see Fuller, D. B.

Parry, Richard. Bonnot Gang: The Story of the French Illegalists. (Illus.). 190p. (Orig.). (C). 1987. pap. 12.00 (*0-946061-04-1*) Left Bank.

— Ice Warrior. Grad, Doug, ed. 288p. (Orig.). 1991. mass mkt. 4.50 (*0-671-70008-1*) PB.

Parry, Richard, jt. ed. see Brown, Alice.

***Parry, Richard D.** Plato's Craft of Justice. LC 95-3471. (SUNY Series in Ancient Greek Philosophy). 1995. write for info. (*0-7914-2731-5*); pap. write for info. (*0-7914-2732-3*) State U NY Pr.

***Parry, Richard L.** Japan. (Cadogan Guides Ser.). (Illus.). 512p. 1995. pap. 21.95 (*0-947754-72-5*) Globe Pequot.

Parry, Robert. In Defense of Astrology: Astrology's Answers to Its Critics. LC 91-16850. (Illus.). 224p. 1992. reprint ed. pap. 9.95 (*0-87542-596-8*) Llewellyn Pubns.

— Tai Chi. (Headway Lifeguides Ser.). (Illus.). 116p. 1995. pap. 13.95 (*0-340-60008-X*, Pub. by Headway UK) Trafalgar.

— Trick or Treason: The October Surprise Mystery. 380p. 1993. 24.95 (*1-879823-08-X*) Sheridan Sq Pr.

Parry, Robert W. & Kodama, Goji. Boron Chemistry-4: Fourth International Meeting on Boron Chemistry, Salt Lake City & Snowbird, Utah, 8-13 July 1979. (IUPAC Symposium Ser.). 150p. 1980. 68.00 (*0-08-025256-7*, Pub. by Pergamon Repr UK) Franklin.

Parry, Ruth S. Custody Disputes: Evaluation & Intervention. 224p. 1986. text ed. 29.95 (*0-669-11975-X*) Free Pr.

Parry, S. Thomas & Stansfield, Charles W. Language Aptitude Reconsidered. 272p. 1990. pap. write for info. (*0-13-521360-6*) P-H.

Parry, Scott B. From Managing to Empowering: An Action Guide to Developing Winning Facilitation Skills. LC 93-47184. (Illus.). 192p. 1994. pap. 19.95 (*0-527-76232-6*) Qual Resc.

Parry, Susan J. Activation Spectrometry in Chemical Analysis. (Chemical Analysis: a Series of Monographs on Analytical Chemistry & Its Applications: No. 1075). 264p. 1991. text ed. 99.95 (*0-471-63844-7*) Wiley.

Parry, Thomas G. The Multinational Enterprise: International Investment & Host-Country Impacts. Altman, Edward I. & Walter, Ingo, eds. LC 77-24394. (Contemporary Studies in Economic & Financial Analysis: Vol. 20). 1980. lib. bdg. 73.25 (*0-89232-092-3*) Jai Pr.

Parry, W. E., ed. Essays in Theoretical Physics: In Honor of Dirk ter Haar. (Illus.). 352p. 1984. 140.00 (*0-08-026523-5*, Pub. by Pergamon Repr UK) Franklin.

Parry, W. H. Three Centuries of English Church Music. 1977. lib. bdg. 59.95 (*0-8490-2745-4*) Gordon Pr.

Parry, Wendy, jt. auth. see Parry, Colin.

Parry, William E. Journal of Voyage of Discovery to Arctic Regions. (Shorey Historical Ser.). 118p. reprint ed. pap. 8.95 (*0-8466-0046-3*, S46) Shorey.

Parry, William J. Chipped Stone Tools in Formative Oaxaca, Mexico: Their Procurement, Production & Use. (Memoirs Ser.: No. 20). (Illus.). xvi, 178p. (Orig.). 1987. pap. 18.00 (*0-915703-10-6*) U Mich Mus Anthro.

Parry, William J. & Christenson, Andrew L. Prehistoric Stone Technology on Northern Black Mesa, Arizona. LC 87-72676. (Center for Archaeological Investigations Research Paper Ser.: No. 12). (Illus.). xx, 312p. (Orig.). 1988. pap. 23.00 (*0-88104-052-5*) Center Archaeo.

Parry, William J. & Speth, John D. Late Prehistoric Occupation in Southeastern New Mexico. (Technical Reports Ser., Contribution Ten in Research Reports in Archaeology: The Garnsey Spring Campsite: No. 15). (Illus.). 228p. (Orig.). 1984. pap. text ed. 8.00 (*0-932206-99-9*) U Mich Mus Anthro.

Parry, William J., jt. ed. see Christenson, Andrew L.

Parry, William J., jt. auth. see Speth, John D.

Parry, William T. & Hacker, Edward A. Aristotelian Logic. LC 90-44126. 555p. (C). 1991. 59.50 (*0-7914-0689-X*); pap. 19.95 (*0-7914-0690-3*) State U NY Pr.

Parry-Wingfield, Maurice, jt. auth. see Davey, Nigel.

Pars, L. A. Introduction to Dynamics. LC 54-354. 523p. reprint ed. pap. 149.10 (*0-317-08553-0*, 2051462) Bks Demand.

— A Treatise on Analytical Dynamics. LC 79-87498. 1979. reprint ed. 95.00 (*0-918024-07-2*) Ox Bow.

Parsa, Misagh. Economic Development & Political Transformation. (Special Studies on Social, Political, & Economic Development). (C). 1929. text ed. 32.50 (*0-8133-7504-5*) Westview.

— Social Origins of the Iranian Revolution. LC 88-31285. (Social Foundations of the Policy Process Ser.). 256p. (C). 1989. pap. text ed. 15.00 (*0-8135-1412-6*) Rutgers U Pr.

***Parsa-Stay, Flora.** The Complete Book of Dental Remedies: A Practical Guide to Nutritional & Conventional Dental Care. 220p. 1995. pap. 12.95 (*0-89529-657-8*) Avery Pub.

Parsaei, H. E. & Mital, Anil, eds. Economics of Advanced Manufacturing Systems. 336p. 1992. 89.95 (*0-442-31516-3*) Chapman & Hall.

Parsaei, H. R. & Sullivan, W. G., eds. Concurrent Engineering: Contemporary Issues & Modern Design Tools. LC 93-14639. 1993. write for info. (*0-412-46510-8*, Chap & Hall NY) Chapman & Hall.

An Asterisk (*) at the beginning of an entry indicates that the title is appearing in BIP for the first time.

Parsaei, H. R., et al, eds. Justification Methods for Computer Integrated Manufacturing Systems. (Manufacturing Research & Technology Ser.: No. 9). 312p. 1990. 100.00 (*0-444-88153-0*) Elsevier.

***Parsaei, Hamid R. & Jamshidi, Mo, eds.** Design & Implementation of Intelligent Manufacturing Systems: From Expert Systems, Neural Networks, to Fuzzy Logic. LC 95-4068. (Environmental & Intelligent Manufacturing Systems Ser.). 1995. text ed. 75.00 (*0-13-192030-8*) P-H.

Parsaei, Hamid R., et al, eds. Economic & Financial Justification of Advanced Manufacturing Technologies. LC 92-26070. (Manufacturing Research & Technology Ser.: Vol. 14). 1992. write for info. (*0-444-89398-9*) Elsevier.

Parsan, Elizabeth. South-South Trade in Global Development. 193p. 1993. 59.95 (*1-85628-432-8*, Pub. by Avebury Technical UK) Ashgate Pub Co.

— South-South Trade Options & Development. 1991. text ed. 59.00 (*0-86187-163-4*, Pub. by Pinter Pubs UK) St Martin.

Parsaye, Kamran & Chignell, Marc. Expert Systems for Experts. LC 87-32620. 462p. 1988. text ed. 53.95 (*0-471-60175-6*); pap. text ed. 29.95 (*0-471-60721-5*) Wiley.

Parsaye, Kamran & Chignell, Mark. Intelligent Database Tools & Applications: Hyperinformation Access, Data Quality, Visualization, Automatic Discovery. 560p. 1993. text ed. 55.95 (*0-471-57065-6*); pap. text ed. 34.95 (*0-471-57066-4*) Wiley.

Parsaye, Kamran, et al. Intelligent Databases: Object Oriented Deductive Hypermedia Technologies. 496p. 1989. pap. text ed. 39.95 (*0-471-50345-2*) Wiley.

Parscoe, G. & Foster-Lynam, Craig. Sand-Small Book. 8p. (J). 1987. 2.95 (*0-88679-554-0*) Educ Insights.

— Sand-Tall Book. 8p. (J). 1987. 17.95 (*0-88679-553-2*) Educ Insights.

Parscoe, G., jt. auth. see Kenneth, David.

Parse, Rosemarie R. Nursing Science: Major Paradigms, Theories & Critiques. (Illus.). 224p. 1987. text ed. 38.95 (*0-7216-1803-0*) Saunders.

***Parse, Rosemarie Rizzo, ed.** Illuminations: The Human Becoming Theory in Practice & Research. 1995. 35.95 (*0-88737-637-1*) Natl League Nurse.

Parsell, David B. Louis Auchincloss. (United States Authors Ser.: No. 534). 152p. 1988. text ed. 20.95 (*0-8057-7516-1*, Twayne) Macmillan.

— Michel de Ghelderode. (Twayne's World Authors Ser.). 128p. 1993. text ed. 22.95 (*0-8057-4303-0*, Twayne) Macmillan.

Parsell, Neal. Knight's Rule: A Tale of Modern Wilderness. LC 90-62374. 226p. (Orig.). 1990. pap. 9.95 (*0-945519-12-5*) Mountn Meadw Pr.

Parsell, Roger, jt. auth. see Breuer, Hans-Peter.

Parsenow, Gunter. Swedish & German Economics & Law Dictionary: Fachwoerterbuch Fuer Recht und Wirtschaft. 2nd ed. 520p. (GER & SWE.). 1985. 195.00 (*0-8288-0825-2*, M7399) Fr & Eur.

Parsey, J. M., Jr., ed. see International Conference on Defects in Semiconductors Staff.

Parshall, B & Wang, J. Quantum Linear Groups. rev. ed. LC 90-19310. (MEMO Ser.: Vol. 89/439). 157p. 1993. reprint ed. pap. text ed. 24.00 (*0-8218-2501-1*, MEMO 89/439) Am Math.

Parshall, Brian J., jt. ed. see Haboush, William J.

Parshall, George W. Homogeneous Catalysis: The Applications & Chemistry of Catalysis by Soluble Transition Metal Complexes. LC 79-27696. (Wiley-Interscience Publication Ser.). 254p. reprint ed. pap. 72.40 (*0-7837-2370-9*, 2040056) Bks Demand.

Parshall, George W. & Ittel, Steven D. Homogeneous Catalysis: The Applications & Chemistry of Catalysis by Soluble Transition Metal Complexes. 2nd ed. 360p. 1992. text ed. 64.95 (*0-471-53829-9*) Wiley.

Parshall, J. C. The History of the Parshall Family from 1066 to the Close of the Nineteenth Century. (Illus.). 309p. 1989. reprint ed. lib. bdg. 54.50 (*0-8328-0938-1*); reprint ed. pap. 46.50 (*0-8328-0939-X*) Higginson Bk Co.

Parshall, Karen H. & Rowe, David E. The Emergence of the American Mathematical Research Community, 1876-1900: J.J. Sylvester, Felix Klein, & E.H. Moore. LC 94-2218. 1994. write for info. (*0-8218-9004-2*) Am Math.

Parshall, Linda B., jt. auth. see Parshall, Peter W.

Parshall, Peter W. & Parshall, Linda B. Art & the Reformation: An Annotated Bibliography. (Reference Books-Reference Publications in Art History). 320p. 1986. lib. bdg. 45.00 (*0-8161-8602-2*) G K Hall.

Parshall, Peter W., jt. auth. see Landau, David.

Parshall, Phil. Beyond the Mosque: Christians Within Muslin Community. 256p. 1991. pap. 10.99 (*0-8010-7089-9*) Baker Bk.

— The Cross & the Crescent. 1989. pap. 10.99 (*0-8423-0473-8*) Tyndale.

— La Fortaleza y el Fuego: Christ & Muslims. (SPA.). 3.95 (*84-7645-055-9*, 223118, Pub. by Edit Clie SP) TSELF.

— Inside the Community: Understanding Muslims Through Their Traditions. LC 94-2526. 256p. (Orig.). 1994. pap. 13.99 (*0-8010-7132-1*) Baker Bk.

— New Paths in Muslim Evangelism: Evangelical Approaches to Contextualization. 200p. (Orig.). 1980. pap. 10.99 (*0-8010-7056-2*) Baker Bk.

***Parshchikov, Alexei.** Blue Vitriol. Chadwick, Cydney, ed. Palmer, Michael et al, trs. 64p. 1994. pap. text ed. 9.50 (*1-880713-02-0*) AVEC Bks.

Parshin, A. N. & Shafarevich, I. R., eds. Algebra Seven: Combinatorial Group Theory. Applications to Geometry. LC 92-13652. (Encyclopaedia of Mathematical Sciences Ser.: Vol. 58). 1993. 89.00 (*0-387-54700-2*) Spr-Verlag.

— Algebraic Geometry IV: Linear Algebraic Groups, Invariant Theory. LC 93-13928. (Encyclopaedia of Mathematical Sciences Ser.: Vol. 55). (Illus.). 291p. 1994. 99.00 (*0-387-54682-0*) Spr-Verlag.

— Number Theory I: Fundamental Problems, Ideas & Theories. LC 94-46819. (Encyclopedia of Mathematical Sciences Ser.: Vol. 49). 1995. write for info. (*0-387-53384-2*) Spr-Verlag.

Parshin, A. N., ed. see Koch, H.

Parshley, H. M., tr. see De Beauvoir, Simone.

Parsifal-Charles, Nancy. The Dream: Four Thousand Years of Theory & Practice - A Critical, Descriptive, & Encylopedic Bibliography, 2 vols., 1. LC 86-15335. 1986. lib. bdg. write for info. (*0-933951-05-1*) Locust Hill Pr.

— The Dream: Four Thousand Years of Theory & Practice - A Critical, Descriptive, & Encylopedic Bibliography, 2 vols., 2. LC 86-15335. 1986. lib. bdg. write for info. (*0-933951-06-X*) Locust Hill Pr.

— The Dream: Four Thousand Years of Theory & Practice - A Critical, Descriptive, & Encylopedic Bibliography, 2 vols., Set. LC 86-15335. 1986. lib. bdg. 69.95 (*0-933951-07-8*) Locust Hill Pr.

Parsigian, Elise. The Dynamics of Media Writing. (Communication Textbook Journalism Ser.). 376p. (C). 1992. text ed. 79.95 (*0-8058-1130-3*); pap. 27.50 (*0-8058-1131-1*) L Erlbaum Assocs.

Parsinejad, Iraj. Akhundzadeh As a Modern Literary Critic. (Middle Eastern Ser.: No. 17). (Illus.). 125p. (Orig.). 1986. pap. 9.00 (*0-936665-03-3*) Jahan Bk Co.

Parsley, Bonnie M. The Choice Is Yours: A Teenager's Guide to Self-Discovery, Relationships, Values, & Spiritual Growth. 160p. (Orig.). (YA). 1992. pap. 9.00 (*0-671-75046-1*, Fireside) S&S Trade.

Parsley, Jamie. The Loneliness of Blizzards: Poems. LC 94-13799. 64p. 1995. pap. 12.95 (*0-7734-0011-7*, Mellen Poetry Pr) E Mellen.

Parsley, Jamie A. Paper Doves, Falling. Smith, James C., Jr., ed. LC 91-38890. 48p. (Orig.). 1992. pap. 6.95 (*0-86534-172-9*) Sunstone Pr.

Parsley, Karen & Corrigan, Philomena. A Practical Approach to Quality Improvement. LC 93-36305. 1993. write for info. (*0-412-48360-2*) Chapman & Hall.

— A Practical Approach to Quality Improvement. LC 93-36305. 1993. 38.25 (*1-56593-236-6*, 0556) Singular Publishing.

Parsley, Reed. Sugar Ships. LC 91-16984. (Illus.). (J). 1991. 12.95 (*0-671-74956-0*, Green Tiger S&S) S&S Childrens.

***Parsley, Rod.** The Backside of Calvary: Where Healing Stained the Cross. 107p. 1991. pap. 5.99 (*1-880244-01-2*) Wrld Harvest Church.

— The Best of Both Worlds. 32p. (Orig.). 1986. pap. 0.75 (*0-88144-083-3*) Christian Pub.

— The Commanded Blessing: Overtaken by God's Provision for a Life Without Lack, Acts 4:34. 212p. (Orig.). 1994. pap. 8.99 (*1-880244-17-9*) Wrld Harvest Church.

— Financial Abundance: What God Opens No Man Can Close. 32p. (Orig.). 1992. pap. 0.75 (*1-880244-05-5*) Wrld Harvest Church.

— Free at Last. 144p. (Orig.). 1994. pap. 7.99 (*1-880244-18-7*) Wrld Harvest Church.

— God's Answer to Insufficient Funds. 94p. (Orig.). 1992. pap. 5.99 (*1-880244-06-3*) Wrld Harvest Church.

— Holiness: Living Leaven Free. 273p. (Orig.). 1993. pap. 11.99 (*1-880244-11-X*) Wrld Harvest Church.

— I See an Underground Church. 61p. (Orig.). 1986. pap. 4.00 (*0-88144-067-1*) Christian Pub.

— If God Hadn't Wanted to Heal You, He Shouldn't Have! 48p. (Orig.). 1992. pap. 0.75 (*1-880244-04-7*) Wrld Harvest Church.

— I'm Glad You Asked: Biblical Answers to Some of Life's Toughest Questions. 114p. (Orig.). 1993. pap. text ed. 10.00 (*1-880244-12-8*) Wrld Harvest Church.

— My Promise Is the Palace: So What Am I Doing in the Pit? 155p. (Orig.). 1993. pap. 8.99 (*1-880244-14-4*) Wrld Harvest Church.

— New Direction. 41p. (Orig.). 1994. pap. 0.75 (*1-880244-16-0*) Wrld Harvest Church.

— Refiner's Fire: Living Holy in a World of Compromise. 78p. (Orig.). 1992. pap. 5.95 (*0-89274-903-2*) Christian Pub.

— Renamed & Redeemed: Operating in the Name of Jesus. 69p. (Orig.). 1991. pap. text ed. 10.00 (*1-880244-02-0*) Wrld Harvest Church.

— Repairers of the Breach: There Is Much to Be Gained by a Return to the Discarded Values of the Past. 410p. (Orig.). 1992. pap. 12.99 (*1-880244-09-8*) Wrld Harvest Church.

— Serious Survival Strategies: For Victory. 229p. (Orig.). 1992. pap. 9.99 (*1-880244-08-X*) Wrld Harvest Church.

— The Someday Syndrome. 37p. 1986. pap. 2.95 (*0-88144-069-8*) Christian Pub.

— Strengthening the Roots of Your Family Tree: A Teaching Syllabus. 110p. (Orig.). 1991. pap. 10.00 (*1-880244-03-9*) Wrld Harvest Church.

— Tribulation to Triumph: A Mandate for Today's Church. (Illus.). 116p. (Orig.). 1991. pap. 6.99 (*0-89274-881-8*, HH881) Harrison Hse.

— Worshipping the Unknown God. 31p. 1986. pap. 2.75 (*0-88144-070-1*) Christian Pub.

— You're a New Species of Being. 32p. (Orig.). 1991. pap. 0.75 (*1-880244-00-4*) Wrld Harvest Church.

***Parsley, Rod, ed.** Ten Keys to Your Increase Study Guide. 57p. 1995. pap. 10.00 (*1-880244-19-5*) Wrld Harvest Church.

***Parsley, Rod & Brown, Clint.** Praise, The Ultimate Experience: Worship, The Ultimate Relationship. 124p. (Orig.). 1992. pap. 6.99 (*1-880244-10-1*) Wrld Harvest Church.

Parsley, Ronald B. Silver Sunset for the Lazy T. 1994. pap. 10.95 (*0-533-11003-3*) Vantage.

Parsloe, C. The Commissioning of Air Systems in Buildings. 1989. 120.00 (*0-86022-231-4*, Pub. by Build Servs Info Assn UK) St Mut.

— The Commissioning of Water Systems in Building. 1992. 160.00 (*0-86022-230-6*, Pub. by Build Servs Info Assn UK) St Mut.

— Design Briefing Manual. 1990. 120.00 (*0-86022-266-7*, Pub. by Build Servs Info Assn UK) St Mut.

— Design for Maintainability. (C). 1992. 110.00x (*0-86022-308-6*, Pub. by Build Servs Info Assn UK) St Mut.

— Design Responsibilities. (C). 1994. 115.00x (*0-86022-371-X*, Pub. by Build Servs Info Assn UK) St Mut.

Parsloe, C., jt. auth. see Hejab, M.

Parsloe, C. J. European Commissioning Procedures. 1990. 72.00 (*0-86022-249-7*, Pub. by Build Servs Info Assn UK) St Mut.

— Pre-Commission Cleaning of Water Systems. 1991. 160.00 (*0-86022-291-8*, Pub. by Build Servs Info Assn UK) St Mut.

***Parsloe, Eric.** Coaching Mentoring & Assessing. 2nd ed. 1995. pap. text ed. 29.95 (*0-89397-442-0*) Nichols Pub.

— Coaching, Mentoring, & Assessing: A Practical Guide to Developing Competence. 220p. (C). 1993. pap. text ed. 25.95 (*0-89397-381-5*) Nichols Pub.

— Coaching, Mentoring, & Assessing: A Practical Guide to Developing Competence. LC 92-44135. 1992. pap. 23.95 (*0-7494-0664-X*, Pub. by Kogan Page Educ UK) Taylor & Francis.

***Parslow, Christopher C.** Rediscovering Antiquity: Karl Weber & the Excavation of Herculaneum, Pompeii & Stabiae. (Illus.). 416p. (C). 1995. 90.00 (*0-521-47150-8*) Cambridge U Pr.

Parslow, G. R. Geochemical Exploration, 1982. (Developments in Economic Geology Ser.: Vol. 17). 1984. 128.25 (*0-444-42268-4*) Elsevier.

Parslow, Percy. Hamsters. (Illus.). 128p. 1989. 9.95 (*0-86622-831-4*, KW-015) TFH Pubns.

Parslow, Robert D. Geometric Modelling & Computer Graphics: Techniques & Applications. (Technical Press-Unicom AIT Ser.: Vol. 7). Orig. Title: Three D Graphics & Geometric Modelling. 250p. 1987. pap. text ed. 104.95 (*0-291-39731-X*, Pub. by Avebury Pub UK) Ashgate Pub Co.

— Information Technology for the Eighties: BCS '81: Proceedings of the British Computer Society Conference, London, 1-3 July, 1981. LC 84-36784. (Illus.). 784p. reprint ed. pap. 180.00 (*0-685-44434-1*, 2032674) Bks Demand.

Parson. Short Wave Length Microscopy, Vol. 306. 1978. 45.00 (*0-89072-062-2*) NY Acad Sci.

Parson, Dwayne, ed. see Samuelson, Don W.

Parson, Erwin R., jt. auth. see Brende, Joel O.

Parson, Frank A. Psychology of Dress. (Illus.). 1995. reprint ed. 48.00 (*1-55888-215-4*) Omnigraphics Inc.

Parson, Harry, ed. see Johnson, Dawn M.

***Parson, L. M., et al, eds.** Hydrothermal Vents & Processes. (Geological Society Special Publication Ser.: No. 87). (Illus.). 416p. 1995. 108.00 (*1-897799-25-X*, Pub. by Geol Soc Pub Hse UK) AAPG.

— Ophiolites & Their Modern Oceanic Analogues. (Geological Society Special Publications: No. 60). (Illus.). vi, 330p. (C). 1992. 92.00 (*0-903317-69-9*, Pub. by Geol Soc Pub Hse UK) AAPG.

Parson, Malcolm. Diagnostic Picture Tests in Clinical Neurology. (Illus.). 128p. 1987. pap. text ed. 14.95 (*0-8151-6616-8*, Yr Bk Med Pubs) Mosby Yr Bk.

Parson, Maria. Up-Lot Reveries: A Sense of Place. 22.95 (*0-8488-0186-5*) Amereon Ltd.

— Up-Lot Reveries: An Oral History of the North Fork. 20.95 (*0-8488-0122-9*, Amereon Hse) Amereon Ltd.

Parson, Mary J. An Executive's Coaching Handbook. LC 85-20524. 297p. reprint ed. pap. 84.70 (*0-8357-4251-2*, 2037041) Bks Demand.

— The Single Solution: A Taxpayer's Guide to Sheltering More of the 20,000, 50,000, or 100,000 Dollars You Make As a Single Person. LC 86-13561. (Illus.). 192p. reprint ed. pap. 54.80 (*0-8357-4253-9*, 2037042) Bks Demand.

Parson, Nels A. Missiles & the Revolution in Warfare. LC 62-19221. (Illus.). 255p. reprint ed. pap. 72.70 (*0-317-08249-3*, 2002825) Bks Demand.

Parson, T. E. How to Dance. (Ballroom Dance Ser.). 1986. lib. bdg. 79.95 (*0-8490-3390-X*) Gordon Pr.

— How to Dance. (Ballroom Dance Ser.). 1985. lib. bdg. 79.00 (*0-87700-690-3*) Revisionist Pr.

Parsonage, M. J., jt. auth. see Kerr, James A.

Parsonage, Maurice, ed. see Epilepsy International Symposium Staff.

Parsonage, N. G., jt. auth. see Nicholson, D.

Parsonnet, Mia. What's Really in Our Food: Facts Everyone Should Know about Foods & Vitamins. 1991. pap. 12.95 (*1-56171-034-2*) Sure Sellers.

Parsonovich, jt. auth. see Chin.

Parsons. Canadian Mining Taxation. 2nd ed. 272p. 1990. 82.00 (*0-409-89384-6*) Butterworth Legal Pubs.

— How to Do Your Student Project in Geography, Earth & Environmental Science. 1995. pap. (*0-412-55950-1*) Chapman & Hall.

— Introduction to Computers. (C). 1994. Instr.'s Manual. teacher ed, text ed. write for info. (*0-7167-8289-8*) W H Freeman.

Parsons, et al. Utah Environmental Law Handbook. (State Environmental Law Ser.). 180p. 1991. pap. 72.00 (*0-86587-341-0*) Gov Insts.

Parsons, A. J. Hillslope Form. 160p. 1988. lib. bdg. 49.95 (*0-415-00905-7*) Routledge.

Parsons, A. J., jt. auth. see Meadows, R. G.

Parsons, A. J., jt. ed. see Meadows, R.

Parsons, A. W. Compaction of Soils & Granular Materials. 340p. 1993. 95.00 (*0-11-551091-5*, HM10915, Pub. by HMSO UK) UNIPUB.

Parsons, Albert R. Parsifal: The Finding of Christ Through Art. 2nd ed. 113p. 1974. reprint ed. spiral bd. 6.60 (*0-7873-0659-2*) Mokelumne.

— Parsifal: The Finding of Christ Through Art or Richard Wagner As Theologian. 113p. 1993. pap. 12.95 (*1-56459-368-1*) Kessinger Pub.

— Parsifal & the Finding of Christ Through Art: Richard Wagner As Theologian. 1991. lib. bdg. 79.95 (*0-8490-4934-2*) Gordon Pr.

***Parsons, Alex.** An Amazing Machine. (Life Education Ser.). (Illus.). (J). (gr. 5-8). 1995. lib. bdg. 12.25 (*0-531-14380-5*) Watts.

— Being Me. (Life Education Ser.). (Illus.). (J). (gr. 5-8). 1995. lib. bdg. 12.25 (*0-531-14381-3*) Watts.

— Fit for Life. (Life Education Ser.). (Illus.). (J). (gr. 5-8). 1995. lib. bdg. 12.25 (*0-531-14372-4*) Watts.

— Me & My World. (Life Education Ser.). (Illus.). (J). (gr. 5-8). 1995. lib. bdg. 12.25 (*0-531-14375-9*) Watts.

Parsons, Alexandra. Amazing Birds. (J). (ps-3). 1990. lib. bdg. 9.99 (*0-679-90223-6*); pap. 7.99 (*0-679-80223-1*) Knopf Bks Yng Read.

— Amazing Cats. LC 90-31885. (Eyewitness Juniors Ser.: No. 5). (Illus.). 32p. (Orig.). (J). (gr. 1-5). 1990. lib. bdg. 9.99 (*0-679-90690-8*); pap. 7.99 (*0-679-80690-3*) Knopf Bks Yng Read.

— Amazing Mammals. LC 89-38831. (Eyewitness Juniors Ser.). (Illus.). 32p. (J). (gr. 1-5). 1990. 7.99 (*0-679-80224-X*) Knopf Bks Yng Read.

— Amazing Mammals. LC 89-38831. (Eyewitness Juniors Ser.). (Illus.). 32p. (J). (gr. 1-5). 1990. lib. bdg. 9.99 (*0-679-90224-4*) Knopf Bks Yng Read.

— Amazing Poisonous Animals. LC 90-31883. (Eyewitness Juniors Ser.: No. 8). 32p. (Orig.). (J). (gr. 1-5). 1990. pap. 7.99 (*0-679-80699-7*) Knopf Bks Yng Read.

— Amazing Poisonous Animals. LC 90-31883. (Eyewitness Juniors Ser.: No. 8). 32p. (Orig.). (J). (gr. 1-5). 1991. lib. bdg. 9.99 (*0-679-90699-1*) Knopf Bks Yng Read.

— Amazing Snakes. LC 89-38944. (Eyewitness Juniors Ser.). (Illus.). 32p. (J). (gr. 1-5). 1990. 7.99 (*0-679-80225-8*) Knopf Bks Yng Read.

— Amazing Snakes. LC 89-38944. (Eyewitness Juniors Ser.). (Illus.). 32p. (J). (gr. 1-5). 1990. lib. bdg. 9.99 (*0-679-90225-2*) Knopf Bks Yng Read.

— Amazing Spiders. LC 89-38833. (Eyewitness Juniors Ser.). (Illus.). 32p. (J). (gr. 1-5). 1990. 7.99 (*0-679-80226-6*); lib. bdg. 9.99 (*0-679-90226-0*) Knopf Bks Yng Read.

— Arctic Peoples. LC 95-10399. (Make It Work! Ser.: History Ser.). (J). 1995. 18.95 (*1-56847-138-6*) Thomson Lrning.

— Earth. (Make It Work! Science Ser.). (Illus.). 48p. (YA). 1995. reprint ed. 15.95 (*1-56847-468-7*) Thomson Lrning.

— Electricity. (Make It Work! Science Ser.). (Illus.). 48p. (J). (gr. 5-9). 1995. reprint ed. 15.95 (*1-56847-469-5*) Thomson Lrning.

— Facts & Phalluses: A Collection of Bizarre & Intriguing Truths, Legends, & Measurements. 80p. (Orig.). 1990. pap. 6.95 (*0-312-04670-7*) St Martin.

— Sound. (Make It Work! Science Ser.). (Illus.). 48p. (J). (gr. 5-9). 1995. reprint ed. 15.95 (*1-56847-471-7*) Thomson Lrning.

Parsons, Alexandra, jt. auth. see Haslam, Andrew.

Parsons, Alexandra, jt. auth. see Watts, Claire.

Parsons, Alice B. Woman's Dilemma. LC 74-3966. (Women in America Ser.). 320p. 1974. reprint ed. 28.95 (*0-405-06115-3*) Ayer.

Parsons, Alyce & Parente, Diane. Universal Style: Dress for Who You Are & What You Want. (Illus.). (Orig.). 1991. pap. 19.95 (*0-9627405-0-0*) A Parsons.

Parsons, Alyce, et al. Universal Style for Men: Dress for Who You Are & What You Want. (Illus.). (Orig.). 1992. pap. 12.95 (*0-9627405-1-9*) A Parsons.

Parsons, Anthony, ed. Antarctica: The Next Decade. (Studies in Polar Research). (Illus.). 176p. 1987. 59.95 (*0-521-33181-1*) Cambridge U Pr.

Parsons, Anthony J. & Abrahams, Athol D., eds. Overland Flow: Hydraulics & Erosion Mechanics. 450p. 1992. 99.50 (*0-412-03721-1*, A9671, Chapman & Hall) Chapman & Hall.

Parsons, Anthony J., jt. ed. see Abrahams, Athol D.

Parsons, Arthur, jt. auth. see Parsons, Particia.

Parsons, B., ed. ASHRAE Handbook - Applications 1991: IP Edition. (Illus.). 682p. 1991. text ed. 119.00 (*0-910110-80-8*) Am Heat Ref & Air Eng.

— ASHRAE Handbook - Refrigeration 1994: I-P Edition. (Illus.). 437p. 1994. text ed. 119.00 (*0-910110-69-7*) Am Heat Ref & Air Eng.

— ASHRAE Handbook - Refrigeration 1994: SI Edition. (Illus.). 437p. 1994. text ed. 119.00 (*0-910110-70-0*) Am Heat Ref & Air Eng.

— ASHRAE Terminology of Heating, Ventilation, Air Conditioning & Refrigeration. 2nd ed. 180p. (C). 1991. pap. 38.00 (*0-910110-77-8*) Am Heat Ref & Air Eng.

— Design Guide for Cool Thermal Storage. (Illus.). 1993. pap. 72.00 (*1-883413-07-9*) Am Heat Ref & Air Eng.

Parsons, B., ed. see McQuiston, F. & Spitler, J.

***Parsons, Bill.** Electronic Prepress: A Hands-On Introduction. 192p. 1994. 29.95 (*0-8273-6449-0*) Delmar.

— Graphic Design with PageMaker for Windows Version 5.0. LC 93-33684. 1993. 30.95 (*0-8273-6451-2*) Delmar.

— PageMaker: Graphic Design with Pagemaker Macintosh Version 5.0. LC 93-37661. 337p. 1994. pap. text ed. 36.95 (*0-8273-5751-6*) Delmar.

PQ

Parsons, Bob, ed. ASHRAE Handbook--Heating, Ventilating, & Air-Conditioning Systems & Equipment, 1992: I-P Edition. (Illus.). 650p. (C). 1992. text ed. 119. 00 (*0-910110-86-7*) Am Heat Ref & Air Eng.

— ASHRAE Handbook--Heating, Ventilating, & Air-Conditioning Systems & Equipment, 1992: SI Edition. (Illus.). 650p. 1992. text ed. 119.00 (*0-910110-87-5*) Am Heat Ref & Air Eng.

***Parsons, Bonnie & Mazik, James M.** Touring Jacob's Ladder Trail by Bicycle or Car. 126p. 1994. pap. 10.00 (*0-9643910-0-7*) Pioneer Valley.

***Parsons, Brian & Time Life Books, eds.** 101 Money-Saving Household Repairs. LC 94-42181. (Illus.). 96p. 1995. write for info. (*0-8094-9177-X*) Time-Life.

Parsons, Brinckerhoff, Quade & Douglas, Inc. Staff. Bridge Inspection & Rehabilitation: A Practical Guide. 312p. 1992. text ed. 84.95 (*0-471-53262-2*) Wiley.

Parsons, Burke A. British Trade Cycles & American Bank Credit: Some Aspects of Economic Fluctuations in the United States, 1815-1840. Bruchey, Stuart, ed. LC 76-39839. (Nineteen Seventy-Seven Dissertations Ser.). (Illus.). 1977. lib. bdg. 37.95 (*0-405-09919-3*) Ayer.

Parsons, C. G. Inside View of Slavery: Or a Tour Among the Planters. 1969. reprint ed. 20.00 (*0-87266-025-7*) Argosy.

***Parsons, Carl, ed.** Quality Improvement in Education: Case Studies in Schools, Colleges & Universities. 160p. 1994. pap. 27.00x (*1-85346-327-2*, Pub. by D Fulton UK) Taylor & Francis.

Parsons, Charles. Constructive Interpretation of Predicative Mathematics. (Harvard Dissertations in Philosophy Ser.). 350p. 1990. reprint ed. 30.00 (*0-8240-5091-6*) Garland.

— Mathematics in Philosophy: Selected Essays. LC 83-45153. 368p. 1983. 49.50 (*0-8014-1471-7*) Cornell U Pr.

— Montauk Point, Long Island: An 1871 Visit. (Illus.). 15p. (Orig.). 1990. reprint ed. pap. 3.95 (*0-89646-082-7*) Vistabooks.

Parsons, Charles David. History & Records of the Oakland United Mehodist Church, Faulkner Co., Arkansas. (Illus.). 126p. 1993. 24.95 (*1-56869-012-6*); pap. 18.95 (*1-56869-013-4*) Oldbuck Pr.

Parsons, Charles G. Inside View of Slavery or a Tour among the Planters. LC 73-92436. 1970. reprint ed. 9.00 (*0-403-00181-1*) Scholarly.

Parsons, Charles H., comp. An Index of Printed Opera Scores, 2 vols. 1987. 139.95 (*0-88946-418-9*); write for info. (*0-88946-419-7*) E Mellen.

— The Mellen Opera Reference Index, 22 vols. write for info. (*0-318-62169-X*) E Mellen.

— The Mellen Opera Reference Index: Opera Discography, 3 vols., Vol. 10: Composers A-O. LC 89-13814. 360p. 1989. lib. bdg. 149.95 (*0-88946-410-3*) E Mellen.

— The Mellen Opera Reference Index: Opera Discography, 3 vols., Vol. 11: Composers P-Z. LC 89-13814. 376p. 1989. lib. bdg. 149.95x (*0-88946-411-1*) E Mellen.

— The Mellen Opera Reference Index: Opera Discography, Vol. 12: Performers. LC 89-13814. 568p. 1989. lib. bdg. 149.95x (*0-88946-497-9*) E Mellen.

— Miscellanea Opera, Vol. 21. 1987. write for info. (*0-318-62170-3*) E Mellen.

— Opera & the Librarian, Vol. 22. 1987. write for info. (*0-318-62172-X*) E Mellen.

— An Opera Bibliography, Vol. 17. LC 95-1400. (Mellen Opera Reference Index Ser.). 400p. 1995. text ed. 149. 95 (*0-88946-416-2*) E Mellen.

— An Opera Bibliography, Vol. 18. LC 95-1400. (Mellen Opera Reference Index Ser.). 400p. 1995. text ed. 149. 95 (*0-88946-417-0*) E Mellen.

— An Opera Bibliography, Vols. 16 & 17. 1987. write for info. (*0-318-62173-8*) E Mellen.

— Opera Composers & Their Works A-D, 22 Vols., Vol. 1. LC 86-7252. (Mellen Opera Reference Index Ser.: Vol. 1). 534p. 1986. lib. bdg. 149.95 (*0-88946-401-4*) E Mellen.

— Opera Composers & Their Works E-K, Vol. 1. LC 86-7252. (Mellen Opera Reference Index Ser.: Vol. 2). 496p. 1986. Vol.1 of 22 Vols. lib. bdg. 149.95 (*0-88946-402-2*) E Mellen.

— Opera Composers & Their Works L-Q. LC 86-7252. (Mellen Opera Reference Index Ser.: Vol. 3). 480p. 1986. lib. bdg. 149.95 (*0-88946-403-0*) E Mellen.

— Opera Composers & Their Works R-Z. LC 86-7252. (Mellen Opera Reference Index Ser.: Vol. 4). 512p. 1986. One of 22 Vols. lib. bdg. 149.95 (*0-88946-404-9*) E Mellen.

— Opera Librettists & Their Works, 22 vols., Vols. 5 & 6. (Opera Reference Index Ser.). 1987. Vol. 6, M-Z. 149.95 (*0-88946-406-5*); Vol. 5, A-L. write for info. (*0-88946-405-7*) E Mellen.

— Opera Premieres: A Geographical Index A-H, 2 vols., Set. LC 88-12902. (Opera Reference Index Ser.: Vol. 7). 460p. (C). 1988. lib. bdg. 149.95 (*0-88946-407-3*) E Mellen.

— Opera Premieres: A Geographical Index I-Z, 2 vols., Set. LC 88-12902. (Opera Reference Index Ser.: Vol. 8). 450p. (C). 1988. lib. bdg. 149.95 (*0-88946-408-1*) E Mellen.

— Opera Premieres: An Index of Casts, 2 vols., Vol. I. LC 92-9245. (Mellen Opera Reference Index Ser.: Vols. 13-14). 690p. 1992. lib. bdg. 149.95 (*0-88946-412-X*) E Mellen.

— Opera Premieres: An Index of Casts, 2 vols., Vol. II. LC 92-9245. (Mellen Opera Reference Index Ser.: Vols. 13-14). 686p. 1992. lib. bdg. 149.95 (*0-88946-413-8*) E Mellen.

— Opera Premieres: An Index of Casts, 22 vols., Vols. 13 & 14. 1987. write for info. (*0-318-62174-6*) E Mellen.

— Opera Premieres: Reviews, 22 vols., Vols. 15. 1987. write for info. (*0-318-62175-4*) E Mellen.

— Opera Subjects, 22 vols., Vol. 9. 1989. 149.95 (*0-88946-409-X*) E Mellen.

— Opera That Is Not Opera, 22 vols., Vol. 20. 1987. write for info. (*0-318-62176-2*) E Mellen.

Parsons, Charles H., ed. A Benjamin Britten Discography. LC 90-6219. (Studies in History & Interpretation of Music: Vol. 31). 260p. 1990. lib. bdg. 89.95 (*0-88946-486-3*) E Mellen.

— Opera Premieres: An Index of Casts-Performers, 2 vols. LC 93-4741. (Mellen Opera Reference Index Ser.: Vols. 15 & 16). 1993. Vol. 15, 600p. write for info. (*0-88946-414-6*); Vol. 16, 600p. write for info. (*0-88946-415-4*) E Mellen.

— Opera Premieres: An Index of Casts-Performers, 2 vols., Set. LC 93-4741. (Mellen Opera Reference Index Ser.: Vols. 15 & 16). 1993. text ed. 149.95 (*0-685-66623-9*) E Mellen.

Parsons, Christina. Dangerous Marine Animals of the Pacific Coast. LC 85-81586. (Illus.). 96p. 1986. pap. 4.95 (*0-936940-03-4*) Helm Pub.

— Dangerous Marine Animals of the Pacific Coast. LC 85-81586. (Illus.). 96p. 1985. text ed. 5.95 (*0-930118-11-1*) Sea Chall.

Parsons, Christine. Decorating with Marble, Stone & Granite. 1990. 16.98 (*1-55521-576-9*) Bk Sales Inc.

Parsons, Chuck. James Madison Brown: Texas Sheriff, Texas Turfman. (Illus.). xiv, 167p. 1993. write for info. (*0-318-72629-7*) C Parsons.

Parsons, Chuck & Fitterer, Gary P. Captain C. B. McKinney: The Law in South Texas. (Illus.). 160p. 1993. 29.95 (*0-9614936-0-7*) C Parsons.

Parsons, Chuck & Parsons, Marjorie. Bowen & Hardin. LC 91-24946. (Illus.). 112p. 1991. 21.95 (*0-932702-91-0*) Creative Texas.

Parsons, Claire D., ed. Healing Practices in the South Pacific. (Illus.). 288p. 1985. text ed. 22.50 (*0-939154-41-2*) UH Pr.

Parsons, Claude. Flowers: Basic Skills. (How to Draw & Paint Ser.). (Illus.). 32p. (Orig.). 1989. pap. 5.95 (*0-929261-17-8*, HT75) W Foster Pub.

Parsons, Coleman O., ed. The Scottish Enlightenment: An AMS Press Reprint Series. reprint ed. write for info. (*0-404-17120-6*) AMS Pr.

Parsons, Cynthia. The Co-Op Bridge: Cooperative Education - Thoroughly Integrating Study & Work. LC 90-15482. 128p. (Orig.). 1991. pap. 7.95 (*0-88007-186-9*) Woodbridge Pr.

— George Bird Grinnell: A Biographical Sketch. 2nd ed. (Illus.). 205p. 1993. reprint ed. 19.95 (*0-9635190-0-X*) Grinnell & Lawton.

— The Purple Hills. 200p. (Orig.). 1990. pap. 5.00 (*0-9617872-6-0*) VT Schoolhse Pr.

— Seeds: Some Good Ways to Improve Our Schools. LC 84-29160. 224p. (Orig.). 1992. pap. 12.95 (*0-88007-200-8*) Woodbridge Pr.

— Servermont & the U. S. A. 70p. (Orig.). 1988. pap. 6.00 (*0-9617872-2-8*) VT Schoolhse Pr.

Parsons, Cynthia, comp. Spinach & Zwieback: Writings of Newell Martin. LC 93-73174. (Illus.). 512p. 1993. 29.95 (*0-9635190-1-8*) Grinnell & Lawton.

Parsons, Cynthia, ed. What'll You Have: Fifty Plus Non-Alcoholic Drinks for Brunch, Lunch & Dinner. 52p. (Orig.). 1986. pap. 5.00 (*0-9617872-0-1*) VT Schoolhse Pr.

***Parsons, D. Wayne.** Public Policy: An Introduction to the Theory & Practice of Policy Analysis. LC 95-10756. 1996. write for info. (*1-85278-553-5*, Pub. by E Elgar Pub UK); pap. write for info. (*1-85278-554-3*, Pub. by E Elgar Pub UK) Ashgate Pub Co.

Parsons, Dave. Danger. 1991. pap. 12.98 (*0-87938-517-0*) Motorbooks Intl.

Parsons, Dave & Nelson, Derek. Fighter Country: The F-14 Tomcats of NAS Oceana. LC 92-10972. (Illus.). 160p. 1992. 11.98 (*0-87938-442-5*) Motorbooks Intl.

Parsons, Dave & Nelson, Derk. Bandits: Pictorial History of U. S. Navy Adversary & U. S. Air Force Agressor A-C. (MBI Ser.). (Illus.). 96p. 1993. pap. 14.95 (*0-87938-623-1*) Motorbooks Intl.

Parsons, David, tr. see Isaev, P. S.

***Parsons, David K.** Bugles Echo Across the Valley: Northern Oswego County, New York & the Civil War. 250p. 1994. pap. 17.50 (*1-886303-04-5*) Write to Print.

— Bugles Echo Across the Valley: Oswego County, New York & the Civil War. rev. ed. Parsons, Marie K., ed. (Illus.). 250p. 1995. pap. 17.50 (*1-886303-09-6*) Write to Print.

— Bugles Echo Across the Valley Vol. 2: Civil War Muster Rolls for Oswego County, New York. (Illus.). 130p. (Orig.). 1995. pap. 12.50 (*1-886303-10-X*) Write to Print.

— The Saddlebag Patriot: Service of Lt. Underfoot in the War for Independence. 106p. 1992. pap. 10.00 (*1-886303-00-2*) Write to Print.

Parsons, David L. & Nelson, Derek. Sixty Year Nav, U. S. Navy Air Patches: Official & Unofficial. (Illus.). 96p. 1990. pap. 14.95 (*0-87938-447-6*) Motorbooks Intl.

Parsons, Donald F., ed. Ultrasoft X-Ray Microscopy: Its Application to Biological & Physical Sciences. (Annals Ser.: Vol. 342). 402p. 1980. 72.00 (*0-89766-066-8*); pap. 72.00 (*0-89766-067-6*) NY Acad Sci.

Parsons, Donald F., et al, eds. Extended Clinical Consulting by Hospital Computer Networks. LC 92-48843. (Annals Ser.: Vol. 670). 1992. write for info. (*0-89766-751-4*); pap. write for info. (*0-89766-752-2*) NY Acad Sci.

Parsons, Donald O. Poverty & the Minimum Wage. LC 80-24407. (AEI Studies: No. 300). (Illus.). 72p. reprint ed. pap. 25.00 (*0-8357-4525-2*, 2037387) Bks Demand.

Parsons, E. M. The Easy Gun. 128p. 1979. pap. 1.50 (*0-449-14293-0*, GM) Fawcett.

— Fargo. 144p. 1980. pap. 1.95 (*0-449-13874-7*, GM) Fawcett.

Parsons, E. W. Folk-Lore from the Cape Verde Islands. LC 24-4017. (American Folklore Society Memoirs Ser.: Vol. 15). 1972. reprint ed. 56.00 (*0-527-01067-7*) Periodicals Srv.

Parsons, Earl. The Database Experts' Guide to IDEAL. 482p. 1989. text ed. 52.95 (*0-07-048550-X*) McGraw.

Parsons, Edward B. Wilsonian Diplomacy. LC 77-80967. 1978. text ed. write for info. (*0-88273-006-1*) Forum Pr IL.

Parsons, Edward E. Humboldt Homegrown: The Golden Age. LC 85-81069. 604p. 1985. 15.00 (*0-9615730-0-7*) Egret Pub Co.

Parsons, Edwin C. I Flew with the Lafayette Escadrille. LC 74-169432. (Literature & History of Aviation Ser.). 1972. reprint ed. 34.95 (*0-405-03775-9*) Ayer.

Parsons, Ella S., jt. auth. see Kelly, Marguerite.

***Parsons, Elsie C.** Isleta Paintings. (Bureau of American Ethnology Bulletins Ser.). 299p. 1995. lib. bdg. write for info. (*0-7812-4181-2*) Rprt Serv.

— Isleta Paintings. 1988. reprint ed. lib. bdg. 59.00 (*0-7812-0927-7*) Rprt Serv.

— Isleta Paintings. reprint ed. 59.00 (*0-403-03619-4*) Scholarly.

— Notes on Zuni, 2 pts., Pt. I. (American Anthropological Association Memoirs Ser.: No. 20). 1917. 15.00 (*0-527-00518-5*) Periodicals Srv.

— Notes on Zuni, 2 pts., Pt. II. (American Anthropological Association Memoirs Ser.: No. 20). 1917. 15.00 (*0-527-00519-3*) Periodicals Srv.

— The Old-Fashioned Woman: Primitive Fancies about the Sex. LC 72-2618. (American Women Ser.: Images & Realities). 378p. 1974. reprint ed. 26.95 (*0-405-04471-2*) Ayer.

— Pueblo Mothers & Children: Essays by Elsie Clews Parsons, 1915-1924. Babcock, Barbara, ed. LC 89-82082. (Illus.). 150p. 1991. 29.95 (*0-941270-66-1*); pap. 16.95 (*0-941270-65-3*) Ancient City Pr.

— Scalp Ceremonial of Zuni. LC 25-1663. (American Anthropological Association Memoirs Ser.). 1924. pap. 15.00 (*0-527-00530-4*) Periodicals Srv.

— Social Organization of the Tewa of New Mexico. LC 30-5855. (American Anthropological Association Memoirs Ser.). 1929. 35.00 (*0-527-00535-5*) Periodicals Srv.

— Tewa Tales. 304p. 1994. reprint ed. pap. 16.95 (*0-8165-1452-6*) U of Ariz Pr.

Parsons, Elsie C., ed. American Indian Life. LC 91-16847. (Illus.). xvi, 467p. 1991. reprint ed. 35.00 (*0-8032-3651-4*); reprint ed. pap. 12.95 (*0-8032-8728-3*) U of Nebr Pr.

— North American Indian Life: Customs & Traditions of 23 Tribes. unabridged ed. LC 92-22904. Orig. Title: American Indian Life by Several of Its Students. (Illus.). 1993. reprint ed. pap. text ed. 10.95 (*0-486-27377-6*) Dover.

Parsons, Elsie C., ed. see Stephen, Alexander M.

Parsons, Elsie W. Educational Legislation & Administration of the Colonial Governments. LC 79-165741. (American Education Ser., No. 2). 1975. reprint ed. 38.95 (*0-405-03612-4*) Ayer.

— Folk Tales of Andros Island, Bahamas. LC 19-4413. (American Folklore Society Memoirs Ser.: Vol. 13). 1969. reprint ed. 37.00 (*0-527-01065-0*) Periodicals Srv.

— The Pueblo of Jemez. LC 76-43805. (Phillips Academy: No. 3). reprint ed. 67.50 (*0-404-15661-4*) AMS Pr.

— Religious Chastity: An Ethnological Study, by John Main (Pseud.) LC 72-9672. reprint ed. 54.00 (*0-404-57489-0*) AMS Pr.

Parsons, Elsie W., ed. Folk-Lore of the Antilles, French & English, 3 Vols, Set. LC 34-20249. (AFS Memoirs Ser.: Vol. 26, Pt. 1-3). (ENG & FRE.). 1972. reprint ed. 138. 00 (*0-527-01078-2*) Periodicals Srv.

— Folk-Lore of the Sea Islands, South Carolina. LC 23-12312. (AFS Memoirs Ser.: Vol. 16). 1972. reprint ed. 25.00 (*0-527-01068-5*) Periodicals Srv.

Parsons, Eugene, jt. comp. see La Moille, T. G.

Parsons, F. The Earlier Inhabitants of London. 1972. 59.95 (*0-8490-0065-3*) Gordon Pr.

Parsons, Florence M. Garrick & His Circle. LC 78-82837. (Illus.). 1972. 35.95 (*0-405-08836-1*, Pub. by Blom Pubns UK) Ayer.

— Incomparable Siddons. LC 77-84847. (Illus.). 1972. 30.95 (*0-405-08837-X*, Pub. by Blom Pubns UK) Ayer.

— The Incomparable Siddons. LC 74-107824. (Illus.). 298p. reprint ed. lib. bdg. 21.00 (*0-8290-0514-5*) Irvington.

Parsons, Frances D. Solomon Shilling - Come to Court. 1991. reprint ed. 12.00 (*0-87012-492-7*) McClain.

Parsons, Frances M. I Didn't Hear the Dragon Roar. braille ed. 575p. 1990. Braille. vinyl bd. 46.00 (*1-56956-258-X*, BR7652) W A T Braille.

Parsons, Frances T. How to Know the Ferns: A Guide to the Names, Haunts, & Habits of Our Common Ferns. 2nd ed. (Illus.). 1899. pap. 5.95 (*0-486-20740-4*) Dover.

Parsons, Francis. Six Men of Yale. LC 72-156702. (Essay Index Reprint Ser.). 1977. reprint ed. 20.95 (*0-8369-2329-4*) Ayer.

Parsons, Frank. Legal Doctrine & Social Progress. 219p. 1982. reprint ed. lib. bdg. 22.50 (*0-8377-1014-6*) Rothman.

Parsons, Frank & McDaniels, Carl, intros. Choosing a Vocation. LC 89-80556. 165p. (C). 1909. reprint ed. pap. 10.00 (*0-912048-65-4*) Garrett Pk.

Parsons, Gary A., et al. California Lithic Studies, No. 1. Breschini, Gary S. & Haversat, Trudy, eds. (Archives of California Prehistory Ser.: No. 11). (Illus.). iv, 96p. (Orig.). 1987. pap. text ed. 7.45 (*1-55567-044-X*) Coyote Press.

Parsons, Gary L., jt. auth. see Gitisetan, Darrin D.

***Parsons, George.** Intervening in a Church Fight: A Manual for Internal Consultants. Date not set. pap. 11.25 (*1-56699-075-0*, OD60) Alban Inst.

Parsons, George D. & Leas, Speed B. Understanding Your Congregation As a System: The Manual. LC 93-73158. 154p. (Orig.). 1994. pap. 18.95 (*1-56699-118-8*, AL147) Alban Inst.

***Parsons, George W.** Put the Vermonters Ahead: The First Vermont Brigade in the Civil War. (Illus.). 236p. (C). 1995. text ed. 24.95 (*0-942597-97-4*) White Mane Pub.

Parsons, Gerald. The Growth of Religious Diversity: Britain from 1945, 1. LC 94-44326. (Illus.). 304p. 1994. pap. 18. 95 (*0-415-08326-5*, B3941) Routledge.

— The Growth of Religious Diversity: Britain from 1945, 2. LC 94-44326. (Illus.). 304p. 1994. pap. 18.95 (*0-415-08328-1*, B3945) Routledge.

Parsons, Gerald, ed. Religion in Victorian Britain, Vol. I: Traditions. 256p. 1989. text ed. 18.95 (*0-7190-2511-7*, Pub. by Manchester Univ Pr UK) St Martin.

— Religion in Victorian Britain, Vol. II: Controversies. LC 88-12359. (Illus.). 256p. 1989. text ed. 12.95 (*0-7190-2513-3*, Pub. by Manchester Univ Pr UK) St Martin.

— Religion in Victorian Britain, Vol. IV: Interpretations. 208p. 1989. text ed. 49.95 (*0-7190-2945-7*, Pub. by Manchester Univ Pr UK); text ed. 14.95 (*0-7190-2946-5*, Pub. by Manchester Univ Pr UK) St Martin.

Parsons, H. E., ed. see Parsons, S. D.

Parsons, Heather. The Antidote. 173p. (Orig.). 1994. pap. 8.95 (*1-55725-037-5*) Paraclete MA.

Parsons, Henry McIlvaine. Man-Machine System Experiments. LC 71-166483. (Illus.). 632p. 1972. 80.00x (*0-8018-1322-0*) Johns Hopkins.

Parsons, Howard L. Christianity Today in the U. S. S. R. LC 86-27320. 211p. (Orig.). reprint ed. pap. 60.20 (*0-7837-0582-4*, 2040926) Bks Demand.

— Self, Global Issues, & Ethics. 209p. (Orig.). 1980. pap. 27. 00 (*90-6032-178-2*, Pub. by B R Gruener NE) Benjamins North Am.

Parsons, Howard L., ed. Marx & Engels on Ecology. LC 77-71866. (Contributions in Philosophy Ser.: No.8). 262p. 1977. text ed. 59.95 (*0-8371-9538-1*, PME/, Greenwood Pr) Greenwood.

Parsons, Howard L., jt. auth. see Somerville, John.

Parsons, Ian, ed. Feldspars & Their Reactions: Proceedings of the NATO Advanced Study Institute, Edinburgh, United Kingdom, June 29-July 10, 1993. LC 94-2625. (NATO Advanced Study Institutes Series C, Mathematical & Physical Sciences: Vol. 421). 650p. (C). 1994. lib. bdg. 223.00 (*0-7923-2722-5*) Kluwer Ac.

— Origins of Igneous Layering. (C). 1987. lib. bdg. 206.50 (*90-277-2455-5*) Kluwer Ac.

Parsons, J. D. Mobile Communication Systems. 292p. 1989. text ed. 79.00 (*0-470-21213-6*) Halsted Pr.

— The Mobile Radio Propagation Channel. 316p. 1992. text ed. 64.95 (*0-470-21824-X*) Halsted Pr.

Parsons, Jack. Santa Fe & Northern New Mexico. (Illus.). 160p. 1991. 37.50 (*0-8478-1333-9*) Rizzoli Intl.

***Parsons, Jack W.** Freedom Is a Two Edged Sword & Other Essays. Beta, Cameron & Beta, Hymenaeus, eds. LC 89-81555. (Oriflamme Ser.). 100p. (Orig.). 1990. pap. 9.95 (*1-56184-116-1*) New Falcon Pubns.

Parsons, James. The Art Fever: Passages Through the Western Art Trade. Fox, Steve & Schlede, Nancy, eds. LC 81-83141. (Illus.). 111p. 1981. 300.00 (*0-9610550-1-4*); 29.95 (*0-9610550-0-6*) Gallery West.

Parsons, James, tr. see Marias, Julian.

Parsons, James J. Antioqueno Colonization in Western Colombia. 2nd rev. ed. LC 68-58002. (University of California Publications in Social Welfare: No. 32). (Illus.). 260p. reprint ed. pap. 74.10 (*0-8357-5635-1*, 2029959) Bks Demand.

— Antioquia's Corridor to the Sea: An Historical Geography of the Settlement of Uraba. LC 68-1378. 132p. 1983. reprint ed. lib. bdg. 25.00x (*0-89370-766-X*) Borgo Pr.

Parsons, James J., jt. ed. see Davidson, William V.

Parsons, Jeffrey R. Prehistoric Settlement Patterns in the Texcoco Region, Mexico. (Memoirs Ser.: No. 3). (Illus.). 1971. pap. 4.00 (*0-932206-65-4*) U Mich Mus Anthro.

Parsons, Jeffrey R. & Parsons, Mary H. Maguey Utilization in Highland Central Mexico: An Archaeological Ethnography. LC 90-34597. (Anthropological Papers: No. 82). (Illus.). xvi, 388p. (Orig.). 1990. pap. 22.00 (*0-915703-20-3*) U Mich Mus Anthro.

Parsons, Jeffrey R., et al. Archaeological Settlement Pattern Data from the Chalco, Xochimilco, Ixtapalapa, Texcoco, & Zumpango Regions, Mexico. LC 84-21935. (Technical Reports: No. 14). (Illus.). 222p. 1983. pap. 8.00 (*0-932206-98-0*) U Mich Mus Anthro.

— Prehistoric Settlement Patterns in the Southern Valley of Mexico: The Chalco-Xochimilco Report. (Memoirs Ser.: No. 14). (Orig.). 1982. pap. 16.00 (*0-932206-88-3*) U Mich Mus Anthro.

***Parsons, Jill.** Curtain Going Up. (Voices Romance Ser.: No. 6). 224p. (J). (gr. 4-7). 1995. mass mkt. 3.99 (*0-8217-4819-X*) Zebra.

Parsons, John. Deceiving Trout. (Illus.). 176p. (Orig.). 1989. pap. 14.95 (*0-88317-141-4*) Stoeger Pub Co.

— The Official Wimbledon Annual 1995. annuals (Illus.). 160p. 1995. 29.95 (*1-874557-31-4*, Pub. by Hazelton UK) Motorbooks Intl.

Parsons, John A., ed. Endocrinology of Calcium Metabolism. (Comprehensive Endocrinology Ser.). 566p. 1982. 167.00 (*0-89004-344-2*) Raven.

Parsons, John C. Eleanor of Castile. (Illus.). 288p. 1995. text ed. 49.95 (*0-312-08649-0*) St Martin.

— Eleanor of Castile: Queen & Society in Thirteenth-Century England. LC 94-31086. 1994. write for info. (*0-312-86490-6*) St Martin.

Parsons, John C., ed. Medieval Queenship. LC 93-10879. 1993. text ed. 49.95 (*0-312-05217-0*) St Martin.

Parsons, Joy. Days Out in Dorset. (C). 1988. text ed. 29.00 (*0-685-45095-3*, Pub. by Thornhill Pr UK) St Mut.

PQ

An Asterisk (*) at the beginning of an entry indicates that the title is appearing in BIP for the first time.

Parsons, Judith. Math-a-Draw, 6 vols. Incl. Vol. I. Math-a-Draw. (J). (gr. k-2). 1989. pap. 8.95 (*0-8224-4569-7*); Vol. II. Math-a-Draw. (J). (gr. 1-3). 1989. pap. 8.95 (*0-8224-4570-0*); Vol. III. Math-a-Draw. (J). (gr. 2-4). 1989. pap. 8.95 (*0-8224-4571-9*); Vol. IV. Math-a-Draw. (J). (gr. 3-5). 1989. pap. 8.95 (*0-8224-4572-7*); Vol. V. Math-a-Draw. (J). (gr. 3-5). 1989. pap. 8.95 (*0-8224-4573-5*); Vol. VI. Math-a-Draw. (J). 1989. pap. 8.95 (*0-8224-4574-3*); (J). (gr. 1-6). 1983. Set pap. write for info. (*0-318-57165-X*) Fearon Teach Aids.

Parsons, K. F. & Fitzpatrick, J. M. Practical Urology in Spinal Cord Injury. (Clinical Practice in Urology Ser.). (Illus.). xii, 145p. 1991. 98.00 (*0-387-19676-5*) Spr-Verlag.

Parsons, Keith M. God & the Burden of Proof. 156p. (C). 1989. text ed. 40.95 (*0-87975-551-2*) Prometheus Bks.

Parsons, Kenneth C. Human Thermal Environments. LC 93-20570. 450p. 1993. 99.00 (*0-7484-0040-0*, Pub. by Tay Francis Ltd UK); pap. 49.50 (*0-7484-0041-9*, Pub. by Tay Francis Ltd UK) Taylor & Francis.

Parsons, Kenneth O. Strategies for Getting an Overseas Job. LC 83-12186. 32p. (Orig.). 1989. pap. 3.95 (*0-87576-105-4*) Pilot Bks.

Parsons, Kitty. Gloucester Sea Ballads. 2nd rev. ed. (Illus.). 64p. 1981. reprint ed. pap. 4.95 (*0-939792-00-1*) Fermata.

Parsons, Langdon & Sommers, Sheldon C. Gynecology, 2 vols. 2nd ed. LC 75-8184. (Illus.). 1660p. 1978. text ed. 155.00 (*0-7216-7081-4*) Saunders.

Parsons, Langdon B. History of the Town of Rye, New Hampshire, from Its Discovery & Settlement to December 31, 1903. (Illus.). viii, 675p. 1992. reprint ed. pap. 38.50 (*1-55613-668-4*) Heritage Bk.

— History of the Town of Rye, New Hampshire, 1623-1903. (Illus.). 675p. 1988. reprint ed. lib. bdg. 68.00 (*0-8328-0071-6*, NH0018) Higginson Bk Co.

Parsons, Larry. A Funny Thing Happened on the Way to the School Library: A Treasury of Anecdotes, Quotes, & Other Happenings. 204p. 1990. pap. 20.00 (*0-87287-751-5*) Libs Unl.

Parsons, Lee A. Origins of Maya Art: Monumental Stone Sculpture of Kaminaljuyu, Guatemala, & the Southern Pacific Coast. LC 85-31148. (Studies in Pre-Columbian Art & Archaeology: No. 28). (Illus.). 224p. (Orig.). 1986. pap. text ed. 30.00 (*0-88402-148-3*, PAORP) Dumbarton Oaks.

Parsons, Lee A., et al, eds. The Face of Ancient America: The Wally & Brenda Zollman Collection of Precolumbian Art. LC 88-81793. (Illus.). 238p. 1988. 55.00 (*0-936260-23-8*); pap. 35.00 (*0-936260-24-6*) Ind Mus Art.

Parsons, Leonard J., jt. auth. see Dalrymple, Douglas J.

Parsons, Les. Expanding Response Journals: Integrating the Curriculum. LC 93-47193. 96p. (C). 1994. pap. text ed. 13.50 (*0-435-08813-0*) Heinemann.

— Poetry, Themes, & Activities: Exploring the Fun & Fantasy of Language. 112p. 1992. pap. text ed. 14.50 (*0-435-08730-4*, 08730) Heinemann.

— Response Journals. 90p. (Orig.). 1989. pap. text ed. 13.50 (*0-435-08517-4*) Heinemann.

— Writing in the Real Classroom. LC 90-28694. 112p. 1991. pap. text ed. 14.00 (*0-435-08587-5*, 08587) Heinemann.

Parsons, Lucy, ed. Famous Speeches of the Eight Chicago Anarchists in Court. LC 77-90187. (Mass Violence in America Ser.). 1974. reprint ed. 12.95 (*0-405-01330-2*) Ayer.

Parsons, Luke, jt. auth. see Steel, David.

Parsons, Lynn H., comp. John Quincy Adams: A Bibliography. LC 92-33703. (Bibliographies of the Presidents of the United States Ser.: No. 6). 240p. 1993. text ed. 55.00 (*0-313-28164-5*, AP06, Greenwood Pr) Greenwood.

Parsons, Lynn H., jt. ed. see O'Brien, Kenneth P.

Parsons, M. L., et al. Atlas of Spectral Interferences in ICP Spectroscopy. LC 79-24222. 654p. 1980. 145.00 (*0-306-40334-X*, Plenum Pr) Plenum.

Parsons, Malcolm. Color Atlas of Clinical Neurology. 2nd ed. (Illus.). 320p. 1992. 95.00 (*0-8151-6613-3*) Mosby Yr Bk.

— Tuberculous Meningitis; Tuberculomas & Spinal Tuberculosis: A Handbook for Clinicians. 2nd ed. (Illus.). 92p. 1988. 29.95 (*0-19-261721-4*) OUP.

***Parsons, Marie K.** Early Sandy Creek History: Reprint of the 1877 Town History with Notes. (Rural Towns of Oswego County Ser.). 56p. 1993. pap. 9.00 (*1-886303-02-9*) Write to Print.

Parsons, Marie K., ed. see Parsons, David K.

Parsons, Marjorie, jt. auth. see Parsons, Chuck.

Parsons, Marnie. Touch Monkeys: Nonsense Strategies for Reading Twentieth-Century Poetry. LC 93-94817. (Theory - Culture Ser.). 262p. 1993. 50.00 (*0-8020-2983-3*) U of Toronto Pr.

Parsons, Mary E. The Wild Flowers of California. 1992. reprint ed. lib. bdg. 75.00 (*0-7812-5074-9*) Rprt Serv.

Parsons, Mary H., jt. auth. see Parsons, Jeffrey R.

Parsons, Mary P. Farmer Brown's Friends. LC 90-71980. (Illus.). 65p. (Orig.). (J). 1992. pap. 8.00 (*1-56002-040-7*) Aegina Pr.

Parsons, Merribell, ed. see Maciejunes, Nannette V.

Parsons, Merribell, ed. see Rosen, Steven W. & Fergus-Jean, John.

Parsons, Michael. Butterflies of the Bulolo-Wau Valley. 1992. 34.95 (*0-930897-61-7*) Bishop Mus.

Parsons, Michael, jt. auth. see Lyon, Pamela.

Parsons, Michael H. Part-Time Occupational Faculty: A Contribution to Excellence. 40p. 1985. 5.50 (*0-317-01306-8*) Ctr Educ Trng Employ.

Parsons, Michael J. How We Understand Art: A Cognitive Development Account of Aesthetic Experience. (Illus.). 208p. 1987. 39.95 (*0-521-32949-3*) Cambridge U Pr.

— How We Understand Art: A Cognitive Development Account of Aesthetic Experience. (Illus.). 208p. 1989. pap. 16.95 (*0-521-37966-0*) Cambridge U Pr.

Parsons, Michael J. & Blocker, H. Gene. Aesthetics & Education. LC 92-21377. (Disciplines in Art Education Ser.). 208p. 1993. 39.95 (*0-252-01988-1*); pap. 15.95 (*0-252-06293-0*) U of Ill Pr.

***Parsons, Michael L.** Global Warming: The Truth Behind the Myth. 250p. 1995. 27.95 (*0-306-45083-6*, Plenum Pr) Plenum.

Parsons, Michael L., jt. auth. see Wolff, Diane D.

Parsons, Mickey L. Patient Centered Care: A Model for Restructuring. 656p. 1994. 80.00 (*0-8342-0573-4*, 20573) Aspen Pub.

Parsons, Mikeal. Cadbury, Knox, & Talbert: American Contributions to the Study of Acts. (Biblical Scholarship in North America Ser.). 274p. 1992. 39.95 (*1-55540-653-X*, 061118); pap. 24.95 (*1-55540-654-8*) Scholars Pr GA.

Parsons, Mikeal C. & Pervo, Richard I. Rethinking the Unity of Luke & Acts. LC 93-9758. 1993. 13.00 (*0-8006-2750-4*, Fortress Pr) Augsburg Fortress.

Parsons, Mikeal C., jt. ed. see Sloan, Robert B.

Parsons, Nancy S., ed. Stockton Springs Vital Records 1859-1891. LC 79-55454. (Orig.). 1979. pap. 14.95 (*0-918768-02-0*) Cay-Bel.

Parsons, Neil. A New History of Southern Africa. 2nd rev. ed. (Illus.). 360p. (C). 1993. pap. text ed. 20.00 (*0-8419-5319-8*, Africana) Holmes & Meier.

Parsons, Neil, ed. see Rey, Charles.

Parsons, Nicholas T. Hungary: A Traveller's Guide. (Illus.). 366p. (Orig.). 1991. pap. 16.95 (*0-87052-976-5*) Hippocrene Bks.

Parsons, Nicholas T., tr. see Werkner, Patrick.

Parsons, Nicholas T., jt. auth. see Werkner, Patrick.

Parsons, Noel R., ed. N-C Machinability Data Systems. LC 74-153852. (Society of Manufacturing Engineers Numerical Control Ser.). 219p. reprint ed. pap. 62.50 (*0-317-09442-4*, 2015999) Bks Demand.

Parsons, Oscar A., et al, eds. Neuropsychology of Alcoholism: Implications for Diagnosis & Treatment. LC 86-29583. 414p. 1987. lib. bdg. 50.00 (*0-89862-696-X*) Guilford Pr.

Parsons, P., jt. auth. see Sato, Sadakatsu.

***Parsons, Particia & Parsons, Arthur.** Hippocrates Now! Is Your Doctor Ethical? 240p. 1995. 35.00 (*0-8020-0526-8*) U of Toronto Pr.

***Parsons, Patricia & Parsons, Arthur.** Hippocrates Now! Is Your Doctor Ethical? 240p. 1995. pap. 14.95 (*0-8020-6963-0*) U of Toronto Pr.

Parsons, Patrick. Cable Television & the First Amendment. LC 86-45883. 176p. 1987. text ed. 35.00 (*0-669-14459-2*) Free Pr.

Parsons, Patrick R., jt. auth. see Knowlton, Steven R.

Parsons, Patrick R., jt. ed. see Knowlton, Steven R.

Parsons, Paul. Getting Published: The Acquisition Process at University Presses. LC 89-31711. 256p. 1989. text ed. 33.00x (*0-87049-611-5*); pap. 14.95 (*0-87049-612-3*) U of Tenn Pr.

Parsons, Paul F. Inside America's Christian Schools. LC 87-24709. 176p. 1988. 24.95 (*0-86554-294-5*, H258); pap. 12.95 (*0-86554-303-8*, P54) Mercer Univ Pr.

Parsons, Peter, et al, eds. Supplementum Hellenisticum. 863p. (GRE.). 1983. 476.95 (*3-11-008171-7*) De Gruyter.

Parsons, Peter A. The Evolutionary Biology of Colonizing Species. LC 82-19763. (Illus.). 304p. 1983. 49.95 (*0-521-25247-4*) Cambridge U Pr.

***Parsons, Philip, ed.** A Companion to Theatre in Australia. (Illus.). 608p. (C). 1992. write for info. (*0-521-34528-6*) Cambridge U Pr.

Parsons, Philip A. Responsibility for Crime: An Investigation of the Nature & Causes of Crime & a Means of Its Prevention. LC 75-76683. (Columbia University. Studies in the Social Sciences: No. 91). reprint ed. 29.50 (*0-404-51091-4*) AMS Pr.

Parsons, Phillip. Shooting the Pianist: The Role of Government in the Arts. (C). 1990. 45.00 (*0-86819-176-0*, Pub. by Currency Pr AT) St Mut.

Parsons, Polly E. & Wiener-Kronish, Jeanine P., eds. Critical Care Secrets: Questions You Will Be Asked on Rounds, in the ICU, OR, & ER, & on Oral Exams. (Secrets Ser.). (Illus.). 478p. (Orig.). 1992. pap. text ed. 35.95 (*1-56053-015-4*) Hanley & Belfus.

Parsons, R., ed. ASHRAE Handbook - Applications 1991: SI Editions. (Illus.). 682p. 1991. text ed. 119.00 (*0-910110-79-4*) Am Heat Ref & Air Eng.

Parsons, R., jt. ed. see Kalvoda, Robert.

***Parsons, R. D.** The Carpets of Afghanistan. (Oriental Rugs Ser.: Vol. 3). 1992. 59.50 (*1-85149-144-9*) Antique Collect.

— Oriental Rugs, Vol. 3: The Carpets of Afghanistan. (Illus.). 160p. 1983. 59.50 (*1-85149-058-2*) Antique Collect.

Parsons, R. W. Income Taxation in Australia: Principles of Income, Deductibility & Tax Accounting. lxxiii, 901p. 1985. pap. 105.00 (*0-455-20601-5*, Pub. by Law Bk Co) W W Gaunt.

Parsons, Ramon M. La Moral en la Educacion. LC 83-10594. 90p. (SPA.). 1983. 6.00 (*0-8477-2746-7*) U of PR Pr.

Parsons, Reg. Woodcarving: A Manual of Techniques. (Illus.). 192p. 1994. pap. 24.95 (*1-85223-770-8*, Pub. by Crowood Pr UK) Trafalgar.

Parsons, Richard & Brooks, Neal A. Baltimore County Panorama. Phillips, Nancy O., ed. LC 88-22953. (Baltimore County Heritage Publications). (Illus.). 375p. 1988. text ed. 29.95 (*0-937076-03-1*) Baltimore Co Pub Lib.

Parsons, Richard D. The Skills of Helping. LC 94-6038. 1994. pap. text ed. write for info. (*0-205-14713-5*) Allyn.

Parsons, Richard D. & Meyers, Joel. Developing Consultation Skills: A Guide to Training, Development, & Assessment for Human Services Professionals. LC 84-5744. (Social & Behavioral Science Ser.). 279p. 1984. 30.95x (*0-87589-605-7*) Jossey-Bass.

Parsons, Richard D. & Wicks, Robert J. Counseling Strategies & Intervention Techniques for the Human Services. 4th ed. LC 93-1560. 1993. pap. text ed. 30.00 (*0-205-14791-7*) Allyn.

Parsons, Richard D., jt. ed. see Wicks, Robert J.

Parsons, Richard E. Sir Edwyn Hoskyns As a Biblical Theologian. LC 85-25038. 152p. 1986. text ed. 29.95 (*0-312-72647-3*) St Martin.

Parsons, Robert. Conference About the Next Succession to the Crown of England. LC 70-38217. (English Experience Ser.: No. 481). 1972. reprint ed. 32.50 (*90-221-0481-8*) Walter J Johnson.

Parsons, Robert & Costello, William T. The Judgment of a Catholicke English-Man Living in Banishment for His Religion. LC 57-9033. 1978. reprint ed. 50.00 (*0-8201-1240-2*) Schol Facsimiles.

Parsons, Rosamond H. Anglo-Norman Books of Courtesy & Nurture. (English Literature Ser.: No. 33). 1970. reprint ed. pap. 39.95 (*0-8383-0059-6*) M S G Haskell Hse.

Parsons, Ruth J. The Integration of Social Work Practice. LC 93-37937. 1994. text ed. 45.95 (*0-534-22284-6*) Brooks-Cole.

Parsons, Ruth J., jt. auth. see Cox, Enid O.

Parsons, S. A. How to Find Out about Engineering. 285p. (C). 1972. text ed. 121.00 (*0-08-016919-8*, Pub. by Pergamon Repr UK) Franklin.

Parsons, S. D. Putting Profit into Ranching: The Livestock Owner's Guide to Success! Parsons, H. E., ed. (Illus.). 150p. (Orig.). 1988. pap. write for info. (*0-318-63364-7*) Ranch Pubns.

Parsons, Samuel B. Parsons on the Rose. (Old Roses Ser.). 1979. text ed. 15.00 (*0-930576-13-6*) E M Coleman Ent.

Parsons, Sarah B. Choose the Perfect Name for Your Baby. LC 92-10483. 1992. 4.95 (*0-681-41444-8*) Longmeadow Pr.

Parsons, Stanley B. The Populist Context: Rural Versus Urban Power on a Great Plains Frontier. LC 72-824. (Contributions in American History Ser.: No. 22). (Illus.). xviii, 205p. 1973. text ed. 55.00 (*0-8371-6392-7*, PAC/, Greenwood Pr) Greenwood.

Parsons, Stanley B., et al. U. S. Congressional Districts & Data, 1843-1883. LC 85-67582. (Illus.). 254p. 1986. text ed. 79.50 (*0-313-22045-X*, PUN/, Greenwood Pr) Greenwood.

— United States Congressional Districts, 1788-1841. LC 77-83897. (Illus.). 416p. 1978. text ed. 105.00 (*0-8371-9828-3*, PUS/, Greenwood Pr) Greenwood.

— United States Congressional Districts, 1883-1913. LC 89-675315. 464p. 1990. text ed. 105.00 (*0-313-26482-1*, PUC/, Greenwood Pr) Greenwood.

Parsons, Steven L., ed. see Nabokov, Vladimir D.

Parsons, T. Voice & Speech Processing. (Electrical Engineering Ser.). 448p. 1987. text ed. write for info. (*0-07-048541-0*) McGraw.

Parsons, T. R., et al. Biological Oceanographic Processes. 3rd ed. (Illus.). 220p. 1984. text ed. 74.00 (*0-08-030766-3*, Pergamon Pr); pap. text ed. 39.00 (*0-08-030765-5*, Pergamon Pr) Elsevier.

Parsons, Talcott. Action Theory & the Human Condition. LC 77-94084. 1978. text ed. 22.95 (*0-02-923990-7*) Free Pr.

— Age & Sex in the Social Structure of the United States. (Reprint Series in Social Sciences). (C). 1993. reprint ed. pap. text ed. 1.00 (*0-8290-3751-9*, S-217) Irvington.

— The Early Essays. LC 90-19213. (Heritage of Sociology Ser.). 384p. 1991. lib. bdg. 45.00 (*0-226-09236-4*); pap. text ed. 19.95 (*0-226-09237-2*) U Ch Pr.

— Essays in Sociological Theory. rev. ed. 1964. pap. 18.95 (*0-02-924030-1*, 92403) Free Pr.

— Social Structure & Personality. LC 64-11218. 1964. text ed. 24.95 (*0-02-924850-7*) Free Pr.

— Social System. 1964. pap. 22.95 (*0-02-924190-1*) Free Pr.

— Sociological Theory & Modern Society. LC 67-12517. 1967. 35.00 (*0-02-924200-2*) Free Pr.

— Structure of Social Action, 1. LC 49-49353. 1967. pap. 14.95 (*0-02-924240-1*) Free Pr.

— Structure of Social Action, 2. LC 49-49353. 1967. pap. 21.95 (*0-02-924250-9*) Free Pr.

— Talcott Parsons on Institutions & Social Evolution: Selected Writings. Mayhew, Leon H., ed. LC 82-4911. (Heritage of Sociology Ser.). 304p. 1985. pap. text ed. 14.95 (*0-226-64749-8*) U Ch Pr.

Parsons, Talcott, ed. Theories of Society. LC 61-9171. 1965. text ed. 60.00 (*0-02-924450-1*) Free Pr.

Parsons, Talcott & Platt, Gerald M. The American University. LC 73-77470. 477p. reprint ed. pap. 136.00 (*0-7837-1524-2*, 2041801) Bks Demand.

Parsons, Talcott & Shils, Edward A., eds. Toward a General Theory of Action. LC 51-14629. 518p. reprint ed. pap. 147.70 (*0-317-09500-5*, 2017682) Bks Demand.

Parsons, Talcott, tr. see Weber, Max M.

Parsons, Talcott, et al. Socialization & Schools. LC 68-59278. (Reprint Ser.: No. 1). 90p. 1968. pap. 5.95 (*0-916690-00-8*) Harvard Educ Rev.

— Working Papers in the Theory of Action. LC 80-24475. 269p. 1981. reprint ed. text ed. 35.00 (*0-313-22468-4*, PAWP, Greenwood Pr) Greenwood.

Parsons, Terence. Events in the Semantics of English: A Study in Subatomic Semantics. (Illus.). 352p. 1994. pap. 21.00 (*0-262-66093-8*) MIT Pr.

— Nonexistent Objects. LC 79-21682. 280p. 1980. 45.00 (*0-300-02404-5*) Yale U Pr.

Parsons, Terry. Canopy Relative Work for Skydivers. 2nd ed. Orig. Title: Canopy Relative Work. (Illus.). 145p. 1988. reprint ed. pap. text ed. 12.95 (*0-9607814-4-7*) AeroGraphics.

Parsons, Terry D. Iowa Legal Forms: Family Law, 1984-1993. 160p. disk, ring bd. 85.00 (*0-685-49477-2*) Butterworth Legal Pubs.

— Iowa Legal Forms: Family Law, 1984-1993. 160p. 1993. disk, ring bd. 60.00 (*0-86678-171-4*) Butterworth Legal Pubs.

— Iowa Legal Forms: Family Law, 1984-1993. suppl. ed. 160p. 1993. 30.00 (*0-614-03180-X*) Butterworth Legal Pubs.

Parsons, Theophilus. Memoir of Theophilus Parsons. LC 71-118032. (American Constitutional & Legal History Ser). 1970. reprint ed. lib. bdg. 55.00 (*0-306-71939-8*) Da Capo.

— The Personal & Property Rights of a Citizen of the United States: How to Exercise & How to Preserve Them Together with I. a Treatise on the Rules of Organization & Procedure in Deliberative Assemblies; II. a Glossary of Law Terms in Common Use. xvi, 744p. 1992. reprint ed. 65.00 (*0-8377-2519-4*) Rothman.

***Parsons, Thomas.** Art in Focus: London. (Illus.). 128p. 1995. 12.95 (*0-8212-2154-X*) Bulfinch Pr.

— Introduction to Algorithms in Pascal. 1994. text ed. write for info. (*0-471-30594-4*) Wiley.

Parsons, Thomas E. Introduction to Compiler Construction. 359p. (C). 1995. text ed. 47.95 (*0-7167-8261-8*) W H Freeman.

Parsons, Thomas S., jt. auth. see Romer, Alfred S.

Parsons, Thomas W., jt. auth. see Haddad, Richard A.

Parsons, Timothy R., jt. auth. see Lalli, Carol M.

Parsons, Tony, jt. auth. see Bromwich, Peter.

Parsons, Tony, jt. auth. see Burchill, Julie.

Parsons, Troy W. Black Keys Only. Ingram, Wanda, ed. (Illus.). 200p. 1993. 13.95 (*0-9637109-0-7*) Fayette Pub.

— The Twig Is Bent. (Illus.). 230p. (Orig.). 1994. pap. 13.95 (*0-9637109-1-5*) Fayette Pub.

Parsons, Vicki. Developing & Managing a Nursing Home Volunteer Program. (Orig.). (C). 1991. pap. text ed. 14.95 (*1-877735-32-9*, 179) M&H Pub Co TX.

Parsons, Vicki L. A Year of Holidays: A Planning & Idea Book for Holiday Activities in Nursing Homes. (Illus.). 169p. (Orig.). (C). 1993. pap. text ed. 14.95 (*1-877735-41-8*, 225) M&H Pub Co TX.

Parsons, Virgil & Meyer, Beverly. The Nurse As Counselor. (C). 1985. pap. 18.95 (*0-8359-5011-5*, Reston) P-H.

Parsons, Virginia, ed. Donor Resources - Public Relations Manual. LC 90-165. 1990. pap. 35.00 (*0-915355-78-7*) Am Assn Blood.

Parsons, W. J. Improving Marketing Performance. 200p. 1987. text ed. 44.95 (*0-566-02595-7*, Pub. by Gower UK) Ashgate Pub Co.

— Improving Purchasing Performance. 128p. 1982. text ed. 45.00 (*0-566-02271-0*) Ashgate Pub Co.

Parsons, W. T. & Cuthbertson, E. G. Noxious Weeds of Australia. (Illus.). 692p. (C). 1993. text ed. 175.00 (*0-909605-81-5*, Pub. by Inkata Pr AT) Intl Spec Bk.

Parsons, Ward C., jt. auth. see Wentz, Gini.

Parsons, Wayne. The Power of the Financial Press: Journalism & Economic Opinion in Britain & America. LC 89-43066. 300p. 1990. text ed. 24.95 (*0-8135-1497-5*) Rutgers U Pr.

Parsons, Wilfrid. Mexican Martyrdom: Firsthand Experiences of the Religious Persecution in Mexico, 1926-1935. LC 87-51412. 295p. 1987. reprint ed. pap. 8.50 (*0-89555-330-9*) TAN Bks Pubs.

— Which Way, Democracy? LC 72-5747. (Essay Index Reprint Ser.). 1977. reprint ed. 21.95 (*0-8369-7296-1*) Ayer.

Parsons, Wilfrid, tr. see Augustine.

Parsons, William. Lifetime & Testamentary Estate Planning. 9th ed. 228p. 1983. 27.00 (*0-8318-0431-9*, B431) Am Law Inst.

Parsons, William, jt. auth. see Tweed, Harrison.

Parsons, William S. Everyone's Not Here: Families of the Armenian Genocide, a Study Guide. (Illus.). 88p. (YA). (gr. 7-12). 1989. spiral bd. 10.00 (*0-925428-04-3*) Armenian Assembly.

Parsons, William S., jt. auth. see Strom, Margot S.

Parsons, William T., ed. Arms Control & Strategic Stability: Challenges for the Future. 184p. (Orig.). (C). 1986. pap. text ed. 20.00 (*0-8191-5475-X*, Ctr for Law & Natl Security) U Pr of Amer.

Parsons, Y., et al. A Manual of Chemical & Biological Methods for Seawater Analysis. (Illus.). 144p. 1984. text ed. 51.00 (*0-08-030288-2*, Pergamon Pr); pap. text ed. 33.00 (*0-08-030287-4*, Pergamon Pr) Elsevier.

Parsonson, Jack. A Time to Remember. Frisque, Tom, ed. (Illus.). 128p. (Orig.). 1994. pap. write for info. (*0-9623080-4-8*) Aviation Usk.

***Parsowith, B. Scott.** Fundamentals of Quality Auditing. 1995. pap. 26.00 (*0-87389-240-2*) ASQC Qual Pr.

— Transparency Masters to Accompany Fundamentals of Quality Auditing. 1995. pap. 16.00 (*0-87389-342-5*) ASQC Qual Pr.

Parsson, Jens O. Dying of Money: Lessons of the Great German & American Inflations. LC 73-92727. 372p. 1974. 19.95 (*0-914688-01-4*) Wellspring Pr.

Partain, C. Leon, et al. Magnetic Resonance (NMR) Imaging, 2 vols., 1. 2nd ed. (Illus.). 1988. text ed. 220.00 (*0-7216-2516-9*) Saunders.

— Magnetic Resonance (NMR) Imaging, 2 vols., 2. 2nd ed. (Illus.). 1988. text ed. 279.00 (*0-7216-2517-7*) Saunders.

— Magnetic Resonance (NMR) Imaging, 2 vols., Set. 2nd ed. (Illus.). 1988. text ed. 495.00 (*0-7216-1340-3*) Saunders.

Partain, Katherine. Honey Delights: Cooking with Whole Wheat Flour & Honey. Thomson, Thomas, ed. (Illus.). 150p. (Orig.). 1989. pap. 9.95 (*0-912495-02-2*) San Diego Pub Co.

***Partain, Larry D., ed.** Solar Cells & Their Applications. LC 94-29987. 1995. text ed. 79.95 (*0-471-57420-1*) Wiley.

Partan, Daniel G. International Law Process. LC 91-76016. 884p. 1992. 65.00 (0-89089-465-5) Carolina Acad Pr.

Partan, Daniel G., jt. auth. see Baram, Michael S.

Partanen, J. Sociability & Intoxication: Alcohol & Drinking in Kenya, Africa & the Modern World. (Finnish Foundation for Alcohol Studies: Vol. 39). 1991. pap. 35.00 (951-9192-48-4) Rutgers Ctr Alcohol.

Partanen, J., et al. Inheritance of Drinking Behavior. (Finnish Foundation for Alcohol Studies: Vol. 14). 1966. 5.50 (951-9192-05-0) Rutgers Ctr Alcohol.

Partch, Harry. Bitter Music: Collected Journals, Essays, Introductions & Librettos. McGeary, Thomas, ed. (Music in American Life Ser.). (Illus.). 520p. 1991. 44.95 (0-252-01660-2) U of Ill Pr.

— Genesis of a Music. 2nd ed. LC 76-87373. (Music Reprint Ser.). 1974. lib. bdg. 49.50 (0-306-71597-X); pap. 12.95 (0-306-80106-X) Da Capo.

— Genesis of a Music: Music Book Index. 362p. 1993. reprint ed. lib. bdg. 89.00 (0-7812-9645-5) Rprt Serv.

Partee, Barbara H., et al. Mathematical Methods in Linguistics. (C). 1990. lib. bdg. 154.00 (90-277-2244-7); pap. text ed. 35.00 (90-277-2245-5) Kluwer Ac.

Partee, Barbara H., ed. Montague Grammar. 370p. 1987. reprint ed. pap. text ed. 53.00 (0-12-545851-7) Acad Pr.

Partee, Linda. Attribute Pattern Boards. (Illus.). 80p. 1982. 10.95 (0-9607366-4-6, KP114) Kino Pubns.

Partee, Morriss H. Plato's Poetics: The Authority of Beauty. LC 81-3332. 238p. reprint ed. pap. 67.90 (0-8357-6846-5, 2035541) Bks Demand.

Partee, Phillip E. The Layman's Guide to Fasting & Losing Weight: Introduced by Dick Gregory. Levy, H. M., Jr., ed. LC 78-64863. (Illus.). (Orig.). (J). (gr. 10-12). 1979. pap. text ed. 4.95 (0-685-94383-6) United Pr.

Partelpoeg, E. H. & Himmesoete, D. C., eds. Process Control & Automation in Extractive Metallurgy. LC 88-63685. (Illus.). 236p. 1989. pap. 103.00 (0-87339-083-0, 351) Minerals Metals.

Partelpoeg, E. H., jt. auth. see Davenport, W. G.

Partelpoeg, E. H., ed. see Minerals, Metals, & Materials Society Staff.

Parthasarasthi, G. & Chattopadhyaya, D. P., eds. Radhakrishnan: The Centenary Volume. (Illus.). 370p. 1990. 24.95 (0-19-562439-4) OUP.

Parthasarathi, G., ed. see Nehru, Jawaharlal.

Parthasarathy, Indira. Tricky Ground. 191p. 1975. write for info. (0-318-53527-0); pap. 4.95 (0-86578-110-9) Ind-US Inc.

Parthasarathy, K. R. An Introduction to Quantum Stochastic Calculus. (Monographs in Mathematics: Vol. 85). 304p. 1992. 116.00 (0-8176-2697-2) Birkhauser.

Parthasarathy, R., tr. The Cilappatikaram of Ilanko Atikal: An Epic of South India. 448p. 1992. text ed. 35.00 (0-231-07848-X) Col U Pr.

Parthasarathy, R., jt. ed. see Healy, J. J.

Parthasarathy, Rangaswami. Memoirs of a News Editor: Thirty Years with the Hindu. 1983. 17.50 (0-8364-0930-2, Pub. by Naya Prokash IA) S Asia.

Parthasarthy, Rangaswamy. Journalism in India: From the Earliest to the Present Times. 336p. 1989. text ed. 40.00 (81-207-0897-0, Pub. by Sterling Pubs II) Apt Bks.

Parthe, E. Cristallochamie De Structures Tetraedriques. 366p. (FRE.). (C). 1972. text ed. 306.00 (0-677-50280-X) Gordon & Breach.

Parthe, Erwin. Crystal Chemistry of Tetrahedral Structures. 186p. 1964. text ed. 169.00 (0-677-00700-0) Gordon & Breach.

Parthe, Erwin, ed. Modern Perspectives in Inorganic Crystal Chemistry. LC 92-26740. 292p. (C). 1992. lib. bdg. 115.00 (0-7923-1954-0) Kluwer Ac.

Parthe, Kathleen F. Russian Village Prose: The Radiant Past. 216p. 1992. text ed. 37.50 (0-691-06889-5); pap. text ed. 13.95 (0-691-01534-1) Princeton U Pr.

Parthemore, E. W. Genealogy of the Ludwig Bretz Family, 1750-1890. 149p. 1988. reprint ed. lib. bdg. 38.00 (0-8328-0312-X); reprint ed. pap. 30.00 (0-8328-0313-8) Higginson Bk Co.

Parthenius. Erotika Pathemata: The Love Stories of Parthenius. Stern, Jacob, tr. LC 91-43279. (Library of World Literature in Translation: Vol. 28). 126p. (GEC.). 1992. 29.00 (0-8240-0441-8) Garland.

Parthier, B. & Boulter, D., eds. Nucleic Acids & Proteins in Plants II: Structure, Biochemistry, & Physiology of Nucleic Acids. (Encyclopedia of Plant Physiology Ser.: Vol. 14 B). (Illus.). 774p. 1982. 299.00 (0-387-11140-9) Spr-Verlag.

Particle Size Analysis Conference Staff. Particle Size Analysis, 1981: Proceedings of the Fourth Particle Size Analysis Conference, Loughborough University of Technology, 21-24 September 1981. Stanley-Wood, N. & Allen, T., eds. 471p. reprint ed. pap. 134.30 (0-317-30324-4, 2024805) Bks Demand.

— Particle Size Analysis 1988: Proceedings of the Sixth Particle Size Analysis Conference, University of Surrey, Guildford, U. K., 19-20th April, 1988 Organized by the Analytical Division of the Royal Society of Chemistry. fac. ed. Lloyd, P. J., ed. LC 88-5633. (Illus.). 371p. 1994. pap. 105.80 (0-7837-7654-3, 2047407) Bks Demand.

Partido Comunista Del Trabajo (Dominican Republic) Staff. Persistir en Nuestra Linea, Luchar Consecuentemente Por su Aplicacion. (Illus.). 66p. (SPA.). reprint ed. pap. 1.00 (0-86714-016-X) Marxist-Leninist.

Partin, Charlotte C. Daydreams & Sunbeams: An Album of Framable Word Pictures. (Illus.). 18p. (Orig.). (YA). (gr. 7 up). 1987. pap. 4.00 (0-9619816-0-1) C C Partin.

Partin, Earl. And This Is How It Is. LC 77-81768. 1977. 10.00 (0-8187-0028-9) Harlo Press.

Partin, Harry, jt. auth. see Ellwood, Robert S., Jr.

Partin, Malcolm O. Waldeck-Rousseau, Combes, & the Church: The Politics of Anticlericalism, 1899-1905. LC 74-76167. 311p. reprint ed. pap. 88.70 (0-317-20441-6, 2023432) Bks Demand.

Partin, Marjorie, jt. auth. see Forquer, Nancy.

Partin, Nell, ed. see St. Ann's Altar Society Staff.

Partin, Ronald. Social Studies Teachers Book. 1991. pap. 29.95 (0-13-824970-9) P-H.

Partin, Ronald & Lovett, Martha. Social Studies Teacher's Survival Kit: Ready-to-Use Activities for Teaching Specific Skills. 288p. 1988. spiral bd. 29.95 (0-87628-782-8) Ctr Appl Res.

Partinen, Markku, jt. auth. see Guilleminault, Christian.

Partington, Angela, ed. The Concise Oxford Dictionary of Quotations. (Paperback Reference Ser.). 592p. 1995. pap. 9.95 (0-19-280026-4) OUP.

— The Oxford Dictionary of Quotations. 1088p. 1992. 35.00 (0-19-866185-1) OUP.

Partington, David. Making the Break: First Steps in Overcoming Eating Disorders, Pornography, Drugs, Alcohol. 128p. 1992. reprint ed. pap. 6.99 (0-87788-522-2) Shaw Pubs.

Partington, I., jt. auth. see Carter, H. C.

Partington, J. A., jt. auth. see Wragg, E. C.

Partington, J. R. Short History of Chemistry. 1989. pap. 10.95 (0-486-65977-1) Dover.

Partington, James R. An Advanced Treatise on Physical Chemistry, 4 vols. Incl. Vol. 1. Fundamental Principles-The Properties of Gases. LC 49-50157. 985p. pap. 180.00 (0-8357-5134-1); Vol. 2. Properties of Liquid. LC 49-50157. 492p. pap. 140.30 (0-8357-5135-X); Vol. 3. Properties of Solids. LC 49-50157. 699p. pap. 180.00 (0-8357-5136-8); Vol. 5. Molecular Spectra & Structure Dielectrics & Dipole Moments. LC 49-50157. 575p. pap. 163.90 (0-8357-5137-6); LC 49-50157. reprint ed. Set pap. write for info. (0-318-58067-5, 2005890) Bks Demand.

— Origins & Development of Applied Chemistry. LC 74-26284. (History, Philosophy & Sociology of Science Ser.). 1975. reprint ed. 50.95 (0-405-06611-2) Ayer.

Partington, James R. & McKie, Douglas. Historical Studies on the Phlogiston Theory. Cohen, I. Bernard, ed. LC 80-2140. (Development of Science Ser.). (Illus.). 1981. lib. bdg. 15.95 (0-405-13895-4) Ayer.

Partington, John & Wragg, Ted. Schools & Parents. (Education Matters Ser.). 96p. 1989. text ed. 45.00 (0-304-31714-4); pap. text ed. 17.95 (0-304-31712-8) Cassell.

Partington, Jonathan R. An Introduction to Hankel Operators. (London Mathematical Society Student Texts Ser.: No. 13). 112p. (C). 1989. pap. 18.95 (0-521-36791-3) Cambridge U Pr.

— An Introduction to Hankel Operators. (London Mathematical Society Student Texts Ser.: No. 13). 112p. (C). 1989. 47.95 (0-521-36611-9) Cambridge U Pr.

Partington, M., jt. auth. see O'Higgins, P.

Partington, Marta. Tic Tac Type. (Illus.). 126p. (Orig.). 1992. pap. 19.95 (0-672-30215-2) Alpha Bks IN.

***Partington, Michael & Werner, Raymond E.** QR-Harvard Graphics for Windows for Dummies. 1994. pap. 9.99 (1-56884-962-1) IDG Bks.

Partington, Michael, jt. auth. see Kay, David.

Partington, Paul G. The Moon Illustrated Weekly: Black America's First Weekly Magazine. 1986. pap. 10.00 (0-685-14028-8) P G Partington.

— W. E. B. Du Bois: A Bibliography of His Published Writings. 3rd ed. 1985. lib. bdg. 20.00 (0-9602538-3-1) P G Partington.

— W. E. B. Du Bois: A Bibliography of His Published Writings, Supplement. 1984. pap. 10.00 (0-685-08855-3) P G Partington.

— Who's Who on the Postage Stamps of the World, 1840-1984: A Master Index. 1989. lib. bdg. 20.00 (0-685-26477-7) P G Partington.

Partington, Paul G. & McDonnell, Robert W. W. E. B. Du Bois: A Bibliography of Writings about Him. 1989. lib. bdg. 20.00 (0-9602538-5-8) P G Partington.

Partington, T. B. Women & the Chinese Poets. 1972. 59.95 (0-8490-1320-8) Gordon Pr.

Partisan Review Staff. Fifty-Year Cumulative Index, 1934-1983, Vol. 1-50. LC 84-22228. (Studies in Modern Literature: No. 15). 1984. 67.50 (0-404-61585-6) AMS Pr.

Partise, David A., ed. see Dar Systems International Staff.

Partlett, D. F. Professional Negligence. xxxvii, 425p. 1985. 86.50 (0-455-20594-9, Pub. by Law Bk Co) W W Gaunt.

Partlett, David F., jt. auth. see Nurcombe, Barry.

Partlow, Francis. Training of Children in the New Thought. 88p. 1994. pap. 7.00 (0-89540-273-4, SB-273) Sun Pub.

***Partlow, Frank.** Functional Consolidation of Truckee Meadows Fire Protection. 13p. 1992. 7.00 (1-886306-00-1) Nevada Policy.

Partlow, Robert B., Jr. & Moore, Harry T., eds. D. H. Lawrence, The Man Who Lived. Papers. LC 80-15262. 320p. 1980. 18.95 (0-8093-0981-5) S Ill U Pr.

Partlow, Thomas E. The People of Wilson County, Tennessee: 1800-1899. 158p. 1983. 22.00 (0-89308-308-9) Southern Hist Pr.

— Wilson County, Tennessee, Circuit Court Records, 1810-1855. 144p. 1988. pap. 24.50 (0-89308-635-5, TN 109) Southern Hist Pr.

— Wilson County, Tennessee, Deed Books C-M, 1793-1829. 248p. 1984. 25.00 (0-89308-540-5) Southern Hist Pr.

— Wilson County, Tennessee, Deed Books N-Z, 1829-1853. 464p. 1984. 35.00 (0-89308-541-3) Southern Hist Pr.

— Wilson County, Tennessee, Deeds, Marriages & Wills, 1800-1902. 244p. 1987. pap. 32.50 (0-89308-605-3, TN 101) Southern Hist Pr.

— Wilson County, Tennessee, Miscellaneous Records, 1800-1875. 270p. 1982. 25.00 (0-89308-283-X, TN 60) Southern Hist Pr.

Partner, Nancy F., ed. Studying Medieval Women: Sex, Gender, Feminism. (Speculum Book Ser.). (Illus.). vii, 197p. 1993. pap. 15.00 (0-915651-06-8) Medieval Acad.

Partner, Peter. The Knights Templar & Their Myth. 232p. 1990. pap. 12.95 (0-89281-273-7) Inner Tradit.

— The Lands of St. Peter: The Papal State in the Middle Ages & the Early Renaissance. LC 73-182793. (Illus.). 495p. reprint ed. pap. 141.10 (0-685-23579-3, 2029056) Bks Demand.

— The Pope's Men: The Papal Civil Service in the Renaissance. 288p. 1990. 69.00 (0-19-821995-4) OUP.

— Renaissance Rome: A Portrait of a Society, 1500-1559. 1976. pap. 14.00 (0-520-03945-9) U CA Pr.

— Renaissance Rome: A Portrait of a Society, 1500-1559. LC 75-13154. (Illus.). 285p. reprint ed. pap. 81.30 (0-685-23637-4, 2029057) Bks Demand.

Partner, Simon. Mergers & Acquisitions Manual. 432p. 1991. 125.00 (0-13-577263-X) P-H.

— Saying Yes to Japanese Investment: How You Can Benefit by Doing Business with the Japanese. 1992. pap. 19.95 (0-13-785049-2, Busn) P-H.

Partners for Livable Places, et al. The Return of the Livable City: Learning from America's Best. (Illus.). 320p. 1987. 28.50 (0-87491-828-6) Acropolis.

Partners for Livable Places Staff. The Better Community Catalog: A Sourcebook of Ideas, People, & Strategies for Improving the Place Where You Live. (Illus.). 375p. 1989. pap. 24.95 (0-87491-912-6) Acropolis.

Partnow, Elaine. New Quotable Woman: From Eve to the Present. rev. ed. 608p. 1992. 40.00 (0-8160-2134-1) Facts on File.

— The Quotable Woman: Eve to 1799. 550p. 1986. 29.95 (0-87196-307-8) Facts on File.

Partnow, Elaine, ed. The New Quotable Woman: The Definitive Treasury of Notable Words by Women - From Eve to the Present. rev. ed. LC 93-17685. 736p. 1993. reprint ed. pap. 15.00 (0-452-01099-3, Mer) NAL-Dutton.

Partnoy, Alicia. The Little School: Tales of Disappearance & Survival in Argentina. Athey, Lois et al, trs. LC 85-73522. (Illus.). 143p. (Orig.). (C). 1991. reprint ed. 21.95 (0-939416-08-5); reprint ed. pap. 9.95 (0-939416-07-7) Cleis Pr.

— Revenge of the Apple: Venganza de la Manzana. Schaaf, Richard & Kreger, Regina, trs. (Illus.). 100p. (Orig.). (ENG & SPA.). (C). 1992. 24.95 (0-939416-62-X); pap. 8.95 (0-939416-63-8) Cleis Pr.

***Parton.** Dolly: My Life & Other Unfinished Business. 1995. mass mkt. 5.99 (0-06-109236-3, Harp PBks) HarpC.

Parton, jt. auth. see Mikhailov, G. K.

Parton, Anthony. Mikhail Larionov & the Russian Avant-Garde. LC 92-20814. (Illus.). 216p. (C). 1993. text ed. 49.50 (0-691-03603-9) Princeton U Pr.

Parton, Dolly. Coat of Many Colors. LC 93-3866. (Illus.). 32p. (J). (gr. 1 up). 1994. 14.00 (0-06-023413-X); lib. bdg. 13.89 (0-06-023414-8) HarpC Child Bks.

— Dolly: My Life & Other Unfinished Business. LC 94-18714. 1994. 25.00 (0-06-017720-9) HarpC.

— Dolly: My Life & Other Unfinished Business. large type ed. LC 94-39240. 1995. write for info. (0-7862-0363-3); pap. write for info. (0-7862-0364-1) Thorndike Pr.

Parton, J. E., et al. Applied Electromagnetics. 2nd ed. 300p. 1986. 42.00 (0-387-91279-7) Spr-Verlag.

Parton, James. Air Force Spoken Here: General Eaker & the Command of the Air. (Illus.). 557p. 1986. 18.00 (0-89745-108-2) Sunflower U Pr.

— Air Force Spoken Here: General Ira Eaker & the Command of the Air. LC 85-28633. (Illus.). 558p. 1986. 24.95 (0-917561-15-5) Adler & Adler.

— Captains of Industry: Or, Men of Business Who Did Something Besides Making Money; a Book for Young Americans. LC 72-2660. (Essay Index Reprint Ser.). 1977. reprint ed. 27.95 (0-8369-2853-9) Ayer.

— Humorous Poetry of the English Language. LC 70-149109. (Granger Index Reprint Ser.). 1977. 41.95 (0-8369-6234-6) Ayer.

— Life & Times of Benjamin Franklin, 2 vols, Set. LC 72-126603. (American Scene Ser.). (Illus.). 1971. reprint ed. lib. bdg. 125.00 (0-306-70048-4) Da Capo.

— Life of Horace Greeley. LC 70-125711. (American Journalists Ser.). 442p. 1977. reprint ed. 35.95 (0-405-01692-1) Ayer.

— Life of Thomas Jefferson. 1972. 69.95 (0-8490-0538-8) Gordon Pr.

— Life of Thomas Jefferson. LC 76-126604. (American Scene Ser.). (Illus.). 1971. reprint ed. lib. bdg. 79.50 (0-306-70049-2) Da Capo.

— Life of Voltaire, 2 vols. 1972. 400.00 (0-8490-0539-6) Gordon Pr.

Parton, James, et al. Eminent Women of the Age: Being Narratives of the Lives & Deeds of the Most Prominent Women of the Present Generation. LC 74-3968. (Women in America Ser.). 656p. 1974. reprint ed. 50.95 (0-405-06116-1) Ayer.

Parton, K. Digital Computer. LC 64-14147. 1964. 62.00 (0-08-012250-7, Pub. by Pergamon Repr UK) Franklin.

Parton, Nigel. Governing the Family: Child Care, Child Protection & the State. LC 90-28660. 264p. 1991. text ed. 39.95 (0-312-06171-4) St Martin.

Parton, Nigel, jt. ed. see Franklin, Bob.

Parton, Roger, jt. ed. see Wardlaw, Alastair C.

Parton, Sara P. Fern Leaves from Fanny's Port-folio. (American Biography Ser.). 400p. 1991. reprint ed. lib. bdg. 79.00 (0-7812-8307-8) Rprt Serv.

— Fern Leaves from Fannys Port-Folio, Second Series. LC 77-164572. (American Fiction Reprint Ser.). 1977. reprint ed. 35.95 (0-8369-7049-7) Ayer.

***Parton, Stella.** Stella Parton's Country Cookin' (Illus.). 180p. (Orig.). 1995. pap. 7.95 (1-55850-473-7) Adams Pubng.

Parton, V. Z. & Boriskovsky, V. G. Dynamic Fracture Mechanics, Vol. 1: Stationary Cracks. Hetnarski, Richard B., ed. Wadwha, Ram S., tr. 260p. 1989. 131.00 (0-89116-550-9) Hemisp Pub.

— Dynamic Fracture Mechanics, Vol. 2: Propagating Cracks. Hetnarski, Richard B., ed. LC 66-55120. 1989. 152.00 (0-89116-605-X) Hemisp Pub.

Parton, V. Z. & Kudryavtsev, B. A. Electromagnetoelasticity: Piezoelectrics & Electrically Conductive Solids. 480p. 1988. text ed. 344.00 (2-88124-671-0) Gordon & Breach.

Parton, V. Z. & Morozov, E. M. Mechanics of Elastic-Plastic Fracture. 2nd rev. ed. 504p. 1989. 136.00 (0-89116-606-8) Hemisp Pub.

Parton, V. Z., jt. auth. see Mikhailov, G. K.

Parton, V. Z., jt. ed. see Mikhailov, G. K.

Parton, V. Z., et al. Engineering Composite Materials. 750p. 1991. 115.00 (0-89116-965-2) CRC Pr.

— Engineering Mechanics of Composite Structures. 1993. 95.00 (0-8493-9302-7, TA418) CRC Pr.

Parton, W. Julian. The Story of the General Crushed Stone Company. (Illus.). 100p. 1992. text ed. 11.95 (0-930973-13-5) Canal Hist Tech.

Partos, Gabriel. The World That Came in from the Cold. 303p. (C). 1994. pap. 15.95 (0-905031-58-X) Brookings.

Partow, Donna. Homemade Business. 1992. 9.99 (1-56179-043-5) Focus Family.

— No More Lone Ranger Moms: Women Helping Women in the Practical Everyday-ness of Life. 224p. 1995. pap. 8.99 (1-55661-531-0) Bethany Hse.

Partridge, A., et al. Punishments Imposed on Federal Offenders, 2 vols., Set. LC 86-81506. v, 1336p. 1986. reprint ed. lib. bdg. 150.00 (0-89941-469-9, 304270) W S Hein.

Partridge, A. E. Astrology in a Nutshell. 72p. 1969. 1.75 (0-86690-018-7, P2262-034) Am Fed Astrologers.

Partridge, Arthur D. & Miller, Daniel L. Major Wood Decays in the Inland Northwest. (Illus.). 125p. 1974. pap. 5.95 (0-89301-014-6) U of Idaho Pr.

Partridge, Ashley C. A Substantive Grammar of Shakespeare's Non-Dramatic Texts. LC 75-44106. 232p. 1976. 27.50 (0-8139-0619-9) U Pr of Va.

Partridge, Bellamy. Big Freeze. LC 74-26119. reprint ed. 16.00 (0-404-58458-6) AMS Pr.

Partridge, Brian, jt. ed. see Linsell, Tony.

Partridge-Brown, Mary. In-Vitro Fertilization Clinics: A North American Directory of Programs & Services. LC 92-56679. 248p. 1993. pap. 28.50 (0-89950-817-0) McFarland & Co.

Partridge, Bruce, jt. auth. see Child, John.

***Partridge, Chris.** Understanding Objects, Re-Engineering & Re-Use: A Practical Handbook. 250p. 1995. pap. 42.95 (0-7506-2082-X, Digital DEC) Buttrwrth-Heinemann.

Partridge, Clive. Foxholes Farm: A Multi-Period Gravel Site. (Illus.). 244p. 1993. pap. text ed. 48.00 (0-9514334-0-7) A Sutton Pub.

Partridge, Colin. Senso - Visconti's Film & Boito's Novella: A Case Study in the Relation Between Literature & Film. LC 91-38740. 124p. 1992. lib. bdg. 59.95 (0-7734-9746-3) E Mellen.

— Tristana: Bunuel's Film & Galdos' Novel: A Case Study in the Relation Between Literature & Film. LC 94-39161. 244p. 1995. text ed. 89.95 (0-7734-9089-2) E Mellen.

— Yuri Trifonov's The Moscow Cycle: A Critical Study. LC 89-12941. (Studies in Slavic Language & Literature: Vol. 3). 208p. 1990. lib. bdg. 89.95 (0-88946-293-3) E Mellen.

Partridge, Colin, jt. ed. see Coustillas, Pierre.

***Partridge, Craig.** The Descendants of William Andrew of Cambridge, Massachusetts. LC 95-4991. 1995. write for info. (0-89725-226-8, Penobscot Pr) Picton Pr.

— Gigabit Networking. 1994. 45.95 (0-201-56333-9) Addison-Wesley.

Partridge, Craig, ed. Innovations in Internetworking. LC 88-26314. (Artech House Telecommunications Library). 544p. reprint ed. pap. 155.10 (0-7837-0414-3, 2040736) Bks Demand.

Partridge, D. & Hussain, K. M. Knowledge-Based Information Systems. LC 94-20437. 1994. 29.95 (0-07-707624-9) McGraw.

Partridge, Derek. Artificial Intelligence & Software Engineering. (Series in Computational Science). 576p. (C). 1991. text ed. 85.00 (0-89391-606-4) Ablex Pub.

— Computers & Creativity. 192p. (Orig.). 1994. write for info. (1-56750-170-2) Ablex Pub.

— A New Guide to Artificial Intelligence. LC 90-34179. (Series in Computational Science). 576p. (C). 1991. text ed. 72.50 (0-89391-607-2); pap. text ed. 35.00 (0-89391-608-0) Ablex Pub.

— Thought-Provoking Thoughts about Living. 208p. 1994. per. 13.95 (0-8403-9456-X) Kendall-Hunt.

Partridge, Derek & Hussain, K. M. Artificial Intelligence & Business Management. (Series in Computational Science). 368p. (C). 1991. text ed. 69.50 (0-89391-796-6); pap. text ed. 37.50 (0-89391-835-0) Ablex Pub.

Partridge, Derek & Rowe, Jon. Computers & Creativity. 224p. (Orig.). 1994. pap. text ed. 22.95 (1-871516-51-X, Pub. by Intellect Bks UK) Cromland.

Partridge, Derek & Wilks, Yorick, eds. The Foundations of Artificial Intelligence: A Sourcebook. (Illus.). 350p. (C). 1990. 79.95 (0-521-35103-0); pap. 29.95 (0-521-35944-9) Cambridge U Pr.

Partridge, Derek, ed. see Halpern, Mark.

Partridge, Derek, ed. see Schvaneveldt, Roger W.

Partridge, Dixie. Deer in the Haystacks. 2nd ed. Boyer, Dale, ed. LC 83-73659. (Ahsahta Press Modern & Contemporary Poets of the West Ser.). 60p. 1984. pap. 6.95 (0-916272-23-0) Ahsahta Pr.

An Asterisk (*) at the beginning of an entry indicates that the title is appearing in BIP for the first time.

P Q

— Watermark. LC 91-16235. (Eileen W. Barnes Award Ser.). (Illus.). 80p. (Orig.). 1991. pap. 7.00 (0-938158-11-2) Saturday Pr.

Partridge, Edmund. Church in Perspective: Standard Course for Layreaders. rev. ed. LC 68-56918. 113p. 1976. pap. 5.95 (0-8192-1210-5) Morehouse Pub.

Partridge, Edward B. The Broken Compass: A Study of the Major Comedies of Ben Jonson. LC 75-38386. 254p. 1976. reprint ed. text ed. 59.75 (0-8371-8662-5, PABC, Greenwood Pr) Greenwood.

Partridge, Edward B., ed. see Jonson, Ben.

Partridge, Elinore H., ed. American Prose & Criticism, 1820-1900: A Guide to Information Sources. LC 74-11519. (American Literature, English Literature, & World Literatures in English Information Guide Ser.: Vol. 39). 592p. 1983. 68.00 (0-8103-1213-1) Gale.

Partridge, Elizabeth, ed. Dorothea Lange: A Visual Life. (Illus.). 176p. 1994. 55.00 (1-56098-350-7); pap. 24.95 (1-56098-455-4) Smithsonian.

Partridge, Eric. Adventuring among Words. LC 76-39202. (Select Bibliographies Reprint Ser.). 1977. reprint ed. 12.95 (0-8369-6804-2) Ayer.

— A Charm of Words: Essays & Papers on Language. LC 73-167400. (Essay Index Reprint Ser.). 1977. reprint ed. 18.95 (0-8369-2707-9) Ayer.

— Concise Usage & Abusage: A Modern Guide to Good English. LC 73-94615. 219p. 1969. reprint ed. text ed. 55.00 (0-8371-2466-2, PAUA, Greenwood Pr) Greenwood.

— A Covey of Partridge: An Anthology. LC 71-117898. (Select Bibliographies Reprint Ser.). 1977. reprint ed. 26.95 (0-8369-5351-7) Ayer.

— Critical Medley. LC 73-148894. (Select Bibliographies Reprint Ser.). 1977. reprint ed. 21.95 (0-8369-5680-X) Ayer.

— A Dictionary of Catch Phrases: American & British, from the Sixteenth Century to the Present Day. rev. ed. Beale, Paul, ed. LC 85-40997. 408p. 1992. 24.95 (0-8128-3101-2, Scrbrough Hse); pap. 12.95 (0-8128-8536-8, Scrbrough Hse) Madison Bks UPA.

— A Dictionary of Cliches. 5th ed. 1978. reprint ed. pap. 13.95 (0-7100-0049-9, RKP) Routledge.

— Dictionary of Slang & Unconventional English. 1980. 45.00 (0-02-594970-5) Macmillan.

— A Dictionary of Slang & Unconventional English. 8th ed. 1408p. 1985. text ed. 75.00 (0-02-594980-2) Macmillan.

— Eighteenth Century English Romantic Poetry. LC 75-117900. (Select Bibliographies Reprint Ser.). 1977. reprint ed. 24.95 (0-8369-5353-3) Ayer.

— English: A Course for Human Beings. 4th ed. LC 79-117901. (Select Bibliographies Reprint Ser.). 1977. reprint ed. 31.95 (0-8369-5354-1) Ayer.

— Frank Honywood, Private: A Personal Record of the 1914-1918 War. 2nd rev. ed. Serle, Geoffrey, ed. 152p. 1987. 24.95 (0-522-84340-9) Intl Spec Bk.

— The French Romantics' Knowledge of English Literature: 1820-1848. LC 72-117902. (Select Bibliographies Reprint Ser.). 1977. reprint ed. 30.95 (0-8369-5355-X) Ayer.

— From Sanskrit to Brazil. LC 77-94281. (Select Bibliographies Reprint Ser.). 1977. 20.95 (0-8369-5055-0) Ayer.

— Glimpses. LC 70-150194. (Select Bibliographies Reprint Ser.). 1977. 21.95 (0-8369-5707-5) Ayer.

— Here, There & Everywhere. LC 75-86775. (Essay Index Reprint Ser.). 1977. 19.95 (0-8369-1187-3) Ayer.

— Journey to the Edge of Morning. LC 77-84331. (Essay Index Reprint Ser.). 1977. 16.95 (0-8369-1101-6) Ayer.

— Literary Sessions. LC 70-117904. (Select Bibliographies Reprint Ser.). 1977. reprint ed. 21.95 (0-8369-5357-6) Ayer.

— Name into Word. 2nd ed. LC 77-117906. (Select Bibliographies Reprint Ser.). 1977. reprint ed. 44.95 (0-8369-5361-4) Ayer.

— A New Testament Word Book: A Glossary. LC 70-117907. (Select Bibliographies Reprint Ser.). 1977. reprint ed. 21.95 (0-8369-5359-2) Ayer.

— Origins: A Short Etymological Dictionary of Modern English. 992p. 1991. 12.99 (0-517-41425-2) Random Hse Value.

— Partridge's Concise Dictionary of Slang & Unconventional English. Beale, Paul, ed. 560p. 1990. text ed. 35.00 (0-02-605350-0) Macmillan.

— Robert Eyres Landor: A Biographical & Critical Sketch, 2 vols. in 1. Bd. with Selections from Robert Landor. LC 78-117909. LC 78-117909. (Select Bibliographies Reprint Ser.). 1977. reprint ed. 26.95 (0-8369-5362-2) Ayer.

— The Shaggy Dog Story. LC 72-117910. (Select Bibliographies Reprint Ser.). (Illus.). 1977. reprint ed. 18.95 (0-8369-5363-0) Ayer.

— Shakespeare's Bawdy. 3rd ed. 240p. 1990. pap. 15.95 (0-415-05076-6, A4700) Routledge.

— Smaller Slang Dictionary. 521p. 1987. 16.95 (0-88029-107-9) Dorset Pr.

— Smaller Slang Dictionary. 1976. reprint ed. pap. 13.95 (0-7100-8331-9, RKP) Routledge.

— Usage & Abusage: How to Pick the Right Words & Avoid the Wrong Ones in Speech & Writing. 400p. 1995. 27.50 (0-393-03761-4) Norton.

— Words at War, Words at Peace: Essays on Language in General & Particular Words. LC 76-117911. (Select Bibliographies Reprint Ser.). 1977. reprint ed. 20.95 (0-8369-5364-9) Ayer.

— Words, Words, Words! LC 70-117912. (Select Bibliographies Reprint Ser.). 1977. reprint ed. 23.95 (0-8369-5365-7) Ayer.

— The World of Words: An Introduction to Language in General & to English & American in Particular. 3rd ed. LC 73-117913. (Select Bibliographies Reprint Ser.). 1977. reprint ed. 24.95 (0-8369-5366-5) Ayer.

Partridge, Eric, ed. A Book of English Prose: Seventeen Hundred to Nineteen Fourteen. LC 73-119942. (Select Bibliographies Reprint Ser.). 1977. reprint ed. 21.95 (0-8369-5385-1) Ayer.

— Ixion in Heaven & Endymion: Disraeli's Skit & Aytoun's Burlesque. LC 76-117903. (Select Bibliographies Reprint Ser.). 1977. 17.95 (0-8369-5356-8) Ayer.

— Poems of Cuthbert Shaw & Thomas Russell. LC 74-117908. (Select Bibliographies Reprint Ser.). 1977. 19.95 (0-8369-5360-6) Ayer.

— The Three Wartons. LC 71-128881. (Select Bibliographies Reprint Ser.). 1977. reprint ed. 19.95 (0-8369-5501-3) Ayer.

Partridge, Eric & Beale, Paul. Shorter Slang Dictionary. Fergusson, Rosalind, ed. 240p. 1993. pap. 15.95 (0-415-08866-6, B0566) Routledge.

Partridge, Eric & Clark, John W. British & American English since Nineteen Hundred. LC 68-9711. (Illus.). 341p. 1968. reprint ed. text ed. 65.00 (0-8371-0189-1, PABA, Greenwood Pr) Greenwood.

Partridge, Eric, jt. auth. see Brophy, John.

Partridge, Eric, ed. see Grose, Francis.

Partridge, Eric, et al, eds. A Dictionary of Forces' Slang: 1939-1945. LC 75-117899. (Select Bibliographies Reprint Ser.). 1977. reprint ed. 21.95 (0-8369-5352-5) Ayer.

— Martial Medley. LC 73-117905. (Select Bibliographies Reprint Ser.). 1977. 29.95 (0-8369-5358-4) Ayer.

Partridge, Eric F. As Large As Life. 1991. 16.95 (0-533-08806-2) Vantage.

Partridge, Frances, jt. auth. see Asturias, Miguel A.

Partridge, G. E. Studies in the Psychology of Intemperance. Grob, Gerald N., ed. LC 80-1244. (Addiction in America Ser.). 1981. reprint ed. lib. bdg. 27.95 (0-405-13614-5) Ayer.

Partridge, Henry V., jt. auth. see Goddard, M. E.

Partridge, I. K., ed. Advanced Composites. 446p. 1990. 122.50 (1-85166-387-8) Elsevier.

Partridge, J. Arthur. The Making of the American Nation or, the Rise & Decline of Oligarchy in the West. 1977. 27.95 (0-8369-9192-3, 9061) Ayer.

Partridge, James. Changing Faces: The Challenge of Facial Disfigurement. 1990. 11.95 (0-14-011597-8) Phoenix Soc.

Partridge, Karen E., jt. auth. see Partridge, Michael S.

Partridge, L. Donald, jt. auth. see Partridge, Lloyd D.

Partridge, Linda, jt. ed. see Harvey, Paul H.

Partridge, Lloyd D. & Partridge, L. Donald. The Nervous System: Its Function & Its Interaction with the World. (Illus.). 450p. 1992. 65.00 (0-262-16134-6, Bradford Bks); pap. 39.00 (0-262-66079-2, Bradford Bks) MIT Pr.

Partridge, Loren. Michelangelo: The Sistine Ceiling, Rome. (Great Fresco Cycles of the Renaissance Ser.). 104p. 1993. 23.50 (0-8076-1315-0) Braziller.

Partridge, Loren, jt. auth. see Starn, Randolph.

Partridge, Michael. The Duke of Wellington: A Bibliography. LC 90-6574. (Bibliographies of British Statesmen Ser.: No. 10). 150p. 1990. text ed. 59.95 (0-313-28075-4, PDB/, Greenwood Pr) Greenwood.

Partridge, Michael S. Military Planning for Defense of the United Kingdom, 1814-1870. LC 88-20637. (Contributions in Military Studies: No. 91). 248p. 1989. text ed. 59.95 (0-313-26871-1, PMY/, Greenwood Pr) Greenwood.

Partridge, Michael S. & Partridge, Karen E. Lord Palmerston, 1784-1865: A Bibliography. LC 93-43710. (Bibliographies of British Statesmen Ser.: No. 16). 328p. 1994. text ed. 85.00 (0-313-28292-7, Greenwood Pr) Greenwood.

Partridge, P. W. Transport Analysis Using Boundary Elements. 1993. disk, ring bd. 475.00 (1-56252-122-5) Computational Mech MA.

Partridge, P. W., ed. Computer Modelling of Seas & Coastal Regions: Proceedings of the International Conference on Computer Modelling of Seas & Coastal Regions Held in Southampton, UK, April 1992. LC 91-77632. 534p. 1992. 204.00 (1-56252-092-X) Computational Mech MA.

Partridge, P. W., jt. ed. see Brebbia, C. A.

Partridge, P. W., et al. The Dual Reciprocity Boundary Element Method. LC 91-70442. (Computational Engineering Ser.). 300p. 1991. 145.00 (0-945824-82-3) Computational Mech MA.

Partridge, Penny M. How to Buy & Apply Cosmetics. Bourassa, Hester, ed. (Illus.). 48p. (Orig.). 1988. pap. write for info. (0-929164-24-5) Alco Pub.

Partridge, R. B. ThreeK: The Cosmic Microwave Background Radiation. (Cambridge Astrophysics Ser.: No. 25). (Illus.). 416p. (C). 1994. 89.95 (0-521-35254-1) Cambridge U Pr.

Partridge, R. T. Operation Skua. 160p. (C). 1987. 54.00 (0-902633-86-4, Pub. by Picton UK) St Mut.

Partridge, Ralph. Broadmoor: A History of Criminal Lunacy & Its Problems. LC 75-31440. (Illus.). 278p. 1976. reprint ed. lib. bdg. 22.50 (0-8371-8520-3, PABRO, Greenwood Pr) Greenwood.

Partridge, Roy. Sailing the Mirror. (C). 1990. text ed. 59.00 (0-906754-01-1, Pub. by Fernhurst Bks UK) St Mut.

Partridge, S. A., jt. auth. see Amato, P. R.

Partridge, Scott H. Cases in Business & Society. 2nd ed. 384p. (C). 1989. pap. text ed. write for info. (0-13-115536-9) P-H.

Partridge, Susan. AIMS: Developmental Indicators of Emotional Health. 1991. write for info. (0-939561-10-7) Univ South ME.

Partridge, Sylvia, ed. see Phillips, Marjorie.

Partridge, Terence, ed. Molecular & Cell Biology of Muscular Dystrophy. LC 92-48393. (Molecular & Cell Biology of Human Diseases Ser.). (Illus.). 320p. 1993. 85.00 (0-412-43440-7, A9501) Chapman & Hall.

Partridge, Tom. The Castle. (Illus.). (J). 1994. 19.95 (0-312-11156-8) St Martin.

Partridge, Virginia P. & Watkins, Susan F. Transcript of the 1800, 1810 & 1820 Federal Census of Schoharie County, New York. 251p. 1992. lib. bdg. 49.95 (1-56012-112-2) Kinship Rhinebeck.

— Transcript of the 1830 & 1840 Federal Census of Schoharie County, New York. 350p. 1991. lib. bdg. 69.95 (1-56012-113-0) Kinship Rhinebeck.

Partridge, William, jt. ed. see Eddy, Elizabeth.

Partridge, William L. The Hippie Ghetto: The Natural History of a Subculture. (Illus.). 88p. (C). 1985. reprint ed. pap. text ed. 7.95 (0-88133-190-2) Waveland Pr.

Partridge, William L., jt. auth. see Kimball, Solon T.

Parts, C. Estonian-English Dictionary for Schools. 2nd rev. ed. 336p. (ENG & EST.). 1984. 29.95 (0-7859-1090-5, 4602020000) Fr & Eur.

Partsch, H., ed. Progress in Lymphology: Proceedings of the XIth International Congress, Vienna, 24-27. (International Congress Ser.). 744p. 1988. 187.75 (0-444-80985-6, Excerpta Medica) Elsevier.

Partsch, H. A. Specification & Transformation of Programs: A Formal Approach to Software Development. Gries, David, ed. (Texts & Monographs in Computer Science). (Illus.). 512p. 1990. text ed. 51.00 (0-387-52356-1) Spr-Verlag.

— Specification & Transformation of Programs: A Formal Approach to Software Development. Gries, David, ed. (Texts & Monographs in Computer Science). (Illus.). 512p. 1990. pap. 39.00 (0-387-52589-0) Spr-Verlag.

***Partsch, Susanna, ed.** Gustav Klimt: Painter of Women. (Pegasus Library). (Illus.). 120p. 1994. 25.00 (3-7913-1428-9) TeNeues.

Parturier, ed. see Merimee, Prosper.

Paruccini, M., ed. Applying Multiple Criteria Aid for Decision to Environmental Management: Based on the Papers Presented at the 38th Meeting of the European Working Group 'Multicriteria Aid for Decision,' Held at the Joint Research Centre, Ispra, Italy, October 7-8, 1993. LC 94-12573. (Eurocourses: Environmental Management Ser.: Vol. 3). 374p. (C). 1994. lib. bdg. 134.00 (0-7923-2922-8) Kluwer Ac.

***Paruit, Bernard H., ed.** Illustrated Glossary of Process Equipment-Glossaire Illustre des Equipements de Procede. fac. ed. LC 81-18257. 352p. (ENG.). Date not set. pap. 100.40 (0-7837-7420-6, 2047215) Bks Demand.

— Illustrated Glossary of Process Equipment-Glossaire Illustre des Equipements de Procede-Glosario Ilustrado de Equipos de Proceso. fac. ed. LC 81-18257. 352p. (ENG.). Date not set. pap. 100.40 (0-7837-7427-3, 2047222) Bks Demand.

Parulski, George, Jr. A Path to Oriental Wisdom: Introductory Studies in Eastern Philosophy. LC 76-21011. (History & Philosophy Ser.). 1976. pap. 16.95 (0-89750-046-6, 320) Ohara Pubns.

Parulski, George R., Jr. Sword of the Samurai: The Classical Art of Japanese Swordsmanship. (Illus.). 144p. 1985. 34.95 (0-87364-332-1) Paladin Pr.

Parunak, Van Dyke H. Linguistic Density Plots in Ezekiel: The Computer Bible, Vol. XXVII A & B. Baird, Arthur J. & Freedman, David, eds. 528p. 1984. pap. 70.00 (0-935106-22-7) Biblical Res Assocs.

Paruta, A. N. & Piekos, R., eds. Four-Aminobenzenesulfonamides: Non-cyclic Substituents, Pt. I. (Solubility Data Ser.). (Illus.). 372p. 1988. 170.00 (0-08-030742-6, Pergamon Pr) Elsevier.

— Four-Aminobenzenesulfonamides: 5-Membered Heterocyclic Substituents, Pt. II. (Solubility Data Ser.). (Illus.). 369p. 1988. 170.00 (0-08-034708-8, Pergamon Pr) Elsevier.

— Four-Aminobenzenesulfonamides, Pt. III: Six-Membered Heterocyclic Substituents & Miscellaneous Systems. (Solubility Data Ser.). (Illus.). 552p. 1988. 170.00 (0-08-034710-X, Pergamon Pr) Elsevier.

Parv, Valerie. Art of Romance Writing: How to Create, Write & Sell Your Contemporary Romance Novel. 1993. pap. 11.95 (1-86373-424-4, Pub. by Allen & Unwin Aust Pty AT) IPG Chicago.

— Flight of Fantasy. large type ed. 1994. 17.95 (0-263-13769-4, Pub. by Mills & Boon Ltd UK) Chivers N Amer.

— Island of Dreams. large type ed. 1992. reprint ed. lib. bdg. 18.95 (0-263-13092-4, Pub. by Mills & Boon UK) Thorndike Pr.

— P. S. I Love You. (Romance Ser.). 1995. mass mkt. 2.99 (0-373-03366-4, 1-03366-1) Harlequin Bks.

Parvan, Vasile. Dacia: An Outline of the Early Civilizations of the Carpatho-Danubian Countries. Evans, I. L. & Charlesworth, Martin P., trs. LC 78-26364. (Illus.). 1979. reprint ed. text ed. 45.00 (0-313-20798-4, PADA, Greenwood Pr) Greenwood.

Parvatham, R., jt. auth. see Gnanam, A.

Parvathamanna, C. New Horizons & Scheduled Castes. 1985. 18.50 (0-8364-1263-X, Pub. by Ashish II) S Asia.

Parvathamm, C. Scheduled Castes & Tribes: A Socio-Economic Survey. 1985. 37.50 (0-8364-1253-2, Pub. by Ashish II) S Asia.

Parvathamma, C. Scheduled Castes at the Crossroads. (C). 1989. 24.00 (81-7024-257-6, Pub. by Ashish II) S Asia.

Parvathamma, C. & Satyanarayana. Housing Rural Poor & Their Living Condition. 114p. 1987. 7.00 (81-212-0088-1, Pub. by Gian Publng Hse II) S Asia.

Parvati, Jeannine. Hygieia: A Woman's Herbal. LC 78-67918. (Illus.). 1979. pap. 10.00 (0-913512-54-0) Freestone Pub Co.

— Prenatal Yoga & Natural Birth. rev. ed. (Illus.). 64p. 1986. reprint ed. pap. 9.95 (0-938190-89-X) North Atlantic.

Parvati, Jeannine & Medvin, O'Brien. Prenatal Yoga & Natural Birth. LC 74-19553. (Illus.). 1978. reprint ed. pap. text ed. 5.00 (0-913512-52-4) Freestone Pub Co.

Parveen, Walji, jt. auth. see Monsted, Mette.

Parvez, H. Methods in Biogenic Amine Research. Parvez, S. et al, eds. 1020p. 1983. 405.25 (0-444-80496-X) Elsevier.

— Monoamine Oxidase: Basic & Clinical Aspects. Yasuhara, H. et al, eds. 256p. 1993. 137.50 (90-6764-146-4) Coronet Bks.

Parvez, H., jt. auth. see Parvez, S.

Parvez, H., et al, eds. Methods in Neurotransmitter & Neuropeptide Research, Pt. 1. LC 93-13620. 1993. 247.00 (0-444-81369-1); pap. 84.50 (0-444-81674-7) Elsevier.

— Methods in Neurotransmitter & Neuropeptide Research, Pt. 2. LC 93-13620. 1993. 247.00 (0-444-81368-3); pap. 84.50 (0-444-81675-5) Elsevier.

— Progress in HPLC, Vol. 1: Gel Permeation & Ion-Exchange Chromatography of Proteins & Peptides. 231p. 1985. lib. bdg. 123.00 (90-6764-048-4, Pub. by VSP NE) Coronet Bks.

— Progress in HPLC, Vol. 2: Electromechanical Detection in Medicine & Chemistry. 480p. 1987. lib. bdg. 202.00 (90-6764-062-X, Pub. by VSP NE) Coronet Bks.

— Progress in Neuroendocrinology, Vol. 1: Neuroendricrinology of Hormone-Transmitter Interactions. 315p. 1985. lib. bdg. 135.00 (90-6764-049-2, Pub. by VSP NE) Coronet Bks.

Parvez, S. & Parvez, H. Biogenic Amines in Development. 1980. 128.25 (0-444-80215-0) Elsevier.

Parvez, S., ed. see Parvez, H.

Parvez, S., et al, eds. Progress in Alcohol Research, Vol. 1: Alcohol Nutrition & the Nervous System. 340p. 1985. lib. bdg. 144.00 (90-6764-050-6, Pub. by VSP NE) Coronet Bks.

Parvez, S. H., jt. ed. see Naoi, M.

Parvez, Z. Immunoassays in Coagulation Testing. (Illus.). xvi, 173p. 1984. 67.00 (0-387-90932-X) Spr-Verlag.

Parvez, Zaheer, et al. Contrast Media: Biologic Effects & Clinical Application, 3 vols., Set. 688p. 1987. 147.00 (0-8493-4500-6, RS341) CRC Pr.

***Parvin, Rose A.** Answer to Humanity: Reclaiming Individual Power & Dignity, Bk. 2. LC 95-5196. 288p. 1995. lib. bdg. 15.00 (1-885917-01-5) Univrsl Pubng.

— Beyond Patterns: The Psychology of Health & Excellence, Bk. 7. 288p. 1995. lib. bdg. 15.00 (1-885917-06-6) Univrsl Pubng.

— Humanity Held Hostage: The Day America Cried, Bk. 5. 288p. 1995. lib. bdg. 15.00 (1-885917-04-X) Univrsl Pubng.

— Pattern Change Programing: Creating Your Own Destiny, Bk. 1. Brooks, Marlo, ed. LC 94-23106. 768p. 1995. lib. bdg. 40.00 (1-885917-00-7) Univrsl Pubng.

— Pattern Changes: Universal Laws of Success & Spiritual Excellence, Bk. 9. LC 95-130. 288p. 1995. lib. bdg. 15.00 (1-885917-08-2) Univrsl Pubng.

— Power Balance Therapy & Pattern Change Programing, Bk. 3. 288p. 1995. lib. bdg. 15.00 (1-885917-02-3) Univrsl Pubng.

— Preventive Family Therapy: Family Patterns of Change, Bk. 6. 288p. 1995. lib. bdg. 15.00 (1-885917-05-8) Univrsl Pubng.

— Programing Excellence: Individual Power Balance, Bk. 4. 288p. 1995. lib. bdg. 15.00 (1-885917-03-1) Univrsl Pubng.

— Self Programer: The Psychology of Destiny Making, Bk. 8. 288p. 1995. lib. bdg. 15.00 (1-885917-07-4) Univrsl Pubng.

Parvini, R. S. & Brau, J. Colliders Physics: Current Status & Future Prospects: Proceedings of the 8th Vanderbilt High Energy Physics Conference, Nashville, Tennessee, U. S. A. 508p. (C). 1988. pap. 52.00 (9971-5-0544-4) World Scientific Pub.

Parvu, Sorin. The Romanian Novel. 320p. 1992. text ed. 44.50 (0-88033-226-3) Col U Pr.

Parzen, Benjamin. Design of Crystal & Other Harmonic Oscillators. LC 82-13620. (Wiley-Interscience Publication Ser.). 474p. reprint ed. pap. 135.10 (0-7837-2405-5, 2040090) Bks Demand.

Parzen, Emanuel. Modern Probability Theory & Its Applications. (Classics Library: No. 1826). 480p. 1992. pap. text ed. 39.95 (0-471-57278-0) Wiley.

— Stochastic Processes. LC 62-9243. (Illus.). 1962. pap. 26.95 (0-8162-6664-6) Holden-Day.

Parzen, Julia A. & Kieschnick, Michael H. Credit Where It's Due: Development Banking for Communities. 288p. (C). 1992. 49.95 (0-87722-811-6) Temple U Pr.

— Credit Where It's Due: Development Banking for Communities. 288p. (C). 1994. pap. 22.95 (1-56639-185-7) Temple U Pr.

Parzych, Holly G. Why Are You Calling Me LD? Manual. (Orig.). 1989. student ed write for info. (0-944791-90-5, CS102); pap. text ed. write for info. (0-944791-91-3, CS103) Peekan Pubns.

Parzych, Kenneth M. Public Policy & the Regulatory Environment. LC 92-42156. 1993. 47.50 (0-8191-9024-1); pap. 25.50 (0-8191-9025-X) U Pr of Amer.

Parzych, Patricia A., et al. Basic Business English. 429p. (C). 1986. pap. text ed. 22.75 (0-15-504905-4) HB Coll Pubs.

Parzynski, William & Zipse, Philip. Introduction to Mathematical Analysis. (Illus.). 384p. (C). 1982. text ed. write for info. (0-07-048845-2) McGraw.

Pas, Harold, jt. auth. see Denise, J. Paul.

***Pas, Julian F.** Visions of Sukhavati: Shan-Tao's Commentary on the Kuan Wu-Liang-Shou-Fo Ching. (SUNY Series in Buddhist Studies). 416p. (C). 1995. 74.50x (0-7914-2519-3); pap. 24.95x (0-7914-2520-7) State U NY Pr.

Pas, Julian F., ed. The Turning of the Tide: Religion in China Today. (Illus.). 392p. 1990. pap. 14.95 (0-19-585117-X) OUP.

P Q

Pas, Julian F., tr. The Recorded Sayings of Ma-Tsu. LC 87-18536. (Studies in Asian Thought & Religion: Vol. 6). 1987. lib. bdg. 99.95 (*0-88946-058-2*) E Mellen.

Pas, Julian F., tr. see Robinet, Isabelle.

Pasachoff, jt. auth. see Wolfson.

Pasachoff, Jay M. Astronomy: From the Earth to the Universe. 4th ed. (C). 1991. pap. text ed. 43.00 (*0-03-031329-5*) SCP.

— Astronomy, from the Earth to the Universe. 95th ed. LC 94-33449. (Golden Sunburst Ser.). (C). 1994. pap. text ed. 48.75 (*0-03-001667-3*) Saunders.

— A Brief View of Astronomy. 336p. (C). 1986. pap. text ed. 37.25 (*0-03-058422-1*) SCP.

— Contemporary Astronomy. 4th ed. (Illus.). 579p. (C). 1989. pap. text ed. 40.00 (*0-03-023247-3*) SCP.

— Journey Through the Universe. (Illus.). 460p. (C). 1992. pap. text ed. 40.00 (*0-03-075037-7*) SCP.

— Journey Through the Universe. LC 93-34229. 1993. pap. text ed. 41.75 (*0-03-097283-3*) SCP.

— Peterson First Guide to Astronomy. (Illus.). 128p. 1988. pap. 4.95 (*0-395-46790-X*) HM.

— Peterson First Guide to the Solar System. (Peterson Field Guide Ser.). (Illus.). 128p. 1990. pap. 4.95 (*0-395-52451-2*) HM.

***Pasachoff, Jay M., ed.** Proceedings of the 1991 Undergraduate Symposium on Research in Astronomy. 120p. (C). 1992. pap. text ed. write for info. (*1-882334-01-9*) Keck NE Astron.

Pasachoff, Jay M. & Covington, Michael A. The Cambridge Eclipse Photography Guide: How & Where to Observe & Photograph Solar & Lunar Eclipses. (Illus.). 96p. (C). 1993. pap. 16.95 (*0-521-45651-7*) Cambridge U Pr.

Pasachoff, Jay M. & Menzel, Donald H. Field Guide to the Stars & Planets. rev. ed. LC 92-17556. (Peterson Field Guide Ser.). (Illus.). 528p. 1992. 24.95 (*0-395-53764-9*); pap. 16.95 (*0-395-53759-2*) HM.

Pasachoff, Jay M. & Percy, John R., eds. The Teaching of Astronomy: Proceedings of the 105th Colloquium of the International Astronomical Union. 445p. (C). 1992. pap. 34.95 (*0-521-42966-8*) Cambridge U Pr.

Pasachoff, Jay M. & Wolfson, Richard. Physics for Scientists & Engineers. 2nd ed. LC 93-29622. (C). 1994. text ed. 74.50 (*0-673-52041-2*) HarpCollege.

Pasachoff, Jay M., jt. ed. see Parker, Sybil P.

Pasachoff, Jay M., jt. auth. see Wolfson, Richard.

Pasachoff, Jay M., et al. The Farthest Things in the Universe. (Illus.). 160p. (C). 1995. 29.95 (*0-521-45170-1*); pap. 19.95 (*0-521-46931-7*) Cambridge U Pr.

Pasachoff, Naomi. Basic Judaism for Young People Vol. 3: God. (Basic Judaism Ser.). (J). (gr. 6-7). pap. 8.95 (*0-87441-425-3*); teacher ed, pap. 14.95 (*0-87441-472-5*); student ed, pap. 4.50 (*0-87441-473-3*) Behrman.

— Basic Judaism for Young People, Vol. 1: Israel. 90p. (J). (gr. 4-5). 1987. By Lesley Silverstone. student ed 4.25 (*0-87441-440-7*); pap. text ed. 7.95 (*0-87441-423-7*) Behrman.

— Basic Judaism for Young People, Vol 2: Torah. 92p. (J). (gr. 5-6). 1986. By Lois M. Cohn. student ed 4.25 (*0-87441-442-3*); pap. text ed. 7.95 (*0-87441-424-5*) Behrman.

— Great Jewish Thinkers: Their Lives & Work. LC 92-30148. 1992. write for info. (*0-87441-529-2*) Behrman.

— Marie Curie. (Oxford Scientists Ser.). (Illus.). 144p. (J). 1995. lib. bdg. 19.95 (*0-19-509214-7*) OUP.

Pasachoff, Naomi & Littman, Robert J. Jewish History in One Hundred Nutshells. LC 94-6114. 368p. 1995. 30.00 (*1-56821-179-1*) Aronson.

Pasadena Art Alliance Staff. Canvassing L.A., an Artful Guide to Galleries, Museums, & Restaurants. (Illus.). 80p. 1988. pap. text ed. 12.95 (*0-937042-07-2*) Pasadena Art.

Pasadena Junior League Staff. California Heritage Cookbook. 1990. pap. 19.95 (*0-385-41677-6*) Doubleday.

Pasahow, Edward J. Electronics Pocket Reference. 2nd ed. LC 93-5244. 1993. pap. text ed. 24.95 (*0-07-048737-5*) McGraw.

— Learning Digital Electronics Through Experiments. LC 81-2688. (Electro-Skills Ser.). (Illus.). 256p. (C). 1982. pap. text ed. 13.35 (*0-07-048722-7*) McGraw.

— Microcomputer Interfacing for Electronics Technicians. 1981. text ed. 28.95 (*0-07-048718-9*) McGraw.

— Microprocessor Technology & Microcomputers. 416p. 1988. text ed. 31.95 (*0-07-048729-4*) McGraw.

— Microprocessors & Microcomputers for Electronics Technicians. 1981. text ed. 28.95 (*0-07-048713-8*) McGraw.

— Pascal for Electronics. 208p. 1985. text ed. 17.95 (*0-07-048724-3*) McGraw.

— Turbo Pascal for Electronics. 208p. (C). 1988. pap. text ed. 14.95 (*0-07-048732-4*) McGraw.

Pasahow, Lynn H., jt. auth. see American Bar Association. Section of Antitrust Law Staff.

Pasahow, Lynn H., jt. auth. see Schwarzer, William W.

Pasamanick, B., jt. auth. see Kawi, A. A.

Pasamanick, Benjamin, jt. auth. see Knobloch, Hilda.

Pasamanick, Benjamin, et al. Schizophrenics in the Community: An Experimental Study in the Prevention of Hospitalization. LC 66-25455. (Illus.). 1967. 29.50 (*0-89197-390-7*) Irvington.

Pasamanick, Judith & Thoms, Judith J. Folk Tales Told Around the World. LC 92-47128. (Illus.). 48p. (J). (gr. 4-6). 1993. 10.95 (*0-382-24372-2*); lib. bdg. 12.95 (*0-382-24363-3*) Silver Burdett Pr.

Pasamanik, Luisa. The Exiled Angel. Hirschman, Jack, tr. 1973. 2.00 (*0-88031-009-X*) Invisible-Red Hill.

Pasamehmetoglu, A. G., et al, eds. Assessment & Prevention of Failure Phenomena in Rock Engineering: Proceedings, Istanbul, April 1993. (Illus.). 800p. (C). 1993. text ed. 150.00 (*90-5410-309-4*, Pub. by A A Balkema NE) Ashgate Pub Co.

— Mining Planning & Equipment Selection 1994: Proceedings of the 3rd International Symposium, Istanbul, Turkey, 18-20 October 1994. (Illus.). 964p. (C). 1994. text ed. 125.00 (*90-5410-327-2*, Pub. by A A Balkema NE) Ashgate Pub Co.

Pasamontes, Carlos M. Diccionario de Pintores. (SPA.). 1987. pap. 250.00 (*0-7859-5910-6*, 8433310216) Fr & Eur.

Pasanen, M. Russian-Finnish Trade - Business Dictionary: Venalais-Suomalainen Kaupan Sanakirja. 341p. (FIN & RUS.). 1985. 250.00 (*0-8288-0834-1*, F17170) Fr & Eur.

Pasano, Beverly, ed. Irish Wolfhounds. (Illus.). 128p. 1990. 11.95 (*0-685-62701-2*, KW-108) TFH Pubns.

***Pasau-Buck, Shirlee & Jones, Edward M.** Male Ordered Health Care: The Inequities of Women. LC 94-65426. 184p. (Orig.). 1994. pap. 19.95 (*0-9627246-2-9*) Power NY.

Pasca, Sue-Rhee. Your First Canary. (YF Ser.). (Illus.). 36p. (Orig.). (YA). 1991. pap. 1.95 (*0-86622-059-3*, YF-103) TFH Pubns.

Pascal, A. H., et al. EBBF: A Guide to Installing Equitable Beneficiary-Based Finance in Local Government. LC 84-13366. 1984. 4.00 (*0-8330-0582-0*, R-3124-HHS) Rand Corp.

***Pascal, Alana & VanderKar, Lynne.** Kombucha: How to & What It's All About. Maurier, Anina, ed. LC 95-90065. (Illus.). 90p. (Orig.). 1995. pap. text ed. 10.95 (*0-9645352-0-3*) Van der Kar Pr.

Pascal, Blaise. A Concordance to Pascal's "Pensees" Davidson, Hugh M. & Dube, Pierre H., eds. LC 75-16808. (Cornell Concordances Ser.). 1488p. 1975. 97.50 (*0-8014-0972-1*) Cornell U Pr.

— Daily Readings with Blaise Pascal. Van de Weyer, Robert, ed. LC 95-60057. 1995. pap. 4.95 (*0-87243-212-2*) Templegate.

— Extraits des Traites de l'Equilibre des Liqueurs et de la Pesanteur de la Masse de l'A Ir. 64p. 1963. 9.95 (*0-686-54846-9*) Fr & Eur.

— Maximes et Pensees. 9.95 (*0-686-54848-5*) Fr & Eur.

— Oeuvres Completes. deluxe ed. Chevalier, ed. (Pleiade Ser.). (FRE.). 1936. 73.95 (*2-07-010432-X*) Schoenhof.

— Pensees, 2 vols. 4.50 (*0-685-73318-1*); pap. 5.95 (*0-685-34246-8*) Fr & Eur.

— Pensees. Desgranges, ed. (Coll. Prestige). 29.95 (*0-685-34245-X*) Fr & Eur.

— Pensees, 2 vols. 1977. pap. 10.95 (*0-7859-4079-0*); pap. 11.95 (*0-7859-4080-4*) Fr & Eur.

— Pensees. Desgranges, ed. 657p. (FRE.). 1991. pap. 55.00 (*0-7859-4650-0*) Fr & Eur.

— Pensees. Krailsheimer, Alban J., tr. (Classics Ser.). 1966. pap. 8.95 (*0-14-044171-9*, Penguin Classics) Viking Penguin.

— Pensees. Krailsheimer, A. J., tr. & intro. by. 368p. 1995. 9.95 (*0-14-044645-1*, Penguin Classics) Viking Penguin.

— Pensees & Other Writings. Levi, Anthony, ed. Levi, Honor, tr. (World's Classics Ser.). 304p. 1995. pap. 8.95 (*0-19-282990-4*) OUP.

— The Provincial Letters. 304p. 1982. pap. 7.95 (*0-14-044196-4*, Penguin Classics) Viking Penguin.

— Les Provinciales. (FRE.). 1966. 10.95 (*0-8288-9947-9*, F40580) Fr & Eur.

— Selections from The Thoughts. Beattie, Arthur H., ed. & tr. by. (Crofts Classics Ser.). 144p. 1965. pap. text ed. write for info. (*0-88295-065-7*) Harlan Davidson.

— The Thoughts of Blaise Pascal. LC 78-12814. 320p. 1978. reprint ed. text ed. 65.00 (*0-313-20530-2*, PATH, Greenwood Pr) Greenwood.

Pascal, Blaise & Brunschvicg, Leon. Oeuvres, 14 vols., Set. 895.00 (*0-686-54849-3*) Fr & Eur.

Pascal, Blaise & Gobry, Ivan. Pages sur Crist. 128p. (FRE.). 1963. pap. 10.95 (*0-7859-5390-6*) Fr & Eur.

Pascal, Blaise & Lafuma, Louis. Deux Pieces Imparfaites sur la Grace et le Concile de Trente, Extraites du M. S. de l'Abbe Perier. 76p. (FRE.). 1947. pap. 13.95 (*0-686-54845-0*, 2711605930) Fr & Eur.

Pascal, Dominique. British Cars at Le Mans. (Illus.). 148p. 1991. 34.95 (*0-85429-872-X*, Pub. by G T Foulis Ltd) Haynes Pubns.

***Pascal, Dominque.** Grand Dictionnaire des Motos Francaises. 127p. (FRE.). 1988. 59.95 (*0-7859-7926-3*, 2707201340) Fr & Eur.

Pascal, Eugene. Jung to Live By. 288p. (Orig.). 1992. pap. 11.99 (*0-446-39294-4*) Warner Bks.

Pascal, Fabian. SQL & Relational Basics: A Practical Guide for PC Database Users. (Illus.). 336p. (Orig.). 1990. disk 38.95 (*1-55851-064-8*) M&T Bks.

— Understanding Relational Databases: With Examples in SQL-92. 304p. 1993. pap. text ed. 29.95 (*0-471-58538-6*) Wiley.

Pascal, Francine. Against the Odds. large type ed. (Sweet Valley High Ser.: No. 51). 151p. (J). (gr. 5-8). 1989. reprint ed. 9.50 (*1-55905-006-3*, Gareth Stevens Inc); reprint ed. lib. bdg. 10.50 (*1-55905-016-0*, Gareth Stevens Inc) Grey Castle.

— Against the Rules. (Sweet Valley Twins Ser.: No. 9). (Orig.). (J). 1987. 3.25 (*0-553-15676-4*) Bantam.

— All Night Long. large type ed. (Sweet Valley High Ser.: No. 5). 134p. (J). (gr. 5-8). 1989. reprint ed. 9.50 (*1-55905-004-7*, Gareth Stevens Inc); reprint ed. lib. bdg. 10.50 (*1-55905-014-4*, Gareth Stevens Inc) Grey Castle.

— Almost Married. (Sweet Valley High Ser.: No. 102). (YA). (gr. 7 up). 1994. pap. 3.50 (*0-553-29859-3*) Bantam.

— Alone in the Crowd. (Orig.). (YA). 1986. pap. 2.99 (*0-553-28087-2*) Bantam.

— The Amazing Jessica. (Sweet Valley Kids Ser.: No. 60). (J). 1995. pap. 2.99 (*0-553-48212-2*) Bantam.

— Amy Moves In. (Sweet Valley Twins Ser.: No. 44). (J). (gr. 4-7). 1991. 3.50 (*0-553-15837-6*) Bantam.

— Amy's Pen Pal. (Sweet Valley Twins Ser.: No. 35). (J). 1990. pap. 3.25 (*0-553-15772-8*) Bantam.

— Amy's Secret Sister. (Sweet Valley Twins & Friends Ser.: No. 83). (J). (gr. 4-7). 1994. 3.50 (*0-553-48101-0*) Bantam.

— Amy's True Love. (Sweet Valley High Ser.: No. 75). (YA). 1991. pap. 2.99 (*0-553-28963-2*) Bantam.

— Anything for Love. (Sweet Valley Ser.: No. 4). (YA). 1994. pap. 3.50 (*0-553-56311-4*) Bantam.

— April Fool! (Sweet Valley Twins Ser.: No. 28). (J). 1989. pap. 3.50 (*0-553-15688-8*) Bantam.

— Are We in Love. (Sweet Valley High Ser.: No. 94). (YA). 1993. pap. 3.25 (*0-553-29851-8*) Bantam.

— The Arrest. (Sweet Valley High Ser.: No. 96). (YA). 1993. pap. 3.50 (*0-553-29853-4*) Bantam.

— The Best Friend Game. (Unicorn Club Ser.: No. 3). (J). (gr. 4-7). 1994. pap. 3.50 (*0-553-48210-6*) Bantam.

— Best Friends. (Sweet Valley Twins Ser.: No. 1). 112p. (Orig.). (YA). (gr. 7-12). 1986. 3.25 (*0-553-15655-1*, Skylark) Bantam.

— The Best Thanksgiving Ever. (Sweet Valley Kids Ser.: No. 34). (J). (ps-3). 1992. 2.99 (*0-553-48007-3*) Bantam.

— Beware the Babysitter. (Sweet Valley High Ser.: No. 99). (YA). 1993. pap. 3.50 (*0-553-29856-9*) Bantam.

— Beware the Wolfman: Super Thriller Ed. (Sweet Valley High Ser.: No. 106). (YA). 1994. mass mkt. 3.99 (*0-553-56234-7*) Bantam.

— Big Camp Secret. (Sweet Valley Twins Ser.: No. 3). 1989. 3.50 (*0-553-15707-8*) Bantam.

— Big for Christmas. (Sweet Valley Twins & Friends Ser.: No. 3). (J). (gr. 4-7). 1994. mass mkt. 3.99 (*0-553-48249-1*) Bantam.

— The Big Party Weekend. (Sweet Valley Twins & Friends Ser.: No. 54). (J). (gr. 4-7). 1991. pap. 3.25 (*0-553-15952-6*) Bantam.

— The Big Race. (Sweet Valley Kids Ser.: No. 37). (J). (ps-3). 1993. 2.99 (*0-553-48011-1*) Bantam.

— Booster Boycott. (Sweet Valley Twins Ser.). (J). (gr. 4-7). 1991. pap. 3.25 (*0-553-15933-X*) Bantam.

— Bossy Steven. (Sweet Valley Kids Ser.: No. 18). (J). (ps-3). 1991. pap. 2.99 (*0-553-15881-3*) Bantam.

— Boy Trouble. (Sweet Valley Ser.: No. 61). (YA). 1990. 2.95 (*0-553-28317-0*) Bantam.

— The Boyfriend War. (Sweet Valley High Ser.: No. 101). (YA). 1994. pap. 3.50 (*0-553-29858-5*) Bantam.

— Boys Against Girls. (Sweet Valley Twins Ser.). (Orig.). (J). 1988. 3.25 (*0-553-15666-7*) Bantam.

— Brooke & Her Rock Star Mom. (Sweet Valley Twins & Friends Ser.: No. 55). (YA). 1992. pap. 3.25 (*0-553-15965-8*) Bantam.

— Bruce's Story. (Sweet Valley High Super Star Ser.: No. 2). 1990. pap. 3.50 (*0-553-28464-9*) Bantam.

— The Bully, No. 19. (Sweet Valley Twins Ser.: No. 19). 112p. 1988. pap. 3.50 (*0-553-15667-5*) Bantam.

— Buried Treasure. (Sweet Valley Twins Ser.: No. 11). (J). 1987. pap. 3.25 (*0-553-15692-6*) Bantam.

— The Carnival Ghost. (Sweet Valley Twins Super Chiller Ser.: No. 3). (J). (gr. 3-7). 1990. mass mkt. 3.99 (*0-553-15859-7*) Bantam.

— Caroline's Halloween Spell. (Sweet Valley Kids Ser.: No. 33). (J). (ps-3). 1992. pap. 2.99 (*0-553-48006-5*) Bantam.

— Carolyn's Mystery Dolls. (Sweet Valley Kids Ser.: No. 17). (J). (gr. 4-7). 1991. pap. 2.99 (*0-553-15870-8*) Bantam.

— The Case of the Alien Princess. (Sweet Valley Kids Super Snooper Ser.: No. 7). (J). (ps-3). 1994. pap. 3.25 (*0-553-48119-3*) Bantam.

— The Case of the Christmas Thief. (Sweet Valley Kids Super Snooper Ser.: No. 4). (J). (ps-3). 1992. 3.50 (*0-553-48063-4*) Bantam.

— Case of the Haunted Camp. (Sweet Valley Kids Super Snooper Ser.: No. 3). (J). (gr. 4-7). 1992. pap. 3.50 (*0-553-15894-5*) Bantam.

— The Case of the Hidden Treasure. (Sweet Valley Kids Super Snooper Ser.: No. 5). (J). (gr. 1-3). 1993. pap. 3.25 (*0-553-48064-2*) Bantam.

— The Case of the Magic Christmas Bell. (Sweet Valley Kids Super Snooper Ser.: No. 2). (J). (ps-3). 1991. pap. 3.25 (*0-553-15964-X*) Bantam.

— The Case of the Million-Dollar Diamonds. (Sweet Valley Kids Super Snooper Ser.: No. 6). (J). (ps-3). 1993. pap. 3.25 (*0-553-48115-0*) Bantam.

— The Case of the Secret Santa. (Sweet Valley Kids Super Snooper Ser.: No. 1). (J). (gr. k-3). 1990. pap. 3.50 (*0-553-15860-0*) Bantam.

— Caught in the Middle. (Sweet Valley High Ser.: No. 42). 160p. 1988. pap. 2.99 (*0-553-26951-8*) Bantam.

— Center of Attention. 1988. pap. 3.25 (*0-553-15668-3*) Bantam.

— The Charm School Mystery. (Sweet Valley Twins & Friends Ser.: No. 64). (J). (gr. 4-7). 1992. pap. 3.25 (*0-553-48050-2*) Bantam.

— Cheating to Win. (Sweet Valley High Ser.: No. 77). (YA). 1991. pap. 2.99 (*0-553-29145-9*) Bantam.

— Choosing Sides. (Sweet Valley Twins Ser.: No. 4). (Orig.). (J). 1986. pap. 3.25 (*0-553-15658-6*) Bantam.

— Christmas Ghost. No. 1. (YA). (gr. 7-12). 1990. pap. write for info. (*0-318-66852-1*) Bantam.

— A Christmas Without Elizabeth. (Sweet Valley Twins & Friends Magna Ser.: No. 2). (J). (gr. 4-7). 1993. mass mkt. 3.99 (*0-553-15947-X*) Bantam.

— Ciao, Sweet Valley! (Sweet Valley Twins Ser.: No. 60). (J). (gr. 4-7). 1992. pap. 3.25 (*0-553-15940-2*) Bantam.

— Class Trip. (Sweet Valley Twins Super Chiller Ser.: Bk. 1). (Orig.). (YA). (gr. 7 up). 1988. pap. 3.50 (*0-553-15588-1*) Bantam.

— College Cruise. (Sweet Valley University Ser.: No. 12). (J). (gr. 9 up). 1995. mass mkt. 3.99 (*0-553-56657-1*) Bantam.

— College Girls. (Sweet Valley University Ser.: No. 1). (YA). (gr. 6 up). 1993. pap. 3.50 (*0-553-56308-4*) Bantam.

— Cousin Kelly's Family Secret. (Sweet Valley Kids Ser.: No. 24). (J). (ps-3). 1991. pap. 2.99 (*0-553-15920-8*) Bantam.

— Crash Landing. (Sweet Valley High Ser.: No. 20). 1985. 3.25 (*0-553-27454-6*) Bantam.

— Crybaby Lois. (Sweet Valley Kids Ser.: No. 11). (J). (gr. 4 up). 1990. 2.99 (*0-553-15818-X*) Bantam.

— The Curse of the Golden Heart. (Sweet Valley Twins & Friends Super Chiller Ser.: No. 6). (J). (gr. 4-7). 1994. pap. 3.50 (*0-553-56403-X*) Bantam.

— The Curse of the Ruby Necklace. (Sweet Valley Twins & Friends Super Chiller Ser.: No. 5). (J). (gr. 4-7). 1993. pap. 3.99 (*0-553-15949-6*) Bantam.

— A Curse on Elizabeth. (Sweet Valley Kids Hair Raiser Super Special Ser.: No. 3). (J). 1995. pap. 2.99 (*0-553-48284-X*) Bantam.

— Dangerous Love. (Sweet Valley High Ser.: No. 6). (J). (gr. 7 up). 1984. 3.50 (*0-553-27741-3*) Bantam.

— Danny Means Trouble. (Sweet Valley Twins Ser.: No. 40). (J). (gr. 3-6). 1990. 3.25 (*0-553-15806-6*) Bantam.

— Date with a Werewolf. (Young Adults Ser.: No. 105). (YA). 1994. 3.50 (*0-553-56228-2*) Bantam.

— The Dating Game. (Sweet Valley High Ser.: No. 78). (YA). 1991. pap. 2.99 (*0-553-29187-4*) Bantam.

— A Deadly Christmas. (Sweet Valley High Ser.: No. 111). (YA). 1994. 3.99 (*0-553-56629-6*) Bantam.

— Deadly Summer. (Sweet Valley High Super Thriller Ser.: No. 4). (YA). 1989. mass mkt. 3.99 (*0-553-28010-4*) Bantam.

— Dear Sister. (Sweet Valley High Ser.: No. 7). (J). (gr. 7 up). 1984. pap. 3.50 (*0-553-27672-7*) Bantam.

— Death Threat. (Sweet Valley High Ser.: No. 110). (YA). 1994. 3.50 (*0-553-56232-0*) Bantam.

— Decisions. (Sweet Valley High Ser.: No. 46). (YA). (gr. 6 up). 1988. pap. 2.99 (*0-553-27278-0*) Bantam.

— Don't Go Home with John. (Sweet Valley High Ser.: No. 90). (YA). 1993. pap. 3.50 (*0-553-29236-6*) Bantam.

— Double-Crossed. (Sweet Valley High Ser.: No. 109). (YA). 1994. 3.50 (*0-553-56231-2*) Bantam.

— Double Love. large type ed. (Sweet Valley High Ser.: No. 1). 186p. (J). (gr. 5-8). 1989. reprint ed. 9.50 (*1-55905-000-4*, Gareth Stevens Inc); reprint ed. lib. bdg. 10.50 (*1-55905-010-1*, Gareth Stevens Inc) Grey Castle.

— The Easter Bunny Battle: Super Special Edition. (Sweet Valley Kids Ser.: No. 9). (J). (ps-3). 1995. pap. 3.50 (*0-553-48252-1*) Bantam.

— Elizabeth & Jessica Run Away. (Sweet Valley Kids Ser.: No. 31). (J). 1992. 2.99 (*0-553-48004-9*) Bantam.

— Elizabeth & the Tattletale. (Sweet Valley Kids Ser.: No. 47). (J). 1994. pap. 2.99 (*0-553-48110-X*) Bantam.

— Elizabeth Betrayed. (Sweet Valley High Ser.: No. 89). (YA). 1992. 3.25 (*0-553-29235-8*) Bantam.

— Elizabeth the Hero. (Sweet Valley Twins & Friends Ser.: No. 74). (J). (gr. 4-7). 1993. pap. 3.50 (*0-553-48060-X*) Bantam.

— Elizabeth the Impossible. (Sweet Valley Twins Ser.: No. 51). 144p. (J). 1991. pap. 3.50 (*0-553-15927-5*) Bantam.

— Elizabeth the Seventh Grader. (Sweet Valley Twins Ser.: No. 85). (J). (gr. 4-7). 1995. pap. 3.50 (*0-553-48109-6*) Bantam.

— Elizabeth's Broken Arm. (Sweet Valley Kids Ser.: No. 35). (J). (ps-3). 1993. pap. 2.99 (*0-553-48009-X*) Bantam.

— Elizabeth's First Kiss. (Sweet Valley Twins Ser.: No. 43). (J). (gr. 4-7). 1990. pap. 3.25 (*0-553-15835-X*) Bantam.

— Elizabeth's New Hero. (Sweet Valley Twins Ser.: No. 33). (J). 1989. pap. 3.25 (*0-553-15753-1*) Bantam.

— Elizabeth's Piano Lessons. (Sweet Valley Kids Ser.: No. 45). (J). (ps-3). 1994. pap. 2.99 (*0-553-48102-9*) Bantam.

— Elizabeth's Secret Diary. (Sweet Valley High Ser.). (YA). 1994. mass mkt. 3.99 (*0-553-56658-X*) Bantam.

— Elizabeth's Super-Selling Lemonade. (Sweet Valley Kids Ser.: No. 9). (J). 1990. pap. 2.99 (*0-553-15807-4*) Bantam.

— Elizabeth's Valentine, No. 4. (J). 1990. 2.99 (*0-553-15761-2*) Bantam.

— Elizabeth's Video Fever. (Sweet Valley Kids Ser.: No. 36). (J). (ps-3). 1993. pap. 2.99 (*0-553-48010-3*) Bantam.

— Ellen Is Home Alone. (Sweet Valley Kids Ser.: No. 39). (J). (ps-3). 1993. 2.99 (*0-553-48013-8*) Bantam.

— Enid's Story. (Sweet Valley High Super Star Ser.: No. 3). (YA). (gr. 7 up). 1990. pap. 3.50 (*0-553-28576-9*) Bantam.

— The Evil Twin. (Sweet Valley High Ser.: No. 100). (YA). 1993. mass mkt. 3.99 (*0-553-29857-7*) Bantam.

— Family Secrets. (Sweet Valley High Ser.: No. 45). 160p. (Orig.). (YA). (gr. 7 up). 1988. pap. 2.99 (*0-553-27176-8*) Bantam.

— Fearless Elizabeth. (Sweet Valley Kids Ser.: No. 15). (J). (gr. 4-7). 1991. pap. 2.99 (*0-553-15844-9*) Bantam.

— First Place. (Sweet Valley Twins Ser.: No. 8). 1987. pap. 3.25 (*0-553-15662-4*) Bantam.

— Forbidden Love. (Sweet Valley High Ser.: No. 34). (Orig.). (YA). 1987. pap. 2.99 (*0-553-27521-6*) Bantam.

— Friend Against Friend. (Sweet Valley High Ser.: No. 69). (YA). (gr. 9-12). 1990. pap. 3.50 (*0-553-28636-6*) Bantam.

— Get the Teacher! (Sweet Valley Kids Ser.: No. 46). (J). (ps-3). 1994. pap. 2.99 (*0-553-48106-1*) Bantam.

— Ghost in the Bell Tower. (Sweet Valley Twins Super Chiller Ser.: No. 4). (J). (gr. 4-7). 1992. mass mkt. 3.99 (*0-553-15893-7*) Bantam.

— The Ghost of Tricia Martin. (Sweet Valley High Ser.: No. 64). (J). 1990. pap. 3.25 (*0-553-28487-8*) Bantam.

— Ghosts in the Graveyard. (Sweet Valley Twins Super Chiller Ser.: No. 2). (J). (gr. 4-7). 1990. mass mkt. 3.99 (*0-553-15801-5*) Bantam.

— Girl They Both Loved. (Sweet Valley High Ser.: No. 80). (YA). 1991. 3.25 (*0-553-29226-9*) Bantam.

— Good-bye, Eva? (Sweet Valley Kids Ser.: No. 38). (J). (ps-3). 1993. pap. 2.99 (*0-553-48012-X*) Bantam.

P
Q

An Asterisk (*) at the beginning of an entry indicates that the title is appearing in BIP for the first time.

— Good-Bye to Love. (Sweet Valley University Ser.: No. 7). (YA). 1994. 3.50 (*0-553-56652-0*) Bantam.
— The Gossip War. (Sweet Valley Twins & Friends Ser.: No. 80). (J). (gr. 4-7). 1994. pap. 3.25 (*0-553-48112-6*) Bantam.
— The Great Boyfriend Switch. (Sweet Valley Twins & Friends Ser.: No. 66). (J). (gr. 4-7). 1993. pap. 3.50 (*0-553-48053-7*) Bantam.
— The Hand-Me-Down Kid. LC 79-5462. (J). (gr. 5-9). 1980. pap. 12.95 (*0-670-35969-6*) Viking Child Bks.
— Hard Choices. (Sweet Valley High Ser.: No. 43). 160p. 1988. pap. 3.50 (*0-553-27006-0*) Bantam.
— The Haunted Burial Ground. (Sweet Valley Twins & Friends Super Chiller Ser.: No. 7). (J). (gr. 4-7). 1994. pap. 3.50 (*0-553-56404-8*) Bantam.
— Haunted House. (Sweet Valley Twins Ser.: No. 3). (Orig.). (J). 1986. pap. 3.50 (*0-553-15657-8*) Bantam.
— Head over Heels. (Sweet Valley High Ser.: No. 18). (Orig.). (J). (gr. 5). 1985. 3.25 (*0-553-27444-9*) Bantam.
— Heartbreaker. (Sweet Valley High Ser.: No. 8). 176p. (J). (gr. 7 up). 1984. pap. 3.50 (*0-553-27569-0*) Bantam.
— He's Watching You. (Sweet Valley University Thriller Ser.: No. 2). (J). 1995. mass mkt. 3.99 (*0-553-56689-X*) Bantam.
— Holiday Mischief. (Sweet Valley Twins Super Chiller Ser.: No. 2). 144p. (J). 1988. pap. 3.75 (*0-553-15641-1*, Skylark) Bantam.
— Home for Christmas. (Sweet Valley University Ser.: No. 8). (YA). 1994. pap. 3.50 (*0-553-56653-9*) Bantam.
— Hostage! (SVH Ser.: No. 26). (Orig.). (YA). 1986. pap. 3.25 (*0-553-27670-0*) Bantam.
— If Wishes Were Horses. LC 93-25726. 1994. 20.00 (*0-517-59682-2*, Crown) Crown Pub Group.
— In Love Again. (Sweet Valley High Ser.: No. 59). (YA). (gr. 7 up). 1989. pap. 3.50 (*0-553-28193-3*) Bantam.
— In Love with a Prince. (Sweet Valley High Ser.: No. 91). (YA). 1993. pap. 3.25 (*0-553-29237-4*) Bantam.
— It Can't Happen Here. (Sweet Valley Twins Ser.: No. 86). (J). (gr. 4-7). 1995. pap. 3.50 (*0-553-48113-4*) Bantam.
— Jealous Lies. (Sweet Valley High Ser.: No. 30). (Orig.). (YA). 1986. pap. 3.25 (*0-553-27558-5*) Bantam.
— Jessica Against Bruce. (Sweet Valley High Ser.: No. 86). (YA). 1992. pap. 3.50 (*0-553-29232-3*) Bantam.
— The Jessica & Elizabeth Show. (Sweet Valley Kids Ser.: No. 55). (J). (ps-3). 1995. pap. 2.99 (*0-553-48205-X*) Bantam.
— Jessica & Jumbo. (Sweet Valley Kids Ser.: No. 19). (J). (ps-3). 1991. pap. 2.99 (*0-553-15936-4*) Bantam.
— Jessica & the Brat Attack. (Sweet Valley Twins Ser.: No. 29). (J). 1989. 3.50 (*0-553-15695-0*) Bantam.
— Jessica & the Earthquake. (Sweet Valley Twins & Friends Ser.: No. 75). (J). (gr. 4-7). 1994. pap. 3.50 (*0-553-48061-8*) Bantam.
— Jessica & the Money Mix-Up. (Sweet Valley Twins Ser.: No. 39). (J). (gr. 4-7). 1990. pap. 3.50 (*0-553-15798-1*) Bantam.
— Jessica & the Secret Star. (Sweet Valley Twins Ser.: No. 50). (J). (gr. 4-7). 1991. pap. 3.50 (*0-553-15911-9*) Bantam.
— Jessica & the Spelling Bee Surprise. (Sweet Valley Kids Ser.: No. 21). 80p. (J). 1991. pap. 2.99 (*0-553-15917-8*) Bantam.
— Jessica Gets Spooked. (Sweet Valley Kids Ser.: No. 43). (J). (ps-3). 1993. pap. 2.99 (*0-553-48094-4*) Bantam.
— Jessica on Stage. (Sweet Valley Twins Ser.: No. 32). 1989. pap. 3.50 (*0-553-15747-7*) Bantam.
— Jessica Plays Cupid. (Sweet Valley Kids Ser.: No. 56). (J). (ps-3). 1995. pap. 2.99 (*0-553-48207-6*) Bantam.
— Jessica Plus Jessica Equals Trouble. (Sweet Valley Kids Ser.: No. 59). (J). 1995. pap. 2.99 (*0-553-48211-4*) Bantam.
— Jessica Quits the Squad. (Sweet Valley High Ser.: No. 112). (YA). 1995. mass mkt. 3.99 (*0-553-56630-X*) Bantam.
— Jessica Saves the Trees. (Sweet Valley Twins & Friends Ser.: No. 71). (J). (gr. 4-7). 1993. pap. 3.25 (*0-553-15946-1*) Bantam.
— Jessica the Babysitter. (Sweet Valley Kids Ser.: No. 14). (J). (gr. 4-7). 1991. 2.99 (*0-553-15838-4*) Bantam.
— Jessica the Nerd. (Sweet Valley Twins Ser.: No. 61). (J). 1992. pap. 3.50 (*0-553-15963-1*) Bantam.
— Jessica the Rock Star. (Sweet Valley Twins Ser.: No. 34). (J). (gr. 5 up). 1989. 3.25 (*0-553-15766-3*) Bantam.
— Jessica the Thief. (Sweet Valley Twins & Friends Ser.: No. 67). (J). (gr. 4-7). 1993. pap. 3.25 (*0-553-48054-5*) Bantam.
— Jessica the TV Star. (Sweet Valley High Ser.: No. 16). (J). (ps-3). 1991. pap. 2.99 (*0-553-15850-3*) Bantam.
— Jessica's Bad Idea. (Sweet Valley Twins Ser.: No. 31). 1989. pap. 3.25 (*0-553-15727-2*) Bantam.
— Jessica's Big Mistake. (Sweet Valley Kids Ser.: No. 7). (J). (ps-3). 1990. pap. 2.99 (*0-553-15799-X*) Bantam.
— Jessica's Blind. (Sweet Valley Kids Ser.: No. 79). (J). 1994. pap. 3.50 (*0-553-48108-8*) Bantam.
— Jessica's Christmas Carol. (Sweet Valley Twins Chiller Ser.: No. 1). (J). (gr. 4-6). 1989. pap. 3.50 (*0-553-15767-1*) Bantam.
— Jessica's Cookie Disaster. (Sweet Valley Twins Ser.: No. 89). (J). 1995. pap. 3.50 (*0-553-48191-6*) Bantam.
— Jessica's Mermaid. (Sweet Valley Kids Ser.: No. 49). (J). (gr. 1 up). 1994. pap. 2.99 (*0-553-48118-5*) Bantam.
— Jessica's Monster Nightmare. (Sweet Valley Kids Ser.: No. 42). (J). (gr. 1-3). 1993. pap. 2.99 (*0-553-48008-1*) Bantam.
— Jessica's New Look. (Sweet Valley Twins Ser.: No. 47). (J). (gr. 4-7). 1991. pap. 3.25 (*0-553-15869-4*) Bantam.
— Jessica's Secret. (Sweet Valley Twins Ser.: No. 42). (J). (gr. 4-7). 1990. pap. 3.50 (*0-553-15824-4*) Bantam.
— Jessica's Secret Diary. (Sweet Valley High Ser.). (YA). 1994. pap. 3.99 (*0-553-56659-8*) Bantam.
— Jessica's Secret Love. (Sweet Valley High Ser.: No. 107). (YA). 1994. pap. 3.50 (*0-553-56229-0*) Bantam.
— Jessica's Snobby. (Sweet Valley Kids Ser.: No. 26). (J). 1992. pap. 2.99 (*0-553-15922-4*) Bantam.
— Jessica's Unburied Treasure. (Sweet Valley Kids Ser.: No. 30). (J). (ps-3). 1992. pap. 2.99 (*0-553-15926-7*) Bantam.
— Jessica's Zoo Adventure. (Sweet Valley Kids Ser.: No. 8). (J). (ps-3). 1990. pap. 2.99 (*0-553-15802-3*) Bantam.
— Julie the Karate Kid. (Sweet Valley Kids Ser.: No. 52). (J). (ps-3). 1994. pap. 2.99 (*0-553-48103-7*) Bantam.
— Keeping Secrets. (Sweet Valley Twins Ser.: No. 12). 96p. (Orig.). (YA). 1987. pap. 3.25 (*0-553-15702-7*, Skylark) Bantam.
— Kidnapped! (Sweet Valley High Ser.: No. 13). 160p. (Orig.). (J). 1984. pap. 3.25 (*0-553-27877-0*) Bantam.
— Kidnapped by a Cult. (Sweet Valley High Ser.: No. 82). (YA). 1992. pap. 3.25 (*0-553-29228-5*) Bantam.
— A Killer on Board. (Sweet Valley High Thriller Ser.). (J). 1995. mass mkt. 3.99 (*0-553-56714-4*) Bantam.
— Last Chance. (Sweet Valley High Ser.: No. 36). (Orig.). (YA). 1987. pap. 3.50 (*0-553-27662-X*) Bantam.
— Left at the Altar! (Sweet Valley High Ser.: No. 108). (YA). 1994. pap. 3.50 (*0-553-56230-4*) Bantam.
— Left Back. (Sweet Valley Kids Ser.: No. 32). (J). 1992. pap. 2.99 (*0-553-48005-7*) Bantam.
— Left Behind. (Sweet Valley Twins Ser.: No. 21). 112p. (Orig.). (J). 1988. pap. 3.25 (*0-553-15609-8*, Skylark) Bantam.
— Left-Out Elizabeth. (Sweet Valley Kids Ser.: No. 25). (J). (ps-3). 1992. pap. 2.99 (*0-553-15921-6*) Bantam.
— Lila's April Fool. (Sweet Valley Kids Ser.: No. 48). (J). (gr. 4 up). 1994. pap. 2.99 (*0-553-48114-2*) Bantam.
— Lila's Birthday Bash. (Sweet Valley Kids Ser.: No. 58). (J). 1995. pap. 2.99 (*0-553-48209-2*) Bantam.
— Lila's Haunted House Party. (Sweet Valley Kids Ser.: No. 23). (J). (gr. 4-7). 1991. pap. 2.99 (*0-553-15919-4*) Bantam.
— Lila's Little Sister. (Unicorn Club Ser.: No. 4). (J). (gr. 4-7). 1994. 3.50 (*0-553-48214-9*) Bantam.
— Lila's Music Video. (Sweet Valley Twins & Friends Ser.: No. 73). (J). (gr. 4-7). 1993. pap. 3.50 (*0-553-48059-6*) Bantam.
— Lila's Secret, No. 6. (J). 1990. pap. 2.99 (*0-553-15773-6*) Bantam.
— Lila's Secret Valentine: Super Edition. (Sweet Valley Twins Ser.: No. 5). (J). (gr. 4-7). 1995. 3.99 (*0-553-48280-7*) Bantam.
— Lila's Story. (Sweet Valley Stars Ser.: No. 1). (YA). (gr. 7 up). 1989. pap. 3.50 (*0-553-28296-4*) Bantam.
— Lois & the Sleepover. (Sweet Valley Kids Ser.: No. 51). (J). (ps-3). 1994. 2.99 (*0-553-48099-5*) Bantam.
— Lois Strikes Back. (Sweet Valley Twins Ser.: No. 38). (J). 1990. 3.25 (*0-553-15789-2*) Bantam.
— The Long, Lost Brother. (Sweet Valley High Ser.: No. 79). (YA). 1991. pap. 3.25 (*0-553-29214-5*) Bantam.
— Love & Death in London. (Sweet Valley High Ser.: No. 104). (YA). 1994. pap. 3.50 (*0-553-56227-4*) Bantam.
— Love Letters. (SVH Ser.: No. 17). (YA). 1985. 3.25 (*0-553-27931-9*) Bantam.
— Love Letters for Sale. (Sweet Valley High Ser.: No. 88). (J). (gr. 4-7). 1992. pap. 3.25 (*0-553-29234-X*) Bantam.
— Love, Lies & Jessica Wakefield. (Sweet Valley University Ser.: No. 2). (YA). 1993. pap. 3.50 (*0-553-56306-8*) Bantam.
— The Love of Her Life. (Sweet Valley University Ser.: No. 6). (YA). 1994. pap. 3.50 (*0-553-56310-6*) Bantam.
— The Love Potion. (Sweet Valley Twins & Friends Ser.: No. 72). (J). (gr. 4-6). 1993. pap. 3.25 (*0-553-48058-8*) Bantam.
— Lovestruck. (SVH Ser.: No. 27). (Orig.). (YA). 1986. pap. 2.99 (*0-553-27885-1*) Bantam.
— Lucky Takes the Reins. (Sweet Valley Twins Ser.: No. 45). (J). (gr. 4-7). 1991. pap. 3.50 (*0-553-15843-0*) Bantam.
— Mademoiselle Jessica. (Sweet Valley Twins Ser.: No. 46). (J). (gr. 4-7). 1991. pap. 3.25 (*0-553-15849-X*) Bantam.
— The Magic Christmas. (Sweet Valley Twins & Friends Magna Ser.: No. 1). (J). (gr. 4-7). 1992. mass mkt. 3.99 (*0-553-48051-0*) Bantam.
— The Magic Puppets. (Sweet Valley Kids Ser.: No. 53). (J). (ps-3). 1994. 2.99 (*0-553-48107-X*) Bantam.
— Malibu Summer. (Sweet Valley High Ser.). 208p. (Orig.). (J). (gr. 4). 1986. pap. 3.50 (*0-553-26050-2*) Bantam.
— Mansy Miller Fights Back. (Sweet Valley Twins Ser.: No. 48). (J). (gr. 4-7). 1991. pap. 3.50 (*0-553-15880-5*) Bantam.
— Maria's Movie Comeback. (Unicorn Club Ser.: No. 2). (J). (gr. 4-7). 1994. pap. 3.50 (*0-553-48206-8*) Bantam.
— A Married Woman. (Sweet Valley University Ser.: No. 5). (YA). 1994. pap. 3.50 (*0-553-56309-2*) Bantam.
— Mary Is Missing. (Sweet Valley Twins Ser.: No. 36). (J). 1990. pap. 3.25 (*0-553-15778-7*) Bantam.
— Meet the Stars of Sweet Valley High. (J). 1995. mass mkt. 3.99 (*0-553-56731-4*) Bantam.
— Memories. (Sweet Valley High Ser.: No. 24). (YA). 1985. pap. 2.99 (*0-553-27492-9*) Bantam.
— The Middle School Gets Married. (Sweet Valley Twins & Friends Ser.: No. 68). (J). (gr. 4-7). 1993. 3.25 (*0-553-48055-3*) Bantam.
— Miss Teen Sweet Valley. (Sweet Valley High Ser.: No. 76). (YA). 1991. pap. 3.50 (*0-553-29060-6*) Bantam.
— The Missing Tea Set. (Sweet Valley Kids Ser.: No. 41). (J). (gr. 1-3). 1993. pap. 2.99 (*0-553-48015-4*) Bantam.
— The Morning After. (Sweet Valley High Ser.: No. 95). (YA). 1993. pap. 3.50 (*0-553-29852-6*) Bantam.
— The Mother-Daughter Switch. (Sweet Valley Twins Ser.: No. 87). (J). 1995. pap. 3.50 (*0-553-48117-7*) Bantam.
— Ms. Quarterback. (Sweet Valley High Ser.: No. 70). (YA). (gr. 9-12). 1990. pap. 3.25 (*0-553-28767-2*) Bantam.
— Murder in Paradise: Super Edition. (Sweet Valley High Ser.). (YA). 1995. mass mkt. 3.99 (*0-553-56710-1*) Bantam.
— Murder on the Line. (Sweet Valley High Super Thriller Ser.). (YA). 1992. pap. 3.50 (*0-553-29308-7*) Bantam.
— My Best Friend's Boyfriend. (Sweet Valley High Ser.: No. 87). (YA). 1992. pap. 3.50 (*0-553-29233-1*) Bantam.
— My First Love & Other Disasters. (J). (gr. 4-7). 1991. pap. 3.95 (*0-14-034886-7*, Puffin) Puffin Bks.
— New Elizabeth. (Sweet Valley High Ser.: No. 63). (YA). 1990. 2.99 (*0-553-28385-5*) Bantam.
— The New Girl. (Sweet Valley Twins Ser.: No. 6). (Orig.). (J). 1987. pap. 3.50 (*0-553-15660-8*) Bantam.
— New Jessica. (Sweet Valley High Ser.: No. 32). (YA). 1986. 2.99 (*0-553-27560-7*) Bantam.
— A Night to Remember. (Sweet Valley High Prom Magna Ser.). (YA). (gr. 4 up). 1993. mass mkt. 3.99 (*0-553-29309-5*) Bantam.
— Nightmare in Death Valley. (Sweet Valley High Ser.: No. 116). (J). 1995. mass mkt. 3.99 (*0-553-56634-2*) Bantam.
— No Girls Allowed. (Sweet Valley Kids Ser.: No. 57). (J). (ps-3). 1995. pap. 2.99 (*0-553-48208-4*) Bantam.
— No Means No. (Sweet Valley University Ser.: No. 10). (YA). 1995. 3.99 (*0-553-56655-5*) Bantam.
— Nowhere to Run. (Orig.). (YA). 1986. pap. 2.99 (*0-553-27944-0*) Bantam.
— Olivia's Story. (Sweet Valley High Super Star Ser.). (YA). 1991. pap. 3.50 (*0-553-29359-1*) Bantam.
— One of the Gang. (Sweet Valley Twins Ser.: No. 10). (J). 1987. 3.50 (*0-553-15677-2*) Bantam.
— Operation Love. (Young Adults Ser.: No. 103). (YA). (gr. 7 up). 1994. pap. 3.50 (*0-553-29860-7*) Bantam.
— Out of Control. (Sweet Valley High Ser.: No. 35). (Orig.). (YA). 1987. pap. 3.50 (*0-553-27666-2*) Bantam.
— Out of Place. (Sweet Valley Twins Ser.: No. 22). (YA). (gr. 7 up). 1988. 3.50 (*0-553-15628-4*) Bantam.
— Out of Reach. large type ed. (Sweet Valley High Ser.: No. 50). 151p. (J). (gr. 5-8). 1989. reprint ed. 9.50 (*1-55905-005-5*, Gareth Stevens Inc); reprint ed. lib. bdg. 10.50 (*1-55905-015-2*, Gareth Stevens Inc) Grey Castle.
— Outcast. (Sweet Valley High Ser.: No. 41). 160p. (Orig.). 1987. pap. 2.95 (*0-553-27693-X*) Bantam.
— The Parent Plot. (Sweet Valley Twins Ser.: No. 67). (J). 1990. pap. 3.50 (*0-553-28611-0*) Bantam.
— Patty's Last Dance. (Sweet Valley Twins & Friends Ser.: No. 65). (J). (gr. 4-7). 1993. pap. 3.25 (*0-553-48052-9*) Bantam.
— The Perfect Girl. (Sweet Valley High Ser.: No. 74). (YA). 1991. pap. 3.25 (*0-553-28901-2*) Bantam.
— Perfect Shot. (Sweet Valley High Ser.: No. 55). (J). 1989. pap. 2.95 (*0-553-27915-7*) Bantam.
— Perfect Summer. (Sweet Valley High Super Special Ser.: No. 1). 256p. (Orig.). (J). (gr. 6 up). 1985. 3.50 (*0-553-25072-8*) Bantam.
— Playing for Keeps. (Sweet Valley High Ser.: No. 49). (YA). (gr. 7 up). 1988. pap. 3.50 (*0-553-27477-5*) Bantam.
— Playing Hooky. (Sweet Valley Twins Ser.: No. 20). (YA). (gr. 6 up). 1988. 3.25 (*0-553-15606-3*) Bantam.
— Playing with Fire. large type ed. (Sweet Valley High Ser.: No. 3). 149p. (J). (gr. 5-8). 1989. reprint ed. lib. bdg. 10.50 (*1-55905-002-0*) Grey Castle.
— The Pompom Wars. (Sweet Valley High Ser.: No. 113). (YA). 1995. pap. 3.99 (*0-553-56631-8*) Bantam.
— Poor Lila! (Sweet Valley Twins & Friends Ser.: No. 63). (J). (gr. 4-7). 1992. 3.50 (*0-553-15962-3*) Bantam.
— Power Play. (Sweet Valley High Ser.: No. 4). 176p. (Orig.). (J). (gr. 7 up). 1985. pap. 2.99 (*0-553-27493-7*) Bantam.
— Power Play. large type ed. (Sweet Valley High Ser.: No. 4). 150p. (Orig.). (J). (gr. 5-8). 1989. reprint ed. 9.50 (*1-55905-003-9*, Gareth Stevens Inc); reprint ed. lib. bdg. 10.50 (*1-55905-013-6*, Gareth Stevens Inc) Grey Castle.
— Princess Elizabeth. (Sweet Valley Twins Ser.: No. 30). 1989. pap. 3.50 (*0-553-15715-9*) Bantam.
— Promises, No. 15. (Orig.). (YA). 1985. 3.25 (*0-553-27940-8*) Bantam.
— Psychic Sisters. (Sweet Valley Twins & Friends Ser.: No. 70). (J). (gr. 4-6). 1993. pap. 3.50 (*0-553-48057-X*) Bantam.
— Racing Hearts. (SVH Ser.: No. 9). (YA). 1984. mass mkt. 3.99 (*0-553-27878-9*) Bantam.
— Rags to Riches. (Sweet Valley High Ser.: No. 16). 160p. (Orig.). (J). (gr. 5 up). 1985. pap. 3.50 (*0-553-27431-7*) Bantam.
— Regina's Legacy. (Sweet Valley High Ser.: No. 73). (YA). 1991. 3.25 (*0-553-28863-6*) Bantam.
— Robbery at the Mall. (Sweet Valley Twins & Friends Ser.: No. 81). (J). (gr. 4-7). 1994. 3.50 (*0-553-48116-9*) Bantam.
— Robin in the Middle. (Sweet Valley Kids Ser.: No. 40). (J). (gr. 1-3). 1993. pap. 2.99 (*0-553-48014-6*) Bantam.
— Rock Star's Girl. (Sweet Valley High Ser.: No. 72). (YA). (gr. 9-12). 1991. 3.25 (*0-553-28841-5*) Bantam.
— Romeo & 2 Juliets. (Sweet Valley Twins Ser.: No. 84). (J). (gr. 4-7). 1995. pap. 3.50 (*0-553-48105-3*) Bantam.
— Rosa's Lie. (Sweet Valley High Ser.: No. 81). (YA). 1992. pap. 3.50 (*0-553-29227-7*) Bantam.
— Rumors. (SVH Ser.: No. 37). (YA). 1987. pap. 3.25 (*0-553-27884-3*) Bantam.
— Runaway. (Sweet Valley High Ser.: No. 21). (Orig.). (YA). 1985. pap. 3.25 (*0-553-27566-6*) Bantam.
— Runaway Hamster. (Sweet Valley Kids Ser.: No. 2). (J). (ps-3). 1989. pap. 2.99 (*0-553-15759-0*, Skylark) Bantam.
— S. S. Heartbreak. (Sweet Valley University Ser.: No. 13). (J). 1995. mass mkt. 3.99 (*0-553-56692-X*) Bantam.
— Sarah's Dad & Sophia's Mom. (Sweet Valley Twins Ser.: No. 62). (J). 1992. pap. 3.25 (*0-553-15944-5*) Bantam.
— Save the Unicorns! (Unicorn Club Ser.: No. 1). (J). (gr. 4-7). 1994. pap. 3.50 (*0-553-48202-5*) Bantam.
— Say Goodbye. (SVH Ser.: No. 23). (Orig.). (YA). 1985. pap. 3.50 (*0-553-27951-3*) Bantam.
— Second Best. (Sweet Valley Twins Ser.: No. 16). (J). 1988. pap. 3.25 (*0-553-15665-9*) Bantam.
— Second Chance. (Sweet Valley High Ser.: No. 53). (J). (ps-1). 1989. pap. 2.95 (*0-553-27771-5*) Bantam.
— Second Chance. large type ed. (Sweet Valley High Ser.: No. 53). 133p. (J). (gr. 5-8). 1989. reprint ed. 9.50 (*1-55905-008-X*, Gareth Stevens Inc); reprint ed. lib. bdg. 10.50 (*1-55905-018-7*, Gareth Stevens Inc) Grey Castle.
— The Secret of the Magic Pen. (Sweet Valley Twins Super Chiller Ser.: No. 8). (J). 1995. pap. 3.50 (*0-553-48282-3*) Bantam.
— Secrets. large type ed. (Sweet Valley High Ser.: No. 2). 118p. (J). (gr. 5-8). 1989. reprint ed. 9.50 (*1-55905-001-2*, Gareth Stevens Inc); reprint ed. lib. bdg. 10.50 (*1-55905-011-X*, Gareth Stevens Inc) Grey Castle.
— She's Not What She Seems. (Sweet Valley High Ser.: No. 92). (YA). 1993. 3.25 (*0-553-29849-6*) Bantam.
— Shipboard Wedding. (Sweet Valley University Ser.: No. 14). (J). 1995. mass mkt. 3.99 (*0-553-56693-8*) Bantam.
— Showdown. (Sweet Valley High Ser.: No. 19). 160p. (J). (gr. 6). 1985. pap. 3.25 (*0-553-27589-5*) Bantam.
— Slam Book Fever. (Sweet Valley High Ser.: No. 48). 160p. (Orig.). 1988. pap. 3.50 (*0-553-27416-3*) Bantam.
— The Slime That Ate Sweet Valley. (Sweet Valley Twins Ser.: No. 53). (J). (gr. 4-7). 1991. 3.25 (*0-553-15935-6*) Bantam.
— Sneaking Out. (Sweet Valley Twins Ser.: No. 5). (J). 1987. 3.50 (*0-553-15659-4*) Bantam.
— Sorority Scandal. (Sweet Valley University Ser.: No. 9). (YA). 1995. 3.99 (*0-553-56654-7*) Bantam.
— Special Christmas. (Sweet Valley High Ser.: No. 2). 240p. (Orig.). 1985. 3.50 (*0-553-25377-8*) Bantam.
— Spring Fever: Spring Super Edition, No. 2. (Sweet Valley High Ser.). 240p. (Orig.). (YA). (gr. 7-12). 1987. 3.50 (*0-553-26420-6*) Bantam.
— Star of the Parade. (Sweet Valley Kids Ser.: No. 54). (J). (ps-3). 1994. pap. 2.99 (*0-553-48111-8*) Bantam.
— Starring Jessica. (Sweet Valley High Ser.: No. 71). (YA). (gr. 9-12). 1991. pap. 3.25 (*0-553-28796-6*) Bantam.
— Starring Winston. (Sweet Valley Kids Ser.: No. 13). (J). (gr. 4-7). 1990. pap. 2.99 (*0-553-15836-8*) Bantam.
— Starting Over. (SVH Ser.: No. 33). (Orig.). (YA). 1987. pap. 2.95 (*0-553-27491-0*) Bantam.
— Stepsisters. (Sweet Valley High Ser.: No. 93). (YA). 1993. pap. 3.25 (*0-553-29850-X*) Bantam.
— Steven & the Zombie. (Sweet Valley Twins Ser.: No. 78). (J). 1994. pap. 3.50 (*0-553-48104-5*) Bantam.
— Steven Gets Even. (Sweet Valley Twins Ser.: No. 88). (J). 1995. pap. 3.50 (*0-553-48189-4*) Bantam.
— Steven's Bride. (Sweet Valley High Ser.: No. 83). (YA). 1992. pap. 3.25 (*0-553-29229-3*) Bantam.
— Steven's Bride. large type ed. LC 93-1350. (Sweet Valley High Ser.). (J). 1993. 15.95 (*1-56054-756-1*) Thorndike Pr.
— Steven's Enemy. (Sweet Valley Twins & Friends Ser.: No. 82). (J). (gr. 4-7). 1994. pap. 3.50 (*0-553-48097-9*) Bantam.
— Steven's in Love. (Sweet Valley Twins Ser.: No. 57). (J). 1992. pap. 3.50 (*0-553-15943-7*) Bantam.
— Steven's Twin. (Sweet Valley Kids Ser.: No. 50). (J). (ps-3). 1994. pap. 2.99 (*0-553-48095-2*) Bantam.
— A Stranger in the House. (Sweet Valley High Thriller Ser.). (J). 1995. mass mkt. 3.99 (*0-553-56711-X*) Bantam.
— The Substitute Teacher. (Sweet Valley Kids Ser.: No. 3). (J). (gr. k-3). 1990. pap. 2.99 (*0-553-15760-4*, Skylark) Bantam.
— Surprise! Surprise! (Sweet Valley Kids Ser.: No. 1). (J). (ps-3). 1989. pap. 2.99 (*0-553-15758-2*, Skylark) Bantam.
— Sweet Valley. (Sweet Valley Twins Ser.: No. 58). (J). 1992. pap. 3.50 (*0-553-15945-3*) Bantam.
— Sweet Valley. (Sweet Valley High Ser.: No. 84). (YA). 1992. pap. 3.50 (*0-553-29230-7*) Bantam.
— Sweet Valley. (Sweet Valley High Ser.: No. 85). (YA). 1992. pap. 3.25 (*0-553-29231-5*) Bantam.
— Sweet Valley Clean-Up. (Sweet Valley Kids Ser.: No. 27). (J). 1992. pap. 2.99 (*0-553-15923-2*) Bantam.
— Sweet Valley High, No. 68. (Orig.). (YA). 1990. 3.25 (*0-553-28618-8*) Bantam.
— Sweet Valley High, No. 56: Lost at Sea. 1989. pap. 3.50 (*0-553-27970-X*) Bantam.
— Sweet Valley High, No. 57: Teacher Crush. 1989. pap. 2.95 (*0-553-28079-1*) Bantam.
— Sweet Valley High, No. 58: Brokenhearted. 1989. pap. 3.25 (*0-553-28156-9*) Bantam.
— Sweet Valley High Super Edition: Spring Break. (Sweet Valley High Ser.: No. 3). 240p. (Orig.). 1986. 3.50 (*0-553-25537-1*) Bantam.
— Sweet Valley Kids, No. 28: Elizabeth Meets Her Hero. (J). (ps-3). 1992. pap. 2.99 (*0-553-15924-0*) Bantam.
— Sweet Valley Kids, No. 29: Andy & the Alien. (J). (ps-3). 1992. pap. 2.99 (*0-553-15925-9*) Bantam.
— Sweet Valley Slumber Party. (Sweet Valley Kids Ser.: No. 22). (J). (gr. 4-7). 1991. pap. 2.99 (*0-553-15934-8*) Bantam.
— Sweet Valley Trick or Treat. (Sweet Valley Kids Ser.: No. 12). (J). (gr. 4-7). 1990. pap. 2.99 (*0-553-15825-2*) Bantam.
— Sweet Valley Twins. (Sweet Valley Twins Ser.: No. 59). (Orig.). (J). 1992. 3.25 (*0-553-15953-4*) Bantam.
— Take Back the Night. (Sweet Valley University Ser.: No. 11). (YA). 1995. pap. 3.99 (*0-553-56656-3*) Bantam.
— Taking Sides. (Sweet Valley High Ser.: No. 31). (Orig.). (YA). 1986. pap. 3.25 (*0-553-27490-2*) Bantam.
— Teacher's Pet. (Sweet Valley Twins Ser.: No. 2). 112p. (Orig.). 1986. pap. 3.50 (*0-553-15656-X*) Bantam.
— Teamwork. (J). (ps-1). 1989. 3.25 (*0-553-15681-0*, SVT #27) Bantam.

— That Fatal Night. (Sweet Valley High Ser.: No. 60). (YA). (gr. 7 up). 1989. 3.25 (*0-553-28264-6*) Bantam.
— Three's a Crowd. (Sweet Valley Twins Ser.: No. 7). 1987. pap. 3.25 (*0-553-15661-6*) Bantam.
— Todd Runs Away. (Sweet Valley Twins Ser.: No. 77). (J). 1994. pap. 3.50 (*0-553-48100-2*) Bantam.
— Todd's Story. (Sweet Valley High Super Star Ser.: No. 4). (YA). 1992. pap. 3.50 (*0-553-29207-2*) Bantam.
— Too Good to Be True. (SVH Ser.: No. 11). (Orig.). (YA). 1985. 3.25 (*0-553-27941-6*) Bantam.
— Too Much In Love. (SVH Ser.: No. 22). (YA). 1985. pap. 2.99 (*0-553-27952-1*) Bantam.
— Trapped in Toyland. (Sweet Valley Kids Super Ser.: No. 8). (J). (ps-3). 1994. 3.50 (*0-553-48251-3*) Bantam.
— The Treasure of Death Valley. (Sweet Valley High Ser.: No. 115). (J). 1995. mass mkt. 3.99 (*0-553-56633-4*) Bantam.
— Trouble at Home. (Sweet Valley High Ser.: No. 65). (YA). 1990. pap. 2.99 (*0-553-28518-1*) Bantam.
— Troublemaker. (Sweet Valley High Ser.: No. 47). 160p. (Orig.). 1988. pap. 2.99 (*0-553-27359-0*) Bantam.
— Tug of War, No. 16. (Sweet Valley Twins Ser.). 112p. (Orig.). 1988. pap. 2.75 (*0-685-18297-5*, Skylark) Bantam.
— The Twins & the Wild West. (Sweet Valley Kids Ser.: No. 10). (J). (gr. 3-6). 1990. pap. 2.99 (*0-553-15811-2*) Bantam.
— The Twin's Big Pow-Wow. (Sweet Valley Kids Ser.: No. 44). (J). (ps-3). 1993. pap. 2.99 (*0-553-48098-7*) Bantam.
— The Twins Get Caught. (Sweet Valley Twins Ser.: No. 41). (J). (gr. 4 up). 1990. pap. 3.25 (*0-553-15810-4*) Bantam.
— The Twins Go to the Hospital. (Sweet Valley Kids Ser.: No. 20). (J). (gr. 4-7). 1991. pap. 2.99 (*0-553-15912-7*) Bantam.
— The Twins' Little Sister. (Sweet Valley Twins Ser.: No. 49). (J). (gr. 4-7). 1991. 3.25 (*0-553-15899-6*) Bantam.
— Two-Boy Weekend. (Sweet Valley High Ser.: No. 54). (YA). 1989. pap. 2.99 (*0-553-27856-8*) Bantam.
— Two-Boy Weekend. large type ed. (Sweet Valley High Ser.: No. 54). 150p. (J). (gr. 5-8). 1989. reprint ed. 9.50 (*1-55905-009-8*, Gareth Stevens Inc); reprint ed. lib. bdg. 10.50 (*1-55905-019-5*, Gareth Stevens Inc) Grey Castle.
— The Unicorns at War: Special Edition. (Unicorn Club Ser.). (J). (gr. 4-7). 1995. 3.50 (*0-553-48222-X*) Bantam.
— The Unicorns Go Hawaiian. (Sweet Valley Twins & Friends Ser.). (J). (gr. 4-7). 1991. 3.99 (*0-553-15948-8*) Bantam.
— Unicorns in Love. (Unicorn Club Ser.: No. 5). (J). (gr. 4-7). 1995. pap. 3.50 (*0-553-48218-1*) Bantam.
— V for Victory. (Sweet Valley High Ser.: No. 114). (YA). 1995. 3.99 (*0-553-56632-6*) Bantam.
— The Verdict. (Sweet Valley High Ser.: No. 97). (YA). 1993. 3.50 (*0-553-29854-2*) Bantam.
— The Wakefield Legacy: The Untold Story. (Sweet Valley Ser.: Saga No. 2). (YA). (gr. 7 up). 1992. mass mkt. 3.99 (*0-553-29794-5*, Starfire) Bantam.
— The Wakefields of Sweet Valley. (Sweet Valley Ser.: No. 1). 352p. (J). 1991. pap. 3.99 (*0-553-29278-1*) Bantam.
— Wakefields Strike. (Sweet Valley Twins Ser.: No. 56). (J). 1992. pap. 3.25 (*0-553-15950-X*) Bantam.
— Wanted for Murder: Thriller Edition. (Sweet Valley University Ser.). (YA). 1995. mass mkt. 3.99 (*0-553-56688-1*) Bantam.
— War Between the Twins. (Sweet Valley Twins Ser.: No. 37). (J). (gr. 4-7). 1990. pap. 3.25 (*0-553-15779-5*) Bantam.
— The Wedding. (YA). 1993. pap. 3.50 (*0-553-29855-0*) Bantam.
— What Your Parents Don't Know. (Sweet Valley University Ser.: No. 3). (YA). 1994. pap. 3.50 (*0-553-56307-6*) Bantam.
— When Love Dies. (Sweet Valley High Ser.: No. 12). 144p. (Orig.). 1984. mass mkt. 3.99 (*0-553-27755-3*) Bantam.
— White Lies. large type ed. (Sweet Valley High Ser.: No. 52). 137p. (J). (gr. 5-8). 1989. reprint ed. 9.50 (*1-55905-007-1*); reprint ed. lib. bdg. 10.50 (*1-55905-017-9*) Grey Castle.
— Who's to Blame? (Sweet Valley High Ser.: No. 66). (J). 1990. pap. 3.25 (*0-553-28555-6*) Bantam.
— Who's Who. (Spanish Bit Saga Ser.: No. 62). (J). 1990. pap. 3.25 (*0-553-28352-9*) Bantam.
— Winter Carnival. (Sweet Valley Twins Super Chiller Ser.: No. 2). (Orig.). (YA). (gr. 7-12). 1986. pap. 3.50 (*0-553-26159-2*) Bantam.
— Won't Someone Help Anna? (Sweet Valley Twins & Friends Ser.: No. 69). (J). (gr. 4-7). 1993. pap. 3.25 (*0-553-48056-1*) Bantam.
— Wrong Kind of Girl. (Sweet Valley High Ser.: No. 10). (J). (gr. 7 up). 1984. pap. 3.50 (*0-553-27668-9*) Bantam.
— Yours for a Day. (Sweet Valley Twins Ser.: No. 76). (J). (gr. 4-7). 1994. 3.50 (*0-553-48096-0*) Bantam.
Pascal, Francine, creator. Against the Odds. (Sweet Valley High Ser.: No. 51). 160p. (J). 1989. pap. 2.95 (*0-553-27650-6*) Bantam.
— Bitter Rivals. (Sweet Valley High Ser.: No. 29). 160p. (Orig.). 1986. 3.25 (*0-553-27590-9*) Bantam.
— Boys Against Girls. 112p. (Orig.). 1988. pap. 2.50 (*0-318-33018-0*) Bantam.
— Buried Treasure. (Sweet Valley Twins Ser.: No. 11). (J). (gr. 3-7). 1987. pap. 2.50 (*0-553-15533-4*, Skylark) Bantam.
— Double Jeopardy. (Sweet Valley High Super Thriller Ser.: No. 1). 214p. (Orig.). (YA). (gr. 7-12). 1987. 3.50 (*0-553-26905-4*) Bantam.
— Jumping to Conclusions. (Sweet Valley Twins Ser.: No. 24). 112p. (Orig.). (J). 1988. pap. 3.25 (*0-553-15635-7*) Bantam.
— Leaving Home High. (Sweet Valley High Ser.: No. 38). (Illus.). 144p. (YA). (gr. 7-12). 1987. pap. 3.50 (*0-553-27631-X*) Bantam.
— The Older Boy. (Sweet Valley Twins Ser.: No. 15). (J). (gr. 3-7). 1988. 3.25 (*0-553-15664-0*, Skylark) Bantam.
— On the Edge. (Sweet Valley High Ser.: No. 40). 160p. (YA). (gr. 7 up). 1987. 3.25 (*0-553-27692-1*) Bantam.
— On the Run. (Sweet Valley High Super Thriller Ser.: No. 2). 240p. (Orig.). 1988. 3.99 (*0-553-27230-6*) Bantam.
— Pretenses. (Sweet Valley High Ser.: No. 44). 1988. pap. 2.99 (*0-553-27064-8*) Bantam.
— Secret Admirer. (Sweet Valley High Ser.: No. 39). 160p. (YA). (gr. 7 up). 1987. pap. 2.99 (*0-553-27691-3*) Bantam.
— Standing Out. (Sweet Valley Twins Ser.: No. 25). 112p. (J). 1989. 3.25 (*0-553-15653-5*) Bantam.
— Stretching the Truth. (Sweet Valley Twins Ser.: No. 13). (J). (gr. 3-7). 1987. pap. 3.25 (*0-553-15654-3*, Skylark) Bantam.
— Sweet Valley High. (Sweet Valley High Ser.: No. 52). 160p. (Orig.). (J). 1989. 2.95 (*0-553-27720-0*) Bantam.
— Sweet Valley High Super Thriller, No. 3. 240p. (Orig.). (YA). 1988. pap. 3.50 (*0-553-27554-2*) Bantam.
— Taking Charge. (Sweet Valley Twins Ser.: No. 26). 112p. (Orig.). (J). 1989. pap. 3.25 (*0-553-15669-1*) Bantam.
— Tug of War. (Sweet Valley Twins Ser.: No. 14). 112p. (Orig.). (YA). (gr. 7-12). 1987. 3.50 (*0-553-15663-2*, Skylark) Bantam.
Pascal, Francine & Stewart, Molly M. Jessica's Cat Trick. (Sweet Valley Kids Ser.: No. 5). (J). (ps-3). 1990. pap. 2.99 (*0-553-15768-X*, Skylark) Bantam.
Pascal, Jean M. The Political Ideas of James Wilson: 1742-1798. LC 91-10728. (Political Theory & Political Philosophy Ser.). 368p. 1991. 25.00 (*0-8153-0139-1*) Garland.
***Pascal, Jean-Noel.** Les Successeurs De la Fontaine Au Siecle Des Lumieres (1715-1815) (Eighteenth Century French Intellectual History Ser.: Vol. 3). 288p. (FRE.). (C). 1995. text ed. 57.95 (*0-8204-2534-6*) P Lang Pubs.
Pascal, Lawrence J. Virginia Workers' Compensation: Law & Practice. 1986. 55.00 (*0-87473-256-5*) Michie Butterworth.
— Virginia Workers' Compensation: Law & Practice. suppl. ed. 1991. 20.00 (*0-87473-914-4*) Michie Butterworth.
— Virginia Workers' Compensation: Law & Practice. 2nd ed. 378p. 1993. 70.00 (*1-55834-027-0*) Michie Butterworth.
***Pascal, Nanette R. & Rojas, Maria P.** Relaciones Comerciales. 352p. (SPA.). (C). 1995. pap. text ed. write for info. (*0-669-32579-1*) Heath.
Pascal, Paul. Concilium Romarici Montis. (Latin Commentaries Ser.). 28p. (Orig.). (C). 1993. pap. text ed. 5.00 (*0-929524-77-2*) Bryn Mawr Commentaries.
— Hrotsvitha Dulcitius & Paphnutius. (Latin Commentaries Ser.). 83p. (Orig.). (C). 1985. pap. text ed. 6.00 (*0-929524-41-1*) Bryn Mawr Commentaries.
Pascal, Pierre. The Religion of the Russian People. LC 76-24462. 130p. 1976. pap. 8.95 (*0-913836-30-3*) St Vladimirs.
Pascal, Robert A., ed. see Voegelin, Eric.
Pascal, Roy. German Literature in the Sixteenth & Seventeenth Centuries: Renaissance-Reformation-Baroque. LC 79-9993. 274p. 1979. reprint ed. text ed. 59.75 (*0-313-21461-1*, PAGL, Greenwood Pr) Greenwood.
— The German Novel: Studies. LC 57-3904. (Canadian University Paperbooks Ser.: No. 24). 354p. reprint ed. pap. 100.90 (*0-8357-4164-8*, 2036938) Bks Demand.
— Kafka's Narrators: A Study of His Stories & Sketches. LC 81-12202. (Anglica Germanica Ser.: No. 2). 200p. 1982. pap. 16.95 (*0-521-28765-0*) Cambridge U Pr.
Pascal, Sevran. Dictionary of the French Chanson(song) Dictionnaire de la Chanson Francaise. 384p. (FRE.). 1986. 32.50 (*0-8288-2173-9*, M2355) Fr & Eur.
Pascale, Celine-Marie. The Blue Corn Cookbook. (Border Bks.). 103p. (Orig.). 1990. pap. 7.95 (*0-685-66859-2*) Out West Pub.
— The Blue Corn Cookbook. (Chile Pepper Cookbook Ser.). (Illus.). 125p. (Orig.). 1992. pap. 7.95 (*0-9623865-1-0*) Out West Pub.
Pascale, J. & Olson, R. E. Theoretical Methods for Atomic & Molecular Collisions: WS Lecture Notes in Physics, Vol. 14. 450p. (C). 1993. text ed. 77.00 (*9971-5-0424-3*); pap. text ed. 37.00 (*9971-5-0425-1*) World Scientific Pub.
Pascale, Jon S., jt. ed. see McGuigan, Patrick B.
Pascale, Richard T. Managing on the Edge: How the Smartest Companies Use Conflict to Stay Ahead. (Illus.). 352p. 1991. pap. 12.00 (*0-671-73285-4*, Touchstone Bks) S&S Trade.
Pascali, D. & Sburlan, S. Nonlinear Mappings of Monotone Type. 351p. 1979. lib. bdg. 92.00 (*90-286-0118-X*) Kluwer Ac.
***Pascali, Don & Skrypnik, I. V.** Methods for Analysis of Nonlinear Elliptical Boundary Value Problems. LC 94-28558. (Translations of Mathematical Monographs: 140). (ENG.). 1994. write for info. (*0-8218-4616-7*) Am Math.
Pascalis, William K., jt. auth. see Ferguson, S. W.
Pascall, Gillian. Social Policy: A Feminist Analysis. 250p. 1986. text ed. 47.50 (*0-422-78660-8*, 1026, Pub. by Tavistock UK); pap. text ed. 15.95 (*0-422-78670-5*, 1043, Pub. by Tavistock UK) Routledge Chapman & Hall.
Pascall, Gillian & Cox, Roger. Women Returning to Higher Education. LC 93-13275. 169p. 1994. 79.00 (*0-335-19056-1*, Open Univ Pr); pap. 33.00 (*0-335-19055-3*, Open Univ Pr) Taylor & Francis.
Pascall, Glenn. The Trillion Dollar Budget: How to Stop the Bankrupting of America. LC 84-40665. (Illus.). 328p. 1985. pap. 14.95 (*0-295-96237-2*) U of Wash Pr.
Pascarella, Anthony. And the Meek. 218p. 1994. pap. 8.95 (*1-56901-288-1*) NW Pub.
Pascarella, Cesare. The Discovery of America. Duval, John, tr. 120p. 1991. 17.95 (*1-55728-229-3*); pap. 9.95 (*1-55728-230-7*) U of Ark Pr.
Pascarella, Ernest T., ed. Studying Student Attrition. LC 81-48576. (New Directions for Institutional Research Ser.: No. IR 36). 1982. pap. 16.95x (*0-87589-906-4*) Jossey-Bass.
Pascarella, Ernest T. & Terenzini, Patrick T. How College Affects Students: Findings & Insights from Twenty Years of Research. LC 90-46068. (Higher & Adult Education Ser.). 920p. 1991. 80.00 (*1-55542-304-3*); pap. 45.00 (*1-55542-338-8*) Jossey-Bass.
Pascarella, Perry. The New Achievers: Creating a Modern Work Ethic. LC 83-49202. 216p. (C). 1984. 32.95 (*0-02-924870-1*) Free Pr.
Pascarella, Perry & Frohman, Mark A. The Purpose-Driven Organization: Unleashing the Power of Direction & Commitment. LC 89-45591. (Management Ser.). 198p. 1989. 24.95 (*1-55542-176-8*) Jossey-Bass.
Pascarelli, Emil & Quilter, Deborah. Repetitive Strain Injury: A Computer User's Guide. 272p. 1994. pap. text ed. 14.95 (*0-471-59533-0*) Wiley.
— Repetitive Strain Injury: A Computer User's Guide. 272p. 1994. text ed. 32.50 (*0-471-59532-2*) Wiley.
Pascarelli, Peter. Courage of Magic Johnson. 1992. mass mkt. 3.99 (*0-553-29915-8*) Bantam.
— The Toughest Job in Baseball: What Managers Do, How They Do It & Why It Gives Them Ulcers. LC 93-16572. 288p. 1993. 21.00 (*0-671-79331-4*) S&S Trade.
Pascenkova, N. A., et al. Czech-Russian Dictionary of Geology. 248p. (CZE & RUS.). 1960. 39.95 (*0-8288-6833-6*, M-9067) Fr & Eur.
Pasch, Brian & Polk, Jacqueline K. The Readability Machine: Radio Shack, TRS-80 Model 4 (Software & Documentation) 48p. 1986. 84.95 (*0-13-753609-7*) P-H.
— The Readability Machine: The Readability Machine for Apple II; Apple IIe, Apple IIc, & Apple-Compatible Microcomputers. 48p. 1986. 84.95 (*0-13-753617-8*) P-H.
Pasch, Marvin, et al. Teaching As Decision Making: Instructional Practices for the Successful Teacher. 320p. (Orig.). (C). 1991. pap. text ed. 36.95 (*0-8013-0157-2*, 75819) Longman.
— Teaching As Decision-Making: Successful Practices for the Elementary Teacher. 2nd ed. LC 94-27769. 373p. (C). 1995. pap. text ed. 37.95 (*0-8013-1431-3*) Longman.
Pasch, Robert A. Wisconsin Collection Law. LC 79-91165. 1993. 115.00 (*0-317-05728-6*) Lawyers Cooperative.
Pasch, S., ed. see Stadelman, W. J. & Olson, V. M.
Pascha, Werner, jt. ed. see Metzger-Court, Sarah.
Paschal, Andrew G., ed. W. E. B. Du Bois: A Reader. LC 92-30128. 376p. 1993. reprint ed. pap. 12.00 (*0-02-002351-0*) Macmillan.
Paschal, G. W. History of North Carolina Baptists, 2 vols., Set. 1990. reprint ed. 54.00 (*0-685-34316-2*) Stevens Bk Pr.
Paschal, Hugh H. A Formalistic Approach to Freshman Composition, Course One. 368p. (C). 1994. per. 31.95 (*0-8403-9095-5*) Kendall-Hunt.
— A Formalistic Approach to Freshman Composition, Course Two. 2nd ed. 160p. 1991. per. 18.95 (*0-8403-6969-7*) Kendall-Hunt.
Paschal, Huston. Michael Timpson. LC 91-66802. (Illus.). 24p. (Orig.). 1991. pap. 7.95 (*0-88259-964-X*) NCMA.
— Tom Phillips: Selections from the Ruth & Marvin Sackner Archive of Concrete & Visual Poetry. LC 90-63612. (Illus.). 28p. (Orig.). 1990. pap. 4.95 (*0-88259-961-5*) NCMA.
Paschal, Huston, intro. Tom Phillips: Words & Texts. (Illus.). 1993. pap. 34.95 (*0-500-97402-0*) Thames Hudson.
Paschal, John & Dorman, John. Paschal's Principles of Weight Training. (Illus.). 1979. pap. 2.95 (*0-89826-003-5*) Natl Paperback.
Paschal, Mary. The Structure of the Roman De Thebes. LC 80-66540. 96p. 1980. pap. 9.95 (*0-89729-261-8*) Ediciones.
Paschal, R. Wade, Jr. Vidal Adult Learning: Choices to Fit Your Church. LC 93-28212. (Choices to Fit Your Church Ser.). 144p. (Orig.). 1994. pap. 11.95 (*0-687-00773-9*) Abingdon.
Paschal, W. N. Life of a Rich Man. (Illus.). 180p. 1976. pap. 2.50 (*0-89114-075-1*) Baptist Pub Hse.
Paschall, jt. ed. see Hobbs.
Paschall, Dorothy M. Vocabulary of Mental Aberration in Roman Comedy & Petronius. (Language Dissertations Ser.: No. 27). 1939. pap. 16.00 (*0-527-00773-0*) Periodicals Srv.
Paschall, Douglas & Swanson, Alice, eds. Homewords: A Book of Tennessee Writers. LC 85-26394. 408p. (Orig.). (C). 1986. 35.00x (*0-87049-494-5*) U of Tenn Pr.
Paschall, Rod. Critical Incident Management. (Illus.). 104p. (Orig.). 1992. pap. 9.50 (*0-942511-54-9*) OICJ.
— The Defeat of Imperial Germany: 1917-1918. LC 88-29356. (Major Battles & Campaigns Ser.: Vol. I). (Illus.). 245p. 1989. 22.95 (*0-945575-05-X*) Algonquin Bks.
— The Defeat of Imperial Germany, 1917-1918. LC 94-11169. Orig. Title: Major Battles & Campaigns, Vol. 1. (Illus.). 288p. 1994. reprint ed. pap. 13.95 (*0-306-80585-5*) Da Capo.
— Witness to War: Korea. LC 94-39653. 1995. 12.00 (*0-399-51934-3*, Perigree Bks) Berkley Pub.
Pascheles, Wolf, ed. Sippurim, 5 pts. in 2, Set. (Volkskundliche Quellen Ser.: No. IV). 1976. reprint ed. write for info. (*3-487-06035-3*, Pub. by Georg Olms GW) Lubrecht & Cramer.
Paschen, Stephen H. Molding a Legacy: A Centennial History of the Akron Porcelain & Plastics Company. (Illus.). 73p. (Orig.). 1989. pap. 6.95 (*0-9621895-3-7*) Summit Cty Hist Soc.
— Speaking of Summit: An Oral History Handbook. 55p. (Orig.). 1989. pap. 2.95 (*0-9621895-2-9*) Summit Cty Hist Soc.
Paschen, Stephen H., ed. What We Wore: An Exhibit Catalogue Celebrating 150 Years of Summit County Costume. (Illus.). 31p. (Orig.). 1990. pap. 9.50 (*0-9621895-4-5*) Summit Cty Hist Soc.
Pascher, A. Suesswasserflora von Mitteleuropa, Vol. 10: Chlorophyta II Tetrasporales, Chlorococcales, Gloeodendrales. rev. ed. Ettl, H. & Gaertner, G., eds. (Illus.). 436p. (GER.). 1988. lib. bdg. 103.00 (*3-437-30409-7*) Lubrecht & Cramer.
— Suesswasserflora Von Mitteleuropa, Vol. 2 - Pt. 3: Bacillariophyceae: Centrales, Fragilariaceae, Eunotiaceae. Krammer, K. et al, eds. (Illus.). 576p. (GER.). 1991. lib. bdg. 122.20 (*3-437-30541-7*, Pub. by G Fischer Verlag GW) Lubrecht & Cramer.
— Suesswasserflora von Mitteleuropa, Vol. 2, Pt. 2: Bacillariophyceae: Bacillariaceae, Epithemiaceae. rev. ed. Krammer, K. & Lange-Bertalot, H., eds. (Illus.). 596p. (GER.). 1988. lib. bdg. 109.50 (*3-437-30508-5*) Lubrecht & Cramer.
— Suesswasserflora von Mitteleuropa, Vol. 2, Pt. 4: Bacillariophyceae, Achnanthaceae & Index to Pts. 1-4. rev. ed. Krammer, K. & Lange, Bertalot H., eds. (Illus.). 437p. (GER.). 1991. lib. bdg. 112.80 (*3-437-30664-2*, Pub. by G Fischer Verlag GW) Lubrecht & Cramer.
— Suesswasserflora von Mittelieuropa, Vol. 20: Schyzomyceten-Bakterien, von J. Haeisler. Ettl, H. & Gerloff, J., eds. (Illus.). 588p. (GER.). 1982. lib. bdg. 96.50 (*3-437-30344-9*) Lubrecht & Cramer.
— Suesswasserflora von Suedeuropa, Vol. 24: Pteridophyta und Antophyta, Part 2-Saururaceae bis Asteraceae. Ettl, H. et al, eds. (Illus.). 540p. 1981. lib. bdg. 89.95 (*3-437-30341-4*) Lubrecht & Cramer.
Pascher, A., ed. Suesswasserflora von Mitteleuropa: Starmach K. Chrysophyceae und Haptophyceae, Vol. 1. (Illus.). 515p. 1985. lib. bdg. 89.95 (*3-437-30402-X*) Lubrecht & Cramer.
Pascher, A., ed. see Casper, S. J. & Krausch, H. D.
Pascher, A., ed. see Ettl, H.
Pascher, A., ed. see Kadlubowska, J. Z.
Pascher, A., ed. see Krammer, K. & Lange-Bertalot, H.
Pascher, A., ed. see Mrozinska, T.
Pascher, A., ed. see Rieth, A.
Pascher, A, et al, eds. Suesswasserflora von Mitteleuropa: Xanthophyceae, Part 1, Vol. 3. (Illus.). 530p. (GER.). 1978. lib. bdg. 70.00 (*3-437-30250-7*) Lubrecht & Cramer.
Paschich, Ed & Hendricks, Paula. The Timber Reduced Energy Efficient Home. Smith, James C., Jr., ed. LC 93-35704. (Illus.). 128p. (Orig.). 1993. pap. 17.95 (*0-86534-208-3*) Sunstone Pr.
— The Tire House. LC 95-1012. (Illus.). 96p. (Orig.). 1995. pap. 14.95 (*0-86534-215-6*) Sunstone Pr.
Paschke, Barbara & Volpendesta, David, eds. Clamor of Innocence: Central American Short Stories. 224p. (Orig.). 1988. pap. 9.95 (*0-87286-227-5*) City Lights.
Paschke, Barbara, ed. see Dalton, Roque.
Paschke, Barbara, jt. ed. see Murguia, Alejandro.
Paschke, Barbara, jt. ed. see Volpendesta, David.
Paschke, Barbara, tr. see Zamora, Daisy.
Paschke, Donald V., tr. see Garcia, Manuel, II.
Paschke, F., et al, eds. Microcircuit Engineering 'Eighty-Eight: Proceedings of the 14th International Conference on Microlithography, Vienna, Austria, 20-22 September, 1988. 652p. 1989. 159.00 (*0-444-87448-8*, North Holland) Elsevier.
Paschke, V., tr. see Garcia, Manuel, II.
Paschkis. So Sleepy/Wide Awake. (J). 1994. 12.95 (*0-8050-3174-X*) H Holt & Co.
***Paschkis, Julie.** So Happy/So Sad. LC 94-41654. (J). 1995. 12.95 (*0-8050-3862-0*) H Holt & Co.
Paschkoff, A. G., tr. see Leskov, Nikolai S.
Paschos, E. A., jt. ed. see Kleinknecht, K.
Paschos, Jacqueline & Destang, Francoise. Come to School. (Rejoice Ser.). (J). (ps). 1986. pap. 0.35 (*0-8091-6505-8*) Paulist Pr.
Pascin, Jules. Pascin: One Hundred Ten Drawings. Werner, Alfred, ed. LC 71-154346. 1972. pap. 5.95 (*0-486-20299-2*) Dover.
Pasco, Allan. Novel Configurations: A Study of French Fiction. 2nd ed. LC 86-63079. 1993. pap. 24.95 (*1-883479-00-2*) Summa Pubns.
Pasco, Allan H. Allusion: A Literary Craft. (Theory - Culture Ser.). 272p. (C). 1994. 55.00 (*0-8020-0449-0*) U of Toronto Pr.
— Balzacian Montage: Configuring La Comedie Humaine. (Romance Ser.: No. 65). 192p. 1991. text ed. 45.00 (*0-8020-2776-8*) U of Toronto Pr.
Pasco, Britt. Hellfire Town. large type ed. (Linford Western Library). 272p. 1994. pap. 14.95 (*0-7089-7586-0*) Ulverscroft.
Pasco, Duane, illus. The Prince & the Salmon People. LC 92-38394. 48p. (J). 1993. 19.95 (*0-8478-1662-1*) Rizzoli Intl.
Pasco, Elezabeth, ed. see Charles, Rodney & Jordan, Anna.
Pasco, Elizabeth, ed. see Charles, Rodney.
Pasco, Elizabeth, ed. see Vellin, Jerry.
Pasco, Rowanne & Redford, John, eds. Faith Alive: A New Presentation of Catholic Belief & Practice. LC 89-51904. 320p. (Orig.). 1990. pap. 9.95 (*0-89622-408-2*) Twenty-Third.
Pascoe. Catalysis of Organic Reactions. (Chemical Industries Ser.: Vol. 47). 408p. 1991. 190.00 (*0-8247-8573-8*) Dekker.
— Introduction to Properties of Engineering Materials. 3rd ed. 1978. pap. 27.95 (*0-442-30233-9*) Chapman & Hall.
Pascoe, Ann. Story of St. Ives. (C). 1990. pap. 18.00 (*0-85025-303-9*, Pub. by Tor Mark Pr UK) St Mut.
Pascoe, Bruce. Mid Life Vices. 440p. (C). 1990. 60.00 (*0-685-52922-3*, Pub. by Pascoe Pub AT) St Mut.
Pascoe, Charles. Wild Horse. 1993. 4.25 (*0-87129-272-6*, W08) Dramatic Pub.

P
Q

Pascoe, Charles E., ed. The Dramatic List: A Record of the Principal Performances of Living Actors & Actresses on the British Stage with Criticisms from Contemporary Journals. LC 74-145225. 358p. 1879. reprint ed. 39.00 (*0-403-00781-X*) Scholarly.
— Our Actors & Actresses: The Dramatic List. 2nd enl. rev. ed. LC 70-91911. 1972. 30.95 (*0-405-08838-8*) Ayer.
Pascoe, D. & Edwards, R. W., eds. Freshwater Biological Monitoring: Proceedings of a Specialized Conference, Cardiff, U. K., Sept. 12-14, 1984. LC 82-645900. (Advances in Water Pollution Control Ser.). 168p. 1984. 78.00 (*0-08-032313-8*, Pub. by Pergamon Repr UK) Franklin.
Pascoe, David, ed. see Stevenson, Robert L.
Pascoe, David P. Hearing Aids - Who Needs Them? What They Can Do for You, Where to Buy Them, How to Use Them. Pascoe, Muriel S., ed. LC 90-86318. (Illus.). 176p. (Orig.). 1991. pap. 10.50 (*0-9628963-0-6*) Big Bend Bks.
***Pascoe, Elaine.** First Facts about American Presidents. Glassman, Bruce, ed. (First Facts Ser.). (Illus.). 112p. (J). (gr. 3-7). 1995. lib. bdg. 19.95 (*1-56711-167-X*) Blackbirch.
— Freedom of Expression: The Right to Speak Out in America. LC 92-7150. (Issue & Debate Ser.). (Illus.). 128p. (YA). (gr. 7 up). 1992. lib. bdg. 15.90 (*1-56294-255-7*) Millbrook Pr.
— South Africa: Troubled Land. rev. ed. LC 92-13608. (Illus.). 128p. (YA). (gr. 9-12). 1992. lib. bdg. 14.77 (*0-531-11139-3*) Watts.
Pascoe, G. & Kenneth, David. Two Feet-Small Book. 8p. (J). 1987. 2.95 (*0-88679-537-0*) Educ Insights.
— Two Feet-Tall Book. 8p. (J). 1987. 17.95 (*0-88679-536-2*) Educ Insights.
Pascoe, G. & Williams, S. Eeeny, Meeny, Miney Mouse-Small Book. 8p. (J). 1987. 2.95 (*0-88679-535-4*) Educ Insights.
— Eeny, Meeny, Miney Mouse-Tall Book. 8p. (J). 1987. 17. 95 (*0-88679-534-6*) Educ Insights.
***Pascoe, Gwen.** Deep in a Rainforest. 32p. (J). 1995. 12.95 (*1-86374-210-7*, Pub. by ERA Pubns AT) Pubs Dist MI.
— The Sea Where I Swim. LC 93-6647. (J). 1994. write for info. (*0-383-03712-3*) SRA Schl Grp.
Pascoe, K. J. Properties of Materials for Electrical Engineers. LC 72-8612. (Illus.). 336p. reprint ed. pap. 95.80 (*0-7837-1877-2*, 2042078) Bks Demand.
Pascoe, L. C. Teach Yourself Arithmetic: Decimalized & Metricated. (Teach Yourself Ser.). 1972. pap. 5.95 (*0-679-10452-6*) McKay.
Pascoe, Muriel S., ed. see Pascoe, David P.
Pascoe, Peggy. Relations of Rescue: The Search for Female Moral Authority in the American West, 1874-1939. (Illus.). 328p. 1990. 45.00 (*0-19-506008-3*) OUP.
— Relations of Rescue: The Search for Female Moral Authority in the American West, 1874-1939. (Illus.). 328p. 1993. reprint ed. pap. 15.95 (*0-19-508430-6*) OUP.
Pascoe Publ. Pty. Ltd. Staff, ed. The Largest Island Study Guide-Ridgeway et Al Pascoe Publishing Pty. Ltd. 88p. (C). 1990. 33.00 (*0-685-52918-5*, Pub. by Pascoe Pub AT) St Mut.
Pascoe, Reg R., jt. auth. see Knottenbelt, Derek C.
Pascoe, Robin. Culture Shock! Successful Living Abroad - A Wife's Guide. 250p. 1993. pap. 10.95 (*1-55868-123-X*) Gr Arts Ctr Pub.
Pascoe, W. H. Teudar: A King of Cornwall. (C). 1989. 40.00 (*1-85022-001-8*, Pub. by Dyllansow Truran UK) St Mut.
Pascolait, Connie & Fimbrez, Louie. The American Citizenship Handbook: A Powerful Step-by-Step Bilingual Study Guide to Becoming an American Citizen. 2nd rev. ed. Pascolait, Steve, ed. Winicker, Susanne, tr. (Illus.). (SPA.). Date not set. pap. text ed. 39.95 (*1-56813-113-5*) Madera Cinevideo.
Pascolait, Steve, ed. see Pascolait, Connie & Fimbrez, Louie.
Pascolini. Pan XIII - Particles & Nuclei: Procedings of the Thirteenth International Conference. 864p. 1994. text ed. 162.00 (*981-02-1799-4*) World Scientific Pub.
Pascolini, Alessandro, jt. ed. see Rotblat, Joseph.
Pascon, Paul. Capitalism & Agriculture in the Haouz of Marrakesh. Hall, John R., ed. Vaughan, C. Edwin & Ingham, Veronique, trs. 300p. 1986. 59.95 (*0-7103-0189-8*, 01898) Routledge Chapman & Hall.
Pascu, Stefan. A History of Transylvania. Ladd, D. Robert, tr. LC 82-8669. (Illus.). 345p. reprint ed. pap. 98.40 (*0-318-39796-X*, 2033199) Bks Demand.
Pascual, Benjamin M. The Happy Time of an Ilocano Boy & Other Stories. 96p. (Orig.). (C). 1989. pap. 7.50 (*971-10-0352-X*, Pub. by New Day Pub PH) Cellar.
— Selmo Comes Home & Other Stories. 138p. (Orig.). (C). 1989. pap. 8.75 (*971-10-0351-1*, Pub. by New Day Pub PH) Cellar.
Pascual-Castroviejo, Ignacio. Spinal Tumors in Children & Adolescents. (International Review of Child Neurology Ser.). 320p. 1990. 126.00 (*0-88167-576-8*, 2044) Raven.
Pascual, J. A., jt. auth. see Corominas i Vigneaux, Joan.
Pascual, J. A., jt. auth. see Corominas, J.
Pascual, J. F. & Calcagno, P. L., eds. Nephrologic Problems of the Newborn. (Contributions to Nephrology Ser.: Vol. 15). (Illus.). 1979. pap. 26.50 (*3-8055-2947-3*) S Karger.
— Recent Advances in Pediatric Nephrology. (Contributions to Nephrology Ser.: Vol. 27). (Illus.). vi, 98p. 1981. pap. 52.00 (*3-8055-1851-X*) S Karger.
Pascual-Leone, J., tr. see Samuda, R. J. & Kong, S. L.
Pascual, Lope, tr. see Galvez, Alfonso.
***Pascual, Luis D.** What Goes Around Comes Around: The Feedback Loop. LC 94-90701. (Illus.). 99p. (Orig.). 1994. pap. 12.95 (*0-9644398-3-2*) WGACA.
Pascual, Manuel, tr. see Killgallon, James J., et al.
Pascual, P., jt. auth. see Galindo, A.
Pascual, R., jt. auth. see Fernandez, E.
Pascual Recuero, Pascal. Diccionario Basico Ladino - Espanol. 182p. (LAD & SPA.). 1977. pap. 29.95 (*0-7859-3362-X*, 8472130886) Fr & Eur.
Pascual-Sanz, Fabriciano. Historia de Cristobal Colon. (Illus.). 522p. (SPA.). 1986. 19.95 (*84-599-1657-X*, Pub. by Tecnograf SP) Ediciones.
Pascualy, Ralph A. & Soest, Sally W. Snoring & Sleep Apnea: Personal & Family Guide to Diagnosis & Treatment. LC 93-997. 1993. pap. 21.95 (*0-9635945-4-0*) Scope Pub WA.
Pascuzzi, Edward, jt. auth. see Harrington, Phillip.
***Pascuzzo, Sandra F.** A Christmas Tree. LC 94-60623. (Illus.). 44p. (J). (ps-4). 1994. 7.95 (*1-55523-707-X*) Winston-Derek.
***Pasda, Patricia & DiEdwardo, Mary A.** The Animal Sketch Book. 50p. 1995. 6.95 (*0-9641468-2-7*) M DiEdwardo Pubng.
— Write a Book of Haiku. (Illus.). 40p. (J). 1994. student ed write for info. (*0-9641468-1-9*) M DiEdwardo Pubng.
Pasda, Patricia & DiEdwards, Mary A. The Integrated Creative Curriculum Log Book. 100p. 1994. spiral bd. 9.95 (*0-9641468-0-0*) M DiEdwardo Pubng.
Pasdermadjian, Hrant. The Department Store: Its Origins Evolution & Economics. LC 75-39265. (Getting & Spending: the Consumer's Dilemma Ser.). 1976. reprint ed. 20.95 (*0-405-08038-7*) Ayer.
***Pase, Marilyn.** Pharmacology. (Outline Ser.). 300p. (Orig.). (C). 1995. pap. text ed. 16.95 (*1-56930-026-7*) Skidmore Roth Pub.
Pasek, Jan C. Memoirs of the Polish Baroque: The Writings of Jan Chryzostom Pasek, a Squire of the Commonwealth of Poland & Lithuania. Leach, Catherine S., ed. LC 74-77731. 415p. reprint ed. pap. 118.30 (*0-685-17871-4*, 2029590) Bks Demand.
Pasemann, F. & Doebner, H. D., eds. Neurodynamics. (Series in Neural Networks: Vol. 1). 240p. (C). 1991. text ed. 83.00 (*981-02-0811-1*) World Scientific Pub.
Pasetti, Mario, ed. Los Escritos y las Ensenanzas del Bienaventurado Jose Marello. LC 93-78554. 292p. (Orig.). (SPA.). 1993. pap. 14.95 (*1-883839-03-3*) Guard Redeemer.
Pasewark, Sr. Lotus 1-2-3 DOS Version. (C). pap. text ed. 14.00 (*0-13-701574-7*) P-H.
***Pasewark.** Microsoft Works, 3.0 DOS: Tutorial & Applications Text. (DT-Fortran Ser.). 1995. text ed. 23. 95 (*0-538-63435-9*) S-W Pub.
Pasewark, Kyle A. A Theology of Power: Domination & Being. LC 92-19343. 400p. 1992. 22.00 (*0-8006-2605-2*, 1-2605) Augsburg Fortress.
Pasewark, S. R. Claris Works. (C). pap. text ed. 14.00 (*0-13-132861-1*) P-H.
— DBASE DOS Version. (C). pap. text ed. 14.00 (*0-13-096959-1*) P-H.
— Generic Microcomputer Simulation. (C). pap. text ed. 14. 00 (*0-13-096983-4*) P-H.
— Microcomputer Survey. (C). pap. text ed. 14.00 (*0-685-65257-2*) P-H.
Pasewark, William, jt. auth. see Willis, Jerry.
Pasewark, William R. Machine Transcription for Document Processing. 3rd ed. LC 94-15008. 1995. pap. 17.95 (*0-538-71074-8*) S-W Pub.
— WordPerfect 5.1 with Personal, School, Career, & Business Applications. LC 93-37660. 1994. pap. 25.00 (*0-13-097007-7*) P-H.
Pasha, A., jt. ed. see Wyn-Davies, M.
Pasha, Cemal. Memoirs of a Turkish Statesman, 1913-1919. LC 73-6295. (Middle East Ser.). 1973. reprint ed. 25.95 (*0-405-05328-2*) Ayer.
Pasha, Johnson, tr. The Secret Garden. 86p. 1969. 17.00 (*0-900860-38-3*, Pub. by Octagon Pr UK) ISHK Bk Service.
Pasha Publications Editors, ed. Enhanced Recovery Week EOR Project Sourcebook. 156p. 1984. pap. text ed. 185. 00 (*0-935453-03-2*) Pasha Pubns.
Pasha Publications Staff. Investment Opportunities in China: Chemical Industry. 1993. 199.00 (*0-935453-59-8*) Pasha Pubns.
Pashaev, O. K., jt. ed. see Makhankov, V. G.
Pashayan, Hermione, jt. auth. see Feingold, Murray.
Pashi, Lumana & Turnbull, Alan. Lingala-English Dictionary. LC 94-71163. 250p. 1994. text ed. 55.00 (*0-931745-86-1*) Dunwoody Pr.
Pashigian, Peter B. Price Theory & Applications. 1994. pap. text ed. write for info. (*0-07-048741-3*) McGraw.
***Pashin, Jack C. & Ettensohn, Frank R.** Reevaluation of the Bedford-Berea Sequence in Ohio & Adjacent States: Forced Regression in a Foreland Basin. LC 95-3060. (Special Papers: Vol. 298). 1995. pap. write for info. (*0-8137-2298-5*) Geol Soc.
Pashinin, P. P., ed. Formation & Control of Optical Wavefronts. (Proceedings of the Institute of General Physics of the Academy of Sciences of the U. S. S. R. Ser.: Vol. 7). 207p. 1990. text ed. 115.00 (*0-941743-29-2*) Nova Sci Pubs.
— Laser-Induced Raman Spectroscopy in Crystals & Gases. (Proceedings of the Institute of General Physics of the Academy of Sciences of the U. S. S. R. Ser.: Vol. 2). 215p. (C). 1988. text ed. 115.00 (*0-941743-13-6*) Nova Sci Pubs.
Pashkevich, Nicolas. Nicolas Pashkevich. LC 94-77354. (Illus.). 168p. 1995. 35.00 (*0-9617756-8-8*) Galerija.
Pashkov, P. Orders & Badges of the White Armies in the Civil War. limited ed. (Illus.). 31p. 1983. pap. 10.00 (*0-317-06616-1*) Quaker.
— The White Armies' Orders & Badges in the Civil War 1917-1922. Budzilovich, G. N. & Zander, R., trs. (Illus.). vi, 31p. (Orig.). 1983. pap. 8.50 (*0-912671-04-1*) Russian Numis.
Pashkow, Frederic J. Clinical Cardiac Rehabilitation. (Illus.). 416p. 1992. 62.00 (*0-683-06780-X*) Williams & Wilkins.
Pashkow, Fredric & Libov, Charlotte. The Woman's Heart Book: The Complete Guide to Keeping Your Heart Healthy & What to Do If Things Go Wrong. (Illus.). 384p. 1994. pap. 11.95 (*0-452-27212-2*) NAL-Dutton.
Pashkow, Fredric, et al. Successful Cardiac Rehabilitation: The Complete Guide for Building Cardiac Rehab Programs. 39.95 (*0-9619796-0-7*) HeartWatchers Pr.
***Pashkow, Fredric J. & Libov, Charlotte.** 50 Essential Things to Do When the Doctor Says It's Heart Disease. 1995. 10.95 (*0-452-27101-0*, Plume) NAL-Dutton.
Pashley, H. N. Notes on the Birds of Cley Norfolk. 127p. (C). 1992. pap. text ed. 95.00 (*0-9512263-3-9*, Pub. by Enchanted Abiary UK) St Mut.
Pashley, M. D., jt. ed. see Salemink, H. W.
Pashuk, Lauren. Fun with Colors. (Fun with Ser.). (Illus.). 32p. (J). (ps-00). 1985. pap. 2.95 (*0-88625-106-0*) Durkin Hayes Pub.
Pashuk, Lauren, jt. auth. see Winik, J. T.
Pashukanis, Evgeny B. Law & Marxism. 196p. (C). 1989. pap. text ed. 16.95 (*0-86104-740-0*, Pub. by Pluto Pr UK) Westview.
Pasi, Mario. Bellini. (Portraits of Greatness Ser.). (Illus.). 80p. 1989. text ed. 17.50 (*0-918367-33-6*); pap. text ed. 12.50 (*0-918367-32-8*) Elite.
— Mascagni. (Portraits of Greatness Ser.). (Illus.). 48p. 1989. 17.50 (*0-918367-30-1*); pap. text ed. 12.50 (*0-918367-31-X*) Elite.
Pasic, N., et al, eds. Workers' Management in Yugoslavia: Recent Developments & Trends. x, 198p. 1982. 28.00 (*92-2-103034-2*); pap. 20.00 (*92-2-103035-0*) Intl Labour Office.
Pasich, William, ed. see Nitsch, Susan L.
Pasichnyk, Richard, jt. auth. see Johnson, Robert.
Pasick, Robert. Awakening from a Deep Sleep. 288p. 1992. pap. 10.00 (*0-06-250714-1*) Harper SF.
— Awakening from the Deep Sleep: A Powerful Guide for Courageous Men. rev. ed. LC 91-58918. 272p. 1994. pap. 10.00 (*0-06-250650-1*) Harper SF.
— What Every Man Needs to Know. 1994. pap. 7.00 (*0-06-251064-9*, PL) HarpC.
— What Every Man Needs to Know. LC 94-4423. 160p. 1994. pap. 6.00 (*0-685-73021-2*) Harper SF.
Pasierbska, Halina. Doll's Houses. (Shire Album Ser.: No. 271). (Illus.). 32p. 1991. pap. text ed. 6.00 (*0-7478-0135-5*, Pub. by Shire Pubns UK) Lubrecht & Cramer.
Pasik-Duncan, B., jt. ed. see Duncan, T. E.
Pasika, Wallace M., ed. Carbon-13 NMR in Polymer Science. LC 79-13384. (ACS Symposium Ser.: No. 103). 344p. 1979. 38.95 (*0-8412-0505-1*) Am Chemical.
Pasinetti, L., ed. Italian Economic Papers. (Illus.). 320p. 1993. 49.95 (*0-19-828769-0*) OUP.
Pasinetti, Luigi. Structural Economic Dynamics: A Theory of the Economic Consequences of Human Learning. LC 92-13438. (Illus.). 216p. (C). 1993. 44.95 (*0-521-43282-0*) Cambridge U Pr.
Pasinetti, Luigi L. Essays on the Theory of Joint Production. LC 79-20620. 1980. text ed. 58.00 (*0-231-04988-9*) Col U Pr.
— Lectures in the Theory of Production. LC 77-1541. Orig. Title: Lezioni Di Teoria Della Produzione. 1977. text ed. 46.00 (*0-231-04100-4*) Col U Pr.
— Structural Change & Economic Growth: A Theoretical Essay on the Dynamics of the Wealth of Nations. LC 80-41496. 296p. 1983. pap. 22.95 (*0-521-27410-9*) Cambridge U Pr.
Pasinetti, Luigi L., ed. Italian Economic Papers, Vol. 2. 286p. 1995. 45.00 (*0-19-828930-8*) OUP.
Pasinetti, Luigi L. & Solow, Robert M., eds. Economic Growth & the Structure of Long-Term Development: Proceedings of the IEA Conference Held in Verenna, Italy. LC 94-5977. (I.E.A. Conference Ser.: No. 112). 1994. write for info. (*0-312-12182-2*) St Martin.
Pasini, A. Diagram Geometrics. (Mathematical Monographs). 350p. 1994. 95.00 (*0-19-853497-3*) OUP.
Pasiuk-Bronikowska, Wanda, et al. Autoxidation of Sulphur Compounds. 182p. 1992. text ed. 78.00 (*0-13-053521-4*) P-H.
Pasiuk, Joan P. Adventures in Careering: A Twin Cities Field Guide. 187p. 1991. pap. 12.95 (*0-9631399-0-8*) Basswood Pr.
Pask, Joseph A. & Evans, A. G., eds. Ceramic Microstructures '86: Role of Interfaces. LC 87-22758. (Materials Science Research Ser.: Vol. 21). 1002p. 1987. 150.00 (*0-306-42681-1*, Plenum Pr) Plenum.
Pask, Joseph A. & Evans, Anthony, eds. Surfaces & Interfaces in Ceramic & Ceramic-Metal Systems. LC 81-5878. (Materials Science Research Ser.: Vol. 14). 768p. 1981. 125.00 (*0-306-40726-4*, Plenum Pr) Plenum.
Pask, Joseph A., jt. ed. see Fulrath, Richard M.
Pask, Judith M. User Education for Online Systems in Libraries: A Selective Bibliography, 1970-1988. LC 90-9102. 220p. 1990. 25.00 (*0-8108-2378-0*) Scarecrow.
Paska, Jocelyn, tr. see Munoz, Silverio.
Paskaleva, K. Bulgarian Icons Through the Centuries. (Illus.). 332p. (C). 1987. text ed. 350.00 (*0-685-40245-2*, Pub. by Collets) St Mut.
— Icons from Bulgaria. (Illus.). 222p. (C). 1987. text ed. 400.00 (*0-685-40244-4*, Pub. by Collets) St Mut.
Paskaleva, K., ed. Sixteen Most Famous Icons from Bulgaria. (Illus.). (C). 1987. text ed. 150.00 (*0-685-40243-6*, Pub. by Collets) St Mut.
Paskauskas, R. Andrew, ed. The Complete Correspondence of Sigmund Freud & Ernest Jones, 1908-1939. LC 92-23913. (Illus.). 888p. 1993. 42.50 (*0-674-15423-1*) Belknap Pr.
— The Complete Correspondence of Sigmund Freud & Ernest Jones 1908-1939. 896p. (Orig.). (C). 1995. pap. 24.95 (*0-674-15424-X*) Belknap Pr.
Paske, Janet V., jt. auth. see Van Amber, Rita C.
Paske-Smith, Montague, ed. Japanese Traditions of Christianity: Being Some Old Translations from the Japanese, with British Consular Reports of the Persecutions of 1868-1872. LC 79-65368. (Studies in Japanese History & Civilization). 160p. 1979. reprint ed. text ed. 55.00 (*0-313-26983-1*, U6983) Greenwood.
***Paskett, Parley J.** Wild Mustangs. LC 86-13165. (Western Experience Ser.). reprint ed. pap. 43.10 (*0-7837-9256-5*, 2049996) Bks Demand.
Paskevicius, Mykolas. Mykolas Paskevicius. Lapkus, Danas, ed. & intro. by. LC 94-77355. (Illus.). 168p. (LIT.). 1995. 35.00 (*0-9617756-9-6*) Galerija.
Paskevska, Anna. Both Sides of the Mirror: The Science & Art of Ballet. 2nd ed. LC 79-51362. 224p. 1992. pap. 18. 95 (*0-87127-180-X*) Princeton Bk Co.
Paski, Robert B. Shallow Faith. 214p. (Orig.). 1994. pap. 8.95 (*1-56901-146-X*) NW Pub.
Paskins, Barrie, ed. Ethics & European Security. LC 86-3580. 192p. 1986. text ed. 49.95 (*0-86569-146-0*, Auburn Hse) Greenwood.
***Pasko.** Superman Story, Vol. 1. 1987. mass mkt. 3.99 (*0-8125-7742-6*) Tor Bks.
Pasko, jt. auth. see Puckett, Kelly.
Paskoff, L. & Kelletat, D., eds. Geomorphology & Geoecology: Coastal Dynamics & Environments. (Annals of Geomorphology Ser.: Suppl. 81). (Illus.). 199p. 1991. pap. text ed. 82.50 (*3-443-21081-3*, Pub. by Gebrueder Borntraeger GW) Lubrecht & Cramer.
Paskoff, Paul, ed. The Iron & Steel Industry in the Nineteenth Century. (Encyclopedia of American Business History & Biography Ser.). (Illus.). 432p. 1988. 85.00 (*0-8160-1890-1*) Facts on File.
Paskoff, Paul F. & Wilson, Daniel J., eds. The Cause of the South: Selections from De Bow's Review, 1846-1867. LC 81-23680. (Library of Southern Civilization). xii, 306p. (C). 1982. pap. text ed. 12.95 (*0-8071-1039-6*) La State U Pr.
Paskov, Victor. Ballad for Georg Hennig. Sturm, Robert, tr. 144p. 1990. 32.00 (*0-7206-0796-5*, Pub. by Peter Owen Ltd UK) Dufour.
Paskow, Irwin, jt. auth. see Paskow, Joan.
Paskow, Joan & Paskow, Irwin. VIP Investments: How to Make Big Money from Real Estate's Sleeping Giants. 1977. 69.50 (*0-13-942128-9*) Exec Reports.
Paskuly, Steven, ed. see Hoss, Rudolf.
Pasle-green, Jeanne & Haynes, Jim, eds. Hello, I Love You! Voices from Within the Sexual Revolution. LC 77-77389. 175p. (Orig.). 1977. pap. 7.95 (*0-87810-032-6*) Times Change.
Pasler, Friedrich A. Radiology. Hassell, Thomas M. & Hefti, Arthur F., trs. LC 92-49748. (Color Atlas of Dental Medicine Ser.). 1992. 149.00 (*0-86577-460-9*) Thieme Med Pubs.
Pasler, Jann, ed. Confronting Stravinsky: Man, Musician, & Modernist. 1986. pap. 17.00 (*0-520-06466-6*) U CA Pr.
Pasler, Margaret C., jt. auth. see Pasler, Rudolph J.
Pasler, Rudolph J. & Pasler, Margaret C. The New Jersey Federalists. LC 73-22570. 256p. 1975. 36.50 (*0-8386-1525-2*) Fairleigh Dickinson.
Pasley, Dorothy L. Who Is Jesus? 1993. 7.95 (*0-533-10318-5*) Vantage.
Pasley, Fred. Al Capone: The Biography of a Self-Made Man. LC 78-150196. (Select Bibliographies Reprint Ser.). 1977. reprint ed. 30.95 (*0-8369-5709-1*) Ayer.
Pasley, Jane S. Let Me Be Your Friend... (Illus.). 52p. (Orig.). 1989. pap. text ed. 6.95 (*0-685-29398-X*) J S Pasley.
Pasley, Kay & Ihinger-Tallman, Marilyn, eds. Remarriage & Stepparenting: Current Research & Theory. LC 87-17718. (Perspectives on Marriage & the Family Ser.). 323p. 1987. pap. text ed. 20.95 (*0-89862-922-5*) Guilford Pr.
— Stepparenting: Issues in Theory, Research, & Practice. LC 93-25073. (Contributions in Sociology Ser.: No. 108). 304p. 1994. text ed. 59.95 (*0-313-28502-0*, PSO/, Greenwood Pr) Greenwood.
Pasley, Malcolm. Germany: A Companion to German Studies. 2nd ed. 700p. 1982. pap. 23.50 (*0-416-33660-4*, 3698) Routledge Chapman & Hall.
Pasley, Malcolm, ed. see Kafka, Franz.
Pasley, Sally. The Tao of Cooking. LC 82-80235. 240p. (Orig.). 1982. pap. 11.95 (*0-89815-069-8*) Ten Speed Pr.
Pasley, Sally, jt. auth. see Williams, Dorothy.
Pasley, Virginia & Green, Jane. You Can Do Anything with Crepes. write for info. (*0-318-59652-0*) S&S Trade.
Paslick, Robert H., tr. see Gadamer, Hans-Georg.
Pasmantier, Jeanne, jt. auth. see Resnick, Seymour.
Pasmett, Doris. Lies. 336p. (Orig.). 1993. mass mkt. 4.99 (*0-515-10991-6*) Jove Pubns.
Pasmore, William A. Creative Strategic Change: Designing the Flexible, High-performing Organization. LC 93-39202. 1994. text ed. 29.95 (*0-471-59729-5*) Wiley.
— Designing Effective Organizations: The Sociotechnical Systems Perspective. LC 87-29521. (Organizational Assessment & Change Ser.). 200p. 1988. text ed. 52.50 (*0-471-88785-4*) Wiley.
Pasmore, William A., jt. ed. see Woodman, Richard W.
Pasnak, R., jt. ed. see Howe, M. L.
***Pasnak, William.** Exit Stage Left. (Degrassi Book Ser.). (YA). 1995. pap. 4.95 (*1-55028-015-5*) Formac Dist Ltd.
— Mimi & the Ginger Princess. (Blue Kite Adventure Ser.). (Illus.). 96p. (J). (gr. 3-6). Date not set. 16.95 (*1-55028-107-0*, Pub. by J Lorimer CN) Formac Dist Ltd.
— Sink or Swim. (J). (gr. 3-8). 1995. pap. 8.95 (*1-55028-480-0*) Formac Dist Ltd.
— Sink or Swim. (J). (gr. 3-8). 1995. bds. 16.95 (*1-55028-481-9*) Formac Dist Ltd.
Pasnau, Robert O. Diagnosis & Treatment of Anxiety Disorders. LC 84-447. 272p. 1984. text ed. 31.00 (*0-88048-022-X*, 48-022-X) Am Psychiatric.

PQ

Paso, Alfonso. Blue Heaven. 1962. pap. 4.75 (*0-8222-0128-3*) Dramatists Play.
— Oh, Mama! No Papa! adapted ed. 1962. pap. 4.75 (*0-8222-0839-3*) Dramatists Play.
— Recipe for a Crime. adapted ed. 1962. pap. 4.75 (*0-8222-0936-5*) Dramatists Play.
***Pasolini & Mazza.** Pier Paoli Pasolini: Poetry. Date not set. per. 15.95 (*0-920428-73-8*, Pub. by Exile Edits CN) InBook.
Pasolini, Pier P. Heretical Empiricism. Barnett, Louise K., ed. & tr. by. Lawton, Ben, tr. LC 85-45070. 352p. 1988. 39.95 (*0-253-32717-2*) Ind U Pr.
— Roman Poems: Bilingual Edition. Ferlinghetti, Lawrence & Valente, Francesca, trs. (Pocket Poets Ser.: No. 41). (Illus.). 96p. (Orig.). (ENG & ITA.). 1986. pap. 7.95 (*0-87286-187-2*) City Lights.
— A Violent Life. Weaver, William, tr. LC 90-53485. 320p. (Orig.). 1992. reprint ed. pap. 13.00 (*0-679-73505-4*) Pantheon.
Pasolini, Pier-Pado. Oedipus Rex. (Illus.). 150p. (Orig.). 1988. pap. 9.95 (*0-571-12614-6*) Faber & Faber.
Pasour, Ernest C., Jr. Agriculture & the State: Market Processes & Bureaucracy. LC 89-11067. (Independent Institute Ser.). 288p. (Orig.). 1990. 39.95 (*0-8419-1272-6*) Holmes & Meier.
— Agriculture & the State: Market Processes & Bureaucracy. (Independent Studies in Political Economy). 279p. (Orig.). (C). 1993. reprint ed. pap. 16.95 (*0-945999-29-1*) Independent Inst.
Pasqariello, Ron. The Almanac of Quotable Quotes from 1990. 300p. 1991. 29.95 (*0-685-38168-4*, Busn); pap. 9.95 (*0-685-38169-2*, Busn) P-H.
Pasqua, Thomas M., jt. auth. see Robinette, Richard.
Pasquaiello, Ronald D. Almanac of Quotable Quotes from 1991. 1992. pap. 12.95 (*0-13-031717-9*, Busn) P-H.
Pasqual, Jack, jt. auth. see Maloney, Pat, Sr.
Pasqual, Sandra, ed. see Evans, Gwendolyn L.
Pasquale, Bruno, Jr. The Great Chicago-Style Pizza Cookbook. (Illus.). 148p. 1983. pap. 12.95 (*0-8092-5730-0*); pap. 95.40 (*0-8092-5508-1*) Contemp Bks.
Pasquale, Frank. Basic Drafting. LC 79-730980. 1980. student ed 6.00 (*0-8064-0283-0*, 720); audio 299.00 (*0-8064-0284-9*) Bergwall.
— Basic Drafting II. LC 80-730729. 1981. student ed 6.00 (*0-8064-0285-7*, 721); audio 289.00 (*0-8064-0286-5*) Bergwall.
Pasquale, Robert C., Jr. The Car Club Directory. 2nd ed. 1991. 12.95 (*0-9631114-0-X*) Genesis CA.
Pasqualetti, Martin, ed. Nuclear Decommissioning: Public Links to a Technical Task. 272p. 1990. 60.00 (*0-415-03480-9*, A4225) Routledge.
Pasquali. Mental Health Nursing, a Holistic Approach. 3rd ed. (Illus.). 976p. 1989. 43.95 (*0-8016-3578-0*) Mosby Yr Bk.
Pasqualin, A. & Da Pian, R., eds. New Trends in Management of Cerebro-Vascular Malformation: Proceedings of the International Conference, Verona, Italy, June 8-12, 1992. LC 94-7680. 1994. 235.00 (*0-387-82528-2*) Spr-Verlag.
Pasqualin, A. & DaPian, R., eds. New Trends in Management of Cerebro-Vascular Malformation: Proceedings of the International Conference, Verona, Italy, June 8-12, 1992. LC 94-7680. 1994. write for info. (*3-211-82528-2*) Spr-Verlag.
Pasqualini & Scholler. Hormones & Fetal Pathophysiology. 808p. 1992. 199.00 (*0-8247-8651-3*) Dekker.
Pasqualini, J. R., ed. Recent Advances in Steroid Biochemistry, Vol. 2. LC 75-4332. 312p. 1975. pap. 67.00 (*0-08-019709-4*, Pub. by Pergamon Repr UK) Franklin.
— Recent Advances in Steroid Biochemistry, Vol. 3. LC 75-4332. 1977. 149.00 (*0-08-021307-3*, Pub. by Pergamon Repr UK) Franklin.
Pasqualini, Jean. Prisonnier de Mao, 2 vols., 1. 1976. pap. 10.95 (*0-7859-4062-6*) Fr & Eur.
— Prisonnier de Mao, 2 vols., 2. 1976. pap. 10.95 (*0-7859-4063-4*) Fr & Eur.
Pasqualini, Jorge R., ed. Receptors & Mechanism of Action of Steroid Hormones, 2 pts., Pt. 1. LC 76-40597. (Modern Pharmacology-Toxicology Ser.: No. 8). (Illus.). 325p. reprint ed. pap. 87.80 (*0-7837-0679-0*, 2041013) Bks Demand.
— Receptors & Mechanism of Action of Steroid Hormones, 2 pts., Pt. 2. LC 76-40597. (Modern Pharmacology-Toxicology Ser.: No. 8). (Illus.). 439p. reprint ed. pap. 125.20 (*0-7837-0680-4*) Bks Demand.
Pasquarelli, N., jt. auth. see Ibarrola, J.
***Pasquarette, Chris.** Pac-Rim Sourcebook. (Cyberpunk Ser.). (Illus.). 160p. 1994. 12.00 (*0-937279-46-3*, CP3311) R Talsorian.
Pasquariella, Susan K., ed. Union List of Population-Family Planning Periodicals. 135p. 1978. 25.00 (*0-318-03477-8*, LC-78-60528); 10.00 (*0-318-03478-6*) Assn Pop Lib.
Pasquariello, Anthony M., ed. see Lopez-Rubio, Jose.
Pasquariello, Ron. Almanac of Quotable Quotes from 1990. 1991. 29.95 (*0-13-026386-9*); pap. 9.95 (*0-685-47732-0*); pap. 9.95 (*0-13-026378-8*) P-H.
Pasquariello, Ronald. Tax Justice: Social & Moral Aspects of American Tax Policy. LC 85-3250. (Illus.). 132p. (Orig.). 1985. lib. bdg. 41.00 (*0-8191-4606-4*); pap. text ed. 14.00 (*0-8191-4607-2*) U Pr of Amer.
***Pasquella.** Comfort of Dreams: Photographs. Date not set. per. 19.95 (*0-85449-140-6*, Pub. by Gay Mens Pr UK) InBook.
Pasquero, Fedele. I Will Follow You: Meditations on Jesus. Lane, Edmund C., tr. LC 92-3174. 200p. (Orig.). 1992. pap. 9.95 (*0-8189-0647-2*) Alba.
Pasquier, Alain. The Louvre: Greek, Etruscan & Roman Antiquities. (Illus.). 96p. 1991. 19.95 (*1-870248-79-1*) Scala Books.
Pasquier, C., et al, eds. Oxidative Stress, Cell Activation & Viral Infection. LC 93-44396. (Molecular & Cell Biology Updates Ser.). (Illus.). 376p. 1993. 74.00 (*0-8176-2941-6*) Birkhauser.
Pasquier, J. & Trnka, L. Use Radioactive Isotopes in Tuberculosis Research: Proceedings of International Symposium, Prague, May 1963. LC 64-24961. 1965. 84.00 (*0-08-010951-9*, Pub. by Pergamon Repr UK) Franklin.
Pasquier, Jacqueline du. Les Arts Decoratifs Bordelais: Mobiliers et Objets Domestiques (1714-1895) 208p. (FRE.). 1993. lib. bdg. 195.00 (*0-7859-3647-5*, 2859171142) Fr & Eur.
Pasquier, Roger F., ed. Conservation of New World Parrots: Proceedings of the ICBP Parrot Working Group Meeting, St. Lucia, 1980. 486p. 1981. text ed. 22.50 (*0-87474-745-7*, PANPP) Smithsonian.
Pasquier, Roger F. & Farrand, John, Jr. Masterpieces of Bird Art: Seven Hundred Years of Ornithological Illustration. (Illus.). 256p. 1991. 95.00 (*1-55859-134-6*) Abbeville Pr.
***Pasquine, Ruth.** Fantastic & Imaginary Art. 44p. 1994. pap. 12.00 (*1-884240-05-4*) Arkansas Art Ctr.
***Pasquini, Katie.** Design & Make Your Own Contemporary Sampler Quilt. LC 94-22078. (Needlework Ser.). (Illus.). 64p. 1994. pap. text ed. 5.95 (*0-486-28197-3*) Dover.
— Mandala Quilt Designs. LC 94-40103. (Needlework Ser.). (Illus.). 112p. 1995. pap. text ed. 8.95 (*0-486-28491-3*) Dover.
— Three-Dimensional Design. LC 88-70657. (Illus.). 80p. (Orig.). 1988. pap. text ed. 16.95 (*0-914881-19-1*) C & T Pub.
Pasquini, Mark T., jt. auth. see Minkema, Douglas D.
Pasquini-Masopust, Katie. Isometric Perspective. Loft, Randi, ed. LC 92-53798. (Illus.). 80p. 1992. pap. 16.95 (*0-914881-46-9*) C & T Pub.
Pasquino, Gianfranco & McCarthy, Patrick, eds. The End of Post-War Politics in Italy: The Landmark 1992 Elections. 187p. (C). 1993. pap. text ed. 34.50 (*0-8133-8628-4*) Westview.
Pasquino, Gianfranco, jt. ed. see Hellman, Stephen M.
Pasquino, Gianfranco, jt. ed. see Hellman, Stephen.
Pasquino, Gianfranco, jt. ed. see Mershon, Carol.
Pass, Christopher & Lowes, Bryan. Business & Microeconomics: An Introduction to the Market Environment. LC 93-39826. (Elements of Business Ser.). 224p. 1994. 59.95x (*0-415-06845-2*, B3534) Routledge.
— Business & Microeconomics: An Introduction to the Market Environment. LC 93-39826. (Elements of Business Ser.). 1994. pap. 19.95 (*0-415-06846-0*, B0184) Routledge.
***Pass, Christopher, et al.** Business & Macroeconomics. LC 94-42204. (Elements of Business Ser.). 1995. write for info. (*0-415-12399-2*) Routledge.
— Harper Dictionary of Economics. LC 90-55512. (Illus.). 576p. 1991. pap. 14.00 (*0-06-461017-9*) HarpC.
***Pass, Christopher L., et al.** Business & Macroeconomics. LC 94-42204. (Elements of Business Ser.). 1995. pap. text ed. write for info. (*0-415-12400-X*) Routledge.
***Pass, Claudia W., ed. & intro.** Carolina Blessings. (Illus.). 288p. 1995. 17.95 (*0-9643051-0-0*) Chldrns Home Soc.
Pass, Destin. Scenes of Beautiful Japan: Memories of a U. S. Airman's 1969 Tour of Duty. LC 90-45924. (Illus.). 80p. (Orig.). 1990. pap. 9.95 (*0-912526-50-5*) Lib Res.
Pass, Dorie F. Everybody's Doing It...and Here's How to Quit. (Orig.). 1990. pap. 12.95 (*0-9625992-3-9*) Golden One Pub.
Pass, Dorie F. & Tegeler, Dorothy. Arizona Favorites: Southwest Traditional to Light Modern Cooking. LC 92-52501. (Illus.). 176p. (Orig.). 1992. pap. 8.95 (*0-935182-55-1*) Gem Guides Bk.
Pass, Gail. Surviving Sisters. 252p. 1989. reprint ed. pap. 8.95 (*0-941483-16-9*) Naiad Pr.
***Pass, Geoff & LaBossiere, Mike.** Protect & Serve. (Cyberpunk Ser.). (Illus.). 96p. (Orig.). 1992. pap. 10.00 (*0-937279-25-0*, CP3171) R Talsorian.
Pass, Joe. Joe Pass Guitar Chords. 1993. 4.95 (*0-87166-615-4*, 94108) Mel Bay.
— Joe Pass Guitar Style. 1993. 8.95 (*1-56222-005-5*, 94106) Mel Bay.
Pass, Joe & Ellis, Herb. Joe Pass & Herb Ellis Jazz Duets. 1993. 4.95 (*0-685-64242-9*, 94107) Mel Bay.
Pass, Linda D. Accepting the Readiness Idea. 40p. (Orig.). 1992. pap. text ed. 6.00 (*0-935493-84-0*) Programs Educ.
Pass, Michael, jt. auth. see Pass, Susan.
PASS Staff & Massey, Howard. The Complete Guide to MIDI Software. (Illus.). 228p. 1987. pap. 19.95 (*0-8256-1088-5*, AM65715) Music Sales.
Pass, Susan & Pass, Michael. Sexcess: Great Sex--Long Term Love: A Couples Guide. LC 93-23244. 1993. pap. 8.95 (*0-9636462-0-6*) Ivy St Pr.
Pass the Plate, Inc. Staff. Pass the Plate. Underhill, Alice & Stewart, Bobbie, eds. 520p. 1981. pap. 13.95 (*0-939114-13-5*) Pass the Plate.
Passafiume, John & Douglas, Michael. Digital Logic Design: Tutorials & Laboratory Exercises. 128p. 1984. Net. text ed. write for info. (*0-471-60345-7*) Wiley.
Passafiume, John F., jt. auth. see Michta, Andrew.
Passage, Charles E. Friedrich Schiller. LC 74-76129. (Literature & Life Ser.). (Illus.). 180p. (C). 1975. 19.95 (*0-8044-2734-8*, F Ungar Bks) Continuum.
Passage, Charles E., tr. see Goethe, Johann Wolfgang Von.
Passage, Charles E., tr. see Schiller, Friedrich.
Passalacqua, Carlos M. Antologia Poetica. LC 84-7594. (Illus.). 143p. (SPA.). 1985. pap. 5.00 (*0-8477-3234-7*) U of PR Pr.
— Noche, Fuente: Poesia. 2nd ed. LC 79-23317. (Illus.). 98p. 1981. 6.00 (*0-8477-3226-6*) U of PR Pr.
Passalacqua, Juan M. Dignidad y Jaiberia: Temer y Ser. 1993. pap. write for info. (*1-56758-023-8*) Edit Cultl.
Passamaneck, Marge. People Are Different, People Are the Same. 1983. pap. 3.25 (*0-89536-615-0*, 1629) CSS OH.
***Passamaneck, S. M. & Finley, M., eds.** Jewish Law Association Studies, Vol. VII: The Paris Conference Volume. 275p. 1994. 59.95 (*1-55540-899-0*, 150007) Scholars Pr GA.
Passamaneck, Stephen M., ed. see Bazak, Jacob.
Passamaneck, Stephen M., tr. see Karo, Joseph Ben Ephraim.
Passano, Eleanor P. An Index of the Source Records of Maryland: Genealogical, Biographical, Historical. LC 67-17943. 478p. 1994. reprint ed. 28.50 (*0-8063-0271-2*, 4400) Genealog Pub.
Passantino, Bob & Passantino, Gretchen. Satanism. (Guide to Cults & Religious Movements Ser.). 64p. 1994. 4.99 (*0-310-70451-0*) Zondervan.
— Witch Hunt: Biblical Solutions in the Search for Heretics. (Orig.). 1988. pap. 9.95 (*0-317-90599-6*) Lawson-Cook Pub.
Passantino, Erika D., ed. see Phillips Collection Staff.
Passantino, Gretchen, jt. auth. see Passantino, Bob.
Passantino, Gretchen, ed. see Snyder, Tom.
***Passantino, Sally.** Thomas & the Bulldozer. (Illus.). 64p. (Orig.). (J). 1994. pap. text ed. 7.50 (*1-56002-395-3*, Univ Edtns) Aegina Pr.
***Passarella, Lee.** Asrael. 25p. 1995. pap. 4.50 (*0-9647127-1-7*) Coreopsis Bks.
— Working from Memory. 20p. 1992. pap. 4.00 (*0-9647127-0-9*) Coreopsis Bks.
Passarelli, Anne B. Public Relations in Business, Government, & Society: A Bibliographic Guide. Wynar, Lubomyr R., ed. (Reference Sources in the Social Sciences Ser.). 225p. 1989. lib. bdg. 32.00 (*0-87287-741-8*) Libs Unl.
Passas, Nikos. Subsidizing Fraud: The Nature & Control of Subsidy Frauds in the EC. 250p. (C). 1996. text ed. 45.00 (*0-8133-8636-5*) Westview.
Passas, Nikos, ed. Organized Crime. (International Library of Criminology & Criminal Justice). 500p. 1995. 129.95 (*1-85521-437-7*, Pub. by Dartmth Pub UK) Ashgate Pub Co.
Passath, A. & Hoefler, H. Thyrotropin: Ultrasensitive TSH Measurement in Clinical Research & Diagnostics. Leb, G. et al, eds. (Illus.). x, 361p. (C). 1987. 113.85 (*0-89925-209-5*); lib. bdg. 96.00 (*0-685-43896-1*) De Gruyter.
Passauer, L. K., jt. auth. see Christian, N. L.
Passchier, C. W., et al. Field Geology of High-Grade Gneiss Terrains. (Illus.). 160p. 1990. pap. text ed. 20.00 (*0-387-53053-3*) Spr-Verlag.
Passcuant, P., ed. see International Congress of Pharmacology Staff.
Passe, Jeff. Elementary School Curriculum. 432p. (C). 1995. pap. text ed. write for info. (*0-697-20107-4*) Brown & Benchmark.
Passe-Smith, John T., jt. ed. see Seligson, Mitchell A.
Passe-Smith, John T., jt. auth. see Williams, Edward J.
Passek, Jean-Loup. Dictionary of the French Cinema: Dictionnaire du Cinema Francais. 867p. 1987. 28.95 (*0-8288-2602-1*, F11830) Fr & Eur.
— Dictionnaire du Cinema. 867p. (FRE.). 1986. 150.00 (*0-8288-2090-2*, F11830) Fr & Eur.
— Larousse Dictionnaire du Cinema. 800p. (FRE.). 1991. 175.00 (*0-8288-9476-0*) Fr & Eur.
Passekov, Vladimir P., jt. auth. see Svirezhev, Yuri M.
Passel, Anne. Your Words: Public & Private. 2nd ed. LC 81-40773. (Illus.). 248p. 1982. pap. text ed. 22.00 (*0-8191-1867-2*) U Pr of Amer.
***Passel, Charles F.** Ice: The Antarctic Diary of Charles F. Passel. Baughman, T. H., ed. & intro. by. (Illus.). 448p. 1995. 29.95 (*0-89672-347-X*) Tex Tech Univ Pr.
Passell, Jeffrey S., jt. ed. see Edmonston, Barry.
Passell, Peter. Essays in the Economics of Nineteenth Century American Land Policy. LC 75-2590. (Dissertations in American Economic History Ser.). (Illus.). 1975. 19.95 (*0-405-07212-0*) Ayer.
— How to Read the Financial Pages. rev. ed. 160p. 1993. mass mkt. 5.99 (*0-446-36504-1*) Warner Bks.
Passell, Peter, jt. auth. see Lee, Susan P.
Passer, Harold C. The Electrical Manufacturers, 1875-1900: A Study in Competition, Entrepreneurship, Technical Change, & Economic Growth. LC 72-5066. (Technology & Society Ser.). (Illus.). 436p. 1979. reprint ed. 40.95 (*0-405-04717-7*) Ayer.
Passerini, Edward. The Curve of the Future: Food-Trees, Solar Cars, War-Math, the Fun Economy, & Other Essential Knowledge for a... 320p. 1992. pap. text ed. 8.00 (*0-8403-7381-3*) Kendall-Hunt.
Passerini, Luisa. Fascism in Popular Memory: The Cultural Experience of the Turin Working Class. Lumley, Robert & Bloomfield, Jude, trs. (Studies in Modern Capitalism). (Illus.). 246p. 1987. 59.95 (*0-521-30290-0*) Cambridge U Pr.
Passerini, Luisa, et al, eds. International Yearbook of Oral History & Life Stories Vol. 1: Memory & Totalitarianism. (International Yearbook of Oral History & Life Stories). 224p. 1993. 55.00 (*0-19-820248-2*) OUP.
Passeron, Rene. Lexikon des Surrealismus. (GER.). 1975. 45.00 (*0-8288-5923-X*, M7220) Fr & Eur.
Passeron, Rene, jt. auth. see Biro, Adam.
Passeron, Roger. Cathelin Lithographs, 1957-89, 2 vols. (Illus.). Set, 218p., 214p. 400.00 (*1-55660-212-X*) A Wofsy Fine Arts.
— Impressionist Prints. (Illus.). 224p. 1988. 100.00 (*0-914427-11-3*, Tabard Pr) W S Konecky Assocs.
Passeron, Roger & Josselin, Jean-Francois. Cassigneul's Graphic Work, Nineteen Sixty-Five to Eighty-Eight: Catalogue Raisonne. (Illus.). 196p. (ENG & FRE.). 1989. 475.00 (*1-55660-091-7*) A Wofsy Fine Arts.
Passes, David. Dragons: Truth, Myth & Legend. LC 92-44745. (Illus.). 48p. (J). (gr. 7 up). 1993. 12.95 (*0-307-17500-6*, Artsts Writrs) Western Pub.
Passet, Joanne, jt. auth. see Maack, Mary N.
Passet, Joanne E. Cultural Crusaders: Women Librarians in the American West, 1900-1917. LC 93-46764. 227p. 1994. 40.00x (*0-8263-1530-5*) U of NM Pr.
Passett, Barry A. Leadership Development for Public Service. LC 70-149755. 149p. reprint ed. pap. 42.50 (*0-685-23773-7*, 2032855) Bks Demand.
Passfield, Sidney. The History of Trade Unionism. LC 75-173495. reprint ed. 20.00 (*0-404-06885-5*) AMS Pr.
Passfield, Sidney J. & Webb, Beatrice. Methods of Social Study. LC 67-30866. 1968. reprint ed. 37.50 (*0-678-00351-3*) Kelley.
Passfield, Sidney J. & Webb, Beatrice P. Industrial Democracy. LC 79-173496. reprint ed. 35.00 (*0-404-06886-3*) AMS Pr.
Passi, Delia & Biza, Ted. A Couple's Guide to Keeping the Relationship Alive. 1994. pap. write for info. (*0-9641081-2-7*) Tedel Pubns.
— Your Guide to Finding the Right One & Being the Right One, Book 1. (Illus.). 70p. 1994. 8.95 (*0-9641081-0-0*); pap. 5.95 (*0-9641081-1-9*) Tedel Pubns.
Passikoff, Barbara & Witt, Verla. Fitness Workbook: A Step-by-Step Guide to Individualized Fitness. 2nd ed. 80p. (C). 1994. pap. text ed., spiral bd. 16.95 (*0-8403-9264-8*) Kendall-Hunt.
Passin, Herbert. Japanese Education: A Bibliography of Materials in the English Language. LC 74-93507. (Columbia University Publications of the Center for Education in Industrial Nations Ser.). 149p. reprint ed. pap. 42.50 (*0-317-28839-3*, 2017766) Bks Demand.
Passin, Herbert, ed. see Cohen, Theodore.
Passin, Herbert, et al. Japan in the Nineteen Eighties, Vol. II. LC 83-61309. (Papers on International Issues: No. 6). (Illus.). 73p. (Orig.) (C). 1983. pap. text ed. 5.00 (*0-935082-05-0*) Southern Ctr Intl Stud.
Passin, Roy. Sensational Sandwiches. Levine, Marian, ed. 64p. (Orig.). 1990. pap. 3.49 (*0-942320-37-9*) Am Cooking.
Passin, Thomas B., jt. auth. see Reid, Christopher E.
Passingham, Bernard & Harmer, Caroline. Law & Practice in Matrimonial Causes. 4th ed. 1985. 99.00 (*0-406-63708-3*); pap. 60.00 (*0-406-63707-5*, U.K.) Butterworth Legal Pubs.
Passingham, R. The Frontal Lobes & Voluntary Action. (Oxford Psychology Ser.: Vol. 21). (Illus.). 328p. 1993. 59.95 (*0-19-852185-5*) OUP.
***Passingham, R. E.** The Frontal Lobes & Voluntary Action. (Oxford Psychology Ser.: Vol. 21). 304p. 1995. reprint ed. pap. 25.95 (*0-19-852364-5*) OUP.
Passingham, W. J. Romance of London's Underground. LC 72-80705. (Illus.). 1972. reprint ed. 36.95 (*0-405-08839-6*) Ayer.
Passini, Romedi. Wayfinding in Architecture. 234p. 1984. text ed. 49.95 (*0-442-27590-0*) Van Nos Reinhold.
— Wayfinding in Architecture. (Illus.). 240p. 1992. pap. 34.95 (*0-442-01095-8*) Van Nos Reinhold.
Passino, Roberto, jt. ed. see Patterson, James W.
Passion, Rich. Nutrients for Love: A Nutritional Approach for Achieving Optimum Mental & Physical Functioning. 52p. (Orig.). (C). 1989. lib. bdg. write for info. (*0-318-66087-3*); pap. 5.95 (*0-9624054-1-8*) Loveglo & Comfort.
Passioura, J. B., jt. ed. see Turner, N. C.
Passlack, M., et al, eds. Infrared Spectral Data: A Living COM-Microfiche Collection. (Illus.). 1986. lib. bdg. 1, 185.00 (*0-89573-447-8*) VCH Pubs.
Passler, David L. Time, Form & Style in Boswell's Life of Johnson. LC 70-151585. (Yale Studies in English: No. 155). 180p. reprint ed. 51.30 (*0-8357-9591-8*, 2013384) Bks Demand.
Passman, D. Group Rings, Crossed Products & Galois Theory. LC 86-1177. (CBMS Regional Conference Series in Mathematics: No. 64). 71p. 1986. pap. text ed. 18.00 (*0-8218-0714-5*, CBMS-64) Am Math.
Passman, Donald. All You Need to Know. 1994. 25.00 (*0-685-68780-5*) S&S Trade.
— A Course in Ring Theory. (C). 1991. text ed. 60.00 (*0-534-13776-8*) Van Nos Reinhold.
— Infinite Crossed Products. (Pure & Applied Mathematics Ser.). 400p. 1989. text ed. 85.00 (*0-12-546390-1*) Acad Pr.
Passman, Donald S. The Algebraic Structure of Group Rings. LC 84-15403. 750p. (C). 1985. reprint ed. lib. bdg. 73.50 (*0-89874-789-9*) Krieger.
— All You Need to Know about the Music Business. 1991. pap. 24.95 (*0-671-76139-0*) S&S Trade.
— All You Need to Know about the Music Business. 2nd ed. 1994. 25.00 (*0-671-88304-6*) S&S Trade.
— Infinite Group Rings. LC 72-163311. (Pure & Applied Mathematics Ser.: No. 6). 159p. reprint ed. pap. 45.40 (*0-7837-2638-4*, 2042991) Bks Demand.
Passman, S. Scientific & Technological Communication. LC 74-91466. 1969. 67.00 (*0-08-006631-3*, Pub. by Pergamon Repr UK) Franklin.
Passmore, Gregory, jt. ed. see Mundy, Wanda M.
Passmore, J. A. Moore: Ancestors & Descendants of Andrew Moore, 1612-1897. (Illus.). 1599p. 1991. reprint ed. lib. bdg. 189.00 (*0-8328-1799-6*); reprint ed. pap. 179.00 (*0-8328-1800-3*) Higginson Bk Co.
Passmore, J. Laurence, jt. auth. see Horne, Arthur M.
Passmore, Jacki. The Book of Ice Creams & Sorbets. LC 86-81043. 128p. 1987. pap. 9.95 (*0-89586-503-3*) Price Stern.
— Complete Spanish Cookbook. 416p. 1993. 34.95 (*0-8048-1823-1*) C E Tuttle.
— The Noodle Shop Cookbook. LC 94-1218. 1995. text ed. 25.00 (*0-02-594705-2*) Macmillan.

An Asterisk (*) at the beginning of an entry indicates that the title is appearing in BIP for the first time.

Passmore, Jackie. Asia the Beautiful Cookbook. LC 16-4. (Beautiful Cookbook Ser.). 256p. 1992. 45.00 (*0-00-255115-2*) Collins SF.
— Wok Cookbook. LC 87-13605. 1992. 12.99 (*0-517-64756-7*) Random Hse Value.
Passmore, John. Perfectability of Man. LC 77-129625. 1978. text ed. 25.00 (*0-684-15521-4*, Scribners) S&S Trade.
— Recent Philosophers. LC 85-5105. 173p. (C). 1985. 29.95 (*0-87548-448-4*) Open Court.
— Recent Philosophers. 1991. pap. 14.95 (*0-8126-9142-3*) Open Court.
— Recent Philosophers. braille ed. 475p. 1992. vinyl bd. 38.00 (*1-56956-083-8*, BR8754) W A T Braille.
— Serious Art. 302p. (C). 1991. 49.95 (*0-8126-9181-4*); pap. 19.95 (*0-8126-9182-2*) Open Court.
***Passmore, Nancy F., ed.** The Lunar Calendar: Dedicated to the Goddess in Her Many Guises. (Illus.). 32p. 1994. 15.00 (*1-877920-05-3*) Luna Pr MA.
Passmore, R., et al. Handbook on Human Nutritional Requirements. 1974. pap. 4.80 (*92-4-140061-7*) World Health.
Passmore, Reginald, et al, eds. William Cullen & the 18th Century Medical World. (Illus.). 256p. 1991. text ed. 49.00 (*0-7486-0302-6*, Pub. by Edinburgh U Pr UK) Col U Pr.
Passoli, Robert. Book on the Open Theatre. LC 78-81296. 1970. 7.50 (*0-672-50775-7*, Bobbs) Macmillan.
Passonneau, Janet V. & Lowry, Oliver H., eds. Enzymatic Analysis: A Practical Guide. LC 92-28742. (Illus.). 400p. 1993. 79.50 (*0-89603-238-8*) Humana.
Passons, W. Gestalt Approaches in Counseling. LC 74-22223. (C). 1975. pap. text ed. 33.25 (*0-03-089421-2*) HB Coll Pubs.
Passos, John D. Grand Design. 1977. reprint ed. lib. bdg. 26.95x (*0-89244-036-8*) Queens Hse-Focus Serv.
— Streets of Night. Clark, Michael, ed. LC 88-43406. 224p. 1990. 39.50 (*0-945636-02-4*) Susquehanna U Pr.
Passow, A. Harry, jt. ed. see Flaxman, Erwin.
Passow, Harry, ed. Developing Programs for the Educationally Disadvantaged. LC 67-19026. reprint ed. pap. 95.00 (*0-317-41882-3*, 2026051) Bks Demand.
Passow, Harry A., ed. see Work Conference on Curriculum & Teaching in Depressed Urban Areas Staff.
Passow, Harry A., ed. see Work Conference on Urban Education Staff.
Passow, Heidi. But I Can't Eat That: Kitchen Tested Recipes for People with Multiple Allergies. (Illus.). 240p. 1993. pap. 19.99 (*0-9637260-9-9*) Dragon Express.
Passow, Hermann, jt. ed. see Bamberg, Ernst.
***Passport.** Getting to Know the United States. 2nd ed. 1995. 8.95 (*0-8442-0724-1*) NTC Pub Grp.
— Passport's Road Atlas: Europe. 1991. pap. 16.95 (*0-8442-9499-3*, Passport Bks) NTC Pub Grp.
Passport Books Editors. Apredamos Ingles Diccionario Illustrado. (J). (gr. 4-7). 1994. 9.95 (*0-8442-7489-5*, Passport Bks) NTC Pub Grp.
— Let's Learn Hebrew Picture Dictionary. (J). (gr. 4-7). 1993. 11.95 (*0-8442-8490-4*, Natl Textbk) NTC Pub Grp.
Passport Books Staff. California: Trip Planner & Guide. 1994. pap. 14.95 (*0-8442-9216-8*, Passport Bks) NTC Pub Grp.
— Christmas in Russia. 1993. 11.95 (*0-8442-4291-8*, Passport Bks) NTC Pub Grp.
— Complete Multilingual Dictionary of Aviation & Aeronautical Terminology. 1994. 49.95 (*0-8442-9109-9*) NTC Pub Grp.
— Concise Dictionary of Phrase & Fable. 1993. pap. 11.95 (*0-8442-3901-1*, Teach Yourslf) NTC Pub Grp.
— Diccionario Practico de la Lengua Espanola del Nuevo Mundo: Practical Dictionary of the Spanish. 1993. 9.95 (*0-8442-7968-4*, Passport Bks) NTC Pub Grp.
— Egypt: A Complete Guide. 1989. pap. 12.95 (*0-8442-9700-3*, Passport Bks) NTC Pub Grp.
— Essential Amsterdam. (Essential Travel Guides Ser.). 128p. 1994. pap. 7.95 (*0-8442-8900-0*, Passport Bks) NTC Pub Grp.
— Essential California. (Essential Travel Guides Ser.). 128p. 1994. pap. 7.95 (*0-8442-8904-3*, Passport Bks) NTC Pub Grp.
— Essential Czechoslovakia Republic. (Essential Travel Guides Ser.). 128p. 1994. pap. 7.95 (*0-8442-8905-1*, Passport Bks) NTC Pub Grp.
— Essential Denmark. (Essential Travel Guides Ser.). 128p. 1994. pap. 7.95 (*0-8442-8907-8*, Passport Bks) NTC Pub Grp.
— Essential Egypt. (Essential Travel Guides Ser.). 128p. 1994. pap. 7.95 (*0-8442-8908-6*, Passport Bks) NTC Pub Grp.
— Essential Hong Kong. (Essential Travel Guides Ser.). 128p. 1994. pap. 7.95 (*0-8442-8913-2*, Passport Bks) NTC Pub Grp.
— Essential Hungary. (Essential Travel Guides Ser.). 128p. 1994. pap. 7.95 (*0-8442-8914-0*, Passport Bks) NTC Pub Grp.
— Essential Istanbul. (Essential Travel Guides Ser.). 128p. 1994. pap. 7.95 (*0-8442-8916-7*, Passport Bks) NTC Pub Grp.
— Essential Jerusalem. (Essential Travel Guides Ser.). 128p. 1994. pap. 7.95 (*0-8442-8918-3*, Passport Bks) NTC Pub Grp.
— Essential London. (Essential Travel Guides Ser.). 128p. 1994. pap. 7.95 (*0-8442-8919-1*, Passport Bks) NTC Pub Grp.
— Essential Mainland Greece. (Essential Travel Guides Ser.). 128p. 1994. pap. 7.95 (*0-8442-8911-6*, Passport Bks) NTC Pub Grp.
— Essential New York. (Essential Travel Guides Ser.). 128p. 1994. pap. 7.95 (*0-8442-8925-6*, Passport Bks) NTC Pub Grp.
— Essential Orlando & Disney World. (Essential Travel Guides Ser.). 128p. 1994. pap. 7.95 (*0-8442-8926-4*, Passport Bks) NTC Pub Grp.
— Essential Paris. (Essential Travel Guides Ser.). 128p. 1994. pap. 7.95 (*0-8442-8927-2*, Passport Bks) NTC Pub Grp.
— Essential Portugal. (Essential Travel Guides Ser.). 128p. 1994. pap. 7.95 (*0-8442-8928-0*, Passport Bks) NTC Pub Grp.
— Essential Provence. (Essential Travel Guides Ser.). 128p. 1994. pap. 7.95 (*0-8442-8929-9*, Passport Bks) NTC Pub Grp.
— Essential Rome. (Essential Travel Guides Ser.). 128p. 1994. pap. 7.95 (*0-8442-8930-2*, Passport Bks) NTC Pub Grp.
— Essential Scotland. (Essential Travel Guides Ser.). 128p. 1994. pap. 7.95 (*0-8442-8932-9*, Passport Bks) NTC Pub Grp.
— Essential Thailand. (Essential Travel Guides Ser.). 128p. 1994. pap. 7.95 (*0-8442-8935-3*, Passport Bks) NTC Pub Grp.
— Essential Toronto. (Essential Travel Guides Ser.). 128p. 1994. pap. 7.95 (*0-8442-8936-1*, Passport Bks) NTC Pub Grp.
— Everyday Indonesian. 1993. pap. 11.95 (*0-8442-9913-8*, Passport Bks) NTC Pub Grp.
— France: Trip Planner & Guide. 1994. pap. 16.95 (*0-8442-9217-6*, Passport Bks) NTC Pub Grp.
— Greece: Trip Planner & Guide. 1994. pap. 16.95 (*0-8442-9218-4*, Passport Bks) NTC Pub Grp.
— Handbook for Multilingual Business Writing. 360p. (ENG, FRE, GER, ITA & SPA.). 1994. 24.95 (*0-8442-9121-8*, NTC Busn Bks) NTC Pub Grp.
— Handbook for Multilingual Business Writing. 2nd ed. 360p. (ENG, FRE, GER, ITA & SPA.). 1994. pap. 17.95 (*0-8442-9122-6*, NTC Busn Bks) NTC Pub Grp.
— Italy: Trip Planner & Guide. 1994. pap. 16.95 (*0-8442-9219-2*, Passport Bks) NTC Pub Grp.
— Just Enough Hungarian: How to Get by & Be Easily Understood. 1992. pap. 4.95 (*0-8442-9519-1*, Passport Bks) NTC Pub Grp.
— Kenya, Nature's Bounty. 1992. pap. 14.95 (*0-8442-9688-0*, Passport Bks) NTC Pub Grp.
— Koh Samui & Environs: Thailand's Tropical Haven. 1992. pap. 14.95 (*0-8442-9698-8*, Passport Bks) NTC Pub Grp.
— Let's Learn English Picture Dictionary. (Illus.). (J). (gr. 4-7). 1992. 9.95 (*0-8442-9114-5*) NTC Pub Grp.
— Malaysia: A Complete Guide. 1989. pap. 12.95 (*0-8442-9719-4*, Passport Bks) NTC Pub Grp.
— Map of France. 1987. pap. 9.95 (*0-8442-9592-2*) NTC Pub Grp.
— Map of Italy. 1987. pap. 9.95 (*0-8442-9594-9*) NTC Pub Grp.
— New Zealand: A Complete Guide. 1989. pap. 12.95 (*0-8442-9722-4*, Passport Bks) NTC Pub Grp.
— Passport Road Atlas: Europe. 2nd ed. 1994. pap. 16.95 (*0-8442-9474-8*, Passport Bks) NTC Pub Grp.
— Resumes for College Students & Other Recent Graduates. 1992. pap. 9.95 (*0-8442-4150-4*, VGM Career Bks) NTC Pub Grp.
— Singapore: A Complete Guide. 1989. pap. 10.95 (*0-8442-9720-8*, Passport Bks) NTC Pub Grp.
— Teach Yourself Business German: A Complete Course for Beginners. 1993. pap. 12.95 (*0-8442-3783-3*, Teach Yourslf) NTC Pub Grp.
— Teach Yourself Business Japanese: A Complete Course for Beginners. 1993. pap. 14.95 (*0-8442-3808-2*, Teach Yourslf) NTC Pub Grp.
— Teach Yourself Finnish: A Complete Course for Beginners. 1993. pap. 16.95 (*0-8442-3765-5*, Teach Yourslf) NTC Pub Grp.
— Teach Yourself French Grammar: A Modern Guide. 278p. 1994. pap. 7.95 (*0-8442-3772-8*, Teach Yourslf) NTC Pub Grp.
— Teach Yourself Hindi: A Complete Course for Beginners. 302p. 1995. pap. 14.95 (*0-8442-3795-7*, Teach Yourslf) NTC Pub Grp.
— Teach Yourself Icelandic: A Complete Course for Beginners. 1993. pap. 14.95 (*0-8442-3797-3*, Teach Yourslf) NTC Pub Grp.
— Teach Yourself Indonesian: A Complete Course for Beginners. 1993. pap. 12.95 (*0-8442-3798-1*, Teach Yourslf) NTC Pub Grp.
— Teach Yourself Spanish: A Complete Course for Beginners. 314p. 1991. pap. 7.95 (*0-8442-3829-5*, Teach Yourslf) NTC Pub Grp.
— Teach Yourself Spanish: A Complete Course for Beginners. 1993. pap. 12.95 (*0-8442-3833-3*, Teach Yourslf) NTC Pub Grp.
— Teach Yourself Swahili: A Complete Course for Beginners. 224p. 1994. pap. 14.95 (*0-8442-3837-6*, Teach Yourslf) NTC Pub Grp.
— Teach Yourself Swedish: A Complete Course for Beginners. 322p. 1994. pap. 14.95 (*0-8442-3839-2*, Teach Yourslf) NTC Pub Grp.
— Teach Yourself Turkish: A Complete Course for Beginners. 1993. pap. 13.95 (*0-8442-3840-6*, Teach Yourslf) NTC Pub Grp.
— Teach Yourself Yoruba: A Complete Course for Beginners. 1993. pap. 14.95 (*0-8442-3843-0*, Teach Yourslf) NTC Pub Grp.
— Walking London. 1994. pap. 12.95 (*0-8442-9213-3*, Passport Bks) NTC Pub Grp.
— Walking Paris. 1994. pap. 12.95 (*0-8442-9214-1*, Passport Bks) NTC Pub Grp.
Passport Books Staff, ed. Let's Learn English: Picture Dictionary. (Illus.). 72p. (J). 1991. 9.95 (*0-8442-5453-3*, Natl Textbk) NTC Pub Grp.
— Let's Learn Italian: Picture Dictionary. (Illus.). 72p. 1991. 9.95 (*0-8442-8065-8*, Natl Textbk) NTC Pub Grp.
— Let's Learn Spanish: Picture Dictionary. (Illus.). 72p. (J). 1991. 9.95 (*0-8442-7558-1*, Natl Textbk) NTC Pub Grp.
***Passport Publications Staff & Cimperman, Wayne.** Passport to Palm Springs. 120p. 1994. 9.95 (*0-9645114-0-1*) Passprt Publ.
Passport Staff. Andalucia. 120p. 1993. pap. 17.95 (*0-8442-9970-7*, Passport Bks) NTC Pub Grp.
— Brittany. 120p. 1993. pap. 17.95 (*0-8442-9967-7*, Passport Bks) NTC Pub Grp.
— Italian Lakes. 120p. 1993. pap. 17.95 (*0-8442-9972-3*, Passport Bks) NTC Pub Grp.
— Provence & the Cote D'Azur. 120p. 1993. pap. 17.95 (*0-8442-9968-5*, Passport Bks) NTC Pub Grp.
— Swiss Alps. 120p. 1993. pap. 17.95 (*0-8442-9969-3*, Passport Bks) NTC Pub Grp.
— Tuscany & Umbria. 120p. 1993. pap. 17.95 (*0-8442-9971-5*, Passport Bks) NTC Pub Grp.
Passty, Jeanette N. Eros & Androgyny: The Legacy of Rose Macaulay. LC 85-46027. 1988. 34.50 (*0-8386-3284-X*) Fairleigh Dickinson.
Passuth, Krisztina. Moholy-Nagy. LC 83-50107. (Illus.). 300p. 1987. pap. 24.95 (*0-500-27449-5*) Thames Hudson.
Passuth, Laszlo. Tlaloc Weeps for Mexico. Hattyar, Harry, tr. 487p. 1987. 19.95 (*0-918872-02-2*) Pac Pub Hse.
Passwater, Richard. Selenium-Update: Good Health Guide. 1987. 1.95 (*0-87983-393-9*) Keats.
Passwater, Richard, ed. see Bland, Jeffrey.
Passwater, Richard, ed. see Lee, William H.
Passwater, Richard, ed. see Mindell, Earl R.
Passwater, Richard A. The Antioxidants. (Good Health Guide Ser.). (Orig.). 1985. pap. 2.50 (*0-87983-404-8*) Keats.
— A Beginner's Introduction to Vitamins: The Fundamental Necessities for Growth & Maintenance of Life. Mindell, Earl, ed. (Good Health Guide Ser.). 32p. 1983. pap. 2.50 (*0-87983-338-6*) Keats.
— Beta-Carotene. Mindell, Earl, ed. (Good Health Guide Ser.). 32p. 1984. pap. 2.50 (*0-87983-363-7*) Keats.
— Cancer Prevention & Its Nutritional Therapies. rev. ed. LC 78-57646. 250p. 1993. pap. 14.95 (*0-87983-607-5*) Keats.
— Chromium Picolinate. 1992. pap. 2.95 (*0-87983-588-5*) Keats.
— EPA-Marine Lipids: Good Health Guide Ser. Mindell, Earl, ed. 32p. (Orig.). 1982. pap. 1.95 (*0-87983-321-1*) Keats.
— Evening Primrose Oil. (Good Health Guide Ser.). 1982. pap. 2.50 (*0-87983-263-0*) Keats.
— Fish Oils Update. (Good Health Guide Ser.). 1987. pap. 2.50 (*0-87983-432-3*) Keats.
— GTF-Chromium. (Good Health Guide Ser.). 1982. pap. 2.50 (*0-87983-272-X*) Keats.
— The Longevity Factor: Chromium Picolinate. LC 93-5147. Orig. Title: Living Longer, Living Better, Slowing Aging with the Longevity Factor. 96p. (Orig.). 1993. pap. 4.95 (*0-87983-619-9*) Keats.
— New Super Antioxidant Plus. 1992. pap. 2.95 (*0-87983-589-3*) Keats.
— New Supernutrition. 1991. pap. 6.99 (*0-671-70071-5*) PB.
— Selenium As Food & Medicine. LC 80-82325. 200p. 1981. 10.95 (*0-87983-237-1*); pap. 2.95 (*0-87983-229-0*) Keats.
Passwater, Richard A. & Cranton, Elmer M. Trace Elements, Hair Analysis & Nutrition: Fact & Myth. LC 81-83892. 1983. 18.95 (*0-87983-348-3*); pap. 14.95 (*0-87983-265-7*) Keats.
Passwater, Richard A. & Kandaswami, Chithan. Pycnogenol: The Super "Protector" Nutrient. 96p. (Orig.). 1994. pap. 4.95 (*0-87983-648-2*) Keats.
Passwater, Richard A., ed. see Bland, Jeffrey.
Passwater, Richard A., ed. see Challem, Jack J.
Passwater, Richard A., ed. see DiCyan, Erwin.
Passwater, Richard A., ed. see Garrison, Robert, Jr.
Passwater, Richard A., ed. see Goldbeck, Nikki.
Passwater, Richard A., ed. see Heinerman, John.
Passwater, Richard A., ed. see Heyer, Albrecht A.
Passwater, Richard A., ed. see Jones, Susan S.
Passwater, Richard A., ed. see Kugler, Hans.
Passwater, Richard A., ed. see Lee, William.
Passwater, Richard A., ed. see Leviton, Richard.
Passwater, Richard A., ed. see Light, Marilyn.
Passwater, Richard A., ed. see Mervyn, Len.
Passwater, Richard A., ed. see Rose, Jeanne.
Passwater, Richard A., ed. see Rosenberg, Harold S.
Passwater, Richard A., ed. see Sloan, Sara.
Passwater, Richard A., ed. see Vogel, Jerome & Walsh, Richard.
Passwater, Richard A., ed. see Wunderlich, Ray C. & Kalita, Dwight K.
***Passwaters, Sandra.** All on a Saturday Night. 130p. Date not set. pap. 7.95 (*0-7610-0205-7*) NW Pub.
Passy, Jane. Cued Articulation: Cued Vowels. (C). 1990. 59.00 (*0-86431-063-3*, Pub. by Aust Council Educ Res AT); 59.00 (*0-86431-062-5*, Pub. by Aust Council Educ Res AT) St Mut.
Past, Ambar. The Sea on Its Side. Hirschman, Jack, tr. 30p. (Orig.). 1994. pap. 7.00 (*0-942996-19-4*) Post Apollo Pr.
Pasta & Co. Staff. Pasta & Co., the Cookbook. Rosene, Marcella, ed. 223p. (Orig.). 1987. pap. 12.95 (*0-685-19027-7*) Pasta & Co Inc.
Pasta, Elmer. Complete Book of Roasts, Boasts, & Toasts. LC 82-6296. 375p. 1982. pap. 4.95 (*0-13-158329-8*, Parker Publishing Co) P-H.
Pastalan, K. Leon & Cowart, Marie E. Lifestyles & Housing of Older Adults: The Florida Experience. LC 88-32230. (Journal of Housing for the Elderly: Vol. 5, No. 1). (Illus.). 114p. 1989. text ed. 39.95 (*0-86656-872-7*) Haworth Pr.
***Pastalan, Leon, ed.** Housing Decisions for the Elderly: To Move or Not to Move. (Journal of Housing for the Elderly Ser.: Vol. 11, No. 2). 175p. 1995. 29.95 (*1-56024-713-4*); text ed. 17.95 (*0-614-05610-1*) Haworth Pr.
Pastalan, Leon A. Aging in Place: The Role of Housing & Social Supports. LC 90-34022. (Journal of Housing for the Elderly: Vol. 6, Nos. 1-2). 130p. 1990. text ed. 29.95 (*0-86656-981-2*) Haworth Pr.
Pastalan, Leon A., intro. Optimizing Housing for the Elderly: Homes Not Houses. (Journal of Housing for the Elderly). 163p. 1990. text ed. 29.95 (*1-56024-076-8*) Haworth Pr.
Pastan, Ira H. & Willingham, Mark C., eds. Endocytosis. LC 85-3436. 344p. 1985. 85.00 (*0-306-41853-3*, Plenum Pr) Plenum.
Pastan, Ira H., jt. ed. see Jakoby, William B.
Pastan, Ira H., jt. auth. see Willingham, Mark C.
Pastan, Linda. An Early Afterlife: Poems. 72p. 1995. 17.95 (*0-393-03727-4*) Norton.
— An Early Afterlife: Poems. 88p. 1996. pap. 10.00 (*0-393-31381-6*) Norton.
— Heroes in Disguise. 96p. 1992. pap. 8.95 (*0-393-30922-3*) Norton.
— Heroes in Disguise: Poems. 96p. 1991. 17.95 (*0-393-03006-7*) Norton.
— The Imperfect Paradise. 1989. pap. 7.95 (*0-393-30524-4*) Norton.
— The Imperfect Paradise: Poems. 1988. 15.95 (*0-393-02565-9*) Norton.
— PM-AM: New & Selected Poems. 128p. 1982. pap. 9.95 (*0-393-30055-2*) Norton.
Paste, Loomis R. Iatrogenic Diseases I: Medical Subject Analysis & Research Guide with Bibliography. LC 83-45540. 140p. 1984. 37.50 (*0-88164-096-4*); pap. 34.50 (*0-88164-097-2*) ABBE Pubs Assn.
Pasteels, J. M., ed. From Individual to Collective Behavior in Social Insects. (BioSeries-EXS: No. 54). 250p. 1987. 105.00 (*0-8176-1859-7*) Birkhauser.
Pasten-Bedingfeld, Henry. Heraldry. 1993. 15.98 (*1-55521-932-2*) Bk Sales Inc.
Pastene, Jerome. Three-Quarter Time: The Life & Music of the Strauss Family of Vienna. LC 76-91768. (Illus.). 307p. 1971. reprint ed. text ed. 38.50 (*0-8371-3991-0*, PATQ, Greenwood Pr) Greenwood.
***Paster, Donna.** Stars Galore & Even More: Speed-Cut Designs Using Hexagons & Octagons. LC 95-7314. (Contemporary Quilting Ser.). 192p. 1995. pap. 22.95 (*0-8019-8615-X*) Chilton.
Paster, Gail K. The Body Embarrassed: Drama & the Disciplines of Shame in Early Modern England. LC 92-36855. (Illus.). 304p. 1993. 42.95 (*0-8014-2776-2*); pap. 14.95 (*0-8014-8060-4*) Cornell U Pr.
— The Idea of the City in the Age of Shakespeare. LC 85-974. 264p. 1985. 27.50 (*0-8203-0785-8*) U of Ga Pr.
Pasteris, Jill D., jt. ed. see Morris, Ellen M.
Pasternack, Barbara, jt. auth. see Parisi, Barbara.
***Pasternack, Carol B.** The Textuality of Old English Poetry. (Studies in Anglo-Saxon England: No. 13). (Illus.). 243p. (C). 1996. write for info. (*0-521-46549-4*) Cambridge U Pr.
Pasternack, Carol B., jt. ed. see Doane, A. N.
Pasternack, Steve. Mass Communication Law in New Mexico. (State Law Ser.). 110p. (C). 1992. pap. text ed. 8.95 (*0-913507-24-5*) New Forums.
Pasternak. Oeuvres. (FRE.). 1990. lib. bdg. 150.00 (*0-8288-3570-5*, F119390) Fr & Eur.
Pasternak, ed. Monovalent Cations in Biological Systems. 1990. 253.00 (*0-8493-4775-0*, QP531) CRC Pr.
***Pasternak & Rudman.** My Sister--Life. Date not set. per. 12.95 (*0-920428-93-2*, Pub. by Exile Edits CN) InBook.
Pasternak, Alexander. A Vanished Present: The Memoirs of Alexander. Slater, Ann P., ed. & tr. by. LC 88-43305. (Illus.). 238p. 1989. pap. 14.95 (*0-8014-9576-8*) Cornell U Pr.
— A Vanished Present: The Memoirs of Alexander Pasternak. Slater, Ann P., tr. LC 84-6532. (Helen & Kurt Wolff Bk.). (Illus.). 240p. 1985. 17.95 (*0-15-193364-2*) HarBrace.
***Pasternak, Anna.** Princess in Love. 1994. 17.95 (*0-525-94017-0*) NAL-Dutton.
Pasternak, Boris. Adolescence of Zhenya Luvers. pap. 1.25 (*0-8065-0306-8*, Citadel Pr) Carol Pub Group.
— Le Docteur Jivago. (FRE.). 1972. pap. 17.95 (*0-7859-3984-9*) Fr & Eur.
— Doctor Zhivago. 1986. mass mkt. 5.95 (*0-345-34100-7*) Ballantine.
— Doctor Zhivago. LC 90-53445. 592p. 1991. pap. 14.00 (*0-679-73123-7*) Pantheon.
— Doctor Zhivago. 550p. 1991. reprint ed. lib. bdg. 36.95 (*0-89966-839-9*) Buccaneer Bks.
— Dr. Zhivago. 544p. 1991. 20.00 (*0-679-40759-6*, Everymans Lib) Knopf.
— I Remember: Sketch for an Autobiography. Magarshack, David, tr. 204p. 1983. pap. 11.95 (*0-674-43950-3*) HUP.
— Karacsonyi Csillag: Kesei Versek, 1945-1969. LC 64-66430. (HUN.). 1965. pap. 5.00 (*0-911050-25-6*) Occidental.
— My Sister--Life. Boychuk, Bohdan, ed. Rudman, Mark & Boychuk, Bohdan, trs. 106p. 1993. reprint ed. pap. 12.95 (*0-8101-1090-3*) Northwestern U Pr.
— The Poems of Doctor Zhivago. Davie, Donald, ed. & tr. by. LC 76-1980. 204p. 1977. reprint ed. text ed. 38.50 (*0-8371-8294-8*, PAPDZ, Greenwood Pr) Greenwood.
— Safe Conduct. LC 58-12799. 1958. pap. 9.95 (*0-8112-0135-X*, NDP77) New Directions.
— Second Nature: Forty-Six Poems. 128p. 1990. 34.00 (*0-7206-0751-5*, Pub. by Peter Owen Ltd UK) Dufour.
— Selected Poems. Stallworthy, Jon & France, Peter, trs. (Twentieth-Century Classics Ser.). 160p. 1992. pap. 8.95 (*0-14-018466-X*, Penguin Classics) Viking Penguin.

— Seven Poems. 2nd ed. Kline, George L., tr. LC 76-134742. (Keepsake Ser.). 1970. 15.00 (*0-87775-083-1*); pap. 6.95 (*0-87775-005-X*) Unicorn Pr.

Pasternak, Boris, et al. Letters: Summer 1926. Wettlin, Margaret & Arndt, Walter, trs. LC 85-865. (Helen & Kurt Wolff Bk.). (Illus.). 384p. 1985. 24.95 (*0-15-150871-2*) HarBrace.

Pasternak, Burton. Guests in the Dragon. LC 83-5194. (Illus.). 224p. 1983. text ed. 55.00 (*0-231-05610-9*) Col U Pr.

— Kinship & Community in Two Chinese Villages. LC 72-78870. (Illus.). 192p. 1972. 29.50 (*0-8047-0823-1*) Stanford U Pr.

— Marriage & Fertility in Tianjin, China: Fifty Years of Transition. LC 86-16515. (Papers of the East-West Population Institute: No. 99). (Illus.). (Orig.). 1986. pap. 3.00 (*0-86638-080-9*) EW Ctr HI.

Pasternak, Burton & Salaff, Janet. Cowboys & Cultivators. (C). 1993. text ed. 54.00 (*0-8133-1877-7*) Westview.

Pasternak, Charles A., ed. Radioimmunoassay in Clinical Biochemistry. LC 76-675546. 317p. reprint ed. pap. 90.40 (*0-317-29335-4*, 2024025) Bks Demand.

Pasternak, Gavril W., ed. The Opiate Receptors. LC 87-3095. (Receptors Ser.). (Illus.). 520p. 1988. 99.50 (*0-89603-120-9*) Humana.

Pasternak, Gavril W., jt. ed. see Kuhar, Michael J.

Pasternak, Grigory I. & Raleigh, Eugene. To Reach This Season: A Russians Odyssey to the West. LC 84-82476. 241p. 1985. pap. 12.95 (*0-943376-23-8*) Magnes Mus.

Pasternak, Jack J., jt. auth. see Glick, Bernard R.

Pasternak, Joseph F., jt. auth. see Holmes, Deborah L.

***Pasternak, Josephine.** Pasternak Leonid 1862-1945. 1982. pap. 20.00 (*0-905836-34-0*, Pub. by Museum Modern Art UK) St Mut.

***Pasternak, Martin B.** Rise Now & Fly to Arms: The Life of Henry Highland Garnet. rev. ed. LC 94-34525. (Studies in African American History & Culture). (Illus.). 192p. 1994. 43.00 (*0-8153-1869-3*) Garland.

Pasternak, Michael G. Helping Kids Learn Multi-Cultural Concepts: A Handbook of Strategies. LC 79-63052. (Illus.). 260p. (C). 1979. reprint ed. pap. text ed. 14.95 (*0-87822-194-8*, 1948) Res Press.

Pasternak, Monique. Flying on the Wings of Aleph: A Tikkun. 76p. (Orig.). 1988. pap. write for info. (*0-945646-07-0*) Ocean Star Pubns.

Pasternak, Vclvcl, ed. see Friedman, Debbie.

Pastides. Conducting Epidemiological Research. 1995. write for info. (*0-87371-558-6*) Lewis Pubs.

Pastier, John. Cesar Pelli. (Illus.). 120p. 1980. 89.50 (*0-8230-7414-5*) Elliots Bks.

Pastier, John, jt. auth. see Gandelsonas, Mario.

Pastin, Mark. The Hard Problems of Management: Gaining the Ethics Edge. LC 85-45911. (Management Ser.). 265p. 1986. 31.95x (*0-87589-688-X*) Jossey-Bass.

Pastine, Maureen, jt. ed. see Huston, Mary M.

Pastis, Steven, jt. auth. see Levy, Nathan.

Pastman, Robert A., ed. Randax Graduate School Directory. LC 75-41652. 303p. 1976. lib. bdg. 21.50 (*0-914880-06-3*) Educ Guide.

Pasto, Daniel, et al. Experiments & Techniques in Organic Chemistry. 624p. (C). 1991. text ed. 49.00 (*0-13-298860-7*) P-H.

Pasto, Daniel G. & Johnson, Carl R. Organic Structure Determination. (C). 1969. text ed. 55.00 (*0-13-640854-0*) P-H.

Pasto, Daniel J. & Johnson, Carol R. Laboratory Text for Organic Chemistry: A Source Book of Chemical & Physical Techniques. 1979. pap. text ed. write for info. (*0-13-521302-9*) P-H.

Paston, George. Social Caricature in the Eighteenth-Century. LC 67-12467. (Illus.). 1972. reprint ed. 54.95 (*0-405-08840-X*) Ayer.

Paston-Williams, Sara. Art of Dining: A History of Cooking & Eating. 1994. 49.50 (*0-8109-1940-0*) Abrams.

— The National Trust Book of Fish Cookery. (Illus.). 160p. 1988. 17.95 (*0-7078-0093-5*, Pub. by Natl Trust UK) Trafalgar.

Pastor, Beatriz. Roberto Arlt y la Rebelion Alienada. LC 80-70560. 128p. (SPA.). 1980. pap. 8.00 (*0-935318-05-4*) Edins Hispamerica.

Pastor, Jose C., tr. see Smook, Gary.

Pastor, Larry & Pastore, Michael. Child Maintenance Made Simple! How Grown-ups & Children Can Work Creatively & Lovingly Together. LC 92-82025. 128p. (Orig.). 1993. pap. 14.95 (*0-927379-48-1*, ZP 64) Zorba Pr.

Pastor, Larry, jt. auth. see Pastore, Michael.

Pastor, Manuel, Jr. Capital Flight & the Latin American Debt Crisis. 45p. 1990. 12.00 (*0-944826-19-9*) Economic Policy Inst.

Pastor, Marion & Luyet, Ron. Where Freedom Begins: The Process of Personal Change. rev. ed. 200p. 1992. reprint ed. pap. 11.95 (*0-914728-79-2*) Wingbow Pr.

Pastor, Peter. Hungary Between Wilson & Lenin: The Hungarian Revolution of 1918-1919 & the Big Three. 191p. 1976. text ed. 42.00 (*0-914710-13-3*) East Eur Quarterly.

Pastor, Peter, ed. Revolutions & Interventions in Hungary & Its Neighbor States, 1918-1919. 320p. 1988. text ed. 47.00 (*0-88033-137-2*) East Eur Quarterly.

Pastor, Peter & Williamson, Samuel R., Jr. Essays on World War I: Origins & Prisoners of War. (East European Monographs: No. 126). 264p. 1983. text ed. 45.00 (*0-88033-015-5*) East Eur Quarterly.

Pastor, Peter, jt. ed. see Kiraly, B. K.

Pastor, Peter, jt. ed. see Williamson, Samuel R., Jr.

Pastor, R., ed. see Menendez Pidal, Ramon.

Pastor, Reyna & Carle, M. Historia de Espana, Vol. 10: Los Reinos Cristianos En los Siglos XI y XII V.1 Economias, Sociedades, Instituciones. 478p. (SPA.). 1992. 189.50x (*84-239-4812-9*) Elliots Bks.

Pastor, Robert. Whirlpool: U. S. Foreign Policy Toward Latin America & the Caribbean. (Studies in International History & Politics). 353p. 1993. pap. text ed. 14.95 (*0-691-02561-4*) Princeton U Pr.

Pastor, Robert A. Condemned to Repetition: The United States & Nicaragua. LC 87-45531. 352p. 1988. text ed. 55.00 (*0-691-07752-5*); pap. 15.95 (*0-691-02291-7*) Princeton U Pr.

— Congress & the Politics of U. S. Foreign Economic Policy, 1929 to 1976. LC 79-63552. (Studies in International Political Economy: Vol. 5). 416p. 1980. pap. 14.00 (*0-520-04645-5*) U CA Pr.

— Integration with Mexico: Options for U. S. Policy in the 21st Century. LC 92-44930. 1993. 8.95 (*0-87078-328-9*) TCFP-PPP.

— Whirlpool: U.S. Foreign Policy Toward Latin America & the Caribbean. (Studies in International History & Politics). 328p. 1992. text ed. 39.50 (*0-691-08651-6*) Princeton U Pr.

Pastor, Robert A. & Carter, Jimmy, eds. Democracy in the Americas: Stopping the Pendulum. LC 89-1781. 262p. 1989. 49.50 (*0-8419-1182-7*); pap. 24.50 (*0-8419-1183-5*) Holmes & Meier.

Pastor, Robert A. & Castaneda, Jorge G. Limits to Friendship. 1989. pap. 13.00 (*0-679-72543-1*, Vin) Random.

Pastor, Xavier. The Ships of Christopher Columbus. (Anatomy of the Ship Ser.). (Illus.). 128p. 1992. 36.95 (*1-55750-755-4*) Naval Inst Pr.

Pastoral Care Office, Reorganized Church of Jesus Christ of Latter Day Saints Staff. Empowered to Care. 1980. pap. 12.00 (*0-8309-0291-0*) Herald Hse.

— Visiting: A Pastoral Care Ministry. 186p. (Orig.). 1985. pap. 13.00 (*0-8309-0429-8*) Herald Hse.

Pastore, Jose & Haller, Archibald O. Inequality & Social Mobility in Brazil. LC 81-69826. 240p. (C). 1982. reprint ed. text ed. 35.00 (*0-299-08830-8*) U of Wis Pr.

Pastore, Judith L., ed. Confronting AIDS Through Literature: The Responsibilities of Representation. LC 92-31606. 272p. 1993. 34.95 (*0-252-01989-X*); pap. 14.95 (*0-252-06294-9*) U of Ill Pr.

Pastore, Mary & Deneen, Lawrence J. Escape from Disability: Best Kept Secrets, Injured Workers Win. LC 87-63296. 107p. (Orig.). 1988. pap. 8.95 (*0-9614877-2-0*) Rehab Pubns.

Pastore, Michael. Aha! The Ice Cream Koans Answer Book: Solutions to 101 Problems in Child Maintenance. LC 92-82028. (Orig.). 1993. pap. 14.95 (*0-927379-19-8*, ZP 120) Zorba Pr.

— Dynamite Counselors Don't Explode! A Complete Survival Course for Child-Care Workers & Camp Counselors. LC 92-82030. 128p. (Orig.). 1993. pap. 14.95 (*0-927379-64-3*, ZP 50) Zorba Pr.

— Flashes of Light. 100p. (Orig.). 1989. pap. 10.00 (*0-927379-88-0*) Zorba Pr.

— Ice Cream Koans: One Hundred One Problems in Child Maintenance for Everyone Who Works with Kids. LC 92-82029. 128p. (Orig.). 1993. pap. 14.95 (*0-927379-05-8*, ZP 101) Zorba Pr.

— Lark's Magic. LC 89-51204. 113p. (YA). (gr. 4-12). 1990. pap. 10.00 (*0-927379-36-8*, ZP36) Zorba Pr.

— Zenlightenment! Insights into the Art of Living Miraculously. Umeboshi, Hokku, tr. LC 89-50097. (Illus.). 104p. (Orig.). 1989. pap. 10.00 (*0-927379-00-7*) Zorba Pr.

Pastore, Michael & Pastor, Larry. You're Ugly & Your Mother Dresses You Funny: How to Win Love, Respect & Co-Operation from the Children You Live with, Teach & Work With. 108p. (Orig.). 1989. pap. 10.00 (*0-927379-60-0*) Zorba Pr.

— Zen in the Art of Child Maintenance: A Complete Survival Course for Everyone Who Works with Kids. LC 92-82027. 120p. (Orig.). 1990. pap. 14.95 (*0-927379-28-7*, ZP 99) Zorba Pr.

Pastore, Michael & Umeboshi, Hokku. Flashes of Light: The Illuminated Poems of Hokku Umeboshi. LC 92-82031. 160p. (Orig.). 1993. pap. 14.95 (*0-927379-98-8*, ZP 88) Zorba Pr.

Pastore, Michael, jt. auth. see Pastor, Larry.

***Pastore, Michael A.** Test Preparation Guide for Microsoft Windows NT Workstation 3.5 Microsoft Certified Professional. Baker, James C., ed. (Illus.). 208p. 1995. pap. 59.95 (*0-89716-566-7*) P B Pubng.

— Test Preparation Guide for Microsoft Windows 3.1 Microsoft Certified Professional. Baker, James C., ed. (Illus.). 160p. 1995. pap. 59.95 (*0-89716-565-9*) P B Pubng.

Pastore, Nicholas & Adler, Helmut E., eds. Helmholtz's Popular Lectures on Vision. 192p. 1986. 21.95 (*0-03-058692-5*, Praeger Pubs) Greenwood.

Pastorek, Joseph G., II, ed. Obstetric & Gynecologic Infectious Disease. LC 93-24716. 858p. 1994. 129.00 (*0-7817-0023-X*) Raven.

Pastorek, Norman J. Blepharoplasty. 3rd ed. (Self-Instructional Package Ser.). (C). 1994. pap. text ed. 25.00 (*1-56772-012-9*) AAO-HNS.

Pastorek, Sheryl. Caps, Commas, & Other Things. 264p. 1982. pap. 18.00 (*0-87879-325-9*) Acad Therapy.

Pastorelli, Pietro, ed. Carteggio (Political Correspondence), 3 vols. Incl. Vol. Primo, 1891-1913. xvi, 592p. 1982. (*0-7006-0225-9*); Vol. Secondo, 1914-1916. xvi, 776p. 1975. (*0-7006-0139-2*); Vol. Terzo, 1916-1922. xvi, 788p. 1976. (*0-7006-0150-3*); (Opera Omnia di - The Complete Works of Sidney Sonnino Ser.). xvi, 592p. (ITA.). 1982. Set. 50.00 (*0-685-04295-2*) U Pr of KS.

Pastoret, P. P., jt. ed. see Edwards, S.

Pastorius, Francis D. Description of Pennsylvania, Seventeen Hundred. 1993. reprint ed. lib. bdg. 89.00 (*0-7812-5816-2*) Rprt Serv.

***Pastouna, Andrew.** Rolls-Royce State Motor Cars. (Illus.). 240p. 1995. 49.95 (*1-85532-440-7*, Pub. by Osprey Pubng Ltd UK) Motorbooks Intl.

— Royal Rolls-Royce Motor Cars. (Illus.). 240p. 1991. 49.95 (*1-85532-142-4*, Pub. by Osprey Pubng Ltd UK) Motorbooks Intl.

Pastre, Oliver. Multinationals: Bank & Corporate Relationships. Altman, Edward I. & Walter, Ingo, eds. LC 81-80869. (Contemporary Studies in Economic & Financial Analysis: Vol. 28). 275p. 1981. 73.25 (*0-89232-219-5*) Jai Pr.

Pastrovicchi, Angelo. St. Joseph of Copertino. LC 79-91298. 135p. 1980. reprint ed. pap. 4.50 (*0-89555-135-7*) TAN Bks Pubs.

Pastubov, V. D. A Guide to the Practice of International Conferences. (Studies in the Administration of International Law & Organization). 1945. reprint ed. 25.00 (*0-527-00882-6*) Periodicals Srv.

Pastur, L. & Figotin, A. Spectra of Random & Almost Periodic Operators. Berger, M. et al, eds. (Grundlehren der Mathematischen Wissenschaften Ser.: Vol. 297). viii, 587p. 1991. 109.00 (*0-387-50622-5*) Spr-Verlag.

***Pasture, Patrick.** Christian Trade Unionism in Europe Since 1968: Tensions Between Identity & Practice. 197p. 1994. 54.95 (*1-85628-950-8*, Pub. by Avebury Pub UK) Ashgate Pub Co.

Pastuszek, Eric J. & French, Robert B. Is the Fetus Human? LC 92-82132. (Illus.). 87p. 1993. pap. 5.00 (*0-89555-486-0*) TAN Bks Pubs.

Pastva, Loretta. Great Religions of the World. (Illus.). 190p. (Orig.). 1986. teacher ed 14.95 (*0-88489-176-3*); pap. text ed. 11.40x (*0-88489-175-5*) St Marys.

Pastva, M. Loretta. Growing up to God: A Guide for Teenagers on the Sacrement of Reconciliation. LC 83-15538. 82p. (Orig.). 1983. pap. 4.95 (*0-8189-0455-0*) Alba.

Pastva, Mary L. The Catholic Youth Retreat Book: Everything You Need to Plan Prayer Experiences for a Day, an Evening, a Weekend. (Illus.). 87p. 1984. pap. 7.95 (*0-86716-032-2*) St Anthony Mess Pr.

Pastwa, Agnes-Josephine, tr. see De Laussat, Pierre-Clement.

Pasvolsky, Leo. Russia in the Far East. LC 79-2918. 181p. 1981. reprint ed. 19.00 (*0-8305-0087-1*) Hyperion Conn.

Pasvolsky, Leo & Viner, Jacob. Current Monetary Issues. Bd. with Balanced Deflation, Inflation or More Depression. LC 82-48212. LC 82-48212. (Gold, Money, Inflation & Deflation Ser.). 235p. 1983. Set lib. bdg. 28.00 (*0-8240-5250-1*) Garland.

Paszek, Lawrence J. A Guide to Documentary Sources. (Reference Ser.). (Illus.). 245p. 1986. reprint ed. write for info. (*0-912799-21-8*) Off Air Force.

Paszek, Lawrence J., jt. auth. see Dornbusch, Charles E.

Paszkiewicz, H. Origin of Russia. 1978. lib. bdg. 59.95 (*0-8490-2385-8*) Gordon Pr.

Paszkiewicz, Henryk. The Rise of Moscow's Power. 1984. text ed. 63.00 (*0-88033-036-8*, 145) Col U Pr.

Paszkiewicz, T., ed. Physics of Phonons. (Lecture Notes in Physics Ser.: Vol. 285). x, 486p. 1987. 58.00 (*0-387-18244-6*) Spr-Verlag.

Paszkiewicz, T. & Rapcewicz, K., eds. Die Kunst of Phonons: Lectures from the Winter School of Theoretical Physics. (Illus.). 432p. (C). 1994. 110.00 (*0-306-44677-4*) Plenum.

Paszkowski, B., jt. auth. see Mikolajczy, P.

Paszkowski, Jerzy, ed. Homologous Recombination & Gene Silencing in Plants. LC 93-50752. 396p. 1994. lib. bdg. 162.00 (*0-7923-2704-7*) Kluwer Ac.

***Pasztor.** When the Pentagon Was for Sale. 1995. (*0-684-19516-X*, Scribners) S&S Trade.

Pasztor, E. Concise Neurosurgery. (Illus.). 292p. 1980. 75.25 (*3-8055-1431-X*) S Karger.

Pasztor, E., et al, eds. Language & Speech: Proceedings of the Fifth Convention of the Academia Eurasiana Neurochirurgica, Budapest, September 19-12, 1990. (Acta Neurochirugica - Supplementum Ser.: No. 56). (Illus.). 120p. 1993. 100.00 (*0-387-82386-7*) Spr-Verlag.

Pasztor, Eileen M. & Wynne, Susan F. Foster Parent Retention & Recruitment: The State of the Art in Practice & Policy. (Orig.). 1995. pap. text ed. 12.95 (*0-87868-576-6*) Child Welfare.

Pasztory, Esther. Aztec Art. (Illus.). 336p. 1993. 49.50 (*0-8109-0687-2*) Abrams.

— The Iconography of the Teotihuacan Tlaloc. LC 74-16543. (Studies in Pre-Columbian Art & Archaeology: No. 15). (Illus.). 22p. 1974. pap. 6.00 (*0-88402-059-2*) Dumbarton Oaks.

Pasztory, Esther, intro. Aztec Stone Sculpture. (Illus.). 1976. pap. 4.00 (*0-89192-166-4*, Ctr Inter-Am Rel) Interbk Inc.

Pasztory, Esther, jt. ed. see Berrin, Kathleen.

Pat & Wise. Nuevo Atlas Biblico (New Bible Atlas) (SPA.). Date not set. 19.99 (*0-8423-6325-4*, 490405) Editorial Unilit.

Pat, Jacob. Ashes & Fire. Steinberg, Leo, tr. LC 48-1353. 254p. reprint ed. pap. 72.40 (*0-8357-5784-6*, 2010713) Bks Demand.

Pata, E. Baltic Oil Shales: Chemistry & Technology. 368p. 1971. text ed. 88.50 (*0-7065-1064-X*, Pub. by Keter Pub IS) Coronet Bks.

Patata, Jan L. Alaskan Malamute Champions, 1936-1980. (Illus.). 138p. 1987. pap. 36.95 (*0-940808-10-2*) Camino E E & Bk.

— Brittany Champions, 1952-1981. (Illus.). 280p. 1986. 36.95 (*0-940808-20-X*) Camino E E & Bk.

— Clumber Spaniel Champions, 1955-1981. (Illus.). 94p. 1982. pap. 36.95 (*0-940808-15-3*) Camino E E & Bk.

— Doberman Pinscher Champions, 1952-1980. (Illus.). 220p. 1981. pap. 36.95 (*0-940808-01-3*) Camino E E & Bk.

— German Shorthaired Pointer Champions, 1952-1980. (Illus.). 201p. 1986. pap. 36.95 (*0-940808-05-6*) Camino E E & Bk.

— German Wirehaired Pointer Champions, 1959-1980. (Illus.). 75p. 1981. pap. 36.95 (*0-940808-07-2*) Camino E E & Bk.

— Lhasa Apso Champions, 1952-1980. (Illus.). 164p. 1981. pap. 36.95 (*0-940808-09-9*) Camino E E & Bk.

— Pekingese Champions, 1952-1981. (Illus.). 236p. 1987. pap. 36.95 (*0-940808-12-9*) Camino E E & Bk.

— Pointer Champions: 1889-1980. (Illus.). 108p. 1981. pap. 36.95 (*0-940808-00-5*) Camino E E & Bk.

— Rhodesian Ridgeback Champions, 1955-1980. (Illus.). 97p. 1981. pap. 36.95 (*0-940808-04-8*) Camino E E & Bk.

— Siberian Husky Champions, 1952-1980. (Illus.). 151p. 1982. pap. 36.95 (*0-940808-11-0*) Camino E E & Bk.

— Whippet Champions, 1952-1980. (Illus.). 187p. 1987. pap. 36.95 (*0-940808-03-X*) Camino E E & Bk.

— Yorkshire Terrier Champions, 1952-1980. (Illus.). 214p. 1981. pap. 36.95 (*0-940808-08-0*) Camino E E & Bk.

Pataccia, T. Upgrading & Repairing Macs. (Illus.). 650p. (Orig.). 1993. pap. 29.95 (*0-88022-960-8*) Que.

Patach, Heidi. Monkey Stickers. (Illus.). (J). (gr. k-3). 1993. pap. 1.00 (*0-486-27493-4*) Dover.

Patacsil, Priscila, tr. see Waldrop, C. Sybil.

Patacsil, Priscila M. Actividades Educativas para Preescolares. 172p. (J). (ps). 1988. pap. 6.25 (*0-311-11049-5*) Casa Bautista.

Patai, Daphne. Brazilian Women Speak: Contemporary Life Stories. 404p. (Orig.). (C). 1988. text ed. 45.00 (*0-8135-1300-6*); pap. 15.00 (*0-8135-1301-4*) Rutgers U Pr.

— Myth & Ideology in Contemporary Brazilian Fiction. LC 81-71313. 256p. 1983. 37.50 (*0-8386-3132-0*) Fairleigh Dickinson.

— The Orwell Mystique: A Study in Male Ideology. LC 84-8488. 344p. 1984. lib. bdg. 30.00 (*0-87023-446-3*); pap. 17.95 (*0-87023-447-1*) U of Mass Pr.

Patai, Daphne, ed. Looking Backward, Nineteen Eighty-Eight to Eighteen Eighty-Eight: Essays on Edward Bellamy. LC 88-10621. 240p. (Orig.). (C). 1988. lib. bdg. 35.00 (*0-87023-633-4*); pap. 16.95x (*0-87023-634-2*) U of Mass Pr.

Patai, Daphne & Koertge, Noretta. Professing Feminism. 256p. 1994. 24.00 (*0-465-09821-5*) Basic.

Patai, Daphne, ed. see Azevedo, Aluisio.

Patai, Daphne, ed. see De Sena, Jorge.

Patai, Daphne, jt. ed. see Gluck, Sherna B.

Patai, Daphne, jt. ed. see Ingram, Angela.

Patai, Jennifer, jt. auth. see Patai, Raphael.

Patai, Joseph. The Middle Gate: An Hungarian Jewish Boyhood. Patai, Raphael, tr. & intro. by. LC 93-48491. 144p. 1994. 19.95 (*0-8276-0517-X*) JPS Phila.

— Souls & Secrets: Hasidic Stories. Patai, Raphael, tr. LC 94-45339. (Illus.). 272p. 1995. 30.00 (*1-56821-355-7*) Aronson.

Patai, R. On Culture Contact & Its Working in Modern Palestine. LC 48-4054. (American Anthropological Association Memoirs Ser.: No. 67). 1974. reprint ed. pap. 15.00 (*0-527-00566-5*) Periodicals Srv.

***Patai, Raphael.** Apprentice in Budapest: Memories of a World That Is No More. LC 87-37185. 538p. 1988. pap. 153.40 (*0-7837-8561-5*, 2049376) Bks Demand.

— Between Budapest & Jerusalem, Vol. 3: The Patai Letters, 1933-1938. LC 91-51097. (Illus.). 320p. (C). 1992. 29.95 (*0-87480-384-5*) U of Utah Pr.

— Gates to the Old City: A Book of Jewish Legends. LC 80-66154. 859p. reprint ed. pap. 180.00 (*0-318-34857-8*, 2031017) Bks Demand.

— The Hebrew Goddess. enl. ed. LC 89-70488. (Jewish Folklore & Anthropology Ser.). (Illus.). 369p. (C). 1990. reprint ed. pap. text ed. 18.95 (*0-8143-2271-9*) Wayne St U Pr.

— Ignaz Goldziher & His Oriental Diary: A Translation & Psychological Portrait. LC 86-24661. 160p. 1986. 29.95 (*0-8143-1842-8*) Wayne St U Pr.

— Israel Between East & West: A Study in Human Relations. rev. ed. LC 70-98711. 394p. 1970. text ed. 65.00 (*0-8371-3719-5*, PAI/, Greenwood Pr) Greenwood.

— The Jewish Alchemists: A History & Source Book. LC 93-35687. 1994. 35.00 (*0-691-03290-4*) Princeton U Pr.

— The Jews of Hungary: History, Culture, Psychology. (Illus.). 600p. 1995. text ed. 39.95x (*0-8143-2561-0*) Wayne St U Pr.

— Journeyman in Jerusalem, Vol. 2: Memories & Letters, 1933-1947. LC 91-51095. (Illus.). 500p. 1992. 34.95 (*0-87480-383-7*) U of Utah Pr.

— The Kingdom of Jordan. LC 83-22723. (Illus.). ix, 315p. 1984. reprint ed. text ed. 41.50 (*0-313-24396-4*, PAKJ, Greenwood Pr) Greenwood.

— Messiah Texts: Jewish Legends of Three Thousound Years. LC 79-5387. 426p. 1979. pap. 17.95 (*0-8143-1850-9*) Wayne St U Pr.

— Nahum Goldmann: His Missions to the Gentiles. LC 85-24518. (Judaic Studies). 325p. 1987. pap. 92.70 (*0-7837-8397-3*, 2059208) Bks Demand.

— On Jewish Folklore. LC 82-11034. 512p. (C). 1992. pap. text ed. 18.95 (*0-8143-2437-1*) Wayne St U Pr.

— Robert Graves & the Hebrew Myths: A Collaboration. LC 91-20963. (Jewish Folklore & Anthropology Ser.). (Illus.). 468p. 1992. 49.95 (*0-8143-2114-3*) Wayne St U Pr.

— The Seed of Abraham: Jews & Arabs in Contact & Conflict. LC 85-29453. 408p. 1986. pap. 116.30 (*0-7837-8560-7*, 2049375) Bks Demand.

Patai, Raphael, ed. Herzl Year Book: Vol. 5, Studies in the History of Zionism in America. LC 72-117807. (Essay Index Reprint Ser.). 1977. 24.95 (*0-8369-1951-3*) Ayer.

An Asterisk (*) at the beginning of an entry indicates that the title is appearing in BIP for the first time.

Patai, Raphael & Goldsmith, Emanuel S. Thinkers & Teachers of Modern Judaism. LC 94-16063. 256p. 1994. 24.95 (*1-55778-701-8*) Paragon Hse.

***Patai, Raphael & Goldsmith, Emanuel S., eds.** Events & Movements in Modern Judaism. 315p. 1995. 24.95 (*1-55778-707-7*) Paragon Hse.

Patai, Raphael & Patai, Jennifer. Myth of the Jewish Race. rev. ed. LC 88-27721. (Jewish Folklore & Anthropology Ser.). (Illus.). 470p. 1989. reprint ed. 39.95 (*0-8143-1948-3*) Wayne St U Pr.

Patai, Raphael, ed. see Brauer, Erich.

Patai, Raphael, jt. auth. see Graves, Robert.

Patai, Raphael, tr. see Patai, Joseph.

Patai, Raphael, et al. Studies in Biblical & Jewish Folklore. LC 72-6871. (Studies in Comparative Literature: No. 35). 1972. reprint ed. lib. bdg. 75.00 (*0-8383-1665-4*) M S G Haskell Hse.

Patai, Saul. Chemistry of Carboxylic Acids & Esters. LC 70-82547. (Chemistry of Functional Groups Ser.). (Illus.). 1169p. reprint ed. pap. 180.00 (*0-685-23488-6*, 2027888) Bks Demand.

— Chemistry of Cyanates & Their Thio Derivatives, Pt. 1. (Interscience Publication, Chemistry of Functional Groups Ser.). reprint ed. Part l. pap. 158.00 (*0-317-26341-2*, 2025197) Bks Demand.

— Chemistry of Cyanates & Their Thio Derivatives, Pt. 2. (Interscience Publication, Chemistry of Functional Groups Ser.). reprint ed. Part 2. pap. 160.00 (*0-317-26342-0*) Bks Demand.

— The Chemistry of Ether Linkage. LC 66-30401. (Chemistry of Functional Groups Ser.). (Illus.). 795p. reprint ed. pap. 180.00 (*0-317-09310-X*, 2016969) Bks Demand.

Patai, Saul, ed. The Chemistry of Acid Derivatives, Pts. 1 & 2. Suppl. B. (Illus.). 767p. reprint ed. pap. write for info. (*0-318-65330-3*); reprint ed. Pt. 1. pap. 180.00 (*0-8357-8829-6*, 2033325); reprint ed. Pt. 2. pap. 180.00 (*0-8357-8835-0*, 2033325) Bks Demand.

— The Chemistry of Acyl Halides. LC 70-37114. (Chemistry of Functional Groups Ser.). 561p. reprint ed. pap. 159.90 (*0-8357-8830-X*, 2033324) Bks Demand.

— The Chemistry of Amidines & Imidates. LC 75-6913. (Chemistry of Functional Groups Ser.). (Illus.). 691p. reprint ed. pap. 180.00 (*0-8357-8831-8*, 2033320) Bks Demand.

— The Chemistry of Amino, Nitroso, & Nitro Compounds & Their Derivatives, Pts. 1 & 2. LC 81-16153. (Chemistry of Functional Groups Ser.: Supplement F). (Illus.). reprint ed. pap. 160.00 (*0-685-73964-3*, 2030491); reprint ed. pap. 160.00 (*0-685-73965-1*) Bks Demand.

— The Chemistry of Diazonium & Diazo Groups, 2 pts., Pt. 1. LC 75-6913. (Chemistry of Functional Groups Ser.). reprint ed. pap. 131.00 (*0-317-10696-1*, 2022404) Bks Demand.

— The Chemistry of Diazonium & Diazo Groups, 2 pts., Pt. 2. LC 75-6913. (Chemistry of Functional Groups Ser.). reprint ed. pap. 143.00 (*0-317-10697-X*) Bks Demand.

— The Chemistry of Doubled-Bonded Functional Groups, Pts. 1 & 2. Suppl. A. (Illus.). 667p. reprint ed. pap. write for info. (*0-318-65329-X*); reprint ed. Pt. 1. pap. 180.00 (*0-8357-8832-6*, 2033319); reprint ed. Pt. 2. pap. 180.00 (*0-8357-8836-9*, 2033319) Bks Demand.

— The Chemistry of Ethers, Crown Ethers, Hydroxyl Groups & Their Sulphur Analogues, Pt. 1. LC 80-41256. (Chemistry of Functional Groups Ser.: Supplement E). (Illus.). 622p. reprint ed. pap. 177.30 (*0-685-20705-6*, 2030490) Bks Demand.

— The Chemistry of Ethers, Crown Ethers, Hydroxyl Groups & Their Sulphur Analogues, Pt. 2. LC 80-41256. (Chemistry of Functional Groups Ser.: Supplement E). (Illus.). 549p. reprint ed. pap. 156.50 (*0-685-44063-X*, 2030490) Bks Demand.

— The Chemistry of Ketenes, Allenes, & Related Compounds, 2 pts., Pt. 1. LC 79-42899. (Chemistry of Functional Groups Ser.). 499p. reprint ed. pap. 142.30 (*0-318-34953-1*, 2030750) Bks Demand.

— The Chemistry of Ketenes, Allenes, & Related Compounds, 2 pts., Pt. 2. LC 79-42899. (Chemistry of Functional Groups Ser.). 491p. reprint ed. pap. 140.00 (*0-318-34954-X*, 2030750) Bks Demand.

— The Chemistry of Peroxides. LC 83-14844. (Chemistry of Functional Groups Ser.). 1020p. reprint ed. pap. 180.00 (*0-318-34974-4*, 2030785) Bks Demand.

— The Chemistry of the Amino Group. LC 67-31072. (Chemistry of Functional Groups Ser.). (Illus.). 827p. reprint ed. pap. 180.00 (*0-8357-8833-4*, 2033321) Bks Demand.

— The Chemistry of the Azido Group. LC 73-149579. (Chemistry of Functional Groups Ser.). (Illus.). 640p. reprint ed. pap. 180.00 (*0-8357-8834-2*, 2033322) Bks Demand.

— The Chemistry of the Carbon-Carbon Triple Bond, 2 pts., Pt. 1. LC 75-6913. (Chemistry of Functional Groups Ser.). (Illus.). 536p. reprint ed. pap. 152.80 (*0-8357-8837-7*, 2033323) Bks Demand.

— The Chemistry of the Carbon-Carbon Triple Bond, 2 pts., Pt. 2. LC 75-6913. (Chemistry of Functional Groups Ser.). (Illus.). 536p. reprint ed. pap. 159.10 (*0-8357-8838-5*, 2033323) Bks Demand.

— The Chemistry of the Carbon-Nitrogen Double Bond. (Illus.). 808p. reprint ed. Pt. 2. write for info. (*0-318-65331-1*) Bks Demand.

— The Chemistry of the Carbon-Nitrogen Double Bond, Pt. 1. LC 70-104166. (Chemistry of Functional Groups Ser.). (Illus.). 808p. reprint ed. pap. 180.00 (*0-8357-8839-3*, 2033327) Bks Demand.

— The Chemistry of the Hydrazo, Azo, & Azoxy Groups, 2 pts., Pt. 1. LC 75-2194. (Chemistry of Functional Groups Ser.). (Illus.). 611p. reprint ed. pap. 174.20 (*0-8357-8840-7*, 2033326) Bks Demand.

— The Chemistry of the Hydrazo, Azo, & Azoxy Groups, 2 pts., Pt. 2. LC 75-2194. (Chemistry of Functional Groups Ser.). (Illus.). 611p. reprint ed. pap. 173.00 (*0-8357-8841-5*, 2033326) Bks Demand.

— The Chemistry of the Hydroxyl Group, 2 vols., 1. LC 77-116164. (Chemistry of Functional Groups Ser.: Vol. 10). (Illus.). 632p. reprint ed. pap. 160.00 (*0-685-23863-6*, 2056647) Bks Demand.

— The Chemistry of the Hydroxyl Group, 2 vols., 2. LC 77-116164. (Chemistry of Functional Groups Ser.: Vol. 10). (Illus.). 632p. reprint ed. pap. 157.10 (*0-685-23864-4*) Bks Demand.

— The Chemistry of the Quinonoid Compounds, 2 pts., Pt. 1. LC 73-17765. 630p. reprint ed. pap. 179.60 (*0-685-20919-9*, 2052254) Bks Demand.

— The Chemistry of the Quinonoid Compounds, 2 pts., Pt. 2. LC 73-17765. 673p. reprint ed. pap. 180.00 (*0-685-20920-2*, 2052254) Bks Demand.

Patai, Saul & Rappoport, Zvi, eds. The Chemistry of Halides, Pseudo-Halides, & Azides, Pt. 1. LC 82-23908. (Chemistry of Functional Groups Ser.: Supplement No. D). reprint ed. Part 1. pap. 160.00 (*0-8357-5603-3*, 2052312) Bks Demand.

— The Chemistry of Halides, Pseudo-Halides, & Azides, Pt. 2. LC 82-23908. (Chemistry of Functional Groups Ser.: Supplement No. D). 950p. reprint ed. Part 2. pap. 180.00 (*0-8357-5604-1*) Bks Demand.

— The Chemistry of the Quinonoid Compounts, Vol. 2, Pt. 1. LC 86-32494. (The Chemistry of Functional Groups Ser.). 892p. 1988. reprint ed. pap. 180.00 (*0-7837-8489-9*, 2049296) Bks Demand.

— The Chemistry of Triple-Bonded Functional Groups, Pts. 1 & 2. LC 82-17355. (Chemistry of Functional Groups Ser.: Supplement C). (Illus.). reprint ed. pap. 160.00 (*0-685-73962-7*, 2030489); reprint ed. pap. 160.00 (*0-685-73963-5*) Bks Demand.

— Supplement D2: The Chemistry of Halides, Pseudo-Halides & Azides, Vol. 2. (Chemistry of Functional Groups: Vol. 2). Date not set. text ed. 995.00 (*0-471-94209-X*) Wiley.

Patai, Saul & Zabicky, J., eds. The Chemistry of the Carbonyl Group, 2 vols., 1. LC 66-18177. (Chemistry of Functional Groups Ser.: Vol. 2). (Illus.). 1027p. reprint ed. pap. 160.00 (*0-685-23861-X*, 2056646) Bks Demand.

— The Chemistry of the Carbonyl Group, 2 vols., 2. LC 66-18177. (Chemistry of Functional Groups Ser.: Vol. 2). (Illus.). 1027p. reprint ed. pap. 120.70 (*0-685-23862-8*) Bks Demand.

Patai, Saul & Zabicky, Jacob, eds. The Chemistry of Alkenes, 2 vols., Vol. 1. LC 64-25218. (Chemistry of Functional Groups Ser.: Vol. 1). (Illus.). 616p. reprint ed. pap. 160.00 (*0-685-23859-8*, 2056645) Bks Demand.

— The Chemistry of Alkenes, 2 vols., Vol. 2. LC 64-25218. (Chemistry of Functional Groups Ser.: Vol. 1). (Illus.). 616p. reprint ed. pap. 160.00 (*0-685-23860-1*) Bks Demand.

Patai, Saul E. The Chemistry of Alkanes & Cycloalkanes. (Chemistry of Functional Groups Ser.: No. 1078). 1092p. 1992. text ed. 795.00 (*0-471-92498-9*) Wiley.

— Patai's Guide to the Chemistry of Functional Groups, 1992. (Chemistry of Functional Groups Ser.: No. 1078). 524p. 1992. text ed. 150.00 (*0-471-93022-9*) Wiley.

Patai, Saul E., ed. The Chemistry of Acid Derivatives, Vol. 2: Supplement B, Pts. 1 & 2. (Chemistry of Functional Groups Ser.). 2723p. 1992. text ed. 1,460.00 (*0-471-93111-X*) Wiley.

— The Chemistry of Double-Bonded Functional Groups: Supplement A, Vol. 2. (Chemistry of Functional Groups Ser.). 891p. 1989. text ed. 795.00 (*0-471-92493-8*) Wiley.

— The Chemistry of Organic Arsenic, Antimony, & Bismuth Compounds. LC 93-3145. (Chemistry of Functional Groups Ser.). 1200p. 1994. text ed. 425.00 (*0-471-93044-X*) Wiley.

— The Chemistry of Organic Selenium & Tellurium Compounds, Vol. 1. (Chemistry of Functional Groups Ser.). 939p. 1986. text ed. 995.00 (*0-471-90425-2*) Wiley.

— The Chemistry of Sulphenic Acids & Their Derivatives. 819p. 1990. text ed. 795.00 (*0-471-92373-7*) Wiley.

— The Chemistry of Sulphinic Acids, Esters & Derivatives. (Chemistry of Functional Groups). 728p. 1990. text ed. 695.00 (*0-471-91918-7*) Wiley.

— The Chemistry of Triple-Bonded Functional Groups, Vol. 2. LC 93-21238. (Chemistry of Functional Groups, Supplementary Ser.: Vol. C2). 1200p. 1994. text ed. 600.00 (*0-471-93559-X*) Wiley.

— Supplement E: The Chemistry of Hydroxyl, Ether & Peroxide Groups, Vol. 2. (Chemistry of Functional Groups Ser.). 1250p. 1993. text ed. 990.00 (*0-471-93045-8*) Wiley.

— Supplement to the Chemistry of Double-Bonded Functional Groups, Vol. 2. (Chemistry of Functional Groups Ser.). 797p. 1989. text ed. 690.00 (*0-471-91719-2*) Wiley.

Patai, Saul E. & Rappoport, Zui, eds. Chemistry of Organic Silicon Compounds, Pt. 1. (Chemistry of Functional Groups Ser.). 892p. 1989. text ed. 895.00 (*0-471-91441-X*) Wiley.

Patai, Saul E. & Rappoport, Zvi. Supplement C: The Chemistry of Triple Bonded Groups, Pt. 1. (Chemistry of Functional Groups Ser.). 736p. 1983. reprint ed. text ed. 598.00 (*0-471-28030-5*) Wiley.

Patai, Saul E. & Rappoport, Zvi, eds. The Chemistry of Amidines & Imidates, Vol. 2. (Chemistry of Functional Groups Ser.: No. 1078). 918p. 1991. text ed. 915.00 (*0-471-92457-1*) Wiley.

— The Chemistry of Enones, Vol. 2. (Chemistry of Functional Groups Ser.). 670p. 1989. text ed. 720.00 (*0-471-92289-7*) Wiley.

— The Chemistry of Organic Selenium & Tellurium Compounds, Vol. 2. (Chemistry of Functional Groups Ser.). 864p. 1987. text ed. 895.00 (*0-471-91020-1*) Wiley.

— The Chemistry of Sulphonic Acids, Esters & Their Derivatives. (Chemistry of Functional Groups Ser.). 1121p. 1991. text ed. 1,150.00 (*0-471-92201-3*) Wiley.

— Supplement S: The Chemistry of Sulphur-Containing Functional Groups. LC 92-23016. (Chemistry of Functional Groups Ser.). 1122p. 1993. text ed. 795.00 (*0-471-93046-6*) Wiley.

Patai, Saul E., jt. ed. see Hartley, Frank R.

Patai, Saul E., ed. see Ogliaruso, Michael A. & Wolfe, James F.

Patai, Saul E., ed. see Schank, K., et al.

Patai, Saul E., et al. Chemistry of Enones & Related Compounds. 597p. 1989. text ed. 615.00 (*0-471-91563-7*) Wiley.

Patajo-Legasto, Priscelina, jt. ed. see Pantoja-Hidalgo, Cristina.

Pataki, Caroly, ed. see Kaplan, Harold I. & Sadock, Benjamin J.

Pataki, Eva. Dominican Painting: Masters & Novices. 2nd rev. ed. LC 89-91748. (Illus.). 102p. (C). 1989. pap. 15.00 (*0-9615932-1-0*) E Pataki.

— Haitian Painting, Art & Kitsch. LC 85-73136. (Illus.). x, 172p. 1986. 25.00 (*0-9615932-0-2*) E Pataki.

Pataki, L. & Zapp, E. Basic Analytical Chemistry. (Analytical Chemistry Ser.: Vol. 2). (Illus.). 1981. 191.00 (*0-08-023850-5*, Pub. by Pergamon Repr UK) Franklin.

Pataki-Schweizer, K. J. A New Guinea Landscape: Community, Space & Time in the Eastern Highlands. LC 78-21211. (Anthropological Studies in the Eastern Highlands of New Guinea: Vol. 4). (Illus.). 188p. 1980. 40.00 (*0-295-95656-9*) U of Wash Pr.

Pataky-Brestyanszky, I. Kovacs, Margit. 194p. (C). 1989. 130.00 (*0-685-34438-X*, Pub. by Collets) St Mut.

Pataky, Sophie. Lexikon Deutscher Frauen der Feder, 2 vols., Set. 1983. fiche write for info. (*0-318-71938-X*, Pub. by Georg Olms GW) Lubrecht & Cramer.

Patalas, E., jt. auth. see Gregor, U.

Patan, Federico. Perfiles: Perfiles Ensayos Sobre Literatura Mexicana Reciente. 1992. 36.00 (*0-89295-066-8*) Society Sp & Sp-Am.

Patani, A., tr. see Samsonov, G. V., ed.

***Patanian, Antranik.** Arabe-Express Dictionnaire, Guide de Conversation et Grammaire de l'Arabe Moderne. 4th ed. 159p. (ARA & FRE.). 1989. pap. 32.95 (*0-7859-7947-6*, 2716310076) Fr & Eur.

Patanjali. How to Know God Patanjali. 1993. 12.95 (*0-87481-010-8*) Vedanta Pr.

— Patanjali's Yoga Sutras. 2nd ed. Prasada, Rama, tr. 318p. 1981. reprint ed. 24.00 (*0-89744-220-2*, Pub. by Orient Reprint II) Auromere.

— Patanjali's Yoga Sutras. (the Aphorisms of Yoga, by Patanjali.) with the Commentary of Vyasa & the Gloss of Vachaspati Misra. Rama Prasada, tr. LC 73-3789. reprint ed. 29.00 (*0-404-57804-7*) AMS Pr.

— Raja Yoga Sutras. Swami Jyotir Maya Nanda, tr. (Illus.). 1978. pap. 6.99 (*0-934664-38-2*) Yoga Res Foun.

— Yoga Sutras of Patanjali. 2nd rev. ed. Johnston, Charles, tr. 1993. pap. 10.00 (*0-914732-08-0*) Bro Life Inc.

Patanjali, Shri & Yeats, William Butler, trs. The Ten Principal Upanishads. 160p. (Orig.). 1970. pap. 8.95 (*0-571-09363-9*) Faber & Faber.

Patanjali, V. Thoughts on Indian Mysticism. 226p. 1978. 14.95 (*0-318-36391-7*) Asia Bk Corp.

Patanjali, V. & Muralidhar, A., eds. Modern Telugu Short Stories: An Anthology. Muralidhar, A., tr. 261p. 1968. pap. 2.45 (*0-88253-065-8*) Ind-US Inc.

Patankar, S. V. Numerical Heat Transfer & Fluid Flow. 197p. 1980. 59.50 (*0-89116-522-3*) Hemisp Pub.

Patankar, S. V., et al, eds. Numerical Prediction of Flow, Heat Transfer Turbulence, & Combustion: Selected Works of Professor D. Brian Spalding. LC 83-12172. 444p. 1983. pap. 178.00 (*0-08-030937-2*, 11, Pub. by Pergamon Repr UK) Franklin.

***Patargias.** English-Greek Dictionary of Biology & Medical Terms. 413p. (ENG & GRE.). Date not set. pap. 95.00 (*0-7859-9051-8*) Fr & Eur.

Patashinskii, A. Z., et al. Fluctuation Theory of Phase Transitions. Shepherd, P. J., ed. (International Series in Natural Philosophy: Vol. 98). (Illus.). 1979. 133.00 (*0-08-021664-1*, Pub. by Pergamon Repr UK) Franklin.

Patat, Jean-Pierre & Lutfalla, Michel. A Monetary History of France in the Twentieth Century. Martindale, Patrick & Cobham, David, trs. LC 89-6284. 290p. 1990. text ed. 59.95 (*0-312-03257-9*) St Martin.

Patavino, Rolandino. The Chronicles of the Trevisan March. Berrigan, Joseph R., ed. & tr. by. 1980. 15.00 (*0-87291-133-0*) Coronado Pr.

Patch, C. K. & Wilson, Stephen B. Psychology: A Self-Directed Approach. (Illus.). 206p. 1990. pap. 10.00 (*0-939249-01-4*) Minds Eye Illinois.

Patch, Cecilia & Moynihan, Brendan. Con Games 101: The Essential Primer to Avoiding Cons, Frauds, & Swindles. 80p. 1992. pap. 7.95 (*0-9635794-0-1*) Infrared Pr.

Patch, Diana C. Reflections of Greatness: Ancient Egypt at the Carnegie Museum of Natural History. LC 89-62543. (Illus.). 128p. (Orig.). (C). 1990. pap. text ed. 24.95 (*0-911239-14-6*) Carnegie Mus.

Patch, Diana C. & Haldane, Cheryl W. The Pharaoh's Boat at the Carnegie. LC 89-85819. (Illus.). 52p. (Orig.). (C). 1990. pap. text ed. 7.95 (*0-911239-22-7*) Carnegie Mus.

***Patch, Elizabeth P.** Plant Closings & Employment Loss in Manufacturing: The Role of Local Economic Conditions. (Studies in the History of American Labor). 137p. 1995. 43.00 (*0-8153-2028-0*) Garland.

Patch, Howard R. Chaucer & the Common People. (Studies in Chaucer: No. 6). (C). 1970. reprint ed. pap. 12.95 (*0-8383-0060-X*) M S G Haskell Hse.

Patch, Robert W. Maya & Spaniard in Yucatan, 1648-1812. LC 92-25923. 344p. 1993. 49.50 (*0-8047-2062-2*) Stanford U Pr.

Patch, William L., Jr. The Christian Trade Unions in the Weimar Republic, 1918-1933: The Failure of "Corporate Pluralism" LC 84-27150. (Yale Historical Publications, Miscellany: No. 133). 260p. 1985. text ed. 32.00 (*0-300-03328-1*) Yale U Pr.

Patchen, Aletha, jt. auth. see Patchen, Marvin.

Patchen, Kenneth. Awash with Roses: The Collected Love Poems of Kenneth Patchen. Smith, Laura, ed. (Midwest Authors Ser.). (Illus.). 176p. (Orig.). 1991. 19.95 (*0-933087-19-5*); pap. 9.95 (*0-933087-21-7*) Bottom Dog Pr.

— Before the Brave. LC 74-3035. (Studies in Poetry: No. 38). 1974. lib. bdg. 75.00 (*0-8383-2062-7*) M S G Haskell Hse.

— Collected Poems. LC 67-23487. 512p. 1969. pap. 16.95 (*0-8112-0140-6*, NDP284) New Directions.

— Doubleheader. Incl. Hurrah for Anything. LC 66-17822. 1966. (*0-318-54636-1*); Poemscapes. LC 66-17822. 1966. (*0-318-54637-X*); Letter to God. LC 66-17822. 1966. (*0-318-54638-8*); LC 66-17822. 1966. Set pap. 1.50 (*0-8112-0139-2*, NDP211) New Directions.

— In Quest of Candlelighters. LC 71-183393. 1972. 6.95 (*0-8112-0344-1*); pap. 1.95 (*0-8112-0141-4*, NDP334) New Directions.

— The Journal of Albion Moonlight. LC 68-28283. 1961. pap. 11.95 (*0-8112-0144-9*, NDP99) New Directions.

— Selected Poems. LC 58-590. 1958. pap. 9.95 (*0-8112-0146-5*, NDP160) New Directions.

— Still Another Pelican in the Breadbox. Morgan, Richard, ed. LC 80-82905. 96p. 1981. pap. 5.95 (*0-917530-14-4*) Pig Iron Pr.

— What Shall We Do Without Us? LC 84-4891. (Illus.). 112p. (Orig.). 1984. 25.00 (*0-87156-843-8*); pap. 12.95 (*0-87156-818-7*) Sierra.

— Wonderings. LC 79-148535. (Illus.). (Orig.). 1971. pap. 8.95 (*0-8112-0149-X*, NDP320) New Directions.

Patchen, Martin. Black-White Contact in Schools: Its Social & Academic Effects. LC 80-83511. (Illus.). 400p. 1982. 16.00 (*0-911198-61-X*); pap. 7.50 (*0-911198-64-4*) Purdue U Pr.

— Resolving Disputes Between Nations: Coercion or Conciliation? LC 87-26845. xiii, 365p. (C). 1988. lib. bdg. 48.00 (*0-8223-0764-2*); pap. text ed. 18.95 (*0-8223-0819-3*) Duke.

Patchen, Marvin & Patchen, Aletha. Baja Adventures by Land, Air & Sea. 1981. pap. 9.95 (*0-9605712-0-5*) Baja Trail.

Patchen, Nancy. Journey of a Master: Swami Chinmayananda, the Man, the Path, the Teaching. LC 90-82276. (Illus.). 360p. (Orig.). 1989. pap. 15.00 (*0-89581-922-8*) Chinmaya Pubns.

— Swami Chinmayananda: Journey of a Master. 335p. Date not set. pap. 15.00 (*1-880687-17-8*) Chinmaya Pubns.

Patchett, Ann. The Patron Saint of Liars. 368p. 1992. 21.00 (*0-395-61306-X*, R Todd) HM.

— The Patron Saint of Liars. 1993. mass mkt. 5.99 (*0-8041-1151-0*) Ivy Books.

— The Patron Saint of Liars. large type ed. 586p. 1992. reprint ed. lib. bdg. 20.95 (*1-56054-526-7*) Thorndike Pr.

— Taft. LC 94-9500. 1994. 21.95 (*0-395-69461-2*) HM.

Patchett, Arnold. Some Yorkshire Bridges of Beauty & Romance. 135p. (C). 1989. text ed. 65.00 (*1-872795-86-2*, Pub. by Pentland PR UK) St Mut.

Patchett, Arnold N. Hadrian's Magic Stones. 223p. (C). 1989. text ed. 80.00 (*0-685-63532-5*, Pub. by Pentland Pr UK) St Mut.

Patchett, J. Barry. Real Estate Math. Hedrick, Rebecca C., ed. 110p. (C). 1989. reprint ed. pap. text ed. 18.95 (*0-317-93337-X*) PDIL.

Patchett, K. W. Recognition of Commercial Judgments & Awards in the Commonwealth. 1984. 128.00 (*0-406-40320-1*, U.K.) Butterworth Legal Pubs.

Patchett, Lynne. Glaciers. LC 91-45080. (Our Planet Ser.). (Illus.). 32p. (J). (gr. 4-6). 1993. lib. bdg. 11.59 (*0-8167-2751-1*); pap. text ed. 3.95 (*0-8167-2752-X*) Troll Assocs.

Patchett, Monica, ed. see Wilde, David.

Patchick, Paul. Eruption. 480p. (Orig.). 1980. pap. 2.75 (*0-89083-614-0*) Zebra.

Patching, David C. Practical Soft Systems Analysis. 320p. (Orig.). 1990. pap. 57.50 (*0-273-03237-2*, Pub. by Pitman Pub Ltd UK) Trans-Atl Phila.

Patching, Roger, jt. auth. see Masterton, Murray.

Patchner, Michael A. & Balgopal, Pallassana R. Excellence in Nursing Homes: Care Planning, Quality Assurance & Personnel Management. LC 92-2217. (Illus.). 144p. 1992. 29.95 (*0-8261-8150-3*) Springer Pub.

Patchner, Michael A., jt. auth. see Berger, Raymond M.

Patchwork Quilt Tsushin Staff & Liddell, Jill. The Changing Seasons: Quilt Patterns from Japan. LC 92-52873. (Illus.). 160p. 1992. 35.00 (*0-525-93438-3*, Dutton Studio); pap. 25.00 (*0-525-48601-1*, Dutton Studio) Studio Bks.

Pate, jt. auth. see Breed.

Pate, Alexs. Losing Absalom. 256p. 1994. 19.95 (*1-56689-017-9*) Coffee Hse.

***Pate, Alexs D.** Losing Absalom. 320p. Date not set. pap. text ed. 6.99 (*0-425-15013-5*) Berkley Pub.

Pate, Antony M., et al. Police Use of Force: Official Reports, Citizen Complaints, & Legal Consequences, 2 vols. LC 93-86909. (Illus.). 383p. (Orig.). 1993. pap. text ed. 60.00 (*1-884614-00-0*) Police Found.

— Police Use of Force: Official Reports, Citizen Complaints, & Legal Consequences, 2 vols., Vol. 1. LC 93-86909. (Illus.). 173p. (Orig.). 1993. pap. text ed. write for info. (*1-884614-01-9*) Police Found.

P
Q

— Police Use of Force: Official Reports, Citizen Complaints, & Legal Consequences, 2 vols., Vol. 2. LC 93-86909. (Illus.). 210p. (Orig.). 1993. pap. text ed. write for info. (*1-884614-02-7*) Police Found.

Pate, C. Marvin. Adam Christology As the Exegetical & Theological Substructure of Second Corinthians 4 7-5 21. 184p. (C). 1991. lib. bdg. 47.50 (*0-8191-8188-9*) U Pr of Amer.

— The Glory of Adam & the Afflictions of the Righteous: Pauline Suffering in Context. LC 93-16072. 380p. 1993. text ed. 99.95 (*0-7734-2360-5*) E Mellen.

— Luke. (Gospel Commentary Ser.). 475p. 1995. pap. 19.99 (*0-8024-5622-7*) Moody.

Pate, Carol. Ready-to-Use Illustrations of Toys, Dolls & Games. (Clip Art Ser.). (Illus.). 64p. (Orig.). 1991. pap. 4.95 (*0-486-26671-0*) Dover.

Pate, Deborah M., jt. auth. see Jaeger, Sharon A.

Pate, Don. He Shall Be Like a Tree. (Horizon Ser.). 128p. 1981. pap. 5.95 (*0-8127-0315-4*) Review & Herald.

Pate, Dudley B. DocuMate. 60p. 1991. pap. 9.95 (*0-88415-006-2*) Gulf Pub.

Pate, Edward. Landlord! A True Story. 102p. (Orig.). 1989. pap. 15.95 (*1-877679-02-X*) S Prodns Bks.

Pate, Ernest. Dreams for a Quiet Night. LC 83-73639. 80p. (Orig.). 1984. pap. 4.95 (*0-87516-535-4*) DeVorss.

Pate, James L. & Wertheimer, Michael, eds. No Small Part: A History of Regional Organizations in American Psychology. LC 93-37085. 256p. 1993. text ed. 40.00 (*1-55798-215-5*) Am Psychol.

Pate, J'Nell. North of the River: A Brief History of North Fort Worth. (Chisholm Trail Ser.: No. 11). 192p. (Orig.). (C). 1994. pap. 12.95 (*0-87565-133-X*) Tex Christian.

Pate, J'Nell L. Livestock Legacy: The Fort Worth Stockyards, 1887-1987. LC 88-1116. (Centennial Series of the Association of Former Students: No. 27). (Illus.). 352p. 1992. pap. 14.95 (*0-89096-530-7*) Tex A&M Univ Pr.

— Ranald Slidell Mackenzie: Brave Cavalry Colonel. LC 93-21952. (J). (gr. 4-8). 1994. 14.95 (*0-89015-901-7*) Sunbelt Media.

Pate, J'Nell L., ed. Document Sets for Texas & the Southwest in U. S. History. 171p. (C). 1991. write for info. (*0-669-27109-8*) Heath.

***Pate, Joan, ed.** Eleventh Census of the United States 1890: Oakland County, Michigan. 118p. (Orig.). 1994. pap. 8.00 (*1-879766-21-3*) OCG Society.

— Michigan State Census for Oakland County 1845. 290p. (Orig.). 1985. pap. 15.00 (*1-879766-01-9*) OCG Society.

— Rose Township Cemeteries, Oakland County, Michigan. 72p. 1987. pap. 5.00 (*1-879766-09-4*) OCG Society.

— Roseland Park Cemetery (Military Sections) 59p. (Orig.). 1993. pap. text ed. 5.00 (*1-879766-19-1*) OCG Society.

— Southfield United Presbyterian Church, Early Records. 101p. (Orig.). 1985. pap. 10.00 (*1-879766-02-7*) OCG Society.

— Surname Directory, 1983. 123p. (Orig.). 1991. pap. 10.00 (*1-879766-06-X*) OCG Society.

— Surname Directory, 1986. 194p. (Orig.). 1986. pap. 8.00 (*1-879766-07-8*) OCG Society.

— Surname Directory, 1989. 190p. (Orig.). 1989. pap. 10.00 (*1-879766-08-6*) OCG Society.

— Troy Township Cemeteries, Oakland County, Michigan. 105p. (Orig.). 1988. pap. 7.00 (*1-879766-10-8*) OCG Society.

Pate, Joan, intro. Birmingham & West Bloomfield Cemeteries, Oakland County, Michigan. 182p. (Orig.). 1990. pap. 11.00 (*1-879766-15-9*) OCG Society.

— Commerce Township Cemeteries, Oakland County, Michigan. 200p. (Orig.). 1989. pap. 12.00 (*1-879766-11-6*) OCG Society.

— Farmington & Farmington Hills Cemeteries, Oakland County, Michigan. 149p. (Orig.). 1990. pap. 9.00 (*1-879766-14-0*) OCG Society.

— Federal Census & Mortality Schedule, 1860, Oakland County, Michigan. 689p. (Orig.). 1988. pap. 40.00 (*1-879766-05-1*) OCG Society.

— Holly Township Cemeteries, Oakland County, Michigan. 235p. (Orig.). 1991. pap. 18.00 (*1-879766-17-5*) OCG Society.

— Southfield Township Cemeteries, Oakland County, Michigan. 135p. (Orig.). 1989. pap. 10.00 (*1-879766-12-4*) OCG Society.

— St. Mary's & Royal Oak Cemeteries, Oakland County, Michigan. 136p. (Orig.). 1990. pap. 11.00 (*1-879766-16-7*) OCG Society.

— Surname Directory, 1992, No. 4. 182p. (Orig.). 1992. pap. 10.00 (*1-879766-18-3*) OCG Society.

— White Lake Township Cemeteries, Oakland County, Michigan. 109p. (Orig.). 1990. pap. 8.00 (*1-879766-13-2*) OCG Society.

Pate, John B. History of Turner County. LC 79-10025. (Illus.). 1979. reprint ed. 22.50 (*0-87152-295-0*) Reprint.

Pate, Larry, et al. Developing Organisations. 1985. 210.00 (*0-903763-42-7*, Pub. by MCB UK) St Mut.

***Pate, Marvin.** The End of the Age Has Come: The Theology of Paul. 256p. 1995. 17.99 (*0-310-38301-3*) Zondervan.

Pate, R. Franklin. The Boomerang Poems. LC 90-46508. xiv, 54p. (Orig.). 1990. pap. 6.00 (*0-926487-07-8*) Rowan Mtn Pr.

Pate, Robert H., Jr., jt. auth. see Brown, Jeannette A.

Pate, Russ. Adman: Morris Hite's Methods for Winning the Ad Game. (Illus.). 225p. 1988. 24.95 (*0-935014-12-8*) E-Heart Pr.

Pate, Russ, jt. auth. see Landers, Robert.

Pate, Russ, jt. auth. see Sanders, Doug.

Pate, Russell & Hohn, Richard C., eds. Health & Fitness Through Physical Education. LC 93-39707. (Illus.). 240p. 1994. pap. text ed. 29.00x (*0-87322-490-6*, BPAT0490) Human Kinetics.

Patek, Jan. Quilts for Summer Days: Seasons of the Heart & Home. 1993. pap. 18.95 (*0-89145-818-2*) Collector Bks.

— Quilts for Winter Days. LC 93-33043. (Seasons of the Heart & Home Ser.: No. 2). 1993. 18.95 (*0-89145-824-7*) Collector Bks.

Patel. Dynamics of Offshore Structures. 1989. 99.95 (*0-408-01074-6*) Buttrwrth-Heinemann.

— Multivariable System Theory & Design. (International Series of Monographs on Systems & Control: Vol. 3). 385p. 1982. 155.00 (*0-08-027297-5*, Pub. by Pergamon Repr UK) Franklin.

Patel, et al. Arrhythmias Detection, Treatment & Cardiac Drugs: A Self-Directed Approach. 176p. 1989. pap. text ed. 27.50 (*0-7216-2820-6*) Saunders.

Patel, A. N. & Singh, S. Remote Sensing - Principles & Applications. (C). 1992. text ed. 40.00 (*81-7233-037-5*, Pub. by Scientific Pubs II) St Mut.

Patel, Arthi, jt. auth. see Goddard, Jane.

Patel, B. B. Workers of Closed Textile Mills. (C). 1988. 14.50 (*81-204-0290-1*, Pub. by Oxford IBH II) S Asia.

Patel, B. B., ed. Problems of Home-Based Workers in India. (C). 1989. 32.50 (*81-204-0395-9*, Pub. by Oxford IBH II) S Asia.

Patel, B. R. Collective Bargaining. 1993. text ed. 35.00 (*0-86311-260-9*, Pub. by Orient Longman Ltd II) Apt Bks.

Patel, B. R., ed. see American Society of Mechanical Engineers Staff.

Patel, C. B. Dynastic History of Nalas. (C). 1990. text ed. 56.00 (*81-85094-27-6*, Pub. by Punthi Pus II) S Asia.

Patel, C. N., jt. ed. see Swaminathan, K.

Patel, Chandra. The Complete Guide to Stress Management. (Illus.). 376p. 1991. 23.95 (*0-306-43967-0*, Plenum Pr) Plenum.

***Patel, Chhaya & Denny, Mary.** Cultural Foods & Renal Diets: Section I: For the Clinical Dietitian; Section II: A Multilingual Guide for Renal Patients, 2 vols., Set. 565p. (C). 1988. pap. text ed. 40.00 (*1-883146-53-4*) Coun Renal Nutrit.

Patel, D. Gel Electrophoresis. LC 94-5796. (Essential Data Ser.). 1994. pap. text ed. 19.95 (*0-471-94306-1*) Wiley.

Patel, D., ed. see Sun, Y.

***Patel, Ebrahim.** Worker Rights Vol. 1: From Apartheid to Democracy - What Role for Organized Labour? 203p. 1994. pap. text ed. 28.00 (*0-7021-3076-1*, Pub. by Juta SA) W W Gaunt.

Patel, Essop, ed. The World of Nat Nakasa: Selected Writings of the Late Nat Nakasa. (Staffrider Ser.: No. 27). 150p. (C). 1985. pap. 12.95 (*0-86975-050-X*, Pub. by Ravan Pr ZA) Ohio U Pr.

***Patel, Essop & Nakasa, Nat.** The World of Nat Nakasa. (Writers Ser.). (Illus.). 206p. (C). 1995. reprint ed. pap. text ed. 12.95x (*0-86975-464-5*, Pub. by Ravan Pr ZA) Ohio U Pr.

Patel, Essop, jt. ed. see Couzens, Tim.

Patel, H., jt. ed. see Mehta, Haroobhai.

Patel, Hasu H., jt. auth. see Mazrui, Ali A.

Patel, I. G. Essays in Economic Policy & Economic Growth. LC 86-1773. 288p. 1986. text ed. 39.95 (*0-312-25940-9*) St Martin.

Patel, I. G., ed. Policies for African Development: From the 1890s to the 1990s. LC 92-15526. 293p. 1992. pap. 24.00 (*0-685-70062-3*) Intl Monetary.

Patel, Ishwarbhai, ed. Sciences & the Vedas. 1986. 12.50 (*0-8364-1663-5*, Pub. by Somaiya) S Asia.

Patel, Jagdish K. & Read, Campbell. Handbook of the Normal Distribution. LC 81-17422. (Statistics, Textbooks & Monographs: No. 40). 351p. reprint ed. pap. 100.10 (*0-7837-3550-2*, 2043387) Bks Demand.

Patel, Jagdish K., et al. Handbook of Statistical Distributions. LC 76-48474. (Statistics, Textbooks & Monographs: No. 20). 324p. reprint ed. pap. 92.40 (*0-318-35010-6*, 2030870) Bks Demand.

Patel, Janak H., jt. auth. see Choudhary, Alok N.

Patel, Jay V., jt. auth. see Sinsky, Robert M.

Patel, Jayant. Seeking Home: An Immigrant's Realization. 181p. 1991. write for info. (*0-9631583-0-9*) J C Patel.

Patel, Jitendra, jt. ed. see Conn, P. J.

***Patel, Kant & Rushefsky, Mark E.** Health Care Politics & Policy in America. (Illus.). 324p. 1995. 59.95 (*1-56324-558-2*); pap. 24.95 (*1-56324-559-0*) M E Sharpe.

***Patel, Kishor.** Multicultural Education in All-White Areas. 321p. 1994. 55.95 (*1-85628-969-9*, Pub. by Avebury Pub UK) Ashgate Pub Co.

***Patel, M. L.** Development Dualism of Primitive Tribes: Constraints, Restraints & Fallacies. 298p. (C). 1984. 90.00x (*81-85880-44-1*, Pub. by Print Hse II) St Mut.

— Tribal Development Without Tears. (C). 1994. 38.00x (*81-210-0320-2*, Pub. by Inter-India Pubns) S Asia.

— Tribal Research in India: Approach, Constraints, Structure & Techniques. (C). 1994. text ed. 34.00 (*81-210-0318-0*, Pub. by Inter-India Pubns) S Asia.

Patel, Minoo H. & Witz, Joel A. Compliant Offshore Structures. 416p. 1991. 170.00 (*0-7506-1070-0*) Buttrwrth-Heinemann.

Patel, N. T., jt. auth. see Srivastava, U. K.

Patel, Narendra H. Student Transfers from White to Black Colleges. (National Association for Equal Opportunity in Higher Education Ser.: No. 3). 40p. (Orig.). (C). 1988. pap. text ed. 10.00 (*0-8191-6952-8*, NAEOHE) U Pr of Amer.

Patel, Naresh M., jt. auth. see Harrison, Peter G.

Patel, Pravinchandra J. Patel's Immigration Law Digest, 5 vols., Set. suppl. ed. LC 84-82185. (Immigration Law Ser.). 1985. ring bd. 575.00 (*0-685-59812-8*) Clark Boardman Callaghan.

Patel, R. I. Forest Flora of Melghat. 380p. (C). 1968. 90.00 (*0-685-21863-5*, Pub. by Intl Bk Distr II) St Mut.

Patel, R. V., et al, eds. Numerical Linear Algebra Techniques for Systems & Control. LC 93-27006. (Illus.). 736p. 1994. text ed. 89.95 (*0-7803-0443-8*) Inst Electrical.

Patel, Rajeshwari. W. B. Yeats & the Ideal of "Unity of Being" 200p. 1990. text ed. 27.50 (*81-85218-13-7*, Pub. by Prestige II) Advent Bks Div.

Patel, Rajnikant V., jt. auth. see Balafoutis, Constantinos A.

Patel, Ramesh C., jt. auth. see Zuman, Petr.

Patel, Ramesh N. Philosophy of the Gita. LC 90-40763. (American University Studies: Philosophy: Ser. V, Vol. 105). 311p. (C). 1991. text ed. 47.95 (*0-8204-1416-6*) P Lang Pubs.

Patel, S. Tribal Education in India: A Case Study of Orrissa. (C). 1991. 14.00 (*81-7099-292-3*, Pub. by Mittal II) S Asia.

Patel, S. J. Indian Economy at the Dawn of the Twenty-First Century. 1993. text ed. 17.95 (*0-86131-799-8*, Pub. by Orient Longman Ltd II) Apt Bks.

Patel, S. J., ed. Pharmaceuticals in Developing Countries. 100p. 1983. 94.00 (*0-08-030210-6*, Pub. by Pergamon Repr UK) Franklin.

Patel, Sardar V. The Collected Works of Sardar Vallabhbhai Patel, Vol. II (1926-1929) Chopra, P. N., ed. 432p. (C). 1992. text ed. 60.00 (*81-220-0252-8*, Pub. by Konark Pubs Pvt Ltd II) Advent Bks Div.

— Collected Works of Sardar Vallabhbhai Patel, 1918-1925, Vol. I. (Illus.). 500p. 1990. text ed. 60.00 (*81-220-0179-3*, Pub. by Konark Pubs Pvt Ltd II) Advent Bks Div.

Patel, Sarol K. Cultural History of Early Medieval Orissa. (C). 1991. text ed. 78.00 (*81-85067-71-6*, Pub. by Sundeep Prakashan II) S Asia.

Patel, Satyavrata. Hinduism: Religion & Way of Life. 165p. (gr. 9-12). 1980. 15.95 (*0-940500-25-6*) Asia Bk Corp.

Patel, Shriprakas B. Nuclear Physics: An Introduction. 346p. 1991. text ed. 51.95 (*0-470-21130-X*) Halsted Pr.

***Patel, Sujata & Thorner, Alice, eds.** Bombay: Metaphor for Modern India. (Illus.). 320p. 1995. 24.00 (*0-19-563688-0*) OUP.

— Bombay: Mosaic of Arts & Letters. (Illus.). 256p. 1995. 24.00 (*0-19-563689-9*) OUP.

***Patel, Surendra J., et al.** Development Distance Between Nations. (Illus.). xxiv, 291p. 1995. 35.00 (*81-7024-651-2*, Pub. by Ashish Pub Hse II) Nataraj Bks.

Patel, Surendra J., ed. Africa. (Technological Transformation in the Third World Ser.: Vol. 2). 242p. 1993. 59.95 (*1-85628-470-0*, Pub. by Avebury Pub UK) Ashgate Pub Co.

— Asia. (Technological Transformation in the Third World Ser.: Vol. 1). 344p. 1993. 67.95 (*1-85628-469-7*, Pub. by Avebury Pub UK) Ashgate Pub Co.

— Developed Countries. (Technological Transformation in the Third World Ser.: Vol. 4). 310p. 1993. 59.95 (*1-85628-472-7*, Pub. by Avebury Pub UK) Ashgate Pub Co.

— Latin America. (Technological Transformation in the Third World Ser.: Vol. 3). 346p. 1993. 67.95 (*1-85628-471-9*, Pub. by Avebury Pub UK) Ashgate Pub Co.

— Trademarks in Developing Countries. 122p. 1979. pap. 29.00 (*0-08-025223-0*, Pergamon Pr) Elsevier.

Patel, T. Dayananda. Kesava Temple at Somanathapura: A Cultural Study. 1990. 74.00 (*0-8364-2522-7*, Pub. by Agam Kala Prakashan) S Asia.

Patel, T. S., tr. see Dubinin, G. N. & Avraamov, Yu S.

Patel, Tara. Development of Education among Tribal Women. 1985. 17.50 (*0-8364-1320-2*, Pub. by Mittal II) S Asia.

Patel, Tara, jt. auth. see Shah, V. P.

***Patel, Tulsi.** Fertility Behaviour: Population & Society in a Rajasthan Village. (Illus.). 286p. 1995. text ed. 26.00 (*0-19-563539-6*) OUP.

Patel, V., jt. auth. see Desai, Neera.

Patel, V. I., jt. ed. see Evans, D. A.

Patel, V. T., ed. Problems & Issues in Gandhism. 1990. reprint ed. 48.50 (*81-210-0250-8*, Pub. by Inter-India Pubns) S Asia.

Patel, Vilma, jt. ed. see Evans, David A.

***Patel, Vithal A.** Numerical Analysis. LC 93-86061. 652p. (C). 1993. text ed. 66.50 (*0-03-098330-4*) SCP.

Patell, Cyrus, jt. ed. see Bercovitch, Sacvan.

Patell, Cyrus R. Joyce's View of History in Finnegans Wake. (LeBaron Russell Briggs Prize Honors Essays in English Ser.). 96p. 1985. pap. 5.00 (*0-674-48711-7*) HUP.

Patella, Chris & Oddo, Eileen. Makin Music! (Musical Munchkins Are...Ser.). 75p. (Orig.). (J). (gr. k-2). 1989. teacher ed write for info. (*0-944333-02-8*); audio, lp write for info. (*0-318-64483-5*) Musical Munchkins.

— Marvelous Musical Adventures for Developing Early Musicianship. (Musical Munchkins Presents Ser.). (Illus.). 50p. 1987. pap. 7.95 (*0-944333-00-1*); audio, lp 9.95 (*0-685-19315-2*) Musical Munchkins.

Patella, Rocco. Basic Air Conditioning. 1980. student ed 6.00 (*0-8064-0333-0*, 830); audio 289.00 (*0-8064-0334-9*) Bergwall.

Pateman, Carole. The Disorder of Women: Democracy, Feminism, & Political Theory. LC 89-62425. 236p. 1990. 39.50 (*0-8047-1764-8*); pap. 12.95 (*0-8047-1765-6*) Stanford U Pr.

— Participation & Democratic Theory. LC 71-120193. 1976. pap. 16.95 (*0-521-29004-X*) Cambridge U Pr.

— The Problem of Political Obligation: A Critical Analysis of Liberal Theory. LC 85-8719. 1986. pap. 14.00 (*0-520-05650-7*) U CA Pr.

— The Problem of Political Obligation: A Critical Analysis of Liberal Theory. LC 78-18460. 217p. reprint ed. pap. 61.90 (*0-685-20602-5*, 2030536) Bks Demand.

— The Sexual Contract. LC 87-63007. xii, 264p. 1988. 42.50 (*0-8047-1476-2*); pap. 14.95 (*0-8047-1477-0*) Stanford U Pr.

Pateman, Carole & Gross, Elizabeth, eds. Feminist Challenges: Social & Political Theory. (Northeastern Series in Feminist Theory). 225p. (C). 1986. text ed. 32.50 (*1-55553-003-6*); pap. 12.95 (*1-55553-004-4*) NE U Pr.

Pateman, Carole, jt. ed. see Goodnow, Jacqueline.

Pateman, Carole, jt. ed. see Shanley, Mary L.

Pateman, Neil A. Teaching Mathematics - A Tantalising Enterprise: On the Nature of Mathematics & Mathematics Teaching. (C). 1989. 44.00 (*0-7300-0630-1*, Pub. by Deakin Univ AT) St Mut.

***Pateman, Robert.** Belgium. (Cultures of the World Ser.). 128p. (J). (gr. 3-5). 1995. lib. bdg. 21.95 (*0-7614-0176-8*) Marshall Cavendish.

— Bolivia. (Cultures of the World Ser.). 128p. (J). (gr. 3-5). 1995. lib. bdg. 21.95 (*0-7614-0178-4*) Marshall Cavendish.

— Egypt. LC 92-10209. (Cultures of the World Ser.). (J). 1992. 21.95 (*1-85435-535-X*) Marshall Cavendish.

— Kenya. LC 92-39263. (Cultures of the World Ser.). (J). 1993. 21.95 (*1-85435-572-4*) Marshall Cavendish.

***Pateman, Robert & Seward, Pat.** Denmark. (Cultures of the World Ser.). 128p. (Orig.). (J). (gr. 3-5). 1995. lib. bdg. write for info. (*0-7614-0168-7*) Marshall Cavendish.

Pateman, Roy. Eritrea: Even the Stones Are Burning. LC 90-81664. (Illus.). 260p. 1990. 35.00 (*0-932415-61-X*); pap. 11.95 (*0-932415-62-8*) Red Sea Pr.

Pateman, Trevor. Key Concepts: A Guide to Aesthetics, Criticisms, & the Arts in Education. (Falmer Press Library on Aesthetic Education). 300p. 1991. 85.00 (*1-85000-793-4*, Falmer Pr); pap. 33.00 (*1-85000-794-2*, Falmer Pr) Taylor & Francis.

Patenaude, Bertrand, jt. ed. see Dallin, Alexander.

Patenaude, Bertrand M., ed. The Russian Revolution. LC 91-45133. (Articles on Russian & Soviet History, 1500-1991 Ser.: Vol. 5). 334p. 1992. 56.00 (*0-8153-0562-1*) Garland.

Patenaude, Bertrand M., jt. ed. see Dallin, Alexander.

Patenaude, Bertrand M., jt. ed. see Emmons, Terence.

Patenm, Geoff. Handguns: A Collector's Guide. 1993. 17.98 (*1-55521-916-0*) Bk Sales Inc.

***Patent & Trademark Office Staff.** Manual of Patent Examining Procedure. 16th ed. (IP Ser.). 1993. pap. 60.00 (*0-614-07304-9*) Clark Boardman Callaghan.

Patent, Arnold M. Death, Taxes & Other Illusions. Bolker, Selma, ed. LC 89-60373. 150p. (Orig.). 1989. 16.00 (*0-9613663-3-8*); pap. 10.00 (*0-9613663-2-X*) Celebration Pub.

— Money & Beyond. LC 93-73898. 200p. (Orig.). 1993. pap. 12.00 (*0-9613663-5-4*) Celebration Pub.

— You Can Have It All. rev. ed. LC 90-84993. 200p. 1991. pap. 11.00 (*0-9613663-4-6*) Celebration Pub.

— You Can Have it All. 3rd rev. ed. LC 94-41441. 210p. (C). 1995. 16.95 (*1-885223-05-6*) Beyond Words Pub.

Patent, Dorothy H. African Elephants: Giants of the Land. LC 91-55028. (Illus.). 40p. (J). (gr. 3-7). 1991. lib. bdg. 14.95 (*0-8234-0911-2*) Holiday.

— The American Alligator. LC 93-37704. (J). 1994. 15.95 (*0-395-63392-3*, Clarion Bks) HM.

— Appaloosa Horses. LC 88-4470. (Illus.). 80p. (J). (gr. 3-7). 1988. lib. bdg. 15.95 (*0-8234-0706-3*) Holiday.

— Baby Horses. (Animals Ser.). 56p. (J). (ps-3). 1991. lib. bdg. 17.50 (*0-87614-690-6*, Carolrhoda) Lerner Group.

— Cattle. LC 92-32987. (Illus.). (J). (gr. 4-6). 1993. 19.95 (*0-87614-765-1*, Carolrhoda) Lerner Group.

— The Challenge of Extinction. LC 90-3288. (Environmental Issues Ser.). (Illus.). 64p. (J). (gr. 6 up). 1991. lib. bdg. 15.95 (*0-89490-268-7*) Enslow Pubs.

— Deer & Elk. LC 93-25894. (Illus.). (J). 1994. 15.95 (*0-395-52003-7*, Clarion Bks) HM.

— Dogs: The Wolf Within. LC 92-12334. (Understanding Animal Behavior Ser.). (J). (gr. 4-6). 1992. 19.95 (*0-87614-691-4*, Carolrhoda) Lerner Group.

— Dogs: The Wolf Within. (J). (gr. 4-6). 1993. pap. 7.95 (*0-87614-604-3*, Carolrhoda) Lerner Group.

— Dolphins & Porpoises. LC 87-45332. (Illus.). 96p. (J). (gr. 4 up). 1987. lib. bdg. 15.95 (*0-8234-0663-6*) Holiday.

— Eagles of America. LC 95-6083. (Illus.). 40p. (J). 1995. 15.95 (*0-8234-1198-2*) Holiday.

— A Family Goes Hunting. (Illus.). 64p. (J). (gr. 4-9). 1991. 14.95 (*0-395-52004-5*, Clarion Bks) HM.

— Family Goes Hunting. (J). (gr. 4-7). 1993. pap. 6.95 (*0-395-66507-8*, Clarion Bks) HM.

— Feathers. (Illus.). 64p. (J). (gr. 5 up). 1992. 15.00 (*0-525-65081-4*, Cobblehill Bks) Dutton Child Bks.

— Flowers for Everyone. LC 89-23937. (Illus.). 64p. (J). (gr. 5 up). 1990. 14.95 (*0-525-65025-3*, Cobblehill Bks) Dutton Child Bks.

— Gray Wolf, Red Wolf. (Illus.). 64p. (J). (gr. 4 up). 1990. 15.95 (*0-89919-863-5*, Clarion Bks) HM.

— Gray Wolf, Red Wolf. (J). (gr. 4-7). 1994. pap. 6.95 (*0-395-69627-5*, Clarion Bks) HM.

— Habitats: Saving Wild Places. LC 92-28082. (Better Earth Ser.). (Illus.). 112p. (J). (gr. 6 up). 1993. lib. bdg. 17.95 (*0-89490-401-9*) Enslow Pubs.

— Horses. LC 93-12329. (Understanding Animals Behavior Ser.). (J). (gr. 4-6). 1993. 19.95 (*0-87614-766-X*, Carolrhoda) Lerner Group.

— Horses of America. LC 81-4165. (Illus.). 80p. (J). (gr. 3-7). 1981. lib. bdg. 15.95 (*0-8234-0399-8*) Holiday.

— How Smart Are Animals? 189p. (YA). (gr. 7 up). 1990. 17.95 (*0-15-236770-5*) HarBrace.

— Hugger to the Rescue. LC 93-32031. (J). 1994. 13.99 (*0-525-65161-6*, Cobblehill Bks) Dutton Child Bks.

— Humpback Whales. LC 89-2026. (Illus.). 32p. (J). (ps-3). 1989. lib. bdg. 15.95 (*0-8234-0779-9*) Holiday.

— Killer Whales. LC 92-23949. (Illus.). 32p. (J). (gr. 3-7). 1993. lib. bdg. 15.95 (*0-8234-0999-6*) Holiday.

An Asterisk (*) at the beginning of an entry indicates that the title is appearing in BIP for the first time.

— Looking at Ants. LC 89-1943. (Illus.). 48p. (J). (ps-4). 1989. lib. bdg. 12.95 (*0-8234-0771-3*) Holiday.
— Looking at Bears. LC 94-1834. 40p. (J). (ps-3). 1994. lib. bdg. 15.95 (*0-8234-1139-7*) Holiday.
— Looking at Dolphins & Porpoises. LC 88-39985. (Illus.). 48p. (J). (ps-4). 1989. lib. bdg. 13.95 (*0-8234-0748-9*) Holiday.
— Looking at Penguins. LC 92-37673. (Illus.). 40p. (J). (ps-4). 1993. lib. bdg. 15.95 (*0-8234-1037-4*) Holiday.
— Mosquitoes. LC 86-45387. (Illus.). 40p. (J). (gr. 3-7). 1986. lib. bdg. 12.95 (*0-8234-0627-X*) Holiday.
— Nutrition: What's in the Food We Eat. LC 92-3665. (Illus.). 40p. (J). (gr. 3-7). 1992. 15.95 (*0-8234-0968-6*) Holiday.
— Osprey. LC 92-30103. (Illus.). 64p. (J). (gr. 4-9). 1993. 14.95 (*0-395-63391-5*, Clarion Bks) HM.
— Pelicans. (Illus.). 64p. (J). (gr. 4-7). 1992. 14.95 (*0-395-57224-X*, Clarion Bks) HM.
— Places of Refuge: Our National Wildlife Refuge System. (Illus.). 80p. (J). (gr. 4-9). 1992. 15.95 (*0-89919-846-5*, Clarion Bks) HM.
— Prairie Dogs. LC 92-34724. (Illus.). (J). 1993. 15.95 (*0-395-56572-3*, Clarion Bks) HM.
— The Quetzal: Sacred Bird of the Forest. (Illus.). 1996. write for info. (*0-688-12662-6*); lib. bdg. write for info. (*0-688-12663-4*) Morrow Jr Bks.
— Return of the Wolf. LC 94-26798. (Illus.). (J). 1995. 15.95 (*0-395-72100-8*, Clarion Bks) HM.
— The Vanishing Feast. LC 94-2227. (Gulliver Green Book Ser.). (J). 1994. 17.95 (*0-15-292867-7*) HarBrace.
— Wagon Train: A Journey on the Oregon Trail. LC 94-48233. (Illus.). 32p. (J). (gr. 2-6). 1995. 15.95 (*0-8027-8377-5*); lib. bdg. 16.85 (*0-8027-8378-3*) Walker & Co.
— The Way of the Grizzly. LC 86-17562. (Illus.). 64p. (J). (gr. 4 up). 1987. 13.95 (*0-89919-383-8*, Clarion Bks) HM.
— The Way of the Grizzly. LC 86-17562. (Illus.). 64p. (J). (gr. 4 up). 1991. pap. 5.95 (*0-395-58112-5*, Clarion Bks) HM.
— Whales: Giants of the Deep. LC 84-729. (Illus.). 96p. (J). (gr. 3-7). 1984. lib. bdg. 15.95 (*0-8234-0530-3*) Holiday.
— What Good Is a Tail? LC 92-45639. (Illus.). 32p. (J). (gr. 1-5). 1994. 13.99 (*0-525-65148-9*, Cobblehill Bks) Dutton Child Bks.
— Where Food Comes From. LC 90-49833. (Illus.). 40p. (J). (gr. 3-7). 1991. lib. bdg. 14.95 (*0-8234-0877-9*) Holiday.
— Where the Bald Eagles Gather. LC 83-20852. (Illus.). 64p. (J). (gr. 3-6). 1984. 15.95 (*0-89919-230-0*, Clarion Bks) HM.
— Where the Bald Eagles Gather. (Illus.). 56p. (J). (gr. 3-7). 1990. pap. 5.95 (*0-395-52598-5*) HM.
— Where the Wild Horses Roam. (J). (gr. 4-7). 1993. pap. 6.95 (*0-395-66506-X*, Clarion Bks) HM.
— Where the Wild Horses Roam. 1989. 15.95 (*0-89919-507-5*) Ticknor & Fields.
— Whooping Crane. (J). (gr. 4-7). 1993. pap. 6.95 (*0-395-66505-1*, Clarion Bks) HM.
— The Whooping Crane: A Comeback Story. LC 88-2871. (Illus.). 96p. (J). (gr. 4 up). 1988. 14.95 (*0-89919-455-9*, Clarion Bks) HM.
— Why Mammals Have Fur. LC 94-28064. (Illus.). (J). 1995. 14.99 (*0-525-65141-1*, Cobblehill Bks) Dutton Child Bks.
— Wild Turkey, Tame Turkey. LC 89-613. (Illus.). 64p. (J). (gr. 3-6). 1989. 14.95 (*0-89919-704-3*, Clarion Bks) HM.
— Wild Turkey, Tame Turkey. (J). (gr. 4-7). 1992. pap. 5.95 (*0-395-55275-3*, Clarion Bks) HM.
— Yellowstone Fires: Flames & Rebirth. LC 89-24544. (Illus.). 40p. (J). (gr. 3-7). 1990. lib. bdg. 14.95 (*0-8234-0807-8*) Holiday.

Patent, Greg. Food Processor Cooking: Quick & Easy. 192p. 1992. pap. 16.95 (*0-89815-479-0*) Ten Speed Pr.
— More Big Sky Cooking. (Big Sky Cooking Ser.: No. 2). (Illus.). 151p. (Orig.). 1980. pap. 9.50 (*0-686-29281-2*) Eagle Comm.

Patent, Trademark, & Copyright Law Section Staff. Careers in Patent Law. 12p. 1971. 0.25 (*0-685-14367-8*, 537-0005) Amer Bar Assn.

Pater, Alan F., ed. Anthology of Magazine Verse & Yearbook of American Poetry. 1985. 35.95 (*0-917734-12-2*) Monitor Bk.
— Anthology of Magazine Verse & Yearbook of American Poetry, 1980. 1981. 25.00 (*0-917734-04-1*) Monitor Bk.
— Anthology of Magazine Verse & Yearbook of American Poetry, 1981. LC 80-645223. 1981. 29.95 (*0-917734-05-X*) Monitor Bk.
— Anthology of Magazine Verse & Yearbook of American Poetry, 1986-1988. LC 80-645223. 800p. 1988. 37.50 (*0-917734-14-9*) Monitor Bk.
— Anthology of Magazine Verse for Nineteen Thirty-Five Yearbook of American Poetry. LC 33-27220. 1976. reprint ed. 19.75 (*0-89609-033-7*) Roth Pub Inc.
— United States Battleships: The History of America's Greatest Fighting Fleet. LC 68-17423. 1968. 19.95 (*0-917734-07-6*) Monitor Bk.

Pater, Alan F. & Pater, Jason, eds. United States Embassies: A History. 690p. 1991. 49.95 (*0-917734-23-8*) Monitor Bk.

Pater, Alan F. & Pater, Jason R., eds. Dogs in the News. 1984. 17.50 (*0-917734-11-4*) Monitor Bk.
— What They Said in 1970: The Standard Source Book for the World's Spoken Opinion, Vol. 2. LC 74-111080. 1971. 17.50 (*0-9600252-3-5*) Monitor Bk.
— What They Said in 1971: The Standard Source Book for the World's Spoken Opinion, Vol. 3. LC 74-111080. 1972. 17.50 (*0-9600252-4-3*) Monitor Bk.
— What They Said in 1972: The Standard Source Book for the World's Spoken Opinion, Vol. 4. LC 74-111080. 1973. 17.50 (*0-9600252-5-1*) Monitor Bk.
— What They Said in 1973: The Standard Source Book for the World's Spoken Opinion, Vol. 5. LC 74-111080. 1974. 17.50 (*0-9600252-6-X*) Monitor Bk.
— What They Said in 1974: The Standard Source Book for the World's Spoken Opinion, Vol. 6. LC 74-111080. 640p. 1975. lib. bdg. 17.50 (*0-9600252-7-8*) Monitor Bk.
— What They Said in 1975: The Yearbook of World Opinion, Vol. 7. LC 74-111080. 1976. 17.50 (*0-9600252-8-6*) Monitor Bk.
— What They Said in 1976: The Yearbook of World Opinion, Vol. 8. LC 74-111080. 1977. 19.50 (*0-9600252-9-4*) Monitor Bk.
— What They Said in 1977: The Yearbook of World Opinion, Vol. 9. LC 74-111080. 1978. lib. bdg. 19.50 (*0-917734-01-7*) Monitor Bk.
— What They Said in 1978: The Yearbook of World Opinion, Vol. 10. LC 74-111080. 1979. 19.50 (*0-917734-02-5*) Monitor Bk.
— What They Said in 1981: The Yearbook of Spoken Opinion, Vol. 13. LC 74-111080. 1982. 27.50 (*0-917734-06-8*) Monitor Bk.
— What They Said in 1982: The Yearbook of World Opinion, Vol. 14. LC 74-111080. 1983. 27.95 (*0-917734-08-4*) Monitor Bk.
— What They Said in 1985: The Yearbook of World Opinion, Vol. 17. LC 74-111080. 1986. 35.00 (*0-917734-13-0*) Monitor Bk.
— What They Said in 1986: The Yearbook of World Opinion, Vol. 18. LC 74-111080. 1987. 35.95 (*0-917734-16-5*) Monitor Bk.
— What They Said in 1987: The Yearbook of World Opinion, Vol. 19. LC 74-111080. 600p. 1988. 37.50 (*0-917734-17-3*) Monitor Bk.
— What They Said in 1988: The Yearbook of World Opinion, Vol. 20. LC 74-111080. 592p. 1989. 37.50 (*0-917734-18-1*) Monitor Bk.
— What They Said in 1989: The Yearbook of World Opinion, Vol. 21. 576p. 1990. 37.95 (*0-917734-20-3*) Monitor Bk.
— What They Said in 1990: The Yearbook of World Opinion, Vol. 22. LC 74-111080. 556p. 1991. 39.75 (*0-917734-21-1*) Monitor Bk.
— What They Said in 1991: The Yearbook of World Opinion, Vol. 23. 480p. 1992. 41.00 (*0-917734-24-6*) Monitor Bk.
— What They Said in 1992: The Yearbook of World Opinion, Vol. 24. 488p. 1993. 41.00 (*0-917734-25-4*) Monitor Bk.
— What They Said in 1993: The Yearbook of World Opinion, Vol. 25. 544p. 1994. 41.00 (*0-917734-26-2*) Monitor Bk.

Pater, Anton S. Personal Education: About General Learning, Motivation, Development & Progress. LC 76-56540. 1977. 20.00 (*0-918210-01-1*, GL-1A); pap. 15.00 (*0-918210-00-3*, GL-1) Multi Spectral.

Pater, Calvin A. Karlstadt As the Father of the Baptist Movements: The Emergence of Lay Protestantism. LC 84-166680. (Illus.). 364p. reprint ed. pap. 103.80 (*0-8357-3783-7*, 2036513) Bks Demand.
— Karlstadt As the Father of the Baptist Movements: The Emergence of Lay Protestantism. LC 93-32132. (Illus.). 364p. 1993. reprint ed. text ed. 99.95 (*0-7734-9357-3*) E Mellen.

Pater, Jason, jt. ed. see Pater, Alan F.

Pater, Jason R., ed. The Great Libraries of America: A Pictorial History. 1983. 35.00 (*0-917734-03-3*) Monitor Bk.

Pater, Jason R., jt. ed. see Pater, Alan F.

Pater, Robert. The Black Belt Manager: Martial Arts Strategies for Power, Creativity, & Control. Orig. Title: Martial Arts & Arts of Management. 224p. 1989. pap. 10.95 (*0-89281-295-8*, Park St Pr) Inner Tradit.
— How to Make High Impact Safety & Health Presentations. 70p. 1988. pap. 25.00 (*0-939874-81-4*) ASSE.

Pater, Walter. Essays on Literature & Art. 203p. 1973. pap. 7.95 (*0-460-87009-2*, Everyman's Classic Lib) C E Tuttle.
— Gaston de Latour: The Revised Text. rev. ed. Monsman, Gerald, ed. & intro. by. LC 94-62118. (1880-1920 British Authors Ser.). (Illus.). 350p. 1995. lib. bdg. 40.00 (*0-944318-09-6*) ELT Pr.
— Marius the Epicurean. Levey, Michael, ed. (Classics Ser.). 320p. 1986. mass mkt. 10.95 (*0-14-043236-1*, Penguin Classics) Viking Penguin.
— Marius the Epicurean: His Sensations & Ideas. 224p. 1985. reprint ed. pap. 18.95 (*0-948166-02-9*, Pub. by Soho Bk Co UK) Dufour.
— The Renaissance. (World's Classics Ser.). 192p. 1987. pap. 4.95 (*0-19-281737-X*) OUP.
— The Renaissance. LC 77-12308. 239p. 1977. reprint ed. pap. 9.00 (*0-915864-35-5*) Academy Chi Pubs.
— The Renaissance: Studies in Art & Poetry. Hill, Donald L., ed. 1980. pap. 16.00 (*0-520-03664-6*) U CA Pr.

Pater, Walter H. Essays from 'The Guardian' LC 73-99717. (Essay Index Reprint Ser.). 1977. 19.95 (*0-8369-1370-1*) Ayer.
— Gaston De Latour: An Unfinished Romance. Shadwell, Charles L., ed. LC 79-8429. reprint ed. 44.50 (*0-404-62093-0*) AMS Pr.
— Imaginary Portraits. LC 75-30036. reprint ed. 29.50 (*0-404-14038-6*) AMS Pr.
— Plato & Platonism. LC 69-14031. 282p. 1970. reprint ed. text ed. 79.50 (*0-8371-1151-X*, PAPP, Greenwood Pr) Greenwood.
— Sketches & Reviews. LC 77-99718. (Essay Index Reprint Ser.). 1977. 19.95 (*0-8369-1371-X*) Ayer.

***Patera, Charlotte.** Schoolhouse Applique: Reverse Techniques & More. Townsend, Louise, ed. (Illus.). 80p. 1995. pap. text ed. 19.95 (*0-914881-99-X*, 10121) C & T Pub.

Patera, J., jt. auth. see McKay, W. G.

Patera, Tatiana, comp. A Concordance to the Poetry of Anna Akhmatova. LC 94-7867. 353p. 1995. 60.00 (*0-87501-111-X*) Ardis Pubs.

Paterculus, Velleius. Concordantia in Velleium Paterculum. Elefante, Maria, ed. (Alpha-Omega, Reihe A Ser.: Bd. LXXVI). vi, 524p. (GER.). 1992. write for info. (*3-487-09506-8*, Pub. by Georg Olms GW) Lubrecht & Cramer.
— Velleii Paterculi Quae Supersunt Ex Historiae Romanae Libris Duobus. cxliv, 638p. (GER.). reprint ed. write for info. (*0-318-70527-3*, Pub. by Georg Olms GW) Lubrecht & Cramer.

Paterek, Josephine. Encyclopedia of American Indian Costume. 516p. 1994. lib. bdg. 75.00 (*0-87436-685-2*) ABC-CLIO.
— Encyclopedia of American Indian Costume. (Illus.). 536p. 1995. 19.95 (*0-393-31382-4*) Norton.

Paternite, David, jt. ed. see Paternite, Stephen.

Paternite, Stephen & Paternite, David, eds. American Infrared Survey. LC 82-6160. (Illus.). 88p. (C). 1982. 21.95 (*0-9609812-0-9*) Photo Survey.

Paterno, Cynthia, jt. auth. see Lackner, Marie.

Paterno, Fred. The Literate Bassist. 1993. 6.95 (*0-87166-958-7*, 93822) Mel Bay.

Paterno, Gianfranco, jt. auth. see Barone, Antonio.

Paterno, Joe. Paterno: By the Book. 1991. mass mkt. 5.95 (*0-425-12909-8*) Berkley Pub.

Paterno, Joe & Asbell, Bernard. The Paterno Principle. 1989. 18.95 (*0-394-56501-0*) Random.

Paterno, Salvatore. The Liturgical Context of Early European Drama. 1990. 33.50 (*0-916379-62-0*) Scripta.

Paterra, Mary E. Cambridge Stratford Study Skills Course, 20 Hour Edition. (Illus.). 196p. (J). (gr. 6-8). 1986. teacher ed 64.95 (*0-935637-03-6*); student ed 12.95 (*0-935637-02-8*); trans. 60.00 (*0-935637-00-1*); audio 40.00 (*0-935637-01-X*) Cambridge Strat.
— Cambridge Stratford Study Skills Course, 30 Hour Edition. (Illus.). (YA). (gr. 9-11). 1986. teacher ed 64.95 (*0-935637-07-9*); student ed 12.95 (*0-935637-06-0*); trans. 120.00 (*0-935637-04-4*); audio 40.00 (*0-935637-05-2*) Cambridge Strat.

Paterson. Consider the Lilies. (J). 1986. lib. bdg. 14.89 (*0-690-04463-1*, Crowell Jr Bks) HarpC.

Paterson, jt. auth. see Stephens.

Paterson, et al. Using PC Tools for Windows. (Using Ser.). (Illus.). 800p. (Orig.). 1993. pap. 27.95 (*1-56529-229-4*) Que.

Paterson, A. Amenability. LC 88-14485. (SURV Ser.: No. 29). 452p. 1988. 110.00 (*0-8218-1529-6*, SURV-29) Am Math.

Paterson, A., jt. ed. see Piggott, J. R.

Paterson, A. B. The Man from Snowy River. (Illus.). 32p. (J). (ps-1). 1992. 7.95 (*0-207-15708-1*) HarperColl Wrld.
— The Man from Snowy River & Other Verses. 198p. 1989. reprint ed. lib. bdg. 25.95 (*0-89966-589-6*) Buccaneer Bks.
— Selected Poems: A. B. Paterson. 160p. (Orig.). 1993. pap. 10.00 (*0-207-17626-4*, Pub. by Angus & Robertson AT) HarpC.
— Waltzing Matilda. (Illus.). 32p. (J). (ps-1). 1991. 7.95 (*0-207-17098-3*) HarperColl Wrld.

Paterson, A. K., ed. see De Molina, Tirso.

Paterson, A. R. A First Course in Fluid Dynamics. LC 82-23437. 350p. 1984. pap. 39.95 (*0-521-27424-9*) Cambridge U Pr.

Paterson, A. Tony. Offshore Fire Safety. LC 93-12103. 300p. 1993. 85.95 (*0-87814-381-5*, S4516) PennWell Bks.

Paterson, Alan J. How Glass Is Made. (How It Is Made Ser.). (Illus.). 32p. (YA). (gr. 7 up). 1986. 12.95 (*0-8160-0038-7*) Facts on File.

Paterson, Alan M. Land Water & Power: A History of the Turlock Irrigation District, 1887-1987. LC 87-70947. (Western Lands & Waters Ser.: Vol. XIV). (Illus.). 420p. 1989. 26.50 (*0-87062-177-7*) A H Clark.

Paterson, Allan, jt. auth. see George, Dick.

Paterson, Allen. Designing a Garden: A Guide to Planning & Planting Through the Seasons. (Illus.). 160p. 1992. pap. 19.95 (*0-921820-45-3*, Pub. by Camden Hse CN) Firefly Bks Ltd.
— Herbs in the Garden. 370p. 1993. pap. 16.95 (*0-460-86015-1*, J M Dent & Sons) Trafalgar.
— Plants for Shade: A Complete Guide to What to Grow in Shade & Woodland. (Illus.). 160p. 1994. pap. 16.95 (*0-460-86096-8*, J M Dent & Sons) Trafalgar.

Paterson, Anna, tr. see Enquist, Per O.

Paterson, B. Donald, jt. auth. see Govindasamy, Devin.

Paterson, Bettina. Scaredy-Ghost. (Die-Cut Board Bks.). (Illus.). 12p. (J). (ps). 1993. bds. 2.50 (*0-448-40574-1*, G&D) Putnam Pub Group.

Paterson, Bettina, illus. Baby's ABC. (So Tall Board Bks.). 18p. (J). 1992. bds. 4.95 (*0-448-40130-4*, G&D) Putnam Pub Group.
— Baby's 1, 2, 3. (So Tall Board Bks.). 18p. (J). (ps). 1992. bds. 4.95 (*0-448-40265-3*, G&D) Putnam Pub Group.
— Busy Witch. (Die-Cut Board Bks.). 12p. (J). (ps). 1993. bds. 2.50 (*0-448-40573-3*, G&D) Putnam Pub Group.
— Duckling's Surprise. 12p. (J). (ps). 1995. bds. 2.50 (*0-448-40587-3*, G&D) Putnam Pub Group.
— Happy Easter, Bunny! 12p. (J). (ps). 1995. bds. 2.50 (*0-448-40588-1*, G&D) Putnam Pub Group.
— Jolly Snowman. (Die-Cut Board Bks.). 12p. (J). (ps). 1992. bds. 2.50 (*0-448-40575-X*, G&D) Putnam Pub Group.
— Merry ABC. (Wee Pudgy Board Bks.). 24p. (J). (ps). 1993. bds. 2.95 (*0-448-40553-9*, G&D) Putnam Pub Group.
— Merry Christmas, Santa! (Die-Cut Board Bks.). 12p. (J). (ps). 1992. bds. 2.50 (*0-448-40576-8*, G&D) Putnam Pub Group.
— Potty Time. (Teddy Board Bks.). 12p. (J). (ps). 1993. bds. 4.95 (*0-448-40539-3*, G&D) Putnam Pub Group.

Paterson, Brian, jt. auth. see Paterson, Cynthia.

Paterson, Bronwyn. Excellence & Expertise in Nursing. (C). 1991. pap. 33.00x (*0-7300-1266-2*, NPR300, Pub. by Deakin Univ AT) St Mut.

Paterson-Brown, Simon & Eckersley, Rupert. Aids to Anatomy. (Illus.). 288p. 1988. pap. text ed. 23.00 (*0-443-03624-1*) Churchill.

Paterson-Brown, Simon, jt. ed. see Ellis, Brian W.

Paterson, Colin R. & MacLennan, W. J. Bone Disease in the Elderly. LC 84-3716. (Wiley Series on Disease Management in the Elderly: No. 3). (Illus.). 224p. reprint ed. pap. 63.90 (*0-8357-3926-0*, 2036661) Bks Demand.

Paterson, Cynthia. The Foxwood Kidnap. 32p. (J). (ps-3). 1986. 6.95 (*0-8120-5771-6*) Barron.

Paterson, Cynthia & Paterson, Brian. The Foxwood Smugglers. (Foxwood Tales Ser.). (Illus.). 32p. (J). (ps-3). 1988. 6.95 (*0-8120-5984-0*) Barron.
— The Foxwood Surprise. (Illus.). 32p. (J). (ps-3). 1988. 6.95 (*0-8120-5986-7*) Barron.
— Robbery at Foxwood. (Foxwood Tales Ser.). (Illus.). 32p. (J). (ps-3). 1985. 6.95 (*0-8120-5665-5*) Barron.

Paterson, D. G. British Direct Investment in Canada, 1890-1914. LC 76-22429. 159p. reprint ed. pap. 45.40 (*0-8357-7421-X*, 2056122) Bks Demand.

Paterson, Dale, ed. Intelligent Schoolhouse: Readings on Computers & Learning. 1984. text ed. 27.00 (*0-8359-3108-0*, Reston) P-H.

Paterson, David & Palmer, Mary, eds. The Status of Animals: Ethics, Education & Welfare. 268p. (Orig.). 1989. pap. text ed. 31.00 (*0-85198-650-1*) CAB Intl.

Paterson, Debi, jt. auth. see Brown, Cathy J.

Paterson, Diane. Someday. LC 92-11401. (Illus.). 40p. (J). (gr. 1-3). 1993. text ed. 12.95 (*0-02-770565-X*, Bradbury S&S) S&S Childrens.

Paterson, Diane, illus. Stone Soup. LC 80-27947. 32p. (J). (gr. 1-4). 1981. lib. bdg. 9.79 (*0-89375-478-1*); pap. text ed. 2.50 (*0-89375-479-X*) Troll Assocs.

***Paterson, Don.** Nil Nil. 64p. (Orig.). 1995. pap. 9.95 (*0-571-16808-6*) Faber & Faber.

Paterson, Donald G. Physique & Intellect. LC 73-98866. 304p. 1970. reprint ed. text ed. 59.75 (*0-8371-2886-2*, PAPI, Greenwood Pr) Greenwood.

Paterson, Donald R. M., ed. see Elsworth, John Van Varick.

Paterson, Ellen R., comp. Anabolic Steroids & Sports: A Selected, Annotated Bibliography 1979-1990. LC 90-83684. 77p. 1991. 10.00 (*0-87875-389-3*) Whitston Pub.

Paterson, Evangeline. A Way Through Stone. LC 93-13725. 1993. pap. 4.00 (*0-940895-10-2*) Cornerstone IL.

Paterson, Fiona & Fewell, Judith, eds. Girls in Their Prime: Scottish Education Revisited. 180p. 1991. reprint ed. pap. 28.00 (*0-7073-0578-0*, Falmer Pr) Taylor & Francis.

Paterson, H., jt. auth. see Roy, J.

Paterson, Helena. The Celtic Lunar Zodiac: How to Interpret Your Moon Sign. (Illus.). 160p. 1992. pap. 19.95 (*0-8048-1821-5*) C E Tuttle.
— The Handbook of Celtic Astrology: The 13-Sign Lunar Zodiac of the Ancient Druids. LC 94-42390. (Illus.). 256p. 1995. pap. 15.00 (*1-56718-509-6*) Llewellyn Pubns.

Paterson, Helena, jt. auth. see Davis, Courtney.

Paterson, Hugh E. Evolution & the Recognition Concept of Species: Collected Writings. McEvey, Shane F., ed. 224p. 1993. text ed. 32.95 (*0-8018-4409-6*) Johns Hopkins.

Paterson, I., jt. ed. see Hubner, Heinz.

Paterson, Isabel. The God of the Machine. rev. ed. LC 92-32935. (Library of Conservative Thought). 292p. (C). 1993. pap. text ed. 21.95 (*1-56000-666-8*) Transaction Pubs.

Paterson, Isabel B. God of the Machine. LC 77-172225. (Right Wing Individualist Tradition in America Ser.). 1972. reprint ed. 25.50 (*0-405-00434-6*) Ayer.
— God of the Machine. LC 72-4510. (Essay Index Reprint Ser.). 1979. reprint ed. 29.95 (*0-8369-2966-7*) Ayer.

Paterson, J. Gaelic Made Easy, Vol. 1. 1991. pap. 7.95 (*0-8288-3348-6*, M4308) Fr & Eur.
— Gaelic Made Easy, Vol. 2. 1991. pap. 7.95 (*0-8288-3349-4*, M4309) Fr & Eur.
— Gaelic Made Easy, Vol. 3. 1991. pap. 7.95 (*0-7859-0644-4*, M4310) Fr & Eur.
— The Homes of Tennyson. LC 72-3621. (Studies in Tennyson: No. 27). (Illus.). 1972. reprint ed. lib. bdg. 61.95 (*0-8383-1579-8*) M S G Haskell Hse.
— Vertebral Manipulation - A Part of Orthodox Medicine. 128p. (C). 1995. lib. bdg. 39.00 (*0-7923-8885-2*) Kluwer Ac.

Paterson, J., jt. auth. see Burn, Loic.

Paterson, J. D. Primate Behavior: An Exercise Workbook. (Illus.). 105p. (Orig.). (C). 1992. pap. text ed. 10.95x (*0-88133-618-1*) Waveland Pr.

Paterson, J. H. North America: A Geography of the United States & Canada. 9th ed. (Illus.). 544p. (C). 1994. text ed. 45.00 (*0-19-508058-0*) OUP.

Paterson, J. R. A Faith for the 1980s. 3.95 (*0-7152-0433-5*) Outlook.

Paterson, James. Commentaries on the Liberty of the Subject & the Laws of England Relating to the Security of the Person, 2 vols., Set. 1010p. 1980. reprint ed. lib. bdg. 75.00 (*0-8377-1005-7*) Rothman.
— The Contemporaries of Burns, & the More Recent Poets of Ayrshire, with Selections from Their Writings. LC 70-144468. reprint ed. 57.50 (*0-404-08524-5*) AMS Pr.
— The Liberty of the Press, Speech & Public Worship: Being Commentaries on the Liberty of the Subject & the Laws of England. xxxi, 568p. 1985. reprint ed. lib. bdg. 42.50 (*0-8377-1019-7*) Rothman.

P Q

***Paterson, Janet M.** Postmodernism & the Quebec Novel. Homel, David & Phillips, Charles, trs. (Theory-Culture Ser.). 168p. 1994. 35.00 (*0-8020-0530-6*); pap. 14.95 (*0-8020-6968-1*) U of Toronto Pr.

Paterson, Janet M., jt. ed. see Lennox, John.

Paterson, Jennifer. Feast Days: Recipes from the Spectator. (Illus.). 178p. 1991. 34.95 (*0-7195-4848-9*, Pub. by John Murray UK) Trafalgar.

Paterson, John. David Harvey's Geography. LC 83-22293. 232p. 1984. 56.00 (*0-389-20441-2*, N8003) B&N Imports.

— Real Truth about Baptism in Jesus' Name. 32p. 1995. pap. 1.50 (*1-56722-035-5*) Word Aflame.

Paterson, John & Paterson, Katherine. Consider the Lilies: Flowers of the Bible. LC 85-43603. (Illus.). 48p. (YA). (gr. 7 up). 1986. 14.95 (*0-690-04461-5*, Crowell Jr Bks) HarpC Child Bks.

Paterson, John, ed. see Eliot, George.

Paterson, John K. & Burn, Loic. Examination of the Back: An Introduction. 1986. lib. bdg. 41.00 (*0-85200-930-5*) Kluwer Ac.

Paterson, John K. & Burn, Loic, eds. Back Pain: An International Review. (C). 1990. lib. bdg. 162.00 (*0-7923-8912-3*) Kluwer Ac.

Paterson, John M. Gaelic Made Easy, 4 texts. 1992. 69.95 (*0-88432-443-5*, AFSG20) Audio-Forum.

Paterson, Josephine & Zderad, Loretta. Humanistic Nursing. 136p. 1988. pap. 19.95 (*0-88737-398-4*, 41-2218) Natl League Nurse.

***Paterson, Judith H.** Sweet Mystery: A Book of Remembering. LC 95-13113. 288p. 1996. 23.00 (*0-374-27226-3*) FS&G.

Paterson, Katherine. Angels & Other Strangers: Family Christmas Stories. LC 79-63797. 128p. (J). (gr. 1 up). 1979. 14.00 (*0-690-03992-1*, Crowell Jr Bks) HarpC Child Bks.

— Angels & Other Strangers: Family Christmas Stories. LC 79-63797. 128p. (YA). (gr. 7 up). 1991. lib. bdg. 13.89 (*0-690-04911-0*, Crowell Jr Bks) HarpC Child Bks.

— Angels & Other Strangers: Family Christmas Stories. LC 79-63797. (Trophy Bk.). 128p. (YA). (gr. 7 up). 1988. reprint ed. pap. 3.95 (*0-06-440283-5*, Trophy) HarpC Child Bks.

— Bridge to Terabithia. LC 77-2221. (Illus.). (J). (gr. 5 up). 1977. 14.95 (*0-690-01359-0*, Crowell Jr Bks) HarpC Child Bks.

— Bridge to Terabithia. braille ed. 182p. (J). 1992. vinyl bd. 14.56 (*1-56956-199-0*, BR8631) W A T Braille.

— Bridge to Terabithia. LC 77-2221. (Illus.). 144p. (J). (gr. 5 up). 1987. reprint ed. lib. bdg. 14.89 (*0-690-04635-9*, Crowell Jr Bks) HarpC Child Bks.

— Bridge to Terabithia. LC 77-2221. (Trophy Bk.). (Illus.). 144p. (J). (gr. 5-9). 1987. reprint ed. pap. 3.95 (*0-06-440184-7*, Trophy) HarpC Child Bks.

— Bridge to Terabithia: (Puente Hasta Terabithia) (SPA.). (J). (gr. 1-6). 8.95 (*84-204-3633-X*) Santillana.

— Come Sing, Jimmy Jo. 192p. (J). (gr. 5 up). 1986. mass mkt. 3.99 (*0-380-70052-2*, Flare) Avon.

— Come Sing, Jimmy Jo. LC 84-21123. 208p. (J). (gr. 5 up). 1985. 14.99 (*0-525-67167-6*, Lodestar Bks) Dutton Child Bks.

— Come Sing, Jimmy Jo. 208p. (J). 1995. pap. 3.99 (*0-14-037397-7*) Puffin Bks.

— Flip-Flop Girl. 128p. (J). (gr. 3-7). 1994. 13.99 (*0-525-67480-2*, Lodestar Bks) Dutton Child Bks.

— Gates of Excellence: On Reading & Writing Books for Children. LC 81-9698. 144p. 1988. pap. 9.95 (*0-525-67249-4*, Lodestar Bks) Dutton Child Bks.

— The Great Gilly Hopkins. LC 77-27075. (J). (gr. 5 up). 1978. 14.00i (*0-690-03837-2*, Crowell Jr Bks); lib. bdg. 14.89 (*0-690-03838-0*, Crowell Jr Bks) HarpC Child Bks.

— The Great Gilly Hopkins. LC 77-27075. (Trophy Bk.). 192p. (J). (gr. 5-9). 1987. reprint ed. pap. 3.95 (*0-06-440201-0*, Trophy) HarpC Child Bks.

— The Great Gilly Hopkins: (La Gran Gilly Hopkins) (SPA.). (J). (gr. 1-6). 8.95 (*84-204-3222-9*) Santillana.

— Jacob Have I Loved. (YA). (gr. 7 up). 1981. pap. 2.95 (*0-380-56499-8*, Flare) Avon.

— Jacob Have I Loved. LC 80-668. 228p. (YA). (gr. 7 up). 1980. 14.95 (*0-690-04078-4*, Crowell Jr Bks); lib. bdg. 14.89 (*0-690-04079-2*, Crowell Jr Bks) HarpC Child Bks.

— Jacob Have I Loved. LC 80-668. (Trophy Bk.). 256p. (J). (gr. 5 up). 1990. reprint ed. pap. 3.95 (*0-06-440368-8*, Trophy) HarpC Child Bks.

— The King's Equal. LC 90-30527. (Illus.). 64p. (J). (gr. 2-5). 1992. 17.00 (*0-06-022496-7*); lib. bdg. 16.89 (*0-06-022497-5*) HarpC Child Bks.

— Lyddie. 240p. (J). (gr. 5-9). 1991. 15.00 (*0-525-67338-5*, Lodestar Bks) Dutton Child Bks.

— Lyddie. LC 92-20304. 192p. (YA). (gr. 7 up). 1992. pap. 3.99 (*0-14-034981-2*) Puffin Bks.

— Lyddie. 192p. (J). 1995. pap. 3.99 (*0-14-037389-6*) Puffin Bks.

— Lyddie. large type ed. 277p. (YA). 1993. reprint ed. bds. 15.95 (*1-56054-616-6*) Thorndike Pr.

— The Master Puppeteer. (Illus.). 180p. (J). (gr. 5 up). 1981. pap. 2.95 (*0-380-53322-7*, Camelot) Avon.

— The Master Puppeteer. LC 75-8614. (Illus.). 192p. (J). (gr. 6 up). 1976. 15.00 (*0-690-00913-5*, Crowell Jr Bks) HarpC Child Bks.

— The Master Puppeteer. LC 75-8614. 192p. (YA). (gr. 7 up). 1991. lib. bdg. 14.89 (*0-690-04905-6*, Crowell Jr Bks) HarpC Child Bks.

— The Master Puppeteer. LC 75-8614. (Trophy Bk.). (Illus.). 192p. (J). (gr. 4 up). 1989. reprint ed. pap. 3.95 (*0-06-440281-9*, Trophy) HarpC Child Bks.

— A Midnight Clear: Twelve Family Stories for the Christmas Season. (Illus.). 192p. (J). 1995. 16.00 (*0-525-67529-9*, Lodestar Bks) Dutton Child Bks.

— Of Nightingales That Weep. LC 74-8294. (Illus.). (J). (gr. 5 up). 1974. 14.00 (*0-690-00485-0*, Crowell Jr Bks) HarpC Child Bks.

— Of Nightingales That Weep. LC 74-8294. (Trophy Bk.). (Illus.). 192p. (J). (gr. 4 up). 1989. reprint ed. pap. 3.95 (*0-06-440282-7*, Trophy) HarpC Child Bks.

— Park's Quest. LC 87-32422. 160p. (J). (gr. 5 up). 1988. 13.99 (*0-525-67258-3*, Lodestar Bks) Dutton Child Bks.

— Park's Quest. (Horn Book "Fanfare" Ser.). 160p. (J). (gr. 5 up). 1989. pap. 3.99 (*0-14-034262-1*, Puffin) Puffin Bks.

— Rebels of the Heavenly Kingdom. 240p. (J). (gr. 7 up). 1984. pap. 2.95 (*0-380-68304-0*, Flare) Avon.

— Rebels of the Heavenly Kingdom. LC 83-1529. 224p. (YA). (gr. 12 up). 1983. 14.99 (*0-525-66911-6*, Lodestar Bks) Dutton Child Bks.

— Rebels of the Heavenly Kingdom. 240p. (YA). (gr. 7 up). 1995. pap. 3.99 (*0-14-037610-0*) Puffin Bks.

— A Sense of Wonder: On Reading & Writing Books for Children. 352p. 1995. pap. 12.95 (*0-452-27476-1*, Plume) NAL-Dutton.

— Sign of the Chrysanthemum. LC 72-7553. 128p. (YA). (gr. 7 up). 1991. lib. bdg. 14.89 (*0-690-04913-7*, Crowell Jr Bks) HarpC Child Bks.

— The Sign of the Chrysanthemum. LC 72-7553. (Trophy Bk.). (Illus.). 128p. (J). (gr. 6 up). 1988. reprint ed. pap. 3.95 (*0-06-440232-0*, Trophy) HarpC Child Bks.

— The Smallest Cow in the World. LC 90-30521. (I Can Read Bk.). (Illus.). 64p. (J). (gr. k-3). 1991. 14.95 (*0-06-024690-1*); lib. bdg. 14.89 (*0-06-024691-X*) HarpC Child Bks.

— Smallest Cow in the World. LC 90-30521. (Trophy I Can Read Bk.). (Illus.). 64p. (J). (gr. k-3). 1993. pap. 3.50 (*0-06-444164-4*, Trophy) HarpC Child Bks.

— The Tale of the Mandarin Ducks. (Illus.). (J). (gr. k-3). 1990. 15.00 (*0-525-67283-4*, Lodestar Bks) Dutton Child Bks.

— The Tale of the Mandarin Ducks. (Illus.). 40p. 1995. 5.99 (*0-14-055739-3*, Puff Unicorn) Puffin Bks.

— Who Am I? (Illus.). 96p. (Orig.). (J). 1992. pap. 7.99 (*0-8028-5072-3*) Eerdmans.

Paterson, Katherine, tr. see Ishii, Momoko.

Paterson, Katherine, jt. auth. see Paterson, John.

Paterson, Katherine, tr. see Yagawa, Sumiko.

Paterson, Kathy, ed. see Kearns, Thomas F.

Paterson, Lee T. California Unemployment Insurance Handbook. 5th ed. 160p. 1991. pap. 39.50 (*1-55943-093-1*) Michie Butterworth.

— Documenting Employee Discipline. 170p. 1994. pap. 42.00 (*0-250-47241-4*) Michie Butterworth.

— Employer's Compliance Audit: California. Johnson, Margaret L., ed. 163p. (Orig.). 1989. pap. 79.50 (*0-932823-02-5*) Am Somerset.

— Employer's Compliance Review: California. 2nd ed. 190p. 1993. pap. 39.50 (*1-55943-198-9*) Michie Butterworth.

— Employer's Compliance Review: Federal. 2nd ed. 160p. 1993. pap. 54.00 (*1-55943-199-7*) Michie Butterworth.

— Employer's Wage Manual (Federal) 380p. 1992. pap. 65.00 (*1-55943-172-5*) Michie Butterworth.

— Federal Mandatory Workplace Posters. 3rd ed. 1992. pap. 30.00 (*1-55943-177-6*) Michie Butterworth.

— Mandatory Workplace Posters in California. 140p. 1994. pap. 35.00 (*0-250-47242-2*) Michie Butterworth.

— Mandatory Workplace Posters in California. 4th ed. 1992. pap. 30.00 (*1-55943-094-X*) Butterworth Legal Pubs.

— Mandatory Workplace Posters in California. 4th ed. 1992. pap. 30.00 (*1-55943-195-4*) Parker Pubns.

— Negotiating Employee Resignations. 2nd ed. 120p. 1991. pap. 29.50 (*1-55943-125-3*) Michie Butterworth.

— Public Employer's Compliance Audit. Johnson, Margaret L., ed. 156p. 1990. pap. 79.50 (*0-932823-07-6*) Am Somerset.

— Public Employer's Compliance Review. 150p. 1993. pap. 39.50 (*1-55943-200-4*) Michie Butterworth.

— Public Employer's Wage Manual. 400p. 1991. pap. 39.50 (*1-55943-066-4*) Michie Butterworth.

— The Strike Manual. 114p. 1987. pap. text ed. 15.00 (*0-943397-04-9*) Assn Calif Sch Admin.

— Supervisor's Guide to Documenting Employee Discipline. 60p. 1993. pap. 19.00 (*0-250-47232-5*) Michie Butterworth.

Paterson, Lee T. & Deblieux, Michael R. Supervisor's Guide to Documenting Employee Discipline. 3rd ed. 1991. pap. 19.00 (*1-55943-091-5*) Butterworth Legal Pubs.

— Supervisor's Guide to Employee Performance Reviews. 2nd ed. 110p. 1993. pap. 19.00 (*1-55943-176-8*) Michie Butterworth.

Paterson, Lee T., jt. auth. see Cowan, Ari.

Paterson, Lee T., jt. ed. see Cowan, Ari.

***Paterson, Linda.** The World of the Troubadours: Medieval Occitan Society, c. 1100-c. 1300. (Illus.). 381p. (C). 1995. pap. write for info. (*0-521-55832-8*) Cambridge U Pr.

Paterson, Linda M. The World of the Troubadours: Medieval Occitan Society, c.1100-c.1300. LC 92-37723. (Illus.). 352p. (C). 1993. 59.95 (*0-521-35240-1*) Cambridge U Pr.

Paterson, M. S., ed. Boolean Function Complexity. (London Mathematical Society Lecture Note Ser.: No. 164). 300p. (C). 1992. pap. 42.95 (*0-521-40826-1*) Cambridge U Pr.

Paterson, M. S., et al, eds. Automata, Languages & Programming: Proceedings 17th International Colloquium Warwick University, England, July 16-20, 1990. (Lecture Notes in Computer Science Ser.: Vol. 443). ix, 781p. 1990. pap. 77.00 (*0-387-52826-1*) Spr-Verlag.

Paterson, Neil. Something Like a Poem. 32p. 1986. 20.00 (*0-7223-1988-6*, Pub. by A H S Ltd UK) St Mut.

Paterson, R. C., et al. Modern Concepts in the Management of Fissure Caries. 80p. 1991. text ed. 40.00 (*1-85097-013-0*) Quint Pub Co.

Paterson, R. M. Dangerous River. LC 89-71264. (Illus.). 240p. (Orig.). 1990. reprint ed. pap. 12.95 (*0-930031-26-1*) Chelsea Green Pub.

***Paterson, R. R. & Bridge, P. D.** Biochemical Techniques for Filamentous Fungi. (IMI Technical Handbooks Ser.: No. 1). 125p. 1994. pap. 30.00x (*0-85198-899-7*) CAB Intl.

Paterson, Richard, jt. ed. see Drummond, Phillip.

Paterson, Robin. Your Baby Book: Birth to Six Years. (Illus.). 120p. 1993. 32.00 (*0-9638231-0-8*) Pacific Eagle.

Paterson, Russell. An Introduction to Ion Exchange. LC 75-104789. 117p. reprint ed. pap. 33.40 (*0-317-09893-4*, 2022545) Bks Demand.

Paterson, Stanley, jt. auth. see Seaburg, Carl.

Paterson, Stuart & Stevenson, Savourna. The Snow Queen. 86p. (Orig.). 1991. pap. 4.95 (*0-87129-065-0*, S84) Dramatic Pub.

***Paterson, Thomas, et al.** American Ascendant: American Foreign Relations Since 1939. 320p. (C). 1995. pap. text ed. write for info. (*0-669-39361-4*) Heath.

Paterson, Thomas G. Contesting Castro: The United States & the Triumph of the Cuban Revolution. (Illus.). 304p. 1994. 30.00 (*0-19-508630-9*) OUP.

— Contesting Castro: The United States & the Triumph of the Cuban Revolution. (Illus.). 284p. 1995. pap. 13.95 (*0-19-510120-0*) OUP.

— Kennedy's Quest for Victory: American Foreign Policy, 1961-1963. 432p. 1989. 42.50 (*0-19-504585-8*); pap. 14.95 (*0-19-504584-X*) OUP.

— Meeting the Communist Threat: Truman to Reagan. 352p. 1988. 29.95 (*0-19-504533-5*) OUP.

— Meeting the Communist Threat: Truman to Reagan. 336p. 1989. pap. 10.95 (*0-19-504532-7*) OUP.

— On Every Front: The Making & Unmaking of the Cold War. rev. ed. 256p. 1992. 24.95 (*0-393-03060-1*) Norton.

— The Origins of the Cold War. 2nd ed. (Problems in European Civilization Ser.). 1990. pap. text ed. 8.50 (*0-669-91447-9*) Heath.

— Soviet-American Confrontation: Postwar Reconstruction & the Origins of the Cold War. LC 73-8120. 302p. reprint ed. pap. 86.10 (*0-7837-5387-X*, 2045151) Bks Demand.

Paterson, Thomas G., ed. Major Problems in American Foreign Policy: Documents & Essays, 2 vols., Vol. I. 3rd ed. LC 88-80720. (Major Problems in American History Ser.). 541p. (C). 1990. pap. text ed. 15.50 (*0-669-15856-9*) Heath.

— Major Problems in American Foreign Policy: Documents & Essays, 2 vols., Vol. II. 3rd ed. LC 88-80720. (Major Problems in American History Ser.). 721p. (C). 1990. pap. text ed. 15.50 (*0-669-15857-7*) Heath.

Paterson, Thomas G. & Clifford, J. Garry. American Foreign Policy, Vol. 2: A History since 1900. 3rd rev. ed. LC 90-82956. 502p. (C). 1991. pap. text ed. write for info. (*0-669-24678-6*) Heath.

Paterson, Thomas G. & McMahon, Robert J., eds. The Origins of the Cold War. 3rd ed. LC 90-82002. (Problems in American Civilization Ser.). 367p. (C). 1991. pap. text ed. write for info. (*0-669-24445-7*) Heath.

***Paterson, Thomas G. & Merrill, Dennis J.** Major Problems in American Foreign Relations Vol. I: To 1920: Documents & Essays, 2 vols. 4th ed. (Major Problems in American History Ser.). 592p. (C). 1995. pap. text ed. write for info. (*0-669-35077-X*) Heath.

— Major Problems in American Foreign Relations Vol. II: Since 1914: Documents & Essays, 2 vols. 4th ed. (Major Problems in American History Ser.). 592p. (C). 1995. pap. text ed. write for info. (*0-669-35078-8*) Heath.

Paterson, Thomas G. & Rabe, Stephen G., eds. Imperial Surge: The United States Abroad, the 1890s-Early 1900s. (Problems in American Civilization Ser.). 211p. (C). 1992. pap. text ed. write for info. (*0-669-26915-8*) Heath.

Paterson, Thomas G., jt. ed. see Hogan, Michael J.

Paterson, Thomas G., et al. American Foreign Policy: A History, 2 vols., Vol. 1 to 1914. 3rd ed. LC 87-81183. 255p. (C). 1988. Vol. I: To 1914, 255 p. pap. text ed. 15.50 (*0-669-12664-0*) Heath.

— American Foreign Policy: A History, 2 vols., Vol. II since 1900. 3rd ed. LC 87-81183. 507p. (C). 1988. Vol. II: Since 1900, 507 p. pap. text ed. 16.50 (*0-669-12665-9*) Heath.

— American Foreign Relations Vol. I: A History: To 1920. 4th ed. 352p. (C). 1995. pap. text ed. write for info. (*0-669-35155-5*) Heath.

— American Foreign Relations Vol. II: A History: Since 1895. 4th ed. 554p. (C). 1995. pap. text ed. write for info. (*0-669-35156-3*) Heath.

Paterson, Thomas T., jt. auth. see Terra, Hellmut D.

Paterson, Torquil, jt. ed. see England, Frank.

Paterson, W., jt. auth. see Guile, A. E.

Paterson, W. S. The Physics of Glaciers. (Illus.). vii, 380p. 1981. pap. text ed. 27.00 (*0-08-024004-6*, Pergamon Pr) Elsevier.

— The Physics of Glaciers. 2nd ed. (Illus.). vii, 380p. 1981. text ed. 96.00 (*0-08-024005-4*, Pergamon Pr) Elsevier.

***Paterson, W. S. B.** The Physics of Glaciers. 3rd ed. LC 94-30918. 1994. text ed. 110.00 (*0-08-037945-1*, Pergamon Pr) Elsevier.

Paterson, William. Writings of William Paterson: Of Dumfriesshire, & a Citizen of London, Founder of the Bank of England, & of the Darien Colony, 3 Vols, Set. 2nd ed. Bannister, Saxe, ed. LC 68-54311. (Library of Money & Banking History). 1968. reprint ed. 150.00 (*0-678-00427-1*) Kelley.

Paterson, William & Padgett, Stephen. A History of Social Democracy in Postwar Europe. (Post War World Ser.). (C). 1991. text ed. 58.95 (*0-582-49173-8*, 789602); pap. text ed. 27.50 (*0-582-49174-6*, 78961) Longman.

***Paterson, William & Southern, David.** Governing Germany. Orig. Title: Modern Governments. (Illus.). 256p. 1989. pap. 19.95 (*0-631-17101-0*) Blackwell Pubs.

Paterson, William, jt. auth. see Bulmer, Simon.

***Paterson, William D.** Highway Design & Maintenance Standards Model Vol. 3: Road Deterioration & Maintenance Effects: Models for Planning & Management. 456p. Date not set. 32.95 (*0-614-02803-5*, 43590) World Bank.

— Highway Design & Maintenance Standards Model Vol. 3: Road Deterioration & Maintenance Effects: Models for Planning & Management, 4 vols., Set. Date not set. 125.00 (*0-614-02804-3*, 43668) World Bank.

— Road Deterioration & Maintenance Effects: Models for Planning & Management. LC 87-22177. (Highway Design & Maintenance Standards Ser.). 352p. (Orig.). 1988. pap. text ed. 32.95 (*0-8018-3590-9*) Johns Hopkins.

Paterson, William E. & Smith, Gordon, eds. West German Model: Perspectives on a Stable State. (Illus.). 184p. 1981. 35.00 (*0-7146-3180-9*, Pub. by F Cass Pubs UK); pap. 12.50 (*0-7146-4034-4*, Pub. by F Cass Pubs UK) Intl Spec Bk.

Paterson, William E. & Southern, David. Governing Germany: The Government & Politics of the Federal Republic. Peele, Gillian, ed. (Comparative Modern Government Ser.). (Orig.). (C). 1991. pap. text ed. 13.95 (*0-393-96041-2*) Norton.

Paterson, William E., jt. ed. see Gillespie, Richard.

Paterson, William E., jt. ed. see Urwin, Derek W.

Paterson, William P. The Nature of Religion. LC 77-27202. (Gifford Lectures: 1924-25). reprint ed. 75.00 (*0-404-60476-5*) AMS Pr.

Paterson, Wilma. A Fountain of Gardens: Plants & Herbs of the Bible. (Illus.). 160p. 1992. 35.00 (*0-87951-461-2*) Overlook Pr.

Paterson, Wilma & Behan, Peter. Salmon & Women: The Feminine Angle. (Illus.). 160p. 1991. 34.95 (*0-85493-201-1*, Pub. by V Gollancz UK) Trafalgar.

Paterson, Yvonne, jt. ed. see Levinson, Arnold I.

Patey, Douglas L. Probability & Literary Form: Philosophic Theory & Literary Practice in the Augustan Age. LC 83-7819. 464p. 1984. 74.95 (*0-521-25456-6*) Cambridge U Pr.

Patey, Douglas L. & Keegan, Timothy, eds. Augustan Studies: Essays in Honor of Irvin Ehrenpreis. LC 85-40084. (Illus.). 272p. 1986. 38.50 (*0-87413-272-X*) U Delaware Pr.

***Patey, R. L.** The Illustrated Rules of Football. (Illustrated Rules of the Game Ser.). (Illus.). 32p. (J). (gr. 1-4). Date not set. lib. bdg. 19.93 (*1-884756-11-5*) Davidson Titles.

— The Illustrated Rules of Football. LC 95-8118. (Illustrated Sports Ser.). (Illus.). 32p. (Orig.). (J). 1995. pap. 6.95 (*1-57102-049-7*, Ideals Child) Hambleton-Hill.

***Patfoort, Pat.** Uprooting Violence: Building Nonviolence. (Illus.). 1995. pap. 10.00 (*0-89166-015-1*) Cobblesmith.

Path Works Staff. Feeling Good about Me. (Illus.). 20p. (J). (gr. 3-5). 1993. 1.95 (*1-56456-218-2*, 741) W Gladden Found.

— Feelings: Having Them, Sharing Them. (Illus.). 20p. (J). (gr. 3-5). 1993. 1.95 (*1-56456-217-4*, 740) W Gladden Found.

Pathak, Aditi. Caste Status & Socialization among the Students. (C). 1989. 20.00 (*0-8364-2468-9*) S Asia.

***Pathak, Akhileshwar.** Contested Domains: The State, Peasants & Forests in Contemporary India. 244p. 1995. 26.00 (*0-8039-9184-3*) Sage.

Pathak, Bindeshwar. Road to Freedom: A Sociological Study on the Abolition of Scavenging in India. (C). 1991. 34.00 (*81-208-0704-9*, Pub. by Motilal Banarsidass II) S Asia.

***Pathak, Bindeshway.** Rural Violence in Bihar. (C). 1993. 18.00x (*81-7022-474-8*, Pub. by Concept II) S Asia.

Pathak, Dayananda. George Bernard Shaw: His Religion & Values. vi, 176p. 1985. 12.00 (*0-685-67633-1*, Pub. by Mittal Pubs Dist II) Nataraj Bks.

Pathak, Dev S., et al, eds. Promotion of Pharmaceuticals: Issues, Trends, Options. LC 92-49617. (Journal of Pharmaceutical Marketing & Management: Vol. 7, No. 1). (Illus.). 203p. 1993. lib. bdg. 39.95 (*1-56024-383-X*); pap. text ed. 14.95 (*1-56024-384-8*) Haworth Pr.

Pathak, J. P., ed. Insect Immunity. LC 92-41646. (Entomologica Ser.: Vol. 48). 204p. 1993. lib. bdg. 98.00 (*0-7923-2086-7*) Kluwer Ac.

Pathak, K. B. & Ram, F. Techniques of Demographic Analysis. (Illus.). 1992. 40.00 (*81-7040-418-5*, Pub. by Himalaya II) Apt Bks.

Pathak, K. K. Nuclear Policy of India. 276p. 1980. 24.95 (*0-318-37256-8*) Asia Bk Corp.

— Nuclear Policy of India. 1983. 18.50 (*0-8364-1024-6*, Pub. by Gitanjali Prakashan) S Asia.

Pathak, K. N., jt. auth. see Prakash, Shamsher.

Pathak, Mahesh T., ed. Sardar Sarovar Project. (C). 1991. 12.50 (*81-204-0545-5*, Pub. by Oxford IBH II) S Asia.

Pathak, Manjushree. Crimes, Customs & Justice in Tribal India. (C). 1991. 34.00 (*81-7099-283-4*, Pub. by Mittal II) S Asia.

Pathak, Mohan, ed. Flood Plains & Agricultural Occupance. (C). 1991. 26.00 (*81-7100-289-7*, Pub. by Ashish II) S Asia.

Pathak, P. K., jt. ed. see Ghosh, M.

Pathak, Pratul. The Infinite Passion of Finite Hearts: Robert Browning & Failure in Love. LC 91-32994. (American University Studies: English Language & Literature: Ser. IV, Vol. 141). 224p. (C). 1992. text ed. 39.95 (*0-8204-1776-9*) P Lang Pubs.

Pathak, R. C. Bhargava's Concise Hindi-English Dictionary. 6th ed. 1040p. 1981. 22.95 (*0-8288-1744-8*, M9437) Fr & Eur.

— Concise English Hindi Dictionary. (ENG & HIN.). 1979. 6.00 (*0-89744-972-X*) Auromere.

An Asterisk (*) at the beginning of an entry indicates that the title is appearing in BIP for the first time.

— Concise Hindi-English Dictionary. (ENG & HIN.). 1979. 6.00 (*0-89744-971-1*) Auromere.
— English-Hindi (Concise) Dictionary. 11th ed. 879p. 11.00 (*0-88431-357-3*) IBD Ltd.
— Hindi-English (Concise) Dictionary. 7th ed. 759p. 11.00 (*0-88431-227-5*) IBD Ltd.
— Hindi-English Dictionary. (ENG & HIN.). 1979. 22.00 (*0-89744-969-X*) Auromere.
Pathak, R. C., comp. English-Hindi Dictionary. (ENG & HIN.). 1981. 42.50 (*0-87557-034-8*, 034-8); 35.00 (*0-685-04464-5*, 034-8X) Saphrograph.
Pathak, R. S., ed. Generalized Functions & Their Applications. LC 92-42065. (Illus.). 316p. (C). 1993. 85.00 (*0-306-44404-6*, Plenum Pr) Plenum.
Pathak, R. S., jt. ed. see Dhokalia, R. P.
Pathak, Raj K. Environmental Planning Resources & Development. 1990. 40.00 (*81-85076-91-X*, Pub. by Chugh Pubns II) S Asia.
Pathak, S. C. Recent Advances in Insect Physiology Morphology & Ecology. (Illus.). xiii, 324p. 1986. 39.00 (*1-55528-079-X*, Pub. by Today & Tomorrows P & P II) Scholarly Pubns.
Pathak, S. N. Land Reforms & Change in Rural Society. (C). 1987. 35.00 (*81-85076-26-X*, Pub. by Chugh Pubns II) S Asia.
Pathak, V. M. Medicinal Plants of Gwalior. (C). 1987. 130.00 (*0-685-21862-7*, Pub. by Intl Bk Distr II) St Mut.
Pathak, Vijay & Ramaiah, L. S. Bibliography of Research in Library & Information Science in India. 1986. 18.00 (*0-8364-1827-1*, Pub. by Indian Doc Serv II) S Asia.
Pathan, B. Gandhian Myth in English Literature in India. 1987. 29.95 (*81-7100-006-1*) Asia Bk Corp.
Pathan, B. A. Gandhian Concept of Beauty. (C). 1989. 12.75 (*81-202-0224-4*, Pub. by Ajanta II) S Asia.
Pathania, B. S. Goldsmith & Sentimental Comedy. 152p. 1989. text ed. 22.50 (*81-85218-00-5*, Pub. by Prestige II) Advent Bks Div.
Pathasarathy, Sampath. Modified Lipoproteins in the Pathogenesis of Atherosclerosis. (Medical Intelligence Unit Ser.). 115p. 1994. 89.95 (*1-57059-080-X*, LN9080) R G Landes.
Pathelin, Pierre. Farce du Quinzieme Siecle. 131p. 1970. 14.95 (*0-8288-7492-1*) Fr & Eur.
Pathfinder Press Staff, ed. see Mandel, Ernest.
Pathmanaban, S., jt. auth. see Berkeley, K. G.
Pathmanathan, I. & Nik-Safiah, N. I. Training of Trainers for Health Systems Research. (Health Systems Research Training Ser.: Vol. 5). 282p. 1992. pap. 17.00 (*0-88936-589-X*, IDRC290, Pub. by IDRC CN) UNIPUB.
***Pathobiology Annual Staff.** Pathobiology Annual Vol. 12. fac. ed. Ioachim, Harry L., ed. LC 78-151816. (Illus.). 368p. pap. 104.90 (*0-7837-7231-9*, 2047067) Bks Demand.
Pathria, R. K. Advanced Statistical Mechanics. (International Series on Natural Philsophy). 1972. text ed. 76.00 (*0-08-016747-0*, Pergamon Pr) Elsevier.
— The Theory of Relativity. 2nd ed. 1974. 138.00 (*0-08-018032-9*, Pub. by Pergamon Repr UK) Franklin.
Pathria, R.K. Advanced Statistical Mechanics. (International Series on Parallel Computation: No. 45). 1972. pap. text ed. 50.00 (*0-08-018994-6*, Pergamon Pr) Elsevier.
Pathy, Jaganath. Anthropology of Development: Demystification & Relevance. 214p. 1987. 13.00 (*81-212-0081-4*, Pub. by Gian Publng Hse II) S Asia.
— Ethnic Minorities in the Process of Development. (C). 1988. 28.50 (*81-7033-055-6*, Pub. by Rawat II) S Asia.
Pathy, M. S., ed. Principles & Practice of Geriatric Medicine. 2nd ed. 1607p. 1991. text ed. 239.95 (*0-471-92403-2*, Wiley-Liss) Wiley.
Pathy, M. S. & Finucane, P., eds. Geriatric Medicine. (Illus.). xix, 383p. 1989. 101.00 (*0-387-19525-4*) Spr-Verlag.
Pati, J. C., et al. High Energy Physics & Cosmology. (ICTP Ser. in Theoretical Phys.: Vol. 7). 732p. 1991. text ed. 129.00 (*981-02-0469-8*) World Scientific Pub.
— Superstrings, Unified Theories & Cosmology, 1988. (ICTP Series in Theoretical Physics: Vol. 5). 1989. pap. 53.00 (*9971-5-0871-0*) World Scientific Pub.
Pati, J. C., et al, eds. Current Topics in Condensed Matter & Particle Physics: Non-Perturbative Phenomena & Strongly Correlated Systems, 19 May-14 June 1991. LC 93-7576. (Kathmandu Summer School Lecture Notes: Vol. 2). 332p. 1993. text ed. 121.00 (*981-02-1376-X*); pap. 58.00 (*981-02-1386-7*) World Scientific Pub.
— Current Trends in Condensed Matter, Particle Physics & Cosmology. 400p. (C). 1990. text ed. 86.00 (*981-02-0114-1*); pap. text ed. 43.00 (*981-02-0115-X*) World Scientific Pub.
— High Energy Physics & Cosmology. 708p. (C). 1990. pap. 44.00 (*981-02-0347-0*) World Scientific Pub.
Pati, R. N. Health, Environment & Development. (C). 1992. 38.00 (*81-7024-460-9*, Pub. by Ashish II) S Asia.
— Population Family & Culture. 1987. 31.95 (*81-7024-151-0*) Asia Bk Corp.
Pati, R. N., ed. Rehabilitation of Child Labourers in India. (C). 1991. 30.00 (*81-7024-361-0*, Pub. by Ashish II) S Asia.
Pati, R. N. & Jagatleg, Lalitendu. Tribal Demography in India. (C). 1991. 29.00 (*81-7024-445-5*, Pub. by Ashish II) S Asia.
Pati, R. N. & Jena, B. Aged in India. 1989. 38.50 (*81-7024-264-9*, Pub. by Ashish II) S Asia.
Pati, R. N. & Jena, B., eds. Tribal Development in India. (C). 1989. 34.00 (*81-7024-228-2*, Pub. by Ashish II) S Asia.
Pati, Rabindra N., jt. auth. see Jena, Basantibala.
Patience, J. The Land of Nursery Rhymes. (Illus.). (J). (ps-1). 1985. 1.98 (*0-517-43878-X*) Random Hse Value.
Patience, John. Adventures in Fern Hollow. (Illus.). 64p. (J). (ps-1). 1985. 2.98 (*0-517-45856-X*) Random Hse Value.
— Dragon Tales. (Happy Ending Stories Ser.). (Illus.). 32p. (J). (gr. k-6). 1991. 3.99 (*0-517-02329-6*) Random Hse Value.
— Hubble Bubble. (Happy Ending Stories Ser.). (Illus.). 32p. (J). (gr. k-6). 1991. 3.99 (*0-517-02333-4*) Random Hse Value.
— Little Merlin's Book of Magic Pets. LC 93-87506. (Illus.). 12p. (J). (gr. 3 up). 1994. 14.95 (*0-8431-3750-9*) Price Stern.
— The Little People. (Happy Ending Stories Ser.). (Illus.). 32p. (J). (gr. k-6). 1991. 3.99 (*0-517-02334-2*) Random Hse Value.
— The Roarasaurus. (Pop-up Book Ser.). (Illus.). 12p. (J). (ps up). 1994. 14.95 (*0-8431-3686-3*) Price Stern.
— The Seasons in Fern Hollow. (Illus.). 64p. (J). (ps-1). 2.98 (*0-517-45857-8*) Random Hse Value.
— Tall Stories. (Happy Ending Stories Ser.). (Illus.). 32p. (J). (gr. k-6). 1991. 3.99 (*0-517-02327-X*) Random Hse Value.
Patient Care Magazine Editors. Medical Abbreviations Handbook. 2nd ed. 200p. 1983. pap. 15.95 (*0-87489-309-7*) Med Economics.
Patient Care Publications Staff. Emergency Medical Procedures for the Outdoors. LC 87-18508. (Illus.). 120p. 1987. reprint ed. pap. 6.95 (*0-89732-051-4*) Menasha Ridge.
Patient, Derrick A. Healthcare Equipment International: Market Trends, Companies, Statistics. 342p. 1989. pap. text ed. 150.00 (*0-582-03683-6*) Churchill.
Patient, Matthew, jt. auth. see Fleck, Richard.
Patient, Matthew, jt. auth. see Morgan, Chris.
Patil, B. S. Civil Engineering Contracts & Estimates. (Illus.). 586p. 1981. pap. text ed. 20.00 (*0-86125-036-2*, Pub. by Orient Longman Ltd II) Apt Bks.
Patil, D. K. Pakistan's Islamic Bomb. 150p. 1979. 14.95 (*0-7069-0911-9*) Asia Bk Corp.
Patil, G. P. Random Counts in Scientific Work, 3 vols. Incl. Vol. 1. Random Counts in Models & Structures. LC 73-114351. 276p. 1970. 25.00 (*0-271-00114-3*); Vol. 2. Random Counts in Biomedical & Social Sciences. LC 73-114351. 232p. 1970. 25.00 (*0-271-00115-1*); Vol. 3. Random Counts in Physical Science, Geoscience, & Business. LC 73-114351. 215p. 1970. 25.00 (*0-271-00116-X*); LC 73-114351. (Illus.). write for info. (*0-318-54929-8*) Pa St U Pr.
Patil, G. P. & Rao, C. R., eds. Environmental Statistics. LC 93-33430. (Handbook of Statistics Ser.: No. 12). 1994. write for info. (*0-444-89803-4*, North Holland) Elsevier.
— Multivariate Environmental Statistics. LC 93-27385. (North-Holland Series in Statistics & Probability: Vol. 6). 1993. write for info. (*0-444-89804-2*, North Holland) Elsevier.
Patil, G. P. & Rosenzweig, M. L., eds. Contemporary Quantitive Ecology & Related Ecometrics. (Statistical Ecology Ser.: Vol. 12). 1979. 60.00 (*0-89974-009-X*) Intl Co-Op.
Patil, S. H. Gandhi & Swaraj. 1984. 12.50 (*0-8364-1227-3*, Pub. by Deep) S Asia.
Patil, S. S., et al, eds. Molecular Strategies of Pathogens & Host Plants. (Illus.). 264p. 1991. 54.00 (*0-387-97448-2*) Spr-Verlag.
Patil, V. K., et al. Grape Research in India, 1981-1986. 134p. 1987. 29.95 (*81-200-0247-4*) Asia Bk Corp.
Patil, V. T. New Dimensions & Perspectives in Gandhism. 1989. 60.00 (*81-210-0230-3*, Pub. by Inter-India Pubns) S Asia.
Patil, V. T., ed. Explorations in Nehruvian Thought. (C). 1992. 38.00 (*81-210-0282-6*, Pub. by Inter-India Pubns) S Asia.
— Studies on Gandhi. viii, 296p. 1984. text ed. 30.00 (*0-86590-520-7*, Pub. by Sterling Pubs II) Apt Bks.
— Studies on Nehru. 421p. 1987. text ed. 45.00 (*81-207-0624-2*, Pub. by Sterling Pubs II) Apt Bks.
Patil, Vimla. A Cook's Tour of South India. 160p. 1988. text ed. 15.95 (*0-685-21868-6*, Pub. by Sterling Pubs II) Apt Bks.
— Cook's Tour of South India. (C). 1993. 6.00 (*81-207-0947-0*, Pub. by Sterling Plns Pvt II) S Asia.
— Entertaining Indian Style Recipes for All Occasions. (C). 1992. pap. 10.00 (*81-85674-16-7*, Pub. by UBS Pubs Dist II) S Asia.
Patilla, B., ed. see Dallas, D. & Jenks, J.
Patilla, Peter. Clixi: Exploring Shape & Space. Stillman, Meg, ed. 48p. (YA). 1994. student ed 7.95 (*1-884461-09-3*) NES Arnold.
***Patilla, Peter & Stone, Bob.** Multilink: Rediscovering Fractions. Brady, Cathleen, ed. (Middle School Math Ser.). (Illus.). 37p. (J). (gr. 5-9). Date not set. student ed 8.95 (*1-884461-12-3*) NES Arnold.
— Multilink: Shape & Space. Brady, Cathleen, ed. (Middle School Math Ser.). (Illus.). 36p. (J). (gr. 5-9). Date not set. student ed 8.95 (*1-884461-13-1*) NES Arnold.
— Multilink: Towards Algebra Through Structure. Brady, Cathleen, ed. (Middle School Math Ser.). (Illus.). 28p. (J). (gr. 5-9). Date not set. student ed 8.95 (*1-884461-15-8*) NES Arnold.
Patin, Douglas L., jt. auth. see Shean, Owen J.
Patin, Sally M. Our Dawson Family. 232p. 1981. 20.00 (*0-89308-215-5*) Southern Hist Pr.
Patin, Sylvie. Monet: The Ultimate Impressionist. Roberts, Anthony, tr. (Discoveries Ser.). (Illus.). 182p. 1993. pap. 12.95 (*0-8109-2883-3*) Abrams.
***Patinkin.** African Journey: Stories & Photographs. (Illus.). 1985. pap. 4.95 (*0-8028-0162-5*) Eerdmans.
Patinkin, Don. Anticipations of the General Theory & Other Essays on Keynes. LC 81-21929. 1982. 25.00 (*0-226-64873-7*) U Ch Pr.
— Anticipations of the General Theory & Other Essays on Keynes. LC 81-21929. 1985. pap. text ed. 15.00 (*0-226-64874-5*) U Ch Pr.
— Essays on & in the Chicago Tradition. LC 79-55770. (Illus.). xii, 315p. 1981. 39.50 (*0-8223-0439-2*) Duke.
— Money, Interest, & Prices: An Integration of Monetary & Value Theory. 2nd ed. 576p. 1989. 65.00 (*0-262-16114-1*) MIT Pr.
Patinkin, Mark. An African Journey. LC 85-15987. (Illus.). 52p. reprint ed. pap. 25.00 (*0-8357-5236-4*, 2030070) Bks Demand.
Patinkin, Mark, jt. auth. see Magaziner, Ira.
***Patino, Diogenes.** Asentamientos Prehispanicos en la Costa Pacifica Caucana. (Illus.). 160p. (SPA.). 1988. pap. 8.50 (*1-877812-19-6*) UPLAAP.
Patitu, Carol L., jt. auth. see Tack, Martha W.
Patitucci, Frank M. & Lichtenstein, Michael H. Improving Cash Management in Local Government: A Comprehensive Approach. LC 76-52518. (Illus.). 1977. pap. 6.00 (*0-89125-003-4*) Municipal.
Patitucci, Karen. Three-Minute Dramas for Worship. LC 89-30342. 272p. (C). 1989. pap. 11.95 (*0-89390-143-1*) Resource Pubns.
Patka, Frederick, ed. Existentialist Thinkers & Thought. 1962. pap. 2.45 (*0-8065-0157-X*, 101, Citadel Pr) Carol Pub Group.
Patkaniowska, M., jt. auth. see Corbridge.
Patkau, Karen. In the Sea. (Illus.). 24p. (J). (ps). 1990. 15.95 (*1-55037-067-7*, Pub. by Annick CN); pap. 5.95 (*1-55037-066-9*, Pub. by Annick CN) Firefly Bks Ltd.
Patkin, Max & Hochman, Stan. The Clown Prince of Baseball. LC 93-43574. (Illus.). 192p. 1994. 19.95 (*1-56796-036-7*, B0367) WRS Group.
Patkus, Ronald D. From Generation to Generation II: The Roman Catholic Archbishop of Boston, a Corporation Sole. LC 91-76158. 1992. pap. 10.95 (*0-8158-0480-6*) Chris Mass.
Patla, A. E., ed. Adaptability of Human Gait: Implications for the Control of Locomotion. (Advances in Psychology Ser.: No. 78). 456p. 1991. 137.25 (*0-444-88364-9*, North Holland) Elsevier.
Patlagean, E. Pauvrete Economique et Pauvrete Social a Byzance 4e-7e Siecles. 1977. 107.70 (*90-279-7933-2*) Mouton.
Patler, Louis, jt. auth. see Kriegel, Robert J.
Patman, Robert. The Soviet Union in the Horn of Africa: The Diplomacy of Intervention & Disengagement. (Cambridge Russian, Soviet & Post-Soviet Studies: No. 71). (Illus.). 250p. (C). 1990. 69.95 (*0-521-36022-6*) Cambridge U Pr.
Patmore, Angela & Couzens, Tim. Your Natural Dog: A Guide to Behavior & Health Care. LC 93-17397. (Illus.). 128p. 1993. 18.95 (*0-88184-947-2*) Carroll & Graf.
Patmore, Coventry K. Courage in Politics & Other Essays, 1885-1896. LC 68-26464. (Essay Index Reprint Ser.). 1977. reprint ed. 19.95 (*0-8369-0774-4*) Ayer.
— Rod, the Root & the Flower. Patmore, Derek, ed. LC 68-16966. (Essay Index Reprint Ser.). 1977. 19.95 (*0-8369-0775-2*) Ayer.
Patmore, Coventry K., ed. The Children's Garland: From the Best Poets. LC 73-167478. (Granger Index Reprint Ser.). 1977. reprint ed. 19.95 (*0-8369-6283-4*) Ayer.
Patmore, Derek, ed. see Patmore, Coventry K.
Patmore, J. Allan. Land & Leisure in England & Wales. LC 75-164656. 332p. 1971. 39.50 (*0-8386-1024-2*) Fairleigh Dickinson.
— Recreation & Resources: Leisure Patterns & Leisure Places. (Illus.). 288p. 1996. 55.00x (*0-631-17229-7*); 55.00 (*0-631-19249-2*) Blackwell Pubs.
Patmore, Ruth & Ross, Elizabeth. Rossmore Appliances. 50p. (C). 1972. write for info. (*0-686-66706-9*) Macmillan.
Patnaik, B. K., ed. Ageing in Cold-Blooded Vertebrates. (Journal: Gerontology Ser.: Vol. 40, Nos. 2-4, 1994). (Illus.). 166p. 1994. pap. 121.00 (*3-8055-5995-X*) S Karger.
***Patnaik, Himanshu S.** Lord Jagannath: His Temple, Cult & Festivals. (Illus.). 196p. (C). 1994. 67.00 (*81-7305-051-1*, Pub. by Aryan Bks Intl IA) Nataraj Bks.
Patnaik, K. U. Industrial Planning, Productivity & Technical Progress in India. (C). 1991. 25.00 (*0-8364-2661-4*, Pub. by Chugh Pubns II) S Asia.
Patnaik, Lalit N. Environmental Impacts of Industrial & Mining Activities. (New World Environment Ser.). 1990. 36.50 (*81-7024-333-5*, Pub. by Ashish II) S Asia.
Patnaik, N. R. History & Culture of Khond Tribes. (C). 1992. 44.00 (*81-7169-199-4*, Commonwealth) S Asia.
Patnaik, Prabhat. Time, Inflation & Growth: Some Macroeconomic Themes in an Indian Perspective. (R C Dutt Lectures). 56p. (C). 1988. pap. 4.95 (*0-86131-878-1*, Pub. by Orient Longman Ltd II) Apt Bks.
***Patnaik, Prabhat, ed.** Macroeconomics. (Oxford in India Readings Ser.). (Illus.). 256p. 1995. 24.95 (*0-19-563534-5*) OUP.
Patnaik, Pradyot. A Comprehensive Guide to the Hazardous Properties of Chemical Substances. 800p. 1992. text ed. 99.95 (*0-442-00191-6*) Van Nos Reinhold.
Patnaik, Prebhat, ed. Lenin & Imperialism: An Appraisal of Theories & Contemporary Reality. 512p. (C). 1986. text ed. 40.00 (*0-86131-502-2*, Pub. by Orient Longman Ltd II) Apt Bks.
Patnaik, S. C. Industrial Development in a Backward Region: Dynamics of Policy. (C). 1988. 26.00 (*81-7024-202-9*, Pub. by Ashish II) S Asia.
Patnaik, Satyendra. Brahmanical Religion in Ancient Orissa. 1987. 42.00 (*0-317-61786-9*, Pub. by Ashish II) S Asia.
Patnaik, Tandra. Sabda: A Study of Bhartrharti's Philosophy of Language. (C). 1994. text ed. 19.00 (*81-246-0028-7*, Pub. by DK Pubs Dist II) S Asia.
Patnaik, Utes & Dingwaney, Manjari, eds. Chains of Servitude: Bondage & Slavery in India. 392p. 1985. text ed. 40.00 (*0-86131-491-3*, Pub. by Sangam Bks II) Apt Bks.
Patnaik, Utsa, ed. Agrarian Relations & Accumulation: The "Mode of Production" Debate in India. 280p. 1991. 24.95 (*0-19-562565-X*) OUP.
***Patneaude, David.** Dark, Starry Morning: Stories of This World & Beyond. LC 95-770. 1995. write for info. (*0-8075-1474-8*) A Whitman.
— Someone Was Watching. Mathews, Judith, ed. LC 92-39130. 240p. (J). (gr. 6-9). 1993. lib. bdg. 13.95 (*0-8075-7531-3*) A Whitman.
***Patner, Andrew, ed.** Alternative Futures: Challenging Designs for Arts Philanthropy. LC 94-79005. 117p. (Orig.). 1994. pap. 11.95 (*0-9643011-0-5*) Grantmakers Arts.
Patni, M. J., jt. auth. see Srivastava, C. M.
Patni, M. J., jt. ed. see Srivastava, C. M.
Patnode, Darwin. A History of Parliamentary Procedure. 3rd ed. LC 81-86047. 85p. (Orig.). 1982. pap. 9.95 (*0-942302-00-1*) Parliamentarians.
Patnode, Gladys. Patckwork Quilt: Stories of My Childhood. (Stories We Tell Ser.). 31p. 1993. pap. 4.00 (*1-884983-03-0*) Homegrown Bks.
Patnoe, S. A Narrative History of Experimental Social Psychology. (Recent Research in Psychology Ser.). 295p. 1988. pap. 43.00 (*0-387-96850-4*) Spr-Verlag.
Patnoi, Melinda, ed. see Gentle World.
Patnuker, B. W. Grasses of Marathwada. (C). 1980. text ed. 50.00 (*81-85046-05-0*, Pub. by Scientific Pubs II) St Mut.
Pato, Hilda. Los Finales Poematicos en la Obra de Luis Cernuda. LC 87-62377. 118p. (SPA.). 1988. pap. 30.00 (*0-89295-052-8*) Society Sp & Sp-Am.
Pato, Michele A. & Zohar, Joseph, eds. Current Treatments of Obsessive-Compulsive Disorder. LC 90-14497. (Clinical Practice Ser.: No. 18). 270p. 1991. text ed. 30.00 (*0-88048-351-2*) Am Psychiatric.
Patocka, J. Le Monde Naturel Comme Probleme Philosophique. (Phaenomenologica Ser.: No. 68). 1976. lib. bdg. 65.50 (*90-247-1795-7*) Kluwer Ac.
Patodia, D. N. Winds of Change: The New Economic Challenges, India. 150p. 1987. 21.00 (*0-8364-2060-8*, Pub. by Allied II) S Asia.
***Paton.** Competition & Planning in the NHS: The Danger of Unplanned Markets. 174p. 1992. pap. 57.50 (*1-56593-058-4*, 0364) Singular Publishing.
— Lifespan Health Psychology: Nursing Problems & Interventions. 288p. 1992. pap. 43.25 (*1-56593-008-8*, 0249) Singular Publishing.
Paton, A. A., et al. Civil Engineering Design for Decommissioning of Nuclear Installations. 104p. 1984. pap. text ed. 67.50 (*0-86010-614-4*) G & T Inc.
Paton, Alan. Ah, but Your Land Is Beautiful. 280p. 1983. pap. 13.95 (*0-684-17830-3*, Scribners) S&S Trade.
— Cry, the Beloved Country. 22.95 (*0-89190-379-8*, Am Repr) Amereon Ltd.
— Cry, the Beloved Country. 304p. 1940. pap. 9.95 (*0-684-71863-4*, Scribners) S&S Trade.
— Cry, the Beloved Country. 1985. pap. 12.00 (*0-684-51544-X*, Scribners) S&S Trade.
— Cry, the Beloved Country. 304p. 1987. pap. 5.95 (*0-02-053210-5*, Collier S&S) S&S Trade.
— Cry the Beloved Country. 304p. 1977. text ed. 35.00 (*0-684-15559-1*, Scribners) S&S Trade.
— Cry, the Beloved Country. abr. ed. (Bridge Ser.). 115p. (YA). 1991. pap. text ed. 5.95 (*0-582-53009-1*, 79129) Longman.
— Cry, the Beloved Country. 300p. 1991. reprint ed. lib. bdg. 25.95x (*0-89966-788-0*) Buccaneer Bks.
— Instrument of Thy Peace. large type ed. 124p. 1985. reprint ed. pap. text ed. 8.95 (*0-8027-2494-9*) Walker & Co.
— Save the Beloved Country. 336p. 1989. text ed. 22.50 (*0-684-19127-X*, Scribners) S&S Trade.
— Tales from a Troubled Land. 128p. 1977. text ed. 20.00 (*0-684-15135-9*, Scribners) S&S Trade.
— Too Late the Phalarope. 21.95 (*0-89190-392-5*, Am Repr) Amereon Ltd.
— Too Late the Phalarope. 1950. pap. 7.95 (*0-684-71866-9*, Scribners) S&S Trade.
— Too Late the Phalarope. 1983. pap. 7.95 (*0-684-10455-5*, Scribners) S&S Trade.
— Too Late the Phalarope. 288p. 1985. reprint ed. pap. 5.95 (*0-684-18500-8*, Scribners) S&S Trade.
— Towards the Mountain. 1988. 19.75 (*0-8446-6322-0*) Peter Smith.
— Towards the Mountain: An Autobiography. 336p. 1987. pap. 9.95 (*0-684-18892-9*, Scribners) S&S Trade.
Paton, Alex. ABC of Alcohol. 3rd ed. 48p. 1994. pap. text ed. 17.00 (*0-7279-0812-X*, BMJ Pubng Grp) Amer Coll Phys.
Paton, Alex, ed. ABC of Alcohol. (Illus.). 35p. 1982. pap. 16.00 (*0-7279-0192-3*, Pub. by British Med Jrnl UK) Amer Coll Phys.
Paton, Andrew. Stendhal. 1972. 59.95 (*0-8490-1124-8*) Gordon Pr.
Paton, B. E. & Nazarenko, O. K. Welding & Surfacing Reviews: Electron Beam Welding: Achievements & Problems (a Review) (Soviet Technology Reviews Ser.: Vol. 1, Pt. 1). ii, 54p. 1989. pap. text ed. 39.00 (*3-7186-4946-2*) Gordon & Breach.
Paton, B. E., ed. see Gladkii, P. V., et al.
Paton, B. E., ed. see Kuchuk-Yatsenko, S. I. & Cherednichok, V. T.
Paton, B. E., ed. see Medovar, B. I., et al.
Paton, B. E., ed. see Pokhodnaya, I. K. & Podgaetsky, V. V.
Paton, C. R. U. S. Health Politics: Public Policy & Political Theory. 240p. 1990. text ed. 63.95 (*0-566-07101-0*, Pub. by Avebury Pub UK) Ashgate Pub Co.
Paton, Calum. Ethics & Politics: Theory & Practice. 139p. 1992. 68.95 (*1-85628-382-8*, Pub. by Avebury Pub UK) Ashgate Pub Co.
Paton, Caroline, jt. auth. see Paton, Sandy.

P Q

An Asterisk (*) at the beginning of an entry indicates that the title is appearing in BIP for the first time.

Paton, D. M., ed. The Transport of Neurotransmitters. (Journal: Pharmacology: Vol. 21, No. 2). (Illus.). 74p. 1980. pap. 19.25 (3-8055-1316-X) S Karger.

Paton, David, ed. see Allen, Roland.

Paton, David F. Fractures & Orthopaedics. 2nd ed. LC 92-12316. (Student Notes Ser.). (Illus.). 248p. 1993. pap. 24.95 (0-443-04707-3) Churchill.

Paton, David M., ed. Adenosine & Adenine Nucleotides: Physiology & Pharmacology. 350p. 1988. 125.00 (0-85066-416-0) Taylor & Francis.

— Methods in Pharmacology, Vol. 6: Methods Used in Adenosine Research. LC 84-26638. 400p. 1985. 89.50 (0-306-41872-X, Plenum Pr) Plenum.

— The Release of Catecholamines from Adrenergic Neurons. 1979. 170.00 (0-08-021536-X, Pub. by Pergamon Repr UK) Franklin.

Paton, Garth, jt. auth. see Haggerty, Terry.

Paton, George E., jt. ed. see Powell, Chris.

Paton, George W. A Textbook of Jurisprudence. 4th ed. Dorham, David P., ed. (C). 1973. text ed. 49.95 (0-19-825314-1) OUP.

Paton, H. J., jt. ed. see Klibansky, R.

Paton, Herbert J. Kant's Metaphysics of Experience, 2 vols., Set. (Muirhead Library of Philosophy). (C). 1970. reprint ed. pap. 50.00 (0-391-00673-8) Humanities.

Paton, Herbert J., tr. see Kant, Immanuel.

Paton, J., see Ruth Kittson, pseud..

Paton, J., see Ruthena H. Kittson, pseud..

Paton, J. E., jt. ed. see Aitchison, Ian J.

Paton, Jean. The Adopted Break Silence. (Adoption Ser.). 1954. pap. 8.00 (0-318-36159-0) Orphan Voyage.

Paton, Jean, ed. see Weyman, Ronald C.

Paton, Jessie, jt. ed. see Rickert, Edith.

Paton, John. The Kingfisher Children's Encyclopedia. LC 92-4785. (Illus.). 816p. (J). (gr. 3-9). 1992. 32.95 (1-85697-800-1, Kingfisher LKC) LKC.

Paton, John G. L' Aria Barocca: Medium High Voice. 110p. (Orig.). 1986. pap. text ed. 8.95 (0-9602296-5-5) Leyerle Pubns.

— L' Aria Barocca: Medium Low Voice. 110p. 1987. pap. text ed. 8.95 (0-9602296-7-1) Leyerle Pubns.

— Twenty-Six Italian Songs & Arias: For Medium Low Voice. 152p. (Orig.). (C). 1991. pap. 7.95 (0-88284-490-3, 3403) Alfred Pub.

Paton, John G., jt. auth. see Christy, Van A.

Paton, John G., ed. see Mendelssohn, Felix & Mendelssohn, Fanny.

Paton, John G., ed. see Mozart, Wolfgang Amadeus.

Paton, John Glenn. Twenty-Six Italian Songs & Arias: For Medium High Voice. 152p. (Orig.). (C). 1991. pap. 7.95 (0-88284-489-X, 3402) Alfred Pub.

Paton, Jonathan. The Land & People of South Africa. LC 89-2477. (Portraits of the Nations Ser.). (Illus.). 304p. (J). (gr. 6 up). 1990. 19.00 (0-397-32361-1, Better Bk Getter) HarpC Child Bks.

— The Land & People of South Africa. LC 89-2477. (Portraits of the Nations Ser.). (Illus.). 304p. (J). (gr. 6 up). 1990. lib. bdg. 18.89 (0-397-32362-X, Lipp Jr Bks) HarpC Child Bks.

Paton, Joseph N. Poems by a Painter. LC 73-112941. reprint ed. 32.00 (0-404-04905-2) AMS Pr.

Paton, Kathleen, ed. Poems to Share. (Real Mother Goose Library). (Illus.). 24p. (J). (ps-3). 1990. 4.95 (1-56288-050-0) Checkerboard.

Paton, L. A. Studies in the Fairy Mythology of Arthurian Romance. 1972. 69.95 (0-8490-1150-7) Gordon Pr.

Paton, Lewis B. The Early History of Syria & Palestine. LC 79-2878. (Illus.). 302p. 1981. reprint ed. 28.50 (0-8305-0046-4) Hyperion Conn.

— Esther: Critical Exegetical Commentary. Driver, Samuel R. et al, eds. LC 08-30156. (International Critical Commentary Ser.). 360p. 1908. 36.95 (0-567-05009-2, Pub. by T & T Clark UK) Bks Intl VA.

— Jerusalem in Bible Times. Davis, Moshe, ed. LC 77-70733. (America & the Holy Land Ser.). (Illus.). 1977. reprint ed. lib. bdg. 23.95 (0-405-10277-1) Ayer.

Paton, Lucy A. Elizabeth Cary Agassiz: A Biography. LC 74-3969. (Women in America Ser.). (Illus.). 454p. 1974. reprint ed. 35.95 (0-405-06117-X) Ayer.

Paton, Mena. System 1032 PCI Guide. Stone, Shirley, ed. 50p. (Orig.). pap. text ed. 20.00 (0-912055-24-3) CompuServe Data Tech.

Paton, N. E., jt. ed. see Hamilton, C. H.

Paton, N. E., ed. see Metallurgical Society of AIME Staff.

Paton, Neil E., ed. see International Conference on Superplasticity & Superplastic Forming Staff.

Paton, Norman W. & Williams, M. Howard, eds. Rules in Database Systems: Proceedings of the 1st International Workshop on Rules in Database Systems, Edinburgh, Scotland, 30 August-1 September 1993. LC 93-27566. (Workshops in Computing Ser.). 1994. 71.00 (0-387-19846-6) Spr-Verlag.

Paton, Patricia. A Medical Gentleman: James J. Waring, M. D. LC 93-23589. 1993. write for info. (0-942576-02-0); pap. write for info. (0-942576-33-0) CO Hist Soc.

*__Paton, Priscilla.__ Howard & the Babysitter Surprise. (Illus.). (J). 1996. write for info. (0-395-71814-7) HM.

Paton, R. Business Case Studies: German. 124p. (ENG & GER.). 1980. pap. 17.95 (0-8288-0991-7, M 9204) Fr & Eur.

Paton, Rob, ed. Reluctant Entrepreneurs. 192p. 1990. 95.00 (0-335-09233-0, Open Univ Pr); pap. 39.00 (0-335-09232-2, Open Univ Pr) Taylor & Francis.

Paton, Robert A., jt. auth. see McCalman, James.

Paton, Roderick. Business Case Studies: French. 124p. (ENG & FRE.). 1980. pap. 19.95 (0-8288-0986-0, M 14377) Fr & Eur.

Paton, Sandy & Paton, Caroline. I've Got a Song! A Collection of Songs for Youngsters. 2nd ed. (Illus.). 40p. (Orig.). (J). (gr. k-4). 1989. pap. 10.98 (0-938702-05-X) Folk-Legacy.

— When the Spirit Says Sing: A Read-along, Sing-along, Coloring Book. (Illus.). 40p. (Orig.). (J). (gr. k-8). 1989. pap. 13.98 (0-938702-06-8) Folk-Legacy.

Paton, Thomas R. Perspectives on a Dynamic Earth. 176p. 1986. text ed. 55.00 (0-04-550042-8); pap. text ed. 21.95 (0-04-550043-6) Routledge Chapman & Hall.

Paton, Valerie. Creative Lace Patterns. (Illus.). 1988. 19.95 (0-85219-705-5) Branford.

Paton, W. A. Corporate Profits As Shown by Audit Reports. (General Ser.: No. 28). 165p. 1935. reprint ed. 42.90 (0-87014-027-2); reprint ed. mic. film 21.50 (0-685-61167-1) Natl Bur Econ Res.

— Down the Islands: A Voyage to the Caribbees. 1976. lib. bdg. 59.95 (0-8490-1731-9) Gordon Pr.

Paton, W. A. & Littleton, A. C. An Introduction to Corporate Accounting Standards. (Monograph: No. 3). 156p. 1940. 12.00 (0-86539-000-2) Am Accounting.

Paton Walsh, Jill. Birdy & the Ghosties. 1989. 10.95 (0-374-30716-4) FS&G.

— Birdy & the Ghosties. 1991. pap. 4.95 (0-374-40675-8) FS&G.

— A Chance Child. (Illus.). 192p. (J). (gr. 5 up). 1991. pap. 3.95 (0-374-41174-3, Sunburst Bks) FS&G.

— Gaffer Samson's Luck. LC 84-10180. (Illus.). 112p. (J). (gr. 5 up). 1984. 11.95 (0-374-32498-0) FS&G.

— Gaffer Samson's Luck. (Illus.). 128p. (J). (gr. 3-7). 1990. pap. 3.50 (0-374-42513-2, Sunburst Bks) FS&G.

— Goldengrove. LC 72-81484. (Sunburst Ser.). 130p. (J). (gr. 6 up). 1985. pap. 3.50 (0-374-42587-6) FS&G.

— Grace. 256p. (YA). (gr. 7 up). 1992. 16.00 (0-374-32758-0) FS&G.

— The Green Book. LC 81-12620. (Illus.). 80p. (J). (gr. 5 up). 1982. 13.00 (0-374-32778-5) FS&G.

— Green Book. LC 81-12620. (Illus.). 80p. (J). (gr. 5 up). 1986. pap. 3.95 (0-374-42802-6) FS&G.

— Matthew & the Sea Singer. (J). (ps-3). 1993. 13.00 (0-374-34869-3) FS&G.

— Parcel of Patterns. (YA). 1992. pap. 3.95 (0-374-45743-3) FS&G.

— Torch. LC 87-45995. 176p. (YA). 1988. 15.00 (0-374-37684-0) FS&G.

— Unleaving. 1990. pap. 3.50 (0-374-48068-0) FS&G.

Paton-Walsh, Jill P. Fireweed. (J). (gr. 6 up). 1988. pap. 3.50 (0-374-42316-4, Sunburst Bks) FS&G.

Paton, William. Man & Mouse: Animals in Medical Research. 2nd ed. (Illus.). 304p. 1993. pap. 14.95 (0-19-286146-8) OUP.

Paton, William A. Down the Islands: A Voyage to the Caribbees. LC 69-19360. (Illus.). 301p. 1970. reprint ed. text ed. 59.75 (0-8371-1129-3, PAD&, Negro U Pr) Greenwood.

— Paton on Accounting: Selected Writings of W. A. Paton. Taggart, Herbert F., ed. LC 64-64728. 729p. reprint ed. pap. 180.00 (0-317-28339-1, 2022093) Bks Demand.

Paton, William A. & Dixon, Robert L. Make-or-Buy Decisions in Tooling for Mass Production. LC 61-63325. (Michigan Business Papers: No. 35). 40p. reprint ed. pap. 25.00 (0-317-28341-3, 2022091) Bks Demand.

Paton, William A. & Stevenson, Russell A. Principles of Accounting. Brief, Richard P., ed. LC 77-87284. (Contemporary Accounting Thought Ser.). 1978. reprint ed. lib. bdg. 59.95 (0-405-10912-1) Ayer.

— Principles of Accounting. LC 75-18479. (History of Accounting Ser.). 1978. reprint ed. 18.95 (0-405-07561-8) Ayer.

Paton, William D., ed. see International Congress of Pharmacology Staff.

Paton, William R. & Hicks, Edward L. The Inscriptions of Cos. (Subsidia Epigraphica Ser.). (Illus.). liv, 407p. (GER.). 1990. reprint ed. 89.70 (3-487-09288-3, Pub. by Georg Olms GW) Lubrecht & Cramer.

Patonay, Gabor, ed. Advances in Near IR Measurements, Vol. 1. 1991. 90.25 (1-55938-173-6) Jai Pr.

— HPLC Detection: Newer Methods. LC 92-26716. 240p. 1993. 95.00 (0-89573-327-7) VCH Pubs.

Patons. Supplement Ser, 1974. 1973. 18.00 (0-316-69344-8) Little.

Patorski, K. Handbook of the Moire Fringe Technique. LC 92-37210. 1992. write for info. (0-444-88823-3) Elsevier.

Patoski, Christina. Merry Christmas, America: A Front-Yard View of the Holidays. LC 94-15297. (Illus.). 112p. 1994. 16.95 (1-56566-071-4) Thomasson-Grant.

Patoski, Joe N. Stevie Ray Vaughan: Caught in the Crossfire. 1994. pap. 11.95 (0-316-16069-5) Little.

Patoski, Margaret, tr. see Denikin, Anton I.

Patouillard, Narcisse-Theophile. Essai Taxonomique sur les Familles et les Genres des Hymenomycetes. 1963. reprint ed. 20.00 (90-6123-119-1) Lubrecht & Cramer.

Patout, Alex. Patout's Cajun Home Cooking. 1986. 25.00 (0-394-54725-X) Random.

Patraka, Vivian M. & Siegel, Mark. Sam Shepard. LC 85-70129. (Western Writers Ser.: No. 69). (Illus.). 49p. (Orig.). 1985. pap. 3.95 (0-88430-043-9) Boise St U W Writ Ser.

Patrascu. Construction Cost Engineering Handbook. (Cost Engineering Ser.: Vol. 12). 520p. 1988. 160.00 (0-8247-7827-8) Dekker.

*__Patray, Stuart.__ The Root of All Evil. abr. ed. 320p. 1995. pap. 9.95 (1-56901-451-5) NW Pub.

*__Patri, Angelo.__ Pinocchio in Africa. Orig. Title: Cherubini. (Illus.). 150p. Date not set. pap. write for info. (0-87556-781-9) Saifer.

Patri, Umesh. Hindu Scriptures & American Transcendentalists. (C). 1987. 21.00 (81-7076-005-4, Pub. by Intellectual Pub Hse II) S Asia.

*__Patriarca, Gianna.__ Italian Women & Other Tragedies. (Essay Ser.). 77p. 1995. pap. (1-55071-001-X) Guernica Editions.

*__Patrias, Carmela.__ Patriots & Proletarians: Politicizing Hungarian Immigrants in Interwar Canada. (McGraw & Arnold's Atlas of Muscle & Musculocutaneous Flaps Ser.). 336p. 1994. 39.95 (0-7735-1174-1, Pub. by McGill CN) U of Toronto Pr.

Patric, Beth S. The Splintered Eye. LC 87-12192. 1987. 15.95 (0-88282-031-1) New Horizon NJ.

Patric, John. Yankee Hobo in the Orient: Why Japan Was Strong. 1979. 250.00 (0-685-96533-3) Revisionist Pr.

Patricca, Nicholas. The Fifth Sun. 1986. pap. 4.95 (0-87129-207-6, F38) Dramatic Pub.

— The Fifth Sun. 1993. 2.75 (0-87129-217-3, F53) Dramatic Pub.

*__Patricca, Nicholas A.__ The Idea of Chaos: Sex, Death, Life & Order in Key West. Sturm, Robert, ed. (Illus.). 96p. (Orig.). 1994. pap. 12.00 (0-9640343-5-2) Traditional Arts.

— Oh, Holy Allen Ginsberg. 1995. 5.00 (0-87129-510-5, O52) Dramatic Pub.

— El Quinto Sol. Date not set. 5.00 (0-87129-596-2, E33) Dramatic Pub.

— An Uncertain Hour. Date not set. 5.00 (0-87129-534-2, U17) Dramatic Pub.

— Where Shadows Fall. Sturm, Robert, ed. 50p. (Orig.). 1994. pap. 12.00 (0-9640343-9-5) Traditional Arts.

Patricelli, Dick. Nature's Pantry Cookbook. 131p. 1990. spiral bd. 19.95 (0-9629224-0-4) Natures Pantry.

Patricelli, Leslie & Gruening, Michelle. Espresso Served Here: The Official Espresso Humor Book. 60p. 1993. pap. 6.95 (0-9639085-0-2) Good Dog Pr.

Patrich, Joseph. The Formation of Nabatean Art: Prohibition of a Graven Image among the Nabateans. LC 90-1846. (Illus.). 231p. 1990. 54.50 (90-04-09285-4) E J Brill.

— Sabas, Leader of Palestinian Monasticism: A Comparative Study in Eastern Monasticism, Fourth to Seventh Centuries. LC 93-49099. (Dumbarton Oaks Studies: No. 32). 1995. 50.00 (0-88402-221-8) Dumbarton Oaks.

Patricia. Jesus I: The Man. Morningland Publications, Inc. Staff, ed. (Series of Three Books Called Jesus). (Illus.). 439p. 1980. pap. 10.00 (0-935146-15-6) Morningland.

— Jesus II: The Mission. Morningland Publications, Inc. Staff, ed. (Series of Three Books Called Jesus). (Illus.). 461p. 1980. pap. 10.00 (0-935146-17-2) Morningland.

— Jesus III: The Return. Morningland Publications, Inc. Staff, ed. (Illus.). 470p. (Orig.). 1980. pap. 10.00 (0-935146-18-0) Morningland.

— Morningland Astrology, Bk. 3. Morningland Publications, Inc. Staff, ed. (Astrology Ser.). (Illus.). 301p. (Orig.). 1980. pap. 7.95 (0-935146-07-5) Morningland.

— Osiris & Isis. (Illus.). 267p. (Orig.). 1980. pap. 7.95 (0-935146-19-9) Morningland.

— Thinis. (Illus.). 330p. (Orig.). 1980. spiral bd. 7.95 (0-935146-12-1) Morningland.

— The Way Out of Vietnam. 166p. (Orig.). 1980. pap. 3.00 (0-935146-21-0) Morningland.

Patricia & Gyan, Gopi. Oneness, Vol. II. (Orig.). 1980. spiral bd. 7.95 (0-935146-24-5) Morningland.

Patricia, De Man, jt. auth. see Van Straten, Roelof.

Patricia Dougherty. American Diplomats & the Franco-Prussian War: Perceptions from Paris & Berlin. 54p. (C). 1985. reprint ed. pap. text ed. 11.50 (0-8191-5056-8, Inst Study Diplomacy) U Pr of Amer.

Patricia, Sri & Gyan, Gopi. Oneness, Vol. I. (Orig.). 1979. pap. 3.95 (0-935146-11-3) Morningland.

Patricios, Nicholas N. Building Marvelous Miami. (Illus.). 376p. 1994. 49.95 (0-8130-1299-6) U Press Fla.

Patricios, Nicholas N., ed. International Handbook on Land Use Planning. LC 84-29018. (Illus.). 699p. 1986. text ed. 165.00 (0-313-23950-9, PHL/, Greenwood Pr) Greenwood.

Patrick. Confession of St. Patrick. pap. 2.95 (0-89981-014-4) Eastern Orthodox.

— Kingdom of the Flies. 19.95 (0-8488-1536-X) Amereon Ltd.

— Treatise on Adhesion & Adhesives, Vol. 5. 416p. 1981. 175.00 (0-8247-1399-0) Dekker.

— Treatise on Adhesion & Adhesives, Vol. 6. 304p. 1989. 125.00 (0-8247-7587-2) Dekker.

Patrick & Fiacc. Writings of St. Patrick, with the Metrical Life of St. Patrick. pap. 2.95 (0-89981-109-4) Eastern Orthodox.

Patrick, Alison. The Men of the First French Republic: Political Alignments in the National Convention of 1792. LC 72-4018. 425p. reprint ed. pap. 121.20 (0-8357-4329-2, 2037129) Bks Demand.

Patrick, Ann. Betting on Love. 224p. (Orig.). 1993. pap. 2.95 (1-56597-081-0, Kismet) Meteor Pub.

— Comfort & Joy. 224p. (Orig.). 1993. pap. 2.95 (1-56597-105-1, Kismet) Meteor Pub.

— For Services Rendered. 224p. (Orig.). 1991. pap. 2.95 (1-878702-61-0, Kismet) Meteor Pub.

— Hearts Collide. 224p. (Orig.). 1991. pap. 2.75 (1-878702-37-8, Kismet) Meteor Pub.

— Let's Make Piano Music with Marvin, Bk. 1. 40p. (J). (gr. k-7). 1985. pap. text ed. 6.95 (0-931759-06-4) Centerstream Pub.

— Lets Make Piano Music with Marvin, Bk. 2. 48p. (J). (gr. k-7). 1986. pap. text ed. 6.95 (0-931759-13-7) Centerstream Pub.

— Let's Make Piano Music with Marvin: Primer. 40p. (J). (gr. k-7). 1985. pap. text ed. 6.95 (0-931759-05-6) Centerstream Pub.

— Opening Act. 224p. (Orig.). 1990. pap. 2.75 (1-878702-16-5, Kismet) Meteor Pub.

Patrick, Bert, ed. see Galindo, Sergio.

Patrick, Beverly H. Uncivil Wars: Men & Women in the Office of the 90's. 144p. 1994. boxed 24.95 (0-8403-9261-3) Kendall-Hunt.

Patrick, Bill. The Food & Drug Administration. (Know Your Government Ser.). (Illus.). 96p. (J). (gr. 5 up). 1989. lib. bdg. 14.95 (0-87754-822-6) Chelsea Hse.

Patrick, Carmen. Making Liqueurs at Home. 74p. (Orig.). 1989. pap. 9.95 (0-919574-76-9) Gordon Soules Bk.

Patrick, Charles. This Book Is Different: A Book of Dreams, Memories & Nonsense. LC 90-92240. (Illus.). 64p. (Orig.). 1991. pap. 7.95 (0-9628764-0-2) Patrick-Po.

Patrick, Christian C. Infections in Immunocompromised Infants & Children. (Illus.). 979p. 1992. text ed. 175.00 (0-443-08857-8) Churchill.

Patrick, Colleen. Mind over Media: Everybody's Ultimate Authority on Media Access from an Insider's Point of View. 184p. (Orig.). 1988. pap. 13.00 (0-935529-04-7) Comprehen Health Educ.

— The One Hundred Percent Solution: Solve Every Problem, Positively! 1992. pap. 11.95 (0-9634281-0-1) Meadow Brook.

Patrick, Dale. The Rendering of God in the Old Testament. LC 80-2389. (Overtures to Biblical Theology Ser.: No. 10). 174p. (Orig.). reprint ed. pap. 49.60 (0-685-23638-2, 2029110) Bks Demand.

Patrick, Dale R. Electronic Instruments: Instrumentation Training Course. 4th ed. 320p. 1991. pap. text ed. 59.00 (0-13-251208-4) P-H.

Patrick, Dale R. & Fardo, Stephen W. Electricity & Electronics: A Survey. 2nd ed. 604p. 1990. text ed. 39.60 (0-13-247875-7) P-H.

— Electricity & Electronics: A Survey. 3rd ed. LC 94-45125. 1995. text ed. 68.00 (0-13-360074-2) P-H.

— Industrial Electrical Experimentation. 2nd ed. (Illus.). 271p. (C). 1983. reprint ed. pap. 14.95 (0-89917-385-3) Tichenor Pub.

— Industrial Electronics: Devices & Systems. (C). 1986. write for info. (0-8359-3198-6, Reston) P-H.

— Understanding AC Circuits. 144p. 1989. pap. text ed. 52.00 (0-13-942954-9) P-H.

— Understanding Electricity & Electronics. 550p. 1989. pap. text ed. 58.00 (0-13-943242-6) P-H.

— Understanding Semiconductor Devices. 272p. 1989. pap. text ed. 52.00 (0-13-943192-6) P-H.

Patrick, Dale R. & Patrick, Steven R. Pneumatic Instrumentation. 3rd ed. LC 92-31773. 434p. 1993. text ed. 34.95 (0-8273-5482-7) Delmar.

Patrick, Dave. California's Nude Beaches: Plus Hawaii, Oregon & Washington. 4th ed. 1994. pap. 14.95 (0-9614880-3-4) Bold Type.

— California's Nude Beaches: The Clothes-Free-Hassle-Free Guide. 1991. pap. 12.95 (0-9614880-2-6) Bold Type.

— California's Nude Beaches: The Clothes-Free Hassle-Free Guide. 2nd ed. 1988. pap. 8.95 (0-9614880-1-8) Bold Type.

— Radio Control Aerobatics for Everyone. Atwood, Tom, ed. (Illus.). 74p. (Orig.). 1994. pap. 12.95 (0-911295-31-3) Air Age.

Patrick, David. Word for Windows 2 Super Book. 1992. pap. 39.95 (0-672-30139-3) Sams.

— WordPerfect 6.0 Super Book. 1993. pap. 34.95 (0-672-30260-8) Sams.

*__Patrick, David R.__ Facility Manager's Guide to Clean Air Compliance. LC 94-29008. 293p. 1995. 75.00 (0-87179-857-3) BNA.

Patrick, David R., ed. Toxic Air Pollution Handbook. LC 93-21545. (Environmental Engineering Ser.). 1994. text ed. 99.95 (0-442-00903-8) Van Nos Reinhold.

*__Patrick, Delaney, et al.__ Electronic GAAP. 1995. pap. text ed. 59.00 (0-471-05656-1) Wiley.

Patrick, Denice. Look Inside a House. (Poke & Look Learning Bks.). (Illus.). 16p. (J). (ps-1). 1989. 11.95 (0-448-19351-5, G&D) Putnam Pub Group.

— Look Inside a Ship. (Poke & Look Learning Bks.). (Illus.). 16p. (J). (ps-1). 1989. 11.95 (0-448-19352-3, G&D) Putnam Pub Group.

— Look Inside Your Body. (Poke & Look Learning Bks.). (Illus.). 16p. (J). (ps-1). 1989. bds. 11.95 (0-448-21033-9, G&D) Putnam Pub Group.

Patrick, Denice, jt. auth. see Ingoglia, Gina.

Patrick, Denise L. The Car Washing Street. LC 92-9229. (Illus.). 32p. (J). (ps up). 1993. 14.00 (0-688-11452-0, Tambourine Bks); lib. bdg. 13.93 (0-688-11453-9, Tambourine Bks) Morrow.

— Disney's Peek-a-Boo Bambi. (Golden Sturdy Shape Bks.). (Illus.). 14p. (J). (ps-00). 1992. write for info. (0-307-12392-8, 12392) Western Pub.

— Disney's The Little Mermaid: Ariel's Secret. (Golden Sturdy Shape Bks.). (Illus.). 14p. (J). (ps-00). 1992. bds. write for info. (0-307-12393-6, 12393, Golden Pr) Western Pub.

— Ghostwriter: The Mini Book of Kid's Puzzles Sports Issue. (J). (ps-3). 1992. pap. 2.50 (0-553-37073-1) Bantam.

— Good Night, Baby. (My First Golden Board Bks.). (Illus.). 24p. (J). (ps). 1993. bds. 3.50 (0-307-06144-2, 6144, Golden Pr) Western Pub.

— Red Dancing Shoes. LC 91-32666. (Illus.). 32p. (J). (ps up). 1993. 14.00 (0-688-10392-8, Tambourine Bks); lib. bdg. 13.93 (0-688-10393-6, Tambourine Bks) Morrow.

— Walt Disney's the Jungle Book. (J). (ps). 1994. 3.95 (0-307-12548-3, Golden Pr) Western Pub.

Patrick, Diane. Coretta Scott King. LC 91-17032. (Impact Biographies Ser.). (Illus.). 144p. (YA). (gr. 9-12). 1991. lib. bdg. 15.47 (0-531-13005-3) Watts.

— The Executive Branch. LC 94-963. (First Bks.). (J). 1994. lib. bdg. 13.93 (0-531-20179-1) Watts.

— Family Celebrations. LC 93-18456. (Family Ties Ser.). (Illus.). 64p. (J). (ps-4). 1993. lib. bdg. 12.95 (1-881889-04-1) Silver Moon.

— Martin Luther King, Jr. LC 89-24800. (First Bks.). (Illus.). (J). 1990. lib. bdg. 13.93 (0-531-10892-9) Watts.

P Q

An Asterisk (*) at the beginning of an entry indicates that the title is appearing in BIP for the first time.

— A Missing Portrait on Sugar Hill. (Mysteries in Time Ser.). (Illus.). 80p. (J). (gr. 4-6). 1995. lib. bdg. 12.95 (*1-881889-66-1*) Silver Moon.

Patrick, Donald L. & Erickson, Pennifer. Health Status & Health Policy: Allocating Resources to Health Care. (Illus.). 504p. 1993. 65.00 (*0-19-505027-4*) OUP.

Patrick, Donald L. & Peach, Hedle. Disablement in the Community. (Illus.). 248p. 1989. pap. 39.95 (*0-19-261434-7*) OUP.

Patrick, E. A. & Costello, J. P. Unsupervised Estimation & Processing of Unknown Signals. LC 71-136727. 207p. 1970. 19.00 (*0-403-04528-2*) Scholarly.

Patrick, Edward & Fattu, James. Artificial Intelligence with Statistical Pattern Recognition. 363p. 1986. text ed. 59. 95 (*0-13-049131-4*, Busn) P-H.

Patrick, Edward A. Decision Analysis in Medicine: Methods & Applications. 352p. 1979. 119.00 (*0-8493-5255-X*, R723, CRC Reprint) Franklin.

Patrick, Elizabeth N., intro. An Interview with William J. Moore. (Illus.). 110p. 1985. lib. bdg. 29.00 (*1-56475-296-8*); fiche write for info. (*1-56475-297-6*) U NV Oral Hist.

***Patrick, Ellen.** Aunt Sally's Cornpone Remedies & Claptrap Cures: 307 Tonics for What Ails You. 96p. 1995. pap. 5.95 (*1-881548-29-5*) Crane Hill AL.

— Help! I'm Southern & I Can't Stop Eating. LC 94-33287. 128p. 1994. pap. 5.95 (*1-881548-13-9*) Crane Hill AL.

Patrick, Floyd A. Personnel - Human Resource Management. 432p. (C). 1994. per. 43.95 (*0-685-72188-4*) Kendall-Hunt.

Patrick, Freda, jt. auth. see Rollins, Kay D.

Patrick, Gay D. Building the Reference Collection: A How-to-Do-It Manual for School & Public Librarians. (How-to-Do-It Ser.). 160p. 1992. 32.50 (*1-55570-105-1*) Neal-Schuman.

***Patrick, George.** George Thomas White Patrick. (American Autobiography Ser.). 180p. 1995. reprint ed. lib. bdg. 69. 00 (*0-7812-8607-7*) Rprt Serv.

Patrick, George Z. Popular Poetry in Soviet Russia. LC 74-174378. 1972. reprint ed. 20.95 (*0-405-08841-8*, Pub. by Blom Pubns UK) Ayer.

— Roots of the Russian Language. 1989. pap. 16.95 (*0-8442-4267-5*, Natl Textbk) NTC Pub Grp.

Patrick, Georgie, jt. auth. see Duncan, Cyndi.

***Patrick, Graham L.** An Introduction to Medicinal Chemistry. (Illus.). 320p. 1995. 69.95 (*0-19-855872-4*); pap. 28.95 (*0-19-855871-6*) OUP.

Patrick, Heather, jt. auth. see Patrick, Ross.

Patrick, Hugh & Rosovsky, Henry, eds. Asia's New Giant: How the Japanese Economy Works. LC 75-42304. 957p. reprint ed. pap. 180.00 (*0-8357-5791-9*, 2030002) Bks Demand.

Patrick, Hugh, jt. ed. see Aoki, M.

Patrick, Hugh T., ed. Pacific Basin Industries in Distress. 560p. 1991. text ed. 55.00 (*0-231-07570-7*) Col U Pr.

Patrick, Hugh T. & Meissner, Larry, eds. Japan's High Technology Industries & Industrial Policy. LC 85-40973. 296p. (C). 1986. 40.00 (*0-295-96342-5*) U of Wash Pr.

Patrick, Hugh T. & Park, Yung C., eds. The Financial Development of Japan, Korea, & Taiwan: Growth, Repression, & Liberalization. LC 93-31448. (Illus.). 432p. 1994. 55.00 (*0-19-508766-6*) OUP.

Patrick, Hugh T. & Tachi, Ryuichiro, eds. Japan & the United States Today: Exchange Rates, Macroeconomic Policies & Financial Market Innovations. 200p. 1987. text ed. 34.50 (*0-231-06576-0*) Col U Pr.

Patrick, Hugh T., jt. ed. see Bhagwati, Jagdish.

Patrick, J. Hearthrobs: And Other Stories. LC 92-62453. 448p. 1994. 12.95 (*1-877978-47-7*) Woldt.

— Trees for Town & City Gardens. Patrick, John, ed. (Lothian Australian Garden Ser.). (Illus.). 64p. (Orig.). 1995. pap. 9.95 (*0-85091-387-X*, Pub. by Lothian Pub AT) Seven Hills Bk.

***Patrick, J., ed.** Dangerous Boys. 512p. (Orig.). 1995. pap. text ed. 14.95 (*1-877978-53-1*, STARbks Pr) Woldt.

— Natural Beauty: An Anthology. 4th ed. LC 90-70649. 284p. 1993. pap. 14.95 (*1-877978-60-4*, STARbks Pr) Woldt.

— Runaways - Kid Stuff. 448p. (Orig.). 1994. pap. 12.95 (*1-877978-52-3*) Woldt.

— Seduced: An Anthology. LC 92-62454. 448p. (Orig.). 1994. pap. 13.95 (*1-877978-67-1*) Woldt.

Patrick, J. & Duncan, K. D., eds. Training, Human Decision Making & Control. 408p. 1988. 115.50 (*0-444-70381-0*, North Holland) Elsevier.

Patrick, J., jt. ed. see Walker, A.

***Patrick, J. James.** Stat Jordan: The Complete Statistical Career of Michael Jordan & Other Basketball Facts. 1995. pap. 7.95 (*0-533-11322-9*) Vantage.

Patrick, J. Max & Sundell, Roger H. Milton & the Art of Sacred Song. LC 78-65014. 248p. 1979. 32.50 (*0-299-07830-2*) U of Wis Pr.

Patrick, J. Max, ed. see Robert Herrick Memorial Conference, University of Michigan Staff.

Patrick, James. Architecture in Tennessee, 1768-1897. LC 80-21089. (Illus.). 228p. 1981. 45.00x (*0-87049-223-3*) U of Tenn Pr.

— Architecture in Tennessee, 1768-1897. 1990. pap. 19.50 (*0-87049-631-X*) U of Tenn Pr.

— Buyer Be Aware: The Complete Car Buyer's Text. 1993. pap. 8.95 (*0-533-10654-0*) Vantage.

— The Magdalen Metaphysicals: Idealism & Orthodoxy at Oxford, 1901-1945. LC 84-20751. xl, 192p. 1985. 18.95 (*0-86554-145-0*, MUP/H135) Mercer Univ Pr.

Patrick, James, jt. ed. see Heinemann, Steve.

Patrick, James, jt. ed. see Walker, Andrew.

Patrick, James B., ed. see Bradley, David.

Patrick, James B., ed. see Dunwell, Steve.

Patrick, James B., ed. see Gannon, Thomas.

Patrick, James B., ed. see Llewellyn, Robert.

Patrick, James B., ed. see McCord, David.

Patrick, James B., ed. see Smith, Clyde H.

Patrick, Jane, ed. A Handwoven Treasury. LC 89-7567. (Illus.). 144p. (Orig.). 1989. pap. 17.95 (*0-934026-46-7*) Interweave.

Patrick, John. Angel: The Complete Quintet. 5th ed. LC 90-7008. (Illus.). 640p. 1991. pap. 14.95 (*1-877978-08-6*, STARbks Pr) Woldt.

— Anybody Out There? 1972. pap. 4.75 (*0-8222-0058-9*) Dramatists Play.

— A Bad Year for Tomatoes. 1975. pap. 4.75 (*0-8222-0089-9*) Dramatists Play.

— A Barrel Full of Pennies. 1970. pap. 4.75 (*0-8222-0095-3*) Dramatists Play.

— Beautiful Gardens with Less Water. (Lothian Austalian Garden Ser.). (Illus.). 64p. (Orig.). 1995. pap. 9.95 (*0-85091-657-7*, Pub. by Lothian Pub AT) Seven Hills Bk.

— Cheating Cheaters. 1985. pap. 4.75 (*0-8222-0199-2*) Dramatists Play.

— The Curious Savage. 1950. pap. 4.75 (*0-8222-0260-3*) Dramatists Play.

— The Dancing Mice. 1972. pap. 4.75 (*0-8222-0267-0*) Dramatists Play.

— Divorce-Anyone? 1976. pap. 4.75 (*0-8222-0316-2*) Dramatists Play.

— Doctor Will See You Now: Four One Act Plays. 1991. pap. 4.75 (*0-8222-0317-0*) Dramatists Play.

— The Enigma. 1974. pap. 4.75 (*0-8222-0361-8*) Dramatists Play.

— Everybody Loves Opal. 1962. pap. 4.75 (*0-8222-0367-7*) Dramatists Play.

— Everybody's Girl. 1968. pap. 4.75 (*0-8222-0368-5*) Dramatists Play.

— The Gay Deceiver. 1988. pap. 4.75 (*0-8222-0433-9*) Dramatists Play.

— The Girls of the Garden Club. 1979. pap. 4.75 (*0-8222-0448-7*) Dramatists Play.

— Great Garden, No Sweat! (Lothian Australian Garden Ser.). (Illus.). 64p. (Orig.). 1995. pap. 9.95 (*0-85091-568-6*, Pub. by Lothian Pub AT) Seven Hills Bk.

— The Hasty Heart. 1945. pap. 4.75 (*0-8222-0501-7*) Dramatists Play.

— It's Been Wonderful. 1976. pap. 4.75 (*0-8222-0580-7*) Dramatists Play.

— John Patrick on Slots: More Than Twenty Ways to Beat the Machine. LC 93-45562. 1994. 12.95 (*0-8184-0574-0*, L Stuart) Carol Pub Group.

— John Patrick's Blackjack. 1991. pap. 12.95 (*0-8184-0555-4*, L Stuart) Carol Pub Group.

— John Patrick's Craps. 1991. pap. 14.95 (*0-8184-0554-6*, L Stuart) Carol Pub Group.

— Love Is a Time of Day. 1970. pap. 4.75 (*0-8222-0692-7*) Dramatists Play.

— Macbeth Did It. 1972. pap. 4.75 (*0-8222-0711-7*) Dramatists Play.

— The Magenta Moth. 1983. pap. 4.75 (*0-8222-0716-8*) Dramatists Play.

— Opal Is a Diamond. 1992. pap. 4.75 (*0-8222-0857-1*) Dramatists Play.

— Opal's Baby. 1974. pap. 4.75 (*0-8222-0858-X*) Dramatists Play.

— Opal's Husband. 1975. pap. 4.75 (*0-8222-0859-8*) Dramatists Play.

— Opal's Million Dollar Duck. 1980. pap. 4.75 (*0-8222-0860-1*) Dramatists Play.

— The Reluctant Rogue: or Mother's Day. 1984. pap. 4.75 (*0-8222-0942-X*) Dramatists Play.

— The Savage Dilemma. 1972. pap. 4.75 (*0-8222-0989-6*) Dramatists Play.

— Scandal Point: Manuscript Edition. 1969. pap. 13.00 (*0-8222-0994-2*) Dramatists Play.

— Sense & Nonsense. 200p. 1990. write for info. (*0-573-64232-X*) French.

— So You Wanna Be a Gambler: Baccarat. (Illus.). 256p. (Orig.). 1985. pap. 9.95 (*0-930911-03-2*) Gambler.

— So You Wanna Be a Gambler: Blackjack. (Illus.). (Orig.). 1983. pap. 9.95 (*0-930911-01-6*) Gambler.

— So You Wanna Be A Gambler: Card Counting. (Illus.). (Orig.). 1986. pap. 14.95 (*0-317-61500-9*) Gambler.

— So You Wanna Be a Gambler: Craps. (Illus.). (Orig.). 1984. pap. 14.95 (*0-930911-00-8*) Gambler.

— So You Wanna Be a Gambler: Roulette-Slots. (Illus.). (Orig.). 1983. pap. 9.95 (*0-930911-02-4*) Gambler.

— The Story of Mary Surratt. 1947. pap. 4.75 (*0-8222-1086-X*) Dramatists Play.

— Suicide Anyone? 1976. pap. 4.75 (*0-8222-1096-7*) Dramatists Play.

— The Willow & I: Manuscript Edition. 1943. pap. 13.00 (*0-8222-1258-7*) Dramatists Play.

***Patrick, John, ed.** Barely Legal. 512p. (Orig.). 1995. pap. text ed. 14.95 (*1-877978-71-X*, STARbks Pr) Woldt.

— Best of the Superstars, 1994. (Illus.). 160p. (Orig.). 1993. pap. 11.95 (*1-877978-54-X*, STARbks Pr) Woldt.

— Best of the Superstars, 1995. (Illus.). 512p. (Orig.). 1995. pap. text ed. 10.95 (*1-877978-73-6*, STARbks Pr) Woldt.

— Big Boys, Little Lies. LC 92-82591. 448p. (Orig.). 1994. pap. 14.95 (*1-877978-65-5*) Woldt.

— Huge: An Anthology. LC 90-70652. 160p. (Orig.). 1992. pap. 14.95 (*1-877978-63-9*, STARbks Pr) Woldt.

— Training Research & Practice. (Illus.). 585p. 1992. text ed. 69.95 (*0-12-546660-9*) Acad Pr.

Patrick, John, ed. see Aldous, David.

Patrick, John, ed. see Aldous.

Patrick, John, ed. see Bailey, Ralph & Lake, Julie.

Patrick, John, ed. see Burnett.

Patrick, John, ed. see Campbell, Colin.

Patrick, John, ed. see Carruthers, Steven.

Patrick, John, ed. see Edmanson.

Patrick, John, ed. see Elliot, Rodger.

Patrick, John, ed. see Elliot, W. Rodger.

Patrick, John, ed. see Elliot.

Patrick, John, ed. see Gilbert, Allen.

Patrick, John, ed. see Gilbert.

Patrick, John, ed. see Green, Michael.

Patrick, John, ed. see Lawrence, Lorrie.

Patrick, John, ed. see Moore, Greg.

Patrick, John, ed. see Patrick, J.

Patrick, John, ed. see Reed, Virginia.

Patrick, John, ed. see Smith, Keith.

Patrick, John, ed. see Stewart.

Patrick, John, ed. see Taylor, Janet.

Patrick, John, ed. see Taylor.

Patrick, John, ed. see Thompson, Paul.

Patrick, John, ed. see Wilkinson, Jennifer.

Patrick, John J. Ideas of the Founders on Constitutional Government: Resources for Teachers of U. S. History & Government. (Illus.). 159p. (Orig.). 1991. pap. text ed. 12.00 (*1-878147-02-1*) Am Political.

— Lessons on the Northwest Ordinance of 1787. (Illus.). (gr. 9-12). 1987. pap. text ed. 8.50 (*0-941339-02-5*) Ind U SSDC.

— Lessons on the Northwest Ordinance of 1787: Learning Materials for Secondary School Courses in American History, Government, & Civics. 1987. pap. 8.50 (*1-885323-52-2*) IN Hist Bureau.

— The Young Oxford Companion to the Supreme Court of the United States. LC 93-6467. (J). (gr. 5 up). 1994. 35. 00 (*0-19-507877-2*) OUP.

***Patrick, John J., ed.** Founding the Republic: A Documentary History. LC 95-7537. 312p. 1995. text ed. 49.95 (*0-313-29226-4*, Greenwood Pr) Greenwood.

— James Madison & the Federalist Papers. 188p. 1991. pap. text ed. 15.00 (*0-941339-11-4*) Ind U SSDC.

Patrick, John J. & Keller, Clair W. Lessons on the Federalist Papers. (Illus.). 95p. (gr. 9-12). 1987. pap. text ed. 10.00 (*0-941339-00-9*) Ind U SSDC.

Patrick, John J. & Remy, Richard C. Lessons on the Constitution: Supplements to High School Courses in American History, Government & Civics. (Orig.). 1985. pap. 13.00 (*0-89994-302-0*) Soc Sci Ed.

***Patrick, John W., ed.** Porosity in Carbons Characterisation & Applications. LC 94-35529. 1994. 89.95 (*0-470-23454-7*) Halsted Pr.

Patrick, Johnstone G. The Wishing Tree of Honey Hill Wood. (J). 1993. 12.95 (*0-533-10617-6*) Vantage.

Patrick, Ken L., ed. Bleaching Technology: For Chemical & Mechanical Pulps. (Illus.). 174p. 1991. pap. 52.00 (*0-87930-246-1*) Miller Freeman.

— Modern Mechanical Pulping: In the Pulp & Paper Industry. LC 89-80421. (Illus.). 247p. (Orig.). 1989. pap. 45.00 (*0-87930-218-6*) Miller Freeman.

— New Maintenance Strategies: Organizing, Implementing & Managing Effective Mill Programs. (Illus.). 200p. 1992. pap. 49.00 (*0-87930-189-9*) Miller Freeman.

— Paper Coating Trends: In the Worldwide Paper Industry. (Illus.). 172p. 1991. pap. 58.00 (*0-87930-247-X*) Miller Freeman.

— Paper Recycling: Strategies, Economics, & Technology. (Illus.). 202p. (Orig.). 1991. pap. 45.00 (*0-87930-231-3*) Miller Freeman.

Patrick, Kenneth G. Perpetual Jeopardy: The Texas Gulf Sulphur Affair. LC 70-143515. (Studies of the Modern Corporation). 1972. 19.95 (*0-02-924890-6*) Macmillan.

Patrick, Kenneth L., ed. see Lavigne, John R.

Patrick, Laurie & Hill, Janis. From Kids with Love. (J). (ps-3). 1987. pap. 9.99 (*0-8224-3166-1*) Fearon Teach Aids.

Patrick, Lawrence M., ed. see Stapp Car Crash Conference Staff.

Patrick, Lewis. Walt Disney's Snow White & the Seven Dwarfs Counting Book. (J). (ps). 1993. 3.95 (*0-307-12529-7*, Golden Pr) Western Pub.

Patrick, Lura L., ed. see Galindo, Sergio.

Patrick, Lynn, ed. see Savannah Junior Auxiliary Staff.

Patrick, Marc. Entrepreneurs Are Like Dandelions: No Matter How Many Times You Mow Them Down They Keep Coming Back Up. (Orig.). (C). 1989. pap. write for info. (*0-318-65072-X*) NEI Seattle.

Patrick, Maxine, ed. see Carnevali, Doris L.

Patrick, Maxine, et al. Medical-Surgical Nursing: Pathophysiological Concepts. 2nd ed. (Illus.). 2238p. 1991. text ed. 69.95 (*0-397-54730-7*) Lippincott.

***Patrick, Michael, et al.** We Are a Part of History: The Story of the Orphan Trains. 1994. write for info. (*0-89865-921-3*) Donning Co.

Patrick, Michael D. & Steel, Richard D., eds. Employment-Based Immigration: New Law & New Strategies. 254p. (Orig.). (C). 1993. pap. text ed. 48.00 (*1-878677-48-9*) Amer Immi Law Assn.

Patrick, Michael D., jt. ed. see Steel, Richard D.

***Patrick, Natalie.** Wedding Bells & Diaper Pins. (Romance Ser.). 1995. mass mkt. 2.99 (*0-373-19095-6*, 1-19095-8) Silhouette.

Patrick, Priscilla. To Life! Yoga with Priscilla Patrick. LC 82-71187. (Illus.). 76p. (Orig.). 1982. pap. 9.95 (*0-943274-00-1*) SC Ed Comm Inc.

Patrick Publishing Staff, jt. auth. see Smith, Jeffrey H.

Patrick, R. S. Color Atlas of Liver Pathology. (Oxford Color Atlases of Pathology Ser.). (Illus.). 1983. 85.00 (*0-19-921033-0*) OUP.

***Patrick, Randal.** White Trash in a Trailer Park. Owensby, Craig, ed. 300p. (Orig.). 1995. pap. 14.95 (*1-886371-15-6*) Eggman Pub.

Patrick, Randal, jt. auth. see Kramer, Phil.

Patrick, Rembert W. Jefferson Davis & His Cabinet. LC 83-45832. reprint ed. 43.50 (*0-404-20197-0*) AMS Pr.

— Opinions of the Confederate Attorneys General, 1861-1865. xxiv, 608p. 1950. lib. bdg. 52.50 (*0-89941-617-9*, 500470) W S Hein.

Patrick, Robert. Mutual Benefit Life. 1979. pap. 4.75 (*0-8222-0795-8*) Dramatists Play.

— My Cup Ranneth Over. 1979. pap. 4.75 (*0-8222-0798-2*) Dramatists Play.

— Temple Slave. 1994. pap. 12.95 (*1-56333-191-8*) Masquerade.

— Untold Decades: Seven Comedies of Gay Romance. (Stonewall Inn Editions Ser.). (Illus.). 240p. 1989. pap. 7.95 (*0-312-03447-4*) St Martin.

Patrick, Robert L. Treatise on Adhesion & Adhesives, Vol. 3. LC 66-11285. 271p. reprint ed. pap. 77.30 (*0-8357-3575-3*, 2026808) Bks Demand.

Patrick, Robert L., ed. Treatise on Adhesion & Adhesives, Vol. 2: Materials. LC 66-11285. (Illus.). 568p. reprint ed. pap. 161.90 (*0-8357-3574-5*, 2026808) Bks Demand.

Patrick, Roslynn. Princess Royale. 1991. mass mkt. 4.95 (*0-06-104024-X*, Harp PBks) HarpC.

Patrick, Ross & Patrick, Heather. Exiles Undaunted: The Irish Rebels Kevin & Eva O'Doherty. 1989. pap. 17.95 (*0-7022-2223-2*, Pub. by Univ Queensland Pr AT) Intl Spec Bk.

Patrick, Ruth. Rivers of the United States. LC 93-27583. 1994. text ed. 89.00 (*0-471-30345-3*) Wiley.

— Rivers of the United States: Chemical & Physical Characteristics, Vol. 2. 1995. text ed. 89.00 (*0-471-10752-2*) Wiley.

— Surface Water Quality: Have the Laws Been Successful? (Illus.). 247p. 1991. text ed. 37.50 (*0-691-08769-5*) Princeton U Pr.

Patrick, Ruth & Reimer, Charles W. The Diatoms of the United States (Exclusive of Alaska & Hawaii), Set. LC 65-29113. (Monograph: No. 13-1). (Illus.). 688p. 1966. 50.00 (*0-910006-19-9*) Acad Nat Sci Phila.

— The Diatoms of the United States (Exclusive of Alaska & Hawaii), Vol. 1. LC 65-29113. (Monograph: No. 13-1). (Illus.). 688p. 1966. lib. bdg. 30.00 (*0-910006-20-2*) Acad Nat Sci Phila.

— The Diatoms of the United States (Exclusive of Alaska & Hawaii), Vol. 2, Pt. 1. (Monograph: No. 13-2). (Illus.). 213p. 1975. lib. bdg. 20.00 (*0-910006-21-0*) Acad Nat Sci Phila.

Patrick, Ruth, jt. ed. see Cairns, John, Jr.

Patrick, Ruth, jt. ed. see Paddock, Todd.

Patrick, Ruth, et al. The Catherwood Foundation Peruvian-Amazon Expedition: Limnological & Systematic Studies. (Monograph: No. 14). (Illus.). 495p. (Orig.). 1966. pap. 15.00 (*0-910006-22-9*) Acad Nat Sci Phila.

— Groundwater Contamination in the United States. 2nd ed. LC 87-19143. 538p. 1987. 58.95x (*0-8122-8079-2*); pap. 24.95x (*0-8122-1256-8*) U of Pa Pr.

***Patrick, S. & Larkin, M.J.** Immunology & Molecular Aspects of Bacterial Virulence. 1995. text ed. 45.95 (*0-471-95251-6*) Wiley.

Patrick, Sally, et al. The Month by Month Treasure Box. LC 86-82599. (Illus.). 80p. (Orig.). (J). (ps-1). 1988. 7.95 (*0-86530-124-7*, IP 130-1) Incentive Pubns.

Patrick, Sam J. Presidents: Washington to Bush. 1989. 14. 99 (*0-517-67896-9*) Random Hse Value.

Patrick, Sean. Patrick's Corner. LC 91-33634. 272p. 1992. 16.95 (*0-88289-878-7*) Pelican.

Patrick, Steven R., jt. auth. see Patrick, Dale R.

Patrick, Steven R., et al. Energy Conservation Guidebook. LC 93-13523. 1993. 68.00 (*0-88173-154-4*) Fairmont Pr.

Patrick, Sue C. Reform of the Federal Reserve System in the Early 1930s: The Politics of Money & Banking. LC 92-35097. (Financial Sector of the American Economy Ser.). 368p. 1992. 60.00 (*0-8153-0970-8*) Garland.

Patrick, Terry. World Class Exporting: A Strategic Guide to Export Market Entry. (Financial Times Management Ser.). 320p. 1994. 90.00x (*0-273-60522-4*, Pub. by Pitman Pubng UK) St Mut.

Patrick, Thomas S., ed. see Benson, Betty L.

Patrick, Toni. One Hundred Ways to Make Ramen Noodles: Creative Cooking When You Can Only Afford Ten-for-One-Dollar Pasta. (Illus.). 96p. (Orig.). 1993. spiral bd. 9.95 (*0-9626335-2-6*) C&G Pub CO.

Patrick, Vanessa E., ed. An Illustrated Glossary of Early Southern Architecture & Landscape. (Illus.). 448p. (C). 1994. 75.00 (*0-19-507992-2*) OUP.

Patrick, W. B. Letter to the Ghosts. LC 77-17153. 53p. 1977. 3.50 (*0-87886-091-6*, Greenfld Rev Pr) Greenfld Rev Lit.

Patrick, W. H., jt. ed. see DeDatta, S. K.

Patrick, Walton R. Ring Lardner. (Twayne's United States Authors Ser.). 1963. pap. 13.95 (*0-8084-0261-7*, T32) NCUP.

***Patrick-Wexler, Diane.** Barbara Jordan. LC 95-12611. (Contemporary African Americans Ser.). (J). 1995. write for info. (*0-8172-3976-6*) Raintree Steck-V.

Patrick, William. Roxa. 1989. 20.00 (*0-918526-68-X*); pap. 12.50 (*0-918526-69-8*) BOA Edns.

***Patrick, William B.** These Upraised Hands. (American Poets Continuum Ser.: No. 34). 1995. 20.00 (*1-880238-26-8*); pap. 12.50 (*1-880238-27-6*) BOA Edns.

Patrides, ed. Figures in a Renaissance Context. 1989. 42.50 (*0-472-10119-6*) U of Mich Pr.

Patrides, C. A. An Annotated Critical Bibliography of Milton. 190p. 1987. text ed. 39.95 (*0-312-00480-X*) St Martin.

— Premises & Motifs in Renaissance Thought & Literature. LC 81-47940. (Illus.). 256p. 1982. 37.50x (*0-691-06505-5*) Princeton U Pr.

Patrides, C. A., ed. Approaches to Sir Thomas Browne: The Ann Arbor Tercentenary Lectures & Essays. LC 81-13017. 200p. 1982. text ed. 23.00 (*0-8262-0357-4*) U of Mo Pr.

— John Milton: Selected Prose. rev. ed. LC 85-1027. 464p. 1986. pap. text ed. 14.95 (*0-8262-0484-8*) U of Mo Pr.

Patrides, C. A. & Wittreich, Joseph A., eds. The Apocalypse in English Renaissance Thought & Literature. LC 84-71281. 452p. (C). 1985. pap. 22.95 (*0-8014-9893-7*) Cornell U Pr.

Patrides, C. A., ed. see Herbert, George.

Patrides, C. A., ed. see Smith, John.

Patrides, G. A., ed. George Herbert: The Critical Heritage. (Critical Heritage Ser.). 390p. 1983. 69.50 (*0-7100-9240-7*, RKP) Routledge.

Patridge, Derek. Engineering Artificial Intelligence Software. LC 90-26630. 212p. 1992. 37.50 (*0-89391-778-8*) Ablex Pub.

Patridge, Frances, tr. see Carpentier, Alejo.

Patridge, Ray. The Deer Hunter Log Book. 36p. 1984. pap. 9.95 (*0-317-68270-9*) Bootstrap Pubns.

Patrignani. A Manual of Practical Devotion to St. Joseph. LC 82-50594. 328p. (J). 1982. reprint ed. pap. 13.50 (*0-89555-175-6*) TAN Bks Pubs.

Patrignani, Roberto, jt. auth. see Colombo, Mario.

Patrik, Arakel. The Embroidery of Ourha. 1985. 40.00 (*0-317-61254-9*, Pub. by Collets UK) Pro-Am Music.

Patrikalakis, N. M., ed. Scientific Visualization of Physical Phenomena. (Illus.). c, 706p. 1991. 179.00 (*0-387-70081-1*) Spr-Verlag.

Patrinos, Harry A., jt. auth. see Psacharopoulous, George.

Patrioli, Tony. Sunbeams. (Orig.). 1989. pap. 15.00 (*1-55583-145-1*) Alyson Pubns.

Patrizio, Giorgio, jt. auth. see Abate, Marco.

Patrizzi, Francesco, tr. see Julianus.

Patro, P. S., jt. auth. see Hari Hara Das.

Patrol Craft Sailors Association Staff. Patrol Craft Sailors. LC 90-70481. (Illus.). 128p. 1990. 45.00 (*0-938021-89-3*) Turner Pub KY.

***Patron.** Dictionnaire des Communes Vol. 2: Departement du Loiret. fac. ed. 586p. (FRE.). 1991. pap. 115.00 (*0-7859-8248-5*, 2909112012); pap. 125.00 (*0-7859-8249-3*, 2909112020) Fr & Eur.

Patron, Susan. Bobbin Dustdobbin. LC 92-25099. (Illus.). 32p. (J). (ps-2). 1993. 14.95 (*0-531-05468-3*); lib. bdg. 14.99 (*0-531-08618-6*) Orchard Bks Watts.

— Burgoo Stew. LC 90-43791. (Illus.). 32p. (J). (ps-1). 1991. 14.95 (*0-531-05916-2*); 14.99 (*0-531-08516-3*) Orchard Bks Watts.

— Dark Cloud Strong Breeze. LC 93-4873. (Illus.). 32p. (J). (ps-1). 1994. 15.95 (*0-531-06815-3*); lib. bdg. 15.99 (*0-531-08665-8*) Orchard Bks Watts.

— Five Bad Boys, Billy Que, & the Dustdobbin. LC 91-736. (Illus.). 32p. (J). (ps-1). 1992. 14.95 (*0-531-05989-8*); lib. bdg. 14.99 (*0-531-08589-9*) Orchard Bks Watts.

— Maybe Yes, Maybe No, Maybe Maybe. (J). (gr. 4-7). 1995. pap. 3.50 (*0-440-40969-1*) Dell.

— Maybe Yes, Maybe No, Maybe Maybe. LC 92-34067. (Richard Jackson Bk.). (Illus.). 96p. (J). (gr. 3-5). 1993. 14.95 (*0-531-05482-9*); lib. bdg. 14.99 (*0-531-08632-1*) Orchard Bks Watts.

***Patrone, Nadia.** Principe y Mecenas: Alfonso V En Los "Dichos y Hechos" De A. Beccadelli. (Currents in Comparative Romance Languages & Literatures Ser.: Vol. 17). 120p. (SPA.). (C). 1995. text ed. 36.95 (*0-8204-2150-2*) P Lang Pubs.

Patrons Association of the Collegiate School Staff, ed. Stuffed Cougar. (Illus.). 375p. (Orig.). 1973. pap. 12.95 (*0-681-21703-0*) Collegiate Schls.

— The Stuffed Cougar, Too. (Illus.). 362p. (Orig.). 1992. pap. 12.95 (*0-9634044-0-7*) Collegiate Schls.

Patros, Philip G. Depression & Suicide in Children & Adolescents. 1988. text ed. 36.95 (*0-205-11670-1*, H16702) Allyn.

Patros, Philip G., jt. auth. see Shamoo, Tonia K.

Patrucco, Armand. The Critics of the Italian Parliamentary System, 1860-1915. LC 91-44343. (Modern European History Ser.). 336p. 1992. 75.00 (*0-8153-0738-1*) Garland.

***Patruno, Nicholas.** Understanding Primo Levi. Date not set. 34.95 (*1-57003-026-X*) U of SC Pr.

Patry, Gilles G. & Chapman, David T. Dynamic Modeling & Expert Systems in Wastewater Engineering. (Illus.). 450p. 1989. 89.95 (*0-87371-174-2*, TD755) Lewis Pubs.

Patry, Philippe, jt. auth. see Carpenter, Edwin.

***Patry, William F.** Copyright & the GATT - an Interpretation & Legislative History of the Uruguay Round Agreements Act: 1995 Supplement to Copyright Law & Practice. LC 95-10477. 1995. pap. write for info. (*0-87179-886-7*) BNA.

— Copyright Law & Practice. 6th ed. LC 88-17494. 687p. 1986. text ed. 75.00 (*0-87179-506-X*, 0506) BNA.

— Copyright Law & Practice, 3 vols., 1. LC 94-12208. 1994. write for info. (*0-87179-854-9*) BNA.

— Copyright Law & Practice, 3 vols., 2. LC 94-12208. 1994. write for info. (*0-87179-855-7*) BNA.

— Copyright Law & Practice, 3 vols., 3. LC 94-12208. 1994. 225.00 (*0-87179-856-5*) BNA.

— Copyright Law & Practice, 3 vols., Set, Vols. I, II, & III. 7th ed. LC 94-12208. 2238p. 1994. text ed. 225.00 (*0-87179-685-6*, S685) BNA.

— The Fair Use Privilege in Copyright Law. 576p. 1985. text ed. 88.00 (*0-87179-451-9*, 0451) BNA.

— The Fair Use Privilege in Copyright Law. 2nd ed. LC 85-4088. 675p. 1995. text ed. 115.00 (*0-87179-831-X*) BNA.

Patrylick, Carol. Bank Loan Pools: Financial Structures for Business Development. Murphy, Jenny, ed. 30p. (Orig.). 1987. pap. 17.00 (*0-317-04817-1*) Natl Coun Econ Dev.

— Downtown Retail Revitalization: Strategies to Maximize Your Market. Murphy, Jenny, ed. 42p. (Orig.). 1989. pap. 21.50 (*0-317-04898-8*) Natl Coun Econ Dev.

— Retail Incubators: Linking Entrepreneurship & Commercial Development. Murphy, Jenny, ed. 38p. (Orig.). 1988. pap. 18.00 (*0-317-04810-4*) Natl Coun Econ Dev.

Patsalis, Toula. Joys of Pressure Cooking. Wadlington, Vickie, ed. 245p. 1990. pap. write for info. (*0-318-68123-4*) Kitchen Glamor.

Patsie, Nichols, ed. see Bureau of Mining & Reclamation Staff & Bureau of Deep Mine Safety Staff.

Patsis, jt. auth. see Parfitt.

Patsis, A. V., ed. Advances in Organic Coatings Science & Technology, Vol. 11: Proceedings of the 13th Conference. LC 89-50154. 265p. 1989. 49.00 (*0-87762-603-0*) Technomic.

Patsis, Angelos V., ed. Advances in Organic Coatings Science & Technology, Vol. 10: Proceedings of the Conference, 12th. LC 86-643074. 220p. 1988. 49.00 (*0-87762-563-8*) Technomic.

— Advances in Organic Coatings Science & Technology, Vol. 9: Proceedings of the Eleventh Conference. 215p. 1987. 49.00 (*0-87762-525-5*) Technomic.

— Advances in the Stabilization & Controlled Degradation of Polymers, Vol. 1. LC 88-50962. 248p. 1989. 55.00 (*0-87762-572-7*) Technomic.

— Advances in the Stabilization & Controlled Degradation of Polymers, Vol. 2. 128p. 1989. 49.00 (*0-87762-588-3*) Technomic.

***Patsoulis, Toula.** The Pressure Cooker Cookbook. 208p. (Orig.). 1994. pap. 12.00 (*1-55788-189-8*, HP Books) Berkley Pub.

***Patsouras, Louis.** Jean Grave & the Anarchist Tradition in France. LC 94-46629. (C). 1995. text ed. 29.95 (*0-391-03911-3*) Humanities.

— Simone Weil & the Socialist Tradition. LC 91-42735. 120p. 1992. pap. text ed. 39.95 (*0-7734-9913-X*) E Mellen.

Patsouras, Louis, ed. The Crucible of Socialism. LC 87-7286. 436p. (C). 1987. text ed. 55.00 (*0-391-03373-5*) Humanities.

— Debating Marx. LC 93-44821. 280p. 1994. pap. 29.95 (*0-7734-1934-9*) E Mellen.

Patsouras, Louis & Thomas, Jack R., eds. Essays on Socialism. LC 92-32173. 420p. 1992. pap. text ed. 39.95 (*0-7734-9911-3*) E Mellen.

Patsouras, Louis, jt. ed. see Ensign, Russell L.

Patt & Nozick. Generation Eighteen Ninety-Eight & After. 1960. pap. 30.95 (*0-8384-3755-9*) Heinle & Heinle.

Patt, B. P., jt. ed. see Florit, Eugenio.

Patt, Beatrice & Nozick, Martin, eds. Spanish Literature: 1700-1900. 463p. (C). 1989. reprint ed. pap. text ed. 16.95 (*0-88133-454-5*) Waveland Pr.

Patt, David. A Strange Liberation: Tibetan Lives in Chinese Hands. LC 92-44590. 1992. pap. 12.95 (*1-55939-013-1*) Snow Lion Pubns.

— Wheel of Time. 1983. pap. write for info. (*0-318-62752-3*) Deer Park Bks.

Patt, Richard B. Cancer Pain. LC 92-49630. 1992. 85.00 (*0-397-51138-8*) Lippincott.

— Manual of Cancer Pain Management. (Illus.). 450p. 1992. write for info. (*0-318-69535-9*) Lippincott.

Patt, Richard B., jt. auth. see Lang, Susan S.

Patt, Richard W. Partners in the Impossible. 1984. 5.00 (*0-89536-678-9*, 4854) CSS OH.

Patt, Ruth M. Uncommon Lives: Eighteen Extraordinary New Jersey Jews. 1994. 17.95 (*0-533-10970-1*) Vantage.

Pattabhiraman, P. Handbook of Tax on Salaries. (C). 1990. 80.00 (*0-89771-266-8*) St Mut.

Pattak, Evan M. & Wilson, Andrew G. Pittsburgh: A Portrait of Progress. Robertson, Scott, ed. LC 92-64401. (Illus.). 160p. 1993. text ed. 49.95 (*0-9634100-0-8*, 08) Wyndham Pubns.

Pattallo, Polly. Judging Women. (C). 1988. 21.00 (*0-946088-07-1*, Pub. by NCCL UK) St Mut.

Pattan, Bruno. Satellite Systems. LC 92-27438. 1993. text ed. 74.95 (*0-442-01357-4*) Van Nos Reinhold.

Pattanaik, P., jt. ed. see Gaertner, W.

Pattanaik, P. K. & Salles, M., eds. Social Choice Welfare. (Contributions to Economic Analysis Ser.: Vol. 145). 324p. 1983. 97.50 (*0-444-86487-3*, North Holland) Elsevier.

Pattanaik, S. N., jt. ed. see Mudur, S. P.

Pattanayak, Debi P., ed. Multilingualism in India. (Multilingual Matters Ser.: No. 61). 116p. 1990. 69.00 (*1-85359-073-8*); pap. 24.95 (*1-85359-072-X*) Taylor & Francis.

Pattangall, William R. Great Maine Men. LC 84-72331. 1985. pap. 8.00 (*0-941216-16-0*) Cay-Bel.

***Pattarozzi, Chris.** Private Sector Participation in Public Transit Systems. (State Legislative Report Ser.: Vol. 18, No. 4). 7p. 1993. 5.00 (*1-55516-298-3*, 7302-1804) Natl Conf State Legis.

— Recreational Boating Safety: State Policies & Programs. 40p. 1992. pap. text ed. 10.00 (*1-55516-989-9*, 9348) Natl Conf State Legis.

Pattarozzi, Michelle M. Uniquely Yours: A Collection of over 700 Suggestions to Individualize Your Wedding. 104p. 1983. 9.95 (*0-317-00911-7*) M M Pattarozzi.

Patte, Daniel. Early Jewish Hermeneutic in Palestine. LC 75-22225. (Society of Biblical Literature. Dissertation Ser.: No. 22). 358p. reprint ed. pap. 102.10 (*0-8357-9570-5*, 2017666) Bks Demand.

— Ethics of Biblical Interpretation: A Reevaluation. 160p. (Orig.). 1995. pap. 16.99 (*0-664-25568-X*) Westminster John Knox.

— The Gospel According to Matthew: A Structural Commentary on Matthew's Faith. LC 86-45218. 432p. 1986. pap. 26.00 (*0-8006-1978-1*, 1-1978, Fortress Pr) Augsburg Fortress.

— The Religious Dimensions of Biblical Texts. 410p. 1990. 31.95 (*1-55540-385-9*); pap. 20.95 (*1-55540-386-7*) Scholars Pr GA.

Pattee, Abigail, ed. see Healy, Gene.

Pattee, F. L., ed. see Brown, Charles B.

Pattee, Fred L. The Development of the American Short Story. LC 66-13477. 1923. 20.00 (*0-8196-0175-6*) Biblo.

— The Development of the American Short Story: An Historical Survey. (BCL1-PS American Literature Ser.). 388p. 1992. reprint ed. lib. bdg. 89.00 (*0-7812-6638-6*) Rprt Serv.

— A History of American Literature since 1870. (BCL1-PS American Literature Ser.). 449p. 1992. reprint ed. lib. bdg. 99.00 (*0-7812-6617-3*) Rprt Serv.

— The New American Literature, 1890-1930. (BCL1-PS American Literature Ser.). 507p. 1992. reprint ed. lib. bdg. 99.00 (*0-7812-6622-X*) Rprt Serv.

— Tradition & Jazz. LC 68-22937. (Essay Index Reprint Ser.). 1977. reprint ed. 23.95 (*0-8369-0776-0*) Ayer.

Pattee, James J. & Otteson, Orlo J. Medical Direction in the Nursing Home: Principles & Concepts for Physician-Administrators. 405p. 1991. 49.50 (*0-9629614-0-X*) N Ridge Pr.

Pattee, Richard, tr. see Ramos, Artur.

Pattee, William S. The Essential Nature of Law or the Ethical Basis of Jurisprudence. xxv, 264p. 1982. reprint ed. lib. bdg. 27.50 (*0-8377-1011-1*) Rothman.

Patten, B. C., ed. Wetlands & Shallow Continental Water Bodies, Vol. 1: Natural & Human Relationships. (Illus.). xiii, 759p. 1990. 180.00 (*90-5103-046-0*, Pub. by SPB Acad Pub NE) Koeltz Sci Bks.

Patten, Bernard C., ed. Systems Analysis & Simulation in Ecology, 4 vols. 1975. write for info. (*0-318-50375-1*) Acad Pr.

Patten, Bernard C. & Jorgensen, Sven E. Complex Ecology. 737p. 1994. text ed. 99.00 (*0-13-161506-8*) P-H.

Patten, Bill V., et al. Destinos Homeviewer's Guide & Audiocassettes: An Introduction to Spanish. 1993. Incl. audiocassettes. audio, pap. text ed. write for info. (*0-07-911479-2*) McGraw.

Patten, Bradley M., et al. Science in Progress, Seventh Series. Baitsell, George A., ed. LC 78-37534. (Essay Index Reprint Ser.). 1977. reprint ed. 44.95 (*0-8369-2532-7*) Ayer.

Patten, Chris. The Tory Case. LC 82-17085. (Jossey-Bass Higher Education Ser.). 208p. reprint ed. pap. 59.30 (*0-317-08605-7*, 2022524) Bks Demand.

Patten, Christine T. & Cardona-Hine, Alvaro. Miss O'Keeffe. LC 91-22431. 212p. (C). 1992. 18.95 (*0-8263-1322-1*) U of NM Pr.

Patten, Christopher. Great Britain & the World: Three Talks at Berkeley. LC 89-26964. 52p. 1990. pap. 6.95 (*0-87772-322-2*) UCB IGS.

Patten, Claudius B. The Methods & Machinery of Practical Banking. Bruchey, Stuart, ed. LC 80-1164. (Rise of Commercial Banking Ser.). (Illus.). 1981. reprint ed. lib. bdg. 49.95 (*0-405-13673-0*) Ayer.

Patten, David A. Newspapers & New Media. LC 84-26139. (Communications Library). 175p. 1985. lib. bdg. 38.95 (*0-86729-137-0*) G K Hall.

Patten, Dennis. My Magic Book. (Fun to Do Ser.). 64p. (J). 1994. write for info. (*0-307-16753-4*) Western Pub.

Patten, Donald W. The Mars - Earth Catastrophes. 1988. 19.95 (*0-685-20125-2*); pap. 14.95 (*0-685-20126-0*) Pacific Mer.

— Symposium on Creation VI. 1977. pap. 3.95 (*0-685-52492-2*) Pacific Mer.

Patten, Edith. Beach Seiners. 1986. pap. 3.00 (*0-942396-38-3*) Blackberry ME.

***Patten, J. M.** Acid Rain. LC 94-24207. (Eye on the Environment Ser.). (J). 1995. write for info. (*1-55916-099-3*) Rourke Bk Co.

— Acids & Bases. LC 95-6213. (Let's Wonder About Science Ser.). (J). 1995. write for info. (*1-55916-128-0*) Rourke Bk Co.

— The Atoms' Family. LC 94-47598. (Let's Wonder About Science Ser.). (J). 1995. write for info. (*1-55916-125-6*) Rourke Bk Co.

— The Big Three: Solids, Liquids & Gases. LC 94-47599. (Let's Wonder About Science Ser.). (J). 1995. write for info. (*1-55916-126-4*) Rourke Bk Co.

— Go & Stop. LC 95-10536. (Energy & Action Ser.). (J). 1995. write for info. (*1-55916-152-3*) Rourke Bk Co.

— Liquid to Gas & Back. LC 95-6214. (Let's Wonder about Science Ser.). (J). 1995. write for info. (*1-55916-129-9*) Rourke Bk Co.

— Matter Really Matters. LC 94-47601. (Let's Wonder about Science Ser.). (J). 1995. write for info. (*1-55916-124-8*) Rourke Bk Co.

— Mix It Up: Elements, Compounds & Mixtures. LC 95-4203. (J). 1995. write for info. (*1-55916-127-2*) Rourke Bk Co.

— Oil Spills. LC 94-37162. (Eye on the Environment Ser.). (J). 1995. write for info. (*1-55916-096-9*) Rourke Bk Co.

— Poisoned Water. LC 94-37163. (Eye on the Environment Ser.). (J). 1995. write for info. (*1-55916-097-7*) Rourke Bk Co.

— Polluted Air. (Eye On the Environment Ser.). 1995. write for info. (*1-55916-098-5*) Rourke Bk Co.

— Toxic Wastes. (Eye On the Environment Ser.). 1995. write for info. (*1-55916-100-0*) Rourke Bk Co.

— Trash. LC 94-42670. (Eye on the Environment Ser.). (J). 1995. write for info. (*1-55916-101-9*) Rourke Bk Co.

Patten, J. P. Neurological Differential Diagnosis: An Illustrated Approach. (Illus.). 292p. 1987. reprint ed. 75.00 (*0-387-90264-3*) Spr-Verlag.

Patten, Jennie M. The Argyle Patent: And Accompanying Documents. 68p. 1991. reprint ed. pap. 9.00 (*0-685-60412-8*, 4520) Clearfield Co.

Patten, Jim, jt. auth. see Ferguson, Donald L.

***Patten, John.** Neurological Differential Diagnosis. 2nd ed. LC 95-14336. 1995. pap. text ed. write for info. (*3-540-19937-3*) Spr-Verlag.

Patten, John, ed. The Expanding City: Essays in Honour of Jean Gottman. 1983. text ed. 112.00 (*0-12-547250-1*) Acad Pr.

Patten, Leslie & Patten, Terry. Biocircuits: Amazing New Tools for Energy Health. Armstrong, Gregory & Lipsett, Suzanne, eds. LC 88-81720. (Illus.). 240p. 1988. pap. 10.95 (*0-915811-13-8*) H J Kramer Inc.

Patten, Lewis. The Best Western Stories of Lewis Patten. Pronzini, Bill & Greenberg, Martin H., eds. LC 86-26144. (Western Writers Ser.). 180p. 1989. reprint ed. pap. 12.95 (*0-8040-0925-2*) Swallow.

Patten, Lewis B. The Cheyenne Pool. Bd. with Tired Gun. 272p. 1983. Set pap. 2.95 (*0-451-12492-8*, Sig) NAL-Dutton.

— Gun Proud. large type ed. LC 93-43544. (General Ser.). 1994. pap. 15.95 (*0-8161-5924-6*, Large Print Bks) Hall.

— Guns at Gray Butte. large type ed. LC 94-33679. 198p. 1995. 17.95 (*0-7838-1157-8*, Large Print Bks) Hall.

— Hunt the Man Down. Bd. with Cheyene Captives. 1984. Set pap. 3.50 (*0-451-13282-3*, Sig) NAL-Dutton.

— The Killings at Coyote Springs - The Trail of the Apache Kid, 2 vols. in 1. 336p. 1994. mass mkt., pap. text ed. 4.99 (*0-8439-3638-X*) Dorchester Pub Co.

— The Law in Cottonwood. 1994. 14.95 (*0-7451-4596-5*, Gunsmoke) Chivers N Amer.

— The Law in Cottonwood: Prodigal Gunfighter. 336p. 1994. pap. text ed. 4.99 (*0-8439-3691-6*) Dorchester Pub Co.

— Lynching at Broken Butte-Sunblade. 320p. 1995. mass mkt., pap. text ed. 4.99 (*0-8439-3792-0*) Dorchester Pub Co.

— Massacre at White River. LC 94-477. 1994. 18.95 (*0-7927-2068-7*, Curley Lrg Print); pap. 17.95 (*0-7927-2067-9*, Curley Lrg Print) Chivers N Amer.

— Rifles of Revenge. 1979. pap. 1.95 (*0-89083-568-3*) Zebra.

— Rifles of Revenge - Red Runs the River. 352p. 1994. pap. 4.99 (*0-8439-3598-7*) Dorchester Pub Co.

— The Ruthless Range - Death Rides a Black Horse. 320p. 1995. mass mkt. 4.99 (*0-8439-3741-6*) Dorchester Pub Co.

— Showdown at War Cloud. 1994. 15.95 (*0-7451-4627-9*, Gunsmoke) Chivers N Amer.

— Track of the Hunter. Bd. with Guilty Guns. 1985. Set pap. 3.50 (*0-451-13413-3*, Sig) NAL-Dutton.

— Villa's Rifles. 18.95 (*0-89190-420-4*, Am Repr) Amereon Ltd.

— Villa's Rifles. large type ed. LC 94-20140. 235p. 1994. pap. 15.95 (*0-8161-7424-5*) Hall.

— The Younger Man Guns. 1986. pap. 2.75 (*0-451-14266-7*, Sig) NAL-Dutton.

Patten, M. N., ed. Information Sources in Metallic Materials. (Guides to Information Sources Ser.). 528p. 1990. lib. bdg. 75.00 (*0-408-01491-1*) Bowker-Saur.

Patten, Malcolm C. Patten Genealogy: One Line Descending from William Patten of Cambridge, 1635. LC 90-62211. (Illus.). 402p. 1990. 25.00 (*0-9627321-0-9*) Powell & Taylor.

Patten, Marjorie. Arts Workshop of Rural America. LC 37-15722. reprint ed. 20.00 (*0-404-04907-9*) AMS Pr.

Patten, Michael. Designing Windows Help. 350p. 1995. pap. text ed. 39.95 (*0-12-547140-8*) Acad Pr.

Patten, Mildred L., ed. Educational & Psychological Research: A Cross-Section of Journal Articles for Analysis & Evaluation. 224p. (C). 1991. pap. text ed. 19.95x (*0-9623744-2-3*) Pyrczak Pub.

Patten, Priscilla, jt. auth. see Patten, Rebecca.

Patten, Priscilla C. & Patten, Rebecca. The World of the Early Church: A Companion to the New Testament. LC 90-44322. 296p. 1991. lib. bdg. 89.95 (*0-88946-598-3*) E Mellen.

Patten, Rebecca & Patten, Priscilla. Before the Times. LC 80-36848. (Illus.). 1980. pap. 6.95 (*0-89407-038-X*); boxed 9.95 (*0-89407-047-9*) Strawberry Hill.

Patten, Rebecca, jt. auth. see Patten, Priscilla C.

Patten, Richard H. & Rosengard, Jay K. Progress with Profits: The Development of Rural Banking in Indonesia. 114p. 1991. pap. 9.95 (*1-55815-140-0*) ICS Pr.

Patten, Robert L. Charles Dickens & His Publishers. LC 77-30164. (Illus.). 1978. 104.00 (*0-19-812076-1*) OUP.

— George Cruikshank's Life, Times, & Art: 1792-1835, Vol. 1. LC 91-40344. (Illus.). 550p. 1992. 50.00 (*0-8135-1813-X*) Rutgers U Pr.

— George Cruikshank's Life, Times, & Art Vol. II: 1835-1878. (Illus.). 500p. (C). 1996. text ed. 55.00 (*0-8135-1814-8*) Rutgers U Pr.

Patten, Robert L., ed. George Cruikshank: A Revaluation. LC 92-12258. (Illus.). 300p. 1992. pap. text ed. 19.95 (*0-691-00293-2*) Princeton U Pr.

— George Cruikshank; a Revaluation. (Illus.). 258p. 1974. 30.00 (*0-87811-018-6*) Princeton Lib.

Patten, Robert L., ed. see Dickens, Charles.

Patten, Robert L., jt. ed. see Jordan, John O.

Patten, S. F. Diagnostic Cytopathology of the Uterine Cervix. 2nd ed. (Monographs in Clinical Cytology: Vol. 3). (Illus.). 1977. 78.50 (*3-8055-2194-4*) S Karger.

Patten, Simon . Premises of Political Economy: Being a Re-Examination of Certain Fundamental Principles of Economic Science. LC 68-30540. (Reprints of Economic Classics Ser.). 1968. reprint ed. 35.00 (*0-678-00446-3*) Kelley.

Patten, Simon N. The Economic Basis of Protection. LC 73-2528. (Big Business; Economic Power in a Free Society Ser.). 1973. reprint ed. 15.95 (*0-405-05107-7*) Ayer.

— New Basis for Civilization. Fox, Daniel M., ed. LC 68-25622. (John Harvard Library). 267p. 1968. 32.00 (*0-674-60901-8*) HUP.

— The Theory of Dynamic Economics. LC 79-1587. 1981. 17.50 (*0-88355-892-0*) Hyperion Conn.

Patten, Stephen C., jt. ed. see Nielsen, Kai.

Patten, Terry. Systemic Text Generation As Problem Solving. (Studies in Natural Language Processing). (Illus.). 275p. 1988. 49.95 (*0-521-35076-X*) Cambridge U Pr.

Patten, Terry, jt. auth. see Patten, Leslie.

Patten, Thomas. Martin Luther: Reformer or Heretic? 1991. pap. write for info. (*1-55673-407-7*, 9220) CSS OH.

Patten, Thomas E. The Twisted Cross & Dietrich Bonhoffer. 1992. pap. 5.75 (*1-55673-475-1*, 7925) CSS OH.

An Asterisk (*) at the beginning of an entry indicates that the title is appearing in BIP for the first time.

Patten, Thomas H., Jr. Fair Pay: The Managerial Challenge of Comparable Job Worth & Job Evaluation. LC 88-42796. (Management Ser.). 294p. 1988. 35.95 (*1-55542-120-2*) Jossey-Bass.

Patten, Thomas H. Manpower Planning & the Development of Human Resources. LC 76-137109. 747p. reprint ed. pap. 180.00 (*0-317-27959-9*, 2055760) Bks Demand.

***Pattenden, G.** General & Synthetic Methods Vol. 16. 620p. 1994. 287.00 (*0-85186-834-7*, R6834) CRC Pr.

Pattenden, G., ed. General & Synthetic Methods, Vol. 15. 450p. 1993. 280.00 (*0-85186-974-2*) CRC Pr.

Pattenden, G., jt. auth. see Ansell, M. F.

Pattenden, Rosemary. Judicial Discretion & Criminal Litigation. 2nd ed. 496p. 1990. 89.00 (*0-19-825567-5*) OUP.

Pattengale, P. K., et al, eds. Lymphoproliferative Diseases: Pathogenesis, Diagnosis, Therapy. (Developments in Oncology Ser.). 1985. lib. bdg. 97.50 (*0-89838-725-6*) Kluwer Ac.

Patterns by Alfreda Staff. Crafts & More Rhyming Instructions & Patterns. 1992. pap. text ed. 21.95 (*0-318-04425-0*, Patterns Alfreda) Prosperity & Profits.

— Herbal Quilts: A Rhyming Pattern Reference. 1991. pap. text ed. 9.00 (*0-318-04426-9*, Patterns Alfreda) Prosperity & Profits.

— Kimono Fashions Poetry Recital. 1984. pap. text ed. 2.00 (*0-318-04427-7*, Patterns Alfreda) Prosperity & Profits.

— Mitten Recycling Pattern, Royal Neck Attire & String Potpourri Pattern Poems. 1984. pap. text ed. 5.00 (*0-318-04428-5*) Prosperity & Profits.

Patterosn, John. Exploring Maori Values. (Orig.). 1992. pap. 26.00 (*0-86469-156-4*) Intl Spec Bk.

Pattersen, M. Divorce Guide for Washington: Step-by-Step Guide for Obtaining Your Own Divorce. 8th ed. (Legal Ser.). 1992. 21.95 (*0-88908-751-2*) Self-Counsel Pr.

Patterson. Chlorinated Dioxins & Furans: Exposed Populations 1994. 1995. write for info. (*0-87371-879-8*) Lewis Pubs.

— Diagnostic Picture Tests in Cardiology. 1990. 14.95 (*0-8151-6623-0*, Yr Bk Med Pubs) Mosby Yr Bk.

— Jurisprudence, Men & Ideas of the Law. 1953. text ed. 25.00 (*0-88277-362-3*) Foundation Pr.

— Living Freshwater Protozoa. 1992. 83.95 (*0-8493-7735-8*, QL366) CRC Pr.

— Newts. 1995. pap. text ed. (*0-7938-0274-1*) TFH Pubns.

— Recent Developments in Urban Gaming. (Simulations Series of Bks.). 120p. 1972. 36.00 (*0-685-66844-4*, SS02-2) Soc Computer Sim.

— Red Eared Slider Turtles. 1995. pap. text ed. (*0-7938-0253-9*) TFH Pubns.

— Sound of the Dove: Singing in Appalachian Primitive Baptist Churches. 1995. audio 45.00 (*0-252-02174-6*) U of Ill Pr.

Patterson, ed. Non-Verbal Intimacy & Exchange: A Special Issue of Journal of Nonverbal Behavior. (Illus.). 169p. (Orig.). 1985. pap. 14.95 (*0-89885-224-2*) Human Sci Pr.

Patterson & Metzloff. Legal Ethics: The Law of Professional Responsibility. 3rd ed. 1989. write for info. (*0-8205-0216-2*, 396); teacher ed write for info. (*0-8205-0217-0*) Bender.

Patterson & Moses. Readings in Rehabilitation Counseling. 1971. pap. 8.60 (*0-87563-034-0*) Stipes.

Patterson, A. M. Hermogenes & the Renaissance: Seven Ideas of Style. 1970. 39.50 (*0-691-05182-8*) Princeton U Pr.

***Patterson, Alec & Couraud, Louis, eds.** Lung Transplantation. LC 94-43203. (Current Topics in General Thoracic Surgery Ser.: Vol. 3). 1994. write for info. (*0-444-81567-8*) Elsevier.

Patterson, Alex. A Field Guide to Rock Art Symbols of the Greater Southwest. LC 92-883. 220p. (Orig.). 1992. pap. 15.95 (*1-55566-091-6*) Johnson Bks.

— Hopi Pottery Symbols. LC 94-2295. (Illus.). 308p. 1994. pap. 17.95 (*1-55566-120-3*) Johnson Bks.

— Spike Lee. 248p. (Orig.). 1992. mass mkt. 4.99 (*0-380-76994-8*) Avon.

***Patterson, Alexander, et al.** Antievolutionism Before World War I. Numbers, Ronald L., ed. & intro. by. LC 94-45044. (Creationism in Twentieth-Century America Ser.: Vol. 1). 424p. 1995. 72.00 (*0-8153-1802-2*) Garland.

Patterson, Alexander Z. Famous Last Words: Deathbed Thoughts of the Great & the Near-Great. LC 92-38809. 1993. 10.95 (*0-8065-1385-3*, Citadel Pr) Carol Pub Group.

***Patterson, Andrew.** The Hypocrites: An Epic Novel about the Middle East from 1959-1989. Date not set. 19.95 (*0-9641679-0-5*) A Patterson.

Patterson, Andrew R. A Celtic Saga: Whithorn, Iona & Lindisfarne. (C). 1989. pap. 32.00 (*0-685-60707-0*, Pub. by St Andrew UK) St Mut.

— A Celtic Saga: Whithorn, Iona & Lindisfarne. (C). 1991. pap. text ed. 29.00 (*86-15-30647-8*, Pub. by St Andrew UK) St Mut.

— A Celtic Saga: Whithorn, Iona & Lindisfarne. 1993. pap. 21.00 (*0-7152-0647-8*) St Mut.

Patterson, Anna G., ed. Index to American Reference Books Annual, 1985-1989: A Cumulative Index to Subjects, Authors, & Titles. 1989. lib. bdg. 55.00 (*0-87287-793-0*) Libs Unl.

— Index to American Reference Books Annual, 1990-1994: Cumulative Index to Subjects, Authors, & Titles. 350p. 1994. lib. bdg. 65.00 (*1-56308-272-1*) Libs Unl.

Patterson, Anna G., jt. ed. see Wynar, Bohdan S.

Patterson, Annabel. Andrew Marvell. 1990. 40.00 (*0-7463-0710-1*, Pub. by Northcote UK); pap. 21.00 (*0-7463-0715-2*, Pub. by Northcote UK) St Mut.

— Fables of Power: Aesopian Writing & Political Theory. LC 90-46299. (Post-Contemporary Interventions Ser.). (Illus.). 184p. 1991. lib. bdg. 31.95 (*0-8223-1106-2*); pap. text ed. 14.95 (*0-8223-1118-6*) Duke.

— Pastoral & Ideology: Virgil to Valery. 425p. (C). 1987. 55.00 (*0-520-05862-3*) U CA Pr.

— Reading Between the Lines. LC 92-50257. 350p. (Orig.). (C). 1993. lib. bdg. 48.50 (*0-299-13540-3*); pap. 17.95 (*0-299-13544-6*) U of Wis Pr.

— Reading Holinshed's Chronicles. LC 93-47629. (C). 1994. lib. bdg. 43.00 (*0-226-64911-3*); pap. text ed. 16.95 (*0-226-64912-1*) U Ch Pr.

Patterson, Annabel, ed. Roman Images: Selected Papers from the English Institute, 1982. LC 83-17560. 208p. 1984. text ed. 31.00x (*0-8018-3127-X*) Johns Hopkins.

Patterson, Annabel, intro. John Milton. LC 92-12385. (Longman Critical Readers Ser.). 248p. (C). 1992. text ed. 49.50 (*0-582-04550-9*, 79370) Longman.

— John Milton. LC 92-12385. (Longman Critical Readers Ser.). 248p. (C). 1993. pap. text ed. 17.95 (*0-582-04539-8*) Longman.

Patterson, Annabel, ed. see Shakespeare, William.

Patterson, Annabel M. Censorship & Interpretation: The Conditions of Writing & Reading in Early Modern England. LC 84-40156. (Illus.). 296p. 1984. text ed. 27.50 (*0-299-09950-4*) U of Wis Pr.

— Censorship & Interpretation: The Conditions of Writing & Reading in Early Modern England. LC 84-40156. (Illus.). 296p. 1990. pap. 14.95 (*0-299-09954-7*) U of Wis Pr.

— Marvell & the Civic Crown. LC 77-85555. (Illus.). 275p. reprint ed. pap. 78.40 (*0-8357-6202-5*, 2034299) Bks Demand.

Patterson, Annette H. Fairbanks Blanket Toss: Your Guide to Bed & Breakfasts in Interior Alaska. LC 93-84312. (Illus.). 176p. (Orig.). (ENG & JPN.). 1993. pap. text ed. 14.95 (*0-9636113-7-2*) RWPP Pr.

Patterson, Archibald L. Public Pension Administration. 116p. (Orig.). 1982. pap. 9.50 (*0-89854-082-8*) U of GA Inst Govt.

Patterson, Austin M., ed. Greene County (Ohio), Eighteen Hundred Three to Nineteen Hundred Eight. (Illus.). 244p. 1990. reprint ed. pap. 20.00 (*1-55613-319-7*) Heritage Bk.

Patterson, Becky. Concentration: Strategies for Attaining Focus. 128p. (C). 1993. per., pap. text ed. 16.95 (*0-8403-8685-0*) Kendall-Hunt.

Patterson, Ben. Serving God: The Grand Essentials of Work & Worship. rev. ed. 192p. 1994. pap. 9.99 (*0-8308-1399-3*, 1399) InterVarsity.

— Waiting: Finding Hope When God Seems Silent. LC 89-15342. 170p. 1988. reprint ed. pap. 9.99 (*0-8308-1296-2*, 1296, Saltshaker Bk) InterVarsity.

— Work. (Christian Basics Bible Studies). 64p. 1994. pap. 4.99 (*0-8308-2007-8*, 2007) InterVarsity.

— Worship. (Christian Basics Bible Studies). 64p. (Orig.). 1994. pap. 4.99 (*0-8308-2008-6*, 2008) InterVarsity.

Patterson, Benton R. Write to Be Read: A Practical Guide to Feature Writing. LC 85-31842. 156p. (C). 1986. text ed. 23.95 (*0-8138-1943-1*) Iowa St U Pr.

Patterson, Bessie. A Living Sacrifice. 1985. pap. 6.25 (*0-89137-436-1*) Quality Pubns.

— The Wise Woman Builds Her House. 1979. pap. 6.25 (*0-89137-413-2*) Quality Pubns.

— The Wise Woman Knows. 1982. 6.25 (*0-89137-422-1*) Quality Pubns.

— Wisely Train the Younger Women. 1973. pap. 6.25 (*0-89137-406-X*) Quality Pubns.

***Patterson, Bette.** Physicalizing FE Principle. 44p. 1994. per., pap. text ed. 9.95 (*0-9643532-0-2*) Teel & Co.

Patterson, Betty. Index to "Memorial & Genealogical Record of Dodge & Jefferson Counties, Wis.", 1894. 15p. (Orig.). 1984. pap. 4.00 (*0-910255-44-X*) Wisconsin Gen.

Patterson, Betty, ed. Some Pioneer Families of Wisconsin, Vol 2. 139p. 1988. pap. 8.00 (*0-910255-49-0*) Wisconsin Gen.

Patterson, Betty, rev. Index to Names in the Portrait & Biographical Record of Waukesha County, Wisconsin, 1894. rev. ed. 42p. 1990. pap. 5.25 (*0-910255-51-2*) Wisconsin Gen.

Patterson, Betty K. & Rossi, Miram. Patterson & Pattersons: Fifty Years of the Patterson Function. Glusker, Jenny P. et al, eds. (IUCr Crystallographic Symposia Ser.). (Illus.). 752p. 1987. 49.95 (*0-19-855230-0*) OUP.

Patterson, Beverly B. The Sound of the Dove: Singing in Appalachian Primitive Baptist Churches. LC 94-1697. (Music in American Life Ser.). 1995. write for info. (*0-252-02123-1*) U of Ill Pr.

Patterson, Bill. The Growing Christian. (Growing Christian Disciples Ser.). 96p. 1989. student ed 4.95 (*1-56794-025-0*, C2287); teacher ed 29.95 (*1-56794-026-9*, C2287T) Star Bible.

— The Growing Christian Teacher, 5 vols. (Growing Christian Disciples Ser.). 126p. 1989. teacher ed 25.00 (*1-56794-028-5*, C2288T) Star Bible.

— The Growing Christian Teacher, 5 vols., Set. (Growing Christian Disciples Ser.). 126p. 1989. Set. student ed 40.00 (*1-56794-027-7*, C2288) Star Bible.

— Qualities of Discipleship: Quarter 1 Workbook. (Growing Christian Disciples Ser.). 75p. (Orig.). 1984. teacher ed 4.95 (*1-56794-015-3*, C2281T); student ed, pap. 3.95 (*1-56794-014-5*, C2281) Star Bible.

— Sacredness & Authority of the Bible: Quarter 2 Workbook. (Growing Christian Disciples Ser.). 96p. (Orig.). 1989. teacher ed 4.95 (*1-56794-017-X*, C2282T); student ed, pap. 3.95 (*1-56794-016-1*, C2282) Star Bible.

— Search for True Discipleship in Church History, Pt. I: Quarter 3. (Growing Christian Disciples Ser.). 96p. 1989. student ed 3.95 (*1-56794-018-8*, C2283); teacher ed 4.95 (*1-56794-019-6*, C2283T) Star Bible.

— Search for True Discipleship in Church History, Pt. II: Quarter 4. (Growing Christian Disciples Ser.). 96p. 1989. student ed 3.95 (*1-56794-020-X*, C2284); teacher ed 4.95 (*1-56794-021-8*, C2284T) Star Bible.

— Search for True Discipleship in Church History, Pt. II: Quarter 4. abr. ed. (Growing Christian Disciples Ser.). 199p. 1989. 5.95 (*0-940999-39-0*, C2151) Star Bible.

— The Task of Interpretation: Quarter 5. (Growing Christian Disciples Ser.). 126p. 1989. student ed 3.95 (*1-56794-022-6*, C2285); teacher ed 4.95 (*1-56794-023-4*, C2285T); teacher ed 4.95 (*1-56794-024-2*, C2286) Star Bible.

Patterson-Black, Gene, tr. see Schwab, Raymond.

Patterson, Bobbie, et al. With a Servant Heart: Perspectives on Women in Leadership. Howard, Gina, ed. 86p. (Orig.). 1992. pap. text ed. 3.95 (*1-56309-048-1*) Womans Mission Union.

***Patterson, Bruce.** Canadians on Everest. (Illus.). 241p. 1990. 29.95 (*1-55059-015-4*) Temeron Bks.

Patterson, C., ed. Molecules & Morphology in Evolution: Conflict or Compromise? 232p. 1987. 69.95 (*0-521-32271-5*); pap. 24.95 (*0-521-33860-3*) Cambridge U Pr.

Patterson, C. H. Plato's the Republic Notes. 1963. pap. 3.75 (*0-8220-1129-8*) Cliffs.

— Rehabilitation Counseling: Collected Papers. 1969. pap. 7.80 (*0-87563-015-4*) Stipes.

— Theories of Counseling & Psychotherapy. 4th ed. 608p. (C). 1990. pap. text ed. 63.00 (*0-06-045053-3*) HarpCollege.

— The Therapeutic Relationship: Foundations for an Electic Psychotherapy. LC 84-29326. (Counseling Ser.). 272p. (C). 1985. pap. 22.95 (*0-534-04944-3*) Brooks-Cole.

Patterson, C. H., jt. auth. see Moses, H.

Patterson, C. Stuart, et al. Principles of Chemistry. LC 66-28993. (Illus.). (C). 1967. 37.00 (*0-89197-530-6*) Irvington.

Patterson, Caleb P. The Constitutional Principles of Thomas Jefferson. LC 77-157352. (Select Bibliographies Reprint Ser.). 1977. reprint ed. 24.95 (*0-8369-5813-6*) Ayer.

Patterson, Catherine M., et al. Nutrition & Eating Disorders: Guidelines for the Patient with Anorexia Nervosa & Bulimia Nervosa. 34p. (Orig.). 1989. pap. 5.95 (*0-9608846-6-1*) PM Inc.

Patterson, Ce C., ed. see Loughrin, Judy.

Patterson, Charles. Animal Rights. LC 92-44286. (Illus.). 112p. (J). (gr. 6 up). 1993. lib. bdg. 17.95 (*0-89490-468-X*) Enslow Pubs.

— Anti-Semitism: The Road to the Holocaust & Beyond. 160p. (J). (gr. 8). 1989. pap. 9.95 (*0-8027-7318-4*) Walker & Co.

— The Civil Rights Movement. LC 95-3027. (Social Reform Movements Ser.). 1995. 17.95 (*0-8160-2968-7*) Facts on File.

— Down with Lawyer Power...Let's Get America Back on Track. LC 93-72960. 284p. 1994. pap. 7.95 (*0-9637926-5-2*) Comm for Pract IPD.

— Eating Disorders. LC 94-32116. (Teen Hot Line Ser.). (J). 1995. lib. bdg. write for info. (*0-8114-3813-9*) Raintree Steck-V.

— Hafiz Al-Asad of Syria. (In Focus Biographies Ser.). (Illus.). 128p. (YA). (gr. 8 up). 1991. lib. bdg. 13.98 (*0-671-69468-5*, Julian Messner); pap. 7.95 (*0-671-69469-3*) Silver Burdett Pr.

— Marian Anderson. LC 88-10695. (Impact Biographies Ser.). (Illus.). 160p. (YA). (gr. 7 up). 1988. lib. bdg. 15.47 (*0-531-10568-7*) Watts.

— The Oxford 50th Anniversary Book of the United Nations. (Illus.). 240p. (YA). (gr. 7 up). 1995. lib. bdg. 30.00 (*0-19-508280-X*) OUP.

Patterson, Charles B. New Thought Essays. 103p. 1994. pap. 9.00 (*0-89540-271-8*, SB-271) Sun Pub.

— The Will to Be Well. 255p. 1994. pap. 20.00 (*0-89540-275-0*, SB-275) Sun Pub.

Patterson, Charles H. Moral Standards: An Introduction to Ethics. 2nd ed. LC 57-6801. 545p. reprint ed. pap. 155.40 (*0-317-07870-4*, 2012523) Bks Demand.

— New Testament Notes. 1965. pap. 3.95 (*0-8220-0880-7*) Cliffs.

— Old Testament Notes. 1965. pap. 3.95 (*0-8220-0949-8*) Cliffs.

— Plato's Euthyphro, Apology, Crito & Phaedo: Notes. 61p. (Orig.). 1975. pap. text ed. 3.75 (*0-8220-1044-5*) Cliffs.

Patterson, Charles I., Jr. The Daemonic in the Poetry of John Keats. LC 71-94399. 1970. 20.00 (*0-252-00079-X*) Lib Soc Sci.

Patterson, Charles W. Psychotherapy: The Mystery Solved. LC 84-61941. 118p. (Orig.). 1984. pap. 8.00 (*0-9614334-1-8*) Passages.

Patterson, Charlotte J., jt. ed. see D'Augelli, Anthony R.

***Patterson, Christopher.** Queens Pawn. 340p. 1995. pap. 9.95 (*1-56901-782-4*) NW Pub.

Patterson, Clair C., jt. auth. see Gilfillan, S. Colum.

Patterson, Claire. It's OK To Be You: A Frank & Funny Guide to Growing Up. LC 94-17791. (Illus.). 70p. (J). (gr. 3-7). 1994. pap. 8.95 (*1-883672-16-3*) Tricycle Pr.

— Let's Celebrate Math. (Illus.). 82p. (J). (gr. 4-9). 1991. pap. 9.95 (*0-9623835-6-2*) Pieces of Lrning.

***Patterson, Cleveland S.** The Cost of Capital: Theory & Estimation. LC 94-32081. 344p. 1995. text ed. 75.00 (*0-89930-862-7*, Quorum Bks) Greenwood.

Patterson, Cynthia. Pericles' Citizenship Law of Four Fifty-One to Four Fifty B. C. 25.00 (*0-405-14046-0*) Ayer.

Patterson, D. H., jt. auth. see Brenes, Edin.

Patterson, D. J., jt. auth. see Corliss, J. O.

Patterson, D. Williams. Brockway Family, Descendants of Wolston Brockway. (Illus.). 167p. 1989. reprint ed. lib. bdg. 44.00 (*0-8328-0326-X*); reprint ed. pap. 34.00 (*0-8328-0327-8*) Higginson Bk Co.

***Patterson, Dan.** Artificial Neural Networks. 1995. pap. text ed. 48.00 (*0-13-295353-6*) P-H.

Patterson, Dan, photos. The Lady: Boeing B-17 Flying Fortress. (Living History Ser.: No. 1). (Illus.). 58p. 1993. pap. 15.95 (*0-943231-58-2*) Howell Pr VA.

— Mustang: North American P-51. (Living History Ser.: No. 3). (Illus.). 64p. 1995. pap. 15.95 (*0-943231-75-2*) Howell Pr VA.

— The Soldier: Consolidated B-24 Liberator. (Living History Ser.: No. 2). (Illus.). 64p. 1993. pap. 15.95 (*0-943231-61-2*) Howell Pr VA.

Patterson, Dan & Merva, George. Shoo-Shoo Baby: A Lucky Lady of the Sky. (Illus.). 1988. pap. 10.00 (*0-9622271-0-2*) Patterson Productions.

Patterson, Daniel & Zugg, Charles G., III, eds. Arts in Earnest: North Carolina Folklife. LC 89-1212. (Illus.). 324p. (Orig.). 1989. lib. bdg. 45.50 (*0-8223-0943-2*); pap. text ed. 20.95 (*0-8223-1021-X*) Duke.

Patterson, Daniel W. Gift Drawing & Gift Song: A Study of Two Forms of Shaker Inspiration. (Illus.). xii, 112p. (Orig.). 1983. 34.95 (*0-915836-17-3*); pap. 24.95 (*0-318-32857-7*) United Soc Shakers.

— The Shaker Spiritual. LC 77-85557. (Illus.). 583p. 1979. reprint ed. pap. 166.20 (*0-7837-8178-4*, 2047883) Bks Demand.

Patterson, Daniel W., ed. Sounds of the South. LC 91-30427. (Illus.). 240p. pap. text ed. 13.95 (*0-8223-1343-X*) Duke.

Patterson, Dave, jt. auth. see Hennessey, John.

Patterson, David. The Affirming Flame: Religion, Language, Literature. LC 87-30026. (Illus.). 192p. 1988. 29.95 (*0-8061-2109-2*) U of Okla Pr.

— Exile: The Sense of Alienation in Modern Russian Letters. LC 94-16230. 224p. 1994. lib. bdg. 21.95x (*0-8131-1888-3*) U Pr of Ky.

— In Dialogue & Dilemma with Elie Wiesel. LC 91-3489. 1992. text ed. 30.00 (*0-89341-674-6*, Longwood Academic) Hollowbrook.

— Literature & Spirit: Essays on Bakhtin & His Contemporaries. LC 88-9743. 176p. 1988. 19.00 (*0-8131-1647-3*) U Pr of Ky.

— A Phoenix with Fetters: Studies in 19th & Early 20th Century Hebrew Fiction. (Oxford Centre for Postgraduate Hebrew Studies). 200p. 1988. 46.75 (*0-8476-7564-5*) Rowman.

— Pilgrimage of a Proselyte: From Auschwitz to Jerusalem. LC 93-13626. 1993. 19.95 (*0-8246-0363-X*) Jonathan David.

— The Shriek of Silence: A Phenomenology of the Holocaust Novel. LC 91-17269. 192p. 1991. text ed. 24.00 (*0-8131-1768-2*) U Pr of Ky.

— The Way of the Child. LC 86-83410. 280p. (Orig.). 1994. pap. 9.95 (*0-89896-168-8*) Larksdale.

Patterson, David, ed. & tr. The Gospel According to Tolstoy. LC 91-41087. 280p. 1992. 27.95 (*0-8173-0590-4*) U of Ala Pr.

Patterson, David & Abramson, Glenda, eds. Tradition & Trauma: Studies in the Fiction of S. J. Agnon. LC 93-43704. (Modern Hebrew Classics Ser.). 216p. 1994. text ed. 59.50 (*0-8133-2024-0*) Westview.

— Tradition & Trauma: Studies in the Fiction of S. J. Agnon. LC 93-43704. (Modern Hebrew Classics Ser.). 216p. (C). 1994. pap. text ed. 21.50 (*0-8133-2025-9*) Westview.

Patterson, David & Rock, Joe. Thomas Begbie's Edinburgh. 200p. (C). 1989. text ed. 96.00 (*0-85976-337-4*, Pub. by J Donald) St Mut.

Patterson, David, ed. see Bradley, Pamela.

Patterson, David, tr. see Dostoyevsky, Fyodor.

Patterson, David, tr. see Shamir, Moshe.

Patterson, David, tr. see Tolstoy, Leo.

Patterson, David, tr. see Turgenev, Ivan S.

Patterson, David A. & Hennessy, John L. Computer Organization & Design: The Hardware-Software Interface. 800p. (C). 1993. text ed. 69.95 (*1-55860-281-X*) Morgan Kaufmann.

Patterson, David A., jt. auth. see Hennessy, John L.

Patterson, David A., et al. Computing Unbound: Hands-on Exercises for the Macintosh. (C). 1988. pap. text ed. 24.95 (*0-393-95668-7*) Norton.

— Computing Unbound: Using Computers in the Arts & Sciences. 400p. (Orig.). (C). 1988. pap. text ed. 41.95 (*0-393-95664-4*) Norton.

— Computing Unbound: Using Computers in the Arts & Sciences. 400p. (Orig.). (C). 1989. Instr's. manual. teacher ed, pap. text ed. write for info. (*0-393-95665-2*) Norton.

Patterson, David J. & Larsen, Jacob, eds. The Biology of Free-Living Heterotrophic Flagellates. (Systematics Association Special Volume Ser.: Vol. 45). (Illus.). 450p. 1992. 135.00 (*0-19-857747-8*) OUP.

Patterson, David S. Toward a Warless World: The Travail of the American Peace Movement, 1887-1914. LC 75-28916. 350p. reprint ed. pap. 99.80 (*0-317-27843-6*, 2056050) Bks Demand.

Patterson, David S., ed. American Foreign Policy: Current Documents, 1985. (Department of State Publication Ser.: No. 9485). 1179p. 1986. text ed. 31.00 (*0-16-004431-6*, S/N 044-000-02136-6) USGPO.

Patterson, David S., jt. ed. see Glennon, John P.

Patterson, David S., et al, eds. American Foreign Policy Current Documents, 1986. (State Department Publications: No. 9620). 887p. 1987. 26.00 (*0-16-004464-2*, S/N 044-000-02194-3) USGPO.

Patterson, Dean, intro. Coastal & Ocean Engineering, Eleventh Australasian Conference, 1993: Coastal Engineering - a Partnership with Nature, 2 vols., Set. (National Conference Publication Ser.: No. 93-4). (Illus.). (Orig.). 1993. pap. 120.00 (*0-85825-574-X*, Pub. by Inst Engrs Aust-EA Bks AT) Accents Pubns.

Patterson, Debbie, jt. auth. see Ganderton, Lucinda.

Patterson, Debra, ed. see Wyman, J. N.

Patterson, Dennis. Postmodernism & Law. Campbell, Tom D., ed. (International Library of Essays in Law & Legal Theory). 500p. 1994. 150.00 (0-8147-6550-5) NYU Pr.

Patterson, Dennis M. Lender Liability: Definitions - Theories - Applications. 350p. 1990. boxed 75.00 (0-88063-279-8) Butterworth Legal Pubs.

Patterson, Dennis M., ed. Wittgenstein & Legal Theory. 256p. 1992. text ed. 64.50 (0-8133-0107-6) Westview.

Patterson, Diane A. The Computer Documentation Kit. 176p. 24.95 (0-685-09668-8) P-H.

— The Computer Documentation Kit. 1984. text ed. 42.00 (0-8359-0841-0, Reston); pap. 29.95 (0-8359-0845-3, Reston) P-H.

Patterson, Dolly K., ed. Questions of Faith: Contemporary Thinkers Respond. LC 90-47636. (Illus.). 128p. (Orig.). (C). 1990. pap. 14.95 (0-334-02484-6) TPI PA.

Patterson, Don. A Child's Trip to Christmas in Santa Fe: A Photographic Documentary. LC 91-62868. (Illus.). 120p. (J). (gr. k-3). 1991. 29.95 (0-9629093-2-7) MyndSeye.

— Ski Vacation. (Illus.). 40p. (J). (gr. k-6). 1991. 13.95 (0-9629093-3-5) MyndSeye.

— Virginia Democrats: A Photographic Portrait. LC 91-61019. (Illus.). 144p. 1991. 34.95 (0-9629093-0-0); pap. 24.95 (0-9629093-1-9) MyndSeye.

Patterson, Donald L. & Patterson, Janet L. Vincent Persichetti: A Bio-Bibliography. LC 88-25084. (Bio-Bibliographies in Music Ser.: No. 16). 352p. 1988. text ed. 69.50 (0-313-25334-X, PPE/, Greenwood Pr) Greenwood.

Patterson, Doris T. & Shelley, Violet M. Be Your Own Psychic. 81p. 1975. pap. 4.95 (0-87604-079-2) ARE Pr.

Patterson, Dorothy K. A Woman Seeking God. 1992. pap. 8.99 (0-8054-5351-2) Broadman.

Patterson, Edna & Beebe, Louise. Halleck Country: A Story of the Land & Its People. LC 82-51317. (Helen Marye Thomas Memorial Ser.: No. 4). 1982. pap. 12.95 (0-317-52265-5) U of Nev Pr.

Patterson, Edna, et al. Nevada's Northeast Frontier. LC 91-2182. (Illus.). 732p. 1991. 45.00x (0-87417-171-7) U of Nev Pr.

Patterson, Edwin W. Essentials of Insurance Law: An Outline of Legal Doctrines in Their Relations to Insurance Practices. 2nd ed. LC 56-13399. 572p. reprint ed. pap. 163.10 (0-317-29997-2, 2051847) Bks Demand.

Patterson, Eldon. A Visitor from Orion. 165p. (Orig.). 1988. pap. 12.75 (0-9623403-0-8) Human Possibilities.

Patterson, Elizabeth B., ed. Saint Francis & the Poet. 163p. 11.95 (0-8159-6802-7) Devin.

Patterson, Elizabeth C. Mary Somerville & the Cultivation of Science, 1815-1848. 1983. lib. bdg. 39.50 (90-247-2433-3) Kluwer Ac.

***Patterson, Ella M.** For Women Who Live Alone. Ennix, Lucille, ed. LC 94-75720. (Illus.). 600p. 1995. 19.95 (1-884331-02-5) Knowledge Concepts.

— One Thousand Reasons to Think. (Illus.). 1993. lib. bdg. 9.95 (0-685-69193-4) Knowledge Concepts.

— One Thousand Reasons to Think. LC 94-75365. (Illus.). 200p. (J). (ps-12). 1993. 14.95 (1-884331-00-9) Knowledge Concepts.

— Will the Real Men Please Stand Up. (Illus.). 400p. 1995. 19.95 (1-884331-11-4) Knowledge Concepts.

— Will the Real Women Please Stand Up. Ennix, Lucille & Whaley, Marvin, eds. LC 94-75061. (Illus.). 280p. (Orig.). (C). 1994. 14.95 (1-884331-01-7) Knowledge Concepts.

***Patterson, Ella M. & Jones, Herbert L., Jr.** For the Sake of Women. (Illus.). 1000p. 1995. 19.95 (1-884331-10-6) Knowledge Concepts.

Patterson, Ellen Tate, jt. auth. see Freda, Margaret Comerford.

Patterson, Elsie E. A Portrait of Everyday Life in Wisconsin. Hoffmann, Susan J., ed. 256p. 1988. 35.95 (0-9620583-0-0) Patterson Comns.

Patterson, Ernest M. & Wilkins, Mira, eds. America's Changing Investment Market. LC 76-29983. (European Business Ser.). (Illus.). 1977. reprint ed. lib. bdg. 31.95 (0-405-09748-4) Ayer.

Patterson, Ernest M., jt. auth. see Conway, Thomas, Jr.

Patterson, F. W. Los Evangelicos Frente al Siglo Veintiuno. 160p. (Orig.). (SPA.). 1992. pap. 3.50 (0-311-29012-4, Edit Mundo) Casa Bautista.

— Manual de Finanzas Para Iglesias. (Illus.). 118p. 1986. reprint ed. pap. 3.75 (0-311-17005-6) Casa Bautista.

Patterson, Fiona M. Out of Place: Public & the Emergence of Truancy. 220p. 1989. 70.00 (1-85000-510-9, Falmer Pr); pap. 35.00 (1-85000-511-7, Falmer Pr) Taylor & Francis.

Patterson, Francine. Colloquial Spanish. 1979. pap. 13.95 (0-415-05908-9) Routledge.

— Koko's Kitten. 50p. (J). (gr. k up). 1985. pap. 13.95 (0-590-40952-2) Scholastic Inc.

— Koko's Kitten. (J). 1987. pap. 4.95 (0-590-44425-5) Scholastic Inc.

— Koko's Story. (Illus.). 40p. (J). 1988. pap. 5.95 (0-590-41364-3) Scholastic Inc.

Patterson, Frank A. Middle English Penitential Lyric. LC 11-26002. reprint ed. 31.50 (0-404-04908-7) AMS Pr.

Patterson, Frank A., ed. see Milton, John.

Patterson, Frank E., 3rd. Afghanistan, Its Twentieth Century Postal Issues. (Illus.). 208p. 1965. 18.00 (0-912574-18-6, HE6185,A32P3) Collectors.

Patterson, Frank W. A Short History of Christian Missions. 176p. 1985. pap. 13.95 (0-311-72663-1) Casa Bautista.

Patterson, Franklin K. Colleges in Consort: Institutional Cooperation Through Consortia. LC 73-20964. (Jossey-Bass Higher Education Ser.). 200p. reprint ed. pap. 57.00 (0-317-41809-2, 2025666) Bks Demand.

Patterson, Frederick C. A Systems Approach to Recreation Programming. LC 87-12682. (Illus.). 181p. (Orig.). (C). 1991. reprint ed. pap. text ed. 13.95x (0-88133-593-2) Waveland Pr.

Patterson, Freeman. Namaqualand: Garden of the Gods. 2nd ed. (Illus.). 128p. 1993. 35.00 (0-919493-37-8, Pub. by Key Porter Bks CN) Natl Bk Netwk.

— Photography & the Art of Seeing. rev. ed. (Illus.). 156p. 1989. pap. 17.95 (1-55013-099-4, Pub. by Key Porter Bks CN) Natl Bk Netwk.

— Photography for the Joy of It. LC 88-30837. (Paperback Library). (Illus.). 168p. 1989. pap. 16.95 (0-87156-697-4) Sierra.

— Photography for the Joy of It. rev. ed. (Illus.). 168p. 1989. pap. 17.95 (1-55013-095-1, Pub. by Key Porter Bks CN) Natl Bk Netwk.

— Portraits of Earth. LC 87-4795. (Illus.). 180p. 1987. 35.00 (0-87156-717-2) Sierra.

Patterson, Freeman, jt. auth. see Canadian Nature Federation Staff.

Patterson, G. A. Basic Fluid System Analysis: With HP-25 & SR-56 Pocket Calculator Programs. LC 76-21585. 95p. 1977. 12.95 (0-917410-00-9) Basic Sci Pr.

— Energy Analysis with a Pocket Calculator. 2nd ed. LC 77-88128. (Illus.). 138p. 1981. 16.95 (0-917410-04-1) Basic Sci Pr.

— Engine Thermodynamics with a Pocket Calculator. 2nd ed. 149p. 1983. 14.95 (0-917410-07-6) Basic Sci Pr.

Patterson, G. R., jt. auth. see Capaldi, D.

Patterson, Gardner. Discrimination in International Trade, the Policy Issues: 1945-1965. 1966. 65.00 (0-691-04119-9) Princeton U Pr.

***Patterson, Gareth.** Last of the Free. (Illus.). 176p. 1995. 21.95 (0-312-13109-7, Pub. by Thomas Dunne Bks) St Martin.

Patterson, Gary B. Find It in the Yellow Pages. Coffen, Richard W., ed. (Better Living Ser.). 32p. (Orig.). 1986. pap. 0.75 (0-8280-0350-5) Review & Herald.

Patterson, Gary K., jt. ed. see Ulbrecht, Jaromir J.

Patterson, Geoffrey. Jonah & the Whale. (Illus.). (J). (ps-3). 1992. 14.00 (0-688-11238-2); lib. bdg. 13.93 (0-688-11239-0) Lothrop.

Patterson, George & Scoggins, Richard. Church Multiplication Guide: Helping Churches to Reproduce Locally & Abroad. LC 93-40678. 128p. 1994. pap. 5.95 (0-87808-245-X) William Carey Lib.

Patterson, George J., Jr. The Unassimilated Greeks of Denver. LC 88-36704. (Immigrant Communities & Ethnic Minorities in the U. S. & Canada Ser.: No. 41). 1989. 49.50 (0-404-19451-6) AMS Pr.

***Patterson, George S.** Preparing Tris (2, 4-Pentanedionato) Iron (III), an Iron Coordination Complex. Neidig, H. A., ed. (Modular Laboratory Program in Chemistry Ser.). 8p. (C). 1993. pap. text ed. 1.25x (0-87540-431-6) Chem Educ Res.

— Synthesizing & Analyzing a Coordination Compound of Nickel (II) Ion, Ammonia, & Chloride Ion. Neidig, H. A., ed. (Modular Laboratory Program in Chemistry Ser.). 16p. (C). 1994. pap. text ed. 1.25x (0-87540-433-2) Chem Educ Res.

Patterson, George S., jt. auth. see Good, William E., Jr.

Patterson, Gerald & Forgatch, Marion. Parents & Adolescents Living Together: The Basics, Pt. 1. 286p. 1987. 12.95 (0-916154-16-5) Castalia Pub.

Patterson, Gerald, jt. auth. see Forgatch, Marion.

Patterson, Gerald, et al. Antisocial Boys. (Social Interactional Approach Ser.: Vol. 4). (Illus.). xiii, 193p. (C). 1992. text ed. 32.95 (0-916154-03-3) Castalia Pub.

Patterson, Gerald G. How to Pass a Road Test for Your Driver's License. 72p. 1994. pap. 8.95 (0-9641406-0-8) Red Rock WI.

Patterson, Gerald R. Depression & Aggression in Family Interaction: Developmental Perspectives. 352p. (C). 1988. text ed. 69.95 (0-8058-0137-5) L Erlbaum Assocs.

— Families: Applications of Social Learning to Family Life. rev. ed. (Illus.). 180p. (Orig.). (C). 1975. pap. text ed. 11.95 (0-87822-156-5, 0020) Res Press.

— Living with Children: New Methods for Parents & Teachers. rev. ed. LC 76-23974. 132p. (C). 1976. pap. text ed. 9.95 (0-87822-130-1, 0003) Res Press.

— Social Learning Approach to Family Intervention: Coercive Family Process, Vol. 3. 386p. 1982. text ed. 39.95 (0-916154-02-5) Castalia Pub.

Patterson, Glenn W. & Nes, W. David, eds. Physiology & Biochemistry of Sterols. 395p. (C). 1992. 80.00 (0-935315-38-1) AOCS Pr.

Patterson, Gordon, jt. auth. see Rodwell, John.

Patterson, Graeme. History & Communications. 258p. 1990. 40.00 (0-8020-2764-4); pap. 15.95 (0-8020-6810-3) U of Toronto Pr.

Patterson, H. B. Bleaching & Purifying Fats & Oils: Theory & Practice. LC 92-30226. 256p. 1993. 70.00 (0-935315-42-X) AOCS Pr.

— Handling & Storage of Oilseeds, Oils, Fats, & Meal. 396p. 1989. 99.00 (1-85166-248-0) Elsevier.

— Hydrogenation of Fats & Oils: Theory & Practice. LC 94-35070. 288p. 1994. 75.00 (0-935315-55-1) AOCS Pr.

Patterson, H. Robert, et al. Current Drug Handbook 1984-1986. 1984. text ed. 34.50 (0-7216-1223-7) Saunders.

Patterson, H. W. Small Boat Building. 144p. 1985. reprint ed. pap. 20.00 (0-87556-691-X) Saifer.

Patterson, Hal. Mapping Your Career: A Working Guide. 100p. 1993. write for info. (1-56829-031-4) Med Group Mgmt.

Patterson, Henry, jt. auth. see Bew, Paul.

Patterson, Henry, jt. auth. see Mead, Michael.

Patterson, Horace L. Clean but Empty. Teasley, Jamie, ed. LC 89-51628. 149p. 1990. pap. 6.95 (1-55523-282-5) Winston-Derek.

— Climbing the Sacred Ladder. LC 91-74114. (Illus.). 70p. 1992. pap. 6.95 (1-55523-468-2) Winston-Derek.

Patterson, Ian, ed. see Fourier, Charles.

Patterson, Ian, tr. see Goubert, Pierre.

Patterson, Ian, tr. see Touraine, Alain, et al.

Patterson, Ian, tr. see Vaneigem, Raoul.

Patterson, J. B. The Life of Blackhawk, Dictated by Himself. enl. ed. 1975. 12.00 (0-87770-137-7) Ye Galleon.

Patterson, J. B., ed. see Black Hawk.

Patterson, J. G. A Zola Dictionary. 1972. 75.00 (0-8490-1350-X) Gordon Pr.

— A Zola Dictionary: The Characters of the Rougon-Macquart Novels of Emile Zola. xi, 232p. 1973. reprint ed. 42.90 (3-487-04854-X, Pub. by Georg Olms GW) Lubrecht & Cramer.

Patterson, J. H. The Man-Eaters of Tsavo. (Peter Capstick Library). (Illus.). 384p. 1985. 15.95 (0-312-51010-1) St Martin.

Patterson, J. K. Turning Troubles into Triumphs. LC 88-62641. 144p. (Orig.). 1988. pap. 7.95 (1-55725-003-0) Paraclete MA.

Patterson, Jack & Stevenson, George B. Native Trees of the Bahamas. (Illus.). pap. 5.95 (0-916224-42-2) Banyan Bks.

Patterson, James. Along Came a Spider. 512p. 1993. mass mkt. 5.99 (0-446-36419-3) Warner Bks.

— Along Came a Spider. large type ed. LC 92-46704. (General Ser.). 1993. 22.95 (0-8161-5752-9, Large Print Bks) Hall.

— Along Came a Spider. large type ed. LC 92-46704. (General Ser.). 1994. pap. 17.95 (0-8161-5753-7, Large Print Bks) Hall.

— Along Came a Spider: A Novel. LC 92-24581. 1993. 21.95 (0-316-69364-2) Little.

— America in the Twentieth Century. 4th ed. 1993. pap. 30.75 (0-15-500502-2) HarBrace.

— America since Nineteen Forty One: A History. 1994. pap. 15.00 (0-15-501113-8) HarBrace.

— Black Market. 368p. 1994. mass mkt. 5.99 (0-446-60046-6) Warner Bks.

— Kiss the Girls. 464p. 1995. mass mkt. 6.99 (0-446-60124-1) Warner Bks.

— Kiss the Girls: A Novel. LC 94-14177. 1995. 22.95 (0-316-69370-7) Little.

— The Midnight Club. 256p. 1990. mass mkt. 5.99 (0-8041-0597-9) Ivy Books.

— Season of the Machete. 352p. 1995. mass mkt. 5.99 (0-446-60047-4, Warner Vision) Warner Bks.

— Simplified Design for Building Fire Safety. (Parker Series of Simplified Design Guides). 344p. 1993. text ed. 49.95 (0-471-57236-5) Wiley.

Patterson, James & Kim, Peter. The Second American Revolution: The People's Agenda for Fixing America - Before It's Too Late: Nine Solutions to Our Most Threatening Problems. LC 93-48960. 1994. 25.00 (0-688-11730-9) Morrow.

Patterson, James, tr. see Gero, Andras.

Patterson, James, jt. auth. see Masterson, Michael.

***Patterson, James G.** Benchmarking: Finding & Using Best Practices. Gerould, Philip, ed. (50-Minute Ser.). (Illus.). 100p. (Orig.). 1995. pap. 9.95 (1-56052-356-5) Crisp Pubns.

— ISO 9000: Worldwide Quality Standard. Gerould, Philip, ed. (Fifty Minute Ser.). (Illus.). viii, 128p. (Orig.). 1995. pap. 9.95 (1-56052-291-7) Crisp Pubns.

Patterson, James H., jt. auth. see Pfaffenberger, Roger C.

Patterson, James M., jt. auth. see Allvine, Fred C.

Patterson, James M., ed. see Obayashi, Alan W. & Gorgan, Joseph M.

Patterson, James T. America in the Twentieth Century: A History. 3rd ed. 534p. (C). 1988. pap. text ed. 30.75 (0-15-502264-4) HB Coll Pubs.

— America's Struggle Against Poverty, 1900-1985. rev. ed. 320p. 1986. pap. 15.95 (0-674-03122-9) HUP.

— America's Struggle Against Poverty, 1900-1994. LC 94-22736. 323p. 1995. pap. text ed. 16.95 (0-674-03123-7, PATAMZ) HUP.

— Congressional Conservatism & the New Deal: The Growth of the Conservative Coalition in Congress, 1933 to 1939. LC 81-4195. (Illus.). ix, 369p. 1981. reprint ed. text ed. 59.75 (0-313-22676-8, PACC, Greenwood Pr) Greenwood.

— The Dread Disease: Cancer & Modern American Culture. LC 87-160. (Illus.). 416p. 1987. 38.00 (0-674-21625-3) HUP.

— The Dread Disease: Cancer & Modern American Culture. (Illus.). 416p. 1989. pap. 17.95 (0-674-21626-1) HUP.

— The New Deal & the States: Federalism in Transition. LC 80-29606. viii, 226p. 1981. reprint ed. text ed. 55.00 (0-313-22841-8, PAND, Greenwood Pr) Greenwood.

Patterson, James W., ed. & intro. Metals Speciation, Separation, & Recovery, Vol. I. (Illus.). 779p. 1987. 103.95 (0-87371-034-7, TD196) Lewis Pubs.

Patterson, James W. & Passino, Roberto, eds. Metals Speciation, Separation & Recovery, Vol. II. (Illus.). 700p. 1990. 104.95 (0-87371-268-4, TD196) Lewis Pubs.

Patterson, Jane, jt. auth. see Madaras, Lynda.

Patterson, Janet L., jt. auth. see Patterson, Donald L.

Patterson, Janice H., jt. auth. see Patterson, Jerry L.

Patterson, Jerry. The Delta & Other Poems. 90p. 1988. per., pap. 6.95 (0-89697-312-3) Intl Univ Pr.

— Moral of the Story & the Last Hero. 50p. per., pap. 7.95 (0-89697-311-5) Intl Univ Pr.

— One Hundred Prayers for Contemporary Life. LC 92-61370. 100p. 1993. pap. 5.95 (1-55523-561-1) Winston-Derek.

— Teacher, Oh Teacher. 180p. 1988. pap. 8.95 (0-89697-300-X) Intl Univ Pr.

— Upside down Leadership: The Rules Have Changed! 112p. (Orig.). 1995. pap. write for info. (0-9646020-0-8) Transit Pr WI.

Patterson, Jerry & Patterson, Nancy. Casino Gambler's Winning Edge: How to Get in, Get the Money & Get Out. (Illus.). 144p. (Orig.). 1989. pap. text ed. 3.95 (0-318-42764-8) Echelon Gaming.

Patterson, Jerry E. The Vanderbilts. (Illus.). 304p. 1989. 49.50 (0-8109-1748-3) Abrams.

Patterson, Jerry L. Blackjack: A Winner's Handbook. 208p. 1990. pap. 10.00 (0-399-51598-4, Perigree Bks) Berkley Pub.

— Blackjack's Winning Formula. (Illus.). 160p. 1982. pap. 10.95 (0-399-50617-9, Perigree Bks) Berkley Pub.

— Leadership for Tomorrow's Schools. LC 93-19133. 1993. 11.95 (0-87120-209-3) Assn Supervision.

Patterson, Jerry L. & Jaye, Walter. Casino Gambling: Winning Techniques for Craps, Roulette, Baccarat & Blackjack. 224p. 1983. pap. 10.00 (0-399-50656-X, Perigree Bks) Berkley Pub.

Patterson, Jerry L. & Olsen, Eddie. Break the Dealer: Winning Strategies for Today's Blackjack. 1986. pap. 10.00 (0-399-51233-0, Perigree Bks) Berkley Pub.

Patterson, Jerry L. & Patterson, Janice H. Putting Computer Power in Schools: A Step-by-Step Approach. 1984. 17.95 (0-317-38248-9, Parker Publishing Co); pap. 12.95 (0-317-38249-7, Parker Publishing Co) P-H.

— Putting Computer Power in Schools: A Step-by-Step Approach. LC 83-8017. 227p. 1983. 17.95 (0-13-744474-5, Busn); pap. 12.95 (0-13-744467-2, Busn) P-H.

Patterson, Jerry L., et al. Productive School Systems for a Nonrational World. LC 86-71233. 125p. (Orig.). 1986. pap. text ed. 7.50 (0-87120-136-4, 611-86022) Assn Supervision.

Patterson, Jo, tr. see Dadie, Bernard B.

***Patterson, Joe A.** God Will Make This Child a Blessing! The Jamie Coulter Story. 100p. 1994. pap. 12.00 (0-9641696-2-2) Heritage TX.

— Pulpit Echoes. 181p. 1988. 12.00 (0-9641696-0-6) Heritage TX.

***Patterson, John.** Child Abuse Prevention Primer. Date not set. write for info. (0-614-03627-5) Nonprof Risk Mgmt Ctr.

— Child Abuse Prevention Primer for Your Organization. LC 95-67770. (Illus.). 1995. 12.00 (0-9637120-2-0) Nonprof Risk Mgmt Ctr.

— Screening Tool Kit: Keeping Bad Apples Out of Your Organization. LC 94-68617. 1994. pap. 15.00 (0-9637120-1-2) Nonprof Risk Mgmt Ctr.

Patterson, John, jt. auth. see Bumann, Joan.

Patterson, John M., jt. auth. see Bliss, Edward, Jr.

Patterson, John W. My Father's Book: The Rights of Men. LC 87-70654. (Chastening Rod Ser.: Vol. I). (Illus.). 110p. 1987. reprint ed. 14.95 (0-944698-00-X); reprint ed. pap. 8.95 (0-944698-01-8) New Genesis Pub.

Patterson, Jose. Angels, Prophets, Rabbis & Kings: From the Stories of the Jewish People. (World Mythology Ser.). (Illus.). 132p. (J). (gr. 6 up). 1991. 22.50 (0-87226-912-4) P Bedrick Bks.

— Mazal-Tov: A Jewish Wedding. (Way We Live Ser.). (Illus.). 25p. (J). (gr. 2-4). 1991. 12.95 (0-237-60140-0, Pub. by Evans Bros Ltd UK) Trafalgar.

Patterson, Joseph, jt. ed. see Lamb, Donald Q.

Patterson, Joseph M. A Little Brother of the Rich. LC 68-57545. (Muckrakers Ser.). (Illus.). reprint ed. lib. bdg. 19.50 (0-8398-1553-0) Irvington.

— Little Brother of the Rich. (Muckrakers Ser.). (C). 1987. reprint ed. pap. text ed. 7.95 (0-8290-2377-1) Irvington.

Patterson, Joy D. Death Bed Miracles. LC 89-50862. 50p. 1990. pap. 5.95 (1-55523-245-0) Winston-Derek.

Patterson, K. D. & Ryding, J. Deriving & Testing Rate of Growth & Higher Order Growth Effects in Dynamic Economic Models. (Bank of England. Discussion Papers: No. 21). 40p. pap. 25.00 (0-317-26765-5, 2024345) Bks Demand.

Patterson, K. D., jt. auth. see Hall, S. G.

Patterson, K. D., jt. ed. see Henry, G. B.

Patterson, K. David. Health in Colonial Ghana: Disease, Medicine, & Socio-Economic Change, 1900-1955. 187p. 1981. 20.00 (0-918456-42-8) African Studies Assn.

— Infectious Diseases in Twentieth-Century Africa: A Bibliography of Their Distribution & Consequences. (Archival & Bibliographic Ser.). 251p. (Orig.). 1979. pap. 25.00 (0-918456-29-0, Crossroads) African Studies Assn.

— Pandemic Influenza Seventeen Hundred to Nineteen Hundred: A Study in Historical Epidemiology. (Illus.). 128p. (C). 1987. 45.00 (0-8476-7512-2, R7512) Rowman.

Patterson, K. David & Hartwig, Gerald. Cerebrospinal Meningitis in West Africa & the Sudan in the Twentieth Century. 1984. pap. 15.00 (0-918456-55-X) African Studies Assn.

— Schistosomiasis in Twentieth Century Africa: Historical Studies on West Africa & Sudan. 1984. pap. 15.00 (0-918456-54-1) African Studies Assn.

Patterson, Keith L. Evaluating Your Liturgical Music Ministry. LC 92-44562. 152p. (Orig.). (C). 1993. pap. text ed. 19.95 (0-89390-258-6) Resource Pubns.

Patterson, Kerry D. Growth Coefficients in Error Correction & Autoregressive Distributed Log Models. LC 84-4308. (Bank of England. Discussion Papers. Technical Ser.: No. 2). 33p. reprint ed. pap. 25.00 (0-318-34693-1, 2031765) Bks Demand.

Patterson, L. Ray & Lindberg, Stanley W. The Nature of Copyright: A Law of Users' Rights. LC 90-28430. 288p. 1991. 30.00 (0-8203-1347-5); pap. 12.95 (0-8203-1362-9) U of Ga Pr.

Patterson, Lee. Chaucer & the Subject of History. LC 90-50651. 504p. (Orig.). (C). 1991. pap. 16.95 (0-299-12834-2) U of Wis Pr.

— Negotiating the Past: The Historical Understanding of Medieval Literature. LC 87-40144. 256p. 1987. text ed. 35.00 (0-299-11040-0); pap. text ed. 15.95 (0-299-11044-3) U of Wis Pr.

Patterson, Lee, ed. Literary Practice & Social Change in Britain, 1380-1530. 1989. 45.00 (0-520-06486-0) U CA Pr.

An Asterisk (*) at the beginning of an entry indicates that the title is appearing in BIP for the first time.

Patterson, Lee T. & Deblieux, Michael R. Documenting Employee Discipline. LC 88-61702. 1988. pap. 39.50 (*0-911110-61-5*) Butterworth Legal Pubs.

Patterson, Leslie, et al. Teacher Research: From Promise to Power. LC 90-36504. 123p. (Orig.). (C). 1991. pap. text ed. 12.95 (*1-878450-09-3*) R Owen Pubs.

Patterson, Leslie, et al, eds. Teachers Are Researchers: Reflection & Action. 248p. 1993. pap. 24.00 (*0-87207-748-9*) Intl Reading.

Patterson, Lewis E. & Welfel, Elizabeth R. The Counseling Process. 4th ed. LC 93-37295. 1994. pap. 29.95 (*0-534-23268-X*) Brooks-Cole.

Patterson, Lewis E., jt. auth. see Eisenberg, Sheldon.

Patterson, Lillie. Francis Scott Key: Poet & Patriot. (Discovery Biographies Ser.). (Illus.). 80p. (J). (gr. 2-6). 1991. reprint ed. lib. bdg. 12.95 (*0-7910-1461-4*) Chelsea Hse.

— Frederick Douglass: Freedom Fighter. (Discovery Biographies Ser.). (Illus.). 80p. (J). (gr. 2-6). 1991. reprint ed. lib. bdg. 12.95 (*0-7910-1410-X*) Chelsea Hse.

— Martin Luther King, Jr. & the Freedom Movement. (Makers of America Ser.). (YA). 1989. 16.95 (*0-8160-1605-4*) Facts on File.

— Martin Luther King, Jr. & the Freedom Movement. 1993. pap. 8.95 (*0-8160-2997-0*) Facts on File.

Patterson, Lillie & Wright, Cornelia H. Oprah Winfrey: Talk Show Host & Actress. LC 89-17002. (Contemporary Women Ser.). (Illus.). 128p. (J). (gr. 6 up). 1990. lib. bdg. 17.95 (*0-89490-289-X*) Enslow Pubs.

Patterson, Lily, jt. auth. see Norman, Winifred L.

Patterson, Lori A. Self-Publishing Made Simple: Step-by-Step Guide No Thinking Required. LC 94-65050. 320p. (Orig.). 1996. 29.95 (*1-884573-04-5*); pap. 19.95 (*1-884573-15-0*) S-By-S Pubns.

Patterson, Lotsee & Snodgrass, Mary E. Indian Terms of the Americas. (Illus.). 150p. 1994. lib. bdg. 35.00 (*1-56308-133-4*) Libs Unl.

Patterson, Lyman R. Copyright in Historical Perspective. LC 68-22415. 1968. 19.95 (*0-8265-1120-1*) Vanderbilt U Pr.

Patterson, M., jt. auth. see Maloy, K.

***Patterson, Margaret C.** Literary Research Guide. 2nd fac. ed. LC 82-20386. 685p. 1984. reprint ed. pap. 180.00 (*0-7837-8032-X*, 2047788) Bks Demand.

Patterson, Margaret C., ed. Author Newsletters & Journals. LC 79-63742. (American Literature, English Literature, & World Literatures in English Information Guide Ser.: Vol. 19). 520p. 1979. 68.00 (*0-8103-1432-0*) Gale.

Patterson, Margaret J., jt. ed. see Russell, Robert H.

Patterson, Mark R. Authority, Autonomy, & Representation in American Literature, 1776-1865. 320p. 1989. 42.50 (*0-691-06743-0*) Princeton U Pr.

***Patterson, Mark W.** Real Estate Portfolios: Acquisition, Management & Disposition. LC 94-37097. (Real Estate Practice Library). 1995. text ed. 115.00 (*0-471-58702-8*, Pub. by Wiley Law Pubns) Wiley.

— Restructuring Troubled Real Estate Loans. (Real Estate Practice Library: No. 1836). 360p. 1992. text ed. 138.00 (*0-471-57466-X*) Wiley.

***Patterson Marketing Staff.** SmARTbook: The Smart Mart to the Arts. (Orig.). 1994. pap. 34.00 (*0-9643197-0-5*) Patterson Mktg.

Patterson, Martha F. The Backyard Bomber of Pacific Palisades: A Love Story. LC 84-52475. (Illus.). 237p. 1984. 9.95 (*0-9614294-0-2*) Seamount Pubns.

Patterson, Martha P. The Working Woman's Guide to Retirement Planning: Saving & Investing NOW for a Secure Future. LC 92-42610. 1993. pap. 15.95 (*0-13-952813-X*) P-H.

Patterson, Marva. Braiding. (Illus.). 192p. 1991. pap. 22.95 (*0-87350-386-4*) Milady Pub.

Patterson, Marvin L. Accelerating Innovation. LC 92-34006. 1993. text ed. 29.95 (*0-442-01378-7*) Van Nos Reinhold.

Patterson, Mary Ann, jt. auth. see Jackson, Sarah.

Patterson, Maureen L. South Asian Civilizations: A Bibliographic Synthesis. LC 81-52518. (Illus.). 900p. 1981. lib. bdg. 70.00 (*0-226-64910-5*) U Ch Pr.

Patterson, Maurice, jt. ed. see Covert, William V.

Patterson, Maurice L. Pioneers of Quarry Hill. (Illus.). 280p. 1984. 19.75 (*0-932334-40-7*); pap. 16.00 (*0-932334-42-3*) Hrt of the Lakes.

Patterson, Mavis, ed. Ladies' Choice: A Collection of Humor by Maine Women. LC 89-5533. (Illus.). 95p. (Orig.). 1982. pap. 4.95 (*0-945980-15-9*) Nrth Country Pr.

Patterson, Michael. Operations Management. 75p. 1983. pap. 5.00 (*0-930204-14-X*) Lord Pub.

Patterson, Michael, ed. see Buchner, Georg.

Patterson, Miles, jt. auth. see Heslin, Richard.

***Patterson, Nancy.** South Sound Places. (Illus.). 64p. (Orig.). 1993. pap. 11.95 (*0-9627201-2-7*) Patcha Pubng.

Patterson, Nancy, jt. auth. see Eskew, Mike.

Patterson, Nancy, jt. auth. see Patterson, Jerry.

Patterson, Nancy R. The Christmas Cup. LC 88-29112. (Illus.). 80p. (J). (gr. 3-5). 1989. 14.95 (*0-531-05821-2*); lib. bdg. 14.99 (*0-531-08421-3*) Orchard Bks Watts.

— The Christmas Cup. 80p. (J). 1991. pap. 2.95 (*0-590-43870-0*, Apple Paperbacks) Scholastic Inc.

— The Shiniest Rock of All. (Illus.). 80p. (J). (gr. 3 up). 1991. 13.00 (*0-374-36805-8*) FS&G.

— Shiniest Rock of All. (J). (ps-3). 1994. pap. 3.95 (*0-374-46615-7*) FS&G.

***Patterson, Neil.** Chalkstream Chronicle. (Illus.). 320p. 1995. 35.00 (*1-55821-425-9*) Lyons & Burford.

Patterson, Nerys. Cattle Lords & Clansmen: The Social Structure of Early Ireland. 2nd ed. (C). 1994. reprint ed. pap. text ed. 21.95 (*0-268-00800-0*) U of Notre Dame Pr.

Patterson-Oriel, Patricia, ed. see Quell, Lawrence A.

Patterson, Orlando. Freedom, Vol. 1. 1992. pap. 15.00 (*0-465-02532-3*) Basic.

— Freedom: Freedom in the Modern World, Vol. II. LC 90-55593. 448p. 1992. 30.00 (*0-465-02537-4*) Basic.

— Slavery & Social Death: A Comparative Study. LC 82-1072. (Illus.). 528p. 1982. 39.95 (*0-674-81082-1*) HUP.

— Slavery & Social Death: A Comparative Study. 528p. 1985. pap. 19.95 (*0-674-81083-X*) HUP.

— Sociology of Slavery. LC 70-84198. 310p. 1975. 35.00 (*0-8386-7469-0*) Fairleigh Dickinson.

***Patterson, P.** Fal: The Dragon Harper. (Illus.). 326p. (Orig.). (YA). 1992. pap. text ed. 19.95 (*1-869890-43-4*) Anthroposophic.

Patterson, P. G. & Pettit, D. G. Ciento Cincuenta Cosas Que Hacer Con Papel. Orig. Title: One Hundred & Fifty Things to Make with Paper. 64p. 1985. reprint ed. pap. 3.50 (*0-311-26604-5*) Casa Bautista.

Patterson, P. R., et al. Psychosocial Aspects of Cystic Fibrosis: A Model for Chronic Lung Disease. LC 72-9893. 1973. text ed. 42.00 (*0-88238-702-2*) Col U Pr.

Patterson, Paige. Song of Solomon. (Everyman's Bible Commentary Ser.). (Orig.). 1986. pap. 7.99 (*0-8024-2057-5*) Moody.

— The Troubled Triumphant Church: An Exposition of I Corinthians. 2nd ed. 326p. reprint ed. pap. 7.95 (*0-317-93397-3*) Criswell Pubns.

***Patterson, Pat.** Sacred Cows in the OR, Vol. II. 1994. pap. 28.00 (*0-945970-03-X*) O R Manager.

Patterson, Pat, ed. see Fernsebner, Billie.

Patterson, Patricia J. Way of Faithfulness: Study Guide to Christians in Japan. (Orig.). 1991. pap. 5.95 (*0-377-00220-8*) Friendship Pr.

Patterson, Paul, et al, eds. Psychosocial Aspects of Cystic Fibrosis: A Model for Chronic Lung Disease. LC 72-9893. 234p. 1973. 12.50 (*0-930194-33-0*) Ctr Thanatology.

***Patterson, Paul E.** Triple Crown. 224p. (Orig.). 1996. pap. 14.95 (*0-86534-240-7*) Sunstone Pr.

Patterson, Paul H. & Purves, Dale, eds. Readings in Developmental Neurobiology. LC 81-68892. 700p. 1982. pap. text ed. 44.00 (*0-87969-144-1*) Cold Spring Harbor.

Patterson, Paul R., et al, eds. Psychosocial Aspects of Cystic Fibrosis: A Model for Chronic Lung Disease. LC 72-9893. 246p. reprint ed. pap. 70.20 (*0-8357-4573-2*, 2037482) Bks Demand.

Patterson, Pernet. The Road to Canaan. 1977. 17.95 (*0-8369-9193-1*, 9062) Ayer.

Patterson, Perry L., ed. Capitalist Goals, Socialist Past: The rise of the Private Sector in Command Economies. LC 93-20305. (C). 1993. pap. text ed. 41.50 (*0-8133-8402-8*) Westview.

Patterson, Philip. Come unto Me. (Illus.). (Orig.). Date not set. pap. 8.99 (*0-89900-613-2*) College Pr Pub.

— The Electronic Millstone: Christian Parenting in a Media Age. 230p. (Orig.). 1992. pap. 9.99 (*0-89900-420-2*) College Pr Pub.

Patterson, Philip & Wilkins, Lee C. Media Ethics: Issues & Cases. 2nd ed. 304p. 1994. pap. write for info. (*0-697-17099-3*) Brown & Benchmark.

Patterson, Philip, jt. ed. see Wilkins, Lee.

***Patterson, Philip D.** Redeeming the Time: The Christian Walk in a Hurried World. LC 94-44044. 1995. 8.99 (*0-89900-726-0*) College Pr Pub.

Patterson, R. D., et al. Expositor's Bible Commentary, Vol. 4. 1988. 37.99 (*0-88469-192-6*) BMH Bks.

Patterson, R. F. Ben Jonson's Conversations with Drummond of Hawthornden. LC 73-22023. (English Literature Ser.: No. 33). 1974. lib. bdg. 47.95 (*0-8383-1835-5*) M S G Haskell Hse.

— Home Medical Dictionary. 256p. (Orig.). 1989. pap. 5.95 (*0-938261-99-1*) PSI & Assocs.

— New Webster's Expanded Dictionary. 384p. (Orig.). 1994. pap. write for info. (*1-884907-01-6*) Paradise Miami.

Patterson, R. F., ed. New Webster's Dictionary. 256p. (Orig.). 1993. pap. 5.95 (*0-938261-80-0*) PSI & Assocs.

— New Webster's Dictionary. 256p. (Orig.). 1994. pap. write for info. (*1-884907-02-4*) Paradise Miami.

— New Webster's Dictionary - Roget's Thesaurus. 512p. 1994. pap. write for info. (*1-884907-00-8*) Paradise Miami.

— New Webster's Dictionary & New Roget's Thesaurus. 512p. (Orig.). 1990. pap. 12.95 (*0-938261-39-8*) PSI & Assocs.

— New Webster's Expanded Dictionary. 384p. (Orig.). 1988. pap. 6.95 (*0-938261-79-7*) PSI & Assocs.

— New Webster's Giant Print Dictionary. 288p. (Orig.). 1990. pap. 5.95 (*0-938261-81-9*) PSI & Assocs.

— New Webster's Large Print Dictionary. large type ed. 256p. 1994. pap. write for info. (*1-884907-03-2*) Paradise Miami.

— New Webster's Pocket Pal Dictionary. 192p. (Orig.). 1989. pap. 3.95 (*0-938261-20-7*) PSI & Assocs.

— Webster's French-English English-French Dictionary. 256p. (Orig.). 1993. pap. 5.95 (*0-938261-15-0*) PSI & Assocs.

— Webster's Spanish-English English-Spanish Dictionary. 192p. (Orig.). (ENG & SPA.). 1993. pap. 2.95 (*0-938261-02-9*) PSI & Assocs.

Patterson, R. Gary. The Walrus Was Paul: The Great Beatle Death Clues of 1969. (Illus.). 162p. (Orig.). 1994. pap. 19.95 (*0-9641163-0-8*) Excursion Prods.

Patterson, R. L., ed. Biochemical Identification of Meat Species: Proceedings of a Seminar in the CEC Programme of Coordination of Livestock Productivity Management, Brussels, Belgium, 27-28 November, 1984. 224p. 1986. 57.75 (*0-85334-408-6*, Pub. by Elsevier Applied Sci UK) Elsevier.

Patterson, R. Michael. Fort Worth: New Frontiers in Excellence. 1990. 32.95 (*0-89781-355-3*) Preferred Mktg.

Patterson, Radha, jt. auth. see Maw, Mary.

Patterson, Ray. House Beautiful. (Illus.). 118p. 1987. pap. 3.95 (*0-936369-05-1*) Son-Rise Pubns.

Patterson, Raymond. The Negro & His Needs. LC 74-178480. (Black Heritage Library Collection). 1977. reprint ed. 25.95 (*0-8369-8929-5*) Ayer.

Patterson, Raymond R. Elemental Blues. Barkan, Stanley H., ed. (Review Chapbook Ser.: No. 19). (Illus.). 48p. 1983. 15.00 (*0-89304-817-8*); 15.00 (*0-89304-842-9*); 5.00 (*0-89304-843-7*); pap. 5.00 (*0-685-49061-0*) Cross-Cultrl NY.

Patterson, Raymond R., jt. auth. see Barkan, Stanley H.

***Patterson, Richard.** Aristotle's Modal Logic: Essence & Entailment in the Organon. (Illus.). 304p. (C). 1995. 54.95 (*0-521-45168-X*) Cambridge U Pr.

— Degree of Guilt. 1994. pap. 5.98 (*0-517-13072-6*) Random Hse Value.

— Effectively Leading. 96p. 1992. pap. text ed. 7.95 (*0-910566-53-4*) Evang Trg Assn.

— Historical Atlas of the Outlaw West. LC 84-82543. (Illus.). 250p. (Orig.). 1984. pap. 16.95 (*0-933472-89-7*) Johnson Bks.

— Image & Reality in Plato's Metaphysics. LC 83-26654. 232p. (C). 1985. lib. bdg. 29.50 (*0-915145-72-3*); pap. text ed. 14.00 (*0-915145-73-1*) Hackett Pub.

Patterson, Richard & White, Dana, eds. Electronic Production Techniques. (Illus.). 100p. (Orig.). (C). 1984. reprint ed. pap. 7.95 (*0-935578-04-8*) ASC Holding.

Patterson, Richard, jt. auth. see Mathias, Harry.

***Patterson, Richard B.** Becoming a Modern Contemplative: A Psychospiritual Model for Personal Growth. LC 94-37758. 106p. 1995. pap. 11.95 (*0-8294-0814-2*, Campion Bks) Loyola Univ Pr.

— Encounters with Angels: The Interplay of Psyche & Spirit in the Counseling Situation. LC 92-24256. 179p. 1992. 10.95 (*0-8294-0736-7*) Loyola Univ Pr.

— In Search of the Wounded Healer. 1990. pap. 9.95 (*0-87193-269-5*) Dimension Bks.

Patterson, Richard D. Nahum, Habakkuk, & Zephaniah: Wycliffe Exegetical Commentary. 1991. 27.99 (*0-8024-9264-9*) Moody.

Patterson, Richard N. Degree of Guilt. LC 92-54446. 1992. 23.00 (*0-679-42064-9*) Knopf.

— Degree of Guilt. 1993. 25.00 (*0-679-42211-0*) Random.

— Degree of Guilt. 1993. reprint ed. mass mkt. 6.99 (*0-345-38184-X*) Ballantine.

— Escape the Night. 384p. 1986. mass mkt. 4.99 (*0-345-33401-9*) Ballantine.

— Eyes of a Child. LC 94-28630. 1995. 24.00 (*0-679-42988-3*) Knopf.

— Eyes of a Child: A Novel. 1995. 23.00 (*0-679-76031-8*) Random.

— The Lasko Tangent. 208p. 1985. mass mkt. 5.99 (*0-345-32532-X*) Ballantine.

— The Lasko Tangent. 1994. mass mkt. 5.99 (*0-345-90128-2*) Ballantine.

— The Outside Man. 240p. 1982. pap. 6.99 (*0-345-30020-3*) Ballantine.

— The Outside Man. 1995. mass mkt. 6.99 (*0-345-90514-8*) Ballantine.

— Private Screening. 448p. 1986. mass mkt. 5.99 (*0-345-31139-6*) Ballantine.

— Private Screening. 1993. pap. 12.00 (*0-345-38572-1*, Ballantine Trade) Ballantine.

— Private Screening. 1994. mass mkt. 5.99 (*0-345-90276-9*) Ballantine.

Patterson, Richard S., jt. ed. see Rutz, Donald A.

***Patterson, Robert B., ed.** The Haskins Society Journal: Studies in Medieval History, Vol. 6, 1994. 240p. 1995. text ed. 53.00 (*0-85115-604-5*) Boydell & Brewer.

— The Haskins Society Journal, No. 5, 1993: Studies in Medieval History. (Illus.). 256p. (C). 1994. text ed. 53.00 (*0-85115-550-2*) Boydell & Brewer.

Patterson, Robert L. The Conception of God in the Philosophy of Thomas Aquinas. 508p. 1977. reprint ed. lib. bdg. 30.00 (*0-915172-27-5*) Richwood Pub.

— Philosophy of William Ellery Channing. LC 76-153342. reprint ed. 23.50 (*0-404-04916-8*) AMS Pr.

Patterson, Robert M., jt. auth. see Hitchcock, Timothy.

Patterson, Robert P., ed. The Haskins Society Journal, Vol. 4, 1992. (Studies in Medieval History). 160p. 1993. text ed. 53.00 (*0-85115-333-X*) Boydell & Brewer.

Patterson, Rod. Reptiles of Southern Africa. (Illus.). 128p. 1989. 39.50 (*0-88359-024-7*) R Curtis Pubng.

Patterson, Roger L. Overcoming Deficits of Aging: A Behavioral Approach. (Applied Clinical Psychology Ser.). 306p. 1982. 55.00 (*0-306-40947-X*, Plenum Pr) Plenum.

Patterson, Roy, et al, eds. Allergic Diseases: Diagnosis & Management. 4th ed. LC 92-19774. 1992. 98.00 (*0-397-51126-4*) Lippincott.

***Patterson, Roy, et al.** Drug Allergy & Protocols for Management of Drug Allergies. 2nd ed. LC 94-69157. 55p. (C). 1995. pap. 33.50 (*0-936587-06-7*) Oceanside Pubns.

Patterson, Roy D., jt. ed. see Moore, Brian C.

Patterson-Rudolph, Carol. Petroglyphs & Pueblo Myths of the Rio Grande. LC 90-49025. (Illus.). 156p. 1990. 29.95 (*0-936755-13-X*) Avanyu Pub.

— Petroglyphs & Pueblo Myths of the Rio Grande. rev. ed. (Illus.). 174p. reprint ed. pap. 29.95 (*0-936755-22-9*) Avanyu Pub.

Patterson, Russell. A View from the Pit. LC 87-46008. (Illus.). 113p. 1987. pap. 12.50 (*0-932845-25-8*) Lowell Pr.

Patterson, Ruth P. The Seed of Sally Good'n: A Black Family of Arkansas, 1833-1953. LC 85-6117. 200p. 1985. 21.00 (*0-8131-1541-8*) U Pr of Ky.

Patterson, S. J. An Introduction to the Theory of the Riemann Zeta-Function. (Cambridge Studies in Advanced Mathematics: No. 14). 176p. 1988. 54.95 (*0-521-33535-3*) Cambridge U Pr.

— An Introduction to the Theory of the Riemann Zeta-Function. (Studies in Advanced Mathematics: No. 14). 170p. (C). 1995. pap. 22.95 (*0-521-49905-4*) Cambridge U Pr.

Patterson, Samuel. Illinois Lobbyists Study, 1964. 2nd ed. LC 75-38490. 1975. write for info. (*0-89138-006-X*) ICPSR.

Patterson, Samuel C. Reaction to the Kennedy Assassination among Political Leaders. 1967. 1.00 (*1-55614-101-7*) U of SD Gov Res Bur.

Patterson, Samuel C. & Wahlke, John C., eds. Comparative Legislative Behaviour: Frontiers of Research. LC 72-3387. (Comparative Studies in Behavioral Science). 323p. reprint ed. pap. 92.10 (*0-317-09357-6*, 2055106) Bks Demand.

Patterson, Samuel C., jt. ed. see Copeland, Gary W.

Patterson, Samuel C., jt. auth. see Jewell, Malcolm E.

Patterson, Samuel C., jt. auth. see Loewenberg, Gerhard.

Patterson, Samuel C., ed. see Loewenberg, Gerhard.

Patterson, Samuel C., jt. ed. see Mughan, Anthony.

Patterson, Samuel W. Horatio Gates: Defender of American Liberties. LC 41-10193. reprint ed. 20.00 (*0-404-04917-6*) AMS Pr.

Patterson, Sandra R. & Thompson, Lawrence S. Medical Terminology from Greek & Latin. LC 77-93780. (GRE & LAT.). 1978. 18.50 (*0-87875-138-6*) Whitston Pub.

Patterson, Sarah. The Distant Summer. large type ed. 1978. 12.00 (*0-7089-0134-4*) Ulverscroft.

Patterson, Seymour. The Microeconomics of Trade. LC 88-29228. (Illus.). 232p. (C). 1989. lib. bdg. 45.50 (*0-943549-02-7*) TJU Pr.

Patterson, Sharon C. I Want to Be Ready: Meditation Based on Quotes from Famous Black Persons. 64p. (Orig.). 1994. pap. 5.95 (*0-687-24133-2*) Abingdon.

Patterson, Sheila. The Last Trek: A Study of the Boer People & the Afrikaner Nation. LC 81-13242. vii, 336p. 1982. reprint ed. text ed. 59.75 (*0-313-23244-X*, PALT, Greenwood Pr) Greenwood.

Patterson, Sheridan. The Patterson Family. LC 93-71855. (Illus.). 367p. 1993. pap. 30.00 (*0-938041-17-7*) Arc Pr AR.

Patterson, Sheron C. Ministry with Black Single Adults. LC 90-80746. 64p. 1990. pap. 4.95 (*0-88177-087-6*, DR087) Discipleship Res.

— Single Principles: The Single Woman's 10 Step Guide to Power. 111p. (Orig.). 1993. pap. 9.95 (*0-9638853-0-8*) Persever Pr.

***Patterson, Sherri, et al.** No No & the Secret Touch: The Gentle Story of a Little Seal Who Learns to Stay Safe, Say "No" & Tell! (Illus.). (J). (gr. 1-6). 1993. pap. 11.95 (*0-614-06765-0*); teacher ed, pap. 14.95 (*0-614-06766-9*); audio, pap. 14.95 (*0-9632276-2-9*); audio 10.95 (*0-614-06767-7*) Natl Self Esteem.

Patterson, Shirley & Zimmerman, Ben. Transitions: The Emergence, Growth & Development of the School of Social Welfare. (Illus.). xii, 192p. (Orig.). 1987. pap. 12.95 (*0-9619225-0-8*) U KS Schl Soc Welfare.

Patterson, Stella W. Dear Mad'm. LC 82-22432. (Illus.). 261p. 1982. lib. bdg. 15.95 (*0-87961-130-8*); pap. 7.95 (*0-87961-131-6*) Naturegraph.

Patterson, Stephen, et al. The Search for Jesus: Modern Scholarship Looks at the Gospels. LC 92-53232. 152p. (Orig.). (C). 1994. pap. text ed. 11.95 (*1-880317-14-1*, 7H44); audio 32.95 (*1-880317-15-X*, 7HC3) Biblical Arch Soc.

Patterson, Stephen E. Political Parties in Revolutionary Massachusetts. LC 72-7991. 312p. 1973. 35.00 (*0-299-06260-0*) U of Wis Pr.

Patterson, Stephen J. The Gospel of Thomas & Jesus: Thomas Christianity, Social Radicalism, & the Quest of the Historical Jesus. LC 91-35781. (Foundations & Facets: New Testament Reference Ser.). 224p. (C). 1992. 26.95 (*0-944344-31-3*); pap. 17.95 (*0-944344-32-1*) Polebridge Pr.

Patterson, Steve & Forrest, Kenton. Rio Grande Ski Train. (Illus.). 64p. 1984. pap. 9.95 (*0-932497-00-4*) Tramway Pr.

Patterson, Susan. I Wish the Hitting Would Stop. (Illus.). 32p. (Orig.). 1987. student ed 3.00 (*0-914633-15-5*) Rape Abuse Crisis.

— I Wish the Hitting Would Stop. rev. ed. (Orig.). 1990. pap. text ed. 19.95 (*0-914633-16-3*) Rape Abuse Crisis.

— I Wish the Hitting Would Stop: A Workbook for Children Living in Violent Homes. rev. ed. 1990. pap. text ed. 3.00 (*0-914633-17-1*) Rape Abuse Crisis.

Patterson, Suzanne, jt. auth. see Beck, Simone.

Patterson, T. J., jt. auth. see Singhal, G. D.

Patterson, T. J., tr. see Zeis, Eduard.

Patterson, T. William. Land Use Planning: Techniques of Implementation. rev. ed. LC 86-2751. 368p. 1988. reprint ed. text ed. 36.50 (*0-89874-944-1*) Krieger.

Patterson, Tanna. Exploring the Creston Valley. (Illus.). 120p. (Orig.). 1989. pap. 9.95 (*0-920641-14-8*) Gordon Soules Bk.

***Patterson-Taylor, Joan.** Free to Be Me: An "in-House" Alternative Approach to Educating the "at Risk" Child. 80p. (Orig.). 1994. pap. 29.95 (*1-56167-180-0*) Am Literary Pr.

Patterson, Ted. The Baltimore Orioles: Forty Years of Magic from 33rd Street to Camden Yards. 192p. 1994. 29.95 (*0-87833-865-9*) Taylor Pub.

— Baltimore Orioles: Forty Years of Magic from 33rd Street to Camden Yards; "the Bible of Bird Base..." 1994. 75.00 (*0-87833-873-X*) Taylor Pub.

Patterson, Terry. Frank Lloyd Wright & the Meaning of Materials. (Architecture Ser.). 1994. text ed. 39.95 (*0-442-01298-5*) Van Nos Reinhold.

Patterson, Thomas. At a Theater Near You: Screen Entertainment from a Christian Perspective. LC 94-13363. (Wheaton Literary Ser.). 216p. 1994. pap. 9.99 (*0-87788-041-7*) Shaw Pubs.

P Q

An Asterisk (*) at the beginning of an entry indicates that the title is appearing in BIP for the first time.

— Why the Campaign Fails. LC 93-9374. 1993. 23.00 (*0-679-41929-2*) Knopf.

Patterson, Thomas C. Archaeology: The Historical Development of Civilizations. 2nd ed. LC 92-16556. 416p. 1992. pap. text ed. 40.00 (*0-13-044298-4*) OUP.

— The Inca Empire: The Formation & Disintegration of a Pre-Capitalist State. 222p. 1991. 49.95 (*0-85496-714-1*) Berg Pubs.

— Inca Empire: The Formation & Disintegration of a Pre-Capitalist State. 256p. 1992. pap. 19.95 (*0-85496-348-0*) Berg Pubs.

— Toward a Social History of Archaeology in the United States. Quilter, Jeffrey, ed. (Case Studies in Archaeology Ser.). 231p. (C). 1994. pap. text ed. write for info. (*0-15-500824-2*) HB Coll Pubs.

Patterson, Thomas C. & Gailey, Christine, eds. Power Relations & State Formation. (Illus.). 169p. (C). 1992. reprint ed. pap. text ed. 10.95 (*1-879215-12-8*) Sheffield WI.

Patterson, Thomas C., jt. ed. see Schmidt, Peter R.

Patterson, Thomas E. The American Democracy. 2nd ed. LC 92-17429. 1993. text ed. write for info. (*0-07-048835-5*) McGraw.

— Out of Order. 1994. pap. 12.00 (*0-679-75510-1*, Vin) Random.

— We the People: A Concise Introduction to American Politics. LC 94-22659. 1994. write for info. (*0-07-048894-0*) McGraw.

Patterson, Tom, jt. auth. see Finster, Howard.

Patterson, Tom, jt. auth. see Terra Museum of American Art Staff.

Patterson, Veronica. How to Make a Terrarium. (CSU Poetry Ser.: Vol. XXIII). 92p. (Orig.). 1987. pap. 6.00 (*0-914946-62-5*) Cleveland St Univ Poetry Ctr.

Patterson, Veronica, ed. see Reiter, Mary J.

Patterson, Veronica, jt. auth. see Stone, Ronda.

Patterson, Vicky, jt. auth. see MacDonald, Dave.

Patterson, W. F., tr. see Robertson, A. T.

Patterson, W. R. Colloquial Spanish. rev. ed. (Colloquial Ser.). pap. 13.95 (*0-7100-6385-7*, RKP) Routledge.

— Language - Students Manual. 1973. 59.95 (*0-8490-0485-3*) Gordon Pr.

— Learn French for English Speakers. 230p. (ENG & FRE.). pap. 19.50 (*0-87557-023-2*, 023-2) Saphrograph.

Patterson, Walt. Rebuilding Romania: Energy, Efficiency, & Economic Transition. 144p. (C). Date not set. pap. 19.95 (*1-85383-207-3*) Brookings.

Patterson, Walt, et al. Power from Plants: The Global Implications of New Technologies for Electricity from Biomass. 80p. (C). 1994. pap. 14.95 (*1-85383-208-1*) Brookings.

Patterson, Walter C., ed. The Energy Alternative. 192p. (C). 1990. 65.00 (*1-85283-284-3*, Pub. by Boxtree Ltd UK) St Mut.

Patterson, Walter C. & Griffin, Richard. Fluidized-Bed Energy Technology: Coming to a Boil. LC 78-60484. (INFORM Report Ser.). 144p. reprint ed. pap. 41.10 (*0-7837-0330-9*, 2040649) Bks Demand.

Patterson, Wanda K. Cobblestones. (Illus.). 66p. 1983. 10.95 (*0-9618774-0-5*) W K Patterson.

Patterson, Ward. Under His Wings. LC 86-70646. (Creative Praise Ser.: No. 1). 160p. 1986. pap. 7.99 (*0-89636-216-7*, LifeJourney) Chariot Family.

Patterson, Wayne. The Korean Frontier in America: Immigration to Hawaii, 1896-1910. LC 88-1163. (Illus.). 288p. 1988. text ed. 30.00 (*0-8248-1090-2*); pap. text ed. 19.95 (*0-8248-1650-1*) UH Pr.

— Koreans in America. (J). 1992. pap. 5.95 (*0-8225-1045-6*, Lerner Publctns) Lerner Group.

— Koreans in America. rev. ed. (Illus.). 64p. (J). (gr. 5 up). 1992. 17.50 (*0-8225-0248-8*, Lerner Publctns) Lerner Group.

— Mathematical Cryptology for Computer Scientists & Mathematicians. 336p. 1987. 68.00 (*0-8476-7438-X*) Rowman.

Patterson, Wayne, ed. see Charr, Easurk E.

Patterson, Wayne A. Bertrand Russell's Philosophy of Logical Atomism. LC 91-17584. (American University Studies: Philosophy: Ser. V, Vol. 89). 364p. 1993. 29.95 (*0-8204-1235-X*) P Lang Pubs.

Patterson, William. Detective's Private Investigation Training Manual. (Illus.). 160p. 1979. pap. 14.95 (*0-87364-161-2*) Paladin Pr.

Patterson, William & Urrutibeheity, Hector. The Lexical Structure of Spanish. LC 73-77744. (Janua Linguarum, Ser. Practica: No. 198). 162p. 1975. pap. text ed. 42.35 (*90-279-3207-7*) Mouton.

Patterson, William B. Fetal Adrenal Hyperplasia: Its Relationship to Late Toxemia. LC 73-90025. (Illus.). 81p. 1973. 6.00 (*0-9606968-0-6*) W B Patterson.

— From the Isle of Skye to the Isle of Maui: A Doctor's Personal Story Including Plantation Medicine & the Cause of High Blood Pressure. (Illus.). 385p. (Orig.). 1991. pap. 20.00 (*0-685-65584-9*) W B Patterson.

Patterson, William D. The Probate Records of Lincoln County Maine. LC 90-64096. 448p. 1991. reprint ed. 39.50 (*0-929539-77-X*) Picton Pr.

Patterson, William H. A Glossary of Words in Use in the Counties of Antrim & Down. (English Dialect Society Publications Ser.: No. 28). 1969. reprint ed. pap. 15.00 (*0-8115-0456-5*) Periodicals Srv.

Patterson, William L. The Man Who Cried Genocide. LC 91-18360. 232p. 1991. pap. 7.95 (*0-7178-0685-5*) Intl Pubs Co.

***Patterson, William L., ed.** Lao-English Dictionary. 1995. write for info. (*1-881265-17-X*) Dunwoody Pr.

Patterson, William L., ed. see Civil Rights Congress Staff.

Patterson, William L., jt. auth. see Lightfoot, Claude.

Patterson, William P. Eating the "I" An Account of the Fourth Way-The Way of Transformation in Ordinary Life. Allen, Barbara C., ed. 368p. (Orig.). 1992. pap. 19.95 (*1-879514-77-X*); boxed 34.95 (*1-879514-76-1*) Arete Commns.

— Struggle of the Magicians: Why Uspenski Left Gurdjieff Exploring the Student-Teacher Relationship. Bodian, Stephen, ed. 168p. (Orig.). Date not set. pap. write for info. (*1-879514-80-X*) Arete Commns.

— Struggle of the Magicians: Why Uspenski Left Gurdjieff Exploring the Student-Teacher Relationship. Bodian, Stephen, ed. 168p. (Orig.). Date not set. write for info. (*1-879514-81-8*) Arete Commns.

Patterson, William R. Learn Spanish for English Speakers. rev. ed. MacAndrew, Ronald, ed. (ENG & SPA.). 19.50 (*0-87557-078-X*, 078-X) Saphrograph.

Patterson, Yvonne. Doubting Thomas. (Arch Bks.). (J). (gr. k-4). 1981. pap. 1.99 (*0-570-06144-X*, 59-1261) Concordia.

***Patteson, Mark.** Equine Cardiology. (Illus.). 224p. 1994. pap. (*0-632-03299-5*, Pub. by Blckwell Sci Pubns UK) Blackwell Sci.

Patteson, Nelda. Clara Driscoll: Savior of the Alamo: Her Life Story Presented Through the Clothes She Wore. (Women of Texas Ser.: Bk. 1). (Illus.). 32p. (J). (gr. 4-7). 1991. pap. 14.95 (*0-9629001-0-9*) Smiley Originals.

— Miriam Amanda Ferguson: First Woman Governor of Texas: Her Life Story Presented Through the Clothes She Wore. (Women of Texas Ser.: 2). (Illus.). p. (Orig.). (J). (gr. 4-8). 1994. pap. 14.95 (*0-9629001-1-7*) Smiley Originals.

Patteson, Richard F. Critical Essay on Donald Barthelme. (Critical Essays on American Literature Ser.). 190p. (C). 1991. text ed. 45.00 (*0-8161-7305-2*, Hall Reference) G K Hall.

— A World Outside: The Fiction of Paul Bowles. 167p. 1987. pap. 7.95 (*0-292-79035-X*) U of Tex Pr.

***Patthy, Laszlo.** Protein Evolution by Exon-Shuffling. (Molecular Biology Intelligence Unit Ser.). 139p. 1995. write for info. (*1-57059-257-8*) R G Landes.

Patti, Archimedes L. Why Vietnam? Prelude to America's Albatross. LC 80-51242. (Illus.). 700p. 1980. pap. 15.00 (*0-520-04783-4*) U CA Pr.

Patti, Charles H. & Frazer, Charles F. Advertising: A Decision-Making Approach. (Illus.). 592p. (C). 1988. text ed. 56.00 (*0-03-071687-X*) Dryden Pr.

Patti, Charles H., et al. Business-to-Business Advertising: A Marketing Management Approach. LC 90-47970. (Illus.). 320p. 1991. 39.95 (*0-8442-3471-0*, NTC Busn Bks) NTC Pub Grp.

Patti, Paul. Silhouettes. 256p. 1991. mass mkt. 3.99 (*0-312-92672-3*) St Martin.

Patti, Rino, et al, eds. Managing for Service Effectiveness in Social Welfare Organizations. LC 87-22930. (Administration in Social Work Ser.: Vol. 11, Nos. 3 & 4). 295p. 1989. text ed. 49.95 (*0-86656-687-2*) Haworth Pr.

***Patti, Sandi.** Merry Christmas with Love. LC 94-20487. (Illus.). (J). (gr. 1 up). 1994. 14.99 (*0-8499-1003-X*) Word Inc.

— Le Voyage. LC 93-7191. (Illus.). 50p. 1993. 12.99 (*0-8499-1065-X*) Word Inc.

Patti, Sebastian T., jt. auth. see Zimmerman, John L.

Pattie, Alice, jt. auth. see Kreis, Bernadine.

Pattie, Alice, jt. auth. see Kreis, Bernardine.

Pattie, D. A. Poetic Reflections. LC 87-72042. 58p. (Orig.). 1987. pap. 1.95 (*0-911789-02-2*) Pattie Prop Inc.

— To Cock a Cannon: A Pilots View of World War II Through the Eyes of a Naval Aviator. LC 82-91126. (Illus.). 164p. 1983. 7.95 (*0-911789-01-4*); pap. 4.95 (*0-911789-00-6*) Pattie Prop Inc.

Pattie, Frank A. Mesmer & Animal Magnetism: A Chapter in the History of Medicine. LC 93-41168. (Illus.). 320p. 1994. 39.95 (*0-9622393-5-6*) Edmonston Pub.

Pattie, James O. Personal Narrative of James O. Pattie. Batman, Richard, ed. LC 88-5221. (Classics of the Fur Trade Ser.). 216p. (Orig.). 1988. 24.95 (*0-87842-206-4*); pap. 14.00 (*0-87842-205-6*) Mountain Pr.

— Personal Narrative of James O. Pattie. (American Biography Ser.). 300p. (Orig.). 1991. reprint ed. lib. bdg. 69.00 (*0-7812-8308-6*) Rprt Serv.

— The Personal Narrative of James O. Pattie: The 1831 Edition. unabridged ed. LC 83-27406. 285p. reprint ed. pap. 81.30 (*0-7837-6011-6*, 2045822) Bks Demand.

— The Personal Narrative of James O. Pattie of Kentucky. Flint, Timothy, ed. LC 72-9464. (Far Western Frontier Ser.). (Illus.). 314p. 1973. reprint ed. 23.95 (*0-405-04992-7*) Ayer.

Pattie, Jane. Cowboy Spurs & Their Makers. LC 90-10889. (Centennial Series of the Association of Former Students: No. 37). (Illus.). 192p. 1991. 39.95 (*0-89096-343-6*) Tex A&M Univ Pr.

Pattie, Steven. For Fathers of Sons. (Illus.). 48p. 1991. 7.95 (*0-8378-1987-3*) Gibson.

***Pattie, T. S.** Manuscripts of the Bible: Greek Bibles in the British Library. rev. ed. (Illus.). 48p. (C). 1995. pap. 9.95 (*0-7123-0403-7*, Pub. by Brit Library UK) U of Toronto Pr.

Pattillo, Craig W. Christmas on Record: Best Selling Xmas Singles & Albums of the Past 40 Years. 220p. 1983. pap. 14.50 (*0-9612044-0-0*) Braemar OR.

— TV Theme Soundtrack Directory & Discography with Cover Versions. 287p. 1990. pap. 14.50 (*0-9612044-2-7*) Braemar OR.

Pattillo, James. Skim: A Novel. LC 91-6442. 1991. 19.95 (*0-939149-50-8*) Soho Press.

Pattillo, James W. Zero-Base Budgeting: A Planning, Resource Allocation & Control Tool. 83p. pap. 9.95 (*0-86641-042-2*, 401) Inst Mgmt Account.

Pattillo, Janice & Vaughan, Elizabeth. Learning Centers for Child-Centered Classrooms. 112p. 1992. 15.95 (*0-8106-0357-8*) NEA.

Pattillo, Manning M., Jr. Private Higher Education in the United States. 46p. (Orig.). (C). 1990. pap. 6.00 (*1-880647-02-8*) U GA Inst High Educ.

Pattinson, James. Across the Narrow Seas. large type ed. (General Ser.). 1993. 20.95 (*0-7089-2811-0*) Ulverscroft.

— Contact Mr. Delgado. large type ed. 1994. 20.95 (*0-7089-3155-3*) Ulverscroft.

— Last in Convoy. 1958. 10.95 (*0-8392-1060-4*) Astor-Honor.

— Silent Voyage. 1959. 10.95 (*0-8392-1105-8*) Astor-Honor.

— The Stalking-Horse. large type ed. LC 94-12704. 272p. 1994. pap. 15.95 (*0-8161-7420-2*) Hall.

— The Wheel of Fortune. large type ed. (Adventure Suspense Ser.). 1991. 21.95 (*0-7089-2376-3*) Ulverscroft.

— Wild Justice. large type ed. (Linford Mystery Library). 1989. pap. 11.95 (*0-7089-6752-3*, Trailtree Bookshop) Ulverscroft.

Pattinson, James A. The Saigon Merchant. large type ed. 274p. 1994. pap. 16.95 (*1-85389-468-0*, Dales) Ulverscroft.

Pattiruhu, Maureen, tr. see Muller, Kal.

Pattis, Anne-Francoise. The French Culture Coloring Book. (Illus.). 64p. (J). 1994. pap. 4.95 (*0-8442-1377-2*, Natl Textbk) NTC Pub Grp.

Pattis, Richard E. Karel the Robot: A Gentle Introduction to the Art of Programming. LC 80-26748. 106p. (C). 1981. Net. pap. text ed. write for info. (*0-471-08928-1*) Wiley.

— Karel the Robot: A Gentle Introduction to the Art of Programming. 2nd ed. LC 94-8087. 1994. text ed. write for info. (*0-471-59725-2*) Wiley.

Pattis, Richard E., jt. auth. see Marateck, Samuel L.

***Pattis, Richard P., et al.** Karel the Robot & Karel the Genie: IBM Software. 1994. disk, pap. text ed. write for info. (*0-471-11734-X*) Wiley.

— Karel the Robot & Karel the Genie: MAC Software. 2nd ed. 1994. pap. text ed. write for info. (*0-471-11733-1*) Wiley.

Pattis, S. William. Advertising. (VGM Career Planner Ser.). 128p. 1989. pap. 7.95 (*0-8442-8675-3*, VGM Career Bks) NTC Pub Grp.

— Careers in Advertising. 1990. pap. 12.95 (*0-8442-8697-4*, VGM Career Bks) NTC Pub Grp.

— Careers in Advertising. 160p. 1991. 16.95 (*0-8442-8696-6*, VGM Career Bks) NTC Pub Grp.

— Opportunities in Advertising Careers. rev. ed. LC 94-49545. 1995. write for info. (*0-8442-4442-2*, VGM Career Bks); pap. write for info. (*0-8442-4443-0*, VGM Career Bks) NTC Pub Grp.

— Opportunities in Magazine Publishing Careers. (Opportunities in...Ser.). (Illus.). 160p. 1992. 13.95 (*0-8442-8179-4*, VGM Career Bks); pap. 10.95 (*0-8442-8180-8*, VGM Career Bks) NTC Pub Grp.

***Pattis, S. William & Carter, Robert A.** Opportunities in Publishing Careers. LC 94-49618. 1995. write for info. (*0-8442-4431-7*, VGM Career Bks); pap. write for info. (*0-8442-4432-5*) NTC Pub Grp.

Pattishall & Hilliard. Trademarks. 1987. write for info. (*0-8205-0501-3*, 725); teacher ed write for info. (*0-8205-0502-1*) Bender.

***Pattishall, Beverly W., et al.** Trademarks & Unfair Competition. LC 94-21711. (Cases & Materials Ser.). 1994. write for info. (*0-256-16475-4*) Bender.

Pattishall, Evan G., Jr. Behavioral Sciences: PreTest Self-Assessment & Review. 6th ed. (Basic Sciences PreTest Ser.). (Illus.). 264p. 1993. pap. text ed. 16.95 (*0-07-051996-X*) Hlth Prof Div.

***Pattishall, Evan G., Jr., ed.** Behavioral Sciences: PreTest Self-Assessment & Review. 7th ed. LC 95-5754. 1995. pap. text ed. 16.95 (*0-07-052084-4*) McGraw.

Pattison, Andrew S. Hegelianism & Personality. 1975. lib. bdg. 59.95 (*0-8490-0288-5*) Gordon Pr.

Pattison, Anna & Pattison, Gordon. Periodontal Instrumentation. 2nd ed. (Illus.). 485p. (C). 1991. pap. text ed. 36.95 (*0-8385-7804-7*, A7804-6) Appleton & Lange.

Pattison, Bruce. Music & Poetry of the English Renaissance. LC 70-127278. (Music Ser.). (Illus.). 1971. reprint ed. lib. bdg. 29.50 (*0-306-71298-9*) Da Capo.

Pattison, Darcy. The River Dragon. LC 90-49931. (Illus.). 32p. (J). (gr. k up). 1991. 13.95 (*0-688-10426-6*); lib. bdg. 13.88 (*0-688-10427-4*) Lothrop.

Pattison, E. Mansell, ed. Selection of Treatment for Alcoholics. LC 79-620007. (NIAAA-RUCAS Alcoholism Treatment Ser.: No. 1). 1982. pap. 22.50 (*0-911290-47-8*) Rutgers Ctr Alcohol.

Pattison, E. Mansell & Kaufman, Edward, eds. Encyclopedic Handbook of Alcoholism. LC 81-24196. 1256p. 1982. 120.00 (*0-89876-017-8*) Gardner Pr.

Pattison, E. Mansell, jt. ed. see Galanter, Marc.

Pattison, E. Scott, ed. Fatty Acids & Their Industrial Applications. 390p. 1968. 10.00 (*0-318-16523-6*) Soap & Detergent.

— Fatty Acids & their Industrial Applications. LC 68-12437. (Illus.). 402p. reprint ed. pap. 114.60 (*0-317-07984-0*, 2055004) Bks Demand.

Pattison, Eugene, jt. auth. see Howells, William Dean.

Pattison, F. L. Granville Sharp Pattison Anatomist & Antagonist, 1791-1851. LC 87-10835. (History of American Science & Technology Ser.). (Illus.). 304p. 1987. 29.50 (*0-8173-0375-8*) U of Ala Pr.

Pattison, George. Art, Modernity & Faith: Towards a Theology of Art. LC 90-48916. 208p. 1991. text ed. 45.00 (*0-312-05707-5*) St Martin.

Pattison, George, ed. Kierkegaard on Art & Communications. LC 91-30318. 192p. 1993. text ed. 49.95 (*0-312-07478-6*) St Martin.

Pattison, Gordon, jt. auth. see Pattison, Anna.

Pattison, Harry C. & D'Appolonia, Elio, eds. RETC Proceedings, Nineteen Seventy-Four, 2 vols. LC 74-84644. (Illus.). 1843p. 1974. reprint ed. 60.00 (*0-89520-024-4*) SMM&E Inc.

Pattison, Iain. History of the British Veterinary Profession, 1791-1948. 222p. 1990. 38.00 (*0-85131-379-5*, Pub. by J A Allen & Co UK) St Mut.

— John McFadyean. 240p. 1990. 32.00 (*0-85131-352-3*, Pub. by J A Allen & Co UK) St Mut.

— ProfessorJames Beart Simonds: A Great British Veterinarian Forgotten. 172p. 1990. 64.00 (*0-85131-491-0*, Pub. by J A Allen & Co UK) St Mut.

Pattison, J. B., jt. auth. see Woods, George.

***Pattison, J. R., et al.** A Practical Guide to Clinical Bacteriology. LC 94-39451. 1995. pap. text ed. 24.95 (*0-471-95288-5*) Wiley.

Pattison, James B. A Programmed Introduction to Gas-Liquid Chromatography. 2nd ed. (Illus.). 320p. reprint ed. pap. 91.20 (*0-685-20641-6*, 2030427) Bks Demand.

Pattison, John R., ed. Parvoviruses & Human Disease. 208p. 1988. 117.00 (*0-8493-5956-2*, QR201, CRC Reprint) Franklin.

Pattison, Joseph E. Acquiring the Future: America's Survival & Success in the Global Economy. 350p. 1989. text ed. 30.00 (*1-55623-184-9*) Irwin Prof Pubng.

— Antidumping & Countervailing Duty Laws. LC 84-14463. (International Business & Law Ser.). 1984. ring bd. 145.00 (*0-87632-446-4*) Clark Boardman Callaghan.

Pattison, Mansell E., ed. Clinical Applications of Social Network Theory: A Special Issue of International Journal of Family Therapy, Vol. 3. LC 81-84340. 88p. 1982. pap. 16.95 (*0-89885-126-2*) Human Sci Pr.

Pattison, Mark. Memoirs. 30.00 (*0-87556-231-0*) Saifer.

— Milton. Morley, John, ed. LC 68-58393. (English Men of Letters Ser.). reprint ed. lib. bdg. 27.50 (*0-404-51725-0*) Madison Bks UPA.

— Milton. (BCL1-PR English Literature Ser.). 227p. 1992. reprint ed. lib. bdg. 79.00 (*0-7812-7388-9*) Rprt Serv.

— Suggestions on Academical Organisation with Especial Reference to Oxford. Metzger, Walter P., ed. (Academic Profession Ser.). 1977. lib. bdg. 29.95 (*0-405-10027-2*) Ayer.

Pattison, Mary Ann. Buffalo County: A Pictorial History. LC 93-4366. 1993. write for info. (*0-89865-870-5*) Donning Co.

Pattison, Pat. Managing Lyric Structure. 112p. 1992. pap. 11.95 (*0-7935-1180-1*, 50481582, Berklee Pr) H Leonard.

— Rhyming Techniques & Strategies. 76p. 1992. pap. 10.95 (*0-7935-1181-X*, 50481583, Berklee Pr) H Leonard.

— Writing Better Lyrics. 192p. 1995. 19.99 (*0-89879-682-2*) Writers Digest.

Pattison, Philippa. Algebraic Models for Social Networks. (Structural Analysis in the Social Sciences Ser.: No. 7). (Illus.). 272p. (C). 1993. 39.95 (*0-521-36568-6*) Cambridge U Pr.

Pattison, Polly. How to Design a Nameplate: A Guide for Art Directors & Editors. LC 81-86058. (Communications Library). 64p. 1982. pap. 19.95 (*0-931368-07-3*) Ragan Comm.

Pattison, Robert. The Great Dissent: John Henry Newman & the Liberal Heresy. 256p. 1991. 37.50 (*0-19-506730-4*) OUP.

— Tennyson & Tradition. LC 79-13247. 178p. 1980. 25.95 (*0-674-87415-3*) HUP.

Pattison, Rodney. Tactics. (Sail to Win Ser.). (Illus.). 64p. 1987. pap. 10.95 (*0-87742-233-8*) Intl Marine.

Pattison, Stephen. Alive & Kicking: Towards a Practical Theology of Illness & Healing. 208p. (C). 1989. pap. text ed. 15.95 (*0-334-01871-4*, SCM Pr) TPI PA.

— A Critique of Pastoral Care. 224p. (C). 1988. 16.95 (*0-334-00280-X*, SCM Pr) TPI PA.

— Pastoral Care & Liberation Theology. (Cambridge Studies in Ideology & Religion: No. 5). 321p. (C). 1994. 59.95 (*0-521-41822-4*) Cambridge U Pr.

Pattison, Stephen, jt. ed. see Seale, Clive.

Pattison, W. T. Life & Works of the Troubadour Raimbaut D'Orange. LC 80-2182. reprint ed. 35.00 (*0-404-19015-4*) AMS Pr.

Pattison, Walter T. Emilia Pardo Bazan. LC 70-120497. (Twayne's World Authors Ser.). 1971. lib. bdg. 17.95 (*0-8057-2120-7*) Irvington.

Pattison, Walter T. & Bleznick, Donald W., eds. Representative Spanish Authors, Vol. 1: From the Middle Ages Through the Eighteenth Century. 3rd ed. (C). 1971. text ed. 27.95 (*0-19-501326-3*) OUP.

— Representative Spanish Authors, Vol. 2: The Nineteenth Century to the Present. 3rd ed. (C). 1971. text ed. 29.95 (*0-19-501433-2*) OUP.

Pattison, William D. Beginnings of the American Rectangular Land Survey Systems, 1704-1800. Bruchey, Stuart, ed. LC 78-56654. (Management of Public Lands in the U. S. Ser.). (Illus.). 1979. reprint ed. lib. bdg. 23.95 (*0-405-11350-1*) Ayer.

Pattisson, Rodney. Boatspeed. 64p. (C). 1990. text ed. 59.00 (*0-906754-25-9*, Pub. by Fernhurst Bks UK) St Mut.

Pattisson, Rodney, ed. Tactics. 2nd ed. 96p. (C). 1993. text ed. 65.00 (*0-906754-75-5*, Pub. by Fernhurst Bks UK) St Mut.

***Pattnaik, Binay K.** Scientific Temper: An Empirical Study. (C). 1992. 22.00x (*81-7033-176-5*, Pub. by Rawat II) S Asia.

Pattnaik, D. D. Political Philosophy of Subash Chandra Bose. 1990. text ed. 22.50 (*81-7045-066-7*, Pub. by Associated Pub Hse II) Advent Bks Div.

Patton. Jersey in Prehistory. 1987. 39.95 (*0-86120-017-9*, Pub. by Aris & Phillips UK) David Brown.

— War As I Knew It. (War Ser.). 1983. pap. 5.99 (*0-553-25991-1*) Bantam.

Patton & Schauf. Introduction to Human Physiology. 736p. 53.95 (*0-8016-6337-7*) Mosby Yr Bk.

P Q

— Study Guide to Accompany Human Physiology. 320p. 1989. pap. 16.95 (*0-8016-4279-5*) Mosby Yr Bk.
Patton & Seeley. Anatomy & Physiology Essentials Lab Manual. 320p. 1991. spiral bd. 24.95 (*0-685-65100-2*) Mosby Yr Bk.
Patton, jt. auth. see Thibodeau, Gary A.
Patton, jt. auth. see Thibodeau.
Patton, et al. Textbook of Physiology, 2 vols., Set. 21th ed. 1989. text ed. 132.50 (*0-7216-1990-8*) Saunders.
Patton, Alex. Patton Ninety-Four Predictions for Rotisser. Date not set. 9.99 (*0-517-10018-5*) Random Hse Value.
— Patton's Nineteen Ninety-Five Predictions for Rotisserie Baseball. 1995. 9.99 (*0-517-12303-7*) Random Hse Value.
Patton, Barbara. Introducing Frederic Chopin. (Introducing the Composers Ser.). (Illus.). (Orig.). (J). (gr. 3-9). 1990. pap. 6.95 (*1-878636-00-6*) Soundboard Bks.
Patton, Barbara W. Introducing Johann Sebastian Bach. (Introducing the Composers Ser.). (Illus.). 48p. (Orig.). (J). (gr. 3-9). 1992. pap. 6.95 (*1-878636-01-4*) Soundboard Bks.
— Introducing Wolfgang Amadeus Mozart. (Introducing the Composers Ser.). (Illus.). 48p. (Orig.). (J). (gr. 3-9). 1991. pap. 6.95 (*1-878636-03-0*) Soundboard Bks.
Patton, Beatrice A. Love Without End. (Illus.). 175p. (Orig.). 1987. pap. 10.00 (*0-914916-79-3*) Ku Paa.
Patton, Bobby R. & Giffin, Kim. Interpersonal Communication in Action: Basic Text & Readings. 2nd ed. (Auer Ser.). (C). 1977. pap. text ed. 14.50 (*0-06-042316-1*) HarpCollege.
Patton, Bobby R., jt. auth. see Griffin, Kim.
Patton, Bobby R., et al. Decision-Making Group Interaction. 3rd ed. 208p. (C). 1990. pap. text ed. 33.50 (*0-06-045066-5*) HarpCollege.
Patton, Boggs & Blow Staff. Emergency Planning & Community Right-to-Know Handbook: Law & Regulations. 4th ed. 192p. 1991. pap. text ed. 67.00 (*0-86587-272-4*) Gov Insts.
— Environmental Law Handbook. Vanderver, Timothy A., Jr., ed. LC 93-47638. 725p. 1994. 115.00 (*0-87179-811-5*) BNA.
Patton, C. V., jt. ed. see Checkoway, B.
Patton, Carl V. Academia in Transition: Mid-Career Change or Early Retirement. (Illus.). 230p. 1984. reprint ed. lib. bdg. 47.50 (*0-8191-4100-3*) U Pr of Amer.
Patton, Carl V., ed. Spontaneous Shelter: International Perspectives & Prospects. LC 87-10002. (Illus.). 256p. (C). 1987. 39.95 (*0-87722-507-9*) Temple U Pr.
Patton, Carl V. & Sawicki, David S. Basic Methods of Policy Analysis & Planning. 2nd ed. 512p. (C). 1993. pap. text ed. write for info. (*0-13-060948-X*) P-H.
Patton, Carl V., jt. auth. see Page, G. William.
Patton, Carole. Os 2.2.1 Secrets with CD ROM. 1994. pap. 44.95 (*1-56884-084-5*) IDG Bks.
Patton, Charles M., jt. auth. see Dick, Thomas P.
Patton, Christopher J. God Is Not a Slot Machine: The Bible on Salvation & Tithing. (Illus.). 112p. (Orig.). 1989. pap. text ed. 7.95 (*0-9623465-0-0*) Sentinel FL.
Patton, Cindy. Inventing AIDS. 160p. 1990. 42.50 (*0-415-90256-8*, A4273, Routledge NY); pap. 13.95 (*0-415-90257-6*, A4277, Routledge NY) Routledge.
— Last Served? Gendering the HIV Pandemic. LC 94-11502. (Social Aspects of AIDS). 1994. write for info. (*0-7484-0189-X*, Pub. by Tay Francis Ltd UK); pap. 17.95 (*0-7484-0190-3*) Taylor & Francis.
— Sex & Germs: The Politics of AIDS. LC 85-26240. 182p. (Orig.). (C). 1985. 35.00 (*0-89608-260-1*); pap. 12.00 (*0-89608-259-8*) South End Pr.
Patton, Cliff. Ghost Rig. (Orig.). 1981. pap. 3.50 (*0-89083-865-8*) Zebra.
— The Omni Strain. (Illus.). 432p. (Orig.). 1981. pap. 2.75 (*0-89083-689-2*) Zebra.
Patton, Cliff & Temple, Leah. Fatal Analysis. 400p. 1988. pap. 3.95 (*0-8217-2351-0*) Zebra.
Patton, Curtis, jt. auth. see Murphy, Dale.
***Patton, D. Keith.** Petroleum Exploration Opportunities in Africa & Countries Beyond. LC 95-3072. 1995. write for info. (*0-87814-440-4*) PennWell Bks.
Patton, David, ed. see Beyer-Machule, Charles & Von Noorden, Gunter K.
Patton, David, ed. see Freeman, H. M. & Tolentino, F.
Patton, David, ed. see Spaeth, George I. & Koch, Douglas D.
Patton, David R. Wildlife Habitat Relationships in Forested Ecosystems. LC 91-14076. (Illus.). 350p. 1992. 45.00 (*0-88192-202-1*) Timber.
Patton, Deborah. Bed & Breakfasts & Country Inns of New England. 2nd ed. 1991. pap. 12.95 (*0-89909-225-X*, 80-650-3) Yankee Bks.
— Bed & Breakfasts & Country Inns of New England. 3rd ed. LC 93-1287. (Travel Guide Ser.). (Illus.). 256p. 1993. pap. 12.95 (*0-89909-367-1*) Yankee Bks.
***Patton, Dick.** Life with Wine: A Practical Guide to the Basice. LC 94-92254. (Illus.). 128p. (Orig.). 1994. pap. 9.95 (*0-9642885-0-8*) R J Patton.
***Patton, Don.** Armadillos. (Nature Bks.). (Illus.). 32p. (J). (gr. 2-6). 1995. lib. bdg. 22.79 (*1-56766-182-3*) Childs World.
— Flamingoes. (Nature Bks.). (Illus.). 32p. (J). (gr. 2-6). 1995. lib. bdg. 22.79 (*1-56766-184-X*) Childs World.
— Funnel Web Spiders. (Nature Bks.). (Illus.). 32p. (J). (gr. 2-6). 1995. lib. bdg. 21.36 (*1-56766-188-2*) Childs World.
— Iguanas. (Nature Bks.). (Illus.). 32p. (J). (gr. 2-6). 1995. lib. bdg. 22.79 (*1-56766-190-4*) Childs World.
— Pythons. (Nature Bks.). (Illus.). 32p. (J). (gr. 2-6). 1995. lib. bdg. 22.79 (*1-56766-180-7*) Childs World.
— Turtles. (Nature Bks.). (Illus.). (J). (gr. 2-6). 1995. lib. bdg. 15.95 (*0-614-04749-8*) Childs World.
Patton, Donald J., jt. ed. see Fernald, Edward A.
Patton, Douglas. Badr al-Din Lu'lu' Atabeg of Mosul, 1211-1259. LC 91-27342. (Occasional Papers, Middle East Center Ser.: No. 3). 122p. (C). 1992. pap. text ed. 12.95 (*0-295-97156-8*) U of Wash Pr.
Patton, F. Lester. Diminishing Returns in Agriculture. LC 68-57575. (Columbia University. Studies in the Social Sciences: No. 284). reprint ed. 20.00 (*0-404-51284-4*) AMS Pr.
Patton, Frances G. Good Morning, Miss Dove. 19.95 (*0-88411-879-7*, Aeonian Pr) Amereon Ltd.
Patton, Frances L. Summary of Christian Doctrine: Sumario de Doctrina Christiana. (SPA.). 4.95 (*84-7228-958-3*, 223039, Pub. by Edit Clie SP) TSELF.
Patton, Fred. The History of Fort Smith, 1817 Through 1992. 468p. 1993. 24.95 (*0-9614629-0-6*); pap. 14.95 (*0-9614629-1-4*) J F Patton.
Patton, Gary M. & Sale-Tinney, Lindsay, eds. Golfing America: Western Edition. 265p. (Orig.). 1993. pap. 16.95 (*0-9636438-0-0*) Golfing Am.
Patton, George S., Jr. The Poems of General George S. Patton, Jr. Lines of Fire. Prioli, Carmine A., ed. LC 90-30990. (Studies in American Literature: Vol. 8). 232p. 1991. 89.95 (*0-88946-162-7*) E Mellen.
Patton, George S. Speech of General George S. Patton to His Third Army. 1982. pap. 2.50 (*0-910746-03-6*, SOG01) Hope Farm.
— War As I Knew It. 1995. pap. 15.95 (*0-395-73529-7*) HM.
Patton, Gerald W. War & Race: The Black Officer in the American Military, 1915 to 1941. LC 80-24629. (Contributions in Afro-American & African Studies: No. 62). (Illus.). 232p. 1981. text ed. 55.00 (*0-313-22176-6*, PWR/, Greenwood Pr) Greenwood.
Patton, Grant W., Jr. & Kistner, Robert W. Atlas of Infertility. 368p. 1984. 99.00 (*0-316-69387-1*, Little Med Div) Little.
Patton, Harold S. Grain Growers' Cooperation in Western Canada. LC 71-100529. reprint ed. 57.50 (*0-404-00630-2*) AMS Pr.
Patton-Hulce, Vicki. Contemporary Legal Issues: Enviornmental Pollution. (Contemporary World Issues Ser.). 300p. 1995. lib. bdg. 39.50 (*0-87436-749-2*) ABC-CLIO.
Patton, Isolde M. My Three Worlds. 167p. 1985. 10.00 (*0-87770-316-7*) Ye Galleon.
Patton, James L. & Smith, Margaret F. The Evolutionary Dynamics of the Pocket Gopher Thomomys bottae, with Emphasis on California Populations. LC 90-11136. (Publications in Zoology: Vol.123). (Illus.). 177p. 1991. pap. 25.00 (*0-520-09761-0*) U CA Pr.
Patton, James M., jt. ed. see Chan, James L.
Patton, James M., et al. A Framework for Evaluating Internal Audit Risk. Holman, Richard, ed. (Research Reports: No. 25). (Illus.). 48p. 1982. pap. text ed. 13.50 (*0-89413-094-3*) Inst Inter Aud.
Patton, James R. Exceptional Children in Focus. 5th ed. 288p. (C). 1990. pap. write for info. (*0-675-21285-5*, Merrill Pub Co) Macmillan.
— Fundamentals of Bank Accounting. (C). 1983. text ed. 37.00 (*0-8359-2119-0*, Reston) P-H.
***Patton, James R. & Polloway, Edward A., eds.** Learning Disabilities: The Challenges of Adulthood. LC 95-14293. 1995. pap. write for info. (*0-89079-581-9*) PRO-ED.
Patton, James R., jt. auth. see Cronin, Mary E.
Patton, James R., jt. auth. see Hoover, John J.
Patton, James R., jt. auth. see Polloway, Edward A.
Patton, James R., et al. Mental Retardation. 3rd ed. 656p. (C). 1990. write for info. (*0-675-21210-3*, Merrill Pub Co) Macmillan.
Patton, James W., jt. ed. see Crabtree, Beth G.
Patton, James W., ed. see Greenville Ladies' Association Staff.
Patton, James W., jt. auth. see Simkins, Francis B.
Patton, Jean. Color to Color: The Black Woman's Guide to the Rainbow for Fashion & Beauty. (Illus.). 128p. (Orig.). 1991. pap. 13.00 (*0-671-69386-7*, Fireside) S&S Trade.
Patton, Jim. Il Basket d'Italia: A Season in Italy with Great food, Good Friends & Some Very Tall Americans. LC 94-16163. 1994. 22.00 (*0-671-86849-7*) S&S Trade.
— Rookie: When Michael Jordan Came to the Minor Leagues. 256p. 1995. 22.12 (*0-201-40959-3*) Addison-Wesley.
Patton, John. Is Human Forgiveness Possible? A Pastoral Care Perspective. LC 85-9191. 192p. (Orig.). 1985. pap. 13.95 (*0-687-19704-X*) Abingdon.
— Pastoral Care in Context: An Introduction to Pastoral Care. LC 93-3262. 288p. 1993. text ed. 20.00 (*0-664-22034-7*) Westminster John Knox.
Patton, John P. Divine Unity: A Universal Spirituality. 303p. (Orig.). 1994. 24.95 (*0-9639382-3-1*); student ed 20.00 (*0-9639382-1-5*); lib. bdg. 29.95 (*0-9639382-2-3*); pap. 14.95 (*0-9639382-0-7*) Ctr Creat Power.
***Patton, Joseph D.** Maintainability & Maintenance Management. 2nd enl. fac. rev. ed. LC 88-13043. (Illus.). 460p. 1994. pap. 131.10 (*0-7837-7633-0*, 2047386) Bks Demand.
Patton, Joseph D., Jr. Maintainability & Maintenance Management. 3rd ed. LC 94-50673. 460p. 1994. 70.00 (*1-55617-510-8*) Instru Soc.
— Preventive Maintenance. LC 82-48557. 208p. 1983. pap. text ed. 30.00 (*0-87664-639-9*, 1639-9) Instru Soc.
— Preventive Maintenance. 2nd ed. LC 94-47619. 1995. pap. write for info. (*1-55617-533-7*) Instru Soc.
— Preventive Maintenance. LC 82-48557. (Illus.). reprint ed. pap. 59.30 (*0-7837-9043-0*, 2049794) Bks Demand.
— Service Parts Management. LC 84-19163. 293p. 1984. text ed. 50.00 (*0-87664-811-1*, 1811-1) Instru Soc.
Patton, Joseph D., Jr., ed. Instrument Maintenance Managers' Sourcebook. 2nd ed. LC 80-83407. (Illus.). 331p. reprint ed. pap. 94.40 (*0-7837-5148-6*, 2044876) Bks Demand.
Patton, Joseph D., jt. auth. see Bleuel, William H.
Patton, Joseph D., Jr.
Patton, Judd W. Missing Dimensions in Economics: Understanding the World Through Economic & Moral Principles. 176p. (Orig.). 1989. pap. text ed. 10.00 (*0-9624095-0-2*) Bellevue College Pr.
Patton, L. T. The Geology of Potter County. (Bulletin Ser.: BULL 2330). (Illus.). 180p. 1923. 0.50 (*0-686-29343-6*) Bur Econ Geology.
— The Geology of Stonewall County, Texas. (Bulletin Ser.: BULL 3027). (Illus.). 77p. 1930. 0.50 (*0-686-29347-9*) Bur Econ Geology.
Patton, Laurie L., ed. Authority, Anxiety, & Canon: Essays in Vedic Interpretation. LC 93-25748. (SUNY Series in Hindu Studies). (Illus.). 334p. 1994. 64.50x (*0-7914-1937-1*); pap. 21.95x (*0-7914-1938-X*) State U NY Pr.
Patton, Mark. Statements in Stone: Monuments & Society in Neolithic Europe. LC 92-30505. (Illus.). 272p. 1993. 59.95 (*0-415-06729-4*, B0308) Routledge.
Patton, Mark A. Visions. LC 90-70313. 49p. 1990. 5.95 (*1-55523-335-X*) Winston-Derek.
***Patton, Marvyl L.** Guide-Lines & God-Lines for Facing Cancer: Mind, Body & Faith Connections. Hermanson, Renee, ed. LC 94-26046. (Illus.). 256p. (Orig.). 1994. pap. 13.95 (*1-880292-12-2*) LangMarc.
***Patton, Mary.** Off to Grandma's House. 2nd ed. (Let Me Read, Level 2, Ser.). (Illus.). (J). 1995. bds. 2.95 (*0-673-36269-8*) GdYrBks.
Patton, Mary, jt. ed. see Archibald, David.
Patton, Michael J. & Meara, Naomi M. Psychoanalytic Counseling. (Series in Psychotherapy & Counselling). 363p. 1992. text ed. 56.95 (*0-471-93421-6*) Wiley.
Patton, Michael J., jt. auth. see Pepinsky, Harold B.
Patton, Michael Q. How to Use Qualitative Methods in Evaluation. 2nd ed. (Program Evaluation Kit Ser.: Vol. 4). 176p. (C). 1987. pap. text ed. 12.95 (*0-8039-3129-8*) Sage.
— Practical Evaluation. (Illus.). 320p. 1982. 44.00 (*0-8039-1904-2*); pap. 21.50 (*0-8039-1905-0*) Sage.
— Qualitative Evaluation & Research Methods. 2nd ed. (Illus.). 536p. (C). 1990. text ed. 48.00 (*0-8039-3779-2*) Sage.
— Utilization-Focused Evaluation. 2nd ed. LC 85-27817. 352p. (C). 1986. text ed. 49.95 (*0-8039-2779-7*); pap. text ed. 24.00 (*0-8039-2566-2*) Sage.
Patton, Michael Q., ed. Family Sexual Abuse: Frontline Research & Evaluation. (Illus.). 248p. 1991. 46.00 (*0-8039-3960-4*); pap. 21.95 (*0-8039-3961-2*) Sage.
Patton, Paul, ed. Nietzsche, Feminism, & Political Theory. LC 92-33978. 264p. 1993. 59.95 (*0-415-08255-2*, B0695, Routledge NY); pap. 16.95 (*0-415-08256-0*, B0699, Routledge NY) Routledge.
Patton, Paul, tr. see Deleuze, Gilles.
Patton, Peter C. & Kent, James M. A Moveable Shore: The Fate of the Connecticut Coast. LC 91-9822. (Living with the Shore Ser.). (Illus.). 159p. 1991. lib. bdg. 52.95 (*0-8223-1128-3*); pap. 21.95 (*0-8223-1147-X*) Duke.
Patton, Phil. Made in U. S. A. The Secret Histories of the Things That Made America Great. (Illus.). 352p. 1992. 24.95 (*0-8021-1276-5*) Grove-Atltic.
— Made in U. S. A. The Secret Histories of the Things That Made America Great. 416p. 1993. pap. 12.50 (*0-14-017588-1*, Penguin Bks) Viking Penguin.
— Technofollies. 1995. 24.95 (*0-8050-3319-X*) H Holt & Co.
Patton, Rob D., ed. The American Family: Life & Health. LC 84-50757. 664p. 1986. text ed. 22.95 (*0-89914-014-9*) Third Party Pub.
Patton, Robert D. & Cissell, William B., eds. Community Organization: Traditional Principles & Modern Applications. (Illus.). 372p. (C). 1990. pap. text ed. 36.50 (*0-9625490-1-0*) Latchpins Pr.
***Patton, Robert F.** Sojourners in Faith: The First 35 Years of Covenant Presbyterian Church, Madison, Wisconsin, 1954-1989. 288p. 1994. 19.95 (*1-881576-25-6*) Providence Hse.
Patton, Robert H. Pattons: A Personal History of an American Family. LC 93-31592. 1994. 25.00 (*0-517-59068-9*, Crown) Crown Pub Group.
Patton, Robert W., et al. Developing & Managing Health-Fitness Facilities. LC 88-13428. (Illus.). 376p. 1989. text ed. 42.00 (*0-87322-203-2*, BPAT0203) Human Kinetics.
— Implementing Health-Fitness Programs. LC 85-10660. (Illus.). 304p. 1986. text ed. 42.00 (*0-87322-038-2*, BPAT0038) Human Kinetics.
Patton, Ron, et al. Fault Diagnosis in Dynamic Systems: Theory & Applications. 464p. 1989. text ed. 97.00 (*0-13-308263-6*) P-H.
Patton, Rosemary & Cooper, Sheila. Ergo: Thinking Critically & Writing Logically. LC 92-24997. (C). 1992. 24.00 (*0-06-500264-4*, HarpT) HarpC.
Patton, Sally J. Alphabetics: A History of Our Alphabet. rev. ed. 92p. (J). (gr. 2-8). 1989. reprint ed. pap. text ed. 14.95 (*0-913705-40-3*) Zephyr Pr AZ.
Patton, Sally J. & Maletis, Margaret. Inventors: A Source Guide for Self-Directed Units. rev. ed. 72p. (J). (gr. 2-6). 1989. reprint ed. pap. text ed. 14.95 (*0-913705-35-7*) Zephyr Pr AZ.
Patton, Sally J. & Maxon, Dianne. Architexture: A Shelter Word. rev. ed. 56p. (J). (gr. 2-6). 1989. reprint ed. pap. text ed. 14.95 (*0-913705-38-1*) Zephyr Pr AZ.
Patton, Sally J., ed. see Madigan, Margaret.
Patton, Sara, ed. see Feldman, Victoria L.
Patton, Sara, ed. see Nielsen, Ashleea.
Patton, Sara, ed. see Taylor, Ted M.
Patton, Sarah, ed. see Pysz, Stephen.
Patton, Stuart & Jensen, Robert G. Biomedical Aspects of Lactation. LC 75-42461. (C). 1976. pap. 60.00 (*0-08-020192-X*, Pub. by Pergamon Repr UK) Franklin.
Patton, Susan O., jt. auth. see Ingersoll, Sandra.
Patton, Temple C. Paint Flow & Pigment Dispersion: A Rheological Approach to Coating & Ink Technology. 2nd ed. LC 78-10774. 631p. 1979. text ed. 189.00 (*0-471-03272-7*, Wiley-Interscience) Wiley.
Patton, Thomas E. & Saunders, Terry R. Securities Fraud: Litigating under Rule 10b-5. 1994. ring bd. 125.00 (*0-8342-0130-5*) Michie Butterworth.
— Securities Fraud: Litigating under Rule 10b-5. suppl. ed. 1993. ring bd. 75.00 (*0-685-74475-2*) Butterworth Legal Pubs.
Patton, Tim & Manno, Karen. PB: SPA Recipes from the Spa at Palm-Aire. (Illus.). 192p. 1989. pap. 8.95 (*0-912608-72-2*) Mid Atlantic.
Patton, Timothy. Summary Judgments in Texas: Practice, Procedure & Review. 400p. 1994. ring bd. 115.00 (*0-409-25573-4*) Michie Butterworth.
— Summary Judgments in Texas: Practice, Procedure & Review. suppl. ed. 400p. 1993. 60.00 (*0-685-74458-2*) Butterworth Legal Pubs.
Patton, Wayne. God Steps Down. 1992. pap. 5.95 (*1-55673-465-4*, 7918) CSS OH.
***Patton, Wesley E.** Sales Force: A Sales Management Simulation. 110p. (C). 1994. pap. 23.95 (*0-256-15009-5*) Irwin.
Patton, William J. Kinematics. (Illus.). 1979. text ed. write for info. (*0-8359-3693-7*, Reston); student ed write for info. (*0-8359-3694-5*, Reston) P-H.
— Materials in Industry. 3rd ed. (Illus.). 480p. (C). 1986. text ed. 52.00 (*0-13-560749-3*) P-H.
— Mechanical Power Transmission. 1980. text ed. 43.00 (*0-13-569905-3*) P-H.
Pattou, E. Hero's Song. (J). (gr. 3-7). 1991. 16.95 (*0-15-233807-1*, HB Juv Bks) HarBrace.
Pattow, Donald & Wresch, William. Communicating Technical Information: A Guide for the Electronic Age. 688p. (C). 1992. pap. text ed. write for info. (*0-13-898669-X*) P-H.
Pattrick, R. A. & Polya, D., eds. Mineralization in the British Isles. 400p. 1992. 85.00 (*0-412-31200-X*, A9626) Chapman & Hall.
Pattrick, R. A., jt. ed. see Vaughan, D. J.
Patty, C. Wayne. Foundations of Topology. LC 92-26369. 368p. 1993. pap. 62.95 (*0-534-93264-9*) PWS Pubs.
Patty, C. Wayne, jt. auth. see Fletcher, Peter.
Patty, C. Wayne, ed. see Fletcher, Peter & Hoyle, Hughes B.
Patty, Catherine. Basic Skills Career Exploration Workbook. (Basic Skills Workbooks). 32p. (gr. 9-12). 1983. 1.98 (*0-8209-0585-2*, CEW-1) ESP.
— Basic Skills Encyclopedia Workbook. (Basic Skills Workbooks). 32p. (gr. 5-9). 1983. 1.98 (*0-8209-0537-2*, UEW-1) ESP.
— Basic Skills Science Workbook: Grade 4. (Basic Skills Workbooks). 32p. (gr. 4). 1982. 1.98 (*0-8209-0403-1*, SW-E) ESP.
— Basic Skills Social Studies Workbook: Grade 3. (Basic Skills Workbooks). 32p. (gr. 3). 1982. 1.98 (*0-8209-0398-1*, SSW-D) ESP.
— Basic Skills Social Studies Workbook: Grade 4. (Basic Skills Workbooks). 32p. (gr. 4). 1982. 1.98 (*0-8209-0399-X*, SSW-E) ESP.
— Basic Skills Social Studies Workbook: Grade 6. (Basic Skills Workbooks). 32p. (gr. 6). 1982. 1.98 (*0-8209-0401-5*, SSW-G) ESP.
— Basic Skills Thinking Development Workbook. (Basic Skills Workbooks). 32p. (gr. 4-7). 1983. 1.98 (*0-8209-0584-4*, TDW-1) ESP.
— Career Exploration. (Social Studies Ser.). 24p. (gr. 9-12). 1979. student ed 5.00 (*0-8209-0260-8*, SS-27) ESP.
— Career Exploration. (Sound Filmstrip Kits Ser.). (gr. 5-8). 1981. teacher ed 34.00 (*0-8209-0440-6*, FCW-17) ESP.
— Community Spirit. (Social Studies Ser.). 24p. (gr. 3-5). 1976. student ed 5.00 (*0-8209-0251-9*, SS-18) ESP.
— Comprehension Development. (Language Arts Ser.). 24p. (gr. 3-5). 1980. student ed 5.00 (*0-8209-0318-3*, LA-4) ESP.
— Developing Citizenship. (Sound Filmstrip Kits Ser.). (gr. 3-6). 1981. teacher ed 34.00 (*0-8209-0439-2*, FCW-16) ESP.
— Electricity. (Sound Filmstrip Kits Ser.). (gr. 3-6). 1981. teacher ed 34.00 (*0-8209-0437-6*, FCW-14) ESP.
— The Healthy Body. (Sound Filmstrip Kits Ser.). (gr. 3-6). 1980. teacher ed 34.00 (*0-8209-0431-7*, FCW-8) ESP.
— The Human Body. (Sound Filmstrip Kits Ser.). (gr. 3-6). 1980. teacher ed 34.00 (*0-8209-0428-7*, FCW-5) ESP.
— Jumbo Science Yearbook: Grade 4. (Jumbo Science Ser.). 96p. (gr. 4). 1978. 18.00 (*0-8209-0025-7*, JSY 4) ESP.
— Jumbo Social Studies Yearbook: Grade 3. (Jumbo Social Studies Ser.). 96p. (gr. 3). 1980. 18.00 (*0-8209-0075-3*, JSSY 3) ESP.
— Jumbo Social Studies Yearbook: Grade 4. (Jumbo Social Studies Ser.). 96p. (gr. 4). 1981. 18.00 (*0-8209-0076-1*, JSSY 4) ESP.
— Jumbo Social Studies Yearbook: Grade 6. (Jumbo Social Studies Ser.). 96p. (gr. 6). 1981. 18.00 (*0-8209-0078-8*, JSSY 6) ESP.
— Learning to Listen. (Language Arts Ser.). 24p. (gr. 4-7). 1980. student ed 5.00 (*0-8209-0317-5*, LA-3) ESP.
— Life's Senses. (Science Ser.). 24p. (gr. 4-8). 1979. student ed 5.00 (*0-8209-0152-0*, S-14) ESP.
— The Orchestra. (Music Ser.). 24p. (gr. 5-9). 1977. student ed 5.00 (*0-8209-0273-X*, MU-2) ESP.
Patty, James S., ed. see Giraudoux, Jean.

P Q

***Patty, L. & Friedrich, P., eds.** Multidomain Proteins: Proceedings of the UNESCO Workshop on Structure & Function of Proteins, Budapest, Sept. 13-15, 1984. 221p. (C). 1986. 78.00x (*963-05-4306-0*, Pub. by Akad Kiado HU) St Mut.

Patty, Robert. Managing Sales People. 2nd ed. (Illus.). 464p. (C). 1982. teacher ed write for info. (*0-8359-4223-6*, Reston); text ed. 34.00 (*0-8359-4221-X*, Reston) P-H.

Patty, Teresa. Discover Your Business Potential: A Comprehensive Self-Evaluation. 96p. 1992. student ed write for info. (*0-9633989-0-3*) New Start Cnslting.

Patunker, B. W. Grasses of Marathwada. 300p. (C). 1979. 100.00 (*0-317-62224-2*, Scientific) St Mut.

Paturas, James & Weinberg, Andrew. Advanced Cardiac Life Support. (Emergency Care Ser.). (C). 1995. pap. text ed. 29.95 (*0-86720-819-8*) Jones & Bartlett.

Paturas, James L. & Werdmann, Michael J. First Aid & Safety for Day Care Providers. Reinberg, Steven E., ed. (Illus.). 100p. (C). 1994. pap. text ed. 15.00 (*1-884225-03-9*) Communs Skills.

Paturas, James L., jt. auth. see Weinberg, Andrew D.

Paturas, James L., jt. ed. see Weinberg, Andrew D.

Paturau, J. M. By-Products of the Cane Sugar Industry: An Introduction to Their Industrial Utilization. 3rd rev. ed. (Sugar Ser.: No. 11). 436p. 1989. 146.25 (*0-444-88214-6*) Elsevier.

Patursson, Trondur. The Faroe Islands: Liv Kjorsvik Schei & Gunnie Moberg. (Illus.). 256p. 1992. 24.95 (*0-7195-5009-2*, Pub. by John Murray UK) Trafalgar.

Patvardhan, V. S. Growth of Indigenous Entrepreneurship, Vol. 1: The House of Garwares India. 1990. 28.00 (*0-685-48709-1*, Pub. by Popular Prakashan II) S Asia.

Patwardhan, jt. auth. see Bunch.

Patwardhan, M. S. Oil & Other Multinationals in India. 170p. 1986. 26.00 (*0-8364-2044-6*, Pub. by Popular Prakashan II) S Asia.

Patwari, A. B. Fundamental Rights & Personal Liberty in India, Pakistan & Bangladesh. (C). 1990. 163.00 (*0-89771-200-5*) St Mut.

Paty, M. La Matiere Derobee: L'Appropriation Critique de l'Objet de la Physique Contemporaine. xx, 442p. 1988. pap. text ed. 72.00 (*2-88124-186-7*) Gordon & Breach.

Paty, Michel, jt. ed. see Lopes, Jose L.

***Patz, N.** To Annabella-Pelican Farmer. 1994. pap. 4.99 (*0-517-13310-5*) Random.

Patz, Nancy. Moses Supposes His Toeses Are Roses. 1989. pap. 4.95 (*0-15-255691-5*) HarBrace.

— Moses Supposes His Toeses Are Roses: And Seven Other Silly Old Rhymes. LC 82-3099. 32p. (J). (ps-3). 1983. 13.95 (*0-15-255690-7*, HB Juv Bks) HarBrace.

— No Thumping No Bumping No Rumpus Tonight! LC 88-7717. (Illus.). 32p. (J). (gr. k-3). 1990. text ed. 13.95 (*0-689-31510-4*, Atheneum Bks Young) S&S Childrens.

— Sarah Bear & Sweet Sidney. LC 88-21300. (Illus.). 32p. (J). (ps-2). 1989. text ed. 13.95 (*0-02-770270-7*, Four Winds Pr) S&S Childrens.

— To Annabella Pelican from Thomas Hippopotamus. LC 90-30038. (Illus.). 32p. (J). (ps-3). 1991. lib. bdg. 13.95 (*0-02-770280-4*, Four Winds Pr) S&S Childrens.

Patz, Naomi & Perman, Jane. In the Beginning: The Jewish Baby Book. (Illus.). 64p. 1983. 13.95 (*0-8074-0258-3*, 510500) UAHC.

Patz, Naomi, jt. auth. see Borowitz, Eugene.

Patzelt, Lawrence H. & Berends, Nancy L. Coronary Artery Bypass Surgery. Grin, Oliver D. & Bouwman, Dorothy, eds. (Patient Education Ser.). (Illus.). 34p. (Orig.). 1991. pap. text ed. 3.00 (*0-929689-41-0*) Ludann Co.

— Heart Valve Surgery. Grin, Oliver D. & Bouwman, Dorothy L., eds. (Patient Education Ser.). (Illus.). 30p. (Orig.). 1991. pap. text ed. 3.00 (*0-929689-42-9*) Ludann Co.

Patzer, Andreas, ed. Franz Overbeck - Erwin Rohde: Briefwechsel. (Supplementa Nietzscheana Ser.: Vol. 1). xxxiii, 652p. (C). 1990. lib. bdg. 173.10x (*3-11-011895-5*) De Gruyter.

Patzer, Gordon L. The Physical Attractiveness Phenomena. LC 85-6593. (Perspectives in Social Psychology Ser.). 320p. 1985. 59.50 (*0-306-41783-9*, Plenum Pr) Plenum.

— Using Secondary Data in Marketing Research. LC 94-40460. 184p. 1995. text ed. 49.95 (*0-89930-961-5*, Quorum Bks) Greenwood.

Patzert, Rudolph W. Running the Palestine Blockade: The Last Voyage of the Paducah. LC 93-28122. 244p. 1994. 25.00 (*1-55750-679-5*) Naval Inst Pr.

Patzia, Arthur G. Ephesians, Colossians, Philemon: New International Biblical Commentary. 336p. 1991. pap. 9.95 (*0-943575-19-2*) Hendrickson MA.

— The Making of the New Testament: Origin, Collection, Text & Canon. LC 94-45403. 228p. (Orig.). 1995. pap. text ed. 14.99 (*0-8308-1859-6*, 1859) InterVarsity.

Patzold, Michael, jt. auth. see Gramley, Stephan.

Pau. Failure Diagnosis & Performance Monitoring. (Control & Systems Theory Ser.: Vol. 11). 448p. 1981. 125.00 (*0-8247-1018-5*) Dekker.

Pau, F. L., ed. see Basar, Tamer S.

Pau, H. Differential Diagnosis of Eye Disease. 2nd enl. rev. ed. Blodi, F. C., tr. (Illus.). 560p. 1988. 149.00 (*0-86577-264-9*) Thieme Med Pubs.

Pau, Hana, tr. see Williams, Julie S.

Pau, Hannah H., ed. see Lowe, Ruby H.

Pau, Hannah H., ed. see Williams, Julie S.

Pau, L. F. & Olafsson, R. Fish Quality Control by Computer Vision. (Food Science & Technology Ser.: Vol. 43). 320p. 1991. 135.00 (*0-8247-8426-X*) Dekker.

Pau-Llosa, Ricardo. Bread of the Imagined. LC 91-11914. 88p. 1992. pap. 8.00 (*0-927534-16-9*) Biling Rev-Pr.

— Cuba. LC 92-71503. (Poetry Ser.). 1993. 16.95 (*0-88748-150-7*); pap. 9.95 (*0-88748-151-5*) Carnegie-Mellon.

— Humberto Calzada: A Retrospective of Work from 1979-1990. Echerri, Vincente, tr. LC 91-73400. (Illus.). 96p. (Orig.) (SPA.). 1991. pap. 25.00 (*1-880511-00-2*) Bass Museum.

— Sorting Metaphors. 1983. pap. 8.00 (*0-938078-15-1*) Anhinga Pr.

Pau, Louis & Willums, Jan-Olaf, eds. Manufacturing Automation at the Crossroads: Standardization in CIM Software. LC 93-78479. 181p. 1993. pap. 70.00 (*90-5199-137-1*, Pub. by IOS Pr NE) IOS Press.

Pau, Louis F. Computer Vision for Electronics Manufacturing. LC 89-22910. (Advances in Computer Vision & Machine Intelligence Ser.). (Illus.). 340p. 1990. 65.00 (*0-306-43182-3*, Plenum Pr) Plenum.

Pau, Louis F., ed. Artificial Intelligence in Economics & Management. 292p. 1986. 69.25 (*0-444-87961-7*, North Holland) Elsevier.

— Mapping & Spatial Modelling for Navigation. (NATO ASI Series F: Computer & Systems Sciences, Special Programme AET: Vol. 65). (Illus.). viii, 357p. 1990. 79.00 (*0-387-52711-7*) Spr-Verlag.

Pau, Louis F. & Gianotti, C. Economic & Financial Knowledge-Based Processing. (Illus.). xv, 364p. 1990. 88.00 (*0-387-53043-6*) Spr-Verlag.

Pau, Louis F. & Nahas, M. Y. El. An Introduction to Infrared Image Acquistion & Classification Systems. 268p. 1983. text ed. 124.50 (*0-471-90151-2*, Wiley-Interscience) Wiley.

Pau, Louis F., et al, eds. Expert Systems in Economics, Banking & Management. 476p. 1989. 97.50 (*0-444-88060-7*, North Holland) Elsevier.

Paubert-Braquet, M., et al, eds. Foods, Nutrition & Immunity. (Dynamic Nutrition Research Ser.: Vol. 1). (Illus.). viii, 126p. 1992. 97.75 (*3-8055-5605-5*) S Karger.

— Lipid Mediators in the Immunology of Shock. LC 87-29239. (NATO ASI Series A, Life Sciences: Vol. 139). (Illus.). 540p. 1988. 135.00 (*0-306-42694-3*, Plenum Pr) Plenum.

Pauchant, Thierry C. & Mitroff, Ian I. Transforming the Crisis-Prone Organization: Preventing Individual, Organizational, & Environmental Tragedies. LC 91-37910. (Management Ser.). 275p. 1992. 29.95 (*1-55542-407-4*) Jossey-Bass.

Pauchant, Thierry C., et al. In Search of Meaning: Managing for the Health of Our Organizations, Our Communities, & the Natural World. (Management Ser.). 368p. 1994. 16.95 (*0-7879-0031-1*) Jossey-Bass.

Pauchet, V. & Dupret, S. Atlas Manual de Anatomia. 6th ed. Rodrigo Garcia, Ignacio, ed. 518p. (SPA.). 1978. pap. 29.95 (*0-8288-4863-7*, S12343) Fr & Eur.

Pauchet, Victor & Dupret, S. Atlas de Anatomia. 6th ed. 520p. 1989. pap. 24.95 (*0-7859-5797-9*) Fr & Eur.

Pauck, Wilhelm, ed. Luther: Lectures on Romans. LC 61-13626. (Library of Christian Classics). 502p. 1977. pap. 14.99 (*0-664-24151-4*, Westminster) Westminster John Knox.

— Melanchthon & Bucer. LC 69-12309. (Library of Christian Classics). 422p. 1980. pap. 16.99 (*0-664-24164-6*, Westminster) Westminster John Knox.

Paudel, M., ed. Agriculture & Industrial Finance in Nepal. 147p. (C). 1987. 200.00 (*0-89771-046-0*, Pub. by Ratna Pustak Bhandar) St Mut.

Paudel, M. M., ed. Planning for Agriculture Development in Nepal. 216p. (C). 1985. 250.00 (*0-89771-054-1*, Pub. by Ratna Pustak Bhandar) St Mut.

Paudel, Mehan M. Agriculture & Industrial Finance in Nepal. 1986. 45.00 (*0-7855-0239-4*, Pub. by Ratna Pustak Bhandar) St Mut.

Paudel, Mehar M. Planning for Agriculture Development in Nepal. 1985. 63.00 (*0-7855-0250-5*, Pub. by Ratna Pustak Bhandar) St Mut.

Paudler, William W., jt. auth. see Newkome, George R.

Pauer, Gyula, jt. auth. see Ulack, Richard.

***Pauer-Studer, Herlinde, ed.** Norms, Values, & Society. (Vienna Circle Institute Yearbook Ser.). 360p. (C). 1994. lib. bdg. 115.00 (*0-7923-3071-4*) Kluwer Ac.

Pauerstein, C. J., ed. Seminar on Tubal Physiology & Biochemistry. (Journal: Gynecologic Investigation: Vol. 6, Nos. 3-4). iv, 160p. 1975. reprint ed. 45.00 (*3-8055-2252-5*) S Karger.

Pauerstein, Carl, ed. Clinical Obstetrics. 1050p. 1987. text ed. 58.00 (*0-471-89586-5*) Churchill.

Pauerstein, Carl J., jt. auth. see Woodruff, James D.

Paueti, Charles. Panati's Browser's Book of Beginnings. (Illus.). 430p. 1990. pap. 8.95 (*0-395-56238-4*) HM.

Paugh, Tom, ed. The Sports Afield Treasury of Fly Fishing. (Illus.). 320p. 1989. 24.95 (*1-55821-037-7*) Lyons & Burford.

Pauk, Walter. How to Study in College, 4 Vols. 4th ed. LC 88-81354. 384p. (C). 1988. pap. 25.96 (*0-395-43409-2*) HM.

— How to Study in College. 4th ed. 384p. 1989. teacher ed write for info. (*0-318-63329-9*) HM.

— Six-Way Paragraphs: Advanced Level. 240p. 1983. pap. text ed. 9.75 (*0-89061-303-6*, 731) Jamestown Pubs.

— Six-Way Paragraphs: Middle Level. 240p. 1983. pap. 9.50 (*0-89061-302-8*, 730) Jamestown Pubs.

— Study Skills for Community & Junior Colleges. LC 87-60317. (Illus.). 126p. (C). 1987. pap. text ed. 8.95 (*0-9614487-1-7*) Reston-Stuart Pub.

— A User's Guide to College: Making Notes & Taking Tests: Conversations with Dr. Walter Pauk. (Illus.). 128p. (C). 1988. pap. text ed. 6.75 (*0-89061-481-4*) Jamestown Pubs.

Pauk, Walter & Millman, J. How to Take Tests. 1969. pap. text ed. 6.95 (*0-07-048915-7*) McGraw.

Pauk, Walter, ed. see O. Henry.

Pauker, G. Y., ed. Energy Efficiency & Conservation in the Asia-Pacific Region: Proceedings of the Fourth Workshop, Honolulu, Hawaii, June 2-5, 1981. 200p. 1983. pap. 28.00 (*0-08-030532-6*, Pergamon Pr) Elsevier.

Pauker, Guy J., ed. Current Attitudes & Reactions to Soviet Policies in the Asia-Pacific Region. 155p. (C). 1986. ring bd. 12.50 (*0-317-91350-6*) Pac Forum.

Pauker, John. Angry Candy. (Poetry Ser.). 48p. 1976. pap. 5.95 (*0-917530-01-2*) Pig Iron Pr.

Pauker, Robert, jt. auth. see Krupp, Judy-Arin.

Pauker, Robert, jt. auth. see Portner, Hal.

Pauker, Robert A. Teaching Thinking & Reasoning Skills. Brodinsky, Ben, ed. (Critical Issues Report Ser.). 80p. (Orig.). 1987. pap. text ed. 13.95 (*0-87652-112-X*, 021-00175) Am Assn Sch Admin.

Pauker, Samuel, jt. auth. see Arond, Miriam.

Paukert, F. & Robinson, D., eds. Incomes Policies in the Wider Context: Wage, Price & Fiscal Inititiatives in Developing Countries. v, 259p. (Orig.). 1992. pap. 28.00 (*92-2-107749-7*) Intl Labour Office.

Paukert, Liba & Richards, Peter, eds. Defence Expenditure, Industrial Conversion & Local Employment. ix, 228p. 1991. 32.00 (*92-2-107288-6*); pap. 24.00 (*92-2-107287-8*) Intl Labour Office.

Pauketat, Timothy R. The Ascent of Chiefs: Cahokia & Mississippian Politics in Native North America. LC 93-42734. (Illus.). 256p. (C). 1994. pap. text ed. 28.95 (*0-8173-0728-1*) U of Ala Pr.

Pauketat, Timothy R., jt. auth. see Esarey, Duane.

Pauketat, Timothy R., et al. Temples of Cahokia Lords: Preston Holder's 1955-1956 Excavation of Kunnemann Mound. LC 93-13529. (Memoirs Ser.: No. 26). 1993. pap. 28.00 (*0-915703-33-5*) U Mich Mus Anthro.

Paukovits, ed. Growth Regulation & Carcinogenesis, 2 vols., I. 1990. 205.00 (*0-8493-5960-0*, QH604) CRC Pr.

— Growth Regulation & Carcinogenesis, 2 vols., II. 1990. 217.00 (*0-8493-5961-9*, QH604) CRC Pr.

Paul. Accounting Fundamentals. 2nd ed. 1991. pap. 64.95 (*0-409-10012-9*) Buttrwrth-Heinemann.

— Bad Girls' Money. 1993. mass mkt. 4.50 (*0-06-108158-2*, Harp PBks) HarpC.

— Death of a Salesman (Miller) (Book Notes Ser.). (C). 1984. pap. 2.95 (*0-8120-3410-4*) Barron.

— Practical High-Risk Obstetrics. 1991. 29.95 (*0-8151-6715-6*, Yr Bk Med Pubs) Mosby Yr Bk.

Paul & Houng-Lee. Handbook of Hong Kong Tax Statutes. 1990. pap. 162.00 (*0-409-99582-7*) Butterworth Legal Pubs.

Paul & Solez, eds. Organ Transplantation: Long-Term Results. LC 92-18547. 432p. 1992. 160.00 (*0-8247-8599-1*) Dekker.

Paul, jt. auth. see Feder.

Paul, jt. auth. see McLaren.

Paul, A. A. & Southgate, David A. McCance & Widdowson's Composition of Foods. 4th ed. 418p. 1978. 118.00 (*0-444-80027-1*) Elsevier.

Paul, A. A., et al, eds. McCance & Widdowson's Composition of Food: First Supplement. 114p. 1981. pap. 59.50 (*0-444-80220-7*) Elsevier.

Paul, A. J., et al. Phytoplankton, Zooplankton, & Ichthyoplankton in Resurrection Bay, Northern Gulf of Alaska in 1988. (Alaska Sea Grant Report: No. 91-02). 22p. 1991. pap. 4.00 (*1-56612-002-0*) AK Sea Grant CP.

Paul, Aileen. Coloring Calendar Cookbook for Kids. (Illus.). 24p. (Orig.). (J). (gr. 5 up). 1982. pap. 2.95 (*0-913270-90-3*) Sunstone Pr.

Paul, Allen. Katyn: The Untold Story of Stalin's Polish Massacre. 352p. 1991. text ed. 24.95 (*0-684-19215-2*, Scribners) S&S Trade.

Paul, Amal. Chemistry of Glasses. 2nd ed. (Illus.). 340p. 1989. 75.00 (*0-685-30073-0*) Chapman & Hall.

Paul, Amy C., ed. Managing for Tomorrow: Global Change & Local Futures. (Practical Management Ser.). (Illus.). 188p. 1990. 23.95 (*0-87326-061-9*) Intl City-Cnty Mgt.

***Paul, Anand J. & Sobolewski, Michael, eds.** Concurrent Engineering: Research & Applications Conference Proceedings 1994. 800p. 1994. pap. 40.00 (*0-9642449-0-X*) Concurrent Tech.

Paul, Ann W. Eight Hands Round: A Patchwork Alphabet. LC 88-745. (Illus.). 32p. (J). (gr. 3 up). 1991. 15.00 (*0-06-024689-8*); lib. bdg. 14.89 (*0-06-024704-5*) HarpC Child Bks.

— The Seasons Sewn: A Year in Patchwork. LC 94-35358. (Illus.). (J). 1996. write for info. (*0-15-276918-8*, Browndeer Pr) HarBrace.

— Shadows are About. (Illus.). 32p. (J). 1992. 13.95 (*0-590-44842-0*, Scholastic Hardcover) Scholastic Inc.

Paul, Anne. Paracas Ritual Attire: Symbols of Authority in Ancient Peru. LC 89-48729. (Civilization of the American Indian Ser.: No. 195). (Illus.). 200p. 1990. 49.95 (*0-8061-2230-7*) U of Okla Pr.

Paul, Anne, ed. Paracas Art & Architecture: Object & Context in South Coastal Peru. LC 91-16740. (Illus.). 455p. 1991. text ed. 42.95 (*0-87745-327-6*) U of Iowa Pr.

***Paul, Anthony.** The Tiger Who Lost His Stripes. 2nd ed. LC 95-15472. (Illus.). (J). 1995. write for info. (*0-15-200992-2*) HarBrace.

— The Water Garden. 167p. 1986. pap. 17.00 (*0-14-046756-4*, Penguin Bks) Viking Penguin.

Paul, Anthony M., jt. ed. see Olson, Raymond E.

Paul, Armine. Programmed Topics in General Chemistry. 1981. 13.00 (*0-88252-095-4*) Paladin Hse.

Paul, Armine D. Lab Manual for Introductory College Chemistry. 1981. spiral bd. 14.00 (*0-88252-020-2*) Paladin Hse.

— Programmed Topics in Organic & Biochemistry. 1981. spiral bd. 10.00 (*0-88252-060-1*) Paladin Hse.

Paul, Arnold M. Conservative Crisis & the Rule of Law: Attitudes of Bar & Bench 1887-1895. 18.50 (*0-8446-0839-4*) Peter Smith.

Paul, B., ed. see Symposium on Mechanics of Transportation Suspension Systems Staff.

Paul, Barbara. The Apostrophe Thief: A Mystery with Marian Larch. LC 93-16109. 256p. 1993. text ed. 20.00 (*0-684-19553-4*, Scribners) S&S Trade.

— Cadenza for Caruso. Date not set. pap. 5.95 (*1-55882-134-1*) Intl Polygonics.

— The Curse of Halewood. large type ed. (General Ser.). 496p. 1993. 21.95 (*0-7089-2926-5*) Ulverscroft.

— Fare Play: A Mystery with Marian Larch. 256p. 1995. 20.00 (*0-684-19715-4*, Scribners) S&S Trade.

— In-Laws & Outlaws. large type ed. (General Ser.). 323p. 1991. text ed. 18.95 (*0-8161-5239-X*, Large Print Bks) Hall.

— Liars & Tyrants & People Who Turn Blue. 179p. pap. 5.95 (*1-55882-110-4*) Intl Polygonics.

— You Have the Right to Remain Silent. (Mystery Ser.). 1993. mass mkt. 3.99 (*0-373-26132-2*, 1-26132-0) Harlequin Bks.

— You Have the Right to Remain Silent: A Mystery with Marian Larch. 256p. 1992. text ed. 20.00 (*0-684-19380-9*, Scribners) S&S Trade.

— Your Eyelids Are Growing Heavy. LC 92-70413. 188p. 1992. reprint ed. pap. 5.95 (*1-55882-126-0*, Lib Crime Classics) Intl Polygonics.

Paul, Barbara D. The Germans after WWII. (History-Reference Ser.). 285p. 1990. text ed. 39.00 (*0-8161-8994-3*, Hall Reference) Macmillan.

— The Polish-German Boderlands: An Annotated Bibliography. LC 94-13054. (Bibliographies & Indexes in World History Ser.: Vol. 35). 224p. 1994. text ed. 69.50 (*0-313-29162-4*, Greenwood Pr) Greenwood.

Paul, Benjamin D., ed. Health, Culture & Community: Case Studies of Public Reactions to Health Programs. LC 55-10583. 494p. 1955. pap. 22.50 (*0-87154-653-1*) Russell Sage.

***Paul, Bernard A., et al.** Backyard Archaeology at the Willis Allen House, 1857-1945. Rubach, Bonita K., ed. (Illus.). 28p. (Orig.). 1994. pap. write for info. (*0-913415-08-1*) Am Resources.

***Paul, Bette.** The A-One Scam. LC 94-79392. (Ten-Minute Mysteries Ser.). 32p. (YA). (gr. 6-12). 1994. pap. 2.49 (*1-56103-801-6*) Lake Pub Co.

— The A-One Scam Readalong. LC 94-79392. (Ten-Minute Mysteries Ser.). 32p. (YA). (gr. 6-12). 1994. audio, pap. 12.39 (*1-56103-803-2*) Lake Pub Co.

Paul, Bil. The Pacific Crest Bicycle Trail. (Illus.). 200p. (Orig.). 1991. pap. 13.95 (*0-931255-06-6*) Bittersweet Pub.

— The Tri-X Chronicles. LC 73-86842. (Illus.). 1972. pap. 3.45 (*0-9600650-0-8*) Alchemist-Light.

***Paul, Bill.** Getting In: Inside the College Admissions Process. 256p. 1995. write for info. (*0-201-62256-4*) Addison-Wesley.

Paul, Bobbi, jt. auth. see Mosteller, Lee.

Paul-Boncour, Joseph. Recollections of the Third Republic. 9.95 (*0-8315-0050-6*) Speller.

Paul, C., tr. see Novikov-Priboi, Aleksei S.

Paul, C. Kegan. William Godwin: His Friends & Contemporaries, 2 Vols, 1. LC 73-115359. reprint ed. write for info. (*0-404-04942-7*) AMS Pr.

— William Godwin: His Friends & Contemporaries, 2 Vols, 2. LC 73-115359. reprint ed. write for info. (*0-404-04943-5*) AMS Pr.

— William Godwin: His Friends & Contemporaries, 2 Vols, Set. LC 73-115359. reprint ed. write for info. (*0-404-04941-9*) AMS Pr.

Paul, C. Kegan, ed. see Huysmans, Joris K.

Paul, C. Kegan, tr. see Huysmans, Joris K.

Paul, C. R. & Smith, A. B., eds. Echinoderm Phylogeny & Evolutionary Biology. (Current Geological Concepts Ser.: No. 1). (Illus.). 392p. 1988. 115.00 (*0-19-854491-X*) OUP.

Paul, Candace, jt. auth. see Paul, Shale.

***Paul, Carol.** Revitalizing Apathetic Communities No. 16. 3rd rev. ed. (GAP Report Ser.: No. 16). 16p. (C). 1994. pap. 14.50 (*0-944715-34-6*) CAI.

Paul, Cedar, tr. see De Man, Henri.

Paul, Cedar, tr. see Mussolini, Benito.

Paul, Cedar, tr. see Oechsli, Wilhelm.

Paul, Cedar, tr. see Schnitzler, Arthur.

Paul, Cedar, tr. see Sigerist, Henry E.

Paul, Cedar, tr. see Spann, Othman.

Paul, Cedar, tr. see Wittels, Fritz.

Paul, Cedar, tr. see Zweig, Stefan.

Paul, Christian, ed. see Hoehne, Manfred.

Paul, Christina, tr. see Glowacki, Janusz.

Paul, Clayton R. Analysis of Linear Circuits. 896p. 1988. text ed. 49.95 (*0-07-045919-3*) McGraw.

— Analysis of Linear Circuits. 1989. text ed. write for info. (*0-07-909340-X*) McGraw.

— Analysis of Multiconductor Transmission Lines. LC 94-5704. (Microwave & Optical Engineering Ser.). 1994. text ed. 79.95 (*0-471-02080-X*) Wiley.

— Introduction to Electromagnetic Compatibility. (Series in Microwave & Optical Engineering: No. 1187). 784p. 1992. text ed. 89.95 (*0-471-54927-4*) Wiley.

Paul, Clayton R. & Nasar, Syed A. Introduction to Electrical Engineering. 2nd ed. 1992. text ed. write for info. (*0-07-011322-X*) McGraw.

— Introduction to Electromagnetic Fields. 2nd ed. (Electrical Engineering "Electromagnetics" Ser.). 760p. 1987. text ed. write for info. (*0-07-045908-8*) McGraw.

Paul, Clayton R., jt. auth. see Nasar, Syed A.

***Paul D. Converse Symposium Staff.** Proceedings: 13th Paul D. Converse Symposium, 1992, University of Illinois. Monroe, Kent & Sudharshan, Devanathan, eds. LC 94-46837. (Proceedings Ser.). 1995. 35.00 (*0-87757-254-2*) Am Mktg.

Paul, D. E., jt. auth. see Carter, G. F.

PQ

1995. pap. 9.95 (*0-9642761-0-0*) PakDonald Pubng.
Our inner cities are cesspools of poverty, islands of decay, drugs & crime: no jobs, no money, no escape. No escape, that is, unless someone took a dozen families away out into the countryside & showed them how to establish their own self-sufficient community, a community with its own computerized currency system, where members are paid for their work, where there would be jobs for all, free enterprise, & a chance for new life. Then, when those families were established, they could plan & work to bring out more, to build up a self-reliant group of five or six hundred men, women, & children. Next, close by, when needed, they would start up another. Communities not just for blacks, but for any other group: VietNam vets, seniors on low pensions, unemployed executives, or New-Age enthusiasts wanting to farm organically, to live harmlessly off the land. Dollars will be needed to buy things the community cannot make, but dollars, too, are plentiful; there will be a guaranteed dollar income for all! Utopia? No, NEWTOPIA! This is the book which spells out the details, why the project must be done, & how it can be attained. PakDonald Publishing Inc., P.O. Box 231101, Tigard, OR 97281-1101. ***Publisher Provided Annotation.***

Paul, D. K., ed. Fiber Optics Reliability: Benign & Adverse Environments. 191p. 1987. 45.00 (*0-89252-877-X*, VOL. 0842) SPIE.

Paul, D. K., et al, eds. Fiber Optics Reliability: Benign & Adverse Environments. 1988. 59.00 (*0-8194-0027-0*, 992) SPIE.

Paul, D. R. & Newman, Seymour, eds. Polymer Blends, 1. 1978. text ed. 187.00 (*0-12-546801-6*) Acad Pr.

Paul, D. R. & Sperling, L. H., eds. Multicomponent Polymer Materials. LC 85-20475. (Advances in Chemistry Ser.: No. 211). (Illus.). xii, 352p. 1986. 87.95 (*0-8412-0899-9*) Am Chemical.

Paul, David, tr. The Collected Works of Paul Valery Degas, Manet, Morisot. (Bollingen Ser.). 298p. 1989. pap. text ed. 9.95 (*0-691-01882-0*) Princeton U Pr.

Paul, David, jt. auth. see Fry, Andrew.

Paul, David B., et al, eds. Slurry Walls: Design, Construction, & Quality Control. LC 92-32908. (Special Technical Publication Ser.: 1129). (Illus.). 430p. 1992. text ed. 47.00 (*0-8031-1427-3*, 04-011290-38) ASTM.

Paul, David M., tr. see Anger, Per, et al.

Paul, David M., tr. see Jersild, P. C.

Paul, David M., tr. see Strindberg, August.

Paul, David W. The Cultural Limits of Revolutionary Politics. rev. ed. 1979. text ed. 54.00 (*0-914710-41-9*, 48) Col U Pr.

***Paul-Dene, Simon.** I Am the Eagle Free: A Six Nations Legend. 36p. (Orig.). (J). (gr. 1-5). 1992. pap. 8.95 (*0-919441-34-3*, Pub. by Theytus Bks Ltd CN) Orca Bk Pubs.

Paul, Diana. Women in Buddhism: Images of the Feminine in the Mahayana Tradition. 1985. pap. 15.00 (*0-520-05428-8*) U CA Pr.

Paul, Diana M. The Buddhist Feminine Ideal. LC 79-12031. (American Academy of Religion. Dissertation Ser.: No. 30). 250p. reprint ed. pap. 71.30 (*0-7837-5404-3*, 2045168) Bks Demand.

Paul, Diana Y. Philosophy of Mind in Sixth-Century China: Paramartha's "Evolution of Consciousness" LC 82-42862. 280p. 1984. 37.50 (*0-8047-1187-9*) Stanford U Pr.

Paul, Diane. Living Left-Handed. 239p. 1993. pap. 16.95 (*0-7475-0860-7*, Pub. by Bloomsbury Pub Ltd UK) Trafalgar.

***Paul, Diane B.** Controlling Human Heredity: 1865 to the Present. LC 95-12762. (Control of Nature Ser.). (Illus.). 144p. (C). 1995. text ed. 39.95 (*0-391-03915-6*); pap. 12.50 (*0-391-03916-4*) Humanities.

Paul, Dilip K., ed. Fiber Optics Reliability & Testing: Proceedings of a Conference Held 8-9 September 1993, Boston, Mass. LC 93-46151. (Critical Reviews of Optical Science & Technology Ser.: Vol. CR50). 1994. 91.00 (*0-8194-1342-9*); pap. 76.00 (*0-8194-1343-7*) SPIE.

Paul, Dilip K., jt. ed. see Greenwall, Roger A.

Paul, Don. AmeriModern. Poems. LC 75-785. 82p. 1982. 5.00 (*0-943096-02-2*); pap. 2.50 (*0-943096-03-0*) Harts Spring Wks.

— Everybody's Knife Bible. 3rd rev. ed. LC 92-80509. (Illus.). 150p. (Orig.). 1992. pap. 12.95 (*0-938263-13-7*) Path Finder.

— Everybody's Outdoor Survival Guide: The Green Beret's Guide to Outdoor Survival, Bk. I. 2nd rev. ed. (Illus.). 151p. 1989. pap. 12.95 (*0-938263-05-6*) Path Finder.

— Good Intentions: A Novel about Revolution. 433p. 1986. 7.00 (*0-685-17721-1*) Harts Spring Wks.

— Great Livin' in Grubby Times: The Green Beret's Guide to Outdoor Survival, Bk. II. 2nd rev. ed. 149p. 1988. pap. 12.95 (*0-938263-09-9*) Path Finder.

— The Green Beret's Compass Course: The New Way to Stay Found (Not Lost) Anywhere. 6th rev. ed. (Illus.). 114p. 1991. reprint ed. pap. 9.95 (*0-938263-00-5*) Path Finder.

— How to Write a Book in Fifty Three Days: The Elements of Speed Writing, Necessity & Benefits, Too! LC 92-80122. (Illus.). 121p. 1992. pap. 14.95 (*0-938263-10-2*) Path Finder.

— Just Like You: Poems & Bits Before Hell. 73p. 1986. 4.00 (*0-943096-05-7*) Harts Spring Wks.

— Lawrence & Mann Overarching: Once Upon the County of Ujamaa; Roll Away der Rock & Other Essays. 360p. 1981. 10.00 (*0-943096-00-6*); pap. 5.00 (*0-943096-01-4*) Harts Spring Wks.

— Never Get Lost: The New Way to Stay Found (Not Lost) Anywhere. LC 92-80510. (Illus.). 128p. Date not set. pap. 9.95 (*0-938263-14-5*) Path Finder.

***Paul, Don & Smith, David B.** Ammo Forever: The Complete What to Shoot & How Manual for Rifles & Shotguns. LC 94-69563. (Illus.). 192p. (Orig.). 1995. pap. 14.95 (*0-938263-15-3*) Path Finder.

— Ammo Forever II: The Complete What to Shoot & How Manual for Handguns. (Illus.). 160p. (Orig.). 1995. pap. 14.95 (*0-938263-19-6*) Path Finder.

Paul, Don, jt. auth. see Huber, Craig F.

Paul, Don, jt. ed. see Huber, Craig.

Paul, Donald R. Polymeric Gas Separation Membranes. 1993. write for info. (*0-8493-4415-8*) CRC Pr.

Paul, Donald R. & Harris, F. W., eds. Controlled Release Polymeric Formulations: Symposium, Jointly Sponsored by the Division of Organic Coatings & Plastics Chemistry & the Division of Polymer Chemistry at the 171st Meeting of the American Chemical Society, New York, N.Y., April 7-9, 1976. LC 76-29016. (ACS Symposium Ser.: No. 33). 327p. reprint ed. pap. 93.20 (*0-7837-1450-5*, 2052426) Bks Demand.

Paul, Doris A. The Navajo Code Talkers. (Illus.). 176p. (C). 1973. 14.50 (*0-8059-1870-1*) Dorrance.

Paul, Doris H., jt. ed. see Hammer, Carolyn S.

Paul, E. Adoption Choices: A Guidebook to National & International Adoption Resources. 1991. pap. 24.95 (*0-8103-9403-0*) Visible Ink Pr.

— Adoption Directory. 2nd ed. 1995. 65.00 (*0-8103-7495-1*) Gale.

— Experts Contact Directory, No. 1. 1995. 89.00 (*0-8103-8567-8*, 101379) Gale.

Paul, E., tr. see Novikov-Priboi, Aleksei S.

Paul, E., et al. Elementary Particle Physics. (Tracts in Modern Physics Ser.: Vol. 79). (Illus.). 1976. 41.00 (*0-387-07778-2*) Spr-Verlag.

Paul, E. A. & Clark, F. E., eds. Soil Microbiology & Biochemistry. 470p. 1988. text ed. 49.95 (*0-12-546805-9*) Acad Pr.

Paul, E. C. Fisheries Development & the Food Needs of Mauritius. (Illus.). 224p. 1987. text ed. 95.00 (*90-6191-627-5*, Pub. by A A Balkema NE) Ashgate Pub Co.

Paul, E. J. Paul: Ancestry of Katharine Choate Paul. (Illus.). 386p. 1991. reprint ed. lib. bdg. 70.00 (*0-8328-1762-7*); reprint ed. pap. 60.00 (*0-8328-1763-5*) Higginson Bk Co.

Paul, E. Robert & Hertzsprung-Kapteyn, Henrietta. The Life & Works of J. C. Kapteyn: An Annotated Translation. 90p. (C). 1994. lib. bdg. 38.50 (*0-7923-2603-2*) Kluwer Ac.

Paul, Eden, tr. see De Man, Henri.

Paul, Eden, tr. see Moll, Albert.

Paul, Eden, tr. see Mussolini, Benito.

Paul, Eden, tr. see Oechsli, Wilhelm.

Paul, Eden, tr. see Schnitzler, Arthur.

Paul, Eden, tr. see Sigerist, Henry E.

Paul, Eden, tr. see Spann, Othman.

Paul, Eden, tr. see Wittels, Fritz.

Paul, Eden, tr. see Zweig, Stefan.

Paul, Eldor A. & McLaren, A. Douglas, eds. Soil Biochemistry, Vol. 3. LC 66-27705. (Books in Soils & the Environment). 352p. reprint ed. pap. 100.40 (*0-8357-3540-0*, 2027833) Bks Demand.

Paul, Ellen F. Equity & Gender: The Comparable Worth Debate. 192p. (Orig.). 1988. pap. 18.95 (*0-88738-720-9*) Transaction Pubs.

— Moral Revolution & Economic Science: The Demise of Laissez-Faire in Nineteenth Century British Political Economy. LC 78-73797. (Contributions in Economics & Economic History Ser.: No. 23). 309p. 1979. text ed. 59.95 (*0-313-21055-1*, PMR/) Greenwood.

— Property Rights & Eminent Domain. 276p. 1987. 34.95 (*0-88738-094-8*) Transaction Pubs.

Paul, Ellen F., ed. Totalitarianism at the Crossroads. 196p. (C). 1990. 32.95 (*0-88738-351-3*); pap. 18.95 (*0-88738-850-7*) Transaction Pubs.

Paul, Ellen F. & Dickman, Howard, eds. Liberty, Property, & Government: Constitutional Interpretation Before the New Deal. LC 88-38771. (SUNY Series in the Constitution & Economic Rights). 303p. 1989. 64.50 (*0-7914-0086-7*); pap. 21.95 (*0-7914-0087-5*) State U NY Pr.

— Liberty, Property, & the Foundations of the American Constitution. LC 88-11614. (SUNY Series in the Constitution & Economic Rights). 181p. 1988. 59.50 (*0-88706-914-2*); pap. 19.95 (*0-88706-915-0*) State U NY Pr.

Paul, Ellen F. & Russo, Philip A., eds. Public Policy: Issues, Analysis, & Ideology. LC 81-10027. (Chatham House Series on Change in American Politics). 333p. reprint ed. pap. 95.00 (*0-7837-2600-7*, 2042764) Bks Demand.

Paul, Ellen F., et al, eds. Altruism. LC 93-6963. (Social Philosophy & Policy Ser.: No. 10). 256p. (C). 1993. pap. 19.95 (*0-521-44759-3*) Cambridge U Pr.

— Contemporary Political & Social Philosophy 12:1. (Social Philosophy & Policy Ser.). 256p. (C). 1995. pap. write for info. (*0-521-48399-9*) Cambridge U Pr.

— Crime, Culpability & Remedy. x, 248p. (Orig.). 1990. pap. text ed. 22.95 (*0-631-17304-8*) Blackwell Pubs.

— Cultural Pluralism & Moral Knowledge. (Social Philosophy & Policy Ser.: No. 11: 1). 256p. (C). 1994. pap. 19.95 (*0-521-46614-8*) Cambridge U Pr.

— Economic Rights. (Social Philosophy & Policy Ser.: No. 9, pt. 1). 256p. (C). 1992. pap. 19.95 (*0-521-42873-4*) Cambridge U Pr.

— The Good Life & the Human Good. (Social Philosophy & Policy Ser.: Vol. 9, No. 2). 256p. (C). 1992. pap. 21.95 (*0-521-43759-8*) Cambridge U Pr.

— The Just Society. (Social Philosophy & Policy Ser.: No. 12:2). 256p. (C). Date not set. pap. write for info. (*0-521-55857-3*) Cambridge U Pr.

— Liberalism & the Economic Order. (Social Philosophy & Policy Ser.: No. 10: 2). 256p. (C). 1993. pap. 24.95 (*0-521-45724-6*) Cambridge U Pr.

— Property Rights. (Social Philosophy & Policy Ser.: No. 11-2). 256p. (C). 1994. pap. 19.95 (*0-521-46739-X*) Cambridge U Pr.

***Paul, Elliot.** Ghost Town on the Yellowstone. (American Autobiography Ser.). 341p. 1995. reprint ed. lib. bdg. 89.00 (*0-7812-8608-5*) Rprt Serv.

— The Last Time I Saw Paris. 1993. reprint ed. lib. bdg. 19.95 (*1-56849-157-3*) Buccaneer Bks.

— Linden on the Saugus Branch. (American Autobiography Ser.). 401p. 1995. reprint ed. lib. bdg. 99.00 (*0-7812-8609-3*) Rprt Serv.

— Mayhem in B-Flat: A Homer Evans Murder Mystery. 320p. 1988. reprint ed. pap. 5.95 (*0-486-25621-9*) Dover.

— The Mysterious Mickey Finn. 256p. 1984. reprint ed. pap. 5.95 (*0-486-24751-1*) Dover.

— Narrow Street. (American Autobiography Ser.). 342p. 1995. reprint ed. lib. bdg. 89.00 (*0-7812-8610-7*) Rprt Serv.

Paul, Elliot H. Life & Death of a Spanish Town. LC 79-138171. 427p. (C). 1971. reprint ed. text ed. 35.00 (*0-8371-5628-9*, PAST, Greenwood Pr) Greenwood.

— The Stars & Stripes Forever. LC 74-22802. reprint ed. 24.00 (*0-404-58459-4*) AMS Pr.

Paul, Erich R. The Milky Way Galaxy & Statistical Cosmology, 1890-1924. LC 92-36530. (Illus.). 304p. (C). 1993. 44.95 (*0-521-35363-7*) Cambridge U Pr.

— Science, Religion, & Mormon Cosmology. (Illus.). 312p. (C). 1992. 29.95 (*0-252-01895-8*) U of Ill Pr.

Paul, Eunice M., tr. Jesus Christ & the Faith: A Collection of Studies by Philippe H. Menoud. LC 78-15551. (Pittsburgh Theological Monographs: No. 18). Orig. Title: Jesus-Christ et la Foi. 1978. 10.00 (*0-915138-22-0*) Pickwick.

***Paul F. Kerr Memorial Symposium Staff.** Mineralogy - Applications to the Minerals Industry: Proceedings of the Paul F. Kerr Memorial Symposium, New York, New York, February 28, 1985. fac. ed. Hausen, Donald M. & Kopp, Otto C., eds. LC 85-71781. (Illus.). 295p. 1985. reprint ed. pap. 84.10 (*0-7837-7864-3*, 2047622) Bks Demand.

Paul, Florence J. A Dream Betrayed. abr. ed. 300p. 1995. pap. 8.95 (*1-56901-515-5*) NW Pub.

Paul, Frances. Spruce Root Basketry of the Alaska Tlingit. 80p. 1991. pap. text ed. 5.95 (*1-880475-02-2*) Friends of SJM.

Paul, Frank A. Sign Language Animals. 32p. 1985. 4.50 (*0-685-66554-2*) Dawn Sign.

— Sign Language Feelings. 32p. (J). 1985. 4.50 (*0-915035-05-7*, 4165) Dawn Sign.

— Sign Language Fun. 32p. (J). 1984. 4.50 (*0-915035-02-2*, 4163) Dawn Sign.

— Sign Language Opposites. 32p. (J). 1985. 4.50 (*0-915035-04-9*, 4164) Dawn Sign.

Paul, Frank A. & Bahan, Ben. The American Sign Language Handshape Game Cards. rev. ed. 16.95 (*0-915035-25-1*, 8110) Dawn Sign.

Paul, Frederic, jt. auth. see Wegman, William.

Paul, G. & Almasi, George S., eds. Parallel Systems & Computation: Proceedings of the 1986 IBM Europe Institute, Seminar on Parallel Computing, Oberlech, Austria 11-15 Aug., 1986. 294p. 1988. 92.50 (*0-444-70371-3*, North Holland) Elsevier.

Paul, G., jt. auth. see Hiebert, Frances F.

Paul, Garrett E., tr. see Troeltsch, Ernst.

Paul, Gordon L. Insight vs. Desensitization in Psychotherapy: An Experiment in Anxiety Reduction. 148p. 1966. 22.50 (*0-8047-0282-9*) Stanford U Pr.

Paul, Gordon L., ed. Assessment in Residential Treatment Settings: Principles & Methods to Support Cost-Effective Quality Operations. LC 86-61550. (Assessment in Residential Treatment Settings Ser.: No. 1). 332p. (Orig.). 1986. pap. text ed. 24.95 (*0-87822-275-8*, 2758) Res Press.

— The Staff-Resident Interaction Chronograph: Observational Assessment Instrumentation for Service & Research. LC 87-62117. (Assessment in Residential Treatment Settings Ser.: No. 3). 280p. 1988. pap. text ed. 18.95 (*0-87822-277-4*, 2774) Res Press.

Paul, Gordon L., et al, eds. The Time-Sample Behavioral Checklist: Observational Assessment Instrumentation for Service & Research. LC 87-62116. (Assessment in Residential Treatment Settings Ser.: No. 2). 286p. 1987. pap. text ed. 18.95 (*0-87822-276-6*, 2766) Res Press.

Paul, Gordon L. & Lentz, Robert J. Psychological Treatment of Chronic Mental Patients: Milieu Versus Social-Learning Programs. LC 77-10868. 528p. reprint ed. pap. 150.50 (*0-7837-4174-X*, 2059023) Bks Demand.

Paul, Gordon W., jt. auth. see Guiltinan, Joseph P.

***Paul, Greg.** 60's Flashback. LC 94-35574. 1995. pap. 19.95 (*0-86636-279-7*) PBC Intl Inc.

Paul, Gregor, jt. ed. see Lenk, Hans.

***Paul, Gregory S. & Cox, Earl.** Beyond Humanity: Cyberdescendants & Virtual Extinction. (Illus.). 300p. 1995. 24.95 (*1-886801-22-3*); pap. 20.95 (*1-886801-21-5*) Chrles River Media.

Paul, H. B., ed. see De Constant, D'Estaurnelles.

Paul, H. G., jt. ed. see Baldwin, C.

Paul, H. N. Paul: Joseph Paull of Ilminster, Somerset, Eng., & Some Descendants Who Have Resided in Philadelphia. (Illus.). 157p. 1992. reprint ed. lib. bdg. 34.00 (*0-8328-2702-9*); reprint ed. pap. 24.00 (*0-8328-2703-7*) Higginson Bk Co.

Paul, H. W. From Knowledge to Power: The Rise of the Science Empire in France, 1860-1939. 415p. 1985. 69.95 (*0-521-26504-5*) Cambridge U Pr.

Paul, Harry, jt. auth. see Ulman, Richard.

Paul, Harry G. John Dennis. LC 75-181968. reprint ed. 34.50 (*0-404-04918-4*) AMS Pr.

— John Dennis, His Life & Criticism. (BCL1-PR English Literature Ser.). 229p. 1992. reprint ed. lib. bdg. 79.00 (*0-7812-7345-5*) Rprt Serv.

Paul, Harry W. The Edge of Contingency: French Catholic Reaction to Scientific Change from Darwin to Duhem. LC 78-11168. 223p. reprint ed. pap. 63.60 (*0-7837-5087-0*, 2044785) Bks Demand.

— The Second Ralliement: The Rapprochement Between Church & State in France in the Twentieth Century. LC 67-14435. 246p. reprint ed. pap. 70.20 (*0-685-17841-2*, 2029503) Bks Demand.

— The Sorcerer's Apprentice: The French Scientist's Image of German Science, 1840-1919. LC 77-178986. (University of Florida Monographs: Social Sciences: No. 44). 96p. reprint ed. pap. 27.40 (*0-7837-5086-2*, 2044784) Bks Demand.

Paul, Hastings, Janofsky & Walker Staff. California OSHA Compliance Handbook. 242p. (Orig.). 1992. pap. text ed. 69.00 (*0-86587-289-9*) Gov Insts.

Paul, Haydn. Gate of Rebirth: Astrology, Regeneration & 8th House Mysteries. 320p. (Orig.). 1993. pap. 14.95 (*0-87728-761-9*) Weiser.

— Lord of the Light: Exploring the Astrological Sun. (Illus.). 240p. 1990. pap. 17.95 (*1-85230-188-0*) Element MA.

— Revolutionary Spirit: Exploring the Astrological Uranus. 1990. pap. 15.95 (*1-85230-059-0*) Element MA.

— Your Starchild: An Astrology Guide for You & Your Child. 320p. 1992. mass mkt. 4.99 (*0-380-76355-9*) Avon.

***Paul, Henry A.** When Kids Are Mad, Not Bad: A Guide to Recognizing & Handling Children's Anger. 256p. (Orig.). 1995. pap. text ed. 5.99 (*0-425-14648-0*) Berkley Pub.

Paul, Herbert W. Men & Letters. LC 70-111856. (Essay Index Reprint Ser.). 1977. 21.95 (*0-8369-1622-0*) Ayer.

Paul, Hermann. German Dictionary: Deutsches Woerterbuch. 8th ed. 841p. (GER.). 1981. 75.00 (*0-8288-1979-3*, M7335) Fr & Eur.

Paul, Hugo. Condominium Trap. LC 79-65558. 1985. 8.95 (*0-916620-36-0*) Portals Pr.

Paul, I. H. The Craft of Psychotherapy: Twenty-Seven Studies. LC 89-17492. 320p. 1989. 40.00x (*0-87668-826-1*) Aronson.

— Letters to Simon: On the Conduct of Psychotherapy. LC 72-8792. 341p. 1973. text ed. 47.50x (*0-8236-3010-2*) Intl Univs Pr.

— Studies in Remembering: The Reproduction of Connected & Extended Verbal Material. (Psychological Issues Monograph: No. 2, Vol. 1, No. 2). 152p. (Orig.). 1959. text ed. 26.00 (*0-8236-6240-3*) Intl Univs Pr.

Paul, Iain, jt. ed. see Fennema, Jan.

Paul, J. Ellis. Manual of Four-Handed Dentistry. (Illus.). 155p. 1980. text ed. 56.00 (*0-931386-09-8*) Quint Pub Co.

Paul, J. K., ed. Genetic Engineering Applications for Industry. LC 81-14028. (Chemical Technology Review Ser.: No. 197). (Illus.). 580p. 1982. 72.00 (*0-8155-0869-7*) Noyes.

Paul, J. P., et al, eds. Progress in Bioengineering: Proceedings of an International Seminar Held on the Occasion of the 25th Anniversary of the Strath Clyde Bioengineering Unit, Glasgow in September 1988. (Illus.). 262p. 1989. 98.00 (*0-85274-085-9*) IOP Pub.

Paul, Jack W. Apple Blossom Cologne Company: Audit Case. 3rd ed. 320p. (C). 1990. pap. text ed. 39.95 (*0-256-08237-5*) Irwin.

— Peach Blossom Cologne Company: A Short Audit Case. 2nd ed. 166p. (C). 1993. text ed. 36.95 (*0-256-09546-9*) Irwin.

— Peach Blossom Cologne Company: Short Audit Case. 216p. (C). 1988. pap. text ed. 36.95 (*0-256-05792-3*) Irwin.

Paul, James C. & Schwartz, Murray L. Federal Censorship: Obscenity in the Mail. LC 77-10978. 368p. 1977. reprint ed. text ed. 65.00 (*0-8371-9818-6*, PAFC, Greenwood Pr) Greenwood.

Paul, James C., jt. auth. see Coates, Albert.

Paul, James L. Educating Emotionally Disturbed Children & Youth. 2nd ed. 480p. (C). 1991. write for info. (*0-675-21211-1*, Merrill Pub Co) Macmillan.

Paul, James L., ed. The Exceptional Child: A Guidebook for Churches & Community Agencies. LC 82-16914. 176p. 1983. text ed. 39.95x (*0-8156-2287-2*); pap. text ed. 16.95x (*0-8156-2288-0*) Syracuse U Pr.

Paul, James L. & Simeonsson, Rune J., eds. Children with Special Needs: Family, Culture, & Society. 2nd ed. (Illus.). 352p. (C). 1993. text ed. 29.50 (*0-03-055743-7*) HB Coll Pubs.

Paul, James L., jt. auth. see Epanchin, Betty C.

Paul, James L., jt. ed. see Pappanikou, A. J.

Paul, James L., et al. Mainstreaming: A Practical Guide. (C). 1977. 27.50x (*0-8156-0136-0*) Syracuse U Pr.

P Q

Paul, James L., et al, eds. Child Advocacy Within the System. (Special Education & Rehabilitation Monograph Ser.: No. 11). (C). 1977. 24.95x (*0-8156-0133-6*) Syracuse U Pr.

Paul, James M., et al, eds. Deinstitutionalization: Program & Policy Development. (Special Education & Rehabilitation Monograph Ser.: No. 12). (C). 1977. 24. 95x (*0-8156-0132-8*) Syracuse U Pr.

***Paul, Jan & Pradier, Claire-Marie, eds.** Carbon Dioxide Chemistry: Environmental Issues. 405p. 1994. 129.95 (*0-85186-634-4*) Royal Soc CN.

Paul, Janet, jt. ed. see Locke, Elsie.

Paul, Janis M. The Victorian Heritage of Virginia Woolf. 225p. 1987. 29.95 (*0-937664-73-1*) Pilgrim Bks OK.

Paul, Jean. How to Propose Marriage (in a Romantic Way) Ellett, Virginia et al, eds. LC 90-83800. (Illus.). 150p. (Orig.). 1991. pap. 12.95 (*1-879268-24-8*) Aphrodite Pubns.

Paul, Jean, jt. auth. see Von Kleist, Heinrich.

Paul, Jeffrey, jt. ed. see Epstein, Richard A.

Paul, Jennifer L. Nobody Home. 1977. 7.95 (*0-393-08766-2*) Norton.

Paul, Jeremy. The Musgrave Ritual. (Orig.). 1992. pap. 11. 00 (*0-86025-443-7*, Pub. by Ian Henry Pubns UK) Empire Pub Srvs.

— The Naval Treaty: The Adventures of Sherlock Holmes. (Illus.). 46p. (Orig.). 1991. pap. 11.00 (*0-86025-435-6*, Pub. by Ian Henry Pubns UK) Empire Pub Srvs.

— The Problem of Thor Bridge: The Case-book of Sherlock Holmes. (Illus.). 50p. (Orig.). 1991. pap. 11.00 (*0-86025-434-8*, Pub. by Ian Henry Pubns UK) Empire Pub Srvs.

— The Secret of Sherlock Holmes. 60p. (Orig.). 1991. pap. 11.00 (*0-86025-425-9*, Pub. by Ian Henry Pubns UK) Empire Pub Srvs.

— The Secret of Sherlock Holmes. 60p. (Orig.). 1991. pap. 11.00 (*0-86025-438-0*, Pub. by Ian Henry Pubns UK) Empire Pub Srvs.

— The Speckled Band: The Adventures of Sherlock Holmes. (Illus.). 42p. (Orig.). 1991. pap. 11.00 (*0-86025-436-4*, Pub. by Ian Henry Pubns UK) Empire Pub Srvs.

Paul, Jim. Catapult: Harry & I Build a Seige Weapon. 1991. 17.50 (*0-394-58507-0*, Villard Bks) Random.

— Catapult: Harry & I Build a Siege Weapon. 272p. 1992. pap. 9.00 (*0-380-71840-5*) Avon.

— What's Called Love: A Real Romance. 1993. 19.00 (*0-685-63495-7*, Villard Bks) Random.

— You Dropped It, You Pick It Up! Planas, Joe, ed. LC 83-82572. (Illus.). 222p. 1984. 14.95 (*0-9612822-0-7*) Green Rose.

***Paul, Jim & Moynihan, Brendan.** What I Learned Losing a Million Dollars. 190p. Date not set. 28.95 (*0-9635794-9-5*) Infrared Pr.

***Paul, John, II.** Crossing Threshold. Date not set. pap. write for info. (*0-679-44066-6*); 45.00 (*0-679-44086-0*) Random.

— El Evangelio de la Vida: Evangelium Vitae. 192p. (Orig.). 1995. pap. 7.95 (*1-55586-317-5*) US Catholic.

— The Gospel of Life: Evangelium Vitae. 189p. (Orig.). 1995. pap. 7.95 (*1-55586-316-7*) US Catholic.

***Paul, John, 2nd.** The Gospel of Life. 123p. (Orig.). 1995. pap. text ed. 2.95 (*1-885845-03-0*) Leaflet Missal.

Paul, John E. Catherine of Aragon & Her Friends. LC 66-15774. 285p. reprint ed. pap. 81.30 (*0-7837-0461-5*, 2040784) Bks Demand.

Paul, John R. The Pine Vole in North Carolina. (Reports of Investigations Ser.: No. 20). (Illus.). 28p. 1970. pap. 1.00 (*0-89792-044-9*) Ill St Museum.

Paul, John R. & Parmalee, Paul W. Soft Drink Bottling: A History with Special Reference to Illinois. (Illus.). 121p. 1973. pap. 5.00 (*0-89792-079-1*) Ill St Museum.

Paul, John W. Apple Blossom Cologne Co. (Micro Computer Version) (C). 1987. text ed. 39.95 (*0-256-05984-5*) Irwin.

***Paul, Jordan.** Do I Have to Give up Me to Be Loved by You Workbook. 1992. pap. 13.95 (*1-56838-051-8*) Hazelden.

***Paul, Jordan & Paul, Margaret.** Do I Have to Give up Me to Be Loved by My Kids? Orig. Title: From Conflict to Caring. 1994. pap. 12.95 (*1-56838-068-2*) Hazelden.

— Do I Have to Give up Me to Be Loved by You? 1995. 7.98 (*1-56731-067-2*, MJF Bks) Fine Comms.

— Free to Love. LC 74-27653. 160p. 1983. reprint ed. pap. 5.95 (*0-912389-00-1*) Evolving Pubns.

Paul, Judith E., jt. auth. see Mills, Kenneth H.

Paul, Juergen. Die Politische und Soziale Bedeutung der Naqshbandiyya in Mittelasien Im 15. Jahrhundert. (Studien zur Sprache, Geschichte und Kultur des Islamischen Orients: Bd. 13). x, 275p. (GER.). (C). 1991. lib. bdg. 136.95 (*3-11-012720-2*) De Gruyter.

Paul, K., ed. see Salusbury, John.

Paul, Karen, ed. Contemporary Issues in Business & Society in the United States. LC 91-22282. (Mellen Studies in Business: Vol. 8). 324p. 1991. lib. bdg. 99.95 (*0-7734-9733-1*) E Mellen.

— Contemporary Issues in Business Ethics & Politics. LC 91-18939. (Mellen Studies in Business: Vol. 7). 316p. 1991. lib. bdg. 99.95 (*0-7734-9718-8*) E Mellen.

Paul, Karen, jt. ed. see Ludwig, Dean C.

Paul, Kathleen. Aries. (Sun Sign Ser.). 40p. (J). (gr. 4). 1989. lib. bdg. 13.95 (*0-88682-255-6*) Creative Ed.

— Sonoran Desert Handbook. 1987. 3.95 (*0-9605656-4-7*) Desert Botanical.

— Taurus. (Sun Sign Ser.). 40p. (J). (gr. 4). 1989. lib. bdg. 13.95 (*0-88682-257-2*) Creative Ed.

Paul, Kees, jt. ed. see Rainders, Reinder.

Paul, Kevin. Chairing a Meeting with Confidence: An Easy Guide to Rules & Procedure. 2nd ed. (Reference Ser.). 96p. 1992. 7.95 (*0-88908-992-2*) Self-Counsel Pr.

— Complete Guide to Canadian Universities: How to Select a University & Succeed When You Get There. 3rd ed. (Reference Ser.). 248p. 1994. pap. 14.95 (*0-88908-524-2*) Self-Counsel Pr.

— Your Guide to Canadian Colleges: Select a Program, Choose a College, & Succeed When You Get There. (Reference Ser.). 256p. 1993. pap. 14.95 (*0-88908-291-X*) Self-Counsel Pr.

Paul, Korky. Pop-up Book of Ghost Tales. 24p. (J). (gr. 3 up). 1991. 14.95 (*0-15-200589-7*, HB Juv Bks) HarBrace.

Paul, Korky, jt. auth. see Long, Jonathan.

Paul, Krugman. Peddling Prosperity: Economic Ideas & Ideology in America. 180p. 1994. 22.00 (*0-393-03602-2*) Norton.

Paul, Larry A. ARE Practice Exam, Non-Graphic Divisions: A, D-F, E, G, H, I. 120p. (Orig.). 1994. pap. 24.95 (*0-912045-69-8*) Prof Pubns CA.

Paul, Lawrence E., et al. Geological, Geochemical & Operational Summary, Aurora Well, OCS Y-0943-1, Beaufortr Sea, Alaska. 1994. write for info. (*0-318-72564-9*) US Interior.

Paul, Leslie. Sir Thomas More. LC 75-128882. (Select Bibliographies Reprint Ser.). 1977. reprint ed. 18.95 (*0-8369-5502-1*) Ayer.

Paul, M. & Robinet, B., eds. International Symposium on Programming: Sixth Colloquium, Toulouse, April 17-19, 1984 Proceedings. (Lecture Notes in Computer Science Ser.: Vol. 167). vi, 262p. 1984. pap. 31.00 (*0-387-12925-1*) Spr-Verlag.

Paul, M. & Siegert, H. J., eds. Distributed Systems. (Lecture Notes in Computer Science Ser.: Vol. 190). vi, 573p. 1988. pap. 55.00 (*0-387-15216-4*) Spr-Verlag.

Paul, M., jt. ed. see Neuhold, Erich J.

Paul, M. C. Dimensions of Tribal Movements in India. (C). 1989. 18.00 (*81-210-0219-2*, Pub. by Inter-India Pubns) S Asia.

Paul, M. Eden, tr. see Bloch, Iwan.

Paul, Manfred, jt. ed. see Sommerville, Ian.

Paul, Manmathanath, tr. see Sandilya.

Paul, Margaret. Inner Bonding: Becoming a Loving Adult to Your Inner Child. LC 91-58163. 240p. 1992. pap. 14.00 (*0-06-250710-9*) Harper SF.

Paul, Margaret & Chopich, Erika J. Healing Your Aloneness: Finding Love & Wholeness Through Your Inner Child. LC 89-46151. 1990. pap. 11.00 (*0-06-250149-6*) Harper SF.

Paul, Margaret, jt. auth. see Chopich, Erika J.

Paul, Margaret, jt. auth. see Paul, Jordan.

Paul, Margareta, tr. see Anger, Per, et al.

Paul, Margareta, tr. see Jersild, P. C.

Paul, Margareta, tr. see Strindberg, August.

Paul, Margot, jt. auth. see Stinchecum, Amanda M.

***Paul-Marie of the Cross, OCD.** Carmelite Spirituality. Payne, Steven, ed. Sullivan, Kathryn, tr. LC 94-27728. Date not set. pap. write for info. (*0-935216-50-2*) ICS Pubns.

Paul, Martin, tr. see Alberti, Rafael.

Paul-Matos, Janice. How to Get into College: Step by Step, Vol. 1. 24p. (Orig.). (J). (gr. 9-12). 1985. pap. 5.00 (*0-9615165-0-X*) Coll Acceptance.

Paul, Maureen, ed. Occupational & Environmental Reproductive Hazards. LC 92-13719. (Illus.). 448p. 1993. 85.00 (*0-683-06801-6*) Williams & Wilkins.

Paul, Michael. Plural of Bus Is Buses Isn't It? A Guide to Word Usage. rev. ed. LC 87-91305. (Illus.). 85p. 1988. pap. 3.00 (*0-9616367-2-6*) Michael Paul.

— The Warning Tract: A Guide to Good Writing from Sports Stories. LC 86-90402. 54p. (Orig.). (YA). (gr. 7-12). 1986. pap. 3.50 (*0-9616367-0-X*) Michael Paul.

Paul, Michele. The Women's Pharmacy. pap. 3.50 (*0-318-23489-0*, Pinnacle NY) Windsor NY.

Paul, N. M., tr. see Bergson, Henri.

Paul, Natalie W., ed. A Guide to Human Chromosome Defects. 2nd ed. LC 68-57287. (March of Dimes Birth Defects Foundation Ser.: Vol. 16, No. 6). 1980. 0.50 (*0-686-30821-2*) March of Dimes.

Paul, Nicholas & Croly, Richard. EC Insurance Law. 322p. 1992. text ed. 135.00 (*0-471-93643-X*, Pub. by Wiley Chancery Law UK) Wiley.

Paul, Nirmaljit, jt. auth. see Hay, Jonathan.

Paul, Norman, ed. see Copeau, Jacques.

Paul of Venice. Logica Magna, Fascicule 8, Pt. 2: Tractatus de Obligationibus. Ashworth, E. J., ed. (Classical & Medieval Logic Texts Ser.: V). (Illus.). 426p. 1989. pap. 110.00 (*0-19-726065-9*) OUP.

Paul, Oglesby. Take Heart. LC 86-3170. (Francis A. Countway Library of Medicine). (Illus.). 336p. 1986. 19. 95 (*0-674-86745-9*) HUP.

— Take Heart: The Life & Prescription for Living of Paul Dudley White. (Illus.). 366p. 1986. 18.95 (*0-317-04059-6*) F A Countway.

Paul, Otis, jt. auth. see Sardegna, Jill.

Paul, P. F., et al, eds. Synthetic Fuels from Coal: Status of the Technology. (C). 1988. pap. text ed. 126.50 (*1-85333-103-1*, Pub. by Graham & Trotman UK) Kluwer Ac.

***Paul, Patty. A New Spirituality: Beyond Religion. LC 94-79198. 192p. 1995. pap. 12.95 (*0-9642726-7-9*) Imdex Pub. A NEW SPIRITUALITY: Beyond Religion is about self-empowerment & personal growth which lead the way to spiritual growth. It offers hope, not only for a new life, but for a new world as well. It's based on the concept that each person creates their own reality, &, by using reality as feedback, a person is shown what inner change is needed. Positive inner change creates positive realities - personal & global. This book offers valuable information of human emotions, finding self-value, discovering personal destiny, & healing the wounded inner child & adolescent. It explains the nature of masculine & feminine energies & how internal balancing will produce an external shift from worldwide male chauvinism to equal partnership between men & women, resulting in powerful & harmonious societies. A NEW SPIRITUALITY explains the holographic nature of physical reality & offers a description of Creation far beyond those offered by religion or science. It discusses the differences between religion & spirituality, & how to discover the Soul & awaken the Spirit within. Most importantly, A NEW SPIRITUALITY tells of the return of the unconditionally loving Goddess & True God & the changes taking place in the world that herald Their return. To order contact: IMDEX Publishing, P.O. Box 5283, Huntington Beach, CA 92615-5283. Phone/Fax: 714-964-0684.** *Publisher Provided Annotation.*

Paul, Paula. Geronimo Chino. 1980. pap. 6.95 (*0-89992-080-2*) Coun India Ed.

— The Mistress at Blackwater. (Orig.). 1993. pap. 3.99 (*0-425-13990-5*) Berkley Pub.

— Sarah, Sissy Weed, & the Ships of the Desert. (Illus.). 112p. (J). (gr. 5-6). 1985. 9.95 (*0-89015-504-6*); pap. 5.95 (*0-89015-552-6*) Sunbelt Media.

— Sweet Ivy's Gold. 1993. mass mkt. 4.50 (*0-06-108001-2*, Harp PBks) HarpC.

***Paul, Penelope.** Costume & Clothes. LC 94-44417. (Legacies Ser.). (Illus.). 48p. (J). (gr. 4-6). 1995. 15.95 (*1-56847-274-9*) Thomson Lrning.

Paul, Peter. Fabio. 60p. 1993. pap. 7.95 (*0-941613-40-2*) Stabur Pr.

Paul, Peter C. Easy Pickings: Non-Profits & Charities Regulation in the 50 US States-10 Canadian Provinces, England-Wales & Australia. Fox, L. Christopher, ed. (Selected Directory of Non-profits & Charities Regulation in the U. S., Canada, Australia, England & Wales Ser.). (Illus.). 700p. (Orig.). (C). 1988. text ed. 38. 95 (*0-318-39968-7*); pap. 38.95 (*0-318-39969-5*) Verzola.

Paul, Peter V. Toward a Psychology of Deafness. 368p. Date not set. write for info. (*0-318-71716-6*) Allyn.

Paul, Peter V. & Jackson, Dorothy W. Toward a Psychology of Deafness: Theoretical & Empirical Perspectives. LC 92-31126. 334p. 1992. text ed. 53.00 (*0-205-14112-9*) Allyn.

Paul, Peter V. & Quigley, Stephen P. Language & Deafness. 2nd ed. LC 94-4478. (Illus.). 128p. (C). 1994. teacher ed write for info. (*1-56593-362-1*, 0695); pap. text ed. 34.95 (*1-56593-108-4*) Singular Publishing.

— Study Guide for Language & Deafness. 2nd ed. 192p. (C). 1994. pap. text ed. 24.50 (*1-56593-363-X*, 0700) Singular Publishing.

Paul, Peter V., jt. auth. see Quigley, Stephen.

***Paul, Philip C.** Where to Find Venture Capital: A Resource Guide. LC 95-815. 296p. (Orig.). 1995. pap. 19.95 (*1-56825-028-2*) Rainbow Books.

Paul, Premila. The Novels of Mulk Raj Anand: A Thematic Study. 183p. 1983. 16.95 (*0-86578-178-8*) Ind-US Inc.

Paul, R. Field Theoretical Methods in Chemical Physics. (Studies in Physical & Theoretical Chemistry: Vol. 19). 414p. 1982. 141.00 (*0-444-42073-8*) Elsevier.

Paul, R. Eli, jt. ed. see Buecker, Thomas R.

Paul, R. S., jt. auth. see Corson, John J.

Paul, R. W., ed. see Shinn, Charles.

Paul, Ray J., ed. Artificial Intelligence in Operational Research. (Illus.). 375p. 1992. text ed. 120.00 (*0-333-55117-6*, Pub. by Macmill Press UK) Scholium Intl.

Paul, Raymond. The Bond Street Burlesque. 1987. 16.95 (*0-393-02402-4*) Norton.

Paul Revere Memorial Association Staff. Paul Revere, Artisan, Businessman, & Patriot: The Man Behind the Myth. (Artisans & the Arts Ser.). (Illus.). 192p. 1988. lib. bdg. 30.00 (*0-9619999-0-X*, Univ Pub Assocs); pap. text ed. 15.00 (*0-9619999-1-8*, Univ Pub Assocs) Paul Revere Mem Assn.

Paul, Rhea. Language Disorders in Children & Adolescents: Asse. 400p. 1995. 39.95 (*0-8016-7927-3*) Mosby Yr Bk.

Paul, Rhea, jt. auth. see Miller, Jon F.

Paul, Richard. A Handbook to the Universe: Explorations of Matter, Energy, Space, & Time for Beginning Scientific Thinkers. LC 92-39670. (Illus.). 320p. (Orig.). (J). (gr. 6 up). 1993. pap. 14.95 (*1-55652-172-3*) Chicago Review.

Paul, Richard & Binker, A. J. Critical Thinking Handbook--High School: A Guide for Re-Designing Instruction. LC 89-62293. (Orig.). 1989. pap. text ed. 18.00 (*0-944583-03-2*) Ctr Critical Thinking.

Paul, Richard, jt. ed. see Brady, Michael.

Paul, Richard, et al. Critical Thinking Handbook - 4th-6th Grades: A Guide for Remodelling Lesson Plans in Language Arts, Social Studies, & Science. LC 87-72836. (Orig.). (C). 1987. pap. text ed. 18.00 (*0-944583-01-6*) Ctr Critical Thinking.

— Critical Thinking Handbook--K-3: A Guide for Remodelling Lesson Plans in Language Arts, Social Studies, & Science. LC 87-71979. (Orig.). (C). 1987. pap. text ed. 18.00 (*0-944583-00-8*) Ctr Critical Thinking.

— Critical Thinking Handbook--6th-9th Grades: A Guide for Remodelling Lesson Plans in Language Arts, Social Studies, & Science. LC 88-64125. (Orig.). 1989. pap. text ed. 18.00 (*0-944583-02-4*) Ctr Critical Thinking.

Paul, Richard P. Robot Manipulators: Mathematics, Programming, & Control. (Artificial Intelligence Ser.). (Illus.). 279p. (C). 1981. 45.00 (*0-262-16082-X*) MIT Pr.

— SPARC Architecture Assembly Language Programming & C. LC 93-10038. 1993. text ed. 48.00 (*0-13-876889-7*) P-H Gen Ref & Trav.

Paul, Richard S. & Haeussler, Ernest F., Jr. Algebra & Trigonometry for College Students. 2nd ed. 1983. text ed. write for info. (*0-8359-0178-5*, Reston); write for info. (*0-8359-0179-3*, Reston) P-H.

— Calculus for Business. (C). 1984. teacher ed write for info. (*0-8359-0636-1*, Reston) P-H.

Paul, Richard S. & Shaevel, M. Leonard. Essentials of Technical Mathematics with Calculus. 2nd ed. 1104p. (C). 1988. text ed. 71.00 (*0-13-289091-7*) P-H.

Paul, Richard S. & Shavel. Essentials of Technical Mathematics. 3rd ed. 832p. (C). 1988. text ed. 71.00 (*0-13-288812-2*) P-H.

Paul, Richard S., jt. auth. see Haeussler, Ernest F., Jr.

Paul, Richard W. Critical Thinking: What Every Person Needs to Survive in a Rapidly Changing World. Binker, A. J., ed. LC 90-80195. 704p. 1992. pap. text ed. 19.95 (*0-944583-07-5*) Ctr Critical Thinking.

Paul, Richard W., et al. Critical Thinking Handbook: K-Three: A Guide for Remodelling Lesson Plans in Language Arts, Social Studies & Science. 2nd ed. LC 90-82938. (Illus.). 410p. 1990. pap. text ed. 18.00 (*0-944583-05-9*) Ctr Critical Thinking.

Paul, Rik, jt. auth. see Darlington, Mansur.

Paul, Rik, jt. auth. see Haynes, J. H.

Paul, Robert A., ed. Biological & Cultural Anthropology at Emory University. (Cultural Anthropology Ser.: Vol. 2, No. 1). 1987. 7.50 (*0-317-66356-9*) Am Anthro Assn.

Paul, Robert D. & Disney, Diane M., eds. The Sourcebook on Postretirement Health Care Benefits. LC 88-15194. 603p. 1988. 89.00 (*0-916592-76-6*) Panel Pubs.

Paul, Robert S. The Assembly of the Lord. (Illus.). 624p. 1985. 54.95 (*0-567-09341-7*, Pub. by T & T Clark UK) Bks Intl VA.

— Freedom with Order: The Doctrine of the Church in the United Church of Christ. LC 87-4992. 160p. (Orig.). 1987. pap. 10.95 (*0-8298-0749-7*) Pilgrim OH.

— Whatever Happened to Sherlock Holmes? Detective Fiction, Popular Theology, & Society. LC 90-23719. 256p. (C). 1991. 24.95 (*0-8093-1722-2*) S Ill U Pr.

Paul, Rodman W. California Gold: The Beginning of Mining in the Far West. LC 47-54111. (Bison Book Ser.). (Illus.). 400p. reprint ed. pap. 114.00 (*0-8357-7974-2*, 2029161) Bks Demand.

Paul, Rodman W. & Etulain, Richard W. The Frontier & the American West. LC 76-11622. (Goldentree Bibliographies Series in American History). (C). 1977. pap. text ed. write for info. (*0-88295-542-X*) Harlan Davidson.

Paul, Ronald. Fire in Our Hearts: A Study of the Portrayal of Youth in a Selection of Post-War British Working-Class Fiction. (Gothenburg Studies in English: No. 51). 225p. (Orig.). 1982. pap. 45.00x (*91-7346-110-5*, Pub. by Acta U Gothenburg SW) Coronet Bks.

Paul, Ronald N., jt. auth. see Bernstein, Charles.

Paul, Ross H. Open Learning & Open Management: Leadership & Integrity in Distance Education. 250p. 1991. text ed. 44.95 (*0-89397-374-2*) Nichols Pub.

Paul, S. Dictionary of Aerospace Teledetection: Dictionnaire de Teledetection Aero-Spatiale. 256p. (ENG & FRE.). 1982. 225.00 (*0-8288-0012-X*, M14360) Fr & Eur.

— Illustrator's Reference Manual: Sports. 1992. 22.98 (*1-55521-791-5*) Bk Sales Inc.

— India's Exports: New Imperatives & Newer Vistas. The Emerging Asia-Pacific Nexus. 1992. 64.00 (*81-7169-173-0*, Commonwealth) S Asia.

— Surface Coatings. 740p. 1985. 160.00 (*0-318-37728-4*) T-C Pubns CA.

Paul, S. K. Accountancy, Vol. I. (C). 1989. 85.00 (*0-89771-429-6*, Current Dist) St Mut.

— Accountancy, Vol. II. (C). 1989. 95.00 (*0-89771-430-X*, Current Dist) St Mut.

— Advanced Accountancy. (C). 1989. 125.00 (*0-685-50343-7*, Current Dist) St Mut.

— Financial Management. (C). 1989. 75.00 (*0-89771-432-6*, Current Dist) St Mut.

Paul, Sally. Creative Fabric Frames. (Illus.). 32p. (J). (gr. 7-12). 1981. pap. 6.00 (*0-932946-06-2*) Burdett CA.

Paul, Samuel. Assessment of the Private Sector: A Case Study & Its Methodological Implications. (Discussion Paper Ser.: No. 93). 114p. 1990. 7.95 (*0-8213-1597-8*, 11597) World Bank.

— Institutional Reforms in Sector Adjustment Operations: The World Bank's Experience. (Discussion Paper Ser.: No. 92). 78p. 1990. 7.95 (*0-8213-1596-X*, 11596) World Bank.

— Strategic Management of Development Programmes: Guidelines for Action. (Management Development Ser.: No. 19). vii, 137p. 1990. pap. 16.00 (*92-2-103252-3*) Intl Labour Office.

— Strengthening Public Service Accountability: A Conceptual Framework. (Discussion Paper Ser.: No. 136). 68p. 1991. 7.95 (*0-8213-1970-1*, 11970) World Bank.

Paul, Samuel & Israel, Arturo, eds. Nongovernmental Organizations & the World Bank: Cooperation for Development. 176p. 1991. 10.95 (0-8213-1924-8, 11924) World Bank.

***Paul, Sandra.** His Accidental Angel. (Romance Ser.). 1995. mass mkt. 2.99 (0-373-19087-5, 1-19087-5) Silhouette.

— Last Chance for Marriage. large type ed. 239p. 1992. reprint ed. lib. bdg. 13.95 (1-56054-541-0) Thorndike Pr.

— The Reluctant Hero. 1994. pap. 2.75 (0-373-91016-9, 5-91016-1); pap. 2.75 (0-373-19016-6, 5-19016-0) Harlequin Bks.

Paul, Serge, jt. auth. see Association National Staff.

Paul, Shale. Maybe It's Not Your Fault, but You Can Do Something about It: The Blue Book for Personal Survival. 64p. (Orig.). 1993. per., pap. 4.95 (0-913787-08-6) Delta G Pr.

— The Warrior Within: A Guide to Inner Power. LC 83-72057. (Illus.). 160p. (Orig.). 1984. 12.95 (0-913787-01-9); pap. 9.95 (0-913787-02-7) Delta G Pr.

Paul, Shale & Paul, Candace. Discovering Your Inner Power: A Workbook for the Warrior Within. (Illus.). 208p. (Orig.). 1992. pap. 12.95 (0-913787-07-8) Delta G Pr.

— Tough-Nice: A Manager's Guide to Sustained High Performance. Hey, Mary, ed. LC 88-70842. 200p. 1988. 16.95 (0-913787-03-5) Delta G Pr.

Paul, Shalom. Amos. LC 90-45137. (Hermeneia Ser.). 440p. (Orig.). 1991. text ed. 46.00 (0-8006-6023-4, 1-6023, Fortress Pr) Augsburg Fortress.

Paul, Sharda. General Elections in India. iv, 205p. 1990. text ed. 27.95 (81-7045-060-8, Pub. by Associated Pub Hse II) Advent Bks Div.

Paul, Sharda, jt. auth. see Ahuja, M. L.

Paul, Sherman. Emerson's Angle of Vision: Man & Nature in American Experience. LC 80-2542. reprint ed. 33.50 (0-404-19267-X) AMS Pr.

— For Love of the World: Essays on Nature Writers. LC 92-6160. 274p. 1992. text ed. 34.95x (0-87745-383-7); pap. 15.95 (0-87745-396-9) U of Iowa Pr.

— Hart's Bridge. LC 76-188133. 325p. reprint ed. pap. 92.70 (0-317-29195-5, 2022264) Bks Demand.

— Hewing to Experience: Essays & Reviews on Recent American Poetry & Poetics, Nature & Culture. LC 89-32349. 407p. 1989. text ed. 38.95x (0-87745-247-4) U of Iowa Pr.

— In Love with the Gratuitous: Rereading Armand Schwerner. (Illus.). 72p. (Orig.). 1986. pap. 5.00 (0-940237-01-6) ND Qtr Pr.

— In Search of the Primitive: Rereading David Antin, Jerome Rothenberg, & Gary Snyder. LC 86-2873. ix, 301p. 1986. text ed. 37.50 (0-8071-1292-5) La State U Pr.

— Lost America of Love: Rereading Robert Creeley, Edward Dorn, & Robert Duncan. LC 80-27470. xvi, 232p. 1981. text ed. 34.95 (0-8071-0865-0) La State U Pr.

— Randolph Bourne. LC 66-64593. (University of Minnesota Pamphlets on American Writers Ser.: No. 60). 48p. (Orig.). reprint ed. pap. 25.00 (0-7837-2869-7, 2057586) Bks Demand.

— The Shores of America: Thoreau's Inward Exploration. LC 58-6998. 447p. reprint ed. pap. 127.40 (0-685-23651-X, 2014928) Bks Demand.

Paul, Sherman, ed. Criticism & Culture. (Papers of the Midwest Modern Language Association: No. 2). x, 123p. (Orig.). 1972. pap. 19.00 (0-87352-171-4, MM69) Modern Lang.

Paul, Sherry. Blossom Bird Falls in Love. (See How I Read Ser.). (Illus.). 32p. (Orig.). (J). (ps-2). 1981. pap. 14.10 (0-685-01192-5); pap. 16.20 (0-685-01193-3) CPI Pub.

— Blossom Bird Finds a Family. (See How I Read Ser.). (Illus.). 32p. (Orig.). (J). (ps-2). 1981. 16.20 (0-685-01194-1) CPI Pub.

— Blossom Bird Finds a Family, Set. (See How I Read Ser.). (Illus.). 32p. (Orig.). (J). (ps-2). 1981. pap. 14.10 (0-686-31343-7) CPI Pub.

— Blossom Bird Goes South. (See How I Read Ser.). (Illus.). 32p. (Orig.). (J). (ps-2). 1981. 16.20 (0-685-01195-X) CPI Pub.

— Blossom Bird Goes South, Set. (See How I Read Ser.). (Illus.). 32p. (Orig.). (J). (ps-2). 1981. pap. 14.10 (0-675-01080-2) CPI Pub.

— Finn the Foolish Fish: Trouble with Bubbles, Set. (See How I Read Ser.). (Illus.). 32p. (Orig.). (J). (ps-2). 16.20 (0-685-01196-8); pap. 14.10 (0-675-01084-5) CPI Pub.

— Two-B & the Rock 'n' Roll Band. (See How I Read Ser.). (Illus.). 32p. (Orig.). (J). (ps-2). 16.20 (0-685-01197-6) CPI Pub.

— Two-B & the Rock 'n' Roll Band, Set. (See How I Read Ser.). (Illus.). 32p. (Orig.). (J). (ps-2). pap. 14.10 (0-675-01082-9) CPI Pub.

— Two-B & the Space Visitor. (See How I Read Ser.). (Illus.). 32p. (Orig.). (J). (ps-2). pap. 14.10 (0-685-01198-4); pap. 16.20 (0-685-01199-2) CPI Pub.

Paul, Stephen C. Illuminations: Visions for Change, Growth, & Self-Acceptance. LC 90-55075. (Illus.). 112p. (Orig.). 1990. pap. 11.00 (0-06-250681-1) Harper SF.

— In Love: Visions of Expanding Love. LC 94-7989. 1994. pap. 11.00 (0-06-251127-0) Harper SF.

Paul, Stephen C. & Collins, Gary M. Inneractions: Visions to Bring Your Inner & Outer Worlds into Harmony. LC 91-58142. (Illus.). 112p. 1992. pap. 12.00 (0-06-250711-7) Harper SF.

***Paul, Stephen L.** Ski Now. LC 94-24357. (Spalding Sports Library). (Illus.). (Orig.). 1995. pap. 12.95 (1-57028-017-7) Masters Pr IN.

***Paul, Sudhir.** Antibody Engineering Protocols. (Methods in Molecular Biology Ser.: Vol. 51). (Illus.). 464p. 1995. spiral bd. 69.50 (0-89603-275-2) Humana.

***Paul, Susan.** The Bride's Portion. (Historical Ser.). 1995. mass mkt. 4.50 (0-373-28866-2, 1-28866-1) Harlequin Bks.

***Paul, Swaraj, ed.** Surface Coatings: Science & Technology. 2nd ed. LC 95-10955. 1995. write for info. (0-471-95818-2) Wiley.

***Paul, T. F.** The Law & Administration of Incorporated Societies. 2nd ed. 276p. 1986. pap. 54.00 (0-409-78744-2, NZ) Butterworth Legal Pubs.

Paul, T. Otis, jt. auth. see Sardegna, Jill.

Paul, Ted. The Christmas Collie. LC 89-17994. (Illus.). 42p. (J). (ps-7). 1989. 12.95 (0-89802-548-6) Beautiful Am.

Paul, Tessa. Tiffany. 1992. 12.99 (0-517-07317-X) Random Hse Value.

— Tiles for a Beautiful Home. (Beautiful Home Ser.). 160p. 1990. 19.95 (0-8120-6175-6) Barron.

Paul, Thazha V. Asymmetric Conflicts: War Initiation by Weaker Powers. (Studies in International Relations: No. 33). (Illus.). 272p. (C). 1994. pap. 19.95 (0-521-46621-0) Cambridge U Pr.

— Asymmetric Conflicts: War Initiation by Weaker Powers. (Studies in International Relations: No. 33). (Illus.). 272p. (C). 1994. 54.95 (0-521-45117-5) Cambridge U Pr.

Paul, Thomas, jt. ed. see Baxi, Uprendra.

Paul, Valerie J. Ecological Roles of Marine Natural Products. LC 91-57899. (Explorations in Chemical Ecology Ser.). (Illus.). 264p. 1992. 41.50 (0-8014-2727-4) Cornell U Pr.

Paul VI. On the Development of Peoples: (Populorum Progressio) Encyclical. 50p. 1987. 2.95 (1-55586-260-8) US Catholic.

Paul, W. & Daniel, E. Muscle: Proceedings, Symposium Faculty of Medicine, University of Alberta, June 1964. LC 65-13879. 1965. 240.00 (0-08-011073-8, Pub. by Pergamon Repr UK) Franklin.

Paul, W. & Moss, T. S., eds. Handbook on Semiconductors: Band Theory & Transport Properties, Vol. 1. 842p. 1982. 228.25 (0-444-85346-4, North Holland) Elsevier.

Paul, Warren. Brave New World Notes. (Orig.). 1965. pap. 3.75 (0-8220-0256-6) Cliffs.

Paul, William. Dance of Death. 1992. 18.95 (0-7278-4271-4) Severn Hse.

— Ernst Lubitsch's American Comedy. (Illus.). 367p. 1987. reprint ed. pap. text ed. 16.00 (0-231-05681-8, King's Crown Paperbacks) Col U Pr.

— Laughing, Screaming: Modern Hollywood Horror & Comedy. LC 93-27388. (Film & Culture Ser.). 510p. (C). 1994. 29.50 (0-231-08464-1) Col U Pr.

— Laughing Screaming: Modern Hollywood Horror & Comedy. 512p. 1995. pap. 16.50 (0-231-08465-X) Col U Pr.

Paul, William & Sarris, Andrew X. Ernst Lubitsch's American Comedy. LC 83-5304. 1983. text ed. 42.00 (0-231-05680-X) Col U Pr.

Paul, William E. Immunology Recognition & Response from Scientific American. (Illus.). 176p. (C). 1995. text ed. 13.95 (0-7167-2223-2) W H Freeman.

Paul, William E., ed. Annual Review of Immunology, Vol. 12. (Illus.). 1994. text ed. 48.00 (0-8243-3012-9) Annual Reviews.

— Annual Reviews of Immunology Vol. 13, 1995. (Illus.). 825p. 1995. lib. bdg. 48.00 (0-8243-3013-7) Annual Reviews.

— Fundamental Immunology. 3rd ed. LC 93-9718. 1440p. 1993. 98.00 (0-7817-0022-1) Raven.

— Immunogenetics. 224p. 1984. text ed. 59.00 (0-88167-013-8) Raven.

Paul, William E., et al, eds. Annual Review of Immunology, Vol. 1. (Illus.). 1983. text ed. 41.00 (0-8243-3001-3) Annual Reviews.

— Annual Review of Immunology, Vol. 2. (Illus.). 1984. text ed. 41.00 (0-8243-3002-1) Annual Reviews.

— Annual Review of Immunology, Vol. 3. (Illus.). 1985. text ed. 41.00 (0-8243-3003-X) Annual Reviews.

— Annual Review of Immunology, Vol. 4. (Illus.). 1986. text ed. 41.00 (0-8243-3004-8) Annual Reviews.

— Annual Review of Immunology, Vol. 5. (Illus.). 1987. text ed. 41.00 (0-8243-3005-6) Annual Reviews.

— Annual Review of Immunology, Vol. 6. 1988. text ed. 41.00 (0-8243-3006-4) Annual Reviews.

— Annual Review of Immunology, Vol. 7. (Illus.). 1989. text ed. 41.00 (0-8243-3007-2) Annual Reviews.

— Annual Review of Immunology, Vol. 8. 1990. text ed. 41.00 (0-8243-3008-0) Annual Reviews.

— Annual Review of Immunology, Vol. 9. 1991. text ed. 41.00 (0-8243-3009-9) Annual Reviews.

— Annual Review of Immunology, Vol. 10. (Illus.). 1992. text ed. 45.00 (0-8243-3010-2) Annual Reviews.

— Annual Review of Immunology, Vol. 11. (Illus.). 1993. text ed. 45.00 (0-8243-3011-0) Annual Reviews.

Paul-Wolf, Helen. Personal Lunation Charts. LC 83-71152. 88p. 1984. 8.00 (0-86690-243-0, W2299-014) Am Fed Astrologers.

Paulaha, D. An American Child's Portfolio. 1992. pap. 9.95 (0-8087-7425-5) Burgess MN Intl.

Paulaharju, Samuli. Arctic Twilight: Old Finnish Tales. Matson, Robert W., ed. Pitkanen, Allan M., tr. (Illus.). 1982. 15.00 (0-943478-00-6) Finnish Am Lit.

Paulanka, Betty J., jt. auth. see Kee, Joyce L.

Paulauskas, V. & Rackauskas, A. Approximation Theory in the Central Limit Theorem: Exact Results in Banach Spaces. (C). 1989. lib. bdg. 109.00 (90-277-2825-9) Kluwer Ac.

Paulay, T. Simplicity & Confidence in Seismic Design. LC 93-37388. (Mallet-Milne Lecture Ser.: Vol. 4). 1993. pap. text ed. write for info. (0-471-94310-X) Wiley.

Paulay, Thomas, jt. auth. see Park, Robert.

Paulay, Tom & Priestley, M. J. Seismic Design of Reinforced Concrete & Masonry Buildings. 768p. 1992. text ed. 99.95 (0-471-54915-0) Wiley.

Paulding. Paulding Short Stories. Bendixen, A., ed. (Masterworks of Literature Ser.). 1991. write for info. (0-8084-0442-3) NCUP.

Paulding, James E. Ensemble, V: A Collection of Fiction & Poetry. LC 87-90639. 156p. (Orig.). 1987. pap. text ed. 17.50 (0-9618718-0-6) J E Paulding.

Paulding, James K. The Dutchman's Fireside. O'Donnell, Thomas F., ed. (Masterworks of Literature Ser.). 1966. 19.95x (0-8084-0110-6); pap. 15.95x (0-8084-0111-4) NCUP.

— Koningsmarke. Wells, Daniel, ed. (Masterworks of Literature Ser.). 1992. pap. 12.95 (0-685-71557-4) NCUP.

— Koningsmarke, 2 vols. in 1. LC 71-173932. reprint ed. 45.00 (0-404-04919-2) AMS Pr.

— Koningsmarke: or Old Times in the New World, 2 vols., Set. (BCL1-PS American Literature Ser.). 1992. reprint ed. lib. bdg. 150.00 (0-7812-6824-9) Rprt Serv.

— Koningsmarke, the Long Finne: A Story of the New World. LC 88-80670. 294p. 1988. 24.00 (0-912756-20-9); pap. 7.75 (0-912756-21-7) Union Coll.

— Letters from the South, Written During an Excursion in the Summer of 1816, 2 vols. in 1. LC 75-173933. reprint ed. 59.50 (0-404-00280-3) AMS Pr.

— Lion of the West. Gado, Frank, ed. 1994. 12.95 (0-8084-0428-8) NCUP.

— The Puritan & His Daughter, 2 vols. LC 78-64087. reprint ed. 75.00 (0-404-17350-0) AMS Pr.

— Salmagundi: Second Series, 2 Vols. in 1. LC 70-144669. reprint ed. 49.50 (0-404-04944-3) AMS Pr.

— Salmagundi: Second Series, 2 vols., Set. (BCL1-PS American Literature Ser.). 1992. reprint ed. lib. bdg. 150.00 (0-7812-6825-7) Rprt Serv.

— Stories of St. Nicholas. LC 95-8396. (New York Classics Ser.). Orig. Title: Book of Saint Nicholas. 104p. 1995. 19.95 (0-8156-0325-8) Syracuse U Pr.

— Westward Ho!, 2 vols., Set. (BCL1-PS American Literature Ser.). 1992. reprint ed. lib. bdg. 150.00 (0-7812-6826-5) Rprt Serv.

— Westward Ho: A Tale, 2 vols., Set. LC 06-25598. 1968. reprint ed. 39.00 (0-403-00066-1) Scholarly.

Paule, Jean. The German Settlement at Anaheim. 74p. (Orig.). 1990. pap. 10.00 (1-877959-02-2) D Henson Bks.

***Pauleau, Y., et al, eds.** Chemistry for Electronic Materials: Proceedings of Symposium C, 1992 E-MRS Spring Conference, Strasbourg, France, 2-5 June 1992. (European Materials Research Society Symposia Proceedings Ser.: 33). viii, 206p. 1993. 197.25 (0-444-89907-3) Elsevier.

***Pauleau, Yves, ed.** Materials & Processes for Surface & Interface Engineering: Proceedings of the NATO Advanced Study Institute, Chateau de Bonas, Gers, France, July 18-29, 1994. LC 95-11665. (NATO ASI Ser.: Series E, Applied Sciences: Vol. 290). 660p. (C). 1995. lib. bdg. 299.00 (0-7923-3458-2) Kluwer Ac.

Paulenoff, Michael J., jt. auth. see Kroll, Stanley.

Paules, Greta F. Dishing It Out: Power & Resistance among Waitresses in a New Jersey Restaurant. (Women in the Political Economy Ser.). (C). 1991. 39.95 (0-87722-887-6); pap. 17.95 (0-87722-888-4) Temple U Pr.

***Paulet, Jean-Pierre.** Dictionnaire D'Economie. 265p. (FRE.). 1992. pap. 49.95 (0-7859-7771-6, 2212008082) Fr & Eur.

Paulet, William. The Lord Marques Idlenes: Conteining Mainfold Matters of Acceptable Devise. LC 79-84131. (English Experience Ser.: No. 949). 112p. 1979. reprint ed. lib. bdg. 11.50 (90-221-0949-6) Walter J Johnson.

Pauletto, Bruno. Strength Training for Basketball. LC 93-17540. (Illus.). 144p. 1994. 14.95 (0-87322-433-7, PPAU0433) Human Kinetics.

— Strength Training for Coaches. LC 90-13122. (Illus.). 192p. (Orig.). 1991. pap. text ed. 19.00x (0-88011-371-5, PPAU0371) Human Kinetics.

— Strength Training for Football. LC 92-12982. (Illus.). 141p. 1993. pap. 14.95 (0-87322-398-5, PPAU0398) Human Kinetics.

Pauley, Bruce F. From Prejudice to Persecution: A History of Austrian Anti-Semitism. LC 91-50249. (Illus.). xxx, 426p. (C). 1992. 55.00 (0-8078-1995-6) U of NC Pr.

— Habsburg Legacy, Eighteen Sixty-Seven to Nineteen Thirty-Nine. LC 76-56401. (Berkshire Problem Studies). 204p. 1977. reprint ed. pap. text ed. 12.50 (0-88275-485-8) Krieger.

— Hitler & the Forgotten Nazis: A History of Austrian National Socialism. LC 80-17006. xvi, 292p. 1981. 34.95 (0-8078-1456-3) U of NC Pr.

— Hitler & the Forgotten Nazis: A History of Austrian National Socialism. LC 80-17006. xvi, 292p. 1987. pap. 14.95 (0-8078-4182-X) U of NC Pr.

Pauley, Michael J. Unreconstructed Rebel: The Life of General John McCausland. LC 92-61980. (Illus.). 112p. (Orig.). 1993. pap. 9.95 (0-929521-65-X) Pictorial Hist.

Pauley, Milton. The Do's & Don'ts of Puts & Calls. LC 76-2045. 79p. 1976. 9.95 (0-678-09957-X) Kelley.

Pauley, Steven E. & Riordan, Daniel. Technical Report Writing Today, 3 Vols. 3rd ed. LC 86-81305. 388p. (C). 1987. text ed. 39.56 (0-395-34251-1) HM.

Pauley, Thomas K., jt. auth. see Green, N. Bayard.

Paulhan, Jean. Progress in Love on the Slow Side: Recits. Laennec, Christine M. & Syrotinski, Michael, trs. LC 94-1316. (French Modernist Library). 184p. 1994. text ed. 25.00 (0-8032-3705-7) U of Nebr Pr.

Pauli, E. Speisekarten-Fuer sie Uebersetzt: Menu Reader. 15th ed. 86p. (ENG, FRE & GER.). 1983. 19.95 (0-8288-1302-7, M15238) Fr & Eur.

Pauli, Eugen. Classical Cooking the Modern Way. 2nd ed. 1989. text ed. 49.95 (0-442-27206-5) Van Nos Reinhold.

Pauli, Gunter A. Crusader for the Future: A Portrait of Aurelio Peccei, Founder of the Club of Rome. (Illus.). 110p. 1987. 53.00 (0-08-034861-0, Pergamon Pr) Elsevier.

Pauli, Gunter A., jt. auth. see Wright, Richard W.

Pauli, Karen. The Care & Feeding of Spinning Wheels. LC 81-80903. (Illus.). 84p. 1986. pap. 7.50 (0-934026-04-1) Interweave.

Pauli, Karen L. Insuring High Value Personal Property. 1991. 29.50 (1-56461-016-0, 46040) Rough Notes.

Pauli, Mary, jt. auth. see Theriot, Billie.

Pauli, Reinhold. Life of Alfred the Great. Thorpe, B., tr. LC 68-57869. (Bohn's Antiquarian Library). reprint ed. 46.00 (0-404-50021-8) AMS Pr.

Pauli, Ulf. The Baltic States in Facts, Figures & Maps. (Illus.). 72p. 1994. pap. 8.95 (1-85756-074-4, Pub. by Janus Pubng UK) Paul & Co Pubs.

Pauli, W. General Principles of Quantum Mechanics. 212p. 1990. pap. 28.00 (0-387-09842-9) Spr-Verlag.

Pauli, Wolfgang. Theory of Relativity. xiv, 241p. 1981. reprint ed. pap. 6.95 (0-486-64152-X) Dover.

Pauli, Wolfgang, et al. Writings on Physics & Philosophy. LC 94-15098. 1994. write for info. (0-387-56859-X) Spr-Verlag.

***Pauliat, Paul.** Dictionnaire Bilingue. 1976. write for info. (0-7859-7652-3, 2034017366) Fr & Eur.

Paulick, Mark A., jt. auth. see Turner, Glenn W.

Paulick, Raymond S., ed. Stakes Annual for Nineteen Ninety-Three. (Illus.). 480p. (Orig.). 1994. pap. 24.95 (0-939049-57-0) Blood-Horse.

Paulick, Raymond S. & Mearns, Dan, eds. Auctions of 1993. (Illus.). 350p. (Orig.). 1994. pap. 35.00 (0-939049-56-2) Blood-Horse.

— Auctions of 1994: Annual Supplement to the Blood-Horse. (Blood-Horse Supplement Ser.). (Illus.). 400p. (Orig.). 1995. pap. 40.00 (0-939049-64-3) Blood-Horse.

— Breeder's Guide for 1993: Annual Supplements. (Illus.). 1994. 95.00 (0-939049-69-4) Blood-Horse.

— Sires of Nineteen Ninety-Three. (Illus.). 190p. (Orig.). 1994. pap. 16.95 (0-939049-58-9) Blood-Horse.

— Sires of 1994: Annual Supplement to the Blood-Horse. (Blood-Horse Supplement Ser.). (Illus.). 180p. (Orig.). 1995. pap. 24.95 (0-939049-66-X) Blood-Horse.

— The Source for North American Racing & Breeding, 1994-95. Orig. Title: The List, The Blood-Horse Directory of North American Racing & Breeding. 470p. (Orig.). 1994. pap. 19.95 (0-939049-59-7) Blood-Horse.

— The Source for North American Racing & Breeding, 1995-96: Annual Supplement to the Blood-Horse. (Blood-Horse Supplement Ser.). 515p. (Orig.). 1995. pap. 19.95 (0-939049-67-8) Blood-Horse.

— Stakes Annual for 1994: Annual Supplement to the Blood-Horse. (Blood-Horse Supplement Ser.). (Illus.). 475p. (Orig.). 1995. pap. 35.00 (0-939049-65-1) Blood-Horse.

— Stallion Register for 1996: Annual Supplement to the Blood Horse. (Blood Horse Supplement Ser.). (Illus.). 1500p. (Orig.). 1995. pap. 29.95 (0-939049-68-6) Blood-Horse.

— Stallion Register, 1995. (Illus.). 1500p. (Orig.). 1994. pap. 29.95 (0-939049-60-0) Blood-Horse.

***Paulidis, Stephen J.** The Exuma Guide: A Cruising Guide to the Exuma Cays. LC 94-39266. (Illus.). 224p. 1995. pap. 24.95 (0-9639566-1-2) Seaworthy WI.

Paulien, Jon. Decoding Revelation's Trumpets: Literary Allusions & Interpretation of Revelation 8:7-12. (Andrews University Seminary Doctoral Dissertation Ser.: Vol. 11). 506p. 1988. pap. 19.99 (0-943872-44-8) Andrews Univ Pr.

— Present Truth in the Real World: Can Adventists Keep & Share Their Faith in a Secular Society? LC 92-32316. 1993. pap. 10.95 (0-8163-1127-7) Pacific Pr Pub Assn.

***Paulier, John.** John: Jesus Gives Life to a New Generation. (Abundant Life Bible Amplifier Ser.). 1995. 17.95 (0-8163-1245-1); pap. 12.95 (0-8163-1244-3) Pacific Pr Pub Assn.

Paulik, Helmut. Lexicon of Education Practice: Lexikon der Ausbildungspraxis. 3rd ed. 256p. (GER.). 1982. pap. 49.95 (0-8288-1394-9, M7274) Fr & Eur.

***Paulin, Barbara.** Path of Promise, Path of Peace: How to Hear Your Higher Self Speak. LC 94-28852. 1995. 12.95 (0-87604-328-7, 397) ARE Pr.

Paulin, Mary A. Creative Uses of Children's Literature. LC 81-12405. 730p. 1986. 55.00 (0-208-01861-1, Lib Prof Pubns); pap. 47.50 (0-208-01862-X, Lib Prof Pubns) Shoe String.

— More Creative Uses of Children's Literature, Vol. 1: Introducing Books in All Kinds of Ways. LC 92-8916. xvii, 619p. 1992. lib. bdg. 57.50 (0-208-02202-3, Lib Prof Pubns); pap. text ed. 35.00 (0-208-02203-1, Lib Prof Pubns) Shoe String.

Paulin, Michael. The Ballad of Daniel Shays. (Illus.). 120p. (Orig.). 1986. pap. 12.95 (0-9609404-5-6) J R Greene.

Paulin, Tom. Ireland & the English Crisis. 1988. pap. 18.95 (0-906427-64-9, Pub. by Bloodaxe Bks UK) Dufour.

— Minotaur: Poetry & the Nation State. 298p. (C). 1992. 29.95 (0-674-57637-3) HUP.

— Walking a Line. 128p. (Orig.). 1995. pap. 9.95 (0-571-17081-1) Faber & Faber.

Paulin, Tom, ed. The Faber Book of Political Verse. 480p. 1986. pap. 18.95 (0-571-13667-2) Faber & Faber.

— The Faber Book of Vernacular Verse. 432p. 1994. pap. 14.95 (0-571-17060-9) Faber & Faber.

Paulin, Tom & Connor, Noel. Book of Juniper. 24p. 1981. pap. 6.95 (0-906427-16-9, Pub. by Bloodaxe Bks UK) Dufour.

Paulin, Tom, ed. see James, Henry.

Pauling, Chris. Introducing Buddhism. 80p. (Orig.). 1993. pap. 6.50 (0-904766-63-2, Pub. by Windhorse UK) Windhorse Pubns.

P
Q

An Asterisk (*) at the beginning of an entry indicates that the title is appearing in BIP for the first time.

Pauling, Linus. General Chemistry. (Illus.). 992p. 1988. reprint ed. pap. text ed. 18.95 (*0-486-65622-5*) Dover.

— How to Live Longer & Feel Better. 416p. 1987. mass mkt. 5.99 (*0-380-70289-4*) Avon.

— The Nature of the Chemical Bond & the Structure of Molecules & Crystals: An Introduction to Modern Structural Chemistry. 3rd ed. (George Fisher Baker Non-Resident Lectureship in Chemistry at Cornell University Ser.). (Illus.). 644p. 1960. 65.00 (*0-8014-0333-2*) Cornell U Pr.

Pauling, Linus & Ikeda. Lifelong Quest for Peace. 158p. (C). 1992. pap. text ed. 14.95 (*0-86720-277-7*); boxed 24.95 (*0-86720-278-5*) Jones & Bartlett.

Pauling, Linus & Wilson, E. Bright. Introduction to Quantum Mechanics with Applications to Chemistry. (Physics Ser.). 468p. 1985. reprint ed. pap. 10.95 (*0-486-64871-0*) Dover.

Pauling, Linus, jt. auth. see Cameron, Ewan.

Pauling, Linus C. General Chemistry. 3rd ed. LC 78-75625. (Books in Chemistry Ser.). (Illus.). 975p. reprint ed. pap. 180.00 (*0-317-09083-6*, 2010726) Bks Demand.

Pauling, Sharon, jt. auth. see Prendergast, John.

Paulino, G., jt. ed. see Buck, C.

Paulinus, A. S. & Bartholomaeo, S. Dissertation on the Sanskrit Language. (Studies in History of Linguistics: No. 12). xxviii, 224p. 1977. 59.00x (*90-272-0953-7*) Benjamins North Am.

Paulinus of Nola. Letters of Saint Paulinus of Nola, 1. Quasten & Burqhardt, eds. (Ancient Christian Writers Ser.: Nos. 35-36). 1966. 18.95 (*0-8091-0088-6*) Paulist Pr.

— Letters of Saint Paulinus of Nola, 2. Quasten & Burqhardt, eds. (Ancient Christian Writers Ser.: Nos. 35-36). 1967. 24.95 (*0-8091-0089-4*) Paulist Pr.

Paulis, L. Technique & Design of Cluny Lace. Rutgers, M., tr. 1984. 16.50 (*0-903585-18-9*) Robin & Russ.

Paulisch, F. N. The Design of an Extendible Graph Editor. (Lecture Notes in Computer Science Ser.: Vol. 704). xv, 184p. 1993. pap. write for info. (*3-540-57090-X*) Spr-Verlag.

Paulissen, Maisie & McQueary, Carl. MA: The Story of Governor Miriam Amanda Ferguson, 1875-1961. LC 94-4455. 1994. 27.50 (*0-89015-971-8*) Sunbelt Media.

Paulita, Mary. Half-Pint on Guadalcanal: A Saga of Heroism, Commitment & Love. (Illus.). 144p. (Orig.). (YA). (gr. 8). 1993. pap. 10.00 (*0-9631198-1-8*) Marist Miss Sis.

Paulk, Don. I Laugh . . . I Cry . . . 212p. 1987. 12.95 (*0-917595-17-3*) Kingdom Pubs.

Paulk, Don, jt. auth. see Paulk, Earl.

Paulk, Earl. The Church: Trampled or Triumphant? 240p. (Orig.). 1990. pap. 9.95 (*0-917595-35-1*) Kingdom Pubs.

— El Cuerpo Herido de Cristo. Orig. Title: Wounded Body of Christ. 144p. (Orig.). (SPA.). 1985. pap. 3.50 (*0-917595-05-X*) Kingdom Pubs.

— Divine Runner. LC 78-71967. 142p. (Orig.). 1978. pap. 3.25 (*0-917595-00-9*) Kingdom Pubs.

— Held in the Heavens until . . . 256p. (Orig.). 1985. pap. 7.95 (*0-917595-07-6*) Kingdom Pubs.

— How to Conquer Depression. (Orig.). 1989. mass mkt. 2.50 (*0-917595-30-0*) Kingdom Pubs.

— The Local Church Says "Hell No" 190p. (Orig.). 1991. pap. 9.95 (*0-917595-40-8*) Kingdom Pubs.

— The Prophetic Community. 140p. (Orig.). 1995. pap. 7.99 (*1-56043-841-X*) Destiny Image.

— The Provoker. Weeks, Tricia, ed. 400p. (Orig.). 1986. pap. 9.95 (*0-917595-09-2*) Kingdom Pubs.

— Satan Unmasked. 344p. (Orig.). 1984. pap. 9.95 (*0-917595-03-3*) Kingdom Pubs.

— Sex Is God's Idea. 175p. (Orig.). 1985. pap. 7.95 (*0-917595-04-1*) Kingdom Pubs.

— Spiritual Megatrends. 293p. 1988. 8.95 (*0-917595-16-5*) Kingdom Pubs.

— That the World May Know. 189p. (Orig.). 1987. pap. 7.95 (*0-917595-15-7*) Kingdom Pubs.

— Thrust in the Sickle & Reap. 141p. (Orig.). 1986. pap. 5.95 (*0-917595-11-4*) Kingdom Pubs.

— Turn on the Light at Christmas. 32p. 1987. mass mkt. 1.50 (*0-917595-23-8*) Kingdom Pubs.

— Twenty-Twenty Vision. 1988. pap. 2.50 (*0-917595-24-6*) Kingdom Pubs.

— Ultimate Kingdom. 2nd ed. 264p. (Orig.). 1987. reprint ed. pap. 7.95 (*0-917595-13-0*) Kingdom Pubs.

— El Ultimo Reino. Orig. Title: The Ultimate Kingdom. 268p. (Orig.). (SPA.). 1987. pap. 3.50 (*0-917595-19-X*) Kingdom Pubs.

— Vision Twenty-Twenty: Una Mirada Clara al Reino de Dios. 50p. 1989. mass mkt. 2.50 (*0-917595-26-2*) Kingdom Pubs.

— Winning Spiritual Warfare in the Family. 21p. 1987. mass mkt. 1.50 (*0-917595-20-3*) Kingdom Pubs.

— Wounded Body of Christ. 2nd ed. 160p. 1985. pap. 4.95 (*0-917595-06-8*) Kingdom Pubs.

— Your Guide to Greatness. 64p. 1990. 3.50 (*0-917595-38-6*) Kingdom Pubs.

Paulk, Earl & Paulk, Don. One Hundred One Questions Your Pastor Hopes You Never Ask. 128p. 1990. 12.95 (*0-917595-36-X*) Kingdom Pubs.

Paulk, Mark, et al. The Capability Maturity Model: Guidelines in Improving the Software Process. (SEI Series Software Engineering). (Illus.). 416p. (C). 1995. text ed. 49.50 (*0-201-54664-7*) Addison-Wesley.

Paulk, William B. Basic & Intermediate Celestial Navigation. LC 89-30771. (Illus.). 224p. 1989. 16.95 (*0-688-08939-9*, Hearst Marine Bks) Morrow.

Paull, Bonnie. Winning with Words: An Introduction to the Dictionary. 128p. (C). 1993. per. 20.50 (*0-8403-8706-7*) Kendall-Hunt.

Paull, Bonnie E. Winning with Grammar: Basic Workbook I. 2nd ed. 224p. (C). 1993. per. 22.95 (*0-8403-8554-4*) Kendall-Hunt.

— Winning with Grammar: Basic Workbook II. 2nd ed. 192p. (C). 1993. per. 22.95 (*0-8403-8705-9*) Kendall-Hunt.

**Paull, Donald.* Fitness to Stand Trial. LC 92-35105. (American Series in Behavioral Science & Law). (Illus.). 196p. 1993. pap. 30.95 (*0-398-06316-8*) C C Thomas.

— Fitness to Stand Trial. LC 92-35105. (American Series in Behavioral Science & Law). (Illus.). 196p. 1993. 51.95x (*0-398-05836-9*) C C Thomas.

Paull, Elisabeth M. Paull-Irwin a Family Sketch. (Illus.). viii, 198p. 1993. reprint ed. lib. bdg. 42.50 (*0-8328-2984-6*); reprint ed. pap. 32.50 (*0-8328-2985-4*) Higginson Bk Co.

Paull, Irving S., et al. Trade Association Activities. (Business Enterprises Reprint Ser.). viii, 381p. 1983. reprint ed. lib. bdg. 45.00 (*0-89941-209-2*, 302950) W S Hein.

Paull, Nancy B. Capital Medicine: A Tradition of Excellence. (Illus.). 128p. 1994. 29.95 (*1-882933-02-8*) Cherbo Pub Grp.

Paull, R. E. & Armstrong, J. W., eds. Insect Pests & Fresh Horticultural Products: Treatments & Responses. 370p. 1994. 85.00 (*0-85198-872-5*) CAB Intl.

Paull, Rachel K. & Paull, Richard A. Geology of Wisconsin & Upper Michigan: Including Parts of Adjacent States. 2nd ed. 288p. 1980. per. 28.95 (*0-8403-2142-2*) Kendall-Hunt.

Paull, Richard A., jt. auth. see Paull, Rachel K.

Paull, Robert C., jt. auth. see Brooks, B. David.

Paull, Susan G. Teach an Adult to Read: Tutor Training Workbook. Ringo, Betty, ed. 40p. 1987. 6.95 (*0-910475-36-9*) KET.

Paull, Sylvia L. Rainclouds Study the Ten Commandments: A Bibly Study Drama. (Illus.). 29p. (Orig.). 1993. pap. 2.50 (*0-88680-393-4*) I E Clark.

Paull, Thelma. Kids Skills: A Resource for Discussion Group Leaders. (C). 1990. 75.00 (*0-86431-084-6*, Pub. by Aust Council Educ Res AT) St Mut.

— Talk about Problems. (C). 1990. 60.00 (*0-86431-085-4*, Pub. by Aust Council Educ Res AT) St Mut.

Paulley, J. W. & Pelser, H. E. Psychological Managements for Psychosomatic Disorders. (Illus.). 370p. 1989. pap. 70.00 (*0-387-19298-0*) Spr-Verlag.

Paullin, C. O. & Paxson, F. L. Guide to the Materials in London Archives for the History of the United States Since 1783. (Carnegie Institute Ser.: Vol. 7). 1914. 55.00 (*0-527-00687-4*) Periodicals Srv.

Paullin, Charles. Navy of the American Revolution. LC 73-122997. (American History & Americana Ser.: No. 47). 1970. reprint ed. lib. bdg. 75.00 (*0-8383-1130-X*) M S G Haskell Hse.

Paullin, Charles O. Commodore John Rodgers. LC 79-6127. (Navies & Men Ser.). (Illus.). 1980. reprint ed. lib. bdg. 44.95 (*0-405-13049-X*) Ayer.

— Diplomatic Negotiations of American Naval Officers 1778-1883. 11.75 (*0-8446-1342-8*) Peter Smith.

Paulling, John, jt. auth. see Christy, Dennis T.

Paulos, Dan. He's Put the Whole World in Her Hands: Silhouette Paper-Cuttings. LC 93-78532. 130p. 1993. 19.95 (*0-89870-466-9*) Ignatius Pr.

Paulos, Dan, ed. & illus. He Put the Whole World in Her Hands. 2nd ed. 126p. 1990. text ed. 19.95 (*0-937739-09-X*) Roman IL.

Paulos, John A. Beyond Numeracy. 1992. pap. 12.00 (*0-679-73807-X*, Vin) Random.

— Beyond Numeracy: An Uncommon Dictionary of Mathematics. 1991. 21.50 (*0-394-58640-9*) Knopf.

— Beyond Numeracy: Ruminations of a Numbers Man. 1991. 22.00 (*0-685-48163-8*) Knopf.

— I Think, Therefore I Laugh. LC 89-40602. 1990. pap. 9.00 (*0-679-72954-2*, Vin) Random.

— Innumeracy. 1990. pap. 8.95 (*0-679-72601-2*, Vin) Random.

— Innumeracy: Mathematical Illiteracy & Its Consequences. LC 88-17001. 224p. 1989. 16.95 (*0-8090-7447-8*) Hill & Wang.

— A Mathematician Reads the Newspaper. LC 94-48206. (Illus.). 180p. 1995. 18.00 (*0-465-04362-3*) Basic.

— Mathematics & Humor. LC 80-12742. 1982. pap. 10.95 (*0-226-65025-1*) U Ch Pr.

Paulos, Lonnie E. & Tibone, James E. Operative Techniques in Shoulder Surgery. 208p. 1990. 89.50 (*0-8342-0184-4*) Raven.

Paulos, Martha, ed. Insectasides: Great Poets on Man's Pest Friend. LC 94-19513. 1995. 14.95 (*0-670-85567-7*, Viking) Viking Penguin.

Paulos, Martha, illus. Felines: Great Poets on Notorious Cats. 64p. 1992. 14.95 (*0-8118-0103-9*) Chronicle Bks.

Paulos, Nicholas. The Doll in the Window. 250p. per., pap. 9.95 (*0-89697-291-7*) Intl Univ Pr.

Paulovich, David. Midterm Survey of Churched Developed: 1985-1989. Weaver, Irvin D., ed. 87p. 1990. pap. 5.00 (*1-877736-09-0*) MB Missions.

Paulre, B. E., ed. System Dynamics & the Analysis of Change: Proceedings of the 6th International Conference, University of Paris, Dauphine, November, '80. 382p. 1981. 102.75 (*0-444-86251-X*, North Holland) Elsevier.

**Pauls & Reed.* Quick Reference to Physical Therapy. 688p. 1995. 38.00 (*0-8342-0654-4*) Aspen Pub.

Pauls, Michael, jt. auth. see Facaros, Dana.

Paulsell, Karen, jt. auth. see Emerson, Sandra L.

Paulsell, William & Kelty, Matthew. Letters from a Hermit. 1978. 7.95 (*0-87243-086-3*) Templegate.

Paulsell, William O. Rules for Prayer. LC 93-4387. 160p. 1993. pap. 9.95 (*0-8091-3410-1*) Paulist Pr.

— Taste & See: A Personal Guide to the Spiritual Life. rev. ed. 128p. 1992. pap. 9.99 (*0-8272-3629-8*) Chalice Pr.

— Tough Minds, Tender Hearts: Six Prophets of Social Justice. 256p. 1990. pap. 11.95 (*0-8091-3184-6*) Paulist Pr.

Paulsell, William O., ed. Sermons in a Monastery: Chapter Talks by Matthew Kelty Ocso, No. 59. (Cistercian Studies). 1983. 14.95 (*0-87907-858-8*); pap. 6.00 (*0-87907-958-4*) Cistercian Pubns.

**Paulsen.* Amos Goes Bananas. (Culpepper Adventures Ser.: No. 24). (J). 1995. pap. 3.50 (*0-440-41008-8*) Dell.

— Danger on Midnight River: Gary Paulsen World of Adventure. 1995. pap. 3.50 (*0-440-41028-2*) Dell.

— Dunc & Amos Go to the Dogs. (Culpepper Adventures Ser.: No. 25). (J). 1995. pap. 3.50 (*0-440-41040-1*) Dell.

— River. 1995. mass mkt. 1.99 (*0-440-21958-2*) Dell.

Paulsen, Arvid, tr. see Strindberg, August.

Paulsen, Brendan P. The Luck of the Irish. (J). (gr. 2-4). 1988. 19.97 (*0-8172-2752-0*) Raintree Steck-V.

— The Luck of the Irish. (Publish-a-Book Clippers Ser.). (Illus.). 32p. (J). (gr. 2-4). 1988. audio 29.28 (*0-8172-2467-X*) Raintree Steck-V.

Paulsen, C. Alvin, jt. ed. see Mastroianni, Luigi, Jr.

Paulsen, David W., jt. auth. see Cederblom, Jerry.

Paulsen, Deborah, ed. see Schwartz, Linda K.

Paulsen, Deborah, ed. see Wolf, Charles R.

Paulsen, Deirdre, jt. auth. see Rider, Rowland.

Paulsen, Douglas F. Basic Histology: Examination & Board Review. 2nd ed. (Illus.). 408p. (C). 1993. pap. text ed. 36.95 (*0-8385-0569-4*, A0569-2) Appleton & Lange.

Paulsen, Frank, ed. Contemporary Issues in American Education. LC 66-24302. 130p. reprint ed. pap. 37.10 (*0-317-51989-1*, 2027387) Bks Demand.

Paulsen, Frank R. American Education: Challenges & Images. LC 66-28787. 124p. reprint ed. pap. 35.40 (*0-8357-5363-8*, 2056212) Bks Demand.

— Changing Dimensions in International Education. LC 73-76783. 175p. reprint ed. pap. 49.90 (*0-317-51988-3*, 2027386) Bks Demand.

Paulsen, Friedrich. Autobiography. Lorenz, Theodore, tr. LC 38-38641. reprint ed. 19.00 (*0-404-04945-1*) AMS Pr.

— Die Deutschen Universitaten und das Universitatsstudium. xii, 575p. 1966. reprint ed. write for info. (*0-318-71853-7*, Pub. by Georg Olms GW) Lubrecht & Cramer.

— German Education Past & Present. Lorenz, T., tr. LC 75-41209. reprint ed. 23.00 (*0-404-14693-7*) AMS Pr.

Paulsen, G. Norsk-Tysk Ordbok: Norwegian - German Dictionary. 416p. (GER & NOR.). 1973. 39.95 (*0-8288-6326-1*, M-9466) Fr & Eur.

Paulsen, Gary. Amos & the Alien. (Culpepper Adventures Ser.: No. 19). (J). (gr. 4-7). 1994. 3.50 (*0-440-40990-X*) Dell.

— Amos Gets Famous. (Culpepper Adventures Ser.: No. 8). (J). (gr. 4-7). 1993. pap. 3.25 (*0-440-40749-4*) Dell.

— Amos Gets Married. (Culpepper Adventure Special Ser.: No. 23). (J). (gr. 4-7). 1995. pap. 3.50 (*0-440-40933-0*) Dell.

— Amos's Killer Concert Caper. (Culpepper Adventures Ser.: No. 22). (J). (gr. 4-7). 1995. pap. 3.50 (*0-440-40989-6*) Dell.

— Amos's Last Stand. (Culpepper Adventures Ser.: No. 11). (J). (gr. 4-7). 1993. pap. 3.25 (*0-440-40775-3*) Dell.

— The Boy Who Owned the School. (J). 1991. pap. 3.50 (*0-440-70694-7*) Dell.

— The Boy Who Owned the School. LC 89-23048. 112p. (J). (gr. 6-9). 1990. 14.95 (*0-531-05865-4*); lib. bdg. 14.99 (*0-531-08465-5*) Orchard Bks Watts.

— Boy Who Owned the School. (J). (gr. 4-7). 1991. pap. 3.50 (*0-440-40524-6*, YB) Dell.

— Call Me Francis Tucket. (J). 1995. write for info. (*0-385-32116-3*) Delacorte.

— Canyons. (J). 1990. 15.95 (*0-385-30153-7*) Delacorte.

— Canyons. 1991. mass mkt. 3.99 (*0-440-21023-2*) Dell.

— Canyons. (J). (gr. 4-8). 1992. 17.25 (*0-8446-6590-8*) Peter Smith.

— The Car. LC 93-41834. (YA). (gr. 7 up). 1994. 13.95 (*0-15-292878-2*) HarBrace.

— The Case of the Dirty Bird. (Culpepper Adventures Ser.: No. 1). 96p. (J). (gr. 4-7). 1992. pap. 3.50 (*0-440-40598-X*, YB) Dell.

— A Christmas Sonata. LC 90-46891. (Illus.). 80p. (J). (gr. 3-7). 1992. 14.95 (*0-385-30441-2*) Delacorte.

— Christmas Sonata. 1994. mass mkt. 3.99 (*0-440-40958-6*) Dell.

— Clabbered Dirt: Sweet Grass. 1994. pap. 9.95 (*0-15-600052-0*) HarBrace.

— Clabbered Dirt, Sweet Grass. 144p. 1992. 19.95 (*0-15-118101-2*) HarBrace.

— Coach Amos. (Culpepper Adventures Ser.: No. 18). (J). (gr. 4-7). 1994. 3.50 (*0-440-40930-6*) Dell.

— The Cookcamp. 128p. (J). (gr. 4-7). 1992. pap. 3.99 (*0-440-40704-4*, YB) Dell.

— The Cookcamp. LC 90-7734. 128p. (J). (gr. 5-7). 1991. 14.95 (*0-531-05927-8*); lib. bdg. 14.99 (*0-531-08527-9*) Orchard Bks Watts.

— Cowpokes & Desperadoes. (Culpepper Adventures Ser.: No. 16). (J). (gr. 4-7). 1994. pap. 3.50 (*0-440-40902-0*) Dell.

— The Crossing. (J). (gr. k up). 1990. mass mkt. 3.99 (*0-440-20582-4*, LFL) Dell.

— The Crossing. LC 87-7738. 128p. (J). (gr. 6-8). 1987. 14.95 (*0-531-05709-7*); lib. bdg. 14.99 (*0-531-08309-8*) Orchard Bks Watts.

— Culpepper Adventures: Dunc & Amos Meet the Slasher, No. 20. 1994. pap. 3.50 (*0-440-40939-X*) Dell.

— Culpepper Adventures: Dunc & the Greased Sticks of Doom, No. 21. 1994. pap. 3.50 (*0-440-40940-3*) Dell.

— Culpepper's Cannon. (Culpepper Mystery Adventure Ser.: No. 3). 96p. (J). (gr. 3-7). 1992. pap. 3.50 (*0-440-40617-X*, YB) Dell.

— Dancing Carl. (J). 1987. pap. 3.99 (*0-14-032241-8*, Puffin) Puffin Bks.

— Dancing Carl. LC 86-30245. (J). (gr. 5 up). 1987. pap. 3.95 (*0-685-19101-X*, Puffin) Puffin Bks.

— Dancing Carl. LC 83-2663. 144p. (J). (gr. 6-8). 1983. text ed. 13.95 (*0-02-770210-3*, Bradbury S&S) S&S Childrens.

— Dogsong. (J). (gr. 5-9). 1987. pap. 4.99 (*0-14-032235-3*, Puffin) Puffin Bks.

— Dogsong. LC 84-20443. 192p. (YA). (gr. 7 up). 1985. text ed. 14.95 (*0-02-770180-8*, Bradbury S&S) S&S Childrens.

— Dunc & Amos & the Red Tatoos, No. 12. (J). (gr. 4-7). 1993. pap. 3.50 (*0-440-40790-7*) Dell.

— Dunc & Amos Hit the Big Top. (Culpepper Adventures Ser.: No. 9). (J). (gr. 4-7). 1993. pap. 3.25 (*0-440-40756-7*) Dell.

— Dunc & the Flaming Ghost. (Culpepper Adventures Ser.: No. 7). 96p. (J). (gr. 3-7). 1992. pap. 3.50 (*0-440-40686-2*, YB) Dell.

— Dunc & the Haunted House. (Culpepper Adventures Ser.: No. 15). (J). 1993. pap. 3.50 (*0-440-40893-8*) Dell.

— Dunc Breaks the Record. (Culpepper Adventures Ser.: No. 6). 96p. (Orig.). (J). (gr. 3-7). 1992. pap. 3.25 (*0-440-40678-1*, YB) Dell.

— Dunc Gets Tweaked. (Culpepper Adventures Ser.: No. 4). 96p. (Orig.). (J). (gr. 3-5). 1992. pap. 3.25 (*0-440-40642-0*, YB) Dell.

— Dunc's Doll. (Culpepper Adventures Ser.: No. 2). 80p. (J). (gr. 4-7). 1992. pap. 3.50 (*0-440-40601-3*, YB) Dell.

— Dunc's Dump. (Culpepper Adventures Ser.: No. 10). (J). (gr. 4-7). 1993. pap. 3.25 (*0-440-40762-1*) Dell.

— Dunc's Halloween. (Culpepper Adventures Ser.: No. 5). 96p. (J). (gr. 3-7). 1992. pap. 3.50 (*0-440-40659-5*, YB) Dell.

— Dunc's Undercover. (J). 1993. pap. 3.50 (*0-440-40874-1*) Dell.

— Eastern Sun, Winter Moon: An Autobiographical Odyssey. LC 91-47127. 1993. 22.95 (*0-15-127260-3*) HarBrace.

— Eastern Sun, Winter Moon: An Autobiographical Odyssey. (Illus.). 256p. 1995. pap. 11.00 (*0-15-600203-5*) HarBrace.

— Eastern Sun, Winter Moon: An Autobiographical Odyssey. large type ed. LC 93-11054. 1993. 21.95 (*0-7927-1698-1*, Curley Lrg Print); pap. 19.95 (*0-7927-1697-3*, Curley Lrg Print) Chivers N Amer.

— Escape from Fire Mountain. (Gary Paulsen World of Adventure Ser.). (J). (gr. 4-7). 1995. pap. 3.50 (*0-440-41025-8*) Dell.

— Father Water, Mother Woods: Essays on Fishing & Hunting in the North Woods. LC 94-2737. (Illus.). (YA). (gr. 6 up). 1994. 16.95 (*0-385-32053-1*) Delacorte.

— The Foxman. 128p. (J). (gr. 4 up). 1990. pap. 3.99 (*0-14-034311-3*, Puffin) Puffin Bks.

— The Foxman. 128p. (J). (gr. 4 up). 1990. pap. 11.95 (*0-670-83360-6*) Viking Child Bks.

— Harris & Me. (YA). (gr. 5 up). 1995. pap. 3.99 (*0-440-40994-2*) Dell.

— Harris & Me: A Summer Remembered. LC 93-19788. 1993. 13.95 (*0-15-292877-4*) HarBrace.

— Hatchet. 1986. 12.95 (*0-02-527403-1*) Macmillan.

— Hatchet. (J). (gr. 5-9). 1988. pap. 4.99 (*0-14-032724-X*, Puffin) Puffin Bks.

— Hatchet. LC 87-6416. 208p. (J). (gr. 6-8). 1987. text ed. 14.95 (*0-02-770130-1*, Bradbury S&S) S&S Childrens.

— Hatchet Rack Trim. (J). (gr. 4-7). 1989. pap. 4.99 (*0-14-034371-7*, Puffin) Puffin Bks.

— The Haymeadow. (J). (gr. 4-7). 1992. 15.00 (*0-385-30621-0*) Doubleday.

— Haymeadow. (J). (gr. 4-7). 1994. mass mkt. 3.99 (*0-440-40923-3*) Dell.

— Hook 'Em, Snotty! Gary Paulsen World of Adventure. (Gary Paulsen World of Adventure Ser.). (J). (gr. 3-7). 1995. mass mkt. 3.50 (*0-440-41027-4*) Dell.

— The Island. (J). (gr. k up). 1990. mass mkt. 3.99 (*0-440-20632-4*, LFL) Dell.

— The Island. LC 87-24761. 224p. (YA). (gr. 6-9). 1988. 15.95 (*0-531-05749-6*); lib. bdg. 15.99 (*0-531-08349-7*) Orchard Bks Watts.

— Kill Fee. 1990. 18.95 (*1-55611-203-3*) D I Fine.

— Legend of Red Horse Cavern. 1994. pap. 3.50 (*0-440-41023-1*) Dell.

— The Madonna Stories. 110p. 1989. 15.95 (*0-929431-00-6*) Van Vliet Co Inc.

— Madonna Stories. (J). (gr. 4-7). 1993. pap. 8.95 (*0-15-655116-0*, HB Juv Bks) HarBrace.

— Monument. 1991. 15.00 (*0-385-30518-4*) Delacorte.

— Monument. (YA). 1993. 3.99 (*0-440-40782-6*) Dell.

— Mr. Tucket. LC 93-31180. (J). 1994. 14.95 (*0-385-31169-9*) Delacorte.

— Murphy. 192p. 1987. 14.95 (*0-8027-4068-5*) Walker & Co.

— Murphy's Gold. 1988. 14.95 (*0-8027-4078-2*) Walker & Co.

— Murphy's Herd. 192p. 1989. 17.95 (*0-8027-4094-4*) Walker & Co.

— Murphy's Stand. LC 93-1058. 128p. 1993. 17.95 (*0-8027-1277-0*) Walker & Co.

— Night Rituals. 320p. 1989. 17.95 (*1-55611-129-0*) D I Fine.

— Night the White Deer Died. (YA). 1991. pap. 3.50 (*0-440-21092-5*, YB) Dell.

— Nightjohn. (YA). 1995. pap. 3.99 (*0-440-21936-1*) Dell.

— Nightjohn. LC 92-1222. 96p. (YA). 1993. pap. 14.00 (*0-385-30838-8*) Doubleday.

— Popcorn Days & Buttermilk Nights. 112p. (J). (gr. 5-9). 1989. pap. 3.99 (*0-14-034204-4*, Puffin) Puffin Bks.

— Prince Amos. (Culpepper Adventures Ser.: No. 17). (J). (gr. 4-7). 1994. pap. 3.50 (*0-440-40928-4*) Dell.

— The Rifle. LC 95-730. (J). 1995. write for info. (*0-15-928804-5*) HarBrace.

— The River. (J). 1991. 15.00 (*0-385-30388-2*) Doubleday.

— River. (YA). 1993. mass mkt. 4.50 (*0-440-40753-2*) Dell.

An Asterisk (*) at the beginning of an entry indicates that the title is appearing in BIP for the first time.

— Rock Jockeys. (Gary Paulsen World of Adventure Ser.). (J). (gr. 4-7). 1995. pap. 3.50 (*0-440-41026-6*) Dell.
— Rodomonte's Revenge. 1994. pap. 3.50 (*0-440-41024-X*) Dell.
— Sentries. 1987. pap. 4.99 (*0-14-032239-6*, Puffin) Puffin Bks.
— Sentries. LC 85-26978. 160p. (YA). (gr. 7 up). 1986. text ed. 14.95 (*0-02-770100-X*, Bradbury S&S) S&S Childrens.
— Sentries. (J). (gr. 5-9). reprint ed. pap. 3.95 (*0-317-62279-X*, Puffin) Puffin Bks.
— Sisters Hermanas. (YA). 1993. 10.95 (*0-15-275323-0*, HB Juv Bks); pap. 3.95 (*0-15-275324-9*, HB Juv Bks) HarBrace.
— The Tent. (J). 1995. 14.00 (*0-15-292879-0*) HarBrace.
— Tiltawhirl John. 1992. 17.25 (*0-8446-6535-5*) Peter Smith.
— Tiltawhirl John. (J). 1990. pap. 3.99 (*0-14-034312-1*, Puffin) Puffin Bks.
— The Tortilla Factory. LC 93-48590. (J). 1995. 14.00 (*0-15-292876-6*, HB Juv Bks) HarBrace.
— La Tortilleria. de Aragon Andujar, Gloria, tr. LC 94-18543. (Illus.). 32p. 1995. 14.00 (*0-15-200237-5*, Red Wagon Bks) HarBrace.
— Tracker. 1987. pap. 3.99 (*0-14-032240-X*, Puffin) Puffin Bks.
— Tracker. LC 83-22447. 96p. (J). (gr. 6-8). 1984. lib. bdg. 13.95 (*0-02-770220-0*, Bradbury S&S) S&S Childrens.
— Tracker. (J). (gr. 5-9). reprint ed. pap. 3.95 (*0-317-62280-3*, Puffin) Puffin Bks.
— The Voyage of the Frog. LC 88-15261. (Illus.). 160p. (J). (gr. 6-8). 1989. 15.95 (*0-531-05805-0*); lib. bdg. 15.99 (*0-531-08405-1*) Orchard Bks Watts.
— The Voyage of the Frog. large type ed. LC 93-30238. (Teen Survival Library). (YA). (gr. 9-12). 1993. 15.95 (*0-7862-0060-X*) Thorndike Pr.
— The Voyage of the Frog. (J). 1990. reprint ed. mass mkt. 3.99 (*0-440-40364-2*, Yearling Classics) Dell.
— The Wild Culpepper Cruise, No. 14. 1993. pap. 3.50 (*0-440-40883-0*) Dell.
— The Winter Room. LC 89-42541. 128p. (J). (gr. 6-9). 1989. 14.95 (*0-531-05839-5*); lib. bdg. 14.99 (*0-531-08439-6*) Orchard Bks Watts.
— Winter Room. (J). (gr. 4-7). 1991. pap. 3.50 (*0-440-40454-1*) Dell.
— Winterdance: The Fine Madness of Running the Iditarod. (YA). (gr. 9 up). 1994. 21.95 (*0-15-126227-6*) HarBrace.
— Winterdance: The Fine Madness of Running the Iditarod. (YA). (gr. 9 up). 1995. pap. 10.95 (*0-15-600145-4*) HarBrace.
— Woodsong. 144p. (YA). (gr. 7 up). 1991. pap. 4.50 (*0-14-034905-7*, Puffin) Puffin Bks.
— Woodsong. LC 89-70835. (Illus.). 160p. (YA). (gr. 7 up). 1990. text ed. 14.95 (*0-02-770221-9*, Bradbury S&S) S&S Childrens.

Paulsen, Gary & Burks, Brian. Murphy's Stand. large type ed. LC 93-48427. (Western Ser.). 177p. Date not set. bds. 17.95 (*0-7862-0169-X*) Thorndike Pr.
Paulsen, Gary & Paulsen, Ruth. Dogteam. (J). 1993. pap. 15.95 (*0-385-30550-8*) Delacorte.
***Paulsen, Gery & Burks, Brian.** Murphy's Ambush. 1995. 17.95 (*0-8027-4149-5*) Walker & Co.
Paulsen, Jim, pref. Quality Upstream: Quality Concepts Conference & Exposition, 1992. (Illus.). 1992. 50.00 (*1-56378-009-7*) ESD.
Paulsen, Joanna. Grace Livingston Hill: A Checklist. reprint ed. pap. 10.95 (*0-89190-993-1*, Rivercity Pr) Amereon Ltd.
Paulsen, Kathryn. The Complete Book of Magic & Witchcraft. 1970. pap. 4.99 (*0-451-16832-1*, E92712, Sig) NAL-Dutton.
Paulsen, Michael B., ed. College Choice: Understanding Student Enrollment Behavior. LC 91-60267. (ASHE-ERIC Higher Education Report Ser.: No. 6). 100p. 1990. pap. 17.00 (*1-878380-03-6*) GWU Schl E&HD.
Paulsen, Monrad G. The Problem of Assistance to the Indigent Accused. 103p. 1961. pap. 2.00 (*0-317-30872-6*, B169) Am Law Inst.
— The Problem of Discovery in Criminal Cases. 61p. 1961. pap. 1.00 (*0-317-30874-2*, B170) Am Law Inst.
— The Problem of Sentencing. 123p. 1962. pap. 1.00 (*0-317-30876-9*, B173) Am Law Inst.
— The Problems of Juvenile Courts & the Rights of Children. 174p. 1975. pap. 2.50 (*0-317-30878-5*, B174) Am Law Inst.
***Paulsen, Norman.** The Christ Consciousness: The Pure Self Within You. (Illus.). 496p. (Orig.). 1994. pap. 19.95 (*0-941848-05-1*) Builders Pub.
Paulsen, Ruth, jt. auth. see Paulsen, Gary.
***Paulsen, S. K.** Rainbow Slide: Kowanda Kids. (Illus.). 20p. (J). (ps-2). 1994. pap. 3.95 (*0-9638163-2-2*) Hisel Bk Ends.
Paulsen, Thomas D., jt. auth. see Mack, William P.
Paulsen, Timothy R. Collect Those Debts! How to Get Your Money & Still Keep Your Customers. 3rd ed. (Business Ser.). 112p. 1992. pap. 8.95 (*0-88908-541-2*) Self-Counsel Pr.
Paulsen, W., jt. ed. see Schirokauer, A.
Paulson, jt. ed. see Hutson.
Paulson, jt. ed. see Koller.
Paulson, Arvid, tr. see Strindberg, August.
Paulson, Bonnie L., tr. see Kelsen, Hans.
Paulson, Boyd C., Jr. Computer Applications in Construction. LC 94-2793. (Series in Construction Engineering & Project Management). 1995. text ed. write for info. (*0-07-048967-X*) McGraw.
Paulson, Boyd C. & Barrie, Donald S. Professional Construction Management Control. (Construction Engineering Ser.). (Illus.). 1978. text ed. write for info. (*0-07-003845-7*) McGraw.
Paulson, Boyd C., jt. auth. see Barrie, Donald S.
Paulson, C. Robert. Fiber Optic Technology & Applications in Image Transmission. 300p. 1991. 55.00 (*0-8493-7403-0*, CRC Reprint) Franklin.
Paulson, Daryl S. Walking the Point: Male Initiation & the Vietnam Experience. LC 94-8249. 96p. (Orig.). 1995. pap. 8.95 (*0-942963-49-0*) Distinctive Pub.
Paulson, David. Genitourinary Cancer I. 1982. lib. bdg. 131. 50 (*90-247-2480-5*) Kluwer Ac.
Paulson, David, ed. see Hamilton, Donna.
Paulson, David F., ed. Genitourinary Surgery, Vol. 1. LC 83-18969. (Illus.). 422p. reprint ed. pap. 120.30 (*0-8357-4661-5*, 2037591) Bks Demand.
— Prostatic Disorders. LC 88-9388. 397p. reprint ed. pap. 113.20 (*0-7837-2737-2*, 2043117) Bks Demand.
Paulson, David F., jt. auth. see DeKernion, Jean B.
Paulson, Deborah. How to Use Ami Pro Releases 2 & 3 for Windows. Reid, Christine, ed. 95p. (Orig.). 1992. pap. text ed. 125.00 (*1-56562-018-6*) OneOnOne Comp Trng.
Paulson, Dennis. Exotic Birds. 1989. 14.99 (*0-517-69090-X*) Random Hse Value.
— Shorebirds of the Pacific Northwest. LC 92-19050. (Illus.). 448p. 1993. 40.00 (*0-295-97233-5*) U of Wash Pr.
***Paulson, Ed.** The Complete Communications Handbook. 2nd ed. 1995. pap. 21.95 (*1-55622-476-1*) Wordware Pub.
— Learn CorelDRAW in a Day. (Popular Applications Ser.). (Illus.). 120p. (Orig.). 1991. pap. 12.95 (*1-55622-206-8*) Wordware Pub.
— Learn Freelance Graphics for Windows in a Day. LC 92-36390. (Popular Applications Ser.). (Illus.). 144p. (Orig.). 1993. disk 15.95 (*1-55622-303-X*) Wordware Pub.
— Learn Lotus 1-2-3 Release 4 for Windows in a Day. LC 93-45769. (Popular Applications Ser.). (Illus.). 136p. 1994. pap. 15.95 (*1-55622-408-7*) Wordware Pub.
— Using CorelDraw. (Using Ser.). (Illus.). 750p. (Orig.). 1993. pap. 29.95 (*1-56529-124-7*) Que.
— Using CorelDRAW! 5.0. 1994. pap. 39.99 (*1-56529-764-4*) Que.
***Paulson, Ed & Layton, Marcia.** The Complete Idiot's Guide to Starting Your Own Business. 350p. 1995. 16.99 (*1-56761-529-5*) Alpha Bks IN.
Paulson, Gary D., jt. auth. see Dyer, Lee.
Paulson, Gaylord D., et al, eds. Xenobiotic Conjugation Chemistry. LC 85-32553. (ACS Symposium Ser.: No. 299). (Illus.). x, 358p. 1986. 54.95 (*0-8412-0957-X*) Am Chemical.
— Xenobiotic Metabolism: In Vitro Studies. LC 79-789. (Symposium Ser.: No. 97). 1979. 37.95 (*0-8412-0486-1*) Am Chemical.
Paulson, Genevieve L. Kundalini & the Chakras: A Practical Manual - Evolution in This Lifetime. LC 90-27422. (New Age Ser.). (Illus.). 224p. (Orig.). 1991. pap. 14.95 (*0-87542-592-5*) Llewellyn Pubns.
— Meditation & Human Growth: A Practical Manual for Higher Consciousness. LC 93-42899. (New Age Ser.). (Illus.). 224p. 1994. pap. 14.95 (*0-87542-599-2*) Llewellyn Pubns.
Paulson, George, jt. ed. see Koller, Willaim C.
Paulson, Gerald A. Wetlands & Water Quality: A Citizen's Handbook on How to Review & Comment on Section 404 Permits. 47p. 1985. 3.00 (*0-318-18950-X*) Lake Mich Fed.
Paulson, J. Sig. To Humanity with Love. 2nd ed. LC 74-33594. (Illus.). 124p. 1982. reprint ed. pap. 6.95 (*0-87516-484-6*) DeVorss.
Paulson, Johannes. Index Hesiodeus. 94p. 1972. reprint ed. write for info. (*0-318-70994-5*, Pub. by Georg Olms GW) Lubrecht & Cramer.
Paulson, L. C. Logic & Computation: Interactive Proof with Cambridge LCF. (Tracts in Theoretical Computer Science Ser.: No. 2). 250p. 1987. 54.95 (*0-521-34632-0*) Cambridge U Pr.
— Logic & Computation: Interactive Proof with Cambridge LCF. (Tracts in Theoretical Computer Science Ser.: No. 2). 320p. (C). 1990. pap. 29.95 (*0-521-39560-7*) Cambridge U Pr.
— ML for the Working Programmer. (Illus.). 448p. (C). 1991. 59.95 (*0-521-39022-2*) Cambridge U Pr.
— ML for the Working Programmer. (Illus.). 440p. (C). 1993. pap. 29.95 (*0-521-42225-6*) Cambridge U Pr.
***Paulson, Lawrence C.** Isabelle: A Generic Theorum Prover. Goos, G. & Hartmanis, J., eds. (Lecture Notes in Computer Science: Vol. 828). 1994. pap. 47.00 (*0-387-58244-4*) Spr-Verlag.
***Paulson, Linus.** Build Your Own Web Site for Almost Free: Create a World Wide Web Site with HTML, Perl, & Linux. 600p. 1995. cd-rom, pap. 36.96 (*1-57169-053-0*) Waite Group Pr.
Paulson, Loren, jt. photos see Paulson, Robert.
Paulson, Lynda R. & Watson, Tom. The Executive Persuader: How to Be a Powerful Speaker. Misuraca, Karen, ed. 192p. 1991. 19.95 (*0-9628039-6-0*) Success Strat.
Paulson, Michael G. A Critical Analysis of De La Fayette's "La Princesse De Cleves" As a Royal Novel: Kings, Queens, & Splendor. LC 91-31495. (Studies in French Literature: Vol. 13). 116p. 1991. lib. bdg. 59.95 (*0-7734-9740-4*) E Mellen.
— The Possible Influence of Montaigne's Essais on Descartes' Treatise on the Passions. 138p. (Orig.). (C). 1988. lib. bdg. 38.00 (*0-8191-7027-5*); pap. text ed. 16. 50 (*0-8191-7028-3*) U Pr of Amer.
— The Queens' Encounter: The Mary Stuart Anachronism in Dramas by Diamante, Boursault, Schiller & Donizetti. (Currents in Comparative Romance Languages & Literatures Ser.: Vol. 1). 241p. 1988. 37.00 (*0-8204-0604-X*) P Lang Pubs.
— The Youth & the Beach: A Comparative Study of Thomas Mann's "Der Tod in Venedig" (Death in Venice) & Reinaldo Arena's "Otra Vez el Mar" (Farewell to the Sea) LC 93-73850. (Coleccion Polymita Ser.). 96p. (Orig.). (SPA.). 1994. pap. 12.00 (*0-89729-712-1*) Ediciones.
Paulson, Michael G. & Alvarez-Detrell, Tamara. Cervantes, Hardy, & "La Fuerza de la Sangre" 1985. 25.50 (*0-916379-13-2*) Scripta.
— La Corona Tragica de Lope de Vega. LC 81-51027. (Illus.). 275p. (SPA.). 1982. 17.00 (*0-938972-01-4*) Spanish Lit Pubns.
— A Critical Edition of Juan Bautista Diamante's "La Reina Maria Estuarda" 1990. 44.50 (*0-916379-64-7*) Scripta.
— Madame de la Fayette's The Princess of Cleves: A New Translation. 204p. (Orig.). (C). 1994. pap. text ed. 29.50 (*0-8191-9732-7*) U Pr of Amer.
Paulson, Michael G., jt. ed. see Alvarez-Detrell, Tamara.
Paulson, Moses, ed. Gastroenterologic Medicine. LC 67-29191. (Illus.). 1645p. reprint ed. pap. 180.00 (*0-8357-9404-0*, 2014575) Bks Demand.
Paulson, Nancy. Fun-to-Learn Bible Lessons: Preschoolers, 1. LC 93-35769. 1993. 12.99 (*1-55945-263-3*) Group Pub.
— Fun-to-Learn Bible Lessons Vol. 2: Preschool. Woods, Paul, ed. (Fun-to-Learn Ser.). (Illus.). 96p. 1995. pap. 12. 99 (*1-55945-602-7*) Group Pub.
— Preschool Program, Pt. 1: Loving God - Loving Others. (Illus.). 140p. 1992. audio 19.99 (*1-55945-400-8*) Group Pub.
— Preschool Program, Pt. 1: Loving God - Loving Others. (Illus.). 140p. (J). (ps). 1992. audio 7.99 (*1-55945-816-X*) Group Pub.
Paulson, Pat A., et al. A Matter of Choice. McCleave, Kathe, ed. LC 88-92607. 300p. (Orig.). 1989. pap. 11.95 (*0-944272-01-0*) Phoenix Rsng.
Paulson, Paul L. Guide to Russian Silver Hallmarks. 1976. pap. 18.00 (*0-685-82101-3*) Quaker.
***Paulson, Rachael P.** Johnny & the Old Oak Tree: A Message about Paper Recycling. (Hands on the World Environmental Ser.). (Illus.). 40p. (Orig.). (J). (gr. k-3). 1994. pap. 9.95 (*0-9642296-0-9*) Crestmont Pubng.
Paulson, Robert & Paulson, Loren, photos. Norway. LC 88-82731. (Illus.). 128p. 1988. 39.95 (*0-932575-66-8*) Gr Arts Ctr Pub.
Paulson, Robert J., jt. auth. see Rippley, LaVern J.
***Paulson, Ronald.** The Beautiful, Novel, & Strange: Aesthetics & Heterodoxy. (Illus.). 304p. 1995. text ed. 39.95x (*0-8018-5171-8*) Johns Hopkins.
— Book & Painting: Shakespeare, Milton, & the Bible - Literary Texts & the Emergence of English Painting. LC 82-2769. (Hodges Lectures Ser.). (Illus.). 248p. 1983. text ed. 28.00x (*0-87049-358-2*) U of Tenn Pr.
— Breaking & Re-Making: Aesthetic Practice in England, 1700-1820. LC 89-30375. (Illus.). 350p. (C). 1989. text ed. 45.00 (*0-8135-1439-8*) Rutgers U Pr.
— Breaking & Remaking: Aesthetic Practice in England, 1700-1820. (Illus.). 363p. (Orig.). (C). 1993. reprint ed. pap. text ed. 17.00 (*0-8135-1440-1*) Rutgers U Pr.
— Figure & Abstraction in Contemporary Painting. LC 90-31079. (Illus.). 300p. 1990. 44.95 (*0-8135-1604-8*) Rutgers U Pr.
— Hogarth, Vol. I: The Modern Moral Subject, 1697-1732. LC 90-24569. (Illus.). 552p. (C). 1991. text ed. 65.00 (*0-8135-1694-3*); pap. 24.95 (*0-8135-1695-1*) Rutgers U Pr.
— Hogarth, Vol. III: Art & Politics, 1750-1764. LC 90-24569. (Illus.). 680p. (C). 1993. text ed. 70.00 (*0-8135-1698-6*); pap. text ed. 24.95 (*0-8135-1699-4*) Rutgers U Pr.
— Hogarth, Vol. 2: High Art & Low, 1732-1750. LC 90-24569. (Illus.). 550p. (C). 1992. text ed. 65.00 (*0-8135-1696-X*); pap. text ed. 24.95 (*0-8135-1697-8*) Rutgers U Pr.
— Hogarth's Graphic Works: Catalogue Raisonne. (Illus.). 476p. 1989. 250.00 (*1-55660-804-7*) A Wofsy Fine Arts.
— Popular & Polite Art in the Age of Hogarth & Fielding. LC 79-63358. (Ward-Phillips Lectures in English Language & Literature Ser: No. 10). 1979. text ed. 32.95 (*0-268-01534-1*) U of Notre Dame Pr.
Paulson, Ross E. Language, Science, & Action: Korzybski's General Semantics--A Study in Comparative Intellectual History. LC 83-5490. (Contributions in Intercultural & Comparative Studies: No. 9). (Illus.). viii, 163p. 1983. text ed. 47.95 (*0-313-23732-8*, PAL/) Greenwood.
Paulson, Ross E., ed. see Jackson, Gregory L.
Paulson, Sean D., jt. auth. see Paulson, Terry L.
Paulson, Stanley L., tr. see Kelsen, Hans.
Paulson, Steven K., jt. auth. see Baker, Eugene, III.
Paulson, Suzanne M. Flannery O'Connor. (Twayne's Studies in Short Fiction: No. 2). 232p. 1988. text ed. 22.95 (*0-8057-8301-6*, Pub. by Royal Botanic Garden UK) Macmillan.
— William Trevor: A Study of the Short Fiction. LC 93-16606. (Studies in Short Fiction: No. 48). 160p. 1993. text ed. 23.95 (*0-8057-0858-8*, Pub. by Royal Botanic Garden UK) Macmillan.
Paulson, Terry. Making Humor Work. Crisp, Michael G., ed. LC 88-72262. (Fifty-Minute Ser.). (Illus.). 96p. (Orig.). 1989. pap. 9.95 (*0-931961-61-0*) Crisp Pubns.
— Paulson on Change. (Distilled Wisdom Ser.). 160p. (Orig.). 1995. pap. 12.95 (*1-882180-49-6*) Griffin CA.
Paulson, Terry L. They Shoot Managers Don't They? Making Conflict Work in a Changing World. 192p. 1991. reprint ed. pap. 11.95 (*0-89815-429-4*) Ten Speed Pr.
— They Shoot Managers, Don't They? Managing Yourself & Leading Others in a Changing World. (Illus.). 156p. (Orig.). Date not set. pap. 10.95 (*0-939007-15-0*) Lee Canter & Assocs.
Paulson, Terry L. & Paulson, Sean D. Secrets of Life Every Teen Needs to Know. LC 90-63405. (Illus.). 160p. (Orig.). (YA). (gr. 7-12). 1990. pap. 6.95 (*0-939513-42-0*) Joy Pub SJC.
Paulson, Tim. The Beanstalk Incident. (Upside Down Ser.). (Illus.). (J). 1992. pap. 8.95 (*0-8065-1313-6*, Citadel Pr) Carol Pub Group.
— How to Fly a 747. (Masters of Motion Ser.). (Illus.). 48p. (Orig.). (J). (gr. 3 up). 1992. pap. 9.95 (*1-56261-061-9*) John Muir.
— Jack & the Beanstalk & the Beanstalk Incident. (Illus.). (J). (ps-2). 1990. 12.95 (*0-685-38934-0*, Birch Ln Pr) Carol Pub Group.
Paulson, Timothy J. Days of Sorrow, Years of Glory, 1831-1850: From the Nat Turner Revolt to the Fugitive Slave Law. LC 93-40851. 1994. write for info. (*0-7910-2263-3*); pap. write for info. (*0-7910-2552-7*) Chelsea Hse.
Paulson, William. Sentimental Education: The Complexity of Disenchantment. (Masterwork Studies: No. 85). 160p. (C). 1992. text ed. 21.95 (*0-8057-9428-X*, Pub. by Royal Botanic Garden UK); pap. 12.95 (*0-8057-8568-X*, Pub. by Royal Botanic Garden UK) Macmillan.
Paulson, William, ed. Les Genres de l'Henaurme Siecle. LC 81-50963. (Michigan Romance Studies: Vol. 9). 142p. (Orig.). 1989. pap. 9.00 (*0-939730-08-1*) Mich Romance.
Paulson, William, tr. see Serres, Michael.
Paulson, William R. Enlightenment, Romanticism, & the Blind in France. LC 87-2274. 360p. 1987. text ed. 42.50 (*0-691-06710-4*) Princeton U Pr.
— The Noise of Culture: Literary Texts in a World of Information. LC 87-47822. 208p. 1988. 28.95 (*0-8014-2102-0*) Cornell U Pr.
Paulsson, Bengt. Urban Applications of Satellite Remote Sensing & GIS Analysis. LC 92-33642. (Urban Management Program Ser.: Vol. 9). 71p. 1992. 6.95 (*0-8213-2266-4*, 12266) World Bank.
Paulsson, Martin. The Social Anxieties of Progressive Reform: Atlantic City, 1854-1920. LC 93-47416. (American Social Experience Ser.). 1994. 37.50 (*0-8147-6620-X*) NYU Pr.
Paulston, Christina B. Linguistic Minorities in Multilingual Settings: Implications for Language Policies. LC 93-44796. (Studies in Bilingualism: No. 4). xi, 139p. 1994. lib. bdg. 39.00 (*1-55619-347-5*); pap. 19.95 (*1-55619-540-0*) Benjamins North Am.
— Linguistics & Communicative Competence: Topics in ESL. (Multilingual Matters Ser.: No. 85). 160p. 1992. 69.00 (*1-85359-149-1*, Pub. by Multilingual Matters UK); pap. 24.95 (*1-85359-148-3*, Pub. by Multilingual Matters UK) Taylor & Francis.
— Sociolinguistic Perspectives on Bilingual Education. (Multilingual Matters Ser.: No. 84). 180p. 1992. 79.00 (*1-85359-147-5*, Pub. by Multilingual Matters UK); pap. 29.95 (*1-85359-146-7*, Pub. by Multilingual Matters UK) Taylor & Francis.
Paulston, Christina B., ed. International Handbook of Bilingualism & Bilingual Education. LC 87-263. 614p. 1988. text ed. 135.00 (*0-313-24484-7*, PIB/, Greenwood Pr) Greenwood.
Paulston, Christina B., et al. Writing: Communicative Activities in English. (Illus.). 288p. (C). 1983. pap. text ed. 14.00 (*0-13-970277-6*) P-H.
Paulston, Roland G. Society, Schools & Progress in Peru. 336p. 1971. 143.00 (*0-08-016428-5*, Pub. by Pergamon Repr UK) Franklin.
Paulston, Rolland G., ed. Non-Formal Education: An Annotated International Bibliography. LC 72-186197. (Special Studies in International Economics & Development). 1972. 39.50 (*0-275-28623-1*) Irvington.
Paulte, Francois. Renoir. (Classic Art Ser.). 1988. 9.98 (*0-671-09412-2*) S&S Trade.
Paulu, Burton. British Broadcasting in Transition. LC 61-8399. 260p. reprint ed. pap. 74.10 (*0-8357-7418-X*, 2055896) Bks Demand.
— Radio & Television Broadcasting in Eastern Europe. LC 74-79505. 604p. reprint ed. pap. 172.20 (*0-318-39685-8*, 2033280) Bks Demand.
— Television & Radio in the United Kingdom. LC 80-20870. 490p. reprint ed. pap. 139.70 (*0-7837-2927-8*, 2057527) Bks Demand.
Paulu, Nancy. Dealing with Dropouts: The Urban Superintendents' Call to Action. (Education Department Publication Ser.: PIP 87-201). 87p. (Orig.). 1987. pap. 3.25 (*0-16-006720-0*, S/N 065-000-00321-0) USGPO.
— Experiences in School Improvement: Story of 16 American Districts. 91p. 1988. pap. 4.50 (*0-16-006736-7*, S/N 065-000-00343-1) USGPO.
— Helping Your Child Get Ready for School: With Activities for Children from Birth Through Age 5. Greene, Wilma P., ed. (Illus.). 51p. (Orig.). (C). 1993. pap. text ed. 11.95 (*0-7881-0041-6*) Diane Pub.
— Improving Math & Science Assessment: Report on the Secretary's 3rd Conference on Mathematics & Science Education. 51p. (Orig.). (C). 1994. pap. text ed. 30.00x (*0-7881-1579-0*) Diane Pub.
— Improving Schools & Empowering Parents: Choice in American Education: A Report Based on the White House Workshop on Choice in Education. (Education Department Publication PIP Ser.: No. 89-002). (Illus.). 54p. (Orig.). 1989. pap. 3.00 (*0-16-006768-5*, S/N 065-000-00386-4) USGPO.
Paulu, Norman. On Matters Musical: A Concise Guide for the Listener of Music in Performance. 100p. 1984. pap. 12.95 (*0-912855-28-2*) E Bowers Pub.
***Paulukonis, May A.** Partners in Preparation: Training Married Couples for Marriage Preparation Ministry. (Orig.). 1995. pap. text ed. write for info. (*0-8146-2285-2*, Liturg Pr Bks) Liturgical Pr.
Paulun, Carl L. Let's Be Friends. 1993. 7.95 (*0-533-10571-4*) Vantage.

Paulus, D. A., jt. auth. see Gravenstein, J. S.

***Paulus, David A., et al.** Gas Monitoring in Clinical Practice. 2nd rev. ed. LC 94-32851. 1994. write for info. (*0-7506-9445-9*) Buttrwrth-Heinemann.

Paulus, Harold, et al. Drugs for Rheumatic Disease: Vol. 8, MCP. (Illus.). 488p. 1987. 85.00 (*0-443-08011-9*) Churchill.

Paulus, Harold E., jt. ed. see Famaey, J. P.

Paulus, Ingeborg. Search for Pure Food: A Sociology of Legislation in Britain. (Law in Society Ser.). 144p. 1974. text ed. 8.50 (*0-85520-076-6*) Rothman.

Paulus Orosius. Seven Books of History Against the Pagans. LC 64-8670. (Fathers of the Church Ser.: Vol. 50). 414p. 1964. 22.95 (*0-8132-0050-4*) Cath U Pr.

Paulus, P. B. Prison Crowding: A Psychological Perspective. (Research in Criminology Ser.). (Illus.). 105p. 1988. 65.00 (*0-387-96650-1*) Spr-Verlag.

Paulus, P. B., ed. Basic Group Processes. (Psychology Ser.). (Illus.). 356p. 1983. 64.00 (*0-387-90862-5*) Spr-Verlag.

Paulus, Paul B. Psychology of Group Influence. 2nd ed. 456p. (C). text ed. 79.95 (*0-8058-0445-5*); pap. 36.00 (*0-8058-0545-1*) L Erlbaum Assocs.

Paulus, Paul B., jt. auth. see Baron, Robert A.

***Paulus, Paul B., et al.** Effective Human Relations: A Guide to People at Work. 3rd ed. LC 94-47138. 1995. write for info. (*0-205-16381-5*) Allyn.

Paulus, T. J., jt. auth. see Pierce, J. F.

Paulus, Trina. Esperanza para las Flores: Hope for the Flowers. Landsness, Ruthanne N. & Prucha, David J., trs. 160p. (SPA.). 1992. pap. 8.95 (*0-8091-3369-5*) Paulist Pr.

— Hope for the Flowers. LC 74-179985. (Illus.). 160p. 1972. 11.95 (*0-8091-0174-2*); pap. 8.95 (*0-8091-1754-1*) Paulist Pr.

Paulus, Virginia, ed. Housing: A Bibliography, 1960-1972. LC 73-15863. (Studies in Modern Society: Political & Social Issues: No. 4). 1974. 45.00 (*0-404-10537-8*) AMS Pr.

Paulus, Wilfried. Microbicides for the Protection of Materials: A Handbook. LC 92-31479. 1993. write for info. (*1-85166-949-3*) Elsevier.

Paluzzi, Faust, tr. see Sandri, Giovanna.

Pauly, A. F. & Wissowa, G. Realencyclopaedie der Classischen Altertumswissenschaft, 68 vols & 15 suppl. vols. write for info. (*0-318-50412-X*) Adlers Foreign Bks.

Pauly, D. & Morgan, G. R., eds. Length-Based Methods in Fisheries Research. (Conference Proceedings Ser.: No. 13). 1986. text ed. 32.50 (*971-10-2228-1*, Pub. by ICLARM PH) Intl Spec Bk.

Pauly, D. & Murphy, G. I., eds. Theory & Management of Tropical Fisheries. (Conference Proceedings Ser.: No. 9). (Illus.). 360p. 1983. pap. 28.50 (*971-04-0022-3*, Pub. by ICLARM PH) Intl Spec Bk.

Pauly, D. & Tsukayama, I., eds. The Peruvian Anchoveta & Its Upwelling Ecosystem: Three Decades of Change. (ICLARM Studies & Reviews: No. 15). 351p. 1987. 36.00 (*971-10-2234-6*, Pub. by ICLARM PH) Intl Spec Bk.

Pauly, D., et al, eds. Growth, Mortality & Recruitment of Commercially Important Fishes & Penaeid Shrimps in Indonesian Waters. (ICLARM Technical Reports: No. 17). 91p. 1986. pap. 8.50 (*971-10-2226-5*, Pub. by ICLARM PH) Intl Spec Bk.

— Peruvian Upwelling Ecosystem: Dynamics & Interactions. 1989. pap. 27.00 (*971-10-2247-8*, Pub. by ICLARM PH) Intl Spec Bk.

Pauly, Daniel. Fish Population Dynamics in Tropical Waters: A Manual for Use with Programmable Calculators. (ICLARM Studies & Reviews: No. 8). (Illus.). 325p. 1984. pap. 25.00 (*971-10-2204-4*, Pub. by ICLARM PH) Intl Spec Bk.

— On the Sex of Fish & the Gender of Scientists: A Collection of Essays in Fisheries Science. (Fish & Fisheries Ser.: 14). 250p. 1994. 59.95 (*0-412-59540-0*) Chapman & Hall.

— Theory & Management of Tropical Multispecies Stock: A Review, with Emphasis on the Southeast Asian Demersal Fisheries. (ICLARM Studies & Reviews: No. 1). (Illus.). 35p. 1983. pap. text ed. 6.50 (*0-89955-398-2*, Pub. by ICLARM PH) Intl Spec Bk.

Pauly, Daniel & Mines, Antonio N., eds. Small-Scale Fisheries of San Miguel Bay, Philippines: Biology & Stock Assessment. (ICLARM Technical Reports: No. 7). (Illus.). 124p. (Orig.). 1983. pap. 16.00 (*0-89955-394-X*, Pub. by ICLARM PH) Intl Spec Bk.

Pauly, Daniel & Wade-Pauly, Sandra. An Annotated Bibliography of Slipmouths: Pisces: Leiognathidae. (Bibliographies Ser.: No. 2). 62p. (Orig.). 1983. pap. 7.00 (*0-89955-374-5*, Pub. by ICLARM PH) Intl Spec Bk.

Pauly, Daniel, jt. auth. see Inglese, Jose.

Pauly, Daniel, jt. ed. see Longhurst, Alan R.

Pauly, Daniel, tr. see Peters, Hans M.

Pauly, Daniel, jt. ed. see Thia-Eng, Chua.

Pauly, Edward. Classroom Crucible: What Really Works, What Doesn't, & Why. LC 90-55591. 1992. pap. 14.00 (*0-465-01151-9*) Basic.

***Pauly, Edward, et al.** Homegrown Lessons: Innovative Programs Linking School & Work. (Education Ser.). 326p. 1995. 26.95 (*0-7879-0074-5*) Jossey-Bass.

Pauly, Edward S., jt. auth. see Gueron, Judith M.

Pauly, Louis W. Opening Financial Markets: Banking Politics on the Pacific Rim. LC 88-47740. (Cornell Studies in Political Economy). 280p. 1988. 36.50 (*0-8014-2080-6*) Cornell U Pr.

— Opening Financial Markets: Banking Politics on the Pacific Rim. LC 88-47740. (Cornell Studies in Political Economy). (Illus.). 280p. 1990. reprint ed. pap. 15.95 (*0-8014-9928-3*) Cornell U Pr.

— Regulatory Politics in Japan: The Case of Foreign Banking. (Cornell East Asia Ser.: No. 45). 92p. (Orig.). 1987. pap. 7.00 (*0-939657-45-7*) Cornell East Asia Pgm.

Pauly, Louis W., jt. ed. see Stein, Janice G.

Pauly, M. V., jt. auth. see Finsinger, J.

***Pauly, Mark V.** An Analysis of Medical Savings Accounts: Do Two Wrongs Make a Right? 32p. 1994. pap. 9.95 (*0-8447-7027-2*) Am Enterprise.

— Doctors & Their Workshops: Economic Models of Physician Behavior. LC 80-16112. (National Bureau of Economic Research Ser.). (Illus.). 144p. 1980. lib. bdg. 17.00 (*0-226-65044-8*) U Ch Pr.

Pauly, Mark V., ed. National Health Insurance: What Now, What Later, What Never? LC 80-22761. (AEI Symposia Ser.: No. 80C). 399p. reprint ed. pap. 113.80 (*0-8357-4513-9*, 2037371) Bks Demand.

Pauly, Mark V., jt. auth. see Kunreuther, Howard K.

Pauly, Mark V., et al. Paying Physicians: Options for Controlling Cost, Volume, & Intensity of Services. LC 92-1567. 233p. (Orig.). 1992. pap. text ed. 30.00 (*0-910701-87-3*, 0920) Health Admin Pr.

— Responsible National Health Insurance. 92p. (Orig.). (C). 1992. pap. text ed. 9.75 (*0-8447-7014-0*) Am Enterprise.

Pauly, Mark V., et al, eds. Lessons from the First Twenty Years of Medicare: Research Implications for Public & Private Sector Policy. LC 88-17368. (Health Economics, Health Management, & Health Policy Ser.). 412p. (C). 1989. text ed. 42.95x (*0-8122-8118-7*) U of Pa Pr.

Pauly, Philip J. Controlling Life: Jacques Loeb & the Engineering Ideal in Biology. (Monographs in History & Philosophy of Biology). (Illus.). 260p. 1987. 29.95 (*0-19-504244-1*) OUP.

— Controlling Life: Jacques Loeb & the Engineering Ideal in Biology. 1990. pap. 14.00 (*0-520-06974-9*) U CA Pr.

Pauly, Rebecca M. Le Berceau et la Bibliotheque: Le Paradoxe de l'Ecriture Autobiographique. LC 89-84500. (Stanford French & Italian Studies: Vol. 62). 116p. (FRE.). 1989. pap. 46.50 (*0-915838-77-X*) Anma Libri.

— The Transparent Illusion: Image & Ideology in French Text & Film. LC 92-16539. (Art of Interpretation Ser.: Vol. 3). 495p. (Orig.). (FRE.). (C). 1993. pap. text ed. 41.95 (*0-8204-1930-3*) P Lang Pubs.

Pauly, Reinhard, jt. auth. see Buettner, Steward.

Pauly, Reinhard G. Music in the Classic Period. 2nd ed. (History of Music Ser.). 224p. 1973. pap. text ed. 22.00 (*0-13-607630-0*) P-H.

— Music in the Classic Period. 3rd ed. (History of Music Ser.). (Illus.). 288p. (C). 1987. pap. text ed. 34.00 (*0-13-607623-8*) P-H.

Pauly, Reinhard G., tr. see Fischer-Dieskau, Dietrich.

Pauly, Reinhard G., tr. see Gaertner, Heinz.

Paumgartner & Burhenne. Lithotripsy & Related Techniques for Gallstone, Vol. 3. 283p. 1991. 99.00 (*0-8151-6624-9*, Yr Bk Med Pubs) Mosby Yr Bk.

Paumgartner, G., ed. see Falk Symposium Staff.

Paumgartner, G., et al, eds. Bile Acids & Cholesterol in Health & Disease. 350p. 1983. lib. bdg. 143.00 (*0-85200-729-9*) Kluwer Ac.

— Bile Acids & the Liver. (Falk Ser.: No. 45). (C). 1987. lib. bdg. 150.50 (*0-85200-675-6*) Kluwer Ac.

— Bile Acids As Therapeutic Agents from Basic Science to Clinical Practice. (Falk Symposia Ser.). (C). 1991. lib. bdg. 161.50 (*0-7923-8954-9*) Kluwer Ac.

— Eterohepatic Circulation of Bile Acids & Sterol Metabolism. (Falk Ser.: No. 42). 1985. lib. bdg. 148.00 (*0-85200-905-4*) Kluwer Ac.

— Strategies for the Treatment of Hepatobiliary Disease. (Falk Symposia Ser.). (C). 1990. lib. bdg. 91.00 (*0-7923-8903-4*) Kluwer Ac.

— Trends in Bile Acid Research. (Falk Symposium Ser.). (C). 1989. lib. bdg. 138.00 (*0-7462-0112-5*) Kluwer Ac.

Paumier, Cyril, et al. Designing the Successful Downtown. 116p. 1988. 47.95 (*0-87420-681-2*) Urban Land.

Paun, G., jt. auth. see Dassow, J.

***Paun, Gheorghe, ed.** Mathematical Aspects of Natural & Formal Languages. LC 94-30230. (Series in Computer Science: Vol. 43). 500p. 1994. text ed. 124.00 (*981-02-1914-8*) World Scientific Pub.

Pauncz, R., ed. Spin Eigenfunctions: Construction & Use. LC 78-27632. (Illus.). 386p. 1979. 89.50 (*0-306-40141-X*, Plenum Pr) Plenum.

Pauncz, R., jt. auth. see Matsen, F. A.

Paunio, Jouko, jt. ed. see Koskela, Erkki.

***Paunovic, M.** Electrochemically Deposited Thin Films II. 422p. 1995. 60.00 (*1-56677-090-4*, PV 94-31) Electrochem Soc.

***Paunovic, M., et al, eds.** Proceedings of the Symposium on Electrochemical Deposited Thin Films. LC 93-70064. (Proceedings Ser.: Vol. 93-26). 426p. 1993. 60.00 (*1-56677-061-0*) Electrochem Soc.

Pauphilet, Albert. Aucassin et Nicolette. 171p. 1971. 9.95 (*0-8288-7472-7*) Fr & Eur.

Pauplis, Mary. Heritage Cooking from the Kitchen of Mary Pauplis. 200p. (Orig.). 1993. pap. write for info. (*0-9635383-0-6*) M Pauplis.

— Heritage Cooking from the Kitchen of Mary Pauplis. rev. ed. 200p. (Orig.). 1994. pap. text ed. write for info. (*0-9635383-1-4*) M Pauplis.

Paur, Leo. How to Teach Your Children to Say No to Drugs: And Keep Their Friends. 126p. 1992. 12.95 (*0-929753-00-3*) Paramount Bks.

Pausacker, Jenny. Fast Forward. LC 90-45762. (J). (gr. 4-7). 1991. 12.95 (*0-688-10195-X*) Lothrop.

Pausanias. Description of Greece, 5 vols., 1. (Loeb Classical Library: No. 93, 188, 272, 297-298). 486p. 1918. 18.95 (*0-674-99104-4*) HUP.

— Description of Greece, 5 vols., 2. (Loeb Classical Library: No. 93, 188, 272, 297-298). 560p. 1926. 18.95 (*0-674-99207-5*) HUP.

— Description of Greece, 5 vols., 3. (Loeb Classical Library: No. 93, 188, 272, 297-298). 448p. 1926. 18.95 (*0-674-99300-4*) HUP.

— Description of Greece, 5 vols., 4. (Loeb Classical Library: No. 93, 188, 272, 297-298). 612p. 1935. 18.95 (*0-674-99328-4*) HUP.

— Description of Greece, 5 vols., 5. (Loeb Classical Library: No. 93, 188, 272, 297-298). 290p. 1935. 18.95 (*0-674-99329-2*) HUP.

— Description of Greece, 6 vols., Set. 2nd ed. Frazer, J. G., tr. LC 65-13634. (Illus.). 1897. 150.00 (*0-8196-0144-6*) Biblo.

— Guide to Greece, Vol. 1: Central Greece. rev. ed. Levi, Peter, tr. (Classics Ser.). (Illus.). 560p. 1984. Vol. 1, Central Greece. pap. 12.95 (*0-14-044225-1*, Penguin Classics) Viking Penguin.

— Guide to Greece, Vol. 2: Southern Greece. rev. ed. Levi, Peter, tr. (Classics Ser.). (Illus.). 560p. 1984. Vol. 2, Southern Greece. pap. 12.95 (*0-14-044226-X*, Penguin Classics) Viking Penguin.

***Pausch, Eberhard M.** Wahrheit Zwischen Erschlossenheit und Verantwortung: Die Rezeption und Transformation der Wahrheitskonzeption Martin Heideggers in der Theologie Rudolf Bultmanns. (Theologische Bibliothek Toepelmann Ser.: Bd. 64). 380p. (GER.). (C). 1994. lib. bdg. 136.95 (*3-11-014230-9*) De Gruyter.

Pausch, Georg. Journal of Captain Pausch, Chief of the Hanau Artillery During the Burgoyne Campaign. Stone, William L., tr. LC 79-140876. (Eyewitness Accounts of the American Revolution Ser., No. 1). 1971. reprint ed. 17.95 (*0-405-01200-4*) Ayer.

Pausch, Lois M. A Guide to Library Service in Mathematics: The Non-Trivial Mathematics Librarian. Anderson, Nancy D., ed. LC 93-43482. (Foundations in Library & Information Science: Vol. 30). 1993. 73.25 (*1-55938-745-9*) Jai Pr.

***Pausewang, Gudrun.** Fall-Out. Crampton, Patricia, tr. 176p. (J). (gr. 5-9). 1995. 13.99 (*0-670-86104-9*) Viking Child Bks.

Pausewang, Siegfried, jt. ed. see Zegeye, Zbebe.

Paushkin, Y. & Vishnyakova, T. Production of Olefine-Containing & Fuel Gases. LC 93-10032. 1964. 111.00 (*0-08-010168-2*, Pub. by Pergamon Repr UK) Franklin.

Paushkin, Y. M., et al. Organic Polymeric Semiconductors. 250p. 1974. text ed. 63.50 (*0-7065-1371-1*, Pub. by Keter Pub IS) Coronet Bks.

***Pausini, Anthony J.** The Federalist, Continued. 1995. pap. 15.00 (*0-614-04808-7*) Greenvale.

Pauson, Marian L. Jung the Philosopher: Essays in Jungian Thought. (New Studies in Aesthetics: Vol. 3). 235p. (C). 1989. text ed. 41.95 (*0-8204-0586-8*) P Lang Pubs.

Paust, B., jt. auth. see RaLonde, R.

Paust, Brian, jt. auth. see Crapo, Chuck.

Paust, Jordon J., jt. auth. see Blaustein, Albert P.

Paustenbach, Dennis J., ed. The Risk Assessment of Environmental & Human Health Hazards. LC 87-35056. 1155p. 1989. text ed. 195.00 (*0-471-84998-7*) Wiley.

Paustian, Paul W. Canal Irrigation in the Punjab. LC 68-58614. (Columbia University. Studies in the Social Sciences: No. 322). reprint ed. 20.00 (*0-404-51322-0*) AMS Pr.

Paustovskii, Konstantin G. The Black Gulf. Schimanskaya, Eugenia, tr. LC 75-39008. (Soviet Literature in English Translation Ser.). 124p. 1977. reprint ed. 16.00 (*0-88355-411-9*) Hyperion Conn.

Pautler, Albert J., Jr., ed. High School to Employment Transition: Contemporary Issues. 300p. (Orig.). 1993. pap. 19.50 (*0-911168-88-5*) Prakken.

— Vocational Education in the 1990's: Major Issues. 302p. (Orig.). (C). 1990. pap. text ed. 16.95 (*0-911168-78-8*) Prakken.

Pautler, Albert J., jt. auth. see Sugarman, Michael N.

Pautz, Otto. Muhammeds Lehre von der Offenbarung Quellenmassig Untersucht. 304p. reprint ed. write for info. (*0-318-71550-3*, Pub. by Georg Olms GW) Lubrecht & Cramer.

Pautz, Peter D., jt. ed. see Cramer, Kathryn D.

Pautz, Roger. Teenage Depression: More Than Just "The Blues" 16p. 1989. pap. 1.75 (*0-925190-07-1*, F911008 C) Fairview Press.

Pauw, Berthold A. Religion in a Tswana Chiefdom. LC 85-21881. (Illus.). xii, 274p. 1985. reprint ed. text ed. 95.00 (*0-313-24974-1*, PRTC, Greenwood Pr) Greenwood.

Pauwels, jt. auth. see Wilson.

Pauwels, A. F. Immigrant Dialects & Language Maintenance in Australia: The Cases of the Limburg & Swabia Dialects. (Topics in Sociolinguistics Ser.). 149p. 1986. pap. 42.35 (*90-6765-140-0*) Mouton.

Pauwels, E. K. Bone Scintigraphy. 224p. 1981. lib. bdg. 101.50 (*90-6021-476-5*) Kluwer Ac.

Pauwels, F. Atlas: The Biomechanics of the Normal & Diseased Hip. Furlong, R. J. & Maguet, P., trs. LC 75-31723. (Illus.). 280p. 1976. 261.00 (*0-387-07428-7*) Spr-Verlag.

— Biomechanics of the Locomotor Apparatus. (Illus.). 520p. 1980. 248.00 (*0-387-09131-9*) Spr-Verlag.

Pauwels, H. Minimization of the Volume & PU Content of the Waste Generated at a Plutonium Fuel Fabrication Plant, No. 14019. 88p. 1992. pap. 13.00 (*92-826-3988-6*, CD-NA-14019-EN-C, Pub. by Europ Com) UNIPUB.

Pauwels, Jacques R. Women, Nazis, & Universities: Female University Students in the Third Reich, 1933-1945. LC 83-20161. (Contributions in Women's Studies: No. 50). (Illus.). 288p. 1984. text ed. 49.95 (*0-313-24203-8*, PWU/, Greenwood Pr) Greenwood.

Pauwels, Louis. Blumroch l'Admirable ou le Dejuener du Surhomme. (FRE.). 1978. pap. 10.95 (*0-7859-4104-5*) Fr & Eur.

Pava, Calvin H. Managing New Office Technology: An Organizational Strategy. LC 83-47519. 224p. (C). 1984. 32.95 (*0-02-924970-8*) Free Pr.

***Pava, Moses L. & Krausz, Joshua.** Corporate Responsibility & Financial Performance: The Paradox of Social Cost. LC 94-45284. 192p. 1995. text ed. 55.00 (*0-89930-921-6*, Quorum Bks) Greenwood.

Pava, Moses L., jt. auth. see Epstein, Marc J.

Pavalon, Eugene I. Human Rights & Health Care Law. LC 80-67574. 250p. reprint ed. pap. 71.30 (*0-317-28219-0*, 2019997) Bks Demand.

Pavalon, Eugene I., jt. auth. see Inlander, Charles B.

Pavan, Barbara N., jt. auth. see Anderson, Robert.

Pavan-Langston, Deborah. Handbook of Ocular Drug Therapy & Ocular Side Effects of Systemic Drugs. 1990. 42.95 (*0-316-69545-9*) Little.

— Manual Ocular, No. 3. 1991. 10.95 (*0-316-69548-3*) Little.

— Manual Ocular Diagonisis. 3rd ed. 1991. 31.95 (*0-316-69547-5*) Little.

— Manual of Ocular Diagnosis & Therapy. 2nd ed. 494p. 1985. 24.50 (*0-316-69544-0*, Little Med Div) Little.

Pavao, John. Understanding Book. Perle, Ruth L., ed. (Illus.). (J). (gr. 1). 1977. pap. text ed. 3.25 (*0-89796-863-8*) New Dimens Educ.

***Pavarini, Peter A., ed.** United States Health Care Laws & Rules. 1700p. 1995. 75.00 (*0-314-06827-9*) Natl Health Lawyers.

Pavarotti, Adua. Pavarotti: Life with Luciano. LC 92-54179. (Illus.). 160p. 1992. 35.00 (*0-8478-1573-0*) Rizzoli Intl.

***Pavarotti, Luciano & Wright, William.** Pavarotti: My World. LC 95-14951. 1995. pap. 24.00 (*0-679-76504-2*) Random.

Pavaskar, Madhav. Saga of the Cotton Exchange. 1985. 18.00 (*0-8364-1405-5*, Pub. by Popular Prakashan II) S Asia.

Pavek, Gary, ed. A Guide to the Mind. 378p. 1988. pap. text ed. 14.95 (*0-275-93010-6*, B3010, Praeger Pubs) Greenwood.

Pavek, Richard R. Handbook of Shen. (Illus.). 174p. (Orig.). 1987. pap. text ed. 14.95 (*0-9618646-0-5*) SHEN Therapy Inst.

Pavel. Fundamentals of Pattern Recognition. (Pure & Applied Mathematics Ser.: Vol. 174). 272p. 1993. 110.00 (*0-8247-8883-4*) Dekker.

— Optimal Control of Differential Equations. (Lecture Notes in Pure & Applied Mathematics Ser.: Vol. 160). 384p. 1994. 125.00 (*0-8247-9234-3*) Dekker.

Pavel, Margaret M., jt. auth. see Herbert, Anne.

Pavel, Marilyn. Emergency Exit. (Illus.). 41p. (Orig.). 1988. pap. 7.95 (*0-317-91297-6*) Entrprs Pub.

Pavel, N. H. Nonlinear Evolution Operators & Semigroups. (Lecture Notes in Mathematics Ser.: Vol. 1260). 285p. 1987. pap. 39.30 (*0-387-17974-7*) Spr-Verlag.

Pavel, Ota. How I Came to Know Fish. 2nd ed. Badal, Jindriska & McDowell, Robert, trs. 151p. 1990. 16.95 (*0-934257-41-8*) Story Line.

— How I Came to Know Fish. Badal, Jindriska & McDowell, Robert, trs. LC 90-21045. 160p. 1991. reprint ed. pap. 9.95 (*0-8112-1165-7*, NDP713) New Directions.

Pavel, Paraschiva, jt. auth. see Micula, Gheorghe.

Pavel, Thomas. The Feud of Language: A History of Structuralist Thought. 1992. reprint ed. pap. 19.95 (*0-631-18086-9*) Blackwell Pubs.

Pavel, Thomas G. Fictional Worlds. 192p. 1986. 28.00 (*0-674-29965-5*) HUP.

— Fictional Worlds. 192p. 1989. reprint ed. pap. 12.95 (*0-674-29966-3*) HUP.

— The Poetics of Plot: The Case of English Renaissance Drama. LC 84-15663. (Theory & History of Literature Ser.: Vol. 18). 192p. 1985. text ed. 39.95 (*0-8166-1374-5*); pap. text ed. 12.95 (*0-8166-1375-3*) U of Minn Pr.

Pavela, Gary. The Dismissal of Students with Mental Disorders: Legal Issues, Policy Considerations & Alternative Responses. Gehring, Donald D. & Parker, D. Young, eds. LC 85-13227. (Higher Education Administration Ser.). 108p. (Orig.). 1994. pap. 16.95 (*0-912557-01-X*) Coll Admin Pubns.

Pavelec, Barry J., jt. auth. see Diclerico, James M.

Pavelich, Marnie H., ed. see Lang, Otto.

Pavelich, Matt. Beasts of the Forest, Beasts of the Field. 1990. pap. 10.00 (*0-937669-43-1*) Owl Creek Pr.

Pavelich, Michael, jt. auth. see Abraham, Michael.

Pavelka, M. Functional Morphology of the Golgi Apparatus. (Advances in Anatomy, Embryology & Cell Biology Ser.: Vol. 106). (Illus.). 100p. 1987. pap. 66.70 (*0-387-18062-1*) Spr-Verlag.

Pavelko, Virginia & Scott, L. B. Five Little Speckled Frogs Big Book. (Illus.). (J). (ps-2). 1988. pap. text ed. 14.00 (*0-922053-05-7*) N Edge Res.

Pavella, M. & Murthy, P. G. Transient Stability of Power Systems: Theory & Practice. LC 93-32934. 1994. text ed. 98.00 (*0-471-94213-8*) Wiley.

Pavendham, A., jt. auth. see Doraiswamy, Indra.

Paver, William & Wan, Yiping. Postsecondary Institutions of the People's Republic of China: A Comprehensive Guide to Institutions of Higher Education in China. Wakefield, Henrianne, ed. (World Education Ser.). 627p. (Orig.). 1992. pap. text ed. 50.00 (*0-929851-11-0*) Am Assn Coll Registrars.

Paver, William J., ed. Handbook on the Placement of Foreign Graduate Students. 209p. 1990. pap. 30.00 (*0-912207-50-7*) NAFSA Washington.

Paves-Yashinsky, Palomba, tr. see Zola, Emile.

Pavese, Cesare. Among Women Only. Paige, D. D., tr. 1979. 24.00 (*0-7206-0350-1*) Dufour.

— Cesare Pavese: Selected Letters 1924 to 1950. Murch, A. E., ed. 270p. 1969. 17.95 (*0-8464-1192-X*) Beekman Pubs.

— Devil in the Hills. 1978. 26.00 (*0-7206-2795-8*) Dufour.

— Dialogues with Leuco. Arrowsmith, William, tr. LC 89-83807. 201p. 1989. 17.95 (*0-941419-38-X*, Eridanos Library) Marsilio Pubs.

— House on the Hill. Strachan, W. J., tr. 1977. 25.00 (*0-7206-4286-8*) Dufour.

P Q

An Asterisk (*) at the beginning of an entry indicates that the title is appearing in BIP for the first time.

— La Luna e i Falo. Musa, Mark, ed. LC 68-13431. (Illus.). (Orig.). (ITA.). (C). 1968. pap. text ed. 6.95 (0-89197-281-1) Irvington.

— La Luna e i Falo. (Orig.). 1988. text ed. 12.95 (0-7190-0771-2, Pub. by Manchester Univ Pr UK) St Martin.

— La Luna e i Falo. Thompson, Doug, ed. 240p. 1995. text ed. 17.95 (0-7190-4383-2, Pub. by Manchester Univ Pr UK) St Martin.

— Le Metier de Vivre, 2 vols., 1. 1977. pap. 10.95 (0-7859-4082-0) Fr & Eur.

— Le Metier de Vivre, 2 vols., 2. 1977. pap. 10.95 (0-685-68142-4) Fr & Eur.

— Political Prisoner. Strachan, W. J., tr. 237p. 1969. reprint ed. 26.00 (0-7206-6202-8) Dufour.

— Selected Letters Nineteen Twenty-four to Nineteen Fifty. Murch, A. E., tr. 1969. 30.00 (0-7206-1520-8) Dufour.

— Stories. Murch, A. E., tr. & intro. by. 415p. 1987. pap. 12.95 (0-88001-124-6) Ecco Pr.

Pavese, Edith. American Highlights (Los Estados Unidos) United States History in Notable Works of Art - Grandes Momentos en su Historia a Traves de Prominentes Obras de Arte. Ezcurra, Madela & Kennedy, Roger G., trs. LC 92-30390. 160p. (ENG & SPA.). 1993. 29.95 (0-8109-1930-3) Abrams.

Pavese, F. & Molinar, G., eds. Modern Gas-Based Temperature & Pressure Measurements. (International Cryogenics Monograph). (Illus.). 490p. (C). 1992. 110.00 (0-306-44167-5, Plenum Pr) Plenum.

Pavese, Mike. Federal Civil Judicial Procedure & Rules. 985p. 1993. pap. text ed. write for info. (0-314-02238-4) West Pub.

— Federal Criminal Code & Rules. 1277p. 1993. pap. text ed. write for info. (0-314-02236-8) West Pub.

Pavese, Phyllis, ed. see Sanford, Charles W., Jr.

Pavesic, Max G. & Studebaker, William. Backtracking: Ancient Art of Southern Idaho. (Illus.). 84p. (Orig.). 1993. pap. 19.95 (0-939696-00-2) Idaho Mus Nat Hist.

Pavetto, Carl S. The Business Manager's Guide to Controlling Legal Costs. LC 89-90688. (Business Managers Ser.: Vol. 1). (Orig.). 1989. pap. 34.00 (0-925997-00-5) CSP Assocs Inc.

***Pavey, N. L.** Guide to Legionellosis Temperature Measurements for Hot & Cold Water Services. 96p. (C). 1994. 110.00x (0-86022-366-3, Pub. by Build Servs Info Assn UK) St Mut.

Pavia, Donald L., et al. Intro to Organic Lab Techniques: A Microscale Approach. 650p. (C). 1990. text ed. 50.75 (0-03-025418-3) SCP.

— Introduction to Organic Laboratory Techniques. 3rd ed. 756p. (C). 1988. text ed. 50.75 (0-03-014813-8) SCP.

— Introduction to Spectroscopy: A Guide for Students of Organic Chemistry. LC 77-11348. 367p. (C). 1979. pap. text ed. 39.00 (0-7216-7119-5) SCP.

Pavia, Maria N. Drama del Siglo de Oro: A Study of Magic: Witchcraft & Occult Beliefs. 116p. 1959. 4.00 (0-318-22344-9) Hispanic Inst.

Pavic, Milorad. Dictionary of the Khazars: Female Edition. Pribicevic-Zoric, Christina, tr. 1989. pap. 13.00 (0-679-72754-X, Vin) Random.

— Dictionary of the Khazars: Male Edition. Pribicevic-Zoric, Christina, tr. 1989. pap. 13.00 (0-679-72461-3, Vin) Random.

— Landscape Painted with Tea. Pribicevic-Zoric, Christina, tr. 1990. 21.95 (0-394-58217-9) Knopf.

Pavicevic, M., jt. auth. see Dragovic, Ivan.

Pavicevic, M. K., jt. ed. see Boekstein, A.

Pavich, Paul N. Joseph Wood Krutch. LC 89-60063. (Western Writers Ser.: No. 89). (Illus.). 52p. (Orig.). 1989. pap. 3.95 (0-88430-088-9) Boise St U W Writ Ser.

Pavicic, Marko, tr. see Stojanovic, Radmila, ed.

Pavidek. Toxic Compounds of Foods. 1995. write for info. (0-8493-4623-1) CRC Pr.

Pavie, A. Contes Populaires du Cambodge. LC 78-20136. (Collection de contes et de chansons populaires: Vol. 27). reprint ed. 21.50 (0-404-60377-7) AMS Pr.

Pavilion Books Staff. Claude Monet. (Postcard Bks.). 1989. pap. 9.00 (0-449-90342-7, Columbine) Ballantine.

— Goodness Beans, Peas & Lentils. 1994. pap. 5.99 (0-517-13039-4) Random.

— Goodness of Potatoes. 1994. pap. 5.99 (0-517-13038-6) Random.

— Hollywood Stars of the Fifties. 1989. mass mkt. 5.95 (0-449-90420-2) Fawcett.

— Postcard Book Angels. 64p. (Orig.). 1989. pap. 9.00 (0-449-90418-0, Columbine) Fawcett.

Pavis, Jose, jt. auth. see Steele, Ross.

Pavis, Patrice. Diccionario del Teatro: Dramaturgia, Estetica, Semiologia. 2nd ed. 605p. 1991. pap. 69.95 (0-7859-6227-1, 8475092373) Fr & Eur.

— Languages of the Stage: Essays in the Semiology of Theatre. (PAJ Bks.). (Illus.). 206p. (C). 1993. pap. text ed. 15.95 (0-933826-15-X) Johns Hopkins.

— Theatre at the Crossroads of Culture. Kruger, Loren, tr. 256p. 1991. 74.50 (0-415-06037-0, A6316); pap. 17.95 (0-415-06038-9, A6320) Routledge.

Pavis, Patricia. Dictionary of the Theatre: Dictionnaire du Theatre Termes et Concepts de l'Analyse Theatrale. 477p. (ENG, FRE, GER & SPA.). 1987. 150.00 (0-8288-2188-7, M15589) Fr & Eur.

Pavisich-Ryan, Olga, tr. see Miravalle, Mark I.

***Pavithran, A. K.** Bangladesh. LC 70-183008. 122p. 1971. 22.50 (0-912004-02-9) W W Gaunt.

Pavitranananda, Swami. A Short Life of the Holy Mother. pap. 1.50 (0-87481-122-8, Pub. by Advaita Ashrama II) Vedanta Pr.

Pavitrananda. Hymns & Prayers. 1974. Bilingual ed. pap. 3.95 (0-87481-146-5, Pub. by Advaita Ashrama II) Vedanta Pr.

Pavitrananda, Swami. Common Sense about Yoga. pap. 1.25 (0-87481-105-8, Pub. by Advaita Ashrama II) Vedanta Pr.

Pavitrananda, Swami, tr. see Pushpadanta.

Pavitt, Charles. Small Group Discussion: A Theoretical Approach. 2nd ed. Curtis, Ellen, ed. LC 93-21097. 450p. (Orig.). 1994. pap. text ed. 35.00 (0-89787-350-5) Gorsuch Scarisbrick.

Pavitt, Irene, jt. ed. see Murfin, James V.

Pavitt, K., jt. auth. see Hanson, P.

Pavitt, Kate, jt. auth. see Thomas, William.

Pavka, John, jt. auth. see Corcoran, Eileen L.

Pavkovic, Aleksandar. Slobodan Jovanovic: An Unsentimental Approach to Politics. 320p. 1993. 45.00 (0-88033-268-9, 371) East Eur Quarterly.

***Pavkovic, Aleksandar, et al, eds.** Nationalism & Postcommunism: A Collection of Essays. LC 95-8908. 1995. write for info. (1-85521-625-6, Pub. by Dartmth Pub UK) Ashgate Pub Co.

Pavlak, Stephen A. Classroom Activities for Correcting Specific Reading Problems. LC 84-19001. 192p. 1985. pap. text ed. 24.95 (0-13-136219-4, Busn) P-H.

— Informal Tests for Diagnosing Specific Reading Problems. LC 84-19094. 134p. 1985. pap. text ed. 24.95 (0-13-464801-3, Busn) P-H.

Pavlak, Thomas J., jt. auth. see Pops, Gerald M.

Pavlat, Leo. Bible Stories: From the Old & New Testament. (J). (gr. 1 up). 1994. 12.98 (0-7858-0013-1) Bk Sales Inc.

Pavle, Kalan, jt. auth. see Bajac, Anton.

Pavlenko, Stefan, tr. see Theophan the Recluse.

Pavletic, Michael M. Atlas of Small Animal Reconstructive Surgery. LC 92-15376. 1992. 95.00 (0-397-51119-1) Lippincott.

Pavletich, Aida. Sirens of Song: The Popular Female Vocalist in America. LC 81-22147. (Quality Paperbacks Ser.). (Illus.). 281p. 1982. reprint ed. pap. 7.95 (0-306-80162-0) Da Capo.

Pavlicek, R., jt. auth. see Root, W.

Pavlicek, Richard, jt. auth. see Root, William S.

Pavlich, Walter. Ongoing Portraits. 52p. (Orig.). 1985. pap. 5.95 (0-935306-33-1) Barnwood Pr.

— Running near the End of the World. LC 91-31623. (Edwin Ford Piper Poetry Award Ser.). 100p. 1992. pap. 10.95 (0-87745-358-6) U of Iowa Pr.

Pavlicko, Marie, jt. auth. see Farr, J. Michael.

Pavlidis, George T., ed. Perspectives on Dyslexia, Vol. 1. 279p. 1990. text ed. 130.95 (0-471-92204-8) Wiley.

— Perspectives on Dyslexia, Vol. 2. 331p. 1990. text ed. 130.95 (0-471-92484-9) Wiley.

Pavlidis, George T. & Fisher, Dennis F., eds. Dyslexia: Its Neuropsychology & Treatment. LC 85-16780. 316p. 1986. text ed. 82.95 (0-471-90875-4) Wiley.

***Pavlidis, George T. & Miles, T. R., eds.** Dyslaxia Research & Its Applications to Education. LC 80-49975. (Illus.). 329p. 1981. reprint ed. pap. 93.80 (0-7837-8872-X, 2049583) Bks Demand.

Pavlidis, George T. & Miles, Timothy R. Dyslexia Research & Its Applications to Education. LC 80-49975. 307p. 1981. text ed. 114.95 (0-471-27841-6, Wiley-Interscience) Wiley.

Pavlidis, Stephen J. & Darville, Ray. A Cruising Guide to the Exuma Cays Land & Sea Park. LC 93-86394. (Illus.). 78p. (Orig.). 1994. pap. 14.95 (0-685-69186-1) Night Flyer.

Pavlidis, T. Structural Pattern Recognition. LC 77-21105. (Electrophysics Ser.: Vol. 1). (Illus.). 1977. 46.00 (0-387-08463-0) Spr-Verlag.

Pavlidis, Theo. Algorithms for Graphics & Image Processing. LC 81-9832. (Principles of Computer Science Ser.). (Illus.). 416p. (C). 1995. text ed. 46.95 (0-7167-8106-9, Computer Sci Pr) W H Freeman.

Pavlik, Bruce M., et al. Oaks of California. (Illus.). 184p. (Orig.). 1992. 29.95 (0-9628505-2-7); pap. 21.95 (0-9628505-1-9) Cachuma Pr.

Pavlik, Cheryl. Speak Up, Set 4. 1982. audio 50.00 (0-8384-2960-2, Newbury) Heinle & Heinle.

***Pavlik, Cheryl & Stumpfhauser De Hernandez, Anna.** Speak Up Bk. 1. 2nd ed. 112p. 1995. pap. 15.95 (0-8384-4996-4) Heinle & Heinle.

Pavlik, Ellen L. & Belkaoui, Ahmed R. Determinants of Executive Compensation: Corporate Ownership, Performance, Size, & Diversification. LC 90-26407. 176p. 1991. text ed. 59.95 (0-89930-633-0, PEZ/, Quorum Bks) Greenwood.

Pavlik, Ellen L., jt. auth. see Riahi-Belkaoui, Ahmed.

Pavlik, John V. Public Relations: What Research Tells Us. (CommText Ser.: Vol. 16). (C). 1987. text ed. 37.00 (0-8039-2950-1); pap. text ed. 16.95 (0-8039-2951-X) Sage.

Pavlik, John V. & Dennis, Everette E., eds. Demystifying Media Technology: Readings from the Freedom Forum Center, Additional readings avail. on diskette. LC 92-25132. 194p. (C). 1993. pap. text ed. 26.95 (1-55934-145-9) Mayfield Pub.

Pavlik, John V., jt. ed. see Williams, Frederick.

Pavlik, Norene. One of Them. LC 88-61212. (Illus.). 220p. 1988. pap. 8.95 (0-87973-420-5, 420) Our Sunday Visitor.

***Pavlik, Philip.** Enhancing Your Intelligence. 480p. Date not set. pap. 12.95 (0-7610-0415-7) NW Pub.

Pavlin, Charles J. & Foster, F. Stuart. Ultrasound Biomicroscopy of the Eye. LC 93-40948. (Illus.). 164p. 1994. 89.00 (0-387-94206-8) Spr-Verlag.

Pavlin, Igor, jt. ed. see Prokopenko, Joseph.

Pavlin, R., ed. Goethe: Die Leiden des Jungen Werthers. (GER.). pap. 14.95 (1-85399-323-9, Pub. by Duckworth UK) Focus Info Gr.

Pavlischek, Keith J. John Courtney Murray & the Dilemma of Religious Toleration. LC 94-4765. 290p. (C). 1994. lib. bdg. 58.50 (0-943549-18-3); pap. text ed. 22.50 (0-943549-26-4) TJU Pr.

Pavlock, Barbara. Eros, Imitation, & the Epic Tradition. LC 89-36639. 248p. 1990. 33.95 (0-8014-2321-X) Cornell U Pr.

Pavloff, George. The Man Who Was It. (Illus.). 72p. (J). (gr. 1 up). 1990. 12.95 (0-931474-39-6) TBW Bks.

— A Rainbow for Suzanne. (Illus.). 72p. (J). (gr. 1 up). 1991. 14.95 (0-931474-40-X) TBW Bks.

Pavlos, Andrew J. The Cult Experience. LC 81-13175. (Contributions to the Study of Religion Ser.: No. 6). xvi, 209p. 1982. text ed. 55.00 (0-313-23164-8, PEX/, Greenwood Pr) Greenwood.

Pavloskis, Zoya, ed. The Story of Apollonius: The King of Tyre. 7.50 (0-87291-095-4) Coronado Pr.

Pavlou, K. N., jt. ed. see Simopoulos, A. P.

Pavlou, Konstantinos N., jt. ed. see Simopoulos, Artemis P.

Pavlov, Alexander, ed. see Kazakov.

Pavlov, Boris & Terentyev, Alexander. Organic Chemistry. Belitzky, B., tr. (Illus.). 570p. 1965. text ed. 260.00 (0-677-20290-3) Gordon & Breach.

— Organic Chemistry. 2nd ed. MIR Publishers, tr. (Illus.). 616p. (C). 1975. 29.95 (0-8464-0690-X) Beekman Pubs.

Pavlov, D., ed. see Symposium on Advances in Lead-Acid Batteries Staff.

Pavlov, Dmitriĭ V. Leningrad Nineteen Forty-One: The Blockade. Adams, John C. & Salisbury, Harrison E., trs. LC 65-2479. (Illus.). 210p. reprint ed. pap. 59.90 (0-317-09259-6, 2020140) Bks Demand.

Pavlov, Helene, ed. The Running Athlete: Roentgenograms & Remedies. (Illus.). 320p. 1987. 69.95 (0-8151-6712-1, RR-1, Yr Bk Med Pubs) Mosby Yr Bk.

Pavlov, Ivan P. Conditioned Reflexes: An Investigation of the Physiological Activity of the Cerebral Cortex. Anrep, G. V., ed. 1927. pap. text ed. 9.95 (0-486-60614-7) Dover.

— Psychopathology & Psychiatry. 550p. (C). 1993. pap. text ed. 24.95 (1-56000-707-9) Transaction Pubs.

Pavlov, V. P., tr. see Kulikov, N. V. & Molchanova, I. V.

Pavlov, Vitaly. Memoirs of a Spymaster: My Fifty Years in the KGB. (Illus.). 540p. 1994. 26.95 (0-88184-451-9) Carroll & Graf.

Pavlov, Yuri. Soviet-Cuban Alliance, 1959-1991. LC 93-8292. 240p. (C). 1994. pap. 18.95 (1-56000-691-9, U Miami North-South Ctr) Transaction Pubs.

Pavlov, Z., ed. see International Congress on Electrocardiology Staff.

Pavlova, E. V. Pushkin - A Gallery of Portraits, 2 vols., Set. 374p. 1983. 100.00 (0-317-61357-X, Pub. by Collets UK) Pro-Am Music.

Pavlova, Karolina. A Double Life. 2nd ed. Heldt, Barbara, tr. & intro. by. (Illus.). xxii, 111p. 1986. reprint ed. pap. 8.95 (0-936041-01-3) Barbary Coast Bks.

Pavlova, L. M., jt. auth. see Glazov, V. M.

Pavlova, Z. V. & Isakova, M. E. Oncology Reviews, Vol. 3. (Soviet Scientific Reviews Ser.: Vol. 3, Pt. 3). 66p. 1989. pap. text ed. 45.00 (3-7186-4913-6) Gordon & Breach.

Pavlovic, Karl, jt. auth. see Schaub, James H.

Pavlovic, Karl R., tr. see Lorenzen, Paul.

Pavlovic, M. N., ed. Steel Structures: Recent Research Advances & Their Applications to Design. 604p. 1986. 169.25 (1-85166-046-1) Elsevier.

Pavlovic, Miodrag. The Slavs Beneath Parnassus. 1985. pap. 7.00 (0-89823-062-4) New Rivers Pr.

Pavlovic, Vladimir, jt. auth. see Shaw, T.

Pavlovic, Vukasin, jt. ed. see Seroka, James H.

Pavlovsky, A. A. Vseobshii Illiustrirovannyi Putevoditel' po Sviatym Mestam Rossiiskoi Imperii i Sv. Afonu. LC 88-61819. (Illus.). 900p. (RUS.). 1988. reprint ed. 85.00 (0-911971-35-1); reprint ed. pap. 55.00 (0-911971-34-3) Effect Pub.

***Pavlovsky, Eduardo.** Three Plays by Eduardo Pavlovsky: Slow Motion, Potestad - Paternity, Pablo. Carter, Hilma O., ed. Verdier, Paul, tr. & adapt. by. (Illus.). 160p. (Orig.). 1994. pap. 12.95 (0-9642024-0-9) Stages Theatre.

Pavlovsky, Evgeny N. Natural Nidality of Transmissible Diseases: With Special Reference to the Landscape Epidemiology of Zooanthroponoses. Levine, Norman D., ed. LC 66-11023. 275p. reprint ed. pap. 78.40 (0-317-28739-7, 2020244) Bks Demand.

Pavlow, Al. Hot Charts, 1950. 84p. (Orig.). 1993. pap. 5.95 (0-915529-01-7) Music Hse Pub.

— Hot Charts, 1951. 84p. (Orig.). 1993. pap. 5.95 (0-915529-02-5) Music Hse Pub.

— Hot Charts, 1952. 92p. (Orig.). 1993. pap. 5.95 (0-915529-03-3) Music Hse Pub.

— Hot Charts, 1953. 96p. (Orig.). 1993. pap. 5.95 (0-915529-04-1) Music Hse Pub.

— Hot Charts, 1954. 84p. (Orig.). 1993. pap. 5.95 (0-915529-05-X) Music Hse Pub.

— Hot Charts, 1955. 80p. (Orig.). 1993. pap. 5.95 (0-915529-06-8) Music Hse Pub.

— Hot Charts, 1956. 96p. (Orig.). 1993. pap. 5.95 (0-915529-07-6) Music Hse Pub.

— Hot Charts, 1957. 96p. (Orig.). 1993. pap. 5.95 (0-915529-08-4) Music Hse Pub.

— Hot Charts, 1958. 92p. (Orig.). 1993. pap. 5.95 (0-915529-09-2) Music Hse Pub.

— Hot Charts, 1959. 104p. (Orig.). 1993. pap. 5.95 (0-915529-10-6) Music Hse Pub.

Pavlowitch, Stevan K. The Improbable Survivor: Yugoslavia & Its Problems, 1918-1988. 184p. 1988. reprint ed. pap. 17.50 (0-8142-0505-4) Ohio St U Pr.

— Tito - Yugoslavia's Great Dictator: A Reassessment. LC 92-23760. 128p. 1992. lib. bdg. 35.00 (0-8142-0600-X); pap. 12.95 (0-8142-0601-8) Ohio St U Pr.

***Pavlowitch, Steven K., ed.** Unconventional Perceptions of Yugoslavia. 256p. 1985. 42.00 (0-88033-081-3) East Eur Quarterly.

Pavlychko, Solomea. Letters from Kiev. Kostash, Myrna, tr. 150p. 1992. text ed. 35.00 (0-312-07588-X) St Martin.

Pavlyshyn, Marko, ed. Glasnost in Context: On the Recurrence of Liberalizations in Central & East European Literatures & Cultures. LC 89-39740. (Berg European Studies Ser.). 215p. 1990. 55.00 (0-85496-598-X) Berg Pubs.

Pavon, J., jt. auth. see Ruiz, H.

Pavone-Macaluso, M., jt. auth. see DeKernion, Jean B.

Pavoni, Joseph, et al. Handbook of Solid Waste Disposal: Materials & Energy Recovery. LC 74-26777. 566p. 1975. 42.50 (0-442-23027-3) Van Nos Reinhold.

Pavoni, N. & Green, R., eds. Recent Crustal Movements. (Developments in Geotectonics Ser.: Vol. 29). 552p. 1991. reprint ed. 131.50 (0-444-41420-7) Elsevier.

Pavord, Anna. Anna Pavord's Gardening Companion. (Illus.). 298p. 1993. pap. 19.95 (0-7011-4953-1, Pub. by Chatto & Windus UK) Trafalgar.

— The Border Book. LC 93-28347. (Illus.). 160p. 1994. 29.95 (1-56458-485-2) Dorling Kindersley.

— Flowering Year: A Guide to Seasonal Planting. (Illus.). 168p. 1991. 39.95 (1-55859-240-7, Cross Riv Pr) Abbeville Pr.

— Hidcote Manor Garden: Gloucestershire. (Illus.). 64p. 1993. pap. 10.95 (0-7078-0166-4, Pub. by Natl Trust UK) Trafalgar.

Pavord, Marcy. David Broome's Training Manual. (Illus.). 152p. 1994. 29.95 (1-57076-008-X, Trafalgar Sq Pub) Trafalgar.

Pavord, Tony. Your Horse's Health. (Crowood Equestrian Ser.). (Illus.). 96p. 1992. pap. 17.95 (1-85223-532-2, Pub. by Crowood Pr UK) Trafalgar.

Pavruisini-Gebert, Lizabeth, jt. ed. see Olmus, Margarite F.

Pavry, Jal D. Zoroastrian Doctrine of a Future Life from Death to the Individual Judgment. 2nd ed. LC 79-10518. reprint ed. 16.50 (0-404-50481-7) AMS Pr.

***Pavuk, Pamela P.** The Story of a Lifetime: A Keepsake of Personal Memoirs. Pavuk, Stephen M., ed. (Illus.). 384p. 1995. 29.95 (0-9643032-5-6) Triangel Pubs.

Pavuk, Stephen M., ed. see Pavuk, Pamela P.

Pavuna, Davor, jt. auth. see Cyrot, Michel.

Pawalowski, K., jt. ed. see Jackowski, S.

Pawczuk, Eugene. Robin Hood. Pronk, Mary, ed. (Traditional Fairy Tales Ser.). (Illus.). 32p. (Orig.). (J). (gr. 1-6). 1992. lib. bdg. 15.55 (0-88625-266-0); pap. 5.95 (0-88625-264-4) Durkin Hayes Pub.

Pawel, Ernst. The Labyrinth of Exile: A Life of Theodor Herzl. (Illus.). 572p. 1992. pap. 15.00 (0-374-52351-7, Noonday) FS&G.

— The Labyrinth of Exile: A Life of Theodore Herzl. 1989. 30.00 (0-374-18256-6) FS&G.

— Life in Dark Ages. 1995. 19.95 (0-88064-168-1) Fromm Intl Pub.

— The Nightmare of Reason: A Life of Franz Kafka. (Illus.). 478p. 1992. pap. 15.00 (0-374-52335-5, Noonday) FS&G.

— The Poet Dying: Heinrich Heine's Last Years in Paris. LC 94-40744. 188p. 1995. 21.00 (0-374-23538-4) FS&G.

Pawel, Ernst, tr. see Aron, Raymond.

Pawel, Ernst, tr. see Lehmann, Lotte.

Pawelczynska, Anna. Values & Violence in Auschwitz: A Sociological Analysis. LC 76-3886. 1979. pap. 11.00 (0-520-04242-5) U CA Pr.

Pawelec, W. The Friends of Zofia. 96p. 1985. 24.95 (0-932735-00-2) Melrose Pub Inc.

Pawelek, Anne J. American in Poland. 1967. 3.75 (0-685-09282-8) Endurance.

Pawick. Using dBASE IV for Windows. 1994. pap. 29.99 (1-56529-630-3) Que.

Pawl, Lawrence E., ed. see Haas, Erwin J.

Pawl, Lawrence E., jt. auth. see Melton, Jack W., Jr.

Pawl, Ronald P. Chronic Pain Primer. LC 79-22621. (Illus.). 221p. reprint ed. pap. 63.00 (0-8357-7627-1, 2056950) Bks Demand.

Pawlak, jt. auth. see Hoag.

Pawlak, Mark. All the News. LC 84-12956. 1984. pap. 4.00 (0-914610-37-6) Hanging Loose.

— Special Handling. LC 93-160. 1993. pap. 10.00 (0-685-62321-1); Casebound. boxed 18.00 (0-914610-99-6) Hanging Loose.

Pawlak, Mark, jt. auth. see Lourie, Dick.

***Pawlak, Mark, et al, eds.** Bullseye. LC 95-9866. (High School Age Writing from the Sixties to Now Ser.: Vol. 2). 264p. 1995. pap. 15.00 (1-882413-12-1) Hanging Loose.

— Bullseye: Stories & Poems by Outstanding High School Writers. 264p. 1995. 25.00 (0-614-05448-6) Hanging Loose.

Pawlak, Walter A., Jr., jt. auth. see Litt, Jerome Z.

Pawlak, Zdzislaw. Rough Sets: Theoretical Aspects of Reasoning about Data. 248p. 1991. lib. bdg. 106.50 (0-7923-1472-7) Kluwer Ac.

***Pawlas, George E.** The Administrator's Guide to School-Community Relations. LC 94-25310. (Illus.). 300p. 1995. 39.95x (1-883001-13-7) Eye On Educ.

Pawle, Gerald. Secret Weapons of World War II. 1978. pap. 1.95 (0-345-27895-X) Ballantine.

Pawlenko, Stephan. Organosilicon Chemistry. (Illus.). xii, 186p. 1986. 153.85 (0-89925-202-8) De Gruyter.

— Organosilicon Chemistry. (Illus.). xii, 186p. 1986. 153.85 (3-11-010329-X) De Gruyter.

Pawley, B. The Second Vatican Council: Studies by Eight Anglican Observers. 12.00 (0-8446-2713-5) Peter Smith.

Pawley, G. S., jt. ed. see Kenway, R. D.

Pawley, J. B., ed. Handbook of Biological Confocal Microscopy. (Illus.). 246p. 1990. 55.00 (0-306-43538-1, Plenum Pr) Plenum.

***Pawley, James B., ed.** Handbook of Biological Confocal Microscopy. 2nd ed. LC 94-46208. 575p. 1995. 85.00 (0-306-44826-2, Plenum Pr) Plenum.

Pawley, Margaret. Praying with the English Tradition. 1991. pap. 5.95 (0-687-86043-1) Abingdon.

P Q

Pawley, Martin. Buckminster Fuller. (Design Heroes Ser.). (Illus.). 192p. 1991. 24.95 (*0-8008-1116-X*) Taplinger.

— Future Systems: The Story of Tomorrow. (Illus.). 156p. (C). 1993. pap. 29.95 (*0-7148-2767-3*, Pub. by Phaidon Press UK) Chronicle Bks.

— Theory & Design in the Second Machine Age. (Illus.). 1990. 34.95 (*0-631-15828-6*) Blackwell Pubs.

Pawley, Martin, ed. see Burney, Jan.

Pawley, Michael. Financial Innovation & Monetary Policy. LC 92-13957. 240p. 1993. 79.95 (*0-415-07503-3*, A7673, Routledge NY) Routledge.

Pawley, Thomas D., jt. auth. see Reardon, William R.

Pawlick, Thomas. A Killing Rain: The Global Threat of Acid Precipitation. LC 84-5367. 224p. 1984. 15.95 (*0-87156-823-3*) Sierra.

Pawliczko, Ann L., ed. Ukraine & Ukrainians Throughout the World: A Demographic & Sociological Guide to the Homeland & Its Diaspora. (Illus.). 464p. (C). 1994. 75. 00 (*0-8020-0595-0*); pap. 35.00 (*0-8020-7200-3*) U of Toronto Pr.

Pawlik, Jonathan, jt. auth. see Chase, Pamela L.

Pawlik, Jonathan, jt. auth. see Chase, Pamela.

Pawlik, K., ed. International Directory of Psychologists: Exclusive of the U. S. A. 4th ed. 1182p. 1985. 92.50 (*0-444-87774-6*, North Holland) Elsevier.

Pawlik, Peter S., jt. auth. see Reismann, Herbert.

Pawlikowski & Senior, eds. Economic Justice: The CTU Commentary on the Bishops Letter on the Economy. 200p. 1988. pap. 12.95 (*0-912405-41-4*) Pastoral Pr.

Pawlikowski, John. Jesus & the Theology of Israel. LC 88-82453. (Zacchaeus Studies: Theology). 99p. (Orig.). (C). 1989. pap. 7.95 (*0-8146-5683-8*) Liturgical Pr.

Pawlikowski, John T. & Fragomeni, Richard, eds. The Ecological Challenge. 152p. (Orig.). 1994. pap. text ed. 9.95 (*0-8146-5840-7*, M Glazier) Liturgical Pr.

Pawlikowski, John T. & Wilde, James A. When Catholics Speak about Jews: Notes for Homilists & Catechists. 88p. 1987. pap. 5.95 (*0-930467-60-4*) Liturgy Tr Pubns.

Pawlikowski, M., jt. auth. see Dohler, K. D.

Pawling, Christopher. Christopher Caudwell: Towards a Dialectical Theory of Literature. LC 88-35482. 208p. 1989. text ed. 39.95 (*0-312-03014-2*) St Martin.

Pawling, Jesse R. Dr. Samuel Guthrie, Discoverer of Chloroform. (Illus.). 123p. 1994. reprint ed. lib. bdg. 22. 00 (*0-8328-3628-1*) Higginson Bk Co.

Pawloski, L., et al, eds. Chemistry for Protection of the Environment: Proceedings of the 6th International Conference, Torino, Italy, 15-18 September, 1987. (Studies in Environmental Science: No. 34). 412p. 1989. 164.00 (*0-444-87130-6*) Elsevier.

Pawlow, E. A. & Semjonowa, O. I. Deutsch-Russisches Worterbuch der Forstund Holzwirtschaft: German-Russian Dictionary of Forestry of the Lumber Industry. 477p. (GER & RUS.). 1978. 29.95 (*0-8288-4870-X*, M9058) Fr & Eur.

Pawlowska, Harriet M. & Dehnert, Edmund J., eds. Merrily We Sing: One Hundred Five Polish Folk Songs. LC 60-10960. (Illus.). 256p. 1984. reprint ed. pap. 19.95 (*0-8143-1753-7*) Wayne St U Pr.

Pawlowski, L. Physiochemical Methods for Water & Wastewater Treatment. 1980. 133.00 (*0-08-024013-5*, Pub. by Pergamon Repr UK) Franklin.

Pawlowski, L., ed. Physiochemical Methods for Water & Wastewater Treatment. (Studies in Environmental Science: Vol. 19). 394p. 1982. 131.00 (*0-444-42067-3*) Elsevier.

Pawlowski, L., jt. auth. see Bolto, B. A.

Pawlowski, L., et al, eds. Chemistry for Protection of the Environment: Proceedings of an International Conference, Toulouse, France, 19-25, Sept., 1983. (Studies in Environmental Science: No. 23). 626p. 1984. 200.00 (*0-444-42347-8*, I-227-84) Elsevier.

— Chemistry for the Protection of the Environment. (Environmental Science Research Ser.). (Illus.). 824p. 1991. 159.50 (*0-306-43904-2*, Plenum Pr) Plenum.

— Chemistry for the Protection of the Environment 1985: Proceedings of the 5th International Conference, Leuven, Belgium, September 9-13, 1985. (Studies in Environmental Science: No. 29). 796p. 1986. 251.50 (*0-444-42715-5*) Elsevier.

Pawlowski, Lech. The Science & Engineering of Thermal Spray Coatings. LC 94-19287. 1995. text ed. 95.95 (*0-471-95253-2*) Wiley.

***Pawlowski, M. & Brown, J.** Casebook on the Law of Landlord & Tenant Vol. 1. 1994. pap. text ed. 48.00 (*0-421-50500-1*, Pub. by Sweet & Maxwll) W W Gaunt.

***Pawlowski, Mark & Brown, James.** Q & A Landlord & Tenant. (Questions & Answers Ser.). 230p. 1995. pap. 20.00 (*1-85431-398-3*, Pub. by Blackstone Pr UK) W W Gaunt.

Pawlowski, Tadeusz. Concept Formation in the Humanities & the Social Sciences. (Synthese Library: No. 144). 233p. 1980. lib. bdg. 74.50 (*90-277-1096-1*) Kluwer Ac.

***Pawlowsky, Peter.** Christianity. Bowden, John, tr. LC 94-47515. (Basic Ser.). 112p. (Orig.). (C). 1995. pap. 10.00 (*1-56338-112-5*) TPI PA.

Pawlson, L. Gregory, jt. ed. see Brody, Stanley J.

Pawluch, Dorothy. The New Pediatrics: A Profession in Transition. (Social Problems & Social Issues Ser.). 144p. 1996. lib. bdg. 38.95 (*0-202-30534-1*); pap. 19.95 (*0-202-30535-X*) Aldine de Gruyter.

Pawlucki, W. Points de Nash des Ensembles Sous-Analytiques. LC 89-18471. 76p. 1990. pap. 18.00 (*0-8218-2430-9*, MEMO 84/425) Am Math.

Pawlycn, Cindy. The Fog City Diner Cookbook. 224p. 1992. 24.95 (*0-89815-493-6*) Ten Speed Pr.

***Pawnee Elem. School Third-Graders.** Alien Attack, Big Bk. (Wee Write Bks.: No. 4). (Illus.). 25p. (J). (ps-3). 1994. 32.95 (*1-884987-17-6*) WeWrite.

— The Zookeeper's Bad Day, Big Bk. (Wee Write Bks.: No. 5). (Illus.). 25p. (J). (ps-3). 1994. 32.95 (*1-884987-20-6*) WeWrite.

***Pawnee Elem. School Third-Graders Staff.** The Strange Dream, Big Bk. (Wee Write Bks.: No. 6). (Illus.). 21p. (J). (ps-3). 1994. 32.95 (*1-884987-23-0*) WeWrite.

***Pawnee Elementary School, Mrs. Salisbury's 1994-1995 Third-Grade Class.** The Joke Ghost. (Wee Write Bks.: No. 14). (Illus.). 35p. (J). (ps-3). 1994. lib. bdg. 17.95 (*1-884987-45-1*); pap. 7.95 (*1-884987-46-X*) WeWrite.

— Our Cool Field Trip. (Wee Write Bks.: No. 13). (Illus.). 35p. (J). (ps-3). 1994. lib. bdg. 17.95 (*1-884987-42-7*); pap. 7.95 (*1-884987-43-5*) WeWrite.

***Pawnee Elementary School Third-Graders.** Alien Attack. (Wee Write Bks.: No. 4). (Illus.). 25p. (J). (ps-3). 1994. 17.95 (*1-884987-15-X*) WeWrite.

— Alien Attack. (Wee Write Bks.: No. 4). (Illus.). 25p. (J). (ps-3). 1994. pap. 7.95 (*1-884987-16-8*) WeWrite.

— The Strange Dream. (Wee Write Bks.: No. 6). (Illus.). 21p. (J). (ps-3). 1994. 17.95 (*1-884987-21-4*) WeWrite.

— The Strange Dream. (Wee Write Bks.: No. 6). (Illus.). 21p. (J). (ps-3). 1994. pap. 7.95 (*1-884987-22-2*) WeWrite.

— The Zookeeper's Bad Day. (Wee Write Bks.: No. 5). (Illus.). 25p. (J). (ps-3). 1994. 17.95 (*1-884987-18-4*) WeWrite.

— The Zookeeper's Bad Day. (Wee Write Bks.: No. 5). (Illus.). 25p. (J). (ps-3). 1994. pap. 7.95 (*1-884987-19-2*) WeWrite.

Pawsey, Margaret M. The Demon of Discord: Tensions in the Catholic Church of Victoria, 1853-1864. (Illus.). 200p. 1983. 29.95 (*0-522-84249-6*) Intl Spec Bk.

Pawsey, P., jt. auth. see Parry, P.

Pawson, D., ed. Biology of the Antarctic Seas Twelve. (Antarctic Research Ser.: Vol. 35). (Illus.). 110p. 1982. 20.00 (*0-87590-181-6*) Am Geophysical.

Pawson, D. L., ed. Biology of the Antarctic Seas Five, Paper 3: Bathypelagic Isopid Crustacea from the Antarctic & Southern Seas. (Antarctic Research Ser.: Vol. 23). 59p. 1977. write for info. (*0-87590-127-1*) Am Geophysical.

— Biology of the Antarctic Seas Seven, 4 papers, Set 27-4. (Antarctic Research Ser.: Vol. 27). 302p. 1978. Minibk. Set. 62.00 (*0-685-55230-6*); Paper 1: Systematics & Morphology of the Antarctic Cranchild Squid Galiteuthis Glacialis (Chun), 40p. write for info. (*0-87590-133-6*); Paper 2: Systematics & Ecology of Ciliated Protozoa from King George Island, South Shetland Islands,. write for info. (*0-87590-134-4*); Paper 3: More Planktonic Isopod Crustaceans from Subantarctic & Antarctic Seas, 34p. write for info. (*0-87590-135-2*); Paper 4: Calanoid Copepods (Aetideidae, Euchaetidae) from Anatarctic & Subantarctic Waters, 200p. write for info. (*0-87590-136-0*) Am Geophysical.

— Biology of the Antarctic Seas Six, Set. (Antarctic Research Ser.: Vol. 26). 51.00 (*0-87590-144-1*) Am Geophysical.

— Biology of the Antarctic Seas Six, Paper Four: Polychaeta from the Weddell Sea Quadrant, Antarctica. (Antarctic Research Ser.: Vol. 26). 60p. 1978. write for info. (*0-87590-132-8*) Am Geophysical.

***Pawson, D. L. & Kornicker, L. S., eds.** Biology of the Antarctic Seas Eight, 3 Papers, Papers 2 & 3: Nonasellote Isopod Crustaceans from. (Antarctic Research Ser.). 50p. 1978. write for info. (*0-87590-142-5*) Am Geophysical.

— Biology of the Antarctic Seas Eight, 3 papers, Set 28-3. (Antarctic Research Ser.: Vol. 28). 70p. 1978. Minibk. Set. 20.00 (*0-685-55231-4*) Am Geophysical.

— Biology of the Antarctic Seas Eight: Morphology & Distribution of Species in the Genus Pogonophryne (Pices, Harpagiferidae), 3 Papers, Paper 1: Morphology & Distribution of Species in t. (Antarctic Research Ser.: Vol. 28). 20p. 1978. write for info. (*0-87590-137-9*) Am Geophysical.

Pawson, David L. Molpadiid Sea Cucumbers (Echinodermata: Holothuroidea) of the Antarctic Seas: Paper 3 in Biology of the Antarctic Seas VI. LC 77-2320. (Antarctic Research Ser.: Vol. 26). (Illus.). 28p. 1977. pap. 10.70 (*0-87590-131-X*) Am Geophysical.

Pawson, David L. & Miller, John E. Systematics & Ecology of the Sea-Urchin Genus Centrostephanus Echinodermata: Echinodea) from the Altantic & Eastern Pacific Oceans. LC 83-600054. (Smithsonian Contributions to the Marine Sciences Ser.: No. 20). 20p. reprint ed. pap. 25.00 (*0-317-29916-6*, 2021766) Bks Demand.

Pawson, David L., ed. see Heron, Gayle A.

Pawson, David L., ed. see Lamb, I. Mackenzie & Zimmerman, Martin H.

Pawson, David L., ed. see Lowry, James K.

Pawson, David L., ed. see Schultz, George A.

Pawson, David L., ed. see Tibbs, John F.

Pawson, Ivan G. Physical Anthropology: Human Evolution. LC 77-2412. (Self-Teaching Guides Ser.). 256p. reprint ed. 73.00 (*0-8357-9954-9*, 2011877) Bks Demand.

Pawson, Ray. A Measure for Measures: A Manifesto for Empirical Sociology. 272p. 1989. 49.95 (*0-415-02870-1*); pap. 15.95 (*0-415-02659-8*) Routledge.

Pax, Noel & Thompson, Mary. Simply Christmas: Great Ideas for a Non-Commercial Holiday. LC 92-14674. (Illus.). 116p. 1992. pap. 8.95 (*0-8027-7389-3*) Walker & Co.

— Simply Christmas Nineteen Ninety-Three: Great Ideas for a Non-Commercial Holiday. LC 93-17883. (Illus.). 112p. 1993. pap. 5.95 (*0-8027-7405-9*) Walker & Co.

Paxinos, George, ed. The Rat Nervous System. 2nd ed. (Illus.). 1136p. 1994. boxed 169.00 (*0-12-547635-3*) Acad Pr.

***Paxinos, George & Huang, Xu F., eds.** Atlas of the Human Brainstem. (Illus.). 160p. 1995. spiral bd. write for info. (*0-12-547615-9*) Acad Pr.

Paxinos, George, et al. Atlas of the Developing Rat Nervous System. 2nd ed. Orig. Title: Atlas of the Developing Rat Brain. (Illus.). 438p. 1994. 125.00 (*0-12-547610-8*) Acad Pr.

Paxinos, George T., ed. The Human Nervous System. 1195p. 1990. text ed. 235.00 (*0-12-547625-6*) Acad Pr.

Paxinos, George T. & Watson, Charles. The Rat Brain. 2nd ed. 264p. 1986. text ed. 79.00 (*0-12-547621-3*) Acad Pr.

Paxinos, George T., jt. ed. see Mendelsohn, F. A.

Paxman, David. A Newcomer's Guide to Hawaii. 144p. 1992. pap. 8.95 (*0-935180-32-X*) Mutual Pub HI.

Paxman, J. M. & Zuckerman, R. J. Laws & Policies Affecting Adolescent Health. 310p. 1987. pap. 29.40 (*92-4-156095-9*) World Health.

Paxman, Jeremy & Harris, Robert. A Higher Form of Killing: The Secret Story of Gas & Germ Warfare. 266p. 1983. pap. 10.95 (*0-8090-1507-2*) Hill & Wang.

Paxman, John M., ed. The World Population Crisis: Policy Implications & the Role of Law: Proceedings of the American Society of International Law Regional Meeting & the John Bassett Moore Society of International Law Symposium. LC 80-19753. vi, 179p. 1980. reprint ed. text ed. 52.50 (*0-313-22619-9*, PAWO) Greenwood.

Paxon, Inc. Staff. International Who's Who: The Ultimate Professional Directory. 1994. 299.95 (*1-882952-00-6*) Intl Whos Who.

Paxon, Ruth. Llamados a Ser Santos: Call to Holiness. (SPA.). 3.25 (*84-7228-813-7*, 220541, Pub. by Edit Clie SP) TSELF.

Paxson, Charles L., ed. see Van Leeuwen, Gerard.

Paxson, Christina H., jt. auth. see Deaton, Angus.

Paxson, Christina H., jt. auth. see Gersovitz, Mark.

Paxson, Diana & Martine-Barnes, Adrienne. Master of Earth & Water. (Legends of Fionn MacCumhall Ser.: Vol. 1). 1993. 22.00 (*0-688-12505-0*) Morrow.

***Paxson, Diana L.** The Dragons of the Rhine. LC 94-3198. (J). 1995. 23.00 (*0-688-13986-8*, AvoNova) Avon.

— The Jewel of Fire. (Westria Ser.: No. 7). 1992. mass mkt. 3.99 (*0-8125-1110-7*) Tor Bks.

— The Serpent's Tooth. 400p. 1993. mass mkt. 4.99 (*0-380-75680-3*, AvoNova) Avon.

— Shield Between the Worlds. 1994. 22.00 (*0-688-13176-X*) Morrow.

— The White Raven. 480p. 1989. reprint ed. mass mkt. 4.99 (*0-380-75229-8*, AvoNova) Avon.

— Wind Crystal. 1990. pap. 3.95 (*0-8125-0040-7*) Tor Bks.

— The Wolf & the Raven. 352p. 1994. mass mkt. 4.99 (*0-380-76526-8*, AvoNova) Avon.

— The Wolf & the Raven. LC 92-27416. 1993. 21.00 (*0-688-10821-0*) Morrow.

***Paxson, Diana L. & Martin-Barnes, Adrienne.** Sword of Fire & Shadow. LC 94-49015. 1995. write for info. (*0-688-14156-0*, AvoNova) Avon.

Paxson, Diana L. & Martine-Barnes, Adrienne. Master of Earth & Water. 1993. pap. text ed. 22.00 (*0-380-97219-0*, AvoNova) Avon.

— Master of Earth & Water. 416p. 1994. mass mkt. 4.99 (*0-380-75801-6*, AvoNova) Avon.

— The Shield Between the Worlds. 336p. 1995. mass mkt. 4.99 (*0-380-75802-4*, AvoNova) Avon.

Paxson, F. L., jt. auth. see Paullin, C. O.

Paxson, Frederic L. History of the American Frontier, 1763-1893. LC 90-47732. (Illus.). 615p. 1990. reprint ed. 39. 95 (*0-87797-194-3*) Cherokee.

Paxson, James J. The Poetics of Personification. (Literature, Culture, Theory Ser.: No. 6). 216p. (C). 1994. 49.95 (*0-521-44539-6*) Cambridge U Pr.

Paxson, Jeanette. Basic Tools & Equipment for the Oil Field. (Illus.). 109p. (Orig.). (C). 1982. pap. text ed. 17. 00 (*0-88698-100-X*, 1.80010) PETEX.

Paxson, Jeanette, ed. Casing & Cementing. 2nd rev. ed. (Rotary Drilling Ser.: Unit II, Lesson 4). (Illus.). 53p. (Orig.). 1982. pap. text ed. 14.00 (*0-88698-056-9*, 2. 20420) PETEX.

— Reciprocating Gas Compressors. (Oil & Gas Production Ser.). (Illus.). 107p. (Orig.). 1982. pap. text ed. 15.00 (*0-88698-119-0*, 3.30210) PETEX.

Paxson, Jeanette R., ed. see Cyrus, Cinda.

Paxson, Ruth. Como Vivir en el Plano Superior. Orig. Title: Life on the Highest Plane. 254p. (SPA.). 1984. pap. 5.99 (*0-8254-1551-9*) Kregel.

— Rios de Agua Viva. 96p. 1983. reprint ed. pap. 2.95 (*0-311-46065-8*) Casa Bautista.

— Rios de Agua Viva: Rivers of Living Water. (SPA.). 3.95 (*84-7228-762-9*, 222395, Pub. by Edit Clie SP) TSELF.

Paxson, William C. Business Writing Handbook. 288p. 1984. mass mkt. 5.99 (*0-553-27041-9*, Bantam Classics) Bantam.

— The New American Spelling Dictionary: Easy Access to More Than 45,000 Words, Spelled & Divided. 448p. (Orig.). 1992. pap. 4.99 (*0-451-17377-5*, Sig) NAL-Dutton.

— The Persons, Places, & Things Spelling Dictionary. 528p. (Orig.). 1994. pap. 5.99 (*0-451-17987-0*, Sig) NAL-Dutton.

— Write It Now: A Timesaving Guide to Writing Better. 1985. pap. 10.53 (*0-201-16878-2*) Addison-Wesley.

***Paxton, Albert S.** National Repair & Remodeling Estimator,1995. (Illus.). 416p. (Orig.). 1994. pap. 32.50 (*1-57218-005-6*) Craftsman.

Paxton, E. H., tr. see Hussein, Taha.

Paxton, Frederic L. American Democracy & the World War, 3 vols., 1. Incl. Vol. 1. Pre-War Years, 1913-1917. LC 66-26828. 57.00 (*0-8154-0173-6*); Vol. 2. America at War, 1917-1918. LC 66-26828. 52.25 (*0-8154-0174-4*); Vol. 3. Postwar Years, Normalcy. LC 66-26828. 52.25 (*0-8154-0175-2*); LC 66-26828. reprint ed. write for info. (*0-318-51436-2*) Cooper Sq.

— American Democracy & the World War, 3 vols., 2. Incl. Vol. 1. Pre-War Years, 1913-1917. LC 66-26828. 57.00 (*0-8154-0173-6*); Vol. 2. America at War, 1917-1918. LC 66-26828. 52.25 (*0-8154-0174-4*); Vol. 3. Postwar Years, Normalcy. LC 66-26828. 52.25 (*0-8154-0175-2*); LC 66-26828. reprint ed. write for info. (*0-318-51437-0*) Cooper Sq.

— American Democracy & the World War, 3 vols., 3. Incl. Vol. 1. Pre-War Years, 1913-1917. LC 66-26828. 57.00 (*0-8154-0173-6*); Vol. 2. America at War, 1917-1918. LC 66-26828. 52.25 (*0-8154-0174-4*); Vol. 3. Postwar Years, Normalcy. LC 66-26828. 52.25 (*0-8154-0175-2*); LC 66-26828. reprint ed. write for info. (*0-318-51438-9*) Cooper Sq.

— American Democracy & the World War, 3 vols., Set. Incl. Vol. 1. Pre-War Years, 1913-1917. LC 66-26828. 57.00 (*0-8154-0173-6*); Vol. 2. America at War, 1917-1918. LC 66-26828. 52.25 (*0-8154-0174-4*); Vol. 3. Postwar Years, Normalcy. LC 66-26828. 52.25 (*0-8154-0175-2*); LC 66-26828. reprint ed. 112.50 (*0-685-01203-4*) Cooper Sq.

— Independence of the South-American Republics: A Study in Recognition & Foreign Policy. LC 70-126379. 1971. reprint ed. 50.00 (*0-8154-0348-8*) Cooper Sq.

Paxton, Frederick S. Christianizing Death: The Creation of a Ritual Process in Early Medieval Europe. LC 90-34072. (Illus.). 256p. 1990. 34.95 (*0-8014-2492-5*) Cornell U Pr.

— Liturgy & Anthropology: A Monastic Death Ritual of the Eleventh Century, Vol. II. LC 93-1787. (Chalice of Repose Project: Studies in Music-Thanatology: Vol. 2). 20p. 1993. write for info. (*1-882878-87-6*) Saint Dunstans.

Paxton, Frederick S., tr. & comment. A Medieval Latin Death Ritual: The Monastic Customaries of Bernard & Ulrich of Cluny. (Chalice of Repose Project: Studies in Music-Thanatology: Vol. 1). 115p. (C). 1993. pap. text ed. 23.95 (*1-882878-88-4*) Saint Dunstans.

Paxton, Harold W. & Bain, Edgar C. Alloying Elements in Steel. 2nd ed. LC 65-29304. 301p. reprint ed. pap. 85.80 (*0-8357-5323-9*, 2026990) Bks Demand.

Paxton, J. H., tr. see Morgan, Jacques J.

Paxton, J. M., ed. Manual of Civil Engineering Plant & Equipment. 2nd ed. (Illus.). 592p. 1977. 158.50 (*0-85334-500-7*, Pub. by Elsevier Applied Sci UK) Elsevier.

***Paxton, John.** Companion to Russian History. fac. ed. LC 82-5192. (Illus.). 515p. 1983. reprint ed. pap. 146.80 (*0-7837-7829-5*, 2047585) Bks Demand.

— Companion to the French Revolution. 256p. 1989. pap. 12.95 (*0-8160-1937-1*) Facts on File.

— Encyclopedia of Russian History: From the Christianization of Kiev to the Break-up of the U.S.S.R. 2nd ed. 483p. 1993. lib. bdg. 65.00 (*0-87436-690-9*) ABC-CLIO.

— European Communities. 250p. (C). 1992. 49.95 (*1-56000-052-X*) Transaction Pubs.

— World Legislatures. LC 74-24740. 192p. (C). 1975. text ed. 29.95 (*0-312-89145-8*) St Martin.

Paxton, John, ed. The Statesman's Year-Book: Historical Companion. 350p. 1988. 45.00 (*0-312-00047-2*) St Martin.

— The Statesman's Year-Book: 1975-1976. 1556p. 1975. 16. 95 (*0-312-76020-5*) St Martin.

— The Statesman's Year-Book: 1983-1984. 120th ed. 1749p. 1983. 37.50 (*0-317-03872-9*) St Martin.

— The Statesman's Year-Book World Gazetteer. 4th ed. LC 85-26263. 680p. 1991. 49.95 (*0-312-05597-8*) St Martin.

— The Statesman's Year-Book, 1982-1983. LC 04-3776. 1700p. 1982. 35.00 (*0-312-76097-3*) St Martin.

— The Statesman's Year-Book, 1986-1987. 123th ed. LC 84-3776. 1750p. 1986. 49.95 (*0-312-75726-3*) St Martin.

— The Statesman's Year-Book 1987-88. 124th ed. LC 04-3776. 1691p. 1987. 55.00 (*0-312-00235-1*) St Martin.

— The Statesman's Year-Book, 1988-89. 125th ed. LC 04-3376. 1700p. 1988. 59.95 (*0-312-02094-5*) St Martin.

— Statesman's Yearbook 1978-1979. 1978. 25.00 (*0-312-76091-4*) St Martin.

— The Statesman's Yearbook, 1989-90. 126th rev. ed. LC 04-3776. 1700p. 1989. 65.00 (*0-312-03235-8*) St Martin.

Paxton, John, jt. auth. see Cook, Chris.

Paxton, John, ed. see Steinberg, S. H.

Paxton, John, jt. auth. see Walsh, A. E.

***Paxton, John L.** From the Collection of John & Mary Lou Paxton. 100p. 1994. pap. 50.00 (*0-9642216-0-8*) J L Paxton.

***Paxton, John R. & Eschmeyer, William N., eds.** Encyclopedia of Fishes. (Illus.). 270p. 1995. 29.95 (*0-12-547660-4*) Acad Pr.

Paxton, Jonijane, ed. see Howard, Scott G.

Paxton, Joseph F., ed. Oklahoma Anthology for Nineteen Twenty-Nine. LC 78-116412. (Granger Index Reprint Ser.). 1977. 16.95 (*0-8369-6153-6*) Ayer.

***Paxton, L. & Siadi, P.** Christmas Time of Year: A Sing, Color, 'n Say Fun Book-Tape Package. 2nd ed. (World of Language Ser.). (Illus.). 32p. (J). (ps up). 1994. reprint ed. audio, pap. 7.95 (*1-880449-10-2*) Wrldkids Pr.

— Going to Grandma's: A Sing, Color 'n Say Coloring Book Package. 2nd ed. (World of Language Ser.). (Illus.). 32p. (J). (ps up). 1994. reprint ed. audio, pap. 7.95 (*1-880449-08-0*) Wrldkids Pr.

PQ

An Asterisk (*) at the beginning of an entry indicates that the title is appearing in BIP for the first time.

— Happy B-I-R-T-H-DAY: A Sing, Color, 'n Say Fun Book-Tape Package. 2nd ed. (World of Language Ser.). (Illus.). 32p. (J). (ps-3). 1994. reprint ed. audio, pap. 7.95 (*1-880449-09-9*) Wrldkids Pr.

— His Name Was David, Around the World: The Story of David & Goliath. 2nd ed. (Sing, Color 'n Say Bible Stories Ser.). (Illus.). 32p. (J). (ps up). 1995. reprint ed. digital audio 7.95 (*1-880449-12-9*) Wrldkids Pr.

— World of Language: Noah & the Ark. (Sing, Color 'n Say Bible Story Ser.). (Illus.). 32p. (J). (ps-4). 1994. reprint ed. audio, pap. 7.95 (*1-880449-11-0*) Wrldkids Pr.

Paxton, Nancy L. George Eliot & Herbert Spencer: Feminism, Evolutionism & the Reconstruction of Gender. 296p. 1991. text ed. 35.00 (*0-691-06841-0*) Princeton U Pr.

Paxton, Norman. Teach Yourself German, Basic. (Teach Yourself Ser.). 1992. 12.95 (*0-8288-8339-4*) Fr & Eur.

— Teach Yourself German Grammar. (Teach Yourself Ser.). 1992. 15.95 (*0-8288-8337-8*) Fr & Eur.

Paxton, P., jt. auth. see Blenkinsopp, Alison.

Paxton, Paul, jt. auth. see Blenkinsopp, Alison.

Paxton, R. Locomotives & Railways of South Africa. (Illus.). 1989. 25.00 (*0-87556-732-0*) Saifer.

Paxton, Robert O. Europe in the Twentieth Century. 2nd ed. (Illus.). 694p. (C). 1985. text ed. 41.25 (*0-15-524719-0*) HB Coll Pubs.

— Parades & Politics at Vichy: The French Officer Corps under Marshall Petain. LC 66-10557. 492p. reprint ed. pap. 140.30 (*0-317-09338-X*, 2010571) Bks Demand.

— Vichy France: Old Guard & New Order, 1940-1944. LC 81-15221. (Morningside Bk.). 424p. 1982. reprint ed. text ed. 53.00 (*0-231-05426-2*); reprint ed. pap. text ed. 16.50 (*0-231-05427-0*) Col U Pr.

Paxton, Robert O. & Wahl, Nicholas, eds. De Gaulle & the United States: A Centennial Reappraisal. LC 93-8091. 320p. 1994. 54.95 (*0-85496-998-5*) Berg Pubs.

— De Gaulle & the United States: A Centennial Reappraisal. LC 93-8091. 320p. 1994. pap. 19.95 (*1-85973-066-3*) Berg Pubs.

Paxton, Robert O., jt. auth. see Marrus, Michael R.

Paxton, Roland, ed. One Hundred Years of the Forth Bridge. 166p. 1990. text ed. 29.00 (*0-7277-1600-X*, Pub. by T Telford UK) Am Soc Civil Eng.

Paxton, Ruth. This Man...This Cause...This Hour. pap. 0.10 (*1-56632-079-8*) Revival Lit.

Paxton, Tom. The Animals' Lullaby. LC 92-18841. (Illus.). 40p. (J). (ps up). 1993. 15.00 (*0-688-10468-1*); lib. bdg. 14.93 (*0-688-10469-X*) Morrow Jr Bks.

— Belling the Cat: And Other Aesop's Fables. LC 89-39851. (Illus.). 40p. (J). (ps up). 1990. 13.95 (*0-688-08158-4*); lib. bdg. 13.88 (*0-688-08159-2*) Morrow Jr Bks.

— Birds of a Feather: And Other Aesop's Fables. LC 92-2909. (Illus.). 40p. (J). (ps up). 1993. 15.00 (*0-688-10400-2*); lib. bdg. 14.93 (*0-688-10401-0*) Morrow Jr Bks.

— Elgelbert Joins the Circus. (Illus.). 1996. write for info. (*0-688-09987-4*); lib. bdg. write for info. (*0-688-09988-2*) Morrow Jr Bks.

— Engelbert Moves the House. 2nd ed. (Let Me Read Ser.). (Illus.). 16p. (J). (ps-2). 1995. pap. 2.95 (*0-673-36239-6*) GdYrBks.

— Engelbert the Elephant. LC 89-9376. (Illus.). 32p. (J). (ps up). 1990. 14.95 (*0-688-08935-6*); lib. bdg. 14.88 (*0-688-08936-4*) Morrow Jr Bks.

— Going to the Zoo. (Illus.). 1996. write for info. (*0-688-13800-4*); lib. bdg. write for info. (*0-688-13801-2*) Morrow Jr Bks.

— Jennifer's Rabbit. LC 87-14113. (Illus.). 32p. (J). (ps-1). 1988. 12.95 (*0-688-07431-6*) Morrow Jr Bks.

— The Story of Santa Claus. LC 94-23919. (Illus.). (J). (gr. k up). 1995. 15.00 (*0-688-11364-8*); lib. bdg. 14.95 (*0-688-11365-6*) Morrow Jr Bks.

— The Story of the Tooth Fairy. LC 95-13266. (Illus.). (J). 1996. write for info. (*0-688-12987-0*); pap. write for info. (*0-688-12988-9*) Morrow Jr Bks.

— Tom Paxton Ramblin' Boy & Other Songs. (Illus.). pap. 11.95 (*0-8256-0007-3*, OK61069, Oak) Music Sales.

— Where's the Baby? LC 92-39875. (Illus.). 32p. (J). (ps up). 1993. 15.00 (*0-688-10692-7*); lib. bdg. 14.93 (*0-688-10693-5*) Morrow Jr Bks.

Paxton, Tom & Scharrett, Darcy. A Car Full of Songs. (Illus.). 84p. (Orig.). (J). (ps-6). 1991. 14.95 (*0-89524-632-5*) Cherry Lane.

— Tom Paxton's Children's Songbook. (Illus.). 68p. (Orig.). (J). (ps-5). 1990. 12.95 (*0-89524-563-9*) Cherry Lane.

Paxton, Vicki, ed. see Louizos, Dianna.

Paxton, W. M. Annals of Platte County, Missouri, from Its Exploration down to June 1, 1897: With Genealogies of Its Noted Families, & Sketches of Its Pioneers & Distinguished People. 1188p. 1992. reprint ed. pap. 70. 00 (*1-55613-520-3*) Heritage Bk.

— The Marshall Family: or A Genealogical Chart of the Descendants of John Marshall & Elizabeth Markham, His Wife. (Illus.). 415p. 1989. reprint ed. lib. bdg. 70.00 (*0-8328-0854-7*); reprint ed. pap. 62.00 (*0-8328-0855-5*) Higginson Bk Co.

Pay-Costa, M. Dictionnaire Pratique Mercure: Francais-Espagnol, Espagnol-Francais. 2nd ed. 1024p. (FRE & SPA.). 1966. 24.95 (*0-7859-0762-9*, M-6471) Fr & Eur.

Pay, John & Till, Geoffrey, eds. The East-West Relations in the Nineteen Nineties: The Naval Dimension. LC 90-44047. (Studies in Contemporary Maritime Policy & Strategy). 350p. 1990. text ed. 49.95 (*0-312-04191-8*) St Martin.

Pay, Marty & Donaldson, Hal. Downfall: Secularization of a Christian Nation. LC 91-60131. 240p. (Orig.). 1991. pap. 8.95 (*0-89221-193-8*) New Leaf.

***Paya.** Nina. 64p. 1995. pap. 9.95x (*1-56163-127-2*, Eurotica) NBM.

Payack, Paul J. The Black List. (Illus.). 1977. 1.00 (*0-686-19654-6*) Chthon Pr.

— Land of Orth. 1978. pap. 2.50 (*0-686-05672-8*) Chthon Pr.

— Legend of the Shaman. 1974. pap. 1.00 (*0-686-24158-4*) Chthon Pr.

— Mythomania. Stokes, Daniel M., ed. (Illus.). 1976. pap. 1.50 (*0-686-16726-0*) Chthon Pr.

— A Ripple in Entropy. 80p. 1973. pap. 2.50 (*0-686-15402-9*) Chthon Pr.

— Solstice II. Clifton, Merritt, ed. (Illus.). 1976. pap. 1.00 (*0-686-18735-0*) Chthon Pr.

— Solstice III. Clifton, Merritt, ed. (Illus.). 1977. 1.00 (*0-686-19655-4*) Chthon Pr.

— Solstice, or Star-Tales. Clifton, Merritt, ed. (Illus.). 1976. pap. 1.00 (*0-686-16727-9*) Chthon Pr.

— The Unexpected Twist Series. (Illus.). 1976. pap. 1.00 (*0-686-16728-7*) Chthon Pr.

Payack, Peter. No Free Will in Tomatoes: Speculations by Peter Payack. LC 87-40271. (Illus.). 118p. (Orig.). 1988. 13.95 (*0-944072-00-3*); pap. 7.95 (*0-944072-01-1*) Zoland Bks.

Payan, Jack, jt. ed. see Vinson, Ronald W.

Payant, Katherine B. Becoming & Bonding: Contemporary Feminism & Popular Fiction by American Women Writers. LC 92-39268. (Contributions in Women's Studies: No. 134). 256p. 1993. text ed. 52.95 (*0-313-28574-8*, PWC/) Greenwood.

Payden, Deborah A. Talking with Your Child about Sacraments & Celebrations. LC 94-10150. (Growing Together Series Book). 1994. pap. text ed. 1.95 (*0-8298-1017-X*) Pilgrim OH.

Payden, Deborah A., jt. auth. see Alberswerth, Roy F.

Paye, Anne, jt. auth. see Wassman, Rose.

Paye, Burrall. Basketball's Zone Presses: A Complete Coaching Guide. 228p. 1983. 19.95 (*0-13-069237-9*, Parker Publishing Co) P-H.

Payer, Cheryl. The Debt Trap: The IMF & the Third World. LC 74-24794. 256p. 1975. pap. 10.00 (*0-85345-376-4*) Monthly Rev.

— Lent & Lost: Foreign Credit & Third World Development. LC 90-47484. 176p. (C). 1991. text ed. 49.95 (*0-86232-952-3*, Pub. by Zed Books UK); pap. 15. 00 (*0-86232-953-1*, Pub. by Zed Books UK) Humanities.

— The World Bank: A Critical Analysis. LC 81-84738. 316p. 1982. pap. 14.00 (*0-85345-602-X*) Monthly Rev.

Payer, I. B. Traite D'organogenie Comparee de la Fleur. 1966. reprint ed. 132.00 (*3-7682-0346-8*) Lubrecht & Cramer.

Payer, J. H., ed. see American Society for Testing & Materials Staff.

Payer, Lynn. Disease Mongers: How Doctors, Drug Companies, & Insurers Are Making You Feel Sick. 304p. 1992. text ed. 22.95 (*0-471-54385-3*) Wiley.

— Disease Mongers: How Doctors, Drug Companies & Insurers Are Making You Feel Sick. 1994. pap. text ed. 12.95 (*0-471-00737-4*) Wiley.

— Medicine & Culture. 208p. 1989. pap. 11.95 (*0-14-012404-7*, Penguin Bks) Viking Penguin.

Payer, Pierre J. The Bridling of Desire: Views of Sex in the Later Middle Ages. LC 92-95553. 285p. 1993. 35.00 (*0-8020-2919-1*) U of Toronto Pr.

— Sex & the Penitentials: The Development of a Sexual Code 550-1150. 232p. 1984. 35.00 (*0-8020-5649-0*) U of Toronto Pr.

Payes, Rachel C. The Dark Towers of Trelochen. 1991. pap. 3.95 (*0-8217-3475-X*) Zebra.

***Payette, Douglas A.** So-- You Want to Be a Travel Agent: An Introduction to Domestic Travel. LC 94-33705. 224p. 1994. pap. text ed. 34.80 (*0-13-326000-3*) P-H.

Paykel, E. S., ed. Handbook of Affective Disorders. 2nd ed. LC 92-1553. 1992. reprint ed. lib. bdg. 69.95 (*0-89862-674-9*) Guilford Pr.

Paykel, E. S. & Coppen, Alec J., eds. Psychopharmacology of Affective Disorders. (British Association for Psychopharmacology Monographs). (Illus.). (C). 1981. pap. text ed. 24.95 (*0-19-261278-6*) OUP.

Paykel, E. S., ed. see Collegium Internationale Neuro-Psychopharmacologicum Staff.

Paykel, Eugene. Depression: An Integrative Approach. 255p. 1989. text ed. 95.00 (*0-433-00090-2*) Buttrwrth-Heinemann.

Paykel, Eugene S., ed. Handbook of Affective Disorders. 2nd ed. (Illus.). 700p. 1992. text ed. 168.00 (*0-443-04302-7*) Churchill.

Paykoc, E., jt. ed. see Yuncu, H.

Payler, Frederick. Law Courts, Lawyers & Litigants. xiv, 242p. 1980. reprint ed. lib. bdg. 24.00 (*0-8377-1006-5*) Rothman.

Paylin, Jolie. Cutover Country: Jolie's Story. LC 76-10245. (Illus.). 174p. reprint ed. pap. 49.60 (*0-317-58162-7*, 2029696) Bks Demand.

— The Gill Netters. LC 79-89031. 1979. 8.95 (*0-910726-82-5*) Hillsdale Educ.

***Paylor, Ian.** Housing Needs of Ex-Offenders. 241p. 1995. 55.95 (*1-85628-996-6*, Pub. by Avebury Pub UK) Ashgate Pub Co.

Paylor, W. J., ed. see Overbury, Thomas.

Paylore, Patricia, ed. Arid-Lands Research Institutions: A World Directory, 1977. LC 67-20092. 317p. 1977. pap. 17.95 (*0-8165-0631-0*) U of Ariz Pr.

Paymar, Michael. Violent No More: Helping Men End Domestic Abuse. LC 93-18003. 224p. 1993. 19.95 (*0-89793-139-4*); pap. 10.95 (*0-89793-117-3*) Hunter Hse.

Paymar, Michael, jt. auth. see Pence, Ellen.

Payment & Trudel, eds. Methods & Techniques in Virology. LC 93-1766. 336p. 1993. Alk. paper. 125.00 (*0-8247-9101-0*) Dekker.

Payment, Maggie, jt. auth. see Stern, Nancy.

***Paymer, Marvin.** Instrumental Music. (Complete Works of G. B. Pergolesi). 1993. lib. bdg. 102.00 (*0-945193-46-7*) Pendragon NY.

Paymer, Marvin E., ed. Facts Behind the Songs: A Handbook of American Popular Music from the Nineties to the 90's. LC 93-24342. 592p. 1993. 95.00 (*0-8240-5240-4*, H1300) Garland.

Paymer, Marvin E. & Williams, Hermine W. Giovanni Battista Pergolesi: A Guide to Research. LC 89-16871. (Composer Resource Manuals Ser.: Vol. 26). 208p. 1989. 38.00 (*0-8240-4595-5*, 1058) Garland.

***Payn, Graham.** My Life with Noel Coward. LC 94-42525. (Illus.). 402p. 1994. 24.95 (*1-55783-190-4*) Applause Theatre Bk Pubs.

Payn, James. Lost Sir Massingberd: A Romance of Real Life. LC 75-32794. (Literature of Mystery & Detection Ser.). 1976. reprint ed. 28.95 (*0-405-07891-9*) Ayer.

Payne. Directory of African American Religious Bodies. 1990. pap. 29.95 (*0-88258-065-5*) Howard U Pr.

— History of Costume: From the Ancient Mesopotamians to the Twentieth Century. 2nd ed. 1994. (*0-8230-4958-2*) Watsn-Guptill.

— Payne on Divorce. 2nd ed. 360p. 1988. 115.00 (*0-409-88849-4*) Butterworth Legal Pubs.

— Spousal Property Rights under the Ontario Family Law Act. 280p. 1987. 72.00 (*0-409-80936-5*) Butterworth Legal Pubs.

— Structured BASIC for IBM PC with Business Applications. (C). 1986. pap. 43.95 (*0-87150-990-3*) PWS Pubs.

Payne & Hahn. Drugs: Issues for Today. (Illus.). 400p. (C). 1990. pap. 29.95 (*0-8016-3701-5*) Mosby Yr Bk.

— Focus on Health. (Illus.). 592p. (C). 1990. pap. 29.95 (*0-8016-3910-7*) Mosby Yr Bk.

Payne, jt. auth. see Hahn.

Payne, et al. Drugs: Issues for Today, No. 2. 1994. 29.95 (*0-8016-7912-5*) Mosby Yr Bk.

— Laboratory Studies in Zoology. 4th ed. 210p. 1990. pap. text ed. 19.95 (*0-88725-130-7*) Hunter Textbks.

Payne, A. W., jt. auth. see Ayre, P.

Payne, Adrian. The Essence of Services Marketing. LC 92-33438. (Essence of Management Ser.). 1993. pap. 19.95 (*0-13-284852-X*) P-H.

***Payne, Adrian, ed.** Advances in Relationship Marketing. (Cranfield Management Ser.). 240p. 1995. pap. 32.50 (*0-7494-1636-X*, Pub. by Kogan Pg UK) Cassell.

Payne, Alfred C. A University at Prayer. LC 86-14613. (Illus.). 1987. 13.95 (*0-9617635-0-7*) VA Tech Found.

***Payne, Alfred S.** Learning English, a Career Investment for Successful Living. 1995. 14.95 (*0-533-11156-0*) Vantage.

Payne, Ann. Medieval Beasts. (Illus.). 96p. (C). 1990. 36.00 (*1-56131-018-2*) New Amsterdam Bks.

Payne, Anthony. The International Crisis of the Caribbean. LC 83-49193. 177p. 1984. 28.50 (*0-8018-3239-X*) Johns Hopkins.

— Politics in Jamaica. 226p. 1995. pap. 18.95 (*0-312-12526-7*) St Martin.

— Politics in Jamaica. 2nd ed. 226p. 1995. 45.00 (*0-312-12525-9*) St Martin.

Payne, Anthony & Sutton, Paul, eds. Modern Caribbean Politics. LC 92-14475. 400p. 1993. text ed. 50.00 (*0-8018-4434-7*); pap. text ed. 15.95 (*0-8018-4435-5*) Johns Hopkins.

Payne, Anthony, jt. ed. see Sutton, Paul.

Payne, Anthony J., jt. ed. see Mayall, James.

Payne, Anthony J., et al. Grenada: Revolution & Invasion. LC 83-40511. 233p. 1986. pap. 11.95 (*0-312-35043-0*) St Martin.

Payne, Arlie J. We're Driving Our Kids Crazy: The Shift to Non-Guilt Parenting. Parker, Diane, ed. LC 90-50893. (Illus.). 150p. (Orig.). 1991. pap. 7.95 (*0-88247-864-8*) R & E Pubs.

Payne, B. D., jt. auth. see Sciberras, E.

Payne, Barbara A., jt. ed. see Dunn, Margery G.

Payne, Beverly C. The Quality of Medical Care: Evaluation & Improvement. LC 75-27157. 1976. 10.00 (*0-87914-029-1*, 669153) Hosp Res & Educ.

Payne, Bob & Ellison, Nick. The International Marine Boat Manager: Your Vessel's Custom Handbook of Operating & Service Procedures. 320p. 1992. pap. 24.95 (*0-87742-301-6*, 60284) Intl Marine.

Payne, Bob, jt. auth. see Morris, Reg.

Payne, Burt, III. The World Is Getting to Be a Funner Place: How I Applied to CalArts under Four Aliases & Was Accepted or Denied. LC 92-90633. 95p. (Orig.). 1992. pap. 21.95 (*0-9633321-0-4*) Dryhouse Bks.

Payne, Buryl. The Body Magnetic. abr. ed. (Illus.). 120p. 1991. pap. text ed. 12.00 (*0-9628569-9-1*) Psycho Physics.

— Love & Sex Without Conflict. (Illus.). 64p. 1993. 7.95 (*0-9635600-0-X*) Psycho Physics.

Payne, C., jt. auth. see Oatey, M.

***Payne, C. D.** Youth in Revolt. LC 94-39709. 1995. 22.50 (*0-385-47693-0*) Doubleday.

***Payne, C. H., intro.** Akbar & the Jesuits: An Account of the Jesuit Missions to the Court of Akbar. (Curzon Travellers Ser.). (C). 1995. text ed. 70.00 (*0-7007-0349-7*, Pub. by Curzon Pr UK) Humanities.

Payne, C. J. & White, K. J., eds. Caring for Deprived Children: International Case Studies of Residential Setting. 1979. text ed. 10.95 (*0-312-12166-0*) St Martin.

Payne, Carl, ed. Education in the Age of Information: The Challenge of Technology. LC 92-42834. (Fulbright Papers: Vol. 11). 139p. 1993. text ed. 79.95 (*0-7190-3587-2*, Pub. by Manchester Univ Pr UK) St Martin.

Payne, Carl, jt. auth. see Oatey, Michael.

Payne, Carol. A Pinch of Rosemary: Country Tales of Lust & Passion. LC 93-7983. (Illus.). 64p. 1993. 12.95 (*0-88184-568-X*) Carroll & Graf.

Payne, Charles. Petrouchka's Cry: A Biography. 1992. pap. write for info. (*0-679-40045-1*) McKay.

Payne, Charles A., et al. Physical Science: Principles & Applications. 6th ed. 688p. (C). 1992. boxed write for info. (*0-697-13929-8*) Wm C Brown Pubs.

Payne, Charles M. Getting What We Ask For: The Ambiguity of Success & Failure in Urban Education. LC 83-18623. (Contributions to the Study of Education Ser.: No. 12). ix, 206p. 1984. text ed. 45.00 (*0-313-23520-1*, PGW/, Greenwood Pr) Greenwood.

— I've Got the Light of Freedom: The Organizing Tradition & the Mississippi Freedom Struggle. LC 94-24645. 1995. 28.00 (*0-520-08515-9*) U CA Pr.

Payne, Chris. Better Services for Older People. (C). 1989. 70.00 (*0-7855-0086-3*, Pub. by Natl Inst Soc Work) St Mut.

— Better Services for Older People. (C). 1989. 65.00 (*0-902789-60-0*, Pub. by Natl Inst Soc Work) St Mut.

— Evaluating the Quality of Care: A Self-Assessment Manual. 1994. 68.00 (*0-902789-93-7*, Pub. by Natl Inst Soc Work) St Mut.

Payne, Chris & Douglas, Robin. Developing Residential Practice: Five Role Play & Simulation Games for Staff in Residential Settings. 1981. 50.00 (*0-317-05757-X*, Pub. by Natl Inst Soc Work) St Mut.

Payne, Chris & Scott, Tony. Developing Supervision of Teams in Field & Residential Social Work, 2 pts. (C). 1982. Pt. 1. 50.00 (*0-7855-0074-X*, Pub. by Natl Inst Soc Work); Pt. 2. 25.00 (*0-7855-0075-8*, Pub. by Natl Inst Soc Work) St Mut.

— Developing Supervision of Teams in Field & Residential Social Work, Pt. 1. (C). 1982. 39.00 (*0-902789-24-4*, Pub. by Natl Inst Soc Work) St Mut.

— Developing Supervision of Teams in Field & Residential Social Work, Pt. 2. (C). 1985. 29.00 (*0-685-28589-8*, Pub. by Natl Inst Soc Work); 25.00 (*0-902789-34-1*, Pub. by Natl Inst Soc Work) St Mut.

— Developing Supervision of Teams in Field & Residential Social Work, pt.2. National Institute for Social Work Staff, ed. 1985. 12.50 (*0-317-40576-4*, Pub. by Natl Inst Soc Work) St Mut.

Payne, Chris, jt. auth. see Aplin, Geoff.

Payne, Chris, jt. auth. see Douglas, Robin.

Payne, Chris, jt. ed. see Douglas, Robin.

Payne, Chris, jt. auth. see Peretz, Liz.

Payne, Chris, jt. auth. see Scott, Tony.

***Payne, Chris, et al.** The Home Manager As Trainer: An Approach to Foundation Training. 1994. pap. 35.00 (*0-902789-88-0*, Pub. by Natl Inst Soc Work) St Mut.

Payne, Christiana. Toil & Plenty: Images of the Agricultural Landscape in England, 1780-1890. LC 93-13885. (Agrarian Studies Ser.). (Illus.). 272p. 1993. 45.00 (*0-300-05773-3*) Yale U Pr.

Payne, Christine. Tearing Down the Walls: An Adult Woman's Guide to Educational Financial Aid. 195p. (Orig.). (C). 1993. pap. text ed. write for info. (*0-9635930-0-5*) Bibury Court.

Payne, Christopher. Animals in Bronze. (Illus.). 424p. 1984. 89.50 (*0-907462-45-6*) Antique Collect.

— Nineteenth Century European Furniture. (Illus.). 512p. 1986. 89.50 (*1-85149-001-9*) Antique Collect.

***Payne, Christopher, ed.** Sotheby's Concise Encyclopedia of Furniture. (Illus.). 208p. 1995. pap. 24.95 (*1-85029-649-9*, Pub. by Conran Octop Ltd UK) Antique Collect.

***Payne, Christopher T.** Strategic Financial Planning for Healthcare Organizations: An Executive Guide to Capital Debt. 1994. 60.00 (*1-55738-615-3*) Probus Pub Co.

Payne, Clive, jt. ed. see O'Muircheartaigh, Colm A.

Payne, Cynthia, jt. ed. see Larson, Judy L.

Payne, D. Employment Law Manual for the United Kingdom: Plus Supplements. 1975. ring bd. 65.00 (*0-8464-0374-9*) Beekman Pubs.

Payne, D., ed. An Easy Guide to the Casio Scientific Calculator. 64p. (C). 1991. 50.00 (*1-870941-85-3*) St Mut.

Payne, D., Sr., jt. auth. see Payne, R.

Payne, Daniel A. History of the African Methodist Episcopal Church. LC 69-18573. (American Negro: His History & Literature, Ser. No. 2). 1969. reprint ed. 39.95 (*0-405-01885-1*) Ayer.

— Recollections of Seventy Years. LC 68-29015. (American Negro: His History & Literature, Ser. 1). (Illus.). 1969. reprint ed. 32.95 (*0-405-01834-7*) Ayer.

— The Semi-Centenary & the Retrospection of the African Methodist Episcopal Church. LC 76-37598. (Black Heritage Library Collection). 1977. reprint ed. 25.95 (*0-8369-8974-0*) Ayer.

— Sermons & Addresses, 1853-1891. LC 70-38458. (Religion in America, Ser. 2). 1976. 21.95 (*0-405-04079-2*) Ayer.

— Treatise on Domestic Education. LC 75-157373. (Black Heritage Library Collection). 1977. 21.95 (*0-8369-8811-6*) Ayer.

Payne, Darwin. Big D: Triumphs & Troubles of an American Supercity in the 20th Century. LC 93-60840. 512p. 1994. 29.95 (*0-9637629-0-7*) Three Forks.

— Owen Wister: Chronicler of the West, Gentleman of the East. LC 85-1989. (Illus.). 392p. 1985. lib. bdg. 24.95 (*0-87074-205-1*) SMU Press.

— Texas Chronicles: The Heritage & Enterprise of the Lone Star State. (Illus.). 176p. 1994. 39.95 (*1-882933-04-4*) Cherbo Pub Grp.

Payne, Darwin, ed. Sketches of a Growing Town: Episodes & People of Dallas from Early Days to Recent Times. 208p. 1991. pap. 12.95 (*0-9631492-0-2*) S Meth U Mstr Lib Arts.

Payne, Darwin R. Canterville Ghost. 49p. 1963. reprint ed. pap. 3.45 (*0-87129-044-8*, C71) Dramatic Pub.

— A Christmas Carol: A Playscript. LC 80-18827. (Illus.). 138p. 1981. pap. 9.95 (*0-8093-0999-8*) S Ill U Pr.

An Asterisk (*) at the beginning of an entry indicates that the title is appearing in BIP for the first time.

— Computer Scenographics. LC 93-39696. (Illus.). 272p. (C). 1994. 47.50 (*0-8093-1904-7*); pap. 29.95 (*0-8093-1905-5*) S Ill U Pr.
— Scenographic Imagination. 3rd ed. LC 92-13216. (Illus.). 400p. (C). 1993. 39.95 (*0-8093-1850-4*); pap. 24.95 (*0-8093-1851-2*) S Ill U Pr.
— Theory & Craft of the Scenographic Model. rev. ed. LC 84-5630. (Illus.). 192p. 1985. 29.95 (*0-8093-1193-3*); pap. 19.95 (*0-8093-1194-1*) S Ill U Pr.
Payne, Darwin R., ed. see Lash, James.
Payne, David. Confessions of a Taoist on Wall Street. 864p. 1985. mass mkt. 5.99 (*0-345-32696-2*) Ballantine.
— Coping with Failure: The Therapeutic Uses of Rhetoric. Arnold, Carroll C., ed. (Studies in Rhetoric-Communication). 173p. 1989. text ed. 34.95 (*0-87249-593-0*) U of SC Pr.
— Cronologia Biblica Portavoz. Orig. Title: The Student Bible Timeline. (Illus.). 16p. (SPA.). 1994. pap. 9.99 (*0-8254-1552-7*) Kregel.
— Early from the Dance. 512p. 1991. mass mkt. 5.95 (*0-345-36871-1*) Ballantine.
— Ruin Creek. LC 92-42476. 1993. 22.50 (*0-385-26418-6*) Doubleday.
— Ruin Creek. large type ed. LC 93-45632. 1994. 22.95 (*0-8161-5948-3*, Large Print Bks) Hall.
— Ruin Creek Vol. 1. 1994. pap. 5.50 (*0-312-95389-5*) St Martin.
Payne, David A. The Assessment of Learning: Cognitive & Affective. (C). 1974. text ed. 18.50 (*0-669-85209-0*) Heath.
— Designing Educational Project & Program Evaluations: A Practical Overview Based on Research & Experience. LC 93-38469. (Evaluation in Education & Human Services Ser.). 288p. (C). 1994. lib. bdg. 85.00 (*0-7923-9426-7*) Kluwer Ac.
Payne, David C. Psychological Theories of Learning & Teaching: An Analysis of the Use of the Psychology. Lee, Don Y., ed. LC 87-82508. 270p. (C). 1988. 43.50 (*0-939758-18-0*) Eastern Pr.
Payne, David E., jt. auth. see Wilhite, Stephen C.
Payne, David F. Kingdoms of the Lord: A History of the Hebrew Kingdoms from Saul to the Fall of Jerusalem. LC 81-3197. (Illus.). 340p. reprint ed. pap. 96.90 (*0-317-11122-1*, 2020852) Bks Demand.
— Samuel. 292p. 1993. pap. 22.00 (*0-7152-0521-8*, Pub. by St Andrew UK) St Mut.
Payne, David L. The Phonology & Morphology of Axininca: Apurucayali Campa. LC 81-52739. (Publications in Linguistics: No. 66). (Illus.). 285p. 1981. fiche 12.00 (*0-88312-270-7*) Summer Instit Ling.
Payne, David L., jt. auth. see Burquest, Donald A.
Payne, David S. Myth & Modern Man in Sherlock Holmes: Sir Arthur Conan Doyle & the Uses of Nostalgia. LC 91-70565. 325p. 1992. 25.00 (*0-934468-29-X*) Gaslight.
Payne, Deborah C. & Canfield, J. Douglas, eds. Cultural Readings of Restoration & Eighteenth-Century English Theater. LC 94-8524. 328p. 1995. 60.00 (*0-8203-1681-4*) U of Ga Pr.
Payne, Doris, ed. Pragmatics of Word Order Flexibility. LC 92-5354. (Typological Studies in Language: No. 22). vii, 320p. 1992. 103.00 (*1-55619-408-0*); pap. 29.95 (*1-55619-409-9*) Benjamins North Am.
Payne, Doris L. The Pragmatics of Word Order: Typological Dimensions of Verb Initial Languages. (Empirical Approaches to Language Typology Ser.: No. 7). xiv, 298p. (C). 1990. lib. bdg. 113.85 (*3-11-012207-3*) Mouton.
Payne, Doris L., ed. Amazonian Linguistics: Studies in Lowland South American Languages. (Illus.). 584p. 1990. text ed. 42.50 (*0-292-70414-3*) U of Tex Pr.
Payne, Doris P. Captain Jack, Modoc Renegade. (Illus.). 272p. 1979. pap. 9.95 (*0-8323-0340-2*) Binford Mort.
Payne, Dorothy. Arkansas Pensioners, Eighteen Eighteen to Nineteen Hundred: Records of Some Arkansas Residents Who Applied to the Federal Government for Benefits Arising from Services in Federal Military Organizations. 226p. 1985. 26.50 (*0-89308-537-5*) Southern Hist Pr.
— Life after Divorce. (Looking up Ser.). 24p. (Orig.). 1982. pap. 1.75 (*0-8298-0610-5*) Pilgrim OH.
Payne, Dorothy, jt. auth. see Kosta, Stefan.
Payne, Dorothy, jt. auth. see Kostka, Stefan.
Payne, Douglas, et al. Latin America after the Cold War: Implications for U. S. Policy. (Latin American Affairs (Study Groups) Ser.). (Illus.). 96p. (C). 1991. pap. 9.95 (*1-879128-01-2*) Americas Soc.
Payne, Douglas W. The Democratic Mask: The Consolidation of the Sandinista Revolution. LC 85-81020. (Perspectives on Freedom Ser.: No. 3). 100p. 1985. pap. 13.75 (*0-932088-06-6*) Freedom Hse.
Payne, E. A. & Payne, William F. Easily Applied Principles of Keypunching. LC 72-118315. (C). 1970. text ed. 18.95 (*0-685-03852-1*) P-H.
Payne, E. F., tr. see Schopenhauer, Arthur.
Payne, E. F. J., ed. see Schopenhauer, Arthur.
Payne, Edgar A. Composition of Outdoor Painting. 4th rev. ed. Hatcher, J. B., ed. LC 84-90701. (Illus.). 155p. 1985. reprint ed. 35.00 (*0-939370-03-4*) DeRu's Fine Art.
Payne, Edmund C. & McArthur, Robert. Developing Expert Systems: A Knowledge Engineer's Handbook For Rules & Ojects. 401p. 1990. pap. text ed. 34.95 (*0-471-51413-6*) Wiley.
Payne, Elizabeth. Meet the North American Indians. (Step-up Bks.). (Illus.). (J). (gr. 2-6). 1965. 6.95 (*0-394-80060-5*) Random Bks Yng Read.
— The Pharaohs of Ancient Egypt. LC 80-21392. (Landmark Books Ser.). (Illus.). 192p. (J). (gr. 5-9). 1981. 4.95 (*0-394-84699-0*) Knopf Bks Yng Read.
Payne, Elizabeth A. Reform, Labor, & Feminism: Margaret Dreier Robins & the Women's Trade Union League. LC 87-10794. (Women in American History Ser.). (Illus.). 234p. 1988. 24.95 (*0-252-01445-6*) U of Ill Pr.
Payne, Emmy. Katy No-Pocket. (Illus.). 32p. (J). (gr. k-3). 1973. pap. 5.95 (*0-395-13717-9*, Sandpiper) HM.
— Katy No-Pocket. (J). (gr. 1-3). 1973. 14.95 (*0-395-17104-0*) HM.
Payne, Ernest A., jt. auth. see Robinson, H. Wheeler.
Payne, F. Anne. Chaucer & Menippean Satire. LC 79-5412. 304p. 1981. 29.50 (*0-299-08170-2*) U of Wis Pr.
— King Alfred & Boethius: An Analysis of the Old English Version of the Consolation of Philosophy. LC 68-9834. 161p. reprint ed. pap. 45.90 (*0-317-08843-2*, 2015370) Bks Demand.
Payne, F. William, ed. Advanced Technologies: Improving Industrial Efficiency. LC 84-48433. 300p. 1985. 39.95 (*0-88173-001-7*) Fairmont Pr.
— Efficient Boiler Operations Sourcebook. 3rd ed. (Illus.). 266p. 1991. 67.00 (*0-88173-135-8*, 0275) Fairmont Pr.
Payne, F. William & McGowan, John J. Building Energy Management & Control Systems. 2nd ed. (Illus.). 399p. 1988. text ed. 67.95 (*0-442-23734-0*) Chapman & Hall.
Payne, F. William, jt. auth. see American Gas Association Staff.
Payne, F. William, ed. see Association of Energy Engineers Staff.
Payne, F. William, ed. see Energy Engineers Associations.
Payne, Fiona, ed. The Human Body. LC 92-54481. (Picturepedia Ser.). (Illus.). (J). (gr. k-3). 1993. 12.95 (*1-56458-249-3*) Dorling Kindersley.
Payne, Frank W. John Donne & His Poetry. 1972. 59.95 (*0-8490-0449-7*) Gordon Pr.
— John Donne & His Poetry. LC 70-120991. (Poetry & Life Ser.). reprint ed. 27.50 (*0-404-52528-8*) AMS Pr.
Payne, Franklin E., Jr. Biblical Healing for Modern Medicine: Choosing Life & Health: Or Disease & Death. LC 93-71420. 240p. (Orig.). 1993. pap. 12.95 (*0-9629876-1-1*) Covenant Enter.
— Making Biblical Decisions. 180p. (Orig.). 1989. pap. 9.95 (*0-685-26107-7*) Hosanna HBPC.
Payne, Fred, intro. Microelectronics Conference, 1991: Enabling Technology. (Illus.). 155p. (Orig.). 1991. pap. 72.00 (*0-85825-523-5*) Accents Pubns.
***Payne, G., et al.** Plant Cell & Tissue Culture in Liquid Systems. 1993. text ed. 69.50 (*0-471-03726-5*) Wiley.
Payne, G. C., jt. ed. see Cuff, E. C.
Payne, G. L., jt. auth. see Wallschutzky, I. G.
Payne-Gallway, Ralph. The Crossbow. (C). 1988. 220.00 (*0-900470-69-0*, Pub. by New Holland Pubs UK) St Mut.
Payne-Galway, Ralph. Cross-Bow, Medieval & Modern. pap. 35.00 (*0-87556-232-9*) Saifer.
Payne, Geoff & Abbott, Pamela. The Social Mobility of Women: Beyond Male Mobility Models. 224p. 1990. 60.00 (*1-85000-845-0*, Falmer Pr); pap. 30.00 (*1-85000-846-9*, Falmer Pr) Taylor & Francis.
Payne, Geoff, jt. ed. see Abbott, Pamela.
Payne, Geoff, jt. ed. see Cross, Malcolm.
Payne, Geoffrey, jt. ed. see Cadman, David.
Payne, Gerrye. The Year-God. Trusky, Tom, ed. LC 91-71533. (Ahsahta Press Modern & Contemporary Poets of the West Ser.). 60p. (Orig.). 1992. pap. 6.95 (*0-916272-51-6*) Ahsahta Pr.
Payne, Heidi, ed. see Aslett, Grant.
Payne, Helen, ed. Dance Movement Therapy: Theory & Practice. LC 91-22938. 272p. 1992. 59.95 (*0-415-05659-4*, A5952); pap. 19.95 (*0-415-05660-8*, A5956) Routledge.
— One River, Many Currents: A Handbook of Inquiry in the Arts Therapies. 250p. 1993. pap. 39.50 (*1-85302-153-9*, Pub. by J Kingsley Pubs UK) Taylor & Francis.
Payne, Hettie. Over the Alps Eighty Years Ago. Grace, Betse, ed. (Illus.). 96p. (Orig.). 1989. pap. 4.95 (*1-878374-26-5*) Pac Coast Pubs.
Payne, Hod. A Man, A Woman & A Dream. 290p. (Orig.). 1994. pap. 11.95 (*0-9641574-0-3*) Ski-Lak.
Payne, Howard E., et al. As the Storm Clouds Gathered: European Perceptions of American Foreign Policy in the 1930's. LC 78-7074. (Topics in American Diplomatic History Ser.). 173p. 1980. 16.95 (*0-941690-06-7*); pap. 10.95 (*0-87716-101-1*) Regina Bks.
***Payne, Ian.** The Almain & Other Measures in England: Their History & Choreography. 220p. 1995. 59.95 (*0-85967-965-9*, Pub. by Scolar Pr UK) Ashgate Pub Co.
— The Provision & Practice of Sacred Music at Cambridge Colleges & Selected Cathedrals, c. 1547-c. 1646: A Comparative Study of the Archival Evidence. LC 92-43443. (Outstanding Dissertations in Music from British Universities Ser.). (Illus.). 480p. 1993. 140.00 (*0-8153-0952-X*) Garland.
Payne, J. Mundo Nuevo - a Spanish Revision Course for CXC. (C). 1986. text ed. 50.00 (*0-85950-128-0*, Pub. by S Thornes Pubs UK) St Mut.
— Mundo Nuevo - Teacher's Book. (C). 1986. text ed. 65.00 (*0-85950-634-7*, Pub. by S Thornes Pubs UK) St Mut.
Payne, J. F., ed. see Boghurst, William.
Payne, J. Gregory & Ratzan, Scott C. Tom Bradley: The Impossible Dream. LC 85-52373. (Illus.). 384p. 1986. pap. 24.95 (*0-915677-29-6*) Roundtable Pub.
Payne, J. H. Cogeneration in the Cane Sugar Industry. (Sugar Ser.: No. 12). 338p. 1990. 141.00 (*0-444-88826-8*) Elsevier.
— Unit Operations in Cane Sugar Production. (Sugar Technology Ser.: Vol. 4). 204p. 1982. 77.00 (*0-444-42104-1*) Elsevier.
Payne, J. H., ed. Noel Deerr-Classic Papers of a Sugar Cane Technologist. (Sugar Ser.: Vol. 5). 646p. 1983. 187.25 (*0-444-42149-1*, I-272-83) Elsevier.
Payne, J. M. & Payne, S. The Metabolic Profile Test. 190p. 1987. 45.00 (*0-19-854544-4*) OUP.
Payne, J. P. & Severinghaus, J. W., eds. Pulse Oximetry. (Illus.). 225p. 1986. 65.00 (*0-387-16857-5*) Spr-Verlag.
Payne, J. W. In Vitro Techniques in Research. 176p. 1991. text ed. 149.95 (*0-471-93251-5*, Wiley-Liss) Wiley.
Payne, J. W., ed. In Vitro Techniques in Research: Recent Advances. 224p. 1989. 113.00 (*0-335-15885-4*) Wiley.
— Microorganisms & Nitrogen Sources: Transport & Utilization of Amino Acids, Peptides, Proteins, & Related Substrates. LC 79-42900. (Illus.). 884p. reprint ed. pap. 180.00 (*0-685-20761-7*, 2030404) Bks Demand.
Payne-Jackson, Arvilla & Lee, John. Folk Wisdom & Mother Wit: John Lee - An African American Herbal Healer. LC 92-46396. (Contributions in Afro-American & African Studies: No. 161). 192p. 1993. text ed. 49.95 (*0-313-28868-2*, GM8868, Greenwood Pr) Greenwood.
Payne, James. Stepping Through Windows. LC 93-9770. 150p. 1993. pap. text ed. 19.60 (*0-13-014911-X*) P-H.
— Structured Programming with QuickBASIC. 363p. (C). 1991. pap. 52.95 (*0-534-92563-4*) PWS Pubs.
— Structured Programming with QuickBASIC. 363p. (C). 1991. pap. 43.95 (*0-534-93060-3*) PWS Pubs.
Payne, James, jt. auth. see Prentice, Diana.
***Payne, James E.** Me Too: A Doctor Survives Prostate Cancer. 144p. 1995. pap. 11.95 (*1-56796-086-3*) WRS Group.
***Payne, James E. & Desai, Pramod D.** Properties of Intermetallic Alloys Vol. 1: Aluminides. LC 94-39757. 1994. 400.00 (*0-931682-48-7*) Purdue U Pubns.
Payne, James E. & Sahu, Anandi P., eds. Defense Spending & Economic Growth. LC 93-15757. (C). 1993. pap. text ed. 47.50 (*0-8133-8631-4*) Westview.
Payne, James E., jt. auth. see Blum, Kenneth.
Payne, James L. The American Threat, National Security & Foreign Policy. 344p. (Orig.). 1981. pap. text ed. 19.95 (*0-915728-07-9*) Lytton Pub.
— Costly Returns: Burdens of the U. S. Tax System. LC 92-19854. 272p. 1993. 34.95 (*1-55815-202-4*); pap. 14.95 (*1-55815-215-6*) ICS Pr.
— The Culture of Spending: Why Congress Lives Beyond Our Means. 250p. 1991. 24.95 (*1-55815-134-6*) ICS Pr.
— Foundations of Empirical Political Analysis. viii, 151p. 1984. pap. text ed. 7.95 (*0-915728-08-7*) Lytton Pub.
— Incentive Theory & Political Process: Motivation & Leadership in the Dominican Republic. (Illus.). 165p. 1976. reprint ed. 23.95 (*0-915728-01-X*) Lytton Pub.
— Labor & Politics in Peru. LC 65-22335. 1980. reprint ed. 23.95 (*0-915728-05-2*) Lytton Pub.
— Princess Navina Visits Mandaat. (Illus.). 56p. 1994. pap. 8.95 (*0-915728-10-9*) Lytton Pub.
— Principles of Social Science Measurement. LC 75-7177. 157p. (Orig.). (C). 1975. pap. text ed. 7.95 (*0-915728-02-8*) Lytton Pub.
— Why Nations Arm. LC 88-21684. 247p. (C). 1995. 39.95 (*0-915728-11-7*) Lytton Pub.
Payne, James L., et al. The Motivation of Politicians. LC 83-26853. 216p. 1984. pap. text ed. 18.95 (*0-88229-824-0*) Nelson-Hall.
Payne, James P. & Hill, D. W., eds. The Management of the Acutely Ill: A Symposium Held in July, 1976. LC 77-370280. (Chartridge Symposium Ser.). (Illus.). 187p. reprint ed. pap. 53.30 (*0-8357-8943-8*, 2033458) Bks Demand.
— Real-Time Computing in Patient Management: A Symposium Held in June, 1975. LC 76-367573. (Chartridge Symposium Ser.). 215p. reprint ed. pap. 61.30 (*0-8357-7003-6*, 2033459) Bks Demand.
Payne, James R. Multicultural Autobiography: American Lives. LC 91-27130. 376p. (C). 1992. lib. bdg. 41.00 (*0-87049-739-1*); pap. text ed. 18.95 (*0-87049-740-5*) U of Tenn Pr.
Payne, James R., ed. Joseph Seamon Cotter, Jr. Complete Poems. LC 88-33073. (Illus.). 224p. 1990. pap. 14.00 (*0-8203-1181-2*) U of Ga Pr.
Payne, James S. Differential Management & Motivation: An Advanced Understanding of Human Development & Motivation. rev. ed. 197p. 1994. pap. text ed. 14.95 (*1-57171-000-0*) Lincoln-Rembrandt.
***Payne, James S., et al.** Differential Selling. 124p. (Orig.). 1994. pap. 14.95x (*1-57171-001-9*) Lincoln-Rembrandt.
— Rehabilitation Techniques: Vocational Adjustment for the Handicapped. 208p. (C). 1984. 35.95 (*0-89885-159-9*) Human Sci Pr.
***Payne, Jason.** The Better Mousetrap. 268p. 1995. pap. 8.95 (*1-56901-592-9*) NW Pub.
***Payne, Jean.** Decorative Folk Painting. (Illus.). 128p. 1995. 24.95 (*0-304-34391-9*, Pub. by Cassell UK) Sterling.
Payne, Jerry. Colloquial Hungarian. 1987. pap. 14.95 (*0-7102-0636-4*, RKP) Routledge.
— Colloquial Hungarian. 2nd ed. (Colloquial Ser.). 240p. 1987. audio 29.95 (*0-415-00077-7*, A2575, RKP); pap. 15.95 (*0-415-04589-4*, 06364, RKP); audio 15.95 (*0-7102-0984-3*, 09843, RKP) Routledge.
Payne, Jerry & Kolmel, Rainer, eds. Babel: The Cultural & Linguistic Barriers Between Nations. 195p. 1990. pap. text ed. 30.00 (*0-08-037969-9*, Pub. by Aberdeen U Pr) Macmillan.
Payne, Jerry, et al. Payne's History of Costume. 2nd ed. (C). 1991. text ed. 68.50 (*0-06-047141-7*) HarpCollege.
Payne, Jessie. When Basildon Was Farms & Fields. 1993. pap. 14.00 (*0-86025-416-X*, Pub. by Ian Henry Pubns UK) Empire Pub Srvs.
Payne, Jim. Funk Drumming. 1993. 9.95 (*0-87166-511-5*, 93892); audio 9.98 (*0-87166-512-3*, 93892); audio 18.95 (*0-87166-513-1*, 93892) Mel Bay.
Payne, Joan C. & Ashmolean Museum. Catalog of the Predynastic Egyptian Collection. LC 93-16134. 1994. 120.00 (*0-19-951355-4*) OUP.
***Payne, John.** A Manual of Management Training Exercises. (Illus.). 240p. 1989. text ed. 154.95 (*1-85904-046-2*, Pub. by Gower UK) Ashgate Pub Co.
— A Manual of Management Training Exercises. 1992. ring bd. 139.95 (*0-87425-201-6*) Human Res Dev Pr.
— Poetical Works: Definitive Edition, 2 vols, 1. LC 73-128418. 1973. reprint ed. write for info. (*0-404-04947-8*) AMS Pr.
— Poetical Works: Definitive Edition, 2 vols, 2. LC 73-128418. 1973. reprint ed. write for info. (*0-404-04948-6*) AMS Pr.
— Poetical Works: Definitive Edition, 2 vols, Set. LC 73-128418. 1973. reprint ed. 110.00 (*0-404-04946-X*) AMS Pr.
***Payne, John & Payne, Shirley.** Exercises for Developing First-Line Managers. 1995. 161.95 (*0-566-07519-9*) Ashgate Pub Co.
— Letting Go Without Losing Control: How to Delegate & Do More. (Institute of Management Ser.). 192p. (Orig.). 1994. pap. 45.00x (*0-273-60425-2*, Pub. by Pitman Pubng UK) St Mut.
Payne, John, tr. see Boccaccio, Giovanni.
Payne, John B., tr. see Erasmus, Desiderius.
Payne, John C. Marine Electrical & Electronics Bible. (Illus.). 416p. 1994. 34.95 (*0-924486-72-4*) Sheridan.
Payne, John H. Brutus: or The Fall of Tarquin. (BCL1-PS American Literature Ser.). 56p. 1992. reprint ed. lib. bdg. 59.00 (*0-7812-6828-1*) Rprt Serv.
Payne, John W., jt. auth. see Carroll, John S.
Payne, John W., et al. The Adaptive Decision Maker. LC 92-21581. (Illus.). 285p. (C). 1993. 59.95 (*0-521-41505-5*); pap. 19.95 (*0-521-42526-3*) Cambridge U Pr.
Payne, Johnny. Conquest of the New Word: Experimental Fiction & Translation in the Americas. LC 93-6537. (Texas Pan American Ser.). 304p. (C). 1993. text ed. 35.00 (*0-292-76546-0*) U of Tex Pr.
— Voice & Style. 176p. 1995. 15.99 (*0-89879-693-8*) Writers Digest.
Payne, Joseph A. Befriending: A Self-Guided Retreat for Busy People. LC 92-28398. 176p. 1993. pap. 12.95 (*0-8091-3354-7*) Paulist Pr.
Payne, Joseph F. English Medicine in the Anglo-Saxon Times. LC 75-23749. (Illus.). reprint ed. 30.00 (*0-404-13355-X*) AMS Pr.
Payne, Joseph N., ed. Mathematics for the Young Child. LC 90-42418. (Illus.). 306p. 1990. 39.50 (*0-87353-288-0*) NCTM.
— Mathematics Learning in Early Childhood: 37th Yearbook. LC 75-6631. (Illus.). 316p. 1975. 20.00 (*0-87353-017-9*) NCTM.
Payne, Judith A. & Fitz, Earl E. Ambiguity & Gender in the New Novel of Brazil & Spanish America: A Comparative Assessment. LC 92-37863. 239p. 1993. text ed. 29.95 (*0-87745-405-1*) U of Iowa Pr.
Payne, Junaidi. Wild Malaysia: The Wildlife & Scenery of Peninsular Malaysia, Sarawak and Sabah. (Illus.). 210p. 1990. 39.95 (*0-262-16078-1*) MIT Pr.
Payne, K. R. Chemicals from Coal: New Processes. LC 86-32482. (Critical Reports on Applied Chemistry). 114p. 1987. text ed. 185.00 (*0-471-91325-1*) Wiley.
Payne, K. R., ed. Industrial Biocides. LC 87-7142. (Critical Reports on Applied Chemistry). 118p. 1988. text ed. 225.00 (*0-471-91880-6*) Wiley.
Payne, K. T. & Anderson, Noma B. How to Prepare for the NESPA: National Examination in Speech Pathology & Audiology. (Illus.). 188p. (Orig.). (C). 1991. pap. text ed. 39.95 (*1-879105-33-0*, 0217) Singular Publishing.
Payne, Karen. Between Ourselves. 1984. pap. 12.95 (*0-395-36571-6*) HM.
Payne, Katharine. Elephants Calling. LC 91-34547. (Face to Face with Science Ser.). (Illus.). 36p. (J). (gr. 2-6). 1992. 14.00 (*0-517-58175-2*); lib. bdg. 14.99 (*0-517-58176-0*) Crown Bks Yng Read.
Payne, Keith, jt. auth. see Sharkey, John.
Payne, L. E. Improperly Posed Problems in Partial Differential Equations. (CBMS-NSF Regional Conference Ser.: No. 22). v, 76p. (Orig.). 1975. pap. text ed. 17.00 (*0-89871-019-7*) Soc Indus-Appl Math.
Payne, L. Maggie, jt. auth. see Witter, Dorothy A.
Payne, L. N., ed. Marek's Disease. (Developments in Veterinary Virology Ser.). 1985. lib. bdg. 98.00 (*0-89838-730-2*) Kluwer Ac.
Payne, L. W. Fifty Famous Southern Poems. 1972. 59.95 (*0-8490-0160-9*) Gordon Pr.
Payne, Larry. Healthy Back Exercises for High Stress Professionals. 48p. (Orig.). 1986. pap. 5.00 (*0-9617784-0-7*) Samata Multimedia.
Payne, Lauren M. Just Because I Am: A Child's Book of Affirmation. Espeland, Pamela, ed. (Illus.). 56p. (Orig.). 1994. teacher ed 12.95 (*0-915793-61-X*) Free Spirit Pub.
— Just Because I Am: A Child's Book of Affirmation. Espeland, Pamela, ed. LC 93-30609. (Illus.). 32p. (Orig.). (J). (ps-3). 1994. pap. 6.95 (*0-915793-60-1*) Free Spirit Pub.
Payne, Laurence. Dead for a Ducat. large type ed. (Mystery Ser.). 439p. 1989. 17.95 (*0-7089-1948-0*) Ulverscroft.
— The Nose on My Face. large type ed. (Mystery Ser.). 560p. 1989. 17.95 (*0-7089-2031-4*) Ulverscroft.
Payne, Laurene, jt. auth. see Dockstader, Mary A.
***Payne, Leanne.** The Broken Image: Restoring Personal Wholeness Through Healing Prayer. 192p. 1995. reprint ed. pap. 11.99 (*0-8010-5334-X*) Baker Bk.
— The Healing Presence: How God's Grace Can Work in You to Bring Healing in Your Broken Places & the Joy of Living in His Love. 272p. 1995. reprint ed. pap. 13.99 (*0-8010-5348-X*) Baker Bk.
— Listening Prayer: Learning to Hear God's Voice & Keep a Prayer Journal. LC 94-37753. 210p. 1994. 16.99 (*0-8010-7139-9*) Baker Bk.

P Q

An Asterisk (*) at the beginning of an entry indicates that the title is appearing in BIP for the first time.

— Real Presence: The Glory of Christ with Us & within Us. LC 94-46185. 192p. 1995. pap. 12.99 (*0-8010-5172-X*) Baker Bk.
— Restoring the Christian Soul: Through Healing Prayer. LC 91-23574. 256p. (Orig.). 1991. 16.99 (*0-89107-625-5*) Crossway Bks.
Payne, Lee. Lighter Than Air: An Illustrated History of the Airship. (Illus.). 320p. 1991. 35.00 (*0-517-57476-4*, Orion Bks) Crown Pub Group.
Payne, Leigh A. Brazilian Industrialists & Democratic Change. LC 93-974. 224p. (C). 1993. text ed. 32.50 (*0-8018-4648-X*) Johns Hopkins.
Payne, Leigh A., jt. ed. see Bartell, Ernest.
Payne, Linda. Arkansas Historical Math Facts. LC 90-63448. 72p. (J). (gr. 3-6). 1986. spiral bd. 25.00 (*0-914546-84-8*) Rose Pub.
Payne, Lucille V. Lively Art of Writing. 1969. pap. 4.99 (*0-451-62712-1*, Ment) NAL-Dutton.
Payne, Lynette R. Fountainheads: Selected Poems. LC 90-91730. 56p. (Orig.). 1990. pap. text ed. 5.40 (*0-9626904-0-6*) Linsu Pr.
Payne, M. G., jt. auth. see Hurst, G. S.
Payne, M. G., ed. see International Symposium on Resonance Ionization Spectroscopy & Its Applications Staff.
Payne, Malcolm. Modern Social Work Theory: A Critical Introduction. LC 90-6435. (Illus.). 272p. (Orig.). (C). 1990. pap. text ed. 29.95 (*0-925065-43-9*) Lyceum IL.
Payne, Mark. How to Beat Hayfever. 1993. pap. 8.00 (*0-7225-2829-9*) Thorsons SF.
— How to Take Care of Your Heart. (Illus.). 160p. 1990. pap. 11.95 (*0-7463-0563-X*, H563, Pub. by Northcote House UK) Trans-Atl Phila.
— Superhealth in a Toxic World: The Complete Environmental Medicine Health Plan. (Illus.). 1992. pap. 18.00 (*0-7225-2589-3*) Thorsons SF.
Payne, Marvin. Love & Oranges. 2nd ed. 64p. (YA). (gr. 9 up). 1988. reprint ed. pap. 3.95 (*0-929985-08-7*) Jackman Pubng.
— Love & Oranges. (Keepsake Paperbacks Ser.). 62p. 1988. reprint ed. pap. 3.95 (*0-88494-402-6*) Jackman Pubng.
Payne, Marvin, jt. auth. see Barkdull, Larry.
Payne, Mary. Up & down the Blood Sugar Trail. (Illus.). (Orig.). (J). (gr. k-4). 1987. pap. 1.98 (*0-9619326-0-0*) MstrWorks Pub.
Payne, Mary A. Russell's Journal: Trust. (Illus.). 32p. (J). (gr. k-4). 1993. 7.95 (*0-8059-3334-4*) Dorrance.
Payne, May D., comp. Melodic Index to the Works of Johann Sebastian Bach. LC 74-24035. reprint ed. 27.50 (*0-404-12858-0*) AMS Pr.
Payne, Michael. Reading Theory: An Introduction to Lacan, Derrida & Kristeva. (Illus.). 250p. (C). 1993. 44.95 (*0-631-18288-8*); pap. 19.95 (*0-631-18289-6*) Blackwell Pubs.
***Payne, Michael, ed. & pref.** A Dictionary of Cultural & Critical Theory. 864p. 1996. write for info. (*0-631-17197-5*) Blackwell Pubs.
Payne, Michael & Heath, James M. Text, Interpretation, Theory. LC 85-5893. (Bucknell Review Ser.: Vol. 29. No. 2). 176p. 1985. 22.00 (*0-8387-5097-4*) Bucknell U Pr.
Payne, Michael, jt. ed. see Fleming, Richard.
Payne, Michael, jt. ed. see Neuman, Mark.
Payne, Michael, jt. ed. see Nueman, Mark.
Payne, Michael, ed. see Ostriker, Alicia S.
Payne, Michael, et al. Explorations in Economics. 3rd ed. (C). 1990. pap. text ed. 43.50 (*0-929655-81-8*) CT Pub.
Payne, Michael H., jt. auth. see Trauner, Theodore J., Jr.
Payne, Michael N. & Anderson, Wayne R. Applied Trigonometry. 567p. (C). 1989. text ed. 41.25 (*0-15-502911-8*); pap. text ed. 4.00 (*0-15-502912-6*) SCP.
Payne, Muriel A. Oliver Untwisted. 1972. 34.95 (*0-8490-0761-5*) Gordon Pr.
Payne, Neil F. Wildlife Habitat Management of Wetlands. 250p. 1992. text ed. 80.00 (*0-07-048955-6*) McGraw.
— Wildlife Habitat Management of Wetlands. 250p. 1992. pap. text ed. 34.95 (*0-07-048956-4*) McGraw.
Payne, Neil F. & Bryant, Fred C. Techniques for Wildlife Habitat Management of Uplands. 500p. 1994. text ed. 60.00 (*0-07-048963-7*); pap. text ed. 34.95 (*0-07-048966-1*) McGraw.
Payne, P. A., jt. auth. see Marks, R. M.
Payne, P. L. The Hydro: A Study of the Development of the Major Hydro-Electric Schemes Undertaken by the North of Scotland Hydro-Electric Board. (Illus.). 368p. 1988. text ed. 50.00 (*0-08-036584-1*, Pub. by Aberdeen U Pr) Macmillan.
Payne, P. L., ed. Studies in Scottish Business History. 435p. 1967. 37.50 (*0-7146-1349-5*, Pub. by F Cass Pubs UK) Intl Spec Bk.
Payne-Palacio, June, et al, prods. West's & Wood's Introduction to Foodservice. 7th ed. LC 93-20467. Orig. Title: Foodservice in Institutions. 704p. (C). 1993. text ed. write for info. (*0-02-390390-2*) Macmillan.
Payne, Patricia C., jt. auth. see Levey, Santina M.
***Payne, Peggy.** Revelation. LC 95-75417. 320p. 1995. pap. 12.95 (*0-9635967-1-3*) Banks Channel.
— Teaching for Life-Changing Learning. (Christian Education Ministries Ser.). 94p. (Orig.). 1984. pap. 3.95 (*0-89367-092-8*) Light & Life.
Payne, Peggy, ed. see Richardson, Arleta.
Payne, Peter. Martial Arts: The Spiritual Dimension. LC 86-51575. (Art & Imagination Ser.). (Illus.). 1987. pap. 15.95 (*0-500-81025-7*) Thames Hudson.
Payne, Peter A. Concise Encyclopedia of Biological & Biomedical Measurement Systems. (Advances in Systems Control & Information Engineering Ser.: No. 3). 512p. 1991. 290.00 (*0-08-036188-9*, Pergamon Pr) Elsevier.
Payne, Peter L., ed. Studies in Scottish Business History. LC 67-20815. (Illus.). 1967. 45.00 (*0-678-05076-7*) Kelley.
Payne, Peter L. & Davis, Lance E. The Savings Bank of Baltimore, 1818-1866: A Historical & Analytical Study. LC 75-41778. (Companies & Men: Business Enterprises in America Ser.). (Illus.). 1976. reprint ed. 23.95 (*0-405-08093-X*) Ayer.
Payne, Philip & Lipton, Michael. How Third World Rural Households Adapt to Dietary Energy Stress: The Evidence & the Issues. LC 94-17153. (Food Policy Review: Vol. 2). 1994. write for info. (*0-89629-501-X*) Intl Food Policy.
Payne, Philip, jt. auth. see Gray, Alistair.
Payne, Pierre S. Journey to Red China. LC 75-39031. (China Studies). 1978. reprint ed. 20.50 (*0-88355-387-2*) Hyperion Conn.
***Payne, R.** George E. Barnard's Invention of a Mail Marking Machine. (Illus.). 80p. 1994. pap. 15.00 (*1-880065-11-8*) Machine Cancel Soc.
Payne, R. & Payne, D., Sr. Cooking with Fruit. 1993. pap. 7.99 (*0-517-11278-7*) Random Hse Value.
Payne, R., jt. auth. see Morris, R.
Payne, R. E. Above the Law: The Hidden Career of John Volz, U.S.A. 281p. 1995. pap. 1,795.00 (*1-885308-00-0*) Sr Polit Action.
— Caught in the Crossfire: The R. E. "Gus" Payne Story. Arroyo, Sidney L., ed. (Illus.). 217p. (Orig.). 1995. pap. 14.95 (*1-885308-01-9*) Sr Polit Action.
Payne, R. E., ed. see Williams, Charles H., 3rd.
Payne, R. W. Genstat 5 Reference Manual. (Illus.). 768p. 1987. 75.00 (*0-19-852212-6*) OUP.
Payne, Reba, jt. auth. see Williams, Joe.
***Payne, Richard.** The Management of Pain in Oncology Patients. 1995. write for info. (*1-884065-10-4*) Assocs in Med.
***Payne, Richard & Turner, Drexl.** The Woodlands: Into the Woods. (Illus.). 98p. 1994. 40.00 (*0-9643743-0-7*); pap. 20.00 (*0-9643743-1-5*) Judson Design.
Payne, Richard, jt. auth. see Speck, Lawrence W.
Payne, Richard A. Charlie the Shy Cowboy. (Illus.). 36p. (J). (gr. 1-9). 1993. pap. 4.95 (*0-9636186-2-8*) Blue Sky Grap.
— Collin the Canada Goose. (J). (gr. 1-5). 1993. pap. text ed. 4.95 (*0-9636186-0-1*) Blue Sky Grap.
— How to Get a Better Job Quick. 1991. pap. 5.99 (*0-451-62784-9*, Sig) NAL-Dutton.
— How To Get a Better Job Quicker. 3rd ed. 256p. 1987. 16.95 (*0-8008-3965-X*) Taplinger.
— How to Get A Better Job Quicker. 3rd ed. 352p. 1975. pap. 4.95 (*0-451-62597-8*, Ment) NAL-Dutton.
— Rick & Jim's Real Reel Indians. (Illus.). 32p. (Orig.). 1994. pap. text ed. 7.95 (*0-9636186-8-7*) Blue Sky Grap.
***Payne, Richard J.** The Clash with Distant Cultures: Values, Interests, & Force in American Foreign Policy. 288p. (C). 1995. 24.50x (*0-7914-2647-5*) State U NY Pr.
— The Nonsuperpowers & South Africa: Implications for U. S. Policy. LC 89-46340. (Illus.). 334p. 1990. 35.00 (*0-253-34294-5*) Ind U Pr.
— Opportunities & Dangers of Soviet-Cuban Expansion: Towards a Pragmatic U. S. Policy. LC 87-26778. 261p. (C). 1988. 59.50 (*0-88706-796-4*); pap. 19.95 (*0-88706-797-2*) State U NY Pr.
— The Third World & South Africa: Post-Apartheid Challenges. LC 92-8847. (Contributions in Political Science Ser.: No. 304). 224p. 1992. text ed. 47.95 (*0-313-28542-X*, PTW, Greenwood Pr) Greenwood.
— The West European Allies, the Third World, & U. S. Foreign Policy: Post-Cold War Challenge. LC 91-2563. (Contributions in Political Science Ser.: No. 282). 256p. 1991. pap. text ed. 15.95 (*0-275-93626-0*, B3626, Praeger Pubs) Greenwood.
— The West European Allies, The Third World, & U. S. Foreign Policy: Post-Cold War Challenges. LC 91-11334. (Contributions in Political Science Ser.: No. 282). 256p. 1991. text ed. 59.95 (*0-313-27460-6*, PWN/, Greenwood Pr) Greenwood.
Payne, Richard K. The Tantric Ritual of Japan. (C). 1991. 90.00 (*81-85179-76-X*, Pub. by Aditya Prakashan II) S Asia.
Payne, Robert. The Fathers of the Eastern Church. (Reprints Ser.). 313p. 1990. reprint ed. 17.95 (*0-88029-404-3*) Dorset Pr.
— The Fathers of the Western Church. (Reprints Ser.). 312p. 1990. reprint ed. 17.95 (*0-88029-403-5*) Dorset Pr.
— The Holy Fire. LC 79-27594. 328p. 1980. reprint ed. pap. 11.95 (*0-913836-61-3*) St Vladimirs.
— Life & Death of Adolf Hitler. (Illus.). 623p. 1990. 19.95 (*0-88029-402-7*) Dorset Pr.
— Life & Death of Mahatma. 1994. 12.98 (*0-8317-5870-8*) Smithmark.
Payne, Robert, ed. see Billings, Bart.
Payne, Robert, tr. see Chekhov, Anton P.
Payne, Robert, ed. see Chekhov, Anton P.
Payne, Robert, jt. auth. see Morris, Reg.
Payne, Robert, ed. see Shen Ts'Ung-Wen.
Payne, Robert B. Behavior, Mimetic Songs & Song Dialects, & Relationships of the Parasitic Indigobirds (Vidua) of Africa. 333p. 1973. 12.50 (*0-943610-11-7*) Am Ornithologists.
— Sexual Selection, Lek & Arena Behavior, & Sexual Size Dimorphism in Birds. 52p. 1984. 8.00 (*0-943610-40-0*) Am Ornithologists.
Payne, Robert J., jt. auth. see Morris, Reg.
Payne, Robert O. Geoffrey Chaucer. 2nd ed. (Twayne's English Authors Ser.: No. 1). 160p. (C). 1986. text ed. 21.95 (*0-8057-6908-0*, Pub. by Royal Botanic Garden UK) Macmillan.
— The Key of Remembrance, a Study of Chaucer's Poetics. LC 72-12316. 246p. 1973. reprint ed. text ed. 75.00 (*0-8371-6694-2*, PAKR, Greenwood Pr) Greenwood.
Payne, Roberta L. The Influence of Dante on Medieval English Dream Visions. (American University Studies: Romance Languages & Literature: Ser. II, Vol. 63). 178p. (C). 1989. text ed. 36.30 (*0-8204-0505-1*) P Lang Pubs.
***Payne, Roberta L., tr.** The Novellino. LC 94-36773. (Studies in Italian Culture: Vol. 17). 1995. write for info. (*0-8204-2676-8*) P Lang Pubs.
***Payne, Roger.** Among Whales. 1995. 25.00 (*0-684-80210-4*, Scribners) S&S Trade.
— In the Company of Whales. (Illus.). 288p. 1995. text ed. 24.00 (*0-02-595245-5*) Macmillan.
Payne, Rolce. Cooking with Fruit: The Complete Guide to Using Fruit Throughout the Meal, the Day, the Year. 1992. 22.00 (*0-517-58406-9*, Crown) Crown Pub Group.
***Payne, Rolce R. & Speyer, Dorrit, Jr.** Cooking with Fruit: The Complete Guide to Using Fruit Throughout the Meal, the Day, the Year. LC 94-41545. 1995. write for info. (*0-517-12353-3*) Wings Bks.
Payne, Rolf. Drainage & Sanitation. LC 82-1455. (Illus.). 192p. reprint ed. pap. 54.80 (*0-685-20296-8*, 2030330) Bks Demand.
Payne, Ronald, jt. auth. see Dobson, Christopher.
***Payne, Rosemary A.** Relaxation Techniques: A Practical Handbook for the Health Care Professional. LC 94-33408. 1995. write for info. (*0-443-04933-5*) Churchill.
Payne, Roy & Cooper, Cary L. Groups at Work. LC 80-41586. (Individuals, Groups & Organizations Ser.). 280p. 1981. text ed. 80.95 (*0-471-27934-X*, Wiley-Interscience) Wiley.
Payne, Roy & Cooper, Cary L., eds. Groups at Work. LC 80-41586. (Wiley Series on Individuals, Groups & Organizations). 278p. reprint ed. pap. 79.30 (*0-318-35029-7*, 2030929) Bks Demand.
Payne, Roy & Firth-Cozens, Jenny. Stress in Health Professionals. LC 87-8122. (Studies in Occupational Stress). 288p. 1987. text ed. 132.50 (*0-471-91254-9*) Wiley.
Payne, Roy, jt. ed. see Cooper, Cary L.
Payne, Roy E., jt. ed. see Cooper, Cary L.
Payne, S., jt. auth. see Payne, J. M.
Payne, Sebastian, ed. Instructing Counsel. 190p. 1994. 175.00 (*0-85459-846-4*, Pub. by Tolley Pubng UK) St Mut.
Payne, Sebastian & Bibby, Peter. Judicial Review. 140p. 1994. 120.00 (*0-85459-761-1*, Pub. by Tolley Pubng UK) St Mut.
Payne, Shaun. A Sussex Christmas. (Illus.). 160p. 1991. pap. 15.00 (*0-86299-747-X*) A Sutton Pub.
***Payne, Sheila & Walker, Janet.** Psychology for Nurses & the Caring Professions. LC 95-14761. (Social Science for Nurses & the Caring Professions Ser.). 1995. write for info. (*0-335-19411-7*, Open Univ Pr); pap. write for info. (*0-335-19410-9*, Open Univ Pr) Taylor & Francis.
Payne, Shirley, jt. auth. see Payne, John.
Payne, Silvano, ed. International Satellite Directory, 1989. 4th ed. (Illus.). 1200p. 1989. 240.00 (*0-936361-04-2*) Design Pubs.
— International Satellite Directory, 1990. 5th ed. (Illus.). 1990. 240.00 (*0-936361-05-0*) Design Pubs.
— World Satellite Directory, 1989. 2nd ed. (Illus.). 225p. 1989. 175.00 (*0-936361-10-7*) Design Pubs.
— World Satellite Directory, 1990. 3rd ed. (Illus.). 1990. 125.00 (*0-936361-11-5*) Design Pubs.
Payne Smith, J., ed. see Smith, R. Payne.
Payne, Stanley G. Basque Nationalism. LC 75-15698. (Basque Ser.). (Illus.). xii, 304p. 1975. 30.00x (*0-87417-042-7*) U of Nev Pr.
— Falange: A History of Spanish Fascism. ix, 316p. 1961. 42.50 (*0-8047-0058-3*); pap. 13.95 (*0-8047-0059-1*) Stanford U Pr.
— Fascism: A Comparative Approach Toward a Definition. LC 79-5413. 248p. 1980. 25.00 (*0-299-08060-9*); pap. 9.95 (*0-299-08064-1*) U of Wis Pr.
— The Franco Regime, 1936-1975. LC 87-40139. (Illus.). 704p. (C). 1987. text ed. 30.00 (*0-299-11070-2*) U of Wis Pr.
— A History of Fascism, 1914-1945. LC 95-16723. 1995. write for info. (*0-299-14870-X*) U of Wis Pr.
— A History of Spain & Portugal, Vol. 1. LC 72-7992. 412p. reprint ed. pap. 117.50 (*0-685-15603-6*, 2026567) Bks Demand.
— A History of Spain & Portugal, Vol. 2. LC 72-7992. (Illus.). 422p. reprint ed. pap. 120.30 (*0-8357-6143-6*, 2034281) Bks Demand.
— Politics & Society in Twentieth Century Spain. LC 75-38923. (Modern Scholarship on European History Ser.). (C). 1976. reprint ed. pap. text ed. 8.95 (*0-531-05588-4*) Wiener Pubs Inc.
— Politics & the Military in Modern Spain. xiii, 574p. 1967. 57.50 (*0-8047-0128-8*) Stanford U Pr.
— Spain's First Democracy: The Second Republic, 1931-1936. LC 92-56925. (Illus.). 494p. (Orig.). (C). 1993. lib. bdg. 60.00 (*0-299-13670-1*); pap. 19.95 (*0-299-13674-4*) U of Wis Pr.
— Spanish Catholicism: An Historical Overview. LC 83-25946. 280p. 1984. text ed. 27.50 (*0-299-09800-1*) U of Wis Pr.
Payne, Stephen, jt. ed. see Kline, Benjamin.
Payne, Stephen L. & Charnov, Bruce H., eds. Ethical Dilemmas for Academic Professionals. 264p. 1987. 42.95x (*0-398-05319-7*) C C Thomas.
— Ethical Dilemmas for Academic Professionals. 264p. 1987. pap. 25.95 (*0-398-06317-6*) C C Thomas.
Payne, Steven, ed. John of the Cross: Conferences & Essays by Members of the Institute of Carmelite Studies & Others. LC 92-20477. (Carmelite Studies: Vol. 6). 1992. pap. 9.95 (*0-935216-18-9*) ICS Pubns.
Payne, Steven, ed. see Paul-Marie of the Cross, OCD.
Payne, Steven K. St. John of the Cross. (C). 1990. lib. bdg. 102.50 (*0-7923-0707-0*) Kluwer Ac.
Payne, Suzzy C., jt. auth. see Murwin, Susan A.
Payne, T. R. Rubinstein & the Philosophical Foundations of Soviet Psychology. (Sovietica Ser.: No. 30). 184p. 1968. lib. bdg. 64.00 (*90-277-0062-1*) Kluwer Ac.
Payne, Thomas. Quantitative Techniques for Management: A Practical Approach. (Illus.). 464p. (C). 1981. 15.00 (*0-8359-6118-4*, Reston); write for info. (*0-8359-6119-2*, Reston) P-H.
Payne, Thomas E. The Twins Stories: Participant Coding in Yagua Narrative. LC 92-23632. (Publications in Linguistics: Vol. 120). 236p. 1992. pap. 28.00 (*0-520-09774-2*) U CA Pr.
***Payne, Todd.** Exploring Lightware 3D! (Illus.). 512p. (Orig.). 1995. pap. text ed. 59.95 (*1-884474-12-8*) New Era Press.
Payne, Todd & Drust, Paul. Mastering Three-D Studio, Vol. 2: Animation & Video Post. 375p. 1994. pap. text ed. 49.95 (*1-884474-02-0*) New Era Press.
— The Video Toaster Companion. 450p. 1995. pap. text ed. 49.95 (*1-884474-05-5*) New Era Press.
Payne, Tom. A Company of One: The Power of Independence in the Workplace. LC 92-91095. 118p. (Orig.). 1993. per., pap. 12.95 (*0-9627085-4-2*) Perf Pr Albuquerque.
— From the Inside Out: How to Create & Survive a Culture of Change. 3rd ed. LC 90-91985. (Illus.). 256p. (Orig.). 1991. per. 14.95 (*0-9627085-2-6*) Perf Pr Albuquerque.
Payne, Tony, jt. ed. see Clarke, Colin.
Payne, Trevor. Christian Videos for Children & Young People: For Use in Home, Church, Youth Club, School. (C). 1989. 35.00 (*0-9510086-9-2*, Pub. by Jay Bks UK) St Mut.
Payne, V. Gregory & Isaacs, Larry D. Human Motor Development: A Lifespan Approach. 2nd ed. 383p. (C). 1991. text ed. 41.95 (*0-87484-989-6*) Mayfield Pub.
— Human Motor Development: A Lifespan Approach. 3rd ed. LC 94-31266. 426p. (C). 1994. 41.95 (*1-55934-379-6*) Mayfield Pub.
Payne, Vicky. Alternative Prospects of Universities & Polytechnics. 1989. 60.00 (*0-7045-0288-7*) St Mut.
Payne, W., ed. see Tusser, Thomas.
Payne, W. H. Australian Plants of the Eighties: Series A. 384p. (C). 1991. text ed. 95.00 (*0-7855-0035-9*, Pub. by Surrey Beatty & Sons AT) St Mut.
Payne, W. H., ed. see Compayre, Gabriel.
Payne, W. J. Denitrification. LC 81-3363. 230p. 1981. pap. 39.95 (*0-471-04764-3*, Wiley-Interscience) Krieger.
Payne, W. J. & Williamson, G. An Introduction to Animal Husbandry in the Tropics. 4th ed. (Tropical Agriculture Ser.). (Illus.). 881p. 1991. text ed. 175.00 (*0-470-21569-0*) Wiley.
***Payne, Wardell J., ed.** Directory of African American Religious Bodies: A Compendium by the Howard University School of Divinity. 2nd ed. LC 95-10152. 1995. write for info. (*0-88258-184-8*); pap. write for info. (*0-88258-185-6*) Howard U Pr.
Payne, Wayne A. & Hahn. Understanding Your Health. 3rd ed. 704p. 1991. pap. 35.95 (*0-8016-6373-3*) Mosby Yr Bk.
Payne, Weldon, jt. auth. see Bradley, Michael R.
Payne, Will. The Money Captain. LC 68-57546. reprint ed. lib. bdg. 29.00 (*0-8398-1556-5*); reprint ed. pap. text ed. 8.95 (*0-8290-2381-X*) Irvington.
Payne, William. Embedded Controller Forth for the 8051 Family. 511p. 1990. text ed. 72.00 (*0-12-547570-5*) Acad Pr.
Payne, William F. Creative Financing for Energy Conservation. LC 83-80094. (Illus.). 250p. 1984. text ed. 43.00 (*0-915586-69-X*) Fairmont Pr.
Payne, William F., jt. auth. see Payne, E. A.
Payne, William L., ed. see Syrian Hamster in Toxicology & Carcinogenesis Research Symposium Staff.
Payne, William M. Greater English Poets of the Nineteenth Century. LC 67-22063. (Essay Index Reprint Ser.). 1977. 20.95 (*0-8369-0777-9*) Ayer.
— Leading American Essayists: Biographies of Leading Americans. LC 68-26466. (Essay Index Reprint Ser.). 1977. reprint ed. 28.95 (*0-8369-0778-7*) Ayer.
Payne, William M., ed. American Literary Criticism. LC 68-26465. (Wampum Library of American Literature, Index Reprint Ser.). 1977. reprint ed. 23.95 (*0-8369-0779-5*) Ayer.
Payne, Willie W. The Todd Road Incident. 89p. 1992. pap. 10.00 (*0-9637462-0-0*) Alcus Pub.
Payne, Wilson F. Industrial Demands upon the Money Market, 1919-57: A Study in Fund-Flow Analysis. (Technical Papers: No. 14). 159p. 1961. reprint ed. 41.40 (*0-87014-420-0*); reprint ed. mic. film 20.70 (*0-685-61328-3*) Natl Bur Econ Res.
Payne, Yolanda, jt. auth. see Farmer, James A.
Paynell, Thomas, tr. see Erasmus, Desiderius.
Paynter, Diane E., jt. auth. see Marzano, Robert J.
Paynter, Elizabeth, ed. see Meyer-Denkmann, Gertrud.
Paynter, G. C., jt. ed. see Murthy, S. N.
Paynter, H. M., jt. ed. see Hedrick, J. K.
Paynter, James. Eyes to Wonder, Tongues to Praise. LC 85-80189. (Illus.). 61p. (Orig.). 1985. pap. 12.50 (*0-9614842-0-9*, 209) Fax Pub Co.
Paynter, John. Sound & Structure. (Resources of Music Ser.). (Illus.). 224p. (C). 1992. 65.00 (*0-521-35581-8*); pap. 29.95 (*0-521-35676-8*); pap. 35.00 (*0-521-35677-6*) Cambridge U Pr.
Paynter, John, ed. see Meyer-Denkmann, Gertrud.
Paynter, John, et al. Companion to Contemporary Musical Thought, 2 vol. set. (Companion Encyclopedia Ser.). 1992. 149.95 (*0-415-01990-7*, A7201) Routledge.
Paynter, John H. Fugitives of the Pearl. LC 72-170846. reprint ed. 32.50 (*0-404-00205-6*) AMS Pr.
Paynter, Raymond A., Jr. Ornithological Gazetteer of Argentina. (Illus.). vi, 509p. 1985. 31.00 (*0-910999-23-6*) Mus Comp Zoo.

P
Q

An Asterisk (*) at the beginning of an entry indicates that the title is appearing in BIP for the first time.

— Ornithological Gazetteer of Bolivia. 2nd ed. (Illus.). vi, 187p. 1992. 14.00 (0-910999-28-7) Mus Comp Zoo.
— Ornithological Gazetteer of Chile. (Illus.). v, 331p. 1988. 22.00 (0-910999-25-2) Mus Comp Zoo.
— Ornithological Gazetteer of Ecuador. 2nd ed. (Illus.). xi, 249p. 1993. 20.00 (0-910999-29-5) Mus Comp Zoo.
— Ornithological Gazetteer of Paraguay. 2nd ed. (Illus.). iv, 61p. 1989. 8.00 (0-910999-26-0) Mus Comp Zoo.
— Ornithological Gazetteer of Uruguay. 2nd ed. (Illus.). vi, 113p. 1994. 14.00 (0-910999-30-9) Mus Comp Zoo.
— Ornithological Gazetteer of Venezuela. (Illus.). iii, 245p. 1982. 18.00 (0-910999-21-X) Mus Comp Zoo.

Paynter, Raymond A., Jr., ed. Avian Energetics. (Publications of the Nuttall Ornithological Club: No. 15). (Illus.). 334p. 1974. 17.00 (1-877973-25-4) Nuttall Ornith.

Paynter, Raymond A., Jr. & Traylor, Melvin A., Jr. Ornithological Gazetteer of Brazil. (Ornithological Gazetteers of the Neotropics Ser.). (Illus.). xiii, 789p. (Orig.). 1991. 53.00 (0-910999-27-9) Mus Comp Zoo.
— Ornithological Gazetteer of Colombia. (Illus.). v, 311p. 1981. 19.00 (0-910999-19-8) Mus Comp Zoo.

Paynter, Richard H. & Blanchard, Phyllis. A Study of Educational Achievement of Problem Children. LC 74-160985. (Select Bibliographies Reprint Ser.). 1977. reprint ed. 16.95 (0-8369-5853-5) Ayer.

Paynter, Robert. Models of Spatial Inequality: Settlement Patterns in the Historical Connecticut River Valley. (Studies in Historical Archaeology). 1982. text ed. 63.00 (0-12-547580-2) Acad Pr.

Paynter, Robert, jt. ed. see McGuire, Randall H.

Paynter, Robert L. Introductory Electronic Devices & Circuits (Electron Flow) 2nd ed. 992p. 1990. text ed. 50.67 (0-13-482985-9) P-H.

Paynter, Robert T. Microcomputer Operation, Troubleshooting, & Repair. (Illus.). 448p. (C). 1986. text ed. 64.00 (0-13-580341-1) P-H.

Paynter, Will. British Trade Unions & the Problem of Change. LC 75-123196. 172p. reprint ed. pap. 49.10 (0-8357-7432-5, 2023835) Bks Demand.

Paynton, Clifford, jt. auth. see Blackey, Robert.

Paynton, Clifford T. & Blackey, Robert. Why Revolution? Theories & Analyses. 294p. 1971. pap. 22.95 (0-87073-133-5) Schenkman Bks Inc.

Payor, Terri, illus. Magic of Music Folk Songs. (Magic of Music Ser.). 64p. (Orig.). 1990. 14.95 (0-89524-557-4) Cherry Lane.

Payr, Sabine, jt. ed. see Baumgartner, Peter.

Payrot, Alain H., ed. see National Structural Engineering Conference Staff.

Pays, Isobel. Gardening in Retirement. (C). 1989. 24.00 (0-86242-039-3, Pub. by Age Concern Eng UK) St Mut.

Paysan, Catherine. L' Empire du Taureau. (FRE.). 1982. pap. 10.95 (0-7859-4177-0) Fr & Eur.
— Je M'Appelle Jericho. (FRE.). 1979. pap. 10.95 (0-7859-4125-8) Fr & Eur.
— Nous Autres les Sanchez. (FRE.). 1976. pap. 8.95 (0-7859-4061-8) Fr & Eur.

Payson, George. Golden Dreams & Leaden Realities. LC 75-104537. reprint ed. lib. bdg. 19.00 (0-8290-2370-4) Irvington.
— Golden Dreams & Leaden Realities. 1987. reprint ed. pap. text ed. 6.95 (0-8290-2120-5) Irvington.

Payson, Harold H. Boat Modeling the Easy Way: A Scratch Builder's Guide. (Illus.). 192p. 1992. pap. 17.95 (0-87742-320-2, 60303) Intl Marine.
— Boat Modeling the Easy Way: A Scratch Builder's Guide. 1992. pap. 17.95 (0-07-048962-9) McGraw.
— Boat Modeling with Dynamite Payson: A Step-by-Step Guide to Building Models of Small Craft. (Illus.). 160p. 1989. pap. text ed. 18.95 (0-87742-983-9) Intl Marine.
— Boat Modeling with Dynamite Payson: A Step-by-Step Guide to Building Models of Small Craft. 1989. pap. text ed. 19.95 (0-07-157371-2) McGraw.
— Build the Instant Catboat. (Illus.). 48p. 1987. pap. text ed. 12.95 (0-87742-222-2) Intl Marine.
— Build the Instant Catboat. 1987. pap. text ed. 12.95 (0-07-155839-X) McGraw.
— Build the New Instant Boats. LC 84-81554. (Illus.). 160p. 1987. pap. text ed. 19.95 (0-87742-187-0) Intl Marine.
— Build the New Instant Boats. 1987. pap. text ed. 19.95 (0-07-155966-3) McGraw.
— Go Build Your Own Boat. 128p. 1995. pap. 19.95 (1-887222-00-6) H H Payson.
— How to Build the Gloucester Light Dory. 1991. 7.95 (0-937822-04-3) WoodenBoat Pubns.
— Instant Boats. 152p. 1995. pap. 16.00 (1-887222-02-2) H H Payson.
— Keeping the Cutting Edge: Setting & Sharpening Hand & Power Saws. 1987. pap. text ed. 7.95 (0-07-155139-5) McGraw.
— Keeping the Cutting Edge: Setting & Sharpening Hand & Power Saws. (Illus.). 1991. 7.95 (0-937822-02-7) WoodenBoat Pubns.

***Payson, Herb.** Blown Away. 256p. 1995. pap. 14.95 (0-924486-95-3) Sheridan.

Payson, Huldah S. Museum Collections of the Essex Institute. Farnam, Anne et al, eds. LC 78-67991. (E.I. Museum Booklet Ser.). (Illus.). 1978. pap. 5.95 (0-88389-070-4, Essx Institute) Peabody Essex Mus.

Payson, Patricia. Science Fiction: A Zephyr Learning Packet. 79p. (J). (gr. k-8). 1980. spiral bd. 19.95 (0-913705-18-7) Zephyr Pr AZ.

Payson, Steven. Quality Measurement in Economics: New Perspectives on the Evolution of Goods & Services. 256p. 1994. 59.95x (1-85278-926-3, Pub. by E Elgar Pub UK) Ashgate Pub Co.

***Paysour, Buck.** Fly Fishing in North Carolina. (Illus.). 220p. (Orig.). 1995. pap. 14.95 (1-878086-38-3) Down Home NC.
— Tar Heel Angler: Fresh Water Game Fishing in North Carolina. LC 91-71000. (Illus.). 180p. 1991. pap. 13.95 (1-878086-03-0) Down Home NC.

Paysse, Rachel W., jt. auth. see Cotton, Kathleen L.

***Payter, Judy P.** Dietary Minerals & Dangerous Influences: Index of Modern Authors & Subjects with Guide for Rapid Research. rev. ed. LC 90-56319. 149p. 1995. 44.50 (0-7883-0244-2); pap. 39.50 (0-7883-0245-0) ABBE Pubs Assn.
— Solvents & Health Sciences: Subject Analysis with Bibliography. LC 87-47635. 160p. 1987. 44.50 (0-88164-572-9); pap. 39.50 (0-88164-573-7) ABBE Pubs Assn.

***Payton, Charles E., ed.** Seismic Stratigraphy-Applications to Hydrocarbon Exploration. (AAPG Memoir Ser.: No. 26). (Illus.). vii, 516p. 1977. 42.00 (0-89181-302-0) AAPG.

Payton, Crystal, jt. auth. see Payton, Leland.

Payton, Leland & Payton, Crystal. Branson: Country Themes, Neon Dreams. (Illus.). 144p. 1994. text ed. 29.95 (0-9636666-3-0) Anderson MO.
— Turned On: American Decorative Lamps of the '50s. (Illus.). 96p. 1989. 12.98 (0-89659-916-7) Abbeville Pr.

Payton, Otto D. Research: The Validation of Clinical Practice. 3rd ed. (Illus.). 350p. (C). 1993. pap. text ed. 22.95 (0-8036-6800-7) Davis Co.

Payton, Otto D., et al. Patient Participation in Program Planning: A Manual for Therapists. LC 89-16154. 97p. (Orig.). (C). 1990. pap. text ed. 13.95 (0-8036-6803-1) Davis Co.

Payton, Otto D., et al, eds. Manual of Physical Therapy. (Illus.). 761p. 1989. text ed. 69.95 (0-443-08499-8) Churchill.

Payton, Philip. Cornish Carols from Australia. (C). 1989. 45.00 (0-907566-92-8, Pub. by Dyllansow Truran UK) St Mut.
— The Cornish Farmer in Australia. (C). 1989. 90.00 (1-85022-029-8, Pub. by Dyllansow Truran UK) St Mut.
— The Cornish Miner in Australia: Cousin Jack Down Under. (C). 1989. 90.00 (0-907566-51-0, Pub. by Dyllansow Truran UK); 50.00 (0-907566-52-9, Pub. by Dyllansow Truran UK) St Mut.
— Tregantle & Scraesdon: Their Forts & Railway. (C). 1989. 35.00 (1-85022-038-7, Pub. by Dyllansow Truran UK) St Mut.

Payton, Philip, ed. Cornwall since the War. (C). 1993. 39.00 (1-85022-073-5, Pub. by Dyllansow Truran UK) St Mut.

Payton, Philip, ed. see Noall, Cyril.

Payton, Robert, et al. Philanthropy: Four Views. 100p. (Orig.). 1988. 24.95 (0-912051-20-5); pap. 17.95x (0-912051-21-3) Transaction Pubs.

Payton, Robert L. Major Challenges to Philanthropy. 127p. 1984. 10.00 (0-318-37631-8) Ind Sector.
— Philanthropy: Voluntary Action for the Public Good. (ACE-Oryx Series on Higher Education). 304p. 1989. 21.95 (0-02-896490-X, ACE-Oryx) Oryx Pr.

Payton, Rodney J. A Modern Reader's Guide to Dante's Inferno. (American University Studies: Romance Languages & Literature: Ser. II, Vol. 191). 264p. 1993. pap. 31.95 (0-8204-1827-7) P Lang Pubs.

Payton, Rodney J., tr. see Huizinga, Johan.

Payton, Shelia. African Americans. LC 94-12631. (Cultures of America Ser.). (J). (gr. 4-7). 1994. 19.95 (1-85435-787-5) Marshall Cavendish.

Payton, William, jt. ed. see Callahan, Nathan.

***Payutto, Phra P.** Buddhadhamma: Natural Laws & Values for Life. Olson, Grant A., tr. (Buddhist Studies Ser.). 315p. 1995. text ed. 59.50x (0-7914-2631-9) State U NY Pr.
— Buddhadhamma: Natural Laws & Values for Life. Olson, Grant A., tr. (SUNY Series in Buddhist Studies). 315p. (C). 1995. pap. text ed. 19.95x (0-7914-2632-7) State U NY Pr.

Payzant, Geoffrey. Eduard Hanslick & Ritter Berlioz in Prague: A Documentary Narrative. (Illus.). 89p. 1991. pap. 12.95 (0-919813-81-X, Pub. by Univ Calgary CN) Paul & Co Pubs.

Payzant, Geoffrey, ed. see Hanslick, Edward.

Payzant, Joan. Halifax: Cornerstone of Canada. 224p. 1985. 27.95 (0-89781-149-6) Preferred Mktg.

Paz. Convergences. 1991. pap. 10.95 (0-15-622586-7, Harvest Bks) HarBrace.
— Solution Manual for Structural Dynamics. 6th ed. 1991. pap. 19.95 (0-442-00806-6) Van Nos Reinhold.

Paz, Carlos F. Practica Para el Examen de Ciudadania. 3rd ed. 1991. pap. 8.95 (0-13-677097-5) P-H.
— Practica Para el Examen de Cuidadania. 3rd ed. 128p. (SPA.). 1990. pap. 8.95 (0-685-54072-3, Arco Test) P-H Gen Ref & Trav.
— Practice for the U. S. Citizenship & Legalization of Status Tests. 3rd ed. 128p. 1991. pap. 9.00 (0-13-691288-5, Arco Test) P-H Gen Ref & Trav.

Paz, D. G. Popular Anti-Catholicism in Mid-Victorian England. 368p. (C). 1992. 42.50 (0-8047-1984-5) Stanford U Pr.
— The Priesthoods & Apostasies of Pierce Connally: A Study of Victorian Conversion & Anticatholicism. LC 86-2487. (Studies in American Religion: Vol. 18). 418p. 1986. lib. bdg. 109.95 (0-88946-662-9) E Mellen.

***Paz, Donna & Kaufman, Mark, eds.** Reading Group Choices: Selections for Lively Book Discussions. 62p. (Orig.). 1995. pap. 2.95 (0-9644876-0-8) Paz & Assoc.

Paz-Ligorria, Elizabeth, see Mariabelem, pseud..

Paz, M. Structural Dynamics. 3rd ed. 1990. text ed. 69.95 (0-442-31894-4) Chapman & Hall.

Paz, Noemi, et al. Programming Logic for Business Applications. 1988. pap. text ed. write for info. (0-07-555394-5) McGraw.

Paz, Octavio. Alternating Current. 1991. pap. 9.95 (1-55970-136-6) Arcade Pub Inc.
— The Bow & the Lyre: The Poem. The Poetic Revelation. Poetry & History. Simms, Ruth L., tr. (Texas Pan American Ser.). 293p. (C). 1987. reprint ed. pap. 12.95 (0-292-70764-9) U of Tex Pr.
— Children of the Mire: Modern Poetry from Romanticism to the Avant-Garde. LC 73-88498. (Charles Eliot Norton Lectures: 1970-1971). 192p. 1974. pap. text ed. 5.95 (0-674-11626-7) HUP.
— The Collected Poems, 1957-1987: Bilingual Edition. Weinberger, Eliot, ed. & tr. by. Bishop, Elizabeth et al, trs. LC 87-23989. 688p. 1987. 37.50 (0-8112-1037-5); pap. 21.00 (0-8112-1173-8, NDP719) New Directions.
— Configurations. LC 78-145932. (ENG & SPA.). 1971. pap. (0-8112-0150-3, NDP303) New Directions.
— Conjuctions & Disjunctions. 1991. pap. 8.95 (1-55970-137-4) Arcade Pub Inc.
— Convergences: Essays on Art & Literature. Lane, Helen, tr. 1987. 19.95 (0-15-122585-0) HarBrace.
— The Double Flame: Love & Eroticism. Lane, Helen, tr. LC 94-32282. 1995. 22.00 (0-15-100103-0) HarBrace.
— A Draft of Shadows & Other Poems. Weinberger, Eliot, tr. LC 79-15588. 1979. pap. 8.95 (0-8112-0738-2, NDP489) New Directions.
— Eagle or Sun? Weinberger, Eliot, tr. LC 76-7229. 1976. pap. 8.95 (0-8112-0623-8, NDP422) New Directions.
— Early Poems, Nineteen Thirty-Five to Nineteen Fifty-Five. rev. ed. Rukeyser, Muriel, tr. & pref. by. LC 72-93981. Orig. Title: Selected Poems. 1973. pap. 7.95 (0-8112-0478-2, NDP354) New Directions.
— Essays on Mexican Art. 1993. 22.95 (0-15-129063-6) HarBrace.
— Essays on Mexican Art. 1995. pap. 12.95 (0-15-600061-X) HarBrace.
— In Search of the Present. 1991. pap. 8.95 (0-15-644556-5) HarBrace.
— Labyrinth of Solitude: The Other Mexico, Return to the Labyrinth of Solitude, Mexico & the U. S. A., the Philanthropic Ogre. Kemp, Lysander, tr. 398p. 1989. 13.95 (0-8021-5042-X) Grove-Atltic.
— Marcel Duchamp: Appearance Stripped Bare. 1991. pap. 9.95 (1-55970-138-2) Arcade Pub Inc.
— Mariposa de Obsidiana (with 33 RPM Recording in Spanish) (Ediciones Especiales y de Bibliofilo Ser.). (Illus.). (ENG & SPA.). 1993. 200.00 (84-343-0343-4) Elliots Bks.
— Monkey Grammarian. 1991. pap. 9.95 (1-55970-135-8) Arcade Pub Inc.
— On Poets & Others. 1991. pap. 9.95 (1-55970-139-0) Arcade Pub Inc.
— On Poets & Others. Schmidt, Michael, tr. LC 86-11904. 1986. text ed. 18.95 (0-8050-0003-8) Seaver Bks.
— One Earth, Four or Five Worlds: Reflections on Contemporary History. 1986. pap. 5.95 (0-15-668746-1) HarBrace.
— One Word to the Other. 1991. pap. 7.00 (0-318-41819-3) Latitudes Pr.
— The Other Voice: Essays on Modern Poetry. Lane, Helen, tr. 1991. 16.95 (0-15-170449-X) HarBrace.
— Other Voice: Essays on Modern Poetry. 1992. pap. 9.95 (0-15-670455-2, Harvest Bks) HarBrace.
— Rufino Tamayo: Myth & Magic. Phillips, Rachel, tr. LC 79-63734. (Illus.). (Orig.). 1979. pap. 12.95 (0-89207-019-6) S R Guggenheim.
— Selected Poems of Octavio Paz. Aroul, G. et al, trs. LC 84-9856. 160p. 1984. pap. 8.95 (0-8112-0899-0, NDP574) New Directions.
— Siren & the Seashell: And Other Essays on Poets & Poetry by Octavio Paz. Kemp, Lysander & Peden, Margaret S., trs. (Texas Pan American Ser.). 1991. pap. 9.95 (0-292-77652-7) U of Tex Pr.
— Sor Juana: Or, the Traps of Faith. Peden, Margaret S., tr. LC 88-3002. (Illus.). 560p. 1988. 42.50 (0-674-82105-X) HUP.
— Sor Juana: Or, the Traps of Faith. Peden, Margaret S., tr. 560p. 1990. pap. text ed. 16.95 (0-674-82106-8) HUP.
— Sunstone - Piedra De Sol. deluxe limited ed. Weinberger, Eliot, tr. LC 91-29993. (Illus.). 64p. 1991. 150.00 (0-8112-1194-0) New Directions.
— Sunstone - Piedra De Sol. Weinberger, Eliot, tr. LC 91-29993. (Illus.). 64p. 1991. reprint ed. 18.95 (0-8112-1197-5); reprint ed. pap. 8.95 (0-8112-1195-9, NDP735) New Directions.
— A Tree Within: Bilingual Edition. Weinberger, Eliot, tr. LC 88-19666. 176p. 1988. pap. 9.95 (0-8112-1071-5, NDP661) New Directions.

Paz, Octavio, ed. Mexican Poetry. Beckett, Samuel, tr. LC 85-17684. 214p. (Orig.). 1985. reprint ed. pap. 9.95 (0-8021-5186-8) Grove-Atltic.

Paz, Octavio, intro. Mexico: Esplendores de Treinta Siglos. (Illus.). 728p. (SPA.). (C). 1991. text ed. 90.00 (0-9628860-0-9) Frnds Arts Mexico.
— Mexico: Splendors of Thirty Centuries. (Illus.). 728p. 1990. pap. 75.00 (0-87099-596-0) Metro Mus Art.

Paz, Octavio, jt. auth. see Villaurrutia, Xavier.

Paz, Octavio, jt. auth. see Weinberger, Eliot.

Pazandak, Carol H., ed. Improving Undergraduate Education in Large Universities. LC 85-644752. (New Directions for Higher Education Ser.: No. 66). 1989. 14.95 (1-55542-867-3) Jossey-Bass.

Pazanin. Wissenschaft und Geschichte in der Phanomelogie Edmund Husserls. (Phaenomenologica Ser.: No. 46). 1972. lib. bdg. 62.00 (90-247-1194-0) Kluwer Ac.

Pazano, Patti. Guide to Successful After-School Elementary Foreign-Language Programs. 1991. pap. 9.95 (0-8442-9365-2, Natl Textbk) NTC Pub Grp.

Pazaris, J. & Hayes, J. E., eds. Fiber Optic Datacom & Computer Networks, Vol. 991. 1988. 51.00 (0-8194-0026-2) SPIE.

Pazaris, J., jt. auth. see Arjavalingam, G.

Pazaris, James & Willenbring, Gerald, eds. Optical Interconnects in the Computer Environment. 221p. 1990. 53.00 (0-8194-0214-1, VOL. 1178) SPIE.

Pazdan, Mary M. Joel, Obadiah, Haggai, Zechariah, Malachi. (Collegeville Bible Commentary - Old Testament Ser.: No. 17). 128p. 1986. pap. 3.95 (0-8146-1424-8) Liturgical Pr.
— The Son of Man: A Metaphor for Jesus in the Fourth Gospel. (Zacchaeus Studies: New Testament). 88p. (Orig.). 1992. pap. text ed. 8.95 (0-8146-5677-3) Liturgical Pr.

Pazdziora, J. Design of Underground Hard-Coal Mines. (Advances in Mining Science & Technology Ser.: Vol. 3). 1988. 89.75 (0-444-98938-2) Elsevier.

Pazi, Margarita, ed. Max Brod Eighteen Eighty-Four to Nineteen Eighty-Four: Untersuchungen zu Max Brods Literarischen und Philosophischen Schriften. (New Yorker Studien zur Neueren Deutschen Literaturgeschichte Ser.: Vol. 8). 268p. 1987. 52.00 (0-8204-0571-X) P Lang Pubs.

Pazienza, Marc, jt. ed. see Davis, Mitchell P.

Pazig, Christianus. Bibliotheca Curiosa: A Treatise of Magic Incantations (1700) Goldsmid, Edmund, ed. 54p. 1994. pap. 12.95 (1-56459-437-8) Kessinger Pub.

Pazman, Andrej. Foundations of Optimum Experimental Design. 1986. lib. bdg. 80.50 (90-277-1865-2) Kluwer Ac.
— Nonlinear Statistical Model. LC 93-7412. (Mathematics & Its Applications Ser.: Vol. 254). 1993. lib. bdg. 119.00 (0-7923-2247-9) Kluwer Ac.

Pazmany Aircraft Corporation Staff, ed. see Pazmany, Ladislao.

Pazmany, Ladislao. Landing Gear Design for Light Aircraft, Vol. 1. Pazmany Aircraft Corporation Staff, ed. (Illus.). 256p. (Orig.). 1986. pap. 25.00 (0-9616777-0-8) Pazmany Aircraft.

Pazmino, Robert W. By What Authority Do We Teach? Sources for Empowering Christian Educators. LC 94-1704. 160p. (Orig.). 1994. pap. 10.99 (0-8010-7129-1) Baker Bk.
— Foundational Issues in Christian Education: An Introduction in Evangelical Perspective. LC 88-16753. 264p. (C). 1993. pap. text ed. 12.99 (0-8010-7103-8) Baker Bk.
— Latin American Journey: Insights for Christian Education in North America. LC 94-1621. 208p. (Orig.). 1994. pap. 13.95 (0-8298-0993-7) Pilgrim OH.
— Principles & Practices of Christian Education: An Evangelical Perspective. LC 92-464. 176p. (C). 1992. pap. text ed. 10.99 (0-8010-7120-8) Baker Bk.
— The Seminary in the City: A Study of New York Theological Seminary. LC 88-17250. 146p. (Orig.). (C). 1988. lib. bdg. 35.50 (0-8191-7073-9); pap. text ed. 16.50 (0-8191-7074-7) U Pr of Amer.

Pazner, Micha, et al. Map Two: Map Processor: A Geographic Information System for the Macintosh. LC 08-938322. 408p. (C). 1989. Net. write for info. (0-471-51704-6) Wiley.
— Simple Commputer Imaging & Mapping. LC 93-13616. (Technical Paper Ser.: No. 206). 1993. write for info. (0-8213-2467-5) World Bank.
— Simple Computer Imaging & Mapping. LC 93-31764. (Technical Paper Ser.: No. 231). 152p. 1993. 9.95 (0-8213-2528-0, 12528) World Bank.

Paznik-Bondarin, Jane & Baxter, Milton. Write & Write Again. 675p. (C). 1987. pap. write for info. (0-02-393220-1) Macmillan.

Pazos, Felipe. Chronic Inflation in Latin America. LC 71-180848. (Special Studies in International Economics & Development). 1972. 29.50 (0-275-28282-1) Irvington.

Pazy, A. Semigroups of Linear Operators & Applications to Partial Differential Equations. John, F. et al, eds. (Applied Mathematical Sciences Ser.: Vol. 44). viii, 279p. 1992. 59.00 (0-387-90845-5) Spr-Verlag.

Pazzagli, M., et al, eds. Journal of Bioluminescence & Chemiluminescence, Vol. 4. 646p. 1989. text ed. 365.00 (0-471-92264-1) Wiley.

Pazzaglini, Peter R. & Hawks, Catharine A. Consilia: A Bibliography of Holdings in the Library of Congress & Certain Other Collections in the United States. LC 89-600323. 154p. 1990. 19.00 (0-8444-0672-4, 030-000-00182-6) Lib Congress.

Pazzani, Michael J. Creating a Memory of Casual Relationships: An Integration of Empirical & Explanation-Based Learning Method. 360p. 1990. write for info. (1-56321-040-1) L Erlbaum Assocs.
— Creating a Memory of Causal Relationships: An Integration of Empirical & Explanation-Based Learning Methods. 360p. 1990. 69.95 (0-8058-0629-6); 10.95 (1-56321-037-1); 10.95 (1-56321-038-X); 10.95 (1-56321-039-8); pap. 29.95 (0-8058-0789-6) L Erlbaum Assocs.

Pazzanita, Anthony G. & Hodges, Tony. Historical Dictionary of Western Sahara. 2nd ed. LC 93-48064. (African Historical Dictionaries Ser.: No. 55). (Illus.). 641p. 1994. 69.50 (0-8108-2661-5) Scarecrow.

Pazzelli, Raffaele. The Franciscan Sisters: Outlines of History & Spirituality. Mullaney, Aidan, tr. LC 92-38686. 1993. pap. 15.00 (0-940535-52-1) Franciscan U Pr.

Pazzelli, Raphael. St. Francis & the Third Order. 1989. pap. 14.95 (0-8199-0953-X, Frncscn Herld) Franciscan Pr.

Pazzi, Robert. Adrift in Time. 150p. 1992. 22.95 (0-233-98715-0, Pub. by A Deutsch UK) Trafalgar.

PBC International Editors. California Design. (Illus.). 224p. 1989. 55.00 (0-86636-102-2) PBC Intl Inc.

PBC International, Inc. Editors. Business Cards Dynamic Graphic Design. 1993. pap. 29.95 (0-86636-239-8) PBC Intl Inc.
— Clubs & Resorts. LC 93-30033. 1994. 55.00 (0-86636-230-4) PBC Intl Inc.

An Asterisk (*) at the beginning of an entry indicates that the title is appearing in BIP for the first time.

P'Bitek, Okot. African Religions in European Scholarship. (African Heritage Classical Research Studies). 140p. reprint ed. 15.00 (0-938818-29-5) ECA Assoc.
— Song of a Prisoner. (Illus.). 128p. 1971. 15.95 (0-89388-004-3); pap. 9.95 (0-685-42289-5) Okpaku Communications.
— Song of Lawino & Song of Ocol. (African Writers Ser.: No. 266). (Illus.). 151p. (C). 1984. reprint ed. pap. 9.95 (0-435-90266-0) Heinemann.
P'Brien, Robert W. & Iwasaki, Amy. College Nisei Revisited. (Illus.). 1994. 21.95 (0-87015-254-8) Pacific Bks.
PBS Adult Learning Service Staff. Transformations of Myth Through Time. (Illus.). 496p. (C). 1989. teacher ed write for info. (0-15-592337-4); pap. text ed. 20.00 (0-15-592335-8); Study guide, 183 pgs. student ed, pap. text ed. 15.00 (0-15-592336-6) HB Coll Pubs.
PC Committee Staff. Are You PC? (Illus.). 64p. (Orig.). 1992. pap. 5.95 (0-89815-447-2) Ten Speed Pr.
PC Learning Lab Staff. PC Learning Labs Teaches DOS 6. (PC Learning Labs Ser.). (Illus.). 456p. (Orig.). 1993. disk 22.95 (1-56276-100-5) Ziff-Davis.
— PC Learning Labs Teaches Microsoft Access. (Learning Labs Ser.). (Illus.). 412p. (Orig.). 1993. disk, pap. 22.95 (1-56276-122-6) Ziff-Davis.
— PC Learning Labs Teaches Netware. (Learning Lab Ser.). (Illus.). (Orig.). 1994. disk, pap. 22.95 (1-56276-253-2) Ziff-Davis.
PC Learning Labs. PC Learning Labs Teaches PowerPoint 4.0 for Windows. (Learning Labs Ser.). (Illus.). 464p. (Orig.). 1994. disk, pap. 22.95 (1-56276-229-X) Ziff-Davis.
PC Learning Labs Staff. PC Learning Labs Teaches Ami Pro 3.0. (Learning Labs Ser.). (Illus.). 1993. disk 22.95 (1-56276-134-X) Ziff-Davis.
— PC Learning Labs Teaches Ami Pro 4.0. (Learning Lab Ser.). (Illus.). 1995. disk, pap. 22.95 (1-56276-224-9) Ziff-Davis.
— PC Learning Labs Teaches CorelDRAW! 4.0. (Learning Lab Ser.). (Illus.). 1994. disk, pap. 22.95 (1-56276-188-9) Ziff-Davis.
— PC Learning Labs Teaches DOS 5. (Learning Labs Ser.). (Illus.). 346p. (Orig.). 1992. disk 22.95 (1-56276-042-4) Ziff-Davis.
— PC Learning Labs Teaches Excel 3.0. (Learning Labs Ser.). (Illus.). 332p. (Orig.). 1991. disk 22.95 (1-56276-034-3) Ziff-Davis.
— PC Learning Labs Teaches Excel 4.0 for Windows. (Learning Labs Ser.). (Illus.). 384p. (Orig.). 1992. disk 22.95 (1-56276-074-2) Ziff-Davis.
— PC Learning Labs Teaches Excel 5.0 for Windows. (Learning Lab Ser.). (Illus.). 1994. disk 22.95 (1-56276-141-2) Ziff-Davis.
— PC Learning Labs Teaches Fox Pro 2.5 for Windows. (Learning Lab Ser.). 1993. disk, pap. 22.95 (1-56276-176-5) Ziff-Davis.
— PC Learning Labs Teaches Lotus Notes 3.0. (Learning Lab Ser.). (Illus.). 1993. disk, pap. 22.95 (1-56276-138-2) Ziff-Davis.
— PC Learning Labs Teaches: Mail. (Learning Lab Ser.). (Illus.). 1993. disk, pap. 22.95 (1-56276-135-8) Ziff-Davis.
— PC Learning Labs Teaches Microsoft Access 2.0. 1994. disk, pap. 22.95 (1-56276-225-7) Ziff-Davis.
— PC Learning Labs Teaches Microsoft Office. (Learning Lab Ser.). (Illus.). (Orig.). 1994. disk, pap. 22.95 (1-56276-272-9) Ziff-Davis.
— PC Learning Labs Teaches Microsoft Project 3.0 for Windows. (Learning Labs Ser.). (Illus.). 399p. (Orig.). 1993. disk 22.95 (1-56276-124-2) Ziff-Davis.
— PC Learning Labs Teaches Microsoft Project 4.0 for Windows. (Learning Lab Ser.). 1994. disk, pap. 22.95 (1-56276-226-5) Ziff-Davis.
— PC Learning Labs Teaches OS-2 2.1. 1993. disk 22.95 (1-56276-148-X) Ziff-Davis.
— PC Learning Labs Teaches Powerpoint for Windows. (Learning Lab Ser.). 1993. disk 22.95 (1-56276-154-4) Ziff-Davis.
— PC Learning Labs Teaches Visual Basic 4.0. (Learning Lab Ser.). (Illus.). (Orig.). 1995. disk, pap. 22.95 (1-56276-227-3) Ziff-Davis.
— PC Learning Labs Teaches Windows 3.1. (Learning Labs Ser.). (Illus.). 339p. (Orig.). 1992. disk 22.95 (1-56276-051-3) Ziff-Davis.
— PC Learning Labs Teaches Word for Windows 2.0. (Learning Labs Ser.). (Illus.). 363p. (Orig.). 1992. disk 22.95 (1-56276-065-3) Ziff-Davis.
— PC Learning Labs Teaches Word 6.0 for Windows. (Learning Lab Ser.). 1993. disk, pap. 22.95 (1-56276-139-0) Ziff-Davis.
— PC Learning Labs Teaches WordPerfect 5.1. (Learning Labs Ser.). 287p. (Orig.). 1991. disk 22.95 (1-56276-032-7) Ziff-Davis.
— PC Learning Labs Teaches WordPerfect 6.0. 1993. disk 22.95 (1-56276-105-6) Ziff-Davis.
— PC Learning Labs Teaches WordPerfect 6.0 for Windows. (Learning Lab Ser.). 1993. disk 22.95 (1-56276-020-3) Ziff-Davis.
— PC Learning Labs Teaches WordPerfect 6.1 for Windows. 1995. pap. 22.95 (1-56276-157-9) Ziff-Davis.
— PC Learning Labs Teaches 1-2-3 Release 2.3. (Learning Lab Ser.). (Illus.). 307p. (Orig.). 1991. disk 22.95 (1-56276-033-5) Ziff-Davis.
— PC Learning Labs Teaches 1-2-3 4.0 for Windows. (Learning Lab Ser.). 1994. disk, pap. 22.95 (1-56276-199-4) Ziff-Davis.
— PC Learning Labs Teaches 1-2-3 5.0 for Windows. 350p. 1994. disk 22.95 (1-56276-295-8) Ziff-Davis.
Pc-sig. Encyclopedia of Shareware. 1990. pap. 19.95 (0-915835-19-3) PC Software.
PC-SIG, Inc. Staff. Business Application Software. 1991. pap. 29.95 (0-07-157861-7) McGraw.
— Business Applications Shareware. 304p. 1991. pap. 29.95 (0-8306-2490-2, Windcrest) TAB Bks.
— DOS Shareware Utilities. 1992. pap. 29.95 (0-07-157859-5) McGraw.
— DOS Shareware Utilities. 304p. 1991. pap. 29.95 (0-8306-2488-0, 3012, Windcrest) TAB Bks.
— The PC-SIG Encyclopedia of Shareware. 4th ed. 1992. pap. 19.95 (0-07-048504-6) McGraw.
— The PC-SIG Encyclopedia of Shareware. 4th ed. 640p. 1991. pap. 19.95 (0-8306-2669-7, Windcrest) TAB Bks.
— Programming Tools Shareware. 1991. pap. 29.95 (0-07-157860-9) McGraw.
— Programming Tools Shareware. 304p. 1991. pap. 29.95 (0-8306-2489-9, Windcrest) TAB Bks.
— Windows 3 Shareware Utilities. 216p. 1992. pap. 29.95 (0-8306-2485-6, Windcrest) TAB Bks.
— Windows 3.0 Shareware Utilties. 1992. pap. 29.95 (0-07-157858-7) McGraw.
PC Sig Staff. PC Sig Encyclopedia of Shareware. 4th ed. 1991. pap. 27.75 (0-915835-20-7) PC Software.
PC Software Interest Group, Inc. Staff. PC Software Interest Group Encyclopedia of Shareware. 1989. pap. 17.95 (0-915835-14-2) PC Software.
PC World Editors. Hands On. write for info. (0-318-58694-0) S&S Trade.
PC World Editors & Myers, David. LOGO for IBM Personal Computers. 1985. pap. 16.95 (0-671-49284-5) S&S Trade.
PCDI Staff & Ronan, David T. Practical VCR Repair. LC 94-20858. 592p. 1994. pap. text ed. 38.95 (0-8273-6583-7) Delmar.
Pchiluk, William & Nash, David. Autofacts Yearbook, 1992, Vol. 2. 500p. 1992. text ed. 495.00 (1-879800-03-9) Autofacts.
PcPhail, Helen, tr. see French Ramblers Association Staff.
***PCRCW '94.** Parallel Computer Routing & Communication: Proceedings of the First International Workshop, PCRCW '94, Seattle, Washington, U. S. A., May 16-18, 1994. Snyder, Lawrence & Bolding, Kevin, eds. LC 94-33307. (Lecture Notes in Computer Science: 853). 1994. write for info. (0-387-58429-3); 47.00 (3-540-58429-3) Spr-Verlag.
PCS Associates Inc., ed. Student Version of PC: Solve (3.5 Inch Disk) (Orig.). (C). 1990. pap. 50.00 (1-878437-16-X) Pac Crest Soft.
***PCS Associates Inc. Staff, ed.** Student Version of PC: Solve. (C). 1990. 3.5 hd, pap. 67.00 (1-878437-03-8) Pac Crest Soft.
***PCS Associates Staff.** PC: Users Guide. (C). 1993. disk 30.00 (1-878437-99-2) Pac Crest Soft.
PCS Associates Staff & Apple, Daniel K. Faculty PC: Solve, 3 vols., Set. (Orig.). (C). 1990. pap. text ed. 40.00 (1-878437-14-3) Pac Crest Soft.
PCS Associates Staff, jt. auth. see Apple, Daniel K.
PDA Research Task Force No. 16 on Dry Heat Processes. Validation of Dry Heat Processes Used for Sterlization & Depyrogenation. (Technical Reports Ser.: No. 3). 55p. (Orig.). 1981. pap. 30.00 (0-939459-02-7) PDA.
PDA Research Task Force on Aseptic Filling. Validation of Aseptic Drug Powder Filling Process. (Technical Reports Ser.: No. 6). 30p. 1984. pap. 30.00 (0-939459-05-1) PDA.
PDA Research Task Group No. 15 on Aseptic Filling Staff. Validation of Aseptic Filling for Solution Drug Products. rev. ed. (Technical Monographs: No. 2). 28p. (Orig.). 1980. pap. 30.00 (0-939459-01-9) PDA.
PDA Research Task Group on Steam Sterilization. Validation of Steam Sterilization Cycles. rev. ed. (Technical Monographs: No. 1). 36p. 1978. pap. 30.00 (0-939459-00-0) PDA.
PDA Research Task Group-Quality Control Subcommittee Task Group. Design Concepts for the Validation of a Water for Injection System. (Technical Reports Ser.: No. 4). 1983. pap. 30.00 (0-939459-03-5) PDA.
PDA Task Force on Depyrogenation. Technical Report, No. 7. (Depyrogenation Ser.). 116p. 1985. pap. 35.00 (0-939459-06-X) PDA.
***Pdersen, Frank A., et al.** Mastery Motivation Vol. 12: Origins, Conceptualizations & Applications. MacTurk, Robert H. & Morgan, George A., eds. (Advances in Applied Developmental Psychology Ser.). 1995. write for info. (1-56750-146-X) Ablex Pub.
***Pderzoli, P., ed.** Facing the Pancreatic Dilemma: Update of Medical & Surgical Pancreatology. LC 94-35004. 1994. write for info. (3-540-58284-3) Spr-Verlag.
PDP Research Group, et al. Parallel Distributed Processing: Explorations in the Microstructure of Cognition, Vol. 1: Foundations. (Computational Models of Cognition & Perception Ser.). (Illus.). 550p. 1987. 47.50 (0-262-18120-7, Bradford Bks); pap. 24.95 (0-262-68053-X, Bradford Bks) MIT Pr.
Pe, Hla. Burma: Literature, Historiography, Scholarship, Language, Life & Buddhism. 224p. 1986. pap. text ed. 19.75 (9971-988-00-3, Pub. by Inst SE Asian Studies SI) Ashgate Pub Co.
Pe Maung, Tin, tr. The Expositor. (C). 1976. reprint ed. 48.50 (0-86013-070-3, Pub. by Pali Text) Wisdom MA.
— The Path of Purity, 3 vols. in 1. (C). 1975. reprint ed. 60.00 (0-86013-008-8, Pub. by Pali Text) Wisdom MA.
Pe Maung Tin, tr. see Buddhaghosa.
Pea, Roy D. & Sheingold, Karen, eds. Mirrors of Minds: Patterns of Experience in Educational Computing. LC 87-1274. (Cognition & Computing Ser.). 336p. 1987. text ed. 52.50 (0-89391-422-3); pap. text ed. 24.95 (0-89391-423-1) Ablex Pub.
Peabody, A., tr. see Dianov, Y. M., ed.
Peabody, Al, tr. see Komar, A. A., ed.
Peabody, Al, tr. see Vaynshtein, B. K. & Chernov, A. A., eds.
Peabody, Andrew P. Harvard Reminiscences. LC 72-39149. (Essay Index Reprint Ser.). 1977. reprint ed. 20.95 (0-8369-2708-7) Ayer.
Peabody, Barbara. The Screaming Room: A Mother's Journal of Her Son's Struggle with AIDS. 288p. 1987. mass mkt. 4.99 (0-380-70345-9) Avon.
Peabody, Berkeley. The Winged Word: A Study in the Technique of Ancient Greek Oral Composition As Seen Principally Through Hesiod's Work & Days. LC 75-4842. 562p. 1975. 64.50 (0-87395-059-3) State U NY Pr.
Peabody, Charles N. Zab: Brevet Major Zabdiel Boylston Adams, 1829-1902, Physician. 255p. 1984. 17.50 (0-317-04058-8) F A Countway.
Peabody, Dean. National Characteristics. (European Monographs in Social Psychology). (Illus.). 280p. 1985. 54.95 (0-521-30449-0) Cambridge U Pr.
Peabody, Elizabeth P. Last Evening with Allston, & Other Papers. LC 72-2953. reprint ed. 47.50 (0-404-10718-4) AMS Pr.
— Record of a School. LC 74-89218. (American Education: Its Men, Institutions & Ideas, Ser. 1). 1974. reprint ed. 20.95 (0-405-01457-0) Ayer.
Peabody, Francis G. Education for Life: The Story of Hampton Institute. LC 77-84106. 464p. 1969. reprint ed. 36.95 (0-405-30234-7) Ayer.
— Reminiscences of Present-Day Saints. LC 74-37525. (Essay Index Reprint Ser.). 1977. reprint ed. 25.95 (0-8369-2576-9) Ayer.
***Peabody, George, ed.** Best Maritime Short Stories. (Illus.). 232p. 1995. pap. 14.95 (0-88780-068-8) Formac Dist Ltd.
Peabody, Kathleen L. & Mooney, Margaret L. The Lonely Pain of Cancer: Home Care for the Terminally Ill. Ellison, Bettye, ed. LC 91-90114. (Illus.). 160p. (Orig.). (C). 1991. pap. 15.95 (0-9629350-1-8) Sharp Pub.
— Swinging in the Wind: Kids: Survivors of a Crisis. Ellison, Bettye & Libby, Peter, eds. LC 92-50632. (Illus.). 144p. (Orig.). (C). 1992. pap. text ed. 12.95 (0-9629350-9-3) Sharp Pub.
Peabody, Kathleen L., et al. Widows Are Special: They Know the Sun Will Rise Again. LC 94-17856. 128p. (Orig.). (C). 1994. pap. 10.95 (0-9629350-7-7) Sharp Pub.
Peabody, Larry. Secular Word Is Full-Time Service Study Guide. 1976. pap. 1.50 (0-87508-449-4) Chr Lit.
— Secular Work Is Full Time Service. 1974. pap. 4.95 (0-87508-448-6) Chr Lit.
Peabody Museum of Archaeology & Ethnology Editors. Author & Subject Catalogues of the Library of the Peabody Museum of Archaeology & Ethnology: Fourth Supplement, 7 vols. 1979. lib. bdg. 1,080.00 (0-8161-0253-8, Hall Library) G K Hall.
Peabody, Paul. Blackberry Hollow. LC 92-8968. (Illus.). 160p. (J). (gr. 3-7). 1993. 15.95 (0-399-22500-5, Philomel Bks) Putnam Pub Group.
Peabody, Pichard, jt. ed. see Ebersole, Lucinda.
***Peabody, Richard.** Buoyancy: And Other Myths. LC 94-78592. 70p. (Orig.). 1995. pap. 7.95 (0-945144-06-7) Gut Punch Pr.
— Mondo Marilyn: A Collection of Stories & Poems about Marilyn. 1994. pap. 13.95 (0-312-11853-8) St Martin.
— Paraffin Days. LC 94-72552. 77p. (Orig.). 1995. pap. 7.95 (0-937998-11-7) Cumber Jrnl.
— Sad Fashions. LC 89-85142. 64p. (Orig.). 1990. pap. 7.95 (0-945144-01-6) Gut Punch Pr.
Peabody, Richard, intro. One Thousand One Monday Nights: Stories by Twelve Washington Writers. 206p. (Orig.). 1990. pap. 10.00 (0-9609062-1-5) WA Expatriates Pr.
Peabody, Richard & Ebersole, Lucinda. Mondo Elvis: A Collection of Fiction & Poetry about the King. 208p. 1993. pap. 12.95 (0-312-10505-3) St Martin.
Peabody, Richard, jt. auth. see Ebersole, Lucinda.
***Peabody, Robert E.** Models of American Sailing Ships. rev. ed. Ratte, John, ed. LC 94-78003. (Illus.). 116p. (Orig.). 1994. 18.00 (1-879886-39-1) Addison Gallery.
Peabody, Robert L. & Polsby, Nelson W., eds. New Perspectives on the House of Representatives. rev. ed. 392p. 1992. pap. text ed. 14.95 (0-8018-4158-5) Johns Hopkins.
— New Perspectives on the House of Representatives. 4th rev. ed. 392p. 1992. text ed. 55.00 (0-8018-4157-7) Johns Hopkins.
Peabody, Robert L., jt. auth. see Huitt, Ralph K.
Peabody, S. Peabody (Paybody, Pabody, Pabodie) Genealogy. (Illus.). 614p. 1989. reprint ed. lib. bdg. 100.00 (0-8328-0942-X); reprint ed. pap. 92.00 (0-8328-0943-8) Higginson Bk Co.
Peabody, Susan. Addiction to Love. rev. ed. (Illus.). 132p. (Orig.). 1994. pap. 9.95 (0-89815-715-3) Ten Speed Pr.
Peace. Statistical Issues in Drug Research & Development. (Statistics: Vol. 106). 384p. 1990. 140.00 (0-8247-8290-9) Dekker.
Peace, ed. Biopharmaceutical Sequential Statistical Applications. (Statistics: Vol. 128). 376p. 1992. 125.00 (0-8247-8628-9) Dekker.
***Peace, Beverly & Peace, Philip.** Planning Ahead: A Positive Act of Love for Family & Friends. 32p. (Orig.). 1992. student ed 4.95 (1-881576-00-0) Providence Hse.
Peace Corps Office of Public Affairs Staff. Leadership for Peace: A Challenge from the Peace Corps. 16p. (Orig.). 1987. pap. text ed. write for info. (0-943051-00-2) US Peace Corps.
Peace Corps Office of Returned Volunteer Services. Natural Resource Careers: Career Information for Returned Peace Corps Volunteers. 19p. (Orig.). 1987. pap. text ed. write for info. (0-943051-01-0) US Peace Corps.
Peace, D. McClymont. Key for Identification of Mandibles of Stored-Food Insects. (Illus.). vi, 166p. 1985. pap. 66.00 (0-935584-32-3) AOAC Intl.
***Peace, David.** Eric Gill: The Inscriptions. (Illus.). 208p. 1995. 50.00 (1-56792-027-6) Godine.
Peace, G., jt. auth. see Faulkner, A.
Peace, Glen S. Taguchi Methods: A Hands on Approach. (Illus.). 384p. 1993. 52.95 (0-201-56311-8) Addison-Wesley.
***Peace, John W.** The Book of Peace. 284p. (Orig.). 1995. pap. write for info. (1-885591-58-6) Morris Pubng.
Peace, Mary. Fireflies. 1986. pap. 4.95 (0-932298-45-1) Tri-State Pr Corp.
Peace, P. & Maugham, M. Jet Engine Manual. 160p. (C). 1989. 55.00 (81-7002-014-X, Pub. by Himalayan Bks II) St Mut.
Peace, Philip, jt. auth. see Peace, Beverly.
Peace Pilgrim II Staff. Enjoying the Journey. LC 94-36788. 224p. (Orig.). 1995. pap. 10.00 (0-931892-94-5) B Dolphin Pub.
***Peace, Ray.** Bicycling Around Victoria: With Great New Day & Weekend Rides. (Illus.). 285p. (Orig.). 1995. pap. 14.95 (0-85091-639-9, Pub. by Lothian Pub AT) Seven Hills Bk.
— Ski-Touring Victoria & NSW: Over 40 Great Day Ski Tours. (Illus.). 140p. (Orig.). 1995. pap. 14.95 (0-85091-556-2, Pub. by Lothian Pub AT) Seven Hills Bk.
Peace, Raymond. Bicycling Around Victoria. (Illus.). 192p. 1991. pap. 19.95 (0-85091-448-5, Pub. by Lothian Pub AT) Intl Spec Bk.
Peace, Richard. The Enigma of Gogol. LC 81-3867. (Cambridge Studies in Russian Literature). 320p. 1982. 69.95 (0-521-23824-2) Cambridge U Pr.
***Peace, Richard, et al.** Facing Your Fears about Sharing Your Faith. (Christian Lifestyle Ser.). Date not set. 14.95 (1-55513-382-7, 73825) Cook.
Peace, Richard. Learning to Love God. (Learning to Love Ser.). 96p. (Orig.). 1994. pap. 6.00 (0-89109-841-0) NavPress.
— Learning to Love Others. (Learning to Love Ser.). 96p. (Orig.). 1994. pap. 6.00 (0-89109-840-2) NavPress.
— Learning to Love Ourselves. (Learning to Love Ser.). 96p. (Orig.). 1994. pap. 6.00 (0-89109-842-9) NavPress.
Peace, Richard, ed. see Dostoevsky, Fyodor M.
Peace, Richard, ed. see Gogol, Nikolai V.
Peace, Roger C., III. A Just & Lasting Peace: The U. S. Peace Movement from the Cold War to Desert Storm. LC 90-63425. (Illus.). 344p. (Orig.). 1991. pap. 14.95 (0-9622683-8-0) Noble Pr.
Peace, Sheila. An International Perspective on the Status of Older Women. 100p. (Orig.). 1981. pap. text ed. 5.00 (0-910473-09-9) Intl Fed Ageing.
Peace, Sheila & Nusberg, Charlotte. Shared Living: A Viable Alternative for the Elderly? LC 84-3776. 118p. (Orig.). 1984. pap. text ed. 10.00 (0-910473-13-7) Intl Fed Ageing.
Peace, Sheila M. Researching Social Gerontology: Concepts, Methods & Issues. Norton, Peter G. et al, eds. 224p. (C). 1990. text ed. 47.50 (0-8039-8284-4); pap. text ed. 19.95 (0-8039-8285-2) Sage.
Peace, Walter. Geography of Canada Sourcebook. 112p. (C). 1992. pap. text ed. 8.95 (0-8403-8080-1) Kendall-Hunt.
Peaceman, Donald W. Fundamentals of Numerical Reservoir Simulation. (Developments in Petroleum Science Ser.: Vol. 6). 176p. 1991. 85.75 (0-444-41578-5) Elsevier.
Peach, Andrew, jt. auth. see Cohen, Jonathan.
Peach, Bernard, ed. see Hutcheson, Francis.
Peach, Charles. The Whole Works This Our Home Record Keeping & Joy of Dicscovery Workbook. (Illus.). 200p. 1987. student ed 30.00 (0-942751-33-7) Whole Works.
— Whole Works Wine Tasting & Record Book. 2nd ed. (Illus.). 100p. 1987. student ed 13.00 (0-942751-01-9) Whole Works.
Peach, David A. & Livernash, E. Robert. Grievance Initiation & Resolution: A Study in Steel. 1974. text ed. 10.00 (0-87584-112-0) HUP.
Peach, Emily. The Tarot Workbook: Understanding & Using Tarot Symbolism. (Workbook Ser.). (Illus.). 256p. (Orig.). 1995. pap. 14.95 (0-85030-390-7) Sterling.
— Things That Go Bump in the Night: How to Investigate & Challenge Ghostly Experiences. 1991. pap. 9.95 (0-85030-873-9, Pub. by Aquarian Pr UK) Thorsons SF.
Peach, Hedle, jt. auth. see Patrick, Donald L.
Peach, James T. Demographic & Economic Change in Mexico's Northern Frontier: Evidence from the X Censo General de Poblacion y Vivienda. 47p. (Orig.). (C). 1984. pap. text ed. 5.25 (0-937795-12-7) Border Res Inst.
Peach, James T. & Hughes, William F. Some Implications of the 1984 Tandem Truck Safety Act for the U. S.-Mexico Border Area. 17p. (Orig.). (C). 1985. pap. text ed. 5.25 (0-937795-07-0) Border Res Inst.
Peach, James T., jt. auth. see Jannuzi, F. T.
Peach, Josephine M., jt. auth. see Hornby, Michael.
***Peach, K. J. & vick, L. L. J., eds.** High Energy Phenomenology: Proceedings of the Forty-Second Scottish Universities Summer School in Physics, St. Andrews, August 1993. LC 94-30447. 1994. 180.00 (0-7503-0326-3) IOP Pub.
Peach, K. J., jt. ed. see Frame, D.
Peach, Linden. Ancestral Lines: Culture & Identity in the Work of Six Contemporary Poets. 175p. 1993. 35.00 (1-85411-061-6, Pub. by Seren Bks UK) Dufour.
— British Influence on the Birth of American Literature. LC 81-18429. 1982. text ed. 29.95 (0-312-10309-3) St Martin.
— Toni Morrison. LC 94-46867. (Modern Novelists Ser.). 1995. write for info. (0-312-12595-X) St Martin.

P Q

Peach, Lucinda J. Women at War: The Ethics of Women in Combat. Cuffel, Victoria J., ed. LC 93-655022. (MacArthur Scholar Series, Occasional Paper: No. 20). 133p. (Orig.). 1993. pap. 4.50 (*1-881157-23-7*) In Ctr Global.

Peach, Robert, ed. The IOS Nine Thousand Handbook. 496p. 1992. pap. 85.00 (*1-883337-27-5*) Ctr Energy Envir.

Peach, S. Running Skills. (Superskills Ser.). (Illus.). 48p. (YA). (gr. 6-10). 1988. pap. 5.95 (*0-7460-0165-7*) EDC.

Peach, S. & Butterfield, M. Photography. (Practical Guides Ser.). (Illus.). 48p. (J). (gr. 6 up). 1987. lib. bdg. 14.96 (*0-88110-292-X*); pap. 7.95 (*0-7460-0107-X*) EDC.

Peach, S., jt. auth. see Millard, A.

Peach, Terry. Interpreting Ricardo. 336p. (C). 1993. 59.95 (*0-521-26086-8*) Cambridge U Pr.

Peach, W. Bernard, ed. The Correspondence of Richard Price, Vol. III: February 1786 - February 1791. LC 82-14646. 376p. 1994. text ed. 49.95 (*0-8223-1327-8*) Duke.

— Richard Price & the Ethical Foundations of the American Revolution. LC 77-91081. 1979. 37.50 (*0-8223-0400-7*) Duke.

Peach, W. Bernard, jt. ed. see Thomas, D. O.

Peach, William. The Security Affiliates of National Banks. LC 78-64180. (Johns Hopkins University. Studies in the Social Sciences. Thirtieth Ser. 1912: 3). 192p. 1983. reprint ed. 34.50 (*0-404-61288-1*) AMS Pr.

Peach, William N. Security Affiliates of National Bank. LC 75-2660. (Wall Street & the Security Market Ser.). 1975. reprint ed. 19.95 (*0-405-06984-7*) Ayer.

***Peach, William S.** The South Side of Boston. (Illus.). 128p. (Orig.). 1995. pap. 9.95 (*1-881576-42-6*) Providence Hse.

Peacham, Henry. The Art of Drawing with the Pen, & Limning with Water Colours. LC 71-25631. (English Experience Ser.: No. 230). 70p. 1970. reprint ed. 35.00 (*90-221-0230-0*) Walter J Johnson.

— The Garden of Eloquence. LC 54-11900. 1977. reprint ed. 50.00 (*0-8201-1225-9*) Schol Facsimiles.

— Minerva Britanna, or a Garden of Heroical Devises. LC 73-171783. (English Experience Ser.: No. 407). 232p. 1971. reprint ed. 45.00 (*90-221-0407-9*) Walter J Johnson.

— A Most True Relation of the Affairs of Cleve & Gulick, with the Articles of Peace Propounded at Santen. LC 72-6024. (English Experience Ser.: No. 549). (Illus.). 44p. 1973. reprint ed. 35.00 (*90-221-0549-0*) Walter J Johnson.

Peache, Robert J. & O'Sullivan, Denis, eds. Current Trends in Protective Packaging of Computers & Electronic Components. LC 88-3289. (Special Technical Publication Ser.: No. 994). 80p. 1988. pap. text ed. 19.00 (*0-8031-1171-1*, 04-994000-11) ASTM.

Peacher, Georgiana. Mary Stuart's Ravishment Descending Time: Prose Symphony. LC 75-35307. 117p. 1992. reprint ed. pap. 6.00 (*0-916384-01-2*) P Shedding.

Peacher, William G., ed. see Chang Chung-Ching.

Peachey, J. Lorne. How to Teach Peace to Children. 32p. (Orig.). 1981. pap. 1.95 (*0-8361-1969-X*) Herald Pr.

Peachey, L. D., ed. see Interdisciplinary Conference Staff.

Peachey, Lee D. & Adrian, Richard H., eds. Handbook of Physiology: Section 10, Skeletal Muscle. (American Physiological Society Book). (Illus.). 700p. 1988. 145.00 (*0-19-520685-1*) OUP.

Peachey, Linda G., jt. auth. see Peachey, Titus.

Peachey, Titus & Peachey, Linda G. Seeking Peace. LC 91-74053. 238p. 1991. pap. 11.95 (*1-56148-049-5*) Good Bks PA.

Peachin, Michael. Roman Imperial Titulature & Chronology, A.D. 235-284. xxviii, 515p. 1990. 147.00 (*90-5063-034-0*, Pub. by Gieben NE) Benjamins North Am.

Peachment, Allan. The Business of Government Western Australia 1983-1990. xvi, 240p. 1991. 36.50 (*1-86287-045-4*, Pub. by Federation Pr AU) W W Gaunt.

***Peachment, Allan, ed.** Westminster Inc. A Survey of Three States in the Eighties. 225p. 1995. pap. 39.00 (*1-86287-164-7*, Pub. by Federation Pr AU) W W Gaunt.

Peachtree Road United Methodist Church Preschool Staff. Flavors & Favors. (Illus.). (Orig.). 1988. 9.50 (*0-9620576-0-6*) Peachtree Rd United Meth Ch.

***Peacock & Martin.** Where Feminists Come From. Date not set. per. 7.95 (*0-920813-75-5*, Pub. by Sister Vision CN) InBook.

Peacock, jt. auth. see Richardson.

Peacock, A., ed. X-Ray Astronomy in the Exosat Era. 1985. lib. bdg. 202.50 (*90-277-2099-1*) Kluwer Ac.

Peacock, Alan. Economic Analysis of Government & Related Theories. LC 79-15836. 1980. text ed. 32.50 (*0-312-22678-0*) St Martin.

***Peacock, Alan, ed.** The Achievement of Brian Friel. 267p. (C). 1994. lib. bdg. 67.50 (*0-86140-349-5*, Pub. by C Smythe Ltd UK) B&N Imports.

— Public Choice Analysis in Historical Perspective. (Raffaele Mattioli Lectures on the History of Economic Thought). (Illus.). 234p. (C). 1992. 44.95 (*0-521-43007-0*) Cambridge U Pr.

Peacock, Alan & Bannock, Graham. Takeovers & the Public Interest: The Hume Report on Corporate Takeovers. (Aberdeen University Press Bks.). 156p. 1991. pap. text ed. 25.90 (*0-08-041206-8*, Pub. by Aberdeen U Pr) Macmillan.

Peacock, Alan & Rizzo, Ilde, eds. Cultural Economics & Cultural Policies. LC 94-15817. 196p. (C). 1994. lib. bdg. 87.00 (*0-7923-2868-X*) Kluwer Ac.

Peacock, Alan & Willgerodt, Hans, eds. German Neo-Liberals & the Social Market Economy. LC 89-4145. 400p. 1989. text ed. 59.95 (*0-312-03132-7*) St Martin.

Peacock, Alan, jt. auth. see Bannock, Graham.

Peacock, Alan, jt. ed. see Clayden, Elizabeth.

Peacock, Alan T., ed. Income Redistribution & Social Policy: A Set of Studies. LC 84-29020. 296p. 1985. reprint ed. text ed. 69.50 (*0-313-23867-7*, PINC, Greenwood Pr) Greenwood.

Peacock, Alan T. & Shaw, G. K. The Economic Theory of Fiscal Policy. 2nd ed. LC 76-366919. 192p. reprint ed. pap. 54.80 (*0-317-20051-8*, 2023271) Bks Demand.

Peacock, Alan T. & Wiseman, Jack. The Growth of Public Expenditure in the United Kingdom. (General Ser.: No. 72). 245p. 1961. reprint ed. 63.70 (*0-87014-071-X*) Natl Bur Econ Res.

Peacock, Alan T., jt. ed. see Musgrave, Richard A.

Peacock, Alan T., et al. The Growth of Public Expenditure in the United Kingdom. (Modern Revivals in Economics Ser.). 215p. (C). 1994. text ed. 61.95 (*0-7512-0256-8*, Pub. by Gregg Revivals UK) Ashgate Pub Co.

Peacock, Basil. A Newcastle Boyhood, 1898-1914. (C). 1985. pap. 35.00 (*0-685-37706-7*, Pub. by Sutton Libs & Arts) St Mut.

Peacock, Bonnie. Sylvania: Majestic Forests & Deep, Clear Waters. LC 87-401098. 60p. 1986. 9.95 (*0-9620008-0-9*) Peacock MI.

Peacock, Brian & Karwowski, Waldemar, eds. Automotive Ergonomics. LC 92-32799. 300p. 1993. 99.00 (*0-7484-0005-2*, Pub. by Tay Francis Ltd UK) Taylor & Francis.

Peacock, Christopher M. Rosario Yesterdays. LC 85-51170. (Illus.). 72p. (Orig.). 1985. pap. 9.98 (*0-9614970-0-9*) Rosario Prod.

Peacock, Colin. Classroom Skills in English Teaching: A Self-Appraisal Framework. 256p. 1990. 59.50 (*0-415-03633-X*, A4137); pap. 17.95 (*0-415-03634-8*, A4141) Routledge.

— Teaching Writing: A Systematic Approach. 160p. (Orig.). 1986. pap. 19.95 (*0-7099-4028-9*, Pub. by Croom Helm UK) Routledge Chapman & Hall.

Peacock, D. G., jt. ed. see Brydson, J. A.

Peacock, D. Keith. Radical Stages: Alternative History in Modern British Drama. LC 91-17119. (Contributions in Drama & Theatre Studies: No. 43). 208p. 1991. text ed. 55.00 (*0-313-27888-1*, PRP, Greenwood Pr) Greenwood.

Peacock, D. P. & Williams, D. F. Amphorae & Roman Economy. (Archaeology Ser.). 304p. 1986. text ed. 53.95 (*0-582-49304-8*) Longman.

Peacock, Daniel J. Lee Boo of Belau: A Prince in London. LC 86-27258. (South Sea Bks.). (Illus.). 272p. 1987. text ed. 18.50 (*0-8248-1086-4*) UH Pr.

Peacock, Derek, jt. auth. see Tribe, Michael A.

Peacock, Don. The Emperor's Guest: A British POW of the Japanese in Indonesia. (Illus.). 220p. 1989. 35.00 (*0-906672-55-4*) Oleander Pr.

Peacock, Doug. Grizzly Years. (Illus.). 384p. 1992. reprint ed. mass mkt. 4.99 (*0-8217-3952-2*) Zebra.

— The Grizzly Years: Encounters with the Wilderness. 320p. 1990. 24.95 (*0-8050-0448-3*) H Holt & Co.

Peacock, Earle E. Wound Repair. 3rd ed. (Illus.). 544p. 1984. text ed. 145.00 (*0-7216-7145-4*) Saunders.

Peacock, Edward. A Glossary of Words Used in the Wapentakes of Manley & Corringham, Lincolnshire. (English Dialect Society Publications Ser.: No. 15). 1969. reprint ed. pap. 31.00 (*0-8115-0447-6*) Periodicals Srv.

Peacock, Frederick & Gaston, Thomas E. Automotive Engine Repair & Overhaul. (Illus.). 480p. 1980. teacher ed write for info. (*0-318-55515-8*, Reston); text ed. 40.00 (*0-8359-0276-5*, Reston) P-H.

Peacock, George. Notes on the Isthmus of Panama & Darien, Also on the River San Juan, Lakes of Nicaragua, Etc.... (Illus.). vii, 96p. 1988. reprint ed. pap. 9.00 (*0-913129-20-8*) La Tienda.

Peacock, Graham. Forces. (Science Activities Ser.). (Illus.). 32p. (J). (gr. 2-4). 1994. 14.95 (*1-56847-192-0*) Thomson Lrning.

— Heat. LC 93-34613. (Science Activities Ser.). (Illus.). 32p. (J). (gr. 2-4). 1994. 14.95 (*1-56847-075-4*) Thomson Lrning.

— The History of Electricity. LC 93-3347. (Resources Ser.). 32p. (J). (gr. 3-6). 1993. 13.95 (*1-56847-048-7*) Thomson Lrning.

— The History of Electricity. LC 93-33258. (Science Activities Ser.). (Illus.). 32p. (J). (gr. 2-4). 1994. 14.95 (*1-56847-078-9*) Thomson Lrning.

— Light. LC 93-7522. (Science Activities Ser.). (Illus.). 32p. (J). (gr. 2-4). 1993. 14.95 (*1-56847-073-8*) Thomson Lrning.

— Materials. LC 93-51024. (Science Activities Ser.). (Illus.). 32p. (J). (gr. 2-4). 1994. 14.95 (*1-56847-076-2*) Thomson Lrning.

— Meteorology. (Science Activities Ser.). (Illus.). 32p. (J). (gr. 2-4). 1995. 14.95 (*1-56847-194-7*) Thomson Lrning.

— Sound. LC 93-7521. (Science Activities Ser.). (Illus.). (J). (gr. 2-4). 1993. 14.95 (*1-56847-074-6*) Thomson Lrning.

— Water. LC 93-49799. (Science Activities Ser.). (Illus.). 32p. (J). (gr. 2-4). 1994. 14.95 (*1-56847-077-0*) Thomson Lrning.

Peacock, Graham & Ashton, Dennis. Astronomy. (Science Activities Ser.). (Illus.). 32p. (J). (gr. 2-4). 1994. 14.95 (*1-56847-191-2*) Thomson Lrning.

Peacock, Graham & Chambers, Cally. The Super Science Book of Materials. LC 93-30779. (Super Science Ser.). (Illus.). 32p. (J). (gr. 4-8). 1993. 14.95 (*1-56847-096-7*) Thomson Lrning.

Peacock, Graham & Hudson, Terry. Exploring Habitats. LC 92-29907. (Exploring Science Ser.). (Illus.). 48p. (J). (gr. 4-8). 1992. lib. bdg. 22.80 (*0-8114-2608-4*) Raintree Steck-V.

— The Super Science Book of Our Bodies. LC 93-7519. (Super Science Ser.). (Illus.). 32p. (J). (gr. 4-8). 1993. 14.95 (*1-56847-023-1*) Thomson Lrning.

***Peacock, Graham & Jesson, Jill.** Geology. (Science Activities Ser.). (Illus.). 32p. (J). (gr. 2-4). 1995. 14.95 (*1-56847-193-9*) Thomson Lrning.

Peacock, Graham & Smith, Robin. Pulley Activities. rev. ed. Doyle, Connie, ed. (Design & Make Ser.). (Illus.). 29p. (J). (gr. 3-6). reprint ed. 9.95 (*1-884461-08-5*) NES Arnold.

Peacock, Graham, jt. auth. see Hudson, Terry.

Peacock, Heber F. A Translator's Guide to Selected Psalms. LC 81-176690. (Helps for Translators Ser.). viii, 154p. 1981. 12.00 (*0-8267-0299-6*, 102763) Untd Bible Soc.

— A Translator's Guide to Selections from the First Five Books of the Old Testament. LC 82-130980. (Helps for Translators Ser.). viii, 323p. 1982. 14.00 (*0-8267-0298-8*, 102764) Untd Bible Soc.

***Peacock, Henry W.** Art As Expression. (Illus.). 256p. (Orig.). 1995. pap. 24.95 (*0-929590-14-7*) Whalesback Bks.

Peacock, Howard. Nature Lover's Guide to the Big Thicket. LC 93-38508. (W. L. Moody, Jr. Natural History Ser.: No. 15). (Illus.). 160p. 1994. 29.50 (*0-89096-589-7*); pap. 12.95 (*0-89096-596-X*) Tex A&M Univ Pr.

Peacock, Howard, ed. The Nature of Texas: A Feast of Native Beauty from Texas Highways Magazine. LC 89-20277. (Louise Lindsey Merrick Texas Environement Ser.: No. 11). (Illus.). 144p. 1990. 24.95 (*0-89096-402-5*) Tex A&M Univ Pr.

Peacock, Ian. Airbrushing & Spray Painting Manual. (Illus.). 175p. 1983. pap. 20.95 (*0-85242-802-2*, Pub. by Argus Pubs UK) Motorbooks Intl.

— Introduction to Electric Flight. (Illus.). 144p. (Orig.). 1988. pap. 16.95 (*0-85242-910-X*, Pub. by Argus Pubs UK) Motorbooks Intl.

Peacock, J. A., et al, eds. Physics of the Early Universe: Proceedings of the Thirty Sixth Scottish Universities Summer School in Physics, Edinburgh, July 24-August 11, 1989. (Scottish Universities Summer School in Physics, a NATO Advanced Study Institute Ser.: No. 36). (Illus.). 502p. 1990. 126.00 (*0-905945-19-0*) IOP Pub.

Peacock, James. Purifying the Faith: The Muhammadijah Movement in Indonesian Islam. (Illus.). vii, 109p. 1992. reprint ed. pap. 12.95 (*1-881044-01-7*) ASU Prog SE Asian.

— Rites of Modernization: Symbols & Social Aspects of Indonesian Proletarian Drama. LC 68-15931. (Symbolic Anthropology Ser.). (Illus.). xxvi, 318p. (C). 1987. pap. text ed. 15.95 (*0-226-65131-2*) U Ch Pr.

Peacock, James L. The Anthropological Lens: Harsh Light, Soft Focus. 144p. 1987. 34.95 (*0-521-33160-9*); pap. 12.95 (*0-521-33748-8*) Cambridge U Pr.

Peacock, James L. & Sabella, James C., eds. Sea & Land: Cultural & Biological Adaptations in the Southern Coastal Plain. LC 87-13284. (Southern Anthropological Society Proceedings Ser.: No. 21). 176p. 1988. pap. 10.00 (*0-8203-0978-8*) U of Ga Pr.

Peacock, James L. & Tyson, Ruel W., Jr. Pilgrims of Paradox: Calvinism & Experience among the Primitive Baptists of the Blue Ridge. LC 89-5853. 290p. 1989. 32.50 (*0-87474-924-7*); pap. 14.95 (*0-87474-923-9*) Smithsonian.

Peacock, Jimmy, ed. see Crist, Terry M., Jr.

Peacock, Jimmy, ed. see Crist, Terry.

Peacock, Jimmy, ed. see Hamilton, Margaret W. & Stone, Sophie I.

Peacock, Jimmy, ed. see Speer, Bonnie.

Peacock, John. Book Production. (Illus.). 512p. 1991. 67.95 (*0-948905-33-6*) Chapman & Hall.

— Chronicle of Western Fashion: From Ancient Times to the Present Day. (Illus.). 224p. 1991. 29.95 (*0-8109-3953-3*) Abrams.

— Costume, 1066-1990s. LC 94-60271. (Illus.). 136p. 1994. pap. 16.95 (*0-500-27791-5*) Thames Hudson.

— Multilingual Dictionary of Printing & Publishing Terms. 242p. (DUT, ENG, FRE, GER, ITA, SPA & SWE.). 1992. 225.00 (*0-8288-7928-1*, 221200808905352) Fr & Eur.

— The Stage Designs of Inigo Jones: The European Context. (Illus.). 400p. (C). 1991. write for info. (*0-521-41812-7*) Cambridge U Pr.

— Twentieth Century Fashion. LC 93-60138. (Illus.). 240p. 1993. 29.95 (*0-500-01564-3*) Thames Hudson.

Peacock, John, ed. Multilingual Dictionary of Print & & Publishing Terms. 192p. (DUT, ENG, FRE, GER, ITA, SPA & SWE.). 1991. 99.95 (*0-948905-35-2*) Chapman & Hall.

***Peacock, Judith.** Hans Christian Andersen. (Profiles Ser.). (YA). (gr. 6 up). 1995. 18.95 (*0-88682-742-6*) Creative Ed.

Peacock, Judith, jt. auth. see Wheeler, Leslie.

Peacock, Larry J. Heart & Soul: A Guide for Spiritual Formation in the Local Church. 64p. (Orig.). 1992. pap. 5.00 (*0-8358-0682-0*) Upper Room Bks.

***Peacock, Larry J., et al.** Source Book of Worship Resources. Purdum, Stan, ed. 232p. 1994. pap. 39.95 (*0-930921-05-4*) Comm Res OH.

Peacock-LeJeune, Harriet. Postscripts for Thinking Flutists: Self-Help Techniques for Individualized Optimum Beauty of Sound. 1993. 12.95 (*0-533-10521-8*) Vantage.

Peacock, Linda & Johnson, Willa. Pathways to Teaching: A Laboratory Manual for Beginning Teachers. 176p. (C). 1994. spiral bd. 17.56 (*0-8403-9413-6*) Kendall-Hunt.

Peacock, Lindsay. Pilots. Stefoff, Rebecca, ed. LC 91-39097. (Living Dangerously Ser.). (Illus.). 32p. (J). (gr. 5-9). 1992. lib. bdg. 17.26 (*1-56074-040-X*) Garrett Ed Corp.

— Strike Aces. (Illus.). 160p. 1989. 14.99 (*0-517-68847-6*) Random Hse Value.

— World's Airforces. 1991. 14.99 (*0-517-05242-3*) Random Hse Value.

Peacock, Lindsay, jt. auth. see Debay, Yves.

Peacock, Mabel, jt. ed. see Gutch, E.

Peacock, Mary, jt. auth. see Village Voice Editors.

Peacock, Mary R. Silversmiths of North Carolina,1696-1860. rev. ed. (Illus.). xxix, 301p. 1984. pap. 12.00 (*0-86526-215-2*) NC Archives.

— Silversmiths of North Carolina,1696-1860. rev. ed. (Illus.). xxix, 301p. 1984. 20.00 (*0-86526-201-2*) NC Archives.

Peacock, Mary R., jt. auth. see Walser, Richard.

***Peacock, Molly.** Animals at the Table. limited ed. Wheatcroft, John, ed. (Bucknell University Fine Editions). (Illus.). 60p. 1995. write for info. (*0-916375-20-X*) Press Alley.

— Original Love. 72p. 1995. 17.95 (*0-393-03741-X*) Norton.

— Take Heart. 1989. pap. 12.00 (*0-679-72196-7*) McKay.

Peacock, N. A., jt. auth. see Moles, E.

Peacock, Noel. L' Ecole des Femmes: Critical Monographs in English. 80p. 1993. pap. 32.00 (*0-85261-245-1*, Pub. by Univ of Glasgow UK) St Mut.

Peacock, P. The Great War in German Lyrical Poetry. 1972. 59.95 (*0-8490-0262-1*) Gordon Pr.

Peacock, Primrose. Discovering Old Buttons. 1989. pap. 25.00 (*0-85263-445-5*, Pub. by Shire UK) St Mut.

Peacock, Raymond L. Nightmare Abbey-Crotchet Castle. 1982. pap. 9.95 (*0-14-043045-8*, Penguin Classics) Viking Penguin.

Peacock, Reginald. The Repressor of Overmuch Blaming of the Clergy, by Sometime Bishop of Chichester, 2 vols. Babington, Churchill, ed. (Rolls Ser.: No. 19). 1974. reprint ed. 90.00 (*0-8115-1025-5*) Periodicals Srv.

Peacock, Richard, jt. auth. see Triere, Lynette.

Peacock, Richard D., et al. Data for Room Fire Model Comparisons. (Illus.). 52p. (Orig.). (C). 1993. pap. text ed. 40.00 (*0-7881-0058-0*) Diane Pub.

Peacock, Ronald. The Art of Drama. LC 73-3026. 263p. 1974. reprint ed. text ed. 35.00 (*0-8371-6825-2*, PEAD, Greenwood Pr) Greenwood.

— The Poet in the Theatre. LC 86-22749. 211p. 1986. reprint ed. text ed. 55.00 (*0-313-25220-3*, PPOE, Greenwood Pr) Greenwood.

Peacock, S. M., jt. ed. see Spear, F. S.

Peacock, Sandra J. Jane Ellen Harrison: The Mask & the Self. LC 88-109. (C). 1988. text ed. 35.00 (*0-300-04128-4*) Yale U Pr.

Peacock, Susan J., jt. auth. see Hughes, Roger T.

Peacock, T. & Linnett, J. Electronic Structure of Organic Molecules. LC 72-75315. (International Encyclopedia of Physical Chemistry & Chemical Physics Ser.). 1972. 71.00 (*0-08-016871-X*, Pub. by Pergamon Repr UK) Franklin.

Peacock, Thomas L. Headlong Hall & Gryll Grange. Baron, Michael & Slater, Michael, eds. (World's Classics Ser.). 480p. 1987. pap. 5.95 (*0-19-281693-4*) OUP.

— Nightmare Abbey. 236p. 1992. reprint ed. 48.00 (*0-685-68189-0*, Pub. by Woodstock Bks UK) Cassell.

— Peacock's Memoir of Shelley, with Shelley's Letters to Peacock. (BCL1-PR English Literature Ser.). 219p. 1992. reprint ed. lib. bdg. 79.00 (*0-7812-7655-1*) Rprt Serv.

— Works, 10 vols. (BCL1-PR English Literature Ser.). 1992. reprint ed. Set. lib. bdg. 900.00 (*0-7812-7616-0*) Rprt Serv.

— Works, 10 vols, Set. Brett-Smith, H. B. & Jones, C. E., eds. LC 71-181967. reprint ed. 835.00 (*0-404-04970-2*) AMS Pr.

Peacock, Valerie S. A Family Heritage Workbook. 2nd ed. 94p. (Orig.). 1982. reprint ed. 9.95 (*0-939909-00-6*) Scribe Write.

Peacock, Virginia A. Problems in the Interpretation of Jonathan Edwards' The Nature of True Virtue. LC 90-35441. (Studies in American Religion: Vol. 47). 252p. 1991. lib. bdg. 89.95 (*0-88946-643-2*) E Mellen.

Peacock, Virginia T. Famous American Belles of the Nineteenth Century. LC 73-128284. (Essay Index Reprint Ser.). 1977. 23.95 (*0-8369-1893-2*) Ayer.

Peacock, W. J., jt. ed. see Evans, L. T.

Peacock, Walter G., jt. auth. see Bates, Frederick L.

Peacock, William. English Prose, 5 vols., Set. (BCL1-PR English Literature Ser.). 1992. reprint ed. lib. bdg. 375.00 (*0-7812-7153-3*) Rprt Serv.

Peacocke, Alfred. God & the New Biology. 1994. 27.50 (*0-8446-6776-5*) Peter Smith.

Peacocke, Arthur. Intimations of Reality: Critical Realism in Science & Religion. LC 84-40357. (Mendenhall Lectures). 96p. (C). 1984. pap. text ed. 5.95 (*0-268-01156-7*) U of Notre Dame Pr.

— Theology for a Scientific Age: Being & Becoming - Natural, Divine, & Human. LC 93-30674. (Theology & the Sciences Ser.). 1993. 21.00 (*0-8006-2759-8*, Fortress Pr) Augsburg Fortress.

Peacocke, Arthur, ed. Reductionism in Academic Disciplines. 1985. 46.00 (*1-85059-006-0*) Taylor & Francis.

Peacocke, Arthur, jt. ed. see Andersen, Svend.

Peacocke, Christopher. A Study of Concepts. (Bradford Representation & Mind Ser.). (Illus.). 260p. 1992. 35.00 (*0-262-16133-8*) MIT Pr.

— A Study of Concepts. (Representation & Mind Ser.). (Illus.). 288p. 1995. reprint ed. pap. 15.00x (*0-262-66097-0*, Bradford Bks) MIT Pr.

Peacocke, Christopher, ed. Objectivity, Simulation & the Unity of Consciousness: Current Issues in the Philosophy of Mind. (Proceedings of the British Academy Ser.: Vol. 83). (Illus.). 220p. 1994. 24.00 (*0-19-726142-6*) OUP.

— Understanding & Sense, Set, Vols. I & II. (International Research Library of Philosophy). 872p. 1993. Set. 229.95 (*1-85521-292-7*, Pub. by Dartmth Pub UK) Ashgate Pub Co.

Peacocke, Helen, jt. auth. see Harris, Mollie.

An Asterisk (*) at the beginning of an entry indicates that the title is appearing in BIP for the first time.

Peacocke, T. Atomic & Nuclear Chemistry: Atomic Theory & the Structure of the Atom, Vol. 1. 1967. 70.00 (*0-08-012524-7*, Pub. by Pergamon Repr UK); pap. 72.00 (*0-08-012525-5*, Pub. by Pergamon Repr UK) Franklin.

Peacocke, T. A. Radiochemistry: Theory & Experiment. (Wykeham Science Ser.: No. 50). 274p. 1978. pap. 18.00 (*0-85109-690-5*) Taylor & Francis.

— Radiochemistry: Theory & Experiment. LC 78-57666. (Wykeham Science Ser.: No. 50). 274p. (C). 1979. pap. 18.00 (*0-8448-1360-5*, Crane Russak) Taylor & Francis.

Peadbody, Susan. Addiction to Love. 1994. pap. 9.95 (*0-89087-715-7*) Celestial Arts.

Peaden, Joyce B. Irish Chain Quilts. 1988. pap. 14.95 (*0-89145-936-7*) Collector Bks.

***Peak.** Justice Administration: Police, Courts & Correction Management. (Illus.). 512p. (C). 1994. text ed. 55.00 (*0-13-189986-4*) P-H.

***Peak, Caroline.** A Perfect Surprise. (Special Edition Ser.). 1995. pap. 3.75 (*0-373-09960-6*, 1-09960-5) Silhouette.

Peak, D. W. Developments in the Air Cargo Industry. 98p. (C). 1981. 190.00 (*0-906297-17-6*, Pub. by ICHCA UK) St Mut.

Peak, David & Frame, Michael. Chaos under Control: The Art & Science of Complexity. LC 94-3092. (C). 1995. pap. text ed. 24.95 (*0-7167-2429-4*) W H Freeman.

Peak, Elizabeth. Prints & Drawings. (Illus.). 1982. pap. 5.00 (*0-916606-04-X*) Bowdoin Coll.

Peak, Helen.

Peak, I., jt. auth. see Gecseg, F.

Peak, I., jt. auth. see Gecseq, F.

Peak, Jan & Hennig, Anna. Trash to Treasure Crafts: From Recyclable Materials. (Illus.). 80p. (J). (gr. 3 up). 1992. student ed 8.99 (*0-87403-890-1*, 14-02146) Standard Pub.

Peak, John. Manager's Primer to Employee Rights. 1993. pap. 14.95 (*0-9635289-4-7*) Williams OR.

Peak, John A. Spare Change. 1994. 24.95 (*0-312-11071-5*, Pub. by Thomas Dunne Bks) St Martin.

Peak, Ken. Policing America: Methods, Issues, & Challenges. LC 92-24248. 496p. 1993. text ed. 61.00 (*0-13-726910-2*) P-H.

***Peak, Kenneth J. & Glensor, Ronald W.** Community Policing & Problem Solving: Strategies & Practices. LC 95-10498. 1996. write for info. (*0-13-294687-4*) PH School.

Peak, Kenneth J., jt. auth. see O'Brien, Patrick G.

Peak, Lois. Learning to Go to School in Japan: The Transition from Home to Preschool Life. LC 91-13628. (Illus.). 224p. 1991. 32.00 (*0-520-07151-4*); pap. 13.00 (*0-520-08387-3*) U CA Pr.

Peak Performance Associates Staff. Building Community Support for Schools. 168p. (C). 1994. 49.95 (*0-8403-9289-3*) Kendall-Hunt.

Peak, Robin, jt. ed. see Lucock, John.

Peak, Steve. Troops in Strikes. (C). 1988. 59.00 (*0-900137-22-3*, Pub. by NCCL UK) St Mut.

Peak, William, ed. Guidelines for Radio Promotion: Best of the Best II. (Illus.). 60p. (Orig.). 1991. 30.00 (*0-89324-156-3*) Natl Assn Broadcasters.

Peakall, D. B. Animal Biomarkers As Pollution Indicators. (Ecotoxicology Ser.: No. 1). (Illus.). 336p. (C). 1992. text ed. 77.50 (*0-412-40200-9*, A6762) Chapman & Hall.

Peakall, David B. & Shugart, Lee R., eds. Research & Application in the Assessment of Environmental Health. LC 92-38833. (NATO ASI Series H: Cell Biology: Vol. 68). 1993. 98.00 (*0-387-54612-X*) Spr-Verlag.

Peake. The Dream on the Hill. large type ed. 1991. 17.95 (*0-7451-8064-7*, AH099, Atlantic Lrg Print) Chivers N Amer.

Peake, A. S., et al. Germany in the Nineteenth Century. LC 67-30189. (Manchester University Publications Historical Series No. 13, Essay Index Reprint Ser.: No. 24). 1977. 18.95 (*0-8369-0472-9*) Ayer.

Peake, C. H. James Joyce: The Citizen & the Artist. LC 76-47985. xii, 369p. 1977. reprint ed. 47.50 (*0-8047-0914-9*); reprint ed. pap. 16.95 (*0-8047-1014-7*) Stanford U Pr.

Peake, Charles. Jonathan Swift & the Art of Raillery. (Princess Grace Irish Library Lecture Ser.: Vol. 3). 32p. (Orig.). 1987. pap. 8.95 (*0-86140-264-2*, Pub. by Colin Smythe Ltd UK) Dufour.

Peake, Cyrus H. Nationalism & Education in Modern China. LC 72-80580. 1970. reprint ed. 35.00 (*0-86527-138-0*) Fertig.

Peake, Donald. The Power of Super Thinking. Templar, Thorguard, ed. (Illus.). 105p. 1994. 25.00 (*1-57179-001-2*) Intern Guild ASRS.

Peake, Elaine, jt. auth. see Kwasny, Barbara.

***Peake, Felicity.** Pure Chance. 1994. 31.95 (*1-85310-367-5*, Pub. by Airlife Pub Ltd UK) Voyageur Pr.

Peake, Frank A. The Riddle of the Ages. 80p. 1975. reprint ed. spiral bd. 5.50 (*0-7873-0660-6*) Mokelumne.

Peake, Harold J. The English Village, the Origin & Decay of Its Community: An Anthropological Interpretation. LC 76-44774. reprint ed. 37.50 (*0-404-15876-5*) AMS Pr.

— The Origins of Agriculture. LC 76-44776. reprint ed. 27.50 (*0-404-15960-5*) AMS Pr.

Peake, Harold J. & Fleure, Herbert J. The Corridors of Time: New Haven & London, 1927-1956, 10 vols., Set. Incl. Vol. 1. Apes & Men. (*0-404-18251-8*); Vol. 2. Hunters & Artists. (*0-404-18252-6*); Vol. 3. Peasants & Potters. (*0-404-18253-4*); Vol. 4. Priests & Kings. (*0-404-18254-2*); Vol. 5. Steepe & the Sown. (*0-404-18255-0*); Vol. 6. Way of the Sea. (*0-404-18256-9*); Vol. 7. Merchant Venturers in Bronze. (*0-404-18257-7*); Vol. 8. Horse & the Sword. (*0-404-18258-5*); Vol. 9. Law & the Prophets. (*0-404-18259-3*); Vol. 10. Times & Places. (*0-404-18260-7*); write for info. (*0-404-18250-X*) AMS Pr.

***Peake, Hayden B.** The Admission of Guilt, Restraining Orders, Opposition to Release, & In-Court Statements of CIA Officer Aldrich Hazen Ames. Bancroft, Elizabeth, ed. (Nightmover Case Ser.: Vol. 3). 1994. 24.95 (*1-878292-13-7*) Natl Intel Bk Ctr.

— A Reader's Guide to Intelligence Periodicals. 2nd ed. Bancroft, Elizabeth, ed. (Illus.). 250p. (Orig.). (C). 1992. pap. text ed. 19.95 (*1-878292-00-5*) Natl Intel Bk Ctr.

Peake, Howard, jt. auth. see Overstreet, Robert M.

Peake, Jacquelyn. Every Woman's Guide on...How to Fix Things! (Illus.). 194p. (Orig.). 1984. pap. 7.95 (*0-9613830-0-3*) J Peake Assocs.

— How to Recognize & Refinish Antiques for Pleasure & Profit. 3rd ed. LC 94-38948. (Illus.). 256p. 1995. pap. 12.95 (*1-56440-506-0*) Globe Pequot.

— Publish Your Own Book (& Pocket the Profits!) (Illus.). 96p. (Orig.). 1985. pap. 4.95 (*0-9613830-1-1*) J Peake Assocs.

Peake, Jacquelyn & Petersen, Carol A. Complete Audio-Visual Guide for Teachers & Media Specialists. 224p. 1989. text ed. 27.95 (*0-13-155441-7*) P-H.

Peake-Jones, Kenneth. The Branch Without a Tree: The Centenary History of the Royal Geographical Society of Australasia (South Australian Br.) Inc. 1885-1985. deluxe ed. 208p. (C). 1985. 125.00 (*0-7855-0329-3*, Pub. by Royal Geograp Soc AT) St Mut.

Peake, Lilian. The Dream on the Hill. large type ed. 1991. pap. 15.95 (*0-7927-0522-X*, AS0135, Atlantic Lrg Print) Chivers N Amer.

— Gold Ring of Revenge. (Presents Ser.). 1993. mass mkt. 2.99 (*0-373-11580-6*, 1-11580-7) Harlequin Bks.

— Gold Ring of Revenge. large type ed. 1992. reprint ed. lib. bdg. 18.95 (*0-263-13100-9*, Pub. by Mills & Boon UK) Thorndike Pr.

— Irresistible Enemy. large type ed. 1991. reprint ed. lib. bdg. 18.95 (*0-263-12680-3*) Thorndike Pr.

— Love in Moonlight. large type ed. LC 94-28431. 1994. 18.95 (*0-7927-2130-6*) Chivers N Amer.

— No Promise of Love. 1994. mass mkt. 2.99 (*0-373-11700-0*, 1-11700-1) Harlequin Bks.

— Stranger Passing By. (Presents Ser.). 1994. mass mkt. 2.99 (*0-373-11629-2*, 1-11629-2) Harlequin Bks.

— Undercover Affair. (Presents Ser.). 1993. pap. 2.89 (*0-373-11532-6*, 1-11532-8) Harlequin Bks.

— Undercover Affair. large type ed. (Harlequin Ser.). 1992. reprint ed. lib. bdg. 18.95 (*0-263-12984-5*) Thorndike Pr.

Peake, Linda, jt. ed. see Moser, Caroline.

Peake, Luise E. Conradin Kreutzer's Fruhlingslieder & Wanderlieder. LC 85-754791. 200p. 1990. lib. bdg. 64.00 (*0-918728-58-4*) Pendragon NY.

Peake, Martin. Pacific People & Society. (Pacific in the Twentieth Century Ser.). (Illus.). 80p. (C). 1991. pap. 16.95 (*0-521-37628-9*) Cambridge U Pr.

Peake, Mervyn. A Book of Nonsense. LC 75-4108. 1975. 10.95 (*0-7206-0412-5*) Dufour.

— The Gormenghast Novels: Titus Groan, Gormenghast, Titus Alone. 1168p. (J). 1995. pap. 19.95 (*0-87951-628-3*) Overlook Pr.

— The Gormenghast Trilogy, 3 bks. in 1. LC 85-7909. 1032p. 1988. 35.00 (*0-87951-974-6*) Overlook Pr.

— The Gormenghast Trilogy, Vol. I: Titus Groan. LC 81-18909. (Illus.). 512p. 1982. 25.00 (*0-87951-143-5*) Overlook Pr.

— The Gormenghast Trilogy, Vol. I: Titus Groan. (Illus.). 408p. 1991. pap. 13.95 (*0-87951-425-6*) Overlook Pr.

— The Gormenghast Trilogy, Vol. II: Gormenghast. (Illus.). 264p. 1982. pap. 13.95 (*0-87951-426-4*) Overlook Pr.

— The Gormenghast Trilogy, Vol. II: Gormenghast. LC 81-18902. (Illus.). 524p. 1982. 25.00 (*0-87951-144-3*) Overlook Pr.

— The Gormenghast Trilogy, Vol. III: Titus Alone. LC 81-18908. (Illus.). 264p. 1982. 25.00 (*0-87951-145-1*) Overlook Pr.

— The Gormenghast Trilogy, Vol. III: Titus Alone. (Illus.). 262p. 1991. pap. 10.95 (*0-87951-427-2*) Overlook Pr.

— Mr. Pye. LC 83-19497. (Illus.). 288p. 1984. 15.95 (*0-87951-955-X*) Overlook Pr.

— Peake's Progress: Selected Writings & Drawings of Mervyn Peake. Gilmore, Maeve, ed. LC 80-83054. (Illus.). 592p. 1981. 37.50 (*0-87951-121-4*) Overlook Pr.

— Rhyme of the Flying Bomb. (Illus.). 43p. 1973. 10.95 (*0-317-61324-3*, Pub. by Colin Smythe Ltd UK) Dufour.

— Rhyme of the Flying Bomb. 1973. 12.95 (*0-900675-93-4*) Dufour.

Peake, Michael A. & Blachly, Linda. Nothing Short of a Miracle: A Chronicle of a Head Injury Survivor. LC 93-72608. 126p. 1993. pap. 8.00 (*0-9638254-0-2*) Andrew Pubns.

***Peake, R. J.** Cotton: Raw Material to Finished Product. (Illus.). 135p. 1994. pap. 20.00 (*0-87556-797-5*) Saifer.

Peake, Richard B. Memoirs of the Colman Family, 2 vols., 1. LC 68-20242. 1972. reprint ed. 30.95 (*0-405-08843-4*, Pub. by Blom Pubns UK) Ayer.

— Memoirs of the Colman Family, 2 vols., 2. LC 68-20242. 1972. reprint ed. 30.95 (*0-405-08844-2*, Pub. by Blom Pubns UK) Ayer.

— Memoirs of the Colman Family, 2 vols., Set. LC 68-20242. 1972. reprint ed. 60.95 (*0-405-08842-6*, Pub. by Blom Pubns UK) Ayer.

Peake, Stephen. Transport in Transition: Lessons from the History of Energy Policy. 144p. (C). 1994. pap. 19.95 (*1-85383-209-X*) Brookings.

Peake, Thomas H. & Ball, John D. Psychotherapy Training: Contextual & Developmental Influences in Settings, Stages & Mind Sets. (Clinical Supervisor Ser.). (Illus.). 230p. 1991. text ed. 39.95 (*1-56024-133-0*); pap. text ed. 19.95 (*1-56024-134-9*) Haworth Pr.

Peake, Thomas H., et al. Brief Psychotherapies: Changing Frames of Mind. 280p. (C). 1988. text ed. 36.00 (*0-8039-2829-7*) Sage.

Peake, Tom H., et al, eds. Clinical Training in Psychotherapy. LC 84-15873. (Clinical Supervisor Ser.: Vol. 2, No. 4). 129p. 1985. text ed. 39.95 (*0-86656-334-2*); pap. text ed. 19.95 (*0-86656-335-0*) Haworth Pr.

***Peake, Tony.** Seduction: A Book of Stories. 224p. (Orig.). 1995. pap. 11.99 (*1-85242-314-5*) Serpents Tail.

Peaker, A. R. & Grimmeiss, H. G., eds. Low Dimensional Structures in Semiconductors: From Basic Physics to Applications. (NATO ASI Series B, Physics: Vol. 281). (Illus.). 220p. 1992. 69.50 (*0-306-44086-5*, Plenum Pr) Plenum.

Peaker, M. & Linzell, J. L. Salt Glands in Birds & Reptiles. LC 75-314900. (Monographs of the Physiological Society: No. 32). 318p. reprint ed. pap. 90.70 (*0-317-28146-1*, 2022465) Bks Demand.

***Peal.** Access the Internet! 1995. 19.99 (*0-7821-1721-X*) Sybex.

Peal, David. Access the Internet. LC 94-66406. 240p. 1994. pap. 19.99 (*0-7821-1529-2*) Sybex.

— Access the Internet. 1995. 19.99 (*0-7821-1744-9*) Sybex.

PEale. Peale Shrink Set. 1993. 30.00 (*0-06-066461-4*, HarpT) HarpC.

— Un Pensamiento Positivo para Cada Dia. (SPA.). 1995. pap. 9.00 (*0-684-81553-2*, Fireside) S&S Trade.

Peale, Charles W. The Papers of Charles Willson Peale Vol. 2: The Artist as Museum Keeper 1791-1810. Miller, Lillian S., ed. LC 87-10646. 1318p. 1988. text ed. 130.00 (*0-300-03422-9*) Yale U Pr.

— The Selected Papers of Charles Willson Peale & His Family, Vol. 3: The Belfield Farm Years, 1810-1820. Miller, Lillian B. et al, eds. 832p. (C). 1992. text ed. 135.00 (*0-300-04930-7*) Yale U Pr.

— The Selected Papers of Charles Wilson Peale & His Family: Charles Wilson Peale: Artist in Revolutionary America, 1735 to 1791, Vol. 1. Miller, Lillian B. & Hart, Sidney, eds. LC 82-20155. (Illus.). 676p. 1983. text ed. 75.00 (*0-300-02576-9*) Yale U Pr.

Peale, Constance F. Give Us Forever. large type ed. (Romance Ser.). 480p. 1984. 15.95 (*0-7089-1091-2*) Ulverscroft.

Peale, George C., et al. Antiguedad Y Actualidad de Luis Velez de Guevara: Estudios Criticos. xii, 298p. 1983. 71.00x (*90-272-1720-3*) Benjamins North Am.

Peale, John S. Biblical History & the Quest for Maturity. LC 85-5067. (Symposium Ser.: Vol. 15). 120p. 1985. lib. bdg. 59.95 (*0-88946-706-4*) E Mellen.

Peale, N. V. Seis Actitudes Para Vencer (Six Attitudes for Winners) (SPA.). Date not set. 2.49 (*1-56063-001-9*, 498050) Editorial Unilit.

Peale, Norman & Peale, Vincent. My Favorite Hymns: And the Stories Behind Them. LC 94-5585. 160p. 1994. 16.00 (*0-06-066463-0*) Harper SF.

***Peale, Norman V.** Power of Positive Thinking. 3rd ed. 1987. 20.00 (*0-671-76470-5*) S&S Trade.

— This Incredible Century. 352p. Date not set. pap. 5.99 (*0-8423-7093-5*) Tyndale.

— Treasury of Joy & Enthusiasm. 1987. mass mkt. 5.99 (*0-449-21483-4*) Fawcett.

— Why Some Positive Thinkers Get Powerful Results. 224p. 1987. mass mkt. 4.95 (*0-449-21359-5*, Crest) Fawcett.

Peale, Norman Vincent. Amazing Results of Positive Thinking. 1987. mass mkt. 4.95 (*0-449-21519-9*) Fawcett.

— Build a Great Future. 1987. audio 8.95 (*0-943371-00-7*) Positive Comns.

— Enthusiasm Makes the Difference. 1986. mass mkt. 4.95 (*0-449-21159-2*, Crest) Fawcett.

— Get Confident Living. 1985. mass mkt. 4.95 (*0-449-20920-2*) Fawcett.

— Have a Great Day. 1986. mass mkt. 5.99 (*0-449-20917-2*, Crest) Fawcett.

— Inspirational Writings of Norman Vincent Peale. 1989. 12.98 (*0-88486-024-8*) Arrowood Pr.

— Inspirational Writings of Norman Vincent Peale. 1991. 12.98 (*0-88486-051-5*, Inspirational Pr) Arrowood Pr.

— Inspiring Messages for Daily Living. 1981. pap. 2.50 (*0-449-20894-X*, Crest) Fawcett.

— My Christmas Treasury. LC 91-70041. 160p. 1991. 77.70 (*0-06-066514-9*) Harper SF.

— My Favorite Bible Passages. LC 95-3425. 1995. 16.00 (*0-06-066452-5*) Harper SF.

— My Favorite Prayers. LC 92-56113. 1993. 16.00 (*0-06-066674-9*) Harper SF.

— My Favorite Quotations. LC 89-45895. 144p. 1990. 15.00 (*0-06-066483-5*) Harper SF.

— My Favorite Quotations. large type ed. 145p. 1991. reprint ed. bds. 14.95 (*1-56054-237-3*) Thorndike Pr.

— Norman Vincent Peale: Three Complete Volumes. LC 92-19453. 1992. pap. 12.99 (*0-517-08472-4*, Pub. by Wings Bks) Random.

— Positive Imaging. 1985. mass mkt. 4.95 (*0-449-21114-2*) Fawcett.

— Positive Principles Today. 1983. mass mkt. 5.95 (*0-449-20029-9*) Fawcett.

— Positive Thinking Everyday. 1993. pap. 17.00 (*0-671-86591-9*, Fireside) S&S Trade.

— Positive Thinking Everyday: An Inspiration for Each Day of the Year. LC 93-22576. 1993. pap. 9.00 (*0-671-86891-8*, Fireside) S&S Trade.

— The Power of Positive Living. 1992. mass mkt. 5.99 (*0-449-22107-5*, Crest) Fawcett.

— The Power of Positive Living. braille ed. 488p. 1992. vinyl bd. 39.04 (*1-56956-081-1*, BR8765) W A T Braille.

— Power of Positive Thinking. 1987. mass mkt. 5.99 (*0-449-21493-1*, Crest) Fawcett.

— Power of Positive Thinking. 1987. 12.00 (*0-671-63530-1*) S&S Trade.

— The Power of Positive Thinking. large type ed. 552p. 1985. pap. 12.95 (*0-8027-2465-5*) Walker & Co.

— Power of the Plus Factor. 1988. pap. 3.95 (*0-449-21600-4*, Crest) Fawcett.

— Reaching Your Potential. LC 90-19875. 176p. 1994. pap. 4.99 (*0-8007-8618-1*) Revell.

— Sin, Sex & Self-Control. 1981. pap. 2.95 (*0-449-23921-7*, Crest) Fawcett.

— Six Attitudes for Winners. 88p. pap. 2.99 (*0-8423-5906-0*) Tyndale.

— Stay Alive All Your Life. 1984. mass mkt. 4.95 (*0-449-20480-4*) Fawcett.

— Think Like a Winner. large type ed. 120p. 1990. pap. 3.99 (*0-8423-7085-4*) Tyndale.

— This Incredible Century. 1991. 14.99 (*0-8423-4615-5*); pap. 5.99 (*0-685-69223-X*) Tyndale.

— Tough Minded Optimist. 1986. mass mkt. 4.95 (*0-449-21171-1*) Fawcett.

— The True Joy of Positive Living. 288p. 1985. mass mkt. 4.95 (*0-449-20833-8*, Crest) Fawcett.

— True Joy of Positive Living: An Autobiography. large type ed. (Large Print Inspirational Ser.). 1985. pap. 16.95 (*0-8027-2503-1*) Walker & Co.

— Why Some Positive Thinkers Get Powerful Results. large type ed. (Large Print Inspirational Ser.). 1987. pap. 12.95 (*0-8027-2569-4*) Walker & Co.

— Words I Have Lived By. 1993. Gift boxed. boxed 9.50 (*0-8378-5301-X*) Gibson.

— You Can If You Think You Can. 1988. 8.95 (*0-318-32659-0*); audio 11.00 (*0-671-66072-1*) S&S Trade.

Peale, Norman Vincent, ed. My Inspirational Favorites. LC 91-58989. 1992. 15.00 (*0-06-066453-3*) Harper SF.

— Youth Prints. LC 88-16786. 128p. (Orig.). (YA). 1988. pap. 7.99 (*0-8066-2380-2*, 10-7499, Augsburg) Augsburg Fortress.

Peale, Norman Vincent & Blanchard, Kenneth H. The Power of Ethical Management. 160p. 1989. 4.95 (*0-449-21765-5*, Crest) Fawcett.

Peale, Norman Vincent & Kauffman, Donald T. Bible Power for Successful Living: Helping You Solve Your Daily Problems. LC 93-3984. 192p. 1993. 14.99 (*0-8007-1688-4*) Revell.

Peale, Titian R. United States Exploring Expedition During the Years 1838, 1839, 1840, 1841, 1842 under the Command of Charles Wilkes, U.S.N, Vol. 8. Sterling, Keir B., ed. LC 77-81078. (Biologists & Their World Ser.). (Illus.). 1978. reprint ed. lib. bdg. 35.95 (*0-405-10646-7*) Ayer.

Peale, Vincent, jt. auth. see Peale, Norman.

Peale, W. B., ed. see Hinkle, Joseph D. & Law, Donald F.

Peale, W. B., ed. see Hukle, Joseph D. & Law, Donald F.

Peall, Keith, jt. auth. see Bridwell, Jim.

Peapell, P. N. & Belk, J. A. BASIC Materials Studies. LC 84-19983. (Basic Ser.). 160p. (C). 1985. pap. text ed. 24.95 (*0-408-01374-5*) Buttrwrth-Heinemann.

Peaps, E. The Fall of Constantinople. 432p. 1987. 300.00 (*1-85077-176-6*, Darf Pubs Ltd) St Mut.

Pear, Joseph, jt. auth. see Martin, Garry L.

Pearc, Frank. Falmouth to Helford. (C). 1989. 40.00 (*1-85022-007-7*, Pub. by Dyllansow Truran UK) St Mut.

***Pearce.** Holistic Approach to Cancer. 1995. pap. 9.95 (*0-85207-211-2*) Atrium Pubs.

— Magical Child - Magical Adult. 1995. 16.95 (*1-879323-24-9*) Sound Horizons AV.

— Making Social Worlds in Interpersonal Communication. (C). 1993. text ed. 34.50 (*0-06-500288-1*) HarpCollege.

— Tourism Today: A Geographical Analysis. LC 85-24228. 229p. 1986. pap. text ed. 44.95 (*0-470-20682-9*) Halsted Pr.

Pearce, jt. auth. see McDaniel.

Pearce, et al. Business Communication: Theory & Practice, Study Guide. 2nd ed. 1988. pap. text ed. 17.95 (*0-471-60168-3*) P-H.

Pearce, Alan, jt. auth. see NBC News Division Staff.

Pearce, Alan, jt. auth. see Stewart, Alan.

***Pearce, Andrew.** Farm Welding. (Illus.). 112p. 1992. text ed. 34.95 (*0-85236-230-7*, Pub. by Farming Pr UK) Diamond Farm Bk.

Pearce, B. G., ed. Health Hazards of VDTs? LC 82-21841. (Wiley Series in Information Processing). 254p. reprint ed. pap. 72.40 (*0-685-44428-7*, 2032664) Bks Demand.

Pearce, Barbara. Regionalized Systems as an Approach to Perinatal Health Care: Annotated Bibliography. (CPL Bibliographies Ser.: No. 54). 81p. 1981. 13.00 (*0-86602-054-3*) Coun Plan Librarians.

***Pearce, Barry.** Arthur Boyd: Retrospective. (Illus.). 200p. (C). 1994. 80.00 (*0-947349-08-1*, Pub. by Lund Humphries UK) Antique Collect.

***Pearce, Barry & Whiteley, Wendy.** Brett Whiteley: Art & Life. LC 95-60188. (Illus.). 240p. 1995. 45.00 (*0-500-09252-4*) Thames Hudson.

Pearce, Brian. How Haig Saved Lenin. LC 87-4690. 144p. 1987. text ed. 35.00 (*0-312-00754-X*) St Martin.

Pearce, Brian, tr. see Amin, Samir.

Pearce, Brian, tr. see Bettelheim, Charles.

Pearce, Brian, tr. see Ferro, Marc.

Pearce, Brian, tr. see Giraud, Marcel.

Pearce, Brian, tr. see Godelier, Maurice.

Pearce, Brian, tr. see Kagarlitsky, Boris.

P Q

Pearce, Brian, tr. see Ladurie, Emmanuel L.
Pearce, Brian, tr. see Mandel, Ernest.
Pearce, Brian, tr. see Mousnier, Roland E.
Pearce, Brian, tr. see Mousnier, Roland.
Pearce, Brian L. Coeli et Terra: Poems of Thirty-Five Years. LC 93-1884. 1993. pap. 4.00 (*0-940895-09-9*) Cornerstone IL.
Pearce, Carol A. Amelia Earhart. LC 87-9102. (Makers of America Ser.). (Illus.). 175p. reprint ed. pap. 49.90 (*0-7837-5340-3*, 2045082) Bks Demand.
Pearce, Carol A., jt. auth. see Eid, J. Francois.
Pearce, Charles. The Anatomy of Letters. (Illus.). 128p. 1987. pap. 11.95 (*0-8008-0199-7*) Taplinger.
— The Little Manual of Calligraphy. 32p. 1981. pap. 3.95 (*0-8008-4923-X*) Taplinger.
Pearce, Charles E. Madame Vestris & Her Times. LC 70-77975. (Illus.). 1972. 26.95 (*0-405-08845-0*, Pub. by Blom Pubns UK) Ayer.
— Polly Peachum: The Story of Lavinia Fenton - "The Beggar's Opera" LC 68-21222. (Illus.). 1972. reprint ed. 26.95 (*0-405-08846-9*) Ayer.
— Sims Reeves, Fifty Years of Music in England. LC 79-25066. (Music Reprint Ser.). 1980. reprint ed. lib. bdg. 35.00 (*0-306-76007-X*) Da Capo.
Pearce, Charles S. Los Alamos Before the Bomb & Other Stories. 1990. 9.50 (*0-533-06948-3*) Vantage.
— Los Alamos Before the Bomb. 108p. 1990. 9.50 (*0-533-08477-6*) Vantage.
Pearce, Christopher. Fifties Source Book. 1990. 15.98 (*1-55521-549-1*) Bk Sales Inc.
— Vintage Jukeboxes. 1988. 10.98 (*1-55521-323-5*) Bk Sales Inc.
Pearce, D., et al. New Friends. 272p. (C). 1991. 45.00 (*0-569-09179-9*, Pub. by Collets) St Mut.
Pearce, D. Public Sector Decision-Making. 1980. pap. 24.00 (*0-08-025832-8*, Pergamon Pr) Elsevier.
Pearce, D. & Wagner, G., eds. Logics in AI: European Workshop JELIA '92, Berlin, Germany, September 7-10, 1992, Proceedings. LC 92-26468. (Lecture Notes in Computer Science Ser.: Vol. 633). viii, 410p. 1992. pap. 63.00 (*0-387-55887-X*) Spr-Verlag.
Pearce, D., et al, eds. Nonclassical Logics & Information Processing: International Workshop, Berlin, Germany, November 9-10, 1990 Proceedings. (Lecture Notes in Computer Science, Lecture Notes in Artificial Intelligence Ser.: Vol. 619). vii, 171p. 1992. pap. 38.00 (*0-387-55745-8*) Spr-Verlag.
Pearce, D. C. Commonwealth Administrative Law. 1986. Australia. 74.00 (*0-409-49088-1*); Australia. pap. 72.00 (*0-409-49089-X*) Butterworth Legal Pubs.
— Delegated Legislation in Australia & New Zealand. 1977. Australia. 76.00 (*0-409-31820-5*) Butterworth Legal Pubs.
— Statutory Interpretation in Australia. 3rd ed. 1988. 102.00 (*0-409-49525-5*); pap. 55.00 (*0-409-30810-2*) Butterworth Legal Pubs.
Pearce, D. C., ed. Australian Administrative Law Decisions, 15 vols., Set. 1990. 2,239.00 (*0-409-42141-3*) Butterworth Legal Pubs.
Pearce, D. T., jt. ed. see Lindsay, D. R.
***Pearce, David.** Blueprint No. 3: Msrng. Sustaining Development. 1993. 15.95 (*1-85383-183-2*, Pub. by Erthscan Pubns UK) Island Pr.
— Conservation Today. 256p. 1989. 49.95 (*0-415-00778-X*, A3718); pap. 16.95 (*0-415-03914-2*, A3722) Routledge.
***Pearce, David & Barbier, Edward.** Blueprint No. 4: Sustaining Earth. 1995. 15.95 (*1-85383-184-0*, Pub. by Erthscan Pubns UK) Island Pr.
***Pearce, David & Morgan, D.** Economic Value Biodiversity. 1994. 45.00 (*1-85383-225-1*, Pub. by Erthscan Pubns UK); pap. 21.95 (*1-85383-195-6*, Pub. by Erthscan Pubns UK) Island Pr.
Pearce, David, jt. auth. see Forss, Derek.
Pearce, David, et al. Sustainable Development: Economics & Environment in the Third World. (Illus.). 288p. 1990. text ed. 63.95 (*1-85278-167-X*, Pub. by E Elgar Pub UK) Ashgate Pub Co.
***Pearce, David D.** Wary Partners: Diplomats & the Media. 190p. 1995. 35.95 (*1-56802-067-8*); pap. 23.95 (*1-56802-066-X*) Congr Quarterly.
Pearce, David W. Economic Values & the Natural World. (Illus.). 137p. 1993. 35.00 (*0-262-16138-9*); pap. 15.95 (*0-262-66084-9*) MIT Pr.
— Environmental Economics. LC 75-44207. (Modern Economics Ser.). (Illus.). 212p. reprint ed. pap. 60.50 (*0-317-09690-7*, 2020974) Bks Demand.
— MIT Dictionary of Modern Economics. 4th ed. (Illus.). 496p. 1992. 42.00 (*0-262-16132-X*); pap. 18.95 (*0-262-66078-4*) MIT Pr.
— World Without End: Economics, Environment, & Sustainable Development, a Summary. 52p. 1993. 6.95 (*0-8213-2502-7*, 12502) World Bank.
Pearce, David W. & Rau, Nicholas J., eds. Economic Perspectives: An Annual Survey of Economics, Vol. 4. 375p. 1986. text ed. 90.00 (*3-7186-0362-4*) Gordon & Breach.
Pearce, David W. & Turner, R. Kerry. Economics of Natural Resources & the Environment. LC 89-19855. 320p. 1990. text ed. 55.00x (*0-8018-3986-6*); pap. text ed. 19.50 (*0-8018-3987-4*) Johns Hopkins.
Pearce, David W. & Warford, Jeremy J. Un Monde Sans Fin - World Without End: Economie, Environnement et Developpement Viable, un Resume - Economics, Environment, & Sustainable Development, a Summary. 52p. (FRE.). 1993. 6.95 (*0-8213-2658-9*, 12658) World Bank.
— World Without End: Economics, Environment, & Sustainable Development. LC 92-39551. 456p. 1993. 39.95 (*0-19-520881-1*, 60881) World Bank.
Pearce, David W., jt. ed. see Button, Kenneth J.
Pearce, Diana M. Child Care Workers' Salaries. 13p. 1988. pap. 5.00 (*0-685-29947-3*) Inst Womens Policy Rsch.
— The Family Support Act: An Analysis of Key Components, Draft Federal Regulations & State Options. 6p. 1989. pap. 4.00 (*0-685-29944-9*) Inst Womens Policy Rsch.
— The Feminization of Poverty: A Second Look. 40p. 1989. pap. 10.00 (*0-685-29933-3*) Inst Womens Policy Rsch.
— The Invisible Homeless: Women & Children. 6p. 1988. pap. 4.00 (*0-685-29945-7*) Inst Womens Policy Rsch.
— Permanent Housing for the Homeless. 9p. 1989. pap. 4.00 (*0-685-29946-5*) Inst Womens Policy Rsch.
— Welfare Is Not for Women: Toward a Model of Advocacy to Meet the Needs of Women in Poverty. 17p. 1989. pap. 5.00 (*0-685-29943-0*) Inst Womens Policy Rsch.
Pearce, Diana M., jt. auth. see Hartmann, Heidi.
Pearce, Donald. Para Worlds: Entanglements of Art & History. LC 88-43434. 304p. 1990. lib. bdg. 35.00 (*0-271-00667-6*) Pa St U Pr.
Pearce, Donald, jt. ed. see Essick, Robert N.
Pearce, Donald, ed. see Pound, Ezra.
***Pearce, Douglas.** Tourism Today: A Geographical Analysis. 2nd ed. LC 94-31124. 1995. pap. text ed. 34.95 (*0-470-23473-3*) Halsted Pr.
— Tourist Development. 2nd ed. 1989. pap. text ed. 43.95 (*0-470-21339-6*) Halsted Pr.
Pearce, Douglas & Butler, Richard J., eds. Tourism Research: Critiques & Challenges. (Issues in Tourism Ser.). 256p. 1993. 69.95 (*0-415-08319-2*, A7690) Routledge.
Pearce, Douglas, jt. ed. see Butler, Richard.
Pearce, E. A. & Smith, Gordon. The Times Books World Weather Guide. enl. ed. (Illus.). 1990. pap. 17.95 (*0-8129-1881-9*, Times Bks) Random.
***Pearce, Edward.** Machiavelli's Children. 224p. 1995. 39.95 (*0-575-05514-6*, Pub. by V Gollancz UK) Trafalgar.
Pearce, Eli M., ed. Macromolecular Synthesis: A Periodic Publication of Methods for the Preparation of Macromolecules, Vol. 8. LC 63-18627. 124p. 1982. text ed. 34.50 (*0-471-86876-0*) Wiley.
Pearce, Eli M., jt. auth. see Lin, Shiow-Ching.
Pearce, Elizabeth. Parameters in Old French Syntax: Infinitival Complements. (Studies in Natural Language & Linguistic Theory). 336p. (C). 1990. lib. bdg. 112.50 (*0-7923-0432-2*); pap. text ed. 44.50 (*0-7923-0433-0*) Kluwer Ac.
Pearce, Ellen. Life in (Very) Minor Works: Poems. 1968. 4.50 (*0-8079-0073-7*); pap. 1.95 (*0-8079-0074-5*) October.
Pearce, Elvina T. Four O'Clock Tunes. Clark, Frances & Goss, Louise, eds. (J). (gr. 2 up). 1986. pap. text ed. 3.50 (*0-913277-19-3*) New Schl Mus Study.
— Solo Flight. Clark, Frances & Goss, Louise, eds. (J). (gr. 2 up). 1986. pap. text ed. 3.50 (*0-913277-18-5*) New Schl Mus Study.
Pearce, Eric, jt. auth. see Mui, Linda.
Pearce, Erica L. The Permissive Garden. 102p. 1987. 65.00 (*0-9511795-0-0*, Pub. by Sweethaws Pr UK) St Mut.
Pearce, F. B. Zanzibar: The Island Metropolis of Eastern Africa. (Illus.). 431p. 1967. reprint ed. 40.00 (*0-7146-1098-4*, Pub. by F Cass Pubs UK) Intl Spec Bk.
Pearce, Flora. Essie. large type ed. 1991. 21.95 (*0-7089-2377-1*) Ulverscroft.
— No Work Today. large type ed. 1989. 17.95 (*0-7089-2108-6*) Ulverscroft.
Pearce, Frank. The Radical Durkheim. 216p. 1989. text ed. 49.95 (*0-04-445269-1*); pap. text ed. 16.95 (*0-04-445270-5*) Routledge Chapman & Hall.
— Sea War: Great Naval Battles of World War Two. large type ed. (Illus.). 352p. 1991. 21.95 (*1-85089-505-8*, Pub. by ISIS UK) Transaction Pubs.
***Pearce, Frank & Snider, Laureen, eds.** Corporate Crime: Contemporary Debates. 416p. 1995. 60.00 (*0-8020-0667-1*) U of Toronto Pr.
— Corporate Crime: Contemporary Debates. 416p. 1995. pap. 19.95 (*0-8020-7621-1*) U of Toronto Pr.
Pearce, Frank & Woodiwiss, Michael, eds. Global Crime Connections: Dynamics & Control. 240p. (Orig.). 1992. 50.00 (*0-8020-2838-1*); pap. 16.95 (*0-8020-7716-1*) U of Toronto Pr.
Pearce, Fred. The Damned: Rivers, Dams, & the Coming World Water Crisis. (Illus.). 400p. 1994. 39.95 (*0-370-31609-6*, Pub. by Bodley Head UK) Trafalgar.
Pearce, G., ed. see University of Western Ontario Conference Staff.
Pearce, George F. The U S Navy in Pensacola: From Sailing Ships to Naval Aviation, 1825-1930. LC 80-12167. (Illus.). vii, 207p. 1980. 24.95 (*0-8130-0665-1*) U Press Fla.
Pearce, Gerald. Orphans. 192p. 1990. 18.95 (*0-8027-5764-2*) Walker & Co.
Pearce, Glenn C., et al. Business Communication: Principles & Applications. 2nd ed. 1988. text ed. 41.50 (*0-471-84851-4*) P-H.
Pearce, Howard D., jt. ed. see Collins, Robert A.
Pearce, Howard D., jt. ed. see Hokenson, Jan.
Pearce, J. A., jt. auth. see Roussy, G.
Pearce, J. A., jt. auth. see Roussy, M. G.
Pearce, J. C. Tug of War. LC 93-15037. (Foul Play Ser.: No. 5). 144p. (J). (gr. 3-7). 1993. pap. 3.25 (*0-14-036663-6*, Puffin) Puffin Bks.
Pearce, J. E. Tales That Dead Men Tell. 1993. reprint ed. lib. bdg. 75.00 (*0-7812-5972-X*) Rprt Serv.
— This Place Called Kentucky. Moremen, John S. & Spears, Amy, eds. (Illus.). 138p. 1994. 29.95 (*0-9624086-6-2*) Sulgrave Pr.
Pearce, J. Gordon. Telecommunications Switching. LC 80-20586. (Applications of Communications Theory Ser.). 348p. 1981. 69.50 (*0-306-40584-9*, Plenum Pr) Plenum.
Pearce, J. M. Parkinson's Disease & Its Management. (Illus.). 160p. 1992. 37.50 (*0-19-262177-7*) OUP.
Pearce, J. Malcolm, ed. Doppler Ultrasound in Perinatal Medicine. 362p. 1992. 98.00 (*0-19-262019-3*) OUP.
Pearce, J. R., jt. ed. see Bachrach, A. L.
Pearce, Jack. Reflections of a Rotarian. LC 94-72593. 401p. 1994. 24.95 (*1-885373-03-1*); pap. 19.95 (*1-885373-04-X*) Emerald Ink.
Pearce, Jacqueline. Border Wares. 160p. 1992. pap. 65.00 (*0-11-290494-7*, HM04947, Pub. by HMSO UK) UNIPUB.
***Pearce, James J.** Entering the Entrepreneurial Highway. 150p. (Orig.). 1996. lib. bdg. 13.95 (*0-9640133-3-9*) Rhapsody.
— More Time to File More Time to Pay: 1996 Edition. annuals (Annual Edition 1074-7125 Ser.: No. 1074-7125). 128p. (Orig.). 1996. lib. bdg. 11.95 (*0-9640133-2-0*) Rhapsody.
Pearce, Jane & Newton, Saul. Conditions of Human Growth. 1969. reprint ed. 6.95 (*0-685-08130-3*, Citadel Pr) Carol Pub Group.
Pearce, Janice, jt. auth. see Gappa, Judith.
Pearce, Jean. Foot-Loose in Tokyo: The Curious Traveler's Guide to the 29 Stages of the Yamanote Line. LC 76-23738. (Exploring Japan Ser.). (Illus.). 212p. 1976. pap. 11.95 (*0-8348-0123-X*) Weatherhill.
— More Foot-Loose in Tokyo: The Curious Traveler's Guide to Shitamachi & Narita. LC 83-51221. (Exploring Japan Ser.). (Illus.). 148p. 1984. pap. 11.95 (*0-8348-0190-6*) Weatherhill.
***Pearce, Jim.** Wildfowl Carving Vol. 1: Essential Techniques for Carving, Texturing & Painting Wildfowl. (Illus.). 160p. 1995. pap. 16.95 (*0-946819-53-X*, Pub. by Guild Mstr Craftsman UK) Sterling.
Pearce, John. Introduction to Animal Cognition. 400p. (C). 1987. text ed. 79.95 (*0-86377-056-8*); pap. text ed. 39.95 (*0-86377-057-6*) L Erlbaum Assocs.
***Pearce, John & Robinson, Richard.** Strategic Management: Formulation, Implementation & Control. 4th ed. (C). 1990. text ed. 60.95 (*0-256-08323-1*) Irwin.
Pearce, John A., II & Robinson, Richard. Formulation, Implementation, & Control of Competitive Strategy. 5th ed. 418p. (C). 1993. pap. text ed. 38.95 (*0-256-12634-8*) Irwin.
Pearce, John A., II & Robinson, Richard B., Jr. Business Week Readings in Strategic Management: Strategy Formulation & Implementation. 2nd ed. 1988. pap. write for info. (*0-318-62544-X*) McGraw.
— Cases in Strategic Management. 2nd ed. 576p. (C). 1990. text ed. 37.95 (*0-256-08322-3*, 11-2719-02) Irwin.
— Cases in Strategic Management. 3rd ed. LC 93-27424. 519p. (C). 1993. pap. text ed. 40.95 (*0-256-12633-X*) Irwin Prof Pubng.
— Management. 700p. (C). 1989. text ed. 41.95 (*0-394-35579-2*) Random.
— Strategic Management: Formulation, Implementation & Control. 4th ed. 1056p. (C). 1990. 34.95 (*0-256-08324-X*) Irwin.
— Strategic Management: Formulation, Implementation, & Control. 5th ed. LC 94-41400. 976p. (C). 1994. 66.95 (*0-256-17067-3*) Irwin.
— Strategic Management Practice. 420p. (C). 1990. pap. text ed. 29.50 (*0-256-09452-7*, 11-3384-01) Irwin.
Pearce, John A., II & Robinson, Richard R., Jr. Management. 1989. text ed. write for info. (*0-07-556981-7*) McGraw.
Pearce, John E. Days of Darkness: The Feuds of Eastern Kentucky. LC 94-2773. (Illus.). 240p. 1994. 23.95 (*0-8131-1874-3*) U Pr of Ky.
— Divide & Dissent: Kentucky Politics, 1930-1963. LC 86-28978. (Illus.). 272p. 1987. 15.00 (*0-8131-0804-7*) U Pr of Ky.
— Ohio River. LC 89-14830. (Illus.). 200p. 1989. 45.00 (*0-8131-1693-7*) U Pr of Ky.
Pearce, John K., jt. auth. see Glantz, Kalman.
Pearce, John L., jt. auth. see Carter, Elizabeth.
Pearce, John N., jt. ed. see McDaniel, George W.
Pearce, Jone L. Volunteers: The Organizational Behavior of Unpaid Workers. LC 92-36057. (People & Organizations Ser.). 1993. write for info. (*0-415-09427-5*, Routledge NY) Routledge.
— Volunteers: The Organizational Behaviour of Unpaid Workers. (People & Organizations Ser.). 288p. 1993. 39.95 (*0-04-445098-2*, A8219) Routledge.
Pearce, Joseph C. The Crack in the Cosmic Egg: Challenging Constructs of Mind & Reality. 224p. 1988. pap. 11.00 (*0-517-56661-3*, Harmony) Crown Pub Group.
— Evolution's End: Claming the Potential of Our Intelligence. rev. ed. LC 91-58899. 288p. 1993. pap. 12.00 (*0-06-250732-X*) Harper SF.
— Magical Child: Rediscovering Nature's Plan for Our Children. 276p. 1992. pap. 10.95 (*0-452-26789-7*, Plume) NAL-Dutton.
Pearce, Joseph R. Analytic Sociology: Its Logical Foundations & Relevance to Theory & Empirical Research. LC 94-17653. 210p. (C). reprint ed. lib. bdg. 32.50 (*0-8191-9578-2*) U Pr of Amer.
Pearce, Lynne. Reading Dialogics. (Interrogating Texts Ser.). 192p. 1994. pap. 15.95 (*0-340-55052-X*, B2527, Pub. by E Arnold UK) Routledge Chapman & Hall.
— Woman - Image - Text: Readings in Pre-Raphaelite Art & Literature. 85.00 (*0-8020-5980-5*); pap. 24.95 (*0-8020-6912-6*) U of Toronto Pr.
***Pearce, Lynne & Stacey, Jackie, eds.** Romance Revisited. (Illus.). 310p. 1995. 45.00 (*0-8147-6630-7*); pap. 15.95 (*0-8147-6631-5*) NYU Pr.
Pearce, M., jt. auth. see Chamberlain, G.
Pearce, Malcolm & Stewart, Geoff. British Political History, 1867-1990: Democracy & Decline. LC 91-33613. (Illus.). 464p. 1992. 83.00 (*0-415-07246-8*, A7491); pap. 25.00 (*0-415-07247-6*, A7495) Routledge.
Pearce, Martin, ed. Sociology. 250p. (C). 1991. pap. 60.00 (*1-85352-929-X*, Pub. by HLT Pubns UK) St Mut.
Pearce, Mary E. Cast a Long Shadow. large type ed. 464p. 1988. 15.95 (*0-7089-1790-9*) Ulverscroft.
— The Old House at Railes. LC 94-8760. 595p. 1994. lib. bdg. 22.95 (*0-8161-5989-0*) G K Hall.
— The Old House at Railes. 416p. 1993. 23.95 (*0-312-10514-2*) St Martin.
Pearce, Michael. Don't Shoot the Piano Player. Daper, Peter, ed. 203p. (Orig.). 1994. pap. 19.95 (*0-9640555-0-3*) Spin Pubng.
— The Mamur & the Girl in the Nile. 1995. pap. write for info. (*0-446-40316-4*, Mysterious Paperbk) Warner Bks.
— The Mamur Zapt & the Donkey-Vous. 272p. 1992. 17.95 (*0-89296-486-3*) Mysterious Pr.
— The Mamur Zapt & the Donkey-Vous. 272p. 1993. mass mkt. 4.99 (*0-446-40181-1*, Mysterious Paperbk) Warner Bks.
— The Mamur Zapt & the Men Behind. 256p. 1993. 17.95 (*0-89296-487-1*) Mysterious Pr.
— The Mamur Zapt & the Men Behind. 240p. 1994. mass mkt. 5.50 (*0-446-40183-8*, Mysterious Paperbk) Warner Bks.
— The Mamur Zapt & the Spoils of Egypt. 192p. 1995. write for info. (*0-89296-560-6*) Mysterious Pr.
— Non-Standard Collection Management. 250p. 1992. 71.95 (*1-85742-020-9*, Pub. by Ashgate UK) Ashgate Pub Co.
— Sporting Clays: Expert Techniques for Every Kind of Clays Course. LC 91-8655. (Illus.). 160p. 1991. 16.95 (*0-8117-1914-6*) Stackpole.
Pearce-Moses, Richard, comp. Photographic Collections in Texas: A Union Guide. LC 87-9979. 400p. 1987. pap. 29.50 (*0-89096-351-7*) Tex A&M Univ Pr.
Pearce, N. Shield & the Sabre. 200p. 1992. 39.95 (*0-11-701637-3*, HM7657) UNIPUB.
Pearce, Narsreen. A Guide to Inheritance Claims. 179p. 1989. 48.00 (*1-85190-073-X*, Pub. by Tolley Pubng UK) St Mut.
Pearce, Nasreen. Adoption: The Law & Practice. 544p. (C). 1991. 120.00 (*1-85190-104-3*, Pub. by Tolley Pubng UK) St Mut.
— Adoption Practice & Procedure. 133p. 1984. 90.00 (*0-906840-79-1*, Pub. by Fourmat Pub UK) St Mut.
— Custodianship: The Law & Practice. 77p. 1986. 70.00 (*1-85190-015-2*, Pub. by Fourmat Pub UK) St Mut.
— Name-Changing: A Practical Guide. 94p. 1990. 55.00 (*1-85190-089-6*, Pub. by Tolley Pubng UK) St Mut.
— Wardship: The Law & Practice. 126p. 1986. 104.00 (*0-906840-97-X*, Pub. by Fourmat Pub UK) St Mut.
***Pearce, Neil, et al, eds.** Occupational Cancer in Developing Countries. (IARC Scientific Publications: No. 129). (Illus.). 200p. 1995. pap. 40.00 (*92-832-2129-X*) OUP.
Pearce, P. L. The Social Psychology of Tourist Behaviour. (International Series in Experimental Social Psychology: Vol. 3). 142p. 1982. 75.00 (*0-08-025794-1*, Pub. by Pergamon Repr UK) Franklin.
— The Ulysses Factor: Evaluating Visitors in Tourist Settings. (Recent Research in Psychology Ser.). (Illus.). 275p. 1990. pap. 48.00 (*0-387-96834-2*) Spr-Verlag.
Pearce, Paul. Construction Marketing: A Professional Approach. 138p. 1992. text ed. 54.00 (*0-7277-1652-2*, Pub. by T Telford UK) Am Soc Civil Eng.
Pearce, Philippa. Emily's Own Elephant. LC 87-14039. (Illus.). 32p. (J). (gr. k-3). 1988. 11.95 (*0-688-07678-5*); lib. bdg. 11.88 (*0-688-07679-3*) Greenwillow.
— Here Comes Tod! LC 93-20026. (Illus.). 96p. (J). (gr. k-3). 1994. 14.95 (*1-56402-328-1*) Candlewick Pr.
— Tom's Midnight Garden. LC 69-12008. 240p. (J). (gr. 5-9). 1992. lib. bdg. 13.89 (*0-397-30477-3*, Lipp Jr Bks) HarpC Child Bks.
— Tom's Midnight Garden. LC 69-12008. (Trophy Bk.). (Illus.). 240p. (J). (gr. 3-7). 1992. pap. 4.95 (*0-06-440445-5*, Trophy) HarpC Child Bks.
— The Way to Sattin Shore. (J). (gr. 5-10). 1993. 16.75 (*0-8446-6652-1*) Peter Smith.
— Who's Afraid? & Other Strange Stories. LC 86-14299. 160p. (J). (gr. 5-9). 1987. 10.25 (*0-688-06895-2*) Greenwillow.
***Pearce, Philippa, ed.** Dread & Delight: A Century of Children's Ghost Stories. 372p. (J). 1996. 25.00 (*0-19-212605-9*) OUP.
Pearce, Phillippa. Fresh. (Illus.). 64p. (J). 1987. lib. bdg. 13.95 (*0-88682-125-8*) Creative Ed.
Pearce, Q. L. All about Dinosaurs. (Illus.). (J). (gr. 2 up). 1989. pap. 7.95 (*0-671-64517-X*, Litl Simon S&S) S&S Childrens.
— Amazing Science Series, 8 bks., Set. (Illus.). 256p. (J). (gr. 4-6). 1989. lib. bdg. 77.88 (*0-671-94111-9*, Julian Messner); pap. 35.70 (*0-671-94112-7*, Julian Messner) Silver Burdett Pr.
— Animal Footnotes: A Nature's Footprints Guide. (Illus.). 40p. (J). (ps-3). 1991. lib. bdg. 12.95 (*0-671-69116-3*); pap. 7.95 (*0-671-69117-1*) Silver Burdett Pr.
— Armadillos & Other Unusual Animals. Steltenpohl, Jane, ed. (Amazing Science Ser.). (Illus.). 64p. (J). (gr. 4-6). 1989. lib. bdg. 12.98 (*0-671-68528-7*, Julian Messner); pap. 5.95 (*0-671-68645-3*, Julian Messner) Silver Burdett Pr.
— The Checkerboard Press Kids' Science Dictionary. LC 88-71150. (Illus.). 124p. (J). (gr. 4-6). 1991. reprint ed. 12.95 (*1-56288-003-9*) Checkerboard.
— The Dinosaur Almanac. (Illus.). 96p. (J). (gr. 1 up). 1994. pap. 4.95 (*1-56565-175-8*) Lowell Hse Juvenile.
— Easy Answers to First Science Questions about Animals. 32p. 1992. pap. 4.95 (*1-56565-023-9*) Lowell Hse.
— Easy Answers to First Science Questions about Oceans. 32p. 1992. pap. 4.95 (*1-56565-022-0*) Lowell Hse.

P Q

An Asterisk (*) at the beginning of an entry indicates that the title is appearing in BIP for the first time.

— Even More Scary Stories for Sleep-overs. LC 94-2799. (Scary Stories Ser.). (Illus.). 128p. (J). (gr. 1 up). 1994. pap. 4.95 (*0-8431-3746-0*) Price Stern.
— Giants of the Deep. (Illus.). 48p. (J). (gr. 3-7). 1993. reprint ed. pap. 5.95 (*1-56565-042-5*) Lowell Hse.
— Giants of the Land. (Illus.). 48p. (J). (gr. 3-7). 1993. reprint ed. pap. 5.95 (*1-56565-041-7*) Lowell Hse.
— Great Predators of the Land. (YA). 1995. 16.95 (*0-312-85480-3*) Tor Bks.
— Great Predators of the Land. (YA). 1995. pap. 9.95 (*0-615-00534-9*) Tor Bks.
— Great Predators of the Sea. (YA). 1995. 16.95 (*0-312-85481-1*) Tor Bks.
— Great Predators of the Sea. (YA). 1995. 13.95 (*0-615-00535-7*) Tor Bks.
— How to Talk Dinosaur with Your Child. (Illus.). 1991. pap. 10.95 (*0-929923-48-0*) Lowell Hse.
— Lightning & Other Wonders of the Sky. Steltenpohl, Jane, ed. (Amazing Science Ser.). (Illus.). 64p. (J). (gr. 4-6). 1989. lib. bdg. 12.98 (*0-671-68534-1*, Julian Messner); pap. 5.95 (*0-671-68648-8*, Julian Messner) Silver Burdett Pr.
— More Scary Stories for Sleep-Overs. LC 92-21705. (Illus.). 128p. (Orig.). (J). 1992. pap. 4.95 (*0-8431-3451-8*) Price Stern.
— More Super Scary Stories for Sleep-Overs. (Scary Stories Ser.). (Illus.). 128p. (J). (gr. 1 up). 1995. pap. 4.95 (*0-8431-3916-1*) Price Stern.
— My Favorite Dinosaur: Tyrannosaurus Rex. (Illus.). 32p. (J). 1993. 12.95 (*1-56565-014-X*) Lowell Hse.
— Ocean. (First Science Words Ser.). (Illus.). 48p. (J). 1991. student ed 2.95 (*0-8431-2912-3*) Price Stern.
— Piranhas & Other Wonders of the Jungle. (Amazing Science Ser.). (Illus.). 64p. (J). (gr. 4-6). 1990. lib. bdg. 12.98 (*0-671-70689-6*, Julian Messner); pap. 5.95 (*0-671-70690-X*, Julian Messner) Silver Burdett Pr.
— Prehistoric Mammals. 48p. 1989. 1.95 (*0-8125-9493-2*) Tor Bks.
— Quicksand & Other Earthly Wonders. Steltenpohl, Jane, ed. (Amazing Science Ser.). (Illus.). 64p. (J). (gr. 4-6). 1989. lib. bdg. 12.98 (*0-671-68530-9*, Julian Messner); pap. 5.95 (*0-671-68646-1*, Julian Messner) Silver Burdett Pr.
— Rainbow Book of Birds: A Color-by-Number Book. 1989. pap. 1.95 (*0-8125-9442-8*) Tor Bks.
— Rainbow Book of Snakes, Turtles, Lizards & More: A Color-by-Number Book. 1989. pap. 1.95 (*0-8125-9444-4*) Tor Bks.
— Saber-Toothed Cats - Prehistoric Worlds. (Amazing Science Ser.). (Illus.). 64p. (J). (gr. 4-6). 1991. lib. bdg. 12.98 (*0-671-70691-8*, Julian Messner); pap. 5.95 (*0-671-70692-6*, Julian Messner) Silver Burdett Pr.
— The Stargazer's Guide to the Galaxy. 1991. mass mkt. 4.99 (*0-8125-9423-1*) Tor Bks.
— Still More Scary Stories for Sleep-Overs. LC 93-12822. (Illus.). 128p. (Orig.). (J). (gr. 3-6). 1993. pap. 4.95 (*0-8431-3588-3*) Price Stern.
— Strange Science: Outer Space. 64p. (Orig.). 1994. pap. 3.50 (*0-8125-2364-4*) Tor Bks.
— Strange Science: Planet Earth. 64p. (Orig.). (YA). 1993. pap. 3.50 (*0-8125-2365-2*) Tor Bks.
— Super Scary Stories for Sleep-Overs. (Scary Stories Ser.). 128p. 1995. 4.95 (*0-8431-3915-3*) Price Stern.
— Super Scary Stories for Sleep-Overs. (Scary Stories Ser.). (Illus.). 128p. (J). (gr. 1 up). 1995. pap. 4.95 (*0-614-03671-2*) Price Stern.
— Tell Me About Nature Dictionary. (J). 1990. 5.99 (*0-517-03567-7*) Random Hse Value.
— Tidal Waves & Other Ocean Wonders. Steltenpohl, Jane, ed. (Amazing Science Ser.). (Illus.). 64p. (J). (gr. 4-6). 1989. lib. bdg. 12.98 (*0-671-68532-5*, Julian Messner); pap. 5.95 (*0-671-68647-X*, Julian Messner) Silver Burdett Pr.
— Tyrannosaurus Rex & Other Dinosaur Wonders. (Amazing Science Ser.). (Illus.). 64p. (J). (gr. 4-6). 1990. lib. bdg. 12.98 (*0-671-70687-X*, Julian Messner); pap. 5.95 (*0-671-70688-8*, Julian Messner) Silver Burdett Pr.
— Whales & Other Wonders - Frozen Worlds. (Amazing Science Ser.). (Illus.). 64p. (J). (gr. 4-6). 1991. lib. bdg. 12.98 (*0-671-70693-4*, Julian Messner); pap. 5.95 (*0-671-70694-2*, Julian Messner) Silver Burdett Pr.
— Why Is a Frog Not a Toad? 32p. 1992. 11.95 (*1-56565-025-5*) Lowell Hse.
Pearce, Q. L. & Pearce, W. J. In the Barnyard. Brook, Bonnie, ed. (Nature's Footprints Ser.). (Illus.). 24p. (J). (ps-1). 1990. 4.95 (*0-671-68828-6*); lib. bdg. 6.95 (*0-671-68824-3*) Silver Burdett Pr.
— Nature's Footprints Series, 4 vols., Set. (Illus.). 96p. (J). (ps-1). 1990. 14.85 (*0-671-94431-2*); lib. bdg. 27.80 (*0-671-94430-4*) Silver Burdett Pr.
Pearce, Q. L. & Pearce, W. L. In the African Grasslands. Brook, Bonnie, ed. (Nature's Footprints Ser.). (Illus.). 24p. (J). (ps-1). 1990. 4.95 (*0-671-68831-6*); lib. bdg. 6.95 (*0-671-68827-8*) Silver Burdett Pr.
— In the Desert. Brook, Bonnie, ed. (Nature's Footprints Ser.). (Illus.). 24p. (J). (ps-1). 1990. lib. bdg. 6.95 (*0-671-68825-1*) Silver Burdett Pr.
— In the Forest. Brook, Bonnie, ed. (Nature's Footprints Ser.). (Illus.). 24p. (J). (ps-1). 1990. 4.95 (*0-671-68830-8*); lib. bdg. 6.95 (*0-671-68826-X*) Silver Burdett Pr.
***Pearce, Querida L.** Atlas of the Strange. LC 94-41537. (Illus.). (J). 1995. write for info. (*1-56565-223-1*) Lowell Hse Juvenile.
Pearce, R. D. The Growth & Evolution of Multinational Enterprise: Patterns of Geographical & Industrial Diversification. 256p. 1993. 63.95 (*1-85278-396-6*, Pub. by E Elgar Pub UK) Ashgate Pub Co.
— Turning Point in Africa: British Colonial Policy, 1938-48. 234p. 1982. text ed. 37.50 (*0-7146-3160-4*, Pub. by F Cass Pubs UK) Intl Spec Bk.
Pearce, R. D., jt. auth. see Buckley, P.
Pearce, R. H., ed. see James, Henry.
Pearce, Rhoda M. Thomas Telford. 1989. pap. 30.00 (*0-85263-410-2*, Pub. by Shire UK) St Mut.
Pearce, Richard. The Politics of Narration: James Joyce, William Faulkner & Virginia Woolf. LC 90-8977. 200p. (C). 1991. text ed. 40.00 (*0-8135-1656-0*) Rutgers U Pr.
— William Styron. LC 74-635458. (University of Minnesota Pamphlets on American Writers Ser.: No. 98). 47p. (Orig.). reprint ed. pap. 25.00 (*0-7837-2868-9*, 2057587) Bks Demand.
Pearce, Richard, ed. Molly Blooms: A Polylogue on Penelope & Cultural Studies. LC 93-39641. 1994. 45.00 (*0-299-14120-9*); pap. 24.75 (*0-299-14124-1*) U of Wis Pr.
Pearce, Robert, ed. Then the Wind Changed in Africa: Nigerian Letters of Robert Hepburn Wright. (Illus.). 256p. (C). 1993. text ed. 39.50 (*1-85043-573-1*, Pub. by I B Tauris UK) St Martin.
Pearce, Robert D. Attlee's Labour Governments, 1945-51. LC 93-15764. (Lancaster Pamphlets Ser.). 1994. write for info. (*0-415-08893-3*) Routledge.
— The Internationalisation of Research & Development by Multinational Enterprises. 209p. 1990. text ed. 49.95 (*0-312-03704-X*) St Martin.
Pearce, Robert D. & Singh, Satwinder. Globalizing Research & Development. LC 91-32279. 256p. 1992. text ed. 55.00 (*0-312-07542-1*) St Martin.
Pearce, Robert D., jt. auth. see Dunning, John H.
Pearce, Robert P., jt. auth. see Pielke, Roger A.
Pearce, Robert R. A History of the Inns of Court & Chancery: With Notices of Their Ancient Discipline, Rules, Orders, & Customs, Readings, Moots, Masques, Revels, & Entertainments; Including an Account of the Eminent Men of the Four Learned & Honourable Societies,--Lincoln's Inn, the Temple, the Middle Temple, & Gray's Inn, etc. 440p. 1987. reprint ed. text ed. 42.50 (*0-8377-2512-7*) Rothman.
Pearce, Roy H. The Continuity of American Poetry. LC 87-17638. 464p. 1987. text ed. 40.00 (*0-8195-5155-4*, Wesleyan Univ Pr); pap. 16.95 (*0-8195-6198-3*, Wesleyan Univ Pr) U Pr of New Eng.
— Gesta Humanorum: Studies in the Historicist Mode. LC 87-5091. (Illus.). 208p. 1987. text ed. 23.00 (*0-8262-0637-9*) U of Mo Pr.
— Historicism Once More: Problems & Occasions for the American Scholar. LC 68-56317. Date not set. reprint ed. pap. 105.80 (*0-7837-9417-7*, 2060158) Bks Demand.
— Historicism Once More, Problems & Occasions for the American Scholar. LC 68-56317. 1969. 52.50 (*0-691-06155-6*) Princeton U Pr.
— Savagism & Civilization: A Study of Indians & the American Mind. 1988. pap. 12.00 (*0-520-06227-2*) U CA Pr.
Pearce, Roy H., ed. see Hawthorne, Nathaniel.
Pearce, Ruth L. Russian for Expository Prose, Vol. 1: Introductory Course. 413p. (Orig.). (C). 1983. pap. text ed. 18.95 (*0-89357-121-0*) Slavica.
— Russian for Expository Prose, Vol. 2: Advanced Course. 255p. (Orig.). 1983. pap. text ed. 16.95 (*0-89357-122-9*) Slavica.
Pearce, S., jt. auth. see Knowlton, J.
Pearce, S. C. The Agricultural Field Experiment: A Statistical Examination of Theory & Practice. LC 82-13711. 335p. 1983. text ed. 142.95 (*0-471-10511-2*, Wiley-Interscience) Wiley.
— Field Experimentation with Fruit Trees & Other Perennial Plants. 2nd ed. 182p. (Orig.). 1976. pap. text ed. 40.00 (*0-85198-354-5*) CAB Intl.
Pearce, S. C. & North, P. M. Statistics: An Introduction for Non-Statisticians. 200p. 1993. 49.00 (*1-85070-420-1*) Prthnon Pub.
Pearce, Sarah J. & Eflin, Roxanne. Guide to Historic Aspen & the Roaring Fork Valley. LC 90-2050. (Illus.). 48p. (Orig.). 1990. pap. 5.95 (*0-917895-32-0*) Cordillera CO.
Pearce, Shirley & Wardle, Jane, eds. The Practice of Behavioural Medicine. 336p. 1989. 75.00 (*0-19-261691-9*); pap. 35.00 (*0-19-261689-7*) OUP.
Pearce, Stanley C. The Agricultural Field Experiment: A Statistical Examination of Theory & Practice. LC 82-13711. 351p. reprint ed. pap. 100.10 (*0-7837-4731-4*, 2044516) Bks Demand.
***Pearce, Stephen S.** Flash of Insight: Metaphor & Narrative in Therapy. 1995. 38.95 (*0-205-14572-8*, Longwood Div) Allyn.
***Pearce, Susan.** On Collecting: An Investigation into Collecting in the European Tradition. LC 94-35151. (Collecting Cultures Ser.). (Illus.). 304p. 1995. 49.95 (*0-415-07560-2*, C0035) Routledge.
***Pearce, Susan, ed.** Art in Museums. (New Research in Museum Studies: Vol. 5). 264p. (C). 1995. text ed. 85.00 (*0-485-90005-X*, Pub. by Athlone Pr UK) Humanities.
— Exploring Science in Museums: New Research in Museum Studies. (International Ser.: Vol. 6). 240p. 1996. 90.00 (*0-485-90006-8*, Pub. by Athlone Pr UK) Humanities.
— Interpreting Objects & Collections. LC 94-11658. (Leicester Readers in Museum Studies). 352p. 1994. 65.00x (*0-415-11288-5*, B4591, Routledge NY); pap. 25.00 (*0-415-11289-3*, B4595, Routledge NY) Routledge.
Pearce, Susan M. Archaeological Curatorship. LC 90-9519. (Leicester Museum Studies Ser.). 224p. 1990. 35.00 (*0-87474-813-5*) Smithsonian.
— Bronze Age Metalwork in Southern Britain. 1989. pap. 25.00 (*0-85263-680-6*, Pub. by Shire UK) St Mut.
— Eskimo Carving. 1989. pap. 25.00 (*0-85263-770-5*, Pub. by Shire UK) St Mut.
— Museums, Objects, & Collections: A Cultural Study. (Illus.). 312p. 1993. pap. text ed. 17.95 (*1-56098-330-2*) Smithsonian.
— On Collecting: An Investigation into Collecting in the European Tradition. LC 94-35151. 1995. write for info. (*0-415-07561-0*) Routledge.
Pearce, Susan M., ed. Museum Studies in Material Culture. 280p. 1990. text ed. 42.50 (*0-7185-1288-X*, Pub. by Pinter Pubs UK) St Martin.
— Museum Studies in Material Culture. LC 91-62182. 188p. (C). 1992. pap. 16.95 (*1-56098-124-5*) Smithsonian.
— Museums & Europe, 1992. LC 92-28225. (New Research in Museum Studies: An International Ser.: Vol. 3). 240p. (C). 1992. text ed. 85.00 (*0-485-90003-3*, Pub. by Athlone Pr UK) Humanities.
— Museums & the Appropriation of Culture. LC 93-39430. (New Research in Museum Studies: An International Ser.: Vol. 4). 256p. (C). 1994. text ed. 85.00 (*0-485-90004-1*, Pub. by Athlone Pr UK) Humanities.
— Museums Economics & the Community. LC 91-25711. (New Research in Museum Studies: An International Ser.: Vol. 2). 224p. (C). 1991. text ed. 55.00 (*0-485-90002-5*, Pub. by Athlone Pr UK) Humanities.
— Objects of Knowledge. LC 90-1021. (New Research in Museum Studies: An International Ser.: Vol. 1). 224p. (C). 1990. text ed. 55.00 (*0-485-90001-7*, Pub. by Athlone Pr UK) Humanities.
Pearce, T. M. Mary Hunter Austin. (Twayne's United States Authors Ser.). 1965. lib. bdg. 17.95 (*0-89197-837-2*); pap. text ed. 4.95 (*0-8290-0003-8*) Irvington.
Pearce, T. M., ed. Literary America, 1903-1934: The Mary Austin Letters. LC 78-67914. (Contributions in Women's Studies: No. 5). (Illus.). 296p. 1979. text ed. 49.95 (*0-313-20636-8*, PEL/, Greenwood Pr) Greenwood.
***Pearce, Terry.** Leading Out Loud: The Authentic Speaker, the Credible Leader. LC 95-14574. 1995. 23.00 (*0-614-07336-7*) Jossey-Bass.
— Winning Hearts & Minds. (Management Ser.). 1995. write for info. (*0-7879-0111-3*) Jossey-Bass.
Pearce, Tola & Falola, Toyin. Child Health in Nigeria: The Impact of a Depressed Economy. 168p. 1994. 54.95 (*1-85628-607-X*, Pub. by Avebury Pub UK) Ashgate Pub Co.
Pearce, Tola, jt. ed. see Abonja, Simi.
Pearce, Tola O., jt. ed. see Afonja, Simi.
Pearce, W. Barnett. Communication & the Human Condition. LC 88-30565. 224p. (C). 1989. text ed. 29.95 (*0-8093-1411-8*); pap. text ed. 19.95 (*0-8093-1412-6*) S Ill U Pr.
Pearce, W. Barnett, jt. auth. see Narula, Uma.
Pearce, W. Barnett, jt. ed. see Narula, Uma.
Pearce, W. Barnett, jt. ed. see Weiler, Michael.
Pearce, W. J., jt. auth. see Pearce, Q. L.
Pearce, W. J., jt. auth. see Rouverol, W. S.
Pearce, W. L., jt. auth. see Pearce, Q. L.
Pearce, Wanda. A Bunch of Fun Dramas. LC 89-33094. (Orig.). 1990. pap. 6.99 (*0-8054-7528-1*) Broadman.
Pearce, William, jt. auth. see Yao, James S.
Pearce, William H., jt. auth. see Yao, James S.
Pearcey, Nancy & Thaxton, Charles. The Soul of Science: Christian Faith & Natural Philosophy. LC 93-42580. (Turning Point Christian Worldview Ser.). 224p. (Orig.). 1994. pap. 12.99 (*0-89107-766-9*) Crossway Bks.
Pearcey, Nancy R., jt. auth. see Colson, Charles W.
Pearcey, S., tr. see Dagnini, G.
Pearcey, T., jt. ed. see Bennett, J. M.
Pearcey, T., jt. auth. see Hatt, H. H.
Pearcy, Arthur. Flying the Frontiers: NACA & NASA Experimental Aircraft. (Illus.). 200p. 1993. 36.95 (*1-55750-258-7*) Naval Inst Pr.
— A History of U. S. Coast Guard Aviation. (Illus.). 188p. 1989. 37.95 (*0-87021-261-3*) Naval Inst Pr.
— U. S. Coast Guard Aircraft since 1916. LC 91-62723. (Illus.). 330p. 1992. 37.95 (*1-55750-852-6*) Naval Inst Pr.
Pearcy, C., ed. Topics in Operator Theory. LC 74-8254. (Mathematical Surveys Ser.: No. 13). 235p. 1979. reprint ed. pap. 44.00 (*0-8218-1513-X*, SURV-13) Am Math.
Pearcy, C., jt. auth. see Brown, A.
Pearcy, Carl M. Some Recent Developments in Operator Theory. LC 78-8754. (CBMS Regional Conference Series in Mathematics: No. 36). 73p. 1980. reprint ed. pap. 18.00 (*0-8218-1686-1*, CBMS 36) Am Math.
Pearcy, Carl M., jt. auth. see Brown, Aren.
Pearcy, G. Etzel. Patterns of International Boundaries. LC 72-86145. (Monograph: No.1). 1972. 4.95 (*0-916434-05-2*) Plycon Pr.
— Supercounties, U. S. A. LC 75-36700. (Monograph: No.3). (Illus.). 1976. 11.95 (*0-916434-15-X*) Plycon Pr.
— Thirty-Eight State U. S. A. LC 73-83685. (Monograph: No.2). (Illus.). 1973. 4.95 (*0-916434-09-5*) Plycon Pr.
— World Food Scene. LC 80-80423. (Illus.). 220p. (Orig.). 1980. pap. 13.95 (*0-686-62774-1*) Plycon Pr.
Pearcy, Lee T. The Shorter Homeric Hymns. 53p. (Orig.). (C). 1989. pap. text ed. 6.00 (*0-929524-62-4*) Bryn Mawr Commentaries.
Pearcy, Lee T., jt. auth. see Smith, Peter M.
Pearcy, Robert W., jt. ed. see Caldwell, Martyn M.
Pearcy, Robert W., et al, eds. Plant Physiological Ecology: Field Methods & Instrumentation. (Illus.). 480p. 1991. pap. 35.00 (*0-412-40730-2*, A5331) Chapman & Hall.
Pearcy, Roy D. Studies in the Age of Chaucer, Vol. 1. 1979. 40.00 (*0-933784-00-7*) New Chaucer Soc.
Pearcy, Roy J. Studies in the Age of Chaucer, Vol. 2. 1980. 40.00 (*0-933784-01-5*) New Chaucer Soc.
— Studies in the Age of Chaucer, Vol. 3. 1981. 40.00 (*0-933784-02-3*) New Chaucer Soc.
— Studies in the Age of Chaucer, Vol. 4. 1982. 40.00 (*0-933784-03-1*) New Chaucer Soc.
Pearcy, William G. Ocean Ecology of North Pacific Salmonids. LC 92-6564. (Books in Recruitment Fishery Oceanography). (Illus.). 190p. 1992. 25.00 (*0-295-97192-4*); pap. 15.00 (*0-295-97193-2*) U of Wash Pr.
Peardon, Thomas P., ed. The Second Treatise of Government: Locke. 168p. (C). 1952. pap. write for info. (*0-02-393300-3*) Macmillan.
Peare, Catherine O. The Helen Keller Story. LC 59-10979. 192p. (J). (gr. 4-6). 1990. lib. bdg. 14.89 (*0-690-04793-2*, Crowell Jr Bks) HarpC Child Bks.
— The Helen Keller Story. LC 90-49173. (American Cavalcade Ser.). (Illus.). 176p. (J). (gr. 6-10). 1991. lib. bdg. 9.95 (*1-55905-084-5*) Marshall Cavendish.
Pearen, Shelley J. Exploring Manitoulin. 176p. 1992. pap. 18.95 (*0-8020-6899-5*) U of Toronto Pr.
Pearl, Anita M. Completely Cheese. 365p. 1990. pap. 9.95 (*0-8246-0348-6*) Jonathan David.
Pearl, Arthur J. & Bergfeld, John A., eds. Extraarticular Reconstruction in the Anterior Cruciate Ligament Deficient Knee. LC 92-16257. (Illus.). 72p. 1992. pap. text ed. 20.00x (*0-87322-388-8*, BPEA0388) Human Kinetics.
Pearl, Arthur J., ed. see American Orthopaedic Society for Sports Medicine Staff.
Pearl, Arthur J., jt. ed. see Cahill, Bernard R.
Pearl, Bill. Getting Stronger. 1988. pap. 14.95 (*0-679-73948-3*) Random.
— Keys to the Inner Universe: Encyclopedia on Weight Training. 638p. 1991. reprint ed. text ed. 52.95 (*0-9629910-1-5*); reprint ed. pap. 32.95 (*0-9629910-0-7*) B Pearl Ent.
Pearl, Bill & Moran, Gary T. Getting Stronger: Weight Training for Men & Women. 464p. 1990. pap. 18.00 (*0-679-73269-1*) Random.
Pearl, Chaim. The Medieval Jewish Mind. LC 76-184221. 208p. 1973. 8.95 (*0-87677-043-X*) Hartmore.
Pearl, Chaim & Brookes, Reuben. The Guide to Jewish Knowledge. rev. ed. LC 75-25366. 142p. 1976. 8.95 (*0-87677-138-X*) Hartmore.
Pearl, Cyril. The Girl with the Swansdown Seat: Aspects of Mid-Victorian Morality. 6.95 (*0-686-85784-4*, Pub. by Quartet UK) Charles River Bks.
Pearl, David. A Textbook on Muslim Personal Law. 304p. 1987. pap. 39.95 (*0-7099-4089-0*, Pub. by Croom Helm UK) Routledge Chapman & Hall.
Pearl, David & Gray, Kevin. Social Welfare Law. 308p. 1981. 29.95 (*0-85664-644-X*, Pub. by Croom Helm UK); pap. 14.75 (*0-7099-2004-0*, Pub. by Croom Helm UK) Routledge Chapman & Hall.
Pearl, David, jt. auth. see Hoggett, Brenda.
Pearl, Dennis K. & Stasny, Elizabeth. Experiments in Statistical Concepts. 192p. (C). 1992. per., pap. text ed. 11.99 (*0-8403-8241-3*) Kendall-Hunt.
Pearl, Dennis K. & Stasny, Elizabeth A. Experiments in Statistical Concepts. 192p. 1992. per. 15.95 (*0-8403-7449-6*) Kendall-Hunt.
Pearl, Diane, jt. auth. see Williams, Ellie.
Pearl, Irwin A. The Chemistry of Lignin. LC 67-17005. (Illus.). 352p. reprint ed. pap. 100.40 (*0-317-07828-3*, 2055034) Bks Demand.
Pearl, Jack. The Yellow Rolls Royce. 17.95 (*0-88411-443-0*, Aeonian Pr) Amereon Ltd.
Pearl, Judea. Probabilistic Reasoning in Intelligent Systems: Networks of Plausible Inference. (Representation & Reasoning Ser.). 552p. (C). 1988. text ed. 54.95 (*0-934613-73-7*) Morgan Kaufmann.
Pearl, Judea, jt. ed. see Shafer, Glenn.
Pearl, Lauren & Kennedy, Doris F., eds. Lingua Latina Mortua Non Est! Latin Is Not Dead. 22p. 1991. pap. text ed. 1.70 (*0-939507-31-5*, B5) Amer Classical.
Pearl, Lizzy. The Adventures of Pussycat Wizzy Willums. LC 92-9475. (Illus.). 26p. (J). (ps-3). 1992. 6.98 (*1-56566-020-X*) Thomasson-Grant.
— The Story of Flight. LC 91-33412. (Story of Ser.). (Illus.). 32p. (J). (gr. 1-4). 1993. lib. bdg. 11.89 (*0-8167-2709-0*); pap. text ed. 3.95 (*0-8167-2710-4*) Troll Assocs.
Pearl, Louis. Sudman's Bubble-ology Guide. (Illus.). 32p. (Orig.). 1985. pap. 11.95 (*0-932165-07-9*) Tangent Pr.
Pearl, Mary, jt. ed. see Western, David.
Pearl, Mary, et al. Conservation & Environment in Papua, New Guinea: Establishing Research Priorities. 170p. 1992. pap. text ed. write for info. (*0-9632064-0-0*) Wildlife Conser Intl.
Pearl, Mignon W., jt. ed. see Richard, Pearl.
Pearl, Monica, jt. ed. see Chris, Cynthia.
Pearl, Morris L. William Cobbett: A Bibliographical Account of His Life & Times. LC 78-136079. 266p. 1971. reprint ed. text ed. 59.75 (*0-8371-5229-1*, PEWC, Greenwood Pr) Greenwood.
Pearl, Patricia. Helping Children Through Books: A Selected Booklist. 24p. 1990. reprint ed. pap. 7.25 (*0-915324-28-8*) CSLA.
— Religious Books for Children: An Annotated Bibliography. rev. ed. 40p. 1988. 8.25 (*0-915324-21-0*); 6.50 (*0-685-41042-0*) CSLA.
Pearl, Quinn, jt. auth. see Maurer, David W.
Pearl, Raymond. Alcohol & Longevity. Grob, Gerald N., ed. LC 80-1245. (Addiction in America Ser.). (Illus.). 1981. reprint ed. lib. bdg. 30.95 (*0-405-13615-3*) Ayer.
— The Biology of Death: Series of Lectures Delivered at the Lowell Institute in Boston in Dec. 1920. LC 75-38141. (Demography Ser.). (Illus.). 1976. reprint ed. 24.95 (*0-405-07994-X*) Ayer.
— The Biology of Population Growth. Egerton, Frank N., 3rd, ed. LC 77-74245. (History of Ecology Ser.). 1978. reprint ed. lib. bdg. 24.95 (*0-405-10414-6*) Ayer.
Pearl, Raymond & Pearl, Ruth D. The Ancestry of the Long-Lived. Kastenbaum, Robert, ed. LC 78-22213. (Aging & Old Age Ser.). (Illus.). 1979. reprint ed. lib. bdg. 17.95 (*0-405-11826-0*) Ayer.
Pearl, Richard H. Colorado's Hydrothermal Resource Base-an Assessment: An Assessment. (Resource Ser.: No. 6). (Illus.). 144p. (Orig.). 1979. pap. 3.00 (*1-884216-27-7*) Colo Geol Survey.

P Q

— Proceedings of a Symposium on Geothermal Energy & Colorado. (Bulletin Ser.: No. 35). (Illus.). 102p. (Orig.). 1974. pap. 2.00 (*1-884216-01-3*) Colo Geol Survey.

Pearl, Richard H., et al. Bibliography of Geothermal Reports in Colorado. (Bulletin Ser.: No. 44). 24p. (Orig.). 1981. pap. 1.00 (*1-884216-06-4*) Colo Geol Survey.

Pearl, Richard M. Colorado Gem Trails & Mineral Guide. 3rd rev. ed. LC 65-16515. (Illus.). 222p. 1972. pap. 14. 95 (*0-8040-0956-2*) Swallow.

— Exploring Rocks, Minerals, Fossils in Colorado. rev. ed. LC 64-25339. (Illus.). 215p. 1969. 16.95 (*0-8040-0105-7*) Swallow.

— Nature's Names for Colorado Communities. (Illus.). 24p. 1994. reprint ed. pap. 2.95 (*0-9624008-6-6*) Pulpit Rock.

— Springs of Colorado. (Illus.). 36p. 1994. reprint ed. pap. 2.95 (*0-9624008-7-4*) Pulpit Rock.

— 1,001 Questions Answered about the Mineral Kingdom. LC 95-6204. 1995. pap. write for info. (*0-486-28711-4*) Dover.

Pearl, Russell K. Gastrointestinal Endoscopy for Surgeons. 225p. 1984. 58.00 (*0-316-69615-3*) Little.

Pearl, Ruth D., jt. auth. see Pearl, Raymond.

Pearl, Stephen. The Picture House in East Anglia. 192p. (C). 1988. 60.00 (*0-900963-56-5*, Pub. by T Dalton UK) St Mut.

Pearlberg, Gerry. Women, AIDS & Communities: A Guide for Action. LC 91-17428. (Illus.). 141p. 1991. 27.50 (*0-8108-2470-1*); pap. 19.50 (*0-8108-2450-7*) Scarecrow.

***Pearlberg, Gerry G.** Key to Everything: Great Lesbian Love Poems. LC 94-36025. 1994. 10.00 (*0-312-11842-2*) St Martin.

Pearlman, Alan L. & Collins, Robert C., eds. Neurobiology of Disease. (Illus.). 504p. 1989. 55.00 (*0-19-505318-4*); pap. 39.95 (*0-19-505319-2*) OUP.

Pearlman, Alan S., jt. auth. see Otto, Catherine M.

Pearlman, Cari J. Take New York Home: The First 3-Dimensional Pop-up Map of New York. (Illus.). (YA). (gr. 1-12). 1994. 11.50 (*0-929644-01-8*) MultiMap.

***Pearlman, Daniel.** The Final Dream & Other Fictions. (Illus.). 272p. (Orig.). (C). 1995. pap. 14.95 (*1-882633-05-9*) Permeable.

Pearlman, Daniel D. & Dubose, Anita. Letter Perfect: An ABC for Business Writers. 112p. (Orig.). (C). 1985. pap. text ed. write for info. (*0-672-61623-8*) Macmillan.

Pearlman, Daniel D. & Pearlman, Paula R. Guide to Rapid Revision. 5th ed. LC 92-13092. (Illus.). 144p. (C). 1993. pap. write for info. (*0-02-393332-1*) Macmillan.

Pearlman, Daniel D., et al. Guide to Rapid Revision Workbook. 2nd ed. 208p. (C). 1989. pap. write for info. (*0-02-393330-5*) Macmillan.

Pearlman, David S., jt. auth. see Bierman, C. Warren.

Pearlman, Della. No Choice: Library Services for the Mentally Handicapped. LC 82-181478. 65p. reprint ed. pap. 25.00 (*0-7837-5320-9*, 2045059) Bks Demand.

***Pearlman, Donn.** Best Buys in Rare Coins. rev. ed. 220p. 1994. pap. text ed. 11.95 (*1-56625-023-4*) Bonus Books.

— Best Buys in Rare Coins: What Expert Dealers & Collectors Advise. (Illus.). 196p. (Orig.). 1990. pap. 8.95 (*0-933893-92-2*) Bonus Books.

— Breaking into Broadcasting. 224p. 1986. 17.95 (*0-933893-16-7*) Bonus Books.

— Collecting Baseball Cards. 3rd ed. LC 87-73307. (Illus.). 123p. 1990. pap. 7.95 (*0-929387-20-1*) Bonus Books.

Pearlman, Donn & Green, Paul. Making Money with Baseball Cards: A Handbook of Insider Secrets & Strategies. 215p. 1989. pap. 7.95 (*0-933893-77-9*) Bonus Books.

Pearlman, E. William Shakespeare: The Histories. (Twayne's English Authors Ser.). 150p. 1992. text ed. 22.95 (*0-8057-7020-8*, Pub. by Royal Botanic Garden UK) Macmillan.

Pearlman, Jill. Elvis for Beginners. (Documentary Comic Bks.). (Illus.). 159p. 1991. pap. 7.95 (*0-86316-110-3*) Writers & Readers.

Pearlman, Jill & White, Wayne. Elvis for Beginners. (Writers & Readers Documentary Comic Bks.). (Illus.). 160p. 1986. pap. 7.95 (*0-04-927011-7*) Writers & Readers.

Pearlman, Joanna, jt. ed. see Henriques, Leslie.

Pearlman, Joanna, ed. see Rapoport, Roger, et al.

Pearlman, Joanna, ed. see Ritz, Stacy.

Pearlman, Joanna, ed. see Scarborough, Carolyn, et al.

Pearlman, Joanna, ed. see Stratton, David.

Pearlman, Kenneth, et al, eds. Contemporary Problems in Personnel. LC 82-20316. (Illus.). 588p. reprint ed. pap. 167.60 (*0-7837-3506-5*, 2057839) Bks Demand.

Pearlman, Laurie A. & Saakvitne, Karen W. Trauma & the Therapist: Countertransference & Vicarious Traumatization in Psychotherapy with Incest Survivors. 320p. 1995. 40.00 (*0-393-70183-2*) Norton.

Pearlman, Laurie A., jt. auth. see McCann, I. Lisa.

Pearlman, Lisa A., jt. auth. see Wells, John F.

***Pearlman, Michael, ed. & tr.** The Heroic & Creative Meaning of Socialism: Selected Essays of Jose Carlos Mariategui. (Revolutionary Studies Ser.). 160p. (C). 1995. text ed. 39.95 (*0-391-03927-X*) Humanities.

Pearlman, Michael, tr. see Lowy, Michael, ed.

Pearlman, Michael D. To Make Democracy Safe for America: Patricians & Preparedness in the Progressive Era. LC 83-1107. (Illus.). 294p. 1984. 24.95 (*0-252-01019-1*) U of Ill Pr.

Pearlman, Mickey. Between Friends. 1994. pap. 13.95 (*0-395-65784-9*, HoughtonT) HM.

— Listen to Their Voices: Twenty Interviews with Women Who Write. 1994. pap. 10.95 (*0-395-68197-9*) HM.

— Listen to Their Voices: Twenty Interviews with Women Who Write. LC 92-14025. 224p. 1993. 20.95 (*0-393-03442-9*) Norton.

— Tillie Olsen. (Twayne's United States Authors Ser.: No. 581). 176p. (C). 1991. text ed. 20.95 (*0-8057-7632-X*, Pub. by Royal Botanic Garden UK) Macmillan.

— Voice of One's Own: Conversations with America's Writing Women. 1992. pap. 8.95 (*0-395-59972-5*) HM.

— What to Read. 192p. (Orig.). 1994. pap. 9.00 (*0-06-095061-7*, PL) HarpC.

Pearlman, Mickey, ed. American Women Writing Fiction: Memory, Identity, Family, Space. LC 88-18667. 248p. 1989. 27.00 (*0-8131-1657-0*); pap. 12.00 (*0-8131-0182-4*) U Pr of Ky.

— The Anna Book: Searching for Anna in Literary History. LC 92-8640. (Contributions to the Study of World Literature Ser.: No. 46). 246p. 1992. text ed. 47.95 (*0-313-27585-8*, PAK/, Greenwood Pr) Greenwood.

— Canadian Women Writing Fiction. LC 92-44969. 288p. 1993. text ed. 32.50 (*0-87805-636-X*) U Pr of Miss.

— Mother Puzzle: Daughters & Mothers in Contemporary American Literature. LC 89-11725. (Contributions in Women's Studies: No. 110). 210p. 1989. text ed. 49.95 (*0-313-26414-7*, PMC/, Greenwood Pr) Greenwood.

Pearlman, Mickey & Henderson, Katherine U., eds. Inter-View: Talks with America's Writing Women. LC 90-33308. (Illus.). 224p. 1990. 25.00 (*0-8131-1780-1*) U Pr of Ky.

Pearlman, Myer. Ensenando Con Exito - Edicion. 128p. (SPA.). 1991. pap. 3.95 (*0-8297-0548-1*) Life Pubs Intl.

— Knowing the Doctrines of the Bible. 400p. 1937. 10.95 (*0-88243-534-5*, 02-0534) Gospel Pub.

— The Minister's Service Book. 160p. 1990. 5.95 (*0-88243-551-5*, 02-0551) Gospel Pub.

— Seeing the Story of the Bible. 128p. 1930. pap. 4.95 (*0-88243-581-7*, 02-0581) Gospel Pub.

— Through the Bible Book by Book, 4 vols., Vol. 1. 99p. 1935. pap. 3.50 (*0-88243-660-0*, 02-0660) Gospel Pub.

— Through the Bible Book by Book, 4 vols., Vol. 2. 112p. 1935. 3.50 (*0-88243-661-9*, 02-0661) Gospel Pub.

— Through the Bible Book by Book, 4 vols., Vol. 3. 96p. 1935. 3.50 (*0-88243-662-7*, 02-0662) Gospel Pub.

— Through the Bible Book by Book, 4 vols., Vol. 4. 128p. 1935. 3.50 (*0-88243-663-5*, 02-0663) Gospel Pub.

Pearlman, Paula R., jt. auth. see Pearlman, Daniel D.

Pearlman, R., jt. ed. see Wang, Y. J.

Pearlman, Theodore. The Threatened Medical Identity of Psychiatry: The Winds of Change. (American Series in Behavioral Science & Law). 292p. (C). 1992. text ed. 51. 95x (*0-398-05768-0*) C C Thomas.

Pearlman, W. A., ed. Visual Communications & Image Processing IV. 1989. 149.00 (*0-8194-0238-9*, VOL. 1199) SPIE.

Pearlstein, Elinor, et al. Asian Art in the Art Institute of Chicago. (Illus.). 152p. 1993. pap. 24.95 (*0-86559-095-8*) Art Inst Chi.

— Asian Art in the Art Institute of Chicago. (Illus.). 152p. 1993. 35.00 (*0-8109-1916-8*) Abrams.

Pearlstein, Richard M. The Mind of the Political Terrorist. LC 90-9134. 237p. 1991. 40.00 (*0-8420-2345-3*) Scholarly Res Inc.

Pearlstein, S., ed. Cross-Section Data for Nuclear Reactor Analyses. (Illus.). 216p. 1984. pap. 88.00 (*0-08-031686-7*, Pergamon Pr) Elsevier.

Pearlstein, Toby. Transportation Planning in the Boston Metropolitan Area: A Selected Bibliography, 1930-1982. LC 83-20954. (CPL Bibliographies Ser.: No. 128). 1983. 10.00 (*0-317-00897-8*) CPL Biblios.

— Transportation Planning in the Boston Metropolitan Area: A Selected Bibliography, 1930-1982. (CPL Bibliographies Ser.: No. 128). 53p. 1983. 10.00 (*0-685-18431-5*) Coun Plan Librarians.

Pearlstone, Zena. Ethnic L. A. (Illus.). 186p. 1990. pap. 12. 95 (*0-914589-05-9*) Hillcrest Pr.

Pearlstone, Zena, ed. see Rubin, Arnold.

Pearman, jt. auth. see Dahlem, Konferenzen.

Pearman, A. D., jt. auth. see Button, K. J.

Pearman, A. D., jt. ed. see Button, K. J.

Pearman, Donald V. The Termite Report: The Homeowner & Buyer's Guide to Structural Pest Control. (Illus.). 140p. (Orig.). 1988. pap. 16.95 (*0-943743-00-1*) Pear Pub.

Pearman, Hugh. Rick Mather: Urban Approaches. (Illus.). 112p. 1993. pap. 29.95 (*1-85702-007-3*, Pub. by Fourth Estate UK) Trafalgar.

Pearman, Richard. Solid State Industrial Electronics. (C). 1984. teacher ed write for info. (*0-8359-7042-6*, Reston); text ed. 58.00 (*0-8359-7041-8*, Reston) P-H.

Pearman, Richard A. Electric Machinery & Transformer Technology. LC 93-40123. 1994. text ed. 61.25 (*0-03-097713-4*) SCP.

Pearman, William A. & Starr, Phillip, eds. Medicare: A Handbook in the History & Issues of Health Care Services for the Elderly. LC 88-2423. (Reference Library of Social Science). 166p. 1988. lib. bdg. 28.00 (*0-8240-8391-1*) Garland.

Pearman, William I. Support of State Educational Programs by Dedication of Specific Revenues & by General Revenue Appropriations: A Study of Certain Factors Which Relate to the Adoption & Use of These General Policies by State Governments. LC 75-177147. (Columbia University. Teachers College. Contributions to Education Ser.: No. 591). reprint ed. 37.50 (*0-404-55591-8*) AMS Pr.

Pearn, B. R., ed. see Watson, James K.

Pearn, M. & Kandola, R. Job Analysis: A Practical Guide for Managers. 144p. (C). 1988. 60.00 (*0-85292-368-6*, Pub. by IPM Hse UK) St Mut.

Pearn, Michael & Kandola, Rajvinder. Job Analysis: A Practical Guide for Managers. 144p. 1993. 40.00 (*0-85292-542-5*, Pub. by IPM Hse UK) St Mut.

***Pearn, Michael, et al.** Learning Organizations in Practice. LC 95-5588. 1995. write for info. (*0-7707-744X-7*) McGraw.

Pearosn, Allen. The Teacher: Theory & Practice in Education. rev. ed. LC 88-92216. 200p. 1989. pap. text ed. 30.00 (*0-9620940-0-5*, A2713) Routledge Chapman & Hall.

***Pearring, Joanne M., ed.** When Someone Dies: A Children's Grief Workbook. (Illus.). 16p. (Orig.). 1995. student ed, pap. 1.50 (*0-89622-644-1*) Twenty-Third.

Pearring, Parker F. Human Behavior - Analysis, Therapy & Treatments: Index of New Information with Authors, Subjects & Bibliography. 180p. 1993. 49.50 (*1-55914-788-1*); pap. 39.50 (*1-55914-789-X*) ABBE Pubs Assn.

Pears, D. F., ed. see Wittgenstein, Ludwig.

Pears, David. The False Prison: A Study of the Development of Wittgenstein's Philosophy, Vol. 1. 224p. 1987. pap. 19.95 (*0-19-824770-2*) OUP.

— The False Prison: A Study of the Development of Wittgenstein's Philosophy, Vol. 2. 360p. 1988. 45.00 (*0-19-824487-8*); pap. 21.00 (*0-19-824486-X*) OUP.

— Hume's System: An Examination of the First Book of His Treatise. 224p. 1991. 49.95 (*0-19-875100-1*); pap. 17.95 (*0-19-875099-4*) OUP.

Pears, David, frwd. Wittgenstein. 224p. 1986. pap. 12.95 (*0-674-53951-6*) HUP.

Pears, E. Destruction of the Greek Empire & the Story of the Capture of Constantinople by the Turks. LC 68-25259. (World History Ser.: No. 48). (Illus.). 1969. reprint ed. lib. bdg. 75.00 (*0-8383-0227-0*) M S G Haskell Hse.

Pears, Edwin. Forty Years in Constantinople: Recollections of Sir Edwin Pears, 1873-1915. LC 78-179533. (Select Bibliographies Reprint Ser.). 1977. reprint ed. 26.95 (*0-8369-6662-7*) Ayer.

— Life of Abdul Hamid. LC 73-6296. (Middle East Ser.). 1973. reprint ed. 28.95 (*0-405-05354-1*) Ayer.

— Turkey & Its People. 2nd ed. LC 77-87634. reprint ed. 28.50 (*0-404-16459-5*) AMS Pr.

Pears, Iain. The Bernini Bust. LC 94-14514. 1994. 20.00 (*0-15-111830-2*) HarBrace.

— The Bernini Bust. 1995. write for info. (*0-7862-0367-6*) Thorndike Pr.

— The Discovery of Painting: The Growth of Interest in the Arts in England, 1680-1768. (Illus.). 301p. (C). 1991. reprint ed. pap. text ed. 22.50 (*0-300-05147-6*) Yale U Pr.

— The Raphael Affair. LC 92-18790. 1992. 18.95 (*0-15-178912-6*) HarBrace.

— The Raphael Affair. large type ed. (Linford Mystery Library). 1991. pap. 13.95 (*0-7089-7155-5*) Ulverscroft.

— The Titian Committee. LC 93-404. 1993. 19.95 (*0-15-190472-3*) HarBrace.

— The Titian Committee. large type ed. LC 93-48428. 1994. pap. 17.95 (*0-7862-0170-3*) Thorndike Pr.

Pears, Randolph. British Battleships Eighteen Ninety-Two to Nineteen Fifty-Seven. 1981. 40.00 (*0-906223-14-8*) St Mut.

Pears, Sarah, jt. auth. see Pears, Thomas.

Pears, Thomas & Pears, Sarah. New Harmony, an Adventure in Happiness: Papers of Thomas & Sarah Pears. Pears, Thomas C., Jr., ed. LC 72-77058. 1973. reprint ed. lib. bdg. 25.00 (*0-678-00908-2*) Kelley.

Pears, Thomas C., Jr., ed. see Pears, Thomas & Pears, Sarah.

***Pears, Tim.** In the Place of Fallen Leaves. 1995. 21.95 (*1-55611-423-0*) D I Fine.

Pearsall, Arlene E. Johannes Pauli (1450-1520) on the Church & Clergy. LC 93-48792. 260p. 1994. 89.95 (*0-7734-9108-2*) E Mellen.

Pearsall, Deborah M. Paleoethnobotany: A Handbook of Procedures. 470p. 1989. text ed. 59.95 (*0-12-548040-7*) Acad Pr.

Pearsall, Deborah M., jt. ed. see Voigt, Eric E.

Pearsall, Deborah M., jt. ed. see Zeidler, James A.

Pearsall, Derek. The Canterbury Tales. 380p. 1985. pap. 19. 95 (*0-415-09444-5*, A8672) Routledge.

— The Life of Geoffrey Chaucer: A Critical Biography. (Critical Biographies Ser.). 336p. 1992. text ed. 29.95 (*1-55786-205-2*) Blackwell Pubs.

— The Life of Geoffrey Chaucer: A Critical Biography. 336p. 1995. pap. 18.95 (*1-55786-665-1*) Blackwell Pubs.

Pearsall, Derek, ed. An Annotated Critical Bibliography of Langland. LC 90-50103. 240p. 1990. reprint ed. text ed. 44.50 (*0-472-10185-4*) U of Mich Pr.

— Floure & the Leafe, the Assembly of Ladies, the Isle of Ladies. (TEAMS Middle English Text Ser.). 1992. pap. 6.95 (*0-918720-43-5*) Medieval Inst.

— Manuscripts & Texts: Editorial Problems in Later Middle English Literature-Essays from the 1985 Conference at the University of York. 1987. 71.00 (*0-85991-231-0*) Boydell & Brewer.

— Piers Plowman: A Facsimile of the Bodleian Library, Oxford, MS Douce 104. (Illus.). 256p. (C). 1992. text ed. 260.00 (*0-85991-345-7*) Boydell & Brewer.

— Studies in the Vernon Manuscript. (Illus.). 224p. 1990. 79.00 (*0-85991-310-4*) Boydell & Brewer.

Pearsall, Derek, ed. see Chaucer, Geoffrey.

Pearsall, Derek, jt. ed. see Griffiths, Jeremy.

Pearsall, Derek, ed. see Salter, Elizabeth.

Pearsall, Derek, et al. A Descriptive Catalogue of the Manuscripts of the Works of John Gower. (Literature Ser.). 300p. lib. bdg. 45.00 (*0-8240-9189-2*) Garland.

Pearsall, Derek A. & Salter, Elizabeth. Landscapes & Seasons of the Medieval World. LC 73-85089. 316p. reprint ed. pap. 90.10 (*0-685-16012-2*, 2026406) Bks Demand.

***Pearsall, Jay.** Mystery & Crime: The New York Public Library Book of Answers. 176p. 1995. 5.98 (*1-56865-132-5*, GuildAmerica) Dblday Bk Music.

— Mystery & Crime NYPL Answers. 1995. pap. 11.00 (*0-671-87237-0*, Fireside) S&S Trade.

Pearsall, Margaret. The Pearsall Guide to Successful Dog Training. 3rd ed. LC 80-16840. (Illus.). 352p. 1981. 25. 95 (*0-87605-759-8*) Howell Bk.

Pearsall, Marilyn. Women & Values: Readings in Recent Feminist Philosophy. 2nd ed. LC 92-13426. 413p. (C). 1993. pap. 27.95 (*0-534-19554-7*) Intl Thomson.

Pearsall, Marilyn, jt. ed. see Garry, Ann.

Pearsall, Milo D. & Verbruggen, Hugo. Scent: Training to Track, Search, & Rescue. (Illus.). 240p. 1982. 16.95 (*0-931866-11-1*) Alpine Pubns.

Pearsall, N. M. Solar Electricity: Its Current Role in Overseas Aid (C48) (C). 1987. 100.00 (*0-685-30231-8*, Pub. by Interntl Solar Energy Soc UK) St Mut.

Pearsall, N. M., ed. Solar Electricity: Its Current Role in Overseas Aid. (C). 1987. 120.00 (*0-685-33091-5*, Pub. by Interntl Solar Energy Soc UK) St Mut.

Pearsall, N. M., jt. auth. see Hill, R.

Pearsall, Nancy N. & Weiser, Russell S. The Macrophage. LC 77-85844. (Illus.). 214p. reprint ed. 61.00 (*0-8357-9410-5*, 2014576) Bks Demand.

***Pearsall, Paul.** A Healing Intimacy. 1995. pap. 13.00 (*0-517-88385-6*) Random.

— Sexual Healing: Intimacy, Immunity, & the Connection Factor. LC 93-34559. 1994. 20.00 (*0-517-59440-4*, Crown) Crown Pub Group.

— Super Marital Sex. 448p. 1988. mass mkt. 5.99 (*0-8041-0367-4*) Ivy Books.

— The Ten Laws of Lasting Love. 336p. 1995. pap. 11.00 (*0-380-72307-7*) Avon.

Pearsall, Paul P. Making Miracles: Finding Meaning in Life's Chaos. 320p. 1993. reprint ed. pap. 10.00 (*0-380-71948-7*) Avon.

— Superimmunity: Master Your Emotions & Improve Your Health. 304p. 1988. mass mkt. 5.99 (*0-449-13396-6*, GM) Fawcett.

— Ten Laws of Lasting Love. LC 92-42016. 352p. 1993. 22. 00 (*0-671-76798-4*) S&S Trade.

Pearsall, Priscilla. An Art Alienated from Itself: Studies in Spanish American Modernism. LC 83-17736. (Romance Monographs: No. 43). 103p. 1984. 19.00 (*84-499-6721-X*) Romance.

Pearsall, Robert B. Frank Harris. LC 74-120526. (Twayne's English Authors Ser.). 196p. (C). 1970. lib. bdg. 17.95 (*0-317-38186-5*) Irvington.

— Robert Browning. (English Authors Ser.: No. 168). 200p. 1974. text ed. 21.95 (*0-8057-1065-5*, Twayne) Macmillan.

Pearsall, Ronald. Edwardian Popular Music. LC 75-10734. (Illus.). 207p. 18.00 (*0-8386-1781-6*) Fairleigh Dickinson.

— The Joy of Antiques. (Illus.). 208p. 1992. pap. 19.95 (*0-7153-0028-8*, Pub. by D & C Pub UK) Sterling.

Pearsall, T. P., ed. GaInAsP Alloy Semiconductors. LC 81-15922. 480p. reprint ed. pap. 136.80 (*0-7837-5875-8*, 2045595) Bks Demand.

Pearsall, Thomas E. Teaching Technical Writing Methods for College English Teachers. 1975. pap. 6.00 (*0-914548-13-1*) Soc Tech Comm.

Pearsall, Thomas E. & Cunningham, Donald H. The Fundamentals of Good Writing. 518p. (C). 1988. pap. write for info. (*0-02-477100-7*) Macmillan.

— How to Write for the World of Work. 4th ed. (Illus.). 479p. (C). 1990. text ed. 28.00 (*0-03-030802-X*) HB Coll Pubs.

— How to Write for the World of Work. 5th ed. LC 93-27792. 1993. pap. text ed. 32.25 (*0-15-501121-9*) HB Coll Pubs.

Pearsall, Thomas E., jt. auth. see Brown, James I.

Pearsall, Thomas P., ed. Semiconductors & Semimetals, Vol. 32: Strained-Layer Superlattices: Physics. 276p. 1990. text ed. 105.00 (*0-12-752132-1*) Acad Pr.

— Semiconductors & Semimetals, Vol. 33: Strained-Layer Superlattices: Materials Science & Technology. 431p. 1990. text ed. 118.00 (*0-12-752133-X*) Acad Pr.

Pearse, A. G. Histochemistry, Vol. 1: Theoretical & Applied. 4th ed. (Illus.). 456p. 1980. text ed. 175.00 (*0-443-01998-3*) Churchill.

— Histochemistry, Vol 2: Theoretical & Applied. 4th ed. (Illus.). 624p. 1985. text ed. 210.00 (*0-443-02997-0*) Churchill.

Pearse, Andrew. Latin American Peasant. (Library of Peasant Studies: No. 1). 299p. 1975. 35.00 (*0-7146-3047-0*, Pub. by F Cass Pubs UK); pap. 15.00 (*0-7146-4021-2*, Pub. by F Cass Pubs UK) Intl Spec Bk.

Pearse, Cecilia M. & Hird, Frank. The Romance of a Great Singer: Memoir of Mario. Farkas, Andrew, ed. LC 76-29961. (Opera Biographies Ser.). (Illus.). 1977. reprint ed. lib. bdg. 28.95 (*0-405-09701-8*) Ayer.

Pearse, John. Cooking with Wine. Warde, John, ed. (Illus.). 100p. 1987. pap. 9.95 (*0-318-22777-0*) Buckingham WP.

— The Guitarist's Picture Chord Encyclopedia. (Illus.). 310p. 1978. pap. 16.95 (*0-8256-2199-2*) Music Sales.

Pearse, John & Warde, John. Stringalong. (Illus.). 96p. 1986. pap. 10.95 (*0-9617175-0-5*) J Pearse Mus Pub.

Pearse, John S., jt. ed. see Giese, Arthur C.

Pearse, M. T. Between Known Men & Visible Saints: A Study of Sixteenth Century English Dissent. LC 94-16045. 1995. write for info. (*0-8386-3563-6*) Fairleigh Dickinson.

Pearse, Nancy C. John Fletcher's Chastity Plays: Mirrors of Modesty. LC 72-3258. 255p. 1973. 22.50 (*0-8387-1151-0*) Bucknell U Pr.

Pearse, Padraic. Short Stories. 118p. 1989. pap. 9.95 (*0-85342-883-2*, Pub. by Mercier Pr IE) Dufour.

Pearse, Padraic H. Collected Works of Padraic H. Pearse. LC 75-28838. reprint ed. 35.00 (*0-404-13827-6*) AMS Pr.

Pearse, Patricia. See How You Grow. LC 87-33268. (Illus.). 32p. (J). (gr. 1-4). 1988. 13.95 (*0-8120-5936-0*) Barron.

An Asterisk (*) at the beginning of an entry indicates that the title is appearing in BIP for the first time.

*__Pearse, Patrick, et al.__ The 1916 Poets: Pearse, Plunkett, MacDonagh. Ryan, Desmond, ed. 179p. 1995. reprint ed. pap. 15.95 (*0-7171-2294-8*, Pub. by Gill & MacMill IE) Irish Bks Media.

Pearse, Richard. The Land Beside the Celtic Sea: Aspect of Cornwall's Past. (C). 1989. pap. 30.00 (*0-907566-48-0*, Pub. by Dyllansow Truran UK) St Mut.

Pearse, Robert F., jt. auth. see Fram, Eugene H.

Pearse, Warren H., jt. auth. see Seltzer, Vicki L.

Pearson. Parasite Antigens: Toward New Strategies for Vaccines. (Receptors & Ligands in Intercellular Communications Ser.: Vol. 7). 424p. 1986. 140.00 (*0-8247-7477-9*) Dekker.

— Pyrogens, Endotoxins & LAL Testing & Depyrogenation. (Advances in Parenteral Science Ser.: Vol. 2). 288p. 1985. 110.00 (*0-8247-8018-3*) Dekker.

— Uncle Alphonso & the Greedy Green Dinosuar. LC 90-20340. (J). 1992. pap. 4.99 (*1-55513-424-6*, Chariot Bks) Chariot Family.

— Uncle Alphonso & the Puffy Proud Dinosuar. LC 90-32442. (J). 1992. pap. 4.99 (*1-55513-562-5*, Chariot Bks) Chariot Family.

Pearson & Barrett, eds. Image Understanding & Man-Machine Interface. 192p. 1987. 43.00 (*0-89252-793-5*, 758) SPIE.

Pearson, et al, eds. Aquatic Toxicology & Hazard Assessment (Fifth Conference)- STP 766. 414p. 1982. 44.50 (*0-8031-0796-X*, 04-766000-16) ASTM.

Pearson, A. C., ed. The Fragments of Zeno & Cleanthes. LC 72-9299. (Philosophy of Plato & Aristotle Ser.). 1974. reprint ed. 21.95 (*0-405-04854-8*) Ayer.

Pearson, A. J., ed. Iron Compounds in Organic Synthesis. (Best Synthetic Methods Ser.). (Illus.). 224p. 1994. boxed 52.50 (*0-12-548270-1*) Acad Pr.

Pearson, A. John, ed. see Lindquist, Emory K., et al.

Pearson, A. John, ed. see Lindquist, Emory K.

Pearson, A. M. & Dutson, Thayne R., eds. Meat & Health. (Advances in Meat Research Ser.: Vol. 6). 564p. 1990. 137.00 (*1-85166-452-1*) Elsevier.

Pearson, A. M. & Young, R. B., eds. Muscle & Meat Biochemistry. (Food Science & Technology Ser.). 457p. 1989. text ed. 194.00 (*0-12-548055-5*) Acad Pr.

Pearson, A. W., jt. auth. see Holden, K.

Pearson, Agusta. A Spinster's Tour Through North Wales. (C). 1988. text ed. 34.00 (*0-86383-412-4*, Pub. by Gomer Pr UK) St Mut.

Pearson, Alan. Nursing, from Whence to Where? Professorial Lecture. (C). 1991. pap. 21.00x (*0-7300-1448-7*, Pub. by Deakin Univ AT) St Mut.

— Optimum Staffing Mix in Australian Nursing Homes: A Review of the Literature (DINROO) 92p. 1993. pap. 39.00 (*0-7300-1550-5*, Pub. by Deakin Univ AT) St Mut.

— The Social Reality of Clinical Nursing in a Rural Hospital. 35p. (C). 1989. pap. 51.00x (*0-7300-0694-8*, NPR803, Pub. by Deakin Univ AT) St Mut.

Pearson, Alan, ed. Primary Nursing: Nursing in the Burford & Oxford Nursing Development Units. 160p. 1988. pap. text ed. 25.00 (*0-7099-4066-1*, Pub. by Croom Helm UK) Routledge Chapman & Hall.

*__Pearson, Alan & Baker, Helen.__ Compliance or Alliance? (Case Study on Introducing Research Papers: No. 9). 1992. pap. text ed. 21.00 (*0-614-04014-0*, Pub. by Deakin Univ AT) St Mut.

— Quality of Care: Do Contemporary Nursing Approaches Make a Difference. 1991. pap. 21.00 (*0-7300-1497-5*, Pub. by Deakin Univ AT) St Mut.

Pearson, Alan, jt. auth. see Baker, Helen.

*__Pearson, Alan, et al.__ Food for Thought: Comparing Nurses Assessment of Food Intake. (Research Paper Ser.: No. 4). 1992. pap. 21.00 (*0-7300-1489-4*, Pub. by Deakin Univ AT) St Mut.

— Hospital Carpets: Comfort, Cosiness & Cleanliness. (Research Papers: No. 2). 1992. pap. 21.00 (*0-7300-1482-7*, Pub. by Deakin Univ AT) St Mut.

*__Pearson, Alan, et al, trs.__ Inservice Training in Non-Government Nursing Homes (DINROO) (Research Monographs: No. 3). 1992. pap. 33.00 (*0-7300-1484-3*, Pub. by Deakin Univ AT) St Mut.

Pearson, Alan J. Unified Theory of Refining. (Pulp & Paper Technology Ser.: No. 6). 128p. 1990. 15.00 (*0-919893-79-1*, 0101JT06) TAPPI.

— A Unified Theory of Refining. (Pulp & Paper Technology Ser.: No. 6). (Illus.). reprint ed. pap. 35.40 (*0-8357-4081-1*, 2036771) Bks Demand.

Pearson, Alison, jt. auth. see Pearson, Steve.

Pearson, Anna. The Complete Needlepoint Course. (Illus.). 176p. 1991. 27.95 (*0-8019-8227-8*) Chilton.

Pearson, Anne. Ancient Greece. LC 92-4713. (Eyewitness Bks.). (Illus.). 64p. (J). (gr. 5 up). 1992. 16.00 (*0-679-81682-8*); lib. bdg. 16.99 (*0-679-91682-2*) Knopf Bks Yng Read.

— Everyday Life in Ancient Egypt. LC 93-37520. (Clues to the Past Ser.). (J). 1994. lib. bdg. 12.60 (*0-531-14309-0*) Watts.

— Everyday Life in Ancient Greece. LC 93-37519. (Clues to the Past Ser.). (J). 1994. lib. bdg. 12.60 (*0-531-14310-4*) Watts.

— The Vikings. (See Through History Ser.). (Illus.). 48p. (J). (gr. 3-7). 1994. 15.99 (*0-670-85834-X*) Viking Child Bks.

— What Do We Know about the Greeks? LC 92-9692. (What Do We Know about...? Ser.). (Illus.). 40p. (J). (gr. 3-6). 1992. lib. bdg. 16.95 (*0-87226-356-8*) P Bedrick Bks.

Pearson, Anthony, jt. auth. see Labovitz, Arthur.

Pearson, Anthony J. Metalloorganic Chemistry. LC 84-3702. 398p. 1985. text ed. 295.00 (*0-471-90440-6*) Wiley.

Pearson, Aval, ed. see Kyte, Shekhem-Cwolde.

Pearson, Barrie. Successful Acquisition of Unquoted Companies. 3rd ed. 192p. 1989. text ed. 77.95 (*0-566-02814-X*, Pub. by Gower UK) Ashgate Pub Co.

Pearson, Barry L. Sounds So Good to Me: The Bluesman's Story. LC 83-14764. (Illus.). 186p. 1984. 19.95 (*0-8122-1171-5*) U of Pa Pr.

— Virginia Piedmont Blues: The Lives & Art of Two Virginia Bluesmen. LC 89-28014. (Publications of the American Folklore Society, Bibliographical & Special Ser.). (Illus.). 300p. (C). 1990. text ed. 41.95x (*0-8122-8209-4*); pap. text ed. 19.95 (*0-8122-1300-9*) U of Pa Pr.

*__Pearson, Bill, et al.__ Hands-on Science with Project Smartlab: Science & Math Activity-Related Teaching from Labs in a Box. LC 95-67968. (Illus.). 280p. (J). (gr. 6-8). Date not set. ring bd. write for info. (*0-89089-852-9*) Carolina Acad Pr.

Pearson, Birger A. Gnosticism, Judaism, & Egyptian Christianity. LC 89-48945. (Studies in Antiquity & Christianity). 248p. (Orig.). 1990. lib. bdg. 31.00 (*0-8006-3104-8*, 1-3104) Augsburg Fortress.

Pearson, Birger A., ed. The Future of Early Christianity: Essays in Honor of Helmut Koester. 544p. 1991. 42.00 (*0-8006-2521-8*, 1-2521, Fortress Pr) Augsburg Fortress.

Pearson, Birger A. & Goehring, James E., eds. The Roots of Egyptian Christianity. LC 85-47736. (Studies in Antiquity & Christianity). 336p. 1986. pap. 20.00 (*0-8006-2706-7*, 1-2706, Fortress Pr) Augsburg Fortress.

Pearson, Brian, jt. auth. see Griffiths, Ronno.

Pearson, Brian, et al. Using Environmental Management Systems to Improve Profits. (C). 1992. ring bd. 160.00 (*1-85333-754-4*) Kluwer Ac.

Pearson, Bruce. Standard of Excellence: Full Score, Bk. 1. 660p. 1993. 49.95 (*0-8497-5948-X*, W21F) Kjos.

— Standard of Excellence: Full Score, Bk. 1. 1993. audio 8.95 (*0-614-03107-9*); 12.95 (*0-614-03108-7*) Kjos.

— Standard of Excellence: Full Score, Bk. 1: Parts. 1993. write for info. (*0-614-03106-0*) Kjos.

— Standard of Excellence: Full Score, Bk. 2. 640p. 1994. 49.95 (*0-8497-5950-1*, W22F); 12.95 (*0-318-72755-2*) Kjos.

— Standard of Excellence: Full Score, Bk. 2. 1994. audio 8.95 (*0-614-03111-7*) Kjos.

— Standard of Excellence: Full Score, Bk. 2: Parts. 640p. 1994. write for info. (*0-685-74724-7*) Kjos.

*__Pearson, Bruce, et al.__ Best in Class Bk. 1: Score & Manual, Parts. 1981. write for info. (*0-614-03105-2*) Kjos.

— Best in Class Bk. 1: Score & Manual, Set. 250p. 1981. 19.95 (*0-8497-5850-5*, W3F) Kjos.

— Encore: Conductor Score & Manual. 248p. 1985. 19.95 (*0-8497-5906-4*, W5F) Kjos.

— Encore: Conductor Score & Manual, Parts. 248p. 1985. write for info. (*0-685-74722-0*) Kjos.

Pearson, Bruce L. Introduction to Linguistic Concepts. 1977. pap. text ed. 12.95 (*0-07-553627-7*) McGraw.

Pearson, C. C. Readjuster Movement in Virginia. 11.25 (*0-8446-1344-4*) Peter Smith.

Pearson, C. C. & Hendricks, J. Edwin. Liquor & Anti-liquor in Virginia, 1619-1919. LC 67-18530. 354p. reprint ed. pap. 100.90 (*0-317-20438-6*, 2023433) Bks Demand.

Pearson, C. E. Above & Below the ABSeas. (Illus.). 56p. (Orig.). (J). (gr. k-5). 1994. pap. 9.95 (*0-9640585-0-2*) Mt Hope Pubng.

Pearson, C. J., ed. Control of Crop Productivity. 339p. 1985. text ed. 106.00 (*0-12-548280-9*) Acad Pr.

Pearson, Carl E. Handbook Applied Mathematics. 1990. pap. 46.95 (*0-442-00521-0*) Chapman & Hall.

— Numerical Methods in Engineering & Science. LC 85-22516. (Illus.). 256p. 1986. text ed. 44.95 (*0-442-27344-4*) Chapman & Hall.

— Theoretical Elasticity. LC 59-9283. 230p. reprint ed. pap. 65.60 (*0-317-08681-2*, 2001586) Bks Demand.

Pearson, Carl E., jt. auth. see Carrier, George F.

*__Pearson, Carol.__ Magic at Work: Five Stages to Realizing the Height of Your Creative Power. 1995. 22.50 (*0-385-41729-2*) Doubleday.

Pearson, Carol L. Beginnings. 6.95 (*0-88494-561-8*) Bookcraft Inc.

— Don't Count Your Chickens until They Cry Wolf: Musical. (J). 1979. 5.00 (*0-87602-122-4*) Anchorage.

— Good-bye, I Love You. LC 93-35914. 1995. 9.95 (*1-882723-04-X*) Gold Leaf Pr.

— I Believe in Make Believe. (Orig.). (J). (gr. k up). 1984. pap. 5.00 (*0-87602-255-7*) Anchorage.

— A Stranger for Christmas. pap. 4.95 (*0-88494-552-9*) Bookcraft Inc.

— Women I Have Known & Been. LC 92-9920. 1992. 11.95 (*1-56236-306-9*) Aspen Bks.

— Women I Have Known & Been. 1993. 11.95 (*1-882723-03-1*) Gold Leaf Pr.

Pearson, Carol S. Awakening the Heroes Within: Twelve Archetypes to Help Us Find Ourselves & Transform Our World. LC 90-55296. 288p. (Orig.). 1991. pap. 16.00 (*0-06-250678-1*) Harper SF.

Pearson, Carol S., et al, eds. Educating the Majority: Improving Higher Education for Women. (C). 1987. write for info. (*0-318-63183-0*, 2014) Macmillan.

Pearson, Charles, ed. Multinational Corporations, Environment, & the Third World: Business Matters. LC 86-19810. (Duke Press Policy Studies). xvi, 295p. 1987. pap. 21.95 (*0-8223-0761-8*) Duke.

Pearson, Charles & Johnson, Nils. The New GATT Round. 76p. (Orig.). (C). 1986. pap. text ed. 11.75 (*0-941700-05-4*) JH FPI SAIS.

Pearson, Charles & Riedel, James, eds. The Direction of Trade Policy. 256p. (C). 1990. text ed. 54.95 (*1-55786-080-7*) Blackwell Pubs.

Pearson, Charles, jt. auth. see Johnson, Nils.

Pearson, Charles E. & Hoffman, Paul E. Last Voyage of El Nuevo Constante: Wreck & Recovery of an Eighteenth Century Spanish Ship off the Louisiana Coast. LC 94-27046. (Illus.). 264p. 1994. 29.95 (*0-8071-1918-0*) La State U Pr.

Pearson, Charles H. Russia: By a Recent Traveler. (Russia Through European Eyes Ser.). 1971. reprint ed. lib. bdg. 39.50 (*0-306-77030-X*) Da Capo.

Pearson, Charles S. Down to Business: Multinational Corporations, the Environment, & Development. LC 84-52795. 120p. (Orig.). 1985. pap. text ed. 10.00 (*0-915825-04-X*) World Resources Inst.

— Free Trade, Fair Trade? The Reagan Record. LC 88-39110. (FPI Papers in International Affairs). 90p. (Orig.). (C). 1989. pap. text ed. 16.00 (*0-941700-49-6*) JH FPI SAIS.

Pearson, Charles S. & Pryor, Anthony. Environment: North & South; An Economic Interpretation. LC 77-11143. (Illus.). 377p. reprint ed. pap. 107.50 (*0-317-09692-3*, 2022499) Bks Demand.

Pearson, Cheryl, ed. see Trostel, Scott D.

Pearson, Cheryll A., jt. auth. see Nelson, C. Michael.

Pearson, Christine, jt. auth. see Mitroff, Alan I.

Pearson, Colin. The Conservation of Marine Archaeological Objects. (Conservation & Museology Ser.). (Illus.). 360p. 1988. text ed. 89.95 (*0-408-10668-9*) Buttrwrth-Heinemann.

Pearson, Craig. Make Your Own Games Workshop. (Crafts Workshop Ser.). (J). (gr. 3-8). 1982. pap. 10.99 (*0-8224-9782-4*) Fearon Teach Aids.

Pearson, Craig J. & Ison, Ray L. Agronomy of Grassland Systems. (Illus.). 200p. 1987. pap. 24.95 (*0-521-31009-1*) Cambridge U Pr.

Pearson, Craig M. Food & You. (Independent Living Ser.). (gr. 11-12). 1978. text ed. 11.00 (*0-07-049057-0*) McGraw.

Pearson, Craig M., et al. Independent Living: Being on Your Own. (Independent Living Ser.). (Illus.). 464p. (gr. 11-12). 1979. text ed. 25.84 (*0-07-049061-9*) McGraw.

Pearson, Crystal K. Spicy Singles, Vol. I. (Illus.). 130p. (Orig.). 1992. pap. text ed. 9.50 (*0-9631853-0-6*) Spicy Singles.

Pearson, Cynthia, jt. auth. see Freidlander, John.

Pearson, D. B., ed. Quantum Scattering & Spectral Theory. (Techniques of Physics Ser.). 519p. 1988. text ed. 137.00 (*0-12-548260-4*) Acad Pr.

Pearson, D. E. Image Processing. 394p. 1991. text ed. 60.00 (*0-07-707323-1*) McGraw.

*__Pearson, D. W., et al, eds.__ Artificial Neural Nets & Genetic Algorithms: Proceedings of the International Conference in Ales, France, 1995. LC 95-10560. 1995. write for info. (*3-211-82692-0*) Spr-Verlag.

Pearson, Daniel. Baseball in 1889: Players vs Owners. LC 92-63282. 234p. (C). 1993. 42.95 (*0-87972-618-0*); pap. 15.95 (*0-87972-619-9*) Bowling Green Univ.

Pearson, Daniel M. The Americanization of Carl Aaron Swensson. LC 77-151736. (Augustana Historical Society Publication Ser.: No.25). 169p. 1977. 5.95 (*0-910184-25-9*) Augustana.

Pearson, Darrell W. Death Walk. LC 93-93784. 152p. (Orig.). 1994. pap. 8.00 (*1-56002-319-8*, Univ Edtns) Aegina Pr.

Pearson, David. Earth to Spirit: In Search of Natural Architecture. LC 93-47523. 1995. 29.25 (*0-8118-0702-9*); pap. 17.95 (*0-8118-0731-2*) Chronicle Bks.

— The Naturally House Book: Creating a Healthy, Harmonious & Ecologically Sound Home Environment. 1989. pap. 20.00 (*0-671-66635-5*, Fireside) S&S Trade.

— Provenance Research in Book History: A Handbook. (British Library Studies in the History of the Book). (Illus.). 336p. 1994. 90.00 (*0-7123-0344-8*) U of Toronto Pr.

— Provenance Research in Book History: A Handbook. (The British Library Studies in the History of the Book). (Illus.). 400p. 1994. 100.00 (*0-7123-0318-9*, Pub. by Brit Library UK) U of Toronto Pr.

Pearson, David, jt. auth. see Middleton, David.

Pearson, David P., et al. Handbook of Reading Research. LC 83-26838. 912p. 1984. text ed. 70.95 (*0-582-28119-9*, 71177) Longman.

Pearson-Davis, Susan, ed. see Zeder, Suzan.

*__Pearson, Debora.__ The Alphabake: A Cookbook & Cookie Cutter Set. LC 95-13379. (Illus.). 32p. (J). (ps-3). 1995. 15.99 (*0-525-45461-6*, DCB) Dutton Child Bks.

Pearson, Della A., jt. auth. see Grinaker, Robert L.

Pearson, Diane. Csardas. 608p. 1984. pap. 3.50 (*0-449-20615-7*, Crest) Fawcett.

— The Loom of the Tancred. large type ed. (Romance Ser.). 1974. 21.95 (*0-85456-303-2*) Ulverscroft.

— Marigold Field. 1986. pap. 3.50 (*0-449-20985-7*) Fawcett.

— Sarah. 304p. 1986. pap. 3.50 (*0-449-20984-9*, Crest) Fawcett.

— Summer of the Barshinsley's. 448p. 1985. mass mkt. 4.50 (*0-449-20783-8*, Crest) Fawcett.

— Voices of Summer. large type ed. 524p. 1993. 21.95 (*0-7505-0455-2*) Ulverscroft.

Pearson, Dorothy M., intro. Perspectives on Equity & Justice in Social Work. LC 93-70219. (Carl A. Scott Memorial Lecture Series, 1988-1992). (Illus.). 88p. (Orig.). (C). 1993. pap. text ed. 12.00 (*0-87293-034-3*) Coun Soc Wk Ed.

Pearson, D'Orsay W., ed. & tr. Pedro Ciruelo's A Treatise Reproving All Superstitions & Forms of Witchcraft: Very Necessary & Useful for All Good Christians Zealous for Their Salvation. Maio, Eugene, tr. LC 74-4979. 366p. 1976. 38.50 (*0-8386-1580-5*) Fairleigh Dickinson.

Pearson, Drew & Allen, Robert S. The Nine Old Men. LC 73-21727. (American Constitutional & Legal History Ser). 325p. 1974. reprint ed. lib. bdg. 45.00 (*0-306-70609-1*) Da Capo.

*__Pearson, Durk & Shaw, Sandy.__ Freedom of Informed Choice: FDA Versus Nutrient Supplements. 126p. (Orig.). Date not set. pap. text ed. 6.95 (*0-9636249-0-3*) Com Sense NJ.

— Life Extension. 1987. pap. 15.99 (*0-446-38735-5*) Warner Bks.

— The Life Extension Weight Loss Program. 1994. reprint ed. lib. bdg. 29.95x (*1-56849-543-9*) Buccaneer Bks.

Pearson, E. A. Proceedings of the First International Conference on Waste Disposal in Marine Environment: Waste Disposal in the Marine Environment. LC 60-12817. 1960. 234.00 (*0-08-009534-8*, Pub. by Pergamon Repr UK) Franklin.

Pearson, E. A. & De Fraga Frangipane, E. Marine Pollution & Marine Waste Disposal. 1975. pap. 197.00 (*0-08-019730-2*, Pub. by Pergamon Repr UK) Franklin.

Pearson, E. K., jt. auth. see Neyman, J.

Pearson, E. Norman. Space, Time & Self: Three Mysteries of the Universe. rev. ed. (Illus.). 290p. (C). 1990. pap. 9.95 (*0-8356-0658-9*, Quest) Theos Pub Hse.

Pearson, E. S. Selected Papers. 327p. 1966. lib. bdg. 35.00 (*0-521-05926-7*) Lubrecht & Cramer.

— Student: A Statistical Biography of William Sealy Gosset. Plackett, R. L. & Barnard, G. A., eds. (Illus.). 152p. 1990. 32.00 (*0-19-852227-4*) OUP.

Pearson, E. S., ed. The History of Statistics in the 17th and 18th Centuries, Against the Changing Background of Intellectual, Scientific & Religious Thought: Lectures Given at the University College London During the Academic Sessions 1921-33. 1978. 45.00 (*0-85264-250-4*) Lubrecht & Cramer.

Pearson, E. S. & Hartley, H. O., eds. Biometrika Tables for Statisticians, Vol. 1. 3rd ed. 270p. 1976. lib. bdg. 75.00 (*0-904653-10-2*) Lubrecht & Cramer.

— Biometrika Tables for Statisticians: Reprint with Corrections, Vol. 2. 385p. 1976. reprint ed. lib. bdg. 75.00 (*0-904653-11-0*) Lubrecht & Cramer.

Pearson, E. S., jt. auth. see Neyman, Jerzy.

Pearson, Edgar. Into All the World. (Illus.). 228p. 1993. 19.95 (*1-85756-097-3*, Pub. by Janus Pub UK) Intl Spec Bk.

Pearson, Edmund. Queer Books. (Illus.). 298p. 1990. pap. 25.00 (*0-87556-763-0*) Saifer.

Pearson, Edmund L. Books in Black or Red. LC 77-93371. (Essay Index Reprint Ser.). 1977. 23.95 (*0-8369-1267-5*) Ayer.

— Secret Book, Vol. 1. LC 72-3419. (Short Story Index Reprint Ser.). 1977. reprint ed. 20.95 (*0-8369-4159-4*) Ayer.

Pearson, Edward S. Law for European Business Studies. 480p. (Orig.). 1994. pap. 72.50 (*0-273-60474-0*, Pub. by Pitman Pub Ltd UK) Trans-Atl Phila.

Pearson, Eileen. Hitler's Reich. Yapp, Malcolm et al, eds. (World History Ser.). (Illus.). (YA). (gr. 6-11). 1980. reprint ed. pap. text ed. 3.95 (*0-89908-208-4*) Greenhaven.

Pearson, Elizabeth W., ed. Letters from Port Royal, 1862-1868. LC 69-18547. (American Negro: His History & Literature, Ser. No. 2). 1968. reprint ed. 17.95 (*0-405-01886-X*) Ayer.

Pearson, Emily C. Cousin Franck's Household; or, Scenes in the Old Dominion, by Pochanontas. LC 72-1517. (Black Heritage Library Collection). 1977. reprint ed. 28.95 (*0-8369-9041-2*) Ayer.

— The Poor White: or The Rebel Conscript. LC 72-1822. (Illus.). 326p. 1977. reprint ed. 28.95 (*0-8369-9042-0*) Ayer.

Pearson, Eunice W., ed. see Martin, Janet L. & Todnem, Allen.

Pearson, Eunice W., ed. see Martin, Janet L.

Pearson, F., et al. Geochemical Databases: PMatch - A Program to Manage Thermochemical Data, Pt. 1. (Illus.). 144p. 1993. pap. 25.00 (*92-826-5329-3*, CD-NA-14170-EN-C, Pub. by Europ Com) UNIPUB.

*__Pearson, F. Griffin, et al, eds.__ Thoracic Surgery. LC 94-42025. (J). 1995. write for info. (*0-443-08798-9*) Churchill.

Pearson, F. J., Jr., et al, eds. Applied Isotope Hydrogeology: A Case Study in Northern Switzerland. (Studies in Environmental Science: No. 43). 460p. 1991. 177.00 (*0-444-88983-3*) Elsevier.

*__Pearson, F.Griffith, et al.__ Esophageal Surgery. LC 94-24093. 1995. write for info. (*0-443-08832-2*) Churchill.

Pearson, Frain G. Indian Head. Van Treese, James B., ed. 298p. 1994. 8.95 (*1-56901-129-X*) NW Pub.

Pearson, Fred L., Jr. Spanish-Indian Relations in Florida: A Study of Two Visitas, 1657-1678. LC 90-14048. (Evolution of North American Indians Ser.: Vol. 15). 336p. 1990. reprint ed. 20.00 (*0-8240-2510-5*) Garland.

Pearson, Frederic S. The Global Spread of Arms: Political Economy of International Security. LC 94-8108. (Dilemmas in World Politics Ser.). (C). 1994. pap. text ed. 13.95 (*0-8133-1574-3*) Westview.

— The Global Spread of Arms: Political Economy of International Security. LC 94-8108. (Dilemmas in World Politics Ser.). (C). 1994. text ed. 49.95 (*0-8133-1573-5*) Westview.

Pearson, Frederic S. & Rochester, J. Martin. International Relations: The Global Condition in the late Twentieth Century. 2nd ed. 590p. (C). 1988. pap. text ed. 23.95 (*0-394-36877-0*) Random.

— International Relations: The Global Condition in the Late 20th Century. 3rd ed. 1992. text ed. write for info. (*0-07-049079-1*) McGraw.

Pearson, Frederic S., jt. auth. see Brzoska, Michael.

Pearson, Frederick, II. Map Projection Methods. Junkins, John L., ed. (Applied Mathematics for Science & Engineering Ser.). (Illus.). 304p. 1984. 31.00 (*0-915313-00-6*) Sigma Sci Inc.

— Map Projection Software. Junkins, John L., ed. (Applied Mathematics for Science & Engineering Ser.). (Illus.). 50p. 1984. disk 110.00 (*0-317-06090-2*) Sigma Sci Inc.

Pearson, G., jt. ed. see Arnold, J.

P Q

Pearson, Gardner W. Records of the Massachusetts Volunteer Militia: Called Out by the Governor of Massachusetts to Suppress a Threatened Invasion During the War of 1812-1814. 448p. 1993. reprint ed. pap. 35.00 (*0-685-69925-0*, 9286) Clearfield Co.

Pearson, Gayle. The Fog Doggies & Me. LC 92-41069. 128p. (J). (gr. 4-8). 1993. text ed. 13.95 (*0-689-31845-6*, Atheneum Bks Young) S&S Childrens.

— One Potato, Tu. (J). (gr. 4-7). 1994. pap. 2.95 (*0-590-47100-7*) Scholastic Inc.

— One Potato, Tu: Seven Stories. LC 91-22307. 128p. (J). (gr. 5-9). 1992. text ed. 13.95 (*0-689-31706-9*, Atheneum Bks Young) S&S Childrens.

Pearson, Geoffrey. The Deviant Imagination: Psychiatry, Social Work & Social Change. LC 75-9815. 252p. (C). 1980. pap. 16.50 (*0-8419-0616-5*) Holmes & Meier.

Pearson, Gerald H., jt. auth. see English, Oliver S.

Pearson, Glenn L. The Book of Mormon - Key to Conversion. pap. 3.95 (*0-88494-105-1*) Bookcraft Inc.

***Pearson, Gordon.** Integrity in Organizations: An Alternative Business Ethic. LC 95-1428. 1995. text ed. 24.95 (*0-07-709136-1*) McGraw.

— Strategic Thinking. 320p. 1990. pap. text ed. 44.00 (*0-13-852153-0*) P-H.

Pearson, H. M. Pilot, Diplomat & Garage Rat. (C). 1989. 49.00 (*0-685-52930-4*) St Mut.

***Pearson, Hayden.** Country Flavor. (American Autobiography Ser.). 112p. 1995. reprint ed. lib. bdg. 69.00 (*0-7812-8611-5*) Rprt Serv.

— Countryman's Year. (American Autobiography Ser.). 192p. 1995. reprint ed. lib. bdg. 69.00 (*0-7812-8612-3*) Rprt Serv.

— Sea Flavor. (American Autobiography Ser.). 178p. 1995. reprint ed. lib. bdg. 69.00 (*0-7812-8613-1*) Rprt Serv.

Pearson, Haydn S. Country Flavor. 1977. 18.95 (*0-8369-7324-0*, 8117) Ayer.

— Sea Flavor. LC 68-58809. (Essay Index Reprint Ser.). 1977. 15.95 (*0-8369-0051-0*) Ayer.

Pearson, Helen R. Do What You Have the Power to Do! Studies of Six New Testament Women. LC 91-65727. 144p. 1992. pap. 8.95 (*0-8358-0643-X*) Upper Room Bks.

***Pearson, Henry & Wray, David.** Language for Curriculum Leaders. (Primary Inset Ser.). 128p. 1994. 49.95 (*0-415-10433-5*, B3526) Routledge.

Pearson, Henry, tr. see Bergman, Hjalmar.

Pearson, Henry A., et al, eds. Development or Destruction: The Conversion of Tropical Forest to Pasture in Latin America. 405p. (C). 1992. pap. text ed. 60.50 (*0-8133-7824-9*) Westview.

Pearson, Henry G. An American Railroad Builder: John Murray Forbes. LC 72-29. (Select Bibliographies Reprint Ser.). 1977. reprint ed. 18.95 (*0-8369-9968-1*) Ayer.

Pearson, Hesketh. Dizzy: The Life & Nature of Benjamin Disraeli, Earl of Beaconsfield. LC 74-12579. (Illus.). 284p. 1974. reprint ed. text ed. 59.75 (*0-8371-7729-4*, PEDIZ, Greenwood Pr) Greenwood.

— Gilbert: His Life & Strife. LC 78-3698. 276p. 1978. reprint ed. text ed. 59.75 (*0-313-20364-4*, PEGI, Greenwood Pr) Greenwood.

— Gilbert & Sullivan. 20.95 (*0-89190-868-4*, Am Repr) Amereon Ltd.

— Gilbert & Sullivan. LC 70-175706. (Select Bibliographies Reprint Ser.). 1977. reprint ed. 21.95 (*0-8369-6621-X*) Ayer.

— Last Actor-Managers. LC 77-148225. (Biography Index Reprint Ser.). (Illus.). 1977. 23.95 (*0-8369-8072-7*) Ayer.

— The Life of Oscar Wilde. LC 78-6898. (Illus.). 399p. 1978. reprint ed. text ed. 37.50 (*0-313-20491-8*, PEOW, Greenwood Pr) Greenwood.

— The Smith of Smiths Being the Life, Wit & Humor of Sydney Smith. 1988. reprint ed. lib. bdg. 49.00 (*0-7812-0197-7*) Rprt Serv.

— The Smith of Smiths Being the Life, Wit & Humor of Sydney Smith. LC 73-145230. (Literature Ser.). (Illus.). 338p. 1972. reprint ed. 49.00 (*0-403-01146-9*) Scholarly.

Pearson, Hesketh, ed. see Wilde, Oscar.

Pearson, Hilary & Miller, Clifford. Commercial Exploitation of Intellectual Property. 474p. 1990. pap. 48.00 (*1-85431-044-5*, Pub. by Blackstone Pr UK) W W Gaunt.

Pearson, Hilary E. Computer Contracts: An International Guide to Agreements & Software Protection. 312p. 1984. 70.50 (*90-6544-198-0*) Kluwer Ac.

Pearson, Howard, ed. see Brinegar, Jerry L.

Pearson, Howard, ed. see Douglass, William C.

***Pearson, Hugh.** The Shadow of the Panther: Huey Newton & the Price of Black Power in America. 422p. 1995. pap. 13.46 (*0-201-48341-6*) Addison-Wesley.

— The Shadow of the Panther: Huey Newton, Oakland, and the Price of Power. (Illus.). 422p. 1994. 23.08 (*0-201-63278-0*) Addison-Wesley.

Pearson, Ian. English in Biological Science. (English in Focus Ser.). 1979. teacher ed 12.00 (*0-19-437505-6*); student ed, pap. text ed. 9.95 (*0-19-437513-7*) OUP.

Pearson, J. D. A Guide to Manuscripts & Documents in the British Isles Relating to South & South-East Asia, Vol. 1. 328p. 1989. text ed. 160.00 (*0-7201-1961-8*, Mansell Pub) Cassell.

— A Guide to Manuscripts & Documents in the British Isles Relating to South & South-East Asia, Vol. 2. 352p. 1990. text ed. 160.00 (*0-7201-2011-X*, Mansell Pub) Cassell.

Pearson, J. D., comp. A Guide to Manuscripts & Documents in the British Isles Relating to Africa, 2 vols. LC 93-2886. 1993. Vol. 2: British Isles (Excluding London), 1994, 448p. write for info. (*0-7201-2090-X*, Mansell Pub) Cassell.

— A Guide to Manuscripts & Documents in the British Isles Relating to Africa, 2 vols., Set. LC 93-2886. 1993. text ed. 430.00 (*0-7201-2167-1*, Mansell Pub) Cassell.

— A Guide to Manuscripts & Documents in the British Isles Relating to Africa, 2 vols., Vol. 1: London. LC 93-2886. 320p. 1993. text ed. 200.00 (*0-7201-2088-8*, Mansell Pub) Cassell.

Pearson, J. J., jt. auth. see Barrett, E. B.

Pearson, J. M. Mathematics for Economists: A First Course. LC 81-14309. (Illus.). 220p. reprint ed. pap. 62.70 (*0-8357-2971-0*, 2039233) Bks Demand.

— Nuclear Physics: Energy & Matter, Special Student Edition. (Illus.). 264p. 1986. 38.00 (*0-85274-804-3*) IOP Pub.

Pearson, J. M. & Stolka, M. Poly (N-Vinylcarbazole) (Polymer Monographs: Vol. 6). 184p. 1981. text ed. 190.00 (*0-677-05520-X*) Gordon & Breach.

Pearson, J. Michael. Encyclopedia of American Cut & Engraved Glass, Vol. 1: Geometric Conceptions. LC 74-18615. (Illus.). 272p. 1975. 60.00 (*0-916528-01-4*) J M Pearson.

— Encyclopedia of American Cut & Engraved Glass, Vol. 2: Realistic Patterns. LC 74-18615. (Illus.). 172p. 1977. 25.00 (*0-916528-03-0*) J M Pearson.

— Encyclopedia of American Cut & Engraved Glass, Vol. 3: Geometric Motifs. LC 74-18615. (Illus.). 260p. 1978. 35.00 (*0-916528-05-7*) J M Pearson.

Pearson, J. R. Mechanics of Polymer Processing. (Illus.). 678p. 1985. 248.00 (*0-85334-308-X*, Pub. by Elsevier Applied Sci UK) Elsevier.

— Pearson on the Orchard-House: Hints on the Construction & Management of Orchard-Houses. (Illus.). 63p. 1994. pap. 10.35 (*1-881763-00-5*) C Barnett Bks.

Pearson, J. R. & Richardson, S. M., eds. Computational Analysis of Polymer Processing. (Illus.). 343p. 1983. 93.75 (*0-85334-188-5*, I-100-83, Pub. by Elsevier Applied Sci UK) Elsevier.

Pearson, Jack. Uncle Alphonso & the Frosty, Fibbing Dinosaurs. LC 92-39373. (On My Own Bks.). (Illus.). (J). 1993. pap. 4.49 (*0-7814-0100-3*, Chariot Bks) Chariot Family.

Pearson, Jack W. Cesarian Delivery in Current Obstetric Practice. 1991. 39.95 (*0-8151-6663-X*, Yr Bk Med Pubs) Mosby Yr Bk.

Pearson, Jacqueline. The Prostituted Muse: Images of Women & Women Dramatists, 1642-1737. LC 87-9497. 256p. 1988. text ed. 55.00 (*0-312-00960-7*) St Martin.

Pearson, James C. G. & Turton, Anthony. Statistical Methods in Environmental Health. LC 93-17174. 184p. 1993. pap. 35.50 (*0-412-48450-1*) Chapman & Hall.

Pearson, James D. Bibliography of Africa: Conference Proceedings, 1967. Jones, Ruth, ed. 362p. 1970. 45.00 (*0-7146-2394-6*, Pub. by F Cass Pubs UK) Intl Spec Bk.

Pearson, James E., ed. Optical Technologies for Aerospace Sensing: Proceedings of a Conference Held 16-17 November 1992, Boston, Massachusetts. LC 93-18557. (Critical Reviews of Optical Science & Technology Ser.: Vol. CR47). 1993. write for info. (*0-8194-1042-X*); pap. write for info. (*0-8194-1041-1*) SPIE.

— Selected Papers on Adaptive Optics for Atmospheric Compensation. LC 93-46626. (Milestone Ser.: Vol. MS 92). 1994. write for info. (*0-8194-1510-3*); pap. write for info. (*0-8194-1509-X*) SPIE.

Pearson, Jamie. Digital at Work: Snapshots of the First Thirty-Five Years. 225p. 1992. pap. 19.95 (*0-13-213489-6*) P-H.

Pearson, Jamie P., ed. Digital at Work: Snapshots from the First Thirty-Five Years. (History Ser.). (Illus.). 212p. (Orig.). 1992. pap. 19.95 (*1-55558-092-0*, EY-J826E-DP, Digital DEC) Buttrwrth-Heinemann.

Pearson, Jan, et al. Recognizing & Treating Low Blood Sugar. (Illus.). 1994. pap. write for info. (*1-885115-05-9*) Intl Diabetes.

Pearson, Jean. On Speaking Terms with Earth. 32p. 1988. pap. 4.50 (*0-945251-42-4*) Great Elm.

— On Speaking Terms with Earth. 32p. 1992. reprint ed. pap. 5.00 (*0-9627741-5-4*) Green World Pr.

Pearson, Jean, tr. see Olofsson, Tommy.

Pearson, Jean E. Kurt Kusenberg: Humorist of the Fantastic. LC 90-42186. (Studies in Modern German Literature: Vol. 19). 183p. (C). 1991. text ed. 40.95 (*0-8204-0601-5*) P Lang Pubs.

Pearson, Jeremy D., jt. ed. see Savage, Caroline O.

Pearson, Jerry D., jt. auth. see Smith, Richard E.

Pearson, Jessie. Life & Love. 60p. 1983. 7.95 (*0-87881-108-7*) Mojave Bks.

Pearson, Joan. Memories of Monday (Wash Day Before Advent of Washing Machine) with Added Chapter on Scotland. (C). 1989. pap. 21.00 (*1-85072-053-3*, Pub. by W Sessions UK) St Mut.

Pearson, John. Basic Communication Theory. 304p. 1992. pap. write for info. (*0-13-061078-X*) P-H.

— The Sitwells. LC 80-14371. 528p. 1980. pap. 7.95 (*0-15-682676-3*, Harvest Bks) HarBrace.

— The Ultimate Family: The Making of the Royal House of Windsor. large type ed. (Illus.). 480p. 1987. 23.95 (*0-7089-8389-8*, Charnwood) Ulverscroft.

— Vindiciae Epistolarum Sancti Ignatii, 2 Vols, Set. LC 76-173936. (Library of Anglo-Catholic Theology: No. 16). reprint ed. 57.50 (*0-404-52140-1*) AMS Pr.

Pearson, John, jt. auth. see Tatelbaum, Charles.

Pearson, John C. & Aros, Andrew A. Home Video Yearbook: 1981. 90p. 1980. pap. 7.00 (*0-932352-05-7*) Applause Pubns.

Pearson, John K., et al. Kansas Personal Property Secured Transactions. LC 88-82763. 200p. 1988. 90.00 (*0-942357-22-1*) KS Bar CLE.

Pearson, John K. & Metzger, Emily, eds. Kansas Bankruptcy Handbook. 2nd rev. ed. 1986. 195.00 (*0-942357-29-9*) KS Bar CLE.

Pearson, John K. & Smith, R. Pete. A Guide to Challenging Consumer Bankruptcy: A Key Debt Recovery Process. 190p. (Orig.). 1991. pap. text ed. 128.00 (*0-89982-367-X*) Am Bankers.

Pearson, John K., et al. Bankruptcy Rules & Forms Handbook, 2 vols. (Bankruptcy Practice Library: No. 1961). 992p. 1993. disk 125.00 (*0-471-57648-4*); 5.25 hd 125.00 (*0-471-57516-X*) Wiley.

— Bankruptcy Rules & Forms Handbook, 2 vols. suppl. ed. (Bankruptcy Practice Library: No. 1961). 992p. 1993. ring bd. write for info. (*0-471-58712-5*) Wiley.

— Bankruptcy Rules & Forms Handbook, 2 vols., 1. suppl. ed. (Bankruptcy Practice Library: No. 1961). 992p. 1993. ring bd. 116.00 (*0-471-30610-X*) Wiley.

— Bankruptcy Rules & Forms Handbook, 2 vols. Set, Vol. 2. (Bankruptcy Practice Library: No. 1961). 992p. 1992. Set. ring bd. 232.00 (*0-471-55909-1*) Wiley.

— Bankruptcy Rules & Forms Handbook, 2 vols., Vol. 2. suppl. ed. (Bankruptcy Practice Library: No. 1961). 992p. 1993. ring bd. 116.00 (*0-471-30611-8*) Wiley.

— Drafting Bankruptcy Reorganization Plans, 3 vols., Vol. 3. 2nd ed. LC 93-10016. (Bankruptcy Practice Library). 1616p. 1993. Acid-free paper. text ed. 315.00 (*0-471-59631-0*) Wiley.

— NACM Bankruptcy Reorganization Guide. 2nd ed. Donohue, Teresa, ed. 272p. (Orig.). 1995. pap. text ed. 34.95 (*0-934914-95-8*) NACM.

Pearson, John R., ed. Hiker's Guide to Trails of Big Bend National Park. 2nd ed. (Illus.). 32p. (Orig.). 1978. pap. 1.25 (*0-912001-00-3*) Big Bend.

— River Guide to the Rio Grande, 4 vols. (Illus.). 72p. (Orig.). 1982. pap. 10.00 (*0-912001-08-9*); General Information. write for info. (*0-912001-04-6*); Vol. 1, Colorado & Santa Elena Canyons. write for info. (*0-912001-05-4*); Vol. 2, Mariscal & Boquillas Canyons. write for info. (*0-912001-06-2*); Vol. 3, The Lower Canyons. write for info. (*0-912001-07-0*) Big Bend.

— Road Guide to Backcountry Dirt Roads of Big Bend National Park. (Illus.). 40p. (Orig.). 1980. pap. 1.25 (*0-912001-01-1*) Big Bend.

— Road Guide to Paved & Improved Dirt Roads of Big Bend National Park. (Illus.). 48p. (Orig.). 1980. pap. 1.25 (*0-912001-02-X*) Big Bend.

Pearson, John R., ed. see Deckert, Frank.

Pearson, John R., ed. see Hanks, Rome A.

Pearson, John R., ed. see Maxwell, Ross A.

Pearson, John R., ed. see Rudig, Doug.

Pearson, Jon. Energy Conservation in Small Business: Promoting the Use of New Testament. LC 83-21739. (Illus.). 212p. (Orig.). 1984. lib. bdg. 52.50 (*0-8191-3659-X*) U Pr of Amer.

Pearson, Jonathan. Genealogies of the Descendants of the First Settlers of Schenectady, 1662-1800. 324p. 1992. reprint ed. pap. 29.50 (*0-8328-2372-4*) Higginson Bk Co.

Pearson, Judy. Friday Fun. 265p. 1993. pap. 28.00 (*0-9637103-0-3*) Clear Writing.

— Healthy Mind Healthy Body: Using Your Mind Power to Stay Healthy Overcome Illness. Celia, Jean, ed. 155p. (Orig.). 1994. 12.95 (*0-9635179-0-2*) Awe Bks.

— Marriage after Mourning. 192p. 1994. per., pap. text ed. 7.50 (*0-7872-0205-3*) Kendall-Hunt.

— Myths of Educational Choice. LC 92-19594. 168p. 1992. text ed. 39.95 (*0-275-94169-8*, C4169, Praeger Pubs) Greenwood.

***Pearson, Judy & Nelson, Paul E.** Understanding & Sharing. 6th ed. (C). 1994. audio write for info. (*0-697-26038-0*) Brown & Benchmark.

— Understanding & Sharing: An Introduction to Speech Communication. 6th ed. 496p. (C). 1994. text ed. write for info. (*0-697-13940-9*) Brown & Benchmark.

Pearson, Judy & Spitzberg, Brian H. Interpersonal Communication: Concepts, Components, & Contexts. 2nd ed. 432p. (C). 1990. pap. write for info. (*0-697-00790-1*) Brown & Benchmark.

Pearson, Judy & Turner, Lynn H. Gender & Communication. 2nd ed. 320p. (C). 1991. pap. write for info. (*0-697-03021-0*) Brown & Benchmark.

Pearson, Judy, jt. auth. see Nelson, Paul E.

Pearson, Judy, et al. Gender & Communication. 3rd ed. 320p. (C). 1995. pap. text ed. write for info. (*0-697-20154-6*) Brown & Benchmark.

Pearson, Judy C. Communication in the Family. 2nd ed. (C). 1993. 29.50 (*0-06-500047-1*) HarpCollege.

— Communications in the Family: Seeking Satisfaction in Changing Times. (C). 1990. pap. 19.50 (*0-06-045114-9*) HarpCollege.

Pearson, K. Tables of the Incomplete Beta-Function. 505p. 1968. 160.00 (*0-85264-704-2*) St Mut.

Pearson, Karl. Tables of the Incomplete Beta Function. 205p. 1968. lib. bdg. 37.95 (*0-521-05922-4*) Lubrecht & Cramer.

Pearson, Karl, ed. see Clifford, William K.

Pearson, Kazue, tr. see Barnes, Gina, et al.

Pearson, Kazue, tr. see Pearson, Richard J., et al, eds.

Pearson, Kit. A Handful of Time. (Illus.). 192p. (J). (gr. 3-7). 1991. pap. 3.99 (*0-14-032268-X*, Puffin) Puffin Bks.

— The Lights Go on Again. 202p. (J). (gr. 5-9). 1994. 13.99 (*0-670-84919-7*) Viking Child Bks.

— Looking at the Moon. 224p. (J). (gr. 5-9). 1992. 12.95 (*0-670-84097-1*) Viking Child Bks.

— The Sky Is Falling. 256p. (J). (gr. 5-9). 1995. pap. 3.99 (*0-14-037652-6*) Puffin Bks.

Pearson, Kristin, ed. see Grayslake Historical Society Bk. Committee Staff, et al.

Pearson, L. Butterworths Student Companions: Company Law. 117p. 1986. Australia. pap. 14.00 (*0-409-30319-4*) Butterworth Legal Pubs.

Pearson, L. R., ed. see Mid-America Spectroscopy Symposium (16th: 1965, Chicago).

Pearson, Landon. Children of Glasnost: Growing up Soviet. LC 90-30147. 528p. (Orig.). 1991. pap. 16.95 (*0-295-97090-1*) U of Wash Pr.

Pearson, Larry, ed. see Vantress, Sally.

***Pearson, Laurice.** Cracking the GRE Psychology Test '96. (Princeton Review Ser.). 1995. pap. 16.00 (*0-679-76144-6*, Villard Bks) Random.

Pearson, Leonard. Death & Dying: Current Issues in the Treatment of the Dying Person. LC 67-11483. 247p. reprint ed. pap. 70.40 (*0-317-10622-8*, 2002266) Bks Demand.

Pearson, Lester B. Words & Occasions: An Anthology of Speeches & Articles from His Papers by the Right Honourable Lester B. Pearson. LC 70-135191. 310p. 1970. 34.50 (*0-674-95611-7*) HUP.

Pearson, Linda. Local Government Law in New South Wales. 352p. 1994. pap. 49.00 (*1-86287-127-2*, Pub. by Federation Pr AU) W W Gaunt.

Pearson, Lionel. The Art of Demosthenes. LC 81-16752. (American Philological Association Special Publications Ser.). (C). 1982. pap. 24.00 (*0-89130-551-3*, 40-05-04) Scholars Pr GA.

— Early Ionian Historians. LC 75-136874. 240p. 1975. reprint ed. text ed. 35.00 (*0-8371-5314-X*, PEIH, Greenwood Pr) Greenwood.

— The Greek Historians of the West: Timaeus & His Predecessors. LC 87-4877. (American Philological Association Philological Monographs). 316p. 1988. 22.00 (*1-55540-078-7*, 40-00-35) Scholars Pr GA.

— The Local Historians of Attica. LC 81-16556. (American Philological Association Monograph Ser.). 1981. reprint ed. pap. 19.50 (*0-89130-540-8*, 40 00 11) Scholars Pr GA.

— Popular Ethics in Ancient Greece. 262p. 1962. 32.50 (*0-8047-0102-4*) Stanford U Pr.

Pearson, Lionel, tr. see Aristoxenus.

***Pearson, Lorentz C.** The Diversity & Evolution of Plants. LC 94-37366. 624p. 1995. 59.95 (*0-8493-2483-1*, 2483) CRC Pr.

— The Mushroom Manual - Tops! Complete for College Class: Simple for You & Me. 224p. 1987. pap. 8.95 (*0-87961-161-8*) Naturegraph.

Pearson, Lu E. Elizabethan Love Conventions. 1972. 59.95 (*0-8490-0102-1*) Gordon Pr.

— Elizabethans at Home. LC 57-9305. (Illus.). x, 630p. 1957. 62.50 (*0-8047-0494-5*) Stanford U Pr.

***Pearson, Lynn F.** Amusement Machines. (C). 1989. pap. 25.00x (*0-7478-0179-7*, Pub. by Shire UK) St Mut.

— The Architectural & Social History of Cooperative Living. LC 87-26409. 284p. 1988. text ed. 45.00 (*0-312-01293-4*) St Martin.

Pearson, M., jt. auth. see Gower, R.

Pearson, M. L., jt. ed. see Abel, Emily K.

Pearson, M. N. Pilgrimage to Mecca: The Indian Experience, 1600-1800. (World History Ser.). (Illus.). 296p. (C). 1995. pap. text ed. 18.95 (*1-55876-090-3*) Wiener Pubs Inc.

— Pilgrimage to Mecca: The Indian Experience, 1600-1800. (World History Ser.). (Illus.). 296p. (C). 1995. text ed. 39.95 (*1-55876-089-X*) Wiener Pubs Inc.

— Pious Passengers: The Hajj in Earlier Times. (C). 1994. 26.00 (*81-207-1601-9*, Pub. by Sterling Plns Pvt II) S Asia.

— The Portuguese in India. (New Cambridge History of India Ser.: I: 1). 200p. 1988. 44.95 (*0-521-25713-1*) Cambridge U Pr.

Pearson, M. N., ed. Legitimacy & Symbols: The South Asian Writings of F. W. Buckler. LC 82-72446. (Michigan Papers on South & Southeast Asia: No. 26). xiii, 193p. 1985. 11.95 (*0-89148-032-3*); pap. 4.99 (*0-89148-033-1*) Ctr S&SE Asian.

Pearson, M. N., jt. auth. see Bickerton, Ian J.

Pearson, M. N., jt. auth. see Das Gupta, Ashin.

Pearson, M. N., jt. ed. see Kling, Blair B.

***Pearson, Maggie & Aldous, Kate, eds.** A Treasury of Old Testament Stories. LC 95-1351. 1995. pap. 5.95 (*1-85697-594-0*, Kingfisher LKC) LKC.

Pearson, Margaret J. Wang Fu & the Comments of a Recluse. LC 88-63526. (Monograph Ser.: No. 24). xiii, 195p. 1989. pap. 10.00 (*0-939252-21-X*) ASU Ctr Asian.

Pearson, Margaret M. Joint Ventures in the People's Republic of China: The Control of Foreign Direct Investment under Socialism. 350p. 1992. text ed. 47.50 (*0-691-07882-3*); pap. text ed. 16.95 (*0-691-02768-4*) Princeton U Pr.

Pearson, Mark. Numbat-His Magic Quest. (C). 1990. 45.00 (*0-947333-14-2*, Pub. by Pascoe Pub AT) St Mut.

Pearson, Mark, jt. auth. see Fielder, John.

Pearson, Mark A. Christian Healing: A Practical, Comprehensive Guide. LC 90-35712. 1990. pap. 11.99 (*0-8007-9165-7*) Chosen Bks.

— Christian Healing: A Practical, Comprehensive Guide. 2nd ed. LC 94-16615. 368p. 1995. pap. 11.99 (*0-8007-9221-1*) Chosen Bks.

— Why Can't I Be Me? Understanding How Personality Type Affects Emotional Healing, Relationships, & Spiritual Growth. LC 92-20526. 256p. (Orig.). 1992. pap. 9.99 (*0-8007-9195-9*) Chosen Bks.

Pearson, Mark L. & Epstein, Henry F., eds. Muscle Development: Molecular & Cellular Control. LC 82-72381. 601p. reprint ed. pap. 162.30 (*0-7837-1993-0*, 2042267) Bks Demand.

Pearson, Mary D. Recordings in the Public Library. LC 62-20852. 40p. reprint ed. pap. 25.00 (*0-317-09931-0*, 2011140) Bks Demand.

Pearson, Mary R. All about God. LC 93-7692. (J). 1993. 8.99 (*0-8423-1215-3*) Tyndale.

— Fifty-Two Children's Programs. 224p. (Orig.). 1985. pap. 14.95 (*0-89636-189-6*) Accent CO.

— More Bible Object Lessons. 1992. 5.95 (*0-89636-286-8*) Accent CO.

— Perky Puppets with a Purpose: A Complete Guide to Puppetry & Ventriloquism in Christian Ministry. LC 91-42507. (Illus.). 160p. 1992. pap. 12.95 (*0-88243-677-5*, 02-0677) Gospel Pub.

An Asterisk (*) at the beginning of an entry indicates that the title is appearing in BIP for the first time.

Pearson, Mary Rose. Bible Object Lessons. (J). (gr. 1-6). 1991. 4.95 (*0-89636-303-1*) Accent CO.
— More Children's Church Time. LC 82-70390. 220p. (Orig.). (J). (gr. 1-6). 1982. 14.95 (*0-89636-082-2*) Accent CO.
Pearson, Max. The Trouble with Midas. (Illus.). 30p. (J). (gr. 3 up). 1976. pap. 4.00 (*0-88680-195-8*) I E Clark.
Pearson, Michael. Imagined Places: Journeys into Literary America. LC 91-16920. 1991. 24.95 (*0-87805-526-6*) U Pr of Miss.
— Millennial Dreams & Moral Dilemmas: Seventh-day Adventism & Contemporary Ethics. 330p. (C). 1990. 74.95 (*0-521-36509-0*) Cambridge U Pr.
— A Place That's Known. 280p. 1994. 22.95 (*0-87805-672-6*) U Pr of Miss.
Pearson, Michael P. & Richards, Colin, eds. Architecture & Order: Approaches to Social Space. LC 93-18491. (Material Cultures Ser.). 1993. write for info. (*0-415-06728-6*) Routledge.
***Pearson, Mildred M.** God's Gift, Your Blessing: A Guide to Pastor's Aid Committees. 96-120p. (Orig.). 1995. pap. 9.95 (*1-882581-10-5*) Campbell Rd Pr.
Pearson, Nancy, tr. see Bertela, Giovanna G.
Pearson, Nancy, tr. see Corbin, Henry.
Pearson, Nancy, ed. see Kiliper, R. Smith.
***Pearson, Nathan W.** Goin' to Kansas City. 1994. pap. 14.95 (*0-252-06438-0*) U of Ill Pr.
Pearson, Nathan W., Jr. Goin' to Kansas City. LC 87-5987. (Music in American Life Ser.). (Illus.). 276p. 1987. 24.95 (*0-252-01336-0*) U of Ill Pr.
Pearson, Nicholas M. The State & the Visual Arts. 128p. 1982. pap. 32.00 (*0-335-10109-7*, Open Univ Pr) Taylor & Francis.
Pearson, Noel, jt. auth. see Calley, Karin.
Pearson, Norman, ed. see Devos, Anthony.
Pearson, Norman H. Decade: A Collection of Poems from the First Ten Years of The Wesleyan Poetry Program. LC 72-82542. 302p. reprint ed. pap. 86.10 (*0-7837-0218-3*, 2040526) Bks Demand.
Pearson, Norman H., jt. ed. see Auden, W. H.
Pearson, Norman H., ed. see Doolittle, Hilda.
Pearson, Norman H., ed. see Hawthorne, Nathaniel.
Pearson, Norman H., ed. see Thoreau, Henry David.
Pearson, P. Psycho-Harmonial Philosophy: Music, Mathematics & Geometry. 1991. lib. bdg. 79.95 (*0-8490-5012-X*) Gordon Pr.
Pearson, P., jt. ed. see Van Empel, Martijn.
Pearson, P. David, jt. auth. see Johnson, Dale D.
Pearson, P. David, jt. ed. see Samuels, S. Jay.
Pearson, P. F. An Introduction to Basic Acupuncture: A Practical Guide for GPs & other Medical Personnel. 84p. (C). 1987. lib. bdg. 41.00 (*0-85200-686-1*) Kluwer Ac.
Pearson, Pat. You Deserve the Best. 1991. pap. 12.95 (*0-9629462-0-6*) Connemara Pub.
Pearson, Pat, jt. auth. see Van Meter, Roz.
Pearson, Patrick, jt. auth. see Kallaway, Peter.
Pearson, Patti. North. 208p. 1993. 14.95 (*0-8059-3321-2*) Dorrance.
Pearson, Patti, jt. auth. see Purcell, Kate.
Pearson, Paul B. & Greenwell, J. Richard, eds. Nutrition, Food & Man: An Interdisciplinary Perspective. LC 80-10297. 159p. 1980. pap. 14.95 (*0-8165-0706-6*) U of Ariz Pr.
Pearson, Paul D. Alvar Aalto & the International Style. (Illus.). 240p. 1989. pap. 32.50 (*0-8230-0174-1*, Whitney Lib) Watsn-Guptill.
Pearson, Paul L. The Ark of Jack Pots. LC 94-65022. (Boxy Book Ser.: No. 1). (Illus.). 73p. (Orig.). 1994. pap. 4.99 (*0-9639830-0-8*) Rainbow TX.
Pearson, Paul M. The Speaker: A Collection of the Best Orations, Poems, Stories, Debates & One Net Plays for Public Speaking & Voice training, 4 vols. text ed. 166.95 (*0-8369-9361-6*, 19732) Ayer.
Pearson, Paul M., ed. The Humourous Speaker: A Book of Humourous Selections for Reading & Speaking. LC 77-167479. (Granger Index Reprint Ser.). 1977. reprint ed. 21.95 (*0-8369-6284-2*) Ayer.
— Speaker, 1. LC 72-5498. (Granger Index Reprint Ser.). 1977. reprint ed. 26.95 (*0-8369-6374-1*) Ayer.
— Speaker, 3. LC 72-5498. (Granger Index Reprint Ser.). 1977. reprint ed. 26.95 (*0-8369-6375-X*) Ayer.
— Speaker, 8. LC 72-5498. (Granger Index Reprint Ser.). 1977. reprint ed. 34.95 (*0-8369-6377-6*) Ayer.
— Speaker, Vol. 6. LC 72-5498. (Granger Index Reprint Ser.). 1977. reprint ed. Vol 6. 29.95 (*0-8369-6376-8*) Ayer.
***Pearson, Pearle M.** Anniversary Promise. 290p. Date not set. pap. 8.95 (*0-7610-0302-9*) NW Pub.
***Pearson, Pegi C.** The Yellow Slicker: A Fable for Women. (Illus.). 28p. 1995. 12.95 (*1-879198-16-9*) Knwldg Ideas & Trnds.
Pearson, Peter. Dun Laoghaire - Kingstown. (Illus.). 176p. (Orig.). 1991. pap. 19.95 (*0-86278-256-2*, Pub. by OBrien Pr IE) Dufour.
— Dun Laoghaire-Kingstown. 176p. 1981. 28.00 (*0-905140-83-4*, Pub. by OBrien Pr IE) Dufour.
Pearson, Peter L., jt. ed. see Cuticchia, A. Jamie.
Pearson, Peter T., jt. auth. see Bader, Ellyn.
Pearson, Premi, ed. see Stoecklein, David R.
Pearson, R. A Pattern in the Heavens. pap. 3.95 (*0-88172-170-0*) Believers Bkshelf.
Pearson, R. B. Fasting & Man's Correct Diet. 153p. 1993. spiral bd. 5.50 (*0-7873-0661-4*) Mokelumne.
— Pasteur, Plagiarist, Impostor! The Germ Theory Exploded! 148p. 1964. reprint ed. spiral bd. 5.50 (*0-7873-0662-2*) Mokelumne.
Pearson, R. S. Commercial Guide to the Forest Economic Products of India. 155p. (C). 1980. text ed. 175.00 (*0-89771-619-1*, Pub. by Intl Bk Distr II) St Mut.
— Commercial Guide to the Forest Economic Products of India. (C). 1988. 40.00 (*0-685-22371-X*, Scientific) St Mut.
— Commercial Guide to the Forest Economic Products of India. 155p. (C). 1980. reprint ed. 125.00 (*0-685-21861-9*, Pub. by Intl Bk Distr II) St Mut.
— Commercial Timber of India, Set, Vols. 1 & 2. (C). 1988. Set. 820.00 (*0-685-22370-1*) St Mut.
Pearson, R. W. & Boruch, R. F., eds. Survey Research Designs: Towards a Better Understanding of Their Costs & Benefits. (Lecture Notes in Statistics Ser.: Vol. 38). v, 129p. 1986. pap. 29.00 (*0-387-96428-2*) Spr-Verlag.
Pearson, Ralph, ed. Ohio in Century Three: Quality of Life. (Illus.). 32p. 1977. pap. 2.00 (*0-318-00841-6*) Ohio Hist Soc.
Pearson, Ralph G. Symmetry Rules for Chemical Reactions: Orbital Topology & Elementary Processes. LC 76-10314. 557p. reprint ed. pap. 158.80 (*0-317-28061-9*, 2055771) Bks Demand.
Pearson, Ralph G., jt. auth. see Basolo, Fred.
Pearson, Ralph G., jt. auth. see Moore, John W.
Pearson, Ralph M. Modern Renaissance in American Art: Presenting the Work & Philosophy of 54 Distinguished Artists. LC 68-20329. (Essay Index Reprint Ser.). 1977. 42.95 (*0-8369-0780-9*) Ayer.
Pearson, Raymond. The Longman Companion to European Nationalism 1789-1920. LC 92-46026. (Companions to History Ser.). 352p. (C). 1993. text ed. 53.50 (*0-582-07229-8*, Pub. by Longman UK); pap. text ed. 28.50 (*0-582-07228-X*, Pub. by Longman UK) Longman.
Pearson, Richard. A Band of Arrogant & United Heroes: The Story of the Royal Shakespeare Co. Production of the Wars of the Roses. 168p. (C). 1990. 60.00 (*1-85634-005-8*, Pub. by Excalibur UK) St Mut.
Pearson, Richard, jt. auth. see Rosenbaum, Barbara.
***Pearson, Richard, et al.** Criminal Justice Education: The End of the Beginning. 1980. pap. text ed. 5.50 (*0-614-07045-7*) John Jay Pr.
Pearson, Richard D., jt. auth. see Wilson, Paul I.
Pearson, Richard E. Counseling & Social Support: Perspectives & Practice. (Illus.). 240p. (C). 1990. 46.00 (*0-8039-3210-3*); pap. 21.95 (*0-8039-3211-1*) Sage.
Pearson, Richard J., et al, eds. Windows on the Japanese Past. Pearson, Kazue & Nishimura, Masao, trs. LC 85-16639. (Illus.). xx, 629p. 1986. pap. 29.95 (*0-939512-24-6*) U MI Japan.
Pearson, Richard N., jt. auth. see Henderson, James A., Jr.
Pearson, Ridley. Angel Maker. 1994. mass mkt. 5.99 (*0-440-21632-X*) Dell.
— Angel Maker: A Novel. large type ed. LC 93-19761. 614p. 1993. reprint ed. 22.95 (*1-56054-606-9*); reprint ed. pap. 14.95 (*1-56054-890-8*) Thorndike Pr.
— Blood of the Albatross. 1993. mass mkt. 5.99 (*0-312-95183-3*) St Martin.
— Hard Fall. 1992. mass mkt. 5.99 (*0-440-21262-6*) Dell.
— Hard Fall. large type ed. 659p. 1992. lib. bdg. 21.95 (*1-56054-396-5*) Thorndike Pr.
— Hard Fall. large type ed. 659p. 1992. pap. 13.95 (*1-56054-932-7*) Thorndike Pr.
— Hidden Charges. 1993. mass mkt. 5.99 (*0-312-92959-5*) St Martin.
— Never Look Back. 1993. mass mkt. 4.99 (*0-312-92975-7*) St Martin.
— No Evidence. 384p. 1995. 22.95 (*0-7868-6172-X*) Hyperion.
— No Witnesses. 384p. 1994. 22.95 (*0-7868-6066-9*) Hyperion.
— No Witnesses: A Novel. large type ed. LC 94-37390. 1995. write for info. (*0-7862-0355-2*) Thorndike Pr.
— Probable Cause. 1991. mass mkt. 5.95 (*0-312-92385-6*) St Martin.
Pearson, Robert. Wisley: Gardening in a Small Space. (Illus.). 66p. 1994. pap. 5.95 (*0-304-32034-X*, Pub. by Cassell UK) Sterling.
Pearson, Robert, et al. Courtyard & Terrace Gardens. (Wisley Gardening Companion Ser.). (Illus.). 256p. 1993. 19.95 (*0-304-32044-7*, Pub. by Cassell UK) Sterling.
Pearson, Robert A. Policies & Procedures. 1984. reprint ed. pap. write for info. (*0-9608378-1-7*) B Pearson.
— Success with Parts. (Illus.). 42p. (Orig.). 1976. pap. 4.20 (*0-9608378-0-9*) B Pearson.
Pearson, Robert H. Cost Effective Decision Making. 1973. 6.95 (*0-912164-12-3*) Masterco Pr.
Pearson, Robert M. The Application of Nuclear Magnetic Resonance Spectroscopes to Quality-Control Measurements of Asphalt & Asphalt-Aggregate Mixes. 42p. (Orig.). (C). 1994. pap. text ed. 10.00 (*0-309-05760-4*, SHRP-A-382) SHRP.
***Pearson, Robert P.** Through Middle Eastern Eyes. (Through Eyes Ser.). 300p. (Orig.). (C). 1993. pap. 21.95 (*0-614-02976-7*); teacher ed, pap. 8.95 (*0-614-02977-5*) Amer Forum.
— Through Middle Eastern Eyes: Teaching Strategies. 110p. (C). 1993. pap. text ed. 8.95 (*0-938960-42-3*) CITE.
Pearson, Robert P. & Clark, Leon E. Through Middle Eastern Eyes. 3rd rev. ed. LC 92-44505. (Illus.). 352p. (Orig.). 1993. pap. text ed. 21.95 (*0-938960-41-5*) CITE.
Pearson, Roberta E. Eloquent Gestures: The Transformation of Performance Style in the Griffith Biograph Films. (C). 1992. 35.00 (*0-520-07365-7*); pap. 15.00 (*0-520-07366-5*) U CA Pr.
Pearson, Roberta E. & Uricchio, William, eds. The Many Lives of the Batman: Critical Approaches to a Superhero & His Media. 288p. 1991. 39.50 (*0-415-90346-7*, A4788, Routledge NY); pap. 13.95 (*0-415-90347-5*, A4792, Routledge NY) Routledge.
Pearson, Roberta E., jt. auth. see Uricchio, William.
Pearson, Robin, comp. A Staffordshire Christmas. LC 93-33710. 1993. 15.00 (*0-7509-0312-0*) A Sutton Pub.
Pearson, Robin, ed. A Black Country Christmas. (Christmas Ser.). (Illus.). 160p. 1992. pap. 15.00 (*0-7509-0071-7*) A Sutton Pub.
***Pearson, Robin M., ed.** Connecticut Real Estate Law Journal. 1983. ring bd. 105.00 (*0-88063-018-3*) Michie Butterworth.
Pearson, Roger. Anthropological Glossary. LC 85-195. 286p. (Orig.). 1985. 26.50 (*0-89874-510-1*) Krieger.
— The Fables of Reason: A Study of Voltaires' "Contes Philosophiques" LC 92-39575. 1993. 55.00 (*0-19-815880-7*, Old Oregon Bk Store) OUP.
— Race, Intelligence & Bias in Academe. (Illus.). 304p. 1991. pap. 25.00 (*1-878465-02-3*) Scott-Townsend Pubs.
Pearson, Roger, ed. Ecology & Evolution. (Mankind Quarterly Monographs: No. 1). 92p. (Orig.). (C). 1981. pap. 20.00 (*0-941694-00-3*) Inst Study Man.
— Essays in Medical Anthropology. (Mankind Quarterly Monographs: No. 2). (Orig.). (C). 1981. pap. 12.00 (*0-941694-01-1*) Inst Study Man.
— Perspectives on Indo-European Language, Culture & Religion, Vol. I: Studies in Honor of Edgar C. Polome. (Journal of Indo-European Studies Monograph: No. 7). (Illus.). 256p. (C). 1991. lib. bdg. 55.00 (*0-941694-36-4*) Inst Study Man.
— Sino-Soviet Intervention in Africa. (JSPES Monograph: No. 2). 1977. pap. 15.00 (*0-930690-05-2*) Coun Soc Econ.
Pearson, Roger, intro. Stendhal: The Red & the Black & the Charterhouse of Parma. LC 93-30285. (Modern Literatures in Perspective Ser.). (C). 1994. text ed. 52.50 (*0-582-09617-0*, 76705, Pub. by Longman UK) Longman.
— Stendhal: The Red & the Black & the Charterhouse of Parma. LC 93-30285. (Modern Literatures in Perspective Ser.). (C). 1995. pap. text ed. 20.95 (*0-582-09616-2*, 76704, Pub. by Longman UK) Longman.
Pearson, Roger, ed. see Shockley, William B.
Pearson, Roger, jt. auth. see Voltaire, Francois-Marie de.
Pearson, Roger, tr. see Voltaire, Francois-Marie de.
Pearson, Roger, ed. see Zysk, K. G., et al.
Pearson, Roger C. & Goheen, Austin C., eds. Compendium of Grape Diseases. LC 88-70733. (Disease Compendium Ser.). (Illus.). 121p. (Orig.). 1988. pap. 30.00 (*0-89054-088-8*) Am Phytopathol Soc.
Pearson, Ron. Using Excel Version 5 for Windows. (Illus.). 120p. 1993. pap. 29.95 (*1-56529-459-9*) Que.
Pearson, Ronald W. The American Patented Brace, 1829-1924: An Illustrated Directory of Patents. (Illus.). 192p. (Orig.). 1994. pap. 22.95 (*1-879335-48-4*) Astragal Pr.
Pearson, Roy. Prayers for All Occasions: For Pastors & Lay Leaders. 144p. (Orig.). 1990. pap. 12.00 (*0-8170-1127-7*) Judson.
Pearson, Ryne D. Cloudburst. LC 92-30489. 1993. 23.00 (*0-688-12246-9*) Morrow.
— October's Ghost. 1994. 22.50 (*0-688-12984-6*) Morrow.
— October's Ghost. 464p. 1995. reprint ed. mass mkt. 5.99 (*0-380-72227-5*) Avon.
— Thunder One. 384p. 1994. reprint ed. mass mkt. 5.50 (*0-380-72037-X*) Avon.
Pearson, Sally, jt. auth. see Ashwell, Malcolm.
Pearson, Scott, jt. auth. see Monke, Eric.
***Pearson, Scott, et al.** Agricultural Policy in Kenya: Applications of the Policy Analysis Matrix. (Food Systems & Agrarian Change Ser.). (Illus.). 328p. 1996. 45.00x (*0-8014-3085-2*) Cornell U Pr.
Pearson, Scott R. Petroleum & the Nigerian Economy. LC 76-130830. xviii, 238p. 1970. 32.50 (*0-8047-0749-9*) Stanford U Pr.
Pearson, Scott R., et al. Rice in West Africa: Policy & Economics. LC 80-50906. (Illus.). 512p. 1981. 57.50 (*0-8047-1095-3*) Stanford U Pr.
— Rice Policy in Indonesia. LC 90-55751. (Food Systems & Agrarian Change Ser.). (Illus.). 208p. 1991. 32.50 (*0-8014-2524-7*) Cornell U Pr.
Pearson, Scott R., et al, eds. Portuguese Agriculture in Transition. LC 86-29198. (Illus.). 288p. 1987. 29.95 (*0-8014-1954-9*) Cornell U Pr.
Pearson-Stamps, Pauline. George Sand's Laura: Journey Within the Crystal: A Study & Translation. (American University Studies: Romance Languages & Literature: Ser. II, Vol. 96). 181p. (C). 1989. text ed. 35.95 (*0-8204-0771-2*) P Lang Pubs.
Pearson, Steve & Pearson, Alison. Rainforest Plants of Eastern Australia. (Illus.). 192p. 1993. 45.00 (*0-86417-474-8*, Pub. by Kangaroo Pr AT) Seven Hills Bk.
***Pearson, Stewart.** Building Brands Directly. (Illus.). 288p. 1995. 40.00 (*0-8147-6618-8*) NYU Pr.
Pearson, Sue. The Haunted School. (Illus.). (J). (gr. 3-6). 1992. pap. 7.95 (*1-56680-509-0*) Mad Hatter Pub.
— Miller's Antiques Checklist: Dolls & Teddy Bears. Miller, Judith & Miller, Martin, eds. (Illus.). 1993. 13.95 (*1-85732-946-5*, Pub. by Millers Pubns UK) Antique Collect.
— Teddy Bears. (C). 1989. pap. text ed. 39.00 (*1-85183-024-3*, Silent Bks) St Mut.
***Pearson, Sue & Ayers, Dottie.** Teddy Bears: A Guide to Their History, Collecting & Care. LC 95-11517. 1995. write for info. (*0-02-860417-2*) Macmillan.
Pearson, Susan. The Baby & the Bear. (Illus.). (J). (ps-00). 1987. pap. 3.95 (*0-670-81299-4*) Viking Child Bks.
— The Bogeyman Caper. (Eagle-Eye Ernie Mysteries Ser.). (Illus.). 80p. (J). (gr. 1-3). 1990. pap. 11.95 (*0-671-70565-2*, S&S Bks Young Read); pap. 2.95 (*0-671-70569-5*, S&S Bks Young Read) S&S Childrens.
— The Campfire Ghosts. (Eagle-Eye Ernie Mysteries Ser.). (Illus.). 96p. (J). (gr. 1-3). 1990. pap. 11.95 (*0-671-70567-9*, S&S Bks Young Read); pap. 2.95 (*0-671-70571-7*, S&S Bks Young Read) S&S Childrens.
— The Day Porkchop Climbed the Christmas Tree. (Illus.). (J). (gr. k-3). 9.95 (*0-317-62031-2*) P-H.
— The Day Porkchop Climbed the Christmas Tree. (Illus.). (J). (ps up). 1989. pap. 9.95 (*0-671-66370-4*, S&S Bks Young Read) S&S Childrens.
— Eagle-Eye Ernie Comes to Town. (Eagle-Eye Ernie Mysteries Ser.). (Illus.). 80p. (J). (gr. 1-3). 1990. pap. 11.95 (*0-671-70564-4*, S&S Bks Young Read); pap. 2.95 (*0-671-70568-7*, S&S Bks Young Read) S&S Childrens.
— The Green Magician Puzzle. LC 90-22436. (Eagle-Eye Ernie Mysteries Ser.). (Illus.). (J). 1991. pap. 11.95 (*0-671-74054-7*, S&S Bks Young Read); pap. 2.95 (*0-671-74053-9*, S&S Bks Young Read) S&S Childrens.
— Jack & the Beanstalk. (J). (ps-6). 1993. pap. 5.95 (*0-671-87172-2*, S&S Bks Young Read) S&S Childrens.
— Lenore's Big Break. (Illus.). 32p. (J). (ps-3). 1994. pap. 4.99 (*0-14-054294-9*) Puffin Bks.
— Lenore's Big Break. (Illus.). 32p. (J). (gr. k up). 1992. lib. bdg. 14.00 (*0-670-83474-2*) Viking Child Bks.
— My Favorite Time of Year. LC 87-45296. (Illus.). 32p. (J). (ps-3). 1988. lib. bdg. 13.89 (*0-06-024682-0*) HarpC Child Bks.
— One-Two-Three Zoo Mystery. 1991. pap. 11.95 (*0-671-74052-0*); pap. 2.95 (*0-671-74051-2*) S&S Trade.
— Porkchop's Halloween. LC 88-4427. (Illus.). 32p. (J). (gr. k-3). 1988. pap. 14.00 (*0-671-66732-7*, S&S Bks Young Read) S&S Childrens.
— Porkchop's Halloween. (Illus.). 32p. (J). (ps up). 1989. pap. 4.00 (*0-671-68872-3*, S&S Bks Young Read) S&S Childrens.
— The Spooky Sleepover. (Eagle-Eye Ernie Mysteries Ser.). (Illus.). 64p. (J). (gr. 1-3). 1991. pap. 12.00 (*0-671-74070-9*, S&S Bks Young Read); pap. 3.00 (*0-671-74069-5*, S&S Bks Young Read) S&S Childrens.
— The Spy Code Caper. (Eagle-Eye Ernie Mysteries Ser.). (Illus.). 64p. (J). (gr. 1-3). 1991. pap. 12.00 (*0-671-74071-7*, S&S Bks Young Read); pap. 3.00 (*0-671-74072-5*, S&S Bks Young Read) S&S Childrens.
— The Tap Dance Mystery. (Eagle-Eye Ernie Mysteries Ser.). (Illus.). 96p. (J). (gr. 1-3). 1990. pap. 2.95 (*0-671-70570-9*, S&S Bks Young Read) S&S Childrens.
— Well, I Never! LC 89-48016. (Illus.). 40p. (J). (ps-1). 1990. pap. 15.00 (*0-671-69199-6*, S&S Bks Young Read) S&S Childrens.
Pearson, Susan, ed. see Morris, Ann.
Pearson, Susan, ed. see Sattler, Helen R.
Pearson, Susan, ed. see Spohn, David.
Pearson, Susie, jt. auth. see Wollerton, Linda.
Pearson, Sybille. Sally & Marsha: A Play in Two Acts. 1985. pap. 4.75 (*0-8222-0980-2*) Dramatists Play.
— Unfinished Stories. 1993. 4.75 (*0-8222-1351-6*) Dramatists Play.
***Pearson, T. A., et al.** Primer in Preventive Cardiology. (Illus.). 290p. (C). 1994. pap. write for info. (*0-87493-006-5*) Am Heart.
Pearson, T. H., jt. ed. see Tyson, R. V.
Pearson, T. R. Call & Response. 432p. 1991. pap. 10.95 (*0-380-71163-X*) Avon.
— Cry Me a River. LC 92-13860. 272p. 1993. 22.00 (*0-8050-2200-7*) H Holt & Co.
— Cry Me a River. 1994. pap. 11.00 (*0-8050-3187-1*) H Holt & Co.
— Gospel Hour. 368p. 1992. pap. 11.00 (*0-380-71036-6*) Avon.
— Gospel Hour. LC 90-43837. 384p. 1991. 19.95 (*0-688-09480-5*) Morrow.
— Off for the Sweet Hereafter: A Novel. 384p. 1995. pap. 12.00 (*0-8050-3756-X*, Owl) H Holt & Co.
— A Short History of a Small Place. 1986. mass mkt. 4.95 (*0-345-33263-6*) Ballantine.
— Short History of A Small Place. 1994. pap. 12.00 (*0-8050-3320-3*) H Holt & Co.
Pearson, Ted. Catenary Odes. LC 87-91337. 48p. 1987. 6.00 (*0-917588-17-7*) O Bks.
— Evidence. 208p. (Orig.). (C). 1989. pap. 12.00 (*0-685-26491-2*) Gaz NJ.
— Planetary Gear. LC 91-67074. 72p. (Orig.). 1991. pap. 8.95 (*0-937804-43-6*) Segue NYC.
Pearson, Thomas S. Russian Officialdom in Crisis: Autocracy & Local Self-Government, 1861-1900. (Illus.). 368p. (C). 1989. 64.95 (*0-521-36127-3*) Cambridge U Pr.
Pearson, Timothy J., jt. ed. see Zensus, J. Anton.
Pearson, Tracey C. The Howling Dog. (Illus.). 32p. (J). (ps up). 1991. 13.95 (*0-374-33502-8*) FS&G.
— The Howling Dog. (Sunburst Ser.). (Illus.). 32p. (J). (ps up). 1995. pap. 4.95 (*0-374-43332-1*) FS&G.
— Storekeeper. (J). (ps-3). 1991. pap. 3.95 (*0-8037-1052-6*, Puff Pied Piper) Puffin Bks.
Pearson, Tracey C., illus. We Wish You a Merry Christmas. LC 82-22224. 32p. (J). (ps up). 1983. pap. 3.95 (*0-8037-0310-4*) Dial Bks Young.
***Pearson, Veronica & Leung, Benjamin K., eds.** Women in Hong Kong. (Illus.). 256p. 1995. 59.00 (*0-19-585954-5*); pap. 24.95 (*0-19-585956-1*) OUP.
***Pearson, Virginia.** Everything but Elephants. (American Autobiography Ser.). 178p. 1995. reprint ed. lib. bdg. 69.00 (*0-7812-8614-X*) Rprt Serv.
Pearson, W. & Raynor, G. Handbook of Lattice Spacings & Structures, Metals & Alloys, Vol. 2. LC 57-14965. (International Series of Monographs in Metals Physics & Physical Metallurgy: Vol. 8). 1967. 586.00 (*0-08-011897-6*, Pub. by Pergamon Repr UK) Franklin.
— Handbook of Lattice Spacings & Structures of Metals & Alloys, Vol. 1. LC 57-14965. (International Series of Monographs on Metals Physics & Physical Metallurgy: Vol. 411). 1964. 430.00 (*0-08-009078-8*, Pub. by Pergamon Repr UK) Franklin.
Pearson, William, jt. auth. see Martin, George.
Pearson, William H., ed. Advances in Heterocyclic Natural Product Synthesis, Vol. 1. 193p. 1991. 90.25 (*1-55938-169-8*) Jai Pr.

PQ

— Advances in Heterocyclic Natural Product Synthesis, Vol. 2. 1992. 90.25 (*1-55938-333-X*) Jai Pr.

Pearson, Willie, Jr. & Bechtel, Kenneth, eds. Blacks, Science, & American Education. 1989. 35.00 (*0-8135-1397-9*) Rutgers U Pr.

Pearson, Willie, Jr. & Fechter, Alan, eds. Who Will Do Science? Educating the Next Generation. LC 94-9005. 208p. 1994. text ed. 31.95 (*0-8018-4857-1*) Johns Hopkins.

Pearsons, Edmund, ed. see Tufts, Henry.

Pearsons, Enid. Random House Spell Checker. 1992. 7.00 (*0-679-40520-8*) Random.

Pearsons, H. Gilbert & Sullivan. lib. bdg. 49.00 (*0-685-95443-9*) Scholarly.

Peart-Binns, John S. Defender of the Church of England: A Biography of R. R. Williams, Bishop of Leicester. 172p. 1984. 30.00 (*0-317-43628-7*, Pub. by Amate Pr Ltd UK) St Mut.

— Edwin Morris: Arch-Bishop of Wales. 200p. (C). 1990. 39.00x (*0-86383-636-4*, Pub. by Gomer Pr UK) St Mut.

Peart, Jane. Autumn Encore. LC 93-8419. (International Romance Ser.). 192p. 1993. reprint ed. pap. 7.99 (*0-8007-5480-8*) Revell.

— Brides of Montclair, No. 1: Valiant Bride. 192p. 1989. pap. 8.99 (*0-310-66951-0*) Zondervan.

— Brides of Montclair, No. 2: Ransomed Bride. 195p. 1989. pap. 8.99 (*0-310-66961-8*) Zondervan.

— Destiny's Bride: Brides of Montclair, No. 8. 224p. 1991. pap. 8.99 (*0-310-67021-7*) Zondervan.

— A Distant Dawn. (Westward Dreams Ser.). 256p. 1995. pap. 9.99 (*0-310-41301-X*) Zondervan.

— Dreams of a Longing Heart. LC 90-38382. 192p. (Orig.). (YA). (gr. 10 up). 1990. pap. 7.99 (*0-8007-5373-9*) Revell.

— Folly's Bride. 1994. mass mkt. 3.99 (*0-06-104314-1*, Harp PBks) HarpC.

— Folly's Bride. (Brides of Montclair Ser.: Vol. 4). 192p. 1990. pap. 8.99 (*0-310-66981-2*) Zondervan.

— Fortune's Bride. 1994. mass mkt. 3.99 (*0-06-104315-X*, Harp PBks) HarpC.

— Fortune's Bride. (Brides of Montclair Ser.: Vol. 3). 192p. 1990. pap. 8.99 (*0-310-66971-5*) Zondervan.

— Gallant Bride: Brides of Montclair, No. 6. 192p. 1990. pap. 8.99 (*0-310-67001-2*) Zondervan.

— The Heart's Lonely Secret. LC 94-16722. (Orphan Train West Ser.). 352p. (Orig.). 1994. pap. 9.99 (*0-8007-5542-1*) Revell.

— Hero's Bride. (Brides of Montclair Ser.: No. 11). 208p. 1993. pap. 8.99 (*0-310-67141-8*) Zondervan.

— Homeward the Seeking Heart. LC 90-8710. 192p. (Orig.). (YA). (gr. 10 up). 1990. pap. 7.99 (*0-8007-5374-7*) Revell.

— Jubilee Bride. (Brides of Montclair Ser.: No. 9). 208p. 1992. pap. 8.99 (*0-310-67121-3*) Zondervan.

— Love Takes Flight. LC 94-587. (International Romance Ser.). 192p. 1994. reprint ed. pap. 7.99 (*0-8007-5513-8*) Revell.

— Mirror Bride. (Brides of Montclair Ser.: No. 10). 208p. 1993. pap. 8.99 (*0-310-67131-0*) Zondervan.

— Orphan Train West Trilogy, 3 bks., Set. 1991. Boxed set. boxed 21.99 (*0-8007-5417-4*) Revell.

— Promise of the Valley. (Westward Dreams Ser.). 256p. 1995. pap. 9.99 (*0-310-41281-1*) Zondervan.

— Quest for Lasting Love. LC 90-40569. (Orig.). (YA). (gr. 10 up). 1990. pap. 7.99 (*0-8007-5372-0*) Revell.

— Ransomed Bride. 1994. mass mkt. 3.99 (*0-06-104316-8*, Harp PBks) HarpC.

— Runaway Heart. LC 94-20318. (Westward Dreams Ser.). 1994. pap. 9.99 (*0-310-41271-4*) Zondervan.

— Scent of Heather. (International Romance Ser.). 187p. (Orig.). 1993. pap. 7.99 (*0-8007-5462-X*) Revell.

— Shadow Bride: Brides of Montclair, No. 7. 224p. 1991. pap. 8.99 (*0-310-67011-X*) Zondervan.

— Sign of the Carousel. (International Romance Ser.). 192p. (Orig.). 1993. pap. 7.99 (*0-8007-5461-1*) Revell.

— Valiant Bride. 1994. mass mkt. 3.99 (*0-06-104317-6*, Harp PBks) HarpC.

— Valiant Bride. large type ed. LC 93-13240. (Brides of Montclair - EasyRead Type Ser.: Bk. 1). 224p. 1993. reprint ed. pap. 8.95 (*0-8027-2673-9*) Walker & Co.

— Where Tomorrow Waits. (Westward Dreams Ser.: Bk. 3). 256p. 1995. reprint ed. pap. text ed. 9.99 (*0-310-41291-9*) Zondervan.

— Yankee Bride - Rebel Bride: Montclair Divided - Brides of Montclair, No. 5. 288p. 1990. pap. 8.99 (*0-310-66991-X*) Zondervan.

Peart, Janet. Senator's Bride. (Brides of Montclair Ser.: No. 12). 224p. 1994. pap. 8.99 (*0-310-67151-5*) Zondervan.

Peart, John. Catalog of Existing Small Tools for Surface Preparation & Support Equipment for Blasters & Painters. (Illus.). 106p. 1984. pap. text ed. 30.00 (*0-938477-14-5*) SSPC.

Peart, Olive. Spanish for Nurses: An English - Spanish Pocket Guide. 135p. (Orig.). (ENG & SPA.). 1993. pap. text ed. 14.95 (*1-881795-02-0*) Eastwind Pub.

— Spanish for the X-Ray Technologist: An English-Spanish Pocket Guide. 140p. (ENG & SPA.). (C). 1992. pap. text ed. 13.95 (*0-9628440-3-9*) Eastwind Pub.

Peart, Rudolph A. When Angels Cry. 1994. 15.95 (*0-533-10523-4*) Vantage.

Pearton, Maurice. Diplomacy, War & Technology Since 1830. LC 84-7272. (Studies in Government & Public Policy). 288p. 1984. pap. 9.95 (*0-7006-0254-2*) U Pr of KS.

***Pearton, S. J.** Hydrogen in Compound Semiconductors. (Materials Science Forum Ser.: Vols. 148-9). (Illus.). 546p. (C). 1994. text ed. 160.00 (*0-87849-672-6*, Pub. by Trans Tech SZ) LPS Dist Ctr.

Pearton, S. J., jt. auth. see Jalali, B.

Pearton, S. J., et al. Hydrogen in Crystalline Semiconductors. Gonser, U. et al, eds. (Materials Science Ser.: Vol. 16). (Illus.). 376p. 1992. 54.00 (*0-387-53923-9*) Spr-Verlag.

— Topics in Growth & Device Processing of III-V Semiconductor. 400p. 1995. text ed. 81.00 (*981-02-1884-2*) World Scientific Pub.

Pearton, S. J., et al, eds. Advanced III-V Compound Semiconductor Growth, Processing & Devices. (Symposium Proceedings Ser.: Vol. 240). 1992. text ed. 66.00 (*1-55899-134-4*) Materials Res.

Peary, Danny, ed. We Played the Game: Sixty-Five Players Remember Baseball's Greatest Era, 1947-1964. LC 93-26497. 672p. 1994. 35.00 (*0-7868-6008-1*) Hyperion.

— We Played the Game: Sixty-Five Players Remember Baseball's Greatest Era, 1947-1964. (Illus.). 672p. 1995. pap. 19.95 (*0-7868-8091-0*) Hyperion.

Peary, Gerald, ed. Little Caesar. LC 80-52291. (Warner Bros. Screenplay Ser.). (Illus.). 190p. (Orig.). 1981. 19.95 (*0-299-08450-7*); pap. 9.95 (*0-299-08454-X*) U of Wis Pr.

Peary, Josephine D. My Arctic Journal: A Year Among Ice-Fields & Eskimos. LC 74-5863. reprint ed. 34.50 (*0-404-11669-8*) AMS Pr.

— My Arctic Journal, A Year Among Ice-Fields & Eskimos: With an Account of the Great White Journey Across Greenland by Robert E. Peary. (American Biography Ser.). 240p. 1991. reprint ed. lib. bdg. 69.00 (*0-7812-8309-4*) Rprt Serv.

Peary, Robert E. The North Pole: Its Discovery in 1909 Under the Auspices of the Peary Arctic Club. 480p. 1986. reprint ed. pap. 9.95 (*0-486-25129-2*) Dover.

— Northward over the Great Ice, Vols. 1-2: A Narrative of Life & Work on Greenland, 1886, 1891-97, Set, Vols. 1 & 2. (Illus.). 1993. reprint ed. Set, Vol. 1, 521p.; Vol. 2, 625p. lib. bdg. 125.00 (*0-8328-3133-6*) Higginson Bk Co.

Peary, Warren, jt. auth. see Peavy, William S.

Pease, A. S., jt. auth. see Fiske, D.

Pease, Alfred E. The Book of the Lion. (Peter Capstick Library). (Illus.). 304p. 1986. 15.95 (*0-312-00108-8*) St Martin.

Pease, Allan. Signals. (Orig.). 1984. pap. 9.95 (*0-553-34366-1*) Bantam.

Pease, Antonella & Bini, Daniela. Italiano in Diretta: An Introductory Course. 2nd ed. LC 92-29537. 1993. text ed. write for info. (*0-07-049267-0*); pap. write for info. (*0-07-049268-9*) McGraw.

Pease, Antonella & Carter, Daniela B. Vivere All Italiana. (C). 1985. pap. text ed. write for info. (*0-07-554713-9*) McGraw.

Pease, Bessie, jt. auth. see Prince, Pamela.

Pease, Clifford A., Jr. Calvin Coolidge & His Family: An Annotated Bibliography. LC 87-71283. (Illus.). 48p. (Orig.). (C). 1987. pap. 12.00 (*0-944951-00-7*) C Coolidge Memorial.

Pease, Daniel C., ed. Cellular Aspects of Neural Growth & Differentiation: Proceedings of a Conference Held November, 1969. LC 73-126760. (UCLA Forum in Medical Sciences Ser.: No. 14). 523p. reprint ed. pap. 149.10 (*0-318-34904-3*, 2031312) Bks Demand.

Pease, David. Strength to Strive. 1992. pap. 12.95 (*0-8119-0770-8*) LIFETIME.

Pease, Deborah. Did You Know? Hunting, Constance, ed. 58p. 1993. pap. 8.95 (*0-913006-52-1*) Puckerbrush.

— The Feathered Wind. Hunting, Constance, ed. 80p. (Orig.). 1992. pap. 8.95 (*0-913006-49-1*) Puckerbrush.

— Into the Amazement. Hunting, Constance, ed. 80p. 1993. pap. 8.95 (*0-913006-56-4*) Puckerbrush.

Pease, Donald E., ed. National Identities & Post-Americanist Narratives. LC 93-49689. (New Americanists Ser.). 352p. 1994. lib. bdg. 39.95 (*0-8223-1477-0*); pap. text ed. 14.95 (*0-8223-1492-4*) Duke.

— New Essays on "The Rise of Silas Lapham" (American Novel Ser.). 144p. (C). 1991. 27.95 (*0-521-37311-5*); pap. 11.95 (*0-521-37898-2*) Cambridge U Pr.

— Revisionary Interventions into the Americanist Canon. LC 93-49688. (New Americanists Ser.). 368p. 1994. lib. bdg. 39.95 (*0-8223-1478-9*); pap. text ed. 14.95 (*0-8223-1493-2*) Duke.

— Visionary Compacts: American Renaissance Writings in Cultural Context. LC 86-23371. (Wisconsin Project on American Writers Ser.). 320p. 1987. pap. 17.50 (*0-299-11004-4*) U of Wis Pr.

Pease, Donald E., jt. ed. see Kaplan, Amy.

Pease, Donald E., jt. ed. see Michaels, Walter B.

Pease, Donald E., ed. see Spanos, William V.

Pease, Dudley A. & Pippenger, John E. Basic Fluid Power. 2nd ed. (Illus.). 384p. 1986. text ed. 76.00 (*0-13-061508-0*) P-H.

Pease, Edward, jt. ed. see Dennis, Everette E.

Pease, Edward M. & Wadsworth, George P. Calculus: With Analytic Geometry. LC 63-56150. 1087p. reprint ed. pap. 180.00 (*0-8357-7971-8*, 2012457) Bks Demand.

Pease, Franklin, jt. ed. see Taylor, William B.

Pease, Greg. Sailing with Pride. LC 90-80916. (Illus.). 128p. 1990. 49.95 (*0-9626299-0-1*) C A Baumgartner Pub.

Pease, Jane H. & Pease, William H. Bound with Them in Chains: A Biographical History of the Antislavery Movement. LC 74-175612. (Contributions in American History Ser.: No. 18). 284p. 1972. text ed. 59.95 (*0-8371-6265-3*, PEB/, Greenwood Pr) Greenwood.

— Ladies, Women, & Wenches: Choice & Constraint in Antebellum Charleston & Boston. LC 89-21450. (Gender & American Culture Ser.). xvi, 218p. (C). 1990. 27.50 (*0-8078-1924-7*); pap. 12.95 (*0-8078-4289-3*) U of NC Pr.

— They Who Would Be Free: Blacks' Search for Freedom, 1830-1861. (Blacks in the New World Ser.). 1990. 14.95 (*0-252-06143-8*) U of Ill Pr.

Pease, Jane H., jt. auth. see Pease, William H.

Pease, Jane H., jt. ed. see Pease, William H.

Pease, Jeane H., jt. ed. see Pease, William H.

Pease, John C. & Niles, John M. A Gazetteer of the States of Connecticut & Rhode Island. (Illus.). xii, 407p. 1992. reprint ed. pap. text ed. 27.00 (*1-55613-544-0*) Heritage Bk.

Pease, Joseph G. A Wealth of Happiness & Many Bitter Trials: The Journals of Sir Alfred Edward Pease a Restless Man. 384p. 1990. 85.00 (*1-85072-107-6*, Pub. by W Sessions UK) St Mut.

Pease, Ken, jt. auth. see Bottomley, A. Keith.

Pease, Ken, jt. auth. see Fitzmaurice, Catherine.

Pease, Mark, jt. auth. see Dichter, Carl.

Pease, Marna, tr. see Steiner, Rudolf.

Pease, Marshall. I Ching, the Aquarian. (Illus.). 169p. (Orig.). 1993. pap. 11.95 (*0-914732-30-7*) Bro Life Inc.

Pease, Neal. Poland, the United States, & the Stabilizaton of Europe, 1919-1933. 224p. 1986. 45.00 (*0-19-504050-3*) OUP.

Pease, Otis. The Responsibilities of American Advertising: Private Control & Public Influence, 1920-1940. LC 75-39266. (Getting & Spending: the Consumer's Dilemma Ser.). (Illus.). 1976. reprint ed. 23.95 (*0-405-08039-5*) Ayer.

Pease, Otis, jt. auth. see Fehrenbacher, Don E.

Pease, Patrick F. The Lover's Picnic: How to Prepare the Most Romantic Picnic Ever. 24p. (Orig.). 1989. pap. 3.95 (*0-9624137-0-4*) Spirit Originals.

Pease, Paul L., ed. Color & Color Vision. 136p. 1982. 18.00 (*0-318-41404-X*, RB-33) Am Assn Physics.

Pease, R. S., ed. Pulsed Fusion Reactors: Proceedings of a Symposium, Erice-Trapani, Sicily, 1974. 1975. pap. 315.00 (*0-08-019749-3*, Pub. by Pergamon Repr UK) Franklin.

Pease, Rick. Filling Station Collectibles. LC 94-65623. (Illus.). 144p. (Orig.). 1994. pap. 29.95 (*0-88740-643-2*) Schiffer.

Pease, Rick, jt. auth. see Stenzler, Sonya.

Pease, Robert A. Troubleshooting Analog Circuits. 208p. 1991. text ed. 32.95 (*0-7506-9184-0*) Buttrwrth-Heinemann.

— Troubleshooting Analog Circuits. (EDN Series for Design Engineers). 220p. 1993. pap. 22.95 (*0-7506-9499-8*) Buttrwrth-Heinemann.

Pease, Robert F. O.U.I. Operating under the Influence. 199p. 1993. pap. 12.95 (*0-9637154-0-2*) Flagg Mtn Pr.

Pease, Robert W. Modoc County: A Geographic Time Continuum on the California Volcanic Tableland. LC 66-63867. (University of California Publications in Social Welfare: Vol. 17). 320p. reprint ed. pap. 91.20 (*0-317-29508-X*, 2021274) Bks Demand.

Pease, Roland F., Jr. The Zoland Books Poetry Post Card Collection. LC 88-51097. 20p. (Orig.). 1989. pap. 5.95 (*0-944072-04-6*) Zoland Bks.

Pease, Sara R. Performance Indicators for Permanent Disability: Low-Back Injuries in New Jersey. 1987. 25.00 (*0-935149-10-4*, WC-87-5) Workers Comp Res Inst.

— Performance Indicators for Permanent Disability: Low-Back Injuries in Texas. 1988. 25.00 (*0-935149-15-5*, WC-88-4) Workers Comp Res Inst.

— Performance Indicators for Permanent Disability: Low-Back Injuries in Wisconsin. 1987. 25.00 (*0-935149-09-0*, WC-87-4) Workers Comp Res Inst.

— Workers' Compensation in Washington: Administrative Inventory. 1989. 25.00 (*0-935149-20-1*, WC-89-3) Workers Comp Res Inst.

Pease, Stephen E. Psywar: Psychological Warfare in Korea, 1950-53. LC 92-21511. (Illus.). 192p. 1992. 12.95 (*0-8117-2592-8*) Stackpole.

Pease, Suzanne, tr. see Lancaster, Barbara M.

Pease, T. C. The Leveller Movement. 1988. 11.75 (*0-8446-1345-2*) Peter Smith.

Pease, T. C., ed. Illinois Election Returns: 1818-1848. LC 24-12338. (Illinois Historical Collections: Vol. 18). 1923. 10.00 (*0-912154-06-3*) Ill St Hist Lib.

Pease, Theodore C. The Frontier State, 1818-1848. (Sesquicentennial History of Illinois). 514p. 1987. reprint ed. 29.95 (*0-252-01338-7*) U of Ill Pr.

— The Story of Illinois. 3rd ed. LC 65-17299. 383p. reprint ed. pap. 109.20 (*0-685-15637-0*, 2026738) Bks Demand.

Pease, William D. Playing the Dozens. 432p. 1992. pap. 5.99 (*0-451-16986-7*, Sig) NAL-Dutton.

— The Rage of Innocence. 464p. 1994. pap. 5.99 (*0-451-18031-3*, Sig) NAL-Dutton.

Pease, William H. & Pease, Jane H. Black Utopia: Negro Communal Experiments in America. LC 63-64494. 204p. 1972. pap. 2.95 (*0-87020-066-6*) State Hist Soc Wis.

— James Louis Petigru: Southern Conservative, Southern Dissenter. 248p. 1995. 35.00 (*0-8203-1680-6*) U of Ga Pr.

— The Web of Progress: Private Values & Public Styles in Boston & Charleston, 1828-1843. LC 91-4003. 352p. 1991. pap. 18.00 (*0-8203-1390-4*) U of Ga Pr.

Pease, William H. & Pease, Jane H., eds. The Antislavery Argument. LC 64-66072. 492p. 1965. text ed. 39.50 (*0-8290-0153-0*) Irvington.

Pease, William H. & Pease, Jeane H., eds. The Antislavery Argument. LC 64-66072. 492p. (C). 1985. reprint ed. pap. text ed. 12.95 (*0-8290-1663-5*) Irvington.

Pease, William H., jt. auth. see Pease, Jane H.

Peaslee, Amos J.

Agriculture-Commodities-Fisheries-Food-Plants, Pt. 2. (International Governmental Organizations Constitutional Documents Ser.). 1975. lib. bdg. 257.50 (*90-247-1687-X*) Kluwer Ac.

— Communications, Transport, Travel. (International Governmental Organizations Constitutional Documents Ser.: Pt. 5). 1977. lib. bdg. 281.50 (*90-247-1826-0*) Kluwer Ac.

— Constitutions of Nations. 1986. lib. bdg. 464.00 (*90-247-2905-X*) Kluwer Ac.

— General & Regional-Political-Economic-Social-Legal-Defense, 2 vols. (International Governmental Organizations Constitutional Documents Ser.: Pt. 1). 1974. lib. bdg. 439.00 (*90-247-1601-2*) Kluwer Ac.

— International Governmental Organizations: Constitutional Documents, Pts. 3 & 4. 3rd rev. ed. 1979. pap. text ed. 289.00 (*90-247-2087-7*) Kluwer Ac.

Peaslee, Ann & De Witt, Sorena. Guess What Day It Is? (Illus.). 216p. (J). (gr. 3-6). 1988. pap. 14.50 (*0-89346-305-1*) Heian Intl.

Peaslee, Ann & Kille, Jullien. You Can Make It! You Can Do It! 101 E-Z Holiday Craft-Tivities for Children. (Illus.). 120p. (Orig.). (J). (gr. 3-6). 1991. pap. 9.95 (*0-89346-337-X*) Heian Intl.

Peaslee, D. C., ed. Topics in Hadron Spectroscopy. 285p. (C). 1992. pap. text ed. 95.00 (*1-56072-036-0*) Nova Sci Pubs.

— Topics in Hadron Spectroscopy, Vol. 3. 202p. (C). 1995. lib. bdg. 83.00 (*1-56072-225-8*) Nova Sci Pubs.

— Topics in Hadron Spectroscopy Vol. 2. 247p. (C). 1995. lib. bdg. 87.00 (*1-56072-224-X*) Nova Sci Pubs.

Peaslee, D. C. & Oneda, S., eds. Hadron 91: Proceedings of the International Conference, University of Maryland, College Park, U. S. A., 12-16 August 1991. 500p. 1992. text ed. 135.00 (*981-02-1003-5*) World Scientific Pub.

Peaslee, James M. & Nirenberg, David Z. The Federal Income Taxation of Mortgage-Backed Securities. rev. ed. 600p. 1993. 95.00 (*1-55738-483-5*) Probus Pub Co.

Peaslee, John, ed. see Fox, Hayden.

Peaster, Laura L., ed. see Milam, June M.

Peat. Current Physical Therapy. 296p. (C). 1988. 49.50 (*1-55664-025-0*) Mosby Yr Bk.

Peat, B. Condensing Boilers. (C). 1986. 105.00 (*0-86022-158-X*, Pub. by Build Servs Info Assn UK) St Mut.

Peat, David, jt. auth. see Briggs, John.

Peat, F. David. Artificial Intelligence: How Machines Think. rev. ed. 368p. 1988. mass mkt. 4.95 (*0-671-65377-6*) Baen Bks.

— Einstein's Moon: Bell's Theorem & the Curious Quest for Quanium Reality. 176p. 1991. pap. 11.95 (*0-8092-3965-5*) Contemp Bks.

— Lighting the Seventh Fire: The Science, Healing & Spiritual Ways of the Native Americans. LC 94-16685. 1994. 19.95 (*1-55972-249-5*, Birch Ln Pr) Carol Pub Group.

— Superstrings & the Search for the Theory of Everything. 256p. 1989. pap. 14.95 (*0-8092-4257-5*) Contemp Bks.

— Synchronicity. 1987. 12.95 (*0-553-34676-8*, New Age Bks) Bantam.

Peat, F. David, jt. auth. see Buckley, Paul.

Peat, F. David, jt. ed. see Hiley, Basil.

Peat, F. David, jt. auth. see Sokdowski, Thomas.

Peat, Isabelle, ed. see Westbrook, Gene.

Peat, Isabelle H., ed. see Westbrook, Gene.

Peat, Lindsay. Practical Guide to DBMS Selection. 340p. 1982. 138.50 (*3-11-008167-9*) De Gruyter.

Peat Marwick Auditores Independentes Staff. Investment in Brazil. (Illus.). xiii, 105p. write for info. (*0-318-58175-2*) Peat Marwick.

Peat Marwick International Staff. Worldwide Financial Reporting & Audit Requirements: A Peat Marwick Inventory. 258p. write for info. (*0-318-57848-4*) Peat Marwick.

Peat, Marwick, Mitchell & Co. Staff. Public Sale of Foreign Securities in the United States: A Guide for Foreign Bankers. iv, 133p. write for info. (*0-318-57034-3*) Peat Marwick.

Peat, Marwick, Mitchell & Co. Staff, ed. Taxation of Intercompany Transactions in Selected Countries in Europe & the U. S. A. 119p. 1979. pap. 16.00 (*90-200-0589-8*) Kluwer Ac.

Peat, N. Ross. Salistamba Sutra: Tibetan Original Sanskrit Vreconstruction, English Translation Critical Notes Including Pali Parallels, Chinese Version & Ancient Tibetan Fragments. (C). 1993. 14.50 (*81-208-1135-6*, Pub. by Motilal Banarsidass II) S Asia.

Peat, W. E., jt. auth. see Chapman, G. P.

Peat, W. Leslie & Willbanks, Stephanie J. Federal Estate & Gift Taxation. 265p. (C). 1991. pap. text ed. 21.00 (*0-314-91649-0*) West Pub.

Peat, Wilbur D. Indiana Houses of the Nineteenth Century. LC 63-2411. (Illus.). 195p. 1969. reprint ed. 17.50 (*0-253-32990-6*) Ind Hist Soc.

Peate, I. C., ed. Studies in Regional Consciousness & Environment: Essays Presented to H. J. Fleure. LC 68-26478. (Essay Index Reprint Ser.). (Illus.). 1977. reprint ed. 23.95 (*0-8369-0917-8*) Ayer.

Peate, Wayne F. Baby Fever. LC 90-70171. 372p. 1992. 10.95 (*1-55523-326-0*) Winston-Derek.

— English-Somali Phrase Book of Common & Medical Terms. 2nd ed. Heald, Phyllis, ed. 101p. 1993. pap. text ed. 17.95 (*1-883023-07-6*) Comp Occup.

Peatman, Dora. Home Delivery. (Stories We Tell Ser.). 29p. 1993. pap. 4.00 (*1-884983-06-5*) Homegrown Bks.

Peatman, Dora, et al. Stories We Tell Series, 6 bks. 167p. 1993. pap. 24.00 (*1-884983-00-6*) Homegrown Bks.

Peatman, John B. Design with Microcontrollers. 512p. 1988. text ed. write for info. (*0-07-049238-7*) McGraw.

Peatman, William. The Beginning of the Gospel: Mark's Story of Jesus. 64p. (Orig.). 1992. pap. 4.95 (*0-8146-2068-X*) Liturgical Pr.

Peatross, C. Ford, ed. Historic America: Buildings, Structures, & Sites. LC 83-14422. 708p. 1983. 29.00 (*0-8444-0431-4*, 030-000-00149-4) Lib Congress.

***Peattie, Charles & Healey, Phil.** Incredible Model Dinosaurs. (J). 1994. pap. 9.95 (*0-8362-4235-1*) Andrews & McMeel.

An Asterisk (*) at the beginning of an entry indicates that the title is appearing in BIP for the first time.

Peattie, Donald C. An Almanac for Moderns. LC 79-90410. (Non Pareil Ser.). (Illus.). 416p. 1995. reprint ed. pap. 15.95 (*0-87923-314-1*) Godine.

Peattie, Donald C., Jr. Flowering Earth. LC 90-25484. (Illus.). 272p. 1991. 27.50 (*0-253-34308-9*); pap. 10.95 (*0-253-20662-6*, MB-662) Ind U Pr.

Peattie, Donald C. A Natural History of Trees of Eastern & Central North America. (Illus.). 624p. 1991. pap. 17.95 (*0-395-58174-5*) HM.

— A Natural History of Western Trees. (Illus.). 768p. 1991. pap. 18.95 (*0-395-58175-3*) HM.

Peattie, Edward G., jt. auth. see Parker, Marshall E.

Peattie, Elia W. Mountain Woman. LC 79-98590. (Short Story Index Reprint Ser.). 1977. 20.95 (*0-8369-3164-5*) Ayer.

— Poems You Ought to Know. LC 75-98084. (Granger Index Reprint Ser.). 1977. 20.95 (*0-8369-6085-8*) Ayer.

— The Precipice. (Prairie State Bks.). 272p. 1989. reprint ed. 8.95 (*0-252-06093-8*) U of Ill Pr.

— Shape of Fear & Other Ghostly Tales. LC 72-98591. (Short Story Index Reprint Ser.). 1977. 18.95 (*0-8369-3165-3*) Ayer.

***Peattie, Ken.** Environmental Marketing Management. 352p. 1995. pap. 59.50 (*0-273-60279-9*, Pub. by Pitman Pub Ltd UK) Trans-Atl Phila.

Peattie, L., jt. auth. see Ronco, W.

Peattie, Lisa. Thinking about Development. LC 81-15858. (Environment, Development, & Public Policy: Public Policy & Social Services Ser.). 208p. 1981. 45.00 (*0-306-40761-2*, Plenum Pr) Plenum.

Peattie, Lisa R. Planners & Protesters: Airport Opposition As Social Movement. (Urban Studies Monograph Ser.: No. 9). 40p. 1991. pap. text ed. 6.00 (*0-913749-19-2*) U MD Urban Stud.

— Planning: Rethinking Ciudad Guayana. (Illus.). 208p. 1987. text ed. 37.50 (*0-472-10085-8*); pap. text ed. 17.95 (*0-472-08069-5*) U of Mich Pr.

— View from the Barrio. LC 68-16441. (Illus.). 1968. 21.95 (*0-472-72280-8*); pap. 13.95 (*0-472-06169-0*) U of Mich Pr.

Peattie, Mark R. Nan'yo: The Rise & Fall of the Japanese in Micronesia, 1885-1945. LC 87-19437. (Pacific Islands Monograph Ser.: No. 4). (Illus.). 306p. (Orig.). 1992. reprint ed. pap. text ed. 19.95 (*0-8248-1480-0*) UH Pr.

Peattie, Mark R., jt. ed. see Myers, Ramon H.

***Peattie, Noel.** Amy Rose. 250p. (Orig.). 1995. pap. 19.95 (*0-916147-62-2*) Regent Pr.

— A Passage for Dissent: The Best of Sipapu, 1970-1988. LC 88-43490. (Illus.). 511p. 1989. lib. bdg. 38.50x (*0-89950-399-3*) McFarland & Co.

— Western Skyline. 120p. (Orig.). 1995. pap. 11.95 (*0-916147-73-8*) Regent Pr.

Peattie, Roderick. Mountain Geography: A Critique & Field Study. LC 70-88918. 1970. text ed. 69.50 (*0-8371-2243-0*, PEMG, Greenwood Pr) Greenwood.

Peattie, Roger W. Selected Letters of William Michael Rossetti. LC 89-3838. 704p. 1990. lib. bdg. 55.00 (*0-271-00678-1*) Pa St U Pr.

Peavey, jt. auth. see Edison.

Peavey, Fran. By Life's Grace: Musings on the Essence of Social Change. 192p. 1994. 39.95 (*0-86571-284-0*); pap. 14.95 (*0-86571-285-9*) New Soc Pubs.

— A Shallow Pool of Time: One Woman Grapples with the AIDS Epidemic. (Orig.). 1988. pap. 10.00 (*0-317-93395-7*) Crabgrass Pubs.

Peavey, Fran, et al. Heart Politics. (Illus.). 224p. 1986. lib. bdg. 34.95 (*0-86571-076-7*); pap. 12.95 (*0-86571-077-5*) New Soc Pubs.

Peavey, Michael. Fuel from Water: Energy Independence with Hydrogen. rev. ed. LC 88-188956. (Illus.). 255p. (C). 1995. pap. 20.00 (*0-945516-04-9*) Merit Prods.

Peavler, Terry J. Julio Cortazar. (Twayne's World Authors Ser.: No. 816). 184p. (C). 1990. text ed. 26.95 (*0-8057-8257-5*, Pub. by Royal Botanic Garden UK) Macmillan.

— Texto en llamas: El arte narrative de Juan Rulfo. (University of Texas Studies in Contemporary Spanish-American Fiction: Vol. 1). 198p. (C). 1989. text ed. 35.50 (*0-8204-0673-2*) P Lang Pubs.

Peavy, Fran. A Shallow Pool of Time: One HIV Positive Woman Grapples with the AIDS Epidemic. 268p. 1990. 39.95 (*0-86571-166-6*); pap. 14.95 (*0-86571-167-4*) New Soc Pubs.

Peavy, H. S. & Rowe, D. Environmental Engineering. 1985. text ed. write for info. (*0-07-049134-8*) McGraw.

Peavy, John W. & Sherrerd, Katrina F. Cases in Portfolio Management. (Orig.). (C). 1991. pap. 30.00 (*1-879087-04-9*) Assn I M&R.

Peavy, Linda. Allison's Grandfather. large type ed. 40p. (J). (gr. 3-4). 1984. reprint ed. 9.50 (*0-317-01866-3*, J-00780-00) Am Printing Hse.

Peavy, Linda & Smith, Ursula. Dreams into Deeds: Nine Women Who Dared. LC 85-40295. 160p. (J). (gr. 6-9). 1985. text ed. 14.95 (*0-684-18484-2*, C Scribner Sons Young) S&S Childrens.

— Food, Nutrition, & You. LC 82-5694. (Illus.). 208p. (YA). (gr. 6 up). 1982. text ed. 14.95 (*0-684-17461-8*, C Scribner Sons Young) S&S Childrens.

— The Gold Rush Widows of Little Falls: A Story Drawn from the Letters of Pamelia & James Fergus. LC 89-49409. (Illus.). 305p. 1990. 29.95 (*0-87351-249-9*); pap. 14.95 (*0-87351-250-2*) Minn Hist.

— Women in Waiting: Life on the Home Frontier. LC 93-38832. (Illus.). 400p. 1994. 35.00 (*0-8061-2616-7*); pap. 17.95 (*0-8061-2619-1*) U of Okla Pr.

— Women Who Changed Things. LC 82-21612. (Illus.). 208p. (YA). (gr. 5 up). 1983. text ed. 14.95 (*0-684-17849-4*, C Scribner Sons Young) S&S Childrens.

***Peavy, Madeline G.** A Journey to Heaven: A True Story. 1995. pap. 10.00 (*0-614-04964-4*) Old Mountain.

Peavy, William S. & Peary, Warren. Super Nutrition Gardening: How to Grow Your Own Powercharged Foods. LC 92-25950. 248p. 1993. pap. 14.95 (*0-89529-532-6*) Avery Pub.

Peay, Eugene L. The Lands of Zarahemla. Van Treese, James B., ed. 286p. 1993. pap. 9.95 (*1-880416-77-8*) NW Pub.

Peay, Jill. Tribunals on Trial: A Study of Decision-Making under the Mental Health Act 1983. 272p. 1989. 59.00 (*0-19-825249-8*) OUP.

Peberdy, et al. Fungal Protoplasts: Applications in Biochemistry & Genetics. (Mycology Ser.: Vol. 6). 368p. 1985. 160.00 (*0-8247-7112-5*) Dekker.

Peberdy, J. F., et al. Genetic Manipulation of Fungi: Laboratory Manual. (Illus.). 208p. 1989. 84.95 (*0-7506-1104-9*) Buttrwrth-Heinemann.

Peberdy, J. F., et al, eds. Applied Molecular Genetics of Fungi. (British Mycological Society Symposium Ser.: No. 18). (Illus.). 200p. (C). 1991. 64.95 (*0-521-41571-3*) Cambridge U Pr.

Peberdy, John F., ed. Penicillium & Acremonium. LC 87-12328. (Biotechnology Handbooks Ser.: Vol. 1). 314p. 1987. 65.00 (*0-306-42345-6*, Plenum Pr) Plenum.

Peberdy, Max. Third World Conundrum: A Call to Christian Partnership. 188p. 1986. pap. 7.50 (*0-85364-463-2*, Pub. by Paternoster UK) Attic Pr.

Peberdy, W. Sterilisation & Hygiene: A Practical Guide. 136p. (C). 1988. 75.00 (*0-85950-900-1*, Pub. by S Thornes Pubs UK) St Mut.

Peboli, O. J. & Rivelles, V. O. Particles & Fields: Proceedings of the VII Ja Swieca Summer School. 812p. 1994. text ed. 135.00 (*981-02-1597-5*) World Scientific Pub.

Pebuy, M., ed. see Peguy, Charles.

***Pebworth, Ted-Larry & Summers, Claude J., eds.** Selected Poems of Ben Jonson. LC 95-8284. (Pegasus Paperbks.). 112p. 1995. pap. write for info. (*0-86698-178-0*, P31) MRTS.

Pebworth, Ted-Larry, jt. auth. see Summers, Claude J.

Pebworth, Ted-Larry, jt. ed. see Summers, Claude J.

Pec, Karel, jt. auth. see Bursa, Milan.

Pecan, Erene, jt. ed. see Woodwell, George M.

Pecar, Branko. Business Forecasting for Management. Davis, Glyn & Lillystone, Simon, eds. LC 93-47175. 1994. 14.95 (*0-07-707865-9*) McGraw.

Pecar, Joseph A., et al. The McGraw-Hill Telecommunications Factbook. LC 92-24340. 1993. pap. text ed. 29.95 (*0-07-049183-6*) McGraw.

Pecaric, Josip E., et al. Convex Functions, Partial Orderings & Statistical Applications. (Mathematics in Science & Engineering Ser.). (Illus.). 467p. 1992. text ed. 69.95 (*0-12-549250-2*) Acad Pr.

Pecarve, Reuben. The Hypnosis Book: Mind & Body Power at the Count of Five. (Orig.). 1995. pap. 12.95 (*1-56171-225-6*, S P I Bks) Sure Sellers.

***Peccati, L. & Viren, M.** Financial Modeling. 364p. 1994. 66.00 (*0-387-91487-0*) Spr-Verlag.

Peccei, Aurelio. The Human Quality. LC 76-52496. (Pergamon International Library Science Technology Engineering & Social Studies). 216p. 1977. 98.00 (*0-08-021479-7*, Pub. by Pergamon Repr UK) Franklin.

— One Hundred Pages for the Future: Reflections of the President of the Club of Rome. (Illus.). 150p. 1981. text ed. 89.00 (*0-08-028110-9*, Pub. by Pergamon Repr UK) Franklin.

***Peccei, Jean S.** Child Language. (Language Workbooks Ser.). (Illus.). 128p. 1994. pap. 12.95 (*0-415-08567-5*, B4016) Routledge.

Peccei, R. & Laraneta, M., eds. Trends in Astroparticle Physics. 600p. (C). 1991. text ed. 130.00 (*981-02-0825-1*) World Scientific Pub.

Pecchia, David, comp. Cinematographers, Production Designers, Costume Designers & Film Editors Guide. 3rd ed. 490p. 1991. 49.95 (*0-943728-43-6*) Lone Eagle Pub.

***Pecci, Ernest F.** The Violence Potential: In Our Society Today. (Illus.). 6p. (Orig.). 1994. pap. 14.95 (*0-9642637-2-6*) Pavior Pubng.

Pecci, Ernest F., jt. auth. see Meisterfeld, C. W.

Pecci, Ernest F., ed. see Pecci, Mary F.

Pecci, Mary F. At Last! A Reading Method for Every Child. 4th ed. 342p. 1988. 27.95 (*0-943220-07-6*) Pecci Educ Pubs.

— Color Words. (Super Seatwork Ser.). (Illus.). 130p. 1984. 11.95 (*0-943220-05-X*) Pecci Educ Pubs.

— Content Areas. (Super Seatwork Ser.). (Illus.). 168p. 1984. 11.95 (*0-943220-01-7*) Pecci Educ Pubs.

— How to Discipline Your Class for Joyful Teaching. Pecci, Ernest F., ed. 42p. (Orig.). (C). 1982. pap. text ed. 4.95 (*0-943220-08-4*) Pecci Educ Pubs.

— Letter Recognition. (Super Seatwork Ser.). (Illus.). 104p. 1984. 11.95 (*0-943220-02-5*) Pecci Educ Pubs.

— Linguistic Exercises. (Super Seatwork Ser.). (Illus.). 106p. 1978. 11.95 (*0-943220-03-3*) Pecci Educ Pubs.

— Number Words. (Super Seatwork Ser.). (Illus.). 120p. 1982. 11.95 (*0-943220-06-8*) Pecci Educ Pubs.

— Phonic Grab Bag. (Super Seatwork Ser.). (Illus.). 138p. 1984. 11.95 (*0-943220-09-2*) Pecci Educ Pubs.

— Why Johnny Ain't Never Gonna Read! A Challenge to the Nation. (Illus.). 148p. (Orig.). 1995. pap. 6.95 (*0-943220-10-6*) Pecci Educ Pubs.

— Word Skills. (Super Seatwork Ser.). (Illus.). 238p. 1980. 17.95 (*0-943220-04-1*) Pecci Educ Pubs.

Pecci, Stephen. Building a Better Hitter. 160p. 1991. pap. write for info. (*0-697-11404-X*) Brown & Benchmark.

Peccinotti, Harri, jt. auth. see Hillman, David.

Peccinotti, Harris, jt. comp. see Hillman, David.

Peccorini, Francisco L. Selfhood As Thinking Thought in the Work of Gabriel Marcel: A New Interpretation. LC 86-28549. (Problems in Contemporary Philosophy Ser.: Vol. 3). 200p. 1987. lib. bdg. 79.95 (*0-88946-329-8*) E Mellen.

Pech, J. C., ed. Cellular & Molecular Aspects of the Plant Hormone Ethylene: Proceedings of the International Symposium "Cellular & Molecular Aspects of Biosynthesis & Action Hormone Ethylene," Agen, France August 31 - Sept. 4, 1992. (Current Plant Science & Biotechnology in Agriculture Ser.). 404p. (C). 1993. lib. bdg. 132.50 (*0-7923-2169-3*) Kluwer Ac.

Pech, Maude R., jt. auth. see Hultgren, Thor.

Pech, Maude R., jt. auth. see Kendrick, John W.

Pech, R. P., jt. ed. see Norton, G. A.

Pecham, John. John Pecham & the Science of Optics: Perspectiva Communis. Lindberg, David C., ed. LC 72-98122. (Medieval Science Publications: No. 14). 1970. 45.00 (*0-299-05730-5*) U of Wis Pr.

***Pechan, A.** Esperanto Hungarian Pocket Dictionary. 464p. (C). 1988. 15.00x (*963-205-210-2*, Pub. by Akad Kiado HU) St Mut.

— Esperanto-Hungarian Pocket Dictionary; Ezperanto-Magyar Szotar. 464p. 1983. 12.95 (*0-8288-1740-5*, M13019) Fr & Eur.

— Hungarian-Esperanto Pocket Dictionary. 5th ed. 560p. (ESP & HUN.). 1983. 12.95 (*0-8288-1656-5*, M 13019) Fr & Eur.

***Pechan, A., ed.** Hungarian-Esperanto Pocket Dictionary. 560p. (C). 1988. 15.00x (*963-205-209-9*, Pub. by Akad Kiado HU) St Mut.

***Pechar, Gary & Ng, Nelson.** Personal Fitness. 112p. (C). 1994. pap. text ed., spiral bd. 9.00 (*0-8403-9692-9*) Kendall-Hunt.

Pechar, Gary S. & Ng, Nelson K. Personal Fitness. 96p. (C). 1992. spiral bd. 7.95 (*0-8403-7743-6*) Kendall-Hunt.

***Peche, Wendy W.** Legendary Team Leadership. (Illus.). 144p. (Orig.). 1994. pap. 12.95 (*0-9630727-1-4*) Spring Brook.

Pechenik, Jan A. Biology of the Invertebrates. 2nd ed. 592p. (C). 1991. pap. write for info. (*0-697-14203-5*) Wm C Brown Pubs.

— A Short Guide to Writing about Biology. (C). 1987. pap. text ed. 9.75 (*0-673-39232-5*) HarpCollege.

— A Short Guide to Writing about Biology. 2nd ed. LC 92-10923. (Short Guide Ser.). (C). 1992. 11.00 (*0-673-52128-1*) HarpCollege.

Pecherek, Andrea, jt. auth. see Cowie, Helen.

Pechman, Carl. Regulating Power: The Economics of Electricity in the Information Age. LC 93-10053. (Topics in Regulatory Economics & Policy Ser.: Vol. 15). 256p. (C). 1993. lib. bdg. 85.00 (*0-7923-9347-3*) Kluwer Ac.

Pechman, Joseph. Fulfilling America's Promise: Social Policies for the 1990s. McPherson, Michael S., ed. LC 91-55562. (Williams College Center for the Humanities & Social Sciences Ser.). (Illus.). 272p. 1992. 38.50 (*0-8014-2631-6*); pap. 15.95 (*0-8014-8059-0*) Cornell U Pr.

Pechman, Joseph A. Federal Tax Policy. 4th ed. LC 83-23126. (Studies of Government Finance). 410p. 1984. 26.95 (*0-8157-6964-4*); pap. 9.95 (*0-8157-6963-6*) Brookings.

— Federal Tax Policy. 5th ed. LC 87-13159. (Studies in Government Finance). 430p. 1987. 36.95 (*0-8157-6962-8*); pap. 16.95 (*0-8157-6961-X*) Brookings.

— Tax Reform & the U. S. Economy. LC 87-70178. (Dialogues on Public Policy Ser.). 108p. 1987. pap. 10.95 (*0-8157-6959-8*) Brookings.

— Who Paid the Taxes, 1966-85? LC 84-45845. (Studies of Government Finance). 84p. 1985. 22.95 (*0-8157-6998-9*); pap. 8.95 (*0-8157-6997-0*) Brookings.

Pechman, Joseph A., ed. A Citizen's Guide to the New Tax Reforms: Fair Tax, Flat Tax, Simple Tax. 176p. 1985. 30.25 (*0-8476-7403-7*) Rowman.

— Economics for Policymaking: Selected Essays by Arthur M. Okun. (Illus.). 736p. 1983. 50.00x (*0-262-15025-5*) MIT Pr.

— Options for Tax Reform. LC 84-72269. (Dialogues on Public Policy Ser.). 149p. 1984. pap. 11.95 (*0-8157-6995-4*) Brookings.

— The Promise of Tax Reform. LC 85-1236. 1985. 15.95 (*0-13-731092-7*) Am Assembly.

— What Should Be Taxed, Income or Expenditure? A Report of a Conference Sponsored by the Fund for Public Policy Research & the Brookings Institution. LC 79-22733. (Studies of Government Finance: Second Ser.). 344p. reprint ed. pap. 98.10 (*0-8357-7072-9*, 2033591) Bks Demand.

— World Tax Reform: A Progress Report. LC 88-70469. 294p. 1988. pap. 14.95 (*0-8157-6999-7*) Brookings.

Pechman, Joseph A. & Timpane, P. Michael, eds. Work Incentives & Income Guarantees: The New Jersey Negative Income Tax Experiment. LC 75-2321. (Studies in Social Experimentation). 232p. 1975. pap. 12.95 (*0-8157-6975-X*) Brookings.

Pechman, Joseph A., jt. ed. see Aaron, Henry J.

Pechman, Joseph A., jt. auth. see Break, George F.

Pechman, Joseph A., jt. ed. see Brown, Clair.

Pechman, Joseph A., jt. ed. see Palmer, John L.

Pechoin, Daniel. Thesaurus Larousse. 1146p. (FRE.). 1991. 125.00 (*0-8288-7369-0*, 2033201074) Fr & Eur.

Pechota, Vratislav. The Right to Know One's Human Rights: A Road Toward Marriage & Family. LC 83-72868. 52p. 1983. pap. 2.50 (*0-87495-056-2*) Am Jewish Comm.

Pechota, Vratislav, ed. Central & East European Legal Materials, 9 vols., Set. 1990. ring bd. 725.00 (*0-929179-47-1*) Transnatl Juris Pubns.

— Commercial Arbitration: An International Bibliography, 2 vols. LC 92-23736. 1993. 185.00 (*1-56425-002-4*) Transnatl Juris Pubns.

— Foreign Investment in Central & Eastern Europe. 1000p. 1992. ring bd. 185.00 (*0-929179-45-5*) Transnatl Juris Pubns.

— Privatization in Eastern Europe. 1994. 95.00 (*1-56425-023-7*) Transnatl Juris Pubns.

Pechota, Vratislav, jt. ed. see Hazard, John N.

Pechota, Vratislav, jt. auth. see Smith, Hans.

Pechota, Vratislav, jt. auth. see Szladits, Charles.

Pecht, M. G., jt. ed. see Nguyen, L. T.

Pecht, Michael. Integrated Circuit, Hybrid & Multichip Module Package Design Guidelines: A Focus on Reliability. LC 93-12475. 448p. 1994. pap. text ed. 69.95 (*0-471-59446-6*) Wiley.

Pecht, Michael, ed. Handbook of Electronic Package Design. (Mechanical Engineering Ser.: Vol. 76). 904p. 1991. 195.00 (*0-8247-7921-5*) Dekker.

— Placement & Routing of Electronic Modules. LC 92-44796. (Electrical Engineering & Electronics Ser.: Vol. 82). 352p. 1993. 140.00 (*0-8247-8916-4*) Dekker.

— Product Reliability, Maintainability, & Supportability Handbook. LC 95-5257. 448p. 1995. 89.95 (*0-8493-9457-0*, 9457) CRC Pr.

Pecht, Michael, ed. see Hakim, Edward.

Pecht, Michael, et al, eds. Quality Conformance & Qualification of Microelectronic Packages & Interconnects. LC 93-9709. 375p. 1994. pap. text ed. 69.95 (*0-471-59436-9*) Wiley.

***Pecht, Michael G.** Plastic Encapsulated Microelectronics: Materials, Processes, Quality, Reliability, & Applications. Nguyen, Luu T. et al, eds. 1995. text ed. 69.95 (*0-471-30625-8*) Wiley.

— Soldering Processes & Equipment. LC 92-33770. 312p. 1993. text ed. 69.95 (*0-471-59167-X*) Wiley.

***Pechter, Edward.** What was Shakespeare? Renaissance Plays & Changing Critical Practice. LC 94-25366. 216p. 1995. 29.95x (*0-8014-3065-8*); pap. 12.95x (*0-8014-8229-1*) Cornell U Pr.

Pechter, Kerry, jt. auth. see Resnick, R. Linda.

Pechtimaldjian, Katharine, ed. see Prince, Frank A.

Pechtimaldjian, Katharine, ed. see Richardson, Barrie & Castronovo Fusco, Mary A.

Pechura, Constance M., ed. see Institute of Medicine, Committee on the Survey of the Health Effects of Mustard Gas & Lewisite Staff.

Pecile, A., ed. Calcitonin '84: Chemistry, Physiology, Pharmacology & Clincial Aspects: Proceedings of the International Symposium Calcitonin 1984, Milian, 2-4 October 1984. (International Congress Ser.: No. 663). 498p. 1986. 153.50 (*0-444-80690-3*, Excerpta Medica) Elsevier.

Pecile, A. & De Bernard, B., eds. Bone Regulatory Factors: Morphology, Biochemistry, Physiology & Pharmacology. LC 90-6777. (NATO ASI Series A, Life Sciences: Vol. 184). (Illus.). 302p. 1990. 89.50 (*0-306-43500-4*, Plenum Pr) Plenum.

Pecile, A. & Rescigno, A., eds. Pharmacokinetics: Mathematical & Statistical Approaches. LC 87-36043. (NATO ASI Series A, Life Sciences: Vol. 145). (Illus.). 358p. 1988. 95.00 (*0-306-42806-7*, Plenum Pr) Plenum.

Pecile, C. Proceedings of the International Conference on the Physics & Chemistry of Low-Dimensional Synthetic Metals: A Special Issue of the Journal Molecular Crystals & Liquid Crystals, 5 vols. 2272p. 1985. 1,400.00 (*0-685-27108-0*) Gordon & Breach.

Pecile, C., et al, eds. Proceedings of the International Conference on the Physics & Chemistry of Low-Dimensional Synthetic Metals: Special Issues of the Journal Molecular Crystals & Liquid Crystals, 5 vols., Set. 2272p. 1985. text ed. 1,850.00 (*0-677-06665-1*) Gordon & Breach.

Pecina, Marko. Tunnel Syndromes. (Illus.). 184p. 1991. 104.00 (*0-8493-6933-9*, RC422) CRC Pr.

Pecina, Marko & Bojanic, Ivan. Overuse Injuries of the Musculoskeletal System. LC 93-8061. 1993. 95.00 (*0-8493-4492-1*, RD97) CRC Pr.

***Peck.** Soup Ahoy. 3.99 (*0-679-87617-0*) Random.

— Student Solutions Guide to Accompany Chemistry: The Molecule. 200p. 1993. pap. 14.95 (*0-8016-5071-2*) Mosby Yr Bk.

Peck, A. J. C. I. I. Legal Liabilities, No. 210. (C). 1987. 240.00 (*0-685-33765-0*, Pub. by Witherby & Co UK) St Mut.

— Mastering German. (Mastering Languages Ser.). (Illus.). 340p. (Orig.). 1991. pap. 11.95 (*0-87052-056-3*); audio 12.95 (*0-87052-061-X*) Hippocrene Bks.

Peck, A. L., ed. see Aristotle.

Peck, Abe. Uncovering the Sixties: The Life & Times of the Underground Press. 1991. pap. 12.95 (*0-8065-1225-3*, Citadel Pr) Carol Pub Group.

Peck, Abraham, ed. American Jewish Archives, Cincinnati: The Papers of the World Jewish Congress, 1945-1950. LC 89-16915. (Archives of the Holocaust Ser.: Vols. 8-9). 544p. 1991. Vol. 8, 544p. 135.00 (*0-8240-5490-3*); Vol. 9, 448p. 120.00 (*0-8240-5491-1*) Garland.

Peck, Abraham J., ed. The German-Jewish Legacy in America, 1938-1988: From Bildung to the Bill of Rights. LC 89-16561. 267p. (C). 1989. text ed. 35.00 (*0-8143-2263-8*); pap. text ed. 19.95 (*0-8143-2264-6*) Wayne St U Pr.

— Jews & Christians after the Holocaust. LC 81-70665. 127p. reprint ed. pap. 36.20 (*0-317-55539-1*, 2029611) Bks Demand.

Peck, Abraham J. & Herscher, Uri D., eds. Queen City Refuge. 270p. 1989. 29.95 (*0-87441-486-5*) Behrman.

Peck, Abraham J., jt. ed. see Cohen, Martin A.

Peck, Abraham J., jt. auth. see Marcus, Jacob R.

Peck, Abraham J., jt. ed. see Marcus, Jacob R.

P Q

*Peck, Ada M. A History of the Hanover Society. rev. ed. Swarthout, Douglas, ed. LC 95-77581. (Illus.). 260p. 1995. write for info. (0-9646900-0-4) Berry Hill NY.

Peck, Alan. The Priestly Gift in Mishnah: A Study of Tractate Terumot. LC 81-2764. (Brown Judaic Studies). (C). 1981. pap. 17.50 (0-89130-488-6, 140020) Scholars Pr GA.

Peck, Amelia. American Quilts & Coverlets in the Metropolitan Museum of Art. (Illus.). 264p. 1990. 35.00 (0-87099-592-8) Metro Mus Art.

— American Quilts & Coverlets in the Metropolitan Museum of Art. 256p. 1990. 50.00 (0-525-24912-5, Dutton Studio) Studio Bks.

Peck, Amelia, ed. Alexander Jackson Davis, American Architect, 1803-1892. LC 92-8479. (Illus.). 1992. 45.00 (0-8478-1484-X); pap. 29.95 (0-8478-1485-8) Rizzoli Intl.

Peck, Annie S. Industrial & Commercial South America. 1977. 75.00 (0-8490-2056-5) Gordon Pr.

Peck, Barbara M., et al. The History of Montgomery Illinois: In Words & Pictures. Giles, Wanda H., ed. LC 90-70501. (Illus.). 224p. 1990. 34.95 (0-9626765-0-0) VMHC.

Peck, Bradford. World a Department Store: A Story of Life Under a Cooperative System. LC 70-154457. (Utopian Literature Ser.). (Illus.). 1979. reprint ed. 23.95 (0-405-03539-X) Ayer.

Peck, Bryan & Archer, Ted. Beginning Teaching: Professional Development & Probation in Scotland. (C). 1989. 35.00 (1-85098-140-X, Pub. by Jordanhill College UK) St Mut.

Peck, Bryan, jt. ed. see Archer, Ted.

Peck, Bryan, et al. Staff Development in Secondary Schools. (C). 1989. 60.00 (1-85098-901-X, Pub. by Jordanhill College UK) St Mut.

Peck, Carl C., et al. Bedside Clinical Pharmacokinetics: Simple Techniques for Individualizing Drug Therapy. rev. ed. 120p. 1989. 10.50 (0-915486-10-5) Applied Therapeutics.

*Peck, Charles. Top Executive Compensation: 1994 Edition. (Report Ser.: No. 1099-94-RR). (Illus.). 80p. (Orig.). 1994. pap. text ed. 120.00 (0-8237-0546-3) Conference Bd.

Peck, Charles, jt. auth. see Potter, Frank.

Peck, Charles A., et al, eds. Integrating Young Children with Disabilities into Community Programs: Ecological Perspectives on Research & Implementation. LC 92-17404. 304p. (Orig.). (C). 1992. pap. text ed. 32.00 (1-55766-108-1) P H Brookes.

*Peck, Chauncey E. History of Wilbraham, Mass. (Illus.). 469p. 1995. reprint ed. lib. bdg. 47.50 (0-8328-4470-5) Higginson Bk Co.

— The History of Wilbraham, Massachusetts. (Illus.). 469p. 1994. reprint ed. lib. bdg. 47.50 (0-8328-3959-0) Higginson Bk Co.

Peck, Connie. How to Make Peace with Your Partner. 288p. 1995. mass mkt. 5.99 (0-446-60189-6) Warner Bks.

*Peck, Dale. The Law of Enclosures. 320p. Date not set. 23.00 (0-374-18419-4) FS&G.

— Martin & John. 240p. 1994. reprint ed. pap. 11.00 (0-06-097588-1, PL) HarpC.

— Martin & John: A Novel. LC 92-1622. 1993. 21.00 (0-374-20311-3) FS&G.

*Peck, Daniel. Dear Rachel: The Civil War Letters of Daniel Peck. Stanford, Martha G., ed. LC 93-87081. (Illus.). 69p. (Orig.). 1993. pap. 6.00 (0-9639704-0-2) Devon Press.

Peck, David. Novels of Initiation: A Guidebook for Teaching Literature to Adolescents. 224p. 1989. pap. text ed. 17.95 (0-8077-2951-5) Tchrs Coll.

Peck, David, jt. comp. see Bullock, Chris.

Peck, David F. & Shapiro, Colin M., eds. Measuring Human Problems: A Practical Guide. (Clinical Psychology Ser.). 406p. 1991. text ed. 102.95 (0-471-91206-9) Wiley.

*Peck, David R. American Ethnic Literatures. (Magill Bibliographies Ser.). 218p. 1992. 40.00 (0-8108-2792-1) Scarecrow.

Peck, David W. Decision at Law. LC 76-56082. 303p. 1977. reprint ed. text ed. 59.75 (0-8371-9419-9, PEDL, Greenwood Pr) Greenwood.

Peck, Dennis L., jt. ed. see Murphy, John W.

Peck, Donald. Solos for Flute. (Carl Fischer's "All Time Favorites" Music Ser.). 48p. (Orig.). 1992. pap. 14.95 (0-8258-0346-2, XF1006) Fischer Inc NY.

Peck, Donald, comp. Easy Original Flute Solos, MFM48. (Illus.). 128p. 1967. pap. 9.95 (0-8256-4048-2, AM41682) Music Sales.

Peck, Donald M., jt. auth. see Jencks, Stanley M.

Peck, Douglas R. Ponce De Leon & the Discovery of Florida. LC 93-89738. (Illus.). 104p. (Orig.). 1993. pap. 13.95 (1-880654-02-4) Pogo Pr.

Peck, Douglas T. Cristoforo Colombo: God's Navigator. (Illus.). 148p. (Orig.). 1994. 18.95 (0-9641798-2-2); lib. bdg. 18.95 (0-9641798-1-4); pap. 12.95 (0-9641798-0-6) Columbian Pubs.

Peck, Edson R. Jesus Christ the Lion & Seeing John. 1994. 24.95 (0-533-10861-6) Vantage.

*Peck, Elisabeth S. & Smith, Emily A. Berea's First 125 Years, 1855-1980. fac. ed. LC 82-6955. (Illus.). 308p. 1994. pap. 87.80 (0-7837-7596-2, 2047349) Bks Demand.

Peck, Elizabeth A., jt. auth. see Montgomery, Douglas C.

Peck, Elsie H., et al. Islamic Art from Michigan Collections. Fisher, Alan W., ed. (Illus.). 114p. (Orig.). 1982. pap. 10.00 (1-879147-04-1) Kresge Art Mus.

Peck, Epophroditus. A History of Bristol, Connecticut. (Illus.). 362p. 1994. reprint ed. lib. bdg. 39.50 (0-8328-4022-X) Higginson Bk Co.

Peck, Gail. New River. (Harperprints Chapbook Competition Ser.). 24p. 1993. 5.00 (0-9624274-9-7) NC Writers Network.

Peck, Gene. Chemistry Lab Manual. (C). 1993. student ed 10.00 (1-881592-02-2) Hayden-McNeil.

Peck, Geo W., ed. History of Wisconsin. (Illus.). 423p. 1992. reprint ed. lib. bdg. 42.50 (0-8328-2577-8) Higginson Bk Co.

Peck, George. Christian Perfection, Vol. 1. 1990. pap. 9.99 (0-88019-266-6) Schmul Pub Co.

— Christian Perfection, Vol. 2. 1991. reprint ed. pap. 9.99 (0-88019-271-2) Schmul Pub Co.

— The Psalms Speak. 32p. (Orig.). 1991. pap. 3.00 (0-87574-298-X) Pendle Hill.

— Simplicity: A Rich Quaker's View. LC 72-97851. (Orig.). 1973. pap. 3.00 (0-87574-189-4) Pendle Hill.

— Sketches & Incidents from the Saddlebag of an Itinerant. 1988. pap. 10.99 (0-88019-237-2) Schmul Pub Co.

— The Triple Way. LC 77-79824. 321p. (Orig.). 1977. pap. 3.00 (0-87574-213-0) Pendle Hill.

— What Is Quakerism? A Primer. LC 87-63556. (Orig.). 1988. pap. 3.00 (0-87574-277-7) Pendle Hill.

Peck, George & Hoffman, John S., eds. The Laity in Ministry. 176p. 1984. pap. 10.00 (0-8170-1041-6) Judson.

Peck, George C., jt. ed. see Gruber, Ronald P.

Peck, George W. How Private Geo. W. Peck Put down the Rebellion, or the Funny Experiences of a Raw Recruit. LC 90-38549. (Illus.). x, 350p. 1990. reprint ed. pap. 9.95 (0-940473-20-8) Wm Caxton.

— How Private George W. Peck Put Down the Rebellion. LC 71-91090. (American Humorists Ser.). (Illus.). 328p. 1979. reprint ed. lib. bdg. 34.50 (0-8398-1559-X) Irvington.

— Peck's Bad Boy & His Pa. (Illus.). 250p. 1991. reprint ed. lib. bdg. 25.95 (0-89966-750-3) Buccaneer Bks.

Peck, Girvan. Writing Persuasive Briefs. LC 84-80192. 246p. 1984. 55.00 (0-316-69666-8) Little.

Peck, Graham. Two Kinds of Time. LC 83-45833. (Illus.). reprint ed. 67.50 (0-404-20198-9) AMS Pr.

Peck, H. Daniel. Thoreau's Morning Work: Memory & Perception in a Week on the Concord & Merrimack Rivers, the Journal & Walden. 208p. (C). 1990. text ed. 27.50 (0-300-04823-8) Yale U Pr.

— Thoreau's Morning Work: Memory & Perception in A Week on the Concord & Merrimack Rivers, the Journal, & Walden. 208p. 1994. pap. 13.00 (0-300-06104-8) Yale U Pr.

— A World by Itself: The Pastoral Moment in Cooper's Fiction. LC 76-25868. 227p. reprint ed. pap. 64.70 (0-8357-3755-1, 2036481) Bks Demand.

Peck, H. Daniel, ed. Green American Tradition: Essays & Poems for Sherman Paul. LC 88-27627. (Illus.). 357p. 1989. text ed. 39.95 (0-8071-1513-4) La State U Pr.

— New Essays on "The Last of the Mohicans" (American Novel Ser.). 160p. (C). 1992. 29.95 (0-521-37414-6); pap. 12.95 (0-521-37771-4) Cambridge U Pr.

Peck, Harold L. Stripping: The Assembly of Film Images. 2nd ed. Destree, Thomas M., ed. LC 88-82939. (Illus.). 300p. (C). 1988. pap. text ed. 50.00 (0-88362-117-7) Graphic Arts Tech Found.

Peck, Harry D., Jr. & LeGall, Jean, eds. Methods in Enzymology, Vol. 243: Inorganic Microbial Sulfur Metabolism. (Illus.). 682p. 1994. text ed. 99.00 (0-12-182144-7) Acad Pr.

Peck, Harry T. The Adventures of Mabel. (Illus.). 236p. (J). (gr. k-5). 1986. reprint ed. 21.95 (0-9616844-0-2) Greenhouse Pub.

— A History of Classical Philosophy. 1972. 59.95 (0-8490-0321-0) Gordon Pr.

— The Personal Equation. LC 79-39121. (Essay Index Reprint Ser.). 1977. reprint ed. 24.95 (0-8369-2709-5) Ayer.

— Studies in Several Literatures. LC 68-16967. (Essay Index Reprint Ser.). 1977. 20.95 (0-8369-0781-7) Ayer.

— What Is Good English? And Other Essays. LC 72-39122. (Essay Index Reprint Ser.). 1977. reprint ed. 21.95 (0-8369-2710-9) Ayer.

— William Hickling Prescott. LC 69-14033. 186p. 1969. reprint ed. text ed. 49.75 (0-8371-0614-1, PEWP, Greenwood Pr) Greenwood.

Peck, Harry Th. William Hickling Prescott. (BCL1-PS American Literature Ser.). 186p. 1992. reprint ed. lib. bdg. 69.00 (0-7812-6838-9) Rprt Serv.

Peck, Hazel, jt. auth. see Holme, David J.

Peck, Herbert. The Book of Rookwood Pottery. LC 68-9062. (Illus.). 184p. 1968. reprint ed. pap. 19.95 (0-943633-02-8) Cinc Art Gal.

— Rockwood Pottery, Bk. 2. 1987. 19.95 (0-943633-00-1) Cinc Art Gal.

Peck, Howard. Howard Peck's New Milford Memories of a Connecticut Town. LC 91-34071. (Illus.). 176p. 1991. 25.00 (0-914659-54-5) Phoenix Pub.

Peck, I. A Genealogical History of the Descendants of Joseph Peck Who Emigrated in 1638: Also an Appendix Giving an Account of the Boston & Hingham Pecks, the Descendant of John of Mendon, Mass. (Illus.). 443p. 1989. reprint ed. lib. bdg. 66.50 (0-8328-0946-2); reprint ed. pap. 56.50 (0-8328-0947-0) Higginson Bk Co.

Peck, Ira. The Life & Words of Martin Luther King Jr. (Illus.). 96p. (Orig.). (J). (gr. 3-7). 1991. pap. 2.95 (0-590-43827-1) Scholastic Inc.

Peck, J. L., et al. Past & Present of O'Brien & Osceola Counties, Iowa, 2 vols. (Illus.). 1319p. 1994. reprint ed. lib. bdg. 135.00 (0-8328-3827-6) Higginson Bk Co.

Peck, J. M. A Gazetteer of Illinois in Three Parts: Containing a General View of the State, a General View of Each County, & a Particular Description of Each Town, Settlement, Stream, Prairie, Bottom, Bluff, Etc. Alphabetically Arranged. xii, 356p. (Orig.). 1993. reprint ed. pap. text ed. 24.00 (1-55613-782-6) Heritage Bk.

Peck, Jan. Ballerina Princess. 18p. (J). (ps-2). 1992. 10.95 (1-879680-15-7) About You.

— The Time Travelers. 18p. (J). (ps-2). 1993. 10.95 (1-879680-16-5) About You.

Peck, Jan, jt. auth. see Lay, Kathryn.

Peck, Janet R., jt. ed. see Bailey, Elizabeth E.

Peck, Janice. The Gods of Televangelism: The Crisis of Meaning & the Appeal of Religious Television. Good, Leslie T., ed. LC 92-32476. (Communication Series: Critical Studies in Communication). 288p. (C). 1993. text ed. 52.50 (1-881303-65-9); pap. text ed. 22.95 (1-881303-66-7) Hampton Pr NJ.

Peck, Janice L. & Ochsner, Florence M. Records Retention Guidelines for U. S. Based Real Estate Organizations. 60p. 1993. pap. 36.00 (0-933887-48-5, A4519) Assn Recs Mgrs & Admin.

Peck, Jeffrey M. Culture - Contexture: Explorations in Anthropology & Literary Studies. Daniel, E. Valentine, ed. LC 94-3997. 1995. 50.00 (0-520-08463-2) U CA Pr.

— Culture - Contexture: Explorations in Anthropology & Literary Studies. Daniel, E. Valentine, ed. 405p. 1995. pap. 16.00 (0-520-08464-0) U CA Pr.

Peck, Jeffrey M., jt. auth. see Borneman, John.

Peck, Jeffrey M., jt. ed. see Cohen, Ralph.

Peck, Johanne, ed. see Goldman, Richard, et al.

Peck, Johanne T., et al. Kindergarten Policies: What Is Best for Children? LC 88-61832. 88p. 1988. text ed. 6.00 (0-935989-15-3, NAEYC #141) Natl Assn Child Ed.

Peck, John. Poem & Translations of Hi-Lo. 160p. (Orig.). 1993. pap. 12.95 (1-878818-28-7) Sheep Meadow.

*Peck, John, ed. David Copperfield, Hard Times: Charles Dickens. LC 94-35204. (New Casebooks Ser.). 1995. write for info. (0-312-12492-9) St Martin.

— Middlemarch. LC 91-36461. (New Casebooks Ser.). 208p. 1992. text ed. 45.00 (0-312-07567-7) St Martin.

Peck, John, tr. see Euripides.

Peck, John E., jt. ed. see Swartz, Thomas R.

Peck, John M. Father Clark: Or, The Pioneer Preacher. LC 72-104539. 285p. reprint ed. lib. bdg. 28.00 (0-8398-1560-3) Irvington.

— Father Clark: Or, The Pioneer Preacher. 285p. 1986. reprint ed. pap. text ed. 6.95 (0-8290-1901-4) Irvington.

— Forty Years of Pioneer Life: Memoir of John Mason Peck, D.D. (American Biography Ser.). 360p. 1991. reprint ed. lib. bdg. 79.00 (0-7812-8310-8) Rprt Serv.

— A Guide for Emigrants: Containing Sketches of Illinois, Missouri, & the Adjacent Parts. LC 75-115. (Mid-American Frontier Ser.). 1975. reprint ed. 28.95 (0-405-06881-6) Ayer.

Peck, Judith. Art & Interaction: An Academic Fieldwork Program for Colleges. (Activities Program for Institutions Ser.). (Illus.). 179p. (C). 1990. pap. text ed. 19.95 (0-685-35355-9) Ramapo College.

— Sculpture: A Fifteen-Week Multimedia Program. (Illus.). 144p. 1986. pap. 14.95 (0-671-61426-6) P-H.

— Sculpture As Experience. LC 88-43308. (Illus.). 208p. 1989. pap. 14.95 (0-8019-7978-1) Chilton.

Peck, Juliana. The Reagan Administration & the Palestinian Question: The First Thousand Days. 138p. 1984. pap. 8.95 (0-88728-140-0) Inst Palestine.

Peck, Kay. Folsom Boy. LC 88-51030. 174p. (J). 1989. pap. 6.95 (1-55523-173-X) Winston-Derek.

Peck, Kyle L., jt. auth. see Hannafin, Michael J.

Peck, Larry & Irgolic, Kurt J. Measurement & Synthesis in the Chemistry Laboratory. (Illus.). 448p. (Orig.). (C). 1991. pap. write for info. (0-02-359835-2) Macmillan.

Peck, Lee. Coping with Cliques. Rosen, Ruth, ed. LC 92-12380. (Coping Ser.). (YA). (gr. 7-12). 1992. 15.95 (0-8239-1412-7) Rosen Group.

Peck, Linda L. Court Patronage & Corruption in Early Stuart England. 320p. 1993. pap. 17.95 (0-415-09368-6, B0617) Routledge.

— Court Patronage & Corruption in Early Stuart England. 320p. 1990. text ed. 55.00 (0-04-942195-6) Routledge Chapman & Hall.

— Northampton: Patronage & Policy at the Court of James I. 288p. (C). 1982. text ed. 55.00 (0-04-942177-8) Routledge Chapman & Hall.

Peck, Linda L., ed. The Mental World of the Jacobean Court. (Illus.). 380p. (C). 1991. 69.95 (0-521-37567-3) Cambridge U Pr.

Peck, M. Scott. Bed by the Window. 1991. pap. 12.95 (0-553-35387-X) Bantam.

— The Different Drum: Community Making & Peace. 336p. 1988. pap. 12.00 (0-671-66833-1, Touchstone Bks) S&S Trade.

— Different Drum, Community Making & Peace. 1987. 14.95 (0-671-64633-8) S&S Trade.

— The Friendly Snowflake: A Fable of Faith, Love & Family. (Illus.). 40p. (J). (gr. 3 up). 1992. 14.95 (1-878685-28-7) Turner Pub GA.

— Further Along the Road Less Traveled. 1994. pap. 12.00 (0-671-89288-6, Touchstone Bks) S&S Trade.

— Further along the Road Less Traveled: The Unending Journey Toward Spiritual Growth. 256p. 1993. 21.00 (0-671-78159-6) S&S Trade.

— Further along the Road Less Traveled: The Unending Journey Toward Spiritual Growth. large type ed. 272p. 1994. pap. 13.95 (0-8027-2682-8) Walker & Co.

— The House of Charon. 1990. write for info. (0-318-65587-X) Bantam.

— In Search of Stones: A Pilgrimage of Faith, Reason & Discovery. (Illus.). 416p. 1995. 22.95 (0-7868-6021-9) Hyperion.

— Meditations from the Road. 384p. (Orig.). 1993. pap. 9.00 (0-671-79799-9, Touchstone Bks) S&S Trade.

— People of the Lie: The Hope for Healing Human Evil. 276p. 1985. pap. 11.00 (0-671-52816-5, Touchstone Bks) S&S Trade.

— The Road Less Traveled. 1985. 23.00 (0-671-60559-3) S&S Trade.

— The Road Less Traveled. 320p. 1988. 14.00 (0-671-67300-9, Touchstone Bks) S&S Trade.

— The Road Less Traveled. 1993. reprint ed. lib. bdg. 28.95x (1-56849-158-1) Buccaneer Bks.

— The Road Less Traveled: A New Psychology of Love, Traditional Values & Spiritual Growth. 1980. pap. 12.00 (0-671-25067-1, Touchstone Bks) S&S Trade.

— Road Less Traveled: A New Psychology of Love, Traditional Values & Spiritual Growth. large type ed. 1985. pap. 16.95 (0-8027-2498-1) Walker & Co.

— What Return Can I Make? Dimensions of the Christian Experience. 1985. 12.95 (0-671-52502-6) S&S Trade.

— A World Waiting to Be Born: Rediscovering Civility. LC 92-34012. 1993. 22.95 (0-553-09307-X) Bantam.

— World Waiting to Be Born: Rediscovering Civility. 1994. pap. 12.95 (0-553-37317-X) Bantam.

*Peck, M. Scott & Von Waldner, Marilyn. Gifts for the Journey: Treasures of the Christian Life. rev. ed. LC 95-8245. Orig. Title: What Return Can I Make?. 1995. 20.00 (0-06-066448-7) Harper SF.

Peck, M. Scott, et al. What Return Can I Make? The Dimensions of the Christian Experience. LC 85-11945. 96p. 1985. 24.95 (0-317-38030-3) S&S Trade.

Peck, Marshall H., III, illus. Heavy-Duty Trucks. (Little Wheel Bks.). 14p. (J). (ps-00). 1992. bds. 4.99 (0-679-83244-0) Random Bks Yng Read.

Peck, Mary G. Carrie Chapman Catt. LC 75-23159. (Pioneers of the Woman's Movement: an International Perspective Ser.). (Illus.). 495p. 1976. reprint ed. 32.45 (0-88355-279-5) Hyperion Conn.

Peck, Merton J., ed. World Aluminum Industry in a Changing Era. LC 88-4990. 831p. 1988. 30.00 (0-915707-42-X) Resources Future.

Peck, Merton J. & Richardson, Thomas J. What Is to Be Done? Proposals for the Soviet Transition to the Market. 224p. (Orig.). 1992. text ed. 30.00 (0-300-05466-1); pap. 14.00 (0-300-05468-8) Yale U Pr.

Peck, Michael, et al. Youth Suicide. (Death & Suicide Ser.: Vol. 6). 224p. 1985. pap. 24.95 (0-8261-4481-0) Springer Pub.

Peck, Michael A., jt. auth. see Ratcliff, Ronald E.

Peck, Nancy B. Second Chance. 1981. pap. 2.50 (0-89083-745-7) Zebra.

Peck, Paul L. Basic Spiritual Metaphysics. LC 78-61984. 1978. 14.50 (0-87881-079-X) Mojave Bks.

— Hymns of Power. LC 79-88061. 1979. 9.95 (0-87881-090-0) Mojave Bks.

— Intermediate Spiritual Metaphysics. LC 78-61985. (Spiritual Metaphysics Ser.: Vol. 2). 1979. 15.95 (0-87881-081-1); pap. 13.50 (0-87881-082-X) Mojave Bks.

Peck, Ralph B., jt. auth. see Terzaghi, Karl.

Peck, Ralph B., et al. Foundation Engineering. 2nd ed. LC 73-9877. 514p. 1974. Net. text ed. write for info. (0-471-67585-7) Wiley.

Peck, Rasamond. The Flavor of Waverly. Belin, Susan S., ed. & intro. by. (Illus.). 266p. 1986. 18.95 (0-9616433-0-7) Waverly Comm Hse.

Peck, Richard. Anonymously Yours. (J). 1991. 12.95 (0-671-74162-4, Julian Messner) Silver Burdett Pr.

— Are You in the House Alone? 176p. (gr. k up). 1977. mass mkt. 3.99 (0-440-90227-4, LFL) Dell.

— Bel-Air Bambi & the Mall Rats. LC 92-29377. (J). 1993. 15.95 (0-385-30823-X) Delacorte.

— Bel-Air Bambi & the Mall Rats. (YA). 1995. pap. 3.99 (0-440-21925-6) Dell.

— Blossom Culp & the Sleep of Death. (J). (gr. k-6). 1994. reprint ed. mass mkt. 3.99 (0-440-40676-5, YB) Dell.

— Close Enough to Touch. LC 81-65498. 192p. (J). (gr. 7 up). 1981. 15.00 (0-385-28145-5) Delacorte.

— Close Enough to Touch. (Young Love Romance Ser.). 144p. (J). (gr. 7 up). 1982. pap. 3.50 (0-440-91282-2, LFL) Dell.

— Don't Look & It Won't Hurt. (YA). 1992. pap. 3.50 (0-440-21213-8) Dell.

— The Dreadful Future of Blossom Culp. (J). (gr. 7 up). 1983. 15.00 (0-385-29300-3) Delacorte.

— The Dreadful Future of Blossom Culp. (J). (gr. k-6). 1994. mass mkt. 3.99 (0-440-42154-3, YB) Dell.

— Dreamland Lake. 128p. (J). (gr. 7 up). 1990. pap. 3.50 (0-440-92079-5, LFL) Dell.

— Dreamland Lake. 1992. 16.25 (0-8446-6542-8) Peter Smith.

— Father Figure. (Orig.). (J). (gr. k-12). 1988. mass mkt. 3.99 (0-440-20069-5, LFL) Dell.

— Father Figure. LC 78-7909. 208p. (Orig.). (J). (gr. 7 up). 1978. pap. 15.00 (0-670-30930-3) Viking Child Bks.

— The Ghost Belonged to Me. (Blossom Culp Mystery Ser.). (J). (gr. k-6). 1987. mass mkt. 3.99 (0-440-42861-0, YB) Dell.

— Ghosts I Have Been. 256p. (J). (gr. 5 up). 1979. pap. 3.50 (0-440-92839-7, LFL) Dell.

— Ghosts I Have Been. (J). (gr. k-6). 1987. mass mkt. 3.99 (0-440-42864-5, YB) Dell.

— Ghosts I Have Been. LC 77-9469. 224p. (J). (gr. 7 up). 1977. pap. 15.00 (0-670-33813-3) Viking Child Bks.

— The Last Safe Place on Earth. LC 94-446. (J). 1995. 15.95 (0-385-32052-3) Delacorte.

— Lost in Cyberspace. LC 94-48330. (J). 1995. 14.99 (0-8037-1931-0) Dial Bks Young.

— Love & Death at the Mall: Teaching & Writing for the Literate Young. LC 93-3933. 1994. 16.95 (0-385-31173-7) Delacorte.

— Princess Ashley. (J). (gr. k-12). 1988. pap. 3.50 (0-440-20206-X, LFL) Dell.

— Remembering the Good Times. (J). (gr. 5-12). 1986. mass mkt. 3.99 (0-440-97339-2, LFL) Dell.

— Representing Super Doll. 192p. (YA). (gr. 7 up). 1989. pap. 2.95 (0-440-97362-7, LFL) Dell.

— Rock: Making Musical Choices. 174p. (Orig.). 1985. pap. 6.95 (0-89084-297-3) Bob Jones Univ Pr.

— Secrets of the Shopping Mall. 192p. (J). (gr. k-6). 1980. pap. 3.99 (0-440-98099-2) Dell.

P
Q

An Asterisk (*) at the beginning of an entry indicates that the title is appearing in BIP for the first time.

— Secrets of the Shopping Mall. 192p. (J). (gr. k-6). 1989. mass mkt. 3.99 (*0-440-40270-0*, LFL) Dell.
— Something for Joey. (J). 1983. mass mkt. 3.99 (*0-553-27199-7*) Bantam.
— Those Summer Girls I Never Met. (J). (gr. k up). 1989. pap. 3.50 (*0-440-20457-7*, LFL) Dell.
— Through a Brief Darkness. 144p. (J). (gr. 7 up). 1989. pap. 3.25 (*0-440-98809-8*, LFL) Dell.
— Unfinished Portrait. (J). 1993. mass mkt. 3.99 (*0-440-21886-1*) Dell.
— Voices after Midnight. (J). (gr. 5-9). 1989. 14.95 (*0-385-29779-3*) Delacorte.
— Voices after Midnight. (YA). 1990. reprint ed. mass mkt. 3.99 (*0-440-40378-2*, Yearling Classics) Dell.
— Write a Tale of Terror. (Illus.). 32p. (YA). (gr. 5-10). 1987. pap. 4.95 (*0-913839-60-4*) Bk Lures.

Peck, Robert A. The Amiga Companion. 256p. 1988. pap. 19.95 (*0-928579-00-X*) IDG NH.
— The Amiga Companion. 2nd rev. ed. 306p. 1989. pap. 19. 95 (*0-928579-01-8*) IDG NH.

Peck, Robert D. Future Focusing: An Alternative to Long-Range Planning. 1983. pap. text ed. 9.95 (*0-317-01653-9*) Coun Indep Colleges.

Peck, Robert L. American Meditation & Beginning Yoga. 1976. 6.00 (*0-917828-05-4*) Personal Dev Ctr.

Peck, Robert L. & Peck, Thelma M. The Handbook for Goats. 1985. 8.50 (*0-917828-00-3*) Personal Dev Ctr.
— Philosophy of Patanjali. 1994. 7.95 (*0-917828-04-6*) Personal Dev Ctr.
— Stone of the Philosophers. 1988. 14.95 (*0-917828-02-X*) Personal Dev Ctr.

Peck, Robert M. A Celebration of Birds: The Life & Art of Louis Agassiz Fuertes. (Illus.). 192p. 1982. 30.00 (*0-8027-0716-5*) Walker & Co.
— Headhunters & Hummingbirds: An Expedition into Ecuador. LC 86-15908. (Illus.). 128p. (J). (gr. 11 up). 1987. 14.95 (*0-8027-6645-5*); lib. bdg. 14.85 (*0-8027-6646-3*) Walker & Co.
— Land of the Eagle: A Natural History of North America. (Illus.). 288p. 1991. 30.00 (*0-671-75596-X*) Summit Bks.

Peck, Robert N. Arly. (History Series for Young People). 160p. (J). (gr. 5 up). 1989. 16.95 (*0-8027-6856-3*) Walker & Co.
— Arly's Run. 160p. (J). (gr. 5-9). 1991. 16.95 (*0-8027-8120-9*) Walker & Co.
— A Day No Pigs Would Die. 1972. 20.00 (*0-394-48235-2*) Knopf.
— A Day No Pigs Would Die. LC 72-259. 156p. (J). (gr. 7 up). 1994. pap. 3.99 (*0-679-85306-5*) Random Bks Yng Read.
— Eagle Fur. large type ed. LC 92-971. 361p. 1992. lib. bdg. 16.95 (*1-56054-390-6*) Thorndike Pr.
— Hallapoosa. 1988. 16.95 (*0-8027-1016-6*) Walker & Co.
— Higbee's Halloween. 101p. (J). (gr. 5-7). 1990. 13.95 (*0-8027-6968-3*); lib. bdg. 14.85 (*0-8027-6969-1*) Walker & Co.
— The Horse Hunters. LC 88-42659. (Illus.). 160p. 1988. 15.95 (*0-394-56980-6*) Random.
— Little Soup's Birthday. (J). (ps-3). 1991. pap. 2.99 (*0-440-40551-3*, YB) Dell.
— Little Soup's Bunny. (J). (ps-3). 1993. pap. 2.99 (*0-440-40772-9*) Dell.
— Little Soup's Hayride. (J). (ps-3). 1991. pap. 2.99 (*0-440-40383-9*) Dell.
— Little Soup's Turkey. (Illus.). 80p. (Orig.). (J). (gr. 1-4). 1992. pap. 2.99 (*0-440-40724-9*, YB) Dell.
— A Part of the Sky. LC 93-41741. 1994. 18.00 (*0-679-43277-9*) Knopf.
— Soup. LC 73-15117. (Illus.). 104p. (J). (gr. 3 up). 1974. lib. bdg. 10.99 (*0-394-92700-1*) Knopf Bks Yng Read.
— Soup. (J). (gr. 3 up). 1979. pap. 3.50 (*0-440-48186-4*, YB) Dell.
— Soup Ahoy. LC 93-14097. (Illus.). 144p. (J). (gr. 2-6). 1994. 15.00 (*0-679-84978-5*) Knopf Bks Yng Read.
— Soup Ahoy. LC 93-14097. (Illus.). 144p. (J). (gr. 2-6). 1994. lib. bdg. 15.99 (*0-679-94978-X*) Knopf Bks Yng Read.
— Soup & Me. LC 75-9514. (Illus.). 112p. (J). (gr. 3-6). 1975. lib. bdg. 13.99 (*0-394-93157-2*) Knopf Bks Yng Read.
— Soup for President. LC 77-3548. (Illus.). (J). (gr. 6 up). 1978. lib. bdg. 10.99 (*0-394-93675-2*) Knopf Bks Yng Read.
— Soup for President. (J). (gr. 3-6). 1986. reprint ed. pap. 3.50 (*0-440-48188-0*, YB) Dell.
— Soup in Love. (J). (gr. 4-7). 1992. 14.00 (*0-385-30563-X*) Delacorte.
— Soup in Love. (J). (gr. 4-7). 1993. pap. 3.50 (*0-440-40755-9*) Dell.
— Soup in the Saddle. LC 82-14010. (Illus.). 96p. (J). (gr. 3-6). 1983. lib. bdg. 11.99 (*0-394-95294-4*) Knopf Bks Yng Read.
— Soup on Ice. LC 85-218. (Illus.). 128p. (J). (gr. 3-7). 1985. lib. bdg. 10.99 (*0-394-97613-4*) Knopf Bks Yng Read.
— Soup on Wheels. LC 80-17661. (Illus.). 128p. (J). (gr. 3 up). 1981. lib. bdg. 11.99 (*0-394-94581-6*) Knopf Bks Yng Read.
— Soup 1776. LC 94-23879. (Illus.). (J). 1995. write for info. (*0-679-87320-1*) Knopf.
— Soup's Hoop. (J). (gr. 4-7). 1992. pap. 3.50 (*0-440-40589-0*, YB) Dell.

Peck, Robert S. The Bill of Rights & the Politics of Interpretation. Lippert, ed. 371p. (C). 1992. text ed. 26. 75 (*0-314-90881-1*) West Pub.

Peck, Robert S., ed. To Govern a Changing Society: Constitutionalism & the Challenge of New Technology. LC 89-39868. 228p. (Orig.). 1990. pap. 14.95 (*0-87474-783-X*) Smithsonian.

Peck, Rodney. Drugs & Sports. Rosen, Ruth, ed. LC 92-12359. (Drug Abuse Prevention Library). (YA). (gr. 7-12). 1992. 15.95 (*0-8239-1420-8*) Rosen Group.
— Working Together Against Human Rights Violations. LC 94-8858. (Library of Social Activism Ser.). (J). 1994. write for info. (*0-8239-1778-9*) Rosen Group.

Peck, Rosalie & Stefanics, Charlotte. Learning to Say Goodbye: Dealing with Death & Dying. LC 87-70820. xx, 164p. 1987. 16.95 (*0-915202-71-9*) Accel Devel.

Peck, Roxy, jt. auth. see Devore, Jay.

Peck, Russell, ed. Heroic Women from the Old Testament in Middle English Verse. (TEAMS Middle English Text Ser.). 1991. pap. 8.95 (*1-879288-11-7*) Medieval Inst.

Peck, Russell A. Kingship & Common Profit in Gower's "Confessio Amantis" LC 78-8984. (Literary Structures Ser.). 232p. 1978. 13.95 (*0-8093-0801-0*) S Ill U Pr.

Peck, Russell A., ed. Chaucer's Romaunt of the Rose & Boece, the Treatise on the Astrolabe, the Equatorie of the Planetis, the Lost Works & the Chaucerian Apocrypha: An Annotated Bibliography 1900-1985. (Chaucer Bibliographies Ser.). 402p. 1988. text ed. 75.00 (*0-8020-2493-9*) U of Toronto Pr.

Peck, Russell A., ed. see Gower, John.

Peck, Ruth A. A Century of Ministry: The History of Trinity Lutheran Church. 140p. 1992. pap. 10.00 (*0-9632829-0-5*) Trinity Evang Luth.

*__Peck, Scott.__ All-American Boy: A Gay Son's Search for His Father. LC 94-45480. 1995. 22.00 (*0-02-595362-1*, Scribners) S&S Trade.

Peck, Shelley, jt. ed. see Goetz, Kathy.

Peck, Stephen R. Atlas of Facial Expression. (Illus.). 176p. 1990. pap. 10.95 (*0-19-506322-8*) OUP.
— Atlas of Human Anatomy for the Artist. 1982. pap. 14.95 (*0-19-503095-8*) OUP.

Peck, Steve. Fly Fishing in Middle-Earth. 12p. 1992. pap. 2.50 (*1-881799-02-6*) Am Tolkien Soc.

Peck, Sylvia. Kelsey's Raven. 240p. (J). (gr. 5 up). 1992. 14. 00 (*0-688-09583-6*) Morrow Jr Bks.
— Seal Child. LC 89-33700. (Illus.). 208p. (J). (gr. 4 up). 1989. 12.95 (*0-688-08682-9*) Morrow Jr Bks.
— Seal Child. (J). (gr. 3-7). 1991. reprint ed. mass mkt. 3.99 (*0-553-15868-6*, Skylark) Bantam.

Peck, T. B. Richard Clarke of Rowley, Mass., & His Descendants in the Line of Timothy Clark of Rockingham, Vermont, 1638-1904. (Illus.). 93p. 1993. reprint ed. lib. bdg. 28.00 (*0-8328-1354-0*); reprint ed. pap. 18.00 (*0-8328-1355-9*) Higginson Bk Co.

Peck, T. R., et al, eds. Soil Testing: Correlating & Interpreting the Analytical Results. 117p. 1977. pap. 6.00 (*0-89118-047-8*) Soil Sci Soc Am.

Peck, Thelma M., jt. auth. see Peck, Robert L.

Peck, Theodore P., ed. Chemical Industries Information Sources. LC 76-6891. (Management Information Guide Ser.: No. 29). 624p. 1979. 68.00 (*0-8103-0829-0*) Gale.

Peck, Thomas B. The Bellows Genealogy: John Bellows, the Boy Emigrant of 1635 & His Descendants. (Illus.). 673p. 1988. reprint ed. lib. bdg. 93.50 (*0-8328-0230-1*); reprint ed. pap. 83.50 (*0-8328-0231-X*) Higginson Bk Co.

Peck, Tom, ed. see Youngson, Jeanne.

Peck, W. A., ed. Bone & Mineral Research Annual, No. 6. 350p. 1989. 143.75 (*0-444-81061-7*) Elsevier.
— Bone & Mineral Research Annual, Vol. 5. 470p. 1987. 97. 75 (*0-317-61525-4*) Elsevier.
— Bone & Mineral Research Annual Vol. 3: A Yearly Survey of Developments in the Field of Bone & Mineral Metabolism. 400p. 1985. 95.00 (*0-444-90347-X*) Elsevier.

Peck, W. A., et al. Bone & Mineral Research, Vol. 7. 364p. 1991. 200.00 (*0-444-81371-3*) Elsevier.

Peck, W. A., et al, eds. Engineering Geology of Melbourne: Proceedings of the Seminar on Engineering Geology of Melbourne, Victoria, Australia, 16 September 1992. (Illus.). 418p. (C). 1992. text ed. 95.00 (*90-5410-083-4*, Pub. by A A Balkema NE) Ashgate Pub Co.

Peck, W. E., ed. see Shelley, Percy Bysshe.

Peck, William. The Detroit Institute of Arts: A Brief History. (Illus.). 196p. 1991. pap. 19.95 (*0-89558-136-1*) Wayne St U Pr.

Peck, William J., ed. New Studies in Bonhoeffer's Society. LC 87-7944. (Toronto Studies in Theology: Vol. 30). 284p. 1987. lib. bdg. 89.95 (*0-88946-775-7*) E Mellen.

*__Peck, Wm. E.__ Selleck & Peck Genealogy. (Illus.). 74p. 1994. reprint ed. lib. bdg. 25.00 (*0-8328-4378-4*); reprint ed. pap. 15.00 (*0-8328-4379-2*) Higginson Bk Co.

Peckarsky, Barbara, et al. Freshwater Macroinvertebrates of Northeastern North America. LC 89-17468. (Illus.). 456p. 1990. 62.50 (*0-8014-2076-8*); pap. 27.50 (*0-8014-9688-8*) Cornell U Pr.

Peckenham, Nancy, ed. Sunbelt Blues: Where Have All the Good Jobs Gone? (Illus.). 64p. (Orig.). 1990. pap. 5.00 (*0-943810-46-9*) Inst Southern Studies.

Peckenham, Nancy & Street, Annie, eds. Honduras: Portrait of a Captive Nation. LC 85-9482. 366p. 1985. text ed. 55.00 (*0-275-90219-6*, C0219, Praeger Pubs) Greenwood.

Peckenpaugh, Angela. Designs, Like Branches or Arteries. 20p. (Orig.). 1994. pap. 15.00 (*1-880723-01-8*) Morgan Pr WI.

*__Peckenpaugh, Nancy J. & Poleman, Charlotte M.__ Nutrition: Essentials & Diet Therapy. 7th ed. LC 94-21254. 560p. 1995. pap. text ed. 26.95 (*0-7216-5130-5*) Saunders.

Pecker, Jean-Claude. The Future of the Sun. 1992. pap. text ed. 11.95 (*0-07-049182-8*) McGraw.

Pecker The Cat. A Rug Before My Time: Memoirs of Pecker the Cat. (Illus.). 32p. 1982. pap. 1.25 (*0-9604894-1-X*) Borf Bks.

Pecker-Wimel, C. Introduction a la Spectroscopie Des Plamas. (Cours & Documents de Mathematiques & de Physique Ser.). 168p. (Orig.). 1967. text ed. 145.00 (*0-677-50130-7*) Gordon & Breach.

Peckerar, M. Electron-Beam, X-Ray, & Ion-Beam Submicrometer Lithographies for Manufacturing, Vol. 1465. 1991. 62.00 (*0-8194-0564-7*) SPIE.

Peckerar, M., ed. Electron-Beam, X-Ray, & Ion-Beam Submicrometer Lithographies for Manufacturing II. 1992. 70.00 (*0-8194-0826-3*, 1671) SPIE.

Peckerar, Martin C., jt. auth. see Murarka, Shyam P.

Peckett, Andrew. The Colours of Opaque Minerals. (Illus.). 573p. 1992. text ed. 124.95 (*0-442-30808-6*) Chapman & Hall.

Peckett, C. W. & Munday, A. R. Thrasymachus: New Greek Course. 344p. 1984. reprint ed. 19.95 (*0-86292-139-2*, Pub. by Brstl Class Pr UK) Focus Info Gr.

Peckham, Brian. The Composition of the Deuteronommistic History. (Harvard Semitic Museum Monographs). (C). 1985. 15.95 (*0-89130-909-8*, 04-00-35) Scholars Pr GA.
— History & Prophecy: The Development of Late Judaean Literary Traditions. LC 92-11671. (Anchor Bible Reference Library). 1993. 35.00 (*0-385-42348-9*) Doubleday.

Peckham, Donald C., jt. ed. see O'Shea, Donald C.

Peckham, George. A True Reporte of the Late Discoueries of the Newfound Landes. LC 78-25630. (English Experience Ser.: No. 341). 1971. reprint ed. 11.50 (*90-221-0341-2*) Walter J Johnson.

Peckham, Gladys C., jt. auth. see Freeland-Graves, Jeanne H.

Peckham, H. C. Van Buren: History of Cornelis Maessen Van Buren. (Illus.). 431p. 1990. reprint ed. lib. bdg. 72. 50 (*0-8328-1628-0*); reprint ed. pap. 64.50 (*0-8328-1629-9*) Higginson Bk Co.

Peckham, Herbert, jt. auth. see Leuhrmann, Arthur.

Peckham, Herbert, jt. auth. see Luehrmann, Arthur.

Peckham, Herbert D. BASIC: A Hands-on Method. 2nd ed. (Illus.). 320p. 1981. pap. text ed. 27.95 (*0-07-049160-7*, BYTE Bks) McGraw.
— Hands-on BASIC for the Atari 400, 800 & 1200XL Computers. (Personal Programming Ser.). 352p. 1983. pap. text ed. write for info. (*0-07-049194-1*, BYTE Bks) McGraw.
— Hands-on BASIC for the Commodore 64. 344p. 1984. pap. text ed. 27.95 (*0-07-049154-2*) McGraw.
— Hands-on Basic for the DEC Professional. 1985. pap. text ed. 27.95 (*0-07-049164-X*) McGraw.
— Hands-on BASIC for the TI 99-4A. 352p. 1984. pap. text ed. write for info. (*0-07-049155-0*) McGraw.
— Hands-on BASIC for the TRS-80 Color Computer. (Personal Programming Ser.). 352p. 1983. pap. text ed. write for info. (*0-07-049159-3*, BYTE Bks) McGraw.
— Hands-on BASIC with a PET. (Illus.). 1979. reprint ed. pap. text ed. write for info. (*0-07-049157-7*, BYTE Bks) McGraw.
— Programming in BASIC with the TI Home Computer. 1979. pap. text ed. 27.95 (*0-07-049156-9*, BYTE Bks) McGraw.

Peckham, Herbert D., jt. auth. see Luehrmann, Arthur.

Peckham, Howard, ed. see Byrd, Cecil K. & Dann, John C.

Peckham, Howard H. Colonial Wars, 1689-1762. LC 64-12606. (Chicago History of American Civilization Ser.). (Illus.). 1965. pap. text ed. 13.95 (*0-226-65314-5*, CHAC21) U Ch Pr.
— Indiana, a History. (States & the Nation Ser.). (Illus.). 1978. 14.95 (*0-393-05670-8*) Norton.
— Pontiac & the Indian Uprising. 374p. 1994. pap. text ed. 14.95 (*0-8143-2469-X*) Wayne St U Pr.
— Sources of American Independence: Selected Manuscripts from the Collection of the William L. Clements Library, 2 vols., Set. LC 77-25964. (Clements Library Bicentennial Studies). 1978. lib. bdg. 40.00 (*0-226-65321-8*) U Ch Pr.
— War for Independence: A Military History. LC 58-5685. (Chicago History of American Civilization Ser.). 1958. pap. text ed. 13.95 (*0-226-65316-1*) U Ch Pr.

Peckham, Howard H., ed. Memoirs of the Life of John Adlum in the Revolutionary War. 1968. 12.00 (*0-940550-03-2*) Caxton Club.

Peckham, Howard H. & Gibson, Charles, eds. Attitudes of Colonial Powers Toward the American Indian. LC 77-99793. (University of Utah Publications in the American West: No. 2). 147p. reprint ed. pap. 41.90 (*0-8357-4380-2*, 2037211) Bks Demand.

Peckham, Howard H., jt. ed. see Brown, Lloyd A.

Peckham, Howard H., ed. see Dearborn, Henry.

Peckham, Howard H., ed. see Michigan University, William L. Clements Library Staff.

Peckham, J. Brian. Development of the Late Phoenician Scripts. LC 68-17629. (Semitic Ser.: No. 20). (Illus.). 245p. 1968. 15.00 (*0-674-20050-0*) HUP.

Peckham, John M., 3rd. Master Guide to Income Property Brokerage. 1969. 59.50 (*0-13-559864-8*) Exec Reports.

Peckham, L. P. Prise De Defur & le Voyage D'Alexandre Au Paradis Terrestre. (Elliott Monographs: Vol. 35). 1974. reprint ed. 20.00 (*0-527-02638-7*) Periodicals Srv.

*__Peckham, Michael, et al, eds.__ Oxford Textbook of Oncology, 2 vols., Set. (Illus.). 2500p. 1995. 275.00 (*0-19-261685-4*) OUP.

Peckham, Morse. The Birth of Romanticism: Cultural Crisis, 1790-1815. (Romanticism & Its Consequences: Emergent Culture in the 19th Century Ser.: Vol. I). (Illus.). 400p. 1986. 32.50 (*0-913283-08-8*) Penkevill.
— Explanation & Power: The Control of Human Behavior. LC 87-24220. 319p. 1988. reprint ed. pap. text ed. 15.95 (*0-8166-1657-4*) U of Minn Pr.
— Humanistic Education for Business Executives: An Essay in General Education. LC 60-9884. 149p. reprint ed. pap. 42.50 (*0-8357-8672-2*, 2056828) Bks Demand.
— The Romantic Virtuoso & Meditations on the Consequences of Romanticism. LC 94-26406. 288p. 1994. 39.95 (*0-8195-5280-1*, Wesleyan Univ Pr) U Pr of New Eng.
— Romanticism & Ideology. 400p. 1985. lib. bdg. 32.50 (*0-913283-05-3*) Penkevill.
— Romanticism & Ideology. LC 94-45308. 400p. 1995. pap. 19.95x (*0-8195-6285-8*, Wesleyan Univ Pr) U Pr of New Eng.
— The Uses of the Unfashionable: The Pre-Raphaelites in Nineteenth-Century Culture. LC 92-33625. 1993. 10.95 (*0-935061-50-9*) Contemp Res.

Peckham, Robert D. Francois Villon: A Bibliography. LC 89-17000. (Medieval Bibliographies Ser.: Vol. 3). 560p. 1990. 69.00 (*0-8240-4530-0*, 1059) Garland.

Peckham, S. F. & Weeks, Joseph D. Census of the United States: U. S. Decennial Census Reports, Tenth Census: 1880, Vol. 33, No. 113: Production Technology, & Uses of Petroleum & Its Products; the Manufacture of Coke; Building Stones of the United States & Statistics of Quarry Industry for 1880. Allison, Peter, ed. LC 07-18862. (Illus.). 448p. reprint ed. fiche, lib. bdg. 500.00 (*0-88354-433-4*) N Ross.

Peckham, Stephen F. Peckham Genealogy: English Ancestors & American Descendants of John Peckham of Newport, RI, 1630. (Illus.). 596p. reprint ed. lib. bdg. 101.00 (*0-8328-1650-7*); reprint ed. pap. 91.00 (*0-8328-1651-5*) Higginson Bk Co.

Peckham, Stewart. From This Earth: The Ancient Art of Pueblo Pottery. 1992. pap. 39.95 (*0-89013-205-4*) Museum NM Pr.
— I Am Here: Two Thousand Years of Southwest Indian Culture. 1988. pap. 39.95 (*0-89013-174-0*) Museum NM Pr.

Peckinpah, Sandra L. Chester... the Imperfect All-Star. LC 92-74057. (Imperfect Angels Ser.). (Illus.). (J). (gr. 1-5). 1993. 15.95 (*0-9627806-1-8*); pap. text ed. 8.95 (*0-9627806-2-6*) Dasan Prodns.
— Rosey...the Imperfect Angel. LC 90-63058. (Imperfect Angels Ser.). (Illus.). 32p. (J). (ps-4). 1991. 15.95 (*0-9627806-0-X*) Dasan Prodns.

Peckinpaugh, Angela & Hayna, Lois B. A Book of Charms. LC 82-74406. 80p. (Orig.). 1983. pap. 6.95 (*0-935306-19-6*) Barnwood Pr.

*__Peckmann, Betty.__ Christian Midwifery. 2nd rev. ed. (Illus.). 500p. 1994. pap. 19.95 (*0-934426-63-5*) NAPSAC Reprods.

Peckron. Planning & Working with the Alternative Minimum Tax. suppl. ed. 248p. 1989. pap. 17.50 (*0-685-67021-X*, 5150) Commerce.

Pecktal, Lynn. Costume Design: Techniques of Modern Masters. LC 92-41428. (Illus.). 256p. 1993. 49.95 (*0-8230-8311-X*, Back Stage Bks) Watsn-Guptill.
— Designing & Drawing for the Theatre. LC 94-21038. 1994. 58.00 (*0-07-557232-X*) McGraw.
— Designing & Painting for the Theatre. LC 74-31271. 416p. (C). 1975. text ed. 49.25 (*0-03-011901-4*) HB Coll Pubs.

*__Peckus, Kestutis & Rackauskas, Jonas.__ Uzsienio Lietuviu Svietimo Ir Pedagogines Minties Istorijos Metmenys: A Historical Outline of Lithuanian Educational Thought Outside of Lithuania. LC 94-73757. (Illus.). 78p. (LIT.). 1995. pap. 5.00 (*0-929700-12-0*) Lith Res & Studies.

Peckwas, Edward A. Register of Vital Records of Roman Catholic Parishes from the Region Beyond the Bug River. 44p. 5.95 (*0-317-57777-8*) Polish Genealog.

Pecock, R. The Donet. (EETS, OS Ser.: No. 156). 1972. reprint ed. 43.00 (*0-527-00153-8*) Periodicals Srv.
— The Folewer to the Donet. (EETS, OS Ser.: No. 164). 1972. reprint ed. 65.00 (*0-527-00161-9*) Periodicals Srv.
— The Reule of Crysten Religioun. (EETS, OS Ser.: No. 171). 1974. reprint ed. 34.00 (*0-527-00168-6*) Periodicals Srv.

Pecora, Amy J., ed. see Sullivan, Steve.

Pecora, Ferdinand. Wall Street under Oath: The Story of Our Modern Money Changers. (Library of Money & Banking History). xi, 311p. 1994. reprint ed. lib. bdg. 45. 00x (*0-678-00372-6*) Kelley.

Pecora, Peter J. & Austin, Michael J. Managing Human Services Personnel. (Human Services Guides Ser.: Vol. 48). 160p. (Orig.). 1987. pap. text ed. 17.95 (*0-8039-2685-5*) Sage.

Pecora, Peter J., et al. The Child Welfare Challenge: Policy, Practice, & Research. (Modern Applications of Social Work Ser.). 543p. 1992. lib. bdg. 49.95 (*0-202-36081-4*); pap. text ed. 27.95 (*0-202-36082-2*) Aldine de Gruyter.
— Evaluating Family-Based Services. (Modern Applications of Social Work Ser.). 320p. 1995. lib. bdg. 44.95 (*0-202-36093-8*); pap. 24.95 (*0-202-36094-6*) Aldine de Gruyter.

Pecora, R., jt. ed. see Dorfmueller, T.

Pecora, Robert, ed. Dynamic Light Scattering: Applications of Photon Correlation Spectroscopy. LC 84-24831. 436p. 1985. 95.00 (*0-306-41790-1*, Plenum Pr) Plenum.

Pecora, Robert, jt. auth. see Berne, Bruce J.

Pecora, Vincent P. Self & Form in Modern Narrative. LC 88-46067. 336p. 1989. text ed. 45.00x (*0-8018-3768-5*) Johns Hopkins.

Pecoraro, Vincent L., ed. Manganese Redox Enzymes. (Illus.). 290p. 1992. text ed. 110.00 (*0-89573-729-9*) VCH Pubs.

Pecoraro, Vincent L., ed. see American Chemical Society, Division of Inorganic Chemistry Staff.

Pecorella, Robert F. Community Power in a Postreform City: Politics in New York City. 240p. 1993. 46.95 (*1-56324-136-6*) M E Sharpe.

Pecorini, Daniele & Shu, Tong. The Game of Wei-Chi. rev. ed. 165p. 1991. reprint ed. pap. 12.95 (*9971-4-9259-8*) Heian Intl.

Pecsi, Joszef, photos. Photo & Advertising. (Illus.). 52p. 1992. 35.00 (*3-909158-16-1*, Pub. by Wiese Verlag SZ) Dist Art Pubs.

P
Q

An Asterisk (*) at the beginning of an entry indicates that the title is appearing in BIP for the first time.

Pecsi, Kalman. The Future of Socialist Economic Integration. Hajdu, George & Crane, Keith, trs. LC 81-2524. 207p. reprint ed. pap. 59.00 (0-685-23743-5, 2032784) Bks Demand.

***Pecsi, M.** Environmental & Dynamic Geomorphology Case Studies in Hungary: Contribution to the First International Geomorphological Conference, Mancheser, Sept. 1985. 220p. (C). 1985. 69.00x (963-05-4226-9, Pub. by Akad Kiado HU) St Mut.

— Geomorphological & Geoecological Essays. (Studies in Geography in Hungary: No. 25). 155p. (C). 1989. 57.00x (963-05-5710-X, Pub. by Akad Kiado HU) St Mut.

— Loess & the Quaternary: Chinese & Hungarian Case Studies. (Studies in Geography in Hungary: No. 18). 125p. (C). 1985. 42.00x (963-05-4227-7, Pub. by Akad Kiado HU) St Mut.

Pecsi, M., ed. Studies on Loess. 556p. (C). 1981. 120.00x (963-05-2871-1, 41212, Pub. by Akad Kiado HU) St Mut.

Pecsi, M. & Sarfalvi, B. Physical & Economic Geography of Hungary. 198p. 1977. 45.00 (0-317-89607-5, Pub. by Collets UK) Pro-Am Music.

***Pecsi, M. & Schweitzer, F., eds.** Quaternary Environment in Hungary: Contribution of the Hungarian National Committee to the XIIIth Inqua Congress, Beijing, China, August, 1991. 103p. (C). 1991. 45.00x (963-05-6080-1, Pub. by Akad Kiado HU) St Mut.

Pecsi, M., jt. auth. see Compton, P. A.

Pecsi, M., jt. auth. see Compton, P.

Pecsi, M., jt. ed. see Kretzoi, M.

Pecsi, M., jt. ed. see Lichtenberger, E.

Pecsi, Marton, jt. auth. see Compton, Paul A.

Pecsok, Robert L., jt. auth. see Hajian, Harry G.

Pecsok, Robert L., jt. ed. see Hajian, Harry G.

Pecsok, Robert L., et al, eds. Chemical Technology Handbook. LC 75-22497. 1975. 24.95 (0-8412-0242-7); pap. 14.95 (0-8412-0578-7) Am Chemical.

Pecther, Alese. What's in the Deep. 1991. 14.95 (0-87491-247-4) Acropolis.

Pecuchet, Jean-Pierre R., jt. ed. see Abdulrab, Habib.

Pecujlic, Miroslav, et al, eds. Science & Technology in the Transformation of the World. LC 83-40706. 174p. 1984. text ed. 24.95 (0-312-70265-5) St Martin.

Pecujlit, Miroslav. The University of the Future: The Yugoslav Experience. Lorkovic, Tanja, tr. LC 86-31899. (Contributions to the Study of Education Ser.: No. 22). 211p. 1987. text ed. 49.95 (0-313-25430-3, PUF/, Greenwood Pr) Greenwood.

Pecura, Constance M., ed. see Institute of Medicine, Committee on a National Neural Circuitry Database Staff.

Peczenik, Aleksander. On Law & Reason. (Law & Philosophy Library: No. 8). 456p. 1989. lib. bdg. 120.00 (0-7923-0444-6) Kluwer Ac.

Peczenik, Aleksander, et al. Theory of Legal Science. 1984. lib. bdg. 162.50 (90-277-1834-2) Kluwer Ac.

Pecznick, Ira, jt. auth. see Hoffman, Paul.

Pedak, Johannes, ed. & illus. Korporation Rotalia Voorsil, 1944-1987. 600p. 1988. 50.00 (0-9621533-0-3) Korp Rotalia.

***Pedan, James A.** Vegetarian Cats & Dogs. 2nd rev. ed. LC 90-82536. (Illus.). 240p. 1995. pap. text ed. 13.95 (0-941319-02-4) Harbingers New Age.

Pedatzur, Reuven, jt. auth. see Klieman, Aharon.

Pedder, Jonathan R., jt. auth. see Brown, Dennis G.

***Peddicord, Jo.** Look Like a Winner after Fifty with Care, Color & Style. 2nd ed. LC 94-66013. 192p. (Orig.). 1994. pap. 15.95 (0-88100-082-5) Natl Writ Pr.

Peddicord, Kathleen, ed. The World's Best. 5th enl. rev. ed. 650p. 1992. pap. 29.00 (0-945332-33-5) Agora Inc MD.

***Peddicord, Richard.** A Studied Ambiguity: Catholic Moral Teaching on the Question of Gay & Lesbian Rights Legislation. (Orig.). Date not set. pap. write for info. (0-614-01755-6) Sheed & Ward MO.

Peddie, J. Cameron, ed. The Forgotten Talent. (C). 1990. pap. 24.00 (0-85305-266-2, Pub. by J Arthur Ltd UK) St Mut.

Peddie, Jon. Graphical User Interface & Graphics Standards. 1992. 40.00 (0-07-049215-8) McGraw.

— Graphical User Interfaces & Graphic Standards. 320p. 1991. 39.95 (0-8306-2505-4) TAB Bks.

— Graphics Display Systems. 1994. text ed. 49.95 (0-07-049288-3); pap. text ed. 34.95 (0-07-049289-1) McGraw.

— High-Resolution Graphic Display Systems. LC 92-21418. 1993. text ed. 49.95 (0-8306-4292-7, Windcrest); pap. text ed. 34.95 (0-8306-4291-9, Windcrest) TAB Bks.

— Multimedia & Graphics Controllers. LC 93-41752. 1994. disk, pap. text ed. 34.95 (0-07-049295-6, Windcrest) TAB Bks.

Peddie, Mary, et al. Growing & Using Scented Geraniums. Foster, Kim & Parkinson, Connie, eds. (Country Wisdom Bulletin Ser.). (Illus.). 32p. 1991. 2.95 (0-88266-699-1, Storey Pub) Storey Comm Inc.

Peddie, Robert A. Place-Names in Imprints: An Index to the Latin & Other Forms Used on Title-Pages. 1968. reprint ed. 35.00 (1-55888-207-3) Omnigraphics Inc.

Peddito, Paul. Of All the Wide Torsos in All the Wild Glen. 46p. 1991. pap. 2.50 (0-87129-097-9, O47) Dramatic Pub.

Peddiwell, J. A. The Saber-Tooth Curriculum. 1959. pap. text ed. 5.95 (0-07-049151-8) McGraw.

***Peddle, Francis K.** Cities & Greed. 255p. Date not set. 12.00 (0-9698812-0-7) Schalkenbach.

Peddle, Jon. Graphical User Interfaces & Graphics Standards. 1991. pap. 29.95 (0-07-049254-9) McGraw.

Peddle, Michael T. Public Finance by Hyman: Study Guide. 4th ed. 295p. (C). 1993. student ed, pap. text ed. 21.00 (0-03-078168-X) Dryden Pr.

Peddy, Carolyn P., jt. auth. see Allen, James L.

***Pedelty, Mark.** War Stories: The Culture of Foreign Correspondents. LC 94-23388. 256p. 1995. 55.00x (0-415-91123-0, B4909, Routledge NY); pap. 16.95 (0-415-91124-9, B4913, Routledge NY) Routledge.

***Peden, Allan.** The Monklands: An Illustrated Architectural Guide. (Illus.). 88p. (C). 1992. pap. 35.00x (1-873190-05-0, Pub. by Rutland Pr UK) St Mut.

Peden, Creighton. The Chicago School: Voices in Liberal Religious Thought. LC 87-51605. 220p. (C). 1987. text ed. 29.95 (1-55605-031-3); pap. text ed. 19.95 (1-55605-032-1) Wyndhall Pr.

Peden, Creighton, ed. Philosophy for a Changing Society. (Orig.). (C). 1985. pap. text ed. 13.95 (0-89894-003-6) Advocate Pub Group.

Peden, Creighton & Axel, Larry E., eds. God, Values & Empiricism: Issues in Philosophical Theology. LC 89-28704. (Highlands Institute Ser.: No. 1). vii, 252p. 1990. 31.95 (0-86554-360-7, MUP/H298) Mercer Univ Pr.

Peden, Creighton & Hudson, Yeager, eds. Communitarianism, Liberalism, & Social Responsibility. LC 91-35244. (Studies in Social & Political Theory: Vol. 14). 336p. 1991. lib. bdg. 99.95 (0-7734-9656-4) E Mellen.

— Freedom, Dharma, & Rights. LC 93-32109. 464p. 1993. text ed. 109.95 (0-7734-9363-8) E Mellen.

— Liberalism, Oppression, & Empowerment. LC 94-17270. 306p. 1994. text ed. 99.95 (0-7734-9091-4) E Mellen.

— Terrorism, Justice & Social Values. LC 90-24911. (Studies in Social & Political Theory: Vol. 11). 456p. 1991. lib. bdg. 109.95 (0-88946-739-0) E Mellen.

Peden, Creighton & Roth, John K., eds. Rights, Justice, & Community. LC 92-27955. 496p. 1992. text ed. 109.95 (0-7734-9599-1) E Mellen.

Peden, Creighton, jt. ed. see Hudson, Yeager.

Peden, Creighton, jt. ed. see Speak, David M.

Peden, Creighton, jt. ed. see Sterba, James.

Peden, Creighton, ed. see Wieman, Henry N.

Peden, Creighton W. The Philosopher of Free Religion: Francis Ellingwood Abbot, 1836-1903. LC 91-31769. (American University Studies: Philosophy: Ser. V, Vol. 133). 207p. (C). 1992. text ed. 39.95 (0-8204-1747-5) P Lang Pubs.

Peden, J. R. Teaching Materials & Cases on Commercial Transactions. 2nd ed. 560p. 1983. Australia. 69.00 (0-409-49364-3) Butterworth Legal Pubs.

Peden, Joseph R. & Glahe, Fred R., eds. The American Family & the State. LC 85-63547. (Illus.). 488p. 1984. 34.95 (0-936488-12-3); pap. 14.95 (0-936488-05-0) PRIPP.

***Peden, Lauren D.** The Mystical Arts: Dream Interpretation. 60p. 1995. write for info. (0-446-51905-7) Warner Bks.

— The Mystical Arts: Dream Interpretation. 60p. 1996. 6.95 (0-446-91015-5) Warner Bks.

— The Mystical Arts: I Ching. 60p. 1995. write for info. (0-446-51903-0) Warner Bks.

— The Mystical Arts: I Ching. 60p. 1996. 6.95 (0-446-91013-9) Warner Bks.

— The Mystical Arts: Numerology. 60p. 1995. write for info. (0-446-51902-2) Warner Bks.

— The Mystical Arts: Numerology. 60p. 1996. 6.95 (0-446-91012-0) Warner Bks.

— The Mystical Arts: Palmistry. 60p. 1995. write for info. (0-446-51904-9) Warner Bks.

— The Mystical Arts: Palmistry. 60p. 1996. 6.95 (0-446-91014-7) Warner Bks.

Peden, Margaret S. Out of the Volcano: Portraits of Contemporary Mexican Artists. LC 91-52842. (Illus.). 264p. (C). 1992. 60.00 (1-56098-060-5); pap. 24.95 (1-56098-061-3) Smithsonian.

Peden, Margaret S., ed. The Latin American Short Story: A Critical History. (Critical History of the Modern Short Story Ser.). 164p. 1983. text ed. 23.95 (0-8057-9351-8, Twayne) Macmillan.

Peden, Margaret S., tr. & intro. Sor Juana Ines de la Cruz: Poems. LC 85-71537. 144p. (ENG & SPA.). 1985. pap. text ed. 12.00 (0-916950-60-3) Biling Rev-Pr.

Peden, Margaret S., tr. A Woman of Genius: The Intellectual Autobiography of Sor Juana de la Cruz. (Illus.). 192p. (C). 1982. 37.50 (0-915998-14-9); pap. 7.95 (0-915998-15-7) Lime Rock Pr.

Peden, Margaret S., tr. see Allende, Isabel.

Peden, Margaret S., tr. see Fuentes, Carlos.

Peden, Margaret S., tr. see Neruda, Pablo.

Peden, Margaret S., tr. see Paz, Octavio.

Peden, Margaret S., tr. see Posse, Abel.

Peden, Margaret S., tr. see Quiroga, Horacio.

Peden, Margaret S., tr. see Rodo, Jose E.

Peden, Margaret S., tr. see Velarde, Ramon L.

Peden, Margaret Sayers, tr. see Fuentes, Carlos.

Peden, Murray. Fall of an Arrow. 192p. 1987. pap. 14.95 (0-7737-5105-X, Pub. by Stoddart Pubng CN) Genl Dist Srvs.

Peden, N. R., jt. auth. see MacLennan, W. J.

Peden, W. Creighton. & Axel, Larry E., eds. New Essays in Religious Naturalism. LC 93-37812. 1994. pap. 29.95 (0-86554-426-3, MUP/H346) Mercer Univ Pr.

***Peden, W. Creighton & Tarbox, Everett J., Jr., eds.** The Collected Essays of Francis Ellingwood Abbot (1836-1903), American Philosopher & Free Religionist, Vol. I. LC 94-49064. 424p. 1995. text ed. 109.95 (0-7734-9007-8) E Mellen.

— The Collected Essays of Francis Ellingwood Abbot (1836-1903), American Philosopher & Free Religionist, Vol. II. LC 94-49064. 444p. 1995. text ed. 109.95 (0-7734-9009-4) E Mellen.

— The Collected Essays of Francis Ellingwood Abbot (1836-1903), American Philosopher & Free Religionist, Vol. III. LC 94-49064. 456p. 1995. text ed. 109.95 (0-7734-9011-6) E Mellen.

— The Collected Essays of Francis Ellingwood Abbot (1836-1903), American Philosopher & Free Religionist, Vol. IV. LC 94-49064. 440p. 1995. text ed. 109.95 (0-7734-9013-2) E Mellen.

Peden, W. Creighton, jt. ed. see Hudson, Yeager.

Peden, William. Fragments & Fictions: Workbooks of an Obscure Writer. 125p. 1990. 14.50 (0-922820-10-4) Watermark Pr.

Peden, William, ed. see Jefferson, Thomas.

***Pedersen.** Graphis Advertising Ninety-Five. 1994. (0-8230-6266-X) Watsn-Guptill.

— Graphis Ephemera. 1995. (0-8230-6446-8) Watsn-Guptill.

— Graphis Poster Ninety-Five: The International Annual of Poster Art. 1995. (0-8230-6447-6) Watsn-Guptill.

— Graphistock Catalogue. 1995. pap. text ed. (0-8230-6449-2) Watsn-Guptill.

***Pedersen, Ann.** Kidding Around Atlanta: A Family Guide to the City. 2nd ed. LC 94-44635. 1995. 9.95 (1-56261-222-0) John Muir.

Pedersen, Anne. Kidding Around Atlanta: A Young Person's Guide to the City. (Illus.). 64p. (J). (gr. 3 up). 1989. pap. 9.95 (0-945465-35-1) John Muir.

— Kidding Around Washington, D. C., A Young Person's Guide. 2nd ed. (Kidding Around Travel Ser.). (Illus.). 64p. (J). (gr. 3 up). 1993. pap. 9.95 (1-56261-093-7) John Muir.

— The Kid's Environment Book: What's Awry & Why. (Kids' Environment Ser.). (Illus.). 192p. (Orig.). (J). (gr. 6 up). 1991. pap. 13.95 (0-945465-74-2) John Muir.

— Teens: A Fresh Look. Mothering Magazine Staff, ed. (Illus.). 240p. (Orig.). 1991. pap. 14.95 (0-945465-54-8) John Muir.

***Pedersen, B. Martin.** Graphis Alternative Photography 94. (Illus.). 240p. 1994. 69.00 (0-8230-6382-8) Watsn-Guptill.

— Graphis Packaging Six. (Illus.). 240p. 1994. 75.00 (0-8230-6374-7) Watsn-Guptill.

— Graphis Paper Promotions. (Illus.). 240p. 1994. 69.00 (0-8230-6376-3) Watsn-Guptill.

— Graphis Photo 94: The International Annual of Photography. (Illus.). 240p. 1994. 69.00 (0-8230-6245-7) Watsn-Guptill.

Pedersen, B. Martin, ed. Graphis Annual Reports 4. (Illus.). 240p. 1994. 75.00 (0-8230-6357-7, Watsn-Guptill) Watsn-Guptill.

— Graphis Brochures 95. (Illus.). 240p. Date not set. 75.00 (0-8230-6296-1) Watsn-Guptill.

— Graphis Corporate Identity 2. (Illus.). 240p. 1994. 75.00 (0-8230-6358-5, Watsn-Guptill) Watsn-Guptill.

— Graphis Design 94. (Illus.). 256p. 1994. 69.00 (0-8230-6249-X, Watsn-Guptill) Watsn-Guptill.

— Graphis Design 95. (Illus.). 240p. Date not set. 69.00 (0-8230-6256-2) Watsn-Guptill.

— Graphis Letterhead 2. (Illus.). 256p. 1994. 69.00 (0-8230-6346-1, Watsn-Guptill) Watsn-Guptill.

— Graphis Logo 2. (Illus.). 240p. 1994. 60.00 (0-8230-6347-X, Watsn-Guptill) Watsn-Guptill.

— Graphis Nudes. (Illus.). 271p. 1993. 85.00 (0-8230-6969-9, Graphis Pr) Watsn-Guptill.

— Graphis Poster 94: The International Annual of Poster Art. (Illus.). 240p. 1994. 69.00 (0-8230-6362-3) Watsn-Guptill.

— Graphis T-Shirt Design 1. (Illus.). 256p. 1994. 75.00 (0-8230-6359-3, Watsn-Guptill) Watsn-Guptill.

— Graphis Typography One. (Illus.). 256p. 1993. 75.00 (0-8230-6269-4, Graphis Pr) Watsn-Guptill.

***Pedersen, Bjorn.** Face to Face with God in Your Church: Establishing a Prayer Ministry. LC 95-2308. 1995. write for info. (0-8066-2766-2, Fortress Pr) Augsburg Fortress.

Pedersen, C. Th. & Becher, J., eds. Developments in the Organic Chemistry of Sulfur: Proceedings of the XIII International Symposium on the Organic Chemistry of Sulfur, August 7-12, 1988, Odense, Denmark. 394p. 1989. text ed. 70.00 (0-677-22140-1) Gordon & Breach.

Pedersen, Carl. The Physical Chemistry of 1, 2-Dithiole Compounds: The Question of Aromaticity. (Sulfur Report Ser.). 96p. 1980. pap. text ed. 87.00 (3-7186-0031-5) Gordon & Breach.

Pedersen, Clarence, jt. comp. see Hanson, Virginia.

Pedersen, Cort A., et al, eds. Oxytocin in Maternal, Sexual, & Social Behaviors. 1992. write for info. (0-318-69349-6); pap. write for info. (0-89766-700-X) NY Acad Sci.

Pedersen, David L. Cameral Analysis: A Method of Treating the Psychoneuroses Using Hypnosis. LC 93-37852. (Illus.). 224p. 1994. 59.95x (0-415-10424-6, B3806, Routledge NY); pap. 18.95 (0-415-10425-4, B3910, Routledge NY) Routledge.

***Pedersen, Donald B. & Meyer, Keith G.** Agricultural Law in a Nutshell. (Nutshell Ser.). 460p. (C). 1995. pap. text ed. 19.00 (0-314-06454-0) West Pub.

Pedersen, F. B. Environmental Hydraulics: Stratified Flows. (Lecture Notes on Coastal & Estuarine Studies: Vol. 18). vii, 278p. 1986. pap. 42.00 (0-387-16792-7) Spr-Verlag.

Pedersen, Frank A., ed. The Father-Infant Relationship: Observational Studies in the Family Settings. LC 79-20514. (Praeger Special Studies). 196p. 1980. text ed. 35.95 (0-275-90535-7, C0535, Praeger Pubs) Greenwood.

Pedersen, Frank A., jt. ed. see Berman, Phyllis W.

Pedersen, Franklin D. Modern Algebra: A Conceptual Approach. 224p. (C). 1992. text ed. write for info. (0-697-11926-2) Wm C Brown Pubs.

Pedersen, G. Analysis Now. (Graduate Texts in Mathematics Ser.: Vol. 118). xiv, 277p. 1988. 49.90 (0-387-96788-5) Spr-Verlag.

Pedersen, G. K. C-Algebras & Their Automorphism Groups. 1979. text ed. 178.00 (0-12-549450-5) Acad Pr.

Pedersen, Gordon W. Textbook of Oral Surgery. (Illus.). 528p. 1988. pap. text ed. 48.95 (0-7216-2426-X) Saunders.

***Pedersen, Gorm.** Afghan Nomads in Transition. LC 94-61394. (Carlberg Nomad Ser.). (Illus.). 320p. 1995. 50.00 (0-500-01639-9) Thames Hudson.

Pedersen, Gunnar. The Highway Angler: Fishing Southcentral Alaska. (Illus.). 258p. (Orig.). 1989. pap. 19.95 (0-9621551-0-1) Alaska Viking Pr.

Pedersen, Gunnar, jt. auth. see Limeres, Rene.

Pedersen, Henrik, et al, eds. Biochemical Engineering VII. LC 92-23487. (Annals Ser.: Vol. 665). 1992. write for info. (0-89766-735-2); pap. write for info. (0-89766-736-0) NY Acad Sci.

***Pedersen, Henry F., Jr.** Sadness in Sunshine: The Flood of Estes Park, an Illustrated Journal. (Illus.). 64p. (Orig.). 1995. pap. 8.50 (0-9641585-3-1) H F Pedersen.

Pedersen, Holger, ed. A Glance at the History of Lingustics with Particular Regard to the Historical Study of Phonology. (Studies in History of Linguistics: No. 7). xxxii, 100p. 1983. 35.00x (90-272-0898-0) Benjamins North Am.

***Pedersen, J. H. & Runestad, J. A.** Concrete Manure Storages Handbook. Huffman, C. J., ed. LC 91-26955. (Illus.). 80p. (Orig.). 1994. pap. 20.00 (0-89373-082-3, MWPS-36) MidWest Plan Serv.

Pedersen, Jean, jt. auth. see Hilton, Peter J.

Pedersen, Jens A., ed. Handbook of EPR Spectra from Natural & Synthetic Quinones & Quinols. 392p. 1985. 155.00 (0-8493-2955-8, QC463) CRC Pr.

Pedersen, Jesper S. & Sorensen, Jesper S., eds. Organizational Cultures in Theory & Practice. (Illus.). 135p. 1989. text ed. 59.95 (0-566-07090-1, Pub. by Avebury Pub UK) Ashgate Pub Co.

Pedersen, Johannes. Israel, Vol. 1 & 2: Its Life & Culture. 578p. 1991. 89.95 (1-55540-643-2) Scholars Pr GA.

— Israel, Vol. 3 & 4: Its Life & Culture. 790p. 1991. 98.95 (1-55540-644-0) Scholars Pr GA.

Pedersen, John, jt. auth. see Mills, Robert.

Pedersen, Jon E. & Digby, Annette D. Secondary Schools & Cooperative Learning: Theories, Models & Strategies. LC 94-15326. (Source Books on Education: Vol. 40). 488p. 1995. 65.00 (0-8153-0421-8, SS788) Garland.

Pedersen, Judy, illus. On the Road of Stars: Native American Night Poems & Sleep Charms. LC 92-20001. 40p. (J). (gr. 1 up). 1994. text ed. 15.95 (0-02-709735-8, Mac Bks Young Read) S&S Childrens.

Pedersen, K. George. The Itinerant Schoolmaster: A Socio-Economic Analysis of Teacher Turnover. LC 72-96751. 1973. pap. 6.00 (0-931080-04-5) U Chicago Midwest Admin.

Pedersen, K. S. Properties of Oil & Natural Gases, Vol. 5. (Contributions in Petroleum Geology & Engineering Ser.). 252p. 1989. 59.00 (0-87201-588-2) Gulf Pub.

Pedersen, Ken. Expert Systems Programming. 2298p. 1989. pap. text ed. 24.95 (0-471-60068-7) Wiley.

Pedersen, Knud, et al. Applied Nuclear Power for Practicing Engineers. (Professional Engineering Career Development Ser.). 1972. 29.95 (0-8464-0143-6) Beekman Pubs.

Pedersen, Kristin. The Shadow Shop. Thatch, Nancy R., ed. (Books for Students by Students Ser.). (Illus.). 29p. (J). (gr. 3-6). 1994. lib. bdg. 14.95 (0-933849-53-2) Landmark Edns.

Pedersen, L. G., jt. auth. see Isenhour, Thomas L.

Pedersen, Laura. Street-Smart Career Guide: A Step-by-Step Guide to Your Career Development. LC 92-42690. 1993. 12.00 (0-517-88037-7, Crown) Crown Pub Group.

Pedersen, Laura & Model, F. Peter. Play Money: My Brief but Brilliant Career on Wall Street. 1991. 20.00 (0-517-58227-9, Crown) Crown Pub Group.

Pedersen, Lee G., jt. auth. see Johnson, Charles S., Jr.

***Pedersen, Liz.** Edge of Desire. (Rainbow Romances Ser.). 160p. 1994. 14.95 (0-7090-5022-4, 912, Hale-Parkwest) Parkwest Pubns.

Pedersen, Marguerite. The Cruise of the Skuld. LC 87-61085. 160p. (Orig.). 1987. pap. 7.00 (0-914752-25-1) Sovereign Pr.

— Life's Meaning. LC 89-60446. 112p. (Orig.). 1989. pap. 7.00 (0-914752-27-8) Sovereign Pr.

Pedersen, Marialyce, ed. see Harmonious Technologies Staff.

***Pedersen, Mark.** Nutritional Herbology: A Reference Guide to Herbs. rev. ed. LC 94-60830. 336p. 1994. pap. text ed. 19.95 (1-885653-03-4) W W Whitman.

Pedersen, Mary J. & Burney, Joan. Sharing the Faith with Your Child: From Age Seven to Fourteen. LC 92-81360. 160p. (Orig.). 1992. pap. 4.50 (0-89243-444-9) Liguori Pubns.

Pedersen, N. F., jt. auth. see Parmentier, R. D.

Pedersen, Niels C. Feline Infectious Diseases. Pratt, P. W. & Ariello, Susan, eds. LC 88-72173. (Illus.). 404p. 1988. text ed. 37.50 (0-685-24945-X) Am Vet Pubns.

Pedersen, Niels C., et al. Feline Husbandry: Disease & Management in the Multiple-Cat Environment. LC 90-81326. (Illus.). 453p. 1990. 39.00 (0-939674-29-7) Am Vet Pubns.

***Pedersen, Norman.** Life of a Black Cat. 128p. Date not set. pap. 14.95 (1-57087-026-8) Prof Pr NC.

Pedersen, Olaf. The Book of Nature. (C). 1992. pap. 9.95 (0-268-00690-3) U of Notre Dame Pr.

— Early Physics & Astronomy. 2nd ed. (Illus.). 356p. (C). 1993. pap. 29.95 (0-521-40899-7) Cambridge U Pr.

— Early Physics & Astronomy. 2nd ed. (Illus.). 356p. (C). 1993. 79.95 (0-521-40340-5) Cambridge U Pr.

— A Survey of the Almagest. (Acta Historica Scientarium Ser.: No. 30). (Illus.). 454p. 1974. pap. 57.50 (87-7492-087-1, D-751, Pub. by Odense Universitets Forlag DK) Coronet Bks.

Pedersen, Paul. The Five Stages of Culture Shock: Critical Incidents Around the World. LC 93-49711. (Contributions in Psychology Ser.: Vol. 25). 296p. 1994. text ed. 59.95 (0-313-28782-1, Greenwood Pr) Greenwood.

An Asterisk (*) at the beginning of an entry indicates that the title is appearing in BIP for the first time.

— A Handbook for Developing Multicultural Awareness. 2nd ed. 320p. 1994. 35.95 (*1-55620-133-8*, 72586) Am Coun Assn.

Pedersen, Paul, ed. Handbook of Cross-Cultural Counseling & Therapy. LC 84-12832. xv, 353p. 1985. text ed. 59.95 (*0-313-23914-2*, PRH/, Greenwood Pr); pap. 19.95 (*0-685-10209-2*, Greenwood Pr) Greenwood.

— Handbook of Cross-Cultural Counseling & Therapy. LC 87-9337. 377p. 1987. pap. text ed. 24.95 (*0-275-92713-X*, B2713, Praeger Pubs) Greenwood.

Pedersen, Paul & Carey, John C., eds. Multicultural Counseling in Schools: A Practical Handbook. LC 93-28777. 254p. 1993. text ed. 42.00 (*0-205-14066-1*) Allyn.

Pedersen, Paul & Ivey, Allen E. Culture-Centered Counseling & Interviewing Skills: A Practical Guide. LC 93-15372. 224p. 1993. text ed. 59.95 (*0-275-94668-1*, C4668, Praeger Pubs); pap. text ed. 19.95 (*0-275-94669-X*, B4669, Praeger Pubs) Greenwood.

Pedersen, Paul B. & Hernandez, Daniel. A Student Workbook for Counseling Across Cultures. (Illus.). 88p. (C). 1993. pap. text ed. 7.95 (*0-8248-1524-6*) UH Pr.

Pedersen, Paul B., jt. ed. see Lefley, Harriet P.

Pedersen, Paul B., jt. auth. see Ponterotto, Joseph G.

Pedersen, Paul B., et al, eds. Counseling Across Cultures. 3rd ed. LC 88-39249. (Illus.). 384p. (Orig.). (C). 1989. pap. text ed. 15.95 (*0-8248-1231-X*) UH Pr.

Pedersen, Pauli, ed. Optimal Design with Advanced Materials: The Frithiof Niordson Volume: Proceeding of the IUTAM Symposium on Optimal Design with Advance Materials, Lyngby, Denmark, 18-20 August 1992. LC 93-3295. 1993. write for info. (*0-444-89869-7*) Elsevier.

Pedersen, Peder J. & Lund, Reinhard, eds. Unemployment: Theory, Policy & Structure. (Studies in Organization: No. 10). 353p. (C). 1987. lib. bdg. 113.85 (*3-11-011071-7*) De Gruyter.

*__Pedersen, Peder J., et al, eds.__ Unemployment: Theory, Policy & Structure. (Studies in Organization: No. 10). 353p. (C). 1987. lib. bdg. 105.75 (*0-89925-277-X*) De Gruyter.

Pedersen, Poul. The Parthenon & the Origin of the Corinthian Capital. (Illus.). 48p. (Orig.). 1989. pap. 27.50 (*87-7492-708-6*, Pub. by Almqv & Wiksell SW) Coronet Bks.

Pedersen, Poul, ed. The Maussolleion at Halikarnassos, Vol. 3: Reports of the Danish Archaeological Expedition to Bodrum, Set. (Illus.). 342p. 1991. 145.00 (*87-7288-058-9*, Pub. by Aarhus Univ Pr DK) Coronet Bks.

Pedersen, Poul O., jt. ed. see Baker, Jonathan.

Pedersen, Rita & Andersen, Flemming G., eds. The Concept of Tradition in Ballad Research. 130p. (Orig.). 1985. pap. text ed. 36.50 (*87-7492-562-8*) Coronet Bks.

Pedersen, Roger A., ed. Current Topics in Developmental Biology, Vol. 28. (Illus.). 214p. 1993. text ed. 75.00 (*0-12-153128-7*) Acad Pr.

— Current Topics in Developmental Biology, Vol. 29. (Illus.). 369p. 1994. text ed. 79.00 (*0-12-153129-5*) Acad Pr.

*__Pedersen, Roger A. & Schatten, Gerald P., eds.__ Current Topics in Developmental Biology Vol. 30. (Illus.). 310p. 1995. text ed. 75.00 (*0-12-153130-9*) Acad Pr.

Pedersen, Roger A., jt. ed. see Rossant, J.

Pedersen, Roger A., et al, eds. Animal Applications of Research in Mammalian Development. (Current Communications in Cell & Molecular Biology Ser.: No. 4). (Illus.). 334p. (C). 1991. pap. text ed. 44.00 (*0-87969-333-9*) Cold Spring Harbor.

Pedersen, Roy N. One Europe - One Hundred Nations. 150p. 1992. 39.00 (*1-85359-123-8*, Pub. by Multilingual Matters UK) Taylor & Francis.

*__Pedersen, Sigfred, ed.__ New Directions in Biblical Theology: Papers of the Aarhus Conference, 16-19 September, 1993. Vol. 76. 1994. 71.50 (*90-04-10120-9*) E J Brill.

Pedersen, Stefi. Psychoanalysis in Our Time. LC 70-173220. 1973. 5.95 (*0-672-51411-7*, Bobbs) Macmillan.

Pedersen, Susan. Family, Dependence, & the Origins of the Welfare State: Britain & France, 1914-1945. LC 92-47002. (Illus.). 275p. (C). 1993. 64.95 (*0-521-41989-1*) Cambridge U Pr.

— Family, Dependence, & the Origins of the Welfare State: Britain & France, 1914-1945. (Illus.). 496p. (C). 1995. pap. 18.95 (*0-521-55834-4*) Cambridge U Pr.

Pedersen, Susan, jt. ed. see Mandler, Peter.

Pedersen, Svend S., jt. ed. see Hlby, Niels.

*__Pedersen, Ted & Gilden, Mel.__ Cyberspace Cowboy. LC 95-7898. (Cybersurfers Ser.). (J). 1995. write for info. (*0-8431-3934-X*) Price Stern.

— Pirates on the Internet. LC 95-7158. (Cybersurfers Ser.). (J). 1995. write for info. (*0-8431-3933-1*) Price Stern.

*__Pedersen, Ted & Moss, Francis.__ Internet for Kids: A Beginner's Guide for Surfing the Net. LC 95-11435. (J). 1995. write for info. (*0-8431-3957-9*) Price Stern.

Pedersen, Ted, jt. auth. see Gilden, Mel.

Pedersen, Teresa. Once for Always. 1991. 13.95 (*0-533-08958-1*) Vantage.

Pedersen, Thomas. European Union & the EFTA Countries: Enlargement & Integration. LC 94-1947. 1994. 49.00 (*1-85567-148-4*, Pub. by Pinter Pubs UK) St Martin.

Pedersen, Tom A. & Curtis, James T. Soil Vapor Extraction Technology. LC 91-12465. (Pollution Technology Review Ser.: No. 204). (Illus.). 316p. 1991. 54.00 (*0-8155-1284-8*) Noyes.

Pederson, jt. auth. see Hilton.

Pederson, Ann, jt. auth. see Farr, Gail.

Pederson, Cynthia, jt. auth. see Daniels, Celia.

*__Pederson, Daniel J.__ U. S. Savings Bonds: A Comprehensive Guide for Bond Owners & Financial Professionals. 2nd ed. (Illus.). 208p. (Orig.). 1995. pap. 24.95 (*0-9643020-1-2*) TSBI.

Pederson, David S. & Heintz, Nicholas H. Transcription Factors & the Control of DNA Replication. (Molecular Biology Intelligence Unit Ser.). 125p. 1994. 89.95 (*1-57059-069-9*, LN9069) R G Landes.

Pederson, Donald, jt. auth. see Coates, Marvin.

Pederson, Donald O. & Mayaram, Kartikeya. Analog Integrated Circuits for Communications: Principles, Simulation & Design. 592p. (C). 1990. lib. bdg. 114.50 (*0-7923-9089-X*) Kluwer Ac.

Pederson, Duane E., jt. auth. see Cook, Harvey A.

Pederson, Gale. Key to the Keys Piano Course, Vol. 1. 20p. 1983. student ed, digital audio 15.95 (*0-88432-116-9*, S1550) Audio-Forum.

— Key to the Keys Piano Course, Vol. 2. 24p. 1986. audio 21.95 (*0-88432-141-X*, S1555) Audio-Forum.

*__Pederson, Gary L., ed.__ National Symposium on Water Quality. LC 94-71974. (Technical Publication Ser.: No. 94-4). (Illus.). 322p. (Orig.). 1994. pap. 40.00 (*1-882132-31-9*) Am Water Resources.

Pederson, Gloria. Nighthawk's Embrace. 400p. (Orig.). 1987. pap. 3.95 (*0-8439-2533-7*) Dorchester Pub Co.

Pederson, Jane M. Between Memory & Reality: Family & Community in Rural Wisconsin, 1870-1970. LC 91-45787. (History of American Thought & Culture Ser.). (Illus.). 330p. (Orig.). (C). 1992. lib. bdg. 50.00 (*0-299-13280-3*); pap. 19.95 (*0-299-13284-6*) U of Wis Pr.

*__Pederson, Jay P. & Estell, Kenneth, eds.__ African-American Almanac, Vol. 2. (African-American Reference Library). (Illus.). (J). (gr. 6-9). 1994. write for info. (*0-8103-9241-0*, UXL) Gale.

— African-American Almanac, Vol. 3. (African-American Reference Library). (Illus.). (J). (gr. 6-9). 1994. write for info. (*0-8103-9242-9*, UXL) Gale.

— African-American Almanac, Vol.1. (African-American Reference Library). (Illus.). 576p. (J). (gr. 6-9). 1994. write for info. (*0-8103-9240-2*, UXL) Gale.

Pederson, Joan, ed. see Bradkin, Cheryl G.

Pederson, Johannes. The Arabic Book. Hillenbrand, Robert, ed. French, Geoffrey, tr. LC 82-61379. (Modern Classics in Near Eastern Studies). Orig. Title: Den Arabiske Bog. (Illus.). 220p. 1984. 35.00 (*0-691-06564-0*) Princeton U Pr.

Pederson, Judith, jt. auth. see Ayuso, Agnes.

Pederson, Judith, jt. auth. see Dolin, Eric J.

Pederson, Lee & McDaniel, Susan L., eds. Linguistic Atlas of the Gulf States, Vol. 3: Technical Index for the Linguistic Atlas of the Gulf States. LC 83-24139. (Illus.). 464p. 1989. 60.00 (*0-8203-1182-0*) U of Ga Pr.

Pederson, Lee, et al, eds. The Linguistic Atlas of the Gulf States, Vol. 2: General Index for the Linguistic Atlas of the Gulf States. LC 83-24139. 400p. 1988. 60.00 (*0-8203-0972-9*) U of Ga Pr.

— Linguistic Atlas of the Gulf States, Vol. 4: Regional Matrix for the Linguistic Atlas of the Gulf States. LC 83-24139. (Illus.). 552p. 1990. 65.00 (*0-8203-1231-2*) U of Ga Pr.

— Linguistic Atlas of the Gulf States, Vol. 5: The Regional Pattern for the Linguistic Atlas of the Gulf States. LC 83-24139. (Illus.). 457p. 1991. 60.00 (*0-8203-1276-2*) U of Ga Pr.

— Linguistic Atlas of the Gulf States, Vol. 6: The Social Matrix for the Linguistic Atlas of the Gulf States. LC 83-24139. (Illus.). 584p. 1991. 65.00 (*0-8203-1345-9*) U of Ga Pr.

— Linguistic Atlas of the Gulf States, Vol. 7: The Social Pattern for the Linguistic Atlas of the Gulf States. LC 83-24139. (Illus.). 552p. 1992. 70.00 (*0-8203-1447-1*) U of Ga Pr.

Pederson, Lee A. The Pronunciation of English in Metropolitan Chicago. (Publications of the American Dialect Society: No. 44). 87p. 1965. pap. 8.70 (*0-8173-0644-7*) U of Ala Pr.

Pederson, Loren. Sixteen Men: Understanding Masculine Personality Types. LC 92-56458. 264p. (Orig.). 1993. pap. 14.00 (*0-87773-692-8*) Shambhala Pubns.

Pederson, Lucille M. Katherine Cornell: A Bio-Bibliography. LC 93-32102. (Bio-Bibliographies in the Performing Arts Ser.: No. 46). 264p. 1993. text ed. 59.95 (*0-313-27718-4*, Greenwood Pr) Greenwood.

*__Pederson, Lucille M. & Trigg, Janet M.__ Breast Cancer: A Family Survival Guide. LC 94-37836. 304p. 1995. text ed. 59.95 (*0-89789-293-3*, Bergin & Garvey) Greenwood.

— Breast Cancer: A Family Survival Guide. LC 94-37836. 304p. 1995. pap. text ed. 19.95 (*0-89789-438-3*, Bergin & Garvey) Greenwood.

Pederson, Poul O., et al, eds. Flexible Specialization: The Dynamics of Small-Scale Industries in the South. 186p. (Orig.). 1994. pap. 24.95 (*1-85339-217-0*, Pub. by Intermed Tech UK) Women Ink.

Pederson, Roger A., ed. Current Topics in Developmental Biology, Vol. 27. (Illus.). 397p. 1992. text ed. 79.00 (*0-12-153127-9*) Acad Pr.

Pederson, Roger A., jt. ed. see Bearer, Elaine L.

Pederson, Rolf A. Our Wild Harvest: Sowing, Reaping, Cooking, Eating. Carlson, Nancy, ed. (Illus.). 174p. (Orig.). 1982. pap. 9.95 (*0-910579-00-8*) Rolfs Gall.

— Waterfowl, Vol. 2. (Orig.). 1983. pap. 9.95 (*0-910579-01-6*) Rolfs Gall.

Pederson, Ronald R. How to Stay in Harmony with the Universe. 89p. 1984. pap. write for info. (*0-318-57834-4*) Writers Pub Serv.

Pederson, Sam, jt. auth. see Bruce, Phillip.

Pederson, Sarah, comp. Database Searching in College Libraries. (CLIP Note Ser.: No. 15). 123p. 1993. 29.95 (*0-8389-7651-4*); 24.95 (*0-685-63357-8*) Assn Coll & Res Libs.

Pederson, Steve, ed. see Willow Creek Resources Staff.

Pederson, Steve, ed. see Willow Creek Staff.

Pederson, Steven I. The Tournament Tradition & Staging the Castle of Perseverance. LC 86-25050. (Theater & Dramatic Studies: No. 38). (Illus.). 148p. reprint ed. pap. 42.20 (*0-8357-1768-2*, 2070568) Bks Demand.

Pederson, Ted, et al. The Life & Adventures of Santa Cat. 1990. pap. 9.95 (*1-55698-270-4*) Movie Pubs Servs.

Pederson, Trudy Rodine. A Pioneer Experience. (Illus.). 116p. (Orig.). 1982. 10.00 (*0-686-95352-5*) Directed Media.

Pederson, Westley M. Take Five. 1983. 2.50 (*0-87129-268-8*, T64) Dramatic Pub.

Pederson, William D. The Barberian Presidency: Theoretical & Empirical Readings. (American University Studies: Political Science: Ser. X, Vol. 14). 265p. (C). 1989. text ed. 37.60 (*0-8204-0693-7*) P Lang Pubs.

Pederson, William D., ed. Congressional-Presidential Relations in the United States: Studies in Governmental Gridlock. LC 91-41686. 164p. 1991. lib. bdg. 79.95 (*0-7734-9742-0*) E Mellen.

Pederson, William D. & Prozier, Norman W., eds. Great Justices of the U. S. Supreme Court: Ratings & Case Studies. LC 92-40142. (American University Studies: Political Science: Ser. X, Vol. 39). 388p. (Orig.). (C). 1993. pap. text ed. 32.95 (*0-8204-2066-2*) P Lang Pubs.

Pederson, William D., jt. ed. see Williams, Frank J.

Pederson, William O. & McLaurin, Ann M., eds. The Rating Game in American Politics: An Interdisciplinary Approach. LC 87-4145. 425p. (C). 1987. text ed. 39.50 (*0-8290-1812-3*); pap. text ed. 19.95 (*0-685-16492-6*) Irvington.

Pederzoli, G., jt. ed. see Eiselt, H. A.

*__Pederzoli, P., et al, eds.__ Facing the Pancreatic Dilemma: Update of Medical & Surgical Pancreatology. LC 94-35004. 528p. 1994. 149.00 (*0-387-58284-3*) Spr-Verlag.

— Pancreatic Fistulas. LC 92-49618. 1992. pap. 125.00 (*0-387-55338-X*) Spr-Verlag.

*__Pedestrian, Abby, et al.__ The Incomplete & Aloof Abby Pedestrian: Crossing the Cosmic Crosswalk. (Collected Poetry Ser.). 72p. 1995. pap. 7.00 (*0-9646193-0-X*) Pedestrian Pubns.

Pedhazur, E. & Schmelkin, L. Measurement, Design, & Analysis: An Integrated Approach. 849p. (C). 1991. student ed 49.95 (*0-8058-1063-3*) L Erlbaum Assocs.

Pedhazur, Elazar J. Multiple Regression in Behavioral Research. 2nd ed. 822p. (C). 1982. text ed. 56.00 (*0-03-041760-0*) HB Coll Pubs.

Pediatric Nephrology International Symposium Staff. Pediatric Nephrology: Proceedings of the Pediatric Nephrology International Symposium, 5th, 1980, No. 3. Gruskin, Alan B. & Norman, Michael E., eds. 530p. 1981. lib. bdg. 140.00 (*90-247-2514-3*) Kluwer Ac.

Pedicini, John G. Slow Moe. Serino, John, ed. (Nantucket Nanny & Friends Ser.). (Illus.). 32p. (J). (gr. k-2). 1991. 9.95 (*0-9627436-7-4*) Je Suis Derby.

Pedicord, Harry W. & Bergmann, Fredrick L., eds. The Plays of David Garrick, Vol. 1: Garrick's Own Plays, 1740-1766. LC 79-28443. (Plays of David Garrick). (Illus.). 480p. 1980. 35.00 (*0-8093-0862-2*) S Ill U Pr.

— The Plays of David Garrick, Vol. 2: Garrick's Own Plays, 1767-1775. LC 79-28443. (Illus.). 444p. 1980. 35.00 (*0-8093-0863-0*) S Ill U Pr.

— The Plays of David Garrick, Vol. 3: Garrick's Adaptations of Shakespeare, 1744-1756. LC 80-28443. (Illus.). 496p. 1981. 50.00 (*0-8093-0968-8*) S Ill U Pr.

— The Plays of David Garrick, Vol. 4: Garrick's Adaptions of Shakespeare, 1759-1773. LC 80-28443. (Illus.). 490p. 1981. 50.00 (*0-8093-0969-6*) S Ill U Pr.

— The Plays of David Garrick, Vol. 5: Garrick's Alterations of Others, 1742-1750. LC 80-28443. 485p. 1982. 50.00 (*0-8093-0993-9*) S Ill U Pr.

— The Plays of David Garrick, Vol. 6: Garrick's Alterations of Others, 1751-1756. LC 80-28443. 453p. 1982. 50.00 (*0-8093-0994-7*) S Ill U Pr.

— The Plays of David Garrick, Vol. 7: Garrick's Alterations of Others, 1757-1773. LC 80-28443. 399p. 1982. 50.00 (*0-8093-1051-1*) S Ill U Pr.

Pedicord, Harry W., ed. see Rowe, Nicholas.

Pedigo. Handbook of Sampling Methods for Arthropod Pests in Agriculture. 1993. 195.00 (*0-8493-2923-X*, SB933) CRC Pr.

Pedigo, Kate. When Even the Cows Were Up: Kate's Book of Childhood in the Early 1900s & After. LC 90-71867. (Illus.). 64p. (Orig.). 1990. pap. text ed. 6.95 (*1-877675-06-7*) Midmarch Arts-WAN.

Pedigo, Larry P. Entomology & Pest Management. 904p. (C). 1989. write for info. (*0-02-393310-0*) Macmillan.

Pedigo, Lewis G., jt. auth. see Pedigo, Virginia G.

Pedigo, Marlene M. New Church in the City. LC 88-3867. (Orig.). 1988. pap. 5.95 (*0-944350-05-4*) Friends United.

Pedigo, Virginia G. & Pedigo, Lewis G. Patrick & Henry Counties, Virginia, History of. LC 76-53104. (Illus.). 400p. 1990. reprint ed. 35.00 (*0-8063-8010-1*) Genealog Pub.

Peditto, C. Natale, ed. see Bivins, Charles.

Peditto, C. Natale, ed. see Priestley, Eric.

Pedlar, Dorothy. Divorce Guide for Manitoba: Step-by-Step Guide to Obtaining Your Own Divorce. 2nd ed. (Legal Ser.). 120p. (Orig.). 1991. Canadian ed. pap. 14.95 (*0-88908-516-1*); 14.95 (*0-88908-517-X*) Self-Counsel Pr.

Pedlar, Neil. Imported Pioneers: Westerners Who Helped Build Modern Japan. (C). 1990. text ed. 60.00 (*0-904404-51-X*, Pub. by Paul Norbury Pubns UK) Humanities.

— The Imported Pioneers: Westerners Who Helped Build Modern Japan. 300p. 1991. text ed. 45.00 (*0-312-03663-9*) St Martin.

Pedler, Margaret. The Hermit of Far End. 1976. lib. bdg. 15.75 (*0-89968-216-2*, Lghtyr Pr) Buccaneer Bks.

— The Lamp of Fate. 1976. lib. bdg. 15.25 (*0-89968-217-0*, Lghtyr Pr) Buccaneer Bks.

— Splendid Family. 12.95 (*0-8488-1444-4*) Amereon Ltd.

— The Splendid Folly. 1976. lib. bdg. 13.75 (*0-89968-218-9*, Lghtyr Pr) Buccaneer Bks.

Pedler, Mike. Action Learning in Practice. 2nd ed. 384p. 1991. text ed. 69.95 (*0-566-02859-X*, Pub. by Gower UK) Ashgate Pub Co.

— Learning Company: A Strategy for Sustainable Development. 1993. pap. 24.95 (*0-07-707479-3*) McGraw.

Pedler, Mike, et al. The Community Development Initiative: A Story of the Manor Employment Project in Sheffield. 256p. 1990. text ed. 59.95 (*0-566-07124-X*) Ashgate Pub Co.

— A Manager's Guide to Self-Development. 3rd ed. LC 94-18933. 1994. pap. text ed. 24.95 (*0-07-707829-2*) McGraw.

*__Pedler, Mike, et al, eds.__ Towards the Learning Company: Concepts & Practices. LC 94-103167. 1994. write for info. (*0-07-707802-0*) McGraw.

*__Pedler, Robin & VanSchendelen, M., eds.__ Lobbying in the European Union: Companies, Trade Associations & Issue Groups. 328p. 1994. 59.95 (*1-85521-609-4*) Ashgate Pub Co.

Pedley, A. J. The Manuscript Collections of the Maryland Historical Society. LC 68-23074. 1968. 20.00 (*0-938420-08-9*) MD Hist.

Pedley, Carolyn F., jt. auth. see Bloomfield, Robert L.

Pedley, Carolyn F., et al. Mnemonics, Rhetoric & Poetics for Medics, Vol. II. (Illus.). 175p. (Orig.). 1984. pap. 10.95 (*0-9612242-3-1*) Harbinger Med Pr NC.

Pedley, Evan David, jt. auth. see Vinedresser, Branch.

Pedley, F. Parents' Guide to Examinations: From Primary School to University. LC 63-23424. 1964. 102.00 (*0-08-010366-9*, Pub. by Pergamon Repr UK) Franklin.

Pedley, John G. Ancient Literary Sources on Sardis. LC 72-172327. (Archaeological Exploration of Sardis Monograph: No. 2). 108p. 1972. 21.50 (*0-674-03375-2*) HUP.

— Greek Art: And Archaeology. (Illus.). 368p. 1992. 55.00 (*0-8109-3369-1*) Abrams.

— Greek Art & Archaeology. 368p. 1993. pap. text ed. write for info. (*0-13-365800-7*) P-H.

— Paestum: Greeks & Romans in Southern Italy. LC 89-51868. (New Aspects of Antiquity Ser.). (Illus.). 184p. 1990. 35.00 (*0-500-39027-4*) Thames Hudson.

— Sardis in the Age of Croesus. LC 67-64447. (Centers of Civilization Ser.). 155p. reprint ed. pap. 44.20 (*0-317-28329-4*, 2016247) Bks Demand.

Pedley, T. J. The Fluid Mechanics of Large Blood Vessels. LC 78-73814. (Cambridge Monographs on Mechanics & Applied Mathematics). (Illus.). 1980. 145.00 (*0-521-22626-0*) Cambridge U Pr.

Pedley, Timothy A., jt. auth. see Daly, David D.

Pedlosky, J. Geophysical Fluid Dynamics: Springer Study Edition. 2nd ed. (Illus.). 710p. 1993. pap. 49.95 (*0-387-96387-1*) Spr-Verlag.

Pedlow, Gregory W. The Survival of the Hessian Nobility, 1770-1870. (Illus.). 320p. 1988. text ed. 47.50 (*0-691-05503-3*) Princeton U Pr.

Pedlow, J. C. Windows on the Holy Land. (Illus.). 150p. 1980. pap. 12.50 (*0-227-67839-7*) Attic Pr.

Pedneau, Dave. A. P. B. 1987. pap. 3.95 (*0-345-34205-4*) Ballantine.

— B & E. 320p. (Orig.). 1991. mass mkt. 4.95 (*0-345-36420-1*) Ballantine.

— Dead Witness. 208p. 1987. pap. 2.95 (*0-380-75214-X*) Avon.

— D.O.A. 320p. 1988. mass mkt. 4.99 (*0-345-34677-7*) Ballantine.

— N.F.D. No Further Description. (Orig.). 1992. mass mkt. 4.99 (*0-345-36419-8*) Ballantine.

Pednekar, S. P., tr. see Larikov, L. N., et al.

Pednekar, S. P., tr. see Samsonov, G. V., ed.

Pedoe, D. & Sneddon, I. N. Introduction to Projective Geometry. LC 62-22053. (International Series of Monographs on Pure & Applied Mathematics: Vol. 33). 1963. 94.00 (*0-08-009920-3*, Pub. by Pergamon Repr UK) Franklin.

Pedoe, D., jt. auth. see Hodge, W. V.

Pedoe, Dan. The Gentle Art of Mathematics. (Illus.). 143p. 1973. reprint ed. pap. 4.95 (*0-486-22949-1*) Dover.

— Geometry & the Visual Arts. (Illus.). 353p. 1983. reprint ed. pap. 7.95 (*0-486-24458-X*) Dover.

Pedolsky, Andrea, jt. auth. see Turock, Betty J.

Pedoto, Constance A. Painting Literature: Dostoevsky, Kafka, Pirandello, & Garcia Marquez in Living Color. 122p. (C). 1993. lib. bdg. 28.50 (*0-8191-9099-3*) U Pr of Amer.

Pedotti, A., ed. Electrophysiological Kinesiology: Proceedings of ISEK Conference, Florence, Italy 28-6 - 2-7. LC 92-53264. (Studies in Health Technology & Informatics: Vol. 5). 438p. 1993. 130.00 (*90-5199-095-2*, Pub. by IOS Pr NE) IOS Press.

Pedotti, A. & Andrich, R., eds. Evaluation & Information in the Field of Technical Aids for Disabled Persons: An European Perspective. (International Exchange of Experts & Information in Rehabilitation Ser.: No. 35). 64p. 1986. pap. text ed. 3.00 (*0-685-17270-8*) World Rehab Fund.

Pedotti, Antonio, jt. ed. see Ferrarin, Maurizio.

Pedowitz, ed. Real Estate Titles. 2nd ed. 65p. 1994. reprint ed. pap. text ed. 25.00 (*0-942954-58-0*) NYS Bar.

Pedowitz, James M. Title Insurance, 1990: The Basics & Beyond. 633p. 1990. pap. 17.50 (*0-685-69506-9*) PLI.

Pedowitz, James M., ed. see New York State Bar Association Staff.

Pedraz, Martin A. Diccionario de la Exportacion. 928p. (SPA.). 1986. 150.00 (*0-7859-6212-3*, 8472991709) Fr & Eur.

— Diccionario Medieval Espanol, 2 vols. 784p. (SPA.). 1986. 150.00 (*0-7859-6213-1*, 8472991717) Fr & Eur.

— Diccionario Militar, Vol. 2. 1712p. (SPA.). 1986. 295.00 (*0-7859-6211-5*, 8472991695) Fr & Eur.

Pedraza, Jesus S., jt. auth. see **Bernard, H. Russell.**

Pedraza, Jorge A. Estampillas de Colores. LC 85-82322. 94p. (Orig.). (SPA.). 1986. pap. 9.95 (*0-89729-386-X*) Ediciones.

Pedraza, Pedro, Jr. An Ethnographic Analysis of Language Use in the Puerto Rican Community of East Harlem. 65p. 1987. lib. bdg. 5.00 (*1-878483-44-7*) Hunter Coll CEP.

Pedreira, Antonio S. Bibliografia Puertorriquena, 2 vols. 1976. lib. bdg. 400.00 (*0-8490-1495-6*) Gordon Pr.

— Complete Works of Antonio S. Pedreira, 2 vols., Set. (Puerto Rico Ser.). 1979. lib. bdg. 400.00 (*0-8490-2888-4*) Gordon Pr.

— Hostos, Citizen of America. (Puerto Rico Ser.). 1979. lib. bdg. 59.95 (*0-8490-2939-2*) Gordon Pr.

— Insularism. (Puerto Rico Ser.). 1979. lib. bdg. 59.95 (*0-8490-2949-X*) Gordon Pr.

Pedrero, Manuel, tr. see **Mike Byrnes & Associates Staff.**

Pedres, Melvin J. The Experience of Teaching. 128p. (C). 1994. pap. text ed., spiral bd. 11.96 (*0-8403-9149-8*) Kendall-Hunt.

Pedretti. Occupational Therapy: Practical Skills for Phy Dys. (Illus.). 704p. 1989. 51.95 (*0-8016-3852-6*) Mosby Yr Bk.

Pedretti, Carlo. Leonardo Da Vinci: Nature Studies from the Royal Library at Windsor Castle. 1981. pap. 14.95 (*0-15-149848-2*) HarBrace.

— Leonardo da Vinci: The Royal Palace at Romorantin. LC 76-102673. 176p. 1972. 45.00 (*0-674-52455-1*) Belknap Pr.

Pedretti, Erica. The Stones. Black, Judith, tr. (Swiss Library). 220p. (Orig.). 1982. pap. 9.95 (*0-7145-3942-2*) Riverrun NY.

***Pedrick, Allen R.** Greencove. 310p. 1995. pap. 9.95 (*1-56901-741-7*) NW Pub.

Pedrick, Gale, ed. see **Dunn, Henry T.**

Pedrick, George. A First Course in Analysis. LC 93-5141. (Undergraduate Texts in Mathematics Ser.). (Illus.). 280p. (C). 1994. 39.50 (*0-387-94108-8*) Spr-Verlag.

Pedrick, Jean. Greenfellow. LC 81-846411. 63p. 1981. pap. 3.00 (*0-89823-033-0*) New Rivers Pr.

— Pride & Splendor. LC 75-23818. 72p. 1976. pap. 9.95 (*0-914086-10-3*) Alicejamesbooks.

— Saints. (Chapbook Ser.: No. 1). 40p. (Orig.). 1980. pap. 4.95 (*0-937672-00-9*) Rowan Tree.

— Wolf Moon. LC 73-94067. 72p. 1974. pap. 9.95 (*0-914086-03-0*) Alicejamesbooks.

Pedrini, Arnold. St. Francis de Sales: Don Bosco's Patron. Klauder, Francis J., ed. Cornell, Wallace L., tr. 149p. 1988. 13.95 (*0-89944-096-7*); pap. 8.95 (*0-89944-092-4*, D Bosco Pubns) Don Bosco Multimedia.

Pedrini, Duilio T., jt. auth. see **Pedrini, Lura.**

Pedrini, Lura & Pedrini, Duilio T. Serpent Imagery & Symbolism. 1966. pap. 15.95 (*0-8084-0274-9*) NCUP.

Pedrizet, P. & Lefebvre, G., eds. Inscriptiones Graecae Aegypti, No. 3: Abydos. xxvi, 125p. 1978. 30.00 (*0-89005-243-3*) Ares.

Pedro, Michael J., jt. auth. see **Tiernan, S. Gregory.**

Pedro Silva Ruiz. Derecho Notarial: Casos y Materiales. LC 89-38006. 629p. (C). 1989. pap. text ed. 27.00 (*0-8477-3032-8*) U of PR Pr.

Pedrocco, Filippo. Titian. Madocks, Susan, tr. (Library of Great Masters). (Illus.). 80p. (Orig.). 1993. pap. 12.99 (*1-878351-14-1*) Riverside NY.

Pedroli, Hubert. The American Golfer's Guide: Over 500 of the Best American Golf Courses Open to the Public. Gray, Tim, ed. (Illus.). 304p. 1992. pap. 19.95 (*1-878685-10-4*) Turner Pub GA.

Pedron, Fotini, ed. see **Catala, Rafael.**

Pedroncini, Guy, ed. see **Corvisier, Andre.**

Pedrone, Dino. The Corinthian Catastrophe: How to Ruin a Church Quickly. 63p. (Orig.). 1987. pap. 1.00 (*0-929961-16-1*) Open Door Ch.

— Walking with Jesus. 48p. (Orig.). 1986. pap. 1.00 (*0-929961-01-3*) Open Door Ch.

Pedrone, Dino J. Walking with Jesus, Pt. 2. 47p. (Orig.). 1985. pap. text ed. 1.20 (*0-929961-02-1*) Open Door Ch.

— Walking with Jesus, Pt. 3. 52p. (Orig.). 1985. pap. text ed. 1.20 (*0-929961-03-X*) Open Door Ch.

— Walking with Jesus, Pt. 4. 43p. (Orig.). 1985. pap. text ed. 1.20 (*0-929961-04-8*) Open Door Ch.

— Walking with Jesus, Pt. 5. 52p. (Orig.). 1985. pap. text ed. 1.20 (*0-929961-05-6*) Open Door Ch.

— Walking with Jesus, Pt. 6. 50p. (Orig.). 1985. pap. text ed. 1.20 (*0-929961-06-4*) Open Door Ch.

— Walking with Jesus, Pt. 7. 53p. (Orig.). 1985. pap. text ed. 1.20 (*0-929961-07-2*) Open Door Ch.

— Walking with Jesus, Pt. 8. 49p. (Orig.). 1985. pap. text ed. 1.20 (*0-929961-08-0*) Open Door Ch.

— Walking with Jesus, Pt. 9. 55p. (Orig.). 1985. pap. text ed. 1.20 (*0-929961-09-9*) Open Door Ch.

— Walking with Jesus, Pt. 10. 48p. (Orig.). 1985. pap. text ed. 1.20 (*0-929961-10-2*) Open Door Ch.

— Walking with Jesus, Pt. 11. 51p. (Orig.). 1986. pap. text ed. 1.20 (*0-929961-11-0*) Open Door Ch.

— Walking with Jesus, Pt. 12. 50p. (Orig.). (C). 1989. pap. text ed. 1.20 (*0-929961-12-9*) Open Door Ch.

— Walking with Jesus, Pt. 13. 50p. (Orig.). 1989. pap. text ed. 1.20 (*0-929961-13-7*) Open Door Ch.

— Walking with Jesus, Pt. 14. 69p. (Orig.). 1989. pap. text ed. 1.20 (*0-929961-14-5*) Open Door Ch.

Pedroni, Peter N. The Anti-Naturalist Experience: Federigo Tozzi. (Explorations in the Humanities Ser.: Vol. 1). 93p. (C). 1989. 25.00 (*0-9624254-1-9*) DeSoto Pr Inc.

— Existence As Theme in Carlo Cassola's Fiction. LC 85-18109. (American University Studies: Romance Languages & Literature: Ser. II, Vol. 31). 182p. (C). 1985. text ed. 26.65 (*0-8204-0236-2*) P Lang Pubs.

Pedroni, Peter N., tr. see **Volponi, Paolo.**

Pedrosa, Gary L., tr. see **Taylor, Eldon.**

Pedrosa, Jose R. Memorias de un Desmemoriado: Lena Para el Fuego de la Historia de Cuba. LC 78-67007. (Coleccion Cuba y Sus Jueces Ser.). 1979. 13.00 (*0-89729-207-3*) Ediciones.

***Pedroso de Lima, Maria C., et al, eds.** Trafficking of Intercellular Membranes: From Molecular Sorting to Membrane Fusion. LC 94-49441. (NATO ASI Series: Subseries H: Cell Biology: Vol. 91). 1995. 171.00 (*3-540-58915-5*) Spr-Verlag.

Pedrotti, Frank L. & Pedrotti, Leno S. Introduction to Optics. 2nd ed. 672p. (C). 1992. text ed. write for info. (*0-13-501545-6*) P-H.

Pedrotti, Leno S., jt. auth. see **Pedrotti, Frank L.**

Pedrotti, Louis. Jozef-Julian Sekowski: The Genesis of a Literary Alien. LC 65-63974. (U. C. Publ. in Modern Philology Ser.: Vol. 73). 233p. reprint ed. pap. 66.50 (*0-8357-9630-2*, 2013798) Bks Demand.

Pedrotti, Louis, tr. see **Senkovskii, Osip I.**

Pedrotti, Robin. Lawn Aeration: How to Turn Hard Soil into Cold Cash. LC 91-90418. (Illus.). 208p. (Orig.). 1992. pap. 19.95 (*0-9629928-5-2*) Prego Pr.

Pedrycz, Witold. Fuzzy Control & Fuzzy Systems. 2nd enl. ed. LC 92-41429. (Control Theory & Applications Research Studies). 350p. 1993. text ed. 89.95 (*0-471-93475-5*) Wiley.

***Pedrycz, Witold & Zadeh, Lotfi A.** Fuzzy Sets Engineering. LC 94-22949. 1995. write for info. (*0-8493-9402-3*) CRC Pr.

Pedrys, R., jt. auth. see **Szymonski, M.**

Peduzzi, Kelli. Ralph Nader: Crusader for Safe Consumer Products. LC 90-9924. (People Who Made a Difference Ser.). (Illus.). 64p. (J). (gr. 3-4). 1991. lib. bdg. 21.26 (*0-8368-0455-4*) Gareth Stevens Inc.

— Ralph Nader: Crusader for Safe Consumer Products & Lawyer for Public Interest. LC 89-4282. (People Who Have Helped the World Ser.). (Illus.). 68p. (J). (gr. 5-6). 1990. lib. bdg. 21.26 (*0-8368-0098-2*) Gareth Stevens Inc.

Peduzzi, Kelli & Cummins, Ronnie. Oscar Arias: Peacemaker & Leader among Nations. LC 90-39917. (People Who Have Helped the World Ser.). (Illus.). 64p. (J). (gr. 5-6). 1991. lib. bdg. 19.93 (*0-8368-0102-4*) Gareth Stevens Inc.

Peeaver, Richard, tr. see **Bychkov, Victor.**

Peebles, Betty, jt. auth. see **Peebles, James.**

Peebles, Betty P. Are You Afraid of Death? 23p. (Orig.). 1990. pap. text ed. 5.00 (*0-918925-41-X*) Jericho Chr Trng.

— Are You Falling Prey to Seducing Spirits? 53p. (Orig.). 1989. pap. text ed. 7.00 (*0-918925-28-2*) Jericho Chr Trng.

— The Gift of Discerning of Spirits. 9p. (Orig.). 1990. pap. text ed. 4.00 (*0-918925-31-2*) Jericho Chr Trng.

— The Gift of Divers Kinds of Tongues. 11p. (Orig.). 1990. pap. text ed. 4.00 (*0-918925-37-1*) Jericho Chr Trng.

— The Gift of Interpretation of Tongues. 7p. (Orig.). 1990. pap. text ed. 4.00 (*0-918925-38-X*) Jericho Chr Trng.

— The Gift of Prophecy. 10p. (Orig.). 1990. pap. text ed. 4.00 (*0-918925-35-5*) Jericho Chr Trng.

— The Gift of Special Faith. 10p. (Orig.). 1990. pap. text ed. 4.00 (*0-918925-32-0*) Jericho Chr Trng.

— The Gift of the Word of Knowledge. 8p. (Orig.). 1990. pap. text ed. 4.00 (*0-918925-30-4*) Jericho Chr Trng.

— The Gift of the Word of Wisdom. 8p. (Orig.). pap. text ed. 4.00 (*0-918925-29-0*) Jericho Chr Trng.

— The Gift of the Working of Miracles. 14p. (Orig.). 1990. pap. text ed. 4.00 (*0-918925-34-7*) Jericho Chr Trng.

— The Gifts of Healing. 11p. (Orig.). 1990. pap. text ed. 4.00 (*0-918925-33-9*) Jericho Chr Trng.

— The Ministry of the Prophet. 15p. (Orig.). 1990. pap. text ed. 4.00 (*0-918925-36-3*) Jericho Chr Trng.

— The Origin & Exposure of the Devil. 31p. (Orig.). 1989. pap. text ed. 7.00 (*0-918925-26-6*) Jericho Chr Trng.

— Whatsoever You Doeth Shall Prosper! 96p. (Orig.). 1989. pap. text ed. 3.95 (*0-918925-00-2*) Jericho Chr Trng.

— Wounded. 38p. (Orig.). 1992. pap. text ed. 7.00 (*0-918925-42-8*) Jericho Chr Trng.

— Yoke up with Jesus. 10p. (Orig.). 1989. pap. text ed. 4.00 (*0-918925-27-4*) Jericho Chr Trng.

Peebles, Betty P., jt. auth. see **Peebles, James R.**

Peebles, Catherine & Edge, Denzil. A Natural Curiosity: Taffy's Search for Self. LC 87-36882. (Illus.). (Orig.). (J). 1988. pap. 6.95 (*0-939991-01-2*) Learning KY.

Peebles, Christopher, jt. ed. see **Gardin, Jean-Claude.**

***Peebles, Curtis.** Dark Eagles: A History of Top Secret U. S. Aircraft. 400p. 1995. 24.95 (*0-89141-535-1*) Presidio Pr.

— The Moby Dick Project: Reconnaissance Balloons over Russia. LC 90-21131. (Illus.). 260p. (C). 1991. 40.00 (*1-56098-025-7*) Smithsonian.

— Watch the Skies! A Chronicle of the Flying Saucer Myth. 432p. (Orig.). 1995. pap. 6.99 (*0-425-15117-4*) Berkley Pub.

— Watch the Skies! A Chronicle of the Flying Saucer Myth. LC 93-26819. 368p. (Orig.). 1994. 24.95 (*1-56098-343-4*) Smithsonian.

***Peebles, David.** Introductory Genetics. 324p. (C). 1995. pap. text ed., spiral bd. 34.95 (*0-7872-1056-0*) Kendall-Hunt.

Peebles, Dorothy, illus. Harvest of Gold. LC 72-92720. 96p. 1973. 9.50 (*0-8378-1760-9*) Gibson.

Peebles, Douglas. Landmark Hawaii: Favorite Postcard Views of the Islands. 112p. 1989. pap. 10.95 (*0-935180-81-8*) Mutual Pub HI.

— Viewbook Hawaii. (Illus.). 32p. (Orig.). 1991. pap. 6.95 (*0-9627294-6-9*) Hawaiian Resources.

— Viewbook Hawaii's Volcanos. (Illus.). 32p. (Orig.). 1994. pap. 6.95 (*0-9627294-9-3*) Hawaiian Resources.

— Viewbook Kauai. (Illus.). 32p. (Orig.). 1991. pap. 6.95 (*0-9627294-5-0*) Hawaiian Resources.

— Viewbook Maui. (Illus.). 32p. 1988. pap. 6.95 (*0-9627294-7-7*) Hawaiian Resources.

— Viewbook Oahu. (Illus.). 32p. (Orig.). 1989. pap. 6.95 (*0-9627294-8-5*) Hawaiian Resources.

Peebles, Douglas, photos. From the Skies of Paradise Kauai. 112p. 1992. 24.95 (*0-935180-51-6*) Mutual Pub HI.

— From the Skies of Paradise Maui. 112p. 1991. 24.95 (*0-935180-74-5*) Mutual Pub HI.

— From the Skies of Paradise Oahu. (Illus.). 176p. 1992. 32.95 (*1-56647-011-0*) Mutual Pub HI.

— Hawaii: A Floral Paradise. 64p. 1995. pap. 8.95 (*1-56647-071-4*) Mutual Pub HI.

Peebles, Gavin. Money in the People's Republic of China: A Comparative Perspective. 1992. text ed. 45.00 (*1-86373-033-8*, Pub. by Allen Unwin AT) Paul & Co Pubs.

— A Short History of Socialist Money. 192p. 1992. text ed. 34.95 (*1-86373-113-X*, Pub. by Allen Unwin AT); pap. text ed. 19.95 (*1-86373-071-0*, Pub. by Allen Unwin AT) Paul & Co Pubs.

Peebles, J. M. The General Principles & the Standard Teachings of Spiritualism. 29p. 1969. reprint ed. spiral bd. 3.30 (*0-7873-0664-9*) Mokelumne.

— What Is Spiritualism, Who Are These Spiritualists, & What Has Spiritualism Done for the World? 131p. 1972. reprint ed. spiral bd. 4.40 (*0-7873-0663-0*) Mokelumne.

— Who Are These Spiritualists? 129p. 1972. reprint ed. 4.40 (*0-7873-1080-8*) Mokelumne.

Peebles, J. Winston. My Funny Cloud. LC 81-50915. (Illus.). 36p. (J). (ps-3). 1981. 4.95 (*0-938232-00-2*) Winston-Derek.

Peebles, James, ed. African Heritage Study Bible. 2048p. 1993. 39.99 (*0-529-10067-3*) World Bible.

Peebles, James & Peebles, Betty. Multiplied Prayer Power. 11p. (Orig.). 1990. pap. text ed. 4.00 (*0-918925-40-1*) Jericho Chr Trng.

— Praying in the Spirit. 7p. (Orig.). pap. text ed. 4.00 (*0-918925-39-8*) Jericho Chr Trng.

Peebles, James R. & Peebles, Betty P. Angels. 21p. (Orig.). 1989. pap. 5.00 (*0-918925-25-8*) Jericho Chr Trng.

— Now Let's Send the Troops the Real Weapon THE WORD OF GOD!!! 24p. (Orig.). pap. text ed. 4.00 (*0-918925-43-6*) Jericho Chr Trng.

***Peebles, James W., ed. & intro.** Winston's African Heritage Study Bible Encyclopedia. LC 94-60970. (Illus.). 600p. (Orig.). 1994. 35.00 (*1-55523-715-0*) Winston-Derek.

***Peebles, Joseph.** Hannibal: The Ultimate Warrior: The Untold Story. LC 94-93928. (Illus.). 110p. (Orig.). (YA). (gr. 10-13). 1994. 24.95 (*0-9644758-0-4*) Peebco Pub.

—Hannibal: The Ultimate Warrior: The Untold Story. McMillian, Ben, ed. LC 94-93928. (Illus.). 110p. (Orig.). (YA). (gr. 10-13). 1994. pap. 9.95x (*0-9644758-1-2*) Peebco Pub.
In an era where grunge is the fashion & foul language is the lingo, there comes a writer whose style & sophistication is as debonair as his personal appearance. The originality of Joseph Peebles' writing style is more contemporary than an inclination to be current. Using his strong cinematic background, he employs a fast-paced drama that leaves every page bursting with excitement. HANNIBAL: THE ULTIMATE WARRIOR; THE UNTOLD STORY begins with the year 234 B.C. After the first Punic War, Carthage, Africa, had lost a great deal of its northern provinces to Rome, Italy. As a means of military & economic survival, the Carthaginian senate had chosen to send Hannibal to Spain to defend against continued Roman aggression. This is the untold story of Hannibal, the ultimate Warrior. "Definitely make this book part of your reading repertoire." Recommended reading age is from 16 through 99. To order direct: send $19.95 plus $3.00 s&h to The Peebco Publishing House, P.O. Box 45333, St. Louis, MO 63145. ***Publisher Provided Annotation.***

Peebles, L. H., Jr. Carbon Fibers: Information, Structure, & Properties. LC 94-7765. 1994. write for info. (*0-8493-2450-5*) CRC Pr.

Peebles, Marvin L. Directory of Consultants & Management Training Programs Intended for Local Non-Profit Groups, 1985. 100p. 1985. ring bd. 20.00 (*0-939020-27-0*) MLP Ent.

— Directory of Management Resources for Community Based Organizations. 6th ed. 125p. 1987. ring bd. 20.00 (*0-939020-06-8*) MLP Ent.

— Own Worst Enemies: Local Charity Unmasked. 300p. 1984. ring bd. 32.50 (*0-939020-50-5*) MLP Ent.

Peebles, P. J. The Large-Scale Structure of the Universe. LC 79-84008. (Physics Ser.). 1980. 69.50 (*0-691-08239-1*); pap. 24.95 (*0-691-08240-5*) Princeton U Pr.

— Principles of Physical Cosmology. LC 92-33370. (Physics Ser.). 736p. (C). 1993. text ed. 65.00 (*0-691-07428-3*); pap. text ed. 29.95 (*0-691-01933-9*) Princeton U Pr.

— Quantum Mechanics. 408p. 1992. text ed. 39.50 (*0-691-08755-5*) Princeton U Pr.

Peebles, P. J., jt. ed. see **Abell, George O.**

Peebles, Patrick, jt. auth. see **Nelson, Lynn H.**

Peebles, Peyton Z. Probability, Random Variables, & Random Signal Principles. 3rd ed. 1992. text ed. write for info. (*0-07-049273-5*) McGraw.

Peebles, Peyton Z., Jr. & Giuma, Tayeb A. Principles of Electrical Engineering. 1991. text ed. write for info. (*0-07-049252-2*) McGraw.

Peebles, Robert W. Leonard Covello: A Study of an Immigrants Contribution to New York City. Cordasco, Francesco, ed. LC 77-90551. (Bilingual-Bicultural Education in the U. S. Ser.). 1978. lib. bdg. 41.95 (*0-405-11090-1*) Ayer.

Peed, Joseph W., ed. see **Citation Directories, Ltd., Inc. Staff.**

Peek. This Is San Quentin. (Illus.). 50p. (Orig.). 1991. pap. 3.95 (*0-9630115-0-2*) San Quentin Mus.

Peek, Andrea, comp. ASTC Salary Survey, 1993. 68p. 1993. 125.00 (*0-944040-33-0*) AST Ctrs.

Peek, C. A. Catch Twenty-Two Notes. 48p. 1975. pap. 3.75 (*0-8220-0296-5*) Cliffs.

Peek, Charles A., jt. auth. see **Ferguson, J. M., Jr.**

***Peek, Chester L.** Resurrection of a Jenny. (Illus.). 120p. (Orig.). 1994. per., pap. 22.95 (*1-886196-00-1*) Three Peaks.

Peek, Chet. The Taylorcraft Story. (Illus.). 236p. 1993. pap. text ed. 24.95 (*0-943691-08-7*) Aviation Heritage.

Peek, Gary. Jumpsuit Color Program: Computerized Color Pattern Selection. 1992. disk 14.95 (*0-915516-88-8*, PR-203) Para Pub.

— Rig Color Program: Computerized Harness-Container Color Pattern Selection. 1992. disk 14.95 (*0-915516-87-X*, PR-201) Para Pub.

— Skydiving Logbook Program: Computerized Jump Record. 1992. disk 14.95 (*0-915516-89-6*, PR-204) Para Pub.

***Peek, Glenna.** ACT! 2.0 for Windows at a Glance. (At a Glance Ser.). 112p. (Orig.). 1995. pap. 15.95 (*1-55622-450-8*) Wordware Pub.

Peek, Hedley & Aflalo, F. G., eds. Encyclopaedia of Sport, 2 vols., Set. (Illus.). 1995. reprint ed. 210.00 (*1-55888-966-3*) Omnigraphics Inc.

***Peek-in Board Books Staff.** There's a Bear in the Woods. Date not set. 3.99 (*0-88705-740-3*) Joshua Morris.

— There's a Cat in the Tree. Date not set. 3.99 (*0-88705-742-X*) Joshua Morris.

— There's a Lion in the Jungle. Date not set. 3.99 (*0-88705-743-8*) Joshua Morris.

— There's a Rabbit in the Garden. Date not set. 3.99 (*0-88705-741-1*) Joshua Morris.

***Peek, Jeannette M.** Stepping into Time. 144p. 1994. pap. 19.95 (*1-56647-052-8*) Mutual Pub HI.

Peek, Jerry. MH & XMH: E-Mail for Users & Programmers. 2nd ed. (Nutshell Handbook Ser.). (Illus.). 728p. 1992. pap. 29.95 (*1-56592-027-9*) OReilly & Assocs.

— MH & xmh: Email for Users & Programmers. 3rd ed. O'Reilly, Tim & Willison, Franke, eds. (Illus.). 750p. (Orig.). 1995. pap. 29.95 (*1-56592-093-7*) OReilly & Assocs.

— UNIX Power Tools. 1993. pap. 60.00 (*0-679-79073-X*) Random.

Peek, Jerry, jt. auth. see **Lamb, Linda.**

Peek, Junice S., jt. auth. see **Smyth, Dan.**

Peek, Merle. Mary Wore Her Red Dress, & Henry Wore His Green Sneakers. LC 84-12733. (Illus.). 32p. (J). (ps-2). 1985. 15.95 (*0-89919-324-2*, Clarion Bks) HM.

— Mary Wore Her Red Dress, & Henry Wore His Green Sneakers. (J). 1988. pap. 5.95 (*0-89919-701-9*, Clarion Bks) HM.

— Mary Wore Her Red Dress & Henry Wore His Green Sneakers. (Illus.). (J). 1993. Incl. cassette. audio 7.95 (*0-395-61577-1*, Clarion Bks) HM.

— Roll Over! A Counting Song. (Illus.). 32p. (J). (ps-2). 1981. 14.95 (*0-395-29438-X*, Clarion Bks) HM.

— Roll Over! A Counting Song. (Illus.). 32p. (J). (ps). 1991. reprint ed. pap. 5.95 (*0-395-58105-2*, Clarion Bks) HM.

— Roll Over! A Counting Song. (Illus.). 32p. (J). (ps). 1991. reprint ed. audio 7.95 (*0-395-60117-7*, Clarion Bks) HM.

Peek, Philip M., ed. African Divination Systems: Ways of Knowing. LC 90-39421. (African Systems of Thought Ser.). (Illus.). 240p. 1991. 35.00 (*0-253-34309-7*); pap. 14.95 (*0-253-20653-7*, MB-653) Ind U Pr.

***Peek, Robin P. & Newby, Gregory B.** Scholarly Publishing: The Electronic Frontier. (Illus.). 450p. (C). 1995. 35.00 (*0-262-16157-5*) MIT Pr.

Peek, Stephen. The Game Inventor's Handbook. 2nd rev. ed. (Illus.). 192p. 1993. pap. 18.95 (*1-55870-315-2*) Betterway Bks.

Peek, Werner. Greek Verse Inscriptions. 740p. (Orig.). (GER & GRE.). 1988. reprint ed. pap. 50.00 (*0-89005-479-7*) Ares.

***Peeke, Graham.** Mission & Change: Institutional Mission & Its Application to the Management of Further & Higher Education. LC 94-19796. 160p. 1994. 85.00x (*0-335-19337-4*); pap. 32.00x (*0-335-19338-2*, Open Univ Pr) Taylor & Francis.

Peeke, Margaret B. Born of Flame: A Rosicrucian Story. 299p. 1971. reprint ed. spiral bd. 11.00 (*0-7873-1139-1*) Mokelumne.

— Numbers & Letters: The Thirty-Two Paths of Wisdom. 191p. 1986. reprint ed. spiral bd. 16.50 (*0-7873-0666-5*) Mokelumne.

— Zenia, the Vestal: The Problem of Vibrations. 355p. 1965. reprint ed. spiral bd. 13.75 (*0-7873-0665-7*) Mokelumne.

Peekel, Gerhard. Grammatik der Neu-Mecklenburgischen Sprache, Speziell der Pala-Sprache. LC 75-35147. reprint ed. 18.50 (*0-404-14163-3*) AMS Pr.

Peel. Realtime, Shadowtime. (J). Date not set. 14.00 (*0-671-79894-4*, S&S Bks Young Read) S&S Childrens.

An Asterisk (*) at the beginning of an entry indicates that the title is appearing in BIP for the first time.

Peel, Bill. What God Does When Men Pray. 96p. (Orig.). 1993. pap. 5.00 (*0-89109-729-5*) NavPress.

Peel, Bruce, comp. Bibliography of the Prairie Provinces to Nineteen Fifty Three: With Biographical Index. 2nd ed. LC 72-97930. 1973. 85.00 (*0-8020-1972-2*) U of Toronto Pr.

Peel, Colin D. Covenant of the Poppies. LC 93-1111. 224p. 1993. 17.95 (*0-312-09264-4*, Pub. by Thomas Dunne Bks) St Martin.

Peel, Derek. Pride of Potters. 3.75 (*0-8315-0049-2*) Speller.

Peel, Don. The Phoenix Solutions. 256p. 1990. per. write for info. (*0-8187-0131-5*) Harlo Press.

***Peel, Doris.** Journey to a New Day. Peel, Robert, ed. & pref. by. LC 92-73476. (Illus.). 144p. 1992. 22.95x (*1-885934-00-9*) Andover Green.

Peel, Dorothy. The Eat-Less-Meat Book. 220p. 1973. 250.00 (*0-87968-071-7*) Gordon Pr.

Peel, Edmund, ed. The Painter: Joaquin Sorolla y Bastida. (Illus.). 264p. 1989. 75.00 (*0-85667-351-X*, Pub. by P Wilson Pubs) Sothebys Pubns.

Peel, Edward. Cream School from Sixteen Forty-Five. (C). 1988. 40.00 (*0-904110-02-8*, Pub. by Thornhill Pr UK) St Mut.

Peel, Fred W., et al. Consolidated Tax Returns: A Treatise on the Law of Consolidated Federal Income Tax Returns, 2 vols., Set. 3rd ed. LC 84-23688. 1990. 245.00 (*0-317-14545-2*) Clark Boardman Callaghan.

***Peel, J. D.** Aladura: A Religious Movement. (Classics in African Anthropology Ser.). (C). 1995. text ed. 58.00 (*3-89473-688-7*); pap. text ed. 25.50 (*3-89473-877-4*) Westview.

— Herbert Spencer. (Modern Revivals in Sociology Ser.). 352p. 1993. 59.95 (*0-7512-0094-8*, Pub. by Gregg Pub UK) Ashgate Pub Co.

— Ijeshas & Nigerians: The Incorporation of a Yoruba Kingdom, 1890s -1970s. LC 83-23660. (African Studies: No. 39). 346p. 1983. 79.95 (*0-521-22545-0*) Cambridge U Pr.

Peel, John. Alien Prey. (Shockers Ser.). (Illus.). 144p. (J). (gr. 3-7). 1993. pap. 3.50 (*0-448-40529-6*, G&D) Putnam Pub Group.

— Blood Wolf. (Shockers Ser.). (Illus.). 144p. (J). (gr. 3-7). 1993. pap. 2.95 (*0-448-40527-X*, G&D) Putnam Pub Group.

— Bond: Live & Let Die. Schuster, Hal, ed. (Files Ser.). 60p. pap. 6.95 (*1-55698-003-5*) Movie Pubs Servs.

— Carmen Sandiego: Golden Mini Play Lights. (J). (gr. 4-7). 1993. 14.95 (*0-307-75403-0*, Golden Bks) Western Pub.

— Dead End. (Shockers Ser.). (Illus.). 160p. (J). (gr. 5-9). 1994. pap. 3.50 (*0-448-40530-X*, G&D) Putnam Pub Group.

— Dinotek: Golden Mini Play Lights. (J). (ps-3). 1993. 14.95 (*0-307-75402-2*, Golden Bks) Western Pub.

— Dr. Who: Season 3, Pt. 1. Schuster, Hal, ed. (Files Ser.). 60p. pap. 5.95 (*1-55698-001-9*) Movie Pubs Servs.

— Dr. Who: Season 3, Pt. 2. Schuster, Hal, ed. (Files Ser.). 60p. pap. 5.95 (*1-55698-002-7*) Movie Pubs Servs.

— Evolution. (Dr. Who Ser.). (Illus.). Date not set. pap. 5.95 (*0-426-20422-0*, London Bridge) Genl Dist Srvs.

— Foul Play: Simon Says. (High Flyer Ser.: No. 4). 144p. (J). (gr. 3-7). 1993. pap. 2.99 (*0-14-036055-7*, Puffin) Puffin Bks.

— Ghost Lake. (Shockers Ser.). (Illus.). 160p. (J). (gr. 5-9). 1994. pap. 3.50 (*0-448-40545-8*, G&D) Putnam Pub Group.

— Grave Doubts. (Shockers Ser.). (Illus.). 144p. (J). (gr. 3-7). 1993. pap. 2.95 (*0-448-40528-8*, G&D) Putnam Pub Group.

— Gunsmoke Years. 1989. pap. 14.95 (*1-55698-221-6*, Pioneer Bks) Movie Pubs Servs.

— Hangman. LC 92-19940. (High Flyer Ser.). 128p. (J). (gr. 3-7). 1992. pap. 2.99 (*0-14-036052-2*) Puffin Bks.

— Here There Be Dragons. Ryan, Kevin, ed. (Star Trek: The Next Generation Ser.: No. 28). 288p. (Orig.). 1993. mass mkt. 5.99 (*0-671-86571-4*) PB.

— Hide & Seek. LC 92-3757. (Foul Play Ser.). 128p. (J). (gr. 3-7). 1993. pap. 2.99 (*0-14-036054-9*) Puffin Bks.

— Making Four Track Music. (Illus.). 114p. (Orig.). pap. 12.95 (*0-933224-51-6*, Pub. by Track Record UK) Bold Strummer Ltd.

— Maniac. (YA). (gr. 7 up). 1995. pap. 3.50 (*0-671-88735-1*, Archway) PB.

— New Trek Encyclopedia. 2nd ed. 1992. pap. 19.95 (*1-55698-350-6*) Movie Pubs Servs.

— Night Wings. (Shockers Ser.). (Illus.). 144p. (J). (gr. 3-7). 1993. pap. 2.95 (*0-448-40526-1*, G&D) Putnam Pub Group.

— Outer Limits: Nightmare. Schuster, Hal, ed. (Files Ser.). 60p. pap. 5.95 (*1-55698-008-6*) Movie Pubs Servs.

— Poison. MacDonald, Pat, ed. 256p. (Orig.). (J). 1994. pap. 3.50 (*0-671-88736-X*, Archway) PB.

— Prisoner, Pt. 2. Schuster, Hal, ed. (Files Ser.). 60p. pap. 5.95 (*1-55698-004-3*) Movie Pubs Servs.

— Prisoners of Peace. Clancy, Lisa, ed. (Star Trek: Deep Space Nine Ser.: No. 3). 128p. (Orig.). (J). 1994. mass mkt. 3.99 (*0-671-88288-0*, Minstrel Bks) PB.

— Shattered. 224p. (Orig.). (J). (gr. 7 up). 1993. pap. 3.50 (*0-671-79406-X*, Archway) PB.

— Tag: You're Dead! LC 92-19939. (High Flyer Ser.). 128p. (J). (gr. 3-7). 1992. pap. 2.99 (*0-14-036053-0*) Puffin Bks.

— The Tale of the Restless House. (Are You Afraid of the Dark Ser.). (J). (gr. 3-6). 1995. mass mkt. 3.99 (*0-671-52547-6*, Minstrel Bks) PB.

— The Tale of the Sinister Statues. Clancy, Lisa, ed. (Are You Afraid of the Dark Ser.). 128p. (Orig.). (J). 1995. mass mkt. 3.99 (*0-671-52545-X*, Minstrel Bks) PB.

— Talons. 224p. (Orig.). (YA). 1993. pap. 3.50 (*0-671-79405-1*, Archway) PB.

— Uptime Downtime. LC 90-27570. (J). 1992. pap. 14.00 (*0-671-73274-9*, S&S Bks Young Read) S&S Childrens.

— Where in America Is Carmen Sandiego? (Golden Favorites Ser.). (Illus.). 32p. (J). (gr. 2-5). 1992. write for info. (*0-307-15859-4*, 15859) Western Pub.

— Where in America's Past Is Carmen Sandiego? (Carmen Sandiego Ser.). (Illus.). 96p. (J). (gr. 3-7). 1992. pap. 2.95 (*0-307-22205-5*, 22205, Golden Pr) Western Pub.

— Where in Space Is Carmen Sandiego? (You Are the Detective Ser.). (J). (gr. 4-7). 1993. pap. 3.25 (*0-307-22207-1*, Golden Pr) Western Pub.

— Where in Space Is Carmen Sandiego? A Mark & See Book with Marker. (J). (gr. 4-7). 1993. pap. 3.95 (*0-307-22305-1*, Golden Pr) Western Pub.

— Where in the U. S. A. Is Carmen Dandiego?, Pt. II. (You Are the Detective Ser.). 96p. (J). 1994. write for info. (*0-307-22208-X*, Golden Bks) Western Pub.

— Where in the U. S. A. Is Carmen Sandiego? (J). (gr. 4-7). 1991. pap. 3.95 (*0-307-22304-3*, Golden Pr) Western Pub.

— Where in the World Is Carmen San Diego? 48p. (J). (gr. 4-7). 1991. pap. 3.95 (*0-307-22301-9*, 22301) Western Pub.

— Where in Time Is Carmen San Diego? 48p. (J). (gr. 4-7). 1991. pap. 3.95 (*0-307-22302-7*, 22302) Western Pub.

— Where in Time Is Carmen Sandiego!, Pt. II. (You Are the Detective Ser.). (Illus.). 96p. (J). (gr. 3-7). 1993. pap. 3.25 (*0-307-22206-3*, 22206-00, Golden Pr) Western Pub.

Peel, John & Nation, Terry. The Official Doctor Who & the Daleks Book: The Complete Story of the Time Lord's Greatest Foes. (Illus.). 240p. 1989. pap. 12.95 (*0-312-02264-6*) St Martin.

Peel, John & Rogers, Dave. The Avengers: Too Many Targets. 192p. (Orig.). 1990. pap. 8.95 (*0-312-05003-8*) St Martin.

Peel, Judie B. Three Hundred Sixty-Five Ways to Make Any Occasion Special. LC 94-5580. 1994. 5.99 (*0-8499-3585-7*) Word Pub.

Peel, Kathy. Do Plastic Surgeons Take VISA? 192p. 1992. pap. 9.99 (*0-8499-3348-X*) Word Inc.

— Making Someone's Day; Quick-Me-Ups: 365 Ways to Show You Care. 1994. 5.99 (*0-8499-3574-1*) Word Inc.

— Stomach Virus & Other Forms of Family Bonding. 1993. pap. 9.99 (*0-8499-3475-3*) Word Inc.

— Streamlining Your Life; Quick-Me-Ups: A Year's Worth of Tips You Read in Seconds & Apply in Minutes. 1994. 5.99 (*0-8499-3573-3*) Word Inc.

Peel, Kathy & Byrd, Judie. A Mother's Manual for Holiday Survival. (Orig.). 1991. pap. 9.99 (*1-56179-040-0*) Focus Family.

Peel, Kathy & Mahaffey, Joy. A Mother's Manual for Schoolday Survival. (Illus.). 92p. (Orig.). 1990. pap. 9.99 (*0-929608-88-7*) Focus Family.

— A Mother's Manual for Summer Survival. LC 89-1348. (Illus.). 72p. 1989. reprint ed. pap. 9.99 (*0-929608-31-3*) Focus Family.

Peel, Kathy, jt. auth. see Peel, William C.

Peel, L. & Tribe, D. E. Domestication, Conservation & Use of the Animal Resources. (World Animal Science Ser.: Vol. 1A). 358p. 1983. 120.50 (*0-444-42068-1*) Elsevier.

Peel, L. J., jt. ed. see Guohua, Xu.

Peel, Lee S. Farmington: A Pictorial History. 2nd rev. ed. (Illus.). 256p. 1993. 45.00 (*0-9626618-1-3*) L S Peel.

— Speak Easy - Read Write. (Illus.). 128p. (Orig.). 1988. 7.95 (*0-9626618-0-5*); pap. 4.77 (*0-685-41319-5*) L S Peel.

Peel, Lynnette J. Rural Industry in the Port Phillip Region: 1835-1880. (Illus.). xiv, 196p. 1974. 29.95 (*0-522-84064-7*) Intl Spec Bk.

Peel, Malcolm. Improving Your Communications Skills. 160p. 1990. text ed. 51.00 (*0-8464-1388-4*); pap. text ed. 23.95 (*0-8464-1389-2*) Beekman Pubs.

— Introduction to Management: A Guide to Better Business Performance. (Institute of Management Ser.). 192p. (Orig.). 1993. pap. 45.00x (*0-273-03892-3*, Pub. by Pitman Pubng UK) St Mut.

Peel, Margaret M., jt. auth. see Gardner, Joan F.

Peel, Mark & Silverton, Nancy. Mark Peel & Nancy Silverton at Home: Two Chefs Cook for Family & Friends. 352p. 1994. 24.95 (*0-446-51736-4*) Warner Bks.

Peel, Michael. How to Catch More Fish Everytime: Your Success Guide to the Great Lakes & the Tributaries. 216p. 1994. pap. 12.95 (*0-9640301-0-1*) Global Publishing.

Peel, Michael J. The Liquidation-Merger Alternative. (Illus.). 204p. 1990. text ed. 68.95 (*0-566-05744-1*, Pub. by Avebury Pub UK) Ashgate Pub Co.

Peel, Peter. British Public Opinion & the Wars of German Unification, 1864-71. LC 81-484. 1984. lib. bdg. 79.95 (*0-87700-585-0*) Revisionist Pr.

Peel, R. Christian Science: Its Encounter with American Culture. 1986. pap. 9.95 (*0-933062-24-9*) R H Sommer.

Peel, Robert. Health & Medicine in the Christian Science Tradition. (Health & Medicine in Faith Tradition Ser.). 160p. 1988. 18.95x (*0-8245-0895-5*) Crossroad NY.

— Mary Baker Eddy, Vol. 1: The Years of Discovery. LC 66-14855. (Illus.). 370p. 1966. 24.95 (*0-87510-085-6*) Christian Sci.

— Mary Baker Eddy, Vol. 2: The Years of Trial. LC 77-94951. (Illus.). 391p. 1971. 24.95 (*0-87510-118-6*) Christian Sci.

— Mary Baker Eddy, Vol. 3: The Years of Authority. LC 66-14855. (Illus.). 528p. 1977. 24.95 (*0-87510-142-9*) Christian Sci.

Peel, Robert, ed. see Peel, Doris.

Peel, Robert L., jt. auth. see Barnes, Leon.

Peel, Robin & Bell, Mary. The Primary Language Leader's Book: A Handbook for English Curriculum Leaders at Key Stages 1 & 2. 160p. 1994. pap. 27.50 (*1-85346-249-7*, Pub. by D Fulton UK) Taylor & Francis.

***Peel, Rosemary J.** Astrology & Heredity: The Thread of Life. (Illus.). 128p. 1995. pap. 9.95 (*0-7137-2477-3*, Pub. by Blandford Pr UK) Sterling.

Peel, Roy V. The Campaign, 1932: An Analysis. (History - United States Ser.). 242p. 1993. reprint ed. lib. bdg. 79.00 (*0-7812-4926-0*) Rprt Serv.

Peel, Roy V. & Donnelly, Thomas C. The Nineteen Thirty-Two Campaign: An Analysis. LC 73-454. (FDR & the Era of the New Deal Ser.). 252p. 1973. reprint ed. lib. bdg. 29.50 (*0-306-70567-2*) Da Capo.

— The Nineteen Twenty-Eight Campaign: An Analysis. LC 73-19170. (Politics & People Ser.). (Illus.). 196p. 1974. reprint ed. 17.95 (*0-405-05892-6*) Ayer.

— The Nineteen Twenty-Eight Campaign: An Analysis. LC 74-12758. (Illus.). 183p. 1975. reprint ed. text ed. 35.00 (*0-8371-7749-9*, PENC, Greenwood Pr) Greenwood.

Peel, S. Granulated Metrial Gland Cells. (Advances in Anatomy, Embryology & Cell Biology Ser.). (Illus.). 120p. 1989. pap. 81.00 (*0-387-50390-0*) Spr-Verlag.

Peel, Stanton & Brodsky, Archie. Love & Addiction. 1976. pap. 4.99 (*0-451-15538-6*) NAL-Dutton.

Peel, V. A. Somaliland. 368p. 1986. 250.00 (*1-85077-086-7*, Darf Pubs Ltd) St Mut.

Peel, Vic, jt. ed. see Sheaff, W. R.

Peel, Victoria, et al. A History of Hawthorn. (Illus.). 320p. 1993. text ed. 49.95 (*0-522-84507-X*) Intl Spec Bk.

Peel, William C. Living in the Lions' Den Without Being Eaten. LC 94-11890. 252p. (Orig.). 1994. pap. 10.00 (*0-89109-794-5*) NavPress.

***Peel, William C. & Peel, Kathy.** Where Is Moses When We Need Him? Teaching Your Kids the Ten Values That Matter Most. LC 95-3390. 1995. write for info. (*0-8054-6180-9*); pap. write for info. (*0-8054-6181-7*) Broadman.

Peel, William J., jt. auth. see Dwight, John A.

Peelaert, Guy & Cohn, Nik. Rock Dreams. LC 73-7289. (Illus.). 176p. 1982. 19.95 (*0-394-52870-0*) Knopf.

Peele, A. C. Town & Country Casuals: An Accounting Clerk Practice Set. 1985. 11.55 (*0-07-049197-6*) McGraw.

Peele, George. The Chronicle of King Edward the First, Surnamed Longshanks: With the Life of Lluellen, Rebel in Wales. LC 74-79524. (Illus.). xliii, 96p. 1974. pap. 5.95 (*0-9601000-1-6*) Longshanks Bk.

— The Old Wives' Tale. 176p. 1980. 20.00 (*0-8018-2410-9*) Johns Hopkins.

— Samples from the Love of King David & Fair Bethsabe: With Reference Portions of the Bible. LC 79-56834. 71p. (Orig.). 1980. pap. 4.95 (*0-9601000-2-4*) Longshanks Bk.

Peele, Gillian. Revival & Reaction: The Right in Contemporary America. 280p. 1985. pap. 22.00 (*0-19-821132-5*) OUP.

Peele, Gillian, jt. auth. see Beloff, Max.

Peele, Gillian, ed. see Paterson, William E. & Southern, David.

Peele, Gillian, et al, eds. Developments in American Politics. LC 91-44872. 416p. 1992. text ed. 49.95 (*0-312-07610-X*); pap. text ed. 18.95 (*0-312-07609-6*) St Martin.

— Developments in American Politics 2. 2nd ed. LC 95-6667. 432p. (C). 1995. pap. text ed. 19.95x (*1-56643-023-2*) Chatham Hse Pubs.

Peele, Howard A. APL: An Introduction. 512p. (C). 1986. pap. text ed. 38.75 (*0-03-004953-9*) SCP.

***Peele, Stanton.** Diseasing of America: How We Allowed Recovery Zealots & the Treatment Industry to Convince Us We Are out of Control. LC 95-6377. 1995. pap. 12.00 (*0-02-874014-9*) Free Pr.

— The Meaning of Addiction: Compulsive Experience & Its Interpretations. LC 79-4750. 224p. 1986. pap. 19.95 (*0-669-13835-5*) Free Pr.

Peele, Stanton, ed. Visions of Addiction: Major Contemporary Perspectives on Addiction & Alcoholism. LC 86-45054. 272p. 1987. text ed. 35.00 (*0-669-13092-3*) Free Pr.

Peele, Stanton & Brodsky, Archie. Love & Addiction. 1987. pap. 4.50 (*0-451-14860-6*, Sig) NAL-Dutton.

— Love & Addiction. LC 74-5818. 284p. 1975. 16.95 (*0-8008-5041-6*) Taplinger.

Peele, Stanton, et al. The Truth about Addiction & Recovery. 432p. 1992. pap. 12.00 (*0-671-75530-7*, Fireside) S&S Trade.

Peelen, Julie, ed. see Capes, Richard.

Peeler, Alexandra. Parish Social Ministry: A Vision & Resource. 194p. 1986. 14.95 (*0-318-20492-4*) Catholic Charities.

Peeler, David P. Hope among Us Yet: Social Criticism & Social Solace in Depression America. LC 86-16016. (Illus.). 352p. 1987. 35.00 (*0-8203-0902-8*) U of Ga Pr.

Peeler, E. F., tr. see Gurian, Waldemar.

***Peeler, J. Yorke, Jr.** Talking with Your Child about the Presence of God. (Growing Together Ser.). 32p. (Orig.). 1995. pap. text ed. 1.95 (*0-8298-0995-3*) Pilgrim OH.

Peeler, John A. Latin American Democracies: Colombia, Costa Rica, Venezuela. LC 84-13209. xiii, 193p. (C). 1985. pap. 11.95 (*0-8078-4153-6*) U of NC Pr.

***Peelman, Achiel.** Christ Is a Native American. 285p. (Orig.). 1995. pap. 19.95 (*1-57075-047-5*) Orbis Bks.

***Peelo, Maira T.** Helping Students with Study Problems. LC 94-27677. 160p. 1994. 79.00x (*0-335-19308-0*, Open Univ Pr); pap. text ed. 24.95x (*0-335-19307-2*, Open Univ Pr) Taylor & Francis.

***Peels, Hendrik G.** The Vengeance of God: The Meaning of the Root NQM & the Function of the NQM-Texts in the Context of Divine Revelation in the Old Testament. LC 94-35317. (Oudtestamentische Studien: Vol. 31). 640p. 1994. 77.25 (*90-04-10164-0*) E J Brill.

Peeper, Ima, jt. auth. see Klitz, Seymore.

***Peeperkorn, David, ed.** Limitation of Free Bargaining & Sanctity of Contracts with Performing Artists & Composers. 122p. 1987. pap. 76.00 (*90-6215-169-8*, Pub. by Maklu Uitgevers BE) W W Gaunt.

— Merchandising & Sponsorship in the Music Business. 120p. 1986. pap. 76.00 (*90-6215-167-1*, Pub. by Maklu Uitgevers BE) W W Gaunt.

***Peeperkorn, David & Van Rij, Cees, eds.** Collecting Societies in the Music Business. 160p. 1989. pap. 95.00 (*90-6215-228-7*, Pub. by Maklu Uitgevers BE) W W Gaunt.

— Music & the New Technologies. 216p. 1988. pap. 95.00 (*90-6215-194-9*) W W Gaunt.

Peeples, Edwin A. Hole in the Hill. LC 77-82913. 1969. 6.50 (*0-9600080-2-0*) Peeples.

— Planting an Inheritance: Life on a Pennsylvania Farm. 224p. 1994. 19.95 (*0-8117-1206-0*) Stackpole.

— Professional Storywriter's Handbook. LC 60-6901. 1960. 8.50 (*0-9600080-0-4*) Peeples.

Peeples, Mary G. All We Like Sheep. 104p. 1989. write for info. (*0-9634836-0-9*) Sheep Shoppe.

Peeples, Mary G. & Peeples, Sam L., Jr. Parenting, an Heir Raising Experience: Raising Your Child with Confidence. Lee, Betsy, ed. (Illus.). 190p. 1993. write for info. (*0-9634836-1-7*) Sheep Shoppe.

Peeples, Sam L., Jr., jt. auth. see Peeples, Mary G.

Peeples, Samuel. The Man Who Died Twice. 252p. 1984. pap. 6.00 (*0-89733-121-4*) Academy Chi Pubs.

Peeples, Susan L., jt. auth. see Seabury, Debra L.

Peer. The Impossible Friendship. Date not set. 17.95 (*0-915361-95-7*) Modan-Adama Bks.

PEER Consultants & CalRecovery, Inc. Staff. Material Recovery Facility Design Manual. 1993. 59.95 (*0-87371-944-1*, TD794) CRC Pr.

Peer, George, jt. auth. see Gershgoren, Sid.

Peer, Larry H. The Romantic Manifesto: An Anthology. (American University Studies: Comparative Literature: Ser. III, Vol. 23). 156p. (C). 1988. text ed. 36.50 (*0-318-37856-6*) P Lang Pubs.

Peer, Larry H., jt. auth. see Matteo, Sante.

Pe'er, M. The Story of Maran BetYosef: R'Yosef Karo - Author of the Shulman Aruch. (ArtScroll Youth Ser.). (Illus.). 96p. 1986. 11.95 (*0-89906-400-0*) Mesorah Pubns.

Peer, Sheila, ed. see Bloomfield, Dick.

Peeradina, Saleem. Group Portrait. (India Paperbacks Ser.). 74p. 1992. pap. 4.95 (*0-19-562868-3*) OUP.

Peerenboom, R. P. Law & Morality in Ancient China: The Silk Manuscripts of Huang-Lao. (SUNY Series in Chinese Philosophy & Culture). 380p. 1993. 59.50 (*0-7914-1237-7*); pap. 19.95 (*0-7914-1238-5*) State U NY Pr.

Peerless Engineering Service Staff. C Language Scientific Subroutine Library Version 2.0. 428p. 1988. text ed. 685.00 (*0-471-61233-2*) Wiley.

Peerless Engineering Services Staff. FORTRAN Scientific Subroutine Library: Version 2.0. 414p. 1989. pap. text ed. 575.00 (*0-471-51499-3*); 35.00 (*0-471-52098-5*) Wiley.

Peerman, Dean G., jt. ed. see Marty, Martin E.

Peers, Allison, tr. see Lull, Ramon, pseud.

Peers, C. J. Ancient Chinese Armies, 1500 BC-200 BC. (Men-at-Arms Ser.: No. 218). (Illus.). 48p. 1990. pap. 11.95 (*0-85045-942-7*, 9175, Pub. by Osprey Pubng Ltd UK) Stackpole.

***Peers, Chris J.** Imperial Chinese Armies 100 BC-AD 589. (Men-at-Arms Ser.). (Illus.). 48p. 1995. pap. 12.95 (*1-85532-514-4*, Pub. by Osprey UK) Stackpole.

— Medieval Chinese Armies 1260-1520. (Men-at-Arms Ser.: No. 251). (Illus.). 48p. pap. 11.95 (*1-85532-254-4*, 9222, Pub. by Osprey UK) Stackpole.

Peers, Don. Haynes Stromberg CD Carburetors through 1976, No. 300. (Illus.). 76p. pap. 16.95 (*1-85010-019-5*) Haynes Pubns.

— Haynes SU Carburetors Thru 1988, No. 299. (Illus.). 88p. pap. 16.95 (*1-85010-589-8*) Haynes Pubns.

Peers, E. A. Studies of the Spanish Mystics, 3 vols. 1977. lib. bdg. 300.00 (*0-8490-2706-3*) Gordon Pr.

Peers, E. A., ed. From Cadalso to Ruben Dario. LC 75-41176. reprint ed. 32.50 (*0-404-15031-4*) AMS Pr.

Peers, E. Alison. The Life of Teresa of Jesus. 1991. pap. 12.00 (*0-385-01109-1*, Image Bks) Doubleday.

Peers, E. Allison. The Mystics of Spain. 1977. lib. bdg. 59.95 (*0-8490-2322-X*) Gordon Pr.

— St. John of the Cross & Other Lectures & Addresses. 1977. lib. bdg. 250.00 (*0-8490-2558-3*) Gordon Pr.

Peers, E. Allison, ed. & tr. Ascent of Mount Carmel: A Classic of Mystical Literature St. John of the Cross. LC 90-47993. 386p. 1991. reprint ed. pap. 9.95 (*0-89243-491-0*, Triumph Books) Liguori Pubns.

Peers, E. Allison, ed. A Critical Anthology of Spanish Verse, 2 vols., Set. 1973. lib. bdg. 250.00 (*0-8490-1685-1*) Gordon Pr.

— Liverpool Studies in Spanish Literature, 4 vols. reprint ed. 200.00 (*0-404-15030-6*) AMS Pr.

Peers, E. Allison, ed. & tr. Living Flame of Love: St. John of the Cross. LC 90-47994. 226p. 1991. reprint ed. pap. 9.95 (*0-89243-503-8*, Triumph Books) Liguori Pubns.

Peers, E. Allison, tr. Blanquerna: A Thirteenth Century Romance Translated from the Catalan. 1977. lib. bdg. 59.95 (*0-8490-1515-4*) Gordon Pr.

Peers, Edgar A. Behind That Wall. LC 72-90672. (Essay Index Reprint Ser.). 1977. 18.95 (*0-8369-1210-1*) Ayer.

— Catalonia Infelix. LC 77-109819. 326p. 1970. reprint ed. text ed. 35.00 (*0-8371-4310-1*, PECI, Greenwood Pr) Greenwood.

— The Church in Spain, Seventeen Thirty-Seven to Nineteen Thirty-Seven. 1980. lib. bdg. 44.95 (*0-8490-3149-4*) Gordon Pr.

— A Handbook to the Study & Teaching of Spanish. 1980. lib. bdg. 69.95 (*0-8490-3105-2*) Gordon Pr.

— Ramon Lull: A Biography. 1980. lib. bdg. 75.00 (*0-8490-3186-9*) Gordon Pr.

— A Short History of the Romantic Movement in Spain. LC 76-28478. reprint ed. 32.50 (*0-404-15034-9*) AMS Pr.

P Q

An Asterisk (*) at the beginning of an entry indicates that the title is appearing in BIP for the first time.

— Spanish Golden Age Poetry & Drama. LC 76-28691. reprint ed. 32.50 (0-404-15032-2) AMS Pr.
— The Spanish Tragedy, Nineteen Thirty to Nineteen Thirty-Six. LC 75-8724. 247p. 1975. reprint ed. text ed. 35.00 (0-8371-8048-1, PEST, Greenwood Pr) Greenwood.
— St. John of the Cross, & Other Lectures & Addresses, 1920-1945. LC 70-136650. (Biography Index Reprint Ser.). 1977. 18.95 (0-8369-8045-X) Ayer.
Peers, Edgar A., ed. Cassell's Spanish Dictionary: Spanish-English, English-Spanish. LC 77-7403. 464p. (ENG & SPA.). 1977. text ed. 13.00 (0-02-522660-6) Macmillan.
— Cassell's Spanish Dictionary: Spanish-English, English-Spanish. LC 77-7403. 1136p. (ENG & SPA.). 1978. text ed. 22.95 (0-02-522910-9); text ed. 19.95 (0-02-522900-1) Macmillan.
— Critical Anthology of Spanish Verse. LC 69-10145. 1741p. 1969. reprint ed. text ed. 45.50 (0-8371-0190-5, PESV, Greenwood Pr) Greenwood.
Peers, Edgar Allison, ed. Spanish Golden Age in Poetry & Drama. LC 74-5001. 220p. 1974. reprint ed. 50.00 (0-87753-060-2) Phaeton.
Peers, Frank W. The Politics of Canadian Broadcasting, 1920-1951. LC 78-430275. 474p. reprint ed. pap. 135.10 (0-317-55707-6, 2029342) Bks Demand.
— The Public Eye: Television & the Politics of Canadian Broadcasting, 1952-68. LC 79-311230. 475p. reprint ed. pap. 135.40 (0-8357-6400-1, 2035758) Bks Demand.
***Peers, Laura.** The Ojibwa of Western Canada, 1780 to 1870. LC 94-31544. (Manitoba Studies in Native History: 7). (Illus.). 288p. 1994. 32.95 (0-87351-310-X) Minn Hist.
— The Ojibwa of Western Canada, 1780 to 1870. LC 94-31544. (Manitoba Studies in Native History: Vol. 7). (Illus.). 288p. 1994. pap. 15.95 (0-87351-311-8) Minn Hist.
Peers, Robert. Adult Education - A Comparative Study. (C). 1972. 45.00 (0-7100-7410-7, Pub. by Univ Nottingham UK) St Mut.
Peers, Tom. Fit Function & Flourish. 78p. 1987. pap. 3.50 (0-88144-077-9) Christian Pub.
Peery, David J. & Azar, J. J. Aircraft Structures. 2nd ed. 1982. text ed. write for info. (0-07-049196-8) McGraw.
Peery, Harry E. & Singer, Margaret A. Basic Microbiology Study Guide. 288p. 1986. pap. text ed. write for info. (0-02-304410-1) Macmillan.
Peery, J. C., et al, eds. Music & Child Development. (Illus.). 315p. 1987. 59.00 (0-387-96422-3) Spr-Verlag.
Peery, Janet. Alligator Dance. LC 93-18694. (Southwest Life & Letters Ser.). 224p. (Orig.). 1993. 22.50 (0-87074-353-8); pap. 10.95 (0-87074-366-X) SMU Press.
Peery, Meira, jt. auth. see Winter, Magda.
***Peery, Nelson.** Black Fire: The Making of a Revolutionary. 352p. 1995. pap. 11.95 (1-56584-159-X) New Press NY.
— Black Fire: The Making of an American Revolutionary. 352p. 1994. 22.95 (1-56584-158-1) New Press NY.
— The Negro National Colonial Question. 1975. pap. text ed. 3.95 (0-917348-00-1) Workers Pr.
Peery, Susan M. The Wellesley Cookie Exchange Cookbook. (Illus.). 256p. 1988. pap. 11.00 (0-671-66588-X, Fireside) S&S Trade.
Pees, Samuel T., ed. History of the Petroleum Industry Symposium: Guidebook (Titusville) (Illus.). 84p. (Orig.). 1989. pap. 15.00 (0-89181-813-8) AAPG.
Peesch, R. Ornament in European Folk Art. (Illus.). 210p. (C). 1982. text ed. 303.00 (0-685-40316-5, Pub. by Collets) St Mut.
— Ornament in European Folk Art. (Illus.). 210p. (C). 1988. 300.00 (0-569-19823-2, Pub. by Collets) St Mut.
Peet, Bill. The Ant & the Elephant. LC 74-179918. (Illus.). 48p. (J). (gr. k-3). 1980. 14.95 (0-395-16963-1); pap. 5.95 (0-395-29205-0) HM.
— Big Bad Bruce. LC 76-62502. (Illus.). (J). (gr. k-3). 1977. 14.95 (0-395-25150-8) HM.
— Big Bad Bruce. LC 76-62502. (Illus.). (J). (gr. k-3). 1982. pap. 5.95 (0-395-32922-1) HM.
— Big Bad Bruce. (Book & Cassette Favorites Ser.). (J). (gr. 3 up). 1987. Incl. cass. pap. 8.95 (0-395-45741-6) HM.
— Bill Peet: An Autobiography. (Illus.). (J). (gr. 3 up). 1989. 17.95 (0-395-50932-7) HM.
— Bill Peet: An Autobiography. (J). (gr. 4-7). 1994. pap. 9.95 (0-395-68982-1) HM.
— Buford, the Little Bighorn. (Illus.). 48p. (J). (gr. k-3). 1975. 13.95 (0-395-20337-6) HM.
— Buford, the Little Bighorn. (Illus.). 48p. (J). (gr. k-3). 1983. pap. 5.95 (0-395-34067-5) HM.
— The Caboose Who Got Loose. LC 79-155554. (Illus.). 48p. (J). (gr. k-3). 1980. 14.95 (0-395-14805-7); pap. 5.95 (0-395-28715-4) HM.
— Capyboppy. (Illus.). 62p. (J). (gr. 2-4). 1976. 13.95 (0-395-24378-5) HM.
— Capyboppy. (Illus.). 62p. (J). (gr. 2-4). 1985. pap. 5.95 (0-395-38368-4) HM.
— Chester the Worldly Pig. (Illus.). (J). (gr. k-3). 1978. pap. 5.95 (0-395-27271-8) HM.
— Chester the Worldly Pig. (Illus.). 48p. (J). (gr. k-3). 1980. 13.95 (0-395-18470-3) HM.
— Cock-a-Doodle Dudley. (Illus.). 48p. (J). (gr. k-3). 1990. 14.95 (0-395-55331-8) HM.
— Cock-a-Doodle Dudley. (Illus.). 48p. (J). (gr. k-3). 1993. pap. 4.95 (0-395-65745-8) HM.
— Countdown to Christmas. LC 72-78394. (Illus.). 48p. (J). (gr. k-8). 1972. lib. bdg. 12.00 (0-516-08716-9, Golden Gate) Childrens.
— Cowardly Clyde. (Illus.). 48p. (J). (gr. k-3). 1979. 14.95 (0-395-27802-3) HM.
— Cowardly Clyde. (Illus.). 48p. (J). (gr. k-3). 1984. pap. 5.95 (0-395-36171-0) HM.
— Cyrus the Unsinkable Sea Serpent. LC 74-20646. (Illus.). 48p. (J). (gr. k-3). 1975. 14.95 (0-395-20272-8) HM.
— Cyrus the Unsinkable Sea Serpent. LC 74-20646. (Illus.). 48p. (J). (gr. k-3). 1982. pap. 5.95 (0-395-31389-9) HM.
— Eli. LC 77-17500. (Illus.). 48p. (J). (gr. k-3). 1978. 14.95 (0-395-26454-5) HM.
— Eli. LC 77-17500. (Illus.). 48p. (J). (gr. k-3). 1984. pap. 5.95 (0-395-36611-9) HM.
— Ella. (Illus.). 48p. (J). (gr. k-3). 1964. 13.95 (0-395-17577-1) HM.
— Ella. (Illus.). 48p. (J). (gr. k-3). 1978. pap. 5.95 (0-395-27269-6) HM.
— Encore for Eleanor. (Illus.). 48p. (J). (gr. k-3). 1981. 13.95 (0-395-29860-1); pap. 3.95 (0-317-18520-9) HM.
— Encore for Eleanor Pa. (J). (ps-3). 1985. pap. 5.95 (0-395-38367-6) HM.
— Farewell to Shady Glade. (Illus.). 48p. (J). (gr. k-3). 1981. 14.95 (0-395-18975-6) HM.
— Farewell to Shady Glade. (Illus.). 48p. (J). (gr. k-3). 1991. audio, pap. 7.95 (0-395-60166-5) HM.
— Fly Homer Fly. (Illus.). (J). (gr. k-3). 1976. 14.95 (0-395-24536-2) HM.
— Fly Homer Fly. (Illus.). (J). (gr. k-3). 1979. pap. 5.95 (0-395-28005-2) HM.
— The Gnats of Knotty Pine. LC 75-17024. (Illus.). 48p. (J). (gr. k-3). 1975. 13.95 (0-395-21405-X) HM.
— The Gnats of Knotty Pine. LC 75-17024. (Illus.). 48p. (J). (gr. k-3). 1984. pap. 4.95 (0-395-36612-7) HM.
— How Droofus the Dragon Lost His Head. LC 75-135136. (Illus.). 48p. (J). (gr. k-3). 1983. 14.95 (0-395-15085-X); pap. 5.95 (0-395-34066-7) HM.
— Hubert's Hair-Raising Adventure. (Illus.). 36p. (J). (gr. k-3). 1959. 14.95 (0-395-15083-3) HM.
— Hubert's Hair-Raising Adventure. (Illus.). (J). (gr. k-3). 1979. pap. 5.95 (0-395-28267-5) HM.
— Huge Harold. (Illus.). 48p. (J). (gr. k-3). 1974. 14.95 (0-395-18449-5) HM.
— Huge Harold. (Illus.). (J). (gr. k-3). 1982. pap. 5.95 (0-395-32923-X) HM.
— Jennifer & Josephine. (Illus.). (J). (gr. k-3). 1973. 14.95 (0-395-18225-5) HM.
— Jennifer & Josephine. (Illus.). (J). (gr. k-3). 1980. pap. 5.95 (0-395-29608-0) HM.
— Jethro & Joel Were a Troll. LC 86-20879. (Illus.). 32p. (J). (gr. k-3). 1987. 13.95 (0-395-43081-X) HM.
— Jethro & Joel Were a Troll. LC 86-20879. (Illus.). 32p. (J). (gr. k-3). 1990. pap. 5.95 (0-395-53968-4) HM.
— Kermit the Hermit. (Illus.). (J). (gr. k-3). 1973. 14.95 (0-395-15084-1) HM.
— Kermit the Hermit. (Illus.). (J). (gr. k-3). 1980. pap. 5.95 (0-395-29607-2) HM.
— The Kweeks of Kookatumdee. LC 84-22379. (Illus.). 32p. (J). (gr. k-3). 1985. 13.95 (0-395-37902-4) HM.
— The Kweeks of Kookatumdee. (Illus.). 32p. (J). (gr. k-3). 1988. pap. 5.95 (0-395-48656-4, Sandpiper) HM.
— The Luckiest One of All. (Illus.). (J). (gr. k-3). 1982. 14.95 (0-395-31863-7) HM.
— The Luckiest One of All. (Illus.). (J). (gr. k-3). 1985. pap. 5.95 (0-395-39593-3) HM.
— Merle the High Flying Squirrel. LC 73-18371. (Illus.). 32p. (J). (gr. k-3). 1974. 14.95 (0-395-18452-5) HM.
— Merle the High Flying Squirrel. (Illus.). 30p. (J). (gr. k-3). 1983. reprint ed. pap. 5.95 (0-395-34923-0) HM.
— No Such Things. LC 82-23234. (Illus.). 32p. (J). (gr. k-3). 1983. 13.95 (0-395-33888-3) HM.
— No Such Things. LC 82-23234. (Illus.). 32p. (J). (gr. k-3). 1985. pap. 4.95 (0-395-39594-1) HM.
— Pamela Camel. LC 83-18594. (Illus.). 32p. (J). (gr. k-3). 1984. 14.95 (0-395-35975-9, 5-93025) HM.
— Pamela Camel. (Illus.). (J). (gr. 4-8). 1986. pap. 5.95 (0-395-41670-1, Sandpiper) HM.
— Pinkish, Purplish, Bluish Egg. (Illus.). (J). (gr. k-3). 1973. 13.95 (0-395-18472-X) HM.
— Pinkish, Purplish, Bluish Egg. (Illus.). (J). (gr. k-3). 1984. pap. 5.95 (0-395-36172-9) HM.
— Randy's Dandy Lions. (Illus.). (J). (gr. k-3). 1979. pap. 5.95 (0-395-27498-2) HM.
— Randy's Dandy Lions. (Illus.). (J). (gr. k-3). 1980. 14.95 (0-395-18507-6) HM.
— Smokey. (Illus.). (J). (gr. k-3). 1962. 14.95 (0-395-15992-X) HM.
— Smokey. (Illus.). 48p. (J). (gr. k-3). 1983. reprint ed. pap. 5.95 (0-395-34924-9) HM.
— The Spooky Tail of Prewitt Peacock. LC 72-7930. (Illus.). 32p. (J). (gr. k-3). 1973. 13.95 (0-395-15494-4) HM.
— The Spooky Tail of Prewitt Peacock. (Illus.). (J). (gr. k-3). 1979. pap. 5.95 (0-395-28159-8) HM.
— Whingdingdilly. LC 71-98521. (Illus.). (J). (gr. k-3). 1977. 14.95 (0-395-24729-2) HM.
— Whingdingdilly. LC 71-98521. (Illus.). (J). (gr. k-3). 1982. pap. 5.95 (0-395-31381-3) HM.
— Wump World. LC 72-124999. (Illus.). (J). (gr. 3-5). 1974. 14.95 (0-395-19841-0) HM.
— Wump World. LC 72-124999. (Illus.). (J). (gr. 3-5). 1981. pap. 5.95 (0-395-31129-2) HM.
— The Wump World. (Illus.). (J). 1991. 7.95 (0-395-58412-4) HM.
— Zella, Zack & Zodia. 1986. 14.95 (0-395-41069-X) HM.
— Zella, Zack & Zodiac. (J). (gr. k-3). 1985. 12.95 (0-317-40567-5) HM.
— Zella, Zack, & Zodiac. (Illus.). 32p. (J). (gr. k-3). 1989. pap. 5.95 (0-395-52207-2) HM.
Peet, Eric. Egypt & the Old Testament. 244p. 1990. pap. text ed. 16.00 (0-916157-83-0) African Islam Miss Pubns.
***Peet, H. John.** In the Beginning God Created... 1994. pap. 8.99 (0-85234-531-3, Pub. by Evangel Pr UK) Presby & Reformed.
Peet, Harvey P. Course of Instruction for the Deaf & Dumb. 1971. 69.95 (0-87968-952-8) Gordon Pr.
— Elementary Lessons: A Course of Instruction for the Deaf & Dumb. 1972. 59.95 (0-8490-0100-5) Gordon Pr.
— Notions of the Deaf & Dumb Before Instruction. 1973. 59.95 (0-8490-0740-2) Gordon Pr.
— Scripture Lessons for the Deaf & Dumb. 1972. 59.95 (0-8490-1007-1) Gordon Pr.
Peet, Henry, ed.
Peet, Isaac L. Language Lessons for Young Learners, Deaf Mutes & Foreigners in the English Language. 1972. 59.95 (0-8490-0486-1) Gordon Pr.
Peet, Jennifer B. & Peet, Palmer M. Pediatric Chiropractic Practice Management. 2nd ed. (Illus.). 187p. (C). Date not set. 45.00 (0-9638642-0-3) Baby Adjusters.
Peet, John. Energy & the Ecological Economics of Sustainability. LC 91-41207. 311p. (Orig.). 1992. 40.00 (1-55963-161-9); pap. 21.95 (1-55963-160-0) Island Pr.
— The Long Engagement: Memoirs of a Cold War Legend. (Illus.). 256p. 1990. 34.95 (0-947795-64-2, Pub. by Fourth Estate UK) Trafalgar.
Peet, John, jt. auth. see Benton, John.
Peet, Palmer M., jt. auth. see Peet, Jennifer B.
Peet, Phyllis. American Women of the Etching Revival. Morris, Kelly & Woods, Amanda, eds. (Illus.). 72p. 1988. pap. 10.00 (0-939802-45-7) High Mus Art.
Peet, Richard. Global Capitalism: Theories of Societal Development. (Illus.). 208p. 1991. 69.50 (0-415-01314-3, 9425); pap. 16.95 (0-415-01315-1, 9426) Routledge.
Peet, Richard, ed. International Capitalism & Industrial Restructuring. LC 86-28870. 256p. 1987. text ed. 39.95 (0-04-338132-4); pap. text ed. 21.95 (0-04-338133-2) Routledge Chapman & Hall.
Peet, Richard & Thrift, Nigel J., eds. New Models in Geography: The Political-Economy Perspective, 1. 448p. (Orig.). 1989. text ed. 75.00 (0-685-44712-X); pap. text ed. 22.95 (0-04-910101-3) Routledge Chapman & Hall.
— New Models in Geography: The Political-Economy Perspective, 2. 448p. (Orig.). 1989. pap. text ed. 22.95 (0-04-445420-1); pap. text ed. 29.95 (0-04-445421-X) Routledge Chapman & Hall.
— New Models in Geography: The Political-Economy Perspective, Vols. 1 & 2. 448p. (Orig.). 1989. write for info. (0-04-910100-5) Routledge Chapman & Hall.
Peet, Stephen D. Prehistoric America, 5 vols., 1. LC 74-7993. 1905. write for info. (0-404-11931-X) AMS Pr.
— Prehistoric America, 5 vols., 2. LC 74-7993. 1905. write for info. (0-404-11932-8) AMS Pr.
— Prehistoric America, 5 vols., 3. LC 74-7993. 1905. write for info. (0-404-11933-6) AMS Pr.
— Prehistoric America, 5 vols., 4. LC 74-7993. 1905. write for info. (0-404-11934-4) AMS Pr.
— Prehistoric America, 5 vols., 5. LC 74-7993. 1905. write for info. (0-404-11935-2) AMS Pr.
— Prehistoric America, 5 vols., Set. LC 74-7993. 1905. 187.50 (0-404-11930-1) AMS Pr.
Peet, T. E. A Comparative Study of the Literatures of Egypt, Palestine & Mesopotamia. (British Academy, London, Schweich Lectures on Biblical Archaeology Series, 1930). 1972. reprint ed. pap. 20.00 (0-8115-1271-1) Periodicals Srv.
Peet, T. Eric. Egypt & the Old Testament. (African Heritage Classical Research Studies). 236p. reprint ed. 25.00 (0-938818-43-0) ECA Assoc.
Peet, T. Eric, tr. & comment. The Rhind Mathematical Papyrus. 1990. reprint ed. 69.00 (3-262-00839-7) Periodicals Srv.
Peet, Verda. Sometimes I Prefer to Fuss. 1984. pap. 4.50 (9971-972-22-0) OMF Bks.
Peeters, jt. auth. see Schuiten.
Peeters, Benoit. Tintin & the World of Herge: An Illustrated History. (Illus.). 160p. (J). (gr. 5 up). 1992. 40.00 (0-316-69752-4, Joy St Bks) Little.
Peeters, F. L., jt. ed. see Valk, J.
Peeters, F. M., jt. ed. see Devresse, J. T.
Peeters, Flor. Jubilate Deo Omnis Terra: Psalm 99, Score & Brass Parts Accompaniment 1954. 43p. reprint ed. pap. 25.00 (0-317-09824-1, 2003407) Bks Demand.
— Little Organ Book for Beginners in Organ Playing. 114p. (Orig.). (gr. 3-12). 1957. pap. text ed. 14.95 (0-87487-600-1) Summy-Birchard.
— Magnificat, Opus One Hundred Eight, Score & Eight Parts, (Trumpet, Trombone, Bass Tuba, Kettle Drum, Cymbals) 45p. reprint ed. pap. 25.00 (0-317-09704-0, 2004389) Bks Demand.
— Thirty-Five Miniatures & Other Pieces for Organ. 64p. (Orig.). (gr. 7-12). 1975. pap. text ed. 10.95 (0-87487-602-8) Summy-Birchard.
Peeters, H., ed. Protides of the Biological Fluids: Metal Binding Proteins, Tumour Markers, Monoclonal Antibodies, Vol. 31. LC 58-5908. (Illus.). 1120p. 1984. 457.00 (0-08-030764-7, Pub. by Pergamon Repr UK) Franklin.
— Separation of Cells & Subcellular Elements. (Illus.). 1979. 65.00 (0-08-024957-4, Pub. by Pergamon Repr UK) Franklin.
Peeters, H. & Wright, P. H. Plasma Protein Pathology: A Workshop on Plasma Proteins, Their Availability, Assay & Therapeutic Uses--Proceedings of a Round Table Meeting, Seville, Spain, October-November 1977. LC 78-40994. (Illus.). 72p. 1979. 39.00 (0-08-023766-5, Pub. by Pergamon Repr UK) Franklin.
Peeters, Hans, jt. auth. see Jameson, E. W., Jr.
Peeters, Hans J., jt. auth. see Jameson, E. W., Jr.
***Peeters, Marga.** Time-to-Build: Interrelated Investments & Labour Demand Modelling with Applications to Six OECD Countries. LC 94-43958. (Lecture Notes in Economics & Mathematical Systems Ser.: Vol. 420). 1995. write for info. (0-387-58809-4) Spr-Verlag.
Peeters, Paul, jt. auth. see Meijer, Anton.
Peeters, Ralf. System Identification Based on Riemannian Geometry: Theory & Algorithms. (Tinbergen Institute Ser.). 368p. 1994. pap. 28.50 (90-5170-246-9, Pub. by Thesis Pubs NE) IBD Ltd.
Peeters, Theo, jt. ed. see DeGrauwe, Paul.
Peeters, Theo, jt. ed. see Fratianni, Michele U.
Peeters, Theo, et al, eds. International Trade & Exchange Rates in the Late Eighties. 300p. 1986. 110.25 (0-444-87941-2, North Holland) Elsevier.
Peetre, J., tr. see Ashurov, R. R., et al.
Peetre, J., jt. auth. see Cwikel, M.
Peetre, J., jt. auth. see Lumiste, V.
Peetre, J., tr. see Nikol'skii, N. K.
Peetre, J., tr. see Nikol'skij, S. M. & Gamkrelidze, R. V., eds.
Peets, Elbert, jt. auth. see Hegemann, Werner.
Peets, Leonora. Women of Marrakech. Taagepera, Rein, tr. LC 87-26536. 200p. 1988. lib. bdg. 31.95 (0-8223-0812-6) Duke.
Peeved, I. M. One Thousand Four Hundred One Even More Things That P ss Me Off. Strnad, Ed, ed. LC 94-10197. 288p. (Orig.). 1994. pap. 5.95 (0-399-52123-2, Perigree Bks) Berkley Pub.
Peeved, I. M. Very. One Thousand Four Hundred & One More Things That P-ss Me Off. LC 93-3357. 288p. (Orig.). 1993. pap. 5.95 (0-399-51823-1, Perigree Bks) Berkley Pub.
Pef. Belles Lisses Poires de France. (Folio - Cadet Bleu Ser.: No. 216). 56p. (FRE.). (J). (gr. 1-5). 1990. pap. 8.95 (2-07-031216-X) Schoenhof.
— Dictionnaires des Mots Tordus. (Folio - Cadet Bleu Ser.: No. 192). 79p. (FRE.). (J). (gr. 1-5). 1989. pap. 10.95 (2-07-031192-9) Schoenhof.
— Ivre de Francais. (Folio - Cadet Bleu Ser.: No. 246). 48p. (FRE.). (J). (gr. 1-5). 1986. pap. 7.95 (2-07-031246-1) Schoenhof.
— Livre de Nattes. (Folio - Cadet Bleu Ser.: No. 240). 78p. (FRE.). (J). (gr. 1-5). 1990. pap. 7.95 (2-07-031240-2) Schoenhof.
Pefanis, Julian. Heterology & the Postmodern: Bataille, Baudrillard & Lyotard. LC 90-3381. 200p. (C). 1990. lib. bdg. 32.00 (0-8223-1075-9); pap. text ed. 17.95 (0-8223-1093-7) Duke.
Pefanis, Julian, jt. ed. see Foss, Paul.
Pefanis, Julian, ed. see Lyotard, Jean F.
Pefaur, Jaime E. & Hoffmann, Robert S. Studies of Small Mammal Populations at Three Sites on the Northern Great Plains. (Occasional Papers: No. 37). 27p. 1975. pap. 1.00 (0-317-04897-X) U of KS Mus Nat Hist.
Pefaur, Jaime E., jt. auth. see Humphrey, Philip S.
Peffer, E. Louise. The Closing of the Public Domain: Disposal & Reservation Policies, 1900-50. LC 72-2862. (Use & Abuse of America's Natural Resources Ser.). 388p. 1972. reprint ed. 25.95 (0-405-04528-X) Ayer.
— The Closing of the Public Domain: Disposal & Reservation Policies, 1900-50. 120p. reprint ed. pap. 30.00 (0-317-29829-1, 2051958) Bks Demand.
Peffer, George & Murcko, Terry. Orphan Trees. LC 79-91911. (Poetry Ser.). 80p. 1980. pap. 3.95 (0-917530-08-X) Pig Iron Pr.
Peffer, Nathaniel. The White Man's Dilemma: Climax of the Age of Imperialism. LC 72-4288. (World Affairs Ser.: National & International Viewpoints). 320p. 1972. reprint ed. 23.95 (0-405-04580-8) Ayer.
Peffer, R. G. Marxism, Morality & Social Justice. 487p. (Orig.). 1990. text ed. 75.00 (0-691-07789-4); pap. text ed. 18.95 (0-691-02298-4) Princeton U Pr.
Peffer, Randall S. Watermen. LC 79-9896. (Maryland Paperback Bookshelf Ser.). 208p. 1985. reprint ed. pap. 10.95 (0-8018-2737-X) Johns Hopkins.
Peffer, William A. The Farmer's Side, His Troubles & Their Remedy. LC 75-723. (Radical Tradition in America Ser.). 275p. 1975. reprint ed. 23.65 (0-88355-241-8) Hyperion Conn.
— Populism, Its Rise & Fall. annot. ed. LC 91-18795. (Illus.). viii, 208p. 1992. 25.00 (0-7006-0509-6) U Pr of KS.
Peffers, Hopkins S. Aurora-Elgin Area Streetcars & Interurbans, 4 vols., Set. (Illus.). 776p. 1993. 198.00 (1-883461-05-7) Am Slide-Chart.
— Aurora-Elgin Area Streetcars & Interurbans, Vol. 2: Aurora Elgin & Fox River Electric. (Illus.). 184p. 1993. 49.50 (1-883461-02-2) Am Slide-Chart.
— Aurora-Elgin Area Streetcars & Interurbans, Vol. 1: Fox River Division. (Illus.). 168p. 1993. 49.50 (1-883461-01-4) Am Slide-Chart.
— Aurora-Elgin Area Streetcars & Interurbans, Vol. 4: The Connecting Lines. (Illus.). 200p. 1993. 49.50 (1-883461-04-9) Am Slide-Chart.
— Aurora-Elgin Area Streetcars & Interurbans, Vol. 3: The Third Rail Line. (Illus.). 224p. 1993. 49.50 (1-883461-03-0) Am Slide-Chart.
Peffers, Ken, jt. auth. see Dos Santos, Brian L.
Peffley, Bill. Prayerful Pauses with Jesus & Mary. LC 85-50690. (Illus.). 96p. (Orig.). 1985. pap. 5.95 (0-89622-251-9) Twenty-Third.
***Pefley, Richard K.** Mechanical Engineering: License Review. 5th ed. (Illus.). 378p. 1995. 39.50 (0-910554-00-5, 005) Engineering.
— Mechanical Engineering License Exam File. 4th rev. ed. LC 85-16230. (Exam File Ser.). 378p. (Orig.). 1986. pap. 39.50 (0-910554-52-8) Engineering.
Pefley, Richard K., jt. ed. see Hirao, Osamu.
Pegalis, Steven E. & Wachsman, Harvey F. American Law of Medical Malpractice, 3 vols., Set. 2nd ed. LC 92-90712. 1992. 365.00 (0-685-59872-1) Clark Boardman Callaghan.
Pegden, C. Dennis, et al. Introduction to Simulation Using SIMAN. 1990. text ed. write for info. (0-07-049217-4) McGraw.
— Introduction to Simulation Using SIMAN. 2nd ed. LC 94-41386. 600p. 1995. 69.95 (0-07-049320-0) McGraw.
Pegels, C. C. Systems Analysis for Production Operations. (Studies in Operations Research). 488p. 1976. text ed. 188.00 (0-677-04710-X) Gordon & Breach.

P Q

An Asterisk (*) at the beginning of an entry indicates that the title is appearing in BIP for the first time.

Pegels, C. Carl. Health Care & the Older Citizen: Economic, Demographic, & Financial Aspects. (Health Care Administration Ser.). 278p. 1988. 69.00 (*0-87189-771-7*) Aspen Pub.

Pegels, C. Carl, ed. Management & Industry in China. LC 86-25260. 294p. 1986. text ed. 65.00 (*0-275-92553-6*, C2553, Praeger Pubs) Greenwood.

Pegels, C. Carl, jt. auth. see Goldberg, Alvin.

Pegels, C. Carl, jt. auth. see Lotfi, Vahid.

Pegels, C. Carl, jt. ed. see Mahajan, Vijay.

Pegels, Carl C., jt. auth. see Lotfi, Vahid.

Pegg, Anthony E., jt. ed. see Zappia, V.

Pegg, Barbara. Braidmaking. (Illus.). 80p. 1991. pap. 14.95 (*0-7136-3198-8*, Pub. by A&C Black UK) Talman.

Pegg, Carl H. Evolution of the European Idea, 1914-1932. LC 82-24796. 238p. reprint ed. pap. 67.90 (*0-7837-7076-6*, 2046888) Bks Demand.

Pegg, D. E. & Karow, A. M., Jr., eds. The Biophysics of Organ Cryopreservation. LC 87-36059. (NATO ASI Series A, Life Sciences: Vol. 147). (Illus.). 496p. 1988. 135.00 (*0-306-42812-1*, Plenum Pr) Plenum.

Pegg, David E., jt. ed. see Karow, Armand M., Jr.

***Pegg, Leonard.** Family Law in Hong Kong. 3rd ed. 305p. 1994. write for info. (*0-409-99687-4*) Butterworth Legal Pubs.

— Family Law in Hong Kong. 3rd ed. 305p. 1994. student ed, pap. text ed. write for info. (*0-409-99688-2*) Butterworth Legal Pubs.

Pegg, Mike. Positive Leadership: How to Build a Winning Team. 242p. 1993. pap. 12.95 (*0-89384-251-6*) Pfeiffer & Co.

— Positive Leadership: How to Build a Winning Team. LC 95-10438. 1995. write for info. (*0-88390-410-1*) Pfeiffer & Co.

Pegg, P. F., jt. auth. see Jespersen, Ellen.

Pegge, S. Two Collections of Derbicisms Containing Words & Phrases in a Great Measure... Derby. Skeat, W. & Hallum, T., eds. (English Dialect Society Publications Ser.: No. 78). 1974. reprint ed. pap. 25.00 (*0-8115-0496-4*) Periodicals Srv.

Pegge, Samuel. An Assemblage of Coins Fabricated by the Authority of the Archbishops of Canterbury. (Illus.). 1975. pap. 15.00 (*0-916710-23-8*) Obol Intl.

Peggs, G. N., ed. High Pressure Measurement Techniques. (Illus.). 397p. 1983. 117.00 (*0-85334-189-3*, I-126-83, Pub. by Elsevier Applied Sci UK) Elsevier.

Peggs, Ian D., ed. Geosynthetics: Microstructure & Performance. LC 90-36990. (Special Technical Publication (STP) Ser.: STP 1076). (Illus.). 170p. 1990. text ed. 30.00 (*0-8031-1298-X*, 04-010760-38) ASTM.

Peggs, L. A. Underground Piping Handbook. LC 83-19906. 296p. 1985. lib. bdg. 29.50 (*0-89874-616-7*) Krieger.

Peggy B. Potpourri of Poetry. 1993. pap. 7.95 (*0-533-10440-8*) Vantage.

***Peggy, Ned, contrib.** So Many Bridges. large type ed. 1994. 21.95 (*0-7089-3209-6*) Ulverscroft.

Pegis, Anton C. St. Thomas & Philosophy. LC 64-17418. (Aquinas Lectures). 1964. 10.00 (*0-87462-129-1*) Marquette.

— St. Thomas & the Greeks. (Aquinas Lectures). 1939. 10.00 (*0-87462-103-8*) Marquette.

Pegis, Anton C., ed. see St. Thomas Aquinas.

***Pegler.** Storefronts & Facades. 5th ed. 1995. 59.95 (*0-07-049385-5*) McGraw.

— Stores of the Year. 9th ed. 1995. 50.00 (*0-07-049384-7*) McGraw.

Pegler, jt. auth. see Spicer.

Pegler, D. N. The Genus Lentinus: A World Monograph. (Illus.). 281p. 1983. pap. text ed. 70.00 (*0-11-242627-1*) Lubrecht & Cramer.

***Pegler, D. N., ed.** Fungi of Europe. 300p. 1993. 60.00x (*0-947643-54-0*, Pub. by Royal Botanic Garden UK) Lubrecht & Cramer.

Pegler, David N. Agaric Flora of Sri Lanka. (Kew Bulletin Additional Ser.: No. XII). (Illus.). 519p. 1986. pap. 65.00 (*0-11-250004-8*) Lubrecht & Cramer.

— A Preliminary Agaric Flora of East Africa. (Kew Bulletin Additional Ser.: No. VI). (Illus.). 615p. 1977. pap. text ed. 135.00 (*0-11-241101-0*) Lubrecht & Cramer.

Pegler, Martin. Dictionary of Interior Design. (Illus.). 260p. (C). 1983. 28.50 (*0-87005-447-3*) Fairchild.

— The Language of Store Planning & Display. (Illus.). 235p. (C). 1981. text ed. 20.00 (*0-87005-403-1*) Fairchild.

— U. S. Cavalryman 1865-90. (Warrior Ser.). (Illus.). 64p. 1993. pap. 12.95 (*1-85532-319-2*, 9603, Pub. by Osprey UK) Stackpole.

— Visual Merchandising & Display. 2nd ed. (Illus.). 304p. (C). 1991. teacher ed 2.50 (*0-685-47884-X*); text ed. 35.00 (*0-87005-734-0*, AAF6) Fairchild.

Pegler, Martin M. Christmas Displays & Promotions. 1993. 49.95 (*0-934590-54-0*) Retail Report.

— Food Presentation & Display. (Illus.). 233p. 1991. 49.95 (*0-934590-41-9*) Retail Report.

— Food Retail Design & Display, No. 2. (Illus.). 240p. 1992. 49.95 (*0-934590-51-6*) Retail Report.

— Store Fronts & Facades, No. 3. (Illus.). 224p. 1990. 49.95 (*0-934590-38-9*) Retail Report.

— Store Fronts & Facades - 4. (Illus.). 240p. 1992. 49.95 (*0-934590-48-6*) Retail Report.

— Store Windows, No. 8. 224p. 1995. 59.95 (*0-934590-72-9*) Retail Report.

— Store Windows That Sell, No. 5. (Illus.). 1990. 49.95 (*0-934590-39-7*) Retail Report.

— Store Windows that Sell, No. 6. (Illus.). 224p. 1992. 49.95 (*0-934590-47-8*) Retail Report.

— Storefronts & Facades No. 5. 240p. 1994. 59.95 (*0-934590-67-2*) Retail Report.

— Stores of the Year, Bk. 7. 1993. 49.95 (*0-934590-53-2*) Retail Report.

— Stores of the Year, No. 6. (Illus.). 224p. 1991. 49.95 (*0-934590-42-7*) Retail Report.

— Stores of the Year, No. 9. 224p. 1995. 59.95 (*0-934590-71-0*) Retail Report.

— Stores of the Year V. (Illus.). 256p. 1989. 34.98 (*0-934590-31-1*) Retail Report.

Pegler, Martin M., ed. Food Retail Design & Display, No. 3. (Illus.). 240p. 1994. 49.95 (*0-934590-61-3*) Retail Report.

— Market Supermarket & Hypermarket Design, No. 2. (Illus.). 224p. 1992. 49.95 (*0-934590-44-3*) Retail Report.

— Store Fronts & Facades, No. 2. (Illus.). 192p. 1988. 44.95 (*0-934590-26-5*) Retail Report.

— Store Windows That Sell, No. 4. (Illus.). 192p. 1988. 44.95 (*0-934590-27-3*) Retail Report.

— Store Windows That Sell, No. 7. (Illus.). 240p. 1994. 49.95 (*0-934590-57-5*) Retail Report.

— Stores of the Year, No. 8. (Illus.). 240p. 1994. 49.95 (*0-934590-60-5*) Retail Report.

— Stores of the Year, Vol. II. (Illus.). 176p. 1981. 39.95 (*0-934590-07-9*) Retail Report.

— Stores of the Year, Vol. III. (Illus.). 176p. 1984. 39.95 (*0-934590-11-7*) Retail Report.

— Successful Food Merchandising & Display. (Illus.). 192p. 1989. 49.95 (*0-934590-24-9*) Retail Report.

Pegler, Martin M., intro. Home Furnishings Merchandising & Store Design. (Illus.). 224p. 1990. 49.95 (*0-934590-36-2*) Retail Report.

— Market Supermarket & Hypermarket Design. (Illus.). 224p. 1990. 49.95 (*0-934590-33-8*) Retail Report.

— Stores of the Year, Vol. IV. (Illus.). 192p. 1987. 44.95 (*0-934590-22-2*) Retail Report.

Pegler, Westbrook. George Spelvin, American: And Fireside Chats. LC 75-39112. (Essay Index Reprint Ser.). 1977. reprint ed. 18.95 (*0-8369-2711-7*) Ayer.

Pegoda, Dan, jt. auth. see Sims, Tim.

Pegoraro, Olinto, jt. ed. see McLean, George F.

Pegoretti, Giovanni, jt. ed. see Dallago, Bruno.

Pegram, Amelia B. Echoes Across a Thousand Hills: Poems. (Illus.). 96p. 1994. 24.95 (*0-86543-417-4*); pap. 9.95 (*0-86543-418-2*) Africa World.

Pegram, Elmer, jt. auth. see Pegram, Joan.

Pegram, Joan & Pegram, Elmer. Secrets from the Galley. (Illus.). 1983. 12.95 (*0-9612544-0-8*) Galley Cabinet.

Pegram, Kay L. Marketing & Promotion from A to Z: For Home Fashions Retailers & Interior Designers. 157p. (Orig.). 1992. pap. 22.95 (*0-9634747-0-7*) Kaymar Bks.

***Pegram, Laura.** A Day for Phyllis Mae. LC 94-41555. (Illus.). (J). 1996. write for info. (*0-8037-1557-9*); lib. bdg. write for info. (*0-8037-1558-7*) Dial Bks Young.

— Rainbow Is Our Face. (J). (ps). 1994. 5.95 (*0-86316-217-7*) Writers & Readers.

— Windy Day. (J). (ps). 1994. 5.95 (*0-86316-218-5*) Writers & Readers.

Pegram, Thomas R. Partisans & Progressives: Private Interest & Public Policy in Illinois, 1870-1922. 312p. 1992. 42.50 (*0-252-01847-8*) U of Ill Pr.

***Pegram, Warren.** Solar Path. 150p. 1995. pap. 7.95 (*0-7610-0006-2*) NW Pub.

***Peguero, Leone.** The Ragged Old Bear. 32p. (J). 1995. 12.95 (*1-86374-020-1*, Pub. by ERA Pubns AT); pap. 5.95 (*1-86374-209-3*, Pub. by ERA Pubns AT) Pubs Dist MI.

Pegues, Etta. On Rainbow Wings. (Orig.). 1981. pap. 1.75 (*0-8439-8031-1*) Dorchester Pub Co.

Pegues, Franklin J. The Lawyers of the Last Capetians. LC 62-11962. 268p. reprint ed. pap. 76.40 (*0-317-09343-6*, 2010020) Bks Demand.

Pegues, Guy. The Illustrated SuperCalc Book. (Illus.). 200p. 17.95 (*0-317-13063-3*) P-H.

Pegues, R. P. Catechism of the Summa Theologica of Saint Thomas Aquinas. Whitacre, Aelred, tr. 315p. 1993. reprint ed. text ed. 15.95 (*0-912141-03-4*) Roman Cath Bks.

Peguy, Charles. L' Argent. 252p. (FRE.). 1932. pap. 34.95 (*0-7859-1292-4*, 2070249743) Fr & Eur.

— La Ballade du Coeur: Poeme Inedit. 274p. (FRE.). 1973. pap. 24.95 (*0-7859-1461-7*, 2252015381) Fr & Eur.

— Cinq Prieres dans la Cathedrale de Chartres. 48p. (FRE.). 1947. pap. 10.95 (*0-7859-1295-9*, 2070249921) Fr & Eur.

— Clio. 276p. (FRE.). 1931. pap. 13.95 (*0-7859-1293-2*, 2070249751) Fr & Eur.

— De Jean Coste. 228p. (FRE.). 1937. pap. 10.95 (*0-7859-1294-0*, 2070249832) Fr & Eur.

— Deuxieme Elegie. 440p. (FRE.). 1955. pap. 16.95 (*0-7859-1298-3*, 2070250024) Fr & Eur.

— Les Enfants. 96p. (FRE.). 1952. pap. 10.95 (*0-7859-1296-7*, 2070249972) Fr & Eur.

— L' Esprit de Systeme. 340p. (FRE.). 1953. pap. 11.95 (*0-7859-1297-5*, 2070249999) Fr & Eur.

— Eve. Les Tapisseries. 160p. (FRE.). 1968. pap. 10.95 (*0-7859-1352-1*, 2070302148) Fr & Eur.

— Eve Premiere Mortelle. (Illus.). 328p. (FRE.). 1933. pap. 13.95 (*0-7859-1291-6*, 2070249697) Fr & Eur.

— Jeanne d'Arc: Cinq Poemes. pap. 3.95 (*0-685-37025-9*) Fr & Eur.

— Jeanne d'Arc: Theatre. 8.95 (*0-685-37026-7*) Fr & Eur.

— Lettres et Entretiens. 13.95 (*0-685-37027-5*) Fr & Eur.

— Lumieres d'homme. pap. 6.25 (*0-685-37052-6*) Fr & Eur.

— Marcel: Premier Dialogue de la Cite Harmonieuse. 208p. (FRE.). 1973. pap. 11.95 (*0-686-54858-2*, 2070284638) Fr & Eur.

— Morceaux choisis; Poesie. pap. 6.95 (*0-685-37014-3*) Fr & Eur.

— Le Mystere de la Charite de Jeanne d'Arc. (Gallimard Ser.). (FRE.). pap. 11.95 (*2-07-010656-X*) Schoenhof.

— Note Conjointe: Note sur M. Bergson et la Philosophie Bergsonienne, Note Conjointe sur Descartes et la Philosophie Cartesienne. pap. 8.75 (*0-685-37030-5*) Fr & Eur.

— Notre Jeunesse de la Raison. (Folio Essais Ser.: No. 232). (FRE.). pap. 15.95 (*2-07-032786-8*) Schoenhof.

— Un Nouveau Theologien, M. Laudet. pap. 3.95 (*0-685-37044-5*) Fr & Eur.

— Oeuvres Completes: Paris, 1917-1955, 20 vols. in 10, Set. 9827p. 1974. 1,995.00 (*0-7859-5391-4*) Fr & Eur.

— Oeuvres en Prose: 1898-1908, Vol. 1. deluxe ed. Pebuy, M., ed. (Pleiade Ser.). (FRE.). 1959. 98.95 (*2-07-011114-8*) Schoenhof.

— Oeuvres en Prose: 1909-1914, Vol. 2: 1905-1909. deluxe ed. Peguy, M., ed. (Pleiade Ser.). (FRE.). 1957. Vol. 2, 1905-1909. 99.95 (*2-07-011134-2*) Schoenhof.

— Oeuvres en Prose: 1909-1914, Vol. 3. Peguy, M., ed. (Pleiade Ser.). (FRE.). 1957. 129.95 (*2-07-011231-4*) Schoenhof.

— Oeuvres en Prose Completes, 1900-1914: Index. Burac, Robert, ed. (FRE.). 1988. lib. bdg. 225.00 (*0-7859-3881-8*) Fr & Eur.

— Oeuvres Poetiques Completes. deluxe ed. Peguy, Marcel, ed. 1664p. (FRE.). 1941. 130.00 (*0-7859-3779-X*, 2070104389) Fr & Eur.

— Oeuvres Poetiques Completes. deluxe ed. Peguy, P & Peguy, M, eds. (Pleiade Ser.). (FRE.). 1939. 76.95 (*2-07-010438-9*) Schoenhof.

— Par Ce Demi-clair Matin. pap. 5.95 (*0-685-37033-X*) Fr & Eur.

— Peguy et les Cahiers. pap. 6.95 (*0-685-37034-8*) Fr & Eur.

— Un Poet L'a Dit. pap. 5.95 (*0-685-37045-3*) Fr & Eur.

— Le Porche du Mystere de la Deuxieme Vertu. (FRE.). 1986. pap. 11.95 (*0-7859-2850-2*) Fr & Eur.

— Precis de Climatologie. (Illus.). 468p. (FRE.). 1970. 150.00 (*0-686-54865-5*, 2225615233) Fr & Eur.

— La Republique... Notre Royaume de France. pap. 7.95 (*0-685-37037-2*) Fr & Eur.

— Sainte Genevieve. pap. 4.50 (*0-685-37038-0*) Fr & Eur.

— Saints de France. pap. 1.95 (*0-685-37039-9*) Fr & Eur.

— Situations. (FRE.). pap. 4.50 (*0-685-37040-2*) Fr & Eur.

— Souvenirs. pap. 1.95 (*0-685-37041-0*) Fr & Eur.

— Les Tapisseries. (Poesie Ser.). (FRE.). pap. 7.95 (*2-07-030214-8*) Schoenhof.

— La These. pap. 4.95 (*0-685-37043-7*) Fr & Eur.

— Veronique, Dialoque de L'Histoire et de l'Ame Charnelle. 12.75 (*0-685-37046-1*) Fr & Eur.

— Victor-Marie, Comte Hugo. pap. 5.95 (*0-685-37047-X*) Fr & Eur.

Peguy, Charles & Basstaire, Jean. Pour l'Honneur de l'Esprit: Correspondance, 1898-1914. 352p. (FRE.). 1973. pap. 13.95 (*0-7859-5392-2*) Fr & Eur.

Peguy, Charles & Burac, Robert. Oeuvres en Prose Complete, 1897-1899, 1900-1905, Vol. 1. (FRE.). 1987. lib. bdg. 160.00 (*0-7859-3876-1*) Fr & Eur.

Peguy, Charles & Roche, Anne. Charles Peguy: de Jean Coste: Edition Critique avec le Roman d'Antonin Lavergne. 670p. (FRE.). 1976. pap. 69.95 (*0-7859-1463-3*, 2252017406) Fr & Eur.

Peguy, Charles, jt. auth. see Rolland, Romain.

Peguy, Charles P. Basic Verities: Prose & Poetry. Green, Ann & Green, Julian, trs. LC 72-4493. (Essay Index Reprint Ser.). 1977. reprint ed. 21.95 (*0-8369-2967-5*) Ayer.

Peguy, M., ed. see Peguy, Charles.

Peguy, Marcel, ed. see Peguy, Charles.

Peguy, P, ed. see Peguy, Charles.

Pehe, Jiri, ed. The Prague Spring: A Mixed Legacy. LC 88-16261. (Perspectives on Freedom Ser.: No. 10). (Illus.). 236p. (Orig.). (C). 1988. lib. bdg. 45.50 (*0-932088-27-9*); pap. text ed. 20.50 (*0-932088-28-7*) Freedom Hse.

Peheim, E., tr. see Eastham, R. C.

Pehl, Erich. Microwave Technology. LC 85-70815. (Artech House Microwave Library). (Illus.). 230p. reprint ed. pap. 65.60 (*0-685-20803-6*, 2030129) Bks Demand.

Pehle, Walter H., ed. November, Nineteen Thirty-Eight: From the Reichskristallnacht to Genocide. Templer, William, tr. 269p. 1991. 59.95 (*0-85496-687-0*) Berg Pubs.

Pehnt, Wolfgang. Rudolph Steiner Goetheanum, Dornach. 95p. 1993. 45.00 (*0-685-67851-2*, Pub. by W Ernst Sohn) VCH Pubs.

***Pehnt, Wolfgang & Forster, Kurt W.** Karl Friedrich Schinkel: The Drama of Architecture. Zukowsky, John, ed. & intro. by. (Illus.). 176p. 1994. 60.00 (*3-8030-2822-1*) Art Inst Chi.

Pehnt, Wolfgang, et al. Transforming Vision: Writers on Art. Zukowsky, John, ed. & intro. by. (Illus.). 176p. 1994. pap. 29.95 (*0-86559-105-9*) Art Inst Chi.

Pehoski, jt. auth. see Henderson.

Pehoski, Charlane, jt. ed. see Case-Smith, Jane.

Pehrson, Bjorn, jt. auth. see Holzmann, Gerard.

Pehrsson, Robert S. & Denner, Peter R. Semantic Organizers: A Study Strategy for Special Needs Learners. LC 88-24931. 224p. (C). 1989. 58.00 (*0-87189-778-4*) Aspen Pub.

***Pei.** I. M. Pei. 1995. (*0-517-10299-4*) Random Hse Value.

Pei, Cherie, ed. see Morgan, Ffiona.

Pei Chi Chou & Pagano, Nicholas J. Elasticity: Tensor, Dyadic, & Engineering Aproaches. (Illus.). 304p. 1992. pap. 8.95 (*0-486-66958-0*) Dover.

Pei, Mario. One Language for the World & How to Achieve It. LC 68-56449. 1958. 20.00 (*0-8196-0218-3*) Biblo.

— The Story of Language. LC 83-24990. 512p. 1984. pap. 14.00 (*0-452-00870-0*, Mer) NAL-Dutton.

— Swords of Anjou. 310p. 1953. 8.95 (*0-913298-66-2*) S F Vanni.

Pei, Mario, ed. see Miles, Preston.

Pei, Mario A. French Precursors of the Chanson De Roland. LC 48-9636. reprint ed. 20.00 (*0-404-04967-2*) AMS Pr.

— Voices of Man. LC 71-173940. reprint ed. 20.00 (*0-404-07928-8*) AMS Pr.

Pei, Mario A., tr. see De Fiori, Vittorio E.

Pei, Meg. Salaryman. 304p. 1992. 21.00 (*0-670-83979-5*, Viking) Viking Penguin.

— Salaryman. (Contemporary American Fiction Ser.). 304p. 1993. reprint ed. pap. 11.00 (*0-14-017826-0*, Penguin Bks) Viking Penguin.

Pei, Minxin. From Reform to Revolution: The Demise of Communism in China & the Soviet Union. LC 93-50948. 263p. 1994. text ed. 39.95 (*0-674-32563-X*, PEIFRO) HUP.

Pei, Richard, jt. auth. see Webb, Timothy.

Pei-Yi Wu. The Confucian's Progress: Autobiographical Writings in Traditional China. 297p. 1992. text ed. 45.00 (*0-691-06788-0*); pap. text ed. 16.95 (*0-691-01524-4*) Princeton U Pr.

Peich, Michael. The Red Ozier: A Literacy Fine Press. (Illus.). 102p. 1993. 130.00 (*1-882916-00-X*) Yellow Barn.

Peich, Michael, ed. see Berger, Suzanne E.

Peich, Michael, jt. auth. see McCurdy, Michael.

Peich, Michael, ed. see Steiner, Robert.

Peierls, R., ed. Niels Bohr Collected Works, Vol. 9: Nuclear Physics 1929-1952. 700p. 1986. 213.00 (*0-444-86929-8*, North Holland) Elsevier.

Peierls, Rudolf. Bird of Passage: Recollections of a Physicist. 350p. 1988. reprint ed. pap. text ed. 14.95 (*0-691-02416-2*) Princeton U Pr.

— Surprises in Theoretical Physics. LC 79-84009. (Physics Ser.). 1979. pap. 14.95 (*0-691-08242-1*) Princeton U Pr.

Peierls, Rudolph. More Surprises in Theoretical Physics. (Physics Ser.). 115p. 1991. text ed. 29.50 (*0-691-08576-5*); pap. 12.95 (*0-691-02522-3*) Princeton U Pr.

***Peifeng, Chen.** Ancient Chinese Bronzes: In the Shanghai Museum. (Illus.). 96p. Date not set. 29.95 (*0-302-00664-8*) Scala Books.

Peifer, Charles, Jr. George Patton: Soldier of Destiny: A Biography of George Patton. LC 88-20265. (People in Focus Ser.). (Illus.). 128p. (J). (gr. 5 up). 1988. text ed. 13.95 (*0-87518-395-6*, Dillon Silver Burdett) Silver Burdett Pr.

— Houston. LC 88-20197. (Downtown America Ser.). (Illus.). 60p. (J). (gr. 3 up). 1988. text ed. 13.95 (*0-87518-387-5*, Dillon Silver Burdett) Silver Burdett Pr.

Peifer, Jane. The Biggest Popcorn Party Ever in Center County. LC 86-27063. (Illus.). 32p. (Orig.). (J). (ps-1). 1987. pap. 4.95 (*0-8361-3435-4*) Herald Pr.

Peifer, Jane & Nolt, Marilyn. Good Thoughts about Me. (Good Thoughts Ser.: No. 1). (Illus.). 24p. (Orig.). (J). (ps-2). 1985. pap. 2.95 (*0-8361-3389-7*) Herald Pr.

— Good Thoughts at Bedtime. (Good Thoughts Ser.: No. 2). (Illus.). 24p. (Orig.). (J). (ps-2). 1985. pap. 2.95 (*0-8361-3388-9*) Herald Pr.

Peiffer. Small Animal Ophthalmology: A Problem Oriented Approach. 256p. 1989. pap. text ed. 32.95 (*0-7216-1461-2*) Saunders.

Peiffer, Max H. Five Lives of Mr. Peiff. LC 91-65537. 141p. 1992. 10.95 (*1-55523-437-2*) Winston-Derek.

***Peiffer, V.** More Positive Thinking. 1995. pap. 7.95 (*1-85230-684-X*) Element MA.

— Positive Thinking. 1994. pap. 7.95 (*1-85230-554-1*) Element MA.

Peiffer, Vera. Positively Fearless: Breaking Free of the Fears That Hold You Back. 1993. pap. 12.95 (*1-85230-389-1*) Element MA.

— Positively Single. 1995. pap. 6.95 (*1-85230-712-9*) Element MA.

— Positively Single: How Being Single Can Be the Beginning of the World and Not the End. 176p. 1991. pap. 12.95 (*1-85230-241-0*) Element MA.

Peigler, Richard S. A Revision of the Indo-Australian Genus Attacus. LC 88-82574. (Illus.). 168p. (Orig.). (C). 1989. pap. text ed. 30.00 (*0-9611464-2-7*) Lepidoptera.

Peigne, Jean. Grande Encyclopedie des Histoires Droles. 447p. (FRE.). 1993. pap. 49.95 (*0-7859-5664-6*, 2877061787) Fr & Eur.

Peik, Leander. Camper's Guide to San Diego County. 1992. pap. 3.50 (*0-9620402-6-6*) Peiks Enter.

— Discover San Diego. 16th ed. 1991. pap. 3.50 (*0-9620402-5-8*) Peiks Enter.

Peik, Leander & Peik, Rosalie. Discover San Diego. 15th rev. ed. (Illus.). 136p. 1988. pap. 2.50 (*0-9620402-0-7*) Peiks Enter.

Peik, Rosalie, jt. auth. see Peik, Leander.

Peikin, Steven. Gastrointestinal Health: A Self-Help Nutritional Program to Prevent, Cure or Alleviate Irritable Bowel Syndrome, Ulcers, Heartburn, Gas, Constipation, & Many Other Digestive Disorders. LC 90-55547. 304p. 1992. reprint ed. pap. 12.00 (*0-06-098405-8*, PL) HarpC.

Peikoff, Leonard. Objectivism: The Philosophy of Ayn Rand. 512p. 1993. pap. 14.95 (*0-452-01101-9*, Mer) NAL-Dutton.

— The Ominous Parallels. 1983. pap. 4.95 (*0-451-62560-9*, Ment) NAL-Dutton.

— Ominous Parallels. 1983. pap. 3.95 (*0-451-62210-3*) NAL-Dutton.

Peikoff, Leonard, ed. Ominous Parallels. 1983. pap. 10.00 (*0-452-01117-5*, Mer) NAL-Dutton.

Peikoff, Leonard, ed. see Rand, Ayn.

Peikoff, Leonard, jt. auth. see Rand, Ayn.

Peil, Margaret. Cities & Suburbs: Urban Life in West Africa. LC 80-26440. (New Library of African Affairs). 330p. (C). 1982. 49.50 (*0-8419-0685-8*) Holmes & Meier.

— Consensus & Conflict in African Societies: An Introduction to Sociology. LC 78-312566. (Illus.). 412p. reprint ed. pap. 117.50 (*0-8357-6073-1*, 2034492) Bks Demand.

— Lagos: The City Is the People. (World Cities Ser.). 256p. 1991. text ed. 35.00 (*0-8161-7299-4*, Hall Reference) Macmillan.

P Q

Peil, Margaret & Sada, Pius O. African Urban Society. LC 84-5092. (Social Development in the Third World Ser.). 404p. reprint ed. pap. 115.20 (0-8357-5242-9, 2031761) Bks Demand.

Peil, William. The Big Way. 1983. 2.00 (0-89536-952-4, 7503) CSS OH.

Peile, Colin. The Creative Paradigm: Insight, Synthesis & Knowledge Development. (Philosophy Ser.). 291p. 1994. 68.95 (1-85628-629-0, Pub. by Avebury Pub UK) Ashgate Pub Co.

Peile, James H. The Reproach of the Gospel: An Inquiry into the Apparent Failure of Christianity As a General Rule of Life & Conduct. 1977. lib. bdg. 59.95 (0-8490-2516-8) Gordon Pr.

Peill, E. J. Invention & Discovery of Reality: The Acquisition of Conservation of Amount. LC 74-10243. 211p. reprint ed. pap. 60.20 (0-317-08086-5, 2016159) Bks Demand.

Peillard, Leonce. Sink the Tirpitz! (Illus.). 348p. 1983. pap. 8.00 (0-583-12384-8, Pub. by Granada UK) Academy Chi Pubs.

Peillon, Michel. The Concept of Interest in Social Theory. LC 90-22627. (Studies in Sociology: Vol. 9). 200p. 1990. lib. bdg. 79.95 (0-88946-722-6) E Mellen.

Peim, Nick. Critical Theory & the English Teacher: Transforming the Subject. LC 93-9850. (Teaching Secondary English Ser.). 208p. 1993. 59.95 (0-415-05751-5, B0800); pap. 16.95 (0-415-05752-3, B0804) Routledge.

Peimbert, Manuel & Jugaku, Jun, eds. Star Forming Regions. 1986. lib. bdg. 206.50 (90-277-2388-5); pap. text ed. 88.00 (90-277-2389-3) Kluwer Ac.

***Peimer, Clayton A.** Surgery of the Hand & Upper Extremity, 2 vols., Set. 2336p. 1995. 295.00 (0-07-049293-X) Hlth Prof Div.

Pein, M., jt. auth. see Przewoznik, J.

Pein, Malcom, jt. auth. see Mikhalchishin, Adrian.

Pein, Roland, jt. ed. see Kuo, Kenneth K.

Peinado, Luis & Peinado, Marilyn. Bienvenidos to Our Kitchen: Authentic Mexican Cooking. LC 91-42877. (Illus.). 208p. 1992. 21.95 (0-88289-873-6) Pelican.

Peinado, Marilyn, jt. auth. see Peinado, Luis.

Peinador, E. M., ed. Geometric Aspects of Banach Spaces. (London Mathematical Society Lecture Note Ser.: No. 140). 200p. (C). 1989. pap. 37.95 (0-521-36752-2) Cambridge U Pr.

Peindao, M., et al. Vegetation of Southeastern Spain. (Flora et Vegetatio Mundi Ser.: Vol. 10). (Illus.). 487p. 1992. pap. text ed. 105.00 (3-443-66002-9, Pub. by Cramer-Borntraeger GW) Lubrecht & Cramer.

Peine, Ira. Quality Assurance Compliance: Procedures for Pharmaceutical & Biotechnology Manufacturers. 279p. 1994. ring bd. 192.50 (0-935184-51-1) Interpharm.

Peinke, J., et al. Chaos in Experiment: Self-Organized Hierachical Complexity in Semiconductor Experiments. LC 92-25600. (Illus.). 320p. 1993. write for info. (3-540-55647-8); 59.00 (0-387-55647-8) Spr-Verlag.

— Encounter with Chaos: Self-Organized Hierarchial Complexity in Semiconductor Experiments. LC 92-30273. 1993. 45.00 (0-387-55845-4) Spr-Verlag.

Peinovich, M. P. Old English Noun Morphology: A Diachronic Study. (Linguistic Ser.: Vol. 41). 244p. 1979. 41.00 (0-444-85287-5, North Holland) Elsevier.

Peiny, David C. Fabulae Romanae: Stories of Famous Romans. 1993. student ed, pap. 16.55 (0-685-66000-1) Longman.

Peiper, Howard, jt. auth. see Anderson, Nina.

***Peiperl, Laurence.** Current Clinical Strategies, Manual of HIV-AIDS Therapy: Current Clinical Strategies. 2nd ed. 85p. 1995. pap. 8.75 (1-881528-09-X) Current Clin Strat.

Peirats, Jose. Anarchists in the Spanish Revolution. Slocombe, Ann & Hollow, Paul, trs. (Illus.). 388p. (Orig.). (C). 1990. pap. 15.00 (0-900384-53-0) Left Bank.

Peirce, Bradford K. Half Century with Juvenile Delinquents: Or, the New York House of Refuge & Its Times. LC 69-16242. (Criminology, Law Enforcement, & Social Problems Ser.: No. 91). (Illus.). 1969. reprint ed. 25.00 (0-87585-091-X) Patterson Smith.

Peirce, Charles S. Charles S. Peirce: Selected Writings. Wiener, Philip P., ed. pap. text ed. 9.95 (0-486-21634-9) Dover.

— Collected Papers of Charles Sanders Peirce, 6 vols, Vol. 2. Hartshorne, Charles & Weiss, Paul, eds. Incl. Vol. 1 (bk. 1). Principles of Philosophy. LC 60-9172. 1934. (0-318-53025-2); Vol. 2 (bk. 1). Elements of Logic. LC 60-9172. 1934. (0-318-53026-0); Vol. 3 (bk. 2). Exact Logic. LC 60-9172. 1934. (0-318-53027-9); Vol. 4 (bk. 2). Simplest Mathematics. LC 60-9172. 1934. (0-318-53028-7); Vol. 5 (bk. 3). Pragmatism & Pragmaticism. LC 60-9172. 1934. (0-318-53029-5); Vol. 6 (bk. 3). Scientific Metaphysics. LC 60-9172. 1934. (0-318-53030-9); LC 60-9172. 1934. Bk. 2. 75.00 (0-674-13801-5, Belknap Pr) HUP.

— Collected Papers of Charles Sanders Peirce, 6 vols, Vol. 3. Hartshorne, Charles & Weiss, Paul, eds. Incl. Vol. 1 (bk. 1). Principles of Philosophy. LC 60-9172. 1934. (0-318-53025-2); Vol. 2 (bk. 1). Elements of Logic. LC 60-9172. 1934. (0-318-53026-0); Vol. 3 (bk. 2). Exact Logic. LC 60-9172. 1934. (0-318-53027-9); Vol. 4 (bk. 2). Simplest Mathematics. LC 60-9172. 1934. (0-318-53028-7); Vol. 5 (bk. 3). Pragmatism & Pragmaticism. LC 60-9172. 1934. (0-318-53029-5); Vol. 6 (bk. 3). Scientific Metaphysics. LC 60-9172. 1934. (0-318-53030-9); LC 60-9172. 1934. Bk. 3. 70.00 (0-674-13802-3, Belknap Pr) HUP.

— Collected Papers of Charles Sanders Peirce, 6 vols, Vol. 4. Hartshorne, Charles & Weiss, Paul, eds. Incl. Vol. 1 (bk. 1). Principles of Philosophy. LC 60-9172. 1934. (0-318-53025-2); Vol. 2 (bk. 1). Elements of Logic. LC 60-9172. 1934. (0-318-53026-0); Vol. 3 (bk. 2). Exact Logic. LC 60-9172. 1934. (0-318-53027-9); Vol. 4 (bk. 2). Simplest Mathematics. LC 60-9172. 1934. (0-318-53028-7); Vol. 5 (bk. 3). Pragmatism & Pragmaticism. LC 60-9172. 1934. (0-318-53029-5); Vol. 6 (bk. 3). Scientific Metaphysics. LC 60-9172. 1934. (0-318-53030-9); LC 60-9172. 1934. Bk. 4. 65.00 (0-674-13803-1, Belknap Pr) HUP.

— Collected Papers of Charles Sanders Peirce, Vols. 1 & 2, 5 & 6. Hartshorne, Charles & Weiss, Paul, eds. LC 60-9172. (Illus.). 959p. reprint ed. Vol. 1-2: Principles of Philosophy & Elements of Logic, 667p. pap. 180.00 (0-7837-1682-6, 2057213); reprint ed. Vol. 5-6: Pragmatism & Pragmaticism & Scientific Metaphysics, 667p. pap. 180.00 (0-7837-1683-4, 2057213) Bks Demand.

— Philosophical Writings of Peirce. Buchler, Justus, ed. 1940. pap. 7.95 (0-486-20217-8) Dover.

— The Philosophy of Peirce: Selected Writings. Buchler, Justus, ed. LC 75-41210. reprint ed. 26.50 (0-404-14694-5) AMS Pr.

— Reasoning & the Logic of Things. 297p. 1993. pap. 22.50 (0-674-74967-7) HUP.

— Writings of Charles S. Peirce: A Chronological Edition: Vol. 1, 1857-1866. Moore, Edward C. et al, eds. LC 79-1993. (Illus.). 738p. 1982. 57.50 (0-253-37201-1) Ind U Pr.

— Writings of Charles S. Peirce: A Chronological Edition: Vol. 2, 1867-1871. Kloesel, Christian J. et al, eds. LC 79-1993. (Illus.). 704p. 1984. 57.50 (0-253-37202-X) Ind U Pr.

— Writings of Charles S. Peirce: A Chronological Edition: Vol. 3, 1872-1878. Kloesel, Christian J. et al, eds. LC 79-1993. (Illus.). 672p. 1986. 57.50 (0-253-37203-8) Ind U Pr.

— Writings of Charles S. Peirce: A Chronological Edition, Vol. 4: 1879-1884. LC 79-1993. 768p. 1989. 67.50 (0-253-37204-6) Ind U Pr.

— Writings of Charles S. Peirce: A Chronological Edition, Vol. 5, 1884-1886. LC 79-1993. (Illus.). 592p. 1992. 65.00 (0-253-37205-4) Ind U Pr.

Peirce, Charles S., ed. Studies in Logic: By Members of the Johns Hopkins University (1883) (Foundations of Semiotics Ser.: No. 1). xl, 203p. (C). 1983. reprint ed. 65.00x (90-272-3271-7) Benjamins North Am.

Peirce, Charles S., et al, eds. The Essential Peirce: Selected Philosophical Writings, Vol 1: 1867-1893. LC 91-32113. (Illus.). 448p. 1992. 45.00 (0-253-32849-7); pap. 19.95 (0-253-20721-5, MB-721) Ind U Pr.

Peirce, Donald C. English Ceramics: Frances & Emory Cocke Collection. LC 88-82295. (Illus.). 255p. (Orig.). 1988. 50.00 (0-939802-53-8); pap. 24.95 (0-939802-51-1) High Mus Art.

Peirce, Donald C. & Alswang, Hope. American Interiors: New England & the South. (Illus.). 62p. pap. 4.87 (0-87273-095-6) Bklyn Mus.

Peirce, Donald C. & Hanks, David A. Virginia Carroll Crawford Collection: American Decorative Arts, 1825-1917. LC 83-81102. (Illus.). 96p. (Orig.). 1983. pap. 9.95 (0-939802-16-3) High Mus Art.

Peirce, E. W. The Peirce Family of the Old Colony: or the Lineal Descent of Abraham Peirce, Who Came to America As Early As 1623. (Illus.). 510p. 1989. reprint ed. lib. bdg. 84.50 (0-8328-0948-9); reprint ed. pap. 76.50 (0-8328-0949-7) Higginson Bk Co.

Peirce, Ebenezer W. Indian History, Biography & Genealogy. LC 72-4336. (Select Bibliographies Reprint Ser.). 1977. reprint ed. 23.95 (0-8369-6890-5) Ayer.

Peirce, Elizabeth. Activity Assemblies for Christian Collective Worship 5-11. 224p. 1991. pap. 28.00 (1-85000-729-2, Falmer Pr) Taylor & Francis.

***Peirce, Hayford.** Dinosaur Park Vol. 1. 1994. pap. 4.99 (0-8125-5040-4) Tor Bks.

— Phylum Monsters. 1989. pap. 3.95 (0-8125-4894-9) Tor Bks.

Peirce, Henry A. Biography. 25p. 1983. pap. 2.00 (0-87770-160-1) Ye Galleon.

Peirce, Henry B., jt. auth. see Durrant, Samuel W.

Peirce, Kathleen. Mercy. LC 91-50110. (Poetry Ser.). 64p. (C). 1991. 19.95 (0-8229-3686-0); pap. 10.95 (0-8229-5457-5) U of Pittsburgh Pr.

Peirce, Leslie P. The Imperial Harem: Women & Sovereignty in the Ottoman Empire. (Studies in Middle Eastern History). (Illus.). 400p. 1993. pap. 19.95 (0-19-508677-5) OUP.

Peirce, Lincoln C. Vegetables: Characteristics, Production & Marketing. LC 86-32625. 566p. 1987. Net. text ed. write for info. (0-471-85022-5) Wiley.

Peirce, Liz. Activity Assemblies for Multi-Racial Schools 5-11. 160p. 1992. pap. 27.00 (0-7507-0049-1, Falmer Pr) Taylor & Francis.

Peirce, Michael. Programming with Appletalk. 1991. pap. 24.95 (0-201-57780-1) Addison-Wesley.

Peirce, Neal. Citistates: How Urban America Can Prosper in a Competitive World. LC 93-18709. 359p. 1993. text ed. 24.95 (0-929765-16-8); pap. 18.95 (0-929765-34-6) Seven Locks Pr.

Peirce, Neal, et al. Democratizing the Development Process. Barker, Michael, ed. LC 79-67384. (Studies in State Development Policy: Vol. 6). 49p. 1979. pap. 11.95 (0-934842-05-1) CSPA.

— Economic Development: The Challenge of the Nineteen Eighties. Barker, Michael, ed. LC 79-54266. (Studies in State Development Policy: Vol. 2). 70p. 1979. pap. 11.95 (0-934842-01-9) CSPA.

***Peirce, Neal R.** Over New England. Fraser, Jane & Wertz, Laurie, eds. (Wings over America Ser.). (Illus.). 256p. 1995. reprint ed. pap. 35.00 (1-887451-05-6) Wldon Owen Ref.

Peirce, Neal R. & Guskind, Robert. Breakthroughs: Re-Creating the American City. LC 93-17189. 203p. (C). 1993. text ed. 24.95 (0-88285-145-4) Ctr Urban Pol Res.

Peirce, Neal R. & Longley, Lawrence D. The People's President: The Electoral College in American History & the Direct Vote Alternative. rev. ed. LC 80-24260. (Illus.). 416p. 1981. reprint ed. text ed. 55.00 (0-300-02612-9); reprint ed. pap. 17.00 (0-300-02704-4, Y-395) Yale U Pr.

Peirce, Pam. Golden Gate Gardening: The Complete Guide to Year-Round Food Gardening the San Francisco Bay Area & Coastal California. LC 92-74725. (Illus.). 397p. (Orig.). 1993. pap. 24.95 (0-932857-10-8) Ag Access.

Peirce, Pamela. Environmentally Friendly Gardening: Controlling Vegetable Pests. Putnam, Cindy, ed. LC 90-86161. 160p. (Orig.). 1991. pap. 9.95 (0-89721-230-4) Ortho Info.

Peirce, Paul S. The Freedmen's Bureau: A Chapter in the History of Reconstruction. (BCL1 - U. S. History Ser.). 200p. 1991. reprint ed. lib. bdg. 69.00 (0-7812-6082-5) Rprt Serv.

Peirce, Susan P., comp. Gift Club Programs: A Survey of How Forty-Four Institutions Raise Money. 60p. 1992. pap. 20.00 (0-89964-292-6) Coun Adv & Supp Ed.

Peire Vidal. Poesie: Edizione Critica e Commento a Cura Di D'Arco Silvio Avalle, 2 vols. in 1. LC 80-2186. reprint ed. 72.50 (0-404-19011-1) AMS Pr.

Peires, J. B. The Dead Will Arise: Nongqawuse & the Great Xhosa Cattle-Killing Movement of 1856-57. LC 88-32799. (Illus.). 364p. 1989. 39.95 (0-253-34338-0); pap. 17.95 (0-253-20524-7, MB-524) Ind U Pr.

— The House of Phalo: A History of the Xhosa People in the Days of Their Independence. LC 82-2624. (Perspectives on Southern Africa Ser.: No. 32). (Illus.). 304p. 1982. pap. 16.00 (0-520-04793-1) U CA Pr.

Peiris, H. A. Political Parties in Sri Lanka Since Independence: A Bibliography. (C). 1988. 22.50 (81-7013-027-1, Pub. by Navrang) S Asia.

Peiris, William. The Western Contribution to Buddhism. 372p. 1974. lib. bdg. 79.95 (0-87968-550-6) Krishna Pr.

Peirson, Gwynne. Police Operations. LC 75-44334. (Justice Administration Ser.). 180p. 1976. 34.95 (0-911012-86-9) Nelson-Hall.

Peisa, R., jt. auth. see Loida, A.

Peisach, Max, jt. auth. see Alfassi, Zeev B.

Peischl, Margaret T., jt. auth. see Godwin-Jones, Robert.

Peischl, Margaret T., tr. see Gruber, Marianne.

Peiser, H., jt. auth. see Air Force Cambridge Research Staff.

Peiser, Kenneth B. Thinker's Guide to Recovery: A Rational Approach. 1993. pap. 9.95 (0-8306-4218-8) TAB Bks.

Peiser, Kenneth B. & Sandry, Martin. The Thinker's Guide to Recovery: A Rational Approach. 1993. pap. 9.95 (0-07-049290-5) TAB Bks.

Peiser, Richard & Schwanke, Dean. Professional Real Estate Development: The ULI Guide to Business. 408p. 1992. 59.95 (0-7931-0392-4, 1913-16) Dearborn Finan.

Peiser, Richard B., jt. auth. see Porter, Douglas R.

Peisner-Coxe, Paula. Finding Peace: Letting Go & Liking It. LC 94-18067. 1994. 8.95 (1-57071-014-7) Sourcebks.

Peisner, Paula. Finding Time: Breathing Space for Women Who Do Too Much. LC 91-31620. 246p. 1992. 16.95 (0-942061-35-7, Sourcebooks Trade); pap. 7.95 (0-942061-33-0, Sourcebooks Trade); 16.95 (0-942061-34-9, Sourcebooks Trade) Sourcebks.

Peiss, Kathy. Cheap Amusements: Working Women & Leisure in Turn-of-the-Century New York. LC 85-14783. 256p. 1985. pap. 16.95 (0-87722-500-1) Temple U Pr.

Peiss, Kathy & Clark Smith, Barbara. Men & Women: A History of Costume, Gender, & Power. (Illus.). 80p. (Orig.). 1989. pap. 6.95 (0-929847-02-4) Natl Mus Am.

Peiss, Kathy, et al, eds. Passion & Power: Sexuality in History. LC 88-21670. (Critical Perspectives on the Past Ser.). (Illus.). 326p. (C). 1989. 39.95 (0-87722-596-6); pap. 18.95 (0-87722-637-7) Temple U Pr.

Peissel, M. Mustang a Lost Tibetan Kingdom. (C). 1993. 108.00 (0-7855-0193-2, Pub. by Ratna Pustak Bhandar) St Mut.

Peissel, Michel. Dangerous Mammals. (J). (gr. 4-7). 1992. pap. 9.95 (0-7910-1935-7, Am Art Analog) Chelsea Hse.

— Dangerous Reptilian Creatures. (Encyclopedia of Danger Ser.). (J). (gr. 4-7). 1992. pap. 9.95 (0-7910-1934-9, Am Art Analog) Chelsea Hse.

— Dangerous Water Creatures. (Encyclopedia of Danger Ser.). (J). (gr. 4-7). 1992. pap. 9.95 (0-7910-1932-2, Am Art Analog) Chelsea Hse.

— Zanskar: The Hidden Kingdom. large type ed. 397p. 1981. 12.00 (0-7089-0714-8) Ulverscroft.

Peissel, Michel & Allen, Missy. Dangerous Environments. (Encyclopedia of Danger Ser.). (Illus.). 112p. (J). (gr. 5 up). 1993. lib. bdg. 19.95 (0-7910-1793-1, Am Art Analog) Chelsea Hse.

— Dangerous Flora. (Encyclopedia of Danger Ser.). (Illus.). 112p. (J). (gr. 5 up). 1993. lib. bdg. 19.95 (0-7910-1786-9, Am Art Analog) Chelsea Hse.

— Dangerous Insects. (Encyclopedia of Danger Ser.). (Illus.). 112p. (J). (gr. 5 up). 1993. lib. bdg. 19.95 (0-7910-1785-0, Am Art Analog); pap. 9.95 (0-7910-1933-0, Am Art Analog) Chelsea Hse.

— Dangerous Mammals. (Encyclopedia of Danger Ser.). (Illus.). 112p. (J). (gr. 5 up). 1993. lib. bdg. 19.95 (0-7910-1790-7, Am Art Analog) Chelsea Hse.

— Dangerous Natural Phenomena. (Encyclopedia of Danger Ser.). (Illus.). 112p. (J). (gr. 5 up). 1993. lib. bdg. 19.95 (0-7910-1794-X, Am Art Analog) Chelsea Hse.

— Dangerous Plants & Mushrooms. (Encyclopedia of Danger Ser.). (Illus.). 112p. (J). (gr. 5 up). 1993. lib. bdg. 19.95 (0-7910-1787-7, Am Art Analog) Chelsea Hse.

— Dangerous Professions. (Encyclopedia of Danger Ser.). (Illus.). 112p. (J). (gr. 5 up). 1993. lib. bdg. 19.95 (0-7910-1792-3, Am Art Analog) Chelsea Hse.

— Dangerous Reptilian Creatures. (Encyclopedia of Danger Ser.). (Illus.). 112p. (J). (gr. 5 up). 1993. lib. bdg. 19.95 (0-7910-1789-3, Am Art Analog) Chelsea Hse.

— Dangerous Sports. (Encyclopedia of Danger Ser.). (Illus.). 112p. (J). (gr. 5 up). 1993. lib. bdg. 19.95 (0-7910-1791-5, Am Art Analog) Chelsea Hse.

— Dangerous Sports. LC 92-23546. (Encyclopedia of Danger Ser.). (J). 1993. pap. write for info. (0-7910-1942-X) Chelsea Hse.

— Dangerous Water Creatures. (Encyclopedia of Danger Ser.). (Illus.). 112p. (J). (gr. 5 up). 1993. lib. bdg. 19.95 (0-7910-1788-5, Am Art Analog) Chelsea Hse.

— The Encyclopedia of Danger, 10 vols., Set. (Illus.). (J). (gr. 5 up). 1993. lib. bdg. 199.50 (0-7910-1784-2, Am Art Analog) Chelsea Hse.

Peissner, Elias. American Question in Its National Aspect. LC 71-152928. (Black Heritage Library Collection). 1977. 17.95 (0-8369-8772-1) Ayer.

Peitchinis, Stephen G. Computer Technology & Employment. LC 83-3401. 260p. 1984. text ed. 39.95 (0-312-15875-0) St Martin.

Peitgen, et al. Fractals: An Animated Discussion. (C). 1995. write for info. (0-7167-2213-5) W H Freeman.

Peitgen, Heinz O., jt. auth. see Nussbaum, Roger.

Peitgen, Heinz-Otto, ed. Newton's Method & Dynamical Systems. (C). 1989. lib. bdg. 105.50 (0-7923-0113-7) Kluwer Ac.

Peitgen, Heinz-Otto & Richter, P. H. Beauty of Fractals: Images of Complex Dynamical Systems. (Illus.). 199p. 1991. 39.00 (0-387-15851-0) Spr-Verlag.

Peitgen, Heinz-Otto & Richter, Peter H., eds. Complex Dynamical Systems & Fractals: Max-Planck-Lecture Series in Mathematics. 320p. (C). 1990. pap. 31.00 (3-528-06363-7, Pub. by Vieweg & Sohn GW) Ballen Bkslr.

Peitgen, Heinz-Otto & Saupe, D. The Science of Fractal Images. (Illus.). xiv, 312p. 1991. 39.95 (0-387-96608-0) Spr-Verlag.

Peitgen, Heinz-Otto, et al. Chaos & Fractals: New Frontiers of Science. LC 92-23277. 1992. write for info. (0-387-97345-1) Spr-Verlag.

— Chaos & Fractals: New Frontiers of Science. (Illus.). 1016p. 1993. 49.00 (0-387-97903-4) Spr-Verlag.

— Fractals for the Classroom: Complex Systems & Mandelbrot Set, Pt. 2. (Illus.). 448p. 1992. 29.00 (0-387-97722-8) Spr-Verlag.

— Fractals for the Classroom: Introduction to Fractals & Chaos. (Illus.). 450p. (C). 1993. text ed. 34.00 (0-387-97041-X) Spr-Verlag.

— Fractals for the Classroom: Introduction to Fractals & Chaos, 2 vols. 2nd ed. (Illus.). xv, 450p. 1993. write for info. (3-540-97041-X) Spr-Verlag.

— Fractals for the Classroom: Strategic Activities, 2 vols., Vol. 1. (Illus.). xii, 128p. 1993. pap. 22.00 (0-387-97346-X) Spr-Verlag.

— Fractals for the Classroom: Strategic Activities, 2 vols., Vol. 2. (Illus.). 160p. 1993. pap. 22.00 (0-387-97554-3) Spr-Verlag.

— The Game of Fractal Images. 2nd ed. 1989. disk 39.00 (0-387-14203-7) Spr-Verlag.

Peitsch, Helmut & Williams, Rhys W., eds. Berlin Seit Dem Kriegsende. (New German Texts Ser.). 160p. 1989. text ed. 15.95 (0-7190-2658-X, Pub. by Manchester Univ Pr UK) St Martin.

Peitsch, Helmut, jt. ed. see Williams, Rhys W.

Peitz, Darlene A. Solidarity As Hermeneutics: A Revisionist Reading of the Theology of Walter Rauschenbusch. LC 91-865. (American University Studies: Theology & Religion: Ser. VII, Vol. 122). 236p. (C). 1992. text ed. 46.95 (0-8204-1753-X) P Lang Pubs.

Peitz, Mary. Romeo & Juliet - Study Guide. Friedland, Joyce & Kessler, Rikki, eds. (Novel-Ties Ser.). (YA). (gr. 9-12). 1993. pap. text ed. 15.95 (0-88122-127-9) Lrn Links.

Peitzman, Faye & Gadda, George, eds. With Difference Eyes: Insights into Teaching Language Minority Students Across the Disciplines. LC 93-33727. 1994. 17.95 (0-8013-1311-2) Longman.

Peixoto, J. P., et al. Physics of Climate. 560p. 1992. 97.00 (0-88318-711-6); pap. 45.00 (0-88318-712-4) Am Inst Physics.

Peixoto, Marta. Passionate Fictions: Gender, Narrative, & Violence in Clarice Lispector. LC 93-29690. 1994. text ed. 29.95 (0-8166-2158-6); pap. text ed. 15.95 (0-8166-2159-4) U of Minn Pr.

Peixotto, Jessica B. Getting & Spending at the Professional Standard of Living: A Study of the Costs of Living an Academic Life. LC 75-39267. (Getting & Spending: the Consumer's Dilemma Ser.). (Illus.). 1976. reprint ed. 28.95 (0-405-08040-9) Ayer.

Pejcic, Bogdan & Meyer, Rolf. Pocket Billiards: Fundamentals of Technique & Play. LC 93-8557. 80p. 1993. pap. 8.95 (0-8069-0458-5) Sterling.

Pejova, Zdravka & Horton, Forest W., eds. Consultancy on Strategic Information Planning. 214p. 1993. pap. 30.00 (92-9038-140-X, Pub. by Intl Ctr Pub Ent XV) Kumarian Pr.

Pejova, Zdravka & Subic, Alenka, eds. Bibliography of ICPE: 1987-1989. 1990. 20.00 (92-9038-105-1, Pub. by Intl Ctr Pub Ent XV) Kumarian Pr.

Pejovich, Steve. Industrial Democracy: Conflict or Cooperation. Dethloff, Henry, ed. (Series on Public Issues: No. 12). 10p. 1984. pap. 2.00 (0-86599-022-0) PERC.

An Asterisk (*) at the beginning of an entry indicates that the title is appearing in BIP for the first time.

— Karl Marx in One Lesson (1818-1883) Dethloff, Henry, ed. (Series on Public Issues: No. 6). 10p. (Orig.). 1983. pap. 2.00 (*0-86599-016-6*) PERC.

Pejovich, Steve, ed. see Auernheimer, Leonardo.

Pejovich, Steve, ed. see Dethloff, Henry C. & Bryant, Keith L., Jr.

Pejovich, Steve, ed. see Fraser, Donald R.

Pejovich, Steve, ed. see Greenhut, Melvin L.

Pejovich, Steve, ed. see Greenhut, Melvin & Smithson, Charles W.

Pejovich, Steve, ed. see Hamilton, Billy.

Pejovich, Steve, ed. see Keim, Gerald.

Pejovich, Steve, ed. see Maurice, S. Charles & Smithson, Charles W.

Pejovich, Steve, ed. see Moore, John H.

Pejovich, Steve, ed. see Reynolds, Morgan O.

Pejovich, Steve, ed. see Saving, Thomas R.

Pejovich, Steve, ed. see Walker, Deborah.

Pejovich, Steve, ed. see Wiggins, Steven N.

Pejovich, Svetovar. The Economics of Property Rights: Towards a Theory of Comparative Systems. (C). 1990. lib. bdg. 102.50 (*0-7923-0878-6*) Kluwer Ac.

***Pejovich, Svetozar.** Economic Analysis of Institutions & Systems. LC 94-40239. (International Studies in Economics & Econometrics). 244p. (C). 1995. lib. bdg. 84.00 (*0-7923-3214-8*) Kluwer Ac.

— The Market-Planned Economy of Yugoslavia. LC 66-18868. (Illus.). 172p. reprint ed. pap. 49.10 (*0-318-39686-6*, 2033281) Bks Demand.

Pejovich, Svetozar, ed. Governmental Controls & the Free Market: The U. S. Economy in the 1970's. LC 76-17976. 240p. 1976. 19.50 (*0-89096-020-8*); pap. 8.95 (*0-89096-309-6*) Tex A&M Univ Pr.

Pejovich, Svetozar, ed. see Greenhut, Melvin.

Pejovich, Svetozar, ed. see Maurice, S. Charles & Smithson, Charles W.

Pejovich, Svetozar, ed. see Maurice, S. Charles & Hobson, Jane.

Pejovich, Svetozar, jt. ed. see Maurice, S. Charles.

Pejovich, Svetozar, ed. see Saving, Thomas R.

Pejsa, Arthur. Modern Practical Ballistics. 2nd ed. LC 88-84150. (Illus.). 224p. (C). 1991. 19.95 (*0-9612776-3-7*) Kenwood Pub.

Pejsa, Arthur J. Boy from Custer: The First Twenty Five Years. (Illus.). 164p. (Orig.). 1992. pap. 19.95 (*0-9612776-5-3*) Kenwood Pub.

— Modern Practical Ballistics. LC 88-84150. (Illus.). 200p. 1989. 19.95 (*0-9612776-1-0*) Kenwood Pub.

***Pejsa, Jane.** Gratia Countryman: Her Life, Her Loves & Her Library. (Illus.). 341p. (Orig.). 1995. pap. write for info. (*0-931714-66-4*) Nodin Pr.

— Matriarch of Conspiracy: Ruth von Kleist, 1867-1945. LC 90-92033. (Illus.). 430p. 1991. 24.95 (*0-9612776-2-9*) Kenwood Pub.

— Matriarch of Conspiracy: Ruth Von Kleist 1867-1945. LC 91-46626. (Illus.). 432p. 1992. reprint ed. pap. 21.95 (*0-8298-0931-7*) Pilgrim OH.

— The Molineux Affair. LC 83-82593. (Illus.). 240p. 1984. pap. 12.95 (*0-9612776-0-2*) Kenwood Pub.

— To Pomerania in Search of Dietrich Bonhoeffer: A Traveler's Companion. (Illus.). 40p. (Orig.). 1995. pap. 6.95 (*0-9612776-6-1*) Kenwood Pub.

Pejsachowicz, jt. auth. see Fitzpatrick.

Pekala, Bev. Don't Settle for Less: A Woman's Guide to Getting a Fair Divorce & Custody Settlement. LC 93-4795. 1994. 22.00 (*0-385-42550-3*) Doubleday.

Pekala, R. J. Quantifying Consciousness: An Empirical Approach. (Illus.). 380p. 1990. 52.50 (*0-306-43750-3*, Plenum Pr) Plenum.

Pekalski, A., jt. ed. see Turko, L.

***Pekalski, Andrzej, ed.** Diffusion Processes Vol. 438: Experiment, Theory, Simulations: Proceedings of the Fifth Max Born Symposium, Held at Kudowa, Poland, 1-4 June 1994. LC 94-39108. (Lecture Notes in Physics Ser.). 1994. write for info. (*3-540-58653-9*) Spr-Verlag.

Pekar, Athanasius. The History of the Church in the Carpathian Rus' Hierarchical Structure. Magosi, Paul R. & Krafcik, Patricia A., eds. 320p. 1991. text ed. 44.00 (*0-88033-219-0*) Col U Pr.

Pekar, George M. & Oettmeier, Timothy N. Advanced Short Baton Techniques: Modern Methods Made Easy. fac. ed. (Illus.). 112p. (C). 1984. spiral bd. 21.95 (*0-398-04897-5*) C C Thomas.

— Techniques with a Thirty-Six Inch Baton: Modern Methods Made Easy. (Illus.). 82p. (C). 1983. 16.95 (*0-398-04751-0*) C C Thomas.

Pekar, Harvey. New American Splendor Anthology. LC 91-2987. (Illus.). 300p. (Orig.). 1991. pap. 18.95 (*0-941423-64-6*) FWEW.

Pekar, Harvey & Brabner, Joyce. Our Cancer Year. LC 94-10523. (Illus.). 252p. (Orig.). 1994. pap. 17.95 (*1-56858-011-8*) FWEW.

Pekar, P. M. Catching Lobsters for Food, Fun & Profit. (Illus.). 1985. 3.95 (*0-318-19500-3*); lib. bdg. 4.95 (*0-318-19499-6*) Comtech Pubns.

— How to Build a Lobster Trap. Wendes, ed. (Illus.). 72p. (Orig.). 1986. lib. bdg. write for info. (*0-318-60955-X*) Comtech Pubns.

***Pekarek, Art. The End-Time Holocaust: A Revealing Text Book on Biblical Prophecy. LC 94-73689. (Illus.). 176p. (Orig.). 1994. pap. 8.95 (*0-9639482-3-7*) Lamb Pubns.**

The author sheds light from the prophecies of Jesus, Ezekiel, Daniel & the Apostles, Paul & John which will culminate in an end- time event called the Holocaust. Although it is a prophetical textbook of the Bible & the author uses the Hebrew & Greek words with explanation, yet it is easy to read & understand. The author denotes that the current events of disasters, earthquakes, floods, pandemic diseases, AIDS, wars, anarchy, terrorism will increase until the end of the 20th century. They are all foreshadows toward this End-Time Holocaust. The author details WW III to begin with a northerly invasion into the Holy Land which will be destroyed by the Antichrist who will be acclaimed as the World Ruler & leader of the UN. This ruler is depicted as the 4-Horsemen of the Apocalypse & he will bring order into the world through the great computer called The Beast. Every person in the world who does not receive his Mark will be killed & no one will be able to buy or sell without it. He will stop all violence, anarchy, drug peddling, wars, etc. through a demonic fascist control from his source of power, the Devil. Lamb Publications, Oakland, CA. Phone: 510-482-3868.

Publisher Provided Annotation.

Pekarek, Art L. The Naked Truth about Gays: A Text Book on the Past, Present & Future of Homosexuality. 346p. 1993. 7.95 (*0-9639482-0-2*) Lamb Pubns.

***Pekarik, Andrew.** Japanese Ceramics from Prehistoric Times to the Present. LC 78-61434. (Illus.). 103p. (C). 1978. pap. 10.00 (*0-943526-31-0*) Parrish Art.

— Painting. LC 92-52987. (Behind the Scenes Ser.). (Illus.). 64p. (J). (gr. 3-7). 1992. 18.95 (*1-56282-296-9*); lib. bdg. 18.89 (*1-56282-297-7*) Hyprn Child.

— Painting. LC 92-52987. (Behind the Scenes Ser.). (Illus.). 64p. (J). (gr. 3-7). 1995. pap. 8.95 (*0-7868-1031-9*) Hyprn Ppbks.

— Sculpture. LC 92-52988. (Behind the Scenes Ser.). (Illus.). 64p. (J). (gr. 3-7). 1992. 18.95 (*1-56282-294-2*); lib. bdg. 18.89 (*1-56282-295-0*) Hyprn Child.

— Sculpture. LC 92-52988. (Behind the Scenes Ser.). (Illus.). 64p. (J). (gr. 3-7). 1995. pap. 8.95 (*0-7868-1032-7*) Hyprn Ppbks.

Pekarik, Andrew J. The Thirty-Six Immortal Women Poets. (Illus.). 192p. 1991. 45.00 (*0-8076-1256-1*); pap. 24.95 (*0-8076-1257-X*) Braziller.

Pekarik, Andrew J., ed. Ukifune: Love in the Tale of Genji. LC 82-1157. 264p. 1983. text ed. 42.00 (*0-231-04598-0*) Col U Pr.

Pekarkova, Iva. Truck Stop Rainbows: A Czech Road Novel. Powelstock, David, tr. 1992. 22.00 (*0-374-24065-5*) FS&G.

— The World Is Round. Powelstock, David, tr. LC 94-653. (RUS.). 1994. 22.00 (*0-374-29287-6*) FS&G.

Pekas, Mary. Telephone Mastery: Skills for Business Productivity. (C). 1990. teacher ed 5.45 (*1-56118-020-3*); student ed, audio 4.80 (*1-56118-010-6*); audio 66.00 (*1-56118-018-1*); vhs 79.00 (*1-56118-019-X*) Paradigm MN.

Pekelis, Alexander H. Law & Social Action: Selected Essays of Alexander H. Pekelis. Konvitz, Milton, ed. LC 77-87376. (American Constitutional & Legal History Ser). (Illus.). 1970. reprint ed. lib. bdg. 37.50 (*0-306-71600-3*) Da Capo.

Pekelny, Olga, jt. auth. see Veklerov, Eugene.

Peker, L., jt. auth. see Dzhelepov, B.

Pekhlivanova, K. Russian Grammar in Pictures. (Illus.). 352p. 1987. text ed. 13.95 (*0-8285-3735-6*) Firebird NY.

Pekhlivanova, K. I. Russian Grammar in Illustrations. (Illus.). 352p. (C). 1986. 73.00 (*0-317-92393-5*, Pub. by Collets UK) Pro-Am Music.

Pekic, Borislav. The Houses of Belgrade. Johnson, Bernard, tr. LC 93-47920. (Writings from an Unbound Europe Ser.). 220p. (C). 1994. reprint ed. pap. 12.95 (*0-8101-1141-1*) Northwestern U Pr.

— The Time of Miracles: A Legend. Edwards, Lovett F., tr. LC 93-45889. (Writings from an Unbound Europe Ser.). 332p. (C). 1994. reprint ed. pap. 13.95 (*0-8101-1117-9*) Northwestern U Pr.

Pekier, Alter. From Kletz to Siberia: A Students Wanderings During the Holocaust. Hirschler, Gertrude, ed. (ArtScroll History Ser.). (Illus.). 160p. 1985. 15.95 (*0-89906-470-1*); pap. 12.95 (*0-89906-471-X*) Mesorah Pubns.

Peking University Faculty Staff. Modern Chinese: A Basic Course. LC 78-169835. 1971. reprint ed. pap. text ed. 4.95 (*0-486-22775-3*); reprint ed. audio 15.95 (*0-486-99910-6*) Dover.

— Modern Chinese: A Second Course. rev. ed. 500p. (C). 1981. reprint ed. pap. 10.95 (*0-486-24155-6*) Dover.

Peking University, Western Languages Department, English Faculty, tr. see Ho, Kan-Chih.

Pekkarinen, Jukka, et al, eds. Social Corporatism: A Superior Economic System? (WIDER Studies in Development Economics). (Illus.). 416p. 1992. 95.00 (*0-19-828380-6*) OUP.

Peklenik, J. Advances in Manufacturing Systems - Research & Development. 196p. 1971. 86.00 (*0-08-016497-8*, Pub. by Pergamon Repr UK) Franklin.

Pekonen, O., jt. ed. see Mickelsson, J.

Pelaccio, Mario. Love in a Bare Room. Barkan, Stanley H., ed. Scammacca, Nat & Scammacca, Nina, trs. (Review Italian-American Writers Ser.: No. 1). 48p. 1992. 15.00 (*0-685-49050-5*); 15.00 (*0-685-49051-3*); pap. 5.00 (*0-89304-668-X*); pap. 5.00 (*0-685-49052-1*) Cross-Cultrl NY.

Peladeau, Marius B. Stephen R. Deane: Early Maine Folk Calligrapher. Howells, Jean, ed. (Illus.). 128p. 1991. 24.95 (*0-933858-04-3*); pap. 19.95 (*0-933858-03-5*) Kennebec River.

Pelaez, Martha, jt. auth. see Dluhy, Milan J.

Pelagatti, G., jt. auth. see Ceri, S.

Pelassy, Dominique, jt. auth. see Dogan, Mattei.

Pelc, Jerzy. Studies in Functional Logical Semiotics of Natural Languages. (Janua Linguarum, Ser. Minor: No. 90). 1971. text ed. 52.35 (*90-279-1599-7*) Mouton.

Pelc, Jerzy, ed. Semiotics in Poland, 1894-1969. Wojtasiewicz, Oligierd A., tr. (Synthese Library: No. 119). 1978. lib. bdg. 112.50 (*90-277-0811-8*) Kluwer Ac.

Pelc, Jerzy, et al, eds. Sign, System & Function: Papers of the First & Second Polish-American Semiotics Colloquia. LC 84-3288. (Approaches to Semiotics Ser.: No. 67). xiii, 503p. 1984. 180.80 (*90-279-3270-0*) Mouton.

Pelce, Pierre, ed. Dynamics of Curved Fronts. (Perspectives in Physics Ser.). 450p. 1988. text ed. 118.00 (*0-12-550355-5*) Acad Pr.

Pelcovits, Nathan. The Long Armistice: UN Peacekeeping & the Arab-Israeli Conflict, 1948-1960. LC 93-19519. 1993. text ed. 63.00 (*0-8133-8483-4*) Westview.

Pelcovits, Nathan A. Security Guarantees in a Middle East Settlement. LC 76-2219. (Foreign Policy Papers: Vol. 2, No. 5). 76p. reprint ed. pap. 25.00 (*0-7837-1987-6*, 2042261) Bks Demand.

Pelczar, Michael J., Jr., et al. Microbiology. 5th ed. 928p. 1986. text ed. write for info. (*0-07-049234-4*) McGraw.

— Microbiology: Concepts & Applications. 1993. text ed. write for info. (*0-07-049258-1*) McGraw.

— Microbiology: Concepts & Applications. 1993. Study guide. student ed, pap. text ed. write for info. (*0-07-049260-3*) McGraw.

— Microbiology: Concepts & Applications. 1993. Lab exercises. pap. text ed. write for info. (*0-07-049264-6*) McGraw.

Pelczynski, Aleksander. Banach Spaces of Analytic Functions & Absolutely Summing Operators. LC 77-9884. (CBMS Regional Conference Series in Mathematics: No. 30). 91p. 1990. reprint ed. pap. 17.00 (*0-8218-1680-2*, CBMS30) Am Math.

Pelczynski, Zbigniew & Gray, John, eds. Conceptions of Liberty in Political Philosophy. LC 84-40378. 360p. 1985. text ed. 39.95 (*0-312-16034-8*) St Martin.

***Pelecanos, George P.** Down by the River Where the Dead Men Go. 240p. 1995. 20.95 (*0-312-13056-2*) St Martin.

— Shoedog. 216p. 1994. 19.95 (*0-312-11061-8*) St Martin.

Pelech, Steven L. Protein Kinase Circuitry in Cellular CRegulation. (Molecular Biology Intelligence Unit Ser.). 119p. 1995. 89.95 (*1-57059-121-0*) R G Landes.

Peled, Abraham & Liu, Bede. Digital Signal Processing. LC 85-7984. 320p. 1985. reprint ed. lib. bdg. 34.50 (*0-89874-864-X*) Krieger.

***Peled, Einat & Davis, Diane.** Groupwork with Children of Battered Women: A Practitioner's Manual. (Interpersonal Violence: the Practice Ser.: Vol. 10). 160p. 1994. 42.95 (*0-8039-5514-6*); pap. 18.95 (*0-8039-5515-4*) Sage.

Peled, Einat, et al, eds. Ending the Cycle of Violence: Community Responses to Children of Battered Women. 264p. 1994. 46.00 (*0-8039-5368-2*); pap. 22.95 (*0-8039-5369-0*) Sage.

Peled, Mattityahu. Religion, My Own: The Literary Works of Najib Mahfuz. LC 82-17582. 268p. 1983. 39.95 (*0-87855-135-2*) Transaction Pubs.

Peled, Ruth, jt. ed. see Sussmann, Ayala.

Peled, Yoav. Class & Ethnicity in the Pale: The Political Economy of Jewish Workers' Nationalism in Late Imperial Russia. LC 88-36982. 224p. 1989. text ed. 49.95 (*0-312-03098-3*) St Martin.

Peleg, Dorith E., jt. auth. see Sweetgall, Robert.

Peleg, Ilan. Begin's Foreign Policy, 1977-1983: Israel's Move to the Right. LC 86-15020. (Contributions in Political Science Ser.: No. 164). 247p. 1987. text ed. 42.95 (*0-313-24938-5*, PGF/, Greenwood Pr) Greenwood.

— Human Rights in the West Bank & Gaza. LC 95-7834. (Studies on Peace & Conflict Resolution). 240p. 1995. 34.95 (*0-8156-2682-7*) Syracuse U Pr.

— Human Rights in the West Bank & Gaza. LC 95-7834. (Studies on Peace & Conflict Resolution). 1995. pap. write for info. (*0-8156-2687-8*) Syracuse U Pr.

Peleg, Ilan, ed. Patterns of Censorship Around the World. 224p. (C). 1993. text ed. 64.50 (*0-8133-1185-3*) Westview.

Peleg, Mordecai, jt. auth. see Marianska-Peleg, Miriam.

Pelegrin, Marc & Hollister, Walter M., eds. Concise Encyclopedia of Aeronautics & Space Systems. LC 93-10616. (Advances in Systems Control, & Information Engineering Ser.). 1993. 310.00 (*0-08-037049-7*, Pergamon Pr) Elsevier.

Pelenski, Jaroslaw. The Contest for the Legacy of Kievan Rus' & Related Essays. 300p. 1993. 42.00 (*0-88033-274-3*, 377) East Eur Quarterly.

— Studies in Ukrainian History. 300p. 1993. 42.00 (*0-88033-275-1*, 378) East Eur Quarterly.

Pelensky, Olga A. Isak Dinesen: The Life & Imagination of a Seducer. LC 90-45735. (Illus.). 243p. 1991. text ed. 34.95 (*0-8214-0968-9*) Ohio U Pr.

— Isak Dinesen: The Life & Imagination of a Seducer. LC 90-45735. (Illus.). 243p. 1991. reprint ed. pap. 19.95 (*0-8214-1008-3*) Ohio U Pr.

Pelensky, Olga A., ed. Isak Dinesen: Critical Views. 340p. (C). 1993. text ed. 39.95x (*0-8214-1055-5*) Ohio U Pr.

Pelerents, C., jt. ed. see Cavalloro, R.

Peles, Y. C., jt. auth. see Lanzilloti, Robert F.

Peletminskii, S. V., jt. auth. see Akhiezev, A. I.

Peletskii, V. E., et al. Thermophysical Properties of Titanium & Its Alloys: A Handbook. 110p. 1990. 85.00 (*0-89116-752-8*) Begell Hse.

Peletz, Michael, jt. ed. see Aihwa Ong.

***Peletz, Michael G.** Reason & Passion: Representations of Gender in a Malay Society. LC 94-45698. 1996. write for info. (*0-520-20069-1*); pap. write for info. (*0-520-20070-5*) U CA Pr.

— A Share of the Harvest: Kinship, Property, & Social History among the Malays of Rembau. 448p. 1988. 50.00 (*0-520-06153-5*) U CA Pr.

— Share of the Harvest: Kinship, Property & Social History among the Malays of Rembau. 1992. pap. 17.00 (*0-520-08086-6*) U CA Pr.

— Social History & Evolution in the Interrelationship of Adat & Islam in Rembau, Negeri Sembilan. 59p. (Orig.). 1981. pap. text ed. 10.00 (*9971-902-28-1*, Pub. by Inst SE Asian Studies SI) Ashgate Pub Co.

Pelfer, P. G., jt. auth. see Navarria, F. L.

Pelfrey, Danny. One-Way Choices in a Wrong-Way World: Growing the Fruit of Righteousness. LC 90-85183. 1991. pap. 7.99 (*0-89636-273-6*, LifeJourney) Chariot Family.

***Pelfrey, Robert.** Art & Mass Media. 400p. (C). 1995. pap. text ed. 45.95 (*0-7872-0488-9*) Kendall-Hunt.

Pelfrey, Sandra H. Basic Accounting for Hospital Based Non-Financial Managers. 1992. pap. text ed. 28.95 (*0-8273-4894-0*) Delmar.

Pelfrey, Wanda. Celebrate the Bible. (Celebrate Ser.). 144p. (J). (gr. 1-6). 1988. 11.95 (*0-86653-453-9*, SS847, Shining Star Pubns) Good Apple.

Pelfrey, William V. The Evolution of Criminology. 117p. 1980. pap. 9.95 (*0-87084-698-1*) Anderson Pub Co.

Pelgrin, M., ed. see IFAC-IFORS Symposium Staff.

Pelgrin, Mark. And a Time to Die. Moon, Sheila & Howes, Elizabeth, eds. LC 75-26836. 159p. 1976. reprint ed. pap. 5.25 (*0-8356-0305-9*, Quest) Theos Pub Hse.

Pelgrom, Els. The Acorn Eaters. Prins, Johanna H. & Prins, Johanna W., trs. LC 93-34210. (J). (gr. 4 up). 1994. 16.00 (*0-374-30029-1*) FS&G.

Pelgrum, Willem J. & Plomp, Tjeerd, eds. The IEA Study of Computers in Education. LC 93-23567. (International Studies in Educational Achievement: Vol. 2). 1993. text ed. 99.00 (*0-08-041935-6*, Pergamon Pr) Elsevier.

Pelham. Sams Sandwich. 1990. write for info. (*0-224-03011-6*) Random.

Pelham, Anabel O. & Clark, William F. Managing Home Care for the Elderly: Lessons from Community-Based Agencies. 208p. 1985. 22.95 (*0-8261-4700-3*) Springer Pub.

Pelham, David. A Is for Animals. (J). (ps). 1991. boxed 15.95 (*0-671-72495-9*, S&S Bks Young Read) S&S Childrens.

— Four Krazy Kites: To Make & Fly. (Illus.). 32p. (J). 1994. 6.99 (*0-525-45172-2*) Dutton Child Bks.

— The Penguin Book of Kites. (Illus.). 224p. 1976. pap. 14.50 (*0-14-004117-6*, Penguin Bks) Viking Penguin.

— Sam's Sandwich. (Illus.). 22p. (J). (ps-4). 1991. 9.95 (*0-525-44751-2*, DCB) Dutton Child Bks.

— Sam's Snack. (Illus.). 16p. (J). (ps-4). 1994. 9.99 (*0-525-45266-4*) Dutton Child Bks.

— Sam's Surprise. (Illus.). 22p. (J). (ps-4). 1992. 9.95 (*0-525-44947-7*, DCB) Dutton Child Bks.

— Worms Wiggle. (Illus.). (J). (ps-1). 1989. pap. 9.95 (*0-671-67218-5*, Litl Simon S&S) S&S Childrens.

***Pelham, David, illus.** The Sensational Samburger. 10p. (J). (ps). 1995. 12.99 (*0-525-45426-8*, DCB) Dutton Child Bks.

Pelham, David, ed. see Miller, Jonathan.

Pelham, David, jt. auth. see Miller, Jonathan.

Pelham, Erra, jt. auth. see Axsom, Dora.

Pelham, Henry, jt. auth. see Copley, John S.

Pelham, Howard. Brotherhood of Thieves. 192p. 1994. 17.95 (*0-8034-9049-6*, Avalon Bks) Bouregy.

— Judas Guns. 192p. 1990. 18.95 (*0-8027-4104-5*) Walker & Co.

Pelham, Jackie, ed. Food for Thought: Ez Recipes & Poetry by Texas Poets. (Illus.). 232p. 1990. pap. 12.95 (*0-9627844-0-0*) Page One TX.

Pelham, Jackie, ed. see Stahl, Carmine A.

Pelham, Thomas G. State Land-Use Planning & Regulation: Florida, the Model Code, & Beyond. LC 79-2390. 224p. reprint ed. pap. 63.90 (*0-7837-5773-5*, 2045438) Bks Demand.

Peli, Pinchas H. Jewish Sabbath: A Renewed Encounter. 1991. pap. 13.00 (*0-8052-0998-0*) Schocken.

— Shabbat Shalom: A Renewed Encounter with the Sabbath. 1989. 17.95 (*0-910250-15-4*) Sure Sellers.

Pelias, Ronald J. Performance Studies: The Interpretation of Aesthetic Texts. LC 90-71638. 256p. (Orig.). (C). 1991. pap. text ed. 16.00 (*0-312-04732-0*) St Martin.

Pelican, Fred. From Dachau to Dunkirk. LC 92-21684. 1993. pap. text ed. 19.50 (*0-85303-253-X*, Pub. by Vallentine Mitchell UK) Intl Spec Bk.

Pelican, Suzanne & Bachman-Carter, Karen. Navajo Food Practices, Customs, & Holidays. (Ethnic & Regional Food Practices Ser.). 1992. pap. 5.75 (*0-88091-083-6*, 0867) Am Dietetic Assn.

Pelicier, Yves, ed. Univers de la Psychologie, 1: Champ, Histoire et Methodes de la Psychologie. 512p. (FRE.). 1977. 150.00 (*0-8288-5525-0*, M6537) Fr & Eur.

— Univers de la Psychologie, 2: La Vie Psychologique Normale. 509p. (FRE.). 1977. 150.00 (*0-8288-5526-9*, M6538) Fr & Eur.

— Univers de la Psychologie, 3: Le Development Psychologique Normale, Lavie Psychologie Pathologique. 523p. (FRE.). 1977. 150.00 (*0-8288-5527-7*, M6539) Fr & Eur.

P Q

An Asterisk (*) at the beginning of an entry indicates that the title is appearing in BIP for the first time.

Pelikan. Applications of Numerical Methods: Molecular Spectroscopy. 1993. 79.95 (*0-8493-7322-0*, QD96) CRC Pr.

— Christianity & Classical Culture: The Metamorphsis of Natural Theology in the Christian. 1995. pap. text ed. 17.00 (*0-300-06255-9*) Yale U Pr.

Pelikan, E., jt. ed. see Novak, M.

Pelikan, Jaroslav. The Christian Tradition - a History of the Development of Doctrine Vol. 1: Emergence of the Catholic Tradition, 100-600. LC 79-142042. 1971. 30.00x (*0-226-65370-6*) U Ch Pr.

— The Christian Tradition - a History of the Development of Doctrine Vol. 1: The Emergence of the Catholic Tradition, 100-600. LC 79-142042. 1975. pap. 14.95 (*0-226-65371-4*, P644) U Ch Pr.

— The Christian Tradition - a History of the Development of Doctrine Vol. 2: The Spirit of Eastern Christendom, 600-1700. LC 79-142042. xxv, 432p. 1974. 30.00x (*0-226-65372-2*) U Ch Pr.

— The Christian Tradition - a History of the Development of Doctrine Vol. 2: The Spirit of Eastern Christendom, 600-1700. LC 79-142042. 1977. reprint ed. pap. 13.95 (*0-226-65373-0*, P738) U Ch Pr.

— The Christian Tradition - a History of the Development of Doctrine Vol. 3: The Growth of Medieval Theology, 600-1300. LC 78-1501. 1978. 35.00x (*0-226-65374-9*) U Ch Pr.

— The Christian Tradition - a History of the Development of Doctrine Vol. 3: The Growth of Medieval Theology, 600-1300. LC 78-1501. 1980. pap. 14.95 (*0-226-65375-7*) U Ch Pr.

— The Christian Tradition - a History of the Development of Doctrine Vol. 4: Reformation of Church & Dogma, 1300-1700. LC 79-142042. lii, 426p. 1984. 34.95x (*0-226-65376-5*) U Ch Pr.

— The Christian Tradition - a History of the Development of Doctrine Vol. 4: Reformation of Church & Dogma, 1300-1700. LC 79-142042. lii, 426p. 1985. pap. 15.95 (*0-226-65377-3*) U Ch Pr.

— The Christian Tradition - a History of the Development of Doctrine Vol. 5: Christian Doctrine & Modern Culture, since 1700. LC 88-23658. 416p. 1989. 34.95x (*0-226-65378-1*) U Ch Pr.

— The Christian Tradition - a History of the Development of Doctrine Vol. 5: Christian Doctrine & Modern Culture, since 1700. 416p. 1991. pap. 13.95 (*0-226-65380-3*) U Ch Pr.

— Christianity & Classical Culture: The Metamorphosis of Natural Theology in the Christian Encounter with Hellenism. LC 92-42407. 416p. (C). 1993. 42.50 (*0-300-05554-4*) Yale U Pr.

— Development of Christian Doctrine: Some Historical Prolegomena. LC 69-14864. (St. Thomas More Lectures Ser.: No. 3). 162p. 1969. 25.00 (*0-300-01082-6*) Yale U Pr.

— Eternal Feminines: Three Theological Allegories in Dante's Paridiso. LC 90-8261. 150p. (C). 1990. text ed. 40.00 (*0-8135-1602-1*); pap. text ed. 15.00 (*0-8135-1603-X*) Rutgers U Pr.

— Faust the Theologian. 1995. write for info. (*0-300-06288-5*) Yale U Pr.

— The Idea of the University: A Reexamination. 288p. (C). 1992. 32.50 (*0-300-05725-3*); pap. 10.00 (*0-300-05834-9*) Yale U Pr.

— Imago Dei: The Byzantine Apologia for Icons. (Bollingen Ser.). (Illus.). 196p. (C). 1990. text ed. 45.00 (*0-691-09970-7*) Princeton U Pr.

— Jesus Through the Centuries: His Place in the History of Culture. LC 86-45679. (Illus.). 288p. (C). 1987. pap. 13.00 (*0-06-097080-4*, PL 7080, PL) HarpC.

— Jesus Through the Centuries: His Place in the History of Culture. LC 85-2428. (Illus.). 272p. 1985. 32.00 (*0-300-03496-2*) Yale U Pr.

— The Melody of Theology: A Philosophical Dictionary. LC 88-690. 320p. 1988. 29.95 (*0-674-56472-3*) HUP.

— The Melody of Theology: A Philosophical Dictionary. 288p. 1990. pap. text ed. 10.95 (*0-674-56473-1*) HUP.

— The Mystery of Continuity: Time & History, Memory & Eternity, in the Thought of St. Augustine. LC 86-7788. (Richard Lectures). 225p. 1986. pap. 9.95 (*0-8139-1174-5*) U Pr of Va.

— Scholarship & Its Survival: Questions on the Idea of Graduate Education. LC 83-15211. 93p. 1983. pap. text ed. 6.50 (*0-931050-24-3*) Carnegie Fnd Advan Teach.

— The Vindication of Tradition. LC 84-5132. 94p. 1986. pap. 11.00 (*0-300-03638-8*) Yale U Pr.

Pelikan, Jaroslav, ed. Luther the Expositor. 1959. 19.95 (*0-570-06431-7*, 15-1741) Concordia.

— Luther's Works, Vol. 9. LC 55-9893. 1960. 19.95 (*0-570-06409-0*, 15-1751) Concordia.

— Luther's Works, Vol. 21. LC 55-9893. 1968. 19.95 (*0-570-06421-X*, 15-1763) Concordia.

— Luther's Works, Vol. 22. Bertram, Martin, tr. LC 55-9893. 1957. 19.95 (*0-570-06422-8*, 15-1764) Concordia.

— Luther's Works, Vol. 24. Bertram, Martin H., tr. LC 55-9893. 1961. 19.95 (*0-570-06424-4*, 15-1766) Concordia.

— Luther's Works: Genesis Chapters 1-5, Vol. 1. Schick, George V., tr. LC 55-9893. 1958. 19.95 (*0-570-06401-5*, 15-1743) Concordia.

— Luther's Works: Genesis Chapters 15-20, Vol. 3. Schick, George V., tr. LC 55-9893. 1961. 19.95 (*0-570-06403-1*, 15-1745) Concordia.

— Luther's Works: Genesis Chapters 6-11, Vol. 2. Schick, George V., tr. LC 55-9893. 1960. 19.95 (*0-570-06402-3*, 15-1744) Concordia.

Pelikan, Jaroslav, ed. see Luther, Martin.

Pelikan, Jaroslav, et al, trs. Luther's Works, Vol. 15, Letters On Ecclesiastes, Song of Solomon, LC 55-9893. 1971. 19.95 (*0-570-06415-5*, 15-1757) Concordia.

***Pelikan, Jaroslav J.** Confessor Between East & West: A Portrait of Ukrainian Cardinal Josyf Slipyj. fac. ed. LC 89-27536. (Illus.). 262p. 1990. reprint ed. pap. 74.70 (*0-7837-7970-4*, 2047726) Bks Demand.

— The Shape of Death: Life, Death, & Immortality in the Early Fathers. LC 78-6030. 128p. 1978. reprint ed. text ed. 38.50 (*0-313-20458-6*, PESD, Greenwood Pr) Greenwood.

Pelikan, Jiri, ed. The Czechoslovak Political Trials, 1950-1954: The Suppressed Report of the Dubcek Government's Commission of Inquiry, 1968. 368p. 1971. 47.50 (*0-8047-0769-3*) Stanford U Pr.

***Pelikan, Judy.** Joy. 1994. 8.95 (*1-55670-386-4*) Stewart Tabori & Chang.

— Love. 1994. 8.95 (*1-55670-387-2*) Stewart Tabori & Chang.

— Peace. 1994. 8.95 (*1-55670-388-0*) Stewart Tabori & Chang.

— Trust. 1994. 8.95 (*1-55670-389-9*) Stewart Tabori & Chang.

Pelikan, Judy, jt. auth. see Levy, Judith.

Pelikan, Wilhelm. Secrets of Metals. Lebensart, Charlotte, tr. 189p. reprint ed. pap. 10.95 (*0-88010-257-8*) Anthroposophic.

Pelinka, Anton. Social Democratic Parties in Europe. LC 82-18940. 208p. 1983. text ed. 55.00 (*0-275-91057-1*, C1057, Praeger Pubs) Greenwood.

Pelinka, Anton & Bischof, Gunter, eds. Austria in the New Europe. (Contemporary Austrian Studies: Vol. 1). 250p. (C). 1992. pap. 30.00 (*1-56000-597-1*) Transaction Pubs.

***Pelissier.** Reichen & Robert: Transforming Space. 1994. pap. 59.00 (*0-8176-5052-0*) Birkhauser.

Pelissier, Michael, jt. auth. see Lupson, Peter.

Pelissier, Michel, jt. auth. see Lupson, Peter.

Pelissier, Rene, jt. auth. see Wheeler, Douglas L.

Peliti, L., ed. Biologically Inspired Physics. (NATO ASI Series B, Physics: Vol. 263). (Illus.). 396p. 1991. 120.00 (*0-306-44000-8*, Plenum Pr) Plenum.

Peliti, L. & Vulpiani, A., eds. Measures of Complexity. (Lecture Notes in Physics Ser.: Vol. 314). vii, 150p. 1988. 41.00 (*0-387-50316-1*) Spr-Verlag.

***Pelizza, John J.** The Answers. Niles, Phillip, ed. (Personal Growth Ser.). (Illus.). 34p. 1995. pap. 3.95 (*0-9614872-4-0*) Pelizza & Assocs.

— The Big Secret. Niles, Phillip, ed. (Children's Bks.). (Illus.). 114p. (J). 1994. pap. 10.95 (*0-9614872-3-2*) Pelizza & Assocs.

— Foot in the Door. (Stress Management & Personal Growth Ser.). (Illus.). 152p. (Orig.). 1985. pap. 10.95 (*0-9614872-0-8*) Pelizza & Assocs.

— There's Magic in Discovery! Niles, Phillip, ed. (Illus.). 165p. 1993. pap. 11.95 (*0-9614872-2-4*) Pelizza & Assocs.

— Thoughts to Make You Think & Feel Better. 87p. 1988. pap. 11.95 (*0-9614872-1-6*) Pelizza & Assocs.

Pelizzetti, Ezio & Schiavello, Mario, eds. Photochemical Conversion & Storage of Solar Energy. (C). 1991. lib. bdg. 209.50 (*0-7923-1194-9*) Kluwer Ac.

Pelizzetti, Ezio & Serpone, Nick, eds. Homogeneous & Heterogeneous Photocatalysis. 1986. lib. bdg. 216.00 (*90-277-2221-8*) Kluwer Ac.

Pelizzetti, Ezio, jt. auth. see Serpone, Nick.

***Pelizzoli, Francesca.** Once Long Ago: The Christmas Story As Told in the Gospels. 28p. 1995. 4.95 (*0-687-00128-5*) Abingdon.

Pelizzoli, Francesca, illus. Far & Away: A Notebook for Travellers. 164p. 1992. 14.95 (*0-948751-04-5*) Interlink Pub.

Pelkey, Eddie J. Gifts of the Heart. LC 91-68090. 113p. (YA). (gr. 6 up). 1992. 8.95 (*1-55523-503-4*) Winston-Derek.

Pelkey, Rosemary M. The Adirondack Bridgebuilder from Charleston: Life & Times of Robert Cogdell Gilchrist. LC 93-6165. 1993. pap. 15.00 (*0-925168-23-8*) North Country.

Pelkmand, Jacques & Wagner, Norbert, eds. Privatization & Deregulation in ASEAN & the EC Making Markets More Effective. 259p. 1990. pap. text ed. 25.75 (*981-3035-65-X*, Pub. by Inst SE Asian Studies SI) Ashgate Pub Co.

Pelkmans, Jacques. Market Integration in the European Community. LC 84-8138. (Studies in Industrial Organization: Vol. 5). 1984. lib. bdg. 98.00 (*90-247-2978-5*) Kluwer Ac.

Pelkmans, Jacques, jt. ed. see Alting Von Gesau, Frans A.

Pelkonen, R. O., jt. ed. see Sotaniemi, E. A.

Pelkowski, Robert, jt. auth. see Smith, Alias.

Pell, Adrian, jt. auth. see I'Anson, Colin.

Pell, Arthur R. Diagnosing Your Doctor: A Straightforward Guide to Asking the Right Questions & Getting the Health Care You Deserve. LC 91-28110. 242p. (Orig.). 1991. pap. 9.95 (*0-937721-87-5*) Chronimed.

— Getting the Most from Your People. 64p. 1990. student ed 59.95 (*0-13-345216-6*); audio (*0-318-67224-3*) P-H.

— Recruiting, Training & Motivating Volunteers. rev. ed. LC 71-180210. 62p. 1989. pap. 4.95 (*0-87576-141-0*) Pilot Bks.

— The Supervisor's Infobook: 1000 Quick Answers to your Toughest Problems. LC 94-2702. 1994. text ed. 49.95 (*0-07-049185-2*) McGraw.

Pell, Arthur R., jt. auth. see Harper, Maxwell J.

Pell, B. Ernest Buckler's the Mountain & the Valley. (Canadian Fiction Studies: No. 31). 120p. (C). 1994. pap. text ed. 14.95 (*1-55022-180-9*, Pub. by ECW Press CN) Genl Dist Srvs.

Pell, Derek. Assassination Rhapsody. (Illus.). 124p. 1989. pap. 6.00 (*0-936756-54-3*) Autonomedia.

— Scar Mirror. (Illus.). 1979. pap. 2.50 (*0-916866-05-X*) Cats Pajamas.

Pell, Elsie, ed. see Gide, Andre.

Pell, Erik M., ed. Proceedings: International Conference on Photoconductivity, 3rd, Stanford University, Aug. 12, 1969. 1971. 172.00 (*0-08-016137-5*, Pub. by Pergamon Repr UK) Franklin.

Pell, Jerry, jt. auth. see Hanna, Steven R.

Pell, John. Ethan Allen. LC 72-5515. (Select Bibliographies Reprint Ser.). (Illus.). 1977. reprint ed. 31.95 (*0-8369-6919-7*) Ayer.

Pell, M. Gas Fluidization. (Handbook of Powder Technology Ser.: No. 8). 126p. 1990. 82.00 (*0-444-88335-5*) Elsevier.

Pell, Malcolm, ed. Handbook of Stereotaxy Using the CRW Apparatus. LC 94-1716. (Illus.). 240p. 1994. 95.00 (*0-683-06835-0*) Williams & Wilkins.

Pell, P. S., ed. Developments in Highway Pavement Engineering, Vol. 1. (Illus.). 285p. 1978. 83.00 (*0-85334-781-6*, Pub. by Elsevier Applied Sci UK) Elsevier.

— Developments in Highway Pavement Engineering, Vol. 2. (Illus.). 196p. 1978. 66.75 (*0-85334-804-9*, Pub. by Elsevier Applied Sci UK) Elsevier.

Pell, Robin. Keene Valley: The Landscape & Its Artists. (Illus.). (Orig.). Date not set. pap. text ed. write for info. (*0-935037-53-5*) G Peters Gallery.

Pell, Sarah, jt. auth. see Welker, Matthew.

Pella Historical Society Staff. Pella Community, Iowa, Vol. I. (Illus.). 682p. 1988. 62.50 (*0-88107-106-4*) Curtis Media.

— Pella Community, Iowa, Vol. II. (Illus.). 749p. 1989. 62.50 (*0-88107-138-2*) Curtis Media.

Pella, Judith. Dawning of Deliverance. 1995. pap. 9.99 (*1-55661-359-8*) Bethany Hse.

— Frontier Lady. 400p. (Orig.) (YA). 1993. pap. 9.99 (*1-55661-293-1*) Bethany Hse.

— Heirs of the Motherland. 1993. pap. 9.99 (*1-55661-358-X*) Bethany Hse.

— Stoner's Crossing. 1994. pap. 9.99 (*1-55661-294-X*) Bethany Hse.

Pella, Judith, jt. auth. see Phillips, Michael R.

Pella, Judith, jt. auth. see Phillips, Michael.

Pella, Judith, jt. auth. see Phillips, Michelle.

Pella, Judy, jt. auth. see Phillips, Michael.

Pella, Judy, jt. auth. see Phillips, Mike.

Pellam, Janet. Perry County Pieces. (Illus.). 26p. (Orig.). 1993. pap. 5.00 (*0-930502-09-4*) Pine Pr.

— Three Faces of the River. 67p. (Orig.). 1994. pap. write for info. (*1-879294-06-0*) Warm Spring Pr.

— Together We Weave. (Illus.). 40p. (Orig.). 1994. pap. 8.00 (*0-930502-12-4*) Pine Pr.

***Pellam, Janet, ed. & intro.** More Than Animals: An Anthology. 64p. (Orig.). 1994. pap. 8.00 (*0-930502-13-2*) Pine Pr.

Pellam, John L. 100 Designers' Favorite Rooms: Selected Projects of the World's Finest Designers & Architects. (Illus.). 236p. 1993. 30.00 (*1-882292-00-6*) Barons Whos Who.

— 100 Designers' Favorite Rooms: Selected Projects of the World's Finest Designers & Architects. 2nd ed. (Illus.). 236p. 1994. 45.00 (*1-882292-03-0*) Barons Whos Who.

— 100 Designers' Favorite Rooms: Selected Projects of the World's Finest Designers & Architects. 3rd ed. (Illus.). 236p. 1996. 45.00 (*1-882292-06-5*) Barons Whos Who.

***Pellam, John L., ed.** Who's Who in Interior Design: 1994-1995 Edition. 512p. 1994. 175.00 (*1-882292-02-2*) Barons Whos Who.

— Who's Who in Interior Design: 1996-1997 Edition. 540p. 1996. 210.00 (*1-882292-07-3*) Barons Whos Who.

— Who's Who of the Asian Pacific Rim: 1993-1994 Edition. 403p. 1993. 175.00 (*1-882292-01-4*) Barons Whos Who.

— Who's Who of the Asian Pacific Rim: 1995-1996 Edition. 381p. 1995. 210.00 (*1-882292-05-7*) Barons Whos Who.

Pellant, Chris. Fossils of the World. Charman, Andrew, ed. LC 93-46144. (Science Nature Guides Ser.). (Illus.). 80p. (J). (gr. 3-6). 1994. 12.95 (*1-85028-262-5*) Thunder Bay CA.

— Rocks & Minerals. LC 91-58222. (Eyewitness Handbks.). (Illus.). 300p. 1992. 29.95 (*1-56458-033-4*); 17.95 (*1-56458-061-X*) Dorling Kindersley.

— Rocks & Minerals. (Fact Finders Ser.). (Illus.). 64p. (J). 1990. 7.99 (*0-517-05148-6*) Random Hse Value.

— Rocks, Minerals & Fossils of the World. 1990. pap. 17.95 (*0-316-69796-6*) Little.

Pellaprat, Henri P. The Great Book of French Cuisine. 1173p. 1994. 45.00 (*0-86565-025-X*) Vendome.

Pellat, C. H., jt. auth. see Chouemi, Moustafa.

Pellaton, Jackie, ed. see Grayson, Stan.

Pellatt, A. H., jt. auth. see Freeman, M. A.

Pellauer, David, tr. see Ricoeur, Paul.

Pellauer, David, tr. see Sartre, Jean-Paul.

Pellauer, David, tr. see Veyne, Paul.

Pellauer, Mary D. Toward a Tradition of Feminist Theology: The Religious Social Thought of Elizabeth Cady Stanton, Susan B. Anthony & Anna Howard Shaw. LC 91-28029. (Chicago Studies in the History of American Religion Ser.: Vol. 15). 325p. 1991. 60.00 (*0-926019-51-1*) Carlson Pub.

Pellauer, Mary D., et al. Sexual Assault & Abuse: A Handbook for Clergy & Religious Professionals. Chester, Barbara & Boyajian, Jane, eds. LC 86-45825. 304p. 1991. pap. text ed. 17.00 (*0-06-066507-6*) Harper SF.

Pellaumail, J., jt. auth. see Metivier, Michel.

Pellcovitz, Raphael. Sforno: Commentary on the Torah. (ArtScroll Mesorah Ser.). 1993. 31.95 (*0-89906-238-5*) Mesorah Pubns.

Pelle, Marie-Paule. Valentino: Thirty Years of Magic. (Illus.). 336p. 1991. 95.00 (*1-55859-237-7*) Abbeville Pr.

***Pellecchia, Michael & Brownlee, Nancy.** Fort Worth: Catching the World's Attention. Hughes, Mary S. & Turner, James E., eds. (Illus.). 300p. 1995. 45.00 (*1-885352-18-2*) Community Comm.

Pellechet, M. Catalogue des Incunables et des Livres Imprimes de MD a MDXX. viii, 302p. reprint ed. write for info. (*0-318-71854-5*, Pub. by Georg Olms GW) Lubrecht & Cramer.

— Cataloque Des Incunables et Des Livres Imprimes De MD a MDXX. viii, 302p. reprint ed. write for info. (*0-318-71386-1*, Pub. by Georg Olms GW) Lubrecht & Cramer.

Pellechio, Anthony, jt. auth. see Dunn, David.

Pellegreno, Ann H. Iowa Takes to the Air: 1845-1918, Vol. 1. LC 79-55458. (Illus.). 288p. (J). (gr. 4 up). 1981. 17.95 (*0-935092-01-3*) Aerodrome Pr.

— Iowa Takes to the Air: 1919-1941, Vol. 2. LC 79-55458. (Illus.). 336p. (J). (gr. 4 up). 1986. 24.95 (*0-935092-02-1*) Aerodrome Pr.

***Pellegrin, Karen L.** Fat-Free Desserts. (Illus.). 192p. 1995. pap. 12.95 (*0-8092-3444-0*) Contemp Bks.

Pellegrin, Roland J., jt. auth. see Coates, Charles H.

***Pellegrini, A., et al, eds.** Role of Medroxyprogesterone in Endocrine-Related Tumors Vol. 3. fac. ed. LC 80-5550. (Progress in Cancer Research & Therapy Ser.: No. 15). (Illus.). 191p. Date not set. pap. 54.50 (*0-7837-7150-9*, 2047146) Bks Demand.

Pellegrini, A. D., jt. ed. see Britton, B. K.

Pellegrini, Alessandro. Friedrich Hoelderlin: Sein Bild in der Forschung. (C). 1965. 115.40 (*3-11-000338-4*) De Gruyter.

Pellegrini, Angelo. The Unprejudiced Palate. 256p. 1992. pap. 14.95 (*1-55821-199-3*) Lyons & Burford.

— Vintage Pellegrini: The Collected Wisdom of an American Buongustaio. Ingle, Schuyler, ed. 262p. 1991. text ed. 18.95 (*0-912365-45-5*); pap. 10.95 (*0-912365-44-7*) Sasquatch Bks.

Pellegrini, Angelo M. The Food Lover's Garden. (Illus.). 288p. 1989. reprint ed. pap. 13.95 (*1-55821-025-3*) Lyons & Burford.

***Pellegrini, Anthony D.** Literate Apprenticeships Vol. 54: The Emergence of Language & Literacy in the Preschool Years. Reeder, Kenneth et al, eds. (Advances in Discourse Processes Ser.). 1995. write for info. (*1-56750-148-6*) Ablex Pub.

— Literate Apprenticeships Vol. 54: The Emergence of Language & Literacy in the Preschool Years. Reeder, Kenneth et al, eds. (Advances in Discourse Processes Ser.). 1995. pap. write for info. (*1-56750-149-4*) Ablex Pub.

— Psychological Bases for Early Education. fac. ed. LC 87-18995. (Wiley Series in Developmental Psychology & Its Applications). 296p. 1988. reprint ed. pap. 84.40 (*0-7837-8275-6*, 2049055) Bks Demand.

— School Recess & Playground Behavior: Educational & Developmental Roles. LC 93-50547. (SUNY Series, Children's Play in Society). 224p. 1994. text ed. 59.50 (*0-7914-2183-X*); pap. text ed. 19.95 (*0-7914-2184-8*) State U NY Pr.

Pellegrini, Anthony D., ed. Applied Child Study: A Developmental Approach. 2nd ed. 264p. (C). 1991. text ed. 49.95 (*0-8058-0722-5*); pap. 27.50 (*0-8058-0723-3*) L Erlbaum Assocs.

Pellegrini, Anthony D., et al, eds. The Development of Oral & Written Language in Social Contexts. LC 84-369. (Advances in Discourse Processes Ser.: Vol. 13). 288p. (Orig.). (C). 1984. text ed. 75.00 (*0-89391-171-2*); pap. text ed. 39.50 (*0-89391-172-0*) Ablex Pub.

Pellegrini, Anthony D., jt. ed. see Bloch, Marianne N.

Pellegrini, Anthony D., jt. ed. see Galda, Lee.

Pellegrini, Anthony D., jt. ed. see Yawkey, Thomas D.

Pellegrini, Anthony L., jt. ed. see Bernardo, Aldo S.

Pellegrini, C., ed. Beam-Beam & Beam-Radiation Interactions: High Intensity & Nonlinear Effects: Proceedings of the 7th ICFA Workshop on Beam Dynamics, U.C.L.A., U. S. A. 13-16 May 1991. 200p. 1992. text ed. 98.00 (*981-02-0838-3*) World Scientific Pub.

Pellegrini, Carlos A., jt. auth. see Way, Lawrence M.

Pellegrini, Claudio. Collective Bargaining in the Construction Industry Wages Hours & Vocational... 153p. 1990. pap. 14.00 (*92-826-0145-5*, CB-58-90-166-EN-C) UNIPUB.

***Pellegrini, Claudio & Sessler, Andrew M., eds.** The Development of Colliders. (Key Papers in Physics). 1995. write for info. (*1-56396-349-3*) Am Inst Physics.

Pellegrini, Luca & Reddy, Srinivas K., eds. Marketing Channels: Relationships & Performance. LC 86-45186. (Advances in Retailing Ser.). 224p. 1986. text ed. 45.00 (*0-669-13158-X*) Free Pr.

Pellegrini, Luca & Reddy, Srivanas K., eds. Retail Marketing Channels. 416p. 1990. 59.95 (*0-415-03218-0*, A3502) Routledge.

Pellegrini, Nina. Charlie Claus: Santa's Best Friend. LC 93-1495. (Illus.). (J). (ps-6). 1993. 4.99 (*0-517-09309-X*, Derrydale Bks) Random Hse Value.

— Families Are Different. LC 90-22876. (Illus.). 32p. (J). (ps-3). 1991. lib. bdg. 15.95 (*0-8234-0887-6*) Holiday.

Pellegrini, Nina, jt. auth. see Garcia, Edward.

***Pellegrini, Robert J. & Meyers, Susan J.** Psychology for Correctional Education: Facilitating Human Development in Prison & Court School Settings. (Illus.). 320p. 1992. pap. 34.95 (*0-398-06318-4*) C C Thomas.

— Psychology for Correctional Education: Facilitating Human Development in Prison & Court School Settings. (Illus.). 320p. (C). 1992. text ed. 56.95x (*0-398-05791-5*) C C Thomas.

Pellegrini, U., jt. auth. see Dadda, L.

Pellegrino, Charles. Flying to Valhalla. 352p. 1994. mass mkt. 4.99 (*0-380-71881-2*, AvoNova) Avon.

— Flying to Valhalla. 1993. 22.00 (*0-688-12506-9*) Morrow.

— Return to Sodom & Gomorrah: Bible Stories from Archaeologists. LC 94-2424. 1994. 25.00 (*0-679-40006-0*) Random.

An Asterisk (*) at the beginning of an entry indicates that the title is appearing in BIP for the first time.

***Pellegrino, Charles & Zebrowski, George.** The Killing Star. LC 94-31367. 1995. write for info. (*0-688-13989-2*) Morrow.

Pellegrino, Charles R. Flying to Valhalla. 1993. pap. text ed. 22.00 (*0-380-97220-4*, AvoNova) Avon.

— Her Name, Titanic: The Real Story of the Sinking & Finding of the Unsinkable Ship. 320p. 1990. mass mkt. 6.50 (*0-380-70892-2*) Avon.

— Time Gate: Hurtling Backward Through History. 1985. pap. 16.95 (*0-07-156531-0*) McGraw.

— Time Gate: Hurtling Backward Through History. LC 84-23955. 1985. pap. 16.95 (*0-8306-1863-5*, 1863P) TAB Bks.

— Unearthing Atlantis: An Archaeological Odyssey. 336p. 1991. 22.50 (*0-394-57550-4*) Random.

— Unearthing Atlantis: An Archaeological Odyssey. LC 92-56364. 1993. pap. 12.00 (*0-679-73407-4*, Vin) Random.

Pellegrino, Charles R., jt. auth. see Stoff, Jesse A.

Pellegrino, E. D., et al, eds. Gift of Life: Catholic Scholars Respond to the Vatican Instruction. LC 90-30838. 210p. 1990. 19.95 (*0-87840-499-6*) Georgetown U Pr.

Pellegrino, Edmund D. Humanism & the Physician. LC 78-23174. 263p. reprint ed. pap. 75.00 (*0-7837-3026-8*, 2042914) Bks Demand.

Pellegrino, Edmund D., et al, eds. Transcultural Dimensions in Medical Ethics. 225p. 1992. 35.00 (*1-55572-015-3*) Univ Pub Group.

Pellegrino, Edmund D. & Thomasma, David C. The Christian Virtues in Medical Practice. LC 94-11007. 1995. write for info. (*0-87840-566-6*) Georgetown U Pr.

— For the Patient's Good: The Restoration of Beneficence in Health Care. 256p. 1988. 39.95 (*0-19-504319-7*) OUP.

— A Philosophical Basis of Medical Practice: Toward a Philosophy & Ethic of the Healing Professions. (Illus.). 1981. text ed. 17.95 (*0-19-502789-2*) OUP.

— The Virtues in Medical Practice. LC 92-49073. 1993. 35.00 (*0-19-508289-3*) OUP.

Pellegrino, Edmund D., jt. ed. see Flack, Harley E.

Pellegrino, Edmund D., et al, eds. Catholic Perspectives on Medical Morals: Foundational Issues. (C). 1989. lib. bdg. 84.50 (*1-55608-083-2*) Kluwer Ac.

— Ethics, Trust, & the Professions: Philosophical & Cultural Aspects. LC 90-46368. reprint ed. pap. 85.00 (*0-7837-9251-4*, 2049890) Bks Demand.

— Preserving the Creation: Environmental Theology & Ethics. LC 93-36684. (C). 1994. 40.00 (*0-87840-549-6*) Georgetown U Pr.

Pellegrino, James W., jt. ed. see Dillon, Ronna F.

Pellegrino, L. J., et al. Stereotaxic Atlas of the Rat Brain. 2nd ed. LC 79-9438. 280p. 1979. 49.50 (*0-306-40269-6*, Plenum Pr) Plenum.

Pellegrino, Mary A. Wang Systems Word Processing. 256p. (C). 1986. pap. text ed. 28.75 (*0-03-006077-X*) HB Coll Pubs.

Pellegrino, Michael. Give What You Command. 3.00 (*0-89942-580-1*, 580/04) Catholic Bk Pub.

Pellegrino, Michele. The True Priest: The Priesthood As Preached & Practiced by Saint Augustine. Rotelle, John E., ed. LC 87-71970. (Illus.). 144p. 1988. reprint ed. pap. 7.95 (*0-941491-08-0*) Augustinian Pr.

Pellegrino, Victor C. Maui Art Thoughts: Expressions & Visions. LC 88-92541. (Illus.). 112p. 1988. pap. 9.95 (*0-945045-01-8*) Maui Arthoughts.

— A Slip of Bamboo: A Collection of Haiku from Maui. 136p. 1995. pap. write for info. (*0-945045-04-2*) Maui Arthoughts.

— A Writer's Guide to Using Eight Methods of Transition. LC 93-77683. 52p. (Orig.). (C). 1993. pap. 5.95 (*0-945045-03-4*) Maui Arthoughts.

Pelleier, Linda. English - French Vocabulary of Microwave Ovens. 52p. (ENG & FRE.). 1987. pap. 24.95 (*0-8288-9381-0*) Fr & Eur.

Pelleier, Susann. Immigrant Dream & Other Poems. 48p. 1989. pap. 7.95 (*0-685-46223-4*) Soleil Pr.

— Immigrant Dream & Other Poems. limited ed. 48p. 1989. pap. 10.95 (*0-685-46224-2*) Soleil Pr.

Pellengahr, I., tr. see Faber, M., et al.

Pellens, Mildred, jt. auth. see Terry, Charles E.

***Peller, Beth.** The Family under the Bridge. Friedland, J. & Kessler, R., eds. (Novel-Ties Ser.). (J). (gr. 3-6). 1995. student ed, pap. text ed. 15.95 (*1-56982-286-7*) Lrn Links.

Peller, Jane E., jt. auth. see Walter, John L.

Peller, Jane E., jt. auth. see Walter, John.

***Peller, Marion.** Crisis-Proof Your Career: A Planning Guide for Job Security & Satisfaction in the 90's. 240p. (Orig.). 1994. pap. text ed. 4.99 (*0-425-14497-6*) Berkley Pub.

Pellerin, Bill & Neidhardt, Ralph. Bicycling the Dallas-Ft. Worth Area. 64p. 1990. pap. text ed. 10.95 (*1-882358-02-3*) TX Bicycle Map.

— Bicycling the Houston Area. 70p. 1987. pap. 9.95 (*1-882358-01-5*) TX Bicycle Map.

— Bicycling the Texas Hill Country & West Texas. 72p. 1988. pap. 9.95 (*1-882358-00-7*) TX Bicycle Map.

— Bicycling the Texas Hill Country & West Texas. rev. ed. 1988. reprint ed. pap. 10.95 (*1-882358-04-X*) TX Bicycle Map.

— Mountain Biking the Houston Area. 72p. (Orig.). 1993. pap. text ed. write for info. (*1-882358-03-1*) TX Bicycle Map.

Pellerin, Dave. Practical Design: Using Programmable Logic. 1991. text ed. 57.00 (*0-13-723834-7*) P-H.

***Pellerin, David.** Electronic Design Automation for Windows: A User's Guide. 479p. 1995. cd-rom, pap. 49.00 (*0-13-348988-4*) P-H.

Pellerin, David & Holley, Michael. Digital Design Using ABEL. LC 93-39558. 320p. 1994. disk 55.00 (*0-13-605874-4*) P-H.

Pellerin, R. G. Woodwind Care & Maintenance. (Illus.). 107p. (Orig.). 1979. 6.00 (*0-317-91154-6*) Intro Musicaids.

— Woodwind Care & Maintenance. (Illus.). 107p. (Orig.). (C). 1986. teacher ed 6.50 (*0-685-72228-7*); pap. 6.50 (*0-685-72226-0*); pap. text ed. 6.50 (*0-685-72227-9*) Intro Musicaids.

Pellerin, R. G., ed. see Ramsey, Thomas L.

Pellerite, James J. A Handbook of Literature for the Flute. 3rd rev. ed. LC 77-85443. 1978. pap. text ed. 20.00 (*0-931200-69-5*) Zalo.

— A Modern Guide to Fingerings for the Flute. LC 72-76260. 1972. pap. text ed. 15.00 (*0-931200-68-7*) Zalo.

— A Modern Guide to Fingerings for the Flute. reprint ed. pap. text ed. 15.95 (*0-88284-449-0*, 2887) Alfred Pub.

— A Notebook of Techniques for a Flute Recital. 1967. pap. text ed. 3.50 (*0-931200-50-4*) Zalo.

— Performance Methods for Flutists. 1968. pap. text ed. 4.95 (*0-931200-51-2*) Zalo.

***Pellet, Elias P.** History of the 114th Regiment: New York State Volunteers. (Illus.). 406p. 1995. reprint ed. pap. 34.00 (*1-887530-07-X*) RSG Pub.

— History of the 114th Regiment of New York State Volunteers. (Illus.). 1995. write for info. (*0-9614858-9-2*) RSG Pub.

Pelletan, Camille. Semaine De Mai. LC 75-173941. (FRE.). reprint ed. 54.00 (*0-404-07163-5*) AMS Pr.

Pelleti, Lisa, tr. see Valcanover, Francesco.

Pelletier. Alkaloids: Chemical & Biological Perspectives, Vol. 4. (Chemical & Biological Perspectives Ser.). 460p. 1986. text ed. 100.00 (*0-471-89301-3*) Krieger.

— Alkaloids: Chemical and Biological Perspectives, Vol. 9. (Alkaloids Chemical & Biological). 273p. 1994. text ed. 140.00 (*0-08-042089-3*, Pergamon Pr) Elsevier.

— Rearrangement. 1985. 18.22 (*0-02-595490-3*) Macmillan.

Pelletier, A. J. Bell Aircraft since Nineteen Thirty-Five. (Putnam Aviation Ser.). (Illus.). 288p. 1992. 47.95 (*1-55750-056-8*) Naval Inst Pr.

***Pelletier, Alain J.** Beech Aircraft & Their Predecessors. (Putnam Aviation Ser.). (Illus.). 256p. 1995. 49.95 (*1-55750-062-2*) Naval Inst Pr.

Pelletier, B. R., jt. ed. see Schafer, C. T.

***Pelletier, Carol M.** A Handbook of Techniques & Strategies for Coaching Student Teachers. 1995. pap. text ed. 34.95 (*0-205-15418-2*, Longwood Div) Allyn.

Pelletier, Cathie. The Bubble Reputation. LC 92-25447. 1993. 21.00 (*0-517-59311-4*, Crown) Crown Pub Group.

— The Bubble Reputation. Ng, Donna, ed. 304p. 1994. reprint ed. pap. 12.00 (*0-671-89010-7*, WSP) PB.

— The Funeral Makers. 256p. 1987. pap. 8.00 (*0-02-023610-7*, Pub. by Gebrueder Borntraeger GW) Macmillan.

— A Marriage Made at Woodstock. LC 93-38183. 1994. 22.00 (*0-517-59796-9*, Crown) Crown Pub Group.

— Once Upon a Time on the Banks. Rosenman, Jane, ed. 384p. 1991. reprint ed. pap. 10.00 (*0-671-72447-9*, WSP) PB.

— The Weight of Winter. LC 92-39708. 432p. 1993. reprint ed. pap. 12.00 (*0-671-79387-X*, WSP) PB.

Pelletier, Claire, jt. auth. see Martin, Helene.

Pelletier, David L. An Analysis of the Uses & Limitations of Information in the Iringa Nutrition Program, Tanzania. (Working Paper Ser.). (C). 1991. pap. text ed. 7.00 (*1-56401-105-4*) Cornell Food.

— The Relationship Between Child Antropometry & Mortality in Developing Countries: Implications for Policy, Progress, & Future Research. (Monograph Ser.). (Illus.). 72p. (C). 1991. pap. text ed. 12.00 (*1-56401-012-0*) Cornell Food.

Pelletier, David L. & Msukwa, Louis A. Intervention Planning in Response to Disasters: A Case Study of the Mealy Bug Disaster in Malawi. (Monograph Ser.). (Illus.). 54p. (C). 1990. pap. text ed. 12.00 (*1-56401-006-6*) Cornell Food.

Pelletier, Elaine S. How to Hire a Nanny: A Step by Step Guide for Parents. (Orig.). 1992. pap. 14.95 (*0-9635575-0-5*) Andre & Lanier.

— How to Hire a Nanny: A Step by Step Guide for Parents. 120p. (Orig.). 1993. pap. 9.95 (*0-9635575-7-2*) Andre & Lanier.

Pelletier, Francis J. Parmenides, Plato & the Semantics of Not-Being. LC 89-27650. 200p. 1990. 29.95 (*0-226-65390-0*) U Ch Pr.

Pelletier, Francis J., jt. ed. see Carlson, Greg N.

Pelletier, Henry L. Favorite Patchwork Patterns: Full-Size Templates & Instructions for Twelve Quilts. 1984. pap. 4.50 (*0-486-24753-8*) Dover.

Pelletier, Henry P. Nature's Endless Pulsations. LC 91-36603. 96p. 1992. pap. 8.95 (*0-86534-168-0*) Sunstone Pr.

Pelletier, Ida O. Dynamic Nurse-Patient Relationship. 128p. 1990. 21.95 (*0-88737-489-1*) Natl League Nurse.

Pelletier, J. W., jt. auth. see Kaijser, S. G.

Pelletier, Jacques, jt. ed. see Moisan, Michel.

***Pelletier, James L.** Mariner's Employment Guide: Every Seaman Needs This Valuable Reference. 2nd expanded rev. ed. (Illus.). 350p. 1995. spiral bd., pap. 39.95 (*0-9644915-0-8*) Marine Techn.

Pelletier, Ken. Sound Mind Sound Body. 1994. 23.00 (*0-671-77000-4*) S&S Trade.

Pelletier, Kenneth R. Holistic Medicine: From Stress to Optimum Health. 1984. 24.50 (*0-8446-6092-2*) Peter Smith.

— Mind As Healer Mind As Slayer. 1977. pap. 12.95 (*0-385-30700-4*, Delta) Dell.

— Mind As Healer-Mind As Slayer: A Holistic Approach to Preventing Stress Disorders. 1984. 21.00 (*0-8446-6093-0*) Peter Smith.

— A New Age: Problems & Potential. (Broadside Editions Ser.). 44p. (Orig.). (C). 1985. pap. 3.95 (*0-931191-02-5*) Rob Briggs.

— Sound Mind, Sound Body: A New Model for Lifelong Health. 1995. pap. 13.00 (*0-684-80251-1*, Fireside) S&S Trade.

— Toward a Science of Consciousness. LC 78-15290. 320p. 1985. pap. 7.95 (*0-89087-419-0*) Celestial Arts.

Pelletier, L. Conrad, jt. auth. see Carrier, Michel.

Pelletier, Louise & Perez-Gomez, Alberto, eds. Architecture, Ethics, & Technology. LC 93-90630. (Illus.). 264p. 1994. 49.95 (*0-7735-1148-2*, Pub. by McGill CN) U of Toronto Pr.

Pelletier, Monique A. Readings in Management & Organizations. 2nd ed. 464p. 1991. per. 25.95 (*0-8403-6531-4*) Kendall-Hunt.

Pelletier, Paul A. Prominent Scientists: An Index to Collective Biographies. 2nd ed. LC 85-3079. 380p. 1985. lib. bdg. 45.00 (*0-918212-78-2*) Neal-Schuman.

— Prominent Scientists: An Index to Collective Biographies. 3rd ed. 390p. 1994. 49.95 (*1-55570-114-0*) Neal-Schuman.

Pelletier, Paula, jt. auth. see Rattenbury, Judith.

Pelletier, Robert. Planets in Aspect: Understanding Your Inner Dynamics. LC 74-82711. (Planets Ser.). 1974. pap. 19.95 (*0-914918-20-6*, Whitford Pr) Schiffer.

— Planets in Houses: Experiencing Your Environment Planets. Anderson, Margaret, ed. (Planets Ser.). (Illus.). 1978. pap. 19.95 (*0-914918-27-3*, Whitford Pr) Schiffer.

Pelletier, Robert, jt. auth. see Cataldo, Leonard.

Pelletier, S. William, ed. Alkaloids: Chemical & Biological Perspectives, Vol. 2. LC 82-11071. 504p. 1984. text ed. 63.00 (*0-471-89299-8*) Krieger.

— Alkaloids: Chemical & Biological Perspectives, Vol. 3. 336p. 1990. text ed. 75.00 (*0-471-89302-1*) Krieger.

— Alkaloids: Chemical & Biological Perspectives, Vol. 5. 730p. 1987. text ed. 125.00 (*0-471-85372-0*) Krieger.

— Alkaloids: Chemical & Biological Perspectives, Vol. 6. 542p. 1988. text ed. 199.00 (*0-471-60298-1*) Wiley.

— Alkaloids, Vol. 7: Chemical & Biological Perspectives. (Illus.). 624p. 1991. 129.00 (*0-387-97290-0*) Spr-Verlag.

— Alkaloids, Vol. 8: Chemical & Biological Perspectives. (Illus.). 344p. 1992. 163.00 (*0-387-97787-2*) Spr-Verlag.

Pelletier, S. William & Phagan, Patricia. Bulletin, Vol. 17: John Taylor Arms: His World & Work. 1993. 10.00 (*0-685-66927-0*) Georgia Museum of Art.

Pelletier, S. William, et al. Adriaen Van Ostade: Etchings of Peasant Life in Holland's Golden Age. LC 93-45388. 1994. 30.00 (*0-915977-14-1*) Georgia Museum of Art.

***Pelletier, Sophie & Magnaint-Lopez, Bernard.** Les Petits Points de Casa Lopez. (Illus.). 176p. 1993. write for info. (*2-200-21331-X*) Lacis Pubns.

Pelletiere, George A., jt. auth. see Larson, Jay L.

Pelletiere, Stephen C. The Iran-Iraq War: Chaos in a Vacuum. LC 91-28089. 184p. 1992. text ed. 49.95 (*0-275-93843-3*, C3843, Praeger Pubs) Greenwood.

— Iraqi Power & United States Security in the Middle East. (Illus.). 107p. 1990. per. 3.25 (*0-16-027003-0*, S/N 008-020-01231-9) USGPO.

Pelletiere, Stephen C. & Johnson, Douglas V., II. Lessons Learned: The Iran-Iraq War. (Illus.). 119p. (Orig.). (C). 1994. pap. text ed. 35.00 (*0-7881-0601-5*) Diane Pub.

Pelletiere, Stephen C., et al. Iraqi Power & U. S. Security in the Middle East. (Illus.). 95p. (Orig.). (C). 1994. pap. text ed. 35.00 (*0-7881-0661-9*) Diane Pub.

Pelletreau, W. S. Smith: Wills of the Smith Families of NY & Long Island, 1664-1794, with Genealogy & History Notes. 151p. 1991. reprint ed. lib. bdg. 37.50 (*0-8328-1831-3*); reprint ed. pap. 27.50 (*0-8328-1832-1*) Higginson Bk Co.

Pelletreau, William S. History of Putnam County, New York. LC 88-24387. (Illus.). 944p. 1988. reprint ed. lib. bdg. 50.00 (*1-55787-033-0*, NY40025) Hrt of the Lakes.

— Suffolk County, Early Long Island Wills of Suffolk County, 1691-1703, with Genealogical & Historical Notes. (Illus.). 289p. 1995. reprint ed. lib. bdg. 37.50 (*0-8328-4714-3*) Higginson Bk Co.

Pellett, P. G., jt. auth. see VanDam, Stephan C.

Pellett, Roy, ed. The Best of Jazz Score. (Illus.). 160p. 1994. 17.95 (*0-563-36326-6*, BBC-Parkwest) Parkwest Pubns.

Pellett, W., et al. Otoneurosurgery. (Illus.). 256p. 1990. 193.00 (*0-387-50979-8*) Spr-Verlag.

Pelletti, Lisa, tr. see Angelini, Alessandro.

Pelletti, Lisa, tr. see Jannella, Cecilia.

Pelletti, Lisa, tr. see Paolieri, Annarita.

Pelletti, Lisa, tr. see Paolucci, Antonio.

Pelletti, Lisa C., tr. see Fossi, Gloria.

Pelletti, Lisa C., tr. see Heusinger, Lutz.

Pellew, George. John Jay. Morse, John T., Jr., ed. LC 70-128973. (American Statesmen Ser.: No. 9). reprint ed. 45.00 (*0-404-50859-6*) AMS Pr.

Pellew, Jill. The Home Office, Eighteen Forty-Eight to Nineteen Fourteen: From Clerks to Bureaucrats. LC 82-1533. 261p. 1982. 37.50 (*0-8386-3165-7*) Fairleigh Dickinson.

Pellicane, Patricia. Creole Captive. 1989. pap. 3.95 (*0-8217-2758-3*) Zebra.

— Darkest Heart. 320p. 1994. mass mkt. 4.50 (*0-8217-4565-4*) Zebra.

— Deceptions of the Heart. 512p. 1988. pap. 3.95 (*0-8217-2427-4*) Zebra.

— Desire's Glory. 1992. mass mkt. 4.50 (*0-8217-3989-1*) Zebra.

— Desperado Passion. 448p. 1991. mass mkt. 4.50 (*0-8217-3336-2*) Zebra.

— Embers of Desire. 400p. 1987. reprint ed. pap. 3.95 (*0-8439-2446-2*) Dorchester Pub Co.

— Fires Tender Kiss. 1991. mass mkt. 4.50 (*0-8217-3534-9*) Zebra.

— Frontier Temptress. 480p. 1989. pap. 3.95 (*0-8217-2574-2*) Zebra.

— Nights of Fire. 448p. 1993. mass mkt. 4.50 (*0-8217-4217-5*) Zebra.

— Nights of Passion. 448p. 1994. mass mkt. 4.50 (*0-8217-4524-7*) Zebra.

— Summer Heat. (Lucky in Love Ser.). 304p. 1992. mass mkt. 3.99 (*0-8217-3838-0*) Zebra.

— Sweet Revenge. pap. 3.50 (*0-317-61761-3*) PB.

— Sweet Seduction. 1992. mass mkt. 4.50 (*0-8217-3745-7*) Zebra.

— This Wild Heart. 1990. mass mkt. 4.50 (*0-8217-3067-3*) Zebra.

Pellicani, Luciano. The Genesis of Capitalism & the Origins of Modernity. Milliron, Kerry, ed. Colbert, James G., tr. 24.00 (*0-914386-25-5*) Telos Pr.

Pellicano, Tony A. History of War: Index of Foreign Medical Literature. LC 88-47853. 150p. 1988. 39.50 (*0-88164-950-3*); pap. 34.50 (*0-88164-951-1*) ABBE Pubs Assn.

— Medical Psychosomatics: Index of Modern Authors & Subjects with Guide for Rapid Research. LC 90-56289. 160p. 1991. 44.50 (*1-55914-382-7*); pap. 39.50 (*1-55914-383-5*) ABBE Pubs Assn.

— Psycho-Physiology & Biofeedback: Index of New Information with Authors & Subjects. LC 94-31239. 1994. write for info. (*0-7883-0258-2*); pap. write for info. (*0-7883-0259-0*) ABBE Pubs Assn.

— Psychophysiology & Biofeedback: Index of New Information with Authors & Subjects. 180p. 1992. 49.50 (*1-55914-620-6*); pap. 39.50 (*1-55914-621-4*) ABBE Pubs Assn.

***Pelliccia, Joseph & Perrotto, John.** Human Nutrition Laboratory Manual. (Illus.). 198p. (C). 1995. student ed 17.50 (*1-878045-78-4*) Whittier Pubns.

Pelliccioni, Louis, Jr., jt. auth. see Scott, Michael.

Pellicciotti, Joseph M. An Analysis of the Age Discrimination in Employment Act. (Public Employee Relations Library: No. 71). 84p. 1989. 14.00 (*0-685-33387-6*) Intl Personnel Mgmt.

— Handbook of Basic Trial Evidence: A College Introduction. LC 91-50745. xx, 462p. (Orig.). (C). 1992. pap. 29.95 (*1-55605-191-3*) Wyndhall Pr.

— Handbook on Basic Trial Evidence. 2nd ed. 246p. (Orig.). (C). 1988. lib. bdg. 45.00 (*0-8191-6715-0*) U Pr of Amer.

— Title Seven Liability for Sexual Harassment in the Workplace. (Public Employee Relations Library: No. 69). 64p. 1988. 14.00 (*0-685-33389-2*) Intl Personnel Mgmt.

— Title VII Liability for Sexual Harassment in the Workplace. 2nd ed. (Public Employee Relations Library: No. 75). 126p. 1993. 14.00 (*0-685-69343-0*) Intl Personnel Mgmt.

Pellicer, Leonard, et al. High School Leaders & Their Schools, Vol. II: Profiles of Effectiveness. 110p. (Orig.). 1990. pap. text ed. 8.00 (*0-88210-238-9*) Natl Assn Principals.

***Pellicer, Leonard O. & Anderson, Lorin W.** A Handbook for Teacher Leaders. LC 95-2535. (Illus.). 240p. 1995. 44.95 (*0-8039-6172-3*); pap. 22.95 (*0-8039-6173-1*) Corwin Pr.

Pellicer, Leonard O. & Stevenson, Kenneth R., eds. The Best of the NASSP Bulletin: Readings in Secondary School Administration. 288p. (Orig.). (C). 1985. pap. text ed. 12.00 (*0-88210-168-4*) Natl Assn Principals.

Pellicer, Olga, jt. ed. see Fagen, Richard R.

Pellicia, Joseph. Laboratory Manual in Bionutrition. Perrotto, John, ed. (Illus.). 200p. (Orig.). (C). 1990. 16.00 (*1-878045-01-6*) Whittier Pubns.

Pellier, P. Programming Real Time Games on the TRS-80. Martres, Laurent, tr. 112p. write for info. (*0-318-57946-4*) Blue Cat.

***Pelligrini, Anthony D., ed.** The Future of Play Theory: A Multidisciplinary Inquiry into the Contributions of Brian Sutton-Smith. (SUNY Series, Children's Play in Society). 384p. (C). 1995. text ed. 74.50x (*0-7914-2641-6*) State U NY Pr.

— The Future of Play Theory: A Multidisciplinary Inquiry into the Contributions of Brian Sutton-Smith. (SUNY Series, Children's Play in Society). 384p. (C). 1995. pap. text ed. 24.95x (*0-7914-2642-4*) State U NY Pr.

Pelligrino, James W., jt. ed. see Dillon, Ronna R.

Pelligrino, Victoria, jt. auth. see Napolitane, Catherine.

Pellikaan, Maja & Schroder, Hannelore, eds. Against Patriarchal Thinking: Women Philosophers in Europe 1992; a Future Without Discrimination? 400p. (Orig.). 1993. pap. text ed. 45.00 (*90-5383-102-9*, Pub. by VU Univ Pr NE) Paul & Co Pubs.

Pelling, C. B., ed. see Plutarch.

Pelling, George. Beginning Your Familiy History in Great Britain. 4th rev. ed. (Illus.). 64p. 1989. 7.50 (*0-8063-1253-X*, 4560) Genealog Pub.

Pelling, Henry. American Labor. LC 60-7247. (Chicago History of American Civilization Ser.). (Illus.). 1961. pap. text ed. 10.95 (*0-226-65393-5*, CHAC16) U Ch Pr.

— Britain & the Marshall Plan. LC 88-18160. 192p. 1988. text ed. 49.95 (*0-312-02427-4*) St Martin.

— A Short History of the Labour Party. 9th ed. 215p. 1991. text ed. 49.95 (*0-312-05272-3*) St Martin.

— A Short History of the Labour Party. 10th ed. LC 93-16705. (Illus.). 225p. 1993. text ed. 45.00 (*0-312-09676-3*) St Martin.

— Social Geography of British Elections, 1885-1910. (Modern Revivals in History Ser.). 488p. (C). 1994. text ed. 80.95 (*0-7512-0278-9*, Pub. by Gregg Revivals UK) Ashgate Pub Co.

Pelling, Henry, jt. auth. see Bealey, Frank W.

Pelling, Margaret & Smith, Richard M., eds. Life, Death & the Elderly: Historical Perspectives. (Wellcome Institute Series in the History of Medicine). 288p. 1991. 59.95 (*0-415-05742-6*, A5839) Routledge.

— Life, Death & the Elderly: Historical Perspectives. LC 93-23614. (Studies in the Social History of Medicine). 272p. 1994. pap. 16.95 (*0-415-11135-8*, B3702) Routledge.

Pellingell, Noel. The Pellingell Book of Birding Records. 2nd ed. LC 91-76702. (Illus.). 152p. (Orig.). 1992. pap. 12.95 (*1-878788-27-2*) Amer Birding Assn.

Pelliot, Paul. Les Mongols et la Papaute, 3 pts. in 1 vol. LC 80-2365. reprint ed. 34.50 (*0-404-18913-X*) AMS Pr.

Pelliot, Paul, ed. see Huc & Gabet.

Pellis, Mark, jt. auth. see Ringel, William E.

Pellisier, Georges. The Literary Movement in France During the Nineteenth Century. LC 71-150197. 504p. reprint ed. lib. bdg. 25.00 (*0-8290-0508-0*) Irvington.

Pellissier-Gart, M., jt. auth. see Lecarme, Olivier.

Pellissier, Georges. Les Ecrivains Politiques en France Avant le Revolution. Mayer, J. P., ed. LC 78-67374. (European Political Thought Ser.). (FRE.). 1980. reprint ed. lib. bdg. 15.95 (*0-405-11724-8*) Ayer.

— Literary Movement in France During the Nineteenth Century. LC 71-150197. (Select Bibliographies Reprint Ser.). 1977. reprint ed. 31.95 (*0-8369-5710-5*) Ayer.

Pellissier, R., tr. see De Musset, Alfred.

Pellitero, Ana M., ed. Teatro Medieval. (Nueva Austral Ser.: No. 157). (SPA.). 1991. pap. text ed. 24.95x (*84-239-1957-9*) Elliots Bks.

Pellizzari, Piero. Italian-Spanish, Spanish-Italian Technical & Commercial Dictionary, 2 vols. 1500p. (ITA & SPA.). 1990. 250.00 (*0-8288-7348-8*, 8885158021) Fr & Eur.

Pellizzi, Francesco, ed. Res: Anthropology & Aesthetics. (RES Monographs on Anthropology & Aesthetics: No. 26). (Illus.). 144p. (C). 1994. pap. write for info. (*0-521-47722-0*) Cambridge U Pr.

— Res: Anthropology & Aesthetics. (RES Monographs on Anthropology & Aesthetics: No. 27). (Illus.). 144p. (C). 1995. pap. write for info. (*0-521-48373-5*) Cambridge U Pr.

— RES: Anthropology & Aesthetics, No. 22. (Illus.). 160p. (C). 1992. pap. 24.95 (*0-521-43760-1*) Cambridge U Pr.

— RES: Anthropology & Aesthetics, No. 23. (Illus.). 152p. (C). 1993. pap. 24.95 (*0-521-44741-0*) Cambridge U Pr.

— RES: Anthropology & Aesthetics, No. 25. (Illus.). 152p. (C). 1994. pap. 24.95 (*0-521-46663-6*) Cambridge U Pr.

— Res: Anthropology & Aesthetics, Vol. 28. (RES Monographs on Anthropology & Aesthetics). 144p. (C). 1995. pap. write for info. (*0-521-55858-1*) Cambridge U Pr.

Pellizzi, Francesco & Tambiah, Stanley J., eds. Ethnicities & Nations: Processes of Interethnic Relations in Latin America, Southeast Asia, & the Pacific. LC 88-6471. 416p. (C). 1988. 22.50 (*0-945472-01-3*) Rothko Chapel.

Pellizzi, Francescso, ed. RES: Anthropology & Aesthetics, No. 24. (RES Monographs on Anthropology & Aesthetics). (Illus.). 160p. (C). 1993. pap. 24.95 (*0-521-44742-9*) Cambridge U Pr.

Pellizzi, G., et al, eds. Energy Savings in Agricultural Machinery & Mechanization. 144p. 1988. 47.00 (*1-85166-236-7*) Elsevier.

Pellman, Kathryn A., jt. auth. see Rafalovich, Danita.

Pellman, Kenneth, jt. auth. see Pellman, Rachel T.

Pellman, Kenneth, jt. auth. see Pellman, Rachel.

Pellman, Kenneth, jt. auth. see Scott, Stephen.

Pellman, Leonard J., jt. auth. see Shimabukuro, Shihan M.

Pellman, Rachel & Pellman, Kenneth. Amish Doll Quilts, Dolls & Other Playthings. LC 86-81060. (Illus.). 96p. (Orig.). 1986. pap. 15.95 (*0-934672-35-0*) Good Bks PA.

— A Treasury of Amish Quilts. deluxe ed. LC 90-82488. (Illus.). 128p. 1990. pap. 19.95 (*1-56148-000-2*) Good Bks PA.

— A Treasury of Mennonite Quilts. deluxe ed. LC 92-26505. (Illus.). 128p. 1992. pap. 19.95 (*1-56148-059-2*) Good Bks PA.

— The World of Amish Quilts. LC 84-80651. (Illus.). 128p. 1984. 24.95 (*0-934672-48-2*) Good Bks PA.

— The World of Amish Quilts. deluxe ed. LC 84-80651. (Illus.). 128p. 1984. pap. 19.95 (*0-934672-22-9*) Good Bks PA.

Pellman, Rachel, jt. auth. see Benner, Cheryl.

Pellman, Rachel T. Amish Quilt Patterns. LC 84-80652. (Illus.). 128p. 1984. pap. 12.95 (*0-934672-23-7*) Good Bks PA.

— Favorite Applique Patterns from the Old Country Store, Vol. 1. LC 92-30871. 124p. 1992. pap. 15.95 (*1-56148-073-8*) Good Bks PA.

— Favorite Applique Patterns from the Old Country Store, Vol. 2. LC 92-30871. 124p. 1992. pap. 15.95 (*1-56148-074-6*) Good Bks PA.

— Favorite Applique Patterns from the Old Country Store, Vol. 3. LC 92-30871. 124p. 1992. pap. 15.95 (*1-56148-075-4*) Good Bks PA.

— Small Amish Quilt Patterns. LC 85-70280. (Illus.). 128p. (Orig.). 1985. pap. 12.95 (*0-934672-30-X*) Good Bks PA.

— Tips for Quilters: A Handbook of Hints, Shortcuts, & Practical Suggestions from Experienced Quilters. LC 93-24758. 160p. (Orig.). 1993. pap. 9.95 (*1-56148-080-0*) Good Bks PA.

Pellman, Rachel T. & Pellman, Kenneth. Amish Crib Quilts. deluxe ed. LC 85-70281. (Illus.). 96p. (Orig.). 1985. pap. 15.95 (*0-934672-29-6*) Good Bks PA.

Pellman, Rachel T. & Ranck, Joanne. Quilts among the Plain People. LC 81-82209. (People's Place Book Ser.: No. 4). (Illus.). 96p. (Orig.). 1981. pap. 5.95 (*0-934672-03-2*) Good Bks PA.

Pellman, Rachel T. & Steffy, Jan. Patterns for Making Amish Dolls & Doll Clothes. LC 87-23700. 224p. (Orig.). 1987. pap. 12.95 (*0-934672-47-4*) Good Bks PA.

Pellman, Rachel T., jt. auth. see Benner, Cheryl A.

Pellman, Rachel T., jt. auth. see Good, Phyllis P.

Pellman, Rachel T., jt. ed. see Good, Phyllis P.

Pellman, Rachel T., jt. auth. see Heisey, Craig N.

Pellman, Samuel. An Introduction to the Creation of Electroacoustic Music. 441p. 1994. pap. 37.95 (*0-534-21450-9*) Intl Thomson.

Pellock, jt. auth. see Dodson.

Pellock, John M. & Myer, Edwin C. Neurologic Emergencies in Infancy & Childhood. 2nd ed. (Illus.). 640p. 1993. 85.00 (*0-7506-9419-X*) Buttrwrth-Heinemann.

Pellon, Gustavo. Jose Lezama Lima's Joyful Vision: A Study of Paradiso & Other Prose Works. LC 89-4856. (Texas Pan American Ser.). (Illus.). 165p. 1989. text ed. 22.50 (*0-292-74020-4*) U of Tex Pr.

Pelloso, Pierre. Practical Digital Electronics. Nelson, John C., tr. LC 85-15524. 229p. reprint ed. pap. 65.30 (*0-7837-4408-0*, 2044151) Bks Demand.

— The Practice of Digital Electronics. LC 85-15524. 219p. 1986. pap. text ed. 54.95 (*0-471-90733-2*) Wiley.

Pelloutier, F. Histoire des Bourses du Travail. (Publications Gramma Ser.). 340p. 1971. pap. text ed. 42.00 (*0-677-50725-9*) Gordon & Breach.

Pelloux, R. M., ed. see Metallurgical Society of AIME Staff.

***Pellow, C. Kenneth.** Films As Critiques of Novels: Transformational Criticism. LC 94-31631. 380p. 1995. text ed. 99.95 (*0-7734-9067-1*) E Mellen.

Pellow, C. Kenneth, jt. ed. see Blackburn, Alexander.

Pellow, Deborah. Women in Accra: Options for Autonomy. Kitchen, Cole, ed. LC 77-78740. (Illus.). 1977. 19.95 (*0-917256-03-4*) Ref Pubns.

Pellow, Harry C. The ABCs & Nine Twelves of Porsche Engines: Porsche Engines & the Future of the Human Race. rev. ed. (Illus.). 700p. 1981. per. 29.95 (*0-941210-04-9*) HCP Res.

— The Maestro Chronicles. 1984p. per. 19.50 (*0-941210-08-1*) HCP Res.

— The Maestro's Newsletter. 200p. (Orig.). 1989. 19.95 (*0-941210-12-X*) HCP Res.

— The Maestro's Spec Book & Emergency Breakdown Procedures. 1984. per. 19.95 (*0-941210-09-X*) HCP Res.

— Murphy Is My Co-Pilot. (Illus.). 407p. 1983. 29.95 (*0-941210-07-3*) HCP Res.

— Secrets of the Inner Circle. 3rd ed. 450p. 1983. per. 29.95 (*0-941210-06-5*) HCP Res.

***Pellowe, Susan, ed. & intro.** A Wesley Family Book of Days. (Illus.). 172p. (Orig.). 1994. pap. 12.00 (*0-9623507-1-0*) Renard Prodns.

Pellowe, Susan I. Saffron & Currants: A Cornish Heritage Cookbook. (Illus.). 52p. (Orig.). 1989. pap. 5.00 (*0-9623507-0-2*) Renard Prodns.

Pellowski, Anne. The Family Storytelling Handbook: How to Use Stories, Anecdotes, Rhymes, Handkerchiefs, Paper & Other Objects to Enrich Your Family Traditions. LC 87-7981. (Illus.). 160p. (J). 1987. text ed. 16.95 (*0-02-770610-9*, Mac Bks Young Read) S&S Childrens.

— Hidden Stories in Plants: Unusual & Easy-to-Tell Stories from Around the World Together with Creative Things to Do While Telling Them. LC 89-37166. (Illus.). 176p. (J). (ps up). 1990. text ed. 15.95 (*0-02-770611-7*, Mac Bks Young Read) S&S Childrens.

— The Story Vine: A Source Book of Unusual & Easy-to-Tell Stories from Around the World. LC 83-26756. (Illus.). 128p. (J). 1984. text ed. 15.95 (*0-02-770590-0*, Mac Bks Young Read); pap. 9.95 (*0-02-044690-X*, Mac Bks Young Read) S&S Childrens.

— Tales with a Twist: A Young People's Guide to Storytelling. LC 95-2991. (J). 1995. write for info. (*0-689-80311-7*, Aladdin Paperbacks) S&S Childrens.

— The World of Storytelling: A Practical Guide to the Origins, Development, & Applications of Storytelling. enl. rev. ed. 330p. 1990. 40.00 (*0-8242-0788-2*) Wilson.

Pellowski, Anne, ed. A World of Children's Stories. LC 93-13509. (Children's World Ser.). (Illus.). 192p. (Orig.). (J). (gr. 3-6). 1993. pap. 19.95 (*0-377-00259-3*) Friendship Pr.

Pellowski, Anne, jt. auth. see Miller, Teresa.

Pellowski, Michael. Clara Joins the Circus. LC 80-25602. (Illus.). 48p. (J). (ps-3). 1981. 5.95 (*0-8193-1057-3*); lib. bdg. 5.95 (*0-8193-1058-1*) Parents.

— Clara Joins the Circus. LC 94-34653. (Parents Magazine Read Aloud Original). (J). 1995. write for info. (*0-8368-0998-X*) Gareth Stevens Inc.

— One Hundred Two Cat & Dog Jokes. LC 91-42769. (Illus.). 64p. (J). (gr. 2-6). 1992. pap. text ed. 2.95 (*0-8167-2790-2*) Troll Assocs.

— One Hundred Two Wacky Monster Jokes. LC 91-44702. (Illus.). 64p. (J). (gr. 2-6). 1992. pap. text ed. 2.95 (*0-8167-2746-5*) Troll Assocs.

— One Hundred Two Wild & Wacky Jokes. LC 91-30783. (Illus.). 64p. (J). (gr. 2-6). 1991. pap. text ed. 2.95 (*0-8167-2612-4*) Troll Assocs.

Pellowski, Michael J. Bad News Boyfriend, No. 2. LC 91-19659. (Riverdale High Ser.). (Illus.). 128p. (YA). (gr. 4-8). 1991. pap. 2.99 (*1-56282-108-3*) Hyprn Child.

— Benny's Bad Day. LC 85-14016. (Illus.). 48p. (Orig.). (J). (gr. 1-3). 1986. lib. bdg. 10.59 (*0-8167-0620-4*); pap. text ed. 3.50 (*0-8167-0621-2*) Troll Assocs.

— The Big Breakup, No. 5. LC 91-73839. (Riverdale High Ser.). (Illus.). 128p. (YA). (gr. 4-8). 1992. pap. 2.99 (*1-56282-147-4*) Hyprn Child.

— Class Clown, No. 7. LC 91-74005. (Riverdale High Ser.). (Illus.). 128p. (Orig.). (YA). (gr. 4-8). 1992. pap. 2.99 (*1-56282-143-X*) Hyprn Child.

— Copycat Dog. LC 85-14128. (Illus.). 48p. (Orig.). (J). (gr. 1-3). 1986. lib. bdg. 10.59 (*0-8167-0652-2*); pap. text ed. 3.50 (*0-8167-0653-0*) Troll Assocs.

— Double Trouble. 120p. (J). (gr. 3-5). 1994. pap. 2.99 (*0-87406-700-6*) Willowisp Pr.

— The Duck Who Loved Puddles. LC 85-14058. (Illus.). 48p. (Orig.). (J). (gr. 1-3). 1986. lib. bdg. 10.59 (*0-8167-0578-X*); pap. text ed. 3.50 (*0-8167-0579-8*) Troll Assocs.

— Fire Fighter. LC 88-10353. (What's It Like to Be a...Ser.). (Illus.). 32p. (J). (gr. 1-3). 1989. lib. bdg. 10.89 (*0-8167-1428-2*); pap. text ed. 2.95 (*0-8167-1429-0*) Troll Assocs.

— Forest Ranger. LC 88-10355. (What's It Like to Be a... Ser.). (Illus.). 32p. (J). (gr. 1-3). 1989. lib. bdg. 10.89 (*0-8167-1422-3*); pap. text ed. 2.95 (*0-8167-1423-1*) Troll Assocs.

— Ghost in the Library. LC 88-1236. (Fiddlesticks Ser.). (Illus.). 48p. (Orig.). (J). (gr. 1-4). 1989. lib. bdg. 10.59 (*0-8167-1337-5*); pap. text ed. 3.50 (*0-8167-1338-3*) Troll Assocs.

— Good-bye Millions, No. 10. LC 91-58617. (Riverdale High Ser.). (Illus.). 128p. (Orig.). (YA). (gr. 4-8). 1992. pap. 2.99 (*1-56282-191-1*) Hyprn Child.

— Is That Arabella?, No. 9. LC 91-58614. (Riverdale High Ser.). (Illus.). 128p. (Orig.). (YA). (gr. 4-8). 1992. pap. 2.99 (*1-56282-190-3*) Hyprn Child.

— It's First Love, Jughead Jones, No. 4. LC 91-71804. (Riverdale High Ser.). (Illus.). 128p. (YA). (gr. 4-8). 1991. pap. 2.99 (*1-56282-110-5*) Hyprn Child.

— Joke & Riddle Bonanza. LC 94-49697. (Illus.). 96p. (J). 1995. 13.95 (*0-8069-0960-9*) Sterling.

— Magic Broom. LC 85-14054. (Illus.). 48p. (Orig.). (J). (gr. 1-3). 1986. lib. bdg. 10.59 (*0-8167-0636-0*); pap. text ed. 3.50 (*0-8167-0637-9*) Troll Assocs.

— Maxwell Finds a Friend. LC 85-14085. (Illus.). 48p. (Orig.). (J). (gr. 1-3). 1986. lib. bdg. 10.59 (*0-8167-0586-0*); pap. text ed. 3.50 (*0-8167-0587-9*) Troll Assocs.

— The Messy Monster. LC 85-14064. (Illus.). 48p. (Orig.). (J). (gr. 1-3). 1986. lib. bdg. 10.59 (*0-8167-0570-4*); pap. text ed. 3.50 (*0-8167-0571-2*) Troll Assocs.

— Mixed-up Magic. LC 88-1312. (Fiddlesticks Ser.). (Illus.). 48p. (Orig.). (J). (gr. 1-4). 1989. lib. bdg. 10.59 (*0-8167-1327-8*); pap. text ed. 3.50 (*0-8167-1328-6*) Troll Assocs.

— Moosey Saves Money. LC 85-14053. (Illus.). 48p. (Orig.). (J). (gr. 1-3). 1986. lib. bdg. 10.59 (*0-8167-0628-X*); pap. text ed. 3.50 (*0-8167-0629-8*) Troll Assocs.

— My Father, the Enemy, No. 8. LC 91-58615. (Riverdale High Ser.). (Illus.). 128p. (YA). (gr. 4-8). 1992. pap. 2.99 (*1-56282-189-X*) Hyprn Child.

— No Fleas, Please! LC 85-14066. (Illus.). 48p. (Orig.). (J). (gr. 1-3). 1986. lib. bdg. 10.59 (*0-8167-0608-5*); pap. text ed. 3.50 (*0-8167-0609-3*) Troll Assocs.

— Not So Great Moments in Sports. LC 94-30974. (Illus.). 96p. 1994. 13.95 (*0-8069-1256-1*) Sterling.

— Not-So-Great Moments in Sports. (Illus.). 96p. (Orig.). 1995. pap. 4.95 (*0-8069-1257-X*) Sterling.

— One Hundred Two School Jokes. LC 91-20702. (Illus.). 64p. (J). (gr. 2-6). 1991. pap. 2.95 (*0-8167-2579-9*) Troll Assocs.

— One Last Date with Archie, No. 3. LC 91-25649. (Riverdale High Ser.). (Illus.). 128p. (YA). (gr. 4-8). 1991. pap. 2.99 (*1-56282-109-1*) Hyprn Child.

— Professor Possum's Great Adventure. LC 88-1281. (Fiddlesticks Ser.). (Illus.). 48p. (Orig.). (J). (gr. 1-4). 1988. lib. bdg. 10.59 (*0-8167-1341-3*); pap. text ed. 3.50 (*0-8167-1342-1*) Troll Assocs.

— The Puppy Nobody Wanted. (Illus.). 24p. (J). (ps-3). 1988. 1.95 (*0-87406-338-8*) Willowisp Pr.

— Rich Girls Don't Have to Worry, No. 6. LC 91-73840. (Riverdale High Ser.). (Illus.). 128p. (YA). (gr. 4-8). 1992. pap. 2.99 (*1-56282-148-2*) Hyprn Child.

— Teddy on Time. LC 85-14127. (Illus.). 48p. (Orig.). (J). (gr. 1-3). 1986. lib. bdg. 10.59 (*0-8167-0582-8*); pap. text ed. 3.50 (*0-8167-0583-6*) Troll Assocs.

— Tour Troubles - Betty Cooper, Baseball Star. LC 91-58616. (Riverdale High Ser.). (Illus.). 256p. (Orig.). (YA). (gr. 4-8). 1992. pap. 3.99 (*1-56282-192-X*) Hyprn Child.

— Triple Trouble. 112p. (Orig.). (J). (gr. 3-5). 1995. pap. 2.99 (*0-87406-724-3*) Willowisp Pr.

— The Trouble with Candy, No. 1. LC 91-19654. (Riverdale High Ser.). (Illus.). 128p. (YA). (gr. 4-8). 1991. pap. 2.99 (*1-56282-107-5*) Hyprn Child.

— Wackiest Jokes in The World. LC 93-38242. (Illus.). 96p. (J). 1994. 13.95 (*0-8069-0493-3*) Sterling.

— Wackiest Jokes in the World. (Illus.). 96p. 1995. pap. 3.95 (*0-8069-0494-1*) Sterling.

— What's It Like to Be a Police Officer. LC 89-34395. (What's It Like to Be a...Ser.). (Illus.). 32p. (J). (gr. k-3). 1990. lib. bdg. 10.89 (*0-8167-1811-3*); pap. text ed. 2.95 (*0-8167-1812-1*) Troll Assocs.

— Who Can't Follow an Ant? LC 85-14009. (Illus.). 48p. (Orig.). (J). (gr. 1-3). 1986. lib. bdg. 10.59 (*0-8167-0592-5*); pap. text ed. 3.50 (*0-8167-0593-3*) Troll Assocs.

Pells, Edward G. European, Coloured & Native Education in South Africa, 1652-1928. LC 74-15077. reprint ed. 29.50 (*0-404-12126-8*) AMS Pr.

— Three Hundred Years of Education in South Africa. LC 71-90156. 152p. 1970. reprint ed. text ed. 52.50 (*0-8371-2217-1*, PEEA, Greenwood Pr) Greenwood.

Pells, P. J., ed. Structural Foundations on Rock: Proceedings of the International Conference, Sydney, 7-9th May 1980, 2 vols., Set. 494p. (C). 1981. text ed. 210.00 (*90-6191-072-2*, Pub. by A A Balkema NE) Ashgate Pub Co.

Pells, Richard H. The Liberal Mind in a Conservative Age: American Intellectuals in the 1940s & 1950s. 2nd ed. LC 89-14676. 488p. 1989. pap. 19.95 (*0-8195-6225-4*, Wesleyan Univ Pr) U Pr of New Eng.

— Radical Visions & American Dreams: Culture & Social Thought in the Depression Years. LC 84-10420. 445p. 1984. pap. 19.95 (*0-8195-6122-3*, Wesleyan Univ Pr) U Pr of New Eng.

Pelly, David. Illustrated Encyclopedia to World Sailing. LC 65-18206. 1989. 16.95 (*0-671-10146-3*) S&S Trade.

Pelly, Lewis. Report on a Journey to Riyadh (1865) (Arabia Past & Present Ser.: Vol. 6). (Illus.). 1978. reprint ed. 26.95 (*0-902675-64-8*) Oleander Pr.

Pelly, T. M. Doctor Minor-a Sketch of the Life of Dr. Thomas T. Minor, 1844-1889. (Shorey Historical Ser.). 142p. reprint ed. pap. 8.95 (*0-8466-0204-0*, S204) Shorey.

Pelmear, Kenneth. Carols of Cornwall. (C). 1989. 40.00 (*0-907566-22-7*, Pub. by Dyllansow Truran UK) St Mut.

— Salute to Truro. (C). 1989. 22.00 (*0-907566-31-6*, Pub. by Dyllansow Truran UK) St Mut.

— Songs of Cornwall. (C). 1989. 30.00 (*1-85022-010-7*, Pub. by Dyllansow Truran UK) St Mut.

Pelmear, P. L., et al, eds. Hand-Arm Vibration: A Comprehensive Guide for Occupational Health Professionals. LC 92-13983. 1992. text ed. 59.95 (*0-442-01250-0*) Van Nos Reinhold.

Pelmont, R. A. Paul Valery et les Beaux-Arts. (Harvard Studies in Romantic Languages: Vol. 23). 1949. 20.00 (*0-527-01121-5*) Periodicals Srv.

Pelnar, Premysl V. Health Effects of Asbestos & of Other Minerals & Fibres: An Annotated Compilation of the Worlds' Literature on Asbestos, 1906-1986, 3 vols., Set. Scherr, George H., ed. 2400p. 362.00 (*0-930376-46-3*) Chem-Orbital.

Pelnar, Tom & Weber, Valerie, eds. Tanzania. LC 88-42890. (Children of the World Ser.). (Illus.). 64p. (J). (gr. 5-6). 1989. lib. bdg. 21.26 (*1-55532-210-7*) Gareth Stevens Inc.

Pelofsky, Arnold, ed. Coal Conversion Technology: Problems & Solutions. LC 79-17936. (ACS Symposium Ser.: No. 110). 257p. 1979. 36.95 (*0-8412-0516-7*) Am Chemical.

Pelofsky, Arnold H., ed. Heavy Oil Gasification. LC 77-24338. (Energy, Power, & Environment Ser.: No. 1). (Illus.). 175p. reprint ed. pap. 49.90 (*0-7837-0846-7*, 2041158) Bks Demand.

— Synthetic Fuels Processing: Comparative Economics. LC 76-41472. (Illus.). 487p. reprint ed. pap. 138.80 (*0-7837-3351-8*, 2043309) Bks Demand.

Peloquin, Albert A. Barrier-Free Residential Design. LC 93-9150. 320p. 1993. text ed. 50.00i (*0-07-049326-X*) McGraw.

Pelos, Carollee, photos. Spectacular Vernacular: Traditional Adobe Architecture. (Illus.). 192p. 1989. 35.00 (*0-89381-391-5*) Aperture.

Pelosi, Frank, jt. auth. see Pelosi, Marjorie.

Pelosi, Guiseppe, jt. ed. see Silvester, Peter P.

Pelosi, Marjorie & Pelosi, Frank. Shellcraft Instruction. (Orig.). 1959. pap. 3.95 (*0-8200-0501-0*) Great Outdoors.

Peloubet, S. S. A Collection of Legal Maxims in Law & Equity, with English Translations. (Illus.). ix, 332p. 1985. reprint ed. lib. bdg. 30.00 (*0-8377-1020-0*) Rothman.

Pelowich, Nadia, jt. ed. see Stewart, Janet.

Pelphrey, Jo Ann. Into the Think Tank with Literature. Keeling, Jan, ed. (Illus.). 160p. (Orig.). (J). (gr. k-3). 1992. pap. text ed. 14.95 (*0-86530-192-1*, IP193-6) Incentive Pubns.

Pelroy, R. A., jt. ed. see Park, J. F.

Pels, H. J. & Wortmann, J. C., eds. Integration in Production Management Systems: Proceedings of the IFIP WG 5.7 Working Conference on Integration in Production Management Systems, Eindhove, The Netherlands, 24-27 August 1992. LC 92-44887. (IFIP Transactions B: Applications in Technology Ser.: Vol. B-7). 1992. write for info. (*0-444-89877-8*, North Holland) Elsevier.

Pels, Peter, jt. ed. see Nencel, Lorraine.

Pelser, Frederick & Pelser, Marcia E. Freedom Bridge. (Illus.). 100p. (Orig.). 1984. pap. 5.95 (*0-9612348-0-6*) Fremar Pr.

Pelser, H. E., ed. Psychosomatic Medicine as an Integrated Approach to Life, Education & Doctor-Patient Cooperation: Fourteenth European Conference on Psychosomatic Research, Noordwijkerhout, September 1982. (Journal: Psychotherapy & Psychosomatics: Vol. 40, No. 1-4). (Illus.). 272p. 1983. pap. 112.00 (*3-8055-3785-9*) S Karger.

Pelser, H. E., jt. auth. see Paulley, J. W.

Pelser, Marcia E., jt. auth. see Pelser, Frederick.

Pelsma, Kimberlie H., ed. Ergonomics Sourcebook: A Guide to Human Factors Information. LC 87-9673. 275p. 1987. 72.50 (*0-916313-12-3*) Ergosyst Assocs.

Pelt, Adrian. Libyan Independence & the United Nations: A Case of Planned Decolonization. LC 72-99836. 1046p. reprint ed. pap. 180.00 (*0-8357-8208-5*, 2033853) Bks Demand.

Pelt, Chester H., Sr. Pelt: A Genealogical History of the Pelt Family Branch of the Van Pelt Family Tree. (Illus.). 140p. 1992. lib. bdg. 32.00 (*0-8328-2382-1*); pap. 22.00 (*0-8328-2383-X*) Higginson Bk Co.

Pelt, Ken A. Farewell to Freedom. 124p. (Orig.). 1985. pap. 7.95 (*0-936527-00-5*) Amer Sec Bill.

— Life. (Pocket Library). 73p. (Orig.). 1987. pap. 4.95 (*0-943139-00-7*) Heritage Heirloom.

***Pelta.** California. 1995. pap. text ed. (*0-8225-9668-7*) Lerner Group.

— Texas. (J). (gr. 3-6). 1995. pap. text ed. (*0-8225-9667-9*) Lerner Group.

Pelta, Kathy. Alexander Graham Bell. (Pioneers in Change Ser.). (Illus.). 144p. (J). (gr. 5-9). 1989. lib. bdg. 13.95 (*0-382-09529-4*) Silver Burdett Pr.

— Bridging the Golden Gate. (American Landmarks Ser.). (Illus.). 96p. (J). (gr. 4-8). 1987. pap. 5.95 (*0-8225-9521-4*, Lerner Publctns) Lerner Group.

— Bridging the Golden Gate. (American Landmarks Ser.). (Illus.). 96p. (J). (gr. 4 up). 1987. lib. bdg. 15.95 (*0-8225-1707-8*, Lerner Publctns) Lerner Group.

P
Q

— California. LC 93-1497. (Hello U. S. A. Ser.). (Illus.). 72p. (J). (gr. 3-6). 1993. lib. bdg. 17.50 (*0-8225-2738-3*, Lerner Publctns) Lerner Group.

— Discovering Christopher Columbus: How History Is Invented. (History Ser.). 112p. (J). (gr. 4-9). 1991. lib. bdg. 19.95 (*0-8225-4899-2*, Lerner Publctns) Lerner Group.

— Idaho. LC 94-2235. (Hello U. S. A. Ser.). (Illus.). 72p. (J). (gr. 3-6). 1995. 17.50 (*0-8225-2734-0*, Lerner Publctns) Lerner Group.

— Texas. LC 93-33390. (Hello U. S. A. Ser.). (Illus.). 72p. (J). (gr. 3-6). 1994. lib. bdg. 17.50 (*0-8225-2749-9*, Lerner Publctns) Lerner Group.

— The U. S. Navy. (Armed Services Ser.). (Illus.). 88p. (YA). (gr. 5 up). 1990. lib. bdg. 22.95 (*0-8225-1435-4*, Lerner Publctns) Lerner Group.

— Vermont. LC 93-33389. (Hello U. S. A. Ser.). (Illus.). 72p. (J). (gr. 3-6). 1994. lib. bdg. 17.50 (*0-8225-2729-4*, Lerner Publctns) Lerner Group.

Peltason, J. W. Fifty-Eight Lonely Men: Southern Federal Judges & School Desegregation. LC 61-12350. 288p. 1971. reprint ed. pap. 12.95 (*0-252-00175-3*) U of Ill Pr.

— Understanding the Constitution. 12th ed. 398p. (C). 1991. pap. text ed. 18.75 (*0-15-592869-4*) HB Coll Pubs.

Peltason, Jack W. Understanding the Constitution. 13th ed. 432p. (C). 1994. pap. text ed. 20.00 (*0-15-500721-1*) HarBrace.

Peltason, Timothy. Reading: In Memoriam. (Essays in Literature Ser.). 200p. 1985. text ed. 35.00x (*0-691-06650-7*) Princeton U Pr.

— Reading in Memoriam. LC 85-42698. (Princeton Essays in Literature Ser.). Date not set. reprint ed. pap. 55.10 (*0-7837-9418-5*, 2060159) Bks Demand.

Peltason, Timothy, ed. see Arnold, Matthew.

Peltenberg, E. J., ed. Early Society in Cyprus. (Illus.). 304p. 1989. 55.00 (*0-85224-633-1*, Pub. by Edinburgh U Pr UK) Col U Pr.

Peltenburg. Vrysi: A Subterranean Settlement in Cyprus, With Microfiche. 1991. pap. write for info. (*0-85668-217-9*, Pub. by Aris & Phillips UK) David Brown.

Peltenburg, Edgar. Western Asiatic Antiquities. 1990. text ed. 90.00 (*0-7486-0224-0*, Pub. by Edinburgh U Pr UK) Col U Pr.

Pelter, Andrew. Borane Reagents. (Best Synthetic Methods Ser.). 503p. 1988. text ed. 158.00 (*0-12-549875-6*) Acad Pr.

Pelteret, David A. Catalogue of English Post-Conquest Vernacular Documents. 152p. 1990. 63.00 (*0-85115-259-7*) Boydell & Brewer.

— Slavery in Early Medieval England: From the Reign of Alfred to the Early Twelfth Century. (Studies in Anglo-Saxon History: Vol. 7). 288p. (C). 1995. text ed. 63.00 (*0-85115-399-2*) Boydell & Brewer.

Pelteret, David A., jt. ed. see Woods, J. D.

***Peltier.** Binocular Stargazer: A Beginner's Guide to Exploring the Sky. 160p. 1995. pap. text ed. 19.95 (*0-913135-25-9*, 18544) Kalmbach.

Peltier, A. P., jt. auth. see Kahn, M. F.

Peltier, Althea Y. Psychology & Its Practice: Index of Modern Information. LC 89-78057. 150p. 1990. 44.50 (*1-55914-202-2*); pap. 39.50 (*1-55914-203-0*) ABBE Pubs Assn.

— Psychology of Mental Disorders: Medical Guidebook for Reference & Research. LC 84-45216. 150p. 1985. 37.50 (*0-88164-184-7*); pap. 34.50 (*0-88164-185-5*) ABBE Pubs Assn.

***Peltier-Draine, Elsaida.** What's Up Girlfriend? (Illus.). 170p. (Orig.). 1994. 17.95 (*0-9643320-1-9*); per., pap. 11.95 (*0-9643320-0-0*) Zenon Pubn.

— What's Up Girlfriend? large type ed. (Illus.). 170p. (Orig.). 1994. 17.95 (*0-9643320-2-7*) Zenon Pubn.

Peltier, Jerome. Antoine Plante: Mountain Man, Rancher, Miner, Guide, Hosteler & Ferryman. 1983. 7.50 (*0-87770-286-1*); pap. 4.95 (*0-685-07495-1*) Ye Galleon.

— Background History of the Coeur D'Alene Indian Reservation. 100p. Date not set. write for info. (*0-318-57414-4*) Ye Galleon.

— Black Harris. 158p. 1986. 15.95 (*0-87770-388-4*) Ye Galleon.

— A Brief History of the Coeur d'Alene Indians 1806-1909. 94p. 1987. pap. 6.95 (*0-87770-256-X*) Ye Galleon.

— Felix Warren, Pioneer Stage Driver. 66p. 1988. pap. 4.95 (*0-87770-391-4*) Ye Galleon.

— Madame Dorion. 44p. 1981. 7.50 (*0-87770-240-3*) Ye Galleon.

Peltier, Jerome, ed. Banditti of the Rockies. 1964. 12.50 (*0-87018-048-7*) Ross.

— Journal of Edward Cavileer Hinde. 84p. 1983. 12.00 (*0-87770-305-1*) Ye Galleon.

Peltier, Leonard. Orthopedics: A History & Iconography. (Illus.). 305p. 1993. 225.00 (*0-930405-47-1*) Norman SF.

Peltier, Leonard F. Fractures: A History & Iconography of Their Treatment. (Illus.). 273p. 1990. 210.00 (*0-930405-16-1*) Norman SF.

***Peltier, Leonard F. & Aust, J. Bradley.** L' Etoile dDu Nord: An Account of Owen Harding Wangensteen (1898-1981), Surgeon-Teacher-Scholar. LC 94-78654. (Illus.). 165p. (Orig.). 1994. pap. text ed. 20.00 (*1-880696-07-X*) Am Coll Surgeons.

Peltier, Thomas R. Policies & Procedures for Data Security: A Complete Manual for Computer Systems & Networks. (Illus.). 170p. 1991. ring bd. 97.00 (*0-87930-241-0*, 722) Miller Freeman.

Peltier, W. R. Mantle Convection: Plate Tectonics & Global Dynamics. viii, 882p. 1989. text ed. 237.00 (*0-677-22120-7*) Gordon & Breach.

Peltier, W. R., ed. Mantle Convection: Plate Tectonics & Global Dynamics. 882p. 1988. 198.00 (*0-677-22102-9*) Gordon & Breach.

Peltier, W. Richard, ed. Ice in the Climate System. LC 93-29039. (NATO ASI Series I: Global Environmental Change: Vol. 12). 1994. 225.00 (*0-387-57167-1*) Spr-Verlag.

Pelto, Gretel H., jt. auth. see Pelto, Pertti J.

Pelto, Pertti, jt. ed. see Bernard, H. Russell.

Pelto, Pertti J. The Snowmobile Revolution: Technology & Social Change in the Arctic. (Illus.). 225p. (C). 1987. reprint ed. pap. text ed. 9.95 (*0-88133-287-9*) Waveland Pr.

Pelto, Pertti J & Pelto, Gretel H. Anthropological Research: The Structure of Inquiry. 2nd ed. LC 76-62583. 1978. pap. 19.95 (*0-521-29228-X*) Cambridge U Pr.

Pelton, jt. auth. see Murphy.

Pelton, Barry C. Tennis. 4th ed. (Physical Activities Ser.). (C). 1986. pap. text ed. 10.00 (*0-673-16665-1*) HarpCollege.

Pelton, Charles L. Doctor, My Bill Is Too High. (Illus.). 1978. 18.00 (*0-931470-01-3*); pap. 14.95 (*0-931470-00-5*) Fam Health Media.

— How to Get Rid of Fat. 45p. 1986. pap. 5.00 (*0-931470-02-1*) Fam Health Media.

— The Sex Book for Those Who Think They Know It All. Klinkel, Sheryl, ed. (Illus.). 227p. 1980. lib. bdg. 24.95 (*0-931470-03-X*); pap. 14.95 (*0-931470-04-8*) Fam Health Media.

Pelton, Charles L. & Myers, Lois. How to Emotionally Survive Difficult Times. 103p. 1986. pap. 6.00 (*0-931470-07-2*) Fam Health Media.

Pelton, Charles L. & Myers-Pelton, Lois. Pelton Family in America: Three Hundred Seventy-Five Years of Genealogy. 1167p. 1992. lib. bdg. 84.95 (*0-931470-10-2*) Fam Health Media.

Pelton, Dan. God Invented Safe Sex: He Created Families. Pelton, Jeanette, ed. 50p. (Orig.). 1993. pap. 5.00 (*1-879564-03-3*) Long Acre Pub.

Pelton, Dan, ed. see Pelton, Jeanette & Pelton, Fawn.

Pelton, Dan, ed. see Pelton, Jeanette.

Pelton, Donald. My Love for You. (Illus.). 1984. pap. 5.95 (*0-933169-00-0*) Heldon Pr.

— My Sense of Self. (Illus.). 1984. pap. 7.95 (*0-933169-01-9*) Heldon Pr.

— Spiritual Quest: Variations on a Theme. (Illus.). (Orig.). 1986. pap. 8.95 (*0-933169-02-7*) Heldon Pr.

Pelton, Fawn, jt. auth. see Pelton, Jeanette.

Pelton, Gordon E. Voice Processing. (Computer Communications Ser.). 389p. 1993. text ed. 45.00i (*0-07-049309-X*) McGraw.

Pelton, Howard K. Noise Control Management. LC 92-18950. 1993. text ed. 59.95 (*0-442-00763-9*) Van Nos Reinhold.

Pelton, J. M. Genealogy of the Pelton Family in America, Being a Record of the Descendants of John Pelton, Who Settled in Boston about 1630-1632. (Illus.). 722p. 1989. reprint ed. lib. bdg. 121.00 (*0-8328-0950-0*); reprint ed. pap. 113.00 (*0-8328-0951-9*) Higginson Bk Co.

Pelton, Jeanette. Don't Call Me Emmy! 94p. (J). (gr. 5-8). 1991. pap. 3.50 (*1-879564-02-5*) Long Acre Pub.

— Folks I Wish I'd Known. Pelton, Dan, ed. (Illus.). 75p. (J). (gr. 5-8). 1993. pap. 4.00 (*1-879564-05-X*) Long Acre Pub.

— God Wanted to Write a Best Seller, So in the Beginning Was the Word. LC 91-90003. 52p. (J). (gr. 6 up). 1991. pap. 5.95 (*1-879564-00-9*, GWBS101) Long Acre Pub.

— Kids Grow in My Garden. LC 91-90004. (Growing with God Ser.: No. I). (Illus.). 88p. (J). (gr. 4-6). 1991. pap. 3.50 (*1-879564-01-7*, GWG1) Long Acre Pub.

— Natural Morning. Pelton, Dan, ed. (Illus.). 100p. (Orig.). (J). (gr. 5-7). 1993. pap. 6.00 (*1-879564-06-8*) Long Acre Pub.

Pelton, Jeanette & Pelton, Fawn. Crafts for a Long, Boring, What-Do-I-Do-Now Afternoon. Pelton, Dan, ed. (Illus.). 50p. (Orig.). (J). (gr. 4-7). 1993. pap. 4.00 (*1-879564-04-1*) Long Acre Pub.

Pelton, Jeanette, ed. see Pelton, Dan.

Pelton, Joeph N., jt. ed. see Edelson, Burton I.

Pelton, Joseph. Futuretalk. 1991. pap. 19.95 (*0-923426-90-6*) Smith Micro.

Pelton, Joseph N. Future Talk. (Illus.). 300p. 1990. pap. 24.95 (*0-685-34870-9*) Smith Micro.

— Global Communications Satellite Policy: INTELSAT, Politics & Functionalism. LC 74-77978. 183p. 1974. 24.50 (*0-912338-32-6*); fiche 11.50 (*0-912338-33-4*) Lomond.

— Wireless & Satellite Telecommunications: The Technology, the Market, & the Regulations. 2nd ed. LC 95-7049. (Digital & Wireless Communication Ser.). 1995. text ed. 55.00 (*0-13-140493-8*) P-H.

Pelton, Joseph N., jt. ed. see Edelson, Burton I.

Pelton, Leroy H. The Psychology of Nonviolence. LC 74-2156. 310p. 1974. 122.00 (*0-08-018099-X*, Pub. by Pergamon Repr UK) Franklin.

Pelton, Leroy H., ed. The Social Context of Child Abuse & Neglect. LC 80-13922. 331p. 1981. 45.95 (*0-87705-504-1*); pap. 21.95 (*0-89885-244-7*) Human Sci Pr.

Pelton, Leroy J. For Reasons of Poverty: A Critical Analysis of the Public Child Welfare System in the United States. LC 89-33968. 220p. 1989. text ed. 42.95 (*0-275-93073-4*, C3073, Praeger Pubs) Greenwood.

Pelton, Linda, illus. & intro. The Hatha Yoga Workbook. 224p. (Orig.). 1989. student ed 11.95 (*0-931454-15-8*) Timeless Bks.

Pelton, Mary H. Reading Is Not a Spectator Sport. (Illus.). 200p. 1993. pap. 23.00 (*1-56308-118-0*) Teacher Ideas Pr.

— Staff Development in Small & Rural Schools. 31p. 1983. pap. 4.50 (*0-87652-050-6*, 021-00835) Am Assn Sch Admin.

Pelton, Mary H. & DiGennaro, Jacqueline. Images of a People: Tlingit Myths & Legends. LC 92-20564. (World Folklore Ser.). 170p. 1992. lib. bdg. 22.00 (*0-87287-918-6*) Libs Unl.

Pelton, Mary H., jt. auth. see Kinghorn, Harriet R.

Pelton, Robert. Circling the Sun. 1986. 12.95 (*0-912405-14-7*) Pastoral Pr.

— Loony Laws. rev. ed. (Illus.). 123p. 1990. pap. 8.95 (*0-8027-7339-7*) Walker & Co.

Pelton, Robert D. The Trickster in West Africa: A Study of Mythic Irony & Sacred Delight. LC 77-75396. (Hermeneutics: Studies in the History of Religions: No. 8). 1980. pap. 12.00 (*0-520-06791-6*) U CA Pr.

Pelton, Robert S. From Power to Communion: Toward a New Way of Being Church Based on the Latin American Experience. LC 93-40435. (C). 1994. text ed. 21.95 (*0-268-00989-9*); pap. text ed. 11.95 (*0-268-00990-2*) U of Notre Dame Pr.

Pelton, Robert W. Dead or Alive? LC 92-90483. 208p. (Orig.). 1993. pap. 11.95 (*0-918751-31-4*) J O Flores.

— The Devil & Karen Kingston: The Incredible Three-Day Exorcism That Brought Miraculous Deliverance to a Totally Demonized Young Girl. LC 76-12148. (Illus.). 1976. 7.50 (*0-916620-10-7*) Portals Pr.

— Infernal Revenue: A Jolly Peek at Some of the Scams that Waste Away Your Taxes. (Illus.). 1984. 4.50 (*0-916620-67-0*) Portals Pr.

— Laughable Laws & Courtroom Capers: Loony Legalities & Curious Cases All Around the U. S. A. 194p. 1993. 9.95 (*0-8027-7390-7*) Walker & Co.

— Loony Sex Laws: Rib-Tickling Legalities in the History of Sex. 190p. (Orig.). 1992. 9.95 (*0-8027-7383-4*) Walker & Co.

— Thieves, Con Men & Murderers. LC 91-74147. 180p. (Orig.). 1992. pap. 9.95 (*0-918751-26-8*) J O Flores.

— X-Rated Media Bloopers & Messups: A Choice Collection of Sexy Newsworthy Boners. LC 93-74665. 120p. (Orig.). 1994. pap. 10.00 (*0-918751-38-1*, 38) J O Flores.

Pelton, Robert W., jt. auth. see Farley, G. M.

Pelton, Robert W., jt. auth. see Lynn, Kristie.

***Pelton, Robert Y.** Fielding's Borneo. Knoles, Kathy, ed. (Travel Guides Ser.). (Illus.). 304p. (Orig.). 1995. pap. 16.95 (*1-56952-026-7*) Fielding Wrldwide.

***Pelton, Robert Y. & Dulles, Wink.** Fielding's Southeast Asia. Knoles, Kathy, ed. (Travel Guides Ser.). (Illus.). 560p. (Orig.). 1994. pap. 16.95 (*1-56952-051-8*) Fielding Wrldwide.

Pelton, Robert Y., jt. auth. see Dulles, Wink.

***Pelton, Robert Y., et al.** Fielding's Guide to the World's Most Dangerous Places. Knoles, Kathy, ed. (Travel Guide Ser.). (Illus.). 400p. (Orig.). 1995. pap. 19.95 (*1-56952-031-3*) Fielding Wrldwide.

***Pelton, Robert Young.** Fielding's Seychelles 1995. (Travel Guide Ser.). 352p. 1995. 12.95 (*1-56952-050-X*) Fielding Wrldwide.

Pelton, Ross & Overholser, Lee. Revolution in Cancer Therapy: The Complete Guide to Current Alternative Treatments. LC 93-30140. 1994. 12.00 (*0-671-79623-2*, Fireside) S&S Trade.

Pelton, Ross & Pelton, Taffy C. Mind Food & Smart Pills: A Sourcebook for the Vitamins, Herbs, & Drugs That Can Increase Intelligence, Improve Memory, & Prevent Brain Aging. 1989. pap. 12.95 (*0-385-26138-1*) Doubleday.

Pelton, Sonya T. Awake Savage Heart. 1983. pap. 3.75 (*0-8217-1279-9*) Zebra.

— Captive Caress. 496p. 1986. pap. 3.95 (*0-8217-1923-8*) Zebra.

— Captive Chains. 1988. pap. 3.95 (*0-8217-2304-9*) Zebra.

— Captive Dove. 448p. 1991. mass mkt. 4.95 (*0-8217-3332-X*) Zebra.

— Dakota Flame. 1989. pap. 3.95 (*0-8217-2700-1*) Zebra.

— Ecstasy's Magic. 1992. mass mkt. 5.99 (*0-8217-3623-X*) Zebra.

— Forbidden Dawn. 1985. pap. 3.75 (*0-8217-1602-6*) Zebra.

— Heavensent. 400p. 1995. mass mkt. 4.99 (*0-8217-4859-9*) Zebra.

— Love Hear My Heart. 1990. mass mkt. 4.50 (*0-8217-2913-6*) Zebra.

— Love's Lost Angel. 448p. 1993. mass mkt. 4.99 (*0-8217-4214-0*) Zebra.

— Passion's Paradise. 544p. (Orig.). 1981. pap. 3.25 (*0-89083-765-1*) Zebra.

— Phantom Love. (Orig.). 1982. pap. 3.50 (*0-89083-950-6*) Zebra.

— Secret Jewel. 448p. 1994. mass mkt. 4.99 (*0-8217-4519-0*) Zebra.

— Wild Island Sands. 1983. pap. 3.75 (*0-8217-1135-0*) Zebra.

— Windswept Passion. 1984. pap. 3.75 (*0-8217-1484-8*) Zebra.

— With Only One Kiss. 448p. 1992. mass mkt. 4.99 (*0-8217-3987-5*) Zebra.

Pelton, Sonya Y. Bittersweet Bondage. 1984. pap. 3.75 (*0-8217-1368-X*) Zebra.

Pelton, Taffy C., jt. auth. see Pelton, Ross.

Pelton, Walter J., et al. Epidemiology of Oral Health. LC 77-88811. (Vital & Health Statistics Monographs, American Public Health Association). (Illus.). 189p. 1969. 23.50 (*0-674-25885-1*) HUP.

Pelton, Willis S. Death & Postmortem Changes-Normal, Rare, Bizarre & Mysterious: Index of New Information. 150p. 1994. 44.50 (*0-7883-0054-7*); pap. 39.50 (*0-7883-0055-5*) ABBE Pubs Assn.

***Peltonen, Markku.** Classical Humanism & Republicanism in English Political Thought 1570-1640. (Ideas in Context Ser.: No. 36). 288p. (C). Date not set. write for info. (*0-521-49695-0*) Cambridge U Pr.

Peltonen, S. Teitotekniikan Artikkelisanakirja. 276p. (FIN.). 1985. 195.00 (*0-8288-1368-X*, M 356) Fr & Eur.

Peltre, G., jt. auth. see Paraf, A.

Pelts, Roman & Albrut, Lev. Comprehensive Chess Course Vols. 1 & 2: From Beginner to Advance Player in 24 Lessons, 2 Vols. in 1. 3rd rev. ed. Parr, Larry, ed. (Illus.). 448p. 1992. per. 42.00 (*0-9617207-5-1*) Chess Info Res Ctr.

— Comprehensive Chess Course, Vols. 1 & 2: From Beginner to Advance Player in 24 Lessons, 2 vols. in 1. 3rd enl. rev. ed. Parr, Larry, ed. (Illus.). 448p. reprint ed. per. write for info. (*0-318-70093-X*) Chess Info Res Ctr.

Peltsman, Michael, see Mikhail Armalinsky, pseud..

Peltu, Malcolm. The Electronic Office. 180p. 1986. pap. 5.95 (*0-563-21056-7*, Pub. by BBC UK) Parkwest Pubns.

Peltu, Malcolm, jt. auth. see Otway, Harry J.

Peltz, Carl F. Walking in the Kingdom of God: A Lenten Meditation for the Busy Christian. 80p. (Orig.). 1994. pap. text ed. 4.95 (*0-8146-2256-9*, Liturg Pr Bks) Liturgical Pr.

Peltz, Diane, ed. see Kommedahl, Thor.

Peltz, Leslie R. Fashion Accessories. LC 74-10891. 1974. teacher ed 5.00 (*0-672-96411-2*, Bobbs); pap. text ed. 8.50 (*0-672-96109-1*, Bobbs) Macmillan.

— Fashion Accessories. 2nd ed. 1980. pap. write for info. (*0-672-97275-1*) Macmillan.

— Fashion Color, Line, & Design. LC 79-142515. 1971. teacher ed 5.00 (*0-672-96057-5*, Bobbs); pap. text ed. 9.90 (*0-672-96056-7*, Bobbs) Macmillan.

— Fashion, Color, Line, & Design. 2nd ed. 1980. write for info. (*0-672-97277-8*); teacher ed write for info. (*0-672-97278-6*) Macmillan.

— Merchandising Mathematics. LC 79-494. 1979. pap. write for info. (*0-672-97273-5*) Macmillan.

Peltz, Mary E., jt. auth. see Goldovsky, Boris.

Peltzer, Karl. Enzyklopaedisches Handbuch der Werbung und Publikation, Vol. 1. (GER.). 1961. 49.95 (*0-8288-6821-2*, M-7081) Fr & Eur.

— Enzyklopaedisches Handbuch der Werbung und Publikation, Vol. 2. (GER.). 1963. 49.95 (*0-8288-6790-9*, M-7082) Fr & Eur.

— Das Treffende Reim. 7th ed. 148p. (GER.). 1993. 39.95 (*0-7859-8690-1*, 372256123x) Fr & Eur.

— Das Treffende Wort. 23th ed. 792696p. (GER.). 1993. 75.00 (*0-8288-1980-7*, M15518) Fr & Eur.

Peltzman, Sam, jt. ed. see Fiorentini, Gianluca.

Pelupessy, Wim. Perspectives on the Agro-Export Economy in Central America. LC 91-2232. (Latin American Ser.). 198p. (C). 1991. 49.95 (*0-8229-1164-7*) U of Pittsburgh Pr.

Pelupessy, Wim & Weeks, John, eds. Economic Maladjustment in Central America. LC 92-18016. 1993. text ed. 69.95 (*0-312-08632-6*) St Martin.

Peluso, Anthony P., et al. Basic BASIC Programming: Self-Instructional Manual & Text. (Computer Science Ser.). (C). 1971. pap. write for info. (*0-201-05845-6*) Addison-Wesley.

Peluso, Emanuel. Good Day. 1966. pap. 2.75 (*0-8222-0461-4*) Dramatists Play.

— Hurricane of the Eye. 1969. pap. 2.75 (*0-8222-0544-0*) Dramatists Play.

— Little Fears. 1967. pap. 2.75 (*0-8222-0675-7*) Dramatists Play.

Peluso, Gary, jt. auth. see Portaro, Sam.

Peluso, Luigi A., jt. auth. see Recardo, Ronald J.

***Peluso, Nancy L.** Rich Forests, Poor People: Resource Control & Resistance in Java. 1992. pap. 15.00 (*0-520-08931-6*) U CA Pr.

— Rich Forests, Poor People: Resource Control & Resistance in Java. 336p. (C). 1992. 45.00 (*0-520-07377-0*) U CA Pr.

Peluso, Samuel L. To Live & Die with Dignity: A Guide to Living Wills. Diecker, Mary L., ed. LC 91-75021. 160p. 1991. pap. 19.95 (*1-880254-01-8*) Vista.

Peluso, Samuel P., jt. auth. see Bollenbacher, George H.

Pelz, Dave & Mastroni, Nick. Putt Like the Pros: Dave Pelz's Scientific Way to Improve Your Stroke Reading the Greens, & Lowering Your Score. LC 86-46095. (Illus.). 240p. 1991. reprint ed. pap. 13.00 (*0-06-092078-5*, PL) HarpC.

Pelz, Donald C. & Andrews, Frank M. Scientists in Organizations Revised Edition: Productive Climates for Research & Development. LC 76-620038. 400p. 1976. 22.00 (*0-87944-208-5*) Inst Soc Res.

Pelz, R. B., et al, eds. Parallel Computational Fluid Dynamics '92: Proceedings of the Conference on Parallel CFD '92 - Implementations & Results Using Parallel Computers, New Brunswick, NJ, 18-20 May, 1992. LC 93-16448. 438p. 1993. 162.50 (*0-444-89986-3*, North Holland) Elsevier.

Pelz, Ruth. Black Heroes of the Wild West. LC 89-63500. (Illus.). (gr. 4-12). 1989. 12.95 (*0-940880-25-3*); pap. 6.95 (*0-940880-26-1*) Open Hand.

— Women of the Wild West: Biographies from Many Cultures. (Contributions Ser.). (Illus.). 64p. (Orig.). (J). (gr. 4 up). 1994. text ed. 12.95 (*0-940880-49-0*); pap. text ed. 6.95 (*0-940880-50-4*) Open Hand.

Pelz, Stephen E. Race to Pearl Harbor: The Failure of the Second London Naval Conference & the Onset of World War II. LC 73-89711. (Studies in American-East Asian Relations: No. 5). 416p. 1974. text ed. 25.50 (*0-685-02135-1*) HUP.

Pelz, William. Basic Keyboard Skills: An Introduction to Accompaniment Improvisation, Transposition & Modulation, with an Appendix on Sight Reading. LC 80-22820. vii, 173p. 1981. reprint ed. text ed. 38.50 (*0-313-22882-5*, PEBK) Greenwood.

— Wilhelm Liebknecht & German Social Collections: A Documentary History. Hahn, Erich, tr. LC 93-31636. (Documentary Reference Collections). 480p. 1994. text ed. 85.00 (*0-313-28200-5*, Greenwood Pr) Greenwood.

Pelz, William A. The Spartakusbund & the German Working Class Movement, 1914-1919. LC 87-5637. (Studies in German Thought & History: Vol. 1). (Illus.). 423p. 1987. lib. bdg. 109.95 (0-88946-355-7) E Mellen.

Pelzel, Suzanne, tr. see Voss, Hermann.

Pelzel, Thomas, tr. see Voss, Hermann.

Pelzel, Vernise E. The Story of Orange. Monk, Lenore, ed. (Illus.). 48p. (J). (gr. 3-12). 1987. pap. 6.95 (0-944131-01-8) HPL Pub.

Pelzer, D. J. Structure, Function & Modulation of Striated Muscle Calcium Channels. (Molecular Biology Intelligence Unit Ser.). 115p. 1994. 89.95 (1-57059-057-5) CRC Pr.

***Pelzer, Dave J.** A Child Called "It" An Abused Child's Journey from Victim to Victor. 150p. (Orig.). 1995. pap. 9.95 (1-55874-366-9, 3669) Health Comm.

Pelzer, David J. The Lost Boy, 3 Vols., Vol. 2. LC 94-66665. 190p. (Orig.). 1994. pap. text ed. 10.00 (0-929099-03-6) Omaha Pr Pub.

Pelzer, Karl J. Pioneer Settlement in the Asiatic Tropics: Studies in Land Utilization & Agricultural Colonization in Southeastern Asia. LC 83-1484. (American Geographical Society Ser.-Special publication). (Illus.). xviii, 288p. 1983. reprint ed. text ed. 59.75 (0-313-23853-7, PEPI) Greenwood.

— West Malaysia & Singapore: A Selected Bibliography. LC 72-87853. (Bibliographies Ser.). 400p. 1971. 25.00 (0-87536-235-4) HRAFP.

Pelzer, Louis. Marches of the Dragoons in the Mississippi Valley: 1833-1850. LC 75-116. (Mid-American Frontier Ser.). 1975. reprint ed. 26.95 (0-405-06882-4) Ayer.

Pelzer, Louis, ed. see Carleton, J. Henry.

Pelzer, Trudy, jt. auth. see Gulutzan, Peter.

Pelzl, J., jt. ed. see Hess, P.

Pember, Don R. Mass Media in America. 6th ed. (Illus.). 544p. (C). 1992. pap. write for info. (0-02-393780-7) Macmillan.

— Privacy & the Press: The Law, the Mass Media, & the First Amendment. LC 79-152335. (Washington Paperback Ser.: No. 64). (Illus.). 312p. 1972. reprint ed. pap. 10.00 (0-295-95265-2) U of Wash Pr.

***Pember, Donald R.** Mass Media Law. 656p. (C). 1995. student ed write for info. (0-697-24603-5); pap. write for info. (0-697-24600-0) Brown & Benchmark.

— Mass Media Law. 6th ed. 64p. (C). 1993. write for info. (0-697-24602-7); boxed write for info. (0-697-12936-5) Brown & Benchmark.

Pember, G. H. Earth's Earliest Ages. LC 75-13928. 332p. 1975. pap. 11.99 (0-8254-3533-1) Kregel.

Pember, Phoebe Y. A Southern Woman's Story. Wiley, Bell I., ed. 152p. 1987. pap. 3.95 (0-89176-024-5, 6024, Mckingbird) R Bemis Pub.

— A Southern Woman's Story: Life in Confederate Richmond. Wiley, Bell I., ed. (Illus.). 233p. 1992. reprint ed. 25.00 (0-916107-27-2) Broadfoot.

Pemberton, et al. Mayo Clinic Diet Manual. 6th ed. 1988. pap. 89.50 (1-55664-033-1) Mosby Yr Bk.

Pemberton, C., ed. Elizabeth, Queen of England: Queen Elizabeth's Englishings of Boethius. (EETS, OS Ser.: No. 113). 1972. reprint ed. 30.00 (0-527-00113-9) Periodicals Srv.

Pemberton, Carol. Practical English. (C). 1989. pap. text ed. 18.50 (0-673-39824-2) HarpCollege.

— Writing Essays. LC 92-14216. 1993. pap. text ed. write for info. (0-205-13986-8) Allyn.

— Writing Paragraphs. 2nd ed. LC 93-11812. 1993. pap. text ed. write for info. (0-205-15282-1) Allyn.

Pemberton, Carol A. Lowell Mason: A Bio-Bibliography. LC 87-37569. (Bio-Bibliographies in Music Ser.: No. 11). 224p. 1988. text ed. 49.95 (0-313-25881-3, PLL/, Greenwood Pr) Greenwood.

— Lowell Mason: His Life & Work. Buelow, George, ed. LC 84-28121. (Studies in Musicology: No. 86). 280p. 1991. pap. 25.00 (0-8357-1992-8) Univ Rochester Pr.

Pemberton, Carole, jt. auth. see Herriot, Peter.

Pemberton, Caroline H. Stephen the Black. LC 72-1520. (Black Heritage Library Collection). 1977. reprint ed. 28.95 (0-8369-9044-7) Ayer.

Pemberton, Deloras, jt. auth. see Pemberton, L. Beaty.

Pemberton, E. M. Chai Kheun. Van Treese, James B., ed. 260p. 1994. pap. 8.95 (1-56901-131-1) NW Pub.

Pemberton, Elizabeth G. & Slane, Kathleen W. The Sanctuary of Demeter & Kore: The Greek Pottery. LC 89-15004. (Corinth Ser.: Vol. 18, Pt. 1). (Illus.). xx, 235p. 1989. 65.00 (0-87661-181-1) Am Sch Athens.

Pemberton, Gayle. Hottest Water in Chicago: Essays on Family, Race, Time, & American Culture. 1992. 19.95 (0-571-12936-6) Faber & Faber.

— The Hottest Water in Chicago: Notes of a Native Daughter. LC 92-46919. 1993. reprint ed. pap. 10.95 (0-385-46842-3, Anchor NY) Doubleday.

Pemberton, Gregory, ed. see Edwards, Peter.

Pemberton, H. Earl. Minerals of California. 672p. 1982. text ed. 52.95 (0-442-27488-2) Chapman & Hall.

Pemberton, Henry. Shakespeare & Sir Walter Raleigh. LC 76-174688. (Studies in Shakespeare: No. 24). 1971. reprint ed. lib. bdg. 39.95 (0-8383-1340-X) M S G Haskell Hse.

Pemberton, J. E. British Official Publications. 2nd ed. LC 73-16231. 328p. 1973. 137.00 (0-08-017797-2, Pub. by Pergamon Repr UK) Franklin.

Pemberton, J. E., ed. The Bibliographic Control of Official Publications. (Guides to Official Publications). (Illus.). 172p. 1982. 81.00 (0-08-027419-6, Pub. by Pergamon Repr UK) Franklin.

Pemberton, J. Michael. Policies of Audiovisual Producers & Distributors: A Handbook for Acquisitions Personnel. 2nd ed. LC 89-10950. 395p. 1989. pap. 35.00 (0-8108-2264-4) Scarecrow.

Pemberton, J. Michael & Prentice, Ann, eds. Information Science: The Interdisciplinary Context. 275p. (Orig.). 1990. pap. text ed. 39.50 (1-55570-048-9) Neal-Schuman.

Pemberton, J. Michael, ed. see Ruffner, Henry.

Pemberton, Jeffery K., comp. Online Inc.'s Top Five Hundred Library Microcomputer Software Application Programs. 352p. 1992. pap. 44.95 (0-910965-09-9) Online.

Pemberton, John. On the Subject of "Java" (Illus.). 320p. 1994. 42.95 (0-8014-2672-3); pap. 17.95 (0-8014-9963-1) Cornell U Pr.

Pemberton, John, III, jt. auth. see Drewal, Henry J.

Pemberton, Judy. Let's Get Cooking. (Illus.). 103p. (Orig.). (J). (gr. 3-12). 1984. text ed. 7.95 (0-317-02695-X) King Fisher Pr.

***Pemberton, L. Beaty & Colburn, Gene L.** Workbook of Surgical Anatomy. (Illus.). 320p. 1991. pap. write for info. (0-614-01395-X) Hlth Prof Div.

Pemberton, L. Beaty & Pemberton, Deloras. Treatment of Water, Electrolyte, & Acid-Base Disorders in the Surgical Patient. 432p. 1994. pap. 32.00 (0-07-049363-4) Hlth Prof Div.

Pemberton, L. Beaty, et al. Workbook of Surgical Anatomy. (Pretest Specialty Level Ser.). 320p. 1991. pap. text ed. 39.95 (0-07-049349-9) Hlth Prof Div.

Pemberton, LeRoy A., jt. auth. see Archer, E. C.

Pemberton, Margaret. The Flower Garden. 544p. 1984. pap. 3.95 (0-8217-1396-5) Zebra.

— Moonflower Madness. 256p. 1993. lib. bdg. 20.00 (0-7278-4467-9) Severn Hse.

— Moonflower Madness. large type ed. 386p. 1994. 19.95 (0-7505-0588-5, Pub. by Magna Print Bks) Ulverscroft.

— Party in Peking. large type ed. 319p. 1993. 21.95 (0-7505-0464-1, Pub. by Magna Print Bks) Ulverscroft.

— Rendezvous with Death. large type ed. (Dales Large Print Ser.). 1994. pap. 16.95 (1-85389-493-1, Pub. by Magna Print Bks) Ulverscroft.

Pemberton, Margaret A. Forever. large type ed. (Dales General Fiction Ser.). 293p. 1993. pap. 16.95 (1-85389-419-2, Dales) Ulverscroft.

Pemberton, Max. Jewel Mysteries I Have Known: From a Dealer's Note Book. LC 75-32772. (Literature of Mystery & Detection Ser.). (Illus.). 1976. reprint ed. 24.95 (0-405-07892-7) Ayer.

— Queen of the Jesters & Her Strange Adventures in Old Paris. LC 76-101818. (Short Story Index Reprint Ser.). 1977. 21.95 (0-8369-3206-4) Ayer.

— Signors of the Night. LC 74-132123. (Short Story Index Reprint Ser.). 1977. 20.95 (0-8369-3680-9) Ayer.

— Ward's Worldwide Automotive Decade of Data - Production, 1994: Passenger Car & Commercial Vehicle Production, 1984-1993. (Worldwide Automotive Decade of Data, 1994 Ser.). (Illus.). (Orig.). (C). 1994. pap. 450.00 (0-910589-98-4) Wards Comm.

— Ward's Worldwide Automotive Decade of Data - Sales, 1994: Passenger Car & Commercial Vehicle Sales, 1984-1993. (Worldwide Automotive Decade of Data, 1994 Ser.). (Illus.). (Orig.). (C). 1994. pap. 450.00 (0-910589-99-2) Wards Comm.

— Ward's Worldwide Automotive Decade of Data, 1994. (Illus.). (Orig.). (C). 1994. pap. 750.00 (0-910589-97-6) Wards Comm.

— Ward's 1994 Worldwide Vehicle Parc. (Illus.). (Orig.). (C). Date not set. pap. 950.00 (0-910589-50-X) Wards Comm.

Pemberton, Nancy. Animal Habitats: The Best Home of All. LC 90-30633. (Discovery World Ser.). (Illus.). 32p. (J). (ps-2). 1990. lib. bdg. 21.36 (0-89565-578-0) Childs World.

Pemberton, Nancy & Riehecky, Janet. Responsibility. LC 87-37557. (Values to Live By Ser.). (Illus.). 32p. (ENG & SPA.). (J). (ps-2). 1988. lib. bdg. 21.36 (0-89565-418-0) Childs World.

— Responsibility. LC 87-37557. (Values to Live By Ser.). (Illus.). 32p. (ENG & SPA.). (J). (ps-2). 1988. lib. bdg. 21.36 (0-89565-953-0) Childs World.

Pemberton, Owen. The Truth about the Rapture of the Church. Jones, M. L., ed. 104p. (Orig.). 1994. pap. 8.95 (1-882270-15-0) Old Rugged Cross.

Pemberton, Robert. The Happy Colony. Richardson, Benjamin W. et al, eds. Bd. with Hygeia: A City of Health. LC 84-48277. LC 84-48277. (Rise of Urban Britain Ser.). 264p. 1985. 35.00 (0-8240-6279-5) Garland.

Pemberton, S. George, ed. Applications of Ichnology to Petroleum Exploration. (Illus.). 442p. 1992. pap. 57.50 (0-918985-97-8) SEPM.

Pemberton, T. Edgar. Dicken's London: Or, London in the Works of Charles Dickens. LC 71-39694. (Studies in Dickens: No. 52). 1972. reprint ed. lib. bdg. 75.00 (0-8383-1404-X) M S G Haskell Hse.

Pemberton, Thomas E. The Life of Bret Harte. LC 74-133530. (Select Bibliographies Reprint Ser.). 1977. reprint ed. 23.95 (0-8369-5562-5) Ayer.

***Pemberton, William E.** Bureaucratic Politics: Executive Reorganization During the Truman Administration. LC 78-2990. 270p. 1979. reprint ed. pap. 77.00 (0-7837-8850-9, AU00454) Bks Demand.

— George Bush. LC 92-46768. (Biographies Ser.). (J). 1993. 19.93 (0-86625-478-1); 14.95 (0-685-66539-9) Rourke Pubns.

— Harry S. Truman. 1988. text ed. 26.95 (0-8057-7767-9, Pub. by Royal Botanic Garden UK); pap. 14.95 (0-8057-7783-0, Pub. by Royal Botanic Garden UK) Macmillan.

Pemble, John. The Raj, the Indian Mutiny, & the Kingdom of Oudh, 1801-1859. LC 76-55892. 303p. 1977. 39.50 (0-8386-2092-2) Fairleigh Dickinson.

— Venice Rediscovered. (Illus.). 230p. 1995. 25.00 (0-19-820501-5) OUP.

Pemble, William. A Briefe Introduction to Geography. LC 77-7420. (English Experience Ser.: No. 883). 1977. reprint ed. lib. bdg. 20.00 (90-221-0883-X) Walter J Johnson.

Pembleton, Aaron, jt. auth. see Vorreux, Damien.

Pembleton, Seliesa. The Armadillo. LC 91-43731. (Remarkable Animals Ser.). (Illus.). 60p. (J). (gr. 4 up). 1992. text ed. 13.95 (0-87518-507-X, Dillon Silver Burdett) Silver Burdett Pr.

— The Pileated Woodpecker. LC 88-20220. (Remarkable Animals Ser.). (Illus.). 60p. (J). (gr. 3 up). 1988. text ed. 13.95 (0-87518-392-1, Dillon Silver Burdett) Silver Burdett Pr.

Pembrey, M. E., jt. auth. see Roberts, J. A.

Pement, Isleta L., jt. auth. see Edwards, Paul M.

Pement, Jack, jt. auth. see Keller, Paul.

Pemeranz, Virginia E. & Schultz, Dodi. First Five Years: The Relaxed Approach to Child Care, Vol. 1. 1987. mass mkt. 3.99 (0-312-90921-7) St Martin.

Pemina Yellow Bird, jt. auth. see Allen, Hayward.

Pemno, Karen, ed. see Neff, Rena.

Pempel, T. J. Japan: The Dilemmas of Success. LC 86-50478. (Headline Ser.: No. 277). (Illus.). 80p. (Orig.). 1986. pap. 5.95 (0-87124-106-4) Foreign Policy.

Pempel, T. J., ed. Uncommon Democracies: The One-Party Dominant Regimes. LC 89-22111. (Illus.). 384p. 1990. pap. 18.95 (0-8014-9696-9) Cornell U Pr.

Pempel, T. J., jt. auth. see Ilgen, Thomas L.

Pemsel, Helmut. A History of War at Sea: An Atlas & Chronology of Conflict at Sea from 480 B. C. to the Present. LC 76-45237. Orig. Title: Atlas of Naval Warfare 480 BC - 1975 AD. (Illus.). 176p. 1977. 25.95 (0-87021-803-4) Naval Inst Pr.

Pemsler, J. Paul, ed. see International Symposium on Molten Salts Staff.

***PEN American Center Staff.** Grants & Awards Available to American Writers, 1994-95. 18th rev. ed. Morrone, John, ed. 199p. 1994. pap. 10.00 (0-934638-13-6) PEN Am Ctr.

Pen, J. Among Economists. (Lectures in Economics Ser.: Vol. 5). 1985. pap. 51.50 (0-444-87636-7) Elsevier.

Pen-Min, Lin, jt. auth. see Decarlo, Raymond A.

Pen Notes Staff. Italic Calligraphy Kit. (J). (gr. 3 up). 1979. spiral bd. 9.95 (0-939564-10-6) Pen Notes.

— Learn Handwriting. (J). (gr. 2 up). 1986. 10.95 (0-939564-00-9) Pen Notes.

— Learn to Print Spanish: (Aprendiendo a Escribir las Letras. (J). (ps up). 1989. Bilingual instrns. 10.95 (0-939564-17-3) Pen Notes.

— Learn to Tell Time. (J). (gr. 1 up). 1982. 8.95 (0-939564-02-5) Pen Notes.

— Learn to Write Numbers. (ps up). 1987. 10.95 (0-939564-04-1) Pen Notes.

— Learning to Print. (J). (ps up). 1984. 10.95 (0-939564-01-7) Pen Notes.

Pen, Ronald. Introduction to Music. 1992. pap. text ed. 9.95 (0-07-038068-6) McGraw.

Pen-yeh, Tsao. The Music of Su-chou T'an-tz'u: A Study of the Structural Elements of the Chinese Southern Singing Narrative. 450p. 1986. lib. bdg. 72.50 (962-201-348-1, Pub. by Chinese Univ HK) Coronet Bks.

Pena, A. Atlas of Surgical Management of Anorectal Malformations. (Illus.). xiii, 104p. 1992. 95.00 (0-387-97067-3, 3064) Spr-Verlag.

Pena, A. S., ed. Recent Advances in Crohn's Disease: Developments in Gastroenterology One. 549p. 1981. lib. bdg. 136.50 (90-247-2475-9) Kluwer Ac.

Pena, A. S., jt. auth. see Hekkens, W. T.

Pena, Alfredo C. & Cardona-Hine, Alvaro. Dos Elegias-Two Elegies. 1977. per. 2.50 (0-685-04493-9) Invisible-Red Hill.

Pena, Amado. Pena on Pena. (Illus.). 96p. 1994. 29.95 (1-56796-061-8) WRS Group.

Pena, Amado & Alba, Juanita. Calor. (Illus.). 32p. 1994. 19.95 (1-56796-069-3) WRS Group.

Pena, Betty W. Las Tres Llaves del Exito. Montoya, Ana M., tr. (Illus.). 64p. 1992. pap. text ed. 6.75 (1-882462-00-9) Surpass Your Limit.

Pena, Carlos G. History of Mexican Literature. 3rd enl. rev. ed. LC 68-24078. 552p. reprint ed. pap. 157.40 (0-8357-8908-X, 2033420) Bks Demand.

***Pena, Devon S.** The Terror of the Machine: Technology, Work, Gender, & Ecology on the U. S.-Mexico Border. (Border & Migration Studies Ser.). (Illus.). 412p. (Orig.). 1995. text ed. 45.00x (0-292-76561-4); pap. 19.95x (0-292-76562-2) U of Tex Pr.

Pena, Flora, tr. see Fine, Anne.

***Pena, German A.** Exploraciones Arqueologicas en la Cuenca Media del Rio Bogota. (Illus.). 138p. (SPA.). 1991. pap. 8.50 (1-877812-22-6) UPLAAP.

Pena, Gladys, ed. For a Permanent Public Art: An Exhibition of Murals Commissioned for New York City Hospitals under President Roosevelt's New Deal. (Illus.). 36p. (Orig.). (C). 1988. pap. text ed. write for info. (0-318-63770-7) Hlth & Hosp Corp.

Pena, Humberto J. El Hijo Del Hijo. 200p. (Orig.). 1991. pap. text ed. 12.00 (0-685-54524-5) Saeta.

Pena, Jake. Eight Highly Successful Tips for Breaking into the Modeling & Commercial Business. 192p. 1993. pap. text ed. 19.95 (0-8403-8463-7) Kendall-Hunt.

***Pena, Jesus J.** Justicia Poetica - Poetic Justice: Memorias de un Abogado de Barrio - Memoirs of a Neighborhood Lawyer. 279p. (SPA.). 1995. pap. 13.00 (1-884912-04-4) Latino Pr.

Pena, Jose, jt. ed. see Solana, Rafael.

Pena, Julia. One Hundred & Fifty Songs with Just Three Chords. 1992. pap. 16.95 (0-943748-47-X) Ekay Music.

Pena, L. M. Domingo Fernandez: Un Hombre Usado Por Dios (A Man Used by God) (SPA.). Date not set. 4.99 (1-56063-459-6, 498262) Editorial Unilit.

Pena, Lydia M. The Life & Times of Agnes Tait. (Illus.). (Orig.). 1983. pap. text ed. 14.95 (0-9612982-0-0) Pena Lydia.

Pena, Manuel. The Texas-Mexican Conjunto: History of a Working-Class Music. (Mexican American Monographs: No. 9). (Illus.). 238p. 1985. text ed. 22.95 (0-292-78068-0); pap. 12.95 (0-292-78080-X) U of Tex Pr.

Pena, Manuel S. Criminal Investigation, Practical. 3rd rev. ed. LC 82-70470. (Illus.). 400p. 1993. pap. 29.95 (0-942728-57-2) Copperhouse.

— Deliver Me from Evil. 1993. 16.95 (0-533-10400-9) Vantage.

***Pena, Milagros.** Theologies & Liberation in Peru: The Role of Ideas in Social Movements. 240p. (Orig.). (C). 1995. text ed. 39.95 (1-56639-294-2) Temple U Pr.

Pena, S. D., et al, eds. DNA Fingerprinting: State of the Science. LC 93-22711. 466p. 1993. 140.00 (0-8176-2781-2); pap. 93.00 (0-8176-2906-8) Birkhauser.

Pena, Sylvia C., ed. Kikiriki: Stories & Poems in English & Spanish for Children. 2nd ed. LC 81-68072. (Illus.). 116p. (Orig.). (ENG & SPA.). (J). (gr. k-6). 1989. pap. 8.50 (0-685-34571-8) Arte Publico.

— Tun-Ta-Ca-Tun: More Stories & Poems in English & Spanish for Children. LC 84-72297. 80p. (Orig.). (ENG & SPA.). (J). (ps up). 1985. pap. 9.50 (0-934770-43-3) Arte Publico.

Pena, William. Problem Seeking. 202p. 1987. pap. 21.95 (0-913962-87-2) AIA Press.

***Penalosa, Fernando, ed. & tr.** Tales & Legends of the Q'anjob'al Maya. (Illus.). 178p. (Orig.). 1995. pap. 8.95 (1-886502-03-X) Yax Te Press.

Penalosa, Fernando, tr. see La Farge, Oliver.

Penalosa, Fernando, ed. see Tomas, Jose J. & Tomas, Domingo A.

Penbera, Joseph J., jt. auth. see Betts, Chris A.

Penberthy, I. How to Restore Fuel Systems & Carburetion. (Illus.). 128p. 1988. pap. 19.95 (0-85045-784-X, Pub. by Osprey Pubng Ltd UK) Motorbooks Intl.

Penberthy, Ian. Building Your Garden. 1989. text ed. 17.95 (0-02-595491-1) Macmillan.

— Mustang. 1993. 9.98 (0-681-41828-1) Longmeadow Pr.

Penberthy, Jenny. Niedecker & the Correspondence with Zukofsky, 1931-1970. LC 92-34643. (Illus.). 384p. (C). 1993. 59.95 (0-521-44369-5) Cambridge U Pr.

Penberthy, John. To Bee or Not to Bee. 119p. 1987. pap. 7.95 (0-945153-13-9) Sound Pub CO.

Penberthy, Stephen & Jones, Gary. Step-by-Step to a Classic Fireplace Mantel. LC 94-65609. (Illus.). 64p. (Orig.). 1994. pap. 12.95 (0-88740-653-X) Schiffer.

Pencak, William. For God & Country: The American Legion, 1919-1941. 411p. 1989. text ed. 42.50 (1-55553-050-8) NE U Pr.

— History, Signing In: Essays in History & Semiotics. LC 92-4143. (Semiotics & the Human Sciences Ser.: Vol. 4). 448p. (C). 1993. text ed. 68.95 (0-8204-1838-2) P Lang Pubs.

Pencak, William, jt. ed. see Freidel, Frank.

Pencak, William, jt. ed. see Gilje, Paul A.

***Pencavel, John.** Labor Markets under Trade Unionism: Employment, Wages, & Hours. (Illus.). 288p. 1991. pap. write for info. (1-55786-467-5) Blackwell Pubs.

***Pence.** Cooking up Trouble. 1995. mass mkt. 4.50 (0-06-108200-7, Harp PBks) HarpC.

Pence, Alan, jt. ed. see Moss, Peter.

Pence, Alan R., ed. Ecological Research with Children & Families: From Concepts to Methodology. 256p. (C). 1988. pap. text ed. 18.95 (0-8077-2913-2) Tchrs Coll.

Pence, Alan R., jt. ed. see Peters, Donald F.

Pence, Caprial. Caprial's Cafe Favorites. 1994. 21.95 (0-89815-600-9) Ten Speed Pr.

— Caprial's Seasonal Kitchen: An Innovative Chef's Menus & Recipes for Easy Home Cooking. LC 91-3274. (Illus.). 240p. (Orig.). 1991. pap. 19.95 (0-88240-417-2) Alaska Northwest.

— Caprial's Seasonal Kitchen: An Innovative Chef's Menus & Recipes for Easy Home Cooking. (Orig.). 1992. pap. 12.95 (0-88240-418-0) Alaska Northwest.

Pence, Daniel J., jt. auth. see Ropers, Richard H.

Pence, Danny B. Keys, Species & Host List, & Bibliography for Nasal Mites of North American Birds (Acarina: Rhinonyssinae, Turbinoptinae, Speleognathinae, & Cytoditidae) (Special Publications: No. 8). (Illus.). 148p. (Orig.). 1975. pap. 6.00 (0-89672-033-0) Tex Tech Univ Pr.

Pence, Dennis. Calculus Activities for Graphic Calculators. 280p. (C). 1990. pap. 27.95 (0-534-92431-X) PWS Pubs.

— Calculus Activities for Graphic Calculators. 2nd ed. 1994. pap. 27.95 (0-534-93267-3) PWS Pubs.

— Calculus Activities for the TI-81 Graphic Calculator. 280p. (C). 1992. pap. 22.95 (0-534-92709-2) PWS Pubs.

***Pence, Donna & Wilson, Charles.** The Role of Law Enforcement in the Response to Child Abuse & Neglect. 78p. (Orig.). (C). 1995. pap. text ed. 35.00x (0-7881-1667-3) Diane Pub.

— The Team Investigation of Child Sexual Abuse: The Uneasy Alliance. (Interpersonal Violence: the Practice Ser.: Vol. 6). 176p. 1994. 42.95 (0-8039-5169-8); pap. 18.95 (0-8039-5170-1) Sage.

Pence, Ellen & Paymar, Michael. Education Groups for Men Who Batter: The Duluth Model. LC 92-35954. 212p. 1993. 28.95 (0-8261-7990-8) Springer Pub.

Pence, George. Classic Cases in Medical Ethics. 412p. (C). 1990. pap. text ed. write for info. (0-07-038092-9) McGraw.

— Indiana Boundaries: Territory, State & County. 883p. 1967. pap. 7.50 (1-885323-06-9) IN Hist Bureau.

Pence, Gregory, jt. auth. see Stephens, G. Lynn.

An Asterisk (*) at the beginning of an entry indicates that the title is appearing in BIP for the first time.

***Pence, Gregory E.** Classic Cases in Medical Ethics: Accounts of Cases That Have Shaped Medical Ethics, with Philosophical, Legal, & Historical Backgrounds. 2nd ed. LC 94-41691. 1994. pap. text ed. 20.00 (0-07-038094-5) McGraw.

Pence, Heather, jt. auth. see Bradley, Patrick.

Pence, I. W., Jr., jt. ed. see White, J. A.

Pence, I. W., jt. ed. see White, J. A., Jr.

Pence, Joanne. Something's Cooking. 1993. mass mkt. 4.50 (0-06-108096-9, Harp PBks) HarpC.

— Too Many Cooks. 1994. pap. 4.50 (0-06-108199-X, Harp PBks) HarpC.

***Pence, Laura, ed.** Interpharm Pharmaceutical Managers' Compliance Guide. 2nd ed. 131p. 1994. pap. 39.00 (0-935184-68-6) Interpharm.

Pence, R. W. & Emery, Donald W. Grammar of Present-Day English. 2nd ed. 448p. (C). 1963. pap. write for info. (0-02-393720-3) Macmillan.

Pence, Richard, jt. auth. see Andereck, Paul.

Pence, Richard A. & Dahl, Patrick, eds. The Next Greatest Thing: Fifty Years of Rural Electrification. (Illus.). 256p. 1984. 29.85 (0-917599-00-4) Natl Rural.

***Pence, Roger, et al.** Desktop Guide to RPG - 400. (News 3X-400 Technical Reference Ser.). 200p. (Orig.). 1995. pap. 34.95 (1-882419-18-9, Duke Pr) Duke Commns Intl.

***Pence, Shari A.** Games Galore for Children's Parties & More: Fun Games & Activities for Parties, Classrooms, Youth Groups, Carnivals, Company Picnics, Rainy Days & Special Occasions. LC 95-90159. (Illus.). 120p. 1995. pap. 9.95 (0-9645771-0-0) Funcastle Pubns.

Pence, Sharon, ed. see Classey, Pat.

Pence-Smith, Penny. Reflections of Kauai: A Celebration of the Island of Kauai. (Illus.). 188p. (JPN.). 1989. 34.95 (0-89610-183-5); boxed 39.95 (0-89610-184-3) Island Heritage.

— Under a Maui Sun: A Celebration of the Island of Maui. (Illus.). 188p. (JPN.). 1989. 34.95 (0-89610-181-9); boxed 39.95 (0-89610-182-7) Island Heritage.

Pence, Terry. Ethics in Nursing: An Annotated Bibliography. 2nd ed. 255p. 1986. pap. 16.95 (0-88737-192-2, 20-1936) Natl League Nurse.

Pence, Terry & Cantrall, Janice, eds. Ethics in Nursing: An Anthology. 352p. 1990. 27.95 (0-88737-461-1) Natl League Nurse.

Pence, Wanda J. Be Still & Know That I Am God. 1988. pap. 6.25 (0-89137-332-2) Quality Pubns.

— The Guest. 1994. pap. 4.95 (1-56794-058-7) Star Bible.

Penchansky, David. The Betrayal of God: Ideological Conflict in Job. (Literary Currents in Biblical Interpretation Ser.). 128p. (Orig.). 1990. pap. 11.99 (0-664-25132-3) Westminster John Knox.

Penchansky, Roy, ed. Health Services Administration: Policy Cases & the Case Method. LC 68-15640. 475p. 1968. 38.00 (0-674-38550-0) HUP.

Penchoen, Thomas G. Tamazight of the Ayt Ndhir. LC 73-91702. (Afroasiatic Dialects Ser.: Vol. 1). (Illus.). 122p. 1973. pap. 20.00 (0-89003-000-6) Undena Pubns.

Penczek, S., ed. Polymerization of Heterocycles (Ring-Opening) LC 76-44623. 1977. 70.00 (0-08-021367-7, Pub. by Pergamon Repr UK) Franklin.

Penczek, S., et al. Cationic Ring-Opening Polymerization. (Advances in Polymer Science Ser.: Vols. 68 & 69). (Illus.). 300p. 1985. 131.00 (0-387-13781-5) Spr-Verlag.

Pendagast, Edward L., Jr., jt. auth. see Butman, Alexander M.

Pendakur, Manjunath. Canadian Dreams & American Control: The Political Economy of the Canadian Film Industry. LC 90-12144. (Contemporary Film & Television Ser.). 331p. (C). 1991. 49.95 (0-8143-1998-X); pap. 19.95 (0-8143-1999-8) Wayne St U Pr.

Pendakur, V. Setty. Urban Transport in Asean. 68p. 1984. pap. 13.95 (9971-902-78-8, Pub. by Inst SE Asian Studies SI) Ashgate Pub Co.

Pendar, Kenneth. Adventure in Diplomacy. LC 76-5479. (World War II Ser.). 1976. reprint ed. lib. bdg. 29.50 (0-306-70774-8) Da Capo.

Pendarkar, Sumant. Using Spreadsheets with Databases. 1993. pap. 20.00 (0-679-79161-2) Random.

Pendarvis, Edwina, et al. The Abilities of Gifted Children. 496p. (C). 1989. Casebound. text ed. write for info. (0-13-002072-9) P-H.

Pendas, Miguel. Chicano Liberation & Socialism. 15p. 1976. 2.50 (0-87348-384-7) Pathfinder NY.

— DBASE IV: A Tutorial to Accompany Peter Norton's Introduction to Computers. LC 93-23741. 1994. write for info. (0-02-801327-1) Glencoe.

— Microsoft Word, Version 5.5. LC 92-17123. (Increasing Your Productivity Ser.). 1992. write for info. (0-02-800682-8); disk write for info. (0-02-800683-6) Glencoe.

— Step-by-Step Lotus 1-2-3. LC 94-8944. 1994. write for info. (0-02-800955-X) Macmillan.

***Pende.** Meaning of Tibetan Buddhist Church. 1994. 24.95 (0-8356-4004-3, Quest) Theos Pub Hse.

Pendell, Dale. City Limits Blues. 20p. 1986. 5.00 (1-882623-02-9) Exiled-Am Pr.

— Pharmakopoeia: Plant Powers, Poisons & Herbcraft. 304p. 1995. pap. 16.95 (1-56279-069-2) Mercury Hse Inc.

— Physics for the Heart. 20p. 1986. 5.00 (1-882623-01-0) Exiled-Am Pr.

— Rough Cuts & Kindling. 40p. 1986. 5.00 (1-882623-03-7) Exiled-Am Pr.

— Swirling. 44p. 1986. boxed 5.00 (1-882623-04-5) Exiled-Am Pr.

Pendell, Dale & Sanfield, Steve. Chasing the Cranes: A Cycle of Linked Hoops. 32p. 1986. 5.00 (1-882623-00-2) Exiled-Am Pr.

Pendell, Dale, tr. see Mokujiki.

Pendell, Elmer. Why Civilizations Self-Destruct. LC 76-40801. 196p. 1977. 12.00 (0-914576-07-0) Howard Allen.

Pendelton, Don. Dixie Convoy. (Executioner Ser.: No. 27). 1989. pap. 3.50 (1-55817-294-7, Pinnacle NY) Windsor NY.

Pender, Beatrice C. Joan of Arc in French Romantic Drama. 1972. 59.95 (0-8490-0447-0) Gordon Pr.

Pender Centennial Book Committee, ed. Pender, Nebraska. (Illus.). 549p. 1984. 40.00 (0-88107-021-1) Curtis Media.

— Pender, Nebraska: The First Hundred Years, 1885-1985. (Illus.). 549p. 1985. reprint ed. 50.00 (0-88107-028-9) Curtis Media.

Pender, Daniel J. Practical Otology. (Illus.). 348p. 1992. text ed. 42.95 (0-397-51016-0) Lippincott.

Pender, Harold & Del Mar, William A., eds. Electrical Engineers' Handbook, Vol. 2. 4th ed. LC 49-11664. (Wiley Engineering Handbook Ser.). 1647p. reprint ed. pap. 180.00 (0-317-55640-1, 2056357) Bks Demand.

Pender, J. A. & Masson, J. Welding Projects: A Design Approach. 1976. text ed. 35.95 (0-07-077330-0) McGraw.

Pender, J. Anne, ed. see Harvard Family Research Project Staff.

Pender, Laura. Garden of Deceit. (Intrigue Ser.). 1993. mass mkt. 2.99 (0-373-22240-8, 1-22240-5) Harlequin Bks.

— Midnight Rider. 1994. mass mkt. 2.99 (0-373-22280-7, 1-22280-1) Harlequin Bks.

— Mindgame. (Intrigue Ser.: No. 177). 1992. pap. 2.79 (0-373-22177-0, 1-22177-9) Harlequin Bks.

— Music in the Mist. (Intrigue Ser.). 1993. mass mkt. 2.99 (0-373-22249-1, 1-22249-6) Harlequin Bks.

Pender, Malcolm. Biedermann & die Brandstifter, Frisch: Critical Monographs in English. 68p. 1993. pap. 32.00 (0-85261-258-3, Pub. by Univ of Glasgow UK) St Mut.

Pender, Malcolm, jt. ed. see Butler, Michael.

***Pender, Michael P. & McCombe, Pamela A.** Autoimmune Neurological Disease. (Cambridge Reviews in Clinical Immunology Ser.). 286p. (C). 1994. write for info. (0-521-46113-8) Cambridge U Pr.

Pender, Nola J. Health Promotion in Nursing Practice. 2nd ed. (Illus.). 497p. (C). 1987. pap. text ed. 37.95 (0-8385-3674-3, A3674-7) Appleton & Lange.

Pender, Robert H., jt. auth. see Miller, Glenn A.

Pender, Rose. A Lady's Experiences in the Wild West in 1883. LC 78-17690. xvi, 134p. 1978. reprint ed. pap. 7.95 (0-8032-8711-9, Bison Books) U of Nebr Pr.

Pendergast, David M. Excavations at Altun Ha, Belize, 1964-1970, Vol. 1. 1994. Boxed. boxed 55.00 (0-88854-219-4, Pub. by Royal Ont Mus CN) U of Toronto Pr.

— Excavations at Altun Ha, Belize, 1964-1970, Vol. 2. 1994. Boxed. boxed 75.00 (0-88854-290-9, Pub. by Royal Ont Mus CN) U of Toronto Pr.

— Excavations at Altun Ha, Belize, 1964-1970, Vol. 3. 1994. Boxed. boxed 135.00 (0-88854-355-7, Pub. by Royal Ont Mus CN) U of Toronto Pr.

***Pendergast, Debbie.** Kwitchyerbellyakin: And Other Bits & Pieces of Everyday Living. 110p. (Orig.). 1994. pap. write for info. (1-885591-36-5) Morris Pubng.

Pendergast, James F. The Massawomeck: Raiders & Traders into the Chesapeake Bay in the Seventeenth Century. LC 90-56111. (Transactions Ser.: Vol. 81, Pt. 2). (Illus.). 93p. (C). 1991. pap. 15.00 (0-87169-812-9, T812-PEJ) Am Philos.

Pendergast, James F. & Trigger, Bruce G. Cartier's Hochelaga & the Dawson Site. LC 78-184767. (Illus.). 470p. 1972. 49.95 (0-7735-0070-7, Pub. by McGill CN) U of Toronto Pr.

Pendergast, John. The Bend in the River: A Prehistory & Contact Period History, Lowell, Dracut, Chelmsford, Tyngsborough & Dunstable (Nashua, NH), Massachusetts 17,000 BP to AD1700. (Illus.). xvii, 92p. (Orig.). 1991. pap. text ed. 14.95 (0-9629338-0-5) Merrimack River.

Pendergast, Kathleen. Say Another One about How I Feel. LC 81-90678. (Illus.). 54p. (Orig.). (J). (gr. k-6). 1982. pap. 6.95 (0-942178-00-9) Madison Park Pr.

— Say Another One about My Family. LC 82-61139. (Say Another One Ser.). (Illus.). 54p. (J). (gr. k-6). 1982. pap. 6.95 (0-942178-01-7) Madison Park Pr.

— Say Another One about Playing. LC 83-62129. (Say Another One Ser.). (Illus.). 54p. (J). (gr. k-6). 1983. pap. 6.95 (0-942178-02-5) Madison Park Pr.

***Pendergast, Richard A.** Learn to Use Your Modem in a Day. (Popular Applications Ser.). 136p. (Orig.). 1995. pap. 15.95 (1-55622-445-1) Wordware Pub.

Pendergast, Richard J. Cosmos. LC 72-82897. 223p. reprint ed. pap. 63.60 (0-7837-0462-3, 2040785) Bks Demand.

Pendergast, Susan, jt. auth. see Derencenzi, Jayne.

Penderghast, Thomas F. E.S.P (Entrepreneurial Simulation Program) 150p. (C). 1988. pap. text ed. 16.50 (0-15-522821-8); teacher ed. pap. text ed. 21.50 (0-15-522822-6) Dryden Pr.

Pendergr, Donald. Collision Repair Estimating. 1977. pap. 25.96 (0-02-681230-4) Macmillan.

— Collision Repair Estimating. 1987. 21.28 (0-02-679910-3) Macmillan.

Pendergraft, Lee. Micrographics Techniques. 1982. pap. 10.00 (0-87771-031-7) Grad School.

Pendergraft, Patricia. Miracle at Clement's Pond. (J). (gr. 5 up). 1987. pap. 13.95 (0-399-21438-0, Philomel Bks) Putnam Pub Group.

— Miracle at Clements' Pond. 256p. (J). (gr. 4-7). 1988. pap. 2.50 (0-590-41458-5, Apple Paperbacks) Scholastic Inc.

Pendergraph, Garland. Handbook of Phlebotomy. 3rd ed. (Illus.). 140p. 1992. pap. text ed. 25.95 (0-8121-1564-3) Williams & Wilkins.

Pendergrass, Bonnie B. Public Power, Politics & Technology in the Eisenhower & Kennedy Years: The Hanford Dual-Purpose Reactor Controversy, 1956-1962. Bruchey, Stuart, ed. LC 78-22705. (Energy in the American Economy Ser.). 1979. lib. bdg. 19.95 (0-405-12007-9) Ayer.

Pendergrass, Carol R. Writing Right!, Bk. 1: Manuscript. 96p. 1994. pap. 4.75 (0-88323-261-8, 149) Pendergrass Pub.

— Writing Right!, Bk. 2: Cursive. 96p. (J). (gr. 1 up). 1994. pap. text ed. 4.75 (0-88323-262-6, 150) Pendergrass Pub.

Pendergrass, Donald H. Collision Repair Estimating. 160p. (Orig.). (C). 1985. teacher ed write for info. (0-672-98387-7); pap. text ed. write for info. (0-672-98386-9) Macmillan.

Pendergrass, Edna. Help Yourself to Happiness. 90p. 1988. pap. 5.99 (0-89225-335-5) Gospel Advocate.

Pendergrass, Virginia E., ed. Women Winning: A Handbook for Action Against Sex Discrimination. LC 78-27379. 196p. 1979. 28.95 (0-88229-450-4) Nelson-Hall.

Pendergrast, James T., jt. auth. see Curtis, Rex.

Pendergrast, Mark. For God, Country & Coca-Cola: The Unauthorized History of the Great American Soft Drink & the Company That Makes It. (Illus.). 576p. 1994. pap. 14.00 (0-02-036035-5, Pub. by Gebrueder Borntraeger GW) Macmillan.

— Victims of Memory: Incest Accusations & Shattered Lives. 603p. (Orig.). 1995. pap. 24.95 (0-942679-16-4) Upper Access.

Pendergrast, Mick. Te Aho Tapu - The Sacred Thread: Traditional Maori Weaving. (Illus.). 124p. 1987. pap. 19.95 (0-8248-1143-7) UH Pr.

***Pendergrast, Stephen.** Desktop KornShell Graphical Programming. 800p. (YA). 1995. 42.95 (0-201-63375-2) Addison-Wesley.

Penders, C. L. The Life & Times of Sukarno. LC 74-369. 224p. 1974. 32.50 (0-8386-1546-5) Fairleigh Dickinson.

Penders, Mary C. Color & Cloth: The Quiltmaker's Ultimate Workbook. LC 89-10448. (Illus.). 136p. (Orig.). 1989. pap. 21.95 (0-913327-20-4) Quilt Digest Pr.

— Rectangles. (Quilts from Simple Shapes Ser.). 1991. pap. 9.95 (0-913327-35-2) Quilt Digest Pr.

— Squares. (Quilts from Simple Shapes Ser.). 1992. pap. 9.95 (0-913327-33-6) Quilt Digest Pr.

— Triangles. (Quilts from Simple Shapes Ser.). 1992. pap. 9.95 (0-913327-34-4) Quilt Digest Pr.

Pendey, Rekha. Women in India, Past & Present. (C). 1990. 32.00 (0-685-49091-2, Pub. by Chugh Pubns II) S Asia.

Pendharkar, Sumant & Biegel, Richard. DBASE IV for VMS & UNIX: A Technical Support Approach. (Illus.). 656p. 1992. pap. 49.95 (0-442-00908-9) Van Nos Reinhold.

— DBase IV Programming Language: A Building Block Approach. 560p. 1994. pap. 17.50 (0-13-301870-9) P-H.

— DBase IV 2.0 for DOS. LC 93-2263. 1994. pap. 29.95 (0-442-01680-8) Van Nos Reinhold.

Pendharkar, Sumant, jt. auth. see Biegel, Richard.

Pendharkar, Sumant S. & Biegel, Richard A. DBase IV Programming. LC 94-1530. 1994. 30.00 (0-02-800424-8) Glencoe.

Pendharkar, Sumant S., jt. auth. see Biegel, Richard A.

Pendias, Alina K. & Pendias, Henry K., eds. Trace Elements in Soils & Plants. 336p. 1984. 168.00 (0-8493-6639-9, S592) CRC Pr.

Pendias, Henry K., jt. ed. see Pendias, Alina K.

Pendias, Henryk, jt. ed. see Kabata-Pendias, Alina.

Pendl, G. Pineal & Midbrain Lesions. (Illus.). 280p. 1985. 106.00 (0-387-81858-8) Spr-Verlag.

Pendle, G. Argentina. 1976. lib. bdg. 59.95 (0-8490-1448-4) Gordon Pr.

— Paraguay: A Riverside Nation. 1976. lib. bdg. 59.95 (0-8490-2409-9) Gordon Pr.

Pendle, George. History of Latin America. (Orig.). (YA). (gr. 11 up). 1963. pap. 6.95 (0-14-020620-5) Viking Child Bks.

— Uruguay. LC 85-24780. 136p. 1986. reprint ed. text ed. 49.75 (0-313-24981-4, PEUR, Greenwood Pr) Greenwood.

Pendle, Karin. Eugene Scribe & French Opera of the Nineteenth Century. LC 79-20451. (Studies in Musicology: No. 6). 635p. reprint ed. pap. 180.00 (0-685-20824-9, 2070039) Bks Demand.

Pendle, Karin, ed. Women & Music: A History. LC 91-8413. (Illus.). 372p. 1991. 27.50 (0-253-34321-6) Ind U Pr.

Pendlebury, D. L., tr. see Shah Waliullah.

Pendlebury, David, tr. Jami: Yusuf & Zulaikha. 1980. 22.00 (0-900860-77-4) ISHK Bk Service.

Pendlebury, J. M. Kinetic Theory. (Student Monographs in Physics). (Illus.). 64p. 1985. pap. 11.00 (0-85274-796-9) IOP Pub.

Pendlebury, John D. The Archaeology of Crete. LC 63-18049. (Illus.). 1969. 28.00 (0-8196-0121-7) Biblo.

— Handbook to the Palace of Minos at Knossos. 1979. reprint ed. pap. 10.00 (0-89005-312-X) Ares.

***Pendlebury, Maurice & Groves, Roger.** Company Accounts. 3rd ed. 256p. 1994. pap. 24.95x (0-415-10602-8, B4059) Routledge.

Pendlebury, Maurice, jt. auth. see Jones, Rowan.

Pendlebury, P., jt. auth. see Abbott, A.

***Pendleton.** Stringer. (Stony Man Ser.: Vol. 18). 1995. mass mkt. 4.99 (0-373-61902-2) Harlequin Bks.

Pendleton, tr. see Hahnemann, Samuel.

Pendleton, Amena. The Golden Heart & Other Stories. (Illus.). 79p. 1987. reprint ed. pap. 4.30 (0-910557-19-5) Acad New Church.

Pendleton, Andrew & Winterton, Jonathon, eds. Public Enterprise in Transition: Industrial Relations in State & Privatized Corporations. LC 92-44127. 1993. write for info. (0-415-07572-6, Routledge NY) Routledge.

***Pendleton, Austin.** Uncle Bob. 1995. pap. 4.75 (0-8222-1476-8) Dramatists Play.

Pendleton, Bonnie & Mehling, Betty. Relax! With Self Therap-Ease: A Simple Illustrated Course. (Illus.). 176p. 1984. pap. 7.95 (0-13-772187-0) P-H.

— Relax! with Self-Therap-Ease: Whole-Body Acupressure. (Illus.). 171p. 1976. lib. bdg. 12.50 (0-917306-01-5) Calif Pubns.

Pendleton, Brian F., jt. auth. see Poloma, Margaret M.

Pendleton, David & Hasler, John, eds. Doctor-Patient Communciation. 1983. text ed. 70.00 (0-12-549880-2) Acad Pr.

Pendleton, Don. Acapulco Rampage. (Executioner Ser.: No. 26). 1989. pap. 3.50 (1-55817-284-X, Pinnacle NY) Windsor NY.

— Arizona Ambush. (Executioner Ser.: No. 31). 1990. pap. 3.50 (1-55817-342-0, Pinnacle NY) Windsor NY.

— Battle Mask. (Executioner Ser.: No. 3). 1988. pap. 3.50 (1-55817-026-X, Pinnacle NY) Windsor NY.

— Boston Blitz. (Executioner Ser.: No. 12). 1989. pap. 3.50 (1-55817-071-5, Pinnacle NY) Windsor NY.

— California Hit. (Executioner Ser.: No. 11). 1989. pap. 3.50 (1-55817-070-7, Pinnacle NY) Windsor NY.

— Canadian Crisis. (Executioner Ser.: No. 24). 1989. pap. 3.50 (1-55817-267-X, Pinnacle NY) Windsor NY.

— Caribbean Kill. (Executioner Ser.: No. 10). 1989. pap. 3.50 (1-55817-069-3, Pinnacle NY) Windsor NY.

— Chicago Wipeout. (Executioner Ser.: No. 8). 1989. pap. 3.50 (1-55817-067-7, Pinnacle NY) Windsor NY.

— Colorado Killzone. (Executioner Ser.: No. 25). 1989. pap. 3.50 (1-55817-275-0, Pinnacle NY) Windsor NY.

— Continental Contract. (Executioner Ser.: No. 5). 1988. pap. 3.50 (1-55817-028-6, Pinnacle NY) Windsor NY.

— Copp for Hire. LC 87-81420. 272p. 1987. 16.95 (1-55611-064-2) D I Fine.

— Copp in Deep. 252p. 1989. 17.95 (1-55611-141-X) D I Fine.

— Copp in Deep. 1991. mass mkt. 4.50 (0-06-100248-8, Harp PBks) HarpC.

— Copp in Shock. LC 91-58661. 256p. 1992. 19.95 (1-55611-287-4) D I Fine.

— Copp in Shock. 1993. mass mkt. 4.99 (0-06-100459-6, Harp PBks) HarpC.

— Copp in the Dark. (Joe Copp Ser.: No. 4). 1990. 18.95 (1-55611-210-6) D I Fine.

— Copp in the Dark. 1992. mass mkt. 4.99 (0-06-100347-6, Harp PBks) HarpC.

— Copp on Fire. LC 87-46278. 1988. 16.95 (1-55611-088-X) D I Fine.

— Copp on Fire. 1990. mass mkt. 4.50 (0-06-100036-1, Harp PBks) HarpC.

— Copp on Ice. 1991. 18.95 (1-55611-235-1) D I Fine.

— Copp on Ice. 1992. mass mkt. 4.99 (0-06-100458-8, Harp PBks) HarpC.

— Detroit Deathwatch. (Executioner Ser.: No. 19). 1989. pap. 3.50 (1-55817-218-1, Pinnacle NY) Windsor NY.

— Executioner, No. 29: Command Strike. 1990. pap. 3.50 (1-55817-318-8, Pinnacle NY) Windsor NY.

— Executioner, No. 30: Cleveland Pipeline. 1990. pap. 3.50 (1-55817-327-7, Pinnacle NY) Windsor NY.

— Executioner, No. 32: Tennessee Smash. 1990. pap. 3.50 (1-55817-354-4, Pinnacle NY) Windsor NY.

— Executioner, No. 33: Monday's Mob. 1990. pap. 3.50 (1-55817-371-4, Pinnacle NY) Windsor NY.

— Executioner No. 34: Terrible Tuesday. 1990. pap. 3.50 (1-55817-382-X, Pinnacle NY) Windsor NY.

— Executioner, No. 35: Wednesday's Wrath. 1990. pap. 3.50 (1-55817-425-7, Pinnacle NY) Windsor NY.

— Executioner, No. 36: Thermal Thursday. 1990. pap. 3.50 (1-55817-407-9, Pinnacle NY) Windsor NY.

— The Fiery Cross. (Gold Eagle Ser.). 1988. pap. 2.95 (0-685-19856-1) S&S Trade.

— Firebase Seattle. (Executioner Ser.: No. 21). 1989. pap. 3.50 (1-55817-236-X, Pinnacle NY) Windsor NY.

— Friday Feast. (Executioner Ser.: No. 37). 1990. pap. 3.50 (1-55817-420-6, Pinnacle NY) Windsor NY.

— Hawaiian Heat. (Executioner Ser.: No. 155). 1991. mass mkt. 3.50 (0-373-61155-2) Harlequin Bks.

— Hawaiian Hellground. (Executioner Ser.: No. 22). (Orig.). 1989. pap. 3.50 (1-55817-246-7, Pinnacle NY) Windsor NY.

— Jersey Guns. (Executioner Ser.: No. 17). 1989. pap. 3.50 (1-55817-176-2, Pinnacle NY) Windsor NY.

— New Orleans Knockout. (Executioner Ser.: No. 20). 1989. pap. 3.50 (1-55817-219-X, Pinnacle NY) Windsor NY.

— Nightmare in New York. (Executioner Ser.: No. 7). 1989. pap. 3.50 (1-55817-066-9, Pinnacle NY) Windsor NY.

— Panic in Philly. (Executioner Ser.: No. 15). 1989. pap. 3.50 (1-55817-174-6, Pinnacle NY) Windsor NY.

— San Diego Siege. (Executioner Ser.: No. 14). 1989. pap. 3.50 (1-55817-173-8, Pinnacle NY) Windsor NY.

— Satan's Sabbath. (Executioner Ser.: No. 38). 1990. pap. 3.50 (1-55817-444-3, Pinnacle NY) Windsor NY.

— Savage Fire. (Executioner Ser.: No. 28). 1990. pap. 3.50 (1-55817-309-9, Pinnacle NY) Windsor NY.

— Sicilian Slaughter. (Executioner Ser.: No. 16). 1989. pap. 3.50 (1-55817-175-4, Pinnacle NY) Windsor NY.

— Stony Man, No. III. 1991. mass mkt. 4.99 (0-373-61887-5) Harlequin Bks.

— Texas Storm. (Executioner Ser.: No. 18). 1989. pap. 3.50 (1-55817-177-0, Pinnacle NY) Windsor NY.

— To Dance with Angels: An Amazing Journey to the Heart with the Phenomenal Thomas Jacobson. 400p. 1995. mass mkt. 5.99 (0-7860-0095-3, Pinnacle NY) Windsor NY.

— Washington I.O.U. (Executioner Ser.: No. 13). 1989. pap. 3.50 (1-55817-172-X, Pinnacle NY) Windsor NY.

Pendleton, Don & Pendleton, Linda. To Dance with Angels. 1990. 18.95 (0-8217-3024-X) Zebra.

— To Dance with Angels. 1992. pap. 10.00 (0-8217-3755-4) Zebra.

— To Dance with Angels. 400p. 1995. pap. 5.99 (0-8217-0095-2) Zebra.

Pendleton, E. H. Holloway: William Holloway of Taunton, Mass. (Illus.). 356p. 1991. reprint ed. lib. bdg. 65.00 (*0-8328-2221-3*); reprint ed. pap. 55.00 (*0-8328-2222-1*) Higginson Bk Co.

Pendleton, Erika, ed. see Matthay, Eileen.

Pendleton, Howard. Criminal Justice in England: A Study in Law Administration. LC 87-81959. xv, 436p. 1987. reprint ed. lib. bdg. 42.00 (*0-89941-579-2*, 305340) W S Hein.

Pendleton, James H. Christian Doctrines: A Compendium of Theology. 1957. 21.00 (*0-8170-0037-2*) Judson.

Pendleton, James M. Baptist Church Manual. rev. ed. 1966. reprint ed. 12.99 (*0-8054-2510-1*) Broadman.

Pendleton, Joe. The Joy of Bible Study. (Illus.). 32p. (Orig.). 1981. P. 32. teacher ed 1.50 (*0-89114-107-3*); pap. 1.95 (*0-89114-106-5*) Baptist Pub Hse.

Pendleton, Leila A. A Narrative of the Negro. LC 78-178481. (Black Heritage Library Collection). 1977. reprint ed. 22.95 (*0-8369-8930-9*) Ayer.

Pendleton, Linda, jt. auth. see Pendleton, Don.

Pendleton, Lorann, jt. auth. see Thomas, David H.

Pendleton, Louis. In the Okefenokee: A Story of War Time and the Great Georgia Swamp. LC 72-1558. (Black Heritage Library Collection). 1977. reprint ed. 20.95 (*0-8369-9045-5*) Ayer.

— The Wedding Garment: A Tale of the Life to Come. 191p. 1987. reprint ed. pap. 5.20 (*0-910557-17-9*) Acad New Church.

Pendleton, Madge, et al. Green Book: Guide for Living in Saudi Arabia. 4th ed. LC 83-61986. (Illus.). 264p. 1984. pap. 13.50 (*0-918992-04-4*) Middle East Edit.

Pendleton, Michael D. Intellectual Property Law in the People's Republic of China: A Guide to Patents, Trade Marks & Technology Transfer. 155p. 1986. pap. 45.00 (*0-409-99519-3*) Butterworth Legal Pubs.

— The Law of Intellectual & Industrial Property in Hong Kong. 595p. 1984. pap. 119.00 (*0-406-18117-9*) Butterworth Legal Pubs.

Pendleton, Michalene & Barnes, F. A. Canyon Country Prehistoric Indians. (Canyon Country Ser.). (Illus.). (Orig.). 1979. pap. 7.50 (*0-915272-24-5*) Wasatch Pubs.

Pendleton, Moses & Richards, Terri. Children on the Hill: Labanotation Score. (Educational Performance Collection). 99p. 1987. pap. write for info. (*0-932582-52-4*) Dance Notation.

Pendleton, Nathaniel D. The Glorification: Sermons & Papers. 2nd ed. 221p. 1985. reprint ed. 7.00 (*0-910557-10-1*) Acad New Church.

— Selected Papers & Addresses. 251p. 1985. 7.00 (*0-910557-09-8*) Acad New Church.

***Pendleton, Philip E.** Oley Valley Heritage: The Colonial Years, 1700-1775, Vol. 28. Yoder, Don, ed. (Illus.). 232p. 1995. write for info. (*0-911122-59-1*) Penn German Soc.

Pendleton, Ralph, ed. The Theatre of Robert Edmond Jones. LC 58-5188. (Illus.). 212p. 1977. pap. 20.00 (*0-8195-6053-7*, Wesleyan Univ Pr) U Pr of New Eng.

***Pendleton, Robert.** Graham Greene's Conradian Masterplot: The Arabesques of Influence. LC 94-44448. 1995. write for info. (*0-312-12571-2*) St Martin.

Pendleton, Shaun & Belinorlec. ABCs of Aerobics. 112p. 1993. pap. 12.95 (*0-8403-8608-7*) Kendall-Hunt.

Pendleton, Thomas A. I'm Sorry about the Clock: Chronology, Composition, & Narrative Technique in The Great Gatsby. LC 91-51135. 160p. 1993. 29.50 (*0-945636-38-5*) Susquehanna U Pr.

Pendleton, Thomas A., jt. ed. see Mahon, John.

Pendleton, W. C. History of Tazewell County & Southwest Virginia, 1748-1920. (Illus.). 720p. 1989. reprint ed. 29.95 (*0-932807-39-9*) Overmountain Pr.

***Pendleton, Wade C.** Katutura: a Place Where We Stay: Life in a Post-Apartheid Township in Namibia. (Monographs in International Studies, Africa Ser.: No. 65). (Illus.). 170p. (Orig.). (C). 1995. pap. text ed. 20.00 (*0-89680-188-8*) Ohio U Pr.

***Pendleton, Wendell.** Estate Planning with the Living Trust. LC 95-68483. 120p. (Orig.). 1995. 19.95 (*1-884570-30-5*) Research Triangle.

Pendleton, Willard D. Education for Use. 290p. 1985. 12.00 (*0-910557-11-X*) Acad New Church.

Pendleton, William C. History of Tazewell County & Southwest Virginia, 1748-1920. (Illus.). 700p. 1994. reprint ed. lib. bdg. 69.50 (*0-8328-4021-1*) Higginson Bk Co.

Pendleton, Winston K. Complete Speakers Galaxy of Funny Stories, Jokes & Anecdotes. 1986. 6.95 (*0-13-164491-2*) P-H.

— Handbook of Inspirational & Motivational Stories, Anecdotes & Humor. LC 82-2279. 350p. 1986. 19.95 (*0-13-378604-8*, Parker Publishing Co) P-H.

— How to Make Money Speaking. LC 77-1536. 128p. 1977. 15.00 (*0-88289-172-3*) Pelican.

— How to Stop Worrying-Forever. LC 66-19811. 80p. 1975. reprint ed. 8.95 (*0-88289-083-2*) Pelican.

— Speaker's Handbook of Successful Openers & Closers. 261p. 1984. 21.95 (*0-13-824525-8*, Busn); pap. 7.95 (*0-13-824517-7*, Busn) P-H.

Pendley, Robert E., jt. ed. see Pilat, Joseph F.

Pendley, William, et al. The United States, Australia, & Regional Nation Defense Interactions in Asia Pacific. 1993. write for info. (*1-884296-01-7*) Austlia-NZ Studies.

Pendley, William P. It Takes a Hero: The Grassroots Battle Against Environmental Oppression. Arnold, Ron, ed. xviii, 326p. (Orig.). 1994. pap. 14.95 (*0-939571-16-1*) Free Enter Pr.

— War on the West: Government Tyranny on America's Great Frontier. 224p. 1995. 21.95 (*0-89526-482-X*) Regnery Pub.

Pendo, Stephen. Aviation in the Cinema. LC 84-14169. 414p. 1985. 35.00 (*0-8108-1746-2*) Scarecrow.

Pendola, Angelo. Poesie per i Romeni: Italian Poetry. 99p. 1990. pap. 10.00 (*0-89304-538-1*) Cross-Cultrl NY.

— Poesie per i Romeni: Italian Poetry. 99p. (ITA.). 1990. 20.00 (*0-89304-539-X*) Cross-Cultrl NY.

— Zabut: Italian Poetry. Scammacca, Nat, ed. 40p. 1983. pap. 5.00 (*0-89304-565-9*) Cross-Cultrl NY.

Pendola, Richard. Lab Manual for General Biology - Zoology. (C). 1993. student ed 8.99 (*1-56870-069-5*) RonJon Pub.

Pendray, E. The Earth-Tube. LC 74-15967. (Science Fiction Ser.). 316p. 1975. reprint ed. 25.95 (*0-405-06287-7*) Ayer.

Pendrell, Ernest. Seven Times Monday. 1961. pap. 4.75 (*0-8222-1016-9*) Dramatists Play.

Pendrill, Charles. London Life in the Fourteenth Century. 1976. lib. bdg. 59.95 (*0-8490-2181-2*) Gordon Pr.

Pendrill, D., jt. auth. see Lewis, R. W.

Pendry, E. D., ed. see Marlowe, Christopher.

Pendse, G. S., ed. Recent Advances in Cytochalasans. 202p. 1987. text ed. 89.00 (*0-412-29350-1*) Chapman & Hall.

Pendse, Shripad G., ed. Perspectives on an Economic Future: Forms, Reforms, & Evaluations. LC 90-37841. (Contributions in Economics & Economic History Ser.: No. 116). 216p. 1991. text ed. 55.00 (*0-313-26288-8*, PCG/, Greenwood Pr) Greenwood.

Pene Du Bois, Henri, tr. see France, Anatole.

Pene du Bois, William. Gentleman Bear. LC 84-48320. (Illus.). 80p. (J). (gr. k up). 1985. 14.95 (*0-374-32533-2*) FS&G.

— Gentleman Bear. (Sunburst Ser.). (Illus.). 80p. (J). (ps up). 1988. pap. 5.95 (*0-374-42536-1*) FS&G.

Pene Du Bois, William. Peter Graves. (Illus.). 172p. (J). (gr. 3-7). 1991. pap. 3.95 (*0-14-034784-4*, Puffin) Puffin Bks.

Pene Du Bois, William, illus. Bear in Mind: A Book of Bear Poems. 32p. (J). (ps-3). 1991. pap. 4.99 (*0-14-050799-X*, Puffin) Puffin Bks.

Penecost, J. Dwight. Prophecy for Today: God's Purpose & Plan for Our Future. 1989. 9.99 (*0-929239-11-3*) Discovery Hse Pubs.

***Penelhum.** Reason & Religious Faith. (Focus Ser.). (C). 1995. pap. text ed. 15.95 (*0-8133-2036-4*) Westview.

Penelhum, Terence. David Hume: An Introduction to His Philosophical System. LC 91-9096. (Series in the History of Philosophy). 240p. (C). 1992. 27.00 (*1-55753-012-2*); pap. 13.75 (*1-55753-013-0*) Purdue U Pr.

— Faith. (Philosophical Topics Ser.). (C). 1989. pap. write for info. (*0-02-393721-1*) Macmillan.

— God & Skepticism. 1983. lib. bdg. 74.50 (*90-277-1550-5*) Kluwer Ac.

Penelope, tr. William of St. Thierry: On Contemplating God, Prayer, Meditations. (Cistercian Fathers Ser.: No. 3). 1970. pap. 5.00 (*0-87907-903-7*) Cistercian Pubns.

Penelope, Julia. Call Me Lesbian: Lesbian Lives, Lesbian Theory. 180p. (Orig.). 1992. pap. 12.95 (*0-89594-496-0*) Crossing Pr.

— Speaking Freely: Unlearning the Lies of the Fathers' Tongues. (Athene Ser.). 370p. 1990. text ed. 37.50 (*0-08-036556-6*, Pub. by PPI UK); pap. text ed. 16.95 (*0-08-036555-8*, Pub. by PPI UK) Elsevier.

— Speaking Freely: Unlearning the Lies of the Fathers' Tongues. (Athene Ser.). 328p. (C). text ed. 37.50 (*0-8077-6245-8*); pap. text ed. 18.95 (*0-8077-6244-X*) Tchrs Coll.

— Women's Crossword Puzzles. 20p. 1995. pap. 7.95 (*0-89594-120-1*) Crossing Pr.

Penelope, Julia, ed. Coming Out of the Class Closet: Lesbians Speak. LC 94-17401. 400p. 1994. pap. 14.95 (*0-89594-704-8*) Crossing Pr.

Penelope, Julia & Valentine, Sarah, eds. Finding the Lesbians: Personal Accounts from Around the World. 260p. (Orig.). 1990. pap. 10.95 (*0-89594-426-X*) Crossing Pr.

— International Feminist Fiction. LC 92-16864. 333p. 1992. pap. 12.95 (*0-89594-567-3*) Crossing Pr.

Penelope, Julia & Wolfe, Susan J., eds. Lesbian Culture: An Anthology. 500p. 1993. lib. bdg. 30.00 (*0-89594-592-4*); pap. text ed. 21.95 (*0-89594-591-6*) Crossing Pr.

— The Original Coming Out Stories. 2nd enl. rev. ed. 300p. 1989. pap. 10.95 (*0-89594-339-5*) Crossing Pr.

Penelope, Julia, jt. auth. see Grey, Morgan.

Penelope, Julia, jt. ed. see Wolfe, Susan J.

Penenberg, Brad L. & Chandler, Hugh P. Bone Stock Deficiency in Total Hip Replacement: Classification & Management. LC 85-62643. 190p. 1989. 60.00 (*0-943432-61-8*) SLACK Inc.

Peneneau, Taylor. Dan Walker: The Glory & the Tragedy. 1993. 29.95 (*0-9623414-7-9*); pap. 15.95 (*0-9623414-6-0*) Smith Collins.

***Pener, Michael A.** Discovery - Interviewing & Investigation. 2nd ed. 1995. pap. 36.95 (*0-929563-17-4*) Pearson Pubns.

Penetrante, Bernie M. & Schultheis, Shirley E., eds. Non-Thermal Plasma Techniques for Pollution Control, 2 Vols. LC 93-21307. (NATO ASI Series G: Ecological Sciences: Vol. 34). (Illus.). lxxii, 790p. 1994. Incl. Parts A & B. 363.00 (*0-387-57174-4*) Spr-Verlag.

Penfield. Bon Voyage. 135p. 1992. 12.00 (*0-86690-406-9*) Am Fed Astrologers.

***Penfield & Hill.** Quick Takes: Short Model Essays for Composition. (C). 1994. text ed. 23.00 (*0-06-501338-7*) HarpCollege.

Penfield, Elizabeth. Short Takes: Model Essays for Composition. 3rd ed. (C). 1989. pap. text ed. 16.00 (*0-673-38872-7*) HarpCollege.

— Short Takes: Model Essays for Composition. 4th ed. LC 92-22100. (C). 1992. 18.50 (*0-673-46598-5*, HarpT); 10.00 (*0-673-46599-3*, HarpT) HarpC.

Penfield, Elizabeth & Hill, Theodora. Quick Takes: Short Model Essays for Basic Composition. LC 94-20373. (C). 1994. write for info. (*0-673-99463-5*) HarpCollege.

Penfield, Elizabeth, jt. ed. see Moran, Charles.

***Penfield, Florence B.** Penfield: Genealogy of the Descendants of Samuel Penfield, with a Supplement of Dr. Levi Buckingham Line & the Gridley, Dwight, Burlingham, Dewey & Pyncheon Collateral Lines. 320p. 1994. reprint ed. lib. bdg. 59.50 (*0-8328-4349-0*); reprint ed. pap. 49.50 (*0-8328-4369-5*) Higginson Bk Co.

Penfield, Joyce. Communicating with Quotes: The Igbo Case. LC 82-15626. (Contributions in Intercultural & Comparative Studies: No. 8). (Illus.). xiv, 138p. 1983. text ed. 55.00 (*0-313-23767-0*, PEN/, Greenwood Pr) Greenwood.

Penfield, Joyce, ed. Women & Language in Transition. LC 86-23113. 208p. 1987. 74.50 (*0-88706-485-X*); pap. 24.95 (*0-88706-486-8*) State U NY Pr.

Penfield, Marjorie P. & Campbell, Ada M. Experimental Food Science. 3rd ed. (Food Science & Technology Ser.). 541p. 1990. text ed. 50.00 (*0-12-157920-4*) Acad Pr.

Penfield, Paul, Jr., ed. see Conference on Advanced Research in VLSI (1984: MIT).

Penfield, Paul, Jr., ed. see Massachusetts Institute of Technology, Conference on Advanced Research in VLSI Staff.

Penfield, Thomas. Dig Here. (Illus.). 240p. (Orig.). 1987. reprint ed. pap. 10.00 (*0-918080-38-X*) Treas Chest Bks.

— Directory of Buried Or Sunken Treasures & Lost Mines of the United States. (True Treasure Ser.). (Illus.). 134p. (Orig.). 1979. reprint ed. pap. text ed. 8.95 (*0-941620-06-9*) Carson Ent.

— A Guide to Treasure in Arizona. (True Treasure Ser.). 134p. 1982. reprint ed. pap. 8.95 (*0-941620-01-8*) Carson Ent.

— A Guide to Treasure in California. (Treasure Guide Ser.). 160p. (Orig.). 1983. reprint ed. pap. 8.95 (*0-941620-23-9*) Carson Ent.

— A Guide to Treasure in Montana & Wyoming. (True Treasure Ser.). 84p. (Orig.). 1975. pap. 6.95 (*0-941620-28-X*) Carson Ent.

— A Guide to Treasure in Texas. (Treasure Guide Ser.). 141p. 1972. pap. 8.95 (*0-941620-02-6*) Carson Ent.

— Treasure Guide to Nebraska, Kansas, North & South Dakota. (Treasure Guide Ser.). 87p. 1971. pap. 6.95 (*0-941620-18-2*) Carson Ent.

— Treasure Guide to Nevada. (Treasure Guide Ser.). 74p. 1974. pap. 7.95 (*0-941620-15-8*) Carson Ent.

— Treasure Guide to New Mexico. (Treasure Guide Ser.). 104p. 1974. pap. 7.95 (*0-941620-24-7*) Carson Ent.

— Treasure Guide to Utah. (Treasure Guide Ser.). 56p. 1974. pap. 6.95 (*0-941620-12-3*) Carson Ent.

Penfield, Wilder. The Mystery of the Mind: A Critical Study of Consciousness & the Human Brain. LC 74-25626. 154p. reprint ed. pap. 43.90 (*0-7837-0102-0*, 2040380) Bks Demand.

Penfield, Wilder & Roberts, Lamar. Speech & Brain Mechanisms. LC 59-5602. (Illus.). 304p. (C). 1959. reprint ed. 60.00 (*0-691-08039-9*); reprint ed. pap. 17.95x (*0-691-02366-2*) Princeton U Pr.

Penfold, John W. Microsoft Visual BASIC: The Programmer's Companion. 272p. (Orig.). 1993. pap. 47.50 (*1-85058-292-0*, Pub. by Sigma Press UK) Coronet Bks.

***Penfold, R. A.** Music Mini Projects. (Maplin Ser.). 200p. 1995. pap. 19.95 (*0-7506-2119-2*, Focal) Buttrwrth-Heinemann.

Peng, David D., ed. Insurance & Legal Issues in the Oil Industry. LC 93-23158. (International Energy & Resources Law & Policy Ser.). 208p. (C). 1993. lib. bdg. 90.00 (*1-85333-913-X*, Pub. by Graham & Trotman UK) Kluwer Ac.

Peng, Fang. The Geopotential: Modeling Techniques & Physical Implications with Case Studies in the South & East China Sea & Fennoscandia. (Uppsala Science Dissertations Ser.: No. 25). (Illus.). 146p. (Orig.). 1989. pap. 45.50x (*91-554-2365-5*, Pub. by Almqv & Wiksell SW) Coronet Bks.

Peng, Fei. Chinese Mulian Plays: Resources for Studies of Ritual & Performance. Seaman, Gary, ed. LC 94-71629. (Monographs Ser.). 300p. (Orig.). (C). 1994. pap. text ed. 15.00 (*1-878986-05-8*) Ethnographics Pr.

Peng, H. L., ed. see Liu, Lily.

***Peng, S., et al, eds.** Climate Change & Rice. LC 95-12491. 1995. write for info. (*3-540-58906-6*) Spr-Verlag.

Peng, S. Y. The Biology & Control of Weeds in Sugar Cane. (Developments in Crop Science Ser.: Vol. 4). 250p. 1984. 107.75 (*0-444-42133-5*) Elsevier.

Peng Shi-Kaung & Morin, Robert J. Biological Effects of Cholesterol Oxides. (Illus.). 224p. 1991. 156.00 (*0-8493-6776-X*, QP752) CRC Pr.

P'eng Shu-Tse. The Chinese Communist Party in Power. Evans, Leslie, ed. LC 79-92214. 1980. lib. bdg. 65.00 (*0-913460-75-3*); pap. 28.95 (*0-913460-76-1*) Pathfinder NY.

Peng, Syd S. Surface Subsidence Engineering. LC 92-80558. 161p. (C). 1992. 68.50 (*0-87335-114-2*, 114-2) SMM&E Inc.

Peng, Tan H. Fun with Chinese Festivals. 1991. pap. 7.95 (*0-89346-358-2*) Heian Intl.

***Peng, Wendy W. & Wallace, Dolores R.** Software Error Analysis. LC 94-24763. 1994. write for info. (*0-929306-18-X*) Silicon Pr.

Peng, Xinwei. A Monetary History of China. Kaplan, Edward H., tr. (East Asian Research Aids & Translations Ser.: Vol. 5). l, 932p. (C). 1994. pap. 50.00 (*0-914584-81-2*) WWUCEAS.

Peng Xizhe. Demographic Transition in China: Fertility Trends in China since the 1950s. (Studies on Contemporary China). (Illus.). 334p. 1991. 79.00 (*0-19-828715-1*) OUP.

Peng, Y. & Reggia, J. A. Abductive Inference Models for Diagnostic Problem Solving. Loveland, D. W. et al, eds. (Symbolic Computation - Artificial Intelligence Ser.). (Illus.). xii, 284p. 1990. 44.00 (*0-387-97343-5*) Spr-Verlag.

Pengelley, Daphne, jt. auth. see Pengelley, Eric T.

Pengelley, Eric T. Sex & Human Life. 2nd ed. LC 77-77720. (Life Sciences Ser.). (Illus.). 1978. pap. text ed. write for info. (*0-201-05770-0*) Addison-Wesley.

Pengelley, Eric T. & Pengelley, Daphne. A Traveler's Guide to the History of Biology & Medicine. 238p. 1986. pap. text ed. 12.50 (*0-9616695-0-0*) Trevor Hill Pr.

Pengelly, Paul & Woodhouse, Douglas. Anxiety & the Dynamics of Collaboration. (Aberdeen University Press Bks.). 176p. (C). 1991. pap. text ed. 25.00 (*0-08-040912-1*, Pub. by Aberdeen U Pr) Macmillan.

Pengilley, Warren. The Law of Travel & Tourism. 132p. (C). 1990. pap. 100.00 (*1-875114-12-2*, Blckstone AT) W W Gaunt.

— Local Government & the Trade Practices Act: Do Some Traditionally Held Views Need Re-Evaluation? 92p. 1991. pap. 32.50 (*1-875114-17-3*, Blckstone AT) W W Gaunt.

Pengilly, John, jt. auth. see Lyon, Rod.

Penglase, Charles. Greek Myths & Mesopotamia: Parallels & Influence in the Homeric Hymns & Hesiod. LC 93-14611. Date not set. write for info. (*0-415-08371-0*) Routledge.

Penglis, Gregory M. The Complete Guide to Flight Instruction. LC 93-38698. 550p. 1994. pap. 29.95 (*1-56825-012-6*) Rainbow Books.

***Pengra, Nancy L.** Family Histories: An Easy Step-by-Step Guide to Capturing Your Family's Precious Memories Now...Before They're Lost! abr. ed. 150p. 1995. pap. 19.95 (*0-9645211-0-5*) Fam Hist MN.

Penguin, Inky. The Writing Book. (Illus.). 44p. (gr. 3-6). 1986. student ed, pap. 7.95 (*0-915924-66-8*) Tchrs & Writers Coll.

Penguin Staff. The Time Out Berlin Guide. (Illus.). 296p. 1993. pap. 14.00 (*0-14-023042-4*, Penguin Bks) Viking Penguin.

Penha, James. On the Back of the Dragon. 52p. (Orig.). 1992. pap. 5.00 (*0-9631755-1-3*) Omega Cat Pr.

Penhale, Douglas, illus. Why Seals Blow Their Noses: North American Wildlife in Fact & Fiction. 80p. 1994. pap. 12.95 (*0-89658-250-7*) Voyageur Pr.

Penhale, Polly A., jt. ed. see Weiler, C. Susan.

Penhallow, Samuel. History of the Indian Wars. 208p. 1973. reprint ed. 21.00 (*0-87928-044-1*) Corner Hse.

Penhallurick, R. D. Tin in Antiquity. 272p. 1986. pap. 62.90 (*0-904357-81-3*, Pub. by Inst Materials UK) Ashgate Pub Co.

Penick, Harvey. And If You Play Golf You're My Friend. 1993. 20.00 (*0-671-87188-9*) S&S Trade.

— Harvey Penick, 2 vols., Set. 1994. 40.00 (*0-671-99842-0*) S&S Trade.

Penick, Harvey & Shrake, Ben. Harvey Penick's Little Red Book: Lessons & Teachings from a Lifetime in Golf. large type ed. 1993. 20.95 (*1-56895-016-0*) Wheeler Pub.

***Penick, Harvey & Shrake, Bud.** For All Who Love the Game: Lessons & Teachings for Women. 176p. 1995. 20.00 (*0-684-80058-6*) S&S Trade.

— Harvey Penick's Little Red Book: Lessons & Teachings from a Lifetime in Golf. 192p. 1992. 20.50 (*0-671-75992-2*) S&S Trade.

Penick, James L., Jr. The New Madrid Earthquakes. rev. ed. LC 81-50531. 192p. 1981. pap. 12.95 (*0-8262-0344-2*) U of Mo Pr.

Penick, James L., et al. The Politics of American Science: 1939 to the Present. rev. ed. 480p. 1972. reprint ed. pap. 9.95 (*0-262-66014-8*) MIT Pr.

Penick, Michael. Beginning Bridge Complete. 176p. 1991. pap. 8.95 (*0-910791-06-6*) Devyn Pr.

— Beginning Bridge Quizzes. 1989. pap. 6.95 (*0-910791-67-8*) Devyn Pr.

Penington, Ceraeme R. Introduction to Medical Rehabilitation: An Australian Perspective. 1990. pap. 24.95 (*0-522-84391-3*) Intl Spec Bk.

Penington, Isaac. The Inward Journey of Isaac Penington. Leach, Robert J., ed. LC 44-280. (Orig.). 1944. pap. 3.00 (*0-87574-029-4*) Pendle Hill.

Penington, M. Basil, ed. Towards an Integrated Humanity: Thomas Merton's Journey. 1988. 21.95 (*0-317-68108-7*); pap. 9.95 (*0-317-68109-5*) Cistercian Pubns.

Penionzhkevich, Yu E. & Kalpakchieva, R. Exotic Nuclei: Proceedings of the International Conference. 516p. 1992. text ed. 102.00 (*981-02-1104-X*) World Scientific Pub.

Penisten, John. Hawaii: Making the Most of Your Family Vacation. (Paradise Family Guides Ser.). (Illus.). 256p. (Orig.). 1992. pap. 12.95 (*1-55958-233-2*) Prima Pub.

— Hawaii: The Big Island. 4th ed. LC 94-3640. 1994. pap. 12.95 (*1-55958-563-3*) Prima Pub.

— Hawaii: The Big Island: Making the Most of Your Family Vacation. 4th ed. LC 94-28554. 1994. write for info. (*1-55958-562-5*) Prima Pub.

— Honolulu. LC 89-11973. (Downtown America Ser.). (Illus.). 60p. (J). (gr. 3 up). 1990. text ed. 13.95 (*0-87518-416-2*, Dillon Silver Burdett) Silver Burdett Pr.

Peniston, A. C. Search for Sybil. Hilovsky, Judy, ed. LC 89-316. 1990. 22.95 (*0-87949-291-0*) Ashley Bks.

Penjam, J., jt. ed. see Hermenegildo, M.

Penjam, Jaan, jt. ed. see Bruynooghe, Maurice.

Penka, Klimo & Vasicek. Floodplain Forest Ecosystem, No. 2: After Water Management Measures. 1991. 230.75 (*0-444-98756-8*) Elsevier.

Penka, M., et al. Floodplain Forest Ecosystem I: Before Water Management Measures. (Developments in Agricultural & Managed-Forest Ecology Ser.: Vol. 15A). 468p. 1986. 151.50 (*0-444-99566-8*) Elsevier.

An Asterisk (*) at the beginning of an entry indicates that the title is appearing in BIP for the first time.

Penke, Botond & Torok, Angela, eds. Peptides: Chemistry-Biology-Interactions with Proteins. 467p. (C). 1988. lib. bdg. 211.55 (*0-89925-430-6*) De Gruyter.
— Peptides: Chemistry-Biology-Interactions with Proteins. 467p. (C). 1988. lib. bdg. 211.55 (*3-11-011546-8*) De Gruyter.
Penkower, Monty N. The Emergence of Zionist Thought. LC 91-3416. (American University Studies: History: Ser. IX, Vol. 111). 159p. (C). 1991. text ed. 33.95 (*0-8204-1600-2*) P Lang Pubs.
— From Catastrophe to Sovereignty: The Holocaust & Israel Reborn. LC 93-41078. 360p. 1994. 47.50 (*0-252-02087-1*); pap. 19.95 (*0-252-06378-3*) U of Ill Pr.
— The Jews Were Expendable: Free World Diplomacy & Holocaust. LC 87-24638. 432p. (C). 1987. reprint ed. pap. 19.95 (*0-8143-1952-1*) Wayne St U Pr.
Penland, Ken, jt. auth. see Alexander, George.
Penland, Patrick R. Communication Science & Technology. LC 74-77108. (Communication Science & Technology Ser.: No. 1). (Illus.). 228p. reprint ed. pap. 65.00 (*0-8357-6064-2*, 2034560) Bks Demand.
— Franchised Desert: A Novel of New Age Personality. 1994. pap. 10.95 (*1-884333-47-8*) Passage Communs.
— Heeled Recovery: Femininity in Redemption. 1994. pap. 11.95 (*1-884333-45-1*) Passage Communs.
— Ransomed Phoenix: Overcoming the Dream. 1994. pap. 12.95 (*1-884333-43-5*) Passage Communs.
Penland, Patrick R. & Fine, Sara. Group Dynamics & Individual Development. LC 74-77110. (Communication Science & Technology Ser.: No. 3). 167p. reprint ed. pap. 47.60 (*0-7837-0911-0*, 2041216) Bks Demand.
Penland, Patrick R. & Mathai, Aleyamma. Interpersonal Communication: Counseling, Guidance & Retrieval for Media, Library & Information Specialists. LC 74-77109. (Communication Science & Technology Ser.: No. 2). (Illus.). 187p. reprint ed. pap. 53.30 (*0-8357-6163-0*, 2034562) Bks Demand.
— The Library As a Learning Service Center. LC 78-13491. (Books in Library & Information Science: No. 24). 255p. reprint ed. pap. 72.70 (*0-8357-6191-6*, 2034561) Bks Demand.
Penland, Patrick R. & Williams, James G. Community Psychology & Coordination. LC 74-77111. (Communications Science & Technology Ser.: No. 4). 200p. reprint ed. pap. 57.00 (*0-7837-0727-4*, 2041051) Bks Demand.
Penland, Patrick R., ed. see McCardle, Ellen S.
Penland, Patrick R., ed. see Williams, James G.
Penley, Constance. Close Encounters: Film, Feminism, & Science Fiction. Speigel, Lynn et al, eds. (Camera Obscura Book Ser.). (Illus.). 313p. (C). 1990. reprint ed. pap. text ed. 15.95 (*0-8166-1912-3*) U of Minn Pr.
— The Future of an Illusion: Film, Feminism, & Psychoanalysis. (Media & Society Ser.). (Illus.). 207p. (Orig.). 1989. text ed. 35.95 (*0-8166-1771-6*); pap. text ed. 14.95 (*0-8166-1772-4*) U of Minn Pr.
— Popular Science & Sex in America. (Illus.). 280p. 1995. 64.95x (*0-86091-405-4*, B4279, Pub. by Verso UK); pap. 18.95 (*0-86091-617-0*, B4283, Pub. by Verso UK) Routledge Chapman & Hall.
Penley, Constance, ed. Feminism & Film Theory. 224p. 1988. pap. text ed. 13.95 (*0-415-90108-1*, Routledge NY) Routledge.
Penley, Constance & Ross, Andrew. Technoculture. (Cultural Politics Ser.: Vol. 3). (Illus.). 312p. (C). 1991. text ed. 39.95 (*0-8166-1930-1*); pap. 15.95 (*0-8166-1932-8*) U of Minn Pr.
Penley, Constance & Willis, Sharon, eds. Male Trouble. LC 92-25407. (Camera Obscura Book Ser.: Vol. 3). 336p. (C). 1993. pap. text ed. 16.95 (*0-8166-2172-1*) U of Minn Pr.
— Male Trouble. LC 92-25407. (Camera Obscura Book Ser.: Vol. 3). 336p. (C). 1993. text ed. 39.95 (*0-8166-2171-3*) U of Minn Pr.
Penley, Floe E. Scrap Cotton. 216p. (Orig.). 1991. 14.95 (*0-932298-84-2*) Tri-State Pr Corp.
***Penley, Janet P. & Stephens, Diane W.** The M.O.M.S. Handbook: Understanding Your Personality Type in Mothering. 48p. (Orig.). 1995. pap. text ed. 8.95 (*0-9646974-0-8*, Mothers of Many Styles) Penley & Assocs.
Penley, Larry & Penley, Yolanda. Human Resources Simulation Using Lotus 1-2-3. (C). 1989. student ed, disk write for info. (*0-538-07832-4*) S-W Pub.
Penley, Yolanda, jt. auth. see Penley, Larry.
Penman, A. D., tr. Deterioration of Dams & Reservoirs: Examples & Their Analysis. 368p. (C). 1984. text ed. 130.00 (*90-6191-546-5*, Pub. by A A Balkema NE) Ashgate Pub Co.
Penman, Bruce, ed. Five Italian Renaissance Comedies. (Classics Ser.). 448p. 1978. pap. 9.95 (*0-14-044338-X*, Penguin Classics) Viking Penguin.
Penman, Bruce, tr. see Machiavelli, Niccolo.
Penman, Bruce, tr. see Manzoni, Alessandro.
Penman, Bruce, tr. see Tusquets, Esther.
Penman, Emily J., jt. auth. see Penman, W. Robert.
Penman, James, jt. auth. see Tavner, Peter J.
Penman, Laurie. The Clock Repairer's Handbook. (Illus.). 176p. 1993. 29.95 (*0-7153-0054-7*, Pub. by D & C Pub UK) Sterling.
***Penman, Robbie M.** Call Me Russell. 136p. 1995. pap. 13.00 (*0-8059-3720-X*) Dorrance.
Penman, Sharon K. Falls the Shadow. 1989. pap. 12.50 (*0-345-36033-8*, Ballantine Trade) Ballantine.
— Here Be Dragons. 784p. 1987. mass mkt. 4.95 (*0-380-70181-2*) Avon.
— Here Be Dragons. 720p. 1993. pap. 12.50 (*0-345-38284-6*, Ballantine Trade) Ballantine.
— The Reckoning. 592p. 1991. 24.95 (*0-8050-1014-9*) H Holt & Co.
— The Reckoning: A Novel. 608p. 1992. pap. 12.50 (*0-345-37888-1*, Ballantine Trade) Ballantine.
— The Sunne in Splendour. 944p. 1990. pap. 12.50 (*0-345-36313-2*, Ballantine Trade) Ballantine.
— When Christ & His Saints Slept. LC 94-22593. 1995. 25.00 (*0-8050-1015-7*) H Holt & Co.
Penman, Susanna, jt. auth. see Emily, Peter.
Penman, Susanna, jt. auth. see Newton, Robert.
Penman, W. Robert & Penman, Emily J. Dr. William Goodell & Camp Paoli: The Goodell Collection at West Chester University Including Camp Paoli Documents (Camp Parole) (Illus.). 104p. 1987. pap. 19.95 (*0-9619411-1-1*) Serpentine Pr.
Penn. Mortal Term. 1985. 12.95 (*0-684-18317-X*, Scribners) S&S Trade.
— Seductions. Date not set. pap. 12.00 (*0-06-095029-3*) HarpC.
Penn, ed. Liquid Crystals & Spatial Light Modulator Materials. 127p. 1986. 36.00 (*0-89252-719-6*, 684) SPIE.
Penn & Teller. Cruel Tricks for Dear Friends. 1989. 23.00 (*0-394-75351-8*, Villard Bks) Random.
Penn, Alfred W., jt. auth. see Piekalkiewicz, Jaroslaw.
Penn, Audrey. The Kissing Hand. LC 93-36159. (Illus.). 30p. (J). (gr. k-6). 1993. 14.95 (*0-87868-585-5*) Child Welfare.
— No Bones about Driftiss. LC 89-13326. (Illus.). viii, 146p. (J). (gr. 2-6). 1989. lib. bdg. 14.95 (*0-939923-11-4*); pap. 7.95 (*0-939923-12-2*) M & W Pub Co.
Penn, Audrey & Ewing, C. S. Blue Out of Season. LC 84-13584. (Illus.). (J). (gr. 3-6). 1985. 10.95 (*0-915556-14-6*) Great Ocean.
Penn, Audrey S., et al, eds. Myasthenia Gravis & Related Disorders: Experimental & Clinical Aspects. LC 93-8239. (Annals Ser.: Vol. 681). 1993. write for info. (*0-89766-755-7*); pap. write for info. (*0-89766-756-5*) NY Acad Sci.
Penn-Brown, Adelle. Surviving Your Seasons of Change. Mackell, Phyllis, ed. (Orig.). 1991. pap. 1.95 (*0-9629630-0-3*) V I Christian Min.
Penn, C. Handling Laboratory Microorganisms. 168p. 1991. text ed. 69.00 (*0-471-93253-1*, Wiley-Liss); pap. text ed. 45.95 (*0-471-93252-3*, Wiley-Liss) Wiley.
Penn, C. W., jt. ed. see Birkbeck, T. H.
Penn, Charles. Handling Laboratory Microorganisms. 192p. 1991. 69.00 (*0-335-09204-7*); pap. 30.00 (*0-335-09203-9*) Wiley.
Penn, Christopher N. Noise Control. 1979. 110.00 (*0-7219-0830-6*, Scientific) St Mut.
Penn, Gareth. Times Seventeen: The Amazing Story of the Zodiac Murders in California & Massachusetts, 1966-1981. (Illus.). 380p. 1987. pap. 25.00 (*0-9618494-0-1*) Foxglove Pr.
Penn, Geoffrey. HMS Thunderer. 208p. 1987. 60.00 (*0-85937-321-5*, Pub. by K Mason Pubns Ltd UK) St Mut.
Penn, Graham. Banking Supervision - The Regulation of the U. K. Banking Sector under the Banking Act 1987. 1989. 110.00 (*0-406-13603-3*, U.K.) Butterworth Legal Pubs.
— Practice & Law of International Banking. 1985. 114.00 (*0-85297-137-0*, Pub. by Inst Bankers UK) St Mut.
Penn, Gregory E. Freedom, the Essence of Life. LC 78-75026. 1979. pap. 5.95 (*0-87516-288-6*) DeVorss.
Penn, I., jt. ed. see Schmahl, D.
Penn, I. Garland. Afro-American Press & Its Editors. LC 69-18574. (American Negro: His History & Literature, Ser. No. 2). 1969. reprint ed. 36.95 (*0-405-01887-8*) Ayer.
Penn, Ira A., et al. Records Management Handbook. 2nd ed. 1994. 64.95 (*0-566-07510-5*, Pub. by Gower UK) Ashgate Pub Co.
Penn, Irving. Flowers. (Illus.). 96p. 1987. 50.00 (*0-517-54074-6*, Harmony) Crown Pub Group.
— Passage. LC 91-52709. (Illus.). 300p. 1991. 99.50 (*0-679-40491-0*) Knopf.
Penn, James R. Encyclopedia of Geographical Features in World History. 1995. lib. bdg. 70.00 (*0-87436-760-3*) ABC-CLIO.
Penn, Jean, ed. see Goodwin, Betty.
Penn, John. Accident Prone. large type ed. (Mystery Ser.). 1990. 21.95 (*0-7089-2159-0*) Ulverscroft.
— Barren Revenge. large type ed. (Mystery Ser.). 299p. 1989. 17.95 (*0-7089-1965-0*) Ulverscroft.
— Death's Long Shadow. large type ed. (Mystery Ser.). 304p. 1993. 21.95 (*0-7089-2959-1*) Ulverscroft.
— Deceitful Death. large type ed. (Mystery Ser.). 320p. 1985. 22.95 (*0-7089-1287-7*) Ulverscroft.
— A Feast of Death. large type ed. (Linford Mystery Library). 384p. 1992. pap. 14.95 (*0-7089-7158-X*, Trailtree Bookshop) Ulverscroft.
— A Haven of Danger. large type ed. 1994. 22.95 (*0-7089-3207-X*) Ulverscroft.
— Mortal Term. large type ed. (Mystery Ser.). 352p. 1988. 17.95 (*0-7089-1822-0*) Ulverscroft.
— Outrageous Exposures. large type ed. (Mystery Ser.). 1991. 21.95 (*0-7089-2350-X*) Ulverscroft.
— Unto the Grave. large type ed. (Mystery Ser.). 320p. 1987. 16.95 (*0-7089-1704-6*) Ulverscroft.
— Widow's End. large type ed. 352p. 1995. 23.95 (*0-7089-3246-0*) Ulverscroft.
— A Will to Kill. large type ed. (Mystery Ser.). 272p. 1988. 17.95 (*0-7089-1764-X*) Ulverscroft.
Penn, Julia M. Linguistic Relativity Versus Innate Ideas. LC 77-170003. (Janua Linguarum, Ser. Minor: No. 120). 62p. (Orig.). 1972. pap. text ed. 30.80 (*90-279-2003-6*) Mouton.
Penn-Lewis, Jessie. Awakening in Wales. rev. ed. 128p. 1993. pap. 4.95 (*0-87508-937-2*) Chr Lit.
— Cara A Cara: Face to Face. (SPA.). 3.25 (*84-7645-115-6*, 223169, Pub. by Edit Clie SP) TSELF.
— Centrality of the Cross. 1993. pap. 4.95 (*0-87508-939-9*) Chr Lit.
— Los Cielos Fueron Abiertos: The Heavens Were Opened. (SPA.). 3.25 (*84-7228-907-9*, 222222, Pub. by Edit Clie SP) TSELF.
— Climax of the Risen Life. 1992. pap. 4.95 (*0-87508-941-0*) Chr Lit.
— Como Entender Ensen. y Misterios Cruz: How to Understand the Teachings. (SPA.). 3.25 (*84-7228-888-9*, 222312, Pub. by Edit Clie SP) TSELF.
— La Comunion Con Dios: Communion with God. (SPA.). 2.95 (*84-7228-950-8*, 223028, Pub. by Edit Clie SP) TSELF.
— Conquest of Canaan. 1992. pap. 4.95 (*0-87508-943-7*) Chr Lit.
— Cross: Touchstone of Faith. 1990. pap. 2.95 (*0-87508-994-1*) Chr Lit.
— Cross of Calvary & Its Message. 1979. pap. 4.95 (*0-947788-02-6*) Chr Lit.
— La Cruz Del Calvario y Su Mensaje: The Message of the Cross. (SPA.). 4.25 (*84-7228-731-9*, 220250, Pub. by Edit Clie SP) TSELF.
— La Cruz, Piedra De Toque De la Fe: The Cross Touchstone of Faith. (SPA.). 3.25 (*84-7228-850-1*, 220248, Pub. by Edit Clie SP) TSELF.
— Dying to Live. 1991. pap. 3.95 (*0-87508-945-3*) Chr Lit.
— Face to Face. 1972. pap. 3.95 (*0-87508-942-9*) Chr Lit.
— Fruitful Living. 1991. pap. 4.95 (*0-87508-240-8*) Chr Lit.
— Guerra Contra los Santos: War on the Saints. (SPA.). 6.50 (*84-7228-967-2*, 223031, Pub. by Edit Clie SP) TSELF.
— Life in the Spirit. 1979. pap. 3.95 (*0-87508-956-9*) Chr Lit.
— Life out of Death. 1979. pap. 3.95 (*0-87508-950-X*) Chr Lit.
— Morir para Vivir: Dying to Live. (SPA.). 2.95 (*84-7645-116-4*, 223167, Pub. by Edit Clie SP) TSELF.
— Oracion & Evangelismo: Prayer & Evangelism. (SPA.). 2.95 (*84-7228-828-5*, 222349, Pub. by Edit Clie SP) TSELF.
— Prayer & Evangelism. 1979. pap. 2.95 (*0-87508-952-6*) Chr Lit.
— Soul & Spirit. 1993. pap. 4.95 (*0-87508-953-4*) Chr Lit.
— Spiritual Warfare. 1991. pap. 4.95 (*0-87508-962-3*) Chr Lit.
— War on the Saints. 1993. pap. 6.95 (*0-87508-963-1*) Chr Lit.
— Warfare with Satan. 1993. pap. 4.95 (*0-87508-999-2*) Chr Lit.
Penn-Lewis, Jessie & Roberts, Evan. War on the Saints. 9th ed. 1988. reprint ed. pap. 10.00 (*0-913926-03-5*) T E Lowe.
— War on the Saints. 10th ed. 325p. 1994. 12.50 (*0-614-00008-4*) T E Lowe.
— War on the Saints. 325p. reprint ed. 12.50 (*0-615-00216-1*) T E Lowe.
Penn, Malka. The Hanukkah Ghosts. LC 94-15257. 88p. (J). 1995. pap. 14.95 (*0-8234-1145-1*) Holiday.
— The Miracle of the Potato Latkes. LC 93-29921. (Illus.). 32p. 1994. lib. bdg. 15.95 (*0-8234-1118-4*) Holiday.
— The Miracle of the Potato Latkes. (Illus.). 1995. pap. 6.95 (*0-8234-1204-0*) Holiday.
Penn, Margaret. The Foolish Virgin. 256p. 1981. pap. 18.95 (*0-521-28297-7*) Cambridge U Pr.
— Manchester Fourteen Miles. LC 80-40707. 247p. reprint ed. pap. 70.40 (*0-318-34833-0*, 2031706) Bks Demand.
— The Young Mrs. Burton. 256p. 1981. pap. 18.95 (*0-521-28298-5*) Cambridge U Pr.
Penn, Norgina W., jt. auth. see Starkey, Carolyn M.
Penn, P. The Remnant Seeds of Creation: A Strategy for Survival, or the Preservation of Non-Favoured Races in the Struggle for Life. 256p. 1991. text ed. 24.95 (*0-9629024-1-1*); pap. text ed. 14.95 (*0-9629024-0-3*) Aahaa Bks.
***Penn, Raymond G.** Medicine on Ancient Greek & Roman Coins. (Illus.). 192p. 1995. pap. 39.95 (*0-7134-7670-2*, Pub. by Seaby UK) Trafalgar.
Penn, Roger. Skilled Workers in Britain & America. 220p. 1990. text ed. 49.95 (*0-312-03726-0*) St Martin.
Penn, Roger, jt. auth. see Mandell, Barbara.
Penn, Roger, et al, eds. Skill & Occupational Change. (Social Change & Economic Life Initiative Ser.). (Illus.). 336p. 1994. 65.00 (*0-19-827914-0*) OUP.
Penn State College of Education Staff. Student Teaching Handbook. 160p. 1992. spiral bd. 19.95 (*0-8403-7308-2*) Kendall-Hunt.
Penn State University (Physics) Staff. General Physics 202-204: Laboratory Manual. 208p. (C). 1994. pap. text ed., spiral bd. 30.95 (*0-8403-8347-9*) Kendall-Hunt.
— Introductory Physics 215-265: Laboratory Manual. 192p. (C). 1994. spiral bd. 29.95 (*0-8403-8742-3*) Kendall-Hunt.
Penn, Thomas A. & Foltz, Ramon D. Understanding Patents & Other Protection for Intellectual Property. (Illus.). 100p. (Orig.). (C). 1990. pap. 15.00 (*0-944606-07-5*) Penn Inst.
Penn, Thomas A., jt. auth. see Foltz, Ramon D.
***Penn, W. S.** The Absence of Angels: A Novel. LC 94-34607. (American Indian Literature & Critical Studies: Vol. 14). 272p. 1995. pap. 13.95 (*0-8061-2714-7*) U of Okla Pr.
Penn, William. The Absence of Angels. LC 93-27526. 274p. 1994. 24.00 (*1-877946-42-7*) Permanent Pr.
— All My Sins Are Relatives. (North American Indian Prose Award: Vol. 3). (Illus.). 270p. (C). 1995. 25.00 (*0-8032-3709-X*) U of Nebr Pr.
— Collection of the Works of William Penn, 2 vols. LC 79-173942. reprint ed. 495.00 (*0-404-04982-6*) AMS Pr.
— Correspondence Between William Penn & James Logan & Others, 2 Vols, Set. Logan, Deborah & Armstrong, Edward, eds. LC 72-173943. reprint ed. 115.00 (*0-404-04985-0*) AMS Pr.
— An Essay Towards the Present & Future Peace in Europe: By the Establishment of a European Dyet, Parliament or Estates. (United Nations Library, Geneva, Sources on the History of International Organization: Series F, Vol. 1). 108p. 1983. reprint ed. 19.37 (*3-487-07345-5*, Pub. by Georg Olms GW) Lubrecht & Cramer.
— Fruits of Solitude. (C). 1988. 55.00 (*0-913408-39-5*, Pub. by W Sessions UK) St Mut.
— No Cross, No Crown. abr. rev. ed. Selleck, Ronald, ed. LC 81-69723. 155p. 1982. pap. 8.95 (*0-913408-71-9*) Friends United.
— No Cross, No Crown. (C). 1989. reprint ed. pap. 32.00 (*0-900657-57-X*, Pub. by W Sessions UK); reprint ed. 69.00 (*0-900657-58-8*, Pub. by W Sessions UK) St Mut.
— The Peace of Europe, The Fruits of Solitude: And Other Writings. 376p. 1993. pap. 6.95 (*0-460-87302-4*, Everyman's Classic Lib) C E Tuttle.
— Quaker Classics in Brief. 1978. pap. 8.00 (*0-87574-904-6*) Pendle Hill.
— The Rise & Progress of the People Called Quakers. (C). 1988. 65.00 (*0-913408-32-8*, Pub. by W Sessions UK) St Mut.
Penn, William, ed. Magnetic Resonance: Symposium, Utrech, April 1985. (Journal: Diagnostic Imaging in Clinical Medicine: Vol. 55, No. 1-2, 1986). (Illus.). 108p. (Orig.). 1986. pap. 70.50 (*3-8055-4259-3*) S Karger.
Penn, William & Brinton, Anna. No Cross No Crown. 1944. pap. text ed. 3.00 (*0-87574-030-8*) Pendle Hill.
Penn, William, ed. see Microsymposium Staff.
Penn, William, jt. pref. see Nickalls, John L.
***Penn, William A.** Rattling Spurs & Broad-Brimmed Hats: The Civil War in Cynthiana & Harrison County, Kentucky. 240p. 1995. lib. bdg. 26.00 (*0-9646989-1-9*) Battle Grove.
Penna, David, jt. ed. see Shepherd, George W., Jr.
***Penna, L. Rao, et al, eds.** Current Developments in International Transfers of Goods & Services. (Singapore Conferences on International Business Law Ser.: Vol. 7). liii, 621p. 1994. text ed. write for info. (*0-409-99667-X*) Butterworth Legal Pubs.
Penna, Richard P., jt. ed. see Knowlton, David H.
Penna, Romano. Paul the Apostle: Exegetical & Theological Studies. 700p. (Orig.). 1995. pap. text ed. 19.95 (*0-8146-5835-0*, M Glazier) Liturgical Pr.
Penna, Sandro. Cofused Dream. Scrivani, George, tr. 92p. (Orig.). 1988. 5.95 (*0-937815-15-2*) Hanuman Bks.
— This Strange Joy: Selected Poems of Sandro Penna. Di Piero, W. S., tr. LC 81-22288. 154p. 1982. 18.95 (*0-8142-0328-0*) Ohio St U Pr.
***Pennacchia, Yvette M.** Healing the Whole. 1995. 55.00 (*0-304-33106-6*); pap. 14.95 (*0-304-33111-2*) InBook.
Pennaih, S. K. Women Own: Men Rent! And Other Facts of Life. Green, L. E., ed. (Illus.). 256p. (Orig.). 1992. pap. 9.95 (*0-9633964-0-4*) SRS Ltd.
Pennak, Robert W. Collegiate Dictionary of Zoology. LC 85-23983. 594p. (C). 1987. reprint ed. pap. text ed. 33.50 (*0-89874-921-2*) Krieger.
— Fresh-Water Invertebrates of the United States: Protozoa to Mollusca. 3rd ed. LC 88-18570. 628p. 1989. text ed. 79.95 (*0-471-63118-3*) Wiley.
Pennance, F. G., jt. auth. see Seldon, Arthur.
Pennanen, Judi. Heads or Tails. (J). (ps-8). 1989. pap. 7.95 (*0-921254-11-3*, Pub. by Penumbra Pr CN) U of Toronto Pr.
Pennant, Edmund. Askance & Strangely: New & Selected Poems. LC 93-18473. 176p. 1993. 24.95 (*0-914061-35-6*) Orchises Pr.
— Dream's Navel. 80p. (Orig.). 1982. pap. 4.95 (*0-931642-08-6*) Lintel.
— Misapprehensions & Other Poems. 80p. (Orig.). 1984. pap. 5.95 (*0-931642-15-9*) Lintel.
— The Wildebeest of Carmine Street. LC 90-31457. 72p. (Orig.). 1990. pap. 10.00 (*0-914061-17-8*) Orchises Pr.
Pennant-Rea, Rupert & Emmott, William. The Pocket Economist. LC 83-15054. (Illus.). 194p. 1984. 27.95 (*0-521-26070-1*) Cambridge U Pr.
Pennant, Thomas. Arctic Zoology, 2 vols. in one. LC 73-17835. (Natural Sciences in America Ser.). (Illus.). 1012p. 1974. reprint ed. 76.95 (*0-405-05758-X*) Ayer.
— A Tour of Scotland (Seventeen Ninety-Six) 496p. (C). 1986. 42.00 (*0-685-30236-9*, Pub. by Mercat Pr Bks UK) St Mut.
Pennar, Davis W.
Pennar, Jaan, jt. ed. see Bereday, George Z.
Pennar, Margaret, ed. The Middle East: Five Perspectives. (Information Papers: No. 7). 33p. (Orig.). (C). 1973. pap. 1.00 (*0-937694-23-1*) Assn Arab-Amer U Grads.
Pennaz, Steve, ed. North American Hunting Adventures. (Illus.). 208p. 1988. text ed. 19.95 (*0-317-89521-4*) N Amer Outdoor Grp.
Pennbrook, Lloyd. A Method to Our Madness. 176p. (Orig.). 1992. pap. 5.95 (*0-9632330-3-3*) Pennywise.
Penne, Leo, ed. The New Civics, Vol. 2. (Livability Digest Ser.: No. 2). 78p. 1982. pap. 6.00 (*0-317-44281-3*) Partners Livable.
Penne, R. Leo, et al. The Economics of Amenity: Community Futures & Quality of Life. LC 85-6545. (Illus.). 160p. (Orig.). 1985. pap. 15.00 (*0-941182-15-0*) Partners Livable.
— State Government Associations: A Reconnaissance. LC 86-146573. (National League of Cities State-Local Backgrounder Ser.). (Illus.). 1986. write for info. (*0-933729-07-3*) Natl League Cities.
***Pennebaker.** You're the Reason I'm Traveling On. (J). 1995. write for info. (*0-8050-4407-8*) H Holt & Co.

P Q

An Asterisk (*) at the beginning of an entry indicates that the title is appearing in BIP for the first time.

Pennebaker, James W. Opening Up: The Healing Power of Confiding in Others. 240p. 1991. pap. 8.95 (*0-380-70849-3*) Avon.
— The Psychology of Physical Symptoms. (Illus.). 192p. 1982. 47.00 (*0-387-90730-0*) Spr-Verlag.
***Pennebaker, James W., ed.** Emotion, Disclosure, & Health. 350p. 1995. text ed. 40.00 (*1-55798-308-9*) Am Psychol.
Pennebaker, James W., jt. ed. see Traue, Harald C.
Pennebaker, James W., jt. ed. see Wegner, Daniel M.
Pennebaker, W. JPEG Data Compression Standard. 1993. text ed. 59.95 (*0-442-01272-1*) Van Nos Reinhold.
Pennee, Donna. Moral Metafiction: The Novels of Timothy Findley. 140p. (C). 1991. pap. text ed. 20.00 (*1-55022-138-8*, Pub. by ECW Press CN) Genl Dist Srvs.
— Praying for Rain: Timothy Findley's Not Wanted on the Voyage. (Canadian Fiction Studies: No. 21). 120p. (C). 1993. pap. text ed. 14.95 (*1-55022-121-3*, Pub. by ECW Press CN) Genl Dist Srvs.
Pennekamp, Marianne, jt. auth. see Freeman, Edith M.
Pennell, Allison A., et al, eds. Business & the Environment: A Resource Guide. LC 91-38369. 364p. 1992. text ed. 55.00 (*1-55963-159-7*) Island Pr.
Pennell, Anne & Alexander, David. The Management of Change in the Primary School: Implementing the National Curriculum in Science, Design & Technology. (School Development & the Management of Change Ser.). 192p. 1990. 75.00 (*1-85000-540-0*); pap. 33.00 (*1-85000-541-9*) Taylor & Francis.
Pennell, C. R., ed. Piracy & Diplomacy in Seventeenth-Century North Africa: The Journal of Thomas Baker, English Consul in Tripoli, 1677-1685. LC 86-45999. (Illus.). 264p. 1989. 39.50 (*0-8386-3302-1*) Fairleigh Dickinson.
Pennell, D. J., et al. Thallium Myocardial Perfusion Tomography in Clinical Cardiology. (Illus.). 240p. 1994. 98.00 (*0-387-19675-7*) Spr-Verlag.
Pennell, E. R. Mary Wollstonecraft Godwin. 1972. lib. bdg. 69.95 (*0-8490-0590-6*) Gordon Pr.
Pennell, Elizabeth R. Charles Godfrey Leland: A Biography, 2 vols, Set. LC 76-140370. (Select Bibliographies Reprint Ser.). 1977. reprint ed. 60.95 (*0-8369-5613-3*) Ayer.
Pennell, Elizabeth R. & Pennell, Joseph. Life of James McNeill Whistler, 2 Vols, Set. LC 70-148285. (Illus.). reprint ed. 135.00 (*0-404-04988-5*) AMS Pr.
Pennell, Francis W. The Scrophulariaceae of Eastern Temperate North America. (Monograph: No. 1). (Illus.). 650p. (Orig.). 1935. pap. 7.00 (*0-910006-08-3*) Acad Nat Sci Phila.
— The Scrophulariaceae of the Western Himalayas. (Monograph: No. 5). (Illus.). 163p. (Orig.). 1943. pap. 5.00 (*0-910006-14-8*) Acad Nat Sci Phila.
Pennell, Jeffrey L. Cases & Materials on the Income Taxation of Trusts, Estates, Grantors & Beneficiaries. LC 87-10563. (American Casebook Ser.). 460p. 1987. text ed. 34.50 (*0-314-42565-9*) West Pub.
Pennell, Joe E. From Anticipation to Transfiguration. 1989. pap. 8.65 (*1-55673-126-4*, 9851) CSS OH.
Pennell, Joseph. Haunts of Old London. LC 71-164620. (Select Bibliographies Reprint Ser.). 1977. reprint ed. 17.95 (*0-8369-5903-5*) Ayer.
— The Illustration of Books. 1973. 59.95 (*0-8490-0384-9*) Gordon Pr.
— The Jew at Home: Impressions of Jewish Life in Russia & Austria. 1976. lib. bdg. 134.95 (*0-8490-2098-0*) Gordon Pr.
— Pen Drawings & Pen-Draughtsmen. LC 76-30462. (Quality Paperbacks Ser.). 1977. reprint ed. pap. 10.95 (*0-306-80064-0*) Da Capo.
Pennell, Joseph & Bryant, Edward. Pennell's New York City Etchings: Ninety-One Prints. (Illus.). 112p. (Orig.). 1981. pap. 7.95 (*0-486-23913-6*) Dover.
Pennell, Joseph, jt. auth. see Pennell, Elizabeth R.
Pennell, Joseph S. The History of Rome Hanks & Kindred Matters. LC 81-85726. 363p. (C). 1981. reprint ed. 22.00 (*0-933256-32-9*) Second Chance.
— The History of Rome Hanks & Kindred Matters. LC 81-85726. 363p. (C). 1981. reprint ed. pap. 16.00 (*0-933256-33-7*) Second Chance.
***Pennell, Paul.** Children's Car. (C). 1989. pap. 25.00x (*0-85263-833-7*, Pub. by Shire UK) St Mut.
Pennell, R. Obsolete Banknotes of North Carolina. LC 83-71430. 1985. reprint ed. pap. 8.00 (*0-942666-29-1*) S J Durst.
Pennell, Rosemary V., jt. auth. see Vari, Frank D.
Pennell, W. E., ed. Pressure Vessel Integrity - 1993. (PVP Ser.: Vol. 250). 304p. 1993. 60.00 (*0-7918-0977-3*, H00809) ASME.
Pennell, W. T., jt. auth. see Hiester, T. R.
Pennella, C. R. Managing the Metrology System: An Important Element of Total Quality Management. LC 92-9659. 95p. 1992. pap. 21.95 (*0-87389-181-3*) ASQC Qual Pr.
Pennells, Ernest. Concrete Bridge Designer's Manual. (Viewpoint Publication Ser.). (Illus.). 1978. text ed. 80.00 (*0-7210-1083-0*, Pub. by C & CA UK) Scholium Intl.
***Pennells, Geoff & Bradburne, Jeremy.** Butterworths International Taxation of Financial Instruments & Transactions: Your Definitive International Guide to the Tax Treatment of Financial Instruments, 3 Vols. 2nd ed. 1994. write for info. (*0-406-00855-8*) Butterworth Legal Pubs.
Pennells, Geoffrey. Butterworths International Taxation of Financial Instruments & Transactions. 2nd ed. 610p. 1994. boxed write for info. (*0-406-10660-6*, U.K.) Butterworth Legal Pubs.
***Pennells, Margaret & Smith, Susan C.** The Forgotten Mourners: Guidelines for Working with Bereaved Children. 64p. 1994. pap. 12.95x (*1-85302-264-0*, Pub. by J Kingsley Pubs UK) Taylor & Francis.
Pennells, Margaret, jt. auth. see Smith, Susan C.

***Penner.** Tea Party Book & Miniature China Tea Set. 1995. 14.99 (*0-679-87005-9*) Random.
Penner, Clifford & Penner, Joyce. The Gift of Sex. 352p. 1981. write for info. (*0-8499-2893-1*) Word Inc.
— Sex Facts for the Family. 1992. pap. write for info. (*0-8499-3287-4*) Word Inc.
Penner, Clifford, jt. auth. see Penner, Joyce.
Penner, Clifford L. & Penner, Joyce. Restoring the Pleasure. 1993. pap. 12.99 (*0-8499-3464-8*) Word Inc.
***Penner, Clifford L. & Penner, Joyce J.** Getting Your Sex Life Off to a Great Start: A Guide for Engaged & Newlywed Couples. LC 94-28374. 1994. pap. 10.99 (*0-8499-3515-6*) Word Inc.
Penner, Dick. Countries of the Mind: The Fiction of J. M. Coetzee. LC 88-34731. (Contributions to the Study of World Literature Ser.: No. 32). 167p. 1989. text ed. 45.00 (*0-313-26684-0*, PCD/, Greenwood Pr) Greenwood.
Penner, Donald. The Project Manager's Survival Guide: The Handbook for Real-World Project Management. LC 93-4016. 100p. 1994. pap. text ed. 14.95 (*0-935470-72-7*) Battelle.
Penner, Erwin. The Power of God in a Broken World. (Studies in Ephesians). 196p. (C). 1990. pap. 7.95 (*0-921788-11-8*) Kindred Prods.
Penner, Fred. Fred Penner's Sing along - Play Along. (Illus.). 112p. (Orig.). (J). (ps-4). 1991. 14.95 (*0-89524-625-2*) Cherry Lane.
Penner, Hans H. Impasse & Resolution: A Critique of the Study of Religion. (Toronto Studies in Religion: Vol. 8). 249p. (C). 1989. text ed. 38.95 (*0-8204-0976-6*) P Lang Pubs.
Penner, James. Goliath: The Life of Robert Schuller. 1993. mass mkt. 6.99 (*0-06-104262-5*, Harp PBks) HarpC.
— Goliath: The Life of Robert Schuller. Baltzell, Richard & Adams, Linda, eds. (Illus.). 448p. 1992. 24.95 (*1-879989-06-9*) New Hope Pub.
Penner, Jonathan. The Intelligent Traveler's Guide to Chiribosco. LC 83-81252. (Orig.). 1984. 6.00 (*0-913123-03-X*); pap. 4.00 (*0-913123-01-3*) Galileo.
— Private Parties. LC 83-47825. (Drue Heinz Literature Prize Ser.). 197p. 1983. 22.50 (*0-8229-3488-4*) U of Pittsburgh Pr.
Penner, Joyce & Penner, Clifford. RCC, Vol. 26: Counseling for Sexual Disorders. 1990. write for info. (*0-8499-0482-X*) Word Inc.
Penner, Joyce, jt. auth. see Penner, Clifford L.
Penner, Louis A. Social Psychology: Concepts & Applications. (Illus.). 699p. (C). 1986. text ed. 52.25 (*0-314-93405-7*) West Pub.
Penner, Louis A., et al, eds. The Challenge in Mathematics & Science Education: Psychology's Response. 395p. 1993. text ed. 40.00 (*1-55798-207-4*) Am Psychol.
Penner, Lucille R. Celebration: The Story of American Holidays. LC 92-25871. (Illus.). 80p. (J). (gr. 1 up). 1993. text ed. 15.95 (*0-02-770903-5*, Mac Bks Young Read) S&S Childrens.
— Colonial Cookbook. (Illus.). 128p. (J). (gr. 4 up). 1976. 14.95 (*0-8038-1202-7*) Hastings.
— Cowboys. LC 94-35463. (All Aboard Bks.). (Illus.). (J). 1995. 2.50 (*0-448-40947-X*, G&D) Putnam Pub Group.
— Dinosaur Babies: A Step One Book. LC 90-36045. (Step into Reading Bks.). (Illus.). 32p. (Orig.). (J). (ps-1). 1991. pap. 3.50 (*0-679-81207-5*) Random Bks Yng Read.
— Dinosaur Babies: A Step One Book. LC 90-36045. (Step into Reading Bks.). (Illus.). 32p. (Orig.). (J). (ps-1). 1991. lib. bdg. 7.99 (*0-679-91207-X*) Random Bks Yng Read.
— Eating the Plates: A Pilgrim Book of Food & Manners. LC 90-5918. (Illus.). 128p. (J). (gr. 1-5). 1991. text ed. 14.95 (*0-02-770901-9*, Mac Bks Young Read) S&S Childrens.
— Knights & Castles. LC 93-45710. (That's a Fact Pictureback Ser.). (J). (gr. 4 up). 1994. lib. bdg. 2.50 (*0-679-85095-3*) Random.
— Landing at Plymouth. 1992. pap. 12.00 (*0-679-83201-7*); pap. 12.99 (*0-679-93201-1*) McKay.
— A Native American Feast. LC 94-10336. (Illus.). (J). 1994. text ed. 14.95 (*0-02-770902-7*) Macmillan.
— S-s-s-snakes! LC 93-46799. (Step into Reading Bks.: Step 2). (Illus.). 48p. (J). (gr. k-2). 1994. lib. bdg. 7.99 (*0-679-94777-9*); pap. 3.50 (*0-679-84777-4*) Random Bks Yng Read.
— Sitting Bull. LC 94-46766. (All aboard Reading Ser.). (Illus.). (J). (gr. 1-3). 1995. lib. bdg. write for info. (*0-448-40938-0*, G&D); pap. 3.95 (*0-448-40937-2*, G&D) Putnam Pub Group.
— The Statue of Liberty. LC 95-1854. (Step into Reading Ser.: Step 1 Bks.). (Illus.). (J). 1995. 3.99 (*0-679-86928-X*) Random.
— The Tea Party Book. LC 91-52093. (Illus.). 48p. (J). (ps-4). 1993. 10.00 (*0-679-82440-5*) Random Bks Yng Read.
— The Tea Party Book. LC 91-52093. (Illus.). 48p. (J). (ps-4). 1993. lib. bdg. 10.99 (*0-679-92440-X*) Random Bks Yng Read.
— The Thanksgiving Book. Donnelly, Judy, ed. LC 84-518. (Illus.). (J). (gr. 4 up). 1985. 14.95 (*0-8038-7228-3*) Hastings.
— That's a Fact Picture. Date not set. write for info. (*0-679-96212-3*); 2.50 (*0-679-86212-9*) Random.
— The True Story of Pocahontas: A Step 2 Book. LC 93-45709. (Step into Reading Bks.). (Illus.). 48p. (Orig.). (J). (gr. k-2). 1994. lib. bdg. 7.99 (*0-679-96166-6*); pap. 3.99 (*0-679-86166-1*) Random Bks Yng Read.
***Penner, Lucy.** Little Women Cookbook. Date not set. 12.00 (*0-679-87405-4*) Random.
Penner, Marci, jt. auth. see Penner, Mil.

Penner, Mil. Kansas Weekend Guide. (Orig.). 1990. pap. write for info. (*0-9615597-3-X*); spiral bd. 12.95 (*0-9615597-2-1*) Sounds Kansas.
Penner, Mil & Penner, Marci. Kansas Event Guide. (Kansas Guide Ser.). (Illus.). 128p. 1991. pap. 12.95 (*0-9615597-4-8*) Sounds Kansas.
Penner, Mil & Schmidt, Carol. Kansas Journeys. (Illus.). 128p. 1985. 27.95 (*0-9615597-0-5*) Sounds Kansas.
— Prairie: The Land & Its People. Nielsen, Mary, ed. LC 89-91644. (Illus.). 224p. 1990. 39.95 (*0-9615597-1-3*) Sounds Kansas.
Penner, N. Canadian Left: A Critical Analysis. 1977. pap. 13.67 (*0-13-113126-5*) P-H.
Penner, Peter. No Longer at Arm's Length. 178p. 1987. pap. 12.95 (*0-919797-55-5*) Kindred Prods.
— The Patronage Bureaucracy in North India: The Robert M. Bird & James Thomason School, 1820-1870. 380p. 1986. 35.00 (*81-7001-017-9*, Pub. by Chanakya II) S Asia.
— Robert Needham Cust, 1821-1909: A Personal Biography. LC 86-23821. (Studies in British History: Vol. 5). (Illus.). 360p. 1987. lib. bdg. 99.95 (*0-88946-456-1*) E Mellen.
Penner, Peter & MaClean, Richard. The Rebel Bureaucrat: Frederick John Shore 1799-1837 as Critic of William Bentinck's India. 1982. 24.00 (*0-8364-0920-5*, Pub. by Chanakya II) S Asia.
Penner, R. C. & Harer, J. L. Combinatorics of Train Tracks. (Annals of Mathematics Studies: No. 125). 216p. 1992. text ed. 49.50 (*0-691-08764-4*); pap. text ed. 22.50 (*0-691-02531-2*) Princeton U Pr.
Penner, Rob, jt. auth. see Smith, Ron.
Penner, Robert, jt. ed. see Yau, S. T.
Penner, Rudolph G., ed. The Congressional Budget Process After Five Years. LC 81-8000. (AEI Symposia Ser.: No. 81H). 216p. reprint ed. pap. 61.60 (*0-8357-4453-1*, 2037291) Bks Demand.
— The Great Fiscal Experiment. LC 90-43204. (Illus.). 250p. (Orig.). 1990. lib. bdg. 41.00 (*0-87766-484-6*); pap. text ed. 15.00 (*0-87766-485-4*) Urban Inst.
Penner, Rudolph G. & Abramson, Alan J. Broken Purse Strings: Congressional Budgeting, 1974-88. LC 88-27801. (Illus.). 129p. (Orig.). (C). 1988. lib. bdg. 45.00 (*0-87766-453-6*); pap. text ed. 15.50 (*0-87766-424-2*) Urban Inst.
Penner, S. & Ducarme, J. Chemistry of Propellants: Meeting Organised Agard Combustion & Propulsion Panel Parts, June, 1959. LC 59-13720. (Combustion & Propulsion Researches & Reviews 1959 Ser.). 1960. 276.00 (*0-08-009232-2*, Pub. by Pergamon Repr UK) Franklin.
Penner, S. S. Chemical Rocket Propulsion & Combustion Research. (Illus.). 170p. 1962. text ed. 136.00 (*0-677-00710-8*) Gordon & Breach.
— New Sources of Oil & Gas: Gases from Coal, Liquid Fuels from Coal, Shale, Tar Sands, & Heavy Oil Sources. (Illus.). 120p. 1982. 45.00 (*0-08-029335-2*, Pub. by Pergamon Repr UK) Franklin.
Penner, S. S., ed. Coal Gasification: Direct Applications & Synthesis of Chemicals & Fuels, Vol. 12. (International Journal of Energy: Vol. 12). 296p. 1987. 75.00 (*0-317-66175-2*, Pergamon Pr) Elsevier.
Penner, Samuel. The Four Dimensions of Paradise. LC 92-74667. 200p. 1992. 27.95 (*0-9627145-0-X*, Cyrus Pr) Waterside Prodns.
Pennetti, Michael. Coping with School Age Fatherhood. rev. ed. LC 86-20288. (Coping Ser.). 148p. (gr. 7-12). 1988. lib. bdg. 15.95 (*0-8239-0824-0*) Rosen Group.
***Penney.** Physiology: MEPC. 9th ed. (Illus.). 276p. (C). 1995. pap. text ed. 16.95 (*0-8385-6222-1*) Appleton & Lange.
Penney, Alexandra. How to Make Love to a Man. 1982. mass mkt. 4.99 (*0-440-13529-X*) Dell.
— How to Make Love to a Man. write for info. (*0-318-59623-7*) S&S Trade.
— How to Make Love to a Man...Safely. 1993. 18.00 (*0-517-59423-4*, Carol Southern Bks) Crown Pub Group.
— Sexiest Sex of All. 1994. mass mkt. 8.95 (*0-440-50641-7*) Dell.
Penney, Alexandria. How to Make Love to a Man. 1988. 7.99 (*0-517-60109-5*) Random Hse Value.
***Penney, Allen.** Houses of Nova Scotia. (Illus.). 160p. 1995. pap. 12.95 (*0-88780-072-6*) Formac Dist Ltd.
Penney, C., jt. auth. see Dugas, H.
***Penney, Charles R.** New Guinea Art & Crafts: The Charles Rand Penney Collection. (Illus.). 80p. 1988. 25.00 (*0-9620346-0-6*) C R Penney.
Penney, Clara L. An Album of Selected Bookbindings. (Illus.). 132p. 1967. 11.00 (*0-317-00602-9*, Hispanic Soc) Interbk Inc.
— Printed Books 1468-1700 in the Hispanic Society of America. (Illus.). 614p. 1965. 15.00 (*0-87535-106-9*) Hispanic Soc.
Penney, D. Andrew. Freewill or Predestination? The Battle over Saving Grace in Mid-Tudor England. (Royal Historical Society: Studies in History). 256p. 1991. 70.00 (*0-86193-219-6*) Boydell & Brewer.
Penney, David E., jt. auth. see Edwards, C. H., Jr.
Penney, David E., jt. auth. see Edwards, Henry.
***Penney, David W.** Art of the American Indian Frontier: A Portfolio. LC 94-42820. 24p. 1995. 18.95 (*1-56584-251-0*) New Press NY.
Penney, David W., ed. Great Lakes Indian Art. LC 87-36857. (Illus.). 107p. 1989. 39.95 (*0-8143-1970-X*); pap. 24.95 (*0-8143-1971-8*) Wayne St U Pr.
Penney, David W. & Longfish, George C. Native American Art. (Illus.). 320p. 1994. 85.00 (*0-88363-694-8*) H L Levin.
Penney, Edmund F. The Facts on File Dictionary of Film & Broadcast Terms. 304p. 1991. 29.95 (*0-8160-1923-1*) Facts on File.

— Facts on File Dictionary of Film & Broadcast Terms. 272p. 1992. pap. 14.95 (*0-8160-2782-X*) Facts on File.
Penney, Frances. I Was There. Griffen, Zofia, tr. LC 87-43136. 152p. 1988. 11.95 (*0-88400-127-X*); pap. 8.95 (*0-88400-128-8*) Shengold.
***Penney, Ian.** Ian Penney's Book of Nursery Rhymes. (J). (ps-2). 1994. 14.95 (*0-8109-3733-6*) Abrams.
Penney, J. C. Fifty Years with the Golden Rule. 1993. reprint ed. lib. bdg. 21.95 (*1-56849-162-X*) Buccaneer Bks.
Penney, Norman, et al. Land Financing, Cases & Materials on. 3rd ed. LC 84-24645. (University Casebook Ser.). 1052p. 1984. text ed. 39.95 (*0-88277-199-X*) Foundation Pr.
Penneys. Skin Manifestations of AIDS. (Illus.). 236p. 1989. text ed. 59.95 (*0-397-58315-X*) Lippincott.
Pennick. Rune Magic. 1993. pap. 17.00 (*1-85538-105-2*) Thorsons SF.
Pennick, Nigel. The Ancient Science of Geomancy: Living in Harmony with the Earth. LC 78-65180. (Illus.). 180p. (Orig.). 1987. reprint ed. pap. 15.95 (*0-916360-38-5*) CRCS Pubns CA.
— Magical Alphabets. LC 92-7859. (Illus.). 256p. (Orig.). 1992. pap. 12.95 (*0-87728-747-3*) Weiser.
— Mazes & Labyrinths. (Illus.). 208p. Date not set. 35.00 (*0-7090-4194-2*, Pub. by R Hale Ltd UK) Antique Collect.
— Oracle of Geomancy. 1995. pap. 16.95 (*1-898307-16-4*) Holmes Pub.
— The Pagan Book of Days: Celebrating Festivals & Sacred Days Through the Millenium. (Illus.). 176p. 1992. pap. 9.95 (*0-89281-369-5*) Inner Tradit.
— Secret Games of the Gods: Ancient Ritual Systems in Board Games. LC 88-27786. (Illus.). 256p. 1992. pap. 12.95 (*0-87728-752-X*) Weiser.
Pennick, Nigel & Jackson, Nigel. The Celtic Oracle: The Ancient Art of the Druids. (Illus.). 1992. pap. 26.00 (*1-85538-132-X*, Pub. by Aquarian Pr UK) Thorsons SF.
Pennick, Nigel, jt. auth. see Jones, Prudence.
Pennie. Love Songs for Our Children. (Illus.). 40p. (Orig.). (J). (ps up). 1989. audio 13.95 (*0-9624135-1-8*) Songs & Co.
Pennie, Michael. African Assortment, African Art in Museums in England & Scotland. (Illus.). 303p. (Orig.). 1991. pap. 39.95 (*0-9513023-2-9*, Pub. by Bath Coll High Educ UK) Ethnographic Arts Pubns.
Pennigstore, Werner, jt. auth. see Davidson, Ken.
Penniman, Clara. State Income Taxation. LC 79-20081. 1980. 45.00x (*0-8018-2290-4*) Johns Hopkins.
Penniman, Howard, ed. Canada at the Polls, 1984: A Study of the Federal General Elections. LC 87-27252. (At the Polls Ser.). xiii, 218p. (C). 1988. lib. bdg. 62.95 (*0-8223-0805-3*); pap. text ed. 21.95 (*0-8223-0821-5*) Duke.
— France at the Polls, 1981 & 1986. LC 87-35743. (At the Polls Ser.). xvi, 368p. (C). 1988. lib. bdg. 62.95 (*0-8223-0833-9*); pap. text ed. 21.95 (*0-8223-0845-2*) Duke.
— Italy at the Polls, 1983: A Study of the National Elections. LC 87-6716. (At the Polls Ser.). (Illus.). xii, 216p. (C). 1987. lib. bdg. 62.95 (*0-8223-0755-3*); pap. text ed. 21.95 (*0-8223-0787-1*) Duke.
Penniman, Howard & Farrell, Brian, eds. Ireland at the Polls, 1981, 1982, & 1987: A Study of Four General Elections. LC 87-13513. xv, 275p. 1987. 62.95 (*0-8223-0754-5*); pap. 21.95 (*0-8223-0786-3*) Duke.
Penniman, Howard R., ed. Australia at the Polls: The National Elections of 1980 & 1983. LC 82-73669. 361p. reprint ed. pap. 102.90 (*0-8357-4435-3*, 2037269) Bks Demand.
— Britain at the Polls, 1979: A Study of the General Election. LC 80-27536. (AEI Studies: No. 296). (Illus.). 368p. reprint ed. pap. 104.90 (*0-8357-4439-6*, 2037273) Bks Demand.
— Canada at the Polls, Nineteen Seventy-Nine & Nineteen Eighty: A Study of the General Elections. LC 81-19144. (Illus.). 448p. reprint ed. pap. 127.70 (*0-8357-4443-4*, 2037278) Bks Demand.
— The French National Assembly Elections of 1978. LC 79-28590. (AEI Studies: No. 269). 272p. reprint ed. pap. 77.60 (*0-8357-4483-3*, 2037335) Bks Demand.
— Greece at the Polls: The National Elections of 1974 & 1977. LC 81-8026. (AEI Studies: No. 317). (Illus.). 236p. reprint ed. pap. 67.30 (*0-8357-4485-X*, 2037337) Bks Demand.
— Italy at the Polls: The Parliamentary Elections of 1976. LC 77-90425. (American Enterprise Institutes Studies in Political & Social Processes: No. 169). 402p. reprint ed. pap. 114.60 (*0-8357-4497-3*, 2037350) Bks Demand.
— Italy at the Polls, Nineteen Seventy-Nine: A Study of the Parliamentary Elections. LC 81-8106. (AEI Studies: No. 321). (Illus.). 356p. reprint ed. pap. 101.50 (*0-8357-4498-1*, 2037351) Bks Demand.
— New Zealand at the Polls: The General Election of 1978. LC 80-16464. (AEI Studies: No. 273). (Illus.). 312p. reprint ed. pap. 89.00 (*0-8357-4514-7*, 2037372) Bks Demand.
Penniman, Howard R. & Mujal-Leon, Eusebio M., eds. Spain at the Polls, Nineteen Seventy-Seven, Nineteen Seventy-Nine & Nineteen Eighty-Two: A Study of the National Elections. LC 85-20523. (Illus.). 392p. reprint ed. pap. 111.80 (*0-8357-4536-8*, 2037417) Bks Demand.
— Spain at the Polls, 1977, 1979, & 1982: A Study of the National Elections. LC 85-20523. (At the Polls Ser.). xviii, 372p. 1985. 52.95 (*0-8223-0663-8*); pap. text ed. 21.95 (*0-8223-0695-6*) Duke.
Penniman, Howard R., jt. auth. see Ranney, Austin.
Penniman, Josiah H. War of the Theatres. LC 73-126649. reprint ed. 16.50 (*0-404-04992-3*) AMS Pr.
Penniman, T. K., ed. see Spencer, Baldwin.

An Asterisk (*) at the beginning of an entry indicates that the title is appearing in BIP for the first time.

Penning, F. M. Electrical Discharges in Gases. 128p. 1957. text ed. 76.00 (0-677-61230-3) Gordon & Breach.

Penning, L. & Thijn, C. J. Liber Amicorum Presented to Prof. Dr. J. R. Blickman. (Journal: Diagnostic Imaging in Clinical Medicine: Vol. 53, No. 4). (Illus.). 56p. 1984. 35.25 (3-8055-3934-7) S Karger.

Penning, Martin J. & Humphries, John. Uniplex II Plus Word Processing Guide. 2nd ed. LC 92-21946. 1992. pap. text ed. 36.00 (0-13-953902-6) P-H.

Penning, Martin J., jt. auth. see Humphries, John.

Penning-Roswell, Edmund. Wines of Bordeaux. 704p. (Orig.). 1983. pap. 12.95 (0-932664-51-2) Wine Appreciation.

Penning-Roswell, Edmund C. & Lowenthal, D., eds. Landscape Meanings & Values. (Illus.). 160p. 1986. text ed. 39.95 (0-04-710003-6) Routledge Chapman & Hall.

Penning-Rowsell, Edmund, ed. The Economics of Coastal Zone Management: A Manual of Assessment Techniques "The Yellow Manual" 368p. 1992. text ed. 104.95 (1-85293-161-2, Pub. by Pinter Pubs Ltd UK) CRC Pr.

Penning-Rowsell, Edmund, jt. auth. see Handmer, John.

***Penning-Rowsell, Edmund C., et al.** Economics of Coastal Management: A Manual of Benefit Assessment Techniques. 1994. text ed. 99.00 (0-471-94744-X) Wiley.

— Floods & Drainage: British Policies for Hazard Reduction, Agricultural Improvement & Wetland Conservation. (Risks & Hazards Ser.: No. 2). (Illus.). 192p. (C). 1985. text ed. 80.00 (0-04-627001-9) Routledge Chapman & Hall.

Penning, William H. Gold & Diamonds: South African Facts & Inferences. LC 72-4212. 100p. 1977. reprint ed. 18.95 (0-8369-9101-X) Ayer.

Penninger, Frieda E. Chaucer's Troilus & Criseyda & the Knight's Tale: Fictions Used. LC 93-25225. 126p. (C). 1993. lib. bdg. 39.50 (0-8191-9218-X) U Pr of Amer.

Penninger, J. M., et al, eds. Supercritical Fluid Technology: Process Technology Proceedings, No. 3. 468p. 1986. 159.00 (0-444-42552-7) Elsevier.

Penningroth, Louis P. Horse & Buggy Days. pap. 5.95 (0-933909-00-4) Cornhusker Pr.

Pennings, F. Benefits of Doubt: A Comparative Study of the Unemployment Benefit Schemes & Reintegration Opportunities of Great Britain, France, the Federal Republic of Germany & the Netherlands. 512p. 1991. pap. 79.00 (90-6544-512-9) Kluwer Law Tax Pubs.

Pennings, Johannes M. Interlocking Directorates: Origins & Consequences of Connections Among Organizations' Boards of Directors. LC 80-8001. (Jossey-Bass Social & Behavioral Science Ser.). 238p. reprint ed. pap. 67.90 (0-8357-6883-X, 2037935) Bks Demand.

Pennings, Johannes M., et al. Organizational Strategy & Change. LC 84-47994. (Jossey-Bass Social & Behavioral Science Ser.). 597p. reprint ed. pap. 170.20 (0-7837-0186-1, 2040482) Bks Demand.

Pennington. Bowes & Church's Food Values of Portions Commonly. 16th ed. (Illus.). 328p. 1992. pap. text ed. 29.95 (0-397-55087-1) Lippincott.

— Husband, Lover, Spy. 1995. mass mkt. 5.99 (0-312-95470-0) St Martin.

Pennington, Albert. Big Boy: The Story of a Dog. 320p. 1971. 3.00 (0-685-04706-7); pap. 1.00 (0-685-04707-5) Pennington.

Pennington, Alicia. Royal Toy Spaniels. (Illus.). 160p. 1993. 22.95 (0-948955-70-8, Pub. by Ringpr Bks UK) Seven Hills Bk.

Pennington, Anne & Levi, Peter, trs. Marko the Prince: Serbo-Croat Heroic Songs. LC 83-40589. 160p. 1984. text ed. 24.95 (0-312-51537-5) St Martin.

Pennington, Arthur R. The Life & Character of Erasmus. 1977. lib. bdg. 59.95 (0-8490-2159-6) Gordon Pr.

Pennington, Basil. Awake in the Spirit: A Practical Handbook on Prayer. 160p. (C). 1990. 49.00 (0-85439-421-4, Pub. by St Paul Pubns UK) St Mut.

— Call to the Center: The Gospel's Invitation to Deeper Prayer. 2nd ed. 168p. 1995. reprint ed. pap. 9.95 (1-56548-070-8) New City.

— The Cistercians. 136p. (Orig.). 1992. pap. text ed. 18.95 (0-8146-5720-6, M Glazier) Liturgical Pr.

— The Eucharist Yesterday & Today. (C). 1988. 39.00 (0-85439-241-6, Pub. by St Paul Pubns UK) St Mut.

Pennington, Bill. The Winning Spirit. pap. 5.95 (1-55748-247-0) Barbour & Co.

— Winning Spirit. 1992. pap. 1.99 (1-55748-359-0) Barbour & Co.

***Pennington, Bonnie.** Triumph. 1995. 19.95 (0-8062-5152-2) Carlton.

Pennington, Bruce F. Diagnosing Learning Disorders: A Neuropsychological Framework. LC 91-9558. 224p. 1991. lib. bdg. 26.95 (0-89862-563-7) Guilford Pr.

Pennington, Bruce F., ed. Reading Disabilities: Genetic & Neurological Influences. 240p. (C). 1992. lib. bdg. 90.50 (0-7923-1606-1) Kluwer Ac.

Pennington, Campbell W. The Pima Bajo of Central Sonora Mexico, 2 vols., 1. LC 79-89878. 430p. pap. 111.80 (0-8357-8986-1, 2033363) Bks Demand.

— The Pima Bajo of Central Sonora Mexico, 2 vols., 2. LC 79-89878. 430p. pap. 45.40 (0-8357-8987-X) Bks Demand.

— The Tarahumar of Mexico: Their Environment & Material Culture. LC 64-1645. 299p. reprint ed. pap. 85. 30 (0-317-30111-X, 2025281) Bks Demand.

— The Tepehuan of Chihuahua: Their Material Culture. LC 73-99792. (Illus.). 427p. reprint ed. pap. 121.70 (0-8357-7051-6, 2033364) Bks Demand.

Pennington, Catherine A. Microcomputer Software Selection for the Law Library, Pt. One: General Business Software. (Law Library Information Reports: Vol. 9). 135p. 1987. pap. 100.00 (0-87802-087-X) Glanville.

— Microcomputer Software Selection for the Law Library, Pt. Two: Library & Legal Software. (Law Library Information Reports: Vol. 13). 152p. 1992. pap. 100.00 (0-87802-088-8) Glanville.

Pennington, D. D., jt. auth. see Pennington, Eunice A.

Pennington, D. H. Europe in the Seventeenth Century. 2nd ed. 622p. (C). 1989. pap. text ed. 27.50 (0-582-49388-9, 78027) Longman.

Pennington, Daniel. Itse Selu: Cherokee Harvest Festival. (Illus.). 32p. (J). (ps-4). 1994. 14.95 (0-88106-851-9); lib. bdg. 15.88 (0-88106-852-7); pap. 6.95 (0-88106-850-0) Charlesbridge Pub.

Pennington, David A. & Taylor, Michael B. Pictorial Guide to American Spinning Wheels. LC 75-15298. (Illus.). 100p. (Orig.). 1975. pap. 5.95 (0-915836-01-7) United Soc Shakers.

Pennington, Elisabeth, ed. Curriculum Revisited: An Update of Curriculum Design. 48p. 1986. 14.95 (0-88737-338-0, 15-2165) Natl League Nurse.

***Pennington, Estill C.** Antiquarian Pursuits. LC 92-71543. (Illus.). 88p. (Orig.). 1992. pap. 20.00 (0-9632836-0-X) R M Hicklin.

— Downriver: Currents of Style in Louisiana Painting, 1800-1950. LC 90-6932. (Illus.). 208p. 1991. 49.95 (0-88289-800-0) Pelican.

— John Bodeker Segar: A Georgia Painter Rediscovered. 24p. 1993. pap. 10.95 (0-9618270-8-4) Morris Comms.

— Light of Touch: Works on Paper from the Permanent Collections. (Illus.). 1993. 19.95 (0-9638753-0-2) Morris Mus Art.

— Look Away: Reality & Sentiment in Southern Art. (Illus.). 208p. 1989. 50.00 (0-934601-92-5) Peachtree Pubs.

— Passage & Progress in the Work of William Tylee Ranney. (Illus.). 1993. pap. 14.95 (0-9638753-1-0) Morris Mus Art.

— A Southern Collection. LC 92-23560. (Illus.). 1992. 34.95 (0-9618270-5-X); pap. 19.95 (0-9618270-6-8) Morris Mus Art.

— A Southern Collection: A Publication of the Morris Museum of Art. LC 92-23560. 248p. (C). 1992. 39.95 (0-8203-1534-6); pap. 24.95 (0-8203-1535-4) U of Ga Pr.

— Victorian Visionary: The Art of Elliott Daingerfield. (Illus.). 1994. 29.95 (0-9638753-2-9) Morris Mus Art.

— Will Henry Stevens: From the Mountains to the Sea. (Illus.). 32p. (Orig.). 1994. pap. 8.00 (0-9641350-0-0) Blue Spiral.

— Will Henry Stevens 1881-1949: An Eye Transformed, a Hand Transforming. LC 93-22164. 1993. 10.95 (0-9618270-7-6) Morris Comms.

— With Joy & Wonder: Ante-Bellum Taste in the Bluegrass. (Illus.). 24p. 1992. pap. text ed. 3.50 (1-882007-04-2) Univ KY Art Mus.

Pennington, Estill C., jt. auth. see Mitnick, Barbara J.

Pennington, Estill C., jt. auth. see Speakes, Vera J.

Pennington, Eunice. History of the Ozarks. (Illus.). 5.00 (0-685-19373-X); pap. 2.00 (0-911120-01-7) Pennington.

— The Ladybird Mystery. 1974. 4.50 (0-685-42423-5); pap. 2.50 (0-685-42424-3) Pennington.

— Master of the Mountain. 1971. 4.50 (0-685-47078-4); pap. 2.50 (0-685-47079-2) Pennington.

— Perry, the Pet Pig. (Illus.). (J). (gr. 4-7). 1966. 3.00 (0-685-19374-8, 911120-06-8); pap. 1.00 (0-685-19375-6) Pennington.

Pennington, Eunice A. & Pennington, D. D. Ozark National Scenic Riverways. (Illus.). 80p. (Orig.). 1967. 3.00 (0-685-09252-6); pap. 1.00 (0-685-09253-4) Pennington.

Pennington, G. W. & Naik, Sandra. Hormone Analysis: Methodology & Clinical Intrepretation, 2 vols., I. 320p. 1981. 134.00 (0-8493-5539-7, RD48, CRC Reprint) Franklin.

— Hormone Analysis: Methodology & Clinical Intrepretation, 2 vols., II. 320p. 1981. 134.00 (0-8493-5540-0, RB48, CRC Reprint) Franklin.

Pennington, H., jt. auth. see Shrayer, M.

Pennington, H. C., et al. Getting Started on the Sharp 1500 & Radio Shack PC-2. 280p. 16.95 (0-936200-11-1) Blue Cat.

Pennington, Harvard C. TRS-80 Disk & Other Mysteries. (TRS-80 Information Ser.: Vol. I). (Illus.). 128p. (Orig.). 1979. pap. 22.50 (0-936200-00-6) Blue Cat.

Pennington, Harvard C. & Shrayer, Michael. The Electric Pencil Operating Manual, Version 2.0. (Illus.). 123p. (Orig.). 1981. pap. 29.95 (0-936200-04-9) Blue Cat.

Pennington, James. Currency of the British Colonies. LC 67-18578. (Library of Money & Banking History). 1967. reprint ed. 35.00 (0-678-00260-6) Kelley.

— Textbook of the Origin & History of the Colored People. LC 77-92437. 1841. 29.00 (0-403-00169-2) Scholarly.

Pennington, James E., ed. Respiratory Infections: Diagnosis & Management. 3rd ed. LC 93-48578. 832p. 1994. 99.00 (0-7817-0173-2) Raven.

Pennington, Janice & De Abreu, Carlos. Husband, Lover, Spy: A True Story. LC 93-72895. (Illus.). 304p. 1994. 21.95 (1-884025-03-X); pap. 14.95 (1-884025-00-5) Custos Morum.

Pennington, Joy, ed. Selected Kentucky Literature. 272p. 1980. text ed. 15.00 (0-89097-019-X) Archer Edns.

Pennington, Judith. Creating a Sales Culture in a Community Bank. 1989. pap. 35.00 (1-55520-079-6) Probus Pub Co.

Pennington, Judith A. Smart Selling: Successful Sales Techniques for Bankers. 1990. 30.00 (1-55520-162-8) Probus Pub Co.

Pennington, K. & Morehead, R., eds. Image Processing Algorithms & Techniques. 1990. 70.00 (0-8194-0291-5, VOL. 1244) SPIE.

Pennington, Kenneth. Popes, Canonists, & Texts, 1100-1550. (Collected Studies: Vol. 412). 352p. 1993. 99.50 (0-86078-387-1, Pub. by Variorum UK) Ashgate Pub Co.

— The Prince & the Law, 1200-1600: Sovereignty & Rights in the Western Legal Tradition. LC 92-40544. 1993. 45. 00 (0-520-07995-7) U CA Pr.

Pennington, Kenneth & Somerville, Robert, eds. Law, Church, & Society: Essays in Honor of Stephan Kuttner. LC 76-53199. (Middle Ages Ser.). 352p. reprint ed. pap. 100.40 (0-7837-3003-9, 2042938) Bks Demand.

Pennington, L. A., jt. ed. see Berg, Irwin A.

Pennington, Lee. Songs of Bloody Harlan. 1975. pap. 10.00 (0-87423-017-9) Westburg.

— Thigmotropism. O'Dell, Mary E., ed. (Green River Writers - Poetry Ser.). 54p. (Orig.). 1993. 17.50 (0-9623666-3-3); pap. 11.95 (0-9623666-4-1); boxed 50. 00 (0-9623666-7-6) Green Rvr Writers.

Pennington, Lillian B. Snafu: The Littlest Clown. LC 73-90113. (Illus.). 32p. (J). (gr. 1-6). 1972. lib. bdg. 9.95 (0-913532-00-2); audio 7.94 (0-87783-225-0) Oddo.

Pennington, Lucinda W. The Hundred Forty-Nine Ways to Profit from Your Divorce. LC 82-17789. 324p. 1983. write for info. (0-672-52744-8) Macmillan.

Pennington, M., ed. see Carter, Elizabeth.

Pennington, M. B. A Retreat with Thomas Merton. (Retreat with Bks.). 128p. 1988. pap. 8.95 (0-916349-23-3) Amity Hse Inc.

Pennington, M. Basil. Awake in the Spirit: A Practical Handbook on Prayer. 168p. 1992. 14.95 (0-8245-1167-0) Crossroad NY.

— Breaking Bread: The Table Talk of Jesus. LC 85-51008. 160p. 1986. 10.95 (0-86683-489-3) Harper SF.

— Called: New Thinking on Christian Vocation. 128p. 1983. pap. 7.95 (0-8164-2472-1) Harper SF.

— Centered Living: The Way of Centering Living. LC 85-27474. 1988. mass mkt. 9.95 (0-385-24291-3, Image Bks) Doubleday.

— Centering Prayer: Renewing an Ancient Christian Prayer Form. LC 82-45077. 256p. 1982. mass mkt. 6.50 (0-385-18179-5, Image Bks) Doubleday.

— Lessons from the Monastery. LC 94-31704. (Illumination Bks.). 64p. 1994. pap. 3.95 (0-8091-3515-9) Paulist Pr.

— Light from the Cloister: Monastic Spirituality for Lay People. 1991. pap. 9.95 (0-8091-3171-4) Paulist Pr.

— The Monastic Way. (Illus.). 128p. 1990. 19.95 (0-8245-1048-8) Crossroad NY.

— Pocket Book of Prayers. LC 85-12936. 192p. 1986. mass mkt. 5.95 (0-385-23298-5, Image Bks) Doubleday.

— Praying by Hand: Rediscovering the Rosary As a Way of Prayer. LC 90-55775. 144p. 1991. 16.00 (0-06-066508-4) Harper SF.

— A Retreat with Thomas Merton. (Illus.). 114p. 1995. reprint ed. pap. text ed. 11.95 (0-8264-0774-9) Continuum.

— Vatican II: It Has Only Just Begun! 176p. 1994. pap. 13. 95 (0-8245-1410-6) Crossroad NY.

Pennington, M. Basil, ed. The Cistercian Spirit: A Symposium in Memory of Thomas Merton. (Cistercian Studies: No. 3). xvi, 286p. 1973. reprint ed. 7.95 (0-87907-803-0) Cistercian Pubns.

— One Yet Two: Monastic Tradition East & West. LC 75-26146. (Cistercian Studies: No. 29). 1976. 14.95 (0-87907-800-6) Cistercian Pubns.

— St. Bernard of Clairvaux: Essays Commemorating the Eighth Centenary of His Canonization. LC 77-4487. (Cistercian Studies: No. 28). 1977. 14.95 (0-87907-828-6) Cistercian Pubns.

***Pennington, M. Basil & Katzir, Yael.** Bernard of Clairvaux: A Saint's Life in Word & Image. LC 93-83255. (Illus.). 256p. 1994. 29.95 (0-87973-467-1, 467) Our Sunday Visitor.

Pennington, M. Basil & McNichols, William H. The Fifteen Mysteries: In Image & Word. LC 92-61553. (Illus.). 168p. 1993. pap. 12.95 (0-87973-499-X, 499) Our Sunday Visitor.

Pennington, M. Basil, jt. auth. see Bolshakoff, Sergius.

Pennington, Malcom W., jt. ed. see Allio, Robert J.

Pennington, Martha, ed. Building Better English Language Programs: Perspectives on Evaluation in ESL. 259p. (Orig.). 1991. pap. text ed. 18.00 (0-912207-57-4) NAFSA Washington.

***Pennington, Martha C., ed.** New Ways in Teaching Grammar. 1995. pap. 22.95 (0-939791-56-0) Tchrs Eng Spkrs.

Pennington, Martha C. & Stevens, Vance, eds. Computers in Applied Linguistics: An International Perspective. (Multilingual Matters Ser.: No. 75). 300p. 1991. 99.00 (1-85359-120-3, Pub. by Multilingual Matters UK); pap. 39.95 (1-85359-119-X, Pub. by Multilingual Matters UK) Taylor & Francis.

Pennington, Michael. An Angel for a Martyr: Jacob Epstein's Tomb for Oscar Wilde. 96p. 1987. pap. 15.00 (0-7049-0113-7, WK3, Whiteknights) MRTS.

— Rossya: A Journey Through Siberia. (Travel Bks.: Vol. 9). (Illus.). 96p. (Orig.). 1982. 16.50 (0-906672-10-4) Oleander Pr.

***Pennington, Michael & Dunn, Ben, eds.** Peptide Analysis Protocols Vol. 36. LC 94-22663. (Methods in Molecular Biology: No. 36). (Illus.). 352p. 1994. pap. 64.50 (0-89603-274-4) Humana.

Pennington, Michael W., jt. ed. see Dunn, Ben M.

Pennington, N. Sugar: A User's Guide to Sucrose. 1990. text ed. 65.00 (0-442-00297-1) Chapman & Hall.

Pennington, Patience. A Woman Rice Planter. (Illus.). 496p. (C). 1991. reprint ed. write for info. (0-318-68580-9) Seajay Society.

Pennington, Patience, pseud. A Woman Rice Planter. Sproat, John G., ed. LC 91-35167. (Southern Classics Ser.). (Illus.). 501p. 1992. reprint ed. pap. 16.95 (0-87249-826-3) U of SC Pr.

Pennington, Randy & Bockmon, Marc. On My Honor, I Will: How One Simple Oath Can Lead You to Success in Business. 176p. 1992. 17.95 (0-446-51618-X) Warner Bks.

Pennington, Renee & Harpending, Henry. The Structure of an African Pastoralist Community: Demography, History, & Ecology of the Ngamiland Herero. (Research Monographs on Human Population Biology: No. 11). (Illus.). 288p. 1993. 67.50 (0-19-852286-X) OUP.

Pennington, Richard. Breaking the Ice: The Racial Integration of Southwest Conference Football. LC 87-43030. 192p. 1987. lib. bdg. 27.50x (0-89950-295-4) McFarland & Co.

— A Descriptive Catalogue of the Etched Works of Wenceslaus Hollar, 1607-1677. LC 81-51828. 452p. 1982. 300.00 (0-521-22408-X) Cambridge U Pr.

— For Texas, I Will: The History of Memorial Stadium. (Illus.). 252p. Date not set. 19.95 (1-881825-01-9) Hist Pubns TX.

Pennington, Richard, ed. see Berry, Margaret C.

Pennington, Robert R. The Law of Investment Markets. 928p. (C). 1989. text ed. 199.95 (0-632-02372-4) Blackwell Sci.

— Pennington's Company Law. 6th ed. 1990. U.K. pap. 60. 00 (0-406-51041-5) Butterworth Legal Pubs.

— Pennington's Corporate Insolvency Law. 1991. pap. 40.00 (0-406-00141-3, U.K.) Butterworth Legal Pubs.

Pennington, Roger. British Fire Engines. (Color Library). (Illus.). 128p. 1994. pap. 15.95 (1-85532-426-1, Pub. by Osprey Pubng Ltd UK) Motorbooks Intl.

***Pennington, T. D.** The Genera Sapotaceae. (Illus.). 296p. 1991. 60.00x (0-947643-34-6) Lubrecht & Cramer.

— Meliaceae. LC 81-11131. (Flora Neotropica Monograph Ser.: No. 28). (Illus.). 470p. 1981. pap. 65.00 (0-89327-235-3) NY Botanical.

Pennington, T. D., et al. Sapotaceae: Palynology. (Flora Neotropica Monograph Ser.: No. 52). (Illus.). 770p. 1990. pap. 136.00 (0-89327-344-9) NY Botanical.

Penninx, R., et al. The Impact of International Migration on Receiving Countries: The Case of the Netherlands. 252p. 1993. pap. 39.00 (90-265-1344-5, Pub. by Swets Pub Serv NE) Taylor & Francis.

Pennock, Dee. Who Is God? Who Am I? Who Are You? Introduction to Basic Christian Psychology. (Illus.). 160p. (Orig.). 1973. pap. 4.95 (1-878997-08-4) St Tikhons Pr.

Pennock, J. Roland. Responsiveness, Responsibility, & Majority Rule. (Reprint Series in Social Sciences). (C). 1993. reprint ed. pap. text ed. 1.00 (0-8290-3603-2, PS-226) Irvington.

Pennock, J. Roland & Chapman, John W. Marxism. (Nomos Ser.: Vol. 26). 336p. 1984. 45.00 (0-8147-6586-6) NYU Pr.

Pennock, J. Roland & Chapman, John W., eds. Criminal Justice. LC 84-14776. (Nomos Ser.: Vol. 27). 384p. 1985. 45.00 (0-8147-6588-2) NYU Pr.

— Due Process. LC 76-40511. (Nomos Ser.: Vol. 18). 1977. 45.00 (0-8147-6569-6) NYU Pr.

— Religion, Morality, & the Law. (Nomos Ser.: Vol. 30). 356p. 1988. 45.00 (0-8147-6606-4) NYU Pr.

— Voluntary Associations. (Nomos Ser.: No. XI). 291p. 1969. text ed. 35.00 (0-685-37877-2) Lieber-Atherton.

Pennock, J. Roland, jt. ed. see Chapman, John W.

Pennock, James R. Liberal Democracy: Its Merits & Prospects. LC 77-13903. 403p. 1978. reprint ed. text ed. 38.50 (0-8371-9865-8, PELD, Greenwood Pr) Greenwood.

Pennock, James R., ed. Self-Government in Modernizing Nations. LC 77-167401. (Essay Index Reprint Ser.). 1977. reprint ed. 18.95 (0-8369-2517-3) Ayer.

Pennock, Jonathan R., jt. ed. see Bryant, Tracey L.

Pennock, Judith B. For the Love of Reading. abr. ed. 150p. 1994. pap. 7.95 (1-56901-329-2) NW Pub.

***Pennock, Margaret T. & Bardwell, Lisa V.** Approaching Environmental Issues in the Classroom. Monroe, Martha C. & Cappaert, David, eds. (EEToolbox Resource Manual Ser.). (Illus.). 60p. 1994. 8.00 (1-884782-05-1) Natl Consort EET.

Pennock, Margaret T., jt. auth. see Corcoran, Peter B.

Pennock, Michael. Being Catholic: Believing, Living, Praying. LC 93-73883. (Friendship in the Lord Ser.). (Illus.). 232p. (Orig.). (YA). (gr. 10-12). 1994. teacher ed, pap. 15.95 (0-87793-528-9); pap. text ed. 11.95 (0-87793-527-0) Ave Maria.

— The Catholic Church Story. LC 90-64153. (Friendship in the Lord Ser.). (Illus.). 224p. (Orig.). (YA). (gr. 9-12). 1991. teacher ed 12.95 (0-87793-448-7); pap. text ed. 8.95 (0-87793-447-9) Ave Maria.

— Choosing: Cases in Moral Decision Making. LC 90-85155. (Friendship in the Lord Ser.). 160p. (Orig.). (YA). (gr. 9-12). 1991. spiral bd. 7.95 (0-87793-446-0) Ave Maria.

— Forming a Catholic Conscience. LC 90-84839. (Friendship in the Lord Ser.). (Illus.). 168p. (Orig.). (YA). (gr. 9-12). 1991. teacher ed 11.95 (0-87793-445-2); pap. text ed. 8.95 (0-87793-444-4) Ave Maria.

— Growing in the Catholic Faith. LC 89-82328. (Friendship in the Lord Ser.). (Illus.). 168p. (Orig.). (YA). (gr. 9-12). 1990. teacher ed 10.95 (0-87793-419-3); Student text, 200p. student ed, pap. text ed. 7.95 (0-87793-418-5) Ave Maria.

— Jesus: Friend & Savior. LC 89-82459. (Friendship in the Lord Ser.). 176p. (Orig.). (YA). (gr. 9-12). 1990. teacher ed 10.95 (0-87793-421-5); student ed, pap. text ed. 7.95 (0-87793-420-7) Ave Maria.

— The Sacraments: Celebrating the Signs of God's Love. LC 92-75347. (Friendship in the Lord Ser.). (Illus.). 240p. (Orig.). (YA). (gr. 9-12). 1993. teacher ed 13.95 (0-87793-504-1); pap. 9.95 (0-87793-503-3) Ave Maria.

Pennock, Michael F. Discovering the Promise of the Old Testament. LC 91-76778. (Friendship in the Lord Ser.). (Illus.). 224p. (Orig.). (YA). (gr. 9-12). 1992. teacher ed 12.95 (0-87793-473-8); student ed, pap. text ed. 8.95 (0-87793-472-X) Ave Maria.

— Living the Message of the New Testament. LC 91-77474. (Friendship in the Lord Ser.). (Illus.). 216p. (Orig.). (YA). (gr. 9-12). 1992. teacher ed 12.95 (*0-87793-468-1*); student ed, pap. text ed. 8.95 (*0-87793-469-X*) Ave Maria.
— The Seeker's Catechism: The Basics of Catholicism. LC 94-71886. 132p. (Orig.). 1994. pap. 3.95 (*0-87793-539-4*) Ave Maria.
— This Is Our Faith... A Catholic Catechism for Adults. LC 88-82681. 288p. (Orig.). 1989. pap. 7.95 (*0-87793-389-8*) Ave Maria.
Pennoyer, F. Douglas, jt. comp. see Wagner, C. Peter.
Pennsylvania Academy of Fine Arts Staff. I Tell My Heart: The Art of Horace Pippin Print Book. (Illus.). 1994. 5.00 (*1-55550-913-4*) Universe.
Pennsylvania Academy of the Fine Arts Staff. Searching Out the Best: A Tribute to the Morris Gallery of the Pennsylvania Academy of the Fine Arts. (Illus.). 212p. (Orig.). 1988. pap. 19.95 (*0-943836-09-3*) Penn Acad Art.
Pennsylvania Bar Institute Staff. Developing Your Law Practice. 135p. 1985. 10.00 (*0-318-19035-4*, 315) PA Bar Inst.
— Law Firm Income: Making Money & Dividing the Pie. 126p. 1985. 15.00 (*0-318-19059-1*, 284) PA Bar Inst.
Pennsylvania Bureau of Mining & Reclamation Staff & Bureau of Deep Mine Safety Staff. Annual Report on Mining Activities: 1983. Nichols, Patsie, ed. 420p. (C). 1983. 8.10 (*0-8182-0060-X*) Commonweal PA.
Pennsylvania Colony Staff. Colonial Records of Pennsylvania, 16 Vols. LC 01-10370. student ed 47.50 (*0-404-05020-4*) AMS Pr.
— Colonial Records of Pennsylvania, 16 Vols. LC 01-10370. reprint ed. 95.00 (*0-685-73116-2*) AMS Pr.
— Colonial Records of Pennsylvania, 16 vols., Set. LC 01-10370. reprint ed. 1,520.00 (*0-404-05000-X*) AMS Pr.
Pennsylvania Economy League Staff. Industrial Tax Burdens in Philadelphia & Twenty-Seven Other Municipalities in Southeastern Pa. write for info. (*0-318-61045-0*) PA Econ League.
Pennsylvania Genealogical Magazine Staff. Genealogies of Pennsylvania Families From the Pennsylvania Genealogical Magazine, 3 vols. LC 81-85694. (Illus.). 2894p. 1982. 135.00 (*0-8063-0974-1*) Genealog Pub.
Pennsylvania Health Law Project Staff. Health Care for the Poor in Pennsylvania: An Outline for 1986. 67p. 1986. pap. 7.00 (*0-685-23176-3*, 41,211) NCLS Inc.
Pennsylvania Horticultural Society Staff. Great Recipes from Great Gardeners. LC 93-72675. 1993. write for info. (*0-9637494-0-4*) Favorite Recipes.
Pennsylvania Legislative Reference Bureau Staff. Pennsylvania Consolidated Statutes: Title 75, Vehicles, 1982 Edition. rev. ed. 378p. (C). 1992. pap. 8.34 (*0-8182-0013-8*) Commonweal PA.
Pennsylvania P. U. C. Staff. Pennsylvania Public Utility Commission Decisions, April 1987-August 1987. Sophy, Kathryn G., ed. (PA P.U.C. Decisions Ser.: Vol. 64). 565p. 1988. text ed. 237.00 (*0-8182-0100-2*) Commonweal PA.
***Pennsylvania Poetry Society, Inc. Wallace Stevens Chapter Staff.** Chiaroscuro. Gasser, Ann, ed. & intro. by. 59p. (Orig.). 1994. pap. 2.00 (*1-884257-02-X*) AGEE Keyboard.
— Visions in Verse. Gasser, Ann, ed. & illus. by. 72p. (Orig.). 1995. pap. 3.00 (*1-884257-09-7*) AGEE Keyboard.
Pennsylvania Special Grand Jury Staff. Investigation of Vice, Crime & Law Enforcement. LC 74-3856. (Criminal Justice in America Ser.). 1974. reprint ed. 23.95 (*0-405-06164-1*) Ayer.
Pennsylvania State Data Center Staff. Closing the Male-Female Earnings Gap in Pennsylvania. 16p. (Orig.). 1994. pap. text ed. 15.00 (*0-939667-29-0*, SDC1P2-94) Penn State Data Ctr.
— Commutation Patterns: Pennsylvania, 1990. 114p. 1993. pap. text ed. 25.00 (*0-939667-18-5*) Penn State Data Ctr.
— Detailed Income Characteristics, 1990. 261p. 1992. pap. 25.00 (*0-939667-17-7*) Penn State Data Ctr.
— Detailed State & County Population Estimates, 1992: Pennsylvania. 95p. 1994. pap. 25.00 (*0-939667-23-1*) Penn State Data Ctr.
— Educational Attainment Level of the Civilian Labor Force: Pennsylvania Counties, 1990. 98p. 1993. pap. 25.00 (*0-939667-19-3*) Penn State Data Ctr.
— General Income Characteristics, 1990: Pennsylvania. 276p. 1992. pap. 25.00 (*0-939667-16-9*) Penn State Data Ctr.
— General Population & Housing Characteristics, 1990: Pennsylvania. 291p. 1991. pap. 25.00 (*0-939667-15-0*) Penn State Data Ctr.
— Legislative Districts on Profile: A Demographic & Socio-Economic Data Book. 90p. 1993. pap. write for info. (*0-939667-27-4*) Penn State Data Ctr.
— Marketers Handbook, 1990, Vol. I. 160p. (Orig.). 1993. pap. text ed. 35.00 (*0-939667-31-2*) Penn State Data Ctr.
— Municipal Population Estimates 1992: Pennsylvania. 100p. 1994. pap. 25.00 (*0-939667-30-4*) Penn State Data Ctr.
— PA Migration: Who the State Gains & Loses. 28p. 1995. pap. 20.00 (*1-885925-02-6*) Penn State Data Ctr.
— Pennsylvania Abstract, 1992. 270p. (Orig.). 1992. pap. 35.00 (*0-939667-25-8*) Penn State Data Ctr.
— Pennsylvania County Data Book: Adams County. 200p. (Orig.). 1993. pap. 25.00 (*0-939667-33-9*) Penn State Data Ctr.
— Pennsylvania County Data Book: Allegheny County. 200p. (Orig.). 1993. pap. 35.00 (*0-939667-34-7*) Penn State Data Ctr.
— Pennsylvania County Data Book: Armstrong County. 200p. (Orig.). 1993. pap. 30.00 (*0-939667-35-5*) Penn State Data Ctr.
— Pennsylvania County Data Book: Beaver County. 200p. (Orig.). 1993. pap. 35.00 (*0-939667-36-3*) Penn State Data Ctr.
— Pennsylvania County Data Book: Bedford County. 200p. (Orig.). 1993. pap. 30.00 (*0-939667-37-1*) Penn State Data Ctr.
— Pennsylvania County Data Book: Berks County. 200p. (Orig.). 1993. pap. 35.00 (*0-939667-38-X*) Penn State Data Ctr.
— Pennsylvania County Data Book: Blair County. 200p. (Orig.). 1993. pap. 25.00 (*0-939667-39-8*) Penn State Data Ctr.
— Pennsylvania County Data Book: Bradford County. 200p. (Orig.). 1993. pap. 30.00 (*0-939667-40-1*) Penn State Data Ctr.
— Pennsylvania County Data Book: Bucks County. 200p. (Orig.). 1993. pap. 35.00 (*0-939667-41-X*) Penn State Data Ctr.
— Pennsylvania County Data Book: Butler County. 200p. (Orig.). 1993. pap. 35.00 (*0-939667-42-8*) Penn State Data Ctr.
— Pennsylvania County Data Book: Cambria County. 200p. (Orig.). 1993. pap. 35.00 (*0-939667-43-6*) Penn State Data Ctr.
— Pennsylvania County Data Book: Cameron County. 200p. (Orig.). 1993. pap. 20.00 (*0-939667-44-4*) Penn State Data Ctr.
— Pennsylvania County Data Book: Carbon County. 200p. (Orig.). 1993. pap. 20.00 (*0-939667-46-0*) Penn State Data Ctr.
— Pennsylvania County Data Book: Centre County. 200p. (Orig.). 1993. pap. 25.00 (*0-685-72107-8*) Penn State Data Ctr.
— Pennsylvania County Data Book: Chester County. 200p. (Orig.). 1993. pap. 35.00 (*0-939667-47-9*) Penn State Data Ctr.
— Pennsylvania County Data Book: Clarion County. 200p. (Orig.). 1993. pap. 30.00 (*0-939667-48-7*) Penn State Data Ctr.
— Pennsylvania County Data Book: Clearfield County. 200p. (Orig.). 1993. pap. 30.00 (*0-939667-49-5*) Penn State Data Ctr.
— Pennsylvania County Data Book: Clinton County. 200p. (Orig.). 1993. pap. 25.00 (*0-939667-50-9*) Penn State Data Ctr.
— Pennsylvania County Data Book: Columbia County. 200p. (Orig.). 1993. pap. 25.00 (*0-939667-51-7*) Penn State Data Ctr.
— Pennsylvania County Data Book: Crawford County. 200p. (Orig.). 1993. pap. 35.00 (*0-939667-52-5*) Penn State Data Ctr.
— Pennsylvania County Data Book: Cumberland County. 200p. (Orig.). 1993. pap. 25.00 (*0-939667-53-3*) Penn State Data Ctr.
— Pennsylvania County Data Book: Dauphin County. 200p. (Orig.). 1993. pap. 30.00 (*0-939667-54-1*) Penn State Data Ctr.
— Pennsylvania County Data Book: Delaware County. 200p. (Orig.). 1993. pap. 30.00 (*0-939667-55-X*) Penn State Data Ctr.
— Pennsylvania County Data Book: Elk County. 200p. (Orig.). 1993. pap. 20.00 (*0-939667-56-8*) Penn State Data Ctr.
— Pennsylvania County Data Book: Erie County. 200p. (Orig.). 1993. pap. 30.00 (*0-939667-57-6*) Penn State Data Ctr.
— Pennsylvania County Data Book: Fayette County. 200p. (Orig.). 1993. pap. 30.00 (*0-939667-58-4*) Penn State Data Ctr.
— Pennsylvania County Data Book: Forest County. 200p. (Orig.). 1993. pap. 20.00 (*0-939667-59-2*) Penn State Data Ctr.
— Pennsylvania County Data Book: Franklin County. 200p. (Orig.). 1993. pap. 20.00 (*0-939667-60-6*) Penn State Data Ctr.
— Pennsylvania County Data Book: Fulton County. 200p. (Orig.). 1993. pap. 20.00 (*0-939667-61-4*) Penn State Data Ctr.
— Pennsylvania County Data Book: Greene County. 200p. (Orig.). 1993. pap. 25.00 (*0-939667-62-2*) Penn State Data Ctr.
— Pennsylvania County Data Book: Huntingdon County. 200p. (Orig.). 1993. pap. 30.00 (*0-939667-63-0*) Penn State Data Ctr.
— Pennsylvania County Data Book: Indiana County. 200p. (Orig.). 1993. pap. 30.00 (*0-939667-64-9*) Penn State Data Ctr.
— Pennsylvania County Data Book: Jefferson County. 200p. (Orig.). 1993. pap. 25.00 (*0-939667-65-7*) Penn State Data Ctr.
— Pennsylvania County Data Book: Juniata County. 200p. (Orig.). 1993. pap. 20.00 (*0-939667-66-5*) Penn State Data Ctr.
— Pennsylvania County Data Book: Lackawanna County. 200p. (Orig.). 1993. pap. 30.00 (*0-939667-67-3*) Penn State Data Ctr.
— Pennsylvania County Data Book: Lancaster County. 200p. (Orig.). 1993. pap. 35.00 (*0-939667-68-1*) Penn State Data Ctr.
— Pennsylvania County Data Book: Lawrence County. 200p. (Orig.). 1993. pap. 25.00 (*0-939667-69-X*) Penn State Data Ctr.
— Pennsylvania County Data Book: Lebanon County. 200p. (Orig.). 1993. pap. 25.00 (*0-939667-70-3*) Penn State Data Ctr.
— Pennsylvania County Data Book: Lehigh County. 200p. (Orig.). 1993. pap. 25.00 (*0-939667-71-1*) Penn State Data Ctr.
— Pennsylvania County Data Book: Luzerne County. 200p. (Orig.). 1993. pap. 35.00 (*0-939667-72-X*) Penn State Data Ctr.
— Pennsylvania County Data Book: Lycoming County. 200p. (Orig.). 1993. pap. 35.00 (*0-939667-73-8*) Penn State Data Ctr.
— Pennsylvania County Data Book: McKean County. 200p. (Orig.). 1993. pap. 20.00 (*0-939667-74-6*) Penn State Data Ctr.
— Pennsylvania County Data Book: Mercer County. 200p. (Orig.). 1993. pap. 30.00 (*0-939667-75-4*) Penn State Data Ctr.
— Pennsylvania County Data Book: Mifflin County. 200p. (Orig.). 1993. pap. 20.00 (*0-939667-76-2*) Penn State Data Ctr.
— Pennsylvania County Data Book: Monroe County. 200p. (Orig.). 1993. pap. 20.00 (*0-939667-77-0*) Penn State Data Ctr.
— Pennsylvania County Data Book: Montgomery County. 200p. (Orig.). 1993. pap. 35.00 (*0-939667-78-9*) Penn State Data Ctr.
— Pennsylvania County Data Book: Montour County. 200p. (Orig.). 1993. pap. 20.00 (*0-939667-79-7*) Penn State Data Ctr.
— Pennsylvania County Data Book: Northampton County. 200p. (Orig.). 1993. pap. 30.00 (*0-939667-80-0*) Penn State Data Ctr.
— Pennsylvania County Data Book: Northumberland County. 200p. (Orig.). 1993. pap. 30.00 (*0-939667-81-9*) Penn State Data Ctr.
— Pennsylvania County Data Book: Perry County. 200p. (Orig.). 1993. pap. 25.00 (*0-939667-82-7*) Penn State Data Ctr.
— Pennsylvania County Data Book: Philadelphia County. 200p. (Orig.). 1993. pap. 20.00 (*0-939667-83-5*) Penn State Data Ctr.
— Pennsylvania County Data Book: Pike County. 200p. (Orig.). 1993. pap. 20.00 (*0-939667-84-3*) Penn State Data Ctr.
— Pennsylvania County Data Book: Potter County. 200p. (Orig.). 1993. pap. 25.00 (*0-939667-85-1*) Penn State Data Ctr.
— Pennsylvania County Data Book: Schuylkill County. 200p. (Orig.). 1993. pap. 35.00 (*0-939667-86-X*) Penn State Data Ctr.
— Pennsylvania County Data Book: Snyder County. 200p. (Orig.). 1993. pap. 20.00 (*0-939667-87-8*) Penn State Data Ctr.
— Pennsylvania County Data Book: Somerset County. 200p. (Orig.). 1993. pap. 35.00 (*0-939667-88-6*) Penn State Data Ctr.
— Pennsylvania County Data Book: Sullivan County. 200p. (Orig.). 1993. pap. 20.00 (*0-939667-89-4*) Penn State Data Ctr.
— Pennsylvania County Data Book: Susquehanna County. 200p. (Orig.). 1993. pap. 30.00 (*0-939667-90-8*) Penn State Data Ctr.
— Pennsylvania County Data Book: Tioga County. 200p. (Orig.). 1993. pap. 30.00 (*0-939667-91-6*) Penn State Data Ctr.
— Pennsylvania County Data Book: Union County. 200p. (Orig.). 1993. pap. 20.00 (*0-939667-92-4*) Penn State Data Ctr.
— Pennsylvania County Data Book: Venango County. 200p. (Orig.). 1993. pap. 25.00 (*0-939667-93-2*) Penn State Data Ctr.
— Pennsylvania County Data Book: Warren County. 200p. (Orig.). 1993. pap. 25.00 (*0-939667-94-0*) Penn State Data Ctr.
— Pennsylvania County Data Book: Washington County. 200p. (Orig.). 1993. pap. 35.00 (*0-939667-95-9*) Penn State Data Ctr.
— Pennsylvania County Data Book: Wayne County. 200p. (Orig.). 1993. pap. 25.00 (*0-939667-96-7*) Penn State Data Ctr.
— Pennsylvania County Data Book: Westmoreland County. 200p. (Orig.). 1993. pap. 35.00 (*0-939667-97-5*) Penn State Data Ctr.
— Pennsylvania County Data Book: Wyoming County. 200p. (Orig.). 1993. pap. 25.00 (*0-939667-98-3*) Penn State Data Ctr.
— Pennsylvania County Data Book: York County. 200p. (Orig.). 1993. pap. 35.00 (*0-939667-99-1*) Penn State Data Ctr.
— Pennsylvania Housing Characteristics. 430p. (Orig.). Date not set. pap. 45.00 (*1-885925-01-8*) Penn State Data Ctr.
— Pennsylvania School District Report, 1990. 1994. pap. 45.00 (*0-939667-22-3*) Penn State Data Ctr.
— Sixty-Five Plus in Pennsylvania. 25p. (Orig.). 1993. pap. 10.00 (*0-939667-32-0*) Penn State Data Ctr.
— State & County Detailed Population Estimates, 1990: Pennsylvania. 100p. 1993. pap. 25.00 (*0-939667-21-5*) Penn State Data Ctr.
— Taking Women into the Twenty First Century: Issues Facing Pennsylvania's Women. 103p. (Orig.). 1994. pap. 25.00 (*0-939667-28-2*) Penn State Data Ctr.
— Transportation to Work, 1990. 193p. 1993. pap. text ed. 25.00 (*0-939667-20-7*) Penn State Data Ctr.
— The Well-Being of Children & Youth in Pennsylvania: Demographic Trends. 14p. (Orig.). 1993. pap. 10.00 (*0-939667-26-6*) Penn State Data Ctr.
Pennsylvania State Department Staff. Corporate Guide: A Manual for Filing Corporate Documents in Pennsylvania. 31p. 1985. write for info. (*0-318-58006-3*) Penna Secy.
Pennsylvania State Federation of Labor Staff. American Cossack. LC 76-154583. (Police in America Ser.). (Illus.). 1978. reprint ed. 22.95 (*0-405-03380-X*) Ayer.
Pennsylvania State Grange Staff. The Pennsylvania State Grange Cookbook. LC 92-30345. 1992. write for info. (*0-87197-350-2*) Favorite Recipes.
Pennsylvania State Legislature Staff. Second Class Township Code. 176p. (Orig.). 1982. text ed. 2.00 (*0-8182-0001-4*) Commonweal PA.
— Third Class City Code. 225p. (Orig.). 1990. text ed. 3.75 (*0-8182-0002-2*) Commonweal PA.
Pennsylvania State University. Electrodeposition of Copper from Fused Salts. 128p. 1966. 19.20 (*0-317-34520-6*, 44) Intl Copper.
Pennsylvania State University Nutrition Education Curriculum Study Staff. Nutrition in a Changing World: Grade Four. LC 80-20736. (Illus.). 152p. (Orig.). (gr. 4). 1981. pap. text ed. 11.95 (*0-8425-1864-9*) BYU Scholarly.
Pennsylvania State University Staff. Laboratory Astronomy: Observations & Analysis for Undergraduates. 208p. 1992. pap. text ed. 14.95 (*0-8403-7477-1*) Kendall-Hunt.
— Thermodynamic Properties of Copper-Base Alloys. 134p. 1981. write for info. (*0-318-60071-4*, 245) Intl Copper.
Pennsylvania University - Department of History Staff. Translations & Reprints from the Original Sources of European History, 6 Vols, Set. rev. ed. LC 75-143179. reprint ed. lib. bdg. 135.00 (*0-404-08970-4*) AMS Pr.
Pennsylvania University, Babylonian Expedition. The Babylonian Expedition of the University of Pennsylvania: Researches & Treatises, Vol. 4. Hilprecht, H. V., ed. LC 18-5954. (Series D: Vol. 4). 355p. reprint ed. pap. 101.20 (*0-8357-5937-7*, 2026653) Bks Demand.
Pennsylvania University Library Staff. Changing Patterns of Scholarship & the Future of Research Libraries. LC 68-14910. (Essay Index Reprint Ser.). 1977. 19.95 (*0-8369-0782-5*) Ayer.
Pennsylvania Writers' Project Staff. Northampton County Guide. 1993. reprint ed. lib. bdg. 89.00 (*0-7812-5817-0*) Rprt Serv.
— Picture of Lycoming County. 1993. reprint ed. lib. bdg. 89.00 (*0-7812-5818-9*) Rprt Serv.
Penny, A. J. Studies in Jacob Boehme. 503p. 1992. pap. 30.00 (*1-56459-290-1*) Kessinger Pub.
Penny, Anne, jt. auth. see Mayhew, Susan.
Penny, David W. Art of the American Indian Frontier: The Chandler-Pohrt Collection. LC 91-37736. (Illus.). 368p. 1993. pap. 35.00 (*0-295-97318-8*) U of Wash Pr.
Penny, Edward B., tr. see Saint-Martin, Louis Claude de.
Penny, F. E. Southern India Land, People & Culture. (C). 1992. 75.00 (*81-7305-029-5*, Pub. by Aryan Bks Intl IA) S Asia.
Penny, George. Traditions of Perth. 335p. 1987. 85.00 (*0-317-89980-5*, Pub. by W Culross & Son Ltd UK) St Mut.
Penny, Gillian N., et al, eds. Health Psychology: A Lifespan Perspective. LC 93-17400. 1994. text ed. 48.00 (*3-7186-5416-4*); pap. text ed. 20.00 (*3-7186-5415-6*) Gordon & Breach.
Penny, J. E., jt. auth. see Lindfield, G. R.
Penny, James S., Jr. Archaeological Investigations for the Hard Times Timber Sale, Union County, Illinois. LC 87-71350. (Center for Archaeological Investigations Research Paper Ser.: No. 56). (Illus.). viii, 52p. 1987. pap. 8.50 (*0-88104-067-3*) Center Archaeo.
— Archaeological Investigations in Highway Construction Borrow Pits in Marion & Monroe Counties, Illinois. LC 85-71883. (Center for Archaeological Investigations Research Paper Ser.: No. 50). (Illus.). ix, 57p. 1985. pap. 6.50 (*0-88104-056-8*) Center Archaeo.
— Archaeological Survey of Mineral Prospecting Lands in the Shawnee National Forest, Southern Illinois, 1983. (Center for Archaeological Investigations Research Paper Ser.: No. 45). (Illus.). vii, 86p. 1984. pap. 7.50 (*0-88104-017-7*) Center Archaeo.
— The Prehistoric Peoples of Southern Illinois. (Illus.). ix, 70p. (Orig.). 1986. pap. 3.50 (*0-88104-062-2*) Center Archaeo.
***Penny, John & Lindfield, George.** Numerical Methods Using MATLAB. LC 94-33327. 1994. pap. 40.00 (*0-13-030966-4*) Tavistock-E Horwood.
Penny, Lee, jt. auth. see Browne, Elizabeth W.
Penny, Malcolm. Alligators & Crocodiles. 1991. 14.99 (*0-517-07012-X*) Random Hse Value.
— Birds of Prey. (Remarkable World Ser.). (Illus.). 48p. (J). (gr. 4 up). 1996. 15.95 (*1-56847-414-8*) Thomson Lrning.
— The Monkey & the Ape: Close Relatives. Stefoff, Rebecca, ed. LC 92-10243. (Wildlife Survival Library). (Illus.). 31p. (J). (gr. 3-6). 1992. lib. bdg. 17.26 (*1-56074-051-5*) Garrett Ed Corp.
— Night Creatures. (Remarkable World Ser.). (Illus.). 48p. (J). (gr. 4 up). 1996. 15.95 (*1-56847-371-0*) Thomson Lrning.
— Protecting Wildlife. LC 90-9925. (Conserving Our World Ser.). (Illus.). 48p. (J). (gr. 4-9). 1990. lib. bdg. 22.13 (*0-8114-2389-1*); pap. 5.95 (*0-8114-3455-9*) Raintree Steck-V.
— Rhinos: An Endangered Species. (Illus.). 128p. 1988. write for info. (*0-318-32664-7*) Facts on File.
Penny, Michael. Approaching the Bible. LC 92-70157. 348p. 1992. pap. 15.00 (*1-880573-03-2*) Grace WI.
— David's Son & the Son of David. 20p. (Orig.). 1994. pap. 2.50 (*1-880573-20-2*) Grace WI.
— The Mark of the Beast & the Jerusalem Temple. (Illus.). 24p. (Orig.). 1993. pap. text ed. 2.50 (*1-880573-08-3*) Grace WI.
— Studies in First Thessalonians. 40p. 1992. pap. text ed. 3.00 (*1-880573-02-4*) Grace WI.
***Penny, Michael, ed.** Studies in Jude. 32p. (Orig.). 1995. pap. 3.00 (*1-880573-26-1*) Grace WI.
Penny, Nicholas. Catalogue of European Sculpture in the Ashmolean Museum, 1540 to the Present Day. LC 92-21820. (C). 1992. write for info. (*0-19-951329-5*, Clarendon Pr) OUP.
— Church Monuments in Romantic England. LC 76-58912. (Studies in British Art). (Illus.). 1977. 50.00 (*0-300-02075-9*) Yale U Pr.

P Q

An Asterisk (*) at the beginning of an entry indicates that the title is appearing in BIP for the first time.

— The Materials of Sculpture. (Illus.). 280p. 1994. 45.00 (*0-300-05556-0*) Yale U Pr.

— Tradition & Revolution in French Art. (National Gallery Publications). (Illus.). 1990. 50.00 (*0-300-06198-6*); pap. 25.00 (*0-300-06199-4*) Yale U Pr.

Penny, Nicholas, intro. David Levine: Caricatures & Watercolours. (Illus.). 28p. 1995. pap. 6.96 (*0-907849-83-0*, 830, Pub. by Ashmolean Mus UK) A Schwartz & Co.

Penny, Nicholas & Johnson, Robert F. Lucian Freud Works on Paper. LC 87-51288. (Illus.). 160p. 1988. 40.00 (*0-500-09185-4*) Thames Hudson.

Penny, Nicholas, jt. auth. see Haskell, Francis.

Penny, Nicholas, jt. auth. see Jones, Roger.

Penny, Norman D. & Arias, Jorge R. Insects of an Amazon Forest. LC 81-7665. (Illus.). 328p. 1982. text ed. 65.00 (*0-231-05266-9*) Col U Pr.

Penny Pincher's Almanac Staff, ed. The Penny Pincher's Almanac: The Handbook for Modern Frugality. (Illus.). 192p. (Orig.). 1993. pap. 8.95 (*0-671-79728-X*, Fireside) S&S Trade.

Penny, Ralph. A History of the Spanish Language. 304p. (C). 1991. pap. 19.95 (*0-521-39784-7*) Cambridge U Pr.

Penny, Ralph J. El Habla Pasiega: Ensayo de Dialectologia Montanesa. (Serie A: Monagrafias, XIII). (Illus.). 470p. (Orig.). (SPA.). (C). 1969. pap. 53.00 (*0-900411-05-8*, Pub. by Tamesis Bks Ltd UK) Boydell & Brewer.

Penny, Richard. The Whitewater Sourcebook. rev. ed. LC 88-16932. (Illus.). 400p. 1990. pap. 19.95 (*0-89732-078-6*) Menasha Ridge.

Penny, Rob. Romance Rhythm & Revolution: New & Selected Poetry. 2nd ed. 100p. (YA). (gr. 9-12). 1993. reprint ed. pap. text ed. 9.95 (*0-685-60180-3*) Magnolia PA.

— Romance Rhythm & Revolution: Selected Poetry of Rob Penny. 200p. 1990. 15.95 (*0-929917-00-6*) Magnolia PA.

Penny, Rob & Lawrence, Valerie, eds. Sharpeville Commemoration...the Legacy. LC 88-61292. 60p. (Orig.). 1988. pap. 8.95 (*0-685-22522-4*) Magnolia PA.

Penny, Rogene N. & Vaughn, Patricia A. Seasonal Phonics Fun: Grades K-3. 1989. 5.95 (*0-89108-209-3*, 8905) Love Pub Co.

Penny, Selwyn & Jones, Philip. Operation Fire-Operation Tan. (C). 1988. 21.00 (*0-685-45101-1*, Pub. by NCCL UK) St Mut.

Penny, Simon, ed. Critical Issues in Electronic Media. (SUNY Series in Film History & Theory). 336p. 1995. text ed. 59.50 (*0-7914-2317-4*); pap. 19.95 (*0-7914-2318-2*) State U NY Pr.

Penny Stock News. Penny Stocks: How to Profit with Low-Priced Stocks. 1986. pap. text ed. 8.95 (*0-07-157137-X*) McGraw.

***Penny, Sylvia.** Lying. 24p. 1995. pap. text ed. 2.00 (*1-880573-23-7*) Grace WI.

***Penny, Timothy J. & Garrett, Major.** Common Cents. 1995. 21.95 (*0-316-69912-8*) Little.

Penny, Virginia. How Women Can Make Money, Married or Single, in All Branches of the Arts & Sciences, Professions, Trades, Agricultural & Mechanical Pursuits. LC 75-156439. (American Labor Ser., No. 2). (Illus.). 1975. reprint ed. 47.95 (*0-405-02937-3*) Ayer.

— Think & Act: A Series of Articles Pertaining to Men & Women, Work & Wages. LC 75-156420. (American Labor Ser., No. 2). 1977. reprint ed. 26.95 (*0-405-02938-1*) Ayer.

Penny, William M., ed. see American Micro Systems Staff.

***Pennybacker, Susan D.** A Vision for London 1889-1914: Labour, Everyday Life & the LCC Experiment. LC 94-41561. 1995. write for info. (*0-415-03588-0*) Routledge.

Pennycook, Alastair. The Cultural Politics of English As an International Language. LC 93-45823. 1994. text ed. write for info. (*0-582-23473-5*, Pub. by Longman UK); pap. write for info. (*0-582-23472-7*, Pub. by Longman UK) Longman.

Pennycook, Joan. Terminal Arrrangements. large type ed. (Dales Mystery Ser.). 255p. 1993. pap. 16.95 (*1-85389-395-1*, Medcom-Trainex) Ulverscroft.

Pennycook, K. A., jt. auth. see Pike, P. G.

Pennycook, K. A., jt. ed. see Pike, P. G.

Pennycuick, C. J. Newton Rules Biology: A Physical Approach to Biological Problems. (Illus.). 160p. 1992. pap. 19.95 (*0-19-854021-3*) OUP.

Pennycuick, Colin J. Conversion Factors: SI Units & Many Others. 48p. 1988. pap. text ed. 7.95 (*0-226-65507-5*) U Ch Pr.

Pennycuick, David & Murphy, Roger. The Impact of Graded Tests. 200p. 1988. 65.00 (*1-85000-277-0*, Falmer Pr); pap. 33.00 (*1-85000-278-9*, Falmer Pr) Taylor & Francis.

Pennypacker, Bert, jt. auth. see Staufer, Alvin F.

Pennypacker, Burt. Pennsylvania M-1. (Classic Power Ser.: No. 8). 120p. 1990. 24.95 (*0-934088-21-7*) NJ Intl Inc.

Pennypacker, Burt, jt. auth. see Staufer, Alvin.

Pennypacker, C. Hands-On Astronomy for Education: Proceedings of the Workshop. 172p. 1992. text ed. 33.00 (*981-02-1135-X*) World Scientific Pub.

Pennypacker, Henry S., jt. auth. see Johnston, James M.

Pennypacker, Isaac R. General Meade. 402p. 1987. reprint ed. 30.00 (*0-942211-19-7*) Olde Soldier Bks.

Pennypacker, Samuel W. Settlement of Germantown, Pennsylvania, & the Beginning of German Emigration to North America. LC 69-13248. (Illus.). 1972. reprint ed. 26.95 (*0-405-08847-7*) Ayer.

Pennypacker, Samuel W., tr. see Dock, Christopher.

Pennypacker, Sara. Dumbstruck. (Illus.). 112p. (J). (gr. 4-7). 1994. 14.95 (*0-8234-1123-0*) Holiday.

Pennypincher, A. & Tightwad, A. Factory Outlet Guide to the Mid-Atlantic States. 3rd ed. 320p. 1993. pap. 8.95 (*1-56440-079-4*) Globe Pequot.

— Outlet Guide: Mid Atlantic States. 4th ed. 320p. 1995. pap. 9.95 (*1-56440-526-5*) Globe Pequot.

Pennypincher, A., pseud., jt. auth. see Miser, A., pseud.

Pennypincher, A., jt. auth. see Miser, A.

Pennypincher, A., pseud., jt. auth. see Miser, A., pseud.

Pennypincher, A., jt. auth. see Tightwad, A.

Pennywell, Sylvia C. The Gift of Hope. (Gift of Hope Ser.). (Illus.). 21p. (J). 1992. pap. 12.00 (*0-9637324-0-4*) Silver Grace Pubs.

— The Gift of Peace. (Gift of Hope Ser.). (Illus.). 21p. (Orig.). (J). 1993. pap. 12.00 (*0-9637324-1-2*) Silver Grace Pubs.

Penoff, R. E., ed. Aircrew Survival. (AF Pam Ser.: No. 64-5). (Illus.). 121p. 1985. spiral bd. 6.50 (*0-16-002209-6*, S/N 008-070-00565-4) USGPO.

***Penolope, George W. & Canan, Pring.** SLAPPS: Getting Sued for Speaking Out. LC 95-13610. 352p. (C). 1995. lib. bdg. 59.95 (*1-56639-368-X*); pap. text ed. 24.95 (*1-56639-369-8*) Temple U Pr.

Penoncello, S. G., ed. Computerized Thermophysical Property Packages. (HTD Ser.: Vol. 225). 44p. 1992. 25.00 (*0-7918-1070-4*, G00714) ASME.

Penot-Demetry, Josee, tr. see Bonnemaison, Joel.

Penot, J. P. New Methods in Optimization & Their Industrial Uses. (International Series of Numerical Mathematics: No. 87). 240p. 1989. 77.00 (*0-8176-2286-1*) Birkhauser.

Penovich, Beatrice A., ed. see Witter, Evelyn, et al.

Penoyar, William F. Fedspeak: U. S. Contracting & Grantsmanship Made Easier. 174p. (Orig.). 1985. pap. 12.95 (*0-9615112-2-2*) G T M Co.

Penrice, J. A Dictionary & Glossary of the Koran, with Copious Grammatical References & Explanations of the Text. 176p. 1978. text ed. 26.00 (*0-685-14040-7*) Coronet Bks.

Penrice, James. Crossing Home: The Spiritual Lessons of Baseball. LC 93-4222. 118p. (Orig.). 1993. pap. 5.95 (*0-8189-0675-8*) Alba.

— Goal to Go: The Spiritual Lessons of Football. LC 94-17292. 1994. pap. 5.95 (*0-8189-0702-9*) Alba.

— If There Is a God Why Do I Need Braces? Approach to Adult Faith. (Orig.). (YA). (gr. 8-12). 1996. pap. write for info. (*0-8189-0735-5*) Alba.

Penrice, John. A Dictionary & Glossary of Koran. 167p. 1978. 29.95 (*0-318-37174-X*) Asia Bk Corp.

— Dictionary & Glossary of the Holy Quran. rev. ed. 24.95 (*0-934905-09-6*) Kazi Pubns.

— Dictionary & Glossary of the Koran. (ARA & ENG.). 1968. 20.00 (*0-86685-088-0*) Intl Bk Ctr.

— A Dictionary & Glossary of the Koran. 166p. (ARA & ENG.). 1987. 49.95 (*0-8288-1201-2*, M9962) Fr & Eur.

— A Dictionary & Glossary of the Koran. 180p. (C). 1985. text ed. 39.95 (*0-7007-0001-3*, Pub. by Curzon Pr UK) Humanities.

— A Dictionary & Glossary of the Koran. 1990. reprint ed. 10.00 (*81-85395-89-6*, Pub. by Low Price II) S Asia.

— Dictionary & Glossary of the Koran, with Copious Grammatical References & Explanations. LC 70-90039. (ARA.). 1969. reprint ed. 25.00 (*0-8196-0252-3*) Biblo.

— A Dictionary & Glossary of the Koran with Grammatical References & Explanations. 1980. lib. bdg. 55.00 (*0-8490-3123-0*) Gordon Pr.

Penrioe, John. A Dictionary & Glossary of the Koran. 172p. (Orig.). (C). text ed. 27.50 (*81-85006-16-4*, Pub. by Sterling Pubs II) Apt Bks.

***Penrod.** Helene Cixious. 1994. 26.95 (*0-8057-8284-2*, Twayne) Macmillan.

Penrod, Glen A. Touchy Situations: An Advanced Conversation Text for ESL Students. rev. ed. (Illus.). 160p. (C). 1993. pap. text ed. 16.75 (*0-9637742-0-4*) Dymon Pubns.

Penrod, James & Plastino, Janice G. The Dancer Prepares: Modern Dance for Beginners. 3rd ed. 94p. (C). 1990. pap. text ed. 11.95 (*0-87484-924-1*) Mayfield Pub.

Penrod, James T., jt. auth. see Chaffee, Clarence L.

Penrod, Joan D., jt. auth. see Kane, Rosalie A.

Penrod, John S. Copper Country. (Orig.). 1990. pap. 4.49 (*0-942618-23-8*) Penrod-Hiawatha.

— Indiana, a Pictorial Guide. rev. ed. (YA). (gr. 9 up). 1990. pap. 4.49 (*0-942618-21-1*) Penrod-Hiawatha.

— Michigan, a Pictorial Guide. 1986. pap. 4.49 (*0-942618-03-3*) Penrod-Hiawatha.

— Michigan Lighthouses Book. 1992. pap. 4.49 (*0-942618-36-X*) Penrod-Hiawatha.

— Michigan State University. rev. ed. 1987. pap. 4.49 (*0-942618-10-6*) Penrod-Hiawatha.

— Michigan's Land & Song of Hiawatha. 1986. pap. 4.49 (*0-942618-05-X*) Penrod-Hiawatha.

— Pictured Rocks Cruises. 1988. pap. 4.49 (*0-942618-14-9*) Penrod-Hiawatha.

— Straits of Mackinac & Mackinac Island. rev. ed. (YA). (gr. 7 up). 1989. pap. 4.49 (*0-942618-20-3*) Penrod-Hiawatha.

— Tahquamenon in Michigan's Upper Peninsula. (YA). (gr. 7 up). 1988. pap. 4.49 (*0-942618-12-2*) Penrod-Hiawatha.

— Traverse Region Book. 1992. pap. 4.49 (*0-942618-37-8*) Penrod-Hiawatha.

— The Upper Peninsula of Michigan. rev. ed. (YA). (gr. 7 up). 1988. pap. 4.49 (*0-942618-11-4*) Penrod-Hiawatha.

***Penrod, Lorene.** A Gift from Vietnam. 1995. 9.95 (*0-8062-5141-7*) Carlton.

***Penrod, Paul.** Developing Windows Applications Using Borland's Delphi. Date not set. pap. text ed. 29.95 (*0-471-11017-5*) Wiley.

***Penrod, Samantha.** WordPerfect Version 6 for Windows: The Step-by-Step Approach. 1994. pap. 25.95 (*1-56529-403-3*) Que.

Penrod, Sigrid, tr. see Imhauser, Hedwig.

Penrod, Steven D., jt. auth. see Cutler, Brian L.

Penrose. A Guide to One Hundred Ninety-Nine Michigan Waterfalls. (Illus.). 200p. (Orig.). 1988. pap. 12.95 (*0-9608588-7-3*) Friede Pubns.

— A Traveler's Guide to One Hundred Sixteen Michigan Lighthouses. (Illus.). 128p. 1992. pap. 14.95 (*0-923756-03-5*) Friede Pubns.

Penrose, A. H., jt. auth. see Hough, M. P.

Penrose, Ann M. & Sitko, Barbara M., eds. Hearing Ourselves Think: Cognitive Research in the College Writing Classroom. LC 92-23469. (Social & Cognitive Studies in Writing & Literacy). 232p. 1993. 39.95 (*0-19-507833-0*) OUP.

Penrose, Antony. The Lives of Lee Miller. LC 88-51525. (Illus.). 216p. 1989. pap. 24.95 (*0-500-27509-2*) Thames Hudson.

Penrose, B. Tudor & Early Stuart Voyaging. LC 79-65985. (Folger Guides to the Age of Shakespeare Ser.). 1979. pap. 4.95 (*0-918016-12-6*) Folger Bks.

Penrose, Barrie & Freeman, Simon. Conspiracy of Silence: The Secret Life of Anthony Blunt. 1988. pap. 10.95 (*0-679-72044-8*, Vin) Random.

Penrose, Boies, jt. auth. see Allinson, Edward P.

Penrose, Dina. Occupational Therapy for Orthopaedic Conditions. LC 92-49578. (Therapy in Practice Ser.: Vol. 36). 1992. write for info. (*1-56593-044-4*) Singular Publishing.

Penrose, Edith T. Growth of Firms, Middle East Oil & Other Essays. 336p. 1971. 37.50 (*0-7146-2772-0*, Pub. by F Cass Pubs UK) Intl Spec Bk.

— The Large International Firm in Developing Countries. LC 76-7581. (Illus.). 311p. 1976. reprint ed. text ed. 59.75 (*0-8371-8850-4*, PELI, Greenwood Pr) Greenwood.

— The Theory of the Growth of the Firm. 300p. 1995. 59.00 (*0-19-828978-2*); pap. 19.95 (*0-19-828977-4*) OUP.

— The Theory of the Growth of the Firm. LC 79-91109. 304p. reprint ed. 86.70 (*0-685-16342-3*, 2027623) Bks Demand.

Penrose, Ernest F. European Imperialism & the Partition of Africa. 180p. 1975. 35.00 (*0-7146-3058-6*, Pub. by F Cass Pubs UK) Intl Spec Bk.

Penrose Family. Traveler's Guide to One Hundred Eastern Great Lakes Lighthouses: American & Canadian Lighthouses of the Eastern Great Lakes. (Illus.). 136p. (Orig.). 1994. pap. 14.95 (*0-923756-09-4*) Friede Pubns.

— A Travelers Guide to 116 Western Great Lakes Lighthouses. (Illus.). 176p. (Orig.). 1995. pap. 14.95 (*0-923756-12-4*) Friede Pubns.

Penrose, Gordon. Dr. Zed's Dazzling Book of Science Activities. (Illus.). 48p. (J). 1993. pap. 7.95 (*0-919872-78-6*, Pub. by Greey dePencier CN) Firefly Bks Ltd.

— Dr. Zed's Science Surprises. (J). 1990. pap. 6.95 (*0-671-70541-5*) PB.

— Magic Mud & Other Great Experiments. (Illus.). 48p. (J). 1994. pap. 9.95 (*0-920775-18-7*, Pub. by Greey dePencier CN) Firefly Bks Ltd.

— More Science Surprises from Dr. Zed. LC 91-38935. (Illus.). 32p. (J). (gr. k-3). 1992. pap. 12.00 (*0-671-77810-2*, S&S Bks Young Read); pap. 6.00 (*0-671-77811-0*, S&S Bks Young Read) S&S Childrens.

— Sensational Science Activities with Dr. Zed. LC 90-9724. (Illus.). 48p. (J). (gr. 3-7). 1990. pap. 5.95 (*0-671-72553-X*, S&S Bks Young Read) S&S Childrens.

Penrose, Harald. An Ancient Air: A Biography of John Stringfellow of Chard. LC 88-60696. (Illus.). 176p. 1988. 35.00 (*0-87474-752-X*) Smithsonian.

— No Echo in the Sky. LC 78-169433. (Literature & History of Aviation Ser.). 1979. reprint ed. 35.95 (*0-405-03776-7*) Ayer.

Penrose, Hubert, ed. see Penrose, John.

Penrose, Jan, jt. ed. see Jackson, Peter.

Penrose, John. Letters from Bath, 1766-1767. Mitchell, Brigitte & Penrose, Hubert, eds. (Illus.). 234p. 1993. pap. text ed. 14.00 (*0-86299-112-9*) A Sutton Pub.

Penrose, John, ed. see Huseman, Richard C. & Lahiff, James M.

Penrose, John M., Jr., et al. Advanced Business Communication. 2nd ed. LC 92-28661. 430p. 1993. text ed. 58.95 (*0-534-93259-2*) Intl Thomson.

***Penrose, Mary.** Roots, Deep & Strong: Great Men & Women of the Church. LC 94-39477. 224p. (Orig.). (C). 1995. pap. 12.95 (*0-8091-3538-8*) Paulist Pr.

Penrose, Maryly B. Compendium of Early Mohawk Valley Families, 2 vols., Set. 1173p. 1990. 75.00 (*0-685-54336-6*, 4558) Genealog Pub.

Penrose, O. Foundations of Statistical Mechanics: A Deductive Treatment. LC 70-89513. (International Series in Natural Philosophy: Vol. 22). (Illus.). 1970. 104.00 (*0-08-013314-2*, Pub. by Pergamon Repr UK) Franklin.

Penrose, R. & Isham, C. J., eds. Quantum Concepts in Space & Time. (Illus.). 320p. 1986. 80.00 (*0-19-851972-9*) OUP.

Penrose, Roger. The Emperor's New Mind: Concerning Computers, Minds, & the Laws of Physics. (Illus.). 480p. 1989. 30.00 (*0-19-851973-7*) OUP.

— The Emperor's New Mind: Concerning Computers, Minds, & the Laws of Physics. (Illus.). 480p. 1991. pap. 15.95 (*0-14-014534-6*) Viking Penguin.

— The Emperor's New Mind: Concerning Computers, Minds, & the Laws of Physics. 1999. pap. write for info. (*0-14-770103-1*, Penguin Bks) Viking Penguin.

— Shadows of the Mind: On Consciousness, Computation, & the New Physics of the Mind. (Illus.). 320p. 1994. 25.00 (*0-19-853978-9*) OUP.

— Techniques of Differential Topology in Relativity. (CBMS-NSF Regional Conference Ser.: No. 7). viii, 72p. (Orig.). 1972. reprint ed. pap. text ed. 14.50 (*0-89871-005-7*) Soc Indus-Appl Math.

Penrose, Roger & Rindler, Wolfgang. Spinors & Space-Time, Vol. 1: Two-Spinor Calculus & Relativistic Fields. (Monographs on Mathematical Physics). 450p. 1987. pap. 49.95 (*0-521-33707-0*) Cambridge U Pr.

— Spinors & Space-Time, Vol. 2: Spinor & Twistor Methods in Space-Time Geometry. (Monographs on Mathematical Physics). (Illus.). 500p. 1986. 125.00 (*0-521-25267-9*) Cambridge U Pr.

— Spinors & Space-Time, Vol. 2: Spinor & Twistor Methods in Space-Time Geometry. (Monographs on Mathematical Physics). (Illus.). 512p. 1988. pap. 49.95 (*0-521-34786-6*) Cambridge U Pr.

***Penrose, Roland.** Antoni Tapies. (Grandes Monografias). (Illus.). 280p. (SPA.). 1993. 75.00 (*84-343-0257-8*) Elliots Bks.

— Man Ray. LC 88-51348. (Illus.). 208p. 1989. reprint ed. pap. 15.95 (*0-500-27055-4*) Thames Hudson.

— Miro. LC 85-50751. (World of Art Ser.). (Illus.). 1985. pap. 12.95 (*0-500-20099-8*) Thames Hudson.

— Picasso. (Color Library Ser.). (Illus.). 128p. (C). 1994. reprint ed. pap. 14.95 (*0-7148-2708-8*, Pub. by Phaidon Press UK) Chronicle Bks.

— Picasso. (Color Library). (Illus.). 128p. (C). 1994. reprint ed. 19.95 (*0-7148-3227-8*, Pub. by Phaidon Press UK) Chronicle Bks.

— Picasso: His Life & Work. 3rd ed. (Illus.). 550p. 1981. pap. 14.00 (*0-520-04207-7*) U CA Pr.

Penrose, Roland & Goldberg, John, eds. Pablo Picasso Eighteen Eighty-One to Nineteen Seventy-Three. (Illus.). 284p. 1988. 22.99 (*0-517-66846-7*) Random Hse Value.

Penrose, Roland, jt. ed. see Mesens, E. L.

Penrose, Stephen B., Jr. That They May Have Life: The Story of the American University of Beirut, 1866-1941. 1970. 17.95 (*0-8156-6000-6*, Am U Beirut) Syracuse U Pr.

Penruddocke, A. Conversational English for Chinese Speakers: Learn Idiomatic English at Home or on the Go. 1994. 25.00 (*0-517-59854-X*, Living Language) Crown Pub Group.

— Conversational English for Japanese Speakers: Learn Idiomatic English at Home or on the Go. 1994. 25.00 (*0-517-59832-9*, Living Language) Crown Pub Group.

— Conversational English for Korean Speakers: Learn Idiomatic English at Home or on the Go. 1994. 25.00 (*0-517-59853-1*, Living Language) Crown Pub Group.

— Conversational English for Russian Speakers: Learn Idiomatic English at Home or on the Go. 1994. 25.00 (*0-517-59855-8*, Living Language) Crown Pub Group.

***Penry, Huw.** Bird Atlas of Botswana. (Illus.). 320p. Date not set. 55.75 (*0-86980-894-X*, Pub. by Univ Natal Pr SA); pap. 45.15 (*0-86980-895-8*, Pub. by Univ Natal Pr SA) Intl Spec Bk.

Penry, J. Kiffin, ed. Epilepsy: Diagnosis, Management, Quality of Life. 64p. 1994. pap. text ed. 9.50 (*0-88167-192-4*) Raven.

Penry, J. Kiffin, ed. see International Symposium on Epilepsy Staff.

Penry, J. Kiffin, jt. auth. see Levy, Rene H.

Penry, J. Kiffin, jt. auth. see Newmark, Michael E.

Penry, John. Three Treatises Concerning Wales. xxix, 168p. 1960. 12.50 (*0-7083-0062-6*, Pub. by U of Wales UK) Bks Intl VA.

***Pensack, Myles L. & Gulya, A. Julianna.** Otology & Neurotology: Audiology. Thornton, Aaron R., ed. (Current Opinion in Otolaryngology & Head & Neck Surgery Ser.). (Illus.). 454p. 1994. pap. text ed. 34.95 (*1-85922-634-5*) Current Science.

Pensack, Robert J. & William, Dwight A. Raising Lazarus. LC 94-19010. 304p. 1994. 22.95 (*0-399-14001-8*, Putnam) Putnam Pub Group.

Pensacola Junior Woman's Club Staff. Fiesta. LC 87-62721. (Illus.). 302p. 1987. 12.95 (*0-9619266-0-0*) Pensacola Jr Womans Club.

Pensaert, M. B. & Horzink, M. C., eds. Virus Infections of Porcines. (Virus Infections of Vertebrates Ser.: No. 2). 280p. 1989. 142.00 (*0-318-42731-1*) Elsevier.

Pensak, Myles L. & Nadol, Joseph B., Jr. Otology, Neuro-Otology, & Skull Base Surgery. (Current Opinion in Otolaryngology & Head & Neck Surgery Ser.). (Illus.). 88p. (Orig.). 1993. pap. text ed. 39.95 (*1-85922-042-8*) Current Science.

Pensare, C. Rape of Nations: A Study in Societal Economics. LC 73-88364. (C). 1969. 18.50 (*0-912010-01-0*); spiral bd. 14.50 (*0-912010-00-2*) Goss.

Pense, Beverly. Genealogy & History of the Pense & Allied Families. LC 87-71628. (Illus.). 219p. (C). 1987. 25.00 (*0-938041-00-2*) Arc Pr AR.

***Pensee Editors.** Velikovsky Reconsidered. LC 74-33637. 1994. reprint ed. lib. bdg. 27.95x (*1-56849-530-7*) Buccaneer Bks.

***Penshansky, David.** The Politics of Biblical Theology: A Postmodern Reading. LC 95-5759. (Studies in American Biblical Hermeneutics: Vol. 10). 1995. write for info. (*0-86554-462-X*) Mercer Univ Pr.

Pensinger, Glen, ed. Digital Video Background & Implementation 4: 2: 2. 160p. 1989. pap. 35.00 (*0-940690-16-0*) Soc Motion Pic & TV Engrs.

Pensky, Max. Melancholy Dialectics: Walter Benjamin & the Play of Mourning. LC 92-42229. 296p. 1993. lib. bdg. 32.50x (*0-87023-853-1*) U of Mass Pr.

Pensky, Max, tr. The Past as Future. LC 93-32385. (Modern German Culture & Literature Ser.). 221p. 1994. text ed. 35.00 (*0-8032-2371-4*); pap. 12.50 (*0-8032-7266-9*) U of Nebr Pr.

Penslar, Derek J. Anti-Semitism: The Jewish Response. Siegel, Adam, ed. (Illus.). 62p. (Orig.). 1989. pap. text ed. 4.95 (*0-87441-494-6*) Behrman.

— Zionism & Technocracy: The Engineering of Jewish Settlement in Palestine, 1870-1918. LC 90-25043. (Modern Jewish Experience Ser.). (Illus.). 224p. 1991. 25.00 (*0-253-34290-2*) Ind U Pr.

Penslar, Derek J. & Gersh, Harry. Talmud: Law & Commentary. 64p. (YA). (gr. 9 up). 1986. By Derek J. Penslar. teacher ed 9.95 (*0-87441-435-0*) Behrman.

Penslar, Robin L., ed. Research Ethics: Cases & Materials. LC 94-5971. 1995. 29.95 (*0-253-34312-7*); pap. 12.95 (*0-253-20906-4*) Ind U Pr.

Pensly, Burry, jt. auth. see Golbchick, Leonard.

Penso, Dorothy E. Keyboard, Graphic & Handwriting Skills: Helping People with Motor Disabilities. Campling, Jo, ed. (Therapy in Practice Ser.: No. 15). 160p. 1990. pap. 23.00 (*0-412-32210-2*, A4415) Chapman & Hall.

— Perceptuo-Motor Difficulties: Theory & Strategies to Help Children, Adolescents, & Adults. LC 92-49040. (Therapy in Practice Ser.: Vol. 34). 1992. write for info. (*1-56593-025-8*) Singular Publishing.

***Penson, Jenny & Fisher, Ronald A.** Palliative Care for People with Cancer. 2nd ed. 336p. 1995. pap. text ed. 38.25 (*1-56593-598-5*, 1224) Singular Publishing.

Penson, John B., Jr., et al. Introduction to Agricultural Economics. (Illus.). 496p. (C). 1986. text ed. 51.00 (*0-13-477712-3*) P-H.

Penson, L. M., jt. auth. see Temperley, H. W.

Penson, Lilliam M. Colonial Agents of the British West Indies: A Study in Colonial Administration, Mainly in the Eighteenth Century. 128p. 1971. reprint ed. 37.50 (*0-7146-1944-2*, Pub. by F Cass Pubs UK) Intl Spec Bk.

Penson, Lillian M., jt. auth. see Temperley, H. W.

Penson, Mary. You're an Orphan, Mollie Brown. LC 92-23407. (Illus.). 122p. (J). (gr. 5-8). 1993. pap. 9.95 (*0-87565-111-9*) Tex Christian.

Penson-Ward, Betty. Idaho Women in History, Vol. 1: Big & Little Biographies & Other Gender Stories. Wallace, Eunice & Miller, Beverly, eds. LC 90-63710. (Illus.). 240p. (Orig.). 1990. pap. 18.95 (*0-9625040-2-5*) Legendary Pub.

Pentagram Partners Staff. Pentagram: The Compendium: The Pentagram Partners. (Illus.). 304p. (C). 1993. pap. text ed. 60.00 (*0-7148-2812-2*, Pub. by Phaidon Press UK) Chronicle Bks.

Pentagram Partnership Staff. Ideas on Design. (Illus.). 160p. 1987. 45.00 (*0-571-14585-X*) Faber & Faber.

Pentagram Staff. More Puzzlegrams. 1994. pap. 18.00 (*0-671-51059-2*, Fireside) S&S Trade.

Pentagram Staff, comp. Puzzlegrams: A Colorful Challenging Collection of 178 Classic Puzzles. 1989. pap. 18.00 (*0-671-68740-9*, Fireside) S&S Trade.

***Pentagram Staff, des.** Northlands, New Art from Scandinavias. 80p. 1990. 48.00 (*0-905836-68-5*, Pub. by Museum Modern Art UK) St Mut.

— Pentamagic: An Eye-Opening Collection of Optical Illusions & Visual Magic. LC 92-15505. 1993. pap. 16.99 (*0-671-79185-0*, Fireside) S&S Trade.

Pentar, Michael P. Building a Happy Marriage. LC 86-6349. 1988. pap. 2.95 (*0-8198-1114-9*) Pauline Bks.

Pentecost, Allan. Introduction to Freshwater Algae. (Illus.). 247p. (Orig.). (C). 1984. pap. 19.50x (*0-916422-49-6*) Mad River.

Pentecost, Don. Put 'Em down, Take 'Em Out: Knife Fighting Techniques from Folsom Prison. (Illus.). 64p. 1988. pap. 8.00 (*0-87364-484-0*) Paladin Pr.

Pentecost, Dwight. Profecias Para el Mundo Moderno (Prophecy for Today) (SPA.). 1990. 4.99 (*0-945792-86-7*, 497703) Editorial Unilit.

Pentecost, Dwight J. A Harmony of the Words & Works of Jesus Christ. 272p. 1981. 14.99 (*0-310-30951-4*, 17016P) Zondervan.

— Parables of Jesus. 1987. pap. 12.99 (*0-310-30961-1*) Zondervan.

Pentecost, E. J. A Model of UK Non-Oil ICCs' Direct Investment. (Bank of England. Discussion Papers: No. 30). 58p. reprint ed. pap. 25.00 (*0-7837-5374-8*, 2045138) Bks Demand.

Pentecost, Elizabeth, jt. ed. see Jernigan, Camille M.

Pentecost, Eric J. Exchange Rate Dynamics: A Modern Analysis of Exchange Rate Theory & Evidence. LC 92-28723. 256p. 1992. 69.95 (*1-85278-138-6*, Pub. by E Elgar Pub UK) Ashgate Pub Co.

— Exchange Rate Dynamics: A Modern Analysis of Exchange Rate Theory & Evidence. 1994. pap. 27.95 (*1-85278-903-4*, Pub. by E Elgar Pub UK) Ashgate Pub Co.

Pentecost, Hugh. The Cannibal Who Overate. 191p. 1990. pap. 3.95 (*0-88184-614-7*) Carroll & Graf.

— Kill & Kill Again. large type ed. (Mystery Ser.). 1990. 21.95 (*0-7089-2243-0*) Ulverscroft.

— Murder in Luxury. 224p. 1991. mass mkt. 3.50 (*0-373-26069-5*) Harlequin Bks.

— Nightmare Time. (Worldwide Mystery Ser.). 1988. pap. 3.50 (*0-317-70123-1*) S&S Trade.

— Nightmare Time. large type ed. (Linford Mystery Library). 304p. 1988. pap. 11.95 (*0-7089-6563-6*, Linford) Ulverscroft.

— Pattern for Terror. large type ed. LC 92-30149. (Nightingale Ser.). 208p. 1993. pap. 14.95 (*0-8161-5637-9*, Nightingale) Hall.

Pentecost, J. Dwight. Designed to Be Like Him: New Testament Insight for Becoming Christlike. 1994. pap. 10.99 (*0-929239-88-1*) Discovery Hse Pubs.

— A Faith That Endures: The Book of Hebrews Applied to the Real Issues of Life. LC 92-26390. 1992. 9.99 (*0-929239-66-0*) Discovery Hse Pubs.

— Marchando Hacia la Madurez Espiritual. 384p. (SPA.). 1979. mass mkt., pap. 7.99 (*0-8254-1554-3*) Kregel.

— El Sermon del Monte. 256p. (SPA.). 1981. mass mkt., pap. 5.99 (*0-8254-1555-1*) Kregel.

— Things to Come. 1965. 24.99 (*0-310-30890-9*, 6355) Zondervan.

— Thy Kingdom Come. 256p. 1995. pap. 12.99 (*0-8254-3450-5*) Kregel.

— The Words & Works of Jesus Christ. 576p. 1981. 24.99 (*0-310-30940-9*, 17015) Zondervan.

— Your Adversary, the Devil. 192p. 1990. pap. 10.99 (*0-310-30911-5*) Zondervan.

Pentenero, P. First Dictionary of Welding. 436p. (ENG & ITA.). 1988. 135.00 (*0-8288-7929-X*) Fr & Eur.

Penthouse Magazine Editors. Erotica from Penthouse III. 224p. (Orig.). 1994. mass mkt. 5.99 (*0-446-60057-1*) Warner Bks.

— Letters to Penthouse V. 224p. (Orig.). 1995. mass mkt. 5.99 (*0-446-60195-0*) Warner Bks.

— Letters to Penthouse VI. 304p. (Orig.). 1996. mass mkt. 5.99 (*0-446-60196-9*) Warner Bks.

— More Erotica from Penthouse. 224p. (Orig.). 1992. mass mkt. 5.99 (*0-446-36297-2*) Warner Bks.

Penthouse Magazine Editors, ed. Letters to Penthouse IV. 224p. (Orig.). 1994. mass mkt. 5.99 (*0-446-60056-3*) Warner Bks.

Penthouse Magazine Staff. More Letters from Penthouse. 224p. (Orig.). 1989. mass mkt. 5.99 (*0-446-34515-6*) Warner Bks.

Penthouse Magazine Staff, ed. Letters to Penthouse III. 240p. (Orig.). 1992. mass mkt. 5.99 (*0-446-36296-4*) Warner Bks.

Penti, Marsha, et al. Women Who Dared: The History of Finnish American Women. Ross, Carl & Brown, K. Marianne, eds. LC 86-80998. (Illus.). xi, 164p. (Orig.). 1986. pap. text ed. 10.00 (*0-932833-05-5*) Immig His Res.

Pentico, David. Management Science: Mathematical Programming & Network Models. (HBJ College Outlines Ser.). 319p. (C). 1992. pap. text ed. 13.50 (*0-15-601646-X*) Dryden Pr.

Pentico, David W., jt. auth. see Morton, Thomas E.

Pentikainen, Juha Y. Kalevala Mythology. Poom, Ritva, ed. & tr. by. LC 88-46031. (Folklore Studies in Translation). 288p. 1990. 25.00 (*0-253-34325-9*) Ind U Pr.

Pentland, Alex, ed. From Pixels to Predicates. LC 85-13413. (Ablex Series in Artificial Intelligence: Vol. 3). 416p. 1986. text ed. 65.00 (*0-89391-237-9*) Ablex Pub.

Pentland Press Ltd. Staff. Lu Gwei-Djen: A Commemoration. (C). 1989. text ed. 59.00 (*1-85821-034-8*, Pub. by Pentland Pr UK) St Mut.

Pentney, jt. auth. see Berlin.

Penton, Carl J., ed. see Gluck, Jay & Gluck, Sumi H.

Penton, M. James. Apocalypse Delayed: The Story of Jehovah's Witnesses. (Illus.). 432p. 1988. pap. 19.95 (*0-8020-6721-2*) U of Toronto Pr.

— Apocalypse Delayed: The Story of Jehovah's Witnesses. LC 85-244517. (Illus.). 428p. reprint ed. pap. 122.00 (*0-8357-4733-6*, 2037650) Bks Demand.

***Pentony, B.** Commercial Transactions: Cases & Materials. 700p. 1991. pap. 90.00 (*0-409-30814-5*, Austral) Butterworth Legal Pubs.

Pentre, Barbara, jt. auth. see Weisert, Hilde.

Pentreath, R. J. Nuclear Power, Man & the Environment. (Wykeham Science Ser.: No. 51). 268p. 1977. pap. 18.00 (*0-85109-840-1*) Taylor & Francis.

— Nuclear Power, Man & the Environment. LC 80-20173. (Wykeham Science Ser.: No. 51). 250p. (C). 1981. pap. 18.00 (*0-8448-1381-8*, Crane Russak) Taylor & Francis.

Penttila, Risto E. Finland's Search for Security Through Defence, 1944-89. LC 90-34613. 208p. 1991. text ed. 65.00 (*0-312-04895-5*) St Martin.

Penttonen, Martti, jt. ed. see Farinas del Cerro, Luis.

Pentz, Croft M. The Complete Book of Zingers. 1990. pap. 9.99 (*0-8423-0467-3*) Tyndale.

— Expository Outlines on Hebrews. (Sermon Outline Ser.). 1979. pap. 2.99 (*0-8010-7045-7*) Baker Bk.

— Ministry to the Deaf. 2nd ed. 88p. (C). 1984. pap. 4.95 (*0-912981-11-3*) Hse BonGiovanni.

— Outlines on Bible Characters. 1989. pap. 6.99 (*0-8010-7108-9*) Baker Bk.

Pentz, Croft M. Outlines on Revelation. (Sermon Outline Ser.). 1978. pap. 2.99 (*0-8010-7030-9*) Baker Bk.

— Outlines on the Holy Spirit. (Sermon Outline Ser.). 1978. pap. 2.99 (*0-8010-7029-5*) Baker Bk.

Pentz, Croft M. Outlines on the Parables of Jesus. (Sermon Outline Ser.). (Orig.). 1980. pap. 2.99 (*0-8010-7055-4*) Baker Bk.

— Sermon Outlines for Special Days. (Sermon Outline Ser.). 1979. pap. 2.99 (*0-8010-7046-5*) Baker Bk.

— Sermon Outlines from Acts. (Sermon Outline Ser.). 1978. pap. 2.99 (*0-8010-7039-2*) Baker Bk.

Pentz, Lundy. The Biolab Book. LC 82-49066. (Illus.). 144p. reprint ed. pap. 41.10 (*0-8357-6040-5*, 2034145) Bks Demand.

Pentz, Mike & Shott, Milo. Handling Experimental Data. Aprahamian, Francis, ed. 96p. 1988. 66.00 (*0-335-15897-8*, Open Univ Pr); pap. 20.00 (*0-335-15824-2*, Open Univ Pr) Taylor & Francis.

Pentz, Peter. The Invisible Conquest: The Ontogenesis of 6th & 7th Century Syria. (Illus.). 96p. (Orig.). 1992. pap. 26.50 (*87-7288-504-1*, Pub. by Aarhus Univ Pr DK) Coronet Bks.

Penuel, Arnold. Intertextuality in Garcia Marquez. LC 93-84976. 80p. (C). 1994. 24.00 (*0-938972-20-0*) Spanish Lit Pubns.

Penuelas, Marcelino C. Jacinto Benavente. LC 68-9515. (Twayne's World Authors Ser.). 1968. lib. bdg. 17.95 (*0-8057-2136-3*) Irvington.

Penvenne. African Workers & Colonial Racism: Mozambican Strategies for Survival in Lourenco Marques, 1877-1962. LC 94-10574. 1994. 50.00 (*0-435-08952-8*); pap. 22.95 (*0-435-08954-4*) Heinemann.

Penwarden, Charles. Little Gregory. 288p. 1991. 23.95 (*1-872180-31-0*, Pub. by Fourth Estate UK) Trafalgar.

Penway, Anne. Confidentiality in Libraries: An Intellectual Freedom Modular Education Program. LC 92-38348. 140p. 1993. 12.50 (*0-8389-3425-0*); 12.50 (*0-8389-3422-6*); 12.50 (*0-8389-3423-4*); 12.50 (*0-8389-3424-2*); 12.50 (*0-8389-3421-8*); teacher ed. pap. text ed. 99.00 (*0-8389-3420-X*) ALA.

Penwell, Dan, ed. World's Compact Bible Dictionary & Concordance, Slim. 1990. pap. 4.99 (*0-529-06936-9*) World Bible.

Penwell, Ellen S. & Kulles, George N. The Morton D. Barker Paperweight Collection. (Handbook of Collections: No. 5). (Illus.). 72p. pap. 15.00 (*0-89792-106-2*) Ill St Museum.

Penwill, Roger. Cartoon Aided Design: The Lighter Side of Computing. 100p. 1993. pap. 14.95 (*0-9639305-0-8*) A-E-C Systs.

Penycate, John, jt. auth. see Mangold, Tom.

***Penz, Alton.** Finding Hidden Profits in Occupancy Analysis. 56p. (Orig.). Date not set. pap. text ed. 55.00 (*0-943130-11-5*) Build Own & Man.

Penz, G. Peter. Consumer Sovereignty & Human Interests. (Illus.). 275p. 1986. 54.95 (*0-521-26571-1*) Cambridge U Pr.

Penza, John & Corsi, Tony. Sicilian American Pasta. 1994. pap. 16.95 (*0-685-72948-6*) Ten Speed Pr.

Penzall, Beverly J., et al. Spices, Rices, & Other Vices: A Cookbook from Miami & the Beach. LC 92-46083. 1993. 24.95 (*0-942637-91-7*) Barricade Bks.

Penzato, Sadie. Growing up Sicilian & Female: "In America, in a Small Town, in the 30s" (Illus.). 336p. (Orig.). 1991. pap. 14.95 (*0-9632331-0-6*) Penzato Ent.

Penzel, Klaus, ed. Philip Schaff: Historian & Ambassador of the Universal Church. LC 90-43814. lxviii, 391p. (C). 1991. 29.95 (*0-86554-376-3*, MUP/H308) Mercer Univ Pr.

Penzer, N. M., ed. see Basile, Giovanni B.

Penzer, Norman M. The Harem. LC 77-180304. (Illus.). reprint ed. 49.50 (*0-404-56316-3*) AMS Pr.

— Poisen-Damsels & Other Essays in Folklore & Anthropology. Dorson, Richard M., ed. LC 80-669. (Folklore of the World Ser.). 1981. reprint ed. lib. bdg. 34.95 (*0-405-13336-7*) Ayer.

Penzer, William N. Getting Back up from an Emotional Down. Gross, Myra, ed. (Illus.). 256p. (Orig.). 1989. pap. 11.95 (*0-9622658-0-2*) Esperance Pub.

Penzer, William N. & Goodman, Bonnie. You Have Choices: Recovering from Anxiety, Panic & Phobia. Gross, Myra, ed. Orig. Title: Overcoming Anxiety, Panic, Phobias Through a Support Group. (Illus.). 256p. (Orig.). 1991. pap. 11.95 (*0-9622658-1-0*) Esperance Pub.

Penzes, Bethen & Tolg, Istvan. Goldfish & Ornamental Carp. 1985. 21.95 (*0-8120-5634-5*) Barron.

Penzi, James. Scenes in Black & White. (Chapbook Ser.). (Illus.). 32p. (Orig.). 1982. pap. 3.00 (*0-936556-06-4*) Contact Two.

***Penzias, Arno.** Harmony: Business, Technology & Life after Paperwork. 320p. 1995. 23.00 (*0-88730-724-8*) Harper Busn.

— Ideas & Information: Managing in a High-Tech World. 1989. 17.95 (*0-393-02649-3*) Norton.

Penzias, Arno A. Computer-Enhanced Human Beings. (Grace A. Tanner Lecture in Human Values Ser.). 1987. 10.00 (*0-910153-04-3*) E T Woolf.

Penzien, Joseph, jt. auth. see Clough, Ray W.

Penzler, Otto. Danger! White Water. LC 75-21844. (Illus.). 32p. (J). (gr. 5-10). 1976. lib. bdg. 10.79 (*0-89375-004-2*) Troll Assocs.

— Hang Gliding: Riding the Wind. LC 75-21843. (Illus.). 32p. (J). (gr. 5-10). 1976. lib. bdg. 10.79 (*0-89375-008-5*); pap. 2.95 (*0-89375-024-7*) Troll Assocs.

— Hunting the Killer Shark. LC 75-23409. (Illus.). 32p. (J). (gr. 5-10). 1976. lib. bdg. 10.79 (*0-89375-009-3*); pap. 2.95 (*0-89375-025-5*) Troll Assocs.

Penzler, Otto, ed. The Great Detectives. LC 77-25487. 281p. 1978. 18.95 (*0-316-69883-0*) Boulevard.

Penzlin, Gustav, jt. auth. see Fuhrhop, Juergen.

Penzlin, Gustav, jt. auth. see Fuhrhop, Jurgen-Hinrich.

Penzner, Diana & Forsell, Mary. Everlasting Design: Ideas & Techniques for Dried Flowers. (Illus.). 144p. 1988. pap. 10.95 (*0-395-46728-4*) HM.

Penzo, P. A., et al, eds. Astrodynamics, 1979, Pt. 1. (Advances in the Astronautical Sciences Ser.). (Illus.). 494p. 1980. Part 1, 494pp. lib. bdg. 45.00 (*0-87703-107-X*, Pub. by Am Astro Soc); pap. 35.00 (*0-87703-108-8*, Pub. by Am Astro Soc) Univelt Inc.

— Astrodynamics, 1979, Pt. 2. (Advances in the Astronautical Sciences Ser.). (Illus.). 502p. 1980. Part 2, 502pp. 45.00 (*0-87703-109-6*, Pub. by Am Astro Soc); pap. 35.00 (*0-87703-110-X*, Pub. by Am Astro Soc) Univelt Inc.

— Astrodynamics, 1979, Vol. 40. (Advances in the Astronautical Sciences Ser.). (Illus.). 1980. fiche 20.00 (*0-87703-139-8*, Pub. by Am Astro Soc) Univelt Inc.

Penzo, Paul A., jt. ed. see Rector, William F., III.

People for the Ethical Treatment of Animals Staff. We're All Animals Coloring Book. (Illus.). 16p. (Orig.). (J). (gr. k-5). Date not set. pap. text ed. 3.35 (*0-9622101-0-2*) Peta Pubns.

People for the Ethical Treatment of Animals Staff & Newkirk, Ingrid. The Compassionate Cook: Or Please Don't Eat the Animals! A Vegetarian Cookbook. 256p. (Orig.). 1993. pap. 9.99 (*0-446-39492-0*) Warner Bks.

People Magazine Editors. People: Private Lives. (Annual Ser.). (Illus.). 144p. 1993. write for info. (*1-883013-00-3*) Time Inc.

***People Magazine Staff.** People Entertainment Almanac, 1995. 1994. pap. 12.95 (*0-316-69885-7*) Little.

People of Kent Staff, photos. From Garden to Gateway the Changing Face of Kent. (Illus.). 128p. (C). 1993. 65.00 (*1-874344-00-0*, Pub. by Heathrow Pubns UK) St Mut.

People's Bridge Action Inc. Staff. All My Heroes Are Crazy. 104p. 1992. pap. 9.00 (*1-881467-00-7*) Peoples Bdge Act.

People's Court, Munich Staff & Hitler, Adolph. Hitler Trial: Before the People's Court in Munich, 3 vols., I. Freniere, H. Francis et al, trs. LC 75-24633. 420p. 1976. text ed. 55.00 (*0-313-27111-9*, U7111) Greenwood.

— Hitler Trial: Before the People's Court in Munich, 3 vols., Set. Freniere, H. Francis et al, trs. LC 75-24633. 420p. 1976. text ed. 150.00 (*0-313-27110-0*, U7110) Greenwood.

— Hitler Trial: Before the People's Court in Munich, 3 vols., Vol. 2. Freniere, H. Francis et al, trs. LC 75-24633. 420p. 1976. text ed. 55.00 (*0-313-27112-7*, U7112) Greenwood.

— Hitler Trial: Before the People's Court in Munich, 3 vols., Vol. 3. Freniere, H. Francis et al, trs. LC 75-24633. 420p. 1976. text ed. 55.00 (*0-313-27113-5*, U7113) Greenwood.

Peoples, David A. Presentations Plus: David Peoples' Proven Techniques. 2nd ed. 304p. 1992. text ed. 36.95 (*0-471-55926-1*); pap. text ed. 14.95 (*0-471-55956-3*) Wiley.

— Selling to the Top: David Peoples' Executive Selling Skills. LC 93-526. 256p. 1993. pap. text ed. 16.95 (*0-471-58105-4*) Wiley.

— Selling to the Top: David Peoples' Executive Selling Skills. LC 93-526. 256p. 1993. text ed. 34.95 (*0-471-58104-6*) Wiley.

***Peoples, Edward E.** Juvenile Procedures in California. 240p. (C). 1994. pap. text ed. 19.95 (*0-9641857-0-9*) Meadow Crest.

Peoples, James & Bailey, Garrick. Humanity: An Introduction to Cultural Anthropology. 2nd ed. 473p. (C). 1991. pap. text ed. 42.75 (*0-314-77277-4*) West Pub.

— Humanity: An Introduction to Cultural Anthropology. 3rd ed. Jucha, ed. LC 93-34740. 500p. (C). 1994. pap. text ed. 47.25 (*0-314-02875-7*) West Pub.

People's Medical Publishing House Staff, comp. The Chinese Way to a Long & Healthy Life. (Illus.). 320p. 1991. 4.99 (*0-517-64337-5*) Random Hse Value.

People's Medical Society Staff. Dial 800 for Health. LC 93-27097. 1994. 4.99 (*0-517-10025-8*, Pub. by Wings Bks) Random Hse Value.

— Your Complete Medical Record. 1993. pap. 12.95 (*1-882606-00-0*) Peoples Med Soc.

Peoples Medical Society Staff. Your Heart: Questions You Have, Answers You Need. 1992. pap. 9.95 (*0-9627334-2-3*) Peoples Med Soc.

People's Medical Society Staff, comp. Dial Eight Hundred for Health. LC 92-45044. 1993. pap. 5.95 (*0-9627334-9-0*) Peoples Med Soc.

People's Medical Society Staff & Inlander, Charles B. Consumer's Medical Desk Reference: Information Your Doctor Can't Or Won't Tell You-Everything You Need to Know for the Best in Health Care. 672p. 1995. 24.95 (*0-7868-6056-1*) Hyperion.

Peoples, Morgan D., jt. auth. see Kurtz, Michael L.

Peoples Republic of China Staff. Ten Great Years: Statistics of the Economic & Cultural Achievements of the People's Republic of China. reprint ed. 21.00 (*0-404-56908-0*) AMS Pr.

People's Republic of China, State Statistical Bureau Staff. A Survey of Income & Expenditure of Urban Households in China, 1985. LC 87-36588. 200p. 1988. pap. text ed. 29.95 (*0-86638-105-8*, Eastwest Ctr Pr) UH Pr.

Peoples, William L. Genealogy of the Corrigan Families, Vol. 1. LC 88-62132. (Illus.). 121p. (C). 1988. write for info. (*0-9621801-1-4*) W L Peoples.

— Genealogy of the Peoples Families, Vol. 1: The Irish Genealogy of the Peoples Families. LC 88-63768. (Illus.). 116p. (C). 1988. write for info. (*0-9621801-0-6*) W L Peoples.

Peoria Newspaper Guild Staff. Peoria People. Knight, Bill, ed. (Illus.). 96p. (Orig.). 1988. pap. 5.95 (*0-9621356-0-7*) Peoria Newspaper Guild.

***Pepe.** Yankees. 1995. 39.95 (*0-87833-095-X*) Taylor Pub.

— Yankees: Limited. 1995. 75.00 (*0-87833-096-8*) Taylor Pub.

Pepe, G., jt. ed. see Albrecht, E.

Pepe, John, ed. see Mobley, David F. & Wilson, Steven K.

Pepe, Phil. Wit & Wisdom for Yogi Berra. 1992. mass mkt. 4.99 (*0-312-92837-8*) St Martin.

— The Wit & Wisdom of Yogi Berra. 2nd rev. ed. 150p. 1988. 16.95 (*0-88736-318-0*) Mecklermedia.

Pepe, Phil, jt. auth. see Hurley, Bob, Sr.

Pepe, Philip S. Personal Typing in Twenty-Four Hours: Learn to Type on Your Electric or Manual Typewriter or Personal Computer. 5th rev. ed. 64p. 1984. pap. text ed. 6.95 (*0-07-049306-5*) McGraw.

— Personal Typing Thirty. 5th ed. 64p. 1974. text ed. 15.96 (*0-07-049299-9*) McGraw.

Pepe, Stephen P. & Dunham, Scott H. Avoiding & Defending Wrongful Discharge Claims, 2 vols. LC 87-10345. 1990. 210.00 (*0-685-18521-4*) Clark Boardman Callaghan.

— Avoiding & Defending Wrongful Discharge Claims. suppl. ed. 1990. write for info. (*0-318-62083-9*) Clark Boardman Callaghan.

***Pepels, Werner.** Kleines Lexikon Marketing-Management. 240p. (GER.). 1994. 49.95 (*0-7859-8571-9*, 3928860046) Fr & Eur.

Peper, Erik & Holt, C. F. Creating Wholeness: A Self-Healing Workbook Using Dynamic Relaxation, Images, & Thoughts. (Illus.). 220p. (C). 1993. 35.00 (*0-306-44172-1*, Plenum Pr) Plenum.

Peper, Erik & Williams, Elizabeth A. From the Inside Out: A Self-Teaching & Laboratory Manual for Biofeedback. LC 80-20551. 446p. 1981. spiral bd. 42.50 (*0-306-40535-0*, Plenum Pr) Plenum.

P
Q

An Asterisk (*) at the beginning of an entry indicates that the title is appearing in BIP for the first time.

Peper, Erik, et al, eds. Mind-Body Integration: Essential Readings in Biofeedback. LC 78-27224. (Illus.). 606p. 1979. 59.50 (*0-306-40102-9*, Plenum Pr) Plenum.

Peper, George. Golf Courses of the PGA Tour. LC 94-4099. (Illus.). 1994. write for info. (*0-8109-3380-2*) Abrams.

— Golfwatching: A Viewer's Guide to the World of Golf. LC 94-42152. 1995. write for info. (*0-8109-3385-3*) Abrams.

— Grand Slam Golf: Courses of the Masters, the PGA Championship, the U. S. Open, the British Open. (Illus.). 304p. 1991. 49.50 (*0-8109-3359-4*) Abrams.

Peper, George, ed. Golf in America: The First One Hundred Years. 2nd ed. LC 94-4490. 1994. reprint ed. write for info. (*0-8109-8123-8*, Abradale Pr) Abrams.

Peper, George, jt. auth. see Norman, Greg.

Peperzak, Adriaan. To the Other: An Introduction to the Philosophy of Emmanuel Levinas. LC 91-44845. (History of Philosophy Ser.). 240p. 1992. 30.00 (*1-55753-023-8*); pap. 14.95 (*1-55753-024-6*) Purdue U Pr.

***Peperzak, Adriaan, ed.** Ethics As First Philosophy: The Significance of Emmanuel Levinas for Philosophy, Literature, & Religion. 288p. 1995. 59.95x (*0-415-91142-7*, B4918, Routledge NY) Routledge.

— Ethics As First Philosophy: The Significance of Emmanuel Levinas for Philosophy, Literature, & Religion. 288p. 1995. pap. 18.95 (*0-415-91143-5*, B4922, Routledge NY) Routledge.

Peperzak, Adriaan T. Philosophy & Politics. 1986. pap. text ed. 25.50 (*90-247-3338-3*) Kluwer Ac.

— Philosophy & Politics. 1987. lib. bdg. 69.50 (*90-247-3337-5*) Kluwer Ac.

— System & History in Philosophy: On the Unity of Thought & Time, Text & Explanation, Solitude & Dialogue, Rhetoric & Truth in the Practice of Philosophy & Its History. LC 85-27679. (SUNY Series in Contemporary Continental Philosophy). 172p. (Orig.). 1986. 64.50 (*0-88706-273-3*); pap. 21.95 (*0-88706-275-X*) State U NY Pr.

Pepeu, G., jt. ed. see Hanin, Israel.

Pepeu, G., et al, eds. New Trends in Aging Research. (FIDIA Research Ser.: Vol. 15). viii, 237p. 1989. 54.00 (*0-387-96911-X*) Spr-Verlag.

Pepi, Jerome S. Design Characteristics of Quick Response Sprinklers. 1986. pap. 7.50 (*0-318-22365-1*, TR 86-3) Society Fire Protect.

Pepicello, W. J. & Green, Thomas A. The Language of Riddles: New Perspectives. LC 84-3551. (Illus.). 175p. 1984. 36.50 (*0-8142-0373-6*) Ohio St U Pr.

***Pepin, David & Pepin, Susan.** Oracle Resource Guide, 1994-1995. 1168p. 1994. pap. 30.00 (*0-9643092-3-8*) Visionary Sftware.

Pepin, Jacques. The Art of Cooking, Vol. I. 1993. 35.00 (*0-8446-6718-8*) Peter Smith.

— The Art of Cooking, Vol. II. 1993. 35.00 (*0-8446-6719-6*) Peter Smith.

— Cuisine Economique. 1992. 22.00 (*0-688-11145-9*) Morrow.

— Good Life Cooking: Light Classics from Today's Gourmet. LC 92-27810. Orig. Title: Today's Gourmet II. (Illus.). 192p. (Orig.). 1992. pap. 15.95 (*0-912333-17-0*) KQED.

— Happy Cooking! More Light Classics from "Today's Gourmet" LC 94-29076. (Illus.). 208p. (Orig.). 1994. pap. 16.95 (*0-912333-27-8*) KQED.

— Jacques Pepin: A French Chef Cooks at Home. 1980. 5.95 (*0-686-62874-8*, 25397, Fireside) S&S Trade.

— Jacques Pepin's Simple & Healthy Cooking. LC 94-29177. (Illus.). 1994. write for info. (*0-87596-234-3*) Rodale Pr Inc.

— Jacques Pepin's Table: The Complete Today's Gourmet. (Illus.). 576p. 1995. 35.00 (*0-912333-19-7*) KQED.

— Jacques Pepin's The Art of Cooking, 1. LC 87-4253. 352p. 1992. pap. 30.00 (*0-679-74270-0*) Knopf.

— Jacques Pepin's The Art of Cooking, 2. LC 87-4253. 352p. 1992. pap. 30.00 (*0-679-74271-9*) Knopf.

— The Short-Cut Cook. LC 90-6306. 320p. 1990. 19.95 (*0-688-09448-1*) Morrow.

— La Technique. 1989. pap. 24.00 (*0-671-70711-6*) S&S Trade.

— Today's Gourmet: Light & Healthy Cooking for the 90's. (Illus.). 176p. (Orig.). 1991. pap. 15.95 (*0-912333-08-1*) KQED.

Pepin, Jean. De La Philosophie Ancienne a la Theologie Patristique. (Collected Studies: No. CS233). 348p. (C). 1986. reprint ed. lib. bdg. 99.50 (*0-86078-181-X*, Pub. by Variorum UK) Ashgate Pub Co.

Pepin, Muriel. Brave Little Fox. LC 93-4238. (Little Animal Adventures Ser.). (Illus.). 22p. (J). (ps-3). 1993. 5.98 (*0-89577-541-7*, Readers Digest Kids) RD Assn.

— Little Bear's New Friend. LC 91-40652. (Little Animal Adventures Ser.). (Illus.). 24p. (J). (ps-3). 1992. 6.99 (*0-89577-417-8*, Random) RD Assn.

— Little Puppy Saves the Day. LC 91-46499. (Little Animal Adventures Ser.). (Illus.). 24p. (J). (ps-3). 1993. 6.99 (*0-89577-473-9*) RD Assn.

***Pepin, Pierre-Yves.** American Stories. (Prose Ser.: No. 28). 128p. 1995. 12.00 (*0-920717-96-9*) Guernica Editions.

Pepin, Ronald E., ed. see Bernard of Cluny.

Pepin, Ronald E., tr. see Sergardi, Lodovico.

Pepin, Susan, jt. auth. see Pepin, David.

Pepine, Carl J., ed. Acute Myocardial Infarction. LC 70-6558. (Cardiovascular Clinics Ser.: Vol. 20, No. 1). (Illus.). 329p. (C). 1989. text ed. 75.00 (*0-8036-6858-9*) Davis Co.

Pepine, Carl J., & Associates Staff, et al, eds. Diagnostic & Therapeutic Cardiac Catheterization. 2nd ed. LC 93-14866. 710p. 1994. 95.00 (*0-683-06845-8*) Williams & Wilkins.

Pepinsky, Harold B. People & Information. 1970. 149.00 (*0-08-015624-X*, Pub. by Pergamon Repr UK) Franklin.

Pepinsky, Harold B. & Patton, Michael J. The Psychological Experiment: A Practical Accomplishment. LC 75-134829. 208p. 1971. 86.00 (*0-08-016515-X*, Pub. by Pergamon Repr UK) Franklin.

Pepinsky, Harold E. The Geometry of Violence & Democracy. LC 90-4704. (Illus.). 156p. 1991. 24.95 (*0-253-34343-7*) Ind U Pr.

Pepinsky, Harold E. & Jesilow, Paul. Myths That Cause Crime. 3rd rev. ed. LC 92-18307. 186p. 1992. pap. 12.95 (*0-932020-91-7*) Seven Locks Pr.

Pepinsky, Harold E. & Quinney, Richard, eds. Criminology As Peacemaking. LC 90-42361. (Illus.). 350p. 1991. 39.95 (*0-253-34357-7*); pap. 17.50 (*0-253-20659-6*, MB-659) Ind U Pr.

Pepinsky, Pauline N. Worlds of Common Sense: Equality, Identity & Two Modes of Impulse Management. LC 94-7432. (Contributions in Psychology Ser.: No. 26). 232p. 1994. text ed. 55.00 (*0-313-28991-3*, Greenwood Pr) Greenwood.

***Pepitone, James S.** Future Training: A Roadmap for Restructuring the Training Function. 250p. 1995. pap. 18.50 (*0-9635822-1-6*) AddVantage Lrn.

Pepitone, James S. & Barker, Edwin N. How to Make a Smart Decision - A True Story. 122p. 1992. pap. 7.95 (*0-9635822-0-8*) AddVantage Lrn.

Peplau, Hildegard E. Interpersonal Relations in Nursing: A Conceptual Frame of Reference for Psychodynamic Nursing. LC 91-4846. 360p. 1991. 35.95 (*0-8261-7910-X*) Springer Pub.

Peplau, L. Anne, et al. Readings in Social Psychology. 2nd rev. ed. 384p. (C). 1988. pap. text ed. write for info. (*0-13-761081-5*) P-H.

Peplau, Letitia A. & Perlman, Daniel, eds. Loneliness: A Sourcebook of Current Theory, Research, & Therapy. LC 81-16272. (Wiley Series on Personality Processes). 447p. reprint ed. pap. 127.40 (*0-7837-2807-7*, 2057665) Bks Demand.

Pepler, C. The Basis of the Mysticism of St. Thomas Aquinas. 1977. lib. bdg. 59.95 (*0-8490-1479-4*) Gordon Pr.

Pepler, D. J. & Rubin, K. H., eds. The Play of Children: Current Theory & Research. (Contributions to Human Development Ser.: Vol. 6). (Illus.). x, 158p. 1982. pap. 49.00 (*3-8055-3540-6*) S Karger.

Pepler, Debra & Rubin, Kenneth H., eds. The Development & Treatment of Childhood Aggression. 488p. 1990. 95.00 (*0-8058-0370-X*) L Erlbaum Assocs.

Peploe, Frances. Love Untangled. large type ed. (Linford Romance Library). 1989. pap. 11.95 (*0-7089-6789-2*, Linford) Ulverscroft.

Peplow, Evelyn. Philippines. (Asian Guides Ser.). 316p. 1991. pap. 15.95 (*0-8442-9690-2*, Passport Bks) NTC Pub Grp.

Peplow, Mary. England. LC 89-21786. (World in View Ser.). (Illus.). 96p. (YA). (gr. 6-12). 1990. lib. bdg. 24.26 (*0-8114-2428-6*) Raintree Steck-V.

Peplow, Mary & Shipley, Debra. Ireland. LC 90-32821. (World in View Ser.). (Illus.). 96p. (YA). (gr. 6-12). 1990. lib. bdg. 24.26 (*0-8114-2430-8*) Raintree Steck-V.

Peplow, Mary, jt. ed. see Shipley, Debra.

Pepose, et al. Ocular Infections & Immunity. 850p. 1994. 149.95 (*0-8016-6757-7*) Mosby Yr Bk.

Peppard, Joe, ed. I.T. Strategy for Business. 306p. 1993. pap. 62.50 (*0-273-60024-9*, Pub. by Pitman Pub Ltd UK) Trans-Atl Phila.

Peppard, Joe, jt. ed. see Burke, Gerard.

Peppard, Nancy R. Special Needs Dementia Units: Design, Development & Operations. LC 91-12278. 152p. 1991. 25.95 (*0-8261-5950-8*) Springer Pub.

Peppard, Victor. The Poetics of Yury Olesha. (University of Florida Humanities Monographs: No. 63). 176p. 1989. lib. bdg. 22.95 (*0-8130-0950-2*) U Press Fla.

***Peppas, N. A. & Langer, R. S., eds.** Biopolymers II. (Advances in Polymer Science Ser.: Vol.122). (Illus.). 379p. 1995. 171.00 (*3-540-58788-8*) Spr-Verlag.

Peppas, Nicholas A., jt. ed. see Buchholz, Fredric L.

Peppas, Nicholas A., jt. ed. see Cooper, Stuart L.

Peppas, Nikolaos A., ed. Hydrogels in Medicine & Pharmacy, Vol. I: Fundamentals. 192p. 1987. 105.00 (*0-8493-5546-X*, R857, CRC Reprint) CRC Pr.

— Hydrogels in Medicine & Pharmacy, Vol. II: Polymers. 184p. 1987. 179.00 (*0-8493-5547-8*, CRC Reprint) CRC Pr.

— Hydrogels in Medicine & Pharmacy, Vol. III: Properties & Applications. 240p. 1987. Vol. III, Properties & Applications, 240 pgs. 191.00 (*0-8493-5548-6*, CRC Reprint) CRC Pr.

Pepper, A. T., jt. ed. see Currie, J. C.

Pepper, Allan. Managing the Training & Development Function. 350p. 1992. 65.95 (*0-566-02977-4*, Pub. by Gower UK) Ashgate Pub Co.

Pepper, Art & Pepper, Laurie. Straight Life: The Story of Art Pepper. 2nd rev. ed. (Illus.). 610p. 1994. reprint ed. pap. 16.95 (*0-306-80558-8*) Da Capo.

Pepper, Barbara, jt. auth. see Levy, Jerrold E.

Pepper, Barbara, jt. ed. see Sekaquaptw, Emory.

Pepper, Barbara, ed. see Talashoema, Herschel.

Pepper, Bert & Ryglewicz, Hilary. Lost Souls: Helping Young Adult Chronic Patients. 300p. 1994. text ed. 22.95 (*0-02-924965-1*) Free Pr.

Pepper, Bert & Ryglewicz, Hilary, eds. The Young Adult Chronic Patient. LC 81-48483. (New Directions for Mental Health Services Ser.: No. MHS 14). 1982. pap. 17.95 (*0-87589-908-0*) Jossey-Bass.

Pepper Bird Staff. Copasetic: Adventures of Bojangles Robinson. (Multicultural Historical Fiction Ser.). (Illus.). 48p. (Orig.). (J). (gr. 4-7). 1993. pap. 3.95 (*1-56817-000-9*) Pepper Bird.

— Frozen Fury: Adventures of Matthew Henson. (Multicultural Historical Fiction Ser.). (Illus.). 48p. (Orig.). (J). (gr. 4-7). 1993. pap. 4.95 (*1-56817-001-7*) Pepper Bird.

— Pea Island Rescue. (Multicultural Historical Fiction Ser.). (Illus.). 48p. (Orig.). (J). (gr. 4-7). 1993. pap. 4.95 (*1-56817-002-5*) Pepper Bird.

— Wild Frontier: Adventures of Jean Baptiste Du Sable. (Multicultural Historical Fiction Ser.). (Illus.). 48p. (Orig.). (J). (gr. 4-7). 1993. pap. 4.95 (*1-56817-003-3*) Pepper Bird.

Pepper, Choral. Back to Baja: Retracing the Erle Stanley Gardner Expeditions. 134p. (Orig.). 1992. pap. 12.95 (*1-56672-002-8*) Seabar Pub.

— Desert Lore of Southern California. LC 93-45649. 1994. 12.95 (*0-932653-20-0*) Sunbelt Pubns.

— Treasure Legends of the West. LC 94-18062. (Illus.). 112p. 1994. pap. 21.95 (*0-87905-611-8*) Gibbs Smith Pub.

Pepper, Christina A., ed. see Munzert, Alfred W.

Pepper, Clayton. First Steps in Faith. 1982. pap. 3.95 (*0-89137-206-7*) Quality Pubns.

Pepper, Clayton, ed. Introduction to Soul Winning. 1982. pap. 3.95 (*0-89137-204-0*) Quality Pubns.

— Total Evangelism. 1982. pap. 3.95 (*0-89137-203-2*) Quality Pubns.

Pepper, Clayton, jt. ed. see Dyer, Jerry.

Pepper, D. W., jt. ed. see Blackwell, B.

Pepper, Darrel W., jt. auth. see Baker, A. J.

Pepper, Darrell & Heinrich, Juan C. Finite Element Methods: Basic Concepts & Applications. (Computational Methods in Mechanics & Thermal Sciences Ser.). 250p. 1992. disk 59.50 (*1-56032-104-0*) Hemisp Pub.

Pepper, David. Eco-Socialism: From Deep Ecology to Social Justice. LC 93-16565. 288p. 1993. 49.95 (*0-415-09718-5*, B2343, Routledge NY); pap. 15.95 (*0-415-09719-3*, B2347, Routledge NY) Routledge.

— Roots of Modern Environmentalism. LC 84-19867. 246p. 1986. pap. text ed. 19.95 (*0-685-30336-5*, Pub. by Croom Helm UK) Routledge Chapman & Hall.

Pepper, Dennis, ed. The Oxford Book of Animal Stories. (Illus.). 320p. (J). 1994. 20.00 (*0-19-278134-0*) OUP.

— An Oxford Book of Christmas Stories. (Illus.). 224p. (J). (gr. 3 up). 1988. pap. 10.95 (*0-19-278124-3*) OUP.

— The Oxford Book of Scary Tales. (Illus.). 160p. (J). 1992. 20.00 (*0-19-278131-6*) OUP.

— The Oxford Children's Book of Ghost Stories. (Illus.). 160p. (J). (gr. 7 up). 1994. 20.00 (*0-19-278126-X*) OUP.

Pepper, Elizabeth & Wilcock, John. Magical & Mystical Sites: Europe & the British Isles. LC 92-28748. (Illus.). 300p. (Orig.). 1983. reprint ed. pap. 16.95 (*0-933999-44-5*) Phanes Pr.

— The Witches' Almanac: Aries 1992 to Pisces 1993. (Illus.). 96p. 1992. 5.95 (*1-881098-00-1*) Witches Almanac.

— The Witches' Almanac: Complete Astrological Guide, Spring 1995 to Spring 1996. 1995. pap. text ed. 6.95 (*1-881098-06-0*) Witches Almanac.

— The Witches' Almanac: Spring 1993 to Spring 1994. 1992. pap. 5.95 (*1-881098-02-8*) Witches Almanac.

Pepper, Frank S., ed. The Wit & Wisdom of the Twentieth Century: A Dictionary of Quotations. LC 87-47755. 420p. 1987. 19.95 (*0-87226-165-4*) P Bedrick Bks.

Pepper, G. A., jt. auth. see Wiener, Matthew B.

Pepper, George B. The Boston Heresy Case in View of the Secularization of Religion: A Case Study in the Sociology of Religion. LC 88-9311. (Studies in Religion & Society: Vol. 18). 260p. 1988. lib. bdg. 89.95 (*0-88946-856-7*) E Mellen.

Pepper, George H. & Wilson, Gilbert L. Hidatsa Shrine & the Beliefs Respecting It. LC 09-5503. (American Anthropological Association Memoirs Ser.). 1908. pap. 15.00 (*0-527-00509-6*) Periodicals Srv.

Pepper, Gerald L. Communicating in Organizations: A Cultural Approach. LC 94-6694. 1994. text ed. write for info. (*0-07-049286-7*) McGraw.

Pepper, Gordon. Money, Credit & Inflation. 80p. (C). 1991. text ed. 59.95 (*0-255-36228-5*, Pub. by Inst Economic Affairs UK) St Mut.

Pepper, Gordon T. Money, Credit, & Asset Prices. LC 93-37498. 1994. text ed. 69.95 (*0-312-12038-9*) St Martin.

Pepper, Herman. Four Lives. LC 92-76155. 281p. 1993. pap. 10.95 (*1-879384-23-X*) Cypress Hse.

Pepper, Howard. Children: Standing Them on Our Shoulders: Family & Church in a Nurturing Network. LC 92-62036. 183p. (Orig.). 1993. pap. 9.95 (*0-9634519-2-8*) Nurture Pr.

Pepper, James, ed. see Welles, Orson.

Pepper, Jeffrey. The Golden Retriever. (Dog Breed Ser.: No. 3). (Illus.). 320p. 1984. 16.95 (*0-87666-668-3*, PS-786) TFH Pubns.

— Petit Basset Griffon Vendeen. (KW Ser.). (Illus.). 192p. 1993. text ed. 11.95 (*0-86622-578-1*, KW-208) TFH Pubns.

Pepper, John. John Pepper's Encyclopedia of Ulster Knowledge. (Illus.). 80p. (Orig.). 1984. pap. 6.50 (*0-86281-118-X*, Pub. by Appletree Pr IE) Irish Bks Media.

— Seeing the Light: The Art of Becoming Beautiful. LC 93-36316. 1994. pap. 11.95 (*1-85230-445-6*) Element MA.

Pepper, Laurie, jt. auth. see Pepper, Art.

Pepper, Margot. At This Very Moment - En Este Preciso Momento. Clarke, Ben, ed. Lopez, Adriana F. & Torres, Javier, trs. (Poetry & Prose from San Francisco's Tenderloin District Ser.). (Illus.). 77p. (Orig.). (ENG & SPA.). 1992. pap. text ed. 6.00 (*0-9625153-3-7*) Freedom Voices Pubns.

Pepper, P., ed. Program Transformation & Programming Environments. (NATO ASI Series F: Computer & Systems Sciences, Special Programme AET: No. 8). 400p. 1984. 82.00 (*0-387-12932-4*) Spr-Verlag.

Pepper, Red, pseud. Red Pepper. 125p. (Orig.). 1991. pap. text ed. write for info. (*0-9626578-2-4*) Savage Pubns.

Pepper, Richard. Sounds for Sax Vol. 2: Alto - Tenor. Date not set. pap. 8.95 (*0-7119-2056-7*, Chester Music) Music Sales.

Pepper, Robert D., ed. Four Tudor Books on Education. LC 66-10027. 270p. 1976. lib. bdg. 50.00 (*0-8201-1271-2*) Schol Facsimiles.

Pepper, Robert M. The Formation of the Public Broadcasting Service. Sterling, Christopher H., ed. LC 78-21732. (Dissertations in Broadcasting Ser.). 1980. lib. bdg. 37.95 (*0-405-11769-8*) Ayer.

Pepper, Roger S. Pressure Groups among "Small Businessmen" Bruchey, Stuart & Carosso, Vincent P., eds. LC 78-18973. (Small Business Enterprise in America Ser.). 1979. lib. bdg. 15.95 (*0-405-11476-1*) Ayer.

Pepper, Simon & Adams, Nicholas. Firearms & Fortifications: Military Architecture & Siege Warfare in Sixteenth Century Siena. LC 85-24673. (Illus.). 272p. 1986. 24.95 (*0-226-65534-2*) U Ch Pr.

Pepper, Stephen. Bob Jones University Collection of Religious Art: Italian Paintings. (Illus.). 336p. (Orig.). 1984. pap. 55.00 (*0-89084-263-9*) Bob Jones Univ Pr.

Pepper, Stephen C. Aesthetic Quality: A Contextualistic Theory of Beauty. LC 79-110052. 239p. 1970. reprint ed. text ed. 45.00 (*0-8371-4437-X*, PEAQ, Greenwood Pr) Greenwood.

— World Hypotheses: A Study in Evidence. (C). 1970. pap. 16.00 (*0-520-00994-0*) U CA Pr.

Pepper, Suzanne. China's Education Reform in the 1980s: Policies, Issues, & Historical Perspectives, No. 36. (China Research Monographs). 195p. (Orig.). 1990. pap. 12.00 (*1-55729-020-2*) IEAS.

— China's Universities: Post-Mao Enrollment Policies & Their Impact on the Structure of Secondary Education. LC 83-25277. (Michigan Monographs in Chinese Studies: No. 46). xvi, 155p. (C). 1984. pap. 8.00 (*0-89264-046-4*) Ctr Chinese Studies.

Pepper, Sylvia. The Art of Pressed Flowers. (Illus.). 48p. 1990. 35.00 (*0-89471-858-4*) Running Pr.

— Pressed Flower. (Workstations Ser.). (Illus.). 48p. (J). (gr. 9 up). 1992. 21.95 (*0-8431-3666-9*) Price Stern.

Pepper, Terence. Dorothy Wilding, The Pursuit of Perfection. (Illus.). 120p. 1991. 35.00 (*1-85514-052-7*, Pub. by Natl Port Gall UK) Antique Collect.

— Howard Coster's Celebrity Portraits: 101 Photographs of Personalities. (Illus.). 113p. 1985. pap. 19.95 (*0-904017-63-X*, Pub. by Natl Port Gall UK) Antique Collect.

— Lewis Morley: Photographer of the Sixties. (Illus.). 96p. 1989. pap. 29.50 (*1-85514-003-9*, Pub. by Natl Port Gall UK) Antique Collect.

Pepper, Terence, jt. auth. see Gibson, Robin.

Pepper, Thomas, et al. The Competition: Dealing with Japan. LC 85-6304. 336p. 1985. text ed. 49.95 (*0-275-91754-1*, C1754, Praeger Pubs) Greenwood.

Pepper, Timothy, jt. auth. see Beattie, Andrew.

Pepper, Walter. Look down on Clouds. 1994. 15.95 (*0-8062-5031-3*) Carlton.

Pepper, Wendy J. Travel-Concerning Health Benefits & Dangers, Risks, Warnings & Strategies for Survival & Enjoyment: Index of New Information. (Illus.). 150p. 1994. 44.50 (*0-7883-0016-4*); pap. 39.50 (*0-7883-0017-2*) ABBE Pubs Assn.

Pepper, William. The Medical Side of Benjamin Franklin. (Illus.). 137p. 1970. reprint ed. 15.00 (*0-87266-039-7*) Argosy.

— Orders to Kill. 448p. 1995. 25.00 (*0-7867-0253-2*) Carroll & Graf.

Peppercorn. Therapy of Inflammatory Bowel Disease: New Medical & Surgical Approaches. (Inflammatory Disease & Therapy Ser.: Vol. 2). 312p. 1990. 170.00 (*0-8247-8169-4*) Dekker.

Peppercorn, David. Bordeaux. 2nd ed. (Books on Wine Ser.). 800p. 1991. 39.95 (*0-571-13699-0*); pap. 24.95 (*0-571-13654-0*) Faber & Faber.

— Les Vins de Bordeaux. 312p. (FRE.). 1993. lib. bdg. 49.95 (*0-7859-3635-1*, 2082005755) Fr & Eur.

Peppercorn, Lisa. Villa-Lobos. (Illus.). 144p. Date not set. pap. 11.95 (*0-7119-1688-8*) Omnibus NY.

— Villa-Lobos. (Illustrated Lives of the Great Composers Ser.). (Illus.). 144p. 1989. pap. 14.95 (*0-7119-1689-6*, OP45061) Omnibus NY.

Peppercorn, Lisa M. Villa-Lobos: Collected Studies by L. M. Peppercorn. 200p. 1992. 62.95 (*0-85967-906-3*, Pub. by Scolar Pr UK) Ashgate Pub Co.

— Villa-Lobos the Music: An Analysis of His Style. De Haan, Stefan, tr. 136p. 1992. 21.75 (*0-912483-36-9*) Pro-Am Music.

***Peppercorn, Mark A.** Contemporary Diagnosis & Management of Ulcerative Colitis & Proctitis. LC 94-74425. 1995. write for info. (*1-884065-08-2*) Assocs in Med.

***Pepperday, Mike.** Celestial Navigation with the S Table: A Complete Sight Reduction Method for All Bodies in Nine Pages. (Illus.). 32p. (Orig.). Date not set. reprint ed. pap. 9.95 (*0-939837-09-9*) Paradise Cay Pubns.

Pepperell, C. A. Three-Dimensional Chemical Similarity Searching. LC 93-39096. (Computers & Chemical Structure Information Ser.: Vol. 3). 304p. 1994. text ed. 89.95 (*0-471-94238-3*) Wiley.

Pepperell, P., ed. Who Says So? Communication Skills. (C). 1989. 70.00 (*0-09-173060-0*, Pub. by S Thornes Pubs UK) St Mut.

P Q

An Asterisk (*) at the beginning of an entry indicates that the title is appearing in BIP for the first time.

Pepperell, R. J., ed. New Aspects of Dopamine Agonist Therapy in Menstrual Disorders & Infertility. (Illus.). 80p. (C). 1990. 35.00 (*1-85070-309-4*) Prthnon Pub.

Pepperell, Robert. Beyond Chaos: The Post-Human Condition. 224p. (Orig.). 1994. pap. text ed. 22.95 (*1-871516-45-5*, Pub. by Intellect Bks UK) Cromland.

***Peppers, Don.** Life's a Pitch...& Then You Buy: Then You Buy. LC 95-13882. 1995. write for info. (*0-385-47403-2*) Doubleday.

— One to One Future: Building Relationships One Customer at a Time. 1993. 22.95 (*0-385-42528-7*) Doubleday.

Peppers, Jerome G. History of United States Military Logistics 1935-1985. Crowe, Elizabeth P. & Nesmith, Alisa A., eds. (Illus.). 300p. (Orig.). (C). 1988. pap. text ed. 27.95 (*0-945488-00-9*) Soc Logistics Engrs.

Peppers, Larry C. & Bails, Dale G. Managerial Economics: Theory & Applications for Decision Making. (Illus.). 672p. (C). 1987. text ed. write for info. (*0-13-550055-9*) P-H.

Peppers, Larry C., jt. auth. see Bails, Dale G.

Peppers, Larry G. & Knapp, Ronald J. How to Go on Living after the Death of a Baby. rev. ed. 204p. 1985. pap. 9.95 (*0-931948-69-X*) Peachtree Pubs.

— Motherhood & Mourning: Perinatal Death. LC 80-286. 184p. 1980. text ed. 45.00 (*0-275-91760-6*, C1760, Praeger Pubs) Greenwood.

Peppin. Story of Painting. (Fine Arts Ser.). (Illus.). 32p. (J). 1980. lib. bdg. 13.96 (*0-88110-030-7*); pap. 6.95 (*0-86020-441-3*) EDC.

Peppin, Anthea. Nature in Art. (YA). 1992. pap. 6.96 (*0-395-64555-7*) HM.

— Nature in Art. LC 91-35014. (Millbrook Arts Library Ser.). (Illus.). 48p. (J). (gr. 2-6). 1992. lib. bdg. 14.40 (*1-56294-173-9*); pap. 6.95 (*1-56294-817-2*) Millbrook Pr.

— People in Art. (J). (gr. 4-7). 1992. pap. 6.96 (*0-395-64556-5*) HM.

— People in Art. LC 91-34983. (Millbrook Arts Library Ser.). (Illus.). 48p. (J). (gr. 2-6). 1992. lib. bdg. 14.40 (*1-56294-171-2*); pap. 6.95 (*1-56294-818-0*) Millbrook Pr.

— Places in Art. (J). (gr. 4-7). 1992. pap. 6.96 (*0-395-64557-3*) HM.

— Places in Art. LC 91-34978. (Millbrook Arts Library Ser.). (Illus.). 48p. (J). (gr. 2-6). 1992. lib. bdg. 14.40 (*1-56294-172-0*); pap. 6.95 (*1-56294-819-9*) Millbrook Pr.

Peppin, Anthea, jt. auth. see Armstrong, Carole.

Pepping, Ernst. Seven Pieces for SATB Recorders. Ballinger, Peter, ed. (Contemporary Consort Ser.: No. 4). 34p. 1989. 10.00 (*1-56571-009-6*) PRB Prods.

Pepple, Ted. Expect a Miracle: The Story of Matt Young - A Quadriplegic's Amazing Comeback & the Incredible Faith that Made It Happen. 150p. 1991. pap. 11.95 (*0-9630054-0-5*) T Pepple.

Peppler, Alice S. Divorce, Surviving the Pain: Reflections for the Divorced. rev. ed. LC 93-22209. 96p. 1993. pap. 6.99 (*0-570-04613-0*) Concordia.

Peppler, Cord. Die Borstgrassrasen, Nardetalia, Westdeutschlands. (Dissertationes Botanicae Ser.: Vol. 193). (Illus.). (GER.). 1992. pap. text ed. 133.00 (*3-443-64105-9*, Pub. by Cramer-Borntraeger GW) Lubrecht & Cramer.

Peppler, Ellen G., ed. see Hood, Mary A.

Peppler, Henry J., ed. Microbial Technology. LC 67-26866. 464p. reprint ed. pap. 132.30 (*0-317-10486-1*, 2005811) Bks Demand.

Peppler, Henry J. & Perlman, David, eds. Microbial Technology, Vol. 1: Microbial Processes. 2nd ed. LC 78-67883. 1979. text ed. 103.00 (*0-12-551501-4*) Acad Pr.

Peprnik, J. Dictionary of Americanisms for Czech Speakers. 620p. (C). 1985. 65.00 (*0-685-37237-5*, Pub. by Collets); 60.00 (*0-89771-908-5*, Pub. by Collets) St Mut.

Pepusch, John C. A Treatise on Harmony: Containing the Chief Rules for Composing in Two, Three & Four Parts. 2nd ed. 227p. 1976. reprint ed. 50.70 (*3-487-05930-4*, Pub. by Georg Olms GW) Lubrecht & Cramer.

Pepys, M. B., ed. Acute Phase Proteins in the Acute Phase Response. (Argenteuil Symposia Ser.). (Illus.). xviii, 210p. 1989. 96.00 (*0-387-19582-3*, 3483) Spr-Verlag.

Pepys, Samuel. Diary of Samuel Pepys. Morshead, O. F., ed. (Illus.). 1960. 25.75 (*0-8446-2727-5*) Peter Smith.

— The Diary of Samuel Pepys, 9 vols. Latham, Robert & Matthews, William, eds. Incl. Vol. 1. 1660. 1970. 42.00 (*0-520-01575-4*); Vol. 2. 1661. 1970. 42.00 (*0-520-01576-2*); Vol. 3. 1662. 1970. 42.00 (*0-520-01577-0*); Vol. 4. 1663. 1971. 42.00 (*0-520-01857-5*); Vol. 5. 1664. 1971. 42.00 (*0-520-01858-3*); Vol. 6. 1665. 1972. 42.00 (*0-520-01859-1*); Vol. 7. 1666. 1972. 42.00 (*0-520-02094-4*); Vol. 8. 1667. 1974. 42.00 (*0-520-02095-2*); Vol. 9. 1668-1669. 1976. 42.00 (*0-520-02096-0*); Vol. 10. Companion. 1983. 42.00 (*0-520-02097-9*); Vol. 11. Index. 1983. 42.00 (*0-520-02098-7*); write for info. (*0-318-56007-0*) U CA Pr.

— Diary of Samuel Pepys, 10 Vols, Set. Wheatley, Henry B., ed. Bright, Mynors, tr. LC 68-57227. reprint ed. lib. bdg. 825.00 (*0-404-05030-1*) AMS Pr.

— A Pepys Anthology. Latham, Robert & Latham, Linnet, eds. 350p. 1988. 25.00 (*0-520-06354-6*) U CA Pr.

— Pepys Ballads, 5 vols., Set. Day, W. G., ed. 1987. 990.00 (*0-85991-256-6*) Boydell & Brewer.

— Pepys' Memoires of the Royal Navy. LC 68-25260. (English Biography Ser.: No. 31). 1969. reprint ed. lib. bdg. 75.00 (*0-8383-0228-9*) M S G Haskell Hse.

— Pepys on the Restoration Stage. McAfee, Helen, ed. LC 63-23195. (Illus.). 1972. 20.95 (*0-405-08848-5*) Ayer.

— A Pepysian Garland: Black-Letter Broadside Ballads of the Years 1595-1639, Chiefly from the Collection of Samuel Pepys. Rollins, Hyder E., ed. LC 74-176041. (Illus.). 527p. 1971. 32.50 (*0-674-66185-0*) HUP.

— The Shorter Pepys. Latham, Robert, ed. & sel. by. LC 85-40210. 1152p. 1985. 48.00 (*0-520-03426-0*) U CA Pr.

Pequeño, Mercedes R. Los Formalistas Rusos y la Teoria De los Generos Literarios. Date not set. 43.50 (*0-685-69528-X*) Scripta.

***Pequegnat, W. & Stover, E., eds.** How to Write a Successful Research Grant Application: A Guide for Social & Behavioral Scientists. (Illus.). (C). 1995. pap. write for info. (*0-306-44965-X*, Plenum Pr) Plenum.

Pequeno, Salvatore S. Social Psychology: Index of Modern Authors & Subjects with Guide for Rapid Research. LC 90-56329. 160p. 1991. 44.50 (*1-55914-454-8*); pap. 39.50 (*1-55914-455-6*) ABBE Pubs Assn.

Pequeux, A. & Gilles, R., eds. High Pressure Effects on Selected Biological Systems. (Illus.). xiv, 145p. 1985. pap. 47.00 (*0-387-15630-5*) Spr-Verlag.

Pequigney, Joseph. Such Is My Love: A Study of Shakespeare's Sonnets. LC 85-984. x, 264p. 1987. pap. 9.95 (*0-226-65564-4*) U Ch Pr.

***Per Noste Staff.** Petit Dictionnaire Francais-Occitan (Bearn) 134p. (FRE.). 1984. pap. 19.95 (*0-7859-8163-2*, 2868660002) Fr & Eur.

Per Olov Enquist. The Night of the Tribades. Shideler, Ross, tr. 1978. pap. 4.75 (*0-8222-0824-5*) Dramatists Play.

Per-Olov, Lowdin, ed. International Journal of Quantum Chemistry, Quantum Biology Symposium No. 19: Proceedings of the International Symposium on the Applications of Fundamental Theory to Problems of Biology & Pharmacology - Held at St. Augustine, Florida, March 14-21, 1992. 19th ed. 304p. (Orig.). 1992. pap. text ed. 220.00 (*0-471-59454-7*) Wiley.

— International Journal of Quantum Chemistry Quantum Chemistry Symposium No. 26: Proceedings of the International Symposium on Atomic, Molecular, & Condensed Matter Theory & Computational Methods. 26th ed. 928p. (Orig.). 1992. pap. text ed. 229.00 (*0-471-59463-6*) Wiley.

Per, Schelde. Androids, Humanoids, & Other Folklore Monsters: Science & Soul in Science Fiction Films. LC 93-274. (Illus.). 288p. (C). 1993. text ed. 40.00 (*0-8147-7930-1*) NYU Pr.

Pera, Marcello. The Ambiguous Frog: The Galvani-Volta Controversy on Animal Electricity. Mandelbaum, Jonathan, tr. (Illus.). 262p. 1992. text ed. 32.50 (*0-691-08512-9*) Princeton U Pr.

— The Discourses of Science. Botsford, Clarissa, tr. LC 94-14169. 1994. 29.95 (*0-226-65617-9*) U Ch Pr.

Pera, Marcello, ed. Persuading Science: The Art of Scientific Rhetoric. 224p. 1991. 39.95 (*0-88135-071-0*, Sci Hist) Watson Pub Intl.

Pera, Marcello, jt. ed. see Pitt, Joseph C.

Peracchia, ed. Biophysics of Gap Junction Channels. 1990. 229.00 (*0-8493-6337-3*, QP603, CRC Reprint) Franklin.

Peracchia, Camillo, ed. Handbook of Membrane Channels: Molecular & Cellular Physiology. 591p. 1994. text ed. 150.00 (*0-12-550640-6*) Acad Pr.

Peracci, R. Geometry of Nonlinear Field Theories. 268p. 1986. text ed. 43.00 (*9971-5-0079-5*) World Scientific Pub.

Peradotto, John. Man in the Middle Voice: Name & Narration in the Odyssey. 155p. 1990. text ed. 29.95 (*0-691-06830-5*) Princeton U Pr.

Peradotto, John & Sullivan, J. P., eds. Women in the Ancient World. LC 83-4975. 377p. (C). 1987. pap. 14.95 (*0-87395-773-3*) State U NY Pr.

Peragallo, H & Peragallo, M. Diatomees Marines de France et des Districts Maritimes Voisins. (Illus.). 552p. (FRE.). 1984. reprint ed. lib. bdg. 329.50 (*3-87429-219-3*) Koeltz Sci Bks.

Peragallo, M., jt. auth. see Peragallo, H.

Perakis, Anastassios N., jt. auth. see Nikolaidis, Efstratios.

***Perakyla, Anssi.** AIDS Counselling: Institutional Interaction & Clinical Practice. (Studies in Interactional Sociolinguistics: Ser. 11). 336p. (C). Date not set. write for info. (*0-521-45463-8*) Cambridge U Pr.

Peral, I & De Francia, Rubio J., eds. Recent Progress in Fourier Analysis: Proceedings of the Seminar on Fourier Analysis Held in El Escorial, Spain, June 30 to July 5 1983. (Mathematics Studies: Vol. III). 268p. 1985. 54.00 (*0-444-87745-2*, North Holland) Elsevier.

Perales, Alonso S. Are We Good Neighbors? LC 73-14213. (Mexican American Ser.). (Illus.). 298p. 1975. reprint ed. 24.95 (*0-405-05687-7*) Ayer.

Perales, Andre P. Fanfou dans les Bayous: The Adventures of a Bilingual Elephant in Louisiana. LC 82-15148. (Illus.). 40p. (J). (gr. 1-7). 1982. pap. 6.95 (*0-88289-378-5*); audio 11.95 (*0-88289-410-2*) Pelican.

Perales, Cesar A. & Young, Lauren S. Women, Health, & Poverty. LC 87-26274. (Women & Health Ser.: Vol. 12, Nos. 3-4). 259p. 1989. text ed. 39.95 (*0-86656-684-8*) Haworth Pr.

Perales, Cesar A. & Young, Lauren S., eds. Too Little, Too Late: Dealing with the Health Needs of Women in Poverty. LC 88-908. (Women & Health Ser.: Vol. 12, Nos. 3-4). 259p. 1988. text ed. 17.95 (*0-918393-50-7*) Harrington Pk.

***Perales, T.** English-Spanish Dictionary of Video Terms. (ENG & SPA.). 1992. pap. 15.00 (*0-7859-8859-9*) Fr & Eur.

Perales, T. & Monroy, C. English-Spanish Dictionary of Video Terms. 95p. (ENG & SPA.). 1992. pap. 15.00 (*84-283-1458-6*, Pub. by Paraninfo) IBD Ltd.

Peralta, Carlos I. Fuentes y Proceso de Investigaciun Juridica. 660p. (SPA.). 1991. 55.00 (*0-88063-587-8*) Michie Butterworth.

Peralta-Ramos, Monica. The Political Economy of Argentina: Power & Class since 1930. 191p. (C). 1991. text ed. 59.00 (*0-8133-7556-8*) Westview.

Peralta, Tina. Afternoon Tea & Other Stories. 102p. (Orig.). 1993. pap. 6.50 (*971-10-0457-7*, Pub. by New Day Pub PH) Cellar.

Perangelo, Julie. A Competitive Analysis of Electronic Wire & Cable End-Use Markets: Copper vs. Fiber, 1988-1996 Analysis. (Illus.). 60p. 1991. pap. text ed. 1,600.00 (*1-878218-23-9*) World Info Tech.

— Electronic Wire & Cable - U. S. Markets, Technologies, & Opportunities: 1991-1996 Analysis. (Illus.). 160p. 1991. pap. text ed. 2,400.00 (*1-878218-20-4*) World Info Tech.

— Power & Distribution Transformers - U. S. & Canadian Markets, Competitors, & Materials: 1989-1996 Analysis. (Illus.). 300p. 1992. pap. text ed. 3,000.00 (*1-878218-28-X*) World Info Tech.

Peranteau, Paul M., et al, eds. Proceedings: Papers from the 8th Regional Meeting. 615p. 1972. pap. 6.00 (*0-914203-02-9*) Chicago Ling.

Perard, Victor. Anatomy & Drawing. 1989. 5.99 (*0-517-68018-1*) Random Hse Value.

Perard, Victor, et al. Drawing Animals. (Illus.). 96p. 1987. pap. 9.00 (*0-399-51390-6*, Perigee Bks) Berkley Pub.

Perard, Victor & Hagman, Rune. Drawing People. (Illus.). 96p. 1987. pap. 9.00 (*0-399-51385-X*, Perigee Bks) Berkley Pub.

Perason, Carol S. The Hero Within: Six Archetypes We Live By. 1989. pap. 12.00 (*0-06-254862-X*, PL) HarpC.

***Perata.** Black on Steel. 1996. 27.95 (*0-8057-4520-3*) Macmillan.

Peratis, Kathleen W., jt. auth. see Cary, Eve.

Peratt, A. L. Physics of the Plasma Universe. (Illus.). 250p. 1991. 79.00 (*0-387-97575-6*) Spr-Verlag.

Peray, K. Cement Manufacturer's Handbook. (Illus.). 1979. 58.50 (*0-8206-0245-0*) Chem Pub.

— Rotary Cement Kiln. 2nd enl. rev. ed. (Illus.). 1986. 72.50 (*0-8206-0314-7*) Chem Pub.

Peraza, Elena V. Bio-Bibliografia de Fermin Peraza Sarausa. LC 90-82804. (Coleccion Polymita Ser.). 118p. (Orig.). (SPA.). 1990. pap. 19.00 (*0-89729-572-2*) Ediciones.

Peraza, Fermin, ed. Revolutionary Cuba: A Bibliographical Guide, 1966. LC 68-21369. 1967. 5.95 (*0-87024-075-7*) U of Miami Pr.

— Revolutionary Cuba: A Bibliographical Guide 1967. LC 75-92596. 1969. 5.95 (*0-87024-136-2*) U of Miami Pr.

— Revolutionary Cuba: A Bibliographical Guide 1968. LC 68-21369. 1970. 5.95 (*0-87024-153-2*) U of Miami Pr.

Peraza, Michael, illus. The Little Mermaid: A Holiday Songbook. LC 93-70939. (Little Mermaid Novels Ser.). 48p. (J). 1993. 9.95 (*1-56282-504-6*) Disney Pr.

Percan, S. T. The Complete Book on Housetraining Rabbits: The Only Rabbit Book You'll Need. (Illus.). 37p. (Orig.). 1984. pap. 3.95 (*0-916005-01-1*) Silver Sea.

Percas de Ponseti, Helena. Cervantes the Writer & Painter of Don Quijote. LC 88-10609. 128p. 1989. text ed. 23.00 (*0-8262-0689-1*) U of Mo Pr.

Perce, John A., II & Robinson, Richard B., Jr. Strategic Management: Formulation, Implementation, & Control. 5th ed. LC 93-5598. 960p. (C). 1993. text ed. 66.95 (*0-256-11362-9*) Irwin.

Percefull, Aaron. The Cambridge Program for the GED Writing Skills Test. (GED Preparation Ser.). 304p. (Orig.). 1988. pap. text ed. 6.45 (*0-8428-9387-3*) Cambridge Bk.

***Percelay, James, et al.** Double Snaps: For Advanced Snappers & Those Who Like the Dozens Raw...an All New Book. LC 94-24792. 1995. pap. 9.95 (*0-688-14011-4*, Quill) Morrow.

— Snaps: The African American Art of Verbal Warfare. LC 93-34484. 1994. 8.95 (*0-688-12896-3*) Morrow.

Percell, Roger A. Principles in Biology: Laboratory Manual. 112p. 1993. spiral bd. write for info. (*0-8403-9877-8*) Kendall-Hunt.

Perces, Marjorie, et al. The Dance Technique of Lester Horton. (Illus.). 256p. (Orig.). 1992. pap. 24.95 (*0-87127-164-8*, Dance Horizons) Princeton Bk Co.

Percesepe, Gary. Ethics of Inclusion: An Introduction to Theory & Practice. LC 94-4826. 650p. (C). 1994. pap. write for info. (*0-02-393891-9*) Macmillan.

— Philosophy: An Introduction to the Labor of Reason. 880p. (C). 1991. write for info. (*0-02-393981-8*) Macmillan.

Percesepe, Gary, jt. auth. see Mehuron, Kate.

Percesepe, Gary J. Future(s) of Philosophy: The Marginal Thinking of Jacques Derrida. (American University Studies: Philosophy: Ser. V, Vol. 67). 237p. (C). 1989. text ed. 36.00 (*0-8204-0804-2*) P Lang Pubs.

Perceval, Edward, tr. see Huysmans, Joris K.

Perceval, John. Perceval's Narrative: A Patient's Account of His Psychosis, 1830-1832. Bateson, Gregory, ed. LC 61-14652. 111p. reprint ed. pap. 30.00 (*0-7837-1223-5*, 2041754) Bks Demand.

Perceval-Maxwell, M. The Outbreak of the Irish Rebellion of 1641. 390p. 1994. 49.95 (*0-7735-1157-1*, Pub. by McGill CN) U of Toronto Pr.

Perceval, W. B., pref. Pictorial New Zealand, Eighteen Ninety-Five. 316p. (C). 1986. 85.00 (*0-85091-239-3*) St Mut.

Perchan, Robert J. Perchan's Chorea. 1991. 17.50 (*0-922820-15-5*) Watermark Pr.

Percheron, G., et al, eds. The Basal Ganglia IV: New Ideas & Data on Structure & Function. (Advances in Behavioral Biology Ser.: Vol. 41). (Illus.). 596p. 1994. 125.00 (*0-306-44639-1*, Plenum Pr) Plenum.

Percheron, Maurice. Buddha & Buddhism. Stapleton, Edmund, tr. LC 82-3471. (Spiritual Masters Ser.). (Illus.). 192p. 1984. 18.95 (*0-87951-157-5*); pap. 9.95 (*0-87951-193-1*) Overlook Pr.

Perchik, Simon. Birthmark. limited ed. (Illus.). 12p. 1992. bds. 65.00 (*1-880392-00-3*) Flockophobic Pr.

— Both Hands Screaming. 1975. 16.00 (*0-685-56234-4*) Elizabeth Pr.

— The Club Fits Either Hand. 1979. 12.00 (*0-686-59670-6*); pap. 5.00 (*0-686-59671-4*) Elizabeth Pr.

— The Emptiness Between My Hands. 24p. (Orig.). 1992. pap. 5.95 (*1-879259-03-6*) Dusty Dog.

— The Gandolf Poems. 1988. 7.00 (*0-934834-31-8*) White Pine.

— Hands You Are Secretly Wearing. 1972. 16.00 (*0-685-27713-5*); pap. 8.00 (*0-685-27714-3*) Elizabeth Pr.

— I Counted Only April. 1964. pap. 4.00 (*0-685-01007-4*) Elizabeth Pr.

— Letters to the Dead. 64p. 1994. pap. 8.95 (*1-879934-08-6*) St Andrews Pr.

— Redeeming the Wings. (Dusty Dog Chapbook Ser.: No. 1). 24p. (Orig.). 1991. pap. 3.00 (*1-879259-00-1*) Dusty Dog.

— Snowcat Poems, 1980-1981, to the Photographs of Robert Frank. LC 90-80827. (Illus.). 64p. 1989. reprint ed. pap. 7.95 (*0-943512-24-7*) Linwood Pub.

— Twenty Years of Hands. 1966. 3.00 (*0-685-01008-2*) Elizabeth Pr.

— Which Hand Holds the Brother. 1969. 4.00 (*0-685-01009-0*) Elizabeth Pr.

***Perchuk, Andrew & Posner, Helaine, eds.** The Masculine Masquerade: Masculinity & Representation. (Illus.). 160p. 1995. 25.00 (*0-262-16154-0*) MIT Pr.

Perchuk, L. L., ed. Progress in Metamorphic & Magmatic Petrology: A Memorial Volume in Honour of D. S. Korzhinskiy. (Illus.). 520p. (C). 1991. 125.00 (*0-521-39077-X*) Cambridge U Pr.

Perchuk, L. L. & Kushiro, I., eds. Physical Chemistry of Magmas. (Advances in Physical Geochemistry Ser.: Vol. 9). (Illus.). x, 341p. 1991. 108.00 (*0-387-97500-4*) Spr-Verlag.

Percier, Charles. Empire Stylebook of Interior Design. 1991. pap. 7.95 (*0-486-26754-7*) Dover.

Percier, Charles & Fontaine, Pierre F. Palais, Maisons et Autres Edifices Modernes Dessines A Rome. 1980. reprint ed. write for info. (*3-487-06920-2*, Pub. by Georg Olms GW) Lubrecht & Cramer.

— Residences Des Souverains, 2 vols. in 1. xi, 354p. 1973. reprint ed. write for info. (*3-487-04796-9*, Pub. by Georg Olms GW) Lubrecht & Cramer.

***Percifield, Glen, ed.** Developing Dynamic Disciples: Pentecostal Faith, Prayer & Commitment. LC 94-76668. 144p. (Orig.). 1994. pap. 2.95 (*0-88243-335-0*, 02-0335) Gospel Pub.

Percival. A Color Atlas of Lens Implantation. 1991. 145.00 (*0-8151-6664-8*, Yr Bk Med Pubs) Mosby Yr Bk.

Percival, Anthony. Galdos & His Critics. (Romance Ser.: No. 53). 548p. 1985. 45.00 (*0-8020-5601-6*) U of Toronto Pr.

— Galdos & His Critics. LC 86-215749. (University of Toronto Romance Ser.: No. 53). 547p. reprint ed. pap. 155.90 (*0-8357-4146-X*, 2036919) Bks Demand.

Percival, Donald B. & Walden, Andrew T. Spectral Analysis for Physical Applications: Multitaper & Conventional Univariate Techniques. (Illus.). 580p. (C). 1993. 94.95 (*0-521-35532-X*); pap. 42.95 (*0-521-43541-2*) Cambridge U Pr.

Percival, Fred, jt. ed. see Land, Ray.

Percival, Fred, et al. A Handbook of Educational Technology. 3rd ed. LC 93-8129. 276p. (C). 1993. pap. 39.95 (*0-89397-389-0*) Nichols Pub.

Percival, Fred, et al, eds. The Simulation & Gaming Yearbook 1993: Developing Transferable Skills in Education & Training. 318p. (C). 1993. text ed. 69.95 (*0-7494-0895-2*, Pub. by Kogan Page UK) Nichols Pub.

Percival, Harold W. Adepts, Masters & MAHATMAS. LC 92-82024. (Illus.). 184p. (Orig.). 1993. reprint ed. pap. 14.95 (*0-911650-11-3*, 113) Word Foun.

— Democracy Is Self-Government: A Guide for Right Living in the New Age. LC 52-30629. (Illus.). 234p. 1989. reprint ed. pap. 9.95 (*0-911650-10-5*, 105) Word Foun.

— Man & Woman, & Child. LC 52-6126. 1992. reprint ed. pap. 9.95 (*0-911650-08-3*) Word Foun.

— Masonry & Its Symbols, in Light of "Thinking & Destiny" LC 52-2237. 1991. reprint ed. pap. 5.95 (*0-911650-07-5*) Word Foun.

— Thinking & Destiny. 11th ed. LC 47-1811. (Illus.). 1000p. (C). 1995. 29.95 (*0-911650-09-1*, 091); pap. 19.95 (*0-911650-06-7*) Word Foun.

Percival, Ian C. & Richards, Derek. Introduction to Dynamics. LC 82-15514. (Illus.). 240p. 1983. pap. 29.95 (*0-521-28149-0*) Cambridge U Pr.

Percival, Lloyd. The Hockey Handbook. 320p. 1992. 24.95 (*1-895246-03-2*, Pub. by McClelland & Stewart CN); pap. 19.99 (*1-895246-09-1*, Pub. by McClelland & Stewart CN) Firefly Bks Ltd.

Percival, M. Floral Biology. LC 64-18202. (Pergamon International Library Science Technology Engineering & Social Studies). 1969. text ed. 110.00 (*0-08-010610-2*, Pub. by Pergamon Repr UK) Franklin.

Percival, M. O., jt. ed. see Andrews, C. E.

Percival, Milton O. William Blake's Circle of Destiny. 340p. 1993. pap. text ed. 21.00 (*1-56459-315-0*) Kessinger Pub.

Percival, Olive. Mexico City. 1976. lib. bdg. 59.95 (*0-8490-0625-2*) Gordon Pr.

Percival, P. Percival's English-Tamil Dictionary. (C). 1993. reprint ed. 22.00 (*81-206-0817-8*, Pub. by Asian Educ Servs II) S Asia.

Percival, Robert V., jt. auth. see Friedman, Lawrence M.

Percival, Ronald, tr. see Roques, Henri.

Percival, Thomas. Percival's Medical Ethics. Leake, Chauncey D., ed. LC 75-23750. reprint ed. 39.50 (*0-404-13356-8*) AMS Pr.

An Asterisk (*) at the beginning of an entry indicates that the title is appearing in BIP for the first time.

Percom. How to Comply with the Data Protection Act: Policies, Practice & Procedures. 200p. 1986. text ed. 78. 95 (0-566-02632-5, Pub. by Gower UK) Ashgate Pub Co.

Percy, Ann, ed. see Kerrigan, Maurie.

Percy, C., et al. International Classification of Disease for Oncology (ICD-0) 144p. 1990. 27.00 (92-4-154414-7) World Health.

Percy, Christopher V. Lalique: A Collector's Guide. (Illus.). 192p. 1989. 15.99 (0-517-69095-0) Random Hse Value.

Percy, Dean H. & Barthold, Stephen W. Pathology of Laboratory Rodents & Rabbits. LC 93-17809. (Illus.). 280p. (C). 1993. text ed. 62.95 (0-8138-1309-3) Iowa St U Pr.

Percy, E. C., et al. Sport Medicine: Incidence & Treatment of Athletic Injuries. LC 73-10382. (Sport Medicine Ser.: Vol. 1). 1973. 29.00 (0-8422-7142-2) Irvington.

Percy, Edward & Denham, Reginald. Ladies in Retirement. 1943. pap. 4.75 (0-8222-0624-2) Dramatists Play.

— Trunk Crime. 1940. pap. 13.00 (0-8222-0345-6) Dramatists Play.

Percy, Graham. Arthouse. LC 93-42988. (Illus.). 64p. 1994. 16.95 (0-8118-0497-6) Chronicle Bks.

— Christmas Sticker Book. (Illus.). (J). (ps-1). 1992. 10.00 (1-56021-187-3) W J Fantasy.

— The Cock, the Mouse, & the Little Red Hen. LC 91-71857. 32p. (J). (ps up). 1994. pap. 5.99 (1-56402-268-4) Candlewick Pr.

— The Farm. (Press & Lift Bks.). (Illus.). 16p. (J). (gr. 1-5). 1989. write for info. (1-881469-27-1) Safari Ltd.

— Favorite Fable Special. (J). 1993. 125.00 (0-8050-3083-2) H Holt & Co.

— Fox's Tale. (Animal Tails Ser.). (Illus.). 20p. (J). (ps up). 1995. 5.99 (0-679-86221-8) Random Bks Yng Read.

— Max and the Orange Door. LC 92-45563. (Illus.). 32p. (J). (ps-3). 1993. lib. bdg. 22.79 (1-56766-076-2) Childs World.

— Max & the Very Rare Bird. (Meg & Max Bks.). (Illus.). 32p. (J). 1991. lib. bdg. 22.79 (0-89565-786-4) Childs World.

— Meg & Her Circus Tricks. (Meg & Max Bks.). (Illus.). 32p. (J). 1991. lib. bdg. 22.79 (0-89565-785-6) Childs World.

— Meg & the Great Race. LC 92-44851. (Illus.). (J). (ps-3). 1993. lib. bdg. 22.79 (1-56766-077-0) Childs World.

— The Mountains. (Press & Lift Bks.). (Illus.). 16p. (J). (gr. 1-5). 1989. 6.50 (1-881469-11-5) Safari Ltd.

— Raccoon's Tale. (Animal Tale's Ser.). (Illus.). 20p. (J). (ps up). 1995. 5.99 (0-679-86223-4) Random Bks Yng Read.

— The Squirrel's Tale. (Animal Tails Ser.). (Illus.). 20p. (J). (ps up). 1995. 5.99 (0-679-86222-6) Random Bks Yng Read.

— The Tiger's Tale. (Animal Tails Ser.). (Illus.). 20p. (J). (ps up). 1995. 5.99 (0-679-86220-X) Random Bks Yng Read.

Percy, Graham, illus. The Cock, the Mouse, & the Little Red Hen. LC 91-71857. 32p. (J). (ps up). 1992. 14.95 (1-56402-008-8) Candlewick Pr.

— Elephants Never Forget: Classic Nursery Rhymes. 48p. (J). (ps-1). 1992. 12.95 (0-8118-0239-6) Chronicle Bks.

— Reynard the Fox. LC 90-11105. 80p. (J). (gr. 2-4). 1991. 16.95 (0-688-09949-1, Tambourine Bks); lib. bdg. 16.88 (0-688-10156-9, Tambourine Bks) Morrow.

Percy, Jane. The Phantom of Harley Grange. (C). 1989. 42. 00 (0-7223-2308-5, Pub. by A H S Ltd UK) St Mut.

Percy, John R., ed. The Study of Variable Stars Using Small Telescopes. (Illus.). 272p. 1987. 59.95 (0-521-33300-8) Cambridge U Pr.

Percy, John R., jt. ed. see Pasachoff, Jay M.

Percy, John R., et al, eds. Variable Star Research: An International Perspective: International Cooperation & Coordination of Variable Star Research. (Illus.). 352p. (C). 1991. 59.95 (0-521-40469-X) Cambridge U Pr.

Percy, John W., ed. see Parish, Charles C.

Percy, Keith & Ramsden, Paul. Independent Study: Two Examples from English Higher Education. 79p. 1980. 28.00 (0-900868-75-9) Taylor & Francis.

Percy, Keith, jt. auth. see Withnall, Alexandra.

***Percy, Kevin E., et al, eds.** Air Polutants & the Leaf Cuticle. LC 94-21967. (NATO ASI, Series G, Ecological Sciences: 36). 1994. 168.00 (0-387-58146-4) Spr-Verlag.

Percy, Larry & Rossiter, John R. Advertising Strategy: A Communication Theory Approach. LC 79-25228. 314p. 1980. text ed. 49.95 (0-275-91692-8, C1692, Praeger Pubs) Greenwood.

Percy, Michael B. & Yoder, Christian. The Softwood Lumber Dispute & Canada-U. S. Trade in Natural Resources. 1989. pap. text ed. 20.00 (0-88645-057-8, Pub. by Inst Res Pub CN) Ashgate Pub Co.

Percy, Simpson.

Percy, Stephen L. Disability, Civil Rights, & Public Policy: The Politics of Implementation. LC 89-30317. 328p. (C). 1990. pap. 21.95 (0-8173-0668-4) U of Ala Pr.

Percy, Stephen L. & Scott, Eric J. Demand Processing & Performance in Public Service Agencies. LC 83-9325. (Illus.). xiv, 167p. 1984. 21.50 (0-8173-0204-2) U of Ala Pr.

Percy, Stephen L., jt. auth. see Frantzich, Stephen E.

Percy, Thomas. The Correspondence of Thomas Percy & John Pinkerton: The Percy Letters, Vol. 8. Wood, Harriet H. & Brooks, Cleanth, eds. LC 84-2916. 129p. 1985. text ed. 35.00x (0-300-03344-3) Yale U Pr.

— The Correspondence of Thomas Percy & Robert Anderson, Vol. 9. LC 88-2074. (C). 1989. text ed. 65.00 (0-300-03814-3) Yale U Pr.

— The Correspondence of Thomas Percy & William Shenstone: The Percy Letters, Vol. VII. Brooks, Cleanth, ed. LC 44-9765. 1977. 50.00 (0-300-01924-6) Yale U Pr.

— Reliques of Ancient English Poetry, 2 vols., Set. (BCL1-PR English Literature Ser.). 1992. reprint ed. lib. bdg. 150.00 (0-7812-7132-0) Rprt Serv.

Percy, Walker. Lancelot. (YA). (gr. 7 up). 1978. mass mkt. 4.50 (0-380-01861-6, Bard) Avon.

— Lancelot. 256p. 1989. mass mkt. 5.99 (0-8041-0380-1) Ivy Books.

— Last Gentleman. 1989. mass mkt. 5.99 (0-8041-0379-8) Ivy Books.

— The Last Gentleman. LC 66-18861. 409p. 1966. 22.95 (0-374-18372-4) FS&G.

— The Last Gentlemen. 320p. 1978. mass mkt. 4.50 (0-380-37796-9, Bard) Avon.

— Lost in the Cosmos: The Last Self-Help Book. LC 83-1590. 262p. 1983. 14.95 (0-374-19165-4) FS&G.

— Lost in the Cosmos: The Last Self-Help Book. 262p. 1992. pap. 13.00 (0-374-52346-0) FS&G.

— Love in the Ruins. LC 71-143301. 416p. 1971. 27.95 (0-374-19302-9) FS&G.

— Love in the Ruins. 352p. 1989. mass mkt. 5.99 (0-8041-0378-X) Ivy Books.

— The Message in the Bottle. 352p. 1975. pap. 14.00 (0-374-51338-4) FS&G.

— Moviegoer. 1961. 23.00 (0-394-43703-9) Knopf.

— The Moviegoer. 208p. 1988. reprint ed. mass mkt. 5.99 (0-8041-0290-2) Ivy Books.

— Novel-Writing in an Apocalyptic Time. (Illus.). 40p. 1986. 150.00 (0-685-09100-7) Faust Pub Co.

— Novel-Writing in an Apocalyptic Time. deluxe limited ed. (Illus.). 40p. 1986. 75.00 (0-917905-01-6) Faust Pub Co.

— The Second Coming. 336p. 1990. mass mkt. 5.99 (0-8041-0542-1) Ivy Books.

— Signposts in a Strange Land. 1991. 25.00 (0-374-26391-4) FS&G.

— Signposts in a Strange Land. 428p. 1992. pap. 15.00 (0-374-52345-2) FS&G.

— State of the Novel: Dying Art or New Science. (Illus.). 20p. 1988. 50.00 (0-917905-05-9); 125.00 (0-317-66751-3) Faust Pub Co.

— The Thanatos Syndrome. 1987. 17.95 (0-374-27354-5) FS&G.

— The Thanatos Syndrome. 384p. 1988. reprint ed. mass mkt. 6.99 (0-8041-0220-1) Ivy Books.

***Percy, Walker & Letner, Kenneth L.** A Thief of Peirce: The Letters of Kenneth Laine Ketner & Walker Percy. Samway, Patrick H., ed. LC 95-14835. 350p. 1995. text ed. 45.00x (0-87805-810-9) U Pr of Miss.

Percy, William, jt. auth. see Johansson, Warren.

Percy, William A. Lanterns on the Levee: Recollections of a Planter's Son. LC 73-90687. (Library of Southern Civilization). xxii, 348p. 1974. 24.95 (0-8071-1184-8); pap. 11.95 (0-8071-0072-2) La State U Pr.

— Sewanee. LC 82-60214. (Illus.). 40p. 1982. 14.95 (0-913720-37-2) Beil.

— Sewanee. 16p. 1941. pap. 7.50 (0-918769-35-3) Univ South Pr.

Percy, William A., jt. auth. see Johnson, Jerah.

Percy, William A., ed. see O'Shaughnessy, Arthur E.

Perczel, Csilla F., ed. Ethiopia: Folk Art of a Hidden Empire. LC 83-62245. (Illus.). 72p. 1983. 15.00 (0-914155-00-8) Mingei Intl Mus.

***Perczynski, Maciej, et al, eds.** After the Market Shock: Central & East European Economies in Transition. 1994. 59.95 (1-85521-594-2, Pub. by Dartmth Pub UK) Ashgate Pub Co.

Perdang, J. M. & LeJeune, A. Cellular Automata: Prospects in Astronomy & Astrophysics. 416p. 1993. text ed. 109. 00 (981-02-1346-8) World Scientific Pub.

Perdigo, Luisa M. The Origins of Vicente Huidobro's Creacionismo (1911-1916) & Its Evolution (1917-1947) LC 93-39318. 360p. 1993. text ed. 99.95 (0-7734-2299-4) E Mellen.

Perdikaris, George A. Computer Controlled Systems: Theory & Applications. 496p. (C). 1991. lib. bdg. 142.00 (0-7923-1422-0) Kluwer Ac.

***Perdomo, Willie.** Where a Nickel Costs a Dime. LC 95-12325. 1996. pap. 13.00 (0-393-31383-2) Norton.

Perdrizet, Marie-Pierre. The Cathedral Builders. Raycraft, Mary B., tr. LC 91-24233. (Peoples of the Past Ser.). (Illus.). 64p. (J). (gr. 4-6). 1992. lib. bdg. 15.90 (1-56294-162-3) Millbrook Pr.

Perdu, Charles. Echoes of Valor. (Illus.). 96p. (Orig.). 1993. pap. 10.00 (0-9638779-0-9) Perdido Pr.

Perdue, Charles L., Jr., ed. Outwitting the Devil: Jack Tales from Wise County, Virginia. LC 87-71657. (New Deal & Folk Culture Ser.). (Illus.). 129p. (Orig.). 1987. 19.95 (0-941270-43-2); pap. 9.95 (0-941270-42-4) Ancient City Pr.

— Pig's Foot Jelly & Persimmon Beer: Foodways from Virginia's Writer's Project. LC 92-9356. (New Deal & Folk Culture Ser.). (Illus.). 130p. (Orig.). 1992. pap. 11. 95 (0-941270-74-2) Ancient City Pr.

Perdue, Charles L., Jr., et al, eds. Weevils in the Wheat: Interviews with Virginia Ex-Slaves. LC 79-65433. (Midland Bks.: No. 237). (Illus.). 405p. (C). 1992. reprint ed. pap. text ed. 16.95 (0-8139-1370-5) U Pr of Va.

Perdue, Clive, ed. Adult Language Acquisition: Crosslinguistic Perspectives, Vol. 1: Field Methods. LC 92-35757. (Illus.). 267p. (C). 1993. 64.95 (0-521-41708-2) Cambridge U Pr.

— Adult Language Acquisition: Crosslinguistic Perspectives, Vol. 2: The Results. (Illus.). 300p. (C). 1993. 64.95 (0-521-41709-0) Cambridge U Pr.

Perdue, Clive, jt. auth. see Klein, Wolfgang.

Perdue, Daniel. Debate in Tibetan Buddhism. 938p. 1992. 45.00 (0-937938-84-X); pap. 38.95 (0-937938-76-9) Snow Lion Pubns.

Perdue, E. M. & Gjessing, E. T., eds. Organic Acids in Aquatic Ecosystems. 345p. 1990. text ed. 199.95 (0-471-92631-0) Wiley.

Perdue, Jim M. The Law of Texas Medical Malpractice. LC 85-8205. 660p. 39.50 (0-913797-08-1) Houston Law Review.

— Who Will Speak for the Victim? A Practical Treatise on Plaintiff's Jury Argument. LC 88-63945. 420p. 1989. 74. 00 (0-938160-54-0, 6231) State Bar TX.

Perdue, Leo. Wisdom & Creation. LC 94-17507. 208p. (Orig.). 1994. pap. 21.95 (0-687-45626-6) Abingdon.

Perdue, Leo G. The Collapse of History: Reconstructing Old Testament Theology. LC 94-2824. 1994. 14.00 (0-8006-1563-8, Fortress Pr) Augsburg Fortress.

Perdue, Leo G. & Gilpin, W. Clark, eds. Voices from the Whirlwind: Interpreting the Book of Job. 224p. 1992. pap. 16.95 (0-687-43812-8) Abingdon.

Perdue, Leo G. & Kovacs, Brian W., eds. A Prophet to the Nations: Essays in Jeremiah Studies. LC 83-20648. xv, 399p. 1984. text ed. 35.00 (0-931464-20-X) Eisenbrauns.

Perdue, Leo G., jt. ed. see Gammie, John G.

Perdue, Leo G., et al, eds. In Search of Wisdom: Essays in Memory of John G. Gammie. 352p. (Orig.). 1993. pap. 24.99 (0-664-25295-8) Westminster John Knox.

Perdue, Lewis. Country Inns of Maryland, Virginia & West Virginia. 4th ed. (Illus.). 210p. 1988. pap. 7.95 (0-915168-06-5) Wash Bk Trad.

— The High Technology Editorial Guide & Stylebook: 1991 Edition. 200p. (C). 1991. pap. 40.00 (1-55623-530-5); disk 40.00 (1-55623-531-3) Irwin Prof Pubng.

— The Linz Testament. LC 85-70278. 400p. 1985. 18.95 (0-917657-22-5) D I Fine.

Perdue, Lewis, et al. The French Paradox & Beyond: Live Longer with Wine & the Mediterranean Lifestyle. (Illus.). 244p. (Orig.). (C). 1992. pap. 12.95 (0-9625271-1-4) Renais CA.

Perdue, Mitzi. Perdue Chicken Cookbook. Grose, Bill, ed. 296p. 1991. 18.95 (0-671-69143-0) PB.

— The Perdue Chicken Cookbook. Grose, Bill, ed. 288p. 1994. reprint ed. pap. 12.00 (0-671-69144-9) PB.

Perdue, Peggy K. Diving into Science, Grades Two-Four. 96p. 1989. pap. 7.95 (0-673-38965-0) GdYrBks.

— Schoolyard Science, Grades 2-4: Schoolyard Science, Grades 2-4. 1990. pap. 8.95 (0-673-38967-7) GdYrBks.

— Science Is an Action Word! Grades 1-3. 1990. pap. 8.95 (0-673-38968-5) GdYrBks.

— Small Wonders: Hands-on Science Activities for Young Children. (Illus.). 66p. (Orig.). 1988. pap. 8.95 (0-673-38198-6) GdYrBks.

Perdue, Peggy K. & Vaszily, Diane A. City Science, Grades 3-6. 1990. pap. 11.95 (0-673-46430-X) GdYrBks.

Perdue, Peggy K., jt. auth. see Vaszily, Diane A.

Perdue, Peter C. Exhausting the Earth. (East Asian Monographs: No. 150). 130p. 1987. 28.00 (0-674-27504-7) HUP.

Perdue, Terry A. Heath Nostalgia. LC 93-93530. (Illus.). 124p. 1992. pap. text ed. 9.95 (0-9637627-0-2) Taptron.

Perdue, Thea. The Cherokee. (Indians of North America Ser.). (Illus.). 111p. (Orig.). (YA). (gr. 5 up). 1989. 17.95 (1-55546-695-8); pap. 9.95 (0-7910-0357-4) Chelsea Hse.

Perdue, Theda. Nations Remembered: An Oral History of the Cherokees, Chickasaws, Choctaws, Creeks. LC 92-50726. (C). 1993. pap. 11.95 (0-8061-2523-3) U of Okla Pr.

— Nations Remembered: An Oral History of the Five Civilized Tribes, 1865-1907. LC 79-6828. (Contributions in Ethnic Studies: No. 1). xxiv, 221p. 1980. text ed. 55. 00 (0-313-22097-2, PFN/, Greenwood Pr) Greenwood.

— Native Carolinians: The Indians of North Carolina. (Illus.). xiv, 73p. 1993. reprint ed. pap. 5.00 (0-86526-217-9) NC Archives.

— Slavery & the Evolution of Cherokee Society, 1540-1866. LC 78-16284. 222p. 1979. 28.00 (0-87049-259-4); pap. 14.95 (0-87049-530-5) U of Tenn Pr.

Perdue, Theda, ed. Cherokee Editor: The Writings of Elias Boudinot. LC 82-11110. 254p. 1983. text ed. 30.00x (0-87049-366-3) U of Tenn Pr.

— The Cherokee Removal: A Brief History with Documents. (Bedford Series in History & Culture). 160p. 1995. 35.00 (0-312-12254-3) St Martin.

***Perdue, Theda & Green, Michael.** The Cherokee Removal. 144p. 1995. pap. text ed. 8.65 (0-312-08658-X) St Martin.

Perdue, Tito. Lee. LC 91-9477. 145p. 1991. 18.95 (0-941423-39-5) FWEW.

— The New Austerities. 208p. 1993. 18.95 (1-56145-086-3) Peachtree Pubs.

— Opportunities in Alabama Agriculture. 222p. 1994. 18.00 (1-880909-24-3) Baskerville.

***Perdue, William D.** Modernization of Poland. LC 95-2491. 264p. 1995. text ed. 65.00 (0-275-95009-3, Praeger Pubs) Greenwood.

— Paradox of Change: The Rise & Fall of Solidarity in Poland. LC 95-7551. 1995. text ed. write for info. (0-275-95295-9, Praeger Pubs) Greenwood.

— Sociological Theory. 410p. (C). 1986. text ed. 44.95 (0-87484-693-5) Mayfield Pub.

— Systemic Crisis: Problems in Society, Politics, & World Order. (Illus.). 550p. (C). 1993. pap. text ed. 26.75 (0-03-055347-4) HB Coll Pubs.

— Terrorism & the State. LC 88-34029. 240p. 1989. text ed. 55.00 (0-275-93140-4, Greenwood Pr) Greenwood.

Pere, Vernice W., jt. auth. see Craig, Robert D.

Perea, Floresmiro. Salvemos la Familia De Hoy (Let's Save Today's Family) (SPA.). 1992. 4.50 (1-56063-302-6, 498423) Editorial Unilit.

Perea, Francisco J. Puedes Hablar en Publico. (Illus.). 112p. (SPA.). 1990. pap. text ed. 9.00 (0-929853-03-2) Condor Pubns Inc.

Perea, Karen M., jt. auth. see Guthrie, Jeanne.

Perea, M. A., jt. ed. see Goldsmith, P. A.

***Perea, Robert L.** Stacey's Story. 70p. (Orig.). 1995. pap. 8.95 (0-931122-80-5) West End.

Perea, Sam. Ultimate Victory. LC 91-34231. (Orig.). 1991. pap. 4.00 (0-915541-80-7) Star Bks Inc.

Pereboom, Derk, jt. ed. see Guignon, Charles.

Pereboom, Maarten L. Democracies at the Turning Point: Britain, France & the End of the Postwar Order, 1928-1933. LC 94-13004. (Studies in Modern European History: Vol. 13). 1995. write for info. (0-8204-2535-4) P Lang Pubs.

Perec, Georges. Un Cabinet d'Amateur. (FRE.). 1989. pap. 6.95 (0-7859-3151-1, 2253050598) Fr & Eur.

— Les Choses. (FRE.). 1987. pap. 8.95 (0-7859-3222-4, 2266025791) Fr & Eur.

— Les Choses: Une Histoire des Annees Soixante. Leblon, Jean M., ed. LC 71-84473. (Illus.). (Orig.). (FRE.). (C). 1969. pap. text ed. 14.95 (0-89197-078-9) Irvington.

— Disparition. (Imaginaire Ser.). (FRE.). pap. 15.95 (2-07-071523-X) Schoenhof.

— La Disparition. (FRE.). 1989. pap. 19.95 (0-7859-3394-8) Fr & Eur.

— Homme Qui Dort. (Folio Ser.: No. 2197). 190p. (FRE.). 1990. pap. 8.95 (2-07-038288-5) Schoenhof.

— Un Homme Qui Dort. (FRE.). 1990. pap. 12.95 (0-7859-2921-5) Fr & Eur.

— Life: A User's Manual. Bellos, David, tr. LC 87-8782. 608p. 1988. pap. 16.95 (0-87923-751-1) Godine.

— Quel Petit Velo a Guidon au Fond de la Cour. (FRE.). 1982. pap. 10.95 (0-7859-2902-9) Fr & Eur.

— Quel Petit Velo a Guidon Chrome au Fond de la Cour? (Folio Ser.: No. 1413). (FRE.). pap. 8.95 (2-07-037413-0) Schoenhof.

— Things & A Man Asleep: Two Novels in One Volume. 1990. 19.95 (0-87923-857-7) Godine.

— La Vie Mode d'Emploi. (FRE.). 1980. pap. 17.95 (0-7859-3100-7) Fr & Eur.

— A Void. Adair, Gilbert, tr. 256p. 1994. 25.00 (0-00-271119-2, HarpT) HarpC.

— W: Or the Memory of Childhood. Bellos, David, tr. LC 88-45291. 192p. 1988. 16.95 (0-87923-756-2) Godine.

***Perec, Georges & Bober, Robert.** Ellis Island. Mathews, Harry, tr. (Illus.). 160p. 1995. pap. 18.00 (1-56584-318-5) New Press NY.

Perecman, Ellen. Integrating Theory & Practice in Clinical Neuropsychology. 464p. 1989. 89.95 (0-8058-0285-1) L Erlbaum Assocs.

Perecman, Ellen, ed. Cognitive Processing in the Right Hemisphere. (Perspectives in Neurolinguistics, Neuropsychology & Psycholinguistics Ser.). 1983. text ed. 54.00 (0-12-550680-5) Acad Pr.

— The Frontal Lobes Revisited. 312p. 1988. 79.95 (0-8058-0288-6) L Erlbaum Assocs.

Perecman, Ellen, ed. see Peuser, Gunther.

Pereda, Rafael C. Textos y Pretextos. LC 85-14137. 114p. (SPA.). 1986. pap. 6.00 (0-8477-3516-8) U of PR Pr.

Pereda Valdes, Ildefonso, ed. Antologia de la Poesia Negra Americana. (B. E. Ser.: No. 9). (POR.). 1953. 29.00 (0-8115-2960-6) Periodicals Srv.

Peredo, H. L., jt. auth. see Butin, H.

***Perego, Maria.** Comes to Life Storyplayer & Topo Gigio & the Friends of the Forest Book Set: Comes to Life Storyplayer & Topo Gigio e Gli Animaletti del Bosco. Preziosi, Giochi, tr. (Comes to Life Bks.). 16p. (ITA.). (J). (ps-2). 1994. write for info. (1-57234-004-5) YES Ent.

— Topo Gigio e il Pirata - Topo Gigio & the Pirate with the Beard. Preziosi, Giochi, tr. (Comes to Life Bks.). 16p. (ITA.). (J). (ps-2). 1994. write for info. (1-57234-005-3) YES Ent.

Peregoy. Total Quality in Government. 300p. 1994. 39.95 (1-884015-12-3) St Lucie Pr.

Peregoy, Suzanne & Boyle, Owen F. Reading, Writing, & Learning in ESL: A Resource Book for K-8 Teachers. LC 92-32444. 240p. (C). 1993. pap. text ed. 24.50 (0-8013-0844-5) Longman.

Peregrine, D. H., ed. Floods Due to High Winds & Tides. (IMA Conference Ser.). 1981. text ed. 71.00 (0-12-551820-X) Acad Pr.

Peregrine, Peter N. Mississippian Evolution: A World-System Perspective. LC 92-4142. (Monographs in World Archaeology: No. 9). 144p. (C). 1992. pap. text ed. 22. 50 (1-881094-00-6) Prehistory Pr.

Peregrine, W. T. & Kassim bin Ahmad, eds. Phytopathological Papers, No. 27: Brunei - A First Annotated List of Plant Diseases & Associated Organisms. 87p. (C). 1982. pap. text ed. 25.00 (0-85198-506-8) CAB Intl.

Pereira, jt. ed. see Becker.

Pereira, A. Ethanol, Employment & Development: Lessons from Brazil. xiv, 195p. (Orig.). 1986. pap. 20.00 (92-2-105380-6) Intl Labour Office.

Pereira, Antonio. Cuentos para Lectores Complices. (Nueva Austral Ser.: Vol. 101). (SPA.). 1991. pap. text ed. 24. 95x (84-239-1901-3) Elliots Bks.

Pereira, Armand, et al. Socio-Economic & Policy Implications of Energy Price Increases. Tims, Wouter, ed. 300p. 1987. text ed. 46.95 (0-566-05520-1, Pub. by Avebury Pub UK) Ashgate Pub Co.

Pereira, Bernardo F., tr. see Calvet De Magalhaes, Jose.

Pereira, Carlos E., jt. auth. see Finney, Douglas M.

Pereira, D. F., jt. auth. see Rao, T. V.

Pereira, Fernando & Grosz, Barbara J., eds. Natural Language Processing. (Artificial Intelligence Special Issues Ser.). (Illus.). 500p. 1994. pap. 35.00 (0-262-66092-X, Bradford Bks) MIT Pr.

Pereira, Fernando C. & Shieber, Stuart M. Prolog & Natural Language Analysis. LC 87-70774. (Center for the Study of Language & Information-Lecture Notes Ser.: No. 10). 268p. (Orig.). 1987. 28.95 (0-937073-17-2); pap. 14.95 (0-937073-18-0) Ctr Study Language.

Pereira, H. C. Policy & Practice in the Management of Tropical Watersheds. 237p. 1989. 125.00 (81-7089-123-X, Pub. by Intl Bk Distr II) St Mut.

Pereira, J. G., jt. auth. see Aldrovandi, R.

Pereira, J. S. & Landsberg, J. J., eds. Biomass Production by Fast-Growing Trees. (C). 1989. lib. bdg. 115.50 (*0-7923-0208-7*) Kluwer Ac.

***Pereira, Joao C.** Majocica Tiles: From the National Museum of Azulejos, Lisbon. (Illus.). 128p. 1996. 35.00 (*0-302-00661-3*) Scala Books.

Pereira, Jose. Elements of Indian Architecture. 1986. 48.00 (*0-8364-0868-3*) S Asia.

— Elements of Indian Architecture. 1987. 30.00 (*81-208-0064-8*, Pub. by Motilal Banarsidass II) S Asia.

— Islamic Sacred Architecture: A Stylistic History. (C). 1994. 165.00 (*81-85016-37-2*, Pub. by Aditya Prakashan II) S Asia.

— Monolithic Jinas: The Iconography of the Jain Temples of Ellora. (C). 1977. 11.00 (*0-8364-2632-0*, Pub. by Motilal Banarsidass II) S Asia.

Pereira, Jose, ed. Hindu Theology: Themes Texts & Structures. (C). 1991. 28.00 (*81-208-0715-4*, Pub. by Motilal Banarsidass II) S Asia.

Pereira, Joseph A., jt. auth. see Rossi, Peter H.

Pereira, Kim. August Wilson & the African-American Odyssey. LC 94-25855. Date not set. write for info. (*0-252-02137-1*); pap. write for info. (*0-252-06429-1*) U of Ill Pr.

Pereira, Luis M. & Nerode, Anil. Logic Programming & Non-Monotonic Reasoning: Proceedings of the Second International Workshop. (Illus.). 500p. 1993. 37.50 (*0-262-66083-0*) MIT Pr.

Pereira, Luiz C., et al. Economic Reforms in New Democracies: A Social-Democratic Approach. LC 92-17342. (Illus.). 240p. (C). 1993. 54.95 (*0-521-43259-6*); pap. 15.95 (*0-521-43845-4*) Cambridge U Pr.

Pereira, Manuel F., ed. Computer-Aided Analysis of Rigid & Flexible Mechanical Systems: Proceedings of the NATO Advanced Study Institute, Troia, Portugal, June 27 - July 9, 1993. (NATO Advanced Study Institutes Series E: Applied Sciences Ser.). 640p. (C). 1994. lib. bdg. 262.00 (*0-7923-2839-6*) Kluwer Ac.

***Pereira, Manuel F. O. S. & Ambrosio, Jorge A. C., eds.** Computational Dynamics in Multibody Systems. LC 94-45512. (Diverse Ser.). 324p. (C). 1995. lib. bdg. 144.00 (*0-7923-3304-7*) Kluwer Ac.

Pereira, Michael E. & Fairbanks, Lynn A., eds. Juvenile Primates: Life History, Development, & Behavior. (Illus.). 400p. 1993. 65.00 (*0-19-507206-5*) OUP.

Pereira, Nancy. Creative Drama in the Library. 2nd ed. 94p. 1976. 10.95 (*0-932720-14-5*); pap. 8.95 (*0-932720-13-7*) New Plays Inc.

Pereira, Nino, et al, eds. Dense Z-Pinches. (AIP Conference Proceedings Ser.: No. 195). 568p. 1989. lib. bdg. 80.00 (*0-88318-396-X*) Am Inst Physics.

Pereira, Norman C., jt. ed. see Wang, Lawrence K.

Pereira, Patricia, jt. auth. see Dibbs, Owen.

Pereira, Sam. Brittle Water. (Illus.). 1987. 50.00 (*0-318-41022-2*); pap. 27.50 (*0-318-41023-0*) Abattoir.

— The Marriage of the Portuguese. LC 78-71826. 53p. (Orig.). 1978. pap. 3.75 (*0-934332-09-6*) LEpervier Pr.

***Pereiras Garcia, Manuel.** It Is It Is Not. 57p. 1994. pap. text ed. 3.95 (*1-885901-14-3*) Presbyters Peartree.

***Pereire, Anita.** The Ward Lock Encyclopedia of Parctical Gardening: The Definitive Single-Volume Guide to Garden Plants & Gardening Techniques. (Illus.). 702p. 1995. 35.00 (*0-7063-7409-6*, Pub. by Ward Lock UK) Sterling.

Perejda, jt. auth. see Uitto.

Perek, L., ed. see International Astronomical Union Staff.

Perekalin, M., jt. auth. see Kasatkin, A.

Perekalin, V. V. Unsaturated Nitro Compounds. 344p. 1964. text ed. 96.50 (*0-7065-0526-3*, Pub. by Keter Pub IS) Coronet Bks.

Perekalin, V. V., et al. Nitroalkenes: Conjugated Nitro Compounds. LC 93-39727. 1994. text ed. 95.00 (*0-471-94318-5*) Wiley.

Perel, Azriel & Stock, M. Christine. Handbook of Mechanical Ventilatory Support. (Illus.). 328p. 1992. 39.00 (*0-683-06856-3*) Williams & Wilkins.

Perel, Earl J. Sequestered Soliloquies. 96p. 1994. 10.00 (*0-932616-46-1*) New Poets Chestnut Hills.

Perel, Jane L. Blowing Kisses to the Sharks. 1978. pap. 4.50 (*0-914278-20-7*) Copper Beech.

Perell. The Fusion of Law & Equity. 184p. 1990. 63.00 (*0-409-89664-0*) Butterworth Legal Pubs.

— Remedies & the Sale of Land. 352p. 1988. 79.00 (*0-409-80534-3*) Butterworth Legal Pubs.

Perella, Nicholas J. The Kiss, Sacred & Profane: An Interpretative History of Kiss Symbolism & Related Religio-Erotic Themes. LC 75-83292. (Illus.). 370p. reprint ed. pap. 105.50 (*0-685-23578-5*, 2029058) Bks Demand.

Perella, Nicholas J., tr. see Palazzeschi, Aldo.

Perella, Nicolas. Midday in Italian Literature: Variations on an Archetypal Theme. LC 78-70313. 347p. reprint ed. pap. 98.90 (*0-8357-7895-9*, 2036314) Bks Demand.

Perella, Nicolas J., tr. see Collodi, Carlo.

Perelli, Robert J. Ministry to Persons with AIDS: A Family Systems Approach. LC 90-43093. 112p. (Orig.). 1990. pap. 9.99 (*0-8066-2507-4*, 9-2507) Augsburg Fortress.

Perello, C., et al. Equadiff - Ninety-One: International Conference on Differential Equations, 2 vols., Set. 1000p. 1993. text ed. 178.00 (*981-02-1023-X*) World Scientific Pub.

Perello, Jorge. Lexicon de Comunicologia - Diccinario para Audiologos, Audioprotesistas, Fonitras, Logopedas, Profesores de Sordos y Psicolinguistas: Lexicon of Communications Science. 856p. (ENG, FRE, GER & SPA.). 1977. 75.00 (*0-8288-5485-8*, S50096) Fr & Eur.

Perelman, Bob. A. K. A. 1984. per. 9.00 (*0-935724-18-4*) Figures.

— Braille. LC 75-319972. 61p. 1975. 3.50 (*0-87886-057-6*, Greenfld Rev Pr) Greenfld Rev Lit.

— Captive Audience. 1988. per. 6.00 (*0-935724-36-2*) Figures.

— Face Value. (Roof Bks.). 60p. (Orig.). 1987. pap. 6.00 (*0-937804-26-6*) Segue NYC.

— The First World. 64p. 1986. per. 7.50 (*0-935724-22-2*) Figures.

— Virtual Reality. LC 92-63354. 80p. (Orig.). 1993. pap. 9.95 (*0-937804-49-5*) Segue NYC.

Perelman, Bob, ed. Writing Talks. LC 83-20338. 305p. 1985. pap. 14.95 (*0-8093-1180-1*) S Ill U Pr.

Perelman, Chaim. Justice, Law & Argument: Essays on Moral & Legal Reasoning. (Synthese Library: No. 142). 175p. 1980. lib. bdg. 62.00 (*90-277-1089-9*) Kluwer Ac.

— The Realm of Rhetoric. Kluback, William, tr. LC 79-66378. (C). 1982. pap. text ed. 9.95 (*0-268-01605-4*) U of Notre Dame Pr.

Perelman, Chaim & Olbrechts-Tyteca, L. The New Rhetoric: A Treatise on Argumentation. Wilkinson, John & Weaver, Purcell, trs. LC 68-20440. (C). 1969. pap. text ed. 19.95 (*0-268-00446-3*) U of Notre Dame Pr.

Perelman, Dale. The Regent. LC 89-71381. (Illus.). 144p. (Orig.). 1990. pap. 8.95 (*0-931832-47-0*) Fithian Pr.

Perelman, F. & Towndrow, R. Rubidium & Caesium. LC 64-15739. (International Series of Monographs on Nuclear Energy: Vol. 2). 1965. 68.00 (*0-08-010555-6*, Pub. by Pergamon Repr UK) Franklin.

Perelman, Jerry. The Perfect Harmonica Method. (Illus.). 64p. (Orig.). 1992. pap. text ed. 15.95 (*0-931759-63-3*) Centerstream Pub.

Perelman, Lewis J. The Learning Enterprise: Adult Learning, Human Capital & Economic Development. 62p. 1984. 10.00 (*0-934842-44-2*) CSPA.

— School's Out: The End of Education & the New Technology. 368p. 1993. reprint ed. pap. 12.00 (*0-380-71748-4*) Avon.

— School's Out: The New Technology & the End of Education. LC 92-11361. 356p. 1992. 23.00 (*0-688-11286-2*) Morrow.

— Technology & Transformation of Schools. 274p. (Orig.). 1987. pap. 35.00 (*0-88364-168-2*) Natl Sch Boards.

Perelman, Michael. Farming for Profit in a Hungry World: Capital & the Crisis in Agriculture. LC 76-43229. 250p. 1978. text ed. 31.00 (*0-916672-88-3*) Rowman.

— Information, Social Relations & the Economics of High Technology. 256p. 1991. text ed. 55.00 (*0-312-05676-1*) St Martin.

— Marx's Crises Theory: Scarcity, Labor, Finance. LC 87-6936. 256p. 1987. text ed. 55.00 (*0-275-92372-X*, C2372, Praeger Pubs) Greenwood.

Perelman, Richard B., ed. American Athletics Annual: 1980 Edition. 694p. (Orig.). (YA). (gr. 12 up). 1980. pap. 15.00 (*0-686-29735-0*) Athletics Cong.

— American Athletics Annual: 1981 Edition. 1981. write for info. (*0-318-57618-X*) Athletics Cong.

***Perelman, S. J.** Acres & Pains. LC 94-24655. (Illus.). 128p. 1995. pap. 12.95 (*1-55821-359-7*) Lyons & Burford.

— Favorites of S. J. Perelman. 22.95 (*0-8488-1123-2*) Amereon Ltd.

— Listen to the Mockingbird. 16.95 (*0-89190-422-0*, Am Repr) Amereon Ltd.

— Vinegar Puss. 19.95 (*0-89190-421-2*, Am Repr) Amereon Ltd.

— Westward, Ha! Around the World in 80 Cliches. LC 84-11380. (Quality Paperbacks Ser.). (Illus.). 160p. 1984. reprint ed. pap. 7.95 (*0-306-80229-5*) Da Capo.

Perelman, S. J., et al. The Marx Brothers: Monkey Business, Duck Soup, A Day at the Races. (Classic Screenplay Ser.). (Illus.). 224p. (Orig.). 1993. pap. 13.95 (*0-571-16647-4*) Faber & Faber.

Perelman, Vladimir. How to Turn a Technical Interview into a Winning Battle: For Computer Professionals. 1991. pap. 25.00 (*0-9631774-0-0*) VSP Mgmt Cnslts.

Perelman, Yakov. Mathematics Can Be Fun. 400p. (C). 1985. 50.00 (*0-685-36888-2*, Pub. by Collets) St Mut.

Perelmuter, Hayim. Siblings: Rabbinic Judaism & Early Christianity. 1989. pap. 11.95 (*0-8091-3104-8*) Paulist Pr.

Perelmuter, Hayim G., tr. see Darshan, David.

Perelomov, A. Generalized Coherent States & Their Applications. (Texts & Monographs in Physics). 320p. 1986. 109.00 (*0-387-15912-6*) Spr-Verlag.

Perelomov, A. M. Integrable Systems of Classical Mechanics & Lie Algebras, Vol. I. 320p. 1990. 95.00 (*0-8176-2336-1*) Birkhauser.

Perelomova, N. V. & Tagieva, M. M. Problems in Crystal Physics with Solutions. 336p. 1983. 50.00 (*0-317-46691-7*, Pub. by Collets UK) Pro-Am Music.

Perelson, et al. Cell Surface Dynamics: Concepts & Models. (Receptors & Ligands in Intercellular Communication Ser.: Vol. 3). 584p. 1984. 195.00 (*0-8247-7115-X*) Dekker.

Perelson, A. S., jt. auth. see Macken, C. A.

Perelson, A. S., et al, eds. Nonlinearity in Biology & Medicine: Proceedings of the 17th International Conference of the Center for Nonlinear Studies Los Alamos National Laboratory, Los Alamos, NM, May 18-22, 1987. 534p. 1988. 136.75 (*0-444-01336-9*, North Holland) Elsevier.

Perelson, Alan. Theoretical Immunology, 2 vols. 1988. write for info. (*0-318-63162-8*, Adv Bk Prog) Addison-Wesley.

— Theoretical Immunology, 2 vols. (Santa Fe Institute Ser.). (C). 1988. pap. 34.95 (*0-201-15683-0*) Addison-Wesley.

— Theoretical Immunology, 2 vols., Vol. 2. (Santa Fe Institute Ser.). 420p. (C). 1988. 49.95 (*0-201-15687-3*); pap. 34.95 (*0-201-15688-1*) Addison-Wesley.

Perelson, Alan S. & Kauffman, Stuart A., eds. Molecular Evolution on Rugged Landscapes: Proteins, RNA, & the Immune System. (Santa Fe Institute Ser.). (Illus.). 336p. (C). 1991. 45.95 (*0-201-52149-0*, Adv Bk Prog); pap. 24.95 (*0-201-52150-4*, Adv Bk Prog) Addison-Wesley.

Perelson, Alan S. & Weisbuch, Gerard, eds. Theoretical & Experimental Insights into Immunity. LC 92-27863. (NATO ASI Series H: Cell Biology: Vol. 95). xvii, 480p. 1992. 169.00 (*0-387-54614-6*) Spr-Verlag.

Perenyi, Constance. Growing Wild: Inviting Wildlife into Your Yard. (Illus.). 40p. (J). (gr. 1-3). 1991. 14.95 (*0-941831-60-4*); pap. 9.95 (*0-941831-63-9*) Beyond Words Pub.

— Wild Wild West: Wildlife Habitats of Western North America. LC 92-46995. (Illus.). 32p. (J). (gr. 1 up). 1993. text ed. 14.95 (*0-912365-82-X*); pap. 8.95 (*0-912365-90-0*) Sasquatch Bks.

Perenyi, Eleanor. Green Thoughts. 1992. 22.00 (*0-8446-6629-7*) Peter Smith.

— Green Thoughts: A Writer in the Garden. LC 83-47805. 304p. 1983. pap. 13.00 (*0-394-71714-7*, Vin) Random.

***Perenyi, I.** Town & Environs. 152p. (C). 1978. 78.00x (*963-05-1493-1*) St Mut.

Perepechko, I. I. Low-Temperature Properties of Polymers. 272p. 1980. 124.00 (*0-08-025301-6*, Pub. by Pergamon Repr UK) Franklin.

***Perera.** Scapegoat Complex. 1995. pap. 15.00 (*0-919123-22-8*) Atrium Pubs.

***Perera, E. S.** The Origin & Development of Dhrupad & Its Bearing on Instrumental Music. (C). 1995. 28.50x (*81-7074-111-4*, Pub. by KP Bagchi IA) S Asia.

Perera, Eve L., jt. ed. see Salitan, Lucille.

Perera, Frederica, jt. ed. see Schulte, Paul A.

Perera, Hilda. Cuentos de Apolo. 3rd ed. (Illus.). 103p. (SPA.). (YA). (gr. 6 up). 1975. pap. 5.00 (*0-89729-438-6*) Ediciones.

— Kiki: A Cuban Boy's Adventures in America. 120p. (J). (gr. 5-8). 1992. pap. 12.95 (*0-940495-24-4*) Pickering Pr.

— Plantado: Una Cronica Desnuda y Terrible de la Experiencia de las Carceles Castristas. 183p. (Orig.). (SPA.). 1981. pap. 7.95 (*84-320-3612-9*) Ediciones.

— El Sitio de Nadie. 3rd ed. 329p. (Orig.). (SPA.). 1973. 15.00 (*84-320-5271-X*) Ediciones.

Perera, Katharine. Children's Writing & Reading: Analyzing Classroom Language. Crystal, David, ed. (Language Library). 352p. 1984. pap. 22.95 (*0-631-13654-1*) Blackwell Pubs.

Perera, Katharine, et al, eds. Growing Points in Child Language: Journal of Child Language, Anniversary Issue 21: 1. 256p. (C). 1994. pap. 19.95 (*0-521-46906-6*) Cambridge U Pr.

Perera, L. A. The Rise, the Decline, & the Fall of Hollywood's Mighty Empires. 1992. 12.95 (*0-533-09634-0*) Vantage.

Perera, Lydia, tr. see Soik, Helmut M.

Perera, M. H. Accounting for State Industrial & Commercial Enterprises in a Developing Country. Brief, Richard P., ed. LC 80-1516. (Dimensions of Accounting Theory & Practice Ser.). 1980. lib. bdg. 35.95 (*0-405-13495-9*) Ayer.

Perera, S. C., tr. Temporal & Spiritual Conquest of Ceylon: Sixteenth & Seventeenth Century Account of Ceylon, 3 vols., Set. (C). 1992. reprint ed. 105.00 (*81-206-0764-3*, Pub. by Asian Educ Servs II) S Asia.

Perera, Suvendrini. Reaches of Empire. 224p. 1991. text ed. 39.00 (*0-231-07578-2*) Col U Pr.

Perera, Sylvia B., jt. auth. see Whitmont, Edward C.

***Perera, Victor.** The Cross & the Pear Tree: A Sephardi Journey. LC 94-26788. 1995. 25.00 (*0-394-58351-5*) Knopf.

— Rites: A Guatemalan Boyhood. 192p. 1986. 15.95 (*0-15-177678-4*) HarBrace.

— Rites: A Guatemalan Boyhood. LC 94-13776. 202p. 1994. reprint ed. pap. 12.95 (*1-56279-065-X*) Mercury Hse Inc.

— Unfinished Conquest: The Guatemalan Tragedy. LC 93-12054. (Illus.). 418p. 1993. 27.00 (*0-520-07965-5*) U CA Pr.

— Unfinished Conquest: The Guatemalan Tragedy. 1995. pap. 14.95 (*0-520-20349-6*) U CA Pr.

Perera, Victor & Bruce, Robert D. The Last Lords of Palenque: The Lacandon Mayas of the Mexican Rain Forest. (Illus.). 320p. 1985. pap. 12.00 (*0-520-05309-5*) U CA Pr.

Perera, Victor, tr. see Montejo, Victor.

Peres, ed. Neuronal Factors. 1987. 123.00 (*0-8493-5241-X*, QP363, CRC Reprint) Franklin.

Peres, A., jt. auth. see Kuper, C. G.

Peres, Asher. Quantum Theory: Concepts & Methods. LC 93-32994. (Fundamental Theories of Physics Ser.). 460p. (C). 1993. lib. bdg. 129.00 (*0-7923-2549-4*) Kluwer Ac.

***Peres, Edward R., illus.** Tendrils of the Eye. 58p. (Orig.). 1993. pap. text ed. write for info. (*0-9639765-0-8*) Haiku Moments.

Peres, Richard. Writing in the Information Age: A Sales & Marketing Approach. 224p. (C). 1991. teacher ed 5.80 (*1-56118-326-1*); pap. text ed. 13.25 (*1-56118-324-5*) Paradigm MN.

***Peres, Shimon.** Battling for Peace: A Memoir. Landau, David, ed. (Illus.). 350p. 1995. 25.00 (*0-679-43617-0*) Random.

— The New Middle East. 1993. 25.00 (*0-8050-3323-8*) H Holt & Co.

— The New Middle East. 240p. 1995. pap. 14.95 (*0-8050-3811-6*, Owl) H Holt & Co.

Peres, Yochanan & Yuchtman-Yaar, Ephraim. Trends in Israeli Democracy: The Public's View. LC 91-43887. (Israel Democracy Institute Policy Studies). 62p. 1992. pap. text ed. 9.95 (*1-55587-308-1*) Lynne Rienner.

Peress, Gilles. Farewell to Bosnia. 1994. 60.00 (*1-881616-22-3*, Pub. by Scalo Pubs) Dist Art Pubs.

— Rwanda - The Silence. 1995. pap. 29.50 (*1-881616-38-X*, Pub. by Scalo Pubs) Dist Art Pubs.

Peress, Gilles, et al, illus. Aperture, Issue 97. (Fine Photography Ser.). 80p. pap. 18.50 (*0-89381-155-6*) Aperture.

Peressini, A. L., et al. The Mathematics of Nonlinear Programming. (Undergraduate Texts in Mathematics Ser.). (Illus.). x, 325p. 1994. 42.00 (*0-387-96614-5*) Spr-Verlag.

— The Mathematics of Nonlinear Programming. 2nd ed. (Undergraduate Texts in Mathematics Ser.). x, 273p. 1993. write for info. (*3-540-96614-5*) Spr-Verlag.

Pereszlenyi-Pinter, Martha. Advanced Hungarian 1. (Illus.). 111p. (Orig.). (HUN.). (C). 1987. teacher ed, pap. 8.00 (*0-87415-124-4*, 51A); student ed, pap. text ed. 19.00 (*0-87415-123-6*, 51); audio 5.00 (*0-87415-125-2*, 51B) OSU Foreign Lang.

Pereszlenyi-Pinter, Martha & Ludanyi, Julianna N. Elementary Hungarian 1. (OSU Foreign Language Publications: No. 20). (Illus.). 133p. (Orig.). (HUN.). (C). 1984. teacher ed, pap. 10.00 (*0-87415-038-8*, 20A); student ed, pap. text ed. 18.00 (*0-87415-037-X*); audio 25.00 (*0-87415-039-6*, 20B) OSU Foreign Lang.

— Elementary Hungarian 2. (OSU Foreign Language Publications: No. 21). (Illus.). 140p. (Orig.). (HUN.). (C). 1984. teacher ed, pap. 9.00 (*0-87415-041-8*, 21A); student ed, pap. text ed. 15.00 (*0-87415-040-X*) OSU Foreign Lang.

— Elementary Hungarian 2, 2 cass., Set. (OSU Foreign Language Publications: No. 21). (Illus.). 312p. (Orig.). (HUN.). (C). 1984. audio 10.00 (*0-87415-042-6*, 21B) OSU Foreign Lang.

— Intermediate Hungarian 1. (OSU Foreign Language Publications: No. 22). (Illus.). 124p. (Orig.). (HUN.). (C). 1984. teacher ed, pap. 7.50 (*0-87415-044-2*, 22A) OSU Foreign Lang.

— Intermediate Hungarian 1. (OSU Foreign Language Publications: No. 22). (Illus.). 434p. (Orig.). (HUN.). (C). 1988. student ed, pap. text ed. 19.00 (*0-87415-043-4*) OSU Foreign Lang.

— Intermediate Hungarian 1, 3 cass., Set. (OSU Foreign Language Publications: No. 22). (Orig.). (HUN.). (C). 1984. audio 15.00 (*0-87415-045-0*, 22B) OSU Foreign Lang.

— Intermediate Hungarian 2. (OSU Foreign Language Publications: No. 23). (Illus.). 398p. (Orig.). (HUN.). (C). 1984. teacher ed, pap. 8.00 (*0-87415-047-7*, 23A); student ed, pap. text ed. 16.00 (*0-87415-046-9*) OSU Foreign Lang.

— Intermediate Hungarian 2, 3 cass., Set. (OSU Foreign Language Publications: No. 23). (Orig.). (HUN.). (C). 1984. audio 15.00 (*0-87415-048-5*, 23B) OSU Foreign Lang.

— Reading Hungarian 1. (Illus.). 119p. (Orig.). (HUN.). (C). 1987. teacher ed, pap. 8.00 (*0-87415-149-X*, 60A); student ed, pap. text ed. 18.00 (*0-87415-148-1*, 60) OSU Foreign Lang.

— Reading Hungarian 1, 2 cass., Set. (Orig.). (HUN.). (C). 1987. audio 10.00 (*0-87415-159-7*, 60B) OSU Foreign Lang.

Peret, Benjamin. Death to the Pigs & Other Writings. Stella, Rachel et al, trs. LC 88-27731. (French Modernist Library). (Illus.). 219p. (FRE.). 1988. 25.00 (*0-8032-3685-9*); pap. 8.95 (*0-8032-8721-6*) U of Nebr Pr.

— From the Hidden Storehouse: A Selection of Poems by Benjamin Peret. Hollaman, Keith, tr. (Field Translation Ser.: No. 6). 150p. (Orig.). (C). 1981. 10.95 (*0-932440-10-X*); pap. 5.95 (*0-932440-11-8*) Oberlin Coll Pr.

— Marvelous World. Poems. Jackson, Elizabeth R., tr. LC 80-13631. 97p. 1985. text ed. 25.00 (*0-8071-0664-X*) La State U Pr.

Peretti, Burton W. The Creation of Jazz: Music, Race, & Culture in Urban America. (Music in American Life Ser.). (Illus.). 304p. (C). 1992. 29.95 (*0-252-01708-0*) U of Ill Pr.

Peretti, Frank. All is Well. 1991. 14.99 (*0-8499-0918-X*) Word Inc.

— The Oath. LC 95-14508. 512p. 1995. 23.99 (*0-8499-1178-8*) Word Pub.

Peretti, Frank E. Ce Monde de Tenebres. 456p. (FRE.). 1990. 16.95 (*0-8297-1213-5*) Life Pubs Intl.

— Door in the Dragons Throat. (Cooper Kids Adventure Ser.: No. 1). (J). (gr. 4-7). 1990. pap. 4.99 (*0-89107-591-7*) Crossway Bks.

— Escape from the Island of Aquarius. (Cooper Kids Adventure Ser.: No. 2). (J). (gr. 4-7). 1990. pap. 4.99 (*0-89107-592-5*) Crossway Bks.

— Esta Patente Oscuridad. 442p. 1989. 11.95 (*0-8297-0854-5*) Life Pubs Intl.

— Este Mundo Tenebroso. 420p. (POR.). 1990. pap. 14.95 (*0-8297-1650-5*) Life Pubs Intl.

— Penetrando la Oscuridad. 468p. (SPA.). 1990. 11.95 (*0-8297-0753-0*) Life Pubs Intl.

— Piercing the Darkness. LC 89-50338. 442p. 1989. pap. 10.99 (*0-89107-527-5*) Crossway Bks.

— Piercing the Darkness. large type ed. LC 93-16771. 1993. Acid-free paper. 21.95 (*0-8161-5699-9*) Hall.

— Prophet. LC 92-4850. 416p. (Orig.). 1992. pap. 11.99 (*0-89107-618-2*) Crossway Bks.

— This Present Darkness. LC 86-70282. 416p. (Orig.). 1986. pap. 10.99 (*0-89107-390-6*) Crossway Bks.

— This Present Darkness. large type ed. LC 92-35902. (General Ser.). (Orig.). 1993. 22.95 (*0-8161-5698-0*, Large Print Bks) Hall.

— This Present Darkness & Piercing the Darkness: Boxed Set, 2 vols., Set. 816p. (Orig.). 1991. pap. 21.98 (*0-89107-640-9*) Crossway Bks.

— Tilly. LC 88-70700. 128p. 1988. pap. 6.99 (*0-89107-496-1*) Crossway Bks.

— Tilly. 112p. (FRE.). 1990. 3.95 (*0-8297-1468-5*) Life Pubs Intl.

— Tily. 128p. 1989. 3.95 (*0-8297-0739-5*) Life Pubs Intl.

P
Q

An Asterisk (*) at the beginning of an entry indicates that the title is appearing in BIP for the first time.

— The Tombs of Anak. LC 86-73183. (Cooper Kids Adventure Ser.: No. 3). 144p. (Orig.). (J). (gr. 4-7). 1990. pap. 4.99 (*0-89107-593-3*) Crossway Bks.
— Trapped at the Bottom of the Sea. (Cooper Kids Adventure Ser.: No. 4). (J). (gr. 4-7). 1990. pap. 4.99 (*0-89107-594-1*) Crossway Bks.
Peretto, Pierre. An Introduction to the Modelling of Neural Networks. (Collection Alea - Saclay: Monographs & Texts in Statistical Physics: No. 2). (Illus.). 450p. (C). 1992. 105.00 (*0-521-41451-2*); pap. 42.95 (*0-521-42487-9*) Cambridge U Pr.
Peretz, David, et al, eds. Death & Grief: Selected Readings for the Medical Student. LC 77-6195. 270p. 1977. pap. 6.95 (*0-930194-82-9*) Ctr Thanatology.
Peretz, Don. Israel & the Palestine Arabs. LC 80-1915. reprint ed. 31.00 (*0-404-18984-9*) AMS Pr.
— The Middle East Today. 6th ed. LC 93-26376. 608p. 1994. text ed. 75.00 (*0-275-94575-8*, Praeger Pubs); pap. text ed. 19.95 (*0-275-94576-6*, Praeger Pubs) Greenwood.
— Palestinians, Refugees, & the Middle East Peace Process. LC 93-37820. 1993. pap. 12.95 (*1-878379-32-1*) US Inst Peace.
Peretz, Don, et al. Islam: Legacy of the Past, Challenge of the Future. 1984. 12.95 (*0-88427-048-3*) New Horizon NJ.
Peretz, I. L. The Magician. LC 85-42955. (Illus.). 32p. (J). (gr. k-6). 1985. text ed. 12.95 (*0-02-782770-4*, Mac Bks Young Read) S&S Childrens.
Peretz, Isaac L. Bontshe the Silent. Rappoport, A. S., tr. LC 77-178454. (Short Story Index Reprint Ser.). 1977. reprint ed. 18.95 (*0-8369-4055-5*) Ayer.
— The I. L. Peretz Reader. LC 90-52541. (Library of Yiddish Classics). 416p. 1992. reprint ed. pap. 16.00 (*0-8052-1001-6*) Schocken.
— Peretz. Liptzin, Solomon, ed. & tr. by. LC 72-5689. (Biography Index Reprints - YIVO Bilingual Ser.). 1977. reprint ed. 23.95 (*0-8369-8137-5*) Ayer.
— Stories & Pictures. 1975. 250.00 (*0-87968-376-7*) Gordon Pr.
***Peretz, Liz & Payne, Chris.** Developing Mental Health Services: A Foundation Training for Residential & Community Based Support Workers. 1994. pap. 35.00 (*0-902789-89-9*) St Mut.
Peretz, Paul. The Political Economy of Inflation in the United States. LC 82-24738. 264p. 1983. pap. text ed. 14.00 (*0-226-65672-1*) U Ch Pr.
Peretz, Paul, ed. Politics of American Economic Policy Making. LC 87-12827. 464p. (C). 1987. text ed. 62.95 (*0-87332-406-4*); pap. text ed. 25.95 (*0-87332-407-2*) M E Sharpe.
— The Politics of American Economic Policy Making. 2nd ed. (Illus.). 464p. 1995. 50.00 (*1-56324-566-3*) M E Sharpe.
— The Politics of American Economic Policy Making. 2nd ed. (Illus.). 464p. 1995. pap. text ed. 19.95 (*1-56324-567-1*) M E Sharpe.
Pereverzev, Sergei V. Optimization of Methods for Approximate Solution of Operator Equations. LC 93-25889. (Computational Mathematics & Analysis Ser.). 330p. (C). 1994. lib. bdg. 98.00 (*1-56072-140-5*) Nova Sci Pubs.
Perevodchikova, N. I., et al, eds. Tegafur-Ftorafur. (Beitraege zur Onkologie, Contributions to Oncology Ser.: Vol. 14). (Illus.). viii, 146p. 1983. pap. 37.00 (*3-8055-3653-4*) S Karger.
Pereyra, jt. auth. see Toledo.
Pereyra, V., ed. Numerical Methods. (Lecture Notes in Mathematics Ser.: Vol. 1005). 296p. 1983. pap. 38.70 (*0-387-12334-2*) Spr-Verlag.
***Perez.** Common Sense about Police Review. (C). 1995. pap. text ed. 18.95 (*1-56639-336-1*) Temple U Pr.
Perez, A., jt. auth. see Valle, J. W.
Perez-Abreu, Marilyn, ed. see Levy-Konesky, Nancy & Daggett, Karen.
Perez-Abreu, Marilyn, ed. see Wegmann, Brenda, et al.
Perez-Abreu, Marlyn, ed. see Gill, Mary M., et al.
Perez-Abreu, Victor, jt. ed. see Houdre, Christian.
Perez, Alejandro R. Colon Nunca Estuvo en San Salvador. (Illus.). 150p. 1990. 37.50 (*1-55914-106-9*); pap. 29.50 (*1-55914-107-7*) ABBE Pubs Assn.
— The Columbus Landfall in America & the Hidden Clues in His Journal. LC 87-47679. (Illus.). 113p. 1987. 37.50 (*0-88164-684-9*); pap. 29.50 (*0-88164-685-7*) ABBE Pubs Assn.
— Columbus Was Never in San Salvador. LC 88-47786. (Illus.). 133p. 1988. text ed. 37.50 (*0-88164-876-0*); pap. text ed. 29.50 (*0-88164-877-9*) ABBE Pubs Assn.
Perez-Amor, M., jt. ed. see Soares, Oliverio D.
Perez, Andrea, pseud. Die Landstortzerin Lustina Dietzin Picara Genandt, 2 vols. in 1. (Barockromane Ser.). 1082p. 1975. reprint ed. write for info. (*3-487-05470-1*, Pub. by Georg Olms GW) Lubrecht & Cramer.
Perez, Angeles, et al. Cassell's Contemporary Spanish. (Illus.). 512p. 1994. text ed. 25.00 (*0-02-595915-8*) Macmillan.
***Perez, Arturo.** Earmarking State Taxes. 3rd ed. 108p. 1994. 20.00 (*1-55516-524-9*, 5322) Natl Conf State Legis.
— Popular Catholicism: A Hispanic Perspective. 74p. 1988. pap. 5.00 (*0-8146-1935-5*) Liturgical Pr.
— State Budget Update: March 1994. (Legislative Finance Paper Ser.: No. 93). 18p. 1994. 15.00 (*1-55516-007-7*, 5101-93) Natl Conf State Legis.
— State Fiscal Outlook for 1993. (Legislative Finance Papers: No. 84). 28p. 1993. pap. text ed. 25.00 (*1-55516-082-4*, 5101-84) Natl Conf State Legis.
***Perez, Arturo & Snell, Ronald K.** State Early Retirement Programs in Fiscal Years 1992 & 1993. (State Legislative Report Ser.: Vol. 18, No. 5). 6p. 1993. 5.00 (*1-55516-225-8*, 7302-1805) Natl Conf State Legis.
— State Fiscal Outlook for 1995. (Legislative Finance Paper Ser.: No. 97). 21p. 1994. 25.00 (*1-55516-006-9*, 5101-90) Natl Conf State Legis.
Perez, Astrid. Astrid Janette Presenta: Cocina Internacional. LC 92-60604. (Illus.). 448p. (SPA.). 1992. 19.95 (*0-9633213-1-5*) Veva Pub.
Perez, Barbara, ed. see Moore, Michael.
Perez, Belia. Tres Dramas De Navidad. 24p. 1985. reprint ed. pap. 1.25 (*0-311-08221-1*) Casa Bautista.
Perez, Bernard. The First Three Years of Childhood. Christie, Alice M., ed. LC 74-21425. (Classics in Child Development Ser.). 330p. 1975. reprint ed. 29.95 (*0-405-06474-8*) Ayer.
Perez, Bertha & Torres-Guzman, Maria E. Learning in Two Worlds: An Integrated Spanish - English Biliteracy Approach. 230p. (Orig.). (ENG & SPA.). (C). 1992. text ed. 28.50 (*0-8013-0628-0*, 78592) Longman.
Perez-Blanco, H., jt. auth. see Stoecker, W. F.
Perez Bowie, Jose A., ed. see Baroja, Pio.
Perez-Brignoli, Hector. A Brief History of Central America. Sawrey, Ricardo B. & De Sawrey, Susana S., trs. 1989. 45.00 (*0-520-06049-0*) U CA Pr.
Perez-Brignoll, Hector. Brief History of Central America. 1989. pap. 13.00 (*0-520-06832-7*) U CA Pr.
Perez Bustamante, Ciriaco. Historia de Espana: 24. La Espana de Felipe III: La Politica Interior y los Problemas Internacionales. 660p. 1992. 189.50x (*84-239-4832-3*) Elliots Bks.
Perez-Bustillo, Camilo, tr. see Espada, Martin.
Perez-Bustillo, Camilo, tr. see Velez, Clemente S.
Perez, Candi, jt. auth. see Goodwin, Bob.
Perez, Candi, jt. auth. see Montousse, Juan L.
Perez, Carla. Getting off the Merry-Go-Round: You Can Live Without Compulsive Habits. rev. ed. LC 94-50887. 304p. 1994. reprint ed. pap. 11.95 (*0-915166-85-2*) Impact Pubs CA.
— Without Clothes, We're All Naked: Reflections on Life in the Real Lane. 160p. (Orig.). 1995. pap. 12.95 (*0-915166-87-9*) Impact Pubs CA.
Perez, Carlos A. & Brady, Luther W. Principles & Practice of Radiation Oncology. 2nd ed. (Illus.). 1568p. 1991. text ed. 195.00 (*0-397-51162-0*) Lippincott.
Perez-Carreras, P. & Bonet, J. Barrelled Locally Convex Spaces. (North-Holland Mathematics Studies: No. 131). 500p. 1987. 107.75 (*0-444-70129-X*, North Holland) Elsevier.
Perez, Cecilio. Ita: Mythology of the Yoruba Religion. LC 89-50356. (Illus.). 184p. (Orig.). (C). 1989. pap. 29.95 (*0-926603-00-0*) Obaecun Bks.
— Oricha: Metodologia de la Religion Yoruba. LC 89-92341. 377p. (Orig.). 1985. pap. 20.00 (*0-926603-01-9*) Obaecun Bks.
Perez-Collins, Yvonne. Soft Gardens: Make Flowers with Your Sewing Machine. LC 92-28182. (Creative Machine Arts Ser.). 160p. 1993. pap. 17.95 (*0-8019-8327-4*) Chilton.
Perez, Cristelia, jt. auth. see Kanellos, Nicolas.
Perez-Cruz, Ignacio H. Graciela. LC 93-70607. (Coleccion Caniqui Ser.). 146p. (Orig.). (SPA.). 1993. pap. 16.00 (*0-89729-672-9*) Ediciones.
Perez, Daniel E. Big Footnotes: A Comprehensive Bibliography Concerning Bigfoot, The Abominable Snowmen & Related Beings. 189p. (Orig.). 1988. pap. 10.00 (*0-9618380-0-0*) D Perez.
Perez, Dario E., jt. auth. see Moro, Oscar P.
***Perez, David.** Capitalism, Genetics & the Natural Order. 26p. 1993. pap. 2.50 (*0-89567-121-2*) World View Forum.
— Destruction of the Environment: Racism & the Profit System. 26p. 1993. pap. 2.50 (*0-614-02749-7*) World View Forum.
Perez De Ayala, Ramon. Belarmino & Apolonio. Baumgarten, Murray & Berns, Gabriel, trs. 1971. pap. 10.00 (*0-520-04958-6*) U CA Pr.
— Tigre Juan, el Curandero de su Honra. Lozano Marcos, Miguel A., ed. (Nueva Austral Ser.: Vol. 122). (SPA.). 1991. pap. text ed. 24.95x (*84-239-1922-6*) Elliots Bks.
Perez De Cuellar, Javier. Anarchy or Order: Annual Report, 1982-1991. 362p. 1991. 14.95 (*92-1-100466-7*, 91.I.52); pap. 9.95 (*0-685-53675-0*) UN.
Perez de Emde. Caminando Con Dios: Walking with God. (SPA.). 4.95 (*84-7228-812-9*, 220130, Pub. by Edit Clie SP) TSELF.
Perez de Guzman, Fernan. Generaciones & Semblanzas. LC 73-173946. reprint ed. 41.50 (*0-404-04993-1*) AMS Pr.
Perez De Montalban, Juan. Para Todos Exemplos Morales, Humanos y Divinos. 592p. reprint ed. write for info. (*0-318-71628-3*, Pub. by Georg Olms GW) Lubrecht & Cramer.
Perez de Villagra, Gaspar. Historia de la Nueve Mexico, 1601. Encinias, Miguel et al, eds. Rodriguez, Alfred & Sanchez, Joseph P., trs. LC 92-28780. 410p. 1992. 37.50x (*0-8263-1392-2*) U of NM Pr.
Perez, Demetrio, Jr. Citizens Training Handbook-Manual de Formacion Ciudadana: Discipline-Moral-Covism-Urbanity. (Illus.). 315p. (ENG & SPA.). (J). 1991. 25.00 (*0-9628780-0-6*) Ed Lncln-Mrt.
— La Escuela Privada Cubana. (SPA.). 1994. 20.00 (*0-9628780-1-4*) Ed Lncln-Mrt.
***Perez, Diana.** Roberto Clemente, Athlete & Hero. (Illus.). (J). (gr. 1-4). 1994. lib. bdg. 9.95 (*0-8136-5267-7*); pap. 4.95 (*0-8136-5273-1*) Modern Curr.
— Roberto Clemente, Atleta y Heroe. (Illus.). (SPA.). (J). (gr. 1-4). 1994. pap. 4.95 (*0-8136-5301-0*) Modern Curr.
Perez-Diaz, Victor. Structure & Change of Castilian Peasant Community: A Sociological Inquiry into Rural Castile, 1550-1990. LC 91-22825. (Harvard Studies in Sociology). 266p. 1992. 22.00 (*0-8240-8473-X*) Garland.
Perez-Diaz, Victor M. The Return of Civil Society: The Emergence of Democratic Spain. LC 92-29941. 367p. 1993. 37.50 (*0-674-76688-1*) HUP.
***Perez, Douglas W.** Common Sense about Police Review. LC 93-11192. 328p. 1994. pap. write for info. (*0-614-03052-8*) Temple U Pr.
— Common Sense about Police Review. LC 93-11192. 328p. 1994. 44.95 (*1-56639-132-6*) Temple U Pr.
Perez, Ed. A Look Around Endangered Animals. (Illus.). 32p. (J). (gr. 1-3). 1992. pap. 2.50 (*0-87406-579-8*) Willowisp Pr.
— A Look Around Rain Forests. (Illus.). 32p. (J). (gr. 1-3). 1993. pap. 2.99 (*0-87406-643-3*) Willowisp Pr.
***Perez, Emma.** Mexican American Women in Houston: Work, Family, & Community, 1990-1940. Date not set. write for info. (*0-614-06975-0*) Univ Houston Mex Amer.
Perez-Erdelyi, Mireya. La Picara y la Dama: La Imagen de las Nujeres en las Novelas Picaresco Cortesanas de Maria de Zayas y Sotomayor. LC 78-74597. (Coleccion Polymita Ser.). (Illus.). 128p. (SPA.). 1979. pap. 10.00 (*0-89729-216-2*) Ediciones.
Perez Esclarin, Antonio. Atheism & Liberation. Drury, John, tr. LC 78-731. 208p. reprint ed. pap. 59.30 (*0-8357-4074-9*, 2036764) Bks Demand.
Perez Esquivel, Adolfo. Christ in a Poncho: Testimonials of the Nonviolent Struggles in Latin America. Antoine, Charles, ed. Barr, Robert R., tr. LC 82-18760. 143p. reprint ed. pap. 40.80 (*0-8357-8550-5*, 2034892) Bks Demand.
Perez, Esther, ed. see Liebmann, Lisa.
Perez Fabo, J. A., illus. Espanol Paso a Paso, Nivel 1. 3rd ed. (Paso a Paso Ser.). 112p. (Orig.). (SPA.). (J). (gr. 1). 1991. reprint ed. pap. text ed. 4.95 (*1-56328-011-6*) Edit Plaza Mayor.
— Espanol Paso a Paso, Nivel 2. 3rd ed. (Paso a Paso Ser.). 160p. (Orig.). (SPA.). (J). (gr. 2). 1991. reprint ed. pap. text ed. 5.95 (*1-56328-012-4*) Edit Plaza Mayor.
— Espanol Paso a Paso, Nivel 3. 3rd ed. (Paso a Paso Ser.). 224p. (Orig.). (SPA.). (J). (gr. 3). 1991. reprint ed. pap. text ed. 6.95 (*1-56328-013-2*) Edit Plaza Mayor.
— Espanol Paso a Paso, Nivel 5. 3rd ed. (Paso a Paso Ser.). 288p. (Orig.). (SPA.). (J). (gr. 5). 1991. reprint ed. pap. text ed. 8.95 (*1-56328-015-9*) Edit Plaza Mayor.
— Espanol Paso a Paso, Nivel 6. 3rd ed. (Paso a Paso Ser.). 304p. (Orig.). (SPA.). (J). (gr. 6). 1991. reprint ed. pap. text ed. 8.95 (*1-56328-016-7*) Edit Plaza Mayor.
— Paso a Paso, Nivel 4. 3rd ed. (Paso a Paso Ser.). 256p. (Orig.). (J). (gr. 4). 1991. pap. text ed. 7.95 (*1-56328-014-0*) Edit Plaza Mayor.
Perez, Faustino. La Lolita. 192p. 1984. pap. 3.95 (*0-88184-043-2*) Carroll & Graf.
Perez Fernandez, M., jt. auth. see Bosque, I.
Perez, Fernando. Poemas. LC 88-81563. (Coleccion Espejo de Paciencia Ser.). 89p. (Orig.). (SPA.). 1989. pap. 9.95 (*0-89729-496-3*) Ediciones.
Perez, Fernando C. Dictionary of Related Ideas: Diccionario de Ideas Afines. 3rd ed. 912p. (SPA.). 1990. pap. write for info. (*0-7859-4950-X*) Fr & Eur.
— Gran Diccionario de Sinonimos y Antonimos. 1128p. (SPA.). 1990. 39.95 (*0-8288-8170-7*, S3383) Fr & Eur.
Perez Firmat, Gustavo. Do the Americas Have a Common Literature? LC 90-33990. 404p. (C). 1990. lib. bdg. 52.95 (*0-8223-1054-6*); pap. text ed. 21.95 (*0-8223-1072-4*) Duke.
— Idle Fictions: The Hispanic Vanguard Novel, 1926-1934. LC 82-12773. 200p. 1993. pap. text ed. 15.95 (*0-8223-1423-1*) Duke.
— Life on the Hyphen: The Cuban-American Way. LC 93-33590. (Illus.). 231p. (C). 1994. text ed. 30.00 (*0-292-71153-0*); pap. 12.95 (*0-292-76551-7*) U of Tex Pr.
— Literature & Liminality: Festive Readings in the Hispanic Tradition. LC 85-13077. xxi, 182p. 1986. 31.95 (*0-8223-0658-1*) Duke.
Perez, Francisco G. Como Leer el Lazarillo. Date not set. 43.00 (*0-685-69535-2*) Scripta.
Perez, G. Yvonne, et al. Let's Learn English: Second Language Activities for the Primary Grades, K-3. (Illus.). 91p. (Orig.). 1987. pap. 9.95 (*0-673-18371-8*) GdYrBks.
Perez-Galdos, Benito. Dona Perfecta; Misericordia. (SPA.). 1989. 7.95 (*0-8288-2572-6*) Fr & Eur.
— The Golden Fountain Cafe. Miller, Yvette E., ed. Rubin, Walter, tr. LC 89-8330. 352p. 1989. 17.95 (*0-935480-36-6*) Lat Am Lit Rev Pr.
— Miau y Marianela. (SPA.). 1989. 7.95 (*0-8288-2573-4*) Fr & Eur.
Perez Galdos, Benito. Las Novelas de Torquemada: Torquemada en la Hoguera, Torquemada en la Cruz. (SPA.). 1989. 18.50 (*0-8288-2584-X*) Fr & Eur.
— La Sombra de Galdos: Libra De Lectura, Repaso y Conversacion. Cardona, Rudolph, ed. (C). 1964. Tapes. audio write for info. (*0-393-99114-8*) Norton.
Perez, Genaro J. La Narrativa de Concha Alos: Texto, Pretexto, & Contexto. (Monografias Ser.: No. A 157). 100p. (SPA.). (C). 1994. pap. text ed. 45.00 (*1-85566-032-6*, Pub. by Tamesis Bks Ltd UK) Boydell & Brewer.
Perez, Gilbert, jt. auth. see Weltman, Dennis.
Perez Gomez, Alberto. Architecture & the Crisis of Modern Science. (Illus.). 416p. 1983. reprint ed. pap. 20.00 (*0-262-66055-5*) MIT Pr.
Perez-Gomez, Alberto. Polyphilo or the Dark Forest Revisited: An Erotic Epiphany of Architecture. (Illus.). 344p. 1994. pap. 17.95 (*0-262-66090-3*) MIT Pr.
***Perez-Gomez, Alberto & Parcell, Stephen, eds.** Chora: Intervals in the Philosophy of Architecture, Vol. 1. (Illus.). 288p. 1994. pap. 24.95 (*0-7735-1276-4*, Pub. by McGill CN) U of Toronto Pr.
— Chora - Intervals in the Philosophy of Architecture Vol. I. (Illus.). 288p. 1994. 60.00 (*0-7735-1193-8*, Pub. by McGill CN) U of Toronto Pr.
Perez-Gomez, Alberto, jt. ed. see Pelletier, Louise.
Perez, Guillermo H. Lo Que los Jovenes Deben Saber Acerca de las Drogas. 80p. 1987. reprint ed. pap. 3.25 (*0-311-46070-4*) Casa Bautista.
Perez, Isaac L. Stories & Pictures. Frank, Helena, tr. LC 75-152953. (Short Story Index Reprint Ser.). 1977. reprint ed. 25.95 (*0-8369-3868-2*) Ayer.
Perez, J. Guillent. A Case of Conscience. 370p. (Orig.). 1985. pap. 12.95 (*0-9607590-2-6*) Action Life Pubns.
Perez, Janet & Aycock, Wendell, eds. The Spanish Civil War in Literature. LC 90-10999. (Studies in Comparative Literature: No. 21). 1990. 24.95 (*0-89672-196-5*) Tex Tech Univ Pr.
Perez, Janet & Horn, Paul W. Contemporary Women Writers of Spain. (World Authors Ser.: No. 798). 256p. 1988. text ed. 26.95 (*0-8057-8229-X*, Twayne) Macmillan.
Perez, Janet & Miller, Stephen, eds. Critical Studies on Gonzalo Torrente Ballester. LC 88-61594. 196p. 1988. pap. 40.00 (*0-89295-054-4*) Society Sp & Sp-Am.
Perez, Jeannine. Bulletin Board Basics: Hands on Science. Stranich, Helen & Hogan, Eric, eds. (Illus.). 96p. 1991. pap. 9.95 (*1-878727-09-5*) First Teacher.
— Explore & Experiment. Durkin, Lisa L. & Hayes, Martha A., eds. (Illus.). 120p. 1988. pap. 10.95 (*0-9615005-8-1*) First Teacher.
Perez, Jose & Alsina, Ramon. Diccionario de Vinos Espanoles. 238p. (SPA.). 1991. reprint ed. 19.95 (*0-7859-5894-0*, 8430781358) Fr & Eur.
Perez, Jose & Spence, Wayman R. Perez on Medicine. (Illus.). 64p. 1993. 29.95 (*1-56796-005-7*) WRS Group.
— Perez on Sports. (Illus.). 64p. 1995. 29.92 (*1-56796-125-8*) WRS Group.
Perez, Jose G. Puerto Rico: U. S. Colony in the Caribbean. 23p. 1976. reprint ed. 2.50 (*0-87348-380-4*) Pathfinder NY.
Perez, Joseph. Coping Within the Alcoholic Family. LC 86-70658. xiii, 178p. 1986. pap. text ed. 9.45 (*0-915202-63-8*) Accel Devel.
— Counseling the Alcoholic Woman. 225p. (C). 1993. pap. text ed. 22.95 (*1-55959-055-6*) Accel Devel.
— Relationships: Adult Children of Alcoholics. LC 87-21105. 1989. 23.95 (*0-89876-150-6*) Gardner Pr.
— Tales of an Italian American Family. 1991. 17.95 (*0-89876-167-0*) Gardner Pr.
Perez, Joseph F. Alcoholism: Causes, Effects, & Treatment. LC 92-53191. 312p. 1992. pap. text ed. 21.95 (*1-55959-039-4*) Accel Devel.
— Counseling the Alcoholic Group. 145p. 1986. text ed. 22.95 (*0-89876-131-X*) Gardner Pr.
Perez, Juan A., jt. auth. see Mugny, Gabriel.
Perez, Julio E. Doppler Echocardiography: A Case Studies Approach. (Illus.). 259p. 1987. text ed. 45.00 (*0-07-049322-7*) Hlth Prof Div.
Perez, L. King. Ghoststalking. LC 93-41576. (J). 1994. 18.95 (*0-87614-821-6*, Carolrhoda) Lerner Group.
Perez, L. M. Guide to the Materials for American History in Cuban Archives. (Carnegie Inst. Wash.: Vol. 16). 1907. 35.00 (*0-527-00696-3*) Periodicals Srv.
Perez, Laura, jt. auth. see Taylor, Macey.
Perez-Lizaur, Marisol, jt. auth. see Lomnitz, Larissa A.
Perez-Lopez, Jorge. Cuban Studies XXIII. 288p. (C). 1994. text ed. 39.95 (*0-8229-3765-4*) U of Pittsburgh Pr.
— The Economics of Cuban Sugar. LC 90-40875. (Latin American Ser.). 336p. (C). 1991. 49.95 (*0-8229-3663-1*) U of Pittsburgh Pr.
— The Nineteen Eighty-Two Cuban Joint Venture Law: Context, Assessment & Prospects. 93p. 1985. 14.95 (*1-56000-662-5*, CP307) Transaction Pubs.
— Sugar & the Cuban Economy: An Assessment. 112p. (C). 1987. 8.95 (*0-685-63349-7*, CP320) U Miami N-S Ctr.
Perez-Lopez, Jorge, ed. Cuba at a Crossroads: Politics & Economics after the Fourth Party Congress. LC 94-16203. 288p. 1994. lib. bdg. 39.95 (*0-8130-1310-0*) U Press Fla.
Perez-Lopez, Jorge F. The Cuban State Budget: Concepts & Measurement. 51p. pap. 10.95 (*0-935501-38-X*) U Miami N-S Ctr.
— Cuba's Second Economy: From Behind the Scenes to Center Stage. 221p. (C). 1994. 32.95 (*1-56000-189-5*) Transaction Pubs.
Perez Lopez, Manuel M., ed. see De Torres Villarroel, Diego.
Perez, Louis A. Army Politics in Cuba, 1898-1958. LC 75-35440. (Pitt Latin American Ser.). 256p. reprint ed. pap. 73.00 (*0-8357-5750-1*, 2025443) Bks Demand.
Perez, Louis A., Jr. Cuba: Between Reform & Revolution. (Latin American Histories Ser.). (Illus.). 528p. 1988. 30.00 (*0-19-504587-4*); pap. text ed. 18.95 (*0-19-504586-6*) OUP.
— Cuba: Between Reform & Revolution. 2nd ed. (Latin American Histories Ser.). (Illus.). 544p. (C). 1995. 55.00 (*0-19-509481-6*); pap. text ed. 16.95 (*0-19-509482-4*) OUP.
— Cuba & the United States: Ties of Singular Intimacy. LC 89-20301. (United States & the Americas Ser.). 336p. 1990. 35.00 (*0-8203-1207-X*); pap. 15.00 (*0-8203-1208-8*) U of Ga Pr.
— Cuba Between Empires, Eighteen Seventy-Eight to Nineteen Two. LC 82-11059. (Latin American Ser.). 510p. 1983. 49.95 (*0-8229-3472-8*) U of Pittsburgh Pr.
— Cuba under the Platt Amendment: 1902-1934. LC 85-26451. (Latin American Ser.). 430p. 1986. 49.95 (*0-8229-3533-3*) U of Pittsburgh Pr.
— Cuba under the Platt Amendment, 1902-1934. LC 85-26451. (Latin American Ser.). 430p. (C). 1991. pap. 19.95 (*0-8229-5446-X*) U of Pittsburgh Pr.
— Essays on Cuban History: Historiography & Research. LC 94-29231. 318p. (C). 1995. lib. bdg. 44.95 (*0-8130-1329-1*) U Press Fla.

P Q

— A Guide to Cuban Collections in the United States. LC 91-6684. (Reference Guides to Archival & Manuscript Sources in World History Ser.: No. 1). 192p. 1991. text ed. 45.00 (*0-313-26858-4*, PGC, Greenwood Pr) Greenwood.

— Intervention, Revolution, & Politics in Cuba 1913-1921. LC 78-53601. (Latin American Ser.). 1978. 49.95 (*0-8229-3386-1*) U of Pittsburgh Pr.

***Perez, Louis A.** Jose Marti in the U.S. The Florida Experience. 120p. (Orig.). (C). 1995. pap. 25.00 (*0-87918-081-1*) ASU Lat Am St.

Perez, Louis A., Jr. Lords of the Mountain: Social Banditry & Peasant Protest in Cuba, 1878-1917. LC 88-19815. (Latin American Ser.). 256p. 1989. 49.95 (*0-8229-3601-1*) U of Pittsburgh Pr.

Perez, Louis A., Jr., comp. Cuba: An Annotated Bibliography. LC 87-28017. (Bibliographies & Indexes in World History Ser.: No. 10). 320p. 1988. text ed. 75.00 (*0-313-26162-8*, PZC/, Greenwood Pr) Greenwood.

Perez, Louis A., Jr., ed. Cuban Studies, Vol. 21. LC 75-64935. (Latin American Ser.). 320p. 1992. 39.95 (*0-8229-3691-7*) U of Pittsburgh Pr.

— Cuban Studies XXV. (Latin American Ser.). 296p. (C). 1996. 39.95x (*0-8229-3911-8*) U of Pittsburgh Pr.

— Slaves, Sugar, & Colonial Society: Travel Accounts of Cuba, 1801-1899. LC 91-44977. (Latin American Silhouettes Ser.). 259p. 1992. 40.00 (*0-8420-2354-2*, SR Bks); pap. 14.95 (*0-8420-2415-8*, SR Bks) Scholarly Res Inc.

Perez, Louis C., ed. see Sabato, Ernesto.

Perez, Louis G. The Dalai Lama. LC 92-38325. (Biographies: World Leaders Ser.). (J). 1993. 19.93 (*0-86625-480-3*); 14.95 (*0-685-67761-3*) Rourke Pubns.

Perez, M. A., jt. auth. see Heurta, R.

Perez, M. R., ed. see Van Den Heuvel, E. P.

Perez, Manuel S. Quien Manda En Cuba? Las Estructuras Del Polder. La Elite. LC 89-83374. (Coleccion Cuba y Sus Jueces Ser.). (Illus.). 255p. (SPA.). 1989. 35.00 (*0-89729-551-X*) Ediciones.

Perez-Marchand, Monelisa L. History of Ideas in Puerto Rico. (Puerto Rico Ser.). 1979. lib. bdg. 59.95 (*0-8490-2935-X*) Gordon Pr.

Perez, Maria, jt. auth. see Gomez-Quintero, Ella.

Perez, Maria E. Lo Americano en el Teatro De Sor Juana Ines de la Cruz. 1975. 14.00 (*0-88303-020-9*); pap. 11.00 (*0-685-73221-5*) E Torres & Sons.

Perez, Maria E., jt. auth. see Gomez-Quintero, Ela R.

Perez-Mato, J. M., et al, eds. Methods of Structural Analysis of Modulated Structures & Quasicrystals. 600p. (C). 1991. text ed. 128.00 (*981-02-0692-5*) World Scientific Pub.

Perez, Maya & Latterman, Terry. Born with a Veil: A Mystic. 1991. pap. 9.95 (*1-878901-04-4*) Hampton Roads Pub Co.

Perez, Maya, jt. auth. see Latterman, Terry.

Perez, Miguel E., jt. ed. see Guzman, Carmen.

Perez, N. A. Breaker. LC 87-33891. 216p. (J). (gr. 5-9). 1988. 14.95 (*0-395-45537-5*) HM.

— One Special Year. LC 84-25258. 200p. (J). (gr. 6-9). 1985. 13.95 (*0-395-36693-3*) HM.

— The Slopes of War. (Illus.). 224p. (J). (gr. 7 up). 1984. 14.95 (*0-395-35642-3*, 5-93140) HM.

— The Slopes of War. (Illus.). 224p. (J). (gr. 7 up). 1990. pap. 5.95 (*0-395-54979-5*) HM.

Perez, Nelida & Tirado, Amilcar. Boricuas En el Norte. (Centro Library). 39p. 1987. reprint ed. pap. 5.00 (*1-878483-26-9*) Hunter Coll CEP.

— Boricuas En el Norte, Set. (Centro Library). 39p. 1987. reprint ed. pap. 1.00 (*1-878483-39-0*) Hunter Coll CEP.

Perez, Nelida & Tirado, Amilcar, eds. Pedro Albizu Campos (1891-1965) (Puerto Rican Bibliographies Ser.). (Illus.). 30p. (C). 1986. reprint ed. pap. 1.00 (*1-878483-43-9*) Hunter Coll CEP.

Perez, Nelida, jt. ed. see Tirado, Amilcar.

Perez, Nissan N., jt. auth. see Ollman, Arthur.

Perez-Palacios, G., jt. ed. see Van Look, P. F.

Perez, Paulina & Snedeker, Cheryl. Special Women: The Role of the Professional Labor Assistant. (Illus.). 157p. (Orig.). 1990. pap. 8.95 (*0-937604-10-0*) Pennypress.

— Special Women: The Role of the Professional Labor Assistant. 2nd ed. LC 94-94211. (Illus.). 157p. (Orig.). 1994. pap. 9.95 (*0-9641159-9-9*) Cutting Edge.

Perez-Prendes, Jose M., ed. see Garcia de Valdeavellano, Luis.

Perez Prendes, Jose M., et al. Historia de Espana, Vol. 3: Espana Visigoda V. 2 la Monarquia la Cultura, las Artes. 510p. (SPA.). 1992. 189.50x (*84-239-4996-6*) Elliots Bks.

Perez Priego, Miguel A., ed. see De Mena, Juan.

Perez Priego, Miguel A., ed. see Manrique, Jorge.

Perez, Rachel. Affinities. (Orig.). 1993. pap. text ed. 4.95 (*1-56333-113-6*) Masquerade.

— Odd Women. (Orig.). 1993. pap. text ed. 4.95 (*1-56333-123-3*) Masquerade.

Perez, Rachel L. Ms. Pea's Pet Store & Other Children's Tales. (J). 1994. 7.95 (*0-533-10836-5*) Vantage.

Perez, Ramon. Garabandal-the Village Speaks. Orhelein, Ann, ed. Mathews, Annette L., tr. LC 81-51901. Orig. Title: Garabandal-Le Village Parle. (Illus.). 352p. (Orig.). 1981. pap. 5.00 (*0-686-32902-3*) Workers Lady Mt Carmel.

Perez-Ramon, Joacquin. Self & Non-Self in Early Buddhism. (Religion & Society Ser.: No. 17). 1980. 84.65 (*90-279-7987-1*) Mouton.

Perez, Ramon T. Diary of an Undocumented Immigrant. Reavis, Dick J., tr. LC 91-7869. 1991. pap. 9.50 (*1-55885-032-5*) Arte Publico.

Perez-Ramos, Antonio. Francis Bacon's Idea of Science & the Maker's Knowledge Tradition. (Illus.). 352p. 1989. 85.00 (*0-19-824979-9*) OUP.

***Perez, Reinaldo, ed.** Handbook of Electromagnetic Compatibility. (Illus.). 1024p. 1995. text ed. 149.95 (*0-12-550710-0*) Acad Pr.

Perez-Reverte, Arturo. Flanders Panel. 1994. 21.95 (*0-15-148926-2*) HarBrace.

— The Flandes Panel. Costa, Margaret J., tr. (ENG.). 1994. write for info. (*0-318-71665-8*) HarBrace.

Perez Rioja, Jose A. Diccionario Literario Universal. 994p. (SPA.). 1977. 89.95 (*0-8288-5351-7*, S31441) Fr & Eur.

Perez, Robert C. Inside Investment Banking. LC 84-11713. 220p. 1984. text ed. 45.00 (*0-275-91242-6*, C1242, Praeger Pubs) Greenwood.

— Inside Venture Capital: Past, Present, & Future. LC 86-30146. 202p. 1986. text ed. 55.00 (*0-275-92118-2*, C2118, Praeger Pubs) Greenwood.

— Marketing Financial Services. LC 83-4230. 192p. 1983. text ed. 49.95 (*0-275-91723-1*, C1723, Praeger Pubs) Greenwood.

***Perez, Robert C. & Willett, Edward F.** Clarence Dillon: A Wall Street Enigma. LC 94-48138. 1995. write for info. (*1-56833-050-2*) Madison Bks UPA.

— A Will to Win: The Biography of Ferdinand Eberstadt. LC 89-1898. (Contributions in Economics & Economic History Ser.: No. 96). 181p. 1989. text ed. 45.00 (*0-313-26738-3*, PWB, Greenwood Pr) Greenwood.

Perez, Roberto M. & Encinosa, Enrique G. The Castro Revolution: Crime Without Punishment. Kvederas, Robert, ed. 250p. 1992. 25.00 (*0-944273-10-6*) U S Cuba Inst.

***Perez, Rolando.** The Ideology of Information: Some Considerations for Academic Librarians. 72p. (Orig.). 1995. pap. text ed. 5.00 (*0-9646208-0-4*) Stranger Bks.

— The Lining of Our Souls. (Orig.). 1995. pap. text ed. 5.00 (*0-9646208-1-2*) Stranger Bks.

— The Odyssey. LC 89-61087. 125p. (Orig.). 1990. 15.00 (*0-944657-07-9*); pap. 10.00 (*0-944657-08-7*) Brook Hse Pr.

— On Anarchy & Schizoanalysis. (Illus.). 160p. (Orig.). (C). 1990. pap. text ed. 8.00 (*0-936756-39-X*) Autonomedia.

Perez, Roman C. & Ferrie, Michel F. Introduction to Business Translation: A Handbook in English - Spanish Contrastive Linguistics. 2nd rev. ed. LC 85-8581. 163p. (C). 1985. pap. 7.00 (*0-8477-3342-4*) U of PR Pr.

Perez, Rosanne. The Legend of Eek Iguana. LC 91-71997. 64p. (J). (gr. 3-7). 1993. pap. 7.00 (*1-56002-078-4*, Univ Edtns) Aegina Pr.

Perez, Rosita. The Music Is You. 2nd ed. 1986. 10.00 (*0-685-43015-4*) T Knox Pub.

— The Music Is You: A Guide to Thinking Less & Feeling More. (Illus.). 124p. (Orig.). 1994. write for info. (*0-9611354-1-7*); disk write for info. (*0-9611354-2-5*) T Knox Pub.

— The Music Is You: A Guide to Thinking Less & Feeling More. 3rd ed. (Illus.). (Orig.). 1994. pap. 15.00 (*0-9611354-5-X*) T Knox Pub.

— The Music Is You: A Guide to Thinking Less & Feeling More. 4th ed. 124p. (Orig.). 1994. pap. 12.50 (*0-9611354-7-6*) T Knox Pub.

Perez-Sabido, Jesus. Spanish - English Handbook for Medical Professionals: Compendio en Ingles y Espanol Para Profesionales de la Medicine. 4th ed. Rogers, Gregg, ed. LC 93-37022. 400p. (ENG & SPA.). 1993. 29.95 (*1-878487-61-2*) Practice Mgmt Info.

— Spanish-English Handbook. 3rd ed. 224p. 1988. pap. 29.95 (*0-87489-478-6*) Med Economics.

Perez-Sala, Paulino. Interferencia Linguistica Del Ingles En el Espanol Hablado En Puerto Rico. LC 72-93776. (Working Paper: No. 77-3). 132p. (SPA.). 1973. 7.50 (*0-913480-10-X*) Inter Am U Pr.

Perez Sanchez, Alfonso E., jt. auth. see Sayre, Eleanor A.

Perez-Segura, E. & Jacques-Ayala, C., eds. Studies of Sonoran Geology. (Special Paper Ser.: No. 254). (Illus.). 136p. 1991. pap. 32.50 (*0-8137-2254-3*) Geol Soc.

Perez-Soler, A. Inflammatory & Artresia-Inducing Disease of the Liver & Bile Ducts. (Monographs in Pediatrics: Vol. 8). (Illus.). 1976. 62.50 (*3-8055-2257-6*) S Karger.

Perez-Stable, Maria A., jt. auth. see Cordier, Mary H.

Perez-Stable, Marifeli. The Cuban Revolution: Origins, Course, & Legacy. LC 93-19990. 256p. (C). 1993. 23.00 (*0-19-508406-3*) OUP.

— The Cuban Revolution: Origins, Course, & Legacy. LC 93-19990. 256p. (C). 1993. pap. 14.95 (*0-19-508407-1*) OUP.

Perez-Tamayo, Ruy. Mechanisms of Disease: An Introduction to Pathology. 2nd ed. LC 84-25728. (Illus.). 668p. reprint ed. pap. 180.00 (*0-8357-6315-3*, 2035588) Bks Demand.

Perez-Tamayo, Ruy & Rojkind, Marcos, eds. Molecular Pathology of Connective Tissues. LC 72-86611. (Biochemistry of Disease Ser.: No. 3). (Illus.). 416p. reprint ed. pap. 118.60 (*0-7837-0887-4*, 2041193) Bks Demand.

Perez, Theresa, jt. auth. see Marquez, Nancy.

Perez-Tibi, Dora. Dufy. (Illus.). 336p. 1989. 75.00 (*0-8109-1147-7*) Abrams.

Perez, Tony. Soundscape with Humans. (Orig.). 1974. pap. 1.50 (*0-915242-02-8*) Pygmalion Pr.

***Perez-Torres, Rafael.** Movements in Chicano Poetry: Against Myths, Against Margins. (Studies in American Literature & Culture: No. 88). 225p. (C). 1995. pap. 17.95 (*0-521-47803-0*) Cambridge U Pr.

— Movements in Chicano Poetry: Against Myths, Against Margins. (Studies in American Literature & Culture: No. 88). 225p. (C). 1995. 59.95 (*0-521-47019-6*) Cambridge U Pr.

Perez-Trejo, F. Desertification & Land Degradation in the European Mediterranean. 69p. 1994. pap. 14.00 (*92-826-7059-7*, CG-NA-14850-ENC, Pub. by Europ Com) UNIPUB.

Perez-Vega, Ivette. El Cielo & la Tierra en Sus Manos: Los Grandes Propietarios de Ponce, 1816-1830. LC 85-81454. 123p. (SPA.). 1985. pap. 5.95 (*0-940238-22-5*) Ediciones Huracan.

Perez-Venero, Alex. Before the Five Frontiers: Panama from 1821-1903. LC 77-78317. 32.50 (*0-404-16003-4*) AMS Pr.

Perez-Vidal, Angel. Muchas Gracias...Marielitos...Siete Anos Despues: Una Historia Verdadera y Siete Cuentos Imaginados. LC 87-83680. (Coleccion Caniqui Ser.). 151p. (Orig.). (SPA.). 1988. pap. 12.00 (*0-89729-473-4*) Ediciones.

Perez-Wilson, Mario. The Design of Experiments: A Seven-Stage Methodology. (Variation Reduction Program Ser.). 400p. 1993. 95.00 (*1-883237-05-X*) Adv Systs Cnslts.

— M - PcPs-Cpk Software: Software for Machine - Process Capability Studies. (Variation Reduction Program Ser.). 120p. 1993. 800.00 (*1-883237-02-5*) Adv Systs Cnslts.

— Machine - Process Capability Study: A Five Stage Methodology for Optimizing Manufacturing Processes. rev. ed. (Variation Reduction Program Ser.). 238p. 1993. reprint ed. 74.95 (*1-883237-00-9*) Adv Systs Cnslts.

— Multi-Vari Chart & Analysis. (Variation Reduction Program Ser.). 86p. 1993. 35.00 (*1-883237-01-7*) Adv Systs Cnslts.

Perez y Mena, Andres I. Speaking with the Dead: Development of Afro-Latin Religion among Puerto Ricans in the United States. LC 91-8469. (Immigrant Communities & Ethnic Minorities in the U. S. & Canada Ser.: No. 75). 1991. 55.00 (*0-404-19485-0*) AMS Pr.

Perez y Mena, Andres I., jt. ed. see Stevens-Arroyo, Anthony M.

Perez, Yvonne, jt. auth. see Schenck, N. C.

***Perfecky, George, tr. & intro.** The Galician-Volhynian Chronicle, Vol. 9. (Harvard Library of Early Ukrainian Literature). (Illus.). 220p. 1995. 35.00 (*0-916458-70-9*) Harvard Ukrainian.

Perfect, Christopher. The Complete Typographer. 224p. 1992. pap. text ed. 39.20 (*0-13-045667-5*) P-H.

Perfect, Christopher & Rookledge, Gordon. Rookledge's International Typefinder. 292p. 1991. pap. 34.95 (*1-55921-052-4*) Moyer Bell.

Perfect, T. John, jt. ed. see Denno, Robert F.

Perfect, William. Annals of Insanity: Comprising a Selection of Curious & Interesting Cases in the Different Species of Lunacy, Melancholy, or Madness. LC 75-16726. (Classics in Psychiatry Ser.). 1976. reprint ed. 28.95 (*0-405-07449-2*) Ayer.

Perfecto, Ivette, jt. auth. see Vandermeer, John.

Perfetti, C. A., jt. ed. see Rieben, L.

Perfetti, Charles A. Reading Ability. (Illus.). 1985. 45.00 (*0-19-503501-1*) OUP.

***Perfetti, Charles A., et al.** Text-Based Learning & Reasoning: Studies in History. 240p. 1995. text ed. 49.95 (*0-8058-1643-7*); pap. 22.50 (*0-8058-1977-0*) L Erlbaum Assocs.

Perfetti, Charles A., jt. ed. see Lesgold, Alan M.

Perfetti, Patricia B., jt. auth. see Terrell, Charles R.

Perfetto, Edda, jt. auth. see Ettinger, Blanche.

Perfil'ev, Boris V., et al. Applied Capillary Microscopy: The Role of Microorganisms in the Formation of Iron-Manganese Desposits. LC 65-15003. 130p. reprint ed. pap. 37.10 (*0-8357-5674-2*, 2020669) Bks Demand.

Perfilov, N. A. & Eismont, V. P. Physics of Nuclear Fission. 216p. 1964. text ed. 59.50 (*0-7065-0336-8*, Pub. by Keter Pub IS) Coronet Bks.

Performance Solutions Staff. Supervisory Training Program: Student Modules. rev. ed. Watson, Gail, ed. 380p. 1993. teacher ed write for info. (*0-318-72221-6*); text ed. write for info. (*0-89982-323-8*) Am Bankers.

Performax (FLETCHER) Staff. Management Control in Today's Teamwork Organization: How to Get Things Done Without Exercising Direct Authority. 208p. 1991. per., text ed. 15.95 (*0-8403-6471-7*) Kendall-Hunt.

***Pergallo-Dittko, V., et al, eds.** A Core Curriculum for Diabetes Education. 2nd ed. (Illus.). 732p. (C). 1994. pap. text ed. 85.00 (*1-881876-01-2*) Am Assn Diabetes Ed.

Pergamon-Infotech Staff. Computer State of the Art Reports. write for info. (*0-318-57470-5*, Pergamon Pr) Elsevier.

Pergamon Press Staff, ed. Information Mongolia: The Comprehensive Reference Source of the People's Republic of Mongolia (MPR) Mongolian People's Republic Academy of Sciences Staff, tr. & comp. by. (World Information Ser.: No. 6). (Illus.). 500p. 1990. 150.00 (*0-08-036193-5*, Pergamon Pr) Elsevier.

Pergaud, Louis. De Goupil a Margot. (FRE.). 1982. pap. 10.95 (*0-7859-4162-2*) Fr & Eur.

— Guerre des Boutons. (Folio Ser.: No. 758). (FRE.). 1987. pap. 8.95 (*2-07-036758-4*) Schoenhof.

— La Guerre des Boutons. (FRE.). 1976. pap. 10.95 (*0-7859-4056-1*) Fr & Eur.

— Le Roman de Miraut: Chien de Chasse. (FRE.). 1978. pap. 11.95 (*0-7859-4102-9*) Fr & Eur.

Pergler, Charles. Judicial Interpretation of International Law in the United States. viii, 222p. 1983. reprint ed. lib. bdg. 25.00 (*0-8377-1016-2*) Rothman.

Pergrin, David. The Carver's Handbook I: Woodcarving the Wonders of Nature. LC 84-51192. (Illus.). 60p. 1984. pap. 5.95 (*0-88740-015-9*) Schiffer.

— The Carver's Handbook II: Carving the Wild Life of the Forest & Jungle. LC 84-52153. (Illus.). 60p. 1985. pap. 5.95 (*0-88740-029-9*) Schiffer.

— The Carver's Handbook III: Woodcarving Wild Animals. LC 85-50298. (Illus.). 48p. 1985. pap. 5.95 (*0-88740-039-6*) Schiffer.

Pergrin, David E. & Hammel, Eric. First Across the Rhine: The Story of the 291st Engineer Combat Battalion. 368p. 1990. mass mkt. 4.95 (*0-8041-0615-0*) Ivy Books.

— First Across the Rhine: The Story of the 291st Engineer Combat Battalion in France, Belgium, & Germany. LC 94-27237. (Illus.). 343p. 1994. 25.00 (*0-935553-09-6*) Pacifica Pr.

Perguson, Barbara P. Basic Bible Commentary, Vol. 4: Joshua, Judges, & Ruth. Deming, Lynne M., ed. LC 94-10965. 160p. (Orig.). 1994. pap. 4.95 (*0-687-02623-7*) Abingdon.

Perham, Jane & Sawyer, Laura, eds. Gems & Minerals: A Guide to Rockhounding in Maine. (Maine Geographic Ser.). (Illus.). 1986. pap. 4.95 (*0-89933-059-2*) DeLorme Map.

Perham, M. F. The Economics of Tropical Dependency, 2 vols. 1976. lib. bdg. 200.00 (*0-8490-1748-3*) Gordon Pr.

— Tribes of the Niger Delta: Their Religion & Customs. 1976. lib. bdg. 59.95 (*0-8490-2768-3*) Gordon Pr.

Perham, Margery. Lugard, 2 vols. Incl. Years of Adventure 1858-1898. 1956. 45.00 (*0-318-55722-3*); (Illus.). 1498p. 1968. Set. 79.50 (*0-208-00235-9*) Shoe String.

— Pacific Prelude: A Journey to Samoa & Australasia. LC 88-70563. 272p. 1988. 40.00 (*0-7206-0683-7*, Pub. by P Owen Ltd UK) Dufour.

— West African Passage: A Journey Through Nigeria, Chad & the Cameroons. 245p. 1983. 33.00 (*0-7206-0609-8*, Pub. by P Owen Ltd UK) Dufour.

Perham, Margery F. The Colonial Reckoning: End of Imperial Rule in Africa in the Light of British Experience. LC 76-25998. 203p. 1976. reprint ed. text ed. 55.00 (*0-8371-9016-9*, PECR, Greenwood Pr) Greenwood.

— Native Administration in Nigeria. LC 74-15078. reprint ed. 24.50 (*0-404-12127-6*) AMS Pr.

Perham, Margery F., jt. auth. see Proudfoot, Mary M.

***Perham, Michael & Lloyd, Trevor.** Enriching the Christian Year. 288p. (Orig.). 1993. pap. text ed. 29.95 (*0-8146-2242-9*, Liturg Pr Bks) Liturgical Pr.

Perham, Michael & Stevenson, Kenneth. Welcoming the Light of Christ. 120p. (Orig.). 1991. pap. text ed. 7.95 (*0-8146-2048-5*) Liturgical Pr.

***Perham, Molly.** Cooking for One: Quick & Easy. 1994. pap. 7.99 (*0-572-01980-7*, Pub. by W Foulsham UK) Trans-Atl Phila.

***Perham, Molly & Rowe, Julian.** Food. LC 94-39692. (MapWorlds Ser.). (J). 1995. lib. bdg. 12.60 (*0-531-14374-0*) Watts.

— Landscapes. LC 95-11947. (MapWorlds Ser.). (Illus.). (J). (gr. 5-8). 1995. lib. bdg. 12.60 (*0-531-14373-2*) Watts.

— People. LC 95-2727. (MapWorlds Ser.). (Illus.). (J). 1995. lib. bdg. 12.60 (*0-531-14362-7*) Watts.

— Resources. LC 95-6877. (MapWorlds Ser.). (J). 1995. write for info. (*0-531-14387-2*) Watts.

— Water. LC 94-39691. (MapWorlds Ser.). (Illus.). (J). (gr. 5-8). 1995. lib. bdg. 12.60 (*0-531-14361-9*) Watts.

Perham, Molly & Steele, Philip. The Children's Illustrated World Atlas: A Young Person's Guide to the World. LC 93-70591. (Illus.). 56p. (J). (gr. 1 up). 1993. 9.98 (*1-56138-331-7*) Courage Bks.

Perham, Molly, jt. auth. see Rowe, Julian.

Perham, Molly, jt. auth. see Rowe, Julina.

Peri, Yoram. Between Battles & Ballots: Israeli Military in Politics. (Cambridge Middle East Library: No. 1). 368p. 1983. 69.95 (*0-521-24414-5*) Cambridge U Pr.

Periam, Jonathan. The Groundswell: A History of the Origins, Aims, & Progress of the Farmers' Movement Embracing an Authoritative Account of the Farmers' Clubs Granges Etc. LC 72-89080. (Rural America Ser.). 1973. reprint ed. 40.00 (*0-8420-1493-4*) Scholarly Res Inc.

Periasamy, K., ed. Histochemistry, Development & Structural Anatomy of Angiosperm: A Symposium. 305p. 1980. 40.00 (*1-55528-211-3*, Pub. by Today & Tomorrows P & P II) Scholarly Pubns.

Perica, Esther. The American Woman: Her Role in the Revolutionary War. LC 80-28294. (Cameo Series of Notable Women). (Orig.). 1981. pap. 5.00 (*0-912526-28-9*) Lib Res.

— Newspaper Indexing for Historical Societies, Colleges & High Schools. LC 74-20822. 60p. 1975. pap. 4.00 (*0-912526-15-7*) Lib Res.

— They Took the Challenge: The Story of Rolling Meadows. LC 79-14803. (Illus.). 167p. 1980. 9.75 (*0-9602782-0-6*) Rolling Meadows.

Perich, Richard, ed. see Grear, Robert D.

***Perich, Shawn.** Fly Fishing the North Country. (Illus.). 160p. (Orig.). 1995. pap. 12.95 (*1-57025-063-4*) Pfeifer-Hamilton.

— The North Shore: A Four Season Guide to Minnesota's Favorite Destination. LC 92-70990. (Illus.). 208p. (Orig.). 1992. pap. 14.95 (*0-938586-67-X*) Pfeifer-Hamilton.

Perich, Shawn C. Fishing Lake Superior: A Complete Guide to Stream, Shoreline, & Open-Water Angling. (Illus.). 192p. (Orig.). 1994. pap. 12.95 (*1-57025-022-7*) Pfeifer-Hamilton.

Periegeta, Dionysius. Dionysius Periegeta - Concordantia in Dionysii Periegetae Descriptionem Orbis Terrarum. Tsavari, Isabelle, ed. (Alpha-Omega, Reihe A Ser.: Bd. CXXX). 273p. (GER.). 1992. write for info. (*3-487-09601-3*, Pub. by Georg Olms GW) Lubrecht & Cramer.

Periegeta, Pausanias. Graeciae Descriptio, 6 vols. in 3, Set. xli, 2758p. (GER.). 1983. reprint ed. write for info. (*3-487-07394-3*, Pub. by Georg Olms GW) Lubrecht & Cramer.

Periers, Bonaventure des. Cymbalum Mundi: Four Very Ancient Joyous & Facetious Poetic Dialogues. Knapp, Bettina L., tr. LC 65-14414. 1965. lib. bdg. 24.50 (*0-8057-5631-0*) Irvington.

Perigo, Grace, tr. Letters of Adam of Perseigne. LC 76-15486. (Cistercian Fathers Ser.: No. 21). 1976. 11.95 (*0-87907-621-6*) Cistercian Pubns.

P
Q

An Asterisk (*) at the beginning of an entry indicates that the title is appearing in BIP for the first time.

Perigord, Michel. Achieving Total Quality Management: A Program for Action. LC 90-48163. (Illus.). 392p. 1991. 50.00x (*0-915299-60-7*) Prod Press.
— Dictionnaire De la Qualite: French-English. 351p. (FRE.). 1993. pap. 105.00 (*0-7859-7739-2*, 2124678116) Fr & Eur.
Perihelion Software Staff. The Helios Parallel Operating System. 600p. 1991. pap. text ed. 58.00 (*0-13-381237-5*) P-H.
***Perillo, G. M., ed.** Geomorphology & Sedimentology of Estuaries. LC 95-15247. (Developments in Sedimentology Ser.: Vol. 53). 1995. write for info. (*0-444-88170-0*) Elsevier.
Perillo, Joseph M. Corbin on Contracts: (SS1-108), Vol. 1. rev. ed. 700p. 1993. text ed. write for info. (*0-314-01881-6*) West Pub.
Perillo, Joseph M., jt. auth. see Calamari, John D.
Perillo, Lucia M. Dangerous Life. 61p. 1989. pap. text ed. 9.95 (*1-55553-059-1*) NE U Pr.
Perin, Constance. Belonging in America: Reading Between the Lines. LC 87-40371. (New Directions in Anthropological Writing Ser.). 320p. (C). 1988. pap. 30.00 (*0-299-11580-1*) U of Wis Pr.
— Belonging in America: Reading Between the Lines. LC 87-40371. (New Directions in Anthropological Writing Ser.). 320p. 1990. pap. 13.95 (*0-299-11584-4*) U of Wis Pr.
— Everything in Its Place: Social Order & Land Use in America. LC 77-72133. 1977. text ed. 44.50 (*0-691-09372-5*) Princeton U Pr.
***Perin, James C.** Atman. (Orig.). 1994. pap. 7.00 (*0-9644656-0-4*) Deep Lingo.
Perin, Marie-Madeleine. English - French Business Dictionary. 92p. 1990. pap. 14.95 (*0-8288-9446-9*) Fr & Eur.
Perin, Robert. Rome in Canada: The Vatican & Canadian Affairs in the Late Victorian Age. 300p. 1990. text ed. 45.00 (*0-8020-5854-X*); pap. text ed. 20.95 (*0-8020-6762-X*) U of Toronto Pr.
Perin, Romaine. The Human Heart. 40p. (Orig.). 1983. pap. 3.00 (*0-917061-17-9*) Top Stories.
Perina, Jan. Coherence of Light. (Orig.). 1985. lib. bdg. 145.50 (*90-277-2004-5*) Kluwer Ac.
— Quantum Optics & Fundamentals of Physics. (Fundamental Theories of Physics Ser.). 352p. (C). 1994. lib. bdg. 132.00 (*0-7923-3000-5*) Kluwer Ac.
— Quantum Statistics of Linear & Nonlinear Optical Phenomena. 1984. lib. bdg. 122.50 (*90-277-1512-2*) Kluwer Ac.
— Quantum Statistics of Linear & Nonlinear Optical Phenomena. 2nd rev. ed. (C). 1900. lib. bdg. 180.00 (*0-7923-1171-X*) Kluwer Ac.
Perina, Jan, ed. Selected Papers on Photon Statistics & Coherence in Nonlinear Optics. (Milestone Ser.: Vol. MS39). 512p. 1991. 107.00 (*0-8194-0738-0*); pap. 92.00 (*0-8194-0739-9*) SPIE.
Perinatal Loss Project Staff, ed. see Schwiebert, Pat & Kirk, Paul.
Perinbam, B. Marie. Holy Violence: The Revolutionary Thought of Franz Fanon. LC 81-51664. 224p. (Orig.). 1983. 22.00 (*0-89410-175-7*); pap. 12.00 (*0-89410-176-5*) Three Continents.
Perinbanayagam, R. S. Discursive Acts. (Communication & Social Order Ser.). 223p. (Orig.). 1991. lib. bdg. 43.95 (*0-202-30366-7*); pap. text ed. 23.95 (*0-202-30367-5*) Aldine de Gruyter.
— The Karmic Theater: Self, Society & Astrology in Jaffna. LC 82-6997. 224p. 1982. lib. bdg. 27.50 (*0-87023-374-2*) U of Mass Pr.
— Signifying Acts: Structure & Meaning in Everyday Life. LC 84-5474. 205p. 1985. 29.95 (*0-8093-1181-X*) S Ill U Pr.
***Perinchief, Richard.** The New Breed Church: In Your Face. 96p. Date not set. pap. write for info. (*1-879993-18-X*) Embassy Pub.
Perinchief, Robert. Drug-Free Word Spree. 58p. (J). (ps-12). 1993. 19.95 (*1-882809-01-7*) Perry Pubns.
— Hamel the Camel: A Different Mammal. (Illus.). 21p. (J). (ps-5). 1993. 12.95 (*1-882809-00-9*) Perry Pubns.
Perine, Robert. The California Romantics: Harbingers of Watercolorism. LC 86-73257. (Illus.). 96p. 1987. 18.95 (*0-936725-01-X*) Artra Pub.
— The Characters We Know: A to Z. (Illus.). 16p. 1978. ring bd. 15.00 (*0-932300-00-6*, AP00) Artra Pub.
— Chouinard: An Art Vision Betrayed. LC 86-70036. (Illus.). 260p. 1986. 37.50 (*0-936725-00-1*) Artra Pub.
— Nola Figen Perla Draws the Figure. (Illus.). 64p. (Orig.). 1993. pap. 20.00 (*0-936725-08-7*) Artra Pub.
Perine, Robert & Andrea, I. San Diego Artists. LC 88-70826. (Illus.). 224p. 1988. 35.00 (*0-936725-02-8*) Artra Pub.
Peringian, Lynda. Physical & Occupational Therapists' Job Search Handbook: Your Complete Job Search Strategy: How to Hire; How to Be Hired. LC 89-50592. (Illus.). 160p. (C). 1989. text ed. 25.00 (*0-9622773-0-4*) Therapy Careers.
Perino, Gregory. The Banks Village Site, Crittenden County, Arkansas. Chapman, Carl H., ed. (Memoir Ser.: No. 4). (Illus.). 161p. (Orig.). 1966. pap. 4.50 (*0-943414-19-9*) MO Arch Soc.
***Perino, Joseph G.** I Think I'm Hopeless but I Could Be Wrong: A Guide to Building Self-Confidence. LC 95-70119. 200p. (Orig.). 1995. pap. 15.95 (*0-9647432-0-5*) Riv Pr NY.
Perino, Renato. Call to Holiness: New Frontiers in Spirituality for Today's Religious. LC 85-28621. 160p. (Orig.). 1986. pap. 7.95 (*0-8189-0493-3*) Alba.
Perior Gross, Toni, jt. auth. see Gross, Francis L., Jr.
Perior, Tim, jt. auth. see David, Scott.
Peripatos. Der Fruhe Peripatos. Bd. 37. 400p. Date not set. write for info. (*0-318-70995-3*, Pub. by Georg Olms GW) Lubrecht & Cramer.
Perira, Wilf. RAF Lyneham: Hercules. (Super Station in Action Ser.). (Illus.). 192p. 1991. 31.95 (*0-85429-767-7*, Pub. by G T Foulis Ltd) Haynes Pubns.
Peris, Carme, jt. auth. see Sanchez, Isidro.
Peris, Jose A. Diccionario de Fisica. 464p. (SPA.). 1987. pap. 110.00 (*0-7859-3337-9*, 8420515299) Fr & Eur.
Perish, Melanie. Notes of a Daughter from the Old Country. 15p. (Orig.). (C). 1978. pap. 1.75 (*0-934238-04-9*) Motheroot.
Perissinotto, Giorgio. Reconquista y Literatura Medieval: Cuatro Ensayos. 127p. 1990. 29.50 (*0-916379-48-5*) Scripta.
Peristiany, J. G. & Pitt-Rivers, Julian, eds. Honour & Grace in Anthropology. (Cambridge Studies in Social & Cultural Anthropology: No. 76). (Illus.). 304p. (C). 1991. 69.95 (*0-521-39055-9*) Cambridge U Pr.
Peritore, N. Patrick. Socialism, Communism, & Liberation Theology in Brazil: An Opinion Survey Using Q-Methodology. LC 90-36505. (Monographs in International Studies, Latin America Ser.: No. 15). 274p. reprint ed. pap. 78.10 (*0-7837-6474-X*, 2046478) Bks Demand.
***Peritore, N. Patrick & Galve-Peritore, Ana.** Politics of Biotechnology. LC 95-16955. 229p. 1995. 45.00 (*0-8420-2556-1*); pap. 16.95 (*0-8420-2557-X*) Scholarly Res Inc.
***Peritti, Burton W.** Creation of Jazz: Music, Race, & Culture in Urban America. 1994. pap. 14.95 (*0-252-06421-6*) U of Ill Pr.
Peritts, Vivian. Fresh Paint. (Illus.). 32p. (Orig.). 1994. pap. 8.95 (*1-884555-02-0*) P Depke Bks.
Peritz, E., jt. auth. see Abramson, J. H.
***Peritz, Rudolph.** Competition Policy in America, 1888-1992: History, Rhetoric, Law. 384p. 1996. 45.00 (*0-19-507461-0*) OUP.
***Periwal, Sukumar, ed.** Notions of Nationalism. (Central European University Press Book Ser.). 272p. 1995. 59.00 (*1-85866-021-1*); pap. 21.00 (*1-85866-022-X*) OUP.
Perjes, Geza. The Fall of the Medieval Kingdom of Hungary: Mohacs, 1526, Buda, 1541. (Atlantic Studies on Society in Change, East European Monographs: No. 255). 350p. 1989. text ed. 52.50 (*0-88033-152-6*) East Eur Quarterly.
Perjes, Z., ed. Relativity Today. 308p. (C). 1992. text ed. 117.00 (*1-56072-028-X*) Nova Sci Pubs.
— Relativity Today: Proceedings of the 2nd Hungarian Relativity Workshop. 288p. (C). 1988. pap. 47.00 (*9971-5-0517-7*) World Scientific Pub.
Perjes, Z., jt. ed. see Kerr, R. P.
Perk, Kalman, et al, eds. Advances in Veterinary Science & Comparative Medicine, Vol. 32: Immunodeficiency Disorders & Retroviruses. 262p. 1988. text ed. 99.00 (*0-12-039232-1*) Acad Pr.
Perkal, Adam, jt. ed. see Wilkie, James W.
***Perkampus, Heinz-Helmut.** Encyclopedia of Spectroscopy. Grinter, Heide-Charlotte & Grinter, Roger, trs. LC 95-7227. 1995. write for info. (*3-527-29281-0*, Pub. by Vlg Chemie) VCH Pubs.
— UV-VIS Spectroscopy & Its Applications. Grinter, H. Charlotte & Threlfall, T. L., trs. LC 92-20077. (Illus.). ix, 240p. 1994. 98.00 (*0-387-55421-1*) Spr-Verlag.
Perkarkova, Iva. Truck Stop Rainbows. 1994. pap. 11.00 (*0-679-74675-7*, Vin) Random.
Perkell, Christine. The Poet's Truth: A Study of the Poet in Virgil's Georgics. 1989. 38.00 (*0-520-06323-6*) U CA Pr.
Perkell, Joseph S. & Klatt, D. H., eds. Invariance & Variability in Speech Processes. 632p. (C). 1986. text ed. 125.00 (*0-89859-545-2*) L Erlbaum Assocs.
Perker, L. Craig, jr. Finnish Criminal Justice: An American Perspective. LC 92-32881. 162p. (C). 1992. lib. bdg. 36.50 (*0-8191-8910-3*) U Pr of Amer.
Perkes, Alden. The Santa Claus Book. (Illus.). 144p. 1993. reprint ed. pap. 14.95 (*0-8184-0381-0*, L Stuart) Carol Pub Group.
Perkes, Alona S. Quick & Easy Cooking: A Busy Person's Guide to Simple, Nutritious Meals. LC 89-83432. 64p. 1991. pap. 6.98 (*0-88290-348-9*) Horizon Utah.
Perket, Cary L., ed. Quality Control in Remedial Site Investigation: Hazardous & Industrial Solid Waste Testing, Vol. 5. LC 86-25873. (Special Technical Publication Ser.: No. 925). (Illus.). 227p. 1986. text ed. 29.00 (*0-8031-0451-0*, 04-925000-16) ASTM.
Perkey, Elton A. Perkey's Nebraska Place Names. LC 82-80300. (Illus.). 227p. 1990. reprint ed. pap. 7.95 (*0-934904-17-0*) J & L Lee.
Perkin, Harold. Origins of Modern English Society: 1780-1880. 480p. pap. 13.95 (*0-7448-0026-9*) Routledge Chapman & Hall.
— The Rise of Professional Society: England since 1880. 480p. 1989. 49.95 (*0-415-00890-5*); pap. 7.95 (*0-415-04975-X*) Routledge.
— The Structured Crowd: Essays in English Social History. 250p. 1981. 44.00 (*0-389-20116-2*, N6890) B&N Imports.
Perkin, Harold J. Key Profession: The History of the Association of University Teachers. LC 73-81990. 1969. 35.00 (*0-678-06506-3*) Kelley.
— The Origins of Modern English Society, 1780-1880. LC 76-384509. (Canadian University Paperbooks Ser.: No. 115). 479p. reprint ed. pap. 136.60 (*0-8357-4165-6*, 2036939) Bks Demand.
***Perkin, J. Russell.** A Reception-History of George Eliot's Fiction. 211p. 1995. text ed. 39.95 (*1-878822-50-0*) Univ Rochester Pr.
***Perkin, Joan.** Victorian Women. (Illus.). 273p. 1995. 45.00 (*0-8147-6624-2*); pap. 17.95 (*0-8147-6625-0*) NYU Pr.
— Women & Marriage in Nineteenth Century England. LC 89-8066. 342p. (C). 1989. reprint ed. text ed. 49.95 (*0-925065-18-8*); reprint ed. pap. text ed. 21.95 (*0-925065-16-1*) Lyceum IL.
Perkin, Judy E. Food Allergies & Adverse Reactions. LC 90-684. 320p. 1990. 56.00 (*0-8342-0170-4*) Aspen Pub.
Perkins. Black Dolls 1820-1991. 360p. 1992. pap. 17.95 (*0-89145-515-9*) Collector Bks.
Perkins, jt. auth. see Dawson, D.
Perkins, A. J. & Woolfson, Theresa. Frances Wright, Free Enquirer: The Study of a Temperament. LC 79-187457. (American Utopian Adventure Ser.). 393p. 1972. reprint ed. lib. bdg. 45.00 (*0-87991-008-9*) Porcupine Pr.
Perkins, Agnes, jt. ed. see Helbig, Alethea.

Perkins, Agnes R., jt. auth. see Helbig, Althea K.
Perkins, Al. Diggingest Dog. LC 67-21920. (Illus.). 72p. (J). (gr. k-3). 1967. 7.99 (*0-394-80047-8*) Beginner.
— Diggingest Dog. LC 67-21920. (Illus.). 72p. (J). (gr. k-3). 1967. lib. bdg. 9.99 (*0-394-90047-2*) Beginner.
— Ear Book. LC 68-28464. (Bright & Early Bks.: No. 3). (Illus.). (J). (ps-1). 1968. lib. bdg. 9.99 (*0-394-91199-7*) Random Bks Yng Read.
— Ear Book. LC 68-28464. (Bright & Early Bks.: No. 3). (Illus.). (J). (ps-1). 1968. 6.95 (*0-394-81199-2*) Random Bks Yng Read.
— Hand, Hand, Fingers, Thumb. LC 76-77841. (Bright & Early Bks.). (Illus.). (J). (ps-1). 1969. 6.95 (*0-394-81076-7*) Random Bks Yng Read.
— Hugh Lofting's Travels of Doctor Dolittle. LC 67-25853. (Beginner Bks.). (Illus.). 64p. (J). (ps-2). 1967. 7.99 (*0-394-80048-6*) Random Bks Yng Read.
— Hugh Lofting's Travels of Doctor Dolittle. LC 67-25853. (Beginner Bks.). (Illus.). 64p. (J). (ps-2). 1967. lib. bdg. 7.99 (*0-394-90048-0*) Random Bks Yng Read.
— Nose Book. LC 71-117540. (Bright & Early Bks.: No. 8). (Illus.). (J). (ps-1). 1970. 6.95 (*0-394-80623-9*); lib. bdg. 7.99 (*0-394-90623-3*) Random Bks Yng Read.
— Tubby & the Lantern. LC 70-158390. (Illus.). (J). (gr. k-2). 1971. lib. bdg. 4.99 (*0-394-92297-2*) Beginner.
Perkins, Alan C. & Pimm, Malcolm V. Immunoscintigraphy: Practical Aspects & Clinical Practice. 208p. 1991. text ed. 98.95 (*0-471-56072-3*) Wiley.
Perkins, Alfred J., ed. see Society for Applied Spectroscopy Staff.
Perkins, Alfred J., ed. see Society for Applied Spectroscopy Staff, et al.
Perkins, Ann, jt. auth. see Townsend, Rita.
Perkins, Ann L. The Comparative Archeology of Early Mesopotamia. LC 49-10748. (Studies in Ancient Oriental Civilization: No. 25). (Illus.). xx, 201p. (Orig.). (C). 1949. reprint ed. pap. text ed. 17.00 (*0-226-62396-3*) Orientl Inst Pr IT.
Perkins, Annabel. Vegetarian Food for All: Zesty International Dishes from England's Celebrated Natural Foods Restaurant. McClure, Vimala, ed. (Illus.). 192p. (Orig.). 1995. reprint ed. pap. 12.95 (*0-945934-13-0*) New Wrld Lib.
Perkins, Anne. El Conejo. Ringlstetter, Maria, tr. (Big Books - Mini Bks.). (Illus.). 8p. (SPA.). (J). (ps-k). 1994. 12.00 (*1-884204-09-0*) Teach Nxt Door.
— I Know Lots of Things. (Big Books - Mini Bks.). (Illus.). 16p. (J). (gr. k). 1994. 12.00 (*0-614-04636-X*) Teach Nxt Door.
— Out of the Box. (Big Books - Mini Bks.). (Illus.). 16p. (J). (ps-k). 1994. 12.00 (*1-884204-13-9*) Teach Nxt Door.
— Perros. Ringlstetter, Maria, tr. (Big Books - Mini Bks.). (Illus.). 8p. (SPA.). (J). (ps-k). 1994. 12.00 (*1-884204-10-4*) Teach Nxt Door.
— Que' Es. Ringlstetter, Maria, tr. (Big Books - Mini Bks.). (Illus.). 8p. (SPA.). (J). (ps-k). 1994. 12.00 (*1-884204-11-2*) Teach Nxt Door.
— This Is a Penny. (Big Books - Mini Bks.). (Illus.). 8p. (J). (gr. k). 1995. 12.00 (*1-884204-15-5*) Teach Nxt Door.
Perkins, Anne T. The Bunny. (Big Books - Mini Bks.). (Illus.). 8p. (J). 1993. 12.00 (*1-884204-02-3*) Teach Nxt Door.
— Dogs. (Big Books - Mini Bks.). (Illus.). 8p. (J). (ps-00). 1994. 12.00 (*1-884204-07-4*) Teach Nxt Door.
— Little Eddy Elephant. (Big Books - Mini Bks.). (Illus.). 8p. (J). (ps-00). 1993. 12.00 (*1-884204-06-6*) Teach Nxt Door.
— My Name Is Jack. (Big Books - Mini Bks.). (Illus.). 8p. (J). (ps-00). 1993. 12.00 (*1-884204-05-8*) Teach Nxt Door.
— Nan's Nickel. (Big Books - Mini Bks.). (Illus.). 8p. (J). 1993. 12.00 (*1-884204-04-X*) Teach Nxt Door.
— Turtles. (Big Books - Mini Bks.). (Illus.). 8p. (J). (ps-00). 1993. 12.00 (*1-884204-00-7*) Teach Nxt Door.
— Valentines. (Big Books - Mini Bks.). (Illus.). 8p. (J). (ps-00). 1994. 12.00 (*1-884204-08-2*) Teach Nxt Door.
— What Is It? (Big Books - Mini Bks.). (Illus.). 8p. (J). 1993. 12.00 (*1-884204-03-1*) Teach Nxt Door.
Perkins, Annie. English 102 Communication Skills Study Guide. 48p. (C). 1992. 5.25 (*0-8403-8065-8*) Kendall-Hunt.
Perkins, Barbara & Perkins, George. American Literature since World War II. 900p. (C). 1988. pap. text ed. write for info. (*0-07-554954-9*) McGraw.
— Kaleidoscope: Stories of the American Experience. 688p. (C). 1993. pap. text ed. 19.95 (*0-19-507222-7*) OUP.
Perkins, Barbara, jt. ed. see Perkins, George.
Perkins, Barbara, et al. Language Lessons for the Cirriculum, 3 vols. (Illus.). 1991. Kindergarten Math. spiral bd. 27.95 (*1-55999-160-7*); Kindergarten Language Arts. spiral bd. 27.95 (*1-55999-161-5*); Kindergarten Science - Social Studies. spiral bd. 27.95 (*1-55999-162-3*) LinguiSystems.
— Language Lessons for the Cirriculum, 3 vols., Set. (Illus.). 1991. spiral bd. 74.85 (*1-55999-184-4*) LinguiSystems.
— Women's Works: An Anthology of American Literature. LC 93-26558. 1993. pap. text ed. write for info. (*0-07-049364-2*) McGraw.
***Perkins, Betty.** Lion Taming: The Courage to Deal with Difficult People Including Yourself. 192p. 1995. pap. 14.95 (*0-929999-10-X*) Tzedakah Pubns.
Perkins, Bill. Fatal Attractions. 1991. student ed, pap. 8.99 (*0-89081-921-1*) Harvest Hse.
***Perkins, Bill, ed.** Steeling the Mind of America. 300p. (Orig.). 1995. pap. 11.95 (*0-89221-294-2*) New Leaf.
Perkins, Billie L. Human Anatomy & Physiology: Study Guide to Accompany Gaudin & Jones. 625p. (C). 1989. pap. text ed. 20.00 (*0-15-539706-0*) HB Coll Pubs.
Perkins, Bob F., ed. Aspects of Trinity Division Geology. LC 74-632779. (Geoscience & Man Ser.: Vol. 8). 228p. 1974. pap. 11.50 (*0-938909-07-X*) Geosci Pubns LSU.
Perkins, Bob F., jt. auth. see Turney, W. Jack.
Perkins, Bradford. The Cambridge History of American Foreign Relations: The Creation of a Republican Empire, 1776-1865, Vol. 1. LC 92-36165. 1993. 27.95 (*0-521-38209-2*) Cambridge U Pr.
— Cambridge History of American Foreign Relations Vol. 1: The Creation of a Republican Empire, 1776-1865. (Illus.). 272p. (C). 1995. pap. 15.95 (*0-521-48384-0*) Cambridge U Pr.
Perkins, Bradford, ed. Causes of the War of Eighteen Twelve: National Honor or National Interest? LC 76-3657. (American Problem Studies). 126p. 1976. reprint ed. pap. 9.50 (*0-88275-408-4*) Krieger.
***Perkins, Bruce.** Canadian First Day Cover Handbook, 1950-1959. 172p. (Orig.). 1994. pap. 16.95 (*1-879390-18-3*) Am First Day.
Perkins, C. & Dommasch, D. Flight Test Manual, 4 vols. rev. ed. 1959. write for info. (*0-318-69652-5*, Pub. by Pergamon Repr UK) Franklin.
— Flight Test Manual, 4 vols., Set. 2nd rev. ed. 1959. 960.00 (*0-08-009213-6*, Pub. by Pergamon Repr UK) Franklin.
Perkins, C. R. & Parry, R. B., eds. Information Sources in Cartography. (Guides to Information Sources Ser.). 384p. 1990. lib. bdg. 96.00 (*0-408-02458-5*) Bowker-Saur.
Perkins, C. R., jt. auth. see Parry, R. B.
Perkins-Carpenter, Betty. The Fun of Fitness: A Handbook for the Senior Class. Creative & Co. Staff, ed. (Illus.). 174p. 1988. ring bd. 16.95 (*0-9621031-0-1*) Sr Fitness Prodns.
— How to Prevent Falls. (Illus.). 112p. (Orig.). 1993. pap. 8.95 (*0-312-09825-1*) St Martin.
— How to Prevent Falls: A Comprehensive Guide to Better Balance. Creative & Co. Staff, ed. LC 89-92153. (Illus.). 105p. (Orig.). 1990. spiral bd. 9.95 (*0-9621031-1-X*) Sr Fitness Prodns.
Perkins, Charles C. Cyclopedia of Painters & Painting, 4 vols., Set. Champlin, John, Jr., ed. LC 77-86249. (Illus.). 1978. reprint ed. pap. 77.00 (*0-8046-1824-0*) Irvington.
Perkins, Charles C., jt. ed. see Champlin, John D., Jr.
Perkins, Charles D. Swinging on a Rainbow. LC 91-78393. (Illus.). 32p. (J). (gr. 1-4). 1992. 14.95 (*0-86543-286-4*); pap. 6.95 (*0-86543-287-2*) Africa World.
Perkins, Cheryl. Can't Stop Overeating, Drinking, Working, Shopping or Using Prescription Drugs: Facilitating a Christian 12-Step Group. 200p. 1993. pap. 9.95 (*1-55673-540-5*) CSS OH.
Perkins, Clizabeth. Deaths of Various People Bristol & Plymouth Counties, MA. Townsend, Charles D., ed. 44p. (Orig.). 1993. pap. 10.00 (*0-9607906-9-1*) ACETO Bookmen.
Perkins Coie Product Liability Law Practice Group Staff & Gerrard, Keith. Product Liability in the United States: A Primer for Manufacturers & Their Employees. Winfield, Laurie, ed. LC 91-60104. (Illus.). 96p. (C). 1991. pap. text ed. 9.95 (*1-879650-00-2*) Perkins Coie.
Perkins Coie Product Liability Practice Group Staff & Gerrard, Keith. Product Liability in the United States: A Primer for Japanese Manufacturers & Their Employees. Lough, Mark, ed. LC 91-60104. (Illus.). 96p. (C). 1991. pap. text ed. 9.95 (*1-879650-01-0*) Perkins Coie.
Perkins, Courtland D. & Hage, Robert E. Airplane Performance, Stability & Control. 493p. 1949. Net. text ed. write for info. (*0-471-68046-X*) Wiley.
Perkins, Craig. National Corrections Reporting Program, 1990. (Illus.). 97p. (Orig.). (C). 1993. pap. text ed. 25.00 (*1-56806-490-X*) Diane Pub.
— National Corrections Reporting Program, 1992. (Illus.). 92p. (Orig.). (C). 1994. pap. text ed. 35.00 (*0-7881-1384-4*) Diane Pub.
***Perkins, Craig R. & Perkins, Kelly A.** Personal Health-Care Organizer: The Original Patient Management Workbook. 110p. 1994. write for info. (*0-9642711-1-7*); pap. write for info. (*0-9642711-0-9*) Crakel Pubns.
***Perkins, Cris.** One Hundred Years of BGA Football, 1894-1994. (Illus.). 128p. 1994. 19.95 (*1-881576-38-8*) Providence Hse.
Perkins, D. A. History of O'Brien County, Iowa. (Illus.). 485p. 1993. reprint ed. lib. bdg. 49.50 (*0-685-67358-8*) Higginson Bk Co.
— History of Osceola County, Iowa. (Illus.). 270p. 1993. reprint ed. lib. bdg. 32.50 (*0-8328-2934-X*) Higginson Bk Co.
Perkins, D. C. The Language of the Media. 430p. (C). 1988. 190.00 (*1-85122-026-7*, Pub. by Domino Bks Ltd UK); pap. 100.00 (*1-85122-023-2*, Pub. by Domino Bks Ltd UK) St Mut.
Perkins, D. H. An Introduction to High Energy Physics. 2nd ed. LC 82-3952. (C). 1982. text ed. write for info. (*0-201-05757-3*) Addison-Wesley.
— Introduction to High Energy Physics. 3rd ed. 462p. (C). 1987. text ed. 56.95 (*0-201-12105-0*, Adv Bk Prog) Addison-Wesley.

PQ

An Asterisk (*) at the beginning of an entry indicates that the title is appearing in BIP for the first time.

Perkins, D. N. The Mind's Best Work: A New Psychology of Creative Thinking. 325p. 1983. pap. 14.95 (0-674-57624-1) HUP.

Perkins, D. N., ed. Knowledge As Design. 264p. (C). 1986. pap. text ed. 25.00 (0-89859-863-X) L Erlbaum Assocs.

Perkins, D. N., jt. ed. see Gardner, Howard.

Perkins, David. Is Literary History Possible? LC 91-22516. 208p. 1992. text ed. 32.50x (0-8018-4274-3) Johns Hopkins.

— Is Literary History Possible? 208p. (C). 1993. reprint ed. pap. text ed. 12.95 (0-8018-4715-X) Johns Hopkins.

— Learnable Intelligence: Breaking the IQ Barrier. 1995. 23.00 (0-02-925212-1) Free Pr.

— Outsmarting IQ: The Emerging Science of Learnable Intelligence. 390p. 1995. 23.00 (0-615-00756-2) Free Pr.

— The Quest for Permanence: The Symbolism of Wordsworth, Shelley & Keats. LC 59-11515. 313p. reprint ed. pap. 90.40 (0-7837-4175-8, 2059024) Bks Demand.

— Smart Schools: Better Thinking & Learning for Every Child. 1995. pap. 12.00 (0-02-874018-1) Free Pr.

— Theoretical Issues in Literary History. (English Studies: Vol. No. 16). 303p. 1991. pap. 12.95 (0-674-87913-9) HUP.

Perkins, David, ed. English Romantic Writers. 1265p. (C). 1967. text ed. 45.25 (0-15-522660-6) HB Coll Pubs.

— Raleigh: A Living History of North Carolina's Capital. LC 93-72410. (Illus.). 208p. 1994. 22.95 (0-89587-121-1) Blair.

Perkins, David & Leondar, Barbara, eds. The Arts & Cognition. LC 76-17237. 352p. reprint ed. pap. 100.40 (0-8357-5777-3, 2025863) Bks Demand.

Perkins, David & Tanis, Norman. Native Americans of North America: A Bibliography Based on Collections in the Libraries of California State University, Northridge. (Illus.). 1975. 27.50 (0-8108-0878-1) Scarecrow.

Perkins, David, jt. ed. see Bate, W. Jackson.

Perkins, David, ed. see Morgan, J. W.

Perkins, David, et al, eds. Thinking: The Second International Conference. 552p. 1987. text ed. 99.95 (0-89859-805-2) L Erlbaum Assocs.

Perkins, David D. History of Modern Poetry: From the Eighteen Nineties to the High Modernist Mode. LC 78-6874. 617p. 1979. pap. 20.00 (0-674-39945-5) Belknap Pr.

— A History of Modern Poetry: Modernism & After. LC 86-14904. 704p. 1987. 37.00 (0-674-39946-3) Belknap Pr.

— History of Modern Poetry: Modernism & After. 704p. 1989. pap. 20.00 (0-674-39947-1) Belknap Pr.

— Smart Schools: From Educating Memories to Educating Minds. LC 92-13763. 1992. 22.95 (0-685-57487-3) Free Pr.

— Wordsworth & the Poetry of Sincerity. LC 64-10443. 299p. 1964. 25.00 (0-674-95820-9) Belknap Pr.

Perkins, David D., ed. Theoretical Issues in Literary History. (English Studies: Vol. No. 16). 303p. (C). 1991. 29.95 (0-674-87912-0) HUP.

Perkins, David D., jt. ed. see Engell, James.

Perkins, David D., jt. ed. see Weber, Robert J.

Perkins, David L., jt. auth. see Tanis, Norman E.

Perkins, David N. The Intelligent Eye: Learning to Think by Looking at Art. LC 94-30. (Occasional Papers Ser.: Vol. 4). 812p. 1994. 10.00 (0-89236-274-X) J P Getty Trust.

— Thinking Connections: Learning to Think & Thinking to Learn. (J). (gr. 4-7). 1993. pap. 24.95 (0-201-81998-8) Addison-Wesley.

Perkins, David N., jt. auth. see Lipson, Abigail.

Perkins, David N., et al, eds. Making Sense: Teaching Understanding with Technology. (Illus.). 288p. 1995. 45.00 (0-19-508938-3) OUP.

Perkins, David V., jt. auth. see Levine, Murray.

Perkins, Dexter. The American Approach to Foreign Policy. rev. ed. LC 62-11400. 247p. reprint ed. pap. 72.70 (0-7837-2309-1, 2057397) Bks Demand.

— American Way. LC 77-128285. (Essay Index Reprint Ser.). 1977. 19.95 (0-8369-2011-2) Ayer.

— Charles Evans Hughes & American Democratic Statesmanship. Handlin, Oscar, ed. LC 78-5919. (Library of American Biography Ser.). 200p. 1978. reprint ed. text ed. 35.00 (0-313-20463-2, PECH, Greenwood Pr) Greenwood.

— The Diplomacy of a New Age: Major Issues in U. S. Policy Since 1945. LC 67-13034. 190p. reprint ed. pap. 54.20 (0-8357-9203-X, 2017635) Bks Demand.

— New Age of Franklin Roosevelt, 1932-1945. LC 56-11263. (Chicago History of American Civilization Ser.). 1957. pap. text ed. 10.95 (0-226-65872-4, CHAC17) U Ch Pr.

— The New Age of Franklin Roosevelt, 1932-1945. LC 56-11263. (Chicago History of American Civilization Ser.). 204p. reprint ed. pap. 58.20 (0-317-09695-8, 2020142) Bks Demand.

— The United States & the Caribbean. rev. ed. LC 67-12532. (American Foreign Policy Library). 210p. reprint ed. pap. 59.90 (0-7837-4176-6, 2059025) Bks Demand.

Perkins, Dorothy. The Passionate Wisdom of Henry Miller: The Religious Dimension of His Life & Art. (Orig.). 1980. pap. 3.00 (0-9604742-1-8) D J Perkins.

Perkins, Dwight G., ed. Rural Small-Scale Industry in the People's Republic of China. LC 76-20015. 1977. 50.00 (0-520-03284-5); pap. 12.00 (0-520-04401-0) U CA Pr.

Perkins, Dwight H. China: Asia's Next Economic Giant? LC 86-15786. (Henry M. Jackson Lectures in Modern Chinese Studies). 128p. 1989. pap. 8.95 (0-295-96855-9) U of Wash Pr.

— Market Control & Planning in Communist China. LC 66-10808. (Economic Studies: No. 128). (Illus.). 299p. 1966. 17.50 (0-674-54950-3) HUP.

Perkins, Dwight H., ed. China's Modern Economy in Historical Perspective. LC 74-82779. 360p. 1975. 45.00 (0-8047-0871-1) Stanford U Pr.

Perkins, Dwight H. & Roemer, Michael, eds. Reforming Economic Systems in Developing Countries. (Institute for International Development Ser.). 492p. 1991. 29.95 (0-674-75319-4, PERREF) HUP.

Perkins, Dwight H. & Yusuf, Shahid. Rural Development in China. LC 83-49366. 246p. (C). 1984. text ed. 28.95 (0-8018-3261-6) Johns Hopkins.

— Rural Development in China. LC 83-49366. 246p. 1985. reprint ed. pap. text ed. 14.95 (0-8018-3066-4) Johns Hopkins.

Perkins, Dwight H., jt. ed. see Koo, Bon-Ho.

Perkins, E. G. & Visek, Willard, eds. Dietary Fats & Health. 978p. 1983. 40.00 (0-935315-07-1) AOCS Pr.

Perkins, E. G., jt. ed. see Sebedio, J. L.

Perkins, E. J. The Life & Work of Harold Palmer. 144p. (C). 1988. 90.00 (0-317-91157-0, Pub. by Domino Bks Ltd UK); pap. 70.00 (1-85122-025-9, Pub. by Domino Bks Ltd UK) St Mut.

Perkins, E. S., et al. Atlas of Diseases of the Eye. 3rd ed. (Illus.). 208p. (Orig.). 1986. pap. text ed. 50.00 (0-443-02961-X) Churchill.

Perkins, Ed & Consumer Reports Books Editors. Consumer Reports Travel Buying Guide, 1994. 320p. (Orig.). 1993. pap. 8.99 (0-89043-676-2) Consumer Reports.

Perkins, Ed, jt. auth. see Consumer Reports Travel Letter Editors.

Perkins, Ed, et al. Consumer Reports Travel Buying Guide. 320p. 1994. pap. 8.99 (0-89043-768-8) Consumer Reports.

Perkins, Edward A., jt. auth. see Reigel, Charles E., Jr.

Perkins, Edward A., Jr., et al. Practice for Professional Typing. 1968. text ed. 16.75 (0-07-049301-4) McGraw.

Perkins, Edward G., ed. Analyses of Fats, Oils & Derivatives. 448p. 1993. pap. 45.00 (0-935315-47-0) AOCS Pr.

— Analyses of Fats, Oils, & Lipoproteins. 664p. (C). 1991. 130.00 (0-935315-36-5) AOCS Pr.

— Lipoproteins. 176p. 1993. pap. 35.00 (0-935315-48-9) AOCS Pr.

***Perkins, Edwin.** On the Martingale Problem for Interactive Measure-Valued Branching Diffusions. LC 95-3279. (Memoirs Ser.: Vol. 549). 1995. write for info. (0-8218-0358-1) Am Math.

Perkins, Edwin, ed. see Mercer, Lloyd J.

Perkins, Edwin C., Jr., jt. auth. see Southerton, Alan.

Perkins, Edwin J. American Public Finance & Financial Services, 1700-1815. LC 93-28736. (Historical Perspectives on Business Enterprise Ser.). 448p. 1994. 49.50 (0-8142-0619-0) Ohio St U Pr.

— The Economy of Colonial America. LC 80-16478. 224p. 1980. pap. text ed. 14.50 (0-231-04959-5) Col U Pr.

— The Economy of Colonial America. 2nd ed. (Illus.). 304p. 1988. text ed. 40.50 (0-231-06338-5); pap. text ed. 16.00 (0-231-06339-3) Col U Pr.

— Financing Anglo-American Trade: The House of Brown, 1800-1880. LC 74-34543. (Harvard Studies in Business History: No. 28). 334p. reprint ed. pap. 96.90 (0-7837-2310-5, 2057398) Bks Demand.

Perkins, Edwin J., jt. auth. see Adams, Judith A.

Perkins, Elizabeth, jt. auth. see Sprague, Stuart.

Perkins, Emogene. Homan Crossing. Van Treese, James B., ed. 360p. 1995. pap. 9.95 (1-56901-118-4) NW Pub.

Perkins, Ethel R., tr. see De Vogue, Adalbert.

Perkins, Ethel R., ed. see Vogue, Adalbert de.

Perkins, F. T. & Hennessen, W., eds. Standardization & Control of Biologicals Produced by Recombinant DNA Technology. (Developments in Biological Standardization Ser.: Vol. 59). (Illus.). viii, 216p. 1985. pap. 56.00 (3-8055-4027-2) S Karger.

Perkins, F. T., ed. see International Association of Biological Standardization Staff.

Perkins, F. T, ed. see International Association of Biological Standardization Symposium Staff.

Perkins, F. T., ed. see Permanent Section of Microbiological Standardization, 31st Symposium, Omstotite of Child Health, Ondon, 1969.

Perkins, Frank O. & Cheng, Thomas C., eds. Pathology in Marine Science. 538p. 1990. text ed. 104.00 (0-12-550755-0) Acad Pr.

Perkins-Frederick, Pamela M. A Leaf Gnawed to Lace. (Illus.). 36p. (Orig.). 1992. pap. 5.00 (0-9625348-4-6) P Goodrich.

Perkins, G., jt. auth. see Drummond, David A.

Perkins, G., jt. auth. see Holzman, R.

Perkins, G. A. The Family of John Perkins of Ipswich, Massachusetts. (Illus.). 499p. 1989. reprint ed. lib. bdg. 60.00 (0-8328-0952-7); reprint ed. pap. 50.00 (0-8328-0953-5) Higginson Bk Co.

Perkins, Gary. Silly Animal Jokes. LC 92-20776. 1992. pap. 1.95 (0-8167-2966-2) Troll Assocs.

— Silly Goofy Jokes. LC 92-20779. (Illus.). 64p. (J). (gr. 2-6). 1992. pap. text ed. 1.95 (0-8167-2965-4) Troll Assocs.

— Silly Haunted Jokes. LC 92-20760. (Illus.). 64p. (J). (gr. 2-6). 1992. pap. text ed. 1.95 (0-8167-2963-8) Troll Assocs.

— Silly School Jokes. LC 92-20437. (Illus.). 64p. (J). (gr. 2-6). 1992. pap. text ed. 1.95 (0-8167-2964-6) Troll Assocs.

Perkins, Geoff, ed. Employee Communications in the Public Sector. 96p. (C). 1986. 45.00 (0-85292-369-4, Pub. by IPM Hse UK) St Mut.

Perkins, George & Perkins, Barbara, eds. The American Tradition in Literature. 8th ed. LC 93-42292. 1994. text ed. write for info. (0-07-049369-3); pap. text ed. write for info. (0-07-049370-7) McGraw.

— The American Tradition in Literature, 2 vols., Vol. 2. 8th ed. LC 93-11009. 1993. text ed. write for info. (0-07-049365-0); pap. text ed. write for info. (0-07-049366-9) McGraw.

— The American Tradition in Literature, 2 vols., Vol. 3. 8th ed. LC 93-11009. 1993. text ed. write for info. (0-07-049367-7); pap. text ed. write for info. (0-07-049368-5) McGraw.

Perkins, George, jt. auth. see Perkins, Barbara.

Perkins, George, et al. American Tradition in Literature, 2 vols., 1. 6th ed. (C). 1985. pap. text ed. 20.95 (0-685-08386-1) McGraw.

— The American Tradition in Literature, Vol. 1. 7th ed. 2000p. (C). 1990. pap. text ed. write for info. (0-07-557208-7) McGraw.

Perkins, George, et al, eds. Benet's Reader's Encyclopedia of American Literature. LC 91-55001. 1056p. 1991. 45.00 (0-06-270027-8, Harper Ref) HarpC.

Perkins, George H. Letters of Capt. Geo. Hamilton Perkins, U. S. N. LC 78-107825. (Select Bibliographies Reprint Ser.). 1977. 23.95 (0-8369-5219-7) Ayer.

— Letters of Capt. Geo. Hamilton Perkins, U. S. N. (American Biography Ser.). 254p. 1991. reprint ed. lib. bdg. 69.00 (0-7812-8311-6) Rprt Serv.

Perkins, Gloria O., jt. auth. see Wheat, Ed.

***Perkins, Graham.** Snakes or Ladders? The Ambitious Executive's Guide to Headhunters & How to Handle Them. 240p. 1991. pap. 60.00 (0-273-03285-2, Pub. by Pitman Pubng UK) St Mut.

Perkins, H. C. Northern Editorials on Secession, 2 vols., Set. 30.00 (0-8446-1347-9) Peter Smith.

Perkins, H. R., et al. Microbial Cell Walls. 575p. 1980. 85.00 (0-412-12030-5, NO. 6415) Chapman & Hall.

Perkins, H. V., jt. auth. see Brandt, R. M.

Perkins, Hal. Leadership Multiplication Books: Book A, World Vision. 30p. 1983. pap. 2.50 (0-8341-0858-5) Beacon Hill.

— Leadership Multiplication Books: Book B, Knowing the Father. 40p. (Orig.). 1983. pap. 2.50 (0-8341-0859-3) Beacon Hill.

— Leadership Multiplication Books: Book C, Coming to Jesus. (Orig.). 1983. pap. 2.50 (0-8341-0852-6) Beacon Hill.

— Leadership Multiplication Books: Book D, Following Jesus. 30p. (Orig.). (YA). (gr. 7 up). 1983. pap. 2.50 (0-8341-0860-7) Beacon Hill.

— Leadership Multiplication Books: Book E, Becoming Like Jesus. 30p. (Orig.). 1983. pap. 2.50 (0-8341-0861-5) Beacon Hill.

— Leadership Multiplication Books: Book F, Making Leaders in Families. 48p. (Orig.). (YA). (gr. 7 up). 1983. pap. 2.50 (0-8341-0862-3) Beacon Hill.

— Leadership Multiplication Books: Book G, Making Leaders in the Church. 48p. (Orig.). (YA). (gr. 7 up). 1983. pap. 2.50 (0-8341-0866-6) Beacon Hill.

— Leadership Multiplication Books: Book H, Making Leaders in the World. 32p. (Orig.). (YA). (gr. 9 up). 1983. pap. 2.50 (0-8341-0867-4) Beacon Hill.

Perkins, Hattie L. Humanities: Lecture-Discussion Syllabus. 1977. pap. 7.95 (0-317-17265-4) Banner Pr AL.

Perkins, Hazlehurst B., jt. auth. see Betts, Edwin M.

Perkins, Henry C. Air Pollution. (Illus.). 448p. (C). 1974. text ed. write for info. (0-07-049302-2) McGraw.

Perkins, Henry C., jt. auth. see Reynolds, William C.

Perkins, Howard C. Northern Editorials on Secession, 2 vols., Set. (History - United States Ser.). 1993. reprint ed. lib. bdg. 150.00 (0-7812-4891-4) Rprt Serv.

Perkins, J. Psiconavegacion. 1995. pap. 10.95 (0-89281-461-6) Inner Tradit.

Perkins, J. D. The Deregulation of the Australian Financial System: The Experience of the 1980s. 1989. pap. 17.95 (0-522-84378-6) Intl Spec Bk.

Perkins, J. D., ed. Interactions Between Process Design & Process Control: Preprints of the IFAC Workshop, London, U. K., 7-8 September 1992. LC 92-40440. 1992. pap. 110.00 (0-08-042063-X, Pergamon Pr) Elsevier.

Perkins, J. O. Australian Macroeconomic Policy 1974-1985. 123p. 1987. pap. 14.95 (0-522-84337-9) Intl Spec Bk.

— A General Approach to Macroeconomic Theory. LC 90-34605. 140p. 1990. text ed. 55.00 (0-312-04896-3) St Martin.

— The Macroeconomic Mix in the Industralized World. LC 84-24878. 128p. 1985. text ed. 29.95 (0-312-50319-9) St Martin.

Perkins, J. O. & Sullivan, J. Banks & the Capital Market: An Australian Study. (Illus.). 123p. 1972. pap. 9.95 (0-522-84048-5) Intl Spec Bk.

Perkins, J. R. Trails, Rails, & War: The Life of General G. M. Dodge. Bruchey, Stuart, ed. LC 80-1338. (Railroads Ser.). (Illus.). 1981. reprint ed. lib. bdg. 38.95 (0-405-13810-5) Ayer.

Perkins, Jack. Parasols of Fern: A Book about Wonder. LC 93-10874. (Illus.). 1993. 18.95 (0-934745-17-X) Acadia Pub Co.

Perkins, James, jt. auth. see Crain, Ernest.

Perkins, James, ed. see International Council for Educational Development Staff.

Perkins, James A. Access to Higher Education: Two Perspectives. A Comparative Study of the Federal Republic of Germany & the United States of America. 84p. 1978. pap. 2.50 (0-89192-219-9) Interbk Inc.

— International Programs of U. S. Colleges & Universities. 1971. pap. 1.00 (0-89192-179-6) Interbk Inc.

— Is the University an Agent for Social Reform? (Occasional Paper of ICED: No. 8). 1973. pap. 1.00 (0-89192-149-4) Interbk Inc.

— The University in Transition. LC 66-15804. (Stafford Little Lectures: No. 1965). 100p. reprint ed. pap. 28.50 (0-8357-4651-8, 2037582) Bks Demand.

Perkins, James A. & Oestreich, Nelson. The Amish: Two Perceptions Two. (Illus.). 24p. (Orig.). 1981. pap. 4.00 (0-936014-10-5) Dawn Valley.

Perkins, James B. Richelieu & the Growth of French Power. LC 70-157353. (Select Bibliographies Reprint Ser.). 1977. reprint ed. 35.95 (0-8369-5814-4) Ayer.

Perkins, James S. Through Death to Rebirth. LC 61-13301. (Illus.). 124p. 1974. pap. 4.25 (81-7059-038-8, Quest) Theos Pub Hse.

— Through Death to Rebirth. LC 61-13301. (Illus.). 124p. 1974. pap. 4.25 (0-8356-0451-9, Quest) Theos Pub Hse.

— Visual Meditations on the Universe. LC 83-40233. (Illus.). 136p. 1984. 16.95 (0-8356-0233-8, Quest) Theos Pub Hse.

Perkins, Jan D. Don C. Wallace W6AM: Amateur Radio's Pioneer. LC 91-8094. (Illus.). 296p. 1991. 29.95 (0-911572-99-6) Vestal.

Perkins, Jane & Wulsin, Lucien. An Advocate's Guide to the Medically Needy Program. (Illus.). 120p. 1985. pap. 10.00 (0-941077-01-2, 40,250) NCLS Inc.

Perkins, Jill, ed. Joyce & Hauptmann: Before Sunrise. James Joyce's Translation. LC 77-87870. (Illus.). 172p. 1978. text ed. 15.00 (0-87328-072-5) Huntington Lib.

Perkins, Jimmy L. & Rose, Vernon E., eds. Case Studies in Industrial Hygiene. LC 86-15709. 188p. 1987. text ed. 79.95 (0-471-84263-X) Wiley.

Perkins, John. Justicia para Todos. (Nueva Creacion Ser.). 1988. pap. 7.99 (0-8028-0909-X) Eerdmans.

— Malice in Wonderland. 1993. pap. 15.00 (0-9636328-0-9) ProMotion Pub.

— Morphosis: Architectural Projects. Krause, Carolyn, ed. (Illus.). 7p. 1989. pap. 2.50 (0-917562-53-4) Contemp Arts.

— El Mundo es Como uno lo Suena-The World Is As You Dream It. 1995. pap. 10.95 (0-89281-465-9) Inner Tradit.

— Planning for Museum Automation. (Technical Reports). 70p. (C). 1994. teacher ed, pap. 40.00 (1-885626-05-3); pap. 15.00 (1-885626-06-1) Archives & Mus.

— Psychonavigation: Techniques for Travel Beyond Time. 160p. (Orig.). 1990. pap. 10.95 (0-89281-300-8) Inner Tradit.

— The World Is As You Dream It: Shamanic Teachings from the Amazon. 144p. (Orig.). 1994. pap. 10.95 (0-89281-459-4) Inner Tradit.

Perkins, John, et al. He's My Brother: Former Racial Foes Offer Strategy for Reconciliation. LC 94-4075. 240p. (Orig.). 1994. pap. 14.99 (0-8007-9214-9) Chosen Bks.

Perkins, John, et al, eds. The Historic Taf Valleys, Vol. 2: In the Brecon Beacons National Park. 190p. (C). 1989. 59.00 (0-905928-21-0, Pub. by D Brown & Sons Ltd UK) St Mut.

— The Historic Taf Valleys, Vol. 3: From the Taf Confluence at Cefn-Coed-y-Cymmer to Aberfan. 184p. (C). 1989. 59.00 (0-905928-59-8, Pub. by D Brown & Sons Ltd UK) St Mut.

Perkins, John H. Insects, Experts, & the Insecticide Crisis: The Quest for New Pest Management Strategies. LC 81-22658. 322p. 1982. 65.00 (0-306-40770-1, Plenum Pr) Plenum.

Perkins, John J. Principles & Methods of Sterilization in Health Sciences. 2nd ed. (Illus.). 580p. 1983. 47.95 (0-398-01478-7) C C Thomas.

Perkins, John M. Beyond Charity: The Call to Christian Community Development. LC 93-18862. 1993. pap. 9.99 (0-8010-7122-4) Baker Bk.

— The Stress-Free Habit: Powerful Techniques for Health & Longevity from the Andes, Yucatan, & Far East. 128p. 1989. pap. 8.95 (0-89281-292-3, Heal Arts VT) Inner Tradit.

Perkins, John P., intro. The Beta-Adrenergic Receptors. LC 90-15616. (Receptors Ser.). (Illus.). 416p. 1991. 109.50 (0-89603-173-X) Humana.

Perkins, Joseph, ed. A Conservative Agenda for Black Americans. 2nd ed. 80p. 1987. pap. 8.00 (0-89195-041-9) Heritage Found.

Perkins, Joseph K., ed. Brown Stock Washing Using Rotary Filters. (Illus.). 60p. 1983. 40.00 (0-89852-414-8, 0101R114) TAPPI.

***Perkins, Judith.** The Suffering Self: Pain & Narrative Representation in Early Christianity. LC 94-42650. 1995. write for info. (0-415-11363-6); pap. text ed. write for info. (0-415-12706-8) Routledge.

Perkins, Judith, ed. see Singh, Ajaib.

Perkins, Judy, jt. auth. see Brown, Alan.

Perkins, Juliet. The Feminine in the Poetry of Herberto Helder. (Tamesis Books - Serie A: Monografias: No. 144). 184p. (C). 1991. text ed. 53.00 (1-85566-006-7, Pub. by Tamesis Bks Ltd UK) Boydell & Brewer.

***Perkins, Kathy & Uno, Roberta, eds.** Contemporary Plays by Women of Color: An Anthology. LC 95-7465. 1996. write for info. (0-415-11377-6); pap. write for info. (0-415-11378-4) Routledge.

Perkins, Kathy A., ed. Black Female Playwrights: An Anthology of Plays Before 1950. LC 88-46040. (Blacks in the Diaspora Ser.). (Illus.). 298p. (Orig.). 1989. 35.00 (0-253-34358-5); pap. 14.95 (0-253-20623-5, MB-623) Ind U Pr.

Perkins, Kelly A., jt. auth. see Perkins, Craig R.

Perkins, Kenneth, tr. see Valensi, Lucette.

Perkins, Kenneth J. Historical Dictionary of Tunisia. LC 89-10422. (African Historical Dictionaries Ser.: No. 45). (Illus.). 264p. 1989. 29.50 (0-8108-2226-1) Scarecrow.

— Port Sudan: The Evolution of a Colonial City. (State, Culture, & Society in Arab North Ser.). 264p. (C). 1993. text ed. 54.00 (0-8133-8484-2) Westview.

— Qaids, Captains, & Colons: French Military Administration in the Colonial Maghrib 1844-1934. LC 80-13114. 278p. (C). 1981. 45.00 (0-8419-0564-9, Africana) Holmes & Meier.

P Q

An Asterisk (*) at the beginning of an entry indicates that the title is appearing in BIP for the first time.

Perkins, Kris. Indycars. (Osprey Color Ser.). (Illus.). 128p. 1993. pap. 15.95 (1-85532-399-0, Pub. by Osprey Pubng Ltd UK) Motorbooks Intl.

Perkins, Kyle, ed. see Teachers of English to Speakers of Other Languages Staff.

Perkins, Llewellyn R., ed. see Robinson, Rowland E.

Perkins, Lucy F. The American Twins of Eighteen Twelve. 18.95 (0-89190-473-5, Am Repr) Amereon Ltd.

— The Cave Twins. 17.95 (0-89190-467-0, Am Repr) Amereon Ltd.

— The Dutch Twins. 18.95 (0-89190-468-9, Am Repr) Amereon Ltd.

— The Dutch Twins. 1993. reprint ed. lib. bdg. 16.95 (1-56849-213-8) Buccaneer Bks.

— The Japanese Twins. 18.95 (0-89190-469-7, Am Repr) Amereon Ltd.

— The Norwegian Twins. 16.95 (0-89190-471-9, Am Repr) Amereon Ltd.

— The Pioneer Twins. 19.95 (0-89190-472-7, Am Repr) Amereon Ltd.

— The Pioneer Twins. 1993. reprint ed. lib. bdg. 17.95 (1-56849-214-6) Buccaneer Bks.

— The Spartan Twins. 17.95 (0-89190-470-0, Am Repr) Amereon Ltd.

— The Swiss Twins. 16.95 (0-89190-670-3, Am Repr) Amereon Ltd.

***Perkins, Luisa.** Shannon's Mirror. 150p. (YA). 1994. 10.95 (0-910523-12-6) Grandin Bk Co.

Perkins, Lynn. The Meaning of Masonry. 2nd ed. Von Seggern Enterprises Staff, ed. 188p. 1993. reprint ed. pap. 11.95 (0-9639283-0-9) Von Seggern.

***Perkins, Lynne R.** Home Lovely. LC 94-21917. (Illus.). 32p. (J). 1995. 15.00 (0-688-13687-7); lib. bdg. 14.93 (0-688-13688-5) Greenwillow.

Perkins, M. J., jt. ed. see Butler, A. R.

Perkins, M. Katherine. Production. Distribution, & Growth in Transitional Economies. LC 87-29292. 172p. 1988. text ed. 55.00 (0-275-92104-2, C2104, Praeger Pubs) Greenwood.

Perkins, Malcolm. So Help Me Elmer! 64p. 1990. 10.00 (0-8062-3748-1) Carlton.

Perkins, Margo, jt. auth. see Hall, Betty L.

Perkins, Mary. Day of Glory: The Life of Baha'u'llah. (Illus.). 160p. 1992. 24.95 (0-85398-347-X); pap. 11.95 (0-85398-339-9) G Ronald Pub.

— Growing into Peace: A Manual for Peace-Builders in the 1990s & Beyond. (YA). (gr. 9-12). 1991. pap. 10.95 (0-85398-323-2) G Ronald Pub.

— Hour of the Dawn (the Life of the Bab) 224p. 1987. 19. 95 (0-85398-251-1) G Ronald Pub.

— Percival the Piano. (Illus.). (Orig.). (J). (gr. k-4). 1990. pap. 5.75 (0-85398-287-2) G Ronald Pub.

Perkins, Mary A. Coleridge's Philosophy: The Logos As Unifying Principle. LC 93-43259. 312p. 1994. 47.50 (0-19-824075-9, Old Oregon Bk Store) OUP.

Perkins, Mary E. Old Houses of the Ancient Town of Norwich, 1660-1800. (Illus.). 621p. 1992. reprint ed. lib. bdg. 65.00 (0-8328-2268-X) Higginson Bk Co.

Perkins, Mary J. Birds of Acadia National Park. (Illus.). 8p. 1990. 2.99 (0-934745-23-4) Acadia Pub Co.

Perkins, Maxwell, ed. see DeJong, Dola.

***Perkins, Maxwell, et al.** Father to Daughter: The Family Letters of Maxwell Perkins. 248p. 1995. pap. 12.95 (0-8362-0487-5) Andrews & McMeel.

***Perkins, Melissa. My Million-Dollar Body. LC 95-92133. (Illus.). 175p. 1995. pap. 21.95 (0-9646493-3-0) Mermaid Enter.**
Enlightened & inspiring autobiography of how one woman conquered obesity - after a lifetime of gaining & losing more than 750 pounds. Once a research subject at Rockefeller University, she developed her own regimen, by trial & error, that DEFIES what those experts have publicly proclaimed: we should accept that obesity is ultimately insurmountable. Features photographs that illustrate the author's repeated trips up & down the scale from age four weeks through age thirty-nine. Examines the traditional & more insidious myths/obstacles that most people encounter when dieting, & thoroughly contradicts the notion that even the largest person-man or woman-is HOPELESSLY fat. Frank, informative, & detailed, the author describes her complete step-by-step program & how, with the use of supplements found in almost any health food store, she has changed her body's metabolism: at age 40, she eats more than 2,000 calories a day & still loses weight - with a mild-to-moderate level of exercise. Lists specific products, ingredients, resources, & suggestions that will help everyone reach their optimal fitness level. Offers several full-bodied, extremely lowfat recipes from "Fried & True Chicken Parmigiana" to "Virtual Reality Mississippi Mud Pie." To order, call; 800-462-8768; in New York - 718-647-2971; FAX - 718-647-2754; e-mail: MERMDENT@aol.com. Or write: Mermaid Enterprises, 323 Barbey Street, Brooklyn, NY 11207. *Publisher Provided Annotation.*

Perkins, Merle L. Ordeal of Arms, Air Combat, Europe & the Balkans, WW Two: Foggia 1944. LC 93-84457. (Illus.). 180p. (Orig.). 1993. lib. bdg. 33.39 (0-9637220-3-4); pap. 21.39 (0-9637220-4-2) SHAPE WI.

***Perkins, Michael.** Coming Up: The World's Best Erotic Writing 1995. (Orig.). 1995. pap. 12.95 (1-56333-370-8) Masquerade.

— Evil Companions. (Orig.). 1992. reprint ed. pap. 6.95 (1-56333-067-9) Masquerade.

— The Secret Record: Modern Erotic Literature. (Orig.). reprint ed. pap. 6.95 (1-56333-039-3) Masquerade.

Perkins, Michael, ed. An Anthology of Classic Anonymous Erotic Writing. (Orig.). 1993. pap. text ed. 6.95 (1-56333-140-3) Masquerade.

***Perkins, Michael & Howard, Sara, eds.** Case Studies in Clinical Linguistics. 300p. (Orig.). (C). 1995. pap. text ed. 45.00 (1-56593-387-7, 0813) Singular Publishing.

***Perkins, Michael C.** Kidware: The Parent's Guide; Reviews of the Best 125 Children's Software, Vol. 1. 1994. pap. 14.95 (1-55958-552-8) Prima Pub.

— The Red Herring Guide to the Entertainment, Communications & Computer Industries. 1996. write for info. (0-446-52018-7) Warner Bks.

Perkins, Michael C. & Nunez, Celia. KidWare: A Parent's Guide. LC 93-30882. 1994. pap. 14.60 (0-8306-4488-1, Windcrest) TAB Bks.

Perkins, Michael R. Modal Expressions in English. LC 83-11890. 190p. 1983. text ed. 39.50 (0-89391-209-3) Ablex Pub.

Perkins, Mitali. The Sunita Experiment. LC 93-28525. 180p. (J). (gr. 5-9). 1994. pap. 4.50 (1-56282-671-9) Hyprn Child.

— The Sunita Experiment. LC 92-37267. 144p. (J). (gr. 1-6). 1993. 14.95 (0-316-69943-8, Joy St Bks) Little.

Perkins, Moreland. Sensing the World. LC 83-10825. 352p. (C). 1983. text ed. 16.50 (0-915145-75-8); lib. bdg. 34.95 (0-915145-74-X) Hackett Pub.

Perkins, Myla. Black Dolls: And Indetification & Value Guide, Bk. 2. 1994. pap. 17.95 (0-89145-605-8) Collector Bks.

Perkins, Myrna. Bored Betty's Wish. (Illus.). 32p. (Orig.). (J). (gr. 2-5). 1986. pap. 5.95 (0-937729-02-7) Markins Enter.

— What Does A Spider Do? (Illus.). 20p. (Orig.). (J). (ps-3). 1985. pap. 3.95 (0-937729-00-0) Markins Enter.

— What Is This? (Illus.). 36p. (Orig.). (J). (ps-3). 1986. pap. 4.95 (0-937729-01-9) Markins Enter.

— What Makes Honey? (Illus.). 32p. (Orig.). (J). (ps-3). pap. 3.95 (0-937729-03-5) Markins Enter.

Perkins, N. C., jt. ed. see Pierre, C.

Perkins, Nancy M., jt. auth. see Perkins, William M.

***Perkins, Noriss H. North African Odyssey: Adventures in the Mediterranean Theater of War. (Illus.). 134p. (Orig.). 1995. pap. 14.95 (0-9638442-1-0) Four Mntn Prods.**
8-1/2 X 11, COVER PHOTO, INDEX, OVER 60 remarkable on-the-spot PHOTOS, 5 cartoons, AUTOGRAPHED. American TANK COMMANDER'S long overdue story of distinguished TANK COMPANY in N. AFRICA, SICILY. Justifiably lawless, decorated for EXTRAORDINARY HEROISM, he writes as ADVENTURER with keen eye for EXOTIC SCENES of romance, beauty, INTRIGUE:--CASABLANCA... MOROCCAN cork forest...WILD BOARS, BERBERS, HIGH ATLAS MOUNTAINS...NATIVE FEASTS... DANCING GIRLS...northern SAHARA...spooky TUNISIAN olive grove...AMPHIBIOUS ASSAULT, waterproofed SHERMAN TANKS... MOBILE BATTLES...SMALL BOY interrupts VIOLENT TANK ATTACK.. .FOG OF BATTLE...wounded captain has poignant encounter with BEAUTIFUL GIRL in lofty mountain citadel. REVIEWS: Col. (Ret.) James M. Thayer, Sr., Civilian Aide to the Secretary of the Army, "I found this book very enticing, a must to read." William Marion Page, Esq., "...poignant memoirs of a tank company commander during the 1943 invasion of Sicily & the rigorous preparation & adventures that preceded it in North Africa. Highly recommended for enjoyable reading." TO ORDER: FOUR MOUNTAIN PRODUCTIONS, 1565 SW Upper Hall St., Portland, OR, 97201-2562, (503) 228-7732. $14.95 plus S & H $2.00 & $1.00 each added copy. Discounts available. *Publisher Provided Annotation.*

Perkins, Norris H. Slow Settles the Dust in Oregon: A Memoir. (Illus.). 131p. 1993. pap. 24.95 (0-9638442-0-2) Four Mntn Prods.

Perkins, P. Johannine Epistles. 1989. pap. 21.00 (0-86217-026-5, Pub. by Veritas IE) St Mut.

Perkins, Pamela, tr. see Wilhelm, James J., ed.

Perkins, Patt & Hootman, Marcia. Making the Break. LC 82-6324. (Illus.). 130p. 1982. pap. 5.95 (0-943172-00-4) New Wave.

Perkins, Percy H., Jr. Gemstones of the Bible. 2nd ed. LC 81-90232. (Illus.). 137p. 1986. 18.95 (0-9603090-2-0) P H Perkins Jr.

Perkins, Pheme. The Book of Revelation, 11. Karris, Robert J., ed. (Collegeville Bible Commentary - New Testament Ser.: No. 11). 96p. (C). 1983. pap. 3.95 (0-8146-1311-X) Liturgical Pr.

— First & Second Peter, James & Jude. LC 94-38274. (Interpretation Ser.). 224p. 1995. 20.00 (0-8042-3145-1, John Knox) Westminster John Knox.

— The Gnostic Dialogue: The Early Church & the Crisis of Gnosticism. LC 80-81441. (Theological Inquiries Ser.). 251p. reprint ed. pap. 71.60 (0-8357-2701-7, 2039813) Bks Demand.

— Gnosticism & the New Testament. LC 93-21890. 1993. 17.00 (0-8006-2801-2, Fortress Pr) Augsburg Fortress.

— The Gospel According to St. John: A Theological Commentary. LC 77-12896. (Herald Scriptural Library). 267p. reprint ed. pap. 76.10 (0-317-28173-9, 2022571) Bks Demand.

— Gospel of St. John. (Read & Pray Ser.). 96p. 1975. pap. 1.95 (0-8199-0787-1, Frncscn Herld) Franciscan Pr.

— Gospel of St. John. (Read & Pray Ser.). 96p. 1975. pap. 1.95 (0-8199-0627-1, Frncscn Herld) Franciscan Pr.

— Jesus As Teacher. (Understanding Jesus Today Ser.). 128p. (C). 1990. pap. 9.95 (0-521-36695-X) Cambridge U Pr.

— Jesus As Teacher. (Understanding Jesus Today Ser.). 128p. (C). 1990. 32.95 (0-521-36624-0) Cambridge U Pr.

— Peter: Apostle for the Whole Church. LC 93-5983. 230p. (C). 1994. text ed. 34.95 (0-87249-974-X) U of SC Pr.

— Reading the New Testament: An Introduction. 2nd rev. ed. 368p. 1988. pap. 9.95 (0-8091-2939-6) Paulist Pr.

— What We Believe: A Biblical Catechism of the Apostles Creed. 144p. (Orig.). 1986. pap. 7.95 (0-8091-2764-4) Paulist Pr.

Perkins, Pheme, jt. auth. see Fuller, Reginald.

Perkins, Philip H. Concrete Floors. (Illus.). 144p. 1993. 59. 95 (0-7506-0770-X) Buttrwrth-Heinemann.

— Concrete Floors: Finishes & External Paving. 184p. 1995. pap. 28.95 (0-7506-2334-9, Butterwrth Archit) Buttrwrth-Heinemann.

— Repair, Protection & Waterproofing of Concrete Structures. 324p. 1986. 74.00 (1-85166-008-9, Pub. by Elsevier Applied Sci UK) Elsevier.

— Swimming Pools. 2nd ed. (Illus.). 395p. 1978. 65.00 (0-85334-769-7, Pub. by Elsevier Applied Sci UK) Elsevier.

— Swimming Pools: A Treatise on the Planning, Layout, Design & Construction, Water Treatment & Other Services, Maintenance & Repairs. 3rd ed. 368p. 1989. 65.00 (1-85166-192-1) Elsevier.

Perkins, Philip H., jt. auth. see Green, J. Keith.

Perkins, Phyllis H. The Bible Speaks to Me about My Service & Mission. 128p. 1990. pap. 5.95 (0-8341-1359-7) Beacon Hill.

— Women in Nazarene Missions: Embracing the Legacy. 96p. 1994. pap. write for info. (0-8341-1476-3) Nazarene.

Perkins, Priscilla L., ed. see Leland, Abigail T.

Perkins, R. Nature, Pregnancy, Sexuality. 1985. text ed. 33. 00 (0-275-91321-X, C1321, Praeger Pubs) Greenwood.

Perkins, R., jt. auth. see Wilson, J. W.

Perkins, R. D., jt. auth. see Enos, Paul.

Perkins, R. W., ed. Mechanics of Cellulosic Materials. (AMD Series, Vol. 145: MD: Vol. 36). 84p. 1992. 30.00 (0-7918-1094-1, G00738) ASME.

Perkins, Rachel, jt. auth. see Kitzinger, Celia.

Perkins, Ray, Jr. The ABCs of the Soviet-American Nuclear Arms Race. LC 90-36499. 272p. (C). 1991. pap. 25.95 (0-534-14526-4) Intl Thomson.

— Logic & Mr. Limbaugh. 200p. 1995. pap. text ed. 9.95 (0-8126-9294-2) Open Court.

Perkins, Ray, Jr., ed. see Sylvester, Robert D.

Perkins-Reed, Marcia A. The Career Workbook: A Tool for Self-Discovery. 53p. (Orig.). 1989. pap. 9.95 (1-878482-02-5) High Flight Pr.

— When Nine to Five Isn't Enough: A Guide to Finding Fulfillment at Work. Kramer, Jill, ed. LC 90-80052. 304p. (Orig.). 1990. pap. 10.00 (0-937611-93-X, 126) Hay House.

Perkins, Revere D. Deixis, Grammar & Culture. LC 92-33519. (Typological Studies in Language Ser.: No. 24). x, 245p. 1992. 59.00x (1-55619-412-9); pap. 24.95x (1-55619-413-7) Benjamins North Am.

***Perkins, Richard.** Let's Study the Holy Spirit. 96p. (C). 1995. pap. 7.95 (1-883893-09-7) Wine Pr Pub.

Perkins, Richard J. Onsite Wastewater Disposal. (Illus.). 280p. 1989. 76.95 (0-87371-211-0, TD523) Lewis Pubs.

Perkins, Rita & Alden, Richard. Writing with a Goal: A Workbook & Study Guide. 124p. (C). 1991. pap. text ed. 24.70 (1-56226-073-1) CT Pub.

Perkins, Robert F., et al, eds. The Boston Athenaeum Art Exhibition Index: 1827-1874. (Illus.). 325p. 1980. 75.00 (0-262-16075-7) MIT Pr.

Perkins, Robert L. Fear & Trembling & Repetition. (International Kierkegaard Commentary Ser.: No. 6). 382p. 1993. text ed. 24.95 (0-86554-408-5, MUP/H331) Mercer Univ Pr.

Perkins, Robert L., ed. The Concept of Anxiety: A Commentary. LC 85-11571. (International Kierkegaard Commentary Ser.: Vol. 8). xii, 203p. 1985. 18.95 (0-86554-142-6, MUP/H133) Mercer Univ Pr.

— The Corsair Affair. LC 84-161455. (International Kierkegaard Commentary Ser.: No. 13). xxv, 193p. (C). 1990. 24.95 (0-86554-363-1, MUP-H301) Mercer Univ Pr.

— History & System: Hegel's Philosophy of History. LC 83-24244. (SUNY Series in Hegelian Studies). 256p. 1984. 64.50 (0-87395-814-4); pap. 21.95 (0-87395-815-2) State U NY Pr.

— Philosophical Fragments & Johannes Climacus. LC 93-48223. (International Kierkegaard Commentary Ser.: No. 7). (C). 1994. 24.95 (0-86554-440-9) Mercer Univ Pr.

— Sickness unto Death. LC 87-5614. (International Kierkegaard Commentary Ser.: No. 19). 272p. 1987. 18. 95 (0-86554-271-6, H234) Mercer Univ Pr.

— Two Ages. LC 83-25106. (International Kierkegaard Commentary Ser.: No. 14). xxiv, 266p. 1984. 18.95 (0-86554-081-0, MUP-H59) Mercer Univ Pr.

***Perkins, Roberta, et al, eds.** Sex Work & Sex Workers in Australia. 1995. pap. 24.95 (0-86840-174-9, Pub. by New South Wales Univ Pr AT) Intl Spec Bk.

Perkins, Roger. The Kashmir Gate Lieutenant: Home & the Delhi VCS. 176p. (C). 1987. 91.00 (0-902633-87-2, Pub. by Picton UK) St Mut.

— Operation Paraquat: The Battle for South Georgia. (Illus.). 276p. (C). 1992. 79.95x (0-948251-13-1, Pub. by Picton UK) St Mut.

— The Punjab Mail Murder. 2nd enl. ed. 108p. (C). 1987. 84.00 (0-948251-09-3, Pub. by Picton UK) St Mut.

Perkins, Rollin M. Criminal Law: Adaptable to Courses Utilizing Materials by Perkins. LC 87-118871. (Legalines Ser.). 317p. 12.95 (0-685-18527-3) HarBrace.

Perkins, Rollin M. & Boyce, Ronald N. Criminal Law. 3rd ed. LC 82-15976. (University Textbook Ser.). 1269p. (C). 1991. reprint ed. text ed. 34.50 (0-88277-067-5) Foundation Pr.

Perkins, Rollin M., jt. auth. see Boyce, Ronald N.

Perkins, Romi. Game in Season: The Orvis Cookbook. (Illus.). 224p. 1988. 27.95 (0-8329-0447-3) Lyons & Burford.

Perkins, Ron. How to Find Your Treasure in a Gift Basket. (Illus.). 144p. (Orig.). 1991. pap. 16.95 (0-9627185-1-3) R Perkins.

Perkins, Roswell B. & Bohm, Richard D. Federal Conflict-of-Interest Laws As Applied to Government Service by Partners & Employees of Accounting Firms. LC 81-111954. 64p. reprint ed. pap. 25.00 (0-8357-2812-9, 2037600) Bks Demand.

Perkins, Russell. The Impact of a Saint. LC 80-51959. 256p. 1989. pap. 8.00 (0-89142-037-1) Sant Bani Ash.

Perkins, Russell, ed. Third World Tour of Kirpal Singh. (Illus.). 1974. pap. 2.50 (0-89142-008-8) Sant Bani Ash.

***Perkins, Russell & Hatch, Denison, eds.** The 1995 Directory of Major Mailers & What They Mail: The Most Powerful Databases on Direct Mail Ever Created! 1995. 495.00 (0-912920-12-2) North Am Pub Co.

Perkins, Russell, ed. see Kabir.

Perkins, Russell, ed. see Oberoi, A. S.

Perkins, Russell, ed. see Singh, Ajaib.

Perkins, Russell, ed. see Singh, Kirpal.

Perkins, Ruth. Off-Centered Riding: Or Not So Swift. (Illus.). 192p. 1993. pap. 9.95 (0-943955-81-5) Trafalgar.

Perkins, Salvador T., jt. auth. see Norris, Jeffrey A.

Perkins, Salvador T., jt. auth. see Williams, Robert E.

Perkins, Samuel. Historical Sketches of the United States: From the Peace of 1815 to 1830. LC 72-31. (Select Bibliographies Reprint Ser.). 1977. reprint ed. 28.95 (0-8369-9969-X) Ayer.

***Perkins, Samuel L.** Basic Contracts & Checklists for Petroleum Marketing. 1995. 69.95 (0-9644877-0-5) Petrol Pub Grp.

Perkins, Shirley, ed. see Kuenning, Kym.

Perkins, Simeon. Diary of Simeon Perkins, 1766-1780, Vol. 29. Innes, Harold A., ed. LC 69-14503. 298p. 1969. reprint ed. text ed. 55.00 (0-8371-5067-1, PEDI, Greenwood Pr) Greenwood.

— Diary of Simeon Perkins, 1780-1789, Vol. 36. Harvey, D. C., ed. LC 69-14503. 531p. 1969. reprint ed. text ed. 75. 00 (0-8371-5068-X, PEDJ, Greenwood Pr) Greenwood.

Perkins, Simon. The Audubon Society Pocket Guide to North American Birds of Sea & Shore. LC 93-21251. (Audubon Society Pocket Guides Ser.). (Illus.). 1994. 9.00 (0-679-74921-7) Random.

Perkins, Spencer, jt. auth. see Rice, Chris.

Perkins, Stan. Arvilla & the Tattler Tree. (Illus.). 702p. (J). 1994. boxed 30.00 (0-9614640-9-7) Broadblade Pr.
The era of the fur trade, with support from the War of 1812, provides the mise-en-scene. This was a lawless & unstable period for venturesome people who chose to migrate to the Northwest Territory. Here, for over two centuries, peltry was the commodity for which men toiled, froze, starved, fought & died. It was the sole product that Natives could use in bartering for marvels of civilization. The dealing in furs was grossly unbalanced in favor of the Traders. This irked a knowledgeable birds-eye maple tree. It rustled her leaves. This matron was further distressed by a serious sailing ship disaster upcurrent in the St. Mary's

P
Q

River on the rocks of Neebish. Five survived. Two seamen, a scoundrel, the schooner's housekeeper & a baby girl. Later, this disturbed tree was tapped. With assistance of computerized technology, sap taken was easily decoded because of its variable cellular composition. Thus, the long sought communication link between flora & fauna was discovered. The ice on Gogomain Baie, to date, has only been cracked by the revelations drawn from the heartwood of this Tattler Tree who was inspired by Arvilla, the man-maker, & stabilized by Abigail, the door opener. To order contact: Broadblade Press, 11314 Miller Road, Swartz Creek, MI 48437-8570. ***Publisher Provided Annotation.***

—Arvilla & the Tattler Tree. (Illus.). 702p. (J). 1994. pap. 25.00 (*0-9620249-4-5*) Broadblade Pr.
The era of the fur trade, with support from the War of 1812, provides the mise-en-scene. This was a lawless & unstable period for venturesome people who chose to migrate to the Northwest Territory. Here, for over two centuries, peltry was the commodity for which men toiled, froze, starved, fought & died. It was the sole product that Natives could use in bartering for marvels of civilization. The dealing in furs was grossly unbalanced in favor of the Traders. This irked a knowledgeable birds-eye maple tree. It rustled her leaves. This matron was further distressed by a serious sailing ship disaster upcurrent in the St. Mary's River on the rocks of Neebish. Five survived. Two seamen, a scoundrel, the schooner's housekeeper & a baby girl. Later, this disturbed tree was tapped. With assistance of computerized technology, sap taken was easily decoded because of its variable cellular composition. Thus, the long sought communication link between flora & fauna was discovered. The ice on Gogomain Baie, to date, has only been cracked by the revelations drawn from the heartwood of this Tattler Tree who was inspired by Arvilla, the man-maker, & stabilized by Abigail, the door opener. To order contact: Broadblade Press, 11314 Miller Road, Swartz Creek, MI 48437-8570. ***Publisher Provided Annotation.***

— Itinerant Auctioneering. 2nd ed. LC 81-51758. (Illus.). 349p. 1983. 14.00 (*0-9614640-0-3*) Broadblade Pr.

— Lore of Wolverine Country. 2nd ed. (Illus.). 244p. 1984. 15.00 (*0-940404-08-7*); pap. 12.00 (*0-9614640-3-8*) Broadblade Pr.

— We're from Duffield. 3rd ed. (Illus.). 147p. 1982. 10.00 (*0-9614640-1-1*); pap. 7.50 (*0-9614640-2-X*) Broadblade Pr.

Perkins, Stephen. Marxism & the Proletariat: A Lukacsian Perspective. LC 93-20550. (C). 1993. text ed. 63.00 (*0-7453-0492-3*, Pub. by Pluto Pr UK); pap. text ed. 21.00 (*0-7453-0499-0*, Pub. by Pluto Pr UK) Westview.

Perkins, Suzanne, jt. auth. see Youens, Paula.

***Perkins, Terry & Bock, Douglas.** Intro Speech Communication. 96p. (C). 1994. pap. text ed., spiral bd. 7.95 (*0-7872-0455-2*) Kendall-Hunt.

Perkins, Terry M. & Bock, Douglas G. Introduction to Speech Communication: A Course Guide. 2nd ed. 80p. 1993. spiral bd. 6.95 (*0-8403-8985-X*) Kendall-Hunt.

Perkins, Tessa, jt. auth. see Beechey, Veronica.

Perkins, Thornton. Junior High Champs. (Illus.). 49p. (Orig.). (YA). (gr. 6-9). 1989. pap. 3.00 (*0-9623407-0-7*) NVEM.

***Perkins, Una.** Fulton & Company. 1995. 9.95 (*0-8062-5305-3*) Carlton.

Perkins, Useni. The Black Fairy & Other Plays for Children. LC 92-60054. (Illus.). 200p. (Orig.). (J). 1993. pap. 13.95 (*0-88378-077-1*) Third World.

Perkins, Useni E. The Afrocentric Self-Inventory & Discovery Workbook. 1990. 5.95 (*0-88378-043-7*) Third World.

— Explosion of Chicago Black Street Gangs: 1900 to Present. (Orig.). 1987. pap. 6.95 (*0-88378-120-4*) Third World.

— Harvesting New Generations: The Positive Development of Black Youth. (Orig.). 1986. pap. 12.95 (*0-88378-116-6*) Third World.

— Home Is a Dirty Street: The Social Oppression of Black Children. LC 74-78322. (Orig.). 1975. pap. 9.95 (*0-88378-048-8*) Third World.

Perkins, V. F. Film As Film: Understanding & Judging Movies. LC 93-25278. 204p. 1993. reprint ed. pap. 12.95 (*0-306-80541-3*) Da Capo.

Perkins, W. Language Handicaps in Adults. (Current Therapy of Communication Disorders Ser.: Vol. 3). 1983. 22.00 (*0-86577-406-4*) Thieme Med Pubs.

Perkins, Walter W., ed. Ceramic Glossary. 100p. 1984. pap. text ed. 12.00 (*0-916094-61-8*) Am Ceramic.

Perkins, Wendy. Temporarily Yours, Vol. I. (Illus.). 112p. (Orig.). (C). 1989. 11.95 (*0-9622980-3-4*) Permanently Collectible.

Perkins, Whitney T. Constraint of Empire: The United States & Caribbean Interventions. LC 80-27269. (Contributions in Comparative Colonial Studies: No. 8). 320p. 1981. text ed. 69.50 (*0-313-22266-5*, PCE/, Greenwood Pr) Greenwood.

Perkins, William. Commentary on Galatians: A Facsimile of the 1617 Edition. LC 89-35504. (Classic Commentaries Ser.). 686p. (C). 1989. lib. bdg. 35.00 (*0-8298-0790-X*); pap. 19.95 (*0-8298-0786-1*) Pilgrim OH.

— A Commentary on Hebrews Eleven (1609) Augustine, John H., ed. LC 90-22542. (Classic Commentaries Ser.). 222p. 1990. reprint ed. 39.95 (*0-8298-0856-6*); reprint ed. pap. 29.95 (*0-8298-0857-4*) Pilgrim OH.

— Dysarthria & Apraxia: Current Therapy of Communication Disorders, Vol. 2. 126p. 1983. 22.00 (*0-86577-086-7*) Thieme Med Pubs.

— General Principles of Therapy: Current Therapy of Communication Disorders, Vol. 1. 98p. 1982. 22.00 (*0-86577-401-3*) Thieme Med Pubs.

— Moving to the Positive Side. pap. 15.95 (*1-55673-445-X*, 7905) CSS OH.

— Three Years in California: William Perkins' Journal of Life at Sonora, 1849-1852. (With an Introduction & Annotations by Dale L. Morgan & James P. Scobie) LC 64-21141. (Illus.). 442p. reprint ed. pap. 126.00 (*0-685-23666-8*, 2029059) Bks Demand.

— The Whole Treatise of the Cases of Conscience. LC 74-38218. (English Experience Ser.: No. 482). 690p. 1972. reprint ed. 75.00 (*90-221-0482-6*) Walter J Johnson.

— Works of William Perkins, 3 Vols, 1. LC 74-144670. reprint ed. write for info. (*0-404-05051-4*) AMS Pr.

— Works of William Perkins, 3 Vols, 2. LC 74-144670. reprint ed. write for info. (*0-404-05052-2*) AMS Pr.

— Works of William Perkins, 3 Vols, 3. LC 74-144670. reprint ed. write for info. (*0-404-05053-0*) AMS Pr.

— Works of William Perkins, 3 Vols, Set. LC 74-144670. reprint ed. lib. bdg. 285.00 (*0-404-05050-6*) AMS Pr.

Perkins, William, jt. auth. see Doyle, William.

Perkins, William, jt. ed. see Fraser, Jane.

Perkins, William C., jt. auth. see Martin, Edley W.

Perkins, William D. Chestnuts, Galls, & Dandelion Wine: Useful Wild Plants of the Boston Harbor Islands. LC 81-19867. (Illus.). (Orig.). 1982. pap. 6.95 (*0-940960-00-1*) Plant Pr MA.

***Perkins, William E., ed.** Droppin' Science: Critical Essays on Rap Music & Hip Hop Culture. LC 95-1532. (Critical Perspectives on the Past Ser.). (Illus.). 352p. (C). 1995. lib. bdg. 49.95 (*1-56639-361-2*); pap. text ed. 18.95 (*1-56639-362-0*) Temple U Pr.

Perkins, William H. Stuttering Disorders, Vol. 8: Current Therapy of Communication Disorders. 255p. 1985. text ed. 22.00 (*0-86577-403-X*) Thieme Med Pubs.

— Stuttering Prevented: A Guide for Parents. (Illus.). 160p. (Orig.). (C). 1991. pap. text ed. 24.95 (*1-879105-50-0*, 0235) Singular Publishing.

Perkins, William H., ed. Hearing Disorders. LC 84-51456. (Current Therapy of Communication Disorders Ser.). 170p. 1984. 22.00 (*0-86577-088-3*) Thieme Med Pubs.

— Language Handicaps in Children: Current Therapy of Communication Disorders, Vol. 7. 187p. 1984. 22.00 (*0-86577-405-6*) Thieme Med Pubs.

— Phonologic-Articulatory Disorders: Current Therapy of Communication Disorders, Vol. 5. 114p. 1983. 22.00 (*0-86577-402-1*) Thieme Med Pubs.

— Voice Disorders: Current Therapy of Communication Disorders, Vol. 4. 160p. 1983. 22.00 (*0-86577-407-2*) Thieme Med Pubs.

Perkins, William H. & Kent, Raymond D. Functional Anatomy of Speech, Language, & Hearing: A Primer. (C). 1991. pap. text ed. 59.00 (*0-205-13572-2*) Allyn.

Perkins, William H., jt. ed. see Curlee, Richard F.

Perkins, William M. & McMurtrie-Perkins, Nancy. Raising Drug-Free Kids in a Drug-Filled World. 98p. (Orig.). 1986. pap. 1.95 (*0-89486-316-9*, 5020) Hazelden.

***Perkins, William M. & Perkins, Nancy M.** Hijos Sanos en un Mundo Invadido por las Drogas. 146p. (SPA.). 1994. pap. 10.00 (*968-39-0639-7*) Hazelden.

Perkins, William R. & Wick, Barthinius L. History of the Amana Society: Or, Community of True Inspiration. LC 75-117. (Mid-American Frontier Ser.). 1975. reprint ed. 15.95 (*0-405-06883-2*) Ayer.

— History of the Amana Society, or Community of True Inspiration. LC 75-339. (Radical Tradition in America Ser.). 94p. 1975. reprint ed. 15.00 (*0-88355-242-6*) Hyperion Conn.

Perkinson, Betty J., jt. auth. see Kettlewell, Gail B.

Perkinson, Henry. Getting Better: Television & Moral Progress. 296p. (C). 1991. 34.95 (*0-88738-397-1*) Transaction Pubs.

Perkinson, Henry J. The Imperfect Panacea: American Faith in Education. 3rd ed. 1991. pap. text ed. write for info. (*0-07-049348-0*) McGraw.

— The Imperfect Panacea: American Faith in Education. 4th ed. 1994. pap. text ed. write for info. (*0-07-049371-5*) McGraw.

— Learning from Our Mistakes: A Reinterpretation of Twentieth-Century Educational Theory. LC 83-26670. (Contributions to the Study of Education Ser.: No. 14). (Illus.). xvi, 209p. 1984. text ed. 55.00 (*0-313-24239-9*, PEM/) Greenwood.

— Teachers Without Goals, Students Without Purposes. LC 92-26491. 1992. pap. text ed. write for info. (*0-07-049372-3*) McGraw.

— Two Hundred Years of American Educational Thought. 342p. 1987. reprint ed. pap. text ed. 27.00 (*0-8191-6124-1*) U Pr of Amer.

Perkinson, Kathryn, ed. see Cullinan, Bernice & Bagert, Brad.

Perkinson, Richard C. Data Analysis: The Key to Data Base Design. LC 83-63212. 303p. reprint ed. pap. 86.40 (*0-7837-5887-1*, 2045610) Bks Demand.

Perkinson, Roy, jt. auth. see Clapp, Anne.

Perkinson, Roy L., jt. auth. see Dolloff, Francis W.

Perkio, L. Swedish & Finnish Glossary of Gastronomy: Gastronomisk Ordlista. 90p. (FIN & SWE.). 1985. 35.00 (*0-8288-0846-5*, F34200) Fr & Eur.

Perkis, Philip, photos. Warwick Mountain Series. LC 78-61647. (Illus.). 1978. 24.00 (*0-932526-01-2*) Nexus Pr.

Perko, F. Michael. Catholic & American: A Popular History. LC 88-63547. 372p. (Orig.). 1989. pap. 13.95 (*0-87973-490-6*, 490) Our Sunday Visitor.

— A Time to Favor Zion: The Ecology of Religion & School Development on the Urban Frontier, Cincinnati, 1830-1870. (Illus.). 276p. (Orig.). 1987. lib. bdg. 29.95 (*0-685-13974-3*); pap. 11.95 (*0-934328-05-6*) Educ Studies Pr.

Perko, F. Michael, ed. Enlightening the Next Generation: Catholics & Their School 1830-1980. LC 88-24523. (Heritage of American Catholicism Ser.). 448p. 1988. 20.00 (*0-8240-4078-3*) Garland.

Perko, L. M. Differential Equations & Dynamical Systems. (Texts in Applied Mathematics Ser.: Vol. 7). (Illus.). xii, 403p. 1993. 39.95 (*0-387-97443-1*) Spr-Verlag.

Perko, Margaret. Other Side of Silence. 1984. pap. 3.25 (*0-8439-2086-6*) Dorchester Pub Co.

***Perko, Marko.** Did You Know That...? Surprising but True Facts about History, Science, Art, Technology. 304p. (Orig.). 1994. pap. text ed. 5.50 (*0-425-14343-0*) Berkley Pub.

Perkoff, David, et al. Processionals & Recessionals for Traditional Weddings: Guidebook & Cassette. (Illus.). 20p. (Orig.). 1990. pap. 15.95 (*0-9631377-0-0*) Seven Veils Recs.

Perkoff, Stuart Z. Alphabet. 1973. 4.00 (*0-88031-010-3*) Invisible-Red Hill.

— Love Is the Silence: Poems, 1948-1974. 1975. pap. 4.00 (*0-88031-018-9*) Invisible-Red Hill.

Perkov, Yury, tr. see Afanasiev, Aleksandr A., ed.

Perkovich, George. Thinking about the Soviet Union. (Illus.). 256p. (Orig.). (J). 1989. pap. text ed. 25.00 (*0-942349-00-8*) Eductrs Soc Respons.

Perkowitz, S. Optical Characterization of Semiconductors. (Techniques of Physics Ser.). (Illus.). 220p. 1993. text ed. 69.00 (*0-12-550770-4*) Acad Pr.

***Perkowitz, S., et al.** Optical Characterization in Microelectronics Manufacturing. (Illus.). 50p. (Orig.). (C). 1994. pap. text ed. 35.00 (*0-7881-1539-1*) Diane Pub.

Perkowitz, Sidney. The Empire of Light. 1996. 25.00 (*0-8050-3211-8*) H Holt & Co.

Perkowski, Jan L. The Darkling: A Treatise on Slavic Vampirism. 169p. (Orig.). 1989. pap. 14.95 (*0-89357-200-4*) Slavica.

— Kashubian Idiolect in the United States. LC 68-64529. (Language Science Monographs: Vol. 2). 1969. pap. text ed. 11.50 (*0-87750-135-1*) Res Inst Inner Asian Studies.

Perl. Gallery Going: Four Seasons in the Art World. 1991. 24.95 (*0-15-134260-1*) HarBrace.

Perl, Arnold. Tevya & His Daughters. 1957. pap. 4.75 (*0-8222-1125-4*) Dramatists Play.

— The World of Sholom Aleichem. 1955. pap. 4.75 (*0-8222-1277-3*) Dramatists Play.

Perl, Gisella. I Was a Doctor in Auschwitz. LC 79-12470. 1979. reprint ed. lib. bdg. 25.95 (*0-405-12300-0*) Ayer.

***Perl, James.** Sleep Right in Five Nights: A Clear & Effective Guide for Conquering Insomnia. 1995. pap. 10.00 (*0-688-14064-5*, Quill) Morrow.

— Sleep Right in Five Nights: A Quick & Easy Guide for Conquering Insomnia. LC 93-16379. 1993. 20.00 (*0-688-12248-5*) Morrow.

Perl, Jed. Man Ray. (Masters of Photography Ser.: Vol. 8). (Illus.). 96p. (Orig.). 1988. pap. 12.95 (*0-89381-307-9*) Aperture.

Perl, Jeffrey M. Skepticism & Modern Enmity: Before & After Eliot. LC 89-11057. 256p. 1989. text ed. 37.50x (*0-8018-3853-3*) Johns Hopkins.

— The Tradition of Return. LC 84-42567. (Illus.). 360p. 1984. text ed. 49.50x (*0-691-06621-3*) Princeton U Pr.

Perl, Lewis J., jt. auth. see Heim, John.

Perl, Lila. Don't Sing Before Breakfast, Don't Sleep in the Moonlight: Everyday Superstitions & How They Began. LC 87-24295. (Illus.). 96p. (J). (gr. 3-6). 1988. 14.95 (*0-89919-504-0*, Clarion Bks) HM.

— From Top Hats to Baseball Caps, from Bustles to Blue Jeans: Why We Dress the Way We Do. LC 89-77717. (Illus.). 118p. (J). (gr. 5-8). 1990. 14.95 (*0-89919-872-4*, Clarion Bks) HM.

— From Top Hats to Baseball Caps, from Bustles to Blue Jeans: Why We Dress the Way We Do. (Illus.). 118p. 1990. 16.95 (*0-89919-972-0*) Ticknor & Fields.

— The Great Ancestor Hunt. LC 88-36211. (Illus.). 112p. (J). (gr. 4 up). 1989. 15.95 (*0-89919-745-0*, Clarion Bks) HM.

— Great Ancestor Hunt: The Fun of Finding Out Who You Are. (J). (gr. 4-7). 1990. pap. 7.95 (*0-395-54790-3*, Clarion Bks) HM.

— Hunter's Stew & Hangtown Fry. LC 77-5366. (Illus.). 176p. (J). (gr. 6 up). 1979. 13.95 (*0-395-28922-X*, Clarion Bks) HM.

— Isaac Bashevis Singer: The Life of a Storyteller. LC 93-45275. 112p. (J). 1994. 13.95 (*0-8276-0512-9*) JPS Phila.

— It Happened in America: True Stories from the Fifty States. (Illus.). 304p. (J). (gr. 4-6). 1993. 22.50 (*0-8050-1719-4*, Bks Young Read) H Holt & Co.

— Molly Picon: A Gift of Laughter. (JPS Young Biography Ser.). (Illus.). 64p. (J). (gr. 4-7). 1990. 14.95 (*0-8276-0336-3*) JPS Phila.

— Mummies, Tombs, & Treasure: Secrets of Ancient Egypt. LC 86-17646. (Illus.). 128p. (J). (gr. 4 up). 1987. 15.95 (*0-89919-407-9*, Clarion Bks) HM.

— Mummies, Tombs, & Treasure: Secrets of Ancient Egypt. LC 86-17646. (Illus.). 128p. (J). (gr. 2-5). 1990. pap. 5.95 (*0-395-54796-2*, Clarion Bks) HM.

— Slumps, Grunts, & Snickerdoodles: What Colonial America Ate & Why. LC 75-4894. (Illus.). 128p. (J). (gr. 6 up). 1979. 14.95 (*0-395-28923-8*, Clarion Bks) HM.

Perl, Lila & Ada, Alma F. Pinatas & Paper Flowers-Pinatas y Flores de Papel: Holidays of the Americas in English & Spanish. LC 82-12211. (Illus.). 91p. (J). (gr. 3-6). 1983. pap. 6.95 (*0-89919-155-X*, Clarion Bks) HM.

***Perl, Lila & Lazan, Marian B.** Four Perfect Pebbles: A Holocaust Story. LC 95-9752. (J). 1996. write for info. (*0-688-14294-X*) Greenwillow.

Perl, Martin L., ed. see Conference on Changing Career Opportunities, Pennsylvania State Univ., Aug. 1977.

Perl, Michael. KSU Student Teaching Handbook. 128p. (C). 1993. 9.95 (*0-8403-8446-7*) Kendall-Hunt.

— Teacher Aide Handbook. 64p. (C). 1992. teacher ed 9.95 (*0-8403-8288-X*) Kendall-Hunt.

***Perl, Michael & Burton, Sharon.** Working Windows World. 208p. (C). 1995. pap. text ed. 23.95 (*0-7872-1039-0*) Kendall-Hunt.

Perl, Raphael, ed. Drugs & Foreign Policy: A Critical Review. 256p. (C). 1994. text ed. 58.00 (*0-8133-8786-8*) Westview.

Perl, Raphael & Larson, Everette E. The Falkland Islands Dispute in International Law & Politics: A Documentary Sourcebook. LC 83-25972. 722p. 1983. lib. bdg. 50.00 (*0-379-11251-5*) Oceana.

Perl, Rose. Death Is Not Saying Goodbye. 60p. 1987. pap. 6.50 (*0-910458-60-X*) Select Bks.

Perl, Sondra, ed. Landmark Essays on Writing Process. (Landmark Essays Ser.: Vol. 7). xxx, 242p. (C). 1994. pap. text ed. 15.95 (*1-880393-13-1*) Hermagoras Pr.

Perl, Susan, jt. auth. see Bayley, Monica.

Perl, Susan, jt. auth. see Dutton, June.

Perl, Teri. Women & Numbers: Lives of Women Mathematicians Plus Discovery Activities. 2nd ed. (Illus.). 192p. 1993. pap. 15.95 (*0-933174-87-X*) Wide World-Tetra.

Perl, Teri, jt. auth. see Freedman, Miriam.

Perl, William R. The Holocaust Conspiracy: An International Policy of Genocide. LC 88-29526. 1989. 19.95 (*0-944007-24-4*) Sure Sellers.

Perla, Georges, jt. auth. see Russo, Gloria.

Perla, Georges, jt. auth. see Russo.

Perla, Peter P., III. The Art of Wargaming. LC 89-28818. (Illus.). 416p. 1990. 29.95 (*0-87021-050-5*) Naval Inst Pr.

***Perlas, Nicanor.** Overcoming Illusions about Biotechnology: The Implications of Genetic Engineering for Agriculture. 120p. (C). 1994. text ed. 55.00 (*1-85649-303-2*, Pub. by Zed Books UK); pap. 17.50 (*1-85649-304-0*, Pub. by Zed Books UK) Humanities.

Perlberg, Deborah. Heartaches High School. 1987. pap. 2.50 (*0-449-70242-1*) Fawcett.

Perlberg, Mark, ed. see Bailey, David H. & Gottlieb, Louise.

Perlberg, Mark, ed. see Bailey, David H., et al.

Perlberg, Mark, ed. see Bailey, David H. & Gottlieb, Louise.

Perlberger, Norman. Pennsylvania Divorce Code, with Forms & Form Disks. rev. ed. LC 92-74127. 1992. disk 49.50 (*0-317-05080-X*) Bisel Co.

— Pennsylvania Divorce Code, with Forms & Form Disks. rev. ed. LC 92-74127. 1994. ring bd. 79.50 (*0-317-05079-6*) Bisel Co.

Perle, E. Gabriel & Williams, John T. The Publishing Law Handbook. 2nd ed. 1592p. 1993. 180.00 (*0-13-109364-9*) Aspen Law.

Perle, George. The Listening Composer. 1990. 25.00 (*0-520-06991-9*) U CA Pr.

— The Operas of Alban Berg: Vol. I, Wozzeck. LC 76-52033. 325p. 1980. pap. 18.00 (*0-520-06617-0*) U CA Pr.

— The Operas of Alban Berg, Vol. II: Lulu. LC 76-52033. (Illus.). 352p. 1984. pap. 19.00 (*0-520-06616-2*) U CA Pr.

— The Right Notes: Twenty-Three Selected Essays by George Perle on Twentieth-Century Music. 400p. 1995. lib. bdg. 42.00 (*0-945193-37-8*) Pendragon NY.

— Serial Composition & Atonality: An Introduction to the Music of Schoenberg, Berg, & Webern. 6th rev. ed. (Illus.). 178p. 1991. 30.00 (*0-520-07430-0*) U CA Pr.

— Style & Idea in the Lyric Suite of Alban Berg. (Illus.). 1995. lib. bdg. 36.00 (*0-945193-65-3*) Pendragon NY.

— Twelve-Tone Tonality. 2nd ed. LC 94-40067. 1995. 45.00 (*0-520-20142-6*) U CA Pr.

Perle, Richard N. Blackchannel: A Cold War Novel. 1992. 20.50 (*0-394-56552-5*) Random.

Perle, Richard N., ed. Reshaping Western Security: The United States Faces a United Europe. 171p. (C). 1991. 22.95 (*0-8447-3759-3*) Am Enterprise.

Perle, Ruth L. Teammates: Home Team Book. Bergstrom, Evelyn J., ed. (Arista TeamMates Ser.). (Illus.). (J). (ps-00). 1977. pap. text ed. 4.25 (*0-89796-862-X*) New Dimens Educ.

— Teammates School Team Book. Bergstrom, Evelyn J., ed. (Arista TeamMates Ser.). (Illus.). (J). (ps-00). 1977. pap. text ed. 4.25 (*0-89796-861-1*) New Dimens Educ.

Perle, Ruth L., ed. see Pavao, John.

Perleberg, Max, tr. see Lung, Kung-Sun.

P Q

An Asterisk (*) at the beginning of an entry indicates that the title is appearing in BIP for the first time.

Perlee, ed. see Bardes, Barbara S., et al.
Perlee, ed. see Coon, Dennis.
Perlee, ed. see Dworetzky, John P.
Perlee, ed. see Kriegel, Lorraine P. & Chandler-Vaccaro, Kimberly.
Perlee, ed. see Lamare, James W.
Perlee, ed. see Miller, Roger L. & Jentz, Gaylord A.
Perlee, ed. see Miller, Roger L. & Stafford, Alan D.
Perlee, ed. see Pagano, Robert R.
Perlee, ed. see Wetherbe, James C. & Vitalari, Nicholas P.
Perlee, ed. see Wetherbe, James C. & Vitalari, Nicholas.
Perlee, ed. see Williams, Raburn.
Perlee, ed. see Wyrick, Thomas.
Perlee, Clyde, ed. see Adams, Lynn & Goldbloom, Erwin.
Perlee, Clyde, ed. see Ahrens, C. Donald.
Perlee, Clyde, ed. see Arnold, Roger A.
Perlee, Clyde, ed. see Bagley, Constance E. & Haubegger, Christi A.
Perlee, Clyde, ed. see Bagley, Constance E.
Perlee, Clyde, ed. see Ballatore, Ron & Miller, William.
Perlee, Clyde, ed. see Bardes, Barbara A., et al.
Perlee, Clyde, ed. see Baumann, Susan K.
Perlee, Clyde, ed. see Baumann, Susan K. & Mandell, Steven L.
Perlee, Clyde, ed. see Bohlman, Herbert M. & Dundas, Mary J.
Perlee, Clyde, ed. see Brinkerhoff, David B., et al.
Perlee, Clyde, ed. see Brinkerhoff, David B. & White, Lynne K.
Perlee, Clyde, ed. see Carper, Donald L., et al.
Perlee, Clyde, ed. see Casten, Carole M. & Jordan, Peg.
Perlee, Clyde, ed. see Casten, Carole M.
Perlee, Clyde, ed. see Clarkson, Kenneth W., et al.
Perlee, Clyde, ed. see Conover, Theodore E.
Perlee, Clyde, ed. see Coon, Dennis.
Perlee, Clyde, ed. see Cox, Frank D.
Perlee, Clyde, ed. see Cross, Frank B. & Miller, Roger L.
Perlee, Clyde, ed. see Dunikoski, Robert H.
Perlee, Clyde, ed. see Dunphy, Marv & Wilde, Rod.
Perlee, Clyde, ed. see Dworetzky, John P.
Perlee, Clyde, ed. see France, Diane L. & Horn, Arthur D.
Perlee, Clyde, ed. see Harris, A. Christine.
Perlee, Clyde, ed. see Hitt, Michael A., et al.
Perlee, Clyde, ed. see Hopper, Grace M. & Mandell, Steven L.
Perlee, Clyde, ed. see Jentz, Gaylord A., et al.
Perlee, Clyde, ed. see Kossen, Stan.
Perlee, Clyde, ed. see Kraemer, Richard H. & Newell, Charldean.
Perlee, Clyde, ed. see Lamare, James W.
Perlee, Clyde, ed. see Mandell, Steven L.
Perlee, Clyde, ed. see Mathis, Robert L. & Jackson, John H.
Perlee, Clyde, ed. see Miller, Roger L. & Jentz, Gaylord A.
Perlee, Clyde, ed. see Miller, Roger L.
Perlee, Clyde, ed. see Miller, Roger L. & Benjamin, Daniel K.
Perlee, Clyde, ed. see Miller, Roger L. & Jentz, Gaylord A.
Perlee, Clyde, ed. see Nelson, Harry, et al.
Perlee, Clyde, ed. see Nelson, Harry & Jurmain, Robert.
Perlee, Clyde, ed. see Oberstone, Joelee.
Perlee, Clyde, ed. see Pagano, Robert R.
Perlee, Clyde, ed. see Peterson, Brent D., et al.
Perlee, Clyde, ed. see Rowe, Bruce M.
Perlee, Clyde, ed. see Schmidt, Steffen W., et al.
Perlee, Clyde, ed. see Smith, Ronald E.
Perlee, Clyde, ed. see Spence, J. Wayne & Windsor, John C.
Perlee, Clyde, ed. see Timm, Paul R. & Peterson, Brent D.
Perlee, Clyde, ed. see Timm, Paul R.
Perlee, Clyde, ed. see Toh, Rex & Hu, Michael.
Perlee, Clyde, ed. see Turnbaugh, William A., et al.
Perlee, Clyde, ed. see Wadood, Tariq & Tan, Karlyne.
Perlee, Simon, ed. see Ahrens, C. Donald.
Perlee, Simon, ed. see Jurmain, Robert & Nelson, Harry.
Perlee, Simon, ed. see Mathis, Robert L. & Jackson, John H.
Perleman, Bob. The Trouble with Genius: Reading Pound, Joyce, Stein, & Zukofsky. LC 93-37181. 1994. 40.00 (*0-520-08583-3*); pap. 16.00 (*0-520-08755-0*) U CA Pr.
Perlemuter, L., jt. auth. see Quevauvilliers, J.
Perlemuter, Leo, jt. auth. see Apfelbaum, Marian.
Perlemuter, Leon. Practical Dictionary of Clinical Medicine: Dictionnaire Pratique de Medecine Clinique. 2nd ed. 1856p. (FRE.). 1982. 195.00 (*0-8288-1821-5*, M6440) Fr & Eur.
— Practical Dictionary of Medical Therapy (Dictionnaire Pratique de Therapeutique Medicale) 6th ed. 1824p. (FRE.). 1990. ring bd. 150.00 (*0-7859-4566-0*) Fr & Eur.
Perlemuter, Leon, jt. auth. see Roucoules, Gil.
Perlemuter, Leon, jt. auth. see Touitou, Yvan.
Perlemuter, Vlado & Jourdan-Morhange, Helene. Ravel According to Ravel. Taylor, Harold, ed. Tanner, Frances, tr. 92p. 1988. 16.50 (*0-912483-19-9*) Pro-Am Music.
Perler, Dominik. Pradestination, Zeit und Kontingenz: Philosophisch-Historische Untersuchungen zu Wilhelm von Ockhams. (Bochumer Studien zur Philosophie Ser.: Vol. 12). x, 322p. (GER.). 1988. 63.00x (*90-6032-310-6*, Pub. by B R Gruener NE) Benjamins North Am.
— Der Propositionale Wahreitsbegriff im 14. Jahrundert. (Quellen & Studien zur Philosophie Ser.: Bd. 33). x, 387p. (GER.). (C). 1992. lib. bdg. 144.65 (*3-11-013415-2*) De Gruyter.
Perles, Benjamin M. & Sullivan, C. Freund & Williams' Modern Business Statistics. rev. ed. (C). 1969. text ed. write for info. (*0-13-589580-4*) P-H.
Perles, Benjamin M., jt. auth. see Freund, John E.
Perles, Catherine. Fascicle 3: Les Industries Lithiques Taillees de Franchthi: Presentation Generale et Industries Paleolithiques, Tome 1. LC 86-46039. (Excavations at Franchthi Cave, Greece Ser.: No. 3). (Illus.). 372p. 1989. pap. 57.50 (*0-253-31972-2*) Ind U Pr.
Perles, Catherine, et al. Fascicle Five: Les Industries Lithiques Taillees de Franchthi (Argolide, Grece), Tome 2: LC 86-46039. (Excavations at Franchthi Cave, Greece Ser.). (Illus.). 296p. 1991. pap. 57.50 (*0-253-31973-0*) Ind U Pr.
Perlewitz, Miriam. Gospel of Matthew. (Message of Biblical Spirituality Ser.: Vol. 8). (Orig.). 1988. 16.95 (*0-8146-5558-0*); pap. 12.95 (*0-8146-5574-2*) Liturgical Pr.
Perley, Daniel. Migrating to Open Systems: Taming the Tiger. LC 92-32088. 224p. 1993. text ed. 30.00i (*0-07-707778-4*, M-H Bk Intl Group) McGraw.
Perley, M. V. The History & Genealogy of the Perley Family. (Illus.). 770p. 1989. reprint ed. lib. bdg. 123.00 (*0-8328-0954-3*); reprint ed. pap. 115.00 (*0-8328-0955-1*) Higginson Bk Co.
Perley, M. V. & Waters, Thomas. Linebrook Parish Church Records 1747-1819. 135p. (Orig.). 1995. pap. 25.00 (*1-878545-02-7*) ACETO Bookmen.
Perley, R., jt. ed. see Cornwell, T.
Perley, R. A., et al, eds. Synthesis Imaging in Radio Astronomy: A Collection of Lectures from the Third NRAO Synthesis Imaging Summer School. (ASP Conference Series Publications: Vol. 6). 509p. 1989. 25.00 (*0-937707-23-6*) Astron Soc Pacific.
Perley, Sidney. The History of Boxford from the Earliest Settlement to the Present Time, a Period of about 230 Years. (Illus.). 418p. 1989. reprint ed. lib. bdg. 42.00 (*0-8328-0809-1*, MA0020) Higginson Bk Co.
Perlgut, Mark. Electricity Across the Border: The U. S. - Canadian Experience. LC 78-65560. (Canadian-American Committee Ser.). 76p. 1978. 4.00 (*0-89068-047-7*) Natl Planning.
Perlick. Introduction to Business. 3rd ed. (Plaid Ser.). 1980. 9.95 (*0-256-02352-2*) Irwin Prof Pubng.
Perlick, Deborah, jt. auth. see Silverstein, Brett.
Perlin, D. E. Father Miguel Hidalgo: A Cry for Freedom. LC 90-27375. (Illus.). 32p. (ENG & SPA.). (J). (gr. k-4). 1991. pap. 5.95 (*0-937460-67-2*) Hendrick-Long.
***Perlin, Doris E.** Eight Bright Candles. LC 95-14089. (Women of the West Ser.). 1995. pap. write for info. (*1-55622-390-0*, Rep of TX Pr) Wordware Pub.
Perlin, Frank. The Invisible City: Monetary, Administrative & Popular Infrastructures in Asia & Europe, 1500-1900. (Collected Studies: No. CS387). 380p. 1992. 92.00 (*0-86078-342-1*, Pub. by Variorum UK) Ashgate Pub Co.
— Unbroken Landscape: Commodity, Category, Sign & Identity: Their Production as Myth & Knowledge from 1500. (Collected Studies). 376p. 1994. 89.95 (*0-86078-431-2*, Pub. by Variorum UK) Ashgate Pub Co.
Perlin, George C. The Tory Syndrome: Leadership Politics in the Progressive Conservative Party. LC 80-474879. 262p. reprint ed. pap. 74.70 (*0-7837-1025-9*, 2041336) Bks Demand.
Perlin, John. A Forest Journey: The Role of Wood in the Development of Civilization. LC 90-19301. (Illus.). 448p. 1991. pap. text ed. 14.95 (*0-674-30892-1*, PERFOX) HUP.
Perlin, Marc G. Mottla's Proof of Cases in Massachusetts. 3rd ed. 1992. 105.00 (*0-317-05377-9*) Lawyers Cooperative.
Perlin, Marc G., ed. Massachusetts Actions & Remedies: Family Law. 480p. 1991. ring bd. 95.00 (*0-88063-446-4*) Michie Butterworth.
— The Rules. 1990. 76.00 (*0-318-18709-4*) Lawyers Weekly.
Perlin, Marc G. & Connors, John M. Handbook of Civil Procedure in the Massachusetts District Courts. 341p. (C). 1990. 79.50 (*0-318-03524-3*) Lawyers Weekly.
Perlin, Michael. The Jurisprudence of the Insanity Defense. LC 93-72952. 460p. (C). 1993. 49.95 (*0-89089-555-4*) Carolina Acad Pr.
***Perlin, Michael L.** Law & Mental Disability. 698p. 1994. 45.00 (*1-55834-153-6*) Michie Butterworth.
— Mental Disability Law: Civil & Criminal, 3 vols. suppl. ed. 1991. 95.00 (*0-87473-787-7*) Michie Butterworth.
— Mental Disability Law: Civil & Criminal, 3 vols., Set. 1989. 240.00 (*0-87473-422-3*) Michie Butterworth.
Perlin, Neil. Business Technology for Managers: An Office Automation Handbook. LC 85-223. (Professional Librarian Ser.). 206p. 1986. pap. 24.95 (*0-86729-123-0*, Hall Reference) Macmillan.
Perlin, Neil E. Small Business Guide to Computers & Office Automation. (Illus.). 210p. (Orig.). 1990. pap. 19.95 (*0-942103-14-9*, 5615-36, Enter-Dearbrn) Dearborn Finan.
***Perlin, Seymour, ed.** A Handbook for the Understanding of Suicide. LC 94-22981. 252p. 1994. pap. text ed. 30.00 (*1-56821-369-7*) Aronson.
Perlin, Seymour, jt. auth. see Beauchamp, Tom L.
Perlin, Terry M. Clinical Medical Ethics: Cases in Practice. LC 92-12544. 1992. 33.95 (*0-316-69959-4*) Little.
Perlin, Terry M., ed. Contemporary Anarchism. LC 74-20197. 294p. 1979. 34.95 (*0-87855-097-6*) Transaction Pubs.
Perlin, Terry M., jt. auth. see Cottell, Philip G., Jr.
Perlin Yu, E. & Wagner, M. Modern Problems in Condensed Matter Sciences: The Dynamical Jahn-Teller Effect in Localized Systems. 1985. 274.50 (*0-444-86779-1*) Elsevier.
Perlina, Nina. Varieties of Poetic Utterance: Quotation in the Brothers Kramazov. LC 84-20959. 236p. (Orig.). 1985. pap. text ed. 24.00 (*0-8191-4372-3*) U Pr of Amer.
Perling, Joseph J. Presidents' Sons: The Prestige of Name in a Democracy. LC 70-148226. (Biography Index Reprint Ser.). 1977. 29.95 (*0-8369-8073-5*) Ayer.
Perlingieri. Sofonisba Anguissola: First Great Woman Artist of the Renaissance. LC 91-38245. (Illus.). 224p. 1992. 50.00 (*0-8478-1544-7*) Rizzoli Intl.
Perlis, Alan. Wallace Stevens: A World of Transforming Shapes. LC 74-19631. 160p. 1975. 27.50 (*0-8387-1651-2*) Bucknell U Pr.
Perlis, Alan, et al, eds. Software Metrics. (Computer Science Ser.). (Illus.). 350p. 1981. 50.00 (*0-262-16083-8*) MIT Pr.
Perlis, Alan D. A Return to the Primal Self: Identity in the Fiction of George Eliot. (American University Studies: English Language & Literature: Ser. IV, Vol. 71). 221p. (C). 1989. text ed. 35.50 (*0-8204-0637-6*) P Lang Pubs.
Perlis, Alan J., jt. auth. see Biggerstaff, Ted J.
Perlis, R., jt. auth. see Connor, P. E.
Perlis, Sam. Theory of Matrices. xiv, 237p. reprint ed. pap. 7.95 (*0-486-66810-X*) Dover.
Perlis, Vivian. Charles Ives Remembered: An Oral History. (Illus.). 256p. 1994. reprint ed. pap. 13.95 (*0-306-80576-6*) Da Capo.
— Two Men for Modern Music. (I.S.A.M. Monographs: No. 9). (Illus.). 35p. 1978. pap. 8.00 (*0-914678-09-4*) Inst Am Music.
Perlis, Vivian, ed. see Charles Ives Centennial Festival Conference Staff.
Perlis, Vivian, jt. auth. see Copland, Aaron.
Perlman & Kirpalani. Resident's Handbook of Neonatology. 304p. 1991. pap. 25.95 (*1-55664-114-1*) Mosby Yr Bk.
Perlman, Alan M. Write Choices: New Options for Effective Communication. 82p. 1989. 26.95 (*0-398-05586-6*) C C Thomas.
— Write Choices: New Options for Effective Communication. 82p. 1989. pap. 14.95 (*0-398-06319-2*) C C Thomas.
Perlman, Anne S. Sorting It Out. LC 82-70744. 1982. pap. 9.95 (*0-915604-73-6*) Carnegie-Mellon.
Perlman, Barbara H. Allan Houser: Ha-o-zous. LC 86-26605. (Illus.). 266p. (C). 1991. reprint ed. 75.00 (*1-56098-102-4*) Smithsonian.
Perlman, Baron, et al. The Academic Intrapreneur: Strategy, Innovation, & Management in Higher Education. LC 88-6609. 224p. 1988. text ed. 49.95 (*0-275-92951-5*, C2951, Praeger Pubs) Greenwood.
Perlman, Bennard B. Robert Henri: His Life & Art. 1991. pap. 11.95 (*0-486-26722-9*) Dover.
Perlman, Bernard B. The Immortal Eight & Its Influence. 108p. 10.00 (*0-318-17801-X*) Art Students.
— Painters of the Ashcan School: The Immortal Eight. (Illus.). 215p. 1990. pap. 9.95 (*0-486-25747-9*) Dover.
Perlman, Bob. Life & Love All Not Spectator Sports. 1986. write for info. (*0-318-62747-7*) Dan Eli Pr.
Perlman, D. Fermentation: 1977: Annual Reports. 1977. pap. text ed. 116.00 (*0-12-040301-3*) Acad Pr.
Perlman, D., ed. Annual Reports in Fermentation Processes, Vol. 6. (Serial Publication Ser.). 1983. pap. text ed. 116.00 (*0-12-040306-4*) Acad Pr.
— Annual Reports on Fermentation Processes, Vol. 5. (Serial Publication Ser.). 1982. pap. text ed. 116.00 (*0-12-040305-6*) Acad Pr.
Perlman, D. & Tsao, G. T., eds. Annual Reports on Fermentation Processes, Vol. 2. (Serial Publication Ser.). 1978. pap. text ed. 116.00 (*0-12-040302-1*) Acad Pr.
— Annual Reports on Fermentation Processes, Vol. 3. (Serial Publication Ser.). 1979. pap. text ed. 116.00 (*0-12-040303-X*) Acad Pr.
— Annual Reports on Fermentation Processes, Vol. 7. (Serial Publication Ser.). 1984. pap. text ed. 116.00 (*0-12-040307-2*) Acad Pr.
Perlman, Daniel & Bartholomew, Kim, eds. Advances in Personal Relationships, Vol. 5: Attachment Processes in Adulthood. 300p. 1993. 75.00 (*1-85302-172-5*, Pub. by J Kingsley Pubs UK) Taylor & Francis.
Perlman, Daniel & Duck, Steven. Intimate Relationships: Development, Dynamics & Deterioration. LC 84-51532. (Focus Editions Ser.: Vol. 80). 340p. 1986. text ed. 49.95 (*0-8039-2609-X*); pap. text ed. 24.95 (*0-8039-2610-3*) Sage.
Perlman, Daniel, jt. ed. see Jones, Warren H.
Perlman, Daniel, jt. ed. see Peplau, Letitia A.
Perlman, David, jt. ed. see Peppler, Henry J.
***Perlman, Debbie.** Psalms for a New Day: Tehillim Shel Yom Chadash. LC 94-74827. 150p. (Orig.). 1995. pap. 10.00 (*0-9644570-3-2*) RAD Publ.
Perlman, Eileen, jt. auth. see Bertin, Phyllis.
Perlman, F., jt. auth. see Gregoire, R.
Perlman, Fredy. Against His-Story, Against Leviathan! (Illus.). 1983. pap. 4.00 (*0-934868-25-5*) Black & Red.
— Against History. 1986. lib. bdg. 79.95 (*0-8490-3849-9*) Gordon Pr.
— Anti-Semitism & the Beirut Program. 16p. (Orig.). 1983. pap. 1.75 (*0-939306-07-7*) Left Bank.
— Anything Can Happen. 128p. (Orig.). Date not set. pap. 9.95 (*0-948984-22-8*, Pub. by Phoenix Pr UK) AK Pr Dist.
— Continuing Appeal of Nationalism. 58p. 1985. pap. 1.50 (*0-934868-27-1*) Black & Red.
— Plunder: A Play. 1962. pap. 1.50 (*0-934868-18-2*) Black & Red.
— The Reproduction of Daily Life. 1969. pap. 1.00 (*0-934868-17-4*) Black & Red.
— The Strait: Book of Obenabi, His Songs. 1988. pap. 5.00 (*0-934868-29-8*) Black & Red.
Perlman, Fredy, tr. see Arshinov, Peter.
Perlman, Gary. UNIX for Software Developers. 250p. 1993. pap. 24.00 (*0-13-932997-8*) P-H.
Perlman, Geoff. Inside Fourth Dimension 3.1. 2nd ed. LC 93-86588. 830p. 1993. 29.99 (*0-7821-1455-5*) Sybex.
Perlman, Harvey S., jt. auth. see Ketch, Edmund W.
Perlman, Harvey S., jt. auth. see Kitch, Edmund W.
Perlman, Helen H. The Dancing Clock & Other Childhood Memories. (Illus.). 212p. 1989. 20.00 (*0-89733-343-8*) Academy Chi Pubs.
— Looking Back to See Ahead. LC 89-31900. 288p. 1989. lib. bdg. 39.00 (*0-226-66037-0*); pap. text ed. 12.95 (*0-226-66038-9*) U Ch Pr.
— Persona: Social Role & Personality. LC 68-21892. 1986. pap. text ed. 15.00 (*0-226-66028-1*) U Ch Pr.
— Relationship: The Heart of Helping People. LC 78-19064. x, 236p. 1983. pap. text ed. 11.95 (*0-226-66036-2*) U Ch Pr.
— Social Casework: A Problem-Solving Process. LC 57-6270. 1957. lib. bdg. 12.95 (*0-226-66033-8*) U Ch Pr.
Perlman, James, ed. see Kottler, Dorian B.
Perlman, James, ed. see McGrath, Thomas.
***Perlman, James S.** Science Without Limits: Toward a Theory of Interaction Between Nature & Knowledge. 360p. 1995. 29.95 (*0-87975-962-3*) Prometheus Bks.
***Perlman, Janet.** Cinderella Penguin. (Illus.). 32p. (J). 1995. pap. 4.99 (*0-14-055552-8*) Puffin Bks.
— Cinderella Penguin. (Illus.). 32p. (J). (ps-3). 1993. 13.99 (*0-670-84753-4*) Viking Child Bks.
— The Emperor Penguin's New Clothes. (Illus.). 32p. (J). (ps-3). 1995. 12.99 (*0-670-85864-1*) Viking Child Bks.
Perlman, Janice E. The Myth of Marginality: Urban Poverty & Politics in Rio De Janeiro. LC 73-87246. 250p. 1976. pap. 15.00 (*0-520-03952-1*) U CA Pr.
Perlman, Jim, ed. see Bly, et al.
Perlman, John. Beacons Imaging Within - As Promises. (Chapbook Ser.). 25p. (Orig.). 1990. pap. 4.00 (*0-945112-08-4*) Generator Pr.
— Dinner Six Hundred & Fifty Warburton Avenue Yonkers. 1974. pap. 6.00 (*0-685-40889-2*) Elizabeth Pr.
— Nicole. 1976. 10.00 (*0-685-79205-6*); pap. 5.00 (*0-685-79206-4*) Elizabeth Pr.
— Notes Toward a Family. 1975. pap. 8.00 (*0-685-56236-0*) Elizabeth Pr.
— Self Portrait. 1976. pap. 8.00 (*0-685-79204-8*) Elizabeth Pr.
— Swath. 1978. 20.00 (*0-686-59675-7*); pap. 8.00 (*0-686-59676-5*) Elizabeth Pr.
— Three Years Rings. 1972. 16.00 (*0-685-27715-1*); pap. 8.00 (*0-685-27716-X*) Elizabeth Pr.
Perlman, Kalman I. The Leasing Handbook: Everything Purchasing Managers Need to Know - Complete with Facts, Figures, Forms & Checklists. 350p. 1991. 40.00 (*1-55738-242-5*) Probus Pub Co.
Perlman, Ken. Clawhammer Style Banjo. 2nd ed. 194p. 1989. reprint ed. pap. text ed. 16.95x (*0-931759-33-1*) Centerstream Pub.
— Contemporary Fingerstyle Guitar. 2nd ed. 218p. 1989. pap. text ed. 14.95 (*0-931759-37-4*) Centerstream Pub.
— Fingerstyle Guitar. rev. ed. 242p. 1989. reprint ed. pap. 14.95 (*0-931759-11-0*) Centerstream Pub.
— Melodic Clawhammer. 1979. pap. 12.95 (*0-8256-0226-2*, Oak) Music Sales.
Perlman, Lawrence. Abraham Heschel's Idea of Revelation. LC 89-6191. 171p. 1989. 46.95 (*1-55540-350-6*, 14 01 71) Scholars Pr GA.
Perlman, Leonard, jt. auth. see Feingold, Norman.
Perlman, Lorraine. Having Little, Being Much: A Chronicle of Fredy Perlman's Fifty Years. (Illus.). 155p. 1989. pap. 3.50 (*0-934868-30-1*) Black & Red.
Perlman, Lorraine, tr. see Arshinov, Peter.
Perlman, M., jt. auth. see Morris, N.
Perlman, M., jt. ed. see Van Der Gaag, Jacques.
Perlman, Marc. Movie Classics. LC 92-30909. (YA). (gr. 5 up). 1993. 18.95 (*0-8225-1641-1*, Lerner Publctns) Lerner Group.
— Youth Rebellion Movies. LC 92-5534. (J). (gr. 4 up). 1993. 18.95 (*0-8225-1640-3*, Lerner Publctns) Lerner Group.
Perlman, Mark. Labor Union Theories in America. LC 76-8925. 313p. 1976. reprint ed. text ed. 59.75 (*0-8371-8916-0*, PELU, Greenwood Pr) Greenwood.
— Machinists: A New Study in American Trade Unionism. LC 61-16695. (Wertheim Publications in Industrial Relations). (Illus.). 350p. 1961. 22.50 (*0-674-54050-6*) HUP.
Perlman, Mark, ed. Human Resources in the Urban Economy. LC 63-22775. 279p. reprint ed. pap. 79.60 (*0-317-27700-6*, 2052104) Bks Demand.
Perlman, Mark, jt. auth. see Baker, Timothy D.
Perlman, Mark, jt. ed. see Barfield, Claude E.
Perlman, Mark, jt. ed. see Heertje, Arnold.
Perlman, Mark, jt. ed. see Scherer, Frederic M.
Perlman, Mark, jt. ed. see Shionoya, Yuichi.
Perlman, Mark, jt. ed. see Weiermair, Klaus.
Perlman, Mark, et al, eds. Index of Economic Articles, Vol. 14, 1972. LC 61-8020. (C). 1977. 50.00 (*0-917290-03-8*, Irwin) Am Economic Assn.
— Index of Economic Articles, Vol. 15, 1978. LC 61-8020. (C). 1978. 50.00 (*0-917290-04-6*, Irwin) Am Economic Assn.
— Spatial Regional & Population Economics. 412p. 1972. text ed. 205.00 (*0-677-15020-2*) Gordon & Breach.
Perlman, Martin M., ed. see International Conference on Electrets, Charge Storage, & Transport in Dielectrics Staff.
Perlman, Meg & Dean, Kevin. Syd Solomon: A Dialogue with Nature. Chilson, Kathleen G., ed. LC 90-63244. (Illus.). 1990. pap. 9.95 (*0-916758-31-1*) Ringling Mus Art.
Perlman, Melissa, jt. auth. see Jackson, Joyce.
Perlman, Michael. Imaginal Memory & the Place of Hiroshima. LC 87-22322. 214p. 1988. 59.50 (*0-88706-746-8*); pap. 19.95 (*0-88706-747-6*) State U NY Pr.
— The Power of Trees: The Reforesting of the Soul. LC 94-4552. 265p. (Orig.). 1994. pap. 17.00 (*0-88214-362-X*) Spring Pubns.

P Q

An Asterisk (*) at the beginning of an entry indicates that the title is appearing in BIP for the first time.

Perlman, Moshe. Yiddish As a Language of the People. 17. 85 (*0-317-58555-X*) P-H.

Perlman, Peter. Annotated Opening Statements. rev. ed. ATLA Press Staff, ed. LC 94-15354. (Illus.). 165p. 1994. pap. 42.00 (*0-941916-69-3*) ATLA Pr.

— Components of a Trial: Opening Statements. 100p. 23.00 (*0-941916-57-X*) ATLA Pr.

Perlman, Radia. Interconnections: Bridges & Routers in OSI & TCP-IP. (Illus.). 272p. 1992. 48.95 (*0-201-56332-0*) Addison-Wesley.

Perlman, Richard, jt. auth. see Hughes, James J.

Perlman, Robert. Bridging Three Worlds: Hungarian-Jewish Americans, 1848-1914. LC 90-11224. 320p. (C). 1991. lib. bdg. 40.00 (*0-87023-468-4*) U of Mass Pr.

— Consumers & Social Services. LC 74-13540. 144p. reprint ed. pap. 41.10 (*0-317-07763-5*, 2013115) Bks Demand.

Perlman, Robert, ed. Family Home Care: Critical Issues for Services & Policies. LC 83-81. (Home Health Care Services Quarterly Ser.: Vol. 3, Nos. 3 & 4). 294p. 1983. text ed. 49.95 (*0-86656-220-6*) Haworth Pr.

Perlman, Robert L., jt. ed. see Dun, Nae J.

Perlman, Robert W. & Furst, Arthur Y., eds. Architectural Design Collaborators, No. 3. (Illus.). 256p. 1992. pap. write for info. (*0-9624219-4-4*) Perlman Stearns.

***Perlman, Ruthie.** Daniel My Son. LC 94-70750. 200p. Date not set. write for info. (*1-56062-193-1*) CIS Comm.

— Getting It Right. LC 90-84360. 225p. 1990. 13.95 (*1-56062-050-1*); pap. 10.95 (*1-56062-051-X*) CIS Comm.

Perlman, Ruthy. Working It Out. LC 90-82185. (YA). (gr. 7 up). 1990. 13.95 (*1-56062-033-1*); pap. 9.95 (*1-56062-035-8*) CIS Comm.

***Perlman, Sandra.** Nightwalking: Voices from Kent State. 80p. (Orig.). 1995. pap. 10.00 (*1-885663-01-3*) Franklin Mills.

Perlman, Selig. Selig Perlman's Lectures on Capitalism & Socialism. LC 74-27312. 203p. reprint ed. pap. 57.90 (*0-8357-6791-4*, 2035468) Bks Demand.

— Theory of the Labor Movement. LC 66-18323. (Reprints of Economic Classics Ser.). 1966. reprint ed. 35.00 (*0-678-00025-5*) Kelley.

Perlman-Stearns Inc. Staff, ed. Architectural Design Collaborators Two: The Comprehensive Sourcebook for the Architectural & Design Communities. (Illus.). 320p. 1991. write for info. (*0-318-68296-6*); Japanese version. write for info. (*0-318-68298-2*); spiral bd. write for info. (*0-318-68297-4*) Perlman Stearns.

Perlman, Stephen M., jt. ed. see Green, Stanton W.

Perlman, William J., ed. The Movies on Trial: The Views & Opinions of Outstanding Personalities Anent Screen Entertainment Past & Present. LC 78-160245. (Moving Pictures Ser.). 1971. reprint ed. lib. bdg. 29.95 (*0-89198-046-6*) Ozer.

Perlmann, Joel. Ethnic Differences: Schooling & Social Structure among the Irish, Italians, Jews & Blacks in an American City, 1880-1935. (Interdisciplinary Perspectives on Modern History Ser.). (Illus.). 344p. (C). 1989. pap. 18.95 (*0-521-38975-5*) Cambridge U Pr.

Perlmann, Moshe, ed. & tr. The History of al-Tabari, Vol. 4: The Ancient Kingdoms. LC 85-17282. (SUNY Series in Near Eastern Studies). 205p. (C). 1987. 49.50 (*0-88706-181-8*); pap. 16.95 (*0-88706-182-6*) State U NY Pr.

Perlmann, Moshe, tr. see Yushmanov, N. V.

Perlmann, P., jt. ed. see Wigzell, H.

Perlmnan, J. J., intro. Sears Roebuck Catalog, 1897. (Illus.). 1993. write for info. (*0-87754-045-4*, Am Art Analog); pap. write for info. (*0-7910-1945-4*, Am Art Analog) Chelsea Hse.

Perlmutter, A., jt. ed. see Kursunoglu, B. N.

Perlmutter, A., et al. Coral Gables Conference on Fundamental Interactions at High Energy, Vol. 2. 380p. (C). 1970. text ed. 255.00 (*0-677-14380-X*) Gordon & Breach.

Perlmutter, Amos. Egypt: The Praetorian State. LC 73-85100. (Third World Ser.). 232p. 1974. 34.95 (*0-87855-085-2*) Transaction Pubs.

— FDR & Stalin: A Not So Grand Alliance, 1943-1945. LC 93-4866. (Illus.). 352p. 1993. 29.95 (*0-8262-0910-6*) U of Mo Pr.

— Military & Politics in Israel: Nation Building & Role Expansion. 2nd rev. ed. (Illus.). 161p. 1977. 35.00 (*0-7146-2392-X*, Pub. by F Cass Pubs UK) Intl Spec Bk.

— The Military & Politics in Modern Times: Professionals, Praetorians & Revolutionary Soldiers. LC 76-45769. 1977. 40.00 (*0-300-02045-7*) Yale U Pr.

— The Military & Politics in Modern Times: Professionals, Praetorians & Revolutionary Soldiers. LC 76-45769. 1979. pap. 17.00 (*0-300-02353-7*) Yale U Pr.

— Modern Authoritarianism: A Comparative Institutional Analysis. LC 81-3403. 208p. reprint ed. pap. 59.30 (*0-7837-3306-2*, 2057708) Bks Demand.

— Political Roles & Military Rulers. 314p. 1981. 35.00 (*0-7146-3122-1*, Pub. by F Cass Pubs UK) Intl Spec Bk.

Perlmutter, Amos & Bennett, Valerie P. The Political Influence of the Military: A Comparative Reader. LC 78-26154. 518p. reprint ed. pap. 147.70 (*0-8357-8275-1*, 2033855) Bks Demand.

Perlmutter, Amos & Gooch, John, eds. Strategy & the Social Sciences: Issues in Defense Policy. 102p. 1981. 35.00 (*0-7146-3157-4*, Pub. by F Cass Pubs UK) Intl Spec Bk.

Perlmutter, Amos, jt. ed. see Gooch, John.

Perlmutter, David M., ed. Studies in Relational Grammar 1. LC 82-6945. xvi, 412p. 1983. lib. bdg. 34.00 (*0-226-66050-8*) U Ch Pr.

— Studies in Relational Grammar 1. LC 82-6945. xvi, 412p. 1986. pap. text ed. 15.95 (*0-226-66052-4*) U Ch Pr.

Perlmutter, David M., jt. auth. see Soames, Scott.

Perlmutter, David M., et al. Studies in Relational Grammar 2, No. 2. LC 82-6945. 1984. 35.00 (*0-226-66051-6*) U Ch Pr.

***Perlmutter, Donna.** Shadowplay: The Life of Antony Tudor. LC 94-39957. (Illus.). 432p. 1995. pap. 17.95 (*0-87910-189-X*) Limelight Edns.

Perlmutter, Elsie. Retire Refired: A Guide to Dynamic Retirements. 1988. pap. 12.95 (*0-318-35152-8*) Grad School.

Perlmutter, Felice D. Changing Hats: From Social Work Practice to Administration. LC 90-6436. 161p. 1990. 21. 95 (*0-87101-184-0*) Natl Assn Soc Wkrs.

***Perlmutter, Felice D., ed.** Women & Social Change: Nonprofits & Social Policy. 188p. (Orig.). (C). 1994. lib. bdg. 24.95 (*0-87101-239-1*, 2391) Natl Assn Soc Wkrs.

Perlmutter, Felice D., intro. Alternative Social Agencies: Administrative Strategies. LC 88-4414. (Administration in Social Work Ser.: Vol. 12, No. 2). (Illus.). 128p. 1989. text ed. 39.95 (*0-86656-783-6*) Haworth Pr.

Perlmutter, Felice D. & Slavin, Simon, eds. Leadership in Social Administration: Perspectives for the 1980s. 268p. 1980. 34.95 (*0-87722-172-3*); pap. 19.95 (*0-87722-201-0*) Temple U Pr.

Perlmutter, Howard V. & Sagafi-Nejad, Tagi. International Technology Transfer: Guidelines, Codes & a Muffled Quadrilogue. LC 80-28322. (Policy Studies on Business & Economics). (Illus.). 250p. 1981. 68.00 (*0-08-027519-2*, Pergamon Pr) Elsevier.

Perlmutter, L., jt. ed. see Keren, C.

Perlmutter, Marian, ed. Cognitive Perspectives on Children's Social & Behavioral Development: The Minnesota Symposia on Child Psychology, Vol. 18. 352p. (C). 1986. text ed. 69.95 (*0-89859-546-0*) L Erlbaum Assocs.

Perlmutter, Marion, ed. Development & Policy Concerning Children with Special Needs. (Minnesota Symposia on Child Psychology Ser.: Vol. 16). 272p. (C). 1983. text ed. 49.95 (*0-89859-261-5*) L Erlbaum Assocs.

— Parent-Child Interaction & Parent-Child Relations, Vol. 17. (Minnesota Symposia on Child Psychology Ser.: Vol. 17). 208p. 1984. text ed. 39.95 (*0-89859-380-8*) L Erlbaum Assocs.

— Perspectives on Intellectual Development. (Minnesota Symposia on Child Psychology Ser.: Vol. 19). 280p. (C). 1986. text ed. 59.95 (*0-89859-784-6*) L Erlbaum Assocs.

Perlmutter, Marion & Hall, Elizabeth. Adult Development & Aging. 2nd ed. 608p. (C). 1992. Net. text ed. write for info. (*0-471-51846-8*) Wiley.

Perlmutter, Marion, jt. ed. see Weinert, Franz E.

Perlmutter, Martin. Producer's Guide to Interactive Videodiscs. 206p. 1991. 45.00 (*0-86729-173-7*) Knowledge Indus.

Perlmutter, P. Conjugate Addition Reactions in Organic Synthesis. (Organic Chemistry Ser.: No. 9). 373p. 1992. text ed. 125.00 (*0-08-037066-7*, Pergamon Pr); pap. text ed. 53.00 (*0-08-037067-5*, Pergamon Pr) Elsevier.

Perlmutter, Philip. Divided We Fall: A History of Ethnic, Religious, & Racial Prejudice in America. LC 90-20153. 414p. 1992. text ed. 44.95 (*0-8138-0644-5*) Iowa St U Pr.

***Perlmutter, Tova.** Privitization, Conversion & Enterprise Reform in Russia. McFaul, Michael, ed. LC 94-24412. (C). 1994. text ed. 59.95 (*0-8133-2548-X*) Westview.

Perlo, Victor. American Labor Today. 1968. pap. 0.25 (*0-87898-029-6*) New Outlook.

— Dollar Crisis: What It Means to You. 1969. pap. 0.40 (*0-87898-033-4*) New Outlook.

— Economics of Racism U. S. A. Roots of Black Inequality. LC 75-9911. (Illus.). 296p. reprint ed. pap. 84.40 (*0-8357-4763-8*, 2037690) Bks Demand.

— End Fascist Terror & U. S. Imperialism in Chile! 56p. 1974. pap. 0.75 (*0-87898-110-1*) New Outlook.

— Marines in Santo Domingo! 1965. pap. 0.20 (*0-87898-004-0*) New Outlook.

— Superprofits & Crises: Modern U. S. Capitalism. LC 88-2925. (Illus.). 568p. (C). 1988. 21.00 (*0-7178-0665-0*); pap. 9.95 (*0-7178-0662-6*) Intl Pubs Co.

Perlo, Victor & Monteiro, Anthony. Economics of Racism II. 1995. 18.00 (*0-7178-0697-9*); pap. 9.50 (*0-7178-0698-7*) Intl Pubs Co.

***Perloff, Carol B.** The Asylum: The History of Friends Hospital & the Quaker Contribution to Psychiatry. LC 94-72152. (Illus.). 55p. 1994. write for info. (*0-9642252-0-4*) Frnds Hosp.

Perloff, Harvey S. Planning the Post-Industrial City. 327p. (Orig.). 1980. 25.95 (*0-318-13056-4*) Am Plan Assn.

— Planning the Post-Industrial City. LC 80-67753. (Illus.). 327p. (Orig.). 1980. lib. bdg. 27.95 (*0-918286-21-2*) Planners Pr.

— Puerto Rico's Economic Future: A Study in Planned Development. LC 74-14240. (Puerto Rican Experience Ser.). (Illus.). 484p. 1975. reprint ed. 52.95 (*0-405-06228-1*) Ayer.

Perloff, Harvey S., ed. The Quality of the Urban Environment: Essays on "New Resources" in an Urban Age. LC 69-16858. 332p. 1969. pap. 14.95 (*0-8018-1028-0*) Resources Future.

Perloff, Harvey S. & Dodds, Vera W. How a Region Grows: Area Development in the U. S. Economy. LC 84-691. 147p. (C). 1984. text ed. 49.75 (*0-313-23152-4*, PEHG, Greenwood Pr) Greenwood.

Perloff, Harvey S. & Wingo, Lowdon, eds. Issues in Urban Economics. 668p. 1968. pap. 20.00 (*0-8018-0529-5*) Resources Future.

Perloff, Harvey S., ed. see Heller, Walter, et al.

Perloff, Janet D., et al. Medicaid & Pediatric Primary Care. LC 87-3164. (Series in Contemporary Medicine & Public Health). 208p. 1987. text ed. 45.00x (*0-8018-3452-X*) Johns Hopkins.

Perloff, Joseph K. The Clinical Recognition of Congenital Heart Disease. 4th ed. LC 93-32195. 1994. text ed. 119. 00 (*0-7216-5504-1*) Saunders.

— Physical Examination of the Heart & Circulation. 2nd ed. (Illus.). 304p. 1989. pap. text ed. 33.50 (*0-7216-7189-6*) Saunders.

Perloff, Joseph K. & Child. Congenital Heart Disease in Adults. (Illus.). 352p. 1990. text ed. 91.95 (*0-7216-7192-6*) Saunders.

Perloff, Joseph K., jt. auth. see Carlton, Dennis.

Perloff, Marjorie. The Futurist Moment: Avant-Garde, Avant Guerre, & the Language of Rupture. LC 86-3147. (Illus.). 288p. (C). 1989. pap. 16.95 (*0-226-65732-9*) U Ch Pr.

— Poetic License: Essays on Modernist & Postmodernist Lyric. (Illus.). 352p. 1990. 42.95 (*0-8101-0843-7*); pap. 16.95 (*0-8101-0844-5*) Northwestern U Pr.

— The Poetics of Indeterminacy. 346p. 1981. reprint ed. pap. 14.95 (*0-8101-0661-2*) Northwestern U Pr.

— Poetics of Indeterminacy: Rimbaud to Cage. LC 80-8569. (Illus.). 360p. 1981. 47.50 (*0-691-06462-8*) Princeton U Pr.

— Radical Artifice: Writing Poetry in the Age of Media. (Illus.). 272p. 1992. 27.50 (*0-226-65733-7*) U Ch Pr.

— Radical Artifice: Writing Poetry in the Age of Media. xvi, 248p. 1994. pap. text ed. 13.95 (*0-226-65734-5*) U Ch Pr.

— Rhyme & Meaning in the Poetry of Yeats. LC 78-102959. (De Proprietatibus Litterarum, Ser. Practica). (Illus.). 1970. pap. text ed. 53.85 (*90-279-0510-X*) Mouton.

***Perloff, Marjorie, ed.** Postmodern Genres. LC 89-40220. (Oklahoma Project for Discourse & Theory Ser.). (Illus.). 288p. 1995. pap. 15.95 (*0-8061-2715-5*) U of Okla Pr.

Perloff, Marjorie & Junkerman, Charles, eds. John Cage: Composed in America. LC 93-36325. (C). 1994. lib. bdg. 45.00 (*0-226-66056-7*) U Ch Pr.

— John Cage: Composed in America. LC 93-36325. (C). 1994. pap. 16.95 (*0-226-66057-5*) U Ch Pr.

Perloff, Nancy. Art & the Everyday: Popular Entertainment & the Circle of Erik Satie. (Illus.). 248p. 1991. 65.00 (*0-19-816194-8*) OUP.

— Art & the Everyday: Popular Entertainment & the Circle of Erik Satie. (Illus.). 248p. 1994. reprint ed. pap. 17.95 (*0-19-816398-3*) OUP.

Perloff, Richard. The Dynamics of Persuasion. (LEA Communication Ser.). 424p. (C). 1993. text ed. 89.95 (*0-8058-0490-0*); pap. 29.95 (*0-8058-1377-2*) L Erlbaum Assocs.

Perloff, Richard M., jt. ed. see Kraus, Sidney.

Perloff, Robert, jt. ed. see Pallak, Michael S.

Perloff, Stephen & Callaghan, Charles, photos. Anthonisen: Woodmere Art Museum Exhibit. (Illus.). 36p. (Orig.). 1992. pap. 12.00 (*0-9634109-0-3*) Anthonisen.

Perlongo, Bob. Early American Advertising. LC 84-71519. 192p. 1985. pap. 9.95 (*0-88108-015-2*) Art Dir.

— The Everyday Almanac. 1992. pap. write for info. (*0-345-37434-7*) Ballantine.

***Perlongo, Bob, ed.** Everyday Almanac: An Astonishing Collection of Facts, Fiddle-Faddle, Advice & Information on the Universe, the Zodiac, Nature, the Arts & Much, Much More. (Illus.). 352p. (Orig.). 1995. pap. 15.95 (*0-88496-398-5*) Capra Pr.

Perlot, Jean N. Gold Seeker: Adventures of a Belgian Argonaut During the Gold Rush Years. Lamar, Howard R., ed. Bretnor, Helen H., tr. LC 84-17378. (Western Americana Ser.: No. 31). (Illus.). 512p. 1985. 29.95x (*0-300-01996-3*) Yale U Pr.

Perlov. English Russian Metallurgical Dictionary. (ENG & RUS.). 1985. 150.00 (*0-8288-3927-1*, F35840) Fr & Eur.

Perlov, N. I. English-Russian Metallurgical Dictionary. 842p. (C). 1985. 195.00 (*0-685-36915-3*, Pub. by Collets) St Mut.

Perlove, Shelley. Bernini & the Idealization of Death: The Blessed Ludovica Albertoni & the Altieri Chapel. LC 89-16336. (Illus.). 152p. 1990. lib. bdg. 32.50 (*0-271-00684-6*) Pa St U Pr.

— Impressions of Faith: Rembrandt's Biblical Etchings. (Illus.). 80p. (Orig.). 1989. pap. text ed. 10.00 (*0-933691-02-5*) U Mich-Dearborn.

***Perlove, Shelley K.** Renaissance, Reform, Reflections in the Age of Durer, Bruegel, & Rembrandt. (Illus.). 152p. (Orig.). 1994. pap. 18.00x (*0-933691-05-X*) U Mich-Dearborn.

Perlow, David L. & Perlow, Joan S. Herpes: Coping with the New Epidemic. 191p. 1983. 15.95 (*0-13-387464-8*) P-H.

Perlow, Gilbert J., ed. Workshop on New Directions in Mossbauer Spectroscopy, Argonne National Lab, June 1977. LC 77-90635. (AIP Conference Proceedings Ser.: No. 38). (Illus.). 1977. lib. bdg. 15.00 (*0-88318-137-1*) Am Inst Physics.

Perlow, Joan S., jt. auth. see Perlow, David L.

Perlow, Jon. The Thinking Person's Guide to Permanent Weight Loss. LC 85-52342. 190p. (Orig.). 1986. pap. 9.95 (*0-936877-02-2*) Twining Pr.

***Perlow, Meir.** Understanding Mental Objects. LC 94-45147. (New Library of Psychoanalysis). 224p. 1995. 59. 95x (*0-415-12178-7*, C0224); pap. 17.95 (*0-415-12179-5*, C0225) Routledge.

Perlowin, David. General Care & Maintenance of Common Kingsnakes. 71p. 1993. pap. text ed. 11.50 (*1-882770-20-X*) Adv Vivarium.

— General Care & Maintenance of Garter Snakes & Water Snakes. 71p. 1994. pap. text ed. 7.50 (*1-882770-26-9*) Adv Vivarium.

***Perlroth.** Freedom from Back Pain. 1995. 10.95 (*1-880688-05-0*) New Life Opt.

Perlroth, Mark G. & Weiland, Douglass J. Fifty Diseases, Fifty Diagnoses. LC 81-3318. 346p. reprint ed. pap. 98. 70 (*0-8357-7598-4*, 2056919) Bks Demand.

Perls, Frederick S. Ego, Hunger, & Aggression: A Revision of Freud's Theory & Method. 286p. 1992. reprint ed. pap. 20.00 (*0-939266-18-0*) Gestalt Journal.

— Gestalt Therapy Verbatim. rev. ed. Wysong, Joe, ed. 304p. 1992. pap. 20.00 (*0-939266-17-2*) Gestalt Journal.

— In & Out the Garbage Pail. (Illus.). 288p. 1992. reprint ed. pap. 18.50 (*0-685-60010-6*) Gestalt Journal.

***Perls, Frederick S., et al.** Gestalt Therapy: Excitement & Growth in the Human Personality. rev. ed. (Illus.). 496p. 1994. pap. 25.00 (*0-939266-24-5*) Gestalt Journal.

Perls, Fritz. The Gestalt Approach & Eyewitness to Therapy. 1973. 13.95 (*0-8314-0034-X*) Sci & Behavior.

Perls, Fritz & Baumgardner. Legacy from Fritz: Gifts from Lake Cowichan. Bd. with Gifts from Lake Cowichan. LC 75-23594. LC 75-23594. 1975. 9.95 (*0-8314-0046-3*) Sci & Behavior.

Perls, Laura P. Living at the Boundary: The Collected Works of Laura Perls. 240p. 1991. text ed. 35.00 (*0-939266-15-6*) Gestalt Journal.

Perlson, Michael R. How to Understand & Influence People & Organizations: Practical Psychology for Goal Achievement. LC 81-69357. 300p. reprint ed. pap. 85.50 (*0-317-26957-7*, 2023577) Bks Demand.

Perlstein, Gary R., jt. auth. see Vetter, Harold J.

Perlstein, Marie T., jt. ed. see Chan, Daniel W.

Perlstein, Scott. Essential Tennis. (Illus.). 192p. 1993. pap. 13.95 (*1-55821-220-5*) Lyons & Burford.

— Winning Doubles. (Illus.). 176p. 1995. pap. 14.95 (*1-55821-330-9*) Lyons & Burford.

***Perlstein, Steve.** Rebel Baseball: The Summer the Game Was Returned to the Fans. LC 94-42570. 1995. pap. 12. 95 (*0-8050-3953-8*, Owl) H Holt & Co.

— Rebel Baseball: The Summer the Game Was Returned to the Fans. LC 94-8634. (Illus.). 256p. 1994. 22.00 (*0-9640334-9-6*) Onion Pr.

Perlwitz, Ellen C. Charlie's Little Moon Trip. (Illus.). 32p. (J). (gr. k-3). 1992. 7.95 (*1-880851-01-6*) Greene Bark Pr.

***Perly, Daniel R.** Implementing Open Systems. LC 95-1106. 1995. text ed. 40.00 (*0-07-707948-5*) McGraw.

Perlzweig, Judith. Lamps from the Athenian Agora. (Excavations of the Athenian Agora Picture Bks.: No. 9). (Illus.). 32p. 1964. pap. 3.00 (*0-87661-609-0*) Am Sch Athens.

— Lamps of the Roman Period, First to Seventh Century After Christ. (Athenian Agora Ser.: Vol. 7). (Illus.). xv, 240p. 1971. reprint ed. 35.00 (*0-87661-207-9*) Am Sch Athens.

***Permaloff, Anne & Grafton, Carl.** Political Power in Alabama: The More Things Change. 1995. write for info. (*0-8203-1721-7*) U of Ga Pr.

Perman, Jane, jt. auth. see Patz, Naomi.

Perman, Lauri. The Other Side of the Coin: The Nonmonetary Characteristics of Jobs. LC 90-29089. (Harvard Studies in Sociology: Outstanding Dissertations & Monographs Twenty-Two Distinguished Works from the Past Fifty Years). 392p. 1991. 30.00 (*0-8240-9265-1*) Garland.

Perman, Michael. Emancipation & Reconstruction, 1862-1879. Franklin, John H. & Eisenstadt, Abraham, eds. LC 86-19889. (American History Ser.). 168p. (C). 1987. pap. text ed. write for info. (*0-88295-836-4*) Harlan Davidson.

— Perspectives on the American Past: To 1877, Vol. I. (C). 1989. pap. text ed. 20.00 (*0-673-18616-4*) HarpCollege.

— The Road to Redemption: Southern Politics, 1869-1879. LC 83-12498. (Fred W. Morrison Series in Southern Studies). xiv, 353p. 1985. 39.95 (*0-8078-1526-8*); pap. 12.95 (*0-8078-4141-2*) U of NC Pr.

Perman, Michael, ed. The Coming of the American Civil War. 3rd ed. (Problems in American Civilization Ser.). 322p. (C). 1993. pap. text ed. write for info. (*0-669-27106-3*) Heath.

— Major Problems in the Civil War & Reconstruction: Documents & Essays. LC 90-81121. (Major Problems in American History Ser.). 598p. (C). 1991. pap. text ed. write for info. (*0-669-20148-0*) Heath.

Perman, Victor, et al. Cytology of the Dog & Cat. 159p. 1979. pap. text ed. 35.00 (*0-9616498-1-X*) Am Animal Hosp Assoc.

Permanand. Political Development in South Asia. 304p. 1988. text ed. 40.00 (*81-207-0767-2*, Pub. by Sterling Pubs II) Apt Bks.

Permane, Terry, jt. photos see Mitton, David.

Permanent Bureau of the Conference Staff, ed. The Hague Convention: Taking of Evidence Abroad. 2nd ed. 1990. student ed, ring bd. write for info. (*0-406-65853-6*) Butterworth Legal Pubs.

Permanent Commission & International Association Staff, jt. auth. see IUPAC Staff.

Permanent Court of International Justice Staff. World Court Reports, 1922-1942, 2 vols., Set. Hudson, Manley O., ed. 1969. reprint ed. lib. bdg. 200.00 (*0-379-00428-3*) Oceana.

Permanent International Altaistic Conference Staff. Aspects of Altaic Civilization: Proceedings. Francis, David & Sinor, Denis, eds. LC 80-28299. (Uralic & Altaic Ser.: Vol. 23). ix, 263p. 1981. reprint ed. text ed. 59.75 (*0-313-22945-7*, PIAA) Greenwood.

Permanent International Altaistic Conference, 18th Meeting, Bloomington, June 29-July 5, 1975. Aspects of Altaic Civilization II: Proceedings. Draghi, Paul A. & Clark, Larry V., eds. (Uralic & Altaic Ser.: Vol. 134). 212p. 1978. 34.00 (*0-933070-02-0*) Res Inst Inner Asian Studies.

Permanent International Association of Navigation Congress (PIANC) Staff. Pianc 25th Pianc Tech Papers, Vol. 11. 1982. 114.00 (*0-08-026732-7*, Pub. by Pergamon Repr UK) Franklin.

Permanent International Committee on Linguistics Staff, ed. Bibliographie Linguistique 1939-1975. 1986. lib. bdg. 0.01 (*90-247-3320-0*) Kluwer Ac.

P Q

An Asterisk (*) at the beginning of an entry indicates that the title is appearing in BIP for the first time.

Permanent Section of Microbiological Standardization, 31st Symposium, Omstotite of Child Health, Ondon, 1969. Interferon & Interferon Inducers. Perkins, F. T. & Regamey, R. H., eds. (Immunobiological Standardization Symposia Ser.: Vol. 14). 1970. 24.00 (*3-8055-0637-6*) S Karger.

Permanente, Kaiser. Health Counts: A Fat & Calorie Guide. 258p. 1991. pap. text ed. 12.95 (*0-471-52949-4*) Wiley.

***Permanyer, Lluis.** Clave: Sculptor. (Great Monographs). (Illus.). 288p. 1993. 250.00 (*84-343-0633-6*) Elliots Bks.

— Tapies y la Nueva Cultura. (Grandes Monografias). (Illus.). 216p. (SPA.). 1993. 350.00 (*84-343-0470-8*) Elliots Bks.

Permenter, Diane. Oh Those Little Rascals. 100p. 1991. pap. 7.50 (*1-56770-247-3*) S Scheewe Pubns.

Permenter, Paris & Bigley, John. Kansas City Cuisine. rev. ed. (Illus.). 144p. (Orig.). 1995. pap. 9.95 (*1-878686-15-1*) Two Lane Pr.

— Texas Barbeque. 160p. (Orig.). 1994. pap. 14.95 (*0-925175-20-X*) Pig Out Pubns.

Permenter, Paris, jt. auth. see Bigley, John.

Perminov, Anatoli M., tr. see Goldenberg, L. A.

Permut, Joanna B. Embracing the Wolf: A Lupus Victim & Her Family Learn to Live with Chronic Disease. Selph, Alexa, ed. LC 88-9193. 192p. 1989. 14.95 (*0-87797-166-8*) Cherokee.

Permut, Steven E., ed. American Academy of Advertising Annual Meeting, 21st, Proceedings. 1979. pap. 25.00 (*0-931030-02-1*) Am Acad Advert.

Permut, Steven E., ed. see Mauser, Gary A.

Permut, Steven E., ed. see Mokwa, Michael P., et al.

Permut, Steven E., jt. ed. see Mokwa, Michael P.

***Permut, Susan.** More Adventures in Eating: Denver's Ethnic Restaurants. (Illus.). 160p. 1994. pap. 9.95 (*0-9638153-2-6*) Better Busn Communs.

Permut, Susan E. Adventures in Eating: A Guide to Denver's Ethnic Markets, Bakeries & Gourmet Stores. (Illus.). 160p. (Orig.). 1993. pap. 9.95 (*0-9638153-1-8*) Better Busn Communs.

Permutt, Cyril. Collecting Old Cameras. LC 76-14888. (Photography Ser.). 1977. lib. bdg. 29.50 (*0-306-70855-8*) Da Capo.

Permutt, S., jt. ed. see Macklem, P. T.

Permyakov. Luminescent Spectroscopy of Proteins. 1992. 84.95 (*0-8493-4553-7*, QP551) CRC Pr.

Pern, Stephen. The Great Divide: A Walk along the Continental Divide of the United States. large type ed. (Non-Fiction Ser.). 512p. 1989. 17.95 (*0-7089-2044-6*) Ulverscroft.

Perna, Debi. The Birthday Book: Stickers to Stick & Cards to Create for Every Month of the Year. (Illus.). 36p. (J). (ps up). 1992. 6.95 (*0-920775-57-8*, Pub. by Greey dePencier CN) Firefly Bks Ltd.

Perna, Debi, ed. see Chickadee Magazine Editors.

Perna, Rita. Fashion Forecasting. (Illus.). 250p. 1987. teacher ed 2.50 (*0-87005-547-X*); text ed. 23.50 (*0-87005-468-6*) Fairchild.

Perna, Sharon. Country Cross-Stitch. (Illus.). 144p. 1992. pap. 12.95 (*0-8069-5769-7*) Sterling.

— Cross-Stitch a Beautiful Gift. LC 91-41489. (Illus.). 128p. 1992. 19.95 (*0-8069-8400-7*) Sterling.

— Cross-Stitch a Beautiful Gift. (Illus.). 144p. 1993. pap. 12.95 (*0-8069-8401-5*) Sterling.

Pernak, Janine M., et al, eds. Selected Proceedings from the First & Second Delft Pain Symposia: Journal: Applied Neurophysiology, Vol. 47, No. 4-6. (Illus.). 112p. 1986. pap. 59.25 (*3-8055-4044-2*) S Karger.

Pernal, Andrew B., tr. see Le Vasseur, Guillaume & De Beauplan, Sieur.

Pernanen, Kai. Alcohol in Human Violence. LC 91-16338. (Substance Abuse Ser.). 280p. 1991. lib. bdg. 34.95 (*0-89862-171-2*) Guilford Pr.

Pernecke, Raegene B. & Schreiner, Sara M., comps. Schooling for the Learning Disabled: A Selective Guide to LD Programs in Elementary & Secondary Schools Throughout the United States. LC 83-50934. 173p. 1983. pap. 9.95 (*0-914985-00-0*) S M S Pub.

Perneczky, Alex, et al. Endoscopic Anatomy for Neurosurgery. (Illus.). 350p. 1993. text ed. 399.00 (*0-86577-490-0*) Thieme Med Pubs.

Perner, Bernard & Perner, Majorie. Mount to the Sky Like Eagles. (Heritage Ser.: Vol. 9). 1986. 10.95 (*0-911802-64-9*); pap. 8.95 (*0-685-43713-2*) Free Church Pubns.

Perner, Josef. Understanding the Representational Mind. (Bradford LDCC Ser.). (Illus.). 340p. 1991. 44.00 (*0-262-16124-9*, Bradford Bks) MIT Pr.

— Understanding the Representational Mind. (Learning, Development, & Conceptual Change). (Illus.). 340p. 1993. reprint ed. pap. 18.00 (*0-262-66082-2*, Bradford Bks) MIT Pr.

Perner, Majorie, jt. auth. see Perner, Bernard.

Pernes, Ruffino. The Crown Stamps of the Portugese Colonies. LC 75-36294. (Illus.). 38p. 1976. pap. 6.00 (*0-916170-01-2*) J-B Pub.

Pernet, Henry. Ritual Masks: Deceptions & Revelations. Denny, Frederick M., ed. LC 91-45396. (Studies in Comparative Religion). (Illus.). 211p. 1992. text ed. 29.95 (*0-87249-793-3*) U of SC Pr.

***Pernetta, John, ed.** Atlas of the Oceans. rev. ed. LC 94-22176. 1994. 29.95 (*0-528-83703-6*) Rand McNally.

***Pernetta, John, et al, eds.** Impacts of Climate Change on Ecosystems & Species: Implications for Protected Areas. (Impacts of Climate Change: No. 4). 105p. (C). 1995. pap. text ed. 17.00 (*2-8317-0173-2*, Pub. by IUCN SZ) Island Pr.

— Impacts of Climate Change on Ecosystems & Species: Marine & Coastal Ecosystems. (Impacts of Climate Change on Ecosystems & Species Ser.: No. 3). 110p. (C). 1995. pap. text ed. 17.00 (*2-8317-0172-4*, Pub. by IUCN SZ) Island Pr.

Pernetta, John C., ed. Marine Protected Areas Needs in the South Asian Seas Region, Vol. 1: Bangladesh. 42p. (C). 1993. pap. text ed. 10.00 (*2-8317-0174-0*, Pub. by IUCN SZ) Island Pr.

— Marine Protected Areas Needs in the South Asian Seas Region, Vol. 2: India. 77p. (C). 1993. pap. text ed. 10.00 (*2-8317-0175-9*, Pub. by IUCN SZ) Island Pr.

— Marine Protected Areas Needs in the South Asian Seas Region, Vol. 3: Maldives. 38p. (C). 1993. pap. text ed. 10.00 (*2-8317-0176-7*, Pub. by IUCN SZ) Island Pr.

— Marine Protected Areas Needs in the South Asian Seas Region, Vol. 4: Pakistan. 42p. (C). 1993. pap. text ed. 10.00 (*2-8317-0177-5*, Pub. by IUCN SZ) Island Pr.

— Marine Protected Areas Needs in the South Asian Seas Region, Vol. 5: Sri Lanka. 67p. (C). 1993. pap. text ed. 10.00 (*2-8317-0178-3*, Pub. by IUCN SZ) Island Pr.

— Marine Protected Areas Needs in the South Asian Seas Region, Vol. 6: Development of a System. 72p. (C). 1993. pap. text ed. 1,995.00 (*2-8317-0179-1*, Pub. by IUCN SZ) Island Pr.

— Monitoring Coral Reefs for Global Change. 102p. (C). 1993. pap. text ed. 10.00 (*2-8317-0117-1*, Pub. by IUCN SZ) Island Pr.

Pernety, Antoine-Joseph. Le Dictionnaire Mytho-Hermetique. 548p. (FRE.). 1980. pap. 150.00 (*0-8288-2191-7*, M6441) Fr & Eur.

***Pernety, Antoine-Joseph.** An Alchemical Treatrise on the Great Art. 272p. 1995. pap. 35.00 (*0-87728-725-2*) Weiser.

— Dictionnaire Portatif de Peinture, Sculpture et Gravure. 1972. write for info. (*0-7859-8649-9*, 282660242X) Fr & Eur.

Perng, Ching-Hsi. Double Jeopardy: A Critique of Seven Yuan Courtroom Dramas. LC 78-13029. (Michigan Monographs in Chinese Studies: No. 35). 178p. 1978. pap. 6.00 (*0-89264-035-9*) Ctr Chinese Studies.

Perng, Ching-hsi, jt. ed. see Wang, Chiu-kuei.

Pernia, Ernesto D. Urbanization, Population Growth & Economic Deveopment in the Philippines. LC 77-24588. (Studies in Population & Urban Demography: No. 3). 213p. 1977. text ed. 55.00 (*0-8371-9721-X*, PEU/, Greenwood Pr) Greenwood.

***Pernia, Ernesto M.** Urban Poverty in Asia: A Survey of Critical Issues. 300p. 1995. 55.00 (*0-19-586770-X*) OUP.

Pernici, B. & Verrijn-Stuart, A. A., eds. Office Information Systems - the Design Process: Proceedings of the IFIP WG8.4 Working Conference, Linz Austria, 15-17 August, 1988. 338p. 1989. 84.75 (*0-444-87279-5*, North Holland) Elsevier.

Pernici, B., et al, eds. Automatic Tools for Designing Office Information Systems: The TODOS Approach. (Research Reports ESPRIT, Project 813, TODOS: Vol. 1). ix, 321p. 1990. pap. 39.00 (*0-387-53284-6*) Spr-Verlag.

Pernick, B. J. Handbook of Modern Optics, Vol. 1. (Illus.). 40p. (Orig.). 1993. pap. 11.00 (*0-9636539-1-1*) Peconic Pubs.

— Handbook of Modern Optics, Vol. 2. (Illus.). 40p. (Orig.). 1994. pap. 11.00 (*0-9636539-3-8*) Peconic Pubs.

***Pernick, Martin S.** The Black Stork: Eugenics & the Death of "Defective" Babies in American Medicine & Motion Pictures. (Illus.). 256p. 1995. 34.95 (*0-19-507731-8*) OUP.

— A Calculus of Suffering: Pain, Professionalism & Anesthesia in Nineteenth Century America. 1985. text ed. 55.00 (*0-231-05186-7*) Col U Pr.

— A Calculus of Suffering: Pain, Professionalism & Anesthesia in Nineteenth Century America. 421p. 1987. reprint ed. pap. text ed. 17.00 (*0-231-05187-5*, King's Crown Paperbacks) Col U Pr.

Pernicka, E. & Wagner, G., eds. Archaeometry, '90. 880p. 1990. 163.50 (*0-8176-2522-4*) Birkhauser.

Pernicone, Nunzio. Italian Anarchism, 1864-1892. LC 92-46661. (Illus.). 336p. 1993. text ed. 39.50 (*0-691-05692-7*) Princeton U Pr.

Pernin, A., jt. auth. see Comte, R.

Pernin, Peter. Great Pestigo Fire. (Wisconsin Stories Ser.). (Illus.). 29p. 1971. pap. 2.00 (*0-87020-194-8*) State Hist Soc Wis.

***Perniola, Mario.** Enigmas: The Egyptian Moment in Art & Society. Woodall, Christopher, tr. 144p. 1995. 59.95x (*1-85984-966-0*, C0510, Pub. by Verso UK); pap. 18.95 (*1-85984-061-2*, C0511, Pub. by Verso UK) Routledge Chapman & Hall.

Pernis, B., jt. ed. see Ferrerini, M.

Pernis, Benvenuto, jt. ed. see Celada, Franco.

Pernis, Benvenuto, jt. ed. see Lefkovits, Ivan.

Pernis, Benvenuto, et al, eds. Processing & Presentation Antigens. 324p. 1988. text ed. 119.00 (*0-12-551855-2*) Acad Pr.

Pernkopf, Eduard. Atlas of Topographical & Applied Human Anatomy, 2 vols., Set. 2nd ed. Ferner, Helmut, ed. Monsen, Harry, tr. LC 79-25264. Orig. Title: Atlas der Topographischen und Angewamdten Anatomie Des Menschen. (Illus.). 1981. reprint ed. text ed. 355.00 (*0-7216-7196-9*) Saunders.

— Atlas of Topographical & Applied Human Anatomy, 2 vols., Set. 3rd enl. rev. ed. Platzer, Werner, ed. Monsen, Harry, tr. Orig. Title: Atlas der Topographischen und Angewamdten Anatomie Des Menschen. (Illus.). 804p. 1990. 295.00 (*0-683-06854-7*) Williams & Wilkins.

— Atlas of Topographical & Applied Human Anatomy, 2 vols., Vol. 1: Head & Neck. 2nd ed. Ferner, Helmut, ed. Monsen, Harry, tr. LC 79-25264. Orig. Title: Atlas der Topographischen und Angewamdten Anatomie Des Menschen. (Illus.). 1980. reprint ed. text ed. 179.00 (*0-7216-7198-5*) Saunders.

— Atlas of Topographical & Applied Human Anatomy, 2 vols., Vol. 2: Thorax, Abdomen & Extremities. 2nd ed. Ferner, Helmut, ed. Monsen, Harry, tr. LC 79-25264. Orig. Title: Atlas der Topographischen und Angewamdten Anatomie Des Menschen. (Illus.). 1980. reprint ed. text ed. 179.00 (*0-7216-7199-3*) Saunders.

— Atlas of Topographical & Applied Human Anatomy, Vol. II: Thorax, Abdomen & Extremities. 3rd enl. rev. ed. Platzer, Werner, ed. Monson, Harry, tr. (Illus.). 424p. 1990. text ed. 175.00 (*0-683-06853-9*) Williams & Wilkins.

— Atlas of Topographical & Applied Human Anatomy, Vol. 1: Head & Neck. 3rd enl. rev. ed. Platzer, Werner, ed. Monsen, Harry, tr. (Illus.) 380p. 1989. 175.00 (*0-683-06852-0*) Williams & Wilkins.

Pernoll, Martin L., jt. auth. see Benson, Ralph C.

***Pernon, Gerard.** Dictionnaire de la Musique. 448p. (FRE.). 1992. 75.00 (*0-7859-8013-X*, 2737311853) Fr & Eur.

***Pernon, Laure-Diane.** Nouveau Dictionnaire des Synonymes. 289p. (FRE.). 1986. 32.95 (*0-7859-8658-8*, 285882925x) Fr & Eur.

Pernot, Laurent. Les "Discours Siciliens" d'Aelius Aristede. rev. ed. Connor, W. R., ed. LC 80-2662. (Monographs in Classical Studies). 1981. lib. bdg. 43.95 (*0-405-14047-9*) Ayer.

Pernot, Michel, ed. see De Retz, Jean-Francois.

Pernotto, James. Chuck Close Editions: A Catalogue Raissone. (Illus.). 32p. (Orig.). (C). 1989. pap. text ed. write for info. (*0-9624401-0-8*) Butler Inst.

Pernoud, Mary-Anne. An Investigation of Alexander Solzhenitsyn's Gulag Archipelago According to Various Themes & Types Found Through Literature History. 1983. 3.00 (*0-940604-03-5*) Intl Inst Adv Stud.

— Stalin & the Expansion of Soviet Power. pap. 1.50 (*0-940604-05-1*) Intl Inst Adv Stud.

Pernoud, Regine. Joan of Arc: By Herself & Her Witnesses. LC 66-24807. 1969. pap. 16.95 (*0-8128-1260-3*, Scrbrough Hse) Madison Bks UPA.

Pernow, Bengt, jt. ed. see Carlson, Lars A.

Pernow, Bengt, jt. ed. see Nobel Symposium Staff.

***Pernu, Dennis.** Hot Rods. (Cruisin' Ser.). 48p. (J). (gr. 3-9). 1995. lib. bdg. 13.35 (*1-56065-253-5*) Capstone Pr.

Pernul, G. & Tjoa, A. M., eds. Entity-Relationship Approach - ER '92: Eleventh International Conference. LC 92-32250. (Lecture Notes in Computer Science Ser.: Vol. 645). 1992. 63.00 (*0-387-56023-8*) Spr-Verlag.

Pero, Albert & Moyo, Ambrose, eds. Theology & Black Experience: The Lutheran Heritage Interpreted by African & African-American Theologians. LC 88-7778. 272p. (Orig.). 1988. pap. 16.99 (*0-8066-2353-5*, 10-6284, Augsburg) Augsburg Fortress.

Peroff, Nicholas C. Menominee Drums: Tribal Termination & Restoration, 1954-1974. LC 81-43641. (Illus.). 302p. 1982. 26.95 (*0-8061-1703-6*) U of Okla Pr.

Perol, C., jt. ed. see Le Tirant, P.

Perol, Lucette, jt. auth. see Diderot, Denis.

Perols, S., jt. illus. see Valat, P. M.

Peron, Dennis, jt. auth. see Rathbun, Mary.

Peron, Juan D. The Speeches of Juan Domingo Peron. 698p. 1973. 300.00 (*0-8490-1108-6*) Gordon Pr.

Peron, Juan D., et al. Peron's Argentina. 429p. 1973. 250.00 (*0-8490-0814-X*) Gordon Pr.

Peron, M. Robert-Collins Dictionary of Management (English & French) 1203p. (ENG & FRE.). 1992. 135.00 (*0-8288-6907-3*, 2850361461) Fr & Eur.

Peron, M., et al. French-English - English-French Dictionary of Management. 1022p. 1992. 69.00 (*2-85036-146-1*, Dict Le Roberts) IBD Ltd.

***Peron, Michel.** Larousse Dictionnaire des Affairs: French-English, English-French. 512p. (ENG & FRE.). 1969. 45.00 (*0-7859-7631-0*, 2030206091) Fr & Eur.

Perone, Christopher, jt. auth. see Manard, Barbara.

Perone, James E. Howard Hanson: A Bio-Bibliography. LC 93-2589. (Bio-Bibliographies in Music Ser.: No. 17). 352p. 1993. text ed. 65.00 (*0-313-28644-2*, Greenwood Pr) Greenwood.

***Perone, Jerry & Sanow, Arnold.** Entrepreneur's Boot Camp. 224p. 1994. boxed 24.95 (*0-7872-0253-3*) Kendall-Hunt.

Perone, Karen L. Lukas Foss: A Bio-Bibliography. LC 90-29280. (Bio Bibliographies in Music Ser.: No. 37). 296p. 1991. text ed. 59.95 (*0-313-26811-8*, PLB, Greenwood Pr) Greenwood.

***Perone, N.** Principles of Real-Time Sonography in Modern Obstetrics: A Handbook for the Practicing Physician. LC 83-42848. (Illus.). Date not set. reprint ed. pap. 49.40 (*0-7837-9536-X*, 2060285) Bks Demand.

***Peroni, Gwen, ed.** Canadian Insurance Claims Directory 1995. annuals 63th ed. 400p. (C). 1995. pap. 37.00 (*0-8020-4042-X*) U of Toronto Pr.

Peroni, Laura. Glorious Flowers. (Illus.). 208p. 1990. 24.99 (*0-517-69627-4*) Random Hse Value.

Peroni, Peter A. The Burg: An Italian-American Community at Bay in Trenton. LC 79-63258. 1979. pap. text ed. 19.00 (*0-8191-0724-7*) U Pr of Amer.

Peroni, Robert J., jt. auth. see Dzienkowski, John S.

Peroni, Robert J., jt. auth. see Kuntz, Joel D.

Peronnet, Louise. Le Parler acadien du Sud-Est du Nouveau-Brunswick: Elements grammaticaux et lexicaux. (American University Studies: Foreign Language Instruction: Ser. VI, Vol. 8). 275p. (FRE.). (C). 1989. text ed. 37.50 (*0-8204-0794-1*) P Lang Pubs.

Peroomian, Rubina. Literary Responses to Catastrophe: A Comparison of the Armenian & Jewish Experience. (UCLA Studies in Near Eastern Culture & Society). 248p. 1993. 44.95 (*1-55540-894-X*, 220008); pap. 29.95 (*1-55540-895-8*, 220008) Scholars Pr GA.

Perosa, Alessandro & Sparrow, John, eds. Renaissance Latin Verse: An Anthology. LC 78-10969. 590p. reprint ed. pap. 168.20 (*0-7837-0301-5*, 2040623) Bks Demand.

Perot, F. Folk-Lore Bourbonnais. LC 78-20141. (Collection de contes et de chansons populaires: Vol. 31). reprint ed. 21.50 (*0-404-60381-5*) AMS Pr.

Perot, Ross. Save Your Job, Save Our Country: Why NAFTA Must Be Stopped - Now! 160p. 1993. pap. 6.95 (*1-56282-711-1*) Hyperion.

***Perotto, Aldo O.** Anatomical Guide for the Electromyographer: The Limbs & Trunk. 3rd ed. (Illus.). 328p. 1994. pap. 29.95 (*0-398-06320-6*) C C Thomas.

— Anatomical Guide for the Electromyographer: The Limbs & Trunk. 3rd ed. (Illus.). 328p. (C). 1994. text ed. 47.95 (*0-398-05900-4*) C C Thomas.

Peroutka, Stephen J., ed. Ecstasy: The Clinical Pharmacological & Neurotoxicological Effects of the Drug MDMA. (Topics in Neurosciences Ser.). (C). 1989. lib. bdg. 107.00 (*0-7923-0305-9*) Kluwer Ac.

— Handbook of Receptors & Channels, Vol. I: G Protein-Coupled Receptors. 336p. 1993. 110.00 (*0-8493-8321-8*) CRC Pr.

— Serotonin Receptor Subtypes: Basic & Clinical Aspects. (Receptor Biochemistry & Methodology Ser.: Vol. 15). 246p. 1990. text ed. 119.95 (*0-471-56840-6*) Wiley.

Perov, jt. auth. see Watt.

***Perova, Natasha, ed.** Glas: New Russian Writing No. 3: Women's View. 1992. pap. 9.95 (*0-939010-48-8*) Zephyr Pr.

— Glas: New Russian Writing No. 7: Booker Winners & Others. (Glas Ser.). (Illus.). 248p. 1994. pap. 9.95 (*0-939010-43-7*) Zephyr Pr.

— Glas: New Russian Writing No. 8: Love Without Fear. (Glas Ser.). (Illus.). 240p. 1995. pap. 10.95 (*0-939010-44-5*) Zephyr Pr.

— Glas: New Russian Writing No. 9: The Generation of the Sixties. 1995. pap. 10.95 (*0-939010-49-6*) Zephyr Pr.

— Glas: New Russian Writing, No. 4: Love & Fear. (Illus.). 240p. 1993. pap. 9.95 (*0-939010-35-6*) Zephyr Pr.

— Glas: New Russian Writing, No. 5: Bulgakov & Mandelstam. (Illus.). 192p. 1993. pap. 9.95 (*0-939010-40-2*) Zephyr Pr.

— Glas: New Russian Writing, No. 6: Jews & Strangers. (Illus.). 224p. (Orig.). 1994. pap. 9.95 (*0-939010-42-9*) Zephyr Pr.

***Perova, Natasha & Bromfield, Andrew, eds.** Glas: New Russian Writing No. 1: Inaugural Issues. 1991. pap. 8.95 (*0-939010-46-1*) Zephyr Pr.

— Glas: New Russian Writing No. 2: Soviet Grotesque. 1992. pap. 8.95 (*0-939010-47-X*) Zephyr Pr.

Perova, Natasha, jt. auth. see Kagal, Ayesha.

Perovitch, Milosh. Radiological Evaluation of the Spinal Cord, 2 vols., Vol. 1. 256p. 1981. 95.00 (*0-8493-5041-7*, RC402, CRC Reprint) Franklin.

— Radiological Evaluation of the Spinal Cord, 2 vols., Vol. 2. 192p. 1981. 75.00 (*0-8493-5043-3*, CRC Reprint) Franklin.

Perowine, Stuart. Hadrian. (Classical Lives Ser.). (Illus.). 192p. (Orig.). (C). 1987. reprint ed. pap. text ed. 14.95 (*0-7099-4048-3*, Pub. by Croom Helm UK) Routledge Chapman & Hall.

Perowne, J. J. Commentary on the Psalms, 2 vols. in 1. LC 89-11054. Orig. Title: Book of Psalms. 1144p. 1989. pap. 29.99 (*0-8254-3485-8*) Kregel.

Perowne, Stewart. Hadrian. (Illus.). 192p. 1990. 17.95 (*0-88029-469-8*) Marboro Bks.

— Hadrian. LC 75-43946. (Illus.). 192p. 1976. reprint ed. text ed. 49.75 (*0-8371-8723-0*, PEHAD, Greenwood Pr) Greenwood.

Perozzo, James. The Complete Guide to Electronics Troubleshooting. 850p. 1994. text ed. 52.95 (*0-8273-5045-7*) Delmar.

— The Complete Guide to Electronics Troubleshooting: Instructor's Guide. 29p. 1994. 15.00 (*0-8273-5046-5*) Delmar.

— Practical Electronics Troubleshooting. LC 84-28626. 256p. (C). 1985. teacher ed 15.00 (*0-8273-2434-0*); pap. text ed. 32.95 (*0-8273-2433-2*) Delmar.

— Practical Electronics Troubleshooting. 2nd rev. ed. 448p. 1992. pap. 32.95 (*0-8273-4053-2*) Delmar.

— Practical Electronics Troubleshooting: Instructor's Guide. 2nd ed. 1992. teacher ed 15.00 (*0-8273-4054-0*) Delmar.

Perozzo, Jim. Assembling & Troubleshooting Microcomputers. 2nd ed. 352p. 1990. teacher ed 15.00 (*0-8273-3987-9*); text ed. 32.95 (*0-8273-3986-0*) Delmar.

***Perpection, Inc., Staff.** Microsoft PowerPoint for Windows 95 Step by Step. 1995. 29.95 (*1-55615-829-7*) Microsoft.

Perper, Joshua A. & Wecht, Cyril H. Microscopic Diagnosis in Forensic Pathology. (Illus.). 488p. 1980. 82.95 (*0-398-03969-0*) C C Thomas.

Perper, R. J., ed. Mechanisms of Tissue Injury with Reference to Rheumatoid Arthritis. (Annals Ser.: Vol. 256). 450p. 1975. 54.50 (*0-89072-010-X*) NY Acad Sci.

Perpetua, Saint. Passion of the Holy Martyrs Sts. Perpetua & Felicity. Wallis, R. E., tr. 1991. pap. 2.95 (*0-89981-133-7*) Eastern Orthodox.

Perpich, George, jt. auth. see Gladstone, John.

Perpich, Sandra W. A Hermeneutic Critique of Structuralist Exegesis: With Specific Reference to Lk. 10.29-37. LC 83-21737. (Illus.). 264p. (Orig.). (C). 1984. pap. text ed. 23.00 (*0-8191-3669-7*) U Pr of Amer.

Perr, Harvey. Rosebloom. 1972. pap. 4.75 (*0-8222-0969-1*) Dramatists Play.

Perr, Herb. Making Art Together Step-by-Step. LC 88-6512. (Illus.). 144p. (Orig.). (C). 1988. pap. 14.95 (*0-89390-118-0*) Resource Pubns.

Perraton, Hilary. Alternative Routes to Formal Education. LC 82-7233. 344p. 1985. pap. text ed. 16.95 (*0-8018-2588-1*) Johns Hopkins.

Perraton, Hilary, ed. Distance Education for Teacher Training. LC 93-541. 432p. 1993. 65.00 (*0-415-09465-8*, B0170) Routledge.

P Q

An Asterisk (*) at the beginning of an entry indicates that the title is appearing in BIP for the first time.

Perraton, Jean & Baxter, Richard, eds. Models, Evaluations & Information Systems for Planners. LC 75-326945. (Cambridge University Centre for Land Use & Built Form Studies Conference Proceedings: No. 1). 316p. reprint ed. pap. 90.10 (0-317-27672-7, 2025215) Bks Demand.

Perraud, Louis, jt. ed. see Thomson, Ian.

Perraudin, Michael. Heinrich Heine: Poetry in Context - A Study of Buch der Lieder. LC 88-9512. (Berg Monographs in German Literature). 304p. 1989. 55.00 (0-85496-028-7) Berg Pubs.

Perrault, Anna H., ed. Nature Classics: A Catalogue of the E. A. McIlhenny Natural History Collection at Louisiana State University. LC 86-15399. (Illus.). 312p. 1987. text ed. 42.50 (0-8071-1363-8) La State U Pr.

Perrault, Anna H., jt. auth. see Blazek, Ronald.

***Perrault, Charles.** Anness: Red Riding Hood. (Illus.). 48p. (J). 1995. 7.98 (0-8317-0746-1) Smithmark.

— Anness: Sleeping Beauty. (Illus.). 48p. (J). 1995. 7.98 (0-8317-1719-X) Smithmark.

— Cinderella. (Creative's Collection of Fairy Tales). (Illus.). 32p. (J). (gr. 4 up). 1983. 13.95 (0-87191-945-1) Creative Ed.

— Cinderella. LC 85-1685. (Illus.). 32p. (J). (ps-3). 1985. 16.99 (0-8037-0205-1) Dial Bks Young.

— Cinderella. 55p. (FRE.). (J). (gr. 3-8). 1990. pap. 10.95 (0-7859-1354-8, 2070312224) Fr & Eur.

— Cinderella. (J). (ps-3). 1990. pap. 4.95 (0-8037-0830-0, Puff Pied Piper) Puffin Bks.

— Cinderella. (J). (ps-3). 1993. pap. 5.99 (0-14-054618-9, Puff Pied Piper) Puffin Bks.

— Cinderella. LC 78-18067. (Illus.). 32p. (J). (gr. k-3). 1979. lib. bdg. 9.79 (0-89375-120-0); pap. 2.50 (0-89375-098-0) Troll Assocs.

— Cinderella. (Tell Me a Story Ser.). (Illus.). 26p. (J). (ps). 1988. audio 9.95 (1-55578-911-0) Worlds Wonder.

— Cinderella. 2nd ed. Brown, Marcia, tr. & illus. by. LC 87-34920. 32p. (J). (ps-3). 1988. pap. 4.95 (0-689-71261-8, Aladdin Paperbacks) S&S Childrens.

— Cinderella: And Other Tales from Perrault. (Illus.). 78p. (J). (ps-2). 1989. 18.95 (0-8050-1004-1, Bks Young Read) H Holt & Co.

— Cinderella; or, The Little Glass Slipper. (Picture Puffins Ser.). (Illus.). (J). (gr. 1 up). 1977. pap. 3.95 (0-14-050137-1, Puffin) Puffin Bks.

— Contes. Rouger, ed. 586p. (FRE.). 1981. pap. 10.95 (0-7859-1374-2, 2070372812) Fr & Eur.

— Contes. (Folio Ser.: No. 1281). (FRE.). 1989. pap. 9.95 (2-07-037281-2) Schoenhof.

— Contes de ma Mere l'Oye. (Folio - Junior Ser). (FRE.). pap. 9.95 (2-07-033028-1) Schoenhof.

— Contes de Ma Mere l'Oye. (Folio - Junior Ser.: No. 443). (Illus.). 223p. (FRE.). (J). (gr. 5-10). 1988. pap. 8.95 (2-07-033443-0) Schoenhof.

— El Gato Con Botas: (Puss in Boots) Marcuse, Aida, tr. (Mirasol Ser.). (Illus.). 32p. (SPA.). (J). 1991. 16.00 (0-374-36158-4) FS&G.

— Little Red Riding Hood. (Creative's Collection of Fairy Tales). (Illus.). 32p. (YA). (gr. 9 up). 1983. lib. bdg. 13.95 (0-87191-943-5) Creative Ed.

— The Pancake That Ran Away & Toads & Diamonds. (Upside Down Bks.). (Illus.). 48p. (J). (ps-3). 1985. 5.95 (0-88110-254-7) EDC.

— Perrault's Fairy Tales. LC 72-79522. (Illus.). viii, 117p. (J). (gr. 4-6). 1969. reprint ed. pap. 5.95 (0-486-22311-6) Dover.

— Popular Tales. Dorson, Richard M., ed. LC 77-70607. (International Folklore Ser.). (Illus.). 1977. reprint ed. lib. bdg. 23.95 (0-405-10118-X) Ayer.

— Le Pull-over Rouge. (FRE.). 1980. pap. 12.95 (0-7859-3104-X, 2253025437) Fr & Eur.

— Puss in Boots. Arthur, Malcolm, tr. 32p. (J). 1990. 16.00 (0-374-36160-6) FS&G.

— Puss in Boots. LC 78-18061. (Illus.). 32p. (J). (gr. k-3). 1979. lib. bdg. 9.79 (0-89375-130-8); pap. 2.50 (0-89375-108-1) Troll Assocs.

— Puss in Boots. (Golden Sound Story Books - Classics Ser.). (Illus.). 20p. (J). (ps up). 1992. write for info. (0-307-74705-0, 64705, Golden Pr) Western Pub.

— Puss in Boots: A Classic Tale. Suire, Diane D., tr. LC 88-35316. (Illus.). 32p. (J). (gr. k-2). 1988. lib. bdg. 19.93 (0-89565-482-2) Childs World.

— Puss in Boots: A Fairy Tale. Lewis, Naomi, tr. LC 93-39758. (Illus.). 32p. (J). (gr. k-3). 1994. 14.95 (1-55858-099-9); lib. bdg. 14.88 (1-55858-120-0) North-South Bks NYC.

— Ricky the Tuft: A Classic Tale. Moncure, Jane B., tr. LC 88-36792. (Illus.). 32p. (J). (gr. k-3). 1988. lib. bdg. 19.93 (0-89565-473-3) Childs World.

— Sleeping Beauty: A Classic Tale. Moncure, Jane B., tr. LC 88-35212. (Illus.). 32p. (J). (gr. k-3). 1988. lib. bdg. 19.95 (0-89565-478-4) Childs World.

— Sleeping Beauty & Other Classic French Fairy Tales. (J). 1991. 12.99 (0-517-03706-8) Random Hse Value.

— Sleeping Beauty & Other Stories. LC 88-43558. (Miniature Editions Ser.). 96p. (J). 1989. 4.95 (0-89471-721-9) Running Pr.

— Sleeping Beauty & The Soldier & the Six Giants. (Upside Down Bks.). (Illus.). 48p. (J). (ps-3). 1985. 5.95 (0-88110-255-5) EDC.

— The Sleeping Beauty in the Woods. (Creative's Collection of Fairy Tales). (Illus.). 32p. (J). (gr. 6 up). 1984. lib. bdg. 13.95 (0-87191-944-3) Creative Ed.

— A Storyteller Book: Cinderella. 48p. (J). 1994. 7.98 (0-8317-0883-2) Smithmark.

— Tales from Perrault. (Oxford Illustrated Classics Ser.). (Illus.). 118p. (J). (gr. 3-7). 1989. 18.95 (0-19-274533-6) OUP.

— Three Wishes. LC 78-18060. (Illus.). 32p. (J). (gr. k-3). 1979. lib. bdg. 9.79 (0-89375-129-4); pap. 2.50 (0-89375-107-3) Troll Assocs.

— Tom Thumb: A Classic Tale. Riehecky, Janet, tr. LC 88-35211. (Illus.). 32p. (J). (gr. k-3). 1988. lib. bdg. 19.95 (0-89565-462-8) Childs World.

Perrault, Charles & Kipling, Rudyard. Cinderella & How the Elephant Got Its Trunk. (Upside Down Bks.). (Illus.). 48p. (J). (gr. 1-4). 1985. 5.95 (0-88110-252-0) EDC.

Perrault, Charles, jt. auth. see Brown, Marcia.

Perrault, Charles, jt. auth. see Leprince de Beaumont, Marie.

Perrault, Claude. Ordonnance for the Five Kinds of Columns after the Method of the Ancients. McEwen, Indra K., tr. LC 92-4649. (Texts & Documents Ser.). (Illus.). 208p. 1993. 34.95 (0-89236-232-4); pap. 19.95 (0-89236-233-2) J P Getty Trust.

Perrault, Gilles. Le Derapage. (FRE.). 1989. pap. 10.95 (0-7859-2919-3) Fr & Eur.

— A Man Apart: The Life of Henry Curiel. Cumming, Bob, tr. LC 87-13282. 272p. (C). 1987. text ed. 39.95 (0-86232-659-1, Pub. by Zed Books UK); pap. 15.00 (0-86232-660-5, Pub. by Zed Books UK) Humanities.

— Notre Ami le Roi. (Folio-Actuel Ser.). (FRE.). 1990. pap. 14.95 (2-07-032695-0) Schoenhof.

— L' Orchestre Rouge. 573p. (FRE.). 1989. pap. 65.00 (0-7859-3451-0, 2213023883) Fr & Eur.

Perrault-Mattison, Patricia. The Art of Bill Alexander & Robert Warren, Series 7. (Illus.). 84p. 1989. pap. text ed. write for info. (1-883576-06-7) Alexander Art.

— The Art of Bill Alexander & Robert Warren, Series 8. (Illus.). 84p. 1989. pap. text ed. write for info. (1-883576-07-5) Alexander Art.

— The Art of Bill Alexander & Robert Warren, Series 9. (Illus.). 78p. 1990. pap. text ed. write for info. (1-883576-08-3) Alexander Art.

— The Art of Buck Paulson, Series 1. (Illus.). 96p. 1989. pap. text ed. write for info. (1-883576-16-4) Alexander Art.

— The Art of Buck Paulson, Series 2. (Illus.). 88p. 1990. pap. text ed. write for info. (1-883576-17-2) Alexander Art.

Perrault, Robert D., ed. Paper Machine Steam & Condensate Systems: A Project of the Water Removal Committee of the Engineering Division. 4th rev. ed. LC 90-41195. reprint ed. pap. 25.00 (0-8357-2740-8, 2039849) Bks Demand.

Perreau & Langford. Concise French-American Dictionary of Figurative & Idiomatic Language. (ENG & FRE.). 17.95 (0-685-36686-3) Fr & Eur.

Perreault, Bruce A. Secret Forces. 7p. 1988. reprint ed. spiral bd. 4.40 (0-7873-0667-3) Mokelumne.

Perreault, George. Curved Like an Eye. Trusky, Tom, ed. LC 87-14656. (Ahsahta Press Modern & Contemporary Poets of the West Ser.). 59p. (Orig.). 1988. pap. 6.95 (0-916272-35-4) Ahsahta Pr.

— Trying to Be Round. 64p. (Orig.). 1994. pap. 9.50 (1-880286-20-3) Singular Speech Pr.

Perreault, Jean M., ed. Reclassification-Rationale & Problems, Vol. 1. 1968. pap. 5.00 (0-911808-02-7) U of Md Lib Serv.

***Perreault, Jeanne.** Writing Selves: Contemporary Feminist Autography. 344p. 1995. text ed. 44.95 (0-8166-2654-5); pap. text ed. 17.95 (0-8166-2655-3) U of Minn Pr.

Perreault, John. Hotel Death. (New American Fiction Ser.: No. 16). 213p. 1990. 16.95 (0-940650-87-8); pap. 10.95 (0-940650-88-6) Sun & Moon CA.

— Hotel Death. deluxe ed. (New American Fiction Ser.: No. 16). 213p. 1990. 30.00 (0-940650-86-X) Sun & Moon CA.

— Luck. 7.00 (0-686-09743-2); pap. 3.50 (0-686-09744-0) Kulchur Foun.

Perreault, John, et al, contribs. Diane Burko. LC 87-63191. (Illus.). 48p. (Orig.). 1990. reprint ed. pap. 15.00 (0-9623799-6-4) Locks Gallery.

Perreault, John, jt. comment see Barreras del Rio, Petra.

Perreault, John, jt. auth. see Nahas, Dominique.

Perreault, William, jt. auth. see McCarthy, E. Jerome.

Perreault, William D., Jr., jt. auth. see Mason, Charlotte.

Perreault, William D., jt. auth. see McCarthy, E. Jerome, Jr.

Perreault, William D., jt. ed. see McCarthy, E. Jerome.

Perreiah, Alan, ed. Paul of Venice: Logica Magna, Tractatus De Suppositione. (Text Ser.). 1971. 16.00 (0-686-11560-0) Franciscan Inst.

Perrella, Stephen. Aspects of Modern Architecture. 1991. pap. 21.95 (0-312-06705-4) St Martin.

Perrella, Stephen, ed. see Riley, Terence.

Perrels, Adriaan, jt. auth. see Nijkamp, Peter.

Perren, S. M. & Schneider, E., eds. Biomechanics: Current Interdisciplinary Research. (Developments in Biomechanics Ser.). 1985. lib. bdg. 239.00 (0-89838-755-8) Kluwer Ac.

Perrenod, Virginia M. Special Districts, Special Purposes: Fringe Governments & Urban Problems in the Houston Area. LC 83-40492. 168p. 1984. 18.50 (0-89096-165-4) Tex A&M Univ Pr.

Perrero, Laurie. World of Tropical Flowers. LC 76-12926. (Illus.). 64p. (Orig.). 1976. pap. 4.95 (0-89317-008-9) Windward Pub.

Perrero, Laurie & Perrero, Louis. Tarantulas: In Nature & As Pets. (Illus.). 1979. pap. 2.95 (0-89317-029-1) Windward Pub.

Perrero, Louis, jt. auth. see Perrero, Laurie.

Perret. The Faces of Science Fiction. (Illus.). 164p. 1984. pap. 11.95 (0-685-10347-1) St Martin.

— The Faces of Science Fiction. deluxe ed. (Illus.). 164p. 1985. Collector's ed. 1985. 35.00 (0-685-10348-X) St Martin.

***Perret, Annick.** Painting on Porcelain: Oriental Designs. (Illus.). 96p. (Orig.). 1995. pap. 22.50 (0-85532-786-3, Pub. by Search Pr UK) A Schwartz & Co.

— Painting on Porcelain: Traditional & Contemporary Design. (Illus.). 96p. (Orig.). (YA). 1994. pap. 22.50 (0-85532-766-9, Pub. by Search Pr UK) A Schwartz & Co.

Perret, B. A., et al, eds. Long-Term Intravenous Immunoglobulin Treatment in Patients with AIDS-Related Complex: Journal: Vox Sanguinis, Vol. 59, Suppl. 1, 1990. (Illus.). iv, 60p. 1990. pap. 17.75 (3-8055-5256-4) S Karger.

Perret, C., jt. ed. see Bossart, H.

Perret, C., jt. ed. see Vincent, J. L.

Perret-Clermont, Anne N., ed. see Hinde, Robert A.

Perret-Clermont, Anne-Nelly. Social Interaction & Cognitive Development in Children. (European Monographs in Social Psychology: No. 19). 1980. text ed. 119.00 (0-12-551950-8) Acad Pr.

Perret-Gallix, D. New Computing Techniques in Physics 2. 804p. 1992. text ed. 178.00 (981-02-1122-8) World Scientific Pub.

Perret-Gallix, D., jt. auth. see Becks, K-H.

Perret, Gene. Comedy Writing Step by Step: How to Write & Sell Your Sense of Humor. 2nd ed. LC 90-2907. 281p. 1990. reprint ed. pap. 11.95 (0-573-60605-6) S French Trade.

— Comedy Writing Workbook. LC 94-20150. 1994. reprint ed. pap. 17.00 (0-88734-647-2) Players Pr.

— Funny Comebacks to Rude Remarks. LC 90-37815. (Illus.). 96p. (YA). (gr. 3-9). 1990. pap. 3.95 (0-8069-7240-8) Sterling.

— Laugh-a-Minute Joke Book. (Illus.). 96p. (J). (gr. 3-9). 1991. pap. 3.95 (0-8069-7415-X) Sterling.

— Shift Your Writing Career into High Gear. 240p. 1993. 16.95 (0-89879-539-7) Writers Digest.

— Successful Stand-up Comedy: Advice from a Comedy Writer. 270p. (Orig.). Date not set. pap. 13.95 (0-573-69916-X) French.

— Super Funny School Jokes. LC 91-22501. (Illus.). 96p. (J). (gr. 2-10). 1991. 13.95 (0-8069-8294-2) Sterling.

— Super Funny School Jokes. LC 91-22501. (Illus.). 96p. (J). (gr. 1-7). 1992. pap. 3.95 (0-8069-8295-0) Sterling.

Perret, Gene & Martin, Terry P. Great One-Liners. LC 92-26651. (Illus.). 128p. 1992. pap. 4.95 (0-8069-8514-3) Sterling.

Perret, Gene & Perret, Linda. Bigshots, Pipsqueaks & Windbags: Jokes, Stories & One-Liners About People, Power & Politics. LC 92-34383. 1993. 10.95 (0-13-350331-3) P-H.

— Gene Perret's Funny Business: Speaker's Treasury of Business Humor for All Occasions. 600p. 1990. 29.95 (0-13-352881-2); pap. 12.95 (0-13-352535-X) P-H.

Perret, Gene & Perret Martin, Terry. Classic One-Liners. LC 94-28144. (Illus.). 128p. (J). 1994. pap. 4.95 (0-8069-0722-3) Sterling.

Perret, Geoffrey. A Country Made by War: A Story of America's Rise to Power. 1989. 22.50 (0-394-55398-5) Random.

— Country Made by War: From the Revolution to Vietnam - The Story of America's Rise to Power. LC 89-40548. 640p. 1990. pap. 14.95 (0-679-72698-5, Vin) Random.

— Old Soldiers Never Die: The Life of Douglas MacArthur. LC 95-8586. 1996. 25.00 (0-679-42882-8) Random.

— There's a War to Be Won. 1992. mass mkt. 5.99 (0-345-37924-1) Ballantine.

— There's a War to Be Won, to Be Won: The United States Army in World War II. LC 91-2117. (Illus.). 656p. 1991. 29.50 (0-394-57831-7) Random.

— Winged Victory: The Army Air Forces in World War Two. LC 92-56838. 1993. 30.00 (0-679-40464-3) Random.

Perret, Jacques. Bande a Part. (FRE.). 1973. pap. 8.95 (0-7859-4000-6) Fr & Eur.

— Les Bifflins de Gonesse. (FRE.). 1979. pap. 8.95 (0-7859-4103-7) Fr & Eur.

— Le Caporal Epingle. (FRE.). 1972. pap. 17.95 (0-7859-3993-8) Fr & Eur.

— Les Origines De la Legende Troyenne De Rome (281-31) xxxii, 678p. reprint ed. write for info. (0-318-71387-X, Pub. by Georg Olms GW) Lubrecht & Cramer.

— Role de Plaisance. (FRE.). 1975. pap. 10.95 (0-7859-4037-5) Fr & Eur.

— Roucou. (FRE.). 1984. pap. 11.95 (0-7859-4202-5) Fr & Eur.

— Le Vent dans les Voiles. (FRE.). 1983. pap. 11.95 (0-7859-4182-7) Fr & Eur.

Perret, Linda, jt. auth. see Perret, Gene.

Perret Martin, Terry, jt. auth. see Perret, Gene.

Perret, R., ed. see IFAC Symposium Staff.

Perret, Yvonne M., jt. auth. see Batshaw, Mark L.

***Perrett, Bryan.** At All Costs: Stories of Impossible Victories. (Illus.). 240p. 1995. pap. 14.95 (1-85409-276-6) Sterling.

— The Battle Book: Crucial Conflicts in History from 1469 BC to the Present. 320p. 1993. 24.95 (1-85409-125-5) Sterling.

— Churchill Infantry Tank 1941-51. (New Vanguard Ser.: No. 4). (Illus.). 48p. pap. 11.95 (1-85532-297-8, 9339, Pub. by Osprey UK) Stackpole.

— German Light Panzers 1932-42. (Vanguard Ser.: No. 33). (Illus.). 48p. pap. 10.95 (0-85045-483-2, 9330, Pub. by Osprey UK) Stackpole.

— A Hawk at War: The Peninsular War Reminiscences of General Sir Thomas Brotherton, CB. 84p. (C). 1986. 84.00 (0-948251-22-0, Pub. by Picton UK) St Mut.

— Iron Fist: Classic Armoured Warfare Case Studies. (Illus.). 240p. 1995. 24.95 (1-85409-218-9) Sterling.

— Last Stand! Famous Battles Against the Odds. (Illus.). 240p. 1993. pap. 14.95 (1-85409-188-3) Sterling.

— Mechanised Infantry. (Vanguard Ser.: No. 38). (Illus.). 48p. pap. 10.95 (0-85045-526-X, 9327, Pub. by Osprey UK) Stackpole.

— The PzKpfw V Panther. (Vanguard Ser.: No. 21). (Illus.). 48p. pap. 10.95 (0-85045-397-6, 9310, Pub. by Osprey UK) Stackpole.

— Seize & Hold: Master Strokes on the Battlefield. (Illus.). 240p. 1994. 24.95 (1-85409-187-5) Sterling.

— Seize & Hold: Master Strokes on the Battlefield. (Illus.). 240p. 1995. pap. 14.95 (1-85409-275-8) Sterling.

— World's Armies. 1991. 14.99 (0-517-05240-7) Random Hse Value.

Perrett, Bryan, ed. The Hawks: A Short History of the 14th-20th. 151p. (C). 1987. 91.00 (0-902633-94-5, Pub. by Picton UK) St Mut.

Perrett, Bryon. At All Costs! Stories of Impossible Victories. (Illus.). 240p. 1993. 24.95 (1-85409-157-3) Sterling.

Perrett, Gene. Comedy Writing Workbook. LC 89-39963. (Illus.). 192p. (Orig.). 1990. pap. 12.95 (0-8069-6554-1) Sterling.

Perrett, Geoffrey. Days of Sadness, Years of Triumph: The American People, 1939-1945. LC 72-87594. 512p. 1985. reprint ed. pap. 17.50 (0-299-10394-3) U of Wis Pr.

***Perrett, Jeanne.** Word Bird & the Whirlies. (English Language Teaching Ser.). (Illus.). (J). 1994. 7.50 (0-13-100256-2) P-H Intl.

Perrett, K., jt. auth. see Walmsley, D.

Perrett, Kathryn. RelationShift: The Guide to Building Better Relationships. 192p. 1989. pap. 9.95 (0-936389-19-2) Tudor Pubs.

Perrett, Roy W. Indian Philosophy of Religion. (C). 1989. lib. bdg. 88.00 (0-7923-0437-3) Kluwer Ac.

Perrett, Roy W., jt. ed. see Oddie, Graham.

Perrett, Thomas I. Gold Book of Photography Prices, 1987. LC 86-18756. 300p. (Orig.). 1987. spiral bd. 29.95 (0-915827-04-2) Photo Res Inst Carson Endowment.

— Gold Book of Photography Prices, 1988. 300p. (Orig.). 1988. pap. 39.95 (0-915827-06-9) Photo Res Inst Carson Endowment.

— Gold Book of Photography Prices, 1990. 300p. 1990. 39.95 (0-915827-11-5); pap. 29.95 (0-915827-10-7) Photo Res Inst Carson Endowment.

— Gold Book of Photography Prices, 1991. 300p. 1991. pap. 29.95 (0-915827-12-3); pap. 39.95 (0-915827-13-1) Photo Res Inst Carson Endowment.

— Gold Book of Photography Prices, 1992. 294p. 1992. pap. 29.95 (0-915827-14-X); pap. 39.95 (0-915827-15-8) Photo Res Inst Carson Endowment.

— Gold Book of Photography Prices, 1993. 342p. 1993. pap. 39.95 (0-915827-16-6) Photo Res Inst Carson Endowment.

— Gold Book of Photography Prices, 1994. 325p. 1994. pap. 39.95 (0-915827-17-4) Photo Res Inst Carson Endowment.

— A Guide to Making Photography Profitable. 304p. (Orig.). 1996. pap. 24.95 (0-915827-05-0) Photo Res Inst Carson Endowment.

— Nineteen Eighty-Eight Gold Book of Photography Prices. 300p. (Orig.). 1988. pap. text ed. 29.95 (0-915827-07-7) Photo Res Inst Carson Endowment.

— Nineteen Eighty-Nine Gold Book of Photography Prices. 300p. 1989. spiral bd. 39.95 (0-915827-09-3) Photo Res Inst Carson Endowment.

— 1995 Gold Book of Photography Prices. (Illus.). 328p. 1995. pap. 39.95 (0-915827-18-2) Photo Res Inst Carson Endowment.

Perrett, Thomas I., ed. Gold Book of Photography Prices, 1989. 300p. 1989. pap. write for info. (0-915827-08-5) Photo Res Inst Carson Endowment.

Perrewe, Pamela L., jt. ed. see Crandall, Rick.

Perrez, Meinrad & Reicherts, Michael. Stress, Coping, & Health: A Situation-Behavior Approach - Theory, Methods, Applications. LC 91-35352. (Illus.). 240p. 1992. text ed. 39.00 (0-88937-065-6) Hogrefe & Huber Pubs.

***Perri 6 & Randon, Anita.** Liberty, Charity & Politics: Non-Profit Law & Freedom of Speech. (Illus.). 240p. 1995. text ed. 59.95 (1-85521-507-1, Pub. by Dartmth Pub UK) Ashgate Pub Co.

Perri, Colleen A. Entrepreneurial Women: 23 Kenosha Women Share Their Success Stories. (Kenosha-My Home Town Ser.: No. 1). (Illus.). 140p. (Orig.). 1987. pap. 12.95 (0-941579-00-X) Possibilities Pub.

Perri, Collen A. Entrepreneurial Woman, Bk. 2: Twenty-One More Success Stories. (Illus.). 144p. (Orig.). 1989. pap. 12.95 (0-941579-02-6) Possibilities Pub.

Perri, Michael G., et al. Improving the Long-Term Management of Obesity: Theory, Research, & Clinical Guidelines. 320p. 1992. text ed. 52.50 (0-471-52899-4) Wiley.

***Perriam, Chris.** Desire & Dissent: An Introduction to Luis Antonio de Villena. Flower, John E., ed. (New Directions in European Writing Ser.). 160p. 1995. 39.95 (1-85973-057-4) Berg Pubs.

Perriard, J., jt. ed. see Eppenberger, H. M.

Perricone, Jack. I Like to Dream. (Illus.). 16p. (J). (ps-2). 1993. lib. bdg. 10.95 (1-879567-16-4, Valeria Bks) Wonder Well.

— Me Gusta Sonar. (Illus.). 16p. (J). (ps-2). 1993. lib. bdg. 10.95 (1-879567-17-2, Valeria Bks) Wonder Well.

Perricone, Mike. From Deadlines to Diapers: Journal of an At-Home Father. LC 92-50437. 224p. (Orig.). 1992. pap. 11.95 (1-879360-22-5) Noble Pr.

Perrie, D. W. Cloud Physics. LC 51-9779. (Scholarly Reprint Ser.). 155p. reprint ed. pap. 44.20 (0-317-08820-3, 2020512) Bks Demand.

Perrie, Maureen. The Agrarian Policy of the Russian Socialist-Revolutionary Party from Its Origins Through the Revolution of 1905-1907. LC 76-644. (Soviet & East European Studies). 228p. reprint ed. pap. 65.00 (0-8357-5263-1, 2030613) Bks Demand.

— Pretenders & Popular Monarchism in Early Modern Russia: The False Tsars of the Time of Troubles. (Illus.). 288p. (C). 1995. write for info. (*0-521-47274-1*) Cambridge U Pr.

***Perrie, W., ed.** Non-Linear Ocean Waves. (Advances in Fluid Mechanics Ser.). 300p. 1996. text ed. 118.00 (*1-85312-414-1*) Computational Mech MA.

Perrie, Walter. Roads that Move: A Journey Through Eastern Europe. (Illus.). 223p. 1992. 29.95 (*1-85158-318-1*, Pub. by Mnstream UK) Trafalgar.

Perrier, jt. auth. see Gibaldi.

Perrier, Edmond. The Earth Before History: Man's Origin & the Origin of Life. LC 76-44777. reprint ed. 24.00 (*0-404-15962-1*) AMS Pr.

Perrier, Eugene R. & Salkini, Abdul B., eds. Supplemental Irrigation in the Near East & North Africa. 628p. 1991. lib. bdg. 195.00 (*0-7923-1006-3*) Kluwer Ac.

Perrier, F., jt. auth. see Kayser, B.

Perrier, Joseph. Wind of Change: Cardinal Lavigerie, 1825-1892. 142p. 1993. 29.00 (*0-85439-435-4*, Pub. by St Paul Pubns UK) St Mut.

Perrier, Joseph L. Revival of Scholastic Philosophy in the Nineteenth Century. LC 09-10966. reprint ed. 32.50 (*0-404-04994-X*) AMS Pr.

Perrig, Alexander. Michelangelo's Drawings: The Science of Attribution. Joyce, Michael, tr. (Illus.). 320p. (C). 1991. text ed. 55.00 (*0-300-03948-4*) Yale U Pr.

Perrigo, Evelyn L. Grandies Are Great. (Illus.). 88p. 1980. pap. 5.00 (*0-933992-11-4*) Coffee Break.

Perrigo, Lynn I. Hispanos: Historic Leaders in New Mexico. LC 85-489. 128p. (Orig.). 1985. pap. 9.95 (*0-86534-011-0*) Sunstone Pr.

Perrigo, O. E. Lathe Design-Construction & Operation. 1984. reprint ed. pap. 12.95 (*0-917914-18-X*) Lindsay Pubns.

Perrild, H., jt. ed. see Ambesi-Impiombato, F. S.

Perrill, John H., jt. auth. see Dunlap, Franklin.

Perrin. The Beacon Handbook, 2 Vols. 2nd ed. (C). 1990. pap. 7.16 (*0-395-52688-4*) HM.

— The Beacon Handbook, 2 Vols. 2nd ed. (C). 1990. 89.56 (*0-395-52987-5*) HM.

Perrin, jt. ed. see Brager.

Perrin, A. F. & Meeker, M. F. Purdy: Allied Families of Purdy, Fauconnier (Falconer), Archer & Perrin. 114p. 1991. reprint ed. pap. 16.50 (*0-8328-1759-7*) Higginson Bk Co.

Perrin, Arnold. The Care & Feeding of the Prostate. 1980. pap. 1.00 (*0-939736-49-7*) Wings ME.

— The Essentials of Writing Poetry. 40p. 1992. pap. 7.95 (*0-911666-50-8*) Wings ME.

— Noah. 1993. pap. 4.00 (*0-939736-50-0*) Wings ME.

— Out of Bondage. (Illus.). 52p. 1983. pap. 4.95 (*0-939736-45-4*) Wings ME.

— Speaking Inuit. 1994. pap. 3.00 (*0-939736-51-9*) Wings ME.

— View from Hill Cabin. 1979. pap. 2.95 (*0-89002-119-8*) Wings ME.

— The Wind's Will. 24p. 1993. pap. 4.00 (*0-939736-05-5*) Wings ME.

— You Were Designed to Live for One Hundred & Forty Years. 1979. pap. 1.00 (*0-939736-06-3*) Wings ME.

Perrin, Arnold, ed. The Best of Nineteen-Eighty. 32p. (Orig.). 1981. pap. 2.95 (*0-939736-20-9*) Wings ME.

— Black Washed & Ghost Bright. 1981. pap. 2.00 (*0-939736-22-5*) Wings ME.

— Bury Me Sioux. 1982. pap. 2.00 (*0-939736-46-2*) Wings ME.

— Ecossaise. 1983. pap. 2.00 (*0-939736-47-0*) Wings ME.

— Fingers of the Wind. 1980. pap. 2.00 (*0-939736-13-6*) Wings ME.

Perrin, Carl. Successful Resumes & Interviews: Instructor's Guide. 23p. 1994. 12.00 (*0-8273-5992-6*) Delmar.

Perrin, Carl & Dublin, Peter. Successful Resumes & Interviews. LC 93-4925. 1993. 25.50 (*0-8273-5991-8*) Delmar.

***Perrin, Cathy J.** Recipes from America's Farm Kitchens. 1995. 11.90 (*0-9646525-0-1*) Perrin Prod.

Perrin, Charles E. La Societe Feodale Allemande et Ses Institutions Du Xe Au XIIe Siecle. LC 80-2013. reprint ed. 38.50 (*0-404-18583-5*) AMS Pr.

Perrin, D., jt. ed. see Gross, M.

Perrin, D., jt. ed. see Nivat, Maurice.

Perrin, D. D. Dissociation Constants of Organic Bases in Aqueous Solution, Vol. 12. 524p. 1972. 480.00 (*0-08-020827-4*, Pub. by Pergamon Repr UK) Franklin.

Perrin, D. D., ed. Ionization Constants of Inorganic Acids & Bases in Aqueous Solution, No.29. 2nd ed. (Chemical Data Ser.). 194p. 1982. 84.00 (*0-08-029214-3*, Pub. by Pergamon Repr UK) Franklin.

— Stability Constants of Metal-Ion Complexes, Pt. B: Organic Ligands. (Chemical Data Ser.: No. 22). 1280p. 1979. 513.00 (*0-08-020958-0*, Pub. by Pergamon Repr UK) Franklin.

Perrin, D. D. & Armarego, W. L. Purification of Laboratory Chemicals. 500p. 1988. pap. text ed. 48.00 (*0-08-034714-2*, Pergamon Pr) Elsevier.

Perrin, D. D. & Dempsey, B. Buffers for Pich & Metal Ion Control. 1979. pap. 25.00 (*0-412-21890-9*, NO.6218) Chapman & Hall.

Perrin, D. D., et al. Purification of Laboratory Chemicals. 2nd ed. LC 79-41708. 580p. 1980. 110.00 (*0-08-022961-1*, Pergamon Pr) Elsevier.

***Perrin, David H.** Athletic Taping & Bracing. LC 95-1519. (Illus.). 136p. 1995. text ed. write for info. (*0-87322-502-3*, BPER0502) Human Kinetics.

— Isokinetic Exercise & Assessment. LC 92-39245. (Illus.). 224p. 1993. text ed. 29.00x (*0-87322-464-7*, BPER0464) Human Kinetics.

Perrin, Dominique, jt. auth. see Berstel, Jean.

Perrin, Don, jt. auth. see Weis, Margaret.

Perrin, Fern B. To Make a Dream Come True. 198p. (Orig.). pap. 8.95 (*0-927022-04-4*) CHJ Pub.

Perrin, J. P., ed. Control, Computers, Communications in Transportation: Selected Papers from the IFAC - IFIP - IFORS Symposium, Paris, France, 19-21 September 1989. (IFAC Symposia Ser.: No. 9012). 300p. 1990. 155.00 (*0-08-037025-X*, Pergamon Pr) Elsevier.

Perrin, J. S., jt. auth. see Garner, F. A.

Perrin, James M., jt. ed. see Hobbs, Nicholas.

Perrin, James M., et al. Home & Community Care for Chronically Ill Children. 176p. 1993. 32.95 (*0-19-507120-4*) OUP.

Perrin, Janet & Howlett, Charles F. A Walk Through History: A Community Named Amityville. (Illus.). 125p. (J). (gr. 7-9). 1993. pap. text ed. write for info. (*1-55787-096-9*) Hrt of the Lakes.

Perrin-Jassy, Marie F. Basic Community in the African Churches. LC 72-93342. (Illus.). 275p. reprint ed. pap. 78.40 (*0-8357-8813-X*, 2033466) Bks Demand.

Perrin, Jean. Atoms. Hammick, D. L., tr. LC 90-42918. xvi, 232p. 1990. reprint ed. 42.00 (*0-918024-78-1*); reprint ed. pap. 17.50 (*0-918024-79-X*) Ox Bow.

Perrin, Jean P. History of the Ancient Christians Inhabiting the Valleys of the Alps. 1991. reprint ed. 24.00 (*0-685-40812-4*) Church History.

Perrin, Jim, ed. Eric Shipton: The Six Mountain-Travel Books. LC 84-62263. (Illus.). 800p. 1985. 38.00 (*0-89886-075-X*) Mountaineers.

— Mirrors in the Cliffs: A Hundred Mountaineering Articles. (Illus.). 688p. 1983. 29.95 (*0-906371-95-3*, Pub. by H & S UK) Trafalgar.

Perrin, Marshall L., tr. see Von Sybel, Heinrich.

Perrin, Michel. The Way of the Dead Indians: Guajiro Myths & Symbols. Fineberg, Michael, tr. (Sourcebooks in Anthropology: No. 13). (Illus.). 229p. 1987. text ed. 30.00 (*0-292-79032-5*); pap. 14.95 (*0-292-79039-2*) U of Tex Pr.

Perrin, Nat. Celebration: Manuscript Edition. 1964. pap. 13.00 (*0-8222-0194-1*) Dramatists Play.

Perrin, Noel. Amateur Sugar Maker. 20th aniversary ed. LC 91-50818. (Illus.). 120p. 1992. pap. 9.95 (*0-87451-579-3*) U Pr of New Eng.

— Dr. Bowdler's Legacy: A History of Expurgated Books in England & America. 320p. 1992. pap. 14.95 (*0-87923-861-5*) Godine.

— First Person Rural: Essays of a Sometime Farmer. LC 77-94109. 124p. 1990. reprint ed. pap. 12.95 (*0-87923-833-X*) Godine.

— Giving up the Gun. LC 80-50744. 122p. 1980. pap. 6.95 (*0-394-73949-3*) Random.

— Giving up the Gun: Japan's Reversion to the Sword, 1543-1879. LC 78-74252. (Illus.). 96p. 1978. pap. 10.95 (*0-87923-773-2*) Godine.

— Last Person Rural. 1991. 21.95 (*0-87923-914-X*) Godine.

— Last Person Rural. large type ed. 320p. 1992. reprint ed. bds. 21.95 (*1-56054-364-7*) Thorndike Pr.

— Life with an Electric Car. LC 94-6309. Orig. Title: Solo. 216p. 1994. reprint ed. 12.00 (*0-87156-497-1*) Sierra.

— A Noel Perrin Sampler. LC 90-50907. 153p. 1991. 22.50 (*0-87451-551-3*); pap. 12.95 (*0-87451-676-5*) U Pr of New Eng.

— A Noel Perrin Sampler. braille ed. 303p. 1993. vinyl bd. 24.24 (*1-56956-379-9*, BR9139) W A T Braille.

— A Reader's Delight. LC 87-40507. 220p. 1988. 25.00 (*0-87451-430-4*); pap. 12.95 (*0-87451-432-0*) U Pr of New Eng.

— Second Person Rural: More Essays of a Sometime Farmer. LC 80-66193. 152p. 1990. reprint ed. pap. 9.95 (*0-87923-834-8*) Godine.

— Solo: Life with an Electric Car. 192p. 1992. 18.95 (*0-393-03407-0*) Norton.

Perrin, Norman. Resurrection According to Matthew, Mark, & Luke. LC 76-47913. 96p. (Orig.). 1977. pap. 9.00 (*0-8006-1248-5*, 1-1248, Fortress Pr) Augsburg Fortress.

— What Is Redaction Criticism? Via, Dan O., Jr., ed. LC 72-81529. (Guides to Biblical Scholarship Ser.). 96p. (Orig.). 1969. pap. 8.00 (*0-8006-0181-5*, 1-181, Fortress Pr) Augsburg Fortress.

Perrin, Norman, jt. auth. see Duling, Dennis C.

Perrin, Norman, et al. The New Testament: An Introduction. 2nd ed. (Illus.). 516p. (Orig.). (C). 1982. pap. text ed. 22.00 (*0-15-565726-7*) HB Coll Pubs.

Perrin, Pat, jt. auth. see Coleman, Wim.

Perrin, Penelope. Russia. LC 93-30422. (Discovering Our Universe Ser.). (Illus.). 32p. (J). (gr. 4 up). 1994. text ed. 13.95 (*0-89686-775-7*, Crstwood Hse) Silver Burdett Pr.

Perrin, Porter G. Reference Handbook of Grammar & Usage. 1972. 12.95 (*0-688-00061-4*) Morrow.

Perrin, Rob, ed. Journal of Roman Pottery Studies, Vol. 4, 1991. (Illus.). 124p. 1992. pap. 21.00 (*0-946897-41-7*, Pub. by Oxbow Bks UK) David Brown.

Perrin, Robert G. Herbert Spencer: A Primary & Secondary Bibliography, 2 vols., Set. LC 93-12108. 1024p. 1993. 145.00 (*0-8240-4597-1*, H1061) Garland.

Perrin, Robert G., jt. auth. see Nisbet, Robert A.

Perrin, Robert G., jt. auth. see Nisbet, Robert.

Perrin, Ron. Max Scheler's Concept of the Person: An Ethics of Humanism. LC 90-43341. 176p. 1991. text ed. 39.95 (*0-312-05308-8*) St Martin.

Perrin, Sandra. Organic Gardening in Cold Climates. (Illus.). 156p. 1991. pap. 10.00 (*0-87842-275-7*) Mountain Pr.

Perrin, Steve. Elfquest: The Official Roleplaying Game. 2nd ed. Chodak, Yurek, ed. (Elfquest Roleplaying Game System Ser.). (Illus.). 192p. (YA). (gr. 9 up). 1989. pap. 19.95 (*0-933635-54-0*, 2605) Chaosium.

— Voice of Doom. 32p. (Orig.). (YA). (gr. 10-12). 1987. pap. 6.00 (*0-915795-80-9*, 38) Iron Crown Ent Inc.

Perrin, Steve, jt. auth. see St. Andre, Ken.

***Perrin, Stuart.** The Dancing Man: A Deeper Sense of Surrender. 145p. (Orig.). (YA). 1993. pap. 10.00 (*0-9638401-0-X*) Carvalhosa Grap.

— Leah: A Story of Meditation & Healing. Ribush, Nicholas, ed. LC 88-62125. (Healing Ser.). 120p. 1988. text ed. 15.95 (*0-86171-088-6*) Wisdom MA.

Perrin, Suzanne M. Comparable Worth & Public Policy: The Case of Pennsylvania. LC 85-51721. (Labor Relations & Public Policy Ser.: No. 29). 136p. reprint ed. pap. 38.80 (*0-8357-3155-3*, 2039418) Bks Demand.

Perrin, Thomas W. I Am an Adult Who Grew up in an Alcoholic Family. 144p. (Orig.). 1991. pap. 8.95 (*0-8245-1319-3*) Crossroad NY.

Perrin, Tom. Atlantic Coast Conference Football: A History Through 1991. LC 92-50315. 480p. 1992. lib. bdg. 43.50x (*0-89950-749-2*) McFarland & Co.

— Football: A College History. LC 87-43029. 438p. 1987. lib. bdg. 32.50x (*0-89950-294-6*) McFarland & Co.

***Perrin, Towers.** Handbook of Executive Benefits. LC 94-32794. 336p. 1995. 75.00 (*0-7863-0185-6*) Irwin Prof Pubng.

Perrin, Ursula. The Looking-Glass Lover: A Novel. 256p. 1989. 17.95 (*0-316-69961-6*) Little.

Perrin, W. H. History of Todd County, Kentucky. Battle, J. H., ed. 385p. 1979. reprint ed. 35.00 (*0-89308-162-0*) Southern Hist Pr.

— History of Trigg County, Historical & Biographical. (Illus.). 293p. 1979. 32.50 (*0-89308-164-7*) Southern Hist Pr.

— Southwest Louisiana. 1971. 30.00 (*0-87511-094-0*) Claitors.

Perrin, Wes. Advertising Realities: A Practical Guide to Agency Management. 184p. (C). 1991. pap. text ed. 19.95 (*0-87484-999-3*) Mayfield Pub.

Perrin, William H. County of Christian, Kentucky. (Illus.). 656p. 1993. reprint ed. lib. bdg. 66.00 (*0-8328-2943-9*) Higginson Bk Co.

— History of Stark County, Ohio. 1012p. 1993. reprint ed. lib. bdg. 105.00 (*0-8328-3443-2*) Higginson Bk Co.

— History of Trigg County, Kentucky. (Illus.). 324p. 1994. reprint ed. pap. text ed. 22.50 (*0-7884-0040-1*) Heritage Bk.

Perrin, William H., ed. Christian County Kentucky, Historical & Biographical. 344p. 1993. reprint ed. pap. text ed. 26.50 (*1-55613-825-3*) Heritage Bk.

— History of Effingham County, Illinois. (Illus.). 628p. 1993. reprint ed. lib. bdg. 65.00 (*0-8328-3232-4*) Higginson Bk Co.

— History of Summit County Ohio. 1050p. 1993. reprint ed. lib. bdg. 99.50 (*0-8328-3462-9*) Higginson Bk Co.

***Perrine, Doug.** Sharks. LC 94-42427. 1995. write for info. (*0-89658-270-1*) Voyageur Pr.

Perrine, H. D. Daniel Perrin, "the Huguenot", & His Descendants in America of the Surnames Perrine, Perine, & Prine, 1665-1910. (Illus.). 553p. 1989. reprint ed. lib. bdg. 79.00 (*0-8328-0956-X*); reprint ed. pap. 69.00 (*0-8328-0957-8*) Higginson Bk Co.

Perrine, James O. Slide Rule Handbook. 112p. (C). 1965. 45.00 (*0-677-01060-5*) Gordon & Breach.

Perrine, Laurence. Dimensions of Drama. 567p. (C). 1973. pap. text ed. 24.00 (*0-15-517655-2*) HB Coll Pubs.

— Sense & Nonsense: Original Limericks by Laurence Perrine. LC 93-42068. 64p. (Orig.). 1994. pap. 10.00 (*0-914061-41-0*) Orchises Pr.

— Sound & Sense: An Introduction to Poetry. 7th ed. 345p. (C). 1987. teacher ed, pap. text ed. 2.25 (*0-15-582609-3*) HB Coll Pubs.

Perrine, Laurence & Aro, Thomas R. Literature: Structure, Sound & Sense. 5th ed. 1441p. (C). 1988. text ed. 32.00 (*0-15-551108-4*) HB Coll Pubs.

Perrine, Laurence & Arp, Thomas R. Literature: Structure, Sound, & Sense. 6th ed. 1450p. (C). 1993. text ed. 32.00 (*0-15-551070-3*) HB Coll Pubs.

— Sound & Sense: An Introduction to Poetry. 3rd ed. 350p. (C). 1992. pap. text ed. 3.00 (*0-15-565732-1*) HB Coll Pubs.

— Sound & Sense: An Introduction to Poetry. 8th ed. 350p. (C). 1992. pap. text ed. 21.50 (*0-15-582610-7*) HB Coll Pubs.

— Story & Structure. 8th ed. 663p. (C). 1993. text ed. 21.50 (*0-15-583792-3*) HB Coll Pubs.

Perrine, Laurence, et al. Into the Limerick Grove: 156 Original Limericks by Contemporary Authors. LC 93-60841. (Illus.). 112p. (Orig.). 1993. pap. 6.95 (*1-880964-04-X*) Zapizdat Pubns.

Perrine, Mary. Nannabah's Friend. (Illus.). 32p. (J). (gr. k-3). 1989. pap. 5.95 (*0-395-52020-7*) HM.

***Perrine, Susie.** Follow the Fun: Places to Go, Things to Do: Las Vegas. (Illus.). 100p. (Orig.). (J). 1995. pap. 9.95 (*1-885511-00-0*) Las Vegas Pubng.

Perring, Christina, et al. Families Caring for People Diagnosed As Mentally Ill. (Social Policy Research Unit Paper Ser.). 64p. 1990. pap. 16.00 (*0-11-701495-8*, HM4958) UNIPUB.

Perring, Christine M. The Experience of Psychiatric Hospital Closure: An Anthropological Study. (Studies of Care in the Community). 231p. 1993. pap. 59.95 (*1-85628-422-0*, Pub. by Avebury Pub UK) Ashgate Pub Co.

Perring, Dominic. Roman London. (Illus.). 150p. 1991. 39.95 (*1-85264-039-1*, Pub. by Seaby UK) Trafalgar.

Perring, Dominic, jt. auth. see Perring, Stefania.

Perring, F. H. & Mellanby, K. Ecological Effects of Pesticide. (Linnean Society Symposium Ser.). 1978. text ed. 109.00 (*0-12-551350-X*) Acad Pr.

Perring, Stefania & Perring, Dominic. Then & Now: The Wonders of the Ancient World Brought to Life in Vivid See-Through Reconstructions. (Illus.). 144p. 1991. text ed. 27.50 (*0-02-599461-1*) Macmillan.

***Perrings, C. A., et al, eds.** Biodiversity Conservation: Problems & Policies. LC 94-32553. (Ecology, Economy & Environment Ser.: Vol. 4). 416p. (C). 1994. lib. bdg. 170.00 (*0-7923-3140-0*) Kluwer Ac.

Perrings, Charles. Economy & Environment: A Theoretical Essay on the Interdependence of Economics & Environmental Systems. 180p. 1987. 64.95 (*0-521-34081-0*) Cambridge U Pr.

***Perrings, Charles, et al, eds.** Biodiversity Loss: Economic & Ecological Issues. (Illus.). 320p. (C). 1995. 54.95 (*0-521-47178-8*) Cambridge U Pr.

Perrino, Anthony F. Holyquest. LC 88-63124. 162p. (Orig.). (C). 1988. pap. 8.00 (*0-931104-24-6*) Sunflower Ink.

— The Numbering of Our Days. (Mediation Manuals Ser.). (Orig.). 1988. pap. 3.00 (*0-933840-33-0*) Unitarian Univ.

— One Hundred Percent Half Right. LC 90-31915. 160p. (Orig.). 1990. pap. 9.95 (*0-936784-84-9*) J Daniel.

Perrino, Karen, jt. auth. see Neff, Rena.

Perrins, Bryan. Trade Union Law. 1985. 70.00 (*0-406-25830-9*); U.K. pap. 48.00 (*0-406-25831-7*) Butterworth Legal Pubs.

Perrins, C. M., jt. auth. see Cramp, Stanley.

Perrins, C. M., jt. ed. see Cramp, Stanley.

Perrins, Christopher. New Generation Guide to the Birds of Britain & Europe. (Corrie Herring Hooks Ser.: No. 8). (Illus.). 320p. 1987. 16.95 (*0-292-75532-5*) U of Tex Pr.

Perrins, Christopher & Middleton, Alex L., eds. The Encyclopedia of Birds. (Illus.). 480p. 1985. 45.00 (*0-8160-1150-8*) Facts on File.

Perrins, Christopher, jt. auth. see Birkhead, Michael.

Perrins, Christopher M. The Illustrated Encyclopedia of Birds: The Definitive Reference to Birds of the World. (Illus.). 420p. 1991. 50.00 (*0-13-083635-4*) P-H.

Perrins, Christopher M., jt. ed. see Cramp, Stanley.

Perrins, Christopher M., et al, eds. Bird Population Studies: Relevance to Conservation & Management. (Ornithology Ser.: No. 1). (Illus.). 704p. 1993. pap. 37.50 (*0-19-854082-5*) OUP.

Perrins, Lesley. How Paper Is Made. (How It Is Made Ser.). (Illus.). 32p. (YA). (gr. 7 up). 1986. 12.95 (*0-8160-0036-0*) Facts on File.

Perris, Arnold. Music As Propaganda: Art to Persuade, Art to Control. LC 84-27969. (Contributions to the Study of Music & Dance Ser.: No. 8). x, 247p. 1985. text ed. 49.95 (*0-313-24505-3*, PMP/, Greenwood Pr) Greenwood.

Perris, C., et al, eds. Clinical Neurophysiological Aspects of Psychopathological Conditions. (Advances in Biological Psychiatry Ser.: Vol. 4). (Illus.). viii, 192p. 1980. pap. 49.00 (*3-8055-0604-X*) S Karger.

— Neurophysiological Correlates of Normal Cognition & Psychopathology. (Advances in Biological Psychiatry Ser.: Vol. 13). (Illus.). viii, 232p. 1984. pap. 78.50 (*3-8055-3737-9*) S Karger.

Perris, Carlo. Cognitive Therapy with Schizophrenic Patients. LC 88-24467. 240p. 1989. lib. bdg. 32.00 (*0-89862-737-0*) Guilford Pr.

Perris, Carlo, et al, eds. Parenting & Psychopathology. LC 94-11557. (Clinical Psychology Ser.). 1995. text ed. 49.95 (*0-471-94226-X*) Wiley.

Perris, Carlo, et al. Biological Psychiatry, Nineteen Eighty-One. (Developments in Psychiatry Ser.: Vol. 5). 1982. 300.50 (*0-444-80404-8*) Elsevier.

Perris, Carlo, et al, eds. Cognitive Psychotherapy. (Illus.). 480p. 1988. 111.00 (*0-387-18870-3*) Spr-Verlag.

Perris, Liz & Padrick, Kevin, eds. Bankruptcy Law. 1988. write for info. (*0-318-61748-X*) OR Bar CLE.

Perrissoud, D. & Testa, B., eds. Liver Drugs: From Experimental Pharmacology to Therapeutic Application. 288p. 1988. 216.00 (*0-8493-6734-4*, RC846) CRC Pr.

Perritt, Gerald & Lavine, Alan. Diversify Your Way to Wealth: How to Customize Your Investment Portfolio to Protect & Build. 1993. 22.95 (*1-55738-546-7*) Probus Pub Co.

Perritt, Gerald W. Dollars & Sense: Financial Wisdom in 101 Doses. 312p. 1986. pap. 18.95 (*0-685-14685-5*) Invest Info.

— Expand Your Investment Horizons & Increase Your Stock Market Profits. 288p. 1987. 24.95 (*0-930369-02-5*); pap. 19.95 (*0-930369-03-3*) Invest Info.

— Mutual Funds & Your Investment Portfolio. 2nd ed. 129p. 1987. pap. 8.95 (*0-930369-18-1*) Invest Info.

— Mutual Funds Made Easy! 1995. pap. 9.95 (*0-7931-1335-0*) Dearborn Finan.

— Small Stocks Big Profits: Gerald Perritt on Investing in Small Companies. 304p. 1993. reprint ed. pap. 17.95 (*0-7931-0635-4*, 560883) Dearborn Finan.

Perritt, Henry H. Americans with Disabilities Act Formbook, Vol. 2. 2nd ed. 1994. text ed. 110.00 (*0-471-30919-2*) Wiley.

— Americans with Disabilities Act Handbook. 2nd ed. (Employment Law Library: No. 1816). 576p. 1991. text ed. 128.00 (*0-471-55636-X*) Wiley.

— Americans with Disabilities Act Handbook, 2 vols., Vol. 2. 2nd ed. (Employment Law Library). 1994. text ed. 238.00 (*0-471-01634-9*) Wiley.

***Perritt, Henry H., Jr.** Civil Rights in the Workplace, 2 vols, Vol. 2. 2nd rev. ed. Incl. Vol. 1. Civil Rights in the Workplace. 2nd rev. ed. LC 94-36366. 1994. (*0-471-10626-7*, Pub. by Wiley Law Pubns); Vol.2. Civil Rights in the Workplace. 2nd rev. ed. LC 94-36366. 1994. (*0-471-10624-0*, Pub. by Wiley Law Pubns); LC 94-36366. (Employment Law Library). 1994. Set text ed. 218.00 (*0-471-10632-1*, Pub. by Wiley Law Pubns) Wiley.

Perritt, Henry H. Employee Benefits Claims: Law & Practice. (Employment Law Library). 529p. 1990. text ed. 128.00 (*0-471-62073-4*) Wiley.

— Employee Benefits Claims: Law & Practice. suppl. ed. (Employment Law Library). 96p. 1990. 50.00 (*0-471-57702-2*) Wiley.

P
Q

— Employee Dismissal Law & Practice, 2 vols., 1. 3rd suppl. ed. (Employment Law Library: No. 1816). 136p. 1992. 85.00 (*0-471-57706-5*) Wiley.

— Employee Dismissal Law & Practice, 2 vols., Vol. 2. 3rd ed. (Employment Law Library: No. 1816). 1992. Set. text ed. 238.00 (*0-471-54686-0*) Wiley.

— How to Practice Law with Computers Plus 1990 Supplement. 779p. 1988. text ed. 110.00 (*0-685-46012-6*, G6-1014) PLI.

— Labor Injunctions. LC 86-5639. (Federal Practice Ser.). 730p. 1986. text ed. 125.00 (*0-471-81330-3*) Wiley.

— Labor Injunctions: 1992 Cumulative Supplement Current Through July 20, 1991. 160p. 1991. pap. text ed. 65.00 (*0-471-55778-1*) Wiley.

— Wiley Employment Law Update, 1993. (Employment Law Library). 432p. 1992. pap. text ed. 110.00 (*0-471-58519-X*) Wiley.

— Workplace Torts: Rights & Liabilities. (Employment Law Library). 431p. 1991. text ed. 138.00 (*0-471-51342-3*) Wiley.

Perritt, Henry H., Jr. Your Rights in the Workplace: Everything Employees Need to Know. 1993. pap. 14.95 (*0-87224-049-5*) PLI.

Perritt, Henry H., jt. auth. see Baum, Michael S.

Perritt, Henry H., jt. auth. see Villanova University. Center for Continuing Legal Education Staff.

***Perritt, Henry R.** Wiley Employment Law Update, 1995. (Employment Law Library). 1995. text ed. 115.00 (*0-471-09011-5*) Wiley.

Perrolle, Pierre M., ed. Fundamentals of the Chinese Communist Party. Richardson, Lloyd & Richardson, Chung, trs. LC 75-46228. (China Book Project Ser.). 253p. reprint ed. 72.20 (*0-8357-9435-0*, 2016134) Bks Demand.

Perron, Charles. Normal Accidents: Living with High-Risk Technologies. LC 83-45256. 400p. 1985. pap. text ed. 18.50 (*0-465-05142-1*) Basic.

Perron, Frank E., jt. auth. see Kohn, Alan J.

Perron, John D., jt. auth. see Capron, H. L.

Perron, Lee. Seeking the Hills. 64p. 1992. lib. bdg. 25.00 (*0-9620634-5-2*); pap. 10.00 (*0-9620634-3-6*) Sun Moon Bear Pr.

— Seeking the Hills. limited ed. (Illus.). 64p. 1992. 50.00 (*0-9620634-4-4*) Sun Moon Bear Pr.

— The White Bones of the Year Are Scattered among Jonquils. (Illus.). 52p. 1988. pap. 35.00 (*0-9620634-0-1*) Sun Moon Bear Pr.

Perron, Madeleine. French - English Vocabulary Related to Tax Returns. 37p. (ENG & FRE.). 1988. pap. 19.95 (*0-8288-9408-6*) Fr & Eur.

Perron, Paul & Collins, Frank, eds. Paris School Semiotics: I. Theory. LC 88-24058. (Semiotic Crossroads Ser.). xxviii, 258p. 1989. 76.00x (*1-55619-040-9*) Benjamins North Am.

— Paris School Semiotics II: Practice. LC 88-24058. (Semiotic Crossroads Ser.: No. 3). xvi, 225p. 1989. 71.00x (*1-55619-041-7*) Benjamins North Am.

Perron, Paul, tr. see Greimas, Algirdas J.

Perron, Paul, tr. see Greimas, Algirdas J. & Fontanille, Jacques.

Perron, Robert, jt. auth. see Gauthier-Lafaye, Jean.

Perron, Robert E. The Adventures of Bum & Carey Bear: A Christmas Tale. (Illus.). 48p. (J). 1994. pap. 8.00 (*0-8059-3578-9*) Dorrance.

Perrone, Bobette, et al. Medicine Women Curanderas & Women Doctors. LC 89-4901. (Illus.). 272p. (C). 1993. pap. 12.95 (*0-8061-2512-8*) U of Okla Pr.

Perrone, Charles A. Masters of Contemporary Brazilian Song: MPB, 1965-1985. (Illus.). 293p. 1989. 27.95 (*0-292-75102-8*) U of Tex Pr.

— Masters of Contemporary Brazilian Song: MPB 1965-1985. (Illus.). 293p. (Orig.). (C). 1993. pap. 15.95 (*0-292-76550-9*) U of Tex Pr.

Perrone, Charles A., tr. see Espinola, Adriano.

Perrone, Ed. Astrology: A New Age Guide. LC 83-70690. 219p. (Orig.). 1983. pap. 8.95 (*0-8356-0579-5*, Quest) Theos Pub Hse.

Perrone, Jeff. Ken Price. Thomas, Sissy & Thompson, Lauri, eds. (Illus.). 40p. 1989. 15.00 (*0-942779-01-0*) Greenberg Gallery.

Perrone, Jeff, contrib. Jennifer Bartlett - Recent Work. LC 88-61642. (Illus.). 40p. (Orig.). 1988. pap. 8.00 (*0-944110-16-9*) Milwauk Art Mus.

Perrone, Jeff & Schjeldahl, Peter. Adrian Saxe. (Illus.). 20p. (Orig.). 1987. pap. text ed. 8.00 (*0-914489-05-4*) Univ Miss-KS Art.

Perrone, Lisbeth. Country Christmas Cross-Stitch. (Illus.). 192p. 1986. write for info. (*0-02-595920-4*) Macmillan.

— The New World of Needlepoint: 101 Exciting Designs in Bargello, Quickpoint, Grospoint & Other Repeat Patterns. (Illus.). 1972. 12.95 (*0-394-47265-9*) Random.

— Woman's Day Christmas Cross-Stitch. LC 83-60328. (Illus.). 144p. 1983. write for info. (*0-02-496620-7*) Macmillan.

Perrone, N., jt. ed. see Herrmann, G.

Perrone, Nicholas. Dynamic Response of Biomechanical Systems: Papers Presented at the Winter Annual Meeting of the ASME, N.Y, N.Y., Dec. 2, 1970. LC 78-143213. 156p. reprint ed. pap. 44.50 (*0-317-08321-X*, 2016913) Bks Demand.

Perrone, Nicholas & Pilkey, W., eds. Structural Mechanics Software Series, 5 vols., Vol. 1. LC 77-641779. 640p. 1977. reprint ed. pap. 172.80 (*0-8357-2719-X*, 2039833) Bks Demand.

— Structural Mechanics Software Series, 5 vols., Vol. 2. LC 77-641779. 466p. 1978. reprint ed. pap. 132.90 (*0-8357-2720-3*) Bks Demand.

— Structural Mechanics Software Series, 5 vols., Vol. 3. LC 77-641779. 352p. 1980. reprint ed. pap. 100.40 (*0-8357-2721-1*) Bks Demand.

— Structural Mechanics Software Series, 5 vols., Vol. 4. LC 77-641779. 476p. 1982. reprint ed. pap. 135.70 (*0-8357-2722-X*) Bks Demand.

— Structural Mechanics Software Series, 5 vols., Vol. 5. LC 77-641779. 350p. 1984. reprint ed. pap. 99.80 (*0-8357-2723-8*) Bks Demand.

Perrone, Nicholas, ed. see Applied Mechanics, Bioengineering & Fluids Engineering Conference Staff.

Perrone, Nicholas, ed. see Symposium on Naval Structural Mechanics Staff.

***Perrone, Steve, ed. & pref.** Discovering & Exploring New Jersey's Fishing Streams & the Deleware River. (Illus.). 152p. (Orig.). Date not set. pap. 10.95 (*1-887544-00-3*) NJ Sportsmens Guides.

— New Jersey Lake Survey Fishing Maps Guide. 5th rev. ed. (Illus.). 128p. Date not set. pap. 9.95 (*1-887544-01-1*) NJ Sportsmens Guides.

Perrone, Vito. The Abuses of Standardized Testing. LC 77-72589. (Fastback Ser.: No. 92). (C). 1977. pap. 1.25 (*0-87367-092-2*) Phi Delta Kappa.

— A Letter to Teachers: Reflections on Schooling & the Art of Teaching. LC 90-19890. (Education-Higher Education Ser.). 166p. 1991. 29.95 (*1-55542-327-2*); pap. 16.95 (*1-55542-313-2*) Jossey-Bass.

— 101 Educational Conversations You Should Have with Your Child, 12 vols., Set. (Illus.). 112p. 1993. lib. bdg. 175.45 (*0-7910-1917-9*, Am Art Analog) Chelsea Hse.

— 101 Educational Conversations You Should Have with Your Fifth Grader. (101 Educational Conversations You Should Have with Your Child Ser.). (Illus.). 112p. 1993. lib. bdg. 15.95 (*0-7910-1921-7*, Am Art Analog); pap. 5.95 (*0-7910-1987-X*) Chelsea Hse.

— 101 Educational Conversations You Should Have with Your Fourth Grader. (101 Educational Conversations You Should Have with Your Child Ser.). (Illus.). 112p. 1993. lib. bdg. 15.95 (*0-7910-1920-9*, Am Art Analog); pap. 5.95 (*0-7910-1985-3*) Chelsea Hse.

— 101 Educational Conversations You Should Have with Your Kindergartner-First Grader. (101 Educational Conversations You Should Have with Your Child Ser.). (Illus.). 112p. 1993. lib. bdg. 15.95 (*0-7910-1918-7*, Am Art Analog); pap. 5.95 (*0-7910-1981-0*) Chelsea Hse.

— 101 Educational Conversations You Should Have with Your Second Grader. (101 Educational Conversations You Should Have with Your Child Ser.). (Illus.). 112p. 1993. lib. bdg. 15.95 (*0-7910-1937-3*, Am Art Analog); pap. 5.95 (*0-7910-1982-9*) Chelsea Hse.

— 101 Educational Conversations You Should Have with Your Seventh Grader. (101 Educational Conversations You Should Have with Your Child Ser.). (Illus.). 112p. 1993. lib. bdg. 15.95 (*0-7910-1923-3*) Chelsea Hse.

— 101 Educational Conversations You Should Have with Your Sixth Grader. (101 Educational Conversations You Should Have with Your Child Ser.). (Illus.). 112p. 1994. lib. bdg. 15.95 (*0-7910-1922-5*, Am Art Analog); pap. 5.95 (*0-7910-1989-6*) Chelsea Hse.

— 101 Educational Conversations You Should Have with Your Third Grader. (101 Educational Conversations You Should Have with Your Child Ser.). (Illus.). 112p. 1993. lib. bdg. 15.95 (*0-7910-1919-5*, Am Art Analog); pap. 5.95 (*0-7910-1984-5*) Chelsea Hse.

— 101 Educational Conversations with Your Twelfth Grader. (One-Hundred-One Educational Conversations You Should Have with Your Child Ser.). 112p. 1995. 15.95 (*0-7910-1928-4*); pap. 5.95 (*0-7910-2016-9*) Chelsea Hse.

— 101 Educational Conversations with Your Seventh Grader: A Parent's Guide. (101 Educational Conversations You Should Have with Your Child Ser.). pap. 5.95 (*0-7910-2011-8*) Chelsea Hse.

— 101 Educational Conversations with Your Eighth Grader. (One-Hundred-One Educational Conversations You Should Have with Your Child Ser.). 112p. 1995. 15.95 (*0-7910-1924-1*) Chelsea Hse.

— 101 Educational Conversations with Your Eighth Grader: A Parent's Guide. (101 Educational Conversations You Should Have with Your Child Ser.). 80p. pap. 5.95 (*0-7910-2012-6*) Chelsea Hse.

— 101 Educational Conversations with Your Ninth Grader. (One-Hundred-One Educational Conversations You Should Have with Your Child Ser.). 112p. 1995. 15.95 (*0-7910-1925-X*); pap. 5.95 (*0-7910-2013-4*) Chelsea Hse.

— 101 Educational Conversations with Your Tenth Grader. (One-Hundred-One Educational Conversations You Should Have with Your Child Ser.). 112p. 1995. 15.95 (*0-7910-1926-8*); pap. 5.95 (*0-7910-2014-2*) Chelsea Hse.

— 101 Educational Conversations with Your Eleventh Grader. (One-Hundred-One Educational Conversations You Should Have with Your Child Ser.). 112p. 1995. 15.95 (*0-7910-1927-6*); pap. 5.95 (*0-7910-2015-0*) Chelsea Hse.

— Working Papers: Reflections on Teachers, Schools, & Communities. 256p. (C). 1989. text ed. 34.95 (*0-8077-2945-0*); pap. text ed. 18.95 (*0-8077-2944-2*) Tchrs Coll.

Perrone, Vito, ed. Portraits of High School. LC 85-12809. 658p. 1985. pap. text ed. 22.50 (*0-931050-27-8*) Carnegie Fnd Advan Teach.

— Visions of Peace. (Illus.). 90p. 1988. pap. 5.00 (*0-940237-02-4*) ND Qtr Pr.

***Perrone, Vito, intro.** J. Edgar Hoover. (Library of Biography). (Illus.). 128p. (YA). (gr. 5 up). 1995. 18.95 (*0-7910-1735-4*) Chelsea Hse.

— Joseph Smith. (Library of Biography). (Illus.). 128p. (YA). (gr. 5 up). 1995. 18.95 (*0-7910-1747-8*) Chelsea Hse.

— Martha Graham. (Library of Biography). (Illus.). 128p. (YA). (gr. 5 up). 1995. 18.95 (*0-7910-1733-8*) Chelsea Hse.

— Muhammad. (Library of Biography). (Illus.). 128p. (YA). (gr. 5 up). 1995. 18.95 (*0-7910-1743-5*) Chelsea Hse.

— Norman Schwarzkopf. (Library of Biography). (Illus.). 128p. (YA). (gr. 5 up). 1995. pap. 7.95 (*0-7910-1726-5*) Chelsea Hse.

— Sam Walton. (Library of Biography). (Illus.). 128p. (YA). (gr. 5 up). 1995. 18.95 (*0-7910-1723-0*) Chelsea Hse.

— William Lloyd Garrison. (Library of Biography). (Illus.). 128p. (YA). (gr. 5 up). 1995. 18.95 (*0-7910-1731-1*) Chelsea Hse.

— William Penn. (Library of Biography). (Illus.). 128p. (YA). (gr. 5 up). 1995. 18.95 (*0-7910-1746-X*) Chelsea Hse.

— William Shakespeare. (Library of Biography). (Illus.). 128p. (YA). (gr. 5 up). 1995. 18.95 (*0-7910-2675-2*) Chelsea Hse.

Perrons, Diane, jt. ed. see Shaw, Jenny.

Perros, Harry G. Queuing Networks with Blocking. 288p. 1994. 49.95 (*0-19-508580-9*) OUP.

Perros, Harry G., ed. High-Speed Communication Networks. LC 92-26600. 1992. 79.50 (*0-306-44257-4*, Plenum Pr) Plenum.

Perros, Harry G. & Altiok, T., eds. Queing Networks with Blocking: Proceedings of the First International Workshop, Raliegh, NC, 20-21 May 1988. 358p. 1989. 89.75 (*0-444-87484-4*, North Holland) Elsevier.

Perros, Harry G. & Viniotis, Yannis, eds. High Speed Networks & Their Performance: Proceedings of the IFIP TC6 Task Force Fifth International Conference. LC 94-2623. (IFIP Transactions C: Communication Systems Ser.: Vol. C-21). 1994. write for info. (*0-444-81721-2*, North Holland) Elsevier.

Perros, Harry G., et al, eds. Modelling & Performance Evaluation of ATM Technology: Proceedings of the IFIP TC6 Task Group - WG6.4 International Workshop on Performance of Communication Systems, Martinique, French Caribbean Island. LC 93-22898. (IFIP Transactions C: Communication Systems Ser.: Vol. 15). 1993. write for info. (*0-444-81512-0*, North Holland) Elsevier.

Perrot, jt. auth. see Fraisse.

Perrot, D. V. Teach Yourself Swahili Dictionary. (Teach Yourself Ser.). (SWA.). 1978. 10.00 (*0-679-10015-6*) McKay.

Perrot, Dominique, jt. auth. see Preiswork, Roy.

Perrot, George, et al. Exploration Archeologique de la Galatie et de la Bithynie, d'une Partie de la Mysie, de la Phrygie, de la Cappadocie et du Pont, Set. 394p. reprint ed. write for info. (*3-487-07404-4*, Pub. by Georg Olms GW) Lubrecht & Cramer.

— Exploration Archeologique de la Galatie et de la Bithynie, d'une Partie de la Mysie, de la Phrygie, de la Cappadocie et du Pont, Vol. 1. 394p. 1983. reprint ed. write for info. (*3-487-07405-2*, Pub. by Georg Olms GW) Lubrecht & Cramer.

— Exploration Archeologique de la Galatie et de la Bithynie, d'une Partie de la Mysie, de la Phrygie, de la Cappadocie et du Pont, Vol. 2. 394p. Date not set. reprint ed. write for info. (*3-487-07406-0*, Pub. by Georg Olms GW) Lubrecht & Cramer.

Perrot, Georges. A History of Art in Ancient Egypt, 2 vols. Armstrong, Walter, ed. 1976. lib. bdg. 200.00 (*0-8490-1969-9*) Gordon Pr.

Perrot, Jean, jt. auth. see Magnusson, Boris.

Perrot, Jean-Claude & Woolf, Stuart J. State & Statistics in France, Seventeen Eighty-Nine to Eighteen Fifteen. (Social Orders Ser.: Vol. 2). 194p. 1984. text ed. 69.00 (*3-7186-0201-6*) Gordon & Breach.

Perrot, M. De, ed. European Security. 343p. 1984. pap. 153.00 (*0-08-031322-1*, Pub. by Pergamon Repr UK) Franklin.

Perrot, Michelle. A History of Private Life, Vol. 4: From the Fires of Revolution to the Great War, Vol. 4. 736p. (C). 1994. text ed. 19.95 (*0-674-40003-8*) HUP.

Perrot, Michelle, ed. Writing Women's History. Pheasant, Felicia, tr. 272p. 1992. pap. 18.95 (*0-631-18612-3*) Blackwell Pubs.

Perrot, Michelle, ed. see Duby, Georges.

Perrot, Michelle, jt. auth. see Duby, Georges.

Perrot, Michelle, et al, eds. A History of Private Life, Vol. 4: From the Fires of Revolution to the Great War, Vol. 4. Goldhammer, Arthur, tr. (Illus.). 736p. 1990. text ed. 39.95 (*0-674-39978-1*) Belknap Pr.

Perrot, Philippe & Bienvenu, Richard, trs. The Bourgeoisie Inside Out: A History of Clothing in the Nineteenth Century. LC 93-40094. 1994. 29.95 (*0-691-03383-8*); 16.95 (*0-691-00081-6*) Princeton U Pr.

Perrott, C. Ophthalmic Lens Design & Fabrication. 1992. 42.00 (*0-8194-0657-0*, 1529) SPIE.

Perrott Cartographics Staff, illus. Good Beer Guide to Belgium & Holland: The Best Bars & All the Breweries. 232p. 1992. per. 18.99 (*1-85249-110-8*, Pub. by Camra Bks UK) Info Devels.

***Perrott, D.** Concise Swahili & English Dictionary. (Teach Yourself Bks. Ser.). 184p. 1993. text ed. 18.00x (*0-340-54695-6*, Pub. by Hodder & Stoughton Ltd UK) Lubrecht & Cramer.

Perrott, D. V. Teach Yourself Swahili. (Teach Yourself Ser.). 1979. pap. 6.95 (*0-679-10225-6*) McKay.

— Teach Yourself Swahili. (Teach Yourself Ser.). 1992. 15.95 (*0-8288-8404-8*) Fr & Eur.

— Teach Yourself Swahili Dictionary. (Teach Yourself Ser.). 1992. 15.95 (*0-8288-8405-6*) Fr & Eur.

Perrott, David. Guide to the Western Islands of Scotland. 96p. 1991. pap. 24.95 (*0-9511003-2-7*, Pub. by Kittiwake Pr UK) St Mut.

— The Western Islands Handbook. 1994. 59.00 (*0-9511003-4-3*, Pub. by Kittiwake Pr UK) St Mut.

Perrott, David L. & Pogany, Istvan. Current Issues in International Business Law. 1988. text ed. 65.00 (*0-566-05473-6*, Pub. by Dartmth Pub UK) Ashgate Pub Co.

Perrott, Jeff, ed. see Krakow, Barbara.

Perrott, John. Bush for the Bushman: Need "The Gods Must Be Crazy" Kalahari People Die? LC 92-11105. (Illus.). 222p. (Orig.). 1993. pap. 14.95 (*1-881399-04-4*) Beaver Pond P&P.

Perrott, R. H. Parallel Programming. 256p. (C). 1987. text ed. 25.95 (*0-201-14231-7*) Addison-Wesley.

— Software for Parallel Computers. (UNICOM Applied Information Technology Ser.: No. 9). (Illus.). 304p. 1991. 89.95 (*0-412-39960-1*) Chapman & Hall.

Perrotta, Mary, ed. see Brown, Fern G.

Perrotta, Mary, ed. see Mango, Karin N.

***Perrotta, Tom.** Bad Haircut: Stories of the Seventies. 256p. (Orig.). 1995. pap. 6.99 (*0-425-14942-0*) Berkley Pub.

— Bad Haircut: Stories of the Seventies. LC 93-33687. 197p. (Orig.). 1994. 18.95 (*1-882593-05-7*) Bridge Wrks.

Perrotto, John, jt. auth. see Pelliccia, Joseph.

Perrotto, John, ed. see Pellicia, Joseph.

Perrotto, Richard S. & Culkin. Abnormal Psychology. (C). 1992. 46.50 (*0-673-46413-X*) HarpCollege.

— Abnormal Psychology. (C). 1993. student ed 17.00 (*0-673-46772-4*) HarpCollege.

Perrotto, Richard S., jt. auth. see Culkin, Joseph.

Perrow, Charles. Complex Organizations. 3rd ed. 1986. pap. text ed. write for info. (*0-07-554799-6*) McGraw.

Perrow, Charles & Guillen, Mauro. The AIDS Disaster: The Failure of Organizations in New York & the Nation. 208p. (C). 1990. text ed. 27.00 (*0-300-04879-3*); pap. 12.00 (*0-300-04880-7*) Yale U Pr.

Perroy, Edouard. La Feodalite En France Du X. Au XII. Siecle. LC 80-2012. reprint ed. 28.00 (*0-404-18584-3*) AMS Pr.

Perrucci, Carolyn C., jt. ed. see Haas, Violet B.

***Perrucci, Dorianne.** Morris County: The Progress of It. 1983. 24.95 (*0-89781-075-9*) Preferred Mktg.

Perrucci, Robert. Japanese Auto Transplants in the Heartland: Capital & Community in Transition. LC 93-50053. (Social Institutions & Social Change Ser.). 200p. 1994. lib. bdg. 37.95 (*0-202-30528-7*); pap. 18.95 (*0-202-30529-5*) Aldine de Gruyter.

Perrucci, Robert & Potter, Harry R. Networks of Power. (Social Institutions & Social Change Ser.). 144p. (Orig.). 1989. lib. bdg. 43.95 (*0-202-30342-X*); pap. text ed. 21.95 (*0-202-30343-8*) Aldine de Gruyter.

Perrucci, Robert & Targ, Dena B. Mental Patients & Social Networks. LC 81-20630. 160p. 1982. text ed. 39.95 (*0-86569-095-2*, Auburn Hse) Greenwood.

Perrucci, Robert, et al. Plant Closings: International Context & Social Costs. (Social Institutions & Social Change Ser.). 203p. (Orig.). (C). 1988. lib. bdg. 44.95 (*0-202-30338-1*); pap. text ed. 22.95 (*0-202-30339-X*) Aldine de Gruyter.

***Perruchot, Henri.** Toulouse-Lautrec. (Illus.). 320p. 1994. reprint ed. pap. 33.50x (*0-09-473720-7*, Pub. by Constable Pubs UK) Trans-Atl Phila.

Perruchoud, A. P., ed. Herzog, Heinrich W. on the Occasion of his 65th Birthday. (Journal: Respiration: Vol. 48 No. 3). (Illus.). 92p. 1985. pap. 36.00 (*3-8055-4256-9*) S Karger.

Perruchoud, A. P., jt. ed. see Herzog, H.

***Perry.** Alain Locke. 1997. text ed. 22.95 (*0-8057-4023-6*) Macmillan.

— Care of the Ophthalmic Patient. 2nd ed. 480p. 1995. pap. 79.75 (*1-56593-334-6*, 0664) Singular Publishing.

— Checklists T-A Clinical Nursing Skills & Techniques. 304p. 1993. 12.95 (*0-8016-7747-5*) Mosby Yr Bk.

— Clinical Nursing Skills & Techniques. 3rd ed. 1188p. 1993. 41.95 (*0-8016-7007-1*) Mosby Yr Bk.

— Conan the Formidable. 1990. pap. text ed. 7.95 (*0-8125-0998-6*) Tor Bks.

— Contemporary Society. 7th ed. (C). 1993. text ed. 32.25 (*0-673-99034-6*) HarpCollege.

— Contemporary Society. 7th ed. (C). 1993. Study guide. student ed 14.50 (*0-673-99038-9*) HarpCollege.

— Low Frequency Electromagnetic Design. (Electrical Engineering & Electronics Ser.: Vol. 28). 256p. 1985. 125.00 (*0-8247-7453-1*) Dekker.

— Pocket Guide Basic Skills & Procedures, No. 3. 544p. 1994. spiral bd. 19.95 (*0-8016-6879-4*) Mosby Yr Bk.

— Social Web. 6th ed. (C). 1992. student ed 9.50 (*0-06-501647-5*) HarpCollege.

— Text & Checklists Package to Accompany Clinical Nursing Skills. 304p. 1993. 46.95 (*0-8016-7746-7*) Mosby Yr Bk.

— Treasy of Traditional Wisdom, Vol. 1. 1995. pap. 18.95 (*1-870196-08-2*) Atrium Pubs.

— Western Civilization: A Brief History, Complete. (C). 1989. student ed. pap. 14.76 (*0-395-53221-3*) HM.

Perry, ed. Geometry: Axiomatic Developments with Problem Solving. (Pure & Applied Mathematics Ser.: Vol. 160). 376p. 1992. 49.75 (*0-8247-8727-7*) Dekker.

Perry & Potter. Clinical Nursing Skills & Techniques. 2nd ed. 1088p. 1989. pap. text ed. 39.95 (*0-8016-5493-9*) Mosby Yr Bk.

— Pocket Guide: Basic Skills & Procedures. 2nd ed. (Illus.). 496p. 1990. spiral bd. 19.95 (*0-8016-5527-7*) Mosby Yr Bk.

Perry & Smith. Mild Hypertension: To Treat or Not to Treat, Vol. 304. 1978. 57.00 (*0-89072-059-2*) NY Acad Sci.

Perry, jt. auth. see Potter.

Perry, et al. Tech & Theory of Periodontal Instrumentation. (Illus.). 432p. 1990. pap. text ed. 45.50 (*0-7216-2734-X*) Saunders.

Perry, A. H. & Symons, L. J., eds. Highway Meteorology. 208p. 1991. write for info. (*0-419-15670-4*, E & FN Spon) Routledge Chapman & Hall.

Perry, A. H. & Walker, J. M. The Ocean-Atmosphere System. LC 76-44276. 172p. reprint ed. pap. 49.10 (*0-317-27660-3*, 2025211) Bks Demand.

An Asterisk (*) at the beginning of an entry indicates that the title is appearing in BIP for the first time.

***Perry, A. Thompson, 2nd.** Brief Field of View & Elderly Drivers: A Research Study. (Illus.). 109p. (Orig.). (C). 1995. pap. text ed. 40.00 (*0-7881-1615-0*) Diane Pub.

***Perry, Adrian.** Approaching Economics. 448p. (C). 1989. 59.00x (*0-7478-0370-6*, Pub. by S Thornes Pubs UK) St Mut.

Perry, Anne. Belgrave Square. 1993. mass mkt. 5.99 (*0-449-22227-6*, Crest) Fawcett.

— Belgrave Square. large type ed. 657p. 1992. reprint ed. lib. bdg. 20.95 (*1-56054-446-5*) Thorndike Pr.

— Bethlehem Road. 320p. 1991. mass mkt. 5.99 (*0-449-45316-2*, Crest) Fawcett.

— Bethlehem Road. 1991. mass mkt. 5.99 (*0-449-21914-3*) Fawcett.

— Bluegate Fields. 288p. 1985. mass mkt. 5.99 (*0-449-45317-0*, Crest) Fawcett.

— Bluegate Fields. 1989. mass mkt. 5.99 (*0-449-20766-8*) Fawcett.

— Cain His Brother. LC 95-8680. 1995. 22.95 (*0-449-90847-X*) Fawcett.

— Callander Square. 256p. 1985. mass mkt. 4.95 (*0-449-20999-7*, Crest) Fawcett.

— Callander Square. large type ed. 1981. 12.00 (*0-7089-0718-0*) Ulverscroft.

— Cardington Crescent. 304p. 1988. reprint ed. mass mkt. 5.99 (*0-449-21442-7*, Crest) Fawcett.

— Cater Street Hangman. 1985. mass mkt. 4.95 (*0-449-20867-2*, Crest) Fawcett.

— A Dangerous Mourning. 1992. mass mkt. 5.99 (*0-8041-1037-9*) Ivy Books.

— Death in the Devil's Acre. 272p. 1987. mass mkt. 5.99 (*0-449-21095-2*, Crest) Fawcett.

— Defend & Betray. 1993. mass mkt. 5.99 (*0-8041-1188-X*) Ivy Books.

— Defend & Betray. large type ed. (Cloak & Dagger Ser.). 737p. 1993. reprint ed. lib. bdg. 21.95 (*1-56054-625-5*) Thorndike Pr.

— Face of a Stranger. 1991. mass mkt. 5.99 (*0-8041-0858-7*) Ivy Books.

— The Face of a Stranger. large type ed. 556p. 1991. reprint ed. lib. bdg. 20.95 (*1-56054-113-X*) Thorndike Pr.

— Farriers' Lane. 1994. mass mkt. 5.99 (*0-449-21961-5*) Fawcett.

— Farrier's Lane. large type ed. LC 93-10504. 1993. 22.95 (*1-56054-626-3*) Thorndike Pr.

— Highgate Rise. 1992. mass mkt. 4.99 (*0-449-21959-3*) Fawcett.

— Highgate Rise. large type ed. (Ulverscroft Ser.). 672p. 1994. 21.95 (*0-7089-3013-1*) Ulverscroft.

— The Hyde Park Headsman. 1995. mass mkt. 5.99 (*0-449-22350-7*, Crest) Fawcett.

— Paragon Walks. 1986. mass mkt. 5.99 (*0-449-45319-7*) Fawcett.

— Resurrection Row. 192p. 1986. mass mkt. 5.99 (*0-449-21067-7*, Crest) Fawcett.

— Riders Ready! A Book about BMX...with Advice from the Experts. LC 85-50294. (Illus.). 130p. (Orig.). (J). (gr. 5-8). pap. 8.95 (*0-9615253-0-4*); 12.05 (*0-8479-9930-0*) Tadpole.

— Rutland Place. 224p. 1986. mass mkt. 5.99 (*0-449-45318-9*, Crest) Fawcett.

— Silence in Hanover Close. 1989. mass mkt. 4.99 (*0-449-21686-1*, Crest) Fawcett.

— Silence in Hanover Close. large type ed. (Mystery Ser.). 1990. 21.95 (*0-7089-2324-0*) Ulverscroft.

— The Sins of the Wolf. LC 94-12099. 384p. 1994. 21.50 (*0-449-90638-8*, Columbine) Fawcett.

— The Sins of the Wolf. large type ed. 720p. 1994. lib. bdg. 22.95 (*0-7862-0319-6*) Thorndike Pr.

— A Sudden, Fearful Death. 384p. 1993. 20.00 (*0-449-90637-X*, Columbine) Fawcett.

— A Sudden, Fearful Death. 1994. mass mkt. 5.99 (*0-8041-1283-5*) Ivy Books.

— A Sudden, Fearful Death. large type ed. LC 93-42207. 1994. 21.95 (*0-7862-0130-4*) Thorndike Pr.

— Traitors Gate. LC 94-27624. 416p. 1995. 21.50 (*0-449-90634-5*, Columbine) Fawcett.

— Traitors Gate. LC 95-5610. 706p. 1995. write for info. (*0-7862-0451-6*) Thorndike Pr.

Perry, Anne C. The Evolution of U. S. Trade Intermediaries: The Changing International Environment. LC 92-882. 200p. 1992. text ed. 49.95 (*0-89930-708-6*, PEI/, Quorum Bks) Greenwood.

Perry, Anne M. Bluebonnet Books: Activities for 1993. 144p. (Orig.). 1993. pap. 16.95 (*0-944459-72-2*) ECS Lrn Systs.

Perry, Anne M., ed. see Clarke, A. B.

Perry, Annetta. Progressive Word Processing Assignments. 160p. (Orig.). 1986. text ed. 32.50 (*0-273-02520-1*) Trans-Atl Phila.

Perry, Arthur L. Origin of Williamstown, MA. 2nd ed. (Illus.). 650p. reprint ed. lib. bdg. 65.00 (*0-8328-2554-9*) Higginson Bk Co.

— Origins in Williamstown, Massachusetts, 2 vols. (Illus.). viii, 631p. 1993. reprint ed. pap. text ed. 36.50 (*1-55613-766-4*) Heritage Bk.

Perry, B. E. Origin of the Book of Sindbad. (C). 1960. 35.00 (*3-11-000538-7*) De Gruyter.

Perry, B. E., tr. see Babrius.

Perry, Barbara. American Ceramics Now: The Twenty-Seventh Ceramic National Exhibition. Piche, Thomas, Jr., ed. LC 87-80542. (Illus.). 84p. (Orig.). 1987. pap. write for info. (*0-914407-08-2*) Everson Mus.

— Fragile Blossoms, Enduring Earth: The Japanese Influence on American Ceramics. Piche, Thomas, ed. LC 89-81057. (Illus.). 96p. (Orig.). 1989. pap. text ed. write for info. (*0-914407-12-0*) Everson Mus.

— Magnetic Connections. (Illus.). 198p. (Orig.). 1985. pap. 12.50 (*0-9616312-0-1*, TXV-101-598) Arkbridge Assn.

Perry, Barbara, jt. auth. see Abraham, Henry.

Perry, Barbara, jt. auth. see Anderson, Ross.

Perry, Barbara, et al. The Twenty-Eighth Ceramic National: Clay, Color, Content. Piche, Thomas, ed. LC 90-81161. (Illus.). 88p. (Orig.). 1990. pap. text ed. write for info. (*0-914407-13-9*) Everson Mus.

Perry, Barbara A. A Representative Supreme Court? The Impact of Race, Religion, & Gender on Appointments. LC 91-14336. (Contributions in Legal Studies: No. 66). 176p. 1991. text ed. 45.00 (*0-313-27777-X*, PRC, Greenwood Pr) Greenwood.

Perry Barbara, A. Unfounded Fears: Myths & Realities of a Constitutional Convention. LC 89-7502. (Contributions in Legal Studies: No. 55). 192p. 1989. text ed. 49.95 (*0-313-26717-0*, WKC, Greenwood Pr) Greenwood.

Perry Barbara, A., jt. auth. see Abernathy, M. Glenn.

Perry, Barbara A., jt. auth. see Weber, Paul J.

Perry, Belinda. Texas Springs. 1993. mass mkt. 5.50 (*0-345-37428-2*) Ballantine.

Perry, Ben, jt. auth. see Girard, Frank.

Perry, Ben E. Studies in the Text History of the Life & Fables of Aesop. LC 81-13575. (American Philological Association Monograph Ser.). 1981. reprint ed. pap. 23. 50 (*0-89130-534-3*, 40 00 07) Scholars Pr GA.

Perry, Ben E. & Dorson, Richard M., eds. Aesopica: A Series of Texts Relating to Aesop or Ascribed to Him Closely Connected with the Literary Tradition That Bears His Name, Vol. 1. LC 80-797. (Folklore of the World Ser.). (ENG, GRE & LAT.). 1981. reprint ed. lib. bdg. 81.95 (*0-405-13337-5*) Ayer.

Perry, Bernard J. Instructional Guide for Introduction to Employee Involvement Teams for Potential Members: The Zero Meeting. rev. ed. 31p. 1992. pap. 15.00 (*0-937670-30-8*) QCI Intl.

***Perry, Bill.** Robert & Oliver. (Illus.). 1995. 9.00 (*1-86371-486-3*) Harper SF.

— Rocky Mountain Wildlife of Yellowstone & Grand Teton National Parks. (Illus.). 68p. 1995. pap. 10.95 (*0-943972-41-8*) Homestead WY.

— A Sierra Club Naturalist's Guide to the Middle Atlantic Coast: Cape Hatteras to Cape Cod. LC 83-18691. (Naturalist's Guides Ser.). (Illus.). 448p. (Orig.). 1985. 25.00 (*0-87156-810-1*); pap. 14.00 (*0-87156-816-0*) Sierra.

— Storyteller's Bible Study for Internationals. 160p. 1992. pap. 8.95 (*0-9633645-0-2*) Multi-Lang Media.

Perry, Bliss. Amateur Spirit. LC 70-84332. (Essay Index Reprint Ser.). 1977. 17.95 (*0-8369-1102-4*) Ayer.

— American Spirit in Literature: A Chronicle of Great Interpreters. (BCL1-PS American Literature Ser.). 281p. 1992. reprint ed. lib. bdg. 79.00 (*0-7812-6605-X*) Rprt Serv.

— And Gladly Teach: Reminiscences. (BCL1-PS American Literature Ser.). 315p. 1993. reprint ed. lib. bdg. 89.00 (*0-7812-6998-9*) Rprt Serv.

— Life & Letters of Henry Lee Higginson. LC 72-37905. (Select Bibliographies Reprint Ser.). 1977. reprint ed. 35. 95 (*0-8369-6743-7*) Ayer.

— Park-Street Papers. LC 73-117826. (Essay Index Reprint Ser.). 1977. 21.95 (*0-8369-2012-0*) Ayer.

— Powers at Play. LC 74-110209. (Short Story Index Reprint Ser.). 1977. 20.95 (*0-8369-3360-5*) Ayer.

— The Praise of Folly: And Other Papers. (BCL1-PS American Literature Ser.). 230p. 1992. reprint ed. lib. bdg. 79.00 (*0-7812-6829-X*) Rprt Serv.

— Salem Kittredge, & Other Stories. LC 71-133165. (Short Story Index Reprint Ser.). 1977. 19.95 (*0-8369-3689-2*) Ayer.

— Walt Whitman: His Life & Work. (BCL1-PS American Literature Ser.). 318p. 1992. reprint ed. lib. bdg. 89.00 (*0-7812-6899-0*) Rprt Serv.

— Walt Whitman, His Life & Work. LC 79-86165. reprint ed. 35.00 (*0-404-04995-8*) AMS Pr.

Perry, Bliss, ed. see Emerson, Ralph Waldo.

Perry, Bob. Landscape Plants for Western Regions: An Illustrated Guide to Plants for Water Conservation. (Illus.). 318p. 1995. 62.00 (*0-9605988-3-9*) Land Design.

— Trees & Shrubs for Dry California Landscapes: Plants for Water Conservation. LC 81-81013. (Illus.). 184p. 1995. reprint ed. pap. 25.00 (*0-9605988-2-0*) Land Design.

Perry, Bonnie J. Bare Essentials. 224p. 1994. mass mkt. 4.50 (*0-7860-0036-8*) Windsor NY.

Perry, Brian. No Rhymes for Poets. LC 86-72947. 94p. (Orig.). 1988. pap. text ed. 6.00 (*0-916383-24-5*) Aegina Pr.

Perry, Bruce. Malcolm: A Life of the Man Who Changed Black America. 1991. 24.95 (*0-88268-103-6*) Station Hill Pr.

— Malcolm: The Life of a Man Who Changed Black America. (Illus.). 1992. 14.95 (*0-88268-121-4*) Station Hill Pr.

***Perry, Bruce D.** Maltreated Children: Experience, Brain Development, & the Next Generation. 224p. 1996. 29.00 (*0-393-70212-X*) Norton.

Perry, Bryon A. Seventy-Five Years at Oakland Hills: A Jubilee Celebration. Cook, Shelby, ed. (Illus.). 120p. 1991. 55.00 (*0-9629299-0-5*) Perry & White.

Perry, C. Seat Weaving. 1940. pap. 6.00 (*0-02-665670-1*) Bennett IL.

Perry, C. B. Charles d'Wolf of Guadalupe, His Ancestors & Descendants, Being a Complete Genealogy of the "RI de Wolf's", the Descendants of Simon, with Their Common Descent from Balthasar of Lyme, Conn., 1668. (Illus.). 325p. 1989. reprint ed. lib. bdg. 59.00 (*0-8328-0476-2*); reprint ed. pap. 49.00 (*0-8328-0477-0*) Higginson Bk Co.

— The Perrys of Rhode Island, & Tales of Silver Creek. (Illus.). 115p. reprint ed. lib. bdg. 33.00 (*0-8328-1654-X*); reprint ed. pap. 23.00 (*0-8328-1655-8*) Higginson Bk Co.

Perry, C. Dianne, jt. ed. see Herumin, Wendy W.

Perry, C. Michael, jt. auth. see Zelenak, Nancy.

Perry, C. R. The Victorian Post Office: The Growth of a Bureaucracy. (Royal Historical Society: Studies in History: No. 64). 288p. (C). 1992. text ed. 79.00 (*0-86193-220-X*, Royal Historical Soc) Boydell & Brewer.

Perry, Campbell, jt. auth. see Laurence, Jean-Roch.

Perry, Carmen, ed. see De la Pena, Jose E.

***Perry, Carol D.** Dangerous to Love. (Superromance Ser.). 1995. mass mkt. 3.75 (*0-373-70652-9*, 1-70652-2) Harlequin Bks.

— Wings of Time. (Superromance Ser.). 1993. mass mkt. 3.39 (*0-373-70537-9*, 1-70537-5) Harlequin Bks.

Perry, Carol J. Ten Women: Political Pioneers. 96p. (YA). (gr. 5 up). 1994. pap. 2.99 (*0-87406-642-5*) Willowisp Pr.

Perry, Carol R. The Fine Art of Technical Writing: Key Points to Help You Think Your Way Through Scientific or Technical Publications, Theses, Term Papers & Business Reports. 112p. (Orig.). 1991. pap. 7.95 (*0-936085-24-X*) Blue Heron OR.

Perry, Carole J. Introduction to Amateur Radio. (Illus.). 155p. 1986. ring bd. 99.95 (*0-939863-00-6*) Media Mentors.

Perry, Carolyn, ed. University of Vermont Student Research on Vermont Topics. (Occasional Papers: No. 1). 66p. (Orig.). 1979. pap. text ed. 2.50 (*0-944277-02-0*, U52) U VT Ctr Rsch VT.

Perry, Carolyn, jt. ed. see Weaks, Mary L.

Perry, Cecilia, ed. see Amidei, Nancy.

Perry, Charles. The Haight-Ashbury: A History. LC 83-43187. (Illus.). 310p. 1985. 16.95 (*0-394-41098-X*) Random.

— Peboan & Seegwun. 32p. (J). Date not set. 4.95 (*0-374-45750-6*) FS&G.

— Up the Rough Side. LC 85-61878. (Illus.). 96p. 1985. pap. 5.95 (*0-9615139-0-X*) C Perry Pub.

— The West, Japan, & Cape Route Imports: The Oil & Non-Fuel Mineral Trades. LC 82-80947. (Special Report Ser.). 88p. 1982. 11.95 (*0-89549-042-0*) Inst Foreign Policy Anal.

Perry, Charles A. Effects of Reservoirs on Flood Discharges in the Kansas & the Missouri River Basins. (Circular Series: Floods in the Upper Mississippi River Basin, 1993). 1994. write for info. (*0-318-72619-X*) US Geol Survey.

Perry, Charles E., ed. Founders & Leaders of Connecticut, Sixteen Thirty-Three to Seventeen Eighty-Three. LC 78-177965. (Essay Index Reprint Ser.). 1977. reprint ed. 23. 95 (*0-8369-2518-1*) Ayer.

Perry, Charles M. Henry Philip Tappan: Philosopher & University President. LC 71-165723. (American Education Ser., No. 2). 1972. reprint ed. 26.95 (*0-405-03715-5*) Ayer.

— Toward a Dimensional Reality. LC 39-11737. 188p. reprint ed. pap. 53.60 (*0-317-09342-8*, 2016249) Bks Demand.

Perry, Charles M., ed. The St. Louis Movement in Philosophy: Some Source Material. LC 31-8773. (Illus.). 150p. reprint ed. pap. 42.80 (*0-317-09234-0*, 2016248) Bks Demand.

Perry, Charles M., jt. ed. see Praaning, Rio D.

Perry, Charles M., jt. auth. see Ra'anan, Uri.

Perry, Charles R. Union Corporate Campaigns. LC 86-82727. (Employee Relations & Collective Bargaining Ser.). (Orig.). 1987. pap. 30.00 (*0-89546-065-3*) U PA Wharton Ctr Human Resc.

Perry, Charles R. & Kegley, Delwyn H. Disintegration & Change: Labor Relations in the Meat Packing Industry. LC 88-83309. (Labor Relations & Public Policy Ser.: No. 35). 240p. 1989. pap. 30.00 (*0-89546-073-4*) U PA Wharton Ctr Human Resc.

Perry, Charles R. & Northrup, Herbert R., frwds. Collective Bargaining & the Decline of the United Mine Workers. LC 84-47503. (Major Industrial Research Unit Studies: No. 60). 273p. 1984. 30.00 (*0-89546-043-2*) U PA Wharton Ctr Human Resc.

Perry, Charles R. & Rowan, Richard L. The Impact of Government Manpower Programs in General & on Minorities & Women. LC 74-13177. (Major Industrial Research Unit Ser.: No. 4). 543p. reprint ed. pap. 154.80 (*0-317-41872-6*, 2025908) Bks Demand.

Perry, Charles R., et al. Employee Financial Participation: An International Survey. LC 90-70533. (Multinational Industrial Relations Ser.). 1990. 35.00 (*0-89546-077-7*, MUL12) U PA Wharton Ctr Human Resc.

— Operating During Strikes: Company Experience, NLRB Policies & Governmental Regulations. LC 82-80521. (Labor Relations & Public Policy Ser.: No. 23). 163p. 1982. pap. 20.00 (*0-89546-036-X*) U PA Wharton Ctr Human Resc.

Perry, Cheryl & Faulkner, Hal. Holiday Mathemagic. (Illus.). (J). (gr. 4-10). 1977. pap. text ed. 7.95 (*0-918932-50-5*) Activity Resources.

Perry, Chrsitopher. Listen to the Voice Within. 1991. pap. 15.95 (*0-687-85683-3*) Abingdon.

Perry, Cindy. Activities That Build Young Women, Vol. 1. 48p. (YA). 1993. pap. 6.98 (*0-88290-456-6*) Horizon Utah.

Perry, Clark, jt. auth. see Rowan, Robin H.

Perry, Clark, jt. auth. see Rowan, Robin.

Perry, Clayton R., et al. Handbook of Fractures. (Illus.). 356p. 1995. pap. text ed. 27.00 (*0-07-048590-9*) Hlth Prof Div.

Perry, D. L. Applications of Analytical Techniques to the Characteristics. (Illus.). 190p. (C). 1992. 75.00 (*0-306-44189-6*, Plenum Pr) Plenum.

Perry, D. L., et al, eds. Applications of Synchrotron Radiation Techniques to Materials Science. (Symposium Proceedings Ser.: Vol. 307). 1993. text ed. 72.00 (*1-55899-203-0*) Materials Res.

Perry, D. R., jt. auth. see Farnfield, Carolyn A.

Perry, Dale L. & Phillips, Sidney L., eds. Handbook of Inorganic Compounds. 1995. write for info. (*0-8493-8671-3*) CRC Pr.

Perry, Dame & Co. Staff. Women's & Children's Fashions of 1917: The Complete Perry, Dame & Co., Catalog. LC 92-12621. Orig. Title: New York Styles - Spring & Summer 1917 Catalog, No. 67. (Illus.). 160p. 1992. reprint ed. pap. 12.95 (*0-486-27128-5*) Dover.

Perry, Dane. Understanding the Yacht Racing Rules - 1993-96. 306p. 1993. reprint ed. pap. 19.95 (*1-882502-02-7*) US Sail Assn.

***Perry, Dave.** Dave Perry's 100 Best Racing Rules Quizzes. 168p. 1994. pap. text ed. 16.95 (*1-882502-19-1*) US Sail Assn.

— Little Fox's Airbrush Stencil Techniques. (Illus.). 125p. (Orig.). 1982. pap. text ed. 14.95 (*0-9603530-8-9*) US Screen.

— Winning in One - Designs. (Illus.). 192p. 1984. 17.95 (*0-396-08191-6*, Putnam) Putnam Pub Group.

— Winning in One Designs. 2nd ed. (Illus.). 293p. 1992. pap. text ed. 16.95 (*1-882502-00-0*) US Sail Assn.

***Perry, David.** Jazz Greats. (20th Century Composers Ser.). (Illus.). 240p. (Orig.). (C). 1995. pap. 19.95 (*0-7148-3204-9*, Pub. by Phaidon Press UK) Chronicle Bks.

Perry, David, jt. auth. see Neal, Bill.

Perry, David A. Forest Ecosystems. LC 94-10796. 1994. text ed. 80.00x (*0-8018-4760-5*) Johns Hopkins.

— Forest Ecosystems. LC 94-10796. 1995. pap. text ed. 49. 95x (*0-8018-4987-X*) Johns Hopkins.

Perry, David A., ed. Maintaining the Longterm Productivity of Pacific Northwest Forest Ecosystems. LC 89-20168. (Illus.). 250p. 1989. text ed. 44.95 (*0-88192-144-0*) Timber.

***Perry, David B.** Bike Cult: The Ultimate Guide to Human-Powered Vehicles. (Illus.). 500p. (Orig.). 1995. pap. 18. 95 (*1-56858-027-4*) FWEW.

***Perry, David C., ed.** Building the Public City: The Politics, Governance & Finance of Public Infrastructure. (Urban Affairs Annual Review Ser.: Vol. 43). 280p. 1994. 54.00 (*0-8039-4432-2*) Sage.

— Building the Public City: The Politics, Governance & Finance of Public Infrastructure. (Urban Affairs Annual Review Ser.: Vol. 43). 280p. 1994. pap. 24.00 (*0-8039-4433-0*) Sage.

Perry, David C. & Watkins, Alfred J., eds. The Rise of the Sunbelt Cities. LC 77-93698. (Urban Affairs Annual Reviews Ser.: No. 14). 309p. reprint ed. pap. 88.10 (*0-8357-8504-1*, 2034783) Bks Demand.

Perry, David C., jt. auth. see Liggett, Helen.

Perry, David G. & Bussey, Kay. Social Development. (Illus.). 416p. (C). 1983. text ed. write for info. (*0-13-816034-1*) P-H.

Perry, David J., jt. auth. see Lebet, Philip E.

Perry, Deane Y. Gays & Lesbians & Sports. (YA). 1994. pap. 12.95 (*0-7910-2636-1*) Chelsea Hse.

Perry, Devern J. College Vocabulary Building. 9th ed. LC 92-15515. 1993. pap. 23.95 (*0-538-61413-7*) S-W Pub.

— Word Division & Spelling Manual. 4th ed. 1994. text ed. 11.95 (*0-538-61995-3*) S-W Pub.

— Word Studies. 8th ed. (C). 1989. text ed. 14.95 (*0-538-05813-7*, E81U) S-W Pub.

Perry, Devern J., jt. auth. see Silverthorn, J. E.

Perry, Dewayne E., jt. auth. see Habermann, A. Nico.

Perry, Donald. Life above the Forest Floor. (Illus.). 160p. 1986. 16.95 (*0-685-16651-1*) S&S Trade.

Perry, Donald G. Managing a Wildland Fire: A Practical Perspective. Brooks, Carol C., ed. LC 89-84092. (Illus.). 145p. (Orig.). (C). 1989. pap. text ed. write for info. (*0-941943-01-1*) Fire Pubns.

***Perry, Donna.** Backtalk: Women Writers Speak Out. (Illus.). 360p. 1995. pap. 16.95 (*0-8135-2199-8*) Rutgers U Pr.

Perry, Donna, ed. Backtalk: Women Writers Speak Out. LC 92-41201. (Illus.). 360p. (C). 1993. 24.95 (*0-8135-1991-8*) Rutgers U Pr.

***Perry, Donna & Maglin, Nan B., eds.** Bad Girls - Good Girls: Women, Sex, & Power in the Nineties. (Illus.). 325p. (C). 1996. text ed. 50.00 (*0-8135-2250-1*); pap. 17. 95 (*0-8135-2251-X*) Rutgers U Pr.

Perry, Doreen. Restoring Dolls: A Practical Guide. (Illus.). 94p. 1987. 15.95 (*0-900873-59-0*, Pub. by Bishopsgte Pr UK); pap. 11.95 (*0-900873-61-2*, Pub. by Bishopsgte Pr UK) Intl Spec Bk.

— Restoring Toys: A Practical Guide. (C). 1988. 35.00 (*1-85219-002-7*, Pub. by Bishopsgate Pr Ltd UK) St Mut.

Perry, Dorothy A., jt. auth. see Carranza, Fermin A., Jr.

Perry, Douglas L. VHDL. 2nd ed. LC 93-23153. (Computer Engineering Ser.). 1993. text ed. 50.00 (*0-07-049434-7*) McGraw.

Perry, Duncan M. The Politics of Terror: The Macedonian Revolutionary Movements, 1893-1903. LC 87-33062. (Illus.). 275p. (C). 1988. lib. bdg. 34.50 (*0-8223-0813-4*) Duke.

— Stefan Stambolov & the Emergence of Modern Bulgaria, 1870-1895. LC 92-34704. (Illus.). 328p. 1993. text ed. 39.95 (*0-8223-1313-8*) Duke.

Perry, E. Caswell. Burbank: An Illustrated History. LC 87-8314. 144p. 1987. 22.95 (*0-89781-204-2*) Preferred Mktg.

Perry, E. Caswell, ed. see Perry, Lilla S.

Perry, E. Eugene. It Works for Everybody Else. 1984. pap. 5.00 (*0-88734-312-0*) Players Pr.

Perry, E. G. A Trip Around Buzzards Bay Shores. LC 76-3145. (Illus.). 1976. reprint ed. 25.00 (*0-88492-013-5*) W S Sullwold.

Perry, Earl & Perry, Wilma. Puppets Go to Church. 85p. 1975. pap. 4.95 (*0-8341-0385-0*) Beacon Hill.

P
Q

Perry, Ed. Sanskrit Primer. 230p. (Orig.). 1986. reprint ed. 22.00 (*0-685-35381-8*, Pub. by Motilal Banarsidass II) S Asia.

Perry, Edith W. Altar Guild Manual. 3rd rev. ed. 72p. 1992. reprint ed. pap. 5.95 (*0-8192-1067-6*) Morehouse Pub.

Perry, Edmond S., et al, eds. Separation & Purification Methods, Vol. 3. LC 73-77000. (Illus.). 479p. reprint ed. pap. 136.60 (*0-685-23648-X*, 2029008) Bks Demand.

Perry, Edmund F., jt. auth. see Reat, N. Ross.

Perry, Edward. Descriptive Analyses of Piano Works. 1977. lib. bdg. 59.95 (*0-8490-1708-4*) Gordon Pr.

Perry, Edward D. A Sanskrit Primer. 4th ed. LC 36-19814. 230p. 1969. text ed. 36.50 (*0-231-00858-9*) Col U Pr.

Perry, Edward L. Luyties Homeopathic Practice. 165p. 1974. pap. 1.65 (*0-89378-052-9*) Formur Intl.

Perry, Edward L., jt. auth. see Chapman, J. B.

Perry, Eleanor. The Swimmer. LC 67-17163. 127p. 1967. 16.95 (*0-910278-70-9*) Boulevard.

***Perry, Elilsabeth I.** Women in Action: Rebels & Reformers 1920-1980. 60p. 1995. pap. 6.95 (*0-89959-389-5*, 1019) LWVUS.

Perry, Elisabeth I. Belle Moskowitz: Feminine Politics & the Exercise of Power in the Age of Alfred E. Smith. (Illus.). 304p. 1987. 29.95 (*0-19-504426-6*) OUP.

— Belle Moskowitz: Feminine Politics & the Exercise of Power in the Age of Alfred E. Smith. 1992. pap. 15.95 (*0-415-90545-1*, A6798, Routledge NY) Routledge.

Perry, Elizabeth J. Rebels & Revolutionaries in North China, 1845-1945. LC 79-65179. xvi, 324p. 1980. 42.50 (*0-8047-1055-4*); pap. 14.95 (*0-8047-1175-5*) Stanford U Pr.

— Shanghai on Strike: The Politics of Chinese Labor. LC 92-17774. 352p. (C). 1993. 42.50 (*0-8047-2063-0*) Stanford U Pr.

— Shanghai on Strike: The Politics of Chinese Labor. (Illus.). 344p. (C). 1995. pap. 16.95 (*0-8047-2491-1*) Stanford U Pr.

Perry, Elizabeth J., jt. ed. see Wasserstrom, Jeffrey N.

Perry, Ellen L. Ward Management & Teaching. 3rd ed. (Illus.). 304p. 1988. 26.00 (*0-685-32962-3*, Bailliere-Tindall) Saunders.

Perry, Elliot. Pat Paragraphs. Turner, George T. & Stanton, Thomas E., eds. LC 81-68198. (Illus.). 1982. 55.00 (*0-930412-05-2*) Bureau Issues.

Perry, Erna K., jt. auth. see Perry, John A.

Perry, Erskine. Cases Illustrative of Oriental Life: The Application of English Law to India. (C). 1988. reprint ed. 36.00 (*81-206-0368-0*, Pub. by Asian Educ Servs II) S Asia.

Perry, Erskine, tr. see Von Savigny, Friedrich K.

Perry, Estelle S. Streamlining the United Nations, Pt. A: Wanted: A U. N. Personnel System That Works. (Monograph in CURE Ser.: No. 12A). 68p. 1993. pap. text ed. 5.00 (*1-881520-02-1*) Ctr U N Reform Educ.

Perry, Eugene C., Jr. & Montgomery, Carla W., eds. Isotope Studies of Hydrologic Processes. LC 82-3431. (Illus.). 118p. 1982. 25.00 (*0-87580-082-3*) N Ill U Pr.

Perry, Eugene W. Practical Export Trade Finance & International Business Credit Management. 475p. 1989. text ed. 65.00 (*1-55623-018-4*) Irwin Prof Pubng.

Perry, Evan. Corkscrews & Bottle Openers. (Album Ser.). (Illus.). 32p. 1980. pap. text ed. 5.25 (*0-85263-534-6*, Pub. by Shire Pubns UK) Lubrecht & Cramer.

Perry, F. E. Dictionary of Banking. 3rd ed. 378p. 1988. pap. 27.50 (*0-273-02961-4*, Pub. by MacDonald & Evans UK) Trans-Atl Phila.

Perry, Foster. When Lightning Strikes a Hummingbird: The Awakening of a Healer. LC 93-10285. 192p. (Orig.). 1993. pap. 10.95 (*1-879181-10-X*) Bear & Co.

Perry, Frances. Grown for Their Leaves. 1979. pap. 18.95 (*0-85967-661-7*, Pub. by Scolar Pr UK) Ashgate Pub Co.

Perry, Frances, ed. Simon & Schuster's Complete Guide to Plants & Flowers. (Illus.). 1976. pap. 15.00 (*0-671-22247-3*) S&S Trade.

Perry, Frances B., ed. Let's Sing Together: Favorite Primary Songs. (Illus.). 96p. (J). (ps-6). 1984. 12.98 (*0-941518-02-7*) Perry Enterprises.

— Let's Sing Together: Favorite Primary Songs of Members of the Church of Jesus Christ of Latter-day Saints. (Illus.). 96p. (J). (ps-6). 1981. 10.98 (*0-941518-00-0*) Perry Enterprises.

Perry, Frank, Jr. Afro-American Vocal Music: A Select Guide to Fifteen Composers. LC 91-751616. 142p. (C). 1991. 24.95 (*0-9628916-2-2*) Vande Vere.

***Perry, Frank.** History of Pigeon Point Lighthouse. (Illus.). 88p. 1995. pap. 7.95 (*0-9617681-2-6*) Otter B Bks.

Perry, Frank A. East Brother: History of an Island Light Station. LC 84-82389. (Illus.). 109p. 1984. pap. 10.00 (*0-9614254-0-7*) East Brother.

— Fossil Invertebrates & Geology of the Marine Cliffs at Capitola, California. 30p. 1993. pap. 3.95 (*0-9632480-2-2*) Santa Cruz Mus Assn.

— Fossil Sharks & Rays of the Southern Santa Cruz Mountains, California. (Illus.). 48p. (Orig.). 1994. pap. 4.95 (*0-9632480-1-4*) Santa Cruz Mus Assn.

Perry, Fred. Elements of Banking. 4th ed. 1984. 100.00 (*0-416-36630-9*, Pub. by Inst Bankers UK) St Mut.

Perry, Frederick. Fair Winds & Foul: A Narrative of Daily Life Aboard an American Clipper Ship. (Seafaring Men: Their Ships & Times Ser). (Illus.). 204p. 1980. reprint ed. text ed. 17.50 (*0-930576-25-X*) E M Coleman Ent.

— St. Louis: Louis IX of France, the Most Christian King. LC 73-14462. reprint ed. 49.50 (*0-404-58280-X*) AMS Pr.

Perry, Frederick J. A Reconstruction-Analysis of "Buried Child" by Playwright Sam Shepard. LC 92-865. 172p. 1992. lib. bdg. 79.95 (*0-7734-9810-9*) E Mellen.

Perry, Fredi, ed. Kitsap County: A Centennial History. (Illus.). 120p. (Orig.). 1989. pap. 15.00 (*0-9622337-1-4*) Perry Pub WA.

Perry, Fredi, et al. Seabeck: Tide's Out; Table's Set. (Illus.). 256p. 1993. 26.00 (*0-9622337-2-2*); pap. 16.00 (*0-9622337-3-0*) Perry Pub WA.

Perry, G., ed. Alterations in the Neuronal Cytoskeleton in Alzheimer's Disease. LC 87-29256. (Advances in Behavioral Biology Ser.: Vol. 34). 240p. 1987. 69.50 (*0-306-42766-4*, Plenum Pr) Plenum.

Perry, G. E., jt. auth. see Wilson, J. G.

Perry, G. G., ed. see Rolle, Richard.

Perry, G. W., jt. ed. see Lowe, A. L.

***Perry, Gai.** Impressionistic Quilts. Konzak-Kuhn, Barbara, ed. (Illus.). 128p. 1995. pap. text ed. 24.95 (*1-57120-003-7*, 10125) C & T Pub.

***Perry, Gail.** The Complete Idiot's Guide to Doing Your 1995 Taxes. 350p. 1995. 14.99 (*1-56761-586-4*) Alpha Bks IN.

— The Complete Idiot's Guide to Preparing Your 1996 Taxes. 350p. 1995. 14.99 (*0-614-03572-4*) Alpha Bks IN.

***Perry, Gail R.** Turbo Tax for Windows for Dummies. 1995. pap. 19.99 (*1-56884-228-7*) IDG Bks.

***Perry, Garland.** An American Saga William George Hughes (1859-1902) A Pioneer Texas Rancher: His Life, His Times, His Story. LC 95-75913. 250p. 1995. 24.95 (*0-9646196-0-1*) G Perry.

Perry, Garry P. & Orchard, Janet. Assessment & Treatment of Adolescent Sex Offenders. LC 92-14135. 160p. (Orig.). 1992. pap. 20.20 (*0-943158-75-3*, ATABP, Prof Resc Pr) Pro Resource.

Perry, George. The Complete Phantom of the Opera. (Illus.). 176p. 1988. 29.95 (*0-8050-0657-5*) H Holt & Co.

— The Complete Phantom of the Opera. 168p. 1991. pap. 19.95 (*0-8050-1722-4*, Owl) H Holt & Co.

— The Life of Python: And Now for Something Completely Different. (Illus.). 192p. (Orig.). 1984. pap. 12.95 (*0-316-70015-0*) Little.

— The Life of Python: The History of Something Completely Different. (Illus.). 192p. 1995. pap. 16.95 (*1-56138-568-9*) Running Pr.

— Sunset Boulevard: The Making of the Musical. (Illus.). 176p. 1994. 29.95 (*0-8050-2927-3*) H Holt & Co.

Perry, George A. Ye Are Gods. (Illus.). 1993. 8.95 (*0-533-10649-4*) Vantage.

Perry, George G., ed. Religious Pieces in Prose & Verse. (EETS, OS Ser.: No. 26). 1974. reprint ed. 26.00 (*0-527-00026-4*) Periodicals Srv.

Perry, George L., jt. ed. see Okun, Arthur M.

Perry, George S. Cities of America. LC 70-128286. (Essay Index Reprint Ser.). 1977. 26.95 (*0-8369-1840-1*) Ayer.

— Hold Autumn in Your Hand. LC 75-7473. (Zia Books Ser.). 261p. 1975. reprint ed. pap. 12.95 (*0-8263-0377-3*) U of NM Pr.

— Walls Rise Up: A Novel. LC 93-37785. (Texas Tradition Ser.: No. 21). 154p. 1994. 19.95 (*0-87565-126-7*) Tex Christian.

Perry, George S. & Fuller, Arthur. Texas: A World in Itself. (Illus.). 293p. 1975. reprint ed. 8.95 (*0-88289-094-8*) Pelican.

Perry, Gerald J., jt. auth. see Malinowsky, H. Robert.

***Perry, Gill.** Women Artists & the Parisian Avant-Garde. LC 94-42772. 1995. text ed. write for info. (*0-7190-4164-3*, Pub. by Manchester Univ Pr UK) St Martin.

Perry, Gill & Rossington, Michael, eds. Femininity & Masculinity in Eighteenth-Century Art & Culture. LC 93-28181. Date not set. pap. write for info. (*0-7190-4228-3*, Pub. by Manchester Univ Pr UK) St Martin.

— Femininity & Masculinity in Eighteenth-Century Art & Culture. LC 93-28181. 1994. text ed. 79.95 (*0-7190-4227-5*, Pub. by Manchester Univ Pr UK) St Martin.

Perry, Gill, et al. Primitivism, Cubism, Abstraction: The Early Twentieth Century. (Illus.). 280p. (C). 1993. text ed. 50.00 (*0-300-05515-3*); pap. text ed. 25.00 (*0-300-05516-1*) Yale U Pr.

Perry, Glen C. Dear Bart: Washington Views of World War II. LC 81-13418. (Contributions in Military History Ser.: No. 31). xix, 341p. 1982. text ed. 59.95 (*0-313-23265-2*, PED/, Greenwood Pr) Greenwood.

Perry, Glenn & Fiorenza, Joseph. How to Start a Jukebox & Pinball Business with Little or No Money: Part-Time, Full-Time or Absentee: A Guide to the Electronic Amusement Game Business. LC 80-83931. (Illus.). (Orig.). 1985. 31.95 (*0-9602586-5-5*); pap. 25.95 (*0-9602586-4-7*) Perry Omega.

Perry, Glenn E. The Middle East: Fourteen Islamic Centuries. 2nd ed. 352p. (C). 1991. pap. text ed. 20.00 (*0-13-584459-2*, 680803) P-H.

— The Palestine Question: An Annotated Bibliography. (Bibliography Ser.: No. 6). 138p. (Orig.). 1990. pap. 6.95 (*0-937694-86-X*) Assn Arab-Amer U Grads.

Perry, Glenn E., et al. Palestine: Continuing Dispossession. LC 85-20031. (AAUG Monograph Ser.: No. 21). 145p. (Orig.). 1986. pap. 10.00 (*0-937694-72-X*) Assn Arab-Amer U Grads.

Perry, Graham. The Numbers Game. 128p. (Orig.). 1993. mass mkt. 3.99 (*0-446-60040-7*) Warner Bks.

Perry, Grant E. Musings & Forebodings. LC 93-71088. (Illus.). 60p. (Orig.). 1993. pap. 7.95 (*1-878149-22-9*) Counterpoint Pub.

Perry, Greg. Absolute Beginner's Guide to Access. 336p. 1993. 16.95 (*0-672-30366-3*) Sams.

— Absolute Beginners Guide to Programming. 400p. 1993. pap. 19.95 (*0-672-30269-1*) Sams.

— Access Programming by Example. (By Example Ser.). (Illus.). 608p. (Orig.). 1993. pap. 27.95 (*1-56529-305-3*) Que.

— Access Programming by Example. 2nd ed. (Orig.). 1994. pap. 27.95 (*1-56529-659-1*) Que.

— Borland C Plus Plus by Example. 1994. pap. 29.99 (*1-56529-756-3*) Que.

— Borland Pascal by Example. 1994. pap. 27.99 (*1-56529-757-1*) Que.

— C by Example: Special Edition. 1993. pap. 24.95 (*1-56529-438-6*) Que.

— C Plus Plus by Example. (Illus.). (Orig.). 1992. pap. 24.95 (*1-56529-038-0*) Que.

— C Plus Plus Programming 101. 1992. disk, pap. 29.95 (*0-672-30200-4*) Sams.

— C Programming in 12 Easy Lessons. (Illus.). 800p. (Orig.). 1994. Incl. diskette. pap. 39.95 (*0-672-30522-4*) Sams.

— The Complete Idiot's Guide to Q Basic. 300p. 1994. 19.95 (*1-56761-490-6*) Alpha Bks IN.

— The Complete Idiot's Guide to Visual Basic. 2nd ed. 350p. 1995. 19.99 (*1-56761-520-1*) Alpha Bks IN.

— Crash Course in QBasic. (Illus.). 250p. (Orig.). 1993. pap. 16.95 (*1-56529-165-4*) Que.

— Managing Rental Properties for Maximum Profit. 1994. pap. 14.95 (*1-55958-572-2*) Prima Pub.

— Managing Your Rental Properties for Maximum Profit: Save Time & Money with Greg Perry's Fool-Proof System. 250p. 1993. 22.95 (*1-55958-314-2*) Prima Pub.

— Moving from C to C Plus Plus. (Illus.). (Orig.). 1992. pap. 29.95 (*0-672-30080-X*) Sams.

— Moving from QBasic to C. 500p. 1993. pap. 24.95 (*0-672-30250-0*) Sams.

— QBASIC by Example. (By Example Ser.). (Illus.). 650p. (Orig.). 1992. pap. 21.95 (*0-88022-811-3*) Que.

— QBasic by Example: Special Edition. (Illus.). 704p. (Orig.). 1993. pap. 21.95 (*1-56529-439-4*) Que.

— QBasic Programming 101. 1993. disk 29.95 (*0-672-30281-0*) Sams.

— Teach Yourself Object Oriented Programming with Visual C Plus Plus in 21 Days. 1994. pap. 26.95 (*0-672-30487-2*) Sams.

— Teach Yourself Windows 95 in 24 Hours. 600p. 1995. 24.00 (*0-672-30504-6*) Sams.

— Turbo C Plus Plus by Example: Special Edition. 1993. pap. 27.95 (*1-56529-440-8*) Que.

— Turbo C Plus Plus Programming in 12 Easy Lessons. (Illus.). 800p. (Orig.). 1994. pap. 39.95 (*0-672-30523-2*) Sams.

— Turbo C Plus Plus Programming 101. 1993. pap. 29.95 (*0-672-30280-2*) Sams.

— Turbo Pascal 6 by Example. (By Example Ser.). (Illus.). 650p. (Orig.). 1992. pap. 21.95 (*0-88022-908-X*) Que.

— Using Turbo C Plus Plus for Windows. (Illus.). (Orig.). 1994. pap. 29.99 (*1-56529-837-3*) Que.

— Visual Basic for COBOL Programmers. (Illus.). 608p. (Orig.). 1995. pap. 45.00 (*0-7897-0268-1*) Que.

— Visual Basic Programming in 12 Easy Lessons. (Illus.). 600p. (Orig.). 1995. pap. 45.00 (*0-672-30728-6*) Sams.

— Visual C Plus Plus by Example. 1994. pap. 27.95 (*1-56529-687-7*) Que.

***Perry, Greg & Spencer, Ian.** Visual C Plus Plus Programming in 12 Easy Lessons. (Illus.). 600p. (Orig.). 1995. pap. 49.99 (*0-672-30637-9*) Sams.

Perry, Greg, jt. auth. see Johnson, Marcus.

Perry, Greg M. Teach Yourself Object-Oriented Programming with Turbo C Plus Plus in Twenty-One Days. LC 92-82098. 776p. 1993. pap. 26.95 (*0-672-30307-8*) Sams.

— Using MicroSoft Word Five. 1989. pap. text ed. 22.95 (*0-07-881484-7*) Osborne-McGraw.

Perry, Gregory. Graphics & Sound on the Commodore 64. (Illus.). 304p. 1986. 39.95 (*0-13-363144-3*); disk 18.95 (*0-13-363169-9*) P-H.

***Perry, Guillermo & Herrera, Ana M.** Public Finances, Stabilization & Structural Reform in Latin America. (Inter-American Development Bank Ser.). 134p. (Orig.). 1994. 15.00x (*0-940602-92-X*) IADB.

Perry, H. Mitchell. Lifelong Management of Hypertension. (Developments in Cardiovascular Medicine Ser.). 1983. lib. bdg. 117.00 (*0-89838-582-2*) Kluwer Ac.

Perry, H. W. Deciding to Decide: Agenda Setting in the United States Supreme Court. 316p. (C). 1992. 45.00 (*0-674-19442-X*) HUP.

— Deciding to Decide: Agenda Setting in the United States Supreme Court. 316p. 1994. pap. 17.95 (*0-674-19443-8*) HUP.

Perry, Helen S. Psychiatrist of America: The Life of Harry Stack Sullivan. LC 81-7066. (Illus.). 74p. 1982. 36.50 (*0-674-72076-8*) Belknap Pr.

— Psychiatrist of America: The Life of Harry Stack Sullivan. 474p. 1987. pap. 16.95 (*0-674-72077-6*) Belknap Pr.

Perry, Henry B. & Breitner, Bina. Physician Assistants: Their Contribution to Health Care. LC 81-6260. 331p. 1982. 45.95 (*0-89885-066-5*) Human Sci Pr.

Perry, Henry B., jt. auth. see Carter, Reginald.

Perry, Hilda. Broken Engagement. large type ed. (Linford Romance Library). 1989. pap. 11.95 (*0-7089-6659-4*, Linford) Ulverscroft.

— Depths of Love. large type ed. (Linford Romance Library). 1990. pap. 12.95 (*0-7089-6912-7*, Trailtree Bookshop) Ulverscroft.

Perry, Horace M., III, et al, eds. Aging, Musculoskeletal Disorders, & Care of the Frail Elderly. LC 93-1426. 392p. 1993. 48.95 (*0-8261-7930-4*) Springer Pub.

Perry, Huey L. Democracy & Public Policy. LC 85-51337. 75p. (Orig.). (C). 1985. pap. 14.95 (*0-932269-46-X*) Wyndhall Pr.

***Perry, Huey L. & Parent, Wayne, eds.** Blacks & the American Political System. LC 95-5917. (Illus.). 312p. 1995. lib. bdg. 49.95 (*0-8130-1372-0*); pap. text ed. 21.95 (*0-8130-1373-9*) U Press Fla.

Perry, I. Mac. Indian Mounds You Can Visit: One Hundred Sixty Five Aboriginal Sites on Florida's West Coast. LC 92-42075. (Illus.). 320p. (Orig.). 1993. pap. 12.95 (*0-8200-1038-3*) Great Outdoors.

Perry, Idris, tr. see Baudelaire, Charles, et al.

Perry, Inez E. & Carey, George W. Twelve Lessons in the Astro Biochemic System of Body Building. 80p. 1973. reprint ed. spiral bd. 13.20 (*0-7873-0668-1*) Mokelumne.

Perry, Inez E., jt. auth. see Carey, George W.

Perry, J., jt. tr. see Hamilton, R.

Perry, J., jt. auth. see Palladino, L.

Perry, J. A. Introduction to Analytical Gas Chromatography: History, Principles, & Practice. (Chromatographic Science Ser.: Vol. 14). 448p. 1981. 110.00 (*0-8247-1537-3*) Dekker.

Perry, J. A. & Mould, R. F., eds. RPL Dosimetry: Radiophotoluminscence in Health Physics. (Medical Science Ser.). 192p. 1987. 86.00 (*0-85274-272-X*) IOP Pub.

Perry, J. B. A Season Till Spring. 119p. 1991. pap. 5.95 (*0-8341-1393-7*) Beacon Hill.

Perry, J. Randolph, jt. auth. see Kowalsky, Richard J.

***Perry, Jack.** Clarion Chronicles, a Garden Along the Railroad Tracks: ...and Other Recollections of Growing Up in a Small Midwestern Town During the Depression. Scherban, Debra, ed. & pref. by. (Illus.). 64p. (Orig.). 1994. pap. 7.95 (*0-9618052-5-0*) Daily Hampshire.

Perry, Jackie & Perry, Roger. The P. M. S. Mail Order Catalog: Sensible Survival Products to Help the Hopelessly Harassed. LC 92-15948. (Illus.). 80p. (Orig.). 1993. pap. 6.99 (*0-8431-3433-X*) Putnam Pub Group.

Perry, Jacquelin. Gait Analysis of Normal & Pathological Function. LC 90-50830. 556p. 1992. 55.00 (*1-55642-192-3*) SLACK Inc.

Perry, Jacquelin & Hislop, Helen J. Principles of Lower-Extremity Bracing. 96p. 1970. pap. 5.00 (*0-912452-16-1*) Am Phys Therapy Assn.

Perry, Jacques. Vie d'un Paien. (FRE.). 1984. pap. 15.95 (*0-7859-4217-3*) Fr & Eur.

Perry, James. Oracle 7 Developer's Guide. 1992. pap. 39.95 (*0-672-22794-0*) Sams.

Perry, James L., ed. Handbook of Public Administration. LC 88-46078. (Public Administration Ser.). 696p. 1989. 59.95x (*1-55542-128-8*) Jossey-Bass.

Perry, James R. The Formation of a Society on Virginia's Eastern Shore, 1615-1655. LC 90-11980. (Institute of Early American History & Culture Ser.). xiv, 254p. (C). 1990. 34.95 (*0-8078-1927-1*) U of NC Pr.

Perry, James T. Application Development Using Object Vision. LC 93-43455. 274p. (C). 1994. pap. 21.95 (*0-87709-140-4*, BF1404) S-W Pub.

***Perry, James T. & Schneider, Gary P.** Building Accounting Systems: A Transaction Cycle Approach. 1994. write for info. (*0-538-84454-X*) S-W Pub.

— Building Accounting Systems Access Ed. A Transaction Cycle Approach. LC 95-1160. 1996. pap. 37.95 (*0-538-84897-9*) S-W Pub.

***Perry, Jan F.** Kinesiology Workbook. 2nd ed. 200p. 1995. pap. 21.95 (*0-8036-0046-1*) Davis Co.

Perry, Jan F., et al. The Kinesiology Workbook. (Illus.). 196p. (Orig.). 1992. pap. text ed. 21.95 (*0-8036-6862-7*) Davis Co.

Perry, Jane G., jt. auth. see Perry, John.

Perry, Janet. Counselling for Women. LC 93-15402. (Counselling in Context Ser.). 128p. 1993. pap. 23.00 (*0-335-19034-0*, Open Univ Pr) Taylor & Francis.

***Perry, Jason L.** Bag Visitors. LC 95-60149. 112p. 1995. per., pap. 6.95 (*0-614-06585-2*) TWanda.

Perry, Jean. Make Your Own Horse Clothing. 112p. (C). 1990. pap. 21.00 (*0-85131-383-3*, Pub. by J A Allen & Co UK) St Mut.

— Make Your Own Horse Equipment. 111p. (C). 1990. pap. 21.00 (*0-85131-393-0*, Pub. by J A Allen & Co UK) St Mut.

Perry, Jeb H. Screen Gems: A History of Columbia Pictures Television from Cohn to Coke, 1948-1983. LC 91-33388. 385p. 1991. 42.50 (*0-8108-2487-6*) Scarecrow.

— Variety Obits: An Index to Obituaries in Variety 1905-1978. LC 80-10424. 322p. 1980. 29.50 (*0-8108-1289-4*) Scarecrow.

Perry, Jesse P., Jr. Pines of Mexico & Central America. LC 90-10774. (Illus.). 221p. 1991. 35.95 (*0-88192-174-2*) Timber.

Perry, Jim. Sleeper Awakes: A Journey to Sleep-Awareness. 1992. pap. 11.95 (*0-945806-06-X*) Summit CA.

Perry, Jim, ed. Administering Oregon Estates, 1991. rev. ed. write for info. (*0-318-61743-9*) OR Bar CLE.

***Perry, Jo Ellen & Levin, Harold D.** Object-Oriented Design & Implemetation in C++ 600p. (C). 1996. pap. text ed. write for info. (*0-201-76564-0*) Addison-Wesley.

Perry, John. Exploring the Transfiguration Story. LC 92-26971. (Exploring Scripture Ser.). 64p. (Orig.). (C). 1993. pap. 5.95 (*1-55612-574-7*, LL1574) Sheed & Ward MO.

— Forty Cords of Wood. (American Autobiography Ser.). 459p. 1995. reprint ed. lib. bdg. 99.00 (*0-7812-8615-8*) Rprt Serv.

— James A. Herne: The American Ibsen. LC 77-17931. (Illus.). 344p. 1978. 35.95 (*0-88229-265-X*) Nelson-Hall.

— The Problem of the Essential Indexical: And Other Essays. LC 92-33242. (Illus.). 352p. (C). 1993. 42.00 (*0-19-504999-3*) OUP.

— State of Russia Under the Present Czar. (Russian Through European Eyes Ser.). 1968. reprint ed. lib. bdg. 45.00 (*0-306-77021-0*) Da Capo.

Perry, John, ed. Doing Fieldwork: Eight Personal Accounts of Social Research. 155p. (C). 1989. pap. 69.00x (*0-7300-0786-3*, Pub. by Deakin Univ AT) St Mut.

— Personal Identity. (Topics in Philosophy Ser.: Vol. 2). 246p. 1975. pap. 13.00 (*0-520-02960-7*) U CA Pr.

Perry, John & Bratman, Michael S. Introduction to Philosophy: Classical & Contemporary Readings. 2nd ed. 896p. (C). 1993. text ed. 39.95 (*0-19-506936-6*) OUP.

An Asterisk (*) at the beginning of an entry indicates that the title is appearing in BIP for the first time.

Perry, John & Perry, Jane G. The Nature of Florida. Arnett, Ross H., Jr., ed. LC 94-3146. (Illus.). 246p. (YA). (gr. 6-12). 1994. pap. 15.95 (*1-877743-20-8*) Sandhill Crane.
— The Sierra Club Guide to the Natural Areas of California. LC 82-16939. (Sierra Club Guides to the Natural Areas of the United States Ser.). (Illus.). 352p. (Orig.). 1983. pap. 10.00 (*0-87156-333-9*) Sierra.
— The Sierra Club Guide to the Natural Areas of Colorado & Utah. LC 84-22215. (Guides to the Natural Areas of the United States Ser.). (Illus.). 416p. (Orig.). 1985. pap. 10.00 (*0-87156-832-2*) Sierra.
— The Sierra Club Guide to the Natural Areas of Florida. LC 92-905. (Guides to the Natural Areas of the United States Ser.). 416p. (Orig.). 1992. pap. 12.00 (*0-87156-551-X*) Sierra.
— The Sierra Club Guide to the Natural Areas of Idaho, Montana & Wyoming. LC 87-26312. (Guides to the Natural Areas of the United States Ser.). 416p. (Orig.). 1988. pap. 13.00 (*0-87156-781-4*) Sierra.
— The Sierra Club Guide to the Natural Areas of New England: Maine, Vermont, New Hampshire, Massachusetts, Rhode Island, & Connecticut. LC 89-37536. (Guides to the Natural Areas of the United States Ser.). (Illus.). 400p. 1990. pap. 14.00 (*0-87156-744-X*) Sierra.
— The Sierra Club Guide to the Natural Areas of New Mexico, Arizona, & Nevada. LC 85-18481. (Guides to the Natuareal Areas of the United States Ser.). (Illus.). 448p. 1986. pap. 12.00 (*0-87156-753-9*) Sierra.
— The Sierra Club Guide to the Natural Areas of Oregon & Washington. LC 82-16937. (Guides to the Natural Areas of the United States Ser.). (Illus.). 360p. (Orig.). 1983. pap. 12.00 (*0-87156-334-7*) Sierra.
Perry, John, tr. see Alavi, Bozorg, et al.
Perry, John, ed. see Berkeley, George.
Perry, John, jt. auth. see Dotterweich, Kass.
Perry, John, ed. see Meskoob, Shahrokh.
Perry, John A. & Perry, Erna K. The Social Web: An Introduction to Sociology. 5th ed. 405p. (C). 1990. pap. text ed. 22.25 (*0-06-045123-8*) HarpCollege.
— The Social Web: An Introduction to Sociology. 6th ed. LC 92-28783. (C). 1992. text ed. 28.50 (*0-06-501212-7*) HarpCollege.
Perry, John A., jt. ed. see Domsky, Irving I.
Perry, John C. Facing West: Americans & the Opening of the Pacific. LC 94-11302. 400p. 1994. text ed. 65.00 (*0-275-94920-6*, Praeger Pubs); pap. text ed. 19.95 (*0-275-94965-6*, Praeger Pubs) Greenwood.
Perry, John H. Adventures of Freddie. (C). 1989. 30.00 (*0-7223-2347-6*, Pub. by A H S Ltd UK) St Mut.
***Perry, John M.** Exploring the Evolution of the Lord's Supper in the New Testament. 160p. (Orig.). 1994. pap. 9.95 (*1-55612-721-9*) Sheed & Ward MO.
— Exploring the Genesis Creation & Fall Stories. LC 92-5024. (Exploring Scripture Ser.). 64p. (Orig.). (C). 1992. pap. 5.95 (*1-55612-553-4*, LL1553) Sheed & Ward MO.
— Exploring the Resurrection of Jesus. LC 93-29160. 160p. 1993. pap. 5.95 (*1-55612-670-0*) Sheed & Ward MO.
Perry, John O. Absent Authority: Issues in Contemporary Indian English Criticism. 1993. text ed. 45.00 (*81-207-1506-3*, Pub. by Sterling Pubs II) Apt Bks.
Perry, John O., ed. Voices of Emergency: An All India Anthology of Protest Poetry of the 1975-77 Emergency, India. 1983. 28.50 (*0-317-05076-1*, Pub. by Popular Prakashan II) S Asia.
Perry, John R. A Dialogue on Personal Identity & Immortality. LC 78-52943. 60p. (C). 1978. lib. bdg. 21.50 (*0-915144-91-3*); pap. text ed. 3.95 (*0-915144-53-0*) Hackett Pub.
— Form & Meaning in Persian Vocabulary: The Arabic Feminine Ending. 270p. (C). 1991. lib. bdg. 45.00 (*0-939214-67-9*) Mazda Pubs.
Perry, John W. The Far Side of Madness. LC 89-21572. (Jungian Classics Ser.: No. 12). 177p. 1974. reprint ed. pap. 14.00 (*0-88214-511-8*) Spring Pubns.
— The Heart of History: Individuality in Evolution. LC 86-14428. (SUNY Series in Transpersonal & Humanistic Psychology). 249p. 1987. 59.50 (*0-88706-399-3*); pap. 19.95 (*0-88706-400-0*) State U NY Pr.
— Lord of the Four Quarters: The Mythology of Kingship. 1991. pap. 12.95 (*0-8091-3252-4*) Paulist Pr.
— Roots of Renewal in Myth & Madness: The Meaning of Psychotic Episodes. LC 76-19500. (Jossey-Bass Behavioral Science Ser.). 268p. reprint ed. pap. 76.40 (*0-317-42373-8*, 2052164) Bks Demand.
Perry, Joseph B., Jr. & Pugh, Meredith. Collective Behavior: Response to Social Stress. (Illus.). 324p. 1978. pap. text ed. 27.25 (*0-8299-0158-2*) West Pub.
Perry, Joseph M. The Impact of Immigration on Three American Industries, 1865-1914. LC 77-14788. (Dissertations in American Economic History Ser.). 1978. 23.95 (*0-405-11052-9*) Ayer.
Perry, Josephine. Cookies from Many Lands. (Cookbook Ser.). 160p. (J). (gr. 6-12). 1972. reprint ed. pap. 4.95 (*0-486-22832-0*) Dover.
***Perry, Kate.** Gerbils. LC 94-26049. (Illus.). (J). 1995. write for info. (*0-8120-9081-0*) Barron.
— Pieces of Earth. Lyons Graphic Designs Staff, ed. (Illus.). 159p. (Orig.). 1994. pap. text ed. write for info. (*0-9626823-5-7*) Perry ME.
Perry, Kathleen A. Another Reality. LC 89-12639. (American University Studies: Classical Languages & Literature: Ser. XVII, Vol. 10). 260p. 1990. text ed. 43.50 (*0-8204-1112-4*) P Lang Pubs.
Perry, Katy. Mad Tuesdays. Lyons, Lisa, ed. (Illus.). 160p. (Orig.). 1992. pap. 12.95 (*0-9626823-3-0*) Perry ME.
— My Grandmother Wears Crazy Hats. Minor, Mary E., ed. (Illus.). 16p. (J). (gr. k-5). 1993. pap. 4.95 (*0-9626823-4-9*) Perry ME.
— Only One Ice-Box to Fill. Steele, Robert, ed. (Illus.). 169p. (Orig.). 1990. pap. text ed. 10.00 (*0-9626823-1-4*) Perry ME.
Perry, Larry L. Compilation & Review Manual. 240p. 1987. ring bd. 95.00 (*0-13-162934-4*, Busn) P-H.
— Compilation & Review Manual Documentation. 144p. 1987. text ed. 40.00 (*0-13-162942-5*) P-H.
— Documentation Manual. 512p. 1988. ring bd. 130.00 (*0-13-217175-9*, Busn) P-H.
— Documentation Manual: Supplemental Document Package. 688p. 1988. text ed. 50.00 (*0-13-217209-7*, Busn) P-H.
— Engagement Performance Manual. 248p. 1987. ring bd. 120.00 (*0-13-277195-0*, Busn) P-H.
— Guide to Quality & Efficiency for Prentice Hall's Accounting & Auditing Manual. 148p. 1988. pap. text ed. 19.95 (*0-13-370628-1*, Busn) P-H.
— Guide to Quality & Efficiency for Prentice Hall's Compilation & Review Manual. 64p. 1987. pap. text ed. 19.95 (*0-13-370644-3*, Busn) P-H.
— Guide to Quality & Efficiency for Prentice Hall's Small Business Audit Manual. 116p. 1987. pap. text ed. 24.95 (*0-13-370677-X*) P-H.
— Prospective Financial Statements Documentation Manual. 432p. 1988. ring bd. 69.95 (*0-13-731373-X*, Busn) P-H.
— Reporting Manual. 248p. 1987. ring bd. 95.00 (*0-13-773490-5*, Busn) P-H.
— Small Business Audit Manual Vol. 2. 344p. 1987. 140.00 (*0-13-813155-4*) P-H.
— Small Business Audit Manual Documentation. 176p. 1987. pap. 50.00 (*0-13-813106-6*) P-H.
Perry, Larry L., jt. auth. see Marthinuss, George.
Perry, Laurens B. Juarez & Diaz: Machine Politics in Mexico. LC 76-14671. (Origins of Modern Mexico Ser.). 467p. 1978. 25.00 (*0-87580-058-0*) N Ill U Pr.
Perry, Lee, ed. see Mooney, F. Bentley, Jr.
Perry, Lee T., et al. Real-Time Strategy: Improvised Team-Based Planning for a Fast Changing World. 272p. 1993. text ed. 27.95 (*0-471-58564-5*) Wiley.
Perry, Leslie A., jt. auth. see Fry, Edward B.
Perry, Lewis. Boats Against the Current: American Culture Between Revolution & Modernity, 1820-1860. LC 92-11094. 352p. (C). 1993. 35.00 (*0-19-506091-1*) OUP.
— Intellectual Life in America: A History. LC 88-27770. xxii, 462p. 1989. pap. text ed. 15.95 (*0-226-66101-6*) U Ch Pr.
— Radical Abolitionism: Anarchy & the Government of God in Antislavery Thought. LC 95-4355. 1995. write for info. (*0-87049-899-1*) U of Tenn Pr.
Perry, Lewis & Fellman, Michael, eds. Antislavery Reconsidered: New Perspectives on the Abolitionists. LC 78-10177. 416p. 1979. pap. text ed. 14.95 (*0-8071-0889-8*) La State U Pr.
Perry, Lewis C. Childhood Marriage & Reform: Henry Clarke Wright, 1797-1870. LC 79-13649. 1980. lib. bdg. 28.00 (*0-226-66100-8*) U Ch Pr.
Perry, Lilla S. My Friend Carl Sandburg: The Biography of a Friendship. Perry, E. Caswell, ed. LC 80-21908. 234p. 1981. 25.00 (*0-8108-1367-X*) Scarecrow.
Perry, Linda A., et al, eds. Constructing & Reconstructing Gender: The Links among Communication, Language, & Gender. LC 91-29718. (SUNY Series in Feminist Criticism & Theory). 320p. (C). 1992. 59.50 (*0-7914-1009-9*); pap. 19.95 (*0-7914-1010-2*) State U NY Pr.
Perry, Lloyd M. Biblical Preaching for Today's World. LC 73-7471. 256p. (C). 1973. 19.99 (*0-8024-0715-3*) Moody.
— Manual for Biblical Preaching. 1965. pap. 19.99 (*0-8010-7047-3*) Baker Bk.
— Predicacion Biblica para el Mundo Actual. Carrodeguas, Angel A., tr. Orig. Title: Biblical Preaching for Today's World. 176p. (SPA.). (C). 1986. 6.95 (*0-8297-0957-6*) Life Pubs Intl.
Perry, Lo Sun, jt. auth. see Shou-hsin Teng.
Perry, Lois J. Million Dollar Planning: A Step by Step Plan. LC 93-43155. 108p. (Orig.). 1993. pap. 11.95 (*1-882185-16-1*) Crnrstone Pub.
Perry, Lora, jt. auth. see Perry, Steve.
Perry, Louise M. & Schwengel, Jeanne S. Marine Shells of the Western Coast of Florida. rev. ed. (Illus.). 262p. 1955. 10.00 (*0-87710-370-4*); pap. 8.00 (*0-87710-369-0*) Paleo Res.
***Perry, Lynn E.** Sacramental Cocoa: And Other Stories from the Parish of the Poor. LC 94-43406. 160p. (Orig.). 1995. pap. 12.99 (*0-664-25521-3*) Westminster John Knox.
Perry, M. Aerospace Instrumentation, Vol. 4: Proceedings of the 4th International Aerospace Symposium 1966. LC 61-17510. (International Symposium Ser.: Vol. 9). 1967. 127.00 (*0-08-012048-2*, Pub. by Pergamon Repr UK) Franklin.
— Flight Test Instrumentation, Vol. 3: Proceedings of the 3rd International Symposium 1964. LC 61-17510. (Cranfield International Symposium Ser.: Vol. 6). 1965. 130.00 (*0-08-011074-6*, Pub. by Pergamon Repr UK) Franklin.
Perry, Mac. Landscaping in Florida: A Photo Idea Book. LC 88-28875. (Illus.). 256p. 1993. pap. 21.95 (*1-56164-057-3*) Pineapple Pr.
— Mac Perry's Florida Lawn & Garden Care. LC 84-80148. (Illus.). 128p. 1984. pap. 6.95 (*0-9613236-0-4*) Florida Flair Bks.
Perry, Margaret. Bio-Bibliography of Countee P. Cullen, 1903-1946. LC 75-105995. 134p. 1970. text ed. 47.95 (*0-8371-3325-4*, PCC&, Negro U Pr) Greenwood.
— Silence to the Drums. LC 74-19806. (Contributions in Afro-American & African Studies: No. 18). 194p. 1976. text ed. 27.50 (*0-8371-7847-9*, PSD/, Greenwood Pr) Greenwood.
Perry, Margaret, ed. The Short Fiction of Rudolph Fisher. LC 86-29580. (Contributions in Afro-American & African Studies: No. 107). 242p. 1987. text ed. 49.95 (*0-313-21348-8*, FPF, Greenwood Pr) Greenwood.
Perry, Margaret A. Using Microcomputers with Gifted Students. LC 89-61966. (Fastback Ser.: No. 295). 40p. (Orig.). (C). 1989. pap. 1.25 (*0-87367-295-X*) Phi Delta Kappa.
Perry, Marion. Dishes. Walsh, Joy, ed. (Little Bks.). (Illus.). 25p. (YA). 1988. pap. 5.00 (*0-938838-29-6*) Textile Bridge.
— Establishing Intimacy. Walsh, Joy, ed. (Illus.). 38p. (Orig.). 1982. pap. 3.75 (*0-938838-05-9*) Textile Bridge.
— Getting More with Less: Learning How to Learn. 150p. (Orig.). (C). 1993. pap. text ed. 25.00 (*0-9632200-2-0*) Marienhelz Artisans.
— Icarcus. 1980. write for info. (*0-938838-03-2*) Textile Bridge.
Perry, Marion, ed. Word Worth Anthology of Fiction. 202p. (C). 1992. pap. text ed. 15.00 (*0-9632200-0-4*) Marienhelz Artisans.
Perry, Marion, intro. Artisans Anthology of Drama. 134p. (Orig.). (C). 1994. pap. text ed. 12.00 (*0-9632200-3-9*) Marienhelz Artisans.
— Word Worth Anthology of Poetry. 154p. (Orig.). (C). 1993. pap. text ed. 15.00 (*0-9632200-1-2*) Word Worth.
Perry, Marion, ed. see Crombie, Mildred.
Perry, Mark. Fire in Zion: How Israel & the Palestinians Made Peace. 1994. 25.00 (*0-688-12171-3*) Morrow.
Perry, Mark C. Morigu: The Desecration. 336p. (Orig.). 1986. pap. 3.50 (*0-445-20300-5*) Warner Bks.
Perry, Marvin. Man's Unfinished Journey: A World History. 2nd annot. ed. LC 79-84595. (Illus.). (J). (gr. 10-12). 1980. Activities bk. teacher ed, pap. 16.76 (*0-395-27558-X*) HM.
— Man's Unfinished Journey: A World History. 2nd ed. LC 79-84595. (Illus.). (J). (gr. 10-12). 1980. teacher ed, pap. 29.92 (*0-395-27557-1*) HM.
— Man's Unfinished Journey: A World History. 2nd ed. LC 79-84595. (Illus.). (J). (gr. 10-12). 1980. pap. 13.40 (*0-395-27562-8*) HM.
Perry, Marvin & Scweitzer, Frederick M., eds. Jewish-Christian Encounters over the Centuries: Symbiosis, Prejudice, Holocaust, Dialogue, Vol. 136. LC 93-31044. (American University Studies: History: Ser. IX, Vol. 136). 436p. (C). 1994. text ed. 52.95 (*0-8204-2082-4*) P Lang Pubs.
Perry, Marvin, jt. ed. see McIntire, C. T.
Perry, Marvin, et al. Sources of the Western Tradition, 2 vols., 1. 2nd ed. (C). 1991. write for info. (*0-395-47304-7*) HM Soft Schl Col Div.
— Sources of the Western Tradition, 2 vols., 2. 2nd ed. (C). 1991. write for info. (*0-395-47305-5*) HM Soft Schl Col Div.
— Sources of the Western Tradition, Vol. 2. LC 86-81593. (C). 1987. pap. text ed. 19.16 (*0-685-17245-7*) HM.
— Western Civilization: Ideas, Politics, & Society. 3rd ed. 1989. teacher ed write for info. (*0-318-63330-2*) HM.
— Western Civilization: Ideas, Politics, & Society, 4 Vols. 4th ed. (C). 1991. pap. 55.16 (*0-395-59330-1*) HM.
— Western Civilization: Ideas, Politics & Society: From the 1400s, 4 Vols. 4th ed. (C). 1991. pap. 47.96 (*0-395-59333-6*) HM.
— Western Civilization: Ideas, Politics & Society, Vol. One: To 1789, 4 Vols. 4th ed. (C). 1991. pap. 39.96 (*0-395-59331-X*) HM.
— Western Civilization: Ideas, Politics & Society, Vol. Two: From the 1600s, 4 Vols. 4th ed. (C). 1991. pap. 39.96 (*0-395-59332-8*) HM.
Perry, Mary E. Crime & Society in Early Modern Seville. LC 79-66452. 311p. reprint ed. pap. 88.70 (*0-7837-2617-1*, 2042952) Bks Demand.
— Gender & Disorder in Early Modern Seville. (Illus.). 202p. (C). 1990. text ed. 45.00 (*0-691-03143-6*); pap. text ed. 13.95 (*0-691-00854-X*) Princeton U Pr.
Perry, Mary E. & Cruz, Anne J., eds. Cultural Encounters: The Impact of the Inquisition in Spain & the New World. LC 90-22450. (Publications of the Center for Medieval & Renaissance Studies: No. 24). (Illus.). 320p. 1991. 35.00 (*0-520-07098-4*) U CA Pr.
Perry, Mary E., jt. ed. see Cruz, Anne J.
Perry, Mary E., jt. auth. see Green, Harvey.
Perry, Matthew C. Narrative of the Expedition of an American Squadron to the China Seas & Japan, 3 Vols, Set. Hawks, Francis L., ed. LC 01-4228. (Illus.). reprint ed. write for info. (*0-404-05060-3*) AMS Pr.
Perry, Matthew C., et al. Narrative of the Expedition of an American Squadron to the China Seas & Japan Performed in the Years 1852, 1853, & 1854 under the Command of Commodore M. C. Perry, United States Navy, by Order of the Government of the United States, Vol. 1. 1968. 60.95 (*0-405-18940-0*, 17148) Ayer.
— Narrative of the Expedition of an American Squadron to the China Seas & Japan Performed in the Years 1852, 1853 & 1854, Under the Command of Commodore M. C. Perry, United States Navy, by Order of the Government of the United States, Vol. 3. 1968. 60.95 (*0-405-18942-7*, 17150) Ayer.
— Narrative of the Expedition of an American Squadron to the China Seas & Japan Performed in the Years 1852, 1853, & 1854 under the Command of Commodore M. C. Perry, United States Navy, by Order of the Government of the United States, Vol. 4. 1968. 60.95 (*0-405-18943-5*, 17151) Ayer.
— Narrative of the Expedition of an American Squadron to the China Seas & Japan Performed in the Years 1852, 1853, 1854, under the Command of Commodore M. C. Perry, United States Navy, by Order of the Government of the United States, Vol. 2. 1968. 60.95 (*0-405-18941-9*, 17149) Ayer.
Perry, Michael. The Dramatized New Testament. LC 93-23807. 440p. 1993. reprint ed. kivar 22.99 (*0-8010-7123-2*) Baker Bk.
— The Dramatized Old Testament Vol. 1: Genesis to Esther. 400p. 1994. pap. 22.99 (*0-8010-7136-4*) Baker Bk.
— Singing to God. 312p. (Orig.). 1995. pap. 16.95 (*0-916642-59-3*) Hope Pub.
Perry, Michael, et al, eds. Come Rejoice! 107p. (Orig.). 1989. pap. 11.95 (*0-916642-38-0*) Hope Pub.
Perry, Michael C. The Chemotherapy Source Book. (Illus.). 1192p. 1992. 140.00 (*0-683-06859-8*) Williams & Wilkins.
Perry, Michael J. The Constitution in the Courts: Law or Politics? LC 93-18539. 1994. Acid-free paper. 35.00 (*0-19-508347-4*) OUP.
— The Constitution, the Courts, & Human Rights: An Inquiry into the Legitimacy of Constitutional Policymaking by the Judiciary. LC 82-40164. 242p. 1984. reprint ed. pap. 14.00 (*0-300-03238-2*, Y-497) Yale U Pr.
— Love & Power: The Role of Morality & Religion in American Politics. 240p. 1991. 35.00 (*0-19-506860-2*) OUP.
— Love & Power: The Role of Religion & Morality in American Politics. 240p. 1993. reprint ed. pap. 14.95 (*0-19-508355-5*) OUP.
— Morality, Politics, & Law. 336p. 1990. reprint ed. pap. 15.95 (*0-19-506456-9*) OUP.
Perry, Michael R. The Groom's Survival Manual. Marrow, Linda, ed. 224p. (Orig.). 1991. pap. 12.00 (*0-671-69357-3*) PB.
— Skelter. Chellus, Jane, ed. 560p. (Orig.). 1994. mass mkt. 5.99 (*0-671-73496-2*, Pocket Star Bks) PB.
— The Stranger Returns. Marrow, Linda, ed. 432p. (Orig.). 1992. mass mkt. 5.50 (*0-671-73495-4*, Pocket Star Bks) PB.
Perry, Michalann. Captive Surrender. 496p. 1987. pap. 3.95 (*0-8217-1986-6*) Zebra.
— Defiant Splendor. 512p. 1988. pap. 3.95 (*0-8217-2374-X*) Zebra.
— Fortune's Choice. 512p. 1988. pap. 3.95 (*0-8217-2481-9*) Zebra.
— Love's Windswept Embrace. 1990. mass mkt. 4.50 (*0-8217-3065-7*) Zebra.
— Rapture's Deception. (Hologram Romances Ser.). 1987. pap. 3.95 (*0-8217-2204-2*) Zebra.
— Savage Rogue. 1989. pap. 3.95 (*0-8217-2619-6*) Zebra.
— Touched by Fire. 448p. 1991. mass mkt. 4.50 (*0-8217-3388-5*) Zebra.
Perry, Milton F. Infernal Machines: The Story of Confederate Submarine & Mine Warfare. LC 85-9706. (Illus.). 231p. 1985. pap. 9.95 (*0-8071-1285-2*) La State U Pr.
Perry, Milton F., et al. The Kansas City Archaeologist. (Kansas City Archaeologists Special Bulletin Ser., 1986: No. 1). (Illus.). 104p. (Orig.). 1986. pap. 5.95 (*0-318-22802-5*) KC Archaeol Soc.
Perry, Murvin H. Murv's Motoring Memories. (Illus.). 160p. 1993. pap. 9.95 (*0-932807-72-0*) Overmountain Pr.
Perry, Nancy W. & Wrightsman, Lawrence S. The Child Witness: Legal Issues & Dilemmas. (Illus.). 280p. 1991. text ed. 49.95 (*0-8039-3771-7*); pap. text ed. 24.00 (*0-8039-3772-5*) Sage.
Perry, Natalie. Teaching the Mentally Retarded Child: Enlarged to Survey All Trainable Retardates & Their Social Needs. 2nd ed. LC 73-20246. 750p. 1974. text ed. 50.00 (*0-231-03652-3*) Col U Pr.
Perry, Nathan W., jt. auth. see Belar, Cynthia D.
Perry, Nell, ed. see Barnes, T. W. & Freeman, Nona.
Perry, Nell, ed. see Freeman, Nona.
Perry, Newman S. Business, Government, & Society: Managing Competitiveness, Ethics & Social Issues. (Illus.). 825p. (C). 1994. text ed. write for info. (*0-02-393401-8*) Macmillan.
Perry, Nicholas. Ruskin's Drawings in the Ashmolean Museum. (Illus.). 79p. text ed. 19.95 (*1-879504-74-X*, Pub. by Ashmolean Mus UK); pap. 17.95 (*0-685-71009-2*, Pub. by Ashmolean Mus UK) A Schwartz & Co.
— Ruskin's Drawings in the Ashmolean Museum. (Illus.). 79p. 1995. 19.95 (*1-85444-039-X*, 741, Pub. by Ashmolean Mus UK); pap. 17.95 (*0-907849-74-1*, 741P, Pub. by Ashmolean Mus UK) A Schwartz & Co.
Perry, Nicholas & Echeverria, Loreto. Under the Heel of Mary. 336p. 1989. 39.95 (*0-415-01296-1*) Routledge.
Perry, Oliver H. Hunting Expeditions of Oliver Hazard Perry: As Recorded in the Diaries Kept from 1836 Through 1855 by Oliver Hazard Perry of Cleveland, Ohio. deluxe ed. LC 94-4228. (Illus.). 299p. 1994. 150.00 (*0-9633094-3-9*) St Huberts Pr.
— Hunting Expeditions of Oliver Hazard Perry: As Recorded in the Diaries Kept from 1836 Through 1855 by Oliver Hazard Perry of Cleveland, Ohio. LC 94-4228. (Illus.). 299p. 1994. reprint ed. 45.00 (*0-9633094-2-0*) St Huberts Pr.
Perry, P. Approaching Economics. (C). 1989. 120.00 (*0-685-37700-8*, Pub. by S Thornes Pubs UK) St Mut.
— Scattering Theory by the Enss Method. (Mathematical Reports: Vol. 1, No. 1). 347p. 1983. text ed. 205.00 (*3-7186-0093-5*) Gordon & Breach.
Perry, Patricia, jt. auth. see Lynch, Marietta.
Perry, Paul. Fasting Safely. LC 78-68564. 128p. (Orig.). 1980. pap. 4.95 (*0-89037-217-9*) Anderson World.
— Fear & Loathing: The Strange & Terrible Saga of Hunter S. Thompson. (Illus.). 288p. 1993. 22.95 (*1-56025-012-7*); pap. 11.95 (*1-56025-065-8*) Thunders Mouth.
— Insiders Guide to Software Development. 1994. pap. 24.99 (*1-56529-864-0*) Que.

— Multimedia Developer's Guide with CD-ROM. 1994. pap. 49.95 (*0-672-30160-1*) Sams.
— Teach Yourself More Visual Basic 3 in 21 Days. 1994. disk, pap. 35.00 (*0-672-30495-3*) Sams.
— World Wide Web Secrets. 1995. pap. 39.99 (*1-56884-456-5*) IDG Bks.
Perry, Paul & Babbs, Ken. On the Bus: The Complete Guide to the Legendary Trip of Ken Kesey & the Merry Pranksters & the Birth of the Counterculture. (Non-Fiction - Photo Ser.). (Illus.). 224p. 1990. pap. 21.95 (*0-938410-91-1*) Thunders Mouth.
Perry, Paul, jt. auth. see Brinkley, Dannion.
Perry, Paul, jt. auth. see Moody, Raymond.
Perry, Paul, jt. auth. see Morse, Melvin.
Perry, Paul, jt. auth. see Que Development Group Staff.
Perry, Paul J. C for Rookies. (Illus.). 250p. (Orig.). 1993. Incl. disk. disk, pap. 19.95 (*1-56529-280-4*) Que.
— Crash Course in C. (Illus.). 250p. (Orig.). 1993. pap. 16. 95 (*1-56529-149-2*) Que.
— Do It Yourself Turbo C Plus Plus. (Illus.). (Orig.). 1992. pap. 24.95 (*0-672-30107-5*) Sams.
— Windows Programming for Beginners with Turbo C Plus Plus for Windows. 1993. pap. 39.95 (*0-672-30229-2*) Sams.
Perry, Paul J., jt. auth. see Callahan, Roger.
Perry, Paul J., jt. auth. see Morse, Melvin L.
Perry, Paul J., jt. auth. see Phaigh, Rich.
Perry, Paul J., et al. Psychotropic Drug Handbook. 6th ed. LC 90-71835. (Illus.). vi, 358p. 1991. pap. text ed. 38.75 (*0-929375-06-8*) H W Bks.
***Perry, Peter C.** Hours into Minutes. (C). 1983. pap. 30.00x (*0-905675-02-9*, Pub. by IPM Hse UK) St Mut.
Perry, Philip. Birds of Prey. 1990. 19.99 (*0-517-03167-1*) Random Hse Value.
— Opportunities in Banking. (Opportunities in...Ser.). (Illus.). 160p. 1993. 13.95 (*0-8442-4049-4*, VGM Career Bks); pap. 10.95 (*0-8442-4050-8*, VGM Career Bks) NTC Pub Grp.
Perry, Philip & Weiss, Ellen. Facts America: Birds. LC 92-9403. (Illus.). 64p. (J). (gr. 2-6). 1993. 7.98 (*0-8317-2315-7*) Smithmark.
***Perry, Philippa.** Amazing Animals. Clayton, Caroline & Kelleher, Damian, eds. (Info Adventure Ser.). (Illus.). 32p. (J). (gr. 4-6). 1995. pap. 5.95 (*1-56847-314-1*) Thomson Lrning.
— Amazing Animals. Clayton, Caroline & Kelleher, Damian, eds. (Info Adventure Ser.). (Illus.). 32p. (J). (gr. 4-6). 1995. 12.95 (*1-56847-407-5*) Thomson Lrning.
— Mega Machines. Carmichael, Nicole, ed. (Info Adventure Ser.). (Illus.). (J). (gr. 4-6). 1995. 12.95 (*1-56847-410-5*); pap. 5.95 (*1-56847-317-6*) Thomson Lrning.
Perry, Phillip A., ed. see Calhoun, W. L.
***Perry, Phyllis J.** Colorado History: Creative Activities for Curious Kids. 85p. 1994. ring bd. 12.00 (*0-931510-55-4*) Hi Willow.
— The Fiddlehoppers: Crickets, Katydids, & Locusts. (First Bks.). (Illus.). 64p. (J). (gr. 4-6). 1995. lib. bdg. 13.93 (*0-531-20209-7*) Watts.
— Getting Started in Science Fairs: From Planning to Judging. LC 94-44103. (J). 1995. pap. text ed. 14.95 (*0-07-049526-2*) TAB Bks.
— A Teacher's Science Companion: Resources & Activities in Science & Math. LC 93-43620. 1994. text ed. 24.95 (*0-07-049518-1*); pap. text ed. 14.95 (*0-07-049519-X*) TAB Bks.
— The World of Water: Linking Fiction to Nonfiction. LC 94-44426. (Literature Bridges to Science Ser.). xvi, 149p. (J). (gr. 4-9). 1995. pap. text ed. 21.50 (*1-56308-321-3*) Teacher Ideas Pr.
— The World's Regions & Weather: Linking Fiction to Nonfiction. (Literature Bridges to Science Ser.). 150p. 1995. pap. text ed. 22.00 (*1-56308-338-8*) Teacher Ideas Pr.
Perry, Phyllis J. & Hoback, John R. A Guide to Independent Research. 69p. 1986. pap. 9.95 (*0-937659-33-9*) GCT.
Perry, R., ed. see Institute of Criminology, University of Cambridge, England Staff.
Perry, R. A., jt. ed. see Goodall, D. W.
Perry, R. L., jt. auth. see Henderson, S. M.
Perry, R. Scott, ed. see Fischer, Fred.
***Perry, Rachel.** Reverse the Aging Process of Your Face: A Simple Technique That Works. 1994. pap. 12.95 (*0-89529-625-X*) Avery Pub.
Perry, Rae. Wild Friends. 1987. pap. 7.95 (*0-930096-82-7*) G Gannett.
Perry, Ralph B. Characteristically American. LC 73-134125. (Essay Index Reprint Ser.). 1977. 20.95 (*0-8369-2013-9*) Ayer.
— The Free Man & the Soldier. LC 73-24250. (Select Bibliographies Reprint Ser.). 1977. reprint ed. 18.95 (*0-8369-5438-6*) Ayer.
— General Theory of Values: Its Meaning & Basic Principles Construed in Terms of Interest. 720p. reprint ed. pap. 180.00 (*0-317-08109-8*, 2006422) Bks Demand.
— In the Spirit of William James. LC 78-31937. 211p. 1979. reprint ed. text ed. 55.00 (*0-313-20715-1*, PEIN, Greenwood Pr) Greenwood.
— Philosophy of the Recent Past: An Outline of European & American Philosophy Since 1860. LC 75-3314. reprint ed. 29.00 (*0-404-59295-3*) AMS Pr.
— Present Philosophical Tendencies. LC 68-21318. 383p. 1968. reprint ed. text ed. 65.00 (*0-8371-0191-3*, PEPT, Greenwood Pr) Greenwood.
— Puritanism & Democracy. 1980. 24.50 (*0-8149-0180-8*) Random.
Perry, Rebecca, illus. Lots of Limericks. LC 91-329. 144p. (J). (gr. 3 up). 1991. text ed. 13.95 (*0-689-50531-0*, McElderry) S&S Childrens.
— Riddle-Me Rhymes. LC 93-25179. 96p. (J). (gr. 3-7). 1994. text ed. 13.95 (*0-689-50602-3*, McElderry) S&S Childrens.
Perry, Regenia A. Free Within Ourselves: African-American Artists in the Collection of the National Museum of American Art. LC 92-14815. (Illus.). 206p. 1992. 40.00 (*1-56640-073-2*); pap. 22.95 (*1-56640-072-4*) Pomegranate Calif.
— Harriet Powers Bible Quilts. LC 93-43140. (Rizzoli Art Ser.). 24p. 1994. 7.95 (*0-8478-1653-2*) Rizzoli Intl.
Perry, Rex, ed. see LaBelle, Dave.
Perry, Richard. Changes. LC 73-13224. 1974. 6.95 (*0-672-51850-3*, Bobbs) Macmillan.
— The Demon & the Warlock. LC 93-93906. 200p. (Orig.). 1994. pap. 10.00 (*1-56002-345-7*, Univ Edtns) Aegina Pr.
— Mexico's Fortress Monasteries. (Illus.). 224p. (Orig.). 1992. pap. 19.95 (*0-9620811-1-6*) Espadana Pr.
— No Other Tale to Tell: A Novel. LC 93-42950. 313p. 1994. 25.00 (*0-688-11595-0*) Morrow.
Perry, Richard & Perry, Rosalind W. Maya Missions: Exploring the Spanish Colonial Churches of Yucatan. (Illus.). 256p. (Orig.). 1988. pap. 12.95 (*0-9620811-0-8*) Espadana Pr.
Perry, Richard D. More Maya Missions: Exploring Colonial Chiapas. LC 93-72945. (Illus.). 128p. (Orig.). (C). 1994. pap. 12.95 (*0-9620811-2-4*) Espadana Pr.
Perry, Richard H., ed. see Hawkins, Ian.
Perry, Richard J. Apache Reservation: Indigenous Peoples & the American State. LC 92-37253. (Illus.). 276p. (C). 1993. text ed. 37.50 (*0-292-76542-8*); pap. 15.95 (*0-292-76543-6*) U of Tex Pr.
— Western Apache Heritage: People of the Mountain Corridor. (Illus.). 314p. (C). 1991. text ed. 37.50 (*0-292-76524-X*); pap. 17.95 (*0-292-76525-8*) U of Tex Pr.
Perry, Richard L., ed. Sources of Our Liberties. LC 78-67316. 466p. reprint ed. 47.50 (*0-89941-752-3*, 305030); reprint ed. pap. 37.50 (*0-685-57351-6*, 305030) W S Hein.
Perry, Ritchie. Bishop's Pawn, No. 4. 192p. 1981. pap. 2.25 (*0-345-28971-4*) Ballantine.
— Dead End. 160p. 1983. pap. 2.25 (*0-345-29214-6*) Ballantine.
— The Fall Guy. (Super Secret Agent Thrillers Ser.: No. 1). 1980. pap. 2.25 (*0-345-29055-0*) Ballantine.
— A Hard Man to Kill, No. 2. (Super Secret Agent Thrillers Ser.: No. 2). 1980. pap. 2.25 (*0-345-29056-9*) Ballantine.
— Your Money & Your Wife. (Orig.). 1981. pap. 2.25 (*0-345-29060-7*) Ballantine.
Perry, Robert. Focus on Nicotine & Caffeine. (Drug-Alert Ser.). (Illus.). 64p. (J). (gr. 2-4). 1991. lib. bdg. 14.98 (*0-8050-2217-1*) TFC Bks NY.
Perry, Robert H., ed. Perry's Biblioteca del Ingeniero Quimico. 6th ed. 1992. text ed. 118.50 (*0-07-104151-6*) McGraw.
Perry, Robert H. & Green, Donald W., eds. Perry's Chemical Engineers' Handbook. 6th ed. (Illus.). 2336p. 1984. text ed. 129.50 (*0-07-049479-7*) McGraw.
Perry, Robert H., jt. ed. see Jones-Parker, Janet.
Perry, Robert L. The Fifty Best Low Investment High-Profit Franchises. 304p. 1990. pap. 12.95 (*0-13-313529-2*) P-H.
— The Fifty Best Low-Investment, High Profit Franchises. LC 94-1569. 1994. write for info. (*0-13-300393-0*) P-H.
— Guide to Self-Employment. LC 89-31828. (Alternatives to College Ser.). (Illus.). 128p. (YA). (gr. 7-12). 1989. lib. bdg. 14.21 (*0-531-10774-4*) Watts.
Perry, Roger, jt. auth. see Perry, Jackie.
Perry, Roland. Lethal Hero: The Mel Gibson Biography. 256p. 1993. 22.95 (*1-870049-79-9*) Oliver Bks.
Perry, Ronald F. & Hoover, Stewart V. Simulation: A Problem Solving Approach. (Illus.). 550p. (C). 1989. text ed. 65.75 (*0-201-16880-4*) Addison-Wesley.
Perry, Ronald W. Comprehensive Emergency Management: Evacuating Threatened Populations. LC 84-12616. (Contemporary Studies in Applied Behavioral Science: Vol. 3). 1985. 73.25 (*0-89232-436-8*) Jai Pr.
Perry, Ronald W. & Greene, Marjorie. Citizen Response to Volcanic Eruption: The Case of Mt. St. Helens. 145p. 1983. text ed. 19.50 (*0-8290-1050-5*) Irvington.
Perry, Ronald W. & Lindell, Michael K. Behavioral Foundations of Community Emergency Response Planning. (Illus.). 630p. 1992. 75.00 (*0-89116-620-3*) Hemisp Pub.
— Living with Mt. St. Helens: Human Adjustment to Volcano Hazards. LC 90-59721. (Illus.). x, 220p. 1990. pap. text ed. 20.00 (*0-87422-053-X*) Wash St U Pr.
Perry, Ronald W. & Mushkatel, Alvin H. Disaster Management: Warning Response & Community Relocation. LC 83-17729. (Illus.). xvi, 280p. 1984. text ed. 59.95 (*0-89930-078-2*, PDM/, Quorum Bks) Greenwood.
Perry, Rosalie S. Charles Ives & the American Mind. LC 74-620003. (Illus.). 157p. reprint ed. 44.80 (*0-8357-9360-5*, 2017296) Bks Demand.
Perry, Rosalind W., jt. auth. see Perry, Richard.
Perry, Roz. Rose Penski. 192p. 1989. pap. 8.95 (*0-941483-37-1*) Naiad Pr.
Perry-Rudolph, Polly S. Home Cookin' Cookin' Like Grandma. 113p. 1992. Spiral bdg. spiral bd. 10.00 (*0-9636540-0-4*) P S Perry-Rudolph.
Perry, Rufus L. The Cushite: or The Children of Ham. 49p. (Orig.). 1887. pap. 4.00 (*0-916157-20-2*) African Islam Miss Pubns.
— The Cushite: Or the Children of Ham (the Negro Race) Obaba, Al I., ed. 49p. (Orig.). (YA). 1991. pap. text ed. 4.00 (*0-916157-32-6*) African Islam Miss Pubns.
Perry, Ruth. The Celebrated Mary Astell: An Early English Feminist. LC 82-28922. (Illus.). 576p. 1986. pap. text ed. 19.95 (*0-226-66095-8*) U Ch Pr.
— Materials for English 207. 32p. (C). 1992. 5.25 (*0-8403-8085-2*) Kendall-Hunt.
— Women, Letters & the Novel. LC 79-8637. (Studies in the Eighteenth Century: No. 4). (Illus.). 1980. 39.50 (*0-404-18025-6*) AMS Pr.
Perry, Ruth & Brownley, Martine W., eds. Mothering the Mind: Twelve Studies of Writers & Their Silent Partners. LC 83-10849. (Illus.). 261p. (C). 1984. 39.95 (*0-8419-0892-3*); pap. 19.95 (*0-8419-0893-1*) Holmes & Meier.
***Perry, Ruth & Kelly, Tim.** Ladies of the Tower. 1971. 3.00 (*0-87129-586-5*, L11) Dramatic Pub.
Perry, Ruth & Milne, A. A. The Red House Mystery. 96p. 1956. pap. 4.95 (*0-87129-115-0*, R34) Dramatic Pub.
Perry, Ruth & Toliver, Johnny. Variations on Humankind Valuepack. 1168p. (C). 1993. 39.36 (*0-8403-9288-5*) Kendall-Hunt.
Perry, Ruth, ed. see Ballard, George.
Perry, Ruth, et al. Joy! Christmas Musical. 1973. 4.25 (*0-87129-138-X*, J01) Dramatic Pub.
Perry, S., jt. auth. see Tatlock, John.
Perry, S. D. Time Cop. 208p. (Orig.). 1994. pap. text ed. 4.99 (*0-425-14652-9*) Berkley Pub.
Perry, Samuel, et al. A DSM-III-R Casebook of Treatment Selection. 2nd ed. LC 90-1317. 416p. 1990. 47.95 (*0-87630-572-9*) Brunner-Mazel.
Perry, Samuel W., III, jt. ed. see Price, Richard W.
Perry, Sara. The Chocolate Book. (Illus.). 72p. 1992. 9.95 (*0-8118-0246-9*) Chronicle Bks.
— The Tea Book: A Gourmet Guide to Buying, Brewing, & Cooking. LeBlond, Bill, ed. LC 92-38967. (Illus.). 157p. 1993. pap. 12.95 (*0-8118-0336-8*) Chronicle Bks.
***Perry, Sarah.** If... LC 94-35108. (J). 1995. 16.95 (*0-89236-321-5*, J P Getty Museum) J P Getty Trust.
— Living with Multiple Sclerosis: Personal Accounts of Coping & Adaptation. (Developments in Nursing & Health). 267p. 1994. 54.95 (*1-85628-893-5*, Pub. by Avebury Pub UK) Ashgate Pub Co.
Perry, Sarah, et al. The Complete Coffee Book. (Illus.). 96p. (Orig.). 1991. 19.95 (*0-87701-899-5*); pap. 12.95 (*0-87701-820-0*) Chronicle Bks.
Perry, Shauneille & Jackson, Donald. Mio & Other Plays for Young People. LC 73-92790. (J). (gr. 4 up). 1976. 5.95 (*0-89388-154-6*) Okpaku Communications.
Perry, Steve. Albino Knife. 1991. mass mkt. 4.99 (*0-441-01391-0*) Ace Bks.
— Aliens vs. Predator Prey. 1994. mass mkt. 4.99 (*0-553-56555-9*) Bantam.
— Black Steel. 1992. mass mkt. 4.99 (*0-441-06698-4*) Ace Bks.
— Brother Death. 256p. (Orig.). 1992. mass mkt. 4.99 (*0-441-54476-2*) Ace Bks.
— Conan the Defiant. 256p. 1987. pap. 6.95 (*0-8125-4264-9*) Tor Bks.
— Conan the Formidable. 1991. mass mkt. 3.99 (*0-8125-1377-0*) Tor Bks.
— Conan the Free Lance. 1990. pap. 3.95 (*0-8125-0690-1*) Tor Bks.
— Conan the Indomitable. 1989. pap. 7.95 (*0-8125-0295-7*) Tor Bks.
— Conan the Indomitable. 1990. pap. 3.95 (*0-8125-0860-2*) Tor Bks.
— Earth Hive. (Aliens Ser.: No. 1). 1992. mass mkt. 4.99 (*0-553-56120-0*, Spectra) Bantam.
— The Female War. (Aliens Ser.: No. 3). 1993. mass mkt. 4.99 (*0-553-56159-6*) Bantam.
— The Forever Drug. 304p. (Orig.). 1995. pap. text ed. 5.50 (*0-441-00142-4*) Ace Bks.
— Mask. 1994. mass mkt. 4.99 (*0-553-56929-5*) Bantam.
— Matador Trilogy, No. 2: Matadora, No. 7. 224p. 1986. mass mkt. 4.99 (*0-441-52207-6*) Ace Bks.
— Matador Trilogy, No. 3: Machiavelli Interface. 208p. 1991. mass mkt. 4.99 (*0-441-51356-5*) Ace Bks.
— Spindoc. 272p. (Orig.). 1994. mass mkt. 4.99 (*0-441-00008-8*) Ace Bks.
— Stellar Ranger. 224p. (Orig.). 1994. mass mkt. 4.99 (*0-380-77301-5*, AvoNova) Avon.
— Steller Ranger: Lone Star. (Steller Ranger Ser.). 224p. (Orig.). 1995. mass mkt. 4.99 (*0-380-77302-3*) Avon.
— The Tularemia Gambit. 224p. (Orig.). 1981. pap. 2.25 (*0-449-14411-9*, GM) Fawcett.
Perry, Steve, ed. Another Dimension. (Illus.). (Orig.). Date not set. pap. write for info. (*0-9640954-9-1*) TFCP.
— Another Dimension: The Big Book. (Illus.). 16p. (Orig.). Date not set. pap. write for info. (*0-9640954-4-0*, 2136691022) TFCP.
Perry, Steve & Perry, Lora. Boating Fiascos: Adventures in Yachting. 232p. 1989. pap. 12.95 (*0-685-29176-6*) Robinhood Pub Co.
Perry, Steve, ed. see Twenty-First Century Publishing Staff.
Perry, Steven. Matador Trilogy, No. 1: Man Who Never Missed, No. 1. 1985. pap. 4.50 (*0-441-51918-0*) Ace Bks.
— Nightmare Asylum. (Aliens Ser.: No. 2). 1993. mass mkt. 4.99 (*0-553-56158-8*) Bantam.
— Ninety-Seventh Step. 1989. mass mkt. 4.99 (*0-441-58105-6*) Ace Bks.
Perry, Stewart E. Building a Model Black Community: The Roxbury Action Program. 100p. 1978. pap. text ed. 12. 95 (*0-87855-773-3*) Transaction Pubs.
— Communities on the Way: Rebuilding Local Economies in the United States & Canada. LC 86-30069. 254p. 1987. 64.50 (*0-88706-526-0*); pap. 21.95 (*0-88706-525-2*) State U NY Pr.
Perry-Sumwalt, Jo, jt. auth. see Sumwalt, John.
Perry, Susan. The Body Bandits. (Umbrella Bks.). (Illus.). (J). (gr. 2-6). 1992. lib. bdg. 21.36 (*0-89565-875-5*) Childs World.
— A Cold Is Nothing to Sneeze At. (Umbrella Bks.). (Illus.). (J). (gr. 2-6). 1992. lib. bdg. 21.36 (*0-89565-819-4*) Childs World.
— Ecology. (Science Fair Projects Ser.). (Illus.). 48p. (J). (gr. 3-6). Date not set. lib. bdg. 12.95 (*1-56065-117-2*) Capstone Pr.
— Getting in Step. (Umbrella Bks.). (Illus.). (J). (gr. 2-6). 1992. lib. bdg. 21.36 (*0-89565-872-0*) Childs World.
— How Are You Feeling Today? (Umbrella Bks.). (Illus.). (J). (gr. 2-6). 1992. lib. bdg. 21.36 (*0-89565-876-3*) Childs World.
— Scientists. (Faces of America Ser.). (Illus.). 128p. (J). (gr. 3-6). Date not set. 19.95 (*1-56065-122-9*) Capstone Pr.
— Women. (Faces of America Ser.). (Illus.). 128p. (J). (gr. 3-6). Date not set. 19.95 (*1-56065-123-7*) Capstone Pr.
— Zoology. (Science Fair Projects Ser.). (Illus.). 48p. (J). (gr. 3-6). Date not set. lib. bdg. 12.95 (*1-56065-111-3*) Capstone Pr.
Perry, Susan & O'Hanlan, Katherine. Natural Menopause: The Complete Guide ot a Woman's Most Misunderstood Passage. (Illus.). 240p. 1992. 19.18 (*0-201-58142-6*) Addison-Wesley.
Perry, Susan & O'Hanlan, Katherine A. Natural Menopause: The Complete Guide to a Woman's Most Misunderstood Passage. (Illus.). 224p. 1993. pap. 10.53 (*0-201-62477-X*) Addison-Wesley.
Perry, Susan, tr. see Ela, Jean Marc.
Perry, Susan K. Playing Smart: A Parent's Guide to Enriching, Offbeat Learning Activities for Ages 4 to 14. Espeland, Pamela, ed. LC 90-40224. (Illus.). 224p. (Orig.). 1990. pap. 12.95 (*0-915793-22-9*) Free Spirit Pub.
Perry, Susan K., jt. auth. see Herman, Barry.
Perry, T. A. The Moral Proverbs of Santob de Carrion: Jewish Wisdom in Christian Spain. 200p. 1987. text ed. 35.00 (*0-691-06721-X*) Princeton U Pr.
— Wisdom Literature & the Structure of Proverbs. LC 92-33650. 160p. 1993. 29.50 (*0-271-00929-2*) Pa St U Pr.
Perry, T. A., tr. & comment. Dialogues with Kohelet: The Book of Ecclesiastes, Translation & Commentary. LC 92-16256. 256p. (C). 1993. 25.00 (*0-271-00882-2*) Pa St U Pr.
Perry, T. Anthony, ed. Proverbios Morales Santob de Carrion. (Spanish Ser.: No. 21). 1986. 17.00 (*0-942260-63-5*) Hispanic Seminary.
***Perry, T. M.** Music Lessons for Children with Special Needs. 140p. 1995. pap. 19.95 (*1-85302-295-0*, Pub. by J Kingsley Pubs UK) Taylor & Francis.
Perry, Ted, ed. Performing Arts Resources, Vol. 3. 175p. 1976. 25.00 (*0-910482-84-5*) Theatre Lib.
Perry, Ted & Prieto, Rene. Michelangelo Antonioni: A Guide to References & Resources. (Reference Books - The Directors). 350p. (C). 1986. lib. bdg. 50.00 (*0-8161-8566-2*, Hall Reference) Macmillan.
Perry, Ted, ed. see Bowser, et al.
Perry, Theodore, jt. auth. see Parkhill, Joe M.
***Perry, Theresa, ed.** Teaching Malcolm X: Popular Culture & Literacy. 224p. 1995. 55.00x (*0-415-91154-0*, B4925, Routledge NY) Routledge.
— Teaching Malcolm X: Popular Culture & Literacy. 224p. 1995. pap. 16.95 (*0-415-91155-9*, B4929, Routledge NY) Routledge.
Perry, Theresa & Fraser, James W., eds. Freedom's Plow: Teaching in the Multicultural Classroom. LC 92-29648. 1993. 55.00 (*0-415-90699-7*, A9786, Routledge NY); pap. 16.95 (*0-415-90700-4*, A9790, Routledge NY) Routledge.
Perry, Thomas. Sleeping Dogs. 1992. 21.50 (*0-679-41064-3*) McKay.
— Sleeping Dogs: A Novel of Suspense. 1993. mass mkt. 5.99 (*0-8041-1160-X*) Ivy Books.
— Vanishing Act. LC 94-17413. 1995. 22.50 (*0-679-43536-0*) Random.
— Vanishing Act. large type ed. 1995. pap. 21.95 (*1-56895-234-1*) Wheeler Pub.
Perry, Thomas, ed. Evidence & Argumentation in Linguistics. (Grundlagen der Kommunikation Ser.). (C). 1979. 108.50 (*3-11-007272-6*) De Gruyter.
Perry, Thomas D. Professional Philosophy. 1985. lib. bdg. 85.50 (*90-277-2071-1*); pap. text ed. 42.50 (*90-277-2072-X*) Kluwer Ac.
Perry, Thomas K. Textile League Baseball: South Carolina's Mill Teams, 1880-1955. LC 92-56680. (Illus.). 1993. lib. bdg. 28.50 (*0-89950-875-8*) McFarland & Co.
Perry, Thomas L., ed. Peacemaking in the Nineteen Nineties: A Guide for Canadians. (Illus.). 312p. (Orig.). 1991. pap. 14.95 (*0-919574-93-9*) Gordon Soules Bk.
Perry, Thomas L. & Foulks, James G., eds. End the Arms Race, Fund Human Needs. 240p. 1986. 14.95 (*0-919574-96-3*) Gordon Soules Bk.
Perry, Thomas S. English Literature in the Eighteenth Century. LC 70-39124. (Essay Index Reprint Ser.). 1977. reprint ed. 26.95 (*0-8369-2712-5*) Ayer.
— Selections from the Letters of Thomas Sergeant Perry. (American Biography Ser.). 255p. 1991. reprint ed. lib. bdg. 69.00 (*0-7812-8312-4*) Rprt Serv.
— Selections from the Letters of Thomas Sergeant Perry. (BCL1-PS American Literature Ser.). 255p. 1992. reprint ed. lib. bdg. 79.00 (*0-7812-6830-3*) Rprt Serv.
— Selections from the Letters of Thomas Sergeant Perry. Robinson, Edwin A., ed. LC 78-131797. 1971. reprint ed. 25.00 (*0-403-00684-8*) Scholarly.
Perry, Thomas W. Public Opinion, Propaganda, & Politics in Eighteenth Century England: A Study of the Jew Bill of 1753. LC 62-17222. (Historical Monographs: No. 51). 215p. 1962. 20.00 (*0-674-72400-3*) HUP.
Perry, Tilden W. Animal Life Cycle Feeding & Nutrition. (Animal Feeding & Nutrition Ser.). 1984. text ed. 66.00 (*0-12-552060-3*) Acad Pr.
— Beef Cattle Feeding & Nutrition. 383p. 1980. text ed. 72. 00 (*0-12-552050-6*) Acad Pr.

An Asterisk (*) at the beginning of an entry indicates that the title is appearing in BIP for the first time.

*__Perry, Tilden W. & Cecava, Michael, eds.__ Beef Cattle Feeding & Nutrition. 2nd ed. (Animal Feeding & Nutrition Ser.). (Illus.). 384p. 1995. boxed write for info. (*0-12-552052-2*) Acad Pr.

Perry, Tim. The Practical Mock Scene Manual. 60p. 1986. student ed 59.95 (*0-915837-02-1*) Palladium Pubns.

Perry, Timothy. Basic Patrol Procedures. (Illus.). 215p. (C). 1993. reprint ed. pap. text ed. 17.95 (*1-879215-18-7*) Sheffield WI.

Perry, Timothy A. Basic Patrol Procedures: A Foundation for the Law Enforcement Student, a Review for the Veteran. (Illus.). 218p. (C). 1984. text ed. 27.00 (*0-915837-01-3*); pap. text ed. 18.00 (*0-915837-00-5*) Palladium Pubns.

Perry, Todd. Kevin Costner. LC 91-77802. 256p. 1991. 20.00 (*1-870049-34-9*) Oliver Bks.

Perry, Troy D. Don't Be Afraid Anymore: The Story of Reverend Troy D. Perry & the Metropolitan Community Churches. 1990. 19.95 (*0-312-04691-X*) St Martin.

Perry, Troy D. & Swicegood, Thomas L. Don't Be Afraid Anymore: The Story of Reverend Troy D. Perry & the Metropolitan Community Churches. (Stonewall Inn Editions Ser.). (Illus.). 384p. 1992. pap. 12.95 (*0-312-06954-5*) St Martin.

— Profiles in Gay & Lesbian Courage. (Stonewall Inn Editions Ser.). (Illus.). 256p. 1992. pap. 10.95 (*0-312-08281-9*) St Martin.

Perry, V. G., ed. see Society of Nematologists Staff.

Perry, V. H. Macrophages & the Nervous System. (Neuroscience Intelligence Unit Ser.). write for info. (*1-57059-173-3*) R G Landes.

Perry, V. Hugh. Macrophages & the Nervous System. (Molecular Biology Intelligence Unit Ser.). 118p. 1994. 89.95 (*1-57059-044-3*, LN9044) R G Landes.

*__Perry, Victoria.__ Built for a Better Future: The Brynmawr Rubber Factory. (Illus.). 96p. 1995. pap. 25.00 (*1-873487-04-5*, Pub. by White Cockade UK) Paul & Co Pubs.

Perry, Vincent G. Skitch. LC 75-20788. (Other Dog Bks.). 1975. 8.95 (*0-87714-032-4*) Denlingers.

Perry, Vincent J., intro. Ken Keeley: Is It Real? (Illus.). 68p. (Orig.). 1993. write for info. (*1-883269-03-2*); pap. write for info. (*1-883269-04-0*) Sunstorm Arts.

Perry, W. Brazil's Foreign Policy. write for info. (*0-275-90004-5*, C0004, Praeger Pubs) Greenwood.

Perry, W. D. Experiments in General Chemistry. 4th ed. (Illus.). 267p. 1993. pap. text ed. 19.95 (*0-89892-110-4*) Contemp Pub Co of Raleigh.

Perry, W. J., Jr., jt. ed. see Schmidt, C. J.

Perry, Walter. The Open University. LC 76-55917. (Illus.). 316p. reprint ed. pap. 90.10 (*0-8357-4693-3*, 2052348) Bks Demand.

*__Perry, Whitall.__ The Widening Beach: Evolutionism in the Mirror of Cosmology. 1995. pap. 9.95 (*1-870196-13-9*) Atrium Pubs.

Perry, Wilhelmina. Sociology of Minority Groups Courses: Syllabi & Related Materials. 145p. 1981. 9.50 (*0-317-36345-X*) Am Sociological.

Perry, William. How to Develop Competency-Based Vocational Education. LC 82-80093. (Illus.). 180p. 1982. pap. 8.95 (*0-911168-48-6*) Prakken.

*__Perry, William & Bailey, Norman A.__ Venezuela 1994: Challenges for the Caldera Administration. LC 94-44043. (CSIS Report Ser.). 24p. (C). 1994. pap. 9.95 (*0-89206-310-6*) CSI Studies.

Perry, William E. Handbook of Diagnosing & Solving Computer Problems. (Illus.). 276p. 1989. 25.95 (*0-8306-9233-9*, TAB/TPR) TAB Bks.

— Hatching the EDP Quality Assurance Function. 2nd ed. (Illus.). 104p. 1986. pap. 24.95 (*0-318-20490-8*) Quality Assurance.

— How to Test Software Packages: A Step-by-Step Guide to Assuring They Do What You Want. LC 85-31572. 231p. 1986. text ed. 55.00 (*0-471-81784-8*) Wiley.

— Management Strategies for Computer Security. 193p. 1985. text ed. 15.00 (*0-409-95135-8*) Buttrwrth-Heinemann.

— Managing Systems Maintenance. LC 81-51630. (Illus.). 382p. reprint ed. pap. 108.90 (*0-8357-8573-4*, 2034939) Bks Demand.

— Quality Assurance for Information Systems: Methods, Tools & Techniques. 1991. 59.95 (*0-89435-347-0*) Wiley.

— Quality Assurance for Information Systems: Methods, Tools, & Techniques. 1993. text ed. 64.95 (*0-471-58804-0*, GD3470) Wiley.

Perry, William E. Quality Assurance System Development Reviews. (Illus.). 1981. pap. 24.95 (*0-318-20493-2*) Quality Assurance.

Perry, William E. Report Writing for Quality Assurance Analysts. (Illus.). 1981. pap. 24.95 (*0-318-20494-0*) Quality Assurance.

— Standards for Auditing Computer Applications. 2nd ed. 1990. Supplemented semi-annually. ring bd. 168.00 (*0-87769-288-2*) Warren Gorham & Lamont.

— Standards for Auditing Computer Applications, No. 1. 2nd suppl. ed. 1991. Supplement, 1991-1. 49.00 (*0-685-45022-8*) Warren Gorham & Lamont.

— Standards for Auditing Computer Applications, No. 2. 2nd suppl. ed. 1991. Supplement, 1991-2. 54.00 (*0-685-45023-6*) Warren Gorham & Lamont.

— A Structured Approach to Systems Testing. 2nd ed. 1993. text ed. 64.95 (*0-471-58805-9*, GD2334) Wiley.

— A Structured Approach to Systems Testing. 2nd rev. ed. 560p. 1988. 49.95 (*0-89435-233-4*) Wiley.

Perry, William E. & Birenbaum, Eric, eds. EDP Auditing. 1992. ring bd. 425.00 (*0-87769-268-8*) Warren Gorham & Lamont.

Perry, William E. & Davis, Keagle W. Handbook for Internal Auditors, 2 vols. 1985. ring bd. write for info. (*0-8205-1390-3*) Bender.

Perry, William E. & Kuong, Javier F. Developing & Implementing an Integrated Test Facility for Testing Computerized Systems. 1979. 35.00 (*0-940706-09-1*, MAP-12) Management Advisory Pubns.

— EDP Risk Analysis & Controls Justification. 1981. 46.00 (*0-940706-10-5*) Management Advisory Pubns.

— Generalized Computer Audit Software-Selection & Application. 1980. 35.00 (*0-940706-15-6*, MAP-14) Management Advisory Pubns.

— How to Test Internal Control & Integrity in Computerized Systems. 1980. 40.00 (*0-940706-13-X*, MAP-15) Management Advisory Pubns.

Perry, William G. Forms of Intellectual & Ethical Development in the College Years. LC 70-107334. (C). 1970. text ed. 40.25 (*0-03-081326-3*) HB Coll Pubs.

Perry, William J. Children of the Sun: A Study in the Early History of Civilization. 551p. 1968. reprint ed. 59.00 (*0-403-00065-3*) Scholarly.

— The Megalithic Culture of Indonesia. LC 77-86999. (Manchester, University. Publications. Ethnological Ser.: No. 3). reprint ed. 21.50 (*0-404-16773-X*) AMS Pr.

Perry, William J., jt. auth. see Carnegie Commission on Science, Technology,.

*__Perry, William J., et al, eds.__ North American Thrust-Faulted Terranes. (AAPG Reprint Ser.: No. 27). (Illus.). xi, 466p. 1984. pap. 8.00 (*0-89181-548-1*) AAPG.

Perry, William L. Elementary Linear Algebra. 512p. 1988. text ed. write for info. (*0-07-049431-2*) McGraw.

Perry, William S. Historical Collections Relating to the American Colonial Church, 5 Pts. in 4 Vols, 1. LC 75-99948. reprint ed. write for info. (*0-404-05071-9*) AMS Pr.

— Historical Collections Relating to the American Colonial Church, 5 Pts. in 4 Vols, 2. LC 75-99948. reprint ed. write for info. (*0-404-05072-7*) AMS Pr.

— Historical Collections Relating to the American Colonial Church, 5 Pts. in 4 Vols, 3. LC 75-99948. reprint ed. write for info. (*0-404-05073-5*) AMS Pr.

— Historical Collections Relating to the American Colonial Church, 5 Pts. in 4 Vols, 4. LC 75-99948. reprint ed. write for info. (*0-404-05074-3*) AMS Pr.

— Historical Collections Relating to the American Colonial Church, 5 Pts. in 4 Vols, Set. LC 75-99948. reprint ed. 375.00 (*0-404-05070-0*) AMS Pr.

Perry, Williams & Wehner, Peter, eds. The Latin American Policies of U. S. Allies: Balancing Global Interests & Regional Concerns. LC 85-12259. 208p. 1985. text ed. 55.00 (*0-275-90220-X*, C0220, Praeger Pubs) Greenwood.

Perry, Wilma, jt. auth. see Perry, Earl.

Perry, Y., ed. Data Communications in the ISDN Era: Proceedings of the IFIP TC6 International Conference on Data Communications in the ISDN Era Tel-Aviv, Israel, 4-5 March, 1985. 188p. 1985. 48.75 (*0-444-87720-7*, North Holland) Elsevier.

Perry, Yvonne N. The Other Side of the Island: Stories. (Illus.). 112p. (Orig.). 1994. pap. 10.00 (*1-880284-06-5*) J Daniel.

Perryman, Andrew. Gabon. (Let's Visit Places & Peoples of the World Ser.). (Illus.). 96p. (J). (gr. 5 up). 1988. 14.95 (*0-7910-0122-9*) Chelsea Hse.

Perryman, F. J. How to Resist the Devil. 48p. pap. 0.75 (*0-686-29122-0*) Faith Pub Hse.

Perryman, M. R., jt. auth. see Anderson, O. D.

Perryman, M. R., jt. ed. see Anderson, O. D.

Perryman, M. Ray. The Measurement of Monetary Policy. 1983. lib. bdg. 40.50 (*0-89838-117-7*) Kluwer Ac.

Perryman, Mark, ed. Altered States: Postmodernism, Politics, Culture. 192p. (C). 1994. pap. 25.00 (*0-85315-793-6*, Pub. by Lawrence & Wishart UK) Humanities.

Persac, A. Plantations on the Mississippi River: From Natchez to New Orleans. 1931. 25.00 (*0-911116-26-5*) Pelican.

Persad, E. & Rakoff, V., eds. Use of Drugs in Psychiatry: A Handbook. LC 86-15371. 180p. 1987. text ed. 29.90 (*0-920887-09-0*) Hogrefe & Huber Pubs.

Persad, Emmanuel, jt. auth. see Endler, Norman E.

Persad, Sandra. We Rarely Close Our Eyes When We Kiss Any More. LC 89-91975. 104p. (Orig.). 1990. pap. 9.95 (*0-9624227-0-3*) Sealed Kiss.

Persak, James. Savage Trail. 1985. pap. 2.25 (*0-8217-1594-1*) Zebra.

Persall, Holli C. The Magic Corn. (Illus.). 24p. (J). (gr. k-4). 1990. 10.95 (*0-9628486-0-3*) Rhyme Time.

Persaud, Bishnodat, jt. ed. see Cable, Vincent.

Persaud, Nancy. Bible Children Puzzles. (Bible Baffler Ser.). 48p. (J). (gr. 3 up). 1990. 7.95 (*0-86653-534-9*, SS891, Shining Star Pubns) Good Apple.

— Bible Number Puzzles. (Bible Baffler Ser.). 48p. (J). (gr. 3 up). 1989. 7.95 (*0-86653-491-1*, SS889, Shining Star Pubns) Good Apple.

*__Persaud, Rajen.__ Making It Through College: The Multicultural Guide for Success & Surviving the Real Deal. 182p. (Orig.). (YA). (gr. 9-12). 1995. pap. 7.95 (*0-9642713-8-9*) D & R Pub CA.

Persaud, T. V., jt. auth. see Moore, Keith L.

Persaud, T. V., et al. Key Facts in Gross Anatomy. (Illus.). 331p. (Orig.). (C). 1985. pap. text ed. 21.00 (*0-443-08311-8*) Churchill.

Persaud, Thakoor. Conflicts Between Multinational Corporations & Less Developed Countries: The Case of Bauxite Mining in the Caribbean with Special Reference to Guyana. Bruchey, Stuart, ed. LC 80-587. (Multinational Corporations Ser.). 1981. lib. bdg. 31.95 (*0-405-13378-2*) Ayer.

Persaud, Winston D. The Theology of the Cross & Marx's Anthropology: A View from the Caribbean. LC 90-40423. (American University Studies: Theology & Religion: Ser. VII, Vol. 84). 298p. (C). 1991. text ed. 48.95 (*0-8204-1409-3*) P Lang Pubs.

Perschbacher, Rex, jt. auth. see Oakley, John.

Perschbacher, Rex R., jt. auth. see Berger, Moise E.

Perschbacher, Rex R., ed. see Schwartz, Mortimer D. & Wydick, Richard C.

Perschbacher, Rex R., jt. auth. see Wydick, Richard C.

Perschbacher, Rex R., ed. see Wydick, Richard C.

Perschbacher, Ruth. Assessment: The Cornerstone of Activity Programs. LC 93-85327. 145p. (C). 1993. pap. 24.95 (*0-910251-62-2*) Venture Pub PA.

Perschbacher, Wesley. Refresh Your Greek. 1989. 59.99 (*0-8024-3352-9*) Moody.

Perschbacher, Wesley J., ed. The New Analytical Greek Lexicon. LC 90-23777. 512p. 1990. 29.95 (*0-943575-33-8*) Hendrickson MA.

*__Perschke, Susan.__ Client-Server Primer. 416p. 1995. disk, pap. 27.95 (*1-55851-440-6*) M&T Bks.

*__Perschke, Walter.__ Restructure Your Life: How to Apply Successful Business Strategies to Achieve Your Personal Life Goals. 1995. pap. 10.95 (*1-886414-00-9*) Atrium Pubs.

Perse, John. St. John Perse: Letters. Knodel, Arthur J., ed. LC 79-9080. (Bollingen Ser.: LXXXVII: 2). (Illus.). 712p. 1979. reprint ed. 65.00 (*0-691-09868-9*); reprint ed. pap. 25.00x (*0-691-01836-7*) Princeton U Pr.

Perse, Saint-John. Selected Poems. Caws, Mary A., ed. Eliot, T. S. et al, trs. LC 82-8305. 160p. (Orig.). (C). 1982. pap. 9.95 (*0-8112-0855-9*, NDP547) New Directions.

— Vents Chroniques. Bd. with Chronique. (Poesie Ser.). (FRE.). Set pap. 6.95 (*2-07-030247-4*) Schoenhof.

Perse, St. John. Anabasis. Eliot, T. S., tr. LC 49-48962. 109p. 1970. reprint ed. pap. 2.95 (*0-15-607406-0*, Harvest Bks) HarBrace.

Persell, Caroline H. Education & Inequality. LC 76-46707. 1979. pap. 16.95 (*0-02-925130-3*) Free Pr.

— Quality, Careers & Training in Educational & Social Research. LC 76-9294. (Illus.). 321p. 1976. pap. text ed. 19.95 (*0-930390-31-8*) Gen Hall.

— Understanding Society. 3rd ed. 688p. (C). 1990. text ed. 54.50 (*0-06-045163-7*) HarpCollege.

Persell, Caroline H. & Cookson, Peter W., Jr. Making Sense of Society. LC 92-10738. (C). 1992. text ed. 11.00 (*0-06-045135-1*) HarpCollege.

Persell, Caroline H., jt. auth. see Cookson, Peter W., Jr.

Persell, Roger A. Principles of Biology: Laboratory Manual. 112p. (C). 1993. spiral bd. 12.95 (*0-8403-8977-9*) Kendall-Hunt.

Persen, L. N. Rock Dynamics & Geophysical Exploration. LC 74-21865. (Developments in Geotechnical Engineering Ser.: Vol. 8). 276p. 1975. 102.75 (*0-444-41284-0*) Elsevier.

Pershad, Chitra. The Raging Moon. 6.75 (*0-89253-716-7*); 4.80 (*0-89253-717-5*) Ind-US Inc.

Pershan, P. S. Structure of Liquid Crystal Phases. (Lecture Notes in Physics Ser.: Vol. 23). 440p. 1988. text ed. 93.00 (*9971-5-0668-8*); pap. text ed. 55.00 (*9971-5-0705-6*) World Scientific Pub.

Pershing, Betty, jt. auth. see Hirschmann, Maria A.

*__Pershing, John J.__ My Experiences in the First World War. (Illus.). 868p. 1995. reprint ed. pap. 19.95 (*0-306-80616-9*) Da Capo.

— My Experiences in the World War. (Military Classics Ser.: Vol. 1). 1989. 16.95 (*0-318-41505-4*) TAB Bks.

— My Experiences in the World War. (Military Classics Ser.: Vol. 2). 472p. 1989. reprint ed. 24.95 (*0-8306-9407-2*) TAB Bks.

Pershing, Karen E., ed. see Garris, Anne.

*__Pershing, Linda.__ Sew to Speak: The Fabric Art of Mary Milne. (Folk Art & Artists Ser.). (Illus.). 72p. 1995. 29.95 (*0-87805-786-2*); pap. 15.95 (*0-87805-787-0*) U Pr of Miss.

*__Pershy, Mary.__ Helping Teens Work Through Grief. 192p. Date not set. write for info. (*0-89944-353-2*) Don Bosco Multimedia.

*__Persia, Juan de.__ Relaciones de Don Juan de Persia. Alonso Cortes, Narciso, ed. 280p. (SPA.). 1968. pap. 100.00 (*0-614-00118-8*) Elliots Bks.

Persichetti, Vincent. Twentieth-Century Harmony. (Illus.). (C). 1961. text ed. 19.95 (*0-393-09539-8*) Norton.

Persico, Enrico, ed. see Levi-Civita, Tullio.

Persico, John, Jr., ed. The TQM Transformation: A Model for Organizational Change. 224p. 1992. text ed. 24.95 (*0-527-91654-4*, 916544) Qual Resc.

Persico, Joseph. Nuremberg: Infamy on Trial. (Illus.). 576p. 1994. 25.95 (*0-670-84276-1*, Viking) Viking Penguin.

— Piercing the Reich. 1979. pap. 2.50 (*0-345-28280-9*) Ballantine.

Persico, Joseph E. Casey: From the OSS to the CIA. braille ed. 1539p. 1990. vinyl bd. 123.12 (*1-56956-207-5*, BR8453) W A T Braille.

— Nuremberg: Infamy on Trial. 544p. 1995. pap. 14.95 (*0-14-016622-X*, Penguin Bks) Viking Penguin.

Persico, V. Richard, Jr., jt. auth. see Platt, Larry A.

Persidsky, Andre, jt. auth. see Kobler, Helmut.

*__Persigout, Jean-Paul.__ Dictionnaire de Mythologie Celte Dieux et Heros. 2nd ed. 319p. (FRE.). 1990. pap. 55.00 (*0-7859-7879-8*, 2268009688) Fr & Eur.

— Dictionnaire de Mythologie Celtique. (FRE.). 1985. pap. 32.95 (*0-7859-7876-3*, 2268003507) Fr & Eur.

Persily, Nancy A. Eldercare: Positioning Your Hospital for the Future. LC 90-14473. 387p. (Orig.). 1991. pap. 47.95 (*1-55648-062-8*, 130102) AHPI.

Persin, Margaret. Recent Spanish Poetry & the Role of the Reader. LC 85-43247. 176p. 1987. 36.50 (*0-8387-5100-8*) Bucknell U Pr.

Persing, David H., et al, eds. Diagnostic Molecular Microbiology: Principles & Applications. LC 92-38523. 700p. 1993. spiral bd. 65.00 (*1-55581-056-X*) Am Soc Microbio.

Persing, Gary. Advanced Practitioner Respiratory Care Review: Written Registry & Clinical Simulation Exam. LC 93-20774. 1994. pap. text ed. 36.95 (*0-7216-4963-7*) Saunders.

— Entry-Level Respiratory Care Review: Study Guide & Workbook. (Illus.). 352p. 1992. pap. text ed. 35.50 (*0-7216-4533-X*) Saunders.

Persing, Louisa, ed. Ever, Never & Sometimes: A Collection of Modern Poetry. (Illus.). 1978. 5.95 (*0-686-24291-2*) Palomar.

— Life Is a Moody Rainbow: A Collection of Modern Poetry. LC 72-87102. (Illus.). 130p. 1972. 5.50 (*0-686-01303-4*) Palomar.

— Shades & Shadows: An Anthology of Modern Poetry. (Illus.). 1973. 5.50 (*0-686-05276-5*) Palomar.

— Stepping Stones: A Collection of Modern Poetry. (Illus.). 1977. 5.95 (*0-686-20028-4*) Palomar.

— To Banbury Cross & Back: A Collection of Modern Poetry. (Illus.). 1976. 5.95 (*0-686-17956-0*) Palomar.

— Windfall: A Collection of Modern Poetry. 1975. 5.95 (*0-686-10961-9*) Palomar.

Persing, Virginia. New Jersey Hospital Association: Celebrating Innovative Leadership in Healthcare. LC 93-3473. 1993. 34.95 (*0-89781-470-3*) Preferred Mktg.

Persinger, Joseph. The Life of Jacob Persinger. 23p. 1983. pap. 3.50 (*0-87770-296-9*) Ye Galleon.

Persinger, Michael A. Neuropsychological Bases of God Beliefs. LC 87-14689. 192p. 1987. text ed. 55.00 (*0-275-92648-6*, C2648, Praeger Pubs) Greenwood.

— The Paranormal: Mechanisms & Models, Pt. 2. LC 74-19227. 195p. 1974. 27.50 (*0-8422-5211-8*); pap. text ed. 9.95 (*0-8422-0476-8*) Irvington.

— The Paranormal: The Patterns, Pt. 1. LC 74-19227. 248p. (C). 1974. 29.50 (*0-8422-5212-6*); pap. text ed. 10.95 (*0-8422-0477-6*) Irvington.

— Weather Matrix & Human Behavior. LC 80-18422. 346p. 1980. text ed. 65.00 (*0-275-90536-5*, C0536, Praeger Pubs) Greenwood.

Persinger, Michael A. & Lafreniere, Gyslaine F. Space-Time Transients & Unusual Events. LC 76-12634. 224p. 1977. 29.95 (*0-88229-334-6*) Nelson-Hall.

Persinger, Michael A., et al. TM & Cult Mania. 208p. (C). 1980. 12.95 (*0-8158-0392-3*) Chris Mass.

Persius. The Satires of Persius Flaccus. Connor, W. R. & Gildersleeve, Basil L., eds. LC 78-67138. (Latin Texts & Commentaries Ser.). (ENG & LAT.). 1979. reprint ed. lib. bdg. 19.95 (*0-405-11605-5*) Ayer.

Persius & Jenkinson. The Satires. 1981. 49.95 (*0-85668-159-8*, Pub. by Aris & Phillips UK); pap. 19.95 (*0-85668-173-3*, Pub. by Aris & Phillips UK) David Brown.

Persius & Juvenal. A. Persi Flacci et D. Invini Ivvenalis Saturae. rev. ed. (Oxford Classical Texts Ser.). 212p. 1992. 22.00 (*0-19-814798-8*) OUP.

Persius, jt. auth. see Juvenal.

Persius Flaccus, Aulus. Auli Persii Flacci Lexicon. Bo, Domenico, ed. Vol. VIII. xiii, 199p. 1967. write for info. (*0-318-71191-5*, Pub. by Georg Olms GW) Lubrecht & Cramer.

— Index Verborum Quae in Saturis Auli Persi Flacci Reperiuntur. Berkowitz, Luci & Brunner, Theodore F., eds. Vol. VII. xvi, 160p. 1967. write for info. (*0-318-71192-3*, Pub. by Georg Olms GW) Lubrecht & Cramer.

— Persius Flaccus, Aulus: Konkordanz zu den Satiren des Persius Flaccus. Bouet, P. et al, eds. (Alpha-Omega, Reihe A Ser.: Bd. XXXVI). 280p. 1978. write for info. (*3-487-06557-6*, Pub. by Georg Olms GW) Lubrecht & Cramer.

— Satirarum Liber. ccxvi, 418p. 1967. reprint ed. write for info. (*0-318-71193-1*, Pub. by Georg Olms GW) Lubrecht & Cramer.

— The Satires of A. Persius Flaccus. Nettleship, H., ed. Conington, John, tr. & comment by. xxxix, 149p. 1987. reprint ed. 29.12 (*3-487-01781-4*, Pub. by Georg Olms GW) Lubrecht & Cramer.

Perske, J., jt. auth. see Witt, U.

Perske, Robert. Circles of Friends: People with Disabilities & Their Friends Enrich the Lives of One Another. LC 88-14616. (Illus.). 96p. 1988. pap. 11.95 (*0-687-08390-7*) Abingdon.

— Deadly Innocence. 128p. (Orig.). 1995. pap. 12.95 (*0-687-00615-5*) Abingdon.

— Don't Stop the Music. LC 86-17426. (YA). (gr. 12 up). 1986. pap. 9.95 (*0-687-11060-2*) Abingdon.

— Hope for the Families: New Directions for Parents of Persons with Retardation or Other Disabilities. LC 81-5700. (Illus.). 112p. (Orig.). 1981. pap. 11.95 (*0-687-17380-9*) Abingdon.

— New Life in the Neighborhood: How Persons with Retardation & Other Disabilities Can Help Make a Good Community Better. LC 80-15517. (Illus.). 80p. (Orig.). 1980. pap. 11.95 (*0-687-27800-7*) Abingdon.

— Show Me No Mercy: A Compelling Story of Remarkable Courage. LC 83-21384. 144p. (Orig.). (YA). (gr. 12 up). 1984. pap. 9.95 (*0-687-38435-4*) Abingdon.

— Unequal Justice. 1991. pap. 11.95 (*0-687-42983-8*) Abingdon.

Perskin, Pamela S., jt. auth. see Noblitt, James R.

*__Persky.__ Buddy's: Meditations on Desire. Date not set. per. 9.95 (*0-921586-19-1*, Pub. by New Star Bks CN) InBook.

Persky, Barry & Golubchick, Leonard H., eds. Early Childhood Education. 2nd ed. 424p. (Orig.). (C). 1991. pap. text ed. 29.00 (*0-8191-8296-6*) U Pr of Amer.

Persky, Harold. Gram Press, The: Gram Pr., The. LC 87-6976. (Sexual Medicine Ser.: Vol. 6). 272p. 1987. text ed. 95.00 (*0-275-92526-9*, C2526, Praeger Pubs) Greenwood.

P
Q

Persky, Joseph, et al. Does America Need Cities? An Urban Investment Strategy for National Prosperity. 1992. 12.00 (*0-944826-47-4*) Economic Policy Inst.

Persky, Joseph J. The Burden of Dependency: Colonial Themes in Southern Economic Thought. LC 92-10844. 192p. 1993. text ed. 29.50x (*0-8018-4422-3*) Johns Hopkins.

Persky, R. S., ed. The Photographic Art Market: Auction Prices 1992. 96p. 1995. pap. 49.95 (*0-913069-44-2*) Consultant Pr.

Persky, Robert S. The Artist's Guide to Getting & Having a Successful Exhibition. LC 85-72702. 120p. (Orig.). 1985. pap. 24.95 (*0-913069-04-3*) Consultant Pr.

— The Guide to Tax Benefits for Collectors, Dealers & Investors. 2nd ed. 176p. 1994. pap. 49.95 (*0-913069-32-9*) Consultant Pr.

Persky, Robert S., ed. Big Apple Street Smarts. 128p. 1992. pap. 14.95 (*0-913069-33-7*) Consultant Pr.

— The Photographer's Complete Guide to Exhibition & Sales Spaces. 2nd ed. 277p. 1989. pap. 24.95 (*0-913069-19-1*) Consultant Pr.

— The Photographic Art Market: Auction Price Results 1982-85. 1987. 69.95 (*0-913069-09-4*) Consultant Pr.

— Photographic Art Market: Auction Price Results 4-93. 96p. 1994. pap. 49.95 (*0-913069-47-7*) Consultant Pr.

— Photographic Art Market: Auction Price Results 5-91. 80p. 1992. pap. 49.95 (*0-913069-40-X*) Consultant Pr.

— Photographic Art Market: Auction Price Results 5/88. 64p. 1989. pap. 49.95 (*0-913069-21-3*) Consultant Pr.

— The Photographic Art Market: Auction Prices 1986. 64p. 1987. pap. 49.95 (*0-913069-15-9*) Consultant Pr.

— Photographic Art Market: Auction Prices 1987. 64p. 1988. pap. 49.95 (*0-913069-16-7*) Consultant Pr.

— The Photographic Art Market: Auction Prices 1989. 96p. 1990. pap. 49.95 (*0-913069-25-6*) Consultant Pr.

— The Photographic Art Market: Auction Prices 1990. LC 81-68613. 96p. 1991. pap. 49.95 (*0-913069-27-2*) Consultant Pr.

— The Photographic Art Market 1994. 96p. 1995. pap. 49.95 (*0-913069-51-5*) Consultant Pr.

— Stock Photo Deskbook. 360p. 1995. pap. 39.95 (*0-913069-43-4*) Consultant Pr.

Persky, Robert S. & Falk, Peter H., eds. The Photograph Collector's Resource Directory. 3rd ed. 267p. 1989. pap. 24.95 (*0-913069-18-3*) Consultant Pr.

Persky, Robert S. & Levy, Susan P. The Photographer's Guide to Getting & Having a Successful Exhibition. 124p. (Orig.). 1987. pap. 24.95 (*0-913069-10-8*) Consultant Pr.

Persky, Robert S., jt. auth. see Cisek, Eugene.

Persky, Serge M. Contemporary Russian Novelists. Eisemann, Frederick, tr. LC 68-26468. (Essay Index Reprint Ser.). 1977. 20.95 (*0-8369-0784-1*) Ayer.

Persky, Stan. America, the Last Domino. (Illus.). 284p. 1984. pap. 2.50 (*0-919573-37-1*) Left Bank.

— At the Lenin Shipyard: Poland & the Rise of the Solidarity Trade Union. 271p. (Orig.). 1982. reprint ed. pap. 4.00 (*0-919888-45-3*) Left Bank.

Persky, Stan, jt. ed. see Jackson, Ed.

Persley, G., jt. ed. see Buddenhagen, I. W.

Persley, G. J. Agricultural Biotechnology: Country Case Studies. 450p. Date not set. write for info. (*0-85198-816-4*) CAB Intl.

Persley, G. J. & Ferrar, P. South Pacific Agriculture Challenges & Opportunities for ACIAR & Its Research Partners. 87p. (C). 1987. text ed. 72.00 (*0-949511-45-5*, Pub. by ACIAR) St Mut.

Persley, Gabrielle J. Agricultural Biotechnology: Opportunities for International Development. (Biotechnology in Agriculture Ser.: No. 2). 528p. 1991. text ed. 119.50 (*0-85198-643-9*) CAB Intl.

— Beyond Mendel's Garden: Biotechnology in the Service of World Agriculture, No. 1. (Biotechnology in Agriculture Ser.). 176p. (Orig.). 1990. pap. text ed. 24.50 (*0-85198-682-X*) CAB Intl.

— Replanting the Tree of Life: Towards An International Agenda for Coconut Palm Research. (Illus.). 150p. 1992. 47.50 (*0-85198-815-6*) CAB Intl.

Persobke & Liozbanski. Access for Windows Power Programming. 1993. pap. 45.00 (*1-56529-194-8*) Que.

Persoglia, S., jt. auth. see Rocca, F.

Person, Ann. Stretch & Sew Guide to Sewing Knits. 144p. 1994. pap. 19.95 (*0-8019-8593-5*) Chilton.

Person, Ann B., jt. auth. see Schiff, Isaac.

Person, Carl E. The Lizard's Trail. LC 74-22755. (Labor Movement in Fiction & Non-Fiction Ser.). reprint ed. 38.50 (*0-404-58508-6*) AMS Pr.

Person, Cheryl, ed. see Trostel, Scott D.

Person, Diane G., jt. ed. see Freeman, Evelyn B.

***Person, Ethel S.** By Force of Fantasy: How We Make Our Lives. LC 95-8649. 1995. 23.00 (*0-465-02359-2*) Basic.

— Dreams of Love & Fateful Encounters: The Power of Romantic Passion. 384p. 1989. pap. 12.00 (*0-14-012055-6*, Penguin Bks) Viking Penguin.

Person, Ethel S., jt. ed. see Gaylin, Willard.

Person, Ethel S., jt. ed. see Stimpson, Catherine R.

***Person, Ethel S., et al, eds.** On Freud's "Creative Writers & Day-Dreaming" LC 94-48270. (Contemporary Freud Ser.). 1995. write for info. (*0-300-06266-4*) Yale U Pr.

— On Freud's "Observations on Transference-Love" (Contemporary Freud: Turning Points & Critical Issues Ser.). 224p. (C). 1993. text ed. 27.00 (*0-300-05437-8*) Yale U Pr.

***Person, James, ed.** Literature Criticism from 1400 to 1800, Vol. 27. 535p. 1995. 122.00 (*0-8103-8943-6*) Gale.

Person, James E., Jr. Essentials of Mathematics. 5th ed. 1989. text ed. 43.50 (*0-471-80044-9*) P-H.

— Literary Criticism from 1400 to 1800, Vol. 16. 1991. 122.00 (*0-8103-6115-9*) Gale.

— Literary Criticism from 1400 to 1800, Vol. 17. 1991. 122.00 (*0-8103-6116-7*) Gale.

— Literary Criticism from 1400 to 1800, Vol. 18. 1992. 122.00 (*0-8103-7960-0*) Gale.

— Literary Criticism from 1400 to 1800, Vol. 21. 1993. 122.00 (*0-8103-7963-5*) Gale.

— Literary Criticism from 1400 to 1800, Vol. 22. 1993. 122.00 (*0-8103-7964-3*) Gale.

— Literary Criticism from 1400 to 1800, Vol. 23. 1993. 122.00 (*0-8103-7965-1*) Gale.

— Literary Criticism from 1400 to 1800, Vol. 24. 1994. 122.00 (*0-8103-8462-0*) Gale.

— Literary Criticism from 1400 to 1800, Vol. 25. 1994. 122.00 (*0-8103-8463-9*) Gale.

— Literary Criticism from 1400 to 1800, Vol. 26. 1994. 122.00 (*0-8103-8464-7*) Gale.

— Literature Criticism from 1400 to 1800, Vol. 14. 1990. 122.00 (*0-8103-6113-2*) Gale.

— Literature Criticism from 1400 to 1800, Vol. 15. 1991. 122.00 (*0-8103-6114-0*) Gale.

— Literature Criticism from 1400 to 1800, Vol. 19. 1992. 122.00 (*0-8103-7961-9*) Gale.

— Literature Criticism from 1400 to 1800, Vol. 20. 1992. 122.00 (*0-8103-7962-7*) Gale.

— Vibrational Intensities in Infrared & Raman Spectroscopy. (Studies in Physical & Theoretical Chemistry: Vol. 20). 466p. 1982. 154.00 (*0-444-42115-7*) Elsevier.

Person, James E., Jr., ed. Literature Criticism from 1400 to 1800, Vol. 1. 1984. 122.00 (*0-8103-6100-0*) Gale.

— Literature Criticism from 1400 to 1800, Vol. 2. 600p. 1985. 122.00 (*0-8103-6101-9*) Gale.

— Literature Criticism from 1400 to 1800, Vol. 3. 600p. 1986. 122.00 (*0-8103-6102-7*) Gale.

— Literature Criticism from 1400 to 1800, Vol. 4. 567p. 1986. 122.00 (*0-8103-6103-5*) Gale.

— Literature Criticism from 1400 to 1800, Vol. 5. 555p. 1987. 122.00 (*0-8103-6104-3*) Gale.

— Literature Criticism from 1400 to 1800, Vol. 6. 545p. 1987. 122.00 (*0-8103-6105-1*) Gale.

— Literature Criticism from 1400 to 1800, Vol. 7. LC 83-20504. 600p. 1988. 122.00 (*0-8103-6106-X*) Gale.

— Literature Criticism from 1400 to 1800, Vol. 9. 600p. 1988. 122.00 (*0-8103-6108-6*) Gale.

— Literature Criticism from 1400 to 1800, Vol. 10. 1989. 122.00 (*0-8103-6109-4*) Gale.

— Literature Criticism from 1400 to 1800, Vol. 8, Vol. 8. 600p. 1988. 122.00 (*0-8103-6107-8*) Gale.

Person, James E., Jr. & Draper, James P., eds. Literature Criticism from 1400-1800, Vol. 12. 1990. 122.00 (*0-8103-6111-6*) Gale.

Person, James E., Jr. & Pollock, Sean R., eds. Statistical Forecasts of the United States. LC 93-7565. 1993. Acid-free paper. 95.00 (*0-8103-8922-3*) Gale.

Person, James E., Jr. & Williamson, Sandra L., eds. Literature Criticism from 1400-1800, Vol. 11. 535p. 1989. 122.00 (*0-8103-6110-8*) Gale.

— Shakespearean Criticism, Vol. 10. 1989. 127.00 (*0-8103-6134-5*) Gale.

Person, James E., Jr., jt. ed. see Draper, James P.

Person, James E., Jr., jt. ed. see Williamson, Sandra L.

Person, Leland S., Jr. Aesthetic Headaches: Women & a Masculine Poetics in Poe, Melville, & Hawthorne. LC 87-12536. 208p. 1988. 25.00 (*0-8203-0985-0*) U of Ga Pr.

Person, Matthew M., III. The Smart Hospital: A Case Study in Hospital Computerization. LC 88-71149. 244p. 1988. lib. bdg. 29.95 (*0-89089-338-1*) Carolina Acad Pr.

Person, R. J. & Newman, G. C. Selection of the University Librarian. 1988. pap. 25.00 (*0-918006-56-2*, OP#13) ARL.

Person, R. J. & Thies, R., eds. Physiology. (Oklahoma Notes Ser.). viii, 263p. 1991. pap. 17.95 (*0-387-97039-8*) Spr-Verlag.

Person, R. J., jt. ed. see Thies, R.

Person, Robert B., jt. auth. see Trenk, Henry C.

Person, Roland C. A New Path: Undergraduate Libraries at United States & Canadian Universities, 1949-1987. LC 87-29553. (New Directions in Information Management Ser.: No. 17). (Illus.). 184p. 1988. text ed. 39.95 (*0-313-25303-X*, PNU/) Greenwood.

Person, Ron. Excel for the Mac Hot Tips. (Hot Tips Ser.). (Illus.). 224p. (Orig.). 1993. pap. 12.99 (*1-56529-162-X*) Que.

— Excel for Windows Hot Tips. (Hot Tips Ser.). (Illus.). 224p. (Orig.). 1993. pap. 12.99 (*1-56529-164-6*) Que.

— Using Excel 4 for Windows: Special Edition. (Illus.). 1034p. (Orig.). 1992. pap. 29.95 (*0-88022-916-0*) Que.

Person, Ron & Rose, Karen. Using Windows 3.1. 1992. pap. 27.95 (*1-56529-109-3*) Que.

— Using Word for Windows 2, Special Edition. (Using Ser.). (Illus.). 800p. 1992. pap. 27.95 (*0-88022-832-6*) Que.

— Windows 3.1 Quickstart. 1992. pap. 21.95 (*0-88022-730-3*) Que.

***Person, Ron & Tow.** Browsing the World Wide Web with Word for Windows. (Illus.). 384p. (Orig.). 1995. pap. 27.99 (*0-7897-0243-6*) Que.

Person, Ron, jt. auth. see Jennings, Roger.

Person, Ron, et al. Using Word for Windows. 2nd ed. 1200p. 1993. pap. 29.95 (*1-56529-469-6*) Que.

Person, Ruth, jt. auth. see Rogers, Sharon.

Person, Ruth J., ed. The Management Process: A Selection of Readings for Librarians. LC 83-3788. 431p. reprint ed. pap. 122.90 (*0-7837-5923-1*, 2045722) Bks Demand.

Person, Ruth J., jt. auth. see McCabe, Gerard B.

Person, Samuel. How to Prepare for the Certified Public Accountant Examination - CPA. 4th ed. 540p. 1992. pap. 18.95 (*0-8120-4839-3*) Barron.

— How to Prepare for the CPA - Certified Public Accountant Examination. 5th ed. 1995. student ed, pap. 18.95 (*0-8120-2865-1*) Barron.

Person, Willis B., jt. auth. see Mulliken, Robert S.

Personal Counselors, Inc. Staff. Postulates of Re-Evaluation Counseling. rev. ed. 1990. pap. 2.00 (*0-913937-43-6*) Rational Isl.

***Personal Crafting Staff.** The Basic Quality Tool System. 1994. ring bd. 35.00 (*0-87425-973-8*) Human Res Dev Pr.

— The Quality Managing & Planning Tool System. 1994. ring bd. 35.00 (*0-87425-972-X*) Human Res Dev Pr.

Personal Narratives Group Staff. Interpreting Women's Lives: Feminist Theory & Personal Narratives. LC 88-45445. (Illus.). 286p. 1989. 39.95 (*0-253-33070-X*); pap. 14.95 (*0-253-20501-8*, MB-501) Ind U Pr.

Personick, Stewart D. Fiber Optics: Technology & Applications. LC 85-12370. (Applications of Communications Theory Ser.). 270p. 1985. 59.50 (*0-306-42079-1*, Plenum Pr); write for info. (*0-318-60148-6*, Plenum Pr) Plenum.

— Optical Fiber Transmission Systems. LC 80-20684. (Applications of Communications Theory Ser.). 192p. 1981. 49.50 (*0-306-40580-6*, Plenum Pr) Plenum.

Personick, Stewart D., jt. ed. see Henry, Paul S.

Personius, Lynne, jt. auth. see Kenney, Anne R.

Personius, Lynne, jt. auth. see Kenney, Anne.

Personke, Carl R. & Johnson, Dale D. Language Arts Instruction & the Beginning Teachers: A Practical Guide. (Illus.). 304p. (C). 1987. text ed. write for info. (*0-13-521675-3*) P-H.

Personnel Management Services, Ltd. Staff. Recruitment. 150p. (C). 1990. 125.00 (*0-85292-449-6*, Pub. by IPM Hse UK) St Mut.

Persons, Albert C. Bay of Pigs: A Firsthand Account of the Mission by a U. S. Pilot in Support of the Cuban Invasion Force in 1961. LC 89-13566. 176p. 1990. pap. 21.95x (*0-89950-483-3*) McFarland & Co.

Persons, Albert C., ed. see Carter, Vincent A.

Persons, Billie, jt. auth. see Holman, David.

***Persons, Georgia A.** The Making of Energy & Telecommunications Policy. LC 94-34318. 208p. 1995. text ed. 55.00 (*0-275-95039-5*, Praeger Pubs) Greenwood.

Persons, Georgia A., ed. Dilemmas of Black Politics: Issues of Leadership & Strategy. LC 92-19599. (C). 1992. text ed. 24.00 (*0-06-500509-0*) HarpCollege.

Persons, Hal. How-to of Great Speaking: Stage Techniques to Tame Those Butterflies. 1992. 18.95 (*0-9632786-1-4*); pap. 10.95 (*0-9632786-0-6*) Black & Taylor.

Persons, Harriet. Australian National Playwrights Conference: A Retrospective. (C). 1990. 45.00 (*0-86819-241-4*, Pub. by Currency Pr AT) St Mut.

Persons, Jacqueline B. Cognitive Therapy in Practice: A Case Formulation Approach. (C). 1989. 25.95 (*0-393-70077-1*) Norton.

Persons, Mark D., ed. Personnel Record Keeper. (Illus.). 400p. 1991. ring bd. 86.00 (*1-878375-31-8*) Panel Pubs.

Persons, Mark D., ed. see Castagnera, James O. & Derewicz, Kristine G.

Persons, Mark D., ed. see Chadwick, Joseph T., Sr.

Persons, Mark D., jt. auth. see DeLuca, Matthew J.

Persons, Mark D., ed. see Farber, Phillip.

Persons, Mark D., ed. see McNeil, Bruce J.

Persons, Mark D., jt. auth. see McNeil, Bruce J.

Persons, Mark D., ed. see Shrader, J. Carl & Weisberg, Stuart A.

Persons, Mark D., ed. see Wertman, Janet A. & Kuraitis, V. P.

Persons, Stow. American Minds: A History of Ideas. rev. ed. LC 74-12326. 540p. 1975. 49.00 (*0-88275-203-0*) Krieger.

— The Decline of American Gentility. LC 73-534. 336p. 1976. text ed. 63.00 (*0-231-03015-0*); pap. text ed. 19.50 (*0-231-08347-5*) Col U Pr.

— Ethnic Studies at Chicago, Nineteen Five to Nineteen Forty-Five. LC 86-11416. 168p. 1987. 24.95 (*0-252-01344-1*) U of Ill Pr.

— The University of Iowa in the Twentieth Century: An Institutional History. LC 90-10771. (Illus.). 354p. 1990. 38.95 (*0-87745-282-2*) U of Iowa Pr.

Persons, Stow, jt. ed. see Egbert, Donald D.

Persons, Todd, ed. see Zagat, Eugene H., Jr. & Zagat, Nina S.

Persons, W. Scott. American Ginseng: Green Gold. rev. ed. (Illus.). 224p. (Orig.). 1994. pap. 15.95 (*0-914875-23-X*) Bright Mtn Bks.

Persson. Mechanics of Cutting Plant Material. LC 87-70989. 280p. (C). 1987. 49.50 (*0-916150-86-0*, M0487) Am Soc Ag Eng.

Persson, A. E. & Boberg, U., eds. The Juxtaglomerular Apparatus. (Fernstrom Foundation Ser.: No. 11). 482p. 1988. 179.50 (*0-444-80982-1*) Elsevier.

Persson, Ake, ed. see Kennelly, Brendan.

***Persson, Alfred V. & Skudder, Paul A., Jr., eds.** Visceral Vascular Surgery. fac. ed. LC 87-6882. (Science & Practice of Surgery Ser.: No. 13). 303p. 1987. reprint ed. pap. 86.40 (*0-7837-8326-4*, 2049113) Bks Demand.

Persson, Axel W. Staat und Manufaktur im Romischen Reiche. Finley, Moses, ed. LC 79-4998. (Ancient Economic History Ser.). (GER.). 1979. reprint ed. lib. bdg. 17.95 (*0-405-12387-6*) Ayer.

Persson, Bertil R. & Stahlberg, Freddy. Health & Safety of Clinical NMR Examinations. 208p. 1988. 109.00 (*0-8493-6096-X*, RC78, CRC Reprint) Franklin.

Persson, C. G., jt. ed. see Anderson, K. E.

Persson, C. G., jt. auth. see O'Donnell, S.

Persson, C. G., et al, eds. Inflammatory Indices in Chronic Bronchitis. (Agents & Actions Supplements Ser.: Vol. 30). 296p. 1990. 67.00 (*0-8176-2370-1*) Birkhauser.

Persson, Conrad. The U. S. A. Travel Phone Book: A Quick-Help Guide to Essential Addresses & Telephone Numbers for Business & Vacation Travellers. 192p. 1991. pap. 8.95 (*1-878446-03-7*) Bon A Tirer Pub.

Persson, Dorothy M. & Winter, Michael F., eds. Psychology & Psychiatry Serials: A Bibliographic Aid for Collection Development. LC 90-39559. (Behavioral & Social Sciences Librarian Ser.). 124p. 1990. text ed. 29.95 (*1-56024-048-2*) Haworth Pr.

Persson, Elwy, jt. auth. see Blomqvist, Gun.

Persson, Eric. Net Power: Resource Guide to Online Computer Services. 812p. 1994. pap. 39.95 (*1-56523-031-0*) Fox Chapel Pub.

Persson, Esther, ed. Gari Melchers: A Retrospective Exhibition. LC 89-63393. (Illus.). 240p. (Orig.). (C). 1991. pap. text ed. 25.00 (*1-878390-00-7*, U of Wash Pr) Mus St Pete.

Persson, Gunnar. Meanings, Models & Metaphors: A Study in Lexical Semantics in English. (Umea Studies in the Humanities: No. 92). (Illus.). 205p. (Orig.). 1990. pap. 43.50x (*91-7174-478-9*, Pub. by Almqv & Wiksell SW) Coronet Bks.

Persson, Gunnar & Jansson, Mats, eds. Phosphorus in Freshwater Ecosystems. (Developments in Hydrobiologia Ser.). (C). 1989. lib. bdg. 193.50 (*90-6193-657-8*) Kluwer Ac.

Persson, Gunnar, jt. ed. see Edlund, Lars-Erik.

Persson, Gunnar, jt. auth. see Magnusson, Ulf.

Persson, Gunnar, jt. ed. see Odenstedt, Bengt.

Persson, H. & McMichael, B. L. Plant Roots & Their Environment: Proceedings of an ISSR-Symposium. (Developments in Agricultural & Managed-Forest Ecology Ser.: Vol. 24). 1991. 192.50 (*0-444-89104-8*) Elsevier.

Persson, Jonas & Jungert, Erland. Generation of Multi-Resolution Maps. (Illus.). 66p. (Orig.). (C). 1993. pap. text ed. 35.00 (*0-7881-0158-7*) Diane Pub.

Persson, Karl G., ed. Economic Development of Denmark & Norway. (Economic Development of Modern Europe since 1870 Ser.). 545p. 1993. 179.95 (*1-85278-683-3*, Pub. by E Elgar Pub UK) Ashgate Pub Co.

Persson, L., jt. ed. see Benman, B. E.

Persson, Lars E., jt. ed. see Gyllenberg, Mats.

Persson, Lars O., jt. auth. see Lundgvist, Lars.

Persson, Leonard N. The Handbook of Job Evaluations & Job Pricing. 1986. pap. 24.95 (*1-55645-401-5*) Busn Legal Reports.

Persson, P. World Forest Resources. (C). 1992. 287.50 (*81-7136-034-3*, Pub. by Periodical Expert India) St Mut.

Persson, P. B. & Kirchheim, H. R., eds. Baroreceptor Reflexes: Integrative Functions & Clinical Aspects. xi, 322p. 1991. 149.00 (*0-387-53588-8*) Spr-Verlag.

Persson, P. E., et al. Off-Flavours in the Aquatic Environment: Proceedings of the 2nd IAWPRC International Symposium held in Kagoshima, Japan, 14-16 October, 1987. LC 82-645900. (Water Science & Technology Ser.: No. 20). (Illus.). 294p. 1988. pap. 112.00 (*0-08-036887-5*, Pergamon Pr) Elsevier.

Persson, P. E., et al, eds. Taste & Odour in Waters & Aquatic Organisms. (Water Science & Technology Ser.: No. 15). (Illus.). 340p. 1983. pap. 91.00 (*0-08-029713-7*, Pergamon Pr) Elsevier.

Persson, Per A., et al. Rock Blasting & Explosives Engineering: A Textbook for Students & a Handbook for Scientists & Engineers Covering the Science & Engineering of the Industrial Use of Explosives with Major Emphasis on Rock Blasting. LC 93-28150. 1993. 69.95 (*0-8493-8978-X*) CRC Pr.

Persson, Richard J. The Stock Photographer's Marketing Guide. (Illus.). (Orig.). 1984. pap. 2.50 (*0-9608486-0-6*) R J Persson Ent.

***Persson, Torsten & Tabellini, Guido, eds.** Monetary & Fiscal Policy: Politics, Vol. 2. LC 93-35772. (Illus.). 500p. 1994. 39.95 (*0-262-16141-9*) MIT Pr.

— Monetary & Fiscal Policy: Politics, Vol. 2. LC 93-35772. (Illus.). 500p. 1994. pap. 23.00 (*0-262-66088-1*) MIT Pr.

— Monetary & Fiscal Policy, Vol. 1: Credibility. LC 93-35772. 1994. 39.95 (*0-02-621614-0*); pap. 23.00 (*0-262-66087-3*) MIT Pr.

Persson, U. On Degenerations of Algebraic Surfaces. LC 77-8972. (Memoirs Ser.: No. 11/189). 144p. 1977. pap. 22.00 (*0-8218-2189-X*, MEMO 11/189) Am Math.

Persson, W., jt. ed. see Svanberg, Sune.

Persun, Terry. Dandelion Soul. Zarucchi, Roy & Page, Carolyn, eds. (Chapbook Ser.). (Illus.). 28p. (Orig.). 1990. pap. 5.00 (*0-9623862-6-X*) Nightshade Pr.

***Persun, Terry L.** Plant-Animal-I. Bixby, Robert, ed. 26p. 1994. pap. text ed. 6.00 (*1-882983-17-3*) March Street Pr.

Perszyk, Kenneth J. Nonexistent Objects: Meinong & Contemporary Philosophy. LC 93-11875. (Nijhoff International Philosophy Ser.). 324p. (C). 1993. lib. bdg. 109.00 (*0-7923-2461-7*) Kluwer Ac.

***Pertersen, Rodney L., ed.** Christianity & Civil Society: Theological Education for Public Life. LC 94-43405. (Boston Theological Institute Ser.: Vol. 4). 184p. (Orig.). 1995. pap. 16.95 (*1-57075-009-2*) Orbis Bks.

Perth, James D. Letters from James Earl of Perth, Lord Chancellor of Scotland, to His Sister the Countess of Erroll, & Other Members of His Family. Jerdan, William, ed. (Camden Society, London. Publications, First Ser.: No. 33). reprint ed. 30.00 (*0-404-50133-8*) AMS Pr.

Perthame, B. Advances in Kinetic Theory: Selected Papers. (Series on Advances in Mathematics). 200p. 1994. text ed. 61.00 (*981-02-1671-8*) World Scientific Pub.

Perthes, Clemens T. Das Deutsche Staatsleben Vor der Revolution. Mayer, J. P., ed. LC 78-67375. (European Political Thought Ser.). (GER.). 1979. lib. bdg. 28.95 (*0-405-11725-6*) Ayer.

Perthuisot, J. P., jt. ed. see Sonnenfeld, P.

Perticara, Bonnie, ed. see Snyder, Judy.

P Q

An Asterisk (*) at the beginning of an entry indicates that the title is appearing in BIP for the first time.

Pertierra, Raul, ed. Remittances & Returnees: The Cultural Economy of Migration in Ilocos. (Illus.). 162p. (Orig.). 1992. pap. 10.75 (*971-10-0476-3*, Pub. by New Day Pub PH) Cellar.

Pertile, Lino, jt. ed. see Baranski, Zygmunt G.

Pertsch, Erich. Langenscheidt Latin-German Dictionary: Langenscheidt Handwoerterbuch Lateinisch-Deutsch. 703p. (GER & LAT.). 1983. 59.95 (*0-8288-1029-X*, F58020) Fr & Eur.

Pertsch, Wilhelm. Die Orientalischen Handschriften der Herzoglichen Bibliothek Zu Gotha, 5 vols. xlviii, 2601p. reprint ed. write for info. (*0-318-71551-1*, Pub. by Georg Olms GW) Lubrecht & Cramer.

Pertschuk, Louis & Lee, Sin H., eds. Localization of Putative Steroid Receptors, 2 vols., Vol. I: Experimental Systems. 200p. 1985. 116.00 (*0-8493-6048-X*, RC268, CRC Reprint) Franklin.

— Localization of Putative Steroid Receptors, 2 vols., Vol. II: Clinically Oriented Studies. 184p. 1985. 156.00 (*0-8493-6049-8*, CRC Reprint) Franklin.

Pertschuk, Louis P. Immunocytochemistry for Steroid Receptors. 240p. 1990. 167.00 (*0-8493-6943-6*, RC280) CRC Pr.

***Pertschuk, Mark, ed.** Major Local Tobacco Control Ordinances in the United States. (Illus.). 139p. (Orig.). (C). 1994. pap. text ed. 30.00x (*0-7881-1457-3*) Diane Pub.

Pertschuk, Michael. Giant Killers. 1987. pap. 7.95 (*0-393-30435-3*) Norton.

— Revolt Against Regulation: The Rise & Pause of the Consumer Movement. LC 82-40108. 192p. 1982. pap. 12.00 (*0-520-05074-6*) U CA Pr.

Pertsin, A. J. & Kitaigorodsky, A. I. The Atom-Atom Potential Method for Organic Molecular Solids. (Chemical Physics Ser.: Vol. 43). (Illus.). 400p. 1987. 91.00 (*0-387-16246-1*) Spr-Verlag.

Pertsov, Nikolai V., jt. auth. see Mel'cuk, Igor K.

Perttu, K. L., ed. Modelling of Energy Forestry: Growth, Water, Relations & Economics. 209p. (C). 1991. text ed. 250.00 (*81-7089-134-5*, Pub. by Intl Bk Distr II) St Mut.

Perttula, Timothy K. The Caddo Nation: Archaeological & Ethnohistoric Perspectives. LC 91-46225. (Texas Archaeology & Ethnohistory Ser.). (Illus.). 344p. 1992. text ed. 40.00x (*0-292-71150-6*) U of Tex Pr.

Pertuiset, Nicole, tr. see Le Corbusier Staff.

Pertwee, Bill. Stars in Battledress. large type ed. (Illus.). 384p. 1993. 23.95 (*0-7089-8717-6*, Trail West Pubs) Ulverscroft.

— The Station Now Standing. (Illus.). 128p. 1992. 34.95 (*0-340-54685-9*, Pub. by H & S UK) Trafalgar.

Pertwee, Ernest. Reciters Treasury of Verse: Serious & Humerous. LC 77-37018. (Granger Index Reprint Ser.). 1977. reprint ed. 42.95 (*0-8369-6317-2*) Ayer.

Pertwee, Roger, ed. Cannabinoid Receptors. (Neuroscience Perspectives Ser.). (Illus.). 288p. 1995. boxed 69.95 (*0-12-551460-3*) Acad Pr.

***Pertz, Emma.** Through the Fire. (Folktales for Children Ser.). 58p. (J). (gr. 6-8). 1994. pap. 7.95 (*1-882427-18-1*) Aspasia Inc.

***Pertzig, F.** Messes of Dresses. Rosenfeld, D., ed. (Illus.). 32p. (J). (gr. 4-8). 1995. write for info. (*0-922613-75-3*); pap. write for info. (*0-922613-76-1*) Hachai Pubns.

Pertzman, F. & Gadder, G. With Different Eyes: Insights into Teaching Language Minority Students. 137p. 1994. pap. text ed. 20.70 (*0-8013-1282-5*) Longman.

Perucho, Juan. Rosas, Diablos y Sonrisas. La Sonrisa de Eros. (Nueva Austral Ser.: Vol. 137). (SPA.). 1991. pap. text ed. 24.95x (*84-239-1937-4*) Elliots Bks.

Peruggia, Mario. Discrete Iterated Function Systems. LC 93-20664. (Illus.). 200p. (C). 1993. text ed. 39.95 (*1-56881-015-6*) AK Peters.

Perugini, Donna. Don't Hug a Grudge. (Orig.). (J). (gr. k-3). 1987. 3.98 (*0-89274-433-2*) Harrison Hse.

— The Flight of Orville Wright Caterpillar. (Illus.). 32p. (Orig.). (J). (gr. k-6). 1983. pap. 3.98 (*0-89274-297-6*) Harrison Hse.

Perugorria, Ricardo, tr. see Stewart, Deborah D.

Perun & Propst. Computer-Aided Drug Design: Methods & Applications. 516p. 1989. 140.00 (*0-8247-8037-X*) Dekker.

Perun, Thomas, jt. ed. see Propst, C.

***Perusek, Glenn & Worcester, Kent, eds.** Trade Union Politics: American Unions & Economic Change, 1960s-1990s. LC 94-37802. 264p. (C). 1995. text ed. 45.00 (*0-391-03886-9*); pap. 17.50 (*0-391-03887-7*) Humanities.

Perushek, Diane E., ed. The Griffis Collection of Japanese Books: An Annotated Bibliography. LC 82-874115. (Cornell East Asia Ser.: No. 28). 118p. 1982. 8.00 (*0-939657-28-7*) Cornell East Asia Pgm.

***Perusse, Roland I.** Haitian Democracy Restored, 1991-1995. LC 95-8761. 1995. write for info. (*0-8191-9951-6*); pap. write for info. (*0-8191-9952-4*) U Pr of Amer.

— The United States & Puerto Rico: Decolonization Options & Prospects. 192p. (Orig.). (C). 1987. pap. text ed. 22.00 (*0-8191-6658-8*) U Pr of Amer.

— United States & Puerto Rico: The Struggle for Equality. LC 89-48583. (Anvil Ser.). 188p. (C). 1990. pap. 11.50 (*0-89464-396-7*) Krieger.

Perusse, Roland I., ed. Directory of Caribbean Scholars. 1978. lib. bdg. 300.00 (*0-8490-1394-1*) Gordon Pr.

Perusse, Yvon. Bushwalking in Papua New Guinea. 2nd ed. (Illus.). 208p. 1993. pap. 14.95 (*0-86442-052-8*) Lonely Planet.

Perutz, Kathrin. Writing for Love & Money. 144p. 1991. 17.95 (*1-55728-211-0*); pap. 9.95 (*1-55728-212-9*) U of Ark Pr.

Perutz, Leo. The Master of the Day of Judgement. Mosbacher, Eric, tr. LC 94-14353. 148p. 1994. 19.95 (*1-55970-171-4*) Arcade Pub Inc.

— The Swedish Cavalier. 192p. 1993. 19.95 (*1-55970-170-6*) Arcade Pub Inc.

Perutz, Max. Is Science Necessary? Essays on Science & Scientists. (Illus.). 304p. 1991. pap. 9.95 (*0-19-286118-2*) OUP.

— Protein Structure. LC 92-928. (C). 1995. pap. text ed. write for info. (*0-7167-7022-9*) W H Freeman.

Perutz, Max F. Cooperativity & Allosteric Regulation in Proteins. (Illus.). 110p. (C). 1990. pap. 22.95 (*0-521-38648-9*) Cambridge U Pr.

Perutz, Vivien. Edouard Manet: The Janus of Mid-Nineteenth-Century French Painting. LC 89-46405. (Illus.). 284p. 1993. 95.00 (*0-8387-5195-4*) Bucknell U Pr.

Peruvian Bishops' Commission for Social Action. Between Honesty & Hope: Documents from & about the Church in Latin America. LC 78-143185. (Maryknoll Documentation Ser.). 271p. reprint ed. pap. 77.30 (*0-8357-7150-4*, 2025116) Bks Demand.

Pervan, Anthony S. Natural Hair Growth: Abnormal Hair Loss Prevention, Scalp Hair Restoration; A Self-Administered Therapy. Leth, Kathryn B., ed. 240p. (Orig.). 1988. pap. 9.95 (*0-8119-0715-5*) LIFETIME.

Pervan, Tomislav. Queen of Peace, Echo of the Eternal Word. (Illus.). 58p. (Orig.). 1988. pap. 3.50 (*0-940535-05-X*, UP104) Franciscan U Pr.

— Reina de la Paz: Eco de la Palabra Eterna. 55p. 1988. pap. 3.50 (*0-940535-16-5*, UP114) Franciscan U Pr.

Pervear, tr. see Marshak.

Perveen, Talot. Growth of Soviet Technical Intelligentsia. 1987. 21.00 (*0-8364-2244-9*, Pub. by Mittal II) S Asia.

Pervical, Mary, jt. auth. see Cohen, Stan B.

Pervin, David J., jt. auth. see Spiegel, Steven L.

Pervin, David J., jt. ed. see Spiegel, Steven L.

Pervin, L. A., ed. Goal Concepts in Personality & Social Psychology. 520p. 1989. 110.00 (*0-8058-0069-7*); pap. 34.50 (*0-8058-0383-1*) L Erlbaum Assocs.

Pervin, Lawrence A. Current Controversies & Issues in Personality. 2nd ed. LC 83-23246. 357p. (C). 1984. Net. pap. text ed. write for info. (*0-471-88086-8*) Wiley.

— Current Controversies & Issues in Personality. LC 78-15361. 323p. reprint ed. pap. 92.10 (*0-7837-3499-9*, 2057832) Bks Demand.

— Personality: Theory & Research. 6th ed. LC 92-21052. 592p. (C). 1993. Net. text ed. write for info. (*0-471-57170-9*) Wiley.

— The Science of Personality. LC 95-5144. 1995. text ed. write for info. (*0-471-57850-9*) Wiley.

Pervin, Lawrence A., ed. Handbook of Personality: Theory & Research. LC 90-37936. 738p. 1990. lib. bdg. 75.00 (*0-89862-430-4*) Guilford Pr.

— Handbook of Personality: Theory & Research. 738p. 1992. pap. text ed. 37.50 (*0-89862-593-9*) Guilford Pr.

Pervin, Lawrence A., et al, eds. The College Dropout & the Utilization of Talent. LC 66-11976. (Illus.). 268p. reprint ed. pap. 76.40 (*0-8357-8849-0*, 2033385) Bks Demand.

Pervo, Richard I. Lesser Festivals Three. LC 85-18756. (Proclamation 3, Ser.: 3). 64p. 1987. pap. 4.50 (*0-8006-4135-3*, 1-4135, Fortress Pr) Augsburg Fortress.

— Luke's Story of Paul. LC 89-27342. 96p. (Orig.). (C). 1989. pap. 9.00 (*0-8006-2405-X*, 1-2405, Fortress Pr) Augsburg Fortress.

— Proclamation Five: Lent, Series C. 1994. pap. 4.50 (*0-8006-4195-7*, Fortress Pr) Augsburg Fortress.

Pervo, Richard I., jt. auth. see Parsons, Mikeal C.

Pervushin, Nikolai V. Stranitsy Russkoi Istorii. LC 89-11104. 192p. (Orig.). 1989. pap. 14.00 (*1-55779-017-5*) Hermitage.

Perweiler, Gary. Secrets of Studio Still Life Photography. (Illus.). 144p. 1984. pap. 18.95 (*0-8174-5898-0*, Amphoto) Watsn-Guptill.

Peryt, T., ed. Coated Grains. (Illus.). 600p. 1983. 107.00 (*0-387-12071-8*) Spr-Verlag.

Peryt, T., jt. ed. see Fuechtbauer, H.

Peryt, T. M., ed. Evaporite Basins. (Lecture Notes in Earth Sciences Ser.: Vol. 13). v, 188p. 1988. 33.00 (*0-387-18679-4*) Spr-Verlag.

— The Zechstein Facies in Europe. (Lecture Notes in Earth Sciences Ser.: Vol. 10). x, 272p. 1987. pap. 54.00 (*0-387-17710-8*) Spr-Verlag.

Peryt, T. M., jt. ed. see Scholle, P. A.

Perz, Walter G. Anon. 176p. 1992. 7.95 (*1-55523-513-1*) Winston-Derek.

Perzaao, Jose M., tr. see Carruthers, Peter.

Perzow, Sidney, jt. ed. see Kets de Vries, Manfred F.

PES Staff, jt. auth. see ARI Staff.

Pesala, Bhikkhu. The Debate of King Milinda. (C). 1991. 14.00 (*81-208-0893-2*, Pub. by Motilal Banarsidass II) S Asia.

Pesando, F. J. Sisters of the Black Moon. 432p. (Orig.). 1994. pap. 4.99 (*0-451-40440-8*, Onyx) NAL-Dutton.

Pesando, James E. & Rea, S. A. Public & Private Pensions in Canada: An Economic Analysis. LC 77-376564. (Ontario Economic Council Research Studies: No. 9). 193p. reprint ed. pap. 55.10 (*0-8357-4001-3*, 2036702) Bks Demand.

Pesantubbee, Michelene A. Encyclopedia of Native American Ceremonies. 1995. lib. bdg. 65.00 (*0-87436-780-8*) ABC-CLIO.

Pesaran, A. A., jt. ed. see Worek, W. M.

Pesaran, M. H., jt. auth. see Barker, T. S.

Pesaran, M. Hashem. The Limits to Rational Expectations. 280p. 1987. pap. text ed. 34.95 (*0-631-16885-0*) Blackwell Pubs.

Pesaran, M. Hashem & Potter, Simon M., eds. Nonlinear Dynamics, Chaos & Econometrics. LC 93-21758. 244p. 1993. text ed. 59.95 (*0-471-93942-0*) Wiley.

***Pesaran, M. Hashem & Wickers, Mike, eds.** Handbook of Applied Econometrics Vol. I: Macroeconomics & Finance. (Illus.). 360p. (C). 1995. write for info. (*1-55786-208-7*) Blackwell Pubs.

Pesatrice, Terri, ed. see Musser, Sandra K.

Pescador de Umpierre, Paquita. Manual De Bailes Folkloricos. 290p. (C). 1981. pap. 5.00 (*0-8477-2501-4*) U of PR Pr.

Pescador, Manuel L., jt. auth. see Berner, Lewis.

Pescar, Susan C. & Nelson, Christine A. Where Does It Hurt? A Guide to Symptoms & Illnesses. LC 83-5663. 323p. reprint ed. pap. 92.10 (*0-7837-1573-0*, 2041865) Bks Demand.

Pescatello, Ann, ed. Female & Male in Latin America: Essays. LC 72-81794. (Latin American Ser.). (Illus.). 362p. (C). 1979. pap. 19.95 (*0-8229-5306-4*) U of Pittsburgh Pr.

Pescatello, Ann M. Charles Seeger: A Life in American Music. LC 92-4679. (Illus.). 360p. (C). 1992. text ed. 34.95 (*0-8229-3713-1*) U of Pittsburgh Pr.

— Power & Pawn: The Female in Iberian Families, Societies & Cultures. LC 75-35352. (Council on Intercultural & Comparative Studies: No. 1). 320p. 1976. text ed. 38.50 (*0-8371-8583-1*, PPP/, Greenwood Pr) Greenwood.

Pescatello, Ann M., ed. Old Roots in New Lands: Historical & Anthropological Perspectives on Black Experiences in the Americas. LC 76-50409. (Contributions in Afro-American & African Studies: No. 31). (Illus.). 301p. 1977. text ed. 55.00 (*0-8371-9476-8*, PEA/) Greenwood.

Pescatore, John. Family Bicycling Guide in the Washington - Baltimore Area. LC 93-26389. (Illus.). 168p. (Orig.). 1993. pap. 10.95 (*0-939009-72-2*) EPM Pubns.

Pescatore, Pierre, et al. Handbook of GATT Dispute Settlement. 1991. ring bd. 225.00 (*0-929179-48-X*) Transnatl Juris Pubns.

Pesce, jt. auth. see Kaplan.

Pesce, Amadeo J. & First, Martin R. Proteinuria: An Integrated Review. LC 79-20352. (Kidney Disease Ser.: No. 1). (Illus.). 310p. reprint ed. pap. 88.40 (*0-7837-0633-2*, 2040977) Bks Demand.

Pesce, Amadeo J., jt. ed. see Kaplan, Lawrence A.

Pesce, Amadeo J., jt. auth. see Pesce, John.

Pesce, Amadeo J., et al, eds. Fluorescence Spectroscopy: An Introduction for Biology & Medicine. LC 76-154611. 262p. reprint ed. pap. 74.70 (*0-317-29566-7*, 2021509) Bks Demand.

Pesce, Angelo. Colours of the Arab Fatherland. 144p. (C). 1990. 150.00 (*0-907151-16-7*, Pub. by IMMEL Pubng UK) St Mut.

— Jiddah Portrait of an Arabian City. 240p. (C). 1990. 150.00 (*0-907151-25-6*, Pub. by IMMEL Pubng UK) St Mut.

— Makkah a Hundred Years Ago. 128p. (C). 1990. 150.00 (*0-907151-36-1*, Pub. by IMMEL Pubng UK); 150.00 (*0-907151-44-2*, Pub. by IMMEL Pubng UK) St Mut.

— Taif the Summer Capital of Saudi Arabia. 120p. (C). 1990. 150.00 (*0-907151-27-2*, Pub. by IMMEL Pubng UK) St Mut.

Pesce, Angelo & Pesce, Elvira G. Marvel of the Desert: The Camel in Saudi Arabia. 112p. (C). 1990. 125.00 (*0-907151-21-3*, Pub. by IMMEL Pubng UK) St Mut.

Pesce, Angelo, ed. see Guarmani, Carlo.

Pesce, Angelo, jt. auth. see Ward, Philip.

Pesce, Celestino. Oil Palms & Other Oilseeds of the Amazon. 2nd ed. Johnson, Dennis V., ed. & tr. by. LC 85-11958. (Studies in Economic Botany). (Illus.). 200p. 1985. 24.95 (*0-917256-28-X*) Ref Pubns.

Pesce, Dolores. The Affinities & Medieval Transposition. LC 86-45398. (Music: Scholarship & Performance Ser.). (Illus.). 256p. 1987. 17.95 (*0-253-30460-1*) Ind U Pr.

Pesce, Elvira G., jt. auth. see Pesce, Angelo.

Pesce, G. Costs & Taxations in Family Law. xxi, 201p. 1988. 45.50 (*0-455-20796-8*, Pub. by Law Bk Co) W W Gaunt.

Pesce, John & Pesce, Amadeo J. The Lead Paint Primer: Questions & Answers on Lead Paint Poisoning. (Illus.). 150p. (Orig.). 1991. pap. 9.95 (*0-9628220-1-9*) Star Industries.

***Pesch, E., et al, eds.** Learning in Automated Manufacturing: A Local Search Approach. (Production & Logistics Ser.). 257p. 1994. pap. text ed. 61.00 (*3-7908-0792-3*) Spr-Verlag.

Pesch, Roland H., jt. auth. see Stallman, Richard M.

Peschansky, V., jt. auth. see Gokhfel'd, V.

Peschar, J., jt. ed. see Niessen, M.

Peschek, Joseph G., jt. ed. see Grover, William F.

Peschel & Spurgeon. Federal Taxation of Trust Grantors & Beneficiaries, No. 2734. rev. ed. 608p. 1989. boxed 155.00 (*0-7913-0370-5*); Supplemented annually; write for info. write for info. (*0-318-67196-4*) Warren Gorham & Lamont.

Peschel, Enid, et al, eds. Neurobiological Disorders in Children & Adolescents. LC 85-644993. (New Directions for Mental Health Services Ser.: No. MHS 54). 160p. 1992. 17.95 (*1-55542-758-8*) Jossey-Bass.

Peschel, Enid R., ed. Medicine & Literature. 1980. 17.95 (*0-685-03475-5*) Watson Pub Intl.

Peschel, Enid R., jt. auth. see Peschel, Richard E.

Peschel, Enid R., tr. see Rimbaud, Arthur.

Peschel, K., ed. Infrastructure & the Space-Economy: Essays in Honor of Rolf Funck. (Illus.). xiv, 447p. 1990. 99.00 (*0-387-52388-X*) Spr-Verlag.

Peschel, Lisa. A Practical Guide to the Runes: Their Uses in Divination & Magick. LC 89-2246. (New Age Ser.). (Illus.). 192p. (Orig.). 1989. pap. 3.95 (*0-87542-593-3*) Llewellyn Pubns.

Peschel, M. & Mende, W. The Predator-Prey Model: Do We Live in a Volterra World? (Illus.). 260p. 1986. 44.00 (*0-387-81848-0*) Spr-Verlag.

Peschel, M., jt. auth. see Ebeling, W.

Peschel, Max, jt. auth. see Mercurio, Gian.

Peschel, Maxymilian L., jt. auth. see Mercurio, Gian.

Peschel, Richard E. & Peschel, Enid R. When a Doctor Hates a Patient: Chapters from a Young Physicians Life. (C). 1986. pap. 12.00 (*0-520-06343-0*) U CA Pr.

***Peschka, V.** Die Eigenart des Rechts. 199p. (C). 1989. pap. 45.00x (*963-05-4987-5*, Pub. by Akad Kiado HU) St Mut.

Peschka, W. Liquid Hydrogen-Fuel of the Future. Wilhelm, E., tr. (Illus.). 256p. 1992. 98.00 (*0-387-82250-X*) Spr-Verlag.

Peschke, Donald B. Woodsmith, 4 vols., Set. (Illus.). 2000p. Date not set. write for info. (*0-9634375-0-X*) Woodsmith Pub.

Peschke, Erhard, ed. August Hermann Francke: Schriften und Predigten. (Texte zur Geschichte des Pietismus Ser.: Vol. 10, Sec. 2). xxvi, 639p. (C). 1989. lib. bdg. 273.10 (*3-11-007143-6*) De Gruyter.

Peschle, Cesare, ed. Normal & Neoplastic Blood Cells: From Genes to Therapy. (Annals Ser.: Vol. 511). 491p. 1987. 123.00 (*0-89766-442-6*) NY Acad Sci.

Pesci, David, ed. see Connolly, Frank B.

Pesci, Marton, ed. see Compton, P. A.

Pescia, G. & Nguyen The, H., eds. Chorionic Villi Sampling (CVS) (Contributions to Gynecology & Obstetrics Ser.: Vol. 15). (Illus.). viii, 116p. 1986. 64.00 (*3-8055-4326-3*) S Karger.

***Pescio, Claudio.** Rembrandt: And Dutch Painting of the 17th Century. (Masters of Art Ser.). (Illus.). 64p. 1995. lib. bdg. 19.95 (*0-87226-317-7*) P Bedrick Bks.

Pescod, M. B., jt. auth. see Arar, A.

Pescod, Michael. Takeover Bids. 1989. write for info. (*0-406-10369-0*) Butterworth Legal Pubs.

Pescok, Robert L., jt. auth. see Hajian, Harry G.

Pescow, Jerome, ed. see Prentice-Hall Editorial Staff.

Pesek, Boris P. Gross National Product of Czechoslovakia in Monetary & Real Terms, 1946-58. LC 65-14429. (Studies in Economics of the Economics Research Center of the University of Chicago). 72p. reprint ed. pap. 25.00 (*0-317-42261-8*, 2025787) Bks Demand.

***Pesek, J. & Hojda, Z.** The Palaces of Prague. 1995. write for info. (*0-86565-958-3*) Vendome.

Pesek, Joseph J. & Leigh, Ivan E., eds. Chemically Modified Surfaces. 240p. 1994. 85.00 (*0-85186-595-X*, R6595) CRC Pr.

Pesek-Marous, Eduard. Salvatore: Bull of Salvation. Tau Editors, ed. LC 76-49340. (Illus.). 111p. 1976. pap. 4.95 (*0-916453-00-6*) TAU Pr.

Pesek-Marous, Georgia. The Bull: A Religious & Secular History of Phallus Worship & Male Homosexuality. (Illus.). 185p. (Orig.). 1984. pap. 9.95 (*0-916453-01-4*) TAU Pr.

Peseroff, Joyce. A Dog in the Lifeboat. (Poetry Ser.). 64p. (Orig.). (C). 1991. lib. bdg. 16.95 (*0-88748-113-2*); pap. 9.95 (*0-88748-114-0*) Carnegie-Mellon.

— The Hardness Scale. LC 77-82224. 72p. 1977. pap. 9.95 (*0-914086-18-9*) Alicejamesbooks.

Peseroff, Joyce, ed. & intro. The Ploughshares Poetry Reader. LC 86-6319. 336p. 1987. 25.00 (*0-933277-02-4*) Ploughshares.

Peseschkian, N. In Search of Meaning. (Illus.). 240p. 1985. pap. 16.00 (*0-387-15766-2*) Spr-Verlag.

— Positive Family Therapy. Rohlfing, R., tr. 340p. 1985. pap. 23.00 (*0-387-15768-9*) Spr-Verlag.

— Psychotheraphy of Everyday Life. (Illus.). 265p. 1986. pap. 16.00 (*0-387-15767-0*) Spr-Verlag.

Peset, Jose L., ed. The Ethics of Diagnosis. (Philosophy & Medicine Ser.). 300p. (C). 1992. lib. bdg. 112.50 (*0-7923-1544-8*) Kluwer Ac.

Pesetsky, Bette. Cast a Spell. 1993. 21.95 (*0-15-116072-4*) HarBrace.

— Confessions of a Bad Girl. 192p. 1990. mass mkt. 3.95 (*0-8041-0572-3*) Ivy Books.

— Digs. LC 85-9432. (Contemporary American Fiction Ser.). 304p. 1985. mass mkt. 6.95 (*0-14-008318-9*, Penguin Bks) Viking Penguin.

— The Late Night Muse: A Novel. LC 90-56367. 272p. 1993. pap. 10.00 (*0-06-098416-3*, PL) HarpC.

Pesetsky, David. Zero Syntax: Experiences & Cascades. (Current Studies in Linguistics: No. 27). 250p. 1994. 39.95x (*0-262-16145-1*) MIT Pr.

Pesez, Maurice & Bartos, J. Colorimetric & Fluorimetric Analysis of Organic Compounds & Drugs. LC 73-84815. (Clinical & Biochemical Analysis Ser.: No. 1). 688p. reprint ed. pap. 180.00 (*0-7837-5176-1*, 2044906) Bks Demand.

Peshawaria, Reeta. Managing Behavior Problems in Children: A Guide for Parents. 1991. pap. text ed. 4.95 (*0-7069-5322-3*, Pub. by Vikas II) S Asia.

Peshef, Robert J. TMJ Therapy Balances Body Chemistry. 1983. 65.00 (*0-9605902-6-9*) Color Coded Charting.

Peshek, Robert J. Clinical Nutrition Using the Seven Lines of Defense Against Disease. 1980. 10.00 (*0-9605902-3-4*) Color Coded Charting.

— Cross Index. 1982. 10.00 (*0-9605902-5-0*) Color Coded Charting.

— Nutrition for a Healthy Heart. (Illus.). 1979. 20.00 (*0-9605902-2-6*) Color Coded Charting.

— Searching for Health. 1982. 15.95 (*0-9605902-4-2*) Color Coded Charting.

— Student's Manual for Balancing Body Chemistry with Nutrition. 1977. 20.00 (*0-9605902-1-8*) Color Coded Charting.

Peshev, Tsolo C., et al. The International History of Mammalogy. Sterling, Keir B., ed. LC 82-18865. (Eastern Europe & Fennoscandia Ser.: Vol. I). (Illus.). 200p. (C). 1987. pap. 25.00 (*0-910485-01-1*) One World Pr.

Peshkin, Alan. The Color of Strangers, the Color of Friends: The Play of Ethnicity in School & Community. LC 90-19765. 320p. 1991. pap. text ed. 15.95 (*0-226-66201-2*) U Ch Pr.

— God's Choice: The Total World of a Fundamentalist Christian School. LC 85-24524. x, 350p. (C). 1986. 24.95 (*0-226-66198-9*) U Ch Pr.

— God's Choice: The Total World of a Fundamentalist Christian School. LC 85-24524. x, 350p. (C). 1988. pap. text ed. 14.95 (*0-226-66199-7*) U Ch Pr.

— Growing up American: Schooling & the Survival of Community. LC 78-5849. 1982. 10.95 (*0-685-04985-X*) U Ch Pr.

— Growing Up American: Schooling & the Survival of Community. (Illus.). 256p. (C). 1994. pap. text ed. 9.95x (*0-88133-825-7*) Waveland Pr.

Peshkin, Alan, jt. ed. see Eisner, Elliot W.

Peshkin, Alan, jt. auth. see Glesne, Corrine.

Peshkin, M. & Tonomura, A. The Aharonov-Bohm Effect. (Lecture Notes in Physics Ser.: Vol. 340). vi, 152p. 1989. 31.00 (*0-387-51567-4*, 3455) Spr-Verlag.

PeshKova, I. M. The Art of the Kasli Masters: Iskusstvo Kaslinskikh Masterov, 2 vols. (RUS.). 1983. Vol. II, 160 pgs. write for info. (*0-318-61835-4*, Pub. by Collets UK) St Mut.

— The Art of the Kasli Masters: Iskusstvo Kaslinskikh Masterov, 2 vols., Vol. I. 160p. (RUS.). 1983. 212.00 (*0-317-57273-3*, Pub. by Collets UK) St Mut.

Peshkova, V. M. & Savostina, V. M. Nickel. (Analytical Chemistry of the Elements Ser.). 220p. 1970. text ed. 51.00 (*0-7065-0756-8*) Coronet Bks.

Pesic, Slobodan, jt. auth. see Gottlieb, Annie.

Pesina, Jaroslav. The Master of the Hohenfurth Alterpiece. (Illus.). 260p. 1989. 95.00 (*0-85667-339-0*) Sothebys Pubns.

Pesiri, Evelyn. Learn to Hear. (Learn to ... Ser.). 64p. (J). (gr. k-3). 1986. student ed 7.95 (*0-86653-337-0*, GA 675) Good Apple.

— Learn to See. (Illus.). 64p. (J). (gr. k-3). 1985. student ed 7.95 (*0-86653-286-2*, GA 674) Good Apple.

— Learn to Think. (Learn to ... Ser.). 64p. (J). (gr. k-3). 1986. student ed 7.95 (*0-86653-343-5*, GA 676) Good Apple.

Pesiri, Evelyn, ed. & illus. Learn to Write. (Learn to ... Ser.). 64p. (J). (gr. k-3). 1986. student ed 7.95 (*0-86653-342-7*, GA 791) Good Apple.

Pesiri, Evelyn & Cheney, Martha. Gifted & Talented Dictionary: A Reference Workbook for Ages 4-6. 80p. (J). (ps-1). 1994. pap. 3.95 (*1-56565-183-9*) Lowell Hse Juvenile.

— Gifted & Talented Word Book: A Reference Workbook for Ages 6-8. 80p. (J). (gr. 1-3). 1994. pap. 3.95 (*1-56565-182-0*) Lowell Hse Juvenile.

Pesiri, Salina, jt. auth. see Ventimiglia, Sebastian B.

Peskett, Howard. Isaiah: Trusting God in Troubled Times. (LifeGuide Bible Studies). 112p. (Orig.). 1991. pap. 4.99 (*0-8308-1029-3*, 1029) InterVarsity.

Peskett, Pamela, jt. auth. see Gibson, J. S.

Peskin, Allan. Garfield. LC 77-15630. 720p. 1978. 35.00x (*0-87338-210-2*) Kent St U Pr.

Peskin, Allan, ed. Volunteers: The Mexican War Journals of Private Richard Coulter & Sergeant Thomas Barclay, Company E, Second Pennsylvania Infantry. LC 90-47704. (Illus.). 456p. 1991. 35.00 (*0-87338-432-6*) Kent St U Pr.

Peskin, C. S., jt. auth. see Hoppensteadt, Frank F.

Peskin, Dean B. The Corporate Casino: How Managers Win & Lose at the Biggest Game in Town. LC 78-12779. 251p. reprint ed. pap. 71.60 (*0-317-19937-4*, 2023570) Bks Demand.

— Human Behavior & Employment Interviewing. LC 78-130915. (Illus.). 256p. reprint ed. pap. 73.00 (*0-317-09787-3*, 2011736) Bks Demand.

— Sacked! What to Do When You Lose Your Job. LC 79-13522. 191p. reprint ed. pap. 54.50 (*0-317-19932-3*, 2023575) Bks Demand.

— Womaning: Overcoming Male Dominance of Executive Row. Ashton, Sylvia, ed. LC 80-13060. 1981. 22.95 (*0-87949-165-5*) Ashley Bks.

Peskin, Henry M., et al, eds. Environmental Regulation & the U. S. Economy. LC 81-47620. 163p. 1981. 19.95 (*0-8018-2711-6*); pap. 12.95 (*0-8018-2712-4*) Resources Future.

Peskin, Michael E. & Schroeder, Daniel V. An Introduction to Quantum Field Theory. 656p. (C). 1994. write for info. (*0-201-50397-2*, Adv Bk Prog); pap. write for info. (*0-201-50934-2*, Adv Bk Prog) Addison-Wesley.

Peskin, Nancy, ed. Angle of Repose. 100p. (Orig.). 1986. pap. 5.95 (*0-936739-01-0*) Hallwalls Inc.

Peskin, Stephan H. How to Settle for Top Dollar. 566p. 1989. 65.00 (*0-87473-441-X*) Michie Butterworth.

— What's It Worth? A Guide to Current Personal Injury Awards & Settlements, 1991: A Guide to Current Personal Injury Awards & Settlements. (Kluwer Damages Library). 1066p. 1991. 70.00 (*0-87473-819-9*) Michie Butterworth.

***Peskine, Christian.** An Algebraic Introduction to Complex Projective Geometry Vol. 1: Commutative Algebra. (Studies in Advanced Mathematics: No. 47). 240p. (C). Date not set. write for info. (*0-521-48072-8*) Cambridge U Pr.

Peskoff, Joel. Beat NYC Parking Tickets - Z System: Beat the Pub at Its Own Game. Bolofsky, Glen, ed. 8p. 1992. student ed write for info. (*0-931579-25-2*) J F Caroll Pub.

— The Original-How to Beat a Parking Ticket - NYC Edition. Ornstein, Judy, ed. 40p. (Orig.). 1991. pap. write for info. (*0-931579-16-3*) J F Caroll Pub.

Peskov, Vassily. Lost in the Taiga: One Russian Family's Fifty-Year Struggle for Survival & Religious Freedom in the Siberian Wilderness. Schwartz, Marian, tr. LC 93-29260. (ENG & RUS.). 1994. 26.95 (*0-385-47209-9*) Doubleday.

Pesman, Curtis. What She Wants. 1992. pap. 10.00 (*0-345-36653-0*) Ballantine.

Pesman, M. Walter. Meet the Natives: A Beginner's Field Guide to Rocky Mountain Wildflowers, Trees & Shrubs. 9th ed. (Illus.). 248p. pap. 12.95 (*1-879373-31-9*) R Rinehart.

Pesmen, Curtis, jt. auth. see Esquire Magazine Editors.

Pesmen, Sandy. Writing for the Media. LC 82-72510. 160p. 1983. pap. 19.95 (*0-8442-3076-6*, Crain Bks) NTC Pub Grp.

Pesola, Carol A., jt. auth. see Curtain, Helena.

Pesonen, N. Medical & Scientific Terms Dictionary: English-Latin-French-German into Finnish. 525p. 1987. 220.00 (*951-0-12511-3*) IBD Ltd.

Pesonen, Niilo & Ponteva, E. Laaketieteen Sanakirja. 8th ed. 525p. (ENG, FRE & SWE.). 1987. 125.00 (*0-8288-1886-X*, M9984) Fr & Eur.

Pesonen, Pertti. An Election in Finland: Party Activities & Voter Reactions. LC 68-13925. 436p. reprint ed. pap. 124.30 (*0-317-29289-7*, 2022029) Bks Demand.

Pesotta, Rose. Bread upon the Waters. 464p. (Orig.). 1987. reprint ed. 39.00 (*0-87546-126-3*); reprint ed. pap. 15.95 (*0-87546-127-1*) ILR Pr.

— Bread upon the Waters. (American Autobiography Ser.). 435p. 1995. reprint ed. lib. bdg. 99.00 (*0-7812-8616-6*) Rprt Serv.

Pesquera, Beatriz M., jt. ed. see De La Torre, Adela.

Pesquera, L. & Rodriguez, M. A., eds. International School on Stochastic Processes Applied to Physics: Proceedings, 1984. 332p. 1985. 70.00 (*9971-978-20-2*) World Scientific Pub.

Pessagno, E. A., Jr. Radiolarian Zonation & Stratigraphy of the Upper Cretaceous Portion of the Great Valley Sequence, California Coast Ranges. (Micropaleontology Special Publications: No. 2). 95p. 1976. 20.00 (*0-686-84250-2*) Am Mus Natl Hist.

Pessanha, Ricardo, jt. auth. see McGowan, Chris.

Pessar, Patricia R., ed. When Borders Don't Divide: Labor Migration & Refugee Movements in the Americas. LC 87-20856. 1988. 19.50 (*0-934733-26-0*); pap. 14.50 (*0-934733-27-9*) Ctr Migration.

Pessar, Patricia R., jt. auth. see Grasmuck, Sherri.

***Pessarakli, Mohammad, ed.** Handbook of Plant & Crop Physiology. LC 94-32077. (Books in Soils, Plants, & the Environment). 1004p. 1994. 175.00 (*0-8247-9250-5*) Dekker.

— Handbook of Plant & Crop Stress. (Books in Soils, Plants, & the Environment: Vol. 29). 720p. 1994. 165.00 (*0-8247-8987-3*) Dekker.

Pessemier, Edgar A., jt. auth. see Moore, William L.

Pessen, D. & Hubl, W. The Design & Application of Programmable Sequence Controllers for Automation Systems. LC 78-40456. 128p. reprint ed. pap. 36.50 (*0-317-07930-1*, 2020976) Bks Demand.

Pessen, David W. Industrial Automation Systems Control. 507p. 1989. text ed. 89.95 (*0-471-60071-7*) Wiley.

Pessen, Edward. Jacksonian America: Society, Personality, & Politics. LC 85-1100. 400p. (C). 1985. reprint ed. pap. 14.95 (*0-252-01237-2*) U of Ill Pr.

— Losing Our Souls: The American Experience in the Cold War. LC 93-11241. 256p. 1993. 24.95 (*1-56663-037-1*) I R Dee.

— Losing Our Souls: The American Experience in the Cold War. 264p. 1995. pap. 12.95 (*1-56663-096-7*) I R Dee.

— The Many-Faceted Jacksonian Era: New Interpretations. LC 77-24621. (Contributions in American History Ser.: No. 67). (Illus.). 331p. 1977. text ed. 59.95 (*0-8371-9720-1*, PJE/, Greenwood Pr) Greenwood.

— Riches, Class, & Power: The United States Before the Civil War. 467p. 1989. pap. 21.95 (*0-88738-806-X*) Transaction Pubs.

Pessen, Edward, ed. Jacksonian Panorama. LC 75-20140. (AHS Ser: No. 85). 1976. pap. 8.95 (*0-672-60142-7*, Bobbs) Macmillan.

Pessereau, Jennifer, ed. see Rinpoche, Bokar.

Pessey, Christian & Samson, Remy. Bonsai Basics: A Step-by-Step Guide to Growing, Training & General Care. LC 92-38557. (Illus.). 120p. 1993. pap. 10.95 (*0-8069-0327-9*) Sterling.

Pessin, Allan. The Illustrated Encyclopedia of the Securities Industry. 1988. 69.95 (*0-13-450306-6*) NY Inst Finance.

Pessin, Allan H. Fundamentals of the Securities Industries. rev. ed. (Illus.). 1985. text ed. 35.00 (*0-317-01037-9*) NY Inst Finance.

— Fundamentals of the Securities Industry: An Inside View from Wall Street. 1986. 39.95 (*0-685-43079-0*) S&S Trade.

— Securities Law Compliance: A Guide for Brokers, Dealers & Investors. 320p. 1989. text ed. 70.00 (*1-55623-228-4*) Irwin Prof Pubng.

Pessin, Allan H. & Ross, Joseph A. More Words of Wall Street: Two Thousand More Investment Terms Defined. 297p. 1986. text ed. 25.00 (*0-87094-701-X*) Irwin Prof Pubng.

— Words of Wall Street: Two Thousand Investment Terms Defined. LC 82-73632. 225p. 1983. pap. 17.00 (*0-87094-417-7*) Irwin Prof Pubng.

***Pessin, Andrew & Goldberg, Sanford, eds.** The Twin Earth Chronicles: Twenty Years of Reflection on Hilary Putnam's "The Meaning of Meaning" LC 95-10001. 1995. write for info. (*1-55778-720-4*); pap. write for info. (*1-55778-721-2*) Paragon Hse.

Pessin, Deborah. Aleph-Bet Story Book. (Illus.). (J). (gr. 1-3). 1989. pap. 7.95 (*0-8276-0337-1*) JPS Phila.

— History of the Jews in America. (Illus.). (J). (gr. 8-10). 1957. pap. 4.95 (*0-8381-0189-5*) United Syn Bk.

— Jewish People, 3 Vols. (Illus.). (J). (gr. 5-8). 1953. write for info. (*0-318-56293-6*); 4.25 (*0-318-56294-4*) United Syn Bk.

— Jewish People, 3 Vols, I. (Illus.). (J). (gr. 5-8). 1953. 4.25 (*0-8381-0182-8*) United Syn Bk.

— Jewish People, 3 Vols, II. (Illus.). (J). (gr. 5-8). 1953. 4.25 (*0-8381-0185-2*) United Syn Bk.

— Jewish People, 3 Vols, III. (Illus.). (J). (gr. 5-8). 1953. 4.25 (*0-8381-0187-9*) United Syn Bk.

— Jewish People, 3 Vols, Vol. I. (Illus.). (J). (gr. 5-8). 1953. 4.25 (*0-8381-0183-6*) United Syn Bk.

— Jewish People, 3 Vols, Vol. II. (Illus.). (J). (gr. 5-8). 1953. 4.25 (*0-8381-0186-0*) United Syn Bk.

— Jewish People, 3 Vols, Vol. III. (Illus.). (J). (gr. 5-8). 1953. 4.25 (*0-8381-0188-7*) United Syn Bk.

Pessireron, Sylvia, tr. see Caldwell, Ian & Volkman, Toby A., eds.

Pessis-Pasternak, Guitta. Dictionnaire de l'Audio-Visuel: Francais-Anglais, Anglais-Francais. 384p. (ENG & FRE.). 1976. pap. 39.95 (*0-8288-5639-7*, M6442) Fr & Eur.

Pessissiron, Sylvia, tr. see Oey, Eric, ed.

Pesso, Albert. Experience in Action: A Psychomotor Psychology. LC 72-96481. 263p. 1973. 50.00x (*0-8147-6559-9*) NYU Pr.

Pesso, Albert, ed. see Crandell, John S.

Pessoa, Fernando. Always Astonished: Selected Prose. Honig, Edwin, tr. 160p. (Orig.). 1988. pap. 8.95 (*0-87286-228-3*) City Lights.

— Antologia Poetica. El Poeta es un Fingidor. Crespo, Angel, ed. & tr. by. (Nueva Austral Ser.: Vol. 67). (SPA.). 1991. pap. text ed. 24.95x (*84-239-1867-X*) Elliots Bks.

— The Book of Disquiet. MacAdam, Alfred, tr. LC 90-53484. 320p. 1991. 25.00 (*0-679-40234-9*) Pantheon.

— The Book of Disquiet. De Lancastre, Maria J., ed. Costa, Margaret J., tr. 320p. 1992. pap. 14.99 (*1-85242-204-1*) Serpents Tail.

— Poems of Fernando Pessoa. Honig, Edwin & Brown, Susan M., eds. Brown, Susan M., tr. (Modern European Poets Ser.). 215p. 1987. pap. 10.50 (*0-88001-123-8*) Ecco Pr.

— The Surprise of Being. Greene, James & Azevedo Mafra, Clara de, trs. LC 86-82063. 64p. 1987. 25.00 (*0-946162-23-9*, Pub. by Angel Bks UK); pap. 13.95 (*0-946162-24-7*, Pub. by Angel Bks UK) Dufour.

Pessolano, F. John, jt. ed. see Mendell, Jay S.

Pessoneaux, Emile. Dictionnaire Grec-Francais: Greek - French Dictionary. 896p. (FRE & GRE.). 1953. 59.95 (*0-8288-6877-8*, M-6443) Fr & Eur.

Pest Publications Staff. Shepherd's Purse: Organic Pest Control Handbook. rev. ed. LC 92-25525. (Illus.). 80p. 1993. pap. 9.95 (*0-913990-98-1*) Book Pub Co.

Pestalozza, Giulio, jt. ed. see Fior, Renato.

Pestalozzi, et al. Business Law Guide to Switzerland. 690p. 1992. 112.50 (*0-685-67808-3*, 5593) Commerce.

Pestalozzi, J. Leonard & Gertrude. 1976. lib. bdg. 250.00 (*0-8490-0507-8*) Gordon Pr.

Pestalozzi, Johann H. Education of Man, Aphorisms. LC 79-88920. 93p. 1969. reprint ed. text ed. 45.00 (*0-8371-2107-8*, PEEM, Greenwood Pr) Greenwood.

— How Gertrude Teaches Her Children: How Mothers Teach Their Own Children. 1973. 250.00 (*0-87968-066-0*) Gordon Pr.

— Pestalozzi. Anderson, Lewis F., ed. LC 73-10877. 283p. 1975. reprint ed. text ed. 35.00 (*0-8371-7046-X*, PEP, Greenwood Pr) Greenwood.

— Pestalozzi's Educational Writings, Vol. 2. Green, John A., tr. Bd. with How Gertrude Teaches Her Children. LC 77-72191. (Contributions to the History of Psychology Ser.: Vol. II, Pt. B, Psychometrics). 424p. 1977. reprint ed. Set text ed. 85.00 (*0-313-26937-8*, U6937, Greenwood Pr) Greenwood.

Pestalozzi, Karl, jt. ed. see Mueller-Lauter, Wolfgang.

Pestana, Carla G. Liberty of Conscience & the Growth of Religious Diversity in Early America, 1636-1786. (Illus.). 102p. 1986. pap. 30.00 (*0-916617-02-5*) J C Brown.

— Quakers & Baptists in Colonial Massachusetts. 240p. (C). 1991. 54.95 (*0-521-41111-4*) Cambridge U Pr.

Pestana, Carlos. Fluids & Electrolytes in the Surgical Patients. 4th ed. 240p. 1989. pap. text ed. 32.00 (*0-683-06862-8*) Williams & Wilkins.

— An Illustrated Diet Book for Humans: With Sensible Medical Advice & a Running Commentary by a Very Smart Dog. LC 92-380. 1992. pap. 16.95 (*0-935834-82-6*) Rainbow Books.

Pestana, Emily. Circles. Bixby, Robert, ed. 17p. 1993. pap. 6.00 (*1-882983-03-3*) March Street Pr.

Pestelli, Giorgio. The Age of Mozart & Beethoven. Cross, Eric, tr. (Storia de la Musica Ser.). 300p. (C). 1984. pap. 24.95 (*0-521-28479-1*) Cambridge U Pr.

Pester, Albert E. Letter to the Editor: Collection of Short Stories, Essays & Poems. 1992. text ed. 16.95 (*0-533-10080-1*) Vantage.

***Pestereau, Gilbert.** Dictionnaire des Personnages Vian. 426p. (FRE.). 1993. pap. 28.95 (*0-7859-7874-7*, 2267012006) Fr & Eur.

Pesti, Gene M. & Miller, Bill R. Animal Food Formulation: Economics & Computer Applications. LC 92-17575. 1993. pap. 49.95 (*0-442-01335-3*) Van Nos Reinhold.

Pestieau, Joseph. Essai Contre le Defaitisme Politique: Imagination Politique et Intelligence Economique. LC 74-180539. 255p. (FRE.). reprint ed. pap. 72.70 (*0-7837-6939-3*, 2046768) Bks Demand.

***Pestis, Gene.** Raising Healthy Poultry under Primitive Conditions. rev. ed. 1994. pap. text ed. 7.50 (*1-886532-02-8*) Christian Vet.

Pestka, Ralph, jt. auth. see Schwei, Priscilla.

Pestka, Sidney, jt. ed. see Colowick, Sidney P.

Pestle, R. Knowing the Elderly in Your Community Through Home Economics. 1979. 2.00 (*0-911365-14-1*, A261-08438) Home Econ Educ.

Pestle, Ruth. Voluntary Simplicity: A Lifestyle Option. 1984. 4.00 (*0-911365-23-0*, A261-08460) Home Econ Educ.

Pestman, P. W., ed. The New Papyrological Primer. 5th ed. (Illus.). xxii, 318p. 1990. pap. 41.25 (*90-04-09348-6*) E J Brill.

Pestoff, Victor A. Between Markets & Politics: Co-Operatives in Sweden. (C). 1991. pap. text ed. 59.50 (*0-8133-8294-7*) Westview.

Pestolesi, Robert A. & Baker, Cindi. Introduction to Physical Education: A Contemporary Careers Approach. (C). 1983. text ed. 29.00 (*0-673-16592-2*) HarpCollege.

— Introduction to Physical Education: A Contemporary Careers Approach. 2nd ed. (C). 1990. text ed. 37.50 (*0-673-16719-4*) HarpCollege.

Peston, M. H. & Quandt, R. E., eds. Prices, Competition & Equilibrium. LC 86-3549. 352p. 1986. 72.50 (*0-389-20626-1*, N8184) B&N Imports.

Pestonjee, D. M. Second Handbook of Psychological & Social Instruments. (C). 1990. 56.00 (*81-7022-193-5*, Pub. by Concept II) S Asia.

— Stress & Coping: The Indian Experience. 224p. (C). 1992. 32.00 (*0-8039-9400-1*) Sage.

Pestre, D. Physique et Physiciens en France 1918-1940. 356p. 1984. pap. text ed. 77.00 (*2-903928-08-8*) Gordon & Breach.

Pestrikov, Dmitri & Dikansky, Nikolai. The Physics of Intense Beams & Storage Rings. LC 93-19889. 1994. 70.00 (*1-56396-107-5*) Am Inst Physics.

Pestryakov, E. M., tr. see Dobrovolsky, V. N. & Litovchenko, V. G.

Pet-Edwards, J., et al. Risk Assessment & Decision Making Using Test Results: The Carcinogenicity Predicition & Battery Selection Approach. (Illus.). 220p. 1989. 65.00 (*0-306-43067-3*, Plenum Pr) Plenum.

Peta People for the Ethical Treatment of Animals Staff, comp. Shopping Guide for Caring Consumers, 1995: A Guide to Products That Are Not Tested on Animals. 128p. 1994. pap. 7.95 (*1-57067-000-5*) Book Pub Co.

Petaccia, Mario A. Walking on Water. (Illus.). 64p. 1986. 15.00 (*0-89304-075-4*, CCC195); pap. 7.50 (*0-89304-076-2*) Cross-Cultrl NY.

Petach, Heidi. Frog Stickers. (Illus.). (J). (gr. k-3). 1994. pap. 1.00 (*0-486-28067-5*) Dover.

— Goldilocks & the Three Hares. LC 94-24495. (J). 1995. 9.95 (*0-399-22828-4*, Grosset-Putnam) Putnam Pub Group.

— Jonah: The Inside Story. (Happy Day Bks.). (Illus.). 32p. (J). (gr. k-2). 1989. 2.50 (*0-87403-594-5*, 3854) Standard Pub.

— One, Two, Buckle My Shoe: A Counting Rhyme. (J). (ps). 1994. 3.95 (*0-307-06146-9*, Golden Pr) Western Pub.

Petaja. Stardrift & Other Fantastic Flotsam. 6.50 (*0-686-00172-9*) Fantasy Pub Co.

Petak, Joseph A. Never Plan Tomorrow. LC 91-78112. (Illus.). 524p. (Orig.). 1992. pap. 19.95 (*0-9631609-6-6*) Aquataur.

Petak, W. J. & Atkisson, A. A. Natural Hazard Risk Assessment & Public Policy: Anticipating the Unexpected. (Environmental Management Ser.). (Illus.). 489p. 1982. 108.00 (*0-387-90645-2*) Spr-Verlag.

Petak, William J., ed. Emergency Management: A Challenge for Public Administration. 176p. 1985. 9.50 (*0-685-25269-8*) Am Soc Pub Admin.

Petak, William J., jt. auth. see Alesch, Daniel J.

Petar, Prince, 2nd. The Mountain Wreath of P. P. Nyegosh, Prince Bishop of Montenegro. Wiles, James W., tr. LC 71-109820. 250p. 1970. reprint ed. text ed. 47.50 (*0-8371-4311-X*, PEMW, Greenwood Pr) Greenwood.

Petch, Alison. At Home in the Community: An Evaluation of Supported Accomodation for People with Mental Health Problems. (Evaluative Studies in Social Work). 240p. 1992. 59.95 (*1-85628-316-X*, Pub. by Avebury Pub UK) Ashgate Pub Co.

Petch, James R., jt. auth. see Haines-Young, Roy H.

Petchenkine, Youry. Buying a Business in Russia: A Handbook for Westerners on Russian Privatization. 182p. 1993. 89.00 (*0-9637388-0-1*) D N Yng & Assocs.

— Ghana: In Search of Stability, 1957-1992. LC 92-9113. 264p. 1993. text ed. 52.95 (*0-275-94326-7*, C4326, Praeger Pubs) Greenwood.

— The United Nations Industrial Development Organization: UNIDO & Problems of International Industrial Development. LC 93-2859. 224p. 1993. text ed. 55.00 (*0-275-94496-4*, C4496, Praeger Pubs) Greenwood.

Petchesky, Rosalind P. Abortion & Woman's Choice: The State, Sexuality & Reproductive Freedom. rev. ed. (Northeastern Series in Feminist Theory). 412p. 1990. pap. text ed. 14.95 (*1-55553-075-3*) NE U Pr.

Petchsiri, Apirat. Eastern Importation of Western Criminal Law: Thailand As a Case Study. LC 86-24821. (Publications of the Comparative Criminal Law Project: Vol. 17). xix, 208p. 1987. 32.50 (*0-8377-1054-5*) Rothman.

Pete, Geradino A. Electric Power Systems Manual. 1992. text ed. 47.00 (*0-07-049530-0*) McGraw.

Pete, Jacelen D. Just Another Busy Day. (Illus.). 32p. (J). 1989. 8.95 (*0-934601-93-3*) Peachtree Pubs.

Pete, Moustache. Road Noise & Sentiments. (Illus.). 65p. (Orig.). 1987. pap. 6.95 (*0-939303-03-5*) Educ Lrn Syst.

Petee, Frank, jt. auth. see Stauffer, Carol.

Peteet, Julie M. Gender in Crisis. 1990. text ed. 35.00 (*0-685-39136-1*) Col U Pr.

— Gender in Crisis: Women & the Palestinian Resistance Movement. 224p. 1991. text ed. 37.50 (*0-231-07446-8*) Col U Pr.

— Gender in Crisis: Women & the Palestinian Resistance Movement. 245p. (C). 1992. pap. text ed. 13.50 (*0-231-07447-6*) Col U Pr.

P Q

An Asterisk (*) at the beginning of an entry indicates that the title is appearing in BIP for the first time.

Petegorsky, David W. Left-Wing Democracy in the English Civil War. LC 72-2021. (British History Ser.: No. 30). 1972. reprint ed. lib. bdg. 75.00 (*0-8383-1472-4*) M S G Haskell Hse.

Petek, Daniel J. Spokane Centennial Cookbook. (Illus.). 144p. (Orig.). 1988. pap. 6.95 (*0-9615201-5-9*) BCG Ltd.

— Spokane Light Cookbook. (Illus.). 144p. (Orig.). 1987. pap. 5.95 (*0-9615201-4-0*) BCG Ltd.

— Spokane Style Cookbook. (Illus.). 72p. (Orig.). 1985. pap. 4.95 (*0-9615201-0-8*) BCG Ltd.

— Spokane Too! Cookbook. (Illus.). 120p. (Orig.). 1986. pap. 4.95 (*0-9615201-3-2*) BCG Ltd.

Petek, Danita, jt. auth. see Kile, Sibyl.

Petelin, Carol. The Country Diary Book of Flowers: Drying, Pressing, & Pot Pourri. (Illus.). 160p. 1991. 24.95 (*0-8050-1770-4*) H Holt & Co.

— The Creative Guide to Dried Flowers. (Illus.). 108p. 1990. pap. 18.95 (*0-7181-3392-7*, Penguin Bks) Viking Penguin.

Petelin, Joseph B., jt. auth. see Klaiber, Christian.

***Petellat, John.** Moving Beyond Trauma. Jaeger, Joseph, ed. (Orig.). 1995. pap. 14.95 (*1-880254-24-7*) Vista.

***Petelle, Joey.** The Southwest Creative Sourcebook. (Illus.). 1996. spiral bd., pap. 50.00 (*1-886295-01-8*) Everest Pubng.

***Petelle, Joey, ed.** Chicago Creative Sourcebook. (Illus.). 1996. spiral bd., pap. 50.00 (*1-886295-04-2*) Everest Pubng.

— The Rocky Mountain Creative Sourcebook. (Illus.). 1995. spiral bd. 50.00 (*1-886295-02-6*) Everest Pubng.

— Texas Creative Sourcebook. (Illus.). 1995. 50.00 (*1-886295-03-4*) Everest Pubng.

— Twin Cities Creative Sourcebook. (Illus.). 1996. spiral bd., pap. 50.00 (*1-886295-05-0*) Everest Pubng.

— U. S. A. Sourcebook. (Illus.). 1995. pap. 50.00 (*1-886295-00-X*) Everest Pubng.

Peteni, R. L. Hill of Fools. (African Writers Ser.). 151p. 1976. pap. 8.95 (*0-435-90178-8*) Heinemann.

— Towards Tomorrow: The Story of the African Teachers Association of South Africa. Kitchen, Cole, ed. LC 78-59714. 1979. pap. 7.95 (*0-917256-08-5*) Ref Pubns.

Peter, jt. auth. see Flight, Graham.

Peter, Chris M. Human Rights in Africa: A Comparative Study of the African Human & People's Rights Charter & the New Tanzanian Bill of Rights. LC 89-17126. (Studies in Human Rights: No. 10). 160p. 1990. text ed. 45.00 (*0-313-26863-0*, PHR/, Greenwood Pr) Greenwood.

Peter-Contesse, Rene & Ellington, John. A Handbook on Leviticus. LC 92-20509. (UBS Handbook Ser.). Orig. Title: Translator's Handbook on Leviticus. ix, 458p. 1990. 16.00 (*0-8267-0110-8*, 104588) Untd Bible Soc.

— A Handbook on the Book of Daniel. LC 93-33287. (UBS Handbook Ser.). 1994. 15.00 (*0-8267-0126-4*, 105036) Untd Bible Soc.

Peter Damian, St. Letters, 1-30. Blum, Owen, tr. LC 88-25802. (Fathers of the Church: Mediaeval Continuation Ser.: Vol. 1). 312p. 1989. 37.95 (*0-8132-0702-9*) Cath U Pr.

Peter Damien, St. Letters, 31-60: Mediaeval Continuation. LC 88-25802. (Fathers of the Church: Mediaeval Continuation Ser.: Vol. 2). 422p. 1990. 37.95 (*0-8132-0707-X*) Cath U Pr.

***Peter, Emmett.** Lake County, Florida: A Pictorial History. LC 94-24867. 1994. write for info. (*0-89865-905-1*) Donning Co.

Peter, Gilbert M. & Peterson, Daniel R. An Understandable Approach to Basic Mathematics. (C). 1982. text ed. 25.75 (*0-673-16045-9*) HarpCollege.

Peter, Gilbert M. & Welch, C. Lee. Algebra for College Students. (C). 1988. text ed. 58.00 (*0-673-18798-5*) HarpCollege.

— Elementary Algebra. LC 94-44473. 650p. 1995. text ed. write for info. (*0-314-04385-3*) West Pub.

— Intermediate Algebra. 650p. 1995. text ed. write for info. (*0-314-04158-3*) West Pub.

Peter, Gilbert M., jt. auth. see Welch, C. Lee.

Peter, Herbert & Schiffer, Nancy. China for America: Export Porcelain of the 18th & 19th Centuries. LC 79-88254. (Illus.). 224p. 1979. 27.50 (*0-916838-23-4*) Schiffer.

Peter, Hermann. Die Geschichtliche Literatur Uber die Romische Kaiserzeit Bis Theodosius I. und Ihre Quellen, 2 vols., Set. xxii, 888p. 1967. reprint ed. write for info. (*0-318-71194-X*, Pub. by Georg Olms GW) Lubrecht & Cramer.

— Wahrheit und Kunst, Geschichtsschreibung und Plagiat Im Klassischen Altertum. xii, 490p. 1965. reprint ed. write for info. (*0-318-70813-2*, Pub. by Georg Olms GW) Lubrecht & Cramer.

Peter, Iain, jt. auth. see Fyffe, Allen.

Peter, Isaac, ed. Six Centuries of the Provincial Book Trade in Britain. 212p. 1990. 28.00 (*0-906795-96-6*) Oak Knoll.

***Peter J., Frost, et al, eds.** Managerial Reality: Balancing Technique, Practice & Values. LC 94-27813. (C). 1995. 24.00 (*0-673-99183-0*) HarpCollege.

Peter, J. H., et al, eds. Sleep & Health Risk. (Illus.). 560p. 1991. pap. 125.00 (*0-387-53083-5*) Spr-Verlag.

Peter, J. Pal, ed. see Certo, Samuel C.

Peter, J. Paul. Marketing for the Manufacturer. (APICS Ser.). 270p. 1992. 45.00 (*1-55623-648-4*) Irwin Prof Pubng.

Peter, J. Paul & Donnelly, James H., Jr. Marketing Management: Knowledge & Skills. 3rd ed. 928p. (C). 1991. text ed. 66.95 (*0-256-09225-7*, 09-1687-03) Irwin.

— A Preface to Marketing Management. 5th ed. 336p. (C). 1990. pap. text ed. 31.95 (*0-256-09445-4*) Irwin.

— A Preface to Marketing Management. 6th ed. LC 93-19853. (Marketing Ser.). 368p. (C). 1993. pap. text ed. 34.95 (*0-256-12251-2*) Irwin.

Peter, J. Paul & Olson, Jerry C. Consumer Behavior & Marketing Strategy. 3rd ed. LC 92-20169. (Series in Marketing). 800p. (C). 1992. text ed. 65.95 (*0-256-10567-7*) Irwin.

— Understanding Consumer Behavior. LC 93-13484. 512p. (C). 1993. text ed. 63.95 (*0-256-12278-4*) Irwin.

Peter, J. Paul & Ray, Michael L. Measurement Readings for Marketing Research. LC 84-9385. (Reading Ser.). 374p. (Orig.). (C). 1984. pap. text ed. 58.00 (*0-87757-168-6*) Am Mktg.

Peter, J. Paul, jt. auth. see Certo, Samuel C.

Peter, J. Paul, jt. auth. see Churchill, Gilbert A.

Peter, Jennifer A., jt. ed. see Crosier, Louis M.

Peter, John. The Oral History of Modern Architecture: Interviews with the Greatest Architects of the Twentieth Century. LC 94-1472. 1994. write for info. (*0-8109-3669-0*) Abrams.

— The Therapist. Cheney, Audrey, ed. LC 89-6699. 202p. (Orig.). 1989. pap. 18.95 (*0-929551-04-4*); audio 9.95 (*0-929551-10-9*) Ability Workshop Pr.

— Vladimir's Carrot: Modern Drama & the Modern Imagination. LC 87-5838. xii, 372p. 1987. 24.95 (*0-226-66265-9*) U Ch Pr.

Peter, Katherine. Nats'ats'a' Ch'adhah Ahkhii: How I Tan Hides. (Illus.). 22p. 1980. pap. 5.00 (*1-55500-012-6*) Alaska Native.

— Neets'aii Gwiindaii: Living in the Chandalar Country. Raboff, Adeline, tr. (Illus.). xii, 108p. (Orig.). 1992. pap. 12.00 (*0-933769-11-3*) Alaska Native.

Peter, Katherine & McGary, Jane M., eds. John Fredson Edward Sapir Haa Googwandak: Stories Told by John Fredson to Edward Sapir. (Illus.). 113p. (Orig.). (C). 1982. pap. 12.00 (*0-933769-02-4*) Alaska Native.

Peter, Laszlo, ed. Historians & the History of Transylvania. 280p. 1992. text ed. 39.00 (*0-88033-229-8*) Col U Pr.

Peter, Laszlo & Pynsent, Robert B. Intellectuals & the Future in the Habsburg Monarchy, 1890-1914. LC 87-21642. 224p. 1988. text ed. 39.95 (*0-312-01547-X*) St Martin.

Peter, Laurence J. Peter's Quotations: Ideas for Our Time. 1993. pap. 12.00 (*0-688-11909-3*, Quill) Morrow.

Peter, Laurence J. & Hull, Raymond. The Peter Principle. 1993. reprint ed. lib. bdg. 18.95 (*1-56849-161-1*) Buccaneer Bks.

— The Peter Principle: Why Things Always Go Wrong. (Illus.). 1971. pap. 9.45 (*0-688-27544-3*, Quill) Morrow.

Peter, Lily. In the Beginning: Myths of the Western World. LC 82-20274. (Illus.). 76p. 1983. 19.00 (*0-938626-15-9*); pap. 7.95 (*0-938626-18-3*) U of Ark Pr.

Peter, Margo I., jt. auth. see Darling, Rosalyn B.

***Peter, Melanie.** Drama for All: Developing Drama in the Curriculum with Pupils with Special Educational Needs. 96p. 1994. pap. 19.95x (*1-85346-315-9*, Pub. by D Fulton UK) Taylor & Francis.

— Making Drama Special: Developing Drama Practice for Special Educational Needs. 176p. 1995. pap. 24.95x (*1-85346-316-7*, Pub. by D Fulton UK) Taylor & Francis.

***Peter, Melanie, ed.** Art for All: Developing Art in the Curriculum with Students with Special Educational Needs. 60p. 1995. pap. text ed. 16.95x (*1-85346-317-5*, Pub. by D Fulton UK) Taylor & Francis.

Peter Nahum Ltd. Staff. Burne-Jones -- A Quest for Love: Works by Sir Edward Burne-Jones BT & Related Works by Contemporary Artists. (Illus.). (C). 1993. pap. 60.00 (*1-872508-03-0*) St Mut.

Peter, Nancy & Schiffer, Herbert F. The Brass Book: American, English & European, 15th Century Thru 1850. LC 78-63428. 1978. 60.00 (*0-916838-17-X*) Schiffer.

Peter Norton Computing Group Staff & Holzner, Steven. Turbo Pascal for Windows Programming. (Illus.). (Orig.). 1992. pap. 39.95 (*1-56686-010-5*) Brady Compu Bks.

Peter Norton Computing Group Staff & Jourdian, Robert. Hard Disk Companion. 2nd ed. 1991. 24.95 (*0-13-658782-8*) Brady Compu Bks.

Peter Norton Computing Group Staff & Qualline, Steven. Advanced C Programming: Practical Solutions to Advanced Programming Problems. 1991. disk, pap. 39.95 (*0-13-663170-3*); pap. 29.95 (*0-13-663188-6*) Brady Compu Bks.

Peter Norton Computing Group Staff, jt. auth. see Holzner, Steven.

Peter Norton Programming Group Staff & Holzner, Steven. Quick C for Windows. (Illus.). (Orig.). 1992. pap. 26.95 (*0-13-747551-9*); disk 39.95 (*0-13-747569-1*) Brady Compu Bks.

Peter, O. Herder-Lexikon Chemie. 3rd ed. 256p. (GER.). 1975. pap. 35.00 (*0-8288-5896-9*, M7454) Fr & Eur.

Peter, P. Canal & River Levees. (Developments in Geotechnical Engineering Ser.: Vol. 29). 540p. 1982. 148.75 (*0-444-99726-1*) Elsevier.

Peter, Paul & Donnelly, James H., Jr. Marketing Management: Knowledge & Skills. 4th ed. LC 94-7621. (Marketing Ser.). 864p. (C). 1909. text ed. 66.95 (*0-256-13727-7*) Irwin.

Peter Pauper Staff. I Love You Because: A Love Quiz. (Personals Ser.). (Illus.). 80p. 1994. pap. 5.99 (*0-88088-607-2*) Peter Pauper.

Peter Peregrinus, Ltd. Staff, jt. auth. see Institution of Electrical Engineers (UK) Staff.

Peter-Raoul, Mar, et al, eds. Yearning to Breathe Free: Liberation Theologies in the U. S. LC 90-46164. 1991. pap. 16.95 (*0-88344-732-0*) Orbis Bks.

Peter, Rozsa. Playing with Infinity: Mathematical Explorations & Excursions. LC 75-26467. 288p. 1976. reprint ed. pap. text ed. 5.95 (*0-486-23265-4*) Dover.

Peter, Salm. The Poem As a Plant: A Biological View of Goethe's Faust. LC 71-141461. 169p. reprint ed. pap. 48.20 (*0-317-08241-8*, 2003259) Bks Demand.

Peter, Sarah. Sarah Peter: Thirty-Six Drawings. (Illus.). 80p. 1994. write for info. (*0-9639922-0-1*) S Peter.

***Peter Seldin & Associates Staff.** Improving College Teaching. 273p. (C). 1995. text ed. 32.95 (*1-882982-08-8*) Anker Pub.

Peter, T. J., et al, eds. Ophiolites - Genesis & Evolution of Oceanic Lithosphere. (C). 1991. lib. bdg. 61.50 (*0-7923-1176-0*) Kluwer Ac.

Peter The Venerable. Letters of Peter the Venerable, 2 Vols, Set. Constable, Giles, ed. LC 67-10086. (Historical Studies: No. 78). 897p. 1967. 60.00 (*0-674-52775-5*) HUP.

Peter, Val J. I Think of My Homelessness: Stories from Boys Town. 102p. (Orig.). 1991. pap. 4.95 (*0-938510-26-6*, 19-004) Boys Town Pr.

— Twenty-Five Thoughts on Parenting from Boys Town. 56p. (Orig.). 1991. pap. text ed. 2.98 (*0-938510-28-2*) Boys Town Pr.

— Twenty-Five Tips on Parenting from Boys Town. 56p. (Orig.). 1991. pap. text ed. 2.98 (*0-938510-29-0*) Boys Town Pr.

— What Makes Boys Town So Special? 150p. (Orig.). (C). 1986. pap. 5.95 (*0-938510-36-3*, 19-003) Boys Town Pr.

***Peter, Wolfgang.** Arbitration & Renegotiation of International Investment Agreements: A Study with Particular Reference to Means of Conflict Avoidance under Natural Resources Investment Agreements. 2nd enl. rev. ed. LC 95-15795. 1995. write for info. (*90-411-0037-7*) Kluwer Ac.

Peteraf, Nancy J. A Plant Called Spot. LC 92-27474. (J). 1994. 13.95 (*0-385-30885-X*) Doubleday.

Peteraitis, V. Lithuanian - English Dictionary. 1991. 49.95 (*0-8288-2626-9*, F58440) Fr & Eur.

Peteraitis, Vilius. Lithuanian-English Dictionary. (ENG & LIT.). 42.50 (*0-87559-037-3*); 47.50 (*0-87559-038-1*) Shalom.

Peterajova, L'udmila. Brunovsky, Albin. 44p. (C). 1985. 195.00 (*0-685-22613-1*, Pub. by Collets UK) Pro-Am Music.

Peterborough Field Naturalists. Kawarthas Nature. Hudson, Noel, ed. 120p. (Orig.). 1995. pap. 19.95 (*1-55046-058-7*, Pub. by Stoddart Publng CN) Pubs Dist MI.

Peterdi. Printmaking. 1986. pap. 27.95 (*0-02-596060-1*) Macmillan.

Peterfreund, Emanuel. Information, Systems & Psychoanalysis. LC 71-141662. (Psychological Issues Monograph: No. 25-26, Vol. 8, No. 1-2). 397p. 1971. text ed. 47.00 (*0-8236-2658-X*); pap. text ed. 42.00 (*0-8236-2659-8*) Intl Univs Pr.

— The Process of Psychoanalytic Therapy: Models & Strategies, Vol. 1. (C). 1983. text ed. 32.50 (*0-88163-003-9*) Analytic Pr.

Peterfreund, Herbert & McLaughlin, Joseph M. New York Practice, Cases & Other Materials. 4th ed. (University Casebook Ser.). 1583p. 1991. reprint ed. text ed. 34.50 (*0-88277-434-4*) Foundation Pr.

Peterfreund, Sheldon P., jt. auth. see Denise, Theodore C.

Peterfreund, Stuart. The Hanged Knife & Other Poems. 52p. 1970. 2.95 (*0-87886-000-2*, Greenfld Rev Pr) Greenfld Rev Lit.

— Harder Than Rain. LC 77-23857. 82p. 1977. 3.50 (*0-87886-084-3*, Greenfld Rev Pr) Greenfld Rev Lit.

Peterfreund, Stuart, ed. Culture-Criticism-Ideology. (Proceedings of the Northeastern University Center for Literary Studies: Vol. 4). 75p. 1986. pap. text ed. 6.95 (*0-930350-97-9*) NE U Pr.

— Literature & Science Theory & Practice. (Illus.). 248p. 1989. text ed. 40.00 (*1-55553-058-3*) NE U Pr.

Peteri, Gyorgy. The Effects of World War I: War Communism in Hungary. 229p. 1984. text ed. 40.00 (*0-88033-059-7*) East Eur Quarterly.

***Peteri, Z.** Legal Theory - Comparative Law: Studies in Honour of Professor Imre Szabo. 463p. (C). 1984. 108.00x (*963-05-3992-6*, Pub. by Akad Kiado HU) St Mut.

***Peteri, Z. & Lamm, V.** Legal Development & Comparative Law 1986: Selected Essays for the 12th Intl. Congress of Comparative Law. 330p. (C). 1986. 87.00x (*963-05-4434-2*, Pub. by Akad Kiado HU) St Mut.

Peteri, Z., jt. auth. see Szabo, I.

Peteri, Zoltan & Lamm, Vanda, eds. General Reports to the Tenth International Congress of Comparative Law, 8 Vols. 1050p. 1981. 230.00 (*0-569-08701-5*, Pub. by Collets UK) St Mut.

Peterich, Eckart, ed. Athens. (Panorama Bks.). (Illus.). (FRE.). 1966. 3.95 (*0-685-11018-4*) Fr & Eur.

Peterjohn, Bruce G. The Birds of Ohio. LC 89-45202. (Illus.). 256p. 1989. 49.95 (*0-253-34183-3*) Ind U Pr.

Peterjohn, Bruce G., et al. Abundance & Distribution of the Birds of Ohio. Cafazzo, Veda M., ed. LC 86-63244. (Biological Notes Ser.). (Illus.). 52p. (Orig.). 1987. pap. 7.00 (*0-86727-103-5*) Ohio Bio Survey.

***Peterken, George.** Natural Woodlands. (Illus.). 446p. (C). 1995. write for info. (*0-521-36613-5*); pap. write for info. (*0-521-36792-1*) Cambridge U Pr.

— Woodland Conservation & Management. 2nd ed. LC 94-107989. 374p. 1994. pap. 47.50 (*0-412-55730-4*) Chapman & Hall.

Peterkiewicz, Jerzy. In the Scales of Fate: An Autobiography. LC 92-27591. (Illus.). 208p. 1993. 30.00 (*0-7145-2960-5*) M Boyars Pubs.

Peterkin, Allan. What about Me? When Brothers & Sisters Get Sick. LC 92-20035. (Illus.). 32p. (J). 1992. 16.95 (*0-945354-48-7*); pap. 8.95 (*0-945354-49-5*) Magination Pr.

Peterkin, Gail L., et al, eds. Hunting & Animal Exploitation in the Later Palaeolithic & Mesolithic of Eurasia. LC 93-40095. (Archeological Papers of the American Anthropological Association: No. 4). 1993. write for info. (*0-913167-61-4*) Am Anthro Assn.

Peterkin, Julia. Black April. 22.95 (*0-89190-527-8*, Am Repr) Amereon Ltd.

— Bright Skin. 19.95 (*0-89190-676-2*, Am Repr) Amereon Ltd.

— A Plantation Christmas. LC 72-4563. (Black Heritage Library Collection). (Illus.). (YA). (gr. 7 up). 1977. reprint ed. 13.95 (*0-8369-9119-2*) Ayer.

— A Plantation Christmas. LC 78-22014. (Illus.). (J). (gr. 6 up). 1978. reprint ed. pap. 2.95 (*0-89783-007-5*) Cherokee.

— Scarlet Sister Mary. LC 90-27635. 352p. 1991. reprint ed. 29.95 (*0-87797-227-3*) Cherokee.

Peterkin, Karen & Black, Donald V. The Directory of Online Healthcare Databases. 5th rev. ed. 80p. 1990. spiral bd. 35.00 (*0-931712-10-6*) Alpine Guild.

Peterkin, Karen & Black, Donald V., eds. The Directory of Online Healthcare Databases. 4th ed. 62p. 1989. spiral bd. 26.00 (*0-931712-09-2*) Alpine Guild.

Peterkin, Mike, illus. Three Little Pigs: Pop-up Book. LC 93-70940. 10p. (J). (ps-3). 1993. 11.95 (*1-56282-513-5*) Disney Pr.

Peterkin, Morris. Gang Leader, PH. D. 1995. 12.95 (*0-8062-5113-1*) Carlton.

Peterkops, Raimonds. Theory of Ionization of Atoms by Electron Impact. Hummer, D. G., ed. Aronson, Elliot, tr. LC 77-81310. (Illus.). 273p. reprint ed. pap. 77.90 (*0-317-09233-2*, 2012203) Bks Demand.

Peterle, Elmo A. Starting to Plan for Lifetime Financial Independence. 1993. pap. 17.95 (*1-882180-10-0*) Griffin CA.

Peterle, Tony J. Wildlife Toxicology. 384p. 1991. text ed. 64.95 (*0-442-00462-1*) Van Nos Reinhold.

Peterle, Tony J., ed. International Congress of Game Biologists: Proceedings, 13th, Atlanta, 11-15 March 1977. (Illus.). 538p. (Orig.). 1977. pap. 6.00 (*0-933564-04-X*) Wildlife Soc.

Peterman, James F. Philosophy As Therapy: An Interpretation & Defense of Wittgenstein's Later Philosophical Project. LC 91-18277. (SUNY Series in Philosophy & Psychotherapy). 158p. 1992. 59.50 (*0-7914-0981-3*); pap. 19.95 (*0-7914-0982-1*) State U NY Pr.

Peterman, Larry I. & Weschler, Louis F., eds. American Political Thought: Readings. LC 78-184069. (C). 1972. pap. text ed. 16.95 (*0-89197-015-0*) Irvington.

Peterman, M. B. & Carrasquillo, R. L. Production of High Strength Concrete. LC 85-25924. (Illus.). 278p. 1986. 36.00 (*0-8155-1057-8*) Noyes.

Peterman, Michael. Robertson Davies. (Twayne's World Authors Ser.: No. 780). 208p. 1986. lib. bdg. 22.95 (*0-8057-6629-4*, Twayne) Macmillan.

***Peterman, Michael A. & Ballstadt, Carl, eds.** Forest & Other Gleanings: The Fugitive Writings of Catherine Parr Traill. (Canadian Short Story Library). 264p. 1995. pap. 18.00 (*0-7766-0391-4*, Pub. by Univ Ottawa Pr CN) Paul & Co Pubs.

Peterman, Phylis J., jt. auth. see Blake, Richard.

Petermann, Erwin. Wilhelm Lehmbruck: The Complete Graphic Work. (Illus.). 428p. (GER.). 1985. 275.00 (*1-55660-005-4*) A Wofsy Fine Arts.

Petermann, J. Kleines Woerterbuch der Kroatisch-Serbischen Idiomatischen Redewendungen: Small Dictionary of Croatian & Serbian Idiomatic Expressions. 144p. (GER & SER.). 1980. 35.00 (*0-8288-1052-4*, M15172) Fr & Eur.

Petermann, K. Laser Diode Modulation & Noise. (C). 1988. lib. bdg. 129.50 (*90-277-2672-8*) Kluwer Ac.

Peternel, Carolyn R. & Ahern, James. The I Like to Go to School Book. (Illus.). 36p. (Orig.). (J). (gr. k-2). 1983. pap. 2.95 (*0-9612060-0-4*) Primary Progs.

***Peternel, Joan.** Hampton Sampler. 48p. (Orig.). 1995. pap. 7.95 (*0-9646718-0-8*) Whelks Walk Pr.

Peters. Cabinetmaking. 1986. 29.95 (*0-684-18520-2*, Scribners) S&S Trade.

— Color Atlas of Arthropods in Clinical Medicine. (Illus.). 256p. 1992. 140.00 (*0-8151-6679-6*, Yr Bk Med Pubs) Mosby Yr Bk.

— Dictionary of Herpetology. 1985. 16.95 (*0-02-850230-2*) Macmillan.

— Most Asked Questions. 1995. pap. 14.00 (*0-679-75764-3*) Random.

— October Smiled Back. (J). 1997. 14.95 (*0-8050-1776-3*) H Holt & Co.

— San Francisco Giants Almanac. 1990. pap. 9.95 (*1-55643-082-5*) North Atlantic.

Peters, ed. Intersatellite Links: IJ Satellite Communications. 240p. 1988. pap. text ed. 140.00 (*0-471-92048-7*) Wiley.

Peters, jt. ed. see Lampman.

Peters, A. & Rockland, K. S., eds. Cerebral Cortex, No. 10. (Illus.). 440p. 1993. 115.00 (*0-306-44605-7*, Plenum Pr) Plenum.

Peters, A., jt. ed. see Brebbia, C. A.

Peters, A. J. British Further Education. 1967. 164.00 (*0-08-011893-3*, Pub. by Pergamon Repr UK) Franklin.

Peters, A. R., ed. Vaccines for Vet Applications. (Illus.). 304p. 1993. 95.00 (*0-7506-1126-X*) Buttrwrth-Heinemann.

Peters, A. R. & Ball, P. J. Reproduction in Cattle. 2nd ed. 224p. 1994. 69.95 (*0-632-03827-6*, Pub. by Blckwell Sci Pubns UK) Blackwell Sci.

Peters, A. T. & Freeman, H. S., eds. Color Chemistry: The Design & Synthesis of Organic Dyes & Pigments. (Advances in Color Chemistry Ser.). 286p. 1991. 140.00 (*1-85166-577-3*) Elsevier.

Peters, Alan A. & Jones, Edward G., eds. Cerebral Cortex, Vol. 1: Cellular Components of the Cerebral Cortex. LC 84-1982. 580p. 1984. 110.00 (*0-306-41544-5*, Plenum Pr) Plenum.

— Cerebral Cortex, Vol. 3: Visual Cortex. LC 84-1982. 438p. 1985. 95.00 (*0-306-42025-2*, Plenum Pr) Plenum.

— Cerebral Cortex, Vol. 4: Association & Auditory Cortices. LC 84-1982. 376p. 1985. 89.50 (*0-306-42040-6*, Plenum Pr) Plenum.

P Q

— Cerebral Cortex, Vol. 6: Further Aspects of Cortical Function, Including Hippocampus. LC 84-1982. 478p. 1987. 110.00 (0-306-42503-3, Plenum Pr) Plenum.

— Cerebral Cortex, Vol. 7: Development & Maturation of Cerebral Cortex. LC 84-1982. (Illus.). 536p. 1988. 110.00 (0-306-42881-4, Plenum Pr) Plenum.

— Cerebral Cortex, Vol. 9: Normal & Altered States of Function. LC 84-1982. (Illus.). 530p. 1991. 110.00 (0-306-43648-5, Plenum Pr) Plenum.

Peters, Alan A., jt. auth. see Brebbia, Carlos A.

Peters, Alan A., ed. see Brebbia, Carlos A., et al.

Peters, Alan A., jt. ed. see Jones, Edward G.

Peters, Alan A., et al. The Fine Structure of the Nervous System: The Neurons & Their Supporting Cells. 3rd ed. (Illus.). 528p. 1990. 65.00 (0-19-506571-9) OUP.

Peters, Alexander, et al, eds. Computational Methods in Water Resources X. LC 94-17902. (Water Science & Technology Library). 1600p. (C). 1994. lib. bdg. 419.00 (0-7923-2937-6) Kluwer Ac.

Peters, Andrew. Salt is Sweeter Than Gold: A Czech Folk Tale. LC 94-7572. 32p. 1994. 16.00 (1-56957-933-4) Barefoot Bks.

Peters, Ann. Rings of Green. 84p. 1982. 19.95 (0-86140-124-7, Pub. by Colin Smythe Ltd UK); pap. 9.95 (0-86140-129-8, Pub. by Colin Smythe Ltd UK) Dufour.

Peters, Anna, jt. auth. see Ney, Philip G.

Peters, Anne. Accidental Dad. (Silhouette Romance Ser.). 1993. pap. 2.75 (0-373-08946-5, 5-08946-1) Silhouette.

— Along Comes Baby (First Comes Marriage) 1995. mass mkt. 2.99 (0-373-19116-2, 1-19116-2) Silhouette.

— His Only Deception. (Silhouette Romance Ser.). 1994. pap. 2.75 (0-373-08995-3, 5-08995-8) Silhouette.

— McCullough's Bride. (Silhouette Romance Ser.). 1994. pap. 2.75 (0-373-19031-X, 1-19031-3) Harlequin Bks.

— The Pursuit of Happiness. 1993. pap. 2.69 (0-373-08927-9, 5-08927-1) Silhouette.

— The Pursuit of Happiness. large type ed. LC 93-30342. 1993. pap. 13.95 (0-7862-0058-8) Thorndike Pr.

— Stand-in Husband. 1995. mass mkt. 2.99 (0-373-19110-3, 1-19110-5) Silhouette.

Peters, Anne L. A Life. 1992. pap. 4.95 (0-87129-143-6, L73) Dramatic Pub.

Peters, Anthony, ed. see Haigh, Robert, et al.

Peters, Anthony R. Anthony Eden at the Foreign Office, 1931-1938. LC 85-24994. 410p. 1987. text ed. 45.00 (0-312-04236-1) St Martin.

Peters, Arlene, jt. auth. see Peters, David.

Peters, Arthur, ed. Jean Cocteau & the French Scene. LC 83-73421. (Illus.). 224p. 1984. 35.00 (0-89659-412-2) Abbeville Pr.

Peters, Arthur K. Jean Cocteau & His World. 1987. 40.00 (0-86565-068-3) Vendome.

Peters, B. Practical Timber Formwork. 1991. pap. 44.95 (0-442-31386-1) Chapman & Hall.

— Practical Timber Formwork. (Illus.). 192p. 1991. pap. 44.95 (0-419-17010-3, E & FN Spon) Routledge Chapman & Hall.

Peters, B. & Kocheril, G. P. Diagnostic Medical Ultrasound Examination Review. 2nd ed. (Allied Health Ser.). 300p. 1988. pap. 37.00 (0-444-01334-2) Elsevier.

Peters, B. F., jt. auth. see Barer, R. D.

Peters, B. Guy. American Public Policy: Promise & Performance. 3rd ed. LC 92-25245. 400p. (Orig.). 1993. pap. text ed. 33.95x (0-934540-87-X) Chatham Hse Pubs.

— American Public Policy: Promise & Performance. 4th ed. LC 95-13597. (Orig.). 1995. write for info. (1-56643-024-0) Chatham Hse Pubs.

— Comparing Public Bureaucracies: Problems of Theory & Method. LC 87-5077. 240p. 1988. pap. 14.95 (0-8173-0368-5) U of Ala Pr.

— European Politics Reconsidered. LC 90-40211. x, 303p. 1991. 39.95 (0-8419-1160-6); pap. 19.95 (0-8419-1161-4) Holmes & Meier.

— The Politics of Bureaucracy. 3rd ed. 300p. (C). 1989. pap. text ed. 25.95 (0-8013-0066-5, 75730) Longman.

— The Politics of Bureaucracy. 4th ed. LC 94-41283. 320p. (C). 1995. pap. text ed. 28.50 (0-8013-1168-3) Longman.

Peters, B. Guy & Hollifield, James F., eds. Democracy & the State: The Rise of Administrative Politics in Britain & the U. S. 288p. (C). 1996. text ed. 65.00 (0-8133-8319-6) Westview.

***Peters, B. Guy & Savoie, Donald J., eds.** Governance in a Changing Environment. (Canadian Centre for Management Development Governance & Public Management Ser.). 304p. 1995. 49.95 (0-7735-1320-5) U of Toronto Pr.

— Governance in a Changing Environment. (Canadian Centre for Management Development Governance & Public Management Ser.). 304p. 1995. pap. 22.95 (0-7735-1321-3) U of Toronto Pr.

Peters, B. Guy, jt. ed. see Barker, Anthony.

Peters, B. Guy, jt. auth. see Hogwood, Brian W.

Peters, B. Guy, jt. ed. see Hood, Christopher.

Peters, Barbara H. & Peters, Jim L., eds. Total Quality Management. (Report Ser.: No. 963). (Illus.). 63p. (Orig.). 1991. pap. text ed. 100.00 (0-8237-0410-6) Conference Bd.

Peters, Barbara J., jt. auth. see Peters, George A.

Peters, Barbara J., jt. ed. see Peters, George A.

Peters, Barbarba & Samuels, Victoria, eds. Dialogue on Diversity: A New Agenda for Women. 88p. 1978. pap. 1.95 (0-87495-003-1) Am Jewish Comm.

Peters, Barry, ed. see Peters, Ronnie.

Peters, Basil, jt. auth. see Edwards, Anthony J.

Peters, Bernard C., ed. Lake Superior Journal: Bela Hubbard's Account of the 1840 Houghton Expedition. LC 82-60622. 1982. 8.95 (0-918616-11-5) Northern Mich.

Peters, Bette D., et al. Denver's City Park. rev. ed. (Illus.). 67p. 1986. pap. 7.95 (0-937859-01-X) Univ CO Dept Hist.

Peters, Betty-Ann. Returning Back to Eden. 124p. (Orig.). 1993. spiral bd. 9.95 (0-945383-55-X, 945-5838) Teach Servs.

Peters, Bonnie H., jt. auth. see McDonald, Winnie P.

Peters, Brent R., jt. auth. see Feltman, Linda C.

Peters, Bruce. Between the Bumpas: That's Franchising. 233p. (C). 1990. 90.00 (0-646-05589-5, Pub. by Boolarong Pubns AT) St Mut.

***Peters, C.** Mathematics, the Gas Laws & the Respiratory Practitioner. 33p. (C). 1988. pap. 15.00 (0-933195-37-0) Allied Hlth Pubns.

Peters, C. D., ed. see Dunlap, Hank.

Peters, C. D., ed. see Peters, Maggie & Peters, Madelyn K.

Peters, C. H., jt. comp. see Johnson, R. C.

Peters, C. J. Clinical Simulations - The Right Way! The Complete Guide to Respiratory Care. 370p. 1990. pap. text ed. 49.95 (0-931657-20-2) Learning Proc Ctr.

Peters, Calvin B., jt. ed. see Loy, James.

Peters, Carl. Eldorado of the Ancients: Archaeology, Ethnology & History of Africa. 1976. lib. bdg. 69.95 (0-8490-1754-8) Gordon Pr.

Peters, Carl C., ed. Managed Futures: Performance, Evaluation & Analysis of Commodity Funds, Pools & Accounts. 400p. 1992. 65.00 (1-55738-291-3) Probus Pub Co.

Peters, Carl C. & Gitlin, Andrew W., eds. Strategic Currency Investing: Trading & Investing in the Foreign Exchange Markets. 400p. 1993. 65.00 (1-55738-466-5) Probus Pub Co.

Peters, Catherine. The King of Inventors: A Life of Wilkie Collins. (Illus.). 523p. 1994. text ed. 35.00 (0-691-03392-7) Princeton U Pr.

Peters, Catherine, ed. see Collins, Wilkie.

***Peters, Celeste.** Don't Be Sad: Fight the Winter Blues - Your Guide to Conquering Seasonal Affective Disorder. 256p. 1995. pap. 14.95 (1-896015-01-8, Pub. by Script Pubng CN) Pubs Dist MI.

Peters, Charles. How Washington Really Works. LC 82-20629. 160p. (Orig.). (C). 1983. pap. 8.61 (0-201-14661-4) Addison-Wesley.

— How Washington Really Works. (Orig.). 1992. pap. write for info. (0-201-57085-8) Addison-Wesley.

— How Washington Really Works. 4th ed. LC 92-44602. (Illus.). (Orig.). 1993. pap. 10.53 (0-201-62470-2) Addison-Wesley.

— Tilting at Windmills. 1990. pap. 12.45 (0-201-52415-5) Addison-Wesley.

— Tilting at Windmills: An Autobiography. Washington Monthly Staff, ed. LC 87-35903. 1988. 18.22 (0-201-05657-7) Addison-Wesley.

Peters, Charles C. Motion Pictures & Standards of Morality. LC 72-124030. (Literature of Cinema Ser.). 1970. reprint ed. 15.95 (0-405-01648-4) Ayer.

Peters, Charles S. & Yoder, Paul. Master Theory, 6 bks. Incl. Bk. 1. Beginning Theory. 1963. pap. text ed. 3.45 (0-8497-0154-6, L173); Bk. 2. Intermediate Theory. 1964. pap. text ed. 3.45 (0-8497-0155-4, L174); Bk. 3. Advanced Theory. 1965. pap. text ed. 3.45 (0-8497-0156-2, L175); Bk. 4. Elementary Harmony. 1966. pap. text ed. 3.45 (0-8497-0157-0, L179); Bk. 5. Intermediate Harmony. 1967. pap. text ed. 3.45 (0-8497-0158-9, L181); Bk. 6. Advanced Harmony & Arranging. 1968. pap. text ed. 3.45 (0-8497-0159-7, L185); (Master Theory Ser.). 1967. Set pap. text ed. write for info. (0-318-53987-X) Kjos.

***Peters, Clarice.** London Tangle. 1995. mass mkt. 4.50 (0-449-28697-5, Crest) Fawcett.

Peters, Colette. Colette's Cakes: The Art of Cake Decorating. 1991. 24.95 (0-316-70205-6) Little.

— Colette's Christmas. LC 92-45279. 1993. 24.95 (0-316-70206-4) Little.

— Colette's Wedding Cakes. LC 94-5299. (Illus.). 1995. 35.00 (0-316-70256-0) Little.

Peters Corporation, Gerald Peters Gallery Staff. Modernist Themes in New Mexico: Works by Early Modernist Painters. Rowley, Michael C., ed. LC 89-84573. (Illus.). 62p. 1990. pap. text ed. 12.00 (0-935037-29-2) G Peters Gallery.

Peters, Cortez W., Jr. Cortez Peters Championship Formatting. LC 92-21574. 1992. write for info. (0-02-802300-5) Glencoe.

— Cortez Peters Championship Keyboarding. (Illus.). 192p. 1988. text ed. 19.96 (0-07-049635-8) McGraw.

— Cortez Peters Championship Typing Drills. 1979. text ed. 14.96 (0-07-049590-4) McGraw.

— The Cortez Peters Championship Typing Drills. 2nd ed. 112p. 1987. pap. text ed. 13.84 (0-07-049607-2) McGraw.

Peters, Curtis H. Kant's Philosophy of Hope. LC 90-35439. (American University Studies: Philosophy: Ser. V, Vol. 103). 190p. (C). 1991. text ed. 37.95 (0-8204-1386-0) P Lang Pubs.

Peters, Cynthia, ed. Collateral Damage: The New World Order at Home & Abroad. 448p. (Orig.). 1992. 40.00 (0-89608-423-X); pap. 16.00 (0-89608-422-1) South End Pr.

Peters, D., ed. Geology in Coal Resource Utilization. (Illus.). 850p. (C). 1991. text ed. 95.00 (1-878907-22-0) TechBooks.

Peters, D. E. Brown: Genealogical Record of the Descendants of Brown, Runyan, Peters, Needham & Ackerman Families, with Historical & Biographical Sketches. 137p. 1993. reprint ed. lib. bdg. 31.00 (0-8328-3274-X); reprint ed. pap. 21.00 (0-8328-3275-8) Higginson Bk Co.

Peters, D. K., ed. Advanced Medicine Twelve: Proceedings of the 12th Annual Symposium of Advanced Medicine, 1976. (Illus.). 1976. pap. 42.00 (0-8464-0117-7) Beekman Pubs.

Peters, Dan, et al. Rock's Hidden Persuader: The Truth about Back Masking. LC 85-71475. 128p. 1985. pap. 3.99 (0-87123-857-8) Bethany Hse.

— What about Christian Rock? LC 86-24472. 240p. (Orig.). 1986. pap. 7.99 (0-87123-672-9) Bethany Hse.

— Why Knock Rock? LC 84-12515. 272p. (Orig.). 1984. pap. 7.99 (0-87123-440-8) Bethany Hse.

Peters, Daniel. The Incas: A Magical Epic about a Lost World. (Illus.). 1060p. write for info. (0-318-68908-1) Random.

— Lawn Animals of Gods. 1995. 24.00 (0-679-43306-6) Random.

— The Luck of Huemac: A Novel About the Aztec World. LC 81-40221. (Illus.). 688p. 1981. 16.95 (0-394-51313-4) Random.

— Tikal: A Novel about the Maya. LC 83-3273. 422p. 1983. 16.95 (0-394-53278-3) Random.

***Peters, Daniel J.** Rising from the Ruins. 1995. 24.00 (0-615-00090-8) Random.

Peters, David. From the Beginning: The Story of Human Evolution. LC 90-19187. (Illus.). 128p. (J). (gr. 3 up). 1991. 14.95 (0-688-09476-7) Morrow Jr Bks.

— Giants of Land, Sea & Air - Past & Present: A Sierra Club Book Series. LC 86-2719. (Illus.). 64p. (J). (gr. 3 up). 1986. lib. bdg. 15.99 (0-394-97805-6) Knopf Bks Yng Read.

— Strange Creatures. LC 91-36205. (Illus.). 48p. (J). (gr. 3 up). 1992. 16.00 (0-688-10154-2); lib. bdg. 15.93 (0-688-10155-0) Morrow Jr Bks.

***Peters, David & Peters, Arlene.** By an Unfamiliar Path: The Story of David & Arlene Peters. (Jaffray Collection of Missionary Portraits: Bk. 13). 164p. 1995. pap. 7.99 (0-87509-580-1) Chr Pubns.

Peters, David W. The Status of the Married Woman Teacher. LC 77-177150. (Columbia University. Teachers College. Contributions to Education Ser.: No. 603). reprint ed. 37.50 (0-404-55603-5) AMS Pr.

Peters, Deanna & Strohm, Richard L. Divorce & Child Custody. 2nd ed. (Layman's Law Guides Ser.). 128p. 1994. pap. 8.95 (1-56414-084-9) Career Pr Inc.

Peters, Deanna, jt. auth. see Strohm, Richard L.

Peters, Dennis G., et al. Chemical Separations & Measurements: Theory & Practice of Analytical Chemistry. LC 73-87385. (Illus.). 749p. (C). 1974. text ed. 53.25 (0-7216-7203-5) SCP.

Peters, DeWitt C. Life & Adventures of Kit Carson, the Nestor of the Rocky Mountains from Facts Narrated by Himself. LC 76-109631. (Select Bibliographies Reprint Ser.). 1977. 36.95 (0-8369-5240-5) Ayer.

Peters, Diana L. S., tr. see Von Kleist, Heinrich.

Peters, Diana S., tr. see Sterner, Gabriele.

Peters, Donald, et al, eds. Continuity & Discontinuity of Experience in Child Care. LC 85-645444. (Advances in Applied Developmental Psychology Ser.: Vol. 2). 224p. 1987. 55.00 (0-89391-406-1) Ablex Pub.

Peters, Donald C. The Democratic System in the Eastern Caribbean. LC 91-33502. (Contributions in Political Science Ser.: No. 298). 256p. 1992. text ed. 55.00 (0-313-28428-8, PDN, Greenwood Pr) Greenwood.

Peters, Donald F. & Pence, Alan R., eds. Family Day Care: Current Research for Informed Policy. (Early Childhood Education Ser.). 304p. (C). 1992. text ed. 36.00 (0-8077-3202-8) Tchrs Coll.

Peters, Donald F., jt. auth. see Carpenter, Gerald.

Peters, Donald F., jt. ed. see Carpenter, Gerald.

Peters, Donald J. A Contrarian Strategy for Growth Stock Investing: Theoretical Foundations & Empiracal Evidence. LC 92-1748. 208p. 1992. text ed. 55.00 (0-89930-803-1, Q803, Quorum Bks) Greenwood.

Peters, Donald L. Counseling Kids. LC 91-70334. 348p. (Orig.). 1991. pap. text ed. 27.95 (1-55959-030-0) Accel Devel.

Peters, E. African Openings to the Tree of Life. 71p. (Orig.). 1987. pap. 9.95 (0-916147-06-1) Regent Pr.

— Peters of New England: A Genealogy & Family History. (Illus.). 470p. 1989. reprint ed. lib. bdg. 78.00 (0-8328-0958-6); reprint ed. pap. 70.00 (0-8328-0959-4) Higginson Bk Co.

Peters, Edgar E. Chaos & Order in the Capital Markets. 256p. 1991. text ed. 55.00 (0-471-53372-6) Wiley.

— Market Analysis: Applying Chaos Theory to Investment & Economics. (Financial Editions Ser.). 256p. 1994. text ed. 49.95 (0-471-58524-6) Wiley.

Peters, Edward. The Magician, the Witch & the Law. LC 78-51341. (Middle Ages Ser.). 216p. 1982. pap. text ed. 16.95 (0-8122-1101-4) U of Pa Pr.

Peters, Edward, ed. Christian Society & the Crusades, 1198-1229: Sources in Translation, Including the Capture of Damietta. LC 78-163385. (Middle Ages Ser.). 192p. (C). 1971. pap. text ed. 16.95 (0-8122-1024-7) U of Pa Pr.

— First Crusade: The Chronicle of Fulcher of Chartres & Other Source Materials. LC 74-163384. (Middle Ages Ser.). 288p. (C). 1971. 33.95x (0-8122-7643-4); pap. text ed. 15.95 (0-8122-1017-4) U of Pa Pr.

— Heresy & Authority in Medieval Europe. LC 79-5262. (Middle Ages Ser.). 312p. 1980. pap. text ed. 19.95 (0-8122-1103-0) U of Pa Pr.

Peters, Edward, jt. ed. see Kors, Alan C.

Peters, Edward I. Basic Chemical Principles. 400p. (C). 1988. text ed. 34.75 (0-03-004809-5) SCP.

— Introduction to Chemical Principles. 4th ed. 624p. (C). 1986. student ed 25.00 (0-685-14159-4) SCP.

— Introduction to Chemical Principles. 5th ed. 525p. (C). 1990. text ed. 52.00 (0-03-030264-1) SCP.

— Problem Solving for Chemistry. 2nd ed. LC 75-12493. (Illus.). 326p. (C). 1976. pap. text ed. 21.50 (0-7216-7206-X) SCP.

Peters, Edward I. & Scroggins, William T. Chemical Skills. 4th ed. 1992. pap. text ed. write for info. (0-07-049562-9) McGraw.

Peters, Edward I., jt. auth. see Weiner, Susan A.

Peters, Edward M. Europe & the Middle Ages. 2nd ed. 416p. (C). 1989. pap. text ed. write for info. (0-13-291931-1) P-H.

— Inquisition. 208p. 1988. 35.00 (0-02-924980-5) Free Pr.

— Inquisition. 1989. pap. 14.00 (0-520-06630-8) U CA Pr.

Peters, Edward N. Home Schooling & the New Code of Canon Law. 48p. (Orig.). 1988. pap. 2.95 (0-318-39833-8) Christendom Pr.

Peters, Edwin. Echoes from Beautiful Feet. (Illus.). 168p. 1975. pap. 1.95 (0-89114-073-5) Baptist Pub Hse.

Peters, Eleanor B. Bradley of Essex County: Early Records, 1643-1746. (Illus.). 213p. 1991. reprint ed. lib. bdg. 45.00 (0-8328-2099-7); reprint ed. pap. 35.00 (0-8328-2100-4) Higginson Bk Co.

Peters, Elisabeth T., intro. Gerald Gleeson (1915-1986) California Watercolorist. (Illus.). 30p. (Orig.). 1990. pap. text ed. 10.00 (0-9626611-1-2) Montgomery Gallery.

Peters, Elizabeth. Borrower of the Night. large type ed. 1992. pap. 15.95 (0-7927-0652-8, Paragon Lrg Print) Chivers N Amer.

— Borrowers of Night. 1994. reprint ed. lib. bdg. 20.00 (0-7278-4664-7) Severn Hse.

— The Camelot Caper. 320p. 1990. mass mkt. 4.99 (0-8125-1241-3) Tor Bks.

— The Camelot Caper. large type ed. 352p. 1991. text ed. 19.95 (0-8161-5165-2) G K Hall.

— The Copenhagen Connection. 224p. 1994. mass mkt. 5.50 (0-446-36483-5) Warner Bks.

— Crocodile on the Sandbank. 288p. 1988. mass mkt. 5.99 (0-445-40651-8, Mysterious Paperbk) Warner Bks.

— Crocodile on the Sandbank. limited ed. LC 90-613. 272p. 1990. reprint ed. 75.00 (0-922890-38-2) Armchair Detective.

— Crocodile on the Sandbank. LC 90-613. 272p. 1990. reprint ed. 18.95 (0-922890-36-6); reprint ed. 25.00 (0-922890-37-4) Armchair Detective.

— The Curse of the Pharaohs. LC 90-680. 296p. 1990. 19.95 (0-922890-39-0); 25.00 (0-922890-40-4) Armchair Detective.

— The Curse of the Pharaohs. 1988. mass mkt. 5.99 (0-445-40648-8, Mysterious Paperbk) Warner Bks.

— The Curse of the Pharaohs. limited ed. LC 90-680. 296p. 1990. 75.00 (0-922890-41-2) Armchair Detective.

— Dead Sea Cipher. 224p. 1988. pap. 4.99 (0-8125-0756-8) Tor Bks.

— The Deeds of the Disturber. 304p. 1989. mass mkt. 5.99 (0-446-35333-7) Warner Bks.

— Devil-May-Care. 1989. mass mkt. 4.50 (0-8125-0789-4) Tor Bks.

— Devil-May-Care. large type ed. (General Ser.). 381p. 1990. lib. bdg. 19.95 (0-8161-4907-0) G K Hall.

— Die for Love. 288p. 1992. mass mkt. 4.50 (0-8125-2470-5) Tor Bks.

— Die for Love. 288p. 1993. reprint ed. lib. bdg. 20.00 (0-7278-4491-1) Severn Hse.

— The Hippopotamus Pool. 1996. write for info. (0-446-51833-6) Warner Bks.

— Jackal's Head. 1988. pap. 3.95 (0-8125-0002-4) Tor Bks.

— The Last Camel Died at Noon. 480p. 1992. mass mkt. 5.99 (0-446-36338-3) Warner Bks.

— The Last Camel Died at Noon. large type ed. (General Ser.). 574p. 1992. text ed. 21.95 (0-8161-5357-4, Large Print Bks) Hall.

— The Last Camel Died at Noon. large type ed. (General Ser.). 576p. 1992. pap. 16.95 (0-8161-5358-2, Large Print Bks) Hall.

— Legend in Green Velvet. 1995. reprint ed. lib. bdg. 20.00 (0-7278-4721-X) Severn Hse.

— Lion in the Valley. 320p. 1990. reprint ed. mass mkt. 4.99 (0-8125-1242-1) Tor Bks.

— Love Talker. 1994. 20.00 (0-7278-4579-9) Severn Hse.

— Love Talker. 1990. pap. 4.99 (0-8125-0727-4) Tor Bks.

— The Mummy Case. 336p. (Orig.). 1995. mass mkt. 5.99 (0-446-60193-4) Warner Bks.

— The Murders of Richard III. 240p. 1986. mass mkt. 5.50 (0-445-40229-6, Mysterious Paperbk) Warner Bks.

— Naked Once More. 1990. mass mkt. 5.99 (0-446-36032-5, Mysterious Paperbk) Warner Bks.

— Naked Once More. large type ed. (General Ser.). 550p. 1990. 20.95 (0-8161-4939-9, Large Print Bks); pap. 13.95 (0-8161-4940-2, Large Print Bks) Hall.

— Night of Four Hundred Rabbits. 1989. mass mkt. 4.50 (0-8125-0773-8) Tor Bks.

— Night of Four Hundred Rabbits. large type ed. 1992. pap. 15.95 (0-7927-1000-2, Paragon Lrg Print) Chivers N Amer.

— Night Train to Memphis. 368p. 1994. 21.95 (0-446-51586-8) Warner Bks.

— Night Train to Memphis. 336p. 1995. mass mkt. 5.99 (0-446-60248-5) Warner Bks.

— Night Train to Memphis. LC 94-26645. 1995. write for info. (0-8161-7483-0) Thorndike Pr.

— The Seventh Sinner. 256p. 1989. mass mkt. 5.50 (0-445-40778-6, Mysterious Paperbk) Warner Bks.

— Silhouette in Scarlet. 224p. 1994. mass mkt. 5.50 (0-446-36482-7) Warner Bks.

— The Snake, the Crocodile & the Dog. 448p. 1994. mass mkt. 5.99 (0-446-36478-9) Warner Bks.

— The Snake, the Crocodile, & the Dog. large type ed. LC 92-35900. (General Ser.). 555p. 1993. 22.95 (0-8161-5681-6, Large Print Bks) Hall.

— The Snake, the Crocodile, & the Dog. large type ed. LC 92-35900. (General Ser.). 555p. 1994. pap. 16.95 (0-8161-5682-4, Large Print Bks) Hall.

— Street of the Five Moons. 1990. mass mkt. 4.50 (0-8125-1244-8) Tor Bks.

An Asterisk (*) at the beginning of an entry indicates that the title is appearing in BIP for the first time.

— Street of the Five Moons. large type ed. (General Ser.). 350p. 1991. text ed. 18.95 (*0-8161-4906-2*) G K Hall.

— Summer of the Dragon. 256p. 1980. pap. 2.25 (*0-449-24291-9*, Crest) Fawcett.

— Summer of the Dragon. 288p. 1989. pap. 4.99 (*0-8125-0754-1*) Tor Bks.

Peters, Ellie R. Home Child Care: The Tender Business. LC 90-82384. 105p. (Orig.). 1990. pap. 5.95 (*0-937779-16-4*) Greenlawn Pr.

Peters, Ellis. The Benediction of Brother Cadfael. 364p. 1992. 35.00 (*0-89296-449-9*) Mysterious Pr.

— Black Is the Color of My True Love's Heart. 208p. 1992. mass mkt. 4.99 (*0-446-40072-6*, Mysterious Paperbk) Warner Bks.

— Brother Cadfael's Penance. 1994. 18.95 (*0-89296-599-1*) Mysterious Pr.

— Brother Cadfael's Penance. 272p. 1996. mass mkt. 5.99 (*0-446-40453-5*, Mysterious Paperbk) Warner Bks.

— Brother Cadfael's Penance: The Twentieth Chronicle of Brother Cadfael. large type ed. LC 94-39590. 1995. write for info. (*0-7838-1175-6*) Hall.

— The Confession of Brother Haluin. large type ed. (General Ser.). 282p. 1990. 19.95 (*0-8161-4859-7*, Large Print Bks) Hall.

— The Confessions of Brother Haluin. 1989. mass mkt. 5.50 (*0-445-40855-3*, Mysterious Paperbk) Warner Bks.

— Confessions of Brother Haluin. 1989. 15.95 (*0-89296-349-2*) Mysterious Pr.

— Death & the Joyful Woman. 224p. 1995. mass mkt. 5.50 (*0-446-40068-8*, Mysterious Paperbk) Warner Bks.

— Death & the Joyful Woman. large type ed. LC 92-24308. 1992. 18.95 (*0-7927-1404-0*, Eagle Lrg Print) Chivers N Amer.

— Death & the Joyful Woman. large type ed. 1993. pap. 16.95 (*0-7927-1403-2*, Paragon Lrg Print) Chivers N Amer.

— An Excellent Mystery. Williams, Jennifer, ed. 224p. 1986. reprint ed. 15.95 (*0-688-06250-4*) Morrow.

— Fallen into the Pit. 336p. 1994. 17.95 (*0-89296-519-3*) Mysterious Pr.

— Fallen into the Pit. 1996. mass mkt. write for info. (*0-446-40318-0*, Mysterious Paperbk) Warner Bks.

— Fallen into the Pit. large type ed. LC 94-19116. 1994. 23.95 (*1-56895-116-7*) Wheeler Pub.

— Flight of a Witch. 1991. 16.95 (*0-89296-404-9*) Mysterious Pr.

— Flight of a Witch. 240p. 1992. mass mkt. 4.99 (*0-446-40146-3*, Mysterious Paperbk) Warner Bks.

— Flight of a Witch: An Inspector George Felse Mystery. large type ed. (General Ser.). 320p. 1992. text ed. 19.95 (*0-8161-5315-9*) G K Hall.

— The Heretic's Apprentice. 1990. 16.95 (*0-89296-381-6*) Mysterious Pr.

— Heretic's Apprentice. 1991. mass mkt. 5.50 (*0-446-40000-9*, Mysterious Paperbk) Warner Bks.

— The Hermit of Eyton Forest. 1989. mass mkt. 5.99 (*0-445-40347-0*, Mysterious Paperbk) Warner Bks.

— Hermit of Eyton Forest. 1988. 15.95 (*0-89296-290-9*) Mysterious Pr.

— The Hermit of Eyton Forest. large type ed. (General Ser.). 329p. 1989. 19.95 (*0-8161-4677-2*, Large Print Bks) Hall.

— The Holy Thief. 256p. 1993. 17.95 (*0-89296-524-X*) Mysterious Pr.

— The Holy Thief. 256p. 1994. mass mkt. 5.50 (*0-446-40363-6*, Mysterious Paperbk) Warner Bks.

— The Holy Thief. large type ed. LC 93-21377. 1994. pap. 18.95 (*0-7927-1743-0*, Paragon Lrg Print) Chivers N Amer.

— The Holy Thief. large type ed. LC 93-21377. 1994. 19.95 (*0-7927-1744-9*, Eagle Lrg Print) Chivers N Amer.

— The Horn of Rowland. large type ed. (Magna Mystery Ser.). 1992. 18.95 (*0-7505-0380-7*, Pub. by Magna Print Bks) Ulverscroft.

— The House of Green Turf. large type ed. 1993. 18.95 (*0-7927-1583-7*, Eagle Lrg Print) Chivers N Amer.

— The House of Green Turf. large type ed. LC 93-11999. 1993. pap. 16.95 (*0-7927-1582-9*, Paragon Lrg Print) Chivers N Amer.

— The Knocker on Death's Door. 208p. 1992. mass mkt. 5.99 (*0-446-40016-5*, Mysterious Paperbk) Warner Bks.

— Monk's Hood. 224p. 1992. mass mkt. 5.50 (*0-446-40300-8*, Mysterious Paperbk) Warner Bks.

— A Morbid Taste for Bones. 224p. 1985. mass mkt. 4.95 (*0-449-20700-5*, Crest) Fawcett.

— A Morbid Taste for Bones. 208p. 1994. mass mkt. 5.99 (*0-446-40015-7*, Mysterious Paperbk) Warner Bks.

— A Nice Derangement of Epitaphs. 208p. 1992. mass mkt. 5.99 (*0-446-40069-6*, Mysterious Paperbk) Warner Bks.

— A Nice Derangement of Epitaphs. large type ed. 1993. 18.95 (*0-7505-0311-4*, Pub. by Magna Print Bks) Ulverscroft.

— One Corpse Too Many. 224p. 1994. mass mkt. 5.50 (*0-446-40051-3*, Mysterious Paperbk) Warner Bks.

— The Piper on the Mountain. 192p. 1996. mass mkt. 5.99 (*0-446-40071-8*, Mysterious Paperbk) Warner Bks.

— The Potter's Field. 240p. 1990. 16.95 (*0-89296-419-7*) Mysterious Pr.

— The Potter's Field. 1991. mass mkt. 5.99 (*0-446-40058-0*, Mysterious Paperbk) Warner Bks.

— The Potter's Field. large type ed. (General Ser.). 303p. 1991. text ed. 19.95 (*0-8161-5194-6*, Large Print Bks) Hall.

— Rainbow's End. 208p. 1992. mass mkt. 4.99 (*0-446-40017-3*, Mysterious Paperbk) Warner Bks.

— A Rare Benedictine. 1989. 19.95 (*0-89296-397-2*) Mysterious Pr.

— A Rare Benedictine. 1991. mass mkt. 5.99 (*0-446-40088-2*, Mysterious Paperbk) Warner Bks.

— Raven in the Foregate. braille ed. 342p. 1991. Braille. vinyl bd. 27.36 (*1-56956-307-1*, BR8413) W A T Braille.

— The Sanctuary Sparrow. 224p. 1984. pap. 3.95 (*0-449-20613-0*, Crest) Fawcett.

— The Sanctuary Sparrow. 1995. mass mkt. 5.50 (*0-446-40429-2*, Mysterious Paperbk) Warner Bks.

— Smart Moves. 224p. 1995. mass mkt. 5.50 (*0-446-40437-3*, Mysterious Paperbk) Warner Bks.

— St. Peter's Fair. 1987. mass mkt. 4.95 (*0-449-21354-4*) Fawcett.

— St. Peter's Fair. 224p. 1992. mass mkt. 5.99 (*0-446-40301-6*, Mysterious Paperbk) Warner Bks.

— The Summer of the Danes. LC 91-11621. 256p. 1991. 16.95 (*0-89296-448-0*) Mysterious Pr.

— The Summer of the Danes. 256p. 1992. mass mkt. 5.99 (*0-446-40018-1*, Mysterious Paperbk) Warner Bks.

— Virgin in the Ice. 1984. mass mkt. 4.95 (*0-449-21121-5*) Fawcett.

— The Virgin in the Ice. 208p. 1995. mass mkt. 5.50 (*0-446-40428-4*, Mysterious Paperbk) Warner Bks.

Peters, Ellis & Morgan, Roy. Shropshire. LC 92-13684. 168p. 1993. 35.00 (*0-89296-516-9*) Mysterious Pr.

— Strongholds & Sanctuaries: The Borderland of England & Wales. LC 93-17979. (Illus.). 192p. 1993. 33.99 (*0-7509-0200-0*) A Sutton Pub.

Peters, Ellis, et al. Thou Shalt Not Kill: Father Brown, Father Dowling & Other Ecclesiastical Sleuths. Chesterton, Gilbert K. & McInerny, Ralph, eds. 256p. (Orig.). 1992. pap. 3.99 (*0-451-17298-1*, Sig) NAL-Dutton.

Peters, Ellis A. The Piper on the Mountain. large type ed. 342p. 1993. 21.95 (*0-7505-0584-2*, Pub. by Magna Print Bks) Ulverscroft.

Peters, Emilie. Muffin, a Palm Beach Pooch. (Muffin Ser.: No. 1). 30p. (J). (gr. 3-8). 1992. pap. write for info. (*0-9635568-0-0*) Muffin Pubns.

Peters, Emrys. The Bedouin of Cyrenaica: Studies in Personal & Corporate Power. Goody, Jack & Marx, Emanuel, eds. (Cambridge Studies in Social & Cultural Anthropology: No. 72). (Illus.). 320p. (C). 1991. 64.95 (*0-521-38561-X*) Cambridge U Pr.

Peters, Erskine. African Americans in the New Millennium: Blueprinting the Future. (Orig.). 1991. pap. 9.95 (*0-916147-18-5*) Regent Pr.

— Fundamentals of Essay Writing: An Orientation Manual. 53p. (Orig.). (C). 1987. pap. text ed. 9.95 (*0-916147-05-3*) Regent Pr.

— Lyrics of the Afro-American Spiritual: A Documentary Collection. LC 92-27574. (Encyclopedia of Black Music Ser.). 480p. 1993. text ed. 65.00 (*0-313-26238-1*, PLY/, Greenwood Pr) Greenwood.

Peters, Eugene H. Hartshorne & Neoclassical Metaphysics: An Interpretation. LC 77-116531. 151p. reprint ed. pap. 43.70 (*0-8357-8683-8*, 2056840) Bks Demand.

Peters, F. E. The Children of Abraham: Judaism, Christianity, Islam. LC 81-47941. 240p. 1983. pap. 12.95 (*0-691-02030-2*) Princeton U Pr.

— The Hajj: The Muslim Pilgrimmage to Mecca & the Holy Places. LC 93-47292. 1994. 29.95 (*0-691-02120-1*) Princeton U Pr.

— Jerusalem: The Holy City in the Eyes of Chroniclers, Visitors, Pilgrims, & Prophets from the Days of Abraham to the Beginnings of Modern Times. LC 85-42699. (Illus.). 712p. 1985. 49.50 (*0-691-07300-7*) Princeton U Pr.

— Judaism, Christianity & Islam: The Classical Texts & Their Interpretation, 3 vols. (Orig.). 1990. 95.00 (*0-691-07356-2*) Princeton U Pr.

— Judaism, Christianity & Islam: The Classical Texts & Their Interpretation, 3 vols., Vol. I. 436p. (Orig.). 1990. pap. text ed. 16.95 (*0-691-02044-2*) Princeton U Pr.

— Judaism, Christianity & Islam: The Classical Texts & Their Interpretation, 3 vols., Vol. II. 434p. (Orig.). 1990. pap. text ed. 16.95 (*0-691-02054-X*) Princeton U Pr.

— Judaism, Christianity & Islam: The Classical Texts & Their Interpretation, 3 vols., Vol. III. 450p. (Orig.). 1990. pap. text ed. 16.95 (*0-691-02055-8*) Princeton U Pr.

— Mecca: A Literary History of the Muslim Holy Land. LC 94-20923. 1994. 29.95 (*0-691-03267-X*) Princeton U Pr.

— Muhammad & the Origins of Islam. LC 93-10568. (SUNY Series in Near Eastern Studies). 334p. 1994. 59.50 (*0-7914-1875-8*); pap. 19.95 (*0-7914-1876-6*) State U NY Pr.

— A Reader on Classical Islam. 440p. 1994. text ed. 55.00 (*0-691-03394-3*); pap. text ed. 19.95 (*0-691-00040-9*) Princeton U Pr.

— The Two Hundred Dollar Look. 1987. 14.95 (*0-8184-0434-5*) Carol Pub Group.

Peters, Francis E. The Distant Shrine: The Islamic Centuries in Jerusalem. LC 89-45876. (Studies in Modern Society: No. 22). 275p. 1993. 39.50 (*0-404-61629-1*) AMS Pr.

Peters, Frank, jt. auth. see McCue, George.

Peters, Frederick G. Robert Musil, Master of the Hovering Life: A Study of the Major Fiction. LC 78-5158. 286p. 1978. text ed. 50.00 (*0-231-04476-3*) Col U Pr.

Peters, Frederick G., tr. see Sterner, Gabriele.

Peters, Frederick G., tr. see Von Kleist, Heinrich.

Peters, Fritz. Finistere. 320p. 1986. pap. 7.95 (*0-452-25884-7*, Plume) NAL-Dutton.

— My Journey with a Mystic. Weaver, Richard & Baron, Ron, eds. 312p. 1989. reprint ed. 22.50 (*0-942139-00-3*); reprint ed. pap. 11.95 (*0-942139-10-0*) Tale Weaver.

Peters, G. David. CMSAP Users' Manual, 2 disks, Set. 1992. disk 20.00 (*0-317-05166-0*) U IL Sch Music.

— Musical Skills: A Computer-Based Assessment. 1992. 8.00 (*0-317-05525-9*) U IL Sch Music.

Peters, G. David & Eddins, John M. A Planning Guide to Successful Computer Instruction. (C). 1981. 19.95 (*0-942132-00-9*) Electron Course.

Peters, G. H. Agriculture. (Reviews of U. K. Statistical Sources Ser.). 224p. 1988. text ed. 79.50 (*0-412-31670-6*) Chapman & Hall.

Peters, G. H., et al. Sustainable Agricultural Development: the Role of International Cooperation: Proceedings of the Twenty-First International Conference of Agricultural Economists. (International Association of Agricultural Economists Ser.). 736p. 1992. 59.95 (*1-85521-272-2*, Pub. by Dartmth Pub UK) Ashgate Pub Co.

Peters, Gary L. Wines & Vines of California. (Illus.). 200p. (Orig.). 1989. pap. 16.95 (*0-89863-136-X*) Star Pub CA.

Peters, Gary L. & Larkin, Robert P. Population Geography: Problems, Concepts, & Prospects. 4th ed. 400p. 1993. per. 40.95 (*0-8403-6590-X*) Kendall-Hunt.

Peters, Gary L., jt. auth. see Larkin, Robert P.

Peters, Geoff, jt. auth. see Fortune, Joyce.

Peters, Geoffrey. The Eye of a Serpent. large type ed. 1972. 12.00 (*0-85456-127-7*) Ulverscroft.

Peters, George. A Biblical Theology of Missions. LC 72-77952. 384p. (C). 1972. 16.99 (*0-8024-0706-4*) Moody.

Peters, George, illus. The Compleat Rokkaku Kite Chronicles & Training Manual. (Best of Kite Lines Ser.). 20p. (Orig.). 1991. reprint ed. pap. 6.95 (*0-937315-00-1*) Aeolus Pr.

Peters, George & Greuter, Henri. Novi: The Legendary Indianapolis Race Car. (Illus.). 224p. 1991. pap. 24.95 (*0-9630227-0-9*) Bar Jean Enter.

Peters, George A. Automotive Engineering & Litigation, Vol. 5. 509p. 1993. text ed. 132.00 (*0-471-58540-8*) Wiley.

— Sourcebook on Asbestos Diseases. 3500p. 1989. boxed 500.00 (*0-614-05965-8*) Michie Butterworth.

Peters, George A., ed. Readings in Product Liability & Civil Liability. 65p. 1985. 10.00 (*0-939874-64-4*) ASSE.

Peters, George A. & Peters, Barbara J. Automotive Engineering & Litigation, Vol. 4. (Personal Injury Library: No. 1810). 552p. 1991. text ed. 118.00 (*0-471-55563-0*) Wiley.

— Sourcebook on Asbestos Diseases: Asbestos Control & Medical Treatment, Vol. 7. 1993. 95.00 (*0-88063-797-8*) Butterworth Legal Pubs.

— Sourcebook on Asbestos Diseases: Asbestos Medical Research, Vol. 4. 1989. boxed 75.00 (*0-88063-759-5*) Butterworth Legal Pubs.

— Sourcebook on Asbestos Diseases Vol. Medical, Legal & Engineering Aspects, Vol. 1. 1980. boxed 75.00 (*0-88063-756-0*) Butterworth Legal Pubs.

— Sourcebook on Asbestos Diseases Vol. Medical, Legal & Engineering Aspects, Vol. 2. 1986. boxed 75.00 (*0-88063-757-9*) Butterworth Legal Pubs.

— Sourcebook on Asbestos Diseases Vol. Medical, Legal & Engineering Aspects, Vol. 3. 1988. boxed 75.00 (*0-88063-758-7*) Butterworth Legal Pubs.

— Sourcebook on Asbestos Diseases Vol. 9: Medical, Legal & Engineering Aspects. 1994. boxed 95.00 (*0-614-03169-9*) Butterworth Legal Pubs.

— Sourcebook on Asbestos Diseases, Vol. 5: Asbestos Abatement, Vol. 5. 800p. 1991. boxed 85.00 (*0-88063-792-7*) Butterworth Legal Pubs.

— Sourcebook on Asbestos Diseases, 1980-1993: Medical, Legal & Engineering Aspects, 8 vols., Set. 7100p. 1993. boxed 500.00 (*0-8240-7175-1*) Butterworth Legal Pubs.

Peters, George A. & Peters, Barbara J., eds. Automotive Engineering & Litigation, Vol. 1. 897p. 1991. text ed. 115.00 (*0-471-55319-0*) Wiley.

— Automotive Engineering & Litigation, Vol. 2. 868p. 1991. text ed. 115.00 (*0-471-55320-4*) Wiley.

— Automotive Engineering & Litigation, Vol. 3. 775p. 1991. text ed. 118.00 (*0-471-55321-2*) Wiley.

— International Directory of Experts & Consultants in Automotive Engineering, Vol. 6. (Automotive Engineering & Litigation Ser.: Vol. 6). 369p. 1993. pap. text ed. 110.00 (*0-471-59276-5*) Wiley.

— Sourcebook on Asbestos Diseases: International Asbestos Medical Research, Vol. 6. 600p. 1991. boxed 95.00 (*0-88063-796-X*) Butterworth Legal Pubs.

Peters, George F. Der Grosse Heide Nr. 2: Heinrich Heine & the Levels of His Goethe Reception. (North American Studies in Nineteenth-Century German Literature: Vol. 4). 322p. (C). 1989. text ed. 49.95 (*0-8204-0880-8*) P Lang Pubs.

***Peters, George H., ed.** Agricultural Economics. LC 95-13218. (International Library of Critical Writings in Economics: Vol. 55). 1995. 115.00 (*1-85278-301-X*, Pub. by E Elgar Pub UK) Ashgate Pub Co.

Peters, George N. H. The Theocratic Kingdom, 3 vols., Set. LC 88-12845. (Kregel Limited Edition Library). 2180p. 115.99 (*0-8254-3540-4*) Kregel.

Peters, George W. El Despertamiento En Indonesia: Indonesia Revival: Focus on Timor. (SPA.). 4.25 (*84-7228-171-X*, 220275, Pub. by Edit Clie SP) TSELF.

— Foundations of Mennonite Brethren Missions. LC 83-72078. 262p. (Orig.). 1984. pap. 7.95 (*0-935196-13-7*) Kindred Prods.

Peters, Gerald. Classic Western American Paintings. LC 78-58003. 22p. 1979. pap. 15.00 (*0-933052-00-6*) G Peters Gallery.

— The Mutilating God: Authorship & Authority in the Narrative of Conversion. LC 93-22151. 224p. 1993. lib. bdg. 29.95 (*0-87023-891-4*) U of Mass Pr.

Peters, Gerald P., III, intro. George Carlson: The Strength of the Spirit. LC 92-73101. (Illus.). 60p. 1992. pap. 15.00 (*0-935037-45-4*) G Peters Gallery.

Peters, Gerald P., intro. Georgia O'Keeffe. LC 90-63231. (Illus.). 48p. 1990. pap. 18.00 (*0-935037-39-X*) G Peters Gallery.

Peters, Gerald P., 3rd & Fox, Megan. Paul Strand: An Extraordinary Vision. LC 94-75850. (Illus.). 40p. (Orig.). 1994. pap. 30.00 (*0-935037-56-X*) G Peters Gallery.

Peters, Gerald P. & Maxon, Gayle, intros. Frankenthaler: Santa Fe Series - Pastels & Other Works on Paper. LC 90-63314. (Illus.). 32p. 1990. pap. 10.00 (*0-935037-35-7*) G Peters Gallery.

***Peters, Gerald R., ed.** Healthcare Integration: A Legal Manual for Constructing Integrated Organizations. 615p. 1995. 75.00 (*0-918945-17-8*) Natl Health Lawyers.

— Healthcare Joint Ventures: The Next Generation. 369p. 1991. 45.00 (*0-918945-12-7*) Natl Health Lawyers.

Peters, Gerald R., jt. auth. see Zirkle, Thomas E.

Peters, Glen. Benchmarking Customer Service. (Financial Times Management Ser.). 256p. 1995. 67.50x (*0-273-61069-4*, Pub. by Pitman Pub Ltd UK) Trans-Atl Phila.

Peters-Golden, Holly. Culture Sketches: Case Studies in Anthropology. 1993. pap. text ed. write for info. (*0-07-035954-7*) McGraw.

***Peters, Greg, text.** Images of Vulnerability: The Art of George Wallace. (Illus.). 128p. 1995. lib. bdg. 37.00 (*0-8095-4916-6*) Borgo Pr.

Peters, Guy & Barker, Anthony, eds. Advising West European Governments: Inquiries, Expertise, & Public Policy. (Policy & Institutional Studies). 240p. (C). 1993. text ed. 49.95 (*0-8229-1172-8*); pap. text ed. 19.95 (*0-8229-6099-0*) U of Pittsburgh Pr.

Peters, Guy B., jt. ed. see Campbell, Colin.

Peters, H. F. Rainer Maria Rilke: Masks & the Man. LC 77-24731. 240p. 1977. reprint ed. 45.00 (*0-87752-198-0*) Gordian.

Peters, H. F. & Hulstijn, W., eds. Speech Motor Dynamics in Stuttering. (Illus.). xv, 420p. 1987. 74.00 (*0-387-81971-1*) Spr-Verlag.

Peters, H. F., et al, eds. Speech Motor Control & Stuttering: Proc. of the 2nd Internat. Conf., Held in Nijmegen, The Netherlands, June 13-16, 1990. (International Congress Ser.: No. 950). 608p. 1991. 251.25 (*0-444-81408-6*, Excerpta Medica) Elsevier.

Peters, H. J. Axiomatic Bargaining Game Theory. LC 92-21620. (Theory & Decision Library: No. C). 1992. lib. bdg. 112.50 (*0-7923-1873-0*) Kluwer Ac.

Peters, Hans F. Zarathustra's Sister: The Case of Elizabeth & Friedrich Nietzsche. LC 85-40728. 242p. 1985. reprint ed. pap. 9.95 (*0-910129-37-1*) Wiener Pubs Inc.

Peters, Hans J. The Maritime Transport Crisis. LC 93-41296. (Discussion Paper Ser.). 60p. 1993. 6.95 (*0-8213-2714-3*) World Bank.

— Seatrade, Logistics, & Transport. (Policy & Research Series Paper: No. 6). 24p. 1989. 6.95 (*0-614-02849-3*, 11364) World Bank.

Peters, Hans M. Fecundity, Egg Weight & Oocyte Development in Tilapias: Cichlidae, Teleostei. Pauly, Daniel, tr. (ICLARM Translations Ser.: No. 2). (Illus.). 28p. (Orig.). 1983. pap. 5.50 (*0-89955-381-8*, Pub. by ICLARM PH) Intl Spec Bk.

Peters, Harold E. The Foreign Debt of the Argentine Republic. LC 78-64290. (Johns Hopkins University. Studies in the Social Sciences. Thirtieth Ser. 1912: 21). 200p. 1983. reprint ed. 37.50 (*0-404-61390-X*) AMS Pr.

Peters, Harry T. America on Stone: The Other Printmakers to the American People. LC 75-22832. (America in Two Centuries Ser.). (Illus.). 1977. reprint ed. 71.95 (*0-405-07703-3*) Ayer.

— California on Stone. LC 75-22833. (America in Two Centuries Ser.). (Illus.). 1977. reprint ed. 55.95 (*0-405-07704-1*) Ayer.

— Currier & Ives: Printmakers to the American People, 2 vols., 1. LC 75-22834. (America in Two Centuries Ser.). (Illus.). 1977. reprint ed. 66.95 (*0-405-07742-4*) Ayer.

— Currier & Ives: Printmakers to the American People, 2 vols., 2. LC 75-22834. (America in Two Centuries Ser.). (Illus.). 1977. reprint ed. 71.95 (*0-405-07743-2*) Ayer.

— Currier & Ives: Printmakers to the American People, 2 vols., Set. LC 75-22834. (America in Two Centuries Ser.). (Illus.). 1977. reprint ed. 137.95 (*0-405-07741-6*) Ayer.

— Printmakers: Currier & Ives; American on Stone; California on Stone. 240.00 (*0-405-07705-X*, 93) Ayer.

Peters, Heather, jt. auth. see Lyons, Elizabeth.

Peters, Helen J., ed. Ground Water in the Pacific Rim Countries. LC 91-21069. 183p. 1991. pap. text ed. 21.00 (*0-87262-812-4*) Am Soc Civil Eng.

Peters, Helene. The Existential Woman. LC 90-41034. (American University Studies: Feminist Studies: Ser. XXVII, Vol. 3). 152p. (C). 1990. text ed. 32.95 (*0-8204-1331-3*) P Lang Pubs.

***Peters, Henrietta.** Mary Ward. 1994. pap. 40.00 (*0-85244-268-8*, Pub. by Gracewing UK) Morehouse Pub.

Peters, Howard K., Jr., jt. auth. see Peters, Jean M.

Peters, Howard M., jt. auth. see Maynard, John T.

Peters, Ivo, photos. The Train Now Departing: Personal Memories of the Last Days of Steam. (Illus.). 168p. 1988. 25.95 (*0-563-20696-9*, Pub. by BBC UK) Parkwest Pubns.

Peters, J., jt. auth. see Bauschinger, J.

Peters, J. Douglas, jt. auth. see Gilbert, Ronald R.

Peters, J. E. Discovering Traditional Farm Buildings. 1989. pap. 25.00 (*0-85263-556-7*, Pub. by Shire UK) St Mut.

Peters, J. H. & Baumgarten, H., eds. Monoclonal Antibodies: A Practical Guide. LC 92-30163. (Laboratory Ser.). (Illus.). 480p. 1992. 69.00 (*0-387-50843-0*) Spr-Verlag.

Peters, J. M., comp. Bow Angle Tables. (C). 1987. 40.00 (*0-85174-135-5*, Pub. by Brwn Son Ferg) St Mut.

Peters, J. Rose. Economics of the Canadian Corporate Bond Market. LC 78-135414. 133p. reprint ed. pap. 38.00 (*0-317-26039-1*, 2023837) Bks Demand.

Peters, Jacob & Smith, Doreen L. Organizational & Interorganizational Dynamics: An Annotated Bibliography. LC 92-10773. (Library of Sociology: Vol. 25). 288p. 1992. 42.00 (*0-8240-5304-4*, SS641) Garland.

***Peters, Jacqueline S.** Music Therapy: An Introduction. 186p. 1987. pap. 19.95 (*0-398-06321-4*) C C Thomas.

— Music Therapy: An Introduction. 186p. (C). 1987. 35.95x (*0-398-05284-0*) C C Thomas.

P Q

An Asterisk (*) at the beginning of an entry indicates that the title is appearing in BIP for the first time.

Peters, James, jt. auth. see Pittman, Thomas.
Peters, James, jt. auth. see Salloum, Habeeb.
Peters, James E. Arlington National Cemetery: Shrine to America's Heros. LC 86-50284. 335p. 1988. pap. 13.95 (0-933149-04-2) Woodbine House.
Peters, James F., III. UNIX Programming: Methods & Tools. 449p. (C). 1988. pap. text ed. 8.50 (0-15-593022-2) SCP.
— UNIX Programming: Methods & Tools. 449p. (C). 1988. pap. text ed. 33.25 (0-15-593021-4); 7.00 (0-15-593023-0) SCP.
Peters, James F. & Holmay, Patrick. VAX-VMS User's Guide. (VAX Users Ser.). (Illus.). 304p. (Orig.). (C). 1989. pap. 29.95 (1-55558-014-9, EY-6739E-DP, Digital DEC) Buttrwrth-Heinemann.
*Peters, James S., II. The Epic of a Proud Black Family: An Allegorical History. 1994. 64.95 (1-883255-79-1); pap. 44.95 (1-883255-78-3) Intl Scholars.
Peters, James S., III. Memoirs of a Black Southern New Englander. (Illus.). 208p. 1994. pap. 13.95 (0-8059-3474-X) Dorrance.
Peters, Jane. Cancer: A Beginner's Guidebook of Hope. rev. ed. 96p. 1991. pap. 6.95 (0-9628806-1-2) Encouraging Words.
Peters, Jane S., ed. Illustrated Bartsch, Vol. 18: German Masters of the Sixteenth Century. LC 79-50679. 1982. 140.00 (0-89835-018-2) Abaris Bks.
— Illustrated Bartsch, Vol. 19, Pt. 1: German Masters of the Sixteenth Century. 1987. 140.00 (0-89835-019-0) Abaris Bks.
— Illustrated Bartsch, Vol. 19, Pt. 2: German Masters of the Sixteenth Century. 1988. 140.00 (0-89835-316-5) Abaris Bks.
— Illustrated Bartsch, Vol. 20, Pt. 1: German Masters of the Sixteenth Century. 1985. 140.00 (0-89835-119-7) Abaris Bks.
Peters, Janice G., jt. ed. see Peters, William L.
Peters, Jean, ed. Book Collecting: A Modern Guide. LC 77-8785. (Illus.). 288p. 1977. 39.95 (0-8352-0985-7) Bowker.
— The Bookman's Glossary. 6th ed. 223p. 1983. 39.95 (0-8352-1686-1) Bowker.
Peters, Jean M. & Peters, Howard K., Jr. The Flexibility Manual. 2nd ed. LC 92-85429. (Illus.). 100p. 1995. 32.00 (0-9633896-0-2) Spts Kinetics.
Peters, Jeff G., ed. AIDS: A Comprehensive Manual of Legal & Policy Issues: A Legal & Policy Manual Designed to Provide Attorneys, AIDS Services Organizations, Activists, & Volunteers with the Tools Necessary to Respond to the Needs of People with AIDS-Related Legal Problems. (Illus.). 1326p. 1992. 85.00 (0-9626786-1-9) FL AIDS LD&EF.
Peters, Jeffrey H. & DeMeester, Tom R. Minimally Invasive Surgery of the Foregut. LC 94-31703. 1994. 115.00 (0-942219-62-7) Quality Med Pub.
Peters, Jennifer. A Promise Broken. 288p. (Orig.). 1985. pap. 3.25 (0-8439-2230-3) Dorchester Pub Co.
— The Video Gift Book, Spring 1988. rev. ed. (Illus.). 200p. 1988. pap. 4.95 (0-942251-02-4) Videotakes.
— The Video Gift Book, 1989. rev. ed. (Illus.). 144p. 1988. pap. 4.95 (0-942251-03-2) Videotakes.
Peters, Jens. Philippines: A Travel Survival Kit. 5th ed. (Illus.). 528p. (Orig.). 1994. pap. 15.95 (0-86442-224-5) Lonely Planet.

***Peters, Jim. Market It Write: Entrepreneur's Guide to Publicity in the Chicago Area Press. LC 95-90279. 149p. (Orig.). 1995. pap. 15.95 (0-9646583-0-5) Eastview Pub.**
An insider's guide for getting FREE publicity in the Chicago area, written for small business owners doing business in metro Chicago, but adaptable to any market. Author is longtime business editor at the Aurora, IL Beacon News, a Chicago area daily newspaper. MARKET IT WRITE gives straight, insightful answers on getting news to editors who will use it. To succeed, entrepreneurs must first understand why different publications have different yardsticks for what is newsworthy. Other topics: how to pitch story ideas to editors, work with reporters, alter news releases for use in different types of publications & keep editors coming back. Essential for entrepreneurs & small businesses, libraries, public relations professionals, business organizations. MARKET IT WRITE is packed with real-life examples & anecdotes, discussing news release writing (with critiques of actual news releases), crisis management & the press, hiring publicity professionals & details such as photographs, press conferences, off the record. Appendixes provide key information for every general circulation newspaper & general business periodical in Chicago. Order directly from East-view Publishing, P.O. Box 666, Aurora, Ill 60507 (708) 897-7158. *Publisher Provided Annotation.*

— The Nigerian Military & the State. (Military & Security Studies). 224p. 1995. text ed. 59.50 (1-85043-874-9) St Martin.
Peters, Jim B. Catacombs of the Bear Cult. 1981. 3.95 (0-940244-55-1) Flying Buffalo.
— Dungeon of the Bear Set. 1982. 6.95 (0-940244-58-6) Flying Buffalo.
— Grimtooth's Dungeon of Doom. (Illus.). 80p. (Orig.). 1992. pap. 9.95 (0-940244-88-8) Flying Buffalo.
Peters, Jim L., jt. ed. see Peters, Barbara H.
Peters, Joan. From Time Immemorial: The Origins of the Arab-Jewish Conflict over Palestine. LC 93-77505. xii, 601p. (C). 1993. pap. 16.95 (0-9636242-0-2) JKAP Pubns.
Peters, Joanne K. Certain Uncertainties: New Literacy & the Evaluation of Student Writing. (Concept Paper Ser.: No. 5). 53p. 1992. pap. 6.95 (0-8141-0526-2) NCTE.
Peters, Joel, jt. ed. see Kyle, Keith.
Peters, Johannes A. Metaphysics, a Systematic Survey. LC 63-8144. (Duquesne Studies, Philosophical Ser.: No. 16). 547p. reprint ed. pap. 155.90 (0-317-09337-1, 2051342) Bks Demand.
Peters, John. Elements of Critical Reading. 192p. (C). 1991. pap. write for info. (0-02-394601-6) Macmillan.
Peters, John & Guttridge, Roger, eds. Bournemouth Then & Now: A Pictorial Past. (C). 1989. 39.00 (1-85455-024-1, Pub. by Ensign Pubns & Print UK) St Mut.
Peters, John E. The U. S. Military: Ready for the New World Order? LC 92-25627. (Contributions in Military Studies: No. 133). 192p. 1993. text ed. 49.95 (0-313-28591-8, PUM, Greenwood Pr) Greenwood.
Peters, John F., jt. auth. see Early, John D.
Peters, John G., Jr. Tactical Handcuffing for Chain- & Hinged-Style Handcuffs. (Illus.). 304p. (Orig.). (C). 1989. pap. 15.00 (0-923401-00-8) Reliapon Police Prods.
Peters, John G., Jr. & Kubota, Takayuki. Realistic Defensive Tactics. (Illus.). 104p. (Orig.). 1982. pap. 18.25 (0-935878-02-5) Calibre Pr.
Peters, John G., jt. ed. see Hibbing, John.
Peters, John M., jt. ed. see Bierbaum, Philip J.
Peters, John M., et al. Adult Education: Evolution & Achievements in a Developing Field of Study. LC 91-13977. (Higher & Adult Education Ser.). 525p. 1991. 42.00 (1-55542-381-7) Jossey-Bass.
— Building an Effective Adult Education Enterprise. LC 78-62573. (Adult Education Association Handbook Series in Adult Education). 200p. reprint ed. pap. 57.00 (0-8357-4959-2, 2037891) Bks Demand.
*Peters, John O. & Peters, Margaret T. Virginia's Historic Courthouses. LC 94-41510. (Illus.). 246p. (C). 1995. 39.95 (0-8139-1604-6) U Pr of Va.
*Peters-Johnson, Cassandra, et al, eds. Communication, Creativity, Collaboration: Current Challenges for School Supervisors & Administrators. 500p. 1995. pap. text ed. 45.00 (0-614-06523-2, 0111964) Am Speech Lang Hearing.
Peters, Jonathan A. A Dance of Masks: Senghor, Achebe, Soyinka. LC 77-3839. 300p. 1978. 18.00 (0-914478-23-0); pap. 7.00 (0-914478-24-9) Three Continents.
Peters, Joseph, jt. auth. see Harlow, George E.
Peters, Joseph P., comp. Indian Battles & Skirmishes on the American Frontier 1790-1898. LC 66-29882. 256p. 1972. 33.95 (0-405-03676-0) Ayer.
Peters, Joyce & Teaching Research Early Childhood Training Department Staff. Supporting Children with Disabilities in Community Programs: The Teaching Research Integrated Preschool. (Illus.). 165p. (Orig.). (C). 1993. pap. text ed. 20.00 (0-685-64739-0) Teaching Res.
*Peters, Judith M. & Peters, Robert M. College Accounting. 2nd ed. LC 95-10475. (Introductory Accounting Ser.). (C). 1995. text ed. write for info. (0-256-09053-X); teacher ed. text ed. write for info. (0-256-19476-9) Irwin.
— College Accounting. 2nd ed. LC 95-10475. (Introductory Accounting Ser.). (C). 1995. text ed. write for info. (0-256-09052-1); text ed. write for info. (0-256-09051-3) Irwin.
— College Accounting, Chapters 1-10. 374p. (C). 1989. text ed. 32.95 (0-256-06926-3) Irwin.
— College Accounting, Chapters 1-15. 580p. (C). 1989. text ed. 38.95 (0-256-06927-1) Irwin.
— College Accounting, Chapters 1-15, No. 1. 328p. (C). 1989. student ed 18.95 (0-256-07073-3); 19.95 (0-256-07075-X) Irwin.
— College Accounting, Chapters 1-29. 1093p. (C). 1989. text ed. 52.95 (0-256-06928-X) Irwin.
— College Accounting, Chapters 1-29. 156p. (C). 1989. Computerized practice set, 1-7. 18.95 (0-256-07187-X); Computerized practice set 2, incl. IBM disk. 18.95 (0-256-07188-8) Irwin.
— College Accounting, Chapters 1-29, No. 2. 160p. (C). 1989. 19.95 (0-256-07076-8) Irwin.
— College Accounting, Chapters 1-29, No. 2. 384p. (C). 1990. student ed 18.95 (0-256-07074-1) Irwin.
Peters, Julie A. B.J.'s Billion Dollar Bet. LC 93-36132. (J). 1994. 12.95 (0-316-70254-4) Little.
— Risky Friends. 144p. (J). (gr. 5-8). 1993. pap. 2.99 (0-87406-646-8) Willowisp Pr.
— Stinky Sneakers Contest. (J). (ps-3). 1992. 13.95 (0-316-70214-5) Little.
— The Stinky Sneakers Contest. 64p. (J). 1994. pap. 3.50 (0-380-72278-X, Camelot Young) Avon.
Peters, Julie S. Congreve, the Drama, & the Printed Word. LC 89-26167. (Illus.). 302p. 1991. 35.00 (0-8047-1751-6) Stanford U Pr.
Peters, Julie S. & Wolper, Andrea, eds. Women's Rights, Human Rights: International Feminist Perspectives. LC 94-15775. 450p. 1994. pap. 17.95 (0-415-90995-3, B3886, Routledge NY) Routledge.
— Women's Rights, Human Rights: International Feminist Perspectives. LC 94-15775. 450p. 1994. 65.00 (0-415-90994-5, B3882, Routledge NY) Routledge.
*Peters, K. Confirmation. 1994. pap. 6.95 (1-55713-154-6) Sun & Moon CA.
Peters, Kathleen, ed. see Bingham, Mindy, et al.
Peters, Kathleen, ed. see Edmondson, Judy, et al.
Peters, Kathryn M. Love Is My Only Master: Affirmations & Reflections for the Heart & Soul. 316p. 1993. pap. 14.95 (0-9638490-0-X) Heartlght Prodns.
Peters, Kenneth E. & Moldowan, J. Michael. The Biomarker Guide: Interpreting Molecular Fossils in Petroleum & Ancient Sediments. 352p. 1992. text ed. 75.00 (0-13-086752-7) P-H.
Peters, Klaus. Wolfgang Willrich: War Artist. (Illus.). 304p. 1990. 42.95 (0-912138-42-4) Bender Pub CA.
Peters, Klaus J. Pictorial History of Fallschirm-Jager Rgt. 3 (Parachute Rgt. 3) (Illus.). 272p. 1992. 32.95 (0-912138-46-7) Bender Pub CA.
Peters, Kurt. Credit Card Management - Card Industry Directory: The Blue Book of Credit & Debit Card in the United States, 1990. 1989. pap. 295.00 (0-685-29402-1) Faulkner & Gray.
— Credit Card Management, Card Industry Directory: The Blue Book of Credit & Debit Card in the United States, 1990. 1989. pap. 295.00 (0-9624775-0-8) Faulkner & Gray.
Peters, Kurt, ed. Automated Medical Payments Projects Sourcebook. 235p. 1993. 175.00 (1-881393-18-6) Faulkner & Gray.
— Automated Medical Payments Projects Sourcebook. 436p. 1994. 195.00 (0-614-02582-6) Faulkner & Gray.
Peters, L. This Way Home. (J). (gr. 4 up). 1994. 14.95 (0-8050-1368-7, Bks Young Read) H Holt & Co.
Peters, Lauren. Problems at the North Pole. Thatch, Nancy R., ed. LC 90-5929. (Books for Students by Students Ser.). (Illus.). 26p. (J). (ps-2). 1990. lib. bdg. 14.95 (0-933849-25-7) Landmark Edns.
Peters, Lawrence H. & Gray, J. Brian. Business Cases in Statistical Decision Making: Computer Based Applications. LC 93-5828. 1993. text ed. write for info. (0-13-285834-7) P-H.
*Peters, Lawrence H., et al. Managing Human Resource Decisions. 2nd ed. 128p. (C). 1993. text ed., disk 25.95 (0-256-12921-5) Irwin.
Peters, Lawrence J. Software Design: Methods & Techniques. LC 80-50609. 248p. (Orig.). (C). 1986. pap. text ed. 52.00 (0-13-821828-5, Yourdon) P-H.
Peters, Lenrie. Selected Poetry. (African Writers Ser.). 143p. (Orig.). (C). 1981. pap. 10.95 (0-435-90238-5) Heinemann.
Peters, Leonard J., jt. auth. see Kane, Thomas S.
Peters, Leonard J., jt. ed. see Kane, Thomas S.
Peters, Lisa, et al. In the Sunlight: The Floral & Figurative Art of John Henry Twachtman. (Illus.). 104p. 1989. pap. 15.00 (0-945936-03-6) Spanierman Gallery.
Peters, Lisa W. Burgess Shale Book. (J). 1995. 15.95 (0-8050-2419-0) H Holt & Co.
— The Hayloft. LC 93-18718. (Illus.). (J). 1995. 12.99 (0-8037-1490-4); lib. bdg. 12.89 (0-8037-1491-2) Dial Bks Young.
— Meg & Dad Discover Treasure in the Air. (J). 1995. 15.95 (0-8050-2418-2) H Holt & Co.
— Purple Delicious Blackberry Jam. (Illus.). 32p. (J). (ps-3). 1992. 14.95 (1-55970-167-6) Arcade Pub Inc.
— The Room. LC 92-39807. (Illus.). (J). 1994. 14.99 (0-8037-1431-9); lib. bdg. 14.89 (0-8037-1432-7) Dial Bks Young.
— Serengeti. LC 89-7859. (National Parks Ser.). (Illus.). 48p. (J). (gr. 4-5). 1989. text ed. 13.95 (0-89686-433-2, Crstwood Hse) Silver Burdett Pr.
— The Sun, the Wind & the Rain. LC 87-23808. (Illus.). 32p. (J). (ps-2). 1988. 13.95 (0-8050-0699-0, Bks Young Read) H Holt & Co.
— The Sun, the Wind & the Rain. LC 87-23808. (Illus.). 32p. (J). (ps-2). 1990. reprint ed. pap. 5.95 (0-8050-1481-0, Owlet BYR) H Holt & Co.
— Tania's Trolls. 64p. (J). (gr. 3). 1992. pap. 2.99 (0-380-71444-2, Camelot Young) Avon.
— Water's Way. (Illus.). 32p. (J). (ps-2). 1991. 14.95 (1-55970-062-9) Arcade Pub Inc.
Peters, Lloyd. Lionhead Lodge. 180p. 1976. 9.95 (0-87770-167-9); pap. 5.95 (0-685-82038-6) Ye Galleon.
Peters, Loren W. Construction Engineering Evidence. suppl. ed. 152p. 1993. pap. 55.00 (0-471-59149-1) Wiley.
Peters, Louise F. Not by Coincidence. 1993. 10.95 (0-8062-4658-8) Carlton.
Peters, M. A. The Club Treasurer's Handbook. 128p. 1982. 50.00 (0-907313-00-0) St Mut.
Peters, M. C., jt. auth. see Francis, W.
Peters, Madelyn K., jt. auth. see Peters, Maggie.
Peters, Madison C. Seven Secrets of Success & Other Talks on Making Good. 108p. 1994. pap. 9.00 (0-89540-289-0, SB-289) Sun Pub.
Peters, Madison C., ed. Wit & Wisdom of the Talmud. 169p. 1995. pap. 14.00 (0-89540-290-4, SB-290) Sun Pub.
Peters, Maggie & Peters, Madelyn K. Dutch Eagle: An Illustrated B iography. Peters, C. D., ed. & illus. by. 300p. 1992. per. 25.00 (0-922484-04-X) Poligion Pub.
Peters, Manfred & Winkler, Peter, eds. Aluminum-Lithium, Vols. 1 & 2: Proceedings of the 6th International Aluminum-Lithium Conference, 2 vols., Set. 1395p. Date not set. lib. bdg. 275.00 (3-88355-180-5, Pub. by DGM Metallurgy Info GW) IR Pubns.
*Peters, Mardy, ed. & illus. The Renal Gourmet: or What to Cook When Your Kidneys Quit. 196p. 1991. spiral bd. 17.80 (0-9641730-0-X) Emonar.
Peters, Margaret. Christmas Traditions from the Heart, Vol. 2. Nadel, Harold & Kuhn, Barbara K., eds. LC 92-71399. (Illus.). 80p. (Orig.). 1994. pap. 18.95 (0-914881-79-5) C & T Pub.
— Christmas Traditions from the Heart: Quilts, Dolls, Crafts & Recipes for Your Family. Nadel, Harold, ed. LC 92-71399. 96p. (Orig.). 1992. pap. 18.95 (0-914881-48-5) C & T Pub.
Peters, Margaret T., jt. auth. see Peters, John O.
Peters, Margaret W. The Ebony Book of Black Achievement. rev. ed. LC 79-128544. (Illus.). 128p. (J). (gr. 4-8). 1974. reprint ed. 10.95 (0-87485-040-1) Johnson Chi.
Peters, Margot. The House of Barrymore. (Illus.). 656p. 1991. pap. 15.00 (0-671-74799-1, Touchstone Bks) S&S Trade.
Peters, Mary A. Write from the Start: Process & Practice. 504p. (C). 1992. write for info. (0-03-025479-5); pap. text ed. 23.50 (0-03-025478-7) HB Coll Pubs.
Peters, Mary E., et al. Handbook of Breast Imaging. Voegeli, Dawn R. & Scanlan, Kathleen A., eds. (Handbooks of Diagnostic Imaging Ser.: Vol. 4). (Illus.). 344p. 1989. text ed. 82.00 (0-443-08620-6) Churchill.
Peters, Mary E., et al, eds. Handbook of Breast Imaging. LC 89-15760. (Handbooks of Diagnostic Imaging Ser.). (Illus.). 354p. reprint ed. pap. 100.90 (0-7837-6820-6, 2046652) Bks Demand.
Peters, Maureen. Incredible Fierce Desire. large type ed. (Dales Romance Ser.). 279p. 1993. pap. 16.95 (1-85389-383-8, Medcom-Trainex) Ulverscroft.
— Kate Alanna. large type ed. 1994. 20.95 (0-7089-3171-5) Ulverscroft.
— Katheryn the Wanton Queen. large type ed. (Shadows of the Crown Ser.). 1973. 12.00 (0-85456-635-X) Ulverscroft.
— Patchwork. large type ed. (Romance Ser.). 1991. 21.95 (0-7089-2378-X) Ulverscroft.
— Tansy. large type ed. 288p. 1995. 23.95 (0-7089-3227-4) Ulverscroft.
— The Vinegar Blossom. large type ed. (General Fiction Ser.). 1991. 21.95 (0-7089-2436-0) Ulverscroft.
— The Vinegar Seed. large type ed. (General Fiction Ser.). 1990. 21.95 (0-7089-2339-9) Ulverscroft.
— The Vinegar Tree. large type ed. (General Fiction Ser.). 384p. 1992. 21.95 (0-7089-2682-7) Ulverscroft.
Peters, Max. College Algebra. rev. ed. LC 61-18891. (Orig.). Date not set. reprint ed. pap. 12.95 (0-8120-0048-X) Barron.
— How to Prepare for the High School Entrance Examinations SSAT & ISEE. 7th ed. 1992. pap. 11.95 (0-8120-4954-3) Barron.
Peters, Max & Shostak, Jerome. How to Prepare for Catholic High School Entrance Examinations - COOP & HSPT. 576p. (YA). 1992. pap. 11.95 (0-8120-4955-1) Barron.
Peters, Max S. Elementary Chemical Engineering. 2nd ed. 1984. text ed. write for info. (0-07-049586-6) McGraw.
Peters, Max S. & Timmerhaus, Klaus D. Plant Design & Economics for Chemical Engineers. 4th ed. 928p. 1991. text ed. write for info. (0-07-049613-7) McGraw.
Peters, Maxine W. Foundations of Pharmacologic Therapy. LC 77-3582. (Wiley Nursing Concept Modules Ser.). (Illus.). 179p. reprint ed. pap. 51.10 (0-317-09216-2, 2017837) Bks Demand.
Peters, Melody, jt. auth. see Enstice, Wayne.
Peters, Melvin K. A Critical Edition of the Coptic (Bohairic) Pentateuch, Vol. 5. LC 83-3260. (Society of Biblical Literature Septuagint & Cognate Studies Ser.). 126p. (C). 1983. pap. 16.95 (0-89130-617-X, 06 04 15) Scholars Pr GA.
— A Critical Edition of the Coptic (Bohairic) Pentateuch: Society of Biblical Literature. LC 83-3260. (Septugaint & Cognate Studies, Exodus: Vol. 2). 122p. (C). 1986. 20.95 (1-55540-030-2, 06-04-22); pap. 15.95 (1-55540-031-0) Scholars Pr GA.
Peters, Melvin K., ed. A Critical Edition of the Coptic (Bohairic) Pentateuch: Genesis, Vol. 1. (C). 1985. pap. 11.95 (0-89130-924-1) Scholars Pr GA.
Peters, Michael. Education & the Postmodern Condition. LC 94-21996. (Critical Studies in Education & Culture). 225p. 1995. text ed. 55.00 (0-89789-373-5, Bergin & Garvey) Greenwood.
Peters, Michael D., jt. auth. see Hisrich, Robert D.
Peters, Michael P., jt. auth. see Hisrich, Robert D.
Peters, Mike. Four-Wheel Grimmy. 128p. 1989. pap. 5.95 (0-88687-557-9, Pharos) Wrld Almnc.
— Grimmy & the Temple of Groom, No. 5. (Illus.). 128p. (Orig.). 1992. pap. 8.95 (0-88687-520-X, Pharos) Wrld Almnc.
— Grimmy Come Home. 128p. 1990. pap. 6.95 (0-88687-508-0, Pharos) Wrld Almnc.
— Mother Goose & Grimm: Bone in the U. S. A. 1992. pap. 3.50 (0-8125-1526-9) Tor Bks.
— Mother Goose & Grimm: Grimmy-Best in Show. 1990. pap. 3.50 (0-8125-0712-6) Tor Bks.
— Mother Goose & Grimm: On the Move. 1992. pap. 3.50 (0-8125-1527-7) Tor Bks.
— Mother Goose & Grimm: Pick of the Litter. 1990. pap. 2.95 (0-8125-1080-1) Tor Bks.
— Mother Goose & Grimm: Top Dog. (Illus.). 128p. (Orig.). 1991. pap. 3.50 (0-8125-1511-0) Tor Bks.
— Mother Goose & Grimm's: Night of the Living Vacuum. (Illus.). 128p. (Orig.). 1991. pap. 8.95 (0-88687-519-6, Pharos) Wrld Almnc.
— Oh God: It's Grimm. 1988. pap. 8.95 (1-55824-064-0) Day Dream SBCA.
— Steel-Belted Grimm. 128p. 1988. pap. 6.95 (0-88687-366-5, Pharos) Wrld Almnc.
Peters, Mollie C., tr. see Rauch, Erich.
Peters, Mollie C., tr. see Schreiner, Claus, ed.
Peters, Molly, tr. see Kohlein, Fritz.
Peters, Nancy, jt. ed. see Ferlinghetti, Lawrence.
Peters, Nancy, ed. see Herron, Don.

P
Q

Peters, Nancy J. It's in the Wind. (Surrealist Research & Development Monographs). (Illus.). 16p. (Orig.). 1977. pap. 7.00 (*0-941194-10-8*) Black Swan Pr.

Peters, Nancy J., jt. ed. see Ferlinghetti, Lawrence.

Peters, Nancy J., et al, eds. War after War. (City Lights Review Ser.: No. 5). (Illus.). 256p. (Orig.). 1992. pap. 11.95 (*0-87286-260-7*) City Lights.

***Peters, Nell & Peters, Robert.** Nell's Story: A Woman from Eagle River. LC 94-24164. (Illus.). 176p. (C). 1995. 22.95 (*0-299-14470-4*) U of Wis Pr.

— Nell's Story: A Woman from Eagle River. LC 94-24164. 1995. pap. write for info. (*0-299-14474-7*) U of Wis Pr.

Peters, Nick. San Francisco Giants Almanac: Thirty Years of Baseball by the Bay. (Illus.). 200p. (Orig.). 1988. 30. 00 (*1-55643-041-8*); pap. 8.95 (*1-55643-040-X*) North Atlantic.

Peters, Norbert & Rogg, Bernd, eds. Reduced Kinetic Mechanisms for Applications in Combustion Systems. LC 92-42967. (Lecture Notes in Physics Ser.: Vol. M15). 1993. write for info. (*3-540-56372-5*); 55.00 (*0-387-56372-5*) Spr-Verlag.

Peters, O. E. Peters: Conrad Peters & Wife Clara Snidow: Their Descendants & Ancestry. (Illus.). 229p. 1991. reprint ed. lib. bdg. 45.00 (*0-8328-1884-4*); reprint ed. pap. 35.00 (*0-8328-1885-2*) Higginson Bk Co.

Peters, P. W., ed. Congenital Malformations Worldwide: A Report from the International Clearing House for Birth Defects Monitoring Systems. 230p. 1991. 97.50 (*0-444-89137-4*) Elsevier.

Peters, P. W., jt. auth. see Ruitenberg, E. J.

Peters, Pam. The Cambridge Australian English Style Guide. (Illus.). 864p. (C). 1995. 79.95 (*0-521-43401-7*) Cambridge U Pr.

Peters, Pamela. Strategies for Student Writers: Guide to Writing Essays, Tutorial Papers, Exam Papers & Reports. 141p. 1987. text ed. 9.95 (*0-471-33406-5*) Wiley.

Peters, Pamela M. Biotechnology: A Guide to Genetic Engineering. 272p. (C). 1992. pap. write for info. (*0-697-12063-5*) Wm C Brown Pubs.

Peters, Patricia, jt. auth. see Lazzari, Andrea.

***Peters, Patricia C.** Early Morning on Castaway Street. LC 94-32411. 64p. 1995. pap. 12.95 (*0-7734-0001-X*, Mellen Poetry Pr) E Mellen.

— When Last I Saw You: Poems. Schultz, Patricia, ed. LC 91-34456. (Lewiston Poetry Ser.: Vol. 18). 78p. 1992. pap. 12.95 (*0-7734-9619-X*) E Mellen.

Peters, Patricia M., jt. auth. see Lazzari, Andrea M.

Peters, Patricia M., jt. auth. see Lazzari, Andrea.

Peters, Paul, jt. auth. see Ball, Robert.

***Peters, Paulette.** Borders by Design: Creative Ways to Border Your Quilt. White, Janet, ed. (Joy of Quilting Ser.). (Illus.). 56p. (Orig.). 1994. pap. 9.95 (*1-56477-082-6*) That Patchwork.

— Corners in the Cabin. LC 92-8659. 1992. 12.95 (*1-56477-011-7*) That Patchwork.

Peters, Pauline E. Dividing the Commons: Politics, Policy, & Culture in Botswana. 320p. (C). 1994. text ed. 49.50 (*0-8139-1547-3*); pap. text ed. 18.95 (*0-8139-1551-1*) U Pr of Va.

Peters, Plym, tr. see Zoeteman, Kees.

Peters, R., jt. auth. see Schmidt, W.

Peters, R. D. Times, Thoughts...Words. LC 93-93900. 160p. (Orig.). 1994. pap. 10.00 (*1-56002-339-2*, Univ Edtns) Aegina Pr.

Peters, R. DeV., jt. ed. see McMahon, R. J.

Peters, Ralph. Bravo Romeo. McCarthy, Paul, ed. 320p. 1990. mass mkt. 4.95 (*0-671-68166-4*) PB.

— Flames of Heaven. McCarthy, Paul, ed. 464p. 1994. reprint ed. mass mkt. 5.99 (*0-671-73739-2*) PB.

— The Perfect Soldier. LC 94-45908. 1995. 23.00 (*0-671-86583-8*) PB.

— Red Army. McCarthy, Paul, ed. 416p. 1990. mass mkt. 5.50 (*0-671-67669-5*) PB.

— Red Army. braille ed. 777p. 1991. Braille. vinyl bd. 62.16 (*1-56956-308-X*, BR8209) W A T Braille.

— The War in 2020. McCarthy, Paul, ed. 624p. (Orig.). 1992. reprint ed. mass mkt. 6.50 (*0-671-75172-7*, Pocket Star Bks) PB.

Peters, Ray D. & McMahon, Robert J. Aggression & Violence Throughout the Life Span. (Illus.). 342p. (C). 1992. 52.00 (*0-8039-4550-7*); pap. 24.00 (*0-8039-4551-5*) Sage.

— Social Learning & Systems Approaches to Marriage & the Family. LC 87-18214. 340p. 1988. 41.50 (*0-87630-477-3*) Brunner-Mazel.

Peters, Ray D., jt. auth. see McMahon, Robert J.

Peters, Raymond H. Textile Chemistry, Vols. 2 & 3. Incl. Vol. 2: Impurities in Fibres. 374p. 1967. 100.00 (*0-444-40452-X*); Vol. 3: The Physical Chemistry of Dyeing. 890p. 1975. 205.25 (*0-444-41120-8*); write for info. (*0-318-51826-0*) Elsevier.

Peters, Reiner, ed. Nucleo-Cytoplastic Transport. 184p. 1989. pap. text ed. 40.00 (*0-12-552100-6*) Acad Pr.

Peters, Reiner & Alexander, P. Biochemical Lesions & Lethal Synthesis. LC 63-11698. (International Series of Monographs on Pure & Applied Mathematics: Vol. 18). 1963. 141.00 (*0-08-013779-2*, Pub. by Pergamon Repr UK) Franklin.

Peters, Reiner & Trendelenburg, M., eds. Nucleo-Cytoplasmic Transport. (Illus.). 315p. 1986. 69. 00 (*0-387-17050-2*) Spr-Verlag.

Peters, Richard, jt. auth. see Agazarian, Yvonne.

Peters, Richard M. & Toledo, Jose, eds. Perioperative Care. LC 92-49794. (Current Topics in General Thoracic Surgery: an International Ser.: Vol. 2). 1992. write for info. (*0-444-89660-0*) Elsevier.

Peters, Richard M., jt. ed. see Ying-Kai, Wu.

Peters, Robert. The Blood Countess, Erzebet of Hungary (1560-1614) LC 86-17570. (Illus.). 120p. 1987. 16.00 (*0-916156-80-X*); pap. 8.00 (*0-916156-81-8*) Cherry Valley.

— Breughel's Pig. (Orig.). 1988. pap. 9.95 (*0-89807-139-9*) Illuminati.

— Cool Zebras of Light. LC 73-87666. (Hip-Pocket Ser.: No. 4). (Illus.). 64p. (Orig.). 1974. pap. 2.75 (*0-685-38810-7*) Christophers Bks.

— Crunching Gravel: A Wisconsin Boyhood in the Thirties. LC 93-19801. (North Coast Bks.). 128p. 1993. reprint ed. lib. bdg. 40.00 (*0-299-14100-4*); reprint ed. pap. 10. 95 (*0-299-14104-7*) U of Wis Pr.

— The Drowned Man to the Fish. (Illus.). (Orig.). 1978. pap. 3.00 (*0-89823-002-0*) New Rivers Pr.

— For You, Lili Marlene: A Memoir of World War II. LC 95-13155. 1995. write for info. (*0-299-14810-6*) U of Wis Pr.

— The Gift to Be Simple: A Garland for Mother Ann Lee. 114p. (Orig.). 1975. pap. 4.95 (*0-87140-103-7*) Liveright.

— Good Night, Paul. 75p. (Orig.). 1992. pap. 8.95 (*1-879194-06-6*) GLB Pubs.

— The Great American Poetry Bake-Off. LC 79-16090. 290p. 1979. 27.50 (*0-8108-1231-2*) Scarecrow.

— The Great American Poetry Bake-Off, Series No. 4. LC 91-12621. (Illus.). 306p. 1991. 32.50 (*0-8108-2410-8*) Scarecrow.

— The Great American Poetry Bake-Off: Second Series. LC 81-18536. 409p. 1982. 29.50 (*0-8108-1502-8*) Scarecrow.

— The Great American Poetry Bake-Off, Third Series. LC 86-28003. 292p. 1987. 29.50 (*0-8108-1960-0*) Scarecrow.

— Hawker. 116p. (Orig.). 1984. 20.00 (*0-87775-165-X*); pap. 9.95 (*0-87775-166-8*) Unicorn Pr.

— Hawthorne: Poems Adapted from Journals. (Illus.). 1977. 15.00 (*0-88031-048-0*); 6.00 (*0-88031-047-2*) Invisible-Red Hill.

— Haydon. (Illus.). 110p. (Orig.). 1989. 20.00 (*0-87775-219-2*); pap. 9.95 (*0-87775-220-6*) Unicorn Pr.

— Holy Cow: Parable Poems. 1974. pap. 2.50 (*0-88031-014-6*) Invisible-Red Hill.

— Kane. (Illus.). 110p. (Orig.). 1985. 20.00 (*0-87775-168-4*); pap. 9.95 (*0-87775-169-2*) Unicorn Pr.

— Love Poems for Robert Mitchum. Hathaway, Michael, ed. 32p. (Orig.). 1992. pap. 6.00 (*0-943795-20-6*) Chiron Rev.

— Ludwig of Bavaria: A Verse Biography & a Play for Single Performer. 128p. (Orig.). 1986. pap. 7.00 (*0-916156-82-6*) Cherry Valley.

— Peters Third Black & Blue Guide to Literary Journals. 3rd ed. 164p. 1987. pap. 5.95 (*0-916685-03-9*) Dustbooks.

— Poems: Selected & New, 1967-1991. LC 92-71208. 190p. (Orig.). 1992. 20.00 (*1-878580-30-2*); pap. 11.95 (*1-878580-31-0*) Asylum Arts.

— Shaker Light. 127p. 1987. 20.00 (*0-87775-200-1*); pap. 9.95 (*0-87775-201-X*) Unicorn Pr.

— Snapshots for a Serial Killer: A Fiction & a Play. 125p. (Orig.). 1992. pap. 10.95 (*1-879194-07-4*) GLB Pubs.

— The Sow's Head & Other Poems. LC 68-24447. 91p. reprint ed. 26.00 (*0-685-16224-9*, 2027600) Bks Demand.

— Where the Bee Sucks: Workers, Drones & Queens of Contemporary American Poetry. LC 94-70673. 300p. (Orig.). 1994. pap. 14.95 (*1-878580-63-9*) Asylum Arts.

— Zapped: Two Novellas: Asbestos: a Book for Lepers, How to Make Love to a Foot. 135p. (Orig.). 1993. pap. 11.95 (*1-879194-10-4*) GLB Pubs.

Peters, Robert, ed. Letters to a Tutor: The Tennyson Family Letters to Henry Graham Dakyns (1861-1911), with the Audrey Tennyson Death-Bed Diary. LC 87-32368. (Illus.). 324p. 1988. 29.50 (*0-8108-2103-6*) Scarecrow.

Peters, Robert, ed. see Murphy, Dan.

Peters, Robert, jt. auth. see Peters, Nell.

Peters, Robert B., ed. see Ratch, Jerry.

Peters, Robert B., ed. see Ratner, Rochelle.

Peters, Robert C., ed. see Prokop, Michael S.

Peters, Robert H. A Critique for Ecology. (Illus.). 400p. (C). 1991. 89.95 (*0-521-40017-1*); pap. 32.95 (*0-521-39588-7*) Cambridge U Pr.

— Ecological Implications of Body Size. 352p. 1986. pap. 29.95 (*0-521-28886-X*) Cambridge U Pr.

Peters, Robert L. The Crowns of Apollo: Swinburne's Principles of Literature & Art: A Study in Victorian Criticism & Aesthetics. LC 65-10769. (Illus.). 226p. reprint ed. pap. 64.50 (*0-7837-3610-X*, 2043476) Bks Demand.

— Getting What You Came For: The Smart Student's Guide to Earning an M.A. or a Ph.D. LC 92-27763. 1992. pap. 12.00 (*0-374-52361-4*, Noonday) FS&G.

Peters, Robert L. & Lovejoy, Thomas E. Global Warming & Biological Diversity. (Illus.). 448p. (C). 1992. pap. 17.00 (*0-300-05930-2*) Yale U Pr.

Peters, Robert L., ed. see Symonds, John A.

***Peters, Robert M.** When Physicians Fail As Managers: An Exploratory Analysis of Career Change Problems. 48p. (Orig.). 1994. pap. text ed. 25.00 (*0-924674-31-8*) Am Coll Phys Execs.

Peters, Robert M., jt. auth. see Peters, Judith M.

Peters, Roger. Dance of the Wolves. 208p. 1986. pap. 3.95 (*0-345-32870-1*) Ballantine.

Peters, Roger, ed. see Michigan Legislative Council Staff.

Peters, Roger W., intro. Michigan Administrative Code 1979: 1988 Annual Supplement. (Illus.). 1050p. 1988. pap. 27.00 (*1-878210-01-7*) Legis Serv Bur.

Peters, Roger W., ed. see Michigan Legislative Council Staff.

Peters, Roger W., jt. auth. see Michigan Legislative Council Staff.

Peters, Ronald M., Jr. The American Speakership: The Office in Historical Perspective. LC 89-20025. 352p. 1990. text ed. 48.50x (*0-8018-3955-6*) Johns Hopkins.

— The Massachusetts Constitution of 1780: A Social Compact. LC 77-90730. 256p. 1978. 30.00x (*0-87023-143-X*) U of Mass Pr.

— The Next Generation: Dialogues Between Leaders & Students. LC 92-54133. 320p. (C). 1992. 19.95 (*0-8061-2426-1*); pap. 9.95 (*0-8061-2430-X*) U of Okla Pr.

Peters, Ronald M., Jr., jt. ed. see Hertzke, Allen D.

***Peters, Ronnie.** Ultimate Claris Works Solutions! for Education. Peters, Barry, ed. (Illus.). 270p. (C). 1994. ring bd. 425.00 (*0-9643120-1-8*); spiral bd. 36.95 (*0-9643120-0-X*) EduPress Pubng.

Peters, Rudolph. Islam & Colonialism. (Religion & Society Ser.). 1984. pap. 29.95 (*3-11-010022-3*) Mouton.

Peters, Rudolph, jt auth. see Zwaini, Laila A.

Peters, Russell. Clambake: A Wampanoag Tradition. (J). (gr. 3-6). 1992. pap. 6.95 (*0-8225-9621-0*, Lerner Publctns) Lerner Group.

Peters, Russell M. Clambake: A Wampanoag Tradition. (We Are Still Here: Native Americans Today Ser.). (Illus.). 48p. (J). (gr. 3-6). 1992. lib. bdg. 19.95 (*0-8225-2651-4*, Lerner Publctns) Lerner Group.

Peters, Ruth A. Who's in Charge? A Positive Parenting Approach to Disciplining Children. LC 89-92329. (Illus.). 144p. (Orig.). 1990. pap. 12.50 (*0-9624728-0-8*) Lindsay FL.

Peters, S. Activated Carbon Technology. (General Engineering Ser.). 1991. text ed. write for info. (*0-442-00810-4*) Van Nos Reinhold.

Peters, Sally. Under the Fang. 352p. (Orig.). 1991. pap. 6.50 (*0-671-69573-8*, Pocket Star Bks) PB.

Peters, Sally, ed. The Autobiography of Special Agent Dale Cooper. 192p. 1991. pap. 8.95 (*0-671-74400-3*) PB.

Peters, Sally, ed. see Alexis, Katina.

Peters, Sally, ed. see Bernstein, Patricia.

Peters, Sally, jt. ed. see Campbell, Ramsey.

Peters, Sally, ed. see Chiel, Deborah.

Peters, Sally, ed. see Cooper, James Fenimore.

Peters, Sally, ed. see Davis, William H.

Peters, Sally, ed. see Dershowitz, Alan M.

Peters, Sally, ed. see Ellison, James.

Peters, Sally, ed. see Engel, Lewis & Ferguson, Tom.

Peters, Sally, ed. see Engelhard, Jack.

Peters, Sally, ed. see Ferguson, Tom & Graedon, Joe.

Peters, Sally, ed. see Geiberger, Al.

Peters, Sally, ed. see Graham, Janis.

Peters, Sally, ed. see Henry, Diane & Horrock, Nicholas.

Peters, Sally, ed. see Hunter, Linda M.

Peters, Sally, ed. see Keane, Maureen B.

Peters, Sally, ed. see Late Night with David Letterman Writers Staff & Letterman, David.

Peters, Sally, ed. see Levin, Ira.

Peters, Sally, ed. see MacLean, Norman.

Peters, Sally, ed. see Malone, Michael.

Peters, Sally, ed. see March, Ray.

Peters, Sally, ed. see McCammon, Robert R.

Peters, Sally, ed. see Minninger, Joan & Dugan, Eleanor.

Peters, Sally, ed. see Morton, Andrew.

Peters, Sally, ed. see Nadel, Jack.

Peters, Sally, ed. see Natow, Annette B. & Hesun, Jo-Ann.

Peters, Sally, ed. see Palmer, Jessica.

Peters, Sally, ed. see Riccero, Delores & Bingham, Joan.

Peters, Sally, ed. see Rincover, Arnold.

Peters, Sally, ed. see Savage, Adrian.

Peters, Sally, ed. see Storm, Jordan.

Peters, Sally, ed. see Strasser, Todd.

Peters, Sally, ed. see Taski, Bob & Flick, Jim.

Peters, Sally, ed. see Toshi, Bob & Flich, Jim.

Peters, Sally, ed. see Watson, Tom.

Peters, Sally, ed. see Watson, Tom & Seitz, Nick.

Peters, Sally, ed. see Watson, Tom & Seltz, Nick.

Peters, Sally, ed. see Weinberg, Robert.

Peters, Sally, ed. see Wilson, F. Paul.

Peters, Samuel A. General History of Connecticut. LC 77-104540. 285p. reprint ed. lib. bdg. 24.50 (*0-8398-1562-X*) Irvington.

— General History of Connecticut, from Its First Settlement Under George Fenwick to Its Latest Period of Amity with Great Britain Prior to the Revolution. LC 71-95073. (Select Bibliographies Reprint Ser.). 1977. 30.95 (*0-8369-5073-9*) Ayer.

Peters, Sarah W. Becoming O'Keeffe: The Early Years. (Illus.). 400p. 1991. 39.95 (*0-89659-907-8*) Abbeville Pr.

— Becoming O'Keeffe: The Early Years. (Illus.). 400p. 1992. pap. 19.95 (*1-55859-362-4*) Abbeville Pr.

Peters, Sharon. Animals at Night. LC 82-19226. (Now I Know Ser.). (Illus.). 32p. (J). (gr. k-2). 1983. lib. bdg. 11. 59 (*0-89375-903-1*); pap. 2.95 (*0-8167-1477-0*) Troll Assocs.

— Champ on Ice. LC 87-10908. (Giant First Start Reader Ser.). (Illus.). 32p. (J). (gr. k-2). 1988. lib. bdg. 11.59 (*0-8167-1093-7*); pap. text ed. 2.95 (*0-8167-1094-5*) Troll Assocs.

— Contento Juan. (Illus.). 32p. (SPA.). (J). (gr. k-2). 1981. lib. bdg. 7.89 (*0-89375-552-4*); pap. 1.95 (*0-685-04945-0*) Troll Assocs.

— Feliz Cumpleanos. (Illus.). 32p. (SPA.). (J). (gr. k-2). 1981. lib. bdg. 7.89 (*0-89375-553-2*); pap. 1.95 (*0-685-04948-5*) Troll Assocs.

— Five Little Kittens. LC 81-2317. (Illus.). 32p. (J). (gr. k-2). 1981. lib. bdg. 11.59 (*0-89375-503-6*); pap. 2.95 (*0-89375-504-4*) Troll Assocs.

— Fun at Camp. (Illus.). 32p. (J). (gr. k-2). 1980. lib. bdg. 7.89 (*0-89375-378-5*); pap. 1.95 (*0-89375-278-9*) Troll Assocs.

— Una Funcion De Titeres. (Illus.). 32p. (SPA.). (J). (gr. k-2). 1981. lib. bdg. 7.89 (*0-89375-551-6*); pap. 1.95 (*0-685-42387-5*) Troll Assocs.

— The Goofy Ghost. LC 81-2573. (Illus.). 32p. (J). (gr. k-2). 1981. lib. bdg. 11.59 (*0-89375-533-8*); pap. 2.95 (*0-89375-534-6*) Troll Assocs.

— Happy Birthday. (Illus.). 32p. (J). (gr. k-2). 1980. lib. bdg. 7.89 (*0-89375-379-3*); pap. 1.95 (*0-89375-279-7*) Troll Assocs.

— Happy Jack. (Illus.). 32p. (J). (gr. k-2). 1980. lib. bdg. 7.89 (*0-89375-380-7*); pap. 1.95 (*0-89375-280-0*) Troll Assocs.

— Here Comes Jack Frost. LC 81-4093. (Illus.). 32p. (J). (gr. k-2). 1981. lib. bdg. 11.59 (*0-89375-513-3*); pap. text ed. 2.95 (*0-89375-514-1*) Troll Assocs.

— Listos, En Sus Marcas, Adelante! (Illus.). 32p. (SPA.). (J). (gr. k-2). 1981. lib. bdg. 7.89 (*0-89375-550-8*); pap. 1.95 (*0-89375-957-0*) Troll Assocs.

— The Marching Band Mystery. LC 84-8783. (Illus.). 48p. (J). (gr. 2-4). 1985. lib. bdg. 10.89 (*0-8167-0406-6*); pap. text ed. 3.50 (*0-8167-0407-4*) Troll Assocs.

— Maxie the Mutt. LC 87-10914. (Illus.). 32p. (J). (gr. k-2). 1988. lib. bdg. 11.59 (*0-8167-1087-2*); pap. text ed. 2.95 (*0-8167-1088-0*) Troll Assocs.

— Messy Mark. (Illus.). 32p. (J). (gr. k-2). 1980. lib. bdg. 7.89 (*0-89375-381-5*); pap. 1.95 (*0-89375-281-9*) Troll Assocs.

— On a Roll: A Conversation & Listening Text. 160p. (C). 1990. pap. text ed. 15.25 (*0-13-155326-7*) P-H.

— Puppet Show. (Illus.). 32p. (J). (gr. k-2). 1980. lib. bdg. 7.89 (*0-89375-385-8*); pap. 1.95 (*0-89375-286-X*) Troll Assocs.

— Pussycat Kite. LC 84-8632. (Giant First Start Reader Ser.). (Illus.). 32p. (J). (gr. k-2). 1985. lib. bdg. 11.59 (*0-8167-0358-2*); pap. text ed. 2.95 (*0-8167-0438-4*) Troll Assocs.

— Ready, Get Set, Go! (Illus.). 32p. (J). (gr. k-2). 1980. lib. bdg. 7.89 (*0-89375-386-6*); pap. 1.95 (*0-89375-285-1*) Troll Assocs.

— The Rooster & the Weather Vane. LC 86-30838. (Illus.). 32p. (J). (gr. k-2). 1988. lib. bdg. 7.89 (*0-8167-0980-7*); pap. text ed. 1.95 (*0-8167-0981-5*) Troll Assocs.

— Rub-a-Dub Suds. LC 86-30856. (Illus.). 32p. (J). (gr. k-2). 1988. lib. bdg. 7.89 (*0-8167-0984-X*); pap. text ed. 1.95 (*0-8167-0985-8*) Troll Assocs.

— Santa's New Sled. LC 81-5028. (Illus.). 32p. (J). (gr. k-2). 1981. lib. bdg. 11.59 (*0-89375-523-0*); pap. text ed. 2.95 (*0-89375-524-9*) Troll Assocs.

— Stop That Rabbit. (Illus.). 32p. (J). (gr. k-2). 1980. lib. bdg. 7.89 (*0-89375-388-2*); pap. 1.95 (*0-89375-288-6*) Troll Assocs.

— The Tiny Christmas Elf. LC 86-30849. (Illus.). 32p. (J). (gr. k-2). 1988. lib. bdg. 7.89 (*0-8167-0988-2*); pap. text ed. 1.95 (*0-8167-0989-0*) Troll Assocs.

— The Tooth Fairy. LC 81-5100. (Illus.). 32p. (J). (gr. k-2). 1981. lib. bdg. 11.59 (*0-89375-519-2*); pap. 2.95 (*0-89375-520-6*) Troll Assocs.

— Trick or Treat Halloween. (Illus.). 32p. (J). (gr. k-2). 1980. lib. bdg. 7.89 (*0-89375-392-0*); pap. 1.95 (*0-89375-292-4*) Troll Assocs.

Peters, Stanley, jt. auth. see Gawron, Jean M.

Peters, Stephen. For Always. LC 91-65705. 72p. 1992. 6.95 (*1-55523-445-3*) Winston-Derek.

Peters, Stephen P., jt. ed. see Glew, Robert H.

Peters, Sue. Maid for Marriage. large type ed. 1992. reprint ed. lib. bdg. 18.95 (*0-263-13134-3*, Pub. by Mills & Boon UK) Thorndike Pr.

— Marriage in Haste. large type ed. (Linford Romance Library). 384p. 1985. pap. 11.95 (*0-7089-6100-2*, Linford) Ulverscroft.

— Tomorrow's Man. large type ed. 1993. 17.95 (*0-263-13581-0*, Pub. by Mills & Boon Ltd UK) Chivers N Amer.

— Tug of War. large type ed. (Linford Romance Library). 384p. 1986. pap. 11.95 (*0-7089-6178-9*, Linford) Ulverscroft.

— Weekend Wife. large type ed. 1992. reprint ed. lib. bdg. 18.95 (*0-263-13038-X*, Pub. by Mills & Boon UK) Thorndike Pr.

Peters, Susan J., ed. Education & Disability in Cross-Cultural Perspective. LC 92-41906. (Reference Library of Social Science, Reference Books in International Education: Vol. 25). 328p. 1993. 49.00 (*0-8240-6988-9*) Garland.

Peters, Susanne. The Germans & the INF Missiles: Getting Their Way in NATO's Strategy of Flexible Response. 334p. 1990. pap. 53.00 (*3-7890-2236-5*, Pub. by Nomos Verlags GW) Intl Bk Import.

Peters, T. & Sjoholm, I. Albumin Structure Biosynthesis Function. LC 77-30609. (Proceedings 11th FEBS Meeting, Copenhagen 1977 Ser.: Vol. 50: B9). 1978. 40. 00 (*0-08-022631-0*, Pub. by Pergamon Repr UK) Franklin.

Peters, Ted. God As Trinity: Relationality & Temporality in the Divine Life. LC 92-17839. 240p. (Orig.). 1993. pap. 14.99 (*0-664-25402-0*) Westminster John Knox.

— God-The World's Future: Systematic Theology for a Postmodern Era. LC 91-43158. 400p. 1992. pap. 22.00 (*0-8006-2542-0*, 1-2542, Fortress Pr) Augsburg Fortress.

— Sin: Radical Evil in Soul & Society. 312p. (Orig.). (C). 1994. 24.99 (*0-8028-3764-6*); pap. 14.99 (*0-8028-0113-7*) Eerdmans.

Peters, Ted, ed. see Pannenberg, Wolfhart.

Peters, Thelma. Biscayne Country, 1870-1926. LC 81-13030. (Illus.). viii, 323p. 1981. pap. 14.95 (*0-916224-65-1*) Banyan Bks.

— Lemon City: Pioneering on Biscayne Bay, 1850-1925. LC 76-48058. (Illus.). 1976. 14.95 (*0-916224-12-0*) Banyan Bks.

Peters, Thelma B., ed. see Maloney, Walter C.

Peters, Theodore & Guitar, Barry. Stuttering: An Integration of Contemporary Therapies, No. 16. LC 80-51679. 1980. pap. 2.00 (*0-933388-15-2*) Stuttering Fnd Am.

Peters, Theodore J. & Guitar, Barry. Stuttering: An Integrated Approach to Its Nature & Treatment. (Illus.). 392p. 1991. 40.00 (0-683-06870-9) Williams & Wilkins.
Peters, Thomas A. The Online Catalog: A Critical Examination of Public Use. LC 90-53602. (Illus.). 280p. 1991. lib. bdg. 38.50x (0-89950-600-3) McFarland & Co.
Peters, Thomas C. Battling for the Modern Mind: A Beginner's Chesterton. LC 94-5963. (Concordia Scholarship Today Ser.). 176p. (Orig.). 1994. pap. 15.99 (0-570-04664-5) Concordia.
Peters, Thomas J. & Austin, Nancy K. A Passion for Excellence: The Leadership Difference. LC 84-45767. 559p. 1985. 30.00 (0-394-54484-6) Random.
Peters, Thomas J. & Waterman, Robert H. In Search of Excellence: Lessons from America's Best Run Companies. write for info. (0-317-17653-6) Macmillan.
Peters, Thomas J. & Waterman, Robert H., Jr. In Search of Excellence. Date not set. pap. write for info. (0-446-36578-5) Warner Bks.
— In Search of Excellence. 384p. 1988. pap. 14.99 (0-446-38507-7) Warner Bks.
— In Search of Excellence: Lessons from America's Best Run Companies. LC 82-47530. (Illus.). xxvi, 360p. 1982. 25.00i (0-06-015042-4, HarpT) HarpC.
Peters, Tim, ed. Little Hopper Catches a Cold. (Children's Doctor Ser.). (Illus.). (J). (ps-2). pap. 4.95 (1-879874-27-X) T Peters & Co.
— Toby Turtle Takes a Tumble. (Illus.). (J). (ps-2). pap. 4.95 (1-879874-29-6) T Peters & Co.
Peters, Tom. Akathistos Hymn. (Illus.). 35p. 1990. pap. 4.95 (1-879516-01-2) Betterpub Pr.
— Beyond Hierarchy: Organizations in the 1990s. 1991. 30.00 (0-685-58667-7) Knopf.
— Fragile People: Stories from Betterway. Scrivo, William, ed. (Illus.). 291p. 1991. pap. 9.95 (1-879516-02-0) Betterpub Pr.
— Hard Time Prayers. (Illus.). 104p. (Orig.). 1991. pap. 3.95 (1-879516-03-9) Betterpub Pr.
— Liberation Management. 1994. pap. 15.00 (0-449-90910-7) Fawcett.
— Liberation Management: Necessary Disorganization for the Nanosecond Nineties. LC 90-53071. 928p. 1992. 27.00 (0-394-55999-1) Knopf.
— Liberation Management: Necessary Disorganization for the Nanosecond Nineties. 880p. 1994. pap. 15.00 (0-449-90888-7, Columbine) Fawcett.
— Naked I Came...And Naked I Shall Go: The Growth & Ending of an Organization. 240p. (Orig.). 1992. pap. write for info. (1-879516-05-5) Betterpub Pr.
— O Felix Culpa...O Happy Fault: How Bad Guys Keep Good Guys Going. (Illus.). 200p. (Orig.). 1991. pap. write for info. (1-879516-04-7) Betterpub Pr.
— O My Soul: The Inside Story. Scrivo, William, ed. (Illus.). 250p. (Orig.). 1991. pap. 15.00 (1-879516-00-4) Betterpub Pr.
— The Pursuit of Wow! Every Person's Guide to Topsy-Turvy Times. 1994. pap. 14.00 (0-679-75555-1, Vin) Random.
— The Skunk Camp Promises. 1987. ring bd. 9.95 (0-317-56480-3) Knopf.
— Thriving on Chaos: Handbook for a Management Revolution. LC 87-45575. 561p. 1987. 30.00 (0-394-56784-6) Knopf.
— Thriving on Chaos: Handbook for a Management Revolution. LC 88-45121. 736p. 1989. pap. 16.00 (0-06-097184-3, PL) HarpC.
— Tuff Time Prayers. (Illus.). 100p. (Orig.). 1991. pap. write for info. (0-318-68596-5) Betterpub Pr.
Peters, Tom F. The Development of Long-Span Bridge Building. (Illus.). 188p. (Orig.). (ENG, FRE & GER.). 1980. pap. text ed. 19.95 (0-686-78178-3) Interbk Inc.
— Transitions in Engineering: Guillaume Henri Dufour & the Early 19th Century Cable Suspension Bridges. 252p. 1987. 100.00 (0-8176-1929-1) Birkhauser.
Peters, Tom J. & Austin, Nancy K. A Passion for Excellence. 608p. 1989. pap. 13.99 (0-446-38639-1) Warner Bks.
Peters, Uwe. Pflanzenoekologische und Bodenkundliche Untersuchungen an Quellwaldstandorten in Bochum. (Dissertationes Botanicae Ser.: Vol. 122). (Illus.). 212p. (GER.). 1988. spiral bd. 48.00 (3-443-64034-6) Lubrecht & Cramer.
Peters, Uwe H. Anna Freud: A Life Dedicated to Children. LC 84-1278. (Illus.). 384p. 1985. 24.95 (0-8052-3910-3) Schocken.
— Dictionary of Psychiatry & Medical Psychology: Woerterbuch der Psychiatrie und Medizinischen Psychologie. 4th ed. 676p. (ENG, FRE & GER.). 1990. 69.95 (0-8288-0586-5, M 6972) Fr & Eur.
Peters, V. P., jt. ed. see Gerwick, Ben C., Jr.
Peters, Victor. All Things Common: The Hutterian Way of Life. LC 65-28661. (Illus.). 245p. reprint ed. pap. 69.90 (0-8357-5315-8, 2033282) Bks Demand.
Peters, W. Chemotherapy & Drug Resistance in Malaria, 2 vols., Vol. 1. 2nd ed. 542p. 1987. text ed. 181.00 (0-12-552721-7) Acad Pr.
— Chemotherapy & Drug Resistance in Malaria, 2 vols., Vol. 2. 2nd ed. 650p. 1987. 161.00 (0-685-18135-9) Acad Pr.
— Peritrophic Membranes. (Zoophysiology Ser.: Vol. 30). (Illus.). xi, 238p. 1992. 153.00 (0-387-53635-3) Spr-Verlag.
Peters, W. & Killick-Kendrick, R., eds. The Leishmaniases: Clinical Aspects & Control, Vol. 2. 400p. 1987. text ed. 189.00 (0-12-552102-2) Acad Pr.
— The Leishmaniases I: Biology & Epidemiology, Vol. 1. 550p. 1987. text ed. 206.00 (0-12-552101-4) Acad Pr.
Peters, W. & Richards, W. H., eds. Antimalarial Drugs. (Handbook of Experimental Pharmacology Ser.: Vol. 68, Pt. 1). (Illus.). 540p. 1984. 247.00 (0-387-12616-3) Spr-Verlag.
— Antimalarial Drugs II: Current Antimalarials & New Drug Developments. (Handbook of Experimental Pharmacology Ser.: Vol. 68). (Illus.). xxiii, 520p. 1984. 261.00 (0-387-12617-1) Spr-Verlag.
Peters, W. A. Gerard Manley Hopkins: A Tribute. 80p. 1984. pap. 4.75 (0-8294-0456-2) Loyola Univ Pr.
Peters, W. J. La Casa di Marcus Lucretius Fronto e le Sue Pitture. (Scrinium (Monographs on History, Archaeology & Art History. Published under the Auspices of the Netherlands Institute & the Foundation of Friends of the Dutch Institute in Rome) Ser.: Vol. V). (Illus.). 400p. (ITA.). 1992. 177.00 (90-5170-163-2) IBD Ltd.
Peters, W. L., jt. auth. see Hubbard, M. D.
Peters, W. S. Counting for Something: Statistical Principles & Personalities. (Texts in Statistics Ser.). (Illus.). 305p. 1986. 39.00 (0-387-96364-2) Spr-Verlag.
Peters, Wallace. A Colour Atlas of Arthropods in Clinical Medicine. 1992. write for info. (0-318-69232-5) Mosby Yr Bk.
Peters, Warren. Mystical Medicine. 96p. (Orig.). 1987. pap. 4.95 (0-923309-08-X) Hartland Pubns.
Peters, Wendy J., jt. auth. see Iannarelli, Cynthia.
***Peters, Werner.** The Existential Runner: On Democracy in America. 1995. 52.50 (1-56324-585-X); pap. 21.95 (1-56324-586-8) M E Sharpe.
Peters, Westberg. Condor. LC 89-28270. (Wildlife Ser.). (Illus.). 48p. (J). (gr. 5). 1990. text ed. 12.95 (0-89686-515-0, Crstwood Hse) Silver Burdett Pr.
Peters, William. A Class Divided. LC 87-50411. 172p. 1987. pap. 11.00 (0-300-04048-2) Yale U Pr.
Peters, William, jt. auth. see Evers, Myrlie.
Peters, William C. Exploration & Mining Geology. 2nd ed. 685p. 1987. Net. text ed. write for info. (0-471-83864-0) Wiley.
— Fire Apparatus Purchasing Handbook. 1994. 47.00 (0-912212-33-0) Fire Eng.
Peters, William E. Ohio Lands & Their History. 3rd ed. Bruchey, Stuart, ed. LC 78-53541. (Development of Public Land Law in the U. S. Ser.). (Illus.). 1979. reprint ed. lib. bdg. 30.95 (0-405-11383-8) Ayer.
Peters, William J. What Your Wedding Can Be. LC 80-65402. 136p. (Orig.). 1980. pap. 2.95 (0-87029-163-7, 20350-5) Abbey.
Peters, William J., jt. auth. see Neuenschwander, Leon F.
Peters, William L. & Peters, Janice G., eds. Ephemeroptera: Proceedings of the First International Conference Held at the Florida Agricultural & Mechanical University, August 1970. (Illus.). 312p. 1973. lib. bdg. 124.00 (90-04-06461-3) Lubrecht & Cramer.
Petersburg Centennial Committee. Petersburg Nebraska. (Illus.). 447p. 1987. 47.50 (0-88107-092-0) Curtis Media.
Petersdorf, Robert G., et al. Harrison's Principles of Internal Medicine, 2. 10th ed. (Illus.). 2240p. 1983. text ed. write for info. (0-07-049609-9) McGraw.
— Harrison's Principles of Internal Medicine, 1. 10th ed. (Illus.). 2240p. 1983. text ed. write for info. (0-07-049608-0) McGraw.
Peterse, Att, jt. auth. see Hoppe, Rob.
Peterse, O. J., jt. ed. see Wierenga, H. K.
Peterseil, Tamar. Aap It! A Microwave Cookbook Just for Kids. (J). (gr. 4-7). 1993. 12.95 (0-943706-13-0) Pitspopany.
Peterseil, Tehila. Secret Files of Lisa Weiss. (J). 1990. 11.95 (0-87306-549-2); pap. 9.95 (0-87306-550-6) Feldheim.
Petersen. Agricultural Field Experiments: Design & Analysis. (Books in Soils, Plants & the Environment: Vol. 31). 416p. 1994. 150.00 (0-8247-8912-1) Dekker.
— Historical Celebrations. pap. 9.95 (0-931406-13-7) Idaho State Soc.
— Leathercrafting. 1980. pap. text ed. (0-8069-8942-4) Sterling.
— On the Track of the Dixie Limited. (Illus.). 64p. 10.00 (0-936610-00-X) Colophon Bk Shop.
— Urologic Pathology. 2nd ed. (Illus.). 800p. 1992. text ed. 135.00 (0-397-51063-2) Lippincott.
Petersen & Bell. Catalyst Deactivation. (Chemical Industries Ser.: Vol. 30). 376p. 1987. 175.00 (0-8247-7741-7) Dekker.
***Petersen & New.** How to Fear God Without Being Afraid of Him. 108p. 1994. pap. 4.99 (1-56476-414-1, 6-3414, Victor Books) SP Pubns.
Petersen, jt. auth. see Andreasen.
Petersen, et al. Binder Characterization & Evaluation, Vol. 4: Test Methods. 193p. (Orig.). (C). 1994. pap. text ed. 15.00 (0-309-05806-6, SHRP-A-370) SHRP.
Petersen, Alan. In a Critical Condition: Health & Power Relations in Australia. 208p. 1994. pap. 22.95 (1-86373-530-5, Pub. by Allen Unwin AT) Paul & Co Pubs.
Petersen, Andrew. Dictionary of Islamic Architecture. (Illus.). 352p. 1995. 75.00 (0-415-06084-2, B0381) Routledge.
Petersen, Anne C. & Mortimer, Jeylan T., eds. Youth Unemployment & Society. (Illus.). 586p. (C). 1994. 44.95 (0-521-44473-X) Cambridge U Pr.
Petersen, Anne C., jt. ed. see Brooks-Gunn, Jeanne.
Petersen, Anne C., jt. ed. see Gibson, Kathleen R.
Petersen, Anne C., jt. ed. see Wittig, Michele A.
Petersen, Antje C. The First Berlin Border-Guard Trial. (MacArthur Scholar Ser.: No. 15). 39p. (Orig.). 1992. pap. 3.50 (1-881157-18-0) In Ctr Global.
Petersen, Arnold. Capital & Labor. 7th ed. 1975. pap. text ed. 0.50 (0-935534-06-7) NY Labor News.
— Daniel De Leon: Social Architect, Vol. 2. 400p. 1953. 2.50 (0-935534-12-1) NY Labor News.
— Democracy...Past, Present & Future. 7th ed. 1971. pap. text ed. 0.50 (0-935534-14-8) NY Labor News.
— Karl Marx & Marxian Science. 1967. 3.00 (0-935534-17-2); pap. 1.00 (0-935534-18-0) NY Labor News.
— Reviling of the Great. 112p. 1949. 1.50 (0-935534-24-5); pap. 0.75 (0-935534-25-3) NY Labor News.
— The Supreme Court. 3rd ed. 1971. pap. text ed. 0.75 (0-935534-30-X) NY Labor News.
Petersen, Arona. Food & Folklore of the Virgin Islands. 300p. (Orig.). (YA). (gr. 9-12). 1990. 20.00 (0-9626577-0-0) A Petersen.
— Herbs & Proverbs. 1974. write for info. (0-318-69480-8) A Petersen.
Petersen, Becky, jt. auth. see Pantiel, Mindy.
Petersen, Bertha I. Eyes That See. Jones, M. L., ed. 171p. (Orig.). 1993. pap. 5.95 (1-882270-05-3) Old Rugged Cross.
Petersen, Bruce L. God's Answer for You: Psalms That Speak to Real-Life Needs. 77p. 1994. pap. 5.95 (0-8341-1493-3) Beacon Hill.
***Petersen, C., et al.** Visual BASIC XX How-To: The All-New Definitive Visual Basic Problem Solver. 800p. 1995. disk, pap. 39.95 (1-57169-001-8) Waite Group Pr.
Petersen, Candyce A. Beauty the Butterfly. (Beginning Science Ser.). 24p. (J). (ps-3). Date not set. 11.95 (1-56065-097-4) Capstone Pr.
— Eggbert the Robin. LC 92-12894. (Beginning Science Ser.). 24p. (J). (ps-3). Date not set. 11.95 (1-56065-099-0) Capstone Pr.
— Lucky Becomes a Frog. LC 92-6417. (Beginning Science - Life Cycles Ser.). (Illus.). (J). Date not set. 11.95 (1-56065-096-6) Capstone Pr.
— Silky the Spider. (Beginning Science Ser.). 24p. (J). (ps-3). Date not set. 11.95 (1-56065-098-2) Capstone Pr.
Petersen, Carol A., jt. auth. see Peake, Jacquelyn.
***Petersen, Carol M.** Bess Streeter Aldrich. (Illus.). 232p. 1995. text ed. 35.00 (0-8032-3700-6) U of Nebr Pr.
Petersen, Carolyn C. Jupiter. (Planetary Exploration Ser.). 48p. 1989. 13.95 (0-8160-2048-5) Facts on File.
***Petersen, Carolyn C. & Brandt, John C.** Hubble Vision: Astronomy with the Hubble Space Telescope. (Illus.). 256p. (C). Date not set. 39.95 (0-521-49643-8) Cambridge U Pr.
Petersen, Charles G. Compiler Writing Made Easy. 340p. (C). 1988. pap. text ed. 25.00 (0-9631838-9-3) P&M Pub Co.
Petersen, Charles G. & Miller, Nancy E. Move up to Ada. 115p. (C). 1991. pap. text ed. 15.00 (0-9631838-8-5) P&M Pub Co.
Petersen, Charlott H. Natufian Chipped Lithic Assemblage from Sunakh Near Petra, Southern Jordan. (Carsten Niebuhr Institute Publications (CNI): No. 18). (Illus.). 120p. 1994. 45.00 (87-7289-281-1, Pub. by Mus Tusculanum DK) Paul & Co Pubs.
Petersen, Christian. Bread & the British Economy, 1770-1870. Jenkins, Andrew, ed. 1995. 84.95 (1-85928-117-6, Pub. by Scolar Pr UK) Ashgate Pub Co.
Petersen, Christian, jt. auth. see Toop, Alan.
Petersen, Christine E. Doctor in French Drama: 1700-1775. LC 39-2239. reprint ed. 20.00 (0-404-04996-6) AMS Pr.
***Petersen, Christopher, et al.** Learned Helplessness: A Theory for the Age of Personal Control. (Illus.). 384p. 1995. reprint ed. pap. 17.95 (0-19-504467-3) OUP.
Petersen, Dan. Analyzing Safety Performance. LC 83-26610. 328p. 1984. reprint ed. 28.50 (0-913690-08-2) Aloray.
— Human Error Reduction & Safety Management. LC 83-26609. 229p. 1984. reprint ed. 26.50 (0-913690-09-0) Aloray.
— Managing Employee Stress. 192p. 1990. 29.95 (0-913690-21-X) Aloray.
— Safe Behavior Reinforcement. Salo, William G., Jr., ed. LC 88-773. (Illus.). 175p. (Orig.). 1989. pap. 28.50 (0-318-42046-5) Aloray.
— Safety Management: A Human Approach. 2nd ed. LC 88-10544. (Illus.). 380p. 1988. 32.50 (0-913690-12-0) Aloray.
— Techniques of Safety Management: A Systems Approach. 3rd ed. (Illus.). 414p. 1989. text ed. 39.50 (0-913690-14-7) Aloray.
Petersen, Dan, ed. Readings in Behavioral Issues in Safety. 106p. 1985. 10.00 (0-939874-63-6) ASSE.
Petersen, David. The Anasazi. LC 91-3036. (New True Bks.). 48p. (J). (gr. k-4). 1991. lib. bdg. 12.90 (0-516-01121-9); pap. 4.95 (0-516-41121-7) Childrens.
— Apatosaurus. LC 88-37654. (New True Bks.). (Illus.). 48p. (J). (gr. k-4). 1989. pap. 4.95 (0-516-41159-4) Childrens.
— Audio, Video, & Data Telecommunications. LC 92-9766. 1992. write for info. (0-07-707427-0) McGraw.
— Canyonlands National Park. LC 91-35274. (New True Bks.). (Illus.). 48p. (J). (gr. k-4). 1992. lib. bdg. 12.90 (0-516-01132-4); pap. 4.95 (0-516-41132-2) Childrens.
— Carlsbad Caverns National Park. LC 93-36997. (New True Bks.). (Illus.). 48p. (J). (gr. k-4). 1994. lib. bdg. 12.90 (0-516-01051-4) Childrens.
— Carlsbad Caverns National Park. LC 93-36997. (J). (ps-2). 1994. pap. 4.95 (0-516-41051-2) Childrens.
— Dinosaur National Monument. LC 94-35655. (New True Bks.). 48p. (J). (gr. k-4). 1995. lib. bdg. 12.90 (0-516-01074-3) Childrens.
— Ghost Grizzlies. LC 94-39887. 256p. 1995. 27.50 (0-8050-3117-0) H Holt & Co.
— Grand Canyon National Park. LC 92-11343. (New True Book Ser.). (Illus.). 48p. (J). (gr. k-4). 1992. lib. bdg. 12.90 (0-516-02197-4) Childrens.
— Grand Canyon National Park. LC 92-11343. (New True Bks.). (Illus.). 48p. (J). (gr. k-4). 1993. pap. 4.95 (0-516-42197-2) Childrens.
— Grand Teton National Park. LC 92-9209. (New True Bks.). (Illus.). 48p. (J). (gr. k-4). 1992. lib. bdg. 12.90 (0-516-01948-1) Childrens.
— Grand Teton National Park. LC 92-9209. (New True Bks.). (Illus.). 48p. (J). (gr. k-4). 1993. pap. 4.95 (0-516-41948-X) Childrens.
— Great Smoky Mountains National Park. LC 92-35049. (New True Book Ser.). (Illus.). 48p. (J). (gr. k-4). 1993. lib. bdg. 12.90 (0-516-01332-7); pap. 4.95 (0-516-41332-5) Childrens.
— Helicopters. LC 82-23502. (New True Bks.). (Illus.). 48p. (J). (gr. k-4). 1983. lib. bdg. 12.90 (0-516-01680-6) Childrens.
— Ishi: The Last of His People. LC 90-28887. (Picture-Story Biographies Ser.). (Illus.). 32p. (J). (gr. 2-4). 1991. lib. bdg. 11.80 (0-516-04179-7); pap. 3.95 (0-516-44179-5) Childrens.
— Mesa Verde National Park. LC 91-35275. (New True Bks.). (Illus.). 48p. (J). (gr. k-4). 1992. lib. bdg. 12.90 (0-516-01136-7); pap. 4.95 (0-516-41136-5) Childrens.
— Moose. LC 94-10948. (New True Bks.). (Illus.). 48p. (J). (gr. k-4). 1994. lib. bdg. 12.90 (0-516-01069-7); pap. 4.95 (0-516-41069-5) Childrens.
— Mountain Lions. LC 94-36353. (New True Bks.). 48p. (J). (gr. k-4). 1995. lib. bdg. 12.90 (0-516-01077-8) Childrens.
— Racks: The Natural History of Antlers & the Animals That Wear Them. LC 91-11391. (Illus.). 176p. (Orig.). 1991. pap. 12.95 (0-88496-323-3) Capra Pr.
— Rocky Mountain National Park. LC 93-798. (New True Bks.). (Illus.). 48p. (J). (gr. k-4). 1993. lib. bdg. 12.90 (0-516-01196-0); pap. 4.95 (0-516-41196-9) Childrens.
— Sequoyah: Father of the Cherokee Alphabet. LC 91-13313. (Picture-Story Biographies Ser.). 32p. (J). (gr. 2-4). 1991. lib. bdg. 11.85 (0-516-04180-0); pap. 3.95 (0-516-44180-9) Childrens.
— Solar Energy at Work. LC 84-23208. (New True Bks.). (Illus.). 48p. (J). (gr. k-4). 1985. lib. bdg. 12.90 (0-516-01942-2) Childrens.
— Submarines. LC 83-26253. (New True Bks.). (Illus.). 48p. (J). (gr. k-4). 1984. lib. bdg. 12.85 (0-516-01728-4) Childrens.
— Tyrannosaurus Rex. LC 88-38054. (New True Bks.). (Illus.). 48p. (J). (gr. k-4). 1989. lib. bdg. 12.90 (0-516-01167-7); pap. 4.95 (0-516-41167-5) Childrens.
— Waterton - Glacier International Peace Park. LC 92-9208. (New True Bks.). (Illus.). 48p. (J). (gr. k-4). 1992. lib. bdg. 12.90 (0-516-01946-5) Childrens.
— Waterton-Glacier International Peace Park. LC 92-9208. (New True Bks.). (Illus.). 48p. (J). (gr. k-4). 1993. pap. 4.95 (0-516-41946-3) Childrens.
— Yellowstone National Park. LC 91-37292. (New True Bks.). (Illus.). 48p. (J). (gr. k-4). 1992. lib. bdg. 12.90 (0-516-01148-0); pap. 4.95 (0-516-41148-9) Childrens.
— Yosemite National Park. LC 92-39156. (New True Bks.). (Illus.). 48p. (J). (gr. k-4). 1993. lib. bdg. 12.90 (0-516-01335-1); pap. 4.95 (0-516-41335-X) Childrens.
— Zion National Park. LC 92-35048. (New True Book Ser.). (Illus.). 48p. (J). (gr. k-4). 1993. lib. bdg. 12.90 (0-516-01336-X); pap. 4.95 (0-516-41336-8) Childrens.
Petersen, David & Coburn, Mark. Meriwether Lewis & William Clark: Soldiers, Explorers, & Partners in History. LC 88-14040. (People of Distinction Ser.). (Illus.). 152p. (J). (gr. 4 up). 1988. lib. bdg. 14.40 (0-516-03264-X) Childrens.
Petersen, David C. Convention Centers, Stadiums, & Arenas. LC 89-50266. 168p. (Orig.). 1989. pap. text ed. 53.95 (0-87420-679-0, C37) Urban Land.
Petersen, David L. Haggai & Zechariah 1-8, a Commentary. LC 84-7477. (Old Testament Library). 320p. 1984. 25.00 (0-664-21830-X, Westminster) Westminster John Knox.
— Zechariah 9-14 & Malachi: A Commentary. LC 94-43410. (Old Testament Library). 272p. 1995. 18.00 (0-664-21298-0) Westminster John Knox.
Petersen, David L., ed. Prophecy in Israel: Search for an Identity. LC 85-45584. (Issues in Religion & Theology Ser.). 176p. 1986. pap. 14.00 (0-8006-1773-8, 1-1773, Fortress Pr) Augsburg Fortress.
Petersen, David L. & Richards, Kent H. Interpreting Hebrew Poetry. LC 92-7934. 112p. 1992. pap. 9.00 (0-8006-2625-7, 1-2625, Fortress Pr) Augsburg Fortress.
Petersen, David M., jt. auth. see Bordner, Diane C.
Petersen, David M., jt. auth. see Thomas, Charles W.
Petersen, Dorothy G. Accrediting Standards & Guidelines: A Current Profile. 168p. 1979. 8.25 (0-318-13851-4) Coun Postsecondary Accredit.
Petersen-Dyggve, Holger N. Chansons Francaises du Treizieme Siecle. LC 80-2167. 1981. 29.50 (0-404-19030-8) AMS Pr.
— Personnages Historiques Figurant Dans la Poesie Lyrique Francaise Des XII et XIIIe Siecles. LC 80-2166. 1981. 67.50 (0-404-19031-6) AMS Pr.
Petersen-Dyggve, Holgern. Trouveres et Protecteurs De Trouveres Dans les Cours Seigneuriales De France. LC 80-2168. reprint ed. 41.50 (0-404-19032-4) AMS Pr.
Petersen, Elizabeth. Maze: How Not to Go into Business. LC 82-62505. 160p. (Orig.). 1983. 14.95 (0-9610200-0-8); pap. 9.95 (0-9610200-1-6) MEDA Pubns.
Petersen, Emma M. Book of Mormon Stories for Young LDS. (J). 9.95 (0-88494-019-5) Bookcraft Inc.
***Petersen, Eugene E.** The Modern Cynic: To Be or Not To Be. LC 94-77719. 104p. 1995. lib. bdg. write for info. (0-9642614-2-1) Knoll Pubs.
Petersen, Eugene E., jt. auth. see Butt, John B.
Petersen, Eugene P. Window in the Rock. LC 93-7109. 1993. 22.50 (0-87770-515-1); pap. 14.95 (0-685-66424-4) Ye Galleon.
Petersen, Eugene T. Mackinac & the Porcelain City. (Illus.). 40p. (Orig.). 1985. pap. 5.00 (0-911872-53-1) Mackinac Island.
— Mackinac Island: Its History in Pictures. LC 74-17184. (Illus.). 103p. (Orig.). 1973. 18.00 (0-911872-13-2) Mackinac Island.
Petersen, Evelyn & Petersen, J. Allan. For Women Only. pap. 5.99 (0-8423-0896-2) Tyndale.

PQ

An Asterisk (*) at the beginning of an entry indicates that the title is appearing in BIP for the first time.

— For Women Only. 1972. pap. 5.99 (*0-8423-0897-0*) Tyndale.

Petersen-Fleming, Judy & Fleming, Bill. Kitten Care & Critters, Too! LC 93-24200. (Illus.). 40p. (J). 1994. 15.00 (*0-688-12563-8*, Tambourine Bks); lib. bdg. 14.93 (*0-688-12564-6*, Tambourine Bks) Morrow.

— Puppy Care & Critters, Too! LC 93-23129. (Illus.). 40p. (J). 1993. 15.00 (*0-688-12565-4*, Tambourine Bks); lib. bdg. 14.93 (*0-688-12566-2*, Tambourine Bks) Morrow.

Petersen-Fleming, Judy, jt. auth. see Fleming, Bill.

Petersen, G. W., jt. auth. see Reybold, W. U.

Petersen, Gary W. & Beatty, Marvin T., eds. Planning Future Land Uses. (ASA Special Publication Ser.). 71p. (C). 1981. pap. 5.50 (*0-89118-067-2*) Am Soc Agron.

Petersen, George & Oppenheimer, Steve. Electronic Musician's Tech Terms: A Practical Dictionary for Audio & Music Production. 56p. 1993. pap. 9.95 (*0-7935-1989-6*, 00183017) H Leonard.

Petersen, George L., et al, eds. Valuing Wildlife Resources in Alaska. 357p. (C). 1991. pap. text ed. 51.00 (*0-8133-8299-8*) Westview.

Petersen, Gerald W. Life in a Mexican Town. (Illus.). 96p. (ENG & SPA.). 1992. pap. 8.65 (*0-8442-7639-1*, Passport Bks) NTC Pub Grp.

Petersen, Grant & Anderson, Mary. Roads to Ride: A Bicyclist's Topographic Guide to Alameda, Contra Costa, & Marin Counties. LC 83-80352. (Illus.). 142p. 1984. pap. 8.95 (*0-930588-07-X*) Heyday Bks.

Petersen, Grant & Kluge, John. Roads to Ride, South: A Bicyclist's Topographic Guide to San Mateo, Santa Clara, & Santa Cruz Counties. LC 84-82439. (Illus.). 160p. 1985. pap. 7.95 (*0-930588-17-7*) Heyday Bks.

Petersen, Grant, et al. Roads to Ride: A Bicyclists' Topographic Guide to Alameda, Contra Costa, & Marin Counties California Bicycling Guides, No. 1. 1991. reprint ed. lib. bdg. 25.00x (*0-8095-4969-7*) Borgo Pr.

— Roads to Ride South: A Bicyclists' Topographic Guide to San Mateo, Santa Clara, & Santa Cruz Counties. (California Bicycling Guide Ser.: No. 2). (Illus.). 1991. reprint ed. lib. bdg. 25.00x (*0-8095-4970-0*) Borgo Pr.

Petersen, Gwen. Yellowstone Pioneers: The Story of Hamilton Stores & Yellowstone National Park. Davis, Linda S., ed. LC 85-50965. (Illus.). 120p. 1989. pap. 9.95 (*0-917859-23-5*) Sunrise SBCA.

***Petersen, Gwen, et al, eds.** Ten Years' Gatherings, Montana Poems & Stories. (Illus.). 192p. (Orig.). 1995. 22.95 (*1-887477-01-2*); pap. 14.95 (*1-887477-02-0*) Ranch Cntry.

Petersen, Gwenn B. The Moon in the Water: Understanding Tanizaki, Kawabata, & Mishima. LC 79-14994. 380p. (C). 1993. reprint ed. pap. text ed. 18.50 (*0-8248-1476-2*) UH Pr.

Petersen, H. Craig. Business & Government. 3rd ed. 560p. (C). 1990. text ed. 39.00 (*0-06-045157-2*) HarpCollege.

— Business & Government. 4th ed. LC 92-11252. (C). 1992. 63.00 (*0-06-501101-5*) HarpCollege.

***Petersen, Hanne & Zahle, Henrik, eds.** Legal Polycentricity: Consequences of Pluralism in Law. (Illus.). 260p. 1995. text ed. 59.95 (*1-85521-662-0*) Ashgate Pub Co.

Petersen, Ingemar, jt. ed. see Kellaway, Peter.

Petersen, J. Allan. Before You Marry. 1974. pap. 4.99 (*0-8423-0104-6*) Tyndale.

— For Men Only. 1982. pap. 4.99 (*0-8423-0892-X*) Tyndale.

— The Myth of the Greener Grass. rev. ed. 222p. 1991. pap. 8.99 (*0-8423-4651-1*) Tyndale.

Petersen, J. Allan, jt. auth. see Petersen, Evelyn.

Petersen, J. L., jt. ed. see Di Vecchia, P.

Petersen, Jack & Petersen, Ruby. The Twelve Years - First & Last. LC 87-81107. (Illus.). 100p. 1987. lib. bdg. 50.00 (*0-87208-203-2*) Island Pr Pubs.

Petersen, James B. Archaeological Testing at the Sharrow Site: A Deeply Stratified Early to Late Holocene Cultural Sequence in Central Maine. (Occasional Publications in Maine Archaeology). (Illus.). 165p. (C). 1991. pap. text ed. 15.00 (*0-935447-08-3*) ME Hist Preserv.

Petersen, James B., ed. Ceramic Analysis in the Northeast Part 11: Contribution to Methodology & Culture History. (Occasional Publications in Northeastern Anthropology: No. 9). (Illus.). 159p. 15.00 (*0-318-23458-0*) F Pierce College.

Petersen, James C., ed. Citizen Participation in Science Policy. LC 84-246. 256p. 1984. lib. bdg. 30.00x (*0-87023-433-1*); pap. 16.95x (*0-87023-434-X*) U of Mass Pr.

Petersen, Jim. Church Without Walls: Moving Beyond Traditional Boundaries. LC 91-67292. 240p. (Orig.). 1991. pap. 10.00 (*0-89109-663-9*) NavPress.

— Evangelism As a Lifestyle: Evangelizacion--Un Estilo de Vida. Armengol, Norma C., tr. (Orig.). (SPA.). 1989. pap. 4.75 (*0-311-13849-7*) Casa Bautista.

— Lifestyle Discipleship: The Challenge of Following Jesus in Today's World. LC 93-39063. 192p. (Orig.). 1994. pap. 10.00 (*0-89109-775-9*, NavPr) NavPress.

— Living Proof: Sharing the Gospel Naturally. rev. ed. LC 88-63874. 252p. 1989. pap. 10.00 (*0-89109-561-6*) NavPress.

Petersen, John E., jt. auth. see Twentieth Century Fund, Task Force on Municipal Bond Credit Ratings Staff.

***Petersen-Jones, Simon M. & Crispin, Sheila M., eds.** Manual of Small Animal Ophthalmology. (Illus.). 304p. 1995. pap. 69.95 (*0-905214-21-8*) Iowa St U Pr.

Petersen, Julius, jt. auth. see Hecker, Max.

Petersen, K., jt. auth. see Lerche, I.

***Petersen, Karen D., contrib.** American Pictographic Images: Historical Works on Paper by Plains Indians. (Illus.). 176p. 1988. 45.00 (*0-614-04592-4*) Morning Star Gal.

Petersen, Karl. Ergodic Theory. (Illus.). 352p. (C). 1990. pap. 37.95 (*0-521-38997-6*) Cambridge U Pr.

***Petersen, Karl E. & Salama, Ibrahim A., eds.** Ergodic Theory & Its Connections with Harmonic Analysis: Proceedings of the 1993 Alexandria Conference. (London Mathematical Society Lecture Note: 205). 448p. (C). 1995. 37.95 (*0-521-45999-0*) Cambridge U Pr.

Petersen, Kate O. On the Sources of the Nonne Prestes Tale. 144p. (C). 1966. text ed. 75.00 (*0-8383-0673-X*) M S G Haskell Hse.

— Sources of the Parson's Tale. LC 72-954. reprint ed. 27.50 (*0-404-04997-4*) AMS Pr.

Petersen, Kathy, ed. Oil Shale: The Environmental Challenges III. (Proceedings of an International Symposium Ser.: No III). (Illus.). 261p. 1983. text ed. 11.00 (*0-918062-54-3*) Colo Sch Mines.

Petersen, Kathy K., jt. ed. see Chappell, Willard R.

Petersen, Keith. Historical Celebrations: A Handbook for Organizers of Diamond Jubilees, Centennials, & Other Community Anniveraries. 142p. 9.95 (*0-685-62671-7*) U of Idaho Pr.

— River of Life, Channel of Death. 250p. (Orig.). 1995. pap. 20.00 (*1-881090-17-5*) Confluence Pr.

Petersen, Keith & Rikoon, J. Sanford. Historic Celebrations: A Handbook for Organizers of Diamond Jubilees, Centennials & Other Community Celebrations. (Illus.). xxiv, 118p. (Orig.). 1986. pap. 10.00 (*0-317-54344-X*) Idaho State Soc.

Petersen, Keith C. Company Town: Potlatch, Idaho, & the Potlatch Lumber Company. LC 87-14980. (Illus.). 284p. (C). 1987. pap. 15.95 (*0-87422-037-8*) Wash St U Pr.

Petersen, Keith C. & Reed, Mary E. Discovering Washington: A Guide to State & Local History. LC 89-5575. (Illus.). 87p. 1989. pap. 7.50 (*0-87422-059-9*) Wash St U Pr.

Petersen, Ken. Choice Adventures: Quarterback Sneak. 160p. (J). (gr. 4-8). 1992. pap. 4.99 (*0-8423-5029-2*) Tyndale.

Petersen, Kenneth, jt. auth. see Lerche, Ian.

***Petersen, Kerry, ed.** Law & Medicine: A Special Issue of Law in Context. Date not set. pap. 19.95 (*1-86324-025-X*, Pub. by LaTrobe Univ AT) Intl Spec Bk.

Petersen, Kerry A. Abortion Regimes. (Medico-Legal Issues Ser.). 201p. 1993. 59.95 (*1-85521-159-9*, Pub. by Dartmth Pub UK) Ashgate Pub Co.

Petersen, Kirsten H., ed. Criticism & Ideology: Second African Writers' Conference, Stockholm, 1986. (Scandinavian Institute of African Studies: No. 20). 223p. 1988. 58.00x (*91-7106-276-9*, Pub. by Nordisk Afrikainstitutet SW) Coronet Bks.

Petersen, Kirsten Holst. Religion, Developement & African Identity, No. 17. (Scandinavian Institute of African Studies). 163p. 1987. text ed. 46.00x (*91-7106-263-7*, Pub. by Nordisk Afrikainstitutet SW) Coronet Bks.

Petersen, Kristen A. & Murphy, Thomas J. Waltham Rediscovered: An Ethnic History of Waltham, MA. (Illus.). 688p. 1988. 30.00 (*0-914339-26-5*) P E Randall Pub.

Petersen, Kurt. The Maquiladora Revolution in Guatemala. LC 92-23067. (Occasional Paper Ser.: Vol. 2). xvi, 244p. (Orig.). (C). 1992. pap. text ed. 7.95 (*1-881862-00-3*) O H Schell Yale Law Schl.

Petersen, Kurt E., ed. Safety & Reliability, 1992. LC 92-16752. 1992. write for info. (*1-85166-875-6*, Pub. by Elsevier Applied Sci UK) Elsevier.

Petersen, Lance W. The Kenai Peninsula College History. 118p. 1992. pap. 5.00 (*0-9641118-0-2*, KPC Pubs) Kenai Peninsula.

Petersen, Laura M. & Lowry, Thea S., eds. A Man of Letters: Montgomery Remembered. LC 93-71932. 125p. (Orig.). 1993. pap. 15.00 (*0-685-67840-7*) Fels & Firn.

Petersen, Lindy & Gannoni, Anne F. Manual for Social Skills Training in Young People with Parent & Teacher Programmes. (C). 1990. 150.00 (*0-86431-116-8*, Pub. by Aust Council Educ Res AT) St Mut.

— Teachers Manual for Training Social Skills While Managing Student Behavior. (C). 1990. 150.00 (*0-86431-117-6*, Pub. by Aust Council Educ Res AT) St Mut.

Petersen, Liz, jt. auth. see Lorentzen, Bob.

Petersen, Marie, jt. auth. see Mueller-Joseph, Laura.

Petersen, Marilyn D. & White, Diana L., eds. Health Care of the Elderly: An Information Sourcebook. 560p. (C). 1989. text ed. 69.95 (*0-8039-3335-5*) Sage.

***Petersen, Marjorie.** Red Sky at Night: Circling the Pacific in Stornoway. LC 94-67446. (Illus.). (Orig.). 1994. pap. 12.95 (*0-9642394-1-8*) Paxi Press.

Petersen, Michael, jt. auth. see Jonsson, Gunilla.

Petersen, Monique, jt. auth. see Klivans, Richard.

Petersen, Morris & Rigby, J. Keith. Interpreting Earth History: A Manual in Historical Geology. 5th ed. 240p. (C). 1993. spiral bd. 34.07 (*0-697-10171-1*) Wm C Brown Pubs.

Petersen, Morris S., et al. Historical Geology - North America. 2nd ed. 240p. (C). 1980. pap. write for info. (*0-697-05062-9*) Wm C Brown Pubs.

Petersen, N. V., ed. Space Rendezvous, Rescue, Recovery, 2 Vols, Pt. 1. (Advances in the Astronautical Sciences Ser.: Vol. 16). 1963. 45.00 (*0-87703-017-0*, Pub. by Am Astro Soc) Univelt Inc.

— Space Rendezvous, Rescue, Recovery, 2 Vols, Pt. 2. (Advances in the Astronautical Sciences Ser.: Vol. 16). 1963. 30.00 (*0-87703-018-9*, Pub. by Am Astro Soc) Univelt Inc.

Petersen, Neal H. American Intelligence, 1775-1990: A Bibliographical Guide. LC 92-16324. (New War - Peace Bibliographical Ser.: Vol. 2). 1992. 49.95 (*0-941690-45-8*) Regina Bks.

Petersen, Niels E., jt. auth. see Jensen, Finn.

Petersen, Nis. Whistlers in the Night: And Other Verse by Nis Petersen. Sorensen, Otto M., tr. LC 82-62386. Orig. Title: Nis Petersen, Samlede Digte. (Illus.). 94p. 1983. 9.95 (*0-933748-04-3*) Nordic Bks.

Petersen, Norman R. Gospel of John & the Sociology of Light: Language & Characterization in the Fourth Gospel. LC 93-2446. 176p. (Orig.). 1993. pap. 15.00 (*1-56338-070-6*) TPI PA.

Petersen, P. J. The Amazing Magic Show. LC 93-34861. (J). 1994. 14.00 (*0-671-86581-1*, S&S Bks Young Read) S&S Childrens.

— The Fireplug Is First Base. LC 92-18956. (Speedsters Ser.). (Illus.). 64p. (J). (gr. 2-5). 1992. pap. 3.99 (*0-14-036165-0*) Puffin Bks.

— I Hate Camping. LC 90-39650. (Illus.). 80p. (J). (gr. 4-7). 1991. 13.00 (*0-525-44673-7*, DCB) Dutton Child Bks.

— I Hate Camping. (Illus.). 96p. (J). (gr. 2-5). 1993. pap. 3.99 (*0-14-036446-3*, Puffin) Puffin Bks.

— I Hate Company. LC 94-2801. (Illus.). 48p. (J). (gr. 2-4). 1994. 12.99 (*0-525-45329-6*, DCB) Dutton Child Bks.

— I Want Answers & a Parachute. LC 92-38262. (YA). (gr. 6 up). 1993. pap. 13.00 (*0-671-86577-3*, S&S Bks Young Read) S&S Childrens.

— Liars. LC 91-28490. 176p. (J). (gr. 5-9). 1992. pap. 15.00 (*0-671-75035-6*, S&S Bks Young Read) S&S Childrens.

— The Sub. LC 92-22269. (Illus.). (J). (gr. 2-5). 1993. 12.99 (*0-525-45059-9*, DCB) Dutton Child Bks.

Petersen, P. S. & Westarp, K. H., eds. British Drama in the Eighties: Texts & Contexts. (Dolphin Ser.: No. 14). 218p. (Orig.). 1986. pap. 29.50 (*0-685-33598-4*, Pub. by Aarhus Univ Pr DK) Coronet Bks.

Petersen, Palle. Inunguak: The Little Greenlander. LC 90-40472. 32p. (J). (gr. 4-7). 1993. 14.00 (*0-688-09876-2*) Lothrop.

— Inunguak: The Little Greenlander. LC 90-40472. (J). (ps-3). 1993. 13.95 (*0-688-09877-0*) Lothrop.

Petersen, Paul, jt. auth. see Hawkins, Jimmy.

Petersen, Paulann. The Animal Bride: Poems by Paulann Petersen. 35p. (Orig.). pap. 7.00 (*0-932264-05-0*) Trask Hse Bks.

Petersen, Per S., ed. Literary Pedagogics after Deconstruction: Scenarios & Perspectives in the Teaching of English Literature. (Dolphin Ser.: No. 22). 110p. (Orig.). 1992. pap. 37.50 (*87-7288-372-3*, Pub. by Aarhus Univ Pr DK) Coronet Bks.

Petersen, Peter L. The Danes in America. (In America Bks.). (Illus.). 96p. (YA). (gr. 5 up). 1987. lib. bdg. 17.50 (*0-8225-0233-X*, Lerner Publctns); pap. 5.95 (*0-8225-1031-6*, Lerner Publctns) Lerner Group.

Petersen, Phil. Good If Not Great Travel with Oxygen. Lee, Mary & Paisley, Pam, eds. 42p. (Orig.). 1993. pap. 5.95 (*0-9621726-2-6*) Raven Pubs.

Petersen, Philip R. Arctic Roads & Summer Sun: (For Older Travelers) (Illus.). 100p. (Orig.). 1988. pap. 14.50 (*0-9621726-0-X*) Raven Pubs.

— Arctic Roads & Summer Sun: Business Supplement. rev. ed. LC 89-831737. (Illus.). 108p. 1990. pap. 9.95 (*0-9621726-1-8*) Raven Pubs.

Petersen, R., jt. auth. see Olgaard, P. L.

Petersen, R. H. A Monograph of Ramaria Subgenus Echinoramaria. (Bibliotheca Mycologica Ser.: No. 79). (Illus.). 150p. 1981. lib. bdg. 48.00 (*3-7682-1290-4*) Lubrecht & Cramer.

— Ramaria, Subgenus Lentoramaria, with Emphasis on North American Taxa. (Bibliotheca Mycologica Ser.: No. 43). 1975. text ed. 30.00 (*3-7682-0961-X*) Lubrecht & Cramer.

Petersen, Randy. Choice Adventure: Appalachian Ambush, No. 15. LC 93-40183. (J). 1994. 4.99 (*0-8423-5133-7*) Tyndale.

— Complete Book of Bible Puzzles, No. 1. 1992. pap. 7.99 (*0-8423-1067-3*) Tyndale.

— Complete Book of Bible Puzzles, No. 2. 1992. pap. 7.99 (*0-8423-1079-7*) Tyndale.

— Family Book of Bible Fun. 1994. pap. 9.99 (*0-8423-1246-3*) Tyndale.

— Fear Not! Be Outrageously Courageous Student Journal. (1995 50-Day Spiritual Adventure Ser.). (Illus.). 80p. (Orig.). (YA). (gr. 7-12). 1994. student ed, pap. text ed. 4.95 (*1-879050-48-X*) Chapel of Air.

— 50 Days to Welcome Christ to Our Church: Youth Journal for the 50-Day Adventure Series. (1991 50-Day Spiritual Adventure Ser.). (Illus.). 64p. (Orig.). (YA). (gr. 7-12). 1990. student ed, pap. text ed. 3.95 (*1-879050-01-3*) Chapel of Air.

— Getting It Together: How to Energize Your Relationships with Other Believers. (1992 50-Day Spiritual Adventure Ser.). (Illus.). 64p. (Orig.). (YA). (gr. 7-12). 1991. student ed, pap. text ed. 4.95 (*1-879050-04-8*) Chapel of Air.

— The Official Frequent Flyer Guidebook. 3rd ed. 495p. (Orig.). 1994. pap. 14.99 (*1-882994-01-9*) AirPress.

— The Official Frequent Flyer Guidebook. 4th ed. 500p. (Orig.). 1995. pap. 14.99 (*1-882994-02-7*) AirPress.

— Survival Skills: Living Strong As a Christian When Times Get Tough. (1993 50-Day Spiritual Adventure Ser.). (Illus.). 64p. (Orig.). (YA). (gr. 7-12). 1992. student ed, pap. text ed. 4.99 (*1-879050-08-0*) Chapel of Air.

***Petersen, Randy & Emmert, Byron.** Beyond Your Wildest Dreams: Daring to Risk with God Student Journal. (1994 50-Day Spiritual Adventure Ser.). (Illus.). 80p. (Orig.). (YA). (gr. 7-12). 1993. student ed, pap. text ed. 4.99 (*1-879050-15-3*) Chapel of Air.

Petersen, Randy, jt. auth. see Matias, Tito.

Petersen, Randy, jt. auth. see Petersen, William J.

Petersen, Randy, ed. see Spurgeon, Charles H.

Petersen, Randy, jt. auth. see Whiteman, Thomas.

***Petersen, Ray.** Consumer Health Decisions. (Health Science Ser.). 512p. 1996. pap. 37.50 (*0-86720-936-4*) Jones & Bartlett.

— Health Issues for Secondary Teachers. 528p. (C). 1991. per. 23.95 (*0-8403-8398-3*) Kendall-Hunt.

Petersen, Renee, jt. auth. see Petersen, William.

Petersen, Richard. Introductory C: Pointers, Functions, & Files. (Illus.). 595p. 1992. pap. text ed. 34.95 (*0-12-552140-5*) Acad Pr.

— The Lost Cities of Cibola. 1985. 22.50 (*0-9616717-0-X*) G & H Bks.

Petersen, Robert & Freedland, Jerold. Advising California Partners & Sole Proprietors. 1992. write for info. (*0-318-69517-0*) Bender.

***Petersen, Robert A. & Curammeng, Jose, Jr.** California Tax Handbook, 1995. rev. ed. 944p. 1994. pap. text ed. 24.95 (*0-7811-0093-3*) Res Inst Am.

Petersen, Robert A. & Plant, Philip. California Taxation, 6 vols. 1983. Including updating service. ring bd. write for info. (*0-8205-1151-X*, 151) Bender.

Petersen, Robert C. Childhood & Adolescent Drug Abuse: A Physicians Guide to Office Practice. rev. ed. LC 87-70131. 55p. 1991. pap. 3.00 (*0-942348-20-6*) Am Council Drug Ed.

Petersen, Robert M. Alleys of the Heart. 130p. 1988. 16.95 (*0-938493-11-6*) Hulogosi Inc.

Petersen, Robert P., jt. ed. see Licata, Salvatore J.

Petersen, Rodney L. Preaching in the Last Days: The Theme of "Two Witnesses" in the Sixteenth & Seventeenth Centuries. LC 92-27964. 336p. 1993. 49.95 (*0-19-507374-6*) OUP.

Petersen, Roger K., jt. auth. see Burr, Carole R.

Petersen, Ronald C., jt. ed. see Yanagihara, Takehiko.

Petersen, Ronald H. B & C: Mycological Association of M. J. Berkeley & M. A. Curtis. (Bibliotheca Mycologica Ser.: No. 72). (Illus.). 120p. 1980. pap. text ed. 19.60 (*3-7682-1258-0*) Lubrecht & Cramer.

— The Clavarioid Fungi of New Zealand. (Illus.). 170p. 1988. pap. 65.00 (*0-477-02514-5*) Lubrecht & Cramer.

— The Genus Clavulinopsis in North America. (Mycologia Memoirs Ser.: No. 3). (Illus.). 39p. 1968. pap. text ed. 12.50 (*0-945345-38-0*) Lubrecht & Cramer.

Petersen, Ronald H., ed. Evolution in the Higher Basidiomycetes: An International Symposium. LC 73-100410. 592p. reprint ed. pap. 168.80 (*0-317-29306-0*, 2022221) Bks Demand.

Petersen, Ruby, jt. auth. see Petersen, Jack.

Petersen, Sandy. Peterson's Field Guide to Creatures of the Dreamland. 1989. pap. 15.95 (*0-933635-53-2*) Chaosium.

Petersen, Sandy, ed. see Barton, William A.

Petersen, Sandy, ed. see Hargrave, et al.

Petersen, Sandy, ed. see Herber, Keith.

Petersen, Sandy, ed. see Love, Penelope, et al.

Petersen, Sandy, et al. Cthulhu Classics: A Full-Length Campaign & Five Adventures. Dunn, Willam G. et al, eds. (Call of Cthulhu Roleplaying Game System Ser.). (Illus.). 152p. (Orig.). 1989. pap. 18.95 (*0-933635-61-3*, 3301) Chaosium.

— Dreamland: Cthulhu Roleplaying Beyond the Wall of Sleep. 2nd ed. Shirley, Sam, ed. (Call of Cthulhu Roleplaying Game System Ser.). (Illus.). 128p. 1992. pap. text ed. 18.95 (*0-933635-97-4*) Chaosium.

Petersen, Sheila. A Special Way to Care: A Guide for Neighbors, Friends, & Community in their Efforts to Provide Financial & Emotional Support for Terminally & Catastrophically Ill Children. 180p. (Orig.). 1988. pap. write for info. (*0-9619785-0-3*) Friends Karen.

Petersen, Steffen B., jt. ed. see Woolley, Paul.

Petersen, Stephanie, jt. auth. see Parente, Diane.

Petersen, Suni & Straub, Ronald. School Crisis Survival Guide: Management Techniques & Materials for Counselors & Administrators. 256p. 1991. spiral bd. 34.95 (*0-87628-806-9*) Ctr Appl Res.

Petersen, Suni, jt. auth. see Wiggins, Frances K.

Petersen, Svend & Filler, Louis. A Statistical History of the American Presidential Elections: With Supplementary Tables Covering 1968 to 1980. LC 81-6348. xxiii, 275p. 1981. reprint ed. text ed. 41.50 (*0-313-22952-X*, PESH, Greenwood Pr) Greenwood.

Petersen, Thor. Using the IBM PC-AT. (Illus.). 144p. 1987. 17.95 (*0-13-939471-0*) P-H.

Petersen, Toni & Molholt, Pat, eds. Beyond the Book: Extending MARC for Subject Access. (Professional Librarian Ser.). 230p. 1990. text ed. 39.95 (*0-8161-1924-4*, Hall Reference); pap. 27.50 (*0-8161-1925-2*, Hall Reference) Macmillan.

Petersen, Ulrich, jt. auth. see Holland, Heinrich D.

Petersen, Verlyn M. & Ambruso, Daniel R. Phagocyte Immunomodulation after Thermal Injury. LC 94-9517. (Medical Intelligence Unit Ser.). 1994. 89.95 (*1-879702-57-6*) R G Landes.

Petersen, Vibeke R. Kursbuch Nineteen Sixty-Five to Nineteen Seventy-Five: Social, Political & Literary Perspectives of West Germany. (Illus.). 205p. (C). 1988. text ed. 35.00 (*0-8204-0737-2*) P Lang Pubs.

Petersen, W. The Politics of Population. 11.25 (*0-8446-0845-9*) Peter Smith.

Petersen, W., jt. auth. see Buck, Carl D.

Petersen, Wayne R. The Audubon Society Pocket Guide to North American SongBirds & Familiar Backyard Birds: Eastern Region. LC 93-21254. (Audubon Society Pocket Guides Ser.). (Illus.). 1994. 9.00 (*0-679-74926-8*) Knopf.

Petersen, Wayne R., jt. auth. see Veit, Richard R.

Petersen, William. Astrologia y Biblia: Astrology & the Bible. (SPA.). 2.95 (*84-7228-232-5*, 220050, Pub. by Edit Clie SP) TSELF.

— Malthus. LC 78-31479. 308p. reprint ed. pap. 89.00 (*0-7837-2311-3*, 2057399) Bks Demand.

— Masonic Quiz. 17.95 (*0-685-22032-X*) Wehman.

Petersen, William, ed. Gospel Traditions in the Second Century: Origins, Recension, Text, & Transmission. LC 89-27807. (Christianity & Judaism in Antiquity Ser.: Vol. 3). 192p. (C). 1990. text ed. 21.95 (*0-268-01022-6*) U of Notre Dame Pr.

An Asterisk (*) at the beginning of an entry indicates that the title is appearing in BIP for the first time.

Petersen, William & Petersen, Renee. Dictionary of Demography: Biographies, 2 vols., 1. LC 83-12567. xx, 1365p. 1985. text ed. 195.00 (*0-313-25137-1*, PDD/01) Greenwood.

— Dictionary of Demography: Biographies, 2 vols., Set. LC 83-12567. xx, 1365p. 1985. text ed. 195.00 (*0-313-21419-0*, PDD/) Greenwood.

— Dictionary of Demography: Biographies, 2 vols., Vol. 2. LC 83-12567. xx, 1365p. 1985. text ed. 195.00 (*0-313-25138-X*, PDD/02) Greenwood.

— Dictionary of Demography: Multilingual Glossary. LC 85-27055. vi, 259p. 1985. text ed. 150.00 (*0-313-25139-8*, PDG/, Greenwood Pr) Greenwood.

— Dictionary of Demography: Terms, Concepts, & Institutions, 2 vols., 1. LC 83-12571. (Illus.). 1772p. 1986. text ed. 125.00 (*0-313-25141-X*, PDE/01) Greenwood.

— Dictionary of Demography: Terms, Concepts, & Institutions, 2 vols., Set. LC 83-12571. (Illus.). 1772p. 1986. text ed. 195.00 (*0-313-24134-1*, PDE/) Greenwood.

— Dictionary of Demography: Terms, Concepts, & Institutions, 2 vols., Vol. 2. LC 83-12571. (Illus.). 1772p. 1986. text ed. 125.00 (*0-313-25142-8*, PDE/02) Greenwood.

Petersen, William, et al. Concepts of Ethnicity. (Dimensions of Ethnicity Ser.). 160p. 1982. pap. 10.50 (*0-674-15726-5*) HUP.

Petersen, William J. O Discipulado de Timoteo. Orig. Title: The Discipling of Timothy. 192p. (POR.). 1986. 4.95 (*0-8297-0685-2*) Life Pubs Intl.

***Petersen, William J. & Petersen, Randy.** The One Year Book of Hymns. Brown, Robert K. & Norton, Mark R., eds. LC 94-43726. 1995. pap. write for info. (*0-8423-5072-1*) Tyndale.

Petersen, William J., ed. see Maclaren, Alexander.

Petersen, William J., ed. see Stalker, James.

***Petersen, William L.** Tatian's Diatessaron: Its Creation, Dissemination, Significance, & History in Scholarship. LC 94-2883. (Supplements to Vigiliae Christianae Ser.: Vol. 25). 1994. 125.75 (*90-04-09469-5*) E J Brill.

Petersham, Maud & Petersham, Miska. Circus Baby. LC 50-9295. (Illus.). 32p. (J). (ps-1). 1968. 13.95 (*0-02-771670-8*, Mac Bks Young Read) S&S Childrens.

— The Circus Baby. LC 88-7369. (Illus.). 32p. (J). (ps-1). 1989. reprint ed. pap. 3.95 (*0-689-71295-2*, Aladdin Paperbacks) S&S Childrens.

— The Rooster Crows: A Book of American Rhymes & Jingles. LC 46-446. (Illus.). 64p. (J). (ps-2). 1969. text ed. 14.95 (*0-02-773100-6*, Mac Bks Young Read) S&S Childrens.

— The Rooster Crows: A Book of American Rhymes & Jingles. LC 87-1138. (Illus.). 64p. (J). (ps-3). 1987. reprint ed. pap. 5.95 (*0-689-71153-0*, Aladdin Paperbacks) S&S Childrens.

Petersham, Miska, jt. auth. see Petersham, Maud.

Petersilia, Joan. Racial Disparities in the Criminal Justice System. LC 83-9777. 128p. 1983. 10.00 (*0-8330-0506-5*, R-2947) Rand Corp.

Petersilia, Joan, jt. auth. see Wilson, James Q.

Petersilia, Joan, et al. Prison vs. Probation in California: Implications for Crime & Offender Recidivism. 63p. 1986. 7.50 (*0-8330-0738-6*, R-3323) Rand Corp.

Petersmann, Ernest-Ulrich & Hilf, Meinhard, eds. The New Gatt Round of Multilateral Trade Negotiations: Legal & Economic Problems. 598p. 1989. 144.00 (*90-6544-365-7*) Kluwer Ac.

Petersmann, Ernst-Ulrich. The GATT World Trade & Legal System after the Uruguay Round. 250p. Date not set. 75.00 (*0-929179-41-2*) Transnatl Juris Pubns.

Petersmann, Ernst-Ulrich & Hilf, Meinhard, eds. The New GATT Round of Multilateral Trade Negotiations: Legal & Economic Problems. 2nd rev. ed. (Studies in Transnational Economic Law: Vol. V). 648p. 1991. 168.00 (*90-6544-518-8*) Kluwer Law Tax Pubns.

Petersmann, Ernst-Ulrich, jt. ed. see Hilf, Meinhard.

***Peterson.** Alberto Moravia. 1995. 26.95 (*0-8057-8296-6*, Twayne) Macmillan.

— Chiropractic: An Illustrated History. 280p. 1994. 59.95 (*0-8016-7735-1*) Mosby Yr Bk.

— Contemporary Oral & Maxillofacial Surgery. 2nd ed. 799p. 1992. 59.95 (*0-8016-6530-2*) Mosby Yr Bk.

— Discover & Introductory Psychology. (C). 1991. text ed. 61.50 (*0-673-52189-3*) HarpCollege.

— Eat to Compete: A Guide to Sports Nutrition. 392p. 1988. pap. 25.95 (*0-8151-6720-2*, Yr Bk Med Pubs) Mosby Yr Bk.

— Introduction to Psychology: Study Guide. (C). 1990. 22.00 (*0-673-39808-0*) HarpCollege.

— Just the Facts: A Pocket Guide to Basic Nursing. 228p. 1994. pap. 19.95 (*0-8016-7877-3*) Mosby Yr Bk.

— Math for Automotive Trade. 320p. 1995. text ed. 24.95 (*0-8273-6712-0*) Delmar.

Peterson, ed. Geology of the Colorado Plateau, No. T130. (IGC Field Trip Guidebooks Ser.). 72p. 1989. 21.00 (*0-87590-644-3*) Am Geophysical.

Peterson & Mountfort, Guy. Birds of Britain & Europe. 1987. 22.95 (*0-685-43762-0*) Viking Penguin.

Peterson & Tate, eds. The Pearl of Great Price: Revelations from God. (Monograph Ser.: Vol. 14). 10.95 (*0-88494-683-5*) Bookcraft Inc.

Peterson, jt. auth. see Gray.

Peterson, ed. see O'Neil, D.

Peterson, jt. auth. see Seligson.

Peterson, et al. Binder Characterization & Evaluation, Vol. 1. 152p. (Orig.). (C). 1994. pap. text ed. 15.00 (*0-309-05809-0*, SHRP-A-367) SHRP.

— Principles of Oral & Maxillofacial Surgery, 3 vols., Set. (Illus.). 2256p. 1992. text ed. 395.00 (*0-397-51011-X*) Lippincott.

Peterson, A. Techniques of Teaching: Primary Education. LC 64-8985. (Pergamon International Library Science Technology Engineering & Social Studies: Vol. 1). 1965. 64.00 (*0-08-012527-1*, Pub. by Pergamon Repr UK) Franklin.

— Techniques of Teaching: Secondary Education. LC 64-8985. (Pergamon International Library Science Technology Engineering & Social Studies: Vol. 2). 1965. 69.00 (*0-08-012529-8*, Pub. by Pergamon Repr UK) Franklin.

— Tertiary Education. LC 64-8985. (Techniques of Teaching Ser.: Vol. 3). 1965. 74.00 (*0-08-012532-8*, Pub. by Pergamon Repr UK) Franklin.

Peterson, A. Brooke, intro. Intensive Orcharding: Managing Your High Production Apple Planting. (Illus.). 208p. (Orig.). 1992. reprint ed. pap. 10.00 (*0-9630659-2-0*) Good Fruit Grow.

Peterson, A. D. Schools Across Frontiers: The Story of the International Baccalaureate & the United World Colleges. 277p. (C). 1986. pap. 17.95 (*0-8126-9145-8*) Open Court.

Peterson, A. E. & Swan, J. B., eds. Universal Soil Loss Equation: Past, Present & Future. 53p. 1979. pap. 3.75 (*0-89118-766-9*) Soil Sci Soc Am.

Peterson, Agnes F. Western Europe: A Survey of Holdings at the Hoover Institution on War, Revolution & Peace. LC 72-142950. (Library Survey Ser.: No. 1). 60p. 1970. pap. 1.20 (*0-8179-5012-5*) Hoover Inst Pr.

Peterson, Agnes F., jt. comp. see Heinz, Grete.

Peterson, Alan H. The American Focus on Business Management: A Guide for Women (& Men), Vol. 1. (Illus.). 235p. (C). 1990. lib. bdg. 34.95 (*1-877858-14-5*) Amer Focus Pub.

— The American Focus on Satanic Crime, 1. 134p. 1989. 34.95 (*1-877858-00-5*) Amer Focus Pub.

— The American Focus on Satanic Crime, 2. 134p. 1989. 49.95 (*1-877858-01-3*) Amer Focus Pub.

— The American Focus on Satanic Crime Series, 10 vols., Set. Marquis, Doc & Peterson, Alan H., eds. Date not set. write for info. (*1-877858-20-X*) Amer Focus Pub.

— The Satanism in Prisons Story, Vol. 1. 100p. 1992. pap. 34.95 (*1-877858-22-6*, TSIPT) Amer Focus Pub.

— Secrets of The Illuminati. Marquis, Doc et al, eds. (American Focus on Satanic Crime Ser.: Vol. 5). (Illus.). 390p. 1994. pap. 44.00 (*1-877858-66-8*) Amer Focus Pub.

Peterson, Alan H., ed. & illus. The American Focus on Satanic Crime, Vol. 4. 300p. 1992. pap. text ed. 54.95 (*1-877858-10-2*, AFSC4) Amer Focus Pub.

Peterson, Alan H. & Cheney, Victor T. The American Focus on Rape, Vol. 1. 450p. 1992. pap. text ed. 75.00 (*1-877858-25-0*, AFR1) Amer Focus Pub.

Peterson, Alan H., ed. see Caldwell, E. S.

Peterson, Alan H., jt. auth. see Collins, Robert.

Peterson, Alan H., ed. see Collins, Robert & Peterson, Alan H.

Peterson, Alan H., ed. see Peterson, Alan H.

Peterson, Alan H., ed. see Willey, Michael R.

Peterson, Alan W., illus. Truth the Poet Sings. LC 83-51133. 220p. 1984. 6.95 (*0-87159-160-X*) Unity Bks.

Peterson, Allan C., jt. auth. see Kelley, Walter G.

Peterson, Allen B., ed. Tree Fruit Nutrition. (Illus.). 224p. (Orig.). 1994. pap. 15.00 (*0-9630659-4-7*) Good Fruit Grow.

***Peterson, Allen D.** Our Father's Family. LC 95-68674. 57p. 1995. pap. 7.50 (*0-9646503-0-4*) A D Peterson.

Peterson, Amy A., tr. see Wilhelm, James J., ed.

Peterson, Ann Z., jt. auth. see Rosenberg, Stephen M.

Peterson, Anne, jt. auth. see Peterson, Cliff.

Peterson, Art & Peterson, Norma. The Unofficial Mother's Handbook. (Illus.). 128p. 1991. mass mkt. 6.95 (*0-452-25213-X*, Plume) NAL-Dutton.

Peterson, Arthur E., jt. auth. see Edwards, George W.

Peterson, Arthur H., jt. auth. see Krambles, George.

Peterson, Audrey. Dartmoor Burial. Isaacson, Dana, ed. 256p. (Orig.). 1992. mass mkt. 5.50 (*0-671-72970-5*) PB.

— Death Too Soon. Isaacson, Dana, ed. 288p. (Orig.). 1994. mass mkt. 4.99 (*0-671-79509-0*) PB.

— Elegy in a Country Graveyard. Isaacson, Dana, ed. 256p. (Orig.). 1990. pap. 3.95 (*0-671-69356-5*) PB.

— Lament for Christobel. Isaacson, Dana, ed. 224p. (Orig.). 1991. mass mkt. 4.50 (*0-671-72969-1*) PB.

— Nocturne Murder. 256p. 1988. pap. 5.50 (*0-671-66102-7*) PB.

Peterson, Axel G. The Training of Elementary & Secondary Teachers in Sweden. LC 70-177151. (Columbia University. Teachers College. Contributions to Education Ser.: No. 575). (C). reprint ed. 37.50 (*0-404-55575-6*) AMS Pr.

***Peterson, B.** Nikon F4-F3. (Magic Lantern Guides Ser.). (Illus.). 176p. (Orig.). 1994. pap. 19.95 (*1-883403-12-X*, H130, Silver Pixel Pr) Saunders Photo.

— Nikon Guide to Wildlife Photography. Ridgway, James, ed. (Illus.). 176p. (Orig.). 1994. pap. 29.95 (*1-883403-06-5*, H700, Silver Pixel Pr) Saunders Photo.

— Nikon Lenses. (Magic Lantern Guides Ser.). (Illus.). 191p. (Orig.). 1994. pap. 19.95 (*1-883403-07-3*, H138, Silver Pixel Pr) Saunders Photo.

***Peterson, B. Moose.** Nikon System Handbook. 4th ed. (Illus.). (C). Date not set. pap. write for info. (*1-883403-32-4*, Silver Pixel Pr) Saunders Photo.

Peterson, B. Moose, photos & intro. California: Vanishing Habitats & Wildlife. (Illus.). 144p. 1993. pap. 21.95 (*0-89802-589-3*) Beautiful Am.

***Peterson, B. Moose & Huber, Michael.** Magic lantern Guide to Nikon SB-26 Flash System. (Magic Lantern Guide Ser.). (Illus.). 176p. (Orig.). (C). 1995. pap. 19.95 (*1-883403-24-3*, Silver Pixel Pr) Saunders Photo.

Peterson, B. Moose, jt. auth. see Huber, Michael.

Peterson, B. R. Buck Peterson's Guide to Deer Hunting. (Illus.). 132p. (Orig.). 1989. pap. 7.95 (*0-89815-291-7*) Ten Speed Pr.

— The Endangered Species Cookbook. LC 93-32497. 1993. pap. 5.95 (*0-89815-556-8*) Ten Speed Pr.

***Peterson, Baird.** Ergonomic PC: Creating a Healthy Computing Environment. 1995. pap. text ed. 27.95 (*0-07-049664-1*, Windcrest) TAB Bks.

— UNIX System Five Libraries: Programmer's Rapid Reference. LC 92-8662. 1992. pap. 34.95 (*0-442-00539-3*) Van Nos Reinhold.

— Unix System V Commands. 1992. pap. 34.95 (*0-442-00998-4*) Van Nos Reinhold.

— UNIX System V Systems Calls: Programmer's Rapid Reference. 192p. 1992. pap. 34.95 (*0-442-00909-7*) Van Nos Reinhold.

— XENIX Commands & Cross Development Services: Programmer's Rapid Reference. 250p. 1992. pap. 34.95 (*0-442-00540-7*) Van Nos Reinhold.

— Xenix System Services. 1992. pap. write for info. (*0-442-00541-5*) Van Nos Reinhold.

Peterson, Barbara B., ed. Notable Women of Hawaii. LC 84-16373. (Illus.). 448p. 1984. text ed. 27.50 (*0-8248-0820-7*) UH Pr.

Peterson, Barbara Sturken. Rapid Descent. 1994. 25.00 (*0-671-76069-6*) S&S Trade.

Peterson, Barry W. & Richmond, Frances J., eds. Control of Head Movement. (Illus.). 336p. 1988. 55.00 (*0-19-504499-1*) OUP.

Peterson, Bernard L. A Century of Musicals in Black & White: An Encyclopedia of Musical Stage Works by, about, or Involving Black Americans. LC 92-41976. 529p. 1993. text ed. 85.00 (*0-313-26657-3*, PEG, Greenwood Pr) Greenwood.

Peterson, Bernard L., Jr. Contemporary Black American Playwrights & Their Plays: A Biographical Directory & Dramatic Index. LC 87-17814. 651p. 1988. text ed. 75.00 (*0-313-25190-8*, PPL/, Greenwood Pr) Greenwood.

— Early Black American Playwrights & Dramatic Writers: A Biographical Directory & Catalog of Plays, Films & Broadcasting Scripts. LC 90-2961. 320p. 1990. text ed. 69.50 (*0-313-26621-2*, PBW/, Greenwood Pr) Greenwood.

Peterson, Bernard W. Briny to the Blue: Memoirs of World War II. LC 91-78372. 462p. 1992. 29.95 (*0-9631875-0-3*) Chuckwalla Pub.

Peterson, Beth. Myrna Never Sleeps. LC 93-8301. (J). (gr. 2-6). 1995. text ed. 11.95 (*0-689-31893-6*, Atheneum Bks Young) S&S Childrens.

Peterson, Betty B. Your Wedding. 1982. pap. 3.00 (*0-89036-211-4*) Hawkes Pub Inc.

Peterson, Bo. Media, Minds & Men: A History of Media in Sweden. (Illus.). 366p. 1988. 71.00x (*91-22-01206-0*, Pub. by Almqv & Wiksell SW) Coronet Bks.

Peterson, Bob. Basketball's High Powered Multiflex Offense. LC 85-30966. 194p. 1986. text ed. 21.95 (*0-13-069220-4*, Parker Publishing Co) P-H.

Peterson, Brenda. Living by Water: Essays on Life, Land & Spirit in the Northwest. LC 90-36821. 125p. (Orig.). 1991. 15.95 (*0-88240-358-3*) Alaska Northwest.

— Living by Water: True Stories of Nature & Spirit. 160p. 1994. reprint ed. pap. 9.00 (*0-449-90919-0*, Columbine) Fawcett.

— Nature & Other Mothers: Personal Stories of Women and the Body of Earth. 256p. 1995. pap. 12.00 (*0-449-90967-0*) Fawcett.

— River of Light. LC 86-81783. 303p. 1986. pap. 8.00 (*0-915308-89-4*) Graywolf.

Peterson, Brent D., jt. auth. see Timm, Paul R.

Peterson, Brent D., et al. The Complete Speaker: An Introduction to Public Speaking. 3rd ed. Perlee, Clyde & Simon, eds. 359p. (C). 1992. pap. text ed. 32.75 (*0-314-93439-1*) West Pub.

Peterson, Brent O. Popular Narratives & Ethnic Identity: Literature & Community in Die Abendschule. LC 91-55070. (Illus.). 320p. 1992. 39.95 (*0-8014-2548-4*) Cornell U Pr.

Peterson, Brent T. & Thilgen, Dean R. Stillwater, Minnesota: A Photographic History. (Illus.). 128p. (Orig.). 1992. pap. 16.95 (*0-9634842-0-6*) Valley Hist Pr.

Peterson, Brian. Buck Peterson's Guide to Indoor Life. (Illus.). 96p. (Orig.). 1992. pap. 6.95 (*0-89815-468-5*) Ten Speed Pr.

Peterson, Brice. Camping & Survival: Step-by-Step Guide to Wilderness Skills & Outdoor Living. LC 94-65054. 320p. (Orig.). 1997. 29.95 (*1-884573-00-2*); pap. 19.95 (*1-884573-19-3*) S-By-S Pubns.

— Meat Lovers: Step-by-Step Guide for the Meat Connoisseur. LC 94-65052. 320p. (Orig.). 1996. 29.95 (*1-884573-02-9*); pap. 19.95 (*1-884573-17-7*) S-By-S Pubns.

Peterson, Brookie. A Woman's Hope. 1991. 9.95 (*0-88494-792-0*) Bookcraft Inc.

***Peterson, Bruce I.** Dinner at Five. LC 94-74643. (Illus.). 32p. (J). (gr. k-3). 1995. 14.95 (*1-885340-12-5*) Coming Age Pr.

Peterson, Bryan. Learning to See Creatively. (Illus.). 144p. 1988. pap. 18.95 (*0-8174-4177-8*, Amphoto) Watsn-Guptill.

— People in Focus: How to Photograph Anyone, Anywhere. (Illus.). 144p. 1993. pap. 22.50 (*0-8174-5388-1*, Amphoto) Watsn-Guptill.

— Understanding Exposure: How to Shoot Great Photographs. (Illus.). 144p. 1990. pap. 22.50 (*0-8174-3712-6*, Amphoto) Watsn-Guptill.

Peterson, Bryan, photos. Germany. (Illus.). 160p. 1991. 39.95 (*1-55868-046-2*) Gr Arts Ctr Pub.

— Holland. (Illus.). 144p. 1992. 39.95 (*1-55868-098-5*) Gr Arts Ctr Pub.

Peterson, Bryan F., photos & text. Photographing Oregon with Professional Results. LC 84-80434. (Illus.). 96p. (Orig.). 1984. pap. 9.95 (*0-912856-90-4*) Gr Arts Ctr Pub.

Peterson, Buck. Buck Peterson's Complete Guide to Fishing. (Illus.). 144p. (Orig.). 1991. pap. 8.95 (*0-89815-405-7*) Ten Speed Pr.

— International Road Kill Cookbook. 1994. pap. 5.95 (*0-89815-567-3*) Ten Speed Pr.

Peterson, C., jt. ed. see McCabe, A.

Peterson, C. Arthur. Teacher's Survival Guide. 1985. pap. 8.95 (*0-452-26399-9*, Plume) NAL-Dutton.

Peterson, C. H., jt. auth. see Conlin, Joseph R.

Peterson, Carl. For Anna Akhmatova & Other Poems. LC 77-3193. 50p. 1977. 3.50 (*0-87886-081-9*, Greenfld Rev Pr) Greenfld Rev Lit.

Peterson, Carl D. How to Leave Your Job & Buy a Business of Your Own. 224p. 1989. audio 9.95 (*0-07-049648-X*) McGraw.

— How to Leave Your Job & Buy a Business of Your Own. 224p. 1992. pap. text ed. 14.95 (*0-07-049653-6*) McGraw.

— How to Sell Your Business. 208p. 1989. audio 9.95 (*0-685-26900-0*) McGraw.

— An Introduction to Business Brokerage: Valuing, Listing & Selling Businesses. 256p. 1991. text ed. 99.95 (*0-471-53996-1*) Wiley.

— Staying in Demand: How to Make Job Offers Come to You. LC 93-9791. 256p. 1993. text ed. 24.95 (*0-07-049655-2*); pap. text ed. 12.95 (*0-07-049656-0*) McGraw.

Peterson, Carl H. & Von Ehrenkrook, Karla. Why Do You Act the Way You Do? 210p. (Orig.). 1988. pap. write for info. (*0-318-62718-3*) C Edla & Assocs.

— Why Do You Act the Way You Do? 247p. (Orig.). 1991. lib. bdg. 9.95 (*0-9619600-0-0*) C Edla & Assocs.

Peterson, Carl R., jt. auth. see Hill, Philip G.

Peterson, Carla L. The Determined Reader: Gender & Culture in the Novel from Napoleon to Victoria. 264p. 1987. pap. text ed. 15.00 (*0-8135-1261-1*) Rutgers U Pr.

— Doers of the Word: African-American Women Reformers in the North (1830-1879) (Race & American Culture Ser.). (Illus.). 256p. 1995. 35.00 (*0-19-508519-1*) OUP.

Peterson, Carol. Macrame Horse Tack. (Illus.). 28p. 1983. pap. 8.95 (*0-910303-04-5*) Writers Pub Serv.

Peterson, Carol A. & Gunn, Scout L. Therapeutic Recreation Program Design: Principles & Procedures. 2nd ed. (Illus.). 368p. 1984. text ed. 57.00 (*0-13-914839-6*) P-H.

Peterson, Carol R. Herbs You Can Master: A Primer for Herbal Enthusiasts. LC 93-91797. (Illus.). 224p. (Orig.). 1994. pap. 11.95 (*0-9639620-0-0*) Mtn Garden.

Peterson, Carole & McCabe, Allyssa. Developmental Psycholinguistics: Three Ways of Looking at a Child's Narrative. (Cognition & Language Ser.). 278p. 1983. 54.50 (*0-306-40964-X*, Plenum Pr) Plenum.

Peterson, Carolyn S. The Mind-Body Partnership in the Treatment of Cancer Patients. 88p. (Orig.). 1993. pap. 7.50 (*0-913545-15-5*) Moonlight FL.

— Story Programs Activities for Older Children. (Illus.). (Orig.). (J). (gr. 3-6). 1987. 20.00 (*0-913545-11-2*) Moonlight FL.

Peterson, Carolyn S. & Fenton, Ann D. Christmas Story Programs. (Illus.). (J). (ps-6). 1981. 10.00 (*0-913545-01-5*) Moonlight FL.

— Reference Books for Children. 4th ed. LC 92-14234. 414p. 1992. 39.50 (*0-8108-2543-0*) Scarecrow.

Peterson, Carolyn S. & Fenton, Ann D., comps. Index to Children's Songs. LC 79-14265. 318p. 1979. 38.00 (*0-8242-0638-X*) Wilson.

Peterson, Carolyn S. & Hall, Brenny. Story Programs: A Source Book of Materials. LC 80-15112. 300p. 1980. pap. 22.50 (*0-8108-1317-3*) Scarecrow.

Peterson, Carrie. The Secrets of Sebastian Beaumont. (Shadows Ser.). 1993. mass mkt. 3.50 (*0-373-27022-4*, 5-27022-8) Silhouette.

Peterson, Carroll V. John Davidson. LC 71-187613. (Twayne's English Authors Ser.). 164p. (C). 1972. lib. bdg. 17.95 (*0-8290-1727-5*) Irvington.

Peterson, Casey, ed. Challenge of Loving: Building Healthy Relationships. 34p. 1986. pap. 2.50 (*0-936098-47-3*) Intl Marriage.

— Grief & Loss: Learning You Are Not Alone. 34p. 1987. pap. 2.50 (*0-936098-56-2*) Intl Marriage.

— Marriage Encounter for Just the Two of You. 50p. 1988. pap. 2.50 (*0-936098-59-7*) Intl Marriage.

Peterson, Cass, jt. auth. see Michalak, Patricia S.

Peterson, Catherine V., jt. auth. see Kielpinski, Penelope.

***Peterson, Charles & Blei, Norbert.** Charles L. Peterson: Of Time & Place. Quale, Mark E. & Peterson, Susan, eds. (Illus.). 96p. 1994. 135.00 (*0-9643438-0-0*) White Door.

— Charles L. Peterson: Of Time & Place. 2nd ed. Quale, Mark E. & Peterson, Susan, eds. (Illus.). 96p. 1994. pap. text ed. 45.00 (*0-9643438-1-9*) White Door.

Peterson, Charles A. How You Can Leave the City Forever. 120p. (Orig.). pap. 10.00 (*0-9614806-0-2*) Peterson Pub CO.

Peterson, Charles C., jt. auth. see Nagy, Kenneth A.

Peterson, Charles E. Colonial St. Louis: Building a Creole Capital. (Illus.). 112p. 1993. reprint ed. pap. 9.95 (*1-880397-00-5*) Patrice Pr.

— The Moore House: The Site of Surrender-Yorktown; A National Park Service Historic Structures Report. 116p. 1981. 8.45 (*0-940091-08-9*); pap. 4.20 (*0-940091-07-0*) Natl Parks & Cons.

Peterson, Charles E., ed. Building Early America. (Illus.). 407p. 1992. reprint ed. 32.95 (*1-879335-30-1*); reprint ed. pap. 19.95 (*1-879335-31-X*) Astragal Pr.

Peterson, Charles E., intro. The Carpenters' Company Seventeen Eighty-Six Rule Book. (Illus.). 158p. reprint ed. 14.95 (*1-879335-28-X*) Astragal Pr.

Peterson, Charles J., jt. ed. see Barber, Dan.

Peterson, Charles L., comp. Agricultural Machinery Management. LC 88-70148. 170p. 1988. spiral bd. 29.00 (*0-916150-90-9*, S1387) Am Soc Ag Eng.

Peterson, Charles M. Diabetes Management in the Nineteen Eighties: The Role of Home Blood Glucose Monitoring & New Insulin Delivery Systems. LC 82-80561. 344p. 1982. text ed. 75.00 (*0-275-91377-5*, C1377, Praeger Pubs) Greenwood.

Peterson, Charles M. & Jovanovic-Peterson, Lois. The Diabetes Self-Care Method: The Breakthrough Program of Self-Management That Will Help You Lead a Better, Freer, More Normal Life. rev. ed. (Illus.). 160p. 1990. reprint ed. pap. 12.95 (*0-929923-29-4*) Lowell Hse.

Peterson, Charles M., ed. see International Sansum Sumposium on Human Fetal Islet Transplantation Staff.

Peterson, Charles M., et al, eds. Fetal Islet Transplantation: Implications for Diabetes. (Illus.). 260p. 1988. 121.00 (*0-387-96587-4*) Spr-Verlag.

Peterson, Charles R., jt. auth. see Koch, Edward D.

Peterson, Charles S. Changing Times: A View from Cache Valley, 1890-1915. LC 93-80099. (Faculty Honor Lecture Ser.: No. 60). 32p. reprint ed. pap. 25.00 (*0-7837-6210-0*, 2045934) Bks Demand.

— Utah: A History. (States & the Nation Ser.). (Illus.). 1977. 14.95 (*0-393-05629-5*) Norton.

Peterson, Christian A., ed. Alfred Stieglitz's Camera Notes. LC 93-12089. (Illus.). 192p. 1993. 39.95 (*0-393-03534-4*) Norton.

Peterson, Christine E. The Second Malaysian Family Life Survey: User's Guide. LC 93-25706. 1993. 9.00 (*0-8330-1357-2*, MR-109) Rand Corp.

Peterson, Christine E. & Campbell, Nancy. The First Malaysian Family Life Survey: Documentation for Subfiles. LC 93-15027. 1993. write for info. (*0-8330-1355-6*, MR-111-NICHD) Rand Corp.

Peterson, Christine E., jt. auth. see Sine, Jeffrey.

Peterson, Christine E., et al. The Second Malaysian Family Life Survey: Codebook. LC 93-18801. 1993. 9.00 (*0-8330-1352-1*, MR-108) Rand Corp.

Peterson, Christopher. Health & Optimism. 224p. 1991. text ed. 19.95 (*0-02-924981-3*) Macmillan.

— Personality. 656p. (C). 1988. text ed. 46.75 (*0-15-569598-3*) HB Coll Pubs.

— Personality. 2nd ed. 700p. (C). 1992. text ed. 45.25 (*0-15-569600-9*) HB Coll Pubs.

— The Psychology of Abnormality. 656p. (C). 1995. text ed. write for info. (*0-15-500092-6*) HB Coll Pubs.

Peterson, Christopher, et al. Learned Helplessness: A Theory for the Age of Personal Control. LC 92-21473. (Illus.). 376p. 1993. 35.00 (*0-19-504466-5*) OUP.

Peterson, Clare G. Perspectives in Surgery. LC 72-115025. 355p. reprint ed. pap. 101.20 (*0-317-07968-9*, 2014577) Bks Demand.

Peterson, Clarence S. Known Military Dead During the American Revolutionary War, 1775-1783. 187p. 1992. reprint ed. pap. 20.00 (*0-685-60347-4*, 4580) Clearfield Co.

— Known Military Dead During the War of 1812. 74p. 1991. reprint ed. pap. 10.00 (*0-685-60351-2*, 9285) Clearfield Co.

Peterson, Clark S. The Goober's Guide to Golf: How to Golf Like a Champ in 10 Minutes (15 If You Read It Twice) (Illus.). 96p. (Orig.). 1992. pap. 8.95 (*0-9634078-0-5*) C S Peterson.

Peterson, Cliff & Peterson, Anne. The Adventures of Sir Wellington Boots. (J). 1993. 7.95 (*0-533-10328-2*) Vantage.

Peterson, Craig. Medisins RX: Your Prescription to Laughter. Parker, Diane, ed. LC 92-50871. (Humor Ser.). 100p. 1993. spiral bd. 7.95 (*0-88247-963-6*, 963-6) R & E Pubs.

Peterson, Craig A. & McCarthy, Claire. Handling Zoning & Land Use Litigation: A Practical Guide with 1987 Cumulative Supplement. 769p. 1982. 60.00 (*0-87215-451-3*) Michie Butterworth.

— Handling Zoning & Land Use Litigation: A Practical Guide with 1987 Cumulative Supplement. suppl. ed. 769p. 1987. 20.00 (*0-87215-832-2*) Michie Butterworth.

Peterson, Craig H. & Lewis, Cris W. Managerial Economics. 2nd ed. (Illus.). 752p. (C). 1990. text ed. write for info. (*0-02-394851-5*); write for info. (*0-02-394701-2*) Macmillan.

Peterson, Cris. Extra Cheese, Please! Mozzarella's Journey from Cow to Pizza. (Illus.). 32p. (J). (ps-3). 1994. 14.95 (*1-56397-177-1*) Boyds Mills Pr.

Peterson, Curt, jt. auth. see Dute, Roland.

Peterson, D. H., ed. Aspects of Climate Variability in the Pacific & the Western Americas. (Geophysical Monograph Ser.: Vol. 55). 445p. 1989. 50.00 (*0-87590-072-0*) Am Geophysical.

Peterson, D. J. Troubled Lands: The Legacy of Soviet Environmental Destruction. (Rand Corporation Research Study Ser.). 276p. (C). 1993. pap. text ed. 21.50 (*0-8133-1674-X*) Westview.

***Peterson, Dale.** Chimpanzee Travels: On & Off the Road in Africa. LC 94-19462. 279p. 1995. 21.15 (*0-201-40737-X*) Addison-Wesley.

— The Deluge & the Ark: A Journey into Primate Worlds. 1991. pap. 11.95 (*0-380-71199-0*) Avon.

— Visions of Caliban: On Chimpanzees & People. 1994. pap. 12.95 (*0-395-70100-7*) HM.

***Peterson, Dale, ed.** A Mad People's History of Madness. LC 81-50430. (Contemporary Community Health Ser.). 382p. 1982. pap. 108.90 (*0-7837-8541-0*, 2049356) Bks Demand.

Peterson, Dan. Safety by Objectives. LC 78-12057. 1978. 28.50 (*0-913690-07-4*) Aloray.

Peterson, Daniel. Roman Legions Recreated in Colour Photographs. (Europa Militaria Ser.) (Illus.). 96p. 1992. pap. 19.95 (*1-872004-06-7*, Pub. by Windrow & Green UK) Motorbooks Intl.

Peterson, Daniel C. Abraham Divided: An LDS Perspective on the Middle East. LC 91-76006. 377p. (Orig.). 1992. pap. 12.95 (*1-56236-203-8*) Aspen Bks.

Peterson, Daniel C. & Ricks, Stephen D. Offenders for a Word: How Anti-Mormons Play Word Games to Attack the Latter-Day Saints. LC 92-32724. 1992. 9.95 (*1-56236-208-9*) Aspen Bks.

Peterson, Daniel R., jt. auth. see Peter, Gilbert M.

Peterson, Darrell J., jt. auth. see Geltner, Peter B.

Peterson, David. Airplanes. LC 81-7671. (New True Bks.). (Illus.). 48p. (J). (gr. k-4). 1981. lib. bdg. 12.90 (*0-516-01606-7*) Childrens.

— Arkansas Historical Dance Series. 80p. 1995. bmax, pap. 25.50 (*0-944436-50-1*) Univ Central AR Pr.

— Engaging with God: A Biblical Theology of Worship. 320p. (Orig.). 1993. pap. 16.99 (*0-8028-0689-9*) Eerdmans.

— Enterprise Network Management: A Guide to IBM's Netview. 1994. text ed. 50.00 (*0-07-049654-4*) McGraw.

— Of Wind, Water & Sand: The Natural Bridges Story. (Illus.). 21p. 1990. 3.50 (*0-937407-02-X*) Canyonlands.

— Racks: The Natural History of Antlers & the Animals that Wear Them. (Illus.). 208p. (C). 1991. reprint ed. lib. bdg. 33.00x (*0-8095-4084-3*) Borgo Pr.

Peterson, David & Denney, Dick. The Vox Story: The History of the Vox Amplifier. Marcinello, Angela, ed. (Guitar History Ser.). (Illus.). 150p. 1993. pap. 19.95 (*0-933224-70-2*) Bold Strummer Ltd.

Peterson, David, jt. auth. see Huff, Larry.

Peterson, David, jt. auth. see Peterson, Joan.

Peterson, David A. Career Paths in the Field of Aging: Professional Gerontology. 128p. 1987. pap. 18.95 (*0-669-15283-8*) Free Pr.

— Career Paths in the Field of Aging: Professional Gerontology. 128p. 1987. text ed. 24.95 (*0-669-15282-X*) Free Pr.

— Facilitating Education for Older Learners. LC 82-49041. (Higher & Adult Education Ser.). 359p. 1983. 39.95x (*0-87589-565-4*) Jossey-Bass.

Peterson, David A. & Hull, Andrew M. Arizona Rental Rights: A Guide Book for Tenants, Landlords, & Mobile Home Users. LC 93-78484. (Illus.). 96p. (Orig.). 1993. pap. 6.95 (*0-935182-63-2*) Gem Guides Bk.

Peterson, David A., et al, eds. Education & Aging. (Illus.). 240p. 1986. text ed. 35.00 (*0-13-235698-8*) P-H.

***Peterson, David M.** TCP/IP Networking: A Guide to the IBM Environment. 1995. text ed. 50.00 (*0-07-049663-3*) McGraw.

Peterson, David R. Mathematics for Business Decisions. (Illus.). 320p. 1983. text ed. 18.75 (*0-07-049620-X*) McGraw.

Peterson, David R. & Miller, Kathleen N. Mathematics for Business. 2nd ed. 1989. text ed. 28.00 (*0-07-049630-7*) McGraw.

Peterson, David W., jt. auth. see Connolly, Walter B., Jr.

Peterson, Dean F. & Crawford, A. Berry, eds. Values & Choices in the Development of the Colorado River Basin. LC 77-13716. 337p. 1978. text ed. 29.95 (*0-8165-0643-4*); pap. 17.95 (*0-8165-0480-6*) U of Ariz Pr.

Peterson, Dean F., jt. ed. see Crawford, A. Berry.

Peterson, Dean R. Hearing Aids New Era. 9.95 (*0-89741-005-X*) Roadrunner Tech.

Peterson, Debora, jt. auth. see King, Thom.

***Peterson, Debra.** Breastfeeding the Adopted Baby. (Illus.). 141p. (Orig.). 1995. pap. 8.95 (*0-931722-43-8*) Corona Pub.

— Things I Couldn't Learn Alone. (Illus.). 122p. Date not set. 40.00 (*0-9637375-1-1*) Pringle Pub.

Peterson, Dennis A. & Wyckoff, Don G., eds. Contributions to Spiro Archeology: Mound Excavations & Regional Perspectives. (Studies in Oklahoma's Past). (Illus.). 285p. (C). 1989. pap. text ed. 11.00 (*1-881346-09-9*) Univ OK Archeol.

***Peterson, Dennis A., et al.** An Archeological Survey of the Spiro Vicinity, Le Flore County, Oklahoma. (Archaeological Resource Survey Report: No. 37). (Illus.). 87p. (C). 1993. pap. text ed. 3.50 (*1-881346-29-3*) Univ OK Archeol.

Peterson, Don. Does a Tiger Wear a Necktie? 1969. pap. 4.75 (*0-8222-0318-9*) Dramatists Play.

— The Masterbook of Portraiture & Studio Management. 5th ed. (Master Ser.: No. 1). (Illus.). 147p. 1989. reprint ed. pap. 29.50 (*0-934420-07-6*) Studio Pr Twain Harte.

Peterson, Donald. Forms of Representation. 224p. (Orig.). 1994. pap. text ed. 29.95 (*1-871516-34-X*, Pub. by Intellect Bks UK) Cromland.

— Wittgenstein's Early Philosophy: Three Sides of the Mirror. 216p. 1990. 40.00 (*0-8020-2770-9*) U of Toronto Pr.

Peterson, Donald, jt. ed. see Hookway, Christopher.

Peterson, Donald A., ed. Progressive Dies: Principles & Practices of Design & Construction. (Illus.). 380p. Date not set. 84.00 (*0-87263-448-5*) SME.

Peterson, Donald I. Relief from Headache. 2nd ed. LC 83-71941. (Illus.). 226p. 1990. pap. 9.95 (*0-913657-00-X*) D E Donel.

Peterson, Donald R., ed. Educating Professional Psychologists. (Rutgers Professional Psychology Review Ser.: Vol. 1). 192p. 1982. text ed. 34.95 (*0-87855-449-1*) Transaction Pubs.

Peterson, Donald R. & Fishman, Daniel B., eds. Assessment for Decision, Vol. I. (Rutgers Symposia on Applied Psychology Ser.). 463p. (C). 1988. pap. text ed. 20.00 (*0-8135-1247-6*) Rutgers U Pr.

Peterson, Doris M., jt. auth. see Peterson, John C.

Peterson, Dorothy W. Choices: The Realistic & Moving Story of a Mother's Decision about Abortion. 9.95 (*0-88494-675-4*) Bookcraft Inc.

Peterson, Douglas E., ed. Oral Complications of Cancer Chemotherapy. 1983. lib. bdg. 54.50 (*0-89838-563-6*) Kluwer Ac.

Peterson, Douglas E., et al, eds. Head & Neck Management of the Cancer Patient. (Developments in Oncology Ser.). 1986. lib. bdg. 151.50 (*0-89838-747-7*) Kluwer Ac.

Peterson, Douglas L. The English Lyric from Wyatt to Donne. 2nd ed. LC 90-82583. xxxi, 391p. 1990. reprint ed. 42.00 (*0-937191-20-5*) Colleagues Pr Inc.

— Time, Tide & Tempest: A Study of Shakespeare's Romances. LC 72-94155. 280p. (C). 1973. 18.00 (*0-87328-058-X*) Huntington Lib.

Peterson, Duncan. Britain on Backroads. 2nd ed. (Illus.). 256p. 1994. pap. 14.95 (*1-55650-638-4*) Hunter NJ.

— Spain on Backroads. (Illus.). 256p. (Orig.). 1994. pap. 14.95 (*1-55650-637-6*) Hunter NJ.

Peterson, E. A. Cellulosic Ion Exchangers. (Laboratory Techniques in Biochemistry & Molecular Biology Ser.: Vol. 2, Pt. 2). 1970. pap. 18.50 (*0-444-10057-1*, North Holland) Elsevier.

Peterson, E. G. Remembering E. G. Peterson: His Life & Our Story. (Illus.). 137p. 1974. 8.95 (*0-87421-070-4*) Utah St U Pr.

Peterson, E. M., jt. auth. see De la Maza, L. M.

Peterson, E. M., jt. ed. see De La Maza, L. M.

Peterson, Edward N. The American Occupation of Germany: Retreat to Victory. LC 77-28965. 377p. reprint ed. pap. 107.50 (*0-8357-5386-7*, 2032018) Bks Demand.

— An Analytical History of World War II, 1. LC 93-46254. (AUS IX: Vol. 154). 480p. (C). 1995. pap. text ed. 29.95 (*0-8204-2395-5*) P Lang Pubs.

— An Analytical History of World War II, 2. LC 93-46254. (AUS IX: Vol. 155). 400p. (C). 1995. pap. text ed. 29.95 (*0-8204-2396-3*) P Lang Pubs.

— An Analytical History of World War II, 2 vols., Set. LC 93-46254. (AUS IX: Vols. 154 & 155). 880p. (C). 1995. pap. text ed. write for info. (*0-8204-2500-1*) P Lang Pubs.

Peterson, Elizabeth A. African American Women: A Study of Will & Success. LC 92-54088. 144p. 1992. pap. 24.95x (*0-89950-730-1*) McFarland & Co.

Peterson, Elizabeth J. Beginning Math at Home, 4 vols., Set. (Illus.). 75p. (J). (ps-1). 1993. 12.95 (*0-938911-01-5*) Indiv Educ Syst.

— Beginning Reading at Home. (Illus.). 136p. (J). (ps-1). 1992. reprint ed. 29.95 (*0-938911-00-7*) Indiv Educ Syst.

— Christina & the Little Red Bird. (Illus.). 23p. (Orig.). (J). (ps-1). 1984. pap. 4.95 (*0-938911-02-3*) Indiv Educ Syst.

Peterson, Elizabeth J., ed. see Skiff, Andrea.

Peterson, Elmer, jt. ed. see Sanouillet, Michel.

Peterson, Elmer G. Remembering E. G. Peterson: His Life & Our Story. LC 74-13517. (Illus.). 149p. reprint ed. pap. 42.50 (*0-7837-7066-9*, 2046878) Bks Demand.

Peterson, Elmer T. Big Dam Foolishness. 1954. 12.95 (*0-8159-5107-8*) Devin.

— Big Dam Foolishness: The Problems of Modern Flood Control & Water Storage. LC 54-10812. 232p. reprint ed. pap. 66.20 (*0-8357-3600-8*, 2022706) Bks Demand.

Peterson, Eric S. Card Modeling: The Art of Creating Scale Models in Paper. (Illus.). 56p. (Orig.). 1994. pap. 14.95 (*0-9637100-0-1*) Caltrop Pub.

Peterson, Ernst, jt. auth. see Chaffin, Glenn M., Jr.

Peterson, Esther. A New Home for Chip. (Illus.). 16p. (J). 1994. 5.95 (*0-8059-3568-1*) Dorrance.

Peterson, Esther A. A Child's Life of Christ. (Illus.). 44p. (J). (gr. 3-8). 1987. 6.95 (*1-55523-045-8*) Winston-Derek.

— Spy Machine. LC 94-72207. (J). (gr. 4-7). 1994. pap. 3.99 (*0-8066-2719-0*, Augsburg) Augsburg Fortress.

Peterson, Eugene. Five Smooth Stones for Pastoral Work. 240p. 1992. reprint ed. pap. 12.99 (*0-8028-0660-0*) Eerdmans.

— The Message: New Testament. LC 92-63203. 656p. (Orig.). 1994. per., pap. 14.00 (*0-89109-853-4*, NavPr) NavPress.

— The Message: New Testament & Psalms. 1994. text ed. 39.00 (*0-89109-860-7*, NavPr) NavPress.

— The Message: The New Testament in Contemporary English. LC 92-63203. 544p. 1993. 20.00 (*0-89109-728-7*) NavPress.

— The Message of Hope. 130p. (Orig.). 1994. per., pap. 0.40 (*0-89109-862-3*, NavPr) NavPress.

— Under the Unpredictable Plant: An Exploration in Vocational Holiness. 208p. 1994. pap. text ed. 10.99 (*0-8028-0848-4*) Eerdmans.

Peterson, Eugene H. Answering God: The Psalms As Tools for Prayer. 1991. pap. 10.00 (*0-06-066512-2*) Harper SF.

— Answering God: The Psalms As Tools for Prayer. LC 88-45992. 160p. 1992. reprint ed. pap. 5.00 (*0-06-066515-7*) Harper SF.

— The Contemplative Pastor: Returning to the Art of Spiritual Direction. 192p. 1993. reprint ed. pap. 14.99 (*0-8028-0114-5*) Eerdmans.

— Like Dew Your Youth: Growing up with Your Teenager. 2nd ed. LC 94-25383. 128p. 1994. pap. 7.99 (*0-8028-0116-1*) Eerdmans.

— A Long Obedience in the Same Direction. LC 79-2715. 192p. 1980. pap. 9.99 (*0-87784-727-4*, 727) InterVarsity.

— The Message: Psalms. LC 94-65384. 192p. (Orig.). 1994. 15.00 (*0-89109-767-8*); pap. 10.00 (*0-89109-788-0*) NavPress.

— The Message: Youth Edition. LC 92-63203. 544p. (Orig.). 1995. pap. 14.00 (*0-89109-793-7*) NavPress.

— Praying with Jesus: A Year of Daily Prayers & Reflections on the Words & Actions of Jesus. LC 92-54533. 400p. 1993. pap. 10.00 (*0-06-066566-1*) Harper SF.

— Praying with Moses: A Year of Daily Prayers & Reflections on the Words & Actions of Moses. LC 93-45696. (Praying with the Bible Ser.). 400p. 1994. pap. 10.00 (*0-06-066518-1*) Harper SF.

— Praying with the Early Christians: A Year of Daily Prayers & Reflections on the Words of the Early Christians. LC 93-45698. (Praying with the Bible Ser.). 400p. 1994. pap. 10.00 (*0-06-066517-3*) Harper SF.

— Praying with the Psalms. 1995. spiral bd. 7.99 (*0-310-96239-0*) Zondervan.

— Praying with the Psalms: A Year of Daily Prayers & Reflections on the Words of David. LC 92-54532. 400p. 1993. pap. 10.00 (*0-06-066567-X*) Harper SF.

— Psalms: Prayers of the Heart. (LifeGuide Bible Studies). 64p. (Orig.). 1987. pap. 4.99 (*0-8308-1034-X*, 1034) InterVarsity.

— Reversed Thunder: The Revelation of John & the Praying Imagination. 1991. pap. 11.00 (*0-06-066503-3*) Harper SF.

— Run with the Horses. LC 83-13005. 213p. (Orig.). 1983. pap. 11.99 (*0-87784-905-6*, 905) InterVarsity.

— Traveling Light: Modern Meditations on St. Paul's Letter of Freedom. LC 88-11258. 204p. 1988. reprint ed. pap. 12.95 (*0-939443-08-2*) Helmers Howard Pub.

— Where Your Treasure Is: Psalms That Summon You from Self to Community. 2nd ed. 176p. 1993. reprint ed. pap. 12.99 (*0-8028-0115-3*) Eerdmans.

— Working the Angles: A Trigonometry for Pastoral Work. 266p. (Orig.). 1987. pap. 12.99 (*0-8028-0265-6*) Eerdmans.

Peterson, Eugene H., ed. see Chrysostom Society Staff.

Peterson, Eugene T. Mackinac in Restoration. Armour, David A., ed. LC 85-129971. (Reports in Mackinac History & Archaeology: No.9). (Illus.). 51p. (Orig.). 1983. pap. 6.00 (*0-911872-48-5*) Mackinac Island.

Peterson, Eugene W., ed. Deafness & Mental Health: Emerging Responses. (Readings in Deafness Ser.: No. 12). 152p. (Orig.). 1985. pap. 5.00 (*0-914494-13-9*) Am Deaf & Rehab.

Peterson, Evan T., jt. ed. see Bahr, Stephen J.

Peterson, Evangeline, jt. auth. see Lewis, Edna.

Peterson, Evelyn H. Who Cares? A Handbook of Christian Counselling. 181p. 1982. pap. text ed. 11.95 (*0-85364-272-9*) Attic Pr.

Peterson, F. P., jt. auth. see Massey, William S.

***Peterson, Fiona & Whittaker, Claire.** Operating Bail - Decision-Making under the Bail Etc. (Scotland) Act 1980. 184p. 1994. pap. 35.00 (*0-11-495173-X*, HM5173X, Pub. by HMSO UK) UNIPUB.

Peterson, Florence. Strikes in the United States. 1988. reprint ed. lib. bdg. 25.00 (*0-7812-0546-8*) Rprt Serv.

— Strikes in the United States, 1880-1936. LC 70-145232. 190p. 1972. reprint ed. 25.00 (*0-403-01148-5*) Scholarly.

Peterson, Francisca E., tr. see Rape & Abuse Crisis Center Staff.

Peterson, Franklynn. The Build-It-Yourself Furniture Catalog. LC 76-6567. 1976. pap. 4.95 (*0-13-085902-8*, Reward) P-H.

— How to Fix Damn Near Everything. 1989. 11.99 (*0-517-66200-0*) Random Hse Value.

Peterson, Franklynn & Kesselman-Turkel, Judi. The Author's Handbook. 248p. 1982. pap. 8.95 (*0-13-053900-7*) P-H.

— The Magazine Writer's Handbook. 263p. 1983. 17.95 (*0-13-543751-2*) P-H.

Peterson, Franklynn, jt. auth. see Kesselman-Turkel, Judi.

Peterson, Fred W. Homes in the Heartland: Balloon Frame Farmhouses of the Upper Midwest, 1850-1920. LC 92-2833. (Rural America Ser.). (Illus.). xii, 300p. 1992. 35.00 (*0-7006-0536-3*) U Pr of KS.

***Peterson, Frederick.** Desert Pioneer Doctor. (American Autobiography Ser.). 130p. 1995. reprint ed. lib. bdg. 69.00 (*0-7812-8617-4*) Rprt Serv.

Peterson, G., jt. auth. see Sakaman, T.

Peterson, G. P. An Introduction to Heat Pipes: Modeling, Testing, & Applications. LC 93-51014. 1994. text ed. 59.95 (*0-471-30512-X*) Wiley.

Peterson, G. P., jt. ed. see Bayazitoglu, Y.

Peterson, Gail, jt. auth. see Diener, Patricia.

Peterson, Gale R., ed. Understanding Biotechnology Law: Protection, Licensing, & Intellectual Property Policies. LC 93-7101. 488p. 1993. 150.00 (*0-8247-8935-0*) Dekker.

***Peterson, Gallen.** The Everlasting Tradition. 160p. 1995. pap. 9.99 (*0-8254-3499-8*, 95-049) Kregel.

Peterson, Garneth O., jt. auth. see Frost, Murray.

***Peterson, Gary & Byrne, David.** Klondike Kalamity. 1978. 5.00 (*0-87129-572-5*, K18) Dramatic Pub.

***Peterson, Gary & Nestor, Larry.** Stone Soup - Musical. 1983. 4.25 (*0-87129-581-4*, S68) Dramatic Pub.

Peterson, Gary A., et al, eds. Technologies for Sustainable Agriculture in the Tropics: Proceedings of an International Symposia Sponsored by Division A-6 of the American Society of Agronomy in San Antonio, TX, & Denver, CO, 1990 & 1991 Respectively. LC 93-21161. (Special Publication Ser.: No. 56). 1993. write for info. (*0-89118-118-0*) Am Soc Agron.

Peterson, Gary B. & Bennion, Lowell C. Sanpete Scenes: A Guide to Utah's Heart. LC 87-72694. (Illus.). 144p. (Orig.). 1987. pap. 16.95 (*0-9617133-0-5*) Basin-Plateau Pr.

Peterson, Gary L., ed. Communicating in Organizations: A Casebook. LC 93-11849. 1993. pap. text ed. 23.00 (*0-89787-349-1*) Gorsuch Scarisbrick.

Peterson, Gary M. & Peterson, Trudy H. Archives & Manuscripts: Law. (Basic Manual Ser.). 96p. 1985. pap. 13.00 (*0-931828-64-3*) Soc Am Archivists.

PQ

Peterson, Gary W., et al. Career Development & Services: A Cognitive Approach. LC 90-39581. 496p. (C). 1991. text ed. 49.95 (*0-534-14496-9*) Brooks-Cole.

Peterson, Gayle. Birthing Normally: A Personal Growth Approach to Childbirth. 2nd ed. (Illus.). 1991. reprint ed. pap. 14.95 (*0-9625231-1-9*) Shadow & Light.

— An Easier Childbirth: A Mother's Guide for Birthing Normally. 2nd ed. (Illus.). 177p. 1993. reprint ed. pap. 14.95 (*0-9625231-4-3*) Shadow & Light.

— An Easier Childbirth: A Mother's Workbook for Health & Emotional Well-Being During Pregnancy & Delivery. 192p. (Orig.). 1991. pap. 11.95 (*0-87477-665-1*) J P Tarcher.

Peterson, Gayle, jt. auth. see Mehl, Lewis.

Peterson, Gayle H., jt. auth. see Mehl, Lewis E.

Peterson, Geoffrey. Conscience & Caring. LC 82-7401. (Creative Pastoral Care & Counseling Ser.). 96p. reprint ed. pap. 27.40 (*0-685-23499-1*, 2029096) Bks Demand.

***Peterson, George.** Modular Digital Multitracks: The Power User's Guide. Jewett, Andy, ed. (Illus.). 120p. 1994. pap. 29.95 (*0-918371-03-1*, MixBooks) Cardinal Busn Media.

Peterson, George A., jt. auth. see Bender, Roger J.

Peterson, George C. Stuck in the Mud, Vol. 1. (Illus.). 208p. (Orig.). (YA). (gr. 9-12). 1988. pap. write for info. (*0-9621320-0-4*) G Peterson.

Peterson, George E., ed. Big City Politics Governance, & Fiscal Constraints. (Urban Opportunity Ser.). 325p. (Orig.). (C). 1994. lib. bdg. 55.00 (*0-87766-572-9*); pap. text ed. 26.50 (*0-87766-573-7*) Urban Inst.

Peterson, George E. & Lewis, Carol W., eds. Reagan & the Cities. (Changing Domestic Priorities Ser.). (Illus.). 251p. (Orig.). 1986. pap. text ed. 23.00 (*0-87766-385-8*) Urban Inst.

Peterson, George E. & Vroman, Wayne, eds. Urban Labor Markets & Job Opportunity. LC 92-10899. (Urban Opportunity Ser.). 342p. (Orig.). (C). 1992. lib. bdg. 61.00 (*0-87766-566-4*); pap. text ed. 26.50 (*0-87766-567-2*) Urban Inst.

Peterson, George E., jt. auth. see Godwin, Stephen R.

Peterson, George E., jt. ed. see Harrell, Adele V.

Peterson, George E., jt. auth. see Hatry, Harry P.

Peterson, George E., jt. auth. see Hochman, Harold M.

Peterson, George E., et al. Guide to Benchmarks of Urban Capital Condition. LC 84-7442. (Guides to Managing Urban Capital Ser.). 40p. (Orig.). 1984. pap. text ed. 13.75 (*0-87766-338-6*) Urban Inst.

— Guide to Financing the Capital Budget & Maintenance Plan. Hatry, Harry P., ed. LC 84-7425. (Guides to Managing Urban Capital Ser.). 39p. (Orig.). 1984. pap. text ed. 13.75 (*0-87766-341-6*) Urban Inst.

— The Reagan Block Grants: What We Have Learned? (Illus.). 134p. (Orig.). 1986. pap. text ed. 23.50 (*0-87766-400-5*) Urban Inst.

Peterson, George H., jt. ed. see McLaren, A. Douglas.

Peterson, George H., jt. ed. see McLaren, Arthur D.

Peterson, George L., et al. Amenity Resource Valuation: Integrating Economics with Other Disciplines. LC 88-50862. 265p. 1988. 27.95 (*0-910251-27-4*) Venture Pub PA.

Peterson, Gerald. Object-Oriented Computing, Vol. 1: Concepts. LC 87-80433. 205p. 1988. pap. 10.95 (*0-8186-0821-8*) IEEE Comp Soc.

— Object-Oriented Computing, Vol. 1: Concepts. LC 87-80433. 205p. 1988. 40.00 (*0-8186-4821-X*) IEEE Comp Soc.

Peterson, Gerald R., jt. auth. see Hill, Frederick J.

Peterson, Gerald W., jt. auth. see Clapp, Steve.

Peterson, Gladys J. Better Photos. 96p. 1994. pap. text ed. 10.95 (*1-884752-06-3*) D C Cook Fnd.

— Pieces - The Story of Elgin in a Quilt. (Illus.). 128p. (Orig.). 1988. write for info. (*0-318-64354-5*); pap. 9.95 (*0-685-24078-9*) Amer Healthcare Ctr.

Peterson, Glen, jt. auth. see Witherspoon, Gary.

Peterson, Gordon M. & Graesser, R. F. Calculus. (Quality Paperback Ser.: No. 51). 321p. (Orig.). 1974. reprint ed. pap. 7.95 (*0-8226-0051-X*) Littlefield.

Peterson, Gregory, tr. see Kora, Takehisa.

Peterson, Grethe, ed. The Tanner Lecture on Human Values, Vol. 13. (Tanner Lecture Ser.). 1992. 30.00 (*0-87480-406-X*) U of Utah Pr.

— The Tanner Lectures on Human Values, Vol. IX: 1988. 320p. 1988. 30.00 (*0-87480-326-8*) U of Utah Pr.

— The Tanner Lectures on Human Values, Vol. X. (Tanner Lecture Ser.). 300p. (C). 1989. text ed. 30.00 (*0-87480-318-7*) U of Utah Pr.

Peterson, Grethe B., ed. Tanner Lectures on Human Values. (Tanner Lecture Ser.: Vol. 15). 400p. (C). 1994. 30.00 (*0-87480-450-7*) U of Utah Pr.

— The Tanner Lectures on Human Values, Vol. XI. (Tanner Lecture Ser.). 500p. 1990. lib. bdg. 30.00 (*0-87480-340-3*) U of Utah Pr.

— The Tanner Lectures on Human Values, Vol. XII. 250p. 1991. lib. bdg. 30.00 (*0-87480-350-0*) U of Utah Pr.

— The Tanner Lectures on Human Values, Vol. 14. (Tanner Lecture Ser.). 320p. (C). 1993. text ed. 30.00 (*0-87480-418-3*) U of Utah Pr.

— The Tanner Lectures on Human Values, Vol. 16. (Tanner Lecture Ser.). 360p. 1995. text ed. 30.00x (*0-87480-476-0*) U of Utah Pr.

Peterson, H. Burke. A Glimpse of Glory. 9.95 (*0-88494-590-1*) Bookcraft Inc.

Peterson, H. Craig & Lewis, W. Cris. Managerial Economics. 3rd ed. (Illus.). 688p. (C). 1993. write for info. (*0-318-69915-X*) Macmillan.

— Managerial Economics. 3rd ed. (Illus.). 688p. (C). 1994. text ed. write for info. (*0-02-394762-4*); student ed. pap. write for info. (*0-02-394766-7*) Macmillan.

***Peterson, H. Donl.** Pearl of Great Price: A History & Commentary. LC 87-15672. xiii, 400p. 1987. pap. 12.95 (*0-87579-665-6*) Deseret Bk.

Peterson, H. E. & Isaksson, A. J., eds. Communication Networks in Health Care: Proceedings of the IFIP-IMIA Working Conference on Communication Networks in Health Care, Ulvsunda Palace, Sweden, 14-18 June, 1982. 366p. 1983. 64.00 (*0-444-86513-6*, 1-495-82, North Holland) Elsevier.

Peterson, H. E. & Schneider, W., eds. Human Computer Communications in Health Care: Proceedings of the IFIP-IMIA Second Stockholm Conference on Communication in Health Care, Stockholm, Sweden, 10-14 June, 1985. 312p. 1986. 64.00 (*0-444-87880-7*) Elsevier.

Peterson, Hans-Inge. Tumor Blood Circulation: Angiogenesis, Vascular Morphology & Blood Flow of Experimental & Human Tumors. 240p. 1979. 139.95 (*0-8493-5695-4*, RC255, CRC Reprint) Franklin.

Peterson, Harold. Historical Treasury of American Guns. LC 66-13822. (Remington Sportsmen's Library). pap. 2.95 (*0-87502-010-0*) Benjamin Co.

— The Last of the Mountain Men. LC 68-57081. 1983. reprint ed. pap. 9.95 (*0-686-46877-5*) Backeddy Bks.

Peterson, Harold A. & Marquardt, Thomas P. Appraisal Diagnosis of Speech & Language Disorders. 3rd ed. LC 93-33657. 1994. text ed. write for info. (*0-13-200149-7*) P-H.

Peterson, Harold F. Diplomat of the Americas: A Biography of William I. Buchanan, 1852-1909. LC 76-22652. 458p. 1977. 59.50 (*0-87395-346-0*) State U NY Pr.

Peterson, Harold I., jt. auth. see Stewart, Watt.

Peterson, Harold L. American Knives. 1980. 24.95 (*0-88227-016-8*) Gun Room.

— The American Sword, Seventeen Seventy-Five to Nineteen Forty-Five. LC 65-25409. (Illus.). 1983. 35.00 (*0-9603094-1-1*) Ray Riling.

— Arms & Armor of the Pilgrims. 1990. reprint ed. 2.00 (*0-940628-04-X*) Pilgrim Soc.

— How Do You Know It's Old? LC 74-13118. (Encore Edition Ser.). (Illus.). 1975. 6.95 (*0-684-15286-X*, Scribners) S&S Trade.

Peterson, Helen S. Oliver Wendell Holmes: Soldier, Lawyer, Supreme Court Justice. LC 78-71848. (Illus.). 91p. 1979. 7.95 (*0-914932-03-9*) Fox Hills Pr.

Peterson, Horace C. & Fite, Gilbert C. Opponents of War, 1917-1918. LC 85-30570. 402p. 1986. reprint ed. text ed. 89.50 (*0-313-25132-0*, FPOP, Greenwood Pr) Greenwood.

Peterson, Houston. Huxley, Prophet of Science. LC 75-30039. reprint ed. 26.00 (*0-404-14040-8*) AMS Pr.

Peterson, Hugh M., jt. auth. see Lewis, Robert T.

Peterson-Hunt, William S. & Woodruff, Evelyn L. Union List of Sanborn Fire Insurance Maps Held by Institutions in the United States & Canada: Volume 2 (Montana to Wyoming, Canada & Mexico, with a Supplement & Corrigenda to Volume 1. rev. ed. LC 76-6129. (Occasional Papers: No. 3). (Illus.). 216p. (Orig.). 1977. pap. 6.00 (*0-939112-03-5*) Western Assn Map.

Peterson, Indira V. Poems to Siva: The Hymns of the Tamil Saints. 368p. 1989. text ed. 57.50 (*0-691-06767-8*) Princeton U Pr.

Peterson, Ingrid. Clare of Assisi: A Biographical Study. LC 93-24140. 1993. 27.95 (*0-685-70885-3*); pap. 20.95 (*0-8199-0964-5*) Franciscan Pr.

***Peterson, Ingrid & Miller, Ramona.** Praying with Clare of Assisi. Koch, Carl, ed. (Companions for the Journey Ser.). (Illus.). 114p. (Orig.). 1994. pap. 6.95 (*0-88489-333-2*) St Marys.

Peterson, Ingrid J. William Nassington: Canon, Mystic, & Poet of the Speculum Vitae. (American University Studies: Theology & Religion: Ser. VII, Vol. 19). 199p. 1987. text ed. 34.00 (*0-8204-0322-9*) P Lang Pubs.

Peterson-Ishaq, Kristin, comp. & pref. Lake Champlain: Reflections on Our Past - a Bibliography. 90p. (Orig.). 1989. pap. text ed. 7.00 (*0-944277-18-7*, U55) U VT Ctr Rsch VT.

Peterson-Ishaq, Kristin, ed. University of Vermont Graduate Theses on Vermont Topics, 1975-1992. (Ocassional Papers: No. 15). 246p. 1993. pap. 15.00 (*0-944277-24-1*) U VT Ctr Rsch VT.

— University of Vermont Graduate Theses on Vermont Topics, 1975-1992. (Ocassional Papers: No. 15). 1993. disk 10.00 (*0-944277-27-6*) U VT Ctr Rsch VT.

***Peterson-Ishaq, Kristin, ed. & pref.** We Vermonters: Perspectives on the Past - A Bibliography. (Illus.). 177p. (Orig.). 1995. pap. 12.50 (*0-944277-29-2*); disk 9.00 (*0-944277-30-6*) U VT Ctr Rsch VT.

Peterson, Ivars. Fatal Defect. 1992. write for info. (*0-679-74027-9*) McKay.

— Fatal Defect. 1995. 25.00 (*0-8129-2023-6*, Times Bks) Random.

— Islands of Truth: A Mathematical Mystery Cruise. LC 89-49501. 325p. (C). 1995. text ed. write for info. (*0-7167-2113-9*) W H Freeman.

— Islands of Truth: A Mathematical Mystery Cruise. 1995. pap. text ed. write for info. (*0-7167-2148-1*) W H Freeman.

— Mathematical Tourist: Snapshots of Modern Mathematics. 1995. pap. text ed. write for info. (*0-7167-2064-7*) W H Freeman.

— Newton's Clock: Chaos in the Solar System. LC 93-7176. 1995. text ed. write for info. (*0-7167-2396-4*) W H Freeman.

— Newton's Clock: Chaos in the Solar System. LC 93-7176. (Illus.). 317p. 1995. pap. text ed. 15.95 (*0-7167-2724-2*) W H Freeman.

Peterson, J., ed. see Royal Swedish Academy of Sciences Staff.

Peterson, J., jt. auth. see Sachs, R.

***Peterson, J. A.** Your Reactions Are Showing. 1980. pap. 2.50 (*0-8474-0999-6*) Back to Bible.

Peterson, J. E. The Arab Gulf States: Steps Toward Political Participation. LC 87-25836. (Washington Papers: No. 131). 176p. 1988. text ed. 45.00 (*0-275-92881-0*, C2881, Praeger Pubs); pap. text ed. 13.95 (*0-275-92882-9*, B2882, Praeger Pubs) Greenwood.

— Historical Dictionary of Saudi Arabia. (Asian Historical Dictionaries Ser.: No. 14). (Illus.). 267p. 1993. 32.50 (*0-8108-2780-8*) Scarecrow.

— U. S. - Arab Relations: Security in the Arabian Peninsula & Gulf States, 1974-84, No. 7. 154p. (Orig.). 1985. pap. 8.00 (*0-916729-12-5*) Natl Coun Arab.

Peterson, J. L., jt. ed. see DiClemente, R. J.

Peterson, Jack. Balance of Power. 560p. (Orig.). 1984. pap. 3.95 (*0-8439-2162-5*) Dorchester Pub Co.

— How to Hire a Development Officer. 66p. (Orig.). 1990. pap. 8.00 (*0-685-47923-4*) Natl Cath Educ.

Peterson, Jack, ed. Industrial Health. (Illus.). (C). 1991. pap. text ed. 60.00 (*0-936712-91-0*) Am Conf Govt Indus Hygienist.

Peterson, Jacqueline. Sacred Encounters: Father De Smet & the Indians of the Rocky Mountain West. (C). 1993. 49.95 (*0-8061-2575-6*); pap. 24.95 (*0-8061-2576-4*) U of Okla Pr.

Peterson, James. Dreams of Chaos, Visions of Order: Understanding the American Avant-Garde Cinema. LC 93-25672. (Contemporary Film & Television Ser.). (Illus.). 212p. 1993. text ed. 44.95 (*0-8143-2456-8*); pap. 19.95 (*0-8143-2457-6*) Wayne St U Pr.

— Employee Stock Ownership Plans. 8p. (Orig.). 1978. pap. 8.00 (*0-317-04829-5*) Natl Coun Econ Dev.

— The Enchanted Alphabet. (Illus.). 160p. (Orig.). 1985. pap. 9.95 (*0-85030-765-1*, Pub. by Aquarian Pr UK) Thorsons SF.

— Sauces: Classical & Contemporary Sauce Making. LC 90-39442. (Illus.). 512p. 1991. text ed. 39.95 (*0-442-23773-1*) Van Nos Reinhold.

— The Secret Life of Kids. LC 87-41026. (Illus.). 237p. (Orig.). 1987. pap. 8.95 (*0-8356-0620-1*, Quest) Theos Pub Hse.

— Splendid Soups. 1993. 29.95 (*0-553-07505-5*) Bantam.

Peterson, James, jt. auth. see Bertucci, Bob.

Peterson, James, tr. see Bilheux, Ronald & Escoffier, Alain.

***Peterson, James, et al.** Perspectives on Politics: Classic to Contemporary. 256p. (C). 1994. per., pap. text ed. 19.95 (*0-8403-9962-6*) Kendall-Hunt.

Peterson, James A. Counseling & Values: A Philosophical Examination. 2nd ed. LC 89-38243. 1989. pap. 21.85 (*0-910328-43-9*) Sulzburger & Graham Pub.

***Peterson, James A., et al.** Strength Training for Women. (Illus.). 392p. (Orig.). 1995. pap. write for info. (*0-87322-752-2*, PPET0752) Human Kinetics.

Peterson, James A., ed. Paleotectonics & Sedimentation in the Rocky Mountain Region, United States. (AAPG Memoir Ser.: No. 41). (Illus.). ix, 693p. 1986. 69.00 (*0-89181-319-5*) AAPG.

— Total Fitness: The Nautilus Way. 2nd ed. LC 81-85623. (Illus.). 288p. 1982. pap. 16.00 (*0-918438-40-3*, PPET0040) Human Kinetics.

Peterson, James A. & Horodyski, Mary B. How to Jump Higher. LC 88-836. 1988. pap. 12.95 (*0-940279-12-6*) Masters Pr IN.

Peterson, James A. & Hronek, Bruce B. Risk Management for Park, Recreation & Leisure Services. 2nd ed. 152p. (Orig.). 1992. pap. text ed. 24.95 (*0-915611-57-0*) Sagamore Pub.

Peterson, James A., jt. auth. see Peterson, Susan L.

Peterson, James A., jt. auth. see Reeves, Steve.

Peterson, James B. Ceramic Analysis in the Northeast, No. 9. Bd. with Nelson Island & Seabrook Marsh Sites. 1985. 15.00 (*0-318-19888-6*) Fund Anthrop.

Peterson, James C., et al. Voluntary Associations: Structure & Process. 272p. 1986. 26.95 (*0-03-061756-1*, Praeger Pubs) Greenwood.

Peterson, James E. Otter Creek: The Indian Road. LC 90-82089. (Illus.). 176p. (Orig.). (YA). (gr. 5 up). 1990. pap. 15.00 (*0-914960-83-0*) Academy Bks.

Peterson, James L. & Silberschatz, Abraham. Operating System Concepts. LC 82-22766. (Computer Science Ser.). (Illus.). 576p. 1983. write for info. (*0-201-06097-3*) Addison-Wesley.

— Operating System Concepts. 2nd ed. (Computer Science Ser.). (C). 1985. teacher ed write for info. (*0-201-06090-6*); text ed. 34.36 (*0-201-06198-8*) Addison-Wesley.

Peterson, James L. & Zill, Nicholas. American Jewish High School Students: A National Profile. LC 84-72249. vi, 32p. (Orig.). 1984. pap. 2.50 (*0-87495-065-1*) Am Jewish Comm.

Peterson, James L., jt. auth. see Silberschatz, Abraham.

***Peterson, James L., et al.** Longitudinal Retirement History Study: Instructor's Manual. (Gerontology Research Toolkit Ser.). 64p. (Orig.). 1994. teacher ed, pap. text ed. 30.00x (*0-8018-5046-0*) Johns Hopkins.

— Longitudinal Study of Aging: Instructor's Manual. (Gerontology Research Toolkit Ser.). 62p. (Orig.). 1994. teacher ed, pap. text ed. 30.00x (*0-8018-5044-4*) Johns Hopkins.

— National Long Term Care Survey: Instructor's Manual. (Gerontology Research Toolkit Ser.). 85p. (Orig.). 1994. teacher ed, pap. text ed. 30.00x (*0-8018-5042-8*) Johns Hopkins.

Peterson, Jan, ed. see Hurst, Jane.

Peterson, Jane, jt. auth. see Lambert, Judith.

Peterson, Janet, jt. auth. see Gaunt, LaRene.

Peterson, Janice & Brown, Doug, eds. The Economic Status of Women under Capitalism: Institutional Economics & Feminist Theory. 240p. 1993. 59.95 (*1-85278-894-1*, Pub. by E Elgar Pub UK) Ashgate Pub Co.

Peterson, Jean. Oneness Remembered - Ultraconsciousness (from: Sananda) Wilkinson, Marilyn J., ed. (Illus.). (Orig.). 1989. pap. 12.00 (*0-685-29784-5*) Meridian Light.

Peterson, Jean R. It Doesn't Grow on Trees. (Illus.). 132p. (Orig.). 1988. pap. 5.95 (*0-932620-96-5*) Betterway Bks.

***Peterson, Jean S.** Talk with Teens about Feelings, Family, Relationships, & the Future: 50 Guided Discussions for School & Counseling Groups. Espeland, Pamela, ed. 224p. (Orig.). (YA). (gr. 7-12). 1995. teacher ed, pap. 21.95 (*0-915793-88-1*) Free Spirit Pub.

— Talk with Teens about Self & Stress: Fifty Guided Discussions for School & Counseling Groups. Espeland, Pamela, ed. LC 93-21514. 192p. (Orig.). 1993. pap. 19.95 (*0-915793-55-5*) Free Spirit Pub.

Peterson, Jeanette F. The Paradise Garden Murals of Malinalco: Utopia & Empire in Sixteenth-Century Mexico. LC 92-7992. (Illus.). 246p. (C). 1993. text ed. 37.50 (*0-292-72750-X*) U of Tex Pr.

— Sacred Gifts: Precolumbian Art & Creativity. LC 94-37480. 1994. write for info. (*0-89951-090-6*) Santa Barb Mus Art.

Peterson, Jeanne W. I Have a Sister, My Sister Is Deaf. LC 76-24306. (Illus.). (J). (gr. k-3). 1977. lib. bdg. 14.89 (*0-06-024702-9*) HarpC Child Bks.

— I Have a Sister, My Sister Is Deaf. LC 76-24306. (Trophy Picture Bk.). (Illus.). 32p. (J). (ps-3). 1984. pap. 4.95 (*0-06-443059-6*, Trophy) HarpC Child Bks.

— My Mama Sings. LC 91-72. (Illus.). 32p. (J). (ps-3). 1994. 15.00 (*0-06-023854-2*) HarpC Child Bks.

— My Mama Sings. LC 91-72. (Illus.). 32p. (J). (ps-3). 1994. lib. bdg. 14.89 (*0-06-023859-3*) HarpC Child Bks.

Peterson, Jim. The Man Who Grew Silent. 88p. 1989. pap. 9.95 (*0-930769-08-2*) Bench Pr SC.

***Peterson, Joan & Peterson, David.** Eat Smart in Brazil: How to Decipher the Menu, Know the Market Foods & Embark on a Tasting Adventure. LC 94-96252. (Illus.). 168p. (Orig.). 1994. pap. 12.95 (*0-9641168-3-9*) Ginkgo Pr.

— Eat Smart in Turkey: How to Decipher the Menu, Know the Market Foods & Embark on a Tasting Adventure. (Illus.). Date not set. pap. 12.95 (*0-9641168-2-0*) Ginkgo Pr.

Peterson, Joan & Peterson, Pete. Summertime Recipes. 36p. (Orig.). 1981. pap. 2.75 (*0-940844-02-8*) Wellspring.

Peterson, Joe & Peterson, Kay. Encyclopedia for RVers. rev. ed. (Illus.). 230p. 1989. 8.95 (*0-685-49342-3*) RoVers Pubns.

— The New Survival of the RV Snowbird. rev. ed. 256p. 1995. 10.95 (*0-614-04797-8*) RoVers Pubns.

Peterson, John. Europe & America in the Nineteen Nineties: Prospects for Partnership. 256p. 1993. 59.95 (*1-85278-536-5*, Pub. by E Elgar Pub UK) Ashgate Pub Co.

— Finite Mathematics. LC 73-10457. 1974. 19.95 (*0-8290-2364-X*) Irvington.

— High Technology & the Competition State: An Analysis of the Eureka Initiative. LC 93-811. 1993. write for info. (*0-415-09562-X*) Routledge.

— Littles. (J). (gr. 4-7). 1993. pap. 2.95 (*0-590-46225-3*) Scholastic Inc.

— Littles & the Big Storm. (J). (gr. 4-7). 1994. pap. 2.75 (*0-590-42276-6*) Scholastic Inc.

— Littles & the Lost Children. (J). (gr. 4-7). 1991. pap. 2.75 (*0-590-43026-2*) Scholastic Inc.

— The Littles & the Terrible Tiny Kid. (J). (gr. 4-7). 1993. pap. 2.75 (*0-590-45578-8*) Scholastic Inc.

— Littles & the Trash Tinies. (J). (gr. 4-7). 1993. pap. 2.75 (*0-590-46595-3*) Scholastic Inc.

— The Littles Give a Party. (J). (gr. 4-7). 1993. pap. 2.75 (*0-590-46597-X*) Scholastic Inc.

— The Littles Go Exploring. (J). (gr. 4-7). 1993. pap. 2.99 (*0-590-46596-1*) Scholastic Inc.

— The Littles Go to School. 80p. (J). (gr. k-3). 1994. pap. 2.50 (*0-590-42129-8*) Scholastic Inc.

— The Littles Have a Wedding. (J). (gr. 4-7). 1993. pap. 2.99 (*0-590-46224-5*) Scholastic Inc.

— The Littles Take a Trip. (J). (gr. 2-5). 1988. 14.50 (*0-8446-6351-4*) Peter Smith.

— Littles Take a Trip. (J). (gr. 4-7). 1993. pap. 2.99 (*0-590-46222-9*) Scholastic Inc.

— The Littles to the Rescue. (J). (gr. 4-7). 1993. pap. 2.95 (*0-590-46223-7*) Scholastic Inc.

— Mystery in the Night Woods. (Illus.). 80p. (J). 1991. pap. 2.75 (*0-590-45224-X*) Scholastic Inc.

— Technical Mathematics. 2nd ed. LC 95-13517. 1996. write for info. (*0-8273-7236-1*) Delmar.

— Tom Little's Great Halloween Scare. (J). 1994. pap. 2.75 (*0-590-42235-9*) Scholastic Inc.

Peterson, John, jt. auth. see Gayton, Tom.

Peterson, John, jt. ed. see Sindelar, Richard.

Peterson, John A., ed. see LeFors, Rufe.

Peterson, John C. Technical Mathematics. LC 92-32234. 846p. 1994. text ed. 39.95 (*0-8273-4575-5*) Delmar.

— Technical Mathematics with Calculus. LC 92-32757. 1342p. 1994. text ed. 43.95 (*0-8273-4577-1*) Delmar.

— Technical Mathematics with Calculus. 2nd ed. LC 95-13516. 1996. write for info. (*0-8273-7243-4*) Delmar.

Peterson, John C. & Herweyer, Alan. Students Solutions Manual to Accompany Technical Mathematics & Technical Mathematics with Calculus. 208p. 1994. 16.95 (*0-8273-6506-3*) Delmar.

— Technical Mathematics & Technical Mathematics with Calculus: Solutions Manual. 647p. 1994. pap. text ed. 18.95 (*0-8273-4582-8*) Delmar.

Peterson, John C. & Peterson, Doris M. Carroll County Indiana Rural Organizations 1828-1979: Vol. I History. LC 80-82231. (Illus.). 400p. 1980. 25.00 (*0-9604376-0-6*) J & D Peterson.

Peterson, John C., jt. auth. see Dobbs, David E.

An Asterisk (*) at the beginning of an entry indicates that the title is appearing in BIP for the first time.

Peterson, John E. Defending Arabia. LC 86-6569. 304p. 1986. text ed. 35.00 (*0-312-19114-6*) St Martin.
— Yemen: The Search for a Modern State. LC 81-48187. 224p. 1982. 25.00 (*0-8018-2784-1*) Johns Hopkins.
***Peterson, John L.** The Road to 2015: Profiles of the Future. LC 94-22027. 372p. 1994. pap. 18.95 (*1-878739-85-9*) Waite Group Pr.
Peterson, Joseph. Early Conceptions & Tests of Intelligence. LC 70-98868. 320p. 1970. reprint ed. text ed. 59.75 (*0-8371-2836-6*, PETI, Greenwood Pr) Greenwood.
Peterson, Joseph L., ed. Forensic Science: Scientific Investigation in Criminal Justice. LC 75-11812. (Studies in Criminal Justice: No. 1). 45.00 (*0-404-13139-5*) AMS Pr.
Peterson, Joyce S. American Automobile Workers, 1900-1933. LC 87-1942. (American Labor History Ser.). 231p. 1987. 64.50 (*0-88706-573-2*); pap. 21.95 (*0-88706-574-0*) State U NY Pr.
Peterson, K., et al. Post-Traumatic Stress Disorder: A Clinician's Guide. LC 90-14309. (Stress & Coping Ser.). (Illus.). 250p. 1990. 37.50 (*0-306-43542-X*, Plenum Pr) Plenum.
Peterson, K., et al, eds. Papers from Twenty-First Regional Meeting of C. L. S., 2 pts., Pt. 1. 438p. (Orig.). 1985. pap. text ed. 9.00 (*0-685-11918-1*) Chicago Ling.
— Papers from Twenty-First Regional Meeting of C. L. S., 2 pts., Pt. 2: Parassession on Causatives & Agentivity. (Orig.). 1985. Pt. 2: Parassession on Causatives & Agentivity. pap. text ed. 9.00 (*0-914203-24-X*) Chicago Ling.
Peterson, K. H., jt. ed. see Rutherford, A.
Peterson, Karon. Why Should I? 29p. 1983. pap. 2.95 (*0-913923-47-8*) Woodland UT.
Peterson, Kathy, ed. Oil Shale: The Environmental Challenges. LC 81-10118. (Proceedings of International Symposium Aug. 11-14, 1980, Vail, Colorado Ser.). (Illus.). 261p. 1981. text ed. 10.00 (*0-918062-43-8*) Colo Sch Mines.
Peterson, Kathy K., ed. Oil Shale: The Environmental Challenges II. LC 82-14759. (Illus.). 392p. 1982. 11.00 (*0-918062-51-9*) Colo Sch Mines.
Peterson, Kay. Home Is Where You Park It. rev. ed. (Illus.). 200p. 1990. reprint ed. pap. 8.95 (*0-910449-00-7*) RoVers Pubns.
— Home Is Where You Park It. (Illus.). 200p. 1992. reprint ed. 8.95 (*0-685-60592-2*) RoVers Pubns.
Peterson, Kay, jt. auth. see Peterson, Joe.
Peterson, Keith, et al. Grasp-It: A General Review & Study Program-Interactive Testing. (C). 1984. 250.00 (*0-06-045147-5*) HarpCollege.
***Peterson, Kenneth D.** Teacher Evaluation: A Comprehensive Guide to New Directions & Practices. (Illus.). 272p. 1995. pap. 18.00 (*0-8039-6244-4*) Corwin Pr.
Peterson, Kenneth L. Climate & the Dolores River Anasazi: A Paleoenvironmental Reconstruction from a 10,000 Year Pollen Record, La Plata Mountains, Southwest Colorado. (Anthropological Papers: No. 113). 160p. (Orig.). 1988. pap. 25.00 (*0-87480-303-9*) U of Utah Pr.
Peterson, Kent D., jt. auth. see Deal, Terrence E.
***Peterson, Kent W. & David, Linda F.** Directory of Occupational Health & Safety Software: Version 8.0. 7th ed. 462p. 1995. pap. 75.00 (*1-885190-02-6*) Comput in Occupat.
Peterson, Kevin. Our Spark of Hope. 168p. (Orig.). 1989. 18.00 (*0-944996-05-1*); pap. text ed. 9.95 (*0-944996-04-3*) Carlsons.
Peterson, Kim, ed. see Diamond, Carlin J.
Peterson, Kim, ed. see Ruiz, Shirley.
Peterson, Kim, ed. see Stearn, Marshall B.
Peterson, Kirk. The Automated Teller Machine As a National Bank under the Federal Law. LC 87-31197. (Legal Research Guides Ser.: Vol. 5). 70p. 1987. lib. bdg. 30.00 (*0-89941-587-3*, 305410) W S Hein.
***Peterson, Kirk L. & Nicod, Pascal, eds.** Cardiac Catheterization. LC 95-3944. 1995. write for info. (*0-7216-3064-2*) Saunders.
Peterson, Kirtland C. Mind of the Ninja: Exploring the Inner Power. (Illus.). 288p. (Orig.). 1986. pap. 14.95 (*0-8092-4951-0*) Contemp Bks.
Peterson, Knut D. The Lost Frontier. LC 79-11657. 1981. 22.95 (*0-87949-172-8*) Ashley Bks.
— When Alaska Was Free. Ashton, Sylvia, ed. LC 77-70299. 1977. 21.95 (*0-87949-081-0*) Ashley Bks.
Peterson, Kolan. Special Effects in Watercolors. (How to Draw & Paint Ser.). (Illus.). 32p. (Orig.). 1989. pap. 5.95 (*0-929261-49-6*, HT207) W Foster Pub.
— Watercolors Step-by-Step. (How to Draw & Paint Ser.). (Illus.). 32p. (Orig.). 1989. pap. 5.95 (*0-929261-47-X*, HT205) W Foster Pub.
Peterson, Kristine. The Strategic Approach to Quality Service in Health Care. (Health Care Administration Ser.). 332p. 1988. 63.00 (*0-87189-764-4*) Aspen Pub.
Peterson, L. A., ed. see Wiesend, Rick.
Peterson, L. A., et al. Brain Fuel: The Book That Improves Your Mind As Well As Your Body! 2nd ed. (Illus.). 256p. 1990. reprint ed. pap. 12.95 (*1-878459-01-5*) Total Rsch Pub.
Peterson, L. E., ed. see Armstong, Ray.
Peterson, Larry, jt. auth. see DePasquale, Dan.
Peterson, Larry, jt. auth. see Gesme, Carole.
Peterson, Larry R. Ignatius Donnelly: A Psychohistorical Study in Moral Development Psychology: Dissertations in American Biography. 1981. 27.95 (*0-405-14102-5*) Ayer.
Peterson, Lars. Sports Injuries. (Illus.). 498p. 1986. text ed. 37.95 (*0-8151-6678-8*, Yr Bk Med Pubs) Mosby Yr Bk.
Peterson, Lee. San Diego. LC 91-73732. (Illus.). 80p. (ENG, ITA, JPN & SPA.). 1991. 18.95 (*0-916251-45-4*) Sunbelt Pubns.
Peterson, Lee A. A Field Guide to Eastern Edible Wild Plants. (Peterson Field Guide Ser.). 1978. 21.95 (*0-395-20445-3*) HM.
— A Field Guide to Eastern Edible Wild Plants. (Peterson Field Guide Ser.). 1982. pap. 15.95 (*0-395-31870-X*) HM.
Peterson, Leonard. They're All Afraid. (Illus.). 161p. 1981. pap. 8.95 (*0-7725-5032-8*, Pub. by Stoddart Pubng CN) Genl Dist Srvs.
Peterson, Leroy J., ed. Yearbook of School Law 1972. 1972. 8.95 (*1-56534-048-5*) NOLPE.
Peterson, Levi S. The Backslider. 2nd ed. LC 90-37395. 361p. 1990. pap. 5.95 (*1-56085-015-9*) Signature Bks.
— Juanita Brooks: Morman Woman Historian. LC 88-17421. (Utah Centennial Ser.: No. 5). 513p. reprint ed. pap. 146.30 (*0-7837-3966-4*, 2043795) Bks Demand.
— Night Soil: New Stories. LC 90-38313. 192p. 1990. 14.95 (*1-56085-002-7*) Signature Bks.
***Peterson, Lewis.** Deliver the Message. LC 94-96297. (Orig.). 1994. audio 12.00 (*1-885721-01-3*) L P Prods.
Peterson, Linda. Careers Without College: Emergencies. Hupping, Carol & Grimaldi, Alicia, eds. LC 93-7077. 96p. (YA). 1993. pap. 7.95 (*1-56079-252-3*) Petersons Guides.
— Careers Without College: Entertainment. (Orig.). (YA). 1994. pap. 7.95 (*1-56079-352-X*) Petersons Guides.
— Starting Out, Starting Over: Finding the Work That's Waiting for You. LC 95-4177. 208p. (Orig.). 1995. pap. 14.95 (*0-89106-073-1*); pap. 14.95 (*0-614-07131-3*, 7230) Davies-Black.
***Peterson, Linda, et al.** Telling Without Telling: A Clinical Guide to Screening Children's Art Productions. LC 95-67176. (Illus.). 144p. 1995. pap. 39.95 (*0-9645604-0-2*) Drawing Conclusions.
Peterson, Linda G. & O'Shanick, G. J., eds. Psychiatric Aspects of Trauma. (Advances in Psychosomatic Medicine Ser.: Vol. 16). (Illus.). x, 238p. 1986. 63.25 (*3-8055-4219-4*) S Karger.
Peterson, Linda H. Victorian Autobiography: The Tradition of Self-Interpretation. LC 85-17964. 240p. 1986. 32.00 (*0-300-03563-2*) Yale U Pr.
Peterson, Linda H., jt. auth. see Casteras, Susan P.
***Peterson, Linda H., et al, eds.** The Norton Reader: An Anthology of Expository Prose. 9th abr. ed. LC 95-2937. 1995. write for info. (*0-393-96827-8*) Norton.
— The Norton Reader: An Anthology of Expository Prose. 9th ed. LC 95-2934. 1995. pap. write for info. (*0-393-96826-X*) Norton.
Peterson, Linda K. & Solt, Marilyn L. Newbery & Caldecott Medal & Honor Books: An Annotated Bibliography. 1982. lib. bdg. 57.50 (*0-8161-8448-8*, Hall Reference) Macmillan.
***Peterson, Linda S.** Birth Expectations of U. S. Women: 1973 to 1988. 9940. write for info. (*0-8406-0501-3*) Natl Ctr Health Stats.
Peterson, Linda W. The Electronic Lifeline: A Media Exploration for Youth. 1990. pap. 3.95 (*0-377-00209-7*) Friendship Pr.
Peterson, Lindy. Stop & Think Parenting. 83p. (Orig.). 1993. pap. 16.95 (*0-86431-131-1*, Pub. by Aust Coun Educ Res AT) Paul & Co Pubs.
Peterson, Liz. Wind in the Willows: (A Musical) (Orig.). (J). 1993. pap. 5.00 (*0-87602-325-1*) Anchorage.
Peterson, Lizette & Harbeck, Cynthia. The Pediatric Psychologist: Issues in Professional Development & Practice. LC 88-61409. (Health Psychology Ser.). 200p. (Orig.). (C). 1988. pap. text ed. 16.95 (*0-87822-296-0*, 2960) Res Press.
Peterson, Lizette, jt. auth. see Gelfand, Donna M.
Peterson, Lorin. The Brutalitarians & the Bomb. LC 87-83304. (Illus.). 160p. 1988. 9.95 (*0-945690-00-2*) Hillside CA.
Peterson, Lorna, comp. PMS: The Premenstrual Syndrome. 76p. 1985. pap. 18.75 (*0-89774-205-2*) Oryx Pr.
Peterson, Lorraine. Anybody Can Be Cool, but Awesome Takes Practice. LC 88-19454. (Devotional for Teens Ser.). (Illus.). 192p. (Orig.). (YA). (gr. 9-12). 1988. pap. 7.99 (*1-55661-040-8*) Bethany Hse.
— Dying of Embarrassment & Living to Tell about It. LC 87-35334. (Devotional Ser.: No. 5). 224p. (Orig.). (YA). (gr. 9-12). 1988. pap. 7.99 (*0-87123-967-1*) Bethany Hse.
— Falling Off Cloud Nine & Other High Places. LC 81-38465. (Illus.). 159p. (Orig.). (J). (gr. 8-12). 1981. pap. 7.99 (*0-87123-167-0*) Bethany Hse.
— If God Loves Me: Teacher's Guide. LC 80-27014. 128p. (Orig.). 1983. pap. 6.99 (*0-87123-586-2*) Bethany Hse.
— If God Loves Me, Why Can't I Get My Locker Open? LC 80-27014. 141p. (Orig.). (J). (gr. 6-12). 1980. pap. 7.99 (*0-87123-251-0*) Bethany Hse.
— If the Devil Made You Do It, You Blew It. 192p. (Orig.). (YA). (gr. 8 up). 1989. pap. 7.99 (*1-55661-052-1*) Bethany Hse.
— If You Really Trust Me, Why Can't I Stay Out Longer? 224p. (Orig.). (YA). 1991. pap. 7.99 (*1-55661-212-5*) Bethany Hse.
— Lord, I Haven't Talked to You since the Last Crisis, But... The Purpose & Power of Prayer. LC 93-40579. (YA). 1994. pap. 7.99 (*1-55661-385-7*) Bethany Hse.
— Please Give Me Another Chance, Lord. 240p. 1995. pap. 7.99 (*1-55661-583-3*) Bethany Hse.
— Radical Advice from the Ultimate Wiseguy. 192p. (Orig.). (YA). (gr. 8-12). 1990. pap. 7.99 (*1-55661-141-2*) Bethany Hse.
— Real Character's in the Making. LC 85-7373. 150p. 1985. pap. 7.99 (*0-87123-824-1*) Bethany Hse.
— Si Dios Me Ama, Por Que Me Sale Todo Mal? Ward, Rhode F., tr. 160p. (SPA.). 1988. reprint ed. pap. 4.95 (*0-88113-269-1*) Edit Betania.
— Trying to Get Toothpaste Back Into the Tube. 192p. (Orig.). (J). (gr. 7-10). 1993. pap. 7.99 (*1-55661-315-6*) Bethany Hse.
— Why Isn't God Giving Cash Prizes? LC 82-17866. (Devitional for Teens Ser.: No. 3). (Illus.). 160p. (J). (gr. 8-12). 1982. pap. 7.99 (*0-87123-626-5*) Bethany Hse.
Peterson, Lynn, jt. auth. see Haseltine, Beth.
Peterson, M. International Interest Organizations & the Transmutation of Postwar Society. 740p. (Orig.). 1979. pap. 71.00x (*91-22-00255-3*, Pub. by Almqv & Wiksell SW) Coronet Bks.
Peterson, M. & Winer, W., eds. Wear Control Handbook. 1500p. 95.00 (*0-317-33640-1*, G00169) ASME.
Peterson, M., jt. auth. see Winn, Charles S.
Peterson, M. J. The General Assembly in World Politics. 240p. 1986. text ed. 55.00 (*0-04-327079-4*) Routledge Chapman & Hall.
Peterson, M. Jeanne. Family, Love, & Work in the Lives of Victorian Gentlewomen. LC 88-45389. (Illus.). 256p. 1989. 39.95 (*0-253-34427-1*); pap. 14.95 (*0-253-20509-3*, MB-509) Ind U Pr.
***Peterson, M. Lewis.** Deliver the Message. rev. ed. (Illus.). 70p. (Orig.). 1994. audio 22.00 (*0-615-00215-3*) L P Prods.
— Deliver the Message. rev. ed. LC 94-96297. (Illus.). 70p. (Orig.). (YA). 1994. pap. 12.00 (*1-885721-00-5*) L P Prods.
Peterson, Mable. No Water: A True, Gripping Story about Demons & Children. 96p. write for info. (*0-936369-08-6*) Son-Rise Pubns.
***Peterson, Marg, ed. & intro.** Going Places: Workshop Proceedings from the 4th National Rails-to-Trails Conference. (Illus.). 320p. (Orig.). 1993. 19.95 (*0-925794-06-6*) Rails Trails.
Peterson, Margaret. Wallace Stevens & the Idealist Tradition. LC 83-4996. (Studies in Modern Literature: No. 24). 199p. reprint ed. pap. 56.80 (*0-8357-1452-7*, 2070517) Bks Demand.
Peterson, Margaret S. Water Resource Planning & Development. (Illus.). 240p. 1984. text ed. 61.00 (*0-13-945908-1*) P-H.
Peterson, Margaret S., jt. auth. see Stephenson, D.
Peterson, Marge & Peterson, Rob. Argentina: A Wild West Heritage. LC 89-11707. (Discovering Our Heritage Ser.). (Illus.). 128p. (J). (gr. 5 up). 1990. text ed. 14.95 (*0-87518-413-8*, Dillon Silver Burdett) Silver Burdett Pr.
Peterson, Marie B. Kaleidoscope. 100p. 1990. 14.99 (*0-925037-13-3*) Great Lks Poetry.
Peterson, Marilyn, jt. ed. see Andrews, Paul, Jr.
Peterson, Marilyn B. Applications in Criminal Analysis: A Sourcebook. LC 94-11219. 336p. 1994. text ed. 79.50 (*0-313-28577-2*, Greenwood Pr) Greenwood.
Peterson, Marilyn R. At Personal Risk: Boundary Violations in Professional-Client Relationships. 200p. (C). 1992. 22.95 (*0-393-70138-7*) Norton.
***Peterson, Marilyn S. & Urquiza, Anthony J.** The Role of Mental Health Professionals in the Prevention & Treatment of Child Abuse & Neglect. 73p. (Orig.). (C). 1995. pap. text ed. 35.00x (*0-7881-1664-9*) Diane Pub.
***Peterson, Marion L.** HIV-AIDS Resources: The National Directory of Resources on HIV Infection-AIDS. 600p. 1994. pap. text ed. 110.00 (*1-885461-00-3*) National Direct.
— National Directory of Children, Youth & Families Services. 10th ed. 800p. 1994. pap. text ed. 84.00 (*1-885461-01-1*) National Direct.
Peterson, Mark. Borland C Plus Plus Developer's Bible. (Illus.). 890p. (Orig.). 1992. pap. 29.95 (*1-878739-16-6*) Waite Group Pr.
Peterson, Mark, jt. ed. see Kendall, Laurel.
Peterson, Mark A. Legislating Together: The White House & Capitol Hill from Eisenhower to Reagan. (Illus.). 352p. 1990. 39.95 (*0-674-52415-2*) HUP.
Peterson, Mark A., jt. auth. see Chin, Audrey.
Peterson, Mark A., jt. auth. see Shanley, Michael G.
Peterson, Mark F., jt. auth. see Smith, Peter B.
Peterson, Marlow, jt. auth. see Castle, Larry.
Peterson, Marquita, jt. auth. see Priestley, Lee.
Peterson, Martha, jt. auth. see Peterson, Robert.
Peterson, Martin. Lift Me to the Sky at Sunrise. abr. ed. 140p. 1995. pap. 6.95 (*1-56901-332-2*) NW Pub.
Peterson, Martin, jt. auth. see Ardinger, Rick.
Peterson, Martin S., jt. ed. see Josephson, Edward S.
Peterson, Marvin, ed. ASHE Reader on Organization & Governance in Higher Education. 4th ed. 1991. 32.50 (*0-536-57981-4*) Ginn Pr.
Peterson, Marvin W. & Mets, Lisa A., eds. Key Resources on Higher Education Governance, Management, & Leadership: A Guide to the Literature. LC 87-45501. (Higher & Adult Education Ser.). 536p. 1987. 52.00x (*1-55542-052-4*) Jossey-Bass.
Peterson, Marvin W., et al. Black Students on White Campuses: The Impacts of Increased Black Enrollments. LC 78-60965. 384p. 1978. 18.00 (*0-87944-221-2*) Inst Soc Res.
Peterson, Mary. Mercy Flights: Stories. LC 84-19490. (Breakthrough Ser.: No. 47). 104p. 1985. pap. 10.95 (*0-8262-0464-3*) U of Mo Pr.
Peterson, Mary E. And I Shall Be Your Ancestor. (Illus.). 48p. (Orig.). 1980. pap. 3.00 (*0-912701-02-1*) Balance Beam Pr.
Peterson, Mary E., ed. The Message in the Mirror. (Illus.). 80p. (Orig.). 1983. pap. 4.70 (*0-912701-00-5*) Balance Beam Pr.
***Peterson, Mary J.** Universal Kitchen Planning: Design That Adapts to People. (Illus.). 220p. (Orig.). (C). 1995. pap. text ed. 50.00 (*1-887127-00-3*) Natl Kit Bath.
Peterson, Meg. Complete Autoharp Songbook. (Complete Book Ser.). 1993. 15.00 (*0-87166-769-X*, 93694) Mel Bay.
— The Complete Method for Autoharp or Chromaharp. 1993. 12.95 (*0-87166-921-8*, 93657); audio 9.98 (*1-56222-593-6*, 93657) Mel Bay.
— Hymns for Auto Harp. 56p. 1978. student ed 4.95 (*0-89228-053-0*) Impact Christian.
— Hymns for Autoharp. 1993. 4.95 (*0-87166-718-5*, 93617) Mel Bay.
— Let's Play the Autoharp. 1993. 4.95 (*0-87166-524-7*, 93701) Mel Bay.
Peterson, Meg & Fox, Dan. Songs of Christmas for Autoharp. 1993. 3.95 (*0-87166-618-9*, 93696) Mel Bay.
Peterson, Melvin N. David's Star Studded Adventures. (Illus.). 58p. (J). (gr. 1-4). 1988. spiral bd. 48.00 (*0-938880-07-1*) MNP Star.
— Flight Deck Uses for the HP-41C: Celestial Navigation, Vol. 3. 58p. (C). 1984. spiral bd. 48.00 (*0-938880-02-0*) MNP Star.
— Flight Deck Uses for the HP-41C Series, Set, Pts. I & II. (Illus.). 63p. (C). 1989. Pt. I, Think Jet & AF36 Zeprom Flight Plan System; Pt. II, Celestial Navigation Intercept Readout Sy. spiral bd. 177.50 (*0-938880-08-X*) MNP Star.
Peterson, Melvin N., ed. Diversity of Oceanic Life: An Evaluative Review. LC 92-39818. (Significant Issues Ser.: Vol. 14, No. 12). 120p. (gr. 13). 1993. pap. text ed. 14.95 (*0-89206-206-1*) CSI Studies.
Peterson, Merrill D. Adams & Jefferson: A Revolutionary Dialogue. LC 76-1145. (Illus.). 1978. pap. 10.95 (*0-19-502355-2*) OUP.
— The Great Triumvirate: Webster, Clay, & Calhoun. 582p. 1987. reprint ed. 35.00 (*0-19-503877-0*) OUP.
— The Great Triumvirate: Webster, Clay, & Calhoun. 582p. 1988. reprint ed. pap. 15.95 (*0-19-505686-8*) OUP.
— Lincoln in American Memory. (Illus.). 496p. 1994. 30.00 (*0-19-506570-0*) OUP.
— Lincoln in American Memory. (Illus.). 496p. 1995. pap. 15.95 (*0-19-509645-2*) OUP.
— Thomas Jefferson & the New Nation: A Biography. LC 70-110394. (Illus.). 1104p. 1986. reprint ed. pap. 22.00 (*0-19-501909-1*) OUP.
Peterson, Merrill D., ed. Democracy, Liberty & Property: The State Constitutional Conventions of the 1820's. LC 65-23013. (Orig.). 1966. pap. 7.35 (*0-672-60062-5*, AHS43, Bobbs) Macmillan.
— The Political Writings of Thomas Jefferson. (Monticello Monograph Ser.). 213p. (Orig.). Date not set. pap. 12.95 (*1-882886-01-1*) T J Mem Fnd.
Peterson, Merrill D., intro. Visitors to Monticello. LC 89-5778. (Illus.). 212p. 1989. 32.50 (*0-8139-1231-8*); pap. 14.95 (*0-8139-1232-6*) U Pr of Va.
Peterson, Merrill D. & Vaughan, Robert C., eds. The Virginia Statute for Religious Freedom: Its Evolution & Consequences in American History. LC 87-13786. (Cambridge Studies in Religious & American Public Life: 1). (Illus.). 420p. 1988. 44.95 (*0-521-34329-1*) Cambridge U Pr.
Peterson, Merrill D., ed. see Jefferson, Thomas.
***Peterson, Michael.** A Bitter Peace. LC 94-37559. 1995. write for info. (*0-671-72695-1*) PB.
— Vocational Assessment of Special Needs Students for Vocational Education: A State-of-the-Art Review. 1988. 8.00 (*0-318-40005-7*, IN 327) Ctr Educ Trng Employ.
***Peterson, Michael, et al, eds.** Philosophy of Religion: Selected Readings. 560p. (C). 1995. pap. text ed. 27.95 (*0-19-508909-X*) OUP.
Peterson, Michael E. The Combined Action Platoons: The U. S. Marines Other War in Vietnam. LC 88-34031. 161p. 1989. text ed. 49.95 (*0-275-93258-3*, C3258, Praeger Pubs) Greenwood.
Peterson, Michael E., et al. Reason & Religious Belief: An Introduction to the Philosophy of Religion. 304p. (C). 1990. pap. text ed. 19.95 (*0-19-506155-1*) OUP.
Peterson, Michael L., ed. The Problem of Evil: Selected Readings. LC 91-50576. (Library of Religious Philosophy: Vol. 8). (C). 1992. text ed. 44.95 (*0-268-01514-7*); pap. text ed. 19.95 (*0-268-01515-5*) U of Notre Dame Pr.
Peterson, Michael P. Interactive & Animated Cartography. LC 94-20878. 1995. text ed. write for info. (*0-13-079104-0*) P-H.
***Peterson, Michael T.** DCE: A Guide to Developing Portable Applications. LC 94-35053. (J. Ramade Workstation Ser.). 1995. cd-rom, text ed. 75.00 (*0-07-911800-3*); pap. text ed. 49.95 (*0-07-911801-1*) McGraw.
Peterson, Molly. The Faith Family: An Allegory about Giving & Receiving. LC 91-41522. (Orig.). 1991. pap. 5.00 (*0-915541-91-2*) Star Bks Inc.
Peterson, Moose. Nikon System Handbook. 164p. 1991. pap. 19.95 (*0-929667-03-4*, 10252) Images NY.
Peterson, N. L. & Harkness, S. D., eds. Radiation Damage in Metals: Papers Presented at a Seminar of the American Society for Metals, Nov. 9-10, 197. LC 76-25094. (Illus.). 415p. reprint ed. pap. 118.30 (*0-317-08178-0*, 2019485) Bks Demand.
Peterson, N. V., ed. Health Freedom: Preventive Medicine Can Save Your Life & Fortune. LC 93-74785. 66p. (Orig.). 1994. pap. 9.00 (*1-57000-028-X*) W S Dawson.
— Health Freedom: Preventive Medicine Can Save Your Life & Fortune. abr. ed. LC 93-74785. 66p. (Orig.). 1994. pap. 2.00 (*1-57000-029-8*) W S Dawson.
Peterson, Nadine & Sofie, Barbara N. Singleness: A Guide to Understanding & Satisfaction. LC 87-50532. 184p. (Orig.). 1987. pap. 9.95 (*0-934955-09-3*) Watercress Pr.
Peterson, Nadya. Living Language Russian Manual. rev. ed. (RUS.). 1993. pap. 6.00 (*0-517-59054-9*, Living Language) Crown Pub Group.
— Living Russian. rev. ed. (Complete Living Language Course Ser.). (ENG & RUS.). 1993. 20.00 (*0-517-59053-0*, Living Language) Crown Pub Group.
— Living Russian: Conversational Manual. rev. ed. (Complete Living Language Course Ser.). (ENG & RUS.). 1993. pap. 6.00 (*0-685-63465-5*, Living Language) Crown Pub Group.

— Living Russian: Dictionary. rev. ed. (Complete Living Language Course Ser.). (ENG & RUS.). 1993. pap. 5.00 (0-517-59055-7, Living Language) Crown Pub Group.

Peterson, Nancy. People of the Old Missury: Years of Conflict. LC 89-10723. (Illus.). 192p. (Orig.). 1989. 29.95 (1-55838-105-8); pap. 16.95 (1-55838-106-6) R H Pub.

Peterson, Nancy L. Early Intervention for Handicapped & At-Risk Children. LC 86-81467. 580p. 1987. text ed. 44.95 (0-89108-129-1) Love Pub Co.

Peterson, Nancy M. People of the Moonshell: A Western River Journal. LC 84-15919. (Illus.). 176p. (Orig.). 1984. 22.95 (0-939650-45-2); pap. 18.95 (0-939650-42-8) R H Pub.

— People of the Troubled Water: A Missouri River Journal. LC 88-26418. (Illus.). 176p. (Orig.). 1988. 24.95 (1-55838-082-5); pap. 15.95 (1-55838-083-3) R H Pub.

Peterson, Nils. The Comedy of Desire. (Illus.). 70p. (Orig.). 1994. pap. 10.00 (0-9638722-0-6) Blue Sofa.

Peterson, Norm, jt. auth. see Harding, Bertrand, Jr.

Peterson, Norma. Teachers: A Survival Guide for the Grown-up in the Classroom. 144p. 1985. mass mkt. 6.95 (0-452-25741-7, Plume) NAL-Dutton.

Peterson, Norma, jt. auth. see Peterson, Art.

Peterson, Norma L. Littleton Waller Tazewell. LC 83-3501. 225p. reprint ed. pap. 64.20 (0-7837-4371-8, 2044081) Bks Demand.

— The Presidencies of William Henry Harrison & John Tyler. LC 89-5341. (American Presidency Ser.). xiv, 330p. 1989. 29.95 (0-7006-0400-6) U Pr of KS.

Peterson, Norman. Photographic Art: Media & Disclosure. LC 83-18127. (Studies in Photography: No. 4). (Illus.). 147p. reprint ed. pap. 41.90 (0-8357-1529-9, 2070569) Bks Demand.

Peterson, O. H. The Electrophysiology of Gland Cells. LC 80-40303. (Physiological Society Monographs: No. 36). 1981. text ed. 145.00 (0-12-552150-2) Acad Pr.

Peterson, Owen. The Divine Discontent: The Life of Nathan S. S. Beman. LC 85-18765. (Illus.). xvii, 224p. 1985. text ed. 21.95 (0-86554-170-1, MUP-H160) Mercer Univ Pr.

Peterson, P., jt. auth. see Sims, Jean.

Peterson, P. F., ed. Proceedings of the Second ASME-JSME Joint Conference on Nuclear Engineering, 2 vols. 1993. 200.00 (0-685-70661-3, IX0343) ASME.

— Proceedings of the Second ASME-JSME Joint Conference on Nuclear Engineering, Vol. 1. 772p. 1993. write for info. (0-7918-0636-7, I0343A) ASME.

— Proceedings of the Second ASME-JSME Joint Conference on Nuclear Engineering, Vol. 2. 916p. 1993. write for info. (0-7918-0637-5, I0343B) ASME.

Peterson, P. F. & Kim, J. H., eds. Transient Phenomena in Nuclear Reactor Systems. (HTD Series, Vol. 245: NE: Vol. 11). 148p. 1993. 40.00 (0-7918-1158-1, G00802) ASME.

Peterson, P. F., jt. ed. see Cheung, F. B.

Peterson, P. J. Some Days, Other Days. LC 93-3871. 32p. (J). 1994. text ed. 14.95 (0-684-19595-X, Scribners) S&S Trade.

Peterson, Pam, jt. auth. see Lick, Carol J.

Peterson, Pamela P. Financial Management & Analysis. LC 93-33419. (Series in Finance). 1994. text ed. write for info. (0-07-049667-6) McGraw.

***Peterson, Pat.** Collector's Guide to Trolls, Identification & Values. 384p. 1995. pap. 18.95 (0-89145-649-X, 3967) Collector Bks.

Peterson, Patricia R. Home Health Care Equipment: A Consumer Guidebook. LC 89-62034. (Illus.). 156p. (Orig.). 1989. 16.95 (0-944871-34-8); pap. 9.95 (0-944871-35-6) Riegel Pub.

— The Know It All: Resource Book for Kids. (Illus.). 144p. (J). (gr. 2 up). 1989. pap. 15.95 (0-913705-45-4) Zephyr Pr AZ.

Peterson, Paul, jt. auth. see Koenig, Mark.

Peterson, Paul, et al. Working in Animal Science. Amberson, Max L., ed. (Illus.). (gr. 9-10). 1978. text ed. 19.96 (0-07-000839-6) McGraw.

Peterson, Paul C., et al. The Feather Mite Family Eustathiidae (Acarina: Sarcoptiformes) (Monograph: No. 21). (Illus.). 143p. 1980. pap. 10.00 (0-910006-29-6) Acad Nat Sci Phila.

Peterson, Paul E. City Limits. LC 80-29043. 288p. (C). 1981. lib. bdg. 27.50 (0-226-66292-6); pap. text ed. 11.95 (0-226-66293-4) U Ch Pr.

— Law in Arkansas Public Schools. LC 94-11805. 1994. 12.95 (0-944436-21-8) Univ Central AR Pr.

— The Politics of School Reform, 1870-1940. LC 85-1042. x, 242p. 1985. pap. text ed. 11.95 (0-226-66295-0) U Ch Pr.

— The Price of Federalism. (Twentieth Century Bks.). 250p. (C). 1995. 36.95x (0-8157-7024-3); pap. 15.95x (0-8157-7023-5) Brookings.

***Peterson, Paul E., ed.** Classifying by Race. LC 95-13494. (Studies in American Politics). 1995. write for info. (0-691-03796-5); pap. write for info. (0-691-00176-6) Princeton U Pr.

— The New Urban Reality. LC 84-45848. 301p. 1985. 35.95 (0-8157-7018-9); pap. 15.95 (0-8157-7017-0) Brookings.

— The President, the Congress & the Making of Foreign Policy. LC 94-11855. 312p. 1994. 34.95x (0-8061-2654-X) U of Okla Pr.

— The President, the Congress & the Making of Foreign Policy. LC 94-11855. 1994. pap. 16.95 (0-8061-2685-X) U of Okla Pr.

Peterson, Paul E. & Rom, Mark C. Welfare Magnets: A New Case for a National Standard. 178p. 1990. 28.95 (0-8157-7022-7); pap. 10.95 (0-8157-7021-9) Brookings.

Peterson, Paul E., jt. ed. see Chubb, John E.

Peterson, Paul E., jt. auth. see Greenstone, J. David.

Peterson, Paul E., jt. ed. see Jencks, Christopher.

Peterson, Paul E., et al. When Federalism Works. LC 86-24467. 243p. 1987. 31.95 (0-8157-7020-0); pap. 12.95 (0-8157-7019-7) Brookings.

Peterson, Paul K., ed. Voices at the Crossroads: First-Person, Dramatic Portrayals of Witnesses to Jesus' Death & Resurrection. LC 91-28518. 80p. (Orig.). 1991. pap. 8.99 (0-8066-2575-9, 9-2575, Augsburg) Augsburg Fortress.

Peterson, Paul M. & Annable, Carol R. Systematics of the Annual Species of Muhlenbergia (Poaceae-Eragrostideae) Anderson, Christiane, ed. (Systematic Botany Monographs: Vol. 31). (Illus.). 109p. 1991. pap. 13.50 (0-912861-31-2) Am Soc Plant.

Peterson, Paul M., jt. auth. see Terrell, Edward E.

Peterson, Paula. Coming Home: An Intimate Glance at a Family Camp in the Adirondack North Country. LC 93-14484. 64p. 1993. pap. 9.95 (0-925168-01-7) North Country.

Peterson, Penelope L. & Walberg, Herbert J., eds. Research on Teaching: Concepts, Findings & Implications. LC 78-62102. (Education Ser.). 1979. 31.50 (0-8211-1518-9); text ed. write for info. (0-685-03236-1) McCutchan.

Peterson, Penelope L., et al, eds. The Social Contexts of Instruction: Group Organization & Group Process. (Educational Psychology Ser.). 1983. text ed. 64.00 (0-12-552220-7) Acad Pr.

Peterson, Pete, ed. see Douglis, Marjie.

Peterson, Pete, jt. auth. see Heddy, Edward J.

Peterson, Pete, jt. auth. see Luts, Jack.

Peterson, Pete, ed. see Oke, Janette.

Peterson, Pete, jt. auth. see Peterson, Joan.

Peterson, Pete, ed. see Springer, Jean.

Peterson, Peter. Facing Up. 1994. pap. 14.00 (0-671-89890-6, Touchstone Bks) S&S Trade.

Peterson, Peter G. Economic Nationalism & International Interdependence: The Global Costs of National Choices. 80p. reprint ed. pap. 25.00 (0-317-41834-3, 2025902) Bks Demand.

— Facing Up. 1993. 22.00 (0-671-79642-9) S&S Trade.

— Social Security. 19.95 (0-394-53318-6) Random.

Peterson, Peter G. & Howe, Neil. On Borrowed Time: How the Growth in Entitlement Spending Threatens America's Future. LC 88-23798. 430p. 1988. 24.95 (1-55815-003-X) ICS Pr.

Peterson, Philip, ed. see Donaldson, John.

Peterson, Philip L. Concepts & Language: An Essay in Generative Semantics & the Philosophy of Language. 1973. pap. 40.00 (90-279-2442-2) Mouton.

Peterson, Phillip J., ed. Corrosion of Electronic & Magnetic Materials. LC 91-42686. (Special Technical Publication Ser.: No. 1148). (Illus.). 120p. 1992. text ed. 49.00 (0-8031-1470-2, 04-011480-27) ASTM.

***Peterson, Phyllis L.** Scott County, Virginia Cemetery Records, 7 vols., Set. 2030p. 1993. pap. 192.00 (0-614-00908-1, 9310) Clearfield Co.

Peterson, Phyllis T., jt. auth. see Peterson, Richard D., 2nd.

***Peterson, Pipi.** Ready, Set, Organize! Get Your Stuff Together. 224p. (Orig.). 1995. pap. 12.95 (1-57112-072-6, P0726, Park Avenue) Park Ave Prods.

Peterson, R. The Classical World. (Atlas of Mankind Ser.: Vol. II). (Illus.). 112p. (C). 1985. 30.00 (0-941694-15-1) Cliveden Pr.

— Modern Europe. (Atlas of Mankind Ser.: Vol. 3). (Illus.). 128p. 1987. 30.00 (0-941694-31-3) Cliveden Pr.

***Peterson, R., ed.** The Racial Origins of the Founders of America. 128p. 1995. pap. 15.00 (0-614-04967-9) Scott-Townsend Pubs.

Peterson, R. & Peterson, V. Tiny Folios: Audubon's Birds of America. (Audubon Society Baby Elephant Folio Ser.). (Illus.). 472p. 1991. 10.95 (1-55859-225-3) Abbeville Pr.

Peterson, R., ed. see Kingsley, Charles.

Peterson, R., jt. auth. see Sayle, A. A.

Peterson, R. A., jt. auth. see Decareau, R. V.

Peterson, R. Dean. A Concise History of Christianity. 334p. (C). 1993. pap. 25.95 (0-534-13278-2) Intl Thomson.

Peterson, R. J. & Strottman, D. D., eds. Pion-Nucleus Physics: Future Directions & New Facilities at Lampf. LC 87-72961. (Conference Proceeding Ser.: No. 163). 592p. 1988. lib. bdg. 75.00 (0-88318-363-3) Am Inst Physics.

Peterson, Ralph. Life in a Crowded Place: Making a Learning Community. LC 92-16468. 142p. 1992. pap. text ed. 16.50 (0-435-08736-3) Heinemann.

Peterson, Ralph H. Did Jesus Know What He Was Talking About? 112p. 1982. 6.95 (0-8187-0045-9) Am Developing.

Peterson, Ralph L. A Place for Caring & Celebration: The School Media Center. LC 78-31809. (School Media Center: Focus on Trends & Issues Ser.: No. 4). 39p. reprint ed. pap. 25.00 (0-685-16424-1, 2027358) Bks Demand.

Peterson, Randolph L. North American Moose. LC 56-1401. 324p. reprint ed. pap. 92.40 (0-317-55710-6, 2029343) Bks Demand.

Peterson, Randy, jt. auth. see Hall, Terry.

Peterson, Raymond H. Accounting for Fixed Assets. (Wiley Institute of Management Accountants Professional Book Ser.). 224p. 1994. text ed. 60.00 (0-471-53703-9) Wiley.

Peterson, Raymond M. & Cleveland, James O. A Guide for State Planning for the Prevention of Mental Retardation & Related Disabilities. 32p. 1987. write for info. (1-55672-020-3) US HHS.

Peterson, Reece L. & Ishii-Jordan, Sharon, eds. Multicultural Education & the Education of Students with Behavioral Disorders. LC 93-31945. 1993. 33.95 (0-914797-89-1) Brookline Bks.

Peterson, Rein, jt. auth. see Silver, Edward.

Peterson, Renno L., jt. auth. see Esperti, Robert A.

Peterson, Richard. Creative Meditation: Inner Peace Is Practically Yours. (Illus.). 240p. (Orig.). 1990. pap. 12.95 (0-87604-255-8, 348) ARE Pr.

— Healing the Child Warrior: A Search for Inner Peace. (Illus.). 200p. (Orig.). 1992. pap. 24.95 (0-9634079-0-2) R W Peterson.

Peterson, Richard A. The Dynamics of Industrial Society. LC 73-10094. (Studies in Sociology). (C). 1973. pap. text ed. write for info. (0-672-61324-7, Bobbs) Macmillan.

Peterson, Richard A., jt. auth. see Gouldner, Alvin W.

Peterson, Richard B., ed. Managers & National Culture: A Global Perspective. LC 92-1747. 474p. 1993. text ed. 65.00 (0-89930-602-0, PMI, Quorum Bks) Greenwood.

Peterson, Richard B. & Tracy, Lane. Systematic Management of Human Resources. LC 78-55826. 1979. text ed. write for info. (0-201-05814-6); write for info. (0-201-05815-4) Addison-Wesley.

Peterson, Richard B., jt. auth. see Bomers, Gerald B.

Peterson, Richard B., jt. auth. see Lewin, David.

Peterson, Richard D., II. A Thelen Family History: The Story of the John & Catherine Thelen Family. LC 92-81557. (Illus.). 250p. (Orig.). 1992. pap. 40.00 (0-941795-01-2) R D Peterson & Sons.

Peterson, Richard D., ed. ASTD Research Ser., 5 vols. (ASTD Research Ser.). 384p. 11.95 (0-318-13264-8); pap. 14.95 (0-318-13263-X, PEDPP) Am Soc Train & Devel.

— Studies in Training & Development, No. 1. (ASTD Research Ser.). 196p. 7.50 (0-318-13284-2); pap. 9.50 (0-318-13283-4, &ESTP) Am Soc Train & Devel.

***Peterson, Richard D., 2nd & Peterson, Phyllis T.** A Davies Family History: The Story of the David & Martha Davies Family. LC 94-73835. (Illus.). 273p. (Orig.). 1994. pap. 40.00 (0-941795-02-0) R D Peterson & Sons.

Peterson, Richard E. & Uhl, Norman P. Formulating College & University Goals: A Guide for Using the Institutional Goals Inventory. 1988. 8.00 (0-317-67884-1) Educ Testing Serv.

Peterson, Richard E., et al. Adult Education & Training in Industrialized Countries. LC 81-84672. 512p. 1981. text ed. 47.95 (0-275-90701-5, C0701, Praeger Pubs) Greenwood.

— Lifelong Learning in America. LC 79-83576. (Jossey-Bass Series in Higher Education). 552p. reprint ed. pap. 157.40 (0-7837-2532-9, 2042691) Bks Demand.

Peterson, Richard F. James Joyce Revisited. (Twayne's English Authors Ser.: No. 490). 170p. (C). 1992. text ed. 22.95 (0-8057-7016-X, Pub. by Royal Botanic Garden UK) Macmillan.

— William Butler Yeats. (English Authors Ser.). 232p. (C). 1982. text ed. 22.95 (0-8057-6815-7, Pub. by Royal Botanic Garden UK) Macmillan.

Peterson, Richard F., et al, eds. Work in Progress: Joyce Centenary Essays. LC 82-16943. 192p. 1983. 22.50 (0-8093-1094-5) S Ill U Pr.

Peterson, Richard G. The Lost Cities of Cibola. 292p. 1980. 5.95 (0-8199-0790-1, Frncscn Herld) Franciscan Pr.

Peterson, Richard H. The Bonanza Kings: The Social Origins & Business Behavior of Western Mining Entrepreneurs, 1870-1900. LC 91-50311. (Illus.). 208p. 1991. reprint ed. pap. 11.95 (0-8061-2389-3) U of Okla Pr.

— Bonanza Rich: Lifestyles of the Western Mining Entrepreneurs. LC 90-25792. 192p. (C). 1991. 21.95 (0-89301-143-6) U of Idaho Pr.

Peterson, Richard J. & Vaughan, Charlotte A., eds. Structure & Process: Readings in Introductory Sociology. 319p. (C). 1986. pap. 21.95 (0-534-05172-3) Intl Thomson.

Peterson, Richard L., jt. auth. see Kidwell, David S.

Peterson, Richard R. Women, Work, & Divorce. LC 88-2133. (SUNY Series in the Sociology of Work). 179p. 1989. 59.50 (0-88706-858-8); pap. 19.95 (0-88706-859-6) State U NY Pr.

Peterson, Richard S. Imitation & Praise in the Poems of Ben Jonson. LC 80-26261. (Illus.). 280p. 1981. 35.00 (0-300-02586-6) Yale U Pr.

Peterson, Richard S. & Bartholomew, George A. The Natural History & Behavior of the California Sea Lion. (ASM Special Publication Ser.: No. 1). (Illus.). ix, 79p. 1967. 6.00 (0-943612-00-4) Am Soc Mammalogists.

Peterson, Richard W. Teaching Physics Safely: Some Practical Guidelines in Seven Areas of Common Concern in Physics Classrooms. 4th ed. 30p. 1985. reprint ed. 10.00 (0-318-41562-3, OP19) Am Assn Physics.

Peterson, Rob, jt. auth. see Peterson, Marge.

Peterson, Robert. California Tax Handbook: 1994 Edition. rev. ed. Curammeng, Jose, Jr., ed. 928p. 1993. pap. text ed. 25.00 (0-7811-0080-1) Res Inst Am.

— The Only Piano Player in La Paz. LC 85-70518. 68p. (Orig.). 1985. pap. 6.95 (0-933525-25-7) Black Dog Pr.

— Only the Ball Was White. (Illus.). 414p. 1992. pap. 12.95 (0-19-507637-0) OUP.

— Only the Ball was White. 23.95 (0-8488-1124-0) Amereon Ltd.

— Waiting for Garbo: 44 Ghazals. LC 87-71660. 52p. (Orig.). 1987. pap. 7.95 (0-933525-30-3) Black Dog Pr.

Peterson, Robert & Peterson, Martha. Roaring Lion. 1989. pap. 4.95 (9971-972-80-8) OMF Bks.

Peterson, Robert & Stradella, Charles. California Tax Handbook: 1993 Edition. rev. ed. 882p. 1992. pap. text ed. 23.00 (0-7811-0063-1) Res Inst Am.

Peterson, Robert, tr. see Della Casa, Giovanni.

Peterson, Robert, jt. ed. see Licata, Salvatore.

Peterson, Robert A. Getting to Know John's Gospel: A Fresh Look at Its Main Ideas. 160p. 1989. pap. 7.99 (0-87552-370-6) Presby & Reformed.

— Hell on Trial: The Case for Eternal Punishment. 224p. (Orig.). 1995. pap. 12.99 (0-87552-372-2) Presby & Reformed.

— Marketing Research. 2nd ed. 592p. (C). 1988. text ed. 63.95 (0-256-03711-6) Irwin.

— Trends in Consumer Behavior Research. LC 76-45657. (American Marketing Association Monograph Ser.: No. 6). 46p. reprint ed. pap. 25.00 (0-317-28135-6, 2022481) Bks Demand.

Peterson, Robert A., ed. The Future of U. S. Retailing: An Agenda for the 21st Century. LC 91-24432. 336p. 1991. text ed. 45.00 (0-89930-679-9, PFU, Quorum Bks) Greenwood.

Peterson, Robert A., jt. auth. see Friedland, Jerold.

Peterson, Robert A., jt. auth. see Kerin, Roger A.

Peterson, Robert A., jt. auth. see Mahajan, Vijay.

Peterson, Robert A., et al. Modern American Capitalism: Understanding Public Attitudes & Perceptions. LC 90-42966. 144p. 1990. text ed. 49.95 (0-89930-625-X, PMJ/, Quorum Bks) Greenwood.

Peterson, Robert D., jt. auth. see Cohen, Joel M.

Peterson, Robert L. & Strauch, Alexander. Agape Leadership: Lessons in Spiritual Leadership from the Life of R. C. Chapman. LC 91-9191. 75p. (Orig.). (C). 1991. pap. 4.99 (0-936083-05-0) Lewis-Roth.

Peterson, Robert O. Information Systems Planning. 1990. 44.95 (0-07-049649-8) McGraw.

Peterson, Robert W. The Boy Scouts: An American Adventure. (Illus.). 256p. 1985. pap. 12.95 (0-685-42998-9) HM.

— Cages to Jump Shots: Pro Basketball's Early Years. (Illus.). 240p. 1991. reprint ed. pap. 9.95 (0-19-507261-8) OUP.

Peterson, Robert W., ed. Agnew: The Coining of a Household Word. LC 70-183844. (Interim History Ser.). 187p. reprint ed. pap. 53.30 (0-8357-5262-3, 2022893) Bks Demand.

Peterson, Roberta. The Elder Pilipino. LC 77-83488. (Elder Minority Ser.). 56p. 1978. pap. 9.50 (0-916304-37-X) SDSU Press.

Peterson, Robin. Principles of Marketing. (College Outline Ser.). 285p. (C). 1989. pap. text ed. 13.50 (0-15-601641-9) HB Coll Pubs.

Peterson, Robin & Phillips, William, eds. Ecology & the Market Place. 1972. 29.50 (0-8422-5019-0) Irvington.

Peterson, Robin T., jt. auth. see Gross, Charles W.

Peterson, Robin T., et al. Marketing in Action: An Experiential Approach. (Illus.). 259p. 1978. teacher ed write for info. (0-8299-0565-0); pap. text ed. 35.50 (0-8299-0204-X) West Pub.

Peterson, Robyn. Managing Successful Learning. 136p. 1992. pap. 34.00 (0-7494-0547-3, Pub. by Kogan Page Educ UK) Taylor & Francis.

Peterson, Robyn G. American Frontier Photography. (Illus.). 36p. 1993. pap. 5.00 (0-9622038-4-X) Rockwell NY.

Peterson, Robyn G., ed. see Hollister, Paul.

Peterson, Rodney D. Political Economy & American Capitalism. 240p. (C). 1991. lib. bdg. 54.00 (0-7923-9142-X) Kluwer Ac.

Peterson, Roger L., jt. auth. see Ziemer, Rodger E.

***Peterson, Roger L., et al.** An Introduction to Spread Spectrum Communications. LC 94-27567. 1995. text ed. 76.00 (0-02-431623-7) P-H.

Peterson, Roger L., et al, eds. The Core Curriculum in Professional Psychology. 187p. 1992. pap. text ed. 30.00 (1-55798-143-4) Am Psychol.

Peterson, Roger T. Audubon's Birds of America. 1993. 100.00 (0-89660-040-8, Artabras) Abbeville Pr.

— Field Giude to Eastern Birds. 4th ed. 1980. pap. 15.95 (0-395-26619-X) HM.

— The Field Guide Art of Roger Tory Peterson, 2 Vols., Set, Vols. 1 & 2. (Illus.). 1992. Set. 300.00 (0-395-64355-4) HM.

— Field Guide to Eastern Birds: A Field Guide to Birds East of the Rockies. (Illus.). 384p. 1984. pap. 16.95 (0-395-36164-8) HM.

— A Field Guide to the Birds: A Completely New Guide to All the Birds of Eastern & Central North America. 4th ed. 1980. 21.95 (0-395-26621-1) HM.

Peterson, Roger T., et al. A Field Guide to the Birds of Britain & Europe. 5th ed. LC 93-22426. (Peterson Field Guide Ser.: No. 8). 1993. 24.95 (0-395-66931-6); pap. 19.95 (0-395-66922-7) HM.

Peterson, Roger T. A Field Guide to the Birds of Texas & Adjacent States. (Peterson Field Guide Ser.). 1979. 24.95 (0-395-08087-8); pap. 21.95 (0-395-26252-6) HM.

— A Field Guide to the Butterflies Coloring Book. (Peterson Field Guide Ser.). 1983. pap. 5.95 (0-395-34675-4) HM.

— Field Guide to Western Birds. 3rd deluxe ed. (Peterson Field Guide Ser.). (Illus.). 432p. 1990. 126.00 (0-395-51748-6) HM.

— Field Guide to Western Birds. 3rd ed. (Peterson Field Guide Ser.). (Illus.). 432p. 1990. 22.95 (0-395-51749-4); pap. 16.95 (0-395-51424-X) HM.

— Peterson's First Guide to Birds. 1986. pap. 4.95 (0-395-40684-6) HM.

— Peterson's First Guide to Wildflowers. 1986. pap. 4.95 (0-395-40777-X) HM.

Peterson, Roger T., illus. & intro. The Field Guide Art of Roger Tory Peterson, Vol. 1, Eastern Birds. LC 92-8460. 356p. 1992. reprint ed. 150.00 (0-395-59358-1) HM.

— The Field Guide Art of Roger Tory Peterson, Vol. 2, Western Birds. LC 92-8460. 356p. 1992. reprint ed. 150.00 (0-395-64356-2) HM.

***Peterson, Roger T., illus. & photos.** Roger Tory Peterson's ABC of Birds: A Book for Little Birdwatchers. LC 95-15540. (J). 1995. write for info. (0-7893-0009-5) Universe.

Peterson, Roger T., photos. Roger Tory Peterson: The Art & Photography of the World's Foremost Birder. LC 94-14288. (Illus.). 208p. 1994. 50.00 (0-8478-1816-0) Rizzoli Intl.

Peterson, Roger T. & Alden, Peter. A Field Guide to Birds Coloring Book. 1982. pap. 5.95 (0-395-32521-8) HM.

An Asterisk (*) at the beginning of an entry indicates that the title is appearing in BIP for the first time.

Peterson, Roger T. & Chalif, Edward L. Field Guide to Mexican Birds. (Peterson Field Guide Ser.). 1973. 24.95 (*0-395-17129-6*) HM.

— Field Guides in Mexican Birds. (Peterson Field Guide Ser.). (Illus.). 298p. 1988. pap. 18.95 (*0-395-48354-9*) HM.

Peterson, Roger T. & Douglas, John. A Field Guide to Shells Coloring Book. 1985. pap. 5.95 (*0-395-37703-X*) HM.

Peterson, Roger T. & McKenny, Margaret. A Field Guide to Wildflowers of Northeastern & North-Central North America. LC 67-13042. (Peterson Field Guide Ser.). 420p. 1975. 24.95 (*0-395-08086-X*); pap. 16.95 (*0-395-18325-1*) HM.

Peterson, Roger T. & Peterson, Virginia M. Audubon's Birds of America: The Audubon Society Baby Elephant Folio. rev. ed. (Illus.). 694p. 1990. 250.00 (*1-55859-128-1*) Abbeville Pr.

Peterson, Roger T. & Tenenbaum, Frances. A Field Guide to Wildflowers Coloring Book. 1982. pap. 5.95 (*0-395-32522-6*) HM.

Peterson, Roger T., jt. auth. see Kaufman, Kenn.

Peterson, Roger T., jt. auth. see Pough, Frederick H.

Peterson, Roger T., ed. see Pough, Frederick H. & Peterson, Roger T.

Peterson, Roger T., jt. auth. see Savage, Candace.

Peterson, Roger T., et al. A Field Guide to Forests Coloring Book. 1983. pap. 5.95 (*0-395-34676-2*) HM.

— A Field Guide to Reptiles & Amphibians Coloring Book. 1985. pap. 5.95 (*0-395-37704-8*) HM.

Peterson, Roland. Everyone Is Right. 352p. (Orig.). 1986. pap. 12.95 (*0-87516-565-6*) DeVorss.

***Peterson, Rolf.** Broken Balance & the Wolves of Isle Royal. (Illus.). 160p. 1995. 29.50 (*1-57223-031-2*, WCP) Outlook Pubng.

Peterson, Ronald E. A History of Russian Symbolism. LC 90-23250. (Linguistic & Literary Studies in Eastern Europe: Vol. 29). xii, 254p. 1990. 89.00x (*90-272-1534-0*) Benjamins North Am.

Peterson, Ronald E., tr. see Borgen, Johan.

Peterson, Rosemary & Felton-Collins, Victoria. The Piaget Handbook for Teachers & Parents: Children in the Age of Discovery, Preschool to 3rd Grade. (Early Childhood Education Ser.). Orig. Title: Piaget: A Handbook for Parents and Teachers in the Age of Discovery. 80p. (C). 1986. pap. text ed. 10.95 (*0-8077-2841-1*) Tchrs Coll.

Peterson, Rosemary, et al. Child-Centered Skiing: The American Teaching System for Children. (Illus.). 543p. (Orig.). (C). 1988. pap. 39.95 (*0-318-39838-9*) Prof Ski Instructors.

Peterson, Rosendo D. Las Novelas de Unamuno. 104p. 1990. 30.00 (*0-916379-44-2*) Scripta.

Peterson, Roy M. The Cults of Campania. LC 23-13673. (American Academy in Rome, Papers & Monographs: Vol. 1). 413p. reprint ed. pap. 117.80 (*0-685-15582-X*, 2026716) Bks Demand.

Peterson, Ruby. Fun with Bible Facts. 1974. pap. 2.75 (*0-89137-620-8*) Quality Pubns.

— More Fun with Bible Facts. 1977. pap. 2.75 (*0-89137-617-8*) Quality Pubns.

Peterson, Rudolph E. Stress Concentration Factors. LC 53-11283. 336p. 1974. text ed. 99.95 (*0-471-68329-9*, Wiley-Interscience) Wiley.

Peterson, Russell W., frwd. Delaware Photographs by Jake Rajs. LC 92-23810. (Illus.). 1992. 50.00 (*0-89802-617-2*) Beautiful Am.

Peterson, Ruth. Before I Die. 32p. 1987. pap. 0.75 (*0-88144-095-7*) Christian Pub.

Peterson, Ruth, jt. ed. see Hagan, John.

Peterson, Ruth C. & Thurstone, Louis L. Motion Pictures & the Social Attitudes of Children. Bd. with Social Conduct & Attitudes of Movie Fans. LC 76-124031. LC 76-124031. (Literature of Cinema: Payne Fund Studies of Motion Pictures & Social Values). 1970. reprint ed. 15.95 (*0-405-01630-1*) Ayer.

Peterson, S., ed. see DeMatteis, M.

Peterson, S., ed. see Dini.

Peterson, Samiha S., tr. see Amin, Qasim.

Peterson, Sandy. Peterson's Field Guide to Cthulhu Monsters. 1989. pap. 15.95 (*0-933635-48-6*) Chaosium.

***Peterson, Sandy & Willis, Lynn.** Call of Cthulhu: Horror Roleplaying in the Worlds of H. P. Lovecraft. 5th ed. (Call of Cthulhu Role Playing Game Ser.). (Illus.). 240p. (Orig.). Date not set. 30.00 (*1-56882-014-3*) Chaosium.

Peterson, Sandy, ed. see Stafford, Greg.

Peterson, Sandy, et al. Call of Cthulhu. 5th ed. (Call of Cthulhu Roleplaying Game System Ser.). (Illus.). 200p. (Orig.). 1992. pap. 21.95 (*0-933635-86-9*, 2336) Chaosium.

Peterson, Scott. Native American Prophecies: Examining the History, Wisdom & Startling Predictions of Visionary Native Americans. 250p. 1991. pap. 12.95 (*1-55778-417-5*) Paragon Hse.

Peterson, Scott K. Face the Music! Jokes about Music. (Make Me Laugh! Joke Bks.). (Illus.). 32p. (J). (gr. 1-4). 1988. lib. bdg. 11.96 (*0-8225-0995-4*, Lerner Publctns) Lerner Group.

— Out on a Limb: Riddles about Trees & Plants. (You Must Be Joking! Riddle Bks.). (Illus.). 32p. (J). (gr. 1-4). 1989. lib. bdg. 13.50 (*0-8225-2328-0*, Lerner Publctns) Lerner Group.

— Out on a Limb: Riddles about Trees & Plants. LC 89-36629. (J). (gr. 1-4). 1991. pap. 3.95 (*0-8225-9582-6*, Lerner Publctns) Lerner Group.

— Plugged In: Electric Riddles. (Illus.). 32p. (J). (gr. 1-4). 1995. pap. 13.50 (*0-8225-9700-4*) Lerner Group.

— Plugged In: Electric Riddles. (You Must Be Joking! Ser.). (Illus.). 32p. (J). (gr. 1-4). 1995. lib. bdg. 13.50 (*0-8225-2344-2*, Lerner Publctns) Lerner Group.

— What's Your Name? Jokes about Names. (Make Me Laugh! Joke Bks.). (Illus.). 32p. (J). (gr. 1-4). 1987. lib. bdg. 11.96 (*0-8225-0994-6*, Lerner Publctns); pap. 2.95 (*0-8225-9520-6*, Lerner Publctns) Lerner Group.

— Wing It! Riddles about Birds. (You Must Be Joking! Ser.). (Illus.). 32p. (J). (gr. 1-4). 1991. lib. bdg. 13.50 (*0-8225-2333-7*, Lerner Publctns) Lerner Group.

— Wing It: Riddles about Birds. (J). (gr. 1-4). 1991. pap. 3.95 (*0-8225-9591-5*, Lerner Publctns) Lerner Group.

Peterson, Scott R., jt. auth. see Bednar, Richard L.

Peterson, Shailer A. Preparing to Enter Dental School. 1979. text ed. 13.95 (*0-13-697326-4*, Spectrum Bks) P-H.

— Preparing to Enter Medical School. 1980. text ed. 14.95 (*0-13-697342-6*, Spectrum Bks) P-H.

Peterson, Sherrie. Help! for Substitutes. (Illus.). 80p. (J). 1985. teacher ed 5.95 (*0-86653-277-3*, GA 642) Good Apple.

Peterson, Sophia, jt. ed. see Hammock, Allan S.

Peterson, Spike & Runyan, Anne S. Global Gender Issues. LC 93-24881. (Dilemmas in World Politics Ser.). 202p. (C). 1993. pap. text ed. 14.95 (*0-8133-1310-4*) Westview.

— Global Gender Issues. LC 93-24881. (Dilemmas in World Politics Ser.). 202p. (C). 1993. text ed. 52.50 (*0-8133-1309-0*) Westview.

Peterson, Spiro. Daniel Defoe: A Reference Guide. (Reference Guides to Literature Ser.). 429p. 1987. text ed. 50.00 (*0-8161-8157-8*, Hall Reference) Macmillan.

Peterson, Steve & McDonald, George, eds. Enemies. (Illus.). 24p. (J). (gr. 10-12). 1986. pap. 6.00 (*0-915795-51-5*, 02) Iron Crown Ent Inc.

Peterson, Steven A., ed. Political Behavior: Patterns in Everyday Life. (Library of Social Research: Vol. 177). 296p. (C). 1990. text ed. 49.95 (*0-8039-3729-6*); pap. text ed. 24.00 (*0-8039-3730-X*) Sage.

Peterson, Steven A. & Maiden, Robert J. The Public Lives of Rural Older Americans. LC 93-13840. 166p. (Orig.). (C). 1993. lib. bdg. 43.50 (*0-8191-9188-4*); pap. text ed. 19.50 (*0-8191-9189-2*) U Pr of Amer.

Peterson, Steven A. & Rasmussen, Thomas H. State & Local Politics. 352p. 1993. pap. text ed. 12.95 (*0-07-049671-4*) McGraw.

Peterson, Steven A. & Somit, Albert. The Political Behavior of Older Americans. LC 94-4762. (Reference Library of Social Science, Issues in Aging: Vol. 972, Vol. 4). 200p. 1994. 30.00 (*0-8153-1321-7*, SS972) Garland.

Peterson, Steven A., jt. ed. see Somit, Albert.

Peterson, Stuart R. Patents, Getting One... A Cost Cutting Primer for Inventors. LC 89-81531. (Illus.). 472p. 1990. 43.95 (*0-914960-75-X*) Academy Bks.

Peterson, Susan. The Craft & Art of Clay. 368p. 1992. pap. text ed. 45.33 (*0-13-188475-1*) P-H.

— Craft & Art of Clay. 1993. 40.00 (*0-13-189598-2*) P-H.

— Fun Places to Go with Kids. 200p. (Orig.). Date not set. pap. 11.95 (*0-9646737-0-3*) Fun Places.

— The Living Tradition of Maria Martinez. rev. ed. LC 77-75373. (Illus.). 300p. 1977. pap. 39.95 (*0-87011-497-2*) Kodansha.

— Lucy Lewis: American Indian Potter. (Illus.). 220p. 1992. reprint ed. pap. 39.95 (*4-7700-1698-0*) Kodansha.

— Lucy M. Lewis: American Indian Potter. (Illus.). 224p. 1984. 65.00 (*0-87011-685-1*) Kodansha.

Peterson, Susan, ed. see Peterson, Charles & Blei, Norbert.

Peterson, Susan C. & Vaughn-Roberson, Courtney A. Women with Vision: The Presentation Sisters of South Dakota, 1880-1985. LC 87-20451. 334p. 1988. 29.95 (*0-252-01493-6*) U of Ill Pr.

***Peterson, Susan J.** Ariel's World: An Exploration of Lake Ontario. (Illus.). 164p. (Orig.). 1995. pap. 11.95 (*0-9646149-0-1*) Ariel Assocs.

Peterson, Susan K. & Tenenbaum, Henry A. Behavior Management: Strategies & Techniques. LC 86-9113. 84p. (Orig.). (C). 1986. lib. bdg. 35.50 (*0-8191-5361-3*); pap. 14.50 (*0-8191-5362-1*) U Pr of Amer.

Peterson, Susan L. Self Defense. (Illus.). 128p. (Orig.). (C). 1988. pap. text ed. 14.95x (*0-89582-185-0*) Morton Pub.

Peterson, Susan L. & Peterson, James A. Sexy Legs: How to Get Them & How to Keep Them. LC 83-80741. (Orig.). 1984. pap. 6.95 (*0-88011-162-3*, Scribners) S&S Trade.

Peterson, Sylvia. From Love That Hurts to Love That's Real: A Recovery Workbook. 298p. 1989. student ed, pap. 12.95 (*0-942421-30-2*) Hazelden.

Peterson, T. Sarah. Acquired Taste: The French Origins of Modern Cooking. (Illus.). 280p. 1994. 24.95 (*0-8014-3053-4*) Cornell U Pr.

Peterson, Thad D., jt. auth. see Klug, John R.

Peterson, Theodore B. Magazines in the Twentieth Century. 2nd ed. LC 64-18668. (Illus.). 498p. reprint ed. pap. 142.00 (*0-8357-6199-1*, 2034458) Bks Demand.

Peterson, Thomas. Doing Something by Doing Nothing. 1985. 6.55 (*0-89536-747-5*, 5853) CSS OH.

Peterson, Thomas E. The Paraphase of an Imaginary Dialogue: The Poetics & Poetry of Pier Pasolini. 356p. (C). 1994. text ed. 48.95 (*0-8204-1529-4*) P Lang Pubs.

Peterson, Thurman S. & Hobby, Charles R. Intermediate Algebra for College Students. 6th ed. 418p. (C). 1990. text ed. 57.00 (*0-06-045185-8*) HarpCollege.

Peterson, Toni, ed. see Getty Art History Information Program.

Peterson, Trudy H. Agricultural Exports, Farm Income, & the Eisenhower Administration. LC 79-15825. 236p. reprint ed. pap. 67.30 (*0-8357-3810-8*, 2036537) Bks Demand.

Peterson, Trudy H., jt. auth. see Peterson, Gary M.

Peterson, V., jt. auth. see Peterson, R.

Peterson, V. Spike, ed. Gendered States: Feminist (Re) Visions of International Relations Theory. LC 91-42673. (Gender & Political Theory Ser.). 226p. 1992. pap. text ed. 17.95 (*1-55587-328-6*) Lynne Rienner.

Peterson, Vicki. The ABCs of My Feelings: A Journal for Recovering & Discovering Human Beings. (Illus.). 60p. (Orig.). 1991. pap. 14.95 (*0-9630195-0-3*) Dynamic Des Pr.

Peterson, Victor P., Jr. Native Trees of Southern California. (California Natural History Guides Ser.: No. 14). (Illus.). 1966. pap. 10.00 (*0-520-01004-3*) U CA Pr.

— Native Trees of the Sierra Nevada. (California Natural History Guides Ser.: No. 36). 1974. pap. 10.00 (*0-520-02666-7*) U CA Pr.

Peterson, Vince, jt. auth. see Folger, Cleve.

Peterson, Virgil. The Mob: Two Hundred Years of Organized Crime in New York. LC 83-8947. 543p. 1985. June, 1985 543 p. pap. 10.95 (*0-89803-156-7*) Green Hill.

Peterson, Virginia M., jt. auth. see Peterson, Roger T.

Peterson, W., ed. see Quintilianus.

Peterson, W. E. Almost Perfect: How a Bunch of Regular Guys Built WordPerfect Corporation. LC 93-34366. 1993. 18.95 (*1-55958-477-7*) Prima Pub.

Peterson, W. H., et al. Peterson. 372p. 1991. reprint ed. lib. bdg. 69.00 (*0-8328-2072-5*); reprint ed. pap. 59.00 (*0-8328-2073-3*) Higginson Bk Co.

Peterson, W. Wesley. Introduction to Economics. 1977. pap. text ed. write for info. (*0-13-481242-5*) P-H.

— Introduction to Programming Languages. 1974. pap. text ed. write for info. (*0-13-493486-5*) P-H.

Peterson, W. Wesley & Weldon, E. J., Jr. Error-Correcting Codes. 2nd rev. ed. 1972. 60.00 (*0-262-16039-0*) MIT Pr.

Peterson, Wade D. The VMEbus Handbook. 332p. 1993. pap. 53.00 (*1-885731-01-9*) VFEA Int Trade.

Peterson, Walfred H. Dormitory Drug Dens & Due Process: The Law of Search in the Federal System. 2nd ed. LC 86-50259. 95p. (C). 1988. text ed. 29.95 (*1-55605-082-8*); pap. text ed. 19.95 (*0-932269-86-9*) Wyndhall Pr.

Peterson, Wallace C. Our Overloaded Economy: Inflation, Unemployment, & the Crisis in American Capitalism. LC 81-51288. 256p. reprint ed. pap. 73.00 (*0-685-23744-3*, 2032785) Bks Demand.

— Silent Depression: The Fate of the American Dream. LC 93-1295. 1994. 25.00 (*0-393-03586-7*) Norton.

— Transfer Spending, Taxes, & the American Welfare State. (C). 1990. lib. bdg. 60.50 (*0-7923-9077-6*) Kluwer Ac.

Peterson, Wallace C., ed. Market Power & the Economy: Industrial, Corporate, Government & Political Aspects. (C). 1988. lib. bdg. 60.50 (*0-89838-267-X*) Kluwer Ac.

***Peterson, Wallace C. & Burgess, Anthony.** Silent Depression: Twenty-Five Years of Wage Squeeze & Middle Class Decline. 320p. 1995. pap. 13.95 (*0-393-31282-8*, Norton Paperbks) Norton.

Peterson, Wallace C. & Estenson, Paul. Income, Employment, & Economic Growth. (C). 1992. pap. text ed. write for info. (*0-393-96184-2*) Norton.

— Income, Employment, & Economic Growth. 7th ed. (C). 1992. text ed. 45.95 (*0-393-96139-7*) Norton.

— Income, Employment, & Economic Growth. 7th ed. (C). 1992. teacher ed write for info. (*0-318-68402-0*) Norton.

***Peterson, Wallace C. & Estenson, Paul S.** Income, Employment, & Economic Growth. 8th ed. LC 95-13314. 1995. write for info. (*0-393-96854-5*) Norton.

Peterson, Walt. Baja Adventure Book. 2nd ed. LC 91-36330. (Illus.). 288p. 1992. pap. 17.95 (*0-89997-130-X*) Wilderness Pr.

— Five Thousand Ways to Say No to Your Child. (Illus.). 112p. (Orig.). 1993. pap. 7.95 (*0-9635892-0-2*) Mendocino Coast.

— Rebuilding the Porch. Zarucchi, Roy & Page, Carolyn, eds. (Chapbook Ser.). (Illus.). 28p. (Orig.). 1990. pap. 5.00 (*1-879205-01-7*) Nightshade Pr.

Peterson, Walter, jt. auth. see Robinson, Bruce R.

Peterson, Walter F. An Industrial Heritage: Allis-Chalmers Corporation. LC 76-57456. (Illus.). 448p. 1978. 17.50 (*0-938076-02-7*) Milwaukee Cty Hist Soc.

Peterson, Warren A. & Quadagno, Jill, eds. Social Bonds in Later Life: Aging & Interdependence. LC 85-1830. (Illus.). 477p. reprint ed. pap. 136.00 (*0-7837-4566-4*, 2044095) Bks Demand.

Peterson, Warren A., jt. ed. see Mangen, David J.

Peterson, Warren A., jt. auth. see Mangen, David.

Peterson, Wayne, ed. see McAllister, Dawson & Altman, Tim.

Peterson, Wilferd A. The Art of Creative Thinking. Olmos, Dan, ed. LC 90-71111. 208p. (Orig.). 1991. pap. 10.00 (*1-56170-004-5*, 131) Hay House.

Peterson, Wilfred. Art of Living: Thoughts on Meeting the Challenge of Life. 1993. 9.98 (*0-88365-831-3*) Galahad Bks.

Peterson, Willard J., et al, eds. The Power of Culture: Studies in Chinese Cultural History. 380p. (Orig.). 1994. 72.50 (*962-201-596-4*, Pub. by Chinese Univ HK) Coronet Bks.

Peterson, William, ed. Advances in Input-Output Analysis: Technology, Planning & Development. (Illus.). 256p. 1991. 55.00 (*0-19-506236-1*) OUP.

***Peterson, William & Archbold, Lawrence W., eds.** French Organ Music: From the Revolution to Franck & Widor. (Eastman Studies in Music: No. 5). 256p. (C). 1995. text ed. 71.00 (*1-878822-55-1*) Univ Rochester Pr.

Peterson, William, jt. ed. see Barker, Terry.

Peterson, William, jt. ed. see Stone, Richard.

Peterson, William N. Mystic Built: Ships & Shipyards of the Mystic River, Connecticut, 1784-1919. (Illus.). xvi, 254p. 1989. 36.00 (*0-913372-51-X*) Mystic Seaport.

Peterson, William N. & Coope, Peter M. Historic Buildings at Mystic Seaport Museum. (Illus.). 136p. 1985. pap. 15.95 (*0-913372-35-8*) Mystic Seaport.

Peterson, William S. A Bibliography of the Kelmscott Press. (Soho Bibliographies Ser.). (Illus.). 1984. 74.00 (*0-19-818199-X*) OUP.

— The Kelmscott Press: A History of William Morris's Typographical Adventure. (Illus.). 385p. 1990. 95.00 (*0-520-06138-1*) U CA Pr.

— Robert & Elizabeth Barrett Browning: An Annotated Bibliography, 1951-1970. LC 74-24915. 224p. 1974. 27.50 (*0-930252-02-0*) Browning Inst.

Peterson, William S., ed. see Morris, William.

Peterson, Willis L. Principles of Economics: Macro. 7th ed. (C). 1988. pap. text ed. 33.95 (*0-256-06795-3*); student ed 15.95 (*0-256-07054-7*) Irwin.

— Principles of Economics: Macro. 8th ed. 440p. (C). 1990. pap. text ed. 35.95 (*0-256-08538-2*, 05-0596-08) Irwin.

— Principles of Economics: Macro. 9th ed. (Illus.). 359p. (C). 1994. pap. text ed. 24.95 (*1-885079-25-7*) Willis Peterson.

— Principles of Economics: Macro. 9th ed. (Illus.). 120p. (C). 1994. teacher ed write for info. (*1-885079-75-3*) Willis Peterson.

— Principles of Economics: Micro. 7th ed. (C). 1988. student ed 15.95 (*0-256-07055-5*) Irwin.

— Principles of Economics: Micro. 8th ed. 410p. (C). 1994. text ed. 35.95 (*0-256-08539-0*, 05-0595-8) Irwin.

— Principles of Economics: Micro. 9th ed. (Illus.). 303p. (C). 1994. pap. text ed. 24.95 (*1-885079-00-1*) Willis Peterson.

— Principles of Economics: Micro. 9th ed. (Illus.). 120p. 1994. teacher ed write for info. (*1-885079-50-8*) Willis Peterson.

Peterson, Zelma, ed. see Browder, Anthony T.

***Petersons.** Top Colleges for Science: A Guide to Leading Four-Year Programs in the Biological, Chemical,.. 292p. 1995. pap. text ed. 16.95 (*1-56079-390-2*, Petersons Pacesetter) Petersons Guides.

***Petersons Guides Staff.** Peterson's Guide to Graduate & Professional Programs Bk. 1: An Overview 1995. 29th rev. ed. Lefferts, Amy, ed. (Graduate Guides Ser.: Bk. 1). 1186p. 1994. pap. 24.95 (*1-56079-380-5*) Petersons Guides.

— Peterson's Guide to Graduate Programs in Business, Education, Health & Law 1995: Graduate & Business Programs, Bk. 6. 29th ed. Lefferts, Amy, ed. (Graduate Guides Ser.: Bk. 6). 1647p. 1994. pap. 24.95 (*1-56079-385-6*) Petersons Guides.

— Peterson's Guide to Graduate Programs in Engineering & Applied Sciences 1995: Graduate & Professional Programs, Bk. 5. 29th ed. Lefferts, Amy, ed. (Graduate Guides Ser.: Bk. 5). 1398p. 1994. pap. 34.95 (*1-56079-384-8*) Petersons Guides.

— Peterson's Guide to Graduate Programs in the Humanities, Arts, & Social Sciences 1995: Graduate & Professional Programs, Bk. 2. 29th ed. Lefferts, Amy, ed. (Graduate Guides Ser.: Bk. 2). 1511p. 1994. pap. 34.95 (*1-56079-381-3*) Petersons Guides.

— Peterson's Guides to Graduate Programs in the Biological & Agricultural Sciences 1995: Graduate & Professional Programs, Bk. 3. 29th ed. Lefferts, Amy, ed. (Graduate Guides Ser.: Bk. 3). 2608p. 1994. pap. 41.95 (*1-56079-382-1*) Petersons Guides.

— Peterson's Guides to Graduate Programs in the Physical Sciences & Mathematics 1995: Graduate & Professional Programs, Bk. 4. 29th ed. Lefferts, Amy, ed. (Graduate Guides Ser.: Bk. 4). 668p. 1994. pap. 31.95 (*1-56079-383-X*) Petersons Guides.

Peterson's Magazine Staff, jt. auth. see Godey's Lady's Book Staff.

Peterson's Staff. Auto Restoration Tips & Techniques. Murray, Spence, ed. (Illus.). 256p. (Orig.). 1977. pap. 17.95 (*1-870642-42-2*) Motorbooks Intl.

***Petersons Staff.** Directory of Overseas Summer Jobs, 95. 26th ed. 192p. 1995. pap. 14.95 (*1-85458-123-6*, Pub. by Vacation-Work UK) Petersons Guides.

— Peterson's Guide to Adventure Holidays, 1995. (Illus.). 176p. 1995. pap. 12.95 (*1-85458-128-7*, Pub. by Vacation-Work UK) Petersons Guides.

Petersson, Bo. The Soviet Union & Peacetime Neutrality in Europe: A Study of Soviet Political Language. (Lund Political Studies: No. 65). 164p. (Orig.). 1990. pap. 54.50x (*91-971458-0-7*, Pub. by Almqv & Wiksell SW) Coronet Bks.

Petersson, C., jt. ed. see Lattin, A. W.

Petersson, Hans, jt. auth. see Ottosen, Niels S.

Petersson, Irmtraud, jt. ed. see Hergenhan, Laurie.

Petersson, O. P., ed. Seminar on Delivery of Child Health Care. (Journal: Paediatrician: Vol. 9, No. 1, 1980). 52p. 1979. pap. 26.50 (*3-8055-0800-X*) S Karger.

Petersson, Torsten. Cicero: A Biography. LC 63-10768. 1920. 25.00 (*0-8196-0119-5*) Biblo.

Peterzell, Jay. Reagan's Secret Wars. LC 83-226461. 100p. 1984. pap. 3.95 (*0-86566-033-6*) Ctr Natl Security.

Peterzen, Elisabet. The Last Draw. Desertrain, Laura, tr. LC 88-19862. (International Women's Crime Ser.). 256p. (Orig.). 1988. pap. 8.95 (*0-931188-67-9*) Seal Pr Feminist.

Petesch, Donald A. A Spy in the Enemy's Country: The Emergence of Modern Black Literature. LC 88-37391. 299p. 1989. reprint ed. pap. 12.95x (*0-87745-322-5*) U of Iowa Pr.

Petesch, Natalie. Soul Clap Its Hands & Sing. LC 81-51386. 206p. 1981. pap. 6.50 (*0-89608-119-2*) South End Pr.

Petesch, Natalie L. After the First Death There Is No Other: The 1974 Iowa Short Fiction Award. LC 74-8851. (Iowa Short Fiction Award Ser.). 208p. 1974. 19.95 (*0-87745-050-1*); pap. 12.95 (*0-87745-064-1*) U of Iowa Pr.

— Justina of Andalusia & Other Stories. LC 90-38575. 120p. 1990. 24.95 (*0-8040-0939-2*) Swallow.

— The Odyssey of Katinou Kalokovich. 199p. (C). 1979. reprint ed. pap. 5.00 (*0-934238-01-4*) Motheroot.

— Wild with All Regret. LC 86-60697. (Illus.). 140p. (Orig.). 1987. 15.95 (*0-930501-06-3*); pap. 10.95 (*0-930501-07-1*) Livingston U Pr.

An Asterisk (*) at the beginning of an entry indicates that the title is appearing in BIP for the first time.

Petesch, Natalie L. M. Duncan's Colony. LC 81-14188. 220p. 1982. 21.95 (0-8040-0401-3); pap. 9.95 (0-8040-0402-1) Swallow.

— Flowering Mimosa. LC 86-23024. 235p. 1987. text ed. 24.95 (0-8040-0870-1); pap. 12.95 (0-8040-0871-X) Swallow.

Petesch, Patti L. North-South Environmental Strategies, Costs & Bargains. LC 92-15158. (Policy Essay Ser.: No. 5). 124p. (C). 1992. pap. text ed. 9.95 (1-56517-005-9) Overseas Dev Council.

Petesch, Patti L. & Williams, Maurice J. Sustaining the Earth: Role of Multilateral Development Institutions. LC 93-5875. (Policy Essay Ser.: No. 9). 112p. (C). 1993. pap. text ed. 9.95 (1-56517-011-3) Overseas Dev Council.

Petev, Valentin. Sozialistisches Zivilrecht. (Sammlung Goeschen Ser.: No. 2851). 246p. (C). 1975. 15.25 (3-11-004697-0) De Gruyter.

Peteves, S. D., ed. Designing Interfaces for Technological Application: Ceramic-Ceramic, Ceramic-Metal Joining - Proceedings of the European Colloquium Organized by the Commission of the European Communities, Joint Research Center, Institute for Advanced Materials, Petten, the Netherlands, 20-21 April 1988. 312p. 1989. 70.25 (1-85166-377-0) Elsevier.

Peth, Howard A. Seven Mysteries...Solved!, Vol. 1. (Illus.). 433p. (Orig.). 1988. pap. 14.95 (0-9618580-0-1); write for info. (0-317-68279-2) Lessons Heaven.

— Seven Mysteries...Solved!, Vol. 2. (Illus.). 545p. (Orig.). 1988. pap. 14.95 (0-9618580-1-X) Lessons Heaven.

Pethel, James, ed. Come, Thou Almighty King. 1986. 8.95 (0-8341-9237-3, MB-560) Lillenas.

Pethel, Stan, contrib. Contemporary Piano. 1988. 7.95 (0-8341-9178-4, MB-591) Lillenas.

— God Leads Us Along. 1984. 7.95 (0-685-68307-9, MB-529) Lillenas.

Petheram, Michel, tr. see Baczko, Bronislaw.

Petheram, Rosemary. Down under from Devon. (C). 1989. pap. text ed. 59.00 (1-85821-021-6, Pub. by Pentland Pr UK) St Mut.

Petherbrdige, D. Art for Architecture: A Handbook on Commissioning. 160p. (Orig.). 1987. pap. text ed. 34.95 (0-11-751794-1, HM679, Pub. by HMSO UK) UNIPUB.

Petherbridge, Dan. How to Get the Most for Your Money: A Consumer's Guide to Year-Round Savings. 130p. (Orig.). 1990. pap. 9.95 (0-9625925-0-1) Sandbridge Pub.

Petherbridge, Deana, intro. Tess Jaray: Prints & Drawings, 1964-1984. 32p. 1984. pap. 9.95 (0-907849-08-3, Pub. by Ashmolean Mus UK) A Schwartz & Co.

— Tess Jaray: Prints & Drawings 1964-1984. (Illus.). 32p. 1995. pap. 9.95 (0-907849-06-7, 067, Pub. by Ashmolean Mus UK) A Schwartz & Co.

Petherbridge, Robin. Turkey & the Dodecanese Cruising Pilot. (Illus.). 128p. 1985. 29.95 (0-229-11716-3, Adlard Coles) Sheridan.

Pethes, G. & Frenyo, V. L. Advances in Animal & Comparative Physiology: Proceedings of the 28th International Congress of Physiological Sciences, Budapest, 1980. LC 80-41894. (Advances in Physiological Sciences Ser.: Vol. 20). (Illus.). 400p. 1981. 182.00 (0-08-027341-6, Pub. by Pergamon Repr UK) Franklin.

Pethes, G., et al, eds. Recent Advances of Avian Endocrinology: Proceedings of a Satellite Symposium of the 28th International Congress of Physiological Sciences, Budapest, Hungary, 1980. LC 80-42007. (Advances in Physiological Sciences Ser.: Vol. 33). (Illus.). 450p. 1981. 200.00 (0-08-027355-6, Pub. by Pergamon Repr UK) Franklin.

***Pethick.** An Introduction to Coastal Geomorphology. 1995. pap. text ed. 29.95 (0-470-24961-7) Wiley.

Pethick, Christopher, jt. auth. see Baym, Gordon.

Pethick, Derek. Vancouver Recalled. (Illus.). 96p. pap. 3.95 (0-919654-09-6) Hancock House.

Pethick-Lawrence, Emmeline. My Part in a Changing World. LC 75-21811. (Pioneers of the Woman's Movement: an International Perspective Ser.). 367p. 1976. reprint ed. 24.75 (0-88355-260-4) Hyperion Conn.

Pethick, Nancy & Norris, Anne. Harnessing Up. (Illus.). 132p. 1990. pap. 21.00 (0-85131-319-1, Pub. by J A Allen & Co UK) St Mut.

Pethig, R. & Schlieper, U., eds. Efficiency, Institutions & Economic Policy. (Illus.). 240p. 1987. 55.00 (0-387-18450-3) Spr-Verlag.

Pethig, R., et al, eds. Conflicts & Cooperation in Managing Environmental Resources. (Microeconomic Studies). (Illus.). xii, 338p. 1992. 98.00 (0-387-54968-4) Spr-Verlag.

Pethig, Ronald. Dielectric & Electronic Properties of Biological Materials. LC 78-13694. (Illus.). 390p. reprint ed. pap. 111.20 (0-8357-3080-8, 2039337) Bks Demand.

Pethig, Rudiger. Valuing the Environment: Methodological & Measurement Issues. LC 93-38948. 376p. (C). 1994. lib. bdg. 137.00 (0-7923-2602-4) Kluwer Ac.

Petho, Attila, et al, eds. Computational Number Theory: Proceedings of the Colloquium on Computational Number Theory. xiii, 342p. (C). 1991. lib. bdg. 98.95 (3-11-012394-0) De Gruyter.

Pethoe, B., ed. DCR Budapest-Nashville in the Diagnosis & Classification of Functional Psychoses. (Journal: Psychopathology: Vol. 21, Nos. 4-5, 1988). (Illus.). 92p. 1989. pap. 60.00 (3-8055-4970-9) S Karger.

Pethrick, R. A. Polymer Yearbook, No. 5. 450p. 1989. 59.00 (3-7186-4858-X); text ed. 180.00 (3-7186-4857-1) Gordon & Breach.

Pethrick, R. A. & Richards, R. W. Static & Dynamic Properties of the Polymeric Solid State. 1982. lib. bdg. 121.50 (90-277-1481-9) Kluwer Ac.

Pethrick, Richard A. Polymer Yearbook, No. 2. 420p. 1985. text ed. 79.00 (3-7186-0274-1); pap. text ed. 31.00 (3-7186-0276-8) Gordon & Breach.

Pethrick, Richard A., ed. Polymer Yearbook, No. 3. 320p. 1986. text ed. 116.00 (3-7186-0342-X); pap. text ed. 44.00 (3-7186-0341-1) Gordon & Breach.

— Polymer Yearbook, No. 4. 400p. 1987. text ed. 144.00 (3-7186-0406-X); pap. text ed. 41.00 (3-7186-0408-6) Gordon & Breach.

— Polymer Yearbook Ten. (Polymer Yearbook Ser.). 1993. text ed. 260.00 (3-7186-5334-6) Gordon & Breach.

— Polymer Yearbook 8. 8th ed. 1991. text ed. 275.00 (3-7186-5154-8) Gordon & Breach.

Pethrick, Richard A., jt. ed. see Elias, Hans-Georg.

Pethukov, B. S. & Polyakov, A. F. Heat Transfer in Turbulent Mixed Convection. Hainsworth, Richard & Rybchinskaya, Galina, trs. (Illus.). 300p. 1988. 68.00 (0-89116-644-0) Hemisp Pub.

Pethybridge, Roger. One Step Backwards, Two Steps Forward: Soviet Society & Politics in the New Economic Policy. (Illus.). 470p. 1990. 105.00 (0-19-821927-X) OUP.

— Witnesses to the Russian Revolution. (Illus.). 1982. pap. 6.95 (0-8065-0018-2, C274, Citadel Pr) Carol Pub Group.

***Petich, Edward J.** Atlas of Florida Fossil Shells. (Illus.). 408p. 1994. text ed. 60.00 (1-886094-04-7) Chicago Spectrum.

Petievich, Gerald. Money Men. 224p. 1988. pap. 3.50 (1-55817-080-4, Pinnacle NY) Windsor NY.

— One-Shot Deal. 224p. 1991. pap. 4.50 (0-451-17046-6, Sig) NAL-Dutton.

— Paramour. 352p. 1992. pap. 5.99 (0-451-17314-7, Sig) NAL-Dutton.

Petig, William E. Literary Antipietism in Germany During the First Half of the Eighteenth Century. LC 83-49223. (Stanford German Studies: Vol. 22). 236p. (Orig.). (C). 1984. pap. text ed. 22.65 (0-8204-0087-4) P Lang Pubs.

Petigru, James L. & Carson, James P. Life, Letters, & Speeches of James Louis Petigru the Union Man of South Carolina. 1977. 24.95 (0-8369-6969-3, 7850) Ayer.

Petillon, Mary & Newman, Sharon. Olympics Made Easy. (Illus.). 202p. (gr. 5-9). 1982. student ed 8.95 (0-685-42542-8); pap. text ed. 8.95 (0-910935-00-9) Olympics Made.

Petiot, G. Le Robert des Sports: Dictionnaire de la Langue des Sports. 553p. (FRE.). 1990. 65.00 (0-7859-4739-6, M14340) Fr & Eur.

Petipa, Marius, et al. Six Fairy Variations. Orig. Title: Sleeping Beauty Prologue. 44p. 1961. pap. 15.00 (0-932582-66-4) Dance Notation.

Petit, ed. see Claudel, Paul.

Petit, ed. see D'Aurevilly.

Petit, A., jt. auth. see Mathieu, Jean P.

Petit, Ann. Secrets to Enliven Learning: How to Develop Extraordinary Self-Directed Training Materials. LC 94-65592. 176p. 1994. pap. 29.95 (0-88390-416-0) Pfeiffer & Co.

Petit Bois, G. Tables of Indefinite Integrals. 1906. pap. text ed. 7.95 (0-486-60225-7) Dover.

Petit, Carlos, jt. ed. see Corfis, Ivy A.

Petit, Charles & Savage, William. Dictionnaire Classique Anglais-Francais et Francais-Anglais. 686p. (ENG & FRE.). 1967. pap. 59.95 (0-8288-6675-9, M-6444) Fr & Eur.

Petit, Charles P. C., ed. New Perspectives on Thomas Hardy. LC 93-36998. 256p. 1994. text ed. 59.95 (0-312-12036-2) St Martin.

Petit, Christopher. Robinson. LC 93-31578. 208p. 1994. 20.95 (0-670-84925-1, Viking) Viking Penguin.

Petit, Diane. Hope to the Rescue. 192p. 1994. 17.95 (0-8034-9062-3, Avalon Bks) Bouregy.

Petit-Dutaillis, C., ed. The French Communes in the Middle Ages. (Europe in the Middle Ages Selected Studies: Vol. 6). 166p. 1978. 69.25 (0-7204-0550-5, North Holland) Elsevier.

Petit-Dutaillis, Charles E. The Feudal Monarchy in France & England from the Tenth to the Thirteenth Century. LC 80-2011. reprint ed. 64.50 (0-404-18585-1) AMS Pr.

Petit, Francis, jt. ed. see Mortreux, Andre.

Petit, Gabriel, et al, eds. Les Allemands et la Science. LC 80-2141. (Develpoment of Science Ser.). (Illus.). 1981. lib. bdg. 38.95 (0-405-13896-2) Ayer.

Petit, Gedeon D. Effects of Dissolved Oxygen on Survival & Behavior of Selected Fishes of Western Lake Erie. (Bulletin New Ser.: Vol. 4, No. 4). 1973. 3.00 (0-86727-063-2) Ohio Bio Survey.

Petit, Genevieve. The Seventh Walnut. LC 92-10588. (J). 1992. 13.95 (0-922984-10-7) Wellington IL.

Petit, Ian. This Is My Body. 96p. (Orig.). 1993. 5.95 (0-8146-2133-3) Liturgical Pr.

Petit, J., et al, eds. Fatigue Crack Growth under Variable Amplitude Loading: Proceedings of the Third International Spring Meeting of the French Metallurgical Society (Societe Francaise de Metallurgie), Held in Paris, France, 15-17 June 1988. 398p. 1989. 81.00 (1-85166-311-8) Elsevier.

Petit, Jacques, ed. see Barbey d'Aurevilly.

Petit, Jacques, ed. see Claudel, Paul.

Petit, Jacques, jt. auth. see Claudel, Paul.

Petit, Jacques, ed. see Claudel, Paul.

Petit, Jacques, ed. see Mauriac, Francois.

Petit, James. Willapa Bay. (Illus.). 22p. (Orig.). 1992. 37.50 (0-9630863-4-0); pap. 20.00 (0-9630863-5-9) Limner Pr.

— Willapa Bay. deluxe ed. (Illus.). 22p. (Orig.). 1992. 50.00 (0-9630863-6-7) Limner Pr.

Petit, Jean-Pierre, jt. auth. see Taine, Jean.

Petit, John D., Jr., jt. auth. see Lesikar, Raymond V.

Petit, K. Marabout. 480p. (FRE.). 1960. pap. 17.95 (0-7859-5541-0, M-6445) Fr & Eur.

Petit, M., jt. auth. see Giraud, A.

Petit, M., et al. Agricultural Policy Formation in the European Community: The Birth of Milk Quotas & CAP Reform. (Developments in Agricultural Economics Ser.: Vol. 4). 176p. 1987. 66.75 (0-444-42894-1) Elsevier.

Petit, Marcel, ed. see Barbey d'Aurevilly.

Petit, Maria L. Control Theory & Dynamic Games in Economic Policy Analysis. (Illus.). 250p. (C). 1991. 59.95 (0-521-38523-7) Cambridge U Pr.

Petit, Norman. The Heart Prepared: Grace & Conversion in Puritan Spiritual Life. 2nd ed. LC 89-5499. 277p. 1989. reprint ed. pap. 16.95 (0-8195-6224-6, Wesleyan Univ Pr) U Pr of New Eng.

Petit, Pascal. Slow Growth & the Service Economy. LC 82-42711. 220p. 1986. text ed. 25.00 (0-312-72947-2) St Martin.

Petit, R. Electromagnetic Theory of Gratings. (Topics in Current Physics Ser.: Vol. 22). (Illus.). 284p. 1980. 70.00 (0-387-10193-4) Spr-Verlag.

Petit, Ronald E. Women & the Career Game: Play to Win! (Illus.). 147p. (Orig.). 1982. pap. 7.95 (0-685-06198-1) Prof Dev Serv.

Petit-Skinner, Solange. The Nauruans. (Illus.). 315p. 1981. 22.80 (0-9606272-0-0) Macduff Pr.

Petit-Skinner, Solange, jt. auth. see Dari, Willie.

Petit, Solange. Les Americains de Paris. (Publications du Censeil International des Sciences Sociales: No. 117). 149p. (Orig.). 1976. pap. text ed. 35.40 (90-279-7506-X) Mouton.

Petit, Susan. Michel Tournier's Metaphysical Fictions. LC 91-40887. (Purdue University Monographs in Romance Languages: No. 37). xvi, 224p. 1992. 71.00x (1-55619-302-5); pap. 27.95 (1-55619-303-3) Benjamins North Am.

Petit, Thomas A. Fundamentals of Management Coordination: Supervisors, Middle Managers, & Executives. LC 74-19474. (Illus.). 525p. reprint ed. pap. 149.70 (0-7837-3462-X, 2057790) Bks Demand.

Petit, Walter W., jt. ed. see Cumming, Caroline K.

Petitfils, Pierre. Rimbaud. Sheridan, Alan, tr. LC 87-6109. (Illus.). 400p. 1988. 37.50 (0-8139-1142-7) U Pr of Va.

Petitjean, Claude, jt. ed. see Schaller, Lukas A.

Petitjean, Patrick, ed. Science & Empires: Historical Studies about Scientific Development & European Expansion. (Boston Studies in the Philosophy of Science). 428p. (C). 1991. lib. bdg. 115.50 (0-7923-1518-9) Kluwer Ac.

Petitt, Dorothy, jt. auth. see McCKay, Sandra L.

Petitti, Diana B. Meta-Analysis, Decision Analysis, & Cost-Effectiveness Analysis: Methods for Quantitative Synthesis in Medicine. LC 93-30258. (Monographs in Epidemiology & Biostatistics: No. 24). (Illus.). 256p. 1994. 45.00 (0-19-507334-7) OUP.

Petitti, Richard E. The American Elegy: The Airs & Graces of Corporate Life. (Self Realization Bks.: Bk. IV). (Illus.). 100p. 1986. pap. 10.00 (0-938582-08-9) Sensitive Man.

— Brighter Leaves of Grass. (Self Realization Bks.: Bk. VI). (Illus.). 100p. 1986. pap. 10.00 (0-938582-11-9) Sensitive Man.

— Executive Notebook: Imbibing the Passion of Adequacy. (Self Realization Bks.: Bk. I). (Illus.). 100p. 1985. pap. 10.00 (0-938582-05-4) Sensitive Man.

— Inyit Scarizot Speaks: Alter Egos Are a Dime a Dozen. (Self Realization Bks.: Bk. VII). (Illus.). 100p. 1986. pap. 10.00 (0-938582-13-5) Sensitive Man.

— No Time for Me. (Illus.). 150p. 1984. pap. 20.00 (0-938582-01-1) Sensitive Man.

— Notions & Reforms: In the Coming of Age. (Self Realization Bks.: Bk. III). (Illus.). 100p. 1986. pap. 10.00 (0-938582-07-0) Sensitive Man.

— On an All Time High: A New Wave Collection for Corporate Seminars. (Self Realization Bks.: Bk. XI). (Illus.). 100p. 1988. write for info. (0-938582-15-1) Sensitive Man.

— Pain Seeks Its Own Solicitor. (Self Realization Bks.: Bk. VIII). (Illus.). 100p. 1986. pap. 7.00 (0-317-45794-2) Sensitive Man.

— Satan Revisited: The Old New England Blues. (Illus.). 150p. 1985. pap. 20.00 (0-938582-02-X) Sensitive Man.

— The Sensitive Man: And It's OK to Be Feminine. (Self Realization Bks.: Bk. II). (Illus.). 150p. 1986. pap. 20.00 (0-938582-03-8) Sensitive Man.

— Snake Charmers Are Made Not Born. (Self Realization Bks.: Bk. V). (Illus.). 100p. 1986. pap. 10.00 (0-938582-09-7) Sensitive Man.

— Swelling My Song in Vagabond Shoes: Re-entering the Corporate Life. (Self Realization Bks.: Bk. IX). (Illus.). 100p. 1986. pap. 10.00 (0-938582-12-7) Sensitive Man.

Petiver, James. Papilionum Britanniae Icones. 1984. 75.00 (0-317-07167-X) St Mut.

***Petkanas, Christopher.** Parish-Hadley: Fifty Years of American Decorating. LC 95-946. 1995. 50.00 (0-316-70032-0) Little.

***Petkeuicius, Jeffrey C.** The Unchained Worker: Principles of Ownership in the Workplace. Smart, Dwain, ed. (Illus.). 154p. (Orig.). 1995. pap. 11.95 (0-9645204-3-5) Cybernetix.

Petkevich, John M. Sports Illustrated Figure Skating. 1989. pap. 10.95 (1-56800-070-7, Pub. by Sports Illus Bks) Natl Bk Netwk.

Petkoff, B., jt. ed. see Bible, W.

Petkov, I. Z. & Stoitsov, M. V. Nuclear Density Functional Theory. (Studies in Nuclear Physics: No. 14). (Illus.). 376p. 1991. 75.00 (0-19-851731-9) OUP.

Petkov, K. & Thirkell, J. E. Labour Relations in Eastern Europe: Organisational Design & Dynamics. (Social Analysis Ser.). 240p. 1991. 74.50 (0-415-00159-5, A5547) Routledge.

Petkov, Nikolay. Systolic Parallel Processing. LC 92-39979. (Advances in Parallel Computing Ser.: Vol. 5). 1992. write for info. (0-444-88769-5, North Holland) Elsevier.

Petkov, P. P., ed. Mathematical Logic. (Illus.). 420p. 1990. 95.00 (0-306-43511-X, Plenum Pr) Plenum.

Petkov, Petko. The United States & Bulgaria in World War I. 224p. 1991. text ed. 31.50 (0-88033-203-4) Col U Pr.

***Petkov, Steven & Mustazza, Leonard.** The Frank Sinatra Reader. (Illus.). 304p. 1995. 25.00 (0-19-509531-6) OUP.

Petkov, V. Scattering Theory for Hyperbolic Operators. (Studies in Mathematics & Its Applications: No. 21). 374p. 1989. 97.50 (0-444-88056-9, North Holland) Elsevier.

Petkov, Vesselin M. & Stoyanov, Luchezar N. Geometry of Reflecting Rays & Inverse Spectral Results. (Pure & Applied Mathematics: A Wiley-Interscience Series of Texts, Monographs & Tracts: No. 1237). 313p. 1992. text ed. 155.00 (0-471-93174-8) Wiley.

Petkovic, Dusan. Mali Leksikon Mikroracunarskih Izraza: Multilingual Computer Dictionary (Serbo-German-English) 268p. (CRO, ENG, GER & SER.). 1990. pap. 95.00 (0-8288-3924-7, F101450) Fr & Eur.

— Small Lexicon of Micro-Accounting Terms, English, German & Serbocroatian: Mali Leksikon Mikroracunarskih Izraza. 202p. (ENG, GER & SER.). 1987. 35.00 (0-8288-0273-4, F44460) Fr & Eur.

Petkovic, M. Iterative Methods for Simultaneous Inclusion of Polynomial Zone. (Lecture Notes in Mathematics Ser.: Vol. 1387). x, 263p. 1989. pap. 37.30 (0-387-51485-6) Spr-Verlag.

Petkun, Lisa B., jt. auth. see Harding, Vicki R.

Petkus, Peggy M. Millionaire's Hill. 1991. mass mkt. 4.99 (0-8217-3573-X) Zebra.

— Millionaires Row. 1989. mass mkt. 4.50 (0-8217-2763-X) Zebra.

Petley, B. W. The Fundamental Physical Constants & the Frontier of Measurement. (Illus.). 358p. 1988. 86.00 (0-85274-388-2) IOP Pub.

— The Fundamental Physical Constants & the Frontiers of Medicine. rev. ed. 356p. 1984. 81.00 (0-85274-427-7) Taylor & Francis.

Petley, H. C. Queen of Slots. 288p. (Orig.). 1990. pap. 4.95 (0-9625559-0-8) Gate Pr Pubs.

Petmesidou, Maria & Tsoulouvis, Lefteris. Planning Technological Change & Economic Development in Greece: High Technology & the Microelectronics Industry. (Progress in Planning Ser.: Vol. 33). (Illus.). 88p. 1990. pap. 45.00 (0-08-040770-6, Pergamon Pr) Elsevier.

Peto, Gloria J. & Medve, William J. EMS Driving: The Safe Way. 224p. 1991. pap. 24.00 (0-89303-828-8) P-H.

Peto, Les. The Dream Lover: Transforming Relationships Through Dreams. LC 90-24119. 192p. 1991. reprint ed. pap. 9.95 (0-87542-595-X) Llewellyn Pubns.

***Peto, Richard.** Mortality from Smoking in Developed Countries: An Analysis from Developed Countries. (Illus.). 678p. 1995. pap. 49.95 (0-19-262619-1) OUP.

Peto, Richard & Hausen, Harald Z., eds. Viral Etiology of Cervical Cancer. LC 86-2227. (Banbury Report Ser.: No. 21). 362p. 1986. text ed. 68.00 (0-87969-221-9) Cold Spring Harbor.

Peto, Richard & Schneiderman, Marvin, eds. Quantification of Occupational Cancer. LC 81-10218. (Banbury Report Ser.: Vol. 9). 756p. (C). 1981. 99.00 (0-87969-208-1) Cold Spring Harbor.

Peto, Richard, jt. ed. see Zaridze, D.

Peto, S. Morton. Resources & Prospects of America: Ascertained During a Visit to the States in the Autumn of 1865. LC 73-2529. (Big Business; Economic Power in a Free Society Ser.). 1973. reprint ed. 29.95 (0-405-05108-5) Ayer.

Petoefi, J., jt. ed. see Van Dijk, T. A.

Petofi, J. S. & Rieser, H., eds. Studies in Text Grammar. LC 73-75766. (Foundations of Language Supplementary Ser.: No. 19). 370p. 1973. lib. bdg. 107.50 (90-277-0368-X) Kluwer Ac.

Petofi, Janos S., ed. Text & Discourse Constitution: Empirical Aspects, Theoretical Approaches. (Research in Text Theory Ser.: Vol. 4). 516p. (C). 1987. lib. bdg. 215.40 (0-89925-326-1) De Gruyter.

— Text & Discourse Constitution: Empirical Aspects, Theoretical Approaches. (Research in Text Theory Ser.: Vol. 4). 516p. (C). 1987. lib. bdg. 215.40 (3-11-007566-0) De Gruyter.

Petofi, Janos S. & Olivi, Terry, eds. Approaches to Poetry: Some Aspects of Textuality, Intertextuality & Intermediality. LC 93-46667. (Research in Text Theory Ser.: No. 20). viii, 300p. (C). 1994. lib. bdg. 149.25 (3-11-013893-X) De Gruyter.

Petofi, Sandor. Works. LC 73-77696. (Literature Ser.). (Illus.). 453p. 1973. 14.90 (0-914648-04-7) Hungarian Cultural.

Petonnet, Colette. Those People: The Subculture of a Housing Project. Smidt, Rita, tr. LC 72-825. (Contributions in Sociology Ser.: No. 10). 293p. 1973. text ed. 29.95 (0-8371-6393-5, PTP/, Greenwood Pr) Greenwood.

Petot, J. M. Melanie Klein, Vol. 1. Trollope, Christine, tr. 324p. 1991. 45.00 (0-8236-3328-4) Intl Univs Pr.

— Melanie Klein, Vol. 2. Trollope, Christine, tr. 300p. 1991. 45.00 (0-8236-3329-2) Intl Univs Pr.

Petr, Boldyrev. Uroki Rossii: Dnevnik Rossiiskogo Separatista. LC 92-47060. 248p. (Orig.). (RUS.). 1993. pap. 16.00 (1-55779-061-2) Hermitage.

Petr, J. Weather & Yield. (Developments in Crop Science Ser.: Vol. 20). 1991. 138.50 (0-444-98803-3) Elsevier.

Petr, J., et al. Yield Formation in the Main Field Crops. (Developments in Crop Science Ser.: No. 13). 336p. 1988. 102.75 (0-444-98954-4) Elsevier.

Petra Press Staff. A Multicultural Portrait of the Move West. LC 93-10317. (Perspectives Ser.). (J). 1993. 18.95 (1-85435-658-5) Marshall Cavendish.

An Asterisk (*) at the beginning of an entry indicates that the title is appearing in BIP for the first time.

Petra ten-Doesschate Chu, ed. Illustrated Bartsch, Vol. 121, Pt. 1: Dominique Vivant Denon. 376p. 1985. 140.00 (*0-89835-220-7*) Abaris Bks.

— Illustrated Bartsch, Vol. 121, Pt. 2: Dominique Vivant Denon. 346p. 1988. 140.00 (*0-89835-315-7*) Abaris Bks.

Petra ten-Doesschate Chu & Weisberg, Gabriel P. The Popularization of Images: Visual Culture under the July Monarchy. LC 93-47332. (Nineteenth-Century Art, Culture, & Society Ser.). 1994. 39.50 (*0-691-03210-6*) Princeton U Pr.

Petra ten-Doesschate Chu, ed. see Courbet, Gustave.

Petracca, Mark P., ed. The Politics of Interests: Interest Groups Transformed. 421p. (C). 1992. pap. text ed. 24. 50 (*0-8133-1001-6*) Westview.

— The Politics of Interests: Interest Groups Transformed. 421p. (C). 1992. text ed. 71.50 (*0-8133-1000-8*) Westview.

Petracca, Michael. Doctor Syntax. 240p. (Orig.). 1989. pap. 9.95 (*0-88739-138-9*, Blk Lizard) Creat Arts Bk.

Petraglia, F., ed. see Genazzani, A. R.

***Petraglia, Joseph, ed.** Reconceiving Writing, Rethinking Writing Instruction. 288p. (C). 1995. text ed. 49.95 (*0-8058-1691-7*) L Erlbaum Assocs.

— Reconceiving Writing, Rethinking Writing Instruction. 288p. (C). 1995. pap. text ed. 22.50 (*0-8058-1692-5*) L Erlbaum Assocs.

Petraglia, Patricia. American Antique Furniture: Styles & Origins, 1640-1840. (Illus.). 176p. 1992. 14.98 (*0-8317-0290-7*) Smithmark.

— American Antique Furniture, 1640-1840. LC 94-27973. 1995. pap. write for info. (*1-56799-147-5*, Friedman-Fairfax) M Friedman Pub Grp Inc.

***Petragnani, Nicola, ed.** Tellerium in Organic Synthesis. (Best Synthetic Methods Ser.). 288p. 1994. text ed. 69. 00 (*0-12-552810-8*) Acad Pr.

Petrak, Cliff. The Art & Science of Aggressive Baserunning. LC 85-30039. 197p. 1986. text ed. 21.95 (*0-13-047671-4*, Parker Publishing Co) P-H.

Petrak, F. & Sydow, H. Die Gattungen der Pyrenomyzeten, Sphaeropsideen und Melanconieen, Pt. 1. (Feddes Repertorium Ser.: Beiheft 27). 551p. (GER.). 1979. reprint ed. lib. bdg. 160.00 (*3-87429-071-9*) Koeltz Sci Bks.

Petrak, Joyce. How to Remember Bach Flower Remedies: or First Get the Elephant off Your Foot. (Illus.). 144p. (Orig.). 1992. pap. 9.95 (*0-9633177-0-9*) Curry-Peterson.

Petrak, Margaret L., ed. Diseases of Cage & Aviary Birds. 2nd ed. LC 81-3792. (Illus.). 720p. reprint ed. pap. 180. 00 (*0-8357-7653-0*, 2056979) Bks Demand.

Petrakis, Gregory J. The New Face of Organized Crime. 192p. 1992. per. 32.95 (*0-8403-7411-9*) Kendall-Hunt.

Petrakis, Harry M. Collected Stories. LC 86-20859. 376p. 1987. 29.95 (*0-941702-14-6*); pap. 14.95 (*0-941702-23-5*) Lake View Pr.

— A Dream of Kings. 1990. pap. 9.95 (*0-312-04306-6*) St Martin.

— The Founder's Touch: The Life of Paul Galvin of Motorola. 3rd ed. 242p. 1991. reprint ed. write for info. (*0-89434-119-7*); reprint ed. pap. write for info. (*0-89434-120-0*) Motorola Univ.

— The Hour of the Bell. LC 75-40738. 384p. 1984. 14.95 (*0-385-04877-7*) Lake View Pr.

— Reflections: A Writer's Life, a Writer's Work. 252p. (Orig.). 1983. reprint ed. 19.95 (*0-941702-04-9*); reprint ed. pap. 9.95 (*0-941702-05-7*) Lake View Pr.

Petrakis, L. & Allen, D. NMR for Liquid Fossil Fuels. (Analytical Spectroscopy Library: No. 1). 242p. 1987. 105.25 (*0-444-42694-9*) Elsevier.

Petrakis, L. & Grandy, D. W. Free Radicals in Coals & Synthetic Fuels. (Coal Science & Technology Ser.: No. 5). 274p. 1983. 100.00 (*0-444-42237-4*, I-306-83) Elsevier.

Petrakis, L., jt. ed. see Cooper, B. R.

Petrakis, Leon & Weiss, F. T., eds. Petroleum in the Marine Environment. LC 79-25524. (ACS Advances in Chemistry Ser.: No. 185). 1980. 60.95 (*0-8412-0475-6*) Am Chemical.

Petrakis, Leonidas & Fraissard, Jacques P., eds. Magnetic Resonance: Introduction, Advanced Topics & Applications to Fossil Energy. 1984. lib. bdg. 98.00 (*0-318-01197-2*) Kluwer Ac.

Petrakis, Leonidas, jt. ed. see Fraissard, Jacques.

Petralia, Joseph F. Flyfishing: First Cast to First Fish. Comer, John et al, eds. LC 94-65404. (Illus.). 248p. (Orig.). 1994. pap. 14.95 (*0-9605890-8-2*, AB1-3) Sierra Trading.

— Gold! Gold! 110p. 1989. pap. 9.95 (*0-88839-118-8*) Hancock House.

— Gold! Gold! A Beginner's Handbook & Recreational Guide: How & Where to Prospect for Gold. 5th rev. ed. Applegate, Jill, ed. LC 81-126200. (Illus.). 144p. (YA). 1992. reprint ed. pap. 9.95 (*0-9605890-5-8*, AB92) Sierra Trading.

Petran, Tabitha. The Struggle over Lebanon. LC 86-18284. 320p. 1987. 27.50 (*0-85345-651-8*) Monthly Rev.

Petranker, Jack, ed. From the Roof of the World: Refugees of Tibet. (Illus.). 285p. (Orig.). (C). 1992. pap. 24.95 (*0-89800-241-9*) Dharma Pub.

Petrarca, Francesco. Letters on Familiar Matters: Rerum Familiarum Libri I-XXIV, 3 vols. Bernardo, Aldo S., tr. LC 75-2418. 352p. 1985. IX-XVI, 352p., 1982. text ed. 50.00 (*0-8018-2750-7*); I-VIII, 472p., 1975. text ed. 50. 00 (*0-8018-2902-X*); XVII-XXIV, 384p., 1985. text ed. 50.00 (*0-8018-2287-4*) Johns Hopkins.

— Letters on Familiar Matters: Rerum Familiarum Libri I-XXIV, 3 vols., Set. Bernardo, Aldo S., tr. LC 75-2418. 1985. 135.00 (*0-8018-2768-X*) Johns Hopkins.

— The Life of Solitude. Zertlin, Jacob, tr. LC 76-48449. (Library of World Literature Ser.). 1985. reprint ed. 29. 50 (*0-88355-594-8*) Hyperion Conn.

— Lord Morley's Tryumphes of Fraunces Petrarcke: The First English Translation of the Trionfi. Carnicelli, D. D., ed. LC 72-164690. 284p. reprint ed. pap. 81.00 (*0-7837-2312-1*, 2057400) Bks Demand.

— Love Rimes of Petrarch. Bishop, Morris, tr. LC 79-12820. (Illus.). 61p. 1980. reprint ed. text ed. 39.75 (*0-313-22002-6*, PELR, Greenwood Pr) Greenwood.

— Petrarch's Africa. Bergin, Thomas G. & Wilson, Alice S., trs. LC 77-75380. 311p. reprint ed. pap. 88.70 (*0-8357-8748-6*, 2033670) Bks Demand.

— Petrarch's Bucolicum Carmen. Bergin, Thomas G., tr. & anno. by. LC 73-94049. 270p. (ENG & LAT.). reprint ed. pap. 77.00 (*0-8357-8749-4*, 2033671) Bks Demand.

— Petrarch's Remedies for Fortune Fair & Foul: A Modern English Translation of "De Remediis Utriusque Fortune," with a Commentary, 5 vols. Rawski, Conrad H., tr. (Illus.). 1991. Vol. 1, Bk. 1: Remedies for Prosperity - Translation, 356p. write for info. (*0-318-68435-7*); Vol. 2, Bk. 1: Remedies for Prosperity - Commentary, 498p. write for info. (*0-318-68436-5*); Vol. 3, Bk. 2: Remedies for Adversity - Translation, 364p. write for info. (*0-318-68437-3*); Vol. 4, Bk. 2: Remedies for Adversity - Commentary, 548p. write for info. (*0-318-68438-1*); Vol. 5: References, Bibliography, Indexes, Tables & Maps, 580p. write for info. (*0-318-68439-X*) Ind U Pr.

— Petrarch's Remedies for Fortune Fair & Foul: A Modern English Translation of "De Remediis Utriusque Fortune," with a Commentary, 5 vols., Set. Rawski, Conrad H., tr. LC 88-46015. (Illus.). 1991. 395.00 (*0-253-34844-7*) Ind U Pr.

— Petrarch's Secret: Or, the Soul's Conflict with Passion. Draper, William H., tr. LC 76-48450. (Library of World Literature Ser.). 1994. reprint ed. 25.00 (*0-88355-596-4*) Hyperion Conn.

— Physicke Against Fortune. Twyne, Thomas, tr. LC 80-22768. 1980. reprint ed. 90.00 (*0-8201-1359-X*) Schol Facsimiles.

— Sonnets & Songs. Armi, Anna M., tr. LC 75-41212. reprint ed. 67.50 (*0-404-14695-3*) AMS Pr.

Petrarca, Francisco. The Revolution of Cola di Rienzo. 2nd rev. ed. Musto, Ronald G, ed. LC 86-80577. Orig. Title: Francesco Petrarca & the Revolution of Cola di Rienzo. 298p. 1986. pap. 12.50 (*0-934977-00-3*) Italica Pr.

Petrarch, Francesco. Selected Sonnets, Odes, & Letters. Bergin, Thomas G., ed. (Crofts Classics Ser.). 160p. 1966. pap. text ed. write for info. (*0-88295-066-5*) Harlan Davidson.

— Selections from the Canzoniere & Other Works. Musa, Mark, ed. & tr. by. (World's Classics Ser.). 128p. 1986. pap. 6.95 (*0-19-281707-8*) OUP.

Petrarch, Francis. Letters of Old Age: Rerum Senilium Libri, No. I-XVIII, 2 vols., Set. Bernardo, Aldo S. et al, trs. 368p. 1992. text ed. 85.00 (*0-8018-4212-3*) Johns Hopkins.

***Petras.** The Only Money Guide You'll Ever Need. 1995. 14.95 (*0-671-75888-8*) S&S Trade.

Petras, James. Politics & Social Structure in Latin America. LC 73-122737. 384p. 1970. reprint ed. pap. 5.95 (*0-85345-195-8*) Monthly Rev.

Petras, James & Morley, Morris. Empire or Republic? American Global Power & Domestic Decay. LC 94-17398. 224p. 1994. 59.95 (*0-415-91064-1*, B4477, Routledge NY); pap. 16.95 (*0-415-91065-X*, B4481, Routledge NY) Routledge.

— Latin America in the Time of Cholera: Electoral Politics, Market Economics, & Permanent Crisis. 240p. 1992. 49. 95 (*0-415-90535-4*, A6756, Routledge NY); pap. 14.95 (*0-415-90536-2*, A6760, Routledge NY) Routledge.

— U. S. Hegemony under Siege: Class Politics & Development in Latin America. 224p. 1990. 45.00 (*0-86091-280-9*, A4499, Pub. by Verso UK); pap. 15.95 (*0-86091-995-1*, A4503, Pub. by Verso UK) Routledge Chapman & Hall.

— The United States & Chile: Imperialism & the Overthrow of the Allende Government. LC 74-21474. (Illus.). 224p. 1975. 10.95 (*0-85345-361-6*); pap. 9.00 (*0-85345-388-8*) Monthly Rev.

Petras, James, jt. auth. see Kurth, James.

Petras, James, et al. Class, State & Power in the Third World: With Case Studies in Class Conflict in Latin America. LC 80-25938. 285p. 1981. pap. text ed. 25.50 (*0-86598-056-X*, R3748) Rowman.

— Democracy & Poverty in Chile. LC 93-43013. (Series in Political Economy & Economic Development in Latin America). 200p. (C). 1994. pap. text ed. 19.95 (*0-8133-8227-0*) Westview.

— Democracy & Poverty in Chile. LC 93-43013. (Series in Political Economy & Economic Development in Latin America). 200p. (C). 1994. text ed. 58.00 (*0-8133-8217-3*) Westview.

Petras, James F. Critical Perspectives on Imperialism & Social Class in the Third World. LC 78-13915. 324p. reprint ed. pap. 92.40 (*0-7837-3901-X*, 2043749) Bks Demand.

— Latin America: Bankers, Generals & the Struggle for Social Justice. LC 86-1885. 200p. (C). 1986. 52.25 (*0-8476-7505-X*) Rowman.

— Politics & Social Structure in Latin America. LC 73-122737. reprint ed. pap. 108.90 (*0-7837-9613-7*, 2060370) Bks Demand.

Petras, James F. & Merino, Hugo Z. Peasants in Revolt: A Chilean Case Study, 1965-1971. Flory, Thomas, tr. LC 72-1578. (Latin American Monographs: No. 28). 168p. reprint ed. pap. 47.90 (*0-8357-7754-5*, 2036112) Bks Demand.

Petras, Kathryn. Jobs 1994. 1993. pap. 16.00 (*0-671-76076-9*, Fireside) S&S Trade.

— Jobs 1995. 1994. pap. 15.00 (*0-671-76077-7*, Fireside) S&S Trade.

Petras, Kathryn & Petras, Ross. Jobs 1993. 592p. (Orig.). 1992. pap. 15.00 (*0-671-76075-0*, Fireside) S&S Trade.

— The Only Job-Hunting Guide You'll Ever Need: The Most Comprehensive Guide for Job Hunters & Career Switchers. 1989. pap. 14.00 (*0-671-63648-0*, Fireside) S&S Trade.

— The Only Job Hunting Guide You'll Ever Need: The Most Comprehensive Guide for Job Hunters & Career Switchers. LC 94-47511. 1995. pap. 15.00 (*0-684-80236-8*, Fireside) S&S Trade.

— The Over-Forty Job Guide. 352p. 1993. pap. 12.00 (*0-671-78078-6*) S&S Trade.

— Seven Hundred Seventy-Six Stupidest Things. 1993. mass mkt. 10.00 (*0-385-41928-7*) Doubleday.

Petras, Kathryn & Petras, Ross, eds. The Whole World Book of Quotations: Wisdom from Women & Men Around the Globe Throughout the Centuries. 576p. 1995. 24.00 (*0-201-62258-0*) Addison-Wesley.

Petras, Kathryn, jt. auth. see Petras, Ross.

Petras, Ross & Petras, Kathryn. Jobs 'Ninety. 320p. (Orig.). 1990. pap. 14.95 (*0-685-31172-4*) P-H.

— The Seven Hundred & Seventy-Six Even Stupider Things Ever Said. LC 93-44804. 224p. (Orig.). 1994. pap. 10.00 (*0-06-095059-5*, PL) HarpC.

— The 776 Nastiest Things Ever Said. 224p. 1995. pap. 7.95 (*0-06-095060-9*, PL) HarpC.

Petras, Ross, jt. auth. see Petras, Kathryn.

Petras, Ross, jt. ed. see Petras, Kathryn.

Petrasch, P., jt. auth. see Adler, J.

Petrascheck, W. E., ed. Ore Mobilization in the Alps & in SE-Europe. (Schriftenreihe der Erdwissenschaftlichen Kommissionen Ser.: Band 6). 106p. (ENG & GER.). 1983. pap. 31.00 (*0-387-86511-X*) Spr-Verlag.

Petrascheck, W. E. & Jankovic, S., eds. Geotectonic Evolution & Metallogeny of the Mediterranean Area & Western Asia: Proceedings of the Final Symposium of IGCP Project 169, Leoben, October, 1984. (Schriftenreihe der Erdwissenschaftlichen Kommissionen Ser.: Band 8). 298p. 1986. pap. 85.00 (*0-387-86527-6*) Spr-Verlag.

Petrasen, G. I., ed. see Steklov Institute of Mathematics, Academy of Sciences, U. S. S. R. Staff.

Petrash, Carol. Earthways: Simple Environment Activities for Young Children. 1992. pap. 14.95 (*0-87659-156-X*) Gryphon Hse.

Petrash, G. G., ed. Metal Vapor & Metal Halide Vapor Lasers. (Proceedings of the Lebedev Physics Institute Ser.: Vol. 181). 261p. 1989. text ed. 115.00 (*0-941743-27-6*) Nova Sci Pubs.

— Optics & Lasers. (Proceedings of the Lebedev Physics Institute Ser.: Vol. 211). 240p. 1994. lib. bdg. 98.00 (*1-56072-197-9*) Nova Sci Pubs.

Petrasouits, G. Proceedings of the Ninth Danube-European Conference on Soil Mechanics & Foundation Engineering. (Illus.). 555p. (C). 1990. text ed. 66.00 (*963-05-5898-X*, Pub. by A K HU) Intl Spec Bk.

Petrasovits, G. Soil Mechanics & Foundation Engineering. 640p. (C). 1984. 405.00 (*0-569-08888-7*, Pub. by Collets) St Mut.

***Petrasovits, G., ed.** Proceedings of the Sixth Budapest Conference on Soil Mechanics & Foundation Engineering. 640p. (C). 1984. 156.00x (*963-05-3962-4*) St Mut.

Petrat, Gerhardt. Einem Besseren Dasein zu Diensten: Die Spur der Aufklarung im Medium Kalender Zwischen 1700 un 1919. (Deutsche Presseforschung Ser.). 242p. (GER.). 1991. pap. 59.00 (*3-598-21628-9*) K G Saur.

Petratca, Francesco. Cancionero, Sonetos y Canciones. Crespo, Angel, tr. & intro. by. (Nueva Austral Ser.: Vol. 42). (SPA.). 1991. pap. text ed. 24.95x (*84-239-1842-4*) Elliots Bks.

***Petrazzini, Ben A.** The Political Economy of Telecommunications Reform in Developing: Privatization & Liberalization in Comparative Perspective. LC 95-7552. (Primary Documents in American History & Contemporary Issues Ser.). 1995. text ed. write for info. (*0-275-95294-0*, Praeger Pubs) Greenwood.

Petre, F. Loraine. Napoleon & the Archduke Charles: A History of the Franco-Austrian Campaign in the Valley of the Danube in 1809. 432p. 40.00 (*1-85367-092-8*, 5558) Stackpole.

— Napoleon at Bay, 1814. LC 93-40524. (Illus.). 240p. 1994. 40.00 (*1-85367-163-0*, 5557) Stackpole.

— Napoleon's Conquest of Prussia, 1806. LC 92-41764. 344p. 1993. 40.00 (*1-85367-145-2*, 5561) Stackpole.

— Napoleon's Last Campaign in Germany, 1813. 424p. 1992. 37.50 (*1-85367-121-5*) Stackpole.

Petre, Francis L. The Republic of Colombia: An Account of the Country, Its People, Its Institutions & Its Resources. 1976. lib. bdg. 39.95 (*0-8490-2517-6*) Gordon Pr.

Petre, G., et al, eds. Capillarity Today: Proceedings of an Advanced Workshop on Capillarity Held In Memoriam Raymond Defay at Brussels, Belgium, 7-10 May 1990. (Lecture Notes in Physics Ser.: Vol. 386). xi, 384p. 1991. 50.00 (*0-387-54367-8*) Spr-Verlag.

Petre, James. Richard the Third: Crown & People. (Illus.). 464p. 1993. text ed. 55.00 (*0-904893-11-1*) A Sutton Pub.

Petre, M. D., ed. see Gorgolini, Pietro.

Petre, Peter, jt. auth. see Schwarzkopf, H. Norman.

Petre, Robert, jt. ed. see Schlegel, Eric M.

Petrecca, Giovanni. Industrial Energy Management: Principles & Applications. LC 92-36761. (International Series in Engineering & Computer Science, VLSI, Computer Architecture, & Digital Screen Processing: Vol. 13). 1992. lib. bdg. 135.00 (*0-7923-9305-8*) Kluwer Ac.

Petrek, Jeanne A., jt. auth. see Robinson, Rebecca Y.

Petrelia, R., jt. ed. see Szalai, A.

Petrella, Carmine. Men of Destiny. (Illus.). 72p. 1994. pap. 8.95 (*0-8059-3460-X*) Dorrance.

Petrella, R., jt. ed. see Kuklinski, Antoni.

***Petrelli.** Italian-English, English-Italian Medical Dictionary. 737p. (ENG & ITA.). 1993. 110.00 (*0-7859-7524-1*, 8871660714) Fr & Eur.

Petrelli, M. Italian-English - English-Italian Medical Dictionary. 737p. 1993. 110.00 (*88-7166-071-4*, Pub. by Le Lettere IT) IBD Ltd.

— Italian-English--English-Italian Medical Dictionary. (ENG & ITA.). 1993. 110.00 (*0-7859-8825-4*) Fr & Eur.

Petrello, George J. In Service to America: The AICS at Seventy-Five. 176p. 1988. pap. text ed. 26.95 (*0-07-049604-8*) McGraw.

Petreman, David A., tr. see Coloane, Francisco.

Petrement, Simone. A Separate God: The Origins & Teachings of Gnosticism. Harrison, Carol, tr. LC 93-19099. 560p. 1993. reprint ed. pap. 18.00 (*0-06-066421-5*) Harper SF.

Petren, Gustaf, et al. Pakistan: Human Rights after Martial Law: Report of a Mission. 157p. reprint ed. pap. 44.80 (*0-318-34908-6*, 2031423) Bks Demand.

Petres, J. & Hundeiker, M. Dermatosurgery. 1978. 66.00 (*0-387-90296-1*) Spr-Verlag.

Petreschi, R., jt. auth. see Bovet, D. P.

Petrescu, M. English & Rumanian Dictionary of Electrical Engineering, Electronic Telecommunication & Cybernetics: Dictionar de Electrotehnica, Electronica, Telecomunicatii, Cibernetica. (ENG & RUM.). 1982. write for info. (*0-8288-0305-6*, M15846) Fr & Eur.

Petreshene, Susan S. Brain Teasers! Over One Hundred Eighty Activities & Worksheets That Make Kids Think. LC 94-11905. (Illus.). 1994. pap. 27.95 (*0-87628-123-4*) Ctr Appl Res.

— Mind Joggers! Five to Fifteen-Minute Activities That Make Kids Think. (Illus.). 1985. pap. 27.95 (*0-87628-583-3*) Ctr Appl Res.

— Research Pleasers. Sussman, Ellen, ed. (Illus.). (Orig.). (J). (gr. 3-6). 1982. pap. text ed. 5.95 (*0-933606-19-2*, MS-618) E Sussman Educ.

Petretschek, Roswitha, ed. see Satchell, Alexis.

Petretti, Allan. Petretti's Coca-Cola Collectibles Price Guide. 6th ed. (Illus.). 384p. 1991. 34.95 (*0-87069-627-0*) Chilton.

— Petretti's Coca-Cola Collectibles Price Guide. 9th ed. 504p. 1994. 39.95 (*0-87069-729-3*) Chilton.

***Petretti, Francesco.** Tropical Rainforest. (Illus.). 144p. 1995. 19.98 (*0-8317-8683-3*) Smithmark.

Petrey, Sandy. History in the Text "Quatrevingt-Treize" & the French Revolution. (Purdue University Monographs in Romance Languages: No 3). viii, 129p. 1980. 35.00x (*90-272-1713-0*) Benjamins North Am.

— Realism & Revolution: Balzac, Stendahl, Zola & the Performances of History. LC 88-18117. 224p. 1989. 29. 95 (*0-8014-2216-7*) Cornell U Pr.

— Speech Acts & Literary Theory. 192p. 1990. 35.00 (*0-415-90181-2*, A3592, Routledge NY); pap. 13.95 (*0-415-90182-0*, A3596, Routledge NY) Routledge.

Petrey, Sandy, intro. The French Revolution, 1789-1989: Two Hundred Years of Rethinking. (Eighteenth Century Ser.). (Illus.). 106p. (C). 1989. 15.95 (*0-89672-198-1*) Tex Tech Univ Pr.

Petrey, Sandy, tr. see Zola, Emile.

Petrey, Susan. Gifts of Blood. 1992. mass mkt. 4.50 (*0-671-72107-0*) Baen Bks.

Petri, Barbara, ed. Kiwi & Emu: An Anthology of Contemporary Poetry by Australian & New Zealand Women. 289p. (C). 1990. 105.00 (*0-947333-05-3*, Pub. by Pascoe Pub AT) St Mut.

Petri, Gyorgi. Night Song of the Personal Shadow: Selected Poems. Wilmer, Clive, tr. & intro. by. 76p. (Orig.). 1991. pap. 14.95 (*1-85224-107-1*, Pub. by Bloodaxe Bks UK) Dufour.

Petri, Herbert L. Motivation: Theory, Research & Applications. 3rd ed. 434p. (C). 1991. text ed. 52.95 (*0-534-14364-4*) Brooks-Cole.

Petri, Mart & Burkhardt, Gina. CaMaPe: An Organizational & Educational Systems Approach to Secondary School Development. 100p. (Orig.). (C). 1992. pap. text ed. 15. 00 (*1-878234-04-8*) Reg Lab Educ IOT NE Isls.

Petri, Peter. Common Foundations of East Asian Success. LC 93-32722. (Lessons of East Asia Ser.). 46p. 1993. 6.95 (*0-8213-2616-3*, 12616) World Bank.

Petri, Peter A. Modeling Japanese-American Trade: A Study of Asymmetric Interdependence. (Economic Studies: No. 156). (Illus.). 232p. 1984. 20.00 (*0-674-57810-4*) HUP.

Petri, Peter A., jt. ed. see Gerlach, Stefan.

Petri, Peter A., jt. auth. see Leipziger, Danny M.

Petri, R. Construction Estimating. 1979. text ed. 74.00 (*0-87909-152-5*, Reston) P-H.

Petric, Vlada. Constructivism in Film: The Man with the Movie Camera. (Studies in Film). (Illus.). 352p. (C). 1993. pap. 19.95 (*0-521-44387-3*) Cambridge U Pr.

Petricciani, J. C., jt. ed. see Hopps, H. E.

Petriccisni, J. C. & Hennessen, W., eds. Cells, Products, Safety. (Developments in Biological Standardization Ser.: Vol. 68). (Illus.). vi, 90p. 1987. pap. 44.00 (*3-8055-4676-9*) S Karger.

Petricic, Dusan, jt. auth. see Shalom, Vivienne.

Petrick, Joseph & Furr, Diana. Total Quality in Human Resources. 300p. 1994. 39.95 (*1-884015-05-0*) St Lucie Pr.

***Petrick, Joseph & Furr, Dianna.** Total Quality in Managing Human Resources. 420p. 1995. 44.95 (*1-884015-24-7*) St Lucie Pr.

***Petrick, Joseph A. & Furr, Diana S.** Total Quality in Organizational Development. 300p. 1995. 39.95 (*1-884015-22-0*) St Lucie Pr.

***Petrick, Neila S.** Jane Long of Texas. (Illus.). 400p. 1995. 23.95 (*0-9642905-0-2*) Prime Time Pr.

Petrick, Neila S., jt. auth. see Dittmer, Lorraine S.

Petrick, Paul J. Fiberglass Repairs. LC 76-17811. (Illus.). 89p. 1976. pap. 8.95 (*0-87033-222-8*) Cornell Maritime.

P Q

Petrick, S. W. Veterinary Eye Surgery. (Illus.). 1986. text ed. 36.95 (*0-409-11265-8*) Buttrwrth-Heinemann.
***Petrick-Steward, Elizabeth.** Beginning Writers in the Zone of Proximal Development. 288p. 1993. pap. 29.95 (*0-8058-1866-9*) L Erlbaum Assocs.
— Beginning Writers in the Zone of Proximal Development. 288p. 1993. text ed. 75.00 (*0-8058-1302-0*) L Erlbaum Assocs.
Petrick, Thomas W., ed. see Powell, Mary C.
Petrick, Tim. Sports Illustrated Skiing. (Illus.). 1989. pap. 9.95 (*1-56800-028-6*, Pub. by Sports Illus Bks) Natl Bk Netwk.
Petricola, Mario, jt. auth. see Jorgensen, Donald G.
Petrides, D. The Latin-American Technique. (Ballroom Dance Ser.). 1986. lib. bdg. 79.95 (*0-8490-3391-8*) Gordon Pr.
— The Latin-American Technique. (Ballroom Dance Ser.). 1980. lib. bdg. 79.50 (*0-87700-689-X*) Revisionist Pr.
Petrides, George A. A Field Guide to Eastern Trees. (Peterson Field Guide Ser.). (Illus.). 1988. 21.95 (*0-395-46731-4*); pap. 14.95 (*0-395-46732-2*) HM.
— Field Guide to Trees & Shrubs. 1973. pap. 14.95 (*0-395-17579-8*) HM.
— Field Guide to Western Trees: Western United States & Canada. 1992. pap. 15.95 (*0-395-46729-2*) HM.
— Peterson First Guide to Trees. LC 92-36586. (Illus.). 128p. (J). 1993. pap. 4.95 (*0-395-65972-8*) HM.
Petrides, Paul. Suzanne Valadon: The Complete Work. (Illus.). 370p. (FRE.). 1971. 475.00 (*1-55660-068-2*) A Wofsy Fine Arts.
Petrides, Ted. Greek Dances: Thirteen Dances of Mainland Greece, the Islands & Crete. rev. ed. (Illus.). 105p. (Orig.). 1975. pap. 10.00 (*960-7269-07-1*, Pub. by Lycabettus Pr GR) Bosphorus Bks.
Petridis, Constantjin, jt. ed. see Herreman, Frank.
Petrie. Cardiovascular & Respiratory Disease Therapy. (Clinically Important Adverse Drug Interactions Ser.: Vol. 1). 244p. 1981. 84.75 (*0-444-80233-9*) Elsevier.
— Funeral Furniture & Stone Vessels. (Petrie Egyptian Collection & Excavations Ser.). reprint ed. 49.95 (*0-85668-036-2*, Pub. by Aris & Phillips UK) David Brown.
— Gizeh & Rifeh. (Petrie Egyptian Collection & Excavations Ser.). reprint ed. 70.00 (*0-85668-037-0*, Pub. by Aris & Phillips UK) David Brown.
— Illahun Kahun & Gurob. 1991. write for info. (*0-913484-10-5*, Pub. by Aris & Phillips UK) David Brown.
— Naqada & Ballas. 1991. write for info. (*0-913484-09-1*, Pub. by Aris & Phillips UK) David Brown.
— Scarabs & Cylinders with Names. reprint ed. 60.00 (*0-85668-010-9*, Pub. by Aris & Phillips UK) David Brown.
— Seven Memphite Tomb Chapels, Vol. 65: British School of Egyptian Archaeology. 1969. 19.95 (*0-85668-116-4*, Pub. by Aris & Phillips UK) David Brown.
— Shabtis. 1935. 39.95 (*0-85668-012-5*, Pub. by Aris & Phillips UK) David Brown.
Petrie, jt. auth. see Meldman.
Petrie, Alexander. An Introduction to Roman History, Literature & Antiquities. 3rd ed. LC 78-25840. (Illus.). 160p. 1979. reprint ed. text ed. 38.50 (*0-313-20848-4*, PEIR, Greenwood Pr) Greenwood.
***Petrie, Asenath.** Oasis in Time: Jerusalem. 111p. (Orig.). 1994. pap. text ed. 8.95 (*965-229-109-9*, Pub. by Gefen Pub Hse IS) Gefen Bks.
Petrie, Barbara. Priscilla Scales & Other Cautionary Tales. (C). 1990. 45.00 (*0-947333-04-5*, Pub. by Pascoe Pub AT) St Mut.
Petrie, Bruce I., Jr. Innovations in Ohio Workplace Injury Law: Intentional Torts, VSSR's, Third-Party Liability, Independent Contractors. Qualls, John R., ed. 128p. 1988. text ed. 21.50 (*0-87084-703-1*) Anderson Pub Co.
Petrie, Catherine. Hot Rod Harry. LC 81-15549. (Rookie Reader Ser.). (Illus.). 32p. (J). (ps-2). 1982. lib. bdg. 10.35 (*0-516-03493-6*); pap. text ed. 2.95 (*0-516-43493-4*) Childrens.
— Hot Rod Harry Big Book. (Rookie Readers Big Bks.). (Illus.). 32p. (J). (ps-2). 1991. lib. bdg. 22.95 (*0-516-49516-X*) Childrens.
— Joshua James Likes Trucks. LC 81-17076. (Rookie Reader Ser.). (Illus.). 32p. (J). (ps-2). 1982. lib. bdg. 10.35 (*0-516-03525-8*); pap. text ed. 2.95 (*0-516-43525-6*) Childrens.
— A Pedro Perez le Gustan los Camiones (Joshua James Likes Trucks) LC 81-17076. (Rookie Readers - Spanish Ser.). (Illus.). 32p. (SPA.). (J). (ps-2). 1988. pap. 2.95 (*0-516-53525-0*) Childrens.
— Sandbox Betty. LC 81-15547. (Rookie Reader Ser.). (Illus.). 32p. (J). (ps-2). 1982. lib. bdg. 10.35 (*0-516-03578-9*); pap. 2.95 (*0-516-43578-7*) Childrens.
***Petrie, Charles.** Carlton Club. 221p. 1955. 69.50 (*0-614-00061-0*) Elliots Bks.
— The Jacobite Movement. 1973. 250.00 (*0-8490-0432-2*) Gordon Pr.
Petrie, Charles A. Diplomatic History, 1713-1933. LC 83-45834. reprint ed. 35.00 (*0-404-20199-7*) AMS Pr.
Petrie, Charles J., Jr., ed. Enterprise Integration Modeling: Proceedings of the First International Conference. (Scientific & Engineering Computation Ser.). (Illus.). 650p. 1992. pap. 45.00 (*0-262-66080-6*) MIT Pr.
Petrie, Chuck, ed. Just Dogs: A Photographic & Literary Tribute to the Great Hunting Breeds. (Illus.). 160p. 1988. 35.00 (*0-932558-47-X*, 1490) Willow Creek Pr.
Petrie, Chuck & Petrie, Tom, eds. Just Dogs. 160p. 1991. pap. 19.95 (*1-55971-117-5*, 1530) NorthWord.
Petrie, Chuck, ed. see Ford, Corey.
Petrie, Chuck, ed. see Grange, Wallace B.
Petrie, Chuck, ed. see Ozoga, John J.
Petrie, Chuck, jt. ed. see Petrie, Tom.
Petrie, Chuck, jt. ed. see Rulseh, Ted.
Petrie, Constance C. Tom Petrie's Reminiscences of Early Queensland. (Orig.). pap. 18.95 (*0-7022-2383-2*, Pub. by Univ Queensland Pr AT) Intl Spec Bk.
Petrie, Dennis W. Ultimately Fiction: Design in Modern American Literary Biography. LC 80-84578. 250p. 1981. 18.00 (*0-911198-62-8*) Purdue U Pr.
Petrie, Duncan, ed. Cinema & the Realms of Enchantment: Lectures, Seminars & Essays by Marina Warner & Others. (Illus.). 144p. 1994. pap. 16.95 (*0-85170-405-0*, Pub. by British Film Inst UK) Ind U Pr.
— New Questions of British Cinema, Vol. 2: Working Papers. (Illus.). 128p. (C). 1993. pap. 16.95 (*0-85170-322-4*, Pub. by British Film Inst UK) Ind U Pr.
— Screening Europe. (Working Papers: Vol. 1). (Illus.). 176p. 1992. pap. 16.95 (*0-85170-321-6*, Pub. by British Film Inst UK) Ind U Pr.
Petrie, Duncan J. Creativity & Constraint in the British Film Industry. LC 90-48652. 240p. 1991. text ed. 39.95 (*0-312-05700-8*) St Martin.
Petrie, Ferdinand. The Big Book of Painting Nature in Watercolor. (Illus.). 400p. 1990. pap. 29.95 (*0-8230-0499-6*, Watsn-Guptill) Watsn-Guptill.
— Drawing Landscapes in Pencil. (Illus.). 144p. 1992. reprint ed. pap. 16.95 (*0-8230-2646-9*, Watsn-Guptill) Watsn-Guptill.
Petrie, Flinders. Decorative Patterns of the Ancient World. (Illus.). 104p. 1991. 12.99 (*0-517-02217-6*) Random Hse Value.
— Decorative Patterns of the Ancient World for Craftsmen. LC 73-79745. (Illus.). 1974. reprint ed. 6.95 (*0-486-22986-6*) Dover.
— Historical Scarabs. (Illus.). 1976. pap. 10.00 (*0-89005-122-4*) Ares.
Petrie, G. Tunis-Kairous-an & Carthage. 360p. 1985. 220.00 (*1-85077-067-0*, Darf Pubs Ltd) St Mut.
Petrie, George L. Simulation of the Maneuverability of Inland Waterway Tows. (University of Michigan, Dept. of Naval Architecture & Marine Engineering, Report Ser.: No. 186). 93p. reprint ed. pap. 26.60 (*0-317-27207-1*, 2023871) Bks Demand.
***Petrie, Glen.** The Hampstead Poisonings. LC 95-13258. 1995. write for info. (*0-88734-915-3*) Players Pr.
Petrie, Gordon. Terrain Modelling in Surveying & Civil Engineering. 345p. 1992. text ed. 69.00 (*0-07-049683-8*) McGraw.
***Petrie, Graham.** Seahorse: A Novel. LC 95-8673. 169p. 1996. 20.00 (*1-56947-077-4*) Soho Press.
— The Siege: A Novel. 232p. 1996. 20.00 (*1-56947-076-6*) Soho Press.
Petrie, Graham & Dwyer, Ruth, eds. Before the Wall Came Down: Soviet & East European Filmakers Working in the West. 254p. (Orig.). (C). 1990. lib. bdg. 50.00 (*0-8191-7858-6*); pap. text ed. 26.50 (*0-8191-7859-4*) U Pr of Amer.
Petrie, Graham, jt. auth. see Johnson, Vida T.
Petrie, Graham, ed. see Sterne, Laurence.
***Petrie, Hugh G., ed.** Professionalizaiton, Partnership, & Power: Building Professional Development Schools. LC 94-39617. (Frontiers in Education Ser.). 288p. (C). 1995. pap. text ed. 19.95 (*0-7914-2606-8*) State U NY Pr.
— Professionalization, Partnership, & Power: Building Professional Development Schools. LC 93-39617. (Frontiers in Education Ser.). 288p. (C). 1995. pap. text ed. 19.95x (*0-7914-2605-X*) State U NY Pr.
Petrie, J. C. Nervous System, Endocrine System & Infusion Therapy, Vol. 2. (Clinically Important Adverse Drug Interactions Ser.). 384p. 1984. 161.00 (*0-444-80529-X*) Elsevier.
Petrie, J. C. & Cluff, L. E. Clinically Important Adverse Drug Interactions, Vol. 3: Gastrointestinal, Haematological & Infectious Disease Therapy. 1985. 153.50 (*0-444-80606-7*) Elsevier.
Petrie, J. C., jt. ed. see Girdwood, Ronald H.
Petrie, J. Howard, jt. auth. see Burton, Paul F.
Petrie, Jennifer, jt. ed. see Barnes, John.
Petrie, Jennifer, jt. ed. see De'Ricci, Catherine.
Petrie, John, tr. see Weil, Simone.
***Petrie, John N., ed.** Essays on Strategy, No. 11. (Illus.). 403p. (Orig.). (C). 1994. pap. text ed. 50.00x (*0-7881-1426-3*) Diane Pub.
Petrie, Joyce. Mainstreaming in the Media Center. LC 82-2182. (Illus.). 232p. (C). 1982. pap. 26.50 (*0-89774-006-8*) Oryx Pr.
Petrie Method Inc. Staff. The Lose Weight Hypnosis Program. 1990. student ed, audio 49.95 (*0-13-540360-X*) P-H.
— The Quit Smoking Hypnosis Program. 16p. 1990. student ed, audio 49.95 (*0-13-748559-X*) P-H.
Petrie, Mildred. Duck-Duck. 1992. 14.95 (*1-877978-41-8*) Woldt.
Petrie, Mildred, ed. The Prima Diner. 2nd ed. (Illus.). 172p. (Orig.). 1984. 7.95 (*0-9605844-0-4*, TX 727-394) Sarasota Opera.
Petrie, Mildred M. Duck, Duck: The Different Duck. LC 87-80921. (Illus.). 40p. (J). 1987. 12.95 (*0-9618241-0-7*) Enfield Pubs.
Petrie, Paul. Light from the Furnace Rising. 1978. pap. 4.50 (*0-914278-19-3*) Copper Beech.
— Strange Gravity: Songs Physical & Metaphysical. LC 84-50796. (Illus.). 77p. (Orig.). 1984. 10.00 (*0-930954-21-1*) Tidal Pr.
— Strange Gravity: Songs Physical & Metaphysical. LC 84-50796. (Illus.). 77p. (Orig.). 1984. pap. 5.00 (*0-930954-22-X*) Tidal Pr.
Petrie, Roy H., ed. Perinatal Pharmacology. 480p. 1989. 57.95 (*0-87489-469-7*) Med Economics.
***Petrie, Ruth, ed.** By the Light of the Silvery Moon. 192p. 1995. pap. 9.95 (*1-85381-775-9*, Pub. by Virago Pr UK) Trafalgar.
Petrie, S. E., jt. ed. see Allen, Geoffrey.
Petrie, Sidney & Stone, Robert B. Helping Yourself with Autogenics. LC 82-14488. 205p. 1983. 17.95 (*0-13-387407-9*, Parker Publishing Co); pap. 4.95 (*0-13-387399-4*, Parker Publishing Co) P-H.
— Hypno-Cybernetics: Helping Yourself to a Rich New Life. 224p. 1973. 4.95 (*0-13-448530-0*, Parker Publishing Co) P-H.
Petrie, Susan W. Lost & Won. 140p. 1990. 15.95 (*0-945942-06-0*); pap. 9.95 (*0-945942-07-9*) Portmanteau Editions.
Petrie, Ted & Randall, John. Connections, Definite Forms, & Four-Manifolds. (Oxford Mathematical Monographs). 144p. 1991. 45.00 (*0-19-853599-6*) OUP.
Petrie, Ted & Randall, John D. Transformation Groups on Manifolds. LC 84-5855. (Monographs & Textbooks in Pure & Applied Mathematics: No. 82). 280p. reprint ed. pap. 79.80 (*0-7837-3384-4*, 2043342) Bks Demand.
Petrie, Ted, jt. auth. see Dovermann, Karl H.
Petrie, Tom. Back Then: Golf Pictorial History. 1990. 29.50 (*1-55971-050-0*) NorthWord.
Petrie, Tom, ed. Back Then Americans Afield. 148p. 1991. pap. 14.95 (*1-55971-118-3*, 1531) NorthWord.
***Petrie, Tom & Petrie, Chuck, eds.** That Reminds Me of the One. 256p. 1995. 25.00 (*1-57223-024-X*) Outlook Pubng.
Petrie, Tom, jt. ed. see Petrie, Chuck.
Petrie, W. M. Historical Scarabs. Obaba, Al I., ed. (Illus.). 100p. 1990. pap. text ed. 6.95 (*0-916157-66-0*) African Islam Miss Pubns.
— Naukratis I. (IGA VI Ser.: No. 1). (Illus.). vi, 98p. (GRE.). (C). 1992. text ed. 35.00 (*0-89005-508-4*) Ares.
— The Religion of Ancient Egypt. (African Heritage Classical Research Studies). 98p. reprint ed. 20.00 (*0-938818-38-4*) ECA Assoc.
— The Revolutions of Civilization. LC 73-158202. (World History Ser.: No. 48). (C). 1972. reprint ed. lib. bdg. 75.00 (*0-8383-1268-3*) M S G Haskell Hse.
Petrie, William. Guide to Orchids of North America. (Illus.). 128p. pap. 9.95 (*0-88839-089-0*) Hancock House.
Petrie, William F. Ancient Egypt & Ancient Israel. 150p. 1982. pap. 20.00 (*0-89005-337-5*) Ares.
— Egyptian Decorative Art. LC 72-8317. (Illus.). 1978. reprint ed. 21.95 (*0-405-08849-3*, Pub. by Blom Pubns UK) Ayer.
— Egyptian Tales, 2 vols. in 1. LC 68-56524. (First & Second Ser.). (Illus.). 1969. reprint ed. 30.00 (*0-405-08850-7*, Pub. by Blom Pubns UK) Ayer.
— Egyptian Tales, 2 vols. in 1, 1. LC 68-56524. (First & Second Ser.). (Illus.). 1972. reprint ed. 18.95 (*0-405-08851-5*, Pub. by Blom Pubns UK) Ayer.
— Egyptian Tales, 2 vols. in 1, 2. LC 68-56524. (First & Second Ser.). (Illus.). 1972. reprint ed. 19.95 (*0-405-08852-3*, Pub. by Blom Pubns UK) Ayer.
— Methods & Aims in Archaeology. LC 68-56525. 1972. reprint ed. 18.95 (*0-405-08853-1*, Pub. by Blom Pubns UK) Ayer.
— Religion & Conscience in Ancient Egypt. LC 72-83176. 1972. reprint ed. 26.95 (*0-405-08854-X*) Ayer.
***Petrie, William L. & Stover, Douglas E.** Bibliography of the Frederick Douglass Library at Cedar Hall. (Illus.). 496p. (Orig.). 1995. pap. 30.00 (*1-887188-00-2*) Silesia Cos.
Petrie, William M. A History of Egypt: During the XVIIth & XVIIIth Dynasties, 1896, with Additons to 1904, Vol. 2. 4th ed. LC 73-39204. (Select Bibliographies Reprint Ser.). (Illus.). 1977. reprint ed. 35.95 (*0-88143-091-9*) Ayer.
— A History of Egypt: From the Earliest Kings to the XVIth Dynasty, Vol. 1. rev. ed. LC 70-39203. (Select Bibliographies Reprint Ser.). (Illus.). 1977. reprint ed. 35.95 (*0-88143-090-0*) Ayer.
— A History of Egypt: From the XIXth to the XXXth Dynasties, Vol. 3. LC 77-39205. (Select Bibliographies Reprint Ser.). 1977. reprint ed. 39.95 (*0-88143-092-7*) Ayer.
— Seventy Years in Archaeology. LC 72-88921. 307p. 1969. reprint ed. text ed. 38.50 (*0-8371-2241-4*, PESA, Greenwood Pr) Greenwood.
Petrik, James. Descartes' Theory of the Will. LC 91-3485. 1994. text ed. 35.00 (*0-89341-678-9*, Longwood Academic) Hollowbrook.
Petrik-Ott, A. J. The Pteridophytes of Kansas, Nebraska, South Dakota & North Dakota, U. S. A. Nova Hedwigia Beiheft, No. 61. 1979. lib. bdg. 50.00 (*3-7682-5461-5*) Lubrecht & Cramer.
Petrik, Paula. No Step Backward: Women & Family on the Rocky Mountain Mining Frontier, Helena Montana, 1865-1900. LC 87-11334. (Illus.). xix, 206p. (C). 1987. 19.95 (*0-917298-13-6*) MT Hist Soc.
— No Step Backward: Women & Family on the Rocky Mountain Mining Frontier, Helena Montana, 1865-1900. LC 87-11334. 206p. 1990. pap. 12.95 (*0-917298-19-5*) MT Hist Soc.
Petrik, Paula, jt. ed. see West, Elliott.
Petrikin, Jonathan S., ed. Environmental Justice. (At Issue Ser.). 112p. (C). 1900. pap. text ed. 19,957.55 (*1-56510-264-9*) Greenhaven.
— Environmental Justice. (At Issue Ser.). 112p. 1995. lib. bdg. 11.95 (*1-56510-297-5*) Greenhaven.
— Male - Female Roles: Opposing Viewpoints. LC 94-4975. (Opposing Viewpoints Ser.). (Illus.). 264p. (YA). (gr. 10 up). 1995. lib. bdg. 19.95 (*1-56510-174-X*); pap. text ed. 11.55 (*1-56510-175-8*) Greenhaven.
Petrikkos, G. L. & Koenig, W., eds. Meeting the Challenge of Community-Acquired Respiratory Tract Infections: The Role of Cephalosporins. (Journal: Respiration: Vol. 60, Suppl. 1, 1993). (Illus.). vi, 58p. 1993. pap. 25.75 (*3-8055-5754-X*) S Karger.
Petrila, John, jt. ed. see Levin, Bruce L.
Petrilli, Ralph S. Kentucky Family Law, 2 vols. 1988. 150.00 (*0-685-07378-5*) Anderson Pub Co.
— Kentucky Family Law with Juvenile Court Practice, 2 vols., Set. 2nd ed. 1988. write for info. (*0-87084-728-7*) Anderson Pub Co.
Petrilli, S., tr. see Deledalle, Gerard.
Petrilli, Susan, tr. see Fano, Giorgio.
Petrilli, Susan, ed. see Rossi-Landi, Ferruccio.
Petrillo, Alan M. British Service Rifles & Carbines 1888-1900. (Illus.). 72p. (Orig.). 1994. pap. 11.95 (*1-880677-05-9*) Excalibur NY.
— The Lee Enfield Number Four Rifles. (Illus.). 64p. (Orig.). 1992. pap. 10.95 (*1-880677-00-8*) Excalibur NY.
— The Lee Enfield Number One Rifles. (Illus.). 64p. (Orig.). 1992. pap. 10.95 (*1-880677-01-6*) Excalibur NY.
— The Number 5 Jungle Carbine. (Illus.). 32p. (Orig.). 1994. pap. 7.95 (*1-880677-06-7*) Excalibur NY.
Petrillo, Anthony J., jt. auth. see Hall, Betty L.
Petrillo, Charles. Anthracite & Slackwater: The North Branch Canal 1828-1901. LC 86-26872. (Orig.). 1987. 28.75 (*0-930973-03-8*); pap. 16.25 (*0-930973-04-6*) Canal Hist Tech.
Petrillo, Daniel J. Robert F. Kennedy. (World Leaders - Past & Present Ser.). (Illus.). 112p. (Orig.). (YA). (gr. 5 up). 1989. 17.95 (*1-55546-840-3*); pap. 9.95 (*0-7910-0581-X*) Chelsea Hse.
Petrillo, Lisa, jt. auth. see Cantlupe, Joe.
***Petrillo, Maureen L.** Creating Technology Awareness. Boulais, Katina, ed. (Illus.). 84p. 1994. ring bd. write for info. (*0-614-00952-9*) E&L Instru.
Petrillo, Robert J. The Complete Arizona Contractors Study Guide-Electrical. 1990. write for info. (*0-318-68031-9*) ACS Assocs Pub.
Petrillo, Robert J., ed. see Holish, James A.
Petrin, Helene. French - English Vocabulary of Collective Agreements. 97p. (ENG & FRE.). 1991. pap. 29.95 (*0-8288-9409-4*) Fr & Eur.
Petrina, Bernard H. How to Sell at a Trade Show. (Orig.). 1990. pap. text ed. 89.95 (*0-940799-02-2*) Exec Mgmt Renew Prog.
— Motivating People to Care. rev. ed. Ickes, James W., ed. 140p. 1989. pap. text ed. 49.00 (*0-940799-01-4*) Exec Mgmt Renew Prog.
Petrina, D. Y., et al. Mathematical Foundations of Classical Statistical Mechanics, Vol. 7. 356p. 1989. text ed. 237.00 (*2-88124-681-8*) Gordon & Breach.
***Petrina, D. Ya.** Mathematical Foundations of Quantum Statistical Mechanics: Continuous Systems. LC 94-39303. (Mathematics Physics Studies: Vol. 15). 1995. lib. bdg. 224.50 (*0-7923-3258-X*) Kluwer Ac.
Petrina, John. Art Work: How Produced, How Reproduced. LC 70-107733. (Essay Index Reprint Ser.). 1977. 20.95 (*0-8369-1531-3*) Ayer.
Petrina, Richard. Workforce Renewal. Gerould, Philip, ed. LC 93-73205. (Illus.). 100p. (Orig.). 1994. pap. 9.95 (*1-56052-270-4*) Crisp Pubns.
***Petrinec, J. N., Jr., ed.** Recertification & Stress Classification Issues: Proceedings of the Pressure Vessels & Piping Conference, Minneapolis, MN, 1994. LC 94-71356. (PVP Ser.: Vol. 277). 169p. 1994. pap. 50.00 (*0-7918-1350-9*) ASME.
Petrini, Elisa, ed. see Burnett, Sarah & Octopus, Conran.
Petrini, Elisa, ed. see Sadd, Eddison, et al.
Petrini, Frank. The Proverbs of Frank Petrini: Food for Thought. Parker, Diane, ed. LC 92-54175. (Inspiration - Proverbs Ser.). 110p. 1992. 10.95 (*0-88247-927-X*, 927) R & E Pubs.
Petrini, John, jt. ed. see Sivak, Michael V., Jr.
Petrini, Orlando & Laursen, Gary A. Arctic & Alphine Mycology 3-4: Proceedings of the Third & Fourth International Symposium on Arctic & Alpine Mycology. (Bibliotheca Mycologica Ser.: Vol. 150). (Illus.). 209p. 1933. pap. 60.00 (*3-443-59051-9*, Pub. by Cramer-Borntraeger GW) Lubrecht & Cramer.
***Petrini, Orlando & Ouellette, Guillemond B., eds.** Host Wall Alterations by Parasitic Fungi. LC 94-78283. (Symposium Ser.). (Illus.). viii, 160p. (Orig.). 1994. pap. 32.00x (*0-89054-168-X*) Am Phytopathol Soc.
Petrino, Bob & Mouat, Marty. Winning Football with the Option Package Offense. 202p. 1985. 19.95 (*0-13-960931-8*, Busn) P-H.
***Petrinovich, Lewis.** Human Evolution, Reproduction, & Morality. LC 95-6514. 339p. 1995. 49.50 (*0-306-44939-0*, Plenum Pr) Plenum.
Petrioli-Tofani, Annamaria & Smith, Graham. Sixteenth Century Tuscan Drawings from the Uffizi. (Illus.). 272p. 1988. 69.00 (*0-19-505597-7*) OUP.
Petrishcheva, P. A., ed. Vectors of Diseases of Natural Foci. 336p. 1965. text ed. 82.00 (*0-7065-0566-2*, Pub. by Keter Pub IS) Coronet Bks.
***Petrisko.** Con los Ojos del Alma: Las Visiones y Profecias de una Nueva Virgin Maria. 1996. pap. 12.00 (*0-684-81555-9*, Fireside) S&S Trade.
***Petrisko, Thomas W.** Call of the Ages. LC 95-69033. 509p. 1995. pap. 11.95 (*1-882972-59-7*) Queenship Pub.
Petriu, Emil, jt. ed. see Archibald, Colin.
Petriwsky, Eugene, jt. auth. see Jacobs, Sonia.
Petrizzi, Michael J., jt. auth. see Shahady, Edward J.
Petro, Jame A., jt. auth. see Nicosia, Joan E.
Petro, L., jt. ed. see Veilleux, R.
Petro, Nicolai, ed. Christianity & Russian Culture in Soviet Society, Vol. 3. 244p. (C). 1990. pap. text ed. 47.50 (*0-8133-7742-0*) Westview.
***Petro, Nicolai N.** The Rebirth of Russian Democracy: An Interpretation of Political Culture. LC 94-45431. (Illus.). 240p. (C). 1995. text ed. 39.95 (*0-674-75001-2*) HUP.
Petro, Pamela. The Newport & Narragansett Bay Book: A Complete Guide. LC 93-44660. (Illus.). 1994. pap. text ed. 16.95 (*0-936399-40-6*) Berkshire Hse.

Petro, Partice. Joyless Streets: Women & Melodramatic Representation in Weimar Germany. 248p. 1989. text ed. 49.50 (0-691-05552-1); pap. text ed. 15.95 (0-691-00830-2) Princeton U Pr.

Petro, Patrice, ed. Fugitive Images: From Photography to Video. LC 93-46701. (Theories of Contemporary Culture Ser.). (C). 1994. 35.00 (0-253-34428-X); pap. 15.95 (0-253-20890-4) Ind U Pr.

Petro, Peter. Modern Satire: Four Studies. (De Proprietatibus Litterarum, Ser. Minor: No. 27). 162p. 1982. 93.10 (90-279-3180-1) Mouton.

Petro, Peter, tr. see Simecka, Martin M.

Petro, Sandy. Spice up Your Life with Joy. 96p. 1990. pap. text ed. 5.99 (0-89693-817-4) SP Pubns.

— Word Pictures Painted by Paul. LC 93-16024. 96p. (Orig.). 1993. pap. 5.99 (1-56476-034-0, Victor Books) SP Pubns.

Petro, Sharon. The Tennis Drill Book. LC 84-47518. (Illus.). 128p. (Orig.). 1986. pap. 13.95 (0-88011-224-7, PPET0224) Human Kinetics.

Petro, Sylvester. The Labor Policy of the Free Society. LC 57-6822. 352p. reprint ed. 100.40 (0-8357-9524-1, 2012368) Bks Demand.

— Power Unlimited: The Corruption of Union Leadership. LC 79-4432. (McClellan Committee Hearings). 323p. 1979. reprint ed. text ed. 35.00 (0-313-20898-0, PEPU, Greenwood Pr) Greenwood.

Petrobelli, Pierluigi. Music in the Theater: Essays on Verdi & Other Composers. Parker, Roger, tr. LC 93-3440. (Opera Studies). (C). 1994. 39.50 (0-691-09134-X) Princeton U Pr.

Petrocchi, Timothy. Crooked Pictures: A Book of Stories. LC 92-91199. 180p. (Orig.). 1994. pap. 9.00 (1-56002-292-2, Univ Edtns) Aegina Pr.

***Petrocelli, Richard W., et al.** Traumatic Brain Injury: Evaluation & Litigation. 643p. 1994. 95.00 (1-55834-172-2) Michie Butterworth.

Petrocelli, Sam R., jt. ed. see Rand, Gary M.

***Petrocelli, William & Repa, Barbara K.** Sexual Harassment on the Job. 2nd ed. LC 94-30168. 1994. pap. 18.95 (0-87337-265-4) Nolo Pr.

Petrocelly, K. L. Facilities Evaluation Manual: Safety, Fire Protection & Environmental Compliance. (Illus.). 271p. 1991. 69.00 (0-88173-114-5, 0286) Fairmont Pr.

— Maintenance Computerization Handbook. LC 92-40191. 1993. write for info. (0-88173-150-1) Fairmont Pr.

— Physical Plant Operations Handbook. (Illus.). 216p. 1991. 69.00 (0-88173-054-8, 0180) Fairmont Pr.

***Petrocelly, Kenneth.** Commercial & Institutional Maintenance Management. LC 94-22856. 1994. write for info. (0-88173-184-6) Fairmont Pr.

— Managing Physical Plant Operations. LC 93-35434. 1993. 68.00 (0-88173-160-9) Fairmont Pr.

Petrocelly, Kenneth & Fairmont, Press. Managing Physical Plant Operations. 332p. 1994. text ed. 68.00 (0-13-147455-3) P-H.

Petrocelly, Kenneth L. Before You Build: One Hundred Home-Building Pitfalls to Avoid. (Illus.). 224p. 1991. 25.95 (0-8306-7712-7, 3712); pap. 15.95 (0-8306-3712-5) TAB Bks.

— Before You Build: One Hundred Home Building Pitfalls to Avoid. 1991. 25.95 (0-07-049661-7); pap. 15.95 (0-07-049662-5) McGraw.

— Build It Right: Supervising the Construction of Your Home. 1990. 24.95 (0-07-156851-4) McGraw.

— Build It Right Supervising Company. (Illus.). 208p. 1990. 24.95 (0-8306-7433-0, 3433); pap. 14.95 (0-8306-3433-9) TAB Bks.

— Stationary Engineering Handbook. LC 88-45795. 300p. 1989. text ed. 67.00 (0-88173-078-5) Fairmont Pr.

Petrocelly, Kenneth L., jt. auth. see Fairmont Press Staff.

Petrochenko, N., jt. auth. see Zagorskaia, A.

Petrochenko, P. F. Defining Dictionary of Business Commerce & Marketing. 64p. (C). 1992. text ed. 60.00 (0-569-07110-0, Pub. by Collets) St Mut.

Petrochenkov, Valerii. Tvorcheskaia Sud'ba Panteleimona Romanova. Krashoshchekova, Elena, ed. LC 88-10990. (Russian Ser.). 208p. (Orig.). 1988. pap. 14.50 (1-55779-002-7) Hermitage.

Petrochenkov, Valery. Osen' Veka. LC 82-84747. (Illus.). 152p. (Orig.). (RUS.). 1983. 8.00 (0-911971-00-9) Effect Pub.

— Sobesednik (Conversationalist) Poems. LC 92-81982. 160p. (Orig.). 1992. pap. 28.00 (0-911971-77-7) Effect Pub.

Petrochilos, Elizabeth A. Stone the Poet. 110p. (Orig.). (YA). 1991. pap. write for info. (0-9629730-0-9) E Petrochilos.

Petrocholis, George A. Foreign Direct Investment & the Development Process: The Case of Greece. (Illus.). 208p. 1989. text ed. 72.95 (0-566-07108-8, Pub. by Avebury Pub UK) Ashgate Pub Co.

Petrocilli, Bobby & Frederick, Chris. Triumph over Tragedy. 180p. 1994. pap. 13.95 (1-56796-067-7) WRS Group.

Petrocokino, Paul. The Heart of It All. 1989. 2.75 (0-901269-70-0) Grosvenor USA.

Petrof, Stephen, jt. auth. see Lawless, Gary.

Petroff, Elizabeth. Consolation of the Blessed. (Illus.). 224p. (C). 1980. 12.95 (0-686-32835-3) Alta Gaia Bks.

Petroff, Elizabeth A. Body & Soul: Essays on Medieval Women & Mysticism. 256p. (C). 1994. 35.00 (0-19-508454-3); pap. text ed. 14.95 (0-19-508455-1) OUP.

Petroff, Elizabeth A., ed. Medieval Women's Visionary Literature. 416p. (Orig.). 1986. pap. text ed. 17.95 (0-19-503712-X) OUP.

Petroff, Ivan, et al. Census of the United States: U. S. Decennial Census Reports, Tenth Census: 1880, Vol. 31, No. 107: The Newspaper & Periodical Press, S. N. D. North Alaska: Its Population, Industries, & Resources; the Seal Islands of Alaska; Ship-building Industry in the United States. Allison, Peter, ed. LC 07-18862. (Illus.). 1120p. reprint ed. fiche, lib. bdg. 500.00 (0-88354-431-8) N Ross.

Petroff, John N. Handbook of MRP II & JIT: Strategies for Total Manufacturing Control. LC 93-16364. 1993. write for info. (0-13-374158-3) P-H.

***Petroff, Lillian.** Sojourners & Settlers: The Macedonian Community in Toronto in 1940. (Multicultural History Society of Ontario Ser.). (Illus.). 256p. 1995. 50.00 (0-8020-0452-0); pap. 19.95 (0-8020-7240-2) U of Toronto Pr.

Petroff, Serge P. Red Eminence: A Biography of Mikhail A. Suslov. LC 87-81055. 273p. (C). 1988. 25.00 (0-940670-13-5) Kingston Pr.

Petroff, Y., ed. Free-Electron Lasers II. 119p. 1989. 42.00 (0-8194-0169-2, VOL. 1133) SPIE.

Petrofske, Mary T. Recollections of Caernarvon Township: A Portrait of a Lancaster County Town. LC 93-33392. (Illus.). 304p. 1993. 35.00 (0-914659-67-7) Phoenix Pub.

Petroianu, A., jt. auth. see Handschin, E.

Petroleo Internacional Staff. Glossary of the Petroleum Industry. 2nd ed. 378p. (ENG & SPA.). 1982. pap. 95.00 (0-8288-0706-X, S 50548) Fr & Eur.

Petroleum Finance Co. Staff. World Petroleum Markets: A Framework for Reliable Projections. (Technical Paper Ser.: No. 92). 190p. 1988. pap. 10.95 (0-8213-1138-7) World Bank.

***Petroleum Marketers Association of America Staff.** Advanced Oil Heat: A Guide. 272p. 1994. per., pap. text ed. 12.81 (0-7872-0395-5) Kendall-Hunt.

Petroleum Mechanical Engineering Conference & Workshop Staff. Petroleum Mechanical Engineering Conference & Workshop: Presented at the 1979 Petroleum Mechanical Engineering Conference & Workshop, Tulsa, Oklahoma, October 28-30, 1979. Collier, S. L., ed. LC 79-54866. (Illus.). 120p. reprint ed. pap. 34.20 (0-8357-2892-7, 2039128) Bks Demand.

Petroleum Mechanical Engineering Workshop & Conference Staff. Refinery-Petrochemical Plant Construction & Maintenance, Plant Operation & Control, Noise & Pollution Control in Refinery-Petrochemical Plants: A Workbook for Engineers: Presented at 38th Petroleum Mechanical Engineering Workshop & Conference, September 12-14, 1982, Philadelphia, Pennsylvania. Reagan, J. E., ed. LC 82-228729. (Illus.). 154p. reprint ed. pap. 43.90 (0-8357-2845-5, 2039080) Bks Demand.

Petroleum Products & Lubricants committee D-2. Multi-Cylinder Test Sequences for Evaluating Automotive Engine Oils, Pt. 3: Sequence V-D - STP 315H. LC 83-68369. 146p. 20.00 (0-8031-0238-0, 04-315100-12) ASTM.

Petron, Angela. The Forgotten Duchess. 199p. (C). 1989. text ed. 49.00 (1-872795-01-3, Pub. by Pentland Pr UK) St Mut.

— The Laird's Casket. large type ed. (Linford Romance Library). 1991. pap. 13.95 (0-7089-6985-2, Trailtree Bookshop) Ulverscroft.

— Prelude to Happiness. large type ed. (Linford Romance Library). 288p. 1989. pap. 11.95 (0-7089-6649-7, Linford) Ulverscroft.

— Villa of Singing Water. large type ed. (Linford Romance Library). 288p. 1988. pap. 11.95 (0-7089-6537-7, Linford) Ulverscroft.

Petrone. Le Satiricon. (FRE.). 1972. pap. 10.95 (0-7859-3983-0) Fr & Eur.

Petrone, Joseph A. Building the High-Performance Sales Force. 224p. 1994. 26.95 (0-8144-0219-4) AMACOM.

***Petrone, Penny.** Breaking the Mould. (Prose Ser.: No. 37). 270p. 1995. 18.00 (1-55071-033-8) Guernica Editions.

— Northern Voices: Inuit Writing in English. (Illus.). 330p. 1988. 27.50 (0-8020-5772-1) U of Toronto Pr.

Petrone, Penny, ed. Canadian Native Literature. 316p. 1990. pap. 19.95 (0-19-540796-2) OUP.

— First People, First Voices. 230p. 1985. pap. 20.95 (0-8020-6562-7) U of Toronto Pr.

— First People, First Voices. LC 83-227895. (Illus.). 256p. reprint ed. pap. 73.00 (0-8357-3770-5, 2036499) Bks Demand.

— Northern Voices: Inuit Writing in English. 332p. 1992. pap. 19.95 (0-8020-7717-X) U of Toronto Pr.

***Petronelli, Paul.** The Desktop Management Interface: Facilitating Application Management. 1995. pap. 42.95 (0-442-02095-3) Van Nos Reinhold.

Petroni, Frank A., et al. Two, Four, Six, Eight, When You Gonna Integrate? 1971. reprint ed. pap. 2.75 (0-87140-241-6) Liveright.

Petronio, C., jt. auth. see Benedetti, R.

Petronio, Sandra, et al. Contemporary Perspectives on Interpersonal Communication. 528p. (C). 1993. pap. text ed. write for info. (0-697-13356-7) Brown & Benchmark.

Petronius. Cena Trimalchionis. Smith, Martin S., ed. 1983. 24.95 (0-19-814459-8) OUP.

— Satiricon. 2nd rev. ed. Sage, Evan T. & Gilleland, Brady B., eds. LC 72-87112. (LAT.). (C). 1969. pap. text ed. 12.95 (0-89197-338-9) Irvington.

— Saturae. Buecheler, Franz, ed. l, 377p. 1963. write for info. (3-296-14900-7, Pub. by Georg Olms GW) Lubrecht & Cramer.

— The Satyricon. 1983. mass mkt. 9.95 (0-452-01005-5, Mer) NAL-Dutton.

— The Satyricon. Arrowsmith, William, tr. 1983. mass mkt. 4.50 (0-452-00964-2, Mer) NAL-Dutton.

— Satyricon. Bd. with Apocolocyntosis. (Loeb Classical Library: No. 15). 15.50 (0-674-99016-1) HUP.

— Satyricon, 2 vols., Set. Burmanno, Petro, ed. 1294p. 1974. reprint ed. write for info. (3-487-05416-7, Pub. by Georg Olms GW) Lubrecht & Cramer.

Petronius & Seneca, Lucius Annaeus. The Satyricon. rev. ed. Sullivan, J. P., tr. Bd. with Apocolocyntosis. 240p. 1986. Set pap. 9.95 (0-14-044489-0, Penguin Classics) Viking Penguin.

Petronius Arbiter. The Works of Petronius Arbiter, in Prose & Verse. LC 73-158324. (Augustan Translators Ser.). reprint ed. 55.00 (0-404-54129-1) AMS Pr.

Petronko, jt. auth. see Schaefer, Charles E.

Petronko, Diane, jt. auth. see Angel, Gerry.

Petropoulos, J. C. Heat & Lust: Hesiod's Midsummer Festival Scene Revisited. LC 93-47916. (Greek Studies: Interdisciplinary Approaches). 1994. write for info. (0-8476-7907-1); pap. write for info. (0-8476-7908-X) Rowman.

— Heat & Lust: Hesiod's Midsummer Festival Scene Revisited. (Greek Studies: Interdisciplinary Approaches). 130p. (C). 1994. lib. bdg. 39.50 (0-8476-7901-2); pap. text ed. 17.95 (0-8476-7902-0) Rowman.

***Petropoulos, Jonathan.** Art as Politics: The National Socialist Leaders' Policies & Collections. LC 95-11738. 1995. write for info. (0-8078-2240-X) U of NC Pr.

Petropoulou, Zoi. L' Espace Sensoriel Chez Albert Camus. LC 93-36149. 160p. (FRE.). 1993. text ed. 79.95 (0-7734-9398-0) E Mellen.

Petropulu, Athina P., jt. auth. see Nikias, Chrysostomos L.

Petros, George. Exploding Hearts, Exploding Stars: The Serial Art & Propagandart of George Petros. (Illus.). 100p. 1992. pap. 11.95 (1-881875-00-8) N Gosney.

Petros, James K., Jr. & Lacy, William J., eds. Hazardous & Industrial Solid Waste Testing: Fourth Symposium, STP 886. LC 85-28730. (Illus.). 365p. 1986. text ed. 52.00 (0-8031-0430-8, 04-886000-16) ASTM.

Petrosian, L. Differential Games of Pursuit. LC 93-24420. (Series on Optimization: Vol. 2). 560p. 1993. text ed. 104.00 (981-02-0979-7) World Scientific Pub.

Petrosian, Levon T. Ancient Armenian Translations. Maksoudian, Krikor & Kupelian, Nubar, trs. LC 92-39098. (ARM & ENG.). 1992. write for info. (0-934728-24-0) D O A C.

Petrosian, Vahe, jt. ed. see Liang, Edison P.

Petrosino, Barbara A., jt. auth. see Daeffler, Reidun.

Petrosino, Barbara M., ed. Nursing in Hospice & Terminal Care: Research & Practice. LC 86-12015. (Hospice Journal Ser.: Vol. 2, No. 1). 138p. 1986. 39.95 (0-86656-567-1) Haworth Pr.

Petroske, Mimi. Boy My Very Special Friend. Caroland, Mary, ed. (Illus.). 44p. (J). (gr. k-3). 1991. 5.95 (1-55523-381-3) Winston-Derek.

Petroski, Catherine. Gravity & Other Stories. LC 81-71003. 120p. (Orig.). 1981. pap. 8.50 (0-931362-05-9) Fiction Intl.

***Petroski, Edward.** The Why of Mankind. 100p. Date not set. pap. 7.95 (0-7610-0425-4) NW Pub.

Petroski, Henry. Design Paradigms: Case Histories of Error & Judgment in Engineering. LC 93-32560. (Illus.). 250p. (C). 1994. 42.95 (0-521-46108-1); pap. 17.95 (0-521-46649-0) Cambridge U Pr.

— Engineers of Dreams: Building Great Bridges. LC 94-48893. (Illus.). 1995. text ed. 30.00 (0-679-43939-0) Knopf.

— The Evolution of Useful Things. LC 91-39524. (Illus.). 256p. 1992. 24.00 (0-679-41226-3) Knopf.

— The Evolution of Useful Things. 1994. pap. 13.00 (0-679-74039-2, Vin) Random.

— Pencil. 1990. 25.00 (0-394-57422-2) Knopf.

— The Pencil: A History of Design & Circumstance. LC 89-45362. 448p. 1992. pap. 15.00 (0-679-73415-5) Knopf.

— To Engineer Is Human: The Role of Failure in Successful Design. 1992. pap. 11.00 (0-679-73416-3, Vin) Random.

Petroski, Richard J. & McCormick, Susan P., eds. Secondary-Metabolite Biosynthesis & Metabolism. LC 92-49318. (Environmental Science Research Ser.: Vol. 44). (Illus.). 358p. (C). 1992. 89.50 (0-306-44309-0, Plenum Pr) Plenum.

Petroski, Richard J., jt. ed. see Conway, Walter D.

Petrosky, Anthony. Red & Yellow Boat: Poems. LC 93-32204. 64p. 1994. text ed. 15.95 (0-8071-1830-3); pap. 8.95 (0-8071-1831-1) La State U Pr.

Petrosky, Anthony, jt. auth. see Bartholomae, David.

Petrosky, Anthony, ed. see Dobler, Patricia.

Petrosky, Anthony, ed. see Ignatow, David.

Petrosky, Anthony R. & Bartholomae, David, eds. The Teaching of Writing. LC 85-62666. (Eighty-Fifth Yearbook of the National Society for the Study of Education Ser.: Pt. 2). x, 212p. 1989. pap. text ed. 11.95 (0-226-59949-3, Natl Soc Stud Educ) U Ch Pr.

Petrosky, Anthony R., jt. auth. see Bartholomae, David.

Petrosky, Arlene B. Two Trees. (Illus.). 62p. 1989. write for info. (0-9623965-0-8) ABR Petrosky.

***Petrosonne, Pierre W.** Crime Analysis--with Medical, Forensic, Political, & Social Involvement: Index of New Information & Research. LC 94-34921. 189p. 1995. 44.50 (0-7883-0450-X); pap. 39.50 (0-7883-0451-8) ABBE Pubs Assn.

Petrosyan, M. I. Rock Breakage by Blasting. Ghose, A. K., ed. (Illus.). 152p. (C). 1994. text ed. 55.00 (90-6191-902-9, Pub. by A A Balkema NE) Ashgate Pub Co.

Petrosy'Ants, A. M. Problems of Nuclear Science & Technology: The Soviet Union As a World Nuclear Power. 4th enl. rev. ed. LC 80-40818. (Illus.). 400p. 1981. 179.00 (0-08-025462-4, Pub. by Pergamon Repr UK) Franklin.

Petrotta, Anthony J. Lexus Ludens: Wordplay & the Book of Micah. LC 91-16769. (American University Studies: Theology & Religion: Ser. VII, Vol. 105). 178p. 1992. 36.95 (0-8204-1539-1) P Lang Pubs.

Petroutsos, Evangelos, jt. auth. see Mansfield, Richard.

Petrov & Marchenko, G. N. Transfer Energy of Semi-Transparent Solids. 1990. 75.00 (0-89116-753-6) CRC Pr.

Petrov, jt. auth. see Ilf.

Petrov, A. A. Catalytic Isomerization of Hydrocarbons. 168p. 1963. text ed. 44.25 (0-7065-0250-7, Pub. by Keter Pub IS) Coronet Bks.

— Einstein Spaces. (C). 1969. 170.00 (0-08-012315-5, Pub. by Pergamon Repr UK) Franklin.

Petrov, Alexander. Lady in an Empty Dress. 1990. pap. 9.95 (0-948259-90-6) Dufour.

Petrov, B. & Csaki, F. The Second International Symposium on Information Theory. 457p. 1973. 89.00 (0-569-08075-4, Pub. by Collets UK) Pro-Am Music.

Petrov, D. F., ed. Apomixis & Its Role in Evolution & Breeding. Sharma, B. R., tr. 275p. (C). 1984. text ed. 55.00 (90-6191-437-X, Pub. by A A Balkema NE) Ashgate Pub Co.

Petrov, Eugene, jt. auth. see Ilf, Ilya.

Petrov, George, tr. see Rudnitsky, Konstantin.

Petrov, K. I., jt. auth. see Elinson, S. V.

Petrov, M. P., et al. Photorefractive Crystals in Coherent Optical Systems. (Optical Sciences Ser.: Vol. 9). (Illus.). 320p. 1991. 90.00 (0-387-52603-X) Spr-Verlag.

***Petrov, Nikolai & Remington, Thomas F., eds.** Russia in the Mid-1990's: The Social & Political Landscape. 650p. 1995. 125.00 (1-56324-517-5) M E Sharpe.

Petrov, R. V., ed. see Borisova, A. A., et al.

Petrov, R. V., ed. see Khaitov, R. M.

Petrov, R. V., ed. see Khakhalin, L. N.

Petrov, R. V., ed. see Lebedev, K. A., et al.

Petrov, R. V., jt. ed. see Zemskov, V. M.

Petrov, R. V., et al. Suppressor B Lymphocytes. Tatarchenko, V. E., tr. (Soviet Medical Reviews, Immunology Series Supplement: Vol. 1). 220p. 1988. text ed. 215.00 (3-7186-4800-8) Gordon & Breach.

Petrov, Rem. V., ed. Immunology: Cell Interactions, Myelopeptides Artificial Immunogens. (Soviet Medical Reviews: Section D, Immunology Reviews Ser.: Vol. 1). 461p. 1987. text ed. 380.00 (3-7186-0315-2) Gordon & Breach.

Petrov-Skitaletz, E. Kronstadt Thesis. 1964. 7.95 (0-8315-0040-9) Speller.

Petrov, V. Artificial Satellites of the Earth. (Illus.). 288p. 1960. text ed. 176.00 (0-677-20540-6) Gordon & Breach.

— India: Spotlight on Population. 276p. (C). 1985. 80.00 (0-685-31699-8, Pub. by Collets UK) Pro-Am Music.

— Vasnetsov, Yury. 196p. (C). 1984. 275.00 (0-685-34413-4, Pub. by Collets) St Mut.

Petrov, V. & Kamensky, A. World of Art Movement in Early Twentieth Century Russia. 332p. (C). 1991. 175.00 (0-569-09298-1, Pub. by Collets) St Mut.

Petrov, V. N. The Russian Fairy Tale in the Art of Yu. A. Vasnetsov. 140p. 1985. 110.00 (0-317-61373-1, Pub. by Collets UK) Pro-Am Music.

Petrov, V. S. & Tulin, S. A. Russian-Czech Polytechnical Dictionary. 639p. (CZE & RUS.). 1962. 125.00 (0-8288-6813-1, M-9074) Fr & Eur.

Petrov, V. V. Sums of Independent Random Variables. Brown, A. A., tr. LC 75-5766. (Ergebnisse der Mathematik Ser.: Vol. 82). 360p. 1975. text ed. 69.00 (0-387-06635-7) Spr-Verlag.

***Petrov, Valentin V.** Limit Theorems of Probability Theory. (Oxford Studies in Probability: No. 4). 256p. 1995. 80.00 (0-19-853499-X) OUP.

Petrov, Victor. Russkie vs. Amerike, XX Vek: Russians in Amerika, XX Century. LC 91-72887. (Illus.). 240p. (Orig.). (RUS.). 1991. pap. 16.00 (0-911971-67-X) Effect Pub.

Petrov, Vladimir. Escape from the Future: The Incredible Adventures of a Young Russian. LC 73-80380. 470p. reprint ed. pap. 134.00 (0-317-27846-0, 2056051) Bks Demand.

— Money & Conquest: Allied Occupation Currencies in World War II. LC 66-26685. (Johns Hopkins University Studies in Historical & Political Science: Series 84: No. 2). 282p. reprint ed. pap. 80.40 (0-317-09096-8, 2020732) Bks Demand.

Petrov, Vladimir, ed. see Borisov, Oleg B. & Koloskov, B. T.

Petrova, A. B. English Self Taught. 8th ed. 365p. (ENG & RUS.). 1992. 29.95 (0-7859-1081-6, 5060029867) Fr & Eur.

***Petrova, Ada & Watson, Peter.** The Death of Hilter: The Full Story with New Evidence from Secret Russian Archives. (Illus.). 1995. 23.00 (0-393-03914-5) Norton.

Petrova, E. Drawings by Russian Artists: Late 18th Early 19th Centuries. (Illus.). (C). 1983. 330.00 (0-685-34446-0, Pub. by Collets) St Mut.

— Drawings by Russian Artists: Late 18th-Early 19th Centuries. (Illus.). (C). 1983. text ed. 360.00 (0-685-40279-7, Pub. by Collets) St Mut.

Petrova, N. Stalin's Doctor, Stalin's Nurse: A Personal Memoir. 107p. 1984. 9.50 (0-940670-22-4) Kingston Pr.

Petrova, Olga. Black Virgin, & Other Stories. LC 72-128746. (Short Story Index Reprint Ser.). 1977. 17.95 (0-8369-3637-X) Ayer.

Petrova, Sylva & Olivie, Jean-Luc, eds. Bohemian Glass, 1400-1989. (Illus.). 240p. 1990. 75.00 (0-8109-1241-4) Abrams.

Petrova, Sylva, et al. Stanislav Libensky & Jaroslava Brychtova: A 40 Year Collaboration in Glass. Buechner, Thomas, ed. (Illus.). 224p. 1994. 99.95 (3-7913-1252-9, Pub. by Prestel) TeNeues.

Petrova, Yevgenia. Traveling Across North America, 1812-1813: Watercolors by the Russian Diplomat Pavel Svinin. (Illus.). 246p. 1992. 29.95 (0-8109-3855-3) Abrams.

Petrovic, Gajo, jt. ed. see Markovic, Mihailo.

Petrovic, J. J., jt. ed. see Vasudevan, A. K.

P Q

Petrovic, R., et al. Hierarchical Spare Parts Inventory Systems. (Studies in Production & Engineering Economics: No. 5). 1986. 100.00 (*0-444-42561-6*) Elsevier.

Petrovic, W. K., ed. see American Society of Mechanical Engineers, Lubrication Division.

Petrovich, Janice, jt. auth. see Witt, Sandi.

Petrovich, Michael B. The Emergence of Russian Panslavism, Eighteen Fifty-Six to Eighteen Seventy. LC 84-25242. xvi, 312p. 1985. reprint ed. text ed. 69.50 (*0-313-24742-0*, PEER, Greenwood Pr) Greenwood.

— A History of Modern Serbia, 1804-1918, 2 vols., Set. LC 76-13227. (Illus.). 1976. 49.50 (*0-15-140950-1*) HarBrace.

Petrovich, Michael B., tr. see Djilas, Milovan.

***Petrovich, Peter. Advanced Conversational English. 230p. 1995. pap. text ed. 25.00 (*0-9647271-4-5*) P Petrovich.**
ADVANCED CONVERSATIONAL ENGLISH by Peter Petrovich is designed to review what students at the intermediate level have already learned & to add to their knowledge of the language at the advanced level. It consists of twenty-four lessons presented in a dialogue form each divided into five sections. Every dialogue has an introduction to the scenario of the dialogue letting the student know beforehand the mood of the conversation. Each lesson has lexical, idiomatic, vocabulary & grammatical ties to the material presented in this book. ADVANCED CONVERSATIONAL ENGLISH also contains a list of 142 irregular verbs - all illustrated by an example sentence, 600 most important idioms, 1500 antonyms (500 verbs, 500 nouns, 500 adjectives) which are absolutely necessary for students of the English language. The answer key at the end of the book will help those students who use this book for self-instruction. ADVANCED CONVERSATIONAL ENGLISH offers an effective approach to the often complicated task of mastering advanced conversational skills in a foreign language. By the end of this course, students will learn advanced grammatical structures, enable themselves to correctly interpret & use many idiomatic expressions, greatly increase vocabulary skills, & effortlessly express themselves like native speakers. The author has written 5 books & is accomplished in 4 languages. Paper (52, 000 words on 230 pages) Price $25. Satisfaction guaranteed. To order ADVANCED CONVERSATIONAL ENGLISH contact Peter Petrovich, 13032 Blodgett Ave., Downey, CA 90242. 310-869-8238. ***Publisher Provided Annotation.***

Petrovich, Tija. Lighten Up! Gourmet Recipes for Lowfat Lifestyles. (Illus.). 211p. (Orig.). 1992. spiral bd. 14.95 (*0-9630679-0-7*) Nutrit Connect.

Petrovich, Z. & Baert, L., eds. Benign Prostatic Hyperplasia: Innovations in the Maanagement. LC 94-527. (Illus.). 384p. 1994. 129.00 (*0-387-56628-7*) Spr-Verlag.

Petrovicky, Ivan. Aquarium Fish of the World: Natural Sciences of the World. (Illus.). 500p. 1989. 22.99 (*0-517-67903-5*) Random Hse Value.

Petrovna, Tanya, jt. auth. see Ferry, Steven.

Petrovsij, A. V. Concise Russian Dictionary of Psychology. 431p. (RUS.). 1985. 24.95 (*0-8288-2211-5*, M15375) Fr & Eur.

Petrovska, Marija. Merope: The Dramatic Impact of a Myth. (American University Studies: Comparative Literature: Ser. III, Vol. 9). 205p. (Orig.). 1984. pap. text ed. 18.95 (*0-8204-0084-X*) P Lang Pubs.

— Prague Diptych. LC 80-52476. 144p. 1981. 6.50 (*0-87141-069-9*) Manyland.

Petrovska, Marija, ed. A Brief Anthology of French Poetry. LC 84-48026. 191p. (C). 1985. text ed. 23.80 (*0-8204-0170-6*) P Lang Pubs.

Petrovskaya, Kyra. Russian Cookbook. LC 92-10473. Orig. Title: Kyra's Secrets of Russian Cooking. 224p. 1992. reprint ed. pap. text ed. 5.95 (*0-486-27329-6*) Dover.

Petrovskih, B. V. Popular Medical Encyclopedia. 704p. (RUS.). 1984. 85.00 (*0-8288-1860-6*, M15422) Fr & Eur.

Petrovskij, B. V. Encyclopedic Dictionary of Medical Terms, 2 vols., Set. 1982. 125.00 (*0-8288-1859-2*, M15410) Fr & Eur.

Petrovsky, A. Age-Group & Pedagogical Psychology. 324p. 1984. 35.00 (*0-317-53830-6*, Pub. by Collets UK) Pro-Am Music.

Petrovsky, A., ed. Concise Psychological Dictionary. 358p. (C). 1987. 60.00 (*0-685-31516-9*) St Mut.

Petrovsky, Boris, et al. Resection & Plastic Surgery of Bronchi. MIR Publishers, tr. (Illus.). 375p. (C). 1975. text ed. 27.95 (*0-8464-0790-6*) Beekman Pubs.

Petrovsky, I. G. Lectures on Partial Differential Equations. (Illus.). x, 245p. 1992. reprint ed. pap. 7.95 (*0-486-66902-5*) Dover.

Petrovsky, V. Nuclear Space Age: The Soviet Viewpoint. 246p. (C). 1987. 35.00 (*0-685-31536-3*, Pub. by Collets UK) Pro-Am Music.

Petrow, Stefan. Policing Morals: The Metropolitan Police & the Home Office 1870-1914. (Illus.). 360p. 1994. 52.00 (*0-19-820165-6*) OUP.

Petrow, Steven. Dancing Against the Darkness: A Journey Through America in the Age of AIDS. 288p. 1990. text ed. 22.95 (*0-669-24309-4*) Free Pr.

***Petrow, Steven & Steele, Nick.** The Essential Book of Gay Manners & Etiquette. 1995. pap. 12.50 (*0-06-095079-X*, PL) HarpC.

Petrow, Steven, et al, eds. Ending the HIV Epidemic: Community Strategies in Disease Prevention & Health Promotion. LC 90-6384. 140p. 1990. 34.95 (*1-56071-033-0*); pap. 24.95 (*1-56071-030-6*) ETR Assocs.

Petrowicz, Lech, tr. see Grudzinski, Tadeusz.

Petrowski, T. & Stolz, A. Wicked Sounds. 1993. pap. 29.95 (*1-55755-168-5*) Abacus MI.

Petrowski, William R. The Kansas Pacific: A Study in Railroad Promotion. Bruchey, Stuart, ed. LC 80-1286. (Railroads Ser.). (Illus.). 1981. lib. bdg. 33.95 (*0-405-13758-3*) Ayer.

Petrozzo, Daniel. Successful Reengineering: An In-Depth Guide to Using Information Technology. (General Engineering Ser.). 1994. text ed. 24.95 (*0-442-01722-7*) Van Nos Reinhold.

Petru, William C., ed. The Library, an Introduction for Library Assistants. LC 66-29578. 85p. reprint ed. pap. 25.00 (*0-8357-2605-3*, 2016137) Bks Demand.

Petrucci, Armando. Public Lettering: Script, Power, & Culture. Lappin, Linda, tr. (Illus.). 256p. 1993. 37.50 (*0-226-66386-8*) U Ch Pr.

— Writers & Readers in Medieval Italy: Studies in the History of Written Culture. Radding, Charles M., ed. & tr. by. LC 94-41633. 1995. write for info. (*0-300-06089-0*) Yale U Pr.

Petrucci, Luigina, jt. auth. see Domel, August W.

Petrucci, Ottaviano. Canti C No Cento Cinquanta. (Monuments of Music & Music Literature in Facsimile: Series I, Vol. 25). (Illus.). 1978. reprint ed. lib. bdg. 60.00 (*0-8450-2025-0*) Broude.

Petrucci, Ralph H. & Harwood, William S. General Chemistry: Principles & Modern Applications. 6th ed. LC 92-13854. (Illus.). 1156p. (C). 1993. text ed. write for info. (*0-02-394931-7*) Macmillan.

Petrucci, Ralph H. & Wismer, Robert K. General Chemistry with Qualitative Analysis. Gordon, Peter, ed. (C). 1987. write for info. (*0-318-60808-1*) Macmillan.

— General Chemistry with Qualitative Analysis. 2nd ed. Gordon, Peter, ed. (C). 1987. write for info. (*0-02-391780-6*) Macmillan.

Petrucci, Raphael. Chinese Painters. Seaver, Frances, tr. LC 79-102253. (Select Bibliographies Reprint Ser.). 1977. 15.95 (*0-8369-5138-7*) Ayer.

Petrucci, Steven J. Cross-Platform Power Tools: Application Development for the Macintosh, Windows, & Windows NT. 1993. pap. 45.00 (*0-679-79147-7*) Random.

Petruccio, Steven J. Tropical Fish Stickers. (Illus.). (J). (gr. k-3). 1994. pap. 1.00 (*0-486-28110-8*) Dover.

Petruccioli, Attilio. Fatehpur Sikri. 55p. 1993. 39.00 (*0-685-67847-4*, Pub. by W Ernst Sohn) VCH Pubs.

Petruccioli, Sandro. Atoms, Metaphors & Paradoxes: Niels Bohr & the Construction of a New Physics. McGilvray, Ian, tr. LC 93-177. 240p. (C). 1994. 54.95 (*0-521-40259-X*) Cambridge U Pr.

Petrucelli. Cher, Reading Level 2. (Reaching Your Goal Bks.: Set II). (Illus.). 24p. (J). (gr. 1-4). 1989. lib. bdg. 14.60 (*0-86592-432-5*) Rourke Corp.

— Consideration, Reading Level 2. (Learn the Value Ser.: Set II). (Illus.). 32p. (J). (gr. 1-4). 1989. lib. bdg. 15.94 (*0-86592-443-0*); lib. bdg. 11.95 (*0-685-58778-9*) Rourke Corp.

— Creativity, Reading Level 2. (Learn the Value Ser.: Set II). (Illus.). 32p. (J). (gr. 1-4). 1989. lib. bdg. 15.94 (*0-86592-444-9*) Rourke Corp.

— Henry Cisneros, Reading Level 2. (Reaching Your Goal Bks.: Set II). (Illus.). 24p. (J). (gr. 1-4). 1989. 10.95 (*0-685-58799-1*); lib. bdg. 14.60 (*0-86592-431-7*) Rourke Corp.

— Jim Henson, Reading Level 2. (Reaching Your Goal Bks.: Set II). (Illus.). 24p. (J). (gr. 1-4). 1989. 10.95 (*0-685-58800-9*); lib. bdg. 14.60 (*0-86592-426-0*) Rourke Corp.

— Loyalty, Reading Level 2. (Learn the Value Ser.: Set II). (Illus.). 32p. (J). (gr. 1-4). 1989. 11.95 (*0-685-58786-X*); lib. bdg. 15.94 (*0-86592-441-4*) Rourke Corp.

— Michael Jordan, Reading Level 2. (Reaching Your Goal Bks.: Set II). (Illus.). 24p. (J). (gr. 1-4). 1989. 10.95 (*0-685-58801-7*); lib. bdg. 14.60 (*0-86592-428-7*) Rourke Corp.

Petrucelli, jt. auth. see Lyons.

Petruck, Marvin, jt. ed. see Levey, Martin.

Petruck, Peninah. Judge Charles Edward Clark, 1889-1963. (New York University School of Law, Ingram Documents in Legal History Ser.). 207p. 1992. lib. bdg. 42.50 (*0-379-20071-6*) Oceana.

Petruk, W., et al, eds. Process Mineralogy IX. (Illus.). 1000p. 1989. 77.00 (*0-87339-103-9*) Minerals Metals.

Petruk, William, intro. Process Mineralogy III. LC 84-71244. (Symposia on Process Mineralogy Ser.). (Illus.). 322p. 1984. pap. 10.00 (*0-89520-426-6*, 426-6) SMM&E Inc.

***Petruk, William & Rule, Albert R., eds.** Process Mineralogy XII: Applications to Environment, Precious Metal, Mineral Beneficiation, Pyrometallurgy, Coal & Refactories. LC 94-75561. 459p. 1994. 110.00 (*0-87339-273-6*) Minerals Metals.

Petrukhin, V. P. Construction of Structures on Saline Soils. Mehta, N. K., tr. (Russian Translation Ser.: Vol. 101). (Illus.). 263p. (C). 1993. text ed. 85.00 (*90-5410-213-6*, Pub. by A A Balkema NE) Ashgate Pub Co.

Petrullo, Luigi, jt. ed. see Tagiuri, Renato.

Petrunis, Sergei. Ieroglify. LC 81-50872. (Russica Poetry Ser.: No. 2). 220p. (RUS.). 1982. pap. 8.95 (*0-89830-040-1*) Russica Pubs.

Petrunkevitch, Alexander. Amber Spiders in European Collections. (Connecticut Academy of Arts & Sciences Ser., Trans.: Vol. 41). 1958. pap. 100.00 (*0-685-22892-4*) Elliots Bks.

— Arachnida from Panama. (Connecticut Academy of Arts & Sciences Ser., Trans.: Vol. 27). 1925. pap. 100.00 (*0-685-22818-5*) Elliots Bks.

— Choice & Responsibility. (Connecticut Academy of Arts & Sciences Ser., Trans.: Vol. 37). 1947. pap. 29.50 (*0-685-22909-2*) Elliots Bks.

— An Inquiry into the Natural Classification of Spiders, Based on a Study of Their Internal Anatomy. (Connecticut Academy of Arts & Sciences Ser., Trans.: Vol. 31). 1933. pap. 75.00 (*0-685-44357-4*) Elliots Bks.

— Russia's Contribution to Science. (Connecticut Academy of Arts & Sciences Ser., Trans.: Vol. 23). 1920. pap. 49.50 (*0-685-22832-0*) Elliots Bks.

— Spiders from the Virgin Islands. (Connecticut Academy of Arts & Sciences Ser., Trans.). 1926. pap. 49.50 (*0-685-44361-2*) Elliots Bks.

— The Spiders of Porto Rico. (Connecticut Academy of Arts & Sciences Ser., Trans.: Vol. 30, Pt. 1). 1929. pap. 75.00 (*0-685-22805-3*) Elliots Bks.

— The Spiders of Porto Rico. (Connecticut Academy of Arts & Sciences Ser., Trans.: Vol. 30, Pt. 2). 1930. pap. 75.00 (*0-685-22804-5*) Elliots Bks.

— The Spiders of Porto Rico. (Connecticut Academy of Arts & Sciences Ser., Trans.: Vol. 31, Pt. 3). 1930. pap. 75.00 (*0-685-44359-0*) Elliots Bks.

— A Study of Amber Spiders. (CT Academy of Arts & Science Transactions Ser.: Vol. 34). 1942. pap. 100.00 (*0-686-51318-5*) Elliots Bks.

— A Study of Palaeozoic Arachnida. (Connecticut Academy of Arts & Sciences Ser., Trans.: Vol. 37). 1949. pap. 100.00 (*0-685-22904-1*) Elliots Bks.

— System Aranearum. (Connecticut Academy of Arts & Sciences Ser., Trans.: Vol. 29). 1928. pap. 75.00 (*0-685-22807-X*) Elliots Bks.

— Tertiary Spiders & Opilionids of North America. (Connecticut Academy of Arts & Sciences Ser., Trans.: Vol. 25). 1922. pap. 75.00 (*0-685-22826-6*) Elliots Bks.

Petrunkevitch, Alexander, et al. Pushkin Centennial Meeting, February 11, 1937: Addresses & Translations of Songs. (Connecticut Academy of Arts & Sciences Ser., Trans.: Vol. 33). 1937. pap. 49.50 (*0-685-22915-7*) Elliots Bks.

Petrunoff, Vance T. Directory of Foreign Trade Organizations in Eastern Europe: Bulgaria, Czechoslovakia, East Germany, Hungary, Poland, Romania & U. S. S. R. LC 88-84163. 300p. (Orig.). 1989. pap. 85.00 (*0-926476-00-9*) Intl Trade Pr.

Petrunoff, Vance T., intro. Directory of Foreign Trade Organizations in Eastern Europe: Bulgaria, Czechoslovakia, East Germany, Hungary, Poland, Romania & U. S. S. R. 2nd ed. LC 89-85034. 325p. (Orig.). 1989. pap. 125.00 (*0-926476-01-7*) Intl Trade Pr.

— Directory of Foreign Trade Organizations in Eastern Europe: Bulgaria, Czechoslovakia, East Germany, Hungary, Poland, Romania & U. S. S. R. 3rd ed. LC 90-80534. 370p. (Orig.). 1990. pap. 125.00 (*0-926476-02-5*) Intl Trade Pr.

Petrus. The New Pearl of Great Price: Treatise Concerning the Treasure & Most Precious Stone of the Philosophers, Vol. 7. LC 74-349. 453p. 1974. reprint ed. 35.95 (*0-405-05911-6*) Ayer.

Petrus of Ferrara Bonus. The New Pearl of Great Price. 441p. 1992. pap. 29.95 (*1-56459-142-5*) Kessinger Pub.

Petruschell, Robert L., et al. Overview of the Total Army Design & Cost System. LC 93-19192. 1993. 7.50 (*0-8330-1371-8*, MR-195-A) Rand Corp.

Petrusha, Ronald, jt. auth. see Nicita, Michael.

Petrushev, P. P. & Popov, V. A. Rational Approximation of Real Functions: Rational Approximation of Real Functions. (Encyclopedia of Mathematics & Its Applications Ser.: No. 28). (Illus.). 300p. 1988. 89.95 (*0-521-33107-2*) Cambridge U Pr.

***Petrushevskaya, Ludmila.** Three Girls in Blue. Mulrine, Stephen, tr. 1991. 5.95 (*0-87129-403-6*, T87) Dramatic Pub.

Petrushevskaya, Ludmilla. The Time... Night. Laird, Sally, tr. LC 94-9076. 1994. 20.00 (*0-679-43616-2*) Pantheon.

Petrushevsky, I. P. Islam in Iran. Evans, Hubert, tr. LC 84-24087. (SUNY Series in Near Eastern Studies). 400p. 1985. 64.50 (*0-88706-070-6*) State U NY Pr.

Petruso, Thomas F. Life Made Real: Characterization in the Novel Since Proust & Joyce. 250p. (C). 1991. text ed. 37.50 (*0-472-10266-4*) U of Mich Pr.

Petrusz, Peter, ed. see Bullock, Gillian R.

Petrusz, Peter, jt. auth. see Bullock, Gillian R.

Petrusz, Peter, ed. see Bullock, Gillian R.

Petruzella, Frank D. Electricity & Electronics Fundamentals, 2 bks., Bk. 1. (Illus.). 256p. 1987. pap. text ed. 19.95 (*0-07-049676-5*) McGraw.

— Essentials of Electronics: A Survey. LC 92-32921. 1993. 44.50 (*0-02-800893-6*) Glencoe.

— Industrial Electronic. LC 94-36563. 1994. write for info. (*0-02-801996-2*) Glencoe.

— Programmable Logic Controllers. 216p. 1989. text ed. 31.95 (*0-07-049687-0*) McGraw.

Petruzzellis, Thomas. The Alarm, Sensor, & Security Circuit Cookbook. LC 93-27562. 1993. 29.95 (*0-8306-4314-1*); pap. 17.95 (*0-8306-4312-5*) TAB Bks.

— The Alarm, Sensor & Security Circuit Cookbook. 1993. pap. text ed. 17.95 (*0-07-049707-9*) McGraw.

— The Alarm, Sensor & Security Circuit Cookbook. 1994. text ed. 29.95 (*0-07-049706-0*) McGraw.

Petruzzelli, Domenico & Helfferich, Friedrich G., eds. Migration & Fate of Pollutants in Soils & Subsoils. LC 92-45284. (NATO ASI Series G: Ecological Sciences: Vol. 32). 1993. 255.00 (*0-387-56041-6*) Spr-Verlag.

Petruzzi, Nancy, jt. auth. see Chenot, Dolores.

Petruzzini, Diane M., ed. see Morley, Laurene S.

***Petry.** Critical Essays on Kate Chopin. 1996. 42.00 (*0-7838-0032-0*) G K Hall.

Petry, Alice H. Critical Essays on Anne Tyler. (Critical Essays on American Literature Ser.). 250p. 1992. text ed. 45.00 (*0-8161-7308-7*, Hall Reference) G K Hall.

— Fitzgerald's Craft of Short Fiction: The Collected Stories, 1920-1935. xiv, 256p. 1991. pap. 16.95 (*0-8173-0547-5*) U of Ala Pr.

— A Genius in His Way: The Art of Cable's Old Creole Days. LC 87-45574. 160p. 1988. 28.50 (*0-8386-3320-X*) Fairleigh Dickinson.

— Understanding Anne Tyler. (Understanding Contemporary American Literature Ser.). 200p. (C). 1990. text ed. 34.95 (*0-87249-716-X*); pap. 14.95 (*0-87249-742-9*) U of SC Pr.

Petry, Ann. Harriet Tubman: Conductor on the Underground Railroad. LC 90-48980. (American Cavalcade Ser.). (Illus.). 176p. (J). (gr. 6-10). 1991. lib. bdg. 9.95 (*1-55905-097-7*) Marshall Cavendish.

— Harriet Tubman: Conductor on the Underground Railroad. (J). (gr. 4-7). 1990. pap. 3.99 (*0-671-73146-7*, S&S Bks Young Read) S&S Childrens.

— Harriet Tubman: Conductor on the Underground Railway. LC 55-9215. 247p. (YA). (gr. 7-11). 1955. 16.95 (*0-690-37236-1*, Crowell Jr Bks) HarpC Child Bks.

— Miss Muriel & Other Stories. LC 88-47664. (Black Women Writers Ser.). 320p. 1989. reprint ed. pap. 12.00 (*0-8070-8311-9*, BP 802) Beacon Pr.

— The Narrows. LC 87-42853. (Black Women Writers Ser.). 464p. (C). 1988. reprint ed. pap. 14.00 (*0-8070-8303-8*, BP 782) Beacon Pr.

— The Street. 448p. 1992. pap. 9.95 (*0-395-57380-7*) HM.

— Tituba of Salem Village. LC 64-20691. 254p. (YA). (gr. 7 up). 1988. lib. bdg. 14.89 (*0-690-04766-5*, Crowell Jr Bks) HarpC Child Bks.

— Tituba of Salem Village. LC 64-20691. (Trophy Bk.). 272p. (J). (gr. 5 up). 1991. pap. 3.95 (*0-06-440403-X*, Trophy) HarpC Child Bks.

Petry, Bonnie F., jt. auth. see Clarke, Peter B.

Petry, Bonnie L., jt. auth. see Clarke, Peter B.

Petry, Bonnie L., jt. auth. see Shorter, Alan W.

Petry, Bonnie L., jt. auth. see Wilkins, James H.

Petry, Carl F. The Civilian Elite of Cairo in the Later Middle Ages. LC 80-8570. (Illus.). 450p. 1981. 70.00 (*0-691-05329-4*) Princeton U Pr.

— Protectors & Praetorians? The Last Mamluk Sultans & Egypt's Waning as a Great Power. LC 94-2925. (SUNY Series in Medieval Middle East History). 280p. 1994. 59.50 (*0-7914-2139-2*); pap. 19.95 (*0-7914-2140-6*) State U NY Pr.

— Twilight of Majesty: The Regions of the Mamluk Sultans al-Ashraf Qaytbay & Qansuh al-Ghawri in Egypt. LC 93-4632. (Occasional Papers, Middle East Center Ser.: No. 4). 264p. 1993. 20.00 (*0-295-97307-2*) U of Wash Pr.

Petry, D. L. Petry, Pettry, Petrey, Pettrey & Allied Families. LC 89-92303. 869p. 1989. 45.00 (*0-9624733-0-8*) McClain.

Petry, Fred, jt. auth. see Nahouraii, Ez.

Petry, Frederick E., jt. auth. see Buckles, Bill P.

Petry, Loren C. A Beachcomber's Botany. LC 68-26716. (Illus.). 160p. 1975. pap. 12.95 (*0-85699-119-8*) Chatham Pr.

Petry, Marvin. Taxation of Intellectual Property: Tax Planning Guide. 1985. Looseleaf updates available. write for info. (*0-8205-1688-0*) Bender.

Petry, Michael, ed. see Spinoza.

Petry, Michael J., ed. G. W. F. Hegel: The Berlin Phenomenology. 256p. 1981. lib. bdg. 84.00 (*90-277-1205-0*) Kluwer Ac.

— Hegel & Newtonianism. LC 93-18478. (Archives Internationales d'Histoire des Idees (International Archives of the History of Ideas) Ser.). 808p. (C). 1993. lib. bdg. 279.00 (*0-7923-2202-9*) Kluwer Ac.

Petry, Ray C. Francis of Assisi. LC 41-25932. reprint ed. 27.50 (*0-404-05017-4*) AMS Pr.

Petry, Ray C., ed. Late Medieval Mysticism. LC 57-5092. (Library of Christian Classics). 420p. 1980. pap. 14.99 (*0-664-24163-8*, Westminster) Westminster John Knox.

***Petry, Ronald D.** Partners in Creation: Stewardship for Pastor & People. fac. ed. LC 79-21770. 126p. 1994. pap. 36.00 (*0-7837-7340-4*, 2047293) Bks Demand.

Petry, S. & Meyer, G., eds. The Perception of Illusory Contours. (Illus.). 345p. 1987. 161.00 (*0-387-96518-1*) Spr-Verlag.

Petryshyn, W. V. Approximation-Solvability of Nonlinear Functional & Differential Equations. (Pure & Applied Mathematics Ser.: Vol. 171). 392p. 1993. 125.00 (*0-8247-8793-5*) Dekker.

***Petryshyn, Wolodymr V.** Generalized Topological Degree & Semilinear Equations. (Cambridge Tracts in Mathematics Ser.: No. 117). 275p. (C). 1995. write for info. (*0-521-44474-8*) Cambridge U Pr.

Petryszyn, Yar, jt. auth. see Cockrum, E. Lendell.

An Asterisk (*) at the beginning of an entry indicates that the title is appearing in BIP for the first time.

Petschauer, Peter. The Education of Women in Eighteenth Century Germany: New Directions from the German Female Perspective. LC 88-26600. (Studies in German Thought & History: Vol. 9). 612p. 1989. lib. bdg. 129.95 (*0-88946-347-6*) E Mellen.

Petschauer, Peter W. Topics in World Civilization: A Key to the Language of Historical Discipline. 176p. (C). 1989. per. 18.95 (*0-8403-5738-9*) Kendall-Hunt.

Petsche, Hellmuth, jt. ed. see Brazier, Mary A.

***Petsche, Thomas, ed.** Computational Learning Theory & Natural Learning Systems Vol. III: Selecting Good Models. 405p. 1995. 45.00 (*0-262-66096-2*, Bradford Bks) MIT Pr.

Petschek, A., et al, eds. Supernovae. (Astronomy & Astrophysics Library). xiii, 293p. 1990. 69.00 (*0-387-97069-X*) Spr-Verlag.

Petschek, Joyce. The Silver Bird: A Tale for Those Who Dream. LC 80-70049. (Illus.). 192p. 1981. pap. 12.95 (*0-89087-359-3*) Celestial Arts.

— Silver Dreams: A Myth of the Sixth Sense. LC 90-82143. (Illus.). 208p. (YA). (gr. 8-12). 1990. 29.95 (*0-89087-619-3*); pap. 19.95 (*0-89087-620-7*) Celestial Arts.

Petschek, Rodolfo, jt. auth. see Bohn, Dave.

Petschulat, Neub & Corinna, Joyce. Stroke...Now What? 240p. (Orig.). 1991. 17.95 (*0-9631426-0-7*) CAM Pub.

Petsinger, Robert E., ed. see Cryogenic Society of America, LNG Terminals & Safety Symposium.

Petska, Darrell E., jt. auth. see Baxa, Donald E.

Petska-Juliussen, Karen, jt. auth. see Juliussen, Eqil.

Petska, Sharon, jt. auth. see Fried, John J.

Petsky, Michael. Competitive Direct Marketing Strategies: Mergers, Acquisitions & Corporate Development Activities, 1992 Edition. Jones, Melissa D., ed. (Illus.). 232p. 1992. pap. 345.00 (*0-9632267-0-3*) Vos Gruppo & Capell.

— The Direct Marketing Mergers, Acquisitions & Strategic Activities Yearbook. Jones, Melissa D., ed. 1995. pap. 345.00 (*0-9632267-1-1*) Vos Gruppo & Capell.

Petsonk, Judy & Remsen, Jim. The Intermarriage Handbook: A Guide for Jews & Christians. 416p. 1991. reprint ed. pap. 12.95 (*0-688-10379-0*, Quill) Morrow.

Petsopoulos, Yanni. Kilims: Masterpieces of Turkey. LC 91-52796. (Illus.). 176p. 1991. 50.00 (*0-8478-1417-3*) Rizzoli Intl.

Petsopoulos, Yanni, ed. Tulips, Arabesques & Turbans: Decorative Arts from the Ottoman Empire. LC 81-20534. (Illus.). 208p. 1982. 75.00 (*0-89659-279-0*) Abbeville Pr.

Pett, Joel W. Rough Sketches: Political Cartoons by Joel Pett, Lexington Herald-Leader. (Illus.). 164p. (Orig.). 1989. pap. write for info. (*0-318-65564-0*) Lex Herald-Leader.

Pett, Steve. Sirens. LC 89-40601. 401p. 1990. pap. 9.95 (*0-394-75712-2*, Vin) Random.

***Pettas, William.** A Sixteenth-Century Spanish Library: The Inventory of Juan de Junta. LC 94-78553. (Transactions Ser.: Vol. 185, Pt. 1). 200p. (C). 1995. pap. 20.00 (*0-87169-851-X*, T851-pew) Am Philos.

Pettas, William A., tr. see Balsamo, Liugi.

Pettavino, Paula J. & Pye, Geralyn. Sport in Cuba: The Diamond in the Rough. LC 93-24372. (Latin American Ser.). 312p. (C). 1994. 49.95 (*0-8229-3764-6*); pap. 19.95 (*0-8229-5512-1*) U of Pittsburgh Pr.

Pettazzoni, Raffaele. The All Knowing God: Researches into the Early Religion & Culture. Bolle, Kees W., ed. LC 77-79150. (Mythology Ser.). (Illus.). 1978. reprint ed. lib. bdg. 44.95 (*0-405-10559-2*) Ayer.

Pettazzoni, Raffaele & Bolle, Kees W., eds. Miti E. Leggende: Myths & Legends, 4 vols. in 1. LC 77-79151. (Mythology Ser.). (ITA.). 1978. reprint ed. lib. bdg. 204.95 (*0-405-10560-6*) Ayer.

Pette, D., ed. Plasticity of Muscle. (C). 1979. 146.15 (*3-11-007961-5*) De Gruyter.

Pette, D., et al. Reviews of Physiology, Biochemistry & Pharmacology, Vol. 116. Blaustein, M. P. et al, eds. (Illus.). 176p. 1990. 87.00 (*0-387-52880-6*) Spr-Verlag.

Pette, Dirk, ed. The Dynamic State of Muscle Fibers: Proceedings of the Int'l Symposium Oct. 1-6, 1989, Konstanz, Fed. Rep. of Germany. (Illus.). xxiv, 729p. (C). 1990. lib. bdg. 288.50 (*3-11-012168-9*) De Gruyter.

Pettee, Ella B. Accent on Delos. 168p. 1994. pap. 10.95 (*0-8059-3527-4*) Dorrance.

Pettegree, Andrew. Emden & the Dutch Revolt: Exile & the Development of Reformed Protestantism. (Illus.). 368p. 1992. 84.00 (*0-19-822739-6*) OUP.

Pettegree, Andrew, ed. The Early Reformation in Europe. 250p. (C). 1992. 59.95 (*0-521-39454-6*); pap. 17.95 (*0-521-39768-5*) Cambridge U Pr.

— The Reformation of the Parishes: The Ministry & the Reformation in Town & Country. LC 93-17868. (C). 1993. text ed. 69.95 (*0-7190-4005-1*, Pub. by Manchester Univ Pr UK) St Martin.

Pettegree, Andrew, jt. ed. see Lewis, Gillian.

Pettegree, Andrew, et al, eds. Calvinism in Europe, 1540-1620. LC 93-37383. (Illus.). 296p. (C). 1995. 59.95 (*0-521-43269-3*) Cambridge U Pr.

Pettegrew, J. W., ed. NMR: Principles & Applications to Biomedical Research. (Illus.). 640p. 1989. 109.00 (*0-387-97094-0*) Spr-Verlag.

Pettegrew, Jay W., jt. ed. see Nasrallah, Henry A.

Pettegrew, Larry D. The New Covenant Ministry of the Holy Spirit: A Study in Continuity & Discontinuity. LC 92-33122. (C). 1993. 47.00 (*0-8191-8913-8*) U Pr of Amer.

Pettegrove, J., tr. see Cassirer, Ernst.

Pettem, Silvia. Boulder: Evolution of a City. (Illus.). 208p. 1994. 29.95 (*0-87081-350-1*) Univ Pr Colo.

— Colorado Traveler: Colorado Mountains & Passes. rev. ed. (American Traveler Ser.). (Illus.). 48p. 1991. pap. 4.95 (*1-55838-117-1*) R H Pub.

— Legend of a Landmark: A History of the Hotel Boulderado. (Illus.). 120p. (Orig.). 1986. pap. 5.95 (*0-9617799-0-X*) Book Lode.

— The Peaceful Valley Story: Fulfillment of a Dream. (Illus.). 64p. (Orig.). 1994. pap. 5.95 (*0-9617799-5-0*) Book Lode.

Pettem, Silvia, jt. auth. see Montgomery, Mabel G.

Pettengell, J. M. & Pope, C. The Pettengell Genealogy. (Illus.). 596p. 1989. reprint ed. lib. bdg. 97.00 (*0-8328-0960-8*); reprint ed. pap. 89.00 (*0-8328-0961-6*) Higginson Bk Co.

Pettengell, Jim. Rottweiler, New. (Illus.). 224p. 1994. 24.95 (*0-7938-0080-3*, TS202) TFH Pubns.

Pettengill, J. S. Labour Unions & Inequality of Earned Income. (Contributions to Economic Analysis Ser.: Vol. 129). 336p. 1980. 66.75 (*0-444-85409-6*, North Holland) Elsevier.

Pettengill, Marian & Young, Lu A. Nursing Practice - Teaching Roles: Faculty-Clinician; Clinician-Faculty. 150p. (Orig.). 1987. pap. 12.50 (*0-942146-13-1*) Midwest Alliance Nursing.

Pettengill, Marian M., ed. Associate Degree Nursing: Facilitating Competency Development. 1987. write for info. (*0-318-68852-2*) Midwest Alliance Nursing.

Pettengill, Marian M. & Schumann, Pamela A., eds. Substance Abuse: Special Needs of Racial - Ethnic Minorities. 52p. (Orig.). 1992. pap. 7.00 (*0-685-62294-0*) Midwest Alliance Nursing.

Pettengill, Marian M. & Young, Lu A. Society in Transition: Impact on Nursing. 150p. (Orig.). 1987. pap. 12.50 (*0-942146-14-X*) Midwest Alliance Nursing.

Pettengill, Marian M. & Young, Lu Ann, eds. Prospective Payment Reimbursement: The Costs to Nursing. 150p. (Orig.). 1988. pap. 12.50 (*0-942146-16-6*) Midwest Alliance Nursing.

Pettengill, Marian M., ed. see Young, Lu Ann.

Pettengill, Samuel B. Hot Oil: The Problem of Petroleum. LC 75-6483. (History & Politics of Oil Ser.). xviii, 308p. 1976. reprint ed. 24.75 (*0-88355-300-7*) Hyperion Conn.

Petter, Hugo. Concordancia Greco-Espanola N. T. Greek-Spanish Concordance. (SPA.). 18.95 (*84-7228-263-5*, 220189, Pub. by Edit Clie SP) TSELF.

Petterle, Elmo A. Getting Your Affairs in Order: Make Life Easier for Those You Leave Behind. Kahn, Robert C. & Rogoff, Marianne, eds. 128p. (Orig.). 1993. pap. 12.95 (*0-89815-547-9*) Shelter Pubns.

Petterle, Joe. Schools Flunk...Kids Don't. (Orig.). 1992. pap. 15.95 (*1-881805-22-0*) Copernicus Systs.

— Schools Flunk...Kids Don't. (Orig.). 1993. pap. 15.95 (*1-882180-16-X*) Griffin CA.

Petterle, Joseph E. ProActive Discipline: Creating a Schoolwide Behavior Management System That Works. 1994. student ed 13.00 (*1-881805-25-5*) Copernicus Systs.

Petters, S. W. Regional Geology of Africa. (Lecture Notes in Earth Sciences Ser.: Vol. 40). (Illus.). xxii, 722p. 1991. pap. 98.00 (*0-387-54528-X*) Spr-Verlag.

Pettersen, Birger, tr. see Kjaer-Hansen, Kai.

Pettersen, Carmen L. The Maya of Guatemala: Their Life & Dress. LC 76-42102. (Illus.). 276p. 1977. 60.00 (*0-295-95537-6*) U of Wash Pr.

Pettersen, Nona. The Miniature World of Pressed Flowers. (Illus.). 96p. 1986. pap. 14.95 (*0-85532-578-X*, Pub. by Search Pr UK) A Schwartz & Co.

Petterson, C. B., jt. ed. see Johnson, A. I.

Petterson, J. A. El Matrimonio a Prueba De Infidelidad (High Fidelity Marriage) (SPA.). Date not set. 2.49 (*0-8423-6513-3*, 498043) Editorial Unilit.

Petterson, Jay, illus. Giants, Witches & Dragons Three-D Coloring Book. 32p. (Orig.). (J). 1990. pap. 3.95 (*0-942025-81-4*) Kidsbks.

Petterson, Ole E., tr. see Jones, Michael P.

Petterson, Steve D. Lost in the Material World: Man's Search for Happiness. Bolinger, Athalie, ed. 215p. (Orig.). 1992. text ed. 17.95 (*1-881353-07-9*); pap. text ed. 12.95 (*1-881353-11-7*) Excaliber Pub.

Petterssen, S., et al. Cloud & Weather Modification: A Group of Field Experiments. (Meteorological Monograph Ser.: Vol. 2, No. 11). (Illus.). 111p. 1957. pap. 17.00 (*0-933876-06-8*) Am Meteorological.

Pettersson, H. & Ringertz, Hans. Measurements in Pediatric Radiology. (Illus.). 192p. 1991. 79.00 (*0-387-19665-X*) Spr-Verlag.

Pettersson, Holger & Lunderquist, Anders, eds. Gastrointestinal & Urogenital Radiology. (Nicer Series on Diagnostic Imaging). (Illus.). 324p. (C). 1991. text ed. 52.00 (*1-873413-05-X*) Merit Pub Intl.

Pettersson, Holger, jt. ed. see Harwood-Nash, Derek C.

Pettersson, Holger, jt. ed. see Harwood-Nash, Derek.

Pettersson, Holger, jt. ed. see Higgins, Charles.

Pettersson, Holger, jt. ed. see Resnick, Donald.

Pettersson, R. F., ed. Expression of Eukaryotic Viral & Cellular Genes. LC 81-68257. 1981. text ed. 136.00 (*0-12-553120-6*) Acad Pr.

Pettersson, Rune. Visual Information. 2nd ed. (Illus.). 400p. 1993. 39.95 (*0-87778-262-8*) Educ Tech Pubns.

Pettersson, T. Retention of Religious Experiences. (Illus.). 158p. (Orig.). 1975. pap. text ed. 22.50x (*0-685-13675-2*, Pub. by Almqv & Wiksell SW) Coronet Bks.

***Pettersson, Thorleif & Riis, Ole, eds.** Scandinavian Values: Religion & Morality in the Nordic Countries. (Psychologia & Sociologia Religionum Ser.: No. 10). 212p. 1994. pap. 38.50 (*91-554-3411-8*, Pub. by Almqv & Wiksell SW) Coronet Bks.

Pettersson, Ulf, jt. auth. see Lindsten, Jan.

Petteruti, Robert E., jt. auth. see Kaplan, Lloyd.

Pettes, Christy L., jt. auth. see Wanamaker, Boyce P.

Pettes, Dorothy E. Staff & Student Supervision: A Task-Centered Approach. 1979. 35.00 (*0-317-05776-6*, Pub. by Natl Inst Soc Work) St Mut.

Pettet, Ben, ed. Current Legal Problems, 1992 Vol. 45, Pt. 1: Annual Review, Vol. 45, Pt. 1. 244p. 1992. pap. 34.00 (*0-19-825721-X*) OUP.

— Current Legal Problems 1993 Vol. 46, Pt. 1: Annual Review. 208p. 1993. pap. 25.00 (*0-19-825860-7*) OUP.

— Current Legal Problems 1994 Vol. 47, Pt. 1: Annual Review. 248p. 1994. pap. 27.00 (*0-19-825904-2*) OUP.

Pettet, E. Shakespeare & the Romance Tradition. LC 75-30806. (Studies in Shakespeare: No. 24). 1975. lib. bdg. 75.00 (*0-8383-2081-3*) M S G Haskell Hse.

Pettet, E. C. On the Poetry of Keats. LC 83-45459. reprint ed. 34.50 (*0-404-20200-4*) AMS Pr.

***Pettet, Simon.** Selected Poems. 120p. (Orig.). 1995. pap. 9.95 (*1-883689-30-9*) Talisman Hse.

— Selected Poems. 120p. (Orig.). 1995. lib. bdg. 29.95 (*1-883689-31-7*) Talisman Hse.

Pettet, Simon, jt. auth. see Burckhardt, Rudy.

Pettett, George. Charles Crawford Pettett: A Plucky Fellow, Vol. 1. LC 89-92192. (Illus.). 300p. 1989. 14.95 (*0-9624353-0-9*) Lochaber Bks.

Petteway, Van H. How to Succeed As a Travel Agent. 375p. 1985. 35.00 (*0-9690625-0-8*) Worldwide Travel.

Pettey, George E. The Narcotic Drug Diseases & Allied Ailments: Pathology, Pathogenesis, & Treatment. Grob, Gerald N., ed. LC 80-1246. (Addiction in America Ser.). (Illus.). 1981. reprint ed. lib. bdg. 49.95 (*0-405-13616-1*) Ayer.

Pettey, John C. Nietzsche's Philosophical & Narrative Styles. LC 91-30171. (North American Studies in German Literature: Vol. 10). 215p. (C). 1992. text ed. 42.95 (*0-8204-1550-2*) P Lang Pubs.

Pettey, Richard J. Asherah: Goddess of Israel. LC 90-35025. (American University Studies: Theology & Religion: Ser. VII, Vol. 74). 233p. (C). 1990. text ed. 41.95 (*0-8204-1306-2*) P Lang Pubs.

Petteys, Chris. Dictionary of Women Artists: An International Dictionary of Women Artists Born Before 1900. LC 84-22511. 872p. 1985. lib. bdg. 75.00 (*0-8161-8456-9*, Hall Reference) Macmillan.

Petti, Anthony, ed. Christmas & Advent. (Chester's Books of Motets: Bk. 6). Date not set. pap. 7.50 (*0-685-69006-7*, Chester Music) Music Sales.

— Christmas & Advent Book. (Chester's Books of Motets: Bk. 12). Date not set. pap. 7.50 (*0-685-69007-5*, Chester Music) Music Sales.

— Christmas & Advent Book. (Chester's Books of Motets: Bk. 16). Date not set. pap. 7.50 (*0-685-69008-3*, Chester Music) Music Sales.

— English School. (Chester's Books of Motets: Bk. 13). Date not set. pap. 7.50 (*0-685-69041-5*, Chester Music) Music Sales.

— English School. (Chester's Books of Motets: Bk. 2). Date not set. pap. 7.50 (*0-685-69039-3*, Chester Music) Music Sales.

— English School. (Chester's Books of Motets: Bk. 9). Date not set. pap. 7.50 (*0-685-69040-7*, Chester Music) Music Sales.

— Flemish & German Schools. (Chester's Books of Motets: Bk. 11). Date not set. pap. 7.50 (*0-685-69045-8*, Chester Music) Music Sales.

— Flemish & German Schools. (Chester's Books of Motets: Bk. 15). Date not set. pap. 7.50 (*0-685-69046-6*, Chester Music) Music Sales.

— Flemish School. (Chester's Books of Motets: Bk. 5). Date not set. pap. 7.50 (*0-685-69047-4*, Chester Music) Music Sales.

— French School. (Chester's Books of Motets: Bk. 8). Date not set. pap. 7.50 (*0-685-69065-2*, Chester Music) Music Sales.

— Motes for Three Voices. (Chester's Books of Motets: Bk. 7). Date not set. pap. 7.50 (*0-685-69096-2*, Chester Music) Music Sales.

Petti, Patricc, ed. Directory of Drug Store & HBC Chains, 1993. pap. 260.00 (*0-86730-576-2*) Lebhar Friedman.

— Directory of High Volume Independent Drug Stores, 1993-94. 1296p. 1992. pap. 285.00 (*0-86730-580-0*, CSG Info Servs) Lebhar Friedman.

Petti, Theodore A., ed. Childhood Depression. LC 83-58. (Journal of Children in Contemporary Society Ser.: Vol. 15, No. 2). 95p. 1983. text ed. 24.95 (*0-917724-95-X*) Haworth Pr.

Petti, Vincent. Swedish-English English-Swedish Dictionary. 750p. 1990. write for info. (*0-87052-871-8*); pap. 18.95 (*0-87052-870-X*) Hippocrene Bks.

Pettibone, Dennis. A Century of Challenge: The Story of Southern College. 356p. (C). 1992. 44.95 (*0-9634258-0-3*) So Coll Seventh-day.

Pettibone, Marian H. Additions to the Family Eulepethidae Chamberlin (Polychaeta: Aphroditacea) LC 86-600055. (Smithsonian Contributions to Zoology Ser.: No. 441). 55p. reprint ed. pap. 25.00 (*0-8357-5097-3*, 2029361) Bks Demand.

— Revision of Some Species Referred to Antinoe, Antinoella, Antinoana, Bylgides, & Harmothoe (Polychaeta: Polynoidae: Harmothinae) LC 93-4229. (Smithsonian Contributions to Zoology Ser.: No. 545). (Illus.). 45p. reprint ed. pap. 25.00 (*0-7837-6292-5*, 2046007) Bks Demand.

— Revision of the Aphroditoid Polychaetes of the Family Acoetidae Kinberg (Polyodontidae Augener) & Reestablishment of Acoetes Audouin & Milne Edwards, 1832, & Euarche Ehlers, 1887. LC 89-600058. (Smithsonian Contributions to Zoology Ser.: No. 464). 142p. reprint ed. pap. 40.50 (*0-8357-7530-5*, 2036240) Bks Demand.

Petticoffer, Dennis. The Decadents (& More Decadence) 56p. 1991. pap. text ed. 9.95 (*1-880402-02-5*) Babble On Pr.

— Maniacs & Mood Pies: Dream, Despair, & Lunatic Prayer. 52p. 1991. pap. text ed. 9.95 (*1-880402-01-7*) Babble On Pr.

— Mosquitoes in My Fez. 50p. (Orig.). Date not set. pap. text ed. write for info. (*1-880402-07-6*) Babble On Pr.

— Power of Babble. 50p. (C). 1992. pap. 29.95 (*1-880402-03-3*) Babble On Pr.

— Tales of Terror. 50p. (C). 1992. pap. 29.95 (*1-880402-04-1*) Babble On Pr.

— The Ten Thousand Dollar Haircut: Assorted Snippets & Barbarities. 56p. (C). 1993. pap. 29.95 (*1-880402-06-8*) Babble On Pr.

— Wholly Babble: The Kingdom of Odd. 56p. (C). 1993. pap. 35.95 (*1-880402-05-X*) Babble On Pr.

— You: Nine Dreamscapes. 52p. 1991. pap. text ed. 12.95 (*1-880402-00-9*) Babble On Pr.

Pettie, George. Petite Pallace of Pettie, 2 Vols. LC 72-124763. reprint ed. 74.50 (*0-404-05025-5*) AMS Pr.

***Pettifer, Adrian.** English Castles: A Guide by Counties. (Illus.). 448p. (C). 1995. text ed. 45.00 (*0-85115-600-2*) Boydell & Brewer.

Pettifer, Ernest W. Punishments of Former Days. (Illus.). 1976. reprint ed. 15.00 (*0-7158-1021-9*) Charles River Bks.

Pettifer, James. Blue Guide: Albania. 192p. 1994. pap. 17.95 (*0-393-31056-6*) Norton.

Pettifer, James, ed. Cockburn in Spain: Despatches from the Spanish Civil War. 208p. (C). 1986. pap. 19.95 (*0-85315-668-9*, Pub. by Lawrence & Wishart UK) Humanities.

***Pettifor, D. G.** Quantum Concepts in the Bonding & Structure of Molecules & Solids. 288p. 1995. 56.00 (*0-19-851787-4*); pap. 29.95 (*0-19-851786-6*) OUP.

Pettifor, D. G. & Cottrell, A. H. Electron Theory in Alloy Design. 312p. 1992. 110.00 (*0-901716-17-0*, Pub. by Inst Materials UK) Ashgate Pub Co.

Pettifor, D. G. & Weaire, D. L., eds. The Recursion Method & Its Applications. (Solid-State Sciences Ser.: Vol. 58). (Illus.). 200p. 1985. 62.00 (*0-387-15173-7*) Spr-Verlag.

Pettifor, D. G., jt. ed. see De Boer, F. R.

Pettigrew, Andrew & Whipp, Richard. Managing Change for Competitive Success. 304p. 1992. text ed. 54.95 (*0-631-18241-1*); pap. 24.95 (*0-631-19142-9*) Blackwell Pubs.

Pettigrew, Andrew, et al. Shaping Strategic Change. (Illus.). 336p. (C). 1992. 65.00 (*0-8039-8778-1*); pap. 27.95 (*0-8039-8779-X*) Sage.

***Pettigrew, David & Raffoul, Francois, eds.** Disseminating Lacan. (SUNY Series in Contemporary Continental Philosophy). 330p. (C). 1996. text ed. 59.50x (*0-7914-2785-4*) State U NY Pr.

— Disseminating Lacan. (SUNY Series in Contemporary Continental Philosophy). 330p. (C). 1996. pap. text ed. 19.95x (*0-7914-2786-2*) State U NY Pr.

Pettigrew, David, tr. see Nancy, Jean-Luc & Lacoue-Labarthe, Philippe.

Pettigrew, Eileen. Night Time. (Illus.). 24p. (J). (ps-1). 1992. lib. bdg. 14.95 (*1-55037-235-1*, Pub. by Annick CN); pap. 4.95 (*1-55037-242-4*, Pub. by Annick CN) Firefly Bks Ltd.

Pettigrew, G. W. & Moore, G. R. Cytochromes C. (Molecular Biology Ser.). (Illus.). xiv, 282p. 1987. 169.00 (*0-387-17843-0*) Spr-Verlag.

Pettigrew, G. W., jt. auth. see Moore, G. R.

Pettigrew, James. The Billboard Guide to Music Publicity. (Illus.). 208p. 1989. pap. 14.95 (*0-8230-7575-3*, Billboard Bks) Watsn-Guptill.

Pettigrew, Jane. An Edwardian Childhood. (Illus.). 160p. 1992. 25.00 (*0-8212-1915-4*) Bulfinch Pr.

— The National Trust Book of Tea-Time Recipes. (Illus.). 160p. 1991. 17.95 (*0-7078-0128-1*, Pub. by Natl Trust UK) Trafalgar.

Pettigrew, John, ed. see Browning, Robert.

***Pettigrew, Joyce M.** The Sikhs of the Punjab: Unheard Voices of the State & Guerrilla Violence. LC 95-13677. (Politics in Contemporary Asia Ser.). (Illus.). 256p. (C). 1995. text ed. 59.95 (*1-85649-355-5*, Pub. by Zed Books UK); pap. 25.00 (*1-85649-356-3*, Pub. by Zed Books UK) Humanities.

Pettigrew, Judith H. Planned Marketing: The Roadmap to Sales. Voiers, Judith S. et al, eds. 58p. 1989. student ed 19.95 (*0-9622899-1-4*) Creative Consort Inc.

— Sure I Can Rollerskate on Jell-O! (Illus.). 108p. (Orig.). 1989. pap. 8.95 (*0-9622899-2-2*) Creative Consort Inc.

Pettigrew, Mary E., ed. see Casey, Mary.

Pettigrew, Richard F. Imperial Washington. LC 78-111704. (American Imperialism: Viewpoints of United States Foreign Policy, 1898-1941 Ser.). 1970. reprint ed. 26.95 (*0-405-02044-9*) Ayer.

Pettigrew, Terence. British Film Character Actors: Great Names & Memorable Moments. LC 82-3913. (Illus.). 208p. (C). 1982. text ed. 38.00 (*0-389-20289-4*, N7112) B&N Imports.

Pettigrew, Thomas F. Negro American Intelligence. 48p. 0.50 (*0-686-74891-3*) ADL.

— The Sociology of Race Relations: Reflection & Reform. LC 79-54666. (Illus.). 1980. pap. 19.95 (*0-02-925110-9*) Free Pr.

Pettigrew, Thomas F. & Alston, Denise A. Tom Bradley's Campaign for Governor: The Dilemma of Race & Political Strategies. 96p. 1988. pap. 16.25 (*0-941410-63-3*) Jt Ctr Pol Studies.

Pettigrew, Thomas F., et al. Prejudice. (Dimensions in Ethnicity Ser.). 128p. 1990. pap. 11.50 (*0-674-70063-5*) HUP.

Pettigrew, Thomas J. Chronicles of the Tombs. LC 68-55555. (Bohn's Antiquarian Library). reprint ed. 46.00 (*0-404-50022-6*) AMS Pr.

— A History of Egyptian Mummies. LC 83-62961. (Classics in Archaeology Ser.). (Illus.). 264p. 1984. reprint ed. 35.00 (*0-915431-00-9*) N American Archives.

Pettigrew, Vera. Fionuala the Glendalough Goat. (Illus.). 112p. (Orig.). (J). (gr. 1-8). 1990. 10.95 (0-947962-42-5, Pub. by Anvil Bks Ltd IE); pap. 7.95 (0-947962-43-3, Pub. by Anvil Bks Ltd IE) Irish Bks Media.

Pettijohn, Bruce. Sixty-Fifth Reunion. 1995. 8.95 (0-8062-5116-6) Carlton.

Pettijohn, F. J., et al. Sand & Sandstone. 2nd ed. (Springer Study Edition Ser.). (Illus.). 500p. 1987. pap. 69.95 (0-387-96350-2) Spr-Verlag.

Pettijohn, F. J., jt. auth. see Krumbein, W. C.

Pettijohn, F. J., jt. auth. see Potter, P. E.

Pettijohn, James B. Profit Plus. (Illus.). 336p. (C). 1987. pap. text ed. 21.50 (0-03-013558-3) Dryden Pr.

Pettijohn, Terry, ed. Sources: Notable Selections in Social Psychology. (Illus.). 336p. (Orig.). 1995. pap. text ed. 14.95 (1-56134-314-5) Dushkin Pub.

Pettijohn, Terry F. Psychology: A Concise Introduction. 3rd ed. LC 91-77531. (Illus.). 496p. (C). 1992. pap. text ed. 25.95 (1-56134-063-4) Dushkin Pub.

— Study Guide to Accompany Psychology: A Concise Introduction. 3rd ed. LC 92-71288. (Illus.). (Orig.). (C). 1992. pap. text ed. 10.95 (1-56134-064-2) Dushkin Pub.

Pettijohn, Terry F., ed. The Encyclopedic Dictionary of Psychology. 4th ed. LC 85-72118. (Illus.). 304p. 1991. pap. text ed. 14.95 (0-87967-885-2) Dushkin Pub.

— Sources: Notable Selections in Psychology. LC 93-34527. 384p. 1994. 14.95 (1-56134-263-7) Dushkin Pub.

Pettinari, Catherine J. Task, Talk & Text in the Operating Room: A Study in Medical Discourse. Freedle, Roy O., ed. LC 88-10396. (Advances in Discourse Processes Ser.: Vol. 33). 208p. 1988. text ed. 45.00 (0-89391-459-2) Ablex Pub.

Pettinati, Helen M., ed. Hypnosis & Memory. LC 87-7597. (Guilford Clinical & Experimental Hypnosis Ser.). 301p. 1988. lib. bdg. 42.00 (0-89862-338-3) Guilford Pr.

Pettinato, Giovanni. Ebla: A New Look at History. Richardson, C. Faith, tr. LC 90-20907. (Illus.). 320p. 1991. text ed. 39.95x (0-8018-4150-X) Johns Hopkins.

Pettingill, Olin S., Jr. A Guide to Bird Finding East of the Mississippi. 2nd ed. LC 76-9253. (Illus.). 1977. 35.00 (0-19-502097-9) OUP.

— A Guide to Bird Finding West of the Mississippi. 2nd ed. LC 80-18666. (Illus.). 1981. 35.00 (0-19-502818-X) OUP.

— Ornithology at the University of Michigan Biological Station & the Birds of the Region. (Illus.). viii, 118p. 1974. pap. text ed. 5.00 (0-939294-00-1, QL-684-M5-P4) Beech Leaf.

— Ornithology in Laboratory & Field. 5th ed. 1985. text ed. 39.95 (0-12-552455-2) Acad Pr.

Pettingill, Olin S., Jr. & Pettingill, Olin S., Jr. My Way to Ornithology. LC 91-50869. (Illus.). 336p. 1992. 26.95 (0-8061-2409-1) U of Okla Pr.

Pettingill, Olin S., Jr., jt. auth. see Pettingill, Olin S., Jr.

Pettingill, W. L. Estudios Sencillos sobre Juan: Believe & Live. (SPA.). 3.25 (84-7645-169-5, 223196, Pub. by Edit Clie SP) TSELF.

— Estudios Sencillos sobre Mateo: Simple Studies on Matthew. (SPA.). 6.95 (84-7645-107-5, 223161, Pub. by Edit Clie SP) TSELF.

— Estudios Sencillos sobre Romanos: Simple Studies in Romans. (SPA.). 5.50 (84-7228-866-8, 222326, Pub. by Edit Clie SP) TSELF.

— Estudios Sobre el Libro De Daniel: Studies on the Book of Daniel. (SPA.). 3.50 (84-7228-994-X, 223065, Pub. by Edit Clie SP) TSELF.

— Estudios sobre la Epistola a Galatas: Studies on Galatians. (SPA.). 3.25 (84-7228-893-5, 222329, Pub. by Edit Clie SP) TSELF.

Pettingill, William L. Nine Hundred Bible Questions Answered. LC 90-20615. Orig. Title: Bible Questions Answered - Enlarged Edition. 566p. 1991. reprint ed. pap. 16.99 (0-8254-3541-2) Kregel.

Pettipher, G. L., jt. ed. see Norris, John R.

Pettis, C. R. Public Use of the Forest Preserve. 17p. 1993. reprint ed. lib. bdg. 69.00 (0-7812-5262-8) Rprt Serv.

***Pettis, Chuck.** Technobrands: How to Create & Use "Brand Identity" to Market, Advertise & Sell Technology Products. LC 94-31044. (Illus.). 208p. 1994. 26.95 (0-8144-0243-7) AMACOM.

***Pettis, Joyce.** Toward Wholeness in Paule Marshall's Fiction. LC 94-48916. 192p. (C). 1995. text ed. 29.50 (0-8139-1614-3) U Pr of Va.

Pettit, Arthur G. Images of the Mexican American in Fiction & Film. Showalter, Dennis E., ed. LC 79-5284. 312p. 1980. 22.50 (0-89096-095-X); pap. 9.95 (0-89096-115-8) Tex A&M Univ Pr.

— Mark Twain & the South. LC 73-86405. 240p. 1974. 26.00 (0-8131-1310-5) U Pr of Ky.

Pettit, D. G., jt. auth. see Patterson, P. G.

Pettit, Eber M. Sketches in the History of the Underground Railroad. LC 73-149875. (Black Heritage Library Collection). 1977. 25.95 (0-8369-8755-1) Ayer.

Pettit, Ed, jt. auth. see Schul, Bill D.

Pettit, F. S., jt. auth. see Blachere, J. R.

Pettit, G. R. Synthetic Peptides, Vol. 5. 404p. 1980. 161.75 (0-444-41895-4) Elsevier.

— Synthetic Peptides, Vol. 6. 512p. 1982. 210.25 (0-444-42080-0) Elsevier.

Pettit, G. R., et al. Biosynthetic Products for Cancer Chemotherapy. 400p. 1989. 148.75 (0-444-88049-6) Elsevier.

Pettit, George R., et al. Anticancer Drugs from Animals, Plants & Microorganisms. LC 93-46997. 1994. text ed. 94.95 (0-471-03657-9) Wiley.

Pettit, J. E., jt. auth. see Hoffbrand, A. V.

Pettit, J. H., et al. Manual of Tropical Dermatology. (Illus.). 270p. 1984. 99.00 (0-387-90987-7) Spr-Verlag.

Pettit, Jan. Utes: The Mountain People. rev. ed. LC 90-91905. 224p. 1990. pap. 11.95 (1-55566-065-7) Johnson Bks.

Pettit, Jayne. Place to Hide: True Stories of Holocaust Rescues. (J). (gr. 4-7). 1993. pap. 2.95 (0-590-45353-X) Scholastic Inc.

Pettit, John, jt. auth. see Lesikar, Raymond V., Sr.

Pettit, John D., jt. auth. see Lesikar, Raymond V.

Pettit, Joseph. Enrollment for Fall, 1988 & Finances & Student Aid Year Ending June 30, 1989 at U. S. Catholic Colleges & Universities. 29p. (Orig.). 1991. pap. 10.00 (1-55833-113-1) Natl Cath Educ.

Pettit, Madge. Pioneers & Residents of West Central Alabama Prior to the Civil War. xvi, 337p. (Orig.). 1988. pap. 27.50 (1-55613-125-9) Heritage Bk.

Pettit, Michael. Cardinal Points: Cowinner of the 1987 Iowa Poetry Prize. LC 88-14797. (Iowa Poetry Prize Ser.). 96p. (Orig.). 1988. pap. 10.95 (0-87745-206-7) U of Iowa Pr.

***Pettit, Michael, ed.** The Writing Path 1: An Annual of Poetry & Prose from Writers' Conferences. 243p. 1995. 32.95 (0-87745-508-2) U of Iowa Pr.

— The Writing Path 1: An Annual of Poetry & Prose from Writers' Conferences. 243p. 1995. pap. 14.95 (0-87745-509-0) U of Iowa Pr.

Pettit, Neila T. & Hardin, Veralee B. Ecological Intervention in Reading & Language Arts. 1982. pap. 9.95 (0-89108-110-0, 8202) Love Pub Co.

Pettit, Norman, ed. see Edwards, Jonathan.

Pettit, P., ed. see Hookway, Christopher.

Pettit, Paul, jt. auth. see Harris, Nathaniel.

Pettit, Philip. The Common Mind: An Essay on Psychology, Society, & Politics. 256p. 1992. 42.00 (0-19-507818-7) OUP.

— Consequentialism. LC 92-36095. (International Research Library of Philosophy). 512p. 1993. 139.95 (1-85521-304-4, Pub. by Dartmth Pub UK) Ashgate Pub Co.

— Contemporary Political Theory. (C). 1991. pap. write for info. (0-02-394955-4) Macmillan.

Pettit, Philip, jt. auth. see Braithwaite, John.

Pettit, Philip, jt. ed. see Goodin, Robert E.

Pettit, Philip, jt. ed. see Hamlin, Alan.

Pettit, Philip, jt. auth. see Kukathas, Chandran.

Pettit, Philip, jt. auth. see MacDonald, Graham.

Pettit, Philip H. Equity & the Law of Trusts. 6th ed. 1989. pap. 58.00 (0-406-51051-2) Butterworth Legal Pubs.

Pettit, Ray H. ECM & ECCM Techniques for Digital Communications Systems. (Systems Engineering Ser.). (Illus.). 178p. 1982. 25.95 (0-534-97932-7) Peninsula CA.

Pettit, Sue S. Coming Home: A Collection. LC 87-62047. 96p. (Orig.). 1988. pap. 4.95 (0-9606896-7-2) Sunrise Pr.

Pettit, T. H. Hospital Administration for Veterinary Staff. LC 93-74972. 200p. 1994. 22.50 (0-939674-53-X) Am Vet Pubns.

Pettitt, Charles, jt. auth. see Orna, Elizabeth.

Pettitt, Deirdre, jt. ed. see Davis, Andrew.

Pettitt, Deirdre, jt. auth. see Palmer, Joy A.

Pettitt, Roland A. Exploring the Jemez Country. 2nd rev. ed. LC 90-33924. (Illus.). 112p. 1990. pap. 8.95 (0-941232-10-7) Los Alamos Hist Soc.

Pettitt, Stephen. Handel. LC 93-39722. (Compact Companions Ser.). 1994. pap. 17.50 (0-671-88790-4) S&S Trade.

Pettler, Pamela & Heckerling, Amy. The No-Sex Handbook. 1990. mass mkt. 6.95 (0-446-39054-2) Warner Bks.

Pettman, Barrie O. Manpower Planning Workbook. 2nd ed. LC 83-18488. 127p. 1984. text ed. 65.00 (0-566-02468-3) Ashgate Pub Co.

Pettman, Jan. Living in the Margins: Racism, Sexism & Feminism in Australia. 220p. (Orig.). 1992. pap. text ed. 19.95 (1-86373-005-2, Pub. by Allen Unwin AT) Paul & Co Pubs.

— Zambia: Security & Conflict, 1964-1973. LC 74-79129. 381p. (C). 1974. text ed. 32.50 (0-312-89845-2) St Martin.

Pettman, Ralph. Human Behavior & World Politics: An Introduction to International Relations. LC 75-10759. 352p. (C). 1976. text ed. 22.50 (0-312-39760-7) St Martin.

— International Politics: Balance of Power, Balance of Productivity, Balance of Ideologies. LC 91-2110. 247p. (C). 1991. pap. text ed. 17.95 (1-55587-281-6) Lynne Rienner.

Pettman, Ralph, ed. Moral Claims in World Affairs. LC 78-11431. 1979. text ed. 29.95 (0-312-54755-2) St Martin.

Pettman, William R. Resources of the United Kingdom: Or the Present Distress Considered. LC 68-56563. (Reprints of Economic Classics Ser.). 1970. reprint ed. 39.50 (0-678-00661-X) Kelley.

Petto, Andrew J., jt. ed. see Novak, Melinda A.

Pettofrezzo, Anthony J. Matrices & Transformations. 1978. reprint ed. pap. text ed. 4.95 (0-486-63634-8) Dover.

Pettorossi, A., ed. Meta-Programming in Logic: Third International Workshop, META-92, Uppsala, Sweden, June 10-12, 1992: Proceedings. LC 92-41020. (Lecture Notes in Computer Science Ser.: Vol. 649). 1992. 57.00 (0-387-56282-6) Spr-Verlag.

Pettrone, Frank A. Athletic Injuries of the Shoulder. 402p. 1994. text ed. 85.00 (0-07-049742-7) Hlth Prof Div.

Petts, C., jt. ed. see Buttler, H.

Petts, G., jt. ed. see Cosgrove, D.

Petts, G. E., jt. auth. see Calow, P.

Petts, G. E., jt. auth. see Carling, Paul A.

Petts, G. E., et al. Historical Change of Large Alluvial Rivers: Western Europe. 355p. 1989. text ed. 175.00 (0-471-92163-7) Wiley.

Petts, Geoff, jt. ed. see Cosgrove, Denis.

Petts, Geoff, jt. ed. see Gurnell, Angela.

Petts, Geoffrey E., jt. ed. see Gore, James A.

Petts, Judith & Eduljee, Gev. Environmental Impact Assessment for Waste Treatment & Disposal Facilities. LC 93-8854. 485p. 1994. text ed. 84.95 (0-471-94112-3) Wiley.

Petts, Kusha. Necklace for a Poor Sod. (C). 1979. 30.00 (0-85088-435-7, Pub. by Gomer Pr UK) St Mut.

Pettus, jt. auth. see Byrd, Donald.

Pettus, Dania, jt. auth. see Lehmann, Peggy.

Pettus, Daniel D., jt. auth. see Pettus, Eloise S.

Pettus, David. Horizontal, Extended-Reach, & Wide-Angle Drilling: An Annotated & Indexed Bibliography. 320p. (Orig.). 1992. 89.00 (0-89896-441-5); pap. 50.00 (0-89896-440-7) Larksdale.

Pettus, Eloise S. & Pettus, Daniel D. Master Index to Summaries of Children's Books: Title & Subject Indexes, 2 Vols. 1985. Vol. I: A-Z; 1054. write for info. (0-318-59798-5); Vol. II: Title & Subject Indexes; 354p. write for info. (0-318-59799-3) Scarecrow.

— Master Index to Summaries of Children's Books: Title & Subject Indexes, 2 Vols., Set. LC 85-1901. 1985. 89.50 (0-8108-1795-0) Scarecrow.

Pettus, Louise & Chepsiuk, Ron. Palmetto State. 1991. 19.95 (0-87844-097-6) Sandlapper Pub Co.

Pettus, Louise, ed. see Bodie, Idella.

Pettus, Theodore. One on One: Win the Interview, Win the Job. LC 81-40211. 200p. 1981. 14.95 (0-394-52138-2) Random.

Petty. Chronic Obstructive Pulmonary Disease. 2nd ed. (Lung Biology in Health & Disease Ser.: Vol. 28). 512p. 1985. 175.00 (0-8247-7385-3) Dekker.

— Swedish-English - English-Swedish Standard Dictionary. rev. ed. 1995. pap. (0-7818-0379-9) Hippocrene Bks.

— Total Joint Replacement. (Illus.). 896p. 1991. text ed. 164.00 (0-7216-3367-6) Saunders.

Petty, Arlie E. Daniel, Gabriel, & Michael: Our Creator. 1992. 11.95 (0-533-10070-4) Vantage.

***Petty, Carolyn A.** Waterdrum Science: Science Through American Indian Arts & Culture. Duranske, Benjamin, ed. LC 94-78267. (Illus.). 290p. (J). (gr. 4-8). 1994. lib. bdg. 28.50 (0-9642898-0-6) Larchmere Ltd.

Petty, Charles E. High Standard Automatic Pistols 1932-1950. 19.95 (0-88227-029-X) Gun Room.

Petty, Clayton. The Anesthesia Machine. LC 86-21574. (Illus.). 246p. reprint ed. pap. 70.20 (0-7837-6809-5, 2046641) Bks Demand.

Petty, Damon H., jt. auth. see Knowles, Harvey C., 3rd.

Petty, Evan R. Martensite: Fundamentals & Technology. LC 70-546066. 217p. reprint ed. pap. 61.90 (0-317-10681-3, 2003648) Bks Demand.

Petty, Frederick C. Italian Opera in London, 1760-1800. LC 79-25564. (Studies in Musicology: No. 16). 441p. reprint ed. pap. 125.70 (0-685-20882-6, 2070227) Bks Demand.

***Petty, Geoffrey.** Teaching Today: A Practical Guide. 384p. (C). 1993. pap. 50.00x (0-7487-1697-1, Pub. by S Thornes Pubs UK) St Mut.

Petty, Gerald. Index of the Ohio Eighteen Thirty-Five Tax Duplicate. 400p. 1988. 100.00 (0-910347-10-7) Chatham Comm Inc.

Petty, Gilbert & Petty, June. A Clean Sweep: A Sailor's Diary in the Pacific World War II. Cornett, June L., ed. (Illus.). 152p. (Orig.). 1988. pap. 9.95 (0-9620646-0-2) Petty Pub.

Petty, H. R. Molecular Biology of Membranes: Structure & Function. (Illus.). 385p. (C). 1993. 59.50 (0-306-44429-1, Plenum Pr) Plenum.

Petty-Hunter, Carol A., ed. see Posey, Alexander.

Petty, James D., jt. auth. see Dempsey, Carla H.

Petty, Jo. An Apple a Day: Treasured Selections from Apples of Gold. 1979. 8.50 (0-8378-5025-8) Gibson.

— Apples of Gold. large type ed. 1985. pap. 8.95 (0-8027-2502-3) Walker & Co.

— Wings of Silver. large type ed. 1986. 9.95 (0-8027-2546-5) Walker & Co.

Petty, Judson, jt. ed. see Hook, Cass.

Petty, Julian J. The Growth & Distribution of Population in South Carolina. LC 74-34438. (Illus.). 242p. 1975. reprint ed. 25.00 (0-87152-200-4) Reprint.

Petty, June, jt. auth. see Petty, Gilbert.

Petty, Kate. Baby Animals: Bears. (Illus.). 24p. (J). (ps-3). 1992. pap. 3.95 (0-8120-4964-0) Barron.

— Baby Animals: Chimpanzees. (Illus.). 24p. (J). (ps-3). 1992. pap. 3.95 (0-8120-4965-9) Barron.

— Baby Animals: Elephants. (Illus.). 24p. (J). (ps-3). 1992. pap. 3.95 (0-8120-4966-7) Barron.

— Baby Animals: Kittens. (Illus.). 24p. (J). (ps-3). 1992. pap. 3.95 (0-8120-4967-5) Barron.

— Baby Animals: Pandas. (Illus.). 24p. (J). (ps-3). 1992. pap. 3.95 (0-8120-4968-3) Barron.

— Baby Animals: Puppies. (Illus.). 24p. (J). (ps-3). 1992. pap. 3.95 (0-8120-4969-1) Barron.

— Baby Animals: Seals. (Illus.). 24p. (J). (ps-3). 1992. pap. 3.95 (0-8120-4970-5) Barron.

— Baby Animals: Tigers. (Illus.). 24p. (J). (ps-3). 1992. pap. 3.95 (0-8120-4971-3) Barron.

— Being Bullied. (Playground Ser.). (Illus.). 24p. (J). (ps-2). 1991. pap. 4.95 (0-8120-4661-7) Barron.

— Cats. (First Pets Ser.). (Illus.). 24p. (J). (ps-3). 1993. pap. 3.95 (0-8120-1485-5) Barron.

— Cobayos. LC 90-71412. (First Pets Ser.). (Illus.). 24p. (SPA.). (J). (gr. k-4). 1991. lib. bdg. 11.62 (0-531-07914-7) Watts.

— Crocodiles & Alligators. (First Library Bks.). (Illus.). (J). 1990. pap. 3.95 (0-531-15153-0) Watts.

— Deserts. (Around & About Ser.). (Illus.). 32p. (J). (gr. 2-4). 1993. pap. 5.95 (0-8120-1762-5) Barron.

— Dogs. (First Pets Ser.). (Illus.). 24p. (J). (ps-3). 1993. pap. 3.95 (0-8120-1484-7) Barron.

— Ducklings. (Baby Animals Ser.). 24p. (J). (gr. k-3). 1993. pap. 3.95 (0-8120-1489-8) Barron.

— Earth. LC 90-31022. (Starting Points Ser.). (Illus.). 32p. (J). (gr. k-4). 1991. lib. bdg. 12.60 (0-531-14098-9) Watts.

— Feeling Left Out. (Playground Ser.). (Illus.). 24p. (J). (ps-2). 1991. pap. 4.95 (0-8120-4658-7) Barron.

— Fire. (Starting Points Ser.). (Illus.). 32p. (J). (gr. k-4). 1990. lib. bdg. 12.60 (0-531-14060-1) Watts.

— Frogs & Toads. (First Library Bks.). 32p. (J). (gr. k-3). 1990. pap. 3.95 (0-531-15154-9) Watts.

— The Ground Below Us. (Around & About Ser.). (Illus.). 32p. (J). (gr. 2-4). 1993. pap. 5.95 (0-8120-1232-1) Barron.

— Guinea Pigs. LC 94-26050. (First Pets Ser.). (Illus.). (J). 1995. write for info. (0-8120-9080-2) Barron.

— Hamsters. (First Pets Ser.). (Illus.). 24p. (J). (ps-3). 1993. pap. 3.95 (0-8120-1472-3) Barron.

— Into Space. (Around & About Ser.). (Illus.). 32p. (J). (gr. 2-4). 1993. pap. 5.95 (0-8120-1761-7) Barron.

— Kangaroos. (Baby Animals Ser.). (Illus.). (J). (gr. k-3). 1993. pap. 3.95 (0-8120-1492-8) Barron.

— Lions. (Baby Animals Ser.). 24p. (J). (gr. k-3). 1993. pap. 3.95 (0-8120-1490-1) Barron.

— Making Friends. (Playground Ser.). (Illus.). 24p. (J). (ps-2). 1991. pap. 4.95 (0-8120-4660-9) Barron.

— Maps & Journals. (Around & About Ser.). (Illus.). 32p. (J). (gr. 2-4). 1993. pap. 5.95 (0-8120-1235-6) Barron.

— Mr. Toad to the Rescue. (Illus.). 24p. (J). (ps-2). 1992. 8.95 (0-8120-6273-6) Barron.

— Mr. Toad's Narrow Escape. (J). (ps-3). 1992. pap. 4.95 (0-8120-1475-8) Barron.

— Mr. Toad's Narrow Escapes. (J). (ps-3). 1992. 8.95 (0-8120-6289-2) Barron.

— My First Atlas, Vol. 1. (J). (ps-8). 1991. 9.95 (1-55782-361-8, Warner Juvenile Bks) Little.

— My First Book of Knowledge. (J). 1990. 5.99 (0-517-05177-X) Random Hse Value.

— New Bike. (Start to Finish Ser.). (Illus.). 32p. (J). (gr. 2 up). 1992. bds. 12.95 (0-7136-3482-0, Pub. by A&C Black UK) Talman.

— New Car. (Start to Finish Ser.). (Illus.). 32p. (J). (gr. 2 up). 1992. bds. 12.95 (0-7136-3484-7, Pub. by A&C Black UK) Talman.

— New Shampoo. (Start to Finish Ser.). (Illus.). 32p. (J). (gr. 2 up). 1992. bds. 12.95 (0-7136-3481-2, Pub. by A&C Black UK) Talman.

— New Shoes. (Start to Finish Ser.). (Illus.). 32p. (J). (gr. 2 up). 1992. bds. 12.95 (0-7136-3483-9, Pub. by A&C Black UK) Talman.

— Our Globe, Our World. (Around & About Ser.). (Illus.). 32p. (J). (gr. 2-4). 1993. pap. 5.95 (0-8120-1236-4) Barron.

— Playing the Game. (Playground Ser.). (Illus.). 24p. (J). (ps-2). 1991. pap. 4.95 (0-8120-4659-5) Barron.

— Ponies & Foals. (Baby Animals Ser.). 24p. (J). (gr. k-3). 1993. pap. 3.95 (0-8120-1487-1) Barron.

— Rabbits. (First Pets Ser.). (Illus.). 24p. (J). (ps-3). 1993. pap. 3.95 (0-8120-1473-1) Barron.

— Rainforests. (Around & About Ser.). (Illus.). 32p. (J). (gr. 2-4). 1993. pap. 5.95 (0-8120-1760-9) Barron.

— The Sky Above Us. (Around & About Ser.). (Illus.). 32p. (J). (gr. 2-4). 1993. pap. 5.95 (0-8120-1234-8) Barron.

— Snakes. (First Library Bks.). 1990. pap. 3.95 (0-531-15156-5) Watts.

— Stop, Look & Listen, Mr. Toad. (Illus.). 24p. (J). (ps-2). 1991. 8.95 (0-8120-6230-2) Barron.

— Under the Sea. (Around & About Ser.). (Illus.). 32p. (J). (gr. 2-4). 1993. pap. 5.95 (0-8120-1759-5) Barron.

Petty, Kyle, jt. auth. see Gaillard, Frye.

Petty, L. Jalik. Black Campus Ministry. 2nd ed. Date not set. pap. text ed. 4.95 (0-942428-01-3) Universal Ministries.

— Reducing Racial Tension in the Schools Through Values Clarification. LC 81-52146. 56p. (Orig.). (C). 1982. pap. 4.95 (0-942428-00-5) Universal Ministries.

***Petty, Michael C.** Langmuir-Blodgett Films: An Introduction. (Illus.). 250p. (C). 1991. write for info. (0-521-41396-6); pap. write for info. (0-521-42450-X) Cambridge U Pr.

***Petty, Michael C., et al.** Introduction to Molecular Electronics. (Illus.). 288p. 1995. pap. text ed. 42.50 (0-19-521156-1) OUP.

Petty, Priscilla H. Under a Lucky Star: The Story of Frederick A. Hauck. LC 86-72173. (Illus.). 180p. 1987. 22.95 (0-9617747-0-3) Cin Oral Hist Foun.

Petty, R. E. & Cacioppo, J. T. Communication & Persuasion. (Social Psychology Ser.). (Illus.). 220p. 1986. 58.00 (0-387-96344-8) Spr-Verlag.

Petty, Richard E. & Cacioppo, John T. Attitudes & Persuasion. 332p. 1981. pap. write for info. (0-697-06551-0) Brown & Benchmark.

***Petty, Richard E. & Krosnick, Jon A., eds.** Attitude Strength: Antecedents & Consequences. 504p. 1995. text ed. 90.00 (0-8058-1086-2) L Erlbaum Assocs.

— Attitude Strength: Antecedents & Consequences. 504p. 1995. pap. 45.00 (0-8058-1087-0) L Erlbaum Assocs.

Petty, Richard E., jt. ed. see Cacioppo, John T.

Petty, Richard E., et al, eds. Cognitive Responses in Persuasion. LC 80-26388. 512p. 1981. text ed. 49.95 (0-89859-025-6) L Erlbaum Assocs.

Petty, Robert, et al. Out of the Shadows: Defeating Disabilities. (Illus.). 149p. (Orig.). 1992. pap. text ed. 8.50 (0-9632731-0-8) Delano Pr.

Petty, Ross D. The Impact of Advertising Law on Business & Public Policy. LC 92-8403. 248p. 1992. text ed. 49.95 (0-89930-617-9, PCQ, Quorum Bks) Greenwood.

Petty, Ross E., jt. auth. see Cassidy, James T.

Petty, Steve. Walk with Jesus: Resources for Holy Week. 48p. 1989. pap. 2.95 (0-687-44005-X) Abingdon.

***Petty, Thomas L. & Nett, Louise M.** Enjoying Life with Chronic Obstructive Pulmonary Disease. Date not set. write for info. (1-886128-04-9) Laennec Pub.

P
Q

Petty, Thomas L., jt. ed. see Casaburi, Richard.
Petty, Thomas L., jt. auth. see Hodgkin, John E.
Petty, Thomas L., jt. ed. see Kira, Shiro.
Petty, Thomas L., jt. auth. see Scoggin, Charles H.
Petty, Thomas L., et al. Intensive & Rehabilitative Respiratory Care: A Practical Approach to the Management of Acute & Chronic Respiratory Failure. 3rd ed. LC 81-23630. 478p. reprint ed. pap. 136.30 (*0-7837-2738-0*, 2043118) Bks Demand.
Petty, Thurman C., Jr. Wreck of the Wild Wave. (Destiny Ser.). 96p. 1991. pap. 2.99 (*0-8163-0937-X*) Pacific Pr Pub Assn.
Petty, Tom. Tom Petty & the Heartbreakers: Greatest Hits (Guitar) Roed, Tom, ed. (Illus.). 100p. (Orig.). 1994. pap. text ed. 18.95 (*0-89898-766-0*) CPP Belwin.
— Tom Petty & the Heartbreakers: Greatest Hits (Piano) Roed, Tom, ed. (Illus.). 80p. (Orig.). 1994. pap. text ed. 16.95 (*0-89898-765-2*) CPP Belwin.
Petty, W. Clayton, jt. auth. see Stanley, Theodore H.
Petty, W. Clayton, jt. ed. see Stanley, Theodore H.
Petty, Walter T., et al. Experience in Language: Tools & Techniques for Language Arts Methods. rev. ed. 550p. 1989. teacher ed write for info. (*0-318-63900-9*, H19334) Allyn.
— Experiences in Language: Tools & Techniques for Language Arts Methods. 6th ed. LC 93-39672. 1994. pap. text ed. write for info. (*0-205-15222-8*) Allyn.
Petty, William. Economic Writings, 2 Vols in 1. Hull, Charles H., ed. LC 63-23521. (Reprints of Economic Classics Ser.). 1968. reprint ed. 57.50 (*0-678-00029-8*) Kelley.
— History of the Survey of Ireland, Commonly Called the Down Survey, 1655-56. Larcom, Thomas A., ed. LC 67-20090. (Reprints of Economic Classics Ser.). 1967. reprint ed. 49.50 (*0-678-00341-6*) Kelley.
— Petty Papers: Some Unpublished Papers of Sir William Petty, 2 Vols. in 1. Landsdowne, ed. LC 66-22634. (Reprints of Economic Classics Ser.). 1967. reprint ed. 57.50 (*0-678-00237-1*) Kelley.
— Petty-Southwell Correspondence, 1676-1687. Marquis Of Landsdowne Staff, ed. LC 67-27557. (Reprints of Economic Classics Ser.). 1967. reprint ed. 39.50 (*0-678-00314-9*) Kelley.
Pettygrove, G. Stuart. How to Perform an Agricultural Experiment. 26p. 1971. English, 26pp. 7.25 (*0-86619-039-2*); Spanish, 31pp. 7.25 (*0-86619-040-6*) Vols Tech Asst.
Pettygrove, G. Stuart & Asano, Takashi. Irrigation with Reclaimed Municipal Wastewater. (Illus.). 518p. 1985. 75.00 (*0-87371-061-4*, TD760) Lewis Pubs.
Pettyjohn, E. S., jt. auth. see Linden, H. R.
Pettyjohn, Wayne A. Introduction to Artificial Ground Water Recharge. (C). 1989. 90.00 (*81-85046-69-7*, Scientific) St Mut.
Pettyjohn, Wayne A., ed. Protection of Public Water Supplies from Ground-Water Contamination. LC 86-31173. (Pollution Technology Review Ser.: No. 141). (Illus.). 177p. 1987. 36.00 (*0-8155-1119-1*) Noyes.
Petuch, Edward J. The Edge of the Fossil Sea: Life Along the Shores of Prehistoric Florida. (Illus.). 156p. (Orig.). 1992. pap. 14.95 (*0-9634264-0-0*) B-M Shell Mus.
— Field Guide to the Ecphoras. (Illus.). 1989. 21.50 (*0-938415-03-4*) CERF Inc.
— Neogene History of Tropical American Mollusks. (Illus.). 1988. 64.95 (*0-938415-02-6*) CERF Inc.
— New Caribbean Molluscan Faunas. (Illus.). 1987. 38.50 (*0-938415-01-8*) CERF Inc.
Petuchowski, Elizabeth, tr. see Breuer, Mordechai.
Petuchowski, Jacob J. Freedom of Expression in the Jewish Tradition. 34p. 1984. pap. 2.50 (*0-87495-062-7*) Am Jewish Comm.
Petuchowski, Jacob J., tr. see Petuchowski, Jakob J., ed.
Petuchowski, Jakob J. Prayerbook Reform in Europe: The Liturgy of European Liberal & Reform Judaism. LC 68-8262. (Illus.). 1969. 13.50 (*0-8074-0091-2*, 387580) UAHC.
— The Theology of Haham David Nieto. 1970. 10.00 (*0-87068-015-3*) Ktav.
Petuchowski, Jakob J., ed. New Perspectives on Abraham Geiger: An HUC-JIR Symposium. LC 75-19131. 64p. reprint ed. pap. 25.00 (*0-7837-3000-4*, 2042941) Bks Demand.
— Theology & Poetry: Studies in the Medieval Piyyut. Petuchowski, Jacob J., tr. (Littman Library of Jewish Civilization). 160p. 1978. 15.00 (*0-19-710014-7*, Pub. by Littman Lib Jew UK) Bnai Brith Bk.
— Understanding Jewish Prayer. 1972. pap. 9.95 (*0-87068-186-9*) Ktav.
— When Jews & Christians Meet. LC 87-9981. 160p. 1988. 59.50 (*0-88706-631-3*) State U NY Pr.
Petukhov, B. S., et al, eds. Heat & Mass Transfer: Convective Heat Exchange in a Homogeneous Medium. 280p. 1967. text ed. 65.00 (*0-7065-0476-3*, Pub. by Keter Pub IS) Coronet Bks.
Petukhov, I. M. & Batugina, I. M. Bibliography of Rockbursts 1900-1979, Pt. I. 308p. (C). 1991. text ed. 135.00 (*90-6191-177-X*, Pub. by A A Balkema NE) Ashgate Pub Co.
Petukhov, I. M., jt. auth. see Batugina, I. M.
Petulengro, Gipsy. Romany Remedies & Recipes. 47p. 1971. reprint ed. spiral bd. 4.40 (*0-7873-0669-X*) Mokelumne.
Petulengro, Gipsy & Starkie, Walter F. Romany Herbal Remedies. 1972. reprint ed. pap. 5.95 (*0-87877-016-X*, H-16) Newcastle Pub.
***Petulengro, Leon.** Herbs, Health & Astrology. LC 94-22265. (Illus.). 1994. 9.95 (*0-87983-640-7*) Keats.
Petulla, Joseph. Crisis to Wellness: Meditations for a Philosophy of Living. LC 92-74018. (Illus.). 155p. (Orig.). 1993. pap. 9.95 (*0-9628464-2-2*) Cmnty Resc Inst.
— Environmental Protection in the United States. LC 87-60733. 208p. 1987. 18.50 (*0-936434-21-X*); pap. 14.50 (*0-936434-22-8*) SF Study Ctr.
Petulla, Joseph M. American Environmental History. 2nd ed. 464p. (C). 1988. pap. write for info. (*0-675-20885-8*, Merrill Pub Co) Macmillan.
Petursson, G., ed. Maedi-Visna & Related Diseases. (Developments in Veterinary Virology Ser.). (C). 1989. lib. bdg. 128.00 (*0-7923-0481-0*) Kluwer Ac.
Petush, Edward J. & Sargent, Dennis M. Atlas of the Living Olive Shells of the World. (Illus.). 1986. 68.50 (*0-938415-00-X*) CERF Inc.
Pety, M. Aquiline, ed. see Jean de la Mote.
Petykiewicz, J. Wave Optics. (C). 1992. lib. bdg. 200.00 (*0-7923-0683-X*) Kluwer Ac.
Petyt, K. M. Dialect & Accent in Industrial West Yorkshire. LC 85-20136. (Varieties of English Around the World General Ser.: 6). viii, 401p. 1985. pap. 87.00x (*90-272-4864-8*) Benjamins North Am.
Petyt, M. Introduction to Finite Element Vibration Analysis. (Illus.). (C). 1990. 140.00 (*0-521-26607-6*) Cambridge U Pr.
Petyt, M., et al, eds. Structural Dynamics: Recent Advances - Proc. of the Fourth Internat. Conf., 15-18 July 1991, Southampton, U. K. 886p. 1991. 161.50 (*1-85166-670-2*) Elsevier.
Petyt, Malcolm, ed. The Growth of Reading. (Illus.). 1994. pap. 14.00 (*0-7509-0330-9*) A Sutton Pub.
Petz, Denes, jt. auth. see Ohya, Masanori.
Petz, Lawrence D. & Garratty, George. Acquired Immune Hemolytic Anemias. LC 79-19235. 478p. reprint ed. pap. 136.30 (*0-7837-3156-6*, 2042829) Bks Demand.
Petz, Lawrence D. & Swisher, Scott, eds. Clinical Practice of Transfusion Medicine. 2nd ed. (Illus.). 790p. 1989. text ed. 142.00 (*0-443-08548-X*) Churchill.
Petz, Richard. Cry Insanity. Welburn, John, ed. 85p. 1988. pap. write for info. (*0-318-62237-8*) RAPCOM Enter.
Petz, Richard, ed. see Cannon, Frances A.
Petz, Richard A. The Impressionable Years: A Play on Social Issues, No. 1. Cannon, Frances A., ed. LC 84-62640. (Illus.). 40p. 1985. pap. 7.00 (*0-317-00954-0*); 5.00 (*0-317-00955-9*) RAPCOM Enter.
Petz, Rita K., ed. see Cannon, Frances A.
Petz, Wolfgang. Iron-Carbene Complexes. LC 92-46132. (Scripts in Inorganic & Organometallic Chemistry Ser.: Vol. 1). 1993. 49.00 (*0-387-56258-3*) Spr-Verlag.
Petzel, Florence E. Textiles of Ancient Mesopotamia, Persia, & Egypt. LC 87-90471. 226p. 1987. pap. text ed. 11.00 (*0-9618476-0-3*) F E Petzel.
Petzel, Todd E. Financial Futures & Options: A Guide to Markets, Applications, & Strategies. LC 89-3775. 254p. 1989. text ed. 55.00 (*0-89930-152-5*, PFF, Quorum Bks) Greenwood.
Petzendorfer, L., ed. Treasury of Authentic Art Nouveau: Alphabets, Decorative Initials, Monograms, Frames & Ornaments. (Lettering, Calligraphy, Typography Ser.). 160p. 1984. reprint ed. pap. 6.95 (*0-486-24653-1*) Dover.
Petzer, J. H. & Hartin, P. J. A South African Perspective on the New Testament: Essays by South African New Testament Scholars Presented to Bruce Manning Metzger During His Vist to South Africa in 1985. (Illus.). xii, 274p. 1986. 52.75 (*90-04-07720-0*) E J Brill.
Petzer, J. H., jt. auth. see Hartin, P. J.
Petzet, Erich & Glauning, Otto. Deutsche Schrifttafeln des IX Bis XVI Jahrhunderts Aus Handschriften der Bayerischen Staatsbibliothek Munchen, 5 pts. in 1. 326p. 1975. reprint ed. write for info. (*3-487-05685-2*, Pub. by Georg Olms GW) Lubrecht & Cramer.
Petzet, Heinrich W. Encounters & Dialogues with Martin Heidegger, 1929-1976. Emad, Parvis & Maly, Kenneth, trs. LC 92-30966. (Illus.). 304p. (C). 1993. 34.95 (*0-226-66441-4*) U Ch Pr.
Petzing, Lawrence N., jt. auth. see Stepp, James O.
Petzinger, E., et al, eds. Hepatic Transport of Organic Substances. (Illus.). 420p. 1989. 90.00 (*0-387-50494-X*) Spr-Verlag.
***Petzinger, Thomas, Jr.** Hard Landing: How the Epic Contest for Power & Profits Plunged the Airlines into Chaos. LC 95-13684. (J). 1995. 42.00 (*0-8129-2186-0*, Times Bks) Random.
Petzke, Karl & Slavin, Sara. Espresso: Culture & Cuisine. LC 93-25397. 96p. 1994. 19.95 (*0-8118-0434-8*); pap. 14.95 (*0-8118-0650-2*) Chronicle Bks.
Petzke, Karl, jt. auth. see Slavin, Sara.
***Petzold, Andreas.** Romanesque Art. LC 94-37842. (Perspectives Ser.). 1995. write for info. (*0-8109-2744-6*) Abrams.
Petzold, Armin. Applied Technical Dictionary: Silicate Technology. 268p. (ENG, FRE, GER & SLO.). (C). 1977. 100.00 (*0-569-08557-8*, Pub. by Collets) St Mut.
Petzold, Charles. OS-2 Presentation Manager Programming. 1994. disk 29.95 (*1-56276-123-4*) Ziff-Davis.
— Programming Graphics for Windows. 1992. 49.95 (*1-55615-380-5*) Microsoft.
— Programming Windows. 3rd ed. 1000p. 1992. cd-rom 49.95 (*1-55615-395-3*) Microsoft.
— Programming Windows 95. 1995. pap. 49.95 (*1-55615-676-6*) Microsoft.
Petzoldt, Julius, ed. Anzeiger fur Bibliographie und Bibliothekswissenschaft, 6 vols. Set incl. 28 microfiches. write for info. (*0-318-71730-1*, Pub. by Georg Olms GW) Lubrecht & Cramer.
— Anzeiger fur Bibliothekswissenschaft, 3 vols. reprint ed. Set incl. 17 microfiches. write for info. (*0-318-71729-8*, Pub. by Georg Olms GW) Lubrecht & Cramer.
— Anzeiger fur Literature der Bibliothekswissenschaft, 40 vols. Set incl. 200 microfiches. write for info. (*0-318-71728-X*, Pub. by Georg Olms GW) Lubrecht & Cramer.
— Neuer Anzeiger fur Bibliographie und Bibliothekswissenschaft, 31 vols., Set. reprint ed. fiche write for info. (*0-318-71731-X*, Pub. by Georg Olms GW) Lubrecht & Cramer.
Petzoldt, Paul. The Wilderness Handbook. rev. ed. (Illus.). 1984. pap. 11.95 (*0-393-30171-0*) Norton.
***Petzoldt, Paul K.** Teton Tale Embracing Life with No Regrets. 1995. 14.95 (*1-57034-015-3*) ICS Bks.
Petzow, G., ed. Ternary Alloys, Vol. 4: Al-Cd-Ce to Al-Dy-Zr. (Illus.). 652p. 1991. lib. bdg. 560.00 (*0-89573-894-5*); 495.00 (*0-685-60602-3*) VCH Pubs.
Petzow, G. & Effenberg, G., eds. Ternary Alloys: A Comprehensive Compendium of Evaluated Constitutional Data & Phase Diagrams. 1989. Vol. 1, 612p. write for info. (*0-89573-846-5*); Vol. 2, 624p. write for info. (*0-89573-847-3*) VCH Pubs.
— Ternary Alloys: A Comprehensive Compendium of Evaluated Constitutional Data & Phase Diagrams, Set. 1989. lib. bdg. 560.00 (*0-685-58395-3*); 495.00 (*0-685-58396-1*) VCH Pubs.
— Ternary Alloys: Al-Ca-Ce to Al-Dy-Zr. (Ternary Alloys, a Comprehensive Compendium of Evaluated Constitutional Data & Phase Diagrams Ser.: Vol. 3). (Illus.). 646p. 1990. lib. bdg. 560.00 (*0-89573-893-7*); 495.00 (*0-685-54384-6*) VCH Pubs.
Petzow, G., jt. ed. see Hoffmann, Michael J.
Petzow, G., et al, eds. Ternary Alloys, Vol. 5: Al-Cu-S to Al-Gd-Sn. (Illus.). 695p. 1992. lib. bdg. 560.00 (*0-89573-895-3*); 495.00 (*0-685-60601-5*) VCH Pubs.
Petzow, Gunter. Metallographic Etching: Metallographic & Ceramographic Methods for Revealing Microstructure. LC 78-8023. 143p. reprint ed. 40.80 (*0-685-16440-3*, 2026987) Bks Demand.
Petzow, Gunter, jt. ed. see Schneider, Gerold A.
Peucker, Brigitte. Incorporating Images: Film & the Rival Arts. LC 94-18110. 1994. 49.50 (*0-691-04098-2*); pap. 16.95 (*0-691-00281-9*) Princeton U Pr.
— Lyric Descent in the German Romantic Tradition. LC 86-23393. 242p. reprint ed. pap. 69.00 (*0-7837-4542-7*, 2080317) Bks Demand.
Peuckert, Detley J. Inside Nazi Germany: Conformity, Opposition, & Racism. LC 86-51431. 288p. (C). 1989. reprint ed. pap. 15.00 (*0-300-04480-1*) Yale U Pr.
— Inside Nazi Germany: Conformity, Opposition, & Racism in Everyday Life. Deveson, Richard, tr. 288p. 1987. 35.00 (*0-300-03863-1*) Yale U Pr.
Peukert, Detlev. The Weimar Republic. Deveson, Richard, tr. 352p. 1992. 28.00 (*0-8090-9674-9*) Hill & Wang.
Peukert, Detlev J. Weimar Republic. 1993. pap. 13.00 (*0-8090-1556-0*) Hill & Wang.
Peukert, Helmut. Science, Action, & Fundamental Theology: Toward a Theology of Communicative Action. Bohman, James, tr. (Studies in Contemporary German Social Thought). 360p. 1986. pap. 14.95 (*0-262-66060-1*) MIT Pr.
Peuquet, Marble. Introductory Reading in Geographic. 1990. pap. 39.50 (*0-85066-857-3*) Taylor & Francis.
***Peura, Robin E. & DeBoer, Carolyn J.** Story Maker: Using Predictable Literature to Develop Communication. LC 94-43564. 1995. pap. 33.00 (*0-930599-33-0*) Thinking Pubns.
Peurifoy, Reneau Z. Anxiety, Phobias & Panic: A Step-by-Step Program for Regaining Control of Your Life. 384p. 1995. pap. 10.99 (*0-446-67053-7*) Warner Bks.
— Anxiety, Phobias & Panic: A Step-by-Step Program for Regaining Control of Your Life. 2nd rev. ed. 304p. 1992. pap. 12.95 (*0-929437-13-6*) LifeSkills.
— Anxiety, Phobias, & Panic: Taking Charge & Conquering Fear. (Orig.). 1988. pap. 12.95 (*0-929437-11-X*) LifeSkills.
Peurifoy, Robert L. & Ledbetter, William B. Construction Planning, Equipment & Methods. 4th ed. (Construction Engineering Ser.). 736p. 1985. text ed. write for info. (*0-07-049763-X*) McGraw.
Peurifoy, Robert L. & Oberlender, Gary. Estimating Construction Costs. 4th ed. (Construction Engineering & Project Management Ser.). 512p. 1989. text ed. write for info. (*0-07-049740-0*) McGraw.
***Peurifoy, Robert L., et al.** Construction Planning, Equipment & Methods. LC 95-10819. 1995. write for info. (*0-07-049836-9*) McGraw.
Peusch, Leonard. The Three Crosses. 1978. 1.95 (*0-8199-0723-5*, Frncscn Herld) Franciscan Pr.
Peuser, Gunther. Language Rehabilitation after Stroke: A Linguistic Model (Monograph No. 24) Perecman, Ellen, ed. (International Exchange of Experts & Information in Rehabilitation Ser.). 64p. 1984. pap. 3.00 (*0-939986-37-X*) World Rehab Fund.
Peusner, L. The Principles of Network Thermodynamics. xv, 255p. 1987. 19.95 (*0-938876-21-X*) Entropy Ltd.
— Studies in Network Thermodynamics. (Studies in Modern Thermodynamics: No. 5). 370p. 1986. 133.50 (*0-444-42580-2*) Elsevier.
Peva, James R., et al. Essential Case Law for Policing America. 393p. (Orig.). 1990. pap. 20.00 (*1-878760-00-9*) Graphics Ltd IN.
Pevar, Stephen L. The Rights of Indians & Tribes: The Basic ACLU Guide to Indian & Tribal Rights. 2nd rev. ed. (ACLU Handbook Ser.). 352p. 1992. pap. 7.95 (*0-8093-1768-0*) S Ill U Pr.
Pevear, D. R. & Mumpton, F. A., eds. Quantitative Mineral Analysis of Clays, Vol. 1. (CMS Workshop Lectures). (Illus.). 171p. (Orig.). (C). 1989. pap. text ed. 14.00 (*1-881208-01-X*) Clay Minerals.
Pevear, David, jt. auth. see Eslinger, Eric.
Pevear, David, jt. ed. see Eslinger, Eric.
Pevear, Richard. Exchanges. 1982. 5.00 (*0-686-34453-7*) S Duyvil.
— Night Talk & Other Poems. LC 77-2533. (Contemporary Poets Ser.). 64p. 1977. 21.95 (*0-691-06347-8*); pap. 9.95 (*0-691-01342-X*) Princeton U Pr.
— Night Talk & Other Poems. LC 77-2533. (Princeton Series of Contemporary Poets). 73p. reprint ed. pap. 25.00 (*0-8357-2778-5*, 2039904) Bks Demand.
— Our King Has Horns! LC 86-23525. (Illus.). 32p. (J). (gr. k-3). 1987. lib. bdg. 14.95 (*0-02-773920-1*, Mac Bks Young Read) S&S Childrens.
Pevear, Richard, tr. see Bonnefoy, Yves.
Pevear, Richard, tr. see Dostoyevsky, Fyodor.
Pevear, Richard, tr. see Kharms, Daniil.
Pevear, Richard, tr. see Marshak, Samuel.
Pevear, Richard, tr. see Savinio, Alberto.
Peveling, Elizabeth, ed. Progress & Problems in Lichenology in the Eighties: Proceedings of an International Symposium at the University of Muenster 1986. (Bibliotheca Lichenologica Ser.: Vol. 25). (Illus.). 497p. 1987. pap. 98.00 (*3-443-58004-1*) Lubrecht & Cramer.
Pevensey Heritage Guides Staff. London. (Illus.). 112p. 1994. pap. 9.95 (*0-907115-78-0*, Pub. by D & C Pub UK) Sterling.
Pevensey Pr. Staff. Bath. (C). 1987. text ed. 100.00 (*0-907115-31-4*, Pub. by Pevensey UK); pap. text ed. 40.00 (*0-907115-32-2*, Pub. by Pevensey UK) St Mut.
— Brighton. (C). 1987. pap. text ed. 35.00 (*0-685-44251-9*, Pub. by Pevensey UK) St Mut.
— Bristol. (C). 1987. text ed. 50.00 (*0-907115-35-7*, Pub. by Pevensey UK); pap. text ed. 40.00 (*0-907115-36-5*, Pub. by Pevensey UK) St Mut.
— Cambridge. (C). 1987. text ed. 60.00 (*0-907115-39-X*, Pub. by Pevensey UK); pap. text ed. 40.00 (*0-907115-40-3*, Pub. by Pevensey UK) St Mut.
— Cambridge Gardens. (C). 1987. text ed. 65.00 (*0-907115-20-9*, Pub. by Pevensey UK) St Mut.
— Chester. (C). 1987. text ed. 50.00 (*0-907115-28-4*, Pub. by Pevensey UK); pap. text ed. 40.00 (*0-907115-29-2*, Pub. by Pevensey UK) St Mut.
— The City of London. (C). 1987. text ed. 50.00 (*0-907115-17-9*, Pub. by Pevensey UK); pap. text ed. 40.00 (*0-907115-18-7*, Pub. by Pevensey UK) St Mut.
— The Cotswolds. (C). 1987. text ed. 45.00 (*0-907115-07-1*, Pub. by Pevensey UK); pap. text ed. 35.00 (*0-907115-08-X*, Pub. by Pevensey UK) St Mut.
— Edinburgh. (C). 1987. text ed. 50.00 (*0-907115-23-3*, Pub. by Pevensey UK); pap. text ed. 40.00 (*0-907115-24-1*, Pub. by Pevensey UK) St Mut.
— Historic Cities of England. (C). 1987. text ed. 75.00 (*0-907115-37-3*, Pub. by Pevensey UK) St Mut.
— London Parks & Gardens. (C). 1987. text ed. 60.00 (*0-907115-30-6*, Pub. by Pevensey UK) St Mut.
— Oxford Gardens. (C). 1987. text ed. 60.00 (*0-907115-27-6*, Pub. by Pevensey UK) St Mut.
— Treasures of the Fitzwilliam Museum. (C). 1987. text ed. 50.00 (*0-907115-19-5*, Pub. by Pevensey UK); pap. text ed. 40.00 (*0-907115-16-0*, Pub. by Pevensey UK) St Mut.
— York. (C). 1987. text ed. 55.00 (*0-907115-21-7*, Pub. by Pevensey UK); pap. text ed. 40.00 (*0-907115-22-5*, Pub. by Pevensey UK) St Mut.
— Yorkshire Moors & Dales. (C). 1987. text ed. 60.00 (*0-907115-33-0*, Pub. by Pevensey UK); pap. text ed. 40.00 (*0-907115-34-9*, Pub. by Pevensey UK) St Mut.
Peverett, E. J. Fire Insurance Law & Claims. (C). 1982. 190.00 (*0-685-32817-1*, Pub. by Witherby & Co UK) St Mut.
Peverill, Jan. Jan Peverill's Inn Places for Bed & Breakfast. 3rd enl. ed. (Illus.). 166p. (Orig.). 1992. pap. 10.95 (*0-9621525-2-8*) Intros Unltd.
— Jan Peverill's Inn Places for Bed & Breakfast, Vol. 2. 2nd ed. (Illus.). 148p. (Orig.). 1990. pap. text ed. 9.95 (*0-9621525-1-X*) Intros Unltd.
— Jan Peverill's Inn Places for Bed & Breakfast in the West. (Illus.). 82p. (Orig.). 1988. pap. 7.95 (*0-9621525-0-1*) Intros Unltd.
Peverill, Sue. Fabric Decorator, Vol. 1. 1990. 29.95 (*0-316-70390-7*) Little.
***Peverley, B. J.** Blackwood. braille ed. 263p. 1991. text ed., vinyl bd. 21.04 (*1-56956-533-3*, BR9433) W A T Braille.
Pevet, Paul, jt. ed. see Ariens-Kappers, J.
Pevet, Paul, jt. auth. see Oksche.
***Pevovar, Eddy H.** Nutrition, the Environment & the Food Chain: Who's Kidding Who...? Gail, Francine, ed. (Therapeutic Nutrition Ser.: Vol. 1). (Illus.). 600p. (Orig.). 1995. pap. text ed. 29.95 (*0-9645077-0-6*) Nutr Res Proj.
Pevsner, Aihud, jt. auth. see Kim, Chung W.
Pevsner, Nikolaus. Academies of Art, Past & Present. LC 78-87379. (Illus.). 332p. 1973. reprint ed. lib. bdg. 49.50 (*0-306-71603-8*) Da Capo.
— A History of Building Types. LC 75-4459. (Bollingen Ser.: No. 35). (Illus.). 1976. 89.50 (*0-691-09904-9*); pap. 29.95 (*0-691-01829-4*) Princeton U Pr.
— Lexikon der Weltarchitektur. 3rd rev. ed. 876p. (GER.). 1992. pap. 295.00 (*0-8288-1195-4*, M7216) Fr & Eur.
— Outline of European Architecture. (Illus.). (Orig.). 1950. pap. 14.95 (*0-14-020109-2*, Penguin Bks) Viking Penguin.
— Pioneers of Modern Design. 1986. pap. 10.95 (*0-14-055211-1*, Penguin Bks) Viking Penguin.
— Sources of Modern Architecture & Design. (World of Art Ser.). (Illus.). 216p. 1985. pap. 14.95 (*0-500-20072-6*) Thames Hudson.
— Studies in Art, Architecture & Design: Victorian & After. LC 81-48077. (Illus.). 288p. (Orig.). (C). 1982. reprint ed. pap. 22.95x (*0-691-00345-9*) Princeton U Pr.
Pevsner, Nikolaus, jt. ed. see Richards, J. M.
Pevsner, Nilkolaus. Diccionario de Arquitectura. 2nd ed. 656p. (SPA.). 1984. 85.00 (*0-7859-5727-8*, 8420652180) Fr & Eur.
Pevsner, Stella. And You Give Me a Pain, Elaine. (J). (gr. 7-9). 1989. pap. 2.99 (*0-671-68838-3*, Archway) PB.
— Cute Is a Four-Letter Word. 176p. (J). (gr. 7 up). 1989. pap. 2.75 (*0-671-68845-6*, Archway) PB.

— I'm Emma, I'm a Quint. LC 92-36952. (J). 1993. 13.95 (*0-395-64166-7*, Clarion Bks) HM.
— Jon, Flora, & the Odd-Eyed Cat. LC 93-41218. (J). 1994. 13.95 (*0-395-67021-7*, Hills Med) HM.
— Me, My Goat & My Sister's Wedding. (J). (gr. 4-7). 1987. pap. 2.75 (*0-671-66206-6*, Minstrel Bks) PB.
— The Night the Whole Class Slept Over. 176p. (J). (gr. 4-9). 1991. 14.95 (*0-89919-983-6*, Clarion Bks) HM.
— The Night the Whole Class Slept Over. McDonald, Patricia, ed. 176p. (J). (gr. 3-6). 1992. reprint ed. pap. 3.50 (*0-671-78157-X*, Minstrel Bks) PB.
Pew, David & Matthews, Jay. Budgeting for Newspapers. rev. ed. (Illus.). 55p. 1989. pap. 49.95 (*1-877888-11-7*) Intl Newspaper.
Pew, John. Guide to Solaris. 1993. pap. 34.95 (*1-56276-087-4*) Ziff-Davis.
Pew, John A., jt. auth. see Young, Douglas A.
Pew, L. Glen, ed. see Alexander, Guy B.
Pew, Stephen, jt. auth. see Kline, Kris.
Pew, William. Second Chance at Life. 1993. pap. 4.99 (*1-56399-013-X*) NewLife Pubns.
Pewe, ed. Quaternary Geology & Permafrost along the Richardson & Glenn Highways Between Fairbanks & Anchorage, Alaska. (IGC Field Trip Guidebooks Ser.). 64p. 1989. 21.00 (*0-87590-603-6*, T102) Am Geophysical.
Pewe, Troy L., ed. Desert Dust: Origin, Characteristics, & Effects on Man. (Special Paper Ser.: No. 186). (Illus.). 1982. pap. 5.00 (*0-8137-2186-5*) Geol Soc.
***Pewe, Troy L., et al.** Origin & Character of Loesslike Silt in the Southern Qinghai-Xizang (Tibet) Plateau, China. 1995. write for info. (*0-615-00035-5*) USGPO.
Pewitt, Jana L. & Bourne, A. Scott. The User-Friendly Computer Dictionary: An Illustrated Guide to 2,000 Hi-Tech Words & Phrases. (Illus.). 320p. (Orig.). 1991. pap. 12.95 (*0-9628538-0-1*) ThunderEgg Pub.
Pewsey, Lynn. A Taste of Essex: Food & Recipes of Essex Through the Ages. LC 93-40448. 1994. 15.00 (*0-88734-902-1*) Players Pr.
Pewsey, Stephen & Brooks, Andrew. East Saxon Heritage: An Essex Gazetteer. LC 93-19606. 1993. 20.00 (*0-7509-0290-6*) A Sutton Pub.
Pexieder, Tomas, ed. Mechanisms of Cardiac Morphogenesis & Teratogenesis. (Perspectives in Cardiovascular Research Ser.: Vol. 5). (Illus.). 528p. 1981. text ed. 146. 50 (*0-89004-460-0*) Raven.
Pexton, Pat. Three Ingredient Cookbook. (Illus.). 76p. 1982. spiral bd. write for info. (*0-9624039-1-1*) DeBry-Pexton.
Pexton, Patricia D. Extravagance of Sentiment. Mead, Irene K., tr. (Illus.). 128p. (Orig.). 1989. pap. 8.00 (*0-685-29174-X*) DeBry-Pexton.
Peyer, Bernd, ed. The Singing Spirit: Early Short Stories by North American Indians. LC 89-32419. (Sun Tracks Ser.). 175p. 1991. reprint ed. pap. 9.95 (*0-8165-1220-5*) U of Ariz Pr.
Peyer, Tom, ed. see Gaiman, Neil.
Peyer, Tom, jt. ed. see Seely, Hart.
Peygambarian, Nassar, et al. Introduction to Semiconductor Optics. 1993. text ed. write for info. (*0-13-638990-2*) P-H.
Peyghambarian, ed. Optical Computing & Nonlinear Materials. 1988. 51.00 (*0-89252-916-4*, 881) SPIE.
Peyhambarian, N., ed. Nonlinear Optical Materials & Devices for Photonic Switching. 1990. 62.00 (*0-8194-0257-5*, VOL. 1216) SPIE.
***Peyman.** Vitreous Substitutes. (C). 1995. text ed. 85.00 (*0-86859-484-9*) Appleton & Lange.
Peyman, Gholam A. & Schulman, Joel A. Intravitreal Surgery. 2nd ed. (Illus.). 1040p. 1994. text ed. 240.00 (*0-8385-4320-0*, A4320-6) Appleton & Lange.
— Vitreous Substitutes. LC 94-39562. 1995. text ed. 85.00 (*0-8385-9484-0*) Appleton & Lange.
Peynado, Celia, tr. see Schubert, Linda.
Peynaud, Emile. Knowing & Making Wine. Spencer, Alan F., tr. LC 84-11936. 391p. 1984. text ed. 59.95 (*0-471-88149-X*, Wiley-Interscience) Wiley.
Peyrard, M., jt. ed. see Remoissenet, M.
Peyrat, Paul & Compton, Linda, eds. California Civil Procedure Before Trial, 3 vols., Set. 3rd rev. ed. LC 90-81348. 2553p. 1990. reprint ed. ring bd. 195.00 (*0-88124-271-3*, CP-31540) Cont Ed Bar-CA.
Peyraud, J., jt. ed. see DeWitt, C.
Peyre, Henri. Historical & Critical Essays. LC 68-12702. 307p. reprint ed. pap. 87.50 (*0-7837-6176-7*, 2045898) Bks Demand.
— Marcel Proust. LC 71-110602. (Columbia Essays on Modern Writers Ser.: No. 48). (Orig.). 1970. pap. text ed. 7.50 (*0-231-03406-7*) Col U Pr.
Peyre, Henri M., ed. Essays in Honor of Albert Feuillerat. LC 75-99633. (Essay Index Reprint Ser.). 1977. 23.95 (*0-8369-1650-6*) Ayer.
Peyrefitte, Alain. The Immobile Empire: The First Great Collision of East & West - The Astonishing History of Britains. Rothschild, Jon, tr. LC 92-329. (Illus.). 624p. 1992. 29.50 (*0-394-58654-9*) Knopf.
***Peyrefitte, Roger.** Hommage a Arno Breker. deluxe ed. (Illus.). 1990. 600.00 (*0-914301-30-6*, Pub. by Marco GW) West-Art.
Peyret, R & Taylor, T. D. Computational Methods for Fluid Flow. (Computational Physics Ser.). (Illus.). x, 358p. 1990. pap. 49.00 (*0-387-13851-X*) Spr-Verlag.
Peyret, Raymond. Marthe Robin: The Cross & the Joy. Faulhaber, Clare W., tr. LC 83-15591. (Illus.). 135p. 1983. pap. 6.95 (*0-8189-0464-X*) Alba.
Peyrous, Pierre. Diccionario de Terminologia Militar Espanol-Frances, 2 vols., Set. 1989. pap. 49.95 (*0-7859-6317-0*, 8478230394) Fr & Eur.
— Diccionario de Terminologia Militar Espanol-Frances, Vol. 1. 2nd ed. 658p. 1991. pap. 29.95 (*0-7859-6318-9*, 8478230408) Fr & Eur.
— Diccionario de Terminologia Militar Espanol-Frances, Vol. 2. 2nd ed. 631p. 1991. pap. 29.95 (*0-7859-6319-7*, 8478230416) Fr & Eur.
— Diccionario de Terminologia Militar Frances-Espanol. 368p. 1976. pap. 49.95 (*0-7859-6044-9*, 8450075289) Fr & Eur.
Peysakhovich, Vladimir. Economics of Automation in the Soviet Machine-Building Industry. Michta, Andrew, ed. (Illus.). (Orig.). 1987. pap. text ed. 75.00 (*1-55831-054-1*) Delphic Associates.
Peyser, Arnold. The Squirrelcage. LC 84-73517. 256p. 1985. 15.95 (*0-917657-29-2*) D I Fine.
Peyser, Herbert, jt. ed. see Gitlow, Stanley E.
Peyser, Herbert F., jt. auth. see Biancolli, Louis L.
***Peyser, James A., ed. & intro.** Agenda for Leadership. (Pioneer Papers). 100p. (Orig.). 1994. pap. 10.00 (*0-929930-12-6*) Pioneer Inst.
Peyser, Joan. The Memory of All That: The Life of George Gershwin. LC 92-44272. (Illus.). 320p. 1993. 25.00 (*0-671-70948-8*) S&S Trade.
— The Music of My Time. (Illus.). 496p. 1995. 35.00 (*0-912483-99-7*) Pro-Am Music.
Peyser, Joseph L., ed. & tr. Letters from New France: The Upper Country, 1686-1783. (Illus.). 264p. 1992. 34.95 (*0-252-01853-2*) U of Ill Pr.
Peyser, Joseph L., jt. auth. see Edmunds, R. David.
Peyster, Robert G. Computed Tomography of the Brain & Spine: An Atlas. 1990. 85.00 (*0-8151-6676-1*, Yr Bk Med Pubs) Mosby Yr Bk.
Peyster, Robert G. & Hoover, Eric D. Computerized Tomography in Orbital Disease & Neurophthalmology. LC 83-12416. (Illus.). 318p. reprint ed. pap. 90.70 (*0-8357-6314-5*, 2035587) Bks Demand.
Peyton, A. J. & Walsh, Y. Analog Electronics with Op Amps: A Source Book of Practical Circuits. LC 92-22691. (Illus.). 300p. (C). 1993. 94.95 (*0-521-33305-9*); pap. 37.95 (*0-521-33604-X*) Cambridge U Pr.
Peyton, David, jt. auth. see Bowen, Charles.
***Peyton, Dennis J.** How to Buy Real Estate in Mexico: A Simple Guide to Buying Property in Mexico. (Law Mexico Ser.). 440p. (Orig.). 1995. pap. 19.95 (*1-885328-25-7*) Law Mexico.
Peyton, J. Lewis. History of Augusta County, Virginia. 418p. 1986. 35.00 (*0-917890-73-6*) Heritage Bk.
Peyton, James W. La Cocina de la Frontera: Mexican-American Cooking from the Southwest. (Illus.). 352p. 1994. pap. 22.50 (*1-878610-34-1*) Red Crane Bks.
— El Norte: The Cuisine of Northern Mexico. rev. ed. (Illus.). (Orig.). 1995. 24.95 (*1-878610-58-9*) Red Crane Bks.
Peyton, Jeffrey L. Puppetools: Introductory Guide. LC 85-19176. Orig. Title: Puppetry: A Tool for Teaching Puppetry & Creative Learning Techniques. (Illus.). 200p. 1986. pap. text ed. 39.00 (*0-9609506-1-3*) Prescott Durrell & Co.
Peyton, Jim. Zions Cause. 232p. 1987. 14.95 (*0-912697-54-7*) Algonquin Bks.
Peyton, John, jt. auth. see Arnold, Ken.
Peyton, John D. The Leadership Way: Management for the Nineties. 254p. 1991. 24.95 (*0-9628901-5-4*) Davidson Manors.
Peyton, John L. Adventures of My Grandfather. LC 65-27156. 270p. 1972. reprint ed. 18.95 (*0-405-03680-9*) Ayer.
— The Birch: Bright Tree of Life & Legend. LC 94-8264. (Illus.). 74p. (Orig.). 1994. 9.95 (*0-939923-42-4*) M & W Pub Co.
— Bright Beat the Water: Memories of a Wilderness Artist. (Illus.). 250p. (Orig.). 1993. pap. 14.95 (*0-939923-30-0*) M & W Pub Co.
— Faces in the Firelight. (Illus.). viii, 268p. 1992. pap. 14.95 (*0-939923-19-X*) M & W Pub Co.
— The Stone Canoe & Other Stories. LC 89-2294. (Illus.). 175p. (Orig.). 1989. 24.95 (*0-939923-06-8*); pap. 14.95 (*0-939923-07-6*) M & W Pub Co.
— Voices from the Ice. (Illus.). 56p. (J). (gr. k-4). 1990. pap. 7.95 (*0-939923-15-7*) M & W Pub Co.
Peyton-Jones, Simon L. & Lester, David. Implementing Functional Languages. 280p. 1992. pap. text ed. 42.00 (*0-13-721952-0*) P-H.
Peyton, Joy K., ed. Students & Teachers Writing Together: Perspectives on Journal Writing. LC 89-51728. 154p. (Orig.). 1990. pap. 11.95 (*0-939791-36-6*) Tchrs Eng Spkrs.
Peyton, Joy K. & Reed, Leslie. Dialogue Journal Writing with Nonnative English Speakers: A Handbook for Teachers. LC 89-51727. 1990. pap. 9.95 (*0-939791-37-4*) Tchrs Eng Spkrs.
Peyton, Joy K. & Staton, Jana. Dialogue Journal Writing with Nonnative English Speakers: An Instructional Packet for Teachers & Workshop Leaders. 152p. 1992. pap. 19.95 (*0-939791-39-0*) Tchrs Eng Spkrs.
— Dialogue Journals in the Multilingual Classroom: Building Language Fluency & Writing Skills Through Written Interaction. Farr, Marcia, ed. LC 92-10058. (Writing Research Ser.). 320p. (C). 1992. text ed. 49.95 (*0-89391-660-9*); pap. text ed. 24.95 (*0-89391-661-7*) Ablex Pub.
Peyton, Joy K., ed. see Rigg, Pat, et al.
Peyton, K. M. The Edge of the Cloud. (YA). (gr. 7 up). 1992. 16.50 (*0-8446-6566-5*) Peter Smith.
Peyton, Leslie. Perfect Health. LC 83-90447. (Illus.). 160p. (Orig.). 1983. pap. 12.95 (*0-317-03499-5*) Getal.
Peyton, Mike. On Passage. (Illus.). 96p. 1991. 16.95 (*0-906754-66-6*) Sheridan.
— Ready About. 96p. (C). 1990. text ed. 59.00 (*0-906754-95-X*, Pub. by Fernhurst Bks UK) St Mut.
Peyton, Patrick. Fr. Peyton's Rosary Prayer Book. 240p. 1991. pap. 7.95 (*1-85390-143-1*, Pub. by Veritas Publns IE) Ignatius Pr.
Peyton, R., sel. At the Track: A Treasury of Racing Stories. 368p. 1991. 3.99 (*0-517-64281-6*) Random Hse Value.
Peyton, Richard. Journey into Fear & Other Great Stories of Horror on the Railways. 1991. 8.99 (*0-517-06007-8*) Random Hse Value.
Peyton, Robert X. & Rubio, Toni C. Construction Safety Practices & Principles. 240p. 1991. text ed. 49.95 (*0-442-23742-1*) Van Nos Reinhold.
Peyton, W. D. Old Oman. 1983. 24.95 (*0-86685-530-0*) Intl Bk Ctr.
Peyton, Wes. San Jose: A Personal View. Muller, Kathleen, ed. (Illus.). 100p. 1989. write for info. (*0-914139-08-8*) San Jose His Mus Assn.
Pezdek, Kathy, jt. auth. see Danks, Joseph H.
Peze, Jacques, jt. auth. see De Coppens, Pierre R.
Pezet, Jean L. Guide to the ECU. 120p. 1993. 24.00 (*1-85573-112-6*, Pub. by Woodhead Pubng UK) St Mut.
Pezinska, Z. & Topulos, A. Polish-English-Russian Data Processing Dictionary. 119p. (ENG, POL & RUS.). 1981. pap. 24.95 (*0-8288-0274-2*, M 9489) Fr & Eur.
Pezzey, John. Sustainable Development Concepts: An Economic Analysis. LC 92-35724. (Environment Paper Ser.: No. 2). 90p. 1992. 7.95 (*0-8213-2278-8*, 12278) World Bank.
Pezzini, Wilma. Italy, 1985. Fisher, Robert C., ed. (Fisher Annotated Travel Guides Ser.). 352p. 1984. 12.95 (*0-8116-0065-3*) NAL-Dutton.
Pezzoli, F. & Mora, E. Farm Animals. (Illus.). 30p. (J). (ps-1). 1986. 3.95 (*0-8120-5723-6*) Barron.
Pezzullo, Lawrence & Pezzullo, Ralph. At the Fall of Somoza. LC 93-1006. (Latin American Ser.). (Illus.). 328p. (C). 1993. text ed. 34.95 (*0-8229-3756-5*) U of Pittsburgh Pr.
Pezzullo, Mary A. Marketing for Bankers. 2nd ed. (Illus.). 564p. (C). 1988. text ed. 45.00 (*0-89982-354-8*) Am Bankers.
— Marketing for Bankers. 4th ed. (Illus.). 570p. (C). 1993. pap. text ed. 45.00 (*0-89982-317-3*) Am Bankers.
Pezzullo, Ralph, jt. auth. see Pezzullo, Lawrence.
Pezzullo, Thomas R., jt. auth. see Brittingham, Barbara E.
Pezzulo, Ted. April Fish, & the Wooing of Lady Sunday: Two Short Plays. 1975. pap. 4.75 (*0-8222-0062-7*) Dramatists Play.
Pezzuti, Ella, ed. see Stewart, Jeffrey R., Jr., et al.
Pezzuto, John M., et al, eds. Biotechnology & Pharmacy. LC 92-49685. 1993. write for info. (*0-412-03861-7*); pap. write for info. (*0-412-03871-4*) Chapman & Hall.
Pfadt, Robert E. Fundamentals of Applied Entomology. 4th ed. 742p. (C). 1985. text ed. write for info. (*0-02-395490-6*) Macmillan.
Pfaelzer, Jean. The Utopian Novel in America, Eighteen Eighty-Six to Eighteen Ninety-Six: The Politics of Form. LC 84-40094. (Critical Essays in Modern Literature Ser.). 223p. 1984. 49.95 (*0-8229-3811-1*) U of Pittsburgh Pr.
— The Utopian Novel in America, 1886-1896: The Politics of Form. LC 84-40094. 223p. (C). 1989. reprint ed. pap. 14.95 (*0-8229-5413-3*) U of Pittsburgh Pr.
***Pfaelzer, Jean, ed.** A Rebecca Harding Davis Reader: "Life in the Iron Mills," Selected Fiction, & Essays. 640p. (C). 1995. pap. 24.95 (*0-8229-5581-4*) U of Pittsburgh Pr.
***Pfaelzer, Jean, ed. & intro.** A Rebecca Harding Davis Reader: "Life in the Iron-Mills," Selected Fiction, & Essays. LC 95-3296. 1995. write for info. (*0-8229-3887-1*) U of Pittsburgh Pr.
Pfaff, Carol W., ed. First & Second Language Acquisition Processes. 288p. 1986. pap. 24.95 (*0-8384-2688-3*, Newbury) Heinle & Heinle.
Pfaff, D. W. Estrogens & Brain Function: Neural Analysis of a Hormone-Controlled Mammalian Reproductive Behavior. (Illus.). 272p. 1980. 65.00 (*0-387-90487-5*) Spr-Verlag.
Pfaff, D. W., ed. Ethical Questions in Brain & Behavior. (Illus.). 190p. 1983. 55.00 (*0-387-90870-6*) Spr-Verlag.
Pfaff, D. W., jt. ed. see Ganten, D.
***Pfaff, Dani B.** Broadsides: Indiana, the Early Years Resource Guide. 424p. Date not set. pap. 6.25 (*1-885323-50-6*) IN Hist Bureau.
Pfaff, Daniel W. Joseph Pulitzer The Second & the Post-Dispatch: A Newspaperman's Life. (Illus.). 448p. 1991. 35.00 (*0-271-00748-6*) Pa St U Pr.
Pfaff, Dieter, jt. auth. see Ordelheide, Dieter.
Pfaff, Donald, ed. Taste, Olfaction & the Central Nervous System: A Festschrift in Honor of Carl Pfaffmann. LC 84-43054. 346p. 1985. 29.95 (*0-87470-039-6*) Rockefeller.
Pfaff, Donn, ed. see Cady, Dale.
Pfaff, Elmer F. Rediscovering Mantua (Portage County, Ohio) (Illus.). 212p. (Orig.). 1985. pap. 10.00 (*0-9615749-0-9*) Mage In Nation.
Pfaff, Eugene E., Jr. & Causey, Michael. Uwharrie. 256p. 1993. 19.95 (*0-936389-30-3*) Tudor Pubs.
Pfaff, Eugene E., Jr. & Emerson, Mark. Meryl Streep: A Critical Biography. LC 87-42516. 158p. 1987. lib. bdg. 27.50x (*0-89950-287-3*) McFarland & Co.
Pfaff, Francoise. The Cinema of Ousmane Sembene: A Pioneer of African Film. LC 84-3842. (Contributions in Afro-American & African Studies: No. 79). (Illus.). xx, 207p. 1984. text ed. 49.95 (*0-313-24400-6*, PCI/, Greenwood Pr) Greenwood.
— Twenty-Five Black African Filmmakers: A Critical Study, with Fimography & Bio-Bibliography. LC 87-15024. 352p. 1988. text ed. 52.95 (*0-313-24695-5*, PBA/, Greenwood Pr) Greenwood.
Pfaff, Henry J. Didactic Verses of an Old-Time Wobbly. 62p. 1983. pap. 3.95 (*0-88286-106-9*) C H Kerr.
Pfaff, Kevin. The Lazarus Man. 90p. (Orig.). 1991. pap. 10. 32 (*0-685-48264-2*) Dayspring Pr.
— Play It Again, Johann Sebastian. 67p. (Orig.). 1991. pap. 7.64 (*0-685-48265-0*) Dayspring Pr.
***Pfaff, Linda.** I Hope They Call Me on a Mission. 24p. (J). 1995. pap. 4.98 (*0-88290-524-4*, 1344) Horizon Utah.
Pfaff, Lucie. The American & German Entrepreneur: Economic & Literary Interplay. (American University Studies: Economics: Ser. XVI, Vol. 4). 183p. (C). 1989. text ed. 32.50 (*0-8204-0807-7*) P Lang Pubs.
Pfaff, Phillip. Financial Modeling. 450p. 1989. write for info. (*0-318-63901-7*, H19847); disk, pap. text ed. 42.00 (*0-205-11983-2*) Allyn.
Pfaff, Richard W. Medieval Latin Liturgy: A Select Bibliography. LC 82-178542. (Toronto Medieval Bibliographies Ser.: No. 9). 151p. reprint ed. pap. 43.10 (*0-685-23593-9*, 2026496) Bks Demand.
***Pfaff, Tim.** Hmong in America: Journey from a Secret War. McLeod, Susan, ed. (Illus.). 100p. (Orig.). 1995. pap. 12. 95 (*0-9636191-3-6*) Chippewa Val Mus.
— Paths of the People: The Ojibwe in the Chippewa Valley. (Illus.). 100p. (Orig.). 1993. pap. text ed. 12.95 (*0-9636191-0-1*) Chippewa Val Mus.
— Settlement & Survival: Building Towns in the Chippewa Valley, 1850-1925. McLeod, Susan, ed. (Illus.). 120p. (Orig.). 1994. pap. 12.95 (*0-9636191-1-X*) Chippewa Val Mus.
Pfaff, William. Barbarian Sentiments: Nationalism & Ideology in the Modern Age. 1989. 19.95 (*0-8090-6665-3*) Hill & Wang.
— Wrath of Nations. 1994. pap. 12.00 (*0-671-89248-7*, Touchstone Bks) S&S Trade.
— Wrath of Nations: Civilization & the Fury of Nationalism. 256p. 1993. 22.00 (*0-671-72829-6*) S&S Trade.
Pfaff, William, jt. auth. see Stillman, Edmund O.
***Pfaffenberger.** Adjustment Processes in Russian Defence Enterprises Within the Framework of Conversion & Transition. Opitz, ed. (Studies on Conversion Research). (C). 1995. pap. text ed. 93.00 (*3-8258-2028-9*) Westview.
— Essentials of dBASE VI with Advanced Applications. (C). 1992. text ed. 6.00 (*0-06-501138-4*) HarpCollege.
— Essentials of DOS. (C). 1992. text ed. 8.50 (*0-06-501135-X*) HarpCollege.
— Essentials of Lotus 1-2-3 with Advanced Applications. (C). 1992. text ed. 9.50 (*0-06-501137-6*) HarpCollege.
— Essentials of Microcomputer Systems. (C). 1992. text ed. 8.50 (*0-06-501134-1*) HarpCollege.
— Essentials of WordPerfect with Advanced Applications. (C). 1992. text ed. 8.50 (*0-06-501136-8*) HarpCollege.
— Microcomputers: Concepts & Applications. (C). 1992. text ed. 45.00 (*0-673-38595-7*) HarpCollege.
Pfaffenberger, Brian, jt. ed. see Manogaran, Chelvadurai.
Pfaffenberger, Bryan. Caste in Tamil Culture: The Religious Foundations of Sudra Domination in Tamil Sri Lanka. LC 82-7321. (Foreign & Comparative Studies Program, South Asian Ser.: No. 7). (Illus.). (Orig.). (C). 1982. pap. 12.00 (*0-915984-84-9*) Syracuse U Foreign Comp.
— Computerizing Your Small Business. 350p. 1991. 19.95 (*0-88022-691-9*) Que.
— Democratizing Information: Online Databases & the Rise of End-User Searching. (Professional Librarian Ser.). 175p. 1989. text ed. 32.50 (*0-8161-1860-4*, Hall Reference); pap. 24.50 (*0-8161-1872-8*, Hall Reference) Macmillan.
— The Elements of Hypertext Style. (Illus.). 140p. 1995. pap. write for info. (*0-12-553142-7*) Acad Pr.
— FoxPro for Windows Solutions. 512p. 1993. pap. text ed. 24.95 (*0-471-59047-9*) Wiley.
— Freelance Graphics for Windows Two Made Easy. 1992. pap. text ed. 29.95 (*0-07-881899-0*) Osborne-McGraw.
— I Hate DOS: A Friendly Guide to DOS. 1993. pap. 16.95 (*1-56529-215-4*) Que.
— I Hate PCs. 2nd ed. (Illus.). 384p. 1994. pap. 16.99 (*1-56529-827-6*) Que.
— I Hate Word for Windows: A Friendly Guide for the Frustrated User. (I Hate! Ser.). (Illus.). 350p. (Orig.). 1993. pap. 16.95 (*1-56529-256-1*) Que.
— I Hate Word Six for Windows, but This Book Made It Easy! The Friendly Guide to Word 6 for Windows. LC 92-86419. 1993. pap. 16.95 (*1-56529-616-8*) Que.
— Internet in Plain English. LC 94-30578. 1994. pap. 19.95 (*1-55828-385-4*) MIS Press.
— Microcomputer Applications in Qualitative Research. (Qualitative Research Methods Ser.: Vol. 14). 96p. (C). 1988. text ed. 21.50 (*0-8039-3119-0*); pap. text ed. 9.50 (*0-8039-3120-4*) Sage.
— Mosaic User's Guide. 1994. disk, pap. 24.95 (*1-55828-409-5*) MIS Press.
— Netscape Navigator (Windows) Surfing the Wev & Exploring the Internet. (Illus.). 220p. 1995. pap. write for info. (*0-12-553132-X*) Acad Pr.
— Netscape Navigator, Macintosh Version: Surfing the Web & Exploring the Internet. (Illus.). 300p. 1995. pap. write for info. (*0-12-553130-3*) Acad Pr.
— PC Tools 7 Made Easy, Second Edition. 2nd ed. 1992. pap. text ed. 19.95 (*0-07-881744-7*) Osborne-McGraw.
— PCs in Plain English. 350p. 1995. pap. 19.95 (*1-55828-384-6*) MIS Press.
— Que's Computer User's Dictionary. 3rd ed. (Illus.). (Orig.). 1992. pap. 12.95 (*1-56529-023-2*) Que.
— Timeslips III Made Easy. 1991. pap. text ed. 19.95 (*0-07-881739-0*) Osborne-McGraw.
— The Usenet Book: Finding, Using, & Surviving Newsgroups on the Internet. LC 94-38690. 468p. 1995. pap. 26.95 (*0-201-40978-X*) Addison-Wesley.
— Using PageMaker 5 for the Mac. LC 93-83293. (Illus.). 1126p. (Orig.). 1993. pap. 34.95 (*1-56529-001-1*) Que.
— Using Word 5.1 for the MAC. LC 92-63327. (Illus.). 1066p. 1993. pap. 29.95 (*1-56529-143-3*) Que.
— Using Word 6 for DOS. (Illus.). 800p. (Orig.). 1993. pap. 29.95 (*1-56529-078-X*) Que.
— World Wide Web Bible. 450p. 1995. disk, pap. text ed. 27.95 (*1-55828-410-9*) MIS Press.

An Asterisk (*) at the beginning of an entry indicates that the title is appearing in BIP for the first time.

Pfaffenberger, Bryan, ed. Que's Computer Users Dictionary. 5th ed. 1994. pap. 12.99 (1-56529-881-0) Que.

Pfaffenberger, Clarence J. New Knowledge of Dog Behavior. LC 63-13674. (Illus.). 208p. 1963. 21.95 (0-87605-704-0) Howell Bk.

Pfaffenberger, Roger. Introductory Operations Research. 169p. (C). 1993. student ed 13.60 (1-56870-052-0) RonJon Pub.

Pfaffenberger, Roger C. & Patterson, James H. Statistical Methods: For Business & Economics. 3rd ed. (C). 1987. text ed. 60.95 (0-256-03664-0) Irwin.

Pfaffenberger, W. E., jt. auth. see Johnsonbaugh, Richard.

Pfaffenbichler, Matthias. Armourers. (Medieval Craftsmen Ser.). (Illus.). 72p. (Orig.). 1992. pap. 18.95 (0-8020-7732-3) U of Toronto Pr.

Pfaffenrath, V., jt. ed. see Lance, J.

Pfaffle, A. E. & Nicosia, Sal. Risk Analysis Guide to Insurance & Employee Benefits. LC 77-10973. 71p. reprint ed. pap. 25.00 (0-317-26314-5, 2055752) Bks Demand.

Pfafflin, James R. & Ziegler, E. N., eds. Encyclopedia of Environmental Science & Engineering, Vol. 1. 2nd ed. xxiv, 404p. 1983. 310.00 (0-677-06400-4) Gordon & Breach.

— Encyclopedia of Environmental Science & Engineering, Vol. 2. 2nd ed. xxiv, 408p. 1983. 398.00 (0-677-06410-1) Gordon & Breach.

— Encyclopedia of Environmental Science & Engineering, Vol. 3. 2nd ed. xxiv, 342p. 1983. 270.00 (0-677-06420-9) Gordon & Breach.

Pfafflin, James R. & Ziegler, Edward N. Advances in Environmental Science & Engineering, Vol. 1. 292p. 1979. text ed. 207.00 (0-677-16070-4) Gordon & Breach.

— Advances in Environmental Science & Engineering, Vol. 2. 228p. 1979. text ed. 207.00 (0-677-14810-0) Gordon & Breach.

— Advances in Environmental Science & Engineering, Vol. 3. 240p. 1980. text ed. 239.00 (0-677-15760-6) Gordon & Breach.

Pfafflin, James R. & Ziegler, Edward N., eds. Advances in Environmental Science & Engineering, Vol. 4. 188p. 1981. text ed. 215.00 (0-677-16250-2) Gordon & Breach.

— Advances in Environmental Science & Engineering, Vol. 5. 220p. 1986. text ed. 206.00 (2-88124-184-0) Gordon & Breach.

— Encyclopedia of Environmental Science & Engineering, 3 Vols., Set. 1350p. 1983. 798.00 (0-677-06430-6) Gordon & Breach.

Pfafflin, Sheila M., jt. ed. see Briscoe, Anne.

Pfafflin, Sheila M., jt. ed. see Sechzer, Jeri A.

Pfahl, John. A Distanced Land: The Photographs of John Pfahl. LC 89-70882. (Illus.). 220p. 1990. 45.00 (0-8263-1214-4); pap. 25.00 (0-8263-1215-2) U of NM Pr.

Pfahl, John K., jt. auth. see Crary, David T.

Pfahl, P. Blair, Jr., jt. auth. see Pfahl, Peter B.

Pfahl, Peter & Kalin, Elwood. American-Style Flower Arranging. (Illus.). 256p. (C). 1981. text ed. 71.00 (0-13-029538-8) P-H.

Pfahl, Peter B. & Pfahl, P. Blair, Jr. The Retail Florist Business. 5th ed. 400p. 1994. 45.25 (0-8134-2967-6); text ed. 33.95 (0-685-06363-1) Interstate.

Pfahler, P., jt. ed. see Kastens, U.

Pfalgerb, Bernhard. Herder Political Lexicon: Herder Lexikon Politik. 4th ed. 380p. (GER.). 1982. 35.00 (0-8288-2257-3, M7450) Fr & Eur.

Pfaller, Alfred, jt. ed. see Gross, Bertram.

Pfaltz, C. R., ed. Neurophysiological & Clinical Aspects of Vestibular Disorders. (Advances in Oto-Rhino-Laryngology Ser.: Vol. 30). (Illus.). xii, 372p. 1983. 157.75 (3-8055-3607-0) S Karger.

— New Aspects of Cochlear Mechanics & Inner Ear Pathophysiology. (Advances in Oto-Rhino-Laryngology Ser.: Vol. 44). (Illus.). x, 170p. 1990. 134.50 (3-8055-5020-0) S Karger.

— New Aspects of Fundamental Problems of Larynology & Otology. (Advances in Oto-Rhino-Laryngology Ser.: Vol. 32). (Illus.). viii, 200p. 1984. 127.25 (3-8055-3701-8) S Karger.

Pfaltz, C. R., jt. ed. see Colman, B. H.

Pfaltz, C. R., ed. see International Congress of Radiology in Oto-Rhine-Laryngology Staff.

Pfaltz, C. R., ed. see International Otoneurological Symposium Staff.

Pfaltz, C. R., jt ed. see Jahnke, K.

Pfaltz, C. R., et al, eds. Bearing of Basic Research on Clinical Otolaryngology. (Advances in Oto-Rhino-Laryngology Ser.: Vol. 46). (Illus.). x, 182p. 1991. 149.00 (3-8055-5338-2) S Karger.

Pfaltzgraff, Diane K., jt. auth. see Dougherty, James E.

Pfaltzgraff, Robert, Jr., ed. National Security Policy for the 1980's. (Annals of the American Academy of Political & Social Science Ser.: Vol. 457). 250p. 1981. 26.00 (0-8039-1705-8); pap. 17.00 (0-8039-1704-X) Sage.

Pfaltzgraff, Robert L., Jr. Energy Issues & Alliance Relationships: The United States, Western Europe & Japan. LC 80-81711. (Special Report Ser.). 71p. 1980. 11.95 (0-89549-021-8) Inst Foreign Policy Anal.

Pfaltzgraff, Robert L., Jr., ed. Study of International Relations: A Guide to Information Sources. LC 73-17511. (International Relations Information Guide Ser.: Vol. 5). 168p. 1977. 68.00 (0-8103-1331-6) Gale.

Pfaltzgraff, Robert L., Jr. & Davis, Jacqueline K. National Security Decisions: The Participants Speak. 1990. text ed. 49.95 (0-669-24488-0); pap. 27.95 (0-669-24494-5) Free Pr.

Pfaltzgraff, Robert L., Jr. & Davis, Jacquelyn K. The Cruise Missile: Bargaining Chip or Defense Bargain? LC 76-51854. (Special Report Ser.). 53p. 1977. 11.95 (0-89549-001-3) Inst Foreign Policy Anal.

Pfaltzgraff, Robert L. & Davis, Jacquelyn K. Japanese-American Relations in a Changing Security Environment. LC 75-37014. (Foreign Policy Papers: Vol. 1, No. 1). 56p. reprint ed. pap. 25.00 (0-7837-1986-8, 2042260) Bks Demand.

Pfaltzgraff, Robert L., Jr. & Schultz, Richard H., Jr. The United States Army: Challenges & Missions in the 1990s. 320p. 1991. text ed. 40.00 (0-669-27562-X) Free Pr.

Pfaltzgraff, Robert L., Jr. & Shultz, Richard H., Jr. U. S. Defense Policy in an Era of Constrained Resources. 416p. 1989. text ed. 55.00 (0-669-21358-6) Free Pr.

Pfaltzgraff, Robert L., Jr., jt. auth. see Davis, Jacquelyn K.

Pfaltzgraff, Robert L.

Pfaltzgraff, Robert L., Jr., jt. auth. see Dougherty, James E.

Pfaltzgraff, Robert L., Jr., jt. auth. see Kintner, William R.

Pfaltzgraff, Robert L., Jr., jt. ed. see Lee, David T.

Pfaltzgraff, Robert L., Jr., ed. see Shultz, Richard H.

***Pfaltzgraff, Robert L., Jr., et al.** Ethnic Conflict & Environmental Tension: Dividing Line or Common Ground? (Institute for Foreign Policy Analysis Special Report Ser.). 130p. (Orig.). 1996. pap. 11.95 (1-57488-045-4) Brasseys Inc.

Pfaltzgraff, Robert L., et al. The Greens of West Germany: Origins, Strategies & Transatlantic Implications. LC 83-48704. (Special Report Ser.). 105p. 1983. 11.95 (0-89549-056-0) Inst Foreign Policy Anal.

Pfaltzgraff, Robert L., Jr., et al, eds. Emerging Doctrines & Technologies: Implications for Global & Regional Political-Military Balances. LC 87-45584. 336p. 1987. text ed. 45.00 (0-669-16755-X) Free Pr.

Pfalzgraf, Beth, jt. auth. see Ewing, Susan A.

***Pfalzgraf, Jochen & Wang, Dongming, eds.** Automated Practical Reasoning. LC 95-1923. (Texts & Monographs in Symbolic Computation). 232p. 1995. 59.00 (0-387-82600-9) Spr-Verlag.

Pfander, Hanspeter, ed. Key to Carotenoids. 2nd ed. 296p. 1987. 107.00 (0-8176-1860-0) Birkhauser.

Pfandl, Ludwig. Geschichte der Spanischen Nationalliteratur in Ihrer Blutezeit. xiv, 618p. 1967. reprint ed. write for info. (0-318-71638-0, Pub. by Georg Olms GW) Lubrecht & Cramer.

Pfann, G. Dynamic Modelling of Stochastic Demand for Manufacturing Employment. Beckmann, Martin J. & Krelle, W., eds. (Lecture Notes in Economics & Mathematical Systems Ser.: Vol. 349). (Illus.). iv, 158p. 1990. pap. 31.00 (0-387-52881-4) Spr-Verlag.

Pfanner, Helmut F. Exile in New York: German & Austrian Writers after 1933. LC 83-10465. 253p. reprint ed. pap. 72.20 (0-7837-3664-9, 2043536) Bks Demand.

Pfannes, C. & Salamone, V. The Great Admirals of World War II: The Germans, Vol. 2. 1984. pap. 3.25 (0-685-07895-7) Zebra.

Pfannes, Charles E. & Salamone, Victor. The Great Commanders of World War II, Vol. II, the British. (YA). (gr. 7 up). 1981. pap. 2.75 (0-89083-786-4) Zebra.

Pfannes, Charles E. & Salamone, Victor A. The Great Admirals of World War II, Vol. I: The Americans. 1983. pap. 3.25 (0-8217-1160-1) Zebra.

— The Great Battles of World War II, Vol. II: The Pacific Naval Battles. 272p. 1986. pap. 3.50 (0-8217-1887-8) Zebra.

— The Great Commanders of World War II. (Germans Ser.: Vol. 1). (YA). (gr. 7 up). 1981. pap. 2.75 (0-89083-727-9) Zebra.

— The Great Commanders of World War II: The Japanese, Vol. IV. (Great Commanders Ser.). (Orig.). 1982. pap. 3.25 (0-8217-1027-3) Zebra.

Pfannes, Charles E. & Salamone, Victor A. The Great Commanders of World War II. (Americans Ser: Vol. III). 1982. pap. 2.95 (0-89083-923-9) Zebra.

Pfannkuch, H. O. Elsevier's Dictionary of Environmental Hydrogeology: In English (with Definitions), French & German. 332p. (ENG, FRE & GER.). 1990. 141.00 (0-444-87269-8) Elsevier.

Pfannkuche, Berd & Baur, Johanna. Dictionary of Ceramics & Earths: English-German, German-English: Worterbuch Keramik und Erden: Englisch-Deutsch, Deutsch-Englisch. LC 93-12989. (ENG & GER.). 1993. 96.00 (1-56081-207-9) VCH Pubs.

***Pfannkuche, Bernd.** Parat Dictionary of Ceramics & Earth: English-German, German-English. 555p. (ENG & GER.). 1993. 225.00 (0-7859-6958-6) Fr & Eur.

Pfannmueller, Gustav. Handbuch der Islam-Literatur. viii, 436p. (GER.). (C). 1974. reprint ed. 173.10 (3-11-002488-8) De Gruyter.

Pfannmuller, Lee, jt. ed. see Coffin, Barbara.

Pfannsteil, Arthur S. & Schuster, Bernard. Modigliani, A Study of His Sculpture. (Illus.). 101p. 1986. write for info. (0-9616170-0-4) Mega Corp.

Pfanstiehl, John. Automotive Paint Handbook. LC 92-14868. (Illus.). 176p. 1992. 14.95 (1-55788-034-4, HP Books) Berkley Pub.

Pfanz, Donald C. The Petersburg Campaign Abraham Lincoln at City Point, March 20-April 9, 1865. (Virginia Civil War Battles & Leaders Ser.). (Illus.). 12.95 (0-930919-76-9) H E Howard.

***Pfanz, Harry W.** Gettysburg. (Civil War Ser.). 60p. (Orig.). 1994. pap. 3.95 (0-915992-63-9) Eastern Acorn.

— Gettysburg: Culp's Hill & Cemetery Hill. LC 93-3323. (Civil War America Ser.). (Illus.). xx, 508p. (C). 1993. 37.50 (0-8078-2118-7) U of NC Pr.

— Gettysburg-The Second Day. LC 87-5965. (Illus.). xxii, 602p. (C). 1987. 37.50 (0-8078-1749-X) U of NC Pr.

Pfanzagel, J. Estimation in Some Semiparametric Models. (Lecture Notes in Statistics Ser.: Vol. 63). iii, 112p. 1990. pap. 21.00 (0-387-97238-2) Spr-Verlag.

Pfanzagl, J. Asymptotic Expansions for General Statistical Models. (Lecture Notes in Statistics Ser.: Vol. 31). vii, 505p. 1985. pap. 59.00 (0-387-96221-2) Spr-Verlag.

— Contributions to a General Asymptotic Statistical Theory. (Lecture Notes in Statistics Ser.: Vol. 13). (Illus.). 315p. 1982. pap. 42.00 (0-387-90776-9) Spr-Verlag.

Pfanzagl, Johann. Allgemeine Methodenlehre der Statistik, Pt. 1. 6th ed. 254p. (GER.). 1983. 17.55 (3-11-009674-9) De Gruyter.

— Parametric Statistical Theory. LC 94-21850. xiii, 374p. 1994. text ed. 89.95 (3-11-014030-6); pap. text ed. 54.95 (3-11-013863-8) De Gruyter.

Pfarr, Richard. Mice As a New Pet. 1991. pap. 5.95 (0-86622-530-7, TU022) TFH Pubns.

***Pfarrer, Chuck.** Virus, Bk. 1. (Illus.). 136p. 1995. pap. 16.95 (1-56971-104-6) Dark Horse Comics.

Pfarrer, Chuck, et al. The Thing from Another World & Climate of Fear Collection. (Illus.). 168p. 1993. pap. 15.95 (1-878574-85-X) Dark Horse Comics.

Pfatteicher, Carl F. John Redford: Organist & Almoner of St. Paul's Cathedral in the Reign of Henry VIII. LC 74-24184. reprint ed. 24.00 (0-404-13088-7) AMS Pr.

Pfatteicher, Philip. A Dictionary of Liturgical Terms. LC 91-22075. 160p. (Orig.). (C). 1991. 15.95 (1-56338-026-9) TPI PA.

— A Dictionary of Liturgical Terms. LC 91-22075. 160p. (Orig.). (C). 1991. pap. 11.00 (1-56338-125-7) TPI PA.

Pfatteicher, Philip H. Commentary on the Occasional Services. LC 82-48542. 336p. 1983. 29.00 (0-8006-0697-3, 1-697, Fortress Pr) Augsburg Fortress.

— Festivals & Commemorations: Handbook to the Calendar in Lutheran Book of Worship. LC 79-54129. 480p. 35.99 (0-8066-1757-8, 10-2295, Augsburg) Augsburg Fortress.

— School of the Church: Worship & Christian Formation. LC 94-47514. 1994. pap. 14.00 (1-56338-110-9) TPI PA.

Pfatteicher, Philip H. & Messerli, Carlos R. Manual on the Liturgy: Lutheran Book of Worship. LC 78-68179. 1979. 25.00 (0-8066-1676-8, 3-2015, Augsburg) Augsburg Fortress.

***Pfau, Michael.** Debate & Argument: A Systems Approach to Advocacy. LC 87-4859. 349p. 1987. reprint ed. pap. 99.50 (0-7837-8852-5, 2049529) Bks Demand.

Pfau, Michael & Kenski, Henry C. Attack Politics: Strategy & Defense. LC 89-29766. (Praeger Series in Political Communication). 216p. 1990. text ed. 47.95 (0-275-93375-X, C3375, Greenwood Pr) Greenwood.

Pfau, Michael W., et al. Debate & Argument: A Systems Approach to Advocacy. (C). 1987. text ed. 20.25 (0-673-18163-4) HarpCollege.

Pfau, Richard. No Sacrifice Too Great: The Life of Lewis L. Strauss. LC 84-13153. (Illus.). 326p. reprint ed. pap. 93.00 (0-7837-4368-8, 2044078) Bks Demand.

Pfau, Richard H. Standardizing Behavioral Measurements Across Cultures, Nations & Time. (TWEC World Education Monographs). 31p. 1984. 3.50 (0-685-09458-8) I N Thut World Educ Ctr.

Pfau, Thomas, ed. & tr. Friedrich Holderlin: Essays & Letters on Theory. LC 87-1882. (SUNY Series, Intersections: Philosophy & Critical Theory). 193p. 1987. 59.50 (0-88706-558-9); pap. 19.95 (0-88706-559-7) State U NY Pr.

Pfau, Thomas, ed. see Schelling, F. W.

Pfau, W. F., jt. auth. see Thiard, A.

Pfau, Werner, jt. auth. see Marx, Siegfried.

Pfautsch, Donna S. Riding the Convection Connection: Teaching Energy: Hot Air Ballons. (Illus.). (Orig.). 1993. teacher ed 10.00 (0-89824-216-9) Trillium Pr.

Pfautsch, Lloyd. Choral Therapy: Vocal Techniques & Exercises for Church Choirs. LC 93-39299. 96p. (Orig.). 1994. pap. 9.95 (0-687-06510-0) Abingdon.

Pfautz, Harold W., ed. see Booth, Charles.

Pfefer, Susanna. Faberge Eggs: Masterpieces from Czarist Russia. 1990. 35.00 (0-88363-090-7) H L Levin.

Pfeffer. Integrals & Measures. (Pure & Applied Mathematics Ser.: Vol. 42). 280p. 1977. 110.00 (0-8247-6530-3) Dekker.

— Twin Troubles. (J). 1994. pap. 4.95 (0-8050-3272-X) H Holt & Co.

Pfeffer, Cynthia R. The Suicidal Child. LC 85-31710. 318p. 1986. lib. bdg. 37.95 (0-89862-664-1) Guilford Pr.

***Pfeffer, Cynthia R., ed.** Severe Stress & Mental Disturbance in Children. 784p. 1995. boxed 69.95 (0-88048-657-0, 8657) Am Psychiatric.

— Suicide among Youth: Perspectives on Risk & Prevention. LC 88-36702. 235p. 1989. text ed. 32.00 (0-88048-167-6) Am Psychiatric.

Pfeffer, David A., jt. auth. see Troutman, Glenn.

Pfeffer, Georg. Status & Affinity in Middle India. vii, 104p. (Orig.). 1982. pap. text ed. 22.00 (3-515-03913-9) Coronet Bks.

Pfeffer, Glen, jt. ed. see Mizel, Mark.

Pfeffer, Glenn B. & Frey, Carol C. Current Practice in Foot & Ankle Surgery, Vol. 2. (Illus.). 208p. 1994. text ed. 55.00 (0-07-049799-0) Hlth Prof Div.

Pfeffer, Glenn B. & Frey, Carol C., eds. Current Practice in Foot & Ankle Surgery, Vol. 1. LC 92-49130. (Current Practice in Foot & Ankle Surgery). 304p. 1993. 49.00 (0-07-049732-X) Hlth Prof Div.

Pfeffer, Irwin, jt. auth. see Abraham, Henry.

Pfeffer, J. Alan & Cannon, Garland, eds. German Loanwords in English: An Historical Dictionary. 400p. (C). 1994. 85.00 (0-521-40254-9) Cambridge U Pr.

Pfeffer, Jeffrey. Competitive Advantage Through People: Unleashing the Power of the Work Force. LC 93-26599. 288p. 1994. 24.95 (0-8458-4413-X) Harvard Busn.

— Competitive Advantage Through People: Unleashing the Power of the Work Force. 1994. text ed. 24.95 (0-07-103577-X) McGraw.

— Managing with Power: Politics & Influence in Organizations. LC 91-26237. 400p. 1992. 24.95 (0-87584-314-X) Harvard Busn.

— Managing with Power: Politics & Influence in Organizations. 400p. 1994. pap. 16.95 (0-87584-440-5) Harvard Busn.

— Managing with Power: Politics & Influence in Organizations. 1992. text ed. 24.95 (0-07-103360-2) McGraw.

— Managing with Power: Power & Influence in Organizations. 1994. pap. text ed. 16.95 (0-07-103452-8) McGraw.

— Organizational Design. Mackenzie, Kenneth D., ed. LC 77-86024. (Organizational Behavior Ser.). (Illus.). (C). 1978. pap. text ed. write for info. (0-88295-453-9) Harlan Davidson.

Pfeffer, Jeremy M. & Waldron, Gillian. Psychiatric Differential Diagnosis. LC 86-26356. (Illus.). 192p. (Orig.). (C). 1987. 40.00 (0-443-03703-5) Churchill.

Pfeffer, K., et al, eds. Function & Specificity of T Cells: International Workshop Schloss Elmau, Bavaria, FRG, October 14-16, 1990. (Current Topics in Microbiology & Immunology Ser.: Vol. 173). (Illus.). xii, 296p. 1991. 110.00 (0-387-53781-3) Spr-Verlag.

Pfeffer, K. H. International Atlas of Karst Phenomena Sheets 8-12. 1990. (Annals of Geomorphology Ser.: Suppl. 77). (Illus.). 105p. 1990. pap. 54.55 (3-443-21077-5, Pub. by Gebrueder Borntraeger GW) Lubrecht & Cramer.

Pfeffer, L. Religious Freedom. Haiman, Franklyn S., ed. (To Protect These Rights Ser.). 192p. 1983. pap. 12.95 (0-8442-6001-0, Natl Textbk) NTC Pub Grp.

Pfeffer, Lawrence M., ed. Mechanisims of Interferon Actions, 2 vols., Set. 224p. 1987. 269.90 (0-8493-6145-1, QR187) CRC Pr.

— Mechanisims of Interferon Actions, 2 vols., Vol. I: Interferons. 176p. 1987. write for info. (0-318-62188-6) CRC Pr.

— Mechanisims of Interferon Actions, 2 vols., Vol. II: Cellular Effects of Interferons. 224p. 1987. write for info. (0-318-62189-4) CRC Pr.

Pfeffer, Leo. Religion, State & the Burger Court. LC 84-43056. 310p. 1985. 30.95 (0-87975-275-0) Prometheus Bks.

Pfeffer, Leo, jt. auth. see Stokes, Anson.

Pfeffer, M. Kleines Woerterbuch zur Arbeits und Sozialpolitik. 396p. (GER.). 1972. pap. 14.95 (0-8288-6403-9, M-7516) Fr & Eur.

Pfeffer, Naomi. The Stork & the Syringe: A Political History of Reproductive Medicine. LC 93-32897. (Feminist Perspectives Ser.). 244p. 1994. 49.95 (0-7456-0821-3); pap. 19.95 (0-7456-1187-7) Blackwell Pubs.

Pfeffer, Paula F. A. Philip Randolph, Pioneer of the Civil Rights Movement. LC 89-38650. 368p. 1990. text ed. 32.50 (0-8071-1554-1) La State U Pr.

Pfeffer, Philip E. & Gerasimowicz, Walter V., eds. Nuclear Magnetic Resonance in Agriculture. 400p. 1989. 239.00 (0-8493-6864-2, S540) CRC Pr.

Pfeffer, Pierre. Bears, Big & Little. Bogard, Vicki, tr. LC 89-8883. (Young Discovery Library). (Illus.). 38p. (J). (gr. k-5). 1989. 5.95 (0-944589-23-5, 023) Young Discovery Lib.

— Elephants: Big, Strong & Wise. Matthews, Sarah, tr. LC 87-33995. (Illus.). 38p. (J). (gr. k-5). 1988. 5.95 (0-944589-04-9, 049) Young Discovery Lib.

Pfeffer, Pierre, ed. Predators & Predation: The Struggle for Life in the Animal World. LC 88-3880. (Illus.). 429p. reprint ed. pap. 122.30 (0-7837-5349-7, 2045092) Bks Demand.

Pfeffer, R., jt. auth. see Institute Advanced Study Geophysics Staff.

Pfeffer, R., jt. ed. see Moser, W. R.

Pfeffer, Richard M. Understanding Business Contracts in China, Nineteen Forty-Nine to Nineteen Sixty-Three. (East Asia Monographs: Vol. No. 53). 147p. 1973. 14.00 (0-674-92095-3) HUP.

Pfeffer, Robert, ed. Fourth International Conference on Physicochemical Hydrodynamics. 1983. 100.00 (0-89766-200-8); pap. 100.00 (0-89766-201-6, VOL. 404) NY Acad Sci.

Pfeffer, Susan B. Family of Strangers. (YA). 1994. mass mkt. 3.99 (0-440-21895-0) Dell.

— Kid Power. 121p. (J). (gr. 3-7). 1988. pap. 2.95 (0-590-42607-9) Scholastic Inc.

— Make Believe. 144p. (J). (gr. 4-7). 1993. 14.95 (0-8050-1754-2, Bks Young Read) H Holt & Co.

— Nobody's Daughter. LC 94-19681. (J). 1995. 14.95 (0-385-32106-6) Delacorte.

— The Riddle Streak. (Illus.). 64p. (J). (gr. 2-4). 1993. 14.95 (0-8050-2147-7, Bks Young Read) H Holt & Co.

— Ring of Truth. (YA). 1994. mass mkt. 3.99 (0-440-21911-6) Dell.

— Sara Kate Saves the World. (J). 1995. 14.95 (0-8050-3148-0) H Holt & Co.

— Sara Kate, Super Kid. (J). 1994. 14.95 (0-8050-3147-2) H Holt & Co.

— Turning Thirteen. LC 88-11347. 144p. (J). (gr. 6-8). 1988. pap. 12.95 (0-590-40764-3, Scholastic Hardcover) Scholastic Inc.

— Twice Taken. LC 93-39010. (J). 1994. 14.95 (0-385-32033-7) Delacorte.

— Twin Surprises. (Redfeather Fiction Ser.). (Illus.). 64p. (J). (gr. 2-4). 1991. 13.95 (0-8050-1850-6, Redfeather BYR) H Holt & Co.

— Twin Surprises. LC 91-13968. (Redfeather Fiction Ser.). (Illus.). 64p. (J). (gr. 2-4). 1993. pap. 4.95 (0-8050-2626-6, Redfeather BYR) H Holt & Co.

— Twin Troubles. LC 92-5773. (Illus.). (J). 1992. 14.95 (0-8050-2146-9, Redfeather BYR) H Holt & Co.

— The Year without Michael. (YA). (gr. 7-12). 1988. mass mkt. 3.99 (0-553-27373-6, Starfire) Bantam.

P
Q

Pfeffer, Susanna. Quilt Masterpieces. 1990. 15.99 (*0-517-03297-X*) Random Hse Value.

Pfeffer, Washek F. The Riemann Approach to Integration. LC 93-18565. (Cambridge Tracts in Mathematics Ser.: No. 109). 292p. (C). 1994. 49.95 (*0-521-44035-1*) Cambridge U Pr.

Pfeffer, Wendy. All about Me: Developing Self Image & Self-Esteem with Hands-On Learning Activities. Minucci, Mary B. & Johansen, Mary L., eds. (Creative Concept Ser.). (Illus.). 48p. 1990. pap. 6.95 (*1-878727-01-X*) First Teacher.

— From Tadpole to Frog. LC 93-3135. (Let's-Read-&-Find-Out Science Bk.). (Illus.). 32p. (J). (ps-1). 1994. pap. 4.95 (*0-06-445123-2*, Trophy) HarpC Child Bks.

— From Tadpole to Frog. LC 93-3135. (Let's-Read-&-Find-Out Science Bk.: Stage 1). (Illus.). 32p. (J). (ps-1). 1994. 15.00 (*0-06-023044-4*) HarpC Child Bks.

— From Tadpole to Frog. LC 93-3135. (Let's-Read-&-Find-Out Science Bk.: Stage 1). (Illus.). 32p. (J). (ps-1). 1994. lib. bdg. 14.89 (*0-06-023117-3*) HarpC Child Bks.

— Marta's Magnets. LC 94-37223. (Illus.). 1995. 13.95 (*0-382-24931-3*); lib. bdg. 15.95 (*0-382-24930-5*); pap. 5.95 (*0-382-24932-1*) Silver Burdett Pr.

— Popcorn Park Zoo. LC 91-3273. (Illus.). 64p. (J). (gr. 2-5). 1992. 14.95 (*0-671-74587-5*, Julian Messner); lib. bdg. 16.98 (*0-671-74589-1*, Julian Messner) Silver Burdett Pr.

— Starting a Child Care Business, a Rewarding Career: A Home Study Course. (Home Study Ser.). 1989. 33.00 (*0-939926-45-8*); audio (*0-939926-44-X*) Fruition Pubns.

— What's It Like to be a Fish? LC 94-6543. (Illus.). (J). (ps-1). 1996. 15.00 (*0-06-024428-3*); lib. bdg. 14.89 (*0-06-024429-1*) HarpC Child Bks.

— The World of Nature. Kranyik, Margery & Johansen, Mary L., eds. (Creative Concept Ser.). (Illus.). 48p. 1990. pap. 6.95 (*1-878727-03-6*) First Teacher.

— Writing Children's Books: Getting Started: A Home Study Course. (Home Study Ser.). 62p. Notebook. ring bd. 33.00 (*0-939926-28-8*); audio (*0-939926-27-X*) Fruition Pubns.

Pfefferblit, Elaine, ed. see Lederer, Richard.

Pfefferblit, Elaine, ed. see Rachlin, Harvey.

Pfefferblit, Elaine, ed. see Thernstrom, Melanie.

Pfefferkorn, Eli, ed. see Nomberg-Przytyk, Sara.

Pfefferkorn, Herman W., jt. ed. see Dutro, J. Thomas, Jr.

Pfefferkorn, Ignaz. Sonora: A Description of the Province. LC 89-5245. (Southwest Center Ser.). 329p. 1990. reprint ed. pap. 12.95 (*0-8165-1144-6*) U of Ariz Pr.

***Pfeffermann, Guy P.** Private Business in Developing Countries: Improved Prospects. (IFC Discussion Paper Ser.: No. 1). 44p. 1988. 6.95 (*0-614-02834-5*, 11130) World Bank.

Pfeffermann, Guy P. & Griffin, Charles C. Nutrition & Health Programs in Latin America: Targeting Social Expenditures. 32p. (ENG & SPA.). 1989. write for info. (*0-318-65542-X*); English edition. 6.95 (*0-8213-1257-X*, 11257); Spanish edition. 6.95 (*0-8213-1258-8*, 11258) World Bank.

***Pfeffermann, Guy P. & Madarassy, Andrea.** Trends in Private Investment in Developing Countries, 1990-91 Edition. (IFC Discussion Paper Ser.: No. 11). 62p. 1991. 6.95 (*0-8213-1695-8*, 11695) World Bank.

— Trends in Private Investment in Developing Countries, 1992. 55p. 1992. 6.95 (*0-8213-2099-8*, 12099) World Bank.

Pfeffinger, Charla R. Holiday Readers Theatre. (Illus.). 120p. 1994. pap. 20.00 (*1-56308-162-8*) Teacher Ideas Pr.

— A Teen's Book of Lists. LC 92-15286. (Illus.). xxii, 114p. 1992. lib. bdg. 12.50 (*0-87287-988-7*) Libs Unl.

Pfeifer, Alenka, tr. see Fornari, Franco.

Pfeifer, Alice A., comp. Let's Pray Together: Thirty-Two Prayer Services for Adults & Teens, Vol. 2. 64p. (Orig.). 1992. pap. 6.95 (*0-937997-23-4*) Hi-Time Pub.

Pfeifer, Carl, jt. auth. see Manternach, Janaan.

Pfeifer, Carl J. & Manternach, Janaan. Questions Catechists Ask & Answers That Really Work. 110p. (Orig.). 1993. pap. 6.95 (*1-55612-620-4*) Sheed & Ward MO.

Pfeifer, Carl J., jt. auth. see Manternach, Janaan.

***Pfeifer, Diane.** The Angel Cookbook: Heavenly Light Cuisine. Poulton, Gail, ed. LC 94-92351. (Illus.). 160p. (Orig.). 1994. pap. 9.95 (*0-9618306-6-2*) Strawberry GA.

— For Popcorn Lovers Only. Blackmun, Susie & McDonald, Marge, eds. LC 87-90472. (Illus.). 160p. (Orig.). 1987. reprint ed. pap. 9.95 (*0-9618306-0-3*) Strawberry GA.

— Gone with the Grits: Gourmet Cookbook. Poulton, Gail, ed. (Illus.). 160p. (Orig.). 1992. pap. 9.95 (*0-9618306-9-7*) Strawberry GA.

— Quick Bytes: Computer Lover's Cookbook. LC 93-83442. (Illus.). 160p. 1993. pap. 9.95 (*0-9618306-7-0*) Strawberry GA.

— Stand by Your Pan: Country Music Cookbook. (Illus.). 160p. 1994. pap. 9.95 (*0-9618306-3-8*) Strawberry GA.

Pfeifer, Diane, ed. see Justice, Jeff.

Pfeifer, Diane, jt. auth. see Justice, Jeff.

Pfeifer, Diane, ed. see Justice, Jeff & Pfeifer, Diane.

Pfeifer, Friedl. Nice Goin: My Life on Skis. 2nd ed. Lund, Morten, ed. LC 93-61670. (Illus.). 244p. 1994. 16.95 (*0-929521-84-6*) Pictorial Hist.

Pfeifer, Jack A. West from Omaha: A Railroader's Odyssey. Pacific Fast Mail Staff, ed. 207p. 1990. 59.50 (*0-915713-20-9*) Pac Fast Mail.

Pfeifer, Jerilyn K. Teenage Suicide: What Can the Schools Do? LC 85-63689. (Fastback Ser.: No. 234). 50p. (Orig.). 1986. pap. 1.25 (*0-87367-234-8*) Phi Delta Kappa.

Pfeifer, Karl. Actions & Other Events: The Unifier-Multiplier Controversy. (American University Studies: Philosophy: Ser. V). 210p. (C). 1989. text ed. 24.95 (*0-8204-1044-6*) P Lang Pubs.

Pfeifer, Kathryn B. Seven Hundred Sixty-First Battalion. (African-American Soldiers Ser.). (Illus.). 80p. (J). (gr. 4-7). 1994. lib. bdg. 14.98 (*0-8050-3057-3*) TFC Bks NY.

Pfeifer, Ken. American Hotel Identity Graphics. (Illus.). 256p. 1993. 84.95 (*4-89239-007-0*, Pub. by Boutique-Sha JA) Bks Nippan.

— CD Packaging & Graphics: The Best Promotional & Retail Packaging for Compact Discs. (Illus.). 192p. 1992. 39.99 (*1-56496-003-X*, 30397) Rockport Pubs.

Pfeifer, Leona, tr. see Beratz, Gottlieb.

Pfeifer, Patricia, illus. Cook's Cupboard. 276p. 1986. 13.95 (*0-9618855-0-5*) NA Benefit Assn.

Pfeifer, Patrick M. Bufotenin (Dimethylserotonin - Mappine) Index of New Information & Medical Research Bible. 160p. 1994. 44.50 (*0-7883-0218-3*); pap. 39.50 (*0-7883-0219-1*) ABBE Pubs Assn.

Pfeifer, R., et al, eds. Connectionism in Perspective. 518p. 1989. 95.00 (*0-444-88061-5*, North Holland) Elsevier.

Pfeifer, Susan K. & Sussman, Marvin B. Families: Intergenerational & Generational Connections. (Marriage & Family Review Ser.: Vol. 16 Nos. 1-4). (Illus.). 174p. 1991. text ed. 59.95 (*0-86656-864-6*) Haworth Pr.

Pfeifer, Walter. The Piano Hammer. Englehardt, J., tr. (Illus.). 120p. (Orig.). 1979. pap. 54.57 (*0-933224-33-8*) Bold Strummer Ltd.

***Pfeifer, Wolfgang.** Etymologisches Woerterbuch des Deutschen, 2 vols. 2nd ed. 1665p. (GER.). 1993. 225.00 (*0-7859-8262-0*, 3050006269) Fr & Eur.

***Pfeiffenberger, Jim.** The Complete Guide to Kenai Fjords National Park, Alaska. (Illus.). 144p. (Orig.). 1995. pap. text ed. 11.95 (*0-936425-26-1*) Greatland Graphics.

***Pfeiffenberger, Jim, et al.** Kenai: Alaska's Kenai Peninsula. Tripp, Angela, ed. (Illus.). 48p. (Orig.). 1993. pap. 10.95 (*1-880352-32-X*) Albion Pub.

Pfeiffenberger, Jim, jt. auth. see Gilroy, Steve.

Pfeiffer. Sensitive Crystallization Processes. LC 68-31125. 1975. pap. 16.00 (*0-910142-66-1*) Anthroposophic.

Pfeiffer & Co Staff. Addressing Sexual Harassment in the Workplace: Trainer's Package. LC 92-93295. 134p. 1992. ring bd. 99.95 (*0-88390-320-2*) Pfeiffer & Co.

Pfeiffer & Co. Staff. Diversity Bingo: An Experiential Learning Event. 65p. 1992. ring bd. 99.95 (*0-88390-332-6*) Pfeiffer & Co.

Pfeiffer & Co Staff. Technical Trainer's Source Book. LC 91-25508. (Illus.). 400p. 1992. ring bd. 99.95 (*0-88390-298-2*) Pfeiffer & Co.

Pfeiffer, A. & Mendelssohn, J. Dialogues of Fundamental Equations of Science & Philosophy. LC 66-30633. 1967. 60.00 (*0-08-012231-0*, Pub. by Pergamon Repr UK) Franklin.

Pfeiffer-Belli, Christian, jt. auth. see Brunner, Gisbert L.

Pfeiffer-Belli, Christian, jt. auth. see Brunner, Gisbert.

Pfeiffer, Bruce. Frank Lloyd Wright Drawings. 1990. 75.00 (*0-8109-1773-4*) Abrams.

Pfeiffer, Bruce B., ed. Collected Writings of Frank Lloyd Wright, 1894-1931, Vol. I. LC 91-40987. (Illus.). 400p. 1992. 60.00 (*0-8478-1546-3*); pap. 40.00 (*0-8478-1547-1*) Rizzoli Intl.

— Collected Writings of Frank Lloyd Wright, 1931-1932, Vol. II. LC 91-40987. (Illus.). 400p. 1992. 60.00 (*0-8478-1548-X*); pap. 40.00 (*0-8478-1549-8*) Rizzoli Intl.

— Frank Lloyd Wright: The Crowning Decade, 1949-1959. (Illus.). 197p. (Orig.). 1989. 22.95 (*0-912201-16-9*) CSU Pr Fresno.

— Frank Lloyd Wright: The Crowning Decade (1949-1959) LC 88-63339. 202p. 1989. 22.95 (*0-8093-1540-8*) S Ill U Pr.

— Frank Lloyd Wright: The Guggenheim Correspondence. LC 86-6520. 320p. (Orig.). 1986. 29.95 (*0-8093-1317-0*) S Ill U Pr.

Pfeiffer, Bruce B. & Nordland, Gerald, eds. Frank Lloyd Wright in the Realm of Ideas. LC 87-20755. (Illus.). 208p. 1988. 60.00 (*0-8093-1421-5*); pap. 29.95 (*0-8093-1422-3*) S Ill U Pr.

Pfeiffer, Bruce B., ed. see Wright, Frank L.

Pfeiffer, Bruce B., ed. see Wright, Frank Lloyd.

Pfeiffer, C. Boyd. Bug Making. (Illus.). 224p. 1993. 22.95 (*1-55821-258-2*) Lyons & Burford.

— Bug Making. 224p. 1995. pap. 14.95 (*1-55821-414-3*) Lyons & Burford.

— The Compleat Surfcaster. (Illus.). 192p. 1989. pap. 14.95 (*1-55821-052-0*) Lyons & Burford.

— Modern Tackle Craft. (Illus.). 1993. 39.95 (*1-55821-184-5*) Lyons & Burford.

— Orvis Guide to Outdoor Photography. LC 86-8370. (Illus.). 200p. 1988. pap. 16.95 (*0-8329-0434-1*) Lyons & Burford.

— Tackle Care: The Tackle Maintenance Handbook. (Illus.). 296p. (Orig.). 1987. pap. 12.95 (*0-941130-56-8*) Lyons & Burford.

Pfeiffer, C. J. Drugs & the Peptic Ulcer, Vol. 1. 224p. 1982. 144.00 (*0-8493-6211-3*, RC821, CRC Reprint) Franklin.

— Drugs & the Peptic Ulcer, Vol. 2. 280p. 1982. 144.00 (*0-8493-6212-1*, CRC Reprint) Franklin.

Pfeiffer, Carl C. Mental & Elemental Nutrients: A Physician's Guide to Nutrition & Health Care. LC 75-19543. 556p. 1976. 24.95 (*0-87983-114-6*) Keats.

— Nutrition & Mental Illness: An Orthomolecular Approach to Balancing Body Chemistry. 128p. 1988. pap. 10.95 (*0-89281-226-5*, Heal Arts VT) Inner Tradit.

— Zinc & Other Micro-Nutrients. LC 77-91321. (Illus.). 1978. pap. 3.50 (*0-87983-169-3*) Keats.

Pfeiffer, Carl C. & Braverman, Eric R. The Healing Nutrients Within: Facts, Findings & New Research on Amino Acids. LC 86-10270. 1987. text ed. 27.95 (*0-87983-384-X*) Keats.

Pfeiffer, Carl C. & Smythies, John R., eds. International Review of Neurobiology, Vol. 25. (Serial Publication Ser.). 1984. text ed. 148.00 (*0-12-366825-5*) Acad Pr.

Pfeiffer, Carl J. Cancer of the Esophagus, Vol. I. 176p. 1982. 110.00 (*0-8493-6213-X*, RC280, CRC Reprint) Franklin.

— Cancer of the Esophagus, Vol. II. 280p. 1982. 119.00 (*0-8493-6214-8*, RC280, CRC Reprint) Franklin.

Pfeiffer, Carl J., ed. Animal Models for Intestinal Disease. 320p. 1985. 191.00 (*0-8493-6215-6*, RC860, CRC Reprint) Franklin.

Pfeiffer, Carl J., jt. ed. see Szabo, Sandor.

Pfeiffer, Charles F. Baker's Bible Atlas. rev. ed. LC 60-15536. (Illus.). 1961. reprint ed. 24.99 (*0-8010-6930-0*) Baker Bk.

— Dead Sea Scrolls & the Bible. enl. rev. ed. LC 72-76780. (Baker Studies in Biblical Archaeology). (Illus.). 1969. pap. 7.99 (*0-8010-6898-3*) Baker Bk.

— Epistle to the Hebrews. (Everyman's Bible Commentary Ser.). (Orig.). (C). 1968. reprint ed. pap. 7.99 (*0-8024-2058-3*) Moody.

— Old Testament History. 1973. 34.99 (*0-8010-6945-9*) Baker Bk.

Pfeiffer, Charles F., ed. Comentario Biblico Moody: Antiguo Testamento. Orig. Title: Wycliffe Bible Commentary: Old Testament. 912p. (SPA.). 1993. 24.99 (*0-8254-1563-2*); pap. 19.99 (*0-8254-1562-4*) Kregel.

— Diccionario Biblico Arqueologico. Gama, Roberto, tr. 768p. (SPA.). 1982. 30.95 (*0-311-03667-8*) Casa Bautista.

Pfeiffer, Charles F., jt. ed. see Harrison, Everett.

Pfeiffer, Charles R. La Epistola a los Hebreos (Comentario Biblico Portavoz) Orig. Title: Epistle to the Hebrews (Everyman's Bible Commentary). 128p. (SPA.). 1981. pap. 5.99 (*0-8254-1564-0*) Kregel.

Pfeiffer, Christine. Chicago. LC 88-20199. (Downtown America Bks.). (Illus.). 60p. (J). (gr. 3 up). 1988. text ed. 13.95 (*0-87518-385-9*, Dillon Silver Burdett) Silver Burdett Pr.

— Germany: Two Nations, One Heritage. LC 86-32954. (Discovering Our Heritage Ser.). (Illus.). 176p. (J). (gr. 5 up). 1987. text ed. 14.95 (*0-87518-361-1*, Dillon Silver Burdett) Silver Burdett Pr.

— Poland: Land of Freedom Fighters. LC 90-26093. (Discovering Our Heritage Ser.). (Illus.). 144p. (J). (gr. 5 up). 1991. text ed. 14.95 (*0-87518-464-2*, Dillon Silver Burdett) Silver Burdett Pr.

Pfeiffer, Chuck. Rebound with Weights. LC 83-70893. (Illus.). 136p. (Orig.). 1983. pap. 6.95 (*0-9611234-0-0*) Beaver Pubns.

Pfeiffer, D. R., et al, eds. Cellular Ca2 Plus Regulation. LC 88-9400. (Advances in Experimental Medicine & Biology Ser.: Vol. 232). (Illus.). 284p. 1988. 79.50 (*0-306-42904-7*, Plenum Pr) Plenum.

Pfeiffer, David, jt. ed. see Watson, Sara.

Pfeiffer-Dennis, Nancy A. Easy-to-Make Patchwork Skirts. (Illus.). (Orig.). 1980. pap. 4.50 (*0-486-23888-1*) Dover.

Pfeiffer, E. Chromatography. 1980. 8.00 (*0-938250-21-3*) Bio-Dynamic Farm.

Pfeiffer, E., et al. Alzheimer's Disease: Caregiver Practices, Programs & Community-Based Strategies. LC 89-60347. 103p. 1989. pap. 15.00 (*0-9622070-0-4*) USF SGC.

Pfeiffer, E. E. Weeds & What They Tell. 96p. 4.50 (*0-938250-04-3*) Bio-Dynamic Farm.

Pfeiffer, Ehrenfried. Bio-Dynamic Gardening & Farming, Vol. 1. 126p. (Orig.). 1983. pap. 8.50 (*0-936132-56-6*) Merc Pr NY.

— Bio-Dynamic Gardening & Farming, 3 vols., Vol. 2. (Illus.). 137p. (Orig.). 1983. pap. 8.50 (*0-936132-60-4*) Merc Pr NY.

— Bio-Dynamic Gardening & Farming, 3 vols., Vol. 3. (Illus.). 131p. (Orig.). 1984. pap. 8.50 (*0-936132-67-1*) Merc Pr NY.

— The Chymical Wedding of Christian Rosenkreutz: A Commentary. 63p. (Orig.). 1984. pap. 6.50 (*0-936132-16-7*) Merc Pr NY.

Pfeiffer, Ehrenfried & Riese, Erika. Grow a Garden & Be Self-Sufficient. 2nd ed. Heckel, Alice, tr. (Illus.). 128p. (Orig.). 1981. pap. 8.50 (*0-936132-37-X*) Merc Pr NY.

Pfeiffer, Enrenfried E., jt. auth. see Bernard, Raymond W.

Pfeiffer, Eric, jt. auth. see Busse, Ewald W.

Pfeiffer, Ernst, ed. see Freud, Sigmund & Andreas-Salome, Lou.

Pfeiffer, Franz. Meister Eckhart, 2 vols. 1977. lib. bdg. 400.00 (*0-8490-2222-3*) Gordon Pr.

— Works of Meister Eckhart; Sermons & Collations; Tractates; Sayings; Liber Positionum; In Collationbus; the Book of Benedictus; Bibliography. 730p. 1992. reprint ed. pap. 49.95 (*1-56459-274-X*) Kessinger Pub.

Pfeiffer, G. & Wieland, B. Telecommunications in Germany: An Economic Perspective. (Illus.). viii, 199p. 1990. pap. 49.00 (*0-387-52360-X*) Spr-Verlag.

Pfeiffer, George J. & Webster, Judith A. WorkCare: A Resource Guide for the Working Person. Piccini, Sara, ed. (Illus.). 398p. 1992. pap. text ed. 19.95 (*0-9634986-0-6*) Workcare Pr.

Pfeiffer, George J. & Williams, Louise. Taking Care of Today & Tomorrow: A Resource Guide for Health, Aging & Long-Term Care. LC 87-71285. (Illus.). 288p. 1989. pap. 14.95 (*0-9616506-1-3*) Ctr Corporate Hlth.

Pfeiffer, Gladys, jt. auth. see Bendure, Zelma.

Pfeiffer, Guy O. & Nikel, Casimir M. The Household Environment & Chronic Illness: Guidelines for Constructing & Maintaining a Less Polluted Residence. (Illus.). 208p. 1980. 36.95 (*0-398-03961-5*) C C Thomas.

— The Household Environment & Chronic Illness: Guidelines for Constructing & Maintaining a Less Polluted Residence. (Illus.). 208p. 1980. pap. 19.95 (*0-398-06322-2*) C C Thomas.

Pfeiffer, H. K. The Diffusion of Electronic Data Interchange. (Contributions to Management Science Ser.). (Illus.). xiv, 257p. 1992. pap. 69.00 (*0-387-91428-5*) Spr-Verlag.

Pfeiffer, Heather D., jt. ed. see Nagle, Timothy E.

Pfeiffer, Herman. For Land's Sake: The Township Plan for Forest Harmony. 200p. 1993. pap. 12.95 (*0-9636194-1-1*) Coyote Pr OR.

Pfeiffer, Hubert, et al. Microscopic Theory of Crystal Growth. (Physical Research Ser.: Vol. II). 400p. 1990. text ed. 60.00 (*3-05-500684-4*, Pub. by Akademie GW) VCH Pubs.

Pfeiffer, Ida R. The Last Travels of Ida Pfeiffer: Inclusive of a Visit to Madagascar. 1977. text ed. 18.95 (*0-8369-9251-2*, 9104) Ayer.

Pfeiffer, J. W. Reference Guide to Handbooks & Annuals: 1994 Edition. LC 93-87780. 304p. 1994. pap. text ed. 9.95 (*0-88390-414-4*) Pfeiffer & Co.

Pfeiffer, J. W., ed. The Annual, Nineteen Ninety-Four: Developing Human Resources. LC 86-643030. 320p. 1994. pap. text ed. 39.95 (*0-88390-413-6*); ring bd. 89.95 (*0-88390-412-8*) Pfeiffer & Co.

— Reference Guide to Handbooks & Annuals. 1,992th ed. LC 75-14661. (Illus.). 265p. 1992. pap. 9.95 (*0-88390-062-9*) Pfeiffer & Co.

— Strategic Planning: Selected Readings. rev. ed. LC 91-61277. 407p. 1991. 34.95 (*0-88390-296-6*) Pfeiffer & Co.

Pfeiffer, J. William, ed. Annual 1987: Developing Human Resources. LC 86-643030. (Human Resource Development Ser.). (Illus.). 294p. (Orig.). 1987. pap. 39.95 (*0-88390-016-5*); ring bd. 89.95 (*0-88390-015-7*) Pfeiffer & Co.

— Annual 1988: Developing Human Resources. LC 86-643030. (Human Resource Development Ser.). (Illus.). 293p. (Orig.). 1988. pap. 39.95 (*0-88390-018-1*); ring bd. 89.95 (*0-88390-017-3*) Pfeiffer & Co.

— Annual, 1989: Developing Human Resources. LC 86-643030. (Human Resource Development Ser.). (Illus.). 291p. (Orig.). 1989. pap. 39.95 (*0-88390-020-3*); ring bd. 89.95 (*0-88390-019-X*) Pfeiffer & Co.

— The Annual, 1990: Developing Human Resources. LC 86-643030. (Human Resource Development Ser.). (Illus.). 294p. (Orig.). 1990. pap. 39.95 (*0-88390-022-X*); ring bd. 89.95 (*0-88390-021-1*) Pfeiffer & Co.

— Annual, 1991: Developing Human Resources. LC 86-643030. (Human Resource Development Ser.). (Illus.). 309p. 1991. pap. text ed. 39.95 (*0-88390-289-3*); ring bd. 89.95 (*0-88390-288-5*) Pfeiffer & Co.

— Annual, 1992: Developing Human Resources. LC 86-643030. (Human Resource Development Ser.). (Illus.). 294p. (Orig.). 1992. pap. 39.95 (*0-88390-305-9*); ring bd. 89.95 (*0-88390-304-0*) Pfeiffer & Co.

— Annual, 1993: Developing Human Resources. LC 86-643030. (Human Resource Development Ser.). (Illus.). 294p. (Orig.). 1993. pap. 39.95 (*0-88390-353-9*); ring bd. 89.95 (*0-88390-352-0*) Pfeiffer & Co.

— The Encyclopedia of Group Activities: 150 Practical Designs for Successful Facilitating. LC 89-4950. 431p. 1989. ring bd. 99.95 (*0-88390-231-1*) Pfeiffer & Co.

— The Encyclopedia of Team-Building Activities. LC 90-48873. (Illus.). 315p. 1991. ring bd. 89.95 (*0-88390-257-5*) Pfeiffer & Co.

— Encyclopedia of Team-Development Activities. LC 90-22868. 348p. 1991. ring bd. 89.95 (*0-88390-258-3*) Pfeiffer & Co.

— Instrumentation Kit. 910p. boxed, ring bd. 295.00 (*0-88390-207-9*) Pfeiffer & Co.

— The University Associates Theories & Models Kit, 4 vols. LC 91-61284. (Illus.). 1000p. 1991. 345.00 (*0-685-70030-5*) Pfeiffer & Co.

— The University Associates Theories & Models Kit, 4 vols., Set. LC 91-61284. (Illus.). 1000p. 1991. ring bd. 395.00 (*0-88390-052-1*) Pfeiffer & Co.

Pfeiffer, J. William, intro. Pfeiffer & Company Library Guide - Index. LC 93-86725. (Illus.). 1994. ring bd. 119.00 (*0-88390-432-2*) Pfeiffer & Co.

— Pfeiffer & Company Library of Experiential Learning Activities: Communication. LC 93-86698. (Illus.). 1994. ring bd. 119.00 (*0-88390-388-1*) Pfeiffer & Co.

— Pfeiffer & Company Library of Experiential Learning Activities: Consulting & Facilitating. LC 93-86708. (Illus.). 1994. ring bd. 119.00 (*0-88390-394-6*) Pfeiffer & Co.

— Pfeiffer & Company Library of Experiential Learning Activities: Groups. LC 93-86711. (Illus.). 1994. ring bd. 119.00 (*0-88390-391-1*) Pfeiffer & Co.

— Pfeiffer & Company Library of Experiential Learning Activities: Individual Development. LC 93-86699. (Illus.). 1994. ring bd. 119.00 (*0-88390-389-X*) Pfeiffer & Co.

— Pfeiffer & Company Library of Experiential Learning Activities: Leadership. LC 93-86709. (Illus.). 1994. ring bd. 119.00 (*0-88390-393-8*) Pfeiffer & Co.

— Pfeiffer & Company Library of Experiential Learning Activities: Problem Solving. LC 93-86712. (Illus.). 1994. ring bd. 119.00 (*0-88390-390-3*) Pfeiffer & Co.

— Pfeiffer & Company Library of Experiential Learning Activities: Teams. LC 93-86710. (Illus.). 1994. ring bd. 119.00 (*0-88390-392-X*) Pfeiffer & Co.

— Pfeiffer & Company Library of Experiential Learning Activities: Training Technologies. LC 93-86700. (Illus.). 1994. ring bd. 119.00 (*0-88390-425-X*) Pfeiffer & Co.

— Pfeiffer & Company Library of Inventories, Questionnaires, & Surveys: Communication. LC 93-86702. (Illus.). 1994. ring bd. 119.00 (*0-88390-395-4*) Pfeiffer & Co.

— Pfeiffer & Company Library of Inventories, Questionnaires, & Surveys: Consulting & Facilitating. LC 93-86706. (Illus.). 1994. ring bd. 119.00 (*0-88390-400-4*) Pfeiffer & Co.

An Asterisk (*) at the beginning of an entry indicates that the title is appearing in BIP for the first time.

— Pfeiffer & Company Library of Inventories, Questionnaires, & Surveys: Groups & Teams. LC 93-86704. (Illus.). 1994. ring bd. 119.00 (0-88390-398-9) Pfeiffer & Co.

— Pfeiffer & Company Library of Inventories, Questionnaires, & Surveys: Individual Development. LC 93-86701. (Illus.). 1994. ring bd. 119.00 (0-88390-396-2) Pfeiffer & Co.

— Pfeiffer & Company Library of Inventories, Questionnaires, & Surveys: Leadership. LC 93-86705. (Illus.). 1994. ring bd. 119.00 (0-88390-399-7) Pfeiffer & Co.

— Pfeiffer & Company Library of Inventories, Questionnaires, & Surveys: Problem Solving. LC 93-86703. (Illus.). 1994. ring bd. 119.00 (0-88390-397-0) Pfeiffer & Co.

— Pfeiffer & Company Library of Inventories, Questionnaires, & Surveys: Training Technologies. LC 93-86707. (Illus.). 1994. ring bd. 119.00 (0-88390-426-8) Pfeiffer & Co.

— Pfeiffer & Company Library of Presentation & Discussion Resources: Communication. LC 93-86714. (Illus.). 1994. ring bd. 119.00 (0-88390-401-2) Pfeiffer & Co.

— Pfeiffer & Company Library of Presentation & Discussion Resources: Consulting. LC 93-86718. (Illus.). 1994. ring bd. 119.00 (0-88390-406-3) Pfeiffer & Co.

— Pfeiffer & Company Library of Presentation & Discussion Resources: Facilitating. LC 93-86719. (Illus.). 1994. ring bd. 119.00 (0-88390-407-1) Pfeiffer & Co.

— Pfeiffer & Company Library of Presentation & Discussion Resources: Groups & Teams. LC 93-86716. (Illus.). 1994. ring bd. 119.00 (0-88390-404-7) Pfeiffer & Co.

— Pfeiffer & Company Library of Presentation & Discussion Resources: Individual Development. LC 93-86713. (Illus.). 1994. ring bd. 119.00 (0-88390-402-0) Pfeiffer & Co.

— Pfeiffer & Company Library of Presentation & Discussion Resources: Leadership. LC 93-86717. (Illus.). 1994. ring bd. 119.00 (0-88390-405-5) Pfeiffer & Co.

— Pfeiffer & Company Library of Presentation & Discussion Resources: Problem Solving. LC 93-86715. (Illus.). 1994. ring bd. 119.00 (0-88390-403-9) Pfeiffer & Co.

— Pfeiffer & Company Library of Presentation & Discussion Resources: Training Technologies. LC 93-86720. (Illus.). 1994. ring bd. 119.00 (0-88390-427-6) Pfeiffer & Co.

— Pfeiffer & Company Library of Theories & Models: Group. LC 93-86722. (Illus.). 1994. ring bd. 119.00 (0-88390-429-2) Pfeiffer & Co.

— Pfeiffer & Company Library of Theories & Models: Individual. LC 93-86721. (Illus.). 1994. ring bd. 119.00 (0-88390-428-4) Pfeiffer & Co.

— Pfeiffer & Company Library of Theories & Models: Management. LC 93-86723. (Illus.). 1994. ring bd. 119.00 (0-88390-430-6) Pfeiffer & Co.

— Pfeiffer & Company Library of Theories & Models: Organization. LC 93-86724. (Illus.). 1994. ring bd. 119.00 (0-88390-431-4) Pfeiffer & Co.

Pfeiffer, J. William & Ballew, Arlette C. Design Skills in Human Resource Development, Set. LC 87-40536. (Training Technologies Set Ser.). 118p. (Orig.). 1988. pap. text ed. 139.00 (0-88390-215-X) Pfeiffer & Co.

— Presentation & Evaluation Skills in Human Resource Development, 7 bks., Set. LC 87-40535. (Training Technologies Set Ser.). 210p. (Orig.). 1988. pap. text ed. 139.00 (0-88390-216-8) Pfeiffer & Co.

— University Associates Training Technologies, 7 vols., Set. 1988. Boxed set. boxed 139.00 (0-88390-286-9) Pfeiffer & Co.

— Using Case Studies, Simulations & Games in Human Resource Developments. LC 88-50384. (Training Technologies Set Ser.). 124p. (Orig.). 1988. Set, 7 bks. & index. pap. 139.00 (0-88390-222-2) Pfeiffer & Co.

— Using Instruments in Human Resource Development. LC 87-40359. (Training Technologies Set Ser.). 116p. (Orig.). 1988. pap. text ed. 139.00 (0-88390-210-9) Pfeiffer & Co.

— Using Lecturettes, Theory, & Models in Human Resource Development. LC 87-40533. (Training Technologies Set Ser.). 92p. (Orig.). 1988. pap. text ed. 139.00 (0-88390-213-3) Pfeiffer & Co.

— Using Role Plays in Human Resource Development. LC 87-40534. (Training Technologies Set Ser.). 129p. (Orig.). 1988. pap. 139.00 (0-88390-214-1) Pfeiffer & Co.

— Using Structured Experiences in Human Resource Development. LC 87-40530. (Training Technologies Set Ser.). 109p. (Orig.). 1988. pap. text ed. 139.00 (0-88390-212-5) Pfeiffer & Co.

Pfeiffer, J. William & Goodstein, Leonard D., eds. Annual for Facilitators, Trainers, & Consultants, 1982. LC 73-92841. (Human Resource Development Ser.). (Illus.). 293p. (Orig.). 1982. pap. 39.95 (0-88390-006-8); ring bd. 89.95 (0-88390-005-X) Pfeiffer & Co.

— The Annual, 1984: Developing Human Resources. LC 73-92841. (Illus.). 292p. (Orig.). 1984. pap. 39.95 (0-88390-010-6); ring bd. 89.95 (0-88390-009-2) Pfeiffer & Co.

— The Annual, 1986: Developing Human Resources. LC 73-92841. (Human Resource Development Ser.). (Illus.). 294p. (Orig.). 1986. pap. text ed. 39.95 (0-88390-014-9); ring bd. 89.95 (0-88390-013-0) Pfeiffer & Co.

Pfeiffer, J. William & Jones, John E., eds. Annual Handbook for Group Facilitators, 1972. LC 73-92841. (Human Resource Development Ser.). (Illus.). 271p. (Orig.). 1972. pap. 39.95 (0-88390-085-8); ring bd. 89.95 (0-88390-072-6) Pfeiffer & Co.

— Annual Handbook for Group Facilitators, 1974. LC 73-92841. (Human Resource Development Ser.). (Illus.). 289p. (Orig.). 1974. pap. 39.95 (0-88390-082-3); ring bd. 89.95 (0-88390-074-2) Pfeiffer & Co.

— Annual Handbook for Group Facilitators, 1976. LC 73-92841. (Human Resource Development Ser.). (Illus.). 292p. (Orig.). 1976. pap. 39.95 (0-88390-088-2); ring bd. 89.95 (0-88390-087-4) Pfeiffer & Co.

— Annual Handbook for Group Facilitators, 1978. LC 73-92841. (Human Resource Development Ser.). (Illus.). 295p. (Orig.). 1978. pap. 39.95 (0-88390-099-8); ring bd. 89.95 (0-88390-098-X) Pfeiffer & Co.

— The Annual Handbook for Group Facilitators, 1980. LC 73-92841. (Human Resource Development Ser.). (Illus.). 296p. (Orig.). 1980. pap. 39.95 (0-88390-097-1); ring bd. 89.95 (0-88390-096-3) Pfeiffer & Co.

— A Handbook of Structured Experiences for Human Relations Training, Set. Incl. Vol. 1. rev. ed. LC 73-92840. 1985. pap. 19.95 (0-88390-041-6); Vol. II. rev. ed. LC 73-92840. 1985. pap. 19.95 (0-88390-042-4); Vol. III. rev. ed. LC 73-92840. 1985. pap. 19.95 (0-88390-043-2); Vol. IV. LC 73-92840. 1985. pap. 19.95 (0-88390-044-0); Vol. V. LC 73-92840. 1985. pap. 19.95 (0-88390-045-9); Vol. VI. LC 73-92840. 1985. pap. 19.95 (0-88390-046-7); Vol. VII. LC 73-92840. 1985. pap. 19.95 (0-88390-047-5); Vol. VIII. LC 73-92840. 1985. pap. 19.95 (0-88390-048-3); Vol. IX. LC 73-92840. 1985. pap. 19.95 (0-88390-049-1); Vol. X. LC 73-92840. 1985. pap. 19.95 (0-88390-184-6); LC 73-92840. (Human Resource Development Ser.). 1985. write for info. (0-88390-040-8) Pfeiffer & Co.

Pfeiffer, J. William, jt. ed. see Goodstein, Leonard D.

Pfeiffer, J. William, jt. ed. see Jones, John E.

Pfeiffer, Janet. The Seedling's Journey. 1994. pap. 3.95 (1-55673-591-X, 7990) CSS OH.

Pfeiffer, John B., ed. Sulfur Removal & Recovery from Industrial Processes. LC 75-11557. (Advances in Chemistry Ser.: No. 139). 1975. 27.95 (0-8412-0217-6) Am Chemical.

Pfeiffer, K. Ludwig, jt. ed. see Gumbrecht, Hans U.

Pfeiffer, K. M., jt. auth. see Heim, U.

Pfeiffer, Katherine S. Word for Windows Design Companion: The Desktop Guide to Creating Great-Looking Brochures, Ads, Newsletters, Catalogs & More. LC 91-35107. (Illus.). 504p. 1992. 21.95 (0-940087-77-4) Ventana Pr.

— Word for Windows Design Companion: The Desktop Guide to Creating Great-Looking Brochures, Ads, Newsletters, Catalogs & More. 2nd ed. 504p. 1994. 21.95 (1-56604-075-2) Ventana Pr.

Pfeiffer, Kenneth & Olson, James N. Basic Statistics for the Behavioral Sciences. LC 80-22778. (C). 1981. text ed. 44.00 (0-03-049866-X) HB Coll Pubs.

Pfeiffer, Laura B. Uprising of June Twentieth, 1792. LC 78-115360. reprint ed. 29.50 (0-404-05019-0) AMS Pr.

Pfeiffer, Lee. The John Wayne Scrapbook. (Citadel Film Ser.). 1989. pap. 17.95 (0-8065-1147-8, Citadel Pr) Carol Pub Group.

— Official Andy Griffith Show Scrapbook. (Illus.). 224p. 1993. pap. 15.95 (0-8065-1449-3, Citadel Pr) Carol Pub Group.

Pfeiffer, Lee & Lisa, Philip. The Films of Sean Connery. LC 92-37561. (Citadel Film Series Paperback Original). (Orig.). 1993. pap. 17.95 (0-8065-1391-8) Carol Pub Group.

— The Incredible World of 007: The Official Celebration of James Bond. (Illus.). 224p. 1992. pap. 16.95 (0-8065-1311-X, Citadel Pr) Carol Pub Group.

Pfeiffer, Lee, jt. auth. see Zmijewsky, Boris.

Pfeiffer, Marlie, jt. auth. see Carpenter, Edwin.

Pfeiffer, Martin. The Agricultural Individuality: A Picture of the Human Being. 64p. (Orig.). (C). 1990. pap. text ed. 4.75 (0-938250-27-2) Bio-Dynamic Farm.

Pfeiffer, P. E. Probability for Applications. (Texts in Statistics Ser.). (Illus.). 695p. 1989. 59.95 (0-387-97138-6) Spr-Verlag.

***Pfeiffer, Paul E.** Basic Probability Topics Using MATLAB. (Bookware Companion Problems Ser.). 160p. 1995. disk, pap. 30.95 (0-534-94536-8) PWS Pubs.

— Concepts of Probability Theory. 1978. pap. text ed. 7.95 (0-486-63677-1) Dover.

Pfeiffer, Peter, ed. Thomas Mann's Doctor Faustus: A Novel at the Margin of Modernism. (Studies in German Literature, Linguistics & Culture: Vol. 49). (Illus.). 210p. 1991. 65.00 (0-938100-73-4) Camden Hse.

Pfeiffer, Peter C., jt. ed. see Eigler, Friederike.

Pfeiffer, Philip A. Pensacola's Currency Issuing Banks & Their Bank Notes, 1833-1935. Romond, Marguerite P., ed. LC 75-6130. (Illus.). 1975. pap. 10.00 (0-9601038-1-3) Pfeiffer.

Pfeiffer, R. Scott, jt. auth. see McLaughlin, Milbrey.

Pfeiffer, Raymond S. & Forsberg, Ralph P. Ethics on the Job: Cases & Strategies. 151p. (C). 1993. pap. 17.95 (0-534-19386-2) Intl Thomson.

Pfeiffer, Ron & Mangus, Brent. Concepts of Athletic Training. (Physical Education Ser.). 400p. (C). 1995. pap. text ed. 38.75 (0-86720-839-2) Jones & Bartlett.

Pfeiffer, Ronald P., jt. auth. see Mangus, Brent C.

Pfeiffer, Rudolfus, ed. see Callimachus.

Pfeiffer, Rudolph. History of Classical Scholarship from 1300 to 1850. 1976. 79.00 (0-19-814364-8) OUP.

Pfeiffer, S. E. & Barbares, E., eds. Remyelination in the Central Nervous System. (Journal: Developmental Neuroscience: Vol. 11, No. 2, 1989). (Illus.). 72p. 1989. pap. 29.00 (3-8055-5033-2) S Karger.

Pfeiffer Staff. Start Your Own Desktop Publishing Business. 240p. 1994. pap. 12.95 (0-89384-245-1) Pfeiffer & Co.

— Start Your Own Import-Export Business. 238p. 1994. pap. 12.95 (0-89384-248-6) Pfeiffer & Co.

— Start Your Own Mail-Order Business. (Start Your Own Ser.). 220p. 1994. pap. 12.95 (0-89384-243-5) Pfeiffer & Co.

— Start Your Own Resume Writing Business. 228p. 1994. pap. 12.95 (0-89384-249-4) Pfeiffer & Co.

— Start Your Own Secretarial Service Business. 240p. 1994. pap. 12.95 (0-89384-244-3) Pfeiffer & Co.

Pfeiffer, Steven. Neuroscience Approached Through Cell Culture, Vol. I. 256p. 1982. 156.00 (0-8493-6340-3, QP356, CRC Reprint) Franklin.

Pfeiffer, Steven E. Neuroscience Approached Through Cell Culture, Vol. II. 192p. 1983. 132.00 (0-8493-6341-1, QP356, CRC Reprint) Franklin.

Pfeiffer, U. J., jt. ed. see Lewis, F. R.

Pfeiffer, Vera. Positive Thinking: Everything You Have Always Known about Positive Thinking But Were Afraid to Put into Practice. LC 92-26000. 1992. pap. 12.95 (1-85230-079-5) Element MA.

Pfeiffer, William. Technical Writing. 1991. pap. write for info. (0-675-21221-9, Merrill Pub Co) Macmillan.

Pfeiffer, William S. Proposal Writing: The Art of Friendly Persuasion. 224p. (C). 1989. pap. write for info. (0-675-20988-9, Merrill Pub Co) Macmillan.

— Technical Writing: A Practical Approach. 2nd ed. LC 93-792. 576p. (C). 1993. pap. write for info. (0-02-395111-7) Macmillan.

***Pfeil.** White Guys: Studies in Postmodern Domination & Difference. 240p. 1995. 64.95x (1-85984-937-7, C0537, Pub. by Verso UK); pap. 18.95 (1-85984-032-9, C0538, Pub. by Verso UK) Routledge Chapman & Hall.

Pfeil, Don, jt. auth. see Haynes, J. H.

Pfeil, E., jt. ed. see Hoffman, E.

Pfeil, Fred. Another Tale to Tell: Essays on Postmodern Culture. 1990. 45.00 (0-86091-277-9, A4297, Pub. by Verso UK); pap. 17.95 (0-86091-992-7, A4301, Pub. by Verso UK) Routledge Chapman & Hall.

— Goodman 2020. LC 84-43153. 240p. 1986. 15.00 (0-253-32617-6) Ind U Pr.

— Shine On. 1987. 14.95 (0-89924-047-X); pap. 7.50 (0-318-32848-8) SPD-Small Pr Dist.

— What They Tell You to Forget: A Novella & Stories. 220p. 1996. 25.00 (0-916366-49-9) Norton.

Pfeil, W. E., jt. ed. see Rollnik, H.

Pfeiler, William K. German Literature in Exile: The Concern of the Poets. LC 57-11322. (University of Nebraska Studies, New Ser.: No. 16). 150p. reprint ed. pap. 42.80 (0-317-08248-5, 2002876) Bks Demand.

— War & the German Mind. LC 41-21951. reprint ed. 19.50 (0-404-05028-X) AMS Pr.

Pfeiler, Wolfgang. Intra-German Relations in a Period of East-West Tensions. (CISA Working Paper Ser.: No. 50). 42p. (Orig.). Date not set. pap. 10.00 (0-86682-063-9) Ctr Intl Relations.

Pfeister, Joseph L. & Pacer, Leonard A. Executive Guide to Federal Income Tax Planning for Life Insurance Companies. LC 81-11413. (Illus.). 303p. 1981. 42.50 (0-942640-01-2) Touche Co.

Pfelpsen, Stephen H., et al. Handbook on ERISA Litigation. 558p. 1992. ring bd. 126.00 (0-13-125493-6) Aspen Law.

Pfenniger, D., ed. see Burton, W. Butler, et al.

Pfenniger, D., jt. ed. see Gurzadyan, V. G.

Pfennigstorf, Werner & Gifford, Donald G. A Comparative Study of Liability Law & Compensation Schemes in Ten Countries & the United States. 224p. (C). 1991. text ed. 45.00 (1-56594-000-8) Ins Res Coun.

Pfennigstorf, Werner & Schwartz, Alec M., eds. Legal Protection Insurance: American & European Approaches. LC 86-71977. ix, 185p. (Orig.). 1986. pap. 18.50 (0-910059-10-1) Am Bar Foun.

***Pfenning, Frank, ed.** Logic Programming & Automated Reasoning: Fifth International Conference, LPAR '94, Kiev, Uraine, July 16-22, 1994. LC 94-21152. (Lecture Notes in Computer Science; Lecture Notes in Artificial Intelligence Ser.). 1994. 52.00 (0-387-58216-9) Spr-Verlag.

— Types in Logic Programming. (Logic Programming Ser.). (Illus.). 325p. 1992. 42.50 (0-262-16131-1) MIT Pr.

Pfenninger & Fowler. Office Procedures for Primary Care. 600p. 1993. pap. 39.95 (0-8016-6384-9) Mosby Yr Bk.

Pfenninger, Karl H., jt. auth. see Widnell, Christopher C.

Pfenninger, Mary A. Gray Wolf. 209p. 1984. 8.95 (0-89697-235-6) Intl Univ Pr.

Pfenningstorf, Werner, ed. Pollution Insurance: International Survey of Coverages & Exclusions. LC 93-32141. (International Environmental Law & Policy Ser.). 272p. (C). 1993. lib. bdg. 110.00 (1-85333-941-5, Pub. by Graham & Trotman UK) Kluwer Ac.

Pfenningstorf, Werner, jt. auth. see Davidson, Ken.

Pferd, William, III. Dogs of the American Indians. Denlinger, William W. & Rathman, R. Annabel, eds. LC 87-432. (Other Dog Bks.). (Illus.). 192p. 1987. 19.95 (0-87714-126-6) Denlingers.

Pfetsch, Frank R. West Germany: Internal Structures & External Relations: Foreign Policy of the Federal Republic of Germany. LC 87-29129. 288p. 1988. text ed. 59.95 (0-275-92868-3, C2868, Praeger Pubs) Greenwood.

***Pfetsch, Frank R., ed.** International Relations & Pan-Europe: Theoretical Approaches & Empirical Findings; Proceedings. 611p. (C). 1994. pap. text ed. 68.00 (3-89473-945-2) Westview.

Pfeufer, Levin M., jt. auth. see Kahn, Robbie P.

Pfeuty, Pierre & Toulouse, Gerard. Introduction to the Renormalization Group & to Critical Phenomena. LC 76-26111. 202p. reprint ed. pap. 57.60 (0-317-29389-3, 2024283) Bks Demand.

Pffeiffer, K. M., jt. auth. see Heim, U.

Pfeiffer, E. E. Using the Bio-Dynamic Compost Preparations & Sprays in Garden, Orchard & Farm. 2nd ed. 64p. (C). reprint ed. pap. 4.75 (0-938250-26-4) Bio-Dynamic Farm.

***Pfiffner.** Earth-Friendly Holidays: How to Make Fabulous Gifts & Decorations from Reusable Objects. (Earth-Friendly Ser.). Date not set. pap. text ed. 12.95 (0-471-12005-7) Wiley.

Pfiffner & Fraser. How Desktop Publishing Works. 1994. pap. 24.95 (1-56276-191-9) Ziff-Davis.

Pfiffner, George. Earth-Friendly Toys: How to Make Fabulous Toys & Games from Reusable Objects. (Illus.). 128p. (J). (gr. 3-7). 1994. pap. text ed. 12.95 (0-471-00822-2) Wiley.

— Earth-Friendly Wearables: How to Make Fabulous Clothes & Accessories from Reusable Objects. (Earth-Friendly Ser.). (J). 1995. pap. text ed. 12.95 (0-471-00823-0) Wiley.

Pfiffner, James P. The Modern Presidency. LC 92-62738. 1993. pap. text ed. 10.00 (0-312-07506-5) St Martin.

Pfiffner, James P., ed. The Presidency in Transition. 550p. (Orig.). (C). 1989. 30.00 (0-938204-00-9); pap. 20.00 (0-318-37937-6) Ctr Study Presidency.

Pfingsten, Ralph & Downs, Floyd L., eds. Salamanders of Ohio. LC 85-60845. (Bulletin New Ser.: Vol. 7, No. 2). (Illus.). 300p. (Orig.). 1989. pap. text ed. 30.00 (0-86727-099-3) Ohio Bio Survey.

Pfingston, Roger. The Circus of Unreasonable Acts: Poems & Photographs. (Illus.). 44p. (Orig.). 1982. pap. 10.00 (0-685-54971-2) Years Pr.

— Hazards of Photography. (Chapbook Series I: No. 3). 32p. 1980. pap. 3.00 (1-880649-03-9) Writ Ctr Pr.

— Something Iridescent. LC 85-72587. 98p. (Orig.). 1987. pap. 7.95 (0-935306-37-4) Barnwood Pr.

Pfister. Papilloma Viruses & Human Cancer. 1990. 205.00 (0-8493-5860-4, RC268) CRC Pr.

***Pfister, Albrecht.** Quadratic Forms with Applications to Algebraic Geometry & Topology. (London Mathematical Society Lecture Note Ser.: No. 217). 220p. (C). 1995. pap. 34.95 (0-521-46755-1) Cambridge U Pr.

Pfister, Arthur. Beer Cans, Bullets, Things & Pieces. 1972. pap. 2.00 (0-910296-29-4) Broadside Pr.

Pfister, D. H., et al. A Bibliography of Taxonomic Literature 1753-1821. (Mycologia Memoirs Ser.: No. 17). 162p. 1991. pap. text ed. 55.00 (3-443-76007-4, Pub. by Cramer-Borntraeger GW) Lubrecht & Cramer.

Pfister, Guenter G. Beginning German: A Way to Self-Awareness. (Illus.). 383p. (C). 1989. text ed. 28.80 (0-87563-302-1) Stipes.

Pfister, Guenter G. & Poser, Yvonne. Culture, Proficiency, & Control in Foreign Language Teaching. LC 87-10594. 174p. (Orig.). (C). 1987. lib. bdg. 43.50 (0-8191-6445-3); pap. text ed. 19.50 (0-8191-6446-1) U Pr of Amer.

Pfister, Joel. The Production of Personal Life: Class, Gender, & the Psychological in Hawthorne's Fiction. LC 91-16686. 288p. 1991. 37.50 (0-8047-1947-0); pap. 14.95 (0-8047-1948-9) Stanford U Pr.

— Staging Depth: The Politics of Psychological Discourse in the Drama of O'Neill. LC 94-26336. (Culture Studies of the United States Ser.). (Illus.). 350p. 1995. lib. bdg. 45.00x (0-8078-2186-1); pap. text ed. 17.95x (0-8078-4496-9) U of NC Pr.

Pfister, Joseph, jt. ed. see Hall, Bob.

Pfister, Judith & Kneedler, Julia A. A Guide to Lasers in the OR. (Illus.). 1983. write for info. (0-9613138-0-3) ED Inc.

Pfister, Judith I., et al. The Nursing Spectrum of Lasers. (Illus.). 156p. (Orig.). (C). 1988. pap. text ed. 32.50 (0-9622255-0-9) ED Inc.

Pfister, Manfred. The Theory & Analysis of Drama. Halliday, John, tr. (European Studies in English Literature). (Illus.). 360p. (C). 1991. pap. 19.95 (0-521-42383-X) Cambridge U Pr.

Pfister, Marcus. Chris & Croc. LC 93-46828. (Illus.). 32p. (J). (gr. k-3). 1994. 14.95 (1-55858-273-8); lib. bdg. 14.88 (1-55858-274-6) North-South Bks NYC.

— The Christmas Star. James, J. Alison, tr. LC 93-15143. (Illus.). 32p. (J). (gr. k-3). 1993. 16.95 (1-55858-203-7); lib. bdg. 16.88 (1-55858-204-5) North-South Bks NYC.

— Dazzle the Dinosaur. James, J. Alison, tr. LC 94-34840. (Illus.). 32p. (J). (gr. k-3). 1994. 16.95 (1-55858-337-8); lib. bdg. 16.88 (1-55858-338-6) North-South Bks NYC.

— Destello el Dinosaurio: Dazzle the Dinosaur. LC 94-42452. (Illus.). 32p. (SPA.). (J). (gr. k-3). 1995. 16.95 (1-55858-387-4); lib. bdg. 16.88 (1-55858-388-2) North-South Bks NYC.

— Hang on, Hopper! Lanning, Rosemary, tr. LC 94-43635. (Illus.). 32p. (J). (gr. k-3). 1995. 14.95 (1-55858-403-X); lib. bdg. 14.88 (1-55858-404-8) North-South Bks NYC.

— Hopper. LC 90-47065. (Illus.). 32p. (J). (ps-00). 1991. 14.95 (1-55858-106-5) North-South Bks NYC.

— Hopper. LC 90-47065. (Illus.). 32p. (J). (gr. k-3). 1994. pap. 5.95 (1-55858-352-1) North-South Bks NYC.

— Hopper Hunts for Spring. Lanning, Rosemary, tr. LC 91-29671. (Illus.). 32p. (J). (gr. k-3). 1992. 14.95 (1-55858-139-1); lib. bdg. 14.88 (1-55858-147-2) North-South Bks NYC.

— Hopper Hunts for Spring. LC 90-47065. (Illus.). (J). (ps-3). 1995. pap. 5.95 (1-55858-416-1) North-South Bks NYC.

— Les Nouveaux Amis De Pit. (Illus.). 32p. (FRE.). (J). (gr. k-3). 1992. 13.95 (3-85539-632-9) North-South Bks NYC.

— Penguin Pete. LC 87-1627. (Illus.). 32p. (J). (gr. k-3). 1987. 14.95 (1-55858-018-2) North-South Bks NYC.

— Penguin Pete. LC 87-1627. (Illus.). 32p. (J). (ps-2). 1994. pap. 5.95 (1-55858-356-4) North-South Bks NYC.

— Penguin Pete, Ahoy! Lanning, Rosemary, tr. LC 93-19921. (Illus.). 32p. (J). (ps-1). 1993. 14.95 (1-55858-220-7); lib. bdg. 14.88 (1-55858-221-5) North-South Bks NYC.

— Penguin Pete & Little Tim. Lanning, Rosemary, tr. LC 94-5093. (J). 1994. 14.95 (1-55858-301-7); lib. bdg. 14.88 (1-55858-302-5) North-South Bks NYC.

— Penguin Pete & Pat. Bell, Anthea, tr. LC 88-25296. (Illus.). 32p. (J). (gr. k-3). 1989. 14.95 (1-55858-003-4) North-South Bks NYC.

P Q

— Penguin Pete's New Friends. LC 87-72037. (Illus.). 32p. (J). (gr. k-3). 1988. 14.95 (*1-55858-025-5*) North-South Bks NYC.

— Penguin Pete's New Friends. LC 87-72037. (Illus.). (J). (ps-3). 1995. pap. 5.95 (*1-55858-414-5*) North-South Bks NYC.

— El Pex Arco Iris. LC 94-30500. (Illus.). 32p. (SPA.). (J). (gr. k-3). 1994. 16.95 (*1-55858-361-0*); lib. bdg. 16.88 (*1-55858-362-9*) North-South Bks NYC.

— Pinguin Pit. (Illus.). 32p. (GER.). (J). (gr. k-3). 1992. 13. 95 (*3-314-00297-1*) North-South Bks NYC.

— Pit et Pat. (Illus.). 32p. (FRE.). (J). (gr. k-3). 1992. 13.95 (*3-85539-657-4*) North-South Bks NYC.

— Pit, le Petit Pingouin. (Illus.). 32p. (FRE.). (J). (gr. k-3). 1992. 13.95 (*3-314-20627-5*) North-South Bks NYC.

— Pit und Pat. (Illus.). 32p. (GER.). (J). (gr. k-3). 1992. 13. 95 (*3-314-00327-7*) North-South Bks NYC.

— Pit's Neue Freunde. (Illus.). 32p. (GER.). (J). (gr. k-3). 1992. 13.95 (*3-85825-301-4*) North-South Bks NYC.

— Rainbow Fish. James, J. Alison, tr. LC 91-42158. (Illus.). 32p. (J). (gr. k-3). 1992. lib. bdg. 16.88 (*1-55858-010-7*) North-South Bks NYC.

— The Rainbow Fish. James, J. Alison, tr. LC 91-42158. (Illus.). 32p. (J). (gr. k-3). 1992. 16.95 (*1-55858-009-3*) North-South Bks NYC.

— The Rainbow Fish Big Book. (Illus.). (J). (gr. k-3). 1995. 25.00 (*1-55858-441-2*) North-South Bks NYC.

— Sun & Moon. (J). (gr. 4-7). 1993. pap. 4.95 (*0-590-44490-5*) Scholastic Inc.

Pfister, Marcus, illus. My Penguin Pete Address Book. (J). 1991. 7.95 (*1-55858-126-X*) North-South Bks NYC.

— My Penguin Pete Birthday Book. (J). 1991. 7.95 (*1-55858-127-8*) North-South Bks NYC.

Pfister, Marcus, jt. auth. see Siegenthaler, Kathrin.

***Pfister, Marucs.** El Pez Arco Iris Libro Grande. (Illus.). (J). (gr. k-3). 1995. 25.00 (*1-55858-440-4*) North-South Bks NYC.

Pfister, Michelle M., jt. auth. see Alderman, Eric.

***Pfister, Patrick.** Tales from the Open Road. 200p. 1995. 20.00 (*0-89733-419-1*) Academy Chi Pubs.

Pfisterer, Bill, ed. see Herbert, Belle.

Pfisterer, Bill, ed. see Martin, Richard.

Pfisterer, F., jt. auth. see Blocks, W. H.

Pfitzer, Donald. The Hiker's Guide to Georgia. (Illus.). 304p. (Orig.). 1993. pap. 12.95 (*1-56044-215-8*) Falcon Pr MT.

Pfitzer, Gregory M. Samuel Eliot Morison's Historical World: In Quest of a New Parkman. 384p. 1991. text ed. 37.50 (*1-55553-101-6*) NE U Pr.

Pfitzer, Peter & Grundmann, Ekkehard, eds. Current Status of Diagnostic Cytology. (Recent Results in Cancer Research Ser.: Vol. 133). (Illus.). 175p. 1993. write for info. (*3-540-56618-X*) Spr-Verlag.

— Current Status of Diagnostic Cytology. LC 93-11295. (Recent Results in Cancer Research Ser.: Vol. 133). 1993. 89.00 (*0-387-56618-X*) Spr-Verlag.

Pfitzner, C. Barry. Mathematical Fundamentals for Microeconomics. LC 92-72588. 1993p. 1993. pap. 16.00 (*1-878975-13-7*) Kolb Pub.

Pflanze, Otto. Bismark & the Development of Germany, Set. (Illus.). 1531p. (C). 1990. 140.00 (*0-691-05673-0*) Princeton U Pr.

— Bismark & the Development of Germany, Vol. 1: The Period of Unification, 1815-1871. (Illus.). 1531p. (C). 1990. Vol. 1; The Period of Unification, 1815-1871. text ed. 55.00 (*0-691-05587-4*) Princeton U Pr.

— Bismark & the Development of Germany, Vol. 2: The Period of Consolidation, 1871-1880. (Illus.). 1531p. (C). 1990. Vol. 2; The Period of Consolidation, 1871-1880. text ed. 55.00 (*0-691-05588-2*) Princeton U Pr.

— Bismark & the Development of Germany, Vol. 3: The Period of Fortification, 1880-1898. (Illus.). 1531p. (C). 1990. Vol. 3; The Period of Fortification, 1880-1898. text ed. 55.00 (*0-691-05589-0*) Princeton U Pr.

Pflanze, Otto, ed. The Unification of Germany, 1848-1871. LC 78-23470. (European Problem Studies). 128p. 1979. reprint ed. pap. 9.50 (*0-88275-803-9*) Krieger.

***Pflanzer, Richard.** Human Physiology. 208p. (C). 1995. pap. text ed. 20.95 (*0-7872-0804-3*) Kendall-Hunt.

— Lecture Notes: N217 Human Physiology. 192p. (C). 1994. spiral bd. 17.95 (*0-8403-9150-1*) Kendall-Hunt.

Pflanzer, Richard G. Experimental & Applied Physiology. 4th ed. 400p. (C). 1989. spiral bd. write for info. (*0-697-01177-1*) Wm C Brown Pubs.

— Experimental & Applied Physiology. 5th ed. 384p. (C). 1994. text ed., spiral bd. 35.00 (*0-697-13786-4*) Wm C Brown Pubs.

Pflanzer, Richard G., jt. auth. see Rhoades, Rodney A.

Pflaum-Connor, Susanna. The Development of Language & Literacy in Young Children. 3rd ed. 256p. (C). 1986. pap. write for info. (*0-675-20447-X*, Merrill Pub Co) Macmillan.

Pflaum-Connor, Susanna, ed. Aspects of Reading Education. LC 77-95250. (National Society for the Study of Education Publication Ser.). 1978. 29.25 (*0-8211-1517-0*); text ed. write for info. (*0-685-03192-6*) McCutchan.

Pflaum, Hans G. Germany on Film: Theme & Content in the Cinema of the Federal Republic of Germany. Richter, Roland & Helt, Richard, trs. LC 89-22661. (Contemporary Film & Television Ser.). 158p. (C). 1990. 27.50 (*0-8143-2258-1*) Wayne St U Pr.

Pflaum, Rosalynd. Marie Curie & Her Daughter Irene. LC 92-2453. (YA). (gr. 5 up). 1993. 21.50 (*0-8225-4915-8*, Lerner Publctns) Lerner Group.

Pflaum, Susanna W., jt. ed. see Pignatelli, Frank.

Pfleeger, Charles P. Machine Organization: An Introduction to the Structure & Programming of Computing. 240p. (C). 1990. reprint ed. 48.50 (*0-471-07970-7*) Krieger.

Pfleeger, Shari L. Software Engineering. 2nd ed. 1991. write for info. (*0-02-395115-X*) Macmillan.

Pfleeger, Shari L. & Straight, David W. Introduction to Discrete Structures. rev. ed. 372p. (C). 1985. lib. bdg. 30.50 (*0-471-80075-9*) Krieger.

Pfleger, Carl, ed. see Strauss, Josef.

Pfleger, Deborah B., jt. auth. see Warren, Sandra.

Pfleger, F. L. & Linderman, R. G., eds. Mycorrhizae & Plant Health. LC 93-72994. (APS Symposium Ser.). 360p. 1994. pap. 34.00 (*0-89054-158-2*) Am Phytopathol Soc.

Pfleger, Helmut. Taktik und Witz Im Schach. (Praxis Schach Ser.: Bd. 8). 182p. (GER.). Date not set. write for info. (*3-283-00252-5*, Pub. by Georg Olms GW) Lubrecht & Cramer.

Pfleger, Karl. Wrestlers with Christ. Watkin, Edward I., tr. LC 68-16968. (Essay Index Reprint Ser.). 1977. 23.95 (*0-8369-0785-X*) Ayer.

Pfleger, Karl, et al. Mass Spectral & GC Data of Drugs, Poisons, Pesticides, Pollutants & Their Metabolites, Pts. I, II & III. enl. rev. ed. LC 92-49331. 3000p. 1992. 675. 00 (*0-685-58974-9*) VCH Pubs.

— Mass Spectral & GC Data of Drugs, Poisons, Pesticides, Pollutants & Their Metabolites, Pts. I, II & III. 2nd enl. rev. ed. LC 92-49331. 3000p. 1992. lib. bdg. 825.00 (*0-89573-855-4*) VCH Pubs.

Pfleger, Margot, jt. ed. see Ranard, Donald A.

***Pfleger, S. & Lefevre, J. P.** Advanced Speech Applications: European Research on Speech Technology. (Project Group Speech Technology Ser.: Vol. 1). 320p. 1994. pap. 50.00 (*0-387-58142-1*) Spr-Verlag.

Pfleger, S., et al, eds. Data Fusion Applications: Workshop Proceedings, Brussels, November 25, 1992. (Research Reports ESPRIT Ser.: Vol. 1). 266p. 1993. pap. 45.00 (*0-387-56973-1*) Spr-Verlag.

Pfleger, T., jt. auth. see Montenbruck, O.

Pfleider, Eugene P., et al, eds. Surface Mining. LC 68-24169. (Seeley W. Mudd Ser.). (Illus.). 1083p. reprint ed. pap. 180.00 (*0-8357-8338-3*, 2033974) Bks Demand.

Pfleiderer, A., ed. Ovarialkarzinom. (Journal: Onkologie: Vol. 7, Suppl. 2). 70p. 1984. pap. 16.00 (*3-8055-3922-3*) S Karger.

— Probleme der Krebsnachsorge. (Beitraege zur Onkologie Ser.: Band 4). (Illus.). 112p. 1980. pap. 26.50 (*3-8055-1378-X*) S Karger.

Pfleiderer, Beatrix & Bibeau, Gilles, eds. Anthropologies of Medicine: A Colloquium on West European & North American Perspectives. (Curare Ser.: Special Vol. 7, 1991). (Illus.). 272p. (C). 1991. pap. 48.00 (*3-528-07820-0*, Pub. by Vieweg & Sohn GW) Ballen Bkslr.

Pfleiderer, Otto. Lectures on the Influence of the Apostle Paul on the Development of Christianity. Smith, J. Frederick, tr. LC 77-27166. (Hibbert Lectures: 1885). reprint ed. 37.50 (*0-404-60406-4*) AMS Pr.

— Philosophy & Development of Religion, 2 vols., Set. LC 77-27229. (Gifford Lectures: 1894). reprint ed. 84.50 (*0-404-60470-6*) AMS Pr.

— Primitive Christianity: Its Writings & Teachings in Their Historical Connections, 4 vols. Morrison, W. D., ed. Montgomery, W., tr. LC 65-22085. (Library of Religious & Philosophical Thought). 1966. reprint ed. lib. bdg. 195.00 (*0-678-09954-5*, Reference Bk Pubs) Kelley.

***Pfleiderer, W., et al, eds.** Biochemical & Clinical Aspects of Pteridines Vol. 5: Cancer - Immunology - Metabolic Diseases. 408p. (C). 1987. lib. bdg. 176.95 (*3-11-011251-5*) De Gruyter.

— Biochemical & Clinical Aspects of Pteridines, Vol. 5: Cancer - Immunology - Metabolic Diseases. 408p. (C). 1987. lib. bdg. 176.95 (*0-89925-334-2*) De Gruyter.

Pfleuger, Al. Fisherman's Handbook. 96p. 1981. pap. 6.95 (*0-89317-035-6*) Windward Pub.

Pflieger, Pat. Beverly Cleary. (Twayne's United States Authors Ser.: No. 572). 232p. (C). 1991. text ed. 20.95 (*0-8057-7613-3*, Twayne) Macmillan.

— Reference Guide to Modern Fantasy for Children. LC 83-10692. 768p. 1984. text ed. 79.50 (*0-313-22886-8*, PFC/, Greenwood Pr) Greenwood.

Pflomm, Phyllis N. Chalk in Hand: The Draw & Tell Book. LC 86-15480. (Illus.). 126p. 1986. pap. 16.50 (*0-8108-1921-X*) Scarecrow.

— Puppet Plays Plus: Hand Puppet Plays for Two Puppeteers. LC 94-4875. (Illus.). 253p. 1994. 29.50 (*0-8108-2738-7*) Scarecrow.

Pfloog, Jan. Asi Son los Gatitos! (Kittens are Like That) Saunders, Paola B., tr. LC 93-19920. (Spanish Translations Picturebacks Ser.). (Illus.). 32p. (J). (ps-3). 1993. pap. 2.25 (*0-679-84719-7*) Random Bks Yng Read.

— Asi Son los Perritos! (Spanish Translations Picturebacks Ser.). (Illus.). 32p. (SPA.). (J). (ps-3). 1993. pap. 2.25 (*0-394-85064-5*) Random Bks Yng Read.

— Asi Son los Perritos - Puppies Are Like That. (J). (ps-3). 1993. pap. 2.25 (*0-394-85604-X*) Random Bks Yng Read.

— The Farm Book. (Golden Super Shape Bks.). (Illus.). 24p. (J). (ps-00). 1989. pap. write for info. (*0-307-58117-9*, Golden Bks) Western Pub.

— The Kitten Book. (Golden Super Shape Bks.). (Illus.). 24p. (J). (ps-00). 1968. pap. write for info. (*0-307-10079-0*, Golden Bks) Western Pub.

— Kittens Are Like That. LC 75-36469. (Pictureback Ser.). (Illus.). 32p. (J). (ps-1). 1976. 2.50 (*0-394-83243-4*) Random Bks Yng Read.

— Puppies Are Like That. LC 74-2542. (Picturebacks Ser.). (Illus.). 32p. (Orig.). (J). (ps-1). 1975. pap. 2.50 (*0-394-82923-9*) Random Bks Yng Read.

— The Puppy Book. (Golden Super Shape Bks.). (Illus.). 24p. (J). (ps-00). 1968. pap. write for info. (*0-307-10078-2*, Golden Bks) Western Pub.

— The Zoo Book. (Golden Super Shape Bks.). (Illus.). 24p. (J). (ps-00). 1989. pap. write for info. (*0-307-58118-7*, Golden Bks) Western Pub.

Pflug, Bernd. Education in Ayurveda: A Re-Constructional Analysis. (C). 1992. 24.00 (*81-212-0399-6*, Pub. by Gian Publng Hse II) S Asia.

Pflug, G., et al, eds. Simulation & Optimization: Proceedings of the International Workshop on Computationally Intensive Methods in Simulation & Optimization Held at the International Institute for Applied Systems Analysis (IIASA) Laxenburg, Austria, August 23-25, 1990. (Lecture Notes in Economics & Mathematical Systems Ser.: Vol. 374). (Illus.). x, 162p. 1992. pap. 39.00 (*0-387-54980-3*) Spr-Verlag.

Pflug, I. J. Selected Papers on the Microbiology & Engineering of Sterilization Processes. 5th ed. 298p. (C). 1988. pap. text ed. write for info. (*0-929340-05-1*) Environ Sterilization Lab.

— Textbook for an Introductory Course in the Microbiology & Engineering of Sterilization Processes. 7th ed. 454p. (C). 1990. pap. write for info. (*0-929340-01-9*) Environ Sterilization Lab.

Pflug, Peter, jt. auth. see Jarnicki, Marek.

Pflug, Warner W., ed. A Guide to the Archives of Labor History & Urban Affairs. LC 73-6004. 196p. reprint ed. pap. 55.90 (*0-7837-3659-2*, 2043530) Bks Demand.

Pfluger, A. Karate: Basic Principles. Kuttner, Paul & Cunningham, Dale S., trs. LC 67-27760. (Illus.). (J). (gr. 8 up). 1969. reprint ed. 6.95 (*0-8069-4432-3*); reprint ed. lib. bdg. 7.49 (*0-8069-4433-1*) Sterling.

Pflugrad, K., et al, eds. Decommissioning of Nuclear Installations: Proceedings of an International Conference Organized by the Commission of the European Communities, Directorate-General Science, Research & Development, Decommissioning Programme, Held in Brussels, Belgium, 24-27 October, 1989. 858p. 1990. 176.50 (*1-85166-523-4*) Elsevier.

***Pfluke, Lillian A.** Breastfeeding & the Active Woman. 160p. 1995. pap. 11.95 (*1-56796-087-1*) WRS Group.

Pflumm, Carol C. Hearthstrings: How to Make Decorative Garlands for All Seasons. LC 93-2140. (Illus.). 128p. 1993. 14.95 (*0-670-84244-3*, Viking Studio) Studio Bks.

***Pfnausch, Edward G.** Codigo, Comunidad, Ministerio. 170p. 1994. pap. 8.00 (*0-943616-66-2*) Canon Law Soc.

Pfnausch, Edward G., ed. Canon Law Digest, Vol. 11: Officially Published Documents Affecting the Code of Canon Law 1984-1985. xi, 433p. 1991. 30.00 (*0-943616-50-6*) Canon Law Soc.

— Code, Community, Ministry. 2nd rev. ed. 145p. 1992. pap. 8.00 (*0-943616-54-9*) Canon Law Soc.

Pfohl, Gerhard. Bibliographie der Griechischen Vers-Inschriften. 62p. (GER.). 1964. write for info. (*0-318-70446-3*, Pub. by Georg Olms GW); write for info. (*0-318-71855-3*, Pub. by Georg Olms GW) Lubrecht & Cramer.

— Bibliographie Der Griechischen Vers-Inschriften. 62p. 1964. write for info. (*0-318-70996-1*, Pub. by Georg Olms GW) Lubrecht & Cramer.

Pfohl, S. J. Deviance & Social Control. 416p. 1985. text ed. write for info. (*0-07-049757-5*) McGraw.

Pfohl, Stephen. Death at the Parasite Cafe: Social Science (Fictions) & the Postmodern. Kroker, Arthur & Kroker, Marilouise, eds. (Culture Texts Ser.). 300p. 1992. pap. 14.95 (*0-312-07573-1*) St Martin.

Pfohl, Stephen J. Images of Deviance & Social Control: A Sociological History. 2nd ed. LC 93-25803. 1993. pap. text ed. write for info. (*0-07-049765-6*) McGraw.

Pfordresher, John. A Variorum Edition of Tennyson's Idylls of the King. LC 73-4852. 1088p. 1973. text ed. 94.00 (*0-231-03691-4*) Col U Pr.

Pfost, Harry, ed. see American Feed Manufacturers Association Staff.

Pfouts, Chris. Lead Poisoning: Twenty-Five True Stories from the Wrong End of a Gun. 184p. 1991. text ed. 21. 95 (*0-87364-620-7*) Paladin Pr.

— True Tales of American Violence. 184p. 1993. text ed. 21. 95 (*0-87364-742-4*) Paladin Pr.

Pfouts, Chris, jt. auth. see MacYoung, Marc.

Pfoutz, Sally. Missing Person. 176p. (J). (gr. 7 up). 1993. 14. 99 (*0-670-84663-5*) Viking Child Bks.

Pfrimmer, Mildred. Books to Learn & Live by, 5 bks., Set. Incl. Bk. ABC's of Creation. 1977. (*0-318-55947-1*); Bk. 2. ABC's of the Flood. 1977. (*0-318-55948-X*); Bk. 3. Aardvark in the Art. 1977. (*0-318-55949-8*); Bk. 4. Elephant in Eden. 1977. (*0-318-55950-1*); Bk. 5. Tale of the Whale. 1977. (*0-318-55951-X*); (Little Talkers Ser.). (J). (gr. 3-9). 1977. 17.50 (*0-685-80546-8*) Triumph Pub.

***Pfrimmer, Vicki M., et al.** Information Management in Insurance Companies. (FLMI Insurance Education Program Ser.). 1995. text ed. 54.00 (*0-939921-70-7*) LOMA.

Pfrogner, J. Gruenlandgesellschaften & Grundwasser der Innaue Suedlich Von Rosenheim. (Dissertationes Botanicae Ser.: Vol. 23). (Illus.). 179p. (GER.). 1973. pap. text ed. 30.00 (*3-7682-0921-0*, Pub. by Cramer GW) Lubrecht & Cramer.

Pfrommer, Michael. Metalwork from the Hellenized East, Catalogue of the Collections: The J. Paul Getty Museum. LC 92-34053. (Illus.). 248p. 1992. 75.00 (*0-89236-218-9*) J P Getty Trust.

Pfuetze, Paul. Self, Society, Existence: Human Nature & Dialogue in the Thought of George Herbert Mead & Martin Buber. LC 72-11743. 400p. 1973. reprint ed. text ed. 65.00 (*0-8371-6708-6*, PFSS, Greenwood Pr) Greenwood.

Pfuhl, Erdwin H., Jr. & Henry, Stuart. The Deviance Process. 3rd ed. LC 93-2942. 296p. 1993. 45.95 (*0-202-30469-8*); pap. 23.95 (*0-202-30470-1*) Aldine de Gruyter.

Pfuhl, Ernst. Masterpieces of Greek Drawing & Painting. Beazley, J. D., tr. LC 79-83879. (Illus.). 1979. reprint ed. lib. bdg. 50.00 (*0-87817-250-5*) Hacker.

Pfund, P. A., ed. see AIAA-ASME Joint Fluids, Plasma, Thermophysics, & Heat Transfer Conference Staff.

Pfund, P. A., ed. see American Society of Mechanical Engineers Staff.

Pfurtscheller, G. & Lopes Da Silva, F. H., eds. Functional Brain Imaging. LC 88-19071. 276p. (C). 1988. text ed. 98.00 (*0-920887-28-7*) Hogrefe & Huber Pubs.

Pfurtscheller, G., et al, eds. Brain Ischemia: Quantitative EEG & Imaging Techniques. (Progress in Brain Research Ser.: Vol. 62). 1985. 151.50 (*0-444-80582-6*) Elsevier.

— Rhythmic EEG Activities & Cortical Function. (Developments in Neuroscience Ser.: Vol. 10). 314p. 1980. 84.00 (*0-444-80028-X*) Elsevier.

***PGA of America Staff.** The Official Guide of the PGA Championships: In-Depth Coverage of Golf's Most Prestigious Events. (Illus.). 456p. (YA). 1995. pap. 16.95 (*1-57243-066-4*) Triumph Bks.

***PGA Senior Tour Staff.** The PGA Senior Tour 1996: Official Media Guide of the PGA Senior Tour. rev. ed. (Illus.). 256p. 1995. pap. 13.95 (*1-57243-078-8*) Triumph Bks.

PGA Staff. The Official Guide of the PGA Championships. 450p. 1994. lib. bdg. 34.95 (*1-880141-66-3*); pap. 16.95 (*1-880141-63-9*) Triumph Bks.

PGA Staff & Wiren, Gary. The PGA Manual of Golf: The Professional Way to Play Better Golf. (Illus.). 480p. 1991. text ed. 39.95 (*0-02-599291-0*) Macmillan.

***PGA Tour Staff.** PGA Tour 1996: Official Media Guide of the PGA Tour. (Illus.). 384p. Date not set. pap. 13.95 (*1-57243-077-X*) Triumph Bks.

PGE Chef's Night Out Committee. PGE Chef's Night Out Cookbook. Otto, Bridget et al, eds. 95p. (Orig.). 1991. pap. 14.95 (*0-9629263-0-2*) PGE Chefs.

PGW Staff. Ban Censorship: The Postcard Activist. 1991. pap. 4.95 (*1-879096-02-1*) Postcard Activist.

— Keep Abortion Safe & Legal: The Postcard Activist. 1991. pap. 4.95 (*1-879096-00-5*) Postcard Activist.

— No Handguns: The Postcard Activist. 1991. pap. 4.95 (*1-879096-01-3*) Postcard Activist.

PH Editorial Staff. Lawyer's Desk Book 1990-1991 Cumulative Supplement. 168p. 1990. pap. 40.00 (*0-13-524208-8*) P-H.

Pha, Mac N., ed. see Phach, Nguyen N.

Phaal, Peter. LAN Traffic Management. LC 94-7848. (Hewlett-Packard Professional Bks.). 170p. 1994. pap. text ed. 32.67 (*0-13-124207-5*) P-H.

Phach, Nguyen N. Vietnam & Meta Revolution. Pha, Mac N., ed. 374p. (C). 1992. 50.00 (*0-9636159-0-4*) Vietnam & Wrld.

Phadke, Arun G. & Thorp, James S. Computer Relaying for Power Systems. 289p. 1988. text ed. 135.00 (*0-471-92063-0*) Wiley.

Phadke, Arun G., jt. auth. see Horowitz, Stanley H.

Phadke, Madhav S. Quality Engineering Using Robust Design. 250p. 1989. text ed. 58.00 (*0-13-745167-9*) P-H.

Phadnis, U. & Malani, I. Women of the World: Illusion & Reality. 285p. 1979. 18.95 (*0-7069-0489-3*) Asia Bk Corp.

Phadnis, Urmila. Domestic Conflicts in South Asia, Vol. 2. 1986. 18.50 (*81-7003-071-4*, Pub. by S Asia Pubs II) S Asia.

— Ethnicity & Nation-Building in South Asia. (Illus.). 352p. (C). 1990. 29.95 (*0-8039-9607-1*) Sage.

Phadnis, Urmilla. Domestic Conflicts in South Asia, Vol. 1: Political Dimensions. 1986. 18.50 (*0-317-68066-8*, Pub. by S Asia Pubs II) S Asia.

Phaedrus. The Fables of Phaedrus. Widdows, P. F., tr. LC 91-9765. (Illus.). 176p. (C). 1991. text ed. 27.00 (*0-292-72470-5*); pap. 12.95 (*0-292-72473-X*) U of Tex Pr.

Phaf, R. Hans. Learning in Natural & Connectionist Systems: Experiments & a Model. LC 93-47517. 312p. (C). 1994. lib. bdg. 112.00 (*0-7923-2685-7*) Kluwer Ac.

Phaff, H. J., et al. The Life of Yeasts. 2nd enl. rev. ed. (Illus.). 320p. 1978. 38.00 (*0-674-53325-9*) HUP.

Phaff, Herman J., ed. A Bibliography of Publications by the Faculty, Staff, & Students of the University of California, 1876-1980, on Grapes, Wines & Related Subjects. (UC Publications in Catalogs & Bibliographies: Vol. 2). 1986. 45.00 (*0-520-09702-5*) U CA Pr.

Phagan, Janice. Communications for Community Associations. (GAP Report Ser.: Vol. 15). (C). 1991. reprint ed. pap. 14.50 (*0-944715-17-6*) CAI.

— Communications for Community Associations, GAP #15. 3rd ed. (Illus.). 16p. (C). 1995. pap. 14.50 (*0-944715-36-2*) CAI.

Phagan, Jesse R. Mastering Electronics Math. 2nd ed. 1991. text ed. 27.95 (*0-07-157622-3*) McGraw.

Phagan, Jesse R. & Spaudling, B. Learning Electronics. 1989. pap. 24.95 (*0-07-156297-4*) McGraw.

Phagan, Jesse R. & Spaudling, Bill. Learning Electronics: Theory & Experiments with Computer-Aided Instruction for the Commodore 64-128. 1988. pap. 16.95 (*0-07-155245-6*) McGraw.

Phagan, Jesse R. & Spaulding, Bill. Learning Electronics: Theory & Experiments with Computer-Aided Instruction for the Commodore 64-128. 1988. text ed. 24.95 (*0-07-155483-1*); pap. text ed. 16.95 (*0-07-155491-2*) McGraw.

— Learning Electronics: Theory & Experiments with Computer-Aided Instruction for the Commodore 64-128. 1988. text ed. 24.95 (*0-07-156725-9*); pap. text ed. 16.95 (*0-07-156731-3*) McGraw.

Phagan, Mary. The Murder of Little Mary Phagan. (Illus.). 300p. 1988. 21.95 (*0-88282-039-7*) New Horizon NJ.

Phagan, Patricia. Charles Meryon & Jean-Francois Millet: Etchings of Urban & Rural 19th-Century France. LC 92-39756. 1992. 25.00 (*0-915977-10-9*) Georgia Museum of Art.

Phagan, Patricia, jt. ed. see Eiland, William U.

Phagan, Patricia, jt. auth. see Pelletier, S. William.

Phagan, R. Jesse. Applied Mathematics. (Illus.). 320p. 1992. text ed. 29.28 (*0-87006-822-9*) Goodheart.
— Mastering Electronics Math. 2nd ed. (Illus.). 352p. 1991. 27.95 (*0-8306-6589-7*, 3589); pap. 17.95 (*0-8306-3589-0*) TAB Bks.
Phagan, R. Jesse & Spaulding, William. Learning Electronics. 1991. 24.95 (*0-8306-6250-2*) TAB Bks.
— Learning Electronics: Theory & Experiments with Computer-Aided Instruction for the Commodore 64-128. (Illus.). 380p. 1988. 24.95 (*0-8306-7882-4*, 2882); pap. 16.95 (*0-8306-2882-7*) TAB Bks.
— Learning Electronics: Theory & Experiments with Computer-Aided Instruction for the Commodore 64-128. (Illus.). 370p. 1988. 24.95 (*0-8306-0182-1*, 2982); pap. 16.95 (*0-8306-2982-3*) TAB Bks.
— Learning Electronics: Theory & Experiments with Computer-Aided Instruction for the Commodore 64-128. (Illus.). 380p. 1989. 24.95 (*0-8306-9082-4*, 3082); pap. 16.95 (*0-8306-9382-3*, 3082) TAB Bks.
— Learning Electronics - C-64. 1991. 24.95 (*0-8306-6431-9*) TAB Bks.
— Learning Electronics Theory. 1991. 24.95 (*0-8306-6677-X*) TAB Bks.
Phagan-Schostok & Maloney. Contemporary Dental Hygiene Practice, Vol. 1. (Illus.). 221p. 1988. Incl. lab manual. student ed, pap. text ed. 68.00 (*0-86715-169-2*) Quint Pub Co.
— Contemporary Dental Hygiene Practice, Vol. 2. (Illus.). 120p. 1989. pap. text ed. 34.00 (*0-86715-170-6*) Quint Pub Co.
***Phaidon Staff.** Art Book: An A-Z of Artists. rev. ed. (C). 1994. 35.00 (*0-7148-2984-6*, Pub. by Phaidon Press UK) Chronicle Bks.
— The Pre-Raphaelite Vision. (Miniature Editions Ser.). (Orig.). (C). 1994. pap. 8.99 (*0-7148-3252-9*, Pub. by Phaidon Press UK) Chronicle Bks.
Phaigh, Rich & Perry, Paul J. Athletic Massage. 176p. 1986. pap. 12.00 (*0-671-60303-5*, Fireside) S&S Trade.
Phair, Charles. Atlantic Salmon Fishing. (Fifty Greatest Bks.). (Illus.). 193p. 1993. reprint ed. 50.00 (*1-56416-049-1*) Derrydale Pr.
Phair, Judith T. William Cullen Bryant & His Critics, 1808-1872: A Bibliography. LC 74-18203. v, 188p. 1974. 12. 50 (*0-87875-064-9*) Whitston Pub.
Phalen, Lane. The Book Lover's Guide to Boston & Cape Cod. (Book Lover's Buide Ser.). 256p. (Orig.). 1992. pap. 14.95 (*1-880339-08-0*) Brigadoon Bay.
— The Book Lover's Guide to Chicagoland. LC 91-74136. (Book Lover's Guide Ser.). (Illus.). 256p. (Orig.). 1991. pap. 14.95 (*1-880339-06-4*) Brigadoon Bay.
— Book Lover's Guide to Washington, D. C. (Book Lover's Guide Ser.). 288p. (Orig.). 1993. pap. 14.95 (*1-880339-09-9*) Brigadoon Bay.
— The New Book Lover's Guide to Chicagoland: Including Southern Wisconsin. expanded ed. LC 95-79486. 288p. 1995. reprint ed. pap. 14.95 (*1-880339-11-0*) Brigadoon Bay.
Phalen, Richard C. In Our Time: Rediscovering America, 1940-90's. LC 93-10742. 1993. 29.95 (*0-912083-64-6*, NO. 64-6) Diamond Communications.
— Our Chicago Cubs: Inside the History & the Mystery of Baseball's Favorite Franchise. LC 92-24663. 1992. 22.95 (*0-912083-60-3*) Diamond Communications.
Phalen, Robert F. Inhalation Studies: Foundations & Techniques. 288p. 1984. 168.00 (*0-8493-5469-2*, RA1270, CRC Reprint) Franklin.
Phalen, Thomas E. Design & Analysis of Single-Ply Roof Systems. 624p. 1993. text ed. 105.00 (*0-13-203407-7*) P-H.
Phalgunadi, I. G., tr. The Indonesian Mahabharata, Adiparva: The First Book. (C). 1990. 59.50 (*81-85179-50-6*, Pub. by Aditya Prakashan II) S Asia.
— Indonesian Mahabharata Udyogaparva. (C). 1994. text ed. 58.00 (*81-85689-96-2*, Pub. by Popular Prakashan II) S Asia.
Phalle, Thibaut D. The Federal Reserve System: An Intentional Mystery. LC 84-15879. 352p. 1984. pap. text ed. 16.95 (*0-275-91803-3*, B1803, Praeger Pubs) Greenwood.
— The Federal Reserve System: An Intentional Mystery. LC 84-15879. 352p. 1985. text ed. 65.00 (*0-275-90083-5*, C0083, Praeger Pubs) Greenwood.
Pham. Proton & Carbon NMR Spectra of Polymers. 1991. 299.95 (*0-8493-7728-5*, QC463) CRC Pr.
Pham, D. T. Robotics & AI: Sensing, Reasoning, Planning, Manipulation, Mobility. (Machine Tools & Manufacture Ser.: Vol. 28). 120p. 1988. 63.00 (*0-08-036627-9*, Pergamon Pr) Elsevier.
Pham, D. T., ed. Artificial Intelligence in Design. (Artificial Intelligence in Industry Ser.). (Illus.). 520p. 1991. 129.00 (*0-387-50634-9*) Spr-Verlag.
— Expert Systems in Engineering. (Artificial Intelligence in Industry Ser.). (Illus.). 450p. 1988. 104.00 (*0-387-19229-8*) Spr-Verlag.
Pham, D. T. & Heginbotham, W. B., eds. Robot Grippers. (International Trends in Manufacturing Technology Ser.). 360p. 1986. 106.00 (*0-387-16004-3*) Spr-Verlag.
***Pham, Duc T. & Xing, Liu.** Neural Networks for Identification, Prediction, & Control. LC 95-12935. 1995. write for info. (*3-540-19959-4*) Spr-Verlag.
Pham, F. Singularites des Systemes Differentiels de Gauss-Manin. (Progress in Mathematics Ser.: No. 2). 340p. (FRE.). 1980. pap. 46.50 (*0-8176-3002-3*) Birkhauser.
Pham, Hoang. Fault-Tolerant Software Systems: Techniques & Applications. LC 92-30945. 128p. 1992. pap. 35.00 (*0-8186-3210-0*, 3210) IEEE Comp Soc.
— Proceedings of the ISSAT International Conference: Reliability & Quality in Design. 436p. (Orig.). (C). 1994. pap. text ed. 60.00 (*0-9639998-0-X*) ISSAT.
***Pham, Hoang, ed.** Software Reliability & Testing (3-95) 148p. 1995. pap. text ed. 35.00 (*0-8186-6852-0*, BP06852) IEEE Comp Soc.
***Pham, Hoangmai, et al.** Understanding the Second Epidemic: The Status of Research on Women & AIDS in the United States. LC 91-81222. 63p. 1992. 15.00 (*1-877966-11-8*) Ctr Women Policy.
***Pham, John-Peter.** Primer for the Catechism of the Catholic Church. 112p. 1994. 4.95 (*0-614-02562-1*) Scepter Pubs.
Pham Kim Vinh. The Vietnhamese Culture: An Introduction. rev. ed. (Illus.). 314p. 1994. pap. 18.00 (*1-882273-25-7*) P K Vinh Res.
***Pham, Mai.** The Best of Vietnamese & Thai Cooking: Favorite Recipes from Lemon Grass Restaurant & Cafe. LC 95-5281. 1995. pap. write for info. (*0-7615-0016-2*) Prima Pub.
Pham, Quang Tho, et al. Proton & Carbon NMR Spectra of Polymers, Vol. 2. 439p. 1983. text ed. 260.00 (*0-471-26263-3*, Wiley-Interscience) Wiley.
***Pham Van Tien.** Le Trinh Nu: Tho. LC 95-90282. 80p. (VIE.). 1995. pap. 6.50 (*0-9645739-1-1*) Van Pham Found.
Phan Huy Ich, jt. auth. see Dang Tran Con.
Phan, Peter C. Eternity in Time: A Study of Karl Rahner's Eschatology. LC 86-43217. 272p. 1988. 39.50 (*0-941664-83-X*) Susquehanna U Pr.
— Grace & the Human Condition. (Message of the Fathers of the Church Ser.: Vol. 15). 317p. (Orig.). 1988. 21.00 (*0-8146-5355-3*); pap. 19.95 (*0-8146-5326-X*) Liturgical Pr.
— Social Thought. LC 83-83156. (Message of the Fathers of the Church Ser.: Vol. 20). 1984. 15.95 (*0-8146-5360-X*); pap. 14.95 (*0-8146-5331-6*) Liturgical Pr.
Phan, Peter C., ed. Church & Theology: Essays in Memory of Carl J. Peter. LC 93-41316. 320p. 1995. 59.95 (*0-8132-0798-3*) Cath U Pr.
— Ethnicity, Nationality, & Religious Experience. (College Theology Society Annual Ser.: Vol. No. 37). 336p. (C). 1995. lib. bdg. 61.00 (*0-8191-9509-X*); pap. text ed. 27. 50 (*0-8191-9524-3*) U Pr of Amer.
***Phan-Phat-Huon.** Ak Va Thap-Gia. 303p. 1994. pap. text ed. 20.00 (*1-885550-06-5*) Du-Sinh St Joseph.
***Phan, Sem H. & Thrall, Roger S., eds.** Pulmonary Fibrosis. LC 94-43568. (Lung Biology in Health & Diseases Ser.: Vol. 80). 1995. write for info. (*0-8247-8851-6*) Dekker.
Phang. The Development of Singapore Law: Historical & Socio-Legal Perspectives. 1990. 252.00 (*0-409-99588-6*) Butterworth Legal Pubs.
Phang, Ruth A., ed. see Green Acres School Staff.
Phanton, Rhona, jt. auth. see Blenkinsopp, Alison.
Pharand, Donat. The Northeast Passage: Arctic Straits. 1984. lib. bdg. 102.00 (*90-247-2979-3*) Kluwer Ac.
— The Waters of the Canadian Arctic. LC 86-26395. (Studies in Polar Research). (Illus.). 300p. 1988. 79.95 (*0-521-32503-X*) Cambridge U Pr.
Pharand, Donat & Leanza, Umberto, eds. The Continental Shelf & the Exclusive Economic Zone - Le Plateau Continental et la Zone Economique Exclusive: Delimitation & Legal Regime - Delimitation et Regime Juridique. LC 92-37816. (Publications on Ocean Development Ser.: Vol. 19). (ENG & FRE.). 1993. lib. bdg. 154.50 (*0-7923-2056-5*) Kluwer Ac.
Phares. Introduction to Personality. 3rd ed. (C). 1991. text ed. 61.50 (*0-673-46424-5*) HarpCollege.
Phares, E. Jerry. Clinical Psychology. 4th ed. 640p. (C). 1992. text ed. 51.95 (*0-534-16830-2*) Brooks-Cole.
Phares, M. I., jt. auth. see Grubb, C. A.
Phares, Ross. Bible in Pocket, Gun in Hand: The Story of Frontier Religion. LC 64-11375. viii, 182p. 1971. pap. 8.95 (*0-8032-5725-2*, Bison Books) U of Nebr Pr.
— Cavalier in the Wilderness. LC 76-1409. (Illus.). 290p. (J). (gr. 6-12). 1976. reprint ed. 18.95 (*0-88289-128-6*); reprint ed. pap. 13.95 (*0-88289-127-8*) Pelican.
— Governors of Texas. LC 76-7013. (Governors of the States Ser.). (Illus.). 184p. 1976. 17.95 (*0-88289-078-6*) Pelican.
— Reverend Devil. (Illus.). 263p. 1974. 17.50 (*0-88289-011-5*) Pelican.
Phares, Tom K., jt. auth. see Jernstedt, George W.
Phares, Walid. Lebanese Christian Nationalism: The Rise & Fall of an Ethnic Resistance. LC 94-28297. 264p. 1994. lib. bdg. 45.00 (*1-55587-535-1*) Lynne Rienner.
Pharies, David A. Charles S. Peirce & the Linguistic Sign. LC 85-11053. (Foundations of Semiotics Ser.: No. 9). vi, 118p. 1985. 39.00x (*90-272-3279-2*) Benjamins North Am.
Pharis, Mary, jt. auth. see Gottesfeld, Mary.
Pharis, R. P. & Reid, D. M., eds. Hormonal Regulation of Development III. (Encyclopedia of Plant Physiology Ser.: Vol. 11). (Illus.). 870p. 1985. 310.00 (*0-387-10197-7*) Spr-Verlag.
Pharma Realm Buddhist University Faculty Staff, comp. Human Roots: Buddhist Stories for Young Readers, Vol. 1. (Illus.). 95p. (Orig.). (J). (gr. 3 up). 1982. pap. 5.00 (*0-88139-500-5*) Buddhist Text.
Pharmaceutical Panel Committee. The Competitive Status of the U. S. Pharmaceutical Industry. LC 83-50568. 102p. 1983. pap. 12.95 (*0-309-03396-9*) Natl Acad Pr.
Pharmaceutical Society of Great Britain. European Pharmacopoeia, Pt. II-5. 2nd ed. 1983. 191.50 (*0-685-04362-2*, Pub. by Pharmaceutical Pr UK) Rittenhouse.
Pharmaceutical Society of Japan. Japanese Pharmaceutical Terms, Japanese-English-Japanese. 508p. 1985. 95.00 (*0-8288-1852-5*) Fr & Eur.
Pharmaceuticals & Cosmetics Manufacturing Expo Staff. Pharmaceuticals & Cosmetics Manufacturing Expo: Proceedings of Technical Program May 13-15, 1980, Rosemont, Illinois. 318p. reprint ed. pap. 90.70 (*0-317-39629-3*, 2020833) Bks Demand.
Pharmacists in Ophthalmic Practice, Inc. Staff. Extemporaneous Ophthalmic Preparations. Closson, Richard G. & Reynolds, Lois A., eds. LC 93-72671. (Illus.). 347p. (Orig.). 1993. pap. 37.50 (*0-915486-18-0*) Applied Therapeutics.
Pharmaco Medical Doc. Inc. Staff. Index Guide - 9. Anzlowar, Rajka, ed. 1992. 590.00 (*0-913210-13-7*) Pharmaco-Med.
Pharmacology of Thermoregulation Symposium Staff. Temperature Regulation & Drug Action: Proceedings of the Pharmacology of Thermoregulation Symposium, 2nd, Paris, 1974. Lommax, P. & Schonbaum, E., eds. 450p. 1975. 119.25 (*3-8055-1756-4*) S Karger.
Pharmacology of Thermoregulation Symposium Staff, et al. Drugs, Biogenic Amines & Body Temperature: Proceedings of the Pharmacology of Thermoregulation Symposium, 3rd, Banff, Alberta, Sept. 1976. Cooper, K. E., ed. (Illus.). 1977. 93.00 (*3-8055-2395-5*) S Karger.
Pharoah, Timothy M., jt. auth. see Collins, Michael F.
***Pharr, Clyde.** Vergil's Aeneid Books, Vol. I-VI. 1995. pap. text ed. 19.00 (*0-86516-272-7*) Bolchazy-Carducci.
Pharr, Clyde & Wright, John. Homeric Greek. rev. ed. LC 84-40698. (Illus.). 416p. 1986. pap. 19.95 (*0-8061-1937-3*) U of Okla Pr.
Pharr, Clyde, tr. see Codex Theodosianus.
Pharr, David. Modern Messages from the Minor Prophets. 1987. pap. 6.25 (*0-89137-330-6*) Quality Pubns.
Pharr, Susan J. Losing Face: Status Politics in Japan. 1990. 32.00 (*0-520-06050-4*) U CA Pr.
— Losing Face: Status Politics in Japan. 1992. pap. 13.00 (*0-520-08092-0*) U CA Pr.
— Political Women in Japan: The Search for a Place in Political Life. LC 80-12984. 275p. 1981. pap. 13.00 (*0-520-04453-3*) U CA Pr.
***Pharr, Susan J. & Krauss, Ellis S., eds.** Media & Politics in Japan. LC 95-8730. 1996. write for info. (*0-8248-1698-6*) UH Pr.
Pharr, Suzanne. Homophobia: A Weapon of Sexism. LC 88-72094. (Illus.). 91p. (Orig.). 1988. pap. 9.95 (*0-9620222-1-7*) Chardon Pr.
***Pharrams, Doris & Charles, Anna.** All Day...All God. 52p. (Orig.). 1995. pap. 5.95 (*0-9645558-0-8*) Gift of Love.
Phased Array Antenna Symposium (1970: Polytechnic Institute of Brooklyn. Phased Array Antennas: Proceedings of the 1970 Phased Array Antenna Symposium. Oliner, Arthur A., ed. (Modern Frontiers in Applied Science Ser.). 393p. reprint ed. pap. 112.10 (*0-685-15315-0*, 2027162) Bks Demand.
Phatak, Arvind V. International Dimensions of Management. 3rd ed. 200p. 1992. pap. 20.95 (*0-534-92812-9*) Intl Thomson.
***Phatak, Avind V.** International Dimensions of Management. 4th ed. LC 94-21634. 1995. text ed. 18.95 (*0-538-84485-X*) S-W Pub.
Phathanothai, Sirin. Dragon's Pearl. 1994. 23.00 (*0-671-79546-5*) S&S Trade.
Phay, Robert E. A Hearings Manual for Faculty Nonreappointment & Other Adversarial Hearings. 84p. (Orig.). (C). 1982. pap. text ed. 7.50 (*1-56011-071-6*, 82. 09) Institute Government.
— Legal Issues in Public School Administrative Hearings. 1982. 4.95 (*1-56534-002-7*) NOLPE.
— Nonreappointment, Dismissal, & Reduction in Force of Teachers & Administrators. 63p. (Orig.). (C). 1982. pap. text ed. 7.50 (*1-56011-107-0*, 81.31) Institute Government.
Phay, Robert E. & Ward, Robert M. Local Acts Creating & Providing for North Carolina City School Administrative Units. 423p. (Orig.). (C). 1972. pap. text ed. 3.50 (*1-56011-173-9*, 72.15) Institute Government.
***Phay, Wilbert L.** John Brown's Family in Red Bluff, 1864-1870. (ANCRR Occasional Publication Ser.: No. 12). 66p. 1986. 6.00 (*0-614-05682-9*) Assn NC Records.
Phayer, Michael. Protestant & Catholic Women in Nazi Germany. LC 89-16574. (Illus.). 287p. (C). 1990. text ed. 34.95 (*0-8143-2211-5*) Wayne St U Pr.
Phayre, Arthur. The Journal of Arthur Phayre, Envoy to the Court of Ava. Bd. with Narrative of the Mission to the Court of Ava in 1855. 31.00 (*0-19-638075-8*) OUP.
Pheanis, D., ed. Computers & Their Applications: Conference Proceedings March 17-19, 1994 Long Beach, CA. 205p. 1994. write for info. (*1-880843-08-0*) Int Soc Comp App.
Pheanise, Suzanne, ed. see Stevenson, Gus.
Phears, William D. Ain't, but It Can Be: Persistence & Faith Overcoming Racist-Related Adversities. LC 93-72874. 323p. 1993. pap. 12.95 (*1-878398-37-7*) Blue Note Pubns.
Pheasant, Felicia, tr. see Perrot, Michelle, ed.
Pheasant, Stephen. Bodyspace: Anthropometry, Ergonomics & Design. 276p. 1986. pap. 44.00 (*0-85066-352-0*) Taylor & Francis.
***Pheasants Forever Staff.** Ringneck. (Illus.). 120p. 1995. 29. 50 (*1-56044-350-2*) Falcon Pr MT.
Pheby, John. Methodology & Economics: A Critical Introduction. LC 90-28626. 145p. (C). 1991. text ed. 46. 95 (*0-87332-851-5*); pap. text ed. 20.95 (*0-87332-852-3*) M E Sharpe.
— New Directions in Post-Keynesian Economics. 1989. text ed. 69.95 (*1-85278-013-4*, Pub. by E Elgar Pub UK) Ashgate Pub Co.
Pheby, John, ed. J. A. Hobson after Fifty Years: Free Thinker of the Social Sciences. LC 93-11883. 1994. text ed. 72.00 (*0-312-10637-8*) St Martin.
Pheby, Keith C. Interventions: Displacing the Metaphysical Subject. (Post Modern Positions Ser.: Vol. 3). 136p. (Orig.). (C). 1988. lib. bdg. 18.95 (*0-944624-04-9*); pap. text ed. 9.95 (*0-944624-05-7*) Maisonneuve Pr.
***Phegan, Barry.** Developing Your Company Culture: The Joy of Leadership - A Handbook for Leaders & Managers. (Illus.). 172p. (Orig.). 1995. pap. 16.95 (*0-9642205-0-4*) Context Pr.
Phegan, C. S., jt. auth. see Cavanaugh, S. W.
Pheifer, Kathleen. Snow. (Short Story Collection Ser.). 100p. 1990. pap. 9.95 (*0-912527-08-0*) Word Beat.
Pheko, Mohau N. Women's Human Rights & Power in Africa. LC 94-65531. 210p. (Orig.). Date not set. write for info. (*1-884921-23-X*) Pheko & Assocs.
Pheko, Motsoko. The Pan Africanist Congress of Azania: Its Role, Achievements, Policies & Ideology. LC 94-65532. 1994. 16.00 (*1-884921-13-2*) Pheko & Assocs.
Pheko, Motsoko, ed. Apartheid: The Story of a Dispossessed People. LC 94-65533. 196p. 1994. 20.00 (*1-884921-02-7*) Pheko & Assocs.
Pheko, S. E. The African People & the Bible. LC 94-65529. 100p. 1995. write for info. (*1-884921-17-5*) Pheko & Assocs.
— The Early Church in Africa: First to Seventh Century & Today. 2nd rev. ed. LC 94-65527. (Illus.). 204p. (C). 1995. 17.00 (*1-884921-05-1*) Pheko & Assocs.
— International Law of Armed Conflict & Guerrilla Warfare. LC 94-65528. 100p. (Orig.). Date not set. write for info. (*1-884921-21-3*) Pheko & Assocs.
— The Land Is Ours: The Political Legacy of Mangaliso Sobukwe. LC 94-65526. (Illus.). 216p. (Orig.). (C). 1994. 20.00 (*1-884921-00-0*) Pheko & Assocs.
— The Law of Succession among the Basotho of Lesotho. LC 94-65530. 200p. 1994. write for info. (*1-884921-08-6*) Pheko & Assocs.
— Selected Speeches to the United Nations. LC 94-65534. 200p. 1994. 17.00 (*1-884921-14-0*) Pheko & Assocs.
Phelan, jt. auth. see Ibsen, Olga A. C.
Phelan, Chas. Dried Fruit: Its Care, Protection from Worms, Packing, Storing, Etc. (Shorey Lost Arts Ser.). 48p. reprint ed. pap. 1.95 (*0-8466-6049-0*, U49) Shorey.
Phelan, Craig. Divided Loyalties: The Public & Private Life of Labor Leader John Mitchell. LC 93-42774. (SUNY Series in American Labor History). 438p. (C). 1994. text ed. 64.50x (*0-7914-2087-6*); pap. text ed. 19.95 (*0-7914-2088-4*) State U NY Pr.
— William Green: Biography of a Labor Leader. LC 88-12356. (SUNY Series in American Labor History). 223p. (Orig.). (C). 1988. 59.50 (*0-88706-870-7*); pap. 19.95 (*0-88706-871-5*) State U NY Pr.
Phelan, Dennis M., jt. ed. see Klain, Ambrose.
***Phelan, Donald J.** Success, Happiness, Independence: Own Your Own Business. LC 94-79175. 200p. 1995. 19.95 (*0-944435-31-9*) Glenbridge Pub.
Phelan, Dorothy. Traditional Bargello: Stitches, Techniques, & Dozens of Pattern & Project Ideas. (Illus.). 96p. (Orig.). 1991. pap. 15.95 (*0-312-06882-4*) St Martin.
***Phelan, Ellen.** Joel Shapiro: Painted Wood Sculpture & Drawings. Newman, Amy, ed. 59p. (Orig.). 1995. pap. write for info. (*1-878283-49-9*) PaceWildenstein.
Phelan, Gerald B. St. Thomas & Analogy. (Aquinas Lectures). 1941. 10.00 (*0-87462-105-4*) Marquette.
Phelan, Gerald B., tr. see Maritain, Jacques.
Phelan, Gerald B., tr. see St. Thomas Aquinas.
Phelan, Gladys, tr. see Fierz-David, Linda.
Phelan, Helene C. And Why Not Every Man? LC 86-90667. (Illus.). 248p. (Orig.). 1987. pap. 12.95 (*0-317-56096-4*) Phelan.
— The Man Who Owned the Pistols. (Illus.). 336p. (Orig.). 1981. pap. 8.50 (*0-9605836-0-2*) Phelan.
— Who Only Stand & Wait. (Illus.). 406p. (Orig.). 1990. pap. 16.95 (*0-9605836-6-1*) Phelan.
Phelan, Helene C., ed. see Kingman, Eugene C.
Phelan, J. P., ed. Clough: Selected Poems. LC 94-20379. (Annotated Texts Ser.). 304p. (C). 1996. text ed. 51.95 (*0-582-05113-4*, 77035, Pub. by Longman UK); pap. text ed. 21.95 (*0-582-05112-6*, 77034, Pub. by Longman UK) Longman.
Phelan, J. P. & Clark, S. L., eds. Cesarean Delivery. 610p. 1988. 63.25 (*0-444-01304-0*) Elsevier.
Phelan, James. Beyond the Tenure Track: Fifteen Months in the Life of an English Professor. 1991. 45.00 (*0-8142-0535-6*); pap. 17.50 (*0-8142-0546-1*) Ohio St U Pr.
— Reading People, Reading Plots: Character, Progression, & the Interpretation of Narrative. LC 88-20840. 256p. 1989. pap. text ed. 13.95 (*0-226-66692-1*) U Ch Pr.
Phelan, James, ed. Reading Narrative: Form, Ethics, Ideology. (Illus.). 336p. (C). 1989. text ed. 42.50 (*0-8142-0458-9*) Ohio St U Pr.
Phelan, James & Rabinowitz, Peter J., eds. Understanding Narrative. (Theory & Interpretation of Narrative Ser.). 256p. 1994. 59.50 (*0-8142-0633-6*); pap. 17.95 (*0-8142-0634-4*) Ohio St U Pr.
Phelan, James, jt. auth. see Graff, Gerald.
Phelan, James, ed. see Twain, Mark, pseud.
Phelan, James R. The Money: The Billon-Dollar Legacy of Howard Hughes. LC 88-42678. (Illus.). 288p. 1989. 17. 95 (*0-394-55637-2*) Random.
Phelan, Jim. The Name's Phelan: The First Part of the Autobiography of Jim Phelan. 298p. 1993. pap. 11.95 (*0-85640-504-3*, Pub. by Blackstaff Pr IE) Dufour.
Phelan, John L. The Hispanization of the Philippines: Spanish Aims & Filipino Responses, 1565-1700. LC 59-8602. (Illus.). 240p. reprint ed. pap. 68.40 (*0-7837-1667-2*, 2052438) Bks Demand.
— The People & the King: The Comunero Revolution in Colombia, 1781. LC 76-53654. (Illus.). 332p. 1978. 32. 50 (*0-299-07290-8*) U of Wis Pr.
***Phelan, Lisa.** Parenting 101. 168p. (Orig.). 1995. pap. 5.95 (*1-56245-188-X*) Great Quotations.
Phelan, Marilyn E. Nonprofit Enterprise: Law & Taxation, 3 vols. LC 85-7870. 1990. 350.00 (*0-685-10477-X*) Clark Boardman Callaghan.

Phelan, Marilyn E. Representing Nonprofit Organizations. 1994. 95.00 (*0-318-72537-1*) Clark Boardman Callaghan.

***Phelan, Michael, et al, eds.** Emergency Mental Health Services in the Community. (Studies in Social & Community Psychiatry). (Illus.). 275p. (C). 1995. write for info. (*0-521-45251-1*) Cambridge U Pr.

Phelan, Nancy. The Romantic Lives of Louise Mack. 1991. pap. 19.95 (*0-7022-2361-1*, Pub. by Univ Queensland Pr AT) Intl Spec Bk.

Phelan, Patricia, ed. Literature & Life: Making Connections in the Classroom. LC 85-644740. (Classroom Practices in Teaching English Ser.: Vol. 25). 182p. (Orig.). 1990. pap. 11.95 (*0-8141-2962-5*) NCTE.

Phelan, Patricia & Davidson, Ann L. Renegotiating Cultural Diversity in American Schools. LC 93-22720. 272p. (C). 1993. text ed. 44.00 (*0-8077-3288-5*); pap. text ed. 18.95 (*0-8077-3287-7*) Tchrs Coll.

Phelan, Patricia J., jt. auth. see Glennie, Angus J.

Phelan, Peggy. Unmarked: The Politics of Performance. LC 92-7895. (Illus.). 224p. 1992. 49.95 (*0-415-06821-5*, A6278); pap. 14.95 (*0-415-06822-3*, A9654) Routledge.

Phelan, Peggy, jt. ed. see Hart, Lynda.

***Phelan, Peter & Reynolds, Peter.** Argument & Evidence: Critical Analysis for the Social Sciences. LC 95-15784. 1995. write for info. (*0-415-11372-5*); pap. write for info. (*0-415-11373-3*) Routledge.

Phelan, Peter D., et al. Respiratory Illness in Children. 3rd ed. 1990. 155.00 (*0-632-02567-0*) Blackwell Sci.

Phelan, Richard M. Fundamentals of Mechanical Design. 3rd ed. LC 79-98487. (C). 1970. text ed. write for info. (*0-07-049776-1*) McGraw.

***Phelan, Shane.** Getting Specific: Postmodern Lesbian Politics. 1994. pap. 17.95 (*0-8166-2110-1*) U of Minn Pr.

— Identity Politics: Lesbian Feminism & the Limits of Community. (Women in the Political Economy Ser.). 256p. (C). 1989. 34.95 (*0-87722-651-2*); pap. 16.95 (*0-87722-902-3*) Temple U Pr.

Phelan, Shane, jt. ed. see Blasius, Mark.

Phelan, Sharon T., et al. Clinical Manual of Obstetrics. 2nd ed. Shaver, David C. et al, eds. LC 92-49503. (Clinical Manual Ser.). (Illus.). 640p. 1993. pap. 32.00 (*0-07-105401-4*) Hlth Prof Div.

Phelan, Susan. Blood Collection: Special Procedures. 1991. vhs 135.00 (*0-89189-309-1*, D47-9-055-VH) Am Soc Clinical.

— Blood Collection: The Pediatric Patient. (NLM Ser.: No. WB382). 1990. vhs 135.00 (*0-89189-302-4*, 47-9-052-VH) Am Soc Clinical.

— Phlebotomy Techniques: A Laboratory Workbook. 1992. 35.00 (*0-89189-343-1*) Am Soc Clinical.

— Phlebotomy Techniques Curriculum Guide. 1993. 20.00 (*0-89189-359-8*) Am Soc Clinical.

Phelan, Thomas. The Hudson: Mohawk Gateway-An Illustrated History. 192p. 1985. 22.95 (*0-89781-118-6*) Preferred Mktg.

Phelan, Thomas W. All about Attention Deficit Disorder: Basic Symptoms, Diagnosis & Treatment Children & Adults. rev. ed. (Illus.). 172p. 1993. pap. 12.95 (*0-9633861-1-5*) Child Mgmt.

— One-Two-Three Magic: Training Your Children to Do What You Want! rev. ed. (Illus.). 1994. pap. 12.95 (*0-9633861-2-3*) Child Mgmt.

— Surviving Your Adolescents: How to Manage & Let Go of Your 13 to 18 Year Olds. rev. ed. (Illus.). 168p. 1993. pap. 12.95 (*0-9633861-0-7*) Child Mgmt.

Phelan, Tom. In the Season of the Daisies. 240p. (Orig.). 1993. pap. 17.95 (*0-946640-97-1*, Pub. by Lilliput Pr Ltd IE) Irish Bks Media.

***Phelan, Virginia.** Praying in Your Own Voice...Through Writing. LC 94-78949. 64p. (Orig.). 1994. pap. 3.95 (*0-89243-682-4*) Liguori Pubns.

Phelan, Virginia B. Two Ways of Life & Death. LC 90-3497. (Studies in Comparative Literature). 272p. 1990. reprint ed. 15.00 (*0-8240-0050-1*) Garland.

Phelan, Walter S. The Christmas Hero & Yuletide Tradition in Sir Gawain & the Green Knight. LC 92-28373. (Illus.). 325p. 1992. text ed. 99.95 (*0-7734-9568-1*) E Mellen.

***Phelizon, Jean-Francois.** Dictionnaire de L'Economie. 4th ed. 352p. (FRE.). 1985. pap. 39.95 (*0-7859-7952-2*, 2717810382) Fr & Eur.

Phelon, Kenneth W., Jr., ed. Phelon's Discount & Jobbing Trade, 1988-1989. 11th ed. 386p. 1989. pap. 95.00 (*0-942239-01-6*) P S & M Inc.

— Sheldon's Retail Directory, 1989. 105th ed. 675p. 1989. pap. 100.00 (*0-942239-03-2*) P S & M Inc.

— Sheldon's Retail Directory, 1990. 106th ed. 656p. 1990. pap. 110.00 (*0-942239-04-0*) P S & M Inc.

Phelon, Mira M., jt. auth. see Phelon, William.

Phelon, W. E. Our Story of Atlantis. 243p. 1972. 7.95 (*0-932785-36-0*) Philos Pub.

Phelon, William & Phelon, Mira M. The Three Sevens. Clymer, R. Swinburne, ed. 212p. 1977. 7.95 (*0-932785-47-6*) Philos Pub.

Phelps. Health Economics. (C). 1991. text ed. 66.50 (*0-673-38746-1*) HarpCollege.

Phelps & Servin. Phelps Family of America & Their English Ancestry, 2 vols. in 1. (Illus.). 1865p. 1989. reprint ed. lib. bdg. 267.00 (*0-8328-0962-4*); reprint ed. pap. 259.00 (*0-8328-0963-2*) Higginson Bk Co.

Phelps, jt. auth. see Wolfe, J. H.

Phelps, Albert. Louisiana: A Record of Expansion. LC 72-3748. (American Commonwealths Ser.: No. 18). reprint ed. 42.50 (*0-404-57218-9*) AMS Pr.

Phelps, Amos A. Lectures on Slavery & Its Remedy. LC 70-92438. 1970. reprint ed. 39.00 (*0-403-00182-X*) Scholarly.

Phelps, Arthur J. The Story of Merwin, Hulbert & Co. Firearms. LC 91-65703. 226p. 1993. 56.00 (*1-882824-00-8*) Graphic Pubs.

Phelps, Arthur L. Canadian Writers. LC 73-38030. (Essay Index Reprint Ser.). 1977. reprint ed. 16.95 (*0-8369-2617-X*) Ayer.

Phelps, Austin, et al. Hymns & Choirs. LC 78-144671. reprint ed. 29.50 (*0-404-07207-0*) AMS Pr.

Phelps, Brian, jt. auth. see Phelps, Erika.

Phelps, Charles, jt. ed. see Burbank, Nelson L.

Phelps, Charles D. & Hansjoerg, E. J., eds. Manual of Common Ophthalmic Surgical Procedures. LC 86-17157. (Illus.). 203p. (Orig.). reprint ed. pap. 57.90 (*0-7837-2557-4*, 2042716) Bks Demand.

Phelps, Christina. The Anglo-American Peace Movement in the Mid-Nineteenth Century. LC 76-37906. (Select Bibliographies Reprint Ser.). 1977. reprint ed. 19.95 (*0-8369-6744-5*) Ayer.

Phelps, Corwin. An Ideal Republic: Or, Way Out of the Fog. LC 76-42793. reprint ed. 28.50 (*0-404-60076-X*) AMS Pr.

Phelps, David S., et al. The Prehistory of North Carolina: An Archaeological Symposium. Mathis, Mark A. & Crow, Jeffrey J., eds. (Illus.). xvi, 206p. 1993. reprint ed. pap. 10.00 (*0-86526-225-X*) NC Archives.

Phelps De Cordova, Loretta. Ponce: Rebirth of a Valuable Heritage. 88p. 1991. pap. 19.95 (*0-89825-001-3*) Pub Resces PR.

— Ponce: Rebirth of a Valuable Heritage. deluxe ed. 88p. 1991. 34.95 (*0-89825-002-1*) Pub Resces PR.

— Ponce: Renacimiento De una Valiosa Herencia. Bizjack, Carmen, tr. 88p. (SPA.). 1991. pap. 19.95 (*0-89825-003-X*) Pub Resces PR.

— Ponce: Renacimiento De una Valiosa Herencia. deluxe ed. Bizjack, Carmen, tr. 88p. (SPA.). 1991. 34.95 (*0-89825-004-8*) Pub Resces PR.

Phelps, Dean. And Now We'll Play a Man's Game: Montana Stories. LC 76-1979. (Illus.). 132p. (Orig.). 1976. pap. 5.95 (*0-914974-10-6*) Holmgangers.

— Serum of the Water. LC 78-12785. 1978. pap. 4.95 (*0-914974-17-3*) Holmgangers.

— Shoshoni River Witching Hour. 2nd ed. 44p. 1975. pap. 3.00 (*0-914974-04-1*) Holmgangers.

Phelps, Donald, ed. Hearing Out James T. Farrell. LC 84-52382. 168p. (Orig.). (C). 1985. 12.95 (*0-912292-75-X*); pap. 8.95 (*0-912292-76-8*) The Smith.

Phelps, E., jt. auth. see Oman, Frydman R.

Phelps, E. R., jt. auth. see Wolfe, John H.

***Phelps, Earl R.** How to Draw Your Own Supercharacters. (J). (gr. 4-12). 1993. pap. 5.95 (*1-887627-00-6*) Phelps Pub.

— How to Draw Your Own Supercharacters, Bk. II. LC 95-92382. (J). (gr. 4-12). 1995. pap. 5.95 (*1-887627-01-4*) Phelps Pub.

— How to Draw Your Own Supermonsters. (J). (gr. 4-12). 1993. pap. 5.95 (*1-887627-02-2*) Phelps Pub.

Phelps, Edmund S. Political Economy: An Introductory Text. (C). 1985. text ed. 37.95 (*0-393-95312-2*) Norton.

— Recent Developments in Macroeconomics, 3 vols., Set. (International Library of Critical Writings in Business History: Vol. 13). 1376p. 1991. text ed. 389.95 (*1-85278-297-8*, Pub. by E Elgar Pub UK) Ashgate Pub Co.

— Seven Schools of Macroeconomic Thought: The Arne Ryde Memorial Lectures. 124p. 1990. 29.95 (*0-19-828333-4*) OUP.

— Structural Slumps: The Modern Equilibrium Theory of Unemployment, Interest, & Assets. LC 93-15775. 436p. 1994. Acid-free paper. 49.95 (*0-674-84373-8*) HUP.

Phelps, Edmund S., ed. Altruism, Morality, & Economic Theory. LC 74-79448. 242p. 1975. 29.95 (*0-87154-659-0*) Russell Sage.

— The Microeconomic Foundations of Employment & Inflation Theory. (C). 1973. pap. text ed. 17.95 (*0-393-09326-3*) Norton.

— Private Wants & Public Needs. rev. ed. (Problems of Modern Economy Ser.). (Orig.). (C). 1965. pap. text ed. 4.95 (*0-393-09496-0*) Norton.

Phelps, Elizabeth S. Chapters from a Life. Baxter, Annette K., ed. LC 79-8822. (Signal Lives Ser.). (Illus.). 1980. reprint ed. lib. bdg. 35.95 (*0-405-12866-5*) Ayer.

— Doctor Zay. LC 87-48. 336p. 1987. reprint ed. pap. 8.95 (*0-935312-72-2*) Feminist Pr.

— A Peep at Number Five; or, a Chapter in the Life of a City Pastor. LC 70-164573. (American Fiction Reprint Ser.). 1977. reprint ed. 25.95 (*0-8369-7050-0*) Ayer.

— The Silent Partner. Bd. with Tenth of January. LC 82-25306. LC 82-25306. 400p. (C). 1983. reprint ed. Set pap. 12.95 (*0-935312-08-0*) Feminist Pr.

Phelps, Elizabeth S., et al. Our Famous Women: An Authorized Record of the Lives & Deeds of Distinguished American Women of Our Times. LC 73-1192. (Essay Index Reprint Ser.). (Illus.). 1977. reprint ed. 38.95 (*0-518-10060-X*) Ayer.

Phelps, Erika & Phelps, Brian. Trampolining. (Skills of the Game Ser.). (Illus.). 112p. 1991. pap. 16.95 (*1-85223-363-X*, Pub. by Crowood Pr UK) Trafalgar.

Phelps, Ethel J. The Maid of the North: Feminist Folk Tales from Around the World. LC 80-21500. (Illus.). 192p. 1982. pap. 9.95 (*0-8050-0679-6*, Owl) H Holt & Co.

Phelps, Ethel J., ed. Tatterhood & Other Tales. LC 78-9352. (Illus.). 192p. (Orig.). (J). (gr. 1 up). 1978. pap. 9.95 (*0-912670-50-9*) Feminist Pr.

Phelps, Frederick M., III, ed. MIT Wavelength Tables: Wavelengths By Element, Vol. 2. 816p. 1982. 95.00 (*0-262-16087-0*) MIT Pr.

Phelps, Geneva M. An Annal Begins with Ezekiel & Margaret (Watkins) Phelps. 179p. 1988. 25.75 (*0-9620925-0-9*) G Phelps.

Phelps, Gilbert. Between Man & Beast: True Tales & Observations of the Animal Kingdom. 1989. 7.99 (*0-517-69038-1*) Random Hse Value.

— Russian Novel in English Fiction. LC 79-158907. 1971. reprint ed. 39.00 (*0-403-01301-1*) Scholarly.

— The Tragedy of Paraguay. LC 74-21750. 300p. (C). 1975. text ed. 29.95 (*0-312-81340-6*) St Martin.

— The Winter People. 1993. reprint ed. lib. bdg. 18.95 (*0-89968-410-6*, Lghtyr Pr) Buccaneer Bks.

Phelps, Glenn A. George Washington & American Constitutionalism. LC 92-21824. (American Political Thought Ser.). x, 238p. 1993. 29.95x (*0-7006-0564-9*) U Pr of KS.

— George Washington & American Constitutionalism. LC 92-21824. 238p. 1994. pap. 14.95x (*0-7006-0683-1*) U Pr of KS.

Phelps, H. P. Hamlet from the Actors Standpoint. LC 76-57925. (Studies in Shakespeare: No. 24). 1977. lib. bdg. 59.95 (*0-8383-2171-2*) M S G Haskell Hse.

Phelps, Henry. Players of a Century: A Record of the Albany Stage. 424p. 1993. reprint ed. lib. bdg. 99.00 (*0-7812-5284-9*) Rprt Serv.

Phelps, Henry P. Players of a Century: A Record of the Albany Stage. LC 78-91562. 1972. 30.95 (*0-405-08855-8*, Pub. by Blom Pubns UK) Ayer.

Phelps, Humphrey. A Suffolk Christmas. (Illus.). 160p. 1991. pap. 15.00 (*0-86299-979-0*) A Sutton Pub.

Phelps, Humphrey, comp. An Essex Christmas. LC 93-33713. 1993. 15.00 (*0-7509-0123-3*) A Sutton Pub.

— A Forest Christmas. LC 93-17680. 1993. 15.00 (*0-7509-0320-1*) A Sutton Pub.

Phelps, J. Alfred. Chappie, America's First Black Four-Star General: The Life & Times of Daniel James, Jr. 1992. pap. 9.95 (*0-89141-464-9*) Presidio Pr.

— They Had a Dream: Story of African-American Astronauts. 1995. pap. 12.95 (*0-89141-540-8*) Presidio Pr.

— They Had a Dream: The Story of African-American Astronauts. LC 93-20956. 304p. 1994. 24.95 (*0-89141-497-5*) Presidio Pr.

Phelps, J. Jacqueline. Contending for the Faith. 1994. 8.75 (*0-8062-4930-7*) Carlton.

Phelps, J. Michael, ed. see Janssen, Ellie.

Phelps, James H. The Illinois State Atlas. (Illus.). 117p. (Orig.). 1988. pap. 9.95 (*0-929998-00-6*) Phelps Map.

— The Indiana State Atlas. (Illus.). 118p. (Orig.). 1990. pap. 9.95 (*0-929998-01-4*) Phelps Map.

Phelps, James T., ed. Black & Catholic: The Challenge & Gift of Black Folk: Contributions of African American Experience & World View to Catholic Theology. (Studies in Theology). (Orig.). 1995. pap. write for info. (*0-87462-629-3*) Marquette.

Phelps, Janice K. & Nourse, Alan E. The Hidden Addiction. 1986. pap. 11.95 (*0-316-70471-7*) Little.

Phelps, Jeana, jt. auth. see Campeau, Frances.

Phelps, Jennifer, ed. see Chek-Chart Staff.

Phelps, Jo L., ed. see Calkins, Michael.

Phelps, Jocelyn, tr. see Corbin, Alain.

Phelps, Jocelyn, tr. see Pardailhe-Galabrun, Annik.

Phelps, John & Gizzi, Julian. Phelps & Gizzi: VAT for Solicitors. 2nd ed. 94p. 1993. pap. 35.00 (*0-406-02008-6*, U.K.) Butterworth Legal Pubs.

— Solicitors & VAT. 1986. pap. 30.00 (*0-406-50360-5*) Butterworth Legal Pubs.

Phelps, John & Philbin, Tom, eds. Complete Building Construction. 2nd ed. LC 82-17789. 1983. text ed. 24.95 (*0-672-23377-0*, Audel) Macmillan.

Phelps, John W. The Island of Madagascar: A Sketch, Descriptive & Historical. LC 72-4155. (Black Heritage Library Collection). 1977. reprint ed. 19.95 (*0-8369-9102-8*) Ayer.

Phelps, Joseph. Stress-Free Golf. 250p. 1989. 15.95 (*0-533-08249-8*) Vantage.

Phelps, L. Allen. An Analysis of Fiscal Policy Alternatives for Serving Special Populations in Vocational Education. 45p. 1984. 4.95 (*0-318-22026-1*, IN278) Ctr Educ Trng Employ.

***Phelps, Lauren.** Boyfriend Blues. (Sweet Dreams Ser.: No. 224). (YA). 1995. 3.50 (*0-553-56678-4*) Bantam.

Phelps, Lauren M. The Love Gamble. 192p. 1992. 13.95 (*0-8034-8972-2*, Avalon Bks) Bouregy.

Phelps, Leland R., intro. The Harold Jantz Collection: Proceedings of a Conference to Introduce the Collection to Specialists in German-American Literary Relations. LC 81-68339. 145p. (Orig.). 1981. pap. text ed. 8.00 (*0-916994-22-8*) Ctr Intl Stud Duke.

Phelps, Leland R., jt. ed. see Loram, Ian C.

Phelps, Louise W. Composition As a Human Science: Contributions to the Self-Understanding of a Discipline. (Illus.). 288p. 1991. pap. 16.95 (*0-19-506782-7*) OUP.

Phelps, Louise W. & Emig, Janet, eds. Feminine Principles & Women's Experience in American Composition & Rhetoric. (Pittsburgh Series in Composition, Literacy, & Culture). 424p. (C). 1995. 59.95 (*0-8229-3863-4*); pap. 22.95 (*0-8229-5544-X*) U of Pittsburgh Pr.

Phelps, Lynn. Your Guide to Medical Hypnosis. (Focus on Health Ser.). (Illus.). 108p. (Orig.). 1993. pap. 9.00 (*0-944838-28-6*) Med Physics Pub.

Phelps, M. Jeana, jt. auth. see Campeau, Frances E.

Phelps, Michael E., jt. ed. see Sorenson, James A.

Phelps, Michael E., et al, eds. Positron Emission Tomography & Autoradiography: Principles & Applications for the Brain & Heart. (Illus.). 704p. 1986. text ed. 132.00 (*0-88167-118-5*) Raven.

Phelps, Myron H. The Master in Akka: Including Recollections of the Greatest Holy Leaf. Orig. Title: Abbas Effendi: His Life & Teachings. (Illus.). 1985. reprint ed. 18.95 (*0-933770-49-9*) Kalimat.

***Phelps, Orra.** When I Was a Girl in the Martin Box. (American Autobiography Ser.). 157p. 1995. reprint ed. lib. bdg. 69.00 (*0-7812-8618-2*) Rprt Serv.

Phelps, P. D. & Lloyd, G. A. Diagnostic Imaging of the Ear. 2nd ed. (Illus.). 234p. 1990. 226.00 (*0-387-19570-X*) Spr-Verlag.

Phelps, P. D., jt. auth. see Stansbie, J. M.

Phelps, Paul B. & Brockman, Paul R. Science & Technology Programs in the States, 1992. 96p. 1992. pap. 30.00 (*0-9632443-0-2*) Adv Develop.

Phelps, R. & Buchanan, I. Interactions in Artificial Intelligence & Statistical Methods. (Technical Press-Unicom AIT Ser.: Vol. 9). Orig. Title: AI Methods in Statistics. 200p. 1987. pap. text ed. 75.00 (*0-291-39743-3*, Pub. by Avebury Pub UK) Ashgate Pub Co.

Phelps, R. R. Convex Functions, Monotone Operators & Differentiability. (Lecture Notes in Mathematics Ser.: Vol. 1364). 115p. 1989. pap. 18.30 (*0-387-50735-3*) Spr-Verlag.

Phelps, Reginald H. & Stein, J. M. The German Heritage. 3rd ed. (C). (gr. 9-12). 1970. text ed. 38.75 (*0-03-084162-3*) HB Coll Pubs.

Phelps, Richard & Scanlon, Pat. Digger Phelps & Notre Dame Basketball. LC 81-43. (Illus.). 216p. 1981. 9.95 (*0-685-03834-3*) P-H.

Phelps, Richard H. History of Newgate of Connecticut, at Simsbury, New East Granby: Its Insurrections & Massacres. LC 74-90189. (Mass Violence in America Ser.). 1969. reprint ed. 24.95 (*0-405-01331-0*) Ayer.

Phelps, Robert. Belles Saisons: A Colette Scrapbook. (Illus.). 304p. 1978. 15.00 (*0-374-11030-1*) FS&G.

— Guitar Workbook. 1993. 9.95 (*0-87166-862-9*, 94329) Mel Bay.

— Heroes & Orators. 1958. 10.95 (*0-8392-1048-5*) Astor-Honor.

Phelps, Robert, ed. Letters from Colette. 208p. 1983. pap. 2.50 (*0-345-30059-9*) Ballantine.

Phelps, Robert, ed. see Wescott, Glenway.

Phelps, Robert G., ed. see Colette.

Phelps, Robert R. Convex Functions, Monotone Operators, & Differentiability. 2nd ed. LC 93-15613. (Lecture Notes in Mathematics Ser.: Vol. 1364). (Illus.). xii, 117p. 1993. pap. 27.00 (*0-387-56715-1*) Spr-Verlag.

Phelps, Roger P., et al. A Guide to Research in Music Education. 4th ed. LC 92-29643. (Illus.). 385p. 1993. 35.00 (*0-8108-2536-8*) Scarecrow.

Phelps, Ruth S. Italian Silhouettes. LC 68-55853. (Essay Index Reprint Ser.). 1977. 19.95 (*0-8369-0786-8*) Ayer.

***Phelps, Sandra S.** Weep for a Madman. 500p. Date not set. pap. 12.95 (*0-7610-0295-2*) NW Pub.

Phelps, Stanlee & Austin, Nancy. The Assertive Woman: A New Look. 2nd rev. ed. LC 87-16794. 256p. 1987. pap. 9.95 (*0-915166-61-5*) Impact Pubs CA.

Phelps, Stephanie J. & Cochran, Emily B. Guidelines for Administration of Intravenous Medications to Pediatric Patients. 4th ed. 136p. 1993. pap. text ed. 35.00 (*1-879907-28-3*) Am Soc Hlth-Syst.

Phelps, Stephen F., jt. auth. see Alvermann, Donna E.

Phelps, Steve. All God's Children Got Gum in Their Hair. LC 94-16538. 1994. write for info. (*0-8308-1822-7*) InterVarsity.

Phelps, Stowe C. Edith Catlin Phelps: A Second Look at an Early Provincetown Painter. (Illus.). 72p. 1990. pap. 5.00 (*0-945135-05-X*) Cape Cod Pilgrim.

***Phelps, T.** Capitol Games. 1994. pap. 4.99 (*0-517-13213-3*) Random Hse Value.

Phelps, Teresa G. The Coach's Wife: A Memoir. LC 93-13148. 1994. 23.00 (*0-393-03470-4*) Norton.

— Problems & Cases for Legal Writing, 4 vols. 33p. 1984. teacher ed 2.50 (*1-55681-057-1*, FBLWT00) Natl Inst Trial Ad.

— Problems & Cases for Legal Writing, 2 vols., Set. rev. ed. 1990. 39.95 (*0-685-74202-4*) Natl Inst Trial Ad.

— Problems & Cases for Legal Writing, 4 vols., Vol. I. 180p. 1984. 10.00 (*1-55681-053-9*, FBLW100) Natl Inst Trial Ad.

— Problems & Cases for Legal Writing, 2 vols., Vol. 1. rev. ed. 1990. 10.00 (*0-685-45129-1*) Natl Inst Trial Ad.

— Problems & Cases for Legal Writing, 4 vols., Vol. II. 585p. 1984. 29.95 (*1-55681-054-7*, FBLW200) Natl Inst Trial Ad.

— Problems & Cases for Legal Writing, 2 vols., Vol. 2. rev. ed. 1990. 10.00 (*1-55681-226-4*) Natl Inst Trial Ad.

— Problems & Cases for Legal Writing, 4 vols., Vol. III. 480p. 1984. 24.95 (*1-55681-055-5*, FBLW300) Natl Inst Trial Ad.

— Problems & Cases for Legal Writing, 4 vols., Vol. IV. 220p. 1984. 12.55 (*1-55681-056-3*, FBLW400) Natl Inst Trial Ad.

Phelps-Tersaki, Diana & Phelps, Tricia. Teaching Written Expression: The Phelps Sentence Guide Program. 112p. 1980. pap. text ed. 15.00 (*0-87879-248-1*); 10.00 (*0-87879-290-2*) Acad Therapy.

Phelps, Thomas C. & O'Donnell, Peggy. Humanities Programming: A How-to-Do-It Manual for Librarians. (How-to-Do-It Ser.). 150p. Date not set. 39.95 (*1-55570-083-7*) Neal-Schuman.

Phelps, Tim, illus. Cytotec: Preclinical & Clinical Review. LC 89-62978. 160p. 1989. text ed. 28.95 (*0-924428-01-5*) Phys Sci Pub.

Phelps, Timothy M. & Winternitz, Helen. Capitol Games: The Inside Story of Clarence Thomas, Anita Hill, & a Supreme Court Nomination. LC 92-54850. 464p. 1993. pap. 14.00 (*0-06-097553-9*, PL) HarpC.

Phelps, Tony. Poisonous Snakes. (Illus.). 272p. 1989. pap. 19.95 (*0-7137-2114-6*, Pub. by Blandford Pr UK) Sterling.

Phelps, Tricia, jt. auth. see Phelps-Tersaki, Diana.

Phelps, W. W., tr. see Christophilopoulou, A.

Phelps, William C. The Foreign Expansion of American Banks: American Branch Banking Abroad. Bruchey, Stuart & Bruchey, Eleanor, eds. LC 76-5028. (American Business Abroad Ser.). 1976. reprint ed. 23.95 (*0-405-09295-4*) Ayer.

Phelps, William D. Alta California, 1840-1842: The Journal & Observations of William Dane Phelps. Busch, Briton C, ed. LC 82-71376. (Western Lands & Waters Ser.: XIII). (Illus.). 364p. 1983. 29.50 (*0-87062-143-2*) A H Clark.

Phelps, William H., Jr., jt. auth. see De Schauensee, M.

Phelps, William L. Advance of the English Novel. LC 74-145233. 1971. reprint ed. 24.00 (*0-403-01149-3*) Scholarly.

— The Advance of the English Novel. (BCL1-PR English Literature Ser.). 334p. 1992. reprint ed. lib. bdg. 89.00 (*0-7812-7114-2*) Rprt Serv.

— Adventures & Confessions. LC 71-121497. (Essay Index Reprint Ser.). 1977. 19.95 (*0-8369-1771-5*) Ayer.

— Autobiography, with Letters. LC 76-29445. reprint ed. 57.50 (*0-404-15320-8*) AMS Pr.

— Beginnings of the English Romantic Movement: A Study in Eighteenth Century Literature. LC 68-57380. 200p. (C). 1968. reprint ed. 50.00 (*0-87752-084-4*) Gordian.

— Essays on Modern Dramatists. LC 77-105032. (Essay Index Reprint Ser.). 1977. 21.95 (*0-8369-1476-7*) Ayer.

— Robert Browning, How to Know Him. (BCL1-PR English Literature Ser.). 381p. 1992. reprint ed. lib. bdg. 89.00 (*0-7812-7466-4*) Rprt Serv.

— Some Makers of American Literature. LC 70-105033. (Essay Index Reprint Ser.). 1977. 20.95 (*0-8369-1477-5*) Ayer.

— Twentieth Century Theatre: Observations on the Contemporary English & American Stage. LC 67-28764. (Essay Index Reprint Ser.). 1977. 18.95 (*0-8369-0787-6*) Ayer.

Phelps, William L., ed. see Riley, James W.

Phelps, Winthrop M., jt. auth. see Stevens, Marvin A.

Phemister, Marilyn B. First John: A Guide to Fellowship with God. LC 88-24762. (Bible Studies). (Orig.). 1988. pap. 5.00 (*0-915541-38-6*) Star Bks Inc.

— The Voice of a Windmill. LC 88-32323. (Illus.). (Orig.). 1988. pap. 7.00 (*0-915541-39-4*) Star Bks Inc.

Phemister, William. The American Piano Concertos: A Bibliography. LC 85-19746. (Bibliographies in American Music Ser.: No. 9). 323p. 1986. 35.00 (*0-89990-026-7*) Info Coord.

Phengsy, Novanta, tr. see Marcus, Russell, ed.

Phenix, Bruce, tr. see Del Granado, Don J.

Phenix, Katharine, et al. On Account of Sex: Annotated Bibliography on the Status of Women in Librarianship, 1982-1986. 152p. 1990. pap. text ed. 10.00 (*0-8389-3375-0*) ALA.

Phenix, Philip H. Man & His Becoming. LC 64-8264. (Brown & Haley Lectures: 1964). 125p. reprint ed. pap. 35.70 (*0-317-08038-5*, 2050625) Bks Demand.

— Religious Concerns in Contemporary Education. LC 59-11329. 118p. reprint ed. 33.70 (*0-8357-9605-1*, 2016949) Bks Demand.

Pherigo, George, ed. see General Dynamics Convair Div. Staff.

Pherigo, Lindsey. The Great Physician Luke: The Healing Stories. LC 90-21917. 144p. 1991. pap. 6.95 (*0-687-15788-9*) Abingdon.

Phero, J. C., jt. ed. see Dionne, R. A.

Pherson, Dave Mac. The Incredible Cover-Up. 1975. 8.95 (*0-88270-143-6*); pap. 3.95 (*0-88270-144-4*) Omega Pubns OR.

Pheterson, Gail, ed. A Vindication of the Rights of Whores: The International Movement for Prostitutes' Rights. LC 88-33060. 320p. (Orig.). 1989. pap. 16.95 (*0-931188-73-3*) Seal Pr Feminist.

Phethean, Richard. The Complete Potter: Throwing. LC 94-12446. (Complete Potter Ser.). (Illus.). 96p. 1994. text ed. 24.95 (*0-8122-3299-2*, Pub. by B T B UK) U of Pa Pr.

Pheto, Molefe. And Night Fell: Memoirs of a Political Prisoner in South Africa. LC 84-234158. (African Writers Ser.). 218p. (C). 1985. reprint ed. pap. 9.95 (*0-435-90258-X*) Heinemann.

Pheysey, Diana C. Organizational Cultures: Types & Transformations. 240p. 1993. 69.95 (*0-415-08291-9*, A3681); pap. 16.95 (*0-415-08292-7*, A9685) Routledge.

Phi Delta Kappa Commission for Developing Public Confidence in Schools Staff, et al. A Handbook for Developing Public Confidence in Schools. LC 88-61690. 144p. (Orig.). 1988. pap. 9.00 (*0-87367-798-6*) Phi Delta Kappa.

Phi Delta Kappa Commission on Teacher-Faculty Morale, et al. Administrator's Handbook for Improving Faculty Morale. LC 85-61680. 70p. 1985. pap. 7.00 (*0-87367-795-1*) Phi Delta Kappa.

Phi Delta Kappa Task Force on Adolescent Suicide Staff. Responding to Adolescent Suicide. LC 88-61773. 29p. (Orig.). 1988. pap. 3.50 (*0-87367-438-3*) Phi Delta Kappa.

Phi Delta Kappan Staff, sel. Prototypes: An Anthology of School Improvement Ideas That Work. LC 89-61103. 150p. 1989. pap. 7.50 (*0-87367-800-1*) Phi Delta Kappa.

Phialas, Peter G. Shakespeare's Romantic Comedies: The Development of Their Form & Meaning. LC 66-25355. 330p. reprint ed. pap. 94.10 (*0-7837-0316-3*, 2040638) Bks Demand.

Phibbs, Kathy, et al. Women Climbing: 1992 Engagement Calendar. (Illus.). 120p. (Orig.). 1991. pap. 12.95 (*0-9630368-7-4*) Women Climbers.

***Phiddian, Robert.** Swift's Parody. (Cambridge Studies in Eighteenth-Century English Literature & Thought Ser.: No. 26). 236p. (C). 1995. write for info. (*0-521-47437-X*) Cambridge U Pr.

Phifer, Edward W., Jr. Burke County: A Brief History. (Illus.). viii, 144p. (Orig.). 1979. pap. 5.00 (*0-86526-130-X*) NC Archives.

Phifer, Kate G. Growing up Small: A Handbook for Short People. LC 78-11290. (Illus.). 1979. 9.95 (*0-8397-3136-1*) Eriksson.

— Tall & Small: A Book about Height. LC 86-32401. (Illus.). 96p. (J). (gr. 5 up). 1987. 11.95 (*0-8027-6684-6*); lib. bdg. 12.85 (*0-8027-6685-4*) Walker & Co.

Phifer, Kenneth G. A Book of Uncommon Faith. LC 90-71862. 144p. (Orig.). 1991. pap. 8.95 (*0-8358-0632-4*) Upper Room Bks.

— A Book of Uncommon Prayer. LC 82-50945. 128p. 1983. reprint ed. pap. 8.95 (*0-8358-0451-8*) Upper Room Bks.

Phifer, Kenneth W. Becoming at Home in the World. 191p. 1992. pap. text ed. 14.95 (*0-9634955-0-X*) Castellio Pr.

Phifer, Paul. Career Planning Q's & A's: A Handbook for Students, Parents, & Professionals. (Illus.). 126p. 1990. pap. 10.95 (*0-912048-83-2*) Garrett Pk.

— College Majors & Careers: A Resource Guide for Effective Life Planning. rev. ed. LC 93-19213. 166p. 1993. 15.00 (*0-912048-46-8*) Garrett Pk.

Phifer, Russell W. & McTigue, William R., Jr. Handbook of Hazardous Waste Management for Small Quantity Generators. (Illus.). 200p. 1988. 69.95 (*0-87371-102-5*, TD811) Lewis Pubs.

Phiffer, Cynthia L. My Body, My Choice. Coy, Stanley C., ed. 40p. (Orig.). (YA). (gr. 7-12). 1994. pap. 2.00 (*1-881459-17-9*) Eagle Pr SC.

Phil, D., jt. ed. see Love, Jack.

Phil, D., jt. auth. see Ramakant, M. A.

Phil, M., ed. Register of York Freemen 1680-1986. 1200p. (C). 1988. 75.00 (*1-85072-054-1*, Pub. by W Sessions UK) St Mut.

Phil, M., ed. see Nutter, Robert S.

Phil, M., jt. auth. see Rose, Jack.

Philabaum, Dabney M. Desert Buddies. (Illus.). 40p. (J). (gr. k-4). 1994. pap. 8.95 (*0-9639215-0-9*) Earth Buddies.

***Philabaum, Dabney M. & Alegret, Nancy L.** Ocean Buddies. (Illus.). 32p. (Orig.). (J). (gr. k-4). Date not set. pap. write for info. (*0-9639215-1-7*) Earth Buddies.

Philadelphia Board of Guardians Staff & Massachusetts General Court Staff. Almshouse Experience: Collected Papers. LC 74-137197. (Poverty U. S. A. Historical Record Ser.). 1974. reprint ed. 23.95 (*0-405-03092-4*) Ayer.

Philadelphia Bronze & Brass Staff. Development of Copper-Base Alloys for Use as Dies & Plungers in the Glass & Plastics Industries. 53p. 1963. 7.95 (*0-317-34509-5*, 27) Intl Copper.

Philadelphia Chamber of Commerce Staff. Giant Houseparty Cookbook. 385p. 1981. pap. 10.95 (*0-686-31495-6*) COC.

***Philadelphia Child Guidance Center Staff & Maguire, Jack.** Your Child's Emotional Health: Adolescence. 1995. pap. 9.95 (*0-02-860003-7*) Macmillan.

— Your Child's Emotional Health: The Early Years. LC 94-34151. 1995. pap. 9.95 (*0-02-860001-0*) Macmillan.

— Your Child's Emotional Health: The Middle Years. 1995. pap. 9.95 (*0-02-860002-9*) Macmillan.

Philadelphia Child Guidance Clinic Staff & Maguire, Jack. Your Child's Emotional Health. LC 92-25481. 418p. 1993. text ed. 25.00 (*0-02-577371-2*) Macmillan.

Philadelphia Inquirer Staff. Weekend Journeys. (Illus.). 336p. 1988. pap. 9.95 (*0-912608-59-5*) Mid Atlantic.

— Weekend Journeys: 62 Getaways Within a Day's Drive of Philidelphia. (Illus.). 240p. 1995. pap. 9.95 (*0-8362-7037-1*) Andrews & McMeel.

— Worst to First: Story of the Nineteen Ninety-Three Phillies. 1993. pap. 8.95 (*0-8362-8062-8*) Andrews & McMeel.

***Philadelphia Inquirer Staff, The, ed.** The Inquirer Regional Almanac 1995. rev. ed. 704p. Date not set. 7.95 (*0-9634709-9-X*) Phila Newspapers.

Philadelphia Institute of Contemporary Art Staff. Group Zero: An American Exhibition. Piene, Otto, ed. LC 68-20081. (Illus.). 1968. reprint ed. 6.00 (*0-405-00389-7*) Ayer.

Philadelphia Institute Staff & Schrader, Barry. Introduction to Estates & Trusts. 2nd ed. Hannan, ed. 500p. (C). 1992. text ed. 57.50 (*0-314-93379-4*) West Pub.

Philadelphia Institute Staff & Warren, Carl S. Introduction to Corporate Law. 2nd ed. Hannan, ed. 481p. (C). 1991. text ed. 57.00 (*0-314-80907-4*) West Pub.

Philadelphia Institute Staff & Weinstein, Mark. Introduction to Civil Litigation. 3rd ed. Hannan, ed. LC 92-42903. (Paralegal Ser.). (Illus.). 450p. (C). 1993. text ed. 52.75 (*0-314-93380-8*) West Pub.

Philadelphia Maritime Museum Staff. George Robert Bonfield: Philadelphia Marine Painter, 1805 to 1898. LC 78-71198. (Illus.). 78p. (Orig.). 1978. pap. text ed. 2.00 (*0-913346-04-7*) Phila Maritime Mus.

— Thomas Birch Seventeen Seventy-Nine to Eighteen Fifty-One: Paintings & Drawings. (Illus.). 64p. 1966. pap. 2.00 (*0-913346-06-3*) Phila Maritime Mus.

Philadelphia Museum of Art Staff. Philadelphia: Three Centuries of American Art. LC 76-3170. (Illus.). 665p. 1990. reprint ed. 35.00 (*0-87633-016-2*) Phila Mus Art.

— Philadelphia Collects: Art since 1940. LC 86-22490. (Illus.). 128p. (Orig.). 1986. pap. 12.95 (*0-87633-066-9*) Phila Mus Art.

***Philadelphia Museum of Art Staff, ed.** Paintings from Europe & the Americas in the Philadelphia Museum of Art: A Concise Catalogue. LC 94-23570. 1994. pap. write for info. (*0-87633-093-6*) Phila Mus Art.

Philadelphia Museum of Art Staff & Winterthur, Henry du Pont Museum Staff, eds. Pennsylvania German Art, Sixteen Eighty-Three to Eighteen Fifty. LC 83-18267. (Chicago Visual Library: No. 43). 264p. (C). 1984. lib. bdg. 90.00 (*0-226-69535-2*) U Ch Pr.

Philadelphia Museum of Art Staff, jt. auth. see Lowe, Sarah M.

Philadelphia Rotary Club Members & Wives. What's Cooking in Philadelphia: A Collection of Favorites Recipes-Cookbook. Brock, Claudie, ed. (Illus.). 224p. 1987. write for info. (*0-9619470-0-4*) Rotary Club Phila.

Philadelphia Schools Students. From the Young at Heart: A Student Anthology. Goodman, Sharon L., ed. (Illus.). 20p. (Orig.). (J). (gr. 1-8). 1989. pap. write for info. (*0-935369-19-8*) In Tradition Pub.

Philadelphia Yearly Meeting Staff. A Collection of Memorials Concerning Diverse Deceased Ministers & Others of the People Called Quakers: In Pennsylvania, New Jersey, & Parts Adjacent, from Nearly the First Settlement Thereof to the Year 1878. 448p. 1990. reprint ed. pap. 25.00 (*1-55613-327-8*) Heritage Bk.

Philalethes, Eirenaeus. Alchemical Works: Eirenaeus Philalethes Compiled. Broddle, S. Merrow, ed. 592p. 1994. 60.00 (*0-9640067-0-7*) Cinnabar.

— Collectanea Chemica. 160p. 1992. reprint ed. pap. 11.95 (*0-922802-81-5*) Kessinger Pub.

— An Open Entrance To the Closed Palace of the King. reprint ed. pap. 6.95 (*0-916411-21-4*) Holmes Pub.

— The Secret of the Immortal Liquor Called Alkahest. 1984. reprint ed. pap. 2.95 (*0-916411-40-0*) Holmes Pub.

Philalethes, Eirenaeus, et al. Collectanea Chemica; Being Certain Select Treatises on Alchemy & Hermetic Literature. Waite, A. E., ed. 1991. reprint ed. pap. 14.95 (*1-55818-149-0*) Holmes Pub.

Philalethes, Eugenius, pseud. The Fame & Confession of the Fraternity of R: C: Commonly of the Rosie Cross with a Preface Annexed Thereto, & a Short Declaration of Their Physical Work. 190p. 1992. reprint ed. pap. 18.00 (*1-56459-257-X*) Kessinger Pub.

Philander, S. George. El Nino, la Nina, & the Southern Oscillation. (International Geophysics Ser.). 293p. 1989. text ed. 85.00 (*0-12-553235-0*) Acad Pr.

Philaretos, S. D. The Idea of the Being. Orthodox Christian Educational Society Staff, ed. Cummings, D., tr. 287p. 1963. 14.95 (*0-938366-09-2*) Orthodox Chr.

Philaretos, Sotirios D. The Decalogue & the Gospel. Orthodox Christian Educational Society Staff, ed. Cummings, D., tr. 62p. (Orig.). 1957. pap. 2.95 (*0-938366-43-2*) Orthodox Chr.

***Philbeam, Pamela M.** Themes in Modern European History, 1780-1830. LC 94-28278. (Themes in Modern European History Ser.). (Illus.). 224p. 1995. pap. 16.95 (*0-415-10173-5*, C0167) Routledge.

— Themes in Modern European History, 1780-1830. LC 94-28278. (Themes in Modern European History Ser.). (Illus.). 224p. 1995. 55.00x (*0-415-10172-7*, C0166) Routledge.

Philbin, Marianne, jt. ed. see McLeese, Don.

Philbin, Regis & Gifford, Kathie L. Cooking with Regis & Kathie Lee: Quick & Easy Recipes from America's Favorite TV Personality. (Illus.). 272p. 1993. 19.95 (*1-56282-930-0*) Hyperion.

— Cooking with Regis & Kathie Lee: Quick & Easy Recipes from America's Favorite TV Personality. (Illus.). 272p. 1993. pap. 9.95 (*1-56282-752-9*) Hyperion.

— Entertaining with Regis & Kathie Lee: Year-Round Holiday Recipes, Entertaining Tips, & Party Ideas. LC 94-14787. (Illus.). 304p. 1994. 19.95 (*0-7868-6067-7*) Hyperion.

— Entertaining with Regis & Kathie Lee: Year-Round Holiday Recipes, Entertaining Tips, & Party Ideas. (Illus.). 304p. 1995. pap. 9.95 (*0-7868-8130-5*) Hyperion.

***Philbin, Regis & Zehme, Bill.** I'm Only One Man! (Illus.). 304p. 1995. 22.95 (*0-7868-6154-1*) Hyperion.

Philbin, Thomas. Plumbing: Installation & Design. 227p. (C). 1988. teacher ed write for info. (*0-15-570676-4*); text ed. 33.25 (*0-15-570675-6*) SCP.

Philbin, Tobias R., III. The Lure of Neptune: German-Soviet Naval Collaboration & Ambitions, 1919-1941. LC 94-3207. (Studies in Maritime History). 1994. write for info. (*0-87249-992-8*) U of SC Pr.

Philbin, Tom. Blink. 1994. pap. 4.50 (*0-515-11397-2*) Jove Pubns.

— Cabinets, Bookcases & Closets. Horowitz, Shirley M., ed. LC 80-69620. (Illus.). 160p. (Orig.). 1980. pap. 9.95 (*0-932944-22-1*) Creative Homeowner.

— Costwise Bathroom Remodeling: A Guide to Renovating or Improving Your Bath. 208p. 1992. text ed. 29.95 (*0-471-52895-1*); pap. text ed. 14.95 (*0-471-52896-X*) Wiley.

— How to Hire a Home Improvement Contractor Without Getting Chiseled. 1991. pap. 13.95 (*0-312-04576-X*) St Martin.

— Jamaica Kill. 1989. pap. 3.50 (*0-449-14508-5*) Fawcett.

— Knock It down, Break It Up: The Definitive Guide to In-Home Demolition. 224p. (Orig.). 1993. pap. 8.00 (*0-380-76850-X*) Avon.

— Murder, U. S. A. (Illus.). 304p. (Orig.). 1992. mass mkt. 4.99 (*0-446-36091-0*) Warner Bks.

— Tom Philbin's Do-It-Yourself Bargain Book. 256p. (Orig.). 1992. pap. 9.99 (*0-446-39339-8*) Warner Bks.

— The Yearbook Killer. (Orig.). 1981. pap. 1.95 (*0-449-14400-3*, GM) Fawcett.

Philbin, Tom & Ettlinger, Steve R. The Complete, Illustrated Guide to Everything Sold in Hardware Stores. (Illus.). 352p. 1988. text ed. 25.95 (*0-02-536310-7*) Macmillan.

Philbin, Tom, jt. auth. see Consumer Reports Books Editors.

Philbin, Tom, jt. auth. see Dezettel, Louis M.

Philbin, Tom, jt. ed. see Phelps, John.

Philbin, Tom, ed. see Stewart, Harry L.

Philbin, Tom, jt. auth. see Stewart, Harry L.

Philbrick, Allen K. This Human World. rev. ed. (Illus.). 500p. (C). 1986. reprint ed. pap. text ed. 39.95 (*1-877751-39-1*) Inst Math Geo.

Philbrick, Charles. Nobody Laughs, Nobody Cries. LC 73-93613. (Illus.). 128p. 1976. 10.00 (*0-912292-33-4*) The Smith.

Philbrick, F. S., ed. The Laws of Illinois Territory: Eighteen Nine to Eighteen Eighteen. LC 50-62758. (Illinois Historical Collections: Vol. 25). 1950. 2.50 (*0-912154-11-X*) Ill St Hist Lib.

— The Laws of Indiana Territory: 1801-1809. (Illinois Historical Collections: Vol. 21). 1930. 7.50 (*0-912154-07-1*) Ill St Hist Lib.

***Philbrick, Francis S.** Laws of Indiana Territory, 1801-1809. 741p. 1931. 4.50 (*1-885323-45-X*) IN Hist Bureau.

Philbrick, Helen & Gregg, Richard B. Companion Plants & How to Use Them. rev. ed. 113p. 1990. pap. 7.95 (*0-8159-5210-4*) Devin.

Philbrick, Helen, jt. auth. see Philbrick, John.

Philbrick, John & Philbrick, Helen. Gardening for Health & Nutrition. LC 79-3595. 96p. 1980. reprint ed. pap. 3.95i (*0-06-066535-1*, RD 402) Harper SF.

— Gardening for Health & Nutrition: The Bio-Dynamic Way. LC 79-150428. (Illus.). 96p. 1973. reprint ed. pap. 10.00 (*0-89345-223-8*, Steinerbks) Garber Comm.

Philbrick, Marianne, ed. see Cooper, James Fenimore.

Philbrick, Nathaniel. Away Offshore: Nantucket Island & Its People. 300p. 1993. text ed. 29.95 (*0-9638910-0-6*); pap. text ed. 19.95 (*0-9638910-1-4*) Mill Hill Pr.

Philbrick, Norman, ed. Trumpets Sounding: Propanda Plays of the American Revolution. LC 77-184007. 1977. reprint ed. lib. bdg. 20.00 (*0-405-11192-4*, Pub. by Blom Pubns UK) Ayer.

Philbrick, Ralph N., ed. Symposium on the Biology of the California Islands: Proceedings. (Illus.). 1967. 12.50 (*0-916436-01-2*) Santa Barb Botanic.

Philbrick, Rodman. Brothers & Sinners. 352p. (Orig.). 1993. pap. 4.99 (*0-451-17677-4*, Onyx) NAL-Dutton.

— Freak the Mighty: A Novel. 176p. (YA). (gr. 7 up). 1995. pap. 3.99 (*0-590-47413-8*, Point) Scholastic Inc.

***Philbrick, Rodman & Harnett, Lynn.** The Final Nightmare. (House on Cherry Street Ser.: Bk. III). (J). (gr. 3-7). 1995. pap. 3.50 (*0-590-25515-0*) Scholastic Inc.

— The Haunting. (House on Cherry Street Ser.: Bk. I). (J). (gr. 3-7). 1995. pap. 3.50 (*0-590-25513-4*) Scholastic Inc.

— The Horror. (House on Cherry Street Ser.: Bk. II). (J). (gr. 3-7). 1995. pap. 3.50 (*0-590-25514-2*) Scholastic Inc.

Philbrick, Stephen. No Goodbye. LC 81-615. 84p. (Orig.). 1981. pap. 6.00 (*0-912292-68-7*) The Smith.

Philbrick, Thomas, ed. see Cooper, James Fenimore.

Philbrick, Thomas, ed. see Dana, Richard H., Jr.

Philbrick, Thomas L., ed. see Cooper, James Fenimore.

Philbrick, W. R. Freak the Mighty. LC 93-19913. 176p. (J). (gr. 5-9). 1993. 13.95 (*0-590-47412-X*) Scholastic Inc.

Philbrook Art Center Staff. Native American Art at Philbrook. LC 80-82374. (Illus.). 96p. 1980. pap. 9.95 (*0-86659-001-3*) Philbrook Mus Art.

Philbrook, Marilyn M., comp. Medical Books for the Layperson: An Annotated Bibliography, Supplement. 1978. pap. 2.00 (*0-89073-060-1*) Boston Public Lib.

Philbrook, Marilyn M., ed. Medical Books for the Layperson: An Annotated Bibliography. 1976. 2.00 (*0-89073-047-4*) Boston Public Lib.

Philby, Harris S. Sheba's Daughters. LC 83-45836. reprint ed. 55.00 (*0-404-20201-2*) AMS Pr.

Philby, Harry. Das Geheimnisvolle Arabien, 2 vols. in 1. (Illus.). 685p. 1985. reprint ed. write for info. (*3-487-07684-5*, Pub. by Georg Olms GW) Lubrecht & Cramer.

Philby, Harry S. Arabia of the Wahhabis. LC 73-6297. (Middle East Ser.). 1977. reprint ed. 36.95 (*0-405-05355-X*) Ayer.

— Sa'udi Arabia. LC 72-4289. (World Affairs Ser.: National & International Viewpoints). (Illus.). 422p. 1978. reprint ed. 26.95 (*0-405-04581-6*) Ayer.

— Sheba's Daughters. (Illus.). xix, 485p. reprint ed. write for info. (*0-318-71552-X*, Pub. by Georg Olms GW) Lubrecht & Cramer.

Philby, J. B. Arabian Highlands. LC 76-10643. (Middle East in the 20th Century Ser.). 1976. reprint ed. lib. bdg. 75.00 (*0-306-70765-9*) Da Capo.

— Arabian Oil Ventures. LC 65-110. 1964. 7.50 (*0-916808-05-X*) Mid East Inst.

Philby, Pamela, jt. auth. see Donaldson, John.

***Philcox.** Florida Where to Stay Book. 1993. pap. text ed. 12.95 (*1-55650-539-6*) Hunter NJ.

— Florida Where to Stay Book. 1995. pap. text ed. 12.95 (*1-55650-682-1*) Hunter NJ.

Philcox, Phil. Executive's Business Information Sourcebook. 512p. 1989. text ed. 39.95 (*0-13-295692-6*) P-H.

— Social Security Update. LC 92-31316. 1992. 5.95 (*0-87576-162-3*) Pilot Bks.

— Where to Stay in America's Heartland. (Where to Stay in America Ser.). 400p. (Orig.). 1994. pap. 13.95 (*1-55650-632-5*) Hunter NJ.

— Where to Stay in Florida. 2nd ed. (Where to Stay Ser.). 400p. 1995. pap. 12.95 (*0-614-03076-5*) Hunter NJ.

— Where to Stay in Mid-Atlantic States. (Where to Stay in America Ser.). 400p. (Orig.). 1994. pap. 12.95 (*1-55650-631-7*) Hunter NJ.

— Where to Stay in Northern California. (Where to Stay Guides Ser.). (Illus.). 400p. (Orig.). 1993. pap. 12.95 (*1-55650-572-8*) Hunter NJ.

— Where to Stay in Southern California. (Where to Stay Guides Ser.). (Illus.). 400p. (Orig.). 1993. pap. 12.95 (*1-55650-573-6*) Hunter NJ.

— Where to Stay in the American Northwest. (Where to Stay Ser.). 450p. (Orig.). 1995. pap. 12.95 (*1-55650-683-X*) Hunter NJ.

— Where to Stay in the American Southeast. (Where to Stay Guides Ser.). 400p. (Orig.). 1994. pap. 12.95 (*1-55650-651-1*) Hunter NJ.

Philcox, Phil & Boe, Beverly. Europe--The Two-Wheeled Adventure. LC 77-95255. (Illus.). 1978. pap. 8.95 (*0-88435-009-6*) Chateau Pub.

Philcox, Phil, jt. auth. see Boe, Beverly.

Philcox, Richard, tr. see Conde, Maryse.

***Philebus & John.** Blue Boys. Date not set. per. 8.95 (*0-85449-144-9*, Pub. by Gay Mens Pr UK) InBook.

Philibert, J. M., jt. ed. see Manning, Frank.

***Philibert, Paul.** Seeing & Believing: Images of the Christian Faith. 150p. (Orig.). 1995. pap. text ed. write for info. (*0-8146-6153-X*, Pueblo Bks); boxed write for info. (*0-8146-6126-2*, Pueblo Bks) Liturgical Pr.

Philibert, Paul J., ed. Living in the Meantime: Concerning the Transformation of Religious Life. LC 94-19036. 192p. 1994. pap. 14.95 (*0-8091-3519-1*) Paulist Pr.

Philibosian, Richard, jt. auth. see Imsand, Shirley.

Philidor, Francois A. D. Ernelinde. Franck, Cesar, ed. (Chefs-d'oeuvre classiques de l'opera francaise Ser.: Vol. 27). (Illus.). 314p. (FRE.). 1970. reprint ed. pap. 35.00 (*0-8450-1127-8*) Broude.

Philidor, Francois-Andre D. Ernelinde: Tragedie Lyrique. Rushton, Julian, ed. LC 92-756279. (French Opera in the 17th & 18th Centuries Ser.: No. 8, Vol. LVI). (Illus.). 1994. lib. bdg. 86.00 (*0-945193-23-8*) Pendragon NY.

***Philip.** Looking for Livingstone: An Odyssey of Silence. Date not set. per. 10.95 (*0-920544-88-6*, Pub. by Mercury Pr CN) InBook.

— She Tries Her Tongue. (NFS Canada Ser.). Date not set. pap. 11.95 (*0-921556-03-9*, Pub. by Gynergy-Ragweed CN) InBook.

Philip, A. Davis, ed. The HR Diagram: The 100th. (Symposia of the International Astronomical Union Ser.: No. 80). (Illus.). 1978. lib. bdg. 117.00 (*90-277-0905-X*); pap. text ed. 80.00 (*90-277-0906-8*) Kluwer Ac.

Philip, A. E., jt. auth. see McCulloch, J. W.

Philip, A. G., jt. auth. see Grindlay, Jonathan E.

Philip, A. G. Davis, ed. X-Ray Symposium 1981. 76p. 1981. pap. 12.00 (*0-9607902-0-9*) L Davis Pr.

Philip, A. G. Davis & Hayes, D. S., eds. Astrophysical Parameters for Globular Clusters: IAU Colloquium, No. 68. 614p. (Orig.). 1982. 31.00 (*0-9607902-2-5*); pap. 27. 00 (*0-9607902-1-7*) L Davis Pr.

Philip, A. G. Davis & Sanduleak, N. A Deep Objective Prism Survey of the Large Magellanic Cloud for OB & Supergiant Stars. 30p. 1983. pap. 12.00 (*0-9607902-3-3*) L Davis Pr.

Philip, A. G. Davis & Upgren, A. R., eds. The Nearby Stars & the Stellar Luminosity Function. (IAU Colloquium Ser.: No. 76). 550p. 1983. 31.00 (*0-9607902-5-X*); pap. 32.00 (*0-9607902-4-1*) L Davis Pr.

Philip, A. T. & Sivaji Rao, K. H. Indian Government & Politics. 299p. 1981. 19.95 (*0-940500-45-0*, Pub. by Sterling II) Asia Bk Corp.

Philip, Alan T., ed. Australian Astronautics Convention Proceedings 1975. (Illus.). 1977. pap. text ed. 18.00 (*0-9596726-1-3*) Univelt Inc.

Philip, Alex. Dicken's Honeymoon & Where He Spent It. LC 72-6507. (Studies in Dickens: No. 52). 1972. reprint ed. lib. bdg. 39.95 (*0-8383-1619-0*) M S G Haskell Hse.

Philip, Alexander. The Business of Bookbinding, Vol. 14. Huttner, Sidney F., ed. (History of Bookbinding & Design Ser.). (Illus.). 272p. 1989. 65.00 (*0-8240-4042-2*) Garland.

Philip, Alexander J. A Dickens Dictionary. (BCL1-PR English Literature Ser.). 375p. 1992. reprint ed. lib. bdg. 89.00 (*0-7812-7514-8*) Rprt Serv.

Philip, Andre, jt. ed. see Cole, G. D.

***Philip B.** Blended Beauty. 128p. 1995. 24.95 (*0-89815-742-0*) Ten Speed Pr.

***Philip C. Crouse & Associates Staff.** Economic Analysis of Horizontal Drilling Investments. fac. ed. LC 90-85985. (Illus.). 118p. Date not set. pap. 33.70 (*0-7837-7433-8*, 2047228) Bks Demand.

Philip, Chris. A Bibliography of Firework Books: Works on Recreative Fireworks from the Sixteenth to the Twentieth Century. (Illus.). xxx, 170p. 1988. reprint ed. text ed. 14.95 (*0-685-44318-3*); reprint ed. write for info. (*0-929931-00-9*) Amer Fireworks.

Philip, Christian, jt. auth. see Barav, Ami.

Philip, Clifford D. Best Book of Foxpro. 1990. pap. 24.95 (*0-672-48487-0*, Bobbs) Macmillan.

Philip, Cynthia Owen. How Bar Associations Evaluate Sitting Judges. 62p. 1976. 2.00 (*0-318-14435-2*) IJA NYU.

Philip, Cynthia Owen, et al. Where Do Judges Come From? 132p. 1976. 3.50 (*0-318-14448-4*) IJA NYU.

Philip, David S. Perceiving India: Views from Far & Near in the Work of Nirad C. Chaudhuri, R. K. Narayan, & Ved Mehta. LC 86-81404. 176p. 1986. text ed. 25.00 (*0-938719-05-X*, Envoy Pr) Apt Bks.

Philip, Frank. Speech Distinct & Pleasing. 162p. 1991. reprint ed. 69.00 (*0-7812-9302-2*) Rprt Serv.

Philip, Franklin & Lane, Harlan, trs. Philosophical Works of Etienne Bonnot, Abbe' de Condillac, Vol. II. 192p. 1986. text ed. 39.95 (*0-89859-616-5*) L Erlbaum Assocs.

Philip, Franklin, tr. see Compagnon, Antoine.

Philip, Franklin, tr. see Constante, Lena.

Philip, Franklin, tr. see Ferry, Luc & Renaut, Alain.

Philip, Franklin, tr. see Ferry, Luc.

Philip, Franklin, tr. see Ferry, Luc & Renaut, Alain.

Philip, Franklin, tr. see Jacob, Francois.

Philip, Franklin, tr. see Lane, Harlan, ed.

Philip, Franklin, tr. see Louder, Dean R. & Waddell, Eric, eds.

Philip, Franklin, tr. see Phillip, F. & Lane, Harlan.

Philip, Franklin, tr. see Picard, Elizabeth.

Philip, Franklin, tr. see Rousseau, Jean-Jacques.

Philip, Franklin, tr. see Walesa, Lech.

***Philip, George.** Encyclopedia World Atlas. (Illus.). 274p. 1994. text ed. 35.00 (*0-19-521090-5*) OUP.

— Oil & Politics in Latin America: Nationalist Movements & State Companies. LC 81-38531. (Cambridge Latin American Studies: No. 40). (Illus.). 608p. 1982. 99.95 (*0-521-23865-X*) Cambridge U Pr.

— The Political Economy of International Oil. (Commodities in the International Economy Ser.). 256p. 1994. 60.00 (*0-7486-0490-1*, Pub. by Edinburgh U Pr UK) Col U Pr.

— The Presidency in Mexican Politics. LC 91-21564. 230p. 1991. text ed. 65.00 (*0-312-06766-6*) St Martin.

Philip, George, ed. The Mexican Economy. 256p. 1988. lib. bdg. 57.50 (*0-415-01265-1*) Routledge.

Philip, George D. E. Mexico. rev. ed. (World Bibliographical Ser.). 1994. lib. bdg. 52.50 (*1-85109-198-X*) ABC-CLIO.

Philip J., Riley. The Phantom of the Opera: The Original Shooting Script. LC 90-61040. (Universal Filmscript Series: Classic Horror Films). (Illus.). (Orig.). 1994. pap. text ed. 24.95 (*1-882127-33-1*) Magicimage Filmbooks.

Philip, James. CC, OT, Vol. 4: Numbers. 364p. 1987. write for info. (*0-8499-0409-9*) Word Inc.

Philip, James A. Pythagoras & Early Pythagoreanism. LC 66-9226. (Phoenix Supplementary Ser.: Supplementary Vol. 7). 232p. reprint ed. pap. 66.20 (*0-317-08752-5*, 2014340) Bks Demand.

Philip, L. F. L. Advances in Coastal & Ocean Engineering, Vol. 1. 300p. 1995. text ed. 86.00 (*981-02-1824-9*) World Scientific Pub.

Philip, Leila. Hidden Dialogue: A Discussion Between Women in Japan & the U. S. 68p. 1992. 12.00 (*0-685-70367-3*) Japan Soc.

— The Road Through Miyama. 1989. 17.95 (*0-394-57818-X*) Random.

— Road Through Miyama. LC 90-50149. (Vintage Departures Ser.). 288p. 1991. pap. 9.95 (*0-679-72501-6*, Vin) Random.

Philip Lief Group. One Thousand Four Hundred & One Things That P-ss Me Off. 1991. pap. 5.95 (*0-399-51670-0*, Perigree Bks) Berkley Pub.

Philip Lief Group, Inc. Staff. Best Home-Based Franchises. LC 92-13458. 1992. pap. 15.00 (*0-385-42196-6*) Doubleday.

Philip Lief Group, Inc Staff & Jones, Constance. The Two Hundred Twenty Best Franchises to Buy. rev. ed. LC 92-28438. 1993. pap. 12.95 (*0-553-35155-9*) Bantam.

Philip Lief Group Staff. Twenty-First Century Mispell. 1993. mass mkt. 5.99 (*0-440-21545-5*, LE) Dell.

Philip Lief Group Staff & Hausman, Carl. Moonlighting: 148 Great Ways to Make Money on the Side. 320p. (Orig.). 1989. pap. 8.95 (*0-380-75485-1*) Avon.

Philip Lief Group Staff, jt. auth. see Lowe, Carl.

Philip Lief Staff. Best Vacation Rentals: Caribbean. 1991. pap. 17.95 (*0-13-928227-0*) P-H.

— Best Vacation Rentals: Europe. 1991. pap. 17.95 (*0-13-928219-X*) P-H.

Philip, Loic. Dictionnaire Encyclopedique des Finances Publiques. 1647p. (FRE.). 1991. 225.00 (*0-8288-9494-9*) Fr & Eur.

Philip, M. S. Measuring Trees & Forests. 2nd ed. 330p. (Orig.). 1993. pap. text ed. 46.50 (*0-85198-883-0*) CAB Intl.

Philip, Marlene N. Harriet's Daughter. (Caribbean Writers Ser.). 150p. (Orig.). (C). 1988. pap. 9.95 (*0-435-98924-3*, 98924) Heinemann.

Philip, N. The Penguin Book of English Folktales. 1994. 22. 00 (*0-8446-6729-3*) Peter Smith.

Philip, Ned, comp. I Have a News. LC 93-32620. (Illus.). (J). (gr. 2 up). 1994. write for info. (*0-688-13367-3*) Lothrop.

***Philip, Neil.** The Illustrated Book of Myths: Tales and Legends of the World. LC 95-2156. (Illus.). 192p. (YA). 1995. 19.95 (*0-7894-0202-5*, 5-70615) Dorling Kindersley.

— The Penguin Book of English Folktales. 464p. 1993. pap. 13.00 (*0-14-013976-1*, Penguin Bks) Viking Penguin.

— The Penguin Book of Scottish Folktales. 512p. 1996. pap. 13.00 (*0-14-013977-X*, Penguin Bks) Viking Penguin.

Philip, Neil, ed. The Book of Christmas. LC 91-12118. (Illus.). 160p. 1991. 27.50 (*1-55670-188-8*) Stewart Tabori & Chang.

— Songs Are Thoughts: Poems of the Inuit. LC 94-27866. 32p. (J). (gr. 1 up). 1995. 15.95 (*0-531-06893-5*) Orchard Bks Watts.

Philip, Neil & Simborowski, Nicoletta, trs. The Complete Fairy Tales of Charles Perrault. LC 92-17781. (Illus.). (J). 1993. 18.95 (*0-395-57002-6*, Clarion Bks) HM.

Philip, Neil, tr. see Andersen, Hans Christian.

Philip, Norman. Shout! The Beatles in Their Generation. LC 81-23. (Illus.). 415p. 1981. pap. 10.00 (*0-671-43253-2*, Fireside) S&S Trade.

Philip, Omana, jt. auth. see Mathew, P. M.

Philip, Robert. Agassi: The Fall & Rise of the Enfant Terrible of Tennis. (Illus.). 224p. 1994. pap. 13.95 (*0-7475-1451-8*, Pub. by Bloomsbury Pub Ltd UK) Trafalgar.

— Early Recordings & Musical Style: Changing Tastes in Instrumental Performance, 1900-1950. (Illus.). 256p. (C). 1992. 64.95 (*0-521-23528-6*) Cambridge U Pr.

Philip, T. & Distler, A., eds. Hypertension: Mechanisms & Management. 279p. 1980. pap. 57.00 (*0-387-10171-3*) Spr-Verlag.

Philip, Thangam. Indian Cuisine. 81p. 1985. 8.95 (*0-318-36295-3*) Asia Bk Corp.

— The Thangam Philip Book of Cooking. 122p. 1982. pap. 3.50 (*0-86131-285-6*) Apt Bks.

Philip, Thangam E. Modern Cookery for Teaching & the Trade, Vol. 1. 3rd ed. (Illus.). 1062p. 1981. pap. text ed. 30.00 (*0-86131-284-8*, Pub. by Orient Longman Ltd II) Apt Bks.

— Modern Cookery for Teaching & the Trade, Vol. 2. (Illus.). 824p. 1982. pap. text ed. 30.00 (*0-86125-158-X*, Pub. by Orient Longman Ltd II) Apt Bks.

Philipchalk, Ronald P. Psychology & Christianity: An Introduction to Controversial Issues. rev. ed. 258p. (Orig.). (C). 1988. pap. text ed. 22.50 (*0-8191-7124-7*) U Pr of Amer.

Philipchalk, Ronald P. & McConnell, James V. Understanding Human Behavior. 8th ed. (Illus.). 704p. (C). text ed. write for info. (*0-15-500991-5*) HB Coll Pubs.

Philipchalk, Ronald P., jt. auth. see McConnell, James V.

Philipe, Anne. Ete pres de la Mer. (Folio Ser.: No. 1152). (FRE.). pap. 8.95 (*2-07-037152-2*) Schoenhof.

Philipon, M. M. Conchita: A Mother's Spiritual Diary. Owen, Aloysius, tr. LC 78-1929. 256p. 1978. pap. 9.95 (*0-8189-0578-6*) Alba.

Philipot. Mammography Exam Review. 1992. 24.95 (*0-397-55019-7*) Lippincott.

***Philipp, B., et al.** Polyelectrolytes: Formation, Characterization & Application. LC 94-26915. 1994. write for info. (*1-56990-127-9*) Hanser-Gardner.

Philipp, Christiane, jt. ed. see Wolfrum, Rudiger.

***Philipp, David P., et al, eds.** Protection of Aquatic Diversity Theme 3: Proceedings of the World Fisheries Congress. 1995. text ed. write for info. (*1-886106-11-8*) Science Pubs.

Philipp, E. E. & O'Dowd, M. J., eds. The History of Obstetrics & Gynaecology. (History of Medicine Ser.). (Illus.). 700p. 1993. 125.00 (*1-85070-224-1*) Prthnon Pub.

Philipp, Elliot E. & Setchell, Marcus E. Scientific Foundations of Obstetrics & Gynecology. 4th ed. 800p. 1991. 275.00 (*0-7506-0184-1*) Buttrwrth-Heinemann.

Philipp, Emanuel L. Political Reform in Wisconsin: A Historical Review of the Subjects of Primary Election, Taxation & Railway Regulation. Caine, Stanley P. & Wyman, Roger, eds. LC 73-620042. (Illus.). 197p. 1973. reprint ed. 12.00 (*0-87020-123-9*) State Hist Soc Wis.

Philipp, Joan A. & Wilkerson, Jerry D. Teaching Team Sports: A Coeducational Approach. LC 89-7533. (Illus.). 320p. (C). 1990. pap. text ed. 30.00x (*0-87322-259-8*, BPHI0259) Human Kinetics.

Philipp, Lillie H. Piano Technique: Tone, Touch, Phrasing & Dynamics. (Illus.). 90p. (J). (gr. 7 up). 1982. reprint ed. pap. 5.95 (*0-486-24272-2*) Dover.

Philipp, Thomas. Syrians in Egypt 1725-1975. (Illus.). 203p. (Orig.). 1985. pap. 48.50 (*3-515-04031-5*) Coronet Bks.

Philipp, Thomas, ed. see Zaidan, Jurji.

Philipp, Walter. Mixing Sequences of Random Variables & Probabilistic Number Theory. LC 52-42839. (Memoirs Ser.: No. 1/114). 102p. 1971. pap. 16.00 (*0-8218-1814-7*, MEMO 1/114) Am Math.

Philipp, Walter & Stout, William. Almost Sure Invariance Principles for Partial Sums of Weakly Dependent Random Variables. (Memoirs Ser.: No. 2/161). 140p. 1987. reprint ed. pap. 26.00 (*0-8218-1861-9*, MEMO 2/ 161) Am Math.

Philippaki-Warburton, Irene, jt. auth. see Joseph, Brian D.

***Philippaki-Warburton, Irene, et al, eds.** Themes in Greek Linguistics: Papers from the First International Conference on Greek Linguistics, Reading, September 1993. LC 94-38050. (Current Issues in Linguistic Theory Ser.: No. 117). xiii, 521p. 1994. lib. bdg. 79.00x (*1-55619-571-0*) Benjamins North Am.

Philippakis, Andreas S. & Kazmier, Leonard J. Structured COBOL. 3rd ed. 440p. (C). 1986. pap. text ed. write for info. (*0-07-049809-1*) McGraw.

Philippakis, Andrew S. & Kazmier, Leonard J. Comprehensive COBOL. 1991. pap. text ed. write for info. (*0-07-049828-8*) McGraw.

Philippart, David, ed. At Home with the Word, 1995. (Illus.). 144p. (Orig.). 1994. pap. 6.00 (*0-685-72805-6*) Liturgy Tr Pubns.

— Preaching about the Mass. (Illus.). 104p. (Orig.). 1992. pap. 8.95 (*0-929650-47-6*) Liturgy Tr Pubns.

Philippart, David, ed. see Buscemi, John.

Philippart, David, ed. see Jones-Frank, Michael.

Philippart, David, ed. see Ryan, Thomas.

Philippart, David, ed. see Smith, Peter E.

Philippart, David, ed. see Sovik, E. A.

Philippatos, George C. Financial Management: Theory & Techniques. LC 72-83249. 661p. (C). 1973. text ed. 36. 95 (*0-8162-6736-7*) Holden-Day.

Philippatos, George C. & Sihler, William W. Financial Management: Intermediate Text & Cases. 2nd ed. 600p. 1990. text ed. 54.00 (*0-205-12439-9*, H24391) Allyn.

— Financial Management: Intermediate Text & Cases. 2nd ed. 600p. 1991. write for info. (*0-318-66340-6*, H24409); write for info. (*0-318-66341-4*, H27014) Allyn.

Philippatos, George C., et al. Cases in Finance. (C). 1985. teacher ed write for info. (*0-8359-0718-X*, Reston); pap. text ed. write for info. (*0-8359-0717-1*, Reston) P-H.

Philippe, Anne. Un Ete pres de la Mer. (FRE.). 1979. pap. 10.95 (*0-7859-4123-1*) Fr & Eur.

— Les Resonances de l'Amour. (FRE.). 1985. pap. 8.95 (*0-7859-4223-8*) Fr & Eur.

***Philippe, Anne & Weelen, Guy.** Arpad Szenes. (Grandes Monografias). (Illus.). 340p. (SPA.). 1993. 300.00 (*84-343-0663-8*) Elliots Bks.

Philippe, Charles-Louis. La Mere et l'Enfant-Le Pere Perdrix. (FRE.). 1983. pap. 13.95 (*0-7859-4194-0*) Fr & Eur.

Philippe De Remi. Roman de la Manekine par Philippe de Reimes. LC 74-174193. (Bannatyne Club, Edinburgh. Publications: No. 68). reprint ed. 37.50 (*0-404-52788-4*) AMS Pr.

— Romance of Blonde of Oxford & Jehan of Dammartin. Le-Roux De Lincy, M., ed. (Camden Society, London. Publications, First Ser.: No. 72). reprint ed. 55.00 (*0-404-50172-9*) AMS Pr.

Philippe, Pierre P. & Spiteri, Laurence J. The Virgin Mary & the Priesthood. LC 93-6682. 158p. (Orig.). (ENG.). 1993. pap. 9.95 (*0-8189-0668-5*) Alba.

Philippe, Thomas. The Contemplative Life. 128p. 1990. 14. 95 (*0-8245-0984-6*) Crossroad NY.

— The Fire of Contemplation: A Guide for Interior Souls. Doran, Verda C., tr. LC 81-8099. 128p. (Orig.). 1981. pap. 4.95 (*0-8189-0414-3*) Alba.

Philippi, Charles, tr. see De Vogue, Adalbert.

Philippi, Charles, tr. see Vogue, Adalbert de.

Philippi, Donald L. Norito: A Translation of the Ancient Japanese Ritual Prayers. (Illus.). 135p. (C). 1990. text ed. 22.95 (*0-691-06859-3*); pap. text ed. 9.95 (*0-691-01489-2*) Princeton U Pr.

— Songs of Gods, Songs of Humans: The Epic Tradition of the Ainu. LC 78-18002. (Illus.). 426p. reprint ed. pap. 121.50 (*0-8357-3704-7*, 2036429) Bks Demand.

Philippi, Donald L., tr. Kojiki. 1977. pap. 40.00 (*0-86008-320-9*, Pub. by U of Tokyo JA) Col U Pr.

Philippides, Dia M. Census of Modern Greek Literature: Check-List of English-Language Sources Useful in the Study of Modern Greek Literature (1824-1987) (Series of Occasional Papers). 300p. (Orig.). (C). 1990. pap. text ed. 3.00 (*0-912105-01-1*) Modern Greek Studies Assn.

— The Iambic Trimeter of Euripides. rev. ed. Connor, W. R., ed. LC 80-2663. 1981. lib. bdg. 35.95 (*0-405-14048-7*) Ayer.

Philippides, Dimitri. Mediterranean Houses: Greece. (Illus.). 144p. 1994. pap. 49.95 (*84-252-1634-6*, Pub. by Gustavo Gili SP) Rizzoli Intl.

Philippides, Marios. Constantine Eleventh Dragas Palaeologus: A Biography of the Last Greek Emperor. (Hellenism: Ancient, Mediaeval, Modern Ser.: No. 17). 600p. (C). 1993. text ed. 85.00 (*0-89241-522-3*) Caratzas.

— Patriarchs, Emperors & Sultans: Short Chronicle of the Sixteenth Century. (Archbishop Iakovos Library of Ecclesiastical & Historical Sources: No. 13). 1987. 24.95 (*0-917653-15-7*); pap. 14.95 (*0-917653-16-5*) Hellenic Coll Pr.

Philippides, Marios, tr. Byzantium, Europe & the Early Ottoman Sultans, 1373-1513: An Anonymous Greek Chronicle of the Seventeenth Century (Codex Barberinus Graecus III) (Late Byzantine & Ottoman Studies: No. 4). 237p. 1990. text ed. 50.00 (*0-89241-430-8*) Caratzas.

Philippides, Marios, ed. see Nestor-Iskander.

Philippides, Marios, tr. see Nestor-Iskander.

Philippides, Mary Z., jt. auth. see Moore, Mary B.

Philippines Commonwealth Constitution 1972 Staff, ed. see Malcolm, George A.

Philippoff, Jennifer, jt. auth. see Maurer-Mathison, Diane V.

Philippon, Patrice, ed. Approximations Diophantiennes et Nombres Transcendants: Diophantine Approximations & Transcendental Numbers. x, 310p. (C). 1992. lib. bdg. 159.95 (*3-11-013486-1*) De Gruyter.

Philippot, Jean R. & Schuber, Francis, eds. Liposomes As Tools in Basic Research & Industry. 288p. 1994. 189.95 (*0-8493-4569-3*, 4569) CRC Pr.

Philippot, Patrick. Turbo Pascal: Procedures & Functions for IBM PCs & Compatibles. Beeson, David & Keith, Seth, eds. LC 87-18797. 204p. reprint ed. pap. 58.20 (*0-7837-0114-4*, 2040391) Bks Demand.

Philippou, A. J., ed. Orthodoxy Life & Freedom: Essays in Honour of Archbishop Iakovos. LC 80-20616. xii, 162p. 1980. reprint ed. lib. bdg. 27.00x (*0-89370-088-6*) Borgo Pr.

Philipps, Eva. Documentation Made Easy: A Library Manual for Nongovernmental Organizations Specializing in Appropriate Technology & Rural Development. Deutsches Zentrum fur Entwicklungstechnologien GATE In: Deutsche Gesellschaft fur Technische Zusammenarbeit (GTZ) GmbH Staff, ed. (Illus.). 207p. 1990. pap. 22.00 (*3-528-02054-7*, Pub. by Vieweg & Sohn GW) Ballen Bkslr.

Philipps, John. The Tragedy of the Soviet Germans. LC 83-61289. (Illus.). 190p. (Orig.). 1983. pap. 6.50 (*0-9611412-0-4*) John Philipps.

Philipps, Myra. Smooth As Silk. 2nd ed. (Illus.). (J). (gr. 3 up). 1979. 1.95 (*0-686-10960-0*) Basin Pub.

Philippsborn, H. E., comp. Dictionary of Industrial Technology: In English, German, & Portuguese. LC 94-1644. (ENG, GER & POR.). 1994. write for info. (*0-444-89945-6*) Elsevier.

Philippson, Robert. Studien Zu Epikur und den Epikureern. Classen, C. Joachim, ed. (Olms GW Studien: Bd. 17). vi, 354p. (GER.). 1983. write for info. (*3-487-07380-3*, Pub. by Georg Olms GW) Lubrecht & Cramer.

Philippus De Thame. Knights Hospitallers in England: Being the Report of Prior Phillip De Thame to the Grand Master Elyan De Villanova for A. D. 1338. Larking, Lambert B., ed. (Camden Society, London. Publications, First Ser.: No. 65). reprint ed. 75.00 (*0-404-50165-6*) AMS Pr.

Philippus, M. J., jt. auth. see Wallace, B. D.

***Philips.** Differential Diagnosis in Speech-Language Pathology. 1999. write for info. (*0-7506-9675-3*, Focal) Buttrwrth-Heinemann.

Philips, jt. auth. see Fess.

Philips, Andrew, ed. see Efiok, Bassey J.

Philips, Barbara. Don't Call Me Fatso. LC 85-24341. (Life & Living from a Child's Point of View Ser.). (Illus.). 32p. (J). (gr. k-6). 1980. lib. bdg. 19.97 (*0-8172-1350-3*) Raintree Steck-V.

Philips, Bill. Professional Locksmithing Techniques. 1991. pap. 25.95 (*0-07-155252-9*) McGraw.

Philips, Bruce A. Brookline: Evolution of an American Jewish Suburb. LC 90-23079. (European Immigrants & American Society Ser.). 200p. 1991. reprint ed. 15.00 (*0-8240-7428-9*) Garland.

Philips, C. H., ed. see Department of Oriental History Staff, University of London.

Philips, C. H., ed. see University of London, Dept. of Oriental & African Studies.

Philips, Carey, jt. ed. see Yates, Katherine.

P Q

An Asterisk (*) at the beginning of an entry indicates that the title is appearing in BIP for the first time.

Philips, Catherine A., tr. see Ugarte, Manuel.

Philips, Christopher L. Guide to the College Library: The Most Useful Resources for Students & Researchers. LC 93-17748. 1993. 49.95 (*0-8027-1283-5*) Walker & Co.

Philips, Clayton. Nature's Sword: A Novel of the Imminent Future. LC 92-45899. 1993. write for info. (*1-880373-04-1*) Pictorial Herit.

Philips, Curt. Love's Journey. LC 84-70262. (Illus.). 139p. (Orig.). (C). 1984. pap. text ed. 6.95 (*0-918899-00-1*) Dragonscales & Mane Pub.

***Philips, D. Z.** Wittgenstein & Religion Vol. 1. 1994. pap. 18.95 (*0-312-12300-0*) St Martin.

Philips, David. Legendary Connecticut. LC 92-24532. (Illus.). 336p. 1992. pap. 14.95 (*1-880684-05-5*) Curbstone.

***Philips, David & Davies, Susanne, eds.** A Nation of Rogues? Crime, Law & Punishment in Colonial Australia. 224p. Date not set. pap. 24.95 (*0-522-84601-7*) Intl Spec Bk.

Philips, Elizabeth D., et al. Intermediate Algebra: Applications & Problem Solving. 2nd ed. LC 93-4030. (C). 1993. text ed. 54.50 (*0-06-045220-X*) HarpCollege.

— Intermediate Algebra: Applications & Problem Solving. 2nd ed. LC 93-4030. (C). 1994. Sale tutorial, Mac. 12.00 (*0-06-502193-2*) HarpCollege.

— Intermediate Algebra: Applications & Problem Solving. 2nd ed. LC 93-4030. (C). 1994. Student study manual. student ed 12.75 (*0-06-501927-X*) HarpCollege.

Philips-Eteng, Etom, ed. see Interspectrum Staff.

***Philips, F. M.** Lust Angeles: An Underground Guide to Greater Los Angeles. Warren, Roger, ed. (Illus.). 300p. (Orig.). 1995. pap. 19.95 (*0-945949-06-5*) Warren Comns.

Philips, Frederick. Forty-Five Years with Philips. 1989. 4.95 (*0-7137-0931-6*) Grosvenor USA.

Philips, George O. Philips Family Record 1978. (Illus.). 520p. (Orig.). 1979. pap. 17.50 (*0-940846-00-4*) Hastings Bks.

Philips, George S. Memoirs of Ebenezer Elliot & the Corn Law Rhymes. 1972. 59.95 (*0-8490-0605-8*) Gordon Pr.

Philips, H. Claire. Psychological Management of Chronic Pain: A Treatment Manual. (Behavior Therapy & Behavioral Medicine Ser.). 240p. (C). 1988. pap. 27.95 (*0-8261-6110-3*) Springer Pub.

Philips IMS Staff. The CD-I Design Handbook. LC 92-15877. (C). 1992. pap. text ed. 24.95 (*0-201-62749-3*) Addison-Wesley.

— The CD-I Production Handbook. LC 92-15878. (C). 1992. pap. text ed. 24.95 (*0-201-62750-7*) Addison-Wesley.

— Introducing CD-I. LC 92-15876. (C). 1992. text ed. 21.50 (*0-201-62748-5*) Addison-Wesley.

Philips, J. G., tr. see Eitel, Wilhelm.

Philips, James M., ed. see Andrews, John C.

Philips, Jim. Caribbean Basin Initiative Guidebook, 1990. 7th ed. (Illus.). 76p. 1990. per., pap. 4.00 (*0-16-028050-8*) USGPO.

Philips, Judson. A Murder Arranged. large type ed. 1981. 12.00 (*0-7089-0591-9*) Ulverscroft.

Philips, Julia, jt. auth. see Philips, Matthew.

Philips, Katherine. Poems by the Most Deservedly Admired Mrs. Katherine Philips: The Matchless Orinda. LC 92-1093. (Scholars' Facsimiles & Reprints Ser.). 200p. 1992. reprint ed. 50.00 (*0-8201-1462-6*) Schol Facsimiles.

Philips, Leslie N., ed. Design with Advanced Composite Materials. (Illus.). 384p. (C). 1989. 59.95x (*0-85072-238-1*, Pub. by Design Council Bks UK) Ashgate Pub Co.

Philips, Louis, jt. ed. see Cole, William.

Philips, Margaret. Genealogical Records Abstracted from the New England Puritan 1840-1841. iv, 275p. (Orig.). 1989. pap. 20.00 (*1-55613-172-0*) Heritage Bk.

Philips, Martha & Hadden, Mary. Behind Stone Walls & Barbed Wire. Lynn, Claire, ed. (Illus.). 176p. (Orig.). (J). (gr. 5 up). 1991. pap. 2.25 (*0-89323-057-X*) Bible Memory.

Philips, Mary E., jt. auth. see Brown, Carol E.

***Philips, Matthew & Philips, Julia.** Witches of Oz. Date not set. pap. 19.95 (*1-898307-18-0*, Pub. by Capall Bann Pubng UK) Holmes Pub.

Philips, Michael. Between Universalism & Skepticism: Ethics As Social Artifact. 224p. 1994. 35.00 (*0-19-508646-5*) OUP.

Philips, Michael, ed. Philosophy & Science Fiction. LC 83-62874. 392p. 1984. pap. 24.95x (*0-87975-248-3*) Prometheus Bks.

Philips, Paul. Time-Space Transcendence. LC 84-71711. 72p. (Orig.). 1984. pap. 8.95 (*0-930149-00-9*) AAP Calif.

— Transpersonal Psychology for Daily Life. LC 80-66662. (Illus.). 98p. (Orig.). 1984. pap. 8.95 (*0-930149-01-7*) AAP Calif.

Philips, Peter, jt. ed. see Mangum, Garth L.

Philips, Ronald J., jt. auth. see Mercer, James L.

Philips, Rosemarie, jt. auth. see Tucker, Stuart K.

Philips, Susan U. The Invisible Culture: Communication in Classroom & Community on the Warm Springs Indian Reservation. rev. ed. 147p. (C). 1993. reprint ed. pap. text ed. 9.95 (*0-88133-694-7*) Waveland Pr.

Philips, Susan U., et al, eds. Language, Gender, & Sex in Comparative Perspective. (Studies in the Social & Cultural Foundations of Language: No. 4). (Illus.). 352p. 1987. pap. 21.95 (*0-521-33807-7*) Cambridge U Pr.

***Philips, Thomas W.** Poems for the Christian Year. LC 93-94028. 96p. (Orig.). 1994. pap. 6.95 (*1-56002-361-9*) Aegina Pr.

Philips University Graduate Seminary Staff, jt. auth. see Hamburger, Roberta.

Philips, V. A., jt. auth. see Moiser, C. H.

Philips, W. Glasgow. Tuscaloosa. LC 93-2481. 1994. 20.00 (*0-688-12861-0*) Morrow.

Philips, William. St. Stephen's Green: Generous Lovers. 1980. 22.00 (*0-85105-367-X*, Pub. by Colin Smythe Ltd UK) Dufour.

Philipsen, Dirk. We Were the People: Voices from East Germany's Revolutionary Autumn of 1989. LC 92-12762. 432p. 1992. lib. bdg. 49.95 (*0-8223-1282-4*); pap. 19.95 (*0-8223-1294-8*) Duke.

Philipsen, Gerry. Speaking Culturally: Explorations in Social Communication. LC 91-33107. 154p. 1992. 49.50 (*0-7914-1163-X*); pap. 16.95 (*0-7914-1164-8*) State U NY Pr.

Philipson, David. The Jew in English Fiction. LC 76-30568. (English Literature Ser.: No. 33). 1977. lib. bdg. 47.95 (*0-8383-2150-X*) M S G Haskell Hse.

— Old European Jewries. LC 74-178586. reprint ed. 41.50 (*0-404-56663-4*) AMS Pr.

Philipson, David, ed. see Wise, Isaac.

Philipson, David, et al. Studies in Jewish Literature Issued in Honor of Professor Kaufmann Kohler, Ph.D. Katz, Steven, ed. LC 79-7167. (Jewish Philosophy, Mysticism & History of Ideas Ser.). 1980. reprint ed. lib. bdg. 29.95 (*0-405-12283-7*) Ayer.

Philipson, Ilene. Ethel Rosenberg: Beyond the Myths. LC 92-23750. 390p. (C). 1993. reprint ed. pap. 14.95 (*0-8135-1917-9*) Rutgers U Pr.

— On the Shoulders of Women: The Feminization of Psychology. LC 93-25404. 177p. 1993. lib. bdg. 21.95 (*0-89862-017-1*) Guilford Pr.

Philipson, Ilene J., jt. ed. see Hansen, Karen V.

Philipson, Julia, jt. auth. see Edes, Shirley.

Philipson, L., et al. Molecular Biology of Adenoviruses. LC 75-6658. (Virology Monographs: Vol. 14). (Illus.). iv, 115p. 1975. 45.00 (*0-387-81284-9*) Spr-Verlag.

Philipson, L., jt. auth. see Lonberg-Holm, K.

Philipson, Morris. Six Stunning Paradoxes: The Present Disadvantages of Certain Unique Improvements. 1968. pap. 2.00 (*0-940550-04-0*) Caxton Club.

Philipson, Morris, ed. see Barzun, Jacques.

Philipson, Morris H. Outline of a Jungian Aesthetics. LC 63-15299. 224p. reprint ed. pap. 63.90 (*0-317-10358-X*, 2006884) Bks Demand.

— Outline of Jungian Aesthetics. 1991. 35.00 (*0-938434-87-X*); pap. 18.95 (*0-938434-88-8*) Sigo Pr.

Philipson, Sten M. A Metaphysics for Theology: A Study of Some Problems in the Later Philosophy of Alfred North Whitehead & Its Applications to Issues in Contemporary Theology. (Studia Doctrinae Christianae Upsaliensia: No. 22). 174p. (Orig.). 1982. pap. 31.00x (*91-554-1246-7*, Pub. by Uppsala Univ Acta Univ Uppsaliensis SW) Coronet Bks.

Philipson, Tomas J. & Posner, Richard A. Private Choices & Public Health: The AIDS Epidemic in an Economic Perspective. LC 93-17417. 276p. 1993. 32.00 (*0-674-70738-9*) HUP.

***Philipson, Trevor.** Carriage by Air. 1994. boxed 209.00 (*0-406-02136-8*, UK) Butterworth Legal Pubs.

Philipson, U. N. Political Slang, Seventeen Fifty to Eighteen Fifty. (Lund Studies in English: Vol. 9). 1974. reprint ed. pap. 35.00 (*0-8115-0552-9*) Periodicals Srv.

Phillabaum, Stephen D. Employee-Employer Rights: The Complete Guide for the Washington Work Force. 2nd ed. (Legal Ser.). 112p. 1992. pap. 8.95 (*0-88908-749-0*) Self-Counsel Pr.

***Phillander, Anthony.** A Poetic Collage of Prose & Poetry. 1995. 9.95 (*0-8062-5279-0*) Carlton.

Phillay, M. Abithana Kosha: The Tamil Classical Dictionary. (ENG & TAM.). 1985. 29.95 (*0-8288-1723-5*, M14481) Fr & Eur.

Philliber, William W. & Obermiller, Phillip J., eds. Too Few Tomorrows: Urban Appalachians in the 1980's. LC 86-28816. 170p. (Orig.). 1987. pap. 8.95 (*0-913239-47-X*) Appalach Consortium.

Philliber, William W., jt. ed. see Obermiller, Phillip J.

Philliber, William W., jt. auth. see Vannoy-Hiller, Dana.

***Philliber, William W., et al, eds.** The Invisible Minority: Urban Appalachians. fac. ed. LC 79-4008. 205p. 1994. pap. 58.50 (*0-7837-7597-0*, 2047350) Bks Demand.

Phillimore, J. Mansfield. (Life & Works: Set II). (Illus.). 112p. (YA). (gr. 7 up). 1990. lib. bdg. 19.94 (*0-86593-020-1*); lib. bdg. 14.95 (*0-685-46451-2*) Rourke Corp.

Phillimore, John G. Private Law among the Romans from the Pandects. xxii, 423p. 1994. reprint ed. lib. bdg. 57.50 (*0-8377-2550-X*) Rothman.

Phillimore, Robert. The Principal Ecclesiastical Judgments Delivered in the Court of Arches 1867 to 1875. xiii, 420p. 1981. reprint ed. lib. bdg. 35.00 (*0-8377-2504-6*) Rothman.

Phillimore, W. P., ed. A Calendar of Wills Relating to the Counties of Northampton & Rutland. Bd. with Calendar of Chancery Proceedings, Bills & Answers.; Index Nominum to the Royalist Composition Papers. (British Record Society Index Library Ser.: Vols. 1,2 & 3). 1972. reprint ed. 67.00 (*0-8115-1452-8*) Periodicals Srv.

— Calendars of Wills & Administrations in the Consistory Court of the Bishop of Lichfield & Coventry, 1516-1652. (British Record Society Index Library Ser.: Vol. 7). 1972. reprint ed. pap. 53.00 (*0-8115-1454-4*) Periodicals Srv.

— An Index to Bills of Privy Signet, Commonly Called Signet Bills: 1584 -1596 & 1603-1624. Bd. with Calendar of Writs of Privy Seal: 1601-1603.; Vol. 2. Calendar of Chancery Proceedings: Bills & Answers.; Vol. 3. Calendar of Chancery Proceedings: Bills & Answers. (British Record Society Index Library Ser.: Vols. 4, 5 & 6). 1969. 67.00 (*0-8115-1453-6*) Periodicals Srv.

— Placita Coram Domino Rege Apud Westmonasterium de Termino Sanocte Trinitatis Anno Regni Regis Edwardii Filii Regis Henrici Vicesimo Quinto: The Pleas of the Count of Kings Bench, Trinity Team, 25 Edward I, 1297. (British Record Society Index Library Ser.: Vol. 19). 1974. reprint ed. pap. 30.00 (*0-8115-1464-1*) Periodicals Srv.

Phillimore, W. P. & Duncan, Leland L., eds. A Calendar of Wills Proved in the Consistory Court of the Bishop of Gloucester, 1541-1650. (British Record Society Index Library Ser.: Vol. 12). 1972. reprint ed. pap. 30.00 (*0-8115-1457-9*) Periodicals Srv.

Phillimore, W. P. & Fry, George S., eds. Abstracts of Inquisitiones Post Mortem for Gloucestershire Returned into the Court of Chancery During the Stuart Period, Pt. III: Miscellaneous Series, 13-18 Charles I, 1637-1642. (British Record Society Index Library Ser.: Vol. 13). 1972. reprint ed. pap. 19.00 (*0-8115-1458-7*) Periodicals Srv.

Phillimore, W. P., jt. ed. see Fry, Edward A.

Phillip, A. J. Dickens Dictionary. 1990. 8.99 (*0-517-02195-1*) Random Hse Value.

Phillip, Clifford. The dBASE IV Developer's Reference Guide. 1989. disk 51.95 (*0-318-42846-6*) MIS Press.

Phillip-Eteng, Eton. Doing Business in Nigeria: Africa's Largest Market Beckons You. 197p. (Orig.). 1992. pap. 19.95 (*0-9629214-3-2*) Intl Spectrum.

Phillip, F. & Lane, Harlan. Philosophical Works of Etienne Bonnot, Abbe de Condillac Vol. I, Vol. 1. Philip, Franklin, tr. 448p. (C). 1982. text ed. 89.95 (*0-89859-181-3*) L Erlbaum Assocs.

Phillip, Franklin, ed. see Walesa, Lech.

Phillip, Jay-Michael, II. The Black Man's Problem Is His Own. Stafford, Marina, ed. 225p. (Orig.). 1994. pap. 11. 95 (*1-884500-00-5*) Dynamic Key.

***Phillip, Neil, ed. & intro.** Singing America: Poems That Define a Nation. (Illus.). 160p. (YA). (gr. 5 up). 1995. 19.99 (*0-670-86150-2*) Viking Child Bks.

Phillip, W., tr. see De Veer, Gerrit.

Phillip Z. A Skeptic's Guide to the Twelve Steps. 242p. (Orig.). 1991. pap. 11.00 (*0-89486-722-9*, 5130A) Hazelden.

Phillipp, Isidor, ed. French Piano Music: An Anthology. (Anthology of French Piano Music Ser.). 188p. 1977. pap. 8.95 (*0-486-23381-2*) Dover.

Phillippe, William R. Bible Stories You Never Heard Before. LC 87-11618. ix, 155p. (Orig.). 1989. pap. 9.95 (*0-940473-06-2*) Wm Caxton.

— A Romp Through the Bible. LC 88-11830. 192p. (Orig.). 1987. 20.00 (*0-940473-01-1*); pap. 9.95 (*0-940473-02-X*) Wm Caxton.

Phillippi, Wendell C. Dear Ike. 274p. 1991. 15.75 (*0-9630859-0-5*); pap. 10.50 (*0-9630859-1-3*) Two-Star. A collection of letters discussing leaders of World War II-- Roosevelt, McArthur, Bradley, Patton, DeGaulle, Montgomery & others in a give & take with Eisenhower about battles & personalities. Kurt Vonnegut, author, after reading it said, "It is the best, authoritative, personalized book on World War II I have read." Son John Eisenhower gives new a new insight into his father's relations with Kay Summerbsy along with others. Good reading to learn about or remember WWII. Written by a soldier who served 2 1/2 years in combat in Italy, France & Germany. Two-Star Press, P.O. Box 817, Nashville, IN 47448. H. $15.75. P. 10.50. PH $2.50 Two-Star Press 317-293-3103. ***Publisher Provided Annotation.***

Phillippo, James M. Jamaica: Its Past & Present State. LC 79-157374. (Black Heritage Library Collection). 1977. 41.95 (*0-8369-8812-4*) Ayer.

— Jamaica: Its Past & Present State. LC 70-109998. (Illus.). 1970. reprint ed. 23.75 (*0-8371-4132-X*, PIA&, Negro U Pr) Greenwood.

Phillippou, Margaret J. Transcendental Dancing. 1982. pap. 3.00 (*0-941500-29-2*) Sharing Co.

Phillipps, Calvin C. & McFadden, David A. Investigating the Fireground. LC 86-4379. (Illus.). 296p. 1986. reprint ed. text ed. 36.75 (*0-912212-14-4*) Fire Eng.

Phillipps, Evelyn M. The Venetian School of Painting. LC 70-37907. (Select Bibliographies Reprint Ser.). 1977. reprint ed. 24.95 (*0-8369-6745-3*) Ayer.

Phillipps, Marilyn. First Aid for a Wounded Marriage. 32p. 1986. pap. text ed. write for info. (*1-884794-00-9*) Eden Pubng.

— Whose Report Will You Believe? 60p. 1993. pap. text ed. write for info. (*1-884794-04-1*) Eden Pubng.

Phillipps, Marilyn, jt. auth. see Phillipps, Mike.

Phillipps, Mike & Phillipps, Marilyn. Casado por Uida. 208p. 1986. pap. text ed. write for info. (*1-884794-05-X*) Eden Pubng.

— Casado por Vida Manual de Liderato. 320p. 1986. pap. text ed. write for info. (*1-884794-06-8*) Eden Pubng.

— Gifta for Livet Ledarhandbok. Smedberg, Jan-Olaf, tr. 322p. (Orig.). (SWE.). 1994. pap. write for info. (*1-884794-08-4*) Eden Pubng.

— Leaders of Leaders Int'l. 100p. (Orig.). 1994. pap. text ed. write for info. (*1-884794-11-4*) Eden Pubng.

— Leader's of Leader's USA. 100p. 1994. pap. text ed. write for info. (*1-884794-10-6*) Eden Pubng.

— Married for Life: Couple's Manual. 208p. 1983. pap. text ed. write for info. (*1-884794-02-5*) Eden Pubng.

— Married for Life: Leader's Manual. 320p. 1983. pap. text ed. write for info. (*1-884794-01-7*) Eden Pubng.

— Married for Life Leder Hanbog. Thorslund, Lena, tr. 322p. (Orig.). (DAN.). 1994. pap. write for info. (*1-884794-07-6*) Eden Pubng.

Phillipps, S. M., contrib. Famous Cases of Circumstantial Evidence, 2 vols. in 1. 1978. reprint ed. lib. bdg. 42.50 (*0-8377-1002-2*) Rothman.

Phillippy, Patricia B. Love's Remedies: Recantation & Renaissance Lyric Poetry. LC 94-21457. 1995. write for info. (*0-8387-5263-2*) Bucknell U Pr.

Phillips. Building Society Finance. 1983. pap. 44.95 (*0-85258-231-5*) Chapman & Hall.

— The Chess Teacher. 1995. pap. 14.95 (*1-85744-161-3*, Scribners) S&S Trade.

— Complete Book of Locks & Locksmithing. 4th ed. 1995. pap. text ed. 24.95 (*0-07-049866-0*) McGraw.

— Ensuring Image Quality Student Workbook. 96p. 1987. pap. 16.95 (*0-8016-3906-9*) Mosby Yr Bk.

— Extra-Sensory Perception of Quarks. 1994. 15.00 (*0-8356-0227-3*, Quest) Theos Pub Hse.

— Great Texas Murder Trail. 1979. 9.95 (*0-02-596150-0*) Macmillan.

— The Heart of the Earth. 1968. boxed 33.75 (*0-685-64773-0*) Jones & Bartlett.

— Natural by Design: Plants for Natural Gardens. 1995. boxed, pap. text ed. 50.00 (*0-89013-278-X*) Museum NM Pr.

— Notting Hill in the Sixties. (C). 1991. pap. 25.00 (*0-85315-751-0*, Pub. by Lawrence & Wishart UK) Humanities.

— Shelter. 1995. pap. (*0-385-31389-6*, Delta) Dell.

Phillips, ed. Analytical Techniques in Immunochemistry. 364p. 1991. 165.00 (*0-8247-8477-4*) Dekker.

— Left & the Erotic. (C). 1983. pap. 18.50 (*0-85315-583-6*, Pub. by Lawrence & Wishart UK) Humanities.

Phillips & Adams. Year Book of Chiropractic, 1993. 352p. 1993. 54.95 (*0-8151-6733-4*, Yr Bk Med Pubs) Mosby Yr Bk.

— Year Book of Chiropractic, 1994. 352p. 1994. 54.95 (*0-8151-6734-2*, Yr Bk Med Pubs) Mosby Yr Bk.

— Year Book of Chiropractic, 1995. 352p. 1995. 54.95 (*0-8151-6735-0*, Yr Bk Med Pubs) Mosby Yr Bk.

— Year Book of Chiropractic, 1996. 352p. 1996. 54.95 (*0-8151-6736-9*, Yr Bk Med Pubs) Mosby Yr Bk.

— Year Book of Chiropractic, 1997. 352p. 1997. 54.95 (*0-8151-6737-7*, Yr Bk Med Pubs) Mosby Yr Bk.

Phillips & Feeney. The Cardiac Rhythms: A Systematic Approach to Interpretation. 3rd ed. (Illus.). 608p. 1990. pap. text ed. 35.50 (*0-7216-2427-8*) Saunders.

Phillips & Finley. Protein Quality & the Effects of Processing. (Food Science & Technology Ser.: Vol. 29). 416p. 1989. 115.00 (*0-8247-7984-3*) Dekker.

***Phillips & Sutherland.** SBS: Container Gardening. (Illus.). 112p. 1995. 14.98 (*0-8317-7790-7*) Smithmark.

Phillips & Wallace. Influence in the Workplace: Maximizing Personal Empowerment. 144p. 1992. pap. text ed. 14.95 (*0-8403-7594-8*) Kendall-Hunt.

Phillips & Washick. U. S. - Mexico Tax Convention: Text & Analysis. 80p. 1993. pap. 39.00 (*0-685-67054-6*, 5404) Commerce.

Phillips, jt. auth. see Denning.

Phillips, jt. auth. see Smith.

Phillips, et al. Bowie Knives of the Ben Palmer Collection. 245p. 1992. 34.95 (*0-932572-24-3*) Phillips Pubns.

— Clinical Chiropractic Care No. 1: Clinical Care. 400p. 1994. pap. 45.00 (*0-8016-6822-0*) Mosby Yr Bk.

Phillips, A. Perspectives on Anti-Trust Policy. 1965. 65.00 (*0-691-04158-X*) Princeton U Pr.

Phillips, A. A. Henry Lawson. (Twayne's World Authors Ser.). (C). 1972. lib. bdg. 17.95 (*0-8057-2512-1*) Irvington.

Phillips, A. A., jt. auth. see Maxwell, I.

Phillips, A. C. The Physics of Stars. LC 93-2079. 175p. 1994. pap. text ed. 32.95 (*0-471-94155-7*) Wiley.

Phillips, A. D. The Underdraining of Farmland in England During the Nineteenth Century. (Cambridge Studies in Historical Geography: No. 15). (Illus.). (C). 1989. 69.95 (*0-521-36444-2*) Cambridge U Pr.

Phillips, A. D., ed. The Potteries: Continuity & Change in a Staffordshire Conurbation. LC 93-10957. 352p. 1993. 36. 00 (*0-7509-0223-X*) A Sutton Pub.

Phillips, A. J. & Stone, J. Contact Lenses: A Textbook for Practitioner & Student. 3rd ed. (Illus.). 1017p. 1989. text ed. 195.00 (*0-407-93275-5*) Buttrwrth-Heinemann.

Phillips, Adam. On Flirtation. LC 94-18821. 252p. 1994. text ed. 19.95 (*0-674-63437-3*, PHIFLI) HUP.

— On Kissing, Tickling, & Being Bored: Psychoanalytic Essays on the Unexamined Life. LC 92-20662. 138p. 1993. text ed. 19.95 (*0-674-63462-4*) HUP.

— On Kissing, Tickling, & Being Bored: Psychoanalytic Essays on the Unexamined Life. 138p. 1994. pap. text ed. 12.00 (*0-674-63463-2*, PHIKAX) HUP.

— Winnicott. LC 88-28390. 192p. 1989. reprint ed. 29.95 (*0-674-95360-6*); reprint ed. pap. 13.95 (*0-674-95361-4*) HUP.

Phillips, Adam, jt. auth. see Eigen, Michael.

Phillips, Alan, pseud. Jazz Improvisation & Harmony. 4th ed. 96p. 1989. reprint ed. pap. text ed. 10.00 (*0-318-41568-2*) CPP Belwin.

Phillips, Albert E., jt. auth. see Bramble, Barry B.

Phillips, Alfred. Phillips: Professional Ethics for Scottish Solicitors. 1990. pap. 37.00 (*0-406-12890-1*) Butterworth Legal Pubs.

Phillips, Allan, jt. auth. see Monson, Gale.

Phillips, Allan R. The Known Birds of North & Middle America Distributions & Variation, Migrations, Changes, Hybrids. etc., Pt. I. (Illus.). 320p. 1986. 60.00 (*0-685-17451-4*) A R Phillips.

P Q

An Asterisk (*) at the beginning of an entry indicates that the title is appearing in BIP for the first time.

— The Known Birds of North & Middle America, Distributions & Variation, Migrations, Changes, Hybrids, Etc., Pt. 2: Bombycillidae; Sylviidae to Sturnidae; Vireonidae. (Illus.). liii, 249p. 1991. lib. bdg. 64.00 (*0-9617402-1-3*) A R Phillips.

Phillips, Allan R., et al. The Birds of Arizona. LC 64-17265. (Illus.). 292p. reprint ed. pap. 83.30 (*0-7837-1910-8*, 2042114) Bks Demand.

Phillips, Allen, ed. see Greenhaw, Wayne.

***Phillips, Almarin, ed.** Perspectives on Antitrust Policy. LC 64-19822. Date not set. reprint ed. pap. 132.90 (*0-7837-9419-3*, 2060160) Bks Demand.

— Promoting Competition in Regulated Markets. LC 74-277. (Studies in the Regulation of Economic Activity). 411p. reprint ed. pap. 117.20 (*0-685-16388-1*, 2027741) Bks Demand.

Phillips, Almarin, et al. Biz Jets: Technology & Market Structure in the Corporate Jet Aircraft Industry. LC 93-42692. (Economics of Science, Technology & Innovation Ser.). 288p. (C). 1994. lib. bdg. 94.50 (*0-7923-2660-1*) Kluwer Ac.

Phillips, Alvin B. Transistor Engineering. LC 81-8432. 400p. 1981. reprint ed. 38.50 (*0-89874-355-9*) Krieger.

Phillips, Amy. Lewis-Gale Medical Center. Harholdt, Phyllis & Nelson, Rodney, eds. (Illus.). 250p. (C). 1993. pap. 40.00 (*0-929690-21-4*); pap. 40.00 (*0-929690-22-2*) Herit Pubs AZ.

Phillips, Amy, ed. see Finnerty, Margaret.

Phillips, Andrew D. The Right & Wrong of Ushering. Smith, Marvin L., ed. LC 92-71668. 84p. (Orig.). 1992. pap. text ed. 5.95 (*0-9625115-7-9*) Campbell Rd Pr.

Phillips, Andy & Dunayevskaya, Raya. The Coal Miner's General Strike of Nineteen Forty-Nine to Fifty & the Birth of Marxist-Humanism in the United States. (Illus.). 50p. 1984. pap. 2.00 (*0-914441-21-3*) News & Letters.

Phillips, Angela. Discrimination. LC 92-39446. (Past & Present Ser.). (Illus.). 48p. (YA). (gr. 6 up). 1993. text ed. 12.95 (*0-02-786881-8*, Mac Bks Young Read) S&S Childrens.

— The Trouble with Boys: A Wise & Symphatetic Guide to the Risky Business of Raising Sons. LC 94-12656. 1994. 23.00 (*0-465-08734-5*) Basic.

— Until They Are Five: A Parents' Guide. 208p. (Orig.). 1989. pap. 10.95 (*0-04-440361-5*) Routledge Chapman & Hall.

Phillips, Ann. A Haunted Year. LC 92-45638. (Illus.). 176p. (J). (gr. 4-8). 1994. text ed. 14.95 (*0-02-774605-4*, Mac Bks Young Read) S&S Childrens.

— The Multiplying Glass. (Illus.). 158p. (J). 1987. 15.00 (*0-19-271455-4*) OUP.

— The Peace Child. (Illus.). 160p. (J). (gr. 5 up). 1988. 15.00 (*0-19-271560-7*) OUP.

***Phillips, Ann & Phillips, Bob.** Make Money from Woodturning. (Illus.). 160p. 1995. pap. 19.95 (*0-946819-50-5*) Sterling.

Phillips, Ann, jt. ed. see Goldberg, Merryl R.

Phillips, Ann L. Soviet Policy Toward East Germany Reconsidered: The Postwar Decade. LC 85-17729. (Contributions in Political Science Ser.: No. 142). (Illus.). 274p. 1986. text ed. 55.00 (*0-313-24671-8*, PSP/, Greenwood Pr) Greenwood.

Phillips, Anne. Democracy & Difference. 176p. 1993. 30.00 (*0-271-01096-7*); pap. 14.95 (*0-271-01097-5*) Pa St U Pr.

— Engendering Democracy. 200p. 1991. 30.00 (*0-271-00783-4*); pap. 14.95 (*0-271-00784-2*) Pa St U Pr.

— The Enigma of Colonialism: British Policy in West Africa. LC 88-13617. 192p. 1989. 29.95 (*0-253-34409-3*) Ind U Pr.

— The Politics of Presence: Democracy & Group Representation. (Oxford Political Theory Ser.). 240p. 1995. 29.95 (*0-19-827942-6*) OUP.

Phillips, Anne, ed. Feminism & Equality. (Readings in Social & Political Theory Ser.). 224p. 1987. 45.00 (*0-8147-6604-8*); pap. 17.50 (*0-8147-6605-6*) NYU Pr.

Phillips, Anne, jt. ed. see Barrett, Michele.

Phillips, Anne D. & Sotiriou, Peter E. Steps to Reading Proficiency. 3rd ed. 340p. (C). 1992. pap. 24.95 (*0-534-16518-4*) Intl Thomson.

Phillips, Anne W. The Ocean. LC 90-36296. (Earth Alert Ser.). (Illus.). 48p. (J). (gr. 6). 1990. text ed. 12.95 (*0-89686-541-X*, Crstwood Hse) Silver Burdett Pr.

***Phillips, Anthony.** Slips & Slipware. (Complete Potter Ser.). (Illus.). 96p. 1995. pap. 19.95 (*0-7134-7713-X*) Trafalgar.

Phillips, Anthony, et al. Basic Accounting for Lawyers. 4th ed. 268p. 1988. text ed. 94.00 (*0-8318-0467-X*, B467) Am Law Inst.

Phillips, Anthony V. & Stone, David A. A Topological Chern-Weil Theory. LC 93-25081. (Memoirs of the American Mathematical Society Ser.: No. 504). 79p. 1993. pap. 28.00 (*0-8218-2566-6*) Am Math.

Phillips, Anthony V., jt. ed. see Goldberg, Lisa R.

Phillips, Ariel, jt. ed. see Rich, Sharon L.

Phillips, Arthur. Survey of African Marriage & Family Life. LC 74-15079. reprint ed. 67.50 (*0-404-12128-4*) AMS Pr.

Phillips, Arthur & Morris, Henry I. Marriage Laws in Africa. LC 75-28914. 239p. reprint ed. pap. 68.20 (*0-8357-3028-X*, 2057115) Bks Demand.

Phillips, Arthur & Phillips, Barbara. High Country Wildflowers. (Illus.). 32p. 1987. 4.95 (*0-89734-061-2*, PL58-3) Mus Northern Ariz.

Phillips, Arthur M., 3rd. Grand Canyon Wildflowers. rev. ed. Priehs, T. J., ed. LC 79-54236. (Illus.). 145p. 1990. 16.95 (*0-938216-01-5*) GCNHA.

Phillips, Arthur S. The Borden Murder Mystery. (Illus.). 40p. (Orig.). 1986. 20.00 (*0-9614811-1-0*) King Philip Pub.

Phillips, Aubrey. Atmospheric Landscapes in Watercolor. 1990. pap. 4.95 (*0-85532-655-7*, Pub. by Search Pr UK) A Schwartz & Co.

— Painting with Pastels. LC 94-9024. (Illus.). 126p. 1994. pap. text ed. 12.95 (*0-486-28159-0*) Dover.

— Painting with Pastels. (Illus.). 128p. 1994. 34.95 (*0-7134-7122-0*, Pub. by Batsford UK) Trafalgar.

Phillips, B. A. Goodbye, Friends: Stories by B. A. Phillips. LC 92-43030. 163p. 1993. 15.95 (*1-882593-01-4*) Bridge Wrks.

Phillips, B. M., jt. auth. see Morton, R. J.

Phillips, Barbara. Don't Call Me Fatso. (Life & Living Ser.). (J). (ps-3). 1993. pap. 3.95 (*0-8114-5203-4*) Raintree Steck-V.

— Spitfire. (Orig.). 1981. pap. 1.95 (*0-8439-8044-3*) Dorchester Pub Co.

Phillips, Barbara, ed. see Maginnis, John.

Phillips, Barbara, jt. auth. see Phillips, Arthur.

Phillips, Barbara, jt. ed. see Ring, Francis J.

Phillips, Barbara, et al. Monitoring the Effects of Recreational Use on Colorado River Beaches in Grand Canyon National Park. (Bulletin Ser.: No. 55). (Illus.). 230p. (Orig.). 1986. pap. 14.95 (*0-89734-057-4*) Mus Northern Ariz.

Phillips, Barbara A. Finding Common Ground: A Field Guide to Mediation. LC 94-75151. 224p. (Orig.). 1994. pap. 16.95 (*0-9633919-7-6*) Hells Canyon.

— Pocket Reference for Medical Intensive Care. 407p. 1986. pap. 38.00 (*0-87189-283-9*) Raven.

Phillips, Barbara G., et al. Annotated Checklist of Vascular Plants of Grand Canyon National Park 1986. (Monographs: No. 7). (Illus.). 96p. (Orig.). 1987. pap. 15.00 (*0-938216-30-9*) GCNHA.

Phillips, Barbara Y. How to Use Section 5 of the Voting Rights Act. 3rd rev. ed. (Illus.). 76p. 1984. pap. 15.25 (*0-941410-27-7*) Jt Ctr Pol Studies.

***Phillips, Barty.** How to Clean Absolutely Everything. 192p. (Orig.). 1995. mass mkt. 4.99 (*0-380-77736-3*) Avon.

— L. Ashley: Decorating with Paint & Paper. 1995. 16.00 (*0-517-88228-0*) Random.

— Tapestry. (Illus.). 240p. (C). 1994. 49.95 (*0-7148-2920-X*, Pub. by Phaidon Press UK) Chronicle Bks.

Phillips, Beeman N. Educational & Psychological Perspectives on Stress in Students, Teachers, & Parents. LC 92-75446. 1993. lib. bdg. 29.95 (*0-88422-122-9*) Clinical Psych.

— School Psychology at a Turning Point: Ensuring a Bright Future for the Profession. LC 89-27510. (Social & Behavioral Sciences Ser.). 324p. 1990. 32.95x (*1-55542-195-4*) Jossey-Bass.

— School Stress & Anxiety. LC 77-21658. 165p. 1978. 32.95 (*0-87705-324-3*) Human Sci Pr.

Phillips, Benny & Phillips, Sheree. Raising Kids Who Hunger for God. LC 91-7367. 251p. (Orig.). 1991. pap. 8.99 (*0-8007-9181-9*) Chosen Bks.

— Walking with the Wise: God's Plan for Parents & Teens. Somerville, Greg, ed. 176p. (Orig.). (YA). (gr. 7-12). 1994. pap. 8.00 (*1-881039-04-8*) People of Destiny.

Phillips, Bernard, ed. see Suzuki, Daisetz T.

***Phillips, Bill.** Hassle-Free Home Security. 128p. 1993. 9.95 (*1-56865-058-2*, GuildAmerica) Dblday Bk Music.

— Home Mechanix Guide to Security: Protecting Your Home, Car, & Family. 240p. 1993. pap. text ed. 16.95 (*0-471-58893-8*) Wiley.

— Professional Locksmithing Techniques. 1991. text ed. 35.95 (*0-07-155243-X*) McGraw.

— Professional Locksmithing Techniques. (Illus.). 400p. 1991. 35.95 (*0-8306-7523-X*, 3523); pap. 25.95 (*0-8306-3523-8*) TAB Bks.

Phillips, Bill, jt. auth. see Roper, C. A.

Phillips, Billie R., jt. auth. see Baker, Rance G.

Phillips, Bob. The All-New Clean Joke Book. LC 90-36617. 192p. (Orig.). 1990. mass mkt. 3.99 (*0-89081-830-4*) Harvest Hse.

— The Awesome Book of Bible Trivia. (Orig.). 1994. pap. 8.99 (*1-56507-294-4*) Harvest Hse.

— Awesome Good Clean Jokes for Kids. LC 92-12109. 207p. (J). 1992. mass mkt. 3.99 (*1-56507-062-3*) Harvest Hse.

— The Best of the Good Clean Jokes. LC 89-32386. 192p. (J). (gr. 5 up). 1989. mass mkt. 4.99 (*0-89081-769-3*) Harvest Hse.

— Best of the Good Clean Jokes Perpetual Calendar. LC 89-32386. 192p. (J). (gr. 5 up). 1993. spiral bd. 10.99 (*1-56507-115-8*) Harvest Hse.

— Bible Brainteasers. Orig. Title: Heavenly Fun. 1993. pap. 5.99 (*1-56507-119-0*) Harvest Hse.

— The Bible Olympics. (Orig.). 1995. pap. 5.99 (*1-56507-296-0*) Harvest Hse.

— Bob Phillips' Encyclopedia of Good Clean Jokes. (Illus.). 385p. (Orig.). 1992. pap. 7.99 (*0-89081-947-5*) Harvest Hse.

— Crazy Good Clean Jokes for Kids. (Orig.). 1994. pap. 4.99 (*1-56507-208-1*) Harvest Hse.

— The Delicate Art of Dancing with Porcupines: Learning to Appreciate the Finer Points of Others. Stewart, Ed, ed. LC 89-31020. 175p. 1989. pap. 7.99 (*0-8307-1333-6*, 5419749) Regal.

— Fifty-Two Offbeat Texas Stops: Traveling with Bob Phillips, Texas Country Reporter. LC 93-92751. 144p. 1993. pap. 10.95 (*0-9636541-1-X*) Phillips Prods.

— Friendship, Love & Laughter. 1993. pap. 4.99 (*1-56507-038-0*) Harvest Hse.

— Good Clean Jokes for Kids. (J). 1991. pap. 3.99 (*0-89081-902-5*) Harvest Hse.

— Goofy Good Clean Jokes for Kids! LC 94-14563. (J). 1994. pap. 4.99 (*1-56507-241-3*) Harvest Hse.

— The Great Bible Challenge. 1994. pap. 5.99 (*1-56507-216-2*) Harvest Hse.

— How Can I Be Sure: A Pre-Marriage Inventory. LC 77-94448. 160p. (Orig.). 1978. pap. 5.99 (*0-89081-073-7*) Harvest Hse.

— KC8 Burma: CBI Air Warning Team, 1942-1943. (Illus.). 194p. (Orig.). 1992. pap. 18.95 (*0-89745-145-7*) Sunflower U Pr.

— The Last of the Good Clean Jokes. LC 74-24851. 1975. pap. 3.99 (*0-89081-005-2*) Harvest Hse.

— Loony Good Clean Jokes for Kids. LC 93-23529. (J). 1994. pap. 4.99 (*1-56507-178-6*) Harvest Hse.

— More Awesome Good Clean Jokes for Kids. LC 94-29224. (Orig.). (J). 1995. mass mkt. 3.99 (*1-56507-270-7*) Harvest Hse.

— More Good Clean Jokes. LC 74-24850. 1979. pap. 3.99 (*0-89081-006-0*) Harvest Hse.

— Nutty Good Clean Jokes for Kids. (Orig.). 1995. mass mkt. 3.99 (*1-56507-374-6*) Harvest Hse.

— Phillip's Book of Great Thoughts & Funny Sayings. LC 92-37072. 1993. 9.99 (*0-8423-5035-7*) Tyndale.

— Redi-Reference. 1975. mass mkt. 2.99 (*0-89081-043-5*) Harvest Hse.

— Redi-Reference Daily Bible Reading Plan. 1992. mass mkt. 2.99 (*0-89081-997-1*) Harvest Hse.

— The Return of the Good Clean Jokes. LC 86-62982. 176p. (Orig.). 1986. mass mkt. 3.99 (*0-89081-568-2*) Harvest Hse.

— Ultimate Good Clean Jokes for Kids. (J). 1993. mass mkt. 3.99 (*1-56507-085-2*) Harvest Hse.

— Unofficial Liberal Joke Book: For the Politically Incorrect. 1994. pap. 7.99 (*1-56507-278-2*) Harvest Hse.

— Wacky Good Clean Jokes for Kids. (J). 1993. pap. 4.99 (*1-56507-141-7*) Harvest Hse.

— What to Do Until the Psychiatrist Comes: How to Counsel Yourself & Others. (Orig.). 1995. pap. 8.99 (*1-56507-231-6*) Harvest Hse.

— The World's Greatest Collection of Clean Jokes. 176p. 1985. reprint ed. mass mkt. 3.99 (*0-89081-456-2*) Harvest Hse.

— The World's Greatest Collection of Heavenly Humor. LC 81-82676. 192p. (Orig.). 1982. mass mkt. 3.99 (*0-89081-297-7*) Harvest Hse.

Phillips, Bob, ed. see Dockery, Wallene T.

Phillips, Bob, jt. auth. see Jones, Charlie T.

Phillips, Bob, jt. auth. see LaHaye, Tim.

Phillips, Bob, jt. auth. see Phillips, Ann.

Phillips, Bob, jt. auth. see Reagan, Michael.

Phillips, Bonnie F. This Is My Life. LC 93-73817. (Illus.). 362p. (Orig.). 1993. pap. write for info. (*0-938041-18-5*) Arc Pr AR.

Phillips, Brad & Helmick, Kyle L. The Helmick Family History. 170p. 1985. pap. 18.00 (*0-9613513-1-4*) B R Phillips.

Phillips, Bradley R. & Helmick, Kyle L. The History of Atlas, W. V. & Vicinity, Upshur County, 1700's-1984. (Illus.). 160p. (Orig.). 1984. pap. text ed. 8.95 (*0-9613513-0-6*) B R Phillips.

Phillips, Bruce F., jt. ed. see Cobb, J. Stanley.

Phillips, C., jt. auth. see Baxter, R. E.

Phillips, C., jt. ed. see Freeman, L.

Phillips, C., jt. auth. see Jones, I.

Phillips, C. A. Functional Electrical Rehabilitation: Technological Restoration after Spinal Cord Injury. (Illus.). 240p. 1991. 108.00 (*0-387-97459-8*) Spr-Verlag.

Phillips, C. A., ed. Effective Upper & Lower Extremity Prostheses: A Special Issue of the Journal Automedica. 276p. 1989. pap. text ed. 543.00 (*0-677-25830-5*) Gordon & Breach.

Phillips, C. A., et al. Banking & the Business Cycle: A Study of the Great Depression in the United States. LC 70-172226. (Right Wing Individualist Tradition in America Ser.). 1976. reprint ed. 24.95 (*0-405-00435-4*) Ayer.

Phillips, C. Abbott, Jr., tr. see Calamandrei, Piero.

Phillips, C. I. & Wolfe, J. N. Clinical Practice & Economics. pap. 25.00 (*0-8464-0251-3*) Beekman Pubs.

Phillips, C. J. America's Funniest Bathroom Graffiti. (Illus.). 80p. (Orig.). 1994. per., pap. 7.95 (*0-9621639-2-9*) Grand Natl Pr.

— The Best Tobacco Cartoons of All Time. Gurian, Mike & Hemeon, Brad, eds. (Illus.). 80p. 1992. pap. 5.95 (*0-9621639-9-6*) Grand Natl Pr.

— The Official Book of Excuses & Related Reasons. Gurian, Philip, ed. (Illus.). 64p. (Orig.). 1989. per., pap. 4.95 (*0-9621639-0-2*) Grand Natl Pr.

Phillips, Calvin & McFadden, David. Investigating the Fireground. LC 82-1290. (Illus.). 288p. 1982. pap. 16.95 (*0-89303-074-0*) P-H.

***Phillips, Carl.** Cortege. 96p. 1995. pap. 12.95 (*1-55597-230-6*) Graywolf.

— Cortege: A Poem. Hickok, Gloria V., ed. 10p. (Orig.). 1994. pap. 3.00 (*1-884235-00-X*) Helicon Nine Eds.

— In the Blood. (Samuel French Morse Poetry Prize Ser.). 69p. 1992. pap. text ed. 9.95 (*1-55553-135-0*) NE U Pr.

Phillips, Carla R. Ciudad Real, 1500-1750: Growth, Crisis, & Readjustment in the Spanish Economy. LC 78-9293. 208p. 1979. 25.00 (*0-674-13285-8*) HUP.

— The Short Life of an Unlucky Spanish Galleon: Los Tres Reyes, 1628-1634. 80p. 1990. text ed. 14.95 (*0-8166-1811-9*) U of Minn Pr.

— Six Galleons for the King of Spain: Imperial Defense in the Early Seventeenth Century. LC 86-45444. (Softshell Bks.). (Illus.). 332p. 1992. pap. text ed. 22.95 (*0-8018-4513-0*) Johns Hopkins.

Phillips, Carla R., ed. see Axtell, James.

Phillips, Carla R., ed. see Kupperman, Karen O.

Phillips, Carla R., ed. see Phillips, William D., Jr.

Phillips, Carla R., jt. auth. see Phillips, William D., Jr.

Phillips, Carla R., ed. see Ronda, James P.

Phillips, Carol. The Household Inventory Guide: Ideas & Lists for Stocking, Restocking, & Taking Stock of Your Home. LC 92-74281. (Illus.). 107p. (Orig.). 1995. pap. 9.95 (*0-9634495-0-8*) IPP Pr.

— In the Bag: Selling in the Salon. LC 94-6811. 320p. 1994. pap. text ed. 29.95 (*1-56253-236-7*) Milady Pub.

Phillips, Carol A. Best of Alaska: The Art of Jon Van Zyle. LC 89-1574. (Illus.). 80p. 1990. 29.95 (*0-945397-06-2*); pap. 19.95 (*0-945397-07-0*) Epicenter Pr.

Phillips, Carol B., ed. Essentials for Child Development Associates. LC 91-71482. (Illus.). 500p. (Orig.). 1991. pap. text ed. 30.00 (*1-879891-00-X*) Council Early Child.

— Field Advisor's Guide to Essentials for Child Development Associates. LC 91-71483. (Illus.). 125p. (Orig.). 1991. pap. text ed. write for info. (*1-879891-01-8*) Council Early Child.

— Seminar Instructor's Guide to Essentials for Child Development Associates. (Illus.). 135p. (Orig.). 1991. pap. text ed. write for info. (*1-879891-02-6*) Council Early Child.

Phillips, Carole. The New Money Workbook for Women. LC 87-27657. 160p. (Orig.). 1988. pap. 9.95 (*0-931790-82-4*) Brick Hse Pub.

***Phillips, Caroline.** The Religious Quest in the Poetry of T. S. Eliot Vol. 14. LC 94-38440. (Studies in Art & Religious Interpretation Ser.). 112p. 1995. text ed. 59.95 (*0-7734-9152-X*) E Mellen.

Phillips, Carolyn E. Michelle. 1989. pap. 2.50 (*0-451-14929-7*) NAL-Dutton.

Phillips, Caryl. Cambridge: A Novel. LC 92-56359. 1993. pap. 10.00 (*0-679-73689-1*) Random.

— Crossing the River. 1994. 22.00 (*0-679-40533-X*) Knopf.

— Crossing the River. 1995. pap. 11.00 (*0-679-75794-5*, Vin) Random.

— The European Tribe. 135p. 1993. reprint ed. pap. 10.95 (*0-571-19803-1*) Faber & Faber.

— The Final Passage. LC 95-14370. 1995. 10.00 (*0-679-75931-X*, Vin) Random.

— Higher Ground: A Novel in Three Parts. LC 95-14371. 1995. 11.00 (*0-679-76376-7*, Vin) Random.

— Higher Ground: A Novel in Three Parts. 224p. 1990. pap. 7.95 (*0-14-011806-3*, Penguin Bks) Viking Penguin.

— A State of Independece. 1988. pap. 6.95 (*0-02-015080-6*, Collier S&S) S&S Trade.

— A State of Independence. 158p. 1986. 13.95 (*0-374-26976-9*) FS&G.

— State of Independence. LC 94-31112. 1995. pap. 10.00 (*0-679-75930-1*, Vin) Random.

Phillips, Casey R., jt. auth. see Steiner, Dale R.

Phillips, Catherina, ed. see Hopkins, Gerard M.

Phillips, Catherine. Robert Bridges: A Biography. (Illus.). 384p. 1992. 55.00 (*0-19-212251-7*) OUP.

Phillips, Catherine, ed. Gerard Manley Hopkins. LC 85-21405. (Authors Ser.). 600p. 1987. pap. 18.95 (*0-19-281386-2*) OUP.

Phillips, Catherine, ed. see Yeats, William Butler.

Phillips, Catherine A., tr. see Basch, Victor.

Phillips, Catherine A., tr. see Moulin-Eckart, Richard D.

Phillips, Catherine A., tr. see Specht, Richard.

Phillips, Catherine Alison, tr. see Grousset, Rene.

***Phillips, Catherine C.** Jessie Benton Fremont: A Woman Who Made History. LC 94-43803. 376p. 1995. pap. 15.00 (*0-8032-8740-2*, Bison Books) U of Nebr Pr.

Phillips, Cecelia. The Best Chicken Recipes. 51p. (Orig.). 1990. pap. 6.95 (*0-9618870-0-1*) L C Ellsworth.

— Natural Solutions: A Guide to a Better Complexion. 30p. (Orig.). 1989. pap. 6.95 (*0-9618870-1-X*) L C Ellsworth.

— Weight Loss Made Easy: Hundreds of Tips for a Weight Loss Life-Style. LC 88-91234. 150p. (Orig.). 1993. write for info. (*0-9618870-3-6*); pap. 14.95 (*0-9618870-2-8*) L C Ellsworth.

Phillips, Cecil E. Cromwell's Captains. LC 73-37908. (Select Bibliographies Reprint Ser.). 1977. reprint ed. 27.95 (*0-8369-6746-1*) Ayer.

Phillips, Celeste R. Family-Centered Maternity-Newborn Care. 3rd ed. 476p. 1991. pap. 29.95 (*0-8016-3935-2*) Mosby Yr Bk.

Phillips, Charles. Archie: His First Fifty Years. 128p. 1993. 15.98 (*0-89660-035-1*, Artabras) Abbeville Pr.

— Heritage of the West. 1991. 19.99 (*0-517-68907-3*) Random Hse Value.

— Missouri: Mother of the American West. 200p. 1988. 19.95 (*0-89781-256-5*, 5284) Preferred Mktg.

Phillips, Charles & Axelrod, Alan. My Brother's Face: Portraits of the Civil War. LC 92-13958. (Illus.). 1993. 27.50 (*0-8118-0386-4*); pap. 16.95 (*0-8118-0162-4*) Chronicle Bks.

Phillips, Charles, jt. auth. see Axelrod, Alan.

Phillips, Charles, tr. see Paterson, Janet M.

Phillips, Charles A. To Grow Spiritually. 312p. 1989. 9.95 (*0-685-26989-2*) C A Phillips.

Phillips, Charles D., jt. ed. see Whitaker, Gordon P.

Phillips, Charles F. The Economics of Regulation: Theory & Practice in the Transportation & Public Utility Industries. rev. ed. LC 69-17160. (Irwin Series in Economics). 790p. reprint ed. pap. 180.00 (*0-317-28462-2*, 2051302) Bks Demand.

Phillips, Charles F., Jr. The Regulation of Public Utilities: Theory & Practice. 3rd ed. 1025p. 1993. 65.00 (*0-910325-45-6*) Public Util.

Phillips, Charles H. The History of the Colored Methodist Episcopal Church in America: Comprising Its Organization, Subsequent Developments & Present Status. LC 73-38459. (Religion in America, Ser. 2). 252p. 1974. reprint ed. 19.95 (*0-405-04080-6*) Ayer.

Phillips, Charles J. Paderewski: The Story of a Modern Immortal. LC 77-17399. (Music Reprint Ser.). (Illus.). 1978. reprint ed. lib. bdg. 55.00 (*0-306-77534-4*) Da Capo.

Phillips, Charles L. Basic Life Support: Skills Manual. LC 77-8351. 1977. pap. 14.95 (*0-87618-883-8*) P-H.

— Basic Life Support Skills. 2nd ed. (Illus.). 224p. 1986. pap. text ed. 30.00 (*0-89303-253-0*) P-H.

— Paramedic Skills Manual. 2nd ed. 256p. 1989. pap. write for info. (*0-318-65460-1*) P-H.

PQ

An Asterisk (*) at the beginning of an entry indicates that the title is appearing in BIP for the first time.

— Specimens of Irish Eloquence. 1977. text ed. 22.95 (0-8369-8171-5, 8311) Ayer.

Phillips, Charles L. & Harbor, Royce D. Basic Feedback Control Systems: Alternate. 2nd ed. 512p. 1990. text ed. 69.00 (0-13-062845-X) P-H.

— Feedback Control Systems. 2nd ed. 704p. 1990. text ed. 72.00 (0-13-313446-6) P-H.

Phillips, Charles L. & Nagle, H. Troy, Jr. Digital Control System Analysis & Design. 2nd ed. 608p. 1989. text ed. 74.00 (0-13-213596-5) P-H.

***Phillips, Charles L. & Nagle, Troy.** Digital Control System Analysis & Design. 3rd ed. LC 94-3482. 1994. text ed. 72.00 (0-13-309832-X) P-H.

Phillips, Charles L. & Parr, John M. Signals, Systems, & Transforms. LC 94-6083. 1994. text ed. 74.00 (0-13-795253-8) P-H.

Phillips, Charles O. Practical Spread Spectrum Bk. IV: Detection, Recognition & Recording of Signals. 154p. 1993. lib. bdg. 58.30 (0-89412-221-5); pap. 48.80 (0-89412-220-7) Aegean Park Pr.

— Practical Spread Spectrum Bk. IV: Detection, Recognition & Recording of Signals, Bk. 2. 152p. 1994. pap. 48.80 (0-89412-224-X) Aegean Park Pr.

Phillips, Charles P. The Law of Copyright in Works of Literature & Art & in the Application of Designs: With the Statutes Relating Thereto. xvi, 261p. 1989. reprint ed. lib. bdg. 37.50 (0-8377-1055-3) Rothman.

Phillips, Charles S. Secrets of Successful Public Relations. LC 85-6426. 315p. 1985. 49.95 (0-317-39230-1) P-H.

Phillips, Charles W. My Life in Archaeology. (Illus.). 190p. 1993. text ed. 30.00 (0-86299-362-8) A Sutton Pub.

Phillips, Cheryl. Quilts Without Corners: Seven Original Circle Quilt Designs for Home & Office Decor. 44p. 1992. 14.95 (0-9630550-0-3) E&P Sewing.

Phillips, Cheryl & Harvey, Bonnie C., eds. My Jesus Pocketbook of God's Fruit. LC 83-50194. (My Jesus Pocketbooks). (Illus.). 32p. (J). (ps-3). 1983. pap. 0.69 (0-937420-08-5) Stirrup Assoc.

Phillips, Cheryl M. & Harvey, Bonnie C., eds. My Jesus Pocketbook of the Lord's Prayer. LC 83-50193. (My Jesus Pocketbooks). (Illus.). 32p. (J). (ps-3). 1983. pap. 0.69 (0-937420-07-7) Stirrup Assoc.

Phillips, Cheryl M., ed. see Stirrup Associates, Inc. Staff.

Phillips, Chester A. Bank Credit. Bruchey, Stuart, ed. LC 80-1165. (Rise of Commercial Banking Ser.). (Illus.). 1981. reprint ed. lib. bdg. 38.95 (0-405-13675-7) Ayer.

Phillips, Chris, jt. auth. see Baker, Christopher T.

Phillips, Chris, jt. auth. see Freeman, Len.

***Phillips, Chris, et al.** International Marketing Strategy. LC 94-43121. 1995. write for info. (0-415-12498-0) Routledge.

Phillips, Christopher. Damned Yankee: The Life of General Nathaniel Lyon. Foley, William E., ed. (Missouri Biography Ser.). (Illus.). 312p. 1990. text ed. 25.95 (0-8262-0731-6) U of Mo Pr.

Phillips, Christopher, ed. Photography in the Modern Era: European Documents & Critical Writings, 1913-1940. (Illus.). 368p. 1989. 39.95 (0-89381-406-7) Aperture.

— Photography in the Modern Era: European Documents & Critical Writings, 1913-1940. (Illus.). 368p. 1989. pap. 14.95 (0-89381-407-5, Aperture) Metro Mus Art.

Phillips, Christopher, jt. auth. see Hambourg, Maria M.

Phillips, Cindy & Williams, Levi. A Positive Steps Approach: A Parent's Guide to Teaching Youth to Be Responsible for Today! Ford, June, ed. LC 93-48830. 240p. (Orig.). 1994. pap. 9.95 (1-56530-124-2) Summit TX.

Phillips, Claude. Emotion in Art. LC 68-29238. (Essay Index Reprint Ser.). 1977. 23.95 (0-8369-0788-4) Ayer.

— Fifty Years of Public School Teaching. (American Autobiography Ser.). 145p. 1995. reprint ed. lib. bdg. 69.00 (0-7812-8619-0) Rprt Serv.

Phillips, Claude S. The Development of Nigerian Foreign Policy. LC 64-13703. (Northwestern University African Studies Ser.: No. 13). 166p. reprint ed. pap. 47.40 (0-317-11319-4, 2015305) Bks Demand.

Phillips, Claudia, ed. Studies in Public Administration: The Berkeley-Hong Kong Project, 1988-1989. (C). 1992. pap. text ed. 20.00 (1-880963-00-0) U of Cal HK Proj.

Phillips, Claudia, et al, eds. Studies in Public Administration: The Berkeley-Hong Kong Project, 1989-1990. LC 93-24207. 1993. write for info. (1-880963-01-9) U of Cal HK Proj.

***Phillips, Clifton J.** Indiana in Transition, 1880-1920. 674p. 1968. 10.00 (1-885323-34-4) IN Hist Bureau.

— Indiana in Transition, 1880-1920. (History of Indiana Ser.). (Illus.). 674p. 1968. 17.50 (0-87195-092-8) Ind Hist Soc.

Phillips, Clifton J., ed. History at DePaul University. (Sesquicentennial Ser.: No. 1). (Illus.). 36p. (Orig.). 1985. pap. text ed. write for info. (0-936631-00-7) DePauw Univ.

— Physics at DePauw University. (Sesquicentennial Ser.: No. 6). (Illus.). 44p. (Orig.). 1987. pap. write for info. (0-936631-05-8) DePauw Univ.

— Psychology at DePauw University. (Sesquicentennial Ser.: No. 2). (Illus.). 32p. (Orig.). 1986. pap. write for info. (0-936631-01-5) DePauw Univ.

— Sociology & Anthropology at DePauw University. (Sesquicentennial Ser.: No. 5). (Illus.). 32p. (Orig.). 1986. pap. write for info. (0-936631-04-X) DePauw Univ.

— Teacher Education at DePauw University. (Sesquicentennial Ser.: No. 4). (Illus.). 32p. (Orig.). 1986. pap. write for info. (0-936631-03-1) DePauw Univ.

— The Teaching & Practice of Art at DePauw. (Sesquicentennial Ser.: No. 3). (Illus.). 32p. (Orig.). 1986. pap. write for info. (0-936631-02-3) DePauw Univ.

***Phillips, Clive.** Cattle Behavior. (Illus.). 224p. 1993. text ed. 34.95 (0-85236-251-X, Pub. by Farming Pr UK) Diamond Farm Bk.

Phillips, Clive & Piggins, David, eds. Farm Animals & the Environment. 430p. 1992. text ed. 99.75 (0-85198-788-5) CAB Intl.

Phillips Collection Staff. A Collection in the Making. LC 76-10817. 1976. fiche, lib. bdg. 45.00 (0-226-69538-7) U Ch Pr.

— Jacob Lawrence. (Migration Ser.). (Illus.). 160p. 1993. write for info. (0-9636129-0-5); pap. write for info. (0-9636129-1-3) Rappahnck Pr.

— The Phillips Collection: A Summary Catalogue. Passantino, Erika D., ed. LC 85-9575. 300p. 1985. pap. 20.00 (0-943044-05-7) Phillips Coll.

Phillips, Connie, ed. see Food & Nutrition Group Staff.

Phillips, Cynthia, jt. auth. see Jones, Iris.

Phillips, D. The Longman TOEFL Preparation Program: (Longman Practice Tests for the TOEFL) 1988. pap. text ed. 15.95 (0-8013-0030-4, 75695); audio 37.95 (0-8013-0032-0, 75697); 48.50 (0-8013-0462-8, 78278) Longman.

— The Longman TOEFL Preparation Program: (Longman Preparation Course for the TOEFL) 1988. 109.00 (0-8013-0461-X, 78277); Complete course. pap. text ed. 20.95 (0-8013-0141-6, 75805); audio 37.95 (0-8013-0031-2, 75696); 8.50 (0-8013-0212-9, 75870) Longman.

Phillips, D. & Desrochers, P., eds. Multimedia Communications: Proceedings of Multimedia Communications Conference, 13-16 April 1993, Banff, Canada. LC 93-78137. 658p. 1993. 98.00 (90-5199-132-0, Pub. by IOS Pr NE) IOS Press.

Phillips, D., jt. auth. see Grice, R.

Phillips, D. A. Subsea Production Systems - Can Engineering Reduce Pipeline Costs? (C). 1989. 95.00 (0-89771-731-7, Pub. by Lorne & MacLean Marine) St Mut.

Phillips, D. C. Philosophy, Science & Social Inquiry: Contemporary Methodological Controversies in Social Science & Related Applied Fields of Research. 245p. 1987. pap. text ed. 28.00 (0-08-033411-3, Pergamon Pr) Elsevier.

— The Social Scientist's Bestiary: A Guide to Fabled Threats to, & Defences of, Naturalistic Social Science. LC 92-21654. 1992. 42.00 (0-08-040254-2, Pergamon Pr) Elsevier.

Phillips, D. C. & Soltis, Jonas F. Perspectives on Learning. 2nd ed. (Thinking about Education Ser.). 128p. (Orig.). (C). 1991. pap. text ed. 11.95 (0-8077-3116-1) Tchrs Coll.

Phillips, D. C., ed. see Bragg, Lawrence.

Phillips, D. C., jt. auth. see Cleverley, John F.

Phillips, D. C., jt. auth. see McLaughlin, Milbrey W.

Phillips, D. C., jt. ed. see McLaughlin, Milbrey W.

Phillips, D. E. Modern Eletronics & Communications. 132p. (C). 1986. 175.00 (0-948691-12-3, Pub. by Witherby & Co UK) St Mut.

***Phillips, D. H. & Venitt, S., eds.** Environmental Mutagenesis: Current Methods for Detecting Mutagens in the Environment. (Human Molecular Genetics Ser.). 350p. 1995. 149.50 (1-872748-19-8, Pub. by Bios Scientific UK) Coronet Bks.

Phillips, D. H., et al, eds. Postlabelling Methods for the Detection of DNA Adducts. (IARC Scientific Publications: No. 124). (Illus.). 416p. 1993. pap. 85.00 (92-832-2124-9) OUP.

Phillips, D. Z. Faith after Foundationalism. 275p. 1988. text ed. 49.95 (0-415-00333-4) Routledge.

— Faith after Foundationalism: Plantinga-Rorty-Lindbeck-Berger: Critiques & Alternatives. LC 95-2371. (C). 1995. pap. text ed. 18.95 (0-8133-2645-1) Westview.

— From Fantasy to Faith: The Philosophy of Religion & Twentieth-Century Literature. 224p. 1991. text ed. 45.00 (0-312-05300-2) St Martin.

— Interventions in Ethics. LC 91-19790. (SUNY Series in Ethical Theory). 300p. (C). 1992. 57.50 (0-7914-0995-3); pap. 18.95 (0-7914-0996-1) State U NY Pr.

— R. S. Thomas: Poet of the Hidden God. LC 85-31998. (Princeton Theological Monograph Ser.: No. 2). 192p. (Orig.). 1986. pap. 15.00 (0-915138-83-2) Pickwick.

Phillips, D. Z. & Winch, Peter, eds. Wittgenstein: Attention to Particulars: Essays in Honour of Rush Rhees. LC 89-34718. 256p. 1990. text ed. 45.00 (0-312-03499-7) St Martin.

Phillips, Dale E. Let Me Introduce You to My Father: A Study on the Nature of God. 120p. 1992. pap. 6.50 (0-9633335-1-8) Dryden Pubs.

Phillips, Daphne. The Great Road to Bath. 192p. 1987. 30.00 (0-905392-26-4) St Mut.

— Reading Old & New. 96p. 1987. pap. 30.00 (0-905392-73-6) St Mut.

— Reminiscences of Reading. 128p. 1987. 30.00 (0-905392-39-6) St Mut.

Phillips, Dave. Animal Mazes. (Illus.). 48p. (J). 1991. pap. 2.95 (0-486-26707-5) Dover.

— Graphic & Op-Art Mazes. (Illus.). 1976. pap. 3.95 (0-486-23373-1) Dover.

— Mind-Boggling Mazes: Forty Graphic & Three-D Labyrinths. (Illus.). 1979. pap. 2.95 (0-486-23798-2) Dover.

— Monster Mazes. 48p. 1989. pap. 2.95 (0-486-26005-4) Dover.

— Mother Goose Mazes. LC 92-17679. (J). 1992. pap. write for info. (0-486-27319-9) Dover.

— Mystifying Mazes. 48p. 1984. pap. 2.95 (0-486-24722-8) Dover.

— Scary Mazes. LC 93-18312. 1993. 2.95 (0-486-27608-2) Dover.

— Space Age Mazes. (J). (gr. 2 up). 1988. pap. 2.95 (0-486-25659-6) Dover.

— Storybook Mazes. (Illus.). 62p. 1978. pap. 2.95 (0-486-23628-5) Dover.

— The World's Most Difficult Maze. 1981. pap. 3.50 (0-486-23970-5) Dover.

Phillips, Dave, illus. Hidden Treasure Maze Book. (Puzzles, Amusements, Recreations Ser.). 48p. (Orig.). (J). (gr. 2 up). 1984. pap. 2.95 (0-486-24566-7) Dover.

Phillips, David. Controlling Iodine Deficiency Disorders in Developing Countries. (C). 1989. pap. text ed. 21.00 (0-85598-107-5, Pub. by Oxfam Pubns UK) St Mut.

— Harvard Graphics for Windows Quick Reference Guide. (Illus.). 1992. spiral bd. 8.95 (1-56243-059-9, HG-17) DDC Pub.

— Health & Health Care in the Third World. 1990. pap. 39.95 (0-582-01418-2, Drumbeat) Longman.

***Phillips, David, ed.** Eating Out in Glasgow 1994. 112p. (C). 1993. pap. 32.00x (1-874640-45-9, Pub. by Argyll Pubng UK) St Mut.

— Education in Germany: Tradition & Reform in Historical Context. LC 94-44701. (International Developments in School Reform Ser.). 1995. write for info. (0-415-11397-0) Routledge.

Phillips, David & Atkinson, George H., eds. Time-Resolved Laser Raman Spectroscopy. 180p. 1987. text ed. 113.00 (3-7186-0343-8) Gordon & Breach.

Phillips, David & Filmer-Sankey, Caroline. Diversification in Modern Language Teaching: Choice & the National Curriculum. LC 92-15265. 208p. 1992. 59.95 (0-415-07200-X, A9807, Routledge NY); pap. write for info. (0-415-07201-8, Routledge NY) Routledge.

Phillips, David & Williams, Allan. Rural Britain: A Social Geography. 288p. 1984. pap. 15.95 (0-631-13237-6) Blackwell Pubs.

Phillips, David, jt. auth. see Booker, Vaughan.

Phillips, David, jt. auth. see Ferry, Steven.

Phillips, David, jt. auth. see Joseph, Alunt.

Phillips, David A. Careers in Secret Operations: How to Be a Federal Intelligence Officer. 104p. 1975. pap. text ed. 21.95 (0-313-27011-2, P7011, Greenwood Pr) Greenwood.

— The Minimax Diet & Nutrition Book: Maximum Nutrition, Minimum Calories. LC 88-6937. 160p. (Orig.). 1988. pap. 8.95 (0-88007-165-6) Woodbridge Pr.

— My Secret Wars Scrapbook: Adventures in Combat, Covert Action & Espionage Operations. 260p. 1988. pap. 15.00 (0-317-90861-8) Stone Trail Pr.

— Writing for Pleasure & Profit in Retirement. (Self Confidence - Self Competence Ser.). 52p. (Orig.). 1985. pap. 6.95 (0-932123-01-5) Stone Trail Pr.

Phillips, David A., ed. see Johnson, William R.

Phillips, David C. Collected Works, 22 vols., Set. 1988. reprint ed. lib. bdg. 2,054.00 (0-7812-1320-7) Rprt Serv.

— The Conflict. (Collected Works of David G. Phillips). 1988. reprint ed. lib. bdg. 79.00 (0-7812-1341-X) Rprt Serv.

— The Cost. (Collected Works of David G. Phillips). 1988. reprint ed. lib. bdg. 79.00 (0-7812-1326-6) Rprt Serv.

— Degarmo's Wife & Other Stories. (Collected Works of David G. Phillips). 1988. reprint ed. lib. bdg. 59.00 (0-7812-1345-2) Rprt Serv.

— The Fashionable Adventure of Joshua Craig. (Collected Works of David G. Phillips). 1988. reprint ed. lib. bdg. 59.00 (0-7812-1337-1) Rprt Serv.

— George Helm. (Collected Works of David G. Phillips). 1988. reprint ed. lib. bdg. 59.00 (0-7812-1344-4) Rprt Serv.

— Golden Fleece. (Collected Works of David G. Phillips). 1988. reprint ed. lib. bdg. 59.00 (0-7812-1324-X) Rprt Serv.

— The Grain of Dust. (Collected Works of David G. Phillips). 1988. reprint ed. lib. bdg. 59.00 (0-7812-1342-8) Rprt Serv.

— The Great God Success. (Collected Works of David G. Phillips). 1988. reprint ed. lib. bdg. 59.00 (0-7812-1321-5) Rprt Serv.

— Her Serene Highness. (Collected Works of David G. Phillips). 1988. reprint ed. lib. bdg. 59.00 (0-7812-1322-3) Rprt Serv.

— The Hungry Heart. (Collected Works of David G. Phillips). 1988. reprint ed. lib. bdg. 79.00 (0-317-90729-8) Rprt Serv.

— The Husband's Story. (Collected Works of David G. Phillips). 1988. reprint ed. lib. bdg. 79.00 (0-7812-1339-8) Rprt Serv.

— Light Fingered Gentry. (Collected Works of David G. Phillips). 1988. reprint ed. lib. bdg. 59.00 (0-7812-1334-7) Rprt Serv.

— The Master-Rogue. (Collected Works of David G. Phillips). 1988. reprint ed. lib. bdg. 59.00 (0-7812-1325-8) Rprt Serv.

— The Mother-Light. (Collected Works of David G. Phillips). 1988. reprint ed. lib. bdg. 59.00 (0-7812-1327-4) Rprt Serv.

— Old Wives for New. (Collected Works of David G. Phillips). 1988. reprint ed. lib. bdg. 59.00 (0-7812-1335-5) Rprt Serv.

— The Plum Tree. (Collected Works of David G. Phillips). 1988. reprint ed. lib. bdg. 59.00 (0-7812-1328-2) Rprt Serv.

— The Price She Paid. (Collected Works of David G. Phillips). 1988. reprint ed. lib. bdg. 59.00 (0-7812-1343-6) Rprt Serv.

— The Reign of Guilt. (Collected Works of David G. Phillips). 1988. reprint ed. lib. bdg. 59.00 (0-7812-1329-0) Rprt Serv.

— The Second Generation. (Collected Works of David G. Phillips). 1988. reprint ed. lib. bdg. 59.00 (0-7812-1333-9) Rprt Serv.

— Susan Lenox: Her Fall & Rise, 2 vols., Set. (Collected Works of David G. Phillips). 1988. reprint ed. lib. bdg. 99.00 (0-7812-1346-0) Rprt Serv.

— White Magic. (Collected Works of David G. Phillips). 1988. reprint ed. lib. bdg. 79.00 (0-7812-1340-1) Rprt Serv.

— Worth of a Woman. (Collected Works of David G. Phillips). 1988. reprint ed. lib. bdg. 59.00 (0-7812-1336-3) Rprt Serv.

Phillips, David G. The Collected Works of David G. Phillips, 11 vols., Set. Incl. Old Wives for New. 1908. reprint ed. 39.00 (0-686-01742-0); Worth of a Woman. 1908. reprint ed. 39.00 (0-686-01743-9); Fashionable Adventures of Joshua Craig. 1909. reprint ed. 39.00 (0-403-03157-5); Hungry Heart. 1909. reprint ed. 40.00 (0-686-01745-5); Husband's Story. 1910. reprint ed. 38.00 (0-686-01746-3); Grain of Dust. 1911. reprint ed. 39.00 (0-685-04693-1); Price She Paid. 1912. reprint ed. 39.00 (0-403-02960-0); George Helm. 1912. reprint ed. 29.00 (0-403-02999-6); Degarmo's Wife & Other Stories. 1913. reprint ed. 26.00 (0-686-01750-1); Susan Lenox: Her Fall & Rise, 2 vols. 1917. reprint ed. 79.00x (0-686-01751-X); 785.00 (0-686-01741-2) Somerset Pub.

— The Conflict. (American Author Ser.). 1981. reprint ed. lib. bdg. 49.00 (0-686-71911-5) Scholarly.

— The Cost. (American Author Ser.). reprint ed. lib. bdg. 69.00 (0-685-47615-4) Scholarly.

— The Deluge. LC 70-104541. (Illus.). 482p. reprint ed. lib. bdg. 15.50 (0-8398-1563-8) Irvington.

— The Deluge. (Illus.). 482p. (C). 1986. reprint ed. pap. text ed. 7.95 (0-8290-1913-8) Irvington.

— The Deluge. 1988. reprint ed. lib. bdg. 75.00 (0-7812-1331-2) Rprt Serv.

— The Deluge. (American Author Ser.). 1981. reprint ed. lib. bdg. 69.00 (0-685-47616-2) Scholarly.

— Fashionable Adventures of Joshua Craig. 23.95 (0-8488-1125-9) Amereon Ltd.

— Federal-State Relations & the Control of Atomic Energy. Bruchey, Stuart, ed. LC 78-22706. (Energy in the American Economy Ser.). 1979. lib. bdg. 18.95 (0-405-12008-7) Ayer.

— The Fortune Hunter. (American Author Ser.). 1981. reprint ed. lib. bdg. 69.00 (0-686-71917-4) Scholarly.

— Golden Fleece. (American Author Ser.). 1981. reprint ed. lib. bdg. 59.00 (0-686-71920-4) Scholarly.

— The Great God Success. (Americans in Fiction Ser.). reprint ed. lib. bdg. 17.00 (0-8398-1564-6); reprint ed. pap. text ed. 6.95 (0-89197-777-5) Irvington.

— The Great God Success. (American Author Ser.). 1981. reprint ed. lib. bdg. 49.00 (0-686-71921-2) Scholarly.

— Her Serene Highness. (American Author Ser.). 1981. reprint ed. lib. bdg. 69.00 (0-686-71923-9) Scholarly.

— Light-Fingered Gentry. (American Author Ser.). 1981. reprint ed. lib. bdg. 69.00 (0-686-71929-8) Scholarly.

— The Master-Rogue. (American Author Ser.). 1981. reprint ed. lib. bdg. 69.00 (0-686-71931-X) Scholarly.

— The Master Rogue: The Confessions of Croesus. LC 68-23724. (Americans in Fiction Ser.). (Illus.). reprint ed. lib. bdg. 18.00 (0-8398-1565-4); reprint ed. pap. text ed. 7.95 (0-89197-841-0) Irvington.

— The Mother-Light. (American Author Ser.). 1981. reprint ed. lib. bdg. 69.00 (0-686-71935-2) Scholarly.

— The Plum Tree. LC 68-57547. (Muckrakers Ser.). (Illus.). 389p. reprint ed. lib. bdg. 17.50 (0-8398-1566-2) Irvington.

— The Plum Tree. (Muckrakers Ser.). (Illus.). 389p. (C). 1986. reprint ed. pap. text ed. 9.95 (0-8290-1884-0) Irvington.

— The Plum Tree. (American Author Ser.). 1981. reprint ed. lib. bdg. 49.00 (0-686-71938-7) Scholarly.

— The Reign of Guilt. (American Author Ser.). 1981. reprint ed. lib. bdg. 49.00 (0-686-71939-5) Scholarly.

— The Second Generation. (American Author Ser.). 1981. reprint ed. lib. bdg. 49.00 (0-686-71943-3) Scholarly.

— The Social Secretary. (Illus.). 1972. reprint ed. lib. bdg. 29.00 (0-8422-8169-X) Irvington.

— The Social Secretary. (Illus.). 1982. reprint ed. pap. text ed. 5.95 (0-8290-1160-9) Irvington.

— Susan Lenox: Her Fall & Rise, 2 vols., Set. LC 68-57548. (Muckrakers Ser.). 1076p. reprint ed. lib. bdg. 16.00 (0-8398-1568-9) Irvington.

— Susan Lenox: Her Fall & Rise, 2 vols., Set. (Muckrakers Ser.). 1076p. 1986. reprint ed. pap. text ed. 12.50 (0-8290-2038-1) Irvington.

— Susan Lenox, Her Fall & Rise, 2 vols. in 1. LC 70-121842. (Illus.). reprint ed. 35.00 (0-404-05029-8) AMS Pr.

— White Magic. (American Author Ser.). 1981. reprint ed. lib. bdg. 49.00 (0-686-71946-8) Scholarly.

— A Woman Ventures. LC 78-104543. (Illus.). 337p. reprint ed. lib. bdg. 27.50 (0-8398-1569-7) Irvington.

— A Woman Ventures. (Illus.). 337p. (C). 1986. reprint ed. pap. text ed. 6.95 (0-8290-1958-8) Irvington.

— A Woman Ventures. (American Author Ser.). 1981. reprint ed. lib. bdg. 49.00 (0-686-71947-6) Scholarly.

Phillips, David J. Quantitative Aquatic Biological Indicators: Their Use to Monitor Trace Metal & Organochlorine Pollution. (Pollution Monitoring Ser.: No. 1). (Illus.). 460p. 1980. 106.25 (0-85334-884-7, Pub. by Elsevier Applied Sci UK) Elsevier.

Phillips, David J. & Rainbow, Philip S. Biomonitoring of Trace Aquatic Contaminants. LC 92-18802. 1992. write for info. (1-85166-884-5) Elsevier.

Phillips, David L. War Diaries: The 1861 Kanawha Valley Campaigns. (Illus.). 479p. (C). 1990. 40.00 (0-9628218-0-2) Gauley Mount Pr.

Phillips, David L., ed. War Stories: Civil War in West Virginia. (Illus.). 490p. (C). 1991. 30.00 (0-9628218-1-0) Gauley Mount Pr.

Phillips, David R. Health & Health Care in the Third World. (Longman Development Studies). 334p. 1990. pap. text ed. 59.95 (0-470-21658-1) Wiley.

Phillips, David R., ed. Ageing in East & Southeast Asia. (Research Studies in Gerontology). 224p. 1992. 59.95 (0-340-54367-1, A9633, Pub. by E Arnold UK) Routledge Chapman & Hall.

Phillips, David R. & Verhasselt, Yola, eds. Health & Development. LC 93-13465. 1994. write for info. (0-415-08528-4); pap. write for info. (0-415-08529-2) Routledge.

Phillips, David R. & Yeh, Anthony G., eds. New Towns in East & South-East Asia. (Illus.). 268p. 1987. 34.00 (0-19-584087-9) OUP.

Phillips, David T. & Wolfkiel, Bill S. Estate Planning Made Easy: Your Step-by-Step Guide to Protecting Your Family, Safeguarding Your Assets & Minimizing the Tax Bite. 227p. (Orig.). 1994. pap. 19.95 (0-7931-0612-5, 560881) Dearborn Finan.

Phillips, Debbie. Hairdos in a Hurry. (Illus.). 32p. (Orig.). 1992. pap. 3.50 (1-56722-004-5) Word Aflame.

Phillips, Debora & Bernstein, Fred. How to Give Your Child a Great Self-Image. 1989. 17.95 (0-394-57478-8) Random.

— How to Give Your Child a Great Self-Image: Proven Techniques to Build Confidence from Infancy to Adolescence. 272p. 1991. pap. 10.95 (0-452-26589-4, Plume) NAL-Dutton.

Phillips, Debora & Judd, Robert. How to Fall Out of Love. 192p. 1985. mass mkt. 5.50 (0-446-31408-0) Warner Bks.

Phillips, Deborah A., ed. Quality in Child Care: What Does Research Tell Us? LC 87-62195. 130p. 1987. pap. text ed. 6.00 (0-935989-08-0, NAEYC #140) Natl Assn Child Ed.

Phillips, Dena, jt. auth. see Beaman, Carol.

Phillips, Denis C. Holistic Thought in Social Science. LC 76-7688. x, 149p. 1976. 22.50 (0-8047-0923-8); pap. 10. 95 (0-8047-1015-5) Stanford U Pr.

Phillips, Dennis. Arena. (New American Poetry Ser.: No. 10). 137p. (Orig.). 1991. pap. 10.95 (1-55713-127-9) Sun & Moon CA.

— The Hero Is Nothing. 88p. (Orig.). 1985. pap. 8.00 (0-9614385-0-9) Kajun Pr.

— Living with Huntington's Disease: A Book for Patients & Families. LC 81-70010. 252p. 1982. 30.00 (0-299-08670-4) U of Wis Pr.

— Twenty Questions. 48p. (Orig.). 1992. pap. 5.95 (0-9629903-0-2) Jahbone Pr.

— A World. (New American Poetry Ser.: No. 3). 80p. 1989. pap. 9.95 (1-55713-057-4) Sun & Moon CA.

Phillips, Dennis, jt. auth. see Morris, Phil.

Phillips, Dennis H. Living with Huntington's Disease: A Book for Patients & Families. LC 81-16492. 251p. reprint ed. pap. 71.60 (0-7837-2645-7, 2042999) Bks Demand.

Phillips, Dennis J. Teaching, Coaching, & Learning Tennis: An Annotated Bibliography. LC 89-10534. 190p. 1989. 19.50 (0-8108-2254-7) Scarecrow.

— The Tennis Sourcebook. LC 95-3842. 1995. write for info. (0-8108-3001-9) Scarecrow.

Phillips, Derek L. Abandoning Method: Sociological Studies in Methodology. LC 72-13598. (Jossey-Bass Behavioral Science Ser.). 218p. 1973. reprint ed. pap. 62.20 (0-8357-5003-5, 2027765) Bks Demand.

— Looking Backward: A Critical Appraisal of Communitarian Thought. LC 92-36381. 280p. (C). 1993. text ed. 29.95 (0-691-07425-9) Princeton U Pr.

— Toward a Just Social Order. LC 85-43303. 450p. 1986. text ed. 72.50x (0-691-09422-5); pap. 18.95x (0-691-02834-6) Princeton U Pr.

Phillips, Derek M., ed. Histones & Nucleohistones. LC 71-161306. 319p. reprint ed. pap. 91.00 (0-685-15772-5, 2026299) Bks Demand.

Phillips, Diane. Keys to Successful Baking. (Illus.). (Orig.). 1984. pap. 3.49 (0-942320-11-5) Am Cooking.

— The Perfect Basket: Make Your Own Special Occasion Baskets. LC 94-6974. 1994. 15.00 (0-688-13031-3) Hearst Bks.

— The Perfect Mix: Bread, soup, dessert, & other homemade mixes from your kitchen. LC 92-41328. 1993. 15.00 (0-688-12104-7) Hearst Bks.

Phillips, Diane, jt. auth. see Cameron, Nonnie.

Phillips, Dianna. A Dog Owner's Guide to the Chow Chow. (Illus.). 95p. 10.95 (0-89356-030-8, 16046) Tetra Pr.

Phillips, Don. Alone with God. 1990. 7.95 (0-8341-9179-2, MB-619) Lillenas.

— A Selected Bibliography of Music Librarianship. (Illinois University Graduate School of Library Science Occasional Papers: No.113). 48p. reprint ed. pap. 25.00 (0-317-10108-0, 2007257) Bks Demand.

Phillips, Don, contrib. Devotional Piano. Date not set. 7.95 (0-8341-9121-0, MB-577) Lillenas.

Phillips, Don T. & Garcia-Diaz, Alberto. Fundamentals of Network Analysis. (Illus.). 474p. (C). 1990. reprint ed. pap. text ed. 32.95 (0-88133-534-7) Waveland Pr.

Phillips, Donald B., jt. auth. see Contis, Ellene T.

Phillips, Donald E. Human Communication Behavior & Information Processing: An Interdisciplinary Sourcebook. LC 91-37399. 960p. 1992. 128.00 (0-8240-3531-3, SS620) Garland.

— Karl Barth's Philosophy of Communication. (Philosophische Texte und Studien Ser.: No. 2). 416p. 1981. text ed. 37.70 (3-487-07154-1, Pub. by Georg Olms GW) Lubrecht & Cramer.

— Student Protest, Nineteen-Sixty to Nineteen-Seventy: An Analysis of the Issues & Speeches-with a Comprehensive Bibliography. rev. ed. 536p. 1985. lib. bdg. 60.00 (0-8191-4652-8) U Pr of Amer.

Phillips, Donald T. Lincoln on Leadership: Executive Strategies for Tough Times. LC 91-50076. 128p. 1992. 17.95 (0-446-51646-5) Warner Bks.

— Lincoln on Leadership: Executive Strategies for Tough Times. 208p. 1993. pap. 10.99 (0-446-39459-9) Warner Bks.

Phillips, Donna-Lee, ed. Eros & Photography. LC 77-81897. (Illus.). pap. 200.00x (0-917986-02-4) NFS Pr.

Phillips, Dorothy B., et al, eds. The Choice Is Always Ours: The Classic Anthology on the Spiritual Way. LC 88-45660. 496p. 1989. pap. 14.00 (0-06-066549-1) Harper SF.

Phillips, Douglas A. & Levi, Steven C. The Pacific Rim Region: Emerging Giant. LC 88-3876. (Illus.). 160p. (J). (gr. 6 up). 1988. lib. bdg. 18.95 (0-89490-191-5) Enslow Pubs.

Phillips, Duncan, ed. Art & Understanding, Nos. 1 & 2. LC 68-9235. (Contemporary Art Ser.). (Illus.). 1968. reprint ed. 20.95 (0-405-00713-2) Ayer.

Phillips, Dwayne. Image Processing in C: Analyzing & Enhancing Didgital Images. 300p. 1994. pap. 40.00 (0-13-104548-2) P-H.

Phillips, E. & Sneddon, I. N. Some Topics in Complex Analysis. (International Series of Monographs on Pure & Applied Mathematics: Vol. 86). 64.00 (0-08-011421-0, Pub. by Pergamon Repr UK) Franklin.

***Phillips, E. Barbara.** City Lights: Urban-Suburban Life in a Global Society. 2nd ed. (Illus.). 544p. (C). 1995. pap. text ed. 35.00 (0-19-505689-2) OUP.

Phillips, E. Barbara & LeGates, Richard T. City Lights: An Introduction to Urban Studies. (Illus.). (C). 1981. pap. text ed. 29.95 (0-19-502797-3) OUP.

Phillips, E. D. Aspects of Greek Medicine. LC 86-72186. 240p. 1987. text ed. 23.95 (0-914783-18-1) Charles.

Phillips, E. F. Beekeeping As a Hobby. (Shorey Lost Arts Ser.). 40p. reprint ed. pap. 1.95 (0-8466-6039-3, U39) Shorey.

Phillips, E. J., jt. auth. see Coulston, J. C.

Phillips, E. L., et al. Intelligence & Personality Factors Associated with Poliomyelitis Among School Age Children. (SRCD M: Vol. 12, No. 2). 1947. pap. 15.00 (0-527-01541-5) Periodicals Srv.

Phillips, E. Lakin. Day to Day Anxiety Management. LC 76-26581. 152p. 1977. 14.50 (0-88275-460-2) Krieger.

— Patient Compliance: New Light on Health Delivery Systems in Medicine & Psychotherapy. LC 88-13068. 370p. (C). 1988. text ed. 38.00 (0-920887-41-4) Hogrefe & Huber Pubs.

— Permissiveness in Child Rearing & Education - A Failed Doctrine? New Trends for the 1990s. LC 92-35833. 134p. (C). 1993. lib. bdg. 34.50 (0-8191-8978-2); pap. text ed. 16.00 (0-8191-8979-0) U Pr of Amer.

— Psychotherapy Revised: New Frontiers in Research & Practice. 264p. (C). 1985. text ed. 39.95 (0-89859-571-1) L Erlbaum Assocs.

— Stress, Health & Psychological Problems in the Major Professions. LC 82-17556. 478p. (Orig.). 1983. lib. bdg. 71.50 (0-8191-2773-6); pap. text ed. 34.00 (0-8191-2774-4) U Pr of Amer.

Phillips, E. Lee. Breaking Silence Before the Lord. (Pulpit Library). 160p. 1986. pap. 5.99 (0-8010-7093-7) Baker Bk.

Phillips, Ed. Crisis in the Atmosphere: The Greenhouse Factor. (Illus.). (Orig.). 1990. pap. 6.95 (0-9625245-0-6) D B Clark & Co Pub.

Phillips, Edgar Giraldus. Functions of a Complex Variable: With Applications. (Longman Mathematical Texts Ser.). 154p. reprint ed. pap. 43.90 (0-317-08527-1, 2013562) Bks Demand.

Phillips, Edward. The New World of English Words: or a General Dictionary. (Anglistica & Americana Ser.: No. 48). 358p. 1969. reprint ed. 76.70 (0-685-66500-3, 05102596, Pub. by Georg Olms GW) Lubrecht & Cramer.

— Sunday's Child. (Stonewall Inn Editions Ser.). 240p. 1988. pap. 7.95 (0-312-02294-8) St Martin.

— Theatrum Poetarum: Or a Compleat Collection of the Poets, Especially the Most Eminent, of All Ages. (Anglistica & Americana Ser.: No. 61). 453p. 1970. reprint ed. 76.70 (0-685-66501-1, 05102475, Pub. by Georg Olms GW) Lubrecht & Cramer.

— Theatrum Poetarum: or Compleat Collection of the Poets, Especially the Most Eminent, of All Ages. No. 61. 453p. 1970. reprint ed. write for info. (0-318-71939-8, Pub. by Georg Olms GW) Lubrecht & Cramer.

Phillips, Edward, ed. Travel Air - Wings over the Prairie. (Illus.). 128p. reprint ed. pap. 21.95 (0-911139-17-6) Flying Bks.

Phillips, Edward H. Beechcraft: Staggerwing to the Starship. LC 86-81230. 1987. 14.95 (0-911139-06-0) Flying Bks.

— CESSNA: A Master's Expression. LC 85-81741. (Illus.). 152p. 1985. 24.95 (0-911139-04-4) Flying Bks.

— The Lower Shenandoah Valley in the Civil War: The Impact of War upon the Civilian Population & upon Civil Institutions. (Virginia Civil War Battles & Leaders Ser.). (Illus.). 224p. 1993. 19.95 (1-56190-042-7) H E Howard.

— Piper: A Legacy Aloft. 1993. write for info. (0-911139-14-1); pap. write for info. (0-911139-15-X) Flying Bks.

— Piper Airplanes: A Legacy Aloft. LC 90-81379. 1990. pap. write for info. (0-911139-10-9) Flying Bks.

— Wings of Cessna: Model 120 to the Citation III. LC 86-72359. (Illus.). 128p. (Orig.). 1986. pap. 12.95 (0-911139-05-2) Flying Bks.

— Wings of Cessna: Model 120 to the Citation X. (Illus.). 128p. 1993. reprint ed. write for info. (0-911139-16-8) Flying Bks.

Phillips, Edward H., ed. Travel Air: Wings Over the Prairie. LC 82-82791. (Illus.). 128p. 1992. 21.95 (0-911139-00-1) Flying Bks.

***Phillips, Edward J.** The Founding of Russia's Navy: Peter the Greatand the Azov Fleet, 1688-1714. LC 94-46941. (Contributions in Military Studies: No. 159). 224p. 1995. text ed. 55.00 (0-313-29520-4, Greenwood Pr) Greenwood.

Phillips, Eleanor. Chung, the China Gold, & Me. 150p. (Orig.). (J). (gr. 6-10). 1990. pap. 7.95 (0-9624210-0-6) Laurelwood Pr.

Phillips, Elizabeth. Emily Dickinson: Personae & Performance. LC 87-43121. 250p. 1988. lib. bdg. 29.50 (0-271-00625-0) Pa St U Pr.

— Marianne Moore. LC 81-71399. (Literature & Life Ser.). 256p. 1982. 19.95 (0-8044-2698-8, F Ungar Bks) Continuum.

Phillips, Elizabeth, jt. auth. see Fortlage, Kate.

Phillips, Elizabeth, et al. Patterns & Functions. Curcio, Frances R., ed. LC 91-18820. (Curriculum & Evaluation Standards for School Mathematics Addenda Ser.: Grades 5-8). (Illus.). 80p. (Orig.). 1991. pap. 13.00 (0-87353-324-0) NCTM.

Phillips, Elizabeth C. Monarch Notes on Faulkner's Absalom, Absalom. (Orig.). (C). pap. 3.95 (0-671-00664-9, Arco Test) P-H Gen Ref & Trav.

Phillips, Ellen. The Tale-Teller Tells All. 1990. write for info. (0-9628226-0-4) Cricket Papers Pr.

Phillips, Ellen & Burrell, C. Colston. Rodale's Illustrated Encyclopedia of Perennials. LC 92-30109. 1993. 26.95 (0-87596-570-9, 01-690-0) Rodale Pr Inc.

***Phillips, Elwood.** Florida Retirees' Handbook: Answers to Your Legal & Financial Questions. 3rd ed. 230p. (Orig.). 1995. pap. 12.95 (1-56164-065-4) Pineapple Pr.

Phillips, Estelle M. & Pugh, D. S. How to Get a PhD. 172p. 1987. pap. 29.00 (0-335-15536-7, Open Univ Pr) Taylor & Francis.

— How to Get a Ph.D: A Handbook for Students & Their Supervisors. 2nd ed. LC 93-32693. 1994. 27.50 (0-335-19214-9, Open Univ Pr) Taylor & Francis.

Phillips, Esther R., ed. An Introduction to Analysis & Integration Theory. 480p. 1984. reprint ed. pap. 13.95 (0-486-64747-1) Dover.

— Studies in the History of Mathematics. LC 87-60581. (Studies in Mathematics: Vol. 26). 320p. 12.00 (0-88385-128-8) Math Assn.

Phillips, Eva. Nodley, the Duck Who Paddled Backwards. LC 91-65791. 44p. (J). (gr. k-3). 1991. pap. 6.95 (1-55523-446-1) Winston-Derek.

— Things We See & Know. LC 89-50580. 54p. 1990. pap. 4.95 (1-55523-230-2) Winston-Derek.

Phillips, Ewing L. Counseling & Psychotherapy: A Behavioral Approach. LC 77-1771. (Wiley Series on Personality Processes). 303p. reprint ed. pap. 86.40 (0-317-08440-2, 2019850) Bks Demand.

Phillips, F. & Warren, Roger. Sin Diego: A Guide to San Diego's Underground. Wilkening, Karen, ed. (Illus.). 280p. (Orig.). 1994. pap. 16.95 (0-945949-05-7) Warren Comns.

Phillips, Faye. Local History Collections in Libraries. 180p. 1994. lib. bdg. 32.00 (1-56308-141-5) Libs Unl.

Phillips, Frances. The Celebrated Running Horse Messenger. (Illus.). 48p. 1979. 5.00 (0-932716-08-3) Kelsey St Pr.

— For a Living. 1981. pap. 7.00 (0-914610-26-0) Hanging Loose.

— Up at Two. 1991. 15.00 (0-914610-90-2); pap. 9.00 (0-914610-89-9) Hanging Loose.

Phillips, Francis R. Creating an Education System for England & Wales. LC 92-12724. (Welsh Studies: Vol. 8). 212p. 1992. lib. bdg. 89.95 (0-7734-9528-2) E Mellen.

***Phillips, Frank.** The Justified Walk. 224p. 1995. per. 8.95 (1-57258-023-2) Teach Servs.

Phillips, Fred. Freedom in the Caribbean: A Study in Constitutional Change. LC 76-49887. 737p. 1977. lib. bdg. 60.00 (0-379-00592-1) Oceana.

Phillips, Fred B., Jr. Closing Officer's Guide: Washington, 1983-1993. 550p. 1994. ring bd. 90.00 (0-409-20149-9) Michie Butterworth.

— Closing Officer's Guide: Washington, 1983-1993. suppl. ed. 550p. 1993. Latest suppl. 12/93. 45.00 (1-56257-816-2) Butterworth Legal Pubs.

Phillips, Fred M. Desert People & Mountain Men: Exploration of the Great Basin 1824-1865. LC 77-23351. (Illus.). 1977. pap. 6.25 (0-912494-25-5) Chalfant Pr.

Phillips, Fred Y., ed. Systems & Management Science by Extremal Methods: Research Honoring Abraham Charnes at Age 70. 608p. (C). 1992. lib. bdg. 177.00 (0-7923-9139-X) Kluwer Ac.

— Thinkwork: Working, Learning, & Managing in a Computer- Interactive Society. LC 91-47085. 300p. 1992. text ed. 49.95 (0-275-93964-2, C3964, Praeger Pubs) Greenwood.

Phillips, Fred Y., jt. auth. see Desai, Chirag.

Phillips, G. Ceramic Packaging of Electronic Circuits. 1992. text ed. write for info. (0-442-00665-9) Van Nos Reinhold.

Phillips, G., jt. auth. see Milner, G. W.

Phillips, G., jt. auth. see Smith, M.J.

Phillips, G. Briggs, ed. see Morrissey, R.

Phillips, G. C., ed. see International Conference on Fast Neutron Physics Staff.

Phillips, G. O., jt. ed. see Inagaki, H.

Phillips, G. O., et al, eds. Gums & Stabilizers for the Food Industry: Interactions of Hydrocolloids. (Illus.). 420p. 1982. 170.00 (0-08-026843-9, Pergamon Pr) Elsevier.

Phillips, G. Robert. Historical Highlights of Charleston: An Overview of the City's 300 Year Past. 56p. 1992. spiral bd. 5.95 (0-9633815-0-4) P&R Enter.

Phillips, Garry D., jt. ed. see Cousins, Michael J.

Phillips, Gary. Commodore 64 Expansion Guide. LC 84-23999. (Illus.). 277p. 1985. pap. 16.60 (0-8306-1961-5, 1961) TAB Bks.

— Violent Spring. 275p. 1994. pap. 9.00 (1-883303-13-3) W Coast Crime.

Phillips, Gary, ed. Reference Encyclopedia for the IBM Personal Computer, 2 Vols. 1984. 69.95 (0-317-03007-8) P-H.

Phillips, Gary, tr. see Entrevernes Group Staff.

Phillips, Gary L., et al. Fishes of the Minnesota Region. 1992. pap. 16.95 (0-8166-0982-9) U of Minn Pr.

Phillips, Gene. Fiction, Film & F. Scott Fitzgerald. 238p. 1986. 3.50 (0-8294-0500-3) Loyola Univ Pr.

Phillips, Gene D. Alfred Hitchcock. LC 83-22786. (Filmmakers Ser.). 233p. 1984. text ed. 22.95 (0-8057-9293-7, Twayne) Macmillan.

— Alfred Hitchcock. LC 83-22786. (Filmmakers Ser.). 233p. 1984. pap. 14.95 (0-8057-9301-1, Twayne) Macmillan.

— Conrad to Cinema: The Art of Adaptation. LC 94-30263. (Ars Interpretandi Ser.: Vol. 4). 1995. write for info. (0-8204-2669-5) P Lang Pubs.

— Evelyn Waugh's Officers, Gentlemen & Rogues: The Fact Behind His Fiction. LC 75-26546. 196p. 1975. 25.95 (0-88229-172-6) Nelson-Hall.

— Fiction, Film, & Faulkner: The Art of Adaptation. LC 87-27201. (Illus.). 240p. 1988. 28.00 (0-87049-564-X) U of Tenn Pr.

— The Films of Tennessee Williams. LC 76-50204. (Illus.). 336p. 1980. 40.00 (0-87982-025-X) Art Alliance.

— Graham Greene: The Films of His Fiction. LC 73-85352. (Studies in Culture & Communication). 222p. reprint ed. pap. 63.30 (0-317-41862-9, 2026056) Bks Demand.

— Major Film Directors of the American & British Cinema. LC 88-46163. (Illus.). 288p. 1990. 49.50 (0-934223-08-4) Lehigh Univ Pr.

Phillips, Geoff. Newnes Electronics Toolkit. (Illus.). 200p. 1993. pap. 23.95 (0-7506-0929-X) Buttrwrth-Heinemann.

Phillips, George. Black Tickets. 1979. pap. 11.95 (0-385-28088-2, Delta) Dell.

— Concise Introduction to Ceramics. (Illus.). 200p. 1991. text ed. 49.95 (0-442-00890-2) Van Nos Reinhold.

Phillips, George H. Indians & Intruders in Central California, 1769-1849. LC 92-54134. (Civilization of the American Indian Ser.: Vol. 207). 1993. 24.95 (0-8061-2446-6) U of Okla Pr.

Phillips, Gerald M. Communication Incompetencies: A Theory of Training Oral Performance Behavior. 360p. (C). 1991. 34.95 (0-8093-1459-2) S Ill U Pr.

— Teaching How to Work in Groups. Dervin, Brenda, ed. LC 90-867. (Communication & Information Science Ser.). 320p. (C). 1990. text ed. 45.00 (0-89391-690-0); pap. text ed. 24.50 (0-89391-730-3) Ablex Pub.

Phillips, Gerald M. & Wood, Julia T., eds. Emergent Issues in Human Decision Making. LC 84-1323. 192p. 1984. 18.95 (0-8093-1151-8) S Ill U Pr.

— Speech Communication: Essays to Commemorate the 75th Anniversary of the Speech Communication Association. LC 89-5875. 256p. (C). 1989. text ed. 29.95 (0-8093-1520-3) S Ill U Pr.

Phillips, Gerald M., ed. see Berge, Zane & Collins, Mauri.

Phillips, Gerald M., ed. see Jones, J. Alfred, et al.

Phillips, Gerald M., jt. auth. see Werman, Robert.

Phillips, Gerald M., jt. auth. see Wyatt, Nancy.

Phillips, Gerald M., jt. auth. see Zolten, Jerome.

Phillips, Gerald M., et al. Development of Oral Communication in the Classroom. LC 71-77821. (C). 1970. text ed. write for info. (0-672-60857-X, Bobbs) Macmillan.

— Speaking in Public & Private. 384p. (Orig.). (C). 1985. teacher ed write for info. (0-672-61613-0); pap. text ed. write for info. (0-672-61612-2); pap. text ed. write for info. (0-02-395740-9); student ed write for info. (0-672-61622-X) Macmillan.

— Survival in the Academy: A Guide for Beginning Academics. LC 93-44472. (Hampton Press - SCA Applied Communication Ser.). 288p. 1994. pap. text ed. 22.95 (1-881303-69-1) Hampton Pr NJ.

Phillips, Gina. First Facts about Giant Sea Creatures. (First Facts about Ser.). (Illus.). 24p. (J). 1991. 2.98 (1-56156-084-7) Kidsbks.

— First Facts about Giant Sea Creatures. (First Facts about Ser.). (Illus.). 24p. (J). 1992. pap. 2.50 (1-56156-156-8) Kidsbks.

— First Facts about Prehistoric Animals. (First Facts about Ser.). (Illus.). 24p. (J). 1991. 2.98 (1-56156-083-9) Kidsbks.

— First Facts about Prehistoric Animals. (First Facts about Ser.). (Illus.). 24p. (J). 1992. pap. 2.50 (1-56156-157-6) Kidsbks.

— First Facts about Snakes & Reptiles. (First Facts about Ser.). (Illus.). 24p. (Orig.). (J). 1991. pap. 2.50 (1-56156-037-5) Kidsbks.

— First Facts about Snakes & Reptiles. (First Facts about Ser.). (Illus.). 24p. (Orig.). (J). 1991. write for info. (1-56156-060-X) Kidsbks.

— First Facts about Wild Animals. (First Facts about Ser.). (Illus.). 24p. (Orig.). (J). 1991. pap. 2.50 (1-56156-038-3) Kidsbks.

— First Facts about Wild Animals. (First Facts about Ser.). (Illus.). 24p. (Orig.). (J). 1991. write for info. (1-56156-061-8) Kidsbks.

Phillips, Gina, ed. Three Minute Aesop's Fables. (Three Minute Bks.). (Illus.). 24p. (J). 1991. 2.98 (1-56156-088-X) Kidsbks.

— Three Minute Bedtime Stories. (Three Minute Bks.). (Illus.). 24p. (J). 1991. 2.98 (1-56156-087-1) Kidsbks.

Phillips, Gloria, et al. A Heart Set Free. LC 85-50700. (Orig.). 1985. pap. 7.00 (0-915541-02-5); student ed write for info. (0-318-58957-5) Star Bks Inc.

Phillips, Gloria A., jt. auth. see Solomon, Eldra P.

Phillips, Glyn, jt. auth. see Hongu, Tatsuo.

PQ

An Asterisk (*) at the beginning of an entry indicates that the title is appearing in BIP for the first time.

***Phillips, Glyn O., et al, eds.** Gums & Stabilisers for the Food Industry No. 7. (Illus.). 448p. 1995. text ed. 115.00 (*0-19-963465-3*, IRL Pr) OUP.
— Gums & Stabilizers for the Food Industry, Vol. 6. (Illus.). 592p. 1992. 115.00 (*0-19-963284-7*) OUP.
Phillips, Gordon. The Rise of the Labour Party 1893-1931. LC 91-28658. (Lancaster Pamphlets Ser.). 1992. pap. 9.95 (*0-415-04051-5*, A7303) Routledge.
Phillips, Gordon M. Increased Debt & Product Market Competition: An Empirical Analysis. (Illus.). 60p. (Orig.). (C). 1993. pap. text ed. 30.00 (*1-56806-914-6*) Diane Pub.
Phillips, Gordon M. & Weiner, Robert. Trading Performance in Forward Markets: Information versus Normal Backwardation. (Illus.). 45p. (Orig.). (C). 1993. pap. text ed. 30.00 (*1-56806-913-8*) Diane Pub.
Phillips, Graham & Keatman, Martin. The Eye of the Fire. 164p. (Orig.). Date not set. pap. 17.95 (*0-8464-4187-X*) Beekman Pubs.
— King Arthur - the True Story: The Truth Behind the Romance & Legends of Excalibur, the Holy Grail & the Site of the Real Avalon. (Illus.). 224p. 1994. pap. 9.95 (*0-09-929681-0*, Pub. by Arrow Bks UK) Trafalgar.
— The Shakespeare Conspiracy. (Illus.). 230p. 1995. 34.95 (*0-7126-5883-1*, Pub. by Century UK) Trafalgar.
Phillips, Greer L. & Washlick, John R. NAFTA Text: Including Supplemental Agreements. Schwartz, Maureen, ed. 96p. (Orig.). 1994. pap. 39.50 (*0-8080-0000-4*) Commerce.
Phillips, Greg & Johnston, Gail. Think Light! Breaking Free from the Diet Prison. 4th ed. 126p. 1989. reprint ed. pap. 6.95 (*0-9625095-1-5*) Speaking Fitness.
Phillips, Gregory D. The Diehards: Aristocratic Society & Politics in Edwardian England. LC 78-16949. (Historical Studies: No. 96). 248p. 1979. 20.00 (*0-674-20555-3*) HUP.
Phillips, H., ed. see Brandes, D.
Phillips, Harold L. Living with Christ. (Eagle Bible Ser.). 1989. pap. 2.50 (*0-87162-500-8*, D9152) Warner Pr.
***Phillips, Harry.** Phillips: Brief History of the Phillips Family, Beginning with the Emigration from Wales & a Detailed Genealogy of the Descendants of John & Benjamin Philips, Pioneer Citizens of Wilson Co. TN. (Illus.). 261p. 1994. reprint ed. lib. bdg. 52.00 (*0-8328-4370-9*); reprint ed. pap. 42.00 (*0-8328-4371-7*) Higginson Bk Co.
Phillips, Harry & Robinson, Jack W. Pritchard on the Law of Wills & Administration of Estates, 3 Vols. 4th suppl. ed. 1991. 75.00 (*0-87473-873-3*) Michie Butterworth.
Phillips, Harry I. The Making (& Occasional Unraveling) of a Sports Car Buff. Thurber, Bruce, ed. (Illus.). 132p. (Orig.). 1991. pap. 10.00 (*0-9629911-0-4*) H I Phillips.
Phillips, Harry R. Growing & Propagating Wild Flowers. Moore, J. Kenneth & Bell, C. Ritchie, eds. LC 84-25734. (Illus.). x, 331p. 1985. pap. 16.95 (*0-8078-4131-5*) U of NC Pr.
Phillips, Harry T. & Gaylord, Susan. Aging & Public Health. LC 85-2815. 352p. 1985. 33.95 (*0-8261-4380-6*) Springer Pub.
Phillips, Harvey, jt. auth. see Winkle, William.
Phillips, Helen, ed. Langland, the Mystics & the Medieval English Religious Tradition: Essays in Honour of S. S. Hussey. 320p. 1990. 79.00 (*0-85991-301-5*) Boydell & Brewer.
Phillips, Henry. American Paper Currency: Series One, Historical Sketches of the Paper Currency of the American Colonies Prior to the Adoption of the Federal Constitution: Series Two, Continental Paper Money, 2 Vols. in 1. LC 68-18223. (Library of Money & Banking History). 1972. reprint ed. lib. bdg. 49.50 (*0-678-00787-X*) Kelley.
Phillips, Henry, Jr., jt. auth. see Chase, Alston H.
Phillips, Henry, Jr., jt. ed. see Chase, Alston H.
Phillips, Henry A. Photodrama. LC 70-124032. (Literature of Cinema, Ser. 1). 1970. reprint ed. 12.95 (*0-405-01632-8*) Ayer.
***Phillips, Henry G.** Remagen: Springboard to Victory. 275p. 1994. write for info. (*0-9637444-1-0*) H G Phillips.
— Sedjenane: The Pay-off Battle. (Illus.). 150p. (Orig.). 1993. pap. 11.25 (*0-9637444-0-2*) H G Phillips.
Phillips, Herbert E. & Ritchie, John C., Jr. Investment Analysis & Portfolio Selection. 2nd ed. (Illus.). 818p. 1992. text ed. 52.95x (*0-912675-16-0*); Tax Reform Act of 1986. write for info. (*0-318-69526-X*) Ardsley.
Phillips, Herbert E., jt. auth. see Frankfurter, George M.
Phillips, Herbert M. Basic Education-a World Challenge: Measures & Innovations for Children & Youth in Developing Countries. LC 74-6995. 270p. reprint ed. pap. 77.00 (*0-8357-5978-4*, 2022405) Bks Demand.
Phillips, Herbert P. The Integrative Art of Modern Thailand. LC 92-81701. 1993. 24.95 (*0-936127-02-3*) P A Hearst Mus.
Phillips, Herbert P., et al. Modern Thai Literature: With an Ethnographic Interpretation. LC 86-30816. 464p. 1987. text ed. 26.00 (*0-8248-1065-1*) UH Pr.
Phillips, Hollibert E. Vicissitudes of the I: An Introduction to the Philosophy of the Mind. LC 94-4967. 176p. 1994. pap. text ed. 21.00 (*0-13-108721-5*) P-H.
Phillips, Howard. Moscow's Challenge to U. S. Vital Interests in Southern Africa. 204p. (Orig.). 1987. pap. 5.95 (*0-940355-01-9*) Policy Analysis.
Phillips, Howard, jt. auth. see Brandes, Donna.
Phillips, Hubert C. My Best Puzzles in Logic & Reasoning. (Orig.). 1961. pap. 3.95 (*0-486-20119-8*) Dover.
— My Best Puzzles in Mathematics. (Orig.). 1961. pap. 4.95 (*0-486-20091-4*) Dover.
Phillips, I. D., jt. auth. see Wareing, P. F.
Phillips, J. Employees' Inventions: A Comparative Study. 212p. 1981. pap. text ed. 60.00 (*0-9507626-0-1*) Cassell.
— Licensing Law Guide. 286p. 1994. pap. text ed. 55.00 (*0-406-02878-8*, UK) Butterworth Legal Pubs.
— Measuring ROI Human Resources. 320p. Date not set. write for info. (*0-88415-492-0*) Gulf Pub.
Phillips, J. A., et al, eds. Planets Around Pulsars. (ASP Conference Series Publications: Vol. 36). 391p. 1993. 40.00 (*0-937707-55-4*) Astron Soc Pacific.
Phillips, J. B. The New Testament in Modern English. 576p. 1973. pap. 9.95 (*0-02-088490-7*) Macmillan.
— The Newborn Christian: 114 Readings. 240p. 1984. pap. 5.95 (*0-02-088270-X*, Collier S&S) S&S Trade.
— The Price of Success: An Autobiography. LC 84-23472. 288p. (Orig.). 1985. pap. 8.99 (*0-87788-659-8*) Shaw Pubs.
— Ring of Truth: A Translator's Testimony. LC 77-80627. 124p. 1977. pap. 7.99 (*0-87788-724-1*) Shaw Pubs.
— Through the Year with J. B. Phillips. (C). 1990. pap. text ed. 30.00 (*0-85305-258-1*, Pub. by J Arthur Ltd UK) St Mut.
— Your God Is Too Small. 1964. pap. 3.50 (*0-02-088540-7*) Macmillan.
Phillips, J. D. & Renwick, W. H., eds. Geomorphic Systems: Proceedings of the 23rd Binghamton Symposium in Geomorphology, Held 25-27 September 1992. LC 92-26714. 1992. reprint ed. write for info. (*0-444-89809-3*) Elsevier.
Phillips, J. F. Town & Village in the Nineteenth Century. (C). 1983. text ed. 45.00 (*0-685-22169-5*, Pub. by Univ Nottingham UK) St Mut.
Phillips, J. H. C. I. I. Interruption Insurance, No. 260. (C). 1981. 230.00 (*0-685-33767-7*, Pub. by Witherby & Co UK) St Mut.
— The Trial of Ned Kelly. xiii, 135p. 1987. 19.50 (*0-455-20759-3*, Pub. by Law Bk Co) W W Gaunt.
Phillips, J. H., ed. Reliability & Risk in Pressure Vessels & Piping. (PVP Ser.: Vol. 251). 172p. 1993. 45.00 (*0-7918-0978-1*, H00810) ASME.
Phillips, J. H. & Bowen, J. K. Forensic Science & the Expert Witness. rev. ed. x, 139p. 1989. 32.50 (*0-455-20958-8*, Pub. by Law Bk Co) W W Gaunt.
Phillips, J. J. Mojo Hand: An Orphic Tale. LC 85-71335. 200p. 1985. reprint ed. pap. 6.95 (*0-933944-12-8*) City Miner Bks.
— Products Liability in a Nutshell. 4th ed. LC 93-1654. (Nut Shell Ser.). 331p. (C). 1993. pap. text ed. 16.00 (*0-314-02252-X*) West Pub.
Phillips, J. M. D. H. Lawrence: An Annotated Bibliography. 1992. lib. bdg. 79.95 (*0-8490-1372-0*) Gordon Pr.
Phillips, J. R. The Medieval Expansion of Europe. (Illus.). 320p. 1988. pap. text ed. 16.95 (*0-19-289123-5*) OUP.
Phillips, J. R., comp. The Justices of the Peace in Wales & Monmouthshire, 1541-1689. 441p. 1975. 38.50 (*0-7083-0563-6*, Pub. by U of Wales UK) Bks Intl VA.
Phillips, J. S. Tax Treaty Networks: 1988-1989 Edition. 734p. 1988. text ed. 142.00 (*2-88316-000-7*) Gordon & Breach.
Phillips, Jack. Freedom in Machinery, Vol. 2: Screw Theory Exemplified. (Illus.). (C). 1990. 99.95 (*0-521-25442-6*) Cambridge U Pr.
Phillips, Jack J. Handbook of Training Evaluation & Measurement Methods. 328p. 1990. text ed. 89.95 (*0-8464-1369-8*) Beekman Pubs.
— Handbook of Training Evaluation & Measurement Methods. 2nd ed. 316p. 1991. 32.95 (*0-87201-174-7*) Gulf Pub.
— Improving Supervisors' Effectiveness. LC 84-43032. (Jossey-Bass Management Ser.). (Illus.). 443p. reprint ed. pap. 126.30 (*0-7837-6524-X*, 2045636) Bks Demand.
— Recruiting, Training, & Retaining New Employees: Managing the Transition from College to Work. LC 86-46332. 346p. reprint ed. pap. 98.70 (*0-7837-6520-7*, 2045632) Bks Demand.
***Phillips, Jack J., ed. & pref.** In Action: Measuring Return on Investment No. 1: Eighteen Case Studies from the Real World of Training. LC 94-78503. (In Action Ser.). 271p. (Orig.). 1994. pap. 50.00 (*1-56286-008-9*) Am Soc Train & Devel.
Phillips, James, tr. see Esteban, Claude.
Phillips, James C. Physics of T-C Superconductors. 403p. 1989. text ed. 73.00 (*0-12-553990-8*) Acad Pr.
Phillips, James D. Pepper & Pirates: Adventures in the Sumatra Pepper Trade of Salem. (Illus.). 141p. 1949. 15.00 (*0-88389-014-3*, Essx Institute) Peabody Essex Mus.
— Salem in the Eighteenth Century. LC 37-36381. (Illus.). 533p. 1969. reprint ed. 30.00 (*0-88389-017-8*, Essx Institute) Peabody Essex Mus.
Phillips, James F. & Ross, John A., eds. Family Planning Programmes & Fertility. (International Studies in Demography). 288p. 1992. 75.00 (*0-19-828385-7*) OUP.
Phillips, James L., ed. see Brown, James A.
Phillips, James M. From the Rising of the Sun: Christians & Society in Contemporary Japan. LC 80-24609. (American Society of Missiology Ser.: No. 3). 320p. (Orig.). reprint ed. pap. 91.20 (*0-8357-2687-8*, 2040223) Bks Demand.
Phillips, James M. & Coote, Robert T., eds. Toward Century Twenty-One in Christian Mission. viii, 376p. (Orig.). pap. 24.99 (*0-8028-0638-4*) Eerdmans.
Phillips, James M., ed. see Yaraborough, William P.
Phillips, James W. Washington State Place Names. rev. ed. LC 73-159435. (Illus.). 186p. 1971. pap. 9.95 (*0-295-95498-1*) U of Wash Pr.
Phillips, Jan. Making Peace: One Woman's Journey Around The World. (Orig.). 1990. pap. 18.95 (*0-377-00200-3*) Friendship Pr.
***Phillips, Jane.** The Magic Daughter: A Memoir of Living with Multiple Personality Disorder. LC 95-7604. 1995. 22.95 (*0-670-85970-2*, Viking) Viking Penguin.
Phillips, Jane E., tr. see Erasmus, Desiderius.
Phillips, Janet. Weaver's Book of Fabric Design. (Illus.). 148p. 1983. pap. 11.95 (*0-312-85980-5*) St Martin.
Phillips, Janet, ed. see Beckwith, Alice.
Phillips, Janine. My Secret Diary. 160p. 1982. 10.95 (*0-317-54333-4*) Dufour.
Phillips, Jayne A. Fast Lanes. (Orig.). 1988. pap. 5.95 (*0-671-64014-3*, WSP) PB.
— Fast Lanes. (Illus.). 56p. (Orig.). 1984. 150.00 (*0-931428-16-5*); pap. 18.00 (*0-931428-17-3*) Vehicle Edns.
— Machine Dreams. Rosenman, Jane, ed. 400p. 1992. reprint ed. pap. 10.00 (*0-671-74235-3*, WSP) PB.
— Shelter. LC 94-8391. 1994. 21.95 (*0-395-48890-7*) HM.
Phillips, Jean A. For Better Reading: Lots You Need to Know about Short Vowels. (Illus.). 56p. 1981. pap. write for info. (*0-911305-00-9*) P Friends Co Inc.
— For Better Reading: Lots You Need to Know about Vowels. (Illus.). 58p. 1983. pap. 5.98 (*0-911305-01-7*) P Friends Co Inc.
Phillips, Jeanne. Shared in an Evil Time. LC 90-72004. 119p. 1992. pap. 10.00 (*1-56002-085-7*, Univ Edtns) Aegina Pr.
Phillips, Jeff. America's First Team in the Gulf. 1993. 24.95 (*0-87833-037-2*) Taylor Pub.
Phillips, Jeff, ed. see Takakjian, Portia.
Phillips, Jeffrey A., ed. see Heinz, John.
Phillips, Jen. The NAG Library: A Beginner's Guide. (Illus.). 260p. 1987. 35.00 (*0-19-853263-6*) OUP.
***Phillips, Jennie.** I Am Responsible. Eldredge, A., ed. 32p. (Orig.). 1994. pap. 4.00 (*1-885857-03-9*) Four Wnds Pubng.
Phillips, Jenny. Symbol, Myth, & Rhetoric: The Politics of Culture in an Armenian-American Population. LC 87-45788. (Immigrant Communities & Ethnic Minorities in the U. S. & Canada Ser.: No. 23). 1989. 47.50 (*0-404-19433-8*) AMS Pr.
Phillips, Jeremy. Butterworths Intellectual Property Law Handbook. 1990. U.K. pap. 60.00 (*0-406-50471-7*) Butterworth Legal Pubs.
— An Introduction to Intellectual Property Law. 2nd rev. ed. 1990. pap. 40.00 (*0-406-51240-X*, U.K.) Butterworth Legal Pubs.
Phillips, Jeremy & Hooke, James. The Debating Book. 120p. pap. 14.95 (*0-86840-325-3*, Pub. by New South Wales Univ Pr AT) Intl Spec Bk.
Phillips, Jerry J., jt. auth. see Cartwright, Robert E.
Phillips, Jerry J., jt. auth. see Christie, George C.
***Phillips, Jerry J., et al.** Products Liability, 3 vols., Set. 2nd ed. 1986. 240.00 (*1-55834-109-9*) Michie Butterworth.
Phillips, Jill. Annus Mirabilis: A Bibliography of Medieval Times. (Bibliographies for Librarians Ser.). 1980. lib. bdg. 250.00 (*0-8490-1398-4*) Gordon Pr.
— George Bernard Shaw: A Bibliography. 1975. lib. bdg. 250.00 (*0-87968-335-X*) Gordon Pr.
— Occult Bibliography. 1975. lib. bdg. 250.00 (*0-8490-0748-8*) Gordon Pr.
Phillips, Jill & Phillips, Leona. D. W. Griffith & His Films. 490p. 1975. lib. bdg. 250.00 (*0-87968-334-1*) Gordon Pr.
Phillips, Jill, jt. auth. see Phillips, Leona.
Phillips, Jill M. Archaeology of the Collective East: Greece, Asia Minor, Egypt, Lebanon, Mesopatamia, Syria, Palestine, an Annotated Bibliography. 1977. lib. bdg. 250.00 (*0-8490-1362-3*) Gordon Pr.
— The Darkling Plain: A Bibliography of Books About World War I. (Bibliographies for Librarians Ser.). 1980. lib. bdg. 250.00 (*0-8490-3207-5*) Gordon Pr.
— The Fate Weaver. 256p. 1992. 17.95 (*1-55972-102-2*, Birch Ln Pr) Carol Pub Group.
— The Good Morning Cook Book. LC 75-31702. 134p. 1976. 8.95 (*0-88289-063-8*) Pelican.
— The Rain Maiden. 570p. 1987. 16.95 (*0-8065-1008-0*, Citadel Pr) Carol Pub Group.
— The Second World War in History, Biography, Diary, Poetry, Literature, & Film: A Bibliography. 1983. lib. bdg. 250.00 (*0-8490-3231-8*) Gordon Pr.
— T. E. Lawrence: A Portrait in Paradox Controversy & Caricature in the Biographies of T. E. Lawrence. 600p. 1975. 250.00 (*0-8490-1172-8*) Gordon Pr.
— Walford's Oak. 386p. 1990. 18.95 (*0-8065-1159-1*, Citadel Pr) Carol Pub Group.
Phillips, Jim. The Devil's Bodyguard. LC 83-61388. (Illus.). 350p. 1986. 19.95 (*0-932572-12-X*) Phillips Pubns.
Phillips, Jim, ed. see Andrews, John C.
Phillips, Jim, ed. see Brunner, John.
Phillips, Jim, jt. ed. see Girard, Philip.
Phillips, Jim, jt. auth. see Moran, William F., Jr.
Phillips, Jim, ed. see White, William.
***Phillips, Jim, et al, eds.** Crime & Criminal Justice: Essays in the History of Canadian Law, Vol. 5. (Osgoode Society for Canadian Legal History Ser.). 584p. 1994. 70.00 (*0-8020-0633-7*) U of Toronto Pr.
— Essays in the History of Canadian Law Vol. 5: Crime & Criminal Justice. (Osgoode Society for Canadian Legal History Ser.). 584p. 1994. pap. 45.00 (*0-8020-7587-8*) U of Toronto Pr.
Phillips, Joan. Lucky Bear. LC 85-14467. (Step into Reading Bks.). (Illus.). 32p. (J). (ps-1). 1986. lib. bdg. 7.99 (*0-394-97987-7*); pap. 3.50 (*0-394-87987-2*) Random Bks Yng Read.
— My New Boy. LC 85-30129. (Step into Reading Bks.). (Illus.). 32p. (J). (ps-1). 1986. 3.50 (*0-394-88277-6*); lib. bdg. 7.99 (*0-394-98277-0*) Random Bks Yng Read.
— Peek-a-Boo! I See You! (Baby's Board Bks.). (Illus.). (J). (ps). 1983. 4.95 (*0-448-03092-6*, G&D) Putnam Pub Group.
— Tiger Is a Scaredy Cat: A Step One Book. LC 85-19673. (Step into Reading Bks.). (Illus.). 32p. (J). (ps-1). 1986. pap. 3.50 (*0-394-88056-0*) Random Bks Yng Read.
— Walt Disney's Bambi's Game. (Golden Very Easy Readers Ser.). (Illus.). (J). (ps-1). 1991. write for info. (*0-307-11599-2*, Golden Pr) Western Pub.
Phillips, Joan, jt. auth. see Vives, Miguel.
Phillips, Joan N., ed. Acronyms & Abbreviations in Government Contracting. LC 93-27383. 1993. 20.00 (*0-935165-24-X*) GWU Gov Contracts.
Phillips, JoAnn. The Run According to Hawkeye. (Illus.). 24p. (Orig.). (J). 1993. pap. 9.95 (*0-9638403-0-4*) Cherokee Strip.
Phillips, Joann, ed. see Zerler, Kathryn S.
Phillips, Joanna, comp. Into the Eighties with Alaskan Environmental Impact Statements: Bibliography. (Elmer E. Rasmuson Library Occasional Papers: No. 11). 234p. (Orig.). 1985. pap. text ed. 12.50 (*0-937592-06-4*) U Alaska Rasmuson Lib.
Phillips, John. The Bible Explorer's Guide. LC 86-18565. 320p. 1987. pap. 11.99 (*0-87213-682-5*) Loizeaux.
— Black-Powder Hunting Secrets. LC 93-79798. (Illus.). 160p. (Orig.). 1993. pap. text ed. 11.95 (*0-936513-38-1*) Larsens Outdoor.
— Carew Manor: A Short Guide. (C). 1985. pap. 30.00 (*0-907335-21-7*, Pub. by Sutton Libs & Arts) St Mut.
— Deer & Fixings. 188p. 1991. pap. 12.00 (*0-937866-23-7*) Atlantic Pub Co.
— Exploring Acts. LC 91-21850. 528p. (Orig.). 1991. reprint ed. 22.99 (*0-87213-668-X*) Loizeaux.
— Exploring Ephesians. LC 93-6579. (Exploring Ser.). 1993. 17.99 (*0-87213-650-7*) Loizeaux.
— Exploring Genesis. LC 92-31406. 1992. reprint ed. 19.99 (*0-87213-659-0*) Loizeaux.
— Exploring Hebrews. LC 91-44909. reprint ed. 17.99 (*0-87213-671-X*) Loizeaux.
— Exploring Proverbs. LC 94-23095. 1994. 24.99 (*0-87213-577-2*) Loizeaux.
— Exploring Revelation. LC 91-18869. 1991. reprint ed. 18.99 (*0-87213-672-8*) Loizeaux.
— Exploring Romans. LC 91-35605. (Exploring Ser.). 1992. reprint ed. 18.99 (*0-87213-669-8*) Loizeaux.
— Exploring the Future. LC 91-39048. (Illus.). 1992. pap. 15.99 (*0-87213-625-6*) Loizeaux.
— Exploring the Gospels: John. LC 88-13345. 425p. 1989. 22.99 (*0-87213-658-2*) Loizeaux.
— Exploring the Psalms, 2 vols., Set. LC 88-12938. 1988. 49.99 (*0-87213-653-1*) Loizeaux.
— Exploring the Psalms, Vol. 1. LC 88-12938. 27.99 (*0-87213-678-7*) Loizeaux.
— Exploring the Psalms, Vol. 2. LC 88-12938. 27.99 (*0-87213-679-5*) Loizeaux.
— Exploring the Scriptures. LC 92-46619. 1993. pap. 14.99 (*0-87213-673-6*) Loizeaux.
— Exploring the Song of Solomon. LC 84-7881. 157p. (C). 1984. pap. 8.99 (*0-87213-683-3*) Loizeaux.
— Exploring the World of the Jew. LC 92-18121. 1993. 14.99 (*0-87213-674-4*) Loizeaux.
— Fish & Fixings. 210p. 1991. pap. 12.00 (*0-937866-29-6*) Atlantic Pub Co.
— How to Live Forever. (Teach Yourself the Bible Ser.). 1964. pap. 3.99 (*0-8024-3700-1*) Moody.
— Introducing People of the Bible, Vol. I. LC 91-39819. 168p. 1992. pap. 8.99 (*0-87213-627-2*) Loizeaux.
— Introducing People of the Bible, Vol. 2. 1993. pap. 8.99 (*0-87213-628-0*) Loizeaux.
— Life on Earth: Its Origin & Succession. Gould, Stephen J., ed. LC 79-8343. (History of Paleontology Ser.). 1980. reprint ed. lib. bdg. 23.95 (*0-405-12733-2*) Ayer.
— The Masters' Secrets of Catfishing. LC 93-79799. (Illus.). 160p. (Orig.). 1993. pap. text ed. 9.95 (*0-936513-44-6*) Larsens Outdoor.
— Masters' Secrets of Deer Hunting. LC 91-90327. (Deer Hunting Library). 160p. (Orig.). 1991. pap. 9.95 (*0-936513-14-4*) Larsens Outdoor.
— Memoirs of William Smith. Albritton, Claude C., Jr., ed. LC 77-6535. (History of Geology Ser.). (Illus.). 1978. reprint ed. lib. bdg. 18.95 (*0-405-10455-3*) Ayer.
— Nathalie Sarraute Vol. 13: Metaphor, Fairy-Tale & the Feminine of the Text. LC 93-40239. (Writing about Women Ser.). 284p. (C). 1994. text ed. 50.95 (*0-8204-2366-1*) P Lang Pubs.
— One Hundred Outlines from the Old Testament. LC 94-16340. 1994. pap. write for info. (*0-87213-575-6*) Loizeaux.
— One Hundred Sermon Outlines from the New Testament. LC 94-16339. 1994. pap. write for info. (*0-87213-576-4*) Loizeaux.
— One Hundred Sermon Outlines from the Old Testament. 2nd ed. pap. 6.99 (*0-8024-7816-6*) Moody.
— Only One Life: The Biography of Stephen F. Olford. LC 94-43087. 1995. write for info. (*0-87213-676-0*) Loizeaux.
— Poet & Pilot: Antoine de Saint-Exupery. (Illus.). 1994. 35.00 (*1-881616-23-1*) Dist Art Pubs.
— Protecting Designs - Law & Litigation. 425p. 1994. 110.00 (*0-455-21275-9*, Pub. by Law Bk Co) W W Gaunt.
— The Science of Deer Hunting. LC 92-71317. (Deer Hunting Library). (Illus.). 160p. (Orig.). 1992. pap. 9.95 (*0-936513-22-5*) Larsens Outdoor.
— Turkey Hunting Tactics. LC 88-63557. (Hunter's Information Ser.). 183p. 1989. write for info. (*0-914697-19-6*) N Amer Outdoor Grp.
Phillips, John, Sr. Why Start a Business When You Can Steal One Instead! 48p. 1994. pap. 7.95 (*0-8059-3481-2*) Dorrance.
Phillips, John & Vines, Jerry. Exploring the Book of Daniel. LC 90-31819. 1990. 18.99 (*0-87213-988-3*) Loizeaux.
Phillips, John, jt. auth. see Jullian, Philippe.
Phillips, John, jt. ed. see Leaska, Mitchell A.
Phillips, John, tr. see Torwesten, Hans.
Phillips, John, jt. auth. see Wilhelm, Henry.
Phillips, John, et al. The Last Edwardians: An Illustrated History of Violet Trefusis & Alice Keppel. LC 85-71852. (Illus.). 93p. (Orig.). 1985. pap. 10.00 (*0-934552-44-4*) Boston Athenaeum.

Phillips, John A. Electoral Behavior in Unreformed England: Plumpers, Splitters, & Straights. LC 82-47608. 375p. reprint ed. pap. 106.90 (0-7837-6772-2, 2046602) Bks Demand.
— The Great Reform Bill in the Boroughs: English Electoral Behaviour, 1818-1841. 352p. 1992. 69.00 (0-19-820296-2) OUP.
Phillips, John B. New Testament in Modern English. rev. ed. 576p. 1972. text ed. 12.95 (0-02-596970-6) Macmillan.
— New Testament in Modern English. 2nd rev. ed. 576p. 1972. pap. 7.95 (0-02-088570-9, 59697) Macmillan.
Phillips, John B., Jr. Tennessee Employment Law. 176p. 1989. ring bd. 89.00 (0-925773-00-X) M Lee Smith.
Phillips, John B. Your God Is Too Small. 2nd ed. 128p. 1987. reprint ed. pap. 3.95 (0-02-088510-5, Pub. by Gebrueder Borntraeger GW) Macmillan.
Phillips, John C. American Game Mammals & Birds: A Catalogue of Books. Sterling, Keir B., ed. LC 77-83129. (Biologists & Their World Ser.). (Illus.). 1978. reprint ed. lib. bdg. 54.95 (0-405-10744-7) Ayer.
— A Bibliography of Sporting Books. 639p. 1991. 75.00 (1-882860-00-4) J Cummins Bksell.
— A Natural History of the Ducks, 2 vols., 1. 1920p. 1986. reprint ed. write for info. (0-486-25141-1) Dover.
— A Natural History of the Ducks, 2 vols., 2. 1920p. 1986. reprint ed. write for info. (0-486-25142-X) Dover.
— A Natural History of the Ducks, 2 vols., Set. 1920p. 1986. reprint ed. 100.00 (0-685-11962-9) Dover.
— Sociology of Sport. LC 92-22181. 1993. pap. text ed. 36.00 (0-205-13983-3) Allyn.
Phillips, John C., jt. auth. see O'Donovan, James.
***Phillips, John E.** Bass Fishing Central Alabama: You Can Find & Catch More & Bigger Bass in Central Alabama Lakes. Ellington, Coke, ed. (Illus.). 160p. (Orig.). 1994. pap. 15.00 (1-882616-05-7) Advertiser.
— How to Make Extra Profits in Taxidermy. LC 84-10409. (Illus.). 160p. (Orig.). 1984. pap. 12.95 (0-8329-0345-0, Winchester Pr) New Win Pub.
— The Masters' Secrets of Bowhunting Deer: Secret Tactics from Master Bowmen. LC 93-78226. (Illus.). 160p. (Orig.). 1993. pap. text ed. 9.95 (0-936513-34-9) Larsens Outdoor.
— The Masters' Secrets of Crappie Fishing. LC 92-74324. (Fishing Library). (Illus.). 160p. (Orig.). (C). 1992. pap. text ed. 9.95 (0-936513-29-2) Larsens Outdoor.
— Masters' Secrets of Turkey Hunting. LC 91-76443. (Turkey Hunting Ser.). (Illus.). 160p. (Orig.). 1991. pap. 9.95 (0-936513-18-7) Larsens Outdoor.
— Monster Bucks, How to Take: Secrets to Finding Trophy Deer. LC 94-72944. 160p. (Orig.). (YA). 1995. pap. 11.95 (0-936513-46-2) Larsens Outdoor.
Phillips, John F. The American Indian in Alabama & the Southeast. (Illus.). 213p. 1986. 10.95 (0-9618289-1-9); pap. 8.95 (0-9618289-2-7) Amer Indian Bks.
— Chief Junaluska of the Cherokee Indian Nation. (Illus.). 88p. 1988. 9.00 (0-9618289-3-5); pap. 6.00 (0-9618289-4-3) Amer Indian Bks.
— The Indian Heritage of Americans. (Illus.). (Orig.). 1981. pap. 2.95 (0-9618289-0-0) Amer Indian Bks.
Phillips, John H. Practical Quantitative Doppler Echocardiography. (Illus.). 192p. 1991. 87.00 (0-8493-4921-4, RC683) CRC Pr.
Phillips, John L. How to Think about Statistics. 2nd ed. (C). 1995. pap. text ed. write for info. (0-7167-2287-9) W H Freeman.
Phillips, John M. & Parker, Barbara N., eds. The Discoveries of Waldron Phoenix Belknap, Jr. Concerning the Influence of the English Mezzotint on Colonial Painting. LC 55-14827. (Illus.). 39p. reprint ed. pap. 25.00 (0-7837-4177-4, 2059026) Bks Demand.
Phillips, John P., Jr., ed. Employment Law Desk Book for Tennessee Employers. 1989. 90.00 (0-925773-03-4) M Lee Smith.
***Phillips, John P., et al, eds.** Organic Electronic Spectral Data, Vol. 30. (Organic Electronic Spectral Data Ser.: Vol. 30). 1994. text ed. 175.00 (0-471-10971-1) Wiley.
Phillips, John P., jt. auth. see Beckman, John E.
Phillips, John P., ed. see Feuer, Henry, et al.
Phillips, John P., jt. ed. see Kessler, M. F.
Phillips, John P., et al. Organic Electronic Spectral Data: 1985, Vol. 27. 944p. 1991. text ed. 270.00 (0-471-55553-3) Wiley.
— Organic Electronic Spectral Data Vol. 29: 1987, Vol. 29. 1993. text ed. 180.00 (0-471-31121-9) Wiley.
Phillips, John P., et al, eds. Organic Electronic Spectral Data, Vol. 5: 1960-61. LC 60-16428. Vol. 5, 1960-61. pap. 160.00 (0-317-11184-1, 2006361) Bks Demand.
— Organic Electronic Spectral Data, Vol. 6: 1962-63. LC 60-16428. Vol. 6, 1962-63. pap. 160.00 (0-317-11185-X) Bks Demand.
— Organic Electronic Spectral Data, Vol. 9: 1967. LC 60-16428. Vol. 9, 1967. pap. 160.00 (0-317-11186-8) Bks Demand.
— Organic Electronic Spectral Data, Vol. 23. 1051p. 1987. text ed. 260.00 (0-471-63557-X) Wiley.
— Organic Electronic Spectral Data, Vol. 24. 984p. 1988. text ed. 243.00 (0-471-61511-0) Wiley.
— Organic Electronic Spectral Data, Vol. 25. 1020p. 1989. text ed. 190.00 (0-471-51505-1) Wiley.
— Organic Electronic Spectral Data, Vol. 26, 1984, Vol. 26. 932p. 1990. text ed. 220.00 (0-471-51941-3) Wiley.
Phillips, John T. Organizing & Archiving Files & Records on Microcomputers. 84p. 1992. pap. 41.00 (0-933887-42-6, A4549) Assn Recs Mgrs & Admin.
Phillips, John T. & Tarrant, Paul. Software Directory for Automated Records Management Systems. 468p. 1994. spiral bd. 48.00 (0-933887-34-5, A4568) Assn Recs Mgrs & Admin.
***Phillips, Jonathon, et al, eds.** The Biology of Disease. LC 94-46340. 1995. write for info. (0-632-03855-1) Blackwell Sci.
***Phillips, Joseph.** Operation Elbow Room. 240p. (Orig.). 1995. pap. 11.95 (1-56474-138-9) Fithian Pr.
Phillips, Joseph D. Little Business in the American Economy. LC 81-4217. (Illinois Studies in the Social Sciences: Vol. 42). (Illus.). ix, 135p. 1981. reprint ed. text ed. 55.00 (0-313-23055-2, PHLB, Greenwood Pr) Greenwood.
***Phillips, Judith.** Natural by Design: Beauty & Balance in Southwest Gardens. (Illus.). 1995. pap. 35.00 (0-89013-277-1) Museum NM Pr.
— Plants for Natural Gardens: Southwestern Native & Adaptive Trees, Shrubs, Wildflowers & Grasses. (Illus.). 1995. pap. 27.50 (0-89013-281-X) Museum NM Pr.
— Private Residential Care: The Admission Process & Reactions of the Public Sector. 278p. 1992. 55.95 (1-85628-188-4, Pub. by Avebury Pub UK) Ashgate Pub Co.
— Southwestern Landscaping with Native Plants. (Illus.). 160p. 1987. pap. 24.95 (0-89013-166-X) Museum NM Pr.
***Phillips, Julia.** Driving under the Affluence. Date not set. 24.00 (0-06-017304-1) HarpC.
— You'll Never Eat Lunch in This Town Again. 656p. 1992. pap. 6.99 (0-451-17072-5, Sig) NAL-Dutton.
— You'll Never Eat Lunch in This Town Again. 573p. 1990. 22.00 (0-394-57574-1) Random.
Phillips, Julie Anne, ed. see Phillips, Trevor M.
Phillips, June K., ed. Reflecting on Proficiency from the Classroom Perspective. (Reports of the Northeast Conference on the Teaching of Foreign Languages). 222p. 1993. pap. 12.95 (0-8442-9271-0) NE Conf Teach Foreign.
Phillips, June K., et al. Chez Vous, Chez Nous: Language in Action: First Year. 608p. (C). 1988. student ed 12.95 (0-685-18204-5); 12.95 (0-685-18205-3); text ed. write for info. (0-07-554123-8) McGraw.
Phillips, K. J. Dying Gods in Twentieth-Century Fiction. LC 88-48036. 256p. 1990. 37.50 (0-8387-5161-X) Bucknell U Pr.
Phillips, Kathleen. Creative Writing. 1985. 23.50 (0-87287-488-5) Libs Unl.
***Phillips, Kathleen C.** How to Write a Story. LC 95-2073. (Speak Out, Write On! Ser.). (Illus.). (YA). (gr. 7-12). 1995. lib. bdg. 14.35 (0-531-11239-X) Watts.
Phillips, Kathleen C. & Steiner, Barbara. Catching Ideas: Activity Book for Creative Writing. (Illus.). 164p. 1988. student ed 20.00 (0-87287-712-4) Libs Unl.
Phillips, Kathleen C., jt. auth. see Steiner, Barbara.
Phillips, Kathryn. Tracking the Vanishing Frogs: An Ecological Mystery. (Illus.). 256p. 1994. 22.95 (0-312-10973-3, Pub. by Thomas Dunne Bks) St Martin.
— Tracking the Vanishing Frogs: An Ecological Mystery. (Illus.). 256p. 1995. pap. 11.95 (0-14-024646-0, Penguin Bks) Viking Penguin.
Phillips, Kathy, jt. auth. see Stewart, Mary.
Phillips, Kathy J. Virginia Woolf Against Empire. (Illus.). 312p. (C). 1994. text ed. 34.95 (0-87049-833-9) U of Tenn Pr.
Phillips, Kay, jt. auth. see Rejai, Hostafa.
Phillips, Kay, jt. auth. see Rejai, Mostafa.
Phillips, Keith. Terror en el Ghetto: Everybody Is Afraid in the Ghetto. (SPA.). 4.95 (84-7228-233-3, 220871, Pub. by Edit Clie SP) TSELF.
Phillips, Keith, jt. ed. see Pitts, Marian.
***Phillips, Kelly A.** Diary of an Anorectic: A Young Woman's Struggle with Anorexia & Her Journey Toward Recovery. Keller, Victoria, ed. 139p. (Orig.). 1995. pap. 12.95 (0-9644527-0-7) Palm Bay Pub.
Phillips, Ken. Koalas: Australia's Ancient Ones. LC 94-14093. 1994. 27.50 (0-671-79777-8) S&S Trade.
Phillips, Kenneth. Open Computings Guide to UnixWare. Date not set. pap. text ed. 29.95 (0-07-882027-8) Osborne-McGraw.
Phillips, Kenneth D., jt. auth. see Burgard, Michael J.
Phillips, Kenneth H. Teaching Kids to Sing. (Illus.). 392p. 1992. text ed. 37.00 (0-02-871795-3) Schirmer Bks.
— Teaching Kids to Sing: Exercise & Vocalize Cards. (C). 1994. ring bd. 49.00 (0-02-871804-6) Schirmer Bks.
***Phillips, Kenneth J.** Guide to the Sun. (Illus.). 400p. (C). 1995. pap. 15.95 (0-521-39788-X) Cambridge U Pr.
Phillips, Kevin. The Arrogant Capital: Washington, Wall Street, & the Frustrations of American Politics. LC 94-10035. 1994. 22.95 (0-316-70618-3) Little.
Phillips, Kevin P. Boiling Point: Republicans, Democrats, & the Decline of Middle-Class Prosperity. 336p. 1994. pap. 13.00 (0-06-097582-2, PL) HarpC.
— The Politics of Rich & Poor: Wealth & the American Electorate in the Reagan Aftermath. 288p. 1990. 19.95 (0-394-55954-1) Random.
— Politics of Rich & Poor: Wealth & the American Electorate in the Reagan Aftermath. LC 90-56095. 320p. 1991. pap. 11.00 (0-06-097396-X, PL) HarpC.
Phillips, Kim T. William Duane, Radical Journalist in the Age of Jefferson. (Outstanding Studies in Early American History). 688p. 1989. reprint ed. 35.00 (0-8240-6193-4) Garland.
Phillips, Kyle M., Jr. In the Hills of Tuscany: Recent Excavations at the Etruscan Site of Poggio Civitate (Murlo, Siena) (Illus.). 144p. 1993. pap. 18.95 (0-934718-96-2) U PA Mus Pubns.
Phillips, Kyle M., Jr., jt. auth. see Ashmead, Ann H.
Phillips, L, intro. Peter Piper's Practical Principles of Plain & Perfect Pronunciation. (Illus.). 1970. reprint ed. pap. 2.95 (0-486-22560-7) Dover.
Phillips, L., jt. auth. see Emsley, James W.
Phillips, L. C. Bloodlines. LC 79-153403. 91p. 1971. 16.95 (0-912282-02-9) Pulse-Finger.
— Disco Candy & Other Stories. LC 78-72027. 210p. 1979. 16.95 (0-912282-07-X) Pulse-Finger.
— Sistine Cartoons. 2nd ed. LC 68-59442. 84p. 1970. 16.95 (0-912282-00-2) Pulse-Finger.
— Twelve Muscle Tones. 104p. 1980. 16.95 (0-912282-08-8) Pulse-Finger.
Phillips, L. K. Aviation for the Private Pilot. 1975. lib. bdg. 250.00 (0-87968-686-3) Gordon Pr.
Phillips, L. M. In the Desert - The Hiterland of Algiers. 352p. 1985. 240.00 (1-85077-072-7, Darf Pubs Ltd) St Mut.
Phillips, L. N., ed. Design with Advanced Composite Materials. (Illus.). 360p. 1990. 77.00 (0-387-51800-2, 3659) Spr-Verlag.
Phillips, Lance. Yonder Comes the Train. 1993. 24.98 (0-88365-715-5) Galahad Bks.
Phillips, Lance G. & Whitehead, Dana M., eds. Structure-Function Properties of Food Proteins. (Food Science & Technology International Ser.). (Illus.). 271p. 1994. text ed. 85.00 (0-12-554360-3) Acad Pr.
***Phillips, Larry W.** Madison Retro. Balousek, Marv, ed. 222p. (Orig.). 1994. pap. 12.95 (1-878569-22-8) Waubesa Pr.
Phillips, Laura. Beginnings. 224p. (Orig.). 1992. pap. 2.95 (1-56597-025-X, Kismet) Meteor Pub.
— Catch a Rising Star. 224p. (Orig.). 1991. pap. 2.75 (1-878702-39-4, Kismet) Meteor Pub.
— Moon Showers. 224p. (Orig.). 1992. pap. 2.95 (1-56597-014-4, Kismet) Meteor Pub.
— Never Let Go. 224p. (Orig.). 1990. pap. 2.75 (1-878702-21-1, Kismet) Meteor Pub.
— To Love a Cowboy. 224p. (Orig.). 1992. pap. 2.95 (1-878702-78-5, Kismet) Meteor Pub.
***Phillips, Lauren.** In the Name of the Patient: Consumer Advocacy in Health Care. 100p. (Orig.). 1995. pap. 45.00 (0-87258-679-0, 157800) Am Hospital.
***Phillips, Laurence.** Paris Scene 1995. 1995. pap. 12.95 (0-85449-220-8) InBook.
Phillips, Lawrence. French Entree: Paris, No. 11. 1993. pap. 11.95 (1-870948-81-5, Pub. by Quiller Pr UK) St Mut.
— French Entree Eleven Paris. 1993. pap. 29.95 (1-870948-83-1, Pub. by Quiller Pr UK) St Mut.
Phillips, Lawrence C., et al. Prentice Hall's Federal Taxation: 1994 Individuals. 1004p. (C). 1993. text ed. write for info. (0-13-720830-8) P-H.
Phillips, Leo A., ed. Viruses Associated with Human Cancer. LC 82-25240. (Illus.). 668p. reprint ed. pap. 180.00 (0-7837-3354-2, 2043312) Bks Demand.
Phillips, Leona. A Christmas Bibliography. 1977. lib. bdg. 250.00 (0-8490-1363-1) Gordon Pr.
— Colonial Days & the Revolutionary War: An Annotated Bibliography. 1976. lib. bdg. 250.00 (0-87968-337-6) Gordon Pr.
— Hitler: An Annotated Bibliography. 1976. lib. bdg. 250.00 (0-8490-1355-0) Gordon Pr.
Phillips, Leona & Phillips, Jill. Chinese History: An Annotated Bibliography. 1978. lib. bdg. 250.00 (0-8490-1391-7) Gordon Pr.
— Film Appreciation: An Outline & Study Guide for Colleges & Universities. 1978. lib. bdg. 250.00 (0-8490-1390-9) Gordon Pr.
Phillips, Leona, jt. auth. see Phillips, Jill.
Phillips, Leona R. Martin Luther & the Reformation: An Annotated Bibliography. 1985. lib. bdg. 250.00 (0-8490-3242-3) Gordon Pr.
— Silent Cinema: An Annotated Critical Bibliography. 1977. lib. bdg. 250.00 (0-8490-1368-2) Gordon Pr.
Phillips, Leonard, Jr. Urban Trees: A Guide for Selection, Maintenance, & Master Planning. LC 92-43723. 1993. text ed. 37.00 (0-07-049835-0) McGraw.
Phillips, Leyson K. Airlines of the World. 1979. lib. bdg. 250.00 (0-8490-1359-3) Gordon Pr.
Phillips, Lila L. Murder Can Be Relative. 242p. 1995. pap. 8.95 (1-56901-218-0) NW Pub.
Phillips, Linda. Concise Guide to Executive Etiquette. 1990. mass mkt. 9.95 (0-385-24766-4) Doubleday.
Phillips, Linda & Phillips, Wayne. Business Etiquette Essentials. 1988. 29.95 (0-87280-200-0, 3402, Asher-Gallant) Caddylak Systs.
Phillips, Linda C., ed. see Stewart, Paul W. & Ponce, Wallace Y.
Phillips, Linda M., jt. ed. see Norris, Stephen P.
***Phillips, Lisa.** Photoplay: Works from the Chase Manhattan Collection. Russell, Emily, ed. Guibert, Rita & Landers, Clifford, trs. (Illus.). 200p. 1992. 42.00 (0-9635340-1-7); pap. text ed. 28.50 (0-9635340-0-9) Chase Manhattan.
— Richard Prince. (Illus.). 192p. 1992. 50.00 (0-8109-6804-5) Abrams.
— Terry Winters. (Illus.). 204p. 1992. 75.00 (0-8109-3963-0) Abrams.
Phillips, Llad & Votey, Harold L. The Economics of Crime Control. LC 81-13588. (Sage Library of Social Research: No. 132). (Illus.). 312p. reprint ed. pap. 89.00 (0-8357-4845-6, 2037776) Bks Demand.
Phillips, Lois B. Wildlife Woodcraft. LC 78-5267. (Illus.). 64p. 1978. 12.95 (0-87961-067-0); pap. 4.95 (0-87961-066-2) Naturegraph.
Phillips, Louis. Alligator Wrestling & You: An Impractical Guide to an Impossible Sport. 96p. (Orig.). (J). (gr. 7-12). 1992. pap. 3.50 (0-380-76303-6, Camelot) Avon.
— Ask Me Anything about Baseball. LC 94-31034. (Avon Camelot Book Ser.). 96p. (Orig.). 1995. pap. 3.99 (0-380-78029-1, Camelot) Avon.
— Ask Me Anything about the Presidents. 144p. (Orig.). (YA). 1992. pap. 3.99 (0-380-76426-1, Camelot) Avon.
— Bulkington. (Hollow Spring Poetry Ser.). (Illus.). 32p. (Orig.). 1982. pap. 4.00 (0-936198-08-7) Hollow Spring Pr.
— The Continuing Education Guide: The CEU & Other Professional Development Criteria. 144p. (C). 1994. per., pap. text ed. 24.95 (0-8403-9351-2) Kendall-Hunt.
— A Dream of Countries Where No One Dare Live. LC 93-24851. 160p. (Orig.). 1993. 19.95 (0-87074-349-X); pap. 9.95 (0-87074-365-1) SMU Press.
— Going Ape: Jokes from the Jungle. (Illus.). 64p. (J). (gr. 2-7). 1988. pap. 10.95 (0-670-81520-9) Viking Child Bks.
— Haunted House Jokes. (Illus.). 64p. (J). (gr. 2-5). 1988. pap. 3.95 (0-14-032062-8, Puffin) Puffin Bks.
— How to Tell if Your Parents Are Aliens. 80p. (J). 1994. pap. 3.50 (0-380-77387-2, Camelot) Avon.
— Invisible Oink. (Illus.). 64p. (J). 1995. pap. 3.99 (0-14-036018-2) Puffin Bks.
— Invisible Oink: Pig Jokes. LC 92-24803. (Illus.). 64p. (J). 1993. 11.99 (0-670-84387-3) Viking Child Bks.
— The Random House Treasury of Best Loved Poems. 2nd ed. 1995. pap. 10.00 (0-679-76315-5, Random Ref) Random.
— The Random House Treasury of Light Verse. 1995. pap. 10.00 (0-679-76316-3, Random Ref) Random.
— School Daze: Jokes Your Teacher Will Hate! LC 93-41484. (Illus.). 64p. (J). (gr. 2-6). 1994. 11.99 (0-670-84929-4) Viking Child Bks.
— Singer in the White Pajamas. 29p. 1991. pap. 2.50 (0-87129-090-1, S97) Dramatic Pub.
— Two Hundred Sixty-Three Brain Busters: Just How Smart Are You, Anyway? LC 85-40446. (Novels Ser.). (Illus.). 87p. (J). (gr. 4-7). 1985. pap. 3.99 (0-14-031875-5, Puffin) Puffin Bks.
— The Upside down Riddle Book. LC 82-73. (Illus.). 32p. (J). (gr. k up). 1982. 14.95 (0-688-00931-X); lib. bdg. 14.88 (0-688-00932-8) Lothrop.
— Wackysaurus: Dinosaur Jokes. LC 93-15134. (Illus.). 64p. (J). (gr. 2-5). 1993. pap. 3.99 (0-14-034687-2, Puffin) Puffin Bks.
— Willie Shoemaker. LC 88-14966. (Sports Close-Ups 2 Ser.). (Illus.). 48p. (J). (gr. 5-6). 1988. text ed. 11.95 (0-89686-381-6, Crstwood Hse) Silver Burdett Pr.
Phillips, Louis, ed. Random House Treasury of Best Loved Poems. 1990. 10.00 (0-394-58688-3) Random.
Phillips, Louis & Holmes, Burnham. Sports Nicknames. LC 93-15170. 1994. 12.00 (0-671-85034-2) P-H Gen Ref & Trav.
— TV Almanac. LC 94-14094. 1994. 10.00 (0-671-88798-X) Macmillan.
Phillips, Louis, jt. auth. see Braden, Vic.
Phillips, Louis, jt. ed. see Cole, William.
Phillips, Louis, jt. auth. see Sweat, Lynn.
***Phillips, Louise.** The First Tulip of Spring. LC 95-60704. (Illus.). 40p. (J). (ps up). 1995. pap. 6.95 (1-883650-22-4) Windswept Hse.
Phillips, Louise S. The First Snowflake of Winter. LC 87-62210. (Illus.). 40p. (J). (gr. 5 up). 1987. pap. 6.95 (0-932433-37-5) Windswept Hse.
— The First Snowflake of Winter. LC 87-62210. (Illus.). 40p. (J). (gr. k-4). 1987. pap. 6.95 (0-932433-36-7) Windswept Hse.
Phillips, Lucinda M., ed. see Tamayo, Reve, pseud.
Phillips, Lynn. Drug Abuse. LC 93-44346. (Life Issues Ser.: Vol. 8). (J). 1994. 14.95 (1-85435-617-8) Marshall Cavendish.
Phillips, Lynn D. Manual of I. V. Therapeutics. (Illus.). 566p. (C). 1993. pap. text ed., spiral bd. 24.95 (0-8036-6911-9) Davis Co.
Phillips, M. Aspects of Text Structure. (Linguistic Ser.: Vol. 52). 1985. 84.75 (0-444-87701-0, North Holland) Elsevier.
Phillips, M. & Tomkinson, W. S. English Women in Life & Letters. LC 72-151974. (Illus.). 1972. reprint ed. 23.95 (0-405-08856-6) Ayer.
Phillips, M. H., ed. Physical Aspects of Stereotactic Radiosurgery. 1993. 59.50 (0-306-44535-2, Plenum Med Bk) Plenum.
Phillips, M. J., jt. auth. see Ansell, J. I.
Phillips, M. James, et al. The Liver: An Atlas & Text of Ultrastructural Pathology. (Illus.). 604p. 1987. text ed. 140.50 (0-88167-302-1) Raven.
Phillips, M. T. & Sechzer, J. A. Animal Research & Ethical Conflict. (Illus.). 250p. 1989. 84.00 (0-387-96935-7, 2512) Spr-Verlag.
Phillips, Maggie & Frederick, Claire. Healing the Divided Self: Clinical & Ericksonian Hypnotherapy for Post-Traumatic & Dissociative Conditions. 384p. 1995. 40.00 (0-393-70184-0) Norton.
Phillips, Maggie, jt. auth. see Sturkie, Joan.
***Phillips, Marcus & Long, Sandra.** Indian Folklore Atlas of Hot Springs National Park. (Illus.). 195p. (Orig.). 1994. pap. 20.00 (0-929604-76-8) Arkansas Ancestors.
Phillips, Margaret. Songs of the Good Earth. LC 79-10731. 62p. 1980. pap. 5.95 (0-88289-221-5) Pelican.
Phillips, Margaret E. Letters to Barbara Bush. 152p. (Orig.). 1992. pap. 9.95 (0-943487-38-2) Sevgo Pr.
Phillips, Margaret I. Governors of Tennessee. LC 77-26845. (Governors of the States Ser.). (Illus.). 193p. (J). (gr. 6-12). 1978. 17.95 (0-88289-169-3) Pelican.
Phillips, Margaret M. Willingly to School. (C). 1989. text ed. 35.00 (0-948929-23-5) St Mut.
Phillips, Margaret M., tr. see Erasmus.
Phillips, Marian, tr. see Von Sacher-Masoch, Wanda.
***Phillips, Marianne O.** Pin-up Poster Book: The Elvgren Collection. (Illus.). 48p. (Orig.). Date not set. pap. 21.95 (0-9635202-5-3) Collectors Pr.
— Pin-up Poster Book: The Elvgren Collection. limited ed. (Illus.). 48p. (Orig.). Date not set. 75.00 (0-9635202-6-1) Collectors Pr.
Phillips, Marilyn, jt. auth. see Phillips, Mike.

An Asterisk (*) at the beginning of an entry indicates that the title is appearing in BIP for the first time.

Phillips, Marion. Colonial Autocracy: New South Wales under Governor Macquarie, 1810-1821. 336p. 1971. reprint ed. 35.00 (*0-7146-2658-9*, Pub. by F Cass Pubs UK) Intl Spec Bk.

Phillips, Marion, jt. auth. see Henderson, Stephanie.

Phillips, Marjorie. Duncan Phillips & His Collection. (Illus.). 1982. 35.00 (*0-393-01608-0*) Norton.

— Duncan Phillips & His Collection. (Illus.). 1982. pap. 18. 95 (*0-393-30041-2*) Norton.

— Marjorie Phillips & Her Paintings. Partridge, Sylvia, ed. (Illus.). 1985. 35.00 (*0-393-02290-0*) Norton.

Phillips, Mark. Francesco Guicciardini: The Historian's Craft. LC 76-56341. 208p. reprint ed. pap. 59.30 (*0-685-16335-0*, 2026439) Bks Demand.

— The Memoir of Marco Parenti. 320p. 1987. text ed. 49.50 (*0-691-05502-5*) Princeton U Pr.

— The Memoir of Marco Parenti: A Life in Medici Florence. 298p. 1989. pap. text ed. 14.95 (*0-691-00833-7*) Princeton U Pr.

Phillips, Mark, ed. Anthrax - Fistful of Metal: Guitar - Vocal. (Illus.). 63p. (Orig.). 1990. pap. text ed. 16.95 (*0-89524-493-4*) Cherry Lane.

— The Authentic Guitar Style of Suzanne Vega. (Illus.). 56p. (Orig.). 1990. pap. text ed. 12.95 (*0-89524-375-X*) Cherry Lane.

— The Best of Quiet Riot (Guitar - Vocal) (Illus.). 63p. (Orig.). 1990. pap. text ed. 12.95 (*0-89524-381-4*) Cherry Lane.

— Best of the Best. (Easy Guitar Ser.). (Illus.). 63p. (Orig.). 1990. pap. text ed. 10.95 (*0-89524-368-7*) Cherry Lane.

— Boston - Third Stage: Guitar Edition. (Illus.). 80p. (Orig.). 1990. pap. text ed. 14.95 (*0-89524-334-2*) Cherry Lane.

— The Erroll Garner Songbook, Vol. 1: Piano - Vocal. (Illus.). 94p. (Orig.). 1990. pap. text ed. 12.95 (*0-89524-030-0*) Cherry Lane.

— The Erroll Garner Songbook, Vol. 2: Piano - Vocal. (Illus.). 77p. (Orig.). 1990. pap. text ed. 14.95 (*0-89524-330-X*) Cherry Lane.

— Faster Pussycat (Guitar - Vocal) (Illus.). 53p. (Orig.). 1990. pap. text ed. 14.95 (*0-89524-399-7*) Cherry Lane.

— Guns n' Roses - Appetite for Destruction: Bass Guitar. (Illus.). (Orig.). 1990. pap. text ed. 14.95 (*0-89524-416-0*) Cherry Lane.

— Guns n' Roses - Appetite for Destruction: Guitar - Vocal. (Illus.). (Orig.). 1990. pap. text ed. 14.95 (*0-89524-564-7*); pap. text ed. 14.95 (*0-89524-386-5*) Cherry Lane.

— Guns n' Roses - The Spaghetti Incident? 1994. pap. 22.95 (*0-89524-826-3*) Cherry Lane.

— Heavy Metal Ballads: Guitar - Vocal. (Illus.). 94p. (Orig.). 1990. pap. text ed. 14.95 (*0-89524-446-2*) Cherry Lane.

— Heavy Metal Guitar, Vol. 3. (Illus.). 111p. (Orig.). 1990. pap. text ed. 14.95 (*0-89524-389-X*) Cherry Lane.

— Heavy Metal in the Hot One Hundred: Guitar - Vocal. (Illus.). 126p. (Orig.). 1990. pap. text ed. 14.95 (*0-89524-521-3*) Cherry Lane.

— Heavy Metal Mixed Bag: Guitar Edition. (Illus.). 118p. (Orig.). 1990. pap. text ed. 16.95 (*0-89524-470-5*) Cherry Lane.

— Hot Metal: Guitar Vocal. (Illus.). 126p. (Orig.). 1990. pap. text ed. 14.95 (*0-89524-412-8*) Cherry Lane.

— Hot Metal (Guitar - Vocal), Vol. II. (Illus.). 111p. (Orig.). 1990. pap. text ed. 14.95 (*0-89524-439-X*) Cherry Lane.

— Lita - Lita Ford (Guitar - Vocal) (Illus.). 51p. (Orig.). 1990. pap. text ed. 12.95 (*0-89524-394-6*) Cherry Lane.

— The Love Songs of John Denver (Piano - Vocal) (Illus.). 79p. (Orig.). 1990. pap. text ed. 9.95 (*0-89524-378-4*) Cherry Lane.

— Metallica - Master of Puppets: Guitar - Vocal. (Illus.). (Orig.). 1990. pap. text ed. 14.95 (*0-89524-565-5*); pap. text ed. 14.95 (*0-89524-358-X*) Cherry Lane.

— Metallica - Master of Puppets (Bass Guitar) (Illus.). 55p. (Orig.). 1990. pap. text ed. 14.95 (*0-89524-408-X*) Cherry Lane.

— Metallica Riff by Riff: Guitar. 1994. pap. 17.95 (*0-89524-840-9*) Cherry Lane.

— The Music of Richard Marx: Easy Guitar. (Illus.). 52p. (Orig.). 1990. pap. text ed. 10.95 (*0-89524-500-0*) Cherry Lane.

— Overkill - The Years of Decay. pap. 17.95 (*0-89524-553-1*); pap. 14.95 (*0-89524-597-3*) Cherry Lane.

— Richard Daniels - Be Dangerous on Rock Guitar. (Illus.). 146p. (Orig.). 1990. pap. text ed. 15.95 (*0-89524-314-8*) Cherry Lane.

— Rock Guitar. (Illus.). 93p. (Orig.). 1990. pap. text ed. 10. 95 (*0-89524-371-7*) Cherry Lane.

— Tesla - Mechanical Resonance: Bass Guitar. (Illus.). 71p. (Orig.). 1990. pap. text ed. 14.95 (*0-89524-429-2*) Cherry Lane.

— Tesla - Mechanical Resonance: Guitar - Vocal. (Illus.). 70p. (Orig.). 1990. pap. text ed. 16.95 (*0-89524-393-8*) Cherry Lane.

— Tom Paxton - Anthology (Piano - Vocal) (Illus.). 63p. 1990. pap. text ed. 10.95 (*0-89524-390-3*) Cherry Lane.

— Van Halen II. pap. 19.95 (*0-89524-715-1*) Cherry Lane.

— Van Halen Live - Right Here, Right Now. 1994. pap. 29. 95 (*0-89524-787-9*) Cherry Lane.

— Van Halen One & Two (Piano - Vocal) (Illus.). 95p. (Orig.). 1990. pap. text ed. 14.95 (*0-89524-436-5*) Cherry Lane.

Phillips, Mark & Aledort, Andy, eds. Heavy Metal Guitar, Vol. 2. (Illus.). 118p. (Orig.). 1990. pap. text ed. 14.95 (*0-89524-356-3*) Cherry Lane.

***Phillips, Mark & Garcia, Frank.** Science Fiction Television Series: Episode Guides, Histories, & Casts & Credits for 62 Prime Time Shows, 1959-1989. 680p. 1995. lib. bdg. 75.00 (*0-7864-0041-2*) McFarland & Co.

Phillips, Mark & Marshall, Wolf, eds. Ozzy Ozbourne - Randy Rhoads Tribute: Guitar - Vocal. (Illus.). 127p. (Orig.). 1990. pap. text ed. 22.95 (*0-89524-347-4*) Cherry Lane.

Phillips, Mark, ed. see Black Crowes.

Phillips, Mark, ed. see Burgie, Irving.

Phillips, Mark, jt. ed. see Chappell, John.

Phillips, Mark, jt. ed. see Crystal, Michael.

Phillips, Mark, ed. see Guns N' Roses.

Phillips, Mark, jt. ed. see Okun, Milt.

Phillips, Mark, et al, eds. America Takes Note: Official Menc Songbook: Piano - Vocal. (Illus.). 112p. (Orig.). (YA). 1988. pap. text ed. 14.95 (*0-89524-369-5*) Cherry Lane.

Phillips, Mark M., jt. ed. see Blanco, Victor M.

Phillips, Marshall, jt. ed. see Jorgenson, James W.

Phillips, Marshall, et al, eds. The Impact of Chemistry on Biotechnology: Multidisciplinary Discussions. LC 87-30751. (Symposium Ser.: No. 362). (Illus.). xiii, 398p. 1987. 87.95 (*0-8412-1446-8*) Am Chemical.

Phillips, Martin A. The Official National Table Hockey League Handbook, Vol. 1. Phillips, Zoe A., ed. LC 89-91696. (Illus.). 66p. (Orig.). (YA). (gr. 12). 1989. write for info. (*0-9623588-0-0*); pap. write for info. (*0-9623588-1-9*) Gnu Wine Pr.

Phillips, Marvin. The Joy Factor of Church Growth. 141p. (Orig.). 1988. pap. 7.95 (*1-878990-01-2*) Howard Pub LA.

— Put Peak in Your Week. 145p. (Orig.). 1985. pap. 6.95 (*1-878990-06-3*) Howard Pub LA.

Phillips, Mary, jt. auth. see MacKenzie, Judith-Anne.

Phillips, Mary W. Creative Knitting. LC 72-110061. 1986. pap. 16.00 (*0-932394-06-X*) Dos Tejedoras.

— Knitting Counterpanes: Traditional Coverlet Patterns for Contemporary Knitters. 1991. 22.50 (*0-8446-6438-3*) Peter Smith.

— Knitting Counterpanes: Traditional Coverlet Patterns for Contemporary Knitters. Timmons, Christine, ed. LC 88-51354. (Illus.). 192p. 1989. pap. 19.95 (*0-918804-98-1*) Taunton.

Phillips, Matt. X-Rated Riddles. 1981. pap. 2.95 (*0-8431-0540-2*) Putnam Pub Group.

Phillips-Matz, Mary J. Verdi: A Biography. LC 92-37841. (C). 1993. 45.00 (*0-19-313204-4*) OUP.

Phillips, Maurice E. Guide to the Manuscript Collections in the Academy of Natural Sciences of Philadelphia. (Special Publication: No. 5). (Illus.). 553p. 1963. lib. bdg. 10.00 (*0-910006-33-4*) Acad Nat Sci Phila.

Phillips, Maurice E., ed. Minutes & Correspondence of the Academy of Natural Sciences of Philadelphia: 1812-1924, Microfilm Publication Guide. (Special Publication: No. 7). 92p. (Orig.). 1967. pap. 5.00 (*0-910006-35-0*) Acad Nat Sci Phila.

***Phillips, McCandlish.** The Bible, the Supernatural & the Jews. 368p. 1995. pap. 10.99 (*0-88965-115-9*, Pub. by Horizon Books CN) Chr Pubns.

Phillips-McClenahan, Sallie. Touchstones. LC 82-11454. (Illus.). 300p. (Orig.). 1982. pap. 8.95 (*0-87233-066-4*) Bauhan.

Phillips, Melanie, jt. auth. see Dawson, John.

Phillips, Melba, ed. The Life & Times of Modern Physics: History of Physics II. LC 92-12669. (Readings from Physics Today Ser.: No. 4). 1992. 40.00 (*0-88318-846-5*) Am Inst Physics.

— On Teaching Physics. 192p. 1980. 18.00 (*0-318-41540-2*, OP17) Am Assn Physics.

— Physics History from AAPT Journals. 240p. 1986. 18.00 (*0-318-41542-9*, OP54) Am Assn Physics.

Phillips, Melba, jt. auth. see Panofsky, Wolfgang K.

Phillips, Melba, jt. intro. see Weart, Spencer.

***Phillips, Michael.** Alternative Man: Poems & Stories by Michael Phillips. 1995. pap. 8.95 (*0-9636829-5-4*) Mother Road.

— Dawn of Liberty. LC 95-14556. (Secret of the Rose Ser.: Vol. 4). 1995. write for info. (*0-8423-5959-1*); pap. write for info. (*0-8423-5958-3*) Tyndale.

— Depths of Destiny. 1992. pap. 11.99 (*0-8024-6319-3*) Moody.

— DisCourses: More Readings for Thinkers on Airplanes. Speer, Tom, ed. LC 89-92418. (Illus.). 142p. (Orig.). 1990. pap. 10.00 (*0-931425-19-0*) Clear Glass.

— The Eleventh Hour. LC 93-4858. (Secret of the Rose Ser.: Vol. 1). 1993. pap. 11.99 (*0-8423-3933-7*) Tyndale.

— The Eleventh Hour. LC 93-4858. (Secret of the Rose Ser.: No. 1). 504p. 1994. 16.99 (*0-8423-3932-9*) Tyndale.

— Escape to Freedom. LC 94-23235. (The Secret of the Rose Ser.: No. 3). 1994. pap. 11.99 (*0-8423-5942-7*) Tyndale.

— Flight from Stonewycke. 1994. pap. 5.99 (*1-55661-453-5*) Bethany Hse.

— A God to Call Father: Discovering Mountaintop Intimacy with God. LC 94-3611. 1994. 14.99 (*0-8423-1392-3*) Tyndale.

— Good Things to Remember. 160p. (Orig.). 1993. 5.99 (*1-55661-337-7*) Bethany Hse.

— Grayfox. 1993. pap. 8.99 (*1-55661-368-7*) Bethany Hse.

— Heather Hills of Stonewycke. (Orig.). 1993. pap. 5.99 (*1-55661-373-3*) Bethany Hse.

— Home for My Heart. 1994. pap. 8.99 (*1-55661-440-3*) Bethany Hse.

— Into the Long Dark Night. (Journals of Corrie Belle Hollister). 304p. (Orig.). 1992. pap. 8.99 (*1-55661-300-8*) Bethany Hse.

— Lady of Stoneswycke. 1994. pap. text ed. 5.99 (*1-55661-521-3*) Bethany Hse.

— Land of the Brave & the Free. (Corrie Belle Hollister Ser.). 304p. (Orig.). (YA). 1993. pap. 8.99 (*1-55661-308-3*) Bethany Hse.

— Mental Snacks: Readings for Thinkers on Airplanes. 2nd ed. LC 87-72261. (Illus.). 152p. 1988. pap. 10.00 (*0-931425-12-3*) Clear Glass.

— Pinnacles of Power. 1991. pap. 10.99 (*0-8024-6327-4*) Moody.

— A Rose Remembered. LC 94-4351. (Secret of the Rose Ser.: Vol. 2). 1994. 11.99 (*0-8423-5929-X*) Tyndale.

— The Seven Laws of Money. LC 93-521. (Pocket Classics Ser.). 288p. 1993. reprint ed. pap. 6.00 (*0-87773-949-8*) Shambhala Pubns.

— Stranger at Stonewycke. 1995. pap. 6.99 (*1-55661-581-7*) Bethany Hse.

— To Be a Father Like the Father. LC 91-76511. 309p. 1992. 8.99 (*0-87509-475-9*) Chr Pubns.

Phillips, Michael & Campbell, Catherine. Simple Living Investments: For True Security & Adventure in Old Age. rev. ed. LC 84-71943. 72p. 1988. pap. 6.00 (*0-931425-00-X*) Clear Glass.

Phillips, Michael & Pella, Judith. The Crown & the Crucible. (Russians Ser.: Bk. 1). 448p. (Orig.). 1991. pap. 9.99 (*1-55661-172-2*) Bethany Hse.

— Daughter of Grace. large type ed. 1995. 20.95 (*0-7838-1179-9*, Large Print Bks) Hall.

— Flight from Stonewycke. LC 85-15836. (Stonewycke Trilogy Ser.). 196p. 1985. pap. 7.99 (*0-87123-837-3*) Bethany Hse.

— A House Divided. (Russians Ser.). 400p. (Orig.). (YA). 1992. pap. 9.99 (*1-55661-173-0*) Bethany Hse.

— Journals of Corrie Belle Hollister, Set. (Orig.). (YA). 1992. Giftset. pap. 44.99 (*1-55661-766-6*) Bethany Hse.

— My Father's World. (Journals of Corrie Belle Hollister). 288p. (Orig.). 1990. pap. 8.99 (*1-55661-104-8*) Bethany Hse.

— My Father's World. large type ed. LC 94-14261. 366p. (Orig.). 1994. 20.95 (*0-8161-5994-7*) Hall.

— On the Trail of Truth: The Journal of Corrie Belle Hollister. 288p. (Orig.). 1991. pap. 8.99 (*1-55661-106-4*) Bethany Hse.

— A Place in the Sun. (Journals of Corrie Belle Hollister: Bk. 5). 320p. (Orig.). (YA). (gr. 9 up). 1991. pap. 8.99 (*1-55661-222-2*) Bethany Hse.

— The Russians 1-3 Giftset. (Russians Ser.). (YA). 1992. 29. 99 (*1-55661-770-4*) Bethany Hse.

— Sea to Shining Sea. (Journals of Corrie Belle Hollister). 304p. (Orig.). (YA). 1992. pap. 8.99 (*1-55661-227-3*) Bethany Hse.

— Shadows over Stonewycke. (Stonewycke Legacy Ser.: Bk. 2). 400p. (Orig.). 1995. mass mkt. 6.99 (*1-55661-632-5*) Bethany Hse.

— The Stonewycke Trilogy, Set. 1989. Boxed set. boxed 23. 99 (*0-87123-971-X*) Bethany Hse.

— Travail & Triumph. (Russians Ser.). 400p. (Orig.). 1992. pap. 9.99 (*1-55661-174-9*) Bethany Hse.

— Travail & Triumph Vol. 3: The Russians. braille ed. 676p. 1994. text ed. 54.08 (*1-56956-480-9*, BR9336) W A T Braille.

— Treasure of Stonewycke. (Stonewycke Legacy Ser.). 352p. (Orig.). (YA). (gr. 11 up). 1988. pap. 8.99 (*0-87123-902-7*) Bethany Hse.

— Treasure of Stonewycke. (Stonewycke Legacy Ser.: Bk. 3). 400p. (Orig.). 1995. mass mkt. 6.99 (*1-55661-634-1*) Bethany Hse.

Phillips, Michael & Pella, Judy. Heather Hills of Stonewycke. LC 84-29771. (Stonewycke Trilogy Ser.). 280p. (Orig.). 1985. pap. 7.99 (*0-87123-803-9*) Bethany Hse.

Phillips, Michael & Rasberry, Salli. Honest Business. 1981. pap. 9.00 (*0-394-74830-1*) Random.

— Marketing Without Advertising. LC 86-62659. (Orig.). 1989. pap. 14.00 (*0-87337-019-8*) Nolo Pr.

Phillips, Michael, ed. see Brown, James B.

Phillips, Michael, jt. auth. see Callenbach, A. Ernest.

Phillips, Michael, ed. see Connor, Ralph.

Phillips, Michael, ed. see MacDonald, George.

Phillips, Michael, jt. auth. see MacDonald, George.

Phillips, Michael, ed. see MacDonald, George.

Phillips, Michael, et al. The Seven Laws of Money. 1974. pap. 9.00 (*0-394-70686-2*) Random.

Phillips, Michael J. The Dilemmas of Individualism: Status, Liberty, & American Constitutional Law. LC 82-15580. (Contributions in American Studies: No. 67). x, 226p. 1983. text ed. 55.00 (*0-313-23690-9*, PSF/, Greenwood Pr) Greenwood.

— Dreamgirls. (Poetry Ser.). (Illus.). 80p. (Orig.). 1989. pap. 7.00 (*0-918342-27-9*) Cambric.

— Selected Concrete Poems. (Cambric Poetry Ser.). 108p. (Orig.). 1986. pap. 11.95 (*0-918342-25-2*) Cambric.

— Superbeasts. 64p. (Orig.). 1983. pap. 5.00 (*0-918342-19-8*) Cambric.

Phillips, Michael J., jt. auth. see Fisher, Bruce D.

Phillips, Michael R. George Macdonald: Scotland's Beloved Storyteller. 1994. pap. 13.99 (*1-55661-403-9*) Bethany Hse.

Phillips, Michael R. & Pella, Judith. A Daughter of Grace. (Journals of Corrie Belle Hollister). 288p. (Orig.). 1990. pap. 8.99 (*1-55661-105-6*) Bethany Hse.

— Robbie Taggart, Highland Sailor. LC 87-29913. (Highland Collection Ser.). 356p. (Orig.). 1987. pap. 7.99 (*0-87123-919-1*) Bethany Hse.

— Shadows over Stonewycke. LC 88-10332. (Stonewycke Legacy Fiction Ser.). 356p. (Orig.). 1988. pap. 8.99 (*0-87123-901-9*) Bethany Hse.

Phillips, Michael R., ed. see Connor, Ralph.

Phillips, Michael R., ed. see MacDonald, George.

Phillips, Michael R., jt. auth. see MacDonald, George.

Phillips, Michael R., ed. see Wright, Harold B.

Phillips, Michelle & Pella, Judith. Stonewycke Legacy Giftset, 3 bks., Set. (Orig.). 1988. pap. 26.99 (*1-55661-755-0*) Bethany Hse.

Phillips, Mike. The Coat Holder. LC 84-24251. 1986. 13.95 (*0-87949-248-1*) Ashley Bks.

— Control Through Planned Budgeting: An Alternative Approach to Inventory Control & Ordering Procedures in the Christian Bookstore. 1978. pap. 12.95 (*0-940652-01-3*) Sunrise Bks.

— Point of Darkness: A Sam Dean Mystery. LC 94-44491. 1995. 21.95 (*0-312-11875-9*) St Martin.

— A Vision for the Church. 110p. 1981. pap. 3.95 (*0-940652-02-1*) Sunrise Bks.

Phillips, Mike & Pella, Judy. Jamie Macleod: Highland Lass. LC 86-33377. 356p. 1987. pap. 7.99 (*0-87123-918-3*) Bethany Hse.

— The Lady of Stonewycke. LC 85-30748. (Stonewycke Trilogy Ser.). 250p. (Orig.). 1986. pap. 7.99 (*0-87123-856-X*) Bethany Hse.

— Stranger at Stonewycke. LC 87-6605. (Stonewycke Legacy Ser.). 356p. (Orig.). 1987. pap. 8.99 (*0-87123-900-0*) Bethany Hse.

***Phillips, Mike & Phillips, Marilyn.** Gifta for Livet. Smedberg, Jan-Olaf, tr. 195p. (Orig.). (SWE.). 1994. pap. text ed. write for info. (*1-884794-09-2*) Eden Pubng.

Phillips, Mike, ed. see MacDonald, George.

Phillips, Mike, jt. auth. see MacDonald, George.

Phillips, Mike, ed. see MacDonald, George.

Phillips, Mildred. The Sign in Mendel's Window. LC 85-5049. (Illus.). 32p. (J). (gr. k-3). 1985. text ed. 13.95 (*0-02-774600-3*, Mac Bks Young Read) S&S Childrens.

Phillips, Millie. What Color Will Bear Wear? 12p. (J). 1989. 4.95 (*0-8167-1602-1*) Troll Assocs.

— What Will Rabbit Do? 12p. (J). 1989. 4.95 (*0-8167-1600-5*) Troll Assocs.

— What's It for Anyhow? 12p. (J). 1989. 4.95 (*0-8167-1603-X*) Troll Assocs.

— Where Does a Pig Live? 12p. (J). 1989. 4.95 (*0-8167-1601-3*) Troll Assocs.

Phillips, N. C. Equivariant K-Theory & Freeness of Group Actions on C Algebras. (Lecture Notes in Mathematics Ser.: Vol. 1274). viii, 371p. 1987. pap. 47.90 (*0-387-18277-2*) Spr-Verlag.

Phillips, N. V., jt. auth. see Hazewindus, Nico.

Phillips, N. V., jt. ed. see Smedema, C. H.

Phillips, Nadezha M., tr. see Goldenberg, L. A.

Phillips, Nancy, ed. see Miller, O. Victor.

Phillips, Nancy H. Choosing Schools & Child Care Options: Answering Parents' Questions. LC 94-19163. (Illus.). 112p. (C). 1994. 34.95 (*0-398-05923-3*) C C Thomas.

— Choosing Schools & Child Care Options: Answering Parents' Questions. LC 94-19163. (Illus.). 112p. (C). 1994. pap. 19.95 (*0-398-05969-1*) C C Thomas.

Phillips, Nancy O., ed. see Parsons, Richard & Brooks, Neal A.

Phillips, Nancy V. & Van Andel, Mary T. Journeying Together: A Study on the Psalms. write for info. (*0-916466-03-5*) Reformed Church.

Phillips, Nancy V., et al. Network Models in Optimization & Their Applications in Practice. (Wiley-Interscience Series in Discrete Mathematics & Optimization). 304p. 1992. text ed. 74.95 (*0-471-57138-5*) Wiley.

***Phillips, Nicola.** Counselling for Change: Coaching & Motivating Your Team. (Institute of Management Ser.). 250p. 1995. pap. 43.50 (*0-273-61176-3*, Pub. by Pitman Pub Ltd UK) Trans-Atl Phila.

— From Vision to Beyond Teamwork: Ten Ways to Wake up & Shake up Your Company. LC 94-3390. 250p. 1994. 25.00 (*0-7863-0318-2*) Irwin Prof Pubng.

— Innovative Management: A Pragmatic Guide to New Technique. (Financial Times Management Ser.). 224p. 1993. 111.00x (*0-273-60025-7*, Pub. by Pitman Pubng UK) St Mut.

— Managing International Teams. 228p. 1993. text ed. 35.00 (*0-7863-0004-3*) Irwin Prof Pubng.

Phillips, Nicola, jt. auth. see Sidney, Elizabeth.

Phillips, Nigel. Sijobang: Sung Narrative Poetry of West Sumatra. LC 80-42227. (Cambridge Studies in Oral & Literate Culture: No. 1). (Illus.). 248p. 1981. 74.95 (*0-521-23737-8*) Cambridge U Pr.

Phillips, Norma. Adventures of a "Wild" Plants Woman: In Pursuit of Native Plant Preservation. LC 88-51160. (Illus.). 236p. (Orig.). (C). 1988. pap. text ed. 12.95 (*0-9622758-1-6*) Little Bridge.

— The Root Book: How to Plant Wildflowers. LC 83-91289. (Illus.). 118p. (Orig.). (C). 1983. spiral bd. 9.50 (*0-9622758-0-8*) Little Bridge.

Phillips, O. M. Flow & Reactions in Permeable Rocks. (Illus.). 208p. (C). 1991. 64.95 (*0-521-38098-7*) Cambridge U Pr.

Phillips, O. M. & Hasselmann, Klaus, eds. Wave Dynamics & Radio Probing of the Ocean Surface. 687p. 1986. 120. 00 (*0-306-41992-0*, Plenum Pr) Plenum.

Phillips, O. S. Isaac Nathan: Jewish Musician & Friend of Byron. 1976. lib. bdg. 34.95 (*0-8490-2078-6*) Gordon Pr.

***Phillips, O. Virginia.** Ashes to Life. Snell, Mikki, ed. (Illus.). 103p. (Orig.). (YA). 1994. lib. bdg. 4.95 (*0-9641507-0-0*) Fmily Connect.

Phillips, Owen R., jt. auth. see Maurice, S. Charles.

Phillips, P. Lee. A List of Books, Magazine Articles & Maps Relating to Central America. 109p. 1984. reprint ed. pap. 12.50 (*0-913129-11-9*) La Tienda.

— Notes on the Life & Works of Bernard Romans. Ware, John, ed. LC 74-20757. (Floridiana Facsimile & Reprint Ser.). (Illus.). 1975. reprint ed. 19.95 (*0-8130-0413-6*) U Press Fla.

Phillips, Pamela I. Heartache & Tears. 48p. 1994. pap. 10. 95 (*0-8059-3498-7*) Dorrance.

— When the Moon Peeps In. (J). 1994. 7.95 (*0-533-10982-5*) Vantage.

Phillips, Patricia. The Constant Flame. 448p. (Orig.). 1993. pap. 4.99 (0-8439-3454-9) Dorchester Pub Co.
— Nightingale. 448p. (Orig.). 1991. pap. 4.50 (0-8439-3078-0) Dorchester Pub Co.
— The Rose & The Flame. 448p. 1992. pap. 4.50 (0-8439-3309-7) Dorchester Pub Co.
***Phillips, Patricia & Mair, George.** Divorce: A Guide for Women: What Every Woman Needs to Know about Getting a Fair Divorce Even When She Thinks She Doesn't Need to Know It. LC 95-5872. 1995. write for info. (0-671-50057-0) Macmillan.
Phillips, Patricia C. Jackie Ferrara: Traversing Space. Nesbitt, Perry L., ed. & intro. by. (Illus.). 6p. (Orig.). 1993. pap. 20.00x (0-941972-13-5) Freedman.
***Phillips, Patricia S.** Life in Illisconsin: 1927-1951. (Illus.). 224p. (Orig.). 1995. pap. write for info. (0-9647032-0-3) Whispering Pn.
Phillips, Patrick L. Developing with Recreational Amenities: Golf, Tennis, Skiing, & Marinas. 257p. 1986. pap. 56.95 (0-87420-664-2, D44) Urban Land.
Phillips, Paul C., ed. see Stuart, Granville.
Phillips, Paul J., jt. auth. see Boyd, Richard H.
***Phillips, Paul T.** A Kingdom on Earth: Anglo-American Social Christianity, 1880-1940. LC 95-14590. 1996. write for info. (0-271-01497-0) Pa St U Pr.
Phillips, Paul T., jt. ed. see Helmstadter, Richard J.
Phillips, Peggy A. Modern France: Theories & Realities of Urban Planning. LC 86-28225. (Illus.). 262p. (Orig.). 1987. pap. text ed. 25.50 (0-8191-6038-5) U Pr of Amer.
— Republican France: Divided Loyalties. LC 92-45075. (Contributions in Political Science Ser.: No. 325). 208p. 1993. text ed. 52.95 (0-313-27503-3, PCJ, Greenwood Pr) Greenwood.
Phillips, Percival. Red Dragon & the Black Shirts: How Italy Found Her Soul, the True Story of the Fascisti Movement. 1982. lib. bdg. 69.95 (0-87700-349-1) Revisionist Pr.
Phillips, Peter & Bunce, Gillian. Repeat Patterns: A Manual for Designers, Artists & Architects. LC 92-70864. (Illus.). 192p. 1993. pap. 19.95 (0-500-27687-0) Thames Hudson.
Phillips, Peter, jt. ed. see Richner, Hans.
Phillips, Peter C., ed. Models, Methods, & Applications of Econometrics: Essays in Honor of A. R. Bergstrom. LC 92-27177. 1993. 74.95 (1-55786-110-2) Blackwell Pubs.
Phillips, Peter W. Wheat, Europe & the GATT: A Political Economy Analysis. LC 90-37799. 272p. 1990. text ed. 49.95 (0-312-05038-0) St Martin.
***Phillips, Phil.** Angels, Angels, Angels - Embraced by the Light...or...Embraced by the Darkness? 320p. 1995. pap. 10.95 (0-914984-65-9) Starburst.
— Dinosaurs: The Bible, Barney & Beyond. 200p. 1995. pap. 9.95 (0-914984-59-4) Starburst.
— Halloween & Satanism. 208p. 1987. pap. 9.95 (0-914984-11-X) Starburst.
— Horror & Violence: The Deadly Duo in the Media. 256p. 1988. pap. 9.95 (0-914984-16-0) Starburst.
— The Truth about Power Rangers. 96p. (Orig.). 1995. pap. 6.95 (0-914984-67-5) Starburst.
— Turmoil in the Box. 1986. vhs 34.95 (0-00-656358-9) Starburst.
— Turmoil in the Box. 208p. 1986. pap. 9.95 (0-914984-04-7) Starburst.
Phillips, Philip L. A List of Books, Magazine Articles & Maps Relating to Brazil. (Brazil Ser.). 1979. lib. bdg. 44.95 (0-8490-2962-7) Gordon Pr.
Phillips, Phillip D. Economic Development for Small Communities & Rural Areas. Kozoll, Charles E., ed. 180p. 1990. pap. 24.95 (1-877847-52-6) Univ IL UCOCE&PS.
Phillips, Phoebe. The Medieval Queens: A Perpetual Day Book. 1990. 12.95 (0-517-58056-X, C P Pubs) Crown Pub Group.
***Phillips, Phyllis.** Cofederate Memories. 520p. 1995. pap. 12.95 (0-7610-0154-9) NW Pub.
Phillips Production, Inc., Staff. Texas Country Reporter Cookbook. 256p. 1990. pap. 13.95 (0-940672-54-5) Shearer Pub.
Phillips, R. D. & Gillis, M. F., eds. Biological Effects of Extremely Low Frequency Electromagnetic Fields: Proceedings. LC 79-607778. (DOE Symposium Ser.). 593p. 1979. pap. 22.50 (0-87079-118-4, CONF-781016); fiche 9.00 (0-87079-148-6, CONF-781016) DOE.
Phillips, R. Hart. Cuba: Island of Paradox. (Illus.). 1960. 23.95 (0-8392-1019-1); pap. 8.95 (0-8392-5012-6) Astor-Honor.
— Cuban Dilemma. 1962. 19.95 (0-8392-1018-3) Astor-Honor.
Phillips, R. S., jt. auth. see Hille, Einar.
***Phillips, R. T., ed.** Coherent Optical Interactions in Semiconductors. (NATO ASI Series B, Physics: Vol. 330). (Illus.). 366p. 1994. 110.00 (0-306-44737-1, Plenum Pr) Plenum.
Phillips, Rachel. Alfonsina Storni: From Poetess to Poet. (Serie A: Monagrafias, LII). 131p. (Orig.). (C). 1975. pap. 36.00 (0-7293-0001-3, Pub. by Tamesis Bks Ltd UK) Boydell & Brewer.
Phillips, Rachel, tr. see Paz, Octavio.
Phillips, Raelene. Freedom in White Mittens. 192p. (Orig.). 1987. pap. 5.99 (0-934998-28-0) Bethel Pub.
— Freedom's Destiny Fulfilled. 164p. (Orig.). 1990. pap. 5.99 (0-934998-36-1) Bethel Pub.
— Freedom's Tremendous Cost. 1993. pap. 5.99 (0-934998-47-7) Bethel Pub.
Phillips, Ralph L., et al. A Handbook for Raising Small Numbers of Sheep. LC 84-72384. (Illus.). 56p. 1985. pap. 5.00 (0-931876-68-0, 21389) ANR Pubns CA.
Phillips, Ralph S., jt. auth. see Lax, Peter D.
Phillips, Ralph S., jt. ed. see Lax, Peter D.
Phillips, Ralph W. Letters from China & India & Other Barnyard Rememberances. 1990. 22.50 (0-9613620-1-4) McClain.
— Skinner's Science of Dental Materials. 9th ed. (Illus.). 624p. 1991. text ed. 55.50 (0-7216-7222-1) Saunders.
— The World Was My Barnyard. (Illus.). 250p. 1986. reprint ed. 15.95 (0-9613620-0-6) McClain.
Phillips, Ralph W. & Moore, B. Keith. Elements of Dental Materials: For Dental Hygienists & Dental Assistants. 5th ed. LC 93-12562. (Illus.). 352p. 1993. pap. text ed. 31.50 (0-7216-4298-5) Saunders.
Phillips, Raphael T. Roots of Strategy: A Collection of Classics. LC 82-11890. 448p. 1982. reprint ed. text ed. 48.50 (0-313-23657-7, PHRS, Greenwood Pr) Greenwood.
Phillips, Ray E. The Bantu in the City. LC 74-15080. reprint ed. 49.50 (0-404-12129-2) AMS Pr.
Phillips, Raymond C., Jr. Struthers Burt. LC 82-74090. (Western Writers Ser.: No. 56). (Illus.). 48p. (Orig.). 1983. pap. 3.95 (0-88430-030-7) Boise St U W Writ Ser.
Phillips, Rene F. Encyclopedic Guide for Professionals in Elementary Education. 556p. (Orig.). (C). 1986. pap. text ed. 42.00 (0-8191-5170-X) U Pr of Amer.
***Phillips, Renee, ed. & intro.** New York Contemporary Art Galleries: The Complete Annual Guide. 254p. 1995. pap. 16.95 (0-9646358-2-8) Manhattan Arts Intl.
Phillips, Richard. Managing for Greater Returns. 1962. 11.95 (0-686-00369-1) AG Pr.
— Numbers: Facts, Figures & Fiction. (Illus.). 96p. (C). 1994. 18.95 (0-521-46481-1) Cambridge U Pr.
Phillips, Richard, ed. see ACA Public Information Committee, 1990-1992 Staff.
Phillips, Richard, et al. Auto Industries of Europe, United States & Japan. LC 82-13856. (Economist Intelligence Ser.). 352p. 1982. 32.00 (0-685-42673-4) Harper Busn.
Phillips, Richard D., jt. auth. see DeVries, John A.
Phillips, Richard E. Farm Buildings: From Planning to Completion. (Illus.). 432p. (Orig.). (C). 1981. 27.95 (0-932250-12-2) Red Wing Busn.
Phillips, Richard H. Bindweed. Fuller, Jean O., ed. (Illus.). 100p. (Orig.). 1988. pap. 7.95 (0-317-92520-2) Ganders Knob.
— Building Big Is Beautiful. 3rd rev. ed. (Illus.). 146p. 1985. pap. 11.95 (0-934575-00-2) Vip Pubs.
Phillips, Richard L. & Dargis, Ann, eds. Correctional Officer Resource Guide. rev. ed. (Illus.). 140p. 1989. pap. 20.95 (0-929310-21-7, 130) Am Correctional.
Phillips, Richard L., ed. see Henderson, James D.
Phillips, Rick. Emergence of the Divine Child: Healing the Emotional Body. LC 89-28386. 204p. (Orig.). 1990. pap. 10.95 (0-939680-67-X) Bear & Co.
Phillips, Rob. Listen, Read & Write Better. 36p. 1992. audio 49.50 (0-685-62450-1, S08100) Audio-Forum.
— Making Tracks. 1981. pap. 2.25 (0-8439-0888-2) Dorchester Pub Co.
— Practical Ways to Improve Your Communication. 38p. 1987. Incl. 6 cass. 49.50 (0-88432-182-7, S08100) Audio-Forum.
Phillips, Robert. Breakdown Lane: Poems. LC 93-43813. (Johns Hopkins Poetry & Fiction Ser.). 1994. 30.00 (0-8018-4854-7); pap. 12.95 (0-8018-4855-5) Johns Hopkins.
— The Confessional Poets. LC 73-8970. (Crosscurrents-Modern Critiques Ser.). 190p. 1973. 6.95 (0-8093-0642-5) S Ill U Pr.
— Denton Welch. LC 73-16129. (Twayne's English Authors Ser.). 190p. (C). 1974. lib. bdg. 17.95 (0-8057-1567-3) Irvington.
— Face to Face. deluxe limited ed. Sofranko, Michael, ed. 32p. 1992. pap. 10.00 (0-930324-26-9) Wings Pr.
— Personal Accounts: New & Selected Poems, 1966-1986. LC 85-28350. (Poetry Ser.). 142p. 1986. pap. 9.95 (0-86538-051-1) Ontario Rev NJ.
— Public Landing Revisited. 208p. 1992. 19.95 (0-934257-78-7) Story Line.
— Singing Cowboy Stars. (Illus.). 96p. 1994. 19.95 (0-87905-593-6, Peregrine Smith) Gibbs Smith Pub.
Phillips, Robert, ed. An Omnibus of Twentieth Century Ghost Stories. 384p. 1991. pap. 10.95 (0-88184-780-1) Carroll & Graf.
Phillips, Robert, ed. see Goyen, William.
Phillips, Robert B. One of God's Children: In the Toe River Valley. LC 83-70886. (Illus.). 176p. (YA). (gr. 9-12). 1983. 7.00 (0-9620577-0-3) R B Phillips Pub.
— Through My Picture Window. LC 88-90639. (Illus.). 256p. (YA). (gr. 9-12). 1988. 9.95 (0-9620577-1-1) R B Phillips Pub.
Phillips, Robert H., Jr. Accounting with New Views: Educational Version. 264p. (Orig.). (C). 1989. pap. text ed. 39.95 (0-8162-6739-1) Holden-Day.
Phillips, Robert H. Coping with An Ostomy: A Guide to Living with an Ostomy. LC 85-22810. 304p. (Orig.). 1986. pap. 9.95 (0-89529-277-7) Avery Pub.
— Coping with Kidney Failure: A Guide to Living with Kidney Failure for You & Your Family. LC 87-17477. 320p. 1987. pap. 12.95 (0-89529-370-6) Avery Pub.
— Coping with Lupus: A Guide to Living with Lupus for You & Your Family. 2nd ed. LC 90-1270. 288p. 1991. pap. 12.95 (0-89529-475-3) Avery Pub.
— Coping with Mitral Valve Prolapse: A Guide to Living with MVP for You & Your Family. LC 91-46165. 286p. 1992. pap. 9.95 (0-89529-514-8) Avery Pub.
— Coping with Osteoarthritis: A Guide to Living with Arthritis for You & Your Family. LC 89-175. 224p. (Orig.). 1989. pap. 9.95 (0-89529-393-5) Avery Pub.
— Coping with Prostate Cancer: A Guide to Living with Prostate Cancer for You & Your Family. LC 93-43373. 294p. 1994. pap. 11.95 (0-89529-564-4) Avery Pub.
— Coping with Rheumatoid Arthritis: A Guide to Living with Arthritis for You & Your Family. LC 88-3450. 272p. 1988. pap. 9.95 (0-89529-371-4) Avery Pub.
— Last & Lost Poem Schwartz. 1980. write for info. (0-394-20917-6) Random.
Phillips, Robert H., jt. auth. see Krumholz, Harlan.
Phillips, Robert H., jt. auth. see McKnight, Thomas W.
Phillips, Robert L., Jr. Shelby Foote: Novelist & Historian. LC 91-26636. 1992. 32.50 (0-87805-531-2) U Pr of Miss.
Phillips, Robert L. & Hunt, James G., eds. Strategic Leadership: A Multiorganizational-Level Perspective. LC 92-8383. 352p. 1992. text ed. 49.95 (0-89930-756-6, PSJ, Quorum Bks) Greenwood.
Phillips, Robert W. Roy Rogers: A Biography, Radio History, Television Career Chronicle, Discography, Filmography, Comicography, Merchandising & Advertising History, Collectibles Description, Bibliography & Index. (Illus.). 382p. 1995. lib. bdg. 55.00 (0-685-72013-6) McFarland & Co.
***Phillips, Rod.** Bible Records. 220p. (Orig.). 1995. pap. 8.95 (0-7610-0062-3) NW Pub.
Phillips, Roderick. Putting Asunder: A History of Divorce in Western Society. (Illus.). 816p. 1988. 64.95 (0-521-32434-3) Cambridge U Pr.
— Untying the Knot: A Short History of Divorce. (Canto Book Ser.). 255p. (C). 1991. pap. 11.95 (0-521-42370-8) Cambridge U Pr.
Phillips, Roger. Guest for the Rose. 1994. 35.00 (0-679-43573-5) Random.
— Mushrooms: The Photographic Guide to Identify Common & Important Mushrooms. 159p. 1986. pap. text ed. 18.00 (0-241-11756-9) Lubrecht & Cramer.
— Mushrooms & Other Fungi of Great Britain & Europe. (Illus.). 288p. (Orig.). 1981. pap. 67.50 (0-330-26441-9, Pub. by Pan Books UK) Trans-Atl Phila.
— Mushrooms of North America: The Most Comprehensive Mushroom Guide Ever. 1991. pap. 29.95 (0-316-70613-2) Little.
— Random House Book of Perennials Vol. 2: Late Perennials. 1991. pap. 25.00 (0-679-73798-7) Random.
— Shrubs. (Illus.). 288p. 1989. pap. 27.50 (0-679-72345-5, Vin) Random.
— Trees of North America & Europe. 1978. pap. 27.50 (0-394-73541-2) Random.
— Wild Food. 24.50 (0-8446-6262-3) Peter Smith.
Phillips, Roger & Foy, Nicky. The Random House Book of Herbs. (Illus.). 1990. pap. 27.50 (0-679-73213-6) Random.
Phillips, Roger & Grant, Sheila. Trees in Britain, Europe & North America. Wellsted, Tom, ed. (Illus.). 224p. (Orig.). 1978. pap. 52.50 (0-330-25480-4, Pub. by Pan Books UK) Trans-Atl Phila.
Phillips, Roger & Rix, Martyn. The Random House Book of Bulbs. LC 89-10361. 256p. 1989. 27.50 (0-679-72756-6) McKay.
— The Random House Book of Perennials, 2 vols. 1991. 25.00 (0-685-74390-X) Random.
— The Random House Book of Perennials, 2 vols., Vol. I. 1991. 25.00 (0-679-73797-9) Random.
— Roses. LC 87-43216. (Illus.). 224p. 1988. pap. 25.00 (0-394-75867-6) Random.
Phillips, Roger, jt. auth. see Rix, Martyn.
Phillips, Roger W. A Concise Russian Review Grammar with Exercises. LC 73-15260. 126p. (ENG & RUS.). reprint ed. pap. 36.00 (0-7837-4386-6, 2044126) Bks Demand.
Phillips, Ron. The Risk Business. (C). 1989. 35.00 (1-871058-05-8, Pub. by Dragonheart Pr UK) St Mut.
Phillips, Ron, jt. auth. see Wittich, John.
Phillips, Ronald C. & Menez, Ernani G. Seagrasses. LC 87-23245. (Smithsonian Contributions to the Marine Sciences Ser.: No. 34). (Illus.). 110p. reprint ed. pap. 31.40 (0-8357-8316-2, 2034077) Bks Demand.
Phillips, Ronald E. No-Tillage Agriculture Principles. Phillips, Shirley H., ed. 320p. 1984. text ed. 57.95 (0-442-27731-8) Chapman & Hall.
Phillips, Ronald L. & Vasil, Indra K., eds. DNA-Based Markers in Plants. LC 93-49927. (Advances in Cellular & Molecular Biology of Plants Ser.: Vol. 1). 380p. (C). 1994. lib. bdg. 177.00 (0-7923-2714-4) Kluwer Ac.
Phillips, Ronnie J. The Chicago Plan & the New Deal Banking Reform. 240p. 1994. text ed. 55.00 (1-56324-469-1); pap. text ed. 21.95 (1-56324-470-5) M E Sharpe.
— Narrow Banking Reconsidered: The Functional Approach to Financial Reform. (Public Policy Briefs Ser.). 52p. (Orig.). 1995. pap. 3.00 (0-941276-05-8, J Levy Econ Inst) Bard Coll Pubns.
Phillips, S. Michael & Escobar, Mario R., eds. The Reticuloendothelial System: A Comprehensive Treatise Vol. 9, Hypersensitivity. LC 79-25933. 512p. 1986. 105.00 (0-306-42305-7, Plenum Pr) Plenum.
Phillips, Sally, jt. ed. see Breem, Wallace.
Phillips, Sandra. Matt Phillips: The Graphic Work. 1976. 7.50 (0-686-24037-5) Bellevue Pr.
Phillips, Sandra S. & Weintraub, Linda, eds. Charmed Places: Hudson River Artists & Their Houses, Studios, & Vistas. (Illus.). 1988. 45.00 (0-8109-1041-1) Abrams.
Phillips, Sarah H. & Williams, Mary H. The Secret Ingredient. (Illus.). 179p. 1987. 10.00 (0-9619306-0-8) M H Williams.
Phillips, Semira A. Mahaska County (Iowa), A Story of the Early Days. 383p. 1993. reprint ed. lib. bdg. 42.00 (0-8328-3520-X) Higginson Bk Co.
Phillips, Sheena, jt. auth. see Tsipis, Kosta.
Phillips, Sheree, jt. auth. see Phillips, Benny.
Phillips, Sherry, ed. see Thoreau, Henry David.
Phillips, Shirley H., ed. see Phillips, Ronald E.
Phillips, Shively W., jt. auth. see Achen, Christopher H.
***Phillips, Sidney & Mulholland, Michael.** Large Intestine: Gastrointestinal Infections. Boedeker, Edgar C., ed. (Current Opinion in Gastroenterology Ser.). (Illus.). 96p. (Orig.). 1995. pap. text ed. 39.95 (1-85922-718-X) Current Science.
Phillips, Sidney F., jt. auth. see Fazio, Victor W.
Phillips, Sidney F., et al. The Large Intestine: Physiology, Pathophysiology, & Diseases. (Illus.). 928p. 1991. 205.00 (0-88167-777-9) Raven.
Phillips, Sidney L., jt. ed. see Perry, Dale L.
Phillips, Sky. Secret Mission to Melbourne: November 1941. (Illus.). 296p. (Orig.). 1992. pap. 18.95 (0-89745-148-1) Sunflower U Pr.
Phillips, Sonia. Venetian Spring. large type ed. 1992. 18.95 (0-7927-1247-1, Curley Lrg Print); pap. 16.95 (0-7927-1248-X, Curley Lrg Print) Chivers N Amer.
Phillips, Stacy. The Art of Hawaiian Steel Guitar. 1993. 15.00 (1-56222-103-5, 94383); 9.98 (1-56222-877-3, 94383) Mel Bay.
— Beginning Dobro. (Illus.). 56p. pap. 4.95 (0-8256-1123-7, AM67497) Music Sales.
— Beginning Fiddle. (Illus.). 64p. 1990. pap. 4.95 (0-8256-2541-6, AM26329) Music Sales.
— Complete Country Fiddler. 1993. 15.00 (1-56222-275-9, 94696); audio 9.98 (1-56222-438-7, 94696) Mel Bay.
— Deluxe Dobro Tune Book. 1993. 15.00 (1-56222-321-6, 94704); audio 9.98 (1-56222-328-3, 94704) Mel Bay.
— The Dobro Book. (Illus.). 96p. 1977. pap. 15.95 (0-8256-0183-5, OK63289, Oak) Music Sales.
— The Dobro Case Chord Book. (Illus.). 40p. pap. 4.95 (0-8256-1124-5, AM67158) Music Sales.
— The Fiddle Case Tunebook: British Isles. LC 66-19062. (Illus.). 52p. (Orig.). 1967. pap. 4.95 (0-8256-2545-9, Oak) Music Sales.
— Fiddle Case Tunebook: British Isles. (Illus.). 48p. 1989. pap. 4.95 (0-685-65792-2, AM71317) Music Sales.
— Fiddle Case Tunebook: Old-Time Southern. (Illus.). 48p. 1989. pap. 4.95 (0-8256-2544-0, AM71309) Music Sales.
— Hot Licks for Bluegrass Fiddle. (Illus.). 144p. 1984. pap. 17.95 (0-8256-0289-0, OK64378, Oak) Music Sales.
Phillips, Stacy & Kosek, Kenny. Bluegrass Fiddle Styles. (Illus.). 112p. pap. 11.95 (0-8256-0185-1, OK63487, Oak) Music Sales.
Phillips, Stacy & O'Connor, Mark, eds. Mark O'Connor - The Championship Years. 1993. 15.00 (0-685-64079-5, 94585) Mel Bay.
Phillips, Starr. I Never Pay Retail: A Guide to Discount Shopping in Orange County, California. 4th ed. 150p. (Orig.). 1985. reprint ed. pap. 7.95 (0-933911-01-7) DC Pub Co.
— Treasure Transfer: A Resale & Consignment Guide for Orange County, Los Angeles County & San Diego County. (Illus.). 170p. (Orig.). 1985. pap. 6.50 (0-933911-00-9) DC Pub Co.
Phillips, Stella. Dear Brother, Here Departed. large type ed. (Linford Mystery Library). 1990. pap. 12.95 (0-7089-6847-3, Trailtree Bookshop) Ulverscroft.
— Death in Arcady. large type ed. (Linford Mystery Library). 331p. 1988. pap. 11.95 (0-7089-6571-7, Linford) Ulverscroft.
— Death in Sheep's Clothing. large type ed. (Linford Mystery Library). 1990. pap. 12.95 (0-7089-6838-4, Trailtree Bookshop) Ulverscroft.
— Down to Death. large type ed. (Linford Mystery Library). 320p. 1988. pap. 11.95 (0-7089-6515-6, Trailtree Bookshop) Ulverscroft.
— The Hidden Wrath. large type ed. (Linford Mystery Library). 304p. 1988. pap. 11.95 (0-7089-6623-3, Linford) Ulverscroft.
— Yet She Must Die. large type ed. (Linford Mystery Library). 352p. 1993. pap. 14.95 (0-7089-7343-4, Linford) Ulverscroft.
Phillips, Stephen & Luehrs, John. Rural Hospitals in Evolution: State Policy Issues & Initiatives. Glass, Karen, ed. 40p. (Orig.). 1989. pap. text ed. 20.00 (1-55877-067-4) Natl Governor.
Phillips, Stephen, jt. auth. see Bonevac, Daniel.
Phillips, Stephen, jt. auth. see Stoffel, Jennifer.
Phillips, Stephen H. Aurobindo's Philosophy of Brahman. xii, 200p. 1986. 41.25 (90-04-07765-0) E J Brill.
— Classical Indian Metaphysics: Refutations of Realism & the Emergence of 'New Logic' 500p. 1995. pap. 19.95 (0-8126-9298-5) Open Court.
Phillips, Stephen H., jt. auth. see Kane, Robert.
Phillips, Steve. Evaluation. 64p. 1993. pap. 35.00 (1-85604-079-8, LAP0798, Pub. by Lib Assn Pub UK) UNIPUB.
— Melinda. LC 93-10062. 1993. 8.95 (0-440-50576-3) Dell.
Phillips, Steve, jt. auth. see Elledge, Robin.
Phillips, Steven. No Heroes, No Villains: The Story of a Murder. 1978. pap. 9.00 (0-394-72531-X, Vin) Random.
— P. M. S. Attacks & Other Inconveniences of Life. 1988. pap. 5.95 (0-89815-239-9) Ten Speed Pr.
— PMS Attacks & Other Inconveniences of Life: The Saga Continues. 1990. pap. 5.95 (0-312-05142-5) St Martin.
Phillips, Steven, jt. auth. see Koen, Vincent.
Phillips, Steven J. Fast Facts on the Fifty Plus Consumer. LC 93-41935. 50p. (Orig.). 1993. pap. 4.95 (0-9621333-3-7, Amrcn Source Bks) Impact Pubs CA.
— Old-House Dictionary: An Illustrated Guide to American Domestic Architecture (1600-1940) (Illus.). 235p. (Orig.). 1992. reprint ed. pap. 12.95 (0-89133-171-9) Preservation Pr.
Phillips, Steven L. & Elledge, Robin L. The Team-Building Source Book. LC 89-5094. 208p. (Orig.). 1989. ring bd. 79.95 (0-88390-232-X) Pfeiffer & Co.
Phillips, Steven L. & Harshman, Carl L. Teaming Up: Achieving Organizational Transformation. 208p. 1993. 19.95 (0-88390-411-X); pap. 14.95 (0-89384-237-0) Pfeiffer & Co.
Phillips, Steven R., jt. auth. see Bergquist, William H.

Phillips, Sue. Gardeners' World Book of Bulbs. (Illus.). 112p. 1992. pap. 9.95 (*0-563-36099-2*, BBC-Parkwest) Parkwest Pubns.
— Well Planned Garden. 1994. 12.99 (*0-517-12018-6*) Random Hse Value.
Phillips, Sue, jt. ed. see Heyward, Carter.
Phillips, Susan E. Fancy Pants. 544p. 1991. reprint ed. mass mkt. 5.95 (*0-671-74715-0*) PB.
— Heaven, Texas: Where Even a Angel Can Raise a Little Hell... 384p. (Orig.). 1995. mass mkt. 5.50 (*0-380-77684-7*) Avon.
— Honey Moon. Zion, Claire, ed. 448p. (Orig.). 1993. mass mkt. 5.99 (*0-671-73593-4*) PB.
— Hot Shot. Zion, Claire, ed. 496p. 1991. mass mkt. 5.95 (*0-671-65831-X*) PB.
— It Had to Be You. 384p. (Orig.). 1994. mass mkt. 5.50 (*0-380-77683-9*) Avon.
Phillips, Susan S. & Benner, Patricia, eds. The Crisis of Care: Affirming & Restoring Caring Practices in the Helping Professions. 256p. 1994. 55.00 (*0-87840-558-5*) Georgetown U Pr.
Phillips, Syd. Unemployment Insurance Handbook for Texas Employers. White, Morley H., ed. LC 92-60755. 489p. 1992. 149.95 (*0-9633768-0-2*) TX Handbk Series.
***Phillips, T. J.** Dance of the Mongoose. 288p. 1995. 19.95 (*0-425-14786-X*, Prime Crime); pap. 9.00 (*0-425-14921-8*) Berkley Pub.
Phillips, Tamara. Day Care ABC. Levine, Abby, ed. LC 88-33911. (Illus.). (J). (ps-2). 1989. lib. bdg. 13.95 (*0-8075-1483-7*) A Whitman.
***Phillips, Theodore & Sandberg, Teena D.** Creative Movement Activities for Preschoolers: Perceptual & Tactile Approach. (Illus.). 177p. (Orig.). (C). 1994. pap. text ed. 12.95x (*0-89641-272-5*) American Pr.
***Phillips, Theodore L. & Pistenmaa, David A., eds.** Radiation Oncology Annual, 1983. LC 84-644857. (Illus.). Date not set. reprint ed. pap. 81.80 (*0-7837-9534-3*, 2060283) Bks Demand.
Phillips, Theodore L. & Wara, William, eds. Radiation Oncology, Vol. 2. 184p. 1987. text ed. 103.00 (*0-89004-957-2*) Raven.
Phillips, Thomas. The Welsh Revival: Its Origins & Development. 168p. 1989. 14.95 (*0-85151-542-8*) Banner of Truth.
Phillips, Thomas, ed. see Vegetius Renatus, Flavia.
Phillips, Thomas R., ed. The Military Institutions of the Romans. Clark, John, tr. LC 83-45853. reprint ed. 24.50 (*0-404-20275-6*, U101) AMS Pr.
— Roots of Strategy: The Five Greatest Military Classics of All Time-Complete in One Volume. LC 84-26826. 448p. 1985. pap. 14.95 (*0-8117-2194-9*) Stackpole.
***Phillips, Timothy R. & Okholm, Dennis L., eds.** Christian Apologetics in the Postmodern World. 240p. (Orig.). 1995. pap. text ed. 15.99 (*0-8308-1860-X*, 1860) InterVarsity.
Phillips, Timothy R., jt. ed. see Okholm, Dennis L.
Phillips, Tom. Dante's Inferno. LC 84-52865. (Illus.). 1985. 19.98 (*0-500-01362-4*) Thames Hudson.
— A Humument. rev. ed. LC 87-50102. (Illus.). 1987. pap. 19.95 (*0-500-97339-3*) Thames Hudson.
Phillips, Toni & Simonich, Juanita. Quilt-A-Saurus. (Illus.). 36p. (Orig.). 1993. 9.95 (*0-9638806-0-8*) Fabric Express.
Phillips, Toni, jt. auth. see Simonich, Junanita.
Phillips, Tony. City of Glass. (Turbo Cowboys Ser.: No. 10). 144p. 1989. pap. 2.95 (*0-345-35925-9*) Ballantine.
— Spin Out-Turbo Cowboy, No. 2. 1988. pap. 2.95 (*0-345-35122-3*) Ballantine.
— Turbo Cowboys: Jump Start, No. 1. (J). (gr. 3 up). 1988. pap. 2.95 (*0-345-35121-5*) Ballantine.
Phillips, Trevor M. Cast of Millions. Young, Paul J., Jr., ed. 1985. write for info. (*0-9622708-7-3*) Zubra Pub.
— Divine Footprints. Phillips, Julie Anne & Young, Paul J., eds. (Illus.). 926p. 1990. 47.95 (*0-9622708-5-7*); pap. 27.95 (*0-9622708-4-9*) Zubra Pub.
— Lose Weight Religiously. 128p. 1990. pap. write for info. (*0-9622708-3-0*) Zubra Pub.
— A New Breeze Is Blowing. 232p. (Orig.). 1989. text ed. 23.96 (*0-9622708-0-6*) Zubra Pub.
— Supercrats. 454p. 1989. write for info. (*0-9622708-1-4*) Zubra Pub.
— Supercrats. 2nd ed. Phillips, Julie Anne, ed. 486p. 1989. write for info. (*0-9622708-2-2*) Zubra Pub.
Phillips, Trevor M., ed. see Young, Paul J., Jr.
Phillips, U. B. Correspondence of Robert Toombs, Alexander H. Stephens, & Howell Cobb. LC 68-54846. (American Scene Ser.). 1970. reprint ed. lib. bdg. 95.00 (*0-306-71191-5*) Da Capo.
Phillips, Ulrich B. American Negro Slavery. 26.75 (*0-8446-1348-7*) Peter Smith.
— American Negro Slavery. (History - United States Ser.). 529p. 1992. reprint ed. lib. bdg. 99.00 (*0-7812-6155-4*) Rprt Serv.
— American Negro Slavery: A Survey of the Supply, Employment, & Control of Negro Labor As Determined by the Plantation Regime. LC 66-31730. (Illus.). xxvi, 530p. 1966. pap. text ed. 16.95 (*0-8071-0109-5*) La State U Pr.
— Georgia & State Rights. LC 83-19635. (Reprints of Scholarly Excellence Ser.). 224p. 1984. 14.95 (*0-86554-103-5*, MUP/H95) Mercer Univ Pr.
— The Slave Economy of the Old South: Selected Essays in Economic & Social History. fac. ed. Genovese, Eugene D., ed. LC 68-21806. 318p. 1968. reprint ed. pap. 90.70 (*0-7837-7814-7*, 2047570) Bks Demand.
Phillips, Ulrich B., ed. see Commons, John R., et al.
Phillips, Ursula, tr. see Maczak, Antoni.
Phillips, Ursula, tr. see Mysliwski, Wieslaw.
Phillips, Utah. The Old Guy Poems. 31p. (Orig.). 1988. pap. 6.00 (*0-317-91179-1*) Brownell Library Pr.
Phillips, V. J. Early Radio-Wave Detectors. (IEE History of Technology Ser.: No. 2). (Illus.). 256p. 1980. boxed 72.00 (*0-906048-24-9*, HT002) Inst Elect Eng.
Phillips, V. N. Bristol, Tennessee - Virginia: A History, 1852-1900. (Illus.). 492p. 1992. 27.95 (*0-932807-63-1*) Overmountain Pr.
Phillips, Velma. Evidence of the Need of Education for Efficient Purchasing. LC 71-177154. (Columbia University. Teachers College. Contributions to Education Ser.: No. 447). reprint ed. 37.50 (*0-404-55447-4*) AMS Pr.
Phillips, Vicki. Personal Development: A One Semester Course Designed to Promote Self-Esteem, Communication Skills, Goal-Setting, Problem-Solving & a Sense of Responsibility in At-Risk High School Students, Group & Individualized Version. rev. ed. 1991. Group curriculum with individualized component. 595.00 (*0-9628482-6-3*) Prsnl Dev.
— Personal Development: A One Semester Course Designed to Promote Self-Esteem, Communication Skills, Goal-Setting, Problem-Solving & a Sense of Responsibility in At-Risk High School Students, Group Version. rev. ed. 1991. Group curriculum. 375.00 (*0-9628482-4-7*) Prsnl Dev.
— Personal Development: A One Semester Course Designed to Promote Self-Esteem, Communication Skills, Goal-Setting, Problem-Solving & a Sense of Responsibility in At-Risk High School Students, Individualized Version. rev. ed. 1991. Individualized curriculum. 350.00 (*0-9628482-5-5*) Prsnl Dev.
— Personal Development: A One Semester Course Designed to Promote Self-Esteem, Communication Skills, Goal-Setting, Problem-Solving & a Sense of Responsibility in At-Risk High School Students, Preview Packet. rev. ed. 1991. 15.00 (*0-9628482-7-1*) Prsnl Dev.
Phillips, Vicki & McCullough, Laura. Student-Staff Support Teams: SST Program Kit, 3 vols. (Illus.). 226p. 1993. teacher ed 125.00 (*0-944584-68-3*); 14.95 (*0-944584-61-6*); 14.95 (*0-944584-60-8*) Sopris.
— Student-Staff Support Teams: SST Program Kit, 3 vols., Set. (Illus.). 390p. 1993. 145.00 (*0-944584-74-8*) Sopris.
Phillips, W. New Common Entrance Mathematics. (C). 1986. text ed. 40.00 (*0-85950-644-4*, Pub. by S Thornes Pubs UK) St Mut.
— New Common Entrance Mathematics - Teacher's Guide. (C). 1986. text ed. 50.00 (*0-85950-650-9*, Pub. by S Thornes Pubs UK) St Mut.
— New Common Entrance Mathematics - Workbook. (C). 1986. text ed. 40.00 (*0-85950-649-5*, Pub. by S Thornes Pubs UK) St Mut.
— Steps to Common Entrance Mathematics One. (C). 1989. text ed. 45.00 (*0-7487-0109-5*, Pub. by S Thornes Pubs UK) St Mut.
Phillips, W., jt. ed. see Adamowicz, W. L.
Phillips, W., ed. see Franklin, Benjamin.
Phillips, W. A., ed. Amorphous Solids. (Topics in Current Physics Ser.: Vol. 24). (Illus.). 167p. 1981. 53.00 (*0-387-10330-9*) Spr-Verlag.
— Selected Poems of Walter Von der Vogel Weide. 69.95 (*0-8490-1020-9*) Gordon Pr.
Phillips, W. A., tr. see Gratz, Gustav & Schuller, Richard.
Phillips, W. A., jt. auth. see Orchard, G. A.
Phillips, W. Andrew, jt. auth. see Sproull, Robert L.
Phillips, W. Gary & Brown, William E. Making Sense of Your World from a Biblical Viewpoint. 1991. pap. 9.99 (*0-8024-0745-5*) Moody.
***Phillips, W. Glasgow.** Tuscaloosa. 192p. 1995. 10.95 (*0-452-27439-7*, Plume) NAL-Dutton.
Phillips, W. Louis. Ohio City & County Directories. 34p. (Orig.). 1986. pap. 5.00 (*1-55613-002-3*) Heritage Bk.
— Warren County, Ohio, Apprenticeship & Indenture Records, 1824-1832, 1864-1867. vi, 51p. (Orig.). 1987. pap. 6.00 (*1-55613-039-2*) Heritage Bk.
Phillips, W. Louis & Stuckey, Ronald L., comps. Index to Plant Distribution Maps in North American Periodicals Through 1972. 1978. lib. bdg. 125.00 (*0-8161-0009-8*, Hall Library) G K Hall.
Phillips, W. S. Social Stratification & Mobility in Urban India. 1990. 23.00 (*81-7033-084-X*, Pub. by Rawat II) S Asia.
— Street Children in India. (C). 1994. 22.50x (*81-7033-188-9*, Pub. by Rawat II) S Asia.
Phillips, W. Scott & Mantock, Jim. Connecting: Sales Rapport Thru NLP. 1993. 65.00 (*1-55552-019-7*) Metamorphous Pr.
Phillips, Wade. The Church of God: History & Prophecy. (Systematic Ecclesiology Ser.). 120p. (Orig.). 1990. pap. 6.95 (*0-934942-82-X*, 2442) White Wing Pub.
Phillips, Wade H. God, the Church & Revelation. 376p. (Orig.). 1986. pap. 8.95 (*0-934942-60-9*, 4048) White Wing Pub.
Phillips, Wally. The Wally Phillips People Book. LC 79-88664. (Illus.). 1979. 7.95 (*0-89803-012-9*) Green Hill.
Phillips, Walter R. Family Farmer & Individual Adjustment of Debts: Chapters 12 & 13 of the Bankruptcy Code. 1987. write for info. (*0-318-66758-4*) Harrison Co GA.
— Reorganizations Under Chapter 11 of the Bankruptcy Code. 1980. write for info. (*0-318-66759-2*) Harrison Co GA.
Phillips, Wanda C. Daily Grams: Guided Review Aiding Mastery Skills. (J). (gr. 6 up). 1987. pap. text ed. 14.50 (*0-936981-05-9*) ISHA Enterprises.
— Daily Grams: Guided Review Aiding Mastery Skills for 2nd & 3rd Grades. 190p. 1991. teacher ed 14.50 (*0-936981-09-1*); pap. text ed. 14.50 (*0-936981-07-5*) ISHA Enterprises.
— Daily Grams: Guided Review Aiding Mastery Skills for 4th & 5th. (J). (gr. 4-5). 1987. pap. text ed. 14.50 (*0-936981-06-7*) ISHA Enterprises.
— Daily Grams: Guided Review Aiding Mastery Skills for 5th & 6th Grades. 210p. 1992. teacher ed 15.50 (*0-936981-10-5*) ISHA Enterprises.
— Easy Grammar. 505p. (Orig.). (J). (gr. 4 up). 1985. pap. 20.95 (*0-936981-00-8*) ISHA Enterprises.
— Easy Grammar: Adverbs. (J). (gr. 4-12). 1987. pap. text ed. 11.50 (*0-936981-04-0*) ISHA Enterprises.
— Easy Grammar: Direct Objects & Indirect Objects. 33p. (J). (gr. 4-12). 1986. pap. text ed. 5.50 (*0-936981-02-4*) ISHA Enterprises.
— Easy Grammar: Level 1. 626p. (Orig.). 1994. teacher ed 24.95 (*0-936981-11-3*) ISHA Enterprises.
— Easy Grammar: Verbs. 130p. (J). (gr. 4-12). 1986. pap. text ed. 12.50 (*0-936981-03-2*) ISHA Enterprises.
— Easy Grammar Workbook. 259p. (J). (gr. 4 up). 1985. 8.95 (*0-936981-01-6*) ISHA Enterprises.
— My Mother Doesn't Like to Cook. (Illus.). 28p. (Orig.). (J). (ps-5). 1993. pap. 6.95 (*0-936981-20-2*) ISHA Enterprises.
Phillips, Warren R. & Rimkunas, Richard. Crisis Warning: The Perception Behavior Interface. 292p. 1983. text ed. 81.00 (*0-677-05940-X*) Gordon & Breach.
Phillips, Wayne, jt. auth. see Phillips, Linda.
Phillips, Wendell. Oman a History. 1968. 16.00 (*0-86685-024-4*) Intl Bk Ctr.
— Review of Lysander Spooner's Essay on the Unconstitutionality of Slavery. LC 76-82220. (Anti-Slavery Crusade in America Ser.). 1970. reprint ed. 11.95 (*0-405-00648-9*) Ayer.
— Speeches, Lectures & Letters: Second Series. LC 79-82210. (Anti-Slavery Crusade in America Ser.). 1970. reprint ed. 41.95 (*0-405-00649-7*) Ayer.
— Unknown Oman. (Arab Background Ser.). 1972. 16.00 (*0-86685-025-2*) Intl Bk Ctr.
Phillips, Wilbur C. Adventuring for Democracy. LC 74-3216. (Children & Youth Ser.). 380p. 1974. reprint ed. 33.95 (*0-405-05994-9*) Ayer.
Phillips, Willard. Manual of Political Economy: With Particular Reference to the Institutions, Resources & Condition of the U. S. LC 65-23673. (Reprints of Economic Classics Ser.). 278p. 1968. reprint ed. 37.50 (*0-678-00278-9*) Kelley.
— Propositions Concerning Protection & Free Trade. LC 67-29515. (Reprints of Economic Classics Ser.). xv, 233p. 1968. reprint ed. 35.00 (*0-678-00369-6*) Kelley.
Phillips, William, jt. ed. see Kurzweil, Edith.
Phillips, William, jt. ed. see Peterson, Robin.
Phillips, William B. Pastoral Transitions: From Endings to New Beginnings. LC 88-71755. 77p. 1988. reprint ed. pap. 9.95 (*1-56699-029-7*, AL108) Alban Inst.
Phillips, William D., Jr. Before 1492: Christopher Columbus's Formative Years. Phillips, Carla R. & Weber, David J., eds. LC 92-81880. (Essays on the Columbian Encounter Ser.). (Illus.). 64p. (Orig.). (C). 1992. 8.00 (*0-87229-065-4*) Am Hist Assn.
— Enrique IV & the Crisis of Fifteenth-Century Castile, 1425-1480. LC 77-89931. 1978. pap. 12.00 (*0-910956-63-4*) Medieval Acad.
Phillips, William D., Jr. & Phillips, Carla R. The Worlds of Christopher Columbus. (Illus.). 336p. (C). 1991. 37.95 (*0-521-35097-2*) Cambridge U Pr.
— The Worlds of Christopher Columbus. (Illus.). 336p. (C). 1993. pap. 14.95 (*0-521-44652-X*) Cambridge U Pr.
Phillips, William H. Analyzing Films. 368p. (C). 1985. pap. text ed. 28.00 (*0-03-063078-9*) HB Coll Pubs.
— St. John Hankin: Edwardian Mephistopheles. LC 77-89783. 150p. 1979. 24.50 (*0-8386-2155-4*) Fairleigh Dickinson.
— Writing Short Scripts. LC 89-21961. (Illus.). 240p. (C). 1990. text ed. 35.00x (*0-8156-2485-9*); pap. text ed. 15.95 (*0-8156-2486-7*) Syracuse U Pr.
Phillips, William J. Carols, Their Origin, Music, & Connection with Mystery-Plays: A Greenwood Archival Edition. LC 75-109821. (Illus.). 134p. 1971. reprint ed. text ed. 45.50 (*0-8371-4312-8*, PHCA, Greenwood Pr) Greenwood.
— An Introduction to Mineralogy for Geologists. LC 79-42898. (Illus.). 374p. reprint ed. pap. 106.60 (*0-8357-2955-9*, 2039211) Bks Demand.
Phillips, William M., Jr. An Unillustrious Alliance: The African American & Jewish American Communities. LC 91-17126. (Contributions in Afro-American & African Studies: No. 146). 176p. 1991. text ed. 49.95 (*0-313-27776-1*, PUL, Greenwood Pr) Greenwood.
Phillips, William R. The Conquest of Kansas, by Missouri & Her Allies. LC 76-161271. (Black Heritage Library Collection). 1977. reprint ed. 31.95 (*0-8369-8830-2*) Ayer.
— The Holocaust. (Illus.). 1992. student ed 35.00 (*0-614-03227-X*) Golden Owl NY.
— The Holocaust. (Illus.). 1992. reprint ed. 27.95 (*1-56696-000-2*) Golden Owl NY.
— An Outline of Mineralogy & Geology: Intended for the Use of Those Who May Desire to Become Acquainted with the Elements of Those Sciences. Albritton, Claude C., Jr., ed. LC 77-6536. (History of Geology Ser.). (Illus.). 1978. reprint ed. lib. bdg. 19.95 (*0-405-10456-1*) Ayer.
Phillips, William R. & Rosenberg, Janet, eds. Changing Patterns of Law: The Courts & the Handicapped: An Original Anthology. LC 79-6009. (Physically Handicapped in Society Ser.). 1980. lib. bdg. 44.95 (*0-405-13101-1*) Ayer.
— Cleveland Symposium on Behavioral Research in Rehabilitation. rev. ed. LC 79-6898. (Physically Handicapped in Society Ser.). 1980. reprint ed. lib. bdg. 25.95 (*0-405-13110-0*) Ayer.
— Education & Occupations of Cripples: Juveniles & Adults. LC 79-6924. (Physically Handicapped in Society Ser.). 1980. reprint ed. lib. bdg. 19.95 (*0-405-13131-3*) Ayer.
— The Origins of Modern Treatment & the Education of Physically Handicapped Children: An Original Anthology. LC 79-6010. (Physically Handicapped in Society Ser.). 1980. lib. bdg. 44.95 (*0-405-13102-X*) Ayer.
— Physically Handicapped in Society Series, 39 bks., Set. 1980. lib. bdg. 965.00 (*0-405-13100-3*) Ayer.
— Social Scientists & the Physically Handicapped: An Original Anthology. LC 79-6011. (Physically Handicapped in Society Ser.). 1980. lib. bdg. 35.95 (*0-405-13103-8*) Ayer.
Phillips, William R., ed. see Anderson, Roy N.
Phillips, William R., ed. see Axford, Wendy A. & McMurtrie, Douglas C.
Phillips, William R., ed. see Barton, George E.
Phillips, William R., ed. see Berkowitz, Edward D.
Phillips, William R., ed. see Carling, Finn & Haecker, Theodor.
Phillips, William R., ed. see Charity Organisation Society Staff.
Phillips, William R., jt. auth. see Conybeare, W. D.
Phillips, William R., ed. see Giralestone, Gathrone R.
Phillips, William R., ed. see Graham, Earl C. & Mullen, Marjorie.
Phillips, William R., ed. see Hathaway, Katharine B.
Phillips, William R., ed. see Hinshaw, David.
Phillips, William R., ed. see Hoyer, Louis & Hay, Charles K.
Phillips, William R., ed. see Hunt, Agnes.
Phillips, William R., ed. see Kenny, Elizabeth.
Phillips, William R., ed. see Kessler, Henry H.
Phillips, William R., ed. see Landis, Carney & Bolles, M. Marjorie.
Phillips, William R., ed. see Leavitt, Moses A.
Phillips, William R., ed. see Macdonald, Mary E.
Phillips, William R., ed. see Mallinson, Vernon.
Phillips, William R., ed. see Mawson, Thomas.
Phillips, William R., ed. see McMurtrie, Douglas C.
Phillips, William R., ed. see Obermann, C. Esco.
Phillips, William R., ed. see Orr, H. Winnett.
Phillips, William R., ed. see Pitner, Rudolf, et al.
Phillips, William R., jt. auth. see Sheppard, David A.
Phillips, William R., ed. see Sullivan, Oscar M. & Snortum, Kenneth O.
Phillips, William R., ed. see Tracy, Susan R.
Phillips, William R., ed. see Watson, Frederick.
Phillips, William R., ed. see Wright, Henry C.
Phillips, William R., ed. see Wurtz, Hans.
Phillips, William R., ed. see Ziegler, Carlos R.
Phillips, Zoe A., ed. see Phillips, Martin A.
Phillipson, Chris, jt. auth. see Laczko, Frank.
Phillipson, Chris, jt. auth. see Walker, Alan.
Phillipson, Chris, et al, eds. Dependency & Interdependency in Old Age. 300p. 1986. 45.00 (*0-7099-3987-6*, Pub. by Croom Helm UK) Routledge Chapman & Hall.
Phillipson, Coleman. The International Law & Custom of Ancient Greece & Rome, Vol. 1. Vlastos, Gregory, ed. LC 78-19383. (Morals & Law in Ancient Greece Ser.). 1979. reprint ed. lib. bdg. 44.95 (*0-405-11565-2*) Ayer.
— Three Criminal Law Reformers: Beccaria, Bentham, Romilly. LC 77-17157. (Criminology, Law Enforcement, & Social Problems Ser.: No. 113). 1970. reprint ed. 25.00 (*0-87585-113-4*); reprint ed. pap. 12.00 (*0-87585-904-6*) Patterson Smith.
Phillipson, David & Grossman, Louis, eds. Selected Writings of Isaac Mayer Wise. LC 71-83433. (Religion in America, Ser. 1). 1975. reprint ed. 31.95 (*0-405-00258-0*) Ayer.
Phillipson, David W. African Archaeology. 2nd ed. LC 92-35021. (Cambridge World Archaeology Ser.). (Illus.). 300p. (C). 1994. 59.95 (*0-521-44103-X*); pap. 19.95 (*0-521-44658-9*) Cambridge U Pr.
Phillipson, H. B., jt. ed. see Brand, E. W.
Phillipson, J. D. & Zenk, M. H., eds. Indole & Biogenetically Related Alkaloids. (Annual Proceedings of the Phytochemical Society of Europe: No. 17). 1981. text ed. 205.00 (*0-12-554450-2*) Acad Pr.
Phillipson, Julia, jt. auth. see Foster, Gayle.
Phillipson, Julia, et al. Towards a Practice Led Curriculum. (C). 1987. text ed. 49.50 (*0-902789-52-X*, Pub. by Natl Inst Soc Work) St Mut.
— Towards a Practice Led Curriculum. (C). 1988. 42.00 (*0-685-28593-6*, Pub. by Natl Inst Soc Work) St Mut.
Phillipson, Julia, et al, eds. Towards a Practice Led Curriculum. (C). 1988. 45.00 (*0-685-40350-5*, Pub. by Natl Inst Soc Work); 65.00 (*0-7855-0080-4*, Pub. by Natl Inst Soc Work) St Mut.
Phillipson, Michael. In Modernity's Wake. 176p. 1989. pap. 9.95 (*0-415-03232-6*, A3636) Routledge.
— Painting, Language & Modernity. 256p. 1985. pap. 35.00 (*0-7102-0480-9*, RKP) Routledge.
Phillipson, N. T. The University in Society. 200p. 1983. 20.00 (*0-85224-461-4*, Pub. by Edinburgh U Pr UK) Col U Pr.
Phillipson, Nicholas & Skinner, Quentin, eds. Political Discourse in Early Modern Britain. (Ideas in Context Ser.: No. 24). 416p. (C). 1993. 64.95 (*0-521-39242-X*) Cambridge U Pr.
Phillipson, Robert. Studien Zu Epikur und Den Epikureern. Bd. 17. write for info. (*0-318-70808-6*, Pub. by Georg Olms GW) Lubrecht & Cramer.
Phillipson, Robert, jt. auth. see Faerch, Claus.
Phillipson, Robert, et al, eds. Foreign - Second Language Pedagogy Research: A Commemorative Volume for Claus Faerch. (Multilingual Matters Ser.: No. 64). 360p. 1991. 39.95 (*1-85359-085-1*, Pub. by Multilingual Matters UK); pap. 39.95 (*1-85359-084-3*, Pub. by Multilingual Matters UK) Taylor & Francis.
Phillipson, William M. Life & Voyages of Wm. M. Phillipson. LC 71-99667. (Select Bibliographies Reprint Ser.). 1977. 20.95 (*0-8369-5096-8*) Ayer.

Phillis, J. W. The Pharmacology of Synapses. 376p. 1970. 156.00 (*0-08-015558-8*, Pub. by Pergamon Repr UK) Franklin.

Phillis, J. W., jt. ed. see Kerkut, G. A.

Phillis, John W. Adenosine & Adenine Nucleotides as Regulators of Cellular Function. (Illus.). 408p. 1991. 236.00 (*0-8493-6928-2*, QP625) CRC Pr.

— The Regulation of Cerebral Blood Flow. 1993. 195.00 (*0-8493-5096-4*, QP108) CRC Pr.

Phillis, Marilyn H. Watermedia Techniques for Releasing the Creative Spirit. LC 92-13481. (Illus.). 144p. 1992. 29.95 (*0-8230-5698-8*, Watsn-Guptill) Watsn-Guptill.

Phillis, Susan, jt. ed. see Jenkins, Betty L.

Phillot. English-Hindustani Vocabulary for Higher Standard & Proficiency Candidates or the Right Word in the Right Place. 2nd ed. 179p. 24.00 (*0-88431-563-0*) IBD Ltd.

Phillott, D. C. English-Hindustani Vocabulary for Higher Standard & Frequency. 1985. 35.00 (*0-8288-1746-4*, M9945) Fr & Eur.

Phillott, D. C. & Harcourt, E. S., trs. Falconry - Two Treatises. 1968. text ed. 45.00 (*0-685-57148-3*) Falcon Head Pr.

Phillpot, Clive, jt. auth. see Medvedow, Jill.

Phillpotts, Adelaide E. Lodgers in London. LC 74-150483. (Short Story Index Reprint Ser.). 1977. reprint ed. 20.95 (*0-8369-3824-0*) Ayer.

Phillpotts, Beatrice. Germany. (People & Places Ser.). (Illus.). 48p. (J). (gr. 4-8). 1989. lib. bdg. 12.95 (*0-382-09794-7*) Silver Burdett Pr.

Phillpotts, Bertha S. Edda & Saga. 1977. lib. bdg. 59.95 (*0-8490-1752-1*) Gordon Pr.

Phillpotts, Eden. Black, White & Brindled. LC 77-142272. (Short Story Index Reprint Ser.). 1977. 21.95 (*0-8369-3756-2*) Ayer.

— Chronicles of St. Tid. LC 78-132124. (Short Story Index Reprint Ser.). 1977. 20.95 (*0-8369-3681-7*) Ayer.

— A Deal with the Devil. Reginald, R. & Menville, Douglas, eds. LC 75-46300. (Supernatural & Occult Fiction Ser.). 1976. reprint ed. lib. bdg. 18.95 (*0-405-08160-X*) Ayer.

— Folk Afield. LC 76-128747. (Short Story Index Reprint Ser.). 1977. 20.95 (*0-8369-3638-8*) Ayer.

— Human Boy. LC 70-170592. (Short Story Index Reprint Ser.). 1977. reprint ed. 20.95 (*0-8369-4021-0*) Ayer.

— Human Boy & the War. LC 70-128748. (Short Story Index Reprint Ser.). 1977. 19.95 (*0-8369-3639-6*) Ayer.

— Peacock House, & Other Mysteries. LC 73-128749. (Short Story Index Reprint Ser.). 1977. 19.95 (*0-8369-3640-X*) Ayer.

— The Red Redmaynes. (Illus.). 384p. (C). 1982. reprint ed. pap. 6.95 (*0-486-24255-2*) Dover.

— Saurus. LC 75-10667. (Classics of Science Fiction Ser.). 281p. 1976. reprint ed. 15.00 (*0-88355-358-9*) Hyperion Conn.

— The Torch, & Other Tales. LC 71-144167. (Short Story Index Reprint Ser.). 1977. reprint ed. 19.95 (*0-8369-3782-1*) Ayer.

— Up Hill, down Dale: A Volume of Short Stories. 2nd ed. LC 79-150558. (Short Story Index Reprint Ser.). 1977. reprint ed. 20.95 (*0-8369-3855-0*) Ayer.

Phillps, G. C., jt. ed. see Gamborg, O. L.

Phillus, J. W., jt. ed. see Kerkut, G. A.

Philmus, Robert M. Into the Unknown: The Evolution of Science Fiction from Frances Godwin to H.G. Wells. 186p. (C). 1983. reprint ed. pap. 12.00 (*0-520-04959-4*) U CA Pr.

Philmus, Robert M., ed. see Wells, H. G.

Philo. Philonis Alexandrini in Flaccum. Connor, W. R., ed. LC 78-18570. (Greek Texts & Commentaries Ser.). 1979. reprint ed. lib. bdg. 25.95 (*0-405-11414-1*) Ayer.

— Philosophical Works. Incl. Vol. 1. 14.50 (*0-674-99249-0*); Vol. 2. 14.50 (*0-674-99250-4*); Vol. 3. 14.50 (*0-674-99272-5*); Vol. 4. 14.50 (*0-674-99287-3*); Vol. 5. 14.50 (*0-674-99303-9*); Vol. 6. 14.50 (*0-674-99319-5*); Vol. 7. 14.50 (*0-674-99353-5*); Vol. 8. 14.50 (*0-674-99376-4*); Vol. 9. 14.50 (*0-674-99400-0*); Vol. 10. 14.50 (*0-674-99417-5*); Suppl. 1. 14.50 (*0-674-99418-3*); Suppl. 2. 14.50 (*0-674-99442-6*); (Loeb Classical Library). write for info. (*0-318-53136-4*) HUP.

Philo, Chris, jt. ed. see Kearns, Gerry.

Philo, Greg. Seeing & Believing: The Influence of Television. 240p. 1990. 65.00 (*0-415-03620-8*, A4236); pap. 17.95 (*0-415-03621-6*, A4240) Routledge.

Philo, Harry M. Lawyers Desk Reference, 3 vols. 8th ed. (Tort Personal Injury Law Ser.). 1993. 345.00 (*0-685-68852-6*) Clark Boardman Callaghan.

— Lawyer's Desk Reference, 3 vols., Set. 8th ed. LC 65-12985. 1993. 365.00 (*0-685-59885-3*) Clark Boardman Callaghan.

— Trial Handbook for Michigan Lawyers. 2nd ed. LC 87-82165. 369p. 1987. 105.00 (*0-317-00477-8*) Lawyers Cooperative.

— Trial Handbook for Michigan Lawyers. 2nd suppl. ed. LC 87-82165. 369p. 1993. Suppl. 1993. 55.00 (*0-317-03182-1*) Lawyers Cooperative.

Philo, Maggie, jt. auth. see Lovric, Michelle.

Philo, Ron & Linner, John H. Guide to Human Anatomy. (Illus.). 335p. 1985. pap. text ed. 33.95 (*0-7216-1203-2*) Saunders.

Philodemos. Uber die Gedichte, Funftes Buch. xi, 178p. 1973. write for info. (*3-296-14930-9*, Pub. by Georg Olms GW) Lubrecht & Cramer.

Philodemus of Garada. The Rhetorica of Philodemus. Hubbell, Harry M., tr. (Connecticut Academy of Arts & Sciences Ser., Trans.: Vol. 23). 1920. pap. 75.00 (*0-685-22831-2*) Elliots Bks.

Philombe, Rene. Tales from Cameroon. Bjornson, Richard, tr. LC 84-50629. (Illus.). 136p. (C). 1984. 18.00 (*0-89410-314-8*) Three Continents.

Philomene, Marie, ed. see Emperor Akihito & Empress Michiko.

Philomusus, S.

Philon, Helen. Early Islamic Ceramics, Vol. 1: Catalogue of Islamic Art in the Benaki Museum. (Illus.). 376p. 1980. 120.00 (*0-85667-098-7*) Sothebys Pubns.

Philoponus. On Aristotle on the Intellect (de Anima 3. 4-8) Charlton, William, tr. LC 91-8806. (Ancient Commentators on Aristotle Ser.). 180p. 1991. 52.50 (*0-8014-2681-2*) Cornell U Pr.

— On Aristotle's Physics 2. Lacey, A. R., tr. (Ancient Commentators on Aristotle Ser.). 1993. 41.50 (*0-8014-2815-7*) Cornell U Pr.

— On Aristotle's "Physics 3" Edwards, M. J., tr. (Ancient Commentators on Aristotle Ser.). 1994. 39.95x (*0-8014-3089-5*) Cornell U Pr.

Philoponus & Simplicius. On Aristotle's "Physics 5-8" with On Aristotle on the Void. Lettinck, Paul & Urmson, J. O., trs. LC 93-31609. (Ancient Commentators on Aristotle Ser.). 288p. 1994. 44.50 (*0-8014-3005-4*) Cornell U Pr.

— Place, Void, & Eternity. Furley, David & Wildberg, Christian, trs. (Ancient Commentators on Aristotle Ser.). 160p. 1991. 47.50 (*0-8014-2634-0*) Cornell U Pr.

Philoponus, Ioannes. De Aeternitate Mundi Contra Proclum. Rabe, Hugo, ed. xiii, 699p. 1984. reprint ed. write for info. (*3-487-00420-8*, Pub. by Georg Olms GW) Lubrecht & Cramer.

Philoponus, John. Against Aristotle on the Eternity of the World. Wildberg, Christian, ed. & tr. by. LC 86-47973. (Ancient Commentators on Aristotle Ser.). 160p. 1987. 39.95 (*0-8014-2052-0*) Cornell U Pr.

Philosophy of Science Association Staff. Boston Studies in the Philosophy of Science, Vol. 20: Proceedings of the Philosophy of Science Association, Biennial Meeting, 1972. Schaffner, Kenneth F. & Cohen, R. S., eds. LC 72-624169. (Synthese Library: Vol. 64). 1974. lib. bdg. 112. 50 (*90-277-0408-2*); pap. text ed. 64.00 (*90-277-0409-0*) Kluwer Ac.

— Boston Studies in the Philosophy of Science, Vol 8: Proceedings of the Philosophy of Science Association, Biennial Meeting, 1970. Buck, R. Creighton & Cohen, R. S., eds. LC 73-20858. (Synthese Library: No. 39). 615p. 1971. lib. bdg. 136.50 (*90-277-0187-3*); pap. text ed. 65. 50 (*90-277-0309-4*) Kluwer Ac.

— PSA 1974: Proceedings of the Philosophy of Science Association, Biennial Meeting, 1974. Michalos, Alex C. & Cohen, R. S., eds. (Synthese Library: No. 91). 1976. lib. bdg. 149.50 (*90-277-0647-6*); pap. text ed. 103.00 (*90-277-0648-4*) Kluwer Ac.

Philostratus, Flavius. Life of Apollonius of Tyana. Epistles of Apollonius & the Treatise of Eusebius, 2 vols., 1. (Loeb Classical Library: No. 16-17). 610p. 1912. text ed. 18.95 (*0-674-99018-8*) HUP.

— Life of Apollonius of Tyana. Epistles of Apollonius & the Treatise of Eusebius, 2 vols., 2. (Loeb Classical Library: No. 16-17). 630p. 1912. text ed. 18.95 (*0-674-99019-6*) HUP.

— Lives of the Sophists. Bd. with Lives of the Philosophers & Sophists. (Loeb Classical Library: No. 134). 15.50 (*0-674-99149-4*) HUP.

— Opera, 2 vols. in 1. Kayser, C. L., ed. lxxxviii, 964p. 1985. reprint ed. write for info. (*3-487-00626-X*, Pub. by Georg Olms GW) Lubrecht & Cramer.

— Vitae Sophistarum. xlii, 416p. 1971. reprint ed. write for info. (*3-487-04155-3*, Pub. by Georg Olms GW) Lubrecht & Cramer.

Philostratus The Elder.

Philotus. Ane Verie Excellent & Delectabill Tratise. Intitulit Philotus Quhairin We May Persave the Greit Inconveineces That Fallis Out in the Marriage Betwene Age & Youth. LC 75-26325. (English Experience Ser.: No. 121). 48p. 1969. reprint ed. 8.00 (*90-221-0121-5*) Walter J Johnson.

Philp & Horn. Plants Are Alive. (Illus.). (Orig.). 1989. pap. text ed. 16.95 (*1-877991-14-7*, AP4286) Flinn Scientific.

Philp, Howard L. Freud & Religious Belief. LC 72-12635. 140p. 1974. reprint ed. text ed. 38.50 (*0-8371-6682-9*, PHFR, Greenwood Pr) Greenwood.

Philp, Kenneth R. John Collier's Crusade for Indian Reform, 1920-1954. LC 76-4427. (Illus.). 320p. reprint ed. pap. 91.20 (*0-7837-1911-6*, 2042115) Bks Demand.

Philp, Kenneth R., ed. Indian Self-Rule: First-Hand Accounts of Indian-White Relations from Roosevelt to Reagan. LC 85-21863. (Current Issues in the American West Ser.: Vol. IV). 350p. 1986. 21.50 (*0-935704-28-0*); pap. 12.50 (*0-935704-29-9*) Howe Brothers.

— Indian Self Rule: First Hand Accounts of Indian-White Relations from Roosevelt to Reagen. LC 94-36862. 352p. 1995. pap. text ed. 19.95 (*0-87421-180-8*) Utah St U Pr.

Philp, Kenneth R. & West, Elliott, eds. Essays on Walter Prescott Webb. LC 75-37672. (Walter Prescott Webb Memorial Lectures: No. 10). 124p. 1976. 10.95 (*0-292-72016-5*) Tex A&M Univ Pr.

Philp, Kenneth R., jt. ed. see Lackner, Bede K.

Philp, Mark. Godwin's Political Justice. LC 86-47538. 288p. 1986. 38.95 (*0-8014-1908-5*) Cornell U Pr.

Philp, Mark, ed. The French Revolution & British Popular Politics. 304p. (C). 1991. 54.95 (*0-521-39123-7*) Cambridge U Pr.

Philp, Mark, ed. see Paine, Thomas.

Philp, Mark, et al, eds. The Collected Novels & Memoirs of William Godwin. (Pickering Masters Ser.). 1992. 575.00 (*1-85196-007-4*, Pub. by Pickering & Chatto UK) Ashgate Pub Co.

— The Political & Philosophical Writings of William Godwin. (Pickering Masters Ser.). 1993. 575.00 (*1-85196-026-0*, Pub. by Pickering & Chatto UK) Ashgate Pub Co.

Philp, R. P. Fossil Fuel Biomarkers: Applications & Spectra: Methods in Geochemistry & Geophysics 23. 296p. 1985. 95.00 (*0-444-42471-7*) Elsevier.

***Philp, Richard B.** Environmental Hazards & Human Health. 304p. 1995. 59.95 (*1-56670-133-3*, L1133) Lewis Pubs.

Philp, Richard B., ed. Mathematical Models in Microbial Population Dynamics. 288p. 1981. 140.00 (*0-8493-6110-9*, RM340, CRC Reprint) Franklin.

Philpin, C. H., ed. Nationalism & Popular Protest in Ireland. (Past & Present Publications). (Illus.). 475p. 1987. 69.95 (*0-521-26816-8*) Cambridge U Pr.

Philpin, C. H., jt. ed. see Aston, T. H.

Philpin, John & Donnelly, John. Beyond Murder: The Inside Account of the Gainesville Student Murders. 416p. (Orig.). 1994. pap. 4.99 (*0-451-40409-2*, Onyx) NAL-Dutton.

***Philpot.** Anthony Ant's Creepy Crawly Party. LC 94-67150. 1995. 7.99 (*0-679-87056-3*) Random.

Philpot, Ed, jt. auth. see Philpot, Jan.

Philpot, Gloria & Gunn, Mildred, eds. Sunday Morning Atlanta Preaching: Sermons, Afro American, Atlanta. 72p. (Orig.). 1994. pap. write for info. (*0-9621362-1-2*) T E Balls Pubns.

Philpot, Graham. The Fabulous Fairy Tale Follies. LC 93-30479. (Illus.). 32p. (J). (gr. k up). 1994. 12.00 (*0-679-85316-2*) Random Bks Yng Read.

Philpot, Graham, jt. auth. see Oivardi, Anne.

Philpot, Graham, jt. auth. see Philpot, Lorna.

Philpot, J. H. The Sacred Tree: The Tree in Religion & Myth. 1977. lib. bdg. 250.00 (*0-8490-2553-2*) Gordon Pr.

— The Seceders. 1970. pap. 4.50 (*0-85151-132-5*) Banner of Truth.

***Philpot, Jan & Philpot, Ed.** Partners in Learning & Growing: Linking the Home, School, & Community Through Curriculum-Based Programs. Britt, Leslie, ed. (Illus.). 80p. (Orig.). (J). (gr. 4-8). 1994. pap. text ed. 8.95 (*0-86530-298-7*) Incentive Pubns.

Philpot, Jan G. Book-a-Tivities! High-Interest Activities to Turn Students into Booklovers. Keeling, Jan, ed. (Illus.). 80p. (Orig.). 1993. teacher ed 8.95 (*0-86530-248-0*) Incentive Pubns.

— Bridging the Gap Between the Media Specialist & the Classroom Teacher. 80p. 1989. pap. text ed. 7.95 (*0-86530-071-2*, IP 166-6) Incentive Pubns.

— Class Act Awards & Motivators: To Encourage School Spirit, Self-Esteem, & Attendance. Keeling, Jan, ed. (Illus.). 80p. (Orig.). 1993. teacher ed 8.95 (*0-86530-214-6*) Incentive Pubns.

— Once upon a Tradition: Using Traditional Literature to Develop Reading, Writing, Thinking, & Research Skills. Keeling, Jan, ed. (Illus.). 80p. (Orig.). 1993. pap. text ed. 8.95 (*0-86530-286-3*) Incentive Pubns.

— Readers' Clubhouse: Organized Reading Programs with a Purpose. Binkley, Margaret, ed. (Illus.). 80p. (Orig.). 1991. pap. text ed. 7.95 (*0-86530-204-9*, IP 192-7) Incentive Pubns.

— Scissor-Tales for Any Day: Storytelling Cutups, Activities, & Extensions. Britt, Leslie, ed. (Illus.). 80p. (Orig.). 1994. pap. text ed. 8.85 (*0-86530-285-5*) Incentive Pubns.

— Scissor-Tales for Special Days: Storytelling Cutups, Activities, & Extensions. Keeling, Jan, ed. (Illus.). 80p. (Orig.). 1994. pap. text ed. 8.95 (*0-86530-284-7*) Incentive Pubns.

— Year of the Reader! Creative Activities to Promote Reading Excitement. Keeling, Jan, ed. (Illus.). 96p. (Orig.). 1993. teacher ed 9.95 (*0-86530-247-2*) Incentive Pubns.

Philpot, Kent. El Libro de la Liberacion: The Deliverance Book. (SPA.). 3.25 (*84-7228-512-X*, 360400, Pub. by Edit Clie SP) TSELF.

Philpot, Lorna & Philpot, Graham. Amazing Anthony Ant. (Illus.). 24p. (J). (gr. k-3). 1994. 13.00 (*0-679-85622-6*) Random Bks Yng Read.

— Anthony Ant Pop-up, No. 1. (Illus.). (J). Date not set. 5.99 (*0-679-87445-3*) Random.

— Anthony Ant Pop-up, No. 2. (Illus.). (J). Date not set. 5.99 (*0-679-87446-1*) Random.

— Anthony Ant Pop-up, No. 3. (Illus.). (J). Date not set. 5.99 (*0-679-87447-X*) Random.

Philpot, Terry & Hanvey, Chris, eds. Practising Social Work. LC 93-28946. 1994. write for info. (*0-415-09236-1*, Routledge NY); pap. write for info. (*0-415-09237-X*, Routledge NY) Routledge.

Philpot, William M. Best Black Sermons. LC 72-75358. 96p. 1972. pap. 9.00 (*0-8170-0533-1*) Judson.

Philpott, A. B., jt. ed. see Anderson, E. J.

Philpott, Adrian. Witnessing Justice in Queensland. 154p. (C). 1990. pap. text ed. 48.00 (*0-646-03848-6*, Pub. by Boolarong Pubns AT) St Mut.

Philpott, Brian & Ott, B. Famous Fighter Aces. (Illus.). 160p. 1990. 26.95 (*1-85260-025-X*, Pub. by Thorsons UK) Motorbooks Intl.

Philpott, Don. The Vineyards of France. LC 88-21427. 441p. 1988. pap. 14.95 (*0-87106-687-4*) Globe Pequot.

Philpott, Fiona A., jt. auth. see Spencer, Michael G.

Philpott, Jane, jt. auth. see Crellin, John K.

***Philpott-Jones, Pamela & McClure, Paul.** Woodworking for Serious Beginners. (Illus.). 160p. (Orig.). 1995. pap. 19.95 (*0-9643999-2-X*) Cambium Pr.

Philpott, Kent. Si el Diablo Escribiera una Biblia: If the Devil Wrote a Bible. (SPA.). 3.25 (*84-7228-417-4*, 220822, Pub. by Edit Clie SP) TSELF.

***Philpott, Peter.** The Art of Wrist-Spin Bowling. (Illus.). 128p. 1995. 24.95 (*1-85223-870-4*, Pub. by Crowood Pr UK) Trafalgar.

Philpott, Thomas L. The Slum & the Ghetto: Immigrants, Blacks, & Reformers in Chicago, 1880-1930. 2nd ed. 437p. (C). 1991. pap. 18.95 (*0-534-14742-9*) Intl Thomson.

Philpott, William, jt. auth. see Kalita, Dwight.

Philpott, William H. & Kalita, Dwight K. Brain Allergies. (Orig.). 1987. pap. 14.95 (*0-87983-426-9*) Keats.

Philpott, William H. & Taplin, Sharon. The BioMagnetic Handbook. 97p. 1989. 17.95 (*0-9636964-0-8*) Enviro-Tech.

Philpotts, Anthony R. Petrography of Igneous & Metamorphic Rocks. 178p. (C). 1988. pap. text ed. write for info. (*0-13-662313-1*) P-H.

— Principles of Igneous & Metamorphic Petrology. (C). 1990. Casebound. text ed. write for info. (*0-13-691361-X*) P-H.

Philps, J. W. The Functional Foot Orthosis. (Illus.). 180p. 1990. pap. text ed. 35.00 (*0-443-04058-3*) Churchill.

— The Functional Foot Orthosis. 2nd ed. 1995. write for info. (*0-443-04991-2*) Churchill.

Phil's Photo Staff, ed. A Typeface Sourcebook: Homage to the Alphabet. rev. ed. 565p. 1990. pap. 39.99 (*0-935603-47-6*, 30254) Rockport Pubs.

Philyaw, Chuck & Lippincott, David. The PC Technical Source-Book, 1988. Kleine, Marty, ed. (Illus.). 76p. (Orig.). 1988. pap. 19.95 (*0-929069-00-5*) Industrial Computer Source.

Phimister, Euan. Savings & Investment in Farm Household: Analysis Using Life Cycles Models. 100p. 1993. 54.95 (*1-85628-596-0*, Pub. by Avebury Pub UK) Ashgate Pub Co.

Phimister, Evelyn J., et al. Sketching at Home & Abroad: British Landscape Drawings, 1750-1850. LC 92-80446. (Illus.). 64p. 1994. pap. 17.50 (*0-87598-094-5*) Pierpont Morgan.

Phinnemore, David, jt. auth. see Church, Clife.

Phinney. Process Your Thoughts with 5.25 Disk IBM. (College ESL Ser.). 1994. pap. 19.20 (*0-8384-5289-2*) Heinle & Heinle.

Phinney, Archie. Nez Perce Texts. LC 73-82344. (Columbia University. Contributions to Anthropology Ser.: Vol. 25). reprint ed. 49.50 (*0-404-50575-9*) AMS Pr.

Phinney, Davis & Carpenter, Connie. Training for Cycling: The Ultimate Guide to Improved Performance. (Illus.). 256p. (Orig.). 1992. pap. 13.00 (*0-399-51731-6*, Perigree Bks) Berkley Pub.

Phinney, E., jt. auth. see Spooner, A.

Phinney, Ed. Cambridge Latin Course, Unit I. 3rd ed. LC 87-10281. 1988. 18.95 (*0-521-34379-8*) Cambridge U Pr.

— Cambridge Latin Course Unit 1. 3rd ed. 232p. (C). 1988. teacher ed, pap. 13.50 (*0-521-34853-6*) Cambridge U Pr.

— Cambridge Latin Course Unit 2. 3rd ed. (C). 1988. teacher ed, pap. 14.95 (*0-521-34855-2*) Cambridge U Pr.

— Cambridge Latin Course, Unit 4: North American. 3rd ed. (C). 1992. student ed, pap. 8.95 (*0-521-34860-9*) Cambridge U Pr.

Phinney, Ed, ed. Cambridge Latin Course, Unit 4: North America. 3rd ed. 1991. 38.95 (*0-521-34380-1*) Cambridge U Pr.

— The History of the American Classical League, 1919-1994. 317p. (Orig.). 1994. per., pap. 40.00 (*0-939507-47-1*) Amer Classical.

Phinney, Ed, jt. auth. see Griffin, M. R.

Phinney, Ed, ed. see Morwood, James & Warman, Mark.

Phinney, Jean S. & Rotheram, Mary. Children's Ethnic Socialization. Society for Research in Child Development Staff, ed. (Focus Editions Ser.: Vol. 81). 400p. (Orig.). 1986. text ed. 49.95 (*0-8039-2815-7*); pap. text ed. 24.95 (*0-8039-2816-5*) Sage.

Phinney, Joanna, jt. auth. see Dodge, Diane T.

Phinney, M. A. Allen: A Brief History of Lewis Allen of Fisher's Island & New London, CT, & His Descendants, from 1699-1954. 207p. 1991. reprint ed. lib. bdg. 44.50 (*0-8328-1803-8*); reprint ed. pap. 34.50 (*0-8328-1804-6*) Higginson Bk Co.

— Isham Genealogy: A Brief History of Jirah Isham. 179p. 1991. reprint ed. lib. bdg. 37.00 (*0-8328-2154-3*); reprint ed. pap. 27.00 (*0-8328-2155-1*) Higginson Bk Co.

Phinney, Margaret. Exploring Land Habitats. LC 94-14058. (Illus.). 24p. (Orig.). (J). (gr. 1-5). 1994. 23.95 (*1-879531-39-9*); lib. bdg. 9.95 (*1-879531-48-8*); pap. 4.95 (*1-879531-38-0*) Mondo Pubng.

***Phinney, Margaret Y.** Baba Yaga: A Russian Folktale. (Illus.). 40p. (J). (gr. 2-6). Date not set. lib. bdg. 13.95 (*1-57255-004-X*) Mondo Pubng.

— Baba Yaga: A Russian Folktale. (Illus.). 40p. (J). (gr. 2-6). Date not set. 25.95 (*1-57255-006-6*) Mondo Pubng.

— Reading with the Troubled Reader. LC 88-11211. (Illus.). 138p. (Orig.). (C). 1988. pap. text ed. 16.00 (*0-435-08480-1*, 08480) Heinemann.

— We're off to Thunder Mountain. LC 95-8418. (J). 1995. write for info. (*1-57255-032-5*); pap. write for info. (*1-57255-031-7*) Mondo Pubng.

Phinney, Marianne. Process Your Thoughts: Writing With Computers. LC 93-39976. 1994. pap. 20.95 (*0-8384-5288-4*) Heinle & Heinle.

— Process Your Thoughts with 3.5 Disk IBM. (College ESL Ser.). 1994. pap. 19.50 (*0-8384-5290-6*) Heinle & Heinle.

Phinney, Robert A., ed. The History of the Earth's Crust: A Symposium. LC 68-20875. (Illus.). 244p. 1968. 65.00 (*0-691-08063-1*); pap. text ed. 19.95x (*0-691-02379-4*) Princeton U Pr.

Phinney, William R., et al, eds. Thomas Ware, a Spectator at the Christmas Conference: A Miscellany on Thomas Ware & the Christmas Conference. LC 84-70457. (Illus.). 320p. (Orig.). 1984. reprint ed. pap. 8.95 (*0-914960-48-2*) Academy Bks.

Phipatseritham, Krirkkiat & Yoshihara, Kunio. Business Groups in Thailand. 39p. (Orig.). 1984. pap. text ed. 16. 95 (*9971-902-69-9*, Pub. by Inst SE Asian Studies SI) Ashgate Pub Co.

Phippen, George. The Life of a Cowboy. LC 70-101102. (Illus.). 104p. reprint ed. 29.70 (*0-8357-9622-1*, 2019352) Bks Demand.

Phippen, George R. Land of Song: Ireland, a Geography. 1993. pap. 17.95 (*0-9638805-1-9*) Esker Pubng.

PQ

Phippen, Mark L. & Wells, Maryann P., eds. Perioperative Nursing: Principles & Practice. LC 92-24341. (Illus.). 944p. 1993. text ed. 57.95 (*0-7216-7233-7*) Saunders.

***Phippen, S., et al, eds.** The Best Maine Stories. LC 94-5391. 320p. 1994. pap. 11.95 (*0-89272-351-3*) Down East.

Phippen, Sanford. People Trying to Be Good. 3rd ed. Hunting, Constance, ed. 150p. 1991. pap. 8.95 (*0-913006-40-8*) Puckerbrush.

— The Police Know Everything: And Other Maine Stories. Hunting, Constance, ed. 149p. (Orig.). 1982. pap. 8.95 (*0-913006-27-0*) Puckerbrush.

Phippen, Sanford, ed. High Clouds Soaring, Storms Driving Low: The Letters of Ruth Moore. (Illus.). 560p. 1993. pap. 16.95 (*0-942396-66-9*) Blackberry ME.

Phipps. Medical-Surgical Nursing: Concepts & Clinical Pr. 1994. 78.95 (*0-8016-7888-9*) Mosby Yr Bk.

— Medical-Surgical Nursing: Concepts & Clinical Practice. 4th ed. (Illus.). 2480p. 1990. 64.95 (*0-8016-6218-4*); disk write for info. (*0-318-67210-3*) Mosby Yr Bk.

— Pulmonary Fibroblast Heterogeneity. 1992. 194.00 (*0-8493-6038-2*, RC776, CRC Reprint) Franklin.

Phipps, jt. auth. see Long.

Phipps, jt. auth. see Sands.

Phipps, Beckey, ed. see Singh, Swayam P.

Phipps, Bonnie. Singing with Young Children: Book & Cassette. (Illus.). 64p. (Orig.). 1991. audio 14.95 (*0-88284-492-X*, 3558) Alfred Pub.

Phipps, Brian. The Catamaran Book. 2nd ed. (C). 1993. text ed. 59.00 (*0-906754-86-0*, Pub. by Fernhurst Bks UK) St Mut.

Phipps, C. & Hawthorne, P. Piano Classics (Blu) (Learn to Play Ser.). (Illus.). 128p. (J). (gr. 2-9). 1994. pap. 16.95 (*0-7460-1967-X*, Usborne) EDC.

Phipps, Clarence A. Variable Speed Drive Fundamentals. LC 93-50689. 1994. 75.00 (*0-88173-191-9*) Fairmont Pr.

Phipps, Denis. The Management of Aviation Security. 384p. (C). 1990. 150.00x (*0-273-03229-1*, Pub. by Pitman Pub Ltd UK) Trans-Atl Phila.

Phipps, Frances. Let Me Be Los: A Code Book for Finnegans Wake. Quasha, George, ed. LC 87-6451. (Illus.). 211p. (C). 1987. reprint ed. pap. 16.95 (*0-88268-042-0*) Station Hill Pr.

— Let Me Be LOS: Codebook for Finnegans Wake. (Illus.). 1987. 43.50 (*0-9606540-5-4*) Classic Nonfic.

Phipps, Frances, jt. auth. see Eldon, Magdalen.

Phipps, Grace M. The Doctor's Three Daughters. large type ed. 1978. 12.00 (*0-7089-0090-9*) Ulverscroft.

Phipps, Graeme, jt. auth. see Stanbury, Peter.

Phipps, J. F., jt. auth. see Cohen, J. M.

Phipps, Jeffrey H. Laparoscopic Hysterectomy & Oopherectomy: A Practical Manual & Colour Atlas. LC 93-7324. (Illus.). 120p. 1993. text ed. 89.00 (*0-443-04929-7*) Churchill.

Phipps, Joe. Summer Stock: Behind the Scenes with LBJ in '48. LC 92-13118. (Illus.). 338p. 1992. 27.95 (*0-87565-107-0*) Tex Christian.

Phipps, John-Francis, jt. auth. see Garrison, Jim.

Phipps, L. B., jt. auth. see Janosik, E. H.

Phipps, Lloyd J. Mechanics in Agriculture Workbook, Pt. 1. 2nd ed. 200p. 1990. pap. 12.95 (*0-8134-2866-1*) Interstate.

— Mechanics in Agriculture Workbook, Pt. 2. 2nd ed. 200p. 1990. pap. 12.95 (*0-8134-2867-X*) Interstate.

Phipps, Lloyd J. & Osborne, Edward. Handbook on Agricultural Education in Public Schools. 5th ed. 596p. 1988. text ed. 29.95 (*0-8134-2774-6*) Interstate.

Phipps, Lloyd J. & Reynolds, Carl L. Mechanics in Agriculture. 4th ed. (Illus.). xi, 765p. 1992. 43.95 (*0-8134-2925-0*); text ed. 32.95 (*0-685-50795-5*); 6.95 (*0-8134-2926-9*) Interstate.

Phipps, Marlynn, et al. Feed a Family of Four for as Low as 10 Dollars Per Week: And Enjoy a Nibble of Independence. 162p. 1992. pap. 15.99 (*0-9631522-0-3*) Phipps AZ.

Phipps, P. Beverley, jt. ed. see Brubaker, George R.

Phipps, Paula, ed. see Burkle, Frank.

Phipps, Paula, ed. see Marshak, David.

Phipps, Phyllis. The Relationship Revolution: A Baby Boomers Guide to Finding Love. 1993. pap. 10.95 (*0-9638341-9-3*) Summer Hill.

Phipps, Ramsay W. The Armies of the First French Republic & the Rise of the Marshals of Napoleon I, 5 vols., 1. LC 79-23801. (Illus.). 1980. reprint ed. text ed. 65.00 (*0-313-22209-6*, PHAR01) Greenwood.

— The Armies of the First French Republic & the Rise of the Marshals of Napoleon I, 5 vols. Set. LC 79-23801. (Illus.). 1980. reprint ed. text ed. 295.00 (*0-313-22208-8*, PHAR) Greenwood.

— The Armies of the First French Republic & the Rise of the Marshals of Napoleon I, 5 vols., Vol. 2. LC 79-23801. (Illus.). 1980. reprint ed. text ed. 65.00 (*0-313-22210-X*, PHAR02) Greenwood.

— The Armies of the First French Republic & the Rise of the Marshals of Napoleon I, 5 vols., Vol. 3. LC 79-23801. (Illus.). 1980. reprint ed. text ed. 65.00 (*0-313-22211-8*, PHAR03) Greenwood.

— The Armies of the First French Republic & the Rise of the Marshals of Napoleon I, 5 vols., Vol. 4. LC 79-23801. (Illus.). 1980. reprint ed. text ed. 65.00 (*0-313-22212-6*, PHAR04) Greenwood.

— The Armies of the First French Republic & the Rise of the Marshals of Napoleon I, 5 vols., Vol. 5. LC 79-23801. (Illus.). 1980. reprint ed. text ed. 65.00 (*0-313-22213-4*, PHAR05) Greenwood.

Phipps, Shirley. Santa Fe & Beyond. LC 93-84179. 1993. 9.95 (*0-916809-61-7*) Scott Pubns MI.

— A Touch of Santa Fe. LC 90-60514. 52p. (Orig.). 1990. pap. 9.95 (*0-916809-41-2*) Scott Pubns MI.

Phipps, Stephen, jt. auth. see Stuebner, Stephen.

Phipps, Thomas E., Jr. Heretical Verities: Mathematical Themes in Physical Description. (Illus.). 632p. 1987. 39.00 (*0-9606540-2-X*) Classic Nonfic.

Phipps, Tim T., et al, eds. Agriculture & the Environment. LC 87-43010. 316p. reprint ed. pap. 90.10 (*0-8357-3282-7*, 2039505) Bks Demand.

Phipps, William E. Assertive Biblical Women. LC 92-3026. (Contributions in Women's Studies: No. 128). 184p. 1992. text ed. 45.00 (*0-313-28498-9*, PAP/, Greenwood Pr) Greenwood.

— Cremation Concerns. (Illus.). 114p. (C). 1989. text ed. 34.95x (*0-398-05532-7*) C C Thomas.

— Death: Confronting the Reality. LC 86-45405. 204p. (Orig.). 1987. pap. 13.99 (*0-8042-0487-X*, John Knox) Westminster John Knox.

— Genesis & Gender: Biblical Myths of Sexuality & Their Cultural Impact. LC 88-27509. 141p. 1989. text ed. 45.00 (*0-275-93200-1*, C3200, Praeger Pubs) Greenwood.

— Muhammad & Jesus: A Comparison of the Prophets & Their Teachings. LC 94-34176. 1995. 16.95 (*1-55778-718-2*) Paragon Hse.

— The Wisdom & Wit of Rabbi Jesus. LC 93-19528. 272p. (Orig.). 1993. pap. 17.99 (*0-664-25232-X*) Westminster John Knox.

Phipps, Wintley & Down, Goldie. The Power of a Dream: The Inspiring Story of a Young Man's Audacious Faith. 176p. 1995. 15.99 (*0-310-47920-7*) Zondervan.

Phipson, Emma. The Animal-Lore of Shakespeare's Time. 1976. lib. bdg. 59.95 (*0-8490-1432-8*) Gordon Pr.

— Animal-Lore of Shakespeare's Time. LC 79-174197. reprint ed. 52.50 (*0-404-05044-1*) AMS Pr.

Phipson, Joan. Bianca. LC 88-13192. 176p. (YA). (gr. 7 up). 1988. text ed. 14.95 (*0-689-50448-9*, McElderry) S&S Childrens.

— Hit & Run. 132p. (YA). (gr. 7 up). 1989. reprint ed. pap. 3.95 (*0-02-044665-9*, Collier Bks Young) S&S Childrens.

***Phister, Montgomery, Jr.** Data Processing Technology & Economics. 1979. 75.00 (*0-917640-04-7*) Santa Monica Pub.

— Data Processing Technology & Economics. 2nd ed. LC 79-25052. (Illus.). 720p. 1979. pap. 50.00 (*0-917640-05-5*) Santa Monica Pub.

— Data Processing Technology & Economics: 1975-1978 Supplement. LC 79-25052. (Illus.). 1979. pap. 10.00 (*0-917640-03-9*) Santa Monica Pub.

— Logical Design of Digital Computers. LC 58-6082. 424p. reprint ed. pap. 120.90 (*0-317-09156-5*, 2016482) Bks Demand.

Phisterer, Frederick. Statistical Record of the Armies of the United States. 343p. 1989. reprint ed. 25.00 (*0-916107-58-2*) Broadfoot.

Phitsanoukanh, Bounta, tr. see Hutchinson, Hanna.

Phizacklea, Annie. Unpacking the Fashion Industry. 128p. 1990. 49.95 (*0-415-00054-8*, A4478); pap. 14.95 (*0-415-00055-6*, A4482) Routledge.

***Phizacklea, Annie & Wolkowitz, Carol.** Homeworking Women: Gender, Race & Class at Work. 160p. 1995. text ed. 55.00 (*0-8039-8873-7*); pap. text ed. 17.95 (*0-8039-8874-5*) Sage.

***Phlegar, Janet & Kaufman, Jill.** Effective Professional Development: A Guide for Youth Apprenticeship & Work-Based Learning Programs. 56p. 1992. pap. 5.00 (*1-887410-73-2*) Jobs for Future.

***Phlegar, Phyllis.** Love Online: A Practical Guide to Digital Dating. 1995. pap. 9.95 (*0-201-40965-8*) Addison-Wesley.

Phleger, Frederick B. Red Tag Comes Back. LC 61-11452. (Science I Can Read Bks.). (Illus.). 64p. (J). (gr. k-3). 1961. lib. bdg. 13.89 (*0-06-024706-1*) HarpC Child Bks.

Phleger, Marjorie. Pilot Down, Presumed Dead. LC 63-16244. (Trophy Bk.). 224p. (J). (gr. 5-9). 1975. pap. 3.95 (*0-06-440067-0*, Trophy) HarpC Child Bks.

Phlegming, I. M. Last of the Secret Agents. 230p. (Orig.). 1986. pap. 7.95 (*0-9614706-0-7*) Thalia Bks.

Philipot, Deborah, jt. auth. see Carlton, Richard R.

Phlips, L. Applied Consumption Analysis. 2nd enl. rev. ed. (Advanced Textbooks in Economics Ser.: Vol. 5). 324p. 1983. 39.50 (*0-444-86531-4*, North Holland) Elsevier.

***Phlips, Louis.** Competition Policy: A Game-Theoretic Perspective. (Illus.). 296p. (C). 1995. write for info. (*0-521-49521-0*); pap. write for info. (*0-521-49871-6*) Cambridge U Pr.

— The Economics of Imperfect Information. (Illus.). 275p. 1989. 64.95 (*0-521-30920-4*); pap. 22.95 (*0-521-31381-3*) Cambridge U Pr.

— The Economics of Price Discrimination: Four Essays in Applied Price Theory. LC 82-14625. 284p. 1983. pap. 24.95 (*0-521-28394-9*) Cambridge U Pr.

Phlips, Louis, ed. Commodity, Futures & Financial Markets. (Advanced Studies in Theoretical & Applied Econometrics). (C). 1990. lib. bdg. 112.50 (*0-7923-1043-8*) Kluwer Ac.

Phlips, Louis & Taylor, Lester D., eds. Aggregation, Consumption & Trade: Essays in Honor of H.S. Houthakker. LC 92-33114. (Advanced Studies in Theoretical & Applied Econometrics: Vol. 27). (C). 1992. lib. bdg. 90.50 (*0-7923-2001-8*) Kluwer Ac.

Phllips, Michael R., ed. see Wright, Harold B.

Pho, Hai B. Vietnamese Public Management in Transition: South Vietnam Public Administration, 1955-1975. LC 89-14648. (Illus.). 210p. (C). 1990. lib. bdg. 42.50 (*0-8191-7517-X*) U Pr of Amer.

Phoa, Sharon S. The Flame That Burns Eternal. LC 93-61288. 147p. 1994. 8.95 (*1-55523-664-2*) Winston-Derek.

Phoenix, ed. see Thompson, Diana L.

Phoenix, Ann. Young Mothers? 250p. 1991. 59.95 (*0-7456-0540-0*); pap. 26.95 (*0-7456-0854-X*) Blackwell Pubs.

***Phoenix, Ann & Tizard, Barbara.** Race, Ethnicity, Gender & Social Class: Social Identities in Adolescence. (Adolescence & Society Ser.). 224p. (Orig.). 1995. 59.95 (*0-415-08329-X*, B4315); pap. 17.95 (*0-415-08330-3*, B4319) Routledge.

Phoenix, Ann, jt. ed. see Bhavnani, Kum-Kum.

Phoenix, Ann, jt. auth. see Tizard, Barbara.

Phoenix, Ann, et al, eds. Motherhood: Meanings, Practices, & Ideologies. (Gender & Psychology Ser.). (Illus.). 240p. 1991. 49.95 (*0-8039-8313-1*); pap. 19.95 (*0-8039-8314-X*) Sage.

Phoenix Art Museum Staff. The Modern Spirit in Chinese Painting: Selections from the Jeannette Shambaugh Elliott Collection. Brown, Claudia & Chou, Ju-hsi, eds. LC 85-72990. (Illus.). (Orig.). 1985. pap. 15.00 (*0-910407-17-7*) Phoenix Art.

— The Popular West: American Illustrators 1900-1940. (Illus.). 55p. (Orig.). 1982. pap. 8.00 (*0-910407-08-8*) Phoenix Art.

Phoenix Arts Commission. Public Art Works: The Arizona Models. LC 93-6893. 1992. spiral bd. 20.00 (*0-9611710-7-3*) Western States.

Phoenix, Clay. Cancer: Memories in Ink & Other Poems. (Illus.). 38p. 1987. pap. 5.00 (*0-9619448-0-3*) Consultantswest Inc.

***Phoenix, Karma.** Secret Powers of Karma: Revenge & Reconciliation in the Sexual Revolution. (Illus.). 350p. (C). 1995. pap. 20.00 (*0-614-04583-5*) Merit Prods.

***Phoenix Mapping Service Staff.** Phoenix Street Atlas: 1995 Assessor. 1995. spiral bd. 25.95 (*0-614-06737-5*, 95892, Phoenix Map Svce) Wide World Maps.

— Phoenix Valley of the Sun Street Guide. 104p. 1995. pap. 3.25 (*0-938448-95-1*, Phoenix Map Svce) Wide World Maps.

***Phoenix Publishing Staff.** Brown County: Paradise in the Hills. (Illus.). 64p. 1994. 29.95 (*1-886154-01-5*) Phoenix IL.

— Brown County: Paradise in the Hills: 1995 Calendar. (Illus.). 26p. 1994. pap. 9.95 (*1-886154-03-1*) Phoenix IL.

Phoenix Staff. The Rape of Emergency Medicine. 288p. (Orig.). 1992. pap. 19.95 (*0-9632237-1-2*) Phoenix.

Phoenix Technologies Staff. ABIOS for IBM PS-2 Computers & Compatibles: The Complete Guide to ROM-Based System Software for OS-2. 1989. pap. 26.95 (*0-201-51805-8*) Addison-Wesley.

— CBIOS for IBM PS-2 Computers & Compatibles: The Complete Guide to ROM-Based System Software for DOS. 1989. pap. 26.95 (*0-201-51804-X*) Addison-Wesley.

— System BIOS for IBM PCs, Compatibles & EISA Computers: The Complete Guide to ROM-Based System Software. 2nd ed. (Illus.). 604p. 1991. pap. 29.95 (*0-201-57760-7*) Addison-Wesley.

Phongpaichit, Pasuk. From Peasant Girls to Bangkok Masseuses. (Women, Work & Development Ser.: No. 2). ix, 80p. 1992. pap. 12.00 (*92-2-103013-X*) Intl Labour Office.

— The New Wave of Japanese Investment in ASEAN: Determinants & Prospects. 136p. 1990. pap. text ed. 13.00 (*981-3035-62-5*, Pub. by Inst SE Asian Studies SI) Ashgate Pub Co.

***Phongpaichit, Pasuk & Baker, Chris.** Thailand: Economy & Politics. (Illus.). 450p. 1995. 55.00 (*967-65-3097-2*) OUP.

Phoon, Wai-On & Chen, P. C. Textbook of Community Medicine in South-East Asia. LC 84-5073. (Wiley-Medical Publication Ser.). (Illus.). 629p. reprint ed. pap. 179.30 (*0-7837-1878-0*, 2042079) Bks Demand.

Phornirunlit, Supon. Best of International Self-Promotion. 1993. 45.00 (*0-942604-32-6*) Madison Square.

— Great Design Using One, Two, & Three Colors. (Illus.). 196p. 1992. 39.95 (*0-942604-24-5*) Madison Square.

— Iconopolis. 1993. 49.95 (*0-685-67211-5*) Madison Square.

— International Logos & Trademarks II, No. II. 1993. 45.00 (*0-942604-26-1*) Madison Square.

— International Women in Design. 1993. 39.95 (*0-942604-30-X*) Madison Square.

***Phornirunlit, Supon, ed.** Innovative Low-Budget Design. (Illus.). 192p. 1996. 45.00 (*0-942604-48-2*) Madison Square.

— International Logos & Trademarks III. (Illus.). 192p. 1995. 45.00 (*0-942604-47-4*) Madison Square.

— The Right Portfolio for the Right Job. (Illus.). 192p. 1994. 45.00 (*0-942604-36-9*) Madison Square.

Phornitzunlit, Supon, ed. World Class Design. (Illus.). 192p. 1996. 45.00 (*0-942604-37-7*) Madison Square.

Photiades, V. Renoir: Nudes. (Rhythem & Color One Ser.). 1970. 9.95 (*0-8288-9503-1*) Fr & Eur.

Photiadis, John D., ed. Religion in Appalachia. 1979. 10.75 (*0-686-26337-5*) W Va U Ctr Exten.

***Photiadis, John D. & Schwarzweller, Harry K., eds.** Change in Rural Appalachia: Implications for Action Programs. 284p. 1971. text ed. 39.95 (*0-8122-7618-3*) U of Pa Pr.

Photiou, Paul. My Conversion to Christ. Orthodox Christian Educational Society Staff, ed. (Orig.). (GRE.). 1970. reprint ed. 2.00 (*0-938366-41-6*) Orthodox Chr.

Photius, Patriarcha C. Epistolae. 851p. 1978. reprint ed. write for info. (*3-487-06675-0*, Pub. by Georg Olms GW) Lubrecht & Cramer.

Photographers Aspen Staff. Aspen, Portrait of a Rocky Mountain Town. Ohlrich, Warren H., ed. LC 92-90947. 112p. (Orig.). 1992. pap. 24.95 (*0-9620046-8-5*) W H O Pr.

Photographic Arts Center N.Y. The Photographic Art Market 1981-82, Vol. 2. 1982. pap. 49.95 (*0-317-59595-4*) Consultant Pr.

Photographic Global Notes Staff, jt. auth. see Eastman Kodak Company Staff.

Photoplay Research Society Staff. Opportunities in the Motion Picture Industry & How to Qualify for Positions in Its Many Branches. LC 73-124033. (Literature of Cinema, Ser. 1). 1970. reprint ed. 12.95 (*0-405-01633-6*) Ayer.

Photosport International Staff, illus. Cyclist's Training Diary. 7th rev. ed. 192p. 1994. pap. 9.95 (*0-941950-32-8*) Vitesse Pr.

Phoutrides, Aristides, jt. tr. see Brown, Demetra V.

Phrynichos. The New Phrynichus Being a Revised Text of the Ecloga of the Grammarian Phrynichus. xi, 539p. 1968. reprint ed. write for info. (*0-318-70998-8*, Pub. by Georg Olms GW) Lubrecht & Cramer.

Phrynichos, Arabius. The New Phrynichus Being a Revised Text of the Ecloga of the Grammarian Phrynichus. xi, 539p. 1968. reprint ed. 83.20 (*0-685-66502-X*, 05101885, Pub. by Georg Olms GW) Lubrecht & Cramer.

Phua, K. H., et al. Optimization Techniques & Applications: International Conference, 2 vols., Set. 1200p. 1992. text ed. 190.00 (*981-02-1062-0*) World Scientific Pub.

Phua, K. K. & Yamaguchi, Y., eds. International Conference on High Energy Physics, 25th. 1576p. (C). 1991. text ed. 273.00 (*981-00-2434-7*); pap. 87.00 (*981-00-2433-9*) World Scientific Pub.

Phua, K. K., et al, eds. High Temperature Superconductivity & Other Related Topics: First Asia-Pacific Conference on Condensed Matter Physics. (Progress in High Temperature Superconductivity: Vol. 12). 328p. 1989. pap. 55.00 (*9971-5-0706-4*) World Scientific Pub.

Phukan, Arvind, ed. Frost in Geotechnical Engineering: Proceedings of the 2nd International Symposium on Frost in Geotechnical Engineering, Anchorage, U. S. A. 28 June - 1 July 1993. (Illus.). 199p. (C). 1993. text ed. 80.00 (*90-5410-319-1*, Pub. by A A Balkema NE) Ashgate Pub Co.

Phukan, Umananda. Agricultural Development in Assam, 1950-85. 1990. 21.50 (*81-7099-202-8*, Pub. by Mittal II) S Asia.

Phul, Raj K. Landmarks of World Civilization. 390p. 1986. 39.95 (*0-318-36971-0*) Asia Bk Corp.

Phuq, K. K., et al, eds. Singapore Super Computing Conference, '90. 500p. (C). 1991. text ed. 104.00 (*981-02-0700-X*) World Scientific Pub.

PhVogel, J., jt. auth. see Hutchison, J.

Phy, Allene S. Mary Shelley. Schlobin, Roger C., ed. LC 86-6502. (Starmont Reader's Guide Ser.: Vol. 36). 124p. (Orig.). 1988. lib. bdg. 25.00x (*0-930261-61-5*) Borgo Pr.

— Presenting Norma Klein. (United States Authors Ser.). 176p. 1988. text ed. 19.95 (*0-8057-8205-2*, TUSAS 538, Twayne) Macmillan.

Phy, Allene S., ed. The Bible & Popular Culture in America. LC 83-11548. (Bible in American Culture Ser.). 1985. 21.95 (*0-89130-640-4*, 06 12 02) Scholars Pr GA.

Phycological Society of America. Algal Biofouling: Proceedings of a Symposium, Gainesville, FL, August, 1985. Hoagland, K. D. & Evans, L. V., eds. (Studies in Environmental Science: No. 28). 328p. 1987. 105.25 (*0-444-42705-8*) Elsevier.

Phye, Gary D. & Andre, Thomas. Cognitive Classroom Learning. (Educational Psychology Ser.). 1986. text ed. 61.00 (*0-12-554252-6*) Acad Pr.

Phye, Gary D., jt. auth. see Klauer, Karl J.

***Phylactou, Takis G.** Brothers of the Cosmos. 1994. pap. 10.00 (*0-533-10793-8*) Vantage.

Phylaktis, Kate & Pradhan, Mahmood, eds. International Finance & the Less Developed Countries. LC 89-70269. 200p. 1990. text ed. 65.00 (*0-312-04506-9*) St Martin.

Phyllis. Along the Path: Loving God. LC 90-21935. (Orig.). 1990. pap. 3.00 (*0-915541-65-3*) Star Bks Inc.

Phylos. Dweller on Two Planets. 1952. pap. 13.50 (*0-87505-088-3*) Borden.

— Earth Dweller Returns. 1940. pap. 13.50 (*0-87505-089-1*) Borden.

— Habitante de Dos Planetas. Garces, Soledad, tr. 438p. (SPA.). 1992. pap. write for info. (*1-883482-06-2*) Edic Gran Dir.

Phylos the Thibetan. A Dweller on Two Planets: The Dividing of the Way. 423p. 1964. reprint ed. spiral bd. 13.20 (*0-7873-0670-3*) Mokelumne.

— A Dweller on Two Planets, or the Dividing of the Way. 2nd ed. (Illus.). 432p. 1991. pap. 15.00 (*0-8334-0022-3*, Spir Lit Lib) Garber Comm.

Phylos the Tibetan. Habitante de Dos Planetas. 438p. 1992. pap. write for info. (*0-318-71306-3*) Edic Gran Dir.

Phylotus. Esoteric Masonry: The Storehouse Unlocked. 77p. 1993. reprint ed. spiral bd. 5.50 (*0-7873-0673-8*) Mokelumne.

— Esoteric Masonry or the Storehouse Unlocked. 80p. 1992. pap. 12.95 (*1-56459-190-5*) Kessinger Pub.

— Private Lessons Interpreting the Inner Meaning of Masonry & the Bible. 78p. 1972. reprint ed. spiral bd. 7.70 (*0-7873-0671-1*) Mokelumne.

Phyrr, Stephen A., jt. auth. see Cooper, James R.

Physical Science for Nonscience Students Project Staff. An Approach to Physical Science: Physical Science for Nonscience Students. Strassenburg, Arnold A., ed. LC 74-1024. (Illus.). 432p. 1974. reprint ed. pap. 123.20 (*0-7837-3463-8*, 2057791) Bks Demand.

Physician Task Force on Hunger in America Staff. Hunger in America: The Growing Epidemic. LC 85-17824. (Illus.). 253p. 1985. text ed. 29.95 (*0-8195-5150-3*, Wesleyan Univ Pr); pap. 14.95 (*0-8195-6158-4*, Wesleyan Univ Pr) U Pr of New Eng.

Physicians for Human Rights - Asia Watch Staff. Thailand - Bloody May: Excessive Use of Lethal Force in Bangkok. 50p. 1992. pap. 7.00 (*1-879707-11-X*) Phy Human Rights.

PQ

An Asterisk (*) at the beginning of an entry indicates that the title is appearing in BIP for the first time.

— Thailand - Bloody May: Excessive Use of Lethal Force in Bangkok: The Events of May 17-20, 1992 (Press Copy) 50p. 1992. pap. 7.00 (*1-879707-10-1*) Phy Human Rights.

Physicians for Human Rights Staff. Cruel & Inhuman Treatment: The Use of Four-Point Restraint in the Onondaga County Public Safety Building, Advance press. LC 93-84902. (Illus.). 90p. 1993. pap. 7.00 (*1-879707-15-2*) Phy Human Rights.

— Cruel & Inhuman Treatment: The Use of Four-Point Restraint in the Onondaga County Public Safety Building, Final copy. LC 93-84902. (Illus.). 90p. 1993. pap. 7.00 (*1-879707-16-0*) Phy Human Rights.

— Health Conditions in Haiti's Prisons. 40p. 1992. pap. text ed. 3.00 (*1-879707-08-X*) Phy Human Rights.

— Hidden Enemies: Land Mines in Northern Somalia. (Illus.). 52p. 1992. pap. 7.00 (*1-879707-12-8*) Phy Human Rights.

— Human Rights on Hold: A Report on Emergency Measures & Access to Health Care in the Occupied Territories. LC 93-83144. 87p. 1992. pap. 10.00 (*1-879707-09-8*) Phy Human Rights.

Physicians for Human Rights Staff & Africa Watch Staff. Somalia: No Mercy in Mogadishu: The Human Cost of Conflict. (Illus.). 30p. 1992. pap. 7.00 (*1-879707-07-1*) Phy Human Rights.

***Physicians for Human Rights Staff & American Refugee Committee.** Health Conditions in Cambodia's Prisons. 65p. 1995. pap. 7.00 (*1-879707-18-7*) Phy Human Rights.

Physicians for Human Rights Staff & Asia Watch Staff. The Crackdown in Kashmir: Torture of Detainees & Assaults on the Medical Community. (Illus.). 38p. 1993. Glossy cover version with photo. pap. text ed. 7.00 (*1-879707-14-4*); Press copy. pap. text ed. 7.00 (*1-879707-13-6*) Phy Human Rights.

Physicians for Human Rights Staff & Cohen, Barend. Yugoslavia: Mistreatment of Ethnic Albanians: A Case Study. 30p. 1991. pap. text ed. 3.00 (*1-879707-03-9*) Phy Human Rights.

***Physicians for Human Rights Staff & Human Rights Watch, Africa Staff.** Mexico: Waiting for Justice in Chiapas. 100p. 1994. pap. text ed. 15.00 (*1-879707-17-9*) Phy Human Rights.

Physicians for Human Rights Staff, jt. auth. see Africa Watch Staff.

***Physics Dept. University of North Texas Staff.** Experiments in College Physics. (C). 1995. 18.27 (*1-56870-203-5*) RonJon Pub.

— Physical Science II. (C). 1995. 16.00 (*1-56870-202-7*) RonJon Pub.

***Physics Dept. UNT Staff.** Engineering Science I. 135p. (C). 1994. 15.95 (*1-56870-160-8*) RonJon Pub.

— Physical Science I. 82p. (C). 1994. 14.00 (*1-56870-159-4*) RonJon Pub.

Physiologus. Icelandic Physiologus. Hermannsson, Halldor, ed. (Islandica Ser.: Vol. 27). 1938. 15.00 (*0-527-00357-3*) Periodicals Srv.

Physiology & Pharmacology of Vascular Neuroeffector Systems Symposium Staff. Vascular Neuroeffector Systems, Physiology & Pharmacology: Proceedings of the Symposium, Interlaken, 1969. Bevan, J. A. et al, eds. (Illus.). viii, 350p. 1971. 57.75 (*3-8055-1184-1*) S Karger.

Phystiklakis, Nicholas G., ed. see Eliopoulos, Nicholas C.

Phythian-Adams, Charles. Desolation of a City. LC 79-9967. (Past & Present Publications). (Illus.). 1980. 79.95 (*0-521-22604-X*) Cambridge U Pr.

Phythian-Adams, Charles, intro. Societies, Cultures, & Kinship, 1580-1850: Cultural Provinces & English Local History. LC 92-36511. (Illus.). 240p. 1993. 65.00 (*0-7185-1453-X*) St Martin.

Phythian, B. A. A Concise Dictionary of Confusables: All Those Impossible Words You Never Get Right. 198p. 1990. pap. text ed. 10.95 (*0-471-52880-3*) Wiley.

Phythian, B. A., ed. A Concise Dictionary of Correct English. (Quality Paperback Ser.: No. 349). 166p. 1979. pap. 6.95 (*0-8226-0349-7*) Littlefield.

— Concise Dictionary of Correct English. 166p. 1979. 17.75 (*0-8476-6212-8*) Rowman.

Phytochemical Society of North America Staff. Recent Advances in Phytochemistry, Vol. 2: Proceedings of the 7th Annual Symposium of. Seikel, Margaret K., ed. 187p. reprint ed. pap. 53.30 (*0-317-26217-3*, 2055689) Bks Demand.

Pi-Kwang Tsung & Hong-Yen Hsu. Allergies & Chinese Herbal Medicine. (Educational Series on Chinese Medicine: No. 3). 40p. (Orig.). (C). 1987. pap. text ed. 5.95 (*0-941942-26-0*) Orient Heal Arts.

Pi-Kwang Tsung & Hong-yen Hsu. Arthritis & Chinese Herbal Medicine. 32p. (Orig.). 1987. pap. 4.95 (*0-941942-25-2*) Orient Heal Arts.

Pi, S. Y., jt. auth. see Abbott, L.

Pi Sigma Alpha Committee on Publications. Major Problems in State Constitutional Revision. Graves, W. Brooke, ed. LC 78-779. xiv, 306p. 1978. reprint ed. text ed. 59.75 (*0-313-20266-4*, PSAM, Greenwood Pr) Greenwood.

Pi, Ying-Hsien, jt. auth. see Jo, Yung-Hwan.

Pia, ed. see De Maupassant, Guy.

Pia, ed. see Leautaud, Paul.

Pia, Albert. A Doll's House. 47p. 1972. pap. 2.50 (*0-87129-102-9*, D19) Dramatic Pub.

Pia, H. W., et al, eds. Spontaneous Intracerebral Haematomas: Advances in Diagnosis & Therapy. (Illus.). 500p. 1981. 133.00 (*0-387-10146-2*) Spr-Verlag.

***Pia, Jacklyn.** Multiple Personality Meditations by Michael: The First Meditation Book Written for Multiples by a Multiple. LC 93-84371. 100p. (Orig.). 1993. spiral bd. 9.95 (*1-56875-067-6*, 067-6) R & E Pubs.

Pia, Jacklyn M. Multiple Personality Gift: A Workbook for You & Your Inside Family. 60p. 1991. pap. 11.95 (*0-88247-890-7*) R & E Pubs.

Pia, Leroy Q. Key to Survival. Van Treese, James B., ed. 300p. 1993. pap. 8.95 (*1-880416-66-2*) NW Pub.

Pia, Simon, told to. Pat Stanton: The Quiet Man. 128p. (C). 1989. text ed. 27.00 (*0-85976-288-2*, Pub. by J Donald) St Mut.

Piacente, Steve, jt. ed. see Trammell, Jeffrey B.

Piacentini, Ernesto. Immaculate Conception: Panorama of the Marian Doctrine of Maximilian Kolbe. Kos, Donald, tr. 64p. (Orig.). 1975. pap. 2.00 (*0-913382-04-3*, 105-3) Prow Bks-Franciscan.

Piacentino, Edward J. T. S. Stribling: Pioneer Realist in Modern Southern Literature. 194p. (Orig.). (C). 1988. pap. text ed. 20.00 (*0-8191-6720-7*) U Pr of Amer.

Piacere, Diana & Piacere, Nicholas. Lovemaking: A No-Nonsense Practical Solution. 64p. 1992. pap. 13.95 (*0-9640117-0-0*) InFour Grp.

Piacere, Nicholas, jt. auth. see Piacere, Diana.

Piade, Lynne, jt. auth. see Cahill, Marie.

Piade, Lynne, jt. ed. see Cahill, Marie.

Piade, Lynne, ed. see Leung, Margaret Y.

Piade, Lynne, ed. see Puliciano, Gina.

Piaget, Gerald & Binkley, Barbara. Overcoming Your Barriers. 236p. 1985. 14.95 (*0-8290-0438-6*) Irvington.

Piaget, Gerald W. & Binkley, Barbara M. Overcoming Your Barriers: A Guide to Personal Reprogramming. 14.95 (*0-88282-005-2*) New Horizon NJ.

Piaget, J., jt. auth. see Beth, E. W.

Piaget, Jean. Adaptation & Intelligence: Organic Selection & Phenocopy. Eames, Steward, tr. LC 79-25592. vi, 124p. (C). 1982. pap. text ed. 8.95 (*0-226-66778-2*) U Ch Pr.

— The Child's Conception of the World. (Quality Paperback Ser.: No. 213). 397p. 1975. reprint ed. pap. 14.95 (*0-8226-0213-X*) Littlefield.

— Le Comportement: Moteur de l'Evolution. (FRE.). 1976. pap. 10.95 (*0-7859-2846-4*) Fr & Eur.

— The Equilibration of Cognitive Structures: The Central Problem of Intellectual Development. Brown, Terence A. & Thampy, Kishore J., trs. (Illus.). 224p. 1985. lib. bdg. 25.00 (*0-226-66781-2*) U Ch Pr.

— Genetic Epistemology. Duckworth, Eleanor, tr. 1971. reprint ed. pap. 5.95 (*0-393-00596-8*) Norton.

— Judgment & Reasoning in the Child. (Quality Paperback Ser.: No. 205). 260p. 1976. reprint ed. pap. 14.95 (*0-8226-0205-9*) Littlefield.

— Logique & Connaissance Scientifique. (Methodique Ser.). 1360p. 55.95 (*0-686-56429-4*) Fr & Eur.

— Logique et Connaissance Scientifique. 1364p. (FRE.). 1973. lib. bdg. 130.00 (*0-7859-3776-5*, 2070104133) Fr & Eur.

— The Moral Judgement of the Child. 1965. pap. 14.95 (*0-317-30591-3*) Free Pr.

— Moral Judgement of the Child. 1985. 19.95 (*0-02-925230-X*) Macmillan.

— The Moral Judgment of the Child. Gabain, Marjorie, tr. 416p. 1965. pap. 15.95 (*0-02-925240-7*) Free Pr.

— Morphisms & Categories: Comparing & Transforming. Brown, Terrance, tr. 248p. 1992. text ed. 49.95 (*0-8058-0300-9*) L Erlbaum Assocs.

— Piaget Sampler: An Introduction to Jean Piaget Through His Own Words. Campbell, Sarah F., ed. LC 75-34129. 168p. reprint ed. pap. 47.90 (*0-317-08167-5*, 2020594) Bks Demand.

— Possibility & Necessity, I. Feider, tr. LC 86-7052. 1987. text ed. 34.95 (*0-8166-1370-2*) U of Minn Pr.

— Psychologie et Pedagogie. (FRE.). 1988. pap. 12.95 (*0-7859-2814-6*) Fr & Eur.

— Psychology of Intelligence. (Quality Paperback Ser.: No. 222). 182p. 1976. reprint ed. pap. 9.95 (*0-8226-0222-9*) Littlefield.

— Six Etudes de Psychologie. (FRE.). 1987. pap. 12.95 (*0-7859-2805-7*) Fr & Eur.

— Six Psychological Studies. Elkind, David, ed. Tenzer, Anita, tr. (Orig.). 1968. pap. 9.00 (*0-394-70462-2*, Vin) Random.

— Sociological Studies. Smith, Leslie, ed. LC 94-27215. 368p. 1995. 49.95 (*0-415-10780-6*, B4388) Routledge.

— Success & Understanding. LC 78-16435. (Illus.). 248p. 1978. 25.00 (*0-674-85387-3*) HUP.

Piaget, Jean, ed. Intelligence & Affectivity: Their Relationship During Child Development. Brown, T. A. & Kaegi, C. E., trs. (Illus.). 1981. text ed. 8.00 (*0-8243-2901-5*) Annual Reviews.

Piaget, Jean & Garcia, Rolando, eds. Toward a Logic of Meanings. Easley, Jack & Davidson, Phil, trs. 200p. 1991. text ed. 39.95 (*0-8058-0301-7*) L Erlbaum Assocs.

Piaget, Jean & Garcia, Rolando V. Psychogenesis & the History of Science. Feider, Helga, tr. (Illus.). 336p. 1989. text ed. 50.50 (*0-231-05992-2*) Col U Pr.

Piaget, Jean & Inhelder, Barbel. Psychology of the Child. Weaver, Helen, tr. LC 78-78449. 192p. 1972. pap. text ed. 16.00 (*0-465-09500-3*) Basic.

Piaget, Jean, et al. The Child's Conception of Geometry. 432p. 1981. reprint ed. pap. 8.95 (*0-393-00057-5*) Norton.

— Epistemology & Psychology of Functions. Castellanos, Javier & Anderson, Vivian, trs. (Synthese Library: No. 83). 1977. lib. bdg. 89.00 (*90-277-0804-5*) Kluwer Ac.

Piaget, Jean M. Psychologie. (FRE.). 1987. lib. bdg. 165.00 (*0-7859-3854-0*) Fr & Eur.

Pialat, M. New Larousse of Scrabble & Word Games: Nouveau Larousse du Scrabble, Dictionnaire des Jeux de Letters. 830p. (FRE.). 1981. pap. 31.95 (*0-8288-2345-6*, M14461) Fr & Eur.

— Nouveau Larousse du Scrabble. 880p. (FRE.). 1981. 52.50 (*0-8288-2344-8*, F82270) Fr & Eur.

Pialorsi, Frank, jt. auth. see Dunkel, Patricia.

Pialorsi, Frank P., ed. Teaching the Bilingual: New Methods & Old Traditions. LC 73-87717. 263p. (C). 1974. pap. 15.95 (*0-8165-0372-9*) U of Ariz Pr.

Piamenta, Moshe. A Dictionary of Post-Classical Yemeni Arabic, Vol. I. LC 90-2137. xxiv, 274p. (ARA & ENG.). 1990. 94.50 (*90-04-09261-7*) E J Brill.

— A Dictionary of Post-Classical Yemeni Arabic, Vol. 2. LC 90-2137. 267p. (ARA & ENG.). 1991. 94.50 (*90-04-09293-5*) E J Brill.

Pian, Rulan C. A Syllabus for Mandarin Primer. (Illus.). 118p. reprint ed. pap. 33.70 (*0-7837-4178-2*, 2059027) Bks Demand.

Piana, Paul. Great Rock Hits of Hueco Tanks: A Climbers Guide. (Illus.). 48p. (Orig.). 1992. pap. 6.95 (*1-879415-03-8*) Mtn n Air Bks.

— Touch the Sky: The Needles in the Black Hills of South Dakota. LC 82-71892. (Illus.). 301p. 1983. pap. 13.50 (*0-930410-16-5*) Amer Alpine Club.

Pianca, Marina. El Teatro de Nuestra America: Un Proyecto Continental, 1959-1989. (Series Towards a Social History of Hispanic & Luso-Brazilian Literatures). 408p. (Orig.). (C). 1990. pap. 14.95 (*1-877660-05-1*) IFTSOIL.

Piani, Andrea L. & Schoenborn, Charlotte A. Health Promotion & Disease Prevention, United States, 1990. LC 92-48186. (Vital & Health Statistics Ser.: No. 184). 1992. write for info. (*0-8406-0474-2*) Natl Ctr Health Stats.

Piani, Gianguido, jt. auth. see Olsson, Gustaf.

Pianka, E. R. Ecology & Natural History of Desert Lizards: Analyses of the Ecological Niche & Community Structure. 1986. 60.00 (*0-691-08148-4*) Princeton U Pr.

***Pianka, Eric R.** Ecology & Natural History of Desert Lizards: Analyses of the Ecological Niche & Community Structure. LC 85-19097. (Illus.). 229p. 1986. reprint ed. pap. 65.30 (*0-7837-8179-2*, 2047884) Bks Demand.

— Evolutionary Ecology. 5th ed. (C). 1993. text ed. 55.50 (*0-06-501225-9*) HarpCollege.

— The Lizard Man Speaks. LC 93-38067. (Corrie Herring Hooks Ser.: No. 26). (Illus.). 224p. (C). 1994. 24.95 (*0-292-76552-5*) U of Tex Pr.

Pianka, Eric R., jt. ed. see Vitt, Laurie J.

Pianka, Phyllis. The Thackery Jewels: Amethyst; Emerald; Topaz. (Regency Romance Ser.). 1994. mass mkt. 5.99 (*0-373-31216-4*, 1-31216-4) Harlequin Bks.

Pianka, Phyllis T. How to Write Romances. 164p. 1988. 15.99 (*0-89879-324-6*) Writers Digest.

Piankoff, A. & Rambova, N., eds. The Tomb of Ramesses VI, 2 vols., Vol. 1 - Texts. LC 54-5646. (Bollingen Ser.: No. 40). reprint ed. Vol. 1- Texts. pap. 145.80 (*0-317-28638-2*, 2051348) Bks Demand.

— The Tomb of Ramesses VI, 2 vols., Vol. 2 - Plates. LC 54-5646. (Bollingen Ser.: No. 40). reprint ed. Vol. 2- Plates. pap. 53.00 (*0-317-28639-0*) Bks Demand.

***Piano, Renzo, ed.** Process Architecture No. 122: Kansai International Airport. (Illus.). 201p. 1995. pap. 36.95 (*4-89331-122-0*, Pub. by Process Archit JA) Bks Nippan.

Piano Teacher Staff. Selections from the Piano Teacher, 1958-1963: A Collection of Articles from the Piano Teacher's First Five Years. Savler, Roberta, ed. LC 64-57578. 136p. reprint ed. pap. 38.80 (*0-317-10057-2*, 2005327) Bks Demand.

Piano Teachers Congress Members. Technical Control for the Modern Pianist: Finger Exercises Used by Members of the Piano Teachers Congress of N.Y., Inc. De Vito, Albert, ed. LC 78-95128. 1978. 9.95 (*0-934286-11-6*) Kenyon.

Pianta, Mario, jt. auth. see Archibugi, Daniele.

Pianta, Robert, ed. Beyond the Parent: The Role of Other Adults in Children's Lives. LC 85-644581. (New Directions for Child Development Ser.: No. CD 57). 110p. 1992. 17.95 (*1-55542-732-4*) Jossey-Bass.

Pianzola, A., jt. auth. see Moody, R. V.

Piar, Carlos R. Jesus & Liberation: A Critical Analysis of the Christology of Latin American Liberation Theology. LC 93-6958. (AUS VII: Vol. 148). 178p. (C). 1995. pap. text ed. 32.95 (*0-8204-2098-0*) P Lang Pubs.

Piard, Christian, jt. auth. see Piard, Joelle.

***Piard, Joelle & Piard, Christian.** Dictionnaire Quartet-Systems du Macintosh. 1990. write for info. (*0-7859-8247-7*, 2-908796-00-7) Fr & Eur.

Piarist Fathers Staff. Constitutions of the Order of the Pious Schools. Cudinach, Salvidor, ed. & tr. by. LC 85-60915. 110p. write for info. (*0-9614908-0-2*) Piarist Father.

Pias, Istavan & Jones, J. B. Handbook of Trace Elements in the Environment. 300p. 1995. 69.95 (*1-884015-34-4*) St Lucie Pr.

Piascik, Chester. Applied Finite Mathematics for Business & the Social & Natural Sciences. Pullins, ed. 795p. (C). 1992. text ed. 63.25 (*0-314-88432-7*) West Pub.

— Applied Mathematics for Business & the Social & Natural Sciences. Pullins, ed. 966p. (C). 1992. text ed. 67.50 (*0-314-83981-X*) West Pub.

— Calculus with Applications for Business & the Social & Natural Sciences. Pullins, ed. LC 92-29638. 900p. (C). 1993. text ed. 66.00 (*0-314-01270-2*) West Pub.

— Calculus with Applications to Management, Economics, & the Social & Natural Sciences. 500p. (C). 1987. write for info. (*0-675-20440-2*, Merrill Pub Co) Macmillan.

Piasco, J. M., jt. auth. see Elloy, J. P.

Piasecki, Anthony A. Estimation of Demand for Emergency Medical Services. (Special Project Report Ser.). 202p. 1986. 8.00 (*0-89940-854-2*) LBJ Sch Pub Aff.

***Piasecki, Bruce W.** Corporate Environmental Strategy: The Avalanche of Change since Bhopal. LC 94-38131. 1995. text ed. 24.95 (*0-471-10627-5*) Wiley.

Piasecki, Bruce W., ed. Toxic Waste: New Strategies for Controlling Toxic Contamination. LC 83-24510. (Quorum Ser.). (Illus.). xix, 239p. 1984. text ed. 59.95 (*0-89930-056-1*, PIT/, Quorum Bks) Greenwood.

Piasecki, Bruce W. & Davis, Gary A. America's Future in Toxic Waste Management: Lesson from Europe. LC 87-2559. 320p. 1987. text ed. 65.00 (*0-89930-113-4*, PMA/, Quorum Bks) Greenwood.

Piasecki, Jerry. They're Torturing Teachers in Room 104. (J). 1992. pap. 3.50 (*0-553-48024-3*) Bantam.

— What Is the Teacher's Toupe Doing in the Fish Tank? (J). (gr. 4-7). 1994. pap. 3.50 (*0-553-48171-1*) Bantam.

Piasek, Martin. Chinese-German Dictionary: Woerterbuch Chinesisch-Deutsch. 6th ed. 336p. (CHI & GER.). 1986. 69.95 (*0-8288-1008-7*, M7320) Fr & Eur.

Piat. Dictionnaire Francais-Langue d'Oc. 1000p. (FRE.). 75.00 (*0-7859-0723-8*, M-6451) Fr & Eur.

***Piat, Stephane-Joseph.** The Story of a Family: The Home of the Little Flower. LC 93-61562. (Illus.). 421p. 1994. pap. 18.50 (*0-89555-502-6*) TAN Bks Pubs.

Piatagorsky, Gregor. Cellist. LC 76-3697. (Music Reprint Ser.). 1976. reprint ed. lib. bdg. 37.50 (*0-306-70822-1*) Da Capo.

Piatetski-Shapiro, Ilya. Complex Representations of GL (2,K) for Finite Fields K. LC 82-24484. (Contemporary Mathematics Ser.: Vol. 16). 71p. 1992. pap. 22.00 (*0-8218-5019-9*, CONM-16) Am Math.

Piatetski-Shapiro, Ilya, jt. auth. see Cogdell, James.

***Piatetsky-Shapiro, Gregory, ed.** Knowledge Discovery in Databases. (Technical Reports). (Illus.). 336p. (Orig.). 1994. pap. 25.00x (*0-929280-49-0*) Amer Artificial.

Piatigorsky, Alexander, jt. auth. see Denwood, Philip.

Piatnitsky, Osip A. Memoirs of a Bolshevik. LC 73-850. (Russian Studies: Perspectives on the Revolution). 244p. 1973. reprint ed. 21.25 (*0-88355-047-4*) Hyperion Conn.

Piatos, Emmanuel. Solo in an Instant. (Illus.). 24p. (Orig.). (C). Date not set. pap. 6.95 (*1-56516-033-9*) Houston IN.

Piatt, Bill. Language on the Job: Balancing Business Needs & Employee Rights. LC 92-28784. 169p. 1993. 27.50 (*0-8263-1410-4*) U of NM Pr.

— Only English? Law & Language Policy in The United States. LC 89-24968. 224p. 1993. reprint ed. pap. 16.95 (*0-8263-1373-6*) U of NM Pr.

Piatt, Emma C. History of Piatt County, Illinois. (Illus.). 643p. 1994. reprint ed. lib. bdg. 65.50 (*0-8328-3985-X*) Higginson Bk Co.

Piatt, Larry. One Thousand One More Questions on the Bible. 96p. 1986. pap. 4.99 (*0-8010-7094-5*) Baker Bk.

— One Thousand One Questions on the Bible. 50p. 1984. pap. 4.99 (*0-8010-7085-6*) Baker Bk.

Piattelli, Massimo P. Inevitable Illusions: How Mistakes of Reason Rule Our Minds. LC 94-12759. 1994. text ed. 24.95 (*0-471-58126-7*) Wiley.

Piattelli-Palmarini, Massimo, ed. Language & Learning: The Debate Between Jean Piaget & Noam Chomsky. 445p. 1984. pap. 18.50 (*0-674-50941-2*) HUP.

Piatti, Alberto, et al. Planning of Geothermal District Heating Systems. LC 92-26787. (C). 1992. lib. bdg. 129.00 (*0-7923-1968-0*) Kluwer Ac.

Piatti, G., ed. Advances in Composite Materials. (Illus.). 405p. 1978. 128.00 (*0-85334-770-0*, Pub. by Elsevier Applied Sci UK) Elsevier.

Piatti, James. Firehouse Memorabilia: Identification & Price Guide. rev. ed. viii, 272p. 1994. reprint ed. pap. 12.00 (*0-380-77092-X*, Confident Collect) Avon.

***Piazza, A. Anthony.** Sue, Settle or Be Silent? 1994. pap. 18.95 (*0-9635237-0-8*) P M C & B.

Piazza, David. Macintosh Step-by-Step. 140p. 1992. 11.99 (*1-56484-002-6*) Intl Society Tech Educ.

***Piazza, G. J., ed.** Lipoxygenase & Lipoxygenase Pathway Enzymes. 1995. write for info. (*0-614-05583-0*) AOCS Pr.

Piazza, Gail. Farberware: World of Wok Cookery. LC 82-71462. (Illus.). 144p. 1982. 10.95 (*0-916752-57-7*) Dorison Hse.

Piazza, Linda. Call of the Deep. 160p. (Orig.). 1994. pap. 3.50 (*0-380-77330-9*, Flare) Avon.

— Evil in the Attic. 176p. (Orig.). (YA). 1995. mass mkt. 3.99 (*0-380-77576-X*, Flare) Avon.

Piazza, Louise D., ed. see Martin, Charles.

Piazza, Michael. Holy Homosexuals: The Truth about Being Gay & Christian. 210p. (Orig.). 1994. pap. write for info. (*1-885591-02-0*) Morris Pubng.

Piazza, Paul. Christopher Isherwood: Myth & Anti-Myth. LC 77-14271. 1978. text ed. 36.50 (*0-231-04118-7*) Col U Pr.

Piazza, Robert, jt. auth. see Buzzell, Judith B.

***Piazza, Theresa J., et al.** The Kaskaskia Manuscripts: St. Louis Mound Group - Prehistoric Mussel Faunas. Wood, W. Raymond, ed. (Missouri Archaeologist Ser.: Vol. 53). (Illus.). iv, 100p. (Orig.). 1995. pap. write for info. (*0-943414-80-6*) MO Arch Soc.

Piazza, Thomas, jt. auth. see Sniderman, Paul M.

***Piazza, Tom.** The Guide to Classic Recorded Jazz. LC 94-36373. 410p. (Orig.). 1995. pap. 22.95 (*0-87745-489-2*) U of Iowa Pr.

— Pantheon Great Jazz. 1991. pap. 14.95 (*0-679-40187-3*) McKay.

***Pibiri, Giovanni.** Maddalena Licheri: Italian Essays. 126p. 1986. pap. 15.00 (*0-89304-579-9*) Cross-Cultrl NY.

Piboubes, Raoul. Dictionary Ocean: Eng - Fr, Ger - Fr, Span - Fr. 761p. (ENG, FRE, GER & SPA.). 1989. write for info. (*0-7859-4578-4*) Fr & Eur.

Piburn, Sidney. Dalai Lama: A Policy of Kindness. 1993. pap. 10.95 (*1-55939-022-0*) Snow Lion Pubns.

Pibworth, Nigel R. Gospel Pedlar: John Berridge & the 18th Century Revival. 1987. pap. 11.99 (*0-85234-236-5*, Pub. by Evangel Pr UK) Presby & Reformed.

***Pica.** Experiences in Movement with Music, Activities & Theory IG. 32p. 1995. teacher ed 14.00 (*0-8273-6479-2*) Delmar.

Pica & Barnes. Teaching Matters. 1990. pap. 20.95 (*0-8384-2788-X*) Heinle & Heinle.

An Asterisk (*) at the beginning of an entry indicates that the title is appearing in BIP for the first time.

Pica, Rae. Dance Training for Gymnastics. LC 87-31862. (Illus.). 160p. (C). 1988. text ed. 25.00x (*0-88011-306-5*, PPIC0306) Human Kinetics.
— Experiences in Movement with Music, Activities, & Theory. LC 94-33269. (Illus.). 416p. 1995. pap. 27.95 (*0-8273-6478-4*) Delmar.
— Let's Move & Learn. 2nd ed. LC 89-29789. (Moving & Learning Ser.). (Illus.). 80p. 1990. audio 19.00x (*0-87322-285-7*, BPIC0285) Human Kinetics.
— Special Themes for Moving & Learning. LC 90-27862. (Illus.). 168p. (Orig.). 1991. pap. text ed. 18.00 (*0-87322-319-5*, BPIC0319) Human Kinetics.
— Toddlers Moving & Learning. 2nd ed. LC 89-24588. (Illus.). 88p. 1990. ring bd. 39.00 (*0-87322-275-X*, BPIC0275) Human Kinetics.
— Upper Elementary Children Moving & Learning. LC 92-43855. (Illus.). 136p. 1993. ring bd. 49.00x (*0-87322-468-X*, BPIC0468) Human Kinetics.
Pica, Rae & Gardzina, Richard. Early Elementary Children Moving & Learning. LC 90-40061. 152p. (Orig.). 1991. audio, ring bd. 49.00x (*0-87322-301-2*, BPIC0301) Human Kinetics.
— More Music for Moving & Learning. 2nd ed. (Illus.). 72p. 1990. audio 39.00x (*0-87322-277-6*, BPIC0277) Human Kinetics.
— Preschoolers Moving & Learning. 2nd ed. LC 89-28483. (Illus.). 144p. 1990. ring bd. 49.00x (*0-87322-276-8*, BPIC0276) Human Kinetics.
Picabia, Francis. Who Knows. Hall, Remy, tr. 168p. (Orig.). 1987. pap. 5.95 (*0-937815-04-7*) Hanuman Bks.
— Yes No. Hall, Remy, tr. 57p. (Orig.). 1990. pap. 5.95 (*0-937815-41-1*) Hanuman Bks.
Picache, Jacqueline. Robert Dictionnaire Etymologique du Francais. 827p. (FRE.). 1991. 45.00 (*0-8288-9432-9*, M5095) Fr & Eur.
Picander. The Coffee Cantata. Hess, Harvey, tr. Bd. with Kona Coffee Cantata. 24p. (GER.). 1986. Set pap. 3.00 (*0-931909-05-8*) Malama Arts.
***Picano, Eugenio.** Stress Echocardiography. 2nd ed. LC 94-29136. 1994. 69.00 (*0-387-58137-5*) Spr-Verlag.
***Picano, Felice.** Ambidextrous. 1995. pap. text ed. 6.95 (*1-56333-275-2*) Masquerade.
— Ambidextrous: The Secret Lives of Children. 200p. 1985. pap. 14.95 (*0-914017-06-3*) Gay Pr NY.
— Dryland's End. (Orig.). Date not set. pap. 12.95 (*1-56333-279-5*) Masquerade.
— Late in the Season. LC 80-39614. 250p. (Orig.). 1985. reprint ed. pap. 7.95 (*0-317-14449-9*) Gay Pr NY.
— Like People in History. LC 94-38159. 1995. 23.95 (*0-670-86047-6*, Viking) Viking Penguin.
— Men Who Loved Me. 1994. pap. text ed. 6.95 (*1-56333-274-4*) Masquerade.
— To the Seventh Power. 320p. 1990. mass mkt. 4.50 (*0-380-70276-2*) Avon.
Picano, Felice, jt. auth. see Silverstein, Charles.
Picard, ed. see Prevost, Abbe F.
Picard, Barbara L. French Legends, Tales & Fairy Stories. (Oxford Myths & Legends Ser.). (Illus.). 216p. (J). (gr. 4 up). 1992. pap. 10.95 (*0-19-274149-7*) OUP.
— Iliad & Odyssey of Homer. 1991. pap. 4.95 (*0-671-08155-1*) S&S Trade.
— The Iliad of Homer. (Oxford Myths & Legends Ser.). (Illus.). 224p. (J). (gr. 4 up). 1991. pap. 10.95 (*0-19-274147-0*) OUP.
— Odyssey by Homer. (Oxford Myths & Legends Ser.). (Illus.). 288p. (J). (gr. 4 up). 1991. pap. 10.95 (*0-19-274146-2*) OUP.
— Selected Fairy Tales. (Illus.). 198p. (J). 1995. pap. 12.95 (*0-19-274162-4*) OUP.
— Tales of Ancient Persia. (Oxford Myths & Legends Ser.). (Illus.). 176p. (J). 1993. pap. 10.95 (*0-19-274154-3*) OUP.
Picard, Barbara L., teller. Tales of the Norse Gods. (Myths & Legends Ser.). (Illus.). 128p. 1994. pap. 10.95 (*0-19-274167-5*) OUP.
Picard, C. F. Graphs & Questionnaires. (Mathematical Studies: Vol. 32). 1980. pap. 61.75 (*0-444-85239-5*, North Holland) Elsevier.
***Picard, Caroline L.** First You Buy a Roux. 28p. (Orig.). 1991. pap. 4.95 (*0-9614228-6-6*) Juliahouse Pubs.
***Picard, Elizabeth.** Lebanon, a Shattered Country: Myths & Realities of the Wars in Lebanon. Philip, Franklin, tr. LC 94-30521. 1994. 29.50 (*0-8419-1233-5*) Holmes & Meier.
Picard, Emile & Simart, G. Theorie des Fonctions Algebriques de Deux Variables Independantes, 2 vols. in 1. LC 67-31156. 1971. 49.50 (*0-8284-0248-5*) Chelsea Pub.
Picard, Frank L. Family Intervention: Positive Action You Can Take to Help a Loved One - & Yourself - to Break the Cycle of Addiction & Codependency. 192p. (Orig.). 1991. pap. 9.95 (*0-942421-37-X*) Hazelden.
Picard, Fred A., jt. ed. see Billigmeier, Robert H.
Picard, G. S., jt. ed. see Sequeira, C. A. C.
Picard, Hymen W. Call of the Goddess: Seven Lives of an Androgyne. 1992. 18.95 (*0-533-09692-8*) Vantage.
Picard, J. M. & De Pontfarcy, Y. The Vision of Tnugdal. (Illus.). 192p. 1989. 35.00 (*1-85182-039-6*, Pub. by Four Cts Pr IE) Intl Spec Bk.
Picard, Jacques, ed. see Racine, Jean.
Picard, Jean-Michel, ed. Aquitaine & Ireland in the Middle Ages. 240p. 1994. boxed, text ed. 39.50 (*1-85182-135-X*, Pub. by Four Cts Pr IE) Intl Spec Bk.
Picard, John & Picard, Ruth. Chevron & Nueva Cadiz Beads. (Beads from the West African Trade Ser.: Vol. VII). (Illus.). 128p. 1993. 35.00 (*0-9622884-2-X*) Picard African.
— Millefiori Beads from the West African Trade. (Beads from the West African Trade Ser.: Vol. VI). (Illus.). 88p. (Orig.). 1991. pap. 25.00 (*0-9622884-1-1*) Picard African.
— Russian Blues, Faceted & Fancy Beads from the West African Trade, Vol. V. (Beads from the West African Trade Ser.). (Illus.). 44p. (Orig.). 1989. pap. 15.00 (*0-9622884-0-3*) Picard African.
Picard, Judith A. College Without Classrooms. 1993. pap. 19.95 (*1-881424-01-4*) Power Programs.
Picard, Judy. Stuffing Envelopes & Mailing Letters. 1992. pap. 9.95 (*1-881424-00-6*) Power Programs.
Picard, Lawrence G., Sr. Fundamentals of Quality Control. 137p. 1992. 25.95 (*0-87389-121-X*) ASQC Qual Pr.
Picard, Louis A. & Garrity, Michele, eds. Policy Reform for Sustainable Development in Africa: The Institutional Imperative. LC 93-14601. 184p. 1993. lib. bdg. 34.00 (*1-55587-449-5*) Lynne Rienner.
Picard, Louis A. & Zariski, Raphael, eds. Subnational Politics in the 1980's: Organization, Reorganization & Economic Development. LC 86-20479. 276p. 1986. text ed. 59.95 (*0-275-92314-2*, C2314, Praeger Pubs) Greenwood.
Picard, M. Dane. Grit & Clay. 358p. 1975. pap. 12.00 (*0-444-41305-7*) Elsevier.
— Mountains & Minerals, Rivers & Rocks: A Geologist's Notes from the Field. LC 92-37492. 224p. 1993. 49.95 (*0-412-03711-4*, A9740, Chap & Hall NY); pap. 17.95 (*0-412-03941-9*, A9919, Chap & Hall NY) Chapman & Hall.
Picard, Marc. Principles & Methods in Historical Phonology: From Proto-Algonkian to Arapaho. 160p. 1994. 55.00 (*0-7735-1171-7*, Pub. by McGill CN) U of Toronto Pr.
Picard, Max. The Flight from God. Kuschnitzky, Marianne & Cameron, J. M., trs. LC 89-38837. 185p. 1989. reprint ed. pap. 9.95 (*0-89526-752-7*) Regnery Pub.
Picard, Nancy. Twenty-Seven Ingredient Chili Con Carne Murders: A Eugenia Potter Mystery. 1994. mass mkt. 4.99 (*0-440-21641-9*) Dell.
Picard, Pierre. Wages & Unemployment: A Study in Non-Walrasian Macroeconomics. LC 92-19475. (Illus.). 312p. (C). 1993. 54.95 (*0-521-35057-3*) Cambridge U Pr.
Picard, R. French Dishes, Easy & Delicious. pap. 4.95 (*0-87557-101-8*, 101-8) Saphrograph.
Picard, Raymond. New Criticism or New Fraud. Towne, Frank, tr. LC 70-5767. 63p. reprint ed. pap. 25.00 (*0-685-24162-9*, 2033036) Bks Demand.
Picard, Robert G. Media Economics: Concepts & Issues. (CommText Ser.: Vol. 22). 160p. (C). 1989. text ed. 37.00 (*0-8039-3501-3*); pap. text ed. 16.95 (*0-8039-3502-1*) Sage.
— The Press & the Decline of Democracy: The Democratic Socialist Response in Public Policy. LC 85-5583. (Contributions to the Study of Mass Media & Communications Ser.: No. 4). (Illus.). xii, 176p. 1985. text ed. 47.95 (*0-313-24915-6*, PPD/) Greenwood.
Picard, Robert G., jt. auth. see Busterna, John C.
Picard, Robert G., et al. Press Concentration & Monopoly. Dervin, Brenda, ed. LC 87-33328. (Communication & Information Science Ser.). 250p. 1988. text ed. 42.50 (*0-89391-464-9*) Ablex Pub.
Picard, Robert J. Media Portrayals of Terrorism: Functions & Meaning of News Coverage. LC 90-20959. (Illus.). 158p. (C). 1993. text ed. 25.95 (*0-8138-1842-7*) Iowa St U Pr.
Picard, Ruth, jt. auth. see Picard, John.
Picarda, Hubert A. The Law Relating to Receivers, Managers, & Administrators. 2nd ed. 1990. 236.00 (*0-406-10501-4*, U.K.) Butterworth Legal Pubs.
— Picarda: The Law & Practice Relating to Charties. 2nd ed. 900p. 1994. write for info. (*0-406-11764-0*) Butterworth Legal Pubs.
Picardello, jt. auth. see Figa-Talamanca.
***Picardello, M. & Baldoni, V., eds.** Representations of Lie Groups & Quantum Groups. (Pitman Research Notes in Mathematics). 1994. pap. text ed. 69.95 (*0-470-23461-X*) Halsted Pr.
Picardello, M. A., ed. Harmonic Analysis & Discrete Potential Theory. (Illus.). 290p. (C). 1992. 75.00 (*0-306-44225-6*, Plenum Pr) Plenum.
***Picardi, Patricia.** Ephesians: Living Towa. 96p. 1995. pap. 4.99 (*1-56476-327-7*, 6-3327, Victor Books) SP Pubns.
Picardt, C. R., ed. Graves' Ophthalmopathy. (Developments in Ophthalmology Ser.: Vol. 20). (Illus.). 230p. 1989. 156.00 (*3-8055-5040-5*) S Karger.
Picariello, Gloria, ed. see Sanchez, Diana V.
Picarski, Ron. Friendly Foods. 258p. (Orig.). 1991. pap. 16.95 (*0-89815-377-8*) Ten Speed Pr.
Picas, ed. see Cota-Robles, Patricia D.
Picascio, Mark, et al, illus. The Pear Tree Trilogy. 1984. 13.95 (*0-916634-10-8*) Double M Pr.
Picasso, Juan R. Senderos de Navidad. 24p. 1980. reprint ed. pap. 1.25 (*0-311-08218-1*) Casa Bautista.
Picasso, Pablo. The Artist & His Model: One Hundred Eighty Drawings. LC 93-37470. 178p. 1993. pap. 12.95 (*0-486-27877-8*) Dover.
— Designs for "The Three-Cornered Hat" (Le Tricorn) Migel, Parmenia, ed. (Illus.). 1978. pap. 7.95 (*0-486-23709-5*) Dover.
— Drawings of Picasso. Longstreet, Stephen, ed. (Master Draughtsman Ser.). (Illus.). (Orig.). 1974. pap. 4.95 (*0-87505-179-0*) Borden.
— Picasso Line Drawings & Prints. (Art Library). (Illus.). 48p. (Orig.). 1982. pap. 3.50 (*0-486-24196-3*) Dover.
— Picasso Lithographs: Sixty-One Works. (Art Library). (Illus.). 64p. (Orig.). 1980. pap. 3.95 (*0-486-23949-7*) Dover.
Picasso, Pablo, jt. auth. see Cesaire, Aime.
Picasso, Pablo, et al. Gongora. Rehl, Beatrice, ed. Trueblood, Alan, tr. (Illus.). 176p. 1985. 50.00 (*0-8076-1133-6*) Braziller.
Picasso Project Staff. Picasso's Paintings, Watercolors, Drawings & Sculputre: A Comprehensive Illustrated Catalogue: Europe at War, 1937-40. (Illus.). 288p. 1995. 150.00 (*1-55660-235-9*) A Wofsy Fine Arts.
— Picasso's Paintings, Watercolors, Drawings & Sculputre: A Comprehensive Illustrated Catalogue: Neo-Classicism I: 1920-21. (Illus.). 288p. 1995. 150.00 (*1-55660-232-4*) A Wofsy Fine Arts.
— Picasso's Paintings, Watercolors, Drawings & Sculputre: A Comprehensive Illustrated Catalogue: Neo-Classicism I: 1920-21. (Illus.). 288p. 1995. 150.00 (*1-55660-231-6*) A Wofsy Fine Arts.
— Picasso's Paintings, Watercolors, Drawings & Sculputre: A Comprehensive Illustrated Catalogue: Toward Surrealism, 1925-29. (Illus.). 288p. 1995. 150.00 (*1-55660-233-2*) A Wofsy Fine Arts.
— Picasso's Paintings, Watercolors, Drawings & Sculpture: A Comprehensive Illustrated Catalogue: From Cubism to Neo-Classicism: 1917-1919. (Illus.). 288p. 1995. 150.00 (*1-55660-230-8*) A Wofsy Fine Arts.
— Picasso's Paintings, Watercolors, Drawings & Sculpture: A Comprehensive Illustrated Catalogue: Liberation & Post War Years, 1944-49. (Illus.). 288p. 1995. 150.00 (*1-55660-237-5*) A Wofsy Fine Arts.
— Picasso's Paintings, Watercolors, Drawings & Sculpture: A Comprehensive Illustrated Catalogue: Nazi Occupation, 1940-44. (Illus.). 288p. 1996. 150.00 (*1-55660-236-7*) A Wofsy Fine Arts.
— Picasso's Paintings, Watercolors, Drawings & Sculpture: A Comprehensive Illustrated Catalogue: Neoclassicism II, 1992-24. (Illus.). 288p. 1995. 150.00 (*0-614-06570-4*) A Wofsy Fine Arts.
— Picasso's Paintings, Watercolors, Drawings & Sculpture: A Comprehensive Illustrated Catalogue: Surrealism, 1930-36. (Illus.). 1995. 150.00 (*1-55660-234-0*) A Wofsy Fine Arts.
Picasso, Sydney, jt. auth. see Baudez, Claude.
Picavet, Francois J. Essais Sur l'Histoire General et Comparee Des Theologies et Des Philosophes Medievales. viii, 415p. reprint ed. write for info. (*0-318-71388-8*, Pub. by Georg Olms GW) Lubrecht & Cramer.
— Les Idealogues: Scientific, Philosophical, & Religious Theories in France Since 1789. LC 74-25774. (European Sociology Ser.). 646p. 1975. reprint ed. 53.95 (*0-405-06528-0*) Ayer.
— Les Ideologues. xiii, 628p. 1972. reprint ed. write for info. (*3-487-04397-1*, Pub. by Georg Olms GW) Lubrecht & Cramer.
Picayune Staff. Picayune Creole Cookbook. (Cookbook Ser.). 1971. pap. 9.95 (*0-486-22678-6*) Dover.
***Picazo, Gloria.** Riera I Arago. (Great Monographs). (Illus.). 464p. 1993. 300.00 (*84-343-0729-4*) Elliots Bks.
Picazo, J., ed. Glucagon in Acute Medicine: Pharmacological, Clinical, & Therapeutic Implications. LC 93-24960. 1993. lib. bdg. 38.50 (*0-7923-8832-1*) Kluwer Ac.
— Glucagon in Gastroenterology & Hepatology: Pharmacological, Clinical & Therapeutic Implications. 160p. 1982. lib. bdg. 67.00 (*0-85200-447-8*) Kluwer Ac.
— Glucagon in Nineteen Eighty-Seven: Gastrointestinal & Hepatobiliaty Physiology, Diagnosis & Treatment. (C). 1989. lib. bdg. 92.00 (*0-7462-0052-8*) Kluwer Ac.
Piccard, Betty J. Introduction to Social Work: A Primer. 4th ed. 196p. (C). 1988. pap. 22.95 (*0-534-10765-6*) Brooks-Cole.
Picchi, F. Italian-English - English-Italian Financial & Commercial Encyclopedia Dictionary. 2nd ed. 1594p. 1990. 124.50 (*88-08-06862-5*) IBD Ltd.
Picchi, F., ed. Economics & Business: Dizionario Enciclopedico Economico Inglese Italiano. 2nd ed. 1350p. (ENG & ITA.). 1990. 135.00x (*0-913298-37-9*) S F Vanni.
***Picchi, Fernando.** Dictionary of Economics & Business & of Modern Language. (ENG & ITA.). Date not set. 100.00 (*0-7859-8874-2*) Fr & Eur.
— English & Italian Encyclopedic Economic & Commercial Dictionary, 2 vols., Set. 2nd ed. 1325p. (ENG & ITA.). 1990. 175.00 (*0-8288-0107-X*, F16130) Fr & Eur.
— A Practical Guide for Mariners English-Italian. 319p. (ENG & ITA.). 1980. pap. 29.95 (*0-8288-4713-4*, M9193) Fr & Eur.
Picchi, Fernando, jt. auth. see Bernabo, M.
Picchio, Antonella. Social Reproduction: The Political Economy of the Labour Market. 208p. (C). 1992. 49.95 (*0-521-41872-0*) Cambridge U Pr.
Picchio, Riccardo. Studies on the Literary Tradition of Medieval Orthodox Slavdom. (Renovatio Ser.: No. 2). 475p. 1990. 35.00 (*0-916458-33-4*) Harvard Ukrainian.
Picchio, Riccardo & Goldblatt, Harvey, eds. Aspects of the Slavic Language Question: Church Slavonic-South Slavic-West Slavic,, Vol. 1. (Yale Russian & East European Publications: No. 4a). 416p. 1984. 35.00 (*0-936586-03-6*) Yale Russian.
— Aspects of the Slavic Language Question: East Slavic, Vol. II. (Yale Russian & East European Publications: No. 4b). 367p. 1984. 35.00 (*0-936586-04-4*) Yale Russian.
Picchione, John & Smith, Lawrence R., eds. Twentieth-Century Italian Poetry: An Anthology. (Italian Linguistics & Language Pedagogy Ser.). 480p. 1992. pap. 35.00 (*0-8020-7368-9*) U of Toronto Pr.
Picchione, Nick, ed. see Dome Financial Services Staff.
Picchione, Richard. Las Vegas-Reno Bartender's Guide. 5th rev. ed. 80p. 1987. pap. 5.95 (*0-317-64218-9*) R Picchione.
Piccialli, Aldo, jt. auth. see De Poli, Giovanni.
Picciani, Ron, jt. auth. see Ginter, Steven J.
Picciano, Anthony G. Computers in the Schools: A Guide to Planning & Administration. 320p. (C). 1993. text ed. write for info. (*0-02-395281-4*, Merrill Pub Co) Macmillan.
Picciano, Mary F. & Lonnerdal, Bo. Mechanisms Regulating Lactation & Infant Nutrient Utilization. (Contemporary Issues in Clinical Nutrition Ser.). 480p. 1992. text ed. 217.95 (*0-471-56134-7*) Wiley.
Picciano, Mary F., jt. auth. see Guthrie, Helen A.
Piccigallo, B., jt. auth. see Bassani, R.
Piccigallo, Philip R. The Japanese on Trial: Allied War Crimes Operations in the East, 1945-1951. (Illus.). 308p. 1979. text ed. 20.00 (*0-292-78033-8*) U of Tex Pr.
Piccini, Sara, ed. see Pfeiffer, George J. & Webster, Judith A.
Piccininni, Livio C., et al. Ordinary Differential Equations in R to the Nth Power. (Applied Mathematical Sciences Ser.: Vol. 39). 386p. 1984. pap. 59.00 (*0-387-90723-8*) Spr-Verlag.
Piccinini, R., ed. Groups of Self-Equivalences & Related Topics: Proceedings of a Conference Held in Montreal, Canada, August 8-12 1988. (Lecture Notes in Mathematics Ser.: Vol. 1425). v, 214p. 1990. pap. 34.80 (*0-387-52658-7*) Spr-Verlag.
Piccinini, R. & Sjerve, D., eds. Conference on Algebraic Topology in Honor of Peter Hilton. LC 84-24518. (Contemporary Mathematics Ser.: Vol. 37). 161p. 1985. pap. text ed. 30.00 (*0-8218-5036-9*, CONM-37) Am Math.
Piccinini, Renzo, jt. auth. see Fritsch, Rudolf.
Piccinni, Niccolo. Atys, Tragedie Lyrique. Rushton, Julian, ed. LC 91-757502. (French Opera in the 17th & 18th Centuries Ser.: No. 7, Vol. LXV). (Illus.). 1991. lib. bdg. 86.00 (*0-945193-21-1*) Pendragon NY.
— Didon. Lefevre, Gustave, ed. (Chefs-d'oeuvre classiques de l'opera francaise Ser.: Vol. 28). (Illus.). 334p. (FRE.). 1970. reprint ed. pap. 35.00 (*0-8450-1128-6*) Broude.
— Roland. Lefevre, Gustave, ed. (Chefs-d'oeuvre classiques de l'opera francaise Ser.: Vol. 29). (Illus.). 390p. (FRE.). 1970. reprint ed. pap. 40.00 (*0-8450-1129-4*) Broude.
***Piccione, Anthony.** For the Kingdom. (American Poets Continuum Ser.: No. 32). 1995. 20.00 (*1-880238-22-5*); pap. 12.50 (*1-880238-23-3*) BOA Edns.
Piccione, Sandi. Polar Sun. LC 79-4685. 1979. pap. 4.00 (*0-918366-12-7*) Slow Loris.
Picciony, M., ed. Diccionario de Alimentacion Animal. 820p. (SPA.). 1970. 85.00 (*0-7859-0586-3*, S-36852) Fr & Eur.
Piccioto, tr. see Nejar, Carlos.
Picciotto, Robert, tr. see Goldemberg, Isaac.
Picciotto, Sol. International Business Taxation: A Study in the Internationalization of Business Regulation. LC 91-47952. 408p. 1992. text ed. 65.00 (*0-89930-777-9*, PIX, Quorum Bks) Greenwood.
Picciotto, Sol, jt. ed. see Holloway, John.
Piccirelli, Annette. New Research Center. 19th ed. Cichonski, ed. 162p. 1994. 260.00 (*0-8103-8508-2*) Gale.
— Research Center Directory, Vol. 1. 19th ed. 1994. write for info. (*0-8103-8357-8*) Gale.
— Research Center Directory, Vol. 2. 19th ed. 1994. write for info. (*0-8103-8358-6*) Gale.
— Research Services Directory. 5th ed. 1992. 325.00 (*0-8103-7631-8*) Gale.
— Research Services Directory. 6th ed. 1995. 335.00 (*0-8103-7905-8*) Gale.
Piccirelli, R. A., ed. see American Institute of Physics.
***Piccirilli, Tom.** Pentacle. (Illus.). 156p. (Orig.). Date not set. pap. 5.99 (*0-9640168-2-6*) Pirate Writings.
***Piccirilli, Tom, et al.** Endings: Four Stories, Sixteen Endings. (Illus.). 48p. (Orig.). Date not set. pap. 3.00 (*0-9640168-3-4*) Pirate Writings.
Piccitto, G., jt. ed. see Pucci, R.
Picco, Elizabeth R. Baby Basics: Children's Activities in How Life Begins. LC 92-20519. (Illus.). 1992. write for info. (*1-56071-126-4*) ETR Assocs.
Piccola, Michael D. Intrepid's Odyssey: The Deception That Haunts the Intrepid Museum. LC 94-92135. (Illus.). 390p. (Orig.). 1994. pap. text ed. 16.95 (*0-9641022-0-X*) Odyssey Pubng.
Piccoli, Terese S., ed. see League of Women Voters of Pennsylvania Education Fund Staff.
Piccolino, F. C., jt. ed. see Zingirian, M.
Piccolo, Lucio. Collected Poems of Lucio Piccolo. Swann, Brian & Feldman, Ruth, eds. LC 74-37576. 215p. reprint ed. pap. 61.30 (*0-7837-1407-6*, 2041761) Bks Demand.
Piccolo, Rina. Stand Back, I Think I'm Gonna Laugh: Cartoons by Rina Piccolo. (Illus.). 96p. (Orig.). 1994. pap. 7.95 (*0-9632526-3-1*) Laugh Lines.
Piccolomini, Enea S. The Tale of Two Lovers. Grierson, Flora, tr. LC 76-48452. (Library of World Literature Ser.). 1993. reprint ed. lib. bdg. 16.50 (*0-88355-598-0*) Hyperion Conn.
Piccolomini, Manfredi. The Brutus Revival: Parricide & Tyrannicide During the Renaissance. LC 89-78134. (Illus.). 200p. (C). 1991. 24.95 (*0-8093-1649-8*) S Ill U Pr.
Piccolpasso, Cipriano. The Three Books of the Potter's Art. 1980. 212.95 (*0-85967-452-5*, Pub. by Scolar Pr UK) Ashgate Pub Co.
Piccone, Anthony. Seeing It Was So. 87p. 1986. 18.00 (*0-918526-50-7*); pap. 10.00 (*0-918526-51-5*) BOA Edns.
Piccone, Paul, ed. see International Telos Conference Staff.
Piccone, Paul, tr. see Paci, Enzo.
Picconi, Marcello. Dictionnaire des Aliments pour les Animaux. 620p. (FRE.). 1965. 65.00 (*0-8288-6741-0*, M-6452) Fr & Eur.
Picconi, Mario J., et al. Business Statistics: Elements & Application. (C). 1992. 12.50 (*0-06-500723-9*); 12.50 (*0-06-500724-7*) HarpCollege.
— Business Statistics: Elements & Application. (C). 1992. student ed 25.00 (*0-06-500175-3*) HarpCollege.

P Q

— Business Statistics: Elements & Application, Minitab Manual IBM. (C). 1992. 21.00 (0-06-501667-X) HarpCollege.

— Business Statistics: Elements & Applications. LC 92-16383. (C). 1993. text ed. 70.50 (0-06-500174-5) HarpCollege.

Picerno, Richard A. Medieval Spanish Ejempla: A Study of Selected Tales from Calila y Dimna, El Libro de los Enganos de las Mujeres & the Libro de los Exemplos por ABC. LC 88-81376. (Coleccion Textos Ser.). 55p. (Orig.). (ENG & SPA.). 1988. pap. 10.00 (0-89729-492-0) Ediciones.

Picerno, Richard A., intro. La Estrella de Sevilla. LC 80-66393. (Coleccion Teatro). 167p. (Orig.). (SPA.). 1984. pap. 14.95 (0-89729-256-1) Ediciones.

Picerno, Vincent J. Dictionary of Musical Terms. LC 76-14903. (Studies in Music: No. 42). (C). 1976. lib. bdg. 75.00 (0-8383-2119-4) M S G Haskell Hse.

Pichal, M. & Sifner, O., eds. Properties of Water & Steam: Proceedings of the 11th International Conference. 704p. 1990. 157.00 (1-56032-042-7) Hemisp Pub.

Pichanick, Valerie. Harriet Martineau: The Woman & Her Work, Eighteen Hundred & Two to Eighteen Seventy-Six. (Women & Culture Ser.). 336p. 1980. 37.50 (0-472-10002-5) U of Mich Pr.

Pichard & Lob. Ulysses, Vol. 1. Koch, Michael, tr. 64p. 1991. pap. 9.95 (1-56163-033-0, Eurotica) NBM.

Pichard, jt. auth. see Vatsyayana.

Pichard, D. Wolinski. Paulette, Tome II. (FRE.). 1981. pap. 11.95 (0-7859-4155-X, 2070373061) Fr & Eur.

Pichard, G. Wolinski. Paulette, Tome I. 1981. pap. 11.95 (0-7859-4140-1) Fr & Eur.

***Pichard, Georges.** Carmen. 64p. 1995. pap. 10.95x (1-56163-123-X, Eurotica) NBM.

— Marie-Gabrielle. 136p. 1995. pap. 14.95x (1-56163-138-8, Eurotica) NBM.

Pichard, Georges & Masoch, Count. The Countess in Red. LeClerc, Jacinthe, tr. 48p. 1994. pap. 9.95 (1-56163-098-5, Eurotica) NBM.

Pichard, J. Brent. Winning with Words: Secrets of the Job Interview. 2nd ed. 77p. (C). 1983. pap. 4.95 (0-9612312-1-1) Magister Inc.

Pichard, Lob. Ulysses, Vol. 2. Koch, M., tr. 64p. 1992. pap. 9.95 (1-56163-043-8, Eurotica) NBM.

Pichard, Pierre. Inventory of Monuments at Pagan, Vol. 1. (Illus.). 432p. (C). 1995. 130.00 (1-870838-01-7, Pub. by Kiscadale UK) Weatherhill.

— Inventory of Monuments at Pagan, Vol. 2. (Illus.). 432p. (C). 1995. 130.00 (1-870838-16-5, Pub. by Kiscadale UK) Weatherhill.

— Inventory of Monuments at Pagan, Vol. 3. (Illus.). 432p. (C). 1995. 130.00 (1-870838-31-9, Pub. by Kiscadale UK) Weatherhill.

— Inventory of Monuments at Pagan, Vol. 4. (Illus.). 432p. 1995. 130.00 (1-870838-86-6, Pub. by Kiscadale UK) Weatherhill.

— The Pentagonoal Monuments of Pagan. (Illus.). 157p. 1991. 35.00 (1-879155-53-2); pap. 22.00 (1-879155-03-6) Lotus WA.

Pichardo, Hector, tr. see Ledbetter, H. & Lomax, John A.

Pichaske. Late Harvest. 1994. pap. 18.95 (1-56924-867-2) Marlowe & Co.

Pichaske, David. Visiting the Father. 1987. 2.50 (0-941127-02-8) Dacotah Terr Pr.

Pichaske, David, jt. ed. see Groen, Gerrit.

Pichaske, David R. A Generation in Motion. 248p. 1989. 15.95 (0-944024-12-2); pap. 10.95 (0-944024-16-5) Ellis Pr.

— The Jubilee Diary: April 10, 1980-April 19, 1981. (Illus.). 240p. (Orig.). 1982. pap. 5.95 (0-933180-42-X) Ellis Pr.

— The Poetry of Rock: The Golden Years. 192p. (Orig.). 1981. pap. 5.95 (0-933180-17-9) Ellis Pr.

— Poland in Transition: 1989-1991. (Illus.). 256p. (Orig.). 1994. pap. 11.95 (0-944024-27-0) Ellis Pr.

— Salem-Peoria, Eighteen Eighty-Three to Nineteen Eighty-Two. (Illus.). 256p. (Orig.). 1982. pap. 6.95 (0-933180-40-3) Ellis Pr.

— Writing Sense: A Handbook of Composition. LC 74-15134. (C). 1975. pap. text ed. 10.95 (0-02-925170-2) Free Pr.

Pichaske, David R., ed. Gates: Poems on the Restoration of Jubilee College. 26p. 1986. pap. 3.00 (0-933180-93-4) Spoon Riv Poetry.

Piche, Denise, jt. ed. see Dagenais, Huguette.

Piche, Thomas. Art Nouveau Glass & Pottery. Meyer, Faith, ed. (Illus.). 16p. (Orig.). 1982. pap. text ed. 4.00 (0-932660-06-1) U of NI Dept Art.

Piche, Thomas, ed. see Doroshenko, Peter & Druckrey, Timothy.

Piche, Thomas, ed. see Doroshenko, Peter.

Piche, Thomas, Jr., ed. see Greengold, Jane.

Piche, THomas, Jr., ed. see Kingsley, April.

Piche, Thomas, ed. see Nahas, Dominique & Perreault, John.

Piche, Thomas, Jr., ed. see Perry, Barbara.

Piche, Thomas

Piche, Thomas, ed. see Perry, Barbara, et al.

Piche, Thomas, Jr., ed. see Sandys, Edwina & Morton, James P.

Piche, Thomas, et al. Fiction, Function, Figuration: The Twenty-Ninth Ceramic National. Herbert, Linda M., ed. 80p. (Orig.). 1993. pap. text ed. write for info. (0-914407-17-1) Everson Mus.

Pichelmaier, H. & Schildberg, F. W., eds. Thoracic Surgery. (Illus.). 480p. 1989. 434.00 (0-387-18464-3) Spr-Verlag.

Picherit, Jean-Louis, ed. & tr. The Journey of Charlemagne. LC 84-52505. 138p. 1985. 12.95 (0-917786-46-7) Summa Pubns.

Pichevin, M. F., et al. Studies on the Self & Social Cognition. 344p. 1993. text ed. 109.00 (981-02-1237-2) World Scientific Pub.

Pichey, Martha. Naples & Campania. 1994. pap. 16.95 (0-8442-9963-4, Passport Bks) NTC Pub Grp.

Pichler, F. R. A. Process in Cybernetics & Systems Research, Vol. 7. 1981. 80.00 (0-07-049847-4) McGraw.

— Progress in Cybernetics & System Research, Vol. 6. 1981. 80.00 (0-07-049846-6) McGraw.

Pichler, Franz R., ed. Advances in Crypotology - Eurocrypt '85. (Lecture Notes in Computer Science Ser.: Vol. 219). ix, 218p. 1986. pap. 36.00 (0-387-16468-5) Spr-Verlag.

— Eurocast Nineteen Eighty-Nine. (Lecture Notes in Computer Science Ser.: Vol. 410). vii, 427p. 1990. pap. 41.80 (0-387-52215-8) Spr-Verlag.

Pichler, Franz R. & Diaz, R. Moreno, eds. Computer Aided Systems Theory, EUROCAST '91: A Selection of Papers from the Second International Workshop on Computer Aided Systems Theory, Krems, Austria, April 15-19, 1991: Proceedings. LC 92-9634. (Lecture Notes in Computer Science Ser.: Vol. 585). x, 761p. 1992. pap. 99.00 (0-387-55354-1) Spr-Verlag.

Pichler, Franz R. & Schwartzel, Heinz, eds. CAST: Methods in Modelling: Computer Aided Systems Theory for the Design of Intelligent Machines. LC 92-8524. (Illus.). 392p. 1992. 98.00 (0-387-55405-X) Spr-Verlag.

Pichler, Joseph A., jt. ed. see DeGeorge, Richard T.

Pichler, Tibor & Gasparikova, Jana, eds. Language, Values, & the Slovak Nation. LC 93-11884. (Cultural Heritage & Contemporary Change Series VI: Foundations of Moral Education,: Vol. 5). 1993. 45.00 (1-56518-036-4); 17.50 (1-56518-037-2) Coun Res Values.

Pichler, W. J., jt. ed. see Stadler, B. M.

Pichler, W. J., et al, eds. Progress in Allergy & Clinical Immunology. LC 89-1678. 600p. 1989. 48.00 (0-920887-45-7) Hogrefe & Huber Pubs.

Pichois, ed. see Colette, Sidonie-Gabrielle.

Pichois, Claude, ed. see Baudelaire, Charles P.

Pichois, Claude, jt. auth. see Baudelaire, Charles P.

Pichois, Claude, ed. see Colette, Sidonie-Gabrielle.

Pichois, Raymond, ed. see Baudelaire, Charles P.

Pichon, Jacqueline, jt. auth. see Wagner, Rene-Louis.

Pichon, Rene. Index Verborum Amatoriorum. iv, 229p. 1991. reprint ed. write for info. (3-487-01411-4, Pub. by Georg Olms GW) Lubrecht & Cramer.

Pichon, Y., ed. Comparative Molecular Neurobiology. LC 92-49315. (Experientia Supplementa Ser.: No. 63). ix, 433p. 1992. write for info. (3-7643-2785-5); 147.50 (0-8176-2785-5) Birkhauser.

Pichot, Andre. La Naissance de la Science: Grece Presocratique, Vol. 2. (FRE.). 1991. pap. 26.95 (0-7859-3972-5) Fr & Eur.

— La Naissance de la Science: Mesopotamie, Egypte, Vol. 1. (FRE.). 1991. pap. 22.95 (0-7859-3971-7) Fr & Eur.

Pichot, P. & Olivier-Martin, R., eds. Psychological Measurements in Psychopharmacology. (Modern Problems of Pharmacopsychiatry Ser.: Vol. 7). (Illus.). 1974. 78.50 (3-8055-1630-4) S Karger.

Pichot, Pierre. Compressor Application Engineering, Vol. 1: Compression Equipment. LC 86-7587. (Illus.). 250p. 1986. 49.00 (0-87201-705-2) Gulf Pub.

— Compressor Application Engineering, Vol. 2: Drivers for Rotating Equipment. LC 86-7587. (Illus.). 230p. 1986. 49.00 (0-87201-706-0) Gulf Pub.

Picinbono, Bernard. Principles of Signals & Systems: Deterministic Signals. (Telecommunications Engineering Library). 240p. 1988. text ed. 19.00 (0-89006-295-1) Artech Hse.

— Random Signals & Systems. 512p. 1993. text ed. 76.00 (0-13-752270-3) P-H.

Picinbono, Bernard, jt. ed. see Longo, G.

Picinelli, Filippo. Mundus Symbolicus, 2 vols. in 1. 1276p. (GER.). 1979. reprint ed. write for info. (3-487-05790-5, Pub. by Georg Olms GW); reprint ed. write for info. (3-487-05970-3, Pub. by Georg Olms GW) Lubrecht & Cramer.

Picirilli, Robert. The Book of Galatians. 1973. pap. 6.95 (0-89265-012-5) Randall Hse.

— The Book of Romans. 324p. (C). 1975. 9.95 (0-89265-026-5) Randall Hse.

— The Book of Romans, 3 vols., 1. 1974. pap. 5.95 (0-89265-015-X) Randall Hse.

— The Book of Romans, 3 vols., 2. 1974. pap. 5.95 (0-89265-016-8) Randall Hse.

— The Book of Romans, 3 vols., 3. 1974. pap. 5.95 (0-89265-017-6) Randall Hse.

— Pauline Writings Notes. 1967. pap. 4.95 (0-89265-001-X) Randall Hse.

— What the Bible Says about Tongues. 1981. pap. 0.95 (0-89265-071-0) Randall Hse.

Picirilli, Robert & Hampton, Ralph, Jr. A Survey of the Major Prophets. 1976. pap. 1.95 (0-89265-034-6) Randall Hse.

Picirilli, Robert, jt. auth. see Harrison, Paul.

Picirilli, Robert E. Church Government & Ordinances. 1973. pap. 1.95 (0-89265-102-4) Randall Hse.

— Fundamentals of the Faith. 30p. 1973. pap. 1.95 (0-89265-106-7) Randall Hse.

— The Gifts of the Spirit. 1980. pap. 1.95 (0-89265-065-6) Randall Hse.

— Paul the Apostle. (Orig.). 1986. pap. 9.99 (0-8024-6325-8) Moody.

— Perseverance. 28p. 1973. pap. 0.95 (0-89265-108-3) Randall Hse.

— Randall House Bible Commentary: 1, 2 Corinthians. Harrison, H. D., ed. 434p. 1987. 24.95 (0-89265-118-0) Randall Hse.

Picirilli, Robert E. & Harrison, H D., eds. Randall House Bible Commentary Series, 6 vols., 4 vols., Set. 1989. write for info. (0-89265-115-6) Randall Hse.

Picirilli, Robert E., ed. see Marberry, Thomas.

Picirilli, Robert E., ed. see Stallings, Jack.

Picirilli, Robert E., et al. Randall House Bible Commentary: I Thessalonians Through Philemon. Harrison, H. D., ed. 1990. 24.95 (0-89265-143-1) Randall Hse.

Pick, A. D., ed. Perception & Its Development: A Tribute to Eleanor J. Gibson. 272p. 1979. text ed. 49.95 (0-89859-409-X) L Erlbaum Assocs.

Pick, A. I. Plasma Cell Dyscrasias. (Journal: Acta Haematologica: Vol. 68, No. 3). (Illus.). vi, 96p. 1982. pap. 47.25 (3-8055-3549-X) S Karger.

Pick, Albert. Standard Catalog of World Paper Money, Vol. II: General Issues. 7th ed. LC 80-81510. (Illus.). 1200p. 1994. 55.00 (0-87341-207-9) Krause Pubns.

Pick, Alfred & Langendorf, Richard. Interpretation of Complex Arrhythmias. LC 79-10741. (Illus.). 598p. 1979. reprint ed. pap. 170.20 (0-7837-1493-9, 2057189) Bks Demand.

Pick, Bernard. The Cabala: Its Influence on Judaism & Christianity. 1991. lib. bdg. 75.00 (0-8490-4257-7) Gordon Pr.

Pick, Bernhard. The Cabala: Its Influence on Judaism & Christianity. 115p. 1993. pap. 9.00 (0-89540-287-4, SB-287) Sun Pub.

Pick, C. Undersea. (Young Scientist Ser.). (Illus.). 32p. (J). 1976. lib. bdg. 13.96 (0-88110-437-X); pap. 6.95 (0-86020-092-2) EDC.

Pick, Christopher. Exploring Rural England & Wales. 1989. pap. 12.95 (0-8442-9464-0, Passport Bks) NTC Pub Grp.

— Landscapes of Scotland. 1991. 14.99 (0-517-06591-6) Random Hse Value.

Pick, Daniel. Faces of Degeneration: Aspects of a European Disorder c. 1848-1918. (Ideas in Context Ser.: No. 15). (Illus.). (C). 1989. 59.95 (0-521-36021-8) Cambridge U Pr.

— Faces of Degeneration: Aspects of a European Disorder c. 1848-1918. (Ideas in Context Ser.: No. 15). (Illus.). 300p. (C). 1993. pap. 19.95 (0-521-45753-X) Cambridge U Pr.

— War Machine: The Rationalization of Slaughter in the Modern Age. (Illus.). 288p. (C). 1993. text ed. 30.00 (0-300-05417-3) Yale U Pr.

Pick, Daniel, ed. see Du Maurier, George.

Pick, Doris J., et al. GuidePak: A Computerized Career Planning Guide Including Your Occupational Interests, Psychological Assessment & Personality Traits. rev. ed. 101p. 1991. pap. 89.00 (1-879858-00-2) Behaviordyne.

Pick, E., tr. see Escarpit, Robert.

Pick, Edgar. Lymphokines Vol. 9: Forum for Immuno-Regulatory Cell Products. 1984. text ed. 138.00 (0-12-432009-0) Acad Pr.

Pick, Edgar, ed. Lymphokine Reports: A Forum for Nonantibody Lymphocyte Products, Vol. 1. 1980. text ed. 85.00 (0-12-432001-5) Acad Pr.

— Lymphokines, Vol. 10. (Serial Publication Ser.). 1985. text ed. 99.00 (0-12-432010-4) Acad Pr.

— Lymphokines, Vol. 12. (Serial Publication Ser.). 1985. pap. text ed. 65.00 (0-12-432012-0) Acad Pr.

— Lymphokines: A Forum for Immunoregulatory Cell Products, Vol. 14. 471p. 1987. text ed. 145.00 (0-12-432014-7) Acad Pr.

Pick, Edgar, et al, eds. Lymphokines Vol. 15: A Forum for Immunoregulatory Cell Products: Interleukin 3 - The Panspecific Hemopoietin. 430p. 1988. text ed. 143.00 (0-12-432015-5) Acad Pr.

— Lymphokines Vol. 13: A Forum for Immunoregulatory Cell Functions: Molecular Cloning & Analysis of Lymphokines. 1987. text ed. 137.00 (0-12-432013-9) Acad Pr.

Pick, F. W., tr. see Riter, Gerhard.

Pick, Franz. The Triumph of Gold. 2nd ed. 150p. 1987. reprint ed. pap. 92.00 (0-938689-01-0) Inst Preserv Wealth.

Pick, Frederick W. The Baltic Nations: Estonia, Latvia, & Lithuania. LC 83-45837. reprint ed. 20.00 (0-404-20202-0) AMS Pr.

Pick, H. L., Jr. & Saltzman, E., eds. Modes of Perceiving & Processing Information. 240p. 1978. text ed. 49.95 (0-89859-354-9) L Erlbaum Assocs.

Pick, Herbert L. & Acredolo, Linda P., eds. Spatial Orientation: Theory, Research, & Application. 398p. 1983. 85.00 (0-306-41255-1, Plenum Pr) Plenum.

Pick, Herbert L., Jr., jt. ed. see Walk, Richard D.

Pick, Herbert L., Jr., et al, eds. Cognition: Conceptual & Methodological Issues. (Illus.). 374p. 1992. text ed. 40.00 (1-55798-165-5) Am Psychol.

Pick, J., jt. auth. see Hala, E.

Pick, James B. & Butler, Edgar W. Mexico Handbook: Economic & Demographic Maps & Statistics. 2nd ed. (C). 1994. pap. text ed. 52.50 (0-8133-1677-4) Westview.

Pick, James B., jt. auth. see Butler, Edgar W.

Pick, John. Gerard Manley Hopkins: Priest & Poet. LC 78-14838. 169p. 1978. reprint ed. text ed. 38.50 (0-313-20589-2, PIGH, Greenwood Pr) Greenwood.

Pick, John, ed. Vile Jelly: The Birth, Life & Lingering Death of the Arts Council of Great Britain. (C). 1989. 45.00 (0-907839-52-5, Pub. by Brynmill Pr Ltd UK) St Mut.

Pick, Joseph R. VHDL: Techniques, Experiments & Caveats. 1994. 45.00 (0-07-049906-3) McGraw.

Pick, Liza, et al, trs. International Tapestry Network. (Illus.). 64p. (Orig.). (C). 1992. pap. 17.00 (0-9625772-1-9) ITNET.

Pick, M. & Machando, M. E., eds. Fundamental Problems in Solar Activity. 472p. 1993. pap. 195.00 (0-08-042339-6, Pergamon Pr) Elsevier.

***Pick, Marc G.** Focal Point Recording: A Universal Approach for Cranial Manipulation. (Illus.). 150p. (C). 1995. spiral bd. 45.00 (0-939616-23-8) Eastland.

Pick, Maritza. How to Save Your Neighborhood, City, or Town: The Sierra Club Guide to Community Organizing. LC 92-25143. (Illus.). 224p. (Orig.). 1993. pap. 12.00 (0-87156-522-6) Sierra.

— League of Liars. LC 86-80648. 270p. 1987. pap. 7.95 (0-935539-16-6) Heroica Bks.

Pick, Otto. Cold War Legacy in Europe: Challenges & Opportunities. 1992. text ed. 55.00 (0-312-06543-4) St Martin.

Pick, Otto, jt. auth. see Busch, Marie.

Pick, Otto, jt. ed. see Maull, Hanns.

Pick, Richard. School of Guitar: The Guitar in Pedagogy, Practice, Performance, 2 vols., Set. LC 92-14177. 1992. pap. 35.00 (0-685-66123-7, RTFT7) Edit Orphee.

— School of Guitar: The Guitar in Pedagogy, Practice, Performance, 2 vols., Vol. 1. LC 92-14177. 1992. pap. 18.95 (0-936186-62-3, RTFT7A) Edit Orphee.

— School of Guitar: The Guitar in Pedagogy, Practice, Performance, 2 vols., Vol. 2. LC 92-14177. 1992. pap. 18.95 (0-936186-69-0, FTFT7B) Edit Orphee.

Pick, Robert M., jt. ed. see Miserendino, Leo J.

Pick, Zuzana M. The New Latin American Cinema: A Continental Project. Schatz, Thomas, ed. LC 93-73. (Film Studies). 264p. (C). 1993. text ed. 37.50 (0-292-76545-2); pap. 16.95 (0-292-76549-5) U of Tex Pr.

Pickar, Arnold D. Preparing for General Physics: Math Skill Drills & Other Useful Help: Calculus Version. LC 92-41812. (C). 1993. pap. text ed. 13.95 (0-201-53802-4) Addison-Wesley.

Pickar, Gloria. Dosage Calculations. 2nd ed. 128p. (C). 1982. disk 149.95 (0-8273-2693-9) Delmar.

— Dosage Calculations. 3rd ed. 144p. 1989. pap. text ed. 23.95 (0-8273-3951-8) Delmar.

Pickar, Gloria D. Dosage Calculations. 4th ed. LC 92-23154. 1992. pap. text ed. 23.95 (0-8273-4982-3) Delmar.

— Dosage Calculations. LC 82-71146. (Illus.). 128p. (C). 1982. reprint ed. pap. text ed. 16.95 (0-8273-2090-6); reprint ed. disk 149.95 (0-8273-2778-1) Delmar.

— Dosage Calculations: Instructor's Guide. 4th ed. 153p. 1993. 14.00 (0-8273-5741-9) Delmar.

Pickar, Roger L. Marketing for Design Firms in the 1990s. 112p. (Orig.). 1991. pap. 20.00 (1-55835-037-3) AIA Press.

Pickard, Ben. Florida's Eden: The History of Alachua County. (Illus.). 180p. 1994. boxed 19.95 (0-929895-12-6) Maupin Hse.

Pickard, Bertram. Peacemakers' Dilemma. (C). 1936. pap. 3.00 (0-87574-016-2) Pendle Hill.

Pickard, Brent K., ed. Skier's Guide to North America. LC 88-50618. (Illus.). 256p. (Orig.). 1988. pap. 11.95 (0-944982-01-8) Wise Guide Pub.

Pickard-Cambridge, A. W. Demoosthenes & the Last Days of Greek Freedom, 384-322 B.C. LC 73-14463. (Heroes of the Nations Ser.). reprint ed. 45.00 (0-404-58281-8) AMS Pr.

Pickard, Christopher. The Insider's Guide to Rio de Janeiro, 1986. 198p. 1986. pap. 11.95 (85-85051-01-9, Pub. by Streamline Lda BL) Luso-Brazilian Bks.

Pickard, Cynthia. The World in an Olive Leaf. 48p. (Orig.). 1985. 25.00 (0-931757-26-6); pap. 15.00 (0-931757-27-4) Pterodactyl Pr.

Pickard, David. Dawn Wind. 1980. pap. 2.50 (0-85363-133-6) OMF Bks.

Pickard, G., jt. auth. see McEwan, S.

Pickard, G. L. & Emery, W. J. Descriptive Physical Oceanography: An Introduction. enl. ed. (Illus.). 320p. 1990. pap. text ed. 26.00 (0-08-037952-4, Pergamon Pr) Elsevier.

— Descriptive Physical Oceanography: An Introduction. 5th enl. ed. (Illus.). 320p. 1990. text ed. 65.00 (0-08-037953-2, Pergamon Pr) Elsevier.

Pickard, G. L. & Emery, W. J., eds. Descriptive Physical Oceanography: An Introduction. 4th ed. enl. ed. (International Series in Geophysics). (Illus.). 265p. 1982. text ed. 61.00 (0-08-026280-5, G145, G125, C145, Pergamon Pr); pap. text ed. 17.95 (0-08-026279-1, Pergamon Pr) Elsevier.

Pickard, G. L. & Pond, S. Introductory Dynamic Oceanography. 2nd ed. LC 77-4427. (Illus.). 368p. 1983. pap. text ed. 25.00 (0-08-028728-X, Pergamon Pr) Elsevier.

Pickard, J. D., et al, eds. Neuroendocrinological Aspects of Neurosurgery. (Acta Neurochirugica - Supplementum Ser.: Supplement 47). (Illus.). 130p. 1990. 102.00 (0-387-82160-0) Spr-Verlag.

— Neurosurgical Aspects of Epilepsy: Proceedings of the Fourth Advanced Seminar in Neurosurgical Research of the European Association of Neurosurgical Societies, May 17-18, 1989, Bressco die Teolo, Padova, Italy. (Acta Neurochirurgica - Supplementum Ser.: No. 50). (Illus.). viii, 144p. 1990. 104.00 (0-387-82227-5) Spr-Verlag.

***Pickard, James.** North American Shortwave Frequency Guide. 1995. pap. 19.95 (0-917963-09-1) Artsci Inc.

Pickard, John B., ed. see Whittier, John Greenleaf.

***Pickard, Kate E.** The Kidnapped & the Ransomed: The Narrative of Peter & Vina Still after Forty Years of Slavery. (Illus.). 528p. 1995. pap. 15.00 (0-8032-9233-3, Bison Books) U of Nebr Pr.

Pickard, Laurens R. Decision Making in Cardiothoracic Surgery. 208p. 1989. text ed. 105.00 (0-7216-1168-0) Saunders.

Pickard, Mary. Feasting Naturally with Our Friends. LC 82-60390. 164p. 1982. spiral bd., pap. 7.95 (0-934474-24-9) Cookbook Pubs.

Pickard, Mary A. Feasting Naturally: From Your Own Recipes. LC 80-68229. 155p. 1980. spiral bd. 7.95 (0-934474-18-4) Cookbook Pubs.

— Feasting...Naturally. LC 79-64450. 159p. 1979. spiral bd., pap. 7.95 (0-934474-05-2) Cookbook Pubs.

Pickard, Nancy. Bum Steer. large type ed. LC 90-40551. 437p. 1990. reprint ed. lib. bdg. 20.95 (1-56054-039-7) Thorndike Pr.

An Asterisk (*) at the beginning of an entry indicates that the title is appearing in BIP for the first time.

— Bum Steer. Marrow, Linda, ed. 288p. 1991. reprint ed. mass mkt. 4.99 (0-671-68042-0) PB.
— But I Wouldn't Want to Die There. Marrow, Linda, ed. 256p. 1994. reprint ed. mass mkt. 5.50 (0-671-72331-6, Pocket Star Bks) PB.
— But I Wouldn't Want to Die There: A Jenny Cain Mystery. large type ed. LC 93-33294. 1993. 19.95 (0-7862-0080-4) Thorndike Pr.
— Confession. 1994. 20.00 (0-671-78261-4) PB.
— Confession: A Jenny Cain Mystery. large type ed. LC 94-37389. 1995. write for info. (0-7862-0344-7) Thorndike Pr.
— Dead Crazy. Marrow, Linda, ed. 1989. mass mkt. 4.99 (0-671-73430-X) PB.
— Generous Death. 330p. 1992. 21.95 (0-913165-67-0); boxed 45.00 (0-685-52690-9) Dark Harvest.
— Generous Death. 1987. pap. 5.50 (0-671-73264-1) S&S Trade.
— I. O. U. large type ed. LC 91-24262. 408p. 1991. reprint ed. bds. 20.95 (1-56054-249-9) Thorndike Pr.
— Marriage Is Murder. Marrow, Linda, ed. 1988. mass mkt. 5.50 (0-671-73428-8) PB.
— Marriage Is Murder. large type ed. (Basic Ser.). 296p. 1988. bds. 7.95 (0-89621-131-2) Thorndike Pr.
— No Body. 1987. mass mkt. 4.99 (0-671-69179-1) PB.
— Say No to Murder. Marrow, Linda, ed. 1988. mass mkt. 4.99 (0-671-73431-8) PB.
— The Twenty Seven Ingredient Chili Con Carne Murders: Based on Characters & a Story Created by Virginia Rich. large type ed. LC 92-46346. 399p. 1993. reprint ed. lib. bdg. 20.95 (1-56054-636-0) Thorndike Pr.

Pickard, Nellie. Just Say It! True Stories about Witnessing Opportunities. 208p. 1992. pap. 8.99 (0-8010-7118-6) Baker Bk.
— What Do You Say When... An Inspirational Guide to Witnessing. LC 88-22284. 192p. 1988. pap. 8.99 (0-8010-7106-2) Baker Bk.
— What Would You Have Said? Witnessing with Confidence & Sensitivity. 176p. (Orig.). 1990. pap. 8.99 (0-8010-7113-5) Baker Bk.

Pickard, Roy. The Oscar Movies. 4th ed. LC 93-8338. 320p. 1994. 35.00 (0-8160-2709-9) Facts on File.

Pickard, Samuel T. Hawthorne's First Diary. LC 72-285. (Studies in Hawthorne: No. 15). 1972. reprint ed. lib. bdg. 75.00 (0-8383-1408-2) M S G Haskell Hse.
— Life & Letters of John Greenleaf Whittier. (BCL1-PS American Literature Ser.). 804p. 1992. reprint ed. lib. bdg. 119.00 (0-7812-6903-2) Rprt Serv.
— Life & Letters of John Greenleaf Whittier, 2 vols., Set. LC 68-24941. (American Biography Ser.: No. 32). 1969. reprint ed. lib. bdg. 89.95 (0-8383-0191-6) M S G Haskell Hse.
— Whittier-Land: A Handbook of North Essex. LC 73-7511. (American Literature Ser.: No. 49). 1973. reprint ed. lib. bdg. 62.95 (0-8383-1698-0) M S G Haskell Hse.

Pickard, Sid. E.C.O. Busted! Five Hundred Thirty-Five Nefutations, Re-Evaluations, Novelties, Improvements & Connections to the Encyclopedia of Chess Openings. Hays, Lou & Hall, John, eds. 240p. 1992. pap. 21.00 (1-880673-92-4) Hays Pub.

***Pickard, Tom.** Tiepin Eros - Typing Errors: New & Selected Poems. 160p. 1994. pap. 16.95 (1-85224-130-6, Pub. by Bloodaxe Bks UK) Dufour.

Pickard, Wayland. Complete Singers Guide: To Becoming a Working Professional. (Illus.). 180p. (Orig.). (C). 1989. 24.95 (0-685-26328-2); pap. text ed. 24.95 (0-685-26329-0) Pickard Pub.
— Complete Singer's Guide to Becoming a Working Professional. 1991. pap. 19.95 (0-9623458-0-6) Pickard Pub.

***Pickarski, Ron.** Eco-Cuisine. 288p. Date not set. pap. 14.95 (0-89815-635-1) Ten Speed Pr.

Pickart, Joan E. Amber, Sing Softly. (Denise Little Presents ser.). 384p. 1994. mass mkt. 4.99 (0-7860-0038-4) Windsor NY.
— Angels & Elves (Man of the Month, Baby Bet) 1995. mass mkt. 3.25 (0-373-05961-2, 1-05961-7) Silhouette.
— The Magic of the Moon. large type ed. (Nightingale Series Large Print Bks.). 211p. 1992. pap. 14.95 (0-8161-5301-9, Nightingale) Hall.
— Tucker Boone. (Loveswept Ser.: No. 285). 192p. 1988. pap. 2.50 (0-318-32847-X) Bantam.

Pickauet, Gary. WordPerfect for Windows QuickStart, New Edition. (QuickStart Ser.). (Illus.). 600p. 1993. pap. 21.95 (1-56529-174-3) Que.

Pickavat, Rairden, et al. Using WordPerfect 6: Special Edition. (Using Ser.). (Illus.). 1200p. (Orig.). 1993. pap. 29.95 (1-56529-077-1) Que.

Pickel, Andreas. Radical Transitions: The Survival & Revival of Entrepreneurship in the GDR. 242p. (C). 1991. pap. text ed. 44.00 (0-8133-8354-4) Westview.

Pickel, Haden H., jt. auth. see Williams, Anne C.

Pickel, Haden H., jt. auth. see Williams, Anne.

Pickel-Hedrick, Susan, jt. auth. see Hedrick, Basil C.

***Pickelhaupt, William R.** Club Rowing on San Francisco Bay, 1869-1939, Featuring the South End Rowing Club. (Illus.). 132p. (Orig.). 1995. pap. 21.95 (0-9647312-0-7) Flyblister Pr.

Pickell, David. Underwater Indonesia: A Guide to the World's Best Diving. 1991. pap. 15.95 (0-8442-9908-1, Passport Bks) NTC Pub Grp.

***Pickell, David & Cooper, Mike, eds.** Sulawesi: The Celebes. 2nd ed. 290p. 1995. pap. 19.95 (962-593-005-1) Periplus.

Pickell, David, ed. see Eiseman, Fred B., Jr.

Pickell, David, ed. see Muller, Kal.

Pickell, Garfield C., jt. auth. see Barrows, Howard S.

Pickell, M. R., jt. ed. see Pickell, P. S.

Pickell, Mark B., ed. Pipeline Infrastructure: Proceedings of the International Conference, San Antonio, Texas, August 16-17, 1993. LC 93-21532. 1993. write for info. (0-87262-923-6) Am Soc Civil Eng.
— Pipelines in Adverse Environments II. 748p. 1983. 59.00 (0-87262-385-8) Am Soc Civil Eng.

***Pickell, P. S. & Pickell, M. R., eds.** Michigan Distributors Directory. 848p. 1991. 131.00 (0-936526-17-3) Pick Pub MI.
— Michigan Distributors Directory. 790p. 1992. 136.00 (0-936526-19-X) Pick Pub MI.
— Michigan Distributors Directory. 804p. 1993. 136.00 (0-936526-20-3) Pick Pub MI.
— Michigan Distributors Directory. 910p. 1994. 141.00 (0-936526-22-X) Pick Pub MI.
— Michigan Distributors Directory. 1995. 146.00 (0-936526-31-9) Pick Pub MI.
— Michigan Manufacturers Directory. 1015p. 1988. 127.00 (0-936526-12-2) Pick Pub MI.
— Michigan Manufacturers Directory. 856p. 1991. 130.00 (0-936526-16-5) Pick Pub MI.
— Michigan Manufacturers Directory. 1168p. 1992. 136.00 (0-936526-18-1) Pick Pub MI.
— Michigan Manufacturers Directory. 1163p. 1993. 136.00 (0-936526-27-0) Pick Pub MI.
— Michigan Manufacturers Directory. 1140p. 1994. 141.00 (0-936526-29-7) Pick Pub MI.
— Michigan Manufacturers Directory. 1108p. 1995. 146.00 (0-936526-30-0) Pick Pub MI.

Pickell, William, ed. see Clausen, Barry & Pomeroy, Dana R.

Pickels, John, ed. GIS & Geography. 248p. 1994. lib. bdg. 40.00 (0-89862-294-8); pap. text ed. 18.95 (0-89862-295-6) Guilford Pr.

Picken, Andrew. The Sectarian: Or, the Church & the Meeting-House, 3 vols. in 2, 1. LC 79-8189. reprint ed. write for info. (0-404-62095-7) AMS Pr.
— The Sectarian: Or, the Church & the Meeting-House, 3 vols. in 2, 2. LC 79-8189. reprint ed. write for info. (0-404-62096-5) AMS Pr.
— The Sectarian: Or, the Church & the Meeting-House, 3 vols. in 2, Set. LC 79-8189. reprint ed. 84.50 (0-404-62094-9) AMS Pr.

Picken, F. & Kahn, A., eds. Medical Librarianship in the Eighties & Beyond: A World Perspective. 440p. 1986. text ed. 110.00 (0-7201-1776-3, Mansell Pub) Cassell.

Picken, Fiona M., jt. auth. see Matthews, David A.

Picken, Laurence, ed. Musica Asiatica, No. 4. 270p. 1984. pap. 69.95 (0-521-27837-6) Cambridge U Pr.

Picken, Laurence & Nickson, Noel J., eds. Music from the Tang Court, Vol. 5. (Illus.). 144p. (C). 1990. pap. 94.95 (0-521-34776-9) Cambridge U Pr.

Picken, Mary B. Old-Fashioned Ribbon Trimmings & Flowers. abr. ed. LC 93-2506. Orig. Title: Ribbon Trimmings & Flowers: Instruction Paper with Examination Questions. (Illus.). 48p. 1993. reprint ed. pap. 2.95 (0-486-27521-3) Dover.

Picken, Nellie B. Fireweed: An American Saga. 400p. 1989. 26.95 (0-9616441-2-5) Melior Dist.

Picken, Stuart D. B. Essentials of Shinto: An Analytical Guide to Principal Teachings. LC 93-40619. 440p. 1994. text ed. 85.00 (0-313-26431-7, Greenwood Pr) Greenwood.

Pickenhagen, W., tr. see Ohloff, Gunther.

Pickens, Buford, notes & pref. The Missions of Northern Sonora: A Nineteen Thirty-Five Field Documentation Relating Piman Indians to the Material Culture of the Hispanic Southwest. LC 92-30728. (Southwest Center Ser.). (Illus.). 250p. (Orig.). 1993. lib. bdg. 26.95 (0-8165-1342-2); pap. 12.95 (0-8165-1356-2) U of Ariz Pr.

Pickens, Donald K. Eugenics & the Progressives. LC 68-28769. 1968. 19.95 (0-8265-1122-8) Vanderbilt U Pr.

Pickens, Elaine. Learn DrawPerfect in a Day. (Popular Applications Ser.). (Illus.). 128p. (Orig.). 1992. disk 15.95 (1-55622-222-X) Wordware Pub.
— Learn WordPerfect 5.1 Plus in a Day. (Popular Applications Ser.). 172p. (Orig.). 1995. pap. 15.95 (1-55622-449-4) Wordware Pub.

Pickens, Elaine E. Learn WordPerfect Presentations in a Day. LC 93-45585. 136p. 1994. 15.95 (1-55622-362-5) Wordware Pub.

Pickens, Ernestine W. Charles W. Chesnutt & the Progressive Movement. LC 93-44758. 152p. (Orig.). 1994. lib. bdg. 52.00 (0-944473-14-8); pap. 21.50 (0-944473-15-6) Pace Univ Pr.

Pickens, James W. The Art of Closing Any Deal: How to Be a "Master Closer" in Everything You Do. LC 89-32619. 1989. 18.95 (0-944007-40-6) Sure Sellers.
— The Art of Closing Any Deal: How to Be a Master Closer in Everything You Do. 1991. pap. 12.99 (0-446-39098-4) Warner Bks.
— The Closers. (Illus.). 1988. reprint ed. pap. 19.95 (0-9620915-7-X) Cobra Pub.
— More Art of Closing Any Deal. 1990. 18.95 (0-944007-58-9) Sure Sellers.

***Pickens, Jasper.** A Visit down Dogwood Lane. 240p. 1995. write for info. (0-614-06925-4) Rountree Pub NC.

Pickens, Jim. The Closers: Sales Closer's Bible. 2nd ed. Gay, Ben, III, ed. LC 87-81170. 320p. 1987. reprint ed. pap. 19.95 (0-942645-00-6) Hampton Hse Pub.
— The Closers: Sales Closer's Bible, 15 cass., Set. 2nd ed. Gay, Ben, III, ed. LC 87-81170. 320p. 1987. reprint ed. audio 99.95 (0-942645-01-4) Hampton Hse Pub.
— Names & Games, Kentucky College Basketball. LC 93-80127. 196p. 1994. 15.95 (0-913383-27-9) McClanahan Pub.

Pickens, Judy, ed. see Mittelstrass, Muriel.

Pickens, Kel, jt. auth. see Meyer, Carolyn.

Pickens, L. Self-Awareness & Drug Abuse & Drug Control. Zak, Therese A., ed. (Lifeworks Ser.). (Illus.). 128p. 1981. text ed. 13.96 (0-07-049910-1) McGraw.

Pickens, Ricky. Chinese Ring Daggers: The Ultimate Close-Quarter Weapons. (Illus.). 104p. 1987. pap. 12.00 (0-87364-444-1) Paladin Pr.

Pickens, Roy, jt. ed. see Glantz, Meyer.

Pickens, Rupert T. The Welsh Knight: Paradoxicality in Chretien's Erec et Enide. LC 76-47499. (French Forum Monographs: No. 6). 163p. (Orig.). 1977. pap. 10.95 (0-917058-05-4) French Forum.

Pickens, Rupert T., ed. Chretien de Troyes: The Story of the Grail or Perceval (Li Contesd del Graal) Kibler, William W., tr. LC 90-3025. (Library of Medieval Literature: Vol. 62A). 576p. 1990. 75.00 (0-8240-4599-8) Garland.
— The Sower & His Seed: Essays on Chretien de Troyes. LC 82-84402. (French Forum Monographs: No. 44). 164p. (Orig.). 1983. pap. 12.95 (0-917058-43-7) French Forum.
— Studies in Honor of Hans-Erich Keller: Medieval French & Occitan Literature & Romance Linguistics. LC 93-12695. (Studies in Medieval Culture). 1993. pap. 25.00 (1-879288-22-2); boxed 45.00 (1-879288-21-4) Medieval Inst.

Pickens, T. Boone. The Second Pearl Harbor: America's Response to the Japan that Can Say No. 160p. 1991. 19.95 (0-915765-94-2) Krantz Co.

Pickens, William. American Aesop: Negro & Other Humor. LC 76-99888. reprint ed. 34.00 (0-404-00206-4) AMS Pr.
— Bursting Bonds: The Heir of Slaves - The Autobiography of a "New Negro" enl. ed. Andrews, William L., ed. LC 91-6847. (Blacks of the Diaspora Ser.). (Illus.). 112p. 1991. 25.00 (0-253-34496-4); pap. 8.95 (0-253-20671-5, MB-671) Ind U Pr.
— New Negro, His Political, Civil & Mental Status & Related Essays. LC 72-95399. reprint ed. 21.50 (0-404-00271-4) AMS Pr.
— The Vengeance of the Gods & Three Other Stories of Real American Color Line Life. LC 73-18564. reprint ed. 24.50 (0-404-11376-1) AMS Pr.
— The Vengeance of the Gods; & Three Other Stories of Real American Color Line Life. LC 72-4612. (Black Heritage Library Collection). 1977. reprint ed. 21.95 (0-8369-9120-6) Ayer.

Picker, Fred. The Zone VI Workshop. (Illus.). 128p. 1978. 13.95 (0-8174-0574-7, Amphoto) Watsn-Guptill.

Picker, Les. Winter Environmental Studies. 176p. (C). 1988. spiral bd. 12.95 (0-8403-4931-9) Kendall-Hunt.

Picker, Martin. Henricus Isaac: A Guide to Research. LC 91-2962. (Composer Resource Manuals Ser.: Vol. 35). 320p. 1991. 45.00 (0-8240-5617-5) Garland.

Picker, Martin, ed. Johannes Ockeghem and Jacob Obrecht: A Guide to Research. LC 88-4175. (Reference Library of the Humanities). 214p. 1988. lib. bdg. 39.00 (0-8240-8381-4) Garland.
— The Motet Books of Andrea Antico. LC 85-754400. (Monuments of Renaissance Music Ser.: Vol. III). (Illus.). 448p. (C). 1987. lib. bdg. 100.00 (0-226-66796-0) U Ch Pr.

Pickerell, Albert G. & Dornin, May. The University of California: A Pictorial History. (Illus.). 1968. 40.00 (0-520-01010-8) U CA Pr.

***Pickerell, James H.** Negotiating Stock Photo Prices. 3rd ed. (Illus.). 188p. 1995. pap. 25.00 (1-886469-03-2) Stock Connect.
— Negotiating Stock Photo Prices, 1992: Buyers Guide. 120p. (Orig.). 1992. pap. write for info. (1-886469-01-6) Stock Connect.
— Negotiating Stock Photo Prices, 1992: Sellers Guide. 120p. (Orig.). Date not set. pap. write for info. (1-886469-00-8) Stock Connect.

***Pickerell, James H. & Child, Andrew.** Marketing Photography in the Digital Environment. 94p. (Orig.). 1994. pap. write for info. (1-886469-02-4) Stock Connect.

Pickering. Putting Process into Practice. (C). 1990. pap. text ed. 26.50 (0-673-38066-1) HarpCollege.

Pickering, A. D., ed. Stress & Fish. LC 81-67907. 1981. text ed. 128.00 (0-12-554550-9) Acad Pr.

Pickering, Andrew. Constructing Quarks: A Sociological History of Particle Physics. LC 84-235. xii, 468p. 1984. lib. bdg. 42.50 (0-226-66798-7) U Ch Pr.
— Constructing Quarks: A Sociological History of Particle Physics. LC 84-235. xii, 468p. 1986. pap. text ed. 19.95 (0-226-66799-5) U Ch Pr.
— The Mangle of Practice: Time, Agency & Science. LC 94-44546. 1995. lib. bdg. 45.00 (0-226-66802-9); pap. text ed. 17.95 (0-226-66803-7) U Ch Pr.
— Science as Practice & Culture. (Illus.). 448p. 1992. lib. bdg. 65.00 (0-226-66800-2); pap. text ed. 22.50 (0-226-66801-0) U Ch Pr.

Pickering, B., jt. auth. see Heller, H.

Pickering, B. T., et al, eds. Neurosecretion: Cellular Aspects of the Production & Release of Neuropeptides. LC 88-12440. (Illus.). 282p. 1988. 75.00 (0-306-42919-5, Plenum Pr) Plenum.

Pickering, C. A. & Jones, W. P. Health & Hygienic Humidification. (C). 1986. 105.00 (0-86022-104-0, Pub. by Build Servs Info Assn UK) St Mut.

Pickering, C. M. Chronological History of Plant (Man's Records) 1222p. (C). 1986. reprint ed. 950.00 (81-7089-042-X, Pub. by Intl Bk Distr II) St Mut.

Pickering, Carolyn. Clear & Simple American History, Vol. I. 176p. 1986. pap. 5.95 (0-671-60111-3) S&S Trade.

***Pickering, Chris.** Grampy's Word to Live By. 96p. 1995. pap. 5.95 (0-9644511-0-7) AISA Pub.

***Pickering, David.** Brewer's Twentieth-Century Music. 480p. 1995. 24.95 (0-304-32049-8, Pub. by Cassell UK) Sterling.

Pickering, David F., et al. Utility Mapping & Record Keeping for Infrastructure. LC 93-10646. (Urban Management Programme Paper Ser.: No. 10). 86p. 1994. 7.95 (0-8213-2426-8, 12426) World Bank.

Pickering, Ernest. For the Hurting Pastor: & Those Who Hurt Him. LC 87-20622. 47p. (Orig.). 1987. pap. 3.95 (0-87227-121-8) Reg Baptist.

Pickering, Ernest D. Biblical Separation: The Struggle for a Pure Church. LC 78-26840. 259p. 1979. pap. 7.95 (0-87227-069-6) Reg Baptist.
— The Theology of Evangelism. LC 74-18174. 65p. (Orig.). (C). 1984. pap. text ed. 2.95 (0-87227-107-2, RBP5131) Reg Baptist.

Pickering, F. B., ed. see American Society for Metals Staff.

Pickering, F. P. Literature & Art in the Middle Ages. LC 79-102698. (Illus.). 1970. 15.95 (0-87024-152-4) U of Miami Pr.

***Pickering, Fran.** Super Secret Code Book. LC 94-23478. (Illus.). 64p. (J). 1995. pap. 5.95 (0-8069-0890-4) Sterling.

Pickering, Frederick P. Essays on Medieval German Literature & Iconography. LC 78-73815. (Anglica Germanica Ser.: No. 2). 240p. reprint ed. pap. 68.40 (0-318-34834-9, 2031707) Bks Demand.

Pickering, George W., jt. auth. see Anderson, Alan B.

Pickering, Glenn. Being a Gentleman: A Resource for Men. LC 93-9723. 192p. 1993. pap. 12.95 (0-938586-75-0) Whole Person.
— Blinding Insights & Blind Alleys. LC 88-62110. 128p. 1989. pap. 6.95 (1-55523-185-3) Winston-Derek.

Pickering, H. G. The Pickering Collection: Neighbors Have My Ducks, Merry Xmas, Mr. Williams Dog Days on Trout Waters & Angling of the Test. (Fifty Greatest Bks.: Bk. 47). (Illus.). 189p. (YA). (gr. 10 up). 1993. reprint ed. 40.00 (1-56416-047-5) Derrydale Pr.

Pickering-Iazzi, Robin. Unspeakable Women: Selected Short Stories Written by Italian Women During Fascism. 176p. 1993. 35.00 (1-55861-062-6); pap. 14.95 (1-55861-063-4) Feminist Pr.

***Pickering-Iazzi, Robin, ed.** Mothers of Invention: Women, Italian Fascism, & Culture. 288p. 1995. text ed. 47.95 (0-8166-2650-2); pap. text ed. 18.95 (0-8166-2651-0) U of Minn Pr.

Pickering-Iazzi, Robin & Baldassaro, Lawrence. In Terza Pagina. LC 88-12834. 224p. (ITA.). (C). 1989. pap. text ed. 22.75 (0-03-013687-3) HB Coll Pubs.

Pickering, J. B., jt. auth. see Rosner, B. S.

Pickering, J. F. Resale Price Maintenance in Practice. LC 66-78485. 236p. 1966. 29.50 (0-678-06025-8) Kelley.

Pickering, J. F & Cockerill, T. A., eds. The Economic Management of the Firm. LC 84-11098. (Illus.). 432p. 1984. 57.00 (0-389-20495-1, N8058) B&N Imports.

Pickering, James H. Fiction Fifty: An Introduction to the Short Story. (Illus.). 736p. (C). 1993. pap. write for info. (0-02-395555-4) Macmillan.
— Fiction Fifty: An Introduction to the Short Story. abr. ed. (Illus.). 736p. (C). 1992. teacher ed write for info. (0-318-69333-X) Macmillan.
— Fiction One Hundred: An Anthology of Short Stories. 6th ed. (Illus.). 1504p. (C). 1992. pap. write for info. (0-02-395463-9) Macmillan.
— Fiction One Hundred: An Anthology of Short Stories. 7th ed. LC 94-8728. (C). 1994. pap. write for info. (0-02-395492-2) Macmillan.

***Pickering, James H., ed.** Frederick Chapin's Colorado: The Peaks about Estes Park & Other Writings. LC 94-47197. (Illus.). 240p. 1995. 29.95 (0-87081-366-8) Univ Pr Colo.
— Frederick Chapin's Colorado: The Peaks about Estes Park & Other Writings. (Illus.). 240p. 1995. pap. 19.95 (0-87081-371-4) Univ Pr Colo.

Pickering, James H., ed. see Cooper, James Fenimore.

Pickering, James H., jt. auth. see Hoeper, Jeffrey D.

Pickering, Jean. Understanding Doris Lessing. (Understanding Contemporary British Literature Ser.). 277p. (C). 1990. text ed. 29.95 (0-87249-710-0); pap. text ed. 14.95 (0-87249-743-7) U of SC Pr.

Pickering, Jerry. Theatre: A Contemporary Introduction. 3rd ed. (Illus.). 389p. (C). 1981. pap. text ed. 40.50 (0-8299-0403-4) West Pub.

Pickering, Jim. Soldier of the Sixth. 200p. (C). 1989. text ed. 60.00 (1-85821-010-0, Pub. by Pentland Pr UK) St Mut.

Pickering, John. The Drummer's Cook Book. 1993. 6.95 (0-87166-826-2, 93301) Mel Bay.
— Interlude of Vice. LC 73-133720. (Tudor Facsimile Texts. Old English Plays Ser.: No. 37). reprint ed. 49.50 (0-404-53337-X) AMS Pr.
— Routes of the Valkyries. 94p. (C). 1987. 49.00 (0-902633-43-0, Pub. by Picton UK) St Mut.
— Studio - Jazz Drum Cookbook. 1993. 8.95 (0-87166-682-0, 93625) Mel Bay.
— Working Man's Political Economy, Founded upon the Principle of Immutable Justice & the Inalienable Rights of Man: Designed for the Promotion of National Reform. LC 79-156421. (American Labor Ser., No. 2). 1977. reprint ed. 21.95 (0-405-02940-3) Ayer.

Pickering, John & Skinner, Martin. From Sentience to Symbols: Readings on Consciousness. 331p. 1991. text ed. 60.00 (0-8020-2795-4); pap. text ed. 18.95 (0-8020-6856-1) U of Toronto Pr.

Pickering, K. T., et al. Deep Marine Environments: Clastic Sedimentation & Tectonics. (Illus.). 352p. 1989. 130.00 (0-04-551122-5); pap. 49.95 (0-04-445201-2) Routledge Chapman & Hall.

Pickering, K. T., jt. ed. see Whateley, M. K.

Pickering, Ken. Beowulf: A Rock Musical. (Illus.). 42p. (Orig.). (YA). (gr. 7 up). 1986. pap. 4.00 (0-88680-248-2); 15.00 (0-88680-249-0) I E Clark.

Pickering, Ken, et al. The Inside Story. 24p. (Orig.). (J). 1992. pap. 4.00 (0-88680-371-3); 15.00 (0-88680-372-1) I E Clark.

Pickering, Kevin T. & Owen, Lewis A. An Introduction to Global Environmental Issues. LC 93-32915. 1994. write for info. (0-415-10227-8, Routledge NY); pap. write for info. (0-415-10228-6, Routledge NY) Routledge.

P
Q

Pickering, Leslie. The Liberal: Lord Byron, Leigh Hunt & the Liberal. LC 68-763. (Studies in Byron: No. 5). 1972. lib. bdg. 75.00 (*0-8383-0609-8*) M S G Haskell Hse.

***Pickering, Marianne.** Lifetimes of Learning. Glassman, Bruce, ed. (Our Human Family Ser.). (Illus.). 64p. (J). (gr. 4-8). 1995. 18.95 (*1-56711-127-0*) Blackbirch.

Pickering, Martin & Ross, Michael. Pedigrees of Leading Winners Nineteen Eighty-One to Nineteen Eighty-Four. 194p. 1986. 65.00 (*0-8131-1601-5*) U Pr of Ky.

— Pedigrees of Leading Winners 1981-1984. 198p. 1990. 120.00 (*0-85131-413-9*, Pub. by J A Allen & Co UK) St Mut.

Pickering, Mary. Auguste Comte: An Intellectual Biography, Vol. 1. LC 92-44510. 800p. (C). 1993. 49.95 (*0-521-43405-X*) Cambridge U Pr.

Pickering, Michael & Green, Tony. Everyday Culture: Popular Song & the Vernacular Milieu. (Popular Music in Britain Ser.). 244p. 1988. 95.00 (*0-335-15289-9*, Open Univ Pr) Taylor & Francis.

Pickering, Michael G. Woman's Self-Defense. LC 78-22054. (Illus.). 144p. 1979. pap. 5.95 (*0-89037-166-0*) Anderson World.

Pickering, Miles. The Rediscovery Book: A General Chemistry Lab Manual. (C). 1989. 29.00 (*0-673-52014-5*) HarpCollege.

Pickering, Morgan. An Introduction to Fast Fourier Transform Methods for Partial Differential Equations with Applications. 178p. 1986. text ed. 114.00 (*0-471-91261-1*) Wiley.

Pickering, Nona M. Never Pay Retail: Chicagoland: Designer Merchandise at Discount Prices. LC 91-90656. 182p. (Orig.). 1992. pap. 9.95 (*0-9631196-0-5*) GuideLines.

Pickering, O. S. & Powell, Susan, eds. Index of Middle English Prose Handlist VI: Yorkshire. 112p. 1989. 53.00 (*0-85991-276-0*) Boydell & Brewer.

Pickering, Paul. Charlie Peace. 1991. 19.50 (*0-394-58544-5*) Random.

***Pickering, Paul A.** Chartism & Chartists in Manchester & Salford. LC 95-8228. 1995. write for info. (*0-312-12727-8*) St Martin.

Pickering, R. I Can Be an Archaeologist. LC 87-14683. (I Can Be Bks.). (Illus.). 32p. (J). (gr. k-3). 1987. lib. bdg. 11.85 (*0-516-01909-0*); pap. 3.95 (*0-516-41909-9*) Childrens.

Pickering, Robert. Lautreamont: Image, Theme & Self-Identity. 88p. 1993. 39.00 (*0-85261-289-3*, Pub. by Univ of Glasgow UK) St Mut.

***Pickering, Robert B.** The People. LC 95-3046. (Illus.). (J). 1995. lib. bdg. write for info. (*1-56294-550-5*) Millbrook Pr.

Pickering, Sam. Trespassing. LC 93-38325. 260p. (C). 1994. 22.50 (*0-87451-640-4*) U Pr of New Eng.

Pickering, Samuel. The Moral Tradition in English Fiction, 1785-1850. LC 74-12540. 194p. reprint ed. pap. 55.30 (*0-7837-0380-5*, 2040700) Bks Demand.

***Pickering, Samuel F.** John Locke & Children's Books in Eighteenth-Century England. fac. ed. LC 80-24899. (Illus.). 300p. Date not set. pap. 85.50 (*0-7837-7359-5*, 2047168) Bks Demand.

Pickering, Samuel F., Jr. Let It Ride. 200p. (C). 1991. 19.95 (*0-8262-0801-0*) U of Mo Pr.

— Let It Ride. 200p. 1992. reprint ed. pap. 10.95 (*0-8262-0869-X*) U of Mo Pr.

— May Days. LC 87-34292. 208p. 1988. 25.95 (*0-87745-204-0*) U of Iowa Pr.

— May Days. LC 87-34292. 208p. 1995. pap. 14.95 (*0-87745-522-8*) U of Iowa Pr.

— Moral Instruction & Fiction for Children, 1749-1820. LC 92-6567. (Illus.). 232p. 1993. 35.00 (*0-8203-1463-3*) U of Ga Pr.

— The Right Distance. LC 86-16012. 204p. 1987. 19.95 (*0-8203-0906-0*) U of Ga Pr.

— Still Life. LC 89-28605. 240p. 1990. 25.00 (*0-87451-515-7*); pap. 12.95 (*0-87451-561-0*) U Pr of New Eng.

Pickering, Susan, jt. auth. see Ackerman, Robert J.

Pickering, Susan E., jt. auth. see Ackerman, Robert J.

Pickering, W. F. Modern Analytical Chemistry. LC 77-138500. 634p. (C). reprint ed. 180.00 (*0-8357-9087-8*, 2055008) Bks Demand.

Pickering, W. J., jt. auth. see Mallows, D. F.

Pickering, W. R., ed. Information Sources in Pharmaceuticals. (Guides to Information Sources Ser.). 528p. 1990. lib. bdg. 100.00 (*0-408-02518-2*) Bowker-Saur.

Pickering, W. R., jt. auth. see Landreau, Anthony N.

Pickering, W. S. Durkheim's Sociology of Religion: Themes & Theories. 576p. 1984. 65.00 (*0-7100-9298-9*, RKP) Routledge.

Pickering, W. S. F., ed. see Durkheim, Emile.

Pickering, Wilbur. A Framework for Discourse Analysis. (Publications in Linguistics: No. 64). 189p. 1980. fiche 8.00x (*0-88312-484-X*) Summer Instit Ling.

Pickering, William. Anglo-Catholicism. 320p. 1989. 59.95 (*0-415-01343-7*, A3475) Routledge.

— Annual Message of the Governor of Washington Territory, Delivered December 17th, 1862. 12p. 1972. pap. 1.00 (*0-87770-098-2*) Ye Galleon.

Pickering, William S. & Martins, Hermino, eds. Debating Durkheim. LC 93-46095. 240p. 1994. 89.95x (*0-415-07720-6*, B3473, Routledge NY) Routledge.

Pickersgill, J. W. My Years with Louis St. Laurent: A Political Memoir. LC 75-24675. (Illus.). 352p. reprint ed. pap. 100.40 (*0-8357-8239-5*, 2034008) Bks Demand.

— The Road Back: By a Liberal in Opposition. 255p. 1986. 30.00 (*0-8020-2598-6*) U of Toronto Pr.

Pickersgill, J. W. & Forster, Donald F., eds. The Mackenzie King Record, Vol. Four: 1947-48. 338p. 1970. text ed. 75.00 (*0-8020-1714-2*) U of Toronto Pr.

— The Mackenzie King Record, Vol. Three: 1945-1946. 424p. 1970. text ed. 75.00 (*0-8020-1713-4*) U of Toronto Pr.

Pickert, G. Projektive Ebenen. 2nd ed. LC 75-9953. (Grundlehren der Mathematischen Wissenschaften Ser.: Vol. 80). (Illus.). 371p. 1975. 94.00 (*0-387-07280-2*) Spr-Verlag.

Pickert, Sarah M. Preparing for a Global Community: Achieving an International Perspective in Higher Education. Fife, Jonathan D., ed. LC 92-85442. (ASHE-ERIC Higher Education Report Ser.: No. 2). 94p. 1992. write for info. (*1-878380-15-X*) GWU Schl E&HD.

Picket, William. The Generic Pizza Tastes Great. 1993. pap. text ed. 23.00 (*0-685-70618-4*) P-H.

Pickett. At Home in Two Lands. 1991. pap. 18.95 (*0-8384-3019-8*) Heinle & Heinle.

Pickett & Hanlon. Public Health Administration & Practice. 10th ed. 1994. 51.95 (*0-8016-7943-5*) Mosby Yr Bk.

Pickett & Laster, Ann A. Technical English. 6th ed. (C). 1993. 45.50 (*0-06-500278-4*) HarpCollege.

Pickett, jt. auth. see Gage.

Pickett, jt. auth. see Hanlon.

Pickett, jt. auth. see Lynch.

Pickett, Albert J. History of Alabama, & Incidentally of Georgia & Mississippi, from the Earliest Period, 2 Vols. in 1. LC 76-146410. (First American Frontier Ser.). (Illus.). 1971. reprint ed. 58.95 (*0-405-02872-5*) Ayer.

Pickett, Anola. Old Enough for Magic. LC 88-30320. (I Can Read Bk.). (Illus.). 64p. (J). (gr. k-3). 1989. lib. bdg. 14.89 (*0-06-024732-0*) HarpC Child Bks.

***Pickett, Arthur.** The Christian Seeker & the Contrary Church. 1994. 12.95 (*0-533-10997-3*) Vantage.

Pickett, Bob, jt. auth. see Allman, Sheldon.

Pickett, Bob, jt. auth. see Brown, J. D.

Pickett, Brian. The Heart of Love. 144p. (C). 1990. 35.00 (*0-85439-366-8*, Pub. by St Paul Pubns UK) St Mut.

Pickett, Calder M. Voices of the Past: Key Documents in the History of American Journalism. LC 76-19674. (Advertising & Journalism Ser.). 496p. (C). 1977. pap. write for info. (*0-02-395790-5*) Macmillan.

Pickett, Cecil, adapt. The Comedy of Errors. (Illus.). 44p. 1986. pap. 2.50 (*0-88680-258-X*) I E Clark.

Pickett, Douglas. Early Persian Tilework: The Medieval Flowering of Kashi. (Illus.). 1990. write for info. (*0-8386-3365-X*) Fairleigh Dickinson.

Pickett, E. E. Atmospheric Pollution. (Arab School of Science & Technology Ser.). 257p. 1987. 99.50 (*0-89116-680-7*) Hemisp Pub.

Pickett, Evelyne, jt. ed. see Schwantes, Carlos A.

Pickett, Fuchsia. For Such a Time As This. 126p. (Orig.). 1992. pap. 7.99 (*1-56043-078-8*) Destiny Image.

— The Next Move of God. 1994. pap. 8.99 (*0-88419-369-1*, Creation Hse) Strang Comms Co.

— Next Move of God. 1994. pap. 8.99 (*0-88419-384-5*, Creation Hse) Strang Comms Co.

— Presenting the Holy Spirit. 196p. (Orig.). 1993. 15.99 (*1-56043-118-0*) Destiny Image.

Pickett, Fuchsia T. God's Dream: His Eternal Plan for You. 154p. (Orig.). 1991. pap. 7.95 (*1-56043-028-1*) Destiny Image.

Pickett, George & Pickett, Terry W. Opportunities in Public Health Careers. 160p. 1988. text ed. 13.95 (*0-8442-6011-8*, VGM Career Bks); pap. 10.95 (*0-8442-6012-6*, VGM Career Bks) NTC Pub Grp.

Pickett, George E. Soldier of the South: General Pickett's War Letters to His Wife. Inman, Arthur C., ed. LC 78-160986. (Select Bibliographies Reprint Ser.). 1977. reprint ed. 25.95 (*0-8369-5854-3*) Ayer.

— Soldier of the South: General Pickett's War Letters to His Wife. (American Biography Ser.). 157p. 1991. reprint ed. lib. bdg. 59.00 (*0-7812-8313-2*) Rprt Serv.

Pickett-Heaps, Jeremy. New Light on the Green Algae. Head, J. J., ed. LC 79-55133. (Carolina Biology Readers Ser.: No. 115). (Illus.). 16p. (gr. 10 up). 1982. pap. 2.75 (*0-89278-315-X*, 45-9715) Carolina Biological.

Pickett-Heaps, Jeremy D. & Pickett-Heaps, Julianne. Living Cells: Structure, Diversity, & Evolution. (Illus.). 1994. teacher ed. pap. write for info. (*0-87893-653-X*); teacher ed, vdisk 350.00 (*0-87893-650-5*) Sinauer Assocs.

Pickett-Heaps, Julianne, jt. auth. see Pickett-Heaps, Jeremy D.

***Pickett, Helen R.** Rejoice Together. 1995. pap. 9.00 (*1-55896-298-0*) Unitarian Univ.

Pickett, J. The Choice of Technology in Developing Countries. 1978. pap. 40.00 (*0-08-023006-7*, Pergamon Pr) Elsevier.

Pickett, J., jt. auth. see Organisation for Economic Cooperation.

Pickett, J. M. The Sound of Speech Communication. (Illus.). 256p. (C). 1991. pap. text ed. 57.00 (*0-205-13542-0*) Allyn.

Pickett, James & Singer, Hans W., eds. Towards Economic Recovery in Sub-Saharan Africa. 288p. (C). 1991. text ed. 74.00 (*0-415-05409-5*, A4706) Routledge.

Pickett, Jeanne, illus. Indian Art Designs. rev. ed. 80p. 1994. pap. text ed. 4.95 (*0-916809-73-0*) Scott Pubns MI.

Pickett, John R. PASCAL Programming for Business. (C). 1991. pap. text ed. 29.00 (*0-87835-503-0*) Boyd & Fraser.

***Pickett, Keri.** Love in the 90s B. B. & Jo: The Story of a Lifelong Love, a Granddaughter's Portrait. (Illus.). 1995. 14.95 (*0-446-52032-2*) Warner Bks.

Pickett, LaSalle. Across My Path. LC 74-128287. (Essay Index Reprint Ser.). 1977. 19.95 (*0-8369-1841-X*) Ayer.

Pickett, Liam E. Organising Development Through Participation Co-Operative Organisation & Services for Land Settlement. 176p. 1988. lib. bdg. 57.50 (*0-7099-5607-X*, Pub. by Croom Helm UK) Routledge Chapman & Hall.

***Pickett, Lynn & Prince, Clive.** Turin Shroud: In Whose Image? The Shocking Truth Revealed. LC 94-29921. 1994. 23.00 (*0-06-017224-X*) HarpC.

Pickett, Margaret E. What's Keeping You, Santa? A Christmas Musical Program Package. (Illus.). 74p. (J). (gr. k-12). 1983. Incl Production Guide with choir arranged songs, cass of songs, thirty slides from bk. student ed, audio 49.95 (*0-913939-01-3*) TP Assocs.

— What's Keeping You, Santa? A Christmas Story Book. LC 83-50122. (Illus.). 64p. (J). (gr. k-5). 1983. lib. bdg. 24.95 (*0-913939-00-5*); audio 4.95 (*0-913939-03-X*) TP Assocs.

Pickett, Mary, et al. Household Equipment in Residential Design. 9th ed. (Illus.). 576p. (C). 1990. reprint ed. text ed. 35.95 (*0-88133-520-7*) Waveland Pr.

Pickett, Nell A. & Laster, Ann A. Technical English: Writing, Reading, & Speaking. 5th ed. 757p. (C). 1989. pap. text ed. 26.50 (*0-06-045204-8*) HarpCollege.

Pickett, Nell A., jt. auth. see Laster, Ann A.

Pickett, O. Gordon. The Coming Star-Shift & Many Prophecies of Bible & Pyramid Fulfilled. 584p. 1981. pap. 65.00 (*0-89540-087-1*, SB-087) Sun Pub.

Pickett, Paul. H-60 Blackhawk in Action. (Aircraft in Action Ser.). (Illus.). 50p. 1993. pap. 8.95 (*0-89747-295-0*, 1133) Squad Sig Pubns.

Pickett, Robert S. House of Refuge: Origins of Juvenile Reform in New York State 1815-1857. LC 69-19745. (New York State Study Ser.). 239p. reprint ed. pap. 68.20 (*0-317-52011-3*, 2027405) Bks Demand.

Pickett, Robert T. Feedback Control Systems for Technicians. (Illus.). 272p. 1988. text ed. 51.00 (*0-13-313933-6*) P-H.

Pickett, Steward T. & White, P. S., eds. The Ecology of Natural Disturbance & Patch Dynamics. 472p. 1986. pap. text ed. 48.00 (*0-12-554521-5*) Acad Pr.

— Natural Disturbance: The Patch Dynamics Perspective. 1985. text ed. 91.00 (*0-12-554520-7*) Acad Pr.

Pickett, Steward T., jt. ed. see McDonnell, Mark J.

Pickett, Steward T., et al. Ecological Understanding: The Nature of Theory & the Theory of Nature. (Illus.). 206p. 1994. text ed. 54.95 (*0-12-554720-X*) Acad Pr.

Pickett, Sue. Little Dog Scooter. 21p. (J). (gr. 4). 1992. pap. text ed. write for info. (*0-9633197-0-1*) Instant Heirloom.

Pickett, Terry W., jt. auth. see Pickett, George.

Pickett, Velma B., jt. auth. see Elson, Benjamin F.

Pickett, W. B., ed. Technology at the Turning Point. (Illus.). 1977. pap. 7.50 (*0-911302-36-0*) San Francisco Pr.

Pickett, William. Dwight David Eisenhower, An American Power. Kraut, Alan M. & Wakelyn, Jon L., eds. (American Biographical History Ser.). (Illus.). 144p. (C). 1995. pap. text ed. 11.95 (*0-88295-918-2*) Harlan Davidson.

— Leaders of the Americas: Short Biographics & Dialogues Book I. 192p. 1994. pap. text ed. 13.25 (*0-13-102484-1*) P-H.

Pickett, William B. Homer E. Capehart: A Senator's Life, 1897-1979. (Illus.). 272p. 1990. 19.95 (*0-87195-054-5*) Ind Hist Soc.

Pickett, William P. The Chicken Smells Good. LC 83-3420. (Illus.). 224p. (C). 1983. pap. text ed. 12.75 (*0-13-130260-4*) P-H.

— Far from Home: Reading & Word Study. 2nd ed. LC 93-25537. 1994. pap. 16.95 (*0-8384-4852-6*) Heinle & Heinle.

— The Pizza Tastes Great: Dialogues & Stories. (Illus.). 176p. (C). 1987. pap. text ed. 13.25 (*0-13-677626-4*) P-H.

***Pickford, Anthony.** Taxation of Intellectual Property. 400p. 1993. pap. text ed. 100.00 (*0-406-01538-4*, UK) Butterworth Legal Pubs.

Pickford, C. E., ed. Gyron le Courtoys. (Illus.). 522p. 1970. 81.00 (*0-85991-152-7*) Boydell & Brewer.

— Gyron le courtoys c. 1501. (French Arthurian Romances Ser.). 1977. 80.00 (*0-85967-353-7*, Pub. by Scolar Pr UK) Ashgate Pub Co.

— L' Hystoire du Sainct Greal. (Illus.). 488p. 1970. 81.00 (*0-85991-154-3*) Boydell & Brewer.

— Meliadus de Leonnoys. fac. ed. 484p. 1970. Facsimile. 81.00 (*0-85991-155-1*) Boydell & Brewer.

— Merlin Fourteen Ninety-Eight. (French Arthurian Romances Ser.). 1975. 130.00 (*0-85967-196-8*, Pub. by Scolar Pr UK) Ashgate Pub Co.

— Tristan. fac. ed. 676p. 1970. Facsimile. 81.00 (*0-85991-157-8*) Boydell & Brewer.

Pickford, C. E., et al, eds. The Arthurian Bibliography II: Subject Index, No. II. (Arthurian Studies: Vol. VI). 144p. 1983. 71.00 (*0-85991-099-7*) Boydell & Brewer.

Pickford, Grace E. Contributions to a Study of South African Microchaetinae (Annedida: Oligochaeta) (Connecticut Academy of Arts & Sciences Ser., Trans.: Vol. 46). 1975. pap. 29.50 (*0-685-22881-9*) Elliots Bks.

— Studies on the Digestive Enzymes of Spiders. (Connecticut Academy of Arts & Sciences Ser., Trans.: Vol. 35). 1942. pap. 49.50 (*0-685-22911-4*) Elliots Bks.

Pickford, Grace E., et al. Studies on the Blood Serum of the Euryhaline Cyprinodont Fish, Fundulus Heteroclitus, Adapted to Fresh or to Salt Water. (Connecticut Academy of Arts & Sciences Ser., Trans.: Vol. 43). 1969. pap. 39.50 (*0-685-22887-8*) Elliots Bks.

Pickford, Ian. Pocket Jackson. 172p. 1991. 25.00 (*1-85149-128-7*) Antique Collect.

— Silver Flatware - English, Irish & Scottish: 1660-1980. (Illus.). 232p. 1983. 59.50 (*0-907462-35-9*) Antique Collect.

Pickford, Ian, ed. Jackson's Silver & Gold Marks of England, Scotland & Ireland. 1989. 99.50 (*0-907462-63-4*) Antique Collect.

— Pocket Edition Jackson's Hallmarks. 172p. 1993. pap. 14.95 (*1-85149-169-4*) Antique Collect.

Pickford, J. Analysis of Water Surge. 214p. 1969. text ed. 169.00 (*0-677-61670-8*) Gordon & Breach.

Pickford, John, et al. Water, Sanitation, Environment & Development: Selected Papers for the 19th WEDC Conference. 176p. (Orig.). 1994. pap. 15.95 (*1-85339-240-5*, Pub. by Intermed Tech UK) Women Ink.

Pickford, Louise. Book of Vegetarian Cooking. 120p. 1993. pap. 12.00 (*1-55788-076-X*, HP Books) Berkley Pub.

— Feasting on Fish. (Illus.). 96p. 1995. 10.98 (*0-8317-3166-4*) Smithmark.

— The Inspired Vegetarian. LC 92-9094. (Illus.). 144p. 1992. 24.95 (*1-55670-230-2*) Stewart Tabori & Chang.

— The Olive Oil Cookbook. LC 94-26713. 96p. 1994. 9.98 (*0-8317-6257-8*) Smithmark.

Pickford, Nigel. The Atlas of Shipwrecks & Treasure. LC 93-48856. 1994. 29.95 (*1-56458-599-9*) Dorling Kindersley.

Pickford, Peter. Wilderness Dawning. 160p. (C). 1988. 170.00 (*1-85368-001-X*, Pub. by New Holland Pubs UK) St Mut.

Pickford, Susan. Barron & Lyla. (Illus.). 38p. (Orig.). (J). (gr. 3-7). 1991. pap. 3.00 (*0-88680-356-X*) I E Clark.

Pickford, Susan T. It's up to You, Griffin! (Illus.). 32p. (J). (gr. k-4). 1993. bds. 10.95 (*0-87033-446-8*, Tidewtr Pubs) Cornell Maritime.

Pickhardt, Carl. Parenting the Adolescent. (Illus.). 200p. (Orig.). 1987. pap. 12.95 (*0-938934-16-3*) LCN.

Pickholz, Marvin G. Securities Crimes, 1 vol. LC 93-14817. (Securities Law Ser.). 1993. ring bd. 145.00 (*0-87632-971-7*) Clark Boardman Callaghan.

Pickin, Chrissie & St. Leger, Selwyn. Assessing Health Need Using the Life Cycle Framework. LC 92-18760. 192p. 1992. 85.00 (*0-335-15743-2*, Open Univ Pr); pap. 27.50 (*0-335-15742-4*, Open Univ Pr) Taylor & Francis.

Pickle, Hal B. & Abrahamson, Royce L. Introduction to Business. 6th ed. (C). 1986. pap. text ed. 26.75 (*0-673-16671-6*) HarpCollege.

— Small Business Management. LC 86-19198. (Wiley Series in Management). (Illus.). 649p. reprint ed. pap. 180.00 (*0-7837-3507-3*, 2057840) Bks Demand.

Pickle, Hal B. & Arahamson, Royce L. Small Business Management. 5th ed. 736p. 1990. Net. text ed. write for info. (*0-471-50071-2*); Net. student ed, pap. text ed. write for info. (*0-471-50240-5*) Wiley.

Pickle, Julianne M. One Hundred Percent Vegetarian: Eating Naturally from Your Grocery Store. LC 90-92224. 121p. (Orig.). 1990. spiral bd., pap. 5.95 (*0-9627645-0-7*) Pickle Pub Co.

***Pickle, Linda S.** Contented Among Strangers: Rural German-Speaking Women & Their Families in the Nineteenth-Century Midwest. Daniels, Roger et al, eds. LC 95-9849. (Statue of Liberty-Ellis Island Centennial Ser.). (Illus.). 360p. (C). 1995. 49.95 (*0-252-02182-7*); pap. 14.95 (*0-252-06472-0*) U of Ill Pr.

Pickle, Linda W., et al. Atlas of United States Cancer Mortality Among Whites: 1950 - 1980. (DHHS Publication NIH Ser.: No. 87-2900). (Illus.). 190p. 1987. 24.00 (*0-16-002552-4*, S/N 017-042-00196-0) USGPO.

Pickleman, Jack, ed. Problems In General Surgery. LC 81-22702. (Reviewing Surgical Topics Ser.). 382p. (C). 1982. 75.00 (*0-306-40765-5*, Plenum Med Bk) Plenum.

Pickles, Dorothy M. The Fifth French Republic. LC 75-32461. 222p. 1976. reprint ed. text ed. 38.50 (*0-8371-8544-0*, PIFF, Greenwood Pr) Greenwood.

Pickles, J., jt. ed. see Dunstan, F.

Pickles, J. D., ed. see Gower, John.

Pickles, J. D., jt. ed. see Shippey, T. A.

Pickles, James O. An Introduction to the Physiology of Hearing. 2nd ed. 567p. 1988. text ed. 73.00 (*0-12-554753-6*); pap. text ed. 39.00 (*0-12-554754-4*) Acad Pr.

Pickles, Sheila. Christmas: A Treasury of Verse & Prose. 1994. 6.50 (*0-517-59900-7*, Harmony) Crown Pub Group.

— Decorating for Christmas. LC 94-642. 1994. 22.50 (*0-517-59697-0*, Harmony) Crown Pub Group.

— The Essence of English Life. LC 93-18044. 1993. 20.00 (*0-517-59280-0*, Harmony) Crown Pub Group.

— The Fragrant Garden: Penhaligon's Scented Treasury of Verse & Prose. 1992. pap. write for info. (*0-517-58942-7*, Harmony) Crown Pub Group.

— Language of Flowers. 1991. 11.00 (*0-517-58676-2*, Harmony); 17.00 (*0-517-58677-0*, Harmony) Crown Pub Group.

— Language of Flowers. 1993. 9.00 (*0-517-58675-4*, Harmony) Crown Pub Group.

— Language of Flowers. 1991. 17.00 (*0-517-58678-9*, Harmony) Random.

— Language of Flowers: A Treasury of Verse & Prose. 1994. 6.50 (*0-517-59899-X*, Harmony) Crown Pub Group.

— The Language of Wildflowers: A Treasury of Verse & Prose Scented by Penhaligon's. 1995. 22.00 (*0-517-59676-8*, Harmony) Crown Pub Group.

— Love: A Treasury of Verse & Prose. 1994. 6.50 (*0-517-59902-3*, Harmony) Crown Pub Group.

— Love Address Book. 1991. 18.00 (*0-517-58291-0*, Harmony) Crown Pub Group.

— Love Birthday Book. 1991. 11.00 (*0-517-58288-0*, Harmony) Crown Pub Group.

— Love Book of Days. 1991. 16.95 (*0-517-58292-9*, Harmony) Crown Pub Group.

— Love Book of Secrets. 1991. 19.95 (*0-517-58290-2*, Harmony) Crown Pub Group.

— Love Notebook. 1991. 8.95 (*0-517-58289-9*, Harmony) Crown Pub Group.

— Morning Glory: Penhaligon's Scented Treasury of Spring Verse & Prose. 1992. 15.00 (*0-517-58941-9*, Harmony) Crown Pub Group.

— Victorian Posy. 1991. 45.00 (*0-517-58213-9*, Ebury Pr Stationery) Crown Pub Group.

 An Asterisk (*) at the beginning of an entry indicates that the title is appearing in BIP for the first time.

— Victorian Posy: A Treasury of Verse & Prose. 1994. 6.50 (*0-517-59901-5*, Harmony) Crown Pub Group.

— Victorian Posy Birthday Book. 1990. 11.00 (*0-517-57854-9*, Harmony) Crown Pub Group.

— Victorian Posy Book of Days. 1990. 17.00 (*0-517-57858-1*, Harmony) Crown Pub Group.

— Victorian Posy Notebook. 1990. 9.95 (*0-517-57855-7*, Harmony) Crown Pub Group.

Pickles, Sheila, ed. Bridal Bouquet: Penhaligon's Scented Treasury of Verse & Prose. (Illus.). 112p. 1991. 25.00 (*0-517-58507-3*, Harmony) Crown Pub Group.

— Christmas: Penhaligon's Scented Treasury of Verse & Prose. 1989. pap. 19.95 (*0-517-57367-9*, Harmony) Crown Pub Group.

— The Language of Flowers: Penhaligon's Scented Treasury of Verse & Prose. 1990. 20.00 (*0-517-57460-8*, Harmony) Crown Pub Group.

— Love: Penhaligon's Scented Treasury of Verse & Prose. (Illus.). 112p. 1988. boxed 20.00 (*0-517-57098-X*, Harmony) Crown Pub Group.

— Love Sonnets: A Treasury of English Verse. (Illus.). 64p. 1995. 13.95 (*1-85793-161-0*, Pub. by Pavilion UK) Trafalgar.

— Mother & Child: A Treasury of Verse & Prose Scented by Penhaligon's. LC 92-54575. 1993. 8.25 (*0-517-59419-6*, Harmony) Crown Pub Group.

— Summer's Cup: A Penhaligon's Book of Potpourri. 1991. 15.00 (*0-517-58464-6*, Harmony) Crown Pub Group.

— Sweet Scented Rose: A Treasure of Verse & Prose. LC 93-25562. 1994. 25.00 (*0-517-59681-4*, Harmony) Crown Pub Group.

— The Winter Garden: Penhaligon's Scented Treasury of Winter Verse & Prose. LC 92-18577. 64p. 1993. 15.00 (*0-517-58940-0*, Harmony) Crown Pub Group.

Pickles, Tim. New Orleans 1815. (Campaign Ser.). (Illus.). 96p. 1994. pap. 14.95 (*1-85532-360-5*, 9527, Pub. by Osprey UK) Stackpole.

Pickles, W., tr. see Blum, Leon.

Pickman, Alan J. The Handbook of Outplacement Counseling. 176p. 1994. 39.95 (*0-8058-1647-X*); pap. 19.95 (*0-8058-1648-8*) L Erlbaum Assocs.

Pickman, James, et al. Producing Lower Income Housing: Local Initiatives. LC 86-26424. 389p. reprint ed. pap. 110.90 (*0-7837-4608-3*, 2044327) Bks Demand.

Picknett, Lynn. Flights of Fancy? One Hundred Years of Paranormal Experiences. 1989. pap. 3.95 (*0-345-35948-8*) Ballantine.

Pickney, Gloria J. The Sunday Outing. LC 93-25383. (Illus.). (J). (gr. k-4). 1994. 14.99 (*0-8037-1198-0*); lib. bdg. 14.89 (*0-8037-1199-9*) Dial Bks Young.

Pickover, Clifford A. Chaos in Wonderland: Visual Adventures in a Fractal World. 256p. 1994. 29.95 (*0-312-10743-9*) St Martin.

— Computers & the Imagination: Visual Adventures Beyond the Edge. (Illus.). 444p. 1992. pap. 19.95 (*0-312-08343-2*) St Martin.

— Computers, Pattern, Chaos & Beauty: Graphics from an Unseen World. LC 89-70068. (Illus.). 415p. 1991. pap. 19.95 (*0-312-06179-X*) St Martin.

— Keys to Infinity. LC 94-45541. 1995. text ed. 24.95 (*0-471-11857-5*) Wiley.

— Mazes for the Mind: Computers & the Unexpected. (Illus.). 448p. 1992. 19.95 (*0-312-08165-0*) St Martin.

— Mazes for the Mind: Computers & the Unexpected. (Illus.). 430p. 1994. pap. 19.95 (*0-312-10353-0*) St Martin.

— The Pattern Book: Recipes for Beauty. 250p. 1995. text ed. 59.00 (*981-02-1426-X*) World Scientific Pub.

— The Visual Display of Biological Information. 300p. 1995. text ed. 74.00 (*981-02-1427-8*) World Scientific Pub.

Pickover, Clifford A., ed. Visions of the Future: Art, Technology & Computing in the Twenty-First Century. 400p. (C). 1993. text ed. 29.95 (*0-312-08481-1*) St Martin.

— Visions of the Future: Art Technology & Computing in the Twenty-First Century. 222p. 1994. pap. 16.95 (*0-312-12212-8*) St Martin.

Pickover, Clifford A., jt. ed. see Hargittai, Istvan.

Pickover, Clifford A., jt. ed. see Tewksbury, Stuart K.

Pickow, Jonathan. Christmas Songs for Children. (Illus.). 56p. 1988. pap. 7.95 (*0-685-65822-8*, AM67117) Music Sales.

Pickow, Peter. Beginning Bass Scales. (Illus.). 48p. 1992. pap. 4.95 (*0-8256-1342-6*, AM87482) Music Sales.

— Hammered Dulcimer. 1979. pap. 14.95 (*0-8256-0174-6*, Oak) Music Sales.

— The Original Guitar Case Chord Book. 48p. pap. 4.95 (*0-8256-2998-5*) Music Sales.

— The Original Guitar Case Scale Book. (Illus.). 48p. 1990. pap. 4.95 (*0-8256-2588-2*, AM86217) Music Sales.

— The Penny Whistle Primer. 1982. pap. 4.95 (*0-8256-0268-8*, Oak) Music Sales.

— You Can Play Guitar. (Illus.). 80p. 1990. pap. 14.95 (*0-8256-2539-4*, AM76159) Music Sales.

Pickow, Peter, jt. auth. see Appleby, Amy.

Pickow, Peter, jt. auth. see Bell, Joe.

Pickow, Peter, jt. auth. see Shulman, Jason.

Pickrahn, H., jt. auth. see Held, P.

Pickrell, Annie D. Pioneer Women in Texas. limited ed. LC 91-24710. 485p. 1991. 60.00 (*0-938349-71-6*) State House Pr.

— Pioneer Women in Texas. LC 91-24710. 485p. 1991. reprint ed. 29.95 (*0-938349-70-8*) State House Pr.

***Pickrell, Jesse.** Group Health Insurance. 2nd ed. (C). 1961. 10.50 (*0-256-00671-7*) Irwin.

Pickrell, John A., ed. Lung Connective Tissue: Location, Metabolism, & Response to Injury. 224p. 1981. 98.95 (*0-8493-5749-7*, RC756) CRC Pr.

Pickron, John E., tr. see Goedan, Juergen C.

Pickston, Margaret. Language of Flowers. 1987. 8.95 (*0-7181-0593-1*, M Joseph) Viking Penguin.

Pickstone, John V., ed. Medical Innovations in Historical Perspective. LC 91-30798. 280p. 1992. text ed. 55.00 (*0-312-07136-1*) St Martin.

Pickthal, M. M. Cultural Side of Islam. 202p. 1981. 14.95 (*0-318-36958-3*) Asia Bk Corp.

— The Meaning of the Glorious Quran. 810p. 1979. 34.95 (*0-318-37187-1*); pap. 7.95 (*0-318-37188-X*) Asia Bk Corp.

— Sadhus of India. 258p. 19.95 (*0-318-37160-X*) Asia Bk Corp.

Pickthal, Muhammad M., tr. see Ghazi, Abdullah.

Pickthall. Glorious Quran: The Arabic Test & English Rendering. 1983. 25.75 (*1-56744-044-4*); pap. 15.95 (*0-933511-24-8*) Kazi Pubns.

— The Meaning of the Glorious Quran. pap. 5.95 (*1-56744-133-5*) Kazi Pubns.

Pickthall, Barry, jt. auth. see Fisher, Bob.

Pickthall, M. Cultural Side of Islam. 12.75 (*0-935782-66-4*) Kazi Pubns.

— The Holy Qur'an Trans. 1990. text ed. 20.00 (*0-685-66725-1*, 35) Tahrike Tarsile Quran.

Pickthall, M., ed. Holy Quran. 1983. reprint ed. 18.50 (*0-8364-0989-2*, Pub. by R Taj Co) S Asia.

Pickthall, M. M. The Meaning of the Holy Quran. 464p. 1989. 12.95 (*81-85274-00-2*) Asia Bk Corp.

Pickthall, M. M., ed. Holy Quran with English Translation. 1976. reprint ed. 19.50 (*0-8364-0415-7*) S Asia.

Pickthall, Mardaduke, tr. Holy Quran. 1986. reprint ed. 20.00 (*0-8364-1623-6*, Pub. by Rajesh) S Asia.

Pickthall, Marjorie. The Worker in Sandalwood: A Christmas Eve Miracle. LC 94-548. (Illus.). 32p. (J). (gr. k-4). 1994. 14.99 (*0-525-45332-6*) Dutton Child Bks.

Pickthall, Marmaduke, ed. The Glorious Koran. 1696p. 1976. text ed. 59.95 (*0-04-297036-9*) Routledge Chapman & Hall.

Pickthall, Marmaduke, tr. The Koran. LC 92-52928. 544p. 1992. 20.00 (*0-679-41736-2*, Everymans Lib) Knopf.

Pickthall, Mohammed M. Meaning of the Glorious Koran. 1993. pap. 5.99 (*0-451-62857-8*, Sig) NAL-Dutton.

— The Meaning of the Holy Quran. (C). 1995. 10.00x (*81-7476-005-9*, Pub. by UBS Pubs Dist II) S Asia.

Pickthall, Mohammed M., tr. Meaning of the Glorious Koran. 1953. pap. 5.99 (*0-451-62745-8*, ME2305, Ment) NAL-Dutton.

Pickthall, Muhammad, tr. The Glorious Koran. 767p. 1983. 20.00 (*0-940368-30-7*, 2) Tahrike Tarsile Quran.

Pickthall, Muhammad M., tr. The Glorious Qur'an. LC 92-64030. 768p. pap. text ed. 8.95 (*0-940368-95-1*) Tahrike Tarsile Quran.

— The Glorious Quran. xxxiv, 605p. 1994. 14.95 (*0-9638962-0-2*) Crescent NY.

Pickthorn, William E., comp. Ministers Manual Ser., 3 vols., Set. Incl. Vol. 1. Services for Special Occasions. LC 65-13222. 134p. 1965. 5.95 (*0-88243-547-7*, 02-0547); Vol. 2. Services for Weddings & Funerals. LC 65-13222. 126p. 1965. 5.95 (*0-88243-548-5*, 02-0548); Vol. 3. Services for Ministers & Workers. LC 65-13222. 134p. 1965. 5.95 (*0-88243-549-3*, 02-0549); LC 65-13222. 1965. 16.95 (*0-88243-544-2*, 02-0544) Gospel Pub.

Pickup, F., jt. auth. see Parker, M. A.

Pickup, J. & Williams, G. Textbook of Diabetes, 2 vols., Set. 1991. 265.00 (*0-632-02594-8*) Blackwell Sci.

Pickup, J. C. Biotechnology of Insulin Therapy. (Frontiers in Pharmacology & Therapeutics Ser.). (Illus.). 186p. 1991. 115.00 (*0-632-03038-0*) Blackwell Sci.

Pickup, J. C. & Williams, G. Textbook of Diabetes Slide Atlas. 1993. 95.00 (*0-632-03569-2*) Blackwell Sci.

Pickup, J. C., jt. auth. see Williams, G.

Pickup, L., jt. auth. see Banister, D.

Pickup, Laurie, et al. Bus Deregulation in the Metropolitan Areas. Kenny, Francesca, ed. (Oxford Studies in Transport). 278p. 1991. text ed. 59.95 (*1-85628-198-1*, Pub. by Avebury Pub UK) Ashgate Pub Co.

Pickup, P. Engineering Drawing with Worked Examples, No. 1. Parker, P., ed. (C). 1976. 70.00 (*0-09-126451-0*, Pub. by S Thornes Pubs UK) St Mut.

Pickup, Ronald, ed. see Morgan, Tom.

Pickus, Bob. Divorce & Family Law in California: A Guide for the General Public. 141p. (Orig.). 1991. pap. 8.95 (*0-9630684-0-7*) B Pickus.

— Fee Agreement Forms Manual: January 1993 Update. LC 88-63608. 172p. 1993. ring bd. 25.00 (*0-88124-585-2*, MI-30442) Cont Ed Bar-CA.

Pickus, Bob & Sanders, Carol S. Fee Agreement Forms Manual: December 1991 Update. LC 88-63608. 74p. 1991. ring bd. 20.00 (*0-88124-455-4*, MI-30441) Cont Ed Bar-CA.

Pickus, Bob, ed. see Walker, Robert L.

Pickvance, C. G. & Preteceille, E. State & Locality: A Comparative Perspective on State Restructuring. 224p. 1991. text ed. 39.00 (*0-86187-983-X*, Pub. by Pinter Pubs UK) St Martin.

Pickvance, C. G., jt. ed. see Gottdiener, M.

Pickvance, Ronald. Van Gogh in Saint Remy & Auvers. (Illus.). 328p. 1986. 18.95 (*0-87099-477-8*, Abrams) Metro Mus Art.

— Vincent Van Gogh: Irises. (Getty Museum Studies on Art). Date not set. pap. 15.95 (*0-89236-226-X*) J P Getty Trust.

Pickvet, Mark. The Definitive Guide to Shot Glasses. (Illus.). 228p. (Orig.). 1993. pap. 19.95 (*0-915410-90-7*) Antique Pubns.

— The Official Price Guide to Glassware. (Illus.). 400p. 1995. pap. 15.00 (*0-87637-953-6*, House of Collect) Ballantine.

— Shot Glasses: An American Tradition. (Illus.). 167p. 1990. pap. 12.95 (*0-915410-62-1*, 3070) Antique Pubns.

Pickwell, George V., jt. auth. see Culotta, Wendy A.

Pickwell, W. D. Binocular Vision Anomalies: Investigation & Treatment. 2nd ed. (Illus.). 181p. 1989. text ed. 80.00 (*0-7506-1488-9*) Buttrwrth-Heinemann.

Pickworth, J., jt. auth. see Pickworth, R.

***Pickworth, R. & Pickworth, J.** Passing HSC Legal Studies. 120p. 1991. pap. 30.00 (*0-409-30194-9*, Austral) Butterworth Legal Pubs.

Picler, F. & Diaz, R. Moreno, eds. Computer Aided Systems Theory - EUROCAST '93: A Selection of Papers from the Third International Workshop on Computer Aided Systems Theory, Las Palmas, Spain, February 1993: Proceedings. LC 93-44606. (Lecture Notes in Computer Science Ser.: Vol. 763). 1994. 58.00 (*0-387-57601-0*) Spr-Verlag.

Pico Della Mirandola, Giovanni. On the Dignity of Man. Wallis, Charles G. et al, trs. Bd. with On Being & UnityLC 65-26540.; Heptaplus. LC 65-26540. LC 65-26540. 1965. Set pap. 7.00 (*0-672-60483-3*, LLA227) Macmillan.

— Oration on the Dignity of Man. Caponigri, A. Robert, tr. 96p. 1956. pap. 8.95 (*0-89526-925-2*) Regnery Pub.

— Pico Della Mirandola: Of Being & Unity. Hamm, Victor M., tr. (Medieval Philosophical Texts in Translation Ser.). 1943. pap. 10.00 (*0-87462-203-4*) Marquette.

Pico Della Mirandola, Giovanni & Pico, Gian F. Opera Omnia, 2 vols., Set. xxvi, 2301p. 1969. reprint ed. write for info. (*0-318-71271-7*, Pub. by Georg Olms GW); reprint ed. write for info. (*0-318-71605-4*, Pub. by Georg Olms GW) Lubrecht & Cramer.

Pico, Fernando. Al Filo del Poder: Subalternos y Dominantes en PR, 1739-1910. (Caribbean Collection). 1993. pap. 11.95 (*0-8477-0180-8*) U of PR Pr.

— Amargo Cafe. LC 81-69788. (Coleccion Semilla Ser.). 162p. 1981. pap. 6.50 (*0-940238-49-7*) Ediciones Huracan.

— El Dia Menospensado: Historia de los Presidiarios en Puerto Rico 1793-1993. 198p. 1994. pap. text ed. 9.95 (*0-929157-27-3*) Ediciones Huracan.

— Don Quijote En Motora y Otras Andanzas. (Illus.). 120p. (Orig.). (SPA.). 1993. pap. 6.75 (*0-929157-24-9*) Ediciones Huracan.

— Los Gallos Peleados. LC 83-83055. (Coleccion Semilla Ser.). 179p. (SPA.). 1983. pap. 6.75 (*0-940238-71-3*) Ediciones Huracan.

— Historia General de Puerto Rico. LC 86-80150. (Huracan Academia Ser.). 300p. (SPA.). 1986. pap. 11.75 (*0-940238-86-1*) Ediciones Huracan.

— Mil Ochocientos Noventa y Ocho: La Guerra Despues de la Guerra. LC 87-80624. (Coleccion Semilla Ser.). 215p. (SPA.). 1987. pap. 7.95 (*0-940238-25-X*) Ediciones Huracan.

— The Red Comb. Palacios, Argentina, tr. LC 94-9832. (Illus.). 48p. (J). (gr. k-4). 1994. lib. bdg. 14.95 (*0-8167-3539-5*); pap. 4.95 (*0-8167-3540-9*) BrdgeWater.

— Vivir en Caimito. LC 88-83372. 185p. 1989. pap. 6.75 (*0-940238-74-8*) Ediciones Huracan.

Pico, Fernando & Izcoa, Carmen R. Puerto Rico, Tierra Adentro y Mar Afuera: Historia y Cultura de los Puertorriquenos. LC 91-71358. 304p. (SPA.). (J). (gr. 7). 1991. text ed. 23.95 (*0-929157-12-5*) Ediciones Huracan.

Pico, Fernando & Ordonez, Maria A. Peineta Colorada. 49p. (SPA.). 1991. 9.95 (*980-257-098-2*) Ediciones Huracan.

Pico, Fernando, et al. Las Vallas Rotas. LC 82-83477. (Nave y el Puerto Ser.). 238p. (SPA.). 1982. pap. text ed. 6.95 (*0-940238-69-1*) Ediciones Huracan.

Pico, Gian F., jt. auth. see Pico Della Mirandola, Giovanni.

Pico, Isabel, ed. Album de la Familia. 45p. 1984. pap. 5.75 (*0-8477-2473-5*) U of PR Pr.

Pico, Isabel & Alegria, Idsa. El Texto Libre de Prejuicios Sexuales y Raciales: Guia para la Preparacion de Materiales de Ensenanza. 56p. (SPA.). 1983. pap. 6.50 (*0-8477-2470-0*) U of PR Pr.

Pico, Isabel, et al. Machismo y Educacion en Puerto Rico. 135p. (SPA.). 1983. pap. 6.25 (*0-8477-2466-2*) U of PR Pr.

Pico, Juan H., jt. auth. see Sobrino, Jon.

Pico, Pancho. Matrimonio Sorprendente. 96p. 1981. reprint ed. pap. 2.75 (*0-311-37022-5*) Casa Bautista.

Picogna, Joseph L. Total Quality Leadership: A Training Approach. LC 93-77639. (Illus.). 364p. (Orig.). (C). 1993. pap. 17.95 (*0-945510-15-2*) Intl Info Assocs.

Picon, ed. see Bernanos, Georges, et al.

Picon, Alice, ed. Pais Foreign Language Index, Vol. 19. 660p. 1989. lib. bdg. 495.00 (*0-685-26609-5*) Pub Aff Info.

Picon, Alice, jt. ed. see Sloan, Gwen.

Picon, Antoine. French Architects & Engineers in the Age of Enlightenment. (Cambridge Studies in the History of Architecture). (Illus.). 452p. (C). 1992. 150.00 (*0-521-38253-X*) Cambridge U Pr.

Picon, G. Panorama de la Nouvelle Litterature Francaise. (FRE.). 1988. pap. 24.95 (*0-7859-2939-8*) Fr & Eur.

Picon, Gaetan. Ingres. LC 90-63791. (Illus.). 1991. pap. 25.00 (*0-8478-1351-7*) Rizzoli Intl.

— Korunk Szellemi Korkepe. LC 66-17649. Orig. Title: Panorama des Idees Contemporaines. (HUN.). 1966. 20.00 (*0-911050-38-8*) Occidental.

Picon, Geotan. Panorama Mysli Wspolczesnych. 713p. 1960. 9.00 (*0-940962-20-9*) Polish Inst Art & Sci.

Picon, Leon, tr. see Inoue, Yasushi.

Picon-Salas, Mariano. A Cultural History of Spanish America: From Conquest to Independence. Leonard, Irving A., tr. LC 82-951. xvii, 192p. 1982. reprint ed. text ed. 38.50 (*0-313-23454-X*, PSCH, Greenwood Pr) Greenwood.

Picornell, Miguel, ed. Measured Performance of Shallow Foundations. (Sessions Proceedings Ser.). 116p. 1988. 16.00 (*0-87262-643-1*) Am Soc Civil Eng.

Picot, Andre, ed. see Prokopetz, Andrew T.

Picot, C. E., jt. ed. see Baumgartner, A.

***Picot, Derek.** Hotel Reservations: Calamities & Hospitality Hiccups from the World's Hotels. 203p. 1995. pap. 11.95 (*0-86051-930-9*, Robson-Parkwest) Parkwest Pubns.

Picot, P. & Johan, Z. Atlas of Ore Minerals. (Illus.). 460p. 1991. 187.50 (*0-444-99684-2*) Elsevier.

Picott, J. Rupert. A Quarter Century of the Black Experience in Elementary & Secondary Education, 1950-1975. (YA). 1990. 9.95 (*0-87498-087-9*) Assoc Pubs DC.

Picott, J. Rupert, ed. Walter Washington. (YA). 1990. 5.95 (*0-87498-094-1*) Assoc Pubs DC.

Picott, R. & Ridley, W. N. History of the Restitution Fund Commission of the Episcopal Diocese of Pennsylvania, a Challenge. (YA). 1990. 15.95 (*0-87498-091-7*) Assoc Pubs DC.

Picoult, Jodi. Harvesting the Heart. LC 93-7190. 416p. 1993. pap. 11.00 (*0-685-64794-3*, Viking) Viking Penguin.

— Harvesting the Heart. 464p. 1995. 10.95 (*0-14-023027-0*, Penguin Bks) Viking Penguin.

— Picture Perfect. 1995. 22.95 (*0-399-14040-9*) Putnam Pub Group.

— Songs of the Humpback Whale: A Novel in Five Voices. 1992. 22.95 (*0-571-12927-7*) Faber & Faber.

***Picq, Jean-Yves.** The Gaspard Meyer Case. Feingold, Michael, tr. 1995. 8.95 (*0-913745-45-6*) Ubu Repertory.

Picquet, D. Cheryn, ed. Computer Law & Software Protection: A Bibliography of Crime, Liability, Abuse, & Security, 1984 Through 1992. LC 92-56631. 253p. 1993. pap. 42.50 (*0-89950-840-5*) McFarland & Co.

Picquet, Louisa, et al. Collected Black Women's Narratives. (Schomburg Library of Nineteenth-Century Black Women Writers). 384p. 1988. 29.95 (*0-19-505260-9*) OUP.

Picraux, S. T., jt. auth. see Nicolet, M. A.

Pictet, Francois J. Traite Elementaire De Paleontologie Histoire Naturelle Des Animaux Fossiles Consideres Ans Leur S Rapports Zoologiques et Geologiques, 4 vols., 1. Gould, Stephen J., ed. LC 79-8344. (History of Paleontology Ser.). (Illus.). (FRE.). 1980. reprint ed. lib. bdg. 47.95 (*0-405-12735-9*) Ayer.

— Traite Elementaire De Paleontologie Histoire Naturelle Des Animaux Fossiles Consideres Ans Leur S Rapports Zoologiques et Geologiques, 4 vols., 2. Gould, Stephen J., ed. LC 79-8344. (History of Paleontology Ser.). (Illus.). (FRE.). 1980. reprint ed. lib. bdg. 47.95 (*0-405-12736-7*) Ayer.

— Traite Elementaire De Paleontologie Histoire Naturelle Des Animaux Fossiles Consideres Ans Leur S Rapports Zoologiques et Geologiques, 4 vols., 3. Gould, Stephen J., ed. LC 79-8344. (History of Paleontology Ser.). (Illus.). (FRE.). 1980. reprint ed. lib. bdg. 47.95 (*0-405-12737-5*) Ayer.

— Traite Elementaire De Paleontologie Histoire Naturelle Des Animaux Fossiles Consideres Ans Leur S Rapports Zoologiques et Geologiques, 4 vols., 4. Gould, Stephen J., ed. LC 79-8344. (History of Paleontology Ser.). (Illus.). (FRE.). 1980. reprint ed. lib. bdg. 47.95 (*0-405-12738-3*) Ayer.

— Traite Elementaire De Paleontologie Histoire Naturelle Des Animaux Fossiles Consideres Ans Leur S Rapports Zoologiques et Geologiques, 4 vols., Set. Gould, Stephen J., ed. LC 79-8344. (History of Paleontology Ser.). (Illus.). (FRE.). 1980. reprint ed. lib. bdg. 191.95 (*0-405-12734-0*) Ayer.

Pictet, Jean. Development & Principles of International Humanitarian Law. 1985. pap. 16.95 (*0-318-18536-9*) Kluwer Ac.

Picthal, M. M. Quranic Advices - Arabic Text with Translation. 154p. 1979. 8.95 (*0-318-37185-5*) Asia Bk Corp.

Picton, Bernard. A Field Guide to the Shallow-Water Echinoderms of the British Isles. 96p. (C). 1990. pap. text ed. 90.00 (*0-907151-88-4*, Pub. by IMMEL Pubng UK) St Mut.

Picton, Bernard & Morrow, Christine. A Field Guide to the Shallow-Water Nudibranchs of the British Isles. 128p. (C). 1990. pap. 125.00 (*0-685-74647-X*, Pub. by IMMEL Pubng UK) St Mut.

Picton, Bernard, jt. auth. see Erwin, David.

Picton, Howard J. The Life & Works of Joseph Anton Steffan (1726-1797) With Special Reference to His Keyboard Concertos, 2 vols., Set. rev. ed. LC 89-23792. (Outstanding Dissertations in Music from British Universities Ser.). 788p. 1990. 75.00 (*0-8240-2345-5*) Garland.

Picton, John. African Textiles. 1989. pap. text ed. 25.00 (*0-06-430190-7*, Icon Edns) HarpC.

***Picton Pub. (Chippenham) Ltd. Staff.** Naval & Military Journal 1895 Vol. 1. 1992. 79.95 (*0-948251-62-X*, Pub. by Picton UK) St Mut.

***Picton Publ. (Chippenham) Ltd. Staff.** Forty Seventh Sikhs War Record: The Great War 1914-1918. 1992. 79.95 (*0-948251-61-1*, Pub. by Picton UK) St Mut.

***Picton Publ. Ltd. Staff.** The Army in India & Its Evolution: Including an Account of the Establishment of the Royal Air Force in India. 1992. 79.95 (*0-948251-68-9*, Pub. by Picton UK) St Mut.

Picton Publishing (Chippenham) Ltd. Staff. Amritsar Legacy: The Dyer Massacre of 1919 & the Effect on Subsequent History. (C). 1987. 75.00 (*0-948251-44-1*, Pub. by Picton UK) St Mut.

— An Anthology of Poems. (C). 1987. 50.00 (*0-948251-21-2*, Pub. by Picton UK) St Mut.

— The Art Gallery & Other Poems. (C). 1987. 50.00 (*0-685-39334-8*, Pub. by Picton UK) St Mut.

— Beyond the Art Gallery. (C). 1987. 50.00 (*0-948251-08-5*, Pub. by Picton UK) St Mut.

— Bombs & Booby Traps: World War II Bomb Clearance. (C). 1987. 75.00 (*0-948251-19-0*, Pub. by Picton UK) St Mut.

— British & Indian Armies in the East Indies (1685-1935) (C). 1987. 125.00 (*0-685-39343-7*, Pub. by Picton UK) St Mut.

P
Q

— British & Indian Armies in the East Indies (1685-1935) deluxe ed. (C). 1987. 475.00 (*0-685-39344-5*, Pub. by Picton UK) St Mut.
— Cautionary Tales & Other Verses. (C). 1987. 50.00 (*0-948251-20-4*, Pub. by Picton UK) St Mut.
— Devizes in Focus: A Town in Photographic Profile. (Illus.). (C). 1987. 75.00 (*0-948251-48-4*, Pub. by Picton UK); pap. 45.00 (*0-948251-47-6*, Pub. by Picton UK) St Mut.
— Gainst All Disaster: The Edward & Albert Medal Conversions to the George Cross. (C). 1987. 75.00 (*0-685-39337-2*, Pub. by Picton UK) St Mut.
— Gannet. (FAA Ser.). (C). 1987. 45.00 (*0-948251-46-8*, Pub. by Picton UK) St Mut.
— Make Your Bets: How To Win at Gambling. (C). 1987. pap. 22.00 (*0-948251-49-2*, Pub. by Picton UK) St Mut.
— Operation Nestegg: The Liberation of Jersey 1945. (C). 1987. 20.00 (*0-948251-26-3*, Pub. by Picton UK) St Mut.
— Operation Skua. (FAA Ser.). (C). 1987. 39.00 (*0-685-39342-9*, Pub. by Picton UK) St Mut.
— Poems Humorous & Inconsequential. (C). 1987. 35.00 (*0-948251-30-1*, Pub. by Picton UK) St Mut.
— Poems Pensive & Peculiar. (C). 1987. 40.00 (*0-685-39333-X*, Pub. by Picton UK) St Mut.
— The Pomprey Train: The Portsmouth Line Explored. (C). 1987. 22.00 (*0-948251-45-X*, Pub. by Picton UK) St Mut.
— Putting the Record Straight: World Helicopter Speed Record. (C). 1987. 22.00 (*0-948251-38-7*, Pub. by Picton UK) St Mut.
— Royal Flying Corps: (Military Wing) Honours & Awards. (C). 1987. 75.00 (*0-685-39335-6*, Pub. by Picton UK) St Mut.
— Satellite TV Installation Guide. (C). 1987. 60.00 (*0-685-39331-3*, Pub. by Picton UK) St Mut.
— Scimitar. (FAA Ser.). (C). 1987. 50.00 (*0-948251-39-5*, Pub. by Picton UK) St Mut.
— Simkin's Soldiers, Vol. 1. (C). 1987. 44.00 (*0-685-39341-0*, Pub. by Picton UK) St Mut.
— Socialist International at Gunpoint: Did the CIA Murder Olaf Palme? (C). 1987. 65.00 (*0-948251-40-9*, Pub. by Picton UK) St Mut.
— Stamps of Alderney. (C). 1987. 50.00 (*0-948251-33-6*, Pub. by Picton UK) St Mut.
— Supplement to the Falkland Islands Catalogue, 1988. (C). 1987. 75.00 (*0-685-39332-1*, Pub. by Picton UK) St Mut.
— Terriers in the Trenches: The Post Office Rifles at War, 1914-1918. (C). 1987. 65.00 (*0-685-39338-0*, Pub. by Picton UK) St Mut.
— The Twenty-Eighth Division in France & Flanders: A History. (C). 1987. 70.00 (*0-948251-36-0*, Pub. by Picton UK) St Mut.
— The Twenty-Eighth Light Cavalry in Persia & Russian Turkistan, 1915-1920. (C). 1987. 90.00 (*0-948251-35-2*, Pub. by Picton UK) St Mut.

Picton Publishing (Chippenham) Ltd. Staff, ed. Prince of Wales Own, the Scinde Horse: A Regimental History. (C). 1987. 150.00 (*0-685-39339-9*, Pub. by Picton UK) St Mut.

Picton Publishing Staff. Angus' Mull. rev. ed. 1987. 30.00 (*0-317-90396-9*, Pub. by Picton UK) St Mut.
— The Army of India Medal Roll, 1799-1826. 123p. (C). 1987. 120.00 (*0-317-90450-7*, Pub. by Picton UK) St Mut.
— The Artwork Interviews. (C). 1987. 35.00 (*0-317-90388-8*, Pub. by Picton UK) St Mut.
— Ben Nevis & Its Observatory. (Illus.). (C). 1987. 30.00 (*0-317-90420-5*, Pub. by Picton UK) St Mut.
— The Celtic-Rangers Joke Book. (Illus.). (C). 1987. 9.00 (*0-317-90419-1*, Pub. by Picton UK) St Mut.
— The Crinan Canal. (Illus.). 40p. 1987. 35.00 (*0-317-90394-2*, Pub. by Picton UK) St Mut.
— Geoff. (C). 1987. 35.00 (*0-317-90387-X*, Pub. by Picton UK) St Mut.
— Glasgow, London: A Traveller's Guide. (C). 1987. 45.00 (*0-317-90390-X*, Pub. by Picton UK) St Mut.
— A Handbook of British & Foreign Orders War Medals & Decorations Awarded to the Army & Navy. (Illus.). 911p. (C). 1987. reprint ed. 287.00 (*0-317-90454-X*, Pub. by Picton UK) St Mut.
— The Highland Line. (Illus.). 118p. (C). 1987. 22.00 (*0-317-90403-5*, Pub. by Picton UK) St Mut.
— HMS Invincible: The Falklands Deployment, 1982. 78p. (C). 1987. 91.00 (*0-317-90377-2*, Pub. by Picton UK) St Mut.
— Honours & Awards Indian Army, August 1914-August 1921. 302p. (C). 1987. 65.00 (*0-317-90457-4*, Pub. by Picton UK) St Mut.
— Jamie Fleeman's Country Cookbook. (Illus.). (C). 1987. 30.00 (*0-317-90401-9*, Pub. by Picton UK) St Mut.
— Kilmartin. 1987. 22.00 (*0-317-90395-0*, Pub. by Picton UK) St Mut.
— The Lochaber Narrow Gauge Railway. (Illus.). (C). 1987. 30.00 (*0-317-90409-4*, Pub. by Picton UK) St Mut.
— Longueval. 62p. (C). 1987. 49.00 (*0-317-90444-2*, Pub. by Picton UK) St Mut.
— Mairi Hedderwick's Views of Scotland. (Illus.). (C). 1987. 35.00 (*0-317-90423-X*, Pub. by Picton UK) St Mut.
— The Mallaign Line. (C). 1987. 22.00 (*0-317-90407-8*, Pub. by Picton UK) St Mut.
— Mallaign Line Steam. (Illus.). (C). 1987. 22.00 (*0-317-90406-X*, Pub. by Picton UK) St Mut.
— Natural History of Loch Lomond. 1987. 30.00 (*0-317-90392-6*, Pub. by Picton UK) St Mut.
— The Old Firm Guide. (C). 1987. 25.00 (*0-317-90418-3*, Pub. by Picton UK) St Mut.
— Old Nooks of Stirling. (Illus.). (C). 1987. 25.00 (*0-317-90424-8*, Pub. by Picton UK) St Mut.
— The Public Enquiry. (C). 1987. 11.00 (*0-317-90391-8*, Pub. by Picton UK) St Mut.
— The Punjab Campaign: Casualty Roll, 1849. 76p. (C). 1987. 105.00 (*0-317-90449-3*, Pub. by Picton UK) St Mut.
— The Rannoch Line. (Illus.). (C). 1987. 22.00 (*0-317-90405-1*, Pub. by Picton UK) St Mut.
— Recipes from Loch Lomond. (C). 1987. 20.00 (*0-317-90400-0*, Pub. by Picton UK) St Mut.
— The Road to the Road to the Isles. (C). 1987. 15.00 (*0-317-90415-9*, Pub. by Picton UK) St Mut.
— Robert Burns. 240p. (C). 1987. 35.00 (*0-317-90413-2*, Pub. by Picton UK) St Mut.
— Robert Burns. limited ed. 240p. (C). 1987. 333.00 (*0-317-90414-0*, Pub. by Picton UK) St Mut.
— Scotland's Distilleries. (Illus.). (C). 1987. 45.00 (*0-317-90427-2*, Pub. by Picton UK) St Mut.
— Scotland's Great Road North. (C). 1987. 20.00 (*0-317-90416-7*, Pub. by Picton UK) St Mut.
— Scotland's Malt Whiskies. (C). 1987. 25.00 (*0-317-90429-9*, Pub. by Picton UK) St Mut.
— Scotland's Stations. (Illus.). 1987. 20.00 (*0-317-90398-5*, Pub. by Picton UK) St Mut.
— Scotland's Threatened Lines. (C). 1987. 28.00 (*0-317-90402-7*, Pub. by Picton UK) St Mut.
— Scottish Farm Animals. (C). 1987. 22.00 (*0-317-90417-5*, Pub. by Picton UK) St Mut.
— Steam Lines. 1987. 30.00 (*0-317-90393-4*, Pub. by Picton UK) St Mut.
— Supplement to the Half-Yearly Army List for the Period Ending 31st December, 1924: War Services of Officers on Retired Pay, Etc. 703p. (C). 1987. 245.00 (*0-317-90447-7*, Pub. by Picton UK) St Mut.
— Tales of the Tay. (Illus.). 1987. 30.00 (*0-317-90399-3*, Pub. by Picton UK) St Mut.
— Tree Life of Argyll. 1987. 25.00 (*0-317-90397-7*, Pub. by Picton UK) St Mut.
— W. D. & H. O. Wills Roll of Honour & War Service Roll, 1914-1918. 46p. (C). 1987. pap. 56.00 (*0-948251-28-X*, Pub. by Picton UK) St Mut.
— West Highland Steam. (C). 1987. 32.00 (*0-317-90389-6*, Pub. by Picton UK) St Mut.

Picton Publishing Staff, ed. The Army of the Sutlej: Casualty Roll, 1845-46. 50p. (C). 1987. 105.00 (*0-317-90445-0*, Pub. by Picton UK) St Mut.
— Casualties Sustained by the British Army in the Korean War, 1950-1953. 85p. (C). 1987. 105.00 (*0-317-90456-6*, Pub. by Picton UK) St Mut.
— It's Angus Again. (C). 1987. 30.00 (*0-317-90411-6*, Pub. by Picton UK) St Mut.
— The South African War Casualty Rolls: Natal Field Force, 20th October, 1899-26th October, 1900. 237p. (C). 1987. 133.00 (*0-317-90430-2*, Pub. by Picton UK) St Mut.

Picton Publishing Staff & Barnard, Alfred. The Whiskey Distillers of Scotland, 1887. (Illus.). 160p. (C). 1987. reprint ed. 60.00 (*0-317-90428-0*, Pub. by Picton UK) St Mut.

Picton Publishing Staff & Keegan, Alan. Scotch in Miniature. rev. ed. (Illus.). (C). 1987. 30.00 (*0-317-90426-4*, Pub. by Picton UK) St Mut.

Picton Publishing Staff & MacBrayne. Summer Tours in Scotland. (C). 1987. reprint ed. 18.00 (*0-317-90421-3*, Pub. by Picton UK) St Mut.

Picton Publishing Staff & MacIntyre, Angus. Angus MacIntyre's Ceilidii Collection. (C). 1987. 22.00 (*0-317-90412-4*, Pub. by Picton UK) St Mut.

Picton Publishing Staff & Weir, Tom. The Oban Line. (Illus.). (C). 1987. 22.00 (*0-317-90404-3*, Pub. by Picton UK) St Mut.

Picton, T. W., ed. Human Event-Related Potentials: Handbook of Electroencephalography & Clinical Neurophysiology. 556p. 1988. 192.50 (*0-444-80929-5*) Elsevier.

Picton, Tom. Old Gotham Theatricals. (Clipper Studies in the American Theater: No. 12). x, 170p. 1995. lib. bdg. 29.00x (*0-89370-362-1*); pap. text ed. 19.00 (*0-89370-462-8*) Borgo Pr.

Pictor, jt. auth. see Johnson.

Picture Me Books Staff. If I Were a California Angel. (Illus.). (J). (ps-3). 1994. 7.95 (*1-878338-59-5*) Picture Me Bks.
— If I Were a Seattle Supersonic. (J). (ps-3). 1994. pap. 5.99 (*1-57151-112-1*) Picture Me Bks.

Picture Me Books Staff & D'Andrea, Joseph C. If I Were a San Francisco Giant. (MLB Ser.). (Illus.). 24p. (Orig.). (J). (ps-5). 1994. pap. 5.99 (*1-878338-64-1*) Picture Me Bks.

Pictureback Books Staff. Topper Debate. 1989. write for info. (*0-679-80319-X*) Random.

Picus, Larry, jt. auth. see Selvin, Molly.

***Picus, Lawrence O. & Wattenbarger, James L.** Where Does the Money Go? Resource Allocation in Elementary Schools. (Yearbook of the American Education Finance Association Ser.). (Illus.). 320p. 1995. 46.95 (*0-8039-6162-6*) Corwin Pr.

Picus, Lawrence O., jt. auth. see Kazlauskas, Edward J.

Picus, Lawrence O., jt. auth. see Odden, Allan R.

Picut, Catherine A., jt. auth. see Lewis, Robert M.

***Pidal, Menendez.** Flor Nueva de Romances Viejos. 33th ed. 264p. 1991. pap. 12.95 (*0-7859-5190-3*) Fr & Eur.

Pidal, Ramon M. Historia de Espana Vol. 10: Los Comienzos de la Reconquista (711-1038) De Urbal, F. J. & Balbas, L. T., eds. 660p. (SPA.). 1992. 195.00 (*0-7859-0515-4*, 8423948080) Fr & Eur.
— Historia De Espana, Vol. 36: La Epoca Del Romanticismo (1808-1874): las Letras, las Artes, la Vida Cotidiana. Zavala, Iris M. et al, eds. 780p. (SPA.). 1992. 195.00 (*0-7859-0539-1*, 8423949931) Fr & Eur.

Pidd, Michael. Computer Simulation in Management Science. 3rd ed. 351p. 1992. pap. text ed. 36.95 (*0-471-93462-3*) Wiley.

Pidd, Michael, ed. Computer Modelling for Discrete Simulation. 274p. 1989. text ed. 94.95 (*0-471-92282-X*) Wiley.

Piddington, H. An English Index to the Plants of India. 243p. 1980. 15.00 (*0-88065-174-1*, Messers Today & Tomorrow) Scholarly Pubns.

Piddington, J. H. Cosmic Electrodynamics. 2nd ed. LC 77-22303. 376p. 1981. lib. bdg. 37.50 (*0-88275-587-0*) Krieger.

Piddington, Ralph, ed. see Williamson, Robert W.

Piderit, John J. The Ethical Foundations of Economics. LC 92-41288. 360p. 1993. 35.00 (*0-87840-535-6*) Georgetown U Pr.

Pidgeon, Alice, jt. ed. see Triffin, Nicholas.

Pidgeon, Harry. Around the World Single-Handed: The Cruise of the Islander. 288p. 1989. pap. 5.95 (*0-486-25946-3*) Dover.

Pidgeon, Mary E. Women in the Economy of the United States of America. Bd. with Employed Women Under NRA CodesLC 75-8784. LC 75-8784. (FDR & the Era of the New Deal Ser.). 1975. reprint ed. Set lib. bdg. 29.50 (*0-306-70731-4*) Da Capo.

Pidgeon, Sue, jt. ed. see Barrs, Myra.

Pidgeon, Walter, jt. auth. see ACA Staff.

***Pidgie, S. Walter.** The Gathering at Charlie's. Champlin, Allen R., Sr., ed. 262p. (Orig.). Date not set. pap. 7.00 (*0-9628802-2-1*) DeChamp CA.

Pidgin, Charles F. & Taylor, J. M. The Chronicles of Quincy Adams Sawyer, Detective. LC 75-32774. (Literature of Mystery & Detection Ser.). (Illus.). 1976. reprint ed. 28.95 (*0-405-07893-5*) Ayer.

Pidgora, V. O., jt. auth. see Belichko, Iu. V.

Pidgora, V. O., jt. auth. see Belichko, Iu V.

Pidoux, Blaise, ed. Eustache du Caurroy, OEuvres Completes. (Gesamtausgaben - Collected Works Ser.: Vol. IX, Pt. 1). 130p. (ENG, FRE & GER.). 1976. lib. bdg. 4.00 (*0-912024-70-4*) Inst Mediaeval Mus.

Pidoux, Pierre, ed. see Goudimel.

Pie Books Staff. C. D. Jacket Collection. (Illus.). 224p. 1994. reprint ed. pap. 49.95 (*4-938586-55-X*, Pub. by PIE Bks JA) Bks Nippan.
— Direct Mail Graphics. (Illus.). 224p. 1994. 79.95 (*4-938586-60-6*, Pub. by PIE Bks JA) Bks Nippan.
— Fashion & Cosmetic Graphics. (Illus.). 224p. 1994. 79.95 (*4-938586-50-9*, Pub. by PIE Bks JA) Bks Nippan.
— Sensual Images. (Illus.). 208p. 1994. pap. 55.00 (*4-938586-57-6*, Pub. by PIE Bks JA) Bks Nippan.
— T-Shirt Graphics. (Illus.). 224p. 1994. pap. 42.95 (*4-938586-58-4*, Pub. by PIE Bks JA) Bks Nippan.
— T-Shirt Print Designs & Logos. (Illus.). 224p. 1994. 79.95 (*4-938586-61-4*, Pub. by PIE Bks JA) Bks Nippan.

Piecemakers Staff. Picking up the Pieces. 128p. 19.95 (*1-881588-02-5*) E-Z Intl.

Piechowski, Carol. Horseman's Guide: Directory to Equestrian Trails & Camping Facilities in Illinois, Indiana, Iowa, Michigan, Minnesota, Nebraska, North Dakota, Ohio, South Dakota, & Wisconsin. (Illus.). 300p. (Orig.). 1990. pap. 7.00 (*0-9625561-1-4*) Horsemans Guide.
— Horseman's Guide: Equestrian Trails & Camping (Iowa, Minnesota, & Wisconsin) Mueller, Julianne, ed. (Illus.). 72p. (Orig.). 1989. pap. 4.00 (*0-9625561-0-6*) Horsemans Guide.

Pieczenik, Steve. Blood Heat. 352p. 1988. 17.95 (*0-15-113216-X*) HarBrace.
— Maximum Vigilance. 448p. 1992. 19.95 (*0-446-51556-6*) Warner Bks.
— Maximum Vigilance. 576p. 1993. mass mkt. 5.99 (*0-446-36468-1*) Warner Bks.
— Pax Pacifica. 1995. write for info. (*0-446-51818-2*); 22.95 (*0-446-51557-4*) Warner Bks.
— Pax Pacifica. 352p. 1995. mass mkt. 5.99 (*0-446-60250-7*) Warner Bks.

Pieczenik, Steve, jt. creator see Clancy, Tom.

Pieczynska, E., jt. ed. see Hillbricht-Ilkowska, A.

Piediscalzi, Nicholas, jt. ed. see Barr, David.

***Piedmont, Donlan.** Peanut Soup & Spoonbread: An Informal History of Hotel Roanoke. Virginia Tech Real Estate Foundation Staff, ed. LC 94-44863. 1994. 19.95 (*0-9617635-1-5*) VA Tech Found.

Piedmont, Ralph L., jt. auth. see Mostofsky, David I.

Piedmonte, Eugene B., jt. auth. see Stamps, Paula L.

Piedra, Joaquin E. Sangre Bajo Las Banderas (de Rusia Vino el Martillo - y la Hoz de Mi Garganta) LC 85-81209. (Coleccion Espejo de Paciencia Ser.). 101p. (Orig.). (SPA.). 1986. pap. 9.95 (*0-89729-382-7*) Ediciones.

Piedracueva, Haydee, ed. A Bibliography of Latin American Bibliographies, 1975 - 1979: Social Sciences & Humanities. LC 82-651. (Bibliography of Latin American Bibliographies Ser.: Supplement 3). 329p. 1982. 35.00 (*0-8108-1524-9*) Scarecrow.

Piegl, Les, ed. Fundamental Developments in Computer-Aided Geometric Modelling. (Illus.). 432p. 1993. text ed. 59.95 (*0-12-554765-X*) Acad Pr.

***Piehl, Frank J.** The Caxton Club, 1895-1995: Celebrating a Century of the Book in Chicago. LC 94-45203. 1995. write for info. (*0-615-00566-7*) Caxton Club.
— The Caxton Club 1895-1995: Celebrating a Century of the Book in Chicago. (Illus.). 224p. 1995. 75.00 (*0-940550-09-1*) Caxton Club.

Piehler, G. Kurt. Remembering War the American Way, 1783-1993. LC 94-10755. 1995. write for info. (*1-56098-461-9*) Smithsonian.

Piek, Tom, ed. Venoms of the Hymenoptera. 1986. text ed. 180.00 (*0-12-554770-6*); pap. text ed. 73.00 (*0-12-554771-4*) Acad Pr.

Piekalkiewicz, Janusz. The Air War, Nineteen Thirty-Nine to Nineteen Forty-Five. Van Heurck, Jan, tr. (Illus.). 436p. 1986. 19.95 (*0-918678-05-6*) Natl Hist Soc.
— The Battle for Cassino. LC 80-51757. 224p. 1980. 16.95 (*0-672-52667-0*, Bobbs) Macmillan.
— BMW Motorcycles in World War Two-R12-R75. LC 91-60854. (Illus.). 192p. 1991. 29.95 (*0-88740-306-9*) Schiffer.
— Cassino: Anatomy of the Battle. (Illus.). 192p. 1988. 19.95 (*0-918678-32-3*) Natl Hist Soc.
— The Cavalry of World War II. LC 80-5800. (Illus.). 256p. (C). 1980. 25.00 (*0-8128-2749-X*, Scrbrough Hse) Madison Bks UPA.
— The Cavalry of World War II. (Illus.). 256p. 1987. 19.95 (*0-918678-31-5*) Natl Hist Soc.
— The German Eighty-Eight Gun in Combat: The Scourge of Allied Armor. Force, Edward, tr. LC 91-62737. (Illus.). 192p. 1992. 29.95 (*0-88740-341-7*) Schiffer.
— Rommel & the Secret War in North Africa 1941-1943: Secret Intelligence in the North African Campaign. Clemens, Fred, tr. LC 91-62740. (Illus.). 240p. 1992. 29.95 (*0-88740-340-9*) Schiffer.
— Sea War: Nineteen Thirty-Nine to Nineteen Forty-Five. Tek Translation & International Print Ltd., tr. Orig. Title: Seekrieg 1939-1945. (Illus.). 353p. 1987. 19.95 (*0-918678-17-X*) Natl Hist Soc.
— Tank War: 1939-1945. Van Heurck, Jan, tr. (Illus.). 332p. 1986. 19.95 (*0-918678-08-0*) Natl Hist Soc.

Piekalkiewicz, Jaroslaw & Bede, Barry. Public Opinion Polling in Czechoslovakia, 1968-1969: Results & Analysis of Surveys Conducted During the Dubcek Era. LC 70-176398. (Special Studies in International Politics & Government). 1972. 29.50 (*0-275-28631-2*) Irvington.

Piekalkiewicz, Jaroslaw & Hamilton, Christopher, eds. Public Bureaucracies Between Reform & Resistance: Legacies, Trends & Effects in China, the U. S. S. R., Poland & Yugoslavia. LC 90-20250. 256p. 1991. 54.95 (*0-85496-295-6*) Berg Pubs.

Piekalkiewicz, Jaroslaw & Penn, Alfred W. Politics of Ideocracy. LC 94-8841. 284p. (C). 1995. 49.50 (*0-7914-2297-6*); pap. 16.95x (*0-7914-2298-4*) State U NY Pr.

Piekarski, Vicki, ed. Westward the Women: An Anthology of Western Stories by Women. LC 87-34238. 186p. 1988. reprint ed. pap. 10.95 (*0-8263-1063-X*) U of NM Pr.

Piekos, R., jt. ed. see Paruta, A. N.

***Piel.** Rebel Wind. 1995. mass mkt. 4.99 (*0-7860-0110-0*, Pinnacle NY) Windsor NY.

Piel Cook, Ellen. Psychological Androgyny. (General Psychology Ser.: No. 133). 256p. 1985. pap. text ed. 25.00 (*0-08-031612-3*, Pergamon Pr) Elsevier.

Piel, Gerard. Only One World: Ours to Make & to Keep. 1995. text ed. write for info. (*0-7167-2316-6*) W H Freeman.

***Piel, Stobie.** Rebel Wind. 416p. 1995. pap. 4.99 (*0-8217-0110-X*) Zebra.

Piele, Philip K. The Politics of Technology Utilization: From Microcomputers to Distance Learning. (Trends & Issues Ser.). vi, 14p. (Orig.). 1989. 6.00 (*0-86552-100-X*) U of Oreg ERIC.

Piele, Philip K., ed. Yearbook of School Law 1975. 1975. 8.95 (*1-56534-046-9*) NOLPE.
— Yearbook of School Law 1977. 1977. 8.95 (*1-56534-045-0*) NOLPE.
— Yearbook of School Law 1978. 1978. 8.95 (*1-56534-044-2*) NOLPE.
— Yearbook of School Law 1979. 1979. 9.95 (*1-56534-043-4*) NOLPE.
— Yearbook of School Law 1980. 1980. 10.95 (*1-56534-042-6*) NOLPE.
— Yearbook of School Law, 1981. 1981. 11.95 (*1-56534-041-8*) NOLPE.
— Yearbook of School Law, 1983. 1983. 13.95 (*1-56534-040-X*) NOLPE.
— Yearbook of School Law, 1984. 1985. 14.95 (*1-56534-039-6*) NOLPE.

Piele, Philip K., jt. ed. see Smith, Stuart C.

Piele, Phillip K., jt. auth. see Farquhar, Robin H.

Pielke, R. A., ed. see Beniston, M.

Pielke, Robert G. Critiquing Moral Arguments. 56p. (C). 1992. pap. text ed. 8.75 (*0-8191-8643-0*) U Pr of Amer.
— Critiquing Moral Arguments. 56p. 1992. lib. bdg. 26.50 (*0-8191-8642-2*) U Pr of Amer.
— Hitler the Cat Goes West. 152p. (Orig.). 1995. pap. 8.00 (*1-56002-452-6*, Univ Edtns) Aegina Pr.
— You Say You Want a Revolution: Rock Music in American Culture. LC 85-25940. 270p. 1986. pap. 19.95 (*0-8304-1201-8*) Nelson-Hall.

Pielke, Roger A. The Hurricane. (Illus.). 192p. 1990. 59.95 (*0-415-03705-0*, A4667) Routledge.
— Mesoscale Meteorological Modeling: An Introductory Survey. LC 83-11757. 1984. text ed. 97.00 (*0-12-554820-6*) Acad Pr.

***Pielke, Roger A. & Pearce, Robert P.** Mesoscale Modeling of the Atmosphere. (Meteorological Monographs: Vol. 25, No. 47). 1994. 65.00 (*1-878220-15-2*) Am Meteorological.

Pielke, Roger A., jt. auth. see Cotton, William R.

Pielmeier, John. Haunted Lives: Three Related Short Plays. 1984. pap. 4.75 (*0-8222-0503-3*) Dramatists Play.
— Impassioned Embraces. 1989. pap. 4.75 (*0-8222-0556-4*) Dramatists Play.

Pielou, E. C. After the Ice Age: The Return of Life to Glaciated North America. LC 90-11024. (Illus.). 368p. 1991. 24.95 (*0-226-66811-8*) U Ch Pr.
— After the Ice Age: The Return of Life to Glaciated North America. LC 90-11024. (Illus.). x, 366p. 1992. pap. 13.95 (*0-226-66812-6*) U Ch Pr.
— Biogeography. LC 92-7291. 366p. (C). 1992. reprint ed. lib. bdg. 49.95 (*0-89464-739-3*) Krieger.

An Asterisk (*) at the beginning of an entry indicates that the title is appearing in BIP for the first time.

— Ecological Diversity. LC 75-9663. 173p. reprint ed. pap. 49.40 (*0-317-55608-8*, 2056349) Bks Demand.
— The Interpretation of Ecological Data: Primer on Classification & Ordination. LC 84-7284. 263p. 1984. text ed. 64.95 (*0-471-88950-4*, Wiley-Interscience) Wiley.
— A Naturalist's Guide to the Arctic. LC 94-2555. 1994. lib. bdg. 57.00 (*0-226-66813-4*) U Ch Pr.
— A Naturalist's Guide to the Arctic. LC 94-2555. 1994. pap. 19.95 (*0-226-66814-2*) U Ch Pr.
— Population & Community Ecology: Principles & Methods. LC 72-86334. (Illus.). 432p. 1974. text ed. 139.00 (*0-677-03580-2*) Gordon & Breach.
— The World of Northern Evergreens. (Illus.). 200p. 1988. 39.95 (*0-8014-2116-0*); pap. 14.95 (*0-8014-9424-9*) Cornell U Pr.

Piemonte, Charles, jt. auth. see Lawrence, Marcia.

Piemonte, G., et al, eds. Developments in Analytical Methods in Pharmaceutical, Biomedical, & Forensic Sciences. LC 87-7180. 340p. 1988. 85.00 (*0-306-42695-1*, Plenum Pr) Plenum.

Piemontes, Grayce. Classic Shirley Temple-Paperdolls. (J). 1989. pap. 3.95 (*0-486-25193-4*) Dover.

Piemontese, Allesio. The Thyrde & Last Parte of the Secretes of Maister Alexis of Piemont. Warde, W., tr. LC 77-6844. (English Experience Ser.: No. 840). 1977. reprint ed. lib. bdg. 17.50 (*90-221-0840-6*) Walter J Johnson.

Pienaar, Kristo, jt. auth. see Johnson-Barker, Carole.

Pienciak, Richard T. Deadly Masquerade: A True Story of High Living, Depravity & Murder. (Signet True-Crime Ser.). 352p. 1991. pap. 5.99 (*0-451-17033-4*, Sig) NAL-Dutton.
— Murder at 75 Birch. 1993. pap. 5.99 (*0-451-40397-5*, Sig) NAL-Dutton.

Piene, Otto & Goldring, Elizabeth, eds. Centerbeam. (Illus.). 144p. (Orig.). 1981. pap. 17.50 (*0-262-66047-4*) MIT Pr.

Piene, Otto, ed. see Philadelphia Institute of Contemporary Art Staff.

Pienemann, Manfred, jt. ed. see Hyltenstam, Kenneth.

Pienkos, Angela. The Imperfect Autocrat: Grand Duke Constantine Pavlovich & the Polish Congress Kingdom. 224p. 1987. text ed. 36.00 (*0-88033-113-5*, 217) East Eur Quarterly.

Pienkos, Donald E. For Your Freedom Through Ours. 400p. 1992. text ed. 56.00 (*0-88033-208-5*) Col U Pr.
— One Hundred Years Young: A History of the Polish Falcons of America, 1887-1987. (East European Monographs: No. 231). 450p. 1987. text ed. 60.00 (*0-88033-128-3*) East Eur Quarterly.
— PNA: A Centennial History of the Polish National Alliance of the U. S. A. 485p. 1984. text ed. 54.00 (*0-88033-060-0*) East Eur Quarterly.

***Pienkowski.** A to Z Sticker Book. 1995. 6.99 (*0-679-87064-4*) Random.
— 1001 Words. 1995. 15.00 (*0-679-87006-7*) Random.

Pienkowski, Jan. ABC. (Illus.). (J). (ps). 1989. 2.95 (*0-671-68133-8*, Litl Simon S&S) S&S Childrens.
— Bronto's Brunch. (Introducing Furrytails Ser.). (J). (ps). 1995. 19.99 (*0-525-45354-7*) Dutton Child Bks.
— Casa Embrujada. (Illus.). 12p. (SPA.). (J). (ps-6). 1992. 14.95 (*0-525-45002-5*, DCB) Dutton Child Bks.
— Colors. (Nursery Board Bks.). (Illus.). 14p. (J). (ps). 1989. 2.95 (*0-671-68134-6*, Litl Simon S&S) S&S Childrens.
— Dinnertime. (Pienkowski Minipops Ser.). (Illus.). 10p. (J). (ps up). 1991. 4.95 (*0-8431-2963-8*); pap. 9.95 (*0-8431-0961-0*) Price Stern.
— Door Bell. (Pienkowski Pop-up Sound Ser.). (Illus.). 10p. (J). (ps up). 1992. 13.95 (*0-8431-3452-6*) Price Stern.
— Faces. (Nursery Board Bks.). (Illus.). 24p. (J). (ps-00). 1991. pap. 2.95 (*0-671-72846-6*, Litl Simon S&S) S&S Childrens.
— Farm. (Nursery Board Bks.). 14p. (J). 1990. pap. 2.95 (*0-671-70476-1*, S&S Bks Young Read) S&S Childrens.
— Farm. (Illus.). 32p. (J). (ps-1). 1985. 13.95 (*0-434-95651-1*, Pub. by W Heinemann Ltd) Trafalgar.
— Ferme. (Folio Ser.). (FRE.). (J). 5.95 (*2-07-056307-3*) Schoenhof.
— Food. (Nursery Board Bks.). (Illus.). 24p. (J). (ps-00). 1991. pap. 2.95 (*0-671-72845-8*, Litl Simon S&S) S&S Childrens.
— Good Night, Moo! (Introducing Furrytails Ser.). (J). (ps). 1995. 19.99 (*0-525-45355-5*) Dutton Child Bks.
— The Haunted House. (Illus.). 12p. (J). (ps up). 1979. 14.95 (*0-525-31520-9*, DCB) Dutton Child Bks.
— Homes. (Nursery Board Bks.). 14p. (J). (ps). 1990. pap. 2.95 (*0-671-70478-8*, Litl Simon S&S) S&S Childrens.
— Little Monsters. (Pienkowski Pop-up Ser.). (Illus.). 10p. (J). (ps up). 1986. 9.95 (*0-8431-1241-7*) Price Stern.
— Little Monsters. (Pienkowski Minipop Ser.). (Illus.). 10p. (J). (ps up). 1991. 4.95 (*0-8431-2964-6*) Price Stern.
— Oh My, a Fly! (Pienkowski Pop-up Ser.). (Illus.). 10p. (J). (ps up). 1989. 9.95 (*0-8431-2765-1*) Price Stern.
— Oh My, a Fly! (Pienkowski Minipop Ser.). (Illus.). 10p. (J). (ps up). 1991. 4.95 (*0-8431-2965-4*) Price Stern.
— One Two Three. (Nursery Board Bks.). (Illus.). 14p. (J). (ps). 1989. 2.95 (*0-671-68136-2*) S&S Trade.
— Pets. (Illus.). 24p. (J). (ps). 1992. pap. 2.95 (*0-671-74518-2*, Litl Simon S&S) S&S Childrens.
— Phone Book. (Pienkowski Pop-up Sound Ser.). (Illus.). 10p. (J). (ps up). 1991. 13.95 (*0-8431-2967-0*) Price Stern.
— Road Hog. (Pienkowski Pop-up Sound Ser.). (Illus.). 10p. (J). (ps up). 1993. 13.95 (*0-8431-3586-7*) Price Stern.
— Shapes. (Nursery Board Bks.). (Illus.). (J). (ps). 1989. 2.95 (*0-671-68135-4*, Litl Simon S&S) S&S Childrens.
— Sizes. (Nursery Board Bks.). (Illus.). 24p. (J). (ps-00). 1991. pap. 2.95 (*0-671-72844-X*, Litl Simon S&S) S&S Childrens.
— Small Talk. (Pop-up Ser.). (Illus.). 10p. (J). (ps up). 1983. 9.95 (*0-8431-0982-3*) Price Stern.
— Small Talk. (Pienkowski Minipop Ser.). (Illus.). 10p. (J). (ps up). 1991. 4.95 (*0-8431-2966-2*) Price Stern.
— Stop Go. (Illus.). 24p. (J). (ps). 1992. pap. 2.95 (*0-671-74519-0*, Litl Simon S&S) S&S Childrens.
— Time. (Nursery Board Bks.). (Illus.). 24p. (J). (ps-00). 1991. pap. 2.95 (*0-671-72847-4*, Litl Simon S&S) S&S Childrens.
— The Toilet Book: Don't Forget to Flush! (Pienkowski Pop-up Sound Ser.). (Illus.). 12p. (J). (ps-3). 1981. 15.95 (*0-8431-3749-5*) Price Stern.
— Weather - Nursery Board Book. (J). (ps). 1990. pap. 2.95 (*0-671-70479-6*, Litl Simon S&S) S&S Childrens.
— Wheels. (Illus.). 24p. (J). (ps). 1992. pap. 2.95 (*0-671-74517-4*, Litl Simon S&S) S&S Childrens.
— Yes No. (Illus.). 24p. (J). (ps). 1992. pap. 2.95 (*0-671-74520-4*, Litl Simon S&S) S&S Childrens.
— Zoo. (Illus.). 32p. (J). (ps-1). 1985. 13.95 (*0-434-95652-X*, Pub. by W Heinemann Ltd) Trafalgar.
— Zoo - Nursery Board Book. (J). (ps). 1990. pap. 2.95 (*0-671-70477-X*, Litl Simon S&S) S&S Childrens.

Pienkowski, Jan, illus. ABC Dinosaurs: And Other Prehistoric Creatures. 10p. (J). (ps-00). 1993. 18.99 (*0-525-67468-3*, Lodestar Bks) Dutton Child Bks.
— Christmas: King James Version. LC 84-5719. 32p. (J). (gr. 1 up). 1984. reprint ed. 18.95 (*0-394-86923-0*) Knopf Bks Yng Read.

Pienkowski, Jan, jt. auth. see Nicoll, Helen.

***Pienta, Norbert J.** Organic Chemistry Toolbox & Study Guide. 5th ed. 256p. 1995. disk 32.95 (*0-534-24901-9*) Brooks-Cole.

Piepenbrink, Arthur. In the Image of God. LC 92-31645. (Illus.). 96p. 1993. pap. 9.95 (*0-942963-28-8*) Distinctive Pub.

Piepenbrink, Linda, ed. The Best of Country Cooking. LC 93-83133. 292p. 1993. 24.98 (*0-89821-106-9*) Reiman Pubns.
— Christmas Country Style. LC 91-62465. 98p. 1991. 14.98 (*0-89821-096-8*) Reiman Pubns.
— A Christmas to Remember. LC 92-60714. 100p. 1992. 14.98 (*0-89821-100-X*) Reiman Pubns.
— Country Ground Beef. LC 93-83939. 100p. 1993. 9.98 (*0-89821-104-2*) Reiman Pubns.
— Country Information. LC 92-63184. 148p. 1993. 8.98 (*0-89821-103-4*) Reiman Pubns.
— God's Country. LC 92-60713. 100p. 1992. 14.98 (*0-89821-101-8*) Reiman Pubns.
— Grandma's Great Desserts. LC 91-68553. 98p. 1992. 10.98 (*0-89821-097-6*) Reiman Pubns.
— Sweet & Scrumptious Chocolate. LC 92-63183. 52p. 1993. 4.98 (*0-89821-102-6*) Reiman Pubns.
— Taste of the Country Five. LC 92-60968. 99p. 1992. 9.98 (*0-89821-098-4*) Reiman Pubns.
— A Taste of the Country Four. LC 91-62226. 99p. 1991. 9.98 (*0-89821-094-1*) Reiman Pubns.
— A Year in the Country Four. LC 91-62330. 98p. 1991. 14.98 (*0-89821-095-X*) Reiman Pubns.
— Year in the Country Three. 98p. 1990. 14.98 (*0-89821-092-5*) Reiman Pubns.

Piepenbrink, Linda, jt. ed. see Mack, Nancy.

***Piepenburg, Robert.** Raku Pottery. rev. ed. (Illus.). 160p. 1994. pap. 26.95 (*0-9628481-1-5*) Pebble Pr.

Piepenburg, Scott. Easy Marc: Pre-Format Integration. 175p. 1994. pap. text ed. 25.00 (*0-931510-51-1*) Hi Willow.

Pieper, August. Isaiah II. 1980. 24.50 (*0-8100-0109-8*, 15N0357) Northwest Pub.

Pieper, Elizabeth. Sticks & Stones Book. 1976. 4.50 (*0-937540-06-4*, HPP-8) Human Policy Pr.

Pieper, Francis. Christian Dogmatics, 4 Vols, 1. Engelder, Theodore et al, trs. 1957. 19.95 (*0-570-06712-X*, 15-1001) Concordia.
— Christian Dogmatics, 4 Vols, 2. Engelder, Theodore et al, trs. 1957. 19.95 (*0-570-06713-8*, 15-1002) Concordia.
— Christian Dogmatics, 4 Vols, 3. Engelder, Theodore et al, trs. 1957. 19.95 (*0-570-06714-6*, 15-1003) Concordia.
— Christian Dogmatics, 4 Vols., Set. Engelder, Theodore et al, trs. 1957. 87.99 (*0-570-06715-4*, 15-1852) Concordia.
— Christian Dogmatics, 4 Vols, Vol. 4. Engelder, Theodore et al, trs. 1957. 28.99 (*0-570-06711-1*, 15-1000) Concordia.

Pieper, H. Variationen uber ein Zahlenthroretisches Them von Carl Friedrich Gauss. (Science & Civilization Ser.: No. 33). 160p. (GER.). 1980. 20.00 (*0-8176-0959-8*) Birkhauser.

Pieper, Irene T. My Culinary Journey. (Illus.). 168p. 1993. 19.93 (*0-9638234-0-X*) I K Pieper.

Pieper, Jeanne. The Catholic Woman: Difficult Choices in a Modern World. 272p. 1993. 23.95 (*1-56565-081-6*, Woman-Woman) Lowell Hse.
— The Catholic Woman: Difficult Choices in a Modern World. 264p. 1994. pap. 13.95 (*1-56565-157-X*) Lowell Hse.
— A Special Place for Santa: A Legend for Our Time. (Illus.). 1991. write for info. (*0-9616286-1-8*) Kneeling Santa.

Pieper, Josef. Abuse of Language, Abuse of Power. Krauth, Lothar, tr. LC 90-85240. 54p. (Orig.). 1992. pap. 5.95 (*0-89870-362-X*) Ignatius Pr.
— Belief & Faith: A Philosophical Tract. Winston, Richard & Winston, Clara, trs. LC 75-31841. 106p. 1975. reprint ed. text ed. 39.75 (*0-8371-8490-8*, PIBF, Greenwood Pr) Greenwood.
— A Brief Reader on the Virtues of the Human Heart. Krauth, Lothar, tr. LC 90-81767. 54p. 1991. pap. 5.95 (*0-89870-303-4*) Ignatius Pr.
— Four Cardinal Virtues. LC 65-14713. 1966. pap. 8.95 (*0-268-00103-0*) U of Notre Dame Pr.
— Guide to St. Thomas. LC 90-86251. 192p. 1991. reprint ed. pap. 14.95 (*0-89870-319-0*) Ignatius Pr.
— Hope & History. 112p. (Orig.). 1994. pap. 9.95 (*0-89870-465-0*) Ignatius Pr.
— In Defense of Philosophy. Krauth, Lothar, tr. LC 91-76072. 128p. (Orig.). 1992. pap. 9.95 (*0-89870-397-2*) Ignatius Pr.
— In Search of the Sacred: Contributions to an Answer. Krauth, Lothar, tr. LC 90-81770. 136p. (Orig.). 1991. pap. 9.95 (*0-89870-301-8*) Ignatius Pr.
— Josef Pieper: An Anthology. LC 88-83748. 255p. (Orig.). 1989. pap. 14.95 (*0-89870-226-7*) Ignatius Pr.
— Leisure: The Basis of Culture. 1964. pap. 2.50 (*0-451-62469-6*, ME2226, Ment) NAL-Dutton.
— Living the Truth. Krauth, Lothar & Lange, Stella, trs. LC 89-84891. 190p. (Orig.). 1989. reprint ed. pap. text ed. 12.95 (*0-89870-261-5*) Ignatius Pr.
— Only the Lover Sings: Art & Contemplation. Krauth, Lothar, tr. LC 90-81771. 76p. (Orig.). 1990. pap. 6.95 (*0-89870-302-6*) Ignatius Pr.
— Problems of Modern Faith: Essays & Addresses. Van Heurck, Jan, tr. 1983. 7.49 (*0-8199-0856-8*, Frncscn Herld) Franciscan Pr.
— What Is a Feast? 66p. (C). 1987. lib. bdg. 16.00 (*0-921075-04-9*) N Waterloo Acad Pr.

Pieper, Josef & Raskop, Heinrich. What Catholics Believe: A Primer of the Catholic Faith. Van Heurck, Jan, tr. LC 82-1411. 116p. 1983. 8.50 (*0-8199-0796-0*, Frncscn Herld) Franciscan Pr.

Pieper, Martha H. & Pieper, William J. Intrapsychic Humanism: An Introduction to a Comprehensive Psychology & Philosophy of Mind. 402p. 1990. 47.50 (*0-9624919-0-X*) Falcon Two Pr.

Pieper, Richard R. TeamPower. LC 88-92255. 70p. (Orig.). (C). 1989. pap. 30.00 (*0-9621149-0-1*) PPC Inc.

***Pieper, Rudiger.** Lexikon Management. 418p. (GER.). 1992. 105.00 (*0-7859-8338-4*, 3409132147) Fr & Eur.

Pieper, Rudiger, ed. Human Resource Management: An International Comparison. (Studies in Organization: No. 26). (Illus.). xii, 285p. (C). 1990. lib. bdg. 54.95 (*3-11-012573-0*) De Gruyter.

Pieper, Thomas I. & Gidney, James B. Fort Laurens, 1778-79: The Revolutionary War in Ohio. LC 75-44712. 128p. 1980. pap. 8.50 (*0-87338-240-4*) Kent St U Pr.

Pieper, Ursula & Stickel, Gerhard. Studia Linguistica Diachronica et Synchronica. 988p. 1985. text ed. 292.30 (*3-11-009664-1*) Mouton.

Pieper, William J., jt. auth. see Pieper, Martha H.

Pieperl, Laurence. Current Clinical Strategies, Handbook of HIV-AIDS Therapy. Chan, Paul D., ed. (Current Clinical Strategies Ser.). 83p. (Orig.). 1992. pap. text ed. 6.50 (*1-881528-01-4*) Current Clin Strat.

Piepers, G. G., ed. Advances in Wind Farming: Proceedings of the International Conference, 13-16 Oct., 1987, Leeuwarden, the Netherlands. 476p. 1988. 138.50 (*0-444-42952-2*) Elsevier.

Piepho, Lee, tr. see Mantuanus, Baptista.

Piepkorn, Arthur C. The Church: Selected Writings of Arthur Carl Piepkorn. Plekon, Michael P. & Wiecher, William S., eds. 304p. (Orig.). (C). Date not set. pap. text ed. 12.00 (*0-9633142-2-X*) Am Luth Pub Bur.
— Profiles in Belief, Vol. 2: Protestantism. LC 76-9971. 1978. 30.00 (*0-06-066582-3*) Harper SF.

Piepmeier, Joseph M., ed. The Outcome Following Traumatic Spinal Cord Injury. (Illus.). 216p. 1992. 42.00 (*0-87993-510-3*) Futura Pub.

Pieprzyk, Josef & Sadeghiyan, Babak. Design of Hashing Algorithms. LC 93-41251. 1994. 39.00 (*0-387-57500-6*) Spr-Verlag.

Pier, A., ed. see Goetz, Friedrich, et al.

Pier, Arthur S. & Forbes, W. Cameron. American Apostles to the Philippines. LC 74-160926. (Biography Index Reprint Ser.). 1977. reprint ed. 20.95 (*0-8369-8089-1*) Ayer.

Pier, J. P., jt. ed. see Eymard, P.

Pierangelo, Roger. Raising Them Right: Three Hundred & One Ways to Be a Loving Parent. 1994. pap. 5.99 (*1-56171-323-6*, S P I Bks) Sure Sellers.
— A Survival Kit for the Special Education Teacher. LC 93-44763. 1994. pap. 29.95 (*0-87628-870-0*) Ctr Appl Res.
— The World's Most Provocative Questions: Rarely Discussed in Public But on Everyone's Mind. 1994. pap. 4.99 (*1-56171-310-4*, S P I Bks) Sure Sellers.

Pieraut-Le Bonniec, Gilberte & Dolitsky, Marlene, eds. Language Bases...Discourse Bases: Some Aspects of Contemporary French-Language Psycholinguistics Research. LC 91-6685. (Pragmatics & Beyond New Ser.: No. 17). viii, 260p. 1991. 59.00x (*1-55619-283-5*) Benjamins North Am.

***Pierce.** Chicken Parts. write for info. (*0-517-70135-9*) Random Hse Value.
— Iron in the Pines. 1980. pap. 13.95 (*0-8135-0267-5*) Rutgers U Pr.

Pierce & Moss. Economics: Study Guide. (C). 1985. write for info. (*0-201-08046-X*) Addison-Wesley.

Pierce, Albert. Scuba Life Saving. LC 86-10308. (Illus.). 192p. 1985. reprint ed. pap. 19.00 (*0-88011-279-4*, PPIE0279) Human Kinetics.

Pierce, Albort F. A History of the Gurnet, Saquish & Clark's Island. (Pilgrim Society Notes Ser.: No. 19). 1969. 2.00 (*0-940628-21-X*) Pilgrim Soc.

Pierce, Alexandra & Pierce, Roger. Expressive Movement: Posture & Action in Daily Life, Sports, & the Performing Arts. (Illus.). 235p. 1989. 19.95 (*0-306-43269-2*, Plenum Insight) Plenum.
— Generous Movement: A Practical Guide to Balance in Action. (Illus.). 171p. (Orig.). 1991. pap. 18.00 (*1-879970-00-7*) Ctr Balance Pr.

Pierce, Alfred R. It Is Finished. rev. ed. 212p. 1993. pap. 14.95 (*0-9641993-0-0*) Radiant Pubns.

Pierce, Allan D. Acoustics: An Introduction to Its Physical Principles & Applications. LC 89-80362. 678p. 1989. pap. 30.00 (*0-88318-612-8*) Acoustical Soc Am.

Pierce, Allan D. & Thurston, Robert N., eds. Physical Acoustics: Underwater Scattering & Radiation, Vol. 22. (Illus.). 384p. 1992. text ed. 99.00 (*0-12-477922-0*) Acad Pr.

Pierce, Allan D., jt. ed. see Thurston, Robert N.

Pierce, Amy E. Language Acquisition & Syntactic Theory: A Comparative Analysis of French & English Child Grammars. 184p. (C). 1992. lib. bdg. 87.50 (*0-7923-1553-7*) Kluwer Ac.

***Pierce, Ann, ed.** 1995 Florida Statistical Abstract. 760p. 1995. lib. bdg. 44.95 (*0-8130-1375-5*); pap. 29.95 (*0-8130-1376-3*) U Press Fla.

Pierce, Ann C., ed. see Sherkyen, Anne H.

Pierce, Anne M. So Many Gifts. (Illus.). (J). (gr. k-6). 1992. audio 8.00 (*0-9623937-1-1*) Forword MN.
— So Many Gifts. (Illus.). 32p. (J). (gr. k-6). 1993. reprint ed. 15.95 (*0-9623937-0-3*) Forword MN.
— So Many Gifts, Miniature edition. (Illus.). 32p. (J). (gr. k-6). 1994. 7.95 (*0-9623937-2-X*) Forword MN.

Pierce, Anne W. Galaxy Girls: Wonder Women Short Stories. LC 93-8411. 1993. pap. 12.95 (*0-9627460-9-6*) Helicon Nine Eds.

***Pierce, AnneMarie.** Pieces of Me. (Illus.). (J). (gr. 1-9). Date not set. write for info. (*0-9623937-3-8*) Forword MN.

Pierce, Arthur & Billips, Connie. Lux Presents Hollywood: A Show-by-Show History of the Lux Radio Theater & the Lux Video Theater, 1934-1959. 740p. 1995. lib. bdg. 85.00 (*0-89950-938-X*) McFarland & Co.

Pierce, Arthur & Swarthout, Douglas. Jean Arthur: A Bio-Bibliography. LC 90-3316. (Bio-Bibliographies in the Performing Arts Ser.: No. 15). 288p. 1990. text ed. 39.95 (*0-313-26699-9*, PJA/, Greenwood Pr) Greenwood.

Pierce, Arthur D. Smugglers Woods. 322p. (C). 1984. reprint ed. pap. 13.95 (*0-8135-0444-9*) Rutgers U Pr.

Pierce Atwood Environmental Department Staff, et al. Maine Environmental & Land Use Statutes Deskbook, 1994. 670p. 1994. 67.50 (*1-56257-346-2*) Butterworth Legal Pubs.
— Maine Environmental & Land Use Statutes Deskbook 1995. Ahrens, Philip F., ed. 670p. 1994. pap. 70.00 (*0-88063-755-2*) Michie Butterworth.

***Pierce, B. Dean.** Reclaim Your Destiny: How to Find Health, Passion & Happiness. Billac, Pete, ed. 176p. (Orig.). 1994. pap. 9.95 (*0-943629-14-4*) Swan Pub.

***Pierce, Barbara, ed. & pref.** The World Under My Fingers: Personal Reflections on Braille. (Illus.). 150p. (Orig.). (C). 1995. pap. text ed. 3.00 (*1-885218-01-X*) Natl Fed Blind.

Pierce, Ben, jt. auth. see Russell, Peter J.

Pierce, Benjamin A. Family Genetic Sourcebook. 340p. 1990. text ed. 14.95 (*0-471-61709-1*) Wiley.

Pierce, Benjamin C. Basic Category Theory for Computer Science. 128p. 1991. pap. 22.00 (*0-262-66071-7*) MIT Pr.

Pierce, Bern D., ed. History of Trempealeau County, Wisconsin. (Illus.). 922p. 1993. reprint ed. lib. bdg. 92.00 (*0-8328-3509-9*) Higginson Bk Co.

Pierce, Bessie L. Civic Attitudes in American School Textbooks. LC 76-165727. (American Education, Ser, No. 2). 1972. reprint ed. 18.95 (*0-405-03716-3*) Ayer.
— Public Opinion & the Teaching of History in the United States. LC 71-107416. (Civil Liberties in American History Ser.). 1970. reprint ed. lib. bdg. 45.00 (*0-306-71883-9*) Da Capo.

Pierce, Bob, ed. Pierce Piano Atlas. 9th enl. rev. ed. LC 65-2545. (Illus.). 416p. (Orig.). Date not set. pap. 17.95 (*0-911138-02-1*) Pierce Piano.

Pierce, Brenda H. Creative Art Picture Starters: General Subjects - Level I. (Illus.). 32p. 1988. teacher ed 3.95 (*0-922694-02-8*) Moons Creat Prods.
— Creative Art Picture Starters: General Subjects - Level II. (Illus.). 32p. (J). (gr. 4-6). 1988. teacher ed 3.95 (*0-922694-03-6*) Moons Creat Prods.
— Creative Art Picture Starters: Landscapes - Level I. (Illus.). 32p. 1988. teacher ed 3.95 (*0-922694-00-1*) Moons Creat Prods.
— Creative Art Picture Starters: Landscapes - Level II. (Illus.). 32p. 1988. teacher ed 3.95 (*0-922694-01-X*) Moons Creat Prods.

***Pierce, Burton W.** Our Glorious Tomorrow. 207p. (Orig.). 1991. pap. 7.95 (*0-9628973-0-2*) Daybreak Pubs.

Pierce, Carl W., et al, eds. Ir Genes: Past, Present, & Future. LC 82-4291. (Experimental Biology & Medicine Ser.). (Illus.). 640p. 1983. 89.50 (*0-89603-050-4*) Humana.

Pierce, Carol & Page, Bill. A Male-Female Continuum: Paths to Colleagueship. 38p. 1986. 8.00 (*0-317-91207-0*) New Dynam Pubns.

Pierce, Carol, jt. auth. see Wishik, Heather.

Pierce, Carol, et al. A Male - Female Continuum: Paths to Colleagueship. 2nd ed. LC 88-92431. (Illus.). 82p. 1994. pap. 12.95 (*0-929767-02-0*) New Dynam Pubns.

Pierce, Carol J. Power Equity & Groups: A Manual for Understanding Equity & Acknowledging Diversity. 118p. 1986. 14.00 (*0-317-91208-9*) New Dynam Pubns.
— The Stages of Awareness for Women & Men Moving Away from Role Stereotyping. rev. ed. 30p. 1983. 7.00 (*0-317-91210-0*) New Dynam Pubns.

Pierce, Carolyn B. Shadows of Love. LC 85-90440. (Illus.). 75p. 1985. 6.95 (*0-9615667-0-1*) Starlight Pubns.

Pierce, Catherine D. Christmas Thief. (Illus.). (Orig.). (J). (ps-00). 1988. pap. text ed. 4.50 (*0-9621397-0-X*) C D Pierce.
— Mrs. Mouse Is Safe. (Illus.). 18p. 1983. 3.25 (*0-933829-06-X*) Ponce Pr.

Pierce, Catherine S., jt. auth. see Cuca, Roberto.

Pierce, Cecil E. Fifty Years a Planemaker & User. LC 92-60195. (Illus.). 80p. 1992. 22.95 (*0-9628001-1-2*) Monmouth Pr.

P Q

Pierce, Charles. Southern Light Cooking: Easy, Healthy, Low-Calorie Recipes from BBQ to Bourbon Peach Shortcake. 192p. 1993. bds. 15.95 (0-399-51808-8, Perigree Bks) Berkley Pub.

— Three Hundred Sixty-Five Ways to Cook Fish & Shellfish. LC 92-54737. (Three Hundred Sixty-Five Ways Ser.). 256p. 1993. 17.95 (0-06-016841-2, HarpT) HarpC.

Pierce, Charles L., ed. The New Settlement Cookbook: The First Collection of American Ethnic Recipes. rev. ed. (Illus.). 640p. 1991. 25.00 (0-671-69336-0) S&S Trade.

Pierce, Charles W. Pioneer Life in Southeast Florida. Curl, Donald W., ed. LC 70-122290. 1981. 13.95 (0-87024-304-7) U of Miami Pr.

Pierce, Chester M., ed. Capital Punishment in the United States. LC 76-5828. (Studies in Modern Society: Political & Social Issues: No. 10). lib. bdg. 42.50 (0-404-10325-1) AMS Pr.

— Television & Education. LC 77-94473. (Sage Contemporary Social Science Issues Ser.: No. 44). 104p. reprint ed. pap. 29.70 (0-317-08983-8, 2021940) Bks Demand.

Pierce, Christine. How to Solve: The Lockheed Case. (Original Papers: No. 5). 50p. (Orig.). 1986. pap. 4.00 (0-912051-11-6) Soc Phil Pol.

Pierce, Christine & Van De Veer, Donald. People, Penguins, & Plastic Trees: Basic Issues in Environmental Ethics. 2nd ed. LC 94-13151. 485p. 1995. pap. 32.95 (0-534-17922-3) Intl Thomson.

Pierce, Christine & VanDeVeer, Donald, eds. AIDS: Ethics & Public Policy. 241p. (C). 1988. pap. 19.95 (0-534-08286-6) Intl Thomson.

Pierce, Christine, jt. auth. see VanDeVeer, Donald.

Pierce, Christine, jt. ed. see VanDeVeer, Donald.

Pierce, Christopher & Chapin, Nicholas. Archaeological Investigations for the West Sinter Project, Southern Cortez Mountains, Eureka County, Nevada. (Social Sciences Center Technical Report Ser.: No. 54). (Illus.). 51p. (Orig.). (C). 1987. pap. 5.00 (0-945920-54-7) Desert Rsch Inst.

Pierce, Christopher, jt. auth. see Livingston, Stephanie D.

Pierce, Clayton C. CryptoPrivacy: A Cryptographer's Manual. LC 89-91620. (Illus.). 139p. 1989. lib. bdg. 19.95 (0-9601564-4-5); pap. 16.95 (0-9601564-5-3) C C Pierce.

— CryptoPrivacy: A Cryptographer's Manual. 2nd rev. ed. (Illus.). 128p. (C). 1992. lib. bdg. 34.95 (0-9601564-6-1) C C Pierce.

— CryptoPrivacy: A Cryptographer's Manual on Classic Ciphers. 3rd rev. ed. LC 89-91620. (Illus.). 130p. 1994. lib. bdg. 39.95 (0-9601564-9-6) C C Pierce.

Pierce, Constance. Philippe at His Bath. 26p. (Orig.). 1983. pap. 5.00 (0-938566-17-2) Adastra Pr.

— When Things Get Back to Normal. LC 86-27870. 256p. 1987. 15.95 (0-932511-00-7); pap. 7.95 (0-932511-01-5) Fiction Coll.

Pierce, Constance, jt. ed. see Sloan, Kay.

Pierce, Cynthia W., jt. auth. see Guthrie, Karen M.

Pierce, Dale. Wild West Characters. LC 91-2039. (Illus.). 144p. (Orig.). 1991. pap. 6.95 (0-914846-53-1) Golden West Pub.

Pierce, David. Forever Yours. (YA). 1994. mass mkt. 3.50 (0-06-106174-3, Harp PBks) HarpC.

— James Joyce's Ireland. (Illus.). 256p. (C). 1992. text ed. 30.00 (0-300-05055-0) Yale U Pr.

— Motion Picture Copyrights & Renewals: 1950-1959. 640p. 1989. 125.00 (0-317-93475-9); pap. 89.00 (0-317-93476-7) Prelinger Assocs.

— Total Quality in Occupational Safety & Health. 300p. 1994. 39.95 (1-884015-20-4) St Lucie Pr.

— Yeats' England & Ireland. LC 95-2457. (Illus.). 1995. write for info. (0-300-06323-7) Yale U Pr.

Pierce, David & Wooding, Don. Rock Priest. (Orig.). 1993. pap. 13.95 (0-85476-412-7) Trans-Atl Phila.

Pierce, David, jt. ed. see Atwell, Robert.

Pierce, David E. Kansas Oil & Gas, Vol. II. LC 88-82765. 400p. 1989. 115.00 (0-942357-24-8) KS Bar CLE.

— Kansas Oil & Gas Handbook, Vol. I. LC 88-82765. 1986. 100.00 (0-942357-07-8) KS Bar CLE.

Pierce, David F. World Air Cargo Forecast. (Illus.). 81p. (Orig.). (C). 1992. pap. text ed. 40.00 (1-56806-133-1) Diane Pub.

— World Air Cargo Forecast, 1994. (Illus.). 74p. (Orig.). (C). 1994. pap. text ed. 65.00x (0-7881-1198-1) Diane Pub.

Pierce, David M. Angels in Heaven. 240p. 1992. 17.95 (0-89296-483-9) Mysterious Pr.

— Angels in Heaven. 208p. 1993. mass mkt. 4.99 (0-446-40163-3, Mysterious Paperbk) Warner Bks.

— Build Me a Castle. 1995. write for info. (0-89296-485-5) Mysterious Pr.

— Write Me a Letter. 272p. 1993. 18.95 (0-89296-484-7) Mysterious Pr.

Pierce, David R., Jr. Project Planning & Control for Construction. (Illus.). 275p. (C). 1988. 59.95 (0-87629-099-3, 67247) R S Means.

Pierce, Deirdre, jt. auth. see Altobello, Patricia.

Pierce, Dianne & Malmstrom, Richard, eds. The Idaho Conversion Kit. (Illus.). 12p. pap. 6.95 (0-9600776-2-6) Idaho First Natl Bank.

Pierce, Donald. Process Safety Pocket Guide. Franklin, Catherine et al, eds. (Illus.). 84p. (Orig.). 1993. pap. text ed. 41.80 (0-931690-56-0) Genium Pub.

Pierce, Donald L., Jr. One Hundred Texas Posters. (Illus.). 1985. 25.00 (0-685-12104-6) Herring Pr.

Pierce, Donna. Vivan las Fiestas. (Illus.). 64p. 1985. pap. text ed. 6.95 (0-89013-159-7) Museum NM Pr.

Pierce, Donna, ed. Cambios: The Spirit of Transformation in Spanish Colonial Art. LC 92-16521. (Illus.). 152p. 1992. 50.00 (0-8263-1408-2); pap. 29.95 (0-8263-1409-0) U of NM Pr.

Pierce, Edward L. Memoir & Letters of Charles Sumner, 4 vols., 1. LC 78-82211. (Anti-Slavery Crusade in America Ser.). 1970. reprint ed. 23.95 (0-405-00675-6) Ayer.

— Memoir & Letters of Charles Sumner, 4 vols., 2. LC 78-82211. (Anti-Slavery Crusade in America Ser.). 1970. reprint ed. 23.95 (0-405-00676-4) Ayer.

— Memoir & Letters of Charles Sumner, 4 vols., 3. LC 78-82211. (Anti-Slavery Crusade in America Ser.). 1970. reprint ed. 23.95 (0-405-00677-2) Ayer.

— Memoir & Letters of Charles Sumner, 4 vols., 4. LC 78-82211. (Anti-Slavery Crusade in America Ser.). 1970. reprint ed. 23.95 (0-405-00678-0) Ayer.

— Memoir & Letters of Charles Sumner, 4 vols., Set. LC 78-82211. (Anti-Slavery Crusade in America Ser.). 1970. reprint ed. 88.95 (0-405-00650-0) Ayer.

— Memoir & Letters of Charles Sumner, 4 vols., Set. (Black Heritage Library Collection). 1977. reprint ed. 96.95 (0-8369-8641-5) Ayer.

Pierce, Elwood W. My Life & Times. LC 90-91579. 389p. 1990. 19.50 (0-9626545-0-7) Power Pub Co.

Pierce, Enid. How Much Farther. 1993. pap. 12.95 (0-685-73047-6, 7935) CSS OH.

Pierce, F. B. Pierce Genealogy, Being the Record of the Posterity of Thomas Pierce, an Early Inhabitant of Charlestown. Pierce, F. C., ed. (Illus.). 369p. 1989. reprint ed. lib. bdg. 74.00 (0-8328-0964-0); reprint ed. pap. 66.00 (0-8328-0965-9) Higginson Bk Co.

Pierce, F. C. Batchelder, Batcheller: Descendants of Rev. Stephen Bachilar of England, a Leading Non-Conformist Who Settled in the Town of New Hampton, N. H., & Joseph, Henry, Joshua, & John Batcheller of Essex Co., Mass. (Illus.). 623p. 1988. reprint ed. lib. bdg. 103.50 (0-8328-0206-9); reprint ed. pap. 93.50 (0-8328-0207-7) Higginson Bk Co.

— The Descendants of John Whitney, Who Came from London, England to Watertown, Massachusetts, in 1635. (Illus.). 692p. 1989. reprint ed. lib. bdg. 95.00 (0-8328-1260-9); reprint ed. pap. 85.00 (0-8328-1261-7) Higginson Bk Co.

— Field Genealogy: Being the Record of All of the Field Family in America Whose Ancestors Were in This Country, 2 vols., Set. (Illus.). 1196p. 1989. reprint ed. lib. bdg. 189.00 (0-8328-0544-0); reprint ed. pap. 179.00 (0-8328-0545-9) Higginson Bk Co.

— Fiske & Fish Family: The Descendants of Symond Fiske, Lord of the Manor of Studhaugh, Suffolk County, England, from the Time of Henry IV to Date, Including All American Members of the Family. (Illus.). 660p. 1989. reprint ed. lib. bdg. 92.00 (0-8328-0548-3); reprint ed. pap. 82.00 (0-8328-0549-1) Higginson Bk Co.

— Foster Genealogy: A Record of the Posterity of Reginald Foster, Early Inhabitant of Ipswich & All Other American Fosters. (Illus.). 1081p. 1989. reprint ed. lib. bdg. 145.00 (0-8328-0550-5); reprint ed. pap. 135.00 (0-8328-0551-3) Higginson Bk Co.

— Pierce Genealogy, Being the Record of the Posterity of Captain Michael, John, & Captain William Pierce, Who Came to This County England, No. IV. 441p. 1989. reprint ed. lib. bdg. 74.00 (0-8328-0966-7); reprint ed. pap. 66.00 (0-8328-0967-5) Higginson Bk Co.

Pierce, F. C., ed. see Pierce, F. B.

***Pierce, F. David.** Total Quality for Safety & Health Professionals. LC 95-8268. 1995. write for info. (0-86587-462-X) Gov Insts.

Pierce, F. E., ed. see Blake, William.

Pierce, F. J., ed. Soil Management for Sustainability. (Illus.). 178p. (Orig.). (C). 1991. pap. text ed. 18.00 (0-935734-23-6) Soil & Water Conserv.

Pierce, F. T. & Womersley, J. R. Cloth Geometry. 70p. (C). 1978. pap. text ed. 90.00 (0-685-36094-6, Pub. by Textile Institue UK) St Mut.

Pierce, Franklin. Federal Usurpation. xx, 437p. 1980. reprint ed. lib. bdg. 35.00 (0-8377-1007-3) Rothman.

Pierce, Frederick C. Batchelder, Batcheller Genealogy. (Illus.). 623p. 1992. reprint ed. pap. 35.00 (1-55613-616-1) Heritage Bk.

— History of Grafton, Worcester Co., Mass., from Early Settlement by the Indians in 1647 to 1879, Including Genealogies of 79 Old Families. 623p. 1989. reprint ed. lib. bdg. 68.00 (0-8328-0827-X, MA0053) Higginson Bk Co.

Pierce, Frederick E. Currents & Eddies in the English Romantic Generation. LC 68-56470. 1972. reprint ed. 26.95 (0-405-08857-4) Ayer.

Pierce, G., ed. Developments in Industrial Microbiology, Vol. 27: Symposia of the 42nd General Meeting 1985 Boston MA. (Illus.). 183p. 1987. text ed. 110.00 (0-444-80870-1) Lubrecht & Cramer.

— Developments in Industrial Microbiology, Vol. 28: Proceedings of Symposium Held August 1986. (Illus.). 181p. 1987. text ed. 120.00 (0-945345-16-X) Lubrecht & Cramer.

— Developments in Industrial Microbiology, Vol. 29: Symposium of the 44th General Meeting 1987. (Illus.). 318p. 1988. text ed. 156.00 (0-945345-17-8) Lubrecht & Cramer.

Pierce, G. A. & Wheeler, W. A. Dickens Dictionary: A Key to the Plots-Characters in the Tales of Charles Dickens. rev. ed. 1914. 39.00 (0-527-71200-0) Periodicals Srv.

Pierce, Gail. Gourmet Meat-Less Entrees for a Month. (Illus.). 36p. (Orig.). 1983. pap. 3.95 (0-9607436-1-8) Sea-Wind Pr.

— The New Age Brown Rice Cookbook. LC 81-84830. (Illus.). 172p. (Orig.). 1982. pap. 7.95 (0-9607436-0-X) Sea-Wind Pr.

Pierce, Gary J., jt. auth. see Zander, Richard H.

Pierce, Gilbert A. The Dickens Dictionary. LC 72-3189. (Studies in Dickens: No. 52). 1972. reprint ed. lib. bdg. 75.00 (0-8383-1526-7) M S G Haskell Hse.

Pierce, Glen, ed. see Bert, Norman.

Pierce, Glen, ed. see Hostetler, Paul.

Pierce, Glen, ed. see Johns, Helen.

Pierce, Glen, ed. see Raser, Lois.

Pierce, Glen A., ed. Our Family Heritage Cookbook. LC 90-80820. 96p. 1990. ring bd. 14.95 (0-916035-39-5) Evangel Indiana.

Pierce, Glen A., ed. see Alderfer, Owen.

Pierce, Glen A., ed. see Bicksler, Harriet.

Pierce, Glen A., ed. see Book, Doyle C.

Pierce, Glen A., ed. see Buckwalter, Leoda.

Pierce, Glen A., ed. see Gaddis, Audie.

Pierce, Glen A., ed. see Johns, Helen & Leadley, Robert.

Pierce, Glen A., ed. see Johns, Helen.

Pierce, Glen A., ed. see Merritt, Bruce.

Pierce, Glen A., ed. see Zercher, David L.

Pierce, Gloria. Peripheral Visions. LC 82-80581. (Illus.). 64p. (Orig.). 1982. pap. 4.95 (0-943148-00-6) Nikki Pr.

Pierce, Grant N., et al. Heart Dysfunction in Diabetes. 256p. 1988. 191.00 (0-8493-6887-1, RC682) CRC Pr.

Pierce, Gregory F. Activism That Makes Sense: Congregations & Community Organization. LC 83-82016. 148p. (Orig.). 1984. reprint ed. pap. 8.95 (0-914070-53-3, 111) ACTA Pubns.

Pierce, Gregory F., ed. Of Human Hands: A Reader in the Spirituality of Work. LC 90-44647. (Christian at Work in the World Ser.). 123p. (Orig.). 1991. pap. 8.95 (0-87946-057-1, 120) ACTA Pubns.

— Of Human Hands: A Reader in the Spirituality of Work. LC 90-44647. (Christian at Work in the World Ser.). 128p. (Orig.). 1991. pap. 9.99 (0-8066-2504-X, 9-2504, Augsburg) Augsburg Fortress.

Pierce, Gregory F., jt. auth. see Droel, William L.

Pierce, Gregory F., jt. auth. see Konieczny, Stanley.

Pierce, Gwendolyn. Exploration into the Applicability of a Psychological Technique for Anthropological Research. 144p. 1973. pap. 4.95 (0-913244-02-3) Hapi Pr.

Pierce, H. A. Preliminary Bibliography of the Geology & Mineral Deposits of Nicaragua. 34p. (Orig.). (C). 1993. pap. text ed. 25.00 (1-56806-360-1) Diane Pub.

Pierce, Harold E., ed. Cosmetic Plastic Surgery in Non-White Patients. 260p. 1982. text ed. 63.95 (0-8089-1495-2, 793303, Grune) Saunders.

Pierce, Hazel. Philip K. Dick. Schlobin, Roger C., ed. LC 82-6005. (Starmont Reader's Guide Ser.: Vol. 12). 64p. (Orig.). 1982. 20.00 (0-916732-34-7); pap. text ed. 10.00 (0-916732-33-9) Borgo Pr.

Pierce, Hazel B. A Literary Symbiosis: Science Fiction-Fantasy Mystery. LC 83-1710. (Contributions to the Study of Science Fiction & Fantasy Ser.: No. 6). ix, 255p. 1983. text ed. 49.95 (0-313-23065-X, PLS/, Greenwood Pr) Greenwood.

Pierce, Henry B., jt. auth. see Durant, Saml. W.

Pierce, Herman & Spencer, Thel. Sheriff Takes the Stand. LC 92-19120. 1992. 12.95 (0-87714-173-8) Denlingers.

Pierce, Ian. The Holistic Approach to Cancer. 152p. (Orig.). Date not set. pap. 14.95 (0-8464-4225-6) Beekman Pubs.

— One Man's Odyssey. 296p. (Orig.). Date not set. pap. 20.95 (0-8464-4263-9) Beekman Pubs.

Pierce, J. Calvin. The Sorceress of Ambermere. 256p. (Orig.). 1993. mass mkt. 4.99 (0-441-33741-4) Ace Bks.

— Wizard of Abermere. 1993. mass mkt. 4.99 (0-441-01959-5) Ace Bks.

Pierce, J. F. Singularity Theory, Rod Theory & Symmetry-Breaking Loads. (Lecture Notes in Mathematics Ser.: Vol. 1377). iv, 177p. 1989. pap. 29.20 (0-387-51304-3) Spr-Verlag.

Pierce, J. F. & Paulus, T. J. Applied Electronics. 688p. (C). Date not set. 55.00 (1-878907-42-5) TechBooks.

Pierce, J. Kingston. San Francisco, You're History: A Chronicle of the Politicians, Proselytizers, Paramours & Performers Who Helped Create California's Wildest City. (Illus.). 320p. (Orig.). 1995. pap. 14.95 (1-57061-007-X) Sasquatch Bks.

Pierce, J. R. The Beginnings of Satellite Communications. (Illus.). 1968. write for info. (0-911302-05-0) San Francisco Pr.

— An Introduction to Information Theory: Symbols, Signals & Noise. 2nd rev. ed. 320p. 1980. reprint ed. pap. 6.95 (0-486-24061-4) Dover.

Pierce, J. Thomas. Study Guide: Fundamentals of Industrial Hygiene. (Occupational Health - Industrial Hygiene Ser.). 192p. (Orig.). 1989. student ed, pap. 15.95 (0-87912-141-6, 15136-0000) Natl Safety Coun.

Pierce, Jack. General Biology 101: Lecture & Laboratory Manual. 324p. (C). 1994. spiral bd. 22.36 (0-8403-9507-8) Kendall-Hunt.

***Pierce, James.** How to Stay Focused on God's Vision for Your Life. 15p. 1994. student ed 5.00 (1-886880-00-X) Life Changers.

Pierce, James A., jt. auth. see Anzaldua, Mike M., Jr.

Pierce, James B. Heart Healthy Magnesium: Your Nutritional Key to Cardiovascular Wellness. LC 94-805. 1994. 12.95 (0-89529-579-2) Avery Pub.

Pierce, James L. The Future of Banking. (Twentieth Century Fund Report Ser.). 192p. (C). 1991. text ed. 32.50 (0-300-05058-5) Yale U Pr.

— The Future of Banking. 192p. (C). 1993. reprint ed. pap. 13.00 (0-300-05371-1) Yale U Pr.

— Monetary & Financial Economics. 784p. (C). 1984. reprint ed. lib. bdg. 54.50 (0-471-08757-2) Krieger.

Pierce, James L., jt. auth. see Hester, Donald D.

***Pierce, James S.** From Abacus to Zeus: A Handbook of Art History. 5th ed. LC 94-37329. 224p. 1995. pap. text ed. write for info. (0-13-324914-X) P-H Gen Ref & Trav.

Pierce, Jan, ed. World Chamber of Commerce Directory, 1989. rev. ed. 362p. 1989. pap. 24.00 (0-943581-02-8) WWCCD.

— World Chamber of Commerce Directory, 1990. rev. ed. 344p. 1990. pap. 24.00 (0-943581-03-6) WWCCD.

— WorldWide Chamber of Commerce Directory: 1987 Edition. 228p. (C). 1987. pap. 22.00 (0-943581-00-1) WWCCD.

— Worldwide Chamber of Commerce Directory, 1988. rev. ed. 250p. (C). 1988. pap. 22.00 (0-943581-01-X) WWCCD.

Pierce, Jan L. & Newstrom, John W. The Manager's Bookshelf. 3rd ed. (C). 1993. 30.00 (0-06-500707-7) HarpCollege.

Pierce, Jan P. The Pilgrim Primer. 2nd ed. 32p. 1992. pap. text ed. 2.00 (0-932050-28-X) New Puritan.

— The Pioneer Primer. 80p. 1995. pap. text ed. 4.00 (0-932050-31-X) New Puritan.

— The Puritan Primer. 37p. 1986. pap. text ed. 2.00 (0-932050-29-8) New Puritan.

Pierce, Jennifer E. The Bottom Line Is Money: A Comprehensive Guide to Songwriting & the Nashville Music Industry. Miccinello, A., ed. (Illus.). 323p. 1994. 29.95 (0-933224-86-9); pap. 19.95 (0-933224-77-X) Bold Strummer Ltd.

***Pierce, Jennifer L.** Gender Trials: Emotional Lives in Contemporary Law Firms. LC 94-24940. Date not set. write for info. (0-520-20107-8); pap. write for info. (0-520-20108-6) U CA Pr.

***Pierce, Jessica.** Flashflood. (Spider's Child Ser.: No. 3). 144p. (J). (gr. 4-7). 1995. mass mkt. 3.50 (0-8217-4852-1) Zebra.

— Keeper. (Spider's Child Ser.: No. 2). 144p. 1994. mass mkt. 3.50 (0-8217-4793-2) Zebra.

— Paintball Warrior. (Spider's Child Ser.: Vol. 4). 144p. 1995. mass mkt. 3.50 (0-8217-4917-X) Zebra.

— Puzzle. (Spider's Child Ser.: No. 5). 144p. 1995. mass mkt. 3.50 (0-8217-4985-4) Windsor NY.

— Someone's Watching. 224p. 1994. pap. 3.50 (0-8217-4579-4) Zebra.

— Trapped. (Spider's Child Ser.: Vol. 1). 144p. 1994. pap. 3.50 (0-8217-4736-3) Zebra.

— Wanted to Rent. (Scream Ser.: No. 3). 224p. 1993. mass mkt. 3.50 (0-8217-4357-0) Zebra.

Pierce, Joe E. Because of August. LC 81-81920. 200p. (Orig.). 1981. pap. 6.95 (0-913244-54-6) Hapi Pr.

— Big Bang? Baloney! LC 91-74062. 137p. (Orig.). 1991. pap. 8.50 (0-913244-27-9) Hapi Pr.

— The Bitter Winds. LC 77-71932. 184p. 1977. 6.95 (0-913244-12-0) Hapi Pr.

— The Curse of Life. 185p. 1980. pap. 6.95 (0-913244-24-4) Hapi Pr.

— Development of a Linguistic System in English Speaking American Children, Vol. 2. LC 77-91612. 125p. (Orig.). 1982. pap. 6.95 (0-913244-56-2) Hapi Pr.

— Fairy Princess. LC 82-83473. 125p. (Orig.). 1982. pap. 6.95 (0-913244-58-9) Hapi Pr.

— How English Really Works. LC 79-202. (Illus.). 1979. pap. 12.95 (0-913244-18-X) Hapi Pr.

— Language: Learning or Acquisition. 55p. (Orig.). 1987. pap. 6.95 (0-913244-70-8) Hapi Pr.

— Language & Dialect Distance in a Space of N-Dimensions. 73p. (Orig.). 1983. pap. 5.95 (0-685-26996-5) Hapi Pr.

— Life in a Turkish Village. Spindler, George & Spindler, Louise, eds. (Case Studies in Cultural Anthropology). (Illus.). 1983. reprint ed. pap. text ed. 7.95 (0-8290-0278-2) Irvington.

— The Nature of Natural Languages. 163p. 1979. pap. 7.95 (0-913244-20-1) Hapi Pr.

— A Practical Guide to the Structure of English for the English Teacher. LC 87-80359. 100p. (Orig.). 1987. pap. 7.50 (0-913244-67-8) Hapi Pr.

— Red Runs the Earth. 2nd ed. LC 70-93459. 1977. pap. 5.95 (0-913244-06-6) Hapi Pr.

— The Sapien Homo. LC 78-71820. 1978. pap. 7.95 (0-913244-01-5) Hapi Pr.

— Shades of Minos. 139p. 1973. pap. 6.95 (0-913244-04-X) Hapi Pr.

— Some Vital Statistics on English Grammar. 600p. 1991. lib. bdg. 40.00 (0-913244-26-0) Hapi Pr.

— Terrorism, the Middle East & You. 132p. 1986. pap. 5.50 (0-913244-65-1) Hapi Pr.

— A Theory of Language, Culture & Human Behavior. 160p. 1972. 9.95 (0-913244-03-1) Hapi Pr.

— Thorns, Thistles & Chrome. 160p. 1984. pap. 6.95 (0-913244-63-5) Hapi Pr.

— Why Terrorism. 160p. (Orig.). 1991. pap. 8.50 (0-913244-25-2) Hapi Pr.

Pierce, Joe E. & Hanna, Ingrid V. The Development of a Phonological System in English Speaking American Children. (Illus.). 120p. 1972. pap. 6.95 (0-913244-09-0) Hapi Pr.

Pierce, Joe E., jt. auth. see Hanna, Inga.

Pierce, John & Barnsely, Roland. Easy Lifelong Gardening: A Practical Guide for Seniors. 256p. 1993. pap. 15.95 (0-943955-72-6, Trafalgar Sq Pub) Trafalgar.

Pierce, John C., et al. Citizens, Political Communication & Interest Groups: Environmental Organizations in Canada & the United States. LC 92-15686. (Praeger Series in Political Communication). 256p. 1992. text ed. 49.95 (0-275-93579-5, C3579, Praeger Pubs) Greenwood.

***Pierce, John E.** Development of Comprehensive Insurance for the Household. (C). 1958. 11.50 (0-256-00673-3) Irwin.

Pierce, John J. Foundations of Science Fiction: A Study in Imagination & Evolution. LC 86-22810. (Contributions to the Study of Science Fiction & Fantasy Ser.: No. 25). 305p. 1987. text ed. 59.95 (0-313-25455-9, PFS/, Greenwood Pr) Greenwood.

— Great Themes of Science Fiction: A Study in Imagination & Evolution. LC 87-8475. (Contributions to the Study of Science Fiction & Fantasy Ser.: No. 29). 264p. 1987. text ed. 59.95 (0-313-25456-7, PTS/, Greenwood Pr) Greenwood.

An Asterisk (*) at the beginning of an entry indicates that the title is appearing in BIP for the first time.

— Odd Genre: A Study in Imagination & Evolution. LC 93-29100. (Contributions to the Study of Science Fiction & Fantasy Ser.: No. 60). 240p. 1994. text ed. 55.00 (0-313-26897-5, Greenwood Pr) Greenwood.

— When World Views Collide: A Study in Imagination & Evolution. LC 88-7708. (Contributions to the Study of Science Fiction & Fantasy Ser.). 255p. 1989. text ed. 55.00 (0-313-25457-5, PWH, Greenwood Pr) Greenwood.

Pierce, John R. Science of Musical Sound. LC 91-46742. 1995. pap. text ed. write for info. (0-7167-6005-3) W H Freeman.

Pierce, John R. & Noll, Michael A. Signals: The Science of Telecommunications. LC 89-70207. (Illus.). (C). 1995. text ed. write for info. (0-7167-5026-0) W H Freeman.

Pierce, John R. & Posner, Edward C. Introduction to Communication Science & Systems. LC 80-14877. (Applications of Communications Theory Ser.). 406p. 1980. 69.50 (0-306-40492-3, Plenum Pr); teacher ed write for info. (0-318-55324-4, Plenum Pr) Plenum.

Pierce, John R., ed. see International Symposium on Visual Science Staff.

Pierce, John R., jt. ed. see Mathews, Max V.

Pierce, John T., Sr. Historical Tracts of the Town of Portsmouth, Rhode Island. LC 91-77837. 120p. (Orig.). 1991. pap. 19.95 (0-9631722-0-4) Hamilton Print.

Pierce, John T., jt. auth. see Furuseth, Owen J.

Pierce-Johnson, Joy, ed. see Singeltary, Theresa, et al.

Pierce, Jon L. & Dunham, Randall B. Managing. (C). 1989. text ed. 68.50 (0-673-46011-8) HarpCollege.

Pierce, Jon L. & Newstrom, John W. Leaders & the Leadership Process: Readings, Self-Assessments, & Applications. LC 94-16990. 331p. (C). 1994. 52.95 (0-256-16311-1) Irwin.

— The Manager's Bookshelf: A Mosaic of Contemporary Views. 2nd ed. (C). 1989. pap. text ed. 17.75 (0-06-045169-6) HarpCollege.

Pierce, Jon L., jt. auth. see Dunham, Randall B.

Pierce, Jon R. Living with Parkinson's Disease: Don't Tush Me! I'm Coping As Fast As I Can. LC 89-63189. 176p. (Orig.). 1989. pap. text ed. write for info. (0-9630559-0-9) J R Pierce.

***Pierce, Joseph A.** Negro Business & Business Education: Their Present & Prospective Development. 350p. 1995. 45.00 (0-306-45073-9) Plenum.

Pierce, Josiah. History of the Town of Gorham (ME) 240p. 1985. reprint ed. pap. 25.00 (0-935207-22-8) Danbury Hse Bks.

Pierce, Jotham D., Jr. Construction Contracts & Litigation, 89. (Real Estate Law & Practice Course Handbook Ser.). 869p. 1989. pap. 17.50 (0-685-69399-6) PLI.

Pierce, Judith, jt. auth. see Saurman, Judith.

Pierce, Kathryn & Gilles, Carol, eds. Cycles of Meaning: Exploring the Potential of Talk in Learning Communities. LC 93-5968. (Illus.). 352p. (C). 1993. pap. text ed. 25.00 (0-435-08797-5, 08797) Heinemann.

Pierce, Kathryn M., jt. ed. see Short, Kathy G.

Pierce, Kathy & Rowland, Lori. Guiding Your Catholic Preschooler. 78p. 1992. pap. 5.00 (0-9638235-0-7) Pierce Pubng.

Pierce, L. Jack. Biology 120: Human Anatomy & Physiology - Lecture & Laboratory Manual. 352p. 1992. spiral bd. 21.95 (0-8403-7514-X) Kendall-Hunt.

— General Biology 102: Lecture & Laboratory Manual. 336p. 1992. spiral bd. 20.95 (0-8403-7513-1) Kendall-Hunt.

Pierce, L. Kay. Year of Terror. LC 86-91612. 234p. 1987. 14.95 (0-941321-00-2) Hogue Pub.

Pierce, Lawrence. Freshman Legislator. 2nd ed. (Illus.). 112p. 1972. pap. 2.00 (0-8323-0210-4) Binford Mort.

Pierce, Linda, ed. see American Institute of Certified Accountants Staff.

Pierce, Linda, ed. see American Institute of Certified Public Accountants Staff.

Pierce, Linda C., ed. see American Institute of Certified Public Accountants.

***Pierce, Lynelle N.** Guide to Mechanical Ventilation & Intensive Respiratory Care. 256p. 1995. pap. text ed., spiral bd. 24.95 (0-7216-6478-4) Saunders.

Pierce, M. Rose. Home Groan: Cynical Puns & Other Wordplay. (Illus.). 160p. 1993. pap. 8.95 (0-7867-0012-2) Carroll & Graf.

Pierce, Maggi K. Keep the Kettle Boiling: Rhymes from a Belfast Childhood. (Illus.). 72p. 1983. pap. 7.95 (0-86281-116-3, Pub. by Appletree Pr IE) Irish Bks Media.

***Pierce, Margret.** Wild Justice. 192p. 1995. 19.95 (0-312-13216-6) St Martin.

Pierce, Marjorie. East of the Gabilans. LC 76-56566. 194p. 1981. reprint ed. pap. 14.95 (0-934136-11-4) Western Tanager.

— San Jose & Its Cathedral. LC 90-71209. (Illus.). 200p. 1990. 12.98 (0-934136-47-5) Western Tanager.

Pierce, Mary F., ed. Town of Weston, Massachusetts: Births, Deaths & Marriages, 1707-1850. 649p. 1993. reprint ed. lib. bdg. 66.00 (0-8328-3145-X) Higginson Bk Co.

Pierce, Matthew D. State Initiatives to Establish Basic Health Insurance Plans. (Working Paper Ser.: No. 61). 23p. 1992. 5.00 (0-685-66568-2) LBJ Sch Pub Aff.

Pierce, Meredith A. Dark Moon. 256p. (YA). (gr. 7 up). 1992. 15.95 (0-685-59346-0, Joy St Bks) Little.

— Dark Moon, Vol. II: Firebringer Trilogy. (Illus.). (YA). (gr. 7 up). 1992. 16.95 (0-316-70744-9, Joy St Bks) Little.

— A Gathering of Gargoyles. 272p. (J). 1985. reprint ed. pap. 2.95 (0-8125-4902-3) Tor Bks.

Pierce, Michael D. The Most Promising Young Officer: A Life of Ranald Slidell Mackenzie. LC 92-32281. (C). 1993. 24.95 (0-8061-2494-6) U of Okla Pr.

Pierce, Milton. How to Collect Your Overdue Bills. LC 80-66023. (Illus.). 224p. reprint ed. pap. 63.90 (0-317-09671-0, 2021649) Bks Demand.

Pierce, N. F., jt. ed. see Kuwahara, S.

Pierce, Neal R. The Creative Partnership: State Power & Local Initiative. 1978. 1.00 (1-55614-031-2) U of SD Gov Res Bur.

— The Great Plains States of America. 1973. 15.95 (0-393-05349-0) Norton.

— The Mountain States of America: People, Politics & Power in the Eight Rocky Mountain States. (Illus.). 320p. 1971. 15.95 (0-393-05255-9) Norton.

— The New England States: People, Politics & Power in the Six New England States. (Illus.). 1976. 15.95 (0-393-05558-2) Norton.

Pierce, Neal R. & Hagstrom, Jerry. The Book of America: Inside Fifty States Today. 1983. 27.50 (0-393-01639-0) Norton.

Pierce, Nona. Garden Getaways: Public Gardens & Special Nurseries in Northern California. LC 89-30775. (Illus.). 176p. 1989. pap. 12.95 (0-935382-70-4) Tioga Pub Co.

Pierce, Olive. No Easy Roses: A Look at the Lives of City Teenagers. (Illus.). 94p. 1986. pap. write for info. (0-9617101-0-1) Olive Pierce.

Pierce, Ovid W. Old Man's Gold, & Other Stories. LC 75-19101. 80p. reprint ed. pap. 25.00 (0-8357-3876-0, 2036608) Bks Demand.

Pierce, Pat. A Pop-Up Book of North American Cities. (Illus.). 20p. (J). (gr. 2-6). 1991. 12.95 (0-8249-8517-6, Ideals Child) Hambleton-Hill.

Pierce, Patricia. Canada, the Missing Years: The Lost Images of Our Heritage. (Illus.). 160p. 1987. 19.95 (0-7737-5120-3, Pub. by Stoddart Pubng CN) Genl Dist Srvs.

— Commonly Computed Rates & Percentages for Hospital Inpatients. 24p. 1987. write for info. (0-318-12836-5, 1017P) Am Hlth Info.

Pierce, Patricia J. Commonly Computed Rates & Percentages for Hospital Inpatients. 24p. 1987. 18.00 (0-317-05427-9) Am Hlth Info.

— The Ultimate Elvis. 1995. pap. 14.00 (0-684-80328-3, Fireside) S&S Trade.

— The Ultimate Elvis: Elvis Presley Day by Day. LC 94-4612. 1994. 30.00 (0-671-87022-X) S&S Trade.

Pierce, Paul. A Baja Love Song. (Illus.). 1985. 5.95 (0-914622-06-4) Baja Trail.

— Freedmen's Bureau: A Chapter in the History of Reconstruction. LC 68-24993. (American History & Americana Ser.: No. 47). 1969. reprint ed. lib. bdg. 75.00 (0-8383-0229-7) M S G Haskell Hse.

Pierce, Paulette. Noncapitalist Development: Struggle to Nationalize the Guyanese Sugar Industry. LC 84-17882. 220p. (C). 1984. 42.00 (0-86598-118-3) Rowman.

***Pierce, Peter.** Australian Melodramas: Thomas Keneally's Fiction. (Studies in Australian Literature Ser.). 222p. 1995. pap. 14.95 (0-7022-2813-3, Pub. by Univ Queensland Pr AT) Intl Spec Bk.

Pierce, Peter, ed. The Oxford Literary Guide to Australia. (Illus.). 516p. 1993. reprint ed. pap. 32.00 (0-19-553447-6) OUP.

Pierce, Peter, jt. ed. see Jordan, Richard.

Pierce, Peter, jt. ed. see Wallace-Crabbe, Chris.

Pierce, Phyllis S. Dow Jones Averages 1885-1990. 3rd ed. 1,500p. 1991. text ed. 80.00 (1-55623-512-7) Irwin Prof Pubng.

— Irwin Investor's Handbook 1994. 13th ed. 228p. 1994. pap. 25.00 (0-7863-0211-9) Irwin Prof Pubng.

Pierce, Phyllis S., ed. The Irwin Investor's Handbook 1993. 12th ed. 200p. 1993. pap. 25.00 (1-55623-673-5) Irwin Prof Pubng.

— The Irwin Investor's Handbook 1995. 14th ed. 200p. 1995. 27.50 (0-7863-0430-8) Irwin Prof Pubng.

***Pierce, Q. L.** Easy Answers to First Science Questions About Space. (Illus.). 1995. pap. 5.95 (1-56565-264-9) Lowell Hse Juvenile.

Pierce, R. A., tr. see Fedorova, Svetlana G.

Pierce, R. A., tr. see Khlebnikov, Kirill T.

Pierce, R. S. Compact Zero-Dimensional Metric Spaces of Finite Type. LC 72-11822. (Memoirs Ser.: No. 1/130). 64p. 1972. pap. 16.00 (0-8218-1830-9, MEMO 1/130) Am Math.

Pierce, R. W. & Hart, G. F. Phytoplankton of the Gulf of Mexico: Taxonomy of Calcareous Nannoplankton. (Geoscience & Man Ser.: Vol. 20). 97p. 1979. pap. 12.00 (0-938909-19-3) Geosci Pubns LSU.

Pierce, Regina & Yackso, Sharon. The Pelican Guide to the Shenandoah. LC 87-6984. (Pelican Guide Ser.). (Illus.). 130p. 1987. pap. 7.95 (0-88289-652-0) Pelican.

Pierce, Richard. Frankenstein's Children: The Creation. 208p. (Orig.). (YA). (gr. 7-12). 1994. pap. text ed. 3.99 (0-425-14361-9) Berkley Pub.

— Frankenstein's Children: The Revenge. 224p. (Orig.). 1994. pap. 3.99 (0-425-14460-7) Berkley Pub.

— Frankenstein's Children - The Curse. 224p. (Orig.). 1995. pap. text ed. 3.99 (0-425-14528-X) Berkley Pub.

Pierce, Richard A. Alaskan Shipping Eighteen Sixty-Seven to Eighteen Seventy-Eight: Arrivals & Departures at the Port of Sitka. (Alaska History Ser.: No. 1). (Illus.). 1972. pap. 3.95 (0-919642-86-1) Limestone Pr.

— Builders of Alaska: The Russian Governors, 1818-1867. (Alaska History Ser.: No. 28). (Illus.). 1985. 11.00 (0-919642-07-1) Limestone Pr.

— Russian America: Seventeen Forty-One to Eighteen Sixty-Seven, a Biographical Dictionary. (Alaska History Ser.: No. 33). (Illus.). 1990. 45.00 (0-919642-45-4) Limestone Pr.

— Russia's Hawaiian Adventure, Eighteen Fifteen to Eighteen Seventeen. (Alaska History Ser.: No. 8). (Illus.). 1976. pap. 18.00 (0-919642-69-1) Limestone Pr.

— Soviet Central Asia, a Bibliography: 1558-1966, 3 pts. 1966. pap. 15.00 (0-919642-94-2) Limestone Pr.

Pierce, Richard A., ed. Journals of Iakov Netsvetov: The Atkha Years, Eighteen Twenty-Eight to Eighteen Forty-Four. Black, Lydia, tr. (Alaska History Ser.: No. 16). (Illus.). 340p. 1980. 24.00 (0-919642-92-6) Limestone Pr.

— The Journals of Iakov Netsvetov: The Yukon Years, 1845-1863. Black, Lydia T., tr. (Alaska History Ser.: No. 26). 514p. 1984. 32.00 (0-919642-01-2) Limestone Pr.

— The Lovtsov Atlas of the North Pacific Ocean, Compiled at Bol'sheretsk, Kamchartka, in 1782. Black, Lydia T., tr. (Alaska History Ser.: No. 38). (Illus.). 62p. 1991. pap. 12.50 (0-919642-31-1) Limestone Pr.

— Round the World Voyage of Hieromonk Gideon, 1803-1809. Black, Lydia T., tr. (Alaska History Ser.: No. 32). (Illus.). 1989. 29.00 (0-919642-20-9) Limestone Pr.

— Siberia & Northwestern America, Seventeen Eighty-Eight to Seventeen Ninety-Two: The Journal of Carl Heinrich Merck. Jaensch, Fritz, tr. (Alaska History Ser.: No. 17). (Illus.). 1980. 18.00 (0-919642-93-4) Limestone Pr.

Pierce, Richard A., tr. Russian-American Company Correspondence: Communications Sent-1818. (Alaska History Ser.: No. 25). (Illus.). 1984. 30.00 (0-919642-02-0) Limestone Pr.

Pierce, Richard A. & Black, Michael. Life-Span Development: A Diversity Reader. 368p. (C). 1993. per. 16.95 (0-8403-8565-X) Kendall-Hunt.

Pierce, Richard A., ed. see Adams, George R.

Pierce, Richard A., ed. see Alekseev, Aleksandr I.

Pierce, Richard A., ed. see Belcher, Edward & Simpkinson, F. G.

Pierce, Richard A., ed. see Gutman, A. Ya.

Pierce, Richard A., ed. see Huggins, Eli L.

Pierce, Richard A., ed. see Ivashintsov, Nikolai A.

Pierce, Richard A., ed. see Kordan, Bohdan S. & Luciuk, Lubomyr Y.

Pierce, Richard A., jt. auth. see Lantzeff, George V.

Pierce, Richard A., ed. see Luciuk, Lubomyr Y. & Kordan, Bohdan S.

Pierce, Richard A., ed. see Luetke, Frederick.

Pierce, Richard A., ed. see Ray, Dorothy J.

Pierce, Richard A., ed. see Shelikhov, Grigorii I.

Pierce, Richard A., ed. see Teben'kov, Mikhail D.

Pierce, Richard A., ed. see Tikhmenev, Petr A.

Pierce, Richard A., tr. see Tikhmenev, Petr A.

Pierce, Richard A., ed. see Veniaminov, Ivan.

Pierce, Richard A., ed. see Von Langsdorff, Georg H.

Pierce, Richard A., ed. see Wrangell, Ferdinand P.

Pierce, Richard D., ed. Records of the First Church in Salem, Massachusetts, 1629-1736. LC 73-93302. 1974. 30.00 (0-88389-050-X, Essx Institute) Peabody Essex Mus.

Pierce, Richard J. Regulated Industries in A Nutshell. 3rd ed. Gellhorn, Ernest, ed. LC 94-8849. (Nutshell Ser.). 372p. 1994. pap. text ed. 17.00 (0-314-03660-1) West Pub.

Pierce, Richard J., ed. Leadership, Perspective, & Restructuring for Total Quality. (Illus.). 235p. 1991. 35.95 (0-87389-101-5) ASQC Qual Pr.

Pierce, Richard J. & Kellner, Paul. Economic Regulation. LC 93-38939. 1994. write for info. (0-87084-275-7) Anderson Pub Co.

Pierce, Richard J., jt. auth. see Gellhorn, Ernest.

Pierce, Richard J., Jr., et al. Administrative Law & Process. 2nd ed. (University Textbook Ser.). 600p. 1992. text ed. 35.95 (0-88277-968-0) Foundation Pr.

Pierce, Richard S. Associative Algebras. (Graduate Texts in Mathematics Ser.: Vol. 88). 416p. 1982. 59.00 (0-387-90693-2) Spr-Verlag.

— Introduction to the Theory of Abstract Algebras. LC 68-16477. 1968. 39.50 (0-03-056010-1) Irvington.

— Modules over Commutative Regular Rings. LC 52-42839. (Memoirs Ser.: No. 1/70). 112p. 1977. reprint ed. pap. 21.00 (0-8218-1270-X, MEMO 1/70) Am Math.

— Translation Lattices. (Memoirs Ser.: No. 1/32). 66p. 1983. reprint ed. pap. 22.00 (0-8218-1232-7, MEMO 1/32) Am Math.

Pierce, Richard S., jt. auth. see Beaumont, Ross A.

Pierce, Robert, et al. Emotional Expression in Psychotherapy. LC 83-5604. 356p. 1983. 29.95 (0-89876-015-1) Gardner Pr.

Pierce, Robert N. A Sacred Trust: Nelson Poynter & the St. Petersburg Times. (Illus.). 408p. 1993. 37.95 (0-8130-1234-1) U Press Fla.

***Pierce, Robyn, ed.** Research on Mature-Age Students Returning to Study Mathematics at Tertiary Level. 67p. 1993. pap. 55.00 (0-7300-2057-6, Pub. by Deakin Univ AT) St Mut.

Pierce, Robyn, jt. auth. see Martin, Peter.

Pierce, Roger, jt. auth. see Pierce, Alexandra.

Pierce, Ronald K. What Are We Trying to Teach Them Anyway? A Father's Focus on School Reform. LC 92-21143. 176p. 1993. 19.95 (1-55815-239-3) ICS Pr.

Pierce, Roxanne H., jt. auth. see Heide, Florence P.

***Pierce, Roy.** Choosing the Chief: Presidential Elections in France & the United States. 326p. 1995. text ed. 39.50x (0-472-10559-0) U of Mich Pr.

Pierce, Roy, jt. auth. see Converse, Philip E.

Pierce, S. K. & Maugel, T. K. Illustrated Invertebrate Anatomy: A Laboratory Guide. (Illus.). 320p. (C). 1989. reprint ed. pap. text ed. 29.95 (0-19-504077-5) OUP.

Pierce, Sally. Whipple & Black: Commercial Photographers in Boston. (Illus.). 132p. 1987. 45.00 (0-934552-49-5, Northeastern Univ Ctr for International); pap. 18.00 (0-934552-50-9, Northeastern Univ Ctr for International) Boston Athenaeum.

Pierce, Sally & Slautterback, Catherina. Boston Lithography, 1825-1880: The Boston Athenaeum Collection. LC 91-73405. (Illus.). 204p. 1991. 48.00 (0-934552-57-6) Boston Athenaeum.

Pierce, Sally & Smith, Temple D. Citizens in Conflict: Prints & Photographs of the American Civil War. LC 81-70895. (Illus.). 50p. (Orig.). 1981. pap. 7.50 (0-934552-38-X) Boston Athenaeum.

Pierce, Sam. Software System Engineering: A First Course. LC 91-29685. (Illus.). 224p. (C). 1992. pap. text ed. 18.95 (0-938661-14-0) Franklin Beedle.

Pierce, Sharon. Making Whirligigs & Other Wind Toys. LC 84-26782. (Illus.). 132p. (Orig.). (YA). (gr. 10-12). 1985. pap. 9.95 (0-8069-7980-1) Sterling.

Pierce, Sharon & Surman, Herb. Making Miniature Country Houses. LC 89-48857. (Illus.). 128p. (Orig.). 1990. pap. 12.95 (0-8069-6984-9) Sterling.

Pierce, Sherri. Expressions in Glass. (Illus.). 51p. 1994. 10.95 (0-936459-26-3) Stained Glass.

Pierce, Steve. Lakes of Yellowstone: A Guide for Hiking, Fishing & Exploring. LC 87-5583. (Illus.). 200p. (Orig.). 1987. pap. 10.95 (0-89886-139-X) Mountaineers.

Pierce, Steven R. & Macpherson, Colin. Blood Group Systems: Duffy, Kidd & Lutheran. LC 88-19267. 1988. 25.00 (0-915355-55-8) Am Assn Blood.

Pierce, Steven R., jt. ed. see Vengelen-Tyler, Virginia.

***Pierce, Stocia.** Hospitality & Greeters Training Manual. 15p. 1994. student ed 5.00 (1-886880-02-6) Life Changers.

— How to Develop a Successful Women's Ministry. 40p. 1994. student ed 10.00 (1-886880-04-2) Life Changers.

— The Image Workshop. 26p. 1994. student ed 15.00 (1-886880-01-8) Life Changers.

— Motivated Women. 15p. 1994. student ed 10.00 (1-886880-03-4) Life Changers.

***Pierce, Sue & Suit, Verna.** Art Quilts: Playing with a Full Deck. LC 94-36681. (Illus.). 152p. (Orig.). 1995. pap. 22.95 (0-87654-300-X) Pomegranate Calif.

Pierce, Susan K., jt. auth. see Humphreys, Robert E.

Pierce, Sydney J., ed. Weeding & Maintenance of Reference Collections. LC 90-30910. (Reference Librarian Ser.: No. 29). 183p. 1990. text ed. 39.95 (1-56024-001-6) Haworth Pr.

— Weeding & Maintenance of Reference Collections. LC 90-30910. (Illus.). 184p. (C). 1995. reprint ed. pap. text ed. 14.95 (1-56024-976-5) Haworth Pr.

Pierce, T. J., ed. Coal Liquid Mixtures: Proceedings of the European Conference, 3rd. (European Federation of Chemical Engineering Ser.). 356p. 1988. 113.00 (0-89116-843-5) Hemisp Pub.

Pierce, Tamora. Alanna: The First Adventure Song of the Lioness, Bk. One. LC 83-2595. 252p. (YA). (gr. 6 up). 1983. text ed. 16.95 (0-689-30994-5, Atheneum Bks Young) S&S Childrens.

— The Emperor Mage. LC 94-23278. (Immortals Ser.). (J). 1995. write for info. (0-689-31989-4, Atheneum S&S) S&S Trade.

— In the Hand of the Goddess. LC 84-2946. 240p. (J). (gr. 5 up). 1990. reprint ed. pap. 3.50 (0-679-80111-1) Random Bks Yng Read.

— In the Hand of the Goddess: Song of the Lioness, Bk. Two. LC 84-2946. 240p. (YA). (gr. 7 up). 1984. text ed. 16.95 (0-689-31054-4, Atheneum Bks Young) S&S Childrens.

— Lioness Rampant: Song of the Lioness, Bk. Four. LC 88-6213. (Song of the Lioness Ser.). 336p. (YA). (gr. 6 up). 1988. text ed. 16.95 (0-689-31116-8, Atheneum Bks Young) S&S Childrens.

— Wild Magic. large type ed. LC 93-8427. (Immortals Ser.). (J). 1993. 15.95 (1-56054-796-0) Thorndike Pr.

— Wild Magic: The Immortals. LC 91-43909. 272p. (YA). (gr. 5 up). 1992. text ed. 16.95 (0-689-31761-1, Atheneum Bks Young) S&S Childrens.

— Wolf-Speaker. LC 93-21909. (Immortals Ser.). 192p. (J). (gr. 4-8). 1994. text ed. 14.95 (0-689-31833-2, Atheneum Bks Young) S&S Childrens.

— The Woman Who Rides Like a Man. LC 85-20054. 256p. (J). (gr. 6 up). 1990. reprint ed. pap. 3.50 (0-679-80112-X) Knopf Bks Yng Read.

— The Woman Who Rides Like a Man: Song of the Lioness, Book Three. LC 85-20054. 288p. (YA). (gr. 7 up). 1986. text ed. 16.95 (0-689-31117-6, Atheneum Bks Young) S&S Childrens.

Pierce, Ted M. Freedom: The Teachings of Jesus. 1992. 16.95 (0-533-10182-4) Vantage.

Pierce, Thomas H., jt. ed. see Hohne, Bruce.

Pierce, Tim, ed. see CGI Staff.

Pierce, Tim, ed. see Long, Jerry H.

Pierce, Tim, ed. see Rupp, Keith & Miller, Dawn.

Pierce, Veronica S. The Chinese Oxymoron. LC 90-81818. (Brown Bag Mystery Line Ser.). 332p. 1990. 14.95 (0-933031-29-7) Coun Oak Bks.

Pierce, Vivienne, ed. Pastoral Responses to Older Adults & Their Families: An Annotated Bibliography. LC 91-43560. (Bibliographies & Indexes in Gerontology Ser.: No. 15). 288p. 1992. text ed. 55.00 (0-313-28039-8, SXD/, Greenwood Pr) Greenwood.

Pierce, W. D., jt. auth. see Epling, W. F.

Pierce, W. David & Epling, W. Frank. Behavior Analysis & Learning. LC 94-20588. 496p. 1994. text ed. write for info. (0-13-175373-8) P-H.

Pierce, W. G., jt. ed. see Melugin, R. K.

Pierce, W. S. Furnishing the Library Interior. (Books in Library & Information Science: Vol. 29). 304p. 1980. 110.00 (0-8247-6900-7) Dekker.

Pierce, Walter, jt. auth. see Lorber, Michael A.

Pierce, Walter M. Oregon Cattleman, Governor, Congressman: Memoirs & Times of Walter M. Pierce. Bone, Arthur H., ed. LC 80-81718. (Illus.). 528p. 1981. pap. 14.95 (0-87595-098-1) Oregon Hist.

Pierce, Wesley G. Goin' Fishin' The Story of the Deep Sea Fishermen of New England. (Illus.). 336p. 1989. text ed. 17.95 (0-87742-251-6) Intl Marine.

Pierce, William, jt. auth. see Adamec, Christine A.

PQ

An Asterisk (*) at the beginning of an entry indicates that the title is appearing in BIP for the first time.

Pierceall, Gregory M. Interiorscapes: Graphics, Planning & Design. (Illus.). 384p. 1987. text ed. 54.20 (*0-8359-3232-X*) P-H.

— Residential Landscapes: Graphics, Planning & Design. (Illus.). 468p. (C). 1994. reprint ed. text ed. 49.95 (*0-88133-788-9*) Waveland Pr.

— Sitescapes. 272p. 1990. text ed. 81.00 (*0-13-812066-8*) P-H.

Piercey, Bertha E. A Widow's Story. LC 92-23311. (Orig.). 1992. pap. 8.95 (*0-9627635-4-3*) Brandylane.

Piercey, Dorothy. Reading Activities in Content Areas: An Ideabook for Middle & Secondary Schools. 2nd ed. 590p. (C). 1981. pap. text ed. 33.95 (*0-205-07372-7*, H73729) Allyn.

***Piercy.** The Coward Does It with a Kiss. Date not set. per. 10.95 (*0-85449-137-6*, Pub. by Gay Mens Pr UK) InBook.

— My Dearest Holmes. 1994. per. 7.95 (*0-85449-081-7*, Pub. by Gay Mens Pr UK) InBook.

Piercy & Barclay Designers, Inc. Staff. Designer Duplex Home Plans. (Illus.). 24p. 1985. 8.95 (*0-929939-08-5*) Piercy Barclay.

— Designer Home Plans, Vol. 4. (Illus.). 63p. 1982. 12.95 (*0-929939-02-6*) Piercy Barclay.

— Designer Home Plans, Vol. 5. (Illus.). 63p. 1985. 12.95 (*0-929939-03-4*) Piercy Barclay.

— Designer Home Plans, Vol. 6. (Illus.). 64p. 1990. pap. text ed. 12.95 (*0-929939-04-2*) Piercy Barclay.

— Designer Leisure Home Plans. (Illus.). 1985. 8.95 (*0-929939-07-7*) Piercy Barclay.

— Designers Book of Home Plans, Vol. 2. (Illus.). 48p. 1976. 12.95 (*0-929939-00-X*) Piercy Barclay.

— Designers Book of Home Plans, Vol. 3. 2nd ed. (Illus.). 1990. 12.95 (*0-929939-09-3*) Piercy Barclay.

— Designers Book of Home Plans: Executive Homes. 4th ed. (Illus.). 64p. 1991. 12.95 (*0-929939-12-3*) Piercy Barclay.

— Designers Book of Home Plans: Narrow Lot Homes. 3rd ed. (Illus.). 64p. 1991. 12.95 (*0-929939-11-5*) Piercy Barclay.

Piercy, C. B. The Shaker Cookbook. 1986. 5.98 (*0-517-62243-2*, 014246) Random Hse Value.

Piercy, Caroline B. & Tolve, Arthur P. The Shaker Cookbook: Recipes & Lore from the Valley of God's Pleasure. rev. ed. (Illus.). 192p. 1984. pap. 12.95 (*0-911861-02-5*) Gabriels Horn.

Piercy, Fred P., ed. Family Therapy Education & Supervision. LC 85-21958. (Journal of Psychotherapy & the Family: Vol. 1, No. 4). 145p. 1986. text ed. 39.95 (*0-86656-510-8*); pap. text ed. 19.95 (*0-86656-511-6*) Haworth Pr.

Piercy, Fred P. & Sprenkle, Douglas H. Family Therapy Sourcebook. LC 86-19588. (Guilford Family Therapy Ser.). 396p. 1986. lib. bdg. 45.00 (*0-89862-071-6*); pap. text ed. 21.95 (*0-89862-913-6*) Guilford Pr.

Piercy, Fred P., jt. auth. see Lobsenz, Norman M.

Piercy, James E., jt. auth. see Forbes, J. Benjamin.

Piercy, Josephine. Studies in Literary Types in Seventeenth Century America. (BCL1-PS American Literature Ser.). 360p. 1993. reprint ed. lib. bdg. 89.00 (*0-7812-6573-8*) Rprt Serv.

Piercy, Josephine K. Anne Bradstreet. (Twayne's United States Authors Ser.). 1964. pap. 13.95x (*0-8084-0051-7*, T72) NCUP.

***Piercy, LaRue W.** Big Island History Makers. 48p. 1994. pap. 3.95 (*1-56647-063-3*) Mutual Pub HI.

— Hawaii: Truth Stranger Than Fiction. 128p. 1994. pap. 6.95 (*1-56647-062-5*) Mutual Pub HI.

— Hawaii This 'n That. 60p. 1994. pap. 4.95 (*1-56647-064-1*) Mutual Pub HI.

— Hawaii's Missionary Saga. 232p. 1992. pap. 16.95 (*0-935180-05-2*) Mutual Pub HI.

Piercy, Marge. Available Light. LC 87-40490. 144p. 1988. pap. 12.00 (*0-394-75691-6*) Knopf.

— Braided Lives. 1986. mass mkt. 4.95 (*0-449-44526-7*, Crest); mass mkt. 5.95 (*0-449-21300-5*, Crest) Fawcett.

— Braided Lives. 1987. 15.50 (*0-685-18687-3*) Summit Bks.

— Braided Lives. LC 81-16695. 441p. 1982. 25.00 (*0-671-43834-4*) Ultramarine Pub.

— Breaking Camp: Poems. LC 68-16007. (Wesleyan Poetry Program Ser.: Vol. 39). 74p. 1968. pap. 10.95 (*0-8195-1039-4*, Wesleyan Univ Pr) U Pr of New Eng.

— Circles on the Water: Selected Poems of Marge Piercy. 320p. 1982. pap. 16.00 (*0-394-70779-6*) Knopf.

— Dance the Eagle to Sleep. 224p. 1982. pap. 3.95 (*0-449-20114-7*, Crest) Fawcett.

— The Earth Shines Secretly: A Book of Days. LC 89-52050. (Illus.). 96p. 1990. 15.95 (*0-944072-10-0*) Zoland Bks.

— Fly away Home. 1988. mass mkt. 5.95 (*0-449-20691-2*, Crest) Fawcett.

— Going down Fast. 1982. mass mkt. 4.95 (*0-449-24480-6*, Crest) Fawcett.

— Gone to Soldiers. 800p. 1988. mass mkt. 5.95 (*0-449-21557-1*, Crest) Fawcett.

— Hard Loving: Poems. LC 70-82544. (Wesleyan Poetry Program Ser.: Vol. 46). 77p. (C). 1969. 22.50 (*0-8195-2046-2*, Wesleyan Univ Pr); pap. 10.95 (*0-8195-1046-7*, Wesleyan Univ Pr) U Pr of New Eng.

— He, She & It. 1993. mass mkt. 5.99 (*0-449-22060-5*) Fawcett.

— He, She & It. Date not set. pap. 4.99 (*0-517-11256-6*) Random Hse Value.

— The High Cost of Living. 1985. mass mkt. 4.50 (*0-449-20879-6*, Crest) Fawcett.

— The Longings of Women. 1995. mass mkt. 6.99 (*0-449-22349-3*, Crest) Fawcett.

— The Longings of Women. large type ed. LC 94-18341. 752p. 1994. 23.95 (*0-8161-7457-1*) Hall.

— The Longings of Women: A Novel. LC 93-34125. 464p. 1994. 22.00 (*0-449-90907-7*, Columbine) Fawcett.

— Mars & Her Children. 1992. pap. 13.00 (*0-679-73877-0*) Knopf.

— The Moon Is Always Female. LC 79-21866. 1980. pap. 11.00 (*0-394-73859-4*) Knopf.

— My Mother's Body. Nicholas, Nancy, ed. LC 84-48661. 160p. 1985. pap. 12.00 (*0-394-72945-5*) Knopf.

— Parti-Colored Blocks for a Quilt: Poets on Poetry. 320p. 1982. pap. 13.95 (*0-472-06338-3*) U of Mich Pr.

— Small Changes. 544p. 1985. mass mkt. 5.95 (*0-449-21083-9*, Crest) Fawcett.

— Stone, Paper, Knife. LC 82-48050. 125p. 1983. pap. 11.00 (*0-394-71219-6*) Knopf.

— Summer People. 416p. 1990. reprint ed. mass mkt. 5.95 (*0-449-21842-2*, Crest) Fawcett.

— Vida. 480p. 1985. mass mkt. 6.99 (*0-449-20850-8*, Crest) Fawcett.

— Woman on the Edge of Time. 384p. 1985. mass mkt. 6.99 (*0-449-21082-0*) Fawcett.

Piercy, Nigel. Market-Led Strategic Change. 416p. 1992. pap. 37.95 (*0-7506-0670-3*) Buttrwrth-Heinemann.

— Marketing Budgeting: A Political & Organisational Model. LC 85-28006. 544p. 1986. 55.00 (*0-7099-2092-X*, Pub. by Croom Helm UK) Routledge Chapman & Hall.

— Marketing Organisation: An Analysis of Information Processing, Power & Politics. (Illus.). 224p. 1985. text ed. 34.95 (*0-04-658245-2*) Routledge Chapman & Hall.

Piercy, Patricia A. The Great Encounter: A Special Meeting Before Columbus. (Illus.). 47p. (J). (gr. 1-7). 1991. pap. 5.95 (*0-913543-26-8*) African Am Imag.

Piercy, Robert, jt. auth. see Mazar, Peter.

Piercy, William, jt. ed. see Wace, Henry.

***Pierian.** Directory of National Helplines: A Guide to Toll-Free Public Service Numbers, 1995. 1995. pap. 7.00 (*0-87650-340-7*) Pierian.

Pierik, R. L. In Vitro Culture of Higher Plants. (C). 1987. lib. bdg. 162.50 (*90-247-3530-0*); pap. text ed. 66.50 (*90-247-3531-9*) Kluwer Ac.

Pierik, R. L. & Prakash, J., eds. Horticulture - New Technologies & Applications: Proceedings of the International Seminar on New Frontiers in Horticulture. (Current Plant Science & Biotechnology in Agriculture Ser.). 428p. 1991. lib. bdg. 115.50 (*0-7923-1279-1*) Kluwer Ac.

Pierik, T., jt. auth. see Prakash, J.

Pierini, Pascal, tr. The Spiritual Canticle of St. John of the Cross. (Illus.). 1991. pap. 25.00 (*0-941179-32-X*) Latitudes Pr.

Pieris, Aloysius. Love Meets Wisdom: A Christian Experience of Buddhism. LC 88-22536. (Faith Meets Faith Ser.). 160p. 1988. pap. 16.95 (*0-88344-371-6*, 371-6) Orbis Bks.

Pieris, Ralph. Asian Development Styles. LC 77-74486. 1977. 7.50 (*0-88386-831-8*) S Asia.

Pierloot, R. A., ed. Recent Research in Psychosomatics. (Psychotherapy & Psychosomatics Journal: Vol. 18, No. 1-6). (Illus.). viii, 376p. 1970. reprint ed. 91.25 (*3-8055-1219-8*) S Karger.

Pierman, Carol J. The Age of Krypton. LC 88-70389. (Carnegie Mellon Poetry Ser.). 1989. pap. 9.95 (*0-685-30813-8*) Carnegie-Mellon.

— The Naturalized Citizen. LC 81-82537. (Illus.). 68p. 1981. pap. 3.00 (*0-89823-032-2*) New Rivers Pr.

Piermattei, D. L. An Atlas of Surgical Approaches to the Bones & Joints of the Dog & Cat. 3rd ed. (Illus.). 336p. 1992. text ed. 49.95 (*0-7216-1012-9*) Saunders.

Piero D. Francesca. De Prospetiva Pingendi, Facsimile of Parma, Biblioteca Palatina, MS 1576. (Documents of Art & Architectural History Ser.: Vol. 2). 420p. (LAT.). 1994. lib. bdg. 125.00 (*0-89371-201-9*) Broude Intl Edns.

Pieron, Henri. Thought & the Brain. LC 73-2981. (Classics in Psychology Ser.). 1980. reprint ed. 25.95 (*0-405-05153-0*) Ayer.

— Vocabulaire de la Psychologie. 8th ed. 608p. (FRE.). 1990. 115.00 (*0-7859-4835-X*) Fr & Eur.

Pieron, Maurice & Graham, George, eds. Sport Pedagogy. LC 85-18113. 226p. (C). 1986. text ed. 36.00x (*0-87322-013-7*, BPIE0013) Human Kinetics.

Pieroni, G. G., ed. Issues on Machine Vision. (Illus.). vi, 339p. 1989. pap. 71.00 (*0-387-82148-1*) Spr-Verlag.

Pieroni, Goffredo G., jt. ed. see Freeman, Herbert.

Pieroni, Robert E. Behavioral Sciences. 2nd ed. (Medical Examination Review Ser.). 248p. 1989. pap. 18.00 (*0-444-01049-1*) Elsevier.

— National Boards Examination Review Pt. II: Clinical Sciences. 3rd ed. 1988. pap. text ed. 38.50 (*0-8385-6656-1*, A6656-1) Appleton & Lange.

— Specialty Board Review: Internal Medicine. 3rd ed. (Illus.). 128p. 1990. pap. text ed. 42.95 (*0-8385-8647-3*, A8647-8) Appleton & Lange.

Pierotti, N. J. Almost Inkfish. 105p. 1993. pap. 10.00 (*0-9638096-0-1*) Inkfish Pr.

Pierpaoli, Walter & Spector, Novera H., eds. Neuroimmunomodulation: Interventions in Aging & Cancer: First Stromboli Conference on Aging & Cancer. (Annals Ser.: Vol. 521). 335p. 1988. 86.00 (*0-89766-431-0*) NY Acad Sci.

***Pierpaoli, Walter, et al.** The Melatonin Miracle: Nature's Age-Reversing, Disease-Fighting, Sex-Enhancing Hormone. 1995. 21.00 (*0-684-81335-1*) S&S Trade.

***Pierpoint, Katherine.** Truffle Beds. 80p. (Orig.). 1995. pap. 10.95 (*0-571-17360-8*) Faber & Faber.

Pierpoint, Richard J. Cam Bridges. (Cambridge Town, Gown & County Ser.: Vol. 3). (Illus.). 40p. 1976. pap. 4.95 (*0-902675-63-X*) Oleander Pr.

Pierpoint, S., jt. auth. see Robb, D. A.

Pierpont, J. S. Jingle Bells. (Sounds of the Season Ser.). (Illus.). 10p. (J). 1994. write for info. (*0-307-17451-4*) Western Pub.

Pierpont, John. Anti-Slavery Poems. LC 71-104544. reprint ed. lib. bdg. 37.50 (*0-8398-1570-0*) Irvington.

Pierpont, Mary E., ed. Genetics of Cardiovascular Disease. 1986. lib. bdg. 170.00 (*0-89838-790-6*) Kluwer Ac.

Pierpont Publishing, Inc. Staff, ed. see Calandro, Ed.

Pierpont, William. What You Can Do About Allergy. 6p. 1965. reprint ed. spiral bd. 4.40 (*0-7873-1107-3*) Mokelumne.

Pierpont, William G., ed. The New Testament in the Original Greek: According to the Byzantine-Majority Textform. LC 91-60094. 576p. (ENG & GEC.). 1991. pap. 24.95 (*0-9626544-3-4*) Original Word.

— The New Testament in the Original Greek: According to the Byzantine-Majority Textform. deluxe limited ed. LC 91-60094. 576p. (ENG & GEC.). 1991. 100.00 (*0-9626544-2-6*) Original Word.

Pierradrd, Pierre. Larousse des Prenoms et des Saints. 256p. (FRE.). 1976. 42.50 (*0-8288-5725-3*, M6454) Fr & Eur.

Pierrakos, Eva. Creating Union: The Pathwork of Relationship. LC 93-86256. (Pathwork Ser.). xx, 184p. (Orig.). 1993. pap. 12.00 (*0-9614777-3-3*) Pathwork Pr.

— Guide Lectures for Self-Transformation. LC 85-134343. 216p. (Orig.). 1985. pap. 7.95 (*0-9614777-1-7*) Pathwork Pr.

Pierrakos, Eva & Thesenga, Donovan. Fear No Evil: The Pathwork Method of Transforming the Lower Self. LC 93-84262. xviii, 269p. 1992. pap. 12.00 (*0-9614777-2-5*) Pathwork Pr.

Pierrakos, Eve. Pathwork of Self Transformation. 1990. pap. 11.95 (*0-553-34896-5*) Bantam.

Pierrakos, John C. Core Energetics: Developing the Capacity to Love & Heal. (Illus.). 304p. 1990. write for info. (*0-940795-00-0*); pap. 18.95 (*0-940795-08-6*) LifeRhythm.

Pierrard, Pierre. Larousse Dictionnaire des Prenoms et des Saints. 224p. (FRE.). 1987. pap. 19.95 (*0-7859-1254-1*, 2037300174) Fr & Eur.

Pierre, Andrew J. The Global Politics of Arms Sales. 353p. 1981. pap. 14.95 (*0-691-02207-0*) Princeton U Pr.

— The Global Politics of Arms Sales. LC 81-15895. (Illus.). Date not set. reprint ed. pap. 106.10 (*0-7837-9420-7*, 2060161) Bks Demand.

Pierre, Andrew J., ed. Cascade of Arms: Controlling Conventional Weapons Proliferation in the 1990s. 385p. (C). Date not set. 42.95x (*0-8157-7064-2*); pap. 18.95 (*0-8157-7063-4*) Brookings.

— The Conventional Defense of Europe: New Technologies & New Strategies. 200p. 1986. pap. 6.95 (*0-87609-015-3*) Coun Foreign.

— A High Technology Gap: Europe, American, & Japan. 114p. 1987. pap. 6.95 (*0-87609-021-8*) Coun Foreign.

— Nuclear Weapons in Europe. 128p. 1984. 5.95 (*0-87609-000-5*) Coun Foreign.

— Third World Instability: Central America As a European-American Issue. 168p. 1985. pap. 5.95 (*0-87609-005-6*) Coun Foreign.

— Unemployment & Growth in the Western Economies. 152p. 1984. pap. 5.95 (*0-87609-001-3*) Coun Foreign.

— Unemployment & Growth in Western Economies. (Europe-America Ser.). 160p. 1985. 35.00x (*0-8147-6589-0*) NYU Pr.

— A Widening Atlantic? Domestic Change & Foreign Policy. 119p. 1984. pap. 5.95 (*0-87609-011-0*) Coun Foreign.

Pierre, Bernard & Pierre, Genevieve. Medical Dictionary for Tropical Regions: Dictionnaire Medical Pour les Regions Tropicales. 2nd ed. 850p. (FRE.). 1988. pap. 75.00 (*0-8288-1823-1*) Fr & Eur.

Pierre, C. & Maurande, G. French-English - English-French Vocabulary of Ecology. 94p. 1989. pap. 26.50 (*2-85608-036-7*, Pub. by La Maison Du Dict FR) IBD Ltd.

Pierre, C. & Perkins, N. C., eds. Structural Dynamics of Large Scale & Complex Systems. LC 93-72635. (DE Ser.: Vol. 59). 160p. 1993. 55.00 (*0-7918-1176-X*, G00820) ASME.

Pierre, Chantal & Pierre, Maurande. Lexique de l'Ecologie: Anglas-Francais, Francais-Anglais. (ENG & FRE.). 1989. pap. 49.95 (*0-7859-3918-0*) Fr & Eur.

Pierre de la Ruffiniere du Prey. The Villas of Pliny from Antiquity to Posterity. LC 93-44209. 1994. 65.00 (*0-226-17300-3*) U Ch Pr.

Pierre, Donald A. Optimization Theory with Applications. LC 69-19239. (Series in Decision & Control). reprint ed. pap. 157.00 (*0-317-08592-1*, 2006317) Bks Demand.

— Optimization Theory with Applications. 640p. 1986. reprint ed. pap. 13.95 (*0-486-65205-X*) Dover.

Pierre du Moulin the Elder. The Anatomy of Arminianisme. LC 76-57380. (English Experience Ser.: No. 797). 1977. reprint ed. lib. bdg. 65.00 (*90-221-0797-3*) Walter J Johnson.

Pierre, Edwards R. Welding Processes & Power Sources. 3rd ed. (Student Study Guide Ser.). (Illus.). 416p. (C). 1984. text ed. write for info. (*0-8087-3369-9*); student ed write for info. (*0-8087-3370-2*) Burgess MN Intl.

Pierre, Genevieve, jt. auth. see Pierre, Bernard.

Pierre, Jon, ed. Bureaucracy in the Modern State: An Introduction to Comparative Public Administration. LC 94-6261. 1995. 69.95 (*1-85278-725-2*, Pub. by E Elgar Pub UK) Ashgate Pub Co.

— Urban & Regional Policy. LC 94-22993. (International Library of Comparative Public Policy: Vol. 2). 500p. 1995. 129.95 (*1-85278-909-3*, Pub. by E Elgar Pub UK) Ashgate Pub Co.

Pierre, Jon, jt. ed. see King, Desmond S.

Pierre, Jose. Investigating Sex: Discussions, 1928-1932. 1992. 24.95 (*0-86091-378-3*, Pub. by Verso UK) Routledge Chapman & Hall.

***Pierre, Jose, ed.** Investigating Sex: Surrealist Discussions 1928-32. Imrie, Malcolm, tr. (Illus.). 220p. 1994. pap. 16.95 (*0-86091-603-0*, B3643, Pub. by Verso UK) Routledge Chapman & Hall.

Pierre, Kenneth J., jt. auth. see Rockers, Dolore.

Pierre, L., jt. ed. see Milne, G. J.

Pierre, Le-Tan, illus. Wit: The Best Things Ever Said by Mark Twain, Oscar Wilde, Disraeli, Voltaire, Dorothy Parker, Winston Churchill, Talleyrand, P. G. Wodehouse, George Bernard Shaw... LC 91-55510. 64p. 1991. 14.00 (*0-06-018223-7*, E Burlingame Bks) HarpC.

Pierre, Maurande, jt. auth. see Pierre, Chantal.

Pierre, Melvin, Sr. How to Get Visa & Mastercards...Even Though You May Have Previously Been Turned Down. 1986. pap. 5.00 (*0-318-36086-1*) RMP Finan Consul.

Pierre, Melvin. How to Manage Your Family Budget During These Troubled Times. rev. ed. 1978. pap. 5.00 (*0-931664-00-4*) RMP Finan Consul.

***Pierre, Michel.** Good Day, Mr. Gauguin. Volk, Carol, tr. LC 94-47282. (Art for Children Ser.). (Illus.). 64p. (ENG & FRE.). (YA). (gr. 3 up). 1995. lib. bdg. 14.95 (*0-7910-2811-9*) Chelsea Hse.

Pierre-Michel, V. Dictionary of the History of France. 464p. (FRE.). 1991. 49.95 (*0-8288-6924-3*, 2203156031) Fr & Eur.

Pierre-Quint, Leon. Marcel Proust: His Life & Work. Miles, Hamish S. et al, trs. 386p. 1986. reprint ed. text ed. 54.00 (*0-8204-0330-X*) P Lang Pubs.

Pierrehumbert, Janet & Beckman, Mary E. Japanese Tone Structure. (Linguistic Inquiry Monographs). 280p. (Orig.). 1988. 30.00 (*0-262-16109-5*); pap. 15.95 (*0-262-66063-6*) MIT Pr.

Pierret, Janine, jt. auth. see Herzlich, Claudine.

Pierret, Paul. Recueil d'Inscriptions Inedites Du Musee Egyptien Du Louvre. ix, 320p. 1978. reprint ed. write for info. (*3-487-06534-7*, Pub. by Georg Olms GW) Lubrecht & Cramer.

Pierret, Robert F. Field Effect Device. LC 81-15035. (Modular Series on Solid State Devices: No. 4). (Illus.). 116p. 1983. pap. write for info. (*0-201-05323-3*) Addison-Wesley.

— Semiconductor Device Fundamentals. 608p. (C). 1995. text ed. write for info. (*0-201-54393-1*) Addison-Wesley.

— Semiconductor Fundamentals. 2nd ed. (Modular Series on Solid State Devices). (Illus.). 128p. (C). 1988. pap. text ed. 18.25 (*0-201-12295-2*) Addison-Wesley.

Pierret, Robert F. & Neudeck, Gerold W. Advanced Semiconductor Fundamentals, Vol. 6. (Modular Series on Solid State Devices). (Illus.). 208p. (C). 1987. pap. text ed. 20.50 (*0-201-05338-1*) Addison-Wesley.

— Modular Series on Solid State Devices: Semiconductor Fundamentals, Vol. I. LC 81-14978. (Electrical Engineering Ser.). (Illus.). 1983. pap. text ed. write for info. (*0-201-05320-9*); write for info. (*0-201-05324-1*) Addison-Wesley.

Pierrot, ed. see De Balzac, Honore.

Pierrot, M., ed. Structure & Properties of Molecular Crystals. (Studies in Physical & Theoretical Chemistry: Vol. 69). 354p. 1990. 146.25 (*0-444-88177-8*) Elsevier.

Piers, F. Orchids of East Africa. 304p. (C). 1984. 80.00 (*0-685-22344-2*, Scientific) St Mut.

Piers, Frank. Orchids of East Africa. 2nd rev. ed. (Illus.). 1984. pap. 50.00 (*3-7682-0569-X*) Lubrecht & Cramer.

Piers, Helen. Puppy's ABC. (Illus.). 32p. (J). (ps-00). 1987. 9.95 (*0-19-520606-1*) OUP.

— Taking Care of Your Cat. (Young Pet Owner's Guides Ser.). (Illus.). 32p. (YA). 1992. pap. 4.95 (*0-8120-4873-3*) Barron.

— Taking Care of Your Dog. (Young Pet Owner's Guides Ser.). (Illus.). 32p. (YA). 1992. pap. 4.95 (*0-8120-4874-1*) Barron.

— Taking Care of Your Gerbils: Young Pet Owner's Guides Ser. Vriends, Matthew M., ed. LC 92-26959. 32p. (J). 1993. pap. 4.95 (*0-8120-1369-7*) Barron.

— Taking Care of Your Goldfish. Vriends, Matthew M., ed. LC 92-32170. (Young Pet Owner's Guides Ser.). 32p. (J). 1993. pap. 4.95 (*0-8120-1368-9*) Barron.

— Taking Care of Your Guinea Pig. (Young Pet Owner's Guides Ser.). 32p. (J). (gr. 3 up). 1993. pap. 4.95 (*0-8120-1367-0*) Barron.

— Taking Care of Your Hamster. (Young Pet Owner's Guides Ser.). 32p. (J). 1992. pap. 4.95 (*0-8120-4695-1*) Barron.

— Taking Care of Your Parakeet. (Young Pet Owner's Guides Ser.). 32p. (J). (gr. 3 up). 1993. pap. 4.95 (*0-8120-1370-0*) Barron.

— Taking Care of Your Rabbit. (Young Pet Owner's Guides Ser.). 32p. (J). 1992. pap. 4.95 (*0-8120-4697-8*) Barron.

Piersanti, Jay. Otto Cartoons. LC 93-80698. (Illus.). 96p. 1994. pap. 5.95 (*0-87341-296-6*) Krause Pubns.

Pierse, D., ed. see Ophthalmic Microsurgery Study Group Symposium Staff.

Pierse, Robert. Pierse: The Law of Road Traffic in the Republic of Ireland. 1989. 62.00 (*1-85475-055-0*) Butterworth Legal Pubs.

Piersel. Photomath. (J). (gr. 3-9). teacher ed 0.29 (*0-87783-201-3*); pap. 1.99 (*0-87783-076-2*) Oddo.

— Photophonics I. (Illus.). (J). (gr. 1-5). 1968. teacher ed 0.29 (*0-685-03702-9*); pap. 1.99 (*0-87783-073-8*) Oddo.

— Photophonics II. (Illus.). (J). (gr. 1-5). 1968. teacher ed 0.29 (*0-685-03703-7*); pap. 2.39 (*0-87783-074-6*) Oddo.

Piersen, William D. Black Legacy: America's Hidden Heritage. LC 92-41003. 280p. (C). 1993. pap. 15.95 (*0-87023-859-0*) U of Mass Pr.

— Black Yankees: The Development of an Afro-American Subculture in Eighteenth-Century New England. LC 87-13862. 256p. (Orig.). (C). 1988. pap. 16.95x (*0-87023-587-7*) U of Mass Pr.

Pierskalla, Carol S. & Heald, Jane D. Help for Families of the Aging: Caregivers Can Express Love & Set Limits. enl. rev. ed. (Illus.). 224p. 1988. student ed 11.95 (*0-9619558-1-3*) Support Source.

— Help for Families of the Aging: Caregivers Can Express Love & Set Limits. 2nd enl. rev. ed. (Illus.). 224p. 1988. 39.95 (*0-9619558-0-5*) Support Source.

Piersma, Mary L., jt. auth. see Allen, Diane D.

An Asterisk (*) at the beginning of an entry indicates that the title is appearing in BIP for the first time.

Piersma, N. Combinatorial Optimization & Empirical Processes. (Tinbergen Institute Ser.). 138p. 1993. pap. 25.00 (*90-5170-211-6*, Pub. by Thesis Pubs NE) IBD Ltd.

Piersma, Paul, et al. Law & Tactics in Juvenile Cases. 3rd ed. 801p. 1977. 15.00 (*0-317-30865-3*, B167) Am Law Inst.

Piersol, Allan G., jt. auth. see Bendat, Julius S.

***Piersol, Mary B.** Van Every - Records of the Van Every Family, United Empire Loyalists, N. Y. State, 1653-1784, Canada, 1784-1947. 131p. 1995. reprint ed. lib. bdg. 34.50 (*0-8328-4565-5*); reprint ed. pap. 24.50 (*0-8328-4566-3*) Higginson Bk Co.

***Pierson.** Greeley Longmont. Date not set. pap. text ed. 2.95 (*0-914449-52-4*) Pierson Graph.

— Voices of Summer. 1994. 3.99 (*0-517-13638-4*) Random Hse Value.

Pierson & Mayer, J. P. La Photographie Consideree Comme Art et Comme Industrie. Bunnell, Peter C. & Sobieszek, Robert A., eds. LC 76-24666. (Sources of Modern Photography Ser.). (FRE.). 1979. reprint ed. lib. bdg. 18.95 (*0-405-09643-7*) Ayer.

Pierson & Stern. Foodborne Microorganisms & Their Toxins (IFT) (IFT Basic Symposium Ser.: Vol. 1). 488p. 1986. 79.75 (*0-8247-7607-0*) Dekker.

Pierson, A. T. Acts of the Holy Spirit. 127p. 1980. pap. 3.99 (*0-87509-274-8*) Chr Pubns.

— El Camino De la Vida Eterna: The Hearth of the Gospel. (SPA.). 4.95 (*84-7228-978-8*, 223054, Pub. by Edit Clie SP) TSELF.

— Los Hechos Del Espiritu Santo: The Acts of the Holy Spirit. (SPA.). 3.25 (*84-7228-926-5*, 223005, Pub. by Edit Clie SP) TSELF.

— Pulpit Legends: Knowing the Scriptures. 1994. 19.99 (*0-89957-203-0*) AMG Pubs.

— World's Guide to Understanding the Bible. 349p. 1994. 12.99 (*0-529-10336-2*) World Bible.

Pierson, Anne. Fifty-Two Simple Things You Can Do to Be Pro-Life. 1991. pap. 5.99 (*1-55661-170-6*) Bethany Hse.

— Mending Hearts, Mending Lives. 166p. (Orig.). 1984. pap. 7.99 (*0-914903-30-6*) Destiny Image.

Pierson, Carlos C., tr. see Tidwell, J. B.

Pierson, Caryl K. & De Voss, Vicki. Level DIV Geometry & Measurement. (Moving with Math Ser.). (Illus.). 100p. 1988. pap. 5.95 (*0-933383-21-5*) Math Teachers Pr.

— Level DV Pre-Algebra. (Moving with Math Ser.). (Illus.). 80p. 1988. pap. 4.95 (*0-933383-22-3*) Math Teachers Pr.

— Skill Builders Using Action Math Level D. (Illus.). 208p. 1988. pap. 29.95 (*0-933383-29-0*) Math Teachers Pr.

Pierson, Caryl K., et al. Skill Builders Using Action Math Level A. 150p. 1987. pap. 29.95 (*0-933383-23-1*) Math Teachers Pr.

Pierson, Christopher. Beyond the Welfare State? The New Political Economy of Welfare. 260p. 1991. text ed. 35.00 (*0-271-00820-2*); pap. text ed. 14.95 (*0-271-00821-0*) Pa St U Pr.

— Socialism After Communism: The New Market Socialism. LC 94-47518. 260p. 1995. pap. 16.95 (*0-271-01479-2*) Pa St U Pr.

— Socialism After Communism: The New Market Socialism. LC 94-47518. 260p. 1995. 45.00 (*0-271-01478-4*) Pa St U Pr.

Pierson, David J. & Kacmarek, Robert M., eds. Foundations of Respiratory Care. LC 92-17459. (Illus.). 1045p. 1992. text ed. 92.00 (*0-443-08509-9*) Churchill.

Pierson, David J., jt. auth. see Luce, John M.

Pierson, Don, jt. auth. see Ditka, Mike.

Pierson, Donna, jt. ed. see Cerutti, Dan.

Pierson, Doug, jt. auth. see Hennech, Michael C.

Pierson, Edna C. The Witch of Turner's Bald. (Illus.). 1971. 5.00 (*0-686-05889-5*) Puddingstone.

Pierson, Elizabeth C. & Pierson, Jan Erik. A Birder's Guide to the Coast of Maine. LC 81-67953. (Illus.). 224p. 1981. pap. 9.95 (*0-89272-118-9*, PIC471) Down East.

Pierson, Frank C. The Minimum Level of Unemployment & Public Policy. LC 80-26536. 194p. 1980. pap. text ed. 12.00 (*0-911558-75-6*) W E Upjohn.

Pierson, Frank M. Principles & Techniques of Patient Care. LC 93-27001. (Illus.). 320p. 1994. pap. text ed. 31.50 (*0-7216-3719-1*) Saunders.

Pierson, George W. The Founding of Yale. (C). 1988. 37.50 (*0-300-04252-3*) Yale U Pr.

Pierson, Hamilton W. Jefferson at Monticello: The Private Life of Thomas Jefferson. LC 71-154161. (Select Bibliographies Reprint Ser.). 1977. reprint ed. 24.95 (*0-8369-5777-6*) Ayer.

— A Letter to Hon. Charles Sumner. LC 78-38018. (Black Heritage Library Collection). reprint ed. 12.50 (*0-8369-8985-6*) Ayer.

Pierson, Herbert, jt. auth. see Giles, Howard.

Pierson, Hugh O. Handbook of Carbon, Graphite, Diamond, & Fullerenes: Properties, Processing, & Applications. LC 93-29744. (Illus.). 405p. 1994. 86.00 (*0-8155-1339-9*) Noyes.

— Handbook of Chemical Vapor Deposition. LC 91-46658. (Illus.). 436p. 1992. 68.00 (*0-8155-1300-3*) Noyes.

Pierson, J. K. & Horn, Jeretta. Structured COBOL Programming. (C). 1986. pap. text ed. 37.00 (*0-673-15913-2*) HarpCollege.

Pierson, Jan Erik, jt. auth. see Pierson, Elizabeth C.

Pierson, Jim. Dark Shadows Resurrected. (Illus.). 176p. (Orig.). 1992. 24.95 (*0-938817-24-8*) Pomegranate Pr.

— Dark Shadows Resurrected. (Orig.). 1993. pap. 15.95 (*0-938817-23-X*) Pomegranate Pr.

— Just Like Everybody Else. (Illus.). 32p. (J). (ps-3). 1993. 10.99 (*0-87403-842-1*, 24-03661) Standard Pub.

Pierson, Jim & Korth, Bob, eds. Reaching out to Special People: A Resource for Ministry with Persons Who Have Disabilities. 320p. 1989. 21.99 (*0-87403-569-4*, 3139) Standard Pub.

Pierson, Jim, ed. see Scott, Kathryn L.

Pierson, Joan K. MIS: Managinng with Computers. (Testbook). 293p. (C). 1993. pap. text ed. 8.00 (*0-15-500815-3*) Dryden Pr.

Pierson, Johann. Moeris Atticista: Lexicon Atticum, 2 vols., Set. 1969. reprint ed. write for info. (*0-318-72055-8*, Pub. by Georg Olms GW) Lubrecht & Cramer.

***Pierson, John.** Spike, Mike, Slackers & Dykes: A Guided Tour Through a Decade of American Cinema. 300p. 1996. 19.95 (*0-7868-6189-4*) Hyperion.

Pierson, John D. Tokutomi Soho, 1863-1957: A Journalist for Modern Japan. LC 79-3226. (Illus.). 496p. 1980. 59.50x (*0-691-04674-3*) Princeton U Pr.

— Tokutomi Soho, 1863-1957: A Journalist for Modern Japan. LC 79-3226. Date not set. reprint ed. pap. 131.70 (*0-7837-9421-5*, 2060162) Bks Demand.

Pierson, John H. Full Employment. 1941. 59.50 (*0-686-83556-5*) Elliots Bks.

— Full Employment Without Inflation. LC 79-5446. 252p. 1980. text ed. 38.00 (*0-916672-39-5*) Rowman.

Pierson, John R. Clock Repair: Part-Time Hours, Full-Time Pay. LC 91-78023. 160p. 1992. 24.95 (*0-9631669-6-4*); pap. 19.95 (*0-9631669-5-6*) Clockwks Pr.

Pierson, John R., frwd. The Keystone Watch Co. Material Catalog. (Illus.). 84p. reprint ed. pap. 12.95 (*0-9631669-0-5*) Clockwks Pr.

Pierson, Judith. Moving Women Up: A Manual for Breaking Down Barriers. LC 83-60668. 201p. reprint ed. pap. 57.30 (*0-7837-6539-8*, 2045676) Bks Demand.

Pierson, Kenn, adapt. Mountain Thunder: The Ballad of Badger Clark. LC 92-44906. (Wayne S. Knutson Dakota Playwriters Ser.: Vol. 4). 1993. 24.95 (*0-929925-23-8*) Univ SD Pr.

Pierson, Lance, jt. auth. see Mandeville, Sylvia.

Pierson, Marcia M., jt. ed. see Kuo, Way.

Pierson, Merle D. & Corlett, Donald A., Jr., eds. HACCP: Principles & Applications. 230p. 1992. text ed. 54.95 (*0-442-00989-5*) Chapman & Hall.

Pierson, Merle D., jt. ed. see Hackney, Cameron R.

Pierson, Michael & Springer, Stephen. Cooperative Education Handbook. 74p. 1990. pap. 17.95 (*0-945483-02-3*) E Bowers Pub.

Pierson, Michael J. & Dorsey, Oscar L. Portfolio Development for Career Planning. 116p. 1987. pap. text ed. 19.95 (*0-912855-71-1*) E Bowers Pub.

Pierson, Mike. In the Wrong Hands. Ingram, tr. 385p. 1994. pap. 9.95 (*1-56901-322-5*) NW Pub.

Pierson, Nancy, ed. David Barbero Recent Paintings: The Paintings of David Barbero. (Illus.). 32p. (C). 1988. write for info. (*0-913763-02-0*) E Mayans Gallery.

— David Barbero Recent Paintings: The Paintings of David Barbero. (Illus.). 32p. (C). 1989. write for info. (*0-913763-05-5*) E Mayans Gallery.

Pierson, Nancy, ed. see Udall, Sharyn.

Pierson, Paul. Dismantling the Welfare State? Reagan, Thatcher, & the Politics of Retrenchment. LC 93-40381. (Cambridge Studies in Comparative Politics). (Illus.). 224p. (C). 1994. 49.95 (*0-521-40382-0*) Cambridge U Pr.

— European Social Policy: Between Fragmentation & Integration. Leibfried, Stephan, ed. (Integrating National Economies: Promise & Pitfalls Ser.). 420p. (C). 1995. 44.95x (*0-8157-5248-2*); pap. 18.95x (*0-8157-5247-4*) Brookings.

Pierson, Peter. Commander of the Armada: A Life of the Seventh Duke of Medina Sidonia, 1549-1615. LC 89-5258. 312p. (C). 1989. 35.00 (*0-300-04408-9*) Yale U Pr.

Pierson, R. H. Guide to Spanish Idioms. 174p. (ENG & SPA.). 1980. pap. 6.95 (*0-8288-2329-4*, S 31738) Fr & Eur.

Pierson, Raymond H. Guide to Spanish Idioms: Guia de Modismos Espanoles. 180p. (ENG & SPA.). 1985. pap. 6.95 (*0-8442-7325-2*, Natl Textbk) NTC Pub Grp.

Pierson, Richard N., Jr., ed. Quantitative Nuclear Cardiology. LC 74-20990. (Illus.). 299p. reprint ed. pap. 85.30 (*0-317-07862-3*, 2012582) Bks Demand.

Pierson, Robert W., Jr., jt. ed. see Tourbier, Joachim T.

Pierson, Ruth & Vik, Susan. Making Sense in English. Sands-Boehmer, Kathleen, ed. 292p. (Orig.). (C). 1987. pap. text ed. 21.94 (*0-201-14585-5*) Addison-Wesley.

Pierson, Ruth R., et al, eds. Women & Peace: Theoretical, Historical & Practical Perspectives. LC 87-6778. 249p. 1987. 45.00 (*0-7099-4068-8*, Pub. by Croom Helm UK) Routledge Chapman & Hall.

Pierson, Stanley. British Socialists: The Journey from Fantasy to Politics. LC 78-25820. 415p. 1979. reprint ed. pap. 118.30 (*0-7837-1720-2*, 2057249) Bks Demand.

— Marxist Intellectuals & the Working-Class Mentality in Germany, 1887-1912. LC 92-41089. 344p. 1993. text ed. 42.50 (*0-674-55123-0*) HUP.

Pierson, Stephanie. Because I'm the Mother, That's Why: Mostly True Confessions of Modern Motherhood. LC 93-5917. (Illus.). 1994. 16.95 (*0-385-31096-X*) Delacorte.

Pierson, Thomas C., jt. auth. see Wright, Thomas L.

Pierson, W. Hispanic-American History: A Syllabus. 1976. lib. bdg. 59.95 (*0-8490-1952-4*) Gordon Pr.

Pierson, William H., Jr. American Buildings & Their Architects, Vol. 1: The Colonial & Neo-Classical Styles. (Illus.). 528p. 1986. pap. 19.95 (*0-19-504216-0*) OUP.

— American Buildings & Their Architects, Vol. 2: Technology & the Picturesque, the Corporate & the Early Gothic Styles. (Illus.). 528p. 1986. pap. 16.95 (*0-19-504217-4*) OUP.

Pierson, William H., Jr. & Davidson, Martha, eds. Arts of the United States: A Pictorial Survey. LC 60-9985. 452p. 1960. 20.00 (*0-8203-0018-7*) U of Ga Pr.

Pierson, William W., jt. ed. see Foerster, Norman.

Pierson, William W., Jr., ed. see Malone, Bartlett Y.

Pierzynski, Gary M., et al. Soils & Environmental Quality. LC 93-23049. 1993. 69.95 (*0-87371-680-9*, TD878) Lewis Pubs.

Pies, Cheri. Considering Parenthood: A Handbook for Lesbians. LC 88-29463. 304p. (Orig.). 1988. pap. 12.95 (*0-933216-17-3*) Spinsters Ink.

Pies, Ronald. Lean Soil. 1984. pap. 3.50 (*0-318-04453-6*) Pudding Hse Pubns.

Pies, Ronald M. Riding Down Dark. Page, Carolyn, ed. & illus. by. (Chapbook Ser.). 32p. (Orig.). 1992. pap. 6.00 (*1-879205-31-9*) Nightshade Pr.

Pies, Ronald W. Clinical Manual of Psychiatric Diagnosis & Treatment: A Biopsychosocial Approach. 1994. boxed 49.95 (*0-88048-534-5*) Am Psychiatric.

Pies, W. & Weiss, A. Crystal Structure Data of Inorganic Compounds, Part B: Key Elements O, S, Se, Te: Pt. B3: Key Elements S, Se, Te. (Landolt-Boernstein Numberical Data & Functional Relationships in Science & Technology Ser.: Group VII, Vol. 7, Pt. B). 460p. 1982. 794.00 (*0-387-11622-2*) Spr-Verlag.

— Crystal Structure Data of Inorganic Compounds, Pt. B: Key Elements O, S, Se, Te; Pt. B2: Substance Numbers B1818...2804. (Landolt-Boernstein Ser.: Group III, Vol. 7). 1979. 255.00 (*0-387-09593-4*) Spr-Verlag.

— Key Elements: N, P, As, Sb, Bi, C - 1: Key Element : N. LC 62-53136. (Landolt-Boernstein Ser.: Group III, Vol. 7, Pt. C). (Illus.). 1978. 315.00 (*0-387-08674-9*) Spr-Verlag.

— Landolt-Boernstein Numerical Data & Functional Relationships in Science & Technology, New Series, Group 3: Crystal & Solid State Physics, Vol. 7, Key Elements O, S, Se, Te, Bl. Substance N. (Illus.). xxiii, 674p. 1974. 818.00 (*0-387-06919-4*) Spr-Verlag.

— Landolt-Boernstein Numerical Data & Functional Relationships in Science & Technology, New Series, Group 3: Crystal & Solid State Physics, Vol. 7a, Structure Data Of Inorganic Compounds. LC 62-53136. 647p. 1973. 782.00 (*0-387-06166-5*) Spr-Verlag.

— Landolt-Boernstein Numerical Data & Functional Relationships in Science & Technology, New Series, Group 3: Crystal & Solid State Physics, Vol. 7g, References. 465p. 1973. 552.00 (*0-387-06541-5*) Spr-Verlag.

— Schluesselelemente. (Landolt-Boernstein Crystal Structure Data of Inorganic Compounds, New Ser.: Group III, Vol. 7e). (Illus.). 780p. 1975. 897.00 (*0-387-07334-5*) Spr-Verlag.

Piesarskas. Lithuanian-English Dictionary. 511p. (ENG & LIT.). 1991. 39.95 (*0-8288-4015-6*, F109070) Fr & Eur.

Piesarskas, B. & Baravykas, V. English-Lithuanian Dictionary. 590p. (ENG & LIT.). 1978. 26.00 (*0-88431-738-2*) IBD Ltd.

— Lithuanian-English Dictionary. (ENG & LIT.). 1978. 26.00 (*0-88431-069-8*) IBD Ltd.

Piesiewicz, Krzysztof, jt. auth. see Kieslowski, Krzysztof.

Piesinger, Gregory H. Nuclear Radiation: What It Is, How to Detect It, How to Protect Yourself from It. LC 80-24001. (Illus.). 127p. (Orig.). (C). 1980. pap. 9.95 (*0-937224-00-6*) Dyco Inc.

***Piesm, Ronald & Weinberg, Andrew D., eds.** Quick Reference Guide to Geriatric Psychopharmacology. 38p. 1990. pap. text ed. 10.00 (*1-887272-01-1*) Amer Med Pub.

***Piesman, Marissa.** Alternate Sides. 1995. write for info. (*0-385-31355-1*) Delacorte.

— Close Quarters. LC 93-42215. 1994. 19.95 (*0-385-30538-9*) Delacorte.

— Heading Uptown. large type ed. LC 93-15034. 1993. 21.95 (*0-7927-1658-2*, Curley Lrg Print); pap. 19.95 (*0-7927-1657-4*, Curley Lrg Print) Chivers N Amer.

— Heading Uptown: A Nina Fischman Mystery. 1994. mass mkt. 4.99 (*0-440-21161-1*) Dell.

— Unorthodox Practices. 224p. 1989. mass mkt. 4.99 (*0-671-67315-7*) PB.

Piesold, David D. Civil Engineering Practice: Engineering Success by Analysis of Failure. 1991. text ed. 49.00 (*0-07-707239-1*) McGraw.

***Piesse, J., et al.** British Financial Markets & Institutions. 2nd ed. LC 95-8631. 1995. pap. write for info. (*0-13-647165-X*) P-H.

Piessens, R. & Mori, M., eds. Numerical Quadrature. 220p. 1987. 66.75 (*0-444-70182-6*, North Holland) Elsevier.

Piessens, R., et al. Quadpack: A Subroutine Package for Automatic Integration. (Computational Mathematics Ser.: Vol. 1). (Illus.). 301p. 1983. pap. 42.00 (*0-387-12553-1*) Spr-Verlag.

Piest, Oskar, ed. Utilitarianism: Mill. 88p. (C). 1957. pap. write for info. (*0-02-395670-4*) Macmillan.

Piest, Oskar, ed. see Cornford, Francis M.

Pieston, Mark. California Mission Cookery. (Border Bks.). 220p. 1993. pap. 15.95 (*0-9623865-5-3*) Out West Pub.

Piet, John H. A Path Through the Bible. LC 81-2258. 318p. reprint ed. pap. 90.70 (*0-7837-2633-3*, 2042983) Bks Demand.

Piet-Pelon, Nancy J. & Hornby, Barbara. Women Overseas: A Practical Guide. 168p. (C). 1986. 50.00 (*0-85292-375-9*); pap. 40.00 (*0-685-60719-4*, Pub. by IPM Hse UK) St Mut.

— Women's Guide to Overseas Living. 2nd rev. ed. LC 92-40422. 210p. 1993. reprint ed. pap. 14.95 (*1-877864-05-6*) Intercult Pr.

Pietarinen, Fred. With Wine & Song & Strange People Rushing Thru Me. (Illus.). 40p. (Orig.). 1983. pap. text ed. 2.50 (*1-879594-07-2*) Androgyne Bks.

Pieters, Albertas. Scofield Bible. pap. 0.99 (*0-87377-070-6*) GAM Pubns.

Pieters, C. M. & Englert, P. A., eds. Remote Geochemical Analysis: Elemental & Mineralogical Composition. LC 92-42655. (Topics in Remote Sensing Ser.: No. 4). (Illus.). 585p. (C). 1993. 79.95 (*0-521-40281-6*) Cambridge U Pr.

Pieters, D. Introduction into the Basic Principles of Social Security. LC 93-42438. 1993. write for info. (*90-6544-787-3*) Kluwer Law Tax Pubs.

Pieters, Danny, ed. Social Security in Europe: Miscellanea of the Erasmus Programme of Studies Relating to Social Security in the European Communities. 295p. 1991. pap. 93.00x (*90-6215-284-8*, Pub. by Maklu Uitgevers BE) W W Gaunt.

Pieters, Danny, et al. Introduction into the Social Security Law of the Member States of the European Community. 2nd ed. 239p. 1993. pap. 63.00 (*90-6215-361-5*, Pub. by Maklu Uitgevers BE) W W Gaunt.

Pieters, Eli. Female Disorders & Symptoms. 1984. 2.95 (*0-8062-1671-9*) Eli Mail.

Pieters, Eli, ed. Healing Herbs. 1978. 5.95 (*0-8062-1493-7*) Eli Mail.

Pieters, J. M., et al. Research on Computer-Based Instruction. 176p. 1990. 37.00 (*90-265-1109-4*, Pub. by Swets Pub Serv NE) Taylor & Francis.

Pieters, J. M., et al, eds. Learning Environments. (Recent Research in Psychology Ser.). ix, 364p. 1990. pap. 41.00 (*0-387-52903-9*) Spr-Verlag.

Pieters, Jos. V. The Discerning Heart. LC 91-34761. (Warbler Cottage Romances Ser.). 192p. 1992. pap. 7.99 (*0-8007-5435-2*) Revell.

— A Gleam of Dawn. LC 91-37647. (Warbler Cottage Romances Ser.). 192p. 1992. pap. 7.99 (*0-8007-5437-9*) Revell.

— A Longing Fulfilled. LC 91-37487. (Warbler Cottage Romances Ser.). 192p. 1992. pap. 7.99 (*0-8007-5436-0*) Revell.

Pieters, Richard S., jt. auth. see Lux, J. Richard.

Pieterse, Arnold H. & Murphy, Kevin J. Aquatic Weeds: The Ecology & Management of Nuisance Aquatic Vegetation. (Illus.). 616p. 1994. reprint ed. pap. 49.95 (*0-19-854840-0*) OUP.

Pieterse, Cosmo & Munro, Donald, eds. Protest & Conflict in African Literature. LC 77-80856. 127p. 1969. pap. 13.50 (*0-8419-0005-1*, Africana) Holmes & Meier.

Pieterse, Cosmo, jt. ed. see House, Amelia B.

***Pieterse, Jan & Parekh, Bhikhu, eds.** The Decolonization of the Imagination: Culture, Knowledge & Power. LC 95-13685. (Illus.). 256p. (C). 1995. text ed. 59.95 (*1-85649-279-6*, Pub. by Zed Books UK) Humanities.

Pieterse, Jan N. Emancipations, Modern & Postmodern. (Illus.). 328p. (C). 1992. 69.96 (*0-8039-8777-3*); pap. 24.95 (*0-8039-8781-1*) Sage.

— Empire & Emancipation: Power & Liberation on a World Scale. LC 88-25302. 436p. 1989. text ed. 69.50 (*0-275-92529-3*, C2529, Praeger Pubs) Greenwood.

— White on Black: Images of Africa & Blacks in Western Popular Culture. LC 91-41603. (C). 1992. 35.00 (*0-300-05020-8*) Yale U Pr.

— White on Black: Images of Africa & Blacks in Western Popular Culture. (Illus.). 242p. 1995. 18.00 (*0-300-06311-3*) Yale U Pr.

Pieterse, Jan N., ed. Christianity & Hegemony: Christianity & Politics on the Frontiers of Social Change. 336p. 1992. 59.95 (*0-85496-749-4*) Berg Pubs.

***Pieterse, Jan N. & Parekh, Bhikhu, eds.** The Decolonization of the Imagination: Culture, Knowledge & Power. LC 95-13685. (Illus.). 256p. (C). 1995. pap. 22.50 (*1-85649-280-X*, Pub. by Zed Books UK) Humanities.

Pietersma, Albert, tr. The Apocryphon of Jannes & Jambres the Magicians: Papyrus Chester Beatty XVI (with New Editions of Papyrus Vindobonensis Greek Inv. 29456-29828 Verso & British Library Cotton Tiberius B. v f. 87) LC 94-4473. (Religions in the Graeco-Roman World Ser.: Vol. 119). (ENG, GEC & LAT.). 1994. 97.25 (*90-04-09938-7*) E J Brill.

Pietersma, Henry, ed. Merleau-Ponty: Critical Essays. LC 89-38160. (Current Continental Research Ser.: No. 553). 300p. (Orig.). (C). 1990. lib. bdg. 49.00 (*0-8191-7588-9*); pap. text ed. 25.50 (*0-8191-7589-7*) U Pr of Amer.

Pietil-Ainen, Pekka, jt. auth. see Chakraborty, Tapash.

Pietila, Hilkka & Vickers, Jeanne, eds. Making Women Mater: The Role of the United Nations. 2nd ed. 224p. (C). 1994. text ed. 49.95 (*1-85649-269-9*, Pub. by Zed Books UK); pap. 17.50 (*1-85649-270-2*, Pub. by Zed Books UK) Humanities.

Pietilainen, P., jt. auth. see Chakraborty, T.

***Pietkiewicz, Karen.** A Lucky Strike for God & Other Stories. 144p. 1995. lib. bdg. 37.00 (*0-8095-4892-5*) Borgo Pr.

***Pietkiewicz, Karen, et al.** Lights over the River: Poetry. 74p. 1995. lib. bdg. 25.00 (*0-8095-4562-4*) Borgo Pr.

Pietra, Francesco. A Secret World: Natural Products & Marine Life. 300p. 1990. 92.50 (*0-8176-2346-9*) Birkhauser.

Pietra, G. G., ed. Pathology of the Lung. (Journal: Applied Pathology: Vol. 4, No. 3, 1986). (Illus.). 96p. 1987. pap. 37.00 (*3-8055-4573-8*) S Karger.

Pietrak, Paul. Buffalo Rochester & Pittsburgh Railway. 2nd ed. LC 92-71876. (Illus.). (C). 1992. reprint ed. pap. 20.00 (*0-9620195-3-4*) S R Ames.

Pietralla, M., ed. Permanent & Transient Networks. (Progress in Colloid & Polymer Science Ser.: Vol. 75). 205p. 1988. 107.00 (*0-387-91310-6*) Spr-Verlag.

Pietralla, M., jt. ed. see Kilian, H. G.

Pietralunga, Mario, tr. see Lajolo, Davide.

***Pietralunga, Mark.** Beppe Fenoglio & English Literature: A Study of the Writer As Translator. LC 86-19300. (University of California Publications in Entomology: No. 118). 255p. 1987. pap. 72.70 (*0-7837-7497-4*, 2049219) Bks Demand.

Pietralunga, Mark, tr. see Lajolo, Davide.

Pietrangeli, Carlo. Raphael: In the Apartments of Julius II & Leo X. 1994. 130.00 (*1-55859-875-8*) Abbeville Pr.

Pietrangeli, Carlo, et al. The Sistine Chapel: The Art, the History, & the Restoration. (Illus.). 272p. 1986. 24.99 (*0-517-05119-2*) Random Hse Value.

Pietrantonj, E. D. Ineffective Erythropoiesis: A Probability Phenomenon. 1987. pap. text ed. 16.00 (*1-57235-059-8*) Piccin NY.

P Q

Pietrasinski, Z. The Psychology of Efficient Thinking. 1969. 93.00 (0-08-012544-1, Pub. by Pergamon Repr UK) Franklin.

***Pietrek, Matt.** Spelunking Windows 95. 1995. pap. 49.99 (1-56884-318-6) IDG Bks.

— Windows Internals: The Design & Implementation of the Windows Operating System. LC 92-46133. 1993. pap. 34.95 (0-201-62217-3) Addison-Wesley.

Pietrewicz, Alexandra T., jt. ed. see Johnston, Timothy D.

Pietri, Pedro. Illusions of a Revolving Door. Rivas, Alfredo M., ed. 261p. 1993. 19.95 (0-8477-3665-2) U of PR Pr.

— Puerto Rican Obituary. LC 73-8058. 128p. 1974. pap. 8.00 (0-85345-330-6, PB3306) Monthly Rev.

Pietrkiewicz, Jerzy & Singer, Burns, comps. Five Centuries of Polish Poetry, 1450-1970. LC 79-15485. 137p. 1979. reprint ed. text ed. 35.00 (0-313-22014-X, PIFC, Greenwood Pr) Greenwood.

Pietrobono, Jean, ed. Coal Mining: A PETEX Primer. (Illus.). 87p. (Orig.). 1985. pap. text ed. 30.00 (0-88698-087-9, 6.00010) PETEX.

— Man Management & Rig Management. (Rotary Drilling Ser.: Unit IV). (Illus.). 75p. (Orig.). 1987. pap. text ed. 24.00 (0-88698-128-X, 2.40000) PETEX.

Pietrobono, Jean T., ed. Open-Hole Fishing. 3rd rev. ed. (Rotary Drilling Ser.: Unit III, Lesson 2). (Illus.). 56p. 1988. pap. text ed. 20.00 (0-88698-126-3, 2.30230) PETEX.

Pietrocini, Thomas W., ed. see National Powder Metallurgy Conference Staff.

Pietrofesa, John J., et al. Counseling: An Introduction, 2 Vols. 2nd ed. LC 83-82703. 544p. (C). 1983. text ed. 58.76 (0-395-35147-2) HM.

Pietromaria. The Reincarnation of the Queen of Port Alberni. 1991. 19.95 (0-533-09533-6) Vantage.

Pietronero, L., ed. Fractals' Physical Origin & Properties. (Ettore Majorana International Science Series, Life Sciences: Vol. 45). (Illus.). 378p. 1990. 75.00 (0-306-43413-X, Plenum Pr) Plenum.

Pietronero, L. & Tossatti, E., eds. Fractals in Physics. 480p. 1986. 62.00 (0-444-86995-6, North Holland) Elsevier.

Pietropaolo, Domenico. Dante Studies in the Age of Vico. 400p. 1989. 12.00 (0-919473-91-1, DH77, Pub. by Dovehouse CN) MRTS.

Pietropaolo, Domenico, ed. The Science of Buffoonery: Theory & History of the Commedia dell'Arte. 310p. 1989. pap. 16.00 (0-919473-67-9, DH81, Pub. by Dovehouse CN) MRTS.

Pietropaolo, James & Pietropaolo, Patricia. Carnivorous Plants of the World. (Illus.). 206p. 1986. 34.95 (0-88192-066-5) Timber.

Pietropaolo, Laura & Testaferri, Ada, eds. Feminisms in the Cinema. LC 94-17548. 1995. 29.95 (0-253-34500-6); pap. 12.95 (0-253-20928-5) Ind U Pr.

Pietropaolo, Laura, tr. see Grassi, Ernesto.

Pietropaolo, Patricia, jt. auth. see Pietropaolo, James.

Pietrusewsky, Michael. Prehistoric Human Skeletal Remains from Papua New Guinea & the Marquesas. LC 76-521. (Asian & Pacific Archaeology Ser.: No. 7). 208p. 1976. pap. text ed. 9.00 (0-8248-0525-9) UH Pr.

Pietrusza, David. Baseball's Canadian-American League: A History of Its Inception, Franchises, Participants, Locales, Statistics, Demise & Legacy, 1936-1951. LC 89-43627. 236p. 1990. lib. bdg. 38.50x (0-89950-508-2) McFarland & Co.

— The Battle of Normandy. LC 95-12205. (Battles of World War II Ser.). (J). 1995. lib. bdg. write for info. (1-56006-413-7) Lucent Bks.

— The End of the Cold War. (World History Ser.). (Illus.). 128p. (J). (gr. 5-9). 1994. lib. bdg. 16.95 (1-56006-280-0, 2800) Lucent Bks.

— Major Leagues: The Formation, Sometimes Absorption & Mostly Inevitable Demise of 18 Professional Baseball Organizations, 1871 to Present. LC 90-53521. (Illus.). 381p. 1991. lib. bdg. 38.50x (0-89950-590-2) McFarland & Co.

— Minor Miracles: The Legend & Lure of Minor League Baseball. (Illus.). 256p. 1995. 22.95 (0-912083-82-4) Diamond Communications.

Pietruszcak, S., ed. Numerical Models in Geomechanics: Proceedings of the 3rd International Symposium on Numerical Models in Geomechanics (NUMOG III) Held in Niagra Falls, 8-11 May 1988. 782p. 1989. 153.00 (1-85166-346-0) Elsevier.

Pietruszczak, S., jt. ed. see Pande, G. N.

Pietruszka, M. & Lambert, P. El Secreto Trimetrico. Baizabal, Candelaria, tr. 320p. (Orig.). (SPA.). 1989. pap. 7.95 (0-318-50089-2) Quail Valley.

Pietruszka, Marvin. El Embarazo, la Infancia y la Ninez: Pregnancy, Infant & Childcare. 1992. pap. 7.95 (0-934249-03-2) Quail Valley.

Pietruszka, Marvin & Lambert, Paulette. The Trimetric Secret. LC 85-61325. (Illus.). 300p. 1986. 9.95 (0-934249-01-6) Quail Valley.

Pietrzak, Jeanne, et al. Practical Program Evaluation: Examples from Child Abuse Prevention. (Sourcebooks for the Human Services Ser.: Vol. 9). 320p. (C). 1989. text ed. 49.95 (0-8039-3495-5); pap. text ed. 24.00 (0-8039-3496-3) Sage.

Pietrzik, K. & Macdonald, I. G., eds. Modern Lifestyles, Lower Energy Intake & Micronutrient Status. (ILSI Human Nutrition Reviews Ser.). (Illus.). 232p. 1991. 107.00 (0-387-19629-3) Spr-Verlag.

Pietrzyk, M. & Lenard, J. G. Thermal-Mechanical Modelling of the Flat Rolling Process. Ilschner, B. & Grant, N. J., eds. (Materials Research & Engineering Ser.). (Illus.). 216p. 1991. 79.00 (0-387-53316-8) Spr-Verlag.

Pietsch, A. Operator Ideals. (Mathematical Library: Vol. 20). 432p. 1980. 128.25 (0-444-85293-X, North Holland) Elsevier.

Pietsch, Albrecht. Eigenvalues & S-Numbers. (Cambridge Studies in Advanced Mathematics: No. 13). 300p. 1987. 84.95 (0-521-32532-3) Cambridge U Pr.

Pietsch, Jim. How to Remember & Tell Jokes. 240p. (Orig.). 1992. mass mkt. 4.99 (0-380-76494-6) Avon.

— The New York City Cab Driver's Joke Book. 1986. mass mkt. 5.50 (0-446-34487-7) Warner Bks.

Pietsch, Paul. Shufflebrain. LC 80-21726. 287p. reprint ed. pap. 81.80 (0-7837-6490-1, AU00447) Bks Demand.

Pietsch, Theodore W. & Grobecker, David B. Frogfishes of the World: Systematics, Zoogeography, & Behavioral Ecology. LC 84-51302. (Illus.). 464p. 1987. 72.50 (0-8047-1263-8) Stanford U Pr.

Pietsch, Theodore W., ed. see Cuvier, Georges.

Pietsch, Theodore W., ed. see Renard, Louis.

Pietsch, William V. Human Be-Ing: How to Have a Creative Relationship Instead of a Power Struggle. Orig. Title: Human Being. 1984. pap. 3.95 (0-451-14683-2, AE2750, Sig) NAL-Dutton.

— Human Being: How to Have a Creative Relationship Instead of a Power Struggle. 1989. pap. 4.50 (0-451-15430-4) NAL-Dutton.

— Serenity Prayer Book. LC 89-46441. 160p. 1992. reprint ed. pap. 10.00 (0-06-250637-4) Harper SF.

Pietsch, Wolfgang. Size Enlargement by Agglomeration. 532p. 1991. text ed. 325.00 (0-471-92991-3) Wiley.

Pietsch, Wolfgang J. Friedrich Von Hagedorn und Horaz. (Studien Zur Vergleichenden Literaturwissenschaft Ser.: Bd. 2). xii, 230p. 1988. write for info. (3-487-09023-6, Pub. by Georg Olms GW) Lubrecht & Cramer.

Pietschmann, H. Formulae & Results in Weak Interactions. (Acta Physica Austriaca Ser.: Suppl. 12). x, 64p. 1974. pap. text ed. 30.00 (0-387-81258-X) Spr-Verlag.

— Weak Interactions: Formulas, Results & Derivations. (Illus.). 202p. 1984. 53.00 (0-387-81783-2) Spr-Verlag.

Pietschmann, M. & Wirth, V. Kritik der Pflanzensoziologischen Klassifikation am Beispiel Calciphytisch-Saxicoler Flechten-und Moosgemein-Schaften Im Bereich des Frankendolomits. (Bibliotheca Lichenologica Ser.: Vol. 33). (Illus.). 156p. (GER.). 1989. pap. text ed. 42.00 (3-443-58012-2, Pub. by Gebruder Borntraeger GW) Lubrecht & Cramer.

Pietschmann, V. Hawaiian Shore Fishes. (BMB Ser.). 1969. reprint ed. 15.00 (0-527-02264-0) Periodicals Srv.

— Remarks on Pacific Fishes. (BMB Ser.). 1974. reprint ed. pap. 15.00 (0-527-02179-2) Periodicals Srv.

Piette, Michael J. & Kulisic, Dubravka. The Americans with Disabilities Act: 101 Questions & Answers. (Illus.). 32p. 1994. pap. text ed. 1.80 (0-88450-617-7, 6117) Lawyers & Judges.

Piette, Nadine, illus. Mi Primer ABC. (Pequenos Libros Ser.). 60p. (SPA.). (J). (ps). 1993. reprint ed. 3.95 (970-607-186-5, Larousse LKC) LKC.

— Mis Primeras Palabras en Ingles. (Pequenos Libros Ser.). 60p. (ENG & SPA.). (J). (ps). 1993. reprint ed. 3.95 (970-607-187-3, Larousse LKC) LKC.

— Mis Primeros Conocimentos. (Pequenos Libros Ser.). 60p. (SPA.). (J). (ps). 1993. reprint ed. 3.95 (970-607-188-1, Larousse LKC) LKC.

Piety, James. Chicago Historical Geographic Laboratory Guide. (Illus.). 140p. (Orig.). (C). 1990. student ed, pap. text ed. 11.80 (0-87563-290-4) Stipes.

— Discover Illinois. (Illus.). 144p. (C). 1990. student ed 11.80 (0-87563-291-2) Stipes.

— Rediscover America. 155p. (C). 1986. student ed 10.80 (0-87563-286-6) Stipes.

Pietz, Linda, et al. Toward Better Blood Pressure. 48p. 1992. student ed write for info. (1-884153-06-2) Prk Nicollet.

Pietz, William, ed. see Apter, Emily.

Pietz, William, jt. ed. see Apter, Emily.

Pietzner, Carlo. Inner Development & the Landscape of the Ego. LC 94-12869. 1994. 14.95 (0-88010-383-3) Anthroposophic.

— Questions of Destiny: Mental Retardation & Curative Education. (Illus.). 60p. (Orig.). 1988. pap. 6.95 (0-88010-264-0) Anthroposophic.

— Who Was Kaspar Hauser? An Essay & a Play. 78p. 1990. pap. 10.95 (0-903540-62-2, 94, Pub. by Floris Books UK) Anthroposophic.

Pietzner, Cornelius, ed. A Candle on the Hill: Images of Camphill Life. (Illus.). 174p. 1990. reprint ed. 31.50 (0-88010-296-9); reprint ed. pap. 19.95 (0-88010-297-7) Anthroposophic.

Pietzschke, F. & Wimmer, F. English-Portuguese Illustrated Dictionary (Brazilian) (New Michaelis) 1151p. 1992. reprint ed. 55.00 (85-06-01599-5, Pub. by Melhoramentos) IBD Ltd.

Pieuchot, M. Seismic Instrumentation. (Handbook of Geophysical Exploration Ser.). 375p. 1984. 140.00 (0-08-036944-8, Pergamon Pr) Elsevier.

Pieuchot, M., jt. auth. see Evenden, B. S.

Pieyre de Mandiargue, Andre. Le Lis de Mer. (FRE.). 1972. pap. 8.95 (0-7859-4051-0) Fr & Eur.

— La Motocyclette. (FRE.). 1973. pap. 10.95 (0-7859-4008-1) Fr & Eur.

Pieyre de Mandiargues, Andre. The Motorcycle. Howard, Richard, tr. LC 76-40432. 187p. 1977. reprint ed. text ed. 49.75 (0-8371-9061-4, MAMC, Greenwood Pr) Greenwood.

Piez, K. A. & Reddi, A. H., eds. Extracellular Matrix Biochemistry. 528p. 1984. 86.50 (0-444-00799-7) Elsevier.

Pifarre, Roque, ed. Anticoagulation, Hemostasis & Blood Preservation in Cardiovascular Surgery. (Illus.). 420p. 1993. text ed. 62.00 (1-56053-098-7) Hanley & Belfus.

***Pifarre, Roque, ed. & intro.** Blood Conservation with Aprotinin. LC 95-6759. (Illus.). 407p. 1995. text ed. 55.00 (1-56053-151-7) Hanley & Belfus.

Pifer, Alan & Bronte, Lydia, eds. Our Aging Society: Paradox & Promise. 1986. pap. 15.95 (0-393-30334-9) Norton.

Pifer, Alan, jt. ed. see Allen, Jessie.

Pifer, Alan, jt. auth. see Chisman, Forrest.

Pifer, Caroline S. & Sandoz, Jules, Jr. Son of Old Jules: Memoirs of Jules Sandoz, Jr. LC 88-19138. (Illus.). xii, 129p. 1989. reprint ed. 26.50 (0-8032-4199-2); reprint ed. pap. 6.50 (0-8032-9190-6) U of Nebr Pr.

Pifer, Drury. Smack. (Contemporary Drama Ser.). 1979. 6.95 (0-912262-58-3); pap. 2.95 (0-912262-59-1) Proscenium.

Pifer, Drury L. Innocents in Africa: An American Family's Story. LC 93-22926. 1994. 24.95 (0-15-107564-6) HarBrace.

Pifer, Ellen. Nabokov & the Novel. LC 80-16197. 208p. 1980. 24.50 (0-674-59840-7) HUP.

— Saul Bellow Against the Grain. LC 89-22596. (Pennsylvania Studies in Contemporary American Fiction). 222p. (C). 1990. pap. text ed. 15.95 (0-8122-1369-6) U of Pa Pr.

Pifer, Ellen, ed. Critical Essays on John Fowles. (Critical Essays on British Literature Ser.). 192p. 1986. lib. bdg. 40.00 (0-8161-8759-2) G K Hall.

Pifer, George W. & Mutoh, Nancy W. Point Counterpoint: Discussion & Persuasion Techniques. 200p. (C). 1988. pap. 17.95 (0-8384-2939-4, Newbury) Heinle & Heinle.

Pifer, Joanne. EarthWise: Earth's Energy. (EarthWise Ser.). (Illus.). 48p. (J). (gr. 5-8). 1993. pap. text ed. 7.95 (0-9633019-3-4) WP Pr.

— EarthWise: Earth's Oceans. (EarthWise Ser.). (Illus.). 48p. (J). (gr. 5-8). 1992. pap. text ed. 7.95 (0-9633019-2-6) WP Pr.

— EarthWise: Environmental Learning Series, Vol. 1. (Illus.). 216p. (J). (gr. 5-8). 1993. Incl. Earth's Trees, Sunlight, Earth's Oceans, Earth's Energy, Earth's Food. pap. text ed. 24.95 (0-9633019-5-0) WP Pr.

— EarthWise: Environmental Learning Series, Vol. II. (Illus.). 192p. (J). (gr. 5-8). Date not set. Incl., Earth's Atmosphere, Earth's Humans, Earth's Wildlife, Earth's Waste. 24.95 (0-9633019-6-9) WP Pr.

Piff, Mike. Discrete Mathematics: An Introduction for Software Engineers. (Illus.). 320p. (C). 1991. 64.95 (0-521-38475-3); pap. 19.95 (0-521-38622-5) Cambridge U Pr.

Piffl, E. Acarcology: Proceedings of the International Congress, 4th. 752p. 1979. 243.00 (0-317-89576-1, Pub. by Collets UK) Pro-Am Music.

— Proceedings of the Fourth International Congress of Acarology, Saalfelden (Austria) 725p. (FRE & GER.). (C). 1979. 180.00x (963-05-1695-0, Pub. by Akad Kiado HU) St Mut.

***Pigafetta, Antonio.** The First Voyage Around the World (1519-1522) Cachey, Theodore, tr. 280p. 1995. 24.00 (1-56886-004-8, Eridanos Library) Marsilio Pubs.

— Magellan's Voyage: A Narrative Account of the First Circumnavigation. (Illus.). 208p. 1994. reprint ed. pap. 8.95 (0-486-28099-3) Dover.

Pigafetta, Antonio, jt. auth. see Columbus, Christopher.

Pigafetta, Filippo. Report of the Kingdom of Congo & of the Surroundings: Countries Drawn Out of the Writings of the Portuguese Duarte Lopez. Hutchinson, Margarite, ed. (Illus.). 174p. 1970. reprint ed. 40.00 (0-7146-1847-0, Pub. by F Cass Pubs UK) Intl Spec Bk.

Pigal, Waldo A. Shortcut to the Italian Language. (Quality Paperback Ser.: No. 165). 286p. 1965. reprint ed. pap. 14.00 (0-8226-0165-6) Littlefield.

Pigdon, Keith & Wooley, Marilyn, eds. The Big Picture. 128p. (C). 1993. pap. text ed. 15.00 (0-435-08792-4, 08792) Heinemann.

***Pigeon.** Dad's Little Instruction Book. 1995. mass mkt. (0-7860-0150-X, Pinnacle NY) Windsor NY.

— Mom's New Little Instruction Book. 1995. mass mkt. (0-7860-0140-2, Pinnacle NY) Windsor NY.

***Pigeon, Annie.** Dad's Little Instruction Book. 96p. 1995. pap. 4.99 (0-8217-0150-9) Zebra.

— Love's Little Instruction Book. 96p. 1994. mass mkt. 4.99 (1-55817-774-4, Pinnacle NY) Windsor NY.

— Mom's Little Instruction Book. 96p. 1994. pap. 4.99 (0-7860-0009-0, Pinnacle NY) Windsor NY.

— Mom's New Little Instruction Book. 96p. 1995. pap. 4.99 (0-8217-0140-1) Zebra.

— More from Love's Little Instruction. 1995. pap. 4.99 (0-7860-0107-0, Pinnacle NY) Windsor NY.

— More of Love's Little Instruction Book. 96p. 1995. pap. 4.99 (0-8217-0107-X) Zebra.

— A Visitor's Guide to the Afterlife: Where to Go, What to Do, Where to Eat, & Other Heavenly Hints. 96p. 1995. 9.95 (0-8217-4987-0) Kensington MI.

Pigeon, R., jt. auth. see Gallagher, C.

Pigeon, Robert, jt. auth. see National Park Service Staff.

Pigeon, Robert F., ed. see AEC Technical Information Center Staff.

Pigford & Baur. Expert Systems for Business: Concepts & Applications. 448p. 1990. 34.50 (0-87835-439-5) Boyd & Fraser.

Pigford, Aretha B. & Tonnsen, Sandra. Women in School Leadership: Survival & Advancement Guidebook. LC 93-60093. 103p. 1993. pap. text ed. 19.50 (1-56676-017-8) Technomic.

Pigford, D., jt. auth. see Baur, G.

Pigford, D. V. Expert Systems for Business. 2nd ed. 1994. Incl. disk. disk 35.95 (0-87709-511-6) Boyd & Fraser.

— Expert Systems for Business: Concepts & Applications. 2nd ed. 1994. pap. 38.95 (0-87709-129-3) Boyd & Fraser.

Pigford, J. N., jt. auth. see Hartmann-Petersen, P.

Pigg, Janice S., et al. Rheumatology Nursing: A Problem-Oriented Approach. LC 84-19551. 462p. 1985. text ed. 38.95 (0-8273-4333-7) Delmar.

Pigge, Fred L. Opinions about Accreditation & Interagency Cooperation: A Nationwide Survey. 93p. 1979. 5.50 (0-318-13854-9) Coun Postsecondary Accredit.

***Pigging Products & Services Association Staff.** Primer of Pipeline Pigging. 128p. 1995. 30.00 (0-88415-405-X) Gulf Pub.

Piggins, Carol A. A Multicultural Portrait of the Civil War. LC 93-10319. (Perspectives Ser.). (J). 1993. 18.95 (1-85435-660-7, Pub. by M Cavendish Bks UK) Marshall Cavendish.

Piggins, Carol A., jt. auth. see Johnson, Rolf E.

Piggins, Carol Ann, jt. auth. see Thurman, Anne H.

Piggins, David, jt. ed. see Phillips, Clive.

Piggly Wiggly Carolina Company Staff. By Special Request. 1993. write for info. (0-9637716-0-4) Piggly Wiggly.

***Piggot, Jan.** Turner's Vignettes. (Illus.). 128p. 1994. pap. 40.00 (1-85437-132-0) U of Wash Pr.

Piggot, John, jt. auth. see Macdonald, John.

Piggot, Patrick J., et al, eds. Regulation of Bacterial Differentiation. LC 93-29794. (Illus.). 300p. (C). 1993. text ed. 72.00 (1-55581-066-7) Am Soc Microbio.

Piggott, Bill. Original Triumph TR2-6: The Restorers Guide. (Illus.). 96p. 1991. 29.95 (1-870979-24-9, Pub. by Bay View Bks UK) Motorbooks Intl.

Piggott, Derek. Gliding: A Handbook on Soaring Flight. 5th ed. LC 87-11459. 276p. 1987. pap. 46.00 (0-389-20748-9, N8304) B&N Imports.

— Gliding Safety. (Illus.). 224p. 1991. pap. 29.95 (0-7136-3397-2, Pub. by A&C Black UK) Talman.

— Going Solo: A Simple Guide to Soaring. (Illus.). 112p. 1978. pap. 17.50 (0-06-495571-0, N6638) B&N Imports.

Piggott, F. T. The Music & Musical Instruments of Japan. LC 70-155234. (Music Ser.). 196p. 1971. reprint ed. lib. bdg. 35.00 (0-306-70160-X) Da Capo.

Piggott, J. & Whalley, J., eds. Applied General Equilibrium. (Studies in Empirical Economics). (Illus.). 160p. 1991. 35.00 (0-387-91397-1) Spr-Verlag.

Piggott, J. R., ed. Sensory Analysis of Foods. 2nd ed. 422p. 1989. 101.00 (1-85166-231-6) Elsevier.

— Statistical Procedures in Food Research. (Illus.). 414p. 1987. 106.25 (1-85166-032-1, Pub. by Elsevier Applied Sci UK) Elsevier.

Piggott, J. R. & Paterson, A., eds. Distilled Beverage Flavour: Recent Developments. LC 88-35234. (Ellis Horwood Series in Food Science & Technology). 352p. 1989. text ed. 155.00 (0-89573-819-8) VCH Pubs.

Piggott, Judith & Cook, Mark. International Business Economics: A European Perspective. LC 92-20202. (C). 1995. pap. text ed. 28.50 (0-582-08576-4) Longman.

Piggott, Judith & Cook, Mark, eds. International Business Economics: A European Perspective. 402p. (C). 1992. pap. text ed. 26.95 (0-582-05876-7, 76770, Pub. by Longman UK) Longman.

Piggott, Juliet. Japanese Mythology. rev. ed. LC 83-71480. (Library of the World's Myths & Legends). (Illus.). 144p. (gr. 8 up). 1983. 24.95 (0-911745-09-2); pap. 14.95 (0-87226-251-0) P Bedrick Bks.

Piggott, Margaret H. Discover Southeast Alaska with Pack & Paddle. 2nd ed. LC 90-36104. (Illus.). 240p. 1990. pap. 12.95 (0-89886-242-6) Mountaineers.

Piggott, Michael R. Load-Bearing Composite Materials. 1980. text ed. 124.00 (0-08-024230-8, Pub. by Pergamon Repr UK) Franklin.

Piggott, Michael R., ed. Interfaces in Composites. 320p. 1991. 136.00 (1-85166-667-2) Elsevier.

Piggott, Stuart. Ancient Britons & Antiquarian Imagination. LC 89-50547. (Illus.). 1989. 19.95 (0-500-01470-1) Thames Hudson.

— Antiquity Depicted: Aspects of Archaeological Illustration. (Ancient Peoples & Places Ser.). (Illus.). 1979. 9.95 (0-500-55010-7) Thames Hudson.

— The Druids. LC 84-51870. (Ancient Peoples & Places Ser.). (Illus.). (C). 1985. pap. 15.95 (0-500-27363-4) Thames Hudson.

— The Earliest Wheeled Transport: From the Atlantic Coast to the Caspian Sea. LC 82-73810. (Illus.). 272p. 1983. 45.00 (0-8014-1604-3) Cornell U Pr.

— Prehistoric India to 1000 B.C. LC 83-45838. reprint ed. 28.00 (0-404-20203-9) AMS Pr.

— Ruins in a Landscape. 212p. 1976. 20.00 (0-85224-303-0, Pub. by Edinburgh U Pr UK); pap. 12.50 (0-85224-311-1, Pub. by Edinburgh U Pr UK) Col U Pr.

— Scotland Before History. (Illus.). 193p. 1983. 21.00 (0-85224-348-0, Pub. by Edinburgh U Pr UK) Col U Pr.

— Wagon, Chariot & Carriage. LC 92-70866. (Illus.). 184p. 1992. 29.95 (0-500-25114-2) Thames Hudson.

Piggott, Stuart, ed. The Agrarian History of England & Wales, Vol. 1, Pt. 1: Prehistory. LC 66-19763. (Agrarian History of England & Wales Ser.). 1981. 125.00 (0-521-08741-4) Cambridge U Pr.

— The Prehistoric Peoples of Scotland. LC 80-27371. (Studies in Ancient History & Archaeology). (Illus.). ix, 165p. 1981. reprint ed. text ed. 52.50 (0-313-22916-3, PIPR, Greenwood Pr) Greenwood.

Piggott, Stuart & Daniel, Glyn E. A Picture Book of Ancient British Art. LC 53-3905. (Illus.). 85p. reprint ed. pap. 25.00 (0-317-10519-1, 2051470) Bks Demand.

Piggott, W. G. Triumph TR2-3-3A. (Super Profile Ser.). (Illus.). 56p. 1987. 11.95 (0-85429-559-3, F559, Pub. by G T Foulis Ltd) Haynes Pubns.

Piggott, W. R., jt. ed. see Rawer, Karl.

Pighetti, Toni. The Children's Organizer: A Calendar System of Daily Tasks for Children. (Illus.). 32p. (Orig.). (J). (gr. k-8). 1983. pap. 7.95 (0-913005-03-7) TAM Assoc.

— Nitty Gritty Bare Bones Method of Housekeeping. (Illus.). 26p. (Orig.). 1985. pap. 6.95 (0-913005-05-3) TAM Assoc.

— Stop the Vacuum! I Want to Get Off. 110p. 1987. pap. 6.95 (0-913005-06-1) TAM Assoc.

P Q

An Asterisk (*) at the beginning of an entry indicates that the title is appearing in BIP for the first time.

Piglia, Ricardo. Artificial Respiration. Balderston, Daniel, tr. LC 93-29571. (Latin America in Translation - En Traduccion - Em Traducao Ser.). 192p. 1994. lib. bdg. 29.95 (*0-8223-1426-6*); pap. 12.95 (*0-8223-1414-2*) Duke.
— Assumed Name. Miller, Yvette E., ed. Waisman, Sergio, tr. (Discoveries Ser.). 160p. Date not set. pap. 15.95 (*0-935480-71-4*) Lat Am Lit Rev Pr.
Pigman, C. W., III. Grief & English Renaissance Elegy. 192p. 1985. 79.95 (*0-521-26871-0*) Cambridge U Pr.
Pigman, G. W., III, ed. see Trollope, Anthony.
Pigman, Ward. Carbohydrates: Chemistry & Biochemistry, Vol. IB. 2nd ed. LC 68-26647. 1980. text ed. 163.00 (*0-12-556351-5*) Acad Pr.
Pigman, Ward & Horton, Derek. The Carbohydrates, 3 Vols. 2nd ed. Incl. Vol. 1A. 1972. text ed. 198.00 (*0-12-556301-9*); Vol. 2A. 1970. text ed. 164.00 (*0-12-556302-7*); Vol. 2B. 1970. text ed. 179.00 (*0-12-556352-3*); write for info. (*0-318-50238-0*) Acad Pr.
Pigman, Ward & Wolfrom, Melville L., eds. Advances in Carbohydrate Chemistry & Biochemistry, Vol. 42. (Serial Publication Ser.). 1984. text ed. 139.00 (*0-12-007242-4*) Acad Pr.
Pignacca, Brizio, text. Alfa Romeo Giulia GT. (Cars That Made History Ser.). (Illus.). 84p. 24.95 (*88-7911-055-1*, Pub. by Giorgio Nada Editore IT) Howell Pr VA.
Pignarre, Robert, jt. auth. see De La Bruyere, Jean.
Pignataro, jt. ed. see Briggs.
Pignataro, M., et al. Stability, Bifurcation & Postcritical Behaviour of Structures. (Developments in Civil Engineering Ser.: Vol. 39). 358p. 1991. 110.50 (*0-444-88140-9*) Elsevier.
Pignatelli, Frank & Pflaum, Susanna W., eds. Celebrating Diverse Voices: Progressive Education & Equity. 276p. 1993. 40.00 (*0-8039-6038-7*); pap. 20.00 (*0-8039-6039-5*) Corwin Pr.
— Experiencing Diversity: Toward Educational Equity. 224p. 1994. 40.00 (*0-8039-6142-1*); pap. 20.00 (*0-8039-6143-X*) Corwin Pr.
Pignato, Jeff T. Can I Really Sell? 72p. (Orig.). 1987. pap. 6.95 (*0-936029-07-2*) Western Bk Journ.
Pignatti, Terisio. Canaletto: Selected Drawings. LC 74-104778. (Illus.). 200p. 1970. Individually boxed. boxed 160.00 (*0-271-00105-4*) A Wofsy Fine Arts.
Pignede, Bernard. The Gurungs. 1993. 325.00 (*0-7855-0228-9*, Pub. by Ratna Pustak Bhandar) St Mut.
Pignolet, Louis M., ed. Homogeneous Catalysis with Metal Phosphine Complexes. LC 83-17609. (Modern Inorganic Chemistry Ser.). 506p. 1983. 120.00 (*0-306-41211-X*, Plenum Pr) Plenum.
Pigoff, Jane & Atkins-Green, R. Word Processing Experience. 176p. (C). 1982. 85.00 (*0-85950-386-0*, Pub. by S Thornes Pubs UK) St Mut.
Pigoff, Janet & Smith, Marion. Office Proofreading. 128p. (C). 1986. 50.00 (*0-85950-550-2*, Pub. by S Thornes Pubs UK) St Mut.
Pigors, Faith, jt. auth. see Pigors, Paul.
Pigors, Paul & Pigors, Faith. The Pigors Incident Process of Case Study. LC 79-23530. (Instructional Design Library). 128p. 1980. 23.95 (*0-87778-149-4*) Educ Tech Pubns.
***Pigoski, Thomas M.** Life Cycle Strategies: Software Support on the Front Line. 107p. 1994. pap. 45.00 (*1-884521-03-7*) Software Maint.
***Pigot, Glenn L. & Block, Richard A.** Workboat Engineers Tally Book. 95p. (Orig.). 1988. pap. text ed. 5.00 (*0-934114-62-5*, BK-496) Marine Educ.
Pigott & Tucker. Seafood: Effects of Technology on Nutrition. (Food Science & Technology Ser.: Vol. 39). 384p. 1990. 125.00 (*0-8247-7922-3*) Dekker.
Pigott, Francis, ed. Free Fall to-? (C). 1989. text ed. 21.00 (*0-902662-01-5*, Pub. by R K Pubns UK) St Mut.
Pigott, Grenville. A Manual of Scandinavian Mythology: Containing a Popular Account of the Two Eddas & of the Religion of Odin. Bolle, Kees W., ed. LC 77-79152. (Mythology Ser.). 1978. reprint ed. lib. bdg. 30.95 (*0-405-10561-4*) Ayer.
Pigott, J., ed. Word Processing Experience - Teacher's Experience: Teacher's Handbook & Solutions. (C). 1982. 75.00 (*0-85950-393-3*, Pub. by S Thornes Pubs UK) St Mut.
Pigott, Rod & Power, Christine, eds. Adhesion Molecules FactsBook. (Facts Book Ser.). (Illus.). 200p. 1993. pap. text ed. 42.00 (*0-12-555180-0*) Acad Pr.
Pigou, A. C., ed. see Marshall, Alfred.
Pigou, Arthur C. Aspects of British Economic History. 251p. 1971. reprint ed. 32.50 (*0-7146-2630-9*, Pub. by F Cass Pubs UK) Intl Spec Bk.
— Economics in Practice: Six Lectures on Current Issues. LC 78-59035. 1991. reprint ed. 22.00 (*0-88355-707-X*) Hyperion Conn.
— The Economics of Welfare. 4th ed. LC 75-41213. reprint ed. 44.50 (*0-404-14583-3*) AMS Pr.
— Essays in Applied Economics. 199p. 1965. reprint ed. 32.50 (*0-7146-1240-5*, BHA-01240, Pub. by F Cass Pubs UK) Intl Spec Bk.
— Essays in Economics. LC 78-20487. 240p. 1988. reprint ed. 25.00 (*0-88355-808-4*) Hyperion Conn.
— Income: An Introduction to Economics. LC 78-21487. 120p. 1979. reprint ed. text ed. 45.00 (*0-313-20665-1*, PIIN, Greenwood Pr) Greenwood.
— Income Revisited, Being a Sequel to Income, an Introduction to Economics. LC 78-20835. viii, 86p. 1956. reprint ed. lib. bdg. 17.50 (*0-678-07010-5*) Kelley.
— Industrial Fluctuations, Nineteen Twenty-Nine. 2nd ed. 425p. 1968. reprint ed. 45.00 (*0-7146-2185-4*, BHA-02185, Pub. by F Cass Pubs UK) Intl Spec Bk.
— Keynes's General Theory: A Retrospective View. LC 76-57702. (Reprints of Economic Classics Ser.). 68p. 1978. reprint ed. lib. bdg. 15.00 (*0-678-01225-3*) Kelley.
— Lapses from Full Employment. LC 76-52488. (Reprints of Economic Classics Ser.). viii, 72p. 1978. reprint ed. lib. bdg. 15.00 (*0-678-01226-1*) Kelley.
— Riddle of the Tariff. LC 74-1328. (Reprints of Economic Classics Ser.). xi, 107p. 1977. reprint ed. 17.50 (*0-678-01227-X*) Kelley.
— Study in Public Finance. 3rd rev. ed. xviii, 285p. 1975. reprint ed. lib. bdg. 37.50 (*0-678-07009-1*) Kelley.
Pigozzi, D., jt. auth. see Blok, W. J.
Pigozzi, Jean. A Short Visit to Planet Earth. (Illus.). 128p. 1991. 40.00 (*0-89381-479-2*) Aperture.
Pigram, Ron. Discovering Walks in the Chilterns. 1989. pap. 25.00 (*0-85263-991-0*, Pub. by Shire UK) St Mut.
Piguet. De l'Esthetique a la Metaphysique. (Phaenomenologica Ser.: No. 3). 1960. pap. text ed. 56.50 (*90-247-0236-4*) Kluwer Ac.
Piguet, Charles & Sentis, Michel. The World at the Turning. Hamilton, Ailsa, tr. 132p. 1989. reprint ed. pap. 8.95 (*0-901269-68-9*) Grosvenor USA.
Piguet, Jacqueline. For the Love of Tomorrow: The Story of Irene Laure. Sciortino, Joanna, tr. (Illus.). 144p. (Orig.). 1986. pap. 5.00 (*0-901269-93-X*) Grosvenor USA.
***Piguet, Olivier & Sorella, Silvio P.** Algebraic Renormalization: Perturbative Renormalization, Symmetries & Anomalies. LC 95-15984. (Lecture Notes in Physics: New Series M, Monographs: Vol. 28). 1995. write for info. (*3-540-59115-X*) Spr-Verlag.
Pihel, K. & Pikamae, A. Finnish-Estonian Dictionary: Soome-Eesti Sonaraamat. 686p. (EST & FIN.). 1986. 95.00 (*0-8288-1690-5*, M2825) Fr & Eur.
Pihl, M. R., tr. see Sung-ok, Kim, et al.
Pihl, Marshall R. The Korean Singer of Tales. LC 93-39953. (Harvard-Yenching Institute Monograph: No. 37). 303p. 1994. text ed. 38.00 (*0-674-50564-6*) HUP.
— Korean Word Book. LC 93-73161. (Illus.). 112p. (ENG & KOR.). (J). (gr. k-6). 1993. 15.95 (*1-880188-53-8*); pap. 11.95 (*1-880188-52-X*) Bess Pr.
Pihl, Marshall R., et al, eds. Land of Exile: Contemporary Korean Fiction. Fulton, Bruce et al, trs. (Illus.). 304p. 1993. text ed. 44.95 (*1-56324-194-3*, East Gate Bk); pap. text ed. 18.95 (*1-56324-195-1*, East Gate Bk) M E Sharpe.
***Pihlaja, Kalevi & Kleinpeter, Erich.** Carbon 13 NMR Chemical Shifts in Structural & Stereochemical Analysis. LC 94-5420. (Methods in Stereochemical Analysis). 1994. write for info. (*0-89573-332-3*) VCH Pubs.
Piiper, J. & Scheid, P., eds. Gas Exchange Function of Normal & Diseased Lungs. (Progress in Respiration Research Ser.: Vol. 16). (Illus.). xvi, 320p. 1981. 158.50 (*3-8055-1638-X*) S Karger.
Piiper, J., jt. ed. see Meyer, M.
Piiper, J., et al, eds. Oxygen Transport to Tissue, No. XII. LC 90-7835. (Advances in Experimental Medicine & Biology Ser.: Vol. 277). (Illus.). 930p. 1990. 175.00 (*0-306-43682-5*, Plenum Pr) Plenum.
Piirainen, Ilpo T. Das Stadtrechtsbuch von Sillein: Einleitung Edition und Glossar. (Quellen und Forschungen zur Sprach und Kulturgeschichte der Germanischen Voelker Ser.: No. 46). (C). 1972. 109.25 (*3-11-003543-X*) De Gruyter.
Piirainen, Timo, ed. Change & Continuity in Eastern Europe. 256p. 1994. 59.95 (*1-85521-499-7*, Pub. by Dartmth Pub UK) Ashgate Pub Co.
Piirma, ed. Polymeric Surfactants. (Surfactant Science Ser.: Vol. 42). 304p. 1992. 150.00 (*0-8247-8608-4*) Dekker.
Piirma, Irja, ed. Emulsion Polymerization. LC 81-17626. 1982. text ed. 128.00 (*0-12-556420-1*) Acad Pr.
Piirma, Irja, ed. see American Chemical Society Staff.
Piirto, Douglas D. Conservation Study Guide. 2nd ed. 352p. 1991. per. 24.95 (*0-8403-7066-0*) Kendall-Hunt.
Piirto, Jane. Gifted Children & Adults: Their Development & Education. LC 93-5945. 448p. (C). 1993. pap. write for info. (*0-02-395775-1*, Merrill Pub Co) Macmillan.
— A Location in the Upper Peninsula: Poems, Stories, Essays. (Illus.). 234p. (Orig.). 1994. pap. text ed. 13.95 (*0-9632975-4-6*) Finnish Amer.
— The Three-Week Trance Diet. 240p. (Orig.). 1985. pap. 12.50 (*0-914140-14-0*) Carpenter Pr.
— Understanding Those Who Create. LC 91-41971. 380p. 1992. pap. 20.00 (*0-910707-19-7*) Ohio Psych Pr.
Piirto, Rebecca. Beyond Mind Games: The Marketing Power of Psychographics. LC 91-58121. 263p. (C). 1991. 34.50 (*0-936889-08-X*) American Demo.
— Beyond Mind Games: The Marketing Power of Psychographics. LC 91-58121. 263p. (C). 1992. pap. 29.95 (*0-936889-10-1*) American Demo.
— Beyond Mind Games: The Marketing Power of Psychographics. abr. ed. (Maro Business Reviews Ser.). 52p. 1993. pap. 7.95 (*0-9627362-1-X*); audio 19.95 (*0-9627362-2-8*) Maro Comns.
Piirto, Rebecca, jt. auth. see Francese, Peter.
Piispanen-Krabbe, Tuula, ed. see Brake, Terence & Walker, Danielle.
Pijanowska, Stanislawa. Przerwany Bieg. 1000p. (Orig.). (POL.). 1988. pap. 18.95 (*0-930401-16-6*) Artex Pub.
Pijanowska, Kate. The Solomon Decision Whose Child Is This? An Adoption Dialogue. LC 88-71629. 234p. (Orig.). 1989. pap. 9.95 (*0-934896-48-8*) Adopt Aware Pr.
Pijanowski, Kathy, ed. see Kehret, Peg.
Pijanowski, Kathy, ed. see Novelly, Maria C.
Pijanowski, Kathy, ed. see Qubein, Nido.
Pijanowski, Kathy, ed. see Toomey, Susie K.
Pijawka, David & Mushkatel, Alvin, eds. Nuclear Waste Policy: Siting the High-Level Nuclear Waste Repository. (Orig.). 1991. pap. 12.00 (*0-944285-27-9*) Pol Studies.
***Pijawka, K. David & Shetter, Kim.** The Environment Comes Home: Arizona Public Service Environmental Showcase Home. (Illus.). 120p. (Orig.). 1995. pap. 12.95 (*1-884320-13-9*) ASU Herberger Ctr.
Pijco, A. B., ed. Application of Non Linear Analysis to Structural Problems. (PVP Ser.: Vol. 76). 141p. 1983. pap. text ed. 30.00 (*0-317-02552-X*, H00262) ASME.
Pijls, Nico H. Maximal Myocardial Perfusion As a Measure of the Functional Significance of Coronary Artery Disease: From a Pathoanatomic to a Pathophysiologic Interpretation of the Coronary Arteriogram. (Developments in Cardiovascular Medicine Ser.). 208p. 1991. lib. bdg. 90.00 (*0-7923-1430-1*) Kluwer Ac.
Pijnappel, Johan, ed. Fluxus. (Art & Design Ser.: No. 28). (Illus.). 96p. (Orig.). 1993. pap. 26.95 (*1-85490-194-X*, Academy Edits) St Martin.
— World Wide Video Art. (Art & Design Ser.: No. 31). (Illus.). 96p. (Orig.). 1993. pap. 26.95 (*1-85490-214-8*, Academy Edits) St Martin.
Pijoan de Van Etten, Teresa. Spanish-American Folktales. (Illus.). 128p. (Orig.). 1990. pap. 9.95 (*0-87483-155-5*) August Hse.
Pijoan, Jose. Arte Barbaro y Preromanico: Desde el Siglo IV Hasta el Ano 1000. (Summa Artis Ser.: Vol. 8). 600p. 1989. 295.00x (*84-239-5208-8*) Elliots Bks.
— El Arte Barroco en Francia, Italia y Aemania, Siglos XVII y XVIII. (Summa Artis Ser.: Vol. 16). 600p. 1989. 295.00x (*84-239-5216-9*) Elliots Bks.
— Arte Cristiano Primitivo. Arte Bizantino: Hasta el Saqueo de Constantinopla por los Cruzados el Ano 1204. (Summa Artis Ser.: Vol. 7). 600p. 1989. 295.00x (*84-239-5207-X*) Elliots Bks.
— Arte de los Pueblos Aborigenes. (Summa Artis Ser.: Vol. 1). 600p. 1989. 295.00x (*84-239-5201-0*) Elliots Bks.
— Arte del Asia Occidental, Sumeria, Babilonia, Asiria, Hititia, Fenicia, Persia, Partia, Sasania, Escitia. (Summa Artis Ser.: Vol. 2). 600p. 1989. 295.00x (*84-239-5202-9*) Elliots Bks.
— Arte del Periodo Humanistico: Trecento y Cuatrocento. (Summa Artis Ser.: Vol. 13). 600p. 1989. 295.00x (*84-239-5213-4*) Elliots Bks.
— El Arte del Renacimiento en el Centro y Norte de Europe. (Summa Artis Ser.: Vol. 15). 600p. 1989. 295.00x (*84-239-5215-0*) Elliots Bks.
— El Arte Egipcio: Hasta la Conquista Romana. (Summa Artis Ser.: Vol. 3). 600p. 1989. 295.00x (*84-239-5203-7*) Elliots Bks.
— Arte Gotico de la Europa Occidental: Siglos XIII, XIV y XV. (Summa Artis Ser.: Vol. 11). 600p. 1989. 295.00x (*84-239-5211-8*) Elliots Bks.
— El Arte Griego: Hasta la Toma de Corinto por los Romanos (146 a. de J. C.) (Summa Artis Ser.: Vol. 4). 600p. 1989. 295.00x (*84-239-5204-5*) Elliots Bks.
— Arte Islamico. (Summa Artis Ser.: Vol. 12). 600p. 1989. 295.00x (*84-239-5212-6*) Elliots Bks.
— Arte Precolombino, Mexicano y Maya. (Summa Artis Ser.: Vol. 10). 600p. 1989. 295.00x (*84-239-5210-X*) Elliots Bks.
— El Arte Prehistorico Europeo. (Summa Artis Ser.: Vol. 6). 600p. 1989. 295.00x (*84-239-5206-1*) Elliots Bks.
— Arte Romanico: Siglos XI y XII. (Summa Artis Ser.: Vol. 9). 5p. 1989. 295.00x (*84-239-5209-6*) Elliots Bks.
— El Arte Romano: Hasta la Muerte de Diocleciano: Arte Etrusco y Arte Helenistico Despues de la Toma de Corinto. (Summa Artis Ser.: Vol. 5). 600p. 1989. 295.00x (*84-239-5205-3*) Elliots Bks.
— Renacimiento Romano y Veneciano: Siglo XVI. (Summa Artis Ser.: Vol. 14). 600p. 1989. 295.00x (*84-239-5214-2*) Elliots Bks.
Pijoan, Jose, ed. Summa Artis, 39 vols., Set. 19200p. (SPA.). 1989. 1,150.00x (*84-239-5200-2*) Elliots Bks.
Pijoan, Jose, et al. Arte Europeo de los Siglos XIX y XX. (Summa Artis Ser.: Vol. 23). 600p. 1989. 295.00x (*84-239-5223-1*) Elliots Bks.
Pijoan, Teresa. La Cuentista: Traditional Tales in Spanish & English. Zimmerman, Nancy, tr. LC 93-38779. (Illus.). 208p. 1994. pap. 13.95 (*1-878610-42-2*) Red Crane Bks.
— Healers on the Mountain. 219p. 1993. pap. 10.00 (*0-87483-269-1*) August Hse.
— White Wolf Woman: And Other Native American Transformation Myths. 160p. 1992. 17.95 (*0-87483-201-2*); pap. 8.95 (*0-87483-200-4*) August Hse.
Pijpers, F. W., jt. auth. see Kateman, G.
***Pijuan, Hernandez.** Hernandez, Pijuan: Dibuixos 1989-1990. Goerg, Charles & Queralt, Rosa, eds. (Illus.). 124p. (SPA.). 1993. 69.50 (*84-343-0325-6*) Elliots Bks.
Pikaev, A. K. The Solvated Electron in Radiation Chemistry. 396p. 1971. text ed. 99.00 (*0-7065-1127-1*, Pub. by Keter Pub IS) Coronet Bks.
Pikaev, A. K., jt. auth. see Vereshchinskii, I. V.
Pikaev, Aleksefi K. Pulse Radiolysis of Water & Aqueous Solutions. Hart, Edwin J., ed. LC 66-14343. (Illus.). 311p. reprint ed. pap. 88.70 (*0-317-09468-8*, 2055226) Bks Demand.
Pikaev, Alexei K., jt. auth. see Woods, Robert J.
Pikale, P. Non-Residents: Taxation & Investment in India. 2nd ed. (C). 1989. 350.00 (*0-685-36449-6*) St Mut.
Pikamae, A., jt. auth. see Pihel, K.
Pikas, Anatol. Abstraction & Concept Formation: An Interpretative Investigation into a Group of Psychological Frames of Reference. Tomkinson, Neil, tr. LC 66-3915. 177p. reprint ed. pap. 50.50 (*0-8357-5023-X*, 2002973) Bks Demand.
Pikcunas, Diane, et al. George Mason & the Legacy of Constitutional Liberty: An Examination of the Influence of George Mason on the American Bill of Rights. Horrell, Joseph & Senese, Donald J., eds. (Illus.). 192p. (Orig.). 1989. write for info. (*0-9623905-0-X*); pap. write for info. (*0-9623905-1-8*) Fairfax Cty Hist Com.
Pikcunas, Diane D. Nations at the Crossroads: Unification Policies for Germany, Korea & China. LC 92-47227. (Journal of Social, Political & Economic Studies Monograph Ser.: No. 22). 96p. (C). 1993. pap. text ed. 10.00 (*0-930690-51-6*) Coun Soc Econ.
Pikcunas, Diane P., jt. auth. see Senese, Donald J.
Pike, et al. Catching the Tune. Armstrong, ed. LC 84-4845. (Illus.). 68p. (Orig.). 1984. pap. 5.00 (*0-943924-08-1*) Mus Stony Brook.
***Pike.** The Howling Ghost. (Spookesville Ser.: No. 2). (J). 1995. mass mkt. 3.99 (*0-671-53726-1*) PB.
Pike, ed. Inverse Problems in Optics. 230p. 1987. 43.00 (*0-89252-843-5*, 808) SPIE.
Pike & Fischer. Administrative Law Decisions Second Series, 1952-1989, 67 vols. rev. ed. LC 51-28517. reprint ed. lib. bdg. 55.00 (*0-685-31150-3*) W S Hein.
— Administrative Law Decisions Second Series, 1952-1989, 67 vols., Set. rev. ed. LC 51-28517. 1978. reprint ed. lib. bdg. 3,283.00 (*0-89941-205-X*, 200900) W S Hein.
— Administrative Law Decisions Third Series 1989-1993, 5 vols., Set. 325.00 (*0-89941-757-4*, 201990) W S Hein.
— Administrative Law Decisions Third Series 1989-1993, Vol. 1-4. 60.00 (*0-685-57352-4*, 201990) W S Hein.
— Radio Regulation First Series: 1948-1963, Set. LC 48-2103. 1980. reprint ed. lib. bdg. 1,325.00 (*0-89941-207-6*, 200920) W S Hein.
— Radio Regulation First Series: 1948-1963, Vol. 1, Pt. 3 & Vol. 3-25. LC 48-2103. 1980. reprint ed. lib. bdg. 65.00 (*0-685-73574-5*) W S Hein.
— Radio Regulation Second Series: 1963-1993, 73 vols., Set, Vols. 1-74 (1963-1994) LC 70-24229. 1963. Set. lib. bdg. 5,032.00 (*0-89941-208-4*, 200930) W S Hein.
— Radio Regulation Second Series: 1963-1993, 72 vols., Vols. 1-49. LC 70-24229. 1963. lib. bdg. 75.00 (*0-685-44965-3*) W S Hein.
— Radio Regulation Second Series: 1963-1993, 72 vols., Vols. 50-74. LC 70-24229. 1963. lib. bdg. 85.00 (*0-685-31162-7*) W S Hein.
Pike & Wilkins. A Comprehensive English Oriya Dictionary. 1988. reprint ed. 30.00 (*81-206-0383-4*, Pub. by Asian Educ Servs II) S Asia.
Pike & Wilkins, N. Comprehensive English & Oriya Dictionary. 688p. 1988. 49.95 (*0-8288-8472-2*) Fr & Eur.
Pike, tr. see Banakh, V. A. & Mironov, V. L.
Pike, jt. auth. see Eager.
Pike & Fischer, Inc. Staff, ed. see Fischer.
Pike & Fischer Staff, ed. Uniform Commercial Code: State Variations Service, 3 vols. LC 82-9735. 1992. 425.00 (*0-317-12222-3*) Clark Boardman Callaghan.
— Uniform Commercial Code Case Digest & Code Service, 33 vols. LC 70-126080. 1992. 1,850.00 (*0-317-11804-8*) Clark Boardman Callaghan.
— Uniform Commercial Code Reporting Service: 1965-1992, 63 vols., Set. 2,650.00 (*0-318-42414-2*) Clark Boardman Callaghan.
Pike, Aebulon M. The Journals of Zebulon Montgomery Pike: With Letters & Related Documents, 2 vols., Set. (American Biography Ser.). 1991. reprint ed. lib. bdg. 148.00 (*0-7812-8315-9*) Rprt Serv.
— Southwestern Expedition of Zebulon M. Pike. (American Biography Ser.). 239p. 1991. reprint ed. lib. bdg. 69.00 (*0-7812-8316-7*) Rprt Serv.
Pike, Albert. The Book of the Lodge: Pike's Blue Lodge Degrees. 1993. pap. 45.00 (*1-56459-308-8*) Kessinger Pub.
— The Book of the Words. 180p. 1992. pap. 24.95 (*1-56459-161-1*) Kessinger Pub.
— Ex Corde Locutiones: Words from the Heart Spoken of His Dead Brethren. 363p. 1993. pap. 29.95 (*1-56459-350-9*) Kessinger Pub.
— Hymns to the Gods & Other Poems. 269p. 1992. reprint ed. pap. 18.50 (*1-56459-034-8*) Kessinger Pub.
— Indo-Aryan Deities & Worship As Contained in the Rig-Veda. 659p. 1992. pap. 70.00 (*1-56459-183-2*) Kessinger Pub.
— Irano-Aryan Faith & Doctrine as Contained in the Zend-Avesta. 700p. 1992. pap. 70.00 (*1-56459-181-6*) Kessinger Pub.
— Lecture on Masonic Symbolism & a Second Lecture on Symbolism on the Omkara & Other Ineffable Words. 500p. 1992. pap. 45.00 (*1-56459-162-X*) Kessinger Pub.
— Lectures of the Arya. 340p. 1992. pap. 45.00 (*1-56459-182-4*) Kessinger Pub.
— The Legenda of the Ancient & Accepted Scottish Rite of Freemasonry. 1993. pap. 45.00 (*1-56459-309-6*) Kessinger Pub.
— The Liturgy of the Ancient & Accepted Scottish Rite of Freemasonry. 1993. pap. 45.00 (*1-56459-310-X*) Kessinger Pub.
— Liturgy of the Blue Degrees of the Ancient & Accepted Scottish Rite of Freemasonry for the Southern Jurisdiction. 227p. 1993. pap. 24.95 (*1-56459-323-1*) Kessinger Pub.
— Lyrics & Love Songs. 260p. (Orig.). 1992. pap. 18.50 (*1-56459-036-4*) Kessinger Pub.
— Magnum Opus: or The Great Work: The Complete Ritual Work of Scottish Rite Freemasonry. 650p. 1992. pap. 45.00 (*1-56459-245-6*) Kessinger Pub.
— Masonic Baptism: Reception of a Louveteau & Adoption. 221p. 1993. pap. 24.95 (*1-56459-348-7*) Kessinger Pub.
— Masonry of Adoption: Albert Pike's Masonic Rituals for Women. 220p. 1992. pap. 19.95 (*1-56459-286-3*) Kessinger Pub.
— The Meaning of Masonry. 66p. 1992. reprint ed. pap. 12.95 (*1-56459-050-X*) Kessinger Pub.
— Morals & Dogma of the Ancient & Accepted Scottish Rite of Freemasonry. (Illus.). 861p. 1992. pap. 45.00 (*1-56459-275-8*) Kessinger Pub.
— The Point Within a Circle: A System of Masonry Veiled in Allegory & Illustrated by Symbols. (Illus.). 1994. pap. 3.95 (*1-55818-305-1*, Sure Fire) Holmes Pub.
— Prose Sketches & Poems: Written in the Western Country. Weber, David J., ed. LC 86-29994. (Southwest Landmark Ser.: No. 6). (Illus.). 336p. 1987. reprint ed. 27.50 (*0-89096-305-3*) Tex A&M Univ Pr.

Pike, Andrew. Practical Building Forms & Agreements. LC 93-3959. 1993. write for info. (*0-419-18150-4*) Chapman & Hall.

Pike, Arthur M., jt. auth. see Popkin, Gary S.

Pike, B. A. Campion's Career a Study of the Novels of Margery Allingham. LC 86-72912. 253p. 1987. 27.95 (*0-87972-379-3*); pap. 14.95 (*0-87972-380-7*) Bowling Green Univ.

Pike, B. A., jt. auth. see Cooper, John.

Pike, Barry A., jt. auth. see Cooper, John.

***Pike, Bill.** Motorboating: A Complete Guide. LC 95-12176. 1995. pap. write for info. (*1-56799-206-4*, Friedman-Fairfax) M Friedman Pub Grp Inc.

***Pike, Bob.** High Impact Presentations. Kirchner, Dave, ed. (AMI How-to Ser.). 100p. 1995. 9.95 (*1-884926-35-5*) Amer Media.

Pike, Bonnie. Three Brass Monkeys. LC 88-9331. 96p. (Orig.). 1988. pap. 7.95 (*0-932419-11-9*) Cherokee.

Pike, Brian, tr. see Quetel, Claude.

Pike, Burton. The Image of the City in Modern Literature. LC 81-47149. (Princeton Essays in Literature Ser.). 183p. reprint ed. pap. 52.20 (*0-8357-6152-5*, 2034292) Bks Demand.

Pike, Burton, tr. see Musil, Robert.

Pike, Burton, ed. see Musil, Robert.

Pike, Christopher. The Ancient Evil. MacDonald, Patricia, ed. (Chain Letter Ser.: No. 2). 240p. (Orig.). (YA). 1992. mass mkt. 3.99 (*0-671-74506-9*, Archway) PB.

— Black Blood. MacDonald, Pat, ed. (Last Vampire Ser.: No. 2). 224p. (Orig.). 1994. 14.00 (*0-671-87258-3*, Archway) PB.

— Black Blood. MacDonald, Pat, ed. (Last Vampire Ser.: No. 2). 224p. (Orig.). (J). 1994. mass mkt. 3.99 (*0-671-87266-4*, Archway) PB.

— Blind Mirror. 1995. 21.95 (*0-312-85895-7*) Tor Bks.

— Bury Me Deep. MacDonald, Patricia, ed. 224p. (Orig.). (J). 1991. mass mkt. 3.99 (*0-671-69057-4*, Archway) PB.

— Chain Letter. 192p. 1986. mass mkt. 3.99 (*0-380-89968-X*, Flare) Avon.

— Christopher Pike, 5 vols. 1989. Boxed. boxed, pap. 11.80 (*0-671-92249-1*) PB.

— Christopher Pike, 4 vols. (YA). 1990. boxed, pap. 11.80 (*0-671-96377-5*) S&S Trade.

— The Cold One. 352p. 1994. 21.00 (*0-312-85117-0*) Tor Bks.

— The Cold One. 416p. 1995. mass mkt. write for info. (*0-614-05506-7*) Tor Bks.

— The Dance. (Final Friends Ser.: No. 2). 1991. mass mkt. 3.99 (*0-671-73679-5*, Archway) PB.

— Die Softly. MacDonald, Patricia, ed. 224p. (Orig.). (J). 1991. mass mkt. 3.99 (*0-671-69056-6*, Archway) PB.

— The Eternal Enemy. MacDonald, Pat, ed. 224p. (Orig.). (J). 1993. mass mkt. 3.99 (*0-671-74509-3*) PB.

— Fall into Darkness. 224p. (J). 1991. mass mkt. 3.99 (*0-671-73684-1*, Archway) PB.

— Gimme a Kiss. 160p. (YA). (gr. 8 up). 1991. mass mkt. 3.99 (*0-671-73682-5*, Archway) PB.

— The Graduation. (Final Friends Ser.: No. 3). (Orig.). (YA). (gr. 9 up). 1991. mass mkt. 3.99 (*0-671-73680-9*, Archway) PB.

— The Immortal. MacDonald, Pat, ed. 256p. (Orig.). (J). 1993. 14.00 (*0-671-87039-4*, Archway); mass mkt. 3.99 (*0-671-74510-7*, Archway) PB.

— The Immortal. large type ed. LC 93-32608. (Teen Scene Ser.). (Orig.). (YA). (gr. 9-12). 1993. pap. 15.95 (*0-7862-0071-5*) Thorndike Pr.

— Last Act. (Orig.). (J). 1991. mass mkt. 3.99 (*0-671-73683-3*, Archway) PB.

— The Last Story. MacDonald, Pat, ed. (Remember Me Ser.: No. 3). 1995. 14.00 (*0-671-87259-1*, Archway) PB.

— The Last Story. MacDonald, Pat, ed. (Remember Me Ser.: No. 3). 224p. (J). 1995. mass mkt. 3.99 (*0-671-87267-2*, Archway) PB.

— The Last Vampire. MacDonald, Pat, ed. (Orig.). 1994. 14.00 (*0-671-87256-7*, Archway) PB.

— The Last Vampire. MacDonald, Pat, ed. (Orig.). (J). 1994. mass mkt. 3.99 (*0-671-87264-8*, Archway) PB.

— The Last Vampire 3: Red Dice. (YA). (gr. 9 up). 1995. 14.00 (*0-671-87260-5*, Archway); mass mkt. 3.99 (*0-671-87268-0*, Archway) PB.

— The Listeners. 352p. (Orig.). 1995. mass mkt. 5.99 (*0-8125-5039-0*) Tor Bks.

— Master of Murder. MacDonald, Pat, ed. (Orig.). (YA). 1992. mass mkt. 3.99 (*0-671-69059-0*, Archway) PB.

— The Midnight Club. MacDonald, Pat, ed. LC 93-20917. 256p. (Orig.). (J). 1994. 14.00 (*0-671-87255-9*, Archway); mass mkt. 3.99 (*0-671-87263-X*, Archway) PB.

— Monster. MacDonald, Pat, ed. 256p. (Orig.). (YA). (gr. 7 up). 1992. mass mkt. 3.99 (*0-671-74507-7*, Archway) PB.

— The Party. (Final Friends Ser.: No. 1). 1991. mass mkt. 3.99 (*0-671-73678-7*, Archway) PB.

— Remember Me. MacDonald, Pat, ed. 224p. (J). 1990. mass mkt. 3.99 (*0-671-73685-X*, Archway) PB.

— Remember Me. (YA). 1994. 14.00 (*0-671-50041-4*, Archway) PB.

— The Return. MacDonald, Pat, ed. (Remember Me Two Ser.). 224p. (Orig.). 1994. 14.00 (*0-671-87257-5*, Archway) PB.

— The Return. MacDonald, Pat, ed. (Remember Me Two Ser.). 224p. (Orig.). (J). 1994. mass mkt. 3.99 (*0-671-87265-6*, Archway) PB.

— Road to Nowhere. MacDonald, Pat, ed. 224p. (Orig.). (YA). (gr. 9 up). 1993. mass mkt. 3.99 (*0-671-74508-5*, Archway) PB.

— Sati. 1991. mass mkt. 4.99 (*0-8125-1035-6*) Tor Bks.

— Scavenger Hunt. (Orig.). 1990. mass mkt. 3.99 (*0-671-73686-8*, Archway) PB.

— The Season of Passage. 480p. 1993. mass mkt. 4.99 (*0-8125-1048-8*) Tor Bks.

— See You Later. MacDonald, Patricia, ed. 240p. (YA). (gr. 8 up). 1991. reprint ed. mass mkt. 3.99 (*0-671-74390-2*, Archway) PB.

— Slumber Party. (Orig.). (J). 1985. pap. 3.50 (*0-590-43014-9*) Scholastic Inc.

— Spellbound. (Orig.). 1990. mass mkt. 3.99 (*0-671-73681-7*, Archway) PB.

— Weekend. (Orig.). (J). 1986. pap. 2.75 (*0-590-42968-X*) Scholastic Inc.

— Weekend. 230p. (Orig.). (YA). (gr. 9 up). 1986. pap. 3.50 (*0-590-44256-2*) Scholastic Inc.

— Whisper of Death. MacDonald, Patricia, ed. 256p. (Orig.). 1991. mass mkt. 3.99 (*0-671-69058-2*, Archway) PB.

— The Wicked Heart. MacDonald, Patricia, ed. 224p. (Orig.). (YA). 1993. 14.00 (*0-671-87314-8*, Archway); mass mkt. 3.99 (*0-671-74511-5*, Archway) PB.

— Witch. MacDonald, Patricia, ed. 240p. (Orig.). (YA). (gr. 8 up). 1990. mass mkt. 3.99 (*0-671-69055-8*, Archway) PB.

Pike, Christopher, ed. Futurists, the Formalists, & Marxist Critique. (C). 1989. text ed. 36.00 (*0-906133-14-9*, Pub. by Pluto Pr UK) Westview.

Pike County Historical Society Staff. History & Families: Pike County, Indiana 1816-1987. LC 87-51612. 236p. 1987. 49.95 (*0-938021-57-5*) Turner Pub KY.

Pike, Cynthia. Miracle of Suggestion: The Story of Jennifer. 176p. 1988. pap. 7.95 (*0-318-35137-4*) InnerVision.

Pike, D., ed. see Ledbetter, H. & Lomax, John A.

***Pike, Dag.** Fast Boat Navigation. (Illus.). 176p. Date not set. 25.00 (*0-229-11859-3*) Sheridan.

— Fishing Boats & Their Equipment. 1978. 40.00 (*0-685-63416-7*) St Mut.

— Fishing Boats & Their Equipment. 3rd ed. (Illus.). 200p. 1992. pap. 42.95 (*0-85238-190-5*) Blackwell Sci.

— Inflatables. (Illus.). 192p. Date not set. pap. 30.00 (*0-7136-3881-8*) Sheridan.

— Motor Sailing: Cruising under Sail & Power. (Illus.). 176p. Date not set. 39.50 (*0-7136-3695-5*) Sheridan.

— Power Boats in Rough Seas. 122p. 1974. 27.95 (*0-8464-1433-3*) Beekman Pubs.

Pike, Dave. Bonsai: Step by Step to Growing Success. (Illus.). 128p. 1990. pap. 16.95 (*1-85223-128-9*, Pub. by Crowood Pr UK) Trafalgar.

— Indoor Bonsai: A Beginner's Step-By-Step Guide. 1992. pap. 16.95 (*1-85223-254-4*, Pub. by Crowood Pr UK) Trafalgar.

Pike, David. German Writers in Soviet Exile, 1933-1945. LC 81-10394. xv, 448p. (C). 1982. 39.95 (*0-8078-1492-X*) U of NC Pr.

— Lukacs & Brecht. LC 84-17406. xviii, 337p. 1985. 39.95 (*0-8078-1640-X*) U of NC Pr.

Pike, David W. In the Service of Stalin: The Spanish Communists in Exile, 1939-1945. LC 92-42791. (Illus.). 484p. (C). 1993. 49.95 (*0-19-820315-2*) OUP.

— The Opening of the Second World War. LC 90-15503. (American University Studies: History: Ser. IX, Vol. 105). 387p. (C). 1991. text ed. 62.95 (*0-8204-1524-3*) P Lang Pubs.

— The Politics of Culture in Soviet-Occupied Germany, 1945-1949. 700p. (C). 1993. 55.00 (*0-8047-2093-2*) Stanford U Pr.

Pike, Deborah, jt. auth. see Thompson, Mary.

Pike, Diane K. Cosmic Unfoldment: The Individualizing Process As Mirrored in the Life of Jesus. LC 76-45344. 99p. 1976. pap. 4.95 (*0-916192-08-3*) L P Pubns.

— Life Is Victorious: How to Grow Through Grief. LC 76-17328. (Illus.). 209p. 1982. 11.95 (*0-916192-20-2*) L P Pubns.

— My Journey into Self Phase One. LC 79-12179. 161p. 1979. pap. 9.95 (*0-916192-13-X*) L P Pubns.

— The Process of Awakening: An Overview, Vol. 1. LC 85-8083. (Illus.). 75p. (Orig.). 1985. pap. 9.95 (*0-916192-29-6*) L P Pubns.

Pike, Diane K., jt. auth. see Lorrance, Arleen.

Pike, Donald & Muench, David. Big Sur. LC 78-51408. (Illus.). 48p. 1979. pap. 6.95 (*0-916122-67-0*) KC Pubns.

Pike, Donald G. & Muench, David. Anasazi: Ancient People of the Rock. LC 73-90795. (Images of America Ser.). 192p. 1986. 17.00 (*0-517-52688-3*, Harmony); pap. 17.00 (*0-517-52690-5*, Harmony) Crown Pub Group.

***Pike, Doris.** Pike's Peek at Boston by Night. 88p. (Orig.). 1994. pap. 10.95 (*0-9641563-0-X*) Edge Publishing.

Pike, Douglas. Australian Dictionary of Biography, 4 vols. Incl. Vol. 1. 1788-1850, A-H. 581p. 1968. reprint ed. 59.95 (*0-522-83516-3*); Vol. 2. 1788-1850, I-Z. 634p. 1967. 59.95 (*0-522-83705-0*); Vol. 3. 1851-1890, A-C. 516p. 1974. 59.95 (*0-522-83909-6*); Vol. 4. 1851-1890, D-J. 1972. 59.95 (*0-522-84034-5*); write for info. (*0-318-53676-5*) Intl Spec Bk.

— Australian Dictionary of Biography, Vol. 5: K-Q, 1851-1890. 550p. 1974. 59.95 (*0-522-84061-2*) Intl Spec Bk.

— PAVN: People's Army of Vietnam. 384p. 1991. pap. 14.95 (*0-306-80432-8*) Da Capo.

— PAVN: People's Army of Vietnam. 408p. 1986. 46.00 (*0-08-033614-0*, Pergamon Pr) Elsevier.

Pike, Douglas, ed. The Bunker Papers: Reports to the President from Vietnam, 1967-1973, 3 vols., Set. (Indochina Research Monograph). 902p. 1990. pap. 35.00 (*1-55729-019-9*) IEAS.

Pike, E. G., jt. auth. see Pike, K. L.

Pike, E. Holly. Family & Society in the Works of Elizabeth Gaskell. LC 93-35970. (American University Studies: English Language & Literature: Ser. IV, Vol. 174). 1994. write for info. (*0-8204-2241-X*) P Lang Pubs.

Pike, E. R. & Lugiato, L. A., eds. Chaos, Noise & Fractals. (Malvern Physics Ser.). (Illus.). 614p. 1987. 75.00 (*0-85274-364-5*) IOP Pub.

Pike, E. R. & Sarkar, S. Frontiers in Quantum Optics. (Malvern Physics Ser.). (Illus.). 600p. 1986. 101.00 (*0-85274-577-X*) IOP Pub.

***Pike, E. R. & Sarkar, Sarben.** The Quantum Theory of Radiation. (International Series of Monographs on Physics: No. 86). (Illus.). 360p. 1995. 86.00 (*0-19-852032-8*) OUP.

Pike, E. R. & Sarker, S., eds. Quantum Measurement & Chaos. LC 87-18934. (NATO ASI Series B, Physics: Vol. 161). (Illus.). 304p. 1987. 79.50 (*0-306-42669-2*, Plenum Pr) Plenum.

Pike, E. R. & Walther, H., eds. Photons & Quantum Fluctuations. (Malvern Physics Ser.). (Illus.). 232p. 1988. 75.00 (*0-85274-240-1*) IOP Pub.

Pike, E. R., jt. ed. see Bertero, M.

Pike, E. R., jt. ed. see Tombesi, P.

Pike, Earl A. Protection Against Bombs & Incendiaries: For Business, Industrial & Educational Institutions. (Illus.). 92p. 1973. 19.95 (*0-398-02517-7*) C C Thomas.

Pike, Eunice V. Dictation Exercises in Phonetics. 188p. 1963. pap. 9.00 (*0-88312-900-0*); fiche 8.00 (*0-88312-382-7*) Summer Instit Ling.

— Ken Pike: Scholar & Christian. LC 81-51058. (Illus.). 270p. (Orig.). 1981. pap. 5.00 (*0-88312-920-5*); fiche 12.00 (*0-88312-986-8*) Summer Instit Ling.

— The Last Five Feet. LC 93-87633. 129p. (Orig.). 1994. pap. 8.00 (*0-88312-709-1*); fiche 12.00 (*1-55671-994-9*) Summer Instit Ling.

— Sarah's Life. LC 93-85571. xi, 53p. 1993. pap. 4.95 (*0-88312-618-4*); fiche 8.00 (*0-88312-855-1*) Summer Instit Ling.

— An Uttermost Part. rev. ed. LC 91-75053. 274p. 1991. fiche 12.00 (*0-88312-714-8*) Summer Instit Ling.

— An Uttermost Part. 2nd rev. ed. LC 91-75053. 274p. 1991. pap. 8.00 (*0-88312-810-1*) Summer Instit Ling.

Pike, Evelyn, jt. auth. see Pike, Kenneth.

Pike, Frank & Dunn, Thomas G. Scenes & Monologues from the New American Theater. 304p. 1988. pap. 5.99 (*0-451-62547-1*, Ment) NAL-Dutton.

Pike, Frank, jt. auth. see Morrow, Lee A.

***Pike, Frederick B.** FDR's Good Neighbor Policy: Sixty Years of Generally Gentle Chaos. LC 94-29811. 1995. 34.95 (*0-292-76557-6*) U of Tex Pr.

— The United States & the Andean Republics: Peru, Bolivia & Ecuador. (American Foreign Policy Library). 493p. 1977. 64.00 (*0-674-92300-6*) HUP.

Pike, Frederick B., jt. ed. see Falcoff, Mark.

Pike, Fredrick B. The Politics of the Miraculous in Peru: Haya de la Torre & the Spiritualist Tradition. LC 85-1162. (Illus.). xviii, 391p. 1986. 35.00 (*0-8032-3672-7*) U of Nebr Pr.

— The United States & Latin America: Myths & Stereotypes of Civilization & Nature. LC 91-42454. (Illus.). 464p. 1992. text ed. 40.00 (*0-292-78523-2*); pap. 19.95 (*0-292-78524-0*) U of Tex Pr.

Pike, G. & Selby, D. Global Teacher, Global Learner. (Illus.). 312p. 1988. pap. text ed. 42.00 (*0-340-40261-X*, Pub. by Hodder & Stoughton Ltd UK) Lubrecht & Cramer.

Pike, G., jt. auth. see Selby, D.

Pike, G. Holden. The Life & Work of Charles Haddon Spurgeon. 608p. 1992. reprint ed. 69.95 (*0-85151-622-X*) Banner of Truth.

Pike, Garnet, jt. auth. see Hendricks, Howard.

Pike, Graham, jt. auth. see Selby, David.

Pike, Gustavus D. Jubilee Singers, & Their Campaign for Twenty Thousand Dollars. LC 72-1692. reprint ed. 36.50 (*0-404-08329-3*) AMS Pr.

— The Singing Campaign for Ten Thousand Pounds. rev. ed. LC 75-164392. (Black Heritage Library Collection). 1977. reprint ed. 29.95 (*0-8369-8851-5*) Ayer.

Pike, James. Scout & Ranger. LC 74-39282. (American Scene Ser.). (Illus.). 164p. 1972. reprint ed. lib. bdg. 25.00 (*0-306-70458-7*) Da Capo.

— Scout & Ranger: Being the Personal Adventures of James Pike of the Texas Tangers in 1859-60. (American Biography Ser.). 164p. 1991. reprint ed. lib. bdg. 59.00 (*0-7812-8314-0*) Rprt Serv.

Pike, James A. Beyond the Law: The Religious & Ethical Meaning of the Lawyer's Vocation. LC 73-10754. 102p. 1973. reprint ed. text ed. 35.00 (*0-8371-7021-4*, PIBL, Greenwood Pr) Greenwood.

Pike, James A. & Pittenger, W. Norman. Faith of the Church. 224p. (Orig.). 1951. pap. 1.00 (*0-8164-2019-X*, SP3) Harper SF.

Pike, Jeff. The Death of Rock & Roll: Untimely Demises, Morbid Preoccupations, & Forecasts of Doom in Rock Music. 250p. (Orig.). 1993. pap. 14.95 (*0-571-19808-2*) Faber & Faber.

Pike, Jeffrey A. Automotive Safety: Anatomy, Injury, Testing & Regulation. 184p. 1990. text ed. 79.00 (*1-56091-007-0*, R103) Soc Auto Engineers.

Pike, John. John Pike Paints Watercolors. (Illus.). 160p. 1986. 29.95 (*0-8230-2577-2*, Watsn-Guptill) Watsn-Guptill.

Pike, John & Barnes, Richard. TQM in Action: A Practical Approach to Continuous Performance Improvement. LC 93-34332. 1993. write for info. (*0-412-48790-X*) Chapman & Hall.

***Pike, John E. & Morton, Douglas R., Jr., eds.** Chemistry of the Prostaglandins & Leukotrienes. LC 84-42772. (Advances in Prostaglandin, Thromboxane & Leukotriene Research Ser.: No. 14). (Illus.). reprint ed. pap. 130.00 (*0-7837-9636-6*, 2060389) Bks Demand.

Pike, Joseph B. Classical Studies & Sketches. LC 67-23259. (Essay Index Reprint Ser.). 1977. 16.95 (*0-8369-0790-6*) Ayer.

Pike, Joyce. Oil Painting: A Direct Approach. (Illus.). 160p. 1992. pap. 22.95 (*0-89134-425-X*, 30439) North Light Bks.

— Painting Flowers with Joyce Pike. (Illus.). 144p. 1992. 27.95 (*0-89134-419-5*, 30361) North Light Bks.

Pike, K. L. & Pike, E. G. Grammatical Analysis. rev. ed. (Publications in Linguistics & Related Fields: No. 53). 463p. 1982. pap. 25.00 (*0-88312-085-2*); fiche 24.00 (*0-88312-533-1*) Summer Instit Ling.

Pike, Kenneth & Pike, Evelyn. Text & Tagmeme. 144p. 1983. text ed. 32.50 (*0-89391-210-7*) Ablex Pub.

Pike, Kenneth L. Conceptos Linguisticos: Linguistic Concepts. Hemingway, Thomas & Langan, Katherine, trs. LC 94-65901. 190p. (SPA.). Date not set. pap. write for info. (*0-88312-710-5*); fiche write for info. (*1-55671-990-6*) Summer Instit Ling.

— The Intonation of American English. LC 78-27696. (University of Michigan Publications, Linguistics: No. 1). (Illus.). 203p. 1979. reprint ed. text ed. 35.00 (*0-313-20910-3*, PIIA, Greenwood Pr) Greenwood.

— Language in Relation to a Unified Theory of the Structure of Human Behavior. (Janua Linguarum, Ser. Major: No. 24). 1967. text ed. 118.50 (*90-279-1869-4*) Mouton.

— Linguistic Concepts: An Introduction to Tagmemics. LC 81-19814. (Illus.). 162p. 1982. reprint ed. pap. 46.20 (*0-7837-6889-3*, 2046719) Bks Demand.

— A Mixtec Lime Oven. LC 80-52480. (International Museum of Cultures Publications: No. 10). (Illus.). 9p. 1980. fiche 4.00 (*0-88312-247-2*) Summer Instit Ling.

— Phonetics: A Critical Analysis of Phonetic Theory & a Technic for the Practical Description of Sounds. 1943. pap. 18.95 (*0-472-08733-9*) U of Mich Pr.

— Tagmemics, Discourse & Verbal Art. LC 81-9541. (Michigan Studies in the Humanities: No. 3). (C). 1981. pap. 6.00 (*0-936534-02-8*) Mich Studies Human.

— Talk, Thought, & Thing: The Emic Road Toward Conscious Knowledge. LC 92-82114. xii, 85p. 1993. pap. 5.00 (*0-88312-610-9*); fiche 8.00 (*0-88312-582-X*) Summer Instit Ling.

Pike, Kenneth L. & Pike, Stephen B. Songs of Fun & Faith by "Fish & Chip" LC 79-115755. (Edward Sapir Monograph Ser. in Language, Culture & Cognition: No. 1). viii, 48p. (Orig.). 1977. pap. 5.00 (*0-933104-00-6*) Jupiter Pr.

Pike, Kenneth L., jt. ed. see Brend, Ruth M.

***Pike, Kenneth L., et al.** The Mystery of Culture Contacts, Historical Reconstruction & Text Analysis: An Emic Approach. Jankowsky, Kurt R., ed. LC 95-14739. 120p. 1995. 29.95 (*0-87840-295-0*) Georgetown U Pr.

Pike, Larry. Killer Instinct. 480p. 1993. mass mkt. 4.50 (*1-55817-749-3*, Pinnacle NY) Windsor NY.

***Pike, Lawrence.** Pierced by Sound: Stories, Sketches & Poems. 2nd rev. ed. 83p. 1994. pap. 9.95x (*1-56439-042-X*) Ridgeway.

Pike, Lionel. Beethoven, Sibelius & "The Profound Logic" Studies in Symphonic Analysis. (Illus.). 240p. (C). 1978. text ed. 56.00 (*0-485-11178-0*, Pub. by Athlone Pr UK) Humanities.

Pike, Louise. Southern Echoes. LC 72-1519. (Black Heritage Library Collection). 1977. reprint ed. 15.95 (*0-8369-9046-3*) Ayer.

Pike, Luke O. A History of Crime in England, 2 vols., Set. Reams, Bernard D., ed. LC 10-19490. (Historical Reprints in Jurisprudence & Classical Legal Literature Ser.). 1984. reprint ed. lib. bdg. 105.00 (*0-89941-256-4*, 303170) W S Hein.

— History of Crime in England, Illustrating the Changes of the Laws in the Progress of Civilization, 2 Vols, Set. LC 68-55779. (Criminology, Law Enforcement, & Social Problems Ser.: No. 19). 1968. 50.00 (*0-87585-019-7*) Patterson Smith.

Pike, Luke O., jt. ed. see Horwood, Alfred J.

Pike, Malcolm C., et al, eds. Hormones & Breast Cancer. LC 80-28015. (Banbury Report Ser.: No. 8). 503p. reprint ed. pap. 143.40 (*0-7837-1999-X*, 2042273) Bks Demand.

Pike, Margaret M. & Wheeler, Sara R. Goodbye My Child. (Illus.). 64p. (Orig.). 1992. pap. 5.50 (*1-56123-052-9*) Centering Corp.

Pike, Mary A. Internet Quickstart. 1994. pap. 21.95 (*1-56529-658-3*) Que.

— Using Mosaic. 1994. pap. 24.99 (*0-7897-0021-2*) Que.

Pike, Mary H. Ida May: A Story of Things Actual & Possible, by Mary Langdon. LC 72-6534. (Black Heritage Library Collection). 1977. reprint ed. 39.95 (*0-8369-9171-0*) Ayer.

Pike, Nelson. Mystic Union: An Essay in the Phenomenology of Mysticism. LC 91-55553. (Cornell Studies in the Philosophy of Religion). (Illus.). 240p. 1992. 34.50 (*0-8014-2684-7*) Cornell U Pr.

— Mystic Union: An Essay in the Phenomonology of Mysticism. (Cornell Studies in the Philosophy of Religion). (Illus.). 240p. 1994. pap. 12.95 (*0-8014-9969-0*) Cornell U Pr.

Pike, Nicholas. Sub-Tropical Rambles in the Land of the Aphanapteryx: Personal Experiences, Adventures & Wanderings in & Around the Island of Mauritius. LC 72-4081. (Black Heritage Library Collection). 1977. reprint ed. 44.95 (*0-8369-9103-6*) Ayer.

Pike, Norman. The Peach Tree. (Illus.). 36p. (J). (ps up). 1984. 12.95 (*0-88045-014-2*) Stemmer Hse.

***Pike, P. G.** BEMS Performance Testing. 109p. (C). 1994. 115.00x (*0-86022-359-0*, Pub. by Build Servs Info Assn UK) St Mut.

— Improved Fresh Air Control. (C). 1994. 110.00 (*0-86022-364-7*, Pub. by Build Servs Info Assn UK) St Mut.

Pike, P. G. & Pennycook, K. A. Installation, Commissioning & Maintenance of Fire & Security Systems. 1992. 240.00 (*0-86022-312-4*, Pub. by Build Servs Info Assn UK) St Mut.

— Installation, Commissioning & Maintenance of Fire & Security Systems, 3 pts., Set, Pts. 1, 2-3. (C). 1992. Set. 110.00x (*0-86022-310-8*, Pub. by Build Servs Info Assn UK) St Mut.

An Asterisk (*) at the beginning of an entry indicates that the title is appearing in BIP for the first time.

— Installation, Commissioning & Maintenance of Fire & Security Systems: Fire Detection Systems, Pt. 2. (C). 1992. 160.00x (*0-86022-311-6*, Pub. by Build Servs Info Assn UK) St Mut.

***Pike, P. G. & Pennycook, K. A., eds.** Installation, Commissioning & Maintenance of Fire & Security Systems Pt. 3: Security Detection Systems. (C). 1992. 160.00 (*0-614-03959-2*, Pub. by Build Servs Info Assn UK) St Mut.

Pike, R. William. Stop, Look, Listen Up! And Other Dramas for Confronting Social Issues in Elementary Schools. LC 93-1816. 128p. (Orig.). (C). 1993. teacher ed, pap. 14.95 (*0-89390-267-5*) Resource Pubns.

Pike, Robert. Creative Training Techniques Handbook. 175p. 1989. 45.50 (*0-943210-06-2*) Lakewood Pubns.

Pike, Robert, jt. auth. see Kernighan, Brian W.

Pike, Robert E. Tall Trees, Tough Men. (Illus.). 320p. 1984. reprint ed. pap. 10.95 (*0-393-30185-0*) Norton.

Pike, Robert L. Bullitt. 184p. 1994. 16.50 (*0-7451-8627-0*, Black Dagger) Chivers N Amer.

Pike, Robert M., et al, eds. Innovation in Access to Higher Education: Ontario, Canada ,England, Wales, & Sweden. (Access to Higher Education Ser.: No. 5). 336p. 1978. pap. 10.00 (*0-89192-217-2*) Interbk Inc.

Pike, Robert W. Winning Checkers for Kids of All Ages. (Illus.). 64p. (Orig.). (J). (gr. 3-8). 1993. pap. 9.95 (*0-9635300-0-3*) C&M Pub MA.

Pike, Royston. The Encyclopaedia of Religion & Religions, Vol. I: Contains Letters A-J. 222p. 1990. pap. text ed. 25.00 (*0-916157-76-8*) African Islam Miss Pubns.

— The Encyclopaedia of Religion & Religions, Vol. II: Contains Letters J-Z. 222p. 1990. pap. text ed. 25.00 (*0-916157-77-6*) African Islam Miss Pubns.

— Round the Year with the World's Religions. (Illus.). 208p. 1993. reprint ed. lib. bdg. 40.00 (*1-55888-996-5*) Omnigraphics Inc.

Pike, Royston E., ed. Human Documents of the Industrial Revolution in Britain. 368p. 1966. pap. text ed. 15.95 (*0-04-942060-7*) Routledge Chapman & Hall.

Pike, Ruth. Penal Servitude in Early Modern Spain. LC 82-70551. (Illus.). 224p. 1983. text ed. 27.50 (*0-299-09260-7*) U of Wis Pr.

Pike, Ruth L. & Brown, Myrtle L. Nutrition: Integrated Approach. 3rd ed. LC 83-16766. 1068p. (C). 1984. write for info. (*0-02-395780-8*) Macmillan.

Pike, Stephen B., jt. auth. see Pike, Kenneth L.

Pike, Ted, et al. The Waite Group's UNIX Communication & the Internet. 3rd ed. 864p. 1995. Incl. diskette. 35.00 (*0-672-30537-2*) Sams.

***Pike, Wilbur L.** Leading the Transition: Management's Role in Creating a Team-Based Culture. LC 94-44928. 1995. write for info. (*0-527-76247-4*) Qual Resc.

Pike, Zebulon M. The Expeditions of Zebulon Montgomery Pike, 1. 1088p. 1987. reprint ed. pap. 12.95 (*0-486-25254-X*) Dover.

— The Expeditions of Zebulon Montgomery Pike, 2. 1088p. 1987. reprint ed. pap. 12.95 (*0-486-25255-8*) Dover.

— Zebulon Pike's Arkansas Journal. Hart, Stephen H. & Hulbert, Archer B., eds. LC 72-138172. (Illus.). 200p. 1972. reprint ed. text ed. 38.50 (*0-8371-5629-7*, PIAJ, Greenwood Pr) Greenwood.

Pikelner, S. B., jt. auth. see Kaplan, Samuil A.

Pikens, Elaine E. WordPerfect 6.0 Survival Skills. LC 93-49551. (Popular Applications Ser.). 144p. (Orig.). 1994. pap. 15.95 (*1-55622-420-6*) Wordware Pub.

Piker, Steven. A Peasant Community in Changing Thailand. (Anthropological Research Papers: No. 30). (Illus.). ix, 157p. 1983. 15.00 (*0-685-73906-6*) AZ Univ ARP.

Piket, Vincent. Louis Auchincloss: The Growth of a Novelist. LC 90-42647. 240p. 1991. text ed. 45.00 (*0-312-05307-X*) St Martin.

Pikin, S. A. Structural Transformations in Liquid Crystals. Alferieff, Michael, tr. 469p. 1991. text ed. 279.00 (*2-88124-296-0*) Gordon & Breach.

Pikin, S. A., et al. Polarization Properties of Liquid Crystals, Vol. 113. (Soviet Scientific Reviews Ser.: Vol. 11, Pt. 3). 90p. 1989. pap. text ed. 66.00 (*3-7186-4904-7*) Gordon & Breach.

Pikl, Barbara H., ed. see Massachusetts General Hospital Department of Nursing Staff.

Pikok, Bob, jt. auth. see Panamarioff, Rob.

***Pikoulakis, Emmanuel.** International Macroeconomics. LC 95-5716. 1995. write for info. (*0-312-12658-1*); pap. write for info. (*0-312-12659-X*) St Martin.

Pikoulis, John. Alun Lewis: A Life. LC 84-62692. (Illus.). 323p. 1984. 30.00 (*0-907476-26-0*, Pub. by Poetry Wales Pr UK) Dufour.

— Alun Lewis: A Life. 322p. (C). 1989. 59.00 (*0-685-61449-2*, Pub. by D Brown & Sons Ltd UK) St Mut.

— Alun Lewis: A Life. rev. ed. (Illus.). 290p. 1992. pap. 24.00 (*1-85411-018-7*, Pub. by Seren Bks UK) Dufour.

Pikunas, Justin. Manual for the Pikunas Graphoscopic Scale. 3rd ed. LC 81-43841. (Illus.). 70p. (Orig.). 1982. 16.50 (*0-8191-2351-X*) U Pr of Amer.

Pikus, Irwin M. & Earnest, David. Breaking down the Barricades: Reforming Export Controls to Increase U. S. Competitiveness. LC 93-44715. (CSIS Panel Report). 82p. (Orig.). (C). (gr. 13). 1994. pap. 21.00 (*0-89206-261-4*) CSI Studies.

***Pikus, P. E. & Ivchenko, E. L.** Superlattices & Other Heterostructures: Symmetry & Optical Phenomena. LC 94-3452. (Springer Series in Solid-State Sciences: Vol. 110). 1995. 98.00 (*0-387-58197-9*) Spr-Verlag.

Pil, Teresita V. Philippine Folk Fiction & Tales. 1977. pap. 5.75 (*971-10-0300-7*, Pub. by New Day Pub PH) Cellar.

***Pila of Hawaii.** Secrets & Mysteries of Hawaii. 300p. 1995. pap. 5.99 (*1-56171-384-8*) Sure Sellers.

— The True Story of the Celestine Prophecy: The Gathering. 250p. 1994. pap. 5.99 (*1-56171-382-1*, S P I Bks) Sure Sellers.

***Pila of Hawaii Staff.** Secrets & Mysteries of Hawaii. 200p. (Orig.). 1995. pap. 10.95 (*1-55874-362-6*, 3626) Health Comm.

Pilachauski, Mel, jt. auth. see Grieco, Peter L., Jr.

***Pilafian, J. Samuel.** Getting It Together. 80p. 1995. pap. 29.99 (*1-887210-02-4*) Summit Bks AZ.

Piland, Sherry. Women Artists: An Historical, Contemporary, & Feminist Bibliography. 2nd ed. LC 93-27248. (Illus.). 497p. 1994. 59.50 (*0-8108-2559-7*) Scarecrow.

Piland, Sherry & Ugucciori, Ellen. The Fountains of Kansas City. LC 85-72962. (Illus.). 336p. 1986. 29.95 (*0-932845-04-5*) Lowell Pr.

Pilant. Elastic Theory of Waves. 2nd ed. write for info. (*0-444-00837-3*) Elsevier.

Pilapil & Studva. Programmed Instruction: Radiation Therapy. 1980. 11.00 (*0-89352-099-3*) Mosby Yr Bk.

Pilapil, Vicente R. Alfonso XIII. LC 78-77035. (Twayne's Rulers & Statesmen of the World Ser.). 242p. (C). 1969. lib. bdg. 17.95 (*0-8290-1749-6*) Irvington.

Pilar, Arlene. Reading Books for Social Studies: A Study Guide. Friedland, Joyce & Kessler, Rikki, eds. (Primary Ser.). (J). (gr. 1-3). 1991. pap. text ed. 20.95 (*0-88122-692-0*) Lrn Links.

Pilar, F. L. Elementary Quantum Chemistry. 2nd ed. 1990. text ed. write for info. (*0-07-050093-2*) McGraw.

Pilarczyk, Daniel. Twelve Tough Issues: What the Church Teaches & Why. 90p. (Orig.). 1989. pap. 4.95 (*0-86716-104-3*) St Anthony Mess Pr.

Pilarczyk, Daniel E. Living in the Lord: The Building Blocks of Spirituality. 88p. 1991. 4.95 (*0-86716-155-8*) St Anthony Mess Pr.

— Our Priests: Who They Are & What They Do. 48p. 1995. pap. 1.50 (*0-614-07223-9*, 665) Our Sunday Visitor.

— The Parish: Where God's People Live. LC 91-42032. 88p. 1992. pap. 4.95 (*0-8091-3299-0*) Paulist Pr.

Pilarczyk, K. W., ed. Coastal Protection: Proceedings of a Short Course, Delft University of Technology, 30 June-1 July 1990. (Illus.). 550p. (C). 1990. text ed. 105.00 (*90-6191-127-3*, Pub. by A A Balkema NE) Ashgate Pub Co.

Pilarski, Michael, ed. Restoration Forestry: An International Guide to Sustainable Forestry Practices. (Illus.). 528p. (Orig.). (C). 1994. pap. 26.95 (*1-882308-51-4*) Kivaki Pr.

***Pilarski, Slawomir & Kameda, Tiko.** A Probabilistic Analysis of Test-Response Compaction. LC 94-27227. 112p. 1995. 40.00 (*0-8186-6532-7*, BP06532) IEEE Comp Soc.

Pilat, Bianca, jt. auth. see Anselmino, Luciano.

Pilat, Dirk. The Economics of Rapid Growth: The Experience of Japan & Korea. LC 94-12017. 352p. 1994. pap. 67.95 (*1-85278-762-7*, Pub. by E Elgar Pub UK) Ashgate Pub Co.

Pilat, Joseph F., ed. The Nonproliferation Predicament. 150p. (C). 1985. 32.95 (*0-88738-047-6*) Transaction Pubs.

***Pilat, Joseph F. & Pendley, Robert E., eds.** 1995: A New Beginning for the NPT? (Issues in International Security Ser.). 310p. 1995. 59.50 (*0-306-45001-1*, Plenum Pr) Plenum.

Pilato, Herbie J. Kung Fu Book of Caine. 192p. 1993. pap. 16.95 (*0-8048-1826-6*) C E Tuttle.

— The Kung Fu Book of Wisdom: Sage Advice from the Original Television Series. (Illus.). 160p. 1995. 14.95 (*0-8048-3044-4*) C E Tuttle.

Pilato, Louis A. & Michno, Michael J. Advanced Composite Materials. LC 94-10694. 1994. write for info. (*3-540-57563-4*); 79.00 (*0-387-57563-4*) Spr-Verlag.

***Pilatowicz, Grazyna.** Eco-Interiors: A Guide to Environmentally Conscious Interior Design. 1994. pap. text ed. 24.95 (*0-471-04045-2*) Wiley.

Pilavachi, P. A. Improved Energy Efficiency in the Process Industries. (EUR Ser.: No. 13541). 312p. 1991. pap. 35.00 (*92-826-2550-8*, CD-NA-13541-2A-C) UNIPUB.

Pilavachi, P. A., ed. Energy Efficiency in Process Technology. LC 93-12183. 1280p. 1993. 336.00 (*1-85861-019-2*, Pub. by Elsevier Applied Sci UK) Elsevier.

Pilavakis. UNIX Workshop. 1989. 30.95 (*0-8493-7104-X*, QA76) CRC Pr.

Pilavczyk, Daniel E. What Must I Do? Morality & the Challenge of God's Word. 83p. 1993. 4.95 (*0-86716-209-0*) St Anthony Mess Pr.

Pilbath, Ferenc. Cohesion Hypothesis: Of the Ultimate & Common-Sense Meaning of Life. LC 84-91759. 229p. 1985. pap. 10.00 (*0-9614411-4-3*) F Pilbat.

Pilbeam, jt. auth. see Youtsey.

Pilbeam, D. J., jt. ed. see Mengel, K.

***Pilbeam, John.** Gymnocalycium: A Collector's Guide. (Illus.). 176p. (C). 1995. text ed. 70.00 (*90-5410-192-X*, Pub. by A A Balkema NE) Ashgate Pub Co.

Pilbeam, Keith. Exchange Rate Management: Theory & Evidence: The U. K. Experience. LC 90-44946. 236p. 1991. text ed. 69.95 (*0-312-05358-4*) St Martin.

Pilbeam, Mavis. Japan. (Focus On Ser.). (Illus.). 32p. (J). (gr. 4-8). 1992. 17.95 (*0-237-60187-7*, Pub. by Evans Bros Ltd UK) Trafalgar.

Pilbeam, Pamela M. The Middle Classes in Europe, 1789-1914: France, Germany, Italy & Russia. LC 89-13220. 328p. (C). 1990. text ed. 49.95 (*0-925065-29-3*); pap. text ed. 21.95 (*0-925065-26-9*) Lyceum IL.

— Republicanism in Nineteenth-Century France, 1814-1871. LC 94-30651. (European Studies Ser.). 1995. write for info. (*0-312-12420-1*); pap. write for info. (*0-312-12421-X*) St Martin.

Pilbeam, Susan P. Mechanical Ventilation. 2nd ed. LC 92-18793. 649p. 1992. pap. 33.95 (*0-8016-6360-1*) Mosby Yr Bk.

— Mechanical Ventilation: Physiological & Clinical Applications. Youtsey, John W., ed. LC 85-61165. (Faculty Lecture Series in Respiratory Care). (Illus.). 384p. (C). 1986. text ed. 29.95 (*0-8016-3872-0*) Mosby Multi-Media.

Pilbrow, J. R. Transition Ion Electron Paramagnetic Resonance. (Illus.). 738p. 1991. 195.00 (*0-19-855214-9*) OUP.

Pilbrow, Richard. Stage Lighting. rev. ed. LC 78-10184. 144p. 1991. reprint ed. 24.95 (*0-89676-005-7*) Drama Bk.

Pilcer, Sonia. Little Darlings. 1980. pap. 2.25 (*0-345-28894-7*) Ballantine.

Pilch, Ernst, ed. see Sophokles.

Pilch, Herbert. Empirical Linguistics. 1978. pap. 6.95 (*3-7720-1090-3*) Adlers Foreign Bks.

***Pilch, John.** Cultural World of Jesus: Sunday by Sunday, Cycle A. 200p. (Orig.). 1995. pap. text ed. write for info. (*0-8146-2286-0*, Liturg Pr Bks) Liturgical Pr.

— Introducing the Cultural Context of the New Testament. 1991. pap. 14.95 (*0-8091-3272-9*) Paulist Pr.

— Introducing the Cultural Context of the Old Testament. 1991. pap. 14.95 (*0-8091-3271-0*) Paulist Pr.

***Pilch, John J.** The Cultural World of Jesus: Sunday by Sunday, Cycle C. 200p. (Orig.). 1995. pap. text ed. write for info. (*0-8146-2288-7*, Liturg Pr Bks) Liturgical Pr.

— Wellness: Your Invitation to Full Life. Frost, Miriam, ed. Orig. Title: Wellness. 128p. (Orig.). 1981. pap. text ed. 5.95 (*0-86683-758-2*) Harper SF.

— Wellness Spirituality. 112p. 1985. pap. 8.95 (*0-8245-0710-X*) Crossroad NY.

Pilch, John J. & Karris, Robert J. Galatians & Romans, No. 6. (Collegeville Bible Commentary - New Testament Ser.). 80p. (C). 1983. pap. 3.95 (*0-8146-1306-3*) Liturgical Pr.

Pilch, John J. & Malina, Bruce J. Biblical Social Values & Their Meaning: A Handbook. LC 93-26041. 1993. 19.95 (*1-56563-004-1*) Hendrickson MA.

Pilch, Michael, jt. auth. see Reddin, Mike.

***Pilcher, Dan.** Learning How to Compete: Workforce Skills & State Economic Development Policies. 40p. 1994. 15.00 (*1-55516-349-1*, 3126) Natl Conf State Legis.

Pilcher, Darryl, ed. Certain Voices: Short Stories about Gay Men. 224p. (Orig.). 1991. pap. 8.95 (*1-55583-194-X*) Alyson Pubns.

Pilcher, Donald M., ed. Data Analysis for the Helping Professions: A Practical Guide. (Sourcebooks for the Human Services Ser.: Vol. 10). 264p. (C). 1990. text ed. 49.95 (*0-8039-3724-5*); pap. text ed. 24.00 (*0-8039-3061-5*) Sage.

Pilcher, Edith. Castorland: French Refugees in the Western Adirondacks 1793-1814. LC 85-5456. (Illus.). 254p. 1985. 24.00 (*0-916346-55-2*) Harbor Hill Bks.

— The Constables: First Family of the Adirondacks. LC 92-8393. 1992. 32.50 (*0-925168-05-X*); pap. 24.95 (*0-925168-04-1*) North Country.

— Up the Lake Road: The First Hundred Years of the Adirondack Mountain Reserve 1887-1987. (Illus.). 208p. 1987. 35.00 (*0-9618456-0-0*); pap. 17.50 (*0-9618456-1-9*) Adk Mtn Reserve.

Pilcher, J. E., jt. ed. see Fabjan, C. W.

***Pilcher, Jane.** Age & Generation in Modern Britain. (Oxford Modern Britain Ser.). 184p. 1995. text ed. 39.95 (*0-19-827961-2*) OUP.

Pilcher, Jeremy, jt. auth. see Etherington-Smith, Meredith.

Pilcher, Larry L. Hospital Philanthropy: The Impact of the Tax Reform Act of 1986, Government Regulations, & Healthcare Trends. LC 92-40119. (Non-profit Institutions in America Ser.). 168p. 1993. 43.00 (*0-8153-0910-4*) Garland.

Pilcher, M. C. Campbell. 444p. 1991. reprint ed. lib. bdg. 78.50 (*0-8328-2043-1*); reprint ed. pap. 68.50 (*0-8328-2044-X*) Higginson Bk Co.

Pilcher, Paul, jt. auth. see Boffey, Barnes.

Pilcher, Rosamunde. Another View. 1989. mass mkt. 4.99 (*0-440-20251-5*) Dell.

— The Blue Bedroom & Other Stories. large type ed. LC 90-48877. 367p. 1991. reprint ed. lib. bdg. 21.95 (*1-56054-094-X*) Thorndike Pr.

— Carousel. 1991. mass mkt. 4.99 (*0-312-92629-4*) St Martin.

— The Carousel. large type ed. LC 91-31107. 233p. 1992. reprint ed. lib. bdg. 19.95 (*1-56054-148-2*) Thorndike Pr.

— The Day of the Storm. 1989. mass mkt. 4.99 (*0-440-20253-1*) Dell.

— The Day of the Storm. large type ed. 313p. 1992. reprint ed. lib. bdg. 19.95 (*1-56054-154-7*) Thorndike Pr.

— The Empty House. 1989. mass mkt. 4.99 (*0-440-20254-X*) Dell.

— The Empty House. large type ed. LC 92-12558. 248p. 1992. reprint ed. lib. bdg. 19.95 (*1-56054-149-0*) Thorndike Pr.

— The End of Summer. 1989. mass mkt. 4.99 (*0-440-20255-8*) Dell.

— The End of Summer. large type ed. 211p. 1991. reprint ed. lib. bdg. 19.95 (*1-56054-153-9*) Thorndike Pr.

— Flowers in the Rain, & Other Stories. 1992. mass mkt. 5.99 (*0-312-92774-6*) St Martin.

— Rosamunde Pilcher, No. 2. 1990. boxed 19.80 (*0-440-36020-X*) Dell.

— Rosamunde Pilcher, No. 3. 1990. boxed 19.80 (*0-440-36021-8*) Dell.

— Rosamunde Pilcher, 3 vols., Set. 1991. pap. 15.97 (*0-312-92620-0*) St Martin.

— Rosamunde Pilcher, 3 vols., Set. 1992. pap. 16.97 (*0-312-92893-9*) St Martin.

— September. 1990. 413.10 (*0-312-04467-4*) St Martin.

— September. 1991. mass mkt. 5.99 (*0-312-92480-1*) St Martin.

— September. large type ed. LC 90-11097. 874p. 1991. pap. 15.95 (*1-56054-089-3*) Thorndike Pr.

— The Shell Seekers. 560p. 1987. 21.95 (*0-312-01058-3*, Pub. by Thomas Dunne Bks) St Martin.

— The Shell Seekers. 1989. reprint ed. mass mkt. 6.99 (*0-440-20204-3*) Dell.

— Sleeping Tiger. 1989. mass mkt. 5.50 (*0-440-20247-7*) Dell.

— Sleeping Tiger. large type ed. LC 93-36820. 1994. 19.95 (*0-7927-1892-5*) Chivers N Amer.

— Sleeping Tiger. large type ed. LC 93-36820. 1994. pap. 18.95 (*0-7927-1891-7*, Paragon Lrg Print) Chivers N Amer.

— Snow in April. 1989. mass mkt. 4.99 (*0-440-20248-5*) Dell.

— Snow in April. large type ed. 239p. 1991. reprint ed. lib. bdg. 19.95 (*1-56054-119-9*) Thorndike Pr.

— Three Complete Novels. 1995. write for info. (*0-517-12190-5*) Wings Bks.

— Under Gemini. large type ed. LC 92-5780. 494p. 1993. reprint ed. lib. bdg. 19.95 (*1-56054-151-2*) Thorndike Pr.

— Under Gemini. 1989. reprint ed. mass mkt. 4.99 (*0-440-20249-3*) Dell.

— Voices in Summer. 1990. mass mkt. 4.99 (*0-312-92527-1*) St Martin.

— Voices in Summer. large type ed. LC 92-6493. 396p. 1992. reprint ed. lib. bdg. 19.95 (*1-56054-150-4*) Thorndike Pr.

— Wild Mountain Thyme. large type ed. LC 93-2471. 1994. 19.95 (*0-7927-1724-4*, Paragon Lrg Print); pap. 17.95 (*0-7927-1723-6*, Paragon Lrg Print) Chivers N Amer.

— Wild Mountain Thyme. 1989. reprint ed. mass mkt. 4.99 (*0-440-20250-7*) Dell.

***Pilcher, V. E.** Early Science & the First Century of Physics at Union College, 1795-1895. LC 94-92379. (Illus.). 114p. 1994. 25.00 (*0-9643133-0-8*) V E Pilcher.

Pilcher, William W. Urban Anthropology: A Research Bibliography, Nos. 944-945. 1975. 10.50 (*0-686-20380-1*) CPL Biblios.

Pilchick, Terry. Jai Bhim! Dispatches from a Peaceful Revolution. 1988. pap. 12.50 (*0-938077-15-5*) Parallax Pr.

Pilcox Cons Svc Staff & Bach, C. Ions for Breathing: Control Air Electrical Climate for Health. LC 67-27480. 1967. 48.00 (*0-08-012463-1*, Pub. by Pergamon Repr UK) Franklin.

Pilditch. Communication by Design: A Study in Corporate Identity. 1970. 19.50 (*0-07-094214-5*) McGraw.

Pile, Frederick D. Better Than Riches. 116p. (C). 1989. text ed. 65.00 (*1-85821-005-4*, Pub. by Pentland Pr UK) St Mut.

Pile, George, ed. see Hess, Rudolf.

Pile, John. Dictionary of Twentieth Century Design. (Illus.). 320p. 1990. 35.00 (*0-8160-1811-1*) Facts on File.

— Dictionary of Twentieth Century Design. LC 93-39780. (Illus.). 320p. 1994. reprint ed. pap. 18.95 (*0-306-80569-3*) Da Capo.

— Modern Furniture. 2nd ed. 312p. 1990. text ed. 75.00 (*0-471-85438-7*) Wiley.

— Perspective for Interior Designers. (Illus.). 160p. 1989. pap. 18.95 (*0-8230-4008-9*, Whitney Lib) Watsn-Guptill.

Pile, John, jt. auth. see Diekman, Norman.

Pile, John F. Interior Design. 2nd ed. LC 94-6342. 1994. write for info. (*0-8109-3463-9*) Abrams.

— Interior Design (ABRAMS) (C). 1988. pap. text ed. 58.95 (*0-13-469248-9*) P-H.

Pile, Kathryne E., jt. auth. see Johnson, David E.

***Pile, Naomi.** Art Experiences for Young Children. (Illus.). 112p. (C). 1990. reprint ed. pap. text ed. 16.50 (*0-87411-444-6*) Copley Pub.

Pile, Robert B. Top Entrepreneurs & Their Businesses. LC 92-38267. (Profiles Ser.). (Illus.). 160p. (YA). (gr. 5-12). 1993. lib. bdg. 14.95 (*1-881508-04-8*) Oliver Pr MN.

— Women Business Leaders. LC 94-46814. (Profiles Ser.). (Illus.). (J). 1995. 14.95 (*1-881508-24-2*) Oliver Pr MN.

Pile, Stephen. The Private Farmer: Transformation & Ligitimation in Advanced Capitalist Agriculture. (Illus.). 218p. 1990. text ed. 52.95 (*1-85521-003-7*, Pub. by Dartmth Pub UK) Ashgate Pub Co.

***Pile, Steve & Thrift, Nigel, eds.** Mapping the Subject: Geographies of Cultural Transformation. LC 94-23747. 1995. 60.00 (*0-415-10225-1*); pap. 19.95 (*0-415-10226-X*) Routledge.

Pile, Steve, jt. ed. see Keith, Michael.

Pile, William. The Department of Education & Science. 247p. (C). 1979. 90.00 (*0-685-06077-2*) St Mut.

— What the Bible Says about Grace. 326p. 1990. 13.99 (*0-89900-265-X*) College Pr Pub.

***Pilegaard, M. & Baden, H.** Danish - English - English - Danish Medical Dictionary. 913p. (DAN.). 1994. 120.00 (*87-12-02240-3*) IBD Ltd.

***Pileggi, Nicholas.** Casino: Love & Honor in Las Vegas. 1995. 24.00 (*0-684-80832-3*) S&S Trade.

— Wise Guy - Good Fellas. 1990. mass mkt. 5.99 (*0-671-72322-7*) PB.

Pileggi, Nicholas, ed. see Ragano, Frank & Raab, Selwyn.

Pileggi, Nicholas, jt. auth. see Scorsese, Martin.

Piles, Roger D. Abrege de la Vie des Peintres. 540p. 1969. reprint ed. write for info. (*0-318-71940-1*, Pub. by Georg Olms GW) Lubrecht & Cramer.

Pilevsky, Philip. Captive Continent: The Stockholm Syndrome in European-Soviet Relations. LC 88-26573. 170p. 1989. text ed. 45.00 (*0-275-93064-5*, C3064, Praeger Pubs) Greenwood.

Pilewski, H., jt. auth. see Cohen, F.

Pilger, Mary A. Crafts Index for Young People. LC 92-12996. (Data Bks.). 288p. 1992. lib. bdg. 32.50 (*1-56308-002-8*) Libs Unl.

— Holidays & Special Days Project Index for Young People. LC 92-12977. 160p. (J). 1992. lib. bdg. 29.50 (*0-87287-998-4*) Libs Unl.

P Q

— Multicultural Projects Index: Things to Make & Do to Celebrate Festivals, Cultures, & Holidays Around the World. (Data Book Ser.). 300p. 1992. pap. text ed. 35.00 (*0-87287-867-8*) Libs Unl.
— Science Experiments Index for Young People. 200p. 1988. lib. bdg. 35.00 (*0-87287-671-3*) Libs Unl.
— Science Experiments Index for Young People: Update 91. 150p. 1992. lib. bdg. 21.00 (*0-87287-858-9*) Libs Unl.
Pilgrim, Adrian. Outline of Manx Language & Literature. pap. 9.95 (*0-89979-064-X*) British Am Bks.
Pilgrim, Anne, jt. auth. see Langton, Mandy.
Pilgrim, Aubrey. Build Your Own IBM Compatible & Save a Bundle. 224p. (Orig.). 1987. 22.95 (*0-8306-0231-3*, 2831); pap. 16.95 (*0-8306-2831-2*) TAB Bks.
— Build Your Own IBM Compatible & Save a Bundle. 2nd ed. (Illus.). 272p. (Orig.). 1991. pap. 19.95 (*0-8306-3804-0*, 3804, Windcrest) TAB Bks.
— Build Your Own LAN & Save a Bundle. 1992. 31.95 (*0-07-050107-6*); pap. 21.95 (*0-07-050108-4*) McGraw.
— Build Your Own LAN & Save a Bundle. LC 92-5692. (Illus.). 256p. 1992. 31.95 (*0-8306-4088-6*, 4210, Windcrest); pap. 21.95 (*0-8306-4089-4*, 4210, Windcrest) TAB Bks.
— Build Your Own Low-Cost PC & Save a Bundle. 1993. 29.95 (*0-07-050105-X*); pap. 19.95 (*0-07-050106-8*) McGraw.
— Build Your Own Low-Cost PC & Save a Bundle. LC 92-26118. (Illus.). 224p. 1992. 29.95 (*0-8306-4086-X*, Windcrest); pap. 18.95 (*0-8306-4087-8*, Windcrest) TAB Bks.
— Build Your Own Multimedia PC. LC 93-21305. 1994. pap. text ed. 36.95 (*0-07-050113-0*, Windcrest) TAB Bks.
— Build Your Own Multimedia PC with CD Rom. 1993. pap. text ed. 36.95 (*0-8306-4566-7*, Windcrest) TAB Bks.
— Build Your Own Pentium Processor. LC 94-6945. 1994. text ed. 32.95 (*0-07-050163-7*, Windcrest) TAB Bks.
— Build Your Own Pentium Processor PC. 1994. pap. text ed. 19.95 (*0-07-050164-5*) McGraw.
— Build Your Own 386 - 386sx & Save a Bundle. 2nd ed. 1992. pap. 18.95 (*0-07-050089-4*) McGraw.
— Build Your Own 486-486SX & Save a Bundle. 2nd ed. (Illus.). 256p. 1992. 29.95 (*0-8306-4217-X*, 4270, Windcrest); pap. 19.95 (*0-8306-4216-1*, 4270, Windcrest) TAB Bks.
— Build Your Own 80286 IBM Compatible & Save a Bundle. (Illus.). 208p. 1988. 24.95 (*0-8306-0331-X*) TAB Bks.
— Build Your Own 80386 Compatible & Save a Bundle. 2nd ed. 1991. write for info. (*0-8306-3752-4*, Windcrest); pap. 18.95 (*0-8306-3750-8*, Windcrest) TAB Bks.
— Build Your Own 80386 IBM Compatble & Save a Bundle. 1988. pap. 17.95 (*0-07-155874-8*) McGraw.
— Build Your Own 80386 IBM Compatible & Save a Bundle. (Illus.). 224p. 1988. 24.95 (*0-8306-9131-6*, 3131); pap. 17.95 (*0-8306-3131-3*, 3131) TAB Bks.
— Build Your Own 80486 & Save a Bundle. 1992. pap. 19.95 (*0-07-050110-6*) McGraw.
— Build Your Own 80486 & Save a Bundle. 2nd ed. 1992. 29.95 (*0-07-050109-2*) McGraw.
— Build Your Own 80486 PC & Save a Bundle. (Illus.). 224p. 1991. pap. 16.95 (*0-8306-7628-7*, Windcrest) TAB Bks.
— Upgrade or Repair Your PC. 4th ed. LC 94-23468. 1995. pap. text ed. 26.95 (*0-07-050114-9*, Windcrest) TAB Bks.
— Upgrade or Repair Your PC & Save a Bundle. 3rd ed. 1993. text ed. 29.95 (*0-07-050111-4*) McGraw.
— Upgrade or Repair Your PC & Save a Bundle. 3rd ed. LC 92-46786. 245p. 1993. 29.95 (*0-8306-4215-3*, Windcrest); pap. 19.95 (*0-8306-4214-5*, Windcrest) TAB Bks.
— Upgrade Your IBM Compatible & Save a Bundle. (Illus.). 240p. 1990. 26.95 (*0-8306-8468-9*, 3468, Windcrest); pap. 16.95 (*0-8306-3468-1*, Windcrest) TAB Bks.
— Upgrade Your IBM Compatible & Save a Bundle. 2nd ed. (Illus.). 272p. 1991. 28.95 (*0-8306-8828-5*, 3828, Windcrest); pap. 19.95 (*0-8306-3828-8*, Windcrest) TAB Bks.
Pilgrim, Constance. Dear Jane. 192p. (C). 1989. text ed. 59.00 (*1-872795-25-0*, Pub. by Pentland Pr UK) St Mut.
— This Is Illyria, Lady. 179p. (C). 1989. text ed. 59.00 (*1-872795-21-8*, Pub. by Pentland Pr UK) St Mut.
Pilgrim, David. Race Relations "Above the Veil" Speeches, Essays & Other Writings. LC 89-40445. 255p. (Orig.). (C). 1989. text ed. 14.95 (*1-55605-108-5*) Wyndhall Pr.
Pilgrim, David, ed. On Being Black: An In-Group Analysis: Essays in Honor of W. E. B. Du Bois. LC 85-52309. 187p. (Orig.). 1986. 29.95 (*0-932269-75-3*); pap. text ed. 19.95 (*0-317-42666-4*) Wyndhall Pr.
— W. E. B. Du Bois in Memoriam: A Centennial Celebration of His Collegiate Education. LC 90-50113. (Illus.). 150p. (C). 1990. text ed. 24.95 (*0-685-35412-1*); pap. text ed. 14.95 (*1-55605-150-6*) Wyndhall Pr.
Pilgrim, David & Rogers, Anne. A Sociology of Mental Health & Illness. LC 93-18726. 1993. 79.00 (*0-335-19014-6*, Open Univ Pr); pap. 27.50 (*0-335-19013-8*, Open Univ Pr) Taylor & Francis.
Pilgrim, David & Treacher, Andy. Clinical Psychology Observed. LC 91-25281. 208p. 1992. write for info. (*0-415-07227-1*, A5927) Routledge.
Pilgrim, G. E. New Siwalik Primates: Their Bearing on the Question of Evolution of Man & the Anthropoidea. Bd. with Sivapithecus Palate. LC 77-86436. LC 77-86436. (India Geological Survey. Records of the Geological Survey of India Ser.: Vol. 45). reprint ed. 15.00 (*0-404-16675-X*) AMS Pr.
Pilgrim, Millie W. Jason's Adventures with the Tuskegee Airmen. (Illus.). 54p. (J). (gr. 3 up). 1992. teacher ed 2.00 (*0-685-60295-8*) H&M Ent.
— Jason's Adventures with the Tuskegee Airmen. rev. ed. (Illus.). 54p. (J). (gr. 3 up). 1992. pap. text ed. 8.00 (*0-685-60294-X*, 133-720) H&M Ent.
Pilgrim, Paul, jt. auth. see Roy, Gerald.
***Pilgrim, Paul D.** Victorian Quilts, 1875-1900: They Aren't All Crazy. 1995. pap. 14.95 (*0-89145-846-8*) Collector Bks.
Pilgrim, Paul D. & Roy, Gerald E. Old & New: A Similar View. LC 93-17523. 1993. 12.95 (*0-89145-817-4*) Collector Bks.
Pilgrim, Peace. Pasos Hacia la Paz Interior: Sugestiones para el Uso de Principios Armonicos para la Vida Humana. Zanelli, Clandio, tr. (Peace Pilgrim Ser.). 64p. (Orig.). (SPA.). 1987. pap. 3.00 (*0-943734-09-6*) Ocean Tree Bks.
— Peace Pilgrim: Her Life & Work in Her Own Words. LC 82-18854. (Illus.). 214p. (Orig.). 1991. 14.95 (*0-943734-20-7*) Ocean Tree Bks.
— Peace Pilgrim: Her Life & Work in Her Own Words. LC 82-18854. (Illus.). 224p. (Orig.). 1994. pap. 12.00 (*0-943734-29-0*) Ocean Tree Bks.
— Steps Toward Inner Peace. (Keepsake Editions Ser.). 64p. 1993. 8.00 (*0-943734-24-X*) Ocean Tree Bks.
Pilgrim, Richard B. Buddhism & the Arts of Japan. rev. ed. LC 93-9361. 78p. (Orig.). 1993. pap. 9.95 (*0-89012-069-2*) Anima Pubns.
Pilgrim, Richard B., jt. auth. see Ellwood, Robert S., Jr.
Pilgrim Society Collection Staff. Arthur Lord Collection. 1971. 2.00 (*0-940628-08-2*) Pilgrim Soc.
***Pilgrim, Susan.** Living in Sync: Creating Your Life with Balance & Purpose. 200p. (Orig.). 1995. pap. 9.95 (*1-55874-340-5*, 3405) Health Comm.
Pilgrim, Thomas A. The Roads Jesus Traveled. 1991. pap. 8.25 (*1-55673-383-6*, 9201) CSS OH.
***Pilgrim, Tim A.** The Seattle JOA & Newspaper Preservation. 288p. 1995. 49.50 (*0-89391-886-5*); pap. 24.50 (*1-56750-050-1*) Ablex Pub.
Pilgrim, Tom. The Master Has Come. (Orig.). 1989. pap. 4.45 (*1-55673-102-7*, 9813) CSS OH.
Piliavin, Jane A. & Callero, Peter L. Giving Blood: The Development of an Altruistic Identity. LC 90-15650. (Series in Contemporary Medicine & Public Health). (Illus.). 320p. 1991. text ed. 50.00 (*0-8018-4152-6*) Johns Hopkins.
Piliavin, Michael A. & Margaryan, Alfred. Germanate Glasses: Structure, Spectroscopy, & Properties. LC 93-13302. 1993. 72.00 (*0-89006-506-3*) Artech Hse.
Piliawsky, Monty. Exit Thirteen: Oppression & Racism in Academia. LC 81-50137. 252p. 1982. 30.00 (*0-89608-097-8*); pap. 7.50 (*0-89608-096-X*) South End Pr.
Pilipenko, A. T., jt. auth. see Samchuk, A. I.
Pilipp, Frank. The Novels of Martin Walser: A Critical Introduction. (Studies in German Literature, Linguistics & Culture: Vol. 64). (Illus.). 298p. 1991. 59.00 (*0-938100-98-X*) Camden Hse.
Pilipp, Frank, ed. New Critical Perspectives on Martin Walser. LC 94-1979. (Literary Criticism in Perspective Ser.). 200p. 1994. 59.00 (*1-879751-67-4*) Camden Hse.
Pilipski, Mark. Les Belles Lettres, Ser. I: Poems of Love. LC 92-62379. 50p. 1993. pap. write for info. (*1-882965-00-0*) Markov Pr.
— Les Belles Lettres, Ser. II: The Marriage of Mark & Marianne. LC 92-62382. 50p. 1993. pap. write for info. (*1-882965-01-9*) Markov Pr.
— Les Belles Lettres, Ser. III: The Vision. LC 92-62391. 50p. 1993. pap. write for info. (*1-882965-02-7*) Markov Pr.
— Les Belles Lettres, Ser. IV: Four Roles for Three Characters. LC 92-62380. 50p. (J). (gr. k-8). 1993. pap. write for info. (*1-882965-03-5*) Markov Pr.
Pilisuk, Marc & Parks, Susan H. The Healing Web: Social Networks & Human Survival. LC 85-26290. (Illus.). 256p. 1986. pap. 14.95 (*0-87451-470-3*) U Pr of New Eng.
Pilisuk, Marc & Pilisuk, Phyllis, eds. How We Lost the War on Poverty. LC 72-91471. 300p. 1973. 27.95 (*0-87855-079-8*); pap. 12.95 (*0-87855-574-9*) Transaction Pubs.
— Poor Americans: How the White Poor Live. 192p. 1971. reprint ed. pap. text ed. 14.95 (*0-685-04923-X*) Transaction Pubs.
Pilisuk, Phyllis, jt. ed. see Pilisuk, Marc.
Pilius, Nancy A. A Manatee Recovers. (J). 1994. 7.95 (*0-533-10835-7*) Vantage.
Piljac, Pamela. You Can Go Home Again: The Career Woman's Guide to Leaving the Work Force. (Illus.). (Orig.). 1985. pap. 9.95 (*0-913339-03-2*) Bryce-Waterton Pubns.
Piljac, Pamela A. The Bride to Bride Book. rev. ed. (Illus.). 160p. 1990. pap. 9.95 (*0-913339-08-3*) Bryce-Waterton Pubns.
— Bride's Thank You Guide. LC 87-24917. 1993. pap. 5.95 (*1-55652-200-2*) Chicago Review.
— Bride's Thank You Guide: Thank You Writing Made Easy. LC 87-24917. (Illus.). 96p. 1988. pap. 4.95 (*0-913339-06-7*) Bryce-Waterton Pubns.
— Newlywed: A Survival Guide to the First Years of Marriage. LC 85-21288. (Illus.). (Orig.). 1985. pap. 8.95 (*0-913339-02-4*) Bryce-Waterton Pubns.
Piljac, Pamela A. & Piljac, Thomas M. Mackinac Island: Historic Frontier, Vacation Resort, Timeless Wonderland. LC 88-4962. (Illus.). (Orig.). 1988. pap. 9.95 (*0-913339-07-5*) Bryce-Waterton Pubns.
Piljac, Thomas M. The Groom to Groom Book. rev. ed. (Illus.). 112p. 1990. pap. 7.95 (*0-913339-09-1*) Bryce-Waterton Pubns.
Piljac, Thomas M., jt. auth. see Piljac, Pamela A.
Pilkey. Mechanics of Structures. 1992. 69.95 (*0-8493-4435-2*, TA407) CRC Pr.
***Pilkey, Dav.** Big Dog, Little Dog Eating & Sleeping. LC 95-3577. (J). Date not set. write for info. (*0-15-200360-6*) HarBrace.
— Big Dog, Little Dog Getting in Trouble. LC 95-3919. (J). Date not set. write for info. (*0-15-200355-X*) HarBrace.
— Big Dog, Little Dog Going for a Walk. LC 95-3917. (J). Date not set. write for info. (*0-15-200352-5*) HarBrace.
— Big Dog, Little Dog Guarding the Picnic. LC 95-3916. (J). Date not set. write for info. (*0-15-200354-1*) HarBrace.
— Big Dog, Little Dog Wearing Sweaters. LC 95-3918. (J). Date not set. write for info. (*0-15-200361-4*) HarBrace.
— Dog Breath! The Horrible Terrible Trouble with Hally Tosis. LC 93-43405. (J). 1994. 12.95 (*0-590-47466-9*, Blue Sky Press) Scholastic Inc.
— Dogzilla. LC 92-37906. (YA). (gr. 4 up). 1993. 10.95 (*0-15-223944-8*); pap. 5.95 (*0-15-223945-6*) HarBrace.
— Dragon Gets By. LC 90-46027. (Illus.). 48p. (J). (gr. 1-3). 1991. 13.95 (*0-531-05935-9*); lib. bdg. 13.99 (*0-531-08535-X*) Orchard Bks Watts.
— Dragon's Fat Cat. LC 91-16369. (Illus.). 48p. (J). (gr. 1-3). 1992. 13.95 (*0-531-05982-0*); lib. bdg. 13.99 (*0-531-08582-1*) Orchard Bks Watts.
— Dragon's Fat Cat. LC 91-16369. (Illus.). 48p. (J). (gr. 1-3). 1995. pap. 4.95 (*0-531-07068-9*) Orchard Bks Watts.
— Dragon's Halloween. LC 91-21107. (Illus.). 48p. (J). (gr. 1-3). 1993. 13.95 (*0-531-05990-1*); lib. bdg. 13.99 (*0-531-08590-2*) Orchard Bks Watts.
— Dragon's Halloween. LC 91-21107. (Illus.). 48p. (J). (gr. 1-3). 1995. pap. 4.95 (*0-531-07069-7*) Orchard Bks Watts.
— Dragon's Merry Christmas. LC 91-1996. (Illus.). 48p. (J). (gr. 1-3). 1991. 13.95 (*0-531-05957-X*); 13.99 (*0-531-08557-0*) Orchard Bks Watts.
— Dragon's Merry Christmas. LC 91-1996. (Illus.). 48p. (J). (gr. 1-3). 1994. pap. 4.95 (*0-531-07055-7*) Orchard Bks Watts.
— A Friend for Dragon. LC 90-45219. (Illus.). 48p. (J). (gr. 1-3). 1991. 13.95 (*0-531-05934-0*); lib. bdg. 13.99 (*0-531-08534-1*) Orchard Bks Watts.
— A Friend for Dragon. LC 90-45219. (Illus.). 48p. (J). (gr. 1-3). 1994. pap. 4.95 (*0-531-07054-9*) Orchard Bks Watts.
— God Bless the Gargoyles. LC 95-2467. (J). 1996. write for info. (*0-15-200248-0*) HarBrace.
— The Hallo-Wiener. LC 94-40949. (J). 1995. 12.95 (*0-590-41703-7*, Blue Sky Press) Scholastic Inc.
— Kat Kong. LC 92-14483. (J). (ps-3). 1993. 10.95 (*0-15-242036-3*); pap. 5.95 (*0-15-242037-1*) HarBrace.
— The Moonglow Roll-O-Rama. LC 94-24846. (Illus.). 32p. (J). (ps-1). 1995. 14.95 (*0-531-06876-5*) Orchard Bks Watts.
— Twas the Night Before Thanksgiving. LC 89-48941. (Illus.). 32p. (J). (ps-2). 1990. 15.95 (*0-531-05905-7*); lib. bdg. 15.99 (*0-531-08505-8*) Orchard Bks Watts.
— When Cats Dream. LC 91-31355. 32p. (J). (ps-2). 1995. lib. bdg. 15.99 (*0-531-08597-X*) Orchard Bks Watts.
— When Cats Dream. LC 91-31355. 32p. (J). (ps-2). 1995. 15.95 (*0-531-05997-9*) Orchard Bks Watts.
— World War Won. LC 87-2711. (Books for Students by Students Ser.). (Illus.). 32p. (J). (gr. 1 up). 1987. lib. bdg. 14.95 (*0-933849-22-2*) Landmark Edns.
***Pilkey, Dave.** The Moonglow Roll-O-Rama. LC 94-24846. (Illus.). 32p. (J). (ps-1). 1995. lib. bdg. 14.99 (*0-531-08726-3*) Orchard Bks Watts.
Pilkey, O. H., et al, eds. Coastal Land Loss. (Short Course Ser.: Vol. 2). 73p. 1989. 13.00 (*0-87590-701-6*) Am Geophysical.
Pilkey, Orrin, Jr., jt. auth. see Kaufman, Wallace.
Pilkey, Orrin H., ed. see Bush, David M., et al.
Pilkey, Orrin H., jt. auth. see Pilkey, Walter D.
Pilkey, Orrin H., Jr., et al. From Currituck to Calabash: Living with North Carolina's Barrier Islands. LC 80-42835. (Living with the Shore Ser.). (Illus.). xi, 258p. 1982. reprint ed. pap. 15.95 (*0-8223-0548-8*) Duke.
Pilkey, Orrin H., et al. Living with the East Florida Shore. LC 84-10297. (Living with the Shore Ser.). xv, 280p. 1985. 31.95 (*0-8223-0514-3*); 16.95 (*0-8223-0515-1*) Duke.
Pilkey, W., jt. ed. see Perrone, Nicholas.
Pilkey, W., et al, eds. Structural Mechanics Computer Programs: Surveys, Assessments, & Availability. LC 74-8300. 1118p. reprint ed. pap. 180.00 (*0-317-28094-5*, 2055728) Bks Demand.
Pilkey, W. D. & Cohen, R., eds. System Identification of Vibrating Structures: Mathematical Models from Test Data Presented at 1972 Winter Annual Meeting of the American Society of Mechanical Engineers. LC 72-92594. (Illus.). 206p. reprint ed. pap. 58.80 (*0-317-08340-6*, 2019473) Bks Demand.
Pilkey, Walter D. Formulas for Stress, Strain, & Structural Matrices. 864p. 1994. text ed. 89.95 (*0-471-52746-7*) Wiley.
Pilkey, Walter D. & Pilkey, Orrin H. Mechanics of Solids. LC 85-46011. 464p. (C). 1986. reprint ed. text ed. 41.50 (*0-89874-917-4*) Krieger.
Pilkington, jt. auth. see Hill.
Pilkington, Ace G. Screening Shakespeare from Richard II to Henry V. LC 90-50310. 216p. 1991. 39.50 (*0-87413-412-9*) U Delaware Pr.
Pilkington, Anna, jt. auth. see Ellis, David.
Pilkington, Anthony E. Bergson & His Influence: A Reassessment. LC 75-22555. 261p. reprint ed. pap. 74.40 (*0-8357-7137-7*, 2031708) Bks Demand.
Pilkington, Brian. Grandpa Claus. (Illus.). 28p. (J). (ps-3). 1990. lib. bdg. 18.95 (*0-87614-436-9*, Carolrhoda) Lerner Group.
Pilkington, Doris. Caprice: A Stockman's Daughter. (Orig.). 1991. pap. 12.95 (*0-7022-2400-6*, Pub. by Univ Queensland Pr AT) Intl Spec Bk.
Pilkington, Evan. Paths to Personal Prayer. LC 88-72018. 64p. (Orig.). 1988. pap. 5.95 (*0-89622-369-8*) Twenty-Third.
Pilkington, Hilary. Russia's Youth & Its Culture: A Nation's Constructors & Constructed. LC 93-26766. 1994. 55.00 (*0-415-09043-1*, Routledge NY); pap. 19.95 (*0-415-09044-X*, Routledge NY) Routledge.
Pilkington, Hilary, tr. see Wolf, Christa.
Pilkington, J. M. His Will Also. (C). 1989. pap. 29.00 (*0-7223-2299-2*, Pub. by A H S Ltd UK) St Mut.
Pilkington, J. Maya. Your Mind over Matter. 160p. 1989. pap. 9.95 (*0-345-36075-3*, Ballantine Trade) Ballantine.
Pilkington, John, Jr. F. Marion Crawford. (Twayne's United States Authors Ser.). 1964. pap. 13.95 (*0-8084-0127-0*, T67) NCUP.
— Francis Marion Crawford. LC 64-20717. (Twayne's United States Authors Ser.). 1964. lib. bdg. 17.95 (*0-89197-763-5*); pap. 3.95 (*0-8290-0004-6*) Irvington.
— Henry Blake Fuller. LC 69-18504. (Twayne's United States Authors Ser.). 1970. lib. bdg. 17.95 (*0-8057-0300-4*); pap. text ed. 6.95 (*0-8290-0005-4*) Irvington.
Pilkington, John D., jt. ed. see McCarthy, Dennis D.
***Pilkington, Laetitia.** Memoirs of Laetitia Pilkington. Elias, A. C., Jr., ed. 1996. write for info. (*0-8203-1719-5*) U of Ga Pr.
Pilkington, Laetitia V. The Celebrated Mrs. Pilkington's Jests; or, the Cabinet of Wit & Humor. LC 73-37707. reprint ed. 27.50 (*0-404-56775-4*) AMS Pr.
Pilkington, Michael. Campion, Dowland & the Lutenist Songwriters. LC 89-11006. (English Solo Song Ser.). 190p. 1989. 25.00 (*0-253-34695-9*) Ind U Pr.
— Gurney, Ireland, Quilter & Warlock. LC 89-11024. (English Solo Song Ser.). 204p. 1989. 25.00 (*0-253-34694-0*) Ind U Pr.
Pilkington, Rachel M. Intelligent Help: Communicating with Knowledge Based Systems. (Illus.). 208p. 1992. 40.00 (*0-19-520940-0*) OUP.
Pilkington, Roger. I Sailed on the Mayflower: The True Story of a Pilgrim Youngster. 1990. 12.95 (*0-533-08820-8*) Vantage.
— Small Boat in the Midi. 210p. (C). 1989. 110.00 (*0-907864-44-9*, Pub. by Imray Laurie Norie & Wilson UK) St Mut.
Pilkington, T. C. & Plonsey, R. Engineering Contributions to Biophysical Electrocardiography. LC 82-9200. 260p. 1982. 49.95 (*0-87942-163-0*, PC01586); pap. 39.95 (*0-87942-164-9*, PP01586) Inst Electrical.
Pilkington, Theo, et al. High Performance Computing in Biomedical Research. 1992. 79.95 (*0-8493-4474-3*, R853) CRC Pr.
Pilkington, Tom, ed. & intro. Careless Weeds: Six Texas Novellas. LC 92-53613. (Southwest Life & Letters Ser.). 352p. 1993. pap. 14.95 (*0-87074-339-2*) SMU Press.
— Careless Weeds: Six Texas Novellas. LC 92-53613. (Southwest Life & Letters Ser.). 352p. 1993. text ed. 35.00 (*0-87074-338-4*) SMU Press.
Pilkington, Tom, jt. ed. see Clifford, Craig.
Pilkington, William T. Imagining Texas: The Literature of the Lone Star State. (Texas History Ser.). (Illus.). 37p. 1981. pap. text ed. 3.95x (*0-89641-095-1*) American Pr.
Pilkis, S. J., ed. Fructose-2,6-Bisphosphate: The Unique Sugar Diphosphate. 1990. 161.00 (*0-8493-4795-5*, QP702) CRC Pr.
Pilkuhn, M., ed. High Excitation & Short Pulse Phenomena: Proceedings of the IUPAP Semiconductor Symposium, 3rd, 26 July, 1984, Trieste, Italy. 606p. 1985. 115.50 (*0-444-86931-X*, North Holland) Elsevier.
Pill Enterprises Staff, ed. see Furlong, Marjorie & Pill, Virginia.
Pill, Virginia, jt. auth. see Furlong, Marjorie.
Pilla, Daniel & Sanders, Franklin. Nineteen Ninety-Four - How to Survive the Economic Fallout of the Next Decade. Engstrom, David M., ed. 200p. (Orig.). 1988. pap. 11.95 (*0-9617124-4-9*) Winning St Paul.
Pilla, Daniel J. Forty-One Ways to Lick the IRS with a Postage Stamp. Date not set. 11.95 (*0-685-68185-8*) Winning St Paul.
— Forty-One Ways to Lick the IRS with a Postage Stamp. Engstrom, David M., ed. LC 90-71404. 224p. 1990. pap. 11.95 (*0-9617124-8-1*) Winning St Paul.
— How Anyone Can Negotiate with the IRS - & Win: A Daring Expose of the Vulnerability of the System & the People Who Run It. Engstrom, David M., ed. (Illus.). 250p. (Orig.). 1990. pap. 12.95 (*0-9617124-5-7*) Winning St Paul.
— How to Fire the IRS: A Plan to Eliminate the Income Tax & the IRS. Engstrom, David M., ed. LC 93-94197. 256p. (Orig.). 1993. pap. 12.95 (*1-884367-00-3*) Winning St Paul.
— How to Get Tax Amnesty: A Guide to the Forgiveness of IRS Debt. LC 92-96839. 224p. (Orig.). 1992. pap. 12.95 (*0-9617124-9-X*) Winning St Paul.
— The Naked Truth: Everything You've Always Wanted to Know about the IRS, but Couldn't Afford to Ask - 163 Questions & Answers about the IRS. LC 86-90235. (Illus.). 210p. (Orig.). 1986. pap. 9.95 (*0-9617124-0-6*) Winning St Paul.
— Tax Amnesty: A Guide to the Forgiveness of IRS Debt Including Penalities & Interest. Date not set. 12.95 (*0-685-68184-X*) Winning St Paul.
— Taxpayers' Ultimate Defense Manual: Nine Devastating Weapons Against I.R.S. Abuse. Engstrom, David M., ed. 224p. (Orig.). 1989. 29.95 (*0-9617124-7-3*) Winning St Paul.
Pilla i, P. S. Law of Torts. (C). 1991. 90.00 (*0-89771-793-7*, Pub. by Eastern Book II) St Mut.
Pilla, Lou, ed. Automating Your Office: Pathways to Management Succcess. (Illus.). 158p. (Orig.). 1984. pap. 13.95 (*0-916323-02-1*) Admin Mgmt.

P Q

An Asterisk (*) at the beginning of an entry indicates that the title is appearing in BIP for the first time.

Pilla, Marianne L. The Best: High-Low Books for Reluctant Readers. (Libraries Unlimited Data Bks.). 100p. 1990. pap. text ed. 12.50 (*0-87287-532-6*); disk 16.50 (*0-87287-775-2*); Apple II 16.00 (*0-87287-780-9*); mac hd 17.00 (*0-87287-790-6*) Libs Unl.

— Resources for Middle-Grade Reluctant Readers: A Guide for Librarians. LC 87-3736. 130p. 1987. lib. bdg. 18.50 (*0-87287-547-4*) Libs Unl.

Pilla, Michael. Barbarian's Quest. 392p. (Orig.). 1992. pap. 9.99 (*1-56043-652-2*) Destiny Image.

Pillado, Francisco. Los Bienes De Dios: God's Property-Should We Tithe? (SPA.). 4.95 (*84-7228-357-7*, 220111, Pub. by Edit Clie SP) TSELF.

***Pillage, Lawrence T.** Electronic Circuit & System Simulation Methods. LC 94-24429. 1995. text ed. 55.00 (*0-07-050169-6*) McGraw.

***Pillai.** Scavenger's Son. (Asian Writers Ser.). 124p. 1994. pap. 9.95 (*0-435-95082-7*) Heinemann.

Pillai, C. N., jt. ed. see Viswanathan, B.

Pillai, C. S. Sahajayoga & Other Meditations. 1987. 8.95 (*0-318-37038-7*) Asia Bk Corp.

Pillai, C. V. Marthanda Varma. Devi, Leela, tr. 292p. 1984. pap. 6.00 (*0-86578-241-5*) Ind-US Inc.

Pillai, G. Narayana. Social Background of Political Leadership in India. 1984. 18.50 (*0-8364-1060-2*, Pub. by Uppal Pub Hse II) S Asia.

Pillai, Gopinadha, jt. auth. see Scheer, Georg.

Pillai, K. C. Light Through an Eastern Window. LC 85-51634. 144p. 1986. 6.75 (*0-910068-63-1*) Am Christian.

— Light Through an Eastern Window. 1963. pap. 4.95 (*0-8315-0057-3*) Speller.

— Orientalisms of the Bible, Vol. I. LC 84-50935. 138p. 1984. 6.75 (*0-910068-55-0*) Am Christian.

— Orientalisms of the Bible, Vol. 1. 1969. 4.95 (*0-912178-02-7*) Mor-Mac.

— Orientalisms of the Bible, Vol. II. LC 84-50935. 164p. 1984. 6.75 (*0-910068-70-4*) Am Christian.

— Orientalisms of the Bible, Vol. 2. 1974. 4.95 (*0-912178-04-3*) Mor-Mac.

Pillai, K. N. Double Jeopardy Protection: A Comparative Overview. (C). 1988. 35.00 (*81-7099-058-0*, Pub. by Mittal II) S Asia.

Pillai, L. D. Indian Chronology (Solar, Lunar & Planetary) 1989. reprint ed. 26.50 (*81-206-0250-1*, Pub. by Asian Educ Servs II) S Asia.

Pillai, M., jt. auth. see James, D. K.

Pillai, M-Arjunan. Ancient Indian History. (C). 1988. 26.00 (*81-7024-188-X*, Pub. by Ashish II) S Asia.

Pillai, M. N., tr. see Sarukhanyan, E. I.

Pillai, M. S. Ravana King of Lanka. (C). 1993. reprint ed. 10.00 (*81-206-0547-0*, Pub. by Asian Educ Servs II) S Asia.

— Tamil Literature. (C). 1995. 24.00x (*81-206-0955-7*, Pub. by Asian Educ Servs II) S Asia.

Pillai, Mary, jt. auth. see James, David.

Pillai, P. Mohanan, jt. auth. see Subrahmanian, K. K.

Pillai, P. S. Jurisprudence & Legal Theory. 1986. 65.00 (*0-317-56729-2*) St Mut.

— Principles of Law of Tort. 1986. 65.00 (*0-317-56727-6*) St Mut.

Pillai, P. S., ed. Law of Tort. (C). 1991. 90.00 (*0-89771-797-X*, Pub. by Eastern Book II) St Mut.

Pillai, Philip N. Companies & Securities Handbook - Singapore & Malaysia. 1401p. 1984. pap. 31.00 (*0-406-18120-9*) Butterworth Legal Pubs.

— Companies & Securities Handbook - Singapore & Malaysia. suppl. ed. 1401p. 1985. 30.00 (*0-409-99507-X*) Butterworth Legal Pubs.

— Company Law & Securities Regulation in Singapore. xxv, 242p. 1987. pap. 48.00 (*0-409-99549-5*) Butterworth Legal Pubs.

— Sourcebook of Singapore & Malaysian Company Law. 1386p. 1986. 277.00 (*0-409-99511-8*) Butterworth Legal Pubs.

Pillai, R. C. Nehru & His Critics. 1986. 28.00 (*0-8364-1540-X*, Pub. by Gitanjali Prakashan) S Asia.

Pillai, R. N. Veerabrahmam: India's Nostradamus Saint. (C). 1991. 19.50 (*81-7017-279-9*, Pub. by Abhinav II) S Asia.

Pillai, S. D. Slums & Urbanization. (C). 1990. 45.00 (*81-7154-259-X*, Pub. by Popular Prakashan II) S Asia.

Pillai, S. K. Analysis of Thyristor Power-Conditioned Motors. 1993. text ed. 25.00 (*0-86311-188-2*, Pub. by Universities Pr II) Apt Bks.

Pillai, S. O. Solid State Electronic Engineering Materials. LC 92-13595. 398p. 1992. text ed. 55.95 (*0-470-21863-0*) Halsted Pr.

Pillai, Sivaraja. The Chronology of the Early Tamils. (Illus.). 284p. 1986. 22.00 (*0-8364-1713-5*, Pub. by Manohar II) S Asia.

Pillai, T. S. Two Measures of Rice. Shakoor, M. A., tr. 118p. 1975. pap. 2.50 (*0-88253-169-7*) Ind-US Inc.

Pillai, Thakazhi S. Chemmeen. Menon, Narayana, tr. 221p. 1964. pap. 4.00 (*0-88253-066-6*) Ind-US Inc.

— Rungs of the Ladder. Verghese, C. Paul, tr. 423p. 1976. pap. 3.50 (*0-86578-146-X*) Ind-US Inc.

— The Unchaste. Bhaskaran, M. K., tr. 112p. 1971. pap. 2.10 (*0-88253-067-4*) Ind-US Inc.

Pillai, U. S. Array Signal Processing. (Illus.). xi, 221p. 1989. 49.50 (*0-318-41905-X*) Spr-Verlag.

Pillai, V. C. The Origins of the Indo-European Races & Peoples. 2 vols. 1990. reprint ed. 110.00 (*81-85326-25-8*, Pub. by Vintage II) S Asia.

Pillai, V. Parameswaran. Temple Culture of South India. 1986. 40.00 (*0-317-53516-1*, Pub. by Manohar II) S Asia.

Pillai, Vijayan K. & Shannon, Lyle W., eds. Developing Areas: A Book of Readings & Research. 450p. 1994. 74.95 (*0-85496-741-9*) Berg Pubs.

Pillaiyar, P. Rice Postproduction Manual. (C). 1988. pap. 10.50 (*81-224-0007-8*, Pub. by Wiley Eastern II) S Asia.

***Pillar, Arlene.** Folk Tales. Friedland, J. & Kessler, R., eds. (Novel-Ties Ser.). (J). (gr. 3-6). 1988. student ed, pap. text ed. 15.95 (*0-88122-867-2*) Lrn Links.

Pillar, Marjorie. Join the Band! LC 90-23261. (Illus.). 32p. (J). (gr. 1-3). 1992. lib. bdg. 14.89 (*0-06-021829-0*) HarpC Child Bks.

Pillar, Paul R. Negotiating Peace: War Termination as a Bargaining Process. LC 83-42572. 272p. 1983. 42.50 (*0-691-07656-1*) Princeton U Pr.

Pillari, Vimala. Family Myths in Therapy. LC 93-74374. 206p. 1994. pap. 27.50 (*1-56821-198-8*) Aronson.

— Human Behavior in the Social Environment. LC 88-14539. 352p. (Orig.). (C). 1988. pap. 22.95 (*0-534-09060-5*) Brooks-Cole.

— Scapegoating in Families: Intergenerational Patterns of Physical & Emotional Abuse. LC 91-3452. 240p. 1991. 27.95 (*0-87630-639-3*) Brunner-Mazel.

— Shadow of Pain. Date not set. write for info. (*1-56821-059-0*) Aronson.

Pillay. Tamil-English Dictionary. 731p. 1988. 19.00 (*81-206-0437-7*) IBD Ltd.

— Tamil-English Dictionary. 731p. (ENG & TAM.). 1988. 19.95 (*0-7859-7525-X*, 8120604377) Fr & Eur.

Pillay, T. V. Aquaculture & the Environment. 189p. 1992. text ed. 69.95 (*0-470-21849-5*) Halsted Pr.

— Planning of Aquaculture Development. 1978. 60.00 (*0-685-63447-7*) St Mut.

Pillay, T. V. R. Aquaculture Development: Progress & Prospects. LC 94-16593. 1994. 59.95 (*0-470-23432-6*) Halsted Pr.

Pillemer, David B., jt. auth. see Light, Richard J.

Pillemer, Karl & McCartney, Kathleen, eds. Parent Child Relations Throughout Life. 304p. 1991. text ed. 59.95 (*0-8058-0822-1*) L Erlbaum Assocs.

Pillemer, Karl A. & Wolf, Rosalie S., eds. Elder Abuse: Conflict in the Family. LC 86-14014. 381p. 1986. text ed. 37.95 (*0-86569-133-9*, Auburn Hse); pap. text ed. 16.95 (*0-86569-134-7*, Auburn Hse) Greenwood.

Pillemer, Karl A., tr. see Gehlen, Arnold.

Pillemer, Karl A., jt. auth. see Wolf, Rosalie S.

***Pillemer, Stanley R., ed. & intro.** The Fibromyalgia Syndrome: Current Research & Future Directions in Epidemiology, Pathogenesis & Treatment. LC 94-35454. (Illus.). 200p. 1994. lib. bdg. 29.95 (*1-56024-714-2*, Hawrth Medical) Haworth Pr.

Pillepich, John A., jt. auth. see Ronzio, Robert A.

Piller, Charles. The Fail-Safe Society: Community Defiance & the End of American Technological Optimism. LC 92-24104. 1993. reprint ed. 13.00 (*0-520-08202-8*) U CA Pr.

Pilleri, G., jt. ed. see Purves, P. E.

Pillet, Roger A., jt. auth. see Dunkel, Harold B.

Pilley, Catherine M. & Wilt, Matthew R., eds. Catholic Subject Headings. rev. ed. ii, 240p. 1981. pap. 25.00 (*0-87507-009-4*) Cath Lib Assn.

Pilley, Christopher. Adult Education, Community Development & Older People: Releasing the Resource. (Council of Europe Ser.). 70p. 1990. text ed. 50.00 (*0-304-32263-6*); pap. text ed. 14.95 (*0-304-32271-7*) Cassell.

***Pilley, H. Robert & Pilley, Lois V.** GPS-Based Airport Operations: Requirements, Analysis & Algorithms. (Engineering Source Book Ser.: Vol. I). (Illus.). 400p. (Orig.). 1994. pap. 150.00 (*0-9643568-0-5*); disk write for info. (*0-9643568-2-1*) DSDC.

Pilley, Lois V., jt. auth. see Pilley, H. Robert.

Pillich, W. Social Dance. (Ballroom Dance Ser.). 1986. lib. bdg. 79.95 (*0-8490-3345-4*) Gordon Pr.

— Social Dance. (Ballroom Dance Ser.). 1985. lib. bdg. 74.00 (*0-87700-688-1*) Revisionist Pr.

Pillider, Sarah, jt. auth. see Rose, John.

Pillin, William. Another Dawn. 54p. (Orig.). 1984. pap. 8.95 (*0-89807-110-0*) Illuminati.

Pilliner, S. Getting Horses Fit. 2nd ed. 1993. pap. 22.95 (*0-632-03476-9*) Blackwell Sci.

— Horse Nutrition & Feeding. 1992. pap. 29.95 (*0-632-03239-1*) Blackwell Sci.

Pilliner, S., jt. auth. see Hodges, J.

Pilliner, S., jt. auth. see Houghton-Brown, J.

Pilliner, Sarah. Care of the Competition Horse: Prepare to Win. (Illus.). 176p. 1994. 24.95 (*0-7134-7090-9*, Pub. by Batsford UK) Trafalgar.

Pilliner, Sarah, jt. auth. see Hodges, Jo.

***Pilling.** The Condition of Britain: Essays to Mark the Centenary of the Death of Frederick Engels. Lea, ed. (C). 1996. text ed. 59.00 (*0-7453-0962-3*, Pub. by Pluto Pr UK) Westview.

Pilling, Ann. Before I Go to Sleep: A Collection of Bible Stories, Poems & Prayers for Children. LC 89-7816. (Illus.). 96p. (J). 1990. lib. bdg. 15.99 (*0-517-58019-5*) Crown Bks Yng Read.

— Considering Helen. large type ed. 1993. 39.95 (*0-7066-1026-1*, Pub. by Remploy Pr CN) St Mut.

— Realms of Gold: Myths & Legends from Around the World. LC 92-30858. (Illus.). (J). 1993. 16.95 (*1-85697-913-X*, Kingfisher LKC) LKC.

Pilling, Arnold R. Aborigine Culture History: A Survey of Publications, 1954-1957. LC 61-12268. (Wayne State University Studies: No. 11: Anthropology). 229p. reprint ed. pap. 65.30 (*0-8357-5013-2*, 2027651) Bks Demand.

Pilling, Donald L. Competition in Defense Procurement. 80p. 1989. pap. 7.95 (*0-8157-7081-2*) Brookings.

Pilling, Doria. Approaches to Case Management for People with Disabilities. (Disability & Rehabilitation Ser.: No. 1). 220p. 1992. 57.00 (*1-85302-099-0*, Pub. by J Kingsley Pubs UK) Taylor & Francis.

***Pilling, Doria & Watson, Graham, eds.** Evaluating Quality in Services for Disabled & Older People. LC 95-7249. (Disability & Rehabilitation Ser.: Vol. 7). 1995. write for info. (*1-85302-289-6*, Pub. by J Kingsley Pubs UK) Taylor & Francis.

Pilling, Doria, jt. auth. see National Children's Bureau Staff.

Pilling, Elaine & Prochak, Michael. Journeys Through Claris Filemaker Pro 2.1. LC 93-49062. (Macintosh Guide Ser.). 1994. pap. 44.95 (*0-201-63158-X*) Addison-Wesley.

***Pilling, Geoff.** Marxist Political Economy: Essays in Retrieval. 1995. pap. 16.50 (*1-899438-06-8*, Pub. by Porcupine Bks UK) Humanities.

Pilling, Geoff, jt. ed. see Brotherstone, Terry.

Pilling, J. C. Bibliography of the Siouan Language. 1977. lib. bdg. 59.95 (*0-8490-1501-4*) Gordon Pr.

Pilling, James C. Bibliographies of the Languages of the North American Indians, 9 Pts. in 3 Vols, Set. LC 76-174200. reprint ed. 125.00 (*0-404-07390-5*) AMS Pr.

— Bibliography of the Algonquian Languages. (Bureau of American Ethnology Bulletins Ser.). 614p. 1995. lib. bdg. 149.00 (*0-7812-4013-1*) Rprt Serv.

— Bibliography of the Algonquian Languages, 2 pts. 1988. reprint ed. lib. bdg. 75.00 (*0-7812-0312-0*) Rprt Serv.

— Bibliography of the Athapascan Languages. (Bureau of American Ethnology Bulletins Ser.). 125p. 1995. lib. bdg. 79.00 (*0-7812-4014-X*) Rprt Serv.

— Bibliography of the Chinookan Languages, Including the Chinook Jargon. (Bureau of American Ethnology Bulletins Ser.). 81p. 1995. lib. bdg. 79.00 (*0-7812-4015-8*) Rprt Serv.

— Bibliography of the Eskimo Languages. (Bureau of American Ethnology Bulletins Ser.). 161p. 1995. lib. bdg. 79.00 (*0-7812-4001-8*) Rprt Serv.

— Bibliography of the Iroquoian Languages. (Bureau of American Ethnology Bulletins Ser.). 208p. 1995. lib. bdg. 89.00 (*0-7812-4006-9*) Rprt Serv.

— Bibliography of the Muskhogean Languages. (Bureau of American Ethnology Bulletins Ser.). 114p. 1995. lib. bdg. 79.00 (*0-7812-4009-3*) Rprt Serv.

— Bibliography of the Salishan Languages. (Bureau of American Ethnology Bulletins Ser.). 86p. 1995. lib. bdg. 79.00 (*0-7812-4016-6*) Rprt Serv.

— Bibliography of the Siouan Language. (Bureau of American Ethnology Bulletins Ser.). 87p. 1995. lib. bdg. 79.00 (*0-7812-4005-0*) Rprt Serv.

— Bibliography of the Wakashan Languages. (Bureau of American Ethnology Bulletins Ser.). 70p. 1995. lib. bdg. 79.00 (*0-7812-4019-0*) Rprt Serv.

Pilling, Jayne, tr. see Malle, Louis & Carriere, Jean-Claude.

Pilling, Jayne, tr. see Truffaut, Francois & Givray, Claude.

Pilling, John. Oxfordshire Houses: An Introduction to Local Traditions. (Illus.). 1993. 26.00 (*0-7509-0222-1*) A Sutton Pub.

— Phase Diagrams & Microstructures: A Computer Aided Learning Guide. 100p. 1992. 192.00 (*0-901716-11-1*, Pub. by Inst Materials UK) Ashgate Pub Co.

Pilling, John, ed. The Cambridge Companion to Beckett. LC 92-47287. (Cambridge Companions to Literature Ser.). (Illus.). 272p. (C). 1994. 59.95 (*0-521-41366-4*) Cambridge U Pr.

— The Cambridge Companion to Beckett. LC 92-47287. (Cambridge Companions to Literature Ser.). (Illus.). 272p. (C). 1994. pap. 16.95 (*0-521-42413-5*) Cambridge U Pr.

Pilling, John & Ridley, Norman. Superplasticity in Crystalline Solids. 214p. 1989. pap. text ed. 36.00 (*0-901462-56-X*, Pub. by Inst Materials UK) Ashgate Pub Co.

***Pilling, Michael J. & Seakins, Paul W.** Reaction Kinetics. (Illus.). 270p. (C). 1995. pap. text ed. 29.95 (*0-19-855527-X*) OUP.

— Reaction Kinetics. (Illus.). 270p. (C). 1995. text ed. 69.95 (*0-19-855528-8*) OUP.

Pilling, R., jt. photos see Miller, Roger C.

Pilling, Ron. Baltimore Captured Memories. Miller, David & Finn, Margaritta, eds. LC 88-81952. (Illus.). 72p. 1988. 9.95 (*0-911897-13-5*) Image Ltd.

— Maryland a Portrait. 2nd ed. Miller, David & Baer, Bonnie, eds. LC 88-81950. (Illus.). 120p. 1988. 34.50 (*0-911897-02-X*); pap. 19.95 (*0-911897-12-7*) Image Ltd.

Pilling, Stella, jt. ed. see Woodward, Hazel.

Pilling, Stephen. Rehabilitation & Community Care. (Strategies for Mental Health Ser.). 224p. 1991. 55.00 (*0-415-05817-1*, A5205); pap. 17.95 (*0-415-01067-5*, A5416) Routledge.

Pillinger, C. T., jt. ed. see Turner, G.

Pillion, jt. auth. see Pootler.

Pilliow, N. Grand Finale. LC 93-79283. 394p. (Orig.). 1994. pap. 11.95 (*1-877978-56-6*, FLF Pr) Woldt.

Pillips, W. R., jt. auth. see Grant, I. S.

Pilliteri, Adele. Maternal & Child Health Nursing: Care of the Childbearing & Childrearing Family. 2nd ed. LC 94-16338. 1994. write for info. (*0-397-55113-4*) Lippincott.

Pillitteri, Adele. Maternal & Child Health Nursing: Care of the Childbearing & Childrearing Family. (Illus.). 1850p. 1992. text ed. 68.95 (*0-397-54862-1*) Lippincott.

— Maternal-Newborn Nursing: Care of the Growing Family. 3rd ed. (Illus.). 1279p. (C). 1985. text ed. 35.25 (*0-673-39401-8*) HarpCollege.

Pillitteri, Joseph. Life Pulse. 1989. mass mkt. 4.50 (*1-55817-280-7*, Pinnacle NY) Windsor NY.

Pillman, Naka. African Diary. LC 89-42868. 304p. 1990. 18.95 (*0-937552-31-3*) Quail Ridge.

Pillman, Naka, ed. Camel Crochet. 32p. 1990. pap. 9.95 (*0-944351-03-4*) N S D Products.

Pillot, Judd, ed. see Fox, Hayden.

Pilloud, Claude, et al, eds. Commentaire des Protocoles Additionnels du 8 Juin 1977 aux Conventions de Geneve du 12 Aout 1949. 1986. lib. bdg. 297.50 (*90-247-3403-7*) Kluwer Ac.

Pillsbury. Operative Challenges in Head & Neck Surgery. 1991. write for info. (*0-8151-6707-5*, Yr Bk Med Pubs) Mosby Yr Bk.

Pillsbury Co. Staff. A Book for a Cook. 1994. reprint ed. 12.95 (*1-55709-225-7*) Applewood.

— Little Book for a Little Cook. (J). 1992. 14.95 (*1-55709-172-2*) Applewood.

Pillsbury Company Editors. The Pillsbury Doughboy's First Cookbook. (Illus.). 72p. (J). (ps-3). 1992. 15.00 (*0-385-23871-1*) Doubleday.

Pillsbury Company Staff. Healthy Baking: Fresh Approaches to More Than 200 Favorite Recipes. (Illus.). 288p. 1994. 22.95 (*0-670-85723-8*, Viking) Viking Penguin.

— Pillsbury Cookbook: The All-Purpose Companion for Today's Cook. 1991. pap. 15.00 (*0-385-41791-8*) Doubleday.

Pillsbury, Dorothy L. Adobe Doorways. LC 52-11521. 208p. 1983. reprint ed. 16.95 (*0-89016-076-7*); reprint ed. pap. 8.95 (*0-89016-070-8*) Lightning Tree.

— No High Adobe. LC 50-10958. 208p. 1983. reprint ed. 16.95 (*0-89016-075-9*) Lightning Tree.

— Roots in Adobe. LC 59-13409. 240p. 1983. reprint ed. 16.95 (*0-89016-077-5*); reprint ed. pap. 8.95 (*0-89016-071-6*) Lightning Tree.

Pillsbury Editors. Pillsbury Kitchens' Family Cookbook. write for info. (*0-318-58126-4*) S&S Trade.

Pillsbury, Edmund P. & Richards, Louise E. The Graphic Art of Federico Barocci. 1978. pap. 6.00 (*0-89467-004-2*) Yale Art Gallery.

Pillsbury, Edmund P., jt. auth. see Riely, John.

Pillsbury, Harold, jt. auth. see Weissler, Mark.

Pillsbury, Harold C., III. Operative Challenges in Otolaryngology - Head & Neck Surgery. (Illus.). 928p. 1990. 159.00 (*0-8151-6708-3*, Yr Bk Med Pubs) Mosby Yr Bk.

Pillsbury, Harold C., III, jt. ed. see Shockley, William W.

Pillsbury, Linda G. Survival Tips for Working Moms: Two Hundred Ninety-Seven Real Tips from Real Moms. LC 93-87732. (Illus.). 192p. (Orig.). 1994. pap. 10.95 (*0-9622036-5-3*) Prspctive Pub.

Pillsbury, Parker. Acts of the Anti-Slavery Apostles. LC 76-82212. (Anti-Slavery Crusade in America Ser.). 1970. reprint ed. 43.95 (*0-405-00651-9*) Ayer.

— Acts of the Anti-Slavery Apostles. LC 70-92758. 503p. 1969. reprint ed. text ed. 59.75 (*0-8371-2183-3*, PIA&, Negro U Pr) Greenwood.

Pillsbury, Richard. From Boarding House to Bistro: The American Restaurant Then & Now. (Illus.). 256p. 1990. text ed. 34.95 (*0-04-445680-8*) Routledge Chapman & Hall.

Pillsbury, Richard, jt. auth. see Rooney, John F., Jr.

Pillsbury, Samuel H. Conviction: A Novel. LC 92-10952. 213p. 1992. 21.95 (*0-8027-1225-8*) Walker & Co.

— The Invasion of Planet Wampetter. LC 95-8432. (Illus.). 144p. (J). (gr. 3-8). 1995. 15.00 (*0-9622036-6-1*) Prspctive Pub.

Pillsbury, Walter B. Attention. LC 73-2982. (Classics in Psychology Ser.). 1980. reprint ed. 28.95 (*0-405-05154-9*) Ayer.

Pilnyak, Boris, pseud. Ivan Moscow. Schwartzman, A., tr. LC 72-90305. (Soviet Literature in English Translation Ser.). 92p. 1973. reprint ed. 15.00 (*0-88355-016-4*) Hyperion Conn.

Pilnyak, Boris. Mahogany & Other Stories. Reck, Vera T. & Green, Michael, trs. 302p. (RUS.). 1993. pap. 16.95 (*0-87501-104-7*) Ardis Pubs.

— The Naked Year. Tulloch, Alexander R., tr. 207p. 1975. pap. 10.95 (*0-88233-078-0*) Ardis Pubs.

— The Naked Year. LC 70-174201. reprint ed. 12.50 (*0-404-06778-6*) AMS Pr.

Pilnyak, Boris, pseud. Tales of the Wilderness. O'Dempsey, F., tr. LC 72-90306. (Soviet Literature in English Translation Ser.). 223p. 1973. reprint ed. 18.50 (*0-88355-017-2*) Hyperion Conn.

— Volga Falls to the Caspian Sea. LC 71-110428. reprint ed. 15.00 (*0-404-05047-6*) AMS Pr.

Pilon, Daniel H. & Bergquist, William H. Consultation in Higher Education: A Handbook for Practitioners & Clients. Quehl, Gary H. & Brodsky, Jean, eds. LC 79-90144. 1980. pap. 10.95 (*0-937012-01-7*) Coun Indep Colleges.

Pilon, Frederick. Essay on the Character of Hamlet. 2nd ed. LC 73-174202. reprint ed. 29.50 (*0-404-05048-4*) AMS Pr.

Pilon, J., jt. auth. see Larouche, L.

***Pilon, Jean-Luc & Morrison, David.** Threads of Arctic Prehistory: Papers on Honour of William E. Taylor, Jr. (Mercury Series: Archeological Survey of Canada: Vol. 149). (Illus.). 436p. 1995. pap. text ed. 29.95x (*0-660-50751-X*) U of Wash Pr.

Pilon, Juliana G. The Bloody Flag: Post-Communist Nationalism in Eastern Europe: Spotlight on Romania. 280p. (C). 1992. 32.95 (*1-56000-062-7*); pap. 17.95 (*1-56000-620-X*) Transaction Pubs.

— Notes from the Other Side of Night. LC 94-7701. 1994. reprint ed. pap. text ed. 14.95 (*0-8191-9510-3*) U Pr of Amer.

Pilon, Juliana G. & Bennett, Ralph K. The U. N. Assessing Soviet Abuses. (C). 1990. 45.00 (*0-907967-90-6*, Pub. by Inst Euro Def & Strat UK) St Mut.

Pilon, Roger. Politics & Law of Term Limits. 1994. 19.95 (*1-882577-12-4*); pap. 10.95 (*1-882577-13-2*) Cato Inst.

***Pilot Books Staff & Small, Samuel.** Directory of Franchising Organizations. LC 62-39831. 80p. 1995. 5.95 (*0-87576-190-9*) Pilot Bks.

Pilot, Kevin. Credit Approved. 144p. 1992. pap. 5.95 (*1-55850-111-8*) Adams Pubng.

— The One Hundred Safest Investments for Retirement. 316p. (Orig.). 1993. pap. 14.95 (*1-56414-071-7*) Career Pr Inc.

Pilot, Michael, jt. auth. see Rosenthal, Neal H.

Pilot, Patricia L. Theron Came Later. 210p. 1984. 7.45 (*0-89697-137-6*) Intl Univ Pr.

Pilot-Raichoor, Christiane, jt. auth. see Hockings, Paul.
Pilot Staff. Your Personal Guide to Pre-Retirement Planning. LC 83-13275. 43p. 1983. pap. 5.00 (0-87576-106-2) Pilot Bks.
Pilotta, Joseph J. & Mickunas, Algis. Science of Communication: Its Phenomenological Foundation. (Communication Textbook Series, General Communication Theory & Methodology Subser.). 200p. 1990. text ed. 39.95 (0-8058-0401-3) L Erlbaum Assocs.
Pilotta, Joseph J., jt. ed. see Golden, James L.
Piloty, R., et al. CONLAN Report. (Lecture Notes in Computer Science Ser.: Vol. 151). 174p. 1983. pap. 24.00 (0-387-12275-3) Spr-Verlag.
Pilowsky, Daniel & Chambers, William, eds. Hallucinations in Children. LC 86-10945. (Clinical Insights Ser.). 140p. reprint ed. pap. 39.90 (0-8357-7836-3, 2036210) Bks Demand.
Pilpay, T. The Fables of Pilpay. 220p. 1987. 78.00 (1-85077-144-8, Darf Pubs Ltd) St Mut.
Pilsbry, H. A., et al. Land Snails from Hawaii, Christmas Island & Samoa. (BMB Ser.: Vol. 47). 1969. reprint ed. pap. 15.00 (0-527-02153-9) Periodicals Srv.
Pilsbry, Henry A. Land Mollusca of North America: North of Mexico, Pt. 1. (Land Mollusca of North America: No. 3). (Illus.). 520p. (Orig.). 1948. reprint ed. pap. 35.00 (0-910006-12-1) Acad Nat Sci Phila.
— Land Mollusca of North America: North of Mexico, Pt. 1. Incl. Pt. 1. Land Mollusca of North America: North of Mexico. (Illus.). 520p. (Orig.). 1948. reprint ed. pap. 35.00 (0-910006-12-1); Pt. 2. Land Mollusca of North America: North of Mexico. (Illus.). 592p. (Orig.). 1948. reprint ed. pap. 35.00 (0-685-73632-6); (Monograph: No. 3). (Illus.). 573p. (Orig.). Set pap. 35.00 (0-910006-11-3) Acad Nat Sci Phila.
— Land Mollusca of North America: North of Mexico, Pt. 2. (Land Mollusca of North America: No. 3). (Illus.). 592p. (Orig.). 1948. reprint ed. pap. 35.00 (0-685-73632-6) Acad Nat Sci Phila.
— Land Mollusca of North America: North of Mexico, Vol. II, Pts. 1 & 2. Incl. Pt. 1. Land Mollusca of North America: North of Mexico. (Illus.). 520p. (Orig.). 1948. reprint ed. pap. 35.00 (0-910006-12-1); Pt. 2. Land Mollusca of North America: North of Mexico. (Illus.). 592p. (Orig.). 1948. reprint ed. pap. 35.00 (0-685-73632-6); (Monograph: No. 3). (Illus.). (Orig.). Pt. 2, 419p. write for info. (0-685-08428-0) Acad Nat Sci Phila.
Pilsbury, D. B. & Getchell, E. A. The Pillsbury Family; Being a History of William & Dorothy Pillsbury (or Pilsbery) of Newbury in New England, & Their Descendants to the Eleventh Generation. (Illus.). 336p. 1989. reprint ed. lib. bdg. 48.25 (0-8328-0968-3); reprint ed. pap. 40.25 (0-8328-0969-1) Higginson Bk Co.
Pilsner, Ray C. Your Health & Life Are in Your Hands. 1974. pap. 2.75 (0-685-57204-8) Byzantine Pr.
Pilson, Michael E. Introduction to the Chemistry of the Sea. 350p. 1992. text ed. 52.00 (0-13-478231-3) P-H.
Pilsudska, Alexandra. Pilsudski: A Biography by His Wife. LC 76-135829. (Eastern Europe Collection Ser.). 1971. reprint ed. 24.95 (0-405-02771-0) Ayer.
Pilsudski Institute of America Staff. Poland in the British Parliament: Documentary Material Relating to the Cause of Poland During World War Two, 3 vols., 2. Jedrzejewicz, Waclaw, ed. 1834p. write for info. (0-940962-26-8) Polish Inst Art & Sci.
— Poland in the British Parliament: Documentary Material Relating to the Cause of Poland During World War Two, 3 vols., 3. Jedrzejewicz, Waclaw, ed. 1834p. write for info. (0-940962-27-6) Polish Inst Art & Sci.
Pilsudski, Jozef. Joseph Pilsudski: The Memories of a Polish Revolutionary & Soldier. Gillie, D. R., ed. LC 70-101275. reprint ed. 27.50 (0-404-05049-2) AMS Pr.
Piltch, Benjamin & Smergut, Peter. Class Trips. (Skyview Ser.). 64p. (J). (gr. 4-8). 1983. 3.95 (0-934618-00-3) Learning Well.
— Money Matters. (Skyview Ser.). 64p. (YA). (gr. 7-12). 1983. 3.95 (0-934618-03-8) Learning Well.
Piltch, Benjamin, ed. see Funes, Marilyn & Lazarus, Alan.
Piltch, Benjamin, ed. see Kaufman, Tanya & Wishny, Judith.
Pilurs, David B. Sun & Storm: The Codex. Caruso, Lenore & Caruso, Sara, eds. (Illus.). 96p. (YA). (gr. 7 up). 1993. per. 12.95 (0-9636551-1-6) Storm Pr.
— Sun & Storm: The Enchiridion. Caruso, Lenore R. & Caruso, Sara L., eds. (Illus.). 96p. (YA). (gr. 7 up). 1993. per. 12.95 (0-9636551-0-8) Storm Pr.
— Sun & Storm: The Terminus. Caruso, Lenore R., ed. (Illus.). 16p. (YA). (gr. 7 up). 1993. 8.95 (0-9636551-2-4, 26635) Storm Pr.
— The Wyrmship Technical Manual. Caruso, Lenore & Caruso, Tom, eds. (Illus.). 144p. (YA). (gr. 7 up). 1994. 16.95 (0-9636551-3-2, 26640) Storm Pr.
Pilutik, Anastasia D., jt. auth. see Seco, Nina.
Pilyugin, S. Y. Introduction to Structurally Stable Systems of Differential Equations. 200p. 1992. 69.00 (0-8176-2574-7) Spr-Verlag.
Pilyugin, Sergei Y. The Space of Dynamical Systems with the C POS-Topology. LC 94-887. (Lecture Notes in Mathematics Ser.: Vol. 1571). (Illus.). x, 188p. 1994. pap. 28.00 (0-387-57702-5) Spr-Verlag.
Pilz, G. Near Rings: The Theory & Its Application. 2nd rev. ed. (Mathematics Studies: Vol. 23). 1983. 59.75 (0-444-86750-3, I-154-83, North Holland) Elsevier.
Pilz, G., jt. auth. see Lidl, R.
Pilz, Jurgen. Bayesian Estimating & Experimental Design in Linear Regression Models. LC 87-27515. (Probability & Mathematical Statistics: Applied Probability & Statistics Section Ser.: No. 1345). 296p. 1991. text ed. 79.95 (0-471-91732-X) Wiley.
***Pilzer, Karl.** The Treasure of the Tear. (Illus.). 40p. (J). 1995. 16.95 (0-936015-51-9) Pocahontas Pr.
Pilzer, Paul Z. Should You Quit Before You're Fired? 64p. 1993. reprint ed. pap. 5.95 (1-883599-00-8) Quantum NV.
— Unlimited Wealth: The Theory & Practice of Economic Alchemy. 1990. 19.95 (0-517-58211-2, Crown) Crown Pub Group.
Pim, Alan. Financial & Economic History of the African Tropical Territories. 1970. reprint ed. 25.00 (0-87266-046-X) Argosy.
Pim, Bedford. Negro & Jamaica. LC 72-157375. (Black Heritage Library Collection). 1977. 15.95 (0-8369-8813-2) Ayer.
Pim, Ralph L. Winning Basketball: Techniques & Drills for Playing Better Basketball. (Illus.). 192p. 1994. pap. 10.95 (0-8092-3553-6) Contemp Bks.
***Pima County Department of Transportation & Flood Control District Staff, contrib.** Channel Change on the Santa Cruz River, Pima County, Arizona, 1936-1986. LC 94-41169. (Water-Supply Papers: Vol. 2429). 1995. write for info. (0-614-03357-8) US Geol Survey.
Pimbley, Joseph M., et al, eds. VLSI Electronics, Vol. 19: Advanced CMOS Process Technology. 296p. 1989. text ed. 116.00 (0-12-234119-8) Acad Pr.
Pimenov, jt. auth. see Novichkov.
Pimenta, Wendy, ed. see LeBell, Gene.
Pimental, David, ed. World Soil Erosion & Conservation. (Studies in Applied Ecology & Resource Management). (Illus.). 360p. (C). 1993. 99.95 (0-521-41967-0) Cambridge U Pr.
Pimental, David & Lehman, Hugh, eds. The Pesticide Question: Environment, Economics, & Ethics. LC 92-13910. 448p. 1992. 45.00 (0-412-03581-2, A7576, Chapman & Hall) Chapman & Hall.
***Pimental, Ken & Teixeira, Kevin.** Virtual Reality: Through the New Looking Glass. 2nd ed. LC 94-3440. 1994. text ed. 36.95 (0-07-050167-X, Windcrest) TAB Bks.
Pimentel, Benjamin. Rebolusyon: A Generation of Struggle in the Philippines. 365p. 1991. 26.00 (0-85345-822-7); pap. 12.00 (0-85345-823-5) Monthly Rev.
Pimentel, David. Handbook of Energy: Utilization in Agriculture. 496p. 1980. 129.00 (0-8493-2661-3, S494, CRC Reprint) Franklin.
Pimentel, David, ed. Food & Natural Resources. 800p. 1989. text ed. 157.00 (0-12-556555-0) Acad Pr.
— Handbook of Pest Management in Agriculture, I. 2nd ed. 1990. 281.95 (0-8493-3844-1, SB950) CRC Pr.
— Handbook of Pest Management in Agriculture, II. 2nd ed. 1990. 281.95 (0-8493-3845-X, SB950) CRC Pr.
— Handbook of Pest Management in Agriculture, III. 2nd ed. 1990. 281.95 (0-8493-3846-8, SB950) CRC Pr.
— Handbook of Pest Management in Agriculture, Vol. 1. 296p. 1981. 314.00 (0-8493-3841-7, SB950, CRC Reprint) CRC Pr.
— Handbook of Pest Management in Agriculture, Vol. 2. 336p. 1981. 146.00 (0-8493-3842-5, CRC Reprint) CRC Pr.
— Handbook of Pest Management in Agriculture, Vol. 3. 672p. 1981. 146.00 (0-8493-3843-3, CRC Reprint) CRC Pr.
Pimentel, David, jt. ed. see Kidd, Charles V.
Pimentel, David, jt. ed. see Sheets, T. J.
Pimentel, Enrique. Handbook of Growth Factors, 1. LC 93-40108. 1994. write for info. (0-8493-2505-6) CRC Pr.
— Handbook of Growth Factors, Vol. 2. 1994. write for info. (0-318-72420-0) CRC Pr.
— Handbook of Growth Factors, Vol. 3. LC 93-40108. 1994. write for info. (0-8493-2507-2) CRC Pr.
— Handbook of Growth Factors, Vol. II: Peptide Growth Factors. 352p. 1994. 99.95 (0-8493-2506-4, 2506) CRC Pr.
— Hormones, Growth Factors & Oncogenes. 256p. 1987. 217.00 (0-8493-5346-7, QP571) CRC Pr.
— Oncogenes. 224p. 1986. 180.00 (0-8493-6566-X, RC268) CRC Pr.
Pimentel, Enrique, ed. Oncogenes, Vol. I. 2nd ed. 528p. 1989. 239.00 (0-8493-6505-8, RC268) CRC Pr.
— Oncogenes, Vol. II. 2nd ed. 448p. 1989. 234.00 (0-8493-6506-6, RC268, CRC Reprint) Franklin.
Pimentel, George C., ed. Chemistry: An Experimental Science. LC 63-18323. (Chemical Education Material Study Ser.). (Illus.). 466p. (C). 1995. pap. text ed. 5.95 (0-7167-0002-6) W H Freeman.
Pimentel, George C. & Coonrod, Janice A. Opportunities in Chemistry: Today & Tomorrow. National Research Council Commission on Physical Sciences, Mathematics, & Applications Staff, ed. 256p. (Orig.). (C). 1987. pap. text ed. 10.00 (0-309-03742-5) Natl Acad Pr.
Pimentel, George C. & Sprately, Richard D. Chemical Bonding Clarified Through Quantum Mechanics. LC 71-75914. 1969. 22.95 (0-8162-6781-2) Holden-Day.
Pimentel, George C. & Spratley, Richard D. Understanding Chemical Thermodynamics. LC 69-13419. (Illus.). (C). 1969. pap. text ed. 22.00 (0-8162-6791-X) Holden-Day.
— Understanding Chemistry. LC 70-142944. (C). 1971. 38.00 (0-8162-6761-8) Holden-Day.
Pimentel, Juan. Communications Networks for Manufacturing. 1990. text ed. 89.67 (0-13-154402-0) P-H.
Pimentel, Ken & Teixeira, Kevin. Virtual Reality: Through the New Looking Glass. (Illus.). 352p. 1992. 32.95 (0-8306-4065-7, 4196, Windcrest); pap. 22.95 (0-8306-4064-9, 4196, Windcrest) TAB Bks.
— Virtual Reality: Through the New Looking Glass. 2nd ed. LC 94-3440. 1994. pap. text ed. 24.95 (0-07-050168-8) TAB Bks.
Pimentel, Ken, jt. auth. see Teixeira, Kevin.
Pimentel, Luz A. Metaphoric Narration: The Paranarrative Dimension of A la Recherche du Temps Perdu. (Romance Ser.). 168p. 1990. text ed. 45.00 (0-8020-2735-0) U of Toronto Pr.
Pimentel, Richard. Developing Jobs for Persons with Disabilities. (C). 1984. 79.00 (0-942071-06-9) M Wright & Assocs.
Pimentel, Richard & Lotito, Michael. The Americans With Disabilities Act: Making the ADA Work for You. 200p. 1991. spiral bd. 39.50 (0-942071-14-X) M Wright & Assocs.
Pimentel, Richard, jt. auth. see Bissonnette, Denise.
Pimentel, Richard, jt. auth. see Bissonnette-Lamendella, Denise.
Pimentel, Richard, et al. The Americans with Disabilities Act: A Comprehensive Guide to Title I. 374p. (C). 1992. text ed. 125.00 (0-942071-17-4) M Wright & Assocs.
— The Americans with Disabilities Act: Making the ADA Work for You. 276p. 1991. teacher ed 775.00 (0-942071-16-6) M Wright & Assocs.
— The Americans with Disabilities Act: Making the ADA Work for You. 2nd ed. 163p. (C). 1992. pap. text ed. 39.50 (0-942071-19-0) M Wright & Assocs.
— The Americans with Disabilities Act: Making the ADA Work for You. 2nd ed. 142p. 1992. 39.50 (0-685-56811-3, PB14) Soc Human Resc Mgmt.
— The Job Placement - ADA Connection: Limiting Liabilities & Maximizing Opportunities for Training & Placement of Persons with Disabilities. Wright, Anita L., ed. 63p. (Orig.). 1993. pap. 24.95 (0-942071-27-1, 242B) M Wright & Assocs.
— Job Placement for the Industrially Injured Worker. 95p. (C). 1988. student ed 28.50 (0-942071-04-2) M Wright & Assocs.
— Performance Based Placement Manual. 52p. 1987. student ed 19.50 (0-942071-01-8) M Wright & Assocs.
— What Managers & Supervisors Need to Know about the ADA: Trainer's Guide. 113p. (C). 1992. 395.00 (0-942071-18-2) M Wright & Assocs.
— The Workers' Compensation-ADA Connection: Supervisory Tools for Workers' Compensation Cost Containment That Reduce ADA Liability. Wright, Anita L., ed. LC 93-12743. 55p. (Orig.). (C). 1993. pap. text ed. 29.50 (0-942071-24-7) M Wright & Assocs.
***Pimentel, Richard K., et al.** The Taking Control Process: Beyond Light Duty. Wexler, Barbara & Wright, Anita L., eds. 135p. (C). 1995. 89.00 (0-942071-31-X) M Wright & Assocs.
Pimentel, Wayne. Dogtown & Ditches: Life on the Westside. LC 87-82867. 134p. 1987. pap. 18.95 (0-944707-00-9) Loose Change.
Pimlott, Ben. Labour & the Left in the Nineteen Thirties. (Illus.). 272p. 1986. reprint ed. pap. text ed. 18.95 (0-04-941016-4) Routledge Chapman & Hall.
Pimlott, Ben & Seaton, Jean. The Media in British Politics. 1987. text ed. 59.50 (0-566-00930-7, Pub. by Dartmth Pub UK) Ashgate Pub Co.
Pimlott, Ben, jt. ed. see MacGregor, Susanne.
Pimlott, J., jt. auth. see Farnham, D.
Pimlott, John. The Military Quiz Book. 128p. 1993. pap. 9.95 (1-85367-151-7, 5425) Stackpole.
Pimlott, John, ed. Rommel: In His Own Words. 192p. 1994. 29.95 (1-85367-185-1, 5439) Stackpole.
Pimlott, John & Badsey, Stephen, eds. The Gulf War Assessed. (Illus.). 288p. 1993. 27.50 (1-85409-146-8) Sterling.
***Pimlott, John & Bullock, Alan, contribs.** The Historical Atlas of World War II. LC 94-39820. (Reference Bks.). 1995. 45.00 (0-8050-3929-5) H Holt & Co.
Pimlott, John, jt. ed. see Beckett, Ian F.
Pimm, David. Speaking Mathematically: Communications in Mathematics Classrooms. 240p. 1989. 44.95 (0-7102-1133-3, 11333, RKP); pap. 14.95 (0-415-03708-5, A3533, RKP) Routledge.
— Symbols & Meanings in School Mathematics. LC 94-39323. 240p. 1995. 55.00x (0-415-11384-9, C0463); pap. 17.95 (0-415-11385-7, C0464) Routledge.
Pimm, June B. & Feist, Joseph R. Psychological Risks of Coronary Bypass Surgery. 226p. 1984. 59.50 (0-306-41586-0, Plenum Pr) Plenum.
Pimm, Malcolm V., jt. auth. see Perkins, Alan C.
Pimm, Stuart L. The Balance of Nature? Ecological Issues in the Conservation of Species & Communities. LC 91-3089. (Illus.). 464p. 1991. pap. text ed. 26.95 (0-226-66830-4) U Ch Pr.
Pimsler, Steven, jt. auth. see Yamada, Yoshimitsu.
Pimsleur, Beverly, jt. auth. see Pimsleur, Paul.
Pimsleur, Meira G., ed. Copyright Society of the U. S. A. Bulletin: Cumulative Index, Vols. 1-20, 1953-1973. LC 74-25274. x, 229p. 1975. text ed. 32.50 (0-8377-0421-9) Rothman.
Pimsleur, Paul & Pimsleur, Beverly. C'est la Vie. 4th ed. 225p. (C). 1987. pap. text ed. 18.00 (0-15-505893-2) HB Coll Pubs.
— C'est la Vie. 5th ed. 225p. (FRE.). (C). 1992. pap. text ed. 20.00 (0-03-055813-1) HB Coll Pubs.
Pimsleur, Paul, ed. see International Congress of Applied Linguistics Staff.
Pimsleur, Paul, et al. Encounters: An ESL Reader. 3rd ed. 192p. (C). 1986. pap. text ed. 18.75 (0-15-522600-2) HB Coll Pubs.
— Sol y Sombra. 3rd ed. (Illus.). 224p. (Orig.). (SPA.). (C). 1983. pap. text ed. 20.00 (0-15-582413-9) HB Coll Pubs.
Pin, Emile J. & Turndorf, Jamie. The Pleasure of Your Company: A Socio-Psychological Analysis of Modern Sociability. 304p. 1985. text ed. 55.00 (0-275-91755-X, C1755, Praeger Pubs) Greenwood.
Pin, J. E. Varieties of Formal Languages. Howie, J. A., tr. (Foundations of Computer Science Ser.). 180p. 1986. 49.50 (0-306-42294-8, Plenum Pr) Plenum.
Pin, J. E., ed. Formal Properties of Finite Automata & Applications. (Lecture Notes in Computer Science Ser.: Vol. 386). viii, 260p. 1989. pap. 37.00 (0-387-51631-X) Spr-Verlag.
Pina-Chan, Roman. A Guide to Mexican Archaeology. (Illus.). 128p. 1979. pap. 5.50 (0-912434-09-0) Ocelot Pr.
Pina da Silva, F. A., jt. ed. see Montalvao e Silva, J. M.
Pina, H. & Brebbia, C. A., eds. Boundary Element Technology VIII. LC 93-71016. (BETECH Ser.: Vol. 8). 383p. 1993. 135.00 (1-56252-173-X) Computational Mech MA.
Pina, Larry. Dead Mac Scrolls. rev. ed. 484p. 1992. 32.00 (1-56609-016-4) Peachpit Pr.
— Mac Classic & SE Repair & Upgrade Secrets. (Illus.). 296p. 1993. pap. 28.00 (1-56609-022-9) Peachpit Pr.
— Mac Printer Secrets. 1990. pap. 34.95 (0-672-48463-3, Bobbs) Macmillan.
— Macintosh II Repair & Upgrade Secrets. (Illus.). (Orig.). 1991. pap. 39.95 (0-13-929530-5) Brady Compu Bks.
— Macintosh Repair & Upgrade Secrets. (Illus.). 300p. (C). 1990. pap. 34.95 (0-672-48452-8) Sams.
Pina, Leslie. Fifties Glass. (Illus.). 224p. 1993. 49.95 (0-88740-548-7) Schiffer.
— Fostoria: Serving the American Table 1887-1986. LC 94-23513. (Illus.). 192p. 1995. 34.95 (0-88740-726-9) Schiffer.
— Popular '50s & '60s Glass: Color along the River. LC 95-10559. (Books for Collectors). (Illus.). 176p. 1995. 29.95 (0-88740-829-X) Schiffer.
— Pottery, Modern Wares 1920-1960. (Illus.). 240p. 1994. 49.95 (0-88740-692-0) Schiffer.
Pina, Leslie A. Louis Rorimer: A Man of Style. LC 90-34121. (Illus.). 158p. 1990. 25.00 (0-87338-418-0) Kent St U Pr.
***Pina, Ravi.** Cracker Jack Collectibles. (Illus.). 112p. (Orig.). 1995. pap. 19.95 (0-88740-847-8) Schiffer.
Pinalie, Pierre. Dictionnaire Elementaire Francais-Creole. 237p. (FRE.). 1992. 59.95 (0-8288-9493-0) Fr & Eur.
***Pinansky, Robert.** After Life, What? A Post-Death Quest. 105p. (Orig.). 1995. pap. 11.95 (1-885395-12-4) Book Tree.
Pinar, Robert, tr. see Spuhler, Friedrich.
Pinar, William. Heightened Consciousness, Cultural Revolution, & Curriculum Theory. LC 73-17615. 1974. 27.00 (0-8211-1511-1); text ed. write for info. (0-685-03222-1) McCutchan.
Pinar, William, ed. Curriculum Theorizing: The Reconceptualists. LC 74-12821. 472p. 1974. 33.25 (0-8211-1513-8); text ed. write for info. (0-685-03199-3) McCutchan.
Pinar, William & Reynolds, William, eds. Understanding Curriculum as Phenomenological & Deconstructed Text. (Critical Issues in Curriculum Ser.: No. 2). 272p. (C). 1991. text ed. 45.95 (0-8077-3114-5); pap. text ed. 21.95 (0-8077-3113-7) Tchrs Coll.
Pinar, William F. Autobiography, Politics, & Sexuality: Essays in Curriculum Theory, 1972-1992, Vol. 2. LC 94-132. (Counterpoints: Studies in the Postmodern Theory of Education: Vol. 2). 278p. (Orig.). (C). 1994. pap. text ed. 24.95 (0-8204-1849-8) P Lang Pubs.
Pinar, William F., jt. ed. see Castenell, Louis A., Jr.
Pinar, William F., jt. ed. see Kincheloe, Joe L.
***Pinar, William F., et al.** Understanding Curriculum: An Introduction to the Study of Historical & Contemporary Discourses. (Counterpoints Ser.: Vol. 17). 1168p. (C). 1995. pap. text ed. 49.95 (0-8204-2601-6) P Lang Pubs.
Pinard, Adrien, jt. auth. see Laurendeau, Monique.
Pinard, Maurice. The Rise of a Third Party: A Study in Crisis Politics. enl. ed. LC 75-329930. 331p. reprint ed. pap. 94.40 (0-7837-1146-8, 2041675) Bks Demand.
Pinatti, Gloria J., ed. see Mozeleski, Peter A.
Pinault, Alain, jt. auth. see Chiche, Gerard.
Pinault, David. The Shiites: Ritual & Popular Piety in a Muslim Community. 224p. 1993. text ed. 17.95 (0-312-10024-8) St Martin.
— Story-Telling Techniques in the Arabian Nights. LC 91-28023. (Journal of Arabic Literature Supplements Ser.: No. 15). 292p. 1992. 65.75 (90-04-09530-6) E J Brill.
Pinault, Jody R. Hippocratic Lives & Legends. LC 91-43634. (Studies in Ancient Medicine: No. 4). x, 160p. 1992. 57.25 (90-04-09574-8) E J Brill.
Pinault, Madeleine. Painter As Naturalist. 288p. 1991. 39.98 (2-08-013516-3, Pub. by Flammarion) Abbeville Pr.
Pinay, Maurice. The Plot Against the Catholic Church: Communism, Free Masonry & the Jewish Fifth Column in the Clergy. 1979. lib. bdg. 69.95 (0-8490-2984-8) Gordon Pr.
— The Plot Against the Church. 1978. 20.00 (0-911038-39-6) Noontide.
Pinborg, Jan, ed. see Augustine.
Pince, David L., jt. auth. see Iacono, Domenic J.
Pincess, Gerald M. & Lockyer, Roger, eds. Shakespeare's World: Background Readings in the English Renaissance. 288p. 1987. reprint ed. pap. text ed. 15.95 (0-8264-0451-0, F Ungar Bks) Continuum.
Pinch. Votive Offerings to Hathor. (Griffith Institute Ser.). 1992. write for info. (0-900416-54-8, Pub. by Aris & Phillips UK) David Brown.
Pinch, Alan & Armstrong, Michael, eds. Tolstoy on Education: Tolstoy's Educational Writings, 1861-62. LC 81-65867. 336p. 1982. 44.50 (0-8386-3121-5) Fairleigh Dickinson.
Pinch, Dorothy H. Happy Horsemanship. 1985. pap. 10.00 (0-671-76321-0) S&S Trade.
Pinch, Enid R. Optimal Control & the Calculus of Variations. LC 92-27772. (Illus.). 248p. 1993. 49.95 (0-19-853217-2) OUP.
***Pinch, Geraldine.** Magic in Ancient Egypt. (Illus.). 192p. (Orig.). 1995. pap. 18.95 (0-292-76559-2) U of Tex Pr.
Pinch, R. G., jt. auth. see Goldie, C. M.
Pinch, Trevor. Confronting Nature. 1986. lib. bdg. 85.50 (90-277-2224-2) Kluwer Ac.

An Asterisk (*) at the beginning of an entry indicates that the title is appearing in BIP for the first time.

Pinch, Trevor, jt. auth. see Collins, Harry M.

Pinchback, jt. ed. see Casper.

Pinchbeck, Ivy. Women Workers & the Industrial Revolution, 1750-1850. 2nd rev. ed. 342p. 1969. 45.00 (*0-7146-1351-7*, Pub. by F Cass Pubs UK) Intl Spec Bk.

Pinchemel, Philippe. France: A Geographical, Social & Economic Survey. Elkins, Dorothy & Elkins, T. H., trs. (Illus.). 668p. 1987. 89.95 (*0-521-24987-2*) Cambridge U Pr.

Pinchemel, Philippe, jt. auth. see Oughton, Marguerita.

***Pincher, Chapman.** My Life As a Real Dog: By Dido. Baker, Deborah, ed. (Illus.). 208p. 1995. 20.00 (*1-56836-116-5*) Kodansha.

Pinchera, A. & Vanhaelst, L., eds. Autoimmunity & Endocrine Diseases. (Journal: Hormone Research: Vol. 16, No. 5). (Illus.). 84p. 1982. pap. 33.00 (*3-8055-3658-5*) S Karger.

Pinchera, A., et al. Thyroid Autoimmunity. LC 87-29258. (Illus.). 654p. 1987. 120.00 (*0-306-42762-1*, Plenum Pr) Plenum.

Pincherle, Marc. Corelli: His Life & His Music. LC 79-9155. (Music Reprint Ser.). 1979. reprint ed. lib. bdg. 32.50 (*0-306-79576-0*) Da Capo.

Pinches, Charles & McDaniel, Jay B. Good News for Animals? Contemporary Christian Approaches to Animal Well-Being. LC 92-41682. (Ecology & Justice Ser.). 250p. 1993. 39.95 (*0-88344-866-1*); pap. 18.95 (*0-88344-859-9*) Orbis Bks.

Pinches, George, jt. auth. see Gordon, Lawrence.

Pinches, George E. Essentials of Financial Management. 3rd ed. 736p. (C). 1989. text ed. 41.50 (*0-06-045198-X*) HarpCollege.

— Essentials of Financial Management. 4th ed. (C). 1991. text ed. 67.50 (*0-06-500072-2*); 25.00 (*0-06-500073-0*) HarpCollege.

— Financial Management. (C). 1994. text ed. 48.00 (*0-06-501369-7*); Study guide. student ed write for info. (*0-06-501370-0*) HarpCollege.

Pinches, George E., jt. auth. see Davis.

Pinches, Michael & Lakha, Salim, eds. Wage Labor & Social Change: The Proletariat in Asia & the Pacific. 283p. (Orig.). 1992. pap. 14.25 (*971-10-0453-4*, Pub. by New Day Pub PH) Cellar.

Pinches, Theophilus G., et al. Late Babylonian Astronomical & Related Texts Copied by J. Schaumberger. Sachs, A. J. & Schaumberger, J., eds. LC 56-1209. (Brown University Studies: No. 18). 326p. reprint ed. pap. 93.00 (*0-317-09132-8*, 2004668) Bks Demand.

Pinchin, Calvin. Issues in Philosophy. (C). 1989. text ed. 50.00 (*0-389-20870-1*, N 8428) B&N Imports.

Pinchin, Jane L. Alexandria Still: Forster, Durrell & Cavafy. LC 76-3014. 1976. 39.50 (*0-691-06283-8*) Princeton U Pr.

Pinchon, Edgcumb. Viva Villa: A Recovery of the Real Pancho Villa, Peon, Bandit, Soldier, Patriot. LC 70-111729. (American Imperialism: Viewpoints of United States Foreign Policy, 1898-1941 Ser.). 1980. reprint ed. 26.95 (*0-405-02045-7*) Ayer.

Pinchon, Edgcumb, jt. auth. see De Lara, L. Gutierrez.

Pinchon, Edgcumb, jt. auth. see Gutierrez De Lara, L.

Pinchon, Jean-Francois, ed. Rob Mallet-Stevens: Architecture, Furniture, Interior Design. (Illus.). 160p. 1989. 35.00 (*0-262-16116-8*) MIT Pr.

Pinchot, Amos R. History of the Progressive Party, 1912-1916. Hooker, Helene M., ed. LC 77-26637. 305p. 1978. reprint ed. text ed. 38.50 (*0-313-20074-2*, PIHP, Greenwood Pr) Greenwood.

Pinchot, Ann. The Luck of the Linscotts. 544p. 1984. pap. 3.95 (*0-8217-1395-7*) Zebra.

Pinchot, Ann, jt. auth. see Gish, Lillian.

Pinchot, Elizabeth, jt. auth. see Pinchot, Gifford.

Pinchot, Gifford. Adirondack Spruce, A Study of the Forest in Ne-Ha-Sa-Ne Park. LC 77-125756. (American Environmental Studies). 1974. reprint ed. 17.95 (*0-405-02682-X*) Ayer.

— Biltmore Forest. LC 70-125757. (American Environmental Studies). 1974. reprint ed. 16.95 (*0-405-02683-8*) Ayer.

— Breaking New Ground. LC 87-82038. (Conservation Classics Ser.). (Illus.). 522p. 1987. reprint ed. pap. 19.95 (*0-933280-42-4*) Island Pr.

— Breaking New Ground. LC 87-82038. (Conservation Classics Ser.). (Illus.). 522p. 1988. reprint ed. 35.00 (*0-933280-50-5*) Island Pr.

— Fishing Talk. 288p. 1993. reprint ed. pap. 12.95 (*0-8117-2512-X*) Stackpole.

Pinchot, Gifford & Pinchot, Elizabeth. The End of Bureaucracy & the Rise of the Intelligent Organization. LC 93-40302. 392p. 1994. 24.95 (*1-881052-34-6*) Berrett-Koehler.

Pinchot, Gifford, III. Intrapreneuring: Why You Don't Have to Leave the Corporation to Become an Entrepreneur. LC 85-4880. (Illus.). 368p. 1986. reprint ed. pap. 15.00 (*0-06-091335-5*, PL1335, PL) HarpC.

Pinchot, Jane. The Mexicans in America. rev. ed. LC 72-3587. (In America Bks.). (Illus.). 104p. (J). (gr. 5 up). 1989. pap. 5.95 (*0-8225-1016-2*, Lerner Publctns) Lerner Group.

— The Mexicans in America. rev. ed. LC 72-3587. (In America Bks.). (Illus.). 104p. (YA). (gr. 5 up). 1989. lib. bdg. 17.50 (*0-8225-0222-4*, Lerner Publctns) Lerner Group.

Pinchover, Yehuda, jt. auth. see Lin, Vladimir.

Pinchuck, Tony, jt. auth. see Clark, Richard.

Pinchuk, Ben-Cion. The Octobrist in the Third Duma. LC 74-2176. (Publications on Russia & Eastern Europe of the School of International Studies: No. 4). 244p. 1974. 25.00 (*0-295-95324-1*) U of Wash Pr.

Pinciroli, Francesco, jt. ed. see Meester, Greert T.

Pinciss, G. M., et al. Explorations in the Arts. 416p. (C). 1985. pap. text ed. 36.00 (*0-03-062939-X*) HB Coll Pubs.

Pinciss, Gerald M. & Lockyer, Roger, eds. Shakespeare's World: Background Readings in the English Renaissance. 288p. 1989. 24.50 (*0-8264-0421-9*) Continuum.

***Pinckaers, Servais.** The Sources of Christian Ethics. 3rd ed. Noble, Mary T., tr. LC 94-28663. Orig. Title: Sources de la Morale Chretienne. 1995. pap. 24.95 (*0-8132-0818-1*) Cath U Pr.

Pincke, Violet, jt. auth. see Steiner, Rudolf.

Pinckernelle, Erdewin, tr. German General Rules of Marine Insurance (ADS) 5th ed. 77p. (C). 1990. pap. 20.00 (*3-11-012666-4*) De Gruyter.

Pinckert, Nell. Taking the Boredom Out of Youth Sunday School. 1992. pap. 10.95 (*1-55673-484-0*, 7934) CSS OH.

Pinckert, Robert C. Pinckert's Practical Grammar. 232p. (Orig.). 1991. pap. 11.95 (*0-89879-441-2*) Writers Digest.

***Pinckey-Harris, Claudette.** Monroe Pinckey, My Father. 135p. (Orig.). (YA). 1995. pap. 12.95 (*0-910671-14-1*) Path Pr Chicago.

Pinckney, Callan. Callanetics: Ten Years Younger in Ten Hours. 208p. 1987. pap. 12.50 (*0-380-70261-4*) Avon.

— Callanetics Countdown: Thirty Days to a Beautiful Body. 192p. 1991. pap. 12.00 (*0-380-71453-1*) Avon.

— Callanetics Countdown: Thirty Days to a Beautiful Body. 1990. 19.95 (*0-394-58613-1*) Random.

— Callanetics for Your Back. 192p. 1990. pap. 11.95 (*0-380-70506-0*) Avon.

Pinckney, Cathey & Pinckney, Edward R. Do-It-Yourself Medical Testing: More Than 240 Tests You Can Do at Home. 3rd ed. 1989. pap. 14.95 (*0-8160-2085-X*) Facts on File.

— The Patient's Guide to Medical Tests. 3rd rev. ed. 432p. 27.95 (*0-8160-1292-X*) Facts on File.

Pinckney, Darryl. High Cotton. 320p. 1992. 21.00 (*0-374-16998-5*) FS&G.

— High Cotton. 320p. 1993. pap. 11.00 (*0-14-017503-2*, Penguin Bks) Viking Penguin.

Pinckney, Edward R., jt. auth. see Pinckney, Cathey.

***Pinckney, Francis M.** Product Comparison Manual Supp. 2. 117p. 1995. text ed. 110.00 (*0-614-01646-0*) BNA.

— Products Comparison Manual, No. 2. suppl. ed. 1994. text ed. 45.00 (*0-685-72838-2*) BNA.

— Products Comparison Manual for Trademark Users with First Supplement, Suppl. 1. 117p. 1991. text ed. 40.00 (*0-87179-688-0*, 0688) BNA.

— Products Comparison Manual for Trademark Users with First Supplement, Suppl. 2. 1995. text ed. 45.00 (*0-87179-813-1*) BNA.

— Products Comparison Manual for Trademark Users with First Supplement: With Most Current Supplement. LC 86-9732. 586p. 1988. text ed. 110.00 (*0-87179-501-9*, 9501) BNA.

Pinckney, Gerrie, jt. auth. see Swenson, Marge.

Pinckney, Jerry, illus. The Tales of Uncle Remus: The Adventures of Brer Rabbit, Vol. I. LC 85-20449. (J). (ps up). 1987. 18.99 (*0-8037-0271-X*); lib. bdg. 16.89 (*0-8037-0272-8*) Dial Bks Young.

Pinckney Stetkevych, Suzanne, ed. Reorientations - Arabic & Persian Poetry. LC 93-6900. 1993. 35.00 (*0-253-35493-5*) Ind U Pr.

***Pincoe, Ruth.** Glenn Gould: Descriptive Catalogue of the Glenn Gould Papers. (Illus.). 318p. (Orig.). 1992. pap. 51.95x (*0-660-57327-X*, Pub. by Canada Commun Grp CN) Accents Pubns.

Pincoffs, Edmund L. Philosophy of Law: A Brief Introduction. 150p. (C). 1991. pap. 19.95 (*0-534-14802-6*) Intl Thomson.

— Quandaries & Virtues: Against Reductivism in Ethics. LC 86-13352. x, 190p. 1986. 25.00 (*0-7006-0308-5*); pap. 9.95 (*0-7006-0363-8*) U Pr of KS.

Pincoffs, Edmund L., ed. see Conference on the Concept of Academic Freedom Staff.

***Pincon, Jacinto O.** Moral Divorce & Other Stories. Fedorchek, Robert M., tr. LC 94-28807. 1995. write for info. (*0-8387-5299-3*) Bucknell U Pr.

Pincus, jt. ed. see Wolfe.

Pincus, Alexis G. Combustion Melting in the Glass Industry. LC 78-55358. (Processing in the Glass Industry Ser.). 300p. 1980. 29.95 (*0-911993-11-8*) Ashlee Pub Co.

— Melting Furnace Design in the Glass Industry. LC 78-55352. (Processing in the Glass Industry Ser.). 269p. 1980. 24.95 (*0-911993-08-8*) Ashlee Pub Co.

— Melting Furnace Operation in the Glass Industry. LC 77-55374. (Processing in the Glass Industry Ser.). 250p. 1980. 24.95 (*0-911993-10-X*) Ashlee Pub Co.

— The Melting Process in the Glass Industry. LC 78-55368. (Processing in the Glass Industry Ser.). 257p. 1980. 24.95 (*0-911993-19-3*) Ashlee Pub Co.

— Refractories in the Glass Industry. LC 78-55364. (Processing in the Glass Industry Ser.). 280p. 1980. 24.95 (*0-911993-09-6*) Ashlee Pub Co.

Pincus, Alexis G., ed. Forming in the Glass Industry, Pt. II: Accessories to Glass Forming, Set. LC 83-70120. (Processing in the Glass Industry Ser.). (Illus.). 254p. 1983. text ed. 69.95 (*0-911993-05-3*) Ashlee Pub Co.

— Forming in the Glass Industry, Pts. I: Forming Machines & Methods, Set. (Processing in the Glass Industry Ser.). (Illus.). 248p. 1983. text ed. 69.95 (*0-911993-03-7*) Ashlee Pub Co.

Pincus, Alexis G. & Chang, S. H. Joining in the Glass Industry. LC 83-73581. (Processing in the Glass Industry Ser.). (Illus.). 282p. 1985. 34.95 (*0-911993-16-9*) Ashlee Pub Co.

— Secondary Manufacturing in the Glass Industry. LC 78-55369. (Processing in the Glass Industry Ser.). 314p. 1978. 34.95 (*0-911993-14-2*) Ashlee Pub Co.

Pincus, Alexis G. & Chang, Shung-Huei, eds. Decorating in the Glass Industry. 2nd ed. LC 84-73283. (Processing in the Glass Industry Ser.). (Illus.). 1985. 39.95 (*0-911993-23-1*) Ashlee Pub Co.

Pincus, Alexis G. & Davies, David H. Batching in the Glass Industry. LC 81-67427. (Processing in the Glass Industry Ser.). 217p. 1981. 24.95 (*0-911993-07-X*) Ashlee Pub Co.

Pincus, Alexis G. & Davies, David H., eds. Raw Materials in the Glass Industry: Minor Ingredients, 2 pts., Set. LC 83-70137. (Processing in the Glass Industry Ser.). (Illus.). 454p. 1983. text ed. 59.90 (*0-911993-02-9*) Ashlee Pub Co.

— Raw Materials in the Glass Industry, Pt. I: Major Ingredients. LC 83-70137. (Processing in the Glass Industry Ser.). (Illus.). 254p. 1983. text ed. 29.95 (*0-911993-00-2*) Ashlee Pub Co.

Pincus, Alexis G. & Holmes, Thomas R., eds. Annealing & Strengthening in the Glass Industry. 2nd ed. LC 87-70822. (Processing in the Glass Industry Ser.). (Illus.). 1988. text ed. 39.95 (*0-911993-24-X*) Ashlee Pub Co.

Pincus, Andrew L. Scenes from Tanglewood. (Illus.). 287p. 1989. pap. text ed. 14.95 (*1-55553-054-0*) NE U Pr.

Pincus, Arthur & Jones, Taylor. How to Talk Football. rev. ed. LC 86-16792. (Illus.). 144p. (Orig.). 1986. pap. 8.95 (*0-934878-83-8*, Dembner NY) Barricade Bks.

Pincus, Debbie. Feeling Good about Others: Activities to Encourage Positive Interaction. (Illus.). 96p. (J). (gr. 3-8). 1994. 9.95 (*0-86653-794-5*, GA1488) Good Apple.

— Feeling Good about Yourself. (Illus.). 96p. (J). (gr. 3-8). 1990. 10.95 (*0-86653-516-0*, GA 1139) Good Apple.

— Interactions. 96p. (J). (gr. 4-9). 1988. student ed 10.95 (*0-86653-448-2*, GA1057) Good Apple.

— Manners Matter. (Illus.). 112p. (J). (gr. 3-7). 1992. student ed 10.95 (*0-86653-688-4*, 1422) Good Apple.

— Sharing. (Illus.). 80p. (J). (gr. 4-8). 1983. student ed 9.95 (*0-86653-117-3*, GA 468) Good Apple.

Pincus, Debbie & Ward, Richard J. Citizenship. 112p. (J). (gr. 4-9). 1991. 10.95 (*0-86653-608-6*, GA 1327) Good Apple.

Pincus, Edward. Guide to Film Making. (Orig.). 1969. pap. 4.95 (*0-451-15172-0*, Sig) NAL-Dutton.

Pincus, Edward & Ascher, Steven. The Filmmaker's Handbook. LC 83-25121. (Illus.). 432p. 1984. pap. 15.95 (*0-452-25526-0*, Plume) NAL-Dutton.

***Pincus, Elizabeth.** The Hangdog Hustle. LC 94-37956. (Nell Fury Mystery Ser.). 224p. (Orig.). 1995. pap. 9.95 (*1-883523-05-2*) Spinsters Ink.

— The Solitary Twist. LC 93-84274. 225p. (Orig.). 1993. pap. 9.95 (*0-933216-93-9*) Spinsters Ink.

— The Two-Bit Tango. LC 92-17511. (Illus.). 193p. (Orig.). 1992. pap. 9.95 (*0-933216-88-2*) Spinsters Ink.

Pincus, Fred L. Race & Ethnic Conflict: Contending Views on Prejudice & Ethnoviolence. 332p. (C). 1994. text ed. 65.00 (*0-8133-1661-8*); pap. text ed. 24.95 (*0-8133-1662-6*) Westview.

Pincus, Fred L. & Archer, Elayne. Bridges to Opportunity. 56p. 1989. pap. 2.00 (*0-685-59931-0*) Acad Educ Dev.

Pincus, Gregory, ed. Recent Progress in Hormone Research, Vol. 40. (Serial Publication Ser.). 1984. text ed. 153.00 (*0-12-571140-9*) Acad Pr.

Pincus, Harold A. & Pardes, Herbert, eds. Clinical Research Careers in Psychiatry. LC 86-17249. (Issues in Psychiatry Ser.). 144p. 1986. pap. text ed. 21.00 (*0-88048-094-7*, 48-094-7) Am Psychiatric.

— The Integration of Neuroscience & Psychiatry. LC 85-11270. (Clinical Insights Ser.). 106p. reprint ed. pap. 30.30 (*0-8357-7827-4*, 2036200) Bks Demand.

Pincus, Harold A., ed. see American Psychiatric Association Office of Research Staff.

Pincus, Howard J. & Hoskins, Earl R., eds. Measurement of Rock Properties at Elevated Pressures & Temperatures-STP 869. LC 84-24558. (Illus.). 162p. 1985. text ed. 30.00 (*0-8031-0237-2*, 04-869000-38) ASTM.

Pincus, J. David. Top Dog: A Different Kind of Book about Becoming an Excellent Leader. 1994. text ed. 24.95 (*0-07-050129-7*) McGraw.

Pincus, Jake. J. S. Bach in Tablature. (Editiones Classicae Ser.). 1993. 4.95 (*1-56222-189-2*, 94581); audio 10.98 (*1-56222-331-3*, 94581) Mel Bay.

Pincus, Joel D. & Zhou, Shaojie. Principal Currents for a Pair of Unitary Operators. LC 94-4146. (Memoirs of the American Mathematical Society Ser.: No. 522). 1994. pap. 32.00 (*0-8218-2609-3*) Am Math.

Pincus, John A. Economic Aid & International Cost Sharing. LC 65-19539. 240p. reprint ed. pap. 68.40 (*0-317-09663-X*, 2020733) Bks Demand.

Pincus, Jonathan H. & Tucker, Gary J. Behavioral Neurology. 3rd ed. (Illus.). 1985. pap. text ed. 19.95 (*0-19-503555-0*) OUP.

Pincus, Laura B., jt. auth. see Bennett-Alexander, Dawn D.

Pincus, Lee. The Songwriters' Success Manual. LC 77-352498. (Illus.). 1976. pap. 9.95 (*0-918318-01-7*) Music Pr.

Pincus, Leo I. Practical Boiler Water Treatment: Including Air-Conditioning Systems. LC 80-29604. 284p. 1981. reprint ed. lib. bdg. 30.50 (*0-89874-255-2*) Krieger.

***Pincus, Leslie.** Authenticating Culture in Interwar Japan: Kuki Shuzo & the Rise of National Aesthetics. LC 95-12978. (Twentieth-Century Japan Ser.: Vol. 5). 1995. write for info. (*0-520-20134-5*) U CA Pr.

Pincus, Marilyn. Projecting a Positive Image. (Business Success Ser.). 112p. 1993. pap. 4.95 (*0-8120-1455-3*) Barron.

Pincus, Robert, et al. Jud Fine: February 1985. Starrels, Josine I. & Lewis, Helen N., eds. LC 85-50180. (Illus.). 52p. (Orig.). 1985. pap. 7.50 (*0-936429-04-6*) LA Municipal Art.

Pincus, Robert L. On a Scale That Competes with the World: The Art of Edward & Nancy Reddin Kienholz. (Illus.). 120p. 1990. 48.00 (*0-520-06730-4*) U CA Pr.

— On a Scale That Competes with the World: The Art of Edward & Nancy Reddin Kienholz. (Illus.). 135p. (C). 1994. pap. 30.00 (*0-520-08446-2*) U CA Pr.

Pincus, Stanley. Respiratory Therapist Manual. LC 74-79838. (Allied Health Ser.). 1975. pap. 7.05 (*0-672-61389-1*, Bobbs) Macmillan.

Pincus, William H. The Problems of Gauguin's Therapist: Language, Madness & Therapy. 134p. 1994. 54.95 (*1-85628-374-7*, Pub. by Avebury Pub UK) Ashgate Pub Co.

Pincus-Witten, Robert. Entries (Maximalism) (Illus.). 250p. 1983. pap. 14.95 (*0-915570-20-3*) Oolp Pr.

— Eye to Eye: Twenty Years of Art Criticism. Kuspit, Donald, ed. LC 83-24121. (Contemporary American Art Critics Ser.: No. 4). 248p. reprint ed. pap. 70.70 (*0-8357-1534-5*, 2070750) Bks Demand.

— Jedd Garet. (Illus.). 162p. 1984. 45.00 (*0-942642-12-0*) Twelvetrees Pr.

— Postminimalism: American Art of the Decade. LC 77-77010. (Illus.). 1981. pap. text ed. 25.00 (*0-915570-07-6*) Oolp Pr.

— Postminimalism into Maximalism: American Art, 1966-1986. LC 86-24925. (Studies in the Fine Arts: Criticism: No. 22). 445p. reprint ed. pap. 126.90 (*0-8357-1763-1*, 2070648) Bks Demand.

Pincus-Witten, Robert, ed. see Fuchs, Rudi.

Pinczes, Elinor J. One Hundred Hungry Ants. (Illus.). 32p. (J). (gr. k-3). 1993. 14.95 (*0-395-63116-5*) HM.

— A Remainder of One. LC 94-5446. (Illus.). (J). 1995. 14.95 (*0-395-69455-8*) HM.

Pinczuk, Aron, jt. ed. see Lockwood, David J.

Pindar. Carmina Cum Fragmentis. Bowra, C. Maurice, ed. (Oxford Classical Texts Ser.). 1935. 24.95 (*0-19-814539-X*) OUP.

— Isthmian Odes of Pindar. 1988. reprint ed. lib. bdg. 59.00 (*0-317-90885-5*) Rprt Serv.

— Odes & Fragments. (Loeb Classical Library: No. 56). 682p. 1915. 18.95 (*0-674-99062-5*) HUP.

— The Odes of Pindar. Bowra, C. Maurice, tr. 1982. pap. 9.95 (*0-14-044209-X*, Penguin Classics) Viking Penguin.

— The Odes of Pindar. 2nd ed. Lattimore, Richmond, tr. LC 75-22336. 184p. 1976. reprint ed. lib. bdg. 12.50 (*0-226-66844-4*) U Ch Pr.

— The Olympian & Pythian Odes. Connor, W. R., ed. LC 78-18577. (Greek Text & Commentaries Ser.). (Illus.). 1979. reprint ed. lib. bdg. 41.95 (*0-405-11420-6*) Ayer.

— Pindar's Odes. Swanson, Roy A., tr. 416p. reprint ed. pap. 12.95 (*0-8290-0332-0*) Irvington.

— Victory Odes: Olympians 2, 7 & 11; Nemean 4; Isthmians 3, 4 & 7. Willcock, M. M., ed. (Cambridge Greek & Latin Classics Ser.). 172p. (C). 1995. 59.95 (*0-521-43055-0*) Cambridge U Pr.

— Victory Odes: Olympians 2, 7 & 11; Nemean 4; Isthmians 3, 4 & 7. Willcock, M. M., ed. (Cambridge Greek & Latin Classics Ser.). 172p. (C). 1995. pap. 19.95 (*0-521-43636-2*) Cambridge U Pr.

Pindarus. Isthmian Odes of Pindar. Bury, John B., ed. 1892. reprint ed. 49.00 (*0-403-00333-4*) Scholarly.

— Nemean Odes of Pindar. 1890. reprint ed. 19.00 (*0-403-00332-6*) Scholarly.

— Pindar, the Olympian & Pythian Odes. Gildersleeve, Basil L., ed. 1885. 59.00 (*0-403-00331-8*) Scholarly.

Pindell, Terry. Good Place to Live. 416p. 1995. 27.50 (*0-8050-2352-6*) H Holt & Co.

— Last Train to Toronto: A Canadian Rail Odyssey. 400p. 1993. pap. 15.95 (*0-8050-2358-5*, Owl) H Holt & Co.

— Making Tracks: An American Rail Odyssey. (Illus.). 416p. 1991. pap. 14.95 (*0-8050-1740-2*, Owl) H Holt & Co.

Pindeo, H. M., et al, eds. Cancer Chemotherapy & Biological Response Modifiers, Vol. 12. 700p. 1991. 214.50 (*0-444-81443-4*) Elsevier.

Pinder, A. C. & Godfrey, G., eds. Food Process Monitoring Systems. LC 92-43492. 1993. write for info. (*0-7514-0099-8*, Pub. by Blackie Acad & Prof UK) Routledge Chapman & Hall.

Pinder, Alan. Quick & Easy Wooden Toys. (Illus.). 128p. 1986. 19.95 (*0-85532-561-5*, Pub. by Search Pr UK) A Schwartz & Co.

Pinder, Alan, jt. auth. see Hinton, Jeremy.

Pinder, Craig C. & Moore, Larry F., eds. Middle Range Theory & the Study of Organizatons. 1980. lib. bdg. 79.00 (*0-89838-021-9*) Kluwer Ac.

Pinder, D. A., jt. ed. see Hoyle, B.

Pinder, David A., ed. Western Europe: Challenge & Change. 290p. 1991. reprint ed. pap. text ed. 30.00 (*0-89862-489-4*) Guilford Pr.

Pinder, David A., jt. auth. see Hoyle, Brian S.

Pinder, G. F., ed. Flow Through Porous Media. (Progress in Engineering Ser.). 125p. 1983. pap. 46.00 (*0-931215-37-4*) Computational Mech MA.

Pinder, George F. & Gray, William G. Finite Element Simulation in Surface & Subsurface Hydrology. 1977. text ed. 99.00 (*0-12-556950-5*) Acad Pr.

Pinder, George F., jt. auth. see Huyakorn, Peter.

Pinder, George F., jt. auth. see Lapidus, Leon.

Pinder, John. European Community: The Building of a Union. 256p. 1991. pap. 15.95 (*0-19-289225-8*) OUP.

— European Community: The Building of a Union. 2nd ed. 272p. 1995. pap. 15.95 (*0-19-289265-7*) OUP.

— The European Community & Eastern Europe. 144p. 1991. pap. 14.95 (*0-87609-112-5*) Coun Foreign.

Pinder, John, jt. auth. see Carter, Charles.

Pinder, John, ed. see Duff, Andrew, et al.

Pinder, L. C. A Key to the Adult Males of the British Chironomidae (Diptera) 1978. 39.00 (*0-900386-32-0*) St Mut.

Pinder, Leslie H. Under the House. LC 87-43217. 184p. 1988. 15.95 (*0-394-56932-6*) Random.

Pinder, Mark & McAdam, Stuart. Be Your Own Management Consultant: The Manager's Guide to Internal Consulting. (Financial Times Management Ser.). 232p. 1994. 75.00x (*0-273-60466-X*, Pub. by Pitman Pubng UK) St Mut.

Pinder, Polly. Home-Made & at a Fraction of the Cost. (Illus.). 128p. 1983. 14.95 (*0-318-23661-3*) Pathway Bk Serv.

— Polly Pinder's Chocolate Cookbook. (Illus.). 144p. (YA). (gr. 7 up). 1988. 24.95 (*0-85532-603-4*, Pub. by Search Pr UK) A Schwartz & Co.

— Polly Pinder's Papercrafts Book. (Illus.). 128p. 1994. pap. write for info. (*0-85532-661-1*, Pub. by Search Pr UK) A Schwartz & Co.

— Polly Pinder's Party Cakes. (Illus.). 128p. 1993. pap. write for info. (*0-85532-769-3*, Pub. by Search Pr UK) A Schwartz & Co.

— Scented Herb Papers: How to Use Natural Scents & Colours in Hand-Made Recycled & Plant Papers. (Illus.). 64p. 1995. pap. 14.95 (*0-85532-789-8*, Pub. by Search Pr UK) A Schwartz & Co.

Pindera, J. T. & Pindera, M. J. Isodyne Stress Analysis. (C). 1989. lib. bdg. 147.50 (*0-7923-0269-9*) Kluwer Ac.

Pindera, M. J., jt. auth. see Pindera, J. T.

Pinderhughes, Dianne M. Race & Ethnicity in Chicago Politics: A Reexamination of Pluralist Theory. LC 86-19297. 339p. reprint ed. pap. 96.70 (*0-8357-3297-5*, 2039520) Bks Demand.

Pinderhughes, Elaine. Understanding Race, Ethnicity, & Power: The Key to Efficacy in Clinical Practice. 256p. 1989. text ed. 35.00 (*0-02-925341-1*) Free Pr.

Pinderhughes, John. Family of the Spirit Cookbook. (Illus.). 320p. (Orig.). 1994. pap. 14.95 (*1-56743-064-3*) Amistad Pr.

Pinderhughes, Raquel, jt. ed. see Moore, Joan.

Pinders, Jerzy T., ed. Modeling Problems in Crack Tip Mechanics. 1984. lib. bdg. 114.50 (*90-247-3067-8*) Kluwer Ac.

Pindur, Wolfgang & Cornetius, Loretta. A Manager's Guide to Informal Complaint Handling. (Public Employee Relations Library: No. 73). 128p. 1990. 14.00 (*0-685-41306-3*) Intl Personnel Mgmt.

Pindyck, Robert S. Econometric Models and Economic Forecasts. 3rd ed. 1991. text ed. write for info. (*0-07-050098-3*) McGraw.

— Optimal Planning for Economic Stabilization. (Contributions to Economic Analysis Ser.: Vol. 81). 168p. 1983. 59.00 (*0-444-10517-4*, North Holland) Elsevier.

— The Structure of World Energy Demand. (Illus.). 1979. 32.50 (*0-262-16074-9*) MIT Pr.

Pindyck, Robert S. & Rubinfeld, Daniel L. Microeconomics. 2nd ed. (Illus.). 752p. (C). 1992. text ed. write for info. (*0-02-395890-1*) Macmillan.

— Microeconomics. 3rd ed. LC 94-11402. 704p. (C). 1994. write for info. (*0-02-395900-2*) Macmillan.

Pindyck, Robert S., jt. auth. see Dixit, Avinash K.

Pindyck, Robert S., et al. Microeconomics: Study Guide. 2nd ed. (Illus.). 256p. (C). 1992. student ed, pap. write for info. (*0-02-349570-7*) Macmillan.

Pindyke, Robert S., ed. Production & Pricing of Energy Resources. (Advances in the Economics of Energy & Resources Ser.: Vol. 2). 250p. 1979. 73.25 (*0-89232-079-6*) Jai Pr.

— The Structure of Energy Markets. (Advances in the Economics of Energy & Resources Ser.: Vol. 1). 310p. 1979. 73.25 (*0-89232-078-8*) Jai Pr.

Pindzola, M. S., jt. ed. see Boyle, James J.

Pine, Ana, jt. auth. see Carbone, Joyce.

***Pine, Arthur.** One Door Closes, Another Door Opens: Turning Your Setbacks into Comebacks. 1995. pap. 8.95 (*0-440-50421-X*) Dell.

— Unexpected Roads: A Personal Success Journal. 160p. (Orig.). 1995. pap. 7.95 (*1-57071-070-8*) Sourcebks.

Pine, Arthur & Houston, Julie. One Door Closes, Another Door Opens. LC 93-20265. 1993. 16.95 (*0-385-31125-7*) Delacorte.

Pine, B. Joseph, II. Mass Customization: The New Frontier in Business Competition. 1992. text ed. 29.95 (*0-07-103385-8*) McGraw.

Pine, Barbara A., et al. Together Again: Family Reunification in Foster Care. 1993. 18.95 (*0-87868-525-1*) Child Welfare.

Pine, Charles. C: A Programming Workshop. LC 85-63275. 302p. (Orig.). (C). 1986. teacher ed write for info. (*0-938188-45-3*); pap. text ed. 29.95 (*0-938188-35-6*) Mitchell Pub.

Pine-Coffin, R. S., tr. see St. Augustine.

Pine, David J. Three Hundred Sixty Five Good Health Hints. Kramer, Jill, ed. LC 94-16934. 192p. (Orig.). 1994. pap. 5.95 (*1-56170-099-1*, 162) Hay House.

Pine, Eli S. How to Enjoy Calculus: With Computer Applications. rev. ed. LC 83-60717. (Illus.). 160p. (C). 1984. reprint ed. pap. 9.95 (*0-917208-02-1*) Steinlitz-Hammacher.

Pine, Fred. Developmental Theory & Clinical Process. LC 84-20841. 272p. 1987. pap. 15.00 (*0-300-04002-4*, Y-661) Yale U Pr.

— Drive, Ego, Object, & Self: A Synthesis for Clinical Work. LC 89-43168. 288p. 1990. text ed. 35.00 (*0-465-01722-3*) Basic.

Pine, Gerald J., jt. auth. see Boy, Angelo V.

***Pine, Jerry, et al.** Zap! No. 2: Hands on E & M. (Physics Ser.). 128p. Date not set. spiral bd., pap. 26.25 (*0-86720-482-6*) Jones & Bartlett.

Pine, Joan, jt. ed. see Geehr, Edward C.

Pine, John C. Block Island. 18p. (Orig.). 1982. pap. 2.50 (*0-943430-01-1*) Moveable Feast Pr.

— Chinese Camp & Other California Poems. 28p. (Orig.). 1982. pap. 2.50 (*0-943430-00-3*) Moveable Feast Pr.

— Chinese Camp & Other California Poems. LC 85-22079. 64p. (Orig.). 1985. pap. 6.95 (*0-86534-078-1*) Sunstone Pr.

— Cliff Walk. LC 84-61838. 96p. 1985. 12.50 (*0-943430-02-X*); pap. 6.95 (*0-943430-03-8*) Moveable Feast Pr.

— Silhouettes at Eventide. 32p. (Orig.). 1989. pap. 4.50 (*0-943430-04-6*) Moveable Feast Pr.

Pine, Jonathan. Backyard Birds. LC 91-45184. (Nature Study Series: A Trophy Nonfiction Bk.). (Illus.). 48p. (J). (gr. 2-5). 1993. pap. 7.95 (*0-06-446150-5*, Trophy) HarpC Child Bks.

— Trees. LC 93-3136. (Nature Study Book Ser.). (Illus.). 48p. (J). (gr. 2-5). 1995. 15.00 (*0-06-021468-6*) HarpC Child Bks.

— Trees. LC 93-3136. (Nature Study Bks.). (Illus.). 48p. (J). (gr. 2-5). 1995. lib. bdg. 14.89 (*0-06-021469-4*) HarpC Child Bks.

Pine, Joseph B., II. Mass Customization: The New Frontier in Business Competition. LC 92-17506. 368p. 1993. 29.95 (*0-87584-372-7*) Harvard Busn.

Pine, L. A., jt. auth. see Lovink, H. J.

Pine, Nicholas. The In-Crowd. (Terror Academy Ser.: No. 10). 192p. (Orig.). (J). (gr. 6 up). 1994. pap. 3.50 (*0-425-14307-4*) Berkley Pub.

— Lights Out. (Terror Academy Ser.: Bk. 1). 192p. (Orig.). 1993. pap. 3.50 (*0-425-13709-0*) Berkley Pub.

— The New Kid. (Terror Academy Ser.: Bk. 5). (YA). 1993. pap. 3.99 (*0-425-13970-0*) Berkley Pub.

— Night School. (Terror Academy Ser.: No. 7). 192p. (Orig.). 1994. pap. 3.50 (*0-425-14151-9*) Berkley Pub.

— The Prom. (Terror Academy Ser.: No. 9). 192p. (Orig.). (YA). 1994. pap. text ed. 3.99 (*0-425-14153-5*) Berkley Pub.

— Science Project. (Terror Academy Ser.: No. 8). 192p. (Orig.). 1994. pap. 3.50 (*0-425-14152-7*) Berkley Pub.

— Student Body. (Terror Academy Ser.: No. 6). (YA). 1993. pap. 3.99 (*0-425-13983-2*) Berkley Pub.

— The Substitute. (Terror Academy Ser.: No. 13). 192p. (Orig.). (YA). 1995. pap. text ed. 3.99 (*0-425-14534-4*) Berkley Pub.

— Terror Academy: Boy Crazy, No. 15. 192p. (Orig.). (YA). 1995. pap. text ed. 3.99 (*0-425-14727-4*) Berkley Pub.

— Terror Academy No. 11: Summer School. 192p. (Orig.). (J). (gr. 4 up). 1994. pap. text ed. 3.50 (*0-425-14338-4*) Berkley Pub.

— Terror Academy No. 12: Breaking Up. 192p. 1994. pap. text ed. 3.50 (*0-425-14398-8*) Berkley Pub.

— Terror Academy No. 14: School Spirit. 192p. (Orig.). 1995. pap. text ed. 3.99 (*0-425-14644-8*) Berkley Pub.

— Terror Academy Four: Spring Break. 208p. (Orig.). 1993. pap. 3.50 (*0-425-13969-7*) Berkley Pub.

— Terror Academy Three: Sixteen Candles. 192p. (Orig.). 1993. pap. 3.50 (*0-425-13841-0*) Berkley Pub.

— Terror Academy Two: Stalker. 192p. (Orig.) 1993. pap. 3.50 (*0-425-13814-3*) Berkley Pub.

Pine, P. Catering Equipment Management. (C). 1989. 130.00 (*0-09-182413-3*, Pub. by S Thornes Pubs UK) St Mut.

Pine, Patricia. Promoting Health Education in Schools: Problems & Solutions. Brodinsky, Ben, ed. (Critical Issues Report Ser.). 96p. (Orig.). 1985. pap. 13.95 (*0-87652-100-6*, 021-00152) Am Assn Sch Admin.

— Raising Standards in Schools: Problems & Solutions. Neill, Shirley B., ed. (Critical Issues Report Ser.). 80p. (Orig.). 1985. pap. 13.95 (*0-87652-099-9*, 021-00145) Am Assn Sch Admin.

Pine, R. J. Management of Technical Change in the Catering. 100p. 1987. text ed. 68.95 (*0-566-05328-4*, Pub. by Avebury Pub UK) Ashgate Pub Co.

Pine, Ray, jt. auth. see Go, Frank M.

Pine, Red, tr. P'u Ming's Oxherding Pictures & Verses. (Illus.). 30p. 1989. ring bd. 5.00 (*0-912887-02-8*) Empty Bowl.

Pine, Red, tr. see bodhidharma.

Pine, Red, pseud., tr. see Po-jen, Sung.

Pine, Richard. Brian Friel & Ireland's Drama. 208p. 1990. 69.95 (*0-415-04753-6*, A4244); pap. 18.95 (*0-415-04754-4*, A4248) Routledge.

— The Dandy & the Herald. 200p. 1988. text ed. 39.95 (*0-312-00521-0*) St Martin.

— Lawrence Durrell: The Mindscape. LC 94-234. 1994. text ed. 39.95 (*0-312-12157-1*) St Martin.

Pine, Richard & Cave, Richard. The Dublin Gate Theatre 1928-1978. (Theatre in Focus Ser.). (Illus.). 124p. 1984. sl., pap. 105.00 (*0-85964-156-2*) Chadwyck-Healey.

Pine, Stanley H. Organic Chemistry. 5th ed. 1184p. 1987. text ed. write for info. (*0-07-050118-1*) McGraw.

Pine, Theodore A., ed. see Schwerin, Julie B.

Pine Tree Legal Assistance, Inc. Staff. Do Your Own Divorce in Maine. (Illus.). 216p. 1991. reprint ed. pap. 16.50 (*0-9610570-0-9*) Bks by Village.

***Pine, Vanderlyn R.** Critical Issues in Dying & Death: Reflections on Death Studies. (Death, Value & Meaning Ser.). 1995. text ed. write for info. (*0-614-02668-7*); pap. write for info. (*0-614-02669-5*) Baywood Pub.

Pine, Wilfred H. Natural Resources Economics. 1977. pap. 4.00 (*0-686-00368-3*) AG Pr.

Pineau, Jean. Mariage, Separation, Divorce: L'Etat Du Droit Au Quebec. 2nd rev. ed. LC 77-565419. 314p. (FRE.). reprint ed. pap. 89.50 (*0-7837-6947-4*, 2046776) Bks Demand.

Pineau, L. Les Contes populaires du Poitou. LC 78-20124. (Collection de contes et de chansons populaires: Vol. 16). reprint ed. 21.50 (*0-404-60366-1*) AMS Pr.

— Le Folk-Lore du Poitou. LC 78-20126. (Collection de contes et de chansons populaires: Vol. 18). reprint ed. 21.50 (*0-404-60368-8*) AMS Pr.

— Le Romancero scandinave. LC 78-20140. (Collection de contes et de chansons populaires: Vol. 30). reprint ed. 21.50 (*0-404-60380-7*) AMS Pr.

Pineau, Roger, tr. see Ito, Masanori.

Pinecrest, R. F. Animal Social Behavior: Index of New Information with Authors, Subjects & Bibliography. rev. ed. 161p. 1994. 49.50 (*0-7883-0168-3*); pap. 45.50 (*0-7883-0169-1*) ABBE Pubs Assn.

Pineda, Ana M., jt. auth. see Schreiter, Robert.

Pineda, Cecile. The Love Queen of the Amazon, Vol. 1. 1993. pap. 9.95 (*0-316-70815-1*) Little.

— Love Queen of the Amazon, Vol. 1. 1992. 19.95 (*0-316-70812-7*) Little.

Pineda, Leonardo A., jt. auth. see Davidson, Alma.

Pineda-Ofreneo, Rosalinda. The Philippine Debt & Poverty. 120p. (C). 1991. text ed. 80.00 (*0-85598-049-4*, Pub. by Oxfam Pubns UK); pap. text ed. 28.00 (*0-85598-050-8*, Pub. by Oxfam Pubns UK) St Mut.

Pineda, Sysy, tr. see Brown, J. Aaron, ed.

Pineda y Ramirez, Antonio de. The Guam Diary of Naturalist Antonio de Pineda y Ramirez, 1792. Driver, Marjorie G., ed. Mallada, Victor F., tr. (Illus.). viii, 85p. (Orig.). (C). 1990. pap. 5.00 (*1-878453-01-7*) Univ Guam MAR Ctr.

Pinedo, H. M., et al, eds. Cancer Chemotherapy & Biological Response Modifiers, Vol. 14. 692p. 1993. 268.50 (*0-444-81509-0*) Elsevier.

Pinedo, Herbert M. & Verweij, Jaap, eds. Treatment of Soft Tissue Sarcomas. (Cancer Treatment & Research Ser.). (C). 1988. lib. bdg. 76.00 (*0-89838-391-9*) Kluwer Ac.

Pinedo, Herbert M., jt. auth. see Potmesil, Milan.

Pinedo, Herbert M., et al, eds. Soft Tissue Sarcomas: New Developments in the Multidisciplinary Approach to Treatment. (C). 1991. lib. bdg. 106.50 (*0-7923-1139-6*) Kluwer Ac.

Pinedo, L. F., jt. ed. see Henriques, J. M.

Pinedo, Michael. Scheduling: Theory, Algorithms & Systems. LC 94-8256. (International Industrial & Sytems Engineering Ser.). 1994. text ed. 60.00 (*0-13-706757-7*) P-H.

Pinegar, Ed J. Preparing for Your Mission. 109p. (Orig.). (YA). (gr. 12 up). 1992. pap. 7.95 (*0-87579-646-X*) Deseret Bk.

— You, Your Family, & the Scriptures. LC 90-82417. 200p. 1990. reprint ed. pap. 5.95 (*0-87579-366-5*) Deseret Bk.

Pinegar, Ed J., jt. auth. see Cannon, Elaine.

***Pineiro, R. J.** The Messenger. 1995. 22.95 (*0-312-85940-6*) Forge NYC.

— Retribution. 1995. 22.95 (*0-614-06177-6*) Forge NYC.

— Siege of Lightning. 320p. (Orig.). 1993. mass mkt. 4.99 (*0-425-13787-2*) Berkley Pub.

— Ultimatum. 384p. 1994. 21.95 (*0-312-85475-7*) Forge NYC.

— Ultimatum. 416p. 1995. mass mkt. 5.99 (*0-8125-2400-4*) Tor Bks.

Pinel, J., ed. Medicaments Essentiels. Guide Pratique d'Utilisation. Pour l'Emploi et la Gestion de Medicaments et Materiel Medical Dans les Dispensaires, les Centres Medicaux et les Camps de Refugies. A l'Usage des Medecins, Infirmier(e) s et Auxiliaries de Sante. (Medecins Sans Frontieres - Hatier Ser.). 255p. (FRE.). 1991. pap. 26.95 (*2-218-02650-3*) Schoenhof.

Pinel, Jane. The Picnic Basket. LC 83-90332. (Illus.). 96p. 1983. pap. 4.95 (*0-915909-00-6*) Ruggles Pub.

Pinel, John P. Biopsychology. 608p. 1989. teacher ed write for info. (*0-318-66398-8*, H20530); text ed. 50.00 (*0-205-12052-0*, H20522); student ed 20.00 (*0-685-29845-0*, H20555); write for info. (*0-318-66399-6*, H22445); write for info. (*0-318-66400-3*, H20548) Allyn.

— Biopsychology. 2nd ed. LC 92-49418. 1992. text ed. 38.25 (*0-205-13897-7*) Allyn.

— Current Research in Biopsychology. 200p. 1991. pap. text ed. 19.00 (*0-205-13000-3*, H3000-0) Allyn.

Pinel, Philippe. The Clinical Training of Doctors: An Essay 1793. Weiner, Dora B., ed. LC 80-14500. (Henry E. Sigerist Supplements to the Bulletin of the History of Medicine, New Ser.: No. 3). 112p. reprint ed. pap. 32.00 (*0-317-51978-6*, 2027378) Bks Demand.

— Traite Medico-Philosophique Sur L'alienation Mentale. 2nd ed. LC 75-16727. (Classics in Psychiatry Ser.). (FRE.). 1976. reprint ed. 46.95 (*0-405-07450-6*) Ayer.

Pinel, Stephen. The Forty Programs of Alexander Guilmant at the St. Louis World's Fair, 1904. 48p. 1985. 5.00 (*0-913499-01-3*) Organ Hist Soc.

Pinel, Stephen L. Old Organs of Princeton: Being an Historical Chronology & Description of All the Known Pipe Organs Installed in the Town of Princeton, New Jersey, from 1760 to 1925, Including Photographs & Stoplists When Available, as Well as Accounts from Newspapers, Church Records, Histories, & Diaries. LC 89-62170. 146p. 1989. 29.95 (*0-9610092-2-5*) Boston Organ Club.

Pinelli, Antonio, jt. ed. see Gambi, Lucio.

Pinelli, Giuseppe, jt. ed. see Di Pasquale, Giuseppe.

Pinelli, Michael A. You & I & Smoking. LC 85-73430. 72p. 1986. pap. 4.25 (*0-936417-01-3*) Axelrod Pub.

***Pinello, Daniel R.** The Impact of Judicial-Selection Method on State-Supreme Court Policy: Innovation, Reaction & Atrophy. (Contributions in Legal Studies: Vol. 80). 1995. text ed. write for info. (*0-313-29243-4*, Greenwood Pr) Greenwood.

Pineo, C. S. & Subrahmanyan, D. V. Community Water Supply & Excreta Disposal Situation in the Developing Countries. (Offset Publication Ser.: No. 15). 1975. pap. 4.80 (*92-4-170015-7*) World Health.

Pineo, Graham F., jt. ed. see Hull, Russell.

Pinera, Angel. Los Cubanos. 1978. pap. 4.50 (*84-400-4714-2*) Ediciones.

Pinera, Estela & Gutierrez de la Solana, Alberto. Humberto Pinera Llera: Pensador, Escritor, Critico y Educador. (Senda de Estudios y Ensayos Ser.). (Illus.). 288p. (SPA.). 1991. pap. 17.95 (*0-918454-83-2*) Senda Nueva.

Pinera, Humberto, et al. Proceso del las Ideas Politicas en Cuba. 132p. (Orig.). (SPA.). 1988. pap. 15.00 (*0-89729-489-0*, Pub. by Laurenty Pub Inc CU) Ediciones.

Pinera-Llera, Humberto. Introduccion E Historia De la Filosofia. 3rd ed. LC 89-65885. (Coleccion Textos Ser.). (Illus.). 348p. (SPA.). 1980. reprint ed. pap. 12.95 (*0-89729-254-5*) Ediciones.

Pinera, Virgilio. Cold Tales. Schafer, Mark, tr. LC 88-80807. 304p. 1988. 24.00 (*0-941419-18-5*, Eridanos Library); pap. 15.00 (*0-941419-80-0*, Eridanos Library) Marsilio Pubs.

— Rene's Flesh. Schafer, Mark, tr. LC 89-83811. 256p. 1992. 17.95 (*0-941419-40-1*, Eridanos Library); pap. 12.00 (*0-941419-76-2*, Eridanos Library) Marsilio Pubs.

Pinera, Virgilio & Gonzales-Cruz, Luis F. Una Caja de Zapatos Vacia. LC 86-80352. (Coleccion Teatro). 83p. (Orig.). (SPA.). 1986. pap. 7.95 (*0-89729-390-8*) Ediciones.

Pineri, Michel & Eisenberg, Adi, eds. Structure & Properties of Ionomers. 1987. lib. bdg. 184.00 (*90-277-2458-X*) Kluwer Ac.

Pinero, A. W. Plays. Rowell, George, ed. (British & American Playwrights Ser.). (Illus.). 315p. 1986. 64.95 (*0-521-24103-0*) Cambridge U Pr.

Pinero, Arthur W. The Collected Letters of Sir Arthur Pinero. Wearing, J. P., ed. LC 74-76742. 314p. reprint ed. pap. 89.50 (*0-318-39674-2*, 2033245) Bks Demand.

— Social Plays, 4 Vols. Hamilton, Clayton, ed. reprint ed. write for info. (*0-318-50716-1*) AMS Pr.

— Social Plays, 4 Vols, 1. Hamilton, Clayton, ed. LC 79-18169. reprint ed. write for info. (*0-404-05081-6*) AMS Pr.

— Social Plays, 4 Vols, 2. Hamilton, Clayton, ed. LC 79-18169. reprint ed. write for info. (*0-404-05082-4*) AMS Pr.

— Social Plays, 4 Vols, 3. Hamilton, Clayton, ed. LC 79-18169. reprint ed. write for info. (*0-404-05083-2*) AMS Pr.

— Social Plays, 4 Vols, 4. Hamilton, Clayton, ed. LC 79-18169. reprint ed. write for info. (*0-404-05084-0*) AMS Pr.

— Social Plays, 4 Vols, Set. Hamilton, Clayton, ed. LC 79-18169. reprint ed. 150.00 (*0-404-05080-8*) AMS Pr.

— Social Plays, 4 vols., Set. (BCL1-PR English Literature Ser.). 1992. reprint ed. lib. bdg. 300.00 (*0-7812-7618-7*) Rprt Serv.

— Trelawny of the "Wells" & Other Plays. Bratton, Jacky, ed. & intro. by. (World's Classics Ser.). 352p. 1995. 49.95 (*0-19-812148-2*); pap. 11.95 (*0-19-282568-2*) OUP.

— Two Plays: Dr. Harmer's Holidays & Child Man. (BCL1-PR English Literature Ser.). 245p. 1992. reprint ed. lib. bdg. 79.00 (*0-7812-7619-5*) Rprt Serv.

Pinero, Eugenio. The Town of San Felipe & Colonial Cacao Economics. LC 94-71251. (Transactions Ser.: Vol. 84, Pt. 3). (Illus.). 190p. (C). 1994. pap. 20.00 (*0-87169-843-9*, T843PIE) Am Philos.

Pinero, Miguel. La Bodega Sold Dreams. LC 79-90765. (Illus.). (Orig.). 1979. pap. 5.00 (*0-934770-02-6*) Arte Publico.

— Bodega Sold Dreams. 2nd ed. LC 79-90765. (Illus.). 1986. pap. 5.00 (*0-685-18634-2*) Arte Publico.

— Outrageous One Act Plays. 160p. (Orig.). 1986. pap. 9.50 (*0-934770-68-9*) Arte Publico.

— Short Eyes. 128p. 1975. pap. 10.00 (*0-374-52147-6*) FS&G.

— The Sun Always Shines for the Cool; Midnight Moon at the Greasy Spoon; Eulogy for a Small Time Thief. LC 83-72582. 128p. (Orig.). (C). 1983. pap. 11.00 (*0-934770-25-5*) Arte Publico.

Pines, jt. ed. see Bell.

Pines, Ayala. Career Burnout. 1989. pap. 12.95 (*0-02-925353-5*) Free Pr.

Pines, Ayala & Aronson, Elliot. Career Burnout: Causes & Cures. 240p. 1988. 27.95 (*0-02-925351-9*) Free Pr.

Pines, Ayala M. & Maslach, Christina. Experiencing Social Psychology: Readings & Projects. 3rd ed. LC 92-11918. (Series in Social Psychology). 1992. pap. text ed. write for info. (*0-07-040773-8*) McGraw.

Pines, Burton Y. & Lamer, Timothy W. Out of Focus: Network Television & the American Economy. LC 93-46426. 384p. 1994. 24.00 (*0-89526-490-0*) Regnery Pub.

Pines, Burton Y., jt. ed. see Heatherly, Charles L.

Pines, Christopher L. Ideology & False Consciousness: Marx & His Historical Progenitors. LC 92-15168. (SUNY Series in the Philosophy of the Social Sciences). 242p. 1993. 49.50 (*0-7914-1431-0*); pap. 16.95 (*0-7914-1432-9*) State U NY Pr.

Pines, David. Elementary Excitations in Solids. (Lecture Notes & Supplements in Physics Ser.: No. 5). 300p. (C). 1963. pap. 34.95 (*0-8053-7913-4*, Adv Bk Prog) Addison-Wesley.

Pines, David, ed. Emerging Syntheses. 1987. 39.95 (*0-317-66911-7*, 15677); pap. 19.95 (*0-317-66912-5*, 15686) Addison-Wesley.

— Emerging Syntheses in Science. (Santa Fe Institute Ser.: Vol. I). 256p. (C). 1988. text ed. write for info. (*0-201-15677-6*, Adv Bk Prog); pap. 29.95 (*0-201-15686-5*, Adv Bk Prog) Addison-Wesley.

— The Many-Body Problem. (Frontiers in Physics Ser.: No. 6). (Illus.). 456p. (C). 1962. pap. 39.95 (*0-8053-7901-0*, Adv Bk Prog) Addison-Wesley.

Pines, David & Nozieres, Philippe. The Theory of Quantum Liquids: Normal Fermi Liquids, Vol. I. (Classics Ser.). (Illus.). 384p. (C). 1989. 44.95 (*0-201-09429-0*, Adv Bk Prog) Addison-Wesley.

Pines, David & Stevens, Benjamin H. Mathematical Programming & Competitive Equilibrium in the Location of Agricultural Production. (Discussion Paper Ser.: No. 23). 1968. pap. 10.00 (*1-55869-073-5*) Regional Sci Res Inst.

PQ

An Asterisk (*) at the beginning of an entry indicates that the title is appearing in BIP for the first time.

Pines, David, jt. ed. see Ventura, Joseph.

Pines, Dinora. A Woman's Unconscious Use of Her Body. 256p. 1994. 25.00 (*0-300-05960-4*) Yale U Pr.

Pines, Eunice & Sabo, Eleanor, eds. Barnum Memorial Cemetery. 2nd ed. (Illus.). 72p. 1987. reprint ed. pap. 8.00 (*0-940133-04-0*) Kinseeker Pubns.

Pines, Herman. The Chemistry of Catalytic Hydrocarbon Conversions. 1981. text ed. 80.00 (*0-12-557160-7*) Acad Pr.

Pines, Jim, ed. Black & White in Colour: Black People in British Television since 1936. (Illus.). 256p. 1992. 55.00 (*0-85170-329-1*, Pub. by British Film Inst UK); pap. 22. 95 (*0-85170-328-3*, Pub. by British Film Inst UK) Ind U Pr.

Pines, Jim & Willemen, Paul, eds. Questions of Third Cinema. (Illus.). 256p. 1989. 29.95 (*0-85170-262-7*, Pub. by British Film Inst UK); pap. 14.95 (*0-85170-230-9*, Pub. by British Film Inst UK) Ind U Pr.

Pines, Malcolm, ed. Bion & Group Psychotherapy. (International Library of Group Psychotherapy & Group Process). 336p. 1985. 49.95 (*0-7100-9949-5*, 99495, RKP) Routledge.

— Bion & Group Psychotherapy. (International Library of Group Psychotherapy & Group Process). 416p. 1991. pap. 19.95 (*0-415-07181-X*, A6940, Tavistock) Routledge.

Pines, Malcolm & Rafaelsen, Lise, eds. The Individual & the Group: Boundaries & Interrelations, 2 vols., Set. LC 81-17924. 1982. 145.00 (*0-685-04077-1*, Plenum Pr) Plenum.

— The Individual & the Group: Boundaries & Interrelations, 2 vols., Vol. 1: Theory. LC 81-17924. 378p. 1982. 65.00 (*0-306-40837-6*, Plenum Pr) Plenum.

— The Individual & the Group: Boundaries & Interrelations, 2 vols., Vol. 2: Practice. LC 81-17924. 700p. 1982. 95.00 (*0-306-40838-4*, Plenum Pr) Plenum.

Pines, Malcolm, jt. ed. see Roberts, Jeff.

Pines, Malcolm, jt. ed. see Schermer, Victor L.

Pines, Maya. Inside the Cell. (Illus.). 62p. (C). 1993. pap. text ed. 17.95 (*1-56806-208-7*) Diane Pub.

Pines, Paul. Hotel Madden Poems. (Illus.). 54p. (Orig.). (C). 1991. pap. 6.00 (*0-936556-25-0*) Contact Two.

— Onion. LC 72-83855. (Illus.). 72p. 1972. pap. 3.00 (*0-913142-00-X*) Mulch Pr.

Pines, Philip A., ed. see Slobody, Evelyn & Slobody, Lawrence B.

Pines, S. & Yovel, Y., eds. Maimonides & Philosophy. (C). 1986. lib. bdg. 88.00 (*90-247-3439-8*) Kluwer Ac.

Pines, Shlomo. Studies in Arabic Versions of Greek Texts & in Mediaeval Science. (Collected Works of Shlomo Pines: Vol. 2). ix, 468p. 1986. 73.25 (*965-223-626-8*) E J Brill.

Pines, Shlomo, tr. see Maimonides, Moses.

Pines, Tonya, ed. Thirteen. 304p. (YA). 1991. pap. 3.99 (*0-590-45256-8*, Point) Scholastic Inc.

***Pineso, H. M., et al, eds.** Cancer Chemotherapy & Biological Response Modifiers. 732p. 1994. 285.75 (*0-444-82056-6*) Elsevier.

***Pinet, B. & Bois, C., eds.** The Potential of Deep Seismic Profiling for Hydrocarbon Exploration: The IFP Exploration & Production Research Conference, Arles, 1989. (Illus.). 502p. (C). 1990. text ed. 123.00 (*2-7108-0590-1*) Technip.

Pinet, Celine & Devlin, Kimberly, eds. Threads: Insights by Women Architects. (Publications in Architecture & Urban Planning: No. R91-1). (Illus.). 53p. 1991. 12.50 (*0-938744-73-9*) U of Wis Ctr Arch-Urban.

Pinet, Helene. Rodin: The Hands of Genius. Palmer, Caroline, tr. (Discoveries Ser.). (Illus.). 144p. 1992. pap. 12.95 (*0-8109-2888-4*) Abrams.

Pinet, Paul. Oceanography: An Introduction to the Planet Oceanus. Pullins, ed. 571p. (C). 1992. text ed. 61.00 (*0-314-77008-9*) West Pub.

Pineus, K. Time-Barred Actions. 2nd ed. Rohreke, H. G., ed. (International Maritime Law Ser.). 1993. boxed 110.00 (*1-85044-027-1*) Lloyds London Pr.

Pineus, Kaj. Ship's Value. 2nd ed. 1986. 85.00 (*1-85044-062-X*) Lloyds London Pr.

Piney, M., et al. Controlling Airborne Contaminants in the Workplace. 173p. (C). 1992. 225.00 (*0-905927-42-7*, Pub. by H&H Sci Cnslts UK) St Mut.

Pinfield, N. Indian Sub-Continent: India, Pakistan & Bangladesh. 1992. pap. text ed. 14.04 (*0-582-20661-8*) Longman.

Pinfold, John. Tibet. (World Bibliographical Ser.). 1991. lib. bdg. 79.25 (*1-85109-158-0*) ABC-CLIO.

Pinfold, Mike. Louis Armstrong. (Illus.). 144p. 1988. pap. 10.95 (*0-7119-1294-7*, OP44486) Omnibus NY.

Pinfold, P., jt. ed. see Sahoo, M.

Pinfold, Wallace, jt. auth. see Hazard, Edith.

Pinford, G. M. Reinforced Concrete Chimneys & Towers. 2nd ed. (Viewpoint Ser.). (Illus.). 176p. 1985. text ed. 60.00 (*0-86310-016-3*, Viewpoint) Scholium Intl.

Ping, April G., ed. see Eames, David.

Ping, April G., ed. see Roberts, George & Roberts, Jan.

Ping, Charles J. Ohio University in Perspective II: The Annual Convocation Addresses of President Charles J. Ping, 1985-1993. LC 94-9002. 1994. 24.95 (*0-8214-1101-2*) Ohio U Pr.

***Ping-Chun Hsiung.** Living Rooms As Factories: Class, Gender, & the Satellite Factory System in Taiwan. (Illus.). 224p. (Orig.). (C). 1995. lib. bdg. 44.95 (*1-56639-389-2*) Temple U Pr.

Ping, Margaret. Looking Back - Moving Forward: History of the Billings YWCA 1907-1988. Schaffer, Rachel, ed. (Orig.). 1991. pap. write for info. (*0-9629912-0-1*) M Ping.

Ping, MariAnn, ed. The Constitution of the United States: La Constitucion de los Estados Unidos. 130p. 1992. 29. 95 (*0-929853-11-3*) Condor Pubns Inc.

Ping, MariAnn & Aldridge, Nilda, eds. The Constitution of the United States: La Constitucion de los Estados Unidos. Figueroa, Minerva, tr. (Illus.). 85p. 1992. teacher ed 29.95 (*0-929853-10-5*); student ed, text ed. 11.95 (*0-929853-07-5*) Condor Pubns Inc.

Ping-Wan. The Chinese System of Public Education. 1977. lib. bdg. 59.95 (*0-8490-1612-6*) Gordon Pr.

***Pingali, Prabhu L. & Roger, Pierre A.** Impact of Pesticides on Farmer Health & the Rice Environment. LC 94-45040. (Natural Resource Management & Policy Ser.). 1995. lib. bdg. write for info. (*0-7923-9521-2*) Kluwer Ac.

— Impact of Pesticides on Farmer Health & the Rice Environment. LC 94-45040. (Natural Resource Management & Policy Ser.). 1995. pap. text ed. write for info. (*0-7923-9522-0*) Kluwer Ac.

Pingali, Prabhu L., et al. Agricultural Mechanization & the Evolution of Farming Systems in Sub-Saharan Africa. LC 86-27523. 208p. 1987. text ed. 25.95 (*0-8018-3502-X*) Johns Hopkins.

Pingaud, Bernard. L' Amour Triste. (FRE.). 1973. pap. 8.95 (*0-7859-4020-0*) Fr & Eur.

***Pingeat, Anne.** Sculpture in the Music d'Orsay. (Illus.). 128p. 1995. 29.95 (*0-302-00670-2*) Scala Books.

Pingel, Volker. Die Vorgeschichtlichen Goldfund der Iberischen Halbinsel: Eine Archaeologische Unterschung zur Auswertung der Spektralanalysen. (Madrider Forschungen Ser.: Bd. 17). (Illus.). xxi, 321p. (GER.). (C). 1992. lib. bdg. 270.80 (*3-11-012337-1*) De Gruyter.

Pingenot, Ben E. Siringo. (Centennial Series of the Association of Former Students: No. 31). (Illus.). 268p. 1989. 29.50 (*0-89096-381-9*) Tex A&M Univ Pr.

Pinger, Robert, jt. auth. see McKenzie, James.

***Pinget, Leonard.** Robert Pinget. (Twayne's World Author Ser.). 1995. lib. bdg. 23.95x (*0-8057-4537-8*, Twayne) Macmillan.

Pinget, Robert. Abel & Bela. Wright, Barbara, tr. LC 87-42246. 48p. 1987. 4.00 (*0-87376-052-2*) Red Dust.

— The Apocrypha. Wright, Barbara, tr. LC 86-61607. 143p. 1987. 12.95 (*0-87376-050-6*) Red Dust.

— Baga. Stevenson, John, tr. 144p. (Orig.). 1985. reprint ed. pap. 9.95 (*0-7145-0099-2*) Riverrun NY.

— Between Fantoine & Agapa. Wright, Barbara, tr. LC 82-60911. (Illus.). 83p. 1983. 8.95 (*0-87376-040-9*) Red Dust.

— A Bizarre Will. Wright, Barbara, tr. 150p. 1989. 10.95 (*0-87376-065-4*) Red Dust.

— Cette Voix. 232p. (FRE.). 1991. pap. 24.95 (*0-7859-1503-6*, 2707300470) Fr & Eur.

— The Enemy. Wright, Barbara, tr. LC 91-62212. 89p. 1992. 12.95 (*0-87376-071-9*) Red Dust.

— Fable. Wright, Barbara, tr. LC 80-50203. 1980. 6.95 (*0-87376-036-0*) Red Dust.

— Graal Flibuste. 240p. (FRE.). 1989. pap. 19.95 (*0-7859-1518-4*, 2707304905) Fr & Eur.

— Identite: Avec: Abel et Bela. 127p. (FRE.). 1992. pap. 16. 95 (*0-7859-1517-6*, 2707303593) Fr & Eur.

— L' Inquisitoire. 512p. (FRE.). 1986. pap. 16.95 (*0-7859-1519-2*, 2707310700) Fr & Eur.

— The Inquisitory. Watson, Donald, tr. 399p. (Orig.). 1982. pap. 12.95 (*0-7145-3911-2*) Riverrun NY.

— Le Libera. 224p. (FRE.). 1984. pap. 24.95 (*0-7859-1516-8*, 2707303488) Fr & Eur.

— The Libera Me Domine. Wright, Barbara, tr. LC 78-53831. (New French Writing Ser.). 1979. 10.50 (*0-87376-025-5*) Red Dust.

— Mahu, or the Material. Sheridan-Smith, Alan, tr. 144p. (Orig.). (C). 1985. pap. 8.95 (*0-7145-0354-1*) Riverrun NY.

— Monsieur Songe. Wright, Barbara, tr. LC 88-61955. 200p. 1989. 12.95 (*0-87376-060-3*) Red Dust.

— Paralchimie: Avec: Architruc, l'Hypothese, Nuit. 2nd ed. 96p. (FRE.). 1990. pap. 17.95 (*0-7859-1520-6*, 2707313289) Fr & Eur.

— Passacaglia. Wright, Barbara, tr. LC 78-53832. 1979. 6.95 (*0-87376-033-6*) Red Dust.

— Passacaille. 136p. (FRE.). 1969. pap. 17.95 (*0-7859-1508-7*, 2707300861) Fr & Eur.

— Quelqu'un. 264p. (FRE.). 1965. pap. 18.95 (*0-7859-1609-1*, 270730347X) Fr & Eur.

— Recurrent Melody. 1986. 11.95 (*0-7145-1088-2*) Riverrun NY.

— Le Renard et la Boussole. 2nd ed. 245p. (FRE.). 1971. pap. 13.95 (*0-7859-1515-X*, 2707303453) Fr & Eur.

— Someone. Wright, Barbara, tr. LC 83-63101. 253p. (C). 1984. 12.95 (*0-87376-043-3*) Red Dust.

— That Voice. Wright, Barbara, tr. LC 82-60910. 114p. 1983. 10.95 (*0-87376-041-7*) Red Dust.

Pingree, Amanda, tr. see De Senarclens, Pierre.

Pingree, Chellie. North Island Designs Five: A Scrapbook of Sweaters from a Maine Island. LC 92-72725. (Illus.). 96p. 1993. pap. 17.95 (*0-89272-329-7*) Down East.

— North Island Designs Four: Sixteen New Patterns from Talented Maine Designers. (Illus.). 96p. 1992. pap. 17.95 (*0-89272-318-1*) Down East.

Pingree, Chellie & Anderson, Debby. Maine Island Classics. (Illus.). 80p. 1992. pap. 15.95 (*0-89272-315-7*) Down East.

— Maine Island Kids. (Illus.). 80p. 1992. pap. 15.95 (*0-89272-316-5*) Down East.

Pingree, D., jt. auth. see Reiner, E.

Pingree, D., jt. auth. see Reiner, Erica.

Pingree, David. The Astronomical Works of Gregory Chioniades, Vol. 1, Pt. 1: The Zij Al-Ala Text, Translation, Commentary. (Corpus des Astronomes Byzantins Ser.: Vol. II). 412p. (Orig.). (C). 1985. pap. 69.00 (*90-70265-65-6*, Pub. by Gieben NE) Benjamins North Am.

— The Astronomical Works of Gregory Chioniades, Vol. 1, Pt. 2: The Zii Al-Ala Tables. (Corpus des Astronomes Byzantins Ser.: Vol. II). 235p. (Orig.). (C). 1986. pap. 85.00 (*90-70265-50-8*, Pub. by Gieben NE) Benjamins North Am.

— Census of the Exact Sciences in Sanskrit, Ser. A, Vol. 1. LC 70-115882. (Memoirs Ser.: Vols. 81, 86, & 146). 1970. pap. 10.00 (*0-87169-081-0*, M081-PID) Am Philos.

— Census of the Exact Sciences in Sanskrit, Ser. A, Vol. 2. LC 70-115882. (Memoirs Ser.: Vols. 81, 86, & 146). 1970. pap. 12.00 (*0-87169-086-1*, M086- PID) Am Philos.

— Census of the Exact Sciences in Sanskrit Ser. A, Vol. 5. LC 94-72374. (Memoirs Ser.: Vol. 213). 756p. (C). 1994. pap. 45.00 (*0-87169-213-9*, M213pid) Am Philos.

Pingree, David, tr. The Yavanajataka of Sphujidhvaja, 2 vols., Set. (Harvard Oriental Ser: No. 48). 1024p. 1978. 90.00 (*0-674-96373-3*) HUP.

Pingree, David, jt. auth. see Goldstein, Bernard.

Pingree, David, ed. see Hashimi, Ali Ibn Sulayman al.

Pingree, David, jt. auth. see Kennedy, Edward S.

Pingree, David E. Census of the Exact Sciences in Sanskrit Series A, Vol. 3. LC 70-115882. (Memoirs of the American Philosophical Society Ser.: Vol. 111). 214p. reprint ed. pap. 61.00 (*0-7837-0541-7*, 2040869) Bks Demand.

Pingry, Julie. Practical Machine Vision. 140p. student ed 77. 00 (*0-943779-00-6*) Cutter Information.

Pingry, Patricia. Story of Daniel & the Lions. (Story of... Ser.). (Illus.). 24p. (Orig.). (J). (ps-2). 1988. pap. 3.95 (*0-8249-8179-0*, Ideals Child) Hambleton-Hill.

— Story of David & the Slingshot. (Story of...Ser.). 24p. (J). (ps-2). 1988. pap. 3.95 (*0-8249-8180-4*, Ideals Child) Hambleton-Hill.

— The Story of Esther. (Story of...Ser.). (Illus.). xp. (J). (ps-2). 1990. pap. 3.95 (*0-8249-8420-X*, Ideals Child) Hambleton-Hill.

— Story of Jonah & the Big Fish. (Story of...Ser.). (Illus.). 24p. (Orig.). (J). (ps-2). 1988. pap. 3.95 (*0-8249-8181-2*, Ideals Child) Hambleton-Hill.

— Story of Joseph & a Dream Come True. (Story of...Ser.). (Illus.). 24p. (Orig.). (J). (ps-2). 1988. pap. 3.95 (*0-8249-8182-0*, Ideals Child) Hambleton-Hill.

— Story of Joshua & the Bugles of Jericho. (Story of...Ser.). (Illus.). 24p. (Orig.). (J). (ps-2). 1988. pap. 3.95 (*0-8249-8178-2*, Ideals Child) Hambleton-Hill.

— The Story of Moses & the Ten Commandments. (Story of...Ser.). (Illus.). (J). (ps-2). 1990. pap. 3.95 (*0-8249-8418-8*, Ideals Child) Hambleton-Hill.

— Story of Noah & the Rainbow. (Story of...Ser.). 24p. (J). (ps-2). 1988. pap. 3.95 (*0-8249-8176-6*, Ideals Child) Hambleton-Hill.

— The Story of Samson & His Great Strength. (Story of... Ser.). (Illus.). 24p. (Orig.). (J). (ps-2). 1994. pap. 3.95 (*0-8249-8655-5*, Ideals Child) Hambleton-Hill.

— The Story of the Garden of Eden. (Story of...Ser.). (Illus.). 24p. (Orig.). (J). (ps-2). 1994. pap. 3.95 (*0-8249-8654-7*, Ideals Child) Hambleton-Hill.

Pings, C. J., jt. auth. see March, Norman H.

Pinguet, Maurice. Voluntary Death in Japan. Morris, Rosemary, tr. (Illus.). 360p. 1993. 27.95 (*0-7456-0870-1*) Blackwell Pubs.

Pinguill, Yves. Da Vinci: The Painter Who Spoke with Birds. (Art for Children Ser.). (Illus.). 64p. (J). (gr. 3 up). 1994. lib. bdg. 14.95 (*0-7910-2808-9*) Chelsea Hse.

Pinhas, Alan R., jt. auth. see Kegley, Susan.

Pinheiro, Aileen F., comp. The Heritage of Balowin Park. (Illus.). 272p. 1981. 10.55 (*0-9607306-0-5*) Hist Soc Baldwin Pk.

Pinheiro, C. U. & Balick, M. J. Brazilian Palms: Notes on Their Uses, & Vernacular Names & Added Illustrations, Contributions from The New York Botanical Garden, Vol. 17. LC 87-12201. (Illus.). 61p. 1987. pap. 8.75 (*0-89327-317-1*) NY Botanical.

Pinheiro, Carlton, jt. auth. see Bray, Maynard.

Pinheiro, Patricia M., jt. auth. see Fryer, Peter.

Pinhey, Elliot C. G. Moths of Southern Africa. (Illus.). 273p. (Orig.). 1975. 41.25 (*0-624-00784-7*) Entomological Repr.

Pinhey, Thomas, jt. auth. see Sanders, William B.

Pini, Richard. Against the Wind. 288p. 1992. mass mkt. 4.99 (*0-8125-2274-5*) Tor Bks.

— Elfquest: Against the Wind, Vol. 4. 1990. pap. 7.95 (*0-8125-4906-6*) Tor Bks.

— Elfquest: Winds of Change, Vol. 3. 1989. pap. 7.95 (*0-8125-4905-8*) Tor Bks.

— Elfquest: Wolfsong, Vol. 2. 1989. mass mkt. 4.50 (*0-8125-0377-5*) Tor Bks.

Pini, Richard, ed. Big Elfquest Gatherum. (Illus.). 244p. (Orig.). 1994. 19.95 (*0-936861-13-4*) Warp Graphics.

— Dark Hours. (Blood of Ten Chiefs Ser.: No. 5). 320p. 1994. mass mkt. 4.99 (*0-8125-2342-3*) Tor Bks.

Pini, Richard, ed. see Asprin, Robert & Foglio, Phil.

Pini, Richard, ed. see Asprin, Robert, et al.

Pini, Richard, jt. auth. see Pini, Wendy.

Pini, Richard, jt. ed. see Pini, Wendy.

Pini, Richard, et al, eds. Elfquest: Blood of Ten Chiefs, Vol. 1. 320p. (Orig.). 1986. pap. 6.95 (*0-8125-3041-1*) Tor Bks.

— Elfquest: Blood of Ten Chiefs, Vol. 1. (Orig.). 1987. pap. 3.50 (*0-8125-3043-8*) Tor Bks.

— Elfquest: Wolfsong, Vol. 2. 320p. 1988. pap. 7.95 (*0-8125-3037-3*) Tor Bks.

Pini, Wendy. Beauty & the Beast, Bk. 2. 1990. pap. 5.95 (*0-915419-75-0*) First Pub IL.

— Beauty & the Beast: Portrait of Love. 1989. pap. 5.95 (*0-915419-50-5*) First Pub IL.

Pini, Wendy & Pini, Richard. The Complete ElfQuest. limited ed. Reynolds, Kay, ed. (ElfQuest Ser.). (Illus.). 652p. 1985. 120.00 (*0-89865-453-X*, Starblaze) Donning Co.

— Elfquest: Captives of Blue Mountain. rev. ed. (Elfquest Graphic Novel Ser.: Vol. 3). (Illus.). 192p. (J). (gr. 4 up). 1994. 19.95 (*0-936861-19-3*, Father Tree Pr) Warp Graphics.

— Elfquest: Fire & Flight. rev. ed. (Elfquest Graphic Novel Ser.: Vol. 1). (Illus.). 192p. (J). (gr. 4 up). 1993. 19.95 (*0-936861-16-9*, Father Tree Pr) Warp Graphics.

— Elfquest: Kings of the Broken Wheel. (Elfquest Graphic Novel Ser.: Vol. 8). (Illus.). 160p. (J). (gr. 4 up). 1994. 19.95 (*0-936861-36-3*, Father Tree Pr) Warp Graphics.

— Elfquest: Quest's End. rev. ed. (Elfquest Graphic Novel Ser.: Vol. 4). (Illus.). 208p. (J). (gr. 4 up). 1994. 19.95 (*0-936861-15-0*, Father Tree Pr) Warp Graphics.

— Elfquest: Rogue's Challenge. (Elfquest Graphic Novel Ser.: Vol. 9). (Illus.). 160p. (Orig.). 1994. 19.95 (*0-936861-26-6*) Warp Graphics.

— Elfquest: Siege at Blue Mountain. (Elfquest Graphic Novel Ser.: Vol. 5). (Illus.). 144p. (Orig.). (J). (gr. 4 up). 1994. 19.95 (*0-936861-34-7*, Father Tree Pr) Warp Graphics.

— Elfquest: The Cry from Beyond. (Graphic Novel Ser.: Vol. 7). (Illus.). 160p. (Orig.). (J). (gr. 4 up). 1993. 19.95 (*0-936861-17-7*, Father Tree Pr) Warp Graphics.

— Elfquest: The Forbidden Grove. (Elfquest Graphic Novel Ser.: Vol. 2). (Illus.). 208p. (J). (gr. 4 up). 1994. 19.95 (*0-936861-18-5*, Father Tree Pr) Warp Graphics.

— Elfquest: The Hidden Years. (Illus.). 160p. (Orig.). 1992. 19.95 (*0-936861-30-4*) Warp Graphics.

— Elfquest: The Secret of Two-Edge. (Elfquest Graphic Novel Ser.: Vol. 6). (Illus.). 144p. (Orig.). (J). (gr. 4 up). 1994. 19.95 (*0-936861-35-5*, Father Tree Pr) Warp Graphics.

Pini, Wendy & Pini, Richard, eds. Elfquest: Bedtime Stories. (Illus.). 128p. (Orig.). 1994. 19.95 (*0-936861-37-1*) Warp Graphics.

— Elfquest: New Blood. (Illus.). 176p. (Orig.). 1993. 19.95 (*0-936861-31-2*) Warp Graphics.

Pinick, Joanna, jt. auth. see Barker, Gayle.

Piniella, J. F., jt. ed. see Jeffrey, G. A.

Pininska, Mary. Little Polish Cookbook. (Illus.). 1992. 7.95 (*0-8118-0262-0*) Chronicle Bks.

Pinion, F. B. A D. H. Lawrence Companion: Life, Thought & Works. LC 78-12348. (Illus.). 316p. 1979. text ed. 45. 00 (*0-06-495574-5*, N6849) B&N Imports.

Pinion, F. B., ed. Browning: Dramatis Personae. 256p. 1969. 22.50 (*0-7121-0139-X*, Pub. by MacDonald & Evans UK) Trans-Atl Phila.

— A George Eliot Companion: Literary Achievement & Modern Significance. LC 81-8044. (Companion Ser.). 290p. 1981. 59.50 (*0-389-20208-8*, N6990) B&N Imports.

— A Thomas Hardy Dictionary. 256p. 1989. 55.00x (*0-8147-6610-2*); pap. text ed. 20.00 (*0-8147-6621-8*) NYU Pr.

Pinion, Frank B. Hardy the Writer: Surveys & Assessments. LC 89-10899. 350p. 1990. text ed. 39.95 (*0-312-04024-5*) St Martin.

— Thomas Hardy: His Life & Friends. LC 91-38715. 396p. 1992. text ed. 39.95 (*0-312-07570-7*) St Martin.

— A Wordsworth Chronology. 160p. 1988. text ed. 38.50 (*0-8161-8950-1*, Hall Reference) Macmillan.

Pinion, Frank B., jt. ed. see Pinion, Marjorie.

Pinion, Marjorie & Pinion, Frank B., eds. The Collected Sonnets of Charles (Tennyson) Turner. LC 87-12521. 256p. 1988. text ed. 35.00 (*0-312-01193-8*) St Martin.

Pink, A. W. & Tell. Camino a la Oracion Ferviente. 200p. 1994. 8.00 (*0-939125-68-4*) Evangelical Lit.

Pink, Arthur. El Anticristo: The Antichrist. (SPA.). 6.95 (*84-7228-835-8*, 220039, Pub. by Edit Clie SP) TSELF.

— Beneficios De la Lectura De la Biblia: Benefits of Bible Reading. (SPA.). 4.25 (*84-7228-621-5*, 220095, Pub. by Edit Clie SP) TSELF.

Pink, Arthur W. The Antichrist. LC 87-29898. 308p. 1988. pap. 11.99 (*0-8254-3539-0*) Kregel.

— The Application of the Scriptures: A Refutation of Dispensationalism. pap. 2.99 (*0-87377-071-4*) GAM Pubns.

— Los Atributos de Dios. 131p. 1990. reprint ed. 4.95 (*0-85151-540-1*) Banner of Truth.

— Attributes of God. 1988. pap. 4.99 (*0-8010-6989-0*) Baker Bk.

— The Beatitudes & the Lord's Prayer. 144p. 1995. reprint ed. pap. 7.99 (*0-8010-7142-9*) Baker Bk.

— Christian Liberty. pap. 0.99 (*0-87377-072-2*) GAM Pubns.

— The Christians in Romans Seven. pap. 0.99 (*0-87377-073-0*) GAM Pubns.

— Comfort for Christians. (Summit Bks.). 122p. 1976. pap. 4.99 (*0-8010-7109-7*) Baker Bk.

— Comfort for Christians. pap. 3.99 (*0-87377-074-9*) GAM Pubns.

— Divine Healing. pap. 0.99 (*0-87377-954-1*) GAM Pubns.

— Divine Inspiration of the Bible. pap. 3.99 (*0-87377-075-7*) GAM Pubns.

— Exposition of Hebrews. LC 54-11076. 1954. 39.99 (*0-8010-6857-6*) Baker Bk.

— Exposition on the Gospel of John, 4 Vols. in 1. 1968. 49. 99 (*0-310-31180-2*, 10566) Zondervan.

— An Exposition on the Sermon on the Mount. 1993. pap. 12.99 (*0-8010-7075-9*) Baker Bk.

— A Fourfold Salvation. pap. 1.59 (*0-87377-953-3*) GAM Pubns.

— Gleanings from Elisha. LC 79-181591. 288p. (C). 1972. pap. 16.99 (*0-8024-3000-7*) Moody.

— Gleanings from Paul. LC 67-14379. (C). 1967. 16.99 (*0-8024-2965-3*); pap. 12.95 (*0-8024-3005-8*) Moody.

P Q

— Gleanings from the Scriptures. LC 73-80942. (C). 1970. pap. 16.99 (*0-8024-3006-6*) Moody.
— Gleanings in Exodus. (C). 1964. pap. 16.99 (*0-8024-3001-5*) Moody.
— Gleanings in Genesis. (C). 1922. pap. 16.99 (*0-8024-3002-3*) Moody.
— Gleanings in Joshua. LC 64-20991. (C). 1964. pap. 16.99 (*0-8024-3004-X*) Moody.
— Gleanings in the Godhead. LC 75-15760. 256p. (C). 1975. 13.99 (*0-8024-2977-7*); pap. 14.99 (*0-8024-3003-1*) Moody.
— Gleanings Series, 7 bks., Set. pap. 113.93 (*0-8024-9582-6*) Moody.
— A Guide to Fervent Prayer. White, Donald R., ed. 224p. 1995. reprint ed. pap. 9.99 (*0-8010-7141-0*) Baker Bk.
— The Holy Spirit. LC 70-107078. 200p. 1995. pap. 7.99 (*0-8010-7041-4*) Baker Bk.
— Letters of A. W. Pink. 1978. pap. 4.95 (*0-85151-262-3*) Banner of Truth.
— The Life of David, 2 vols. in one. (Giant Summit Bks.). 768p. 1981. reprint ed. pap. 19.99 (*0-8010-7061-9*) Baker Bk.
— The Life of Elijah. 313p. 1991. reprint ed. pap. 10.95 (*0-85151-041-8*) Banner of Truth.
— New Birth. pap. 0.99 (*0-87377-076-5*) GAM Pubns.
— Practical Christianity. 232p. 1995. pap. 9.99 (*0-8010-6990-4*) Baker Bk.
— Profiting from the Word. 1977. pap. 5.50 (*0-85151-032-9*) Banner of Truth.
— The Sovereignty of God. 1984. pap. 12.99 (*0-8010-7088-0*) Baker Bk.
— The Sovereignty of God. 1976. pap. 6.50 (*0-85151-133-3*) Banner of Truth.
— Studies in the Scriptures, 1946. 1982. pap. 13.95 (*0-85151-346-8*) Banner of Truth.
— Studies in the Scriptures, 1947. 298p. 1982. pap. 13.95 (*0-85151-347-6*) Banner of Truth.
— The Ten Commandments. 80p. 1995. reprint ed. pap. 6.99 (*0-8010-7140-2*) Baker Bk.
— Tithing. pap. 0.99 (*0-87377-077-3*) GAM Pubns.
— La Vida de Elias. 360p. (SPA.). 1992. reprint ed. pap. 10.95 (*0-85151-424-3*) Banner of Truth.
Pink, Brenda. Twenty-Third Psalm. 1993. pap. 3.99 (*0-529-10029-0*) World Bible.
Pink, Brenda, ed. see Pink, Michael.
Pink, E. & Barhta, L., eds. The Metallurgy of Doped Non-Sag Tungsten. 330p. 1989. 75.75 (*1-85166-390-8*) Elsevier.
***Pink Floyd.** Pink Floyd: Division Bell GT Tab Edition. 1994. 29.95 (*0-8256-1409-0*, AM92188) Omnibus NY.
Pink, Louis H. Gaynor, the Tammany Mayor Who Swallowed the Tiger: Lawyer, Judge, Philosopher. LC 77-124251. (Select Bibliographies Reprint Ser.). 1977. reprint ed. 20.95 (*0-8369-5439-4*) Ayer.
— The New Day in Housing. LC 73-11941. (Metropolitan America Ser.). (Illus.). 262p. 1974. reprint ed. 18.95 (*0-405-05410-6*) Ayer.
Pink, Marilyn M., ed. see Jobe, Frank W.
Pink, Matthew. Paterson's Licensing Acts, 1993. 101th ed. 1993. 230.00 (*0-406-01561-9*) Butterworth Legal Pubs.
***Pink, Michael.** His Little Instruction Book. 160p. (Orig.). 1995. pap. 5.99 (*0-529-10393-1*) World Bible.
— Mosaic Series Beatitudes. 1993. pap. 5.99 (*1-877994-14-6*) Hidden Manna.
— Mosaic Series Lords Prayers. 1993. pap. 5.99 (*1-877994-02-2*) Hidden Manna.
— Mosaic Series Twenty-Third Psalm. 1993. pap. 5.99 (*1-877994-12-X*) Hidden Manna.
— Spiritual Warfare. Pink, Brenda, ed. (Orig.). 1993. pap. 2.99 (*0-529-10016-9*) World Bible.
Pink, Michael, ed. The Bible Incorporated (in Your Life, Job & Business) 1988. 5.99 (*0-529-10010-X*) World Bible.
— Tough Questions, Straight Answers. 1991. pap. 5.99 (*0-8024-8526-X*) Moody.
— The Words in Red. 3.99 (*0-529-10009-6*) World Bible.
Pink, Michael Q. The Bible Incorporated: In Your Life, Job & Business. 320p. 1988. 19.95 (*0-685-74042-0*); Burgundy. write for info. (*0-9621491-0-1*); Mauve. write for info. (*0-9621491-2-8*); Gray. write for info. (*0-9621491-3-6*) Hidden Manna.
— The Words in Red: The Teachings of Christ Compiled. 96p. (Orig.). (C). 1989. pap. 3.95 (*1-877994-01-4*) Hidden Manna.
Pink, William, ed. see Corbett, H. Dickson & Wilson, Bruce L.
Pink, William, ed. see Fox, Thomas.
Pink, William, jt. auth. see Nobli, George W.
Pink, William T., et al, eds. Effective Staff Development for School Change. (Interpretive Perspectives on Education & Policy Ser.). 320p. (C). 1992. text ed. 55.00 (*0-89391-832-6*); pap. text ed. 24.50 (*0-89391-938-1*) Ablex Pub.
Pink, William T., ed. see Corson, David.
Pink, William T., ed. see Kanpol, Barry.
Pink, William T., jt. ed. see Noblit, George W.
Pink, William T., ed. see Tesconi, Charles A.
***Pinkal, Manfred.** Logic & Lexicon: The Semantics of the Indefinite. LC 95-3466. (Studies in Linguistics & Philosophy: Vol. 56). 380p. (C). 1995. lib. bdg. 93.00 (*0-7923-3387-X*) Kluwer Ac.
Pinkard, Terry. Democractic Liberalism & Social Union. LC 86-23088. 240p. 1987. 32.95 (*0-87722-458-7*) Temple U Pr.
— Hegel's Dialectic: The Explanation of Possibility. 272p. (C). 1988. 37.95 (*0-87722-570-2*) Temple U Pr.
— Hegel's Phenomenology: The Sociality of Reason. 496p. (C). 1994. 59.95 (*0-521-45300-3*) Cambridge U Pr.
Pinkard, Terry, jt. ed. see Englehardt, H. Tristram, Jr.
Pinkard, Terry P., jt. ed. see Beauchamp, Tom L.
Pinkau, K. & Sprecher, eds. Umweltstandards: Grundlagen, Tatsachen und Bewertungen Am Beispiel Des Strahlenrisikos. (Akademie der Wissenschaften zu Berlin, Forschungsbericht Ser.: No. 2). xv, 494p. (GER.). (C). 1992. lib. bdg. 75.40 (*3-11-013450-0*) De Gruyter.
Pinkau, K., ed. see NATO Advanced Study Institute Staff.
Pinkava, J. Handbook of Laboratory Units Operations for Chemists & Chemical Engineers. 470p. 1970. text ed. 297.00 (*0-677-60600-1*) Gordon & Breach.
Pinkel, Benjamin. Consciousness, Matter & Energy: The Emergence of Mind in Nature. 221p. 1992. 20.00 (*0-9635403-0-0*) Turover Pr.
— The Existential Adventure: The Roles of Science & Belief. LC 75-36964. 156p. 1976. 12.50 (*0-87516-210-X*) DeVorss.
Pinkel, Sheila & Chang, Kou. Kou Chang's Story. (Artists' Book Ser.). (Illus.). 128p. (Orig.). 1992. pap. 16.00 (*0-89822-103-X*) Visual Studies.
Pinkele, Carl F. & Pollis, Adamantia, eds. The Contemporary Mediterranean World. LC 82-16658. 394p. 1983. text ed. 59.95 (*0-275-91058-X*, C1058, Praeger Pubs) Greenwood.
Pinkele, Carl F., jt. auth. see Musto, Stefan A.
Pinker, Robert. Social Work in an Enterprise Society. 192p. (C). 1991. text ed. 59.95 (*0-415-04491-X*, A5535) Routledge.
Pinker, Steven. The Language Instinct. LC 93-31842. 1994. 23.00 (*0-688-12141-1*) Morrow.
— The Language Instinct: How the Mind Creates Language. 496p. 1995. pap. 14.00 (*0-06-097651-9*, PL) HarpC.
— Language Learnability & Language Development. (Cognitive Science Ser.: No. 7). 456p. 1987. pap. 16.95 (*0-674-51055-0*) HUP.
— Learnability & Cognition: The Acquisition of Argument Structure. (Learning, Development, & Conceptual Change). 296p. 1989. 40.00 (*0-262-16111-7*) MIT Pr.
— Visual Cognition. (Computational Models of Cognition & Perception Ser.). 296p. 1985. pap. 22.50 (*0-262-16103-6*, Bradford Bks) MIT Pr.
Pinker, Steven & Mehler, Jacques, eds. Connections & Symbols. (Cognition Special Issue Ser.). 272p. (Orig.). 1988. pap. 18.50x (*0-262-66064-4*, Bradford Bks) MIT Pr.
— Learnability & Cognition: The Acquisition of Argument Structure. (Illus.). 428p. 1991. pap. 20.00 (*0-262-66073-3*, Bradford Bks) MIT Pr.
Pinkert, Carl A., ed. Transgenic Animal Technology: A Laboratory Handbook. (Illus.). 364p. 1994. pap. 59.95 (*0-12-557165-8*) Acad Pr.
Pinkert, James R. & Wear, Larry L. Operating Systems: Concepts, Policies & Mechanisms. 352p. 1988. boxed, text ed. 69.00 (*0-13-638073-5*) P-H.
Pinkert-Saltzer, Inke, ed. German Hymns & Songs. (German Library: Vol. 53). 324p. 1995. 29.50 (*0-8264-0730-7*); pap. text ed. 14.95 (*0-8264-0731-5*) Continuum.
Pinkerton, A. Molly Maguires & the Detectives. LC 72-2092. (American History & Americana Ser.: No. 47). 1972. 75.00 (*0-8383-1289-6*) M S G Haskell Hse.
Pinkerton, Allan. Criminal Reminiscences & Detective Sketches. LC 70-109632. (Select Bibliographies Reprint Ser.). 1977. 30.95 (*0-8369-5241-3*) Ayer.
— Criminal Reminiscences & Detective Sketches. 1972. reprint ed. 25.00 (*0-8422-8104-5*) Irvington.
— The Expressman & the Detective. LC 75-32775. (Literature of Mystery & Detection Ser.). (Illus.). 1976. reprint ed. 24.95 (*0-405-07894-3*) Ayer.
— Professional Thieves & the Detective. LC 73-156031. reprint ed. 35.00 (*0-404-09133-4*) AMS Pr.
— The Spy of the Rebellion. LC 89-33081. (Illus.). 712p. 1989. 40.00 (*0-8032-3686-7*) U of Nebr Pr.
— The Spy of the Rebellion: A True History of the Spy System of the United States Army. (Illus.). 734p. 1991. reprint ed. pap. 35.00 (*1-55613-441-X*) Heritage Bk.
— Strikers, Communists, Tramps & Detectives. LC 79-90190. (Mass Violence in America Ser.). 1977. reprint ed. 32.95 (*0-405-01332-9*) Ayer.
— Thirty Years a Detective: A Thorough & Comprehensive Expose of Criminal Practices of All Grades & Classes. (Criminology, Law Enforcement, & Social Problems Ser.: No. 154). (Illus.). 1975. reprint ed. Witn Intro. Essay & Index Added. 28.00 (*0-87585-154-1*) Patterson Smith.
Pinkerton, Brian R., jt. auth. see Butler, David.
Pinkerton, C. R., jt. ed. see Plowman, P. N.
Pinkerton, C. R., jt. auth. see Plowman, P. W.
Pinkerton, C. R., et al. Paediatric Oncology in Practice. (Illus.). 256p. 1993. 49.50 (*0-412-41080-X*) Chapman & Hall.
Pinkerton, Edward C. Word for Word. LC 77-20391. xxxii, 432p. 1982. 39.95 (*0-685-05243-5*) Verbatim Bks.
Pinkerton, Elaine. Santa Fe on Foot: Running, Walking & Bicycling Adventures in the City Different. rev. ed. Polese, Richard, ed. LC 86-60510. (Cota Editions Ser.: No. 1). (Illus.). 144p. 1994. pap. 9.95 (*0-943734-25-8*) Ocean Tree Bks.
— The Santa Fe Trail by Bicycle: A Historic Adventure. (Illus.). 176p. 1993. pap. 12.95 (*1-878610-24-4*) Red Crane Bks.
Pinkerton, Elizabeth, jt. auth. see Tsukamoto, Mary.
***Pinkerton, James P.** What Comes Next: The End of Big Government - & the New Paradigm Ahead. 356p. 1995. 21.95 (*0-7868-6105-3*) Hyperion.
Pinkerton, James R., jt. auth. see Hassinger, Edward W.
Pinkerton, John. In Care at Home: Parenting, the State & Civil Society. 180p. 1994. 54.95 (*1-85628-536-7*, Pub. by Avebury Pub UK) Ashgate Pub Co.
Pinkerton, John, ed. Ancient Scottish Poems, Never Before in Print, 2 Vols. LC 77-144530. reprint ed. Set. 35.00 (*0-404-08677-2*); reprint ed. 18.00 (*0-685-73102-2*) AMS Pr.
— Ancient Scottish Poems, Never Before in Print, 2 Vols, 1. LC 77-144530. reprint ed. 18.00 (*0-404-08678-0*) AMS Pr.
— Ancient Scottish Poems, Never Before in Print, 2 Vols, 2. LC 77-144530. reprint ed. 18.00 (*0-404-08679-9*) AMS Pr.
— Scotish Poems, 3 vols., 1. LC 70-144531. reprint ed. 55.00 (*0-685-73146-4*) AMS Pr.
— Scotish Poems, 3 vols., 2. LC 70-144531. reprint ed. 55.00 (*0-685-73147-2*) AMS Pr.
— Scotish Poems, 3 vols., 3. LC 70-144531. reprint ed. 55.00 (*0-685-73148-0*) AMS Pr.
— Scotish Poems, 3 vols., Set. LC 70-144531. reprint ed. 165.00 (*0-404-08680-2*) AMS Pr.
— Select Scottish Ballads, 2 vols. enl. ed. reprint ed. write for info. (*0-318-50712-9*) AMS Pr.
— Select Scottish Ballads, 2 vols, 1. enl. ed. LC 72-144529. reprint ed. 10.50 (*0-404-08675-6*) AMS Pr.
— Select Scottish Ballads, 2 vols, 2. enl. ed. LC 72-144529. reprint ed. 10.50 (*0-404-08676-4*) AMS Pr.
— Select Scottish Ballads, 2 vols, Set. 2nd enl. ed. LC 72-144529. reprint ed. 20.00 (*0-404-08674-8*) AMS Pr.
Pinkerton, Linda F. The Writer's Law Primer. 1990. pap. 12.95 (*1-55821-085-7*) Lyons & Burford.
Pinkerton, Linda F. & Guardalabene, John T. The Art Law Primer. 224p. 1988. pap. 9.95 (*1-55821-002-4*) Lyons & Burford.
Pinkerton, P., tr. see Puccini, Giacomo.
Pinkerton, P. H. & Reis, M. D., eds. Genetic Markers of Haematological Malignancy. (Illus.). iv, 94p. 1990. 38.50 (*3-8055-5341-2*) S Karger.
Pinkerton, Percy, tr. see Artsybashev, Mikhail P.
Pinkerton, Percy, tr. see Masuccio, et al.
Pinkerton, Philip. Childhood Disorder: A Psychosomatic Approach. LC 74-18488. (Illus.). 192p. 1975. text ed. 36.50 (*0-231-03955-7*) Col U Pr.
Pinkerton, Robert. Russia: or Miscellaneous Observations on the Past & Present State of That Country & Its Inhabitants. LC 74-115579. (Russia Observed, Series I). 1970. reprint ed. 28.95 (*0-405-03058-4*) Ayer.
Pinkerton, Robert, tr. see Metropolitan Philaret of Moscow Staff.
Pinkerton, Scott. Mariposa Courthouse: "A Shrine to Justice" (Illus.). 112p. 1989. pap. 5.95 (*0-685-29449-8*) Mariposa Heritage Pr.
Pinkerton, Sharon. German Wirehaired Pointers Today. (Illus.). 160p. 1994. 25.95 (*0-87605-182-4*) Howell Bk.
Pinkerton, Steven D., jt. auth. see Abramson, Paul R.
Pinkerton, Steven D., jt. ed. see Abramson, Paul R.
Pinkerton, SueEllen & Schroeder, Patricia. Commitment to Excellence: Developing a Professional Nursing Staff. 320p. (C). 1987. 62.00 (*0-87189-882-9*) Aspen Pub.
Pinkerton, William A. Train Robberies, Train Robbers, & the Holdup Men. LC 74-15748. (Popular Culture in America Ser.). (Illus.). 88p. 1980. reprint ed. 15.95 (*0-405-06383-0*) Ayer.
Pinkett, Harold T. Gifford Pinchot: Private & Public Forester. LC 74-76830. 180p. reprint ed. pap. 51.30 (*0-317-28983-7*, 2020234) Bks Demand.
Pinkevich, A. & Amelin, B. Diccionario Espanol-Ruso de le Prospeccion y Refinacion del Petroleo. Dobriansky, A. F., ed. 424p. (RUS & SPA.). 1966. 39.95 (*0-8288-6705-4*, S-37368) Fr & Eur.
Pinkham, James R., et al, eds. Pediatric Dentistry: Infancy Through Adolescence. 2nd ed. LC 92-49086. (Illus.). 576p. 1993. text ed. 63.00 (*0-7216-4695-6*) Saunders.
Pinkham, Joan, tr. see Cesaire, Aime.
Pinkham, Joan, tr. see Nizan, Paul.
Pinkham, Joan, tr. see Troyat, Henri.
***Pinkham, Julia.** The InsectAlphabet Coloring Book. (NaturEncyclopedia Ser.). (Illus.). 48p. (Orig.). (J). (gr. 2 up). 1995. pap. 5.95 (*0-88045-134-3*) Stemmer Hse.
Pinkham, Linda, ed. see Bond, Ronald L.
Pinkham, Linda, ed. see Low, Robert J.
Pinkham, Linda, ed. see Powers, Dennis.
Pinkham, Mary E. Mary Ellen's Best of Helpful Hints, Bk. II. (Illus.). 144p. (Orig.). 1981. 4.50 (*0-941298-00-0*) M E Pinkham.
— Mary Ellen's Best of Helpful Hints Library. 1981. pap. 12.50 (*0-941298-03-5*) M E Pinkham.
— Mary Ellen's Best of Helpful Kitchen Hints. (Illus.). 144p. (Orig.). 1980. pap. 4.50 (*0-941298-01-9*) M E Pinkham.
— Mary Ellen's Clean House. 400p. 1993. 20.00 (*0-517-58823-4*, Crown) Crown Pub Group.
— Mary Ellen's Greatest Hints. 352p. 1990. mass mkt. 4.95 (*0-449-21714-0*, Crest) Fawcett.
— Mary Ellen's Help Yourself Diet Plan. 256p. 1985. pap. 2.95 (*0-317-29684-1*) St Martin.
— Mary Ellen's Wow! Ideas That Really Work. 150p. 1992. 6.95 (*0-9631933-0-9*) M Ellen Bks.
Pinkham, Mary Ellen. Mary Ellen's Best of Helpful Hints. (Orig.). 1983. mass mkt. 5.99 (*0-446-38121-7*) Warner Bks.
— Mary Ellen's Clean House. 1994. 12.00 (*0-517-88185-3*) Crown Pub Group.
Pinkney, Alphonso. Black Americans. 4th ed. 256p. 1992. pap. text ed. write for info. (*0-13-034240-8*) P-H.
— The Committed: White Activists in the Civil Rights Movement. 1968. 19.95x (*0-8084-0084-3*) NCUP.
— Lest We Forget: Howard Beach & Other Atrocities. 300p. (Orig.). (C). 1993. pap. 16.95 (*0-88378-088-7*) Third World.
— The Myth of Black Progress. LC 84-1912. 198p. 1986. pap. 14.95 (*0-521-31047-4*) Cambridge U Pr.
Pinkney, Alphonso & Woock, Roger R. Poverty & Politics in Harlem. 1970. 19.95 (*0-8084-0249-8*); pap. 15.95x (*0-8084-0250-1*) NCUP.
***Pinkney, Andrea D.** Alvin Ailey. LC 92-54865. (Illus.). 32p. (J). (gr. k-4). 1995. pap. 4.95 (*0-7868-1077-7*) Hyprn Ppbks.
— Dear Benjamin Banneker. LC 93-31162. (Illus.). (J). 1994. 14.95 (*0-15-200417-3*, Gulliver Bks) HarBrace.
— Hold Fast to Dreams. LC 94-32909. (Illus.). 112p. 1995. 15.00 (*0-688-12832-7*) Morrow Jr Bks.
— Seven Candles for Kwanzaa. LC 92-3698. (Illus.). 32p. (J). (gr. k up). 1993. 14.99 (*0-8037-1292-8*); lib. bdg. 14.89 (*0-8037-1293-6*) Dial Bks Young.
***Pinkney, Brian.** Jojo's Flying Side Kick. (J). 1995. write for info. (*0-671-88111-6*, S&S Bks Young Read) S&S Childrens.
— Max Found Two Sticks. LC 93-12525. (J). 1994. pap. 15.00 (*0-671-78776-4*, S&S Bks Young Read) S&S Childrens.
Pinkney, Brian J., jt. auth. see Wandelmaier, Roy.
Pinkney, David H. Decisive Years in France, 1840-1847. LC 85-43304. 248p. reprint ed. pap. 70.70 (*0-7837-1425-4*, 2041780) Bks Demand.
— The French Revolution of 1830. Halsey, F. D., tr. LC 72-39051. 407p. reprint ed. 116.00 (*0-8357-9498-9*, 2014875) Bks Demand.
Pinkney, David H., ed. see Brooks, Charles W.
Pinkney, David H., ed. see Bundy, Frank J.
Pinkney, David H., ed. see Burney, John M.
Pinkney, David H., jt. auth. see De Bertier de Sauvigny, G.
Pinkney, David H., ed. see Edmonson, James M.
Pinkney, David H., ed. see Hildreth, Martha.
Pinkney, David H., ed. see Nelms, Brenda.
Pinkney, David H., ed. see Segal, Paul H.
Pinkney, David H., ed. see Seid, Roberta P.
Pinkney, David H., ed. see Stein, Margot B.
Pinkney, Edward C. Poems. LC 72-4970. (Romantic Tradition in American Literature Ser.). 76p. 1972. reprint ed. 21.95 (*0-405-04640-5*) Ayer.
Pinkney, Gloria J. Back Home. LC 91-22610. (Illus.). 40p. (J). (gr. k-4). 1992. 15.00 (*0-8037-1168-9*); lib. bdg. 14.89 (*0-8037-1169-7*) Dial Bks Young.
Pinkney, Jerry, illus. The Adventures of Spider: West African Folk Tales. LC 92-444. (J). 1992. 7.95 (*0-316-05107-1*) Little.
— David's Songs: His Psalms & Their Story. LC 90-25459. 64p. (J). 1992. 17.00 (*0-8037-1058-5*); lib. bdg. 16.89 (*0-8037-1059-3*) Dial Bks Young.
— The Last Tales of Uncle Remus. LC 93-7531. (J). (ps-4). 1994. 18.99 (*0-8037-1303-7*); lib. bdg. 18.89 (*0-8037-1304-5*) Dial Bks Young.
— More Tales of Uncle Remus: Further Adventures of Brer Rabbit, His Friends, Enemies & Others. LC 86-32890. 160p. (J). (ps up). 1988. 15.95 (*0-8037-0419-4*); lib. bdg. 15.89 (*0-8037-0420-8*) Dial Bks Young.
— Rabbit Makes a Monkey of Lion: A Swahili Tale. 32p. (J). (ps-3). 1993. pap. 4.99 (*0-14-054593-X*) Puffin Bks.
Pinkney, Jerry, jt. auth. see Gibson, Barbara.
Pinkney, Nathaniel, illus. Conversation Games: Vol. I-People Times. 87p. (Orig.). (J). (ps-6). 1978. pap. 15.00 (*0-939632-17-9*) ILM.
— Conversation Games: Vol. II-Experiences. 87p. (Orig.). (J). (ps-6). 1978. pap. 15.00 (*0-939632-20-9*) ILM.
Pinkney, Robert. Democracy in the Third World. LC 93-16049. (Issues in Third World Politics Ser.). 182p. (C). 1994. pap. text ed. 17.95 (*1-55587-454-1*) Lynne Rienner.
— Right-Wing Military Government. (Twayne's Themes in Right-Wing Ideology & Politics Ser.: No. 3). 256p. (C). 1990. text ed. 30.95 (*0-8057-9554-5*, Twayne); pap. 16.95 (*0-8057-9555-3*, Twayne) Macmillan.
Pinkney, Tony. D. H. Lawrence & Modernism. LC 90-70151. 190p. (Orig.). (C). 1990. text ed. 26.00 (*0-87745-294-6*); pap. 13.95 (*0-87745-295-4*) U of Iowa Pr.
— Raymond Williams. 144p. 1991. 35.00 (*1-85411-047-0*, Pub. by Seren Bks UK); pap. 15.95 (*1-85411-048-9*, Pub. by Seren Bks UK) Dufour.
Pinkney, William, Jr. Life of William Pinkney. LC 75-75276. (Law, Politics & History Ser.). 1969. reprint ed. lib. bdg. 49.50 (*0-306-71307-1*) Da Capo.
Pinkoski, Jim. Discovered: Sodom & Gomorrah. (Illus.). 24p. (Orig.). 1992. 2.95 (*0-945383-40-1*) Teach Servs.
— Discovered: True! The Genesis Story of Creation. (Illus.). 32p. (Orig.). 1992. 2.95 (*0-945383-39-8*) Teach Servs.
Pinkowski, Ben, ed. Proceedings of the Twenty-Third Annual Simulation Symposium. LC 71-149514. (Illus.). 168p. 1990. pap. text ed. 48.00 (*0-8186-2067-6*, ANS23-1) Soc Computer Sim.
Pinkson, Tom. A Quest for Vision. 301p. 1976. pap. 12.50 (*0-318-37564-8*) Freeperson.
Pinkster, Harm. Latin Syntax & Semantics. (Romance Linguistics Ser.). 368p. 1990. 110.00 (*0-415-04682-3*, A4541) Routledge.
Pinkster, Harm, ed. Latin Linguistics & Linguistic Theory: Proceedings of the 1st. International Colloquium on Latin Linguistics. (Studies in Language Companion: 12). xviii, 307p. 1983. 71.00x (*90-272-3011-0*) Benjamins North Am.
Pinkster, Harm & Genee, Inge, eds. Unity in Diversity: Papers Presented to Simon C. Dik on His 50th Birthday. viii, 313p. (Orig.). (C). 1990. pap. text ed. 69.25 (*3-11-013353-9*) Mouton.
Pinksterboer, Hugo. The Cymbal Book. Mattingly, Rick, ed. 200p. 1993. pap. 24.95 (*0-7935-1920-9*, 06621763) H Leonard.
Pinkston. Care of the Elderly. (C). 1984. pap. 19.95 (*0-205-14449-7*, H4449) Allyn.
***Pinkston, Elizabeth & Lussier, Frances M.** Cleaning up the Department of Energy's Nuclear Weapons Complex. (Illus.). 78p. (Orig.). (C). 1994. pap. text ed. 45.00x (*0-7881-0895-6*) Diane Pub.
Pinkston, Elsie M., et al, eds. Effective Social Work Practice. LC 82-48057. (Jossey-Bass Social & Behavioral Science Ser.). 528p. reprint ed. pap. 150.50 (*0-8357-4915-0*, 2037845) Bks Demand.

An Asterisk (*) at the beginning of an entry indicates that the title is appearing in BIP for the first time.

Pinkston, Isabel. Seed-Sower for God's Kingdom. Loehr, Franklin, ed. LC 87-62134. (Illus.). 222p. (Orig.). 1987. pap. 7.25 (0-915151-14-6) Religious Res Pr.

Pinkston, Isabel, ed. see Church of Religious Research, Inc. Staff.

Pinkston, Isabel H. Understanding Homosexuality. Roberts, Helen, ed. LC 92-64453. (Researching the Soul with Dr. John Ser.: No. 3). 122p. (Orig.). 1993. pap. 5.95 (0-915151-17-0) Religious Res Pr.

Pinkston, Isabel H., ed. see Stone, Julita M.

Pinkston, Joan & Tipton, Nancy. Songs of Our Heritage. (Sound Forth Ser.). (Illus.). 80p. (Orig.). (YA). 1991. pap. 7.95 (0-89084-608-1) Bob Jones Univ Pr.

Pinkston, Joseph, jt. auth. see Cromie, Robert.

Pinkston, Oletha M. The Process of Regeneration: Change. LC 90-82451. 112p. (Orig.). 1991. pap. 9.95 (0-9627055-0-0) Pinkston.

Pinkston, Suzi. Grief Walk. Keithley, C. David, ed. (Illus.). 64p. (Orig.). 1992. pap. 6.95 (0-89896-199-8) Larksdale.

Pinkston, William S., Jr. With Wings As Eagles. (English Skills for Christian Schools Ser.). (Illus.). 127p. (J). (gr. 2). 1983. pap. 7.72 (0-89084-231-0) Bob Jones Univ Pr.

Pinkstone, William G. The Abrasive Ages. LC 74-23797. (Illus.). 136p. 1975. 10.00 (0-915010-01-1) Sutter House.

Pinksy, Robert, tr. see Dante Alighieri.

Pinkus, Alan. N-Widths in Approximation Theory. (Ergebnisse der Mathematik und Ihrer Grenzgebiete Ser.: Vol. 7). 300p. 1985. 89.00 (0-387-13638-X) Spr-Verlag.

Pinkus, Alan, jt. ed. see Nevai, Paul.

Pinkus, Allan M. On L1-Approximation. (Cambridge Tracts in Mathematics Ser.: No. 92). 250p. (C). 1989. 59.95 (0-521-36650-X) Cambridge U Pr.

Pinkus, Benjamin. The Jews of the Soviet Union: The History of a National Minority. (Cambridge Russian, Soviet & Post-Soviet Studies: No. 62). 416p. (C). 1990. pap. 24.95 (0-521-38926-7) Cambridge U Pr.

Pinkus, Benjamin, jt. auth. see Ingsborg, Fleischhauer.

Pinkus, Benjamin, jt. ed. see Troen, Selwyn I.

***Pinkus, Karen.** Bodily Regimes: Advertising under Italian Fascism. LC 94-37311. 1995. text ed. 49.95 (0-8166-2562-X); pap. text ed. 19.95 (0-8166-2563-8) U of Minn Pr.

Pinkus, Karen, tr. see Barilli, Renato.

Pinkus, Karen E., tr. see Agamben, Giorgio.

Pinkus, Michael. Pressure Point Therapy: The Complete Do-It-Yourself. LC 94-94008. (At Home Treatment Manual Ser.). (Illus.). 58p. (Orig.). 1994. pap. 39.95 (0-9640393-0-3) Alternat Hlth.

Pinkus, O. & Wilcock, D. F., eds. Strategy for Energy Conservation Through Tribology, Bk. No. H00109. 2nd ed. 1982. 20.00 (0-685-37585-4) ASME.

Pinkus, Oscar. The House of Ashes. rev. ed. LC 89-5220. 272p. 1991. reprint ed. text ed. 24.95 (0-912756-23-3); reprint ed. pap. text ed. 9.95 (0-912756-24-1) Union Coll.

— The Son of Zelman. 176p. 1982. 19.95 (0-87073-548-9); pap. 11.95 (0-87073-549-7) Schenkman Bks Inc.

Pinkus, Oscar, ed. Thermal Aspects of Fluid Film Tribology. 515p. 1990. 94.00 (0-7918-0011-3, 800113) ASME Pr.

Pinkus, Sue, jt. auth. see Robertson, Bruce.

Pinkus, Sue, jt. auth. see Robertson, Jane.

***Pinkwater, Daniel.** The Afterlife Diet. LC 94-21540. 1995. 21.00 (0-679-41936-5) Random.

— Attila the Pun: A Magic Moscow Story. (Illus.). (J). (gr. 3-6). 1995. pap. 3.95 (0-689-71764-4, Aladdin Paperbacks) S&S Childrens.

— Aunt Lulu. LC 88-1736. (Illus.). 32p. (J). (gr. k-3). 1988. text ed. 13.95 (0-02-774661-5, Mac Bks Young Read) S&S Childrens.

— Aunt Lulu. LC 90-39981. (Illus.). 32p. (J). (gr. k-3). 1991. reprint ed. pap. 3.95 (0-689-71413-0, Aladdin Paperbacks) S&S Childrens.

— Author's Day. LC 92-18154. (Illus.). 32p. (J). (gr. k-3). 1993. text ed. 13.95 (0-02-774642-9, Mac Bks Young Read) S&S Childrens.

— Borgel. LC 89-13421. 176p. (YA). (gr. 5 up). 1990. text ed. 13.95 (0-02-774671-2, Mac Bks Young Read) S&S Childrens.

— Borgel. LC 91-42914. 176p. (J). (gr. 3-7). 1992. reprint ed. pap. 3.95 (0-689-71620-6, Aladdin Paperbacks) S&S Childrens.

— Doodle Flute. LC 90-6622. (Illus.). 32p. (J). (gr. k-3). 1991. text ed. 13.95 (0-02-774635-6, Mac Bks Young Read) S&S Childrens.

— Goose Night. LC 94-40898. (Illus.). (J). 1996. lib. bdg. 9.99 (0-679-94654-3); pap. 2.99 (0-679-84654-9) Random.

— Guys from Space. LC 88-13485. (Illus.). 32p. (J). (gr. k-3). 1989. text ed. 13.95 (0-02-774672-0, Mac Bks Young Read) S&S Childrens.

— Guys from Space. LC 91-20100. (Illus.). 32p. (J). (gr. k-3). 1992. reprint ed. pap. 3.95 (0-689-71590-0, Aladdin Paperbacks) S&S Childrens.

— I Was a Second Grade Werewolf. (J). (gr. 1-3). 1986. 19.95 (0-87499-010-6); 27.95 (0-87499-009-2); pap. 12.95 (0-87499-008-4) Live Oak Media.

— Jolly Roger: A Dog of Hoboken. LC 84-12629. (Illus.). 64p. (J). (gr. 4-6). 1984. 13.95 (0-688-03898-0) Lothrop.

— The Magic Moscow. LC 92-27150. (Illus.). 64p. (J). (gr. 3-7). 1993. pap. 3.95 (0-689-71710-5, Aladdin Paperbacks) S&S Childrens.

— The Muffin Fiend. LC 85-10944. (Illus.). 48p. (J). (gr. 3-7). 1986. 12.95 (0-688-04274-0); lib. bdg. 12.88 (0-688-04275-9) Lothrop.

— Ned Feldman, Space Pirate. LC 93-40893. (Illus.). 48p. (J). (gr. k-3). 1994. text ed. 14.95 (0-02-774633-X, Mac Bks Young Read) S&S Childrens.

— The Phantom of the Lunch Wagon. LC 92-3051. (Illus.). 32p. (J). (gr. k up). 1992. text ed. 13.95 (0-02-774641-0, Mac Bks Young Read) S&S Childrens.

— Spaceburger: A Kevin Spoon & Mason Mintz Story. LC 93-6658. (Illus.). 32p. (J). (gr. k-3). 1993. text ed. 13.95 (0-02-774643-7, Mac Bks Young Read) S&S Childrens.

— Tooth-Gnasher Superflash. LC 89-18207. (Illus.). 32p. (J). (gr. k-3). 1990. pap. 3.95 (0-689-71407-6, Aladdin Paperbacks) S&S Childrens.

— Tooth-Gnasher Superflash. 2nd ed. LC 89-18207. (Illus.). 32p. (J). (gr. k-3). 1990. reprint ed. lib. bdg. 13.95 (0-02-774655-0, Mac Bks Young Read) S&S Childrens.

— Wempires. LC 90-46925. (Illus.). 32p. (J). (gr. k-3). 1991. text ed. 13.95 (0-02-774411-6, Mac Bks Young Read) S&S Childrens.

— The Wuggie Norple Story. LC 88-878. (Illus.). 40p. (J). (gr. k-4). 1988. pap. 4.50 (0-689-71257-X, Aladdin Paperbacks) S&S Childrens.

Pinkwater, Daniel M. Big Orange Splot. (J). (ps-3). 1993. pap. 3.95 (0-590-44510-3) Scholastic Inc.

— Big Orange Splot. (Illus.). 32p. (J). 1992. reprint ed. 12.95 (0-8038-9346-9) Hastings.

— Blue Moose & Return of the Blue Moose. 1995. 17.50 (0-8446-6831-1) Peter Smith.

— Blue Moose, & Return of the Moose. LC 93-22614. (Illus.). 112p. (Orig.). (J). (gr. 2-7). 1993. pap. 3.99 (0-679-84717-0, Bullseye Bks) Random Bks Yng Read.

— Chicago Days, Hoboken Nights. 1991. 17.26 (0-201-52359-0) Addison-Wesley.

— Chicago Days, Hoboken Nights. (Illus.). 176p. 1992. pap. 8.61 (0-201-63225-X) Addison-Wesley.

— Fat Men from Space. (Illus.). 64p. (J). (gr. 4-6). 1980. pap. 3.25 (0-440-44542-6, YB) Dell.

— Hoboken Chicken Emergency. LC 76-41910. (Illus.). 94p. (J). (gr. k-3). 1977. pap. 4.95 (0-671-66447-6, S&S Bks Young Read) S&S Childrens.

— Hoboken Chicken Emergency. LC 76-41910. (Illus.). 94p. (J). (gr. k-3). 1990. pap. 12.95 (0-671-73980-8, S&S Bks Young Read) S&S Childrens.

— I Was a Second Grade Werewolf. LC 82-17715. (Unicorn Paperbacks Ser.). (Illus.). 32p. (J). (ps-2). 1985. pap. 3.95 (0-525-44194-8, DCB) Dutton Child Bks.

— Lizard Music. 160p. 1988. mass mkt. 3.99 (0-553-15605-5, Skylark) Bantam.

— Mush, a Dog from Space. LC 94-29212. (Illus.). (J). 1995. write for info. (0-02-774634-8) Macmillan.

— Roger's Umbrella. LC 81-2294. (Illus.). 32p. (J). (gr. 1-3). 1982. 11.95 (0-525-38555-X, DCB) Dutton Child Bks.

— Roger's Umbrella. LC 81-2294. (Unicorn Paperbacks Ser.). (Illus.). 32p. (J). (gr. 1-3). 1985. pap. 3.95 (0-525-44223-5, DCB) Dutton Child Bks.

— The Snarkout Boys & the Avocado of Death. Bd. with Avocado of Death. 160p. 1983. Set pap. 2.50 (0-451-15852-0, Sig Vista) NAL-Dutton.

— The Snarkout Boys & the Baconburg Horror. (J). 1985. pap. 2.50 (0-451-13581-4, Sig Vista) NAL-Dutton.

— Young Adults. (Illus.). 192p. (Orig.). 1991. mass mkt. 3.99 (0-8125-1519-6) Tor Bks.

Pinkwater, Daniel M., jt. auth. see Pinkwater, Jill.

Pinkwater, Jill. Buffalo Brenda. LC 88-31929. 208p. (J). (gr. 5-9). 1989. text ed. 14.95 (0-02-774631-3, Mac Bks Young Read) S&S Childrens.

— Buffalo Brenda. LC 91-14806. 208p. (J). (gr. 3-7). 1992. reprint ed. pap. 3.95 (0-689-71586-2, Aladdin Paperbacks) S&S Childrens.

— Mister Fred. 160p. (J). (gr. 5-8). 1994. 15.99 (0-525-44778-4) Dutton Child Bks.

— Tails of the Bronx: A Tale of the Bronx. LC 90-48914. 208p. (J). (gr. 3-7). 1991. lib. bdg. 14.95 (0-02-774652-6, Mac Bks Young Read) S&S Childrens.

— Tails of the Bronx: A Tale of the Bronx. LC 92-20623. 208p. (J). (gr. 3-7). 1993. pap. 3.95 (0-689-71671-0, Aladdin Paperbacks) S&S Childrens.

Pinkwater, Jill & Pinkwater, Daniel M. Superpuppy: How to Choose, Raise & Train the Best Possible Dog for You. LC 76-8825. (Illus.). 208p. (J). (gr. 6 up). 1982. pap. 7.95 (0-89919-084-7, Clarion Bks) HM.

Pinloche, A. Dictionnaire Francais-Allemand, Deutsch-Franzosisch. 805p. (FRE & GER.). pap. 6.50 (0-7859-0817-X, M-9043) Fr & Eur.

***Pinn.** Why Lord? Suffering & Evil in Black Theology. 256p. 1995. 24.95 (0-8264-0854-0) Continuum.

Pinnacle Communications Staff. Managing a LAN. Jonas, Jacqueline & Menges, Patricia A., eds. (Illus.). 160p. (Orig.). (C). 1990. pap. text ed. 245.00 (0-917792-80-7) OneOnOne Comp Trng.

Pinnell, Norma L., ed. Nursing Pharmacology. LC 94-20441. 1995. text ed. write for info. (0-7216-6482-2) Saunders.

Pinnell, Norma N. & De Meneses, Mary. The Nursing Process: Theory, Application & Related Processes. 432p. 1986. pap. text ed. 30.95 (0-8385-7036-4, A7036-5) Appleton & Lange.

Pinnell, Richard. The Rioplatnense Guitar: The Early Guitar & It's Context in Argentina & Uruguay, Vol. 1. (Illus.). 500p. (Orig.). (C). 1993. 45.00 (0-933224-42-7); pap. 35.00 (0-933224-43-5) Bold Strummer Ltd.

***Pinnell, Robert P.** A Colorimetric Determination of Aspirin in Commercial Preparations. Neidig, H. A., ed. (Modular Laboratory Program in Chemistry Ser.). 12p. (C). 1989. pap. text ed. 1.25x (0-87540-360-3) Chem Educ Res.

Pinnell, William H. Theatrical Scene Painting: A Lesson Guide. LC 86-15500. (Illus.). 160p. (Orig.). (C). 1987. pap. 24.95 (0-8093-1332-4) S Ill U Pr.

Pinner, Felix. Emil Rathenau & das Elektrische Zeitalter. Wilkins, Mira, ed. LC 76-29777. (European Business Ser.). 1977. reprint ed. lib. bdg. 35.95 (0-405-09789-1) Ayer.

Pinner, Frank A., et al. Old Age & Political Behavior: A Case Study. Stein, Leon, ed. LC 79-8678. (Growing Old Ser.). (Illus.). 1980. reprint ed. lib. bdg. 35.95 (0-405-12796-0) Ayer.

Pinner, Mary T. & Shuard, Hilary. In-Service Education in Primary Mathematics. 208p. 1985. pap. 25.00 (0-335-15023-3, Open Univ Pr) Taylor & Francis.

Pinner, S. H., ed. Weathering & Degradation of Plastics. 144p. 1966. text ed. 105.00 (0-677-11830-9) Gordon & Breach.

***Pinney.** Illustrated Veterinary Guide for Dogs, Cats, Birds, & Exotic Pets. (Illus.). 1995. pap. text ed. 19.95 (0-07-050179-3) TAB Bks.

***Pinney, Chris C.** Caring for Your Older Dog. LC 95-6756. 1995. write for info. (0-8120-9149-3) Barron.

— Illustrated Veterinary Guide for Dogs, Cats, Birds & Exotic Pets. 512p. 1992. 29.95 (0-8306-1986-0) TAB Bks.

Pinney, Christopher. Guide to Home Pet Grooming. 144p. 1990. pap. 8.95 (0-8120-4298-0) Barron.

Pinney, Edward C. Orthopaedic Nursing. 6th ed. (Illus.). 368p. 1983. text ed. 18.95 (0-7216-0933-3) Saunders.

***Pinney, Edward L., Jr.** A First Group Psychotherapy Book. 222p. 1995. pap. 30.00 (1-56821-617-3) Aronson.

Pinney, Geoff, jt. auth. see Tarring, Trevor.

Pinney, Peter. The Barbarians: A Soldier's New Guinea Diary. (Orig.). 1989. pap. 15.95 (0-7022-2158-9, Pub. by Univ Queensland Pr AT) Intl Spec Bk.

— The Glass Cannon: A Bougainville Diary 1944-45. 1991. pap. 15.95 (0-7022-2329-8, Pub. by Univ Queensland Pr AT) Intl Spec Bk.

Pinney, Thomas. A History of Wine in America: From the Beginnings to Prohibition. 1989. 50.00 (0-520-06224-8) U CA Pr.

— A Short Handbook & Style Sheet. 58p. (Orig.). (C). 1977. pap. text ed. 8.00 (0-15-580925-3) HB Coll Pubs.

Pinney, Thomas, ed. The Letters of Rudyard Kipling. LC 90-70525. (Illus.). 400p. 1991. text ed. 44.95 (0-87745-306-3); text ed. 44.95 (0-87745-305-5) U of Iowa Pr.

— The Letters of Rudyard Kipling, 2 vols., Set. 80.00 (0-685-39466-2) U of Iowa Pr.

— The Letters of Rudyard Kipling Vol. 3: 1900-10. LC 90-70525. (Illus.). 376p. 1995. text ed. 49.95 (0-87745-495-7) U of Iowa Pr.

Pinney, Thomas, ed. see Kipling, Rudyard.

Pinney, Thomas, ed. see Macaulay, Thomas B.

Pinney, Tor. Outfitting the Modern Cruising Sailboat. 1994. 19.95 (0-930030-79-6) Western Marine Ent.

Pinney, William E. & McWilliams, Donald B. Management Science: An Introduction to Quantitative Analysis for Management. 2nd ed. 620p. (C). 1990. text ed. 40.50 (0-06-045229-3) HarpCollege.

***Pinney, William E. & McWilliams, Donald B.** Management Science: An Introduction to Quantitative Analysis for Management. 2nd ed. (Illus.). xvii, 620p. 1987. 29.95 (0-06-350589-4) Valian Assocs.

Pinnick, Alfred W., jt. auth. see Middlebrook, Stanley M.

Pinnington, Ashly. Using Video in Training & Education. 1991. pap. text ed. 24.95 (0-07-707384-3) McGraw.

Pinnock, Chuck H. & Brown, Delwin. Theological Crossfire: An Evangelical-Liberal Dialogue. 256p. 1991. pap. 14.99 (0-310-51441-X) Zondervan.

Pinnock, Clark, et al. The Openness of God: A Biblical Challenge to the Traditional Understanding of God. LC 94-3575. 240p. (Orig.). 1994. pap. 14.99 (0-8308-1852-9, 1852) InterVarsity.

Pinnock, Clark H. Defense of Biblical Infallibility. LC 66-30703. 1967. pap. 2.50 (0-87552-350-1) Presby & Reformed.

— Grace Unlimited. LC 75-22161. 272p. 1975. pap. 9.99 (0-87123-185-9) Bethany Hse.

— A Witness in God's Mercy: The Finality of Jesus Christ in a World of Religions. 208p. 1992. pap. 16.99 (0-310-53591-3) Zondervan.

Pinnock, Clark H. & Brow, Robert C. Unbounded Love: A Good News Theology for the 21st Century. LC 94-26381. 192p. (Orig.). 1994. pap. 12.99 (0-8308-1853-7, 1853) InterVarsity.

Pinnock, Colin A. & Haden, Robert M. MCQ Tutor in Anaesthesia: Clinical Practice. 304p. (Orig.). 1993. pap. text ed. 34.00 (0-443-04610-7) Churchill.

Pinnock, Colin A. & Jones, Robert P. MCQ Tutor in Anaesthesia: Part 1 FRCA. LC 93-29089. 1993. write for info. (0-443-04963-7) Churchill.

— MCQ Tutor in Basic Sciences for Anaesthesia. 240p. (Orig.). 1992. pap. text ed. 28.00 (0-443-04611-5) Churchill.

Pinnock, J., jt. auth. see Bindloss, H.

***Pinnock, Wilsome.** The Rebirth of Robert Samuels. 96p. (Orig.). 1995. pap. 9.95 (0-571-17662-3) Faber & Faber.

Pinnow, Hermann. History of Germany. Brailsford, Mabel R., tr. LC 74-130563. (Select Bibliographies Reprint Ser.). 1977. reprint ed. 25.95 (0-8369-5536-6) Ayer.

***Pinnow, Marilyn.** Romancing the Mountain: Two Tales of Marin Trails. 224p. (Orig.). 1994. pap. 12.00 (0-9643293-0-1) F I D Ent.

Pino, Edward C. Remaking Our Schools: What Has Gone Wrong & New Ways to Fix It. 200p. (Orig.). (C). 1993. lib. bdg. 19.95 (1-883732-01-8) I G S.

Pino, Laurence J. The Business Success Start-up Kit, 8 bklts., Set. 1990. 99.95 (1-56354-000-2) Open U FL.

— The Desktop Lawyer, 2 vols., Set. 1991. ring bd. 495.00 (1-56354-003-7) Open U FL.

— The Desktop Lawyer Software. 300p. 1991. 139.95 (1-56354-004-5) Open U FL.

— Double Your Income with Your Own Home Business. 1991. write for info. (0-318-68778-X) Open U FL.

— Finding Your Niche: A Handbook for Entrepreneurs. 224p. (Orig.). 1994. pap. 9.00 (0-425-14148-9, Berkley Trade) Berkley Pub.

— How to Choose & Use a Lawyer. 1991. write for info. (0-318-68777-1) Open U FL.

— How to Incorporate in Any State Without a Lawyer. 1991. write for info. (0-318-68779-8) Open U FL.

— Money Makers of America. 1991. student ed, audio 99.95 (1-56354-002-9) Open U FL.

— What You Need to Know About Business Law. 1991. write for info. (0-318-68780-1) Open U FL.

Pino, Ondina, jt. auth. see Yenes, Martha.

Pino, Piero, jt. ed. see Wender, Irving.

Pinola, Lanny, jt. auth. see London, Jonathan.

***Pinola, Rudy.** Techniques for Forecasting Industry & Occupational Employment. 1995. pap. 16.00 (1-883428-02-5) Econ Res Srv.

Pinola, Rudy, jt. auth. see Sher, William.

Pinon, Christopher, jt. ed. see Kanazawa, Makoto.

Pinon, Christopher J., ed. see Johnson, Karen E.

Pinon, Christopher J., jt. ed. see Kanazawa, Makoto.

Pinon, Nelida. The Republic of Dreams: A Novel. Lane, Helen, tr. (Texas Pan American Ser.). 669p. 1991. reprint ed. pap. 17.95 (0-292-77050-2) U of Tex Pr.

Pinot, H. M. Fahnestock Genealogy: Ancestors & Descendants of Johann Diedrich Fahnestock. (Illus.). 442p. 1991. reprint ed. lib. bdg. 77.50 (0-8328-1705-8); reprint ed. pap. 67.50 (0-8328-1706-6) Higginson Bk Co.

Pinot, Pierre, jt. auth. see Auge-Laribe, Michel.

Pinotti, J. A. & Faundes, A. Women & Their Right to a Health Policy. (Illus.). 150p. 1989. 45.00 (1-85070-225-X) Prthnon Pub.

Pinsdorf, Marion K. Communicating When Your Company Is under Siege: Surviving Public Crisis. LC 85-45473. 192p. 1986. text ed. 27.95 (0-669-11790-0) Free Pr.

— German-Speaking Entrepreneurs: Builders of Business in Brazil. (American University Studies: Economics: Ser. XVI, Vol. 6). 411p. (C). 1989. text ed. 77.95 (0-8204-1099-3) P Lang Pubs.

Pinsent, Gordon. By the Way. (Illus.). 272p. 1992. 26.95 (0-7737-2647-0, Pub. by Stoddart Pubng CN) Genl Dist Srvs.

Pinsent, John. Greek Mythology. rev. ed. LC 83-71479. (Library of the World's Myths & Legends). (Illus.). 144p. (gr. 8 up). 1983. pap. 14.95 (0-87226-250-2) P Bedrick Bks.

— Greek Mythology: The Library of the World's Myths & Legends. LC 83-71479. (Illus.). 144p. 1990. pap. 10.95 (0-87226-299-5) P Bedrick Bks.

Pinsent, P. J. Outline of Clinical Diagnosis in the Horse. (Outline Ser.). 200p. 1990. pap. text ed. 42.95 (0-7236-0959-4) Blackwell Sci.

Pinsent, Pat, ed. Language Culture & Young Children: Developing English in the Multi-Ethnic Nursery & Infant School. 144p. 1992. pap. 24.95 (1-85346-184-9, Pub. by D Fulton UK) Taylor & Francis.

— The Power of the Page: Children's Books & Their Readers. 144p. 1993. pap. 27.50 (1-85346-234-9, Pub. by D Fulton UK) Taylor & Francis.

Pinske, J. Orchideen Fuer zu Hause. (Illus.). 127p. (GER.). 1984. pap. text ed. 12.50 (3-405-12923-0) Lubrecht & Cramer.

***Pinsker.** Catcher in the Rye. 128p. 1993. 22.95 (0-8057-7978-7, Twayne) Macmillan.

Pinsker, Harold M. & Willis, William D., Jr., eds. Information Processing in the Nervous System. 378p. 1980. text ed. 97.00 (0-89004-422-8) Raven.

Pinsker, Lev S. Road to Freedom. LC 70-162734. 142p. 1975. reprint ed. text ed. 45.00 (0-8371-6195-9, PIRF, Greenwood Pr) Greenwood.

Pinsker, Richard. Getting Hired. Gerould, W. Philip, ed. LC 93-73202. (Illus.). 100p. (Orig.). 1994. pap. 9.95 (1-56052-252-6) Crisp Pubns.

— Hiring Winners. 192p. 1991. 19.95 (0-8144-5051-2, 040547) AMACOM.

Pinsker, S. Jewish American Fiction. (Twayne's United States Authors Ser.). 200p. 1992. text ed. 22.95 (0-8057-3959-9, Pub. by Royal Botanic Garden UK) Macmillan.

Pinsker, Sanford. Bearing the Bad News: Contemporary American Literature & Culture. LC 90-35570. 195p. 1990. 25.95 (0-87745-292-X) U of Iowa Pr.

— Between Two Worlds: The American Novel in the Nineteen Sixties. LC 79-64168. 139p. 1980. 7.50 (0-87875-169-6) Whitston Pub.

— The Catcher in the Rye: Innocence under Pressure. LC 92-31048. (Masterwork Studies Ser.: No. 114). 107p. 1993. lib. bdg. 21.95 (0-8057-8365-2, Twayne); pap. 12.95 (0-8057-8028-9, Twayne) Macmillan.

— The Schlemiel As Metaphor: Studies in Yiddish & American Jewish Fiction. enl. rev. ed. 216p. (C). 1991. 29.95 (0-8093-1581-5) S Ill U Pr.

— Three Pacific Northwest Poets: William Stafford, Richard Hugo, & David Wagoner. (United States Authors Ser.: No. 506). 160p. 1987. lib. bdg. 21.95 (0-8057-7500-5, Twayne) Macmillan.

— The Uncompromising Fictions of Cynthia Ozick. LC 86-30788. 128p. 1987. pap. 9.95 (0-8262-0635-2) U of Mo Pr.

— Understanding Joseph Heller. Bruccoli, Matthew J., ed. (Understanding Contemporary American Literature Ser.). 200p. 1991. text ed. 34.95 (0-87249-751-8) U of SC Pr.

Pinsker, Sanford & Fischel, Jack, eds. America & the Holocaust, Vol. I. (Holocaust Studies Annual). 200p. (C). 1984. lib. bdg. 15.00 (0-913283-02-9) Penkevill.

— Holocaust Studies Annual 1990. LC 88-648983. 176p. 1990. 27.00 (0-8240-6987-0) Garland.

— Holocaust Studies Annual, 1991: General Essays. LC 88-64893. 176p. 1992. 27.00 (0-8153-0393-9, SS787) Garland.

— Literature, the Arts, & the Holocaust, Vol. III. (Holocaust Studies Annual). (Illus.). 288p. (C). 1987. lib. bdg. 30.00 (0-913283-21-5) Penkevill.

Pinsker, Sanford, jt. ed. see Fischel, Jack R.

Pinsker, Sanford, jt. ed. see Fischel, Jack.

Pinsker, Z. G. Dynamical Scattering of X-Rays in Crystals. (Solid-State Sciences Ser.: Vol. 3). (Illus.). 1978. 58.00 (*0-387-08564-5*) Spr-Verlag.

***Pinskey, Raleigh.** You Can Hype Anything: Creative Tactics & Advice for Anyone with a Product, Business or Talent to Promote. LC 94-45497. 184p. 1995. pap. 10.95 (*0-8065-1630-5*, Citadel Pr) Carol Pub Group.

— The Zen of Hype: An Insider's Guide to the Publicity Game. 208p. (Orig.). 1991. pap. 10.95 (*0-8065-1239-3*, Citadel Pr) Carol Pub Group.

Pinski, David. Temptations: A Book of Short Stories. Goldberg, Isaac, tr. LC 74-163045. (Short Story Index Reprint Ser.). 1977. reprint ed. 23.95 (*0-8369-3959-X*) Ayer.

— Three Plays. Goldberg, Isaac, tr. LC 74-29513. (Modern Jewish Experience Ser.). 1975. reprint ed. 23.95 (*0-405-06739-9*) Ayer.

Pinsky. Stochastic Analysis & Applications. (Advances in Probability & Related Topics Ser.: Vol. 7). 472p. 1984. 140.00 (*0-8247-1906-9*) Dekker.

Pinsky, Laura, et al. Essential HIV Treatment Fact Book. Centrello, Gina, ed. 464p. 1992. pap. 14.00 (*0-671-72528-9*) PB.

Pinsky, M., jt. auth. see Durrett, R.

Pinsky, Mark, jt. ed. see Green, Mark.

Pinsky, Mark, et al. Video Display Terminals: Health & Safety Update, 1983. (Excerpts from Microwave News Ser.). 29p. 1984. pap. 10.00 (*0-9610580-1-3*) Microwave.

Pinsky, Mark A. The Carpal Tunnel Syndrome Book: Preventing & Treating CTS. Orig. Title: Tendinitis & Related Cumulative Trauma Disorders. (Illus.). 224p. (Orig.). 1993. mass mkt. 5.99 (*0-446-36527-0*) Warner Bks.

— Diffusion Processes & Related Problems in Analysis. 600p. 1991. 58.50 (*0-8176-3516-5*) Birkhauser.

— The EMF Book: What You Should Know about Electromagnetic Fields, Electromagnetic Radiation & Your Health. 256p. (Orig.). 1995. pap. 9.99 (*0-446-67004-9*) Warner Bks.

— Lecture Notes on Random Evolution. 150p. (C). 1991. text ed. 36.00 (*981-02-0559-7*) World Scientific Pub.

— Partial Differential Equations & Boundary Value Problems with Applications. 2nd ed. 488p. 1991. text ed. write for info. (*0-07-050128-9*) McGraw.

Pinsky, Mark A. & Wihstutz, V., eds. Diffusion Processes & Related Problems in Analysis, Vol. II: Stochastic Flows. (Progress in Probability Ser.: Vol. 27). ix, 346p. 1991. 68.50 (*0-8176-3543-2*) Birkhauser.

Pinsky, Michael R. & Dhainaut, Jean-Francois A. Pathophysiologic Foundations of Critical Care. LC 92-15867. (Illus.). 1008p. 1993. 120.00 (*0-683-06888-1*) Williams & Wilkins.

Pinsky, Robert. An Explanation of America. LC 79-83974. (Contemporary Poets Ser.). 1979. 8.95 (*0-691-01360-8*) Princeton U Pr.

— History of My Heart. (American Poetry Ser.: Vol. 30). 51p. (Orig.). 1985. 12.50 (*0-88001-037-1*); pap. 9.95 (*0-88001-048-7*) Ecco Pr.

— Poetry & the World. 256p. (C). 1988. 19.95 (*0-88001-216-1*) Ecco Pr.

— Poetry & the World: Selected Prose, 1977-1987. 11th ed. LC 88-4411. 1991. pap. 10.95 (*0-88001-217-X*) Ecco Pr.

— Sadness & Happiness: Poems. LC 75-3486. (Contemporary Poets Ser.). 740p. 1975. pap. 12.95 (*0-691-01322-5*, 358) Princeton U Pr.

— The Situation of Poetry: Contemporary Poetry & Its Traditions. LC 76-3015. (Essays in Literature Ser.). 1977. pap. 12.95 (*0-691-01352-7*) Princeton U Pr.

— The Want Bone. 80p. 1990. 17.95 (*0-88001-250-1*) Ecco Pr.

— Want Bone. 1991. pap. 9.95 (*0-88001-251-X*) Ecco Pr.

Pinsky, Robert, tr. see Milosz, Czeslaw.

***Pinsky, Ross G.** Positive Harmonic Functions & Diffusion. (Studies in Advanced Mathematics: No. 45). 496p. (C). 1995. 79.95 (*0-521-47014-5*) Cambridge U Pr.

Pinsky, Steven M., et al, eds. Imaging of Peripheral Vascular System. 352p. 1984. text ed. 110.00 (*0-8089-1636-X*, 793308, Grune) Saunders.

Pinsky, Susan, jt. auth. see Starkman, David.

***Pinsky, Valerie & Wylie, Alison, eds.** Critical Traditions in Contemporary Archaeology: Essays in the Philosophy, History, & Socio-Politics of Archaeology. LC 94-45894. 180p. 1995. reprint ed. pap. 19.95 (*0-8263-1599-2*) U of NM Pr.

Pinsler. Evidence, Advocacy & the Litigation Process. 1992. 158.00 (*0-409-99612-2*) Butterworth Legal Pubs.

Pinsof, William M., jt. ed. see Greenberg, Leslie S.

Pinson, Arie, ed. The Heart Cell in Culture, 3 vols., Set. 1987. 393.00 (*0-8493-4696-7*, QP114) CRC Pr.

P Q

Pinson, Dar. Sticks 'n' Bones 'n' Chewing Gum: Creating Gifts from Finder's Art. 43p. 1994. spiral bd. 14.95 (*1-886724-00-8*) Pinson Pr. STICKS 'N' BONES 'N' CHEWING GUM is a new release from Pinson Press. It's the Craft Book for you. Creating gifts from "Finder's Art" for just pennies a gift! The book has 22 projects in it & once you know what you're "Looking for" you can create anything you want. Use your imagination. STICKS represents pinecones, grapevine, cinnamon sticks, etc. BONES represents sea shells, eggshells, chicken & turkey neck bones (really!!) 'n' don't forget the 'n'! It can be dough art, macrame cords, etc. It's never ending supplies, plain-talk directions, diagrams, patterns, color photos on the back, all in a spiral bound book that lies flat while you work! Why not chew gum while you make your gifts? Some projects take just a few minutes. Others can challenge you for a few hours, or days. Work on a project alone or get the family involved. (Great for Scouts, Church Groups, Seniors, even the grandkids can do some of these projects.) Turn off that T.V. & get started! Other books in progress by the same author are: The Grandpa Rudy & Grandma Dar Children's Stories. To order: Pinson Press, P.O. 256, Rio Linda, CA 95673.** ***Publisher Provided Annotation.

Pinson, Hermine. ASHE. Whitebird, J., ed. (New Texas Poetry Sampler Ser.). 28p. (Orig.). 1992. pap. text ed. 10.00 (*0-930324-23-4*) Wings Pr.

Pinson, James C. Designing Screen Interfaces in C. 304p. 1991. pap. text ed. 38.60 (*0-13-201583-8*) P-H.

Pinson, James L., jt. auth. see Brooks, Brian S.

Pinson, Joe. Seven Organ Voluntaries. 1993. 4.95 (*0-87166-272-8*, 94291) Mel Bay.

Pinson, Koppel S. Modern Germany: Its History & Civilization. 2nd ed. (Illus.). 682p. (C). 1989. reprint ed. pap. text ed. 25.95 (*0-88133-434-0*) Waveland Pr.

Pinson, Koppel S., tr. see Lichtenberger, Henri.

Pinson, Lewis J. Electro-Optics. LC 85-5397. 282p. 1985. text ed. 56.95 (*0-471-88142-2*) Krieger.

Pinson, Lewis J. & Wiener, Richard S. An Introduction to Object-Oriented Programming & Smalltalk. (Illus.). 430p. (C). 1988. pap. text ed. 36.75 (*0-201-19127-X*) Addison-Wesley.

Pinson, Lewis J., ed. see Wiener, Richard S.

Pinson, Lewis J., jt. auth. see Wiener, Richard S.

Pinson, Lewis S. & Wiener, Richard S. Case Studies in Object-Oriented Programming. (Computer Science Ser.). (Illus.). (C). 1990. text ed. 40.95 (*0-201-50369-7*) Addison-Wesley.

Pinson, Linda & Jinnet, Jerry. Anatomy of a Business Plan. 176p. 1993. pap. 17.95 (*0-7931-0618-4*, 561408, Enter-Dearbrn) Dearborn Finan.

Pinson, Linda & Jinnett, Jerry. The Home-Based Entrepreneur: The Complete Guide to Working at Home. 2nd rev. ed. 192p. 1993. pap. 19.95 (*0-936894-46-6*) Upstart Pub.

— Keeping the Books: Basic Recordkeeping & Accounting for the Small Business. 2nd rev. ed. 208p. 1993. pap. 19.95 (*0-936894-47-4*) Upstart Pub.

— Steps to Small Business Start-Up: Everything You Need to Know to Turn Your Idea into a Successful Business. LC 93-9087. 256p. (Orig.). 1993. pap. 19.95 (*0-936894-50-4*) Upstart Pub.

— Target Marketing for the Small Business: Researching, Reaching & Retaining Your Target Market. LC 93-9086. 176p. (Orig.). 1993. pap. 19.95 (*0-936894-51-2*) Upstart Pub.

— The Woman Entrepreneur. LC 91-90096. 244p. (Orig.). 1993. pap. 14.00 (*0-944205-18-6*) Upstart Pub.

Pinson, Mark, ed. The Muslims of Bosnia-Herzegovina: Their Historic Development from the Middle Ages to the Dissolution of Yugoslavia. (Middle Eastern Monographs). (Orig.). (C). 1994. 14.95 (*0-932885-09-8*) Harvard CMES.

***Pinson, Stephen, contrib.** Prints of the Fort Worth Circle, 1940-1960. (Illus.). 45p. 1992. pap. 10.00 (*0-935213-22-8*) A M Huntington Art.

Pinson, William M., Jr., jt. auth. see Fant, Clyde E., Jr.

Pinson, William W. In White & Black: A Story. LC 72-1560. (Black Heritage Library Collection). 1977. reprint ed. 32.95 (*0-8369-9047-1*) Ayer.

Pinstrup-Andersen, Per. Macroeconomic Policy Reforms, Poverty, & Nutrition: Analytical Methodologies. (Monograph Ser.). (C). 1990. pap. text ed. 12.00 (*1-56401-003-1*) Cornell Food.

Pinstrup-Andersen, Per, ed. The Political Economy of Food & Nutrition Policies. LC 92-25287. (International Food Policy Research Institute Ser.). 352p. 1993. text ed. 38.50 (*0-8018-4480-0*) Johns Hopkins.

Pinstrup-Andersen, Per, et al, eds. Child Growth & Nutrition in Developing Countries: Priorities for Action. (Food Systems & Agrarian Change Ser.). (Illus.). 496p. 1994. 57.00 (*0-8014-3001-1*); pap. 25.00 (*0-8014-8189-9*) Cornell U Pr.

Pinstrup-Anderson, Per. Agricultural Research & Technology in Economic Development. LC 81-14297. (Illus.). 304p. (C). 1982. text ed. 39.95 (*0-582-46048-4*) Longman.

Pinstrup-Anderson, Per, ed. Food Subsidies in Developing Countries: Costs, Benefits, & Policy Options. LC 88-1709. 416p. 1988. text ed. 39.50 (*0-8018-3632-8*) Johns Hopkins.

Pint, Ellen M. & Schmidt, Rachel. Financial Condition of U. S. Military Aircraft Prime Contractors. LC 93-42657. 1994. write for info. (*0-8330-1494-3*, MR-372-AF) Rand Corp.

Pint, Gayle, ed. see Bernard, Don.

Pinta, M. Detection & Determination of Trace Elements. 620p. 1962. text ed. 130.00 (*0-685-43582-2*, Pub. by Keter Pub IS) Coronet Bks.

Pinta, M., jt. auth. see Aubert, H.

Pinta, Maurice. Modern Methods for Trace Element Analysis. 492p. 1978. 24.50 (*0-250-40152-5*) Technomic.

Pinta, Thanom, tr. see Kemvichanuvat, Cherdchai.

Pinta, Thanom, tr. see Rausiri, Supa.

Pintak, Larry. Beirut Outtakes: A TV Correspondent's Portrait of America's Encounter with Terror. 368p. 1989. text ed. 24.95 (*0-669-19512-X*); pap. 12.95 (*0-669-21361-6*) Free Pr.

Pintanich, Kristin, ed. see Siebert, Al.

Pintar, Judith. The Cards of Winds & Changes. 24p. 1990. 12.95 (*0-88079-467-4*) US Games Syst.

— Halved Soul: Retelling the Myths of Romantic Love. 1992. pap. 14.00 (*0-04-440868-4*) Thorsons SF.

Pintauro, Joe. Men's Lives. 1994. pap. 4.75 (*0-8222-1381-8*) Dramatists Play.

— Raft of the Medusa. 1992. pap. 4.75 (*0-8222-1314-1*) Dramatists Play.

Pintauro, Joseph. Cacciatore: Three Short Plays. 1980. pap. 4.75 (*0-8222-0172-0*) Dramatists Play.

Pintchman, Tracy. The Rise of the Goddess in the Hindu Tradition. LC 93-40617. 300p. (FRE.). (C). 1994. pap. 16.95x (*0-7914-2112-0*) State U NY Pr.

— The Rise of the Goddess in the Hindu Tradition. LC 93-40617. 300p. (FRE.). (C). 1994. 49.50x (*0-7914-2111-2*) State U NY Pr.

Pintchovski, F. S., jt. ed. see Cale, T. S.

Pintel, Gerald & Diamond, Jay. Basic Business Mathematics. 4th ed. 432p. (C). 1989. pap. text ed. write for info. (*0-13-058728-1*) P-H.

— Retailing. 5th ed. 544p. 1991. text ed. 72.00 (*0-13-775362-4*) P-H.

Pintel, Gerald, jt. auth. see Diamond, Jay.

Pintelon, R., jt. auth. see Schoukens, J.

Pinter & Nabet. Nonlinear Vision. 1992. 89.95 (*0-8493-4292-9*, QP475) CRC Pr.

Pinter, C. C. A Book of Abstract Algebra. 2nd ed. 1990. text ed. write for info. (*0-07-050138-6*) McGraw.

Pinter, H. African Grey Parrots As a Hobby. (Illus.). 96p. 1994. pap. 7.95 (*0-7938-0093-5*, TT036) TFH Pubns.

Pinter, Harold. Betrayal. 1980. pap. 2.75 (*0-8222-0109-7*) Dramatists Play.

— Betrayal. 144p. 1988. pap. 9.95 (*0-8021-3080-1*) Grove-Atltic.

— The Birthday Party & the Room. (Illus.). 120p. 1989. pap. 8.95 (*0-8021-5114-0*) Grove-Atltic.

— The Caretaker. 1962. pap. 4.75 (*0-8222-0184-4*) Dramatists Play.

— The Caretaker & the Dumbwaiter. (Illus.). 121p. 1989. pap. 8.95 (*0-8021-5087-X*) Grove-Atltic.

— Complete Works, 4 vols. 251p. 1990. Vol. 1, 251p. pap. 10.95 (*0-8021-5096-9*); Vol. 2, 248p. pap. 10.95 (*0-8021-3237-5*); Vol. 3, 248p. pap. 10.95 (*0-8021-5049-7*); Vol. 4, 384p. pap. 10.95 (*0-8021-5050-0*) Grove-Atltic.

— The Dwarfs. 224p. (Orig.). 1991. pap. 11.95 (*0-8021-3266-9*) Grove-Atltic.

— Dwarfs & Eight Review Sketches. 1965. pap. 4.75 (*0-8222-0344-8*) Dramatists Play.

— Five Screenplays: The Servant; The Pumpkin Eater; The Quiller Memorandum; Accident; The Go-Between. 368p. 1989. pap. 18.95 (*0-8021-5119-1*) Grove-Atltic.

— Homecoming. 96p. 1989. pap. 7.95 (*0-8021-5105-1*) Grove-Atltic.

— The Hothouse. 1980. pap. 4.75 (*0-8222-0535-1*) Dramatists Play.

— I Know the Place. (C). 1990. 150.00 (*0-906887-02-X*, Pub. by Greville Pr UK) St Mut.

— The Lover. 1965. pap. 2.75 (*0-8222-0704-4*) Dramatists Play.

— The Lover. Bd. with Tea Party.; Basement. 1967. Set pap. 3.95 (*0-394-17263-9*, E432) Grove-Atltic.

— Moonlight. 1995. pap. 4.75 (*0-8222-1481-4*) Dramatists Play.

— Moonlight: A Play. 112p. 1994. pap. 12.00 (*0-8021-3393-2*) Grove-Atltic.

— Mountain Language. 1988. pap. 4.75 (*0-8222-0777-X*) Dramatists Play.

— Mountain Language. 48p. 1989. pap. 7.95 (*0-8021-3168-9*) Grove-Atltic.

— The New World Order. 1992. pap. 2.50 (*0-8222-1449-0*) Dramatists Play.

— No Man's Land. LC 75-13555. 96p. 1975. pap. 9.95 (*0-8021-5187-6*) Grove-Atltic.

— Old Times. 75p. 1989. pap. 7.95 (*0-8021-5029-2*) Grove-Atltic.

— One for the Road: A Play. 80p. 1986. pap. 7.95 (*0-8021-5188-4*) Grove-Atltic.

— Other Places: Three Plays; A Kind of Alaska; Victoria Station; Family Voices. LC 82-24185. 96p. 1983. pap. 6.95 (*0-8021-5189-2*) Grove-Atltic.

— Other Places: Three Short Plays. 1984. pap. 4.75 (*0-8222-0866-0*) Dramatists Play.

— Party Time & the New World Order. 1993. pap. 12.00 (*0-8021-3352-5*) Grove-Atltic.

— Poems & Prose: 1949-1977. LC 78-56046. 112p. 1989. pap. 8.95 (*0-8021-5190-6*) Grove-Atltic.

— The Proust Screenplay: A la Recherche du Temps Perdu. LC 77-78081. 192p. 1977. pap. 3.95 (*0-8021-5191-4*) Grove-Atltic.

— Tea Party & The Basement: Two Plays. 1969. pap. 4.75 (*0-8222-1115-7*) Dramatists Play.

— Ten Early Poems. (C). 1990. 35.00 (*0-906887-50-X*, Pub. by Greville Pr UK) St Mut.

Pinter, Harold, et al, eds. Ninety-Nine Poems in Translation: An Anthology. 160p. 1994. 16.00 (*0-8021-1557-8*) Grove-Atltic.

Pinter, Harold, et al, sels. One Hundred Poems by One Hundred Poets. 192p. 1987. pap. 9.95 (*0-8021-3279-0*) Grove-Atltic.

Pinter, Helmut. Amazon Parrots in Your Home. (Illus.). 157p. 1988. lib. bdg. 14.95 (*0-86622-901-9*, TS-115) TFH Pubns.

— Labyrinth Fish. (Illus.). 176p. 1986. 18.95 (*0-8120-5635-3*) Barron.

— The Proper Care of Cockatoos. (TW Ser.). (Illus.). 256p. 1993. text ed. 14.95 (*0-86622-387-8*, TS-126) TFH Pubns.

Pinter, I. Hungarian Anti-Fascism & Resistance, 1941-1945. 238p. (C). 1986. 150.00 (*0-569-09000-8*, Pub. by Collets UK) Pro-Am Music.

Pinter, Les. FoxPro Programming. 1990. pap. 21.95 (*0-8306-3525-4*, Windcrest) TAB Bks.

— FoxPro Programming. 2nd ed. 1992. pap. 22.95 (*0-07-050146-7*) McGraw.

— FoxPro 2.0 Applications Programming. (Illus.). 384p. 1992. pap. 24.95 (*0-8306-4268-4*, 4302, Windcrest) TAB Bks.

— FoxPro 2.5 Programming. (Illus.). 400p. 1993. pap. 24.95 (*0-8306-4398-2*, Windcrest) TAB Bks.

— FoxPro(R) Programming. 2nd ed. 384p. 1992. pap. 22.95 (*0-8306-2586-0*, 4057, Windcrest) TAB Bks.

— Microsoft FoxPro 2.5 Applications Programming. LC 93-30187. 1993. pap. text ed. 24.95 (*0-07-050153-X*, Windcrest) TAB Bks.

— Microsoft FoxPro 2.5 Programming. 1993. pap. text ed. 24.95 (*0-07-050152-1*) McGraw.

Pinter, Neil. The Eternal Question...Does God Exist? New Powerful Evidence - Scientific, Historical, Mathematical. LC 91-67660. (Illus.). 246p. (Orig.). 1994. pap. 12.95 (*0-9633317-2-8*) Westhaven Pub.

Pinter, Nicholas, jt. auth. see Keller, Edward A.

Pinter, Robert B., jt. auth. see Nabet, Bahram.

Pinthus, Kurt, ed. Menschheitsdammerung: Dawn of Humanity: a Document of Expressionism with Biographies & Bibliographies. Ratych, Joanna M. et al, trs. LC 93-2165. (Studies in German Literature, Linguistics & Culture). 400p. 1993. 58.50 (*1-879751-48-8*) Camden Hse.

***Pinto, Antonio C., ed.** Modern Portugal. 380p. 1995. 45.00 (*0-930664-14-0*) SPOSS.

Pinto, Brian, jt. auth. see Glen, Jack D.

***Pinto, Celsa.** Trade & Finance in Portuguese India. (C). 1994. text ed. 40.00 (*81-7022-507-8*, Pub. by Concept II) S Asia.

Pinto da Cunha, A., ed. Scale Effects in Rock Masses: Proceedings of the First International Workshop, Loen, 7 - 8 June 1990. (Illus.). 352p. (C). 1990. text ed. 105.00 (*90-6191-126-5*, Pub. by A A Balkema NE) Ashgate Pub Co.

Pinto, Diana, ed. Contemporary Italian Sociology: A Reader. (Illus.). 224p. 1981. 59.95 (*0-521-23738-6*) Cambridge U Pr.

Pinto-Duschinsky, Michael. British Political Finance, Eighteen Thirty to Nineteen Eighty. LC 81-7963. (AEI Studies: No. 330). (Illus.). 368p. reprint ed. pap. 104.90 (*0-8357-4441-8*, 2037275) Bks Demand.

Pinto, E., jt. ed. see Seco, Pedro S.

Pinto, Fernao M. The Travels of Mendes Pinto. Catz, Rebecca D., ed. & tr. by. LC 88-39778. (Illus.). 864p. 1989. 49.95 (*0-226-66951-3*) U Ch Pr.

***Pinto, Jeffrey K.** Successful Information System Implementation: The Human Side. LC 94-24721. (Perspective Ser.). 220p. 1994. pap. 30.00 (*1-880410-37-0*) Proj Mgmt Inst.

Pinto, Jeffrey K., jt. auth. see Obermeyer, Nancy J.

***Pinto, Jefrey K. & Kharbanda, O. P.** Leading Your Team to Success. (Industrial Engineering Ser.). 300p. 1995. text ed. 34.95 (*0-442-01952-1*) Van Nos Reinhold.

Pinto, John A. The Trevi Fountain. LC 85-2480. 320p. 1986. 42.00 (*0-300-03335-4*) Yale U Pr.

Pinto, John A., jt. auth. see MacDonald, William L.

Pinto, John B. Marketing an Orthopedic Practice. 160p. (Orig.). 1991. pap. 19.95 (*1-879952-02-5*) Inst Spine.

Pinto, John D. Behavior & Taxonomy of the Epicauta Maculata Group (Coleoptera, Meloidae) LC 79-27381. (University of California Publications in Social Welfare: No. 89). (Illus.). 117p. reprint ed. pap. 33.40 (*0-8357-7107-5*, 2031584) Bks Demand.

— The Taxonomy of North American Epicauta (Coleoptera: Meloidae) With a Revision of the Nominate Subgenus & a Survey of Courtship Behavior. (Publications in Entomology: Vol. 110). 448p. (C). 1991. pap. 50.00 (*0-520-09764-5*) U CA Pr.

Pinto, Julio C. The Reading of Time: A Semantic-Semiotic Approach. (Approaches to Semiotics Ser.: No. 82). x, 162p. (C). 1989. lib. bdg. 79.25 (*0-89925-354-7*) Mouton.

Pinto, Lelina, tr. see Marcos, Plinio, et al.

Pinto-Lopez, J. Polyporaceae, Contribuicao Rara a Sua Bio-Taxonomia (Broteriana 8) (Illus.). 1968. reprint ed. pap. 36.00 (*3-7682-0555-X*) Lubrecht & Cramer.

Pinto, Magdalena G., tr. see Garcia Pinto, Magdalena.

Pinto, Maria H., et al. Portugal & the East Through Embroidery: 16th to 18th Century Coverlets from the Museu Nacional De Arte Antiga, Lisbon. LC 81-83994. (Illus.). 40p. 1981. pap. 10.80 (*0-88397-038-4*) Art Srvc Intl.

Pinto, Marina. Federalism & Higher Education: The Indian Experience. 192p. 1984. text ed. 27.50 (*0-86131-456-5*, Pub. by Orient Longman Ltd II) Apt Bks.

Pinto-Moisi, Diana, et al, eds. Securing the Euro-Atlantic Bridge: The Council of Europe & the United States. LC 93-1208. 1993. 14.95 (*0-913449-35-0*) Inst EW Stud.

— Securing the Euro-Atlantic Bridge: The Council of Europe & the United States. LC 93-1208. 1993. 14.85 (*0-8133-8785-X*) Westview.

Pinto, Patrick R. & Walker, James W. A Study of Professional Training & Development Roles & Competencies. 124p. 6.95 (*0-318-13286-9*); pap. 9.00 (*0-318-13285-0*, PWBCP) Am Soc Train & Devel.

***Pinto, Ricardo, ed.** Developments in Housing Management & Ownership. LC 94-43135. 1995. text ed. write for info. (*0-7190-3713-1*, Pub. by Manchester Univ Pr UK) St Martin.

An Asterisk (*) at the beginning of an entry indicates that the title is appearing in BIP for the first time.

Pinto, Ricardo R. Estate Action Initiative: A Study of Council Housing Renewal, Management & Effectiveness. 298p. 1993. 59.95 (*1-85628-358-5*, Pub. by Avebury Pub UK) Ashgate Pub Co.

Pinto, Robert. Basic Estate Planning. (Illus.). 200p. 1992. pap. 35.00 (*0-685-14622-7*) NJ Inst CLE.

Pinto, Robert C., jt. auth. see Blair, John A.

Pinto, Robert C., jt. ed. see Hansen, Hans V.

Pinto, Roger. Aspects de l'Evolution Gouvernementale de l'Indochine Francaise. LC 77-179234. reprint ed. 22.50 (*0-404-54861-X*) AMS Pr.

***Pinto, Rogerio F.** Projectizing the Governance Approach to Civil Service Reform: An Environmental Assessment for Preparing a Sectoral Adjustment Loan in the Gambia. LC 94-28328. (World Discussion Papers Africa Technical Department: 252). 1994. write for info. (*0-8213-2966-9*) World Bank.

Pinto, Russ. Somewhere Within: A Journey. LC 91-71772. 98p. (Orig.). 1991. pap. 9.95 (*0-9629316-8-3*) A One Pub.

Pinto, Sousa, jt. auth. see Hoskins.

Pinto, Vivian De Sola. Rochester: Portrait of a Restoration Poet. LC 73-175707. (Select Bibliographies Reprint Ser.). 1977. reprint ed. 23.95 (*0-8369-6622-8*) Ayer.

Pinto, Vivian de Sola. Sir Charles Sedley, 1639-1701: A Study in the Life & Literature of the Restoration. LC 76-85904. reprint ed. 49.50 (*0-404-05056-5*) AMS Pr.

Pinto, Vivian De Sola, ed. The Divine Vision. LC 68-24905. (Studies in Blake: No. 3). 1973. reprint ed. lib. bdg. 75.00 (*0-8383-0790-6*) M S G Haskell Hse.

— English Biography in the Seventeenth Century. LC 72-101833. (Biography Index Reprint Ser.). 1977. 23.95 (*0-8369-8007-7*) Ayer.

Pintoff, Ernest. Bolt from the Blue: A True Story. Van Treese, James B., ed. 232p. 1992. 14.95 (*1-880416-54-9*) NW Pub.

— The Complete Guide to American Film Schools & Cinema & Television Courses. LC 93-30073. 624p. 1994. pap. 15.95 (*0-14-017226-2*, Penguin Bks) Viking Penguin.

— Zachary (A Novel) LC 90-37898. 272p. 1990. 17.95 (*0-8397-9042-2*) Eriksson.

Pinton, Giorgio A., tr. see Vico, Giambattista.

Pintonelli, Deborah. Ego Monkey. LC 90-85075. 112p. 1991. pap. 10.95 (*0-929968-15-8*) Another Chicago Pr.

Pintor, C., et al, eds. Pediatric Endocrinology. (Illus.). 256p. 1993. 175.00 (*0-387-54321-X*) Spr-Verlag.

Pintor Genaro, Mercedes. Eduardo Mallea, Novelista. LC 76-6545. (Coleccion Mente y Palabra). 277p. (SPA.). 1976. 5.00 (*0-8477-0524-2*); pap. text ed. 4.00 (*0-8477-0525-0*) U of PR Pr.

Pintozzi, Frank, et al. Passing the College Placement Examination. 2nd ed. 262p. (C). 1990. pap. text ed. 23.95 (*0-89892-086-8*) Contemp Pub Co of Raleigh.

***Pintrich, Paul R. & Schunk, Dale H.** Student Motivation. 1996. pap. write for info. (*0-02-395621-6*, Merrill Pub Co) Macmillan.

Pintrich, Paul R., et al, eds. Student Motivation, Cognition, & Learning: Essays in Honor of Wilbert J. McKeachie. 400p. 1994. text ed. 69.95 (*0-8058-1376-4*) L Erlbaum Assocs.

Pintur, D. A. Finite Element Beginnings. 200p. 1994. 49.50 (*0-8176-3751-6*) Birkhauser.

Pintur, David. Finite Element Beginnings. 1994. 99.00 (*0-8176-3752-4*) Birkhauser.

Pintz, William S. Ok Tedi: Evolution of a Third World Mining Project. 206p. 1984. 34.00 (*0-685-50784-X*) EW Ctr HI.

Pinus, A G. Boolean Constructions in Universal Algebras. LC 92-44823. (Mathematics & Its Applications Ser.: Vol. 242). 1993. lib. bdg. 149.00 (*0-7923-2117-0*) Kluwer Ac.

Pinus, Lee. The Songwriters' Success Manual. 2nd ed. LC 78-60263. 1978. pap. 9.95 (*0-918318-02-5*) Music Pr.

Pinxten, Rik, ed. Universalism Versus Relativism in Language & Thought: Proceedings of a Colloquium on the Sapir-Whorf Hypothesis. (Contributions to the Sociology of Language Ser.: No. 11). 1977. text ed. 63.10 (*90-279-7791-7*) Mouton.

Pinxten, Rik, jt. ed. see Callebaut, Werner.

Pinxten, Rik, et al. Anthropology of Space: Explorations into the Natural Philosophy & Semantics of the Navajo. LC 82-23703. 252p. reprint ed. pap. 71.90 (*0-7837-3005-5*, 2042936) Bks Demand.

Pinyan, Pamela, jt. auth. see Friendlander, Eva.

Pinyopusarerk, K. Acacia Auriculiformis. 154p. (Orig.). 1990. pap. 10.00 (*0-933595-41-7*) Winrock Intl.

Pinza, Ezio & Magidoff, Robert. Ezio Pinza: An Autobiography. Farkas, Andrew, ed. LC 76-29962. (Opera Biographies Ser.). (Illus.). 1977. reprint ed. lib. bdg. 30.95 (*0-405-09702-6*) Ayer.

Pinzon, Renee, jt. auth. see Pinzon, Scott.

Pinzon, Scott. Tales of Evermore. 90p. (Orig.). (YA). (gr. 7-12). 1991. pap. 4.95 (*0-8474-6621-3*) Back to Bible.

Pinzon, Scott & Pinzon, Renee. Knights of Evermore. 1994. pap. 5.99 (*0-934998-56-6*) Bethel Pub.

Pio, Padre. The Agony of Jesus. 40p. 1974. pap. 1.50 (*0-89555-097-0*) TAN Bks Pubs.

— Meditation Prayer on Mary Immaculate. (Illus.). 28p. 1974. pap. 1.25 (*0-89555-099-7*) TAN Bks Pubs.

Pioli, Richard. Stung by Salt & War: Creative Texts of the Italian Avant-Gardist F.T. Marinetti. (Reading Plus Ser.: Vol. 2). 187p. (C). 1987. text ed. 31.50 (*0-8204-0381-4*) P Lang Pubs.

Piombino, Alfred E. Notary Public Handbook: A Guide for Florida. LC 92-30566. (Illus.). 500p. (Orig.). 1993. pap. 24.95 (*0-944560-33-4*) East Coast NY.

— Notary Public Handbook: A Guide for Maine. LC 91-37769. (Illus.). 504p. 1992. pap. 24.95 (*0-944560-32-6*) East Coast NY.

— Notary Public Handbook: A Guide for New Jersey. LC 90-20150. (Illus.). 296p. (C). 1991. 22.95 (*0-944560-29-6*); pap. 14.95 (*0-944560-26-1*) East Coast NY.

— Notary Public Handbook: A Guide for New York. 3rd rev. ed. LC 92-19416. (Illus.). 284p. 1995. pap. 21.95 (*0-944560-31-8*) East Coast NY.

— Notary Public Register & Recordkeeping Protocols. (Illus.). 64p. (Orig.). 1993. pap. 14.95 (*0-944560-35-0*) East Coast NY.

Piombino, Nick. Boundary of Blur. LC 92-63355. (Language Poetics Ser.: No. 6). 122p. (Orig.). 1993. pap. 13.95 (*0-937804-50-9*) Segue NYC.

— Poems. 88p. (Orig.). 1988. pap. 8.95 (*1-55713-011-6*) Sun & Moon CA.

Piomelli, U., jt. ed. see Ragab, S. A.

Pioneer. Frederick Banting. (J). 1992. lib. bdg. 13.98 (*0-8050-2335-6*) H Holt & Co.

Pioneer Historical Society Staff. Telfair County, Georgia. (Illus.). 574p. 1988. 60.00 (*0-88107-114-5*) Curtis Media.

Pioneer Institute for Public Policy Research Staff. Bay State Auto Rates: What Are the Driving Forces? Edited Remarks. (Dialogue Ser.: No. 2). 25p. (Orig.). 1990. pap. 5.00 (*0-929930-04-5*) Pioneer Inst.

Pioneer Press, ed. see Daniel, Larry J. & Gunter, Riley W.

Pioneer Press Staff, ed. see Reese, Michael, II.

Pioneer Press Staff, ed. see Schreier, Konrad F., Jr.

Pioneers Club of Birmingham Staff. Early Days in Birmingham. 1968. 5.95 (*0-87651-006-3*); pap. 9.95 (*0-87651-007-1*) Southern U Pr.

Piontac, Nechemiah. The Arizal: The Life & Times of Rabbi Yitzchak Luria. Weinbach, Shaindel, tr. (ArtScroll Youth Ser.). (Illus.). 288p. (J). (gr. 5-12). 1988. 12.95 (*0-89906-835-9*); pap. 9.95 (*0-89906-836-7*) Mesorah Pubns.

Piontek, Heinz. Alive or Dead. Exner, Richard, tr. LC 72-77917. (German Ser.: Vol. 4). 64p. 1975. 17.50 (*0-87775-041-6*); pap. 7.95 (*0-87775-089-0*) Unicorn Pr.

— Selected Poems. Osers, Ewald, tr. 80p. 1994. pap. 14.95 (*1-85610-033-2*, Pub. by Forest Bks UK) Dufour.

Piontelli, Alessandra. From Fetus to Child: An Observational & Psychoanalytic Study. LC 91-5236. (New Library of Psychoanalysis). 1992. 59.95 (*0-415-07436-3*, A7369, Pub. by Tavistock UK); pap. 16.95 (*0-415-07437-1*, A7373, Pub. by Tavistock UK) Routledge Chapman & Hall.

Piore, Emanuel. Science & Academic Life in Transition. 96p. (C). 1990. 24.95 (*0-88738-337-8*) Transaction Pubs.

***Piore, Michael J.** Beyond Individualism. LC 94-34909. 223p. 1995. 22.95 (*0-674-06897-1*, PIOBEY) HUP.

— Birds of Passage: Migrant Labor & Industrial Societies. LC 78-12067. 239p. reprint ed. pap. 68.20 (*0-8357-7272-1*, 2024518) Bks Demand.

Piore, Michael J., ed. Unemployment & Inflation: Institutional & Structuralist Views, A Reader in Labor Economics. LC 79-55274. 300p. 1979. pap. 19.95 (*0-87332-165-0*) M E Sharpe.

Piore, Michael J. & Sabel, Charles F. The Second Industrial Divide: Possibilities for Prosperity. LC 83-46080. 366p. 1986. pap. text ed. 19.50 (*0-465-07561-4*) Basic.

Piore, Michael J., jt. auth. see Berger, Suzanne.

Piore, Michael J., jt. auth. see Doeringer, Peter B.

Piore, Nancy K. Lightning: The Poetry of Rene Char. LC 80-22001. (Illus.). 153p. 1981. text ed. 24.95 (*0-930350-08-1*) NE U Pr.

Piorkowski, G. K. Too Close for Comfort: Exploring the Risks of Intimacy. (Illus.). 285p. 1994. 25.95 (*0-306-44641-3*, Plenum Insight) Plenum.

Pioro, I. L., jt. auth. see Pioro, L. S.

Pioro, L. S. & Pioro, I. L. Two-Phase Industrial Thermosyphons. 200p. 1991. 75.00 (*0-89116-765-X*) CRC Pr.

Piot, P., et al. AIDS in Africa: A Manual for Physicians. (Illus.). viii, 125p. 1992. pap. text ed. 14.40 (*92-4-154435-X*) World Health.

Piotrkowski, Chaya S. Work & the Family System: A Naturalistic Study of Working-Class & Lower-Middle-Class Families. LC 79-7478. (Illus.). 1979. 19.95 (*0-02-925340-3*) Free Pr.

Piotrouski, Boris. Treasures of the Hermitage. 1990. 39.99 (*0-517-02725-9*) Random Hse Value.

Piotrovsky, B. Hermitage. (Illus.). 391p. (C). 1989. text ed. 400.00 (*0-569-09215-9*, Pub. by Collets) St Mut.

Piotrovsky, Mikhail B., intro. Great Art Treasures of the Hermitage Museum, St. Petersburg. LC 94-8939. 1994. write for info. (*0-8109-3428-0*) Abrams.

Piotrovsky, T. Scythian Art. (C). 1990. 250.00 (*0-685-34383-9*, Pub. by Collets) St Mut.

— Treasures of the Orthodox Church Museum in Finland. (C). 1990. 500.00 (*0-685-34382-0*, Pub. by Collets) St Mut.

Piotrow, Phyllis T. World Population: The Present & Future Crisis. LC 80-69582. (Headline Ser.: No. 251). (Illus.). 80p. (Orig.). (C). 1980. pap. 5.95 (*0-87124-064-5*) Foreign Policy.

***Piotrow, Phyllis T., et al.** Family Planning Communication: State of the Art. LC 94-78725. 175p. 1995. write for info. (*1-885960-00-X*) JHU Sch Hygiene.

— Strategies for Family Planning Promotion. LC 93-32252. (Technical Paper Ser.: No. 223). 68p. 1994. write for info. (*0-8213-2622-8*) World Bank.

Piotrowska, Irena G. Art of Poland. LC 75-179736. (Biography Index Reprint Ser.). 1977. reprint ed. 38.95 (*0-8369-8104-9*) Ayer.

Piotrowska, Maria, tr. see Bigon, Maria, et al.

Piotrowski. Shaft Alignment Handbook. (Mechanical Engineering Ser.: Vol. 46). 296p. 1986. 99.75 (*0-8247-7432-9*) Dekker.

Piotrowski, Christine M. Interior Design Management. 1992. text ed. 49.95 (*0-442-00760-4*) Van Nos Reinhold.

— Professional Practice for Interior Design. 2nd ed. (Illus.). 448p. 1994. text ed. 49.95 (*0-442-01684-0*) Van Nos Reinhold.

— Professional Practice for Interior Designers. (Illus.). 328p. 1989. text ed. 44.95 (*0-442-27519-6*) Van Nos Reinhold.

Piotrowski, Harry, jt. auth. see McWilliams, Wayne C.

Piotrowski, Maryann V. Effective Business Writings: Strategies & Suggestions; How to Write--& Think--Clearly about a. 1993. pap. 10.00 (*0-06-272048-1*, PL) HarpC.

Piotrowski, R. G., et al. Oil & Gas Developments in Pennsylvania in Nineteen Seventy-Eight. (Progress Report Ser.: No. 192). (Illus.). 61p. 1984. reprint ed. pap. 3.20 (*0-8182-0040-5*) Commonweal PA.

Piotrowski, Roman. Cartels & Trusts: Their Origin & Historical Development, from the Economic & Legal Aspects. LC 78-14461. 376p. 1979. reprint ed. lib. bdg. 45.00 (*0-87991-951-5*) Porcupine Pr.

Piotrowski, Sylvester A. Etienne Cabet & the Voyage En Icarie: A Study in the History of Social Thought. LC 75-340. (Radical Tradition in America Ser.). (Illus.). 173p. 1975. reprint ed. 18.15 (*0-88355-243-4*) Hyperion Conn.

Piotrowski, Tadeusz. Vengeance of the Swallows: Memoir of a Polish Family's Ordeal under Soviet Aggression, Ukrainian Ethnic Cleansing & Nazi Enslavement, & Their Emigration to America. (Illus.). 264p. 1995. lib. bdg. 29.95 (*0-7864-0001-3*) McFarland & Co.

Piotrowski, Z. A. Perceptanalysis. 523p. 1987. text ed. 49.95 (*0-8058-0102-2*) L Erlbaum Assocs.

Piotrowski, Zygmunt A. Dreams: A Key to Self-Knowledge. 200p. 1986. text ed. 39.95 (*0-89859-691-2*) L Erlbaum Assocs.

— Perceptanalysis. LC 57-5067. (Illus.). 505p. (C). 1985. reprint ed. text ed. 29.95 (*0-318-03720-3*) Ex Libris PA.

Piott, Steven L. The Anti-Monopoly Persuasion: Popular Resistance to the Rise of Big Business in the Midwest. LC 84-15694. (Contributions in Economics & Economic History Ser.: No. 60). x, 194p. 1985. text ed. 49.95 (*0-313-24545-2*, PAN/) Greenwood.

Piotti, Vittorio, jt. auth. see Pugh, Harry.

Pioud, G., jt. auth. see Lofmarker, R.

Pious, Richard M. American Politics & Government. 752p. 1986. text ed. 34.95 (*0-07-050121-1*) McGraw.

— Essentials of American Politics & Government. 576p. 1987. pap. text ed. 27.95 (*0-07-050126-2*) McGraw.

— The Presidency. (Ballots & Bandwagons Ser.). (Illus.). 128p. (J). (gr. 5 up). 1991. lib. bdg. 12.95 (*0-382-24316-1*); pap. 7.95 (*0-382-24322-6*) Silver Burdett Pr.

— The Presidency. LC 95-12298. 1996. write for info. (*0-02-395792-1*) Allyn.

— Richard Nixon. (J). (gr. 7 up). 1992. lib. bdg. 13.98 (*0-671-72852-0*, Julian Messner); pap. 7.95 (*0-671-72853-9*, Julian Messner) Silver Burdett Pr.

— Young Oxford Companion to Governments of the World. (Illus.). 512p. (J). 1995. lib. bdg. 70.00 (*0-19-508486-1*) OUP.

— The Young Oxford Companion to the Presidency of the United States. LC 93-19908. (YA). 1994. Alk. paper. 35.00 (*0-19-507799-7*) OUP.

Pious, Richard M., jt. ed. see Pyle, Christopher H.

Piozzi, Hester. Autobiography, Letters, & Literary Remains of Mrs. Piozzi (Thrale), 2 vols., Set. LC 70-178349. reprint ed. 115.00 (*0-404-56776-2*) AMS Pr.

Piozzi, Hester L. Anecdotes of the Late Samuel Johnson. (BCL1-PR English Literature Ser.). 205p. 1992. reprint ed. lib. bdg. 79.00 (*0-7812-7367-6*) Rprt Serv.

— Anecdotes of the Late Samuel Johnson, L.D: During the Last Twenty Years of His Life. Roberts, S. C., ed. LC 70-95109. 205p. 1971. reprint ed. text ed. 55.00 (*0-8371-3138-3*, PIAN, Greenwood Pr) Greenwood.

— The Piozzi Letters: Correspondence of Hester Lynch Piozzi, 1784-1821 (Formerly Mrs. Thrale), Vol. 2: 1792-1798. Bloom, Edward A. & Bloom, Lillian D., eds. LC 87-40231. (Illus.). 592p. 1991. 75.00 (*0-87413-360-2*) U Delaware Pr.

Piozzi, Hesther L. Anecdotes of Samuel Johnson. Roberts, S. C., ed. LC 75-99668. (Select Bibliographies Reprint Ser.). 1980. 15.95 (*0-8369-5097-6*) Ayer.

Pipa, Arshi. Albanian Stalinism: Ideo-Political Aspects. (East European Monographs: No. 287). 240p. 1990. text ed. 29.50 (*0-88033-184-4*) Col U Pr.

— Contemporary Albanian Literature. 224p. 1991. text ed. 31.50 (*0-88033-202-6*) Col U Pr.

— Montale & Dante. LC 68-31650. (Minnesota Monographs in the Humanities: Vol. 4). 227p. reprint ed. pap. 64.70 (*0-318-39688-2*, 2033283) Bks Demand.

— The Politics of Language in Socialist Albania. 288p. 1989. text ed. 46.00 (*0-88033-168-2*) East Eur Quarterly.

Pipa, Joseph A. Leader's Guide for T. Norton Sterrett's "How to Understand Your Bible" A Teaching Manual for Use in Adult Study Groups. (Orig.). 1977. pap. 3.95 (*0-934688-06-0*) Great Comm Pubns.

Pipe, David & Rapley, Linda. Ocular Anatomy & Histology. (C). 1989. 130.00 (*0-900099-19-4*, Pub. by Assn Brit Dispen Opticians UK) St Mut.

Pipe, G. R. & Veenhius, A. A. National Planning for Informatics in Developing Countries: Proceedings of a Conference Held in Baghdad, 1975. 1976. 72.00 (*0-7204-0392-8*, North Holland) Elsevier.

Pipe, G. R., jt. ed. see Rada, J. F.

Pipe, Peter, jt. auth. see Mager, Robert F.

***Pipe, Rhona.** Born in a Stable. (Illus.). 1995. pap. 4.99 (*0-8010-4040-X*) Baker Bk.

— One Christmas Night. Smith, Julie, ed. (Illus.). 24p. (J). (ps-3). Date not set. 4.99 (*0-7814-1511-X*, Chariot Bks); 4.99 (*0-7814-1510-1*, Chariot Bks) Chariot Family.

— Where Is Jesus? An Interactive Bible Storybook. (J). (ps-3). 1993. 7.99 (*1-56507-146-8*) Harvest Hse.

— Where Is Noah? An Interactive Bible Storybook. (J). (ps-3). 1993. 7.99 (*1-56507-144-1*) Harvest Hse.

Pipe, Russell G. & Brown, Chris, eds. The International Information Economy Handbook. 131p. (Orig.). 1985. pap. 27.50 (*0-936107-00-6*) Trans Data Rep.

Pipe, Steve. One Hundred One Ways to Run Your Own Business Profitably. 128p. (Orig.). 1993. pap. text ed. 19.95 (*0-7494-1089-2*, Pub. by Kogan Page UK) Nichols Pub.

Pipeline Supervisory & Control Systems Workshop Staff. Pipeline Supervisory & Control Systems Workshop: Presented at the 5th Annual Energy-Sources Technology Conference, New Orleans, Louisiana, March 8-10, 1982. Seiders, E. J., ed. LC 82-70514. 96p. reprint ed. pap. 27.40 (*0-8357-8750-8*, 2033653) Bks Demand.

Piper. And Then There Were Two. 109p. 1993. pap. text ed. 14.50 (*0-88751-060-4*) Heinemann.

— Regulation of Heme Biosynth by Drugs, Hormones & Toxicants. 1994. 139.95 (*0-8493-6834-0*) CRC Pr.

— Stories from Ugadali: Cherokee Story Teller. 1981. pap. 3.95 (*0-89992-078-0*) Coun India Ed.

Piper & Marbury. Maryland Environmental Law Handbook. 2nd ed. (State Environmental Law Ser.). 275p. 1993. pap. text ed. 85.00 (*0-86587-359-3*) Gov Insts.

Piper, et al. Personal Shorthand for the Executive Secretary: Syllabus. 211p. 1977. pap. text ed. 12.95 (*0-89420-030-5*, 217150); audio 243.95 (*0-89420-171-9*, 217100) Natl Book.

Piper & Marbury Staff, jt. auth. see Waste Management, Inc. Staff.

Piper, A. J., ed. see Beadle, Richard.

Piper, A. J., jt. auth. see Ker, Neil R.

Piper, Adrian, jt. auth. see Sims, Lowery S.

Piper, Andrew, jt. auth. see Samuels, John.

Piper, Beverly. Quick & Easy Healthy Cookery. (Illus.). 136p. (Orig.). 1993. pap. 9.95 (*0-563-36339-8*, BBC-Parkwest) Parkwest Pubns.

Piper, Buddy, jt. auth. see Darnell, Jeanie.

Piper, Charles. Valves: Valves. LC 83-161604. (Mud Equipment Manual Ser.). (Illus.). 56p. (Orig.). 1985. pap. 26.00 (*0-87201-622-6*) Gulf Pub.

Piper, Christine, jt. auth. see King, Michael.

***Piper, D. Z. & Medrano, M. D.** Geochemistry of the Phosphoria Formation at Montpelier Canyon, Idaho: Environment of Deposition. (U. S. Geological Survey Bulletin Ser.: Vol. 2023). 1994. write for info. (*0-615-00202-1*) US Geol Survey.

Piper, D. Z., jt. ed. see Bischoff, J. L.

Piper, David. The English Face. Rogers, Malcolm, ed. (Illus.). 272p. 1992. 85.00 (*1-85514-008-X*, Pub. by Natl Port Gall UK); pap. 49.50 (*1-85514-009-8*, Pub. by Natl Port Gall UK) Antique Collect.

— Language Theories & Educational Practice. LC 92-28795. 472p. 1992. 109.95 (*0-7734-9864-8*) E Mellen.

— Looking at Art: An Introduction to Enjoying the Great Paintings of the World. 256p. (C). 1984. pap. text ed. write for info. (*0-07-554784-8*) McGraw.

— Treasures of the Ashmolean. (Illus.). 112p. 1995. 16.95 (*0-907849-09-1*, TREA, Pub. by Ashmolean Mus UK) A Schwartz & Co.

Piper, David, intro. Michael Ayrton: Exhibition Catalogue. (Illus.). 16p. 1973. pap. 1.00 (*0-911209-01-8*) Palmer Mus Art.

Piper, David, ed. see Meredith, Fred.

Piper, David N. Is Higher Education Fair? SRHE Annual Conference Papers 1981. 194p. 1981. 38.00 (*0-900868-82-1*, Open Univ Pr) Taylor & Francis.

Piper, David W. Are Professors Professional? The Organisation of University Examinations. LC 93-38452. (Higher Education Policy Ser.: No. 25). 252p. 1994. 60.00 (*1-85302-540-2*, Pub. by J Kingsley Pubs UK) Taylor & Francis.

Piper, David W., jt. ed. see Acker, Sandra.

Piper, Don C. The International Law of the Great Lakes: A Study of Canadian-United States Co-operation. LC 66-29860. (Duke University, Commonwealth-Studies Center, Publication Ser.: No. 30). 179p. reprint ed. pap. 51.10 (*0-317-20435-1*, 2023434) Bks Demand.

Piper, Don C. & Terchek, Ronald J., eds. Interaction: Foreign Policy & Public Policy. LC 83-8810. (AEI Studies: No. 381). (Illus.). 255p. pap. 72.70 (*0-8357-4493-0*, 2037346) Bks Demand.

Piper, Doris. Stories of Old New Hampshire. 1987. 7.95 (*0-685-43893-7*) Equity Pubng NH.

Piper, Douglas W., jt. auth. see Powell, Lawrie W.

Piper, Edwin F. Canterbury Pilgrims: Poems. 128p. 1989. 14.95 (*0-944266-06-1*) Maecenas Pr.

Piper, Eloise & Dilligan, Mary. Creating & Crafting Dolls: Patterns, Techniques, & Inspirations for Making Cloth Dolls: Featuring Give Me Color! Doll Patterns. LC 93-45404. (Craft Kaleidoscope Ser.). 128p. 1994. pap. 19.95 (*0-8019-8524-2*) Chilton.

Piper, Evelyn. Bunny Lake Is Missing. large type ed. LC 92-28645. (Nightingale Ser.). 320p. 1993. pap. 15.95 (*0-8161-5634-4*, Nightingale) Hall.

— The Lady & Her Doctor. 320p. 1986. reprint ed. pap. 6.00 (*0-89733-194-X*) Academy Chi Pubs.

— The Nanny. large type ed. LC 92-38586. (General Ser.). 319p. 1993. 16.95 (*0-8161-5610-7*) G K Hall.

Piper, F. C., jt. auth. see Beker, Henry J.

Piper, F. C., jt. ed. see Beker, Henry J.

Piper, H. Beam. Murder in the Gunroom. 272p. 1993. reprint ed. pap. 15.00 (*1-882968-02-6*) Old Earth Bks.

Piper, H. W. The Singing of Mount Abora: Coleridge's Use of Biblical Imagery & Natural Symbolism in Poetry & Philosophy. LC 86-45480. 128p. 1987. 28.50 (*0-8386-3295-5*) Fairleigh Dickinson.

Piper, Hans M., ed. Cell Culture Techniques in Heart & Vessel Research. (Illus.). 375p. 1990. 114.00 (*0-387-51934-3*) Spr-Verlag.

— Pathophysiology of Severe Ischemic Myocardial Injury. 440p. 1990. lib. bdg. 194.50 (*0-7923-0459-4*) Kluwer Ac.

PQ

Piper, Hans M. & Isenberg, Gerrit, eds. Isolated Adult Cardiomyocytes, 2 vols., Vol. I: Structure & Metabolism. 304p. 1989. Vol. I, Structure & Metabolism, 304 pgs. 205.00 (*0-8493-4741-6*, QP114) CRC Pr.
— Isolated Adult Cardiomyocytes, 2 vols., Vol. II. 288p. 1989. 217.00 (*0-8493-4742-4*) CRC Pr.
Piper, Hans M. & Preuse, Claus J., eds. Ischemia-Reperfusion in Cardiac Surgery. LC 93-16723. (Developments in Cardiovascular Medicine Ser.: Vol. 142). 1993. lib. bdg. 180.00 (*0-7923-2241-X*) Kluwer Ac.
Piper, Henry D. Fitzgerald's The Great Gatsby: The Novel, the Critics, the Background. (Research Anthologies Ser.). (Illus.). 235p. (Orig.). (C). 1970. pap. write for info. (*0-02-395710-7*, Scribners) S&S Trade.
Piper, J., jt. ed. see Lundsteen, C.
Piper, J. D. Palaeomagnetic Database. 304p. 1988. 163.00 (*0-335-15211-2*) Wiley.
— Palaeomagnetic Database. 264p. 1991. text ed. 195.00 (*0-471-93255-8*) Wiley.
— Palaeomagnetism & the Continental Crust. 434p. 1991. 84.95 (*0-471-93254-X*) Wiley.
Piper, Jacqueline M. Rice in South-East Asia: Cultures & Landscapes. (Images of Asia Ser.). (Illus.). 108p. 1994. 16.95 (*967-65-3038-7*) OUP.
***Piper, James E.** Handbook of Facility Management: Tools & Techniques, Formulas & Tables. LC 94-33199. 1994. write for info. (*0-13-554296-0*) P-H.
Piper, Janet P. Behind This Mortal Bone: Poems. 160p. 1990. 16.95 (*0-944266-07-X*) Maecenas Pr.
Piper, Joanne. Filing: Syllabus. 2nd ed. 1979. pap. text ed. 8.95 (*0-89420-037-2*, 327007); audio 105.25 (*0-89420-146-8*, 106000) Natl Book.
— Vowel Sounds & Silent Letters: Syllabus. 1975. pap. text ed. 5.95 (*0-89420-023-2*, 240008); audio 22.45 (*0-89420-196-4*, 240000) Natl Book.
Piper, Joanne & Yerian, Theo. Personal Shorthand: Teacher's Manual & Key to Syllabus. 1975. teacher ed 4.95 (*0-89420-094-1*, 217007) Natl Book.
— Personal Shorthand: Syllabus. 1975. pap. text ed. 14.95 (*0-89420-083-6*, 217000); audio 248.60 (*0-89420-172-7*, 178000) Natl Book.
Piper, John. Desiring God: Meditations of a Christian Hedonist. LC 86-23818. 281p. 1987. pap. 10.99 (*0-88070-221-4*, Multnomah Bks) Questar Pubs.
— The Justification of God: An Exegetical & Theological Study of Romans 9: 1-23. 2nd ed. LC 82-74139. 257p. (Orig.). 1992. pap. 14.99 (*0-8010-7079-1*) Baker Bk.
— Let the Nations Be Glad! The Supremacy of God in Missions. LC 93-14327. 240p. (Orig.). 1993. pap. 12.99 (*0-8010-7124-0*) Baker Bk.
— Love Your Enemies: Jesus' Love Command in the Synoptic Gospels & the Early Christian Paraenesis. LC 91-24175. 287p. 1992. pap. text ed. 14.99 (*0-8010-7117-8*) Baker Bk.
— The Supremacy of God in Preaching. LC 90-34898. 128p. (Orig.). 1990. pap. text ed. 7.99 (*0-8010-7112-7*) Baker Bk.
— What's the Difference? Manhood & Womanhood According to the Bible. 64p. (Orig.). (YA). 1990. pap. 3.99 (*0-89107-562-3*) Crossway Bks.
Piper, John, frwd. John Piper's Stowe. (Illus.). (C). 1989. 950.00 (*0-903696-25-8*, Pub. by Hurtwood Pr Ltd) St Mut.
Piper, John & Grudem, Wayne A., eds. Recovering Biblical Manhood & Womanhood. LC 90-20258. 576p. (Orig.). 1991. pap. 19.99 (*0-89107-586-0*) Crossway Bks.
Piper, John T., ed. see American Bar Association, Section of Taxation Staff.
Piper, Jon K., jt. auth. see Soule, Judith D.
Piper, June-el, jt. ed. see Jacobson, LouAnn.
Piper, June-el, ed. see Staski, Edward.
Piper, L. J. Contractors' All Risks & Public Liability Insurance. 80p. 1981. pap. 75.00 (*0-948691-03-4*, Pub. by Witherby & Co UK) St Mut.
Piper, Linda J. The Spartan Twilight. (Illus.). xx, 244p. 1986. lib. bdg. 60.00 (*0-89241-378-6*) Caratzas.
Piper, Margaret A. & Unger, Elizabeth R. Nucleic Acid Probes: A Primer for Pathologists. LC 89-17940. (Illus.). 154p. 1989. pap. text ed. 31.00 (*0-89189-283-4*) Am Soc Clinical.
Piper, Margo. Staying on Top: A Survival Handbook for the Ages of Our Lives. LC 91-17592. 80p. 1991. pap. 9.95 (*0-942963-14-8*) Distinctive Pub.
Piper, Mark, tr. see Decroux, Etienne.
Piper, Martha C. & Darrah, Johanna. Alberta Infant Motor Scale (AIMS) (Illus.). 1994. 20.95 (*0-7216-4721-9*) Saunders.
— Motor Assessment of the Developing Infant. LC 93-24914. (Illus.). 224p. 1994. text ed. 39.95 (*0-7216-4307-8*) Saunders.
Piper, Mel L. Cain & Abel. 48p. 1987. pap. 2.95 (*0-88144-103-1*) Christian Pub.
— Jacob & Esau: The Truth Unfolded. (Heroes of Faith Ser.). 80p. 1992. pap. 4.95 (*1-881477-01-0*) Piper Hse.
Piper, Patricia L., et al. Manual on KF: The Library of Congress Classification Schedule for Law of the United States. LC 72-86471. (American Association of Law Libraries Publications Ser.: No. 11). viii, 135p. 1972. text ed. 22.50 (*0-8377-0109-0*) Rothman.
Piper, Paul, ed. Die Geistliche Dichtung des Mittelalters, 2 vols. in 1. vi, 699p. 1985. reprint ed. write for info. (*3-283-07723-1*, Pub. by Georg Olms GW) Lubrecht & Cramer.
Piper, Priscilla J. SRS-A & Leukotrienes: Proceedings of the Annual Symposium of the Institute of Basic Medical Sciences, Royal College of Surgeons of England, 24th September 1980. LC 80-41758. (Prostaglandins Research Studies Ser.: No. 1). (Illus.). 296p. reprint ed. pap. 84.40 (*0-8357-3549-4*, 2034232) Bks Demand.
Piper, Priscilla J., ed. The Leukotrienes: Their Biological Significance-A Biological Council Symposium. (Illus.). 236p. 1986. text ed. 96.50 (*0-88167-214-9*) Raven.
Piper, Priscilla J., jt. ed. see Costello, John F.
Piper, Priscilla J., ed. see Royal College of Surgeons of England, Institute of Basic Medical Sciences, Symposium Staff.
Piper Pub. Co. Editorial Staff, ed. Kitchen Gourmet (Twin Cities) LC 79-87647. (Illus.). 1979. 10.00 (*0-87832-044-X*) Piper.
Piper, R. K. The Jefferson Square Business Association Area: Profiles & Prospects. (Illus.). 15p. (Orig.). 1983. pap. 1.50 (*1-55719-009-7*) U NE CPAR.
— Kellom Heights Stage II: Trends & Conditions Impacting Commercial & Office Space Development. 49p. (Orig.). 1983. pap. 3.50 (*1-55719-010-0*) U NE CPAR.
— Neighborhood & Community Histories: Their Value & Suggestions for Their Preparation. 33p. (Orig.). 1983. pap. 2.50 (*1-55719-031-3*) U NE CPAR.
— Re-Use of the Muse Theater: A Study of Consumer Preferences. 20p. (Orig.). 1986. pap. 2.00 (*1-55719-089-5*) U NE CPAR.
Piper, R. K. & Ruff, Jack. Omaha's Neighborhood Housing Services Area: A Physical Conditions Inventory. 80p. (Orig.). 1982. pap. 6.50 (*1-55719-032-1*) U NE CPAR.
Piper, R. K., jt. auth. see Ruff, Jack.
Piper, R. K., et al. Legal Aid Clients with General Assistance Problems: A Study of Housing Conditions. 14p. (Orig.). 1984. pap. 1.50 (*1-55719-077-1*) U NE CPAR.
Piper, R. Titus. Fishing in New Mexico. LC 88-33746. (Coyote Books Ser.). (Illus.). 298p. 1989. pap. 14.95 (*0-8263-1138-5*) U of NM Pr.
Piper, Ralph E. Point of No Return: An Aviator's Story. LC 89-27919. (Illus.). 222p. 1990. 24.95 (*0-8138-0158-3*) Iowa St U Pr.
Piper, Robert G., et al. Fish Hatchery Management. 517p. 1982. pap. 43.50 (*0-913235-03-2*) Am Fisheries Soc.
Piper, Robert J. & Rush, Richard D. Opportunities in Architecture Careers. LC 92-20018. (Opportunities in... Ser.). 1993. 13.95 (*0-8442-4038-9*, VGM Career Bks); pap. 10.95 (*0-8442-4039-7*, VGM Career Bks) NTC Pub Grp.
***Piper, Ronald A.** The Gospel Behind the Gospels: Current Studies on Q. LC 94-23349. (Supplements to Novum Testamentum: 75). 1994. 97.25 (*90-04-09737-6*) E J Brill.
— Wisdom in the Q Tradition: The Aphoristic Teaching of Jesus. (Society for New Testament Studies Monographs: No. 61). 296p. 1989. 74.95 (*0-521-35293-2*) Cambridge U Pr.
Piper, Susie S. Season of Inspiration One. (Orig.). 1985. pap. write for info. (*0-9618280-1-3*) S S Piper.
— Seasons of Inspiration Two. (Orig.). 1986. pap. 3.50 (*0-9618280-2-1*) S S Piper.
— Squibbles & Quotes. (Orig.). 1983. pap. write for info. (*0-9618280-0-5*) S S Piper.
Piper, Terry. Language for All Our Children. (Illus.). 416p. (Orig.). (C). 1993. pap. write for info. (*0-675-21362-2*) Macmillan.
Piper, Thomas R. Income Participations on Mortgage Loans by Major Financial Institutions, 1966-1974. (Explorations in Economic Research Three Ser.: No. 4). 43p. 1976. reprint ed. 35.00 (*0-685-61405-0*) Natl Bur Econ Res.
Piper, Thomas R. & Arnold, Jaspar H., III. Warrants & Convertible Debt As Financing Vehicles in the Private Placement Market. (Explorations in Economic Research Four Ser.: No. 2). 26p. 1977. reprint ed. 35.00 (*0-685-61411-5*) Natl Bur Econ Res.
Piper, Thomas R., et al. Can Ethics Be Taught? Perspectives, Challenges & Approaches at Harvard Business School. 1993. text ed. 19.95 (*0-07-103417-X*) McGraw.
— Can Ethics Be Taught? Perspectives, Challenges, & Approaches at the Harvard Business School. LC 92-27077. 208p. 1993. 19.95 (*0-87584-400-6*) Harvard Busn.
Piper, Watty. The Easy-to-Read-Little Engine That Could. (All Aboard Bks.) (Illus.). 32p. (J). (ps-2). 1986. audio 5.95 (*0-448-19088-5*, G&D); pap. 2.25 (*0-448-19078-8*, G&D) Putnam Pub Group.
— The Easy-to-Read Little Engine That Could. (All Aboard Books & Puzzles). (Illus.). (J). (ps-2). 1990. pap. 4.95 (*0-448-34344-4*, Platt & Munk Pubs) Putnam Pub Group.
— The Fast Rolling Little Engine That Could. LC 85-70661. (Fast Rolling Bks.). (Illus.). 12p. (J). (ps). 1985. 6.95 (*0-448-09878-4*, G&D) Putnam Pub Group.
— The Little Engine That Could. LC 99-44044. (Pop-Up Bks.). (Illus.). 12p. (J). (ps-2). 1984. 8.95 (*0-448-18963-1*, Platt & Munk Pubs) Putnam Pub Group.
— Little Engine That Could. (J). 1991. 5.95 (*0-448-40520-2*, Platt & Munk Pubs) Putnam Pub Group.
— The Little Engine That Could. 40p. (J). 1981. reprint ed. lib. bdg. 15.95 (*0-89966-366-4*) Buccaneer Bks.
— The Little Engine That Could. 69p. (J). 1981. reprint ed. lib. bdg. 10.95 (*0-89967-040-7*) Harmony Raine.
— The Little Engine That Could: Miniature Edition. (Illus.). 48p. (J). 1990. pap. 2.95 (*0-448-40071-5*, Platt & Munk Pubs) Putnam Pub Group.
— The Little Engine That Could: Sixtieth Anniversary Edition. (Illus.). 48p. (J). 1990. 12.95 (*0-448-40041-3*, Platt & Munk Pubs) Putnam Pub Group.
— The Little Engine That Could Board Book. (Illus.). 12p. (J). (ps). 1991. bds. 4.95 (*0-448-40101-0*, G&D) Putnam Pub Group.
— The Little Engine That Could Let's Count 123. LC 90-83240. (Illus.). 24p. (J). (ps). 1991. 9.95 (*0-448-40131-2*, G&D) Putnam Pub Group.
Piper, Watty, ret. The Little Engine That Could. (Comes to Life Bks.). 16p. (J). (ps-2). 1993. write for info. (*1-883366-15-1*) YES Ent.
Piper, William, ed. see Swift, Jonathan.
Piper, William B. Evaluating Shakespeare's Sonnets. LC 79-63593. (Rice University Studies: Vol. 65, No. 2). 85p. (C). 1979. pap. 5.50 (*0-89263-241-0*) Rice Univ.
— Immaterialist Aesthetics. LC 88-42619. (Illus.). 189p. 1989. text ed. 27.50 (*0-89263-268-2*) Rice Univ.
Piper, William E., et al. Adaptation to Loss Through Short-Term Group Psychotherapy. LC 92-1424. 219p. 1992. lib. bdg. 27.95 (*0-89862-796-6*) Guilford Pr.
Piperno, Dolores R. Phytolith Analysis: An Archaeological & Geological Perspective. 280p. 1987. text ed. 79.00 (*0-12-557175-5*) Acad Pr.
Pipes. Russia under the Old Regime. 1984. 21.75 (*0-684-14826-9*, Scribners) S&S Trade.
Pipes & Worthington. Nutrition in Infancy & Childhood, No. 5: Nutrition. 1993. 42.95 (*0-8016-7724-6*) Mosby Yr Bk.
Pipes, Alan. Production for Graphic Designers. 224p. 1992. pap. text ed. 41.00 (*0-13-739285-0*) P-H.
Pipes, Daniel. Greater Syria: The History of an Ambition. 256p. 1990. 35.00 (*0-19-506021-0*) OUP.
— Greater Syria: The History of an Ambition. 256p. 1992. pap. 16.95 (*0-19-506022-9*) OUP.
— The Long Shadow: Culture & Politics in the Middle East. 320p. 1988. pap. 34.95 (*0-88738-220-7*) Transaction Pubs.
— The Long Shadow: Culture & Politics in the Middle East. 320p. (C). 1990. pap. 21.95 (*0-88738-849-3*) Transaction Pubs.
— The Rushdie Affair: The Novel, the Ayatollah, & the West. 224p. 1990. 18.95 (*1-55972-025-5*, Birch Ln Pr) Carol Pub Group.
— Slave Soldiers & Islam: The Genesis of a Military System. LC 80-23969. 276p. reprint ed. pap. 78.70 (*0-7837-2990-1*, 2043193) Bks Demand.
Pipes, Daniel, ed. Sandstorm: Middle East Conflicts & America. LC 92-29688. 422p. (Orig.). (C). 1993. lib. bdg. 71.50 (*0-8191-8893-X*); pap. text ed. 19.50 (*0-8191-8894-8*) U Pr of Amer.
Pipes, Louis A. & Hovanessian, Shahen A. Matrix-Computer Methods in Engineering. LC 77-23111. 346p. 1977. reprint ed. 29.50 (*0-88275-591-9*) Krieger.
Pipes, Nancy A. The Pocket Guide to Business Writing. (Illus.). 150p. (Orig.). 1990. pap. write for info. (*0-923768-03-3*) Tekne Pr.
Pipes, Peggy L. Nutrition in Infancy & Childhood. 5th ed. 429p. 1993. pap. 26.95 (*0-8016-6567-1*) Mosby Yr Bk.
Pipes, R. B., ed. Nondestructive Evaluation & Flaw Criticality for Composite Materials - STP 696. 364p. 1979. 34.50 (*0-8031-0527-4*, 04-696000-33) ASTM.
Pipes, R. Byron & Blake, Robert A., Jr. Delaware Composites Design Encyclopedia, Vol. 6: Test Methods, 6 vols. LC 89-51098. 1990. lib. bdg. 195.00 (*0-87762-704-5*) Technomic.
— Delaware Composites Design Encyclopedia, Vol. 6: Test Methods, 6 vols., Set. LC 89-51098. 1990. lib. bdg. 995.00 (*0-685-45597-1*) Technomic.
Pipes, R. Byron & Lagneborg, Rune, eds. Materials Futures: Strategies & Opportunities. (MFSO Conference Proceedings Ser.). 1988. text ed. 40.00 (*1-55899-000-3*) Materials Res.
Pipes, Randolph & Davenport, Donna. Introduction to Psychotherapy. 384p. (C). 1990. Casebound. text ed. write for info. (*0-13-493578-0*) P-H.
***Pipes, Richard.** A Concise History of the Russian Revolution. LC 95-3127. 1995. 27.50 (*0-679-42277-3*) Knopf.
— Legalised Lawlessness: Soviet Revolutionary Justice. (C). 1990. 50.00 (*0-907967-73-6*, Pub. by Inst Euro Def & Strat UK) St Mut.
— Russia under Bolshevik Regime. 1995. pap. 18.00 (*0-679-76184-5*, Vin) Random.
— Russia under the New Regime: Lenin & the Birth of the Totalitarian State. 1994. 35.00 (*0-394-50242-6*) Knopf.
— Social Democracy & the St. Petersburg Labor Movement, 1885-97. 2nd ed. LC 85-27842. xviii, 107p. (C). 1985. 20.00 (*1-884445-13-6*) C Schlacks Pub.
Pipes, Richard, ed. see Conference on the Russian Revolution Staff, et al.
Pipes, Richard E. Formation of the Soviet Union: Communism & Nationalism, 1917-1923. rev. ed. LC 64-21284. (Russian Research Center Studies: No. 13). 377p. 1964. 37.00 (*0-674-30950-2*) HUP.
— History of the Russian Revolution. (Illus.). 1990. 39.50 (*0-394-50241-8*) Knopf.
— Russia under the Old Regime. LC 74-32564. 360p. 1976. pap. write for info. (*0-02-395700-X*, Scribners) S&S Trade.
— Russia under the Old Regime: With a New Foreword by the Author. 392p. (Orig.). 1992. reprint ed. pap. 15.00 (*0-02-036042-8*, Pub. by Gebrueder Borntraeger GW) Macmillan.
— The Russian Revolution. LC 91-50008. 976p. 1991. pap. 22.00 (*0-679-73660-3*, Vin) Random.
— Struve: Liberal on the Left, 1870-1905. (Russian Research Center Studies: No. 64). 429p. 1970. 39.95 (*0-674-84595-1*) HUP.
— Struve: Liberal on the Right, 1905-1944. LC 79-16145. (Russian Research Center Studies: No. 80). 536p. 1980. 47.50 (*0-674-84600-1*) HUP.
Pipes, Robert F. The Playboy: The Story of a B-24 Liberator Bomber. Wordworks Services Staff, ed. (Illus.). 51p. (Orig.). 1989. pap. text ed. 4.95 (*0-9622915-2-8*) C S Hosie Pub.
— The Playboy Crew - Nineteen Forty-Four to Forty-Five: Memoirs of World War II. (Illus.). 176p. 1989. pap. 15.95 (*0-317-93918-1*) C S Hosie Pub.
Pipes, Wesley O. Bacterial Indicators of Pollution. 184p. 1982. 144.00 (*0-8493-5970-8*, QR48, CRC Reprint) Franklin.
Pipes, William H. Say Amen, Brother! Old-Time Negro Preaching: A Study in American Frustration. LC 91-19572. (African American Life Ser.). 232p. 1992. 29.95 (*0-8143-2383-9*); pap. 14.95 (*0-8143-2384-7*) Wayne St U Pr.
— Say Amen Brother, Old-Time Negro Preaching: A Study in American Frustration. LC 73-111585. 210p. 1970. reprint ed. text ed. 35.00 (*0-8371-4611-9*, PSA&, Negro U Pr) Greenwood.
Pipestem, Nan H. The Ecology Cookbook. 1991. pap. 11.95 (*0-89087-632-0*) Celestial Arts.
Pipher, Mary. Hunger Pains: The American Women's Tragic Quest for Thinness. 150p. (Orig.). 1988. pap. 6.50 (*0-9620533-0-9*) M Pipher.
— Reviving Ophelia: Saving the Selves of Adolescent Girls. 304p. 1995. pap. 12.50 (*0-345-39282-5*) Ballantine.
— Reviving Ophelia: Saving the Selves of Adolescent Girls. 320p. 1994. 24.95 (*0-399-13944-3*, Grosset-Putnam) Putnam Pub Group.
Pipics, Z. The Librarian's Practical Dictionary in Twenty-Two Languages. 450p. 1993. 325.00 (*0-686-72094-6*, Pub. by Collets UK) Pro-Am Music.
— Woerterbuch Des Bibliothekars in 22 Sprachen: Librarian's Practical Dictionary in 22 Languages. 6th rev. ed. 385p. 1974. 295.00 (*0-8288-6227-3*, M-7540) Fr & Eur.
Pipikwass. When No One Was Looking. 50p. (Orig.). 1990. pap. 7.00 (*0-9621498-4-5*, Robin Hood) R Hood Little.
Pipili, Maria. Laconian Iconography of the Sixth Century BC. (Illus.). 1987. pap. 46.00 (*0-947816-12-7*, Pub. by Univ Comm Archeology UK) David Brown.
Pipitone, David A., ed. Safe Storage of Laboratory Chemicals. 2nd ed. 297p. 1991. text ed. 105.00 (*0-471-51581-7*) Wiley.
Pipkin. Lab Exercises in Oceanography. 2nd ed. (C). 1995. pap. text ed. write for info. (*0-7167-1917-7*) W H Freeman.
Pipkin, A. C. A Course on Integral Equations. (Texts in Applied Mathematics Ser.: Vol. 9). (Illus.). xiii, 268p. 1991. 39.00 (*0-387-97557-8*) Spr-Verlag.
— Lectures on Viscoelasticity Theory. 2nd ed. (Applied Mathematical Sciences Ser.: Vol. 7). (Illus.). viii, 188p. 1986. pap. 49.00 (*0-387-96345-6*) Spr-Verlag.
Pipkin, Bernard & Cummings, David. Environmental Geology: Practical Exercises. (Illus.). 240p. (C). 1983. pap. 20.95 (*0-89863-058-4*) Star Pub CA.
Pipkin, Bernard & Proctor, Richard, eds. Engineering Geology Practice in Southern California. LC 92-29101. (Illus.). 1992. lib. bdg. 79.95 (*0-89863-171-8*) Star Pub CA.
Pipkin, Bernard W. Geology & the Environment. LC 93-40808. 450p. (C). 1994. pap. text ed. 50.00 (*0-314-02834-X*) West Pub.
Pipkin, Bernard W., et al. Laboratory Exercises in Oceanography. 2nd ed. (Illus.). (C). 1995. teacher ed 5.95 (*0-7167-1845-6*); pap. text ed. write for info. (*0-7167-1810-3*) W H Freeman.
Pipkin, Fiona B. Medical Statistics Made Easy. (Illus.). 148p. (Orig.). 1984. pap. 22.00 (*0-443-02888-5*) Churchill.
Pipkin, George. Pete Aguereberry: Death Valley Prospector. LC 81-84564. (Illus.). 1982. 9.95 (*0-930704-11-8*) Sagebrush Pr.
Pipkin, H. Wayne, comp. A Zwingli Bibliography. LC 73-153549. (Bibliographia Tripotamopolitana Ser.: No. 7). 1972. 7.00 (*0-931222-06-0*) Pitts Theolog.
***Pipkin, H. Wayne, ed.** Essays in Anabaptist Theology. (Text Reader Ser.: No. 5). 271p. (Orig.). 1994. pap. 15.00 (*0-936273-21-6*) Inst Mennonite.
— Seek Peace & Pursue It: Proceedings from the 1988 International Baptist Peace Conference. 222p. (Orig.). 1989. pap. 15.00 (*0-9622896-0-4*) Baptist Peace.
Pipkin, H. Wayne & Yoder, John H., eds. Balthasar Hubmaier. (Classics of the Radical Reformation Ser.: No. 5). 496p. 1989. 49.95 (*0-8361-3103-7*) Herald Pr.
Pipkin, H. Wayne, jt. ed. see Furchs, E. J.
Pipkin, H. Wayne, ed. see Shenk, Wilbert R.
Pipkin, J. J. The Story of a Rising Race. LC 70-173609. (Black Heritage Library Collection). 1977. reprint ed. 38.95 (*0-8369-8901-5*) Ayer.
Pipkin, Turk. Be a Clown: The Complete Guide to Instant Clowning. LC 88-51585. 104p. 1989. pap. 9.95 (*0-89480-347-6*, 1347) Workman Pub.
— Fast Greens. 192p. (Orig.). 1994. pap. 8.95 (*1-881484-06-8*) Softshoe Pub.
— The Winner's Guide to the Texas Lottery. (Illus.). 128p. (Orig.). 1992. pap. 4.95 (*1-881484-03-3*) Softshoe Pub.
Pipkin, Turk & Frech, Marshall, eds. Barton Springs Eternal: The Soul of a City. LC 93-83037. (Illus.). 144p. 1993. 24.95 (*1-881484-05-X*) Softshoe Pub.
Pipkin, Wayne H., tr. Huldrych Zwingli-Writings in Search of True Religion: Reformation, Pastoral & Eucharistic Writings, Vol. 2. LC 84-25454. (Pittsburgh Theological Monographs: No. 13). 1984. pap. 19.95 (*0-915138-59-X*) Pickwick.
Pipoly, J. J. A Systematic Revision of the Genus Cybianthus Subgenus Grammadenia (Myrsinaceae) LC 87-11221. (Memoirs Ser.: Vol. 43). (Illus.). 76p. 1987. pap. 17.50 (*0-89327-314-7*) NY Botanical.
Pippa, Arshi & Repishti, Sami, eds. Studies on Kosova. 279p. 1984. text ed. 48.00 (*0-88033-047-3*) East Eur Quarterly.
Pippa Sales Staff. Alcohol Abuse: How to Help a Loved One. LC 94-94058. 120p. (Orig.). 1994. pap. 10.95 (*1-884633-01-3*) DISA Pubns.
Pippard, A. B. The Dynamics of Conduction Electrons. 158p. 1965. text ed. 114.00 (*0-677-00720-5*) Gordon & Breach.

An Asterisk (*) at the beginning of an entry indicates that the title is appearing in BIP for the first time.

— Reconciling Physics With Reality: An Inaugural Lecture. LC 70-187082. 40p. reprint ed. pap. 25.00 (*0-317-08599-9*, 2051384) Bks Demand.

Pippard, A. Brian. Magnetoresistance in Metals. (Cambridge Studies in Low Temperature Physics: No. 2). (Illus.). 250p. 1989. 84.95 (*0-521-32660-5*) Cambridge U Pr.

— The Physics of Vibration, Vol. 1. (Illus.). 648p. (C). 1989. 79.95 (*0-521-37200-3*) Cambridge U Pr.

— The Physics of Vibration, Vol. 2: The Simple Vibrator in Quantum Mechanics. LC 77-85685. (Illus.). 200p. 1983. 74.95 (*0-521-24623-7*) Cambridge U Pr.

— Response & Stability: An Introduction to the Physical Theory. (Illus.). 238p. 1985. 74.95 (*0-521-26673-4*); pap. 29.95 (*0-521-31994-3*) Cambridge U Pr.

Pippard, John & Ellam, Les. Electroconvulsive Treatment in Great Britain, 1980: A Report to the Royal College of Psychiatrists. 172p. reprint ed. pap. 49.10 (*0-318-34925-6*, 2031461) Bks Demand.

Pippen, Christie. A Very Scraggly Christmas Tree. (J). (gr. 2-4). 1988. 19.97 (*0-8172-2754-7*) Raintree Steck-V.

— A Very Scraggly Christmas Tree. (Publish-a-Book Clippers Ser.). (Illus.). 32p. (J). (gr. 2-4). 1988. 29.28 (*0-8172-2469-6*) Raintree Steck-V.

Pippen, Christine. Very Scraggly Christmas Tree. (J). (ps-3). 1993. pap. 4.95 (*0-8114-5214-X*) Raintree Steck-V.

Pippen, Delois B. The Manager Who Became a Superstar: The Story of Scottie Pippen. 78p. 1994. 10.95 (*0-533-10730-X*) Vantage.

***Pippenger, C. E., et al, eds.** Antiepileptic Drugs: Quantitative Analysis & Interpretation. fac. ed. LC 76-58055. 383p. Date not set. pap. 109.20 (*0-7837-7503-2*, 2047003) Bks Demand.

Pippenger, John E., jt. auth. see Pease, Dudley A.

Pippenger, John H. & Hicks, Tyler G. Industrial Hydraulics. 3rd ed. (Illus.). 1979. text ed. 46.95 (*0-07-050140-8*) McGraw.

***Pippenger, John J.** Fluid Power: The Hidden Giant. (Global Series in Fluid Power). (Illus.). 503p. 1994. 100. 00 (*0-929276-02-7*) Amalgam Pub Co.

— Hydraulic Cartridge Valve Technology. (Global Series in Fluid Power). (Illus.). 347p. 1990. text ed. 84.95 (*0-929276-01-9*) Amalgam Pub Co.

— Hydraulic Valves & Controls: Selection & Application. (Fluid Power & Control Ser.: Vol. 4). (Illus.). 264p. 1984. 99.75 (*0-8247-7087-0*) Dekker.

— Zero Downtime Hydraulics. (Global Series in Fluid Power). (Illus.). 85p. (C). 1989. text ed. 24.95 (*0-929276-00-0*) Amalgam Pub Co.

***Pippenger, John J. & Gordon, Greg P.** Basics for the Fluid Power Mechanic. (Illus.). 238p. 1994. 48.00 (*0-929276-04-3*); teacher ed, pap. 6.00 (*0-929276-05-1*) Amalgam Pub Co.

***Pippenger, John J. & Lansky, Z. J.** Zero Downtime Pneumatics. (Global Series in Fluid Power). (Illus.). 256p. 1994. 48.00 (*0-929276-03-5*) Amalgam Pub Co.

Pipper, Audrey G. Nutrition & Medicine: Scientific Subject Index with Research Bibliography. LC 88-47596. 150p. 1988. 39.50 (*0-88164-748-9*); pap. 34.50 (*0-88164-749-7*) ABBE Pubs Assn.

Pippert, Rebecca & Siemens, Ruth. Evangelism. (LifeGuide Bible Studies). 64p. (Orig.). 1985. pap. 4.99 (*0-8308-1050-1*, 1050) InterVarsity.

Pippert, Rebecca M. Hope Has Its Reasons: Living the Promise of the Cross & the Resurrection. 1989. 14.95 (*0-318-42500-9*) Harper SF.

— Hope Has Its Reasons: Surprised by Faith in a Broken World. LC 93-22640. 32p. (Orig.). 1991. pap. 6.00 (*0-89109-652-3*) NavPress.

— Hope Has Its Reasons: Surprised by Faith in a Broken World. LC 91-70035. 224p. (Orig.). 1991. reprint ed. pap. 9.00 (*0-06-066685-4*) Harper SF.

— Out of the Saltshaker: Evangelism As a Way of Life. LC 79-1995. 192p. 1979. pap. 10.99 (*0-87784-735-5*, 735) InterVarsity.

Pippert, Wesley G. An Ethics of News: A Reporter's Search for Truth. LC 88-24700. 169p. (Orig.). 1989. pap. 10.95 (*0-87840-470-8*) Georgetown U Pr.

— The Hand of the Mighty: Right & Wrong Uses of Our Power. LC 91-6666. 160p. 1991. 14.99 (*0-8010-7115-1*) Baker Bk.

Pippin, James A. Developing Casework Skills. LC 80-18799. (Human Services Guides Ser.: Vol. 15). 149p. 1980. pap. 17.95 (*0-8039-1503-9*) Sage.

Pippin, Lonnie. Archaeological Test Excavations at 4-PLU-369 Near Chester, Plumas County, California. (Illus.). 39p. 1979. 7.00 (*0-945920-09-1*) Desert Rsch Inst.

Pippin, Lonnie & Davis, Jonathan. A Study of Cultural Resources Inventory by Island Park, Reservoir, Fremont County, Idaho. (Social Sciences Center Technical Report Ser.: No. 14). (Illus.). 146p. (C). 1980. spiral bd. 15.00 (*0-945920-14-8*) Desert Rsch Inst.

Pippin, Lonnie & Hattori, Eugene. An Analysis of Prehistoric Artifacts from Lassen National Forest, California. (Social Sciences Center Technical Report Ser.: No. 15). (Illus.). 140p. (C). 1980. spiral bd. 15.00 (*0-945920-15-6*) Desert Rsch Inst.

Pippin, Lonnie & Zerga, Donald. Cultural Resources Overview for the Nuclear Waste Storage Investigations, Nevada Test Site, Nye County, Nevada. (Social Sciences Center Technical Report Ser.: No. 24). (Illus.). 117p. (C). 1981. spiral bd. 10.00 (*0-945920-24-5*) Desert Rsch Inst.

Pippin, Lonnie, et al. Archaeological Investigations at the Pike's Point Site (4-LAS-537) Eagle Lake, Lassen County, California. (Social Sciences Center Technical Report Ser.: No. 7). (Illus.). 182p. (C). 1979. spiral bd. 18.50 (*0-945920-07-5*) Desert Rsch Inst.

— An Archaeological Reconnaissance of the NNWSI Yucca Mountain Project Area Southern Nye County, Nevada. (Social Sciences Center Technical Report Ser.: No. 28). (Illus.). 120p. (C). 1982. spiral bd. 12.00 (*0-945920-28-8*) Desert Rsch Inst.

Pippin, Lonnie C. An Overview of Cultural Resources on Pahute & Rainier Mesas on the Nevada Test Site, Nye County, Nevada. (Social Sciences Center Technical Report Ser.: No. 45). (Illus.). 225p. (Orig.). (C). 1986. pap. text ed. 20.00 (*0-945920-45-8*) Desert Rsch Inst.

— Prehistoric & Historic Patterns of Lower Pinyon-Juniper Woodland Ecotone Exploitation at Borealis, Mineral County, Nevada. (Social Sciences Center Technical Report Ser.: No. 17). (Illus.). 63p. (C). 1980. spiral bd. 7.00 (*0-945920-17-2*) Desert Rsch Inst.

— Prehistory & Paleoecology of Guadalupe Ruin, New Mexico. (Anthropological Papers: No. 112). (Illus.). 272p. (Orig.). 1987. pap. text ed. 25.00 (*0-87480-281-4*) U of Utah Pr.

Pippin, Lonnie C., ed. Limited Test Excavations at Selected Archaeological Sites in the NNWSI Yucca Mountain Project Area, Southern Nye County, Nevada. (Social Sciences Center Technical Report Ser.: No. 40). (Illus.). 307p. (C). 1984. spiral bd. 30.00 (*0-945920-40-7*) Desert Rsch Inst.

Pippin, Lonnie C. & Zerga, Donald L. An Annotated Bibliography of Cultural Resources Literature for the Nevada Nuclear Waste Storage Investigations. (Social Sciences Center Technical Report Ser.: No. 30). (Illus.). 142p. (C). 1981. spiral bd. 14.00 (*0-945920-30-X*) Desert Rsch Inst.

Pippin, Lonnie C., jt. auth. see Henton, Gregory H.

Pippin, Lonnie C., jt. auth. see Reno, Ronald L.

Pippin, Lonnie C., et al. A Class II Archaeological Reconnaissance of a Portion of Area 20, Nevada Test Site, Nye County, Nevada. (Illus.). 46p. 1987. 10.00 (*0-945920-52-0*) Desert Rsch Inst.

***Pippin, Michael J.** Retirement Plans: A Users Guide for Employees & Retirees. LC 94-69148. 192p. 1995. pap. 12.95 (*0-9644272-0-6*) Pension Srv Design.

Pippin, Robert, et al. Marcuse: Critical Theory & the Promise of Utopia. LC 87-20002. 288p. 1987. text ed. 55.00 (*0-89789-106-6*, Bergin & Garvey); pap. text ed. 18.95 (*0-89789-107-4*, Bergin & Garvey) Greenwood.

Pippin, Robert B. Modernism As a Philosophical Problem: On the Dissatisfactions of European High Culture. 224p. (C). 1991. pap. 21.95 (*0-631-17657-8*) Blackwell Pubs.

Pippin, Robert S. Hegel's Idealism: The Satisfactions of Self-Consciousness. 384p. (C). 1989. pap. 22.95 (*0-521-37923-7*) Cambridge U Pr.

Pippin, Tina. Death & Desire: The Rhetoric of Gender in the Apocalypse of John. (Literary Currents in Biblical Interpretation Ser.). 144p. (Orig.). 1992. pap. 18.99 (*0-664-25157-9*) Westminster John Knox.

Pippin, Tina, jt. auth. see Aichele, George.

Pippin, Tina, jt. auth. see Jobling, David.

Pippin, Wilbur & Winters, Marian. Catwise. LC 78-27344. (Illus.). 1979. pap. 5.95 (*0-394-73786-5*) Knopf.

Pippin, Wilbur & Winters, Marion. Catwise. (Illus.). 96p. 1991. reprint ed. 8.99 (*0-517-06506-1*) Random Hse Value.

Pipprek, J. Large German-Polish Dictionary: Grosswoerterbuch Deutsch-Polnisch, 2 vols. 6th ed. 2116p. (GER & POL.). 1984. 150.00 (*0-8288-0484-2*, F33210) Fr & Eur.

— Large Polish-German Dictionary: Grosswoerterbuch Polnisch-Deutsch, 2 vols. 5th ed. 2100p. (GER & POL.). 1984. 125.00 (*0-8288-0485-0*, M9128) Fr & Eur.

Piprell, Collin & Boyd, Ashley. Diving in Thailand. (Illus.). 192p. 1994. 22.50 (*0-7818-0315-2*) Hippocrene Bks.

Pique, Chantal, jt. auth. see Pique, Gil.

Pique, Gil & Pique, Chantal. Papillote Fish, Secrets of Papillote Cooking, Vol. 5: No Mess Gourmet Cooking en Papillote. (Illus.). 112p. 1994. text ed. write for info. (*0-9633688-5-0*) Papillote.

— Papillote Meat, Secret of Papillote Cooking, Vol. 2: No Mess Gourmet Cooking en Papillote. (Illus.). 112p. 1994. text ed. write for info. (*0-9633688-4-2*) Papillote.

— Papillote Poultry, Secret of Papillote Cooking, Vol. 3: No Mess Gourmet Cooking en Papillote. (Illus.). 112p. 1994. text ed. write for info. (*0-9633688-3-4*) Papillote.

— Papillote Vegetable, Secret of Papillote Cooking, Vol. 4: No Mess Gourmet Cooking en Papillote. (Illus.). 112p. 1994. text ed. write for info. (*0-9633688-2-6*) Papillote.

— Papillotes: Secret of Papillote Cooking. (Illus.). 120p. 1993. reprint ed. pap. 15.00 (*0-9633688-1-8*) Papillote.

— Secret of Papillote Cooking, No. 1: No Mess Gourmet Cooking. (Illus.). 112p. Date not set. text ed. 19.95 (*0-9633688-7-7*) Papillote.

Piquet, O. & Sibold, K. Renormalized Supersymmetry: The Perturbation Theory of N-1 Supersymmetric Theories in Flat Space-Time. (Progress in Physics Ser.: Vol. 12). 368p. 1986. 63.50 (*0-8176-3346-4*) Birkhauser.

Pir Oveyssi, Shah M., jt. auth. see Hazrat, Molana-al-Moazam.

PIRA. Paklegis: A Guide to Packaging Legislation. 1983. pap. 40.00 (*0-08-029888-5*, Pub. by Pergamon Repr UK) Franklin.

Pirages, Dennis. Global Technopolitics: The International Politics of Technology & Resources. LC 88-25887. 304p. (C). 1989. pap. 21.95 (*0-534-09912-2*) Intl Thomson.

Pirages, Dennis C. & Sylvester, Christine, eds. Transformations in the Global Political Economy. LC 89-28541. (International Political Economy Ser.). 236p. 1990. text ed. 49.95 (*0-312-04075-X*) St Martin.

Piraino, Anthony. A Psychological Study of Tolstoy's Anna Karenina. LC 93-29917. 172p. 1993. pap. 24.95 (*0-7734-1943-8*) E Mellen.

Piraino, Emil S. When We Dreamed of America: My Boyhood in Cefalu During Italy's Fascist Era. 1992. 18. 95 (*0-533-10267-7*) Vantage.

Pirajno, F. Hydrothermal Mineral Deposits: Principles & Fundamental Concepts for the Exploration Geologist. (Illus.). 728p. 1992. 169.00 (*0-387-52517-3*) Spr-Verlag.

Piramal, Gita, jt. auth. see Herdeck, Margaret.

Piran, Niva & Kaplan, Allan S., eds. A Day Hospital Group Treatment Program for Anorexia Nervosa & Bulimia Nervosa. LC 89-22065. (Eating Disorders Monograph Ser.: No. 3). 168p. 1990. 26.95 (*0-87630-552-4*) Brunner-Mazel.

Piran, T., jt. ed. see Weinberg, S.

Piran, T., et al, eds. Supernovae: Sixth Jerusalem Winter School for Theoretical Physics. 344p. (C). 1990. text ed. 74.00 (*9971-5-0963-6*); pap. text ed. 36.00 (*9971-5-0964-4*) World Scientific Pub.

Pirandello, Luigi. Better Think Twice about It: And Twelve Other Stories. (Short Story Index Reprint Ser.). 1977. reprint ed. 29.95 (*0-8369-4269-8*) Ayer.

— Cap & Bells. 1974. 4.00 (*0-87141-048-6*) Manyland.

— Eleven Short Stories - Undici Novelle: A Dual-Language Book. 224p. (Orig.). (ENG & ITA.). 1994. pap. 8.95 (*0-486-28091-8*) Dover.

— The Late Mattia Pascal. Weaver, William, tr. LC 87-83302. 262p. 1988. reprint ed. 23.00 (*0-941419-08-8*, Eridanos Library); reprint ed. pap. 14.00 (*0-941419-09-6*, Eridanos Library) Marsilio Pubs.

— Naked Masks. 1957. pap. 12.95 (*0-452-01082-9*, Mer) NAL-Dutton.

— Naked Masks: Five Plays. Bentley, Eric, ed. 1957. Incl. It Is So if You Think So; Henry IV; 6 Characters in Search of an Author; Each in His Own Way;. pap. 7.95 (*0-525-48319-5*, Dutton) NAL-Dutton.

— Naked Masks: Five Plays. Bentley, Eric, ed. Incl. It Is So If You Think So. 1957. (*0-318-51786-8*); Henry Fourth. 1957. (*0-318-51787-6*); Six Characters in Search of an Author. 1957. (*0-318-51788-4*); Each in His Own Way. 1957. (*0-318-51789-2*); Liola. 1957. (*0-318-51790-6*); 1957. Set pap. 7.95 (*0-525-47006-9*, 0674-210, Dutton) NAL-Dutton.

— Notebooks of Serafino Gubbio. (Dedalus European Classics Ser.). 356p. 1990. pap. 11.95 (*0-946626-58-8*) Hippocrene Bks.

— Novelle per un Anno. McCormick, C. A., ed. (Italian Texts Ser.). 240p. (ITA.). (C). 1988. text ed. 14.95 (*0-7190-0469-1*, Pub. by Manchester Univ Pr UK) St Martin.

— The Oil Jar & Other Stories. unabridged ed. (Thrift Editions Ser.). 96p. 1995. pap. text ed. 1.00 (*0-486-28459-X*) Dover.

— On Humor. LC 74-4281. (University of North Carolina Studies in Comparative Literature: No. 58). reprint ed. pap. 47.40 (*0-7837-9034-1*, 2049785) Bks Demand.

— One, No One & One Hundred Thousand. Weaver, William, tr. & intro. by. LC 88-83033. 260p. 1990. 18.95 (*0-941419-35-5*, Eridanos Library); pap. 9.95 (*0-941419-74-6*, Eridanos Library) Marsilio Pubs.

— Six Personnages en Quete d'Auteur, la Volupte de l'Honneur. (FRE.). 1978. pap. 10.95 (*0-7859-4105-3*) Fr & Eur.

— The Sounds of the Girgenti Dialect, & Their Development. Bussino, Giovanni R., tr. & intro. by. LC 92-21618. (American University Studies: Linguistics: Ser. XIII, Vol. 18). 228p. (C). 1992. text ed. 45.95 (*0-8204-1457-3*) P Lang Pubs.

— Tales of Suicide. 1988. 11.95 (*0-937832-31-6*) Dante U Am.

— Theatre Complet, Vol. 1. 1536p. 45.00 (*0-686-56547-9*) Fr & Eur.

— Theatre Complet, Vol. 1. deluxe ed. Bouissy, Andre, ed. 1536p. (FRE.). 1977. 120.00 (*0-7859-3832-X*, 2070108791) Fr & Eur.

— Theatre Complet, Vol. 2. Bouissy, Andre, ed. (FRE.). 1985. lib. bdg. 150.00 (*0-7859-3869-9*) Fr & Eur.

— Three Plays: 'Enrico IV', 'Sei Personaggi in Cerca d'Autore', 'La Giara' Firth, F., ed. (Italian Texts Ser.). 308p. (ITA.). (C). 1988. text ed. 14.95 (*0-7190-0346-6*, Pub. by Manchester Univ Pr UK) St Martin.

— Tonight We Improvise & "Leonora, Addio!" Sbrocchi, Leonard G. & Campbell, J. Douglas, trs. (Biblioteca di Quaderni d'Italianistica Ser.: Vol. 3). (Illus.). 122p. (Orig.). 1987. pap. 10.00 (*0-9691979-2-6*, Pub. by Can Soc Ital Stu CN) Speedimpex.

— Vetir Ceux Qui Sont Nus, Comme Avant, Mieux Qu'Avant. (FRE.). 1982. pap. 10.95 (*0-7859-4176-2*) Fr & Eur.

***Pirandello, Luigi, tr.** Tales of Madness. (ITA.). 1984. 14.50 (*0-937832-26-X*) Dante U Am.

Piranesi, Giovanni B. Differentes Vues de Quelques Restes... de l'Ancienne Ville de Pesto. (Illus.). 25p. 1973. 95.00 (*1-55660-198-0*) A Wofsy Fine Arts.

— Giovanni Battista Piranesi: Drawings in the Pierpont Morgan Library. Stampfle, Felice, ed. 1978. pap. 9.95 (*0-486-23714-1*) Dover.

— The Prisons (Le Carceri) The Complete First & Second States. LC 72-92762. (Illus.). 96p. 1974. reprint ed. pap. 8.95 (*0-486-21540-7*) Dover.

Piranesi, Giovanni B. & Levit, Herschel. Views of Rome Then & Now. (Illus.). 96p. (Orig.). 1976. pap. 14.95 (*0-486-23339-1*) Dover.

Pirani, C. L., ed. Ultrastructural Pathology of the Kidney. (Journal: Applied Pathology: Vol. 5, No. 2, 1987). (Illus.). 68p. 1987. pap. 36.00 (*3-8055-4634-3*) S Karger.

Pirani, F. A., jt. auth. see Crampin, M.

Pirani, Felix. Rosalie, Sylvia & Melanie. (I Love to Read Collection). (Illus.). (J). (gr. 3-8). 1992. lib. bdg. 12.79 (*0-89565-888-7*) Childs World.

Pirani, Felix A., et al. Local Jet Bundle Formulation of Backlund Transformations. (Mathematical Physics Studies: No. 1). 1979. pap. text ed. 32.50 (*90-277-1036-8*) Kluwer Ac.

Pirani, G., et al, eds. Advanced Algorithms & Architectures for Speech Understanding. (Research Reports ESPRIT, Project 26 SIP: Vol. 1). xiv, 274p. 1990. pap. 35.00 (*0-387-53402-4*) Spr-Verlag.

Piranian, Deborah, tr. see Shatayev, Vladimir.

Piraro. Glasnost Bizarro. 1990. pap. 5.95 (*0-87701-693-3*) Chronicle Bks.

***Piraro, Dan.** Best of Bizarro Vol. II. 1994. pap. 9.95 (*0-8118-0771-1*) Chronicle Bks.

— The Best of Bizzaro. (Illus.). 144p. 1992. pap. 9.95 (*0-8118-0276-0*) Chronicle Bks.

— Bizarro. (Illus.). 104p. (Orig.). 1986. pap. 5.95 (*0-87701-402-7*) Chronicle Bks.

— Bizarro, No. 9. (Illus.). 112p. (Orig.). 1995. pap. 6.95 (*0-8362-0430-1*) Andrews & McMeel.

— Mondo Bizarro. 1989. pap. 5.95 (*0-87701-711-5*) Chronicle Bks.

— Post-Modern Bizarro. (Illus.). 96p. (Orig.). 1991. pap. 6.95 (*0-87701-854-5*) Chronicle Bks.

— Sumo Bizarro. (Illus.). 104p. (Orig.). 1990. pap. 5.95 (*0-87701-774-3*) Chronicle Bks.

— Too Bizarro. (Illus.). 104p. 1988. pap. 5.95 (*0-87701-536-8*) Chronicle Bks.

Pirasteh, Hassan. Applications of Economics: Contemporary Issues. 1993. pap. text ed. 28.30 (*1-56226-137-1*) CT Pub.

Pirasteh, Hassan, et al. Macroeconomics - Theory & Reality. 1994. pap. 29.95 (*1-56226-171-1*) CT Pub.

— Principles of Microeconomics. 1992. pap. 44.05 (*1-56226-101-0*) CT Pub.

Pirault, J. P., jt. auth. see Collings, Nick.

Piraux, B., et al, eds. Super-Intense Laser-Atom Physics. (NATO ASI Series B, Physics: Vol. 316). (Illus.). 512p. (C). 1994. 129.50 (*0-306-44587-5*, Plenum Pr) Plenum.

Piraux, Henri. Diccionario General de Acustica y Electro Acustica. 374p. (SPA.). 1967. 29.95 (*0-8288-6672-4*, S-50237) Fr & Eur.

— Dictionaire Francais-Anglais d'electro-technique et d'electronique. (FRE.). 75.00 (*0-685-36687-1*) Fr & Eur.

— Dictionary of Electrical Engineering, Electronics & Related Applications: Dictionnaire de l'Electrotechnique, l'Electronique & Applications Connexes. 272p. (FRE & GER.). 1983. 75.00 (*0-8288-0923-2*, M6455) Fr & Eur.

— Dizionario Inglese-Italiano dei Termini Relativi all'Elettrotecnica e Alle Applicazioni Connesse: English-Italian Dictionary of Terms Relative to Electronics, Electrical Engineering & Related Applications. 534p. (ENG & ITA.). 1977. pap. 59.95 (*0-8288-5463-7*, M9195) Fr & Eur.

— English - French Dictionary of Electronics & Related Terms. 16th ed. 401p. (ENG & FRE.). 1992. reprint ed. pap. 125.00 (*0-7859-4630-6*) Fr & Eur.

— French-English Dictionary of Electrical Engineering & Related Terms (Dictionnaire Francais-Anglais des Termes Relatifs a l'Electrotechnique) 11th rev. ed. 218p. 1988. 110.00 (*0-7859-4629-2*) Fr & Eur.

— French-English, English-French Dictionary of Electrotechnic Electronics & Allied Fields, 2 vols. 11th ed. 218p. (ENG & FRE.). 1988. French-English, 11th ed., 1988, 218p. 130.00 (*0-88431-205-4*) IBD Ltd.

Pirazizy, A. A. Mountain Environment: Understanding the Change. (Illus.). x, 194p. 1993. 25.00 (*81-7024-563-X*, Pub. by Ashish Pub Hse II) Nataraj Bks.

Pirbazari, Massoud & Devinny, Joseph S., eds. Environmental Engineering. 810p. 1984. 67.00 (*0-87262-405-6*) Am Soc Civil Eng.

Pirbhai, Imtiaz A., jt. auth. see Hatley, Derek J.

Pirch, Sarah, ed. The Country Music Cookbook: Personal Favorite Recipes of the Greatest Stars in Country Music. (Illus.). 240p. 1994. 19.99 (*1-881649-38-5*) Genl Pub Grp.

— Courtship: The Golden Rules for Modern Romance. (Life's Golden Rules Ser.). 160p. 1995. pap. 5.99 (*1-881649-17-2*) Genl Pub Grp.

— Here I Stand: The Golden Rules for Surviving a Break-up. (Life's Golden Rules Ser.). 160p. 1994. 5.99 (*1-881649-16-4*) Genl Pub Grp.

— Single Parenting: The Golden Rules for Raising Children Alone. (Life's Golden Rules Ser.). 160p. 1994. 5.99 (*1-881649-18-0*) Genl Pub Grp.

Pirch, Sarah, ed. see Barrymore, Jaid.

Pirch, Sarah, ed. see Blackwell.

Pirch, Sarah, ed. see Hill, Kathleen T. & Hill, Gerald N.

Pirch, Sarah, ed. see Muller, Lillian & Coleman, John.

Pirchner, Franz. Population Genetics in Animal Breeding. 2nd ed. Frape, D. L., tr. LC 83-2164. 424p. 1983. 95.00 (*0-306-41201-2*, Plenum Pr) Plenum.

Pirckheimer, Willibald. Opera Politica, Historica, Philologica et Epistolica. Goldast, Melchior, ed. 406p. (GER.). 1969. reprint ed. write for info. (*0-318-70502-8*, Pub. by Georg Olms GW) Lubrecht & Cramer.

— Opera Politica, Historica, Philologica Et Epistolica. Goldast, Melchior, ed. 406p. 1969. reprint ed. write for info. (*0-318-71272-5*, Pub. by Georg Olms GW) Lubrecht & Cramer.

Pireau, A. & Vanderborck, Y. Residual Cold Work Determination by X-Ray Diffraction, No. EUR 12575. 111p. 1990. pap. 12.00 (*92-826-1164-7*, CD-NA-12575-EN-C) UNIPUB.

Pireaux, J. J., et al, eds. Polymer-Solid Interfaces: Proceedings of the First International Conference, 2-6 September 1991, Namur, Belgium. (Illus.). 520p. 1992. 145.00 (*0-7503-0192-9*) IOP Pub.

Pirece, Christine. How to Solve the Lockheed Case. (Studies in Social Philosophy & Policy). 49p. 1986. pap. 14.95 (*0-88738-660-1*) Transaction Pubs.

Pirenne, Henri. Belgian Democracy: Its Early History. LC 73-120219. reprint ed. 42.50 (*0-404-05057-3*) AMS Pr.

— Bibliogrpahie de l'Histoire de Belgique. viii, 440p. 1979. reprint ed. lib. bdg. 63.70 (*3-487-06722-6*, Pub. by Georg Olms GW) Lubrecht & Cramer.

— Economic & Social History of Medieval Europe. Clegg, I. E., tr. LC 37-28587. 239p. 1956. pap. 5.95 (*0-15-627533-3*, Harvest Bks) HarBrace.
— Medieval Cities: Their Origins & the Revival of Trade. Halsey, Frank D., tr. (C). 1952. pap. 12.95 (*0-691-00760-8*) Princeton U Pr.

Pires, Deborah S., jt. auth. see Malkemes, Fred.

Pires-Ferreira, Jane W. Formative Mesoamerican Exchange Networks with Special Reference to the Valley of Oaxaca. Flannery, Kent V., ed. (Prehistroy & Human Ecology of the Valley of Oaxaca Memoirs Ser. No. 8: Vol. 3). (Illus.). 1975. mic. film write for info. (*0-932206-69-7*) U Mich Mus Anthro.

Pires, Manuel. International Juridical Double Taxation of Income. (Series on International Taxation: Vol. 11). 336p. 1990. 100.00 (*90-6544-426-2*) Kluwer Law Tax Pubs.

Piret, John A. How the Universe Was Born: The Big Bang Concept Buried. Parker, Diane, ed. LC 90-50881. 156p. (Orig.). (C). 1991. pap. 11.95 (*0-88247-858-3*) R & E Pubs.

Piret, P. Convolutional Codes: An Algebraic Approach. 360p. 1988. 45.00 (*0-262-16110-9*) MIT Pr.

Pirgl, Les. Book of Nurbs, Vol. 1. (Monographs in Visual Communication). 1994. 79.00 (*0-387-55069-0*) Spr-Verlag.

Pirgo, Helm M. Virgin Mary, Queen of Poland: Historical Essay. 33p. 1966. pap. 2.50 (*0-940962-44-6*) Polish Inst Art & Sci.

Piri, Erkki, ed. see Vilkama, Kirsti.

Pirie, David. Shelley. (Open Guides to Literature Ser.). 128p. 1988. 75.00 (*0-335-15091-8*, Open Univ Pr); pap. 22.00 (*0-335-15082-9*, Open Univ Pr) Taylor & Francis.

Pirie, David B. How to Write Critical Essays: A Guide for Students of Literature. 136p. (C). 1985. pap. 12.95 (*0-416-34290-6*, 4146) Routledge Chapman & Hall.

Pirie, David B., ed. The Romantic Period. (Penguin History of Literature Ser.). 448p. 1994. 12.95 (*0-14-017755-8*, Penguin Bks) Viking Penguin.

Pirie, Donald. National Park Vacations. LC 93-70917. (Illus.). 182p. (Orig.). 1993. pap. 9.95 (*1-56790-012-7*) Cool Hand Comms.

Pirie, Donald, ed. & tr. Young Poets of a New Poland: Anthology. (Illus.). 280p. 1994. pap. 22.00 (*1-85610-010-3*, Pub. by Forest Bks UK) Dufour.

Pirie, James W. Books for Junior College Libraries: A Selected List of Approximately 19,700 Titles. LC 76-82133. 464p. reprint ed. pap. 132.30 (*0-8357-7345-0*, 2023942) Bks Demand.

Pirie, Lynne & Reynolds, Bill. Getting Built. (Illus.). 224p. (Orig.). 1985. pap. 12.50 (*0-446-38289-2*) Warner Bks.

Pirie, M., ed. Elgin International. (Illus.). 70p. 1986. 18.50 (*0-08-032459-2*, Pub. by Aberdeen U Pr); pap. 7.75 (*0-08-032452-5*, Pub. by Aberdeen U Pr) Macmillan.

Pirie, Madsen. The Book of the Fallacy: A Training Manual for Intellectual Subversives. (Illus.). 192p. 1985. 19.95 (*0-7102-0521-X*, RKP) Routledge.
— Micropolitics. 320p. 1988. text ed. 54.95 (*0-7045-3103-8*, Pub. by Avebury Pub UK) Ashgate Pub Co.

Pirie, N. W. Leaf Protein & Its Biproducts in Human & Animal Nutrition. 200p. 1987. 54.95 (*0-521-33030-0*) Cambridge U Pr.

Pirie, Norman W., jt. ed. see Clark, Frederick L.

Pirie, Peter, jt. auth. see Wright, Paul.

Pirie, Peter J. Twentieth Century British Music: A Collector's Guide. (Front Music Publications: No. 2). 20p. (Orig.). 1980. pap. 6.50 (*0-934082-02-2*) Theodore Front.

Pirie, R. Gordon, ed. Oceanography: Contemporary Readings in Ocean Sciences. 2nd ed. (Illus.). (C). 1977. pap. text ed. 16.95 (*0-19-502119-3*) OUP.

Pirie, S. Nurses & Mathematics. 108p. 1987. pap. 20.00 (*0-902606-92-1*) Ishiyaku Euro.

Pirillo, Rose M. Decision Making & Problem Solving: The Process Approach. rev. ed. (Illus.). 1987. student ed 4.99 (*1-55631-002-1*); teacher ed 14.95 (*1-55631-003-X*) Chron Guide.

Pirinci, Akif. Felidae. LC 92-50551. 1993. 19.00 (*0-679-42069-X*, Villard Bks) Random.

Pirinen & Jutikkala. History of Finland. (Reprints Ser.). (Illus.). 257p. 1989. 16.95 (*0-88029-260-1*) Dorset Pr.

Piriou, A., jt. auth. see Chazarain, J.

Piriou, Jean-Pierre, jt. auth. see Walz, Joel.

Pirke, K. M., et al, eds. The Psychobiology of Bulimia Nervosa. (Illus.). 120p. 1988. pap. 53.00 (*0-387-18670-0*) Spr-Verlag.

Pirkey, Jan. A Gift from the Heart: A Profile of Helenka A. Pontileoni American Volunteer. LC 86-83088. (Illus.). 200p. (Orig.). 1988. pap. write for info. (*0-9617147-0-0*) J P Enterprises.

Pirkis, Catherine L. The Experiences of Loveday Brooke, Lady Detective. 112p. 1986. reprint ed. pap. 4.95 (*0-486-25164-0*) Dover.

Pirkl & Babic. Guidelines & Strategies for Designing Transgenerational Products. pap. 19.95 (*0-87411-230-3*); 19.95 (*0-87411-270-2*) Copley Pub.

Pirkl, James J. Transgenerational Design: Products for an Aging Population. LC 93-9870. 260p. 1994. text ed. 49.95 (*0-442-01065-6*) Van Nos Reinhold.

Pirkle & Markland. Hemostasis & Animal Venoms. (Hematology Ser.: Vol. 7). 658p. 1988. 220.00 (*0-8247-7806-5*) Dekker.

***Pirkle, Arthur.** Winchester Lever Action Repeating Rifles Vol. I: The Models of 1866, 1873, & 1876. (For Collectors Only Ser.). (Illus.). 202p. 1995. pap. 19.95 (*1-882391-05-5*) N Cape Pubns.

Pirkle, Arthur K. Valhalla's Child. LC 92-62012. 288p. 1994. pap. 12.95 (*1-56002-232-9*, Univ Edtns) Aegina Pr.

Pirkle, E. C., et al. Natural Landscapes of the United States. 4th ed. 432p. 1992. per. 34.95 (*0-8403-8321-5*) Kendall-Hunt.

Pirmell, Charles. The Trashing of America. 1975. 7.00 (*0-686-11117-6*); pap. 3.50 (*0-686-11118-4*) Kulchur Foun.

Pirner, Connie. Even Little Kids Get Diabetes. Tucker, Kathy, ed. LC 90-12738. (Illus.). 24p. (J). (ps-2). 1991. 10.95 (*0-8075-2158-2*) A Whitman.
— Even Little Kids Get Diabetes. (Albert Whitman Prairie Book Ser.). (J). (ps-3). 1994. pap. 4.95 (*0-8075-2159-0*) A Whitman.

Pirnie, Bruce. Analysis of Special Operations Forces in Decision Aids: Recommendations. LC 94-3128. 1994. write for info. (*0-8330-1510-9*, MR-243-SOCOM) Rand Corp.

Piro, Sal. Creatures of the Night: The Rocky Horror Picture Show Experience. Schneider, Merylene, ed. (Illus.). 160p. (Orig.). 1990. pap. 15.95 (*0-941613-12-7*) Stabur Pr.

Piro, Sal & Hess, Michael. The Rocky Horror Picture Show Audience Participation Guide. 96p. (Orig.). 1991. pap. 9.95 (*0-941613-16-X*) Stabur Pr.

Piro, Stephanie. Men! Ha! Cartoons by Stephanie Piro. (Illus.). 96p. (Orig.). 1993. pap. 7.50 (*0-9632526-2-3*) Laugh Lines.

Piro, Stephanie H. Blank Tapes, Boots & Salads. 64p. 1992. pap. 4.95 (*1-880053-01-2*) Pge One Pubs.

Piroch, Sigrid S. Design Challenges: Monograph One. LC 91-72743. (Illus.). 169p. (Orig.). 1991. pap. 24.95 (*0-9630006-0-8*) Design Orig.

Pirodda, E., ed. Neurophysiology of the Vestibular System. (Advances in Oto-Rhino-Laryngology Ser.: Vol. 41). (Illus.). xii, 244p. 1988. 137.00 (*3-8055-4766-8*) S Karger.

Pirodda, E. & Pompeiano, O., eds. Advances in Oto-Rhino-Laryngology, Vol. 41 & 42, Set. (Illus.). xiv, 556p. 1988. 251.25 (*3-8055-4911-3*) S Karger.

Pirodsky, Donald M. & Cohn, Jerry S. Clinical Primer of Psychopharmacology: A Practical Guide. 2nd ed. (Illus.). 144p. 1992. pap. text ed. 24.95 (*0-07-105388-3*) Hlth Prof Div.

Pirog, Gerald. Aleksandr Blok's Ital'janskie Stixi: Confrontation & Disillusionment. (Illus.). 203p. (Orig.). 1983. pap. 18.95 (*0-89357-095-8*) Slavica.

Pirog-Good, Maureen A. & Stets, Jan E., eds. Violence in Dating Relationships: Emerging Social Issues. LC 88-31894. 302p. 1989. text ed. 57.95 (*0-275-93004-1*, C3004, Praeger Pubs); pap. text ed. 17.95 (*0-275-93353-9*, B3353, Praeger Pubs) Greenwood.

***Pirog, John E.** The Practical Application of Meridian-Style Acupuncture. (Illus.). 400p. (Orig.). 1995. pap. 60.00 (*1-881896-13-7*) Pacific View Pr.

Pirog, Robert L., et al. Energy Economics: Theory & Policy. (Illus.). 384p. (C). 1987. pap. text ed. write for info. (*0-13-277245-0*) P-H.

Pirogov, Nikolai I. Questions of Life: Diary of an Old Physician. LC 89-24332. (Resources in Medical History Ser.). (Illus.). xxii, 480p. 1992. 29.95 (*0-88135-061-3*, Sci Hist) Watson Pub Intl.

Pirogova, L. Aspectual Usage in Modern Russian. 320p. (C). 1988. 50.00 (*0-685-33700-6*, Pub. by Collets) St Mut.
— Conjugation of Russian Verbs. 319p. 1988. text ed. 10.95 (*0-8285-4944-3*) Firebird NY.
— Conjugation of Russian Verbs. 320p. (C). 1988. 60.00 (*0-685-39369-0*, Pub. by Collets) St Mut.

Pirogova, L. I. Complete Handbook of Russian Verbs. 320p. (Orig.). 1991. pap. 16.95 (*0-8442-4270-5*, Natl Textbk) NTC Pub Grp.

***Pirok, Kenneth R.** Commercial Loan Analysis: Principles & Techniques for Credit Analysts & Lenders. 150p. 1994. 42.50 (*1-55738-716-8*) Probus Pub Co.
— The Lender's Toolkit: The Pocket Guide to the Essential Formulas, Ratios & Tables. 150p. 1995. 24.95 (*1-55738-756-7*) Probus Pub Co.
— Managing Credit Department Functions: A Manager's Guide to Improving Loan Analysis, Documentation & Reporting. 225p. 1995. 50.00 (*1-55738-755-9*) Probus Pub Co.

Pirolo, Neal. Serving As Senders: How to Care for Your Missionaries While They Are Preparing to Go, While They Are on the Field, When They Return Home. 207p. (Orig.). 1991. pap. 7.95 (*1-880185-00-8*) Emmaus Rd Intl.

Piron, Claude. Gerda malaperis! Vortlisto - Wordlist. 26p. (YA). 1993. pap. text ed. 3.75 (*1-882251-05-9*) Eldonejo Bero.

Pirone, James & Sweeney, Paula. Jake Montana: A Matter of Destiny. 124p. (Orig.). (YA). 1993. lib. bdg. 15.00 (*0-88092-073-4*); pap. 5.00 (*0-88092-072-6*) Royal Fireworks.
— Jake Montana: Mystery at Deep Ravine. (Orig.). (J). (gr. 7 up). 1995. lib. bdg. 15.00 (*0-88092-296-6*) Royal Fireworks.
— Jake Montana: Mystery at Deep Ravine. (Orig.). (YA). (gr. 7 up). 1995. pap. 5.00 (*0-88092-295-8*) Royal Fireworks.

Pirone, Pascal P. Diseases & Pests of Ornamental Plants. 5th ed. LC 77-26893. 566p. 1978. text ed. 69.95 (*0-471-07249-4*) Wiley.

Pirone, Pascal P., et al. Tree Maintenance. 6th ed. (Illus.). 528p. 1988. 49.95 (*0-19-504370-7*) OUP.

Pirone, T. P. & Shaw, J. G., eds. Viral Genes & Plant Pathogenesis. (Illus.). xvi, 215p. 1990. 54.00 (*0-387-97313-3*) Spr-Verlag.

Pironio, Eduardo. Joyful in Hope. (C). 1988. 39.00 (*0-85439-156-8*, Pub. by St Paul Pubns UK) St Mut.
— We Wish to See Jesus. 214p. 1982. pap. 10.50 (*0-8189-0392-9*) Alba.

Pironio, Eduardo, ed. We Wish to See Jesus. (C). 1988. 39.00 (*0-85439-198-3*, Pub. by St Paul Pubns UK) St Mut.

Pironneau, O. The Finite Element Method for Fluids. 205p. 1989. text ed. 74.95 (*0-471-92255-2*) Wiley.
— Optimal Shape Design for Elliptic Systems. (Computational Physics Ser.). (Illus.). 190p. 1983. 69.00 (*0-387-12069-6*) Spr-Verlag.

Pironneau, O., et al, eds. Numerical Simulation of Unsteady Flows, Transition to Turbulence. (Illus.). 440p. (C). 1992. 64.95 (*0-521-41618-3*) Cambridge U Pr.

***Pirotin.** No Naughty Cats. 1995. mass mkt. 5.99 (*0-06-100902-4*, Harp PBks) HarpC.

Pirotta, Saviour. Chloe on the Jungle Gym. (J). (ps-3). 1992. 13.95 (*0-8120-6269-8*); pap. 5.95 (*0-8120-4829-6*) Barron.
— Follow That Cat! LC 92-38287. (Illus.). 32p. (J). (gr. k-3). 1993. 13.99 (*0-525-45125-0*, DCB) Dutton Child Bks.
— Jerusalem. LC 92-30130. (Holy Cities Ser.). (Illus.). 48p. (J). (gr. 5 up). 1993. text ed. 13.95 (*0-87518-569-X*, Dillon Silver Burdett) Silver Burdett Pr.
— Little Bird. LC 91-25413. (Illus.). 32p. (J). (ps-3). 1992. 14.00 (*0-688-11289-7*, Tambourine Bks); lib. bdg. 13.93 (*0-688-11290-0*, Tambourine Bks) Morrow.
— Monsters of the Deep. (Remarkable World Ser.). (Illus.). 48p. (J). (gr. 3-6). Date not set. write for info. (*1-56847-367-2*) Thomson Lrning.
— Pirates & Treasure. (Remarkable World Ser.). (Illus.). 48p. (J). (gr. 7-9). Date not set. 13.95 (*1-56847-366-4*) Thomson Lrning.
— Rome. LC 92-19685. (Holy Cities Ser.). (Illus.). 48p. (J). (gr. 5 up). 1993. text ed. 13.95 (*0-87518-570-3*, Dillon Silver Burdett) Silver Burdett Pr.

Pirotte, A., et al, eds. Advances in Database Technology - EDBT '92. (Lecture Notes in Computer Science Ser.: Vol. 580). 551p. 1992. pap. 73.00 (*0-387-55270-7*) Spr-Verlag.

Pirotte, Jean & Derroitte, Henri, eds. Churches & Health Care in the Third World. LC 91-9389. (SCM Ser.: No. 5). xxi, 176p. (ENG & FRE.). 1991. 54.50 (*90-04-09470-9*) E J Brill.

Pirotton, S., jt. auth. see Boeynaems, J. M.

Pirouet, M. Louise. Historical Dictionary of Uganda. LC 94-20483. (African Historical Dictionaries Ser.: No. 64). 1995. write for info. (*0-8108-2920-7*) Scarecrow.

Pirow, P. C., et al, eds. Information Systems in Practice & Theory: Proceeding of the IFIP TC8 International Symposium on Information Systems, Johannesburg, South Africa, 22-24 April, 1987. 510p. 1988. 102.75 (*0-444-70462-0*, North Holland) Elsevier.

Piroyan, Wallace. Love Is Forever. 143p. (Orig.). 1983. pap. 2.50 (*0-9613129-1-2*) Chiwaukee Pub Co.

Pirozynski, K. A. & Hawksworth, David L., eds. The Coevolution of Fungi with Plants & Animals. 490p. 1988. text ed. 102.00 (*0-12-557365-0*) Acad Pr.

Pirozzi, Richard C. College Textbook Reading & Study Skills. 277p. (C). 1983. pap. text ed. 20.00 (*0-03-059436-7*) HB Coll Pubs.

Pirozzolo, Fran, jt. auth. see McLean, Jim.

Pirozzolo, Francis J. & Wittrock, Merlin C. Neuropsychological & Cognitive Processes in Reading. (Perspectives in Neurolinguistics & Psycholinguistics Ser.). 1981. text ed. 54.00 (*0-12-557360-X*) Acad Pr.

Pirozzolo, Francis J., jt. ed. see Maletta, Gabe J.

Pirquet, Clemens. Volksgesundheit Im Krieg, 2 Vols., Set. (Wirtschafts-Und Sozialgeschichte des Weltkrieges (Osterreichische Und Ungarische Serie)). (GER.). 1926. 235.00 (*0-317-27641-7*) Elliots Bks.

Pirra, E. S. Guideline for Golf Course Irrigation System Design. 425p. 1989. write for info. (*0-318-69364-X*) Irrigation.

Pirri, A. N. & Piwczyk, B. P., eds. Excimer Beam Applications, Vol. 998. 1988. 38.00 (*0-8194-0033-5*) SPIE.

Pirrie, S. R. & Arnold, J. S., eds. Iran-U. S. Claims Tribunal Reports, Vols. 1-7. (C). 1992. text ed. 310.00 (*0-7855-0124-X*, Pub. by Grotius Pubns UK) St Mut.

Pirrie, S. R., et al, eds. Iran U. S. Claims: Tribunal Reports, 27 vols. (C). 1993. text ed. 368.00 (*0-685-74585-6*, Pub. by Grotius Pubns UK) St Mut.

Pirro, Andre. Johann Sebastian Bach: The Organist & His Works for the Organ. Goodrich, Wallace, tr. LC 74-24185. reprint ed. 15.50 (*0-404-13089-5*) AMS Pr.

Pirronello, V., jt. ed. see Greenberg, J. M.

Pirrong, S. Craig. Grain Futures Contracts: An Economic Appraisal. LC 92-44334. 1993. lib. bdg. 69.95 (*0-7923-9327-9*) Kluwer Ac.

Pirrotta, Nino. Don Giovanni's Progress: A Rake Goes to the Opera. Saunders, Harris, tr. (Illus.). 280p. 1994. 32.00 (*0-685-66912-2*); pap. 17.00 (*0-941419-94-0*) Marsilio Pubs.
— Music & Culture in Italy from the Middle Ages to the Baroque: A Collection of Essays. LC 83-12827. (Studies in the History of Music: No. 1). 499p. reprint ed. pap. 142.80 (*0-7837-2313-X*, 2057401) Bks Demand.
— Paolo Tenorista in a New Fragment of the Italian Ars Nova. (Illus.). 83p. 1961. 18.00 (*0-934082-07-3*, M61-2053, E E Gottlieb CA) Theodore Front.

Pirrwitz, D., jt. auth. see Palz, Wolfgang.

Pirsch, P., ed. VLSI Implementations for Image Communications. LC 93-30175. (Advances in Image Communication Ser.: Vol. 2). 402p. 1993. 154.50 (*0-444-88790-3*) Elsevier.

Pirsein, Robert W. The Voice of America. Sterling, Christopher H., ed. LC 78-21733. (Dissertations in Broadcasting Ser.). 1980. lib. bdg. 44.95 (*0-405-11770-1*) Ayer.

***Pirsig, Maynard E.** Pirsig on Minnesota Pleading, 2 vols., Set. 960p. 1994. boxed 175.00 (*0-614-05945-3*) Michie Butterworth.
— Pirsig on Minnesota Pleading, 1987-1991, 2 vols. 5th ed. 960p. 1991. boxed 175.00 (*0-86678-554-X*) Butterworth Legal Pubs.
— Pirsig on Minnesota Pleading, 1987-1991, 2 vols. 5th suppl. ed. 960p. 1992. 60.00 (*1-56257-835-9*) Butterworth Legal Pubs.

Pirsig, Maynard E. & Kirwin, Kenneth F. Professional Responsibility: Cases & Materials. LC 84-7566. (American Casebook Ser.). 107p. 1986. Tchr's. manual. teacher ed, pap. text ed. write for info. (*0-314-98583-2*) West Pub.
— Professional Responsibility: Cases & Materials. 4th ed. LC 84-7566. (American Casebook Ser.). 603p. 1988. reprint ed. text ed. 38.50 (*0-314-83001-4*) West Pub.

Pirsig, Robert M. Lila: An Inquiry into Morals. 1992. mass mkt. 6.99 (*0-553-29961-1*) Bantam.
— Zen & the Art of Motorcycle Maintenance: An Inquiry into Values. 416p. 1984. pap. 6.99 (*0-553-27747-2*, Bantam Classics) Bantam.
— Zen & the Art of Motorcycle Maintenance: An Inquiry into Values. LC 73-12275. 1974. 23.40 (*0-688-00230-7*) Morrow.
— Zen & the Art of Motorcycle Maintenance: An Inquiry into Values. LC 73-12275. 1979. pap. 13.50 (*0-688-05230-4*) Morrow.

Pirson, A., ed. General Index. (New Encyclopedia of Plant Physiology Ser.: Vol. 20). 320p. 1993. 198.00 (*0-387-18162-8*) Spr-Verlag.

Pirson, Raymond H. Guide to Spanish Idioms. 180p. (C). 1988. 50.00 (*0-85950-334-8*, Pub. by S Thornes Pubs UK) St Mut.

Pirson, Sylvain J. Geologic Well Log Analysis. 3rd ed. LC 82-24218. 476p. 1983. 35.00 (*0-87201-902-0*) Gulf Pub.
— Geologic Well Log Analysis. 3rd suppl. ed. LC 82-24218. 32p. 1983. 62.00 (*0-87201-903-9*) Gulf Pub.
— Handbook of Well Log Analysis: For Oil & Gas Formation Evaluation. 1963. text ed. 85.00 (*0-13-382804-2*) P-H.

***Pirt, S. John.** Control of Foam Formation & Antifoam Action in Aerated Systems. (Pirtferm Papers). (C). 1992. 75.00x (*1-874685-00-2*, Pub. by Pirtferm Ltd UK) St Mut.
— The Penicillin Fermentation: A Model for Secondary Metabolite Production. (Pirtferm Papers). (C). 1993. 75.00x (*1-874685-10-X*, Pub. by Pirtferm Ltd UK) St Mut.
— Stoichiometry & Kinetics of Microbial Growth. (Pirtferm Papers). (C). 1994. 75.00x (*1-874685-20-7*, Pub. by Pirtferm Ltd UK) St Mut.
— Total Biocombustion of Sewage Sludge by the Bicycle Process. (Pirtferm Papers). (C). 1993. 75.00x (*1-874685-05-3*, Pub. by Pirtferm Ltd UK) St Mut.

***Pirt, S. John, ed.** Product Formation in Cultures of Microbes & the Microbial Growth Process. (Pirtferm Papers). (C). 1994. 75.00x (*1-874685-15-0*, Pub. by Pirtferm Ltd UK) St Mut.

Pirtle, Caleb, III, et al, eds. Texas: Generations of Harvest. 96p. Date not set. write for info. (*1-879234-11-4*) Leisure TX.

***Pirtle, Carol.** Where Illinois Began: A Pictorial History of Randolph County. LC 95-11610. (Illus.). 1995. write for info. (*0-89865-939-6*) Donning Co.

Pirtle, Henry. The Lost Word of Freemasonry. 240p. 1993. pap. 19.95 (*1-56459-320-7*) Kessinger Pub.

Pirtle, Thomas R. History of the Dairy Industry. LC 72-89079. (Rural America Ser.). 1973. reprint ed. 42.00 (*0-8420-1494-2*) Scholarly Res Inc.

Pirto, Douglas D. Forestry Study Guide. 440p. 1992. per. 29.95 (*0-8403-8159-X*) Kendall-Hunt.

Pirumov, U. G. & Roslyakov, G. S. Gas Flow in Nozzles. (Chemical Physics Ser.: Vol. 29). (Illus.). 436p. 1986. 107.00 (*0-387-12413-6*) Spr-Verlag.

Pirz, Therese S. Speak French to Your Baby: Easy French Phrases to Teach Your Baby. (Bilingual Baby Ser.). (Illus.). 150p. (Orig.). (ENG & FRE.). 1981. 12.95 (*0-929724-07-0*); pap. 11.95 (*0-929724-06-2*) Command Performance.
— Speak Spanish to Your Baby: Easy Spanish Phrases to Teach Your Baby. (Bilingual Baby Ser.). (Illus.). 160p. (Orig.). (ENG & SPA.). 1985. pap. 11.95 (*0-929724-08-9*) Command Performance.

Pisa, Maria G., jt. auth. see Russel, K. W.

Pisacane, Vincent L. & Moore, Robert C., eds. Space Systems. LC 92-9490. (Johns Hopkins Applied Physics Laboratory Series in Science & Engineering). 1994. 75.00 (*0-19-507497-1*) OUP.

Pisani, Assunta, ed. Euro-Librarianship: Shared Resources, Shared Responsibilities. LC 91-38269. (Collection Management Ser.). 556p. 1992. lib. bdg. 119.95 (*1-56024-266-3*) Harrington Pk.

Pisani, C., et al. Hartree-Fock Ab Initio Treatment of Crystalline Systems. (Lecture Notes in Chemistry Ser.: Vol. 48). 193p. 1988. pap. 31.00 (*0-387-19317-0*) Spr-Verlag.

Pisani, Donald J. To Reclaim a Divided West: Water, Law, & Public Policy, 1848-1902. LC 92-14161. (Histories of the American Frontier Ser.). 508p. 1992. 42.50x (*0-8263-1380-9*); pap. 20.95 (*0-8263-1381-7*) U of NM Pr.

Pisani, Edgard, ed. Health & Social Welfare. (Journal of Contemporary European Affairs Ser.: No. 2). 180p. 1990. pap. 13.75 (*0-08-040234-8*, 2701; 2902; 3002, Pergamon Pr) Elsevier.
— Politics & Religion. (Contemporary European Affairs Ser.: No. 2). 204p. 1990. pap. 12.50 (*0-08-040794-3*, Pergamon Pr) Elsevier.

Pisani, Edgard, et al, eds. Educating Europe. (Contemporary European Affairs Ser.: No. 3). 202p. 1991. pap. 14.50 (*0-08-041390-0*, Pergamon Pr) Elsevier.
— Europe: Two Perspectives. (Journal of Contemporary European Affairs Ser.: No. 2). 174p. 1990. pap. 13.75 (*0-08-040490-1*, Pergamon Pr) Elsevier.
— European Immigration Policy. (Contemporary European Affairs Ser.: No. 3). 190p. 1991. pap. 16.00 (*0-08-041388-9*, Pergamon Pr) Elsevier.

An Asterisk (*) at the beginning of an entry indicates that the title is appearing in BIP for the first time.

— The Gulf Crisis. (Contemporary European Affairs Ser.: No. 4). 190p. 1991. pap. 17.25 (*0-08-041391-9*, Pergamon Pr) Elsevier.

Pisani, Emilia D. The Wellness Daybook: The Personal Health Management Book. 175p. 1993. pap. text ed. 15. 95 (*0-9637571-0-5*) Design Data.

Pisani, F., et al, eds. New Antiepileptic Drugs. (Epilepsy Research Ser.: No. 3). 212p. 1991. 172.50 (*0-444-81392-6*) Elsevier.

Pisani, Mary A. Services for the Seriously Mentally Ill in Texas: Facts & Issues. 39p. (Orig.). 1988. pap. 1.00 (*0-915757-11-7*) League Women Voters TX.

Pisani, Ralph R. Investing in Land: How to Be a Successful Developer. 235p. 1991. pap. text ed. 14.95 (*0-471-53644-X*) Wiley.

Pisani, Robert. Statistics: A Tutorial Workbook. (C). 1985. pap. text ed. 9.95 (*0-393-95457-9*) Norton.

— Statistics: A Tutorial Workbook. 2nd ed. (C). 1993. pap. text ed. 11.95 (*0-393-96369-1*) Norton.

Pisani, Sallie. The CIA & the Marshall Plan. LC 91-16840. x, 190p. 1991. 25.00 (*0-7006-0502-9*) U Pr of KS.

Pisano, A. P., et al, eds. Micromechanical Systems, 1993. LC 93-73713. 107p. 1993. pap. 40.00 (*0-7918-1000-3*) ASME.

Pisano, Beverly. Afghan Hounds. (Illus.). 125p. 1980. 9.95 (*0-87666-682-9*, KW-077) TFH Pubns.

— Boxers. (Illus.). 160p. 1981. 11.95 (*0-86622-160-3*, KW-041) TFH Pubns.

— Chihuahuas. (Illus.). 160p. 1989. 11.95 (*0-86622-506-4*, KW-087) TFH Pubns.

— Chow Chows. (Illus.). 125p. 1989. 11.95 (*0-86622-514-5*, KW089) TFH Pubns.

— Miniature Schnauzer. 1994. 11.95 (*0-7938-1050-7*) TFH Pubns.

— Old English Sheepdogs. (Illus.). 128p. 1990. 11.95 (*0-86622-814-4*, KW-093) TFH Pubns.

— Pekingese. (Illus.). 128p. 1981. 11.95 (*0-86622-799-7*, KW-095) TFH Pubns.

— Shetland Sheepdogs. 1994. 9.95 (*0-7938-1054-X*) TFH Pubns.

— Siberian Huskies. 1990. 11.95 (*0-86622-449-1*, KW-068) TFH Pubns.

Pisano, Beverly, ed. Dalmatians. (Illus.). 128p. 1980. 11.95 (*0-86622-501-3*, KW-090) TFH Pubns.

— English Setters. (Illus.). 128p. 1988. 11.95 (*0-86622-521-8*, KW-102) TFH Pubns.

Pisano, Beverly & Holcombe, A. D. Beagles. (Illus.). 125p. 1979. 11.95 (*0-87666-686-1*, KW-080) TFH Pubns.

Pisano, Beverly & Lewis, Gloria. Miniature Schnauzers. (Illus.). 1979. 11.95 (*0-86622-864-0*, KW-042) TFH Pubns.

Pisano, Beverly & Monte, Evelyn, eds. Brittany Spaniels. (Illus.). 128p. 1989. 11.95 (*0-86622-223-5*, KW-092) TFH Pubns.

Pisano, Beverly & Ricketts, Viva L. Pomeranians. (Illus.). 128p. 1980. 9.95 (*0-86622-500-5*, KW-091) TFH Pubns.

Pisano, Beverly & Taynton, Mark. Shetland Sheepdogs. 125p. 1979. 11.95 (*0-86622-587-0*, KW-079) TFH Pubns.

Pisano, Carmen T., jt. auth. see Lamagna, Joseph.

Pisano, Dominick, jt. auth. see Hardesty, Von.

Pisano, Dominick, et al. Legend, Memory, & the Great War in the Air. LC 92-24189. (Illus.). 144p. 1992. 34.95 (*0-295-97215-7*); pap. 18.95 (*0-295-97216-5*) U of Wash Pr.

Pisano, Dominick A. To Fill the Skies with Pilots: The Civilian Pilot Training Program, 1939-46. LC 92-29061. (Illus.). 248p. 1993. 34.95 (*0-252-01994-6*) U of Ill Pr.

Pisano, Dominick A., frwd. American Airport Designs. (Illus.). 96p. 1990. pap. 12.95 (*1-55835-025-X*) AIA Press.

Pisano, Dominick A., ed. see Jakab, Peter L.

***Pisano, Gary P. & Hayes, Robert H., eds.** Manufacturing Renaissance: A Harvard Business Review Book. LC 94-43320. (Business Review Bks.). 1995. 29.95 (*0-87584-610-6*) Harvard Busn.

Pisano, Jane G. Los Angeles Two Thousand. (Urban Studies Monograph Ser.: No. 8). 48p. (Orig.). 1989. pap. 6.00 (*0-913749-10-9*) U MD Urban Stud.

Pisano, Joseph C., jt. auth. see Epps, Anna C.

Pisano, Lewis, ed. Air & Space History: An Annotated Bibliography. LC 88-342. 571p. 1988. 88.00 (*0-8240-8543-4*, H00834) Garland.

Pisano, Mary B. Going to New Orleans to Visit Weezie Anna. LC 93-34203. (Illus.). 24p. (J). 1994. 8.95 (*0-937552-52-6*) Quail Ridge.

Pisano, Raff, jt. auth. see Lonie, Ian.

***Pisano, Ronald G.** An American Place. LC 81-81364. (Illus.). 40p. (Orig.). (C). 1981. pap. 5.00 (*0-943526-28-0*) Parrish Art.

— Henry & Edith Mitchill Prellwitz & the Peconic Art Colony. (Illus.). 64p. 1995. pap. text ed. 10.00 (*0-943924-20-0*) Mus Stony Brook.

— A Leading Spirit in American Art: William Merritt Chase, 1849-1916. LC 83-82428. (Illus.). 204p. 1983. 25. 00 (*0-935558-14-4*) Henry Art.

— The Long Island Landscape 1914-1946: The Transitional Years. LC 82-81697. (Illus.). 40p. (Orig.). 1982. pap. 4.00 (*0-943526-35-3*) Parrish Art.

— One Hundred Years: A Centennial Celebration of the National Association of Women Artists. LC 88-72138. (Illus.). 95p. Date not set. 20.00 (*0-685-72097-7*) Gal Assn NY.

— Summer Afternoons: The Landscape Paintings of William Merritt Chase. (Illus.). 160p. 1993. 60.00 (*0-8212-1929-4*) Bulfinch Pr.

— William Merritt Chase in the Company of Friends. LC 79-87491. (Illus.). 70p. 1979. 4.00 (*0-943526-06-X*) Parrish Art.

— William Merritt Chase (1849-1916) (Illus.). 25p. (Orig.). (C). 1976. pap. 5.00 (*0-943526-43-4*) Parrish Art.

***Pisano, Ronald G., intro.** American Paintings from the Parrish Art Museum. LC 82-61450. (Illus.). 54p. (Orig.). (C). 1982. pap. 10.00 (*0-943526-27-2*) Parrish Art.

— 17 Abstract Artists of East Hampton: The Pollock Years, 1946-56. LC 80-81980. (Illus.). 32p. (Orig.). 1980. pap. text ed. 4.00 (*0-943526-40-X*) Parrish Art.

Pisano, Ronald G. & Longwell, Alicia G. Photographs from the William Merritt Chase Archives. LC 92-85286. (Illus.). 118p. 1992. pap. 18.00 (*0-943526-22-1*) Parrish Art.

Pisano, Ronald G. & Rood, Beverly. The Art Students League: Selections from the Permanent Collection. (Illus.). 110p. 1987. 20.00 (*0-934483-09-4*) Gal Assn NY.

***Pisano, Ronald G. & Weber, Bruce.** Parodies of the American Masters: Rediscovering the Society of American Fakirs, 1891-1914. (Illus.). 48p. 1993. pap. 5.00 (*0-943924-18-9*) Mus Stony Brook.

Pisano, Vittorfranco S. The Dynamics of Subversion & Violence in Contemporary Italy. 224p. (C). 1987. pap. text ed. 14.95 (*0-8179-8552-2*) Hoover Inst Pr.

Pisano, Vivian M., jt. auth. see Mackay, Nancy.

Pisarenkova, Lubov. Food & Gossip in the Moscow Circus. Klopfer, Fred, ed. (Illus.). 97p. 1994. pap. 9.95 (*0-9638715-1-X*) Vanatech Systs.

Pisarev, Dimitri I. Selected Philosophical, Social, & Political Essays. Dixon, R. & Katzer, J., trs. LC 79-2919. (Illus.). 711p. 1982. reprint ed. 49.50 (*0-8305-0089-8*) Hyperion Conn.

Pisar'kova, Liubov' F. Index to the Publications of the Russian Provincial Archeographic Commissions, 1884-1923, 5 vols., I. Shmidt, Sigurd O., ed. LC 92-60510. 1250p. (RUS.). 1992. lib. bdg. 100.00 (*0-88354-359-1*) N Ross.

— Index to the Publications of the Russian Provincial Archeographic Commissions, 1884-1923, 5 vols., II. Shmidt, Sigurd O., ed. LC 92-60510. 1250p. (RUS.). 1992. lib. bdg. 100.00 (*0-88354-360-5*) N Ross.

— Index to the Publications of the Russian Provincial Archeographic Commissions, 1884-1923, 5 vols., III. Shmidt, Sigurd O., ed. LC 92-60510. 1250p. (RUS.). 1992. lib. bdg. 100.00 (*0-88354-361-3*) N Ross.

— Index to the Publications of the Russian Provincial Archeographic Commissions, 1884-1923, 5 vols., IV. Shmidt, Sigurd O., ed. LC 92-60510. 1250p. (RUS.). 1992. lib. bdg. 100.00 (*0-88354-362-1*) N Ross.

— Index to the Publications of the Russian Provincial Archeographic Commissions, 1884-1923, 5 vols., V. Shmidt, Sigurd O., ed. LC 92-60510. 1250p. (RUS.). 1992. lib. bdg. 100.00 (*0-88354-363-X*) N Ross.

Pisarowicz, James, ed. Proceedings Death Valley Conference on History & Prehistory, 3rd. LC 91-74081. (Death Valley History Conference Ser.). (Illus.). 260p. (Orig.). (C). 1992. pap. 10.95 (*1-878900-26-9*) DVNH Assn.

Pisarowicz, James, jt. ed. see Johnson, Jean.

Pisarowicz, James, jt. ed. see Lingenfelter, Richard.

Pisarski, Cathryn & Smith, Phil, contribs. Robin Hood. (Illus.). 28p. (Orig.). (J). (gr. 1 up). 1988. pap. 3.50 (*0-88680-308-X*); 7.50 (*0-88680-309-8*) I E Clark.

Pisarski, R. D., jt. auth. see Gocksch, A.

***Piscataway Conoy Confereracy & Subtribes, Inc. Staff.** A Piscataway Story: The Legend of Kittimuquinn. Seib-Toup, Rebecca, ed. (Illus.). 96p. (J). (gr. 4-6). 1994. 10. 00 (*0-945253-09-5*) Thornsbury Bailey Brown.

Piscatella, Joseph. Choices for a Healthy Heart. LC 86-40199. 592p. (Orig.). 1987. pap. 15.95 (*0-89480-138-4*, 1138) Workman Pub.

— Don't Eat Your Heart out Cookbook. LC 83-14830. 560p. 1983. pap. 15.95 (*0-89480-488-X*, 488) Workman Pub.

Piscatella, Joseph C. Controlling Your Fat Tooth. LC 90-50361. 544p. 1991. pap. 15.95 (*0-89480-431-6*, 1431) Workman Pub.

— Don't Eat Your Heart Out. 1989. pap. 15.95 (*0-8161-4747-7*) G K Hall.

— Don't Eat Your Heart Out Cookbook. rev. ed. Kovalchick, Sally, ed. LC 94-32730. 664p. 1994. pap. 17.95 (*1-56305-558-9*) Workman Pub.

— Fat Tooth, Fat Gram Counter. 1993. pap. 12.95 (*1-56305-149-4*, 3149) Workman Pub.

Piscatori, James, ed. Islamic Fundamentalisms & the Gulf Crisis: A Fundamentalism Project Report. 267p. (Orig.). (C). 1991. pap. 9.95 (*0-9629608-0-2*) Fundmtal Project.

Piscatori, James P., jt. ed. see Eickelman, Dale F.

Piscatori, James P., jt. auth. see Royal Institute of International Affairs Staff.

Pischel, Dohrmann K. Dohrmann Kaspar Pischel, M. D. American Links with Germanic Ophthalmology Retinal Detachment Surgery San Francisco. (Ophthalmology Oral History Ser.). (Illus.). xxii, 120p. (Orig.). (C). 1988. pap. 35.00 (*0-926866-00-1*) FAAO.

Pischel, Enrica C. China from the 7th to 19th Century. LC 93-40124. (History of the World Ser.). (J). 1994. lib. bdg. 25.67 (*0-8114-3329-3*) Raintree Steck-V.

Pischinger, Alfred. Matrix & Matrix Regulation: Basis for a Holistic Theory in Medicine. Heine, Hartmut, ed. Mac Lean, Norman, tr. (Illus.). 221p. (C). 1991. text ed. 39. 95 (*2-8043-4000-7*, Pub. by Edits Haug Intl) Medicina Bio.

***Pischke, Sibyl J.** Ashes of Roses & War. 900p. 1994. write for info. (*0-614-00095-5*) S J Pischke.

— The Legend of Mammy Jane. 2nd ed. 405p. 1994. pap. 14.95 (*0-9608532-2-7*) S J Pischke.

— Matches at Midnight. (Illus.). 365p. (Orig.). 1987. pap. 4.95 (*0-9608532-1-9*) S J Pischke.

— Sibyl's Legend of Mammy Jane. 1981. 14.95 (*0-9608532-0-0*) S J Pischke.

Piscicelli, U. Respiratory Autogenic Training & Obstetric Psychoprophylaxis. 292p. 1987. pap. text ed. 25.00 (*1-57235-026-1*) Piccin NY.

Pisciotta, Alexander W. Benevolent Repression: Social Control & the American Reformatory-Prison Movement. LC 93-41515. 1994. 35.00 (*0-8147-6623-4*) NYU Pr.

Pisciotto, Patricia T., ed. Blood Transfusion Therapy: A Physician's Handbook. (Illus.). (C). 1993. pap. text ed. 7.00 (*1-56395-027-8*) Am Assn Blood.

Piscitelli, Nicola. Diccionario Atlas de Anatomia Humana. 2nd ed. (Illus.). 256p. (SPA.). 1980. pap. write for info. (*0-7859-5106-7*) Fr & Eur.

Piscitello, Dave. Open Systems Networking, TCP - IP & OSI. 1993. 48.95 (*0-201-56334-7*) Addison-Wesley.

Piscol, K., et al, eds. Neurosurgical Standards, Cerebral Aneurysms, Malignant Gliomas. (Advances in Neurosurgery Ser.: Vol. 20). (Illus.). 360p. 1992. pap. 79. 00 (*0-387-54838-6*) Spr-Verlag.

Piscopo, Joe. The Piscopo Tapes. pap. 5.95 (*0-317-56817-5*) PB.

***Piscopo, Maria.** Marketing & Promoting Your Work. LC 95-6350. 1995. write for info. (*0-89134-608-2*) North Light Bks.

— The Photographer's Guide to Marketing & Self-Promotion. 2nd ed. LC 95-75285. (Illus.). 176p. 1995. pap. 18.95 (*1-880559-24-2*) Allworth Pr.

Piscoya, Francisco M. Estructuras Algebraicas VI: Formas Cuadraticas. Organization of American States General Secretariat Staff, ed. (Mathematics Ser.: Monograph No. 23). 98p. (SPA.). (C). 1981. pap. 3.50 (*0-8270-1359-0*) OAS.

Pise, Charles C. Father Rowland: A North American Tale. 1978. 18.95 (*0-405-10847-8*, 11850) Ayer.

Pisegna, D. Complete American Candymaking. Date not set. 25.00 (*0-06-016972-9*, HarpT) HarpC.

Pisemskii, Aleksei F. One Thousand Souls. Litvinov, Ivy, tr. 1970. reprint ed. text ed. 69.50 (*0-8371-2239-2*, PIOS, Greenwood Pr) Greenwood.

— One Thousand Souls. Litvinov, Ivy, tr. LC 76-23892. (Classics of Russian Literature Ser.). 1989. reprint ed. pap. 22.00 (*0-88355-506-9*) Hyperion Conn.

— The Simpleton. Litvinova, I., tr. LC 76-23893. (Classics of Russian Literature Ser.). (Illus.). 1977. reprint ed. 15.00 (*0-88355-508-5*); reprint ed. pap. 10.00 (*0-88355-507-7*) Hyperion Conn.

Pisetsky, David S., ed. Neurological Manifestations of Rheumatologic Disease. 1991. write for info. (*1-56262-001-0*) PMA Pub Corp.

***Pisetsky, David S. & Trien, Susan F.** The Duke University Medical Center Book of Arthritis. 416p. 1995. pap. 12. 95 (*0-449-90887-9*) Fawcett.

Pisharoti, K. A. Guide to the Integration of Health Education in Environmental Health Programmes. (Offset Publication Ser.: No. 20). 1975. pap. 6.00 (*92-4-170020-3*) World Health.

Pishdad, A. Alan, ed. Hazardous Waste Sites in the U. S. 175p. 1981. pap. 46.00 (*0-08-026274-0*, Pergamon Pr) Elsevier.

Pisier, G. Factorization of Linear Operators & Geometry of Banach Spaces. LC 85-18605. (CBMS Regional Conference Series in Mathematics: No. 60). 154p. 1987. reprint ed. pap. text ed. 25.00 (*0-8218-0710-2*, CBMS-60) Am Math.

Pisier, Gilles. Volume Inequalities in the Geometry of Banach Spaces. (Cambridge Tracts in Mathematics Ser.: No. 93). (Illus.). 224p. (C). 1989. 64.95 (*0-521-36465-5*) Cambridge U Pr.

Pisier, Gilles, jt. auth. see Marcus, Michael B.

Pisk, Litz. The Actor & His Body. LC 76-8369. (Illus.). 1976. pap. 9.95 (*0-87830-553-X*, Theatre Arts Bks) Routledge Chapman & Hall.

Piskac, A., jt. ed. see Bartik, M.

***Piske, Thorsten & Winitz, Harris.** Basic Structures, German: A Textbook for the Learnables. 132p. (Orig.). (GER.). 1993. pap. 45.00 (*0-939990-74-1*) Intl Linguistics.

***Piske, Thorsten, et al.** Wetter. (German Language Ser.). (Illus.). 42p. (Orig.). (GER.). (YA). (gr. 7 up). 1993. pap. 22.00 (*0-939990-86-5*) Intl Linguistics.

Piskin, Erhan & Hoffman, Allan S., eds. Polymeric Biomaterials. 1986. lib. bdg. 115.50 (*90-247-3303-0*) Kluwer Ac.

Piskulich, John P. Collective Bargaining in State & Local Government. LC 91-28142. 144p. 1992. text ed. 45.00 (*0-275-94043-8*, C4043, Praeger Pubs) Greenwood.

Piskunov, Nikolai. Differential & Integral Calculus. 896p. 1965. text ed. 297.00 (*0-677-20600-3*) Gordon & Breach.

Piskurich, George M. Self-Directed Learning: A Practical Guide to Design, Development & Implementation. LC 93-12369. (Management Ser.). 379p. 1993. 35.95 (*1-55542-532-1*) Jossey-Bass.

Piskurich, George M., ed. The ASTD Handbook of Instructional Technology. LC 92-23142. 1992. 59.95 (*0-07-001531-7*) Am Soc Train & Devel.

Pison, Gilles, jt. ed. see Bledsoe, Caroline.

Pisor, Robert L. The End of the Line: The Siege of Khe Sanh. 1985. pap. 3.95 (*0-345-33112-5*) Ballantine.

Pissanetzky, Sergio. Sparse Matrix Technology. 1984. text ed. 113.00 (*0-12-557580-7*) Acad Pr.

Pissard, Hippolyte. La Guerre Sainte en Pays Chretien. LC 78-63357. (Crusades & Military Orders Ser.: Second Series). reprint ed. 47.50 (*0-404-17027-7*) AMS Pr.

Pissarides, Christopher A. Equilibrium Unemployment Theory. (Illus.). 224p. 1990. text ed. 59.95 (*0-631-15213-X*) Blackwell Pubs.

***Pissarro, Camille.** Letters to His Son Lucien. Rewald, John, ed. Abel, Lionel, tr. (Illus.). 431p. 1995. reprint ed. pap. 15.95 (*0-306-80631-2*) Da Capo.

Pissarro, Camille & Rewald, John, eds. Letters to His Son Lucien. 4th enl. rev. ed. (Illus.). 399p. 37.50 (*0-911858-22-9*) Appel.

Pissarro, Joachim. Camille Pissarro. LC 93-12280. 1993. 75. 00 (*0-8109-3724-7*) Abrams.

— Camille Pissarro. LC 92-15547. (Rizzoli Art Ser.). (Illus.). 24p. 1992. 7.95 (*0-8478-1582-X*) Rizzoli Intl.

Pissarro, Joachim, jt. auth. see Brettell, Richard R.

Pissarro, Ludovic-Rodo. Pissarro's Art & Oeuvre: A Catalogue Raisonne, 2 vols., Set. (Illus.). (FRE.). 1989. reprint ed. 295.00 (*1-55660-027-5*) A Wofsy Fine Arts.

Pissart, A. & Terwindt, J. H., eds. Present Day Geomorphological Processes. (Annals of Gemorphology Supplement Ser.: No. 49). (Illus.). 207p. (Orig.). 1984. pap. text ed. 78.50 (*3-443-21049-X*, Pub. by Gebruder Borntraeger GW) Lubrecht & Cramer.

Pissin, Raimund. Almanache der Romantik. Vol. 5. xii, 450p. 1970. reprint ed. write for info. (*0-318-71856-1*, Pub. by Georg Olms GW) Lubrecht & Cramer.

Pissiotis, C., jt. ed. see Androulakis, G.

Pistenmaa, David A., jt. ed. see Phillips, Theodore L.

Pisto, John. Monterey's Cookin' Pisto Style: From Sicily to Monterey. (Illus.). 110p. (Orig.). 1994. pap. 12.95 (*0-9640828-0-2*) Pistos Kitchen.

Pistoia, G., ed. Lithium Batteries: New Materials, Development & Perspectives. LC 93-42028. (Industrial Chemistry Library: Vol. 5). 494p. 1993. 242.75 (*0-444-89957-X*) Elsevier.

Pistole, Jesse R. Criminal Law for Peace Officers. 480p. 1976. 31.00 (*0-87909-163-0*, Reston) P-H.

Pistole, Larry M. The Pictorial History of the Flying Tigers. O'Donnell, Mike & Sylvia, Steve, eds. LC 81-84192. (Illus.). 300p. 1981. 29.95 (*0-943522-05-6*); lib. bdg. 25. 00 (*0-685-03418-6*) Moss Pubns VA.

Pistolese, Clifford. Nerves of Steel: Mastering Your Emotions to Beat the Market. 225p. 1992. 22.95 (*1-55738-467-3*) Probus Pub Co.

— Using Technical Analysis: A Step-by-Step Guide to Understanding & Applying Stock Market. 1994. pap. 24. 95 (*1-55738-527-0*) Probus Pub Co.

Pistolesi, jt. auth. see Milne.

Pistolesi, Roseanna. Let's Celebrate Christmas: A Book of Drawing Fun. LC 87-61376. (Illus.). 32p. (J). (gr. 2-6). 1988. lib. bdg. 10.65 (*0-8167-1133-X*); pap. text ed. 1.95 (*0-8167-1134-8*) Troll Assocs.

— Let's Celebrate Halloween: A Book of Drawing Fun. LC 87-50426. (Illus.). 32p. (J). (gr. 2-6). 1988. lib. bdg. 10. 65 (*0-8167-1002-3*); pap. text ed. 1.95 (*0-8167-1003-1*) Troll Assocs.

Pistoleta. Der Trobador Pistoleta. Bd. with Trobador Guillem Margret. LC 80-2184. LC 80-2184. reprint ed. 27.00 (*0-404-19013-8*) AMS Pr.

Piston, Walter. Counterpoint. (Illus.). (C). 1947. text ed. 23. 95 (*0-393-09728-5*) Norton.

— Orchestration. (Illus.). (C). 1955. text ed. 31.95 (*0-393-09740-4*) Norton.

— Principles of Harmonic Analysis. 1933. pap. 13.00 (*0-911318-05-4*) E C Schirmer.

Piston, Walter, et al. Harmony. 500p. (C). 1987. student ed, pap. text ed. 16.95 (*0-393-95484-6*) Norton.

— Harmony. 500p. (C). 1987. Instr's. manual. teacher ed, pap. text ed. write for info. (*0-393-95681-4*) Norton.

— Harmony. 5th ed. 500p. (C). 1987. text ed. 41.95 (*0-393-95480-3*) Norton.

Piston, William G. Carter's Raid: An Episode of the Civil War in East Tennessee. (Illus.). 92p. (Orig.). 1989. pap. 8.95 (*0-932807-42-9*) Overmountain Pr.

— Lee's Tarnished Lieutenant: James Longstreet & His Place in Southern History. LC 86-16025. 264p. 1987. 24.95 (*0-8203-0907-9*) U of Ga Pr.

— Lee's Tarnished Lieutenant: James Longstreet & His Place in Southern History. LC 86-16025. (Brown Thrasher Bks.). 264p. 1990. pap. 11.95 (*0-8203-1229-0*) U of Ga Pr.

***Pistone, Daniele.** Nineteenth-Century Italian Opera from Rossini to Puccini. Glasow, E. Thomas, tr. LC 94-28692. (Illus.). 276p. 1995. 29.95 (*0-931340-82-9*, Amadeus Pr) Timber.

Pistone, Joseph D. & Woodley, Richard. Donnie Brasco: My Undercover Life in the Mafia. 1989. pap. 5.99 (*0-451-15749-4*, Sig) NAL-Dutton.

Pistorius, Alan. Cutting Hill. 1990. 19.95 (*0-394-57439-7*) Knopf.

— Cutting Hill. 1992. pap. 3.99 (*0-517-09184-4*) Random Hse Value.

Pistorius, Alan & Gartlein, Delight. The Pember Museum of Natural History. (Illus.). 96p. (Orig.). 1986. pap. 9.95 (*0-9616427-0-X*) Pember Lib Mus.

Pistorius, Alan, jt. ed. see Eriksson, Paul S.

Pistorius, Christel & Pistorius, Rolf. Steiff: Sensational Teddy Bears, Animals & Dolls. (Illus.). 160p. 1991. 39. 95 (*0-87588-356-7*) Hobby Hse.

Pistorius, D. Pollak on Jurisdiction. 231p. 1993. write for info. (*0-7021-2953-4*, Pub. by Juta SA) W W Gaunt.

Pistorius, Rolf, jt. auth. see Pistorius, Christel.

***Piszkiewicz, Dennis.** The Nazi Rocketeers: Dreams of Space & Crimes of War. LC 95-10102. 274p. 1995. text ed. 24.95 (*0-275-95217-7*, Praeger Pubs) Greenwood.

Pita, Beatrice, ed. see Ruiz de Burton, Maria A.

Pita, Beatriz, ed. see Ruiz de Burton, Amparo.

Pita, Dianne D. Addictions Counseling: A Practical Guide to Counseling People with Chemical & Other Addictions. 144p. 1994. pap. 18.95 (*0-8245-1386-X*) Crossroad NY.

— The Dumbo Dilemma: Learning to Fly in Spite of Life's Worries. LC 93-21662. 178p. (Orig.). 1993. pap. 11.95 (*0-8245-1367-3*) Crossroad NY.

Pita, E. Air Conditioning Principles & Systems: an Energy Approach. 2nd ed. 1989. text ed. 74.00 (*0-13-018151-X*) P-H.

Pita, Edward G. Air Conditioning Principles & Systems: An Energy Approach. 2nd ed. 1989. text ed. 44.95 (*0-471-86506-0*) P-H.

— Refrigeration Principles & Systems: An Energy Approach. LC 91-14219. 1991. 41.95 (*0-912524-61-8*) Busn News.

P
Q

Pita, Juana R. Florencia Nuestra. Editorial Arcos, Inc. Staff, ed. (Arcos Poetica Ser.: No. 3). (Illus.). 82p. (Orig.). (SPA.). 1992. lib. bdg. 8.00 (*0-937509-07-8*) Edit Arcos.
— Sorbos de Luz - Sips of Light. De Salvatierra, Mario, tr. (Eboli Poetry Ser.). (Illus.). 64p. (Orig.). (ENG & SPA.). 1990. pap. write for info. (*0-932367-09-7*) Ed El Gato Tuerto.

Pita, Juana R., ed. see Ruiz, Enrique L.

Pitaevskii, L. P., ed. Perspectives in Theoretical Physics: The Collected Papers of E. M. Lifshitz. Sykes, J. B., tr. (Illus.). 688p. 1992. 165.00 (*0-08-036364-4*, Pergamon Pr) Elsevier.

Pitaevskii, L. P., jt. ed. see Halperin, W. P.

Pitaevskii, L. P., jt. auth. see Lifshitz, E. M.

Pitanguy, I. Aesthetic Plastic Surgery of Head & Body. (Illus.). 425p. 1981. 654.00 (*0-387-08706-0*) Spr-Verlag.

Pitard, Francis F. Pierre Gy's Sampling Theory & Sampling Practice. 2nd ed. 1993. 89.95 (*0-8493-8917-8*, TN560) CRC Pr.
— Pierre Gy's Sampling Theory & Sampling Practice, 2 Vols., Vol. I. 208p. 1989. 156.00 (*0-8493-6658-5*, TN560) CRC Pr.
— Pierre Gy's Sampling Theory & Sampling Practice, 2 Vols., Vol. II. 288p. 1989. 191.00 (*0-8493-6659-3*, TN560) CRC Pr.

Pitard, J. & Proust, L. Les Iles Canaries. 503p. 1973. reprint ed. pap. 147.00 (*3-87429-050-6*) Koeltz Sci Bks.

Pitas, Ioannis. Digital Image Processing Algorithms. 1993. write for info. (*0-318-70002-6*) P-H.

Pitas, Ioannis, ed. Parallel Algorithms for Digital Image Processing, Computer Vision & Neural Networks. (Parallel Computing Ser.). 395p. 1993. text ed. 59.95 (*0-471-93566-2*) Wiley.

Pitassi, Maria C. Entre Croire et Savoir: Probleme de la Methode Critique chez Jean le Clerc. (Kerkhistorische Bijdragen Ser.: No. 14). 401p. 1987. 48.00 (*90-04-08091-0*) E J Brill.

Pitblado, John R. The North Mkata Plain, Tanzania: A Study of Land Capability & Land Tenure. (University of Toronto, Department of Geography Research Publications: No. 16). (Illus.). 192p. reprint ed. pap. 54.80 (*0-685-23606-4*, 2026497) Bks Demand.

Pitcairn, D. M. & Flahault, D., eds. Medical Assistant: An Intermediate Level of Health Care Personnel. (Public Health Papers: No. 60). 1974. pap. 4.00 (*92-4-130060-4*) World Health.

Pitcairn, Feodor U. & Humann, Paul. Cayman: Underwater Paradise. Pitcairn, Kirstin, ed. LC 79-84293. (Illus.). (Orig.). 1979. 21.95 (*0-9602530-0-9*); pap. 14.95 (*0-685-04291-X*) Reef Dwellers.

Pitcairn, Harold F. & Odhner, Hugo L., eds. A Concordance of Selected Subjects Treated of in the Rational Psychology of Emanuel Swedenborg. 337p. 1960. 12.95 (*0-915221-11-X*) Swedenborg Sci Assn.

Pitcairn, Kirstin, ed. see Pitcairn, Feodor U. & Humann, Paul.

Pitcairn, Richard H. & Hubble Pitcairn, Susan. Dr. Pitcairn's Complete Guide To Natural Health for Dogs & Cats. LC 82-5336. (Illus.). 304p. 1982. pap. 12.95 (*0-87857-395-X*, 13-779-1) Rodale Pr Inc.

***Pitcairn, Richard H. & Pitcairn, Susan H.** Dr. Pitcairn's Complete Guide to Natural Health for Dogs & Cats. rev. ed. (Illus.). 304p. 1995. pap. 15.95 (*0-87596-243-2*) Rodale Pr Inc.

Pitcairn, Robert. Ancient Criminal Trials in Scotland, 3 pts in 4 vols. LC 71-174207. (Maitland Club, Glasgow. Publications: No. 19). reprint ed. Set. 205.00 (*0-404-52748-5*) AMS Pr.

Pitcairn, Robert, ed. Chronicon Coenobit Sanctae Crucis Edinburgensis. LC 75-169478. (Bannatyne Club, Edinburgh. Publications: No. 20). reprint ed. 21.50 (*0-404-52724-8*) AMS Pr.

Pitcairn, Robert, ed. see Bannatyne, Richard.

Pitcairn, Susan H., jt. auth. see Pitcairn, Richard H.

Pitcairn, Theodore. The Beginning & Development of Doctrine in the New Church. 64p. 1968. pap. 3.25 (*1-883270-09-X*) Swedenborg Assn.
— The Bible, or Word of God, Uncovered & Explained: After the Revelation Given Through Emanuel Swedenborg. 96p. 1964. pap. 3.75 (*1-883270-08-1*) Swedenborg Assn.
— My Lord & My God: Essays on Modern Religion, the Bible, & Emanuel Swedenborg. (Illus.). 312p. 1967. 7.50 (*1-883270-03-0*); pap. 5.00 (*1-883270-04-9*) Swedenborg Assn.
— The Ten Commandments: A Series of Sermons. 70p. 1964. pap. 3.75 (*1-883270-05-7*) Swedenborg Assn.

Pitcairne, Archibald. The Assembly. Tobin, Terence, ed. LC 74-171849. 120p. 1972. 5.95 (*0-911198-30-X*) Purdue U Pr.
— Babell. LC 75-174208. (Maitland Club, Glasgow. Publications: No. 6). reprint ed. 11.00 (*0-404-52931-3*) AMS Pr.

Pitch, Anthony S. Congressional Chronicles: Amusing & Amazing Anecdotes of the U. S. Congress & Its Members. LC 90-91538. (Illus.). 200p. (Orig.). 1990. pap. 12.95 (*0-931719-07-0*) Mino Pubns.
— Exclusively First Ladies Trivia. LC 85-60254. 176p. (Orig.). 1994. pap. 3.95 (*0-931719-03-8*) Mino Pubns.
— Exclusively Presidential Trivia. LC 84-62716. 176p. (Orig.). 1994. pap. 3.95 (*0-931719-01-1*) Mino Pubns.
— Exclusively Washington Trivia. LC 84-62046. 176p. (Orig.). 1994. pap. 3.95 (*0-931719-00-3*) Mino Pubns.
— Washington, D. C. Sightseers' Guide. LC 86-70380. (Illus.). 128p. (Orig.). 1994. pap. 4.95 (*0-931719-04-6*) Mino Pubns.

Pitch, Anthony S., jt. auth. see Alvarez, Everett, Jr.

***Pitch, Tamar.** Limited Responsibilities. Lea, John, tr. 240p. 1994. 59.95 (*0-415-08653-1*, B4213); pap. 18.95 (*0-415-08654-X*, B4217) Routledge.

Pitcher, Alvin. Listen to the Crying of the Earth: Cultivating Creation Communities. LC 93-15430. 168p. (Orig.). 1993. pap. 14.95 (*0-8298-0961-9*) Pilgrim OH.

Pitcher, Arthur. Memoirs of Peter. 1981. 4.95 (*0-86544-015-8*) Salv Army Suppl South.

Pitcher, Arthur R. Christmas Remembered. 1985. pap. 5.95 (*0-86544-029-8*) Salv Army Suppl South.
— Holiness in the Traffic. 125p. (Orig.). 1987. pap. 4.95 (*0-86544-046-8*) Salv Army Suppl South.
— People of My Pilgrimage. 1989. 8.95 (*0-86544-052-2*) Salv Army Suppl South.

***Pitcher, Caroline.** Joseph Storm. (J). 1994. 5.99 (*0-517-12016-X*) Random Hse Value.

Pitcher, Diana. The Mischief Maker. (Illus.). 64p. (J). 1990. pap. 5.95 (*0-86486-106-0*, Pub. by D Philip SA) Interlink Pub.
— Tokoloshi: African Folktales Retold. LC 93-26253. (Illus.). 64p. (J). (gr. 4 up). 1993. reprint ed. pap. 8.95 (*1-883672-03-1*) Tricycle Pr.

Pitcher, Don. Berkeley Inside-Out. (Illus.). 384p. (Orig.). 1989. pap. 12.95 (*0-930588-33-9*) Heyday Bks.
— Wyoming Handbook. 2nd ed. LC 92-42315. (Illus.). 430p. (Orig.). 1993. pap. 14.95 (*0-918373-98-0*) Moon Pubns CA.

Pitcher, Don & Margolin, Malcolm. Berkeley Inside-Out. 384p. (Orig.). 1991. reprint ed. lib. bdg. 33.00x (*0-8095-4967-0*) Borgo Pr.

Pitcher, Don, jt. ed. see Castleman, Deke.

Pitcher, E. J. Science & Engineering on Supercomputers: Fifth International Symposium October 22-24, 1990, London, England. ix, 628p. 1990. 180.00 (*0-387-53226-9*) Spr-Verlag.

Pitcher, Eric J., ed. Science & Engineering on Supercomputers. LC 90-84073. 628p. 1990. 165.00 (*0-945824-99-8*) Computational Mech MA.

Pitcher, Evelyn G. & Schultz, Lynn H. Boys & Girls at Play: The Development of Sex Roles. 220p. 1983. text ed. 49.95 (*0-275-91059-8*, C1059, Praeger Pubs) Greenwood.
— Boys & Girls at Play: The Development of Sex Roles. LC 82-16579. 224p. 1985. pap. text ed. 14.95 (*0-89789-055-8*, Bergin & Garvey) Greenwood.

Pitcher, Evelyn G., et al. Helping Young Children Learn. 5th ed. 384p. (C). 1989. pap. write for info. (*0-675-21054-2*, Merrill Pub Co) Macmillan.

Pitcher, Everett. A History of the Second Fifty Years, American Mathematical Society 1939-1988. LC 88-22318. (Centennial Publications: Vol. I). 360p. 1988. 50.00 (*0-8218-0125-2*, HMPITCHERC) Am Math.

Pitcher, Gayle D. & Poland, A. Scott. Crisis Intervention in the Schools. LC 92-1417. (Guilford School Practitioner Ser.). 246p. 1992. lib. bdg. 25.00 (*0-89862-364-2*) Guilford Pr.

***Pitcher, George.** The Dogs Who Came to Stay. LC 95-13629. (Illus.). 156p. 1995. 18.95 (*0-525-94050-2*, Dutton) NAL-Dutton.

Pitcher, George, ed. Berkeley: The Philosophy of Immaterialism. (Philosophy of George Berkeley Ser.). 397p. 1988. lib. bdg. 35.00 (*0-8240-2443-5*) Garland.
— Berkeley & Malebranche: A Study in the Origins of Berkeley's Thought. (Philosophy of George Berkeley Ser.). 248p. 1989. lib. bdg. 25.00 (*0-8240-2442-7*) Garland.
— Berkeley's Theory of Vision: A Critical Examination of Bishop Berkeley's Essay Towards a New Theory of Vision. (Philosophy of George Berkeley Ser.). 128p. 1989. reprint ed. lib. bdg. 20.00 (*0-8240-2448-6*) Garland.
— The Development of Berkeley's Philosophy. (Philosophy of George Berkeley Ser.). 400p. 1988. lib. bdg. 35.00 (*0-8240-2436-2*) Garland.
— George Berkeley Bicentenary: The British Journal for the Philosophy of Science, Vol. 4, No. 13. (Philosophy of George Berkeley Ser.). 92p. 1988. lib. bdg. 15.00 (*0-8240-2438-9*) Garland.
— Life & Letters of George Berkeley: Metaphysical, Descriptive, Theological with Many Writings of Bishop Berkeley Hitherto Unpublished. (Philosophy of George Berkeley Ser.). 672p. 1988. lib. bdg. 75.00 (*0-8240-2437-0*) Garland.
— A Theory of Perceptions. LC 73-120759. 250p. reprint ed. pap. 71.30 (*0-317-10596-5*, 2011399) Bks Demand.

Pitcher, George, jt. ed. see Doney, Willis.

Pitcher, George, jt. ed. see Stephen, Clark R.

Pitcher, H. J., ed. see Gogol.

Pitcher, Harvey. The Chekhov Play: A New Interpretation. 224p. 1984. pap. 12.00 (*0-520-05311-7*) U CA Pr.
— Witnesses of the Russian Revolution. (Illus.). 303p. 1995. 29.95 (*0-7195-5171-4*, Pub. by John Murray UK) Trafalgar.

Pitcher, Harvey, tr. see Chekhov, Anton.

Pitcher, John, ed. see Bacon, Francis.

Pitcher, John, ed. see Daniel, Samuel.

Pitcher, M. A. Management Accounting for the Lending Banker. 176p. 1979. 55.00 (*0-85297-050-1*, Pub. by Inst Bankers UK); pap. 44.00 (*0-85297-047-1*, Pub. by Inst Bankers UK) St Mut.

Pitcher, M. Anne. Politics in the Portuguese Empire: The State, Industry, & Cotton, 1926-1974. LC 92-41457. (C). 1993. 65.00 (*0-19-827373-8*, Clarendon Pr) OUP.

Pitcher, Max G., ed. see International Symposium on Arctic Geology Staff.

Pitcher, Seymour M., et al, eds. Two Creative Traditions in English Poetry. LC 72-450. (Granger Index Reprint Ser.). 1977. reprint ed. 23.95 (*0-8369-6367-9*) Ayer.

Pitcher, T. J., ed. Behaviour of Teleost Fishes. (Fish & Fisheries Ser.). (Illus.). 576p. 1992. 125.00 (*0-412-42930-6*, A9620); pap. 39.95 (*0-412-42940-3*, A9624) Chapman & Hall.

Pitcher, Terry, jt. auth. see Kalinich, David B.

Pitcher, Tony J., ed. The Behavior of Teleost Fishes. LC 85-19887. (Illus.). 554p. reprint ed. pap. 157.90 (*0-7837-1107-7*, 2041637) Bks Demand.

Pitcher, Valerie. Anya Astern, Come Down from the Sky. LC 90-71860. 44p. (J). (gr. 6). 1991. 6.95 (*1-55523-412-7*) Winston-Derek.

Pitcher, W. Alvin, jt. ed. see Amjad-Ali, Charles.

***Pitcher, W. R.** Imaging America: Anecdote, Tale, & Short Story in the Eighteenth Century. Date not set. write for info. (*0-912756-29-2*) Union Coll.

Pitcher, W. R. & Gado, Frank, eds. First Person: Conversations on Writers & Writing. 266p. (C). 1995. text ed. 29.95x (*0-912756-03-9*) Union Coll.

Pitcher, W. S. The Nature & Origin of Granite. 256p. 1993. 64.50 (*0-7514-0080-7*, A6884, Pub. by Blackie Acad & Prof UK) Routledge Chapman & Hall.

Pitcher, W. S. & Aguirre, L., eds. Bibliography of Circum-Pacific Plutonism. (Microform Publication: No. 12). 1982. 1.50 (*0-8137-6012-7*) Geol Soc.

Pitcher, Wayne H., Jr. Immobilized Enzymes for Food Processing. 232p. 1980. 113.95 (*0-8493-5345-9*, TP456, CRC Reprint) Franklin.

Pitchford, Gene. Young Folks' Hawaiian Time. (Illus.). (J). (ps). 1965. pap. 3.00 (*0-87505-275-4*) Borden.

***Pitchford, John.** The Current Account & Foreign Debt. LC 94-46487. 1995. write for info. (*0-415-09401-1*) Routledge.

Pitchford, Kenneth, tr. see Rilke, Rainer Maria.

Pitchford, L. C., et al, eds. Swarm Studies & Inelastic Electron-Molecule Collisions. (Illus.). xi, 403p. 1986. 90.00 (*0-387-96402-9*) Spr-Verlag.

Pitchford, Paul. Healing with Whole Foods: Oriental Traditions & Modern Nutrition. LC 93-87. (Illus.). 656p. (Orig.). 1993. pap. 24.95 (*0-938190-64-4*) North Atlantic.
— Healing with Whole Foods: Oriental Traditions & Modern Nutrition. limited ed. LC 93-87. 656p. (Orig.). (C). 1994. 40.00 (*1-55643-194-5*) North Atlantic.

Pitchford, Polly & Quigley, Delia. Cookin' Healthy with One Foot Out the Door: Quick Meals for Fast Times. LC 93-43471. 160p. 1994. 8.95 (*0-913990-86-8*) Book Pub Co.

Pitchford, Polly, jt. auth. see Quigley, Delia.

Pitchfork, E. D., ed. Tort. 248p. (C). 1990. pap. 60.00 (*1-85352-765-3*, Pub. by HLT Pubns UK) St Mut.

Pite, Ralph. The Circle of Our Vision: Dante's Presence in English Romantic Poetry. (Illus.). 288p. 1994. 45.00 (*0-19-811294-7*) OUP.

Pitel, J., ed. Multicriterion Optimization & Its Application in Agriculture: Developments in Agricultural Economics, No. 6. 247p. 1991. 108.75 (*0-444-98727-4*) Elsevier.

Pitelis, Christos. Market & Non-Market Hierarchies: Theory of Institutional Failure. LC 93-16051. 258p. 1993. reprint ed. text ed. 54.95 (*0-631-15796-4*); reprint ed. pap. 24.95 (*0-631-19061-9*) Blackwell Pubs.

Pitelis, Christos, ed. Surveys in Transaction Costs, Markets & Hierarchies. LC 92-30554. 1993. 54.95 (*0-631-18371-X*); pap. 24.95 (*0-631-18898-3*) Blackwell Pubs.

Pitelis, Christos, jt. ed. see Clarke, Thomas.

Pitelis, Christos N. Corporate Capital: Control, Ownership, Savings & Crisis. 136p. 1987. 49.95 (*0-521-32848-9*) Cambridge U Pr.

Pitelis, Christos N. & Sugden, Roger, eds. The Nature of the Transnational Firm. 256p. 1991. 79.95 (*0-415-05271-8*, A5193); pap. 19.95 (*0-415-05748-5*, A5197) Routledge.

Pitelis, Christos N., jt. ed. see Clarke, Thomas.

Pitelka, D. & Kerkut, G. A. Electron-Microscopic Structure of Protozoa. LC 92-19274. (International Series of Monographs on Pure & Applied Mathematics: Vol. 13). 1963. 120.00 (*0-08-009820-7*, Pub. by Pergamon Repr UK) Franklin.

Piterman, Mark A., tr. see Nigmatulin, R. I.

Piterman, Mark A., tr. see Polyanin, Andrei D. & Dilman, Victor V.

Pitfield, D. E., jt. ed. see Button, K. J.

Pitfield, Michael & Donnelly, Robert. How to Take Exams. 112p. (C). 1980. 60.00 (*0-85292-262-0*, Pub. by IPM Hse UK) St Mut.

Pitfield, P. & Donnelly, D. How to Take Exams. 112p. (C). 1980. 90.00 (*0-685-39809-9*, Inst Pur & Supply) St Mut.

Pithers, William, et al. From Trauma to Understanding: A Guide for Parents of Children with Sexual Behavior Problems. Bear, Euan & Knopp, Fay, eds. (Safer Society Ser.: No. 10). 32p. 1993. pap. text ed. 5.00 (*1-884444-07-5*) Safer Soc.

Pithisaria, M. K., jt. ed. see Chaturvedi, K.

Pithisaria, V., jt. auth. see Chaturvedi, T. N.

Pithouse, A. Social Work: The Social Organisation of an Invisible Trade. 1987. text ed. 55.95 (*0-566-05378-0*, Pub. by Avebury Pub UK) Ashgate Pub Co.

Pitisaria, C. Chaturvediand. Income Tax Law, 6 vols. (C). 1990. 193.00 (*0-89771-275-7*) St Mut.

Pitkanen, Allan M., tr. see Paulaharju, Samuli.

***Pitkeathley, Jill & Emerson, David.** Only Child: How to Survive Being One. 1995. pap. 14.95 (*0-285-63182-9*) Atrium Pubs.

Pitkethly, Alan S., jt. auth. see Fernie, John.

Pitkin, Anne. Yellow. (Orig.). 1989. 22.00 (*0-934847-08-8*); pap. 9.00 (*0-934847-09-6*) Arrowood Bks.

Pitkin, Donald S. The House That Giacomo Built: History of an Italian Family 1898-1978. (Illus.). 208p. 1985. 64.95 (*0-521-30168-8*) Cambridge U Pr.

Pitkin, Gary M. Serials Automation in the United States: A Bibliographic History. LC 76-18116. 157p. 1976. 20.00 (*0-8108-0955-9*) Scarecrow.

Pitkin, Gary M., ed. Cost-Effective Technical Services: How to Track, Manage, & Justify Internal Operations. 325p. (Orig.). 1989. pap. text ed. 39.50 (*1-55570-041-1*) Neal-Schuman.
— The Impact of Emerging Technologies on Reference Service & Bibliographic Instruction. LC 95-3802. (Contributions in Librarianship & Information Science Ser.: No. 87). 192p. 1995. text ed. 49.95 (*0-313-29365-1*, Greenwood Pr) Greenwood.

Pitkin, Hanna F. The Concept of Representation. 1967. pap. 14.00 (*0-520-02156-8*) U CA Pr.
— Fortune Is a Woman: Gender & Politics in the Thought of Niccolo Machiavelli. LC 83-6541. 350p. (C). 1984. pap. 13.00 (*0-520-06176-4*) U CA Pr.

Pitkin, Hanna R. Wittgenstein & Justice: The Significance of Ludwig Wittgenstein for Social & Political Thought. 1972. reprint ed. 42.50 (*0-520-05471-7*); reprint ed. pap. 15.00 (*0-520-02329-3*) U CA Pr.

***Pitkin, Harvey.** Wintu Dictionary. (University of California Publications in Entomology: No. 95). 943p. 1985. pap. 180.00 (*0-7837-7499-0*, 2049221) Bks Demand.
— Wintu Grammar. LC 84-16268. (University of California Publications in Entomology: No. 94). 326p. 1984. pap. 93.00 (*0-7837-7498-2*, 2049220) Bks Demand.

Pitkin, John, jt. auth. see Masnick, George.

Pitkin, Julia M., ed. see Clark, Jim & Beck, Ken.

Pitkin, Julie M., ed. see Maynard, Kitty & Maynard, Lucian.

Pitkin, Olive. My Garden & I. 224p. 1992. 19.95 (*1-55821-180-2*) Lyons & Burford.

Pitkin, Ron, jt. auth. see Ricker, Robert S.

Pitkin, Thomas M. The Black Hand: A Chapter in Ethnic Crime. 274p. 1977. pap. 10.00 (*0-8226-0333-0*) Junius-Vaughn.

Pitkin, Timothy. Political & Civil History of the United States of America from the Year 1763 to the Close of the Administration of President Washington in March, 1797, 2 Vols, Set. LC 79-109613. (Era of the American Revolution Ser.). 1970. reprint ed. lib. bdg. 135.00 (*0-306-71908-8*) Da Capo.
— Statistical View of the Commerce of the United States of America. LC 65-26374. (Library of Early American Business & Industry: No. 13). 1967. reprint ed. 57.50 (*0-678-00219-3*) Kelley.

***Pitkin, Walter B.** Life Begins at Forty. 1994. lib. bdg. 24.95x (*1-56849-381-9*) Buccaneer Bks.

***Pitkin, William.** Qualifications for the Priesthood in the Liberal Catholic Church. rev. ed. 13p. 1994. pap. 2.25 (*0-918980-15-1*) St Alban Pr.

Pitkin, William H., ed. see Sheehan, Edmund W.

Pitlick, William H. Antiepileptic Drug Interactions. LC 88-71752. (Illus.). 338p. 1989. 79.95 (*0-939957-14-0*) Demos Vermande.

Pitman, jt. auth. see Larson.

Pitman, A. J., jt. ed. see Henderson-Sellers, A.

Pitman, Brian. Fencing: Techniques of Foil, Epee & Sabre. (Illus.). 144p. 1989. 34.95 (*1-85223-152-1*, Pub. by Crowood Pr UK) Trafalgar.

Pitman, C. B., tr. see Orleans, Henri P.

Pitman, C. E. Pitman: History & Pedigree of the Family Pitman of Dunchideock, Exeter, & Collaterals, & of the Pitmans of Alphington, Norfolk & Edinburgh. (Illus.). 181p. 1992. reprint ed. lib. bdg. 37.50 (*0-8328-2706-1*); reprint ed. pap. 27.50 (*0-8328-2707-X*) Higginson Bk Co.

Pitman, Carol S., illus. The Feline Muse. LC 86-81933. 92p. 1986. 14.95 (*0-8233-0424-8*) Golden Quill.

Pitman, E. R. Ann H. Judson of Burma. 1988. pap. 3.95 (*0-87508-601-2*) Chr Lit.

Pitman, Elizabeth. This Won't Change Your Life: (But It Might Help!) 140p. 1990. pap. 19.95 (*1-873150-00-8*, Pub. by Multilingual Matters UK) Taylor & Francis.

Pitman, Emma R. Elizabeth Fry. LC 69-14036. 269p. 1969. reprint ed. text ed. 38.50 (*0-8371-1005-X*, PIEF, Greenwood Pr) Greenwood.

Pitman-Gelles, Bonnie. Museums, Magic & Children: Youth Education in Museums. Kendall, Aubyn & Bannerman, Carol, eds. (Illus.). 262p. (Orig.). 1982. pap. 21.00 (*0-944040-13-6*) AST Ctrs.

Pitman, Gerald H. Liposuction & Aesthetic Surgery. LC 92-532. 1993. 245.00 (*0-942219-18-X*) Quality Med Pub.

Pitman, Jim. Probability. LC 92-39051. (Texts in Statistics Ser.). 596p. 1994. 49.00 (*0-387-97974-3*) Spr-Verlag.

Pitman, John. Breechloading Carbines of the United States Civil War Period. LC 87-70171. (Illus.). 94p. 1987. 29.95 (*0-939683-00-8*) Armory Pubns.
— The Pitman Notes on U. S. Martial Small Arms & Ammunition, 1776-1933: Miscellaneous Notes, Vol. 5. (Illus.). 212p. (C). 1993. text ed. 29.95 (*0-939631-35-0*) Thomas Publications.
— The Pitman Notes on U. S. Martial Small Arms & Ammunition, 1776-1933, Vol. 2: Revolvers & Automatic Pistols. (Illus.). 192p. (C). 1991. text ed. 29.95 (*0-939631-32-6*) Thomas Publications.
— The Pitman Notes on U. S. Martial Small Arms & Ammunition, 1776-1933, Vol. 3: Rifles & Carbines, Cal. 45. (Illus.). 192p. 1991. 29.95 (*0-939631-33-4*) Thomas Publications.
— The Pitman Notes on U. S. Martial Small Arms & Ammunition, 1776-1933, Vol. 4: U. S. Magazine Rifles 30 caliber. (Illus.). 194p. (C). 1992. text ed. 29.95 (*0-939631-34-2*) Thomas Publications.

Pitman, John, ed. see Lightfoot, John.

Pitman, John C., jt. auth. see Roueche, John E.

Pitman, Martha B. & Szyfelbein, Wanda M., eds. Fine Needle Aspiration Biopsy of the Liver: A Coloar Atlas. LC 94-15909. (Illus.). 1994. write for info. (*0-7506-9463-7*) Buttrwrth-Heinemann.

Pitman, Mary A., jt. ed. see Fetterman, David M.

Pitman, Mary A., et al. Culture Acquisition: A Holistic Approach to Human Learning. LC 88-27507. 252p. 1989. text ed. 52.95 (*0-275-93031-9*, C3031, Praeger Pubs) Greenwood.

PQ

An Asterisk (*) at the beginning of an entry indicates that the title is appearing in BIP for the first time.

— Culture Acquisition: A Holistic Approach to Human Learning. LC 88-27507. (Illus.). 252p. 1989. lib. bdg. 42.95 (*0-318-41925-4*, C3031, Greenwood Pr) Greenwood.

Pitman, Paul M., III, ed. Turkey: A Country Study. 4th ed. LC 88-8844. (Area Handbook Ser.). (Illus.). 495p. 1989. text ed. 18.00 (*0-16-001710-6*, S/N 008-020-01162-2) USGPO.

Pitman Publishing, Ltd. Editors. Peterborough Postgraduate Symposia: Cardiology. (Pitman Medical Conference Reports). (Illus.). 128p. 1975. pap. text ed. 19.95 (*0-8464-0713-2*) Beekman Pubs.

Pitman Publishing Ltd. Staff, ed. The Pitman Dictionary of English & Shorthand. 850p. 1988. 57.50 (*0-273-36137-6*, Pub. by Pitman Pub Ltd UK) Trans-Atl Phila.

Pitman Publishing Ltd Staff, ed. Pitman New Era Shorthand Pocket Dictionary. 221p. (Orig.). 1985. pap. text ed. 9.95 (*0-273-40954-9*, Pub. by Pitman Pub Ltd UK) Trans-Atl Phila.

Pitman Publishing Ltd. Staff, ed. Pitman Two Thousand Shorthand First Course. 2nd ed. 1902. pap. 19.95 (*0-273-01800-0*, Pub. by Pitman Pub Ltd UK); teacher ed 3.95 (*0-273-01808-6*, Pub. by Pitman Pub Ltd UK) Trans-Atl Phila.

Pitman Publishing Staff, ed. Pitman New Era Shorthand: Anniversary Edition, 2 vols., Set. 192p. (Orig.). 1988. Two-vol. set. student ed, pap. 22.00 (*0-273-02902-9*, Pub. by Pitman Pub Ltd UK) Trans-Atl Phila.

Pitman, Randy. The Video Librarian's Guide to Collection Development & Management. LC 92-15104. (Professional Librarian Ser.). 280p. 1992. text ed. 35.00 (*0-8161-1978-3*, Hall Reference); pap. text ed. 22.50 (*0-8161-1979-1*, Hall Reference) Macmillan.

Pitman, Randy & Swanson, Elliott. Video Movies: A Core Collection for Libraries. 266p. 1990. lib. bdg. 45.00 (*0-87436-577-5*) ABC-CLIO.

***Pitman, Richard.** Hunted. large type ed. (Magna Large Print Ser.). 1994. 26.95 (*0-7505-0725-X*) Ulverscroft.

— Warned Off. large type ed. (Ulverscroft Ser.). 512p. 1994. 21.95 (*0-7089-3048-4*) Ulverscroft.

Pitman, Rod. Reel Extra Money: The Background Actor's Handbook. (Orig.). Date not set. pap. write for info. (*0-9642118-6-6*) Cascade Press.

Pitman, Sally C., intro. The Empty Laugh Book. (Orig.). 1981. pap. text ed. 12.00 (*0-935229-07-8*) Am Assoc Med.

***Pitman, Vicki.** Herbal Medicine: The/ Use of the Herbs for Health & Healing. LC 94-23421. (Health Library). 1995. pap. 9.95 (*1-85230-591-6*) Element MA.

Pitman, Walter C., III, jt. ed. see Talwani, Manik.

Pitman, Walter G. The Baptists & Public Affairs in the Province of Canada: 1840-1867. Gaustad, Edwin S., ed. LC 79-52576. (Baptist Tradition Ser.). 1980. lib. bdg. 23.95 (*0-405-12444-9*) Ayer.

Pitner, Erin C. Stones & Roses. 80p. (Orig.). 1993. pap. 5.95 (*0-9637559-0-0*) Chamisa.

Pitner, Ernst. Maximilian's Lieutenant: A Personal History of the Mexican Campaign, 1864-67. Etherington-Smith, Gordon, tr. LC 92-44670. 216p. 1994. 42.50x (*0-8263-1425-2*) U of NM Pr.

Pitner, Rudolf, et al. The Psychology of the Physically Handicapped. Phillips, William R. & Rosenberg, Janet, eds. LC 79-6922. (Physically Handicapped in Society Ser.). 1980. reprint ed. lib. bdg. 37.95 (*0-405-13130-5*) Ayer.

Pitney, John J., Jr., jt. auth. see Connelly, William F., Jr.

Piton, Camille. The Civil Costumes of France of Thirteenth & Fourteenth Century. (Illus.). 380p. 1986. reprint ed. pap. text ed. 35.00 (*0-87556-387-2*) Saifer.

Pitone, Louise. Absence & Lateness: How to Reduce It, How to Control It. 1987. pap. 24.95 (*1-55645-515-1*) Busn Legal Reports.

— The BLR Encyclopedia of Prewritten Personnel Letters. 436p. 1988. 99.95 (*1-55645-527-5*) Busn Legal Reports.

Pitoniak, Scott. The Buffalo Bills Official All-New Trivia Book II. (Illus.). 112p. (Orig.). 1992. pap. 8.99 (*0-312-08151-0*) St Martin.

— The Buffalo Bills Official Trivia Book. (Illus.). 128p. (Orig.). 1989. pap. 8.95 (*0-312-03737-6*) St Martin.

Pitot. Fundamentals of Oncology. 3rd rev. ed. 544p. 1986. 49.75 (*0-8247-7457-4*) Dekker.

Pitou, N. S. His Majesty's Rebel Captain. 1992. 12.95 (*0-8062-4322-8*) Carlton.

Pitou, Spire. The Paris Opera: An Encyclopedia of Operas, Ballets, Composers & Performers, Genesis & Glory, 1671-1715. LC 82-21140. xii, 364p. 1983. text ed. 59.95 (*0-313-21420-4*, PFO/, Greenwood Pr) Greenwood.

— The Paris Opera: An Encyclopedia of Operas, Ballets, Composers & Performers, Genesis & Glory, 1671-1715. LC 82-21140. xviii, 619p. 1985. text ed. 105.00 (*0-313-24394-8*, POR/, Greenwood Pr) Greenwood.

— The Paris Opera: An Encyclopedia of Operas, Ballets, Composers & Performers, Genesis & Glory, 1671-1715. LC 87-21140. 1608p. 1990. text ed. 185.00 (*0-313-26218-7*, PGH, Greenwood Pr) Greenwood.

— The Paris Opera: An Encyclopedia of Operas, Ballets, Composers, & Performers; Growth & Grandeur, 1815-1914; A-L. LC 82-21140. 816p. 1990. text ed. 185.00 (*0-313-27782-6*, PGH01, Greenwood Pr) Greenwood.

— The Paris Opera: An Encyclopedia of Operas, Ballets, Composers, & Performers; Growth & Grandeur, 1815-1914; A-L, Vol. 2. LC 82-21140. 768p. 1990. text ed. 185.00 (*0-313-27783-4*, Greenwood Pr) Greenwood.

Pitowsky, I., ed. Quantum Probability - Quantum Logic. (Lecture Notes in Physics Ser.: Vol. 321). ix, 209p. 1989. 33.00 (*0-387-50679-9*) Spr-Verlag.

Pitrat, J. An Artificial Approach to Understanding Natural Language. 162p. 1988. 35.00 (*0-87683-945-6*, PR-4) Soc Computer Sim.

Pitre, David W. To Martin Luther King, with Love: A Southern Quaker's Tribute. LC 84-60119. 1984. pap. 3.00 (*0-87574-254-8*) Pendle Hill.

Pitre, Giuseppe. Sicilian Folk Medicine. (Illus.). 320p. 1971. 48.50 (*0-87291-013-X*) Coronado Pr.

Pitre, Glen. Belizaire the Cajun. Shapiro, Dean, ed. LC 88-9820. 1988. 13.95 (*0-88289-711-X*); pap. 7.95 (*0-88289-671-7*) Pelican.

— The Crawfish Book. (Illus.). 160p. 1993. pap. 13.95 (*0-87805-599-1*) U Pr of Miss.

Pitre, Glen & Benoit, Michelle. Great River. LC 93-22333. 224p. 1993. pap. 12.95 (*0-88289-783-7*) Pelican.

Pitre, Marianne R., jt. auth. see Anderson, Anne S.

Pitre, Richard & Adams, Barbara L. Practice Problem in Financial Accounting (Tex-So Company) 1984. 11.95 (*0-931920-87-6*) Dame Pubns.

Pitre, Richard, jt. auth. see Waller, Thomas C.

Pitre, Verne. Cornshucks, Spanish Moss & Feathers: More Tales of the Cajun Wetlands. (Illus.). 96p. (Orig.). (J). (gr. 5-7). 1993. pap. 7.95 (*0-9621724-9-9*) Blue Heron LA.

— Grandma Was a Sailmaker: Tales of the Cajun Wetlands. (Illus.). 160p. (Orig.). (YA). (gr. 7 up). 1991. pap. 6.00 (*0-9621725-6-1*) Blue Heron LA.

— Grandma Was a Sailmaker: Tales of the Cajun Wetlands. (Illus.). 160p. (Orig.). (YA). (gr. 9). 1991. pap. 12.95 (*0-9621724-5-6*) Blue Heron LA.

Pitroda, Sam. Exploding Freedom: Roots in Technology. (C). 1993. 18.00 (*81-7023-270-8*, Pub. by Allied II) S Asia.

Pitrone, Jean M. Hudson's Hub of America's Heartland. 220p. 1991. 24.95 (*1-878005-18-9*) Northmont Pub.

— Jean Hoxie: The Robin Hood of Tennis. LC 85-70768. 130p. 1985. 11.95 (*0-910977-01-1*) Avenue Pub.

Pitrone, Jean M. & Nosis, George J. Tangled Web: Legacy of Auto Pioneer, John F. Dodge. 336p. 1989. 19.95 (*0-910977-05-4*) Avenue Pub.

Pitschmann, Louis A. Scholars' Guide to Washington, D. C., for Northwest European Studies: Belgium, Denmark, Finland, Great Britain, Greenland, Iceland, Ireland, Luxembourg, the Netherlands, Norway, & Sweden. David, Zdenek V., ed. LC 84-600036. 452p. 1984. 29.95 (*0-87474-754-6*, Johns Hopkins); pap. text ed. 15.00 (*0-87474-753-8*, Johns Hopkins) W Wilson Ctr Pr.

Pitseolak, Peter. Peter Pitseolak (1902-1973) Bellman, David, ed. 1982. pap. 24.95 (*0-7735-0400-1*, Pub. by McGill CN) U of Toronto Pr.

Pitseolak, Peter & Eber, Dorothy H. People from Our Side: A Life Story with Photographs & Oral Biography. Hanson, Ann, tr. (Illus.). 168p. 1993. 39.95 (*0-7735-0996-8*, Pub. by McGill CN); pap. 19.95 (*0-7735-1118-0*, Pub. by McGill CN) U of Toronto Pr.

Pitskhelauri, G. Z. The Longliving of Soviet Georgia. Lesnoff-Caravaglia, Gari, tr. LC 81-4176. (Illus.). 158p. 1982. 30.95 (*0-89885-073-8*) Human Sci Pr.

Pitstick, Mark R. Balanced Living: Realizing Your Fullest Potentials. LC 92-31432. 380p. 1993. pap. 16.95 (*0-935834-91-5*) Rainbow Books.

Pitstow, Margaret. The Hand of Destiny. (Rainbow Romances Ser.). 160p. 1993. 14.95 (*0-7090-4897-1*, Hale-Parkwest) Parkwest Pubns.

— The Hand of Destiny. large type ed. (Romance Ser.). 1994. pap. 14.95 (*0-7089-7617-4*, Linford) Ulverscroft.

Pitsvada, Bernard T. The Senate, Treaties & National Security, 1945-1974. 252p. (C). 1991. lib. bdg. 46.00 (*0-8191-8198-6*); pap. text ed. 27.00 (*0-8191-8199-4*) U Pr of Amer.

Pitt, jt. auth. see Yashinsky.

Pitt, A., jt. ed. see Cross, P.

Pitt, Brice. Making the Most of Middle Age. large type ed. 128p. 1991. 17.95 (*1-85089-170-2*, Pub. by ISIS UK) Transaction Pubs.

Pitt, C. W., jt. ed. see Roberts, G. G.

Pitt, D. C., ed. Deforestation: Social Dynamics in Watersheds & Mountain Ecosystems. 224p. 1988. lib. bdg. 55.00 (*0-415-00456-X*) Routledge.

Pitt, D. H., et al. Category Theory & Computer Science. (Lecture Notes in Computer Science Ser.: Vol. 283). v, 300p. 1987. pap. 39.00 (*0-387-18508-9*) Spr-Verlag.

Pitt, D. H., et al, eds. Category Theory & Computer Science. (Lecture Notes in Computer Science Ser.: Vol. 389). vi, 365p. 1989. pap. 43.00 (*0-387-51662-X*, 3506) Spr-Verlag.

— Category Theory & Computer Science: Paris, France, September 3-6, 1991 Proceedings. (Lecture Notes in Computer Science Ser.: Vol. 530). vii, 301p. 1991. pap. 34.00 (*0-387-54495-X*) Spr-Verlag.

Pitt, David & Thompson, Gordon, eds. Nuclear Free Zones. 160p. 1987. lib. bdg. 55.00 (*0-7099-4076-9*, Pub. by Croom Helm UK) Routledge Chapman & Hall.

Pitt, David, jt. ed. see Briceno, Salvano.

Pitt, David, jt. auth. see Nilsson, Sten.

Pitt, David C. Using Historical Sources in Anthropology & Sociology. (George & Louise Spindler Case Studies in Cultural Anthropology). 92p. (C). reprint ed. pap. write for info. (*0-8290-0587-0*) Irvington.

Pitt, David C., ed. Development from Below: Anthropologists & Development Situations. (World Anthropology Ser.). x, 278p. 1976. 36.95 (*90-279-7869-7*) Mouton.

Pitt, David G. E. J. Pratt: The Master Years 1927-1964. (Illus.). 576p. 1987. 40.00 (*0-8020-5753-5*) U of Toronto Pr.

— E. J. Pratt: The Truant Years Eighteen Eighty-Two to Nineteen Twenty-Seven. (Illus.). 448p. 1984. 30.00 (*0-8020-5660-1*); pap. 17.95 (*0-8020-6563-5*) U of Toronto Pr.

***Pitt, Estella M.** A Restoring God. 40p. 1994. pap. 4.95 (*0-9642764-0-2*) E Pitt.

Pitt, G. D., jt. auth. see Parker, H.

Pitt, G. J. & Milward, G. R., eds. Coal & Modern Coal Processing: An Introduction. 1979. text ed. 61.00 (*0-12-557850-4*) Acad Pr.

Pitt, Gwyneth. Butterworths Commercial Law Handbook. 1989. U.K. pap. 41.00 (*0-406-54722-X*) Butterworth Legal Pubs.

Pitt, H. R. Measure & Integration for Use. (Institute of Mathematics & Its Applications Conference Series, New Ser.). 156p. 1985. 28.95 (*0-19-853608-9*) OUP.

Pitt, Harvey L., et al. The Law of Financial Services, 6 vols. 5000p. 1988. write for info. (*0-318-65468-7*, H44003) P-H.

Pitt, Harvey L., jt. auth. see Block, Dennis J.

Pitt, Harvey L., jt. auth. see Greene, Edward F.

Pitt, Harvey L., et al. The Law of Financial Services, 8 vols. 9530p. 1988. ring bd. 695.00 (*0-13-099276-3*) Aspen Law.

Pitt, Harvey L., et al, eds. Twenty-Third Annual Institute on Securities Regulation Transcript - The SEC in a New Environment - Securitization - Troubled Companies - Sharehold Activism Enforcement. 350p. 1992. 105.00 (*0-685-69368-6*) PLI.

***Pitt, Henry A., et al.** Hepatic & Pancreatic Disease: The Team Approach to Management. LC 94-46416. 1995. 99.95 (*0-316-70915-8*) Little.

Pitt, Hy. SPC for the Rest of Us: A Personal Path to Statistical Process Control. LC 93-8311. 1994. 32.95 (*0-201-56366-5*) Addison-Wesley.

Pitt, J. C., ed. The Philosophy of Wilfrid Sellars: Queries & Extensions. (Philosophical Studies in Philosophy Ser.: No. 12). 1978. lib. bdg. 70.00 (*90-277-0903-3*) Kluwer Ac.

Pitt, J. I., jt. ed. see Samson, Robert A.

Pitt, J. I., et al. Regnum Vegetabile, Vol. 128: NCU-2. Names in Current Use in the Families Trichocomataceae, Cladoriaceae, Pinaceae, & Lemnaceae. 152p. 1993. pap. 55.00 (*1-878762-44-3*, 053047) Koeltz Sci Bks.

Pitt, Jo J., ed. see Smothers, Thelma W.

***Pitt, John.** U. S. A. by Rail. (Bradt Guides Ser.). (Illus.). 306p. 1994. 15.95 (*1-56440-563-X*) Globe Pequot.

Pitt, John I. The Genus Penicillium & Its Teleomorphic States: Eupenicillium & Talaromyces, No. 640. LC 79-40923. 1980. text ed. 248.00 (*0-12-557750-8*) Acad Pr.

Pitt, John I., jt. ed. see Samson, Robert A.

Pitt, Joseph C. Galileo, Human Knowledge, & the Book of Nature: Method Replaces Metaphysics. (Western Ontario Ser.). 216p. (C). 1992. lib. bdg. 94.00 (*0-7923-1510-3*) Kluwer Ac.

— Pictures, Images & Conceptual Change: Wilfrid Sellars & the Philosophy of Science. 168p. 1981. lib. bdg. 62.00 (*90-277-1276-X*) Kluwer Ac.

— Theories of Explanation. (Illus.). 234p. 1988. pap. text ed. 15.95 (*0-19-504971-3*) OUP.

Pitt, Joseph C., ed. Philosophy in Economics. 210p. 1981. lib. bdg. 62.00 (*90-277-1210-7*) Kluwer Ac.

Pitt, Joseph C. & Pera, Marcello, eds. Rational Changes in Science. (C). 1987. lib. bdg. 100.00 (*90-277-2417-2*) Kluwer Ac.

Pitt, Joseph C., jt. ed. see Butts, Robert E.

Pitt, Joseph C., jt. ed. see Byrne, Edmund F.

Pitt, Judith. Glass Eggs. 75p. 1984. pap. 5.95 (*0-935684-06-9*) Plumbers Ink Bks.

Pitt, Ken. Bowie: The Pitt Report. (Illus.). 230p. 1985. pap. 12.95 (*0-7119-0619-X*, OP43256) Omnibus NY.

Pitt-Kethley, Fiona. Dogs. 84p. 1994. pap. 16.95 (*1-85619-285-7*, Sinclair-Stevenson) Trafalgar.

— The Literary Companion to Sex. 1994. 25.00 (*0-679-42323-0*) Random.

Pitt, Leonard. The Decline of the Californios: A Social History of the Spanish-Speaking Californians, 1846-1890. 1966. pap. 13.00 (*0-520-01637-8*) U CA Pr.

— Documenting America: A Reader in United States History, Vol. I: Colonial Times to 1877. 320p. 1989. per. 42.95 (*0-8403-5245-X*) Kendall-Hunt.

— Study Guide for We Americans, Vol. I. 3rd ed. 112p. 1989. per. 21.95 (*0-8403-5628-5*) Kendall-Hunt.

— Study Guide for We Americans, Vol. II. 3rd ed. 160p. 1989. per. 24.95 (*0-8403-5629-3*) Kendall-Hunt.

— We Americans. 2nd ed. 984p. 1984. per. 35.95 (*0-8403-3220-3*) Kendall-Hunt.

Pitt, Leonard, ed. California Controversies: Major Issues in the History of the State. 2nd ed. (Illus.). 384p. 1990. pap. text ed. write for info. (*0-88295-879-8*) Harlan Davidson.

Pitt, Leonard, jt. ed. see Haussler, David.

Pitt, Mark M. & Rosenweig, Mark R. The Selectivity of Fertility & the Determinants of Human Capital Investments: Parametric & Semiparametric Estimates. (Living Standards Measurement Study Working Paper Ser.: No. 72). 54p. 1990. 6.95 (*0-8213-1629-X*, 11629) World Bank.

Pitt, Martin, jt. ed. see Loveridge, Raymond.

Pitt, Martyn, jt. ed. see Loveridge, Raymond.

Pitt, Peter. Guide to Building Control by Local Acts, 1987. 128p. 1987. 115.00 (*0-85139-841-3*) Buttrwrth-Heinemann.

Pitt-Rivers. Love of Food, Love of God. (C). 1991. lib. bdg. 34.95 (*0-226-67005-8*) U Ch Pr.

Pitt-Rivers, Augustus H. Antique Works of Art from Benin. LC 68-9011. (Illus.). 1971. 25.00 (*0-87817-017-0*) Hacker.

— Antique Works of Art from Benin, West Africa. LC 74-138344. (Black Heritage Library Collection). 1977. 23.95 (*0-8369-8736-5*) Ayer.

— The Evolution of Culture, & Other Essays. Myres, J. L., ed. LC 76-44719. reprint ed. 49.50 (*0-404-15858-7*) AMS Pr.

— Excavations in Cranborne Chase: Near Rushmore, on the Borders of Dorset & Wilts: 1880-1896, 4 vols. LC 77-86426. reprint ed. 315.00 (*0-404-16640-7*) AMS Pr.

Pitt-Rivers, Julian, jt. ed. see Peristiany, J. G.

Pitt-Rivers, Julian A. The Fate of Shechem: or, The Politics of Sex: Essays in the Anthropology of the Mediterranean. LC 76-27913. (Cambridge Studies in Social Anthropology: No. 19). 207p. reprint ed. pap. 59.00 (*0-318-34835-7*, 2031710) Bks Demand.

— People of the Sierra. 2nd ed. LC 70-153710. 264p. 1972. pap. text ed. 9.95 (*0-226-67010-4*, P55) U Ch Pr.

Pitt-Rivers, R. & Greene, R. Advances in Thyroid Research: Transactions of the 4th International Goitre Conference, London, July, 1960. LC 61-9607. 1961. 232.00 (*0-08-009203-9*, Pub. by Pergamon Repr UK) Franklin.

Pitt-Rivers, Rosalind & Trotter, W. R., eds. The Thyroid Gland, 2 vols., I. LC 64-9966. (Illus.). reprint ed. pap. 114.00 (*0-317-41693-6*, 2025714) Bks Demand.

— The Thyroid Gland, 2 vols., II. LC 64-9966. (Illus.). reprint ed. pap. 84.30 (*0-317-41694-4*) Bks Demand.

***Pitt, Robert, et al.** Investigation of Inappropriate Pollutant Entries into Storm Drainage Systems: A User's Guide. (Illus.). 87p. (Orig.). 1994. pap. text ed. 50.00x (*0-7881-1359-3*) Diane Pub.

— Potential Groundwater Contamination from Intentional & Nonintentional Stormwater Infiltration. (Illus.). 120p. (Orig.). (C). 1994. pap. text ed. 60.00x (*0-7881-1059-4*) Diane Pub.

Pitt, Ruth S., et al. Creatures of Middle Earth. (Middle Earth Ser.). (Illus.). 64p. (Orig.). (C). 1988. pap. 10.00 (*1-55806-019-7*, 8005) Iron Crown Ent Inc.

Pitt, Theodore K. Premarital Counseling Handbook for Ministers. 192p. 1985. pap. 10.00 (*0-8170-1071-8*) Judson.

Pitt, Valeria. Enciclopedia Juvenil de la Ciencia. 260p. (SPA.). (J). 1975. 95.00 (*0-8288-5870-5*, S26475) Fr & Eur.

Pitt, Valerie. Tennyson Laureate. 304p. reprint ed. pap. 86.70 (*0-8357-4166-4*, 2036940) Bks Demand.

Pitt, Valerie, ed. see Eiler, Andrew.

Pitt, Valerie H., ed. The Penguin Dictionary of Physics. (Reference Ser.). 1977. pap. 8.95 (*0-14-051071-0*, Penguin Bks) Viking Penguin.

Pitt-Watson. A Primer for Preachers. LC 86-72370. 112p. 1987. pap. 5.99 (*0-8010-7096-1*) Baker Bk.

Pitt, William. General View of the Agriculture of the County of Worcester: With Observations on the Means of Its Improvement. LC 77-92000. (Illus.). xx, 428p. 1969. reprint ed. 49.50 (*0-678-05545-9*) Kelley.

Pitta, Robert. U. N. Forces, 1948-1994. (Elite Ser.). (Illus.). 64p. 1994. pap. 12.95 (*1-85532-454-7*, 9469, Pub. by Osprey UK) Stackpole.

Pitta, Robert & Fannell, Jeff. South African Special Forces. (Elite Ser.: No. 47). (Illus.). 64p. pap. 12.95 (*1-85532-295-1*, 9462, Pub. by Osprey UK) Stackpole.

Pittam, Jeffery. Voice in Social Interaction: An Interdisciplinary Approach to Vocal Communication. (Language & Language Behaviors Ser.: Vol. 5). 200p. 1994. 39.95 (*0-8039-5750-5*); pap. 18.95 (*0-8039-5751-3*) Sage.

Pittano, Giuseppe. Phraseological Synonym & Antonym Dictionary of Equivalences, Analogous & Contrary Terms: Sinonimi e Contrari Dizionario Fraseologico delle Parole Equivalenti Analoghe e Contrarie. 864p. (ITA.). 1987. lib. bdg. 95.00 (*0-8288-3337-0*, F120160); Small edition. lib. bdg. 85.00 (*0-685-58982-X*) Fr & Eur.

Pittano, Giuseppe & Fatta, Frase. Capo Ha: Dizionario Dei Modi di Dire, Proverbi e Locuzioni. 352p. (ITA.). 1993. 75.00 (*0-8288-9428-0*) Fr & Eur.

Pittard, Kay & Mitchell, Robert W. Comparative Morphology of the Life Stages of Cryptocellus Pelaezi (Arachnida, Ricinulie) (Graduate Studies: No. 1). (Illus.). 77p. (Orig.). 1972. pap. 4.00 (*0-89672-008-X*) Tex Tech Univ Pr.

Pittard, Lynne. More Magic Methods in Oil with Lynne Pittard: Thirteen New Paintings Illustrated in Four Stages, in Full Color. (Illus.). 72p. (Orig.). 1984. pap. 14.95 (*0-943295-05-X*) Graphics Plus FL.

— Paint with Pittard: Thirteen New Paintings by Lynne Pittard in Four Stages & Full Color. (Illus.). 72p. (Orig.). 1985. pap. 14.95 (*0-943295-06-8*) Graphics Plus FL.

— Paint with Pittard III: Twelve New Paintings by Lynne Pittard in Four Stages & Full Color. (Illus.). 72p. (Orig.). 1989. pap. 14.95 (*0-943295-10-6*) Graphics Plus FL.

Pittard, Suzan Z., ed. see Zedick, Mary P.

Pittaro. Cuentos Faciles de Hoy y de Ayer. 1973. pap. text ed. 7.95 (*0-88334-059-3*, 76059) Longman.

Pittas-Hershbach, Mary. Time & Space in Euripides & Racine: The Hippolytos of Euripides & Racine's Phedre. LC 89-29820. (American University Studies: Comparative Literature: Ser. III, Vol. 32). 344p. (C). 1990. text ed. 53.95 (*0-8204-1182-5*) P Lang Pubs.

Pittas, Peggy A. Blow Your Little Tin Whistle: A Biography of Richard Clarke Sommerville. LC 92-11142. 258p. (Orig.). (C). 1992. lib. bdg. 39.50 (*0-8191-8744-5*); pap. text ed. 24.50 (*0-8191-8745-3*) U Pr of Amer.

Pittau, Francisco. Tightrope Walker. LC 92-54429. (J). (ps-3). 1993. 13.00 (*0-688-12379-1*) Lothrop.

— Voyage under the Stars. LC 91-26075. (Illus.). 32p. (J). (ps-3). 1992. 13.00 (*0-688-11328-1*); lib. bdg. 12.93 (*0-688-11329-X*) Lothrop.

Pittau, Joseph. Political Thought in Early Meiji Japan, 1868-1889: 1868-1889. LC 65-22065. (Harvard East Asian Ser.: No. 24). 261p. reprint ed. pap. 74.40 (*0-317-09172-7*, 2003781) Bks Demand.

Pittaway, A. R. Arthropods of Medical & Veterinary Importance: A Checklist of Preferred Names & Allied Terms. 192p. 1991. pap. 59.95 (*0-8288-7365-8*, 851987419) Fr & Eur.

Pittaway, A. R., comp. Arthropods of Medical & Veterinary Importance: A Checklist of Preferred Names & Allied Terms. 160p. 1991. pap. 31.00 (*0-85198-741-9*) CAB Intl.

Pittelman, Susan D., jt. auth. see Heimlich, Joan E.

Pittelman, Susan D., et al. Semantic Feature Analysis: Classroom Application. 66p. 1991. pap. 6.00 (*0-87207-235-5*) Intl Reading.

Pittenger, David J., jt. auth. see Allen, Joseph D.

Pittenger, John, jt. ed. see Valenti, S. Stavros.

Pittenger, Mark. American Socialists & Evolutionary Thought, 1870-1920. LC 92-28041. (History of American Thought & Culture Ser.). 320p. (Orig.). (C). 1993. 60.00 (*0-299-13600-0*); pap. 24.95 (*0-299-13604-3*) U of Wis Pr.

Pittenger, Norman. Before the Ending of the Day. LC 84-62373. 110p. 1985. pap. 6.95 (*0-8192-1365-9*) Morehouse Pub.

— The Lord's Prayer. 74p. (Orig.). 1989. pap. 2.35 (*0-88028-091-3*, 971) Forward Movement.

— The Ministry of All Christians. LC 82-62393. 96p. 1983. pap. 5.95 (*0-8192-1323-3*) Morehouse Pub.

Pittenger, Owen E. & Gooding, C. Thomas. Learning Theories in Educational Practice: An Integration of Psychological Theory & Educational Philosophy. LC 79-140553. 228p. (C). reprint ed. 65.00 (*0-8357-9922-0*, 2051747) Bks Demand.

Pittenger, Peggy J. Reschooling the Thoroughbred. rev. ed. (Illus.). 224p. 1991. 23.95 (*0-929346-09-2*) R Meerdink Co Ltd.

Pittenger, Shari. Listen, Color & Learn: A Coloring Book for Family Devotions, Vol. I, Psalm 1-30. 35p. (Orig.). (J). (ps-6). 1989. pap. text ed. 5.00 (*0-923463-49-6*) Noble Pub Assocs.

— Listen, Color, & Learn, Vol. II: A Coloring Book for Family Devotions, Psalm 31-60. 40p. (J). 1990. student ed 5.00 (*0-923463-75-5*) Noble Pub Assocs.

— Listen, Color, & Learn, Vol. III: A Coloring Book for Family Devotions, Psalm 61-90. 40p. (J). 1991. student ed 5.00 (*0-923463-77-1*) Noble Pub Assocs.

Pittenger, W. Norman, jt. auth. see Pike, James A.

Pittenger, William N. Catholic Faith in a Process Perspective. LC 81-9615. 160p. (Orig.). reprint ed. pap. 45.60 (*0-8357-8825-3*, 2033560) Bks Demand.

— Christian Faith & the Question of History. LC 73-79353. 159p. reprint ed. pap. 45.40 (*0-685-15547-1*, 2026910) Bks Demand.

Pitter. Applications Software Supplement. 1987. pap. text ed. write for info. (*0-07-555298-1*) McGraw.

— Every Student's Guide to the Internet. 1995. pap. text ed. 15.75 (*0-07-051773-8*) McGraw.

Pitter, ed. Biodegradability of Organic Substances in Aquatic Environ. 1990. 190.00 (*0-8493-5131-6*, QH530) CRC Pr.

Pitter, Keiko. Application Software Tutorial. 1987. pap. write for info. (*0-07-556490-4*) McGraw.

— First Look at Works 2.0 for the Mac. 1992. pap. text ed. write for info. (*0-07-050293-5*) McGraw.

— Introducing Microsoft Excel 4.0 for Windows. 125p. 1993. pap. text ed. write for info. (*0-07-051576-X*) McGraw.

— Introducing Microsoft Excel 4.0 for Windows. 100p. 1993. pap. text ed. write for info. (*0-07-051586-7*) McGraw.

— Introducing Microsoft Excel 5.0 for Windows. 1994. pap. text ed. write for info. (*0-07-051596-4*) McGraw.

— Introducing the PC & Windows 3.1. 150p. 1993. pap. text ed. write for info. (*0-07-051584-0*) McGraw.

— Introducing WordPerfect for Windows. 150p. 1993. pap. text ed. write for info. (*0-07-051588-3*) McGraw.

— Introducing WordPerfect 6.0 for Windows. 1994. pap. text ed. write for info. (*0-07-051597-2*) McGraw.

— Using Apple Works. 2nd ed. 300p. (C). 1989. text ed. write for info. (*0-394-39446-1*) Mitchell Pub.

— Using IBM Microcomputers: Word Perfect, dBase III Plus & IV, & Lotus. 3rd ed. 300p. (C). 1989. text ed. write for info. (*0-394-39449-6*) Mitchell Pub.

— Using Lotus 1-2-3, 2.2 for the IBM Pc. 2nd ed. 1990. pap. text ed. write for info. (*0-07-050258-7*) McGraw.

— Using Microcomputers: An Apple Lab Manual. 237p. 1984. pap. text ed. 17.95 (*0-938188-21-6*) Mitchell Pub.

Pitter, Keiko & Pitter, Richard. Using Lotus 1-2-3 for DOS Release 3.1 Plus. 264p. 1993. text ed. write for info. (*0-07-050296-X*) McGraw.

— Using Microcomputers: An IBM PC Lab Manual. 280p. 1984. pap. text ed. 17.95 (*0-938188-22-4*) Mitchell Pub.

— Using Microcomputers: An IBM-PC Lab Manual. 2nd ed. 256p. (Orig.). (C). 1986. pap. text ed. 19.95 (*0-938188-38-0*) Mitchell Pub.

— Using Microsoft Excel 4.0 for Windows: The Basics. 1993. pap. text ed. write for info. (*0-07-050295-1*) McGraw.

— Using Microsoft Excel 5.0 for Windows: Advanced. 1995. pap. text ed. write for info. (*0-07-051593-X*) McGraw.

Pitter, Keiko & Trainor, Timothy N. Introducing Microsoft Works 3.0 for Windows. 1994. pap. text ed. write for info. (*0-07-051595-6*) McGraw.

Pitter, Richard, jt. auth. see Pitter, Keiko.

Pitter, Ruth. Ruth Pitter Collected Poems. 299p. (Orig.). 1990. pap. 22.00 (*1-870612-06-X*, Pub. by Enitha Pr UK) Dufour.

***Pitteway, Les.** Ninety Miles from Cuba: Topical & Tropical Half-Truths from Key West. Murdoch, Robert et al, eds. LC 94-72282. 395p. 1994. 19.95 (*1-885659-47-4*) Bald Head Bks.

Pittfield, E. P. Book of Bere Regis. 1988. 60.00 (*0-686-75650-9*) Dorset Pr.

Pittham, Keith S. Rehabilitation: Index of Modern Information with Bibliography. LC 88-47796. 150p. (Orig.). 1988. 44.50 (*0-88164-884-1*); pap. 39.50 (*0-88164-885-X*) ABBE Pubs Assn.

Pittier de Fabrega, Henri. Ethnographic & Linguistic Notes on the Paez Indians of Tierra Adentro, Cauca, Colombia. LC 08-3129. (American Anthropological Association Memoirs Ser.). 1907. 15.00 (*0-527-00504-5*) Periodicals Srv.

Pittiglio, D. Harmening, jt. auth. see Isbister, James.

Pittiglio, Rabin, Todd & McGrath Staff & McGrath, Michael E. Product Development: Success Through PACE. (Illus.). 272p. 1992. 29.95 (*0-7506-9289-8*) Buttrwrth-Heinemann.

Pittilo, R. M. & Machin, S. J. Platelet-Vessel Wall Interaction. (Bloomsbury Series in Clinical Science). (Illus.). 195p. 1988. 89.50 (*0-387-17488-5*) Spr-Verlag.

Pittinger, Charles B., ed. James Taylor Gwathmey - American Pioneer Anesthesiologist. LC 88-51678. 630p. (C). 1989. 55.00 (*0-9623307-0-1*) Anesthesia Pr.

Pittman, Allan, jt. auth. see Smith, Robert W.

Pittman, Allen, jt. auth. see Smith, Robert W.

Pittman, Anne. Tennis. (Sport for Life Ser.). (C). 1988. pap. text ed. 10.50 (*0-673-18346-7*) HarpCollege.

Pittman, Avril. From Ostpolitik to Reunification: West German-Soviet Political Relations since 1974. (Cambridge Russian, Soviet & Post-Soviet Studies: No. 85). (Illus.). 256p. (C). 1992. 59.95 (*0-521-40166-6*) Cambridge U Pr.

Pittman, Bill. AA: The Way It Began. LC 87-73390. 252p. (Orig.). 1988. pap. 8.95 (*0-934125-08-2*) Glen Abbey Bks.

— Stepping Stones to Recovery. LC 87-73389. 308p. 1988. pap. 8.95 (*0-934125-04-X*) Hazelden.

— Twelve Step Prayer Book. 128p. (Orig.). 1990. pap. 4.95 (*0-934125-11-2*) Hazelden.

Pittman, Bill, intro. Easy Does It: A Book of Daily 12 Step Meditations. 400p. (Orig.). 1990. pap. 7.95 (*0-934125-12-0*, Lakeside Recovery Pr) Hazelden.

Pittman, Bill & Goetsch, Jerry. Let It Ride. 1994. pap. 8.95 (*0-934125-33-3*) Hazelden.

Pittman, Bill & Weber, Todd. Drop the Rock! Removing Character Defects. LC 92-4263. 128p. (Orig.). 1993. pap. 7.95 (*0-934125-27-9*) Hazelden.

Pittman, Bill, jt. auth. see Bishop, Charles, Jr.

Pittman, Bill, jt. auth. see Pittman, Mel B.

Pittman, Blair, photos. The Natural World of the Texas Big Thicket. LC 78-6369. (Louise Lindsey Merrick Texas Environement Ser.: No. 2). (Illus.). 100p. 1978. reprint ed. 24.95 (*0-89096-061-5*); reprint ed. pap. 12.95 (*0-89096-303-7*) Tex A&M Univ Pr.

Pittman, David J. & White, Helene R. Society, Culture, & Drinking Patterns Reexamined. 824p. 1991. pap. 31.95 (*0-911290-22-2*) Rutgers Ctr Alcohol.

Pittman, E. D. & Lewan, M. D., eds. Organic Acids in Geological Processes. LC 94-3819. 1994. 89.00 (*0-387-56953-7*) Spr-Verlag.

Pittman, Eddie B., Jr. Words Chiseled from Rock. LC 87-61254. (Illus.). 80p. (Orig.). 1987. pap. 5.00 (*0-9618791-0-6*) Pub Press.

Pittman, Frank. Private Lies. 1989. 19.95 (*0-393-02634-5*) Norton.

— Private Lies, Infidelity & the Betrayal of Intimacy. 1990. pap. 10.95 (*0-393-30707-7*) Norton.

Pittman, Frank S. Man Enough: Fathers, Sons, & the Search for Masculinity. LC 92-34246. 288p. (Orig.). 1993. 22.95 (*0-399-13819-6*) Putnam Pub Group.

Pittman, Frank S., III. Man Enough: Fathers, Sons, & the Search for Masculinity. LC 94-11093. 336p. (Orig.). 1994. pap. 14.00 (*0-399-51883-5*, Putnam) Putnam Pub Group.

— Turning Points: Treating Families in Transition & Crisis. (Professional Bks.). 1987. 34.95 (*0-393-70040-2*) Norton.

Pittman, H. C. Inside the Third House: A Fifty Year Frolic Through Texas Politics. LC 92-30776. 1992. 24.95 (*0-89015-879-7*) Sunbelt Media.

Pittman, Helena C. Counting Jennie. (J). (ps-3). 19.95 (*0-87614-745-7*, Carolrhoda) Lerner Group.

— A Dinosaur for Gerald. (Gerald Bks.). (Illus.). 32p. (J). (ps-3). 1990. lib. bdg. 18.95 (*0-87614-431-8*, Carolrhoda) Lerner Group.

— Gerald-Not-Practical. (Gerald Bks.). (Illus.). 32p. (J). (ps-3). 1990. lib. bdg. 18.95 (*0-87614-430-X*, Carolrhoda) Lerner Group.

— The Gift of the Willows. (Carolrhoda Picture Bks.). (Illus.). 32p. (J). (ps-3). 1988. 18.95 (*0-87614-354-0*, Carolrhoda) Lerner Group.

— A Grain of Rice. (J). 1992. pap. 3.50 (*0-553-15986-0*) Bantam.

— Miss Hindy's Cats. LC 89-22214. (Carolrhoda Picture Bks.). (Illus.). 32p. (J). (ps-3). 1990. pap. 18.95 (*0-87614-368-0*, Carolrhoda) Lerner Group.

— Miss Hindy's Cats: Picture Book. (J). (ps-3). 1991. pap. 6.95 (*0-87614-538-1*, Carolrhoda) Lerner Group.

— The Moon's Party. LC 92-40866. (J). 1994. 15.95 (*0-399-22541-2*, Putnam) Putnam Pub Group.

— Once When I Was Scared. LC 88-3598. (Illus.). 32p. (J). (gr. k-3). 1988. 14.00 (*0-525-44407-6*, DCB) Dutton Child Bks.

— Once When I Was Scared. (Illus.). 36p. (J). (ps-3). 1993. pap. 4.99 (*0-14-054932-3*, Puff Unicorn) Puffin Bks.

— One Quiet Morning: Story & Pictures. LC 93-49596. (Illus.). (J). 1995. write for info. (*0-87614-838-0*, Carolrhoda) Lerner Group.

Pittman, Holly. Art of the Bronze Age: Southeastern Iran, Western Central Asia, & the Indus Valley. (Orig.). 1994. pap. 7.95 (*0-8109-6446-5*) Abrams.

— Art of the Bronze Age: Southeastern Iran, Western Central Asia, & the Indus Valley. Ekman, Joanna, ed. LC 84-728. 100p. (Orig.). 1984. pap. 4.95 (*0-87099-365-8*) Metro Mus Art.

Pittman, J. F., et al, eds. Numerical Analysis of Forming Processes. LC 83-21600. (Wiley Series in Numerical Methods in Engineering). 462p. reprint ed. pap. 131.70 (*0-7837-4012-3*, 2043842) Bks Demand.

Pittman, Joe F., jt. ed. see Bowman, Gary L.

Pittman, John. Africa Calling: Isolate the Racists! the Liberation Struggle in Southern Africa. 32p. 1973. pap. 0.60 (*0-87898-107-1*) New Outlook.

Pittman, Karen J., jt. auth. see Burt, Martha R.

Pittman-Lindeman, Mary, jt. ed. see Corless, Inge B.

Pittman, Mary, ed. Reports of the United States Tax Court, Vol. 84: Jan. 1, 1985 to June 30, 1985. 1404p. 1985. 38.00 (*0-16-003768-9*, S/N 028-005-00154-3) USGPO.

Pittman, Mary T., ed. United States Reports of Tax Court, Vol. 86, Jan. 1, 1986 to June 30, 1986. 1407p. 1986. 37.00 (*0-16-003770-0*, S/N 028-005-00156-0) USGPO.

Pittman, Mary T. & Fee, John T. Reports of Tax Court of the United States, Vol. 92. (Illus.). 1440p. 1990. boxed 41.00 (*0-16-003776-X*, S/N 028-005-00162-4) USGPO.

Pittman, Mel B. & Pittman, Bill. Seven Key Principles of Successful Recovery. 1994. pap. 7.95 (*0-934125-32-5*) Hazelden.

Pittman, Nancy P. From the Land. LC 88-25551. (Conservation Classics Ser.). (Illus.). 473p. 1988. pap. 19.95 (*0-933280-65-3*) Island Pr.

— From the Land. LC 88-25551. (Conservation Classics Ser.). (Illus.). 473p. 1989. 34.95 (*0-933280-66-1*) Island Pr.

Pittman, Philip M. & Covington, George M. Don't Blame the Treaties. (Fresh Coast Publication Ser.). (Illus.). 500p. 1992. 45.00 (*1-878005-11-1*); pap. 22.95 (*1-878005-59-6*) Northmont Pub.

Pittman, Philip M. & Simonsen, Larry L. North Shore Chinook: Lake Huron Salmon on Light Tackle. (Illus.). 164p. (Orig.). 1993. pap. 16.95 (*0-9620206-4-8*) Avonstoke Pr.

Pittman, Phillip M., jt. ed. see Watson, Jeanie.

Pittman, Rachel N. The Wedding of G. Washington Bear. (Illus.). 42p. (Orig.). (J). (ps-5). 1986. pap. 6.95 (*0-9615382-1-X*) Pittman Pub.

Pittman, Richard S. The Faculty of Letters, 3 fiche, Set. LC 90-72068. (Alphabet Makers Ser.: No. 1). 126p. (Orig.). 1991. fiche 12.00 (*0-88312-263-4*) Summer Instit Ling.

Pittman, Richard S., jt. auth. see Kenicutt, Wally.

Pittman, Riitta H. The Writer's Divided Self in Bulgakov's The Master & Margarita. LC 91-2123. 224p. 1991. text ed. 49.95 (*0-312-06148-X*) St Martin.

***Pittman, Ruth.** Roadside History of California. Greer, Dan, ed. (Roadside History Ser.). (Illus.). 496p. 1995. 30.00 (*0-87842-317-6*); pap. 18.00 (*0-87842-318-4*) Mountain Pr.

Pittman, Sandra. Lord, Let Me Prove That Winning the Lottery Won't Spoil Me! (Illus.). 144p. (Orig.). 1992. pap. 9.95 (*0-940873-92-3*) AKG.

— With Tongue in Cheek. LC 86-72589. (Illus.). 128p. (Orig.). 1986. pap. 6.95 (*0-940873-86-9*) AKG.

Pittman, Sidney E. Glossary of Healthcare Terms for Environmental Services. 78p. (Orig.). 1991. pap. 50.00 (*0-87258-618-9*, 057009) Am Hospital.

Pittman, Steve. The Case for an Illinois Coal Severance Tax. (Illus.). (Orig.). 1984. pap. text ed. 2.00 (*0-943724-08-2*) Illinois South.

Pittman, Thane S., jt. ed. see Boggiano, Ann K.

Pittman, Thane S., jt. ed. see Bornstein, Robert F.

Pittman, Thomas & Peters, James. The Art of Compiler Design: Theory & Practice. 368p. 1991. text ed. 60.00 (*0-13-048190-4*) P-H.

Pittman, Walter E., Jr. Navalist & Progressive: The Life of Richmond P. Hobson. 235p. 1981. pap. 29.00 (*0-89126-100-1*) MA-AH Pub.

Pittmon, Woodrow K. To Be a Man. 1992. 13.95 (*0-533-10107-7*) Vantage.

Pittner, L., jt. ed. see Mitter, H.

Pittock, A. B., et al. Environmental Consequences of Nuclear War, Vol. 1: Physical & Atmospheric Effects. 2nd ed. (Scientific Committee on Problems of the Environment Ser.: No. 28). 359p. 1989. pap. text ed. 74.95 (*0-471-92469-5*) Wiley.

Pittock, Joan, jt. auth. see Carter, Jennifer E.

Pittock, Joan H. & Wear, Andrew, eds. Interpretation & Cultural History. 320p. 1991. text ed. 49.95 (*0-312-05360-6*) St Martin.

Pittock, Murray. The Invention of Scotland: The Stuart Myth & the Scottish Identity, 1638 to the Present. 224p. 1991. 74.50 (*0-415-05586-5*, A5741) Routledge.

Pittock, Murray G. Poetry & Jacobite Politics in Eighteenth-Century Britain & Ireland. LC 93-42500. (Studies in Eighteenth-Century English Literature & Thought: No. 23). 276p. (C). 1995. 59.95 (*0-521-41092-4*) Cambridge U Pr.

— Spectrum of Decadence: The Literature of the 1890s. LC 92-18438. 240p. 1993. 59.95 (*0-415-07757-5*, B0373) Routledge.

Pittoni, Mario. Brief Writing & Argumentation. 3rd ed. (University Textbook Ser.). 217p. 1991. reprint ed. pap. text ed. 11.95 (*0-88277-415-8*) Foundation Pr.

Pitts, et al. Academic Writing: A Brief Guide. 192p. (C). 1992. pap. text ed. 11.95 (*0-8403-8158-1*) Kendall-Hunt.

— Shadowmasters, No.1. 48p. 1989. 3.95 (*0-87135-546-9*) Marvel Entmnt.

Pitts, Alger E. A Work to Be Done. Hill, Renais J., ed. LC 92-52943. 90p. (Orig.). 1992. pap. 8.95 (*1-55666-079-0*) Pubs Grp Toluca.

***Pitts, Alice & Champ, Minnie.** Collin County, Texas. (Illus.). 397p. 1994. 65.00 (*0-88107-246-X*) Curtis Media.

Pitts, Audre. Let Me Keep Laughter. 106p. 1985. pap. 4.95 (*0-8341-1090-3*) Beacon Hill.

— Music Keeps on Playing. 94p. (Orig.). 1988. pap. 4.95 (*0-8341-1250-7*) Beacon Hill.

Pitts, Bill, jt. auth. see Lois, George.

***Pitts, Colin.** Motivating Your Organization: Achieving Business Success Through Reward & Recognition. LC 95-1427. (Quality in Action Ser.). 1995. 22.95 (*0-07-707967-1*) McGraw.

Pitts, David. How in the World Do I Get along With My Parents? 40p. 1982. pap. 0.95 (*0-88144-046-9*) Christian Pub.

Pitts, Donald G. & Kleinstein, Robert N. Environment & Vision. 422p. 1993. 85.00 (*0-7506-9051-8*) Buttrwrth-Heinemann.

Pitts, Donald R. One Thousand Solved Problems in Heat Transfer. 1990. pap. text ed. 19.95 (*0-07-050204-8*) McGraw.

Pitts, Donald R. & Sissam, Leighton E. Heat Transfer. (Schaum's Outline Ser.). (C). 1977. pap. text ed. 12.95 (*0-07-050203-X*) McGraw.

Pitts, Emma T., jt. ed. see Duhon-Sells, Rose M.

***Pitts, Gertrude & Scott, Anne.** Tragedies of Life. LC 94-42140. (African American Women Writers, 1910-1940 Ser.). 1995. write for info. (*0-8161-1634-2*) G K Hall.

Pitts, Greg, jt. auth. see Bowden, Scott.

Pitts, J. N., Jr. Excited State Chemistry. 160p. (C). 1970. text ed. 125.00 (*0-677-14630-2*) Gordon & Breach.

Pitts, J. R. Life & Confession of Noted Outlaw James Copeland. (Illus.). 263p. 1992. pap. 15.95 (*0-87805-611-4*) U Pr of Miss.

Pitts, James, Jr. & Metcalf, Robert L., eds. Advances in Environmental Science & Technology, Vol. 5. LC 74-644364. 382p. 1975. 39.50 (*0-471-69088-0*) Wiley.

Pitts, James M., ed. The Way of Faith: Words of Admonition & Encouragement for the Journey Based on the Letter to the Hebrews. 176p. (Orig.). 1985. pap. 8.95 (*0-913029-10-6*) Stevens Bk Pr.

Pitts, James N., jt. auth. see Finlayson-Pitts, Barbara J.

Pitts, John. A Manual of Geology for Civil Engineers. 228p. 1985. text ed. 48.00 (*9971-978-05-9*); pap. text ed. 23.00 (*9971-978-12-1*) World Scientific Pub.

— The Politics of Juvenile Crime. (Contemporary Criminology Ser.: Vol. 2). 192p. (C). 1988. text ed. 39.95 (*0-8039-8132-5*); pap. text ed. 16.50 (*0-8039-8133-3*) Sage.

Pitts, John D. & Finbow, Malcolm E., eds. The Functional Integration of Cells in Animal Tissues. LC 81-10213. (British Society for Cell Biology Symposium Ser.: No. 5). (Illus.). 400p. 1982. 105.00 (*0-521-24199-5*) Cambridge U Pr.

Pitts, John T. Existence & Regularity of Minimal Surfaces on Riemannian Manifolds. LC 81-47150. (Mathematical Notes Ser.: No. 27). 192p. (Orig.). 1981. pap. 24.95 (*0-691-08290-1*) Princeton U Pr.

Pitts, Judy M., jt. auth. see Stripling, Barbara K.

Pitts, Lawrence & Wagner, Franklin. Craniospinal Trauma. Blaisdell & Trunkey, eds. (Trauma Management Ser.: Vol. 5). (Illus.). 280p. 1989. text ed. 89.00 (*0-86577-322-X*) Thieme Med Pubs.

Pitts, Lawrence H., jt. auth. see Andrews, Brian T.

***Pitts, Lee.** People Who Live at the End of Dirt Roads. (Illus.). 112p. 1995. pap. 10.95 (*0-87905-673-8*) Gibbs Smith Pub.

Pitts, Marian & Phillips, Keith, eds. The Psychology of Health: An Introduction. 304p. (C). 1991. text ed. 69.95 (*0-415-04114-7*, A5413) Routledge.

Pitts, Mark & Fabozzi, Frank J. Interest Rate Futures & Options. 350p. 1987. 65.00 (*0-917253-95-7*) Probus Pub Co.

Pitts, Mary. Hyde Park, Massachusetts This Modern Cannan. (Illus.). 91p. (Orig.). 1988. pap. 12.00 (*0-913553-06-9*) Albert Hse Pub.

Pitts, Mary E. Theodore DwightWeld - This Was A Man! 30p. 1987. pap. 5.00 (*0-913553-05-0*) Albert Hse Pub.

— Toward a Dialogue of Understandings: Loren Eiseley & the Critique of Science. LC 94-46994. 1995. write for info. (*0-934223-37-8*) Assoc Univ Prs.

Pitts, Michael R. Famous Movie Detectives, No. II. LC 90-9083. (Illus.). 357p. 1991. 47.50 (*0-8108-2345-4*) Scarecrow.

— Horror Film Stars. 2nd ed. LC 90-53707. (Illus.). 472p. 1991. pap. 27.50x (*0-89950-507-4*) McFarland & Co.

— Kate Smith: A Bio-Bibliography. LC 87-25154. (Bio-Bibliographies in the Performing Arts Ser.: No. 2). 320p. 1988. text ed. 45.00 (*0-313-25541-5*, PKS/, Greenwood Pr) Greenwood.

— Radio Soundtracks: A Reference Guide. 2nd ed. LC 85-30409. 349p. 1986. 32.50 (*0-8108-1875-2*) Scarecrow.

Pitts, Michael R., jt. auth. see Campbell, Richard H.

Pitts, Michael R., jt. auth. see Parish, James R.

Pitts, Michael S. Making the Holy Spirit Your Partner: Discovering His Plan, Purpose, & Power. 71p. 1992. pap. 7.00 (*0-9633583-0-8*) Pitts Evang Assn.

Pitts, Nolan T. The Message, the Mess, the Mileage. 96p. (Orig.). 1994. pap. 5.95 (*1-883928-08-7*) Longwood.

Pitts, Paul. Crossroads. 160p. (Orig.). (J). (gr. 5). 1994. pap. 3.50 (*0-380-77606-5*, Camelot) Avon.

— For a Good Time, Don't Call Claudia. 128p. (J). (gr. 7 up). 1986. pap. 2.50 (*0-380-75117-8*, Flare) Avon.

— Racing the Sun. 160p. (J). 1988. pap. 3.50 (*0-380-75496-7*, Camelot) Avon.

— The Shadowman's Way. 128p. (Orig.). (J). (gr. 5). 1992. pap. 3.50 (*0-380-76210-2*, Camelot) Avon.

Pitts, Ralph A., jt. auth. see Jenkins, A. Felton, Jr.

Pitts, Robert A. & Snow, Charles C. Strategies for Competitive Success. LC 85-10483. 76p. 1986. Net. pap. text ed. write for info. (*0-471-81656-6*) Wiley.

Pitts, Robert E., Jr. & Woodside, Arch G. Personal Values & Consumer Psychology. LC 83-48123. 336p. 1984. text ed. 27.95 (*0-669-09807-8*) Free Pr.

Pitts, Robert E., jt. ed. see Woodside, Arch G.

Pitts, Sadie T. Sparkle. 1989. pap. 5.95 (*0-913543-12-8*) African Am Imag.

— The Tri Bros. (J). 1994. 7.95 (*0-533-10929-9*) Vantage.

Pitts, Senetta, ed. see Koger, Dorothy P.

Pitts, Terence. Contemporary Photography in Mexico. (Illus.). 16p. 1978. pap. 3.50 (*0-938262-00-9*) Ctr Creat Photog.

— Four Spanish Photographers. (Illus.). 24p. (Orig.). 1988. pap. 8.00 (*0-938262-18-1*) Ctr Creat Photog.

Pitts, Terence, contrib. Arizona Photographers: The Snell & Wilmer Collection. (Illus.). 80p. (Orig.). 1990. pap. 15.00 (*0-938262-19-X*) Ctr Creat Photog.

An Asterisk (*) at the beginning of an entry indicates that the title is appearing in BIP for the first time.

Pitts, Terence, intro. A Portrait Is Not a Likeness. (Illus.). 48p. 1991. pap. 14.00 (*0-938262-22-X*) Ctr Creat Photog.

Pitts, Terence, et al. Edward Weston: Color Photography. (Illus.). 64p. 1986. 15.00 (*0-938262-14-9*); pap. 8.95 (*0-938262-15-7*) Ctr Creat Photog.

Pitts, Teresa A. The Music of a Poet's Heart. (Illus.). 147p. (Orig.). (YA). (gr. 7 up). 1987. pap. 10.00 (*0-9618600-0-6*) T A Pitts.

— Where Freedom Begins. 27p. (Orig.). (J). (gr. 5 up). 1990. pap. 10.00 (*0-9618600-1-4*) T A Pitts.

Pitts, Teresa A., ed. see Lothario.

Pitts, Vincent J. The Man Who Sacked Rome: Charles de Bourbon, Constable of France, 1490-1527. LC 93-18629. (American University Studies: Vol. 142). 614p. 1993. 89.95 (*0-8204-2456-0*) P Lang Pubs.

Pitts, Walter F. Old Ship of Zion: The Afro-Baptist Ritual in the African Diaspora. LC 92-15256. (Religion in America Ser.). 216p. 1993. 32.00 (*0-19-507509-9*) OUP.

Pitts, William W. Commanding WordStar Professional Release 4.0. (Illus.). 310p. 1988. pap. 16.95 (*0-8306-2983-1*, 2983P) TAB Bks.

— Commanding WordStar Release 7.0. 2nd ed. (Illus.). 368p. 1992. pap. 29.95 (*0-8306-3970-5*, 4154, Windcrest) TAB Bks.

— Commanding WordStar, Release 7.0. 2nd ed. 1993. pap. 29.95 (*0-07-050206-4*) McGraw.

Pittsburgh Corning Europe Staff. Foamglas Industrial Insulation Handbook. 512p. 1992. 395.00 (*2-930049-00-6*, Pub. by Edits Technip FR) St Mut.

Pittuck, P., jt. auth. see Hillier, H.

Pittwood, tr. see Martignoni & Schonenberger.

***Pitty, Abelino & Munoz, Rony.** Guia Practica para el Manejo de Malezas. 222p. (C). 1993. pap. text ed. 5.00 (*1-885995-09-1*) Escuela Agricola.

Pitty, Abelino, jt. auth. see Munoz, Roni.

Pitty, Alistair, ed. Geomorphology: Themes & Trends. LC 84-24436. (Illus.). 286p. 1985. 53.00 (*0-389-20537-0*, BNB-08099) B&N Imports.

Pityana, Barney, et al, eds. Bounds of Possibility: The Legacy of Steve Biko & Black Consciousness. 288p. (C). 1991. text ed. 49.95 (*1-85649-047-5*, Pub. by Zed Books UK); pap. 17.50 (*1-85649-048-3*, Pub. by Zed Books UK) Humanities.

Pityn, P. J., jt. auth. see Fraser, T. M.

***Pitz, Henry C.** Drawing Outdoors. LC 95-7137. 1995. write for info. (*0-486-28679-7*) Dover.

Pitz, Henry C., ed. see Remington, Frederic.

Pitz, Mary E. Careers in Government. 1994. pap. 12.95 (*0-8442-4195-4*) NTC Pub Grp.

Pitzele, P. Our Father's Wells. 1995. 22.00 (*0-06-250617-X*, HarpT) HarpC.

— Our Father's Wells. 1995. pap. 12.00 (*0-06-251240-4*, HarpT) HarpC.

Pitzele, Sefra. We Are Not Alone: Learning to Live with Chronic Illness. LC 84-16378. (Illus.). 320p. 1985. pap. 14.95 (*0-918351-01-4*) Thompson Co Inc.

Pitzele, Sefra K. Kind Words for Caring People: Affirmations for Caregivers. 365p. (Orig.). 1992. pap. 7.95 (*1-55874-210-7*) Health Comm.

— One More Day: Daily Meditations for People with Chronic Illness. LC 87-45718. 396p. 1988. pap. 12.00 (*0-06-255473-5*, PL-4258, Hazelden SF) Harper SF.

— One More Day: Daily Meditations for the Chronically Ill. (Meditation Ser.). 400p. (Orig.). 1989. pap. 9.00 (*0-89486-519-6*, 5145A) Hazelden.

— One More Day: Daily Meditations for the Chronically Ill. large type ed. (Large Print Inspirational Ser.). (Orig.). 1989. pap. 12.95 (*0-8027-2638-0*) Walker & Co.

— Surviving Divorce: Daily Affirmations. 1991. 6.95 (*1-55874-118-6*) Health Comm.

— We Are Not Alone: Learning to Live with Chronic Illness. LC 86-40200. 336p. 1986. pap. 9.95 (*0-89480-139-2*, 1139) Workman Pub.

— When You Love Again. 368p. (Orig.). 1992. pap. 7.95 (*1-55874-211-5*) Health Comm.

Pitzer, G. C. Suggestion in the Cure of Diseases & the Correction of Vices. 1991. lib. bdg. 79.95 (*0-8490-4493-6*) Gordon Pr.

Pitzer, George C. Suggestion in the Cure of Diseases & the Correction of Vices. 80p. 1963. reprint ed. spiral bd. 5.50 (*0-7873-1093-X*) Mokelumne.

***Pitzer, Gloria.** The Best of the Better Cookery Cookbook. (Illus.). 120p. 1995. reprint ed. pap. write for info. (*1-886138-05-2*) G Pitzers.

— The Best of the First Twenty Years: A Secret Recipes Newsletter Cookbook. (Illus.). 60p. 1994. pap. 10.00 (*1-886138-01-X*) G Pitzers.

— Copycat Cookbook (of Secret Recipes) (Illus.). 120p. 1995. pap. write for info. (*1-886138-04-4*) G Pitzers.

— The Less Fat Cookbook of Secret Recipes: Updated & Easier. (Illus.). 60p. 1994. 10.00 (*1-886138-00-1*) G Pitzers.

— Make Alike Recipes. (Illus.). 120p. (Orig.). 1994. pap. text ed. 7.50 (*1-886138-02-8*) G Pitzers.

— Secret Fast Food Recipes: The Fast Food Cookbook. rev. ed. (Illus.). 120p. 1995. reprint ed. pap. 7.70 (*1-886161-38-0*) G Pitzers.

Pitzer, Kenneth & Brewer, D. F. Thermodynamics. 2nd ed. (Advanced Chemistry Ser.). 1961. text ed. write for info. (*0-07-037622-0*) McGraw.

Pitzer, Kenneth S. Activity Coefficients in Electrolyte Solutions. 2nd ed. (Illus.). 536p. 1991. 236.00 (*0-8493-5415-3*, QD565) CRC Pr.

— Molecular Structure & Statistical Thermodynamics: Twentieth Century Chemistry Ser. 536p. 1993. text ed. 83.00 (*981-02-1439-1*) World Scientific Pub.

— Thermodynamics. 3rd ed. LC 94-26960. 1994. text ed. write for info. (*0-07-050221-8*) McGraw.

Pitzer, Paul C. Grand Coulee: Harnessing a Dream. (Illus.). 512p. 1994. pap. 24.95 (*0-87422-110-2*) Wash St U Pr.

— Grand Coulee: Harnessing a Dream. (Illus.). 512p. 1994. 42.00 (*0-87422-113-7*) Wash St U Pr.

***Pitzer, Sara.** Dixie: A Traveler's Guide. (Illus.). 384p. (Orig.). 1995. pap. 14.95 (*1-56440-648-2*) Globe Pequot.

— North Carolina: Off the Beaten Path. 2nd ed. LC 92-42523. (Voyager Book Ser.). (Illus.). 144p. (Orig.). 1993. pap. 9.95 (*1-56440-159-6*) Globe Pequot.

— Pennsylvania: Off the Beaten Path: A Guide to Unique Places. 3rd ed. LC 94-8788. (Off the Beaten Path Ser.). (Illus.). 160p. 1994. pap. 9.95 (*1-56440-474-9*) Globe Pequot.

— Recommended Country Inns: The South-AL, AR, FL, GA, KY, LA, MS, NC, SC, TN. 5th ed. LC 92-29446. (Recommended Country Inns Ser.). (Illus.). 352p. 1994. pap. 14.95 (*1-56440-512-5*) Globe Pequot.

— The Southern Hospitality Cookbook: Menus & Recipes for Entertaining Simply & Graciously. 1993. pap. 11.95 (*0-87483-348-5*) August Hse.

— Traveling in South Carolina: A Selective Guide to Where to Go, What to See, What to Do. LC 93-6535. (Illus.). 165p. (Orig.). 1993. pap. 10.95 (*0-87249-868-9*) U of SC Pr.

Pitzer, Sara, jt. auth. see Cline, Don.

***Pitzl, Gerald R., ed.** Annual Editions: Geography, 95-96. 10th rev. ed. (Illus.). 256p. (C). 1995. pap. text ed. 12.95x (*1-56134-356-0*) Dushkin Pub.

Piumini, Roberto. Knot in the Tracks. LC 93-203043. (J). (ps-3). 1994. 14.00 (*0-688-11166-1*, Tambourine Bks); lib. bdg. 13.93 (*0-688-11167-X*, Tambourine Bks) Morrow.

— The Saint & the Circus. Holmes, Olivia, tr. LC 90-23481. (Illus.). 32p. (J). (ps-3). 1991. 14.95 (*0-688-10377-4*, Tambourine Bks); lib. bdg. 14.88 (*0-688-10378-2*, Tambourine Bks) Morrow.

— Store. (J). (ps). 1992. 4.50 (*1-56397-203-4*) Boyds Mills Pr.

Pius, Basil K. Agatha Christie, the Unknown Assyrian, & Baklava. (Illus.). 116p. (Orig.). 1993. pap. 8.00 (*0-9638003-4-5*) Tri-C Printing.

Piva, Michael J. The Borrowing Process: Public Finance in the Province of Canada, 1840-1867. 233p. 1992. pap. 25.00 (*0-7766-0343-4*, Pub. by Univ Ottawa Pr CN) Paul & Co Pubs.

Piva, R., jt. ed. see Morino, L.

Pival, Jean G., jt. auth. see Adelstein, Michael E.

Pivar, Bradley, jt. auth. see Pivar, William.

Pivar, Bradley, jt. auth. see Plvar, William.

Pivar, Bradley A. & Pivar, William H. Power Real Estate Advertising: The Complete Guide for Professionals. LC 91-24520. 188p. 1991. pap. 24.95 (*0-7931-0158-1*, 1907-0501) Dearborn Trade.

Pivar, Bradley A., jt. auth. see Pivar, William H.

Pivar, Corinne E., jt. auth. see Pivar, William H.

Pivar, David J. Purity Crusade: Sexual Morality & Social Control, 1868-1900. LC 70-179650. (Contributions in American History Ser.: No. 23). 308p. 1973. text ed. 38.50 (*0-8371-6319-6*, PPC/, Greenwood Pr) Greenwood.

Pivar, Stuart. Barye Bronzes, A Catalogue Raisonne. 2nd ed. (Illus.). 300p. 1990. reprint ed. 89.50 (*1-85149-142-2*) Antique Collect.

Pivar, William & Pivar, Bradley. Classified Secrets: Writing Real Estate Ads That Work. 2nd ed. 375p. 1989. pap. 29.95 (*0-88462-112-X*, 1926-01) Dearborn Finan.

Pivar, William H. California Real Estate License Preparation Text. 6th rev. ed. (Illus.). 320p. (C). 1984. student ed 17.95 (*0-685-08873-1*) P-H.

— California Real Estate License Preparation Text. 9th ed. LC 93-3893. 1993. pap. text ed. 41.00 (*0-13-220013-9*) P-H.

— Power Real Estate Listing. 2nd ed. LC 88-9129. 232p. 1988. 18.95 (*0-88462-151-0*, 1907-01, Real Estate Ed) Dearborn Finan.

— Power Real Estate Selling. 2nd ed. LC 88-9130. 288p. 1989. 18.95 (*0-88462-152-9*, 1907-02, Real Estate Ed) Dearborn Finan.

— Real Estate Ethics. 2nd ed. 160p. 1989. pap. text ed. 15.95 (*0-88462-431-5*, 1966-01, Real Estate Ed) Dearborn Finan.

— Real Estate Exam Guide: Designed for ASI Sales & Broker Exams. 4th ed. LC 94-24988. 1995. pap. 21.95 (*0-7931-1107-2*, Real Estate Ed) Dearborn Finan.

— Real Estate Exam Guide (A. S. I.) 3rd ed. 240p. 1991. pap. 21.95 (*0-7931-0378-9*, 197006) Dearborn Finan.

— Real Estate Investing from A to Z: The Most Comprehensive Practical & Readable Guide. 1993. pap. 22.95 (*1-55738-535-1*) Probus Pub Co.

Pivar, William H. & Bruss, Robert J. California Real Estate Law. 3rd ed. 528p. 1994. text ed. 39.95 (*0-7931-0731-8*, 1523-02, Real Estate Ed) Dearborn Finan.

***Pivar, William H. & Pivar, Bradley A.** The Big Book of Real Estate Ads: 1001 Ads That Sell. 320p. 1995. pap. 29.95 (*0-7931-1430-6*, 1926-1101, Real Estate Ed) Dearborn Finan.

Pivar, William H. & Pivar, Corinne E. Power Real Estate Letters. 2nd ed. 346p. 1994. pap. 29.95 (*0-7931-1115-3*, 192603-02, Real Estate Ed) Dearborn Finan.

Pivar, William H. & Post, Richard W. Power Real Estate Negotiation. 264p. 1989. 19.95 (*0-88462-898-1*, 1907-04) Dearborn Finan.

Pivar, William H., jt. auth. see Malouf, Doug.

Pivar, William H., jt. auth. see Pivar, Bradley A.

Pivarnik, James M., jt. auth. see Morrow, James R., Jr.

***Pivato, Joseph.** Echo: Essays on Other Literatures. 272p. 1994. pap. 15.00 (*1-55071-004-4*) Guernica Editions.

Pivato, Joseph, ed. Contrasts: Comparative Essays on Italian-Canadian Writing. 1991. pap. 15.00 (*0-920717-35-7*) SPD-Small Pr Dist.

Pivec, Mary, ed. Law Office Economics Handbook. 165p. 1992. pap. write for info. (*1-878677-31-4*) Amer Immi Law Assn.

Piven, Frances F. & Cloward, Richard A. The New Class War: Reagan's Attack on the Welfare State & Its Consequences. 160p. 1982. pap. 8.76 (*0-394-70647-1*) Pantheon.

— Poor People's Movements: Why They Succeed, How They Fail. LC 78-54652. 1978. pap. 7.96 (*0-394-72697-9*, Vin) Random.

— Why Americans Don't Vote. LC 87-43012. 288p. 1988. 15.00 (*0-685-73933-3*) Pantheon.

— Why Americans Don't Vote. 1989. pap. 9.95 (*0-685-37789-X*) Pantheon.

— Why Americans Don't Vote. 1989. pap. 11.96 (*0-679-72318-8*, Publishers Media) Random.

Piven, Frances F. & Cloward, Richard A., eds. Regulating the Poor: The Functions of Public Welfare. LC 93-17460. 1993. 12.00 (*0-679-74516-5*, Vin) Random.

Piver. Manual Gyn-Onc ISE. 1989. 15.95 (*0-316-70937-9*) Little.

— Manual of Gynecologic Oncology & Gynecology. 1989. 31.95 (*0-316-70936-0*) Little.

***Pivert, Francois.** Schism or Not? The Episcopal Consecrations of Archbishop Marcel Lefebore. 50p. 1995. pap. text ed. 3.95 (*0-935952-54-3*) Angelus Pr.

Pivetta, jt. auth. see PPI Staff.

Pivetta, Sue. Emergency Medical Communications: Basics for Emergency Medical Calls. 150p. Date not set. pap. text ed. 10.95 (*1-882960-06-8*) Prof Pride.

— Emergency Radio Dispatching: 911 Dispatchers Guide Procedures, Safety, Technology. 150p. Date not set. pap. text ed. 10.95 (*1-882960-07-6*) Prof Pride.

— Fire Communications: Fire Responses, ICS, Hazmat. 150p. (C). Date not set. pap. text ed. 10.95 (*1-882960-05-X*) Prof Pride.

— Nine-One-One Emergency Call Receiver Guide: Call Taking, E911, CAD, Maps, Officer Safety & Liability. 150p. (C). 1993. pap. text ed. 10.95 (*1-882960-01-7*) Prof Pride.

— Nine-One-One Emergency Communications Manual. 1991. pap. 39.95 (*0-910303-21-5*) Writers Pub Serv.

— Nine-One-One Emergency Communications Manual: Police Fire Medical Communications Call Receiving, Dispatch, Crisis, Career Development. 515p. 1993. pap. text ed. 39.95 (*1-882960-00-9*) Prof Pride.

— Police Communications: Call Taking & Dispatching. 150p. (C). Date not set. pap. text ed. 10.95 (*1-882960-02-5*) Prof Pride.

Pivetti, Massimo. An Essay on Money & Distribution. LC 90-45103. 150p. 1991. text ed. 59.95 (*0-312-05359-2*) St Martin.

Pivevic, Edo. The Concept of Reality. (Modern Revivals in Philosophy Ser.). 312p. 1993. 54.95 (*0-7512-0273-8*, Pub. by Gregg Revivals UK) Ashgate Pub Co.

Pivirotto, Evelyn. The Killer Within. abr. ed. 350p. 1995. pap. 9.95 (*1-56901-501-5*) NW Pub.

Pivovarnick, jt. auth. see Walnum.

***Pivovarnick, John.** The Complete Idiot's Guide to America Online. (Illus.). 350p. (Orig.). 1995. pap. text ed. 19.99 (*1-56761-597-X*) Alpha Bks IN.

— The Complete Idiot's Guide to CD-ROM. 2nd ed. (Illus.). 375p. (Orig.). 1995. pap. 19.99 (*1-56761-606-2*) Alpha Bks IN.

— The Complete Idiot's Guide to the Mac. 2nd ed. 400p. 1994. 16.95 (*1-56761-534-1*) Alpha Bks IN.

— This Mac Is Mine. LC 92-10937. 1992. write for info. (*0-201-63206-3*) Addison-Wesley.

— This Mac Is Mine: Twelve Terrific Tools to Customize Your Macintosh. 1992. pap. 19.95 (*0-201-63267-5*) Addison-Wesley.

Pivovarov, A. A. Thermal Conditions in Freezing Lakes & Rivers. 144p. 1974. text ed. 47.00 (*0-7065-1350-9*, Pub. by Keter Pub IS) Coronet Bks.

Piwczyk, B. P. Excimer Laser Materials Processing & Beam Delivery Systems, Vol. 1377. 1991. 42.00 (*0-8194-0444-6*) SPIE.

Piwczyk, B. P., jt. ed. see Pirri, A. N.

Piwonka, J. Forging Ahead in Life: How to Chart Your Life, Your Physical, Intellectual & Mental Self. 1991. lib. bdg. 69.95 (*0-8490-4178-3*) Gordon Pr.

Piwonka, James M. The Secret of Facial Rejuvenation. 15p. 1994. reprint ed. spiral bd. 2.75 (*0-7873-1052-2*) Mokelumne.

— You Can Help Yourself to Beauty. 31p. 1994. reprint ed. spiral bd. 3.85 (*0-7873-1166-9*) Mokelumne.

Piwonka, T. S., ed. see Int. Conference on Modeling of Casting & Welding Processes Staff.

Piwonka, T. S., et al, eds. Modeling of Casting, Welding, & Advanced Solidification Processing VI. (Illus.). 763p. 1993. 182.00 (*0-87339-209-4*, 467) Minerals Metals.

Piwonski, Shirley, jt. auth. see Marer, Sharon.

Pix, Mary. Inhumane Cardinal. LC 84-5358. 1984. reprint ed. 50.00 (*0-8201-1396-4*) Schol Facsimiles.

***Pixar Animators Staff.** Toy Story: A Postcard Book. (Illus.). 64p. 1995. pap. 8.95 (*0-7868-8138-0*) Hyperion.

— Toy Story: An Animated Flip Book. (Illus.). 96p. 1995. pap. 3.95 (*0-7868-8139-9*) Hyperion.

Pixen, Francis F., ed. Labor Parties in Postindustrial Societies. (Europe & the International Order Ser.). 300p. (C). 1992. text ed. 45.00 (*0-19-520926-5*); pap. 17.95 (*0-19-520927-3*) OUP.

Pixler, Paul. Hiking Trails of Southwestern Colorado: The Revised & Updated Guide to Mountain Trails in the San Juan & Uncompahgre National Forests, Including All-New Material on the Colorado Trail. 2nd ed. LC 92-5699. (Illus.). 249p. 1992. pap. 16.95 (*0-87108-816-9*) Pruett.

Pixley, jt. auth. see Boff.

Pixley, Aristene. Vermont Country Cooking. 1979. reprint ed. pap. 2.95 (*0-486-23803-2*) Dover.

Pixley, Francis W. Auditors: Their Duties & Responsibilities Under the Joint-Stock Companies Acts & the Friendly Societies & Industrial & Provident Societies Acts. LC 75-18480. (History of Accounting Ser.). (Illus.). 1978. reprint ed. 20.95 (*0-405-07562-6*) Ayer.

— The Profession of a Chartered Accountant & Other Lectures: Delivered to the Institute of Chartered Accountants in England & Wales. Brief, Richard P., ed. LC 77-87285. (Development of Contemporary Accounting Thought Ser.). 1978. reprint ed. lib. bdg. 26.95 (*0-405-10913-X*) Ayer.

Pixley, Frank, jt. auth. see Read, Opie.

Pixley, George V. On Exodus: A Liberation Perspective. Barr, Robert R., tr. LC 87-7835. 256p. (Orig.). 1987. pap. 16.95 (*0-88344-559-X*) Orbis Bks.

Pixley, Jocelyn. Citizenship & Employment: Investigating Post-Industrial Options. LC 92-19634. (Illus.). 346p. (C). 1993. 59.95 (*0-521-41793-7*) Cambridge U Pr.

Pixley, Jorge. Biblical Israel: A People's History. LC 92-38146. 176p. (Orig.). 1992. pap. 10.00 (*0-8006-2551-X*, 1-2551, Fortress Pr) Augsburg Fortress.

***Pixton, Paul B.** The German Episcopacy & the Implementation of the Decrees of the Fourth Lateran Council, 1216-1245: Watchmen on the Tower. LC 94-44944. (Studies in the History of Christian Thought: Vol. 64). 1994. 135.00 (*90-04-10262-0*) E J Brill.

Pizam, A. & Gu, Z. Journal of Travel Research Index & Abstracts, Vols. 6-24. 182p. 1988. pap. text ed. 48.00 (*0-318-42765-6*) U CO Busn Res Div.

Pizam, Abraham, jt. auth. see Jones, Peter.

Pizam, Abraham, jt. ed. see Jones, Peter.

Pizar, Kathleen, ed. see Dickens, Charles.

Pizarro, Antonio. Pre-Calculus. (Illus.). 200p. (Orig.). (C). 1994. pap. text ed. 25.00 (*1-878045-32-6*) Whittier Pubns.

***Pizarro, Hayden.** The Genus Characiociopsis Borzi (Mischococcales, Tribophyceae) Taxonomy, Biogeography & Ecology. (Bibliotheca Phycologica Ser.: Vol. 98). (Illus.). 112p. 1995. pap. 60.00 (*3-443-60025-5*, Pub. by Cramer-Borntraeger GW) Lubrecht & Cramer.

Pizarro, Joaquin M. A Rhetoric of the Scene: Dramatic Narrative in the Early Middle Ages. 280p. 1989. text ed. 40.00 (*0-8020-5754-3*) U of Toronto Pr.

— Writing Ravenna: The Liber Pontificalis of Andreas Agnellus. LC 95-8303. (Recentiores Ser.). 1995. write for info. (*0-472-10606-6*) U of Mich Pr.

Pizarro, Jose L. I Like the Way I Am Right Now: A 5th Grade Student Writes About His Feelings for His Class, His Teacher, His Family & His Future. (Illus.). 1974. pap. 0.50 (*0-918374-08-1*) City Coll Wk.

Pizarro, P. Relation of the Discovery & Conquest of the Kingdoms of Peru, 2 Vols. in 1. Means, Philip A., tr. (Cortez Society Ser.). 1974. reprint ed. 50.00 (*0-527-19724-6*) Periodicals Srv.

Pizer, Abigail. It's a Perfect Day. LC 89-37937. (Trophy Picture Bk.). (Illus.). 32p. (J). (ps-3). 1992. pap. 4.95 (*0-06-443302-1*, Trophy) HarpC Child Bks.

***Pizer, Abigail & Day, David.** Tippu. LC 94-28923. (J). 1995. write for info. (*0-8120-6498-4*); pap. write for info. (*0-8120-9183-3*) Barron.

Pizer, Donald. Critical Essays on Stephen Crane's "The Red Badge of Courage" Nagel, James, ed. (Critical Essays on American Literature Ser.). 264p. (C). 1990. text ed. 45.00 (*0-8161-8898-X*) G K Hall.

— Dos Passos' U. S. A. A Critical Study. LC 87-27905. 222p. reprint ed. pap. 63.30 (*0-8357-2570-7*, 2040262) Bks Demand.

— The Novels of Frank Norris. LC 72-6785. (Studies in Fiction: No. 34). 1972. reprint ed. lib. bdg. 75.00 (*0-8383-1666-2*) M S G Haskell Hse.

— The Novels of Theodore Dreiser: A Critical Study. LC 75-20769. 394p. reprint ed. pap. 112.30 (*0-8357-6536-9*, 2035898) Bks Demand.

— Realism & Naturalism in Nineteenth-Century American Literature. rev. ed. LC 83-20406. 176p. 1984. 19.95 (*0-8093-1125-9*) S Ill U Pr.

— Theodore Dreiser: A Primary Bibliography & Reference Guide. (Reference Guides to Literature Ser.). 450p. 1991. text ed. 75.00 (*0-8161-8976-5*, Hall Reference) Macmillan.

— The Theory & Practice of American Literary Naturalism: Selected Essays & Reviews. LC 92-23398. 272p. (C). 1993. 32.50 (*0-8093-1847-4*) S Ill U Pr.

— Twentieth-Century American Literary Naturalism: An Interpretation. LC 81-5606. (Crosscurrents-Modern Critiques, New Ser.). 187p. 1982. 19.95 (*0-8093-1027-9*) S Ill U Pr.

***Pizer, Donald, ed.** The Cambridge Companion to American Realism & Naturalism: From Howells to London. (Cambridge Companions to Literature Ser.). 320p. (C). 1995. 59.95 (*0-521-43300-2*); pap. 17.95 (*0-521-43876-4*) Cambridge U Pr.

— John Dos Passos: The Major Nonfictional Prose. LC 88-18090. 308p. 1988. pap. 18.95 (*0-8143-2058-9*) Wayne St U Pr.

— New Essays on "Sister Carrie" (American Novel Ser.). 133p. (C). 1991. 27.95 (*0-521-38278-5*); pap. 11.95 (*0-521-38714-0*) Cambridge U Pr.

Pizer, Donald, ed. see Crane, Stephen.

Pizer, Donald, ed. see Dreiser, Theodore.

Pizer, Donald, ed. see Garland, Hamlin.

Pizer, Donald, jt. ed. see Harbert, Earl.

Pizer, Donald, ed. see London, Jack.

Pizer, Donald, ed. see Norris, Frank.

Pizer, H. F., jt. auth. see Foley, Conn.

Pizer, H. F., jt. auth. see Massachusetts General Hospital Organ Transplant Team.

Pizer, Harry & Sloan, Stephen. Corporate Aviation Security: The Next Frontier in Aerospace Operations. LC 92-54135. (Illus.). 176p. 1992. 45.00 (*0-8061-2470-9*) U of Okla Pr.

***Pizer, John.** Toward a Theory of Radical Origin: Essays on Modern German Thought. LC 94-45932. (Modern German Culture & Literature Ser.). 224p. 1995. text ed. 35.00 (0-8032-3711-1) U of Nebr Pr.

Pizer, Laurence R. Plymouth in the Nineteenth Century. (Pilgrim Society Notes Ser.: No. 31). 1983. 2.00 (0-940628-48-1) Pilgrim Soc.

— A Primer for Local Historical Societies. 2nd rev. ed. (Illus.). 144p. 1991. pap. 16.95 (0-942063-12-0) AASLH.

Pizer, R., jt. auth. see Moore, J.

Pizer, Russell A. Evaluation Programs for School Bands & Orchestras. 248p. 1990. pap. 27.95 (0-13-292301-7) P-H.

— Instrumental Music Evaluation Kit: Forms & Procedures for Assessing Student Performance. 208p. 1987. pap. text ed. 27.95 (0-13-468117-7) P-H.

***Pizer, Stuart A.** Negotiation of Paradox in Psychoanalysis. (RPBS Ser.). 1997. write for info. (0-88163-170-1) Analytic Pr.

Pizinger, Neal. The Dead Survivor. (Orig.). 1979. pap. 2.50 (0-89083-470-9) Zebra.

Pizurki, H., jt. auth. see Turnbull, L. M.

Pizz Staff, jt. auth. see Zone, Ray.

Pizzarelli, Alan. Zenryu & Other Works, 1974. (Xtras Ser.: No. 2). (Illus.). 36p. (Orig.). 1975. pap. 2.00 (0-89120-001-0) From Here.

Pizzarello, Donald J., ed. Radiation Biology. 312p. 1982. 139.95 (0-8493-6011-0, QP82, CRC Reprint) Franklin.

Pizzarello, Donald J., jt. auth. see Cooper, Jay S.

***Pizzatto, Giuseppe.** Euro 5: Woerterbuch Italien-Franzoesich-Englisch-Deutsch-Spanisch. 511p. (FRE, GER & ITA.). 1990. 39.95 (0-7859-8539-5, 3889750419) Fr & Eur.

***Pizzey.** Swimming with Dolphins. 1995. mass mkt. 5.50 (0-06-100558-4, Harp PBks) HarpC.

Pizzey, E. Morningstar. 1994. mass mkt. 5.99 (0-06-100430-8, Harp PBks) HarpC.

Pizzey, Erin. Consul General's Daughter. 1991. mass mkt. 5.50 (0-06-100151-1, Harp PBks) HarpC.

— First Lady. 1991. mass mkt. 5.50 (0-06-100321-2, Harp PBks) HarpC.

— In the Shadow of the Castle. 1992. mass mkt. 5.50 (0-06-100211-9, Harp PBks) HarpC.

— Other Lovers. 1993. mass mkt. 5.50 (0-06-109032-8, Harp PBks) HarpC.

— The Snow Leopard of Shanghai. 1990. mass mkt. 4.95 (0-06-100037-X, Harp PBks) HarpC.

— The Watershed. 1992. mass mkt. 5.50 (0-06-100396-4, Harp PBks) HarpC.

Pizzey, Graham. A Field Guide to the Birds of Australia. LC 80-8588. (Illus.). 432p. 1988. 79.50 (0-691-08277-4); pap. text ed. 26.95 (0-691-08483-1) Princeton U Pr.

***Pizzi.** Productive Living Strategies. 1994. 17.95 (1-56024-027-X) Haworth Pr.

— Wood Adhesives: Chemistry & Technology, Vol. 2. 424p. 1989. 175.00 (0-8247-8052-3) Dekker.

— Wood Adhesives Vol. 1: Chemistry & Technology. 384p. 1983. 155.00 (0-8247-1579-9) Dekker.

Pizzi, A. & Mittal, K., eds. Handbook of Adhesive Technology. LC 94-4800. 704p. 1994. 195.00 (0-8247-8974-1) Dekker.

Pizzi, Antonio. Advanced Wood Adhesives Technology. LC 94-21042. 304p. 1994. 115.00 (0-8247-9266-1) Dekker.

Pizzi, Emilio. Mario Botta. (Illus.). 248p. (ENG & SPA.). 1992. pap. 18.95 (84-252-1448-3) Rizzoli Intl.

Pizzi, J. R., jt. ed. see Guinet, D.

Pizzi, Linda. Breath of Clarity. LC 90-82582. 55p. (Orig.). 1990. pap. write for info. (0-9627073-0-9) Clarion Word Servs.

Pizzi, Michael, jt. ed. see Johnson, Jerry.

Pizzigati, Sam. The Maximum Wage: A Common-Sense Prescription for Revitalizing America by Taxing the Very Rich. LC 91-33410. (Illus.). 144p. (Orig.). 1992. pap. 11.95 (0-945257-45-7) Apex Pr.

Pizzigati, Sam & Solowey, Fred J., eds. The New Labor Press: Journalism for a Changing Union Movement. LC 92-10352. (Illus.). 256p. (Orig.). 1992. 38.00 (0-87546-189-1); pap. 16.95 (0-87546-190-5) ILR Pr.

Pizzimenti, John J. Evolution of the Prairie Dog Genus Cynomys. (Occasional Papers: No. 39). 73p. 1975. pap. 1.00 (0-317-04900-3) U of KS Mus Nat Hist.

***Pizzini, S., ed.** Defects in Electronic Ceramics. (Materials Science Forum Ser.: Vol. 116). 260p. 1993. text ed. 80. 00 (0-87849-653-X) LPS Dist Ctr.

***Pizzitullo, Peter D.** Pediatric Orthopaedics in Primary Practice. (Illus.). 624p. 1995. text ed. 65.00 (0-07-050252-8) Hlth Prof Div.

Pizzo. Principles & Practice of Pediatric Oncology. 2nd ed. (Illus.). 1993. text ed. 165.00 (0-397-51207-4) Lippincott.

Pizzo, Albert. Doc Pizzo's Nutrition Handbook. 102p. 1980. pap. 4.95 (0-939126-14-1) Back Bay.

Pizzo, Joan. Pelican Bill. (Tales of the Back Bay Ser.). (Illus.). (J). (gr. k-6). 1990. lib. bdg. 11.95 (0-939126-10-9) Back Bay.

Pizzo, Joan E. Amy Avocet. LC 83-70739. (Tales of the Back Bay Ser.). (Illus.). (J). (gr. k-6). 1983. 8.95 (0-939126-06-0) Back Bay.

— Little Crumb: Tales of the Back Bay. (Illus.). 35p. (Orig.). (J). (gr. k-6). 1980. teacher ed 8.95 (0-939126-03-6); lib. bdg. 10.95 (0-939126-00-1); pap. 7.95 (0-939126-01-X) Back Bay.

— Little Crumb Fun Book. (Illus.). 32p. (Orig.). (J). (gr. k-6). 1983. pap. 3.95 (0-939126-04-4) Back Bay.

— Nutrition Handbook Teacher's Manual. 28p. 1983. pap. 5.95 (0-939126-15-X) Back Bay.

Pizzo, P., et al. Lessons Learned: Provision of Technical Assistance to States. Beatty, Noelle, ed. 90p. (Orig.). 1993. pap. 9.00 (0-943657-29-6) Zero To Three.

Pizzo, Philip A. & Wilfert, Catherine M. Pediatric AIDS: The Challenge of HIV Infection in Infants, Children & Adolescents. 2nd ed. (Illus.). 896p. 1994. 99.00 (0-683-06895-4) Williams & Wilkins.

Pizzo, Stephen & Muolo, Paul. Profiting from the Bank & Savings & Loan Crisis: How Anyone Can Find Bargains at America's Greatest Garage Sale. 320p. 1994. pap. 13. 00 (0-88730-665-9) Harper Busn.

Pizzo, Stephen, et al. Inside Job: The Looting of America's Savings & Loans. 443p. 1990. text ed. 19.95 (0-07-050230-7) McGraw.

Pizzo, Stephen P., jt. auth. see Cotchett, Joseph W.

Pizzoferrato, A., et al, eds. Biomaterials & Clinical Applications: Proceedings of the Sixth European Conference on Biomaterials, Bologna, Italy, Sept. 14-17, 1986. (Advances in Biomaterials Ser.: Vol. 7). 808p. 1987. 187.25 (0-444-42883-6) Elsevier.

Pizzorno, Alessandro, jt. ed. see Crouch, Colin.

Pizzorno, Joseph, jt. auth. see Murray, Michael.

Pizzorno, Joseph E., et al. A Textbook of Natural Medicine, 2 vols., Set, Vols. 1-2. rev. ed. (Illus.). 1230p. (C). 1993. Set. ring bd. 295.00 (0-9618764-0-9, K03V2) John Bastyr.

— A Textbook of Natural Medicine, 2 vols., Vol. 1. rev. ed. (Illus.). 750p. (C). 1993. write for info. (0-9618764-1-7) John Bastyr.

— A Textbook of Natural Medicine, 2 vols., Vol. 2. rev. ed. (Illus.). 400p. (C). 1993. write for info. (0-9618764-2-5) John Bastyr.

Pizzorusso, Alessandro, ed. Italian Studies in Law, Vol. II: A Review of Legal Problems. 264p. (C). 1994. lib. bdg. 94. 00 (0-7923-2483-8) Kluwer Ac.

— Italian Studies in Law, 1991, Vol. I: A Review of Legal Problems. 184p. (C). 1992. lib. bdg. 98.00 (0-7923-1564-2) Kluwer Ac.

Pizzuti, John A., jt. auth. see Pizzuti, Mary R.

Pizzuti, Mary R. & Pizzuti, John A. Getting More Hair: How You Can Go from Bald or Thinning to a Full Head of Hair. Lohman, Karen, ed. LC 85-30276. (Illus.). 170p. 1986. 23.95 (0-934941-00-9); pap. 17.95 (0-934941-01-7) Step Ahead Pr.

Pizzuto, Joseph. Fabric Science Instructor's Guide. 64p. 1990. teacher ed 3.50 (0-685-55785-5) Fairchild.

Pjerrou, Joe. Go Ask the Owl. Jacobsen, Steven, ed. & illus. by. 40p. 1990. pap. 6.50 (0-685-47506-9) Guerilla Poetics.

***PKM Publications Staff.** Visitor's Guide to Florida's Suncoast. 1993. pap. 17.95 (0-9633219-0-0) PKM Pubns.

***PKR Foundation Scientific Advisors Staff.** Q & A on PKD Vol. 3. rev. ed. Grantham, Jared J. et al, eds. 96p. (C). 1995. pap. 12.00 (0-9614567-2-8) PKR Foundation.

Pla Dalmau, Jose M. Enciclopedia Autodidactica. 1556p. (SPA.). 1965. 59.95 (0-8288-6746-1, S-11964) Fr & Eur.

— Enciclopedia Autodidactica. 4th ed. 1060p. (SPA.). 1987. 69.95 (0-7859-5049-4) Fr & Eur.

Plaa, G. L., et al, eds. Interactions Between Drugs & Chemicals in Industrial Societies, No. 2. (Esteve Foundation Ser.). 292p. 1987. 98.00 (0-444-80873-6) Elsevier.

Plaass, Peter. Kant's Theory of Natural Science: Translation Analytic Introduction & Commentary by Alfred E. & Maria G. Miller. Miller, Alfred E. & Miller, Maria G., trs. LC 94-5203. (Boston Studies in the Philosophy of Science: Vol. 159). 384p. (C). 1994. lib. bdg. 105.00 (0-7923-2750-0) Kluwer Ac.

Plaat, Otto. Ordinary Differential Equations. LC 70-156869. 350p. 1971. 33.95 (0-8162-6844-4) Holden-Day.

Plaatje, Sol. Mafeking Diary. Comaroff, John, ed. LC 89-22784. (Illus.). 192p. 1990. text ed. 24.95 (0-8214-0944-1); pap. 12.95 (0-8214-0945-X) Ohio U Pr.

Plaatje, Sol T. Native Life in South Africa: Before & since the European War & the Boer Rebellion. LC 90-24402. 437p. (Orig.). (C). 1982. pap. text ed. 17.95x (0-8214-0986-7, Pub. by Ravan Pr ZA) Ohio U Pr.

Plaatje, Solomon T. Native Life in South Africa, Before & since the European War & the Boer Rebellion. 2nd ed. LC 76-78585. (Illus.). 352p. 1970. text ed. 35.00 (0-8371-1420-9, PLN&, Negro U Pr) Greenwood.

Placcius, Vicentius. Theatrum Anonymorum et Pseudonymorum Ex Symbolis et Collatione Virorum Per Europam Doctissimorum Ac Celeberrimorum Post Syntagma Dudum Editum, 2 vols., Set. reprint ed. write for info. (0-318-71941-X, Pub. by Georg Olms GW) Lubrecht & Cramer.

Place, Allen R., jt. ed. see Robb, Frank T.

Place, C. H., jt. auth. see Arrowsmith, D. K.

Place, C. M., jt. auth. see Arrowsmith, D. K.

Place, Charles A. Charles Bulfinch: Architect & Citizen. LC 68-27717. (Architecture & Decorative Art Ser.). (Illus.). 1968. reprint ed. lib. bdg. 45.00 (0-306-71150-8) Da Capo.

Place, Chuck. Ancient Walls: Indian Ruins of the Southwest. LC 91-58636. (Illus.). 112p. (Orig.). 1992. 34.95 (1-55591-125-0); pap. 19.95 (1-55591-126-9) Fulcrum Pub.

Place, Edwin B., tr. see De Segura, Juan.

Place, Edwin B., ed. see Tourney, Gautier de.

Place, Francis. Illustrations & Proofs of the Principle of Population: Being the First Work on Population in the English Language Recommending Birth Control. LC 67-16338. (Reprints of Economic Classics Ser.). 1967. reprint ed. 45.00 (0-678-00210-X) Kelley.

Place, Francois. The Last Giants. 78p. 1993. 15.95 (0-87923-990-5) Godine.

Place, Georges, et al. Bibliographie des Auteurs Modernes de Langue Francaise, 1801-1972: Montfort, Montherlant, Vol. 20. 299p. (FRE.). 1973. 150.00 (0-7859-5387-6) Fr & Eur.

Place, Irene, et al. Executive Secretarial Procedures. 5th ed. LC 79-9097. (Illus.). 1980. text ed. 37.00 (0-07-050255-2) McGraw.

Place, Irene. Keydrills Six: New Office Vocabulary Drills for the Keyboard. 1989. spiral bd. 9.95 (0-88462-838-8, 4800-09) Dearborn Finan.

— Opportunities in Business Management. (Illus.). 160p. 1987. 13.95 (0-8442-6185-8, VGM Career Bks); pap. 10. 95 (0-8442-6186-6, VGM Career Bks) NTC Pub Grp.

— Opportunities in Business Management Careers. rev. ed. LC 90-50738. (Opportunities in...Ser.). 160p. (YA). (gr. 7 up). 1991. 13.95 (0-8442-8158-1, VGM Career Bks); pap. 10.95 (0-8442-8160-3, VGM Career Bks) NTC Pub Grp.

— Women in Management. (Illus.). 160p. 1983. pap. 10.95 (0-8442-6650-7, VGM Career Bks) NTC Pub Grp.

Place, Irene & Higgins, Mary. Keydrills Four: Centering, Tabulating & Formatting Drills for the Keyboard. 96p. 1988. 9.95 (0-88462-754-3, 4800-04) Dearborn Finan.

Place, Irene & Miller, James. Keydrills Five: Keyboarding Numbers & Special Characters. 1989. spiral bd. 9.95 (0-88462-837-X, 4800-08) Dearborn Finan.

Place, Irene & Moreland, Paul A. Keydrills One: Timed Writings. 96p. 1988. 9.95 (0-88462-751-9, 4800-01) Dearborn Finan.

Place, Irene, et al. Keydrills Three: Improving Spelling Skills at the Keyboard. 96p. 1988. 9.95 (0-88462-753-5, 4800-03) Dearborn Finan.

— Keydrills Two: Improving Language Skills at the Keyboard. 96p. 1988. 9.95 (0-88462-752-7, 4800-02) Dearborn Finan.

Place, Irene M., jt. auth. see Hyslop, David.

Place, J. Retail Store Design. 1988. text ed. write for info. (0-442-27558-7) Van Nos Reinhold.

Place, J. A. The Non-Western Films of John Ford. (Illus.). 1979. 17.95 (0-8065-0643-1, Citadel Pr); pap. 9.95 (0-8065-0779-9, Citadel Pr) Carol Pub Group.

— The Western Films of John Ford. (Illus.). 226p. 1974. text ed. 12.00 (0-8065-0445-5, Citadel Pr) Carol Pub Group.

— The Western Films of John Ford. 1977. pap. 9.95 (0-8065-0594-X, Citadel Pr) Carol Pub Group.

***Place, Jennifer.** Creating Logos & Letterheads. LC 95-1851. (Graphic Design Basics Ser.). 1995. write for info. (0-89134-571-X) North Light Bks.

Place, Lew, jt. auth. see Cooper, James Fenimore.

Place, Linna F., jt. ed. see Davis, Allen F.

Place, Robert M., jt. auth. see Guiley, Rosemary E.

***Place, Robin.** Bodies from the Past. (Digging up the Past Ser.). (Illus.). 48p. (J). (gr. 4-6). 1995. 15.95 (1-56847-397-4) Thomson Lrning.

— Excavating People: Archaeology in Britain. (Illus.). 32p. (C). 1992. write for info. (0-521-36224-5) Cambridge U Pr.

— The Romans: Fact & Fiction. (Illus.). 32p. (J). 1989. 13. 95 (0-521-33267-2); pap. 8.25 (0-521-33787-9) Cambridge U Pr.

— The Vikings: Adventures of Young Vikings in Jorvik. (Illus.). 52p. (J). (gr. 2-8). 1987. pap. 8.25 (0-521-31572-7) Cambridge U Pr.

Place, Stan C. The Art & Science of Professional Makeup. (Illus.). 324p. 28.00 (0-87350-361-9) Milady Pub.

Place, Susan E., et al, eds. Tropical Rainforests: Latin American Nature & Society in Transition. LC 93-4335. (Jaguar Books on Latin America: Vol. 2). (Illus.). 222p. (C). 1993. text ed. 40.00 (0-8420-2423-9); pap. text ed. 14.95 (0-8420-2427-1) Scholarly Res Inc.

Placek, J. A., jt. auth. see Mandich, D. R.

***Placencia.** The European Context for Assistive Technology-TIDE 95. LC 95-75770. 1995. 93.00 (0-614-06284-5) IOS Press.

Placencia, Oliver & Welge Staff. Business Owner's Guide to Accounting & Bookkeeping. Crawford, Scott D., ed. (Successful Business Library). 145p. 1991. pap. 19.95 (1-55571-156-1) Oasis Pr OR.

***Plach, Thomas A.** Residential Treatment & the Sexually Abused Child. LC 93-7334. 170p. 1993. pap. 24.95 (0-398-06324-9) C C Thomas.

— Residential Treatment & the Sexually Abused Child. LC 93-7334. 170p. (C). 1993. text ed. 38.95 (0-398-05864-4) C C Thomas.

Plach, Tom. The Creative Use of Music in Group Therapy. (Illus.). 90p. 1980. 27.95 (0-398-04156-3) C C Thomas.

— The Creative Use of Music in Group Therapy. (Illus.). 90p. 1980. pap. 15.95 (0-398-06323-0) C C Thomas.

Placher, William C. A History of Christian Theology: An Introduction. LC 83-16778. 324p. (C). 1983. pap. 16.99 (0-664-24496-3, Westminster) Westminster John Knox.

— Narratives of a Vulnerable God: Christ, Theology, & Scripture. LC 93-47618. 192p. (Orig.). 1994. pap. 14.99 (0-664-25534-5) Westminster John Knox.

— Readings in the History of Christian Theology: From Its Beginnings to the Eve of the Reformation, Vol. 1. LC 87-29540. 204p. (Orig.). 1988. pap. 16.99 (0-664-24057-7, Westminster) Westminster John Knox.

— Readings in the History of Christian Theology: From the Reformation to the Present, Vol. 2. LC 87-29540. 216p. (Orig.). 1988. pap. 16.99 (0-664-24058-5, Westminster) Westminster John Knox.

— Unapologetic Theology: A Christian Voice in a Pluralistic Conversation. LC 88-27706. 178p. 1989. pap. 15.99 (0-664-25064-5) Westminster John Knox.

Placher, William C. & Willis-Watkins, David. Belonging to God: A Commentary on "A Brief Statement of Faith" 224p. (Orig.). 1992. pap. 9.99 (0-664-25296-6) Westminster John Knox.

Placher, William C., ed. see Frei, Hans W.

Plachno, Jackie, ed. The Steam Locomotive Directory of North America, Vol. 1. LC 87-30098. (Illus.). 192p. 1988. pap. 25.00 (0-933449-04-6) Transport Trails.

— The Steam Locomotive Directory of North America, Vol. 2. LC 87-30098. (Illus.). 176p. 1988. pap. 25.00 (0-933449-05-4) Transport Trails.

Plachno, Jackie, ed. see Plachno, Larry.

Plachno, Larry. Beginner's Guide to Converted Coaches. (Illus.). 120p. 1992. pap. 15.00 (0-933449-13-5) Transport Trails.

— The Longest Interurban Charter. Bronsky, Eric, ed. LC 88-24784. (Illus.). 96p. 1988. pap. 16.00 (0-933449-08-9) Transport Trails.

— Sunset Lines: The Story of the Chicago Aurora & Elgin Railroad, Number 1, Trackage. Bronsky, Eric, ed. (Illus.). 160p. 1987. 32.00 (0-933449-02-X) Transport Trails.

— Sunset Lines: The Story of the Chicago Aurora & Elgin Railroad, Number 1, Trackage. (Illus.). 1991. write for info. (0-318-68935-9) Transport Trails.

— Sunset Lines - the Story of the Chicago Aurora & Elgin Railroad, Vol. 2. LC 86-30751. (Sunset Lines Ser.). (Illus.). 352p. 1990. text ed. 64.00 (0-933449-10-0) Transport Trails.

— Used Intercity Bus Pricing 1978-1986. Plachno, Jackie, ed. LC 87-19189. (Illus.). 40p. 1987. pap. 20.00 (0-933449-03-8) Transportation.

Plachno, Larry, ed. see Insull, Samuel.

Plachy, Roger. Building a Fair Pay Program: A Step by Step Guide. LC 86-47595. 315p. 1986. 75.00 (0-8144-7662-7) AMACOM.

Plachy, Roger J. & Plachy, Sandra J. Performance Management: Getting Results from Your Performance Planning & Appraisal System. LC 88-47713. 308p. 1988. 59.95 (0-8144-7705-4) AMACOM.

— Results-Oriented Job Descriptions. 300p. 1993. spiral bd. 65.00 (0-8144-7806-9) AMACOM.

Plachy, Sandra J., jt. auth. see Plachy, Roger J.

Plachy, Sylvia. Unguided Tour. 1990. 39.95 (0-89381-393-1) Aperture.

Plachy, Sylvia, photos. Unguided Tour. (Illus.). 144p. 1991. pap. 29.95 (0-89381-431-8) Aperture.

Plachy, V., jt. auth. see Bata, M.

Placidi, G. F., et al, eds. Recurrent Mood Disorders: New Perspectives in Therapy. LC 92-48355. 1993. 178.00 (3-540-54046-6); 130.00 (0-387-54046-6) Spr-Verlag.

Placido, Bucolo, ed. The Other Pareto. LC 79-24588. 1980. text ed. 39.95 (0-312-58955-7) St Martin.

Placito, P. J., jt. auth. see Mabberley, D. J.

Plackett, R. L. Principles of Regression Analysis. LC 60-50875. 184p. reprint ed. pap. 52.50 (0-317-09179-4, 2051613) Bks Demand.

Plackett, R. L., ed. see Pearson, E. S.

Placksin, Sally. Mothering the New Mother: A Postpartum Resource Guide. LC 93-24989. (Illus.). 352p. 1993. 24. 95 (1-55704-172-5); pap. 14.95 (1-55704-178-4) Newmarket.

Placzek, Adolf K., ed. Macmillan Encyclopedia of Architects, 4 vols. 1982. text ed. 425.00 (0-02-925000-5) Macmillan.

Placzek, Adolph K., jt. auth. see Hitchcock, Henry-Russell.

PLAE, Inc. Staff. Universal Access to Outdoor Recreation: A Design Guide. (Illus.). 300p. 1993. pap. 44.95 (0-944661-25-4) MIG Comns.

— Universal Access to Outdoor Recreation: A Pocket Guide. (Illus.). 64p. (Orig.). 1994. pap. text ed. 9.95 (0-944661-28-9) MIG Comns.

Plaetzer, Ross F., ed. Lincoln for the Defense: The Only Known Transcript of an Abraham Lincoln Criminal Jury Trial. 198p. 1994. pap. 15.95 (0-9641176-0-6) High Hse Pr.

Plaff, Paula, jt. auth. see Meany, Janet.

Plafker, George & Berg, H. C., eds. The Geology of Alaska. (DNAG, Geology of North America Ser.: Vol. G1). (Illus.). 1994. 135.00 (0-8137-5219-1) Geol Soc.

Plaford, Gary. Domine IV. abr. ed. 320p. 1995. pap. 9.95 (1-56901-509-0) NW Pub.

Plageman, jt. auth. see Herbert.

Plageman, Karen. Good, Hearty Soups. LC 78-70972. (Illus.). 1979. pap. 2.95 (0-915942-12-7) SF Design.

— Great Casseroles! LC 80-80567. (Illus.). 1980. pap. 2.95 (0-915942-14-3) SF Design.

— Slow-Crock Cookery. LC 74-24590. (Illus.). 1974. pap. 2.95 (0-915942-02-X) SF Design.

Plagemann, Catherine & Fisher, M. Fine Preserving: Jams & Jellies, Pickles & Relishes, Conserves & Chutneys & Brandied Fruits for City & Country Cooks. rev. ed. (Illus.). 144p. (Orig.). 1986. reprint ed. 17.95 (0-943186-35-8); reprint ed. pap. 9.95 (0-943186-31-5) Aris Bks.

Plagenhoef, Richard & Adler, Carol. Why Am I Still Addicted? A Holistic Approach to Recovery. 1991. pap. 9.95 (0-07-050280-3) McGraw.

— Why Am I Still Addicted? A Holistic Approach to Recovery. 252p. 1991. 17.95 (0-8306-3361-8, 2307, TAB-Human Servs Inst); pap. 9.95 (0-8306-2135-0, TAB-Human Servs Inst) TAB Bks.

Plagens, Peter. DeWain Valentine. 24p. 1975. 7.00 (0-686-99813-8) Mus Contemp Art.

— Moonlight Blues: An Artist's Art Criticism. LC 86-11335. (Contemporary American Art Critics Ser.: No. 9). 355p. reprint ed. pap. 101.20 (0-8357-1753-4, 2070612) Bks Demand.

Plagman, Bernard K., et al. Audit & Control of Systems Programming Activities. (Illus.). 121p. 1985. pap. text ed. 33.00 (0-89413-143-5) Inst Inter Aud.

Plagman, Bernard K. & O'Loughlin, Anne. Telecommunications Management, Control, & Audit. 207p. 1988. pap. text ed. 45.00 (0-89413-181-8) Inst Inter Aud.

Plaice, Neville, tr. see Bering, Dietz.

Plaice, Neville, tr. see Bloch, Ernst.

Plaice, Neville, tr. see Bloch, Ernst, et al.

Plaice, Stephen, tr. see Bloch, Ernst, et al, eds.

Plaid, Ian. Brace Yourself, Bridget! The Official Irish Sex Manual. 96p. 1982. 6.95 (0-312-09430-2); 29.75 (0-312-09431-0) St Martin.

An Asterisk (*) at the beginning of an entry indicates that the title is appearing in BIP for the first time.

Plaidy, Jean. Bastard King. 22.95 (0-8488-0605-0) Amereon Ltd.
— The Battle of the Queens. 384p. 1982. pap. 2.95 (0-449-24565-9, Crest) Fawcett.
— The Captive of Kensington Palace. large type ed. (Shadows of the Crown Ser.). 1975. 21.95 (0-85456-599-X) Ulverscroft.
— Caroline the Queen. large type ed. (Shadows of the Crown Ser.). 1974. 21.95 (0-85456-595-7) Ulverscroft.
— The Courts of Love. 496p. 1989. mass mkt. 4.95 (0-449-21657-8, Crest) Fawcett.
— Follies O. (Plantagenet Saga Ser.: No. 8). 1984. pap. 2.95 (0-449-20043-4) Fawcett.
— Gay Lord Robert. large type ed. (Shadows of the Crown Ser.). 1974. 21.95 (0-85456-608-2) Ulverscroft.
— Hammer of the Scots. 1983. pap. 2.95 (0-449-20046-9) Fawcett.
— A Health Unto His Majesty. 253p. reprint ed. lib. bdg. 21.95 (0-88411-894-0, Aeonian Pr) Amereon Ltd.
— In the Shadow of the Crown. 448p. 1991. mass mkt. 4.95 (0-449-21855-4, Crest) Fawcett.
— It Began in Vaushall Gardens. large type ed. 1995. 22.95 (0-7838-1162-4, Large Print Bks) Hall.
— Katharine, the Virgin Widow. LC 93-21797. 224p. 1993. 22.95 (0-399-13873-0, Putnam) Putnam Pub Group.
— Mary, Queen of Scotland: The Triumphant Year. large type ed. (Shadows of the Crown Ser.). 1974. 21.95 (0-85456-610-4) Ulverscroft.
— Melisande. 1993. mass mkt. 4.99 (0-449-22191-1) Fawcett.
— Myself, My Enemy. 352p. 1985. pap. 3.95 (0-449-20648-3, Crest) Fawcett.
— Passage to Pontefract. 416p. 1984. pap. 3.95 (0-449-20265-8, Crest) Fawcett.
— Passionate Enemies. 22.95 (0-8488-0606-9) Amereon Ltd.
— Perdita's Prince. 304p. 1989. pap. 3.95 (0-449-21658-6, Crest) Fawcett.
— Plantagenet Prelude. 22.95 (0-8488-0607-7) Amereon Ltd.
— The Pleasures of Love. large type ed. LC 92-20784. 1992. 19.95 (0-7927-1382-6, Eagle Lrg Print) Chivers N Amer.
— The Pleasures of Love. large type ed. 1993. pap. 17.95 (0-7927-1381-8, Paragon Lrg Print) Chivers N Amer.
— Prince & Quakeress. 1989. pap. 3.95 (0-449-21443-5) Fawcett.
— Princess of Celle. 25.95 (0-8488-0608-5) Amereon Ltd.
— Princess of Celle. 1987. pap. 3.95 (0-449-21004-9) Fawcett.
— The Princess of Celle. large type ed. (Shadows of the Crown Ser.). 1974. 21.95 (0-85456-594-9) Ulverscroft.
— The Queen & Lord "M" large type ed. (Shadows of the Crown Ser.). 1975. 21.95 (0-85456-600-7) Ulverscroft.
— The Queen & Lord M. 268p. reprint ed. lib. bdg. 20.95 (0-88411-895-9, Aeonian Pr) Amereon Ltd.
— Queen from Provence. 1983. pap. 2.50 (0-449-20052-3) Fawcett.
— Queen in Waiting. 24.95 (0-8488-0609-3) Amereon Ltd.
— The Queen's Husband. large type ed. (Shadows of the Crown Ser.). 1975. 21.95 (0-85456-601-5) Ulverscroft.
— The Reluctant Queen: The Story of Anne of York. large type ed. LC 94-919. 1994. 21.95 (0-8161-7426-1, Large Print Bks) Hall.
— Rise of the Spanish Inquisition. (Illus.). 192p. 1959. text ed. 28.50 (0-7091-5080-6) Trans-Atl Phila.
— The Rose Without a Thorn. LC 93-34598. (Queens of England Ser.). 256p. 1994. 22.95 (0-399-13930-3, Putnam) Putnam Pub Group.
— The Rose Without a Thorn. large type ed. 1994. 23.95 (1-56895-161-2) Wheeler Pub.
— The Scarlet Cloak. 1994. reprint ed. mass mkt. 4.99 (0-449-22240-3) Fawcett.
— The Shadow of the Pomegranate. LC 94-1785. 240p. 1994. 22.95 (0-399-13967-2, Putnam) Putnam Pub Group.
— St. Thomas's Eve. 20.95 (0-8488-0610-7) Amereon Ltd.
— The Sun in Splendour. 352p. 1985. pap. 3.95 (0-449-20628-9, Crest) Fawcett.
— The Third George. (Georgian Saga Ser.). 320p. 1989. pap. 3.95 (0-449-21599-7, Crest) Fawcett.
— The Third George. large type ed. (Shadows of the Crown Ser.). 1974. 21.95 (0-85456-596-5) Ulverscroft.
— Victoria in the Wings. large type ed. (Shadows of the Crown Ser.). 1974. 21.95 (0-85456-598-1) Ulverscroft.
— The Vow on the Heron. 408p. 1984. pap. 3.95 (0-449-20264-X, Crest) Fawcett.
— The Widow of Windsor. large type ed. (Shadows of the Crown Ser.). 1975. 15.95 (0-85456-602-3) Ulverscroft.
— William's Wife. LC 92-32588. (Queen's of England Ser.). 288p. 1993. 22.95 (0-399-13807-2, Putnam) Putnam Pub Group.
— William's Wife. 1995. mass mkt. 5.99 (0-449-22284-5, Crest) Fawcett.
Plain, Belva. Belva Plain: Three Complete Novels: Evergreen - Random Winds - Eden Burning. LC 93-32354. 1993. 11.99 (0-517-10066-5, Pub. by Wings Bks) Random Hse Value.
— Blessings. large type ed. LC 93-45469. 1994. pap. 17.95 (0-8161-5793-6, Large Print Bks) Hall.
— Blessings. 1990. reprint ed. mass mkt. 6.99 (0-440-20652-9) Dell.
— Carousel. 1995. 23.95 (0-385-31107-9) Delacorte.
— The Carousel. large type ed. LC 95-2475. 436p. Date not set. pap. 19.95 (0-7838-1117-9, Large Print Bks) Hall.
— The Carousel. large type ed. LC 95-2475. 436p. 1995. 25.95 (0-7838-1116-0, Large Print Bks) Hall.
— Crescent City. 1987. mass mkt. 6.99 (0-440-11549-3) Dell.
— Daybreak. 1994. 22.95 (0-385-31104-4) Delacorte.
— Daybreak. 1995. mass mkt. 6.99 (0-440-21681-8) Dell.
— Daybreak: A Novel. 1994. 27.95 (0-385-31232-6) Delacorte.
— Eden Burning. 1987. mass mkt. 6.99 (0-440-12135-3) Dell.
— Evergreen. 1987. mass mkt. 6.99 (0-440-13278-9) Dell.
— Evergreen. 598p. 1991. reprint ed. lib. bdg. 38.95 (0-89966-813-5) Buccaneer Bks.
— Evergreen Saga, 3 vols. 1990. boxed 16.50 (0-440-36011-0) Dell.
— The Golden Cup. 384p. 1986. 17.95 (0-385-29508-1) Delacorte.
— The Golden Cup. 1987. mass mkt. 6.99 (0-440-13091-3) Dell.
— Harvest. 1990. 21.95 (0-385-29926-5) Delacorte.
— Harvest. 1991. mass mkt. 6.99 (0-440-20891-2) Dell.
— Harvest. large type ed. 1990. 24.95 (0-385-30236-3, Delacorte LT) BDD LT Grp.
— Random Winds. 1987. mass mkt. 6.99 (0-440-17562-3) Dell.
— Random Winds. large type ed. LC 92-38593. (General Ser.). 816p. 1993. pap. 18.95 (0-8161-5684-0) G K Hall.
— Tapestry. 1989. mass mkt. 6.99 (0-440-20271-X) Dell.
— Treasures. 1992. 21.00 (0-385-29927-3) Delacorte.
— Treasures. 1993. mass mkt. 6.99 (0-440-21400-9) Dell.
— Treasures. large type ed. 1992. pap. 25.00 (0-385-30610-5, Delacorte LT) BDD LT Grp.
— Treasures. large type ed. LC 93-1991. 1993. pap. 17.95 (0-8161-5803-7) Hall.
— Whispers. LC 92-36572. 1993. 22.95 (0-385-29928-1) Delacorte.
— Whispers. 1994. mass mkt. 6.99 (0-440-21674-5) Dell.
— Whispers. large type ed. 1993. pap. 27.50 (0-385-30917-1, Delacorte LT) BDD LT Grp.
— Whispers. large type ed. LC 93-35518. 1994. 17.95 (0-8161-5811-8, Large Print Bks) Hall.
Plain, Nancy. Mary Cassatt, the Life of an Artist. LC 93-46578. (People in Focus Ser.). (J). 1994. text ed. 13.95 (0-87518-597-5, Dillon Silver Burdett) Silver Burdett Pr.
Plains Genealogical Society Staff. Kimball County, Nebraska. (Illus.). 924p. 1988. 65.00 (0-88107-113-7) Curtis Media.
Plaisance, George. Lexique Pedologique Trilingue. 355p. (FRE.). 1958. pap. 39.95 (0-8288-6851-4, M-6458) Fr & Eur.
Plaisance, Georges. Dictionnaire des Forets. 5th ed. (FRE.). 1975. pap. 49.95 (0-8288-5851-9, M6457) Fr & Eur.
***Plaismond, Marcus.** Haitian Days: Ti Djo Remembers. (J). (gr. k-2). 1994. audio 8.95 (0-7608-0488-5); 21.95 (1-56801-362-0); pap. 4.95 (1-56801-360-4) Sundance Pub.
Plaison, ed. Map Projection: Theory & Applications. 1990. 115.00 (0-8493-6888-X, GA110) CRC Pr.
Plaisted, Jon. Sam's Valley Serenade. 80p. (Orig.). 1992. pap. 5.95 (0-9634702-0-5) Goodwin Coffin Pubs.
Plaister, Ted. Developing Listening Comprehension for ESL Students: The Kingdom of Kochen. 1976. pap. text ed. 16.95 (0-13-204479-X) P-H.
— ESOL Case Studies: The Real World of L2 Teaching & Administration. LC 92-21668. 1992. pap. text ed. 22.50 (0-13-118738-4) P-H.
Plaitakis, Andreas, ed. Cerebellar Degenerations: Clinical Neurobiology. (Foundations of Neurology Ser.). 528p. (C). 1992. lib. bdg. 218.50 (0-7923-1490-5) Kluwer Ac.
Plaitakis, Andreas, jt. ed. see Duvoisin, Roger C.
***Plakans, Andrejs.** Latvia & the Latvians: A Short History. (Studies of Nationalities). (Illus.). 390p. (Orig.). (C). 1995. pap. 24.95 (0-8179-9302-9) Hoover Inst Pr.
— Latvia & the Latvians: A Short History. (Studies of Nationalities). (Illus.). 258p. (Orig.). (C). 1995. 39.95 (0-8179-9301-0) Hoover Inst Pr.
Plakans, Andrejs, jt. ed. see Hareven, Tamara.
***Plakida, N. M.** High-Temperature Superconductivity: Experiment & Theory. LC 94-21156. (Lecture Notes in Computer Science Ser.). 1994. 59.00 (0-387-57072-1) Spr-Verlag.
Plakides, Antonios G. Strawberry Diseases. LC 64-21596. (Louisiana State University Studies Biological Science Ser.: No. 5). 207p. reprint ed. pap. 59.00 (0-317-29858-5, 2019566) Bks Demand.
Plaks, Andrew H. Archetype & Allegory in the Dream of the Red Chamber. LC 75-3469. (Illus.). 280p. reprint ed. pap. 79.80 (0-8357-7893-2, 2036312) Bks Demand.
— The Four Masterworks of the Ming Novel: Ssu ta ch'i-shu. (Illus.). 500p. 1987. text ed. 80.00 (0-691-06708-2) Princeton U Pr.
Plaks, Andrew H., ed. Chinese Narrative: Critical & Theoretical Essays. LC 76-45907. 378p. reprint ed. pap. 107.80 (0-7837-6774-9, 2046604) Bks Demand.
Plaks, Andrew H. & Birch, Cyril, eds. Chinese Narrative: Critical & Theoretical Essays. LC 76-45907. 1977. pap. text ed. 19.95 (0-691-10224-4) Princeton U Pr.
Plaksin, I. N., ed. Flotation Properties of Rare Metal Minerals. LC 67-16333. (Illus.). 91p. 1967. 19.25 (0-911184-05-8) Primary.
Plakun, Erik M., ed. New Perspectives in Narcissism. LC 89-17973. (Clinical Practice Ser.: Vol. 13). 250p. 1990. text ed. 31.00 (0-88048-178-1) Am Psychiatric.
Plambeck, Herb. The Way It Was. 300p. (Orig.). 1993. pap. 12.95 (0-9635812-2-8) Sigler Print.
Plambeck, James A. Electroanalytical Chemistry: Basic Principles & Applications. LC 82-2803. (Wiley-Interscience Publication Ser.). 426p. reprint ed. pap. 121.50 (0-7837-2406-3, 2040091) Bks Demand.
Plamenac, D., intro. Dijon: Bibliotheque Publique, Ms. 517. (Veroffentlichungen Mittelalterlicher Musikhandschriften - Publications of Mediaeval Musical Manuscripts Ser.). 1972. 127.00 (0-912024-12-7) Inst Mediaeval Mus.
Plamenatz, John P. German Marxism & Russian Communism. LC 75-1135. 356p. 1975. reprint ed. text ed. 69.50 (0-8371-7986-6, PLGM, Greenwood Pr) Greenwood.
— Man & Society, Vol. II: From Montesquieu to the Early Socialists. 2nd rev. ed. 392p. (C). 1994. pap. text ed. 33.50 (0-582-05546-6, 79207) Longman.
— Man & Society, Vol. III: Hegel, Marx & Engels & the Idea of Progress. 2nd rev. ed. 392p. (C). 1994. pap. text ed. 33.50 (0-582-05541-5, 79209) Longman.
— Man & Society, Vol. 1: From Middle Ages to Locke. 2nd rev. ed. 392p. (C). 1994. pap. text ed. 33.50 (0-582-05540-7, 79208) Longman.
— The Revolutionary Movement in France: Eighteen Fifteen to Eighteen Seventy-One. LC 78-14135. 1986. reprint ed. 20.00 (0-88355-809-2) Hyperion Conn.
Plamenevskii, B. A. Algebras of Pseudodifferential Operators. (C). 1989. lib. bdg. 147.50 (0-7923-0231-1) Kluwer Ac.
PLamenevsky, Boris A., jt. auth. see Nazarov, S. A.
Plamondon. Progress in Automatic Signature Verification. 250p. 1994. text ed. 74.00 (981-02-1852-4) World Scientific Pub.
Plamondon, Ann L. Whitehead's Organic Philosophy of Science. LC 78-7350. 174p. 1979. 49.50 (0-87395-387-8) State U NY Pr.
Plamondon, R. & Leedham, G. Computer Processing of Handwriting. 424p. 1990. pap. 37.00 (981-02-0520-1) World Scientific Pub.
Plamondon, R., et al, eds. Computer Recognition & Human Production of Handwriting. 408p. 1989. text ed. 81.00 (9971-5-0665-3) World Scientific Pub.
— Pattern Recognition: Architectures, Algorithms & Applications. 350p. (C). 1991. text ed. 104.00 (981-02-0604-6) World Scientific Pub.
Plan Econ Inc. Staff. How to Invest in Eastern Europe. 1993. 197.00 (0-935453-54-7) Pasha Pubns.
Planadeball, Marta J., jt. auth. see La Verne, Walker.
Planadeball, Marta J., jt. auth. see Walker, La Verne.
Planas, Joe, jt. auth. see Hunter, Bruce.
Planas, Joe, ed. see Paul, Jim.
Planchart, Alejandro. The Repertory of Tropes at Winchester. LC 76-3033. 1976. text ed. 135.00 (0-691-09121-8) Princeton U Pr.
Planchart, Alejandro E. The Repertory of Tropes at Winchester, 2 vols., Vol. 1. LC 76-3033. 407p. reprint ed. pap. 109.90 (0-8357-3430-7, 2039688) Bks Demand.
— The Repertory of Tropes at Winchester, 2 vols., Vol. 2. LC 76-3033. 408p. reprint ed. pap. 116.30 (0-8357-3431-5) Bks Demand.
Planche, Bernard. Living on a Tropical Island. Matthews, Sarah, tr. LC 87-34592. (Illus.). 38p. (J). (gr. k-5). 1988. 5.95 (0-944589-13-8, 138) Young Discovery Lib.
— Living with the Eskimos. Matthews, Sarah, tr. LC 87-31805. (Illus.). 38p. (J). (gr. k-5). 1988. 5.95 (0-944589-12-X, 12X) Young Discovery Lib.
Planche, James R. Plays. Roy, D., ed. (British & American Playwrights Ser.). 241p. 1986. 64.95 (0-521-24111-1); pap. 22.95 (0-521-28441-4) Cambridge U Pr.
— Recollections & Reflections. LC 78-17733. (Music Reprint Ser.). (Illus.). 1978. reprint ed. lib. bdg. 65.00 (0-306-79501-9) Da Capo.
Planche, Remi. Data Driven Systems Modelling. 450p. 1991. 53.33 (0-13-201179-4) P-H.
Planck, Annika, tr. see Lundkvist, Artur.
Planck, Charles R. The Changing Status of German Reunification in Western Diplomacy, 1955-1966. LC 67-22894. (Washington Center of Foreign Policy Research. Studies in International Affairs: No. 4). 73p. reprint ed. pap. 25.00 (0-317-28471-1, 2020742) Bks Demand.
Planck, H. I., et al. Medical Textiles for Implantation: Proceedings of the 3rd International ITV Conference on Biomaterials, Stuttgart, June 14-16, 1989. (Illus.). 368p. 1991. 96.00 (0-387-52741-9) Spr-Verlag.
— Polyurethanes in Biomedical Engineering. (Progress in Biomedical Engineering Ser.: Vol. 1). 1984. 133.50 (0-444-42399-0) Elsevier.
Planck, H. I., et al, eds. Degradation Phenomena on Polymeric Biomaterials: Proceedings of the 4th International ITV Conference on Biomaterials, Denkendorf, September 3-5, 1991. LC 92-14876. (Illus.). x, 197p. 1992. 89.00 (0-387-55548-X) Spr-Verlag.
— Polyurethanes in Biomedical Engineering II: Proceedings of the 2nd International Conference on Polyurethanes in Biomedical Engineering, Fellbach-Stuttgart, June 18-19, 1986. (Progress in Biomedical Engineering Ser.: No. 3). 272p. 1987. 97.50 (0-444-42759-7) Elsevier.
Planck, Kristi, tr. see Branner, H. C.
Planck, Max. A Survey of Physical Theory. LC 93-6110. 128p. 1994. reprint ed. pap. text ed. 6.95 (0-486-67867-9) Dover.
— The Theory of Heat Radiation. (Illus.). 256p. reprint ed. pap. 7.95 (0-486-66811-8) Dover.
— The Theory of Heat Radiation - Waermestrahlung. Masius, Morton, tr. (History of Modern Physics & Astronomy Ser.: No. 11). (Illus.). 512p. 1989. 45.00 (0-88318-597-0) Am Inst Physics.
— Where Is Science Going? Murphy, James, tr. LC 80-84974. 224p. 1981. reprint ed. 26.00 (0-918024-21-8); reprint ed. pap. 14.00 (0-918024-22-6) Ox Bow.
Planck, Max K. Scientific Autobiography & Other Papers. Gaynor, Frank, tr. LC 68-23319. 192p. 1968. reprint ed. text ed. 35.00 (0-8371-0194-8, PLAP, Greenwood Pr) Greenwood.
— Where Is Science Going? Murphy, James, tr. LC 75-41215. reprint ed. 18.50 (0-404-14696-1) AMS Pr.
Planck, Max, Society for the Advancement of Science, Gmelin Institute for Inorganic Chemistry Staff. B Boron Compounds Vol. II: Boron & Oxygen. 8th ed. (Gmelin Handbuch der Anorganischen Chemie Ser.: Suppl. 4). (Illus.). xvi, 297p. 1993. 1,113.00 (0-387-93673-4) Spr-Verlag.
— Borverbindungen-Boron Compounds. (Gmelin Handbuch der Anorganischen Chemie Ser.: Vol. 23, Pt. 5). (Illus.). 277p. 1975. 344.00 (0-387-93292-5) Spr-Verlag.
— Boverbindungen-Boron Compounds. (Gmelin Handbuch der Anorganischen Chemie Ser.: Vol. 22, Pt. 4). (Illus.). 360p. 1975. 458.00 (0-387-93289-5) Spr-Verlag.
— Manganese, Pt. C: The Compounds: Section 2, Manganate Compounds with Metals, from Li to U. (Gmelin Handbuch der Anorganischen Chemie Ser.). (Illus.). 302p. 1975. 381.00 (0-387-93287-9) Spr-Verlag.
— Nickel-Organische Verbibdunger Register-Organical Compounds Index for Pts. 1 & 2 of the Gmelin Handbuch. (Gmelin Handbuch der Anorganischen Chemie Ser.: Vol. 18). 129p. 1975. 109.00 (0-387-93296-8) Spr-Verlag.
— Organonickel Compounds. (Gmelin Handbuch der Anorganischen Chemie Ser.: Vol. 16, Pt. 1). (Illus.). 419p. 1975. 540.00 (0-387-93294-1) Spr-Verlag.
— Organotin Compounds. 8th ed. (Gmelin Handbuch der Anorganischen Chemie Ser.: Vol. 26, Pt. 1). 182p. 1975. 242.00 (0-387-93291-7) Spr-Verlag.
Planck, Max, Society for the Advancement of Science, Gmelin Institute for Inorganic Chemistry Staff, et al. Oxygen: Walter Desalting. (Gmelin Handbuch der Anorganischen Chemie Ser.). (Illus.). 339p. 1974. 483.00 (0-387-93280-1) Spr-Verlag.
Planck, Max, Society for the Advancement of Science, Gmelin Institute for Inorganic Chemistry Staff. Perfluorhalogenorano-Verbindungen der Haupt Gruppenelemente-Perfluorohalogenorgano-Compounds of Main Group Elements. (Gmelin Handbuch der Anorganischen Chemie Ser.: Vol. 24, Pt. 3). 233p. 1975. 306.00 (0-387-93293-3) Spr-Verlag.
— Register-Index for the Gmelin Handbuch Dev Anorganischen Chemie. (Gmelin Handbuch der Anorganischen Chemie Ser.: Vol. 1, Ac-Au). 254p. 1975. 229.00 (0-387-93295-X) Spr-Verlag.
Planck, Max Society for the Advancement of Science, the Gmelin Institute for Inorganic Chemistry Staff. Th Thorium: Compounds with Si, P, As, Sb, Bi, & Ge. (Gmelin Handbuch der Anorganischen Chemie Ser.). (Illus.). xxiii, 301p. 1993. 1,125.00 (0-387-93675-0) Spr-Verlag.
Planck, Max, Society for the Advancement of Science, Gmelin Institute for Inorganic Chemistry Staff. Tin, Pt. C. (Gmelin Handbuch der Anorganischen Chemie Ser.). (Illus.). 206p. 1975. 282.00 (0-387-93284-4) Spr-Verlag.
— Transurane-Transuranium Elements. (Gmelin Handbuch der Anorganischen Chemie Ser.: Vol. 20d, Pt. 2). (Illus.). 278p. 1975. 365.00 (0-387-93288-7) Spr-Verlag.
— Uranium, Pt. C, Section 3. (Illus.). 360p. 1975. 463.00 (0-387-93290-9) Spr-Verlag.
Plander, I. Artificial Intelligence Information-Control Systems of Robots '94. 432p. 1994. text ed. 109.00 (981-02-1877-X) World Scientific Pub.
Plander, I., ed. Artificial Intelligence & Information-Control Systems of Robots: Proceedings of the International Conference on Artificial Intelligence & Information-Control Systems of Robots, Smolenice, 3rd, Czechoslovakia, June 11-15, 1984. 402p. 1984. 87.25 (0-444-87533-6, North Holland) Elsevier.
— Artificial Intelligence & Information-Control Systems of Robots-87: Proceedings of the 4th International Conference on Artificial Intelligence & Information-Control Systems of Robots Smolenice, Czechoslovakia, 19-23 Oct. 1987. 482p. 1987. 92.50 (0-444-70303-9) Elsevier.
— Artificial Intelligence & Information-Control Systems of Robots, '89: Proc. of the 5th Internat. Conf., Strbske Pleso, Czechoslovakia, 6-10 Nov. 1989. 470p. 1989. 95.00 (0-444-88317-7, North Holland) Elsevier.
***Plane.** Plane & Pilot International Aircraft Directory. 1995. pap. text ed. 24.95 (0-07-050305-2) TAB Bks.
***Plane & Pilot Magazine Staff & Werner, Steve.** Plane & Pilot International Aircraft Directory. 1995. text ed. 34.95 (0-07-050304-4) TAB Bks.
Plane, David A. & Rogerson, Peter A. The Geographical Analysis of Population with Applications to Planning & Business. LC 93-48671. 1994. text ed. write for info. (0-471-51014-9) Wiley.
Plane, Donald R. Management Science: A Spreadsheet Approach. LC 93-48683. (Scientific Press Ser.). 437p. 1994. 64.25 (0-89426-225-4) Boyd & Fraser.
Plane, Donald R. & Crummer, Roy E. Quantitative Tools for Decision Support Using IFPS-Optimum. LC 84-24368. 400p. (C). 1986. pap. text ed. 45.25 (0-201-05844-8) Addison-Wesley.
Planel, Philippe G., tr. see Rouland, Norbert.
Planells, M. Dictionary of the Secrets of Ibiza: Diccionario de Secretos de Ibiza. 345p. (SPA.). 1982. pap. 16.95 (0-8288-1463-5, S39884) Fr & Eur.
Planer, F. E. Superstition. 377p. 1988. pap. 20.95 (0-87975-494-X) Prometheus Bks.
Planes, Kindersley. Planes. LC 91-25688. (Eye Openers Ser.). (Illus.). 24p. (J). (ps-k). 1992. pap. 7.95 (0-689-71564-1, Aladdin Paperbacks) S&S Childrens.
Planes, Peter, jt. auth. see Ehrhardt, Sherry.
Planeta-Agostini. Illustrated Encyclopedia of Cooking, 8 vols., Set. (Illus.). (SPA.). 1987. 595.00 (0-8288-7574-X, 8439501234) Fr & Eur.
***Planeta Staff.** Clasicos del Arte: Classics of Art. 1989. write for info. (0-7859-5232-2) Fr & Eur.
— Diccionario Bompiano de Autores Literarios, Vol. 2. 616p. 1987. 29.95 (0-7859-6005-8, 8439506457) Fr & Eur.
— Diccionario Bompiano de Autores Literarios, Vol. 3. 632p. 1988. 29.95 (0-7859-6006-6, 8439506465) Fr & Eur.
— Diccionario Bompiano de Autores Literarios, Vol. 4. 632p. 1988. 29.95 (0-7859-6007-4, 8439506473) Fr & Eur.
— Diccionario Bompiano de Autores Literarios, Vol. 5. 640p. 1988. 29.95 (0-7859-6008-2, 8439506481) Fr & Eur.

P Q

— Diccionario Larousse de Historia Univeral, Vol. 1. 680p. 1988. 29.95 (*0-7859-6019-8*, 8439507690) Fr & Eur.
— Diccionario Larousse de Historia Univeral, Vol. 2. 760p. 1988. 29.95 (*0-7859-6003-1*, 8439407704) Fr & Eur.
— Diccionario Larousse de Historia Univeral, Vol. 3. 776p. 1988. 29.95 (*0-7859-6020-1*, 8439507712) Fr & Eur.
— Diccionario Larousse de Historia Univeral, Vol 5. 832p. 1988. 29.95 (*0-7859-6022-8*, 8439509731) Fr & Eur.
— Diccionario Larousse de la Pintura, 6 vols. 1988. write for info. (*0-7859-6023-6*, 8439509766) Fr & Eur.
— Diccionario Larousse de la Pintura, Vol. 1. 368p. 1989. 16.95 (*0-7859-6024-4*, 8439509774) Fr & Eur.
— Diccionario Larousse de la Pintura, Vol. 2. 376p. 1989. 16.95 (*0-7859-6025-2*, 8439509782) Fr & Eur.
— Diccionario Larousse de la Pintura, Vol. 3. 360p. 1989. 16.95 (*0-7859-6026-0*, 8439509790) Fr & Eur.
— Diccionario Larousse de la Pintura, Vol. 4. 368p. 1989. 16.95 (*0-7859-6027-9*, 8439509804) Fr & Eur.
— Diccionario Larousse de la Pintura, Vol. 5. 328p. 1989. 16.95 (*0-7859-6028-7*, 8439509812) Fr & Eur.
— Diccionario Larousse de la Pintura, Vol. 6. 344p. 1989. 16.95 (*0-7859-6029-5*, 8439509820) Fr & Eur.
— Diccionario UNESCO de Ciencias Sociales, Vol. 1. 624p. 1987. 29.95 (*0-7859-6009-0*, 8439506619) Fr & Eur.
— Diccionario UNESCO de Ciencias Sociales, Vol. 2. 592p. 1988. 29.95 (*0-7859-6010-4*, 8439506627) Fr & Eur.
— Diccionario UNESCO de Ciencias Sociales, Vol. 3. 616p. 1988. 29.95 (*0-7859-6011-2*, 8439506635) Fr & Eur.
— Diccionario UNESCO de Ciencias Sociales, Vol. 4. 568p. 1988. 29.95 (*0-7859-6012-0*, 8439506643) Fr & Eur.
— Enciclopedia Planeta De las Ciencias Ocultas y Parapsicologia: Planeta Encyclopedia of Occult Sciences & Parapsychology, 8 vols., Set. 300p. (SPA.). 1978. 250.00 (*0-8288-5228-6*, S50576) Fr & Eur.
— Gran Atlas de Espana: Large Atlas of Spain, 7 vols. (Illus.). 1991. write for info. (*0-7859-5229-2*) Fr & Eur.
— Historia de Espana: History of Spain. (SPA.). 1991. write for info. (*0-7859-5230-6*) Fr & Eur.
— Historia Universal del Arte, 10 vols. 1992. write for info. (*0-7859-5227-6*) Fr & Eur.
— Illustrated Encyclopedia of Cooking, 8 vols., Set. (Illus.). (SPA.). 1986. 595.00 (*0-8288-8229-0*, 8439501218) Fr & Eur.
— El Mundo de los Animales: The World of Animals. 1990. write for info. (*0-7859-5228-4*) Fr & Eur.
— Practical Encyclopedia of Pedagogy, 6 vols., Set. (SPA.). 695.00 (*0-8288-8254-1*) Fr & Eur.
Planinc, Zdravko. Plato's Political Philosophy: Prudence in the Republic & the Laws. 328p. (C). 1991. text ed. 37.50 (*0-8262-0798-7*) U of Mo Pr.
Planisek, Sandra, jt. auth. see Crum, Howard.
Plank, Anna. Harrap's Polish Phrase Book. 1991. pap. 4.00 (*0-13-382649-X*) P-H.
Plank, David N. & Ginsberg, Rick, eds. Southern Cities, Southern Schools: Public Education in the Urban South. LC 89-49230. (Contributions to the Study of Education Ser.: No. 38). 296p. 1990. text ed. 49.95 (*0-313-26297-7*, GIB/, Greenwood Pr) Greenwood.
Plank, David N., jt. ed. see Ginsberg, Rick.
Plank, Donald M. Xanta Vele's Dream Numbers Winners Book. Boone, Edgar S., ed. (Illus.). 81p. (Orig.). 1992. 3.95 (*1-881938-02-6*) Economy Pubns.
Plank, Frans, ed. Double Case: Agreement by Suffixaufnahme. (Illus.). 416p. 1995. 75.00 (*0-19-508775-5*) OUP.
— Ergativity: Towards a Theory of Grammatical Relations. LC 78-73889. 1980. text ed. 206.00 (*0-12-558150-5*) Acad Pr.
— Paradigms: The Economy of Inflection. LC 91-33626. (Empirical Approaches to Language Typology Ser.: No. 9). x, 317p. (C). 1991. lib. bdg. 136.95 (*3-11-012761-X*) Mouton.
— Relational Typology. (Trends in Linguistics, Studies & Monographs: No. 28). xii, 443p. 1985. 161.55 (*0-89925-086-6*) Mouton.
Plank, Franz, ed. Objects. 1984. text ed. 101.00 (*0-12-558160-2*) Acad Pr.
Plank, Harry, tr. see Smith, Frank K.
Plank, Karl. Mother of the Wire Fence: Inside & Outside the Holocaust. 192p. (Orig.). 1994. pap. 16.99 (*0-664-25219-2*) Westminster John Knox.
Plank, Karl A. Paul & the Irony of Affliction. LC 87-4844. (Society of Biblical Literature Semeia Studies). 150p. (C). 1987. 18.95 (*1-55540-102-3*, 06-06-17); pap. 15.95 (*1-55540-103-1*) Scholars Pr GA.
Plank, Lois R., jt. ed. see Plank, Tom M.
***Plank, Robert.** George Orwell's Guide Through Hell: A Psychological Study of 1984. rev. ed. LC 94-30950. (Milford Ser.: Vol. 41). 136p. (Orig.). 1994. lib. bdg. 27.00 (*0-89370-313-3*); pap. 17.00 (*0-89370-413-X*) Borgo Pr.
Plank, Roger, jt. auth. see Bell, Trevor.
***Plank, Shane P.** Up the Country: Selected Poems 1992-94. 32p. 1995. pap. 5.00 (*1-885710-10-0*) Geekspeak Unique.
***Plank, Steven.** The Way to Heavens Doore: An Introduction to Liturgical Process & Musical Style. LC 94-34082. (Studies in Liturgical Musicology: No. 2). 183p. 1994. 27.50 (*0-8108-2953-3*); 27.50 (*0-614-02751-9*) Scarecrow.
Plank, Tom M. & Plank, Lois R., eds. Encyclopedia of Accounting Systems. 2nd ed. LC 93-23812. 1993. write for info. (*0-13-276817-8*) P-H Gen Ref & Trav.
Plank, Tom M., jt. auth. see Blensly, Douglas L.
Plank, William. Gulag Sixty-Five: A Humanist Looks at Aging. (American University Studies Anthropology & Sociology: Ser. XI, Vol. 25). 205p. (C). 1989. text ed. 35.30 (*0-8204-0784-4*) P Lang Pubs.
— Sartre & Surrealism. LC 81-431. (Studies in the Fine Arts - Art Theory). 110p. reprint ed. pap. 31.40 (*0-8357-1175-7*, 2070253) Bks Demand.
***Plann, Susan.** Relative Clauses in Spanish Without Overt Antecedents & Related Constructions. LC 78-68838. (University of California Publications in Linguistics: No. 93). 208p. 1980. pap. 59.30 (*0-7837-8420-1*, 2049222) Bks Demand.
Planned Parenthood Federation of America, Inc. Staff. Echoes from the Past. LC 79-90484. (Illus.). 128p. 1979. 11.50 (*0-934586-03-9*) Plan Parent.
Planned Parenthood Federation of America Staff. A Tradition of Choice: Planned Parenthood at 75. LC 91-75358. (Illus.). 108p. 1991. 29.95 (*0-934586-71-3*) Plan Parent.
Planned Pottery Staff. Brick Oven Baking with Planned Pottery Bakeware, Vol. 1. rev. ed. (Illus.). 1988. pap. 6.00 (*0-9620282-0-7*) Planned Pottery.
Planner, John, intro. MECH 'Ninety-One Australia: Engineering for a Competitive World, Conference 5: Cost Effective Bulk Materials Handling. (Illus.). 107p. (Orig.). 1991. pap. 38.50 (*0-85825-529-4*, Pub. by Inst Engrs Aust-EA Bks AT) Accents Pubns.
Plannett, A., jt. auth. see Johnson, N.
Planning Commission Staff. Nehru & Planning in India: Proceedings of the National Seminar on Pandit Jawaharlal Nehru. (C). 1989. 28.00 (*0-8364-2865-X*, Pub. by Manohar II) S Asia.
***Plano, J. P. & Olton, Roy.** Dictionary of International Relations: Diccionario de Relaciones Internacionales. 465p. (SPA.). 1980. pap. 14.95 (*0-8288-2270-0*) Fr & Eur.
Plano, Jack, jt. auth. see Greenberg, Milton.
Plano, Jack C. & Greenberg, Milton. The American Political Dictionary. 8th ed. 700p. (C). 1989. pap. text ed. 22.00 (*0-03-022932-4*) HB Coll Pubs.
Plano, Jack C. & Olton, Roy. The International Relations Dictionary. 4th ed. (Clio Dictionaries in Political Science Ser.). 446p. 1988. lib. bdg. 55.00 (*0-87436-477-9*); pap. text ed. 24.75 (*0-87436-478-7*) ABC-CLIO.
Plano, Jack C., jt. auth. see Chandler, Ralph C.
Plano, Jack C., jt. auth. see Riggs, Robert E.
Plano, Jack C., jt. ed. see Rossi, Ernest E.
Plans Sanz De Bremond, Jose M. Diccionario Practico: Asesor de la Propiedad & Copropiedad Inmobiliaria. 392p. (SPA.). 1975. pap. 24.95 (*0-7859-0649-5*, S50138) Fr & Eur.
Plans y de Gabriel Sanz de Bremond, Fructuoso Staff. Diccionario Ortografico Mikron. 51th ed. 640p. (SPA.). 1978. 9.95 (*0-8288-5147-6*, S50033) Fr & Eur.
Plansquaert, P. & Haggar, R. Legumes in Farming Systems. (Developments in Plant & Soil Science Ser.). (C). 1989. lib. bdg. 67.00 (*0-7923-0134-X*) Kluwer Ac.
Plant, jt. auth. see University of Wisconsin Staff.
Plant, A. MacDonough. Maryland Estate Planning, Will Drafting & Estate Administration Forms. 220p. 1993. disk, ring bd. 159.00 (*0-87189-280-4*) Michie Butterworth.
Plant, Al. Petagwana to Pele: Point Edward to Point Pelee. 2nd ed. (Illus.). 113p. (Orig.). 1983. pap. 9.95 (*0-913611-00-X*) W E C Plant Ent.
— Petagwana to Pele: The Story of Great Lakes Prehistoric & Historic Sites & Their People (Point Edward to Point Pelee) 3rd ed. (Illus.). 116p. (YA). (gr. 7 up). 1995. pap. 17.95 (*0-913611-06-9*) W E C Plant Ent.
— Wahiawa Town. (Hawaii Mini History Ser.). (Illus.). 36p. (Orig.). 1995. pap. 3.95 (*0-913611-04-2*) W E C Plant Ent.
Plant, Al & Plant, Julie. Gourmet Odyssey: Cooking in a Tiny Kitchen from Michigan to Molokai. (Illus.). 192p. 1994. 16.95 (*0-913611-05-0*) W E C Plant Ent.
Plant, Albin M. Maryland Estate Planning, Will Drafting & Estate Administration Forms. suppl. ed. 220p. 1993. disk, ring bd. 79.00 (*1-56257-795-6*) Butterworth Legal Pubs.
Plant, Andrew. Drawing Is Easy. LC 93-16116. (Illus.). (J). 1994. pap. write for info. (*0-383-03692-5*) SRA Schl Grp.
Plant, Arnold, ed. Some Modern Business Problems: A Series of Studies. LC 67-23260. (Essay Index Reprint Ser.). 1977. 23.95 (*0-8369-0792-2*) Ayer.
Plant Breeding Symposium Staff. Plant Breeding: A Symposium, Iowa State University, 1965. Frey, Kenneth J., ed. LC 66-21642. 438p. reprint ed. pap. 124.90 (*0-317-30428-3*, 2024932) Bks Demand.
Plant, Christopher, jt. auth. see Plant, Judith.
Plant, David, jt. auth. see Ross, Alec.
Plant, David W., et al, eds. Patenting of Life Forms. LC 82-4191. (Banbury Report Ser.: No. 10). 351p. reprint ed. pap. 100.10 (*0-7837-2001-7*, 2042275) Bks Demand.
***Plant, Deborah G.** Every Tub Must Sit on Its Own Bottom: The Philosophy & Politics of Zora Neale Hurston. LC 94-47523. 1995. write for info. (*0-252-02183-5*) U of Ill Pr.
Plant, Elton M. Radio's First Broadcaster. (Illus.). 105p. 1989. pap. 9.95 (*0-913611-03-4*) W E C Plant Ent.
Plant, G. T., jt. ed. see Hess, R. F.
***Plant, Geoff & Spens, Karl-Grik, eds.** Profound Deafness & Speech Communication. 600p. (Orig.). (C). 1995. pap. text ed. 75.00 (*1-56593-492-X*, 0715) Singular Publishing.
***Plant, Glen.** Environmental Protection & the Law of War: A Fifth Geneva Convention on the Protection of the Environment in Time of Armed Conflict. LC 09-135125. 1994. text ed. 115.00 (*0-471-94748-2*) Wiley.
Plant, Glen, ed. Environmental Protection & the Law of War. 302p. 1992. text ed. 69.00 (*1-85293-234-1*, Pub. by Pinter Pubs UK) St Martin.
Plant, J. A., jt. ed. see Hale, M.
Plant, Jeffrey G., jt. auth. see Plant, Jeremy F.
Plant, Jeremy F. & Plant, Jeffrey G. Delaware & Hudson In Color, Vol. 2. LC 92-80546. (Illus.). 128p. 1993. 49.95 (*1-878887-27-0*) Morning NJ.
Plant, Jeremy F., jt. auth. see Arnold, David S.
Plant, Judith, ed. Healing the Wounds: The Promise of Ecofeminism. 276p. (Orig.). 1989. lib. bdg. 39.95 (*0-86571-152-6*); pap. 14.95 (*0-86571-153-4*) New Soc Pubs.
Plant, Judith & Plant, Christopher. Green Business: Hope or Hoax. (New Catalyst Bioregional Ser.). 144p. (Orig.). 1991. lib. bdg. 34.95 (*0-86571-195-X*); pap. 9.95 (*0-86571-196-8*) New Soc Pubs.
— Putting Power in Its Place: Developing Community Control of Resources. (New Catalyst Bioregional Ser.). 1991. lib. bdg. 34.95 (*0-86571-216-6*); pap. 9.95 (*0-86571-217-4*) New Soc Pubs.
— Turtle Talk: Voices for a Sustainable Future. (New Catalyst Bioregional Ser.). (Illus.). 144p. (Orig.). 1990. lib. bdg. 34.95 (*0-86571-185-2*); pap. 9.95 (*0-86571-186-0*) New Soc Pubs.
Plant, Julie, jt. auth. see Plant, Al.
Plant, M. Spanish-English Dictionary of Microelectronics. 227p. (ENG & SPA.). 1987. 49.95 (*0-8288-7252-X*, S30009) Fr & Eur.
— Spanish-English Dictionary of Microelectronics with an English-Spanish Vocabulary. 227p. 1987. pap. 29.00 (*84-283-1559-0*) IBD Ltd.
Plant, Martin, ed. AIDS, Drugs, & Prostitution. 256p. 1990. 36.00 (*0-415-04108-2*, A4329) Routledge.
Plant, Martin & Plant, Moira. Risk-Takers: Alcohol, Drugs, Sex & Youth. LC 91-41467. 208p. 1992. 69.95 (*0-415-03538-4*, A7514) Routledge.
Plant, Martin, et al, eds. Alcohol & Drugs. 1991. text ed. 50.00 (*0-7486-0113-9*, Pub. by Edinburgh U Pr UK) Col U Pr.
— Alcohol & Drugs: The Scottish Experience. (Illus.). 216p. 1992. pap. text ed. 24.50 (*0-7486-0377-8*, Pub. by Edinburgh U Pr UK) Col U Pr.
Plant, Mike, jt. auth. see Tinley, Scott.
Plant-Moeller, Jean, ed. Proceedings of the Twelfth National Convention of the Registry of Interpreters for the Deaf. 224p. (Orig.). (C). 1992. pap. 14.95 (*0-916883-11-6*) RID Pubns.
Plant, Moira. Women, Drinking & Pregnancy. 208p. 1985. 45.00 (*0-422-78610-1*, 9483, Pub. by Tavistock UK) Routledge Chapman & Hall.
— Women, Drinking, & Pregnancy. 184p. 1987. pap. 16.95 (*0-422-61750-4*, Pub. by Tavistock UK) Routledge Chapman & Hall.
Plant, Moira, jt. auth. see Plant, Martin.
Plant, Oliver. Woodturning: Step-by-Step Techniques. (Illus.). 128p. 1994. pap. 24.95 (*1-85223-759-7*, Pub. by Crowood Pr UK) Trafalgar.
Plant, Philip, jt. auth. see Petersen, Robert A.
Plant, R. V., jt. auth. see Holloway, J. C.
Plant, Raymond. Modern Political Thought: An Introduction to Political Philosophy. 352p. 1991. pap. 19.95 (*0-631-14224-X*) Blackwell Pubs.
Plant, Raymond, jt. auth. see Hoover, Kenneth.
Plant, Richard. Arabic Coins & How to Read Them. 2nd ed. (Illus.). 151p. 1980. 22.95 (*0-900652-52-7*, Pub. by Seaby UK) Trafalgar.
— Greek Coin Types & Their Identification. (Illus.). 344p. 1979. 39.95 (*0-900652-47-0*, Pub. by Seaby UK) Trafalgar.
— The Pink Triangle: The Nazi War Against Homosexuals. LC 86-346. 272p. 1988. pap. 11.95 (*0-8050-0600-1*) H Holt & Co.
Plant, Richard, jt. auth. see Ball, John.
Plant, Richard E. & Stone, Nicholas D. Knowledge-Based Systems in Agriculture. (Biological Resources Management Ser.). 400p. 1991. text ed. 44.00 (*0-07-050316-8*) McGraw.
Plant, Richard M. Formulae for the Mariner. 2nd ed. LC 86-47710. (Illus.). 107p. 1986. pap. text ed. 12.50 (*0-87033-361-5*) Cornell Maritime.
Plant, Robert. Industries in Trouble. vi, 178p. (Orig.). 1981. 24.00 (*92-2-102678-7*); pap. 16.00 (*92-2-102679-5*) Intl Labour Office.
Plant, Roger. Sugar & Modern Slavery: A Tale of Two Countries. LC 87-13315. 192p. (C). 1987. text ed. 39.95 (*0-86232-572-2*, Pub. by Zed Books UK); pap. 17.50 (*0-86232-573-0*, Pub. by Zed Books UK) Humanities.
Plant, Sadie. The Most Radical Gesture: The Situationist International in the Postmodern Age. LC 91-32553. 272p. (Orig.). 1992. 55.00 (*0-415-06221-7*, A6853); pap. 16.95 (*0-415-06222-5*, A6857) Routledge.
Plant, Tim. Painted Illusions: A Creative Guide to Painting Murals & Trompe-l'Oeil Effects. (Illus.). 128p. 1991. pap. 16.95 (*0-7063-7011-2*, Pub. by Ward Lock UK) Sterling.
Plant, W. J., jt. ed. see Geernaert, G. L.
Planta, Balthasar. How to Select a Bow for the Violin Family of Instruments. 32p. (Orig.). pap. 11.95 (*0-933224-31-1*) Bold Strummer Ltd.
Plantamura, Carol. Woman Composers. (Illus.). 48p. pap. 3.95 (*0-88388-110-1*) Bellerophon Bks.
Plantamura, Vito L., et al, eds. Frontier Decision Support Concepts: Help Desk, Learning, Fuzzy Diagnosis, Quality Evaluation, Prediction, Evolution. LC 93-45486. (Sixth-Generation Computer Technology Ser.). 1994. text ed. 64.95 (*0-471-59256-0*) Wiley.
Plante, Alan R. Western Massachusetts Mineral Localities. (Illus.). 150p. (Orig.). 1992. pap. 11.50 (*0-9616520-2-0*) Val Geol Pubns.
Plante, David. The Accident. 160p. 1991. 18.95 (*0-395-56925-7*) HM.
— Annunciation. LC 93-44724. 1994. 21.95 (*0-395-68091-3*) Ticknor & Fields.
Plante, Edmund. Alone in the House. 176p. (Orig.). (J). (gr. 5). 1991. pap. 3.50 (*0-380-76424-5*, Flare) Avon.
— Garden of Evil. 368p. 1991. pap. 3.95 (*0-8439-2683-X*) Dorchester Pub Co.
— Last Date. 176p. (Orig.). (J). (gr. 5). 1993. pap. 3.50 (*0-380-77154-3*, Flare) Avon.
— Transformation. 352p. (Orig.). 1987. pap. 3.95 (*0-8439-2490-X*) Dorchester Pub Co.
— Trapped. 368p. (Orig.). 1989. pap. 3.95 (*0-8439-2877-8*) Dorchester Pub Co.
Plante, Elena, jt. auth. see Boone, Daniel R.
***Plante, Ellen M.** The History of the American Kitchen. LC 94-33235. 320p. 1995. 27.95 (*0-8160-3038-3*) Facts on File.
— Kitchen Collectibles: An Illustrated Price Guide. LC 91-2104. 176p. 1991. pap. 14.95 (*0-87069-581-9*) Chilton.
Plante, Ellen M. & Plante, Ted. Country Furniture: A Walker-Homestead Price Guide. LC 92-32289. (Illus.). 160p. 1993. pap. 14.95 (*0-87069-640-8*, Wallace-Hmestead) Chilton.
Plante, Julian G. Austrian Monasteries, Part 1: Gottweig, Heiligenkreuz, Herzogenburg,...Seitenstetten, & Wilhering. (Checklists of Manuscripts Microfilmed for the Hill Monastic Manuscript Library Ser.: Vol. I). iv, 52p. (Orig.). 1967. pap. 10.00 (*0-940250-26-8*) Hill Monastic.
— Austrian Monasteries, Part 2: Admont, Altenburg,..." Osterreichische Nationalbibliothek, Universitatsbibliothek, Wilten, Zwettl. (Checklists of Manuscripts Microfilmed for the Hill Monastic Manuscript Library Ser.: Vol. I). viii, 296p. 1974. pap. 20.00 (*0-940250-27-6*) Hill Monastic.
— Spain, Pt. 1. (Checklists of Manuscripts Microfilmed for the Hill Monastic Manuscript Library Ser.: Vol. II). vi, 295p. (Orig.). 1978. pap. 15.75 (*0-8357-0366-5*) Hill Monastic.
Plante, Julian G., ed. Translatio Studii: Manuscript & Library Studies Honoring Oliver L. Kapsner, OSB. LC 73-76553. xii, 288p. (GER & SPA.). 1972. 20.00 (*0-940250-75-6*) Hill Monastic.
Plante, Michael, jt. auth. see McDonnell, Patricia.
Plante, Patricia R. Art of Decision Making: Issues & Cases in Higher Education. (ACE-Oryx Series on Higher Education). 224p. 1987. 27.95 (*0-02-924550-8*, ACE-Oryx) Oryx Pr.
Plante, Patricia R. & Caret, Robert L. Myths & Realities of Academic Administration. (ACE-Oryx Series on Higher Education). 160p. 1990. 27.95 (*0-02-897335-6*, ACE-Oryx) Oryx Pr.
Plante, Pele. Dirty Money: A Cynthia Chenery Scott Suspense Novel. 169p. (Orig.). 1993. pap. 10.95 (*1-878533-04-5*) Clothespin Fever Pr.
— Getting Away with Murder. 189p. (Orig.). 1991. pap. 9.95 (*1-878533-00-2*) Clothespin Fever Pr.
Plante, R. J. Arabic Coins & How to Read Them. (Illus.). 1981. pap. 20.00 (*0-686-45249-6*, Pub. by Seaby UK) S J Durst.
Plante, Ted, jt. auth. see Plante, Ellen M.
Plantigna, Theodore. How Memory Shapes Narratives: A Philosophical Essay on Redeeming the Past. LC 92-24382. 200p. 1992. text ed. 79.95 (*0-7734-9575-4*) E Mellen.
Plantin, Amy & Kurisaki, Yoshiko. Information Technology Outlook, 1992. 48p. (Orig.). 1992. pap. text ed. 30.00 (*92-64-03527-3*, 93-92-01-3) OECD.
Planting, Scott, jt. auth. see Pappas, Anthony.
Plantinga, Alvin. Does God Have a Nature? LC 80-6585. (Aquinas Lectures). 1980. pap. 10.00 (*0-87462-145-3*) Marquette.
— God & Other Minds: A Study of the Rational Justification of Belief in God. 288p. 1990. pap. 13.95 (*0-8014-9735-3*) Cornell U Pr.
— God, Freedom, & Evil. 1978. pap. 8.99 (*0-8028-1731-9*) Eerdmans.
— The Nature of Necessity. (Clarendon Library of Logic & Philosophy). 268p. 1979. pap. 21.00 (*0-19-824414-2*) OUP.
— Warrant: The Current Debate. LC 92-13183. 256p. 1993. 45.00 (*0-19-507861-6*); pap. 19.95 (*0-19-507862-4*) OUP.
— Warrant & Proper Function. LC 92-408. 272p. 1993. pap. 19.95 (*0-685-56686-2*) OUP.
— Warrant & Proper Function. LC 92-408. 272p. 1993. 45.00 (*0-19-507863-2*) OUP.
Plantinga, Alvin & Wolterstorff, Nicholas, eds. Faith & Rationality: Reason & Belief in God. LC 83-14843. 336p. (C). 1984. pap. text ed. 14.95 (*0-268-00965-1*) U of Notre Dame Pr.
Plantinga, Conelius, Jr., jt. ed. see Long, Thomas G.
Plantinga, Cornelius, Jr. Assurances of the Heart: Faith-Building Devotions on Questions Christians Ask. 304p. 1993. reprint ed. pap. 12.99 (*0-310-38641-1*) Zondervan.
— Beyond Doubt: A Devotional Response to Questions of Faith. LC 80-10647. (Illus.). 256p. (Orig.). 1980. pap. text ed. 11.95 (*0-933140-12-6*); teacher ed, pap. text ed. 8.50 (*0-933140-61-4*) CRC Pubns.
— Not the Way It's Supposed to Be: A Breviary of Sin. LC 94-23308. 202p. 1995. 19.99 (*0-8028-3716-6*) Eerdmans.
— A Place to Stand: A Reformed Study of Creeds & Confessions. LC 79-371. (Illus.). 1979. teacher ed 32.95 (*0-685-41992-4*); teacher ed 9.45 (*0-685-41993-2*); pap. text ed. 11.50 (*0-933140-01-0*) CRC Pubns.
— A Sure Thing. LC 86-8280. (Illus.). 300p. (J). (gr. 8-10). 1986. teacher ed 11.95 (*0-930265-28-9*); text ed. 14.95 (*0-930265-27-0*) CRC Pubns.
Plantinga, Cornelius, Jr., jt. auth. see Feenstra, Ronald.
Plantinga, Leon. Clementi: His Life & Music. LC 84-1797. (Music Reprint Ser.). 360p. 1985. reprint ed. lib. bdg. 42.50 (*0-306-76198-X*) Da Capo.
— Romantic Music. LC 83-42653. (Introduction to Music History Ser.). (Illus.). (C). 1985. pap. text ed. 29.95 (*0-393-95196-0*) Norton.
Plantinga, Leon, ed. Anthology of Romantic Music. LC 83-42652. (Introduction to Music History Ser.). (Illus.). 1985. 25.95 (*0-393-01811-3*) Norton.

P
Q

An Asterisk (*) at the beginning of an entry indicates that the title is appearing in BIP for the first time.

— Anthology of Romantic Music. LC 83-42652. (Introduction to Music History Ser.). (Illus.). (C). 1985. pap. text ed. 21.95 (*0-393-95211-8*) Norton.

Plantinga, Leon B. Schumann As Critic. LC 76-7599. (Music Reprint Ser.). 1976. reprint ed. 42.50 (*0-306-70785-3*) Da Capo.

Plantinga, Theodore. Historical Understanding in the Thought of Wilhelm Dilthey. LC 92-45581. (Studies in the History of Philosophy: Vol. 31). 216p. 1993. text ed. 89.95 (*0-7734-9240-2*) E Mellen.

— Historical Understanding in the Thought of Wilhelm Dilthey. LC 79-19240. 215p. reprint ed. pap. 61.30 (*0-8357-6401-X*, 2035759) Bks Demand.

— Learning to Live with Evil. LC 81-22041. 163p. reprint ed. pap. 46.50 (*0-317-30157-8*, 2025339) Bks Demand.

— Public Knowledge & Christian Education. LC 87-35552. (Studies in Religious Education: Vol. 1). 136p. 1988. 69. 95 (*0-88946-477-4*) E Mellen.

— Reading the Bible As History. 110p. (Orig.). 1980. pap. 4.25 (*0-919532-58-6*) Dordt Coll Pr.

— Wait for the Lord: Meditations on the Christian Life. 137p. (Orig.). 1981. pap. 5.75 (*0-932914-12-8*) Dordt Coll Pr.

Plantinga, Theodore, tr. see Boer, Theodore De.

Plantinga, Theodore, tr. see Wagner, Gerrit A.

Plantos, T. Heather Hits Her First Home Run. (Illus.). 24p. (J). (ps-8). 1989. pap. 4.95 (*0-88753-185-7*, Pub. by Black Moss Pr CN) Firefly Bks Ltd.

Plants, Forrest M. A Loving Community. (Eagle Bible Ser.). 1989. pap. 2.50 (*0-87162-551-2*, D9153) Warner Pr.

Plants, Raymond. Ciclo Villa. (Coleccion Rosa Ser.). (Illus.). 60p. (SPA.). (J). (gr. 5 up). 1994. pap. 5.95 (*958-07-0067-2*) Firefly Bks Ltd.

Plants, W. E. The Guyette Story: In Defense of Innocence. 300p. 1995. 29.95 (*1-887297-95-2*) Last Chnce Pub. THE GUYETTE STORY was written to prove the innocence of a young couple who on March 12, 1966 were washing windows at the Carlin Coffee Shop in the early afternoon. While they were thus engaged, a dual murder took place 197 miles away from the Carlin Coffee Shop. Harold Guyette was nineteen years old on Dec. 13, 1966 when the State of Nevada convicted him & sentenced him to prison for life without the possibility of parole for a murder that he could not have committed. The conviction was in 1966 & the first edition of this book was in 1970. By 1972, the book was in the third edition. Each edition has added new evidence of the innocence of Harold Guyette. Knowing as this writer did that Harold was innocent before the murder trial began, it was heart rending to witness how an innocent person can be convicted. This Book reveals the suppressed evidence that would have prevented any jury from finding him guilty. This new edition in 1995 gives an update to show the continuing struggle of Guyette to prove his innocence. Order from "A Last Chance Publisher", P.O. Box 279, Pleasant Garden, NC 27313, Tel. 800-990-9502.** ***Publisher Provided Annotation.

Plantu. Ouverture en Bemol. 174p. (FRE.). 1991. pap. 15.95 (*0-7859-4365-X*, 2070383857) Fr & Eur.

Planty-Bonjour, G. Les Categories du Materialisme Dialectique: L'Ontologie Sovietique Contemporaine. (Sovietica Ser.: No. 21). 206p. (FRE.). 1965. lib. bdg. 45. 50 (*90-277-0063-X*) Kluwer Ac.

— The Categories of Dialectical Materialism: Contemporary Soviet Ontology. (Sovietica Ser.: No. 24). 182p. 1967. lib. bdg. 42.50 (*90-277-0064-8*) Kluwer Ac.

Planty, Earl & Mellone, Michael. Planty's Encyclopedia of Cacheted F. D. C.'s, 10 vols, Set. (Illus.). 1979. pap. 99. 98 (*0-89794-008-3*) FDC Pub.

— Planty's Encyclopedia of Cacheted F. D. C.'s, Vol. 3. (Illus.). 1978. pap. 8.95 (*0-89794-011-3*) FDC Pub.

— Planty's Encyclopedia of Cacheted F. D. C.'s, Vol. 4. (Illus.). 1978. pap. 9.95 (*0-89794-012-1*) FDC Pub.

— Planty's Encyclopedia of Cacheted F. D. C.'s, Vol. 5. (Illus.). 1978. pap. 9.95 (*0-89794-013-X*) FDC Pub.

— Planty's Encyclopedia of Cacheted F. D. C.'s, Vol. 6. (Illus.). 1978. pap. 9.95 (*0-89794-014-8*) FDC Pub.

— Planty's Encyclopedia of Cacheted F. D. C.'s, Vol. 7. (Illus.). 1979. pap. 9.95 (*0-89794-015-6*) FDC Pub.

— Planty's Encyclopedia of Cacheted F. D. C.'s, Vol. 8. (Illus.). 1979. pap. 9.95 (*0-89794-016-4*) FDC Pub.

— Planty's Encyclopedia of Cacheted F. D. C.'s: 1923-28, Vol. 1. (Illus.). 1977. pap. 9.95 (*0-89794-009-1*) FDC Pub.

— Planty's Encyclopedia of Cacheted F. D. C.'s: 1928-1929, Vol. 2. (Illus.). 1977. pap. 9.95 (*0-89794-010-5*) FDC Pub.

— Planty's Encyclopedia of Cacheted F. D. C.'s, Vol. 10. (Illus.). 1978. pap. 9.95 (*0-317-16574-7*) FDC Pub.

— Planty's Encyclopedia of Cacheted F. D. C.'s, Vol. 9. (Illus.). 1978. pap. 9.95 (*0-317-16573-9*) FDC Pub.

Plantz, Scott H., jt. auth. see Cole, Jesse A.

Plantz, Scott H., et al. Getting into Medical School: Strategies for the Nineties. 2nd ed. 160p. 1993. pap. 12. 00 (*0-671-84685-X*, Arco Test) P-H Gen Ref & Trav.

— Getting into Medical School: Strategies for the 90s. 2nd ed. LC 92-18926. 1992. 12.00 (*0-13-355173-3*) P-H Gen Ref & Trav.

Planz, Allen, ed. see Moran, Daniel T.

Plarr, Victor. In the Dorian Mood, 1896. LC 93-41355. (Decadents, Symbolists, Anti-Decadents Ser.). 1994. 43. 00 (*1-85477-154-X*, Pub. by Woodstock Bks UK) Cassell.

Plas, Jeanne M., jt. auth. see Arnold, William W.

Plasa, Carl & Ring, Betty J., eds. The Discourse of Slavery: Aphra Behn to Toni Morrison. LC 93-27522. 1994. write for info. (*0-415-08151-3*, Routledge NY); pap. write for info. (*0-415-08152-1*, Routledge NY) Routledge.

Plaschke, Bill, jt. auth. see Knox, Chuck.

Plaschke, Bill, jt. auth. see Williams, Dick.

Plascik, Chester. Applied Calculus for Business & the Social & Natural Sciences. Pullins, ed. 604p. (C). 1992. text ed. 63.25 (*0-314-91851-5*) West Pub.

Plascott, Roy. Kent Rambles. 64p. 1987. 30.00 (*0-905392-76-0*) St Mut.

Plascov, Avi. Palestinian Refugees in Jordan, 1948-57. (Illus.). 286p. 1981. 45.00 (*0-7146-3120-5*, Pub. by F Cass Pubs UK) Intl Spec Bk.

Plascov, Avi, ed. Modernization, Political Development & Stability. LC 80-28387. (Security in the Persian Gulf Ser.: Vol. 3). 192p. 1982. pap. text ed. 19.50 (*0-86598-046-2*) Rowman.

Plasencia, Jorge R. Pinceladas Criollas. LC 87-83348. (Coleccion Caniqui Ser.). 88p. (Orig.). (SPA.). 1988. pap. 9.95 (*0-89729-472-6*) Ediciones.

Plasil, Ellen. Therapist. 1988. pap. 3.95 (*0-317-65539-6*) St Martin.

***Plasker, James R., ed.** U. S. National Report to FIG, 1990. (Surveying & Land Information Systems Journal Ser.: Vol. 50, No. 2). 124p. 1990. 20.00 (*0-614-06107-5*, SM502) Am Congrs Survey.

Plasketes, George, jt. auth. see Denisoff, R. Serge.

Plaskin, Glenn. The Turning Point: Pivotal Moments in the Lives of Celebrities. (Illus.). 208p. 1992. 18.95 (*1-55972-138-3*, Birch Ln Pr) Carol Pub Group.

Plaskow, Judith. Sex, Sin & Grace: Women's Experience & the Theologies of Reinhold Niebuhr & Paul Tillich. LC 79-5434. 1980. pap. text ed. 21.00 (*0-8191-0882-0*) U Pr of Amer.

— Standing Again at Sinai: Judaism from a Feminist Perspective. 1990. 21.95 (*0-685-31438-3*) Harper SF.

— Standing Again at Sinai: Judaism from a Feminist Perspective. LC 89-45559. 272p. 1991. reprint ed. pap. 15.00 (*0-06-066684-6*) Harper SF.

— Women & Judaism: Judaism From a Feminist Perspective. 1991. pap. 12.95 (*0-00-003404-5*) Harper SF.

— Women & Religion. Arnold, Joan & Romero, Joan A., eds. LC 74-83126. (American Academy of Religion. Aids for the Study of Religion Ser.). 216p. reprint ed. 61.60 (*0-8357-9581-0*, 2017557) Bks Demand.

Plaskow, Judith & Christ, Carol P., eds. Weaving the Visions: New Patterns in Feminist Spirituality. 352p. 1989. pap. 15.00 (*0-06-061383-1*) Harper SF.

Plaskow, Judith, jt. auth. see Christ, Carol P.

***Plaskowski, A.** Imaging Industrial Flows: Applications of Electrical Process Tomography. LC 95-3373. 1995. write for info. (*0-7503-0296-8*) IOP Pub.

Plaskowski, A., jt. auth. see Beck, M. S.

Plasmans, Joseph E., ed. Econometric Modelling in Theory & Practice. 225p. 1982. lib. bdg. 103.00 (*90-247-2553-4*) Kluwer Ac.

Plasmeijer, Rinus & Van Eekelen, Marko. Functional Programming & Parallel Graph Rewriting. LC 93-19724. (C). 1993. text ed. 49.50 (*0-201-41663-8*) Addison-Wesley.

Plass, Ewald. This Is Luther. 1984. pap. 4.95 (*0-570-03942-8*, 12-2875) Concordia.

— What Luther Says: A Practical-in-Home Anthology for the Active Christian. 1696p. 1987. 37.95 (*0-570-04240-2*, 15-1232) Concordia.

Plass, Harold J., Jr., jt. auth. see Cochin, Ira.

***Plass, Paul.** The Game of Death in Ancient Rome: Arena Sport & Political Suicide. LC 94-40884. (Studies in Classics). 296p. (C). 1995. lib. bdg. 48.75 (*0-299-14570-0*) U of Wis Pr.

— Wit & the Writing of History: The Rhetoric of Historiography in Imperial Rome. LC 88-40193. 204p. (Orig.). (C). 1988. pap. text ed. 17.50 (*0-299-11804-5*) U of Wis Pr.

Plass, Richard M., ed. see Kranepool, Harry A.

Plass, Richard M., jt. auth. see Reep, Marianna L.

***Plassard, Marie-France, ed.** Guidelines for Subject Authority & Reference Entries. (UBCIM Publications). 65p. 1993. 35.00 (*3-598-11180-0*) K G Saur.

— ISBD (PM) International Standard Bibliographic Description for Printed Music. 2nd rev. ed. (UBCIM Publications). 73p. 1991. lib. bdg. 36.00 (*3-598-10985-7*) K G Saur.

— Minimal Level Cataloguing by National Bibliographic Agencies. 73p. 1992. 50.00 (*3-598-11102-9*) K G Saur.

— Seminar on Bibliographic Records. 147p. 1992. 55.00 (*3-598-11085-5*) K G Saur.

— UNIMARC & CDS/ISIS. (UBCIM Publications). 92p. 1994. 35.00 (*3-598-11210-6*) K G Saur.

— UNIMARC Manual: Bibliographic Format. (UBCIM Publications). 100p. 1994. 35.00 (*3-598-11211-4*) K G Saur.

***Plassard, Marie-France & Brooking, Diana M., eds.** UNIMARC/CCF: Proceedings of the Workshop Held in Florence, 5-7 June 1991. (UBCIM Publications). 150p. 1993. 60.00 (*3-598-11140-1*) K G Saur.

Plassmann, R., ed. Factitious Disease. (Journal Psychotherapy & Psychosomatics Ser.: Vol. 62, Nos. 1-2, 1994). (Illus.). 140p. 1994. pap. 80.00 (*3-8055-6013-3*) S Karger.

Plassmann, Thomas. The Upper Room: Retreat Readings for Priests. (Spirit & Life Ser.). 1954. 4.50 (*0-686-11565-1*) Franciscan Inst.

Plaster, David R. Ordinances: What Are They? 1985. pap. 7.99 (*0-88469-164-0*) BMH Bks.

Plaster, Edward. Soils: Science & Management. LC 85-4486. 352p. (C). 1985. teacher ed 8.00 (*0-8273-2407-3*); text ed. 39.95 (*0-8273-2406-5*) Delmar.

Plaster, Edward J. Soil Science & Management. 2nd ed. 1991. teacher ed 10.00 (*0-8273-4051-6*); text ed. 39.95 (*0-8273-4050-8*) Delmar.

Plaster, H. J. Blast Cleaning & Allied Processes, 2 vols., Set. 826p. (C). 1989. 370.00 (*0-901994-03-0*, Pub. by Fuel Metallurgical Jrnl UK) St Mut.

Plaster, John L. Ultimate Sniper. (Illus.). 464p. 1993. pap. 39.95 (*0-87364-704-1*) Paladin Pr.

Plasterer, Nicholas N. Assignment Jonesville: A News Reporting Workbook. 2nd ed. xii, 210p. (C). 1971. pap. text ed. 12.95 (*0-8071-0037-4*) La State U Pr.

Plasterer, Nicholas N., jt. auth. see Bowers, David R.

Plastic Design Library Staff, jt. ed. see Woishnis, William A.

Plastic Surgery Educational Foundation Staff. Instructional Courses, Vol. 5. 177p. 1992. 89.00 (*0-8016-6840-9*) Mosby Yr Bk.

— Instructional Courses, Vol. 3: 1990. 308p. 1990. 89.00 (*0-8016-3936-0*) Mosby Yr Bk.

— PSEF Instructional Course Lecture. 4th ed. 304p. 1991. 89.00 (*0-8016-4114-4*) Mosby Yr Bk.

Plastics & Rubber Institute Staff, ed. Carbon Fibers: Technology Uses & Prospects. LC 86-5155. (Illus.). 217p. 1986. 36.00 (*0-8155-1079-9*) Noyes.

— Plastics & Polymer Processing Automation. LC 87-12401. (Illus.). 251p. 1988. 39.00 (*0-8155-1140-X*) Noyes.

Plastics & Rubbers Institute Staff, & the British Plastics Federation Staff, ed. Fillers. 200p. 1986. 68.00 (*0-444-01114-5*) Elsevier.

Plastics Committee D-20, ed. Bibliography on Size Exclusion Chromatography (Gel Permeation Chromatography) - AMD 40-S3. LC 85-6242. (Atomic & Molecular Data Series AMD-S3). 298p. 1985. pap. text ed. 29.00 (*0-8031-0439-1*, PCN10-040030-39) ASTM.

Plastics Design Library Staff. Chemical Compatability, 2 vols. 725p. 1990. Vol. I, 625p. write for info. (*1-884207-01-4*); Vol. ii, 100p. write for info. (*0-318-72167-8*) William Andrew.

— Chemical Compatability, 2 vols., Set. 725p. 1990. 285.00 (*1-884207-00-6*) William Andrew.

— Chemical Resistance Vol. 1: Thermoplastics. 2nd ed. (PDL Handbook Ser.). 1100p. 1994. lib. bdg. 285.00 (*1-884207-12-X*, 6531U) William Andrew.

— Chemical Resistance Vol. 2: Thermoplastic Elastomers, Thermosets & Rubbers. 2nd ed. (PDL Handbook Ser.). 977p. 1994. lib. bdg. 285.00 (*1-884207-13-8*, 6533U) William Andrew.

— Effect of Creep, 2 vols., Set. 525p. 1991. 285.00 (*1-884207-03-0*) William Andrew.

— Effect of Creep, Vol. I. 425p. 1991. write for info. (*1-884207-04-9*) William Andrew.

— Effect of Creep, Vol. II. 100p. 1991. write for info. (*1-884207-05-7*) William Andrew.

— The Effect of Sterilization on Plastics & Elastomers. (PDL Handbook Ser.). 476p. 1994. lib. bdg. 285.00 (*1-884207-10-3*) William Andrew.

— Effect of Temperature, 2 vols., Set. 480p. 1990. 285.00 (*1-884207-06-5*) William Andrew.

— Effect of Temperature, Vol. I. 380p. 1990. write for info. (*1-884207-07-3*) William Andrew.

— Effect of Temperature, Vol. II. 100p. 1990. write for info. (*1-884207-08-1*) William Andrew.

— The Effect of UV Light & Weather on Plastics & Elastomers. (PDL Handbook Ser.). 476p. 1994. lib. bdg. 285.00 (*1-884207-11-1*) William Andrew.

— Fatigue & Tribological Properties of Plastics & Elastomers. (PDL Handbook Ser.). 525p. 1994. lib. bdg. 285.00 (*1-884207-15-4*) William Andrew.

— Permeability & Other Film Properties of Plastics & Elastomers. (PDL Handbook Ser.). 726p. 1994. lib. bdg. 285.00 (*1-884207-14-6*) William Andrew.

Plastics Education Foundation Staff. Curriculum Guide for Plastics Education. LC 77-4080. 1977. pap. write for info. (*0-672-97113-5*) Macmillan.

Plastics Institute of America Staff. FoodPlas VIII-91: Proceedings of the Annual FoodPlas Conference, 8th. 1991. pap. 49.00 (*0-87762-866-1*) Technomic.

Plastino, Janice G., jt. auth. see Penrod, James.

Plastock, R. A. & Kalley, G. Schaum's Outline of Computer Graphics. (Schaum's Outline Ser.). 352p. 1986. pap. text ed. 12.95 (*0-07-050326-5*) McGraw.

Plastow, John R. Football, Pizza & Success! 130p. (Orig.). (J). (gr. 7-12). 1987. pap. 5.95 (*0-937382-03-5*) Rhinos Pr.

Plastow, Michael. Exploring Kiryu, Ashio, & Nikko: Mountain Walks in the Land of Shodo Shonin. (Exploring Japan Ser.). (Illus.). 272p. (Orig.). (C). 1992. pap. 19.95 (*0-8348-0242-2*) Weatherhill.

Plastrik, Peter, jt. auth. see Sykes, Gary.

Plat, Hugh. Floures of Philosophie. LC 81-21324. 1982. reprint ed. 50.00 (*0-8201-1374-3*) Schol Facsimiles.

***Plat, R.** Gravitational & Centrifugal Oil-Water Separators with Plate Pack Internals. 172p. (Orig.). 1994. pap. 52. 50x (*90-6275-985-8*, Pub. by Delft U Pr NE) Coronet Bks.

Plata, Maximino. Assessment, Placement, & Programming of Bilingual Exceptional Pupils: A Practical Approach. 54p. 1982. pap. 9.10 (*0-86586-136-6*, R259) Coun Exc Child.

Plata, Maximino, jt. auth. see Elliot, Norbert.

Plata, Sababu, ed. see Wilson, Ames N.

Plata, Sababu N., jt. auth. see Wilson, Amos N.

Plata, Sababy, ed. see Spencer-Strachan, Louise.

Platanora, T. A. & Goltrovsa, V. V. Nemotodes & Their Role in the Meiobenthos. (C). 1985. 25.00 (*0-8364-2115-9*, Pub. by Oxford IBH II) S Asia.

Platanov, K. K. Concise Dictionary of the System of Psychological Understanding. 2nd ed. 174p. (RUS.). 1984. 12.95 (*0-8288-2212-3*, M15380) Fr & Eur.

Plate, Erich J. Aerodynamic Characteristics of Atmospheric Boundary Layers. LC 70-611329. (AEC Critical Review Ser.). 190p. 1971. pap. 12.75 (*0-87079-132-X*, TID-25465); fiche 9.00 (*0-87079-133-8*, TID-25465) DOE.

Plate, Erich J., ed. Engineering Meteorology. (Studies in Wind Engineering & Industrial Aerodynamics: Vol. 1). 740p. 1982. 207.75 (*0-444-41972-1*, I-272-82) Elsevier.

Plate, Erich J., jt. ed. see Duckstein, Lucien.

Plate, Kenneth H. Management Personnel in Libraries. 1970. 7.95 (*0-685-03095-4*) Am Faculty Pr.

Plate, N. A., ed. Liquid-Crystal Polymers. Schnur, S. L., tr. (Specialty Polymers Ser.). (Illus.). 426p. (C). 1992. 110. 00 (*0-306-44219-1*, Plenum Pr) Plenum.

Plate, N. A. & Shibaev, V. P. Comb-Shaped Polymers & Liquid Crystals. Cowie, J. M., ed. Schnur, S. L., tr. LC 87-18518. (Specialty Polymers Ser.). (Illus.). 428p. 1987. 115.00 (*0-306-42723-0*, Plenum Pr) Plenum.

***Plate, Nicolai A., et al.** Macromolecular Reactions: Pecularities, Theory & Experimental Approach. LC 94-30634. 1995. text ed. 148.00 (*0-471-94392-4*) Wiley.

***Plate, Peter.** Joaquin (in the Fog) (Autofiction Ser.). 70p. (Orig.). (C). 1988. pap. 7.00 (*1-878124-01-3*) Flatland.

— A Kamakaze in Her Eyes. 288p. (Orig.). 1994. pap. 10.00 (*0-9627091-4-X*) Pressure Drop.

— One Foot off the Guitar. 200p. (Orig.). 1995. pap. 13.00x (*1-884615-11-2*, Incommunicado) Rockpress Pub.

Plateaux, L., jt. auth. see Montenat, C.

Platek, R., et al, eds. Small Area Statistics: An International Symposium. 294p. (C). 1987. lib. bdg. 47.95 (*0-471-84456-X*) Krieger.

Platen, E., jt. auth. see Kloeden, P. E.

Plater, Alan. The Beiderbecke Connection. 2nd large type ed. 273p. 1993. 22.95 (*1-85695-360-2*, Pub. by ISIS UK) Transaction Pubs.

***Plater, David D.** The Remarkably Neat Church in the Village of Thibodaux: An Antebellum History of St. John's Episcopal Church. (Illus.). 109p. (Orig.). Date not set. pap. 10.00 (*0-940984-90-3*) U of SW LA Ctr LA Studies.

Plater, J., jt. auth. see Kimbell, R.

Plater, Ormonde. Deacons in the Liturgy. LC 91-39693. 79p. (Orig.). 1992. pap. 8.95 (*0-8192-1585-6*) Morehouse Pub.

— Intercession: A Practical & Theological Guide. xx, 138p. 1995. pap. 11.95 (*1-56101-115-0*) Cowley Pubns.

— Many Servants: An Introduction to Deacons. LC 91-622. 215p. (Orig.). 1991. pap. 13.95 (*1-56101-043-X*) Cowley Pubns.

Plater, William M. The Grim Phoenix: Reconstructing Thomas Pynchon. LC 77-12833. 285p. reprint ed. pap. 82.10 (*0-685-23895-4*, 2056715) Bks Demand.

Plater, Zygmunt J. & Abrams, Robert H. Environmental Law & Policy: Nature, Law & Society As a First Course, Supplementary Manual for Teaching. Goldfarb, William, ed. (American Casebook Ser.). 247p. 1992. reprint ed. pap. text ed. write for info. (*0-314-01382-2*) West Pub.

Plater, Zygmunt J., et al. Environmental Law & Policy: A Coursebook on Nature, Law & Society, Cases, Materials & Text. (American Casebook Ser.). 1039p. 1993. reprint ed. text ed. 49.50 (*0-314-00341-X*) West Pub.

— Environmental Law & Policy: Nature, Law & Society, Teacher's Manual to Accompany. (American Casebook Ser.). 353p. (C). 1992. pap. text ed. write for info. (*0-314-00583-8*) West Pub.

— Environmental Law & Policy: Nature, Law, & Society, 1994. suppl. ed. (American Casebook Ser.). 420p. (C). 1994. pap. text ed. 16.50 (*0-314-04693-3*) West Pub.

Platero, Elaine. Lessons & Lovers. (Orig.). 1994. pap. 4.95 (*1-56333-196-9*) Masquerade.

Plath, jt. auth. see Krueger.

Plath, David W. The After Hours: Modern Japan & the Search for Enjoyment. LC 83-22869. xi, 222p. 1984. reprint ed. text ed. 55.00 (*0-313-24297-6*, PLAF, Greenwood Pr) Greenwood.

— Long Engagements: Maturity in Modern Japan. 248p. 1980. 32.50 (*0-8047-1054-6*); pap. 11.95 (*0-8047-1176-3*) Stanford U Pr.

Plath, David W., et al, eds. Work & Lifecourse in Japan. LC 82-10481. (Illus.). 267p. 1984. 64.50 (*0-87395-704-0*); pap. 21.95 (*0-87395-705-9*) State U NY Pr.

Plath, Iona. Decorative Arts of Sweden. (Illus.). 1965. pap. 9.95 (*0-486-21478-8*) Dover.

— Decorative Arts of Sweden. (Illus.). 15.25 (*0-8446-2745-3*) Peter Smith.

— The Handweaver's Pattern Book: Over One Hundred-Twenty Upholster, Curtains, Place Mats, Etc. Orig. Title: The Craft of Handweaving. (Illus.). 128p. 1981. reprint ed. pap. 5.95 (*0-486-24166-1*) Dover.

— The Handweaver's Pattern Book: Over 120 Designs for Upholstery, Curtains, Place Mats, Etc. (Illus.). 16.50 (*0-8446-5909-6*) Peter Smith.

Plath, James, ed. Conversations with John Updike. (Literary Conversations Ser.). 308p. 1994. 37.50 (*0-87805-699-8*); pap. 15.95 (*0-87805-700-5*) U Pr of Miss.

Plath, Sylvia. Ariel. LC 66-15738. 1981. pap. 10.00 (*0-06-090890-4*, CN890, PL) HarpC.

— Ariel: Poems. 94p. 1991. reprint ed. lib. bdg. 25.00x (0-8095-9056-5) Borgo Pr.
— The Bell Jar. 224p. 1983. mass mkt. 5.99 (0-553-27835-5, Bantam Classics) Bantam.
— The Bell Jar. 300p. 1991. reprint ed. lib. bdg. 25.95 (0-89966-815-1) Buccaneer Bks.
— Collected Poems. LC 75-25075. 288p. 1981. pap. 17.00 (0-06-090900-5, CN 900, PL) HarpC.
— The Colossus. 1991. reprint ed. lib. bdg. 21.95 (1-56849-040-2) Buccaneer Bks.
— Colossus & Other Poems. 96p. 1968. pap. 7.00 (0-394-70466-5, Vin) Random.
— Crossing the Water. LC 71-138756. 1980. pap. 9.00 (0-06-090789-4, CN 789, PL) HarpC.
— Crossing the Water. 62p. 1991. reprint ed. lib. bdg. 25.00x (0-8095-9058-1) Borgo Pr.
— Johnny Panic & the Bible of Dreams. 1994. lib. bdg. 24.95x (1-56849-385-1) Buccaneer Bks.
— Letters Home: Correspondence 1950-1963. LC 91-58567. (Illus.). 512p. 1992. reprint ed. pap. 15.00 (0-06-097491-5, PL) HarpC.
— Sylvia Plath: Collected Poems. Hughes, Ted, ed. 350p. 1991. reprint ed. lib. bdg. 39.00x (0-8095-9057-3) Borgo Pr.

Plath, Tony, jt. ed. see Nunnally, Ben.

Platis, Kerri, jt. ed. see Collinson, Michael P.

Platizky, Roger S. A Blueprint of His Dissent: Madness & Method in Tennyson's Poetry. LC 87-46433. 144p. 1989. 28.50 (0-8387-5151-2) Bucknell U Pr.

Platko, Elizabeth, jt. auth. see Starbuck, Marjorie.

Platnauer, M., ed. see Euripides.

Platnick, A. Joseph. Index to the Code of Jewish Law. 233p. 1989. text ed. 19.95 (0-9626361-0-X) A J Platnick.

Platnick, Kenneth. Great Mysteries of History. 1987. 17.95 (0-88029-157-5) Dorset Pr.

Platnick, Norman, jt. auth. see Nelson, Gareth.

Platnick, Norman I. Advances in Spider Taxonomy 1988-1991: With Synonymies & Transfers 1940-1980. Merrett, P., ed. 864p. 1993. text ed. 75.00 (0-913424-10-2) Am Mus Natl Hist.

Platnick, Norman I. & Funk, Vicki A., eds. Advances in Cladistics: Proceedings of the Second Meeting of the Willi Hennig Society, Vol. 2. 288p. 1983. text ed. 55.00 (0-231-05646-X) Col U Pr.

Platnick, Norman I., jt. auth. see Nelson, Gareth.

Plato. Anonymer Kommentar Zu Platons Theaetet. xxxvii, 62p. (GER.). 1905. write for info. (0-318-70540-0, Pub. by Georg Olms GW) Lubrecht & Cramer.
— The Apologia of Plato. Riddell, James, ed. 244p. (GER.). 1974. reprint ed. 50.70 (3-487-05225-3, Pub. by Georg Olms GW) Lubrecht & Cramer.
— Apology. Stokes, ed. (Classical Texts Ser.). 1992. write for info. (0-85668-371-X, Pub. by Aris & Phillips UK); pap. write for info. (0-85668-372-8, Pub. by Aris & Phillips UK) David Brown.
— The Apology of Plato. LC 72-9300. (Philosophy of Plato & Aristotle Ser.). (ENG & GRE.). 1977. reprint ed. 19.95 (0-405-04855-6) Ayer.
— The Apology of Socrates & Crito. rev. ed. Ash, A. S., ed. Jowett, Benjamin, tr. LC 86-64057. (Humanist Classics Ser.). 48p. 1990. pap. 4.00 (0-942208-05-6) Bandanna Bks.
— Apology of Socrates & Crito. Dyer, Louis, ed. (College Classical Ser.). 246p. (C). 1992. reprint ed. lib. bdg. 32.50 (0-89241-000-0); reprint ed. pap. 17.50 (0-89241-345-X) Caratzas.
— Charmides. West, Thomas G. & West, Grace S., eds. West, Grace S., tr. LC 85-24934. (HPC Classics Ser.). 60p. (Orig.). (C). 1986. lib. bdg. 19.50 (0-87220-011-6); pap. 3.95 (0-87220-010-8) Hackett Pub.
— Charmides, Alcibiades First & Second, Hipparchus, the Lovers, Theages, Minos, Epinomis, Vol. XII. (Loeb Classical Library: No. 201). 512p. 1927. text ed. 18.95 (0-674-99221-0) HUP.
— The Complete Works of Plato. 1995. 19.00 (0-679-60164-3) Random.
— Concordantiae in Platonis Opera Omnia. Siviero, Mauro, ed. Bd. CX. (GER.). Date not set. write for info. (0-318-70541-9, Pub. by Georg Olms GW) Lubrecht & Cramer.
— Cratylus, Parmenides, Greater Hippias, Lesser Hippias, Vol. IV. (Loeb Classical Library: No. 167). 488p. 1926. text ed. 18.95 (0-674-99185-0) HUP.
— Dialogue of the Immortality of the Soul. LC 73-161797. (Augustan Translators Ser.). reprint ed. 49.50 (0-404-54134-8) AMS Pr.
— Dialogues, 2 vols., I. Jowett, Benjamin E., tr. 1937. 25.00 (0-394-42004-7) Random.
— The Dialogues of Plato. 400p. 1986. 5.95 (0-553-21371-7, Bantam Classics) Bantam.
— Dialogues of Plato. Kaplan, Justin E., ed. Jowett, Benjamin E., tr. 400p. (C). 1984. mass mkt. 5.99 (0-671-52524-7, WSP) PB.
— Early Socratic Dialogues. Sauders, Trevor J., ed. & intro. by. 352p. 1987. mass mkt. 9.95 (0-14-044447-5, Penguin Classics) Viking Penguin.
— Euthryphro. Burnet, John, ed. Bd. with Apology of Socrates.; Crito. 1977. 19.95 (0-19-814015-0) OUP.
— The Euthryphro, Apology, Crito, & Phaedo. Jowett, Benjamin, tr. (Great Books in Philosophy). 138p. (C). 1988. pap. text ed. 5.95 (0-87975-496-6) Prometheus Bks.
— Euthydemus. Sprague, Rosamond K., tr. LC 65-26539. (Orig.). 1965. pap. 2.30 (0-672-60478-7, LLA222, Bobbs) Macmillan.
— Euthydemus. Sprague, Rosamond K., tr. LC 93-14427. (Hackett Classics Ser.). 96p. (Orig.). (C). 1993. reprint ed. lib. bdg. 24.95 (0-87220-235-6); reprint ed. pap. text ed. 5.95 (0-87220-234-8) Hackett Pub.
— The Euthydemus of Plato. LC 72-9288. (Philosophy of Plato & Aristotle Ser.). (ENG & GRE.). 1977. reprint ed. 22.95 (0-405-04838-6) Ayer.
— Euthyphro, Apology & Crito. Stawell, Florence M., tr. LC 73-174210. (Temple Greek & Latin Classics: No. 2). reprint ed. 17.50 (0-404-07902-4) AMS Pr.
— Euthyphro, Apology, Crito, Phaedo, Phaedrus, Vol. I. (Loeb Classical Library: No. 36). 600p. 1914. text ed. 18.95 (0-674-99040-4) HUP.
— Euthyphro, Crito, Apology, & Symposium. LC 53-8797. 142p. 1953. reprint ed. pap. 9.95 (0-89526-916-3) Regnery Pub.
— Five Dialogues. Grube, G. M., tr. LC 81-82275. (HPC Classics Ser.). 168p. (C). 1981. text ed. 27.50 (0-915145-23-5); pap. 4.95 (0-915145-22-7) Hackett Pub.
— Gorgias. LC 93-48984. (World's Classics Ser.). 176p. 1994. pap. 5.95 (0-19-283165-8) OUP.
— Gorgias. Hamilton, Walter, tr. (Classics Ser.). 1960. mass mkt. 7.95 (0-14-044094-1, Penguin Classics) Viking Penguin.
— Gorgias. 416p. 1990. reprint ed. pap. 29.95 (0-19-814495-4) OUP.
— The Gorgias of Plato. LC 72-9308. (Philosophy of Plato & Aristotle Ser.). (ENG & GRE.). 1980. reprint ed. 28.95 (0-405-04867-X) Ayer.
— Hippias Major. LC 81-7027. (HPC Classics Ser.). 232p. (C). 1982. 27.95 (0-915145-25-1) Hackett Pub.
— The Hippias Major Attributed to Plato. LC 75-13284. (History of Ideas in Ancient Greece Ser.). (ENG & GRE.). 1978. reprint ed. 21.95 (0-405-07326-7) Ayer.
— Ion & Hippias Major: Two Comic Dialogues. Woodruff, Paul, tr. LC 83-269. (HPC Classics Ser.). 93p. (C). 1983. lib. bdg. 22.50 (0-915145-76-6); pap. text ed. 5.95 (0-915145-77-4) Hackett Pub.
— Laches & Charmides. Sprague, Rosamond K., tr. & intro. by. LC 92-6207. 112p. (C). 1992. reprint ed. lib. bdg. 24.95 (0-87220-135-X); reprint ed. pap. text ed. 5.95 (0-87220-134-1) Hackett Pub.
— Laches, Protagoras, Meno & Euthydemus, Vol. II. (Loeb Classical Library: No. 165). 530p. 1924. 18.95 (0-674-99183-4) HUP.
— The Last Days of Socrates: Euthyphro - The Apology - Crito - Phaedo. Tredennick, Hugh & Tarrant, Harold, trs. 256p. 1993. 8.95 (0-14-044582-X, Penguin Classics) Viking Penguin.
— Laws. Saunders, T. J., tr. (Classics Ser.). 1970. mass mkt. 8.95 (0-14-044222-7, Penguin Classics) Viking Penguin.
— Laws, 2 vols., 1. (Loeb Classical Library: No. 187, 192). 522p. 1926. text ed. 18.95 (0-674-99206-7) HUP.
— Laws, 2 vols., 2. (Loeb Classical Library: No. 187, 192). 590p. 1926. text ed. 18.95 (0-674-99211-3) HUP.
— The Laws of Plato. Pangle, Thomas L., tr. xiv, 562p. 1988. pap. text ed. 19.95 (0-226-67110-0) U Ch Pr.
— The Laws of Plato, 2 vols. LC 75-13285. (History of Ideas in Ancient Greece Ser.). 1979. reprint ed. 82.95 (0-405-07327-5) Ayer.
— Libro Llamadro Fedron. Diaz de Toledo, Pero, tr. (Serie B: Textos: No. 39). 408p. (SPA.). 1993. 71.00 (1-85566-024-5) Boydell & Brewer.
— Lysis, Symposium, Gorgias, Vol. III. (Loeb Classical Library: No. 166). 558p. 1925. text ed. 18.95 (0-674-99184-2) HUP.
— Meno. Sharples, R. W., ed. 49.00 (0-86516-089-9) Bolchazy-Carducci.
— Meno. Sharples, ed. (Classical Texts Ser.). 1985. 49.95 (0-85668-248-9, Pub. by Aris & Phillips UK); pap. 24.95 (0-85668-249-7, Pub. by Aris & Phillips UK) David Brown.
— Meno. 2nd ed. Grube, G. M., tr. LC 76-40412. (HPC Classics Ser.). 48p. (C). 1980. pap. 3.45 (0-915144-24-7) Hackett Pub.
— Meno: Text & Critical Essays. Brown, Malcolm, ed. Guthrie, William K., tr. LC 78-162302. (Text & Commentary Ser.). (C). 1971. pap. write for info. (0-672-61123-6, TC10, Bobbs) Macmillan.
— Oeuvres. (Vol. 1). (FRE.). 1940. lib. bdg. 95.00 (0-8288-3572-1, F17630) Fr & Eur.
— Oeuvres. (Vol. 2). (FRE.). 1977. lib. bdg. 110.00 (0-8288-3573-X, F17180) Fr & Eur.
— Oeuvres Completes: Theetete, Parmenide, Critias, Les Lois, etc., Vol. 2. 1676p. 42.95 (0-686-56549-5) Fr & Eur.
— Opera, 5 vols. Burnet, John, ed. Incl. Vol. 2. Parmenides, Philebus, Symposium, Phaedrus, Alcibiades 1 & 2, Hipparchus, Amatores. 2nd ed. 1922. 29.95 (0-19-814541-1); Vol. 3. Theages, Charmides, Laches, Lysis, Euthydemus, Protagoras, Gorgias, Meno, Hippias Maior, Hippas Minor, Io, Menexenus. 1922. 29.95 (0-19-814542-X); Vol. 4. Clitopho, Respublica, Timaeus, Critias. 1922. 29.95 (0-19-814544-6); Vol. 5. Minos, Leges, Epinomis, Epistulae, Definitiones. 1922. 47.00 (0-19-814546-2); write for info. (0-318-54865-8) OUP.
— Phaedo. Hackforth, R., ed. 200p. (C). 1972. pap. 14.95 (0-521-09702-9) Cambridge U Pr.
— Phaedo. Rowe, C. J., ed. LC 92-33958. (Greek & Latin Classics Ser.). 292p. (C). 1993. 64.95 (0-521-30796-1); pap. 22.95 (0-521-31318-X) Cambridge U Pr.
— Phaedo. Grube, G. M., tr. LC 76-49565. (HPC Classics Ser.). 72p. (C). 1980. pap. 3.45 (0-915144-18-2) Hackett Pub.
— Phaedo. Gallop, David, tr. & notes by. (Clarendon Plato Ser). 1977. pap. 24.95 (0-19-872049-1) OUP.
— Phaedo. Gallop, David, ed. & tr. by. LC 92-29711. (World's Classics Ser.). 136p. 1993. 5.95 (0-19-283090-2) OUP.
— The Phaedo of Plato. LC 72-9280. (Philosophy of Plato & Aristotle Ser.). 1977. reprint ed. 22.95 (0-405-04831-9) Ayer.
— Phaedrus. Hackforth, R., ed. 200p. (C). 1972. pap. 14.95 (0-521-09703-7) Cambridge U Pr.
— Phaedrus. Rowe, ed. (Classical Texts Ser.). 1986. 49.95 (0-85668-313-2, Pub. by Aris & Phillips UK); pap. 24.95 (0-85668-314-0, Pub. by Aris & Phillips UK) David Brown.
— Phaedrus & Letters VII & VIII. Hamilton, Walter, tr. (Classics Ser.). (Orig.). 1973. pap. 9.95 (0-14-044275-8, Penguin Classics) Viking Penguin.
— Philebus. Hackforth, R., ed. 200p. (C). 1972. pap. 14.95 (0-521-09704-5) Cambridge U Pr.
— Philebus. Frede, Dorothea, tr. & intro. by. LC 93-587. 150p. 1993. lib. bdg. 32.50 (0-87220-171-6); pap. text ed. 9.95 (0-87220-170-8) Hackett Pub.
— Philebus. Waterfield, Robin A., tr. 1983. mass mkt. 5.95 (0-14-044395-9, Penguin Classics) Viking Penguin.
— The Philebus of Plato. Bury, Robert G., ed. LC 72-9284. (Philosophy of Plato & Aristotle Ser.). (ENG & GRE.). 1977. reprint ed. 25.95 (0-405-04834-3) Ayer.
— Plato Reader. Levinson, Ronald B., ed. (YA). (gr. 9 up). 1967. pap. 9.96 (0-395-05197-5, RivEd) HM.
— The Platonic Epistles. Harward, J., tr. LC 75-13287. (History of Ideas in Ancient Greece Ser.). 1979. reprint ed. 26.95 (0-405-07330-5) Ayer.
— Platonis Opera, Vol. I: Euthyphro, Apologia, Socratis, Crito, Phaedo, Cratylus, Sophista, Politicus. Duke, E. A. et al, eds. (Classical Texts Ser.). 540p. 1995. 24.00 (0-19-814569-1) OUP.
— Plato's Apology of Socrates: A Literary & Philosophical Study with a Running Commentary. Strycker, Emile de, ed. LC 94-20723. (Mnemosyne, Bibliotheca Classica Batava, Supplementum: Vol. 137). 1994. 103.00 (90-04-10103-9) E J Brill.
— Plato's Apology of Socrates: An Interpretation, with a New Translation. LC 78-11532. 240p. 1979. 31.50 (0-8014-1127-0) Cornell U Pr.
— Plato's Euthyphro. Bd. with Pseudo-Platonica: A Dissertation Presented to the Faculty of Arts, Literature & Science of the University of Chicago in Candidacy for the Degree of Doctor of Philosophy, 1896. LC 75-13272. LC 75-13272. (History of Ideas in Ancient Greece Ser.). (ENG & GRE.). 1978. reprint ed. 16.95 (0-405-07313-5) Ayer.
— Plato's Euthyphro, Apology of Socrates & Crito. Burnet, John, ed. LC 76-29434. reprint ed. 45.00 (0-404-15322-4) AMS Pr.
— Plato's Gorgias. Anderson, Lieselotte, ed. 114p. (Orig.). (C). 1994. pap. text ed. 24.00 (1-887250-01-8) Agora Pubns.
— Plato's Protagoras: A Socratic Commentary. Hubbard, B. A., ed. LC 83-18122. xvi, 172p. 1984. lib. bdg. 20.00 (0-226-67034-1) U Ch Pr.
— Plato's Republic. Jowett, Benjamin, tr. (Airmont Classics Ser.). (J). (gr. 11 up). 1968. pap. 2.75 (0-8049-0172-4, CL-172) Airmont.
— Plato's Republic, Vol. 2: Essays. Jowett, Benjamin E. & Campbell, Lewis, eds. LC 72-9295. (Philosophy of Plato & Aristotle Ser.). (GRE.). 1974. reprint ed. 37.95 (0-405-04846-7) Ayer.
— Plato's Sophist. Cobb, William S., tr. 144p. (C). 1990. text ed. 51.00 (0-8476-7652-8); pap. text ed. 14.50 (0-8476-7653-6) Rowman.
— Plato's Sophist: The Being of the Beautiful, Pt. II. Benardete, Seth, tr. LC 85-28861. xx, 180p. 1986. pap. text ed. 11.95 (0-226-67032-5) U Ch Pr.
— Plato's Statesman: The Being of the Beautiful, Pt. III. Benardete, Seth, tr. LC 85-28827. xx, 156p. 1986. pap. text ed. 12.95 (0-226-67033-3) U Ch Pr.
— Plato's Theaetetus: The Being of the Beautiful, Pt. I. Benardete, Seth, tr. LC 85-28863. xx, 196p. 1986. pap. text ed. 13.95 (0-226-67031-7) U Ch Pr.
— Portable Plato. Buchanan, Scott, ed. (Portable Library: No. 40). 1977. pap. 13.95 (0-14-015040-4, Penguin Bks) Viking Penguin.
— Protagoras. Lombardo, Stanley & Bell, Karen, trs. LC 91-28322. (HPC Classics Ser.). 112p. (C). 1992. lib. bdg. 27.50 (0-87220-095-7); pap. text ed. 5.95 (0-87220-094-9) Hackett Pub.
— Protagoras. (College Classical Ser.). ix, 232p. (C). 1984. reprint ed. pap. text ed. 17.50 (0-89241-387-5) Caratzas.
— Protagoras & Meno. Guthrie, William K., tr. Bd. with Meno. (Classics Ser.). 1957. Set mass mkt. 8.95 (0-14-044068-2, Penguin Classics) Viking Penguin.
— Republic. Irwin, Terence, ed. Lindsay, A. D., tr. 404p. 1993. pap. 7.95 (0-460-87382-2, Everyman's Classic Lib) C E Tuttle.
— Republic. Waterfield, Robin A., tr. LC 92-38853. (World's Classics Ser.). 1993. 25.00 (0-19-212604-0) OUP.
— Republic. Jowett, Benjamin E., tr. 1955. pap. 6.95 (0-394-70128-3, Vin) Random.
— The Republic. Lindsay, Alexander D., tr. LC 92-52932. 368p. (ENG & GRE.). 1992. 17.00 (0-679-41330-8, Everymans Lib) Knopf.
— The Republic. Grube, G. M., tr. & intro. by. LC 73-71951. (HPC Classics Ser.). 288p. (C). 1973. 34.95 (0-915144-04-2) Hackett Pub.
— The Republic. Larson, Raymond, ed. & tr. by. LC 77-86034. (Crofts Classics Ser.). 336p. (C). 1979. pap. text ed. write for info. (0-88295-118-1) Harlan Davidson.
— The Republic. Jowett, B., tr. (Great Books in Philosophy). 397p. 1986. pap. text ed. 9.95 (0-87975-345-5) Prometheus Bks.
— The Republic. Jowett, Benjamin E., tr. LC 41-51966. 1983. 15.50 (0-394-60813-5, Modern Lib) Random.
— The Republic. Jowett, Benjamin E., tr. LC 90-55688. 416p. 1991. pap. 9.00 (0-679-73387-6, Vin) Random.
— Republic. rev. ed. Lee, H. D., tr. (Classics Ser.). (YA). (gr. 9 up). 1955. mass mkt. 6.95 (0-14-044048-8, Penguin Classics) Viking Penguin.
— Republic. 2nd ed. Grube, G. M., tr. LC 92-21578. 320p. (C). 1992. lib. bdg. 34.95 (0-87220-137-6); pap. text ed. 5.95 (0-87220-136-8) Hackett Pub.
— Republic. Waterfield, Robin, tr. & intro. by. (World's Classics Ser.). (Illus.). 560p. 1994. reprint ed. pap. 5.95 (0-19-282909-2) OUP.
— Republic, 2 vols., 1. (Loeb Classical Library: No. 237, 276). 552p. 1930. text ed. 18.95 (0-674-99262-8) HUP.
— Republic, 2 vols., 2. (Loeb Classical Library: No. 237, 276). 614p. 1935. text ed. 18.95 (0-674-99304-7) HUP.
— Republic, 2 vols., Vols. V & VI. No. 237, 276. write for info. (0-318-53175-5) HUP.
— Republic Five. Halliwell, ed. 1992. write for info. (0-85668-535-6, Pub. by Aris & Phillips UK); pap. write for info. (0-85668-536-4, Pub. by Aris & Phillips UK) David Brown.
— Republic of Plato. 1951. pap. 7.95 (0-19-500364-0) OUP.
— Republic 10. Halliwell, ed. (Classical Texts Ser.). 1986. 49.95 (0-85668-405-8, Pub. by Aris & Phillips UK); pap. 24.95 (0-85668-406-6, Pub. by Aris & Phillips UK) David Brown.
— Sophist. White, Nicholas, tr. & intro. by. (Hackett Classics Ser.). 128p. (Orig.). (C). 1993. lib. bdg. 28.95 (0-87220-203-8); pap. text ed. 9.95 (0-87220-202-X) Hackett Pub.
— The Sophistes & Politicus of Plato. LC 72-9286. (Philosophy of Plato & Aristotle Ser.). 1977. reprint ed. 35.95 (0-405-04836-X) Ayer.
— Statesman. Ostwald, Martin, ed. Skemp, B. J., tr. LC 57-14633. 1957. pap. 3.95 (0-672-60230-X, LLA57, Bobbs) Macmillan.
— The Statesman. Annas, Julia & Waterfield, Robin, eds. (Cambridge Texts in the History of Political Thought Ser.). 128p. (C). 1995. 39.95 (0-521-44262-1); pap. 14.95 (0-521-44778-X) Cambridge U Pr.
— Statesman. Skemp, J. B., tr. LC 92-26568. 136p. (C). 1992. reprint ed. 29.50 (0-87220-139-2); reprint ed. pap. 5.95 (0-87220-138-4) Hackett Pub.
— Statesman & Philebus, Vol. VIII. Warmington, E. H., ed. Bd. with Ion (Loeb Classical Library: No. 164). (ENG & GRE.). 15.50 (0-674-99182-6) HUP.
— Symposium. Dover, Kenneth J., ed. LC 78-67430. (Cambridge Greek & Latin Classics Ser.). 1980. pap. 21.95 (0-521-29523-8) Cambridge U Pr.
— Symposium. Woodruff, Paul, tr. LC 89-30960. (HPC Classics Ser.). 110p. (C). 1989. lib. bdg. 21.50 (0-87220-077-9); pap. 4.95 (0-87220-076-0) Hackett Pub.
— Symposium. Waterfield, Robin A., tr. LC 93-566. (World's Classics Ser.). 160p. (ENG & GER.). 1994. pap. 5.95 (0-19-282908-4) OUP.
— Symposium. Hamilton, Walter, tr. (Classics Ser.). 1952. mass mkt. 7.95 (0-14-044024-0, Penguin Classics) Viking Penguin.
— Symposium & Phaedrus. 96p. 1993. reprint ed. pap. text ed. 1.00 (0-486-27798-4) Dover.
— The Symposium & the Phaedo. Larson, Raymond, ed. & tr. by. LC 79-55931. (Crofts Classics Ser.). 144p. (Orig.). (C). 1980. pap. text ed. write for info. (0-88295-122-X) Harlan Davidson.
— The Symposium & The Phaedrus: Plato's Erotic Dialogues. LC 92-35391. (SUNY Series in Ancient Greek Philosophy). 214p. (C). 1993. 29.50 (0-7914-1617-8); pap. 9.95 (0-7914-1618-6) State U NY Pr.
— Symposium of Plato. Jowett, Benjamin, tr. pap. 3.95 (0-8283-1456-X, 17, Intl Pocket Lib) Branden Pub Co.
— Symposium of Plato. Griffith, Tom, tr. (Illus.). 144p. 1993. pap. 15.00 (0-520-06695-2) U CA Pr.
— The Symposium of Plato. Brentlinger, John A., ed. Groden, Suzy Q., tr. LC 79-103478. (Illus.). 144p. (C). 1970. pap. 12.95x (0-87023-076-X) U of Mass Pr.
— Theaetetus. Levett, M. J., tr. LC 92-28261. 128p. (C). 1992. 27.50 (0-87220-159-7); pap. 4.95 (0-87220-158-9) Hackett Pub.
— Theaetetus. McDowell, John, tr. (Clarendon Plato Ser.). 1977. pap. 22.00 (0-19-872083-1) OUP.
— Theaetetus. Waterfield, Robin A., ed. & intro. by. 224p. 1987. mass mkt. 6.95 (0-14-044450-5, Penguin Classics) Viking Penguin.
— Theaetetus, & Sophist, Vol. VII. (Loeb Classical Library: No. 123). 474p. 1923. text ed. 18.95 (0-674-99137-0) HUP.
— The Theaetetus of Plato. LC 72-9287. (Philosophy of Plato & Aristotle Ser.). 1977. reprint ed. 21.95 (0-405-04837-8) Ayer.
— Timaeus & Critias. Lee, H. D., tr. (Classics Ser.). 1972. mass mkt. 8.95 (0-14-044261-8, Penguin Classics) Viking Penguin.
— Timaeus, Critias, Cleitophon, Menexenus, Epistolae, Vol. IX. (Loeb Classical Library: No. 234). 644p. 1929. text ed. 18.95 (0-674-99257-1) HUP.
— The Timaeus of Plato. vii, 358p. (GER.). 1988. write for info. (0-318-70539-7, Pub. by Georg Olms GW) Lubrecht & Cramer.
— The Timaeus of Plato. Archer-Hind, R. D., ed. LC 72-9281. (Philosophy of Plato & Aristotle Ser.). (ENG & GRE.). 1977. reprint ed. 27.95 (0-405-04832-7) Ayer.
— The Tragedy & Comedy of Life: Plato's Philebus. Benardete, Seth, tr. LC 92-44620. (Illus.). 264p. (C). 1993. 37.50 (0-226-04239-1) U Ch Pr.
— The Trial & Death of Socrates. Grube, G. M., tr. LC 75-33058. (HPC Classics Ser.). 64p. (Orig.). (C). 1975. pap. 3.95 (0-915144-15-8) Hackett Pub.
— The Trial & Death of Socrates: Four Dialogues. (Thrift Editions Ser.). 128p. 1992. reprint ed. pap. 1.00 (0-486-27066-1) Dover.
— Works of Plato. Edman, Irwin, ed. Jowett, Benjamin E., tr. 1965. pap. text ed. write for info. (0-07-553651-X, T71) McGraw.
— The Works of Plato. Edman, Irwin, ed. & intro. by. LC 31-2780. 1977. 16.50 (0-394-60420-2, Modern Lib) Random.

An Asterisk (*) at the beginning of an entry indicates that the title is appearing in BIP for the first time.

— Works of Plato, 5 Vols, Set. LC 78-16080. reprint ed. 380.00 (*0-404-16360-2*) AMS Pr.

Plato & Thompson, W. H. The Phaedrus of Plato. LC 72-9307. (Philosophy of Plato & Aristotle Ser.). (ENG & GRE.). 1977. reprint ed. 18.95 (*0-405-04866-1*) Ayer.

Plato, Ann. Essays. (Schomburg Library of Nineteenth-Century Black Women Writers). 177p. 1988. 22.00 (*0-19-505247-1*) OUP.

***Plato Center Grade School Third-Graders.** Plato Center Olympic. (Wee Write Bks.: No. 7). (Illus.). 23p. (J). (ps-3). 1994. pap. 7.95 (*1-884987-25-7*) WeWrite.

— Plato Center Olympics. (Wee Write Bks.: No. 7). (Illus.). 23p. (J). (ps-3). 1994. 17.95 (*1-884987-24-9*) WeWrite.

— Stone Age Soccer. (Wee Write Bks.: No. 8). (Illus.). 23p. (J). (ps-3). 1994. 17.95 (*1-884987-27-3*) WeWrite.

— Stone Age Soccer. (Wee Write Bks.: No. 8). (Illus.). 23p. (J). (ps-3). 1994. pap. 7.95 (*1-884987-28-1*) WeWrite.

— Stone Age Soccer, Big Bk. (Wee Write Bks.: No. 8). (Illus.). 23p. (J). (ps-3). 1994. 32.95 (*1-884987-29-X*) WeWrite.

***Plato Center Third-Graders Staff.** Plato Center Olympic, Big Bk. (Wee Write Bks.: No. 7). (Illus.). 23p. (J). (ps-3). 1994. 32.95 (*1-884987-26-5*) WeWrite.

Plato, Chris C., jt. ed. see Durham, Norris M.

Plato, Chris C., jt. ed. see Wertelecki, Wladimir.

Plato, Chris C., et al. Dermatoglyphics: Science in Transition. (Birth Defects: Original Article Ser.: No. 1903). 348p. 1991. text ed. 239.95 (*0-471-56104-5*, Wiley-Liss) Wiley.

Plato, Timaios. The Timaeus of Plato. vii, 358p. Date not set. write for info. (*0-318-71000-5*, Pub. by Georg Olms GW) Lubrecht & Cramer.

Platon. Apologia de Socrates. Criton. Carta VII. Lopez Castellon, Enrique, ed. & tr. by. (Nueva Austral Ser.: Vol. 164). (SPA.). 1991. pap. text ed. 24.95x (*84-239-1964-1*) Elliots Bks.

— Concordantiae in Platonis Opera Omnia, Pt. I: Euthyphro. Siviero, Mauro, ed. (Alpha-Omega, Reihe A Ser.: Bd. CX). 180p. (GER.). 1990. write for info. (*3-487-09360-X*, Pub. by Georg Olms GW) Lubrecht & Cramer.

— Dialogos (Gorgias - Fedon - el Banquete) Roig de Lluis, Luis, tr. (Nueva Austral Ser.: Vol. 22). (SPA.). 1991. pap. text ed. 24.95x (*84-239-1822-X*) Elliots Bks.

— Oeuvres Completes: Hippias, Protagoras, L'Apologie de Socrates, Criton, Le Banquet, Phedon, La Republique etc., Vol. 1. 1472p. 39.95 (*0-686-56548-7*) Fr & Eur.

— Orthodox Doctrine of the Apostolic Eastern Church. 1973. 5.00 (*0-89981-066-7*) Eastern Orthodox.

— Orthodox Doctrine of the Apostolic Eastern Church: A Compendium of Christian Theology. LC 70-81772. reprint ed. 42.50 (*0-404-05058-1*) AMS Pr.

— Present State of the Greek Church in Russia. LC 75-131031. reprint ed. 49.50 (*0-404-05059-X*) AMS Pr.

— Rules for a Pious Life. 1994. pap. 0.50 (*0-89981-153-1*) Eastern Orthodox.

Platon, Nicholas. Zakros: The Discovery of a Lost Palace of Ancient Crete. 345p. 1985. reprint ed. pap. 67.00 (*90-256-0865-5*, Pub. by A M Hakkert NE) Benjamins North Am.

Platonbild, Das. Zehn Beitrage Zum Platonverstandnis. No. 1. xiii, 326p. (GER.). 1969. write for info. (*0-318-70538-9*, Pub. by Georg Olms GW) Lubrecht & Cramer.

Platonov & Hellie, Richard. Ivan the Terrible. Wieczynski, J. L., ed. reprint ed. pap. 12.50 (*0-87569-054-8*) Academic Intl.

Platonov, Andrei. Vprok (To Profit From) 2nd ed. Poliak, Gregory, ed. (Illus.). 100p. (Orig.). (RUS.). pap. 8.00 (*0-686-88508-2*) Silver Age Pub.

Platonov, Andrey. The Foundation Pit. Ginsburg, Mirra, tr. & intro. by. (European Classics Ser.). 156p. 1994. pap. 12.95 (*0-8101-1145-4*) Northwestern U Pr.

Platonov, Sergei F. Time of Troubles: A Historical Study of the Internal Crisis & Social Struggles in Sixteenth & Seventeenth-Century Muscovy. Alexander, John T., tr. LC 79-97029. xviii, 198p. (C). 1970. pap. 7.95 (*0-7006-0062-0*) U Pr of KS.

Platonov, Vladimir & Rapinchuk, Andrei. Algebraic Groups & Number Theory. Rowen, Rachel, tr. LC 92-35876. (Pure & Applied Mathematics Ser.: Vol. 139). (Illus.). 614p. (ENG & RUS.). 1993. text ed. 99.95 (*0-12-558180-7*) Acad Pr.

Platou, Dode. Chas H. Reinike. McCaffrey, Rosanne, ed. (Illus.). 16p. 1981. pap. 5.50 (*0-917860-07-1*) Historic New Orleans.

Platova, Victoria. Neiarkaia Zhizn' Sani Kornilova: Stories. LC 90-25013. 115p. (Orig.). (RUS.). 1991. pap. 7.50 (*1-55779-031-0*) Hermitage.

Platt. Emergency Case Study, No. 2. 1991. 38.95 (*0-316-70971-9*) Little.

— Police Guide to the Young Offender's Act. 224p. 1991. pap. 27.00 (*0-409-89340-4*) Butterworth Legal Pubs.

— Young Offenders Law in Canada. 352p. 1990. 87.00 (*0-409-80990-X*) Butterworth Legal Pubs.

Platt, jt. auth. see Kass.

Platt, A. M., jt. ed. see Tedder, P. William.

Platt, A. M., et al, eds. Nuclear Fact Book. 192p. 1985. text ed. 50.00 (*3-7186-0273-3*) Gordon & Breach.

Platt, Agnes, tr. see Zenzinov, Vladimir M.

Platt, Alan, ed. Arms Control & Confidence Building in the Middle East. LC 92-18784. (Orig.). 1992. pap. 13.95 (*1-878379-18-6*) US Inst Peace.

Platt, Alan, jt. auth. see Bowie, Christopher J.

Platt, Anthony M. The Child Savers. LC 69-14827. (Phoenix Ser.). 1977. reprint ed. pap. text ed. 10.95 (*0-226-67072-4*, P462) U Ch Pr.

— E. Franklin Frazier Reconsidered. LC 90-36223. (Illus.). 310p. (C). 1991. text ed. 35.00 (*0-8135-1631-5*) Rutgers U Pr.

Platt, Arthur. Nine Essays. LC 68-16969. (Essay Index Reprint Ser.). 1977. reprint ed. 19.95 (*0-8369-0793-0*) Ayer.

Platt, Barbara. Residential Real Estate: How to Find, Buy, Manage, & Sell for a Profit. Bowman, Linda, ed. LC 87-60697. (Illus.). 206p. 1987. 24.95 (*0-941089-17-7*); pap. 14.95 (*0-941089-18-5*) Roscher Hse.

Platt, Brenda & Seldman, Neil. Garbage in Europe: Technologies, Economics & Trends. LC 88-671. (Illus.). 260p. 1988. per. 25.00 (*0-917582-42-X*) Inst Local Self Re.

Platt, Brenda & Zachary, Jill. Co-Collection of Recyclables & Mixed Waste: Problems & Opportunities. LC 92-34141. 60p. 1992. pap. text ed. 15.00 (*0-917582-26-8*) Inst Local Self Re.

Platt, Brenda, jt. auth. see Morris, David.

Platt, Brenda, et al. Directory of Waste Utilization Technologies in Europe & the United States. LC 88-28436. 225p. 1989. pap. text ed. 25.00 (*0-917582-41-1*) Inst Local Self Re.

— Pitfalls & Promise of Resource Recovery in Union County, New Jersey. rev. ed. LC 89-7632. 200p. 1989. pap. text ed. 20.00 (*0-917582-36-5*) Inst Local Self Re.

Platt, Brenda A., et al. In-Depth Studies of Recycling & Composting Programs, Vols. I-III: Designs, Costs, Results, 3 vols., Set. LC 92-9856. (Illus.). (Orig.). 1992. pap. text ed. 45.00 (*0-917582-32-2*) Inst Local Self Re.

— In-Depth Studies of Recycling & Composting Programs, Vols. I-III: Designs, Costs, Results, 3 vols., Vol. I: Rural Communities. LC 92-9856. (Illus.). 127p. (Orig.). 1992. Vol. I, Rural Communities, 127p. pap. text ed. 18.00 (*0-917582-31-4*) Inst Local Self Re.

— In-Depth Studies of Recycling & Composting Programs, Vols. I-III: Designs, Costs, Results, 3 vols., Vol. II: Suburbs & Small Cities. LC 92-9856. (Illus.). 202p. (Orig.). 1992. Vol. II, Suburbs & Small Cities, 202p. pap. text ed. 18.00 (*0-917582-30-6*) Inst Local Self Re.

— In-Depth Studies of Recycling & Composting Programs, Vols. I-III: Designs, Costs, Results, 3 vols., Vol. III: Urban Areas. LC 92-9856. (Illus.). 207p. (Orig.). 1992. Vol. III, Urban Areas, 207p. pap. text ed. 18.00 (*0-917582-29-2*) Inst Local Self Re.

***Platt, Cameron & Wright, John.** Treasure Islands: The Fascinating World of Pirates, Buried Treasure, & Fortune Hunters. LC 94-34454. 1995. 16.95 (*1-55591-190-0*) Fulcrum Pub.

Platt, Carolyn, ed. see Bockhoff, Esther & Fleming, Nancy I.

***Platt, Carolyn V.** Ohio's Natural Landscape: A Rewoven Fabric. LC 94-35409. (Illus.). 200p. 1995. 45.00 (*0-87338-523-3*) Kent St U Pr.

Platt, Cathy, jt. auth. see Schmidbauer, Paul L.

Platt, Charles. Artificial Intelligence in Action: Commodore 64. 1985. pap. 12.99 (*0-89824-119-7*) Trillium Pr.

— Free Zone. 1989. pap. 3.50 (*0-380-75411-8*) Avon.

— The Gas. 160p. (Orig.). 1968. pap. 11.95 (*0-86130-023-8*, Pub. by Savoy Bks UK) AK Pr Dist.

Platt, Charles, Jr. Platt Genealogy in America, from the Arrival of Richard Platt in New Haven, Conn., in 1638. (Illus.). 453p. 1993. reprint ed. lib. bdg. 81.00 (*0-8328-3572-2*); reprint ed. pap. 71.00 (*0-8328-3573-0*) Higginson Bk Co.

Platt, Charles. The Silicon Man. LC 93-60317. 232p. 1993. reprint ed. 19.95 (*0-9623712-7-0*) Tafford Pub.

— Who Writes Science Fiction. 400p. (Orig.). 1981. pap. 3.95 (*0-86130-048-3*, Pub. by Savoy Bks UK) AK Pr Dist.

Platt, Charles A. Italian Gardens. LC 92-33622. (Illus.). 172p. 1993. 34.95 (*0-88192-273-0*) Timber.

Platt, Colin. The Architecture of Medieval Britain: A Social History. (Illus.). 352p. (C). 1991. text ed. 60.00 (*0-300-04953-6*) Yale U Pr.

— Atlas of Medieval Man Vol. 1. 1994. pap. 18.95 (*0-312-11549-0*) St Martin.

— The Great Rebuildings of Tudor & Stuart England: Revolutions in Architectural Taste. LC 94-32050. 1994. 65.00 (*1-85728-315-5*, Pub. by UCL Pr UK); pap. 21.95 (*1-85728-316-3*, Pub. by UCL Pr UK) Taylor & Francis.

— Medieval England: A Social History & Archaeology from the Conquest to 1600 A. D. LC 94-42748. 256p. 1989. pap. text ed. 17.95 (*0-415-00278-8*) Routledge.

— Medieval England: A Social History & Archaeology from the Conquest to 1600 A. D. rev. ed. LC 94-42748. 1995. write for info. (*0-415-11915-4*) Routledge.

— The Monastic Grange in Medieval England: A Reassessment. LC 73-80106. 280p. reprint ed. pap. 79.80 (*0-7837-0463-1*, 2040786) Bks Demand.

Platt, Constance A., jt. auth. see Hoffman, Stephanie B.

Platt, D., ed. Gerontology. (Illus.). 336p. 1990. 84.00 (*0-387-51544-5*) Spr-Verlag.

Platt, D. C., jt. ed. see Di Tella, Guido.

Platt, David. Celluloid Power: Social Film Criticism from the Birth of a Nation to Judgement at Nuremberg. LC 91-35568. (Illus.). 700p. 1992. 72.50 (*0-8108-2442-6*) Scarecrow.

— Intimations of Divinity. (American University Studies: Philosophy: Ser. V, Vol. 72). 248p. (C). 1989. text ed. 35.95 (*0-8204-0856-5*) P Lang Pubs.

— Win Thirty Two from Scratch: A Programm'ers Workbook. 1994. Incl. disk. disk 37.50 (*0-13-121484-5*) P-H.

Platt, David C., jt. auth. see Shaffer, Dale O.

***Platt, David D. & Conkling, Philip W., eds.** Island Journal Vol. XII: An Annual Publication of the Island Institute. (Illus.). 96p. (Orig.). 1995. pap. 14.95 (*0-942719-14-X*) Island Inst.

Platt, David S. The Gift of Contingency. LC 91-8283. (American University Studies: Philosophy: Ser. V, Vol. 120). 210p. 1992. 38.95 (*0-8204-1543-X*) P Lang Pubs.

Platt, Donald. Fresh Peaches, Fireworks, & Guns. LC 93-40660. 88p. (Orig.). 1994. pap. 11.95 (*1-55753-048-3*) Purdue U Pr.

Platt, Dora B. The Miracle on Harding Road. (Illus.). 136p. 1989. lib. bdg. write for info. (*0-9623777-0-8*) St Thomas Hospital.

Platt, Edmund. History of Poughkeepsie, Sixteen Eighty-Three to Nineteen Hundred & Five. 328p. 1987. reprint ed. lib. bdg. 25.00 (*0-932334-83-0*, NY14011) Hrt of the Lakes.

Platt, Eleanor S. Wreaths, Arrangements & Basket Decorations: Using Flowers, Foliage, Herbs & Grasses to Make Colorful Crafts. (Illus.). 176p. 1994. 24.95 (*0-87596-587-3*) Rodale Pr Inc.

Platt, Elizabeth. Scenes from Day Care: How Teachers Teach & What Children Learn. (Early Childhood Education Ser.: No. 35). 128p. (C). 1992. pap. text ed. 16.95 (*0-8077-3131-5*) Tchrs Coll.

***Platt, Ellen S.** The Ultimate Wreath Book: Hundreds of Beautiful Wreaths to Make from Natural Materials. 1995. 27.95 (*0-87596-720-5*) Rand McNally.

Platt, Eugene. Bubba, Missy & Me. LC 92-64263. 128p. (Orig.). 1992. pap. 10.00 (*0-937684-29-5*) Tradd St Pr.

Platt, F. Dewitt, jt. auth. see Matthews, Roy T.

Platt, F. DeWitt

Platt, F. Dewitt

Platt, Frederic W. Conversation Failure: Case Studies in Doctor-Patient Communication. LC 92-15049. 1992. 16.95 (*0-943685-16-8*) Life Sci Pr.

— Conversation Repair. LC 95-835. 1995. 24.95 (*0-316-71082-2*) Little.

Platt, Frederic W., jt. auth. see Markoff, Mortimer.

Platt, Frederick. America's Gilded Age. 25.00 (*0-8453-1322-3*, Cornwall Bks) Assoc Univ Prs.

Platt, G. L. Platt Lineage: A Genealogical Research & Record. (Illus.). 398p. 1989. reprint ed. lib. bdg. 68.00 (*0-8328-0972-1*); reprint ed. pap. 60.00 (*0-8328-0973-X*) Higginson Bk Co.

Platt, Geoffrey. A Writer's Journey. LC 90-82233. 258p. (C). 1991. pap. text ed. write for info. (*0-669-20298-3*); Instr.'s guide. teacher ed write for info. (*0-669-24712-X*) Heath.

— A Writer's Journey. 2nd ed. 320p. (C). 1995. pap. text ed. write for info. (*0-669-35142-3*) Heath.

Platt, George. George Platt Lynes: Portrait, 1927-1955. Woody, Jack, ed. (Illus.). 144p. 1994. 65.00 (*0-944092-27-6*) Twin Palms Pub.

— ISA Guide to Measurement Conversions. LC 93-27095. 172p. 1993. pap. 50.00 (*1-55617-489-6*) Instru Soc.

— Process Control: A Primer for the Nonspecialist & the Newcomer. LC 88-15459. 130p. 1988. pap. 35.00 (*1-55617-096-3*, A096-3) Instru Soc.

Platt, George M. South Dakota's Nineteen Sixty-Five Legislative Session. 1965. 1.00 (*1-55614-004-5*) U of SD Gov Res Bur.

Platt, George M., jt. auth. see Clem, Alan L.

Platt, Gerald, ed. see Harris, Anthony.

Platt, Gerald, ed. see Mortimer, Jeylan, et al.

Platt, Gerald, ed. see Schneider, Joseph & Kitsuse, John I.

Platt, Gerald, ed. see Suttles, Gerald & Zald, Mayer N.

Platt, Gerald M., jt. auth. see Parsons, Talcott.

Platt, Gillian. Suite for Five Viols. (Charney Manor Ser.: No. 7). i, 15p. 1994. 10.00 (*1-56571-083-5*, CM007) PRB Prods.

Platt, H., jt. ed. see Platt, S.

Platt, Harlan D. The First Junk Bond: A Story of Corporate Boom & Bust. LC 93-17066. 224p. 1994. 50.00 (*1-56324-275-3*); pap. 21.95 (*1-56324-276-1*) M E Sharpe.

Platt, Harold L. The Electric City: Energy & the Growth of the Chicago Area, 1880-1930. LC 90-38285. (Illus.). 352p. 1991. 34.95 (*0-226-67075-9*) U Ch Pr.

Platt, Harvey J. Making a Will & Creating Estate Plans. (No Nonsense Guides Ser.). 128p. 1992. pap. 4.95 (*0-681-41399-9*) Longmeadow Pr.

— Your Living Trust & Estate Plan: How to Maximize Your Family's Assets & Protect Your Loved Ones. LC 95-7584. (Orig.). 1995. pap. 12.95 (*1-880559-25-0*) Allworth Pr.

Platt, Howard M. & Warwick, Richard M. Free-Living Marine Nematodes: Synopses of the British Fauna. Kermack, Doris M. & Barnes, R. S., eds. (British Chromadorids Ser.: Pt. II). (Illus.). (Orig.). 1988. pap. 100.75 (*90-04-08595-5*) E J Brill.

Platt, Hugh. A New, Cheape & Delicate Fire of Cole-Balles. LC 72-7838. (English Experience Ser.: No. 550). 32p. 1972. reprint ed. 15.00 (*90-221-0550-4*) Walter J Johnson.

Platt, Janet. Daily Activities after Your Hip Surgery. (Illus.). 20p. (Orig.). 1991. pap. 5.20 (*0-910317-25-9*) Am Occup Therapy.

Platt, Janet V., et al. Actividades Diarias Despues de Tu Reemplazo Total de Rodilla. Irizarry, Dyhalma, tr. (Illus.). (C). 1993. pap. text ed. write for info. (*1-56900-005-0*) Am Occup Therapy.

Platt, Jean S. Ribbons. (Illus.). 96p. (Orig.). 1992. pap. text ed. 11.95 (*0-9634688-0-4*) Persona Pr PA.

Platt, Jeffrey L., ed. Hyperacute Xenograft Rejection. (Medical Intelligence Unit Ser.). 194p. 1995. pap. 79.00 (*1-879702-92-4*, LN0292) R G Landes.

***Platt, Jerome J.** Heroin Addiction, 3 vols., Set. 1074p. 1995. 99.95 (*0-89464-923-X*) Krieger.

— Heroin Addiction: Theory, Research & Treatment, Vol. 1. 2nd ed. LC 88-13253. 464p. (C). 1989. reprint ed. lib. bdg. 46.50 (*0-89464-325-8*) Krieger.

— Heroin Addiction: Theory, Research & Treatment Vol. 2: The Addict, the Treatment Process, & Social Control. (C). 1995. 37.50 (*0-89464-267-7*) Krieger.

— Heroin Addiction: Theory, Research & Treatment Vol. 3: Treatment Advances & Aids. (C). 1995. 39.50 (*0-89464-881-0*) Krieger.

Platt, Jerome J., jt. ed. see Buhringer, Gerhard.

Platt, Jerome J., et al, eds. The Effectiveness of Drug Abuse Treatment: Dutch & American Perspectives. 344p. 1990. 55.00 (*0-89464-266-9*) Krieger.

Platt, John, et al. The New Englishes. 190p. 1984. pap. 12.95 (*0-7102-0194-X*, RKP) Routledge.

Platt, John, jt. auth. see Mitchell, Mitch.

Platt, John, jt. auth. see Owens, Dan.

Platt, John, et al. Singapore & Malaysia. (Varieties of English Around the World Text Ser.: T4). iv, 138p. (Orig.). 1983. pap. 32.00x (*90-272-4712-9*) Benjamins North Am.

Platt, John A. Whispers from Old Genesee & Echoes of the Salmon River. (Illus.). 184p. 1975. 14.95 (*0-87770-143-1*) Ye Galleon.

Platt, John D. Jeremiah Wadsworth, Federalist Entrepreneur. 1981. 27.95 (*0-405-14103-3*) Ayer.

Platt, John P. The Petrology, Structure, & Geologic History of the Catalina Schist Terrain, Southern California. LC 74-22941. (University of California Publications in Social Welfare: Vol. 112). (Illus.). 141p. reprint ed. pap. 40.20 (*0-685-23616-1*, 2014962) Bks Demand.

Platt, John T., jt. auth. see Ho Mian-Lian.

Platt, Joseph. Harvey Mudd College: The First Twenty Years. (Illus.). 224p. 1994. 28.95 (*1-56474-097-8*); pap. 16.95 (*1-56474-100-1*) Fithian Pr.

Platt, Kin. Big Max. LC 91-14742. (I Can Read Bk.). (Illus.). 64p. (J). (gr. k-3). 1965. lib. bdg. 12.89 (*0-06-024751-7*) HarpC Child Bks.

— Big Max. LC 91-14743. (Trophy I Can Read Bk.). (Illus.). (J). (gr. k-3). 1978. pap. 3.50 (*0-06-444006-0*, Trophy) HarpC Child Bks.

— Darwin & the Great Beasts. LC 90-39674. 64p. (J). (gr. 2 up). 1992. 14.00 (*0-688-10030-9*) Greenwillow.

— Flames Going Out. 144p. (gr. 10 up). 1980. 8.95 (*0-416-30621-7*, NO. 0150) Routledge Chapman & Hall.

— Murder in Rosslare. 192p. 1986. 13.95 (*0-8027-5639-5*) Walker & Co.

Platt, Kin, ed. see London, Jack.

Platt, Kin, ed. see Stevenson, Robert Louis.

Platt, Larry, jt. auth. see Negroni, Andrea L.

Platt, Larry A. & Persico, V. Richard, Jr. Grief in Cross-Cultural Perspective: A Casebook. LC 91-25907. 446p. 1992. 70.00 (*0-8240-4565-3*, 557) Garland.

Platt, Larry A., jt. auth. see Branch, Roger G.

***Platt, Laurence E. & Schulman, Phillip L.** A Practical Guide to the Real Estate Settlement Procedures Act. 624p. 1995. pap. 175.00 (*0-7913-2202-5*) Warren Gorham & Lamont.

Platt, LaVonne G. Bela Banerjee, Bringing Health to India's Villages: Bringing Health to India's Villages. LC 87-51688. (Illus.). xi, 178p. (Orig.). 1995. pap. 11.95 (*0-945530-00-5*) Wordsworth KS.

— Hope for the Family Farm: Trust God & Care for the Land. Sheely, Maynard, ed. LC 87-81635. 240p. 1987. pap. 7.95 (*0-87303-126-1*) Faith & Life.

Platt, Naomi D. Word Procesing & Desktop Publishing Applications. 2nd ed. LC 93-8600. 1994. write for info. (*0-02-801021-3*) Glencoe.

Platt, Norman, tr. see Mozart, Wolfgang Amadeus.

***Platt, Pamela.** Pig with a View. 80p. (J). (gr. 2-6). 1995. pap. 9.95 (*0-7022-2589-4*, Pub. by Univ Queensland Pr AT) Intl Spec Bk.

***Platt, Polly.** French or Foe? Getting the Most Out of Living & Working in France. (Illus.). 254p. 1994. reprint ed. pap. 14.95 (*0-9646684-0-8*) Distribks Inc.

Platt, Priscilla. When Kids Get into Trouble: A Guide for Parents & Children, Teachers & Professionals, Including the Young Offenders Act. 208p. 1987. pap. 14.95 (*0-7737-5104-1*, Pub. by Stoddart Pubng CN) Genl Dist Srvs.

Platt, R. H. Forgotten Books of Eden. 1988. 7.99 (*0-517-30886-X*, Crown) Crown Pub Group.

Platt, Randall B. The Four Arrows Fe-As-Ko. LC 90-28802. 240p. 1991. 17.95 (*0-945774-14-1*, PS3566.L29386) Catbird Pr.

— Out of a Forest Clearing: An Environmental Fable. 224p. (Orig.). 1991. pap. 9.95 (*0-936784-89-X*) J Daniel.

Platt, Richard. Cross Sections: Man-of-War. LC 92-21227. (Illus.). 32p. (J). (gr. 3 up). 1993. 16.95 (*1-56458-321-X*) Dorling Kindersley.

— Film. LC 91-53133. (Eyewitness Bks.). (Illus.). 64p. (J). (gr. 5 up). 1992. 16.00 (*0-679-81679-8*); lib. bdg. 16.99 (*0-679-91679-2*) Knopf Bks Yng Read.

— In the Beginning. LC 95-2427. 80p. (J). 1995. 19.95 (*0-7894-0206-8*, 5-70619) Dorling Kindersley.

— Incredible Cross-Sections. LC 91-27439. (Illus.). 48p. (J). 1992. 20.00 (*0-679-81411-6*) Knopf Bks Yng Read.

— The Photographer's Idea Book. (Illus.). 192p. 1988. pap. 22.50 (*0-8174-5420-9*, Amphoto) Watsn-Guptill.

— Pirate. (Illus.). (J). 1995. 17.00 (*0-679-87255-8*); 17.99 (*0-679-97255-2*) Dorling Kindersley.

— The Smithsonian Visual Timeline of Inventions. LC 94-21429. (Illus.). 64p. (J). (gr. 3 up). 1994. 16.95 (*1-56458-675-8*) Dorling Kindersley.

Platt, Roger, jt. auth. see Biesty, Stephen.

Platt, Ron. Cannibal Eyes. LC 91-51145. (Illus.). 24p. (Orig.). 1992. pap. 7.00 (*0-938437-40-2*) MIT List Visual Arts.

— Jno Cook: Radically Recycled Cameras. LC 89-64406. (Illus.). 8p. 1990. pap. 3.50 (*0-938437-30-5*) MIT List Visual Arts.

— Maria Fernanda Cardoso. (Illus.). 32p. (Orig.). 1994. pap. 5.00 (*0-938437-46-1*) MIT List Visual Arts.

Platt, Ron & Halperin, David. Doug Ischar: Orderly. LC 92-56627. (Illus.). 24p. (Orig.). (C). 1993. pap. 7.00 (*0-938437-43-7*) MIT List Visual Arts.

Platt, Ron, et al. Warren Neidich: Historical In(ter) vention. LC 91-14972. (Illus.). 16p. 1991. pap. 5.00 (*0-938437-38-0*) MIT List Visual Arts.

Platt, Rorin M. Virginia in Foreign Affairs, 1933-1941. 270p. (C). 1991. lib. bdg. 43.50 (*0-8191-7803-9*) U Pr of Amer.

Platt, Rutherford. One Thousand-One Questions Answered about Trees. (Illus.). 352p. 1992. reprint ed. pap. 10.95 (*0-486-27038-6*) Dover.

Platt, Rutherford H. Open Land in Urban Illinois: Roles of the Citizen Advocate. LC 78-146641. 132p. 1971. pap. 8.50 (*0-87580-506-X*) N Ill U Pr.

— The Open Space Decision Process: Spatial Allocation of Costs & Benefits. LC 72-85930. (Research Papers Ser.: No. 142). (Illus.). 1972. pap. 12.00 (*0-89065-049-7*, 142) U Chicago Comm Geo.

Platt, Rutherford H., ed. Regional Management of Metropolitan Floodplains. (Program on Environment & Behavior Monograph Ser.: No. 45). 334p. (Orig.). (C). 1987. pap. 10.00 (*0-685-28119-1*) Natural Hazards.

Platt, Rutherford H. & Macinko, George, eds. Beyond the Urban Fringe: Land Use Issues of Nonmetropolitan America. LC 83-3518. 432p. reprint ed. pap. 123.20 (*0-7837-2926-X*, 2057528) Bks Demand.

Platt, Rutherford H., et al. Coastal Erosion: Has Retreat Sounded? LC 92-34852. (Program on Environment & Behavior Monograph Ser.: No. 53). 1992. 10.00 (*1-877943-07-X*) Natural Hazards.

Platt, Rutherford H., et al, eds. Cities on the Beach: Management Issues of Developed Coastal Barriers. LC 86-25051. (Research Papers Ser.: No. 224). 324p. 1987. pap. 10.00 (*0-89065-128-0*) U Chicago Comm Geo.

— The Ecological City: Preserving & Restoring Urban Biodiversity. LC 93-26506. (Illus.). 304p. 1994. lib. bdg. 45.00 (*0-87023-883-3*); pap. 17.95 (*0-87023-884-1*) U of Mass Pr.

Platt, S. & Platt, H., eds. Social Significance of Speech. (North-Holland Linguistic Ser.: Vol. 23). 194p. 1975. pap. 48.75 (*0-444-10972-2*, North Holland) Elsevier.

Platt, Stephen, et al. Teams: A Game to Develop Group Skills. 1988. 129.95 (*0-566-02735-6*, Pub. by Gower UK) Ashgate Pub Co.

Platt, Stephen, et al, eds. Locating Health: Sociological & Historical Explorations. 274p. 1993. 67.95 (*1-85628-367-4*, Pub. by Avebury Pub UK) Ashgate Pub Co.

Platt, Stephen D., jt. ed. see Kreitman, Norman.

Platt, Susan N. Modernism in the Nineteen Twenties: Interpretations of Modern Art in New York from Expressionism to Constructivism. LC 85-1070. (Studies in the Fine Arts: Criticism: No. 17). 203p. reprint ed. pap. 57.90 (*0-8357-1661-9*, 2070597) Bks Demand.

Platt, Suzy, ed. Respectfully Quoted: A Dictionary of Quotations from the Library of Congress. 1992. 44.95 (*0-87187-687-6*) Congr Quarterly.

— Respectfully Quoted: A Dictionary of Quotations from the Library of Congress. 546p. 1992. pap. text ed. 25.95 (*0-87187-674-4*) Congr Quarterly.

Platt, Thomas C. The Autobiography of Thomas Collier Platt. LC 73-19172. (Politics & People Ser.). (Illus.). 580p. 1974. reprint ed. 44.95 (*0-405-05894-2*) Ayer.

— The Autobiography of Thomas Collier Platt. (American Biography Ser.). 556p. 1991. reprint ed. lib. bdg. 99.00 (*0-7812-8317-5*) Rprt Serv.

Platt, Thomas C., ed. see Orr & Reno Staff.

Platt, Thomas C., ed. see Orr & Reno P. A. Staff.

Platt, Tony & Takagi, Paul, eds. Punishment & Penal Discipline: Essays on the Prison & the Prisoner's Movement. 2nd ed. LC 79-90275. (Illus.). (Orig.). 1982. pap. 10.95 (*0-935206-00-0*) Soc Justice.

Platt, W. R. Color Atlas of Hematology: Atlas de Hematologia en Color. 645p. 1982. 175.00 (*0-8288-1873-8*) Fr & Eur.

***Platt, Wendy, ed.** Fort Ross Cookbook: Recipes of Fort Ross & Russia. (Orig.). 1994. pap. text ed. write for info. (*0-9617973-4-7*) Ft Ross Interpret.

Plattard, ed. see D'Aubigne, Agrippa.

Plattard, Jean. Life of Francois Rabelais. Roache, L. D., tr. 308p. 1968. reprint ed. 35.00 (*0-7146-2077-7*, BHA-02077, Pub. by F Cass Pubs UK) Intl Spec Bk.

Plattard, Jean, ed. see Rabelais, Francois.

Platte, Curtis R., III, ed. see Weatherford, John R.

Platteau, Jean-Philippe, jt. auth. see Baland, Jean-Marie.

Platten, J. K. & Legros, J. C. Convection in Liquids. (Illus.). 700p. 1983. 139.00 (*0-387-12637-6*) Spr-Verlag.

***Platter, John.** John Platter's South African Wine Guide 1995. (Illus.). 324p. 1995. 13.95 (*1-85732-613-X*, Pub. by Reed Illust Books UK) Antique Collect.

Plattes, Gabriel. A Discovery of Infinite Treasure, Hidden Since the Worlde's Beginning. LC 74-80202. (English Experience Ser.: No. 682). 96p. 1974. reprint ed. 13.00 (*90-221-0682-9*) Walter J Johnson.

Plattner, B., et al. Message Handling & Data Communications X400: The Standards & Their Applications. (Illus.). 408p. (C). 1992. text ed. 45.25 (*0-201-56503-X*) Addison-Wesley.

Plattner, Bernhard, jt. ed. see Neufeld, Gerald.

Plattner, Helmut, ed. Electron Microscopy of Subcellular Dynamics. 368p. 1989. 228.00 (*0-8493-6079-X*, QH212) CRC Pr.

Plattner, Marc F., jt. ed. see Diamond, Larry J.

Plattner, Marc F., jt. ed. see Diamond, Larry.

Plattner, Robert. Real Estate Investment: Analysis & Management. 464p. (C). 1988. write for info. (*0-675-20524-7*, Merrill Pub Co) Macmillan.

Plattner, Robert H. Real Estate Principles. 607p. (C). 1984. text ed. 48.75 (*0-15-575844-6*) HB Coll Pubs.

Plattner, S., ed. Formal Methods in Economic Anthropology. (American Anthropological Association Special Publication: No. 4). 1975. pap. 7.50 (*0-686-36565-8*); pap. 5.00 (*0-685-06020-9*) Am Anthro Assn.

Plattner, Sandra S. Connecting Around the World. (J). (ps-00). 1991. pap. 10.99 (*0-86653-978-6*) Fearon Teach Aids.

— Connecting with Holidays. (J). (ps-00). 1991. pap. 10.99 (*0-8224-1634-4*) Fearon Teach Aids.

— Connecting with My Community. (J). (ps-00). 1991. pap. 10.99 (*0-8224-3912-3*) Fearon Teach Aids.

— Connecting with Myself. (J). (ps-00). 1991. pap. 10.99 (*0-86653-986-7*) Fearon Teach Aids.

— Connecting with Nature. (J). (ps-00). 1991. pap. 10.99 (*0-86653-976-X*) Fearon Teach Aids.

— Connecting with the Seasons. (J). (ps-00). 1991. pap. 10.99 (*0-86653-977-8*) Fearon Teach Aids.

Plattner, Steven W. Roy Stryker: U. S. A., 1943-1950, The Standard Oil (New Jersey) Photography Project. (Illus.). 144p. 1983. 27.95 (*0-292-77028-6*) U of Tex Pr.

Plattner, Stuart, ed. Economic Anthropology. LC 89-4547. 504p. 1989. 52.50 (*0-8047-1645-5*); pap. 18.95 (*0-8047-1752-4*) Stanford U Pr.

— Markets & Marketing: Proceedings of the 1984 Meeting of the Society for Economic Development. (Monographs in Economic Anthropology: No. 4). (Illus.). 438p. 1985. lib. bdg. 55.00 (*0-8191-4604-8*); pap. text ed. 37.00 (*0-8191-4605-6*) U Pr of Amer.

Platto, Charles. Enforcement of Foreign Judgments. (C). 1989. lib. bdg. 127.50 (*1-85333-315-8*, Pub. by Graham & Trotman UK) Kluwer Ac.

Platto, Charles, ed. Civil Appeal Procedures Worldwide. LC 92-18821. (International Bar Association Ser.). 448p. (C). 1992. lib. bdg. 170.00 (*1-85333-725-0*, Pub. by Graham & Trotman UK) Kluwer Ac.

— Obtaining Evidence in Another Jurisdiction in Business Disputes. 2nd ed. (International Bar Association Ser.). 208p. (C). 1993. lib. bdg. 100.00 (*1-85333-758-7*, Pub. by Graham & Trotman UK) Kluwer Ac.

— Pre-Trial & Pre-Hearing Procedures Worldwide. (C). 1990. lib. bdg. 150.00 (*1-85333-458-8*, Pub. by Graham & Trotman UK) Kluwer Ac.

— Trials & Court Procedures Worldwide. (International Bar Association Ser.). 480p. (C). 1991. lib. bdg. 160.00 (*1-85333-608-4*, Pub. by Graham & Trotman UK) Kluwer Ac.

Platto, Charles & Horton, William G., eds. Enforcement of Foreign Judgments Worldwide. 2nd ed. LC 93-29171. (International Bar Association Ser.). 1993. lib. bdg. 115.00 (*1-85333-757-9*, Pub. by Graham & Trotman UK) Kluwer Ac.

Platts, Dennis R., jt. ed. see Boulous, Edward N.

Platts, Geoffrey. Trek! Man Alone in the Arizona Wild. Grenard, Jack, ed. (Illus.). 208p. (Orig.). 1991. pap. 10.50 (*0-9631487-0-2*) Carefree Comm.

Platts, J. & St. Aubyn, J. D. Uninterruptible Power Supplies. (IEE Power Engineering Ser.: No. 14). 168p. 1992. text ed. 68.00 (*0-86341-263-7*) Inst Elect Eng.

Platts, John T. Dictionary of Urdu, Classical Hindi & English. (ENG, HIN & URD.). 1987. 95.00 (*0-8288-1745-6*, F29960) Fr & Eur.

— A Dictionary of Urdu Classical Hindi & English. 2nd ed. (C). 1988. 52.00 (*0-8364-2410-7*) S Asia.

— The Grammar of the Hindustani or Urdu Language. 1990. reprint ed. 27.00 (*0-685-48703-2*, Pub. by Munshiram Manoharial II) S Asia.

— Grammar of the Hindustani or Urdu Language. (ENG & HIN.). 1992. reprint ed. 49.95 (*0-8288-8473-0*) Fr & Eur.

Platts, Mark. Moral Realities: An Essay in Philosophical Psychology. 288p. (C). 1991. text ed. 72.50 (*0-415-05892-9*, A5551) Routledge.

Platts, Mitchell. Illustrated History of Golf. (Illus.). 1988. 19.99 (*0-517-65837-2*) Random Hse Value.

Plattsmouth Journal Staff. Cass County, Nebraska. (Illus.). 669p. 1989. 62.50 (*0-88107-137-4*) Curtis Media.

Platukis, Joseph G., jt. auth. see Gordon, William R.

Platvoet, J. G. Comparing Religions: A Limitative Approach. (Religion & Reason Ser.: No. 24). xiv, 350p. 1982. 63.25 (*90-279-3170-4*) Mouton.

Platz-Horster, Gertrud. Nil und Euthenia. (Winckelmannsprogramm der Archaologischen Gesellschaft zu Berlin Ser.: No. 133). 47p. (GER.). (C). 1992. pap. text ed. 29.25 (*3-11-013779-8*) De Gruyter.

Platz, Joseph, tr. see Nimzowitsch, Aron.

Platz, Judith R. The Silence of Light. (Salt River Poetry Ser.). 32p. (Orig.). 1990. pap. 6.95 (*1-882021-15-0*) Salt River Pr.

Platz, M. S., ed. Kinetics & Spectroscopy of Carbenes & Biradicals. LC 89-29219. (Illus.). 388p. 1990. 95.00 (*0-306-43282-X*, Plenum Pr) Plenum.

Platz, Theodore A., Jr. Banking. deluxe ed. (Barron's Business Library). 320p. 1991. 14.95 (*0-8120-4542-4*) Barron.

Platz, Tom & Reynolds, Bill. Pro-Style Bodybuilding. LC 84-23950. (Illus.). 1985. pap. 12.95 (*0-8069-7910-0*) Sterling.

Platz, Valerie A., jt. ed. see Kratz, Charles E.

Platzack, Christer, jt. auth. see Holmberg, Anders.

Platzer, B., et al. Thermophysical Properties of Refrigerants. (Illus.). 464p. 1990. 233.00 (*0-387-16112-0*) Spr-Verlag.

Platzer, Steven, tr. see Horio, Teruhisa.

Platzer, W., ed. European Anatomical Congress, 7th, Insbruck, September 1984: Abstracts. (Journal: Acta Anatomica: Vol. 120, No. 1-2). 92p. 1984. pap. 30.50 (*3-8055-3955-X*) S Karger.

Platzer, Werner. Color Atlas & Textbook of Human Anatomy: Locomotor System, Vol. I. 4th ed. (Illus.). 440p. 1992. pap. 27.00 (*0-86577-423-4*) Thieme Med Pubs.

Platzer, Werner, ed. see Pernkopf, Eduard.

Platzky, Laurine & Walker, Cherryl. The Surplus People: Forced Removals in South Africa. LC 82-95958. 250p. 1985. pap. text ed. 16.95 (*0-86975-255-3*, Pub. by Ravan Pr ZA) Ohio U Pr.

Platzmann, Julius. Vezeichniss einer Auswahl Amerikanischer Grammatiken. 1977. reprint ed. 23.95 (*0-518-19010-2*) Ayer.

Platzner, Gloria, jt. auth. see Harris, Stephen L.

Platzner, Robert L. The Metaphysical Novel in England: The Romantic Phase. Varma, Devendra P., ed. LC 79-8468. (Gothic Studies & Dissertations). 1980. lib. bdg. 36.95 (*0-405-12656-5*) Ayer.

Platzner, Robert L. & Harris, Stephen L. Touchstones: Classic Texts in the Humanities. 600p. (C). 1991. pap. text ed. 20.00 (*0-03-047504-X*) HB Coll Pubs.

Platzner, Robert L., jt. auth. see Gersh, Harry.

Platzoder, Renate, ed. The Law of the Sea Documents, 1983-1992: Preparatory Commission for the International Sea-Bed Authority & for the International Tribunal for the Law of the Sea, 15 vols., Set. LC 89-43541. (Second Ser.). 1990. lib. bdg. 1,500.00 (*0-379-20935-7*) Oceana.

— Third United Nations Conference on the Law of the Sea: Documents, 1973-1982, 18 vols., Set. 1982. 1,800.00 (*0-379-20724-9*) Oceana.

Platzoder, Renate, ed. see United Nations Conference on the Law of the Sea Staff.

Platzoder, Renate, jt. auth. see Von Welck, Stephan.

Plauger, P. J. The C Plus Plus Library. 512p. 1994. pap. text ed. 39.00 (*0-13-117003-1*) P-H.

— Programming on Purpose: Essays on Programming Design. LC 92-45905. (Illus.). 256p. (C). 1993. pap. text ed. 30.67 (*0-13-721374-3*) P-H.

— Programming on Purpose III: Essays on Software Technology. 1993. pap. text ed. 30.67 (*0-13-328113-2*) P-H.

— Programming on Purpose 2: Essays on Software People. 224p. (C). 1993. pap. text ed. 30.67 (*0-13-328105-1*) P-H.

— Standard C Library. 1991. text ed. 53.00 (*0-13-838012-0*); pap. text ed. 40.00 (*0-13-131509-9*) P-H.

Plauger, P. J., jt. auth. see Kernighan, Brian W.

***Plauger, P. L. & Brodie, Jim.** Standard C. LC 95-15055. 1995. pap. text ed. 29.95 (*0-13-436411-2*) P-H.

Plauger, P. L., jt. auth. see Kernighan, Brian W.

Plaugher, Gregory, ed. Textbook of Clinical Chiropractic. LC 92-5613. (Illus.). 550p. 1993. 80.00 (*0-683-06897-0*) Williams & Wilkins.

Plaumann, Peter, jt. ed. see Strambach, Karl.

Plaut, Arthur, jt. auth. see Binkoski, Joseph.

Plaut, David. Chasing October: The Dodgers-Giants Pennant Race of 1962. LC 94-9008. (Illus.). 260p. 1994. 22.95 (*0-912083-69-7*) Diamond Communications.

— Start Collecting Baseball Cards. LC 89-43016. (Start Collecting Ser.). (Illus.). 96p. (Orig.). (J). (gr. 4 up). 1989. pap. 9.95 (*0-89471-762-6*) Running Pr.

Plaut, David, ed. Baseball Wit & Wisdom. LC 91-50911. (Miniature Editions Ser.). (Illus.). 144p. 1992. 4.95 (*1-56138-104-7*) Running Pr.

— Speaking of Baseball. LC 92-50793. (Illus.). 384p. 1993. 9.95 (*1-56138-238-8*) Running Pr.

Plaut, Eric A. Grand Opera: Mirror of the Western Mind. LC 93-8351. (Illus.). 336p. 1993. 28.50 (*1-56663-034-7*) I R Dee.

Plaut, Fred. Analysis Analysed. LC 92-49187. (Illus.). 400p. 1993. 39.95 (*0-415-00789-5*, A2430, Routledge NY) Routledge.

Plaut, H. Japanese Conversation - Grammar with Numerous Reading Lessons & Dialogues, 2 vols., Set. 1991. lib. bdg. 98.95 (*0-8490-4512-6*) Gordon Pr.

Plaut, James S., ed. Sources of Modern Painting. LC 79-91372. (Contemporary Art Ser.). 1970. reprint ed. 19.95 (*0-405-00734-5*) Ayer.

Plaut, L., ed. see International Astronomical Union Staff.

Plaut, Mary, ed. see Michael, Christine.

Plaut, Simone. Radiation Protection in the X-Ray Department. LC 92-49239. 192p. 1993. 25.00 (*0-7506-0606-1*) Buttrwrth-Heinemann.

Plaut, Thomas. An Econometric Analysis of Regional Wastepaper Markets. (Discussion Paper Ser.: No. 104). 1978. pap. 10.00 (*1-55869-030-1*) Regional Sci Res Inst.

— The Effects of Urbanization on the Loss of Farmland at the Rural-Urban Fringe: A National & Regional Perspective. (Discussion Paper Ser.: No. 94). 1976. pap. 10.00 (*1-55869-034-4*) Regional Sci Res Inst.

— The Real Property Tax, Differential Assessment, & the Loss of Farmland on the Rural-Urban Fringe. (Discussion Paper Ser.: No. 97). 1977. pap. 10.00 (*1-55869-104-9*) Regional Sci Res Inst.

Plaut, Thomas & Steiker, Gene. Characteristics of Wastepaper Markets & Trends in Scrap Paper Recycling, Prices, Demand & Availability: A National & Regional Overview. (Discussion Paper Ser.: No. 103). 1978. pap. 10.00 (*1-55869-012-3*) Regional Sci Res Inst.

Plaut, Thomas, jt. auth. see Coughlin, Robert E.

***Plaut, Thomas F.** El Asma En un Minuto: Lo Que Usted Necessita Saber. (Illus.). 40p. (YA). (gr. 9-12). 1995. pap. 4.95 (*0-914625-12-8*) Pedipress.

— Children with Asthma: A Manual for Parents. 2nd ed. LC 87-34311. (Illus.). 291p. 1989. pap. 14.95 (*0-914625-03-9*); Pocket-size ed. pap. 7.95 (*0-914625-05-5*) Pedipress.

— One Minute Asthma: What You Need to Know. LC 91-590. (Illus.). 48p. (Orig.). 1991. pap. 4.95 (*0-914625-07-1*) Pedipress.

— One Minute Asthma: What You Need to Know. rev. ed. LC 91-590. (Illus.). 40p. (Orig.). Date not set. pap. 4.95 (*0-914625-11-X*) Pedipress.

— One Minute Asthma: What You Need to Know. 2nd ed. LC 91-47892. (Illus.). 48p. (Orig.). (YA). (gr. 6-12). 1996. pap. 4.95 (*0-914625-13-6*) Pedipress.

***Plaut, W. Gunther.** Asylum: A Moral Dilemma. LC 95-3330. 192p. 1995. text ed. 55.00 (*0-275-95195-2*, Praeger Pubs); pap. text ed. 16.95 (*0-275-95196-0*, Praeger Pubs) Greenwood.

— The Magen David: How the Six-Pointed Star Became the Emblem of the Jewish People. (Illus.). 114p. 1990. 22.50 (*0-910250-16-2*); pap. 12.95 (*0-910250-17-0*) Bnai Brith Intl.

— The Man Who Would Be Messiah: A Biographical Novel. 258p. 1995. lib. bdg. 33.00 (*0-8095-4904-2*) Borgo Pr.

— The Rise of Reform Judaism: A Sourcebook of Its European Origins. Incl. Growth of Reform Judaism: American & European Sources to 1948. 1965. (*0-318-56271-5*); 1963. 10.00 (*0-8074-0089-0*, 382770) UAHC.

Plaut, W. Gunther & Bamberger, Bernard J. Torah: A Modern Commentary. 1824p. 1981. 100.00 (*0-8074-0286-9*, 381597); 55.00 (*0-8074-0333-4*, 381630) UAHC.

— Torah: A Modern Commentary. 1824p. 1981. 40.00 (*0-8074-0165-X*, 381590); 40.00 (*0-8074-0055-6*, 381600) UAHC.

Plaute. Oeuvres Completes. (FRE.). 1971. lib. bdg. 95.00 (*0-8288-3574-8*, F40040) Fr & Eur.

Plaute & Terence. Oeuvres Completes. 1512p. 41.50 (*0-686-56550-9*) Fr & Eur.

Plautus. Amphitryon, Vol. I. Bd. with Comedy of Asses.; Pot of Gold.; Two Bacchises.; Captives. (Loeb Classical Library: No. 60). 15.50 (*0-674-99067-6*) HUP.

— Amphitryon: Index Verborum, Lexiques Inersese, Releves Lexicaux et Grammaticaux. Maniet, Albert & Paquot, Annette, eds. Bd. XIX. vii, 217p. (GER.). 1970. write for info. (*0-318-70439-0*, Pub. by Georg Olms GW) Lubrecht & Cramer.

— Amphitryon & Two Other Plays. Casson, Lionel, ed. 1971. pap. 8.95 (*0-393-00601-8*) Norton.

— Ausgewahlte Komodien, 3 vols. Lorenz, August O., ed. 1981. Bd. 2: Mostellaria, 239p. write for info. (*3-296-15001-3*, Pub. by Georg Olms GW); Bd. 3: Miles Gloriosus, viii, 294p. write for info. (*0-318-71196-6*, Pub. by Georg Olms GW); Bd. 4: Pseudolus, viii, 289p. write for info. (*3-296-15003-X*, Pub. by Georg Olms GW) Lubrecht & Cramer.

— Ausgewahlte Komodien, 3 vols., Set. Lorenz, August O., ed. 1981. write for info. (*0-318-71195-8*, Pub. by Georg Olms GW) Lubrecht & Cramer.

— Bacchides. Barsby, ed. (Classical Texts Ser.). 49.95 (*0-85668-226-8*, Pub. by Aris & Phillips UK); pap. 24.95 (*0-85668-227-6*, Pub. by Aris & Phillips UK) David Brown.

— The Captivi of Plautus. Connor, W. R. & Lindsey, Wallace M., eds. LC 78-67134. (Latin Texts & Commentaries Ser.). (ENG & LAT.). 1979. reprint ed. lib. bdg. 30.95 (*0-405-11608-X*) Ayer.

— Casina, Vol. II. Bd. with Casket Comedy.; Curculio.; Epidicus.; Two Menaechmuses. (Loeb Classical Library: No. 61). 15.50 (*0-674-99068-4*) HUP.

— Comoediae, 2 vols. Leo, Friedrich, ed. 1958. Vol. I, viii, 478p. write for info. (*0-318-71198-2*, Pub. by Georg Olms GW); Vol. II, iv, 575p. write for info. (*0-318-71199-0*, Pub. by Georg Olms GW) Lubrecht & Cramer.

— Comoediae, 2 Vols, 1. Lindsay, W. M., ed. 1922. 39.95 (*0-19-814628-0*) OUP.

— Comoediae, 2 Vols, 2. Lindsay, W. M., ed. 1922. 39.95 (*0-19-814629-9*) OUP.

— Comoediae, 2 vols., Set. Leo, Friedrich, ed. 1958. write for info. (*0-318-71197-4*, Pub. by Georg Olms GW) Lubrecht & Cramer.

— Lexique Inverse: Listes Grammaticales, Releves Divers. Maniet, Albert, ed. Bd. XVIII. viii, 201p. (GER.). 1969. write for info. (*0-318-70440-4*, Pub. by Georg Olms GW) Lubrecht & Cramer.

— Little Carthaginian, Vol. IV. Bd. with Pseudolus.; Rope. (Loeb Classical Library: No. 260). 15.50 (*0-674-99286-5*) HUP.

— Menaechmi. Gratwick, A. S., ed. LC 92-17790. (Greek & Latin Classics Ser.). 304p. (C). 1993. 64.95 (*0-521-34162-0*); pap. 22.95 (*0-521-34970-2*) Cambridge U Pr.

— Plaute, Amphitryon. Index Verborum, Lexiques Inverses, Releves Lexicaux et Grammaticaux. Maniet, Albert & Paquot, Annette, eds. Bd. XIX. vii, 217p. 1970. write for info. (*0-318-71200-8*, Pub. by Georg Olms GW) Lubrecht & Cramer.

— Plaute, Lexique Inverse. Listes Grammaticales. Releves Divers. Maniet, Albert, ed. Bd. XVIII. viii, 201p. 1969. write for info. (*0-318-71201-6*, Pub. by Georg Olms GW) Lubrecht & Cramer.

— Plauti Mercator, 2 vols. in one. Connor, W. R., ed. LC 78-67131. (Latin Texts & Commentaries Ser.). (ENG & LAT.). 1979. reprint ed. lib. bdg. 25.95 (*0-405-11601-2*) Ayer.

— Plauti Truculentus, 2 vols. in one. Connor, W. R., ed. LC 78-67132. (Latin Texts & Commentaries Ser.). (LAT.). 1979. reprint ed. lib. bdg. 28.95 (*0-405-11602-0*) Ayer.

— Rudens. Fay, H. C., ed. & intro. by. (College Classical Ser.). v, 221p. (C). 1983. reprint ed. pap. text ed. 17.50 (*0-89241-386-7*) Caratzas.

— Rudens, Curculio, Casina. Stace, Christopher, tr. LC 81-6086. (Translations from Greek & Roman Authors Ser.). (Illus.). 160p. 1982. pap. 11.95 (*0-521-28046-X*) Cambridge U Pr.

— Stichus, Vol. V. Bd. with Three Bob Day.; Truculentus.; Tale of a Traveling Bag.; Fragments. (Loeb Classical Library: No. 328). 15.50 (*0-674-99362-4*) HUP.

— T. Macci Plauti Aulularia: With Critical & Exegetical Notes & an Introduction. Connor, W. R., ed. LC 78-67156. (Latin Texts & Commentaries Ser.). (ENG & LAT.). 1979. reprint ed. lib. bdg. 19.95 (*0-405-11623-3*) Ayer.

— T. Macci Plauti Epidicus. Connor, W. R., ed. (Latin Texts & Commentaries Ser.). (ENG & LAT.). 1979. reprint ed. lib. bdg. 37.95 (*0-405-11600-4*) Ayer.

An Asterisk (*) at the beginning of an entry indicates that the title is appearing in BIP for the first time.

— T. Macci Plauti Pseudolus. Connor, W. R., ed. LC 78-11622. (Latin Texts & Commentaries Ser.). (ENG & LAT.). 1979. reprint ed. lib. bdg. 15.95 (0-405-11622-5) Ayer.
— T. Macci Plauti Rudens. Connor, W. R. & Sonnenschein, Edward A., eds. LC 78-67153. (Latin Texts & Commentaries Ser.). (ENG & LAT.). 1979. reprint ed. lib. bdg. 25.95 (0-405-11620-9) Ayer.
— Three Comedies. Wind, Robert, ed. & tr. by. LC 94-41092. 1995. write for info. (0-8191-9815-3) U Pr of Amer.
— Three Comedies: Miles Gloriosus - Pseudolus - Rudens. LC 90-41383. (Masters of Latin Literature Ser.). 320p. 1991. 41.95 (0-8014-2355-4); pap. 12.95 (0-8014-9594-6) Cornell U Pr.
Plautus, jt. auth. see Aristophanes.
Plautus, T. Maccius. Menaechmi. rev. ed. Hammond, Mason & Moseley, Nicholas, eds. 140p. 1961. 22.50 (0-674-56725-0) HUP.
— Miles Gloriosus. 2nd rev. ed. Hammond, Mason et al, eds. LC 73-122213. 140p. 1963. 23.50 (0-674-57436-2) HUP.
Plautus, T. Maccus. Fabularum Reliquiae Ambrosianae. xxxii, 524p. (GER.). 1972. reprint ed. write for info. (3-487-04334-3, Pub. by Georg Olms GW) Lubrecht & Cramer.
Plavchan, Ronald J. A History of Anheuser-Busch, Eighteen Fifty-Two to Nineteen Thirty-Three. LC 75-41779. (Companies & Men: Business Enterprises in America Ser.). 1980. 26.95 (0-405-08094-8) Ayer.
Plavec, Mirek J., ed. see International Astronomical Union Staff.
Plavsic, Branko M., et al. Gastrointestinal Radiology: A Concise Text. (Illus.). 576p. 1992. text ed. 95.00 (0-07-105369-7) Hlth Prof Div.
— Gastrointestinal Radiology: A Concise Text. 640p. 1991. 89.01 (0-08-040685-8, Pub. by PPI UK) McGraw.
Plawin, Paul. Careers for Travel Buffs & Other Restless Types. (Careers for You Ser.). 160p. 1992. 12.95 (0-8442-8109-3, VGM Career Bks); pap. 9.95 (0-8442-8127-1, VGM Career Bks) NTC Pub Grp.
Plaxton, Elmer H., ed. North American Terrestrial Orchids: Symposium II - Proceedings & Lectures. LC 82-62805. (Illus.). 144p. 1983. pap. 17.95 (0-9610332-0-7) Mich Orchid Soc.
***Play Bac Publisher Staff.** Boing! Date not set. write for info. (0-679-87486-0) Random.
— Pop! Date not set. write for info. (0-679-87487-9) Random.
***Play Bac Publishing.** TeamTracker NFL Football. (YA). 1994. 24.95 (0-8362-4239-4) Andrews & McMeel.
***Play Bac Publishing Staff.** Team Tracker: NBA Basketball. (Illus.). 64p. (J). (gr. 3 up). 1994. pap. 24.95 (0-8362-4238-6) Andrews & McMeel.
Playboy Enterprises, Inc. Staff. The Playboy Interview: The Best of Three Decades 1962-1992. (Illus.). (Orig.). Date not set. 24.95 (0-87223-909-8); pap. 9.95 (0-87223-908-X) Playboy Ent.
— Playboy Presents: Dian Parkinson. (Illus.). 96p. (Orig.). 1993. pap. 5.95 (0-87223-913-6) Playboy Ent.
— Playboy Presents International Playmates. (Playboy Presents Ser.). (Illus.). 112p. (Orig.). 1992. pap. 5.95 (0-87223-900-4, Playboy Pr) Playboy Ent.
— Playboy Presents Playboy's Playmate Review. (Playboy Presents Ser.). (Illus.). 112p. (Orig.). 1992. pap. 5.95 (0-87223-903-9, Playboy Pr) Playboy Ent.
— Playboy's Bathing Beauties. (Illus.). 112p. (Orig.). 1992. pap. 5.95 (0-87223-902-0, Playboy Pr) Playboy Ent.
— Playboy's Career Girls. (Illus.). 112p. (Orig.). 1992. pap. 5.95 (0-87223-905-5, Playboy Pr) Playboy Ent.
— Playboy's Girls of Summer Ninety-Two. (Illus.). 112p. (Orig.). 1992. pap. 5.95 (0-87223-904-7, Playboy Pr) Playboy Ent.
— Playboy's Girls of the World. (Illus.). 112p. (Orig.). 1992. pap. 5.95 (0-87223-906-3, Playboy Pr) Playboy Ent.
— Playboy's Nudes. (Illus.). 112p. (Orig.). 1992. pap. 5.95 (0-87223-907-1, Playboy Pr) Playboy Ent.
— Playboy's Sisters. (Illus.). 112p. (Orig.). 1992. pap. 5.95 (0-87223-901-2, Playboy Pr) Playboy Ent.
Player, Elaine, ed. The Future of Prisons: Reform in the Post-Woolf Era. LC 93-14816. 1994. write for info. (0-415-07956-X) Routledge.
Player, Elaine, jt. auth. see Genders, Elaine.
Player, Gary. Fit for Golf. LC 94-10738. 1995. pap. 15.00 (0-671-89994-5) S&S Trade.
Player, Gary & Tolhurst, Desmond. Golf Begins at Fifty: Playing the Lifetime Game Better Than Ever. 1989. pap. 14.00 (0-671-68319-5, Fireside) S&S Trade.
Player, Jay & Player, Margaret, comps. Index to the Ninth Federal Census, 1870, Grand Traverse County, Michigan. 104p. 1989. pap. 9.00 (0-9622372-3-X) Grand Traverse.
Player, Jay, jt. comp. see Player, Margaret.
Player, Lesley. My Story. 1993. mass mkt. 5.99 (0-06-109222-3, Harp PBks) HarpC.
***Player, Mack A., et al.** Employment Discrimination Law, Cases & Materials On. 2nd ed. LC 95-16452. (American Casebook Ser.). 743p. (C). 1995. text ed. write for info. (0-314-06393-5) West Pub.
Player, Mack A. Federal Laws of Employment Discrimination in a Nutshell. 3rd ed. (Nutshell Ser.). 338p. 1993. reprint ed. pap. text ed. 15.00 (0-314-00128-X) West Pub.
— The Law of Employment & Discrimination: Practitioner's Edition. (Hornbook Ser.). 951p. 1989. reprint ed. text ed. write for info. (0-314-58666-0) West Pub.
— The Law of Employment & Discrimination: Student Edition. (Hornbook Ser.). 708p. (C). 1988. text ed. 34.50 (0-314-58916-3) West Pub.
Player, Mack A., et al. Employment Discrimination: Third Edition, Cases & Materials. (American Casebook Ser.). 827p. 1990. text ed. 46.00 (0-314-73435-X) West Pub.
— Employment Discrimination Law, Cases & Materials, 1992 Supplement to Accompany. (American Casebook Ser.). 240p. (C). 1992. pap. text ed. 11.00 (0-314-01212-5) West Pub.
— Employment Discrimination, Teacher's Manual to Accompany Cases & Materials On. (American Casebook Ser.). 300p. 1990. pap. text ed. write for info. (0-314-79654-1) West Pub.
Player, Margaret & Player, Jay, comps. Index to the Ninth Federal Census, 1870, Leelanau County, Michigan. 93p. 1990. pap. 9.00 (0-9622372-6-4) Grand Traverse.
Player, Margaret, jt. comp. see Player, Jay.
***Player Picker Staff & Catlin, Mark G.** The Art of Soccer: A Better Way to Play. rev. ed. 206p. (Orig.). 1993. 24.95 (0-9626834-2-6) Soccer Bks.
***Player, R. Steven & Keys, David E.** Activity-Based Management: Arthur Andersen's Lessons from the ABM Battlefield. 224p. 1995. 24.95 (1-57101-054-8) MasterMedia Ltd.
Player, Steve. Win: Lotto & Daily Numbers Playing Techniques. LC 88-81912. (LOMAP Ser.: Vol. 7). (Illus.). 108p. 1988. pap. 9.95 (0-318-37498-6) Intergalactic NJ.
Player, Theresa J., et al. California Trial Techniques. 800p. 1994. ring bd. 115.00 (1-55943-115-6) Michie Butterworth.
— California Trial Techniques, No. 1. suppl. ed. 1993. 45.00 (1-55943-174-1) Butterworth Legal Pubs.
Playfair, Emma, ed. International Law & the Administration of Occupied Territories: Two Decades of Israeli Occupation of the West Bank Gaza Strip. 576p. 1992. 120.00 (0-19-825297-8) OUP.
Playfair, George M. The Cities & Towns of China: A Geographical Dictionary. 1976. lib. bdg. 59.95 (0-8490-1635-5) Gordon Pr.
Playfair, Helen. Flying High. 512p. 1994. mass mkt. 4.99 (0-8217-4564-6) Zebra.
— A Kiss to Remember. 416p. 1993. mass mkt. 4.50 (0-8217-4129-2) Zebra.
— A Kiss to Remember. large type ed. LC 93-5223. 415p. 1993. reprint ed. lib. bdg. 16.95 (0-7862-0011-1) Thorndike Pr.
Playfair, J. H. Immunology at a Glance. 5th ed. (At a Glance Ser.). (Illus.). 96p. 1992. pap. 24.95 (0-632-03315-0) Blackwell Sci.
***Playfair, John H.** Infection & Immunity. (Illus.). 150p. 1995. 39.95 (0-19-854926-1); pap. 17.95 (0-19-854925-3) OUP.
Playfair, Nigel R. Story of the Lyric Theatre, Hammersmith. LC 77-84524. (Illus.). 1972. 24.95 (0-405-08858-2) Ayer.
Playfair, Robert L. The Scourge of Christendom: Annals of British Relations with Algiers Prior to the French Conquest. LC 72-3987. (Black Heritage Library Collection). 1977. reprint ed. 35.95 (0-8369-9104-4) Ayer.
Playfair, William L. & Bryson, George. The Useful Lie. 192p. (C). 1991. pap. 8.95 (0-89107-637-9) Crossway Bks.
Playfoot, Jane, jt. ed. see Gonzalez, Jose L.
Playfoot, Janet, jt. ed. see Gonzalez-Balado, Jose L.
Playford, John & Purcell, Henry. An Introduction to the Skill of Musick. LC 67-27551. (Music Reprint Ser.). 282p. 1972. reprint ed. lib. bdg. 39.50 (0-306-70937-6) Da Capo.
Playko, Marsha A., jt. auth. see Daresh, John C.
Playwright, Young. Inside Out-Upside Down. 40p. 1986. pap. 4.95 (0-87129-153-3, 143) Dramatic Pub.
Plaza & Janes Staff. Gran Diccionario Enciclopedico, 20 vols. 7th ed. 3896p. (SPA.). 1991. 3,500.00 (0-7859-5057-5) Fr & Eur.
Plaza, A. Diccionario de las Americas. 1216p. (SPA.). 1991. 125.00 (0-7859-5684-0, 8401601657) Fr & Eur.
— Diccionario Enciclopedico, 6 vols. 3796p. (SPA.). 1991. 895.00 (0-7859-5686-7, 8401607256) Fr & Eur.
— Gran Diccionario Enciclopedico, Vol. 1. 416p. (SPA.). 1991. 175.00 (0-7859-5687-5, 8401612012) Fr & Eur.
— Gran Diccionario Enciclopedico, Vol. 2. 416p. (SPA.). 1991. 175.00 (0-7859-5688-3, 8401612020) Fr & Eur.
— Gran Diccionario Enciclopedico, Vol. 3. 416p. (SPA.). 1991. 175.00 (0-7859-5689-1, 8401612039) Fr & Eur.
— Gran Diccionario Enciclopedico, Vol. 4. 416p. (SPA.). 1991. 175.00 (0-7859-5690-5, 8401612047) Fr & Eur.
— Gran Diccionario Enciclopedico, Vol. 5. 416p. (SPA.). 1991. 175.00 (0-7859-5691-3, 8401612055) Fr & Eur.
— Gran Diccionario Enciclopedico, Vol. 6. 416p. (SPA.). 1991. 175.00 (0-7859-5692-1, 8401612063) Fr & Eur.
— Gran Diccionario Enciclopedico, Vol. 8. 416p. 1991. 175.00 (0-7859-6443-6) Fr & Eur.
— Gran Diccionario Enciclopedico, Vol. 9. 416p. (SPA.). 1991. 175.00 (0-7859-5694-8, 8401612098) Fr & Eur.
— Gran Diccionario Enciclopedico, Vol. 10. 416p. (SPA.). 1991. 175.00 (0-7859-5695-6, 8401612101) Fr & Eur.
— Gran Diccionario Enciclopedico, Vol. 11. 416p. 1991. 175.00 (0-7859-6444-4) Fr & Eur.
— Gran Diccionario Enciclopedico, Vol. 12. 416p. (SPA.). 1991. 175.00 (0-7859-5696-4, 8401612128) Fr & Eur.
— Gran Diccionario Enciclopedico, Vol. 13. 416p. (SPA.). 1991. 175.00 (0-7859-5697-2, 8401612136) Fr & Eur.
— Gran Diccionario Enciclopedico, Vol. 14. 416p. (SPA.). 1991. 175.00 (0-7859-5698-0, 8401612144) Fr & Eur.
— Gran Diccionario Enciclopedico, Vol. 15. 416p. (SPA.). 1991. 175.00 (0-7859-5699-9, 8401612152) Fr & Eur.
— Gran Diccionario Enciclopedico, Vol. 16. 416p. (SPA.). 1991. 175.00 (0-7859-5700-6, 8401612160) Fr & Eur.
— Gran Diccionario Enciclopedico, Vol. 17. 416p. (SPA.). 1991. 175.00 (0-7859-5701-4, 8401612179) Fr & Eur.
— Gran Diccionario Enciclopedico, Vol. 18. 416p. (SPA.). 1991. 175.00 (0-7859-5702-2, 8401612187) Fr & Eur.
— Gran Diccionario Enciclopedico, Vol. 19. 416p. (SPA.). 1991. 175.00 (0-7859-5703-0, 8401612195) Fr & Eur.
— Gran Diccionario Enciclopedico, Vol. 20. 416p. (SPA.). 1991. 175.00 (0-7859-5704-9, 8401612209) Fr & Eur.
Plaza, Fuensanta. Clint Eastwood: Malpaso. LC 91-71749. (Illus.). 256p. (Orig.). 1991. pap. 24.95 (0-9629481-9-5) Ex Libris CA.
Plaza Janes Staff. Diccionario Familiar Larousse, Vol. 1: Espanol - Ingles. 66p. (ENG & SPA.). 1991. pap. 39.95 (0-7859-5706-5, 8401614074) Fr & Eur.
— Diccionario Familiar Larousse, Vol. 2: Ingles - Espanol. 62p. (ENG & SPA.). 1991. pap. 39.95 (0-7859-5707-3, 8401614082) Fr & Eur.
— Diccionario Manual Auxiliar Basico. 2nd ed. 432p. (SPA.). 1991. write for info. (0-7859-5091-5) Fr & Eur.
Plaza, Lasso G. Problems of Democracy in Latin America. LC 81-36. (Weil Lectures on American Citizenship Ser.). vi, 88p. 1981. reprint ed. text ed. 49.75 (0-313-22877-9, PLPD, Greenwood Pr) Greenwood.
Plazaola, Luis T. Cine y Mujer en America Latina. 304p. 1991. pap. 17.50 (0-8477-2507-3) U of PR Pr.
— South American Cinema: A Dictionary of Film Makers. 236p. 1989. pap. 10.95 (0-8477-2011-X) U of PR Pr.
Plazaola, Luis Trelles. Cine Sudamericano: Diccionario de Directores. (UPREX, Teatro y Cine Ser.: No. 72). 373p. 1985. pap. 6.00 (0-8477-0072-0) U of PR Pr.
Plaziat, J., jt. auth. see Freytet, P.
Plazy, Gilles. A Weekend with Rousseau. LC 93-12187. (Illus.). 64p. (J). 1993. 19.95 (0-8478-1717-2) Rizzoli Intl.
***Plead, Jane.** Worlds Apart. 150p. 1995. 19.95 (0-9646885-0-6) Manoa Valley.
Pleadwell, F. L., ed. see Drake, Joseph R.
***Pleas.** Implementing Ole 2.0 in Visual Basic. 1995. pap. 39.99 (1-56884-311-9) IDG Bks.
Pleasance, Charles A. The Spirit of Independent Telephony: A Chronicle of the Accomplishments, Intrigue, & the Fight for Survival of the Independent Telephone Movement in the United States. LC 88-83741. (Illus.). 320p. 1989. 29.50 (0-9622205-0-7) Ind Tel Bks.
Pleasant, Barbara. Alabama Gardener's Almanac. 64p. 1992. pap. 5.95 (0-9633210-0-5) Southern Ground.
— The Gardener's Bug Book: Earth-Safe Insect Control. Stell, Liz & Balmuth, Deborah, eds. LC 93-36907. (Illus.). 160p. 1994. pap. 9.95 (0-88266-609-6, Garden Way Pub) Storey Comm Inc.
— The Gardener's Guide to Plant Diseases: Earth-Safe Remedies. LC 94-34067. 1995. 16.95 (0-88266-297-X, Storey Pub); pap. 12.95 (0-88266-274-0) Storey Comm Inc.
— Warm-Climate Gardening: Tips - Techniques - Plans - Projects for Humid or Dry Conditions. Steege, Gwen, ed. LC 92-54255. (Illus.). 208p. 1993. pap. 12.95 (0-88266-818-8, Garden Way Pub) Storey Comm Inc.
Pleasant Company Staff. Addy Paper Doll. (American Girls Collection). 24p. (Orig.). (J). (gr. 2-5). 1994. pap. 5.95 (1-56247-126-0) Pleasant Co.
— Addy's Cookbook. (American Girls Collection Ser.). 48p. (Orig.). (J). (gr. 2-5). 1994. pap. 5.95 (1-56247-123-6) Pleasant Co.
— Addy's Craft Book. (American Girls Collection). 48p. (Orig.). (J). (gr. 2-5). 1994. pap. 5.95 (1-56247-124-4) Pleasant Co.
— Addy's Theater Kit. (American Girls Collection). 48p. (Orig.). (J). (gr. 2-5). 1994. pap. 5.95 (1-56247-125-2) Pleasant Co.
— Felicity's Theater Kit. (American Girls Collection). 48p. (Orig.). (J). (gr. 2-5). 1994. pap. 5.95 (1-56247-122-8) Pleasant Co.
— Kirsten's Theater Kit. (American Girls Collection). 48p. (Orig.). (J). (gr. 2-5). 1994. pap. 5.95 (1-56247-113-9) Pleasant Co.
— Molly's Theater Kit. (American Girls Collection). 48p. (Orig.). (J). (gr. 2-5). 1994. pap. 5.95 (1-56247-119-8) Pleasant Co.
— My Trip to Felicity's Williamsburg: An American Girl's Journal. (Illus.). 14p. (J). (gr. 2-5). 1991. 4.95 (1-56247-028-0); 1.95 (1-56247-029-9) Pleasant Co.
— Samantha's Theater Kit. (American Girls Collection). 48p. (Orig.). (J). (gr. 2-5). 1994. pap. 5.95 (1-56247-116-3) Pleasant Co.
Pleasant, Hazen H. A History of Crawford County, Indiana. (Illus.). 644p. 1992. reprint ed. lib. bdg. 65.00 (0-8328-2544-1) Higginson Bk Co.

Pleasant, James W. Doctor Jim's Odyssey. LC 94-60592. 138p. 1994. pap. 8.00 (0-912400-14-5) Western Res Pr. Ohio Veterinarian Jim Pleasant's Multiple Myeloma bone marrow transplant treatment required quiet time. Encouraged by friends to put his journal, of reactions, stories of family & hospitals, animal care at his office, sailing & model train hobbies, into book form, Jim has done so & gone on to becoming active in the Gilda's Club startups. Clinical concerns, his wry grin at life, the sidestepping of internal spins of despair are shared here. Winding through these narratives is his grip on the Myeloma experience as another of life's adventures. He uses Bilbo Baggins of Tolkien's book The Hobbit to gear into survivorship, calls on early interest in a rock band, talks of his wife & sons & their own journeys with his illness. He is a winning skipper on the Great Lakes today, rich in his family, & busy in practice. He sees his book as helping him to talk to others about similar cancer challenges & to using his medical training to track current research. To order contact - Western Reserve Press, Inc., 1046 Locust Drive, P.O. Box 2245, Ashtabula, OH 44005. 216-964-2728. ***Publisher Provided Annotation.***

Pleasant, Mae B. Hampton University, Our Home by the Sea: An Illustrated History. LC 92-22434. (Illus.). 1992. write for info. (0-89865-844-6) Donning Co.
Pleasants, Craig. The Three Little Pigs: As It Was Originally Passed into English Folklore in 1620. (Illus.). 12p. (Orig.). (J). 1994. pap. 5.00 (0-9638129-2-0) Gates of Heck.
***Pleasants, Henry, ed. & anno.** The Great Tenor Tragedy: The Last Days of Adolphe Nourrit, As Told (Mostly) by Himself. LC 94-49112. 1995. 22.95 (0-931340-89-6, Amadeus Pr) Timber.
Pleasants, Henry, ed. The Music Criticism of Hugo Wolf. LC 77-11092. 291p. 1979. 39.50 (0-8419-0331-X) Holmes & Meier.
Pleasants, Henry, ed. see Hanslick, Eduard.
Pleasants, Henry, ed. see Spohr, Louis.
Pleasants, Henry, tr. see Spohr, Louis.
Pleasants, Henry, ed. see Wieck, Friedrich.
Pleasants, Jacob H. Four Late Eighteenth Century Anglo-American Landscape Painters. LC 78-128288. (Essay Index Reprint Ser.). 1977. 20.95 (0-8369-1894-0) Ayer.
Pleasants, Jacob H. & Sill, Howard. Maryland Silversmiths 1715-1830. limited ed. LC 30-31299. (Illus.). 416p. 1972. reprint ed. 50.00 (0-9600266-2-2) R A Green.
Pleasants, Julian M. & Burns, Augustus M., III. Frank Porter Graham & the Nineteen Fifty Senate Race in North Carolina. LC 90-50011. (Fred W. Morrison Series in Southern Studies). (Illus.). xviii, 356p. (C). 1990. 32.50 (0-8078-1933-6) U of NC Pr.
Pleasants, Mary M. Which One? & Other Ante Bellum Days. LC 72-4620. (Black Heritage Library Collection). 1977. reprint ed. 19.95 (0-8369-9121-4) Ayer.
Pleasants, Samuel A. Fernando Wood of New York. LC 48-7608. (Columbia University. Studies in the Social Sciences: No. 536). reprint ed. 20.00 (0-404-51536-3) AMS Pr.
Pleasants, William J. Twice Across the Plains to California 1849-1856. 74p. 1981. 12.00 (0-87770-259-4) Ye Galleon.
Please, Stanley. Sector Adjustment Lending & the Inter-American Development Bank. 22p. 1989. pap. text ed. write for info. (0-940602-29-6) IADB.
Please Touch Museum Staff. Please Touch Cookbook. Brook, Bonnie, ed. (Illus.). 64p. (J). (ps-2). 1990. spiral bd. 6.95 (0-671-70558-X, S&S Bks Young Read) S&S Childrens.
***Pleasure, Mose, Jr. & Lofton, Fred C., eds.** Living in Hell: The Dilemma of African-American Survival. LC 95-12479. 1995. pap. write for info. (0-310-49781-7) Zondervan.
Pleban. Analysis of Trace Metals in Biological Materials. 1981. write for info. (0-85501-624-8) Wiley.
Plebani, M. & Di Mario, F. Gastric Secretion. (Advances in Gastroenterology Ser.: No. 5). 160p. 1992. text ed. 32.00 (1-57235-021-0) Piccin NY.
Plebanke, Barbara, tr. see Lipska, Ewa.
Plebanski, J., jt. auth. see Infeld, L.
Plechanoff, George. Anarchism & Socialism. Aveling, Eleanor M., tr. LC 79-2921. 148p. 1990. reprint ed. 21.00 (0-88350-090-6) Hyperion Conn.
— The Bourgeois Revolution. 3rd ed. Kuhn, Henry, tr. 1968. pap. text ed. 0.50 (0-935534-05-9) NY Labor News.
Plechner, Alfred J. & Zucker, Martin. Pet Allergies: Remedies for an Epidemic. LC 85-51341. 130p. (Orig.). 1986. pap. 6.95 (0-9615452-0-8) Very Healthy Ent.
Pleck, et al. Legacies: A History of Women & the Family in America, 1607-1870. 1987. 65.00 (0-938545-04-3) Jennings & Keefe.
Pleck, Elizabeth H. Domestic Tyranny: The Making of American Social Policy Against Family Violence from Colonial Times to the Present. 292p. 1989. pap. 12.95 (0-19-505926-3) OUP.
Pleck, Elizabeth H., jt. auth. see Cott, Nancy F.
Pleck, Elizabeth H., et al. The Legacies Book: A Companion Volume to the Audiocourse. 288p. (Orig.). 1987. pap. 25.00 (0-89776-206-1) Jennings & Keefe.
Pleck, Joseph H., jt. ed. see Lopata, Helena Z.
Pleck, Joseph H., jt. auth. see Staines, Graham L.
Pleck, M. H., et al. Problems in Engineering Graphics. (Engineering Graphics Ser.: No. 88). (Illus.). 91p. (C). 1989. pap. text ed. 13.80 (0-87563-413-3) Stipes.
Plecki, Gerard. Robert Altman. (Filmmakers Ser.). 1985. lib. bdg. 22.95 (0-8057-9303-8, Twayne) Macmillan.
***Plecnik, John & Zielonka, David M.** A User-Friendly Introduction to Logic. 302p. (Orig.). (C). 1994. pap. text ed. 19.60 (0-87563-514-8) Stipes.
Pledge, H. T. Science since Fifteen-Hundred: A Short History of Mathematics, Physics, Chemistry, Biology. 11.75 (0-8446-0850-5) Peter Smith.
Pledger, Florence M. Pledger Family History. 176p. 1991. 29.95 (0-942407-13-X) Father & Son.
***Pledger, Maurice.** An Adventure with Billy Bunny. (Illus.). 20p. (J). (ps). 1995. 14.50 (1-881445-47-X) Sandvik Pub.
Plee, H. D. Karate: Beginner to Black Belt. (Illus.). 1967. 19.95 (0-685-05344-X) Wehman.
— Karate by Pictures. 19.95 (0-685-22004-4) Wehman.

P Q

Pleeter, Saul. Economics in the News. 2nd ed. (Illus.). 416p. (C). 1993. pap. text ed. 17.25 (0-201-58656-8) Addison-Wesley.

Pleeter, Saul & Way, Philip K. Economics in the News. (Illus.). 320p. (C). 1990. pap. text ed. 13.95 (0-201-50924-5) Addison-Wesley.

Pleger, Wolfgang H. Schleiermachers Philosophie. x, 207p. (GER.). (C). 1988. lib. bdg. 26.15x (3-11-011706-1) De Gruyter.

Plegge, Anne M., ed. see Floyd, Maita.

Pleh, C. S., jt. auth. see Kardos, L.

Plehinger, Russell. Marathon Flyers & the Flights to Nowhere. 1989. 27.00 (0-8187-0112-9) Harlo Press.

Plehn, Jonathan F. Transesophageal Echocardiography. 1994. 100.00 (0-412-04451-X) Chapman & Hall.

Pleijel, Agneta. The Dog Star. 120p. 1992. 30.00 (0-7206-0844-9, Pub. by P Owen Ltd UK) Dufour.

— Eyes from a Dream: Poems. Born, Anne, tr. (Illus.). 49p. (Orig.). 1991. pap. 16.95 (1-85610-015-4, Pub. by Forest Bks UK) Dufour.

Pleil, Nadine M. Free from Bondage: After Forty Years in Bruderhof Communities on Three Continents. Huntington, Gertrude E., ed. (Women from Utopia Ser.). 350p. (Orig.). 1994. pap. 17.00 (1-882260-07-4) Carrier Pigeon.

***Pleiman, H., Jr.** You Be Hoobee. (Illus.). 45p. (YA). 1994. 24.95 (0-9621755-1-X) Metahomin Pub.

— You Be Hoobee. (Illus.). 45p. (YA). 1994. pap. 17.95 (0-9621755-2-8) Metahomin Pub.

Pleiner, Radomir. The Celtic Sword. (Illus.). 256p. 1993. 95.00 (0-19-813411-8) OUP.

Pleins, J. David. The Psalms: Songs of Tragedy, Hope, & Justice. LC 93-17541. (Bible & Liberation Ser.). 160p. (Orig.). 1993. pap. 12.95 (0-88344-928-5) Orbis Bks.

***Pleisch, Bonnita L.** Ridge Ranch. 310p. Date not set. pap. 9.95 (0-7610-0377-0) NW Pub.

Pleit-Kuiper, Angie, tr. see Van der Hart, Onno.

Pleiter, Anneka, jt. auth. see Bredewold, Ank.

Pleiter, Anneke, jt. auth. see Bredewold, Ank.

Pleket, H. W. & Stroud, R. S., eds. SEG, 1982: Supplementum Epigraphicum Graecum. xxi, 550p. (C). 1985. 91.00 (90-70265-19-2, Pub. by Gieben NE) Benjamins North Am.

— SEG, 1983: Supplementum Epigraphicum Graecum. xx, 532p. (C). 1986. 91.00 (90-70265-57-5, Pub. by Gieben NE) Benjamins North Am.

— Supplementum Epigraphicum Graecum, Vol. XXVI. 550p. 1979. 70.00 (0-89005-429-0) Ares.

— Supplementum Epigraphicum Graecum, Vol. XXVII. (SEG Ser.). 389p. 1980. 75.00 (0-89005-430-4) Ares.

— Supplementum Epigraphicum Graecum, Vol. XXIX. (SEG Ser.). 544p. 1982. 95.00 (0-89005-432-0) Ares.

— Supplementum Epigraphicum Graecum, Vol. XXX. (SEG Ser.). 634p. 1983. 95.00 (0-89005-433-9) Ares.

— Supplementum Epigraphicum Graecum, Vol. XXXI. (SEG Ser.). 500p. 1984. 95.00 (0-89005-434-7) Ares.

— Supplementum Epigraphicum Graecum, Vol. XXXII. 2nd ed. (SEG Ser.). xxi, 550p. (GRE.). 1985. 95.00 (0-89005-439-8) Ares.

Plekhanov, George V. Fundamental Problems of Marxism. Katzer, Julius, tr. (ENG.). 1962. pap. 14.95 (0-8464-0435-4) Beekman Pubs.

— Fundamental Problems of Marxism. rev. ed. LC 69-20358. 160p. 1992. pap. text ed. 6.95 (0-7178-0073-3) Intl Pubs Co.

Plekhov, A. Dictionary of Military Terms. 336p. (C). 1988. 125.00 (0-685-37189-1, Pub. by Collets) St Mut.

Plekon, Michael P., ed. see Piepkorn, Arthur C.

Pleming, L. Triumph of Job. 1978. 7.95 (0-933062-00-1) R H Sommer.

Plemmons, Patrick & Myers, David. Personal Computer Buyer's Guide. 184p. (Orig.). pap. 12.95 (0-685-08848-0) Random.

Plemmons, Richard J., jt. ed. see Meyer, Carl D.

Plemmons, Robert, et al. Parallel Algorithms for Matrix Computations. (Miscellaneous Ser.: No. 22). x, 197p. 1990. reprint ed. pap. 16.00 (0-89871-260-2) Soc Indus-Appl Math.

Plemmons, Robert J., jt. auth. see Berman, Abraham.

***Plemons, Marsha.** Short Skits about Bible People. Hayes, Theresa, ed. 64p. 1995. pap. 3.99 (0-7847-0283-7, 14-03351) Standard Pub.

Plemons, Marti. Brooke & the Guilty Secret. (Grace Street Kids Ser.). (Illus.). 128p. (J). (gr. 3-6). 1992. pap. 4.99 (0-87403-938-X, 24-03768) Standard Pub.

— Erin & the Special Promise. (Grace Street Kids Ser.). (Illus.). 128p. (J). (gr. 3-6). 1992. pap. 4.99 (0-87403-935-5, 24-03765) Standard Pub.

— Georgie & the New Kid. (Grace Street Kids Ser.). (Illus.). 128p. (J). (gr. 3-6). 1992. pap. 4.99 (0-87403-687-9, 24-03727) Standard Pub.

— Josh & the Guinea Pig. (Grace Street Kids Ser.). (Illus.). 128p. (J). (gr. 3-6). 1992. pap. 4.99 (0-87403-686-0, 24-03726) Standard Pub.

— Marty & the Mystery Gift. (Grace Street Kids Ser.). (Illus.). 128p. (J). (gr. 3-6). 1992. pap. 4.99 (0-87403-937-1, 24-03767) Standard Pub.

— Megan & the Owl Tree. (Grace Street Kids Ser.). (Illus.). 128p. (J). (gr. 3-6). 1992. pap. 4.99 (0-87403-685-2, 24-03725) Standard Pub.

— Michael & the Dark Cross. (Grace Street Kids Ser.). (Illus.). 128p. (J). (gr. 3-6). 1992. pap. 4.99 (0-87403-936-3, 24-03766) Standard Pub.

— Scott & the Ogre. (Grace Street Kids Ser.). (Illus.). 128p. (J). (gr. 3-6). 1992. pap. 4.99 (0-87403-688-7, 24-03728) Standard Pub.

Plempel, M., jt. auth. see Berg, D.

Plender, Richard. International Migration Law. 1988. lib. bdg. 162.00 (90-247-3604-8) Kluwer Ac.

Plender, Richard, ed. Legal History & Comparative Law: Essays in Honour of Albert Kiralfy. 239p. 1990. text ed. 40.00 (0-7146-3397-6, Pub. by F Cass Pubs UK) Intl Spec Bk.

Plender, Richard & Ushers. Cases & Materials on the Law of the European Communities. 3rd ed. 1993. pap. write for info. (0-406-01624-0) Butterworth Legal Pubs.

Plenderleith, H. J. & Werner, A. E. Conservation of Antiquities & Works of Art: Treatment, Repair, & Restoration. 2nd ed. 1972. 85.00 (0-19-212960-0) OUP.

Plenderleith, H. J., tr. see Mora, L., et al.

Plenderleith, P., jt. ed. see Whyte, W.

***Plenert, Gerhard.** World Class Manager: Olympic Quality Performance in the New Global Economy. LC 95-3860. 1995. write for info. (0-7615-0030-8) Prima Pub.

Plenert, Gerhard J. Plant Operations Handbook: A Tactical Guide to Everyday Management. 528p. 1992. 75.00 (1-55623-707-3) Irwin Prof Pubng.

Plenert, W. & Heine, W. Normalwerte. 6th exp. rev. ed. (Illus.). 518p. 1984. 33.00 (3-8055-3896-0) S Karger.

***Plenielk, W. Charles.** A Survival Guide for Anatomy & Physiology: A Topical Review for Board Examination Review for RN, RT, PA, LPN, PA, PT, OT, DH & MLT Health Occupations. Kleinelp, W., ed. 140p. (Orig.). (C). 1994. 15.95 (0-929941-17-9) Wood River Pubns.

Plenk, Agnes M. Helping Young Children at Risk: A Psychoeducational Approach. LC 93-20303. 232p. 1993. Alk. paper. text ed. 57.95 (0-275-94591-X, C4591, Praeger Pubs); Alk. paper. pap. text ed. 16.95 (0-275-94592-8, Praeger Pubs) Greenwood.

Plenk, Anton. The Obersalzberg & the Third Reich. (Illus.). 87p. pap. 15.00 (3-922590-13-6) Johnson Ref Bks.

Plenk, Dagmar. Sophie & the Incas. LC 90-71979. 72p. (Orig.). (J). (gr. 3-7). 1991. pap. 9.00 (1-56002-039-3) Aegina Pr.

Plenk, H. Osteolathyrismus: Quantitativ-Morphologische Untersuchungen der Experimentellen Skeletterkrankungen bei der Ratte. Wolf-Heidegger, G., ed. (Bibliotheca Anatomica Ser.: No. 14). (Illus.). 104p. 1976. 38.50 (3-8055-2306-8) S Karger.

Plenk, Henry P. & McMurrin, Trudy, eds. Medicine in the Beehive State, 1940-1990. (Illus.). 608p. 1992. 35.00 (0-87480-396-9) U of Utah Pr.

Plenn. El Arbol de la Violeta. 1964. 6.95 (0-87751-015-6) E Torres & Sons.

— La Cancion Verde. 1956. 6.95 (0-87751-014-8) E Torres & Sons.

***Plenty International Staff.** From the Global Kitchen. Haren, Charles T., ed. LC 95-14033. 144p. 1995. 10.95 (1-57067-006-4) Book Pub Co.

Plenzdorf, Ulrich. The New Sufferings of Young W. Wilcox, Kenneth P., tr. LC 78-20928. 200p. 1979. pap. text ed. 7.95 (0-8044-6656-4, F Ungar Bks) Continuum.

Plenzvik, Joseph. What Are They Saying about Paul? (What Are They Saying about...Ser.). 144p. 1986. pap. 5.95 (0-8091-2776-8) Paulist Pr.

Plesa Eyk. Enciclopedia de Nuestro Mundo. 98p. (SPA.). 1979. pap. 19.95 (0-8288-4739-8, S50442) Fr & Eur.

Plesch, P. Chemistry of Cationic Polymerization. LC 63-10034. 1963. 298.00 (0-08-010289-1, Pub. by Pergamon Repr UK) Franklin.

Plesch, P. H. High Vacuum Techniques for Chemical Synthesis & Measurement. (Illus.). 150p. (C). 1989. 74.95 (0-521-25756-5) Cambridge U Pr.

***Plescia, Jeffrey B., et al.** Paleomagnetic Analysis of Miocene Basalt Flows in the Tehachapi Mountains, California. Vol. 2100. 1994. write for info. (0-615-00001-0) US Interior.

***Plescia, Joseph.** The Bill of Rights & Roman Law: A Comparative Study. 300p. (Orig.). 1995. 69.95 (1-57292-005-X); pap. 49.95 (1-57292-004-1) Austin & Winfield.

— The Oath & Perjury in Ancient Greece. LC 73-13540. 124p. reprint ed. pap. 35.40 (0-7837-4903-1, 2044568) Bks Demand.

Plesea, Gabriel. Bitter Be Thy Bread. LC 89-92290. 307p. (Orig.). 1989. pap. 7.00 (0-9624498-0-6) G Plesea.

Plesent, Stanley. Preparing Matrimonial Agreements. (Basic Practice Skills Ser.). 237p. 1989. text ed. 15.00 (0-87224-001-0, Q1-3003) PLI.

Pleshakova, T., jt. ed. see Maslova, N.

Pleshanova, I. & Likhachova, L. Old Russian Decorative & Applied Art. (Illus.). 224p. (C). 1985. text ed. 330.00 (0-685-40317-3, Pub. by Collets) St Mut.

Pleshanova, Iailla. Old Russian Decorative & Applied Art in the Russian Musuem. Likhachova, Liudmila, ed. 224p. 1985. 210.00 (0-317-61334-0, Pub. by Collets UK) Pro-Am Music.

Pleshoyano, Dan V. Colonel Nicolae Plesoianu & the National Regeneration Movement in Walachia. 200p. 1991. text ed. 28.00 (0-88033-207-7) Col U Pr.

***Plesken, W. & Nebe, G.** Finite Rational Matrix Groups. LC 95-15923. (Memoirs Ser.: No. 556). 1995. write for info. (0-8218-0343-3) Am Math.

Plesken, W., jt. auth. see Holt, Derek F.

Pleskin, W., ed. Group Rings of Finite Groups over p-adic Integers. (Lecture Notes in Mathematics Ser.: Vol. 1026). 151p. 1983. pap. 29.60 (0-387-12728-3) Spr-Verlag.

***Plesko, Les.** The Last Bongo Sunset: A Novel. LC 94-22439. 1995. write for info. (0-671-88049-7) S&S Trade.

Pleskov, Yu V. Solar Energy Conversion. (Illus.). x, 163p. 1989. 128.00 (0-387-51474-0) Spr-Verlag.

Pleskov, Yu V. & Gurevich, Y. Y. Semiconductor Photoelectrochemistry. Bartlett, P. N., tr. LC 85-17411. 448p. 1985. 110.00 (0-306-10983-2, Consultants) Plenum.

Pleskov, Yurii V., jt. auth. see Myamlin, Viktor.

Pleskovic, Boris, jt. ed. see Bruno, Michael.

Pleskovitch-Peman, Judi. A Matter of Opinion: Listening & Speaking Exercises. 220p. (C). 1986. pap. text ed. 18.50 (0-03-001518-9) HB Coll Pubs.

Plesl, Evakzen, jt. auth. see Ehrich, Robert W.

Pless, I. A., ed. World-Wide Collaboration for Safe & Peaceful Use of Nuclear Energy: Proceedings of the International Seminar, November 1986. vii, 244p. 1986. text ed. 84.00 (2-88124-209-X) Gordon & Breach.

Pless, Ivan B. The Epidemiology of Childhood Disorders. (Illus.). 552p. 1994. 75.00 (0-19-507516-1) OUP.

Pless, John. How Sweet the Sound. 1992. pap. 4.95 (1-55673-444-1, 7904) CSS OH.

Pless, Vera. Introduction to the Theory of Error-Correcting Codes. 2nd ed. 221p. 1989. text ed. 64.95 (0-471-61884-5) Wiley.

Plessas, W., jt. ed. see Mathelitsch, L.

Plessas, W., jt. ed. see Mitter, H.

Plesset, Isabel R. Noguchi & His Patrons. LC 78-66819. 320p. 1970. 38.50 (0-8386-2347-6) Fairleigh Dickinson.

Plessinger, James, ed. see Tharp, Robert N.

Plessis, Alain. The Rise & Fall of the Second Empire, 1852-1871. Mandelbaum, Jonathan, tr. (Cambridge History of Modern France Ser.: No. 3). (Illus.). 210p. 1988. pap. 17.95 (0-521-35856-6) Cambridge U Pr.

Plessis, F. Horatius Flaccus, Quintus, Odes, Epodes et Chant Seculaire. lxxviii, 396p. (GER.). 1966. reprint ed. write for info. (0-318-70455-2, Pub. by Georg Olms GW) Lubrecht & Cramer.

***Plessis, J. du.** Surface Segregation. (Solid State Phenomena Ser.: Vol. 11). 132p. 1990. text ed. 76.00 (3-908044-06-5, Pub. by Trans Tech SZ) LPS Dist Ctr.

Plessix, jt. auth. see Dieter.

Plessix, Dieter & Plessix, Michel. Grisnoir: Julien Boisvert, Vol. 2. Baisden, Greg, ed. Irwin, Mary, tr. (Illus.). 48p. 1993. reprint ed. 14.95 (0-87816-227-5) Kitchen Sink.

— Neekibo: Julien Boisvert, Vol. 1. Baisden, Greg, ed. Irwin, Mary, tr. (Illus.). 48p. 1993. reprint ed. 14.95 (0-87816-226-7) Kitchen Sink.

Plessix, Michel, jt. auth. see Plessix, Dieter.

Plessman, C. K., jt. auth. see Lynch, R. L.

Plessner, Gerald M. The Encyclopedia of Fund Raising: A Three Volume Work on How to Organize Fund Raising Special Events, Set. (Illus.). 351p. 1980. 100.00 (0-916555-00-3) Fund Raisers Inc.

— The Encyclopedia of Fund Raising: Charity Auction Management Manual. rev. ed. (Illus.). 83p. 1986. 39.00 (0-916555-01-1) Fund Raisers Inc.

— The Encyclopedia of Fund Raising: Golf Tournament Management Manual. rev. ed. (Illus.). 110p. 1986. 39.00 (0-916555-02-X) Fund Raisers Inc.

— The Encyclopedia of Fund Raising: Testimonial Dinner & Industry Luncheon Management Manual. (Illus.). 142p. 1980. 39.00 (0-916555-03-8) Fund Raisers Inc.

Plessner, Helmuth. Die Stufen des Organischen und der Mensch: Einleitung in die philosophische Anthropologie. 3rd ed. (Sammlung Goeschen Ser.: No. 2200). 373p. (C). 1975. 22.95 (3-11-005985-1) De Gruyter.

Plessner, Markus. Vox--Enciclopedia Cultural, Tomo 2: El Hombre. 210p. (SPA.). 1977. 29.95 (0-8288-5546-3, S50509) Fr & Eur.

Plessner, Yakir. The Political Economy of Israel: From Ideology to Stagnation. LC 93-203. (SUNY Series in Israeli Studies). 328p. (C). 1993. 64.50 (0-7914-1741-7); pap. 21.95 (0-7914-1742-5) State U NY Pr.

Plessz, Nicholas G. Problems & Prospects of Economic Integration in West Africa. LC 67-29636. (Centre for Developing-Area Studies, McGill University, Keith Callard Lectures: No. 2). 102p. reprint ed. pap. 29.10 (0-7837-1158-1, 2041687) Bks Demand.

Plesters, Joyce, jt. auth. see Bull, David.

Plestina, Dijana. Regional Development in Communist Yugoslavia: Success, Failure, & Consequences. 223p. (C). 1992. text ed. 46.50 (0-8133-8186-X) Westview.

Plesur, Gregory H. Smart House: Control Your Home with Your PC. 1994. disk 27.95 (0-8306-4506-3, Windcrest) TAB Bks.

Pleszczynska, Elzbieta, jt. ed. see Bromek, Tadeusz.

***Pletcher, Barbara.** Readings in Business Today. (C). 1980. 12.50 (0-256-02376-X) Irwin.

Pletcher, Barbara A. On the Right Track: A Guide to a Successful Sales Career. 144p. (C). 1984. per. 23.95 (0-8403-3486-9) Kendall-Hunt.

Pletcher, D., jt. ed. see Genders, J. D.

***Pletcher, Derek.** A First Course in Electrode Processes. 270p. 1991. 45.00 (0-614-04929-6); pap. 45.00 (0-9517307-0-3) Electrosyn Co.

Pletcher, Derek & Walsh, Frank C. Industrial Electrochemistry. 400p. 1989. 125.00 (0-412-30410-4) Chapman & Hall.

— Industrial Electrochemistry. 2nd ed. LC 93-28740. 1993. write for info. (0-7514-0148-X, Pub. by Blackie Acad & Prof UK) Routledge Chapman & Hall.

Pletcher, Derek, jt. ed. see Genders, J. David.

Pletcher, Jean E., et al. Memories of the Michigan City Lighthouse & Description of the United States Lighthouse Service. (Little Bit of History Ser.: Bk. 5). 24p. (Orig.). (YA). (gr. 6 up). 1991. pap. 2.00 (0-935549-15-3) MI City Hist.

***Pletcher, Larry.** The Hiker's Guide to New Hampshire. (Illus.). 248p. (Orig.). 1995. pap. 14.95 (1-56044-225-5) Falcon Pr MT.

Pletcher, Vincent C., et al. Treating Nicotine Addiction: A Challenge for the Recovery Professional. 60p. (Orig.). 1990. pap. 7.00 (0-89486-645-1, 5531B) Hazelden.

— Treating Nicotine Addiction: A Challenge for the Recovery Professional. 60p. (Orig.). 1990. pap. 7.95 (0-89486-715-6, 5531B) Hazelden.

Pletnev, A., tr. see Nezlin, M. V. & Snezhkin, E. N.

Pleton, Sonya T. Tiger Rose. 1990. mass mkt. 4.95 (0-8217-3116-5) Zebra.

Plets, C., et al. Computer Tomographic Imaging & Anatomic Correlation of the Human Brain. (Series in Radiology). 1987. lib. bdg. 121.50 (0-89838-811-2) Kluwer Ac.

Pletsch, Carl. Young Nietzsche: Becoming a Genius. 261p. 1991. text ed. 27.95 (0-02-925041-2) Free Pr.

— Young Nietzsche Becoming a Genius. 261p. 1992. pap. 12.95 (0-02-925042-0) Free Pr.

Pletsch, Susan, jt. auth. see Palmer, Pati.

Pletsch, William. Integrated Circuits: Making the Miracle Chip. rev. ed. LC 84-90578. (Illus.). 96p. 1984. pap. text ed. 8.00 (0-917927-00-1) Pletsch Assocs.

Pletscher, A. & Ladewig, D., eds. Fifty Years of LSD: Current Status & Perspectives of Hallucinogens. LC 94-8290. (Illus.). 238p. 1994. 75.00 (1-85070-569-0) Prthnon Pub.

Plett, Heinrich, ed. Renaissance-Rhetorik - Renaissance Rhetoric. ix, 391p. (ENG & GER.). (C). 1993. lib. bdg. 161.55 (3-11-013567-1) De Gruyter.

***Plett, Heinrich F., ed.** Renaissance-Poetik - Renaissance Poetics. 449p. (ENG & GER.). (C). 1994. lib. bdg. 155.75 (3-11-013964-2) De Gruyter.

Plett, Henry. Wings of Hope: A Father's Story. 152p. (Orig.). 1990. pap. 8.95 (0-8361-3527-X) Herald Pr.

Plett, Nicole, ed. Eleanor King: Sixty Years in American Dance. LC 88-90581. (Illus.). 80p. 1988. pap. 10.95 (0-8263-1028-1) U of NM Pr.

Plett, P., et al. Training for Older People: A Handbook. v, 217p. (Orig.). 1991. pap. 20.00 (92-2-107294-0) Intl Labour Office.

Plettinger, H. Anne. Table of the Sin Function & Sin Squared Function for Values from 2 Degrees to 87 Degrees. 46p. 1965. pap. 63.00 (0-677-01100-8) Gordon & Breach.

***Pletzke, Jonathon.** Smalltalk Developer's Guide. (Illus.). 800p. (Orig.). 1995. pap. 49.99 (0-672-30720-0) Sams.

Plevan, Kenneth A. & Siroky, Miriam L. Advertising Compliance Handbook. LC 88-62454. 527p. 1988. text ed. 10.00 (0-318-41230-6, G1-1008) PLI.

Plevan, Kenneth A., et al. Advertising Compliance Handbook. 2nd ed. 860p. 1992. text ed. 125.00 (0-87224-025-8, G6-2003) PLI.

Plevin, Arlene. Education As a Career. 64p. 1988. 9.95 (0-8106-1462-6) NEA.

Plevyak, Thomas, jt. ed. see Aidarous, Salah.

Plew, Mark G. An Introduction to the Archaeology of Southern Idaho. (Hemingway Western Studies). (Illus.). 51p. (Orig.). 1986. pap. 4.95 (0-932129-03-X) Heming W Studies.

***Plewa, Franklin & Friedlob, George T.** Understanding Cash Flow. 1995. text ed. 29.95 (0-471-10385-3); pap. text ed. 14.95 (0-471-10386-1) Wiley.

Plewa, Franklin, jt. auth. see Friedlob, George T.

***Plewa, Franklin J. & Friedlob, G. Thomas.** Understanding Income Statements. LC 94-29850. 1995. pap. text ed. 14.95 (0-471-10384-5) Wiley.

— Understanding Income Statements. LC 94-29850. 1995. text ed. 29.95 (0-471-10383-7) Wiley.

Plewig, Gerd & Kligman, Albert M. Acne & Rosacea. 2nd rev. ed. LC 92-49778. 1992. 198.00 (0-387-52277-8) Spr-Verlag.

Plewig, Gerd, jt. ed. see Marks, R. M.

***Plewis, Ian.** Analysing Change: Measurement & Explanation Using Longitudinal Data. fac. ed. LC 84-22044. 194p. 1985. reprint ed. pap. 55.30 (0-7837-8276-4, 2049056) Bks Demand.

— Analysing Change: Methods for the Measurement & Explanation of Change in the Social Sciences. LC 84-22044. 182p. 1985. text ed. 143.00 (0-471-10444-2) Wiley.

Pleyel. Six Easy Violin Duets. Date not set. pap. 11.95 (0-685-69310-4, Chester Music) Music Sales.

Pleyte, E. & Rossi, F. Papyrus De Turin. 253p. reprint ed. write for info. (0-318-71390-X, Pub. by Georg Olms GW) Lubrecht & Cramer.

Pleyte, Willem. Chapitres Supplementaires Du Livre Des Morts 162-174. vii, 178p. reprint ed. write for info. (0-318-71391-8, Pub. by Georg Olms GW) Lubrecht & Cramer.

Plezia, Valerie. Polka Party Dances. (Ballroom Dance Ser.). (Orig.). 1986. lib. bdg. 79.95 (0-8490-3344-6) Gordon Pr.

— Polka Party Dances. (Ballroom Dance Ser.). (Orig.). 1985. lib. bdg. 60.00 (0-87700-687-3) Revisionist Pr.

— Polka Party Dances. (Ethnic Dance Book Ser.: No.280). 130p. (Orig.). 1982. pap. 8.95 (0-9609368-0-7) V Plezia.

Plice, Steven S. Manpower & Merger: The Impact of Merger upon Personnel Policies in the Carpet & Furniture Industries. LC 76-21151. (Manpower & Human Resources Studies: No. 5). 168p. reprint ed. pap. 47.90 (0-317-41877-7, 2025909) Bks Demand.

Plieninger, Helga, ed. see Cous, Hippocrates.

Plievier, Theodore. Stalingrad. Winston, Richard & Winston, Clara, trs. 460p. 1984. pap. 8.95 (0-88184-108-0) Carroll & Graf.

Plikhanou, Georgi. Development of the Monist View of History. 334p. 1972. reprint ed. 25.00 (0-8464-1086-9) Beekman Pubs.

Plimmer, Jack R., ed. Pesticide Residues & Exposure. LC 81-20568. (ACS Symposium Ser.: No. 182). 1982. 32.95 (0-8412-0701-1) Am Chemical.

Plimoth Plantation Staff & Hornblower, Malabar. The Plimoth Plantation New England Cookery Book. 224p. 1990. pap. 12.95 (1-55832-027-X) Harvard Common Pr.

Plimpton, Chet. A Word in Season. 196p. (Orig.). 1993. pap. 8.95 (0-9632190-4-9) Longwood.

Plimpton, Elizabeth B., jt. auth. see Hall, Verne M.

Plimpton, George. Best of Plimpton. 1991. pap. 12.95 (0-87113-503-5) Grove-Atltic.

— The Bogey Man: A Month on the PGA Tour. 320p. 1993. pap. 13.95 (1-55821-241-8) Lyons & Burford.

An Asterisk (*) at the beginning of an entry indicates that the title is appearing in BIP for the first time.

— Curious Case of Sidd Finch. 1987. 14.95 (*0-02-597650-8*) Macmillan.
— Mad Ducks & Bears: Football Revisited. 432p. 1993. pap. 14.95 (*1-55821-240-X*) Lyons & Burford.
— Open Net: A Professional Amateur in the World of Big-Time Hockey. 288p. 1993. pap. 12.95 (*1-55821-242-6*) Lyons & Burford.
— Out of My League. 160p. 1993. pap. 10.95 (*1-55821-238-8*) Lyons & Burford.
— Paper Lion. 368p. 1993. pap. 14.95 (*1-55821-239-6*) Lyons & Burford.
— Paris Review No. 133. 1995. 10.00 (*0-679-76053-9*) Random.
— The Paris Review No. 134: Strippable. 1995. pap. 10.00 (*0-679-76299-X*) Random.
— The Paris Review No. 135: Strippable. 1995. pap. 10.00 (*0-679-76300-7*) Random.
— Paris Review Anthology. 1990. 25.00 (*0-393-02769-4*) Norton.
— Shadow Box. 352p. 1993. pap. 14.95 (*1-55821-276-0*) Lyons & Burford.
— Very Special Art: Profiles in Disability & Creativity. 1993. 23.00 (*0-394-57003-0*) Random.
— The X Factor: A Quest for Excellence. 144p. 1994. 18.95 (*0-393-03484-4*) Norton.
— The X Factor: A Quest for Excellence. Rukeyser, William S. & Kiser, Anthony C., eds. LC 90-70577. (Larger Agenda Ser.). (Illus.). 88p. 1990. 11.95 (*0-9624745-4-1*) Whittle Comns.

Plimpton, George, ed. The Norton Book of Sports. 500p. 1992. 24.95 (*0-393-03040-7*) Norton.
— Women Writers at Work. 512p. 1989. pap. 9.95 (*0-14-011790-3*, Penguin Bks) Viking Penguin.
— The Writer's Chapbook: A Compendium of Fact, Opinion, Wit, & Advice, from the 20th Century's Preeminent Writers. enl. rev. ed. 400p. 1992. reprint ed. pap. 12.50 (*0-14-009878-X*, Penguin Bks) Viking Penguin.

Plimpton, George, intro. The Best of Bad Hemingway: Choice Entries from the Harry's Bar & American Grill Imitation Hemingway Competition. (Illus.). 163p. 1989. pap. 8.95 (*0-15-611861-0*) HarBrace.

Plimpton, George, ed. see Midwood, Barton A.

Plimpton, George, ed. see Stein, Jean.

Plimpton, George A. A Collector's Recollections. Plimpton, Pauline A., ed. (Illus.). 104p. (Orig.). 1993. pap. 10.00 (*0-9607862-6-0*) Columbia U Libs.
— Education of Chaucer. LC 74-160453. reprint ed. 32.50 (*0-404-05064-6*) AMS Pr.
— Education of Shakespeare. LC 76-109658. (Select Bibliographies Reprint Ser.). 1977. 23.95 (*0-8369-5267-7*) Ayer.

Plimpton, Oakes, ed. Stories of Early Twentieth Century Life: An Oral History of Arlington, Massachusetts. LC 92-61076. 192p. 1992. per. 12.00 (*0-89725-082-6*, Penobscot Pr) Picton Pr.

Plimpton, Pauline A. Oakes Ames; Jottings of a Harvard Botanist. LC 79-52949. (Illus.). 401p. 1980. text ed. 12.95 (*0-674-62921-3*) HUP.

Plimpton, Pauline A., ed. A Window on Our World: Plimpton Papers. (Illus.). 314p. 1989. 17.95 (*0-9621510-0-9*) British Amer Pub.

Plimpton, Pauline A., ed. see Plimpton, George A.

Plimpton, Ruth T. Mary Dyer: Biography of a Rebel Quaker. (Illus.). 300p. 1994. 21.95 (*0-8283-1964-2*) Branden Pub Co.

Pline, Marc J. Biology 1110 Laboratory Manual. 128p. (C). 1993. pap. text ed., spiral bd. 15.95 (*0-8403-8990-6*) Kendall-Hunt.
— Biology 1112 Laboratory Manual. 96p. (C). 1993. pap. text ed., spiral bd. 12.95 (*0-8403-8787-3*) Kendall-Hunt.

Pliner, Jayne, ed. see Christie, Agatha.

Plinio, Alex J. & Scanlon, Joanne B. Resource Raising: The Role of Non-Cash Assistance in Corporate Philanthropy. 56p. 1986. pap. 10.00 (*0-685-23210-7*) Ind Sector.

Plinius. Epistularum Libri Duo. Cowan, James, ed. xxxiii, 198p. (GER.). 1982. reprint ed. write for info. (*3-487-07229-7*, Pub. by Georg Olms GW) Lubrecht & Cramer.
— Physica Plinii Bambergensis. Onnerfors, Alf, ed. (Bibliotheca Graeca Et Latina Ser.: Vol. II). 174p. 1975. write for info. (*3-487-05873-1*, Pub. by Georg Olms GW) Lubrecht & Cramer.

Plinius, Secundus. Elder Pliny's Chapters on the History of Art. 1988. reprint ed. lib. bdg. 59.00 (*0-7812-0568-9*) Rprt Serv.

Plinius Secundus, C. Konkordanz Zur Naturalis Historia Des C. Plinius Elder, Set, 3 Vols. Rosumek, Peter & Najock, Dietmar, eds. 1750p. Date not set. Set. write for info. (*0-318-71202-4*, Pub. by Georg Olms GW) Lubrecht & Cramer.
— Naturalis Historia, 6 vols. in 3. 1784p. (GER.). reprint ed. Banden I: Bd. 1, Libri 1-6, 1866. Bd. 2, Libri 7-15, 1867. Zus. 590p. write for info. (*0-318-70424-2*, Pub. by Georg Olms GW); reprint ed. Banden II: Bd. 3, Libri 16-22, 1868. Bd. 4, Libri 23-31, 1871. Zus. 637p. write for info. (*0-318-70425-0*, Pub. by Georg Olms GW); reprint ed. Banden III: Bd. 5, Libri 32-37, 1873. Bd. 6, Index Deorum et Hominum. Index Locorum, 1882. Zus. 557p. write for info. (*0-318-70426-9*, Pub. by Georg Olms GW) Lubrecht & Cramer.
— Naturalis Historia, 6 vols. in 3, Set. 1784p. (GER.). reprint ed. write for info. (*0-318-70423-4*, Pub. by Georg Olms GW) Lubrecht & Cramer.

***Plint, Guy A.** Sedimentary Facies Analysis: A Tribute to the Research & Teaching of Harold G. Reading. LC 94-30445. 1995. write for info. (*0-86542-898-0*) Blackwell Sci.

Plint, M. A. & Boeswirth, L. Fluid Mechanics: A Laboratory Course. (Illus.). 186p. 1978. pap. 25.00 (*0-85264-245-8*) Lubrecht & Cramer.

Plint, M. A. & Boswirth, L. Mechanical Engineering Thermodynamics: A Laboratory Course. 246p. 1986. lib. bdg. 32.50 (*0-85264-276-8*) Krieger.

***Plint, Michael A. & Martyr, Anthony.** Engine Testing: Theory and Practice. LC 94-33331. 1995. pap. write for info. (*0-7506-1668-7*) Buttrwrth-Heinemann.

Plint, Thomas. Crime in England: Its Relation, Character & Extent As Developed from 1801-1848. LC 73-14175. (Perspectives in Social Inquiry Ser.). 192p. 1974. reprint ed. 13.95 (*0-405-05518-8*) Ayer.

Pliny. Epistularum Libri Decem. Mynors, Roger A., ed. (Classical Texts Ser.). 386p. 1963. 24.00 (*0-19-814643-4*) OUP.
— Fifty Letters of Pliny. 2nd ed. Sherwin-White, A. N., ed. 1969. pap. 13.95 (*0-19-912010-2*) OUP.
— Natural History, 1. Warmington, E. H., ed. (Loeb Classical Library: No. 330, 352-353, 370-371). 372p. 1938. text ed. 18.95 (*0-674-99364-0*) HUP.
— Natural History, 2. Warmington, E. H., ed. (Loeb Classical Library: No. 330, 352-353, 370-371). 674p. 1942. text ed. 18.95 (*0-674-99388-8*) HUP.
— Natural History, 3. Warmington, E. H., ed. (Loeb Classical Library: No. 330, 352-353, 370-371). 626p. 1940. text ed. 18.95 (*0-674-99389-6*) HUP.
— Natural History, 4. Warmington, E. H., ed. (Loeb Classical Library: No. 330, 352-353, 370-371). 564p. 1945. text ed. 18.95 (*0-674-99408-6*) HUP.
— Natural History, 5. Warmington, E. H., ed. (Loeb Classical Library: No. 330, 352-353, 370-371). 562p. 1950. text ed. 18.95 (*0-674-99409-4*) HUP.
— Natural History, 6. (Loeb Classical Library: No. 392-394, 418-419). 558p. 1951. text ed. 18.95 (*0-674-99431-0*) HUP.
— Natural History, 7. (Loeb Classical Library: No. 392-394, 418-419). 576p. 1956. text ed. 18.95 (*0-674-99432-9*) HUP.
— Natural History, 8. (Loeb Classical Library: No. 392-394, 418-419). 604p. 1963. text ed. 18.95 (*0-674-99460-4*) HUP.
— Natural History, 9. (Loeb Classical Library: No. 392-394, 418-419). 430p. 1952. text ed. 18.95 (*0-674-99433-7*) HUP.
— Natural History, 10. (Loeb Classical Library: No. 392-394, 418-419). 362p. 1962. text ed. 18.95 (*0-674-99461-2*) HUP.
— Pliny. Greig, C., tr. LC 77-91088. (Illus.). 1979. pap. 10.95 (*0-521-21978-7*) Cambridge U Pr.
— Selections from Pliny's Letters. Fisher, M. B. & Griffen, M. R., eds. LC 73-80489. (Latin Texts Ser.). (Illus.). 64p. 1973. pap. 9.50 (*0-521-20298-1*) Cambridge U Pr.

Pliny the Elder. Natural History. Healy, John F., tr. & intro. by. 448p. 1991. 11.95 (*0-14-044413-0*, Penguin Classics) Viking Penguin.

Pliny The Younger. Letters, 2 vols., 1. (Loeb Classical Library: No. 55, 59). 596p. 1969. text ed. 18.95 (*0-674-99061-7*) HUP.
— Letters, 2 vols., 2. (Loeb Classical Library: No. 55, 59). 592p. 1969. text ed. 18.95 (*0-674-99066-8*) HUP.

Plis, Alexander I., jt. auth. see Shikin, Eugene V.

Plischke, Elmer. Berlin: Development of Its Government & Administration. LC 70-98789. 257p. 1970. reprint ed. text ed. 59.75 (*0-8371-3024-7*, PLB, Greenwood Pr) Greenwood.
— Contemporary U. S. Foreign Policy: Documents & Commentary. LC 90-43385. 872p. 1991. text ed. 115.00 (*0-313-26032-X*, PEF/, Greenwood Pr) Greenwood.
— Foreign Relations: Analysis of Its Anatomy. LC 88-3121. (Contributions in Political Science Ser.: No. 213). 328p. 1988. text ed. 59.95 (*0-313-25245-9*, PFR/, Greenwood Pr) Greenwood.
— Microstates in World Affairs: Policy Problems & Options. LC 77-1351. (AEI Studies: No. 144). 168p. reprint ed. pap. 47.90 (*0-8357-4506-6*, 2037363) Bks Demand.

Plischke, Michael & Bergersen, Birger. Equilibrium Statistical Physics. 368p. 1989. reprint ed. text ed. 55.00 (*0-13-283276-3*) P-H.

Plischke, Michael, jt. auth. see Bergersen, Birger.

Plischke, Michael, jt. auth. see Bergerson, Birger.

***Plischke, Micheal & Bergersen, Birger.** Equilibrium Statistical Physics: Solution Manual. 2nd ed. 112p. 1994. pap. text ed. 21.00 (*981-02-2068-5*) World Scientific Pub.

Plisek, V., jt. auth. see Leskova, T.

Pliska, Greg, jt. auth. see Gill, Madelaine.

Plisken, Berenice & Sargent, Claudia K. Top Twenty-Four Spanish Word Game Hits. 1987. pap. text ed. 18.00 (*0-582-99852-2*, 75277) Longman.

Pliskin, B. & Sargent. Top Twenty-Four French Word Game Hits. 1987. pap. text ed. 18.00 (*0-582-99858-1*, 75283) Longman.

Pliskin, Jacqueline. The Jewish Holiday Game & Workbook. (Illus.). (YA). (gr. 8-12). 1989. pap. 5.95 (*0-933503-85-7*) Sure Sellers.
— My Animated Haggadah & Story of Passover. (Illus.). 48p. (J). (gr. 5-8). 1989. pap. 5.95 (*0-933503-28-8*) Sure Sellers.
— My Very Own Animated Jewish Holiday Activity Book. (Illus.). 96p. (J). (gr. 4-8). 1987. pap. 5.95 (*0-933503-16-4*) Sure Sellers.
— Passover Haggadah. 1986. pap. 9.95 (*0-88125-014-7*) Ktav.

Pliskin, Jacqueline J. The Bible Game & Workbook. 96p. (J). 1990. pap. 5.95 (*0-944007-84-8*) Sure Sellers.
— The Bible Story Activity Book. (Illus.). 96p. (J). (gr. 1-4). 1990. pap. 5.95 (*0-944007-67-8*) Sure Sellers.

Pliskin, Karen L. Silent Boundaries: Cultural Constraints on Sickness & Diagnosis of Iranians in Israel. LC 86-32492. 293p. reprint ed. pap. 83.60 (*0-7837-4551-6*, 2080342) Bks Demand.

Plissner, Martin, jt. auth. see Mitofsky, Warren J.

Plissner, Martin, et al, eds. Campaign Seventy-Six. LC 77-78784. (Individual Publications). (Illus.). 1977. lib. bdg. 51.95 (*0-405-10515-0*) Ayer.

Plitnik, George R., jt. auth. see Strong, William J.

Plivier, Theodore. The Kaiser's Coolies. Green, M., tr. 308p. 1988. reprint ed. lib. bdg. 45.00 (*0-86527-378-2*) Fertig.

Plocek, Joseph. Economic Indicators. 1991. 24.95 (*0-13-626896-X*) P-H.

Ploch, Beth, ed. see Junior League of Memphis Staff.

Plocharski, J. & Roth, S., eds. Electrochemistry of Conducting Polymers 88. (Materials Science Forum Ser.: Vol. 42). 260p. 1989. text ed. 65.00 (*0-87849-585-1*, Pub. by Trans Tech GW) LPS Dist Ctr.

Plocher, Hermann. German Air Force Versus Russia, Nineteen Forty-One. LC 68-22547. (German Air Force in World War 2 Ser.). (Illus.). 1968. reprint ed. 23.95 (*0-405-00044-8*) Ayer.
— German Air Force Versus Russia, Nineteen Forty-Three. LC 68-22549. (German Air Force in World War 2 Ser.). (Illus.). 1968. reprint ed. 20.95 (*0-405-00046-4*) Ayer.
— German Air Force Versus Russia, Nineteen Forty-Two. LC 68-22548. (German Air Force in World War 2 Ser.). (Illus.). 1968. reprint ed. 25.95 (*0-405-00045-6*) Ayer.

Plochmann, George K. Richard McKeon: A Study. LC 89-28254. (Illus.). 272p. 1990. 29.95 (*0-226-67109-7*) U Ch Pr.

Plochmann, George K. & Robinson, Franklin E. A Friendly Companion to Plato's "Gorgias" LC 87-12884. 466p. 1987. text ed. 49.95 (*0-8093-1404-5*) S Ill U Pr.

Plock, Ernest D. East German-West German Relations & the Fall of the GDR. 220p. (C). 1992. pap. text ed. 39.00 (*0-8133-8145-2*) Westview.

Ploetz, Craig T. Milo's Friends in the Dark. (Illus.). 32p. (J). (ps-4). 1992. lib. bdg. 11.95 (*1-882172-00-0*) Milo Prods.
— Milo's Super Heroes. (J). (ps-3). 1994. 11.95 (*1-882172-02-7*) Miller Freeman.
— Milo's Trip to the Museum with Grandpa. (J). (ps-3). 1994. 11.95 (*1-882172-01-9*) Milo Prods.

Ploetz, R. C., ed. Fusarium Wilt of Banana. LC 90-82570. (Illus.). 140p. (Orig.). 1990. pap. 26.00 (*0-89054-112-4*) Am Phytopathol Soc.

Ploetz, R. C., et al, eds. Compendium of Tropical Fruit Diseases. LC 94-70664. (Disease Compendium Ser.). (Illus.). viii, 118p. (Orig.). 1994. pap. 30.00 (*0-89054-162-0*) Am Phytopathol Soc.

Plog, Barbara A., ed. & pref. Fundamentals of Industrial Hygiene. 3rd ed. LC 87-60256. (Occupational Safety & Health Ser.). (Illus.). 915p. 1988. 105.95 (*0-87912-082-7*, 15133-0000N) Natl Safety Coun.

Plog, F., ed. An Analytical Approach to Cultural Resource Management: The Little Colorado Planning Unit. (Anthropological Research Papers: No. 13). (Illus.). xiv, 293p. 1978. 15.00 (*0-685-19298-9*) AZ Univ ARP.

Plog, Fred & Bates, Daniel. Cultural Anthropology. 2nd ed. (Illus.). 256p. (C). 1988. text ed. write for info. (*0-394-36359-0*) Knopf.

Plog, Fred, jt. auth. see Bates, Daniel G.

Plog, Fred, jt. auth. see Bates, Daniel.

Plog, Fred, jt. auth. see Dittert, Alfred E., Jr.

Plog, Fred, jt. auth. see Jolly, Clifford.

Plog, Michael & Stenzel, Norman. The Rainbow Guide to Introductory Statistics. Kirby, Belinda, ed. 150p. (Orig.). 1987. 6.95 (*0-932471-05-6*) Falsoft.

***Plog, Stanley.** Fielding's Vacation Places Rated. Knoles, Kathy, ed. (Travel Guide Ser.). (Illus.). 300p. (Orig.). 1995. pap. 19.95 (*1-56952-062-3*) Fielding Wrldwide.

Plog, Stanley C. Leisure Travel: Making It a Growth Market Again! 244p. 1991. Net. text ed. write for info. (*0-471-52952-4*) Wiley.

Plog, Stephen. Stylistic Variation in Prehistoric Ceramics. (New Studies in Archaeology). (Illus.). 40p. 1980. 54.95 (*0-521-22581-7*) Cambridge U Pr.

Plog, Stephen, ed. Spatial Organization & Exchange: Archaeological Survey on Northern Black Mesa. LC 84-23646. (Illus.). 400p. 1985. text ed. 30.00 (*0-8093-1214-X*) S Ill U Pr.

Plog, Stephen & Powell, Shirley, eds. Papers on the Archaeology of Black Mesa, Arizona, Vol. II. LC 75-32340. (Papers in Archaeology Ser.). (Illus.). 224p. 1984. 29.95 (*0-8093-1149-6*) S Ill U Pr.

Plogg, H. Coating Thickness Measurement. (C). 1988. 150.00 (*0-85218-036-5*, Pub. by Fuel Metallurgical Jrnl UK) St Mut.

Plohn, H. & Preikschat, W. Technical Dictionary of Radio Telecommunication & Installation. LC 63-13529. 1963. 414.00 (*0-08-010593-9*, Pub. by Pergamon Repr UK) Franklin.

Ploman, Edward W. Space, Earth & Communication. LC 84-12969. ix, 237p. 1984. text ed. 49.95 (*0-89930-094-4*, PSE/, Quorum Bks) Greenwood.

Ploman, Edward W., ed. International Law Governing Communications & Information: A Collection of Documents. LC 81-7036. xvi, 367p. 1982. text ed. 45.00 (*0-313-23277-6*, PLC/, Greenwood Pr) Greenwood.

Ploman, Edward W., jt. ed. see Thomas, Alan M.

Plomer, Aurora. Phenomenology, Geometry & Vision: Merleau Ponty's Critique of Classical Theories of Vision. 110p. 1991. text ed. 59.95 (*1-85628-218-X*, Pub. by Avebury Pub UK) Ashgate Pub Co.

Plomer, Henry R., comp. Index of Wills & Administrations Now Preserved in the Probate Registry at Canterbury, 1396-1558 & 1640-1650. (British Record Society Index Library Ser.: Vol. 50). 1969. reprint ed. pap. 48.00 (*0-8115-1495-1*) Periodicals Srv.

Plomer, William C. At Home: Memoirs. LC 79-179737. (Biography Index Reprint Ser.). 1977. reprint ed. 18.95 (*0-8369-8106-5*) Ayer.
— Double Lives: An Autobiography. LC 72-179738. (Biography Index Reprint Ser.). 1977. reprint ed. 20.95 (*0-8369-8105-7*) Ayer.

Plomin, Robert. Development, Genetics, & Psychology. 384p. (C). 1986. text ed. 79.95 (*0-89859-630-0*) L Erlbaum Assocs.
— Genetics & Experience. (Individual Differences & Development Ser.: Vol. 6). (C). 1994. text ed. 42.95 (*0-8039-5420-4*); pap. text ed. 18.95 (*0-8039-5421-2*) Sage.
— Nature & Nuture: An Introduction to Behavioral Genetics. LC 89-9725. 150p. (C). 1990. pap. 13.00 (*0-534-10768-0*) Brooks-Cole.

Plomin, Robert & DeFries, John C. Origins of Individual Differences in Infancy: The Colorado Adoption Project. (Developmental Psychology Ser.). 1985. text ed. 68.00 (*0-12-558280-3*) Acad Pr.

Plomin, Robert & Dunn, Judy, eds. The Study of Temperament: Changes, Continuities & Challenges. 192p. 1986. text ed. 39.95 (*0-89859-670-X*) L Erlbaum Assocs.

Plomin, Robert & McClearn, Gerald E., eds. Nature, Nurture, & Psychology. LC 93-9822. (Illus.). 516p. 1993. text ed. 49.95 (*1-55798-202-3*) Am Psychol.

Plomin, Robert, jt. auth. see Buss, Arnold H.

Plomin, Robert, jt. ed. see Wachs, Theodore D.

Plomin, Robert, et al. Behavioral Genetics: A Primer. 2nd ed. (Psychology Ser.). 416p. (C). 1995. text ed. 39.95 (*0-7167-2056-6*) W H Freeman.
— Nature & Nurture During Infancy & Early Childhood. 320p. 1988. 69.95 (*0-521-34370-4*) Cambridge U Pr.

Plommer, W. H., ed. see Cook, John M.

Plommer, William H. Vitruvius & Later Roman Building Manuals. LC 72-90487. (Cambridge Classical Studies). 125p. reprint ed. pap. 35.70 (*0-317-27568-2*, 2024512) Bks Demand.

Plommet, M., jt. ed. see Verger, J. M.

Plomp, T., et al, eds. CAL for Europe-Computer Assisted Learning for Europe: Proceedings of a Conf. of the European Commission on the Development of Educational Software, Eschede, The Netherlands 25-28-May 1986. 176p. 1987. 46.25 (*0-444-70258-X*, North Holland) Elsevier.

Plomp, T., jt. ed. see Moonen, J.

Plomp, Tjeerd, jt. auth. see Ely, Donald P.

Plomp, Tjeerd, jt. ed. see Pelgrum, Willem J.

Plon, jt. auth. see Mame.

Plonsey, R. & Barr, R. C. Bioelectricity: A Quantitative Approach. LC 88-22418. (Illus.). 326p. 1988. 85.00 (*0-306-42894-6*, Plenum Pr) Plenum.

Plonsey, R., jt. auth. see Pilkington, T. C.

Plonsey, Robert, jt. auth. see Malmivuo, Jaakko.

Plonsky, Lydia, et al. Math for the Very Young: A Handbook of Activities for Parents & Children. LC 94-20861. 1995. text ed. 24.95 (*0-471-01671-3*); pap. text ed. 12.95 (*0-471-01647-0*) Wiley.

Plonus, Martin. Applied Electromagnetics. 2nd ed. (Illus.). 1978. text ed. write for info. (*0-07-050345-1*) McGraw.

***Ploof, Ron.** The Edison Effect: Success Strategies for the Information Age. (Illus.). 262p. 1995. 22.95 (*0-89447-313-1*); pap. 17.95 (*0-89447-338-7*) Cypress.
— The Edison Effect: Success Strategies in the Information Age. (Illus.). 1995. 22.95 (*0-89447-315-8*) Cypress.

Ploog, K. H. & Tapfer, L., eds. Physics & Technology of Semiconductor Quantum Devices: Proceedings of the International School Held in Mesagne, Brindisi, Italy, 21-26 September 1992. (Lecture Notes in Physics Ser.: Vol. 419). (Illus.). viii, 212p. 1993. 56.00 (*0-387-56989-8*) Spr-Verlag.

Ploog, Klaus, jt. ed. see Chang, Leroy L.

Ploog, Michael, jt. auth. see Twain, Mark.

Ploog, Randy. Benjamin West Drawings from the Historical Society of Pennsylvania, (Exhibition Catalogue) 1,987th ed. (Illus.). 66p. (Orig.). 1987. pap. 7.50 (*0-911209-36-0*) Palmer Mus Art.
— Florence Putterman: A Twenty Year Survey, 1970-1990. (Illus.). 40p. 1990. 7.00 (*0-911209-43-3*) Palmer Mus Art.

Plooij, D. Pilgrim Fathers from a Dutch Point of View. LC 71-100509. reprint ed. 20.00 (*0-404-05065-4*) AMS Pr.

Plooij, Daniel. Pilgrim Fathers from a Dutch Point of View. LC 79-131801. 1970. reprint ed. 7.00 (*0-403-00688-0*) Scholarly.

Plooij, Frans X. The Behavioral Development of Free-Living Chimpanzee Babies & Infants. Lipsitt, Lewis P., ed. LC 83-25804. (Monographs on Infancy: Vol. 4). (Illus.). 208p. (Orig.). 1984. text ed. 45.00 (*0-89391-115-1*) Ablex Pub.

Ploos van Amstel, M. J., jt. auth. see Farmer, David.

Plopper, Bruce L. The Problem-Solving Handbook for High School Journalism Advisers. 1992. 8.50 (*0-317-04966-6*) Quill & Scroll.

Ploquin, Max. Dictionnaire de l'Enfantement. 264p. (FRE.). 1974. pap. 39.95 (*0-8288-6012-2*, M6459) Fr & Eur.

***Ploski, Cynthia.** Conversations with My Healers: My Journey to Wellness from Breast Cancer. 240p. 1995. 24.95 (*1-57178-010-6*) Coun Oak Bks.

Ploski, Harry A., comp. Reference Library of Black America, 5 vols., Set. (Illus.). 1600p. 1990. lib. bdg. 179.90 (*0-685-49222-2*) Afro Am Pr.

Ploski, Harry A. & Williams, James, eds. The Negro Almanac: A Reference Work on the Afro American. 4th ed. LC 86-72654. (Illus.). 1550p. 1983. text ed. 99.95 (*0-685-17467-0*) Bellwether Pub.
— Negro Almanac: A Reference Work on the Afro American. 5th ed. (Illus.). 1989. text ed. 99.95 (*0-913144-09-6*) Bellwether Pub.

Ploskonka, Catherine A., ed. see Thacker, Robert M.

Ploss, Douglas A. The Tweens at Deep Lake: An Original American Fantasy. LC 79-90996. (Illus.). 88p. (J). (gr. 3 up). 1979. (*0-9603632-0-3*); pap. 8.50 (*0-9603632-1-1*) OPC.

Ploss, Sidney L. Conflict & Decision-Making in Soviet Russia: A Case Study of Agricultural Policy, 1953-1963. (Center of International Studies Ser.). 1965. 47.50 (*0-691-08706-7*); pap. 14.95 (*0-691-02503-7*) Princeton U Pr.
Ploss, Thomas H. The Nation Pays Again: The Demise of The Milwaukee Road, 1928-1986. 3rd ed. 214p. (C). 1991. 40.00 (*0-685-48875-6*) T H Ploss.
Plosser, Gray G., ed. see White, Marjorie L.
Plossl, George W. Effective Corporate Strategy in Manufacturing. LC 86-90412. (Illus.). 120p. 1986. 21.95 (*0-926219-03-0*) G P Ed Serv.
— Managing in the New World of Manufacturing: How Companies Can Improve Operations to Compete Globally. 256p. 1991. boxed 24.95 (*0-13-617143-5*) P-H.
— Orlicky's Material Requirements Planning. 2nd ed. LC 93-41951. 1994. text ed. 49.00 (*0-07-050459-8*) McGraw.
— Production & Inventory Control: Applications. LC 83-81732. (Illus.). 320p. 1983. 42.67 (*0-926219-04-9*) G P Ed Serv.
Plossl, George W. & Welch, W. Evert. The Role of Top Management in the Control of Inventory. (Illus.). 1978. 35.00 (*0-8359-6697-6*, Reston) P-H.
Plossl, George W. & Wright, Oliver W. Production & Inventory Control: Principles & Techniques. 2nd ed. (Illus.). 448p. 1985. text ed. 78.00 (*0-13-725144-0*) P-H.
Plossl, Keith R. Engineering for the Control of Manufacturing. (Illus.). 240p. (ENG & SPA.). 1987. text ed. 34.95 (*0-317-56749-7*) P-H.
Plossu, Bernard. The African Desert. LC 87-5021. (Illus.). 91p. 1987. pap. 6.95 (*0-8165-0934-4*) U of Ariz Pr.
Plotch, Batia, ed. NewYorkwalks: The Ninety-Second Street Y. (Walks Ser.). (Illus.). 272p. 1992. pap. 12.95 (*0-8050-1660-0*, Owl) H Holt & Co.
Plotch, Batia & Cobe, Patricia, eds. The Kosher Gourmet: The Ninety Second Street Y Kosher Cooking School. 464p. 1994. pap. 12.50 (*0-449-90959-X*) Fawcett.
Plotch, Walter, jt. ed. see Tumin, Melvin M.
Plotikov, N. I. & Roginets, I. I. Hydrogeology of Ore Deposits. (C). 1989. 32.50 (*81-204-0420-3*, Pub. by Oxford IBH II) S Asia.
Plotinus. Are the Stars Causes? 1985. pap. 3.95 (*0-916411-93-1*, Pub. by Alexandrian Pr) Holmes Pub.
— Complete Works of Plotinus with Concordance, 4 vols. Guthrie, K. S., ed. 1977. lib. bdg. 1,000.00 (*0-8490-1659-2*) Gordon Pr.
— Ennead III.6. Fleet, D. B., ed. & tr. by. 336p. (ENG & GRE.). 1995. text ed. 65.00 (*0-19-814965-4*) OUP.
— The Enneads. Dillon, John, ed. MacKenna, Stephen, tr. 688p. 1991. 13.95 (*0-14-044520-X*, Penguin Classics) Viking Penguin.
— The Enneads. MacKenna, Stephen, ed. & tr. by. 768p. 1992. reprint ed. 65.00 (*0-943914-55-8*) Larson Pubns.
— Liber De Pulchritudine. cxlii, 574p. 1976. reprint ed. write for info. (*3-487-06054-X*, Pub. by Georg Olms GW) Lubrecht & Cramer.
— On Nature, Contemplation & the One. Taylor, Thomas, ed. & tr. by. 1989. pap. 5.95 (*1-55818-160-1*, Pub. by Alexandrian Pr) Holmes Pub.
— Opera, Vol. I: Enneades I-III cum vita Porphyrii. Henry, Paul & Schwyzer, H. R., eds. (Oxford Classical Texts Ser.). 1964. 39.95 (*0-19-814561-6*) OUP.
— Opera, Vol. II: Enneades IV-V. Schwyzer, H. R. & Henry, Paul, eds. (Oxford Classical Texts Ser.). 1977. 39.95 (*0-19-814582-9*) OUP.
— Opera, Vol. III: Ennead VI. Schwyzer, H. R. & Henry, Paul, eds. (C). 1983. 45.00 (*0-19-814591-8*) OUP.
— Plotinus: Essay on the Beautiful. Taylor, Thomas, tr. 1984. pap. 7.95 (*0-916411-86-9*, Pub. by Alexandrian Pr) Holmes Pub.
— Works, 7 vols. No. 440-445, & 468. write for info. (*0-318-53221-2*) HUP.
— Works, 7 vols., 1. (Loeb Classical Library: No. 440-445, & 468). 364p. 1966. text ed. 18.95 (*0-674-99484-1*) HUP.
— Works, 7 vols., 2. (Loeb Classical Library: No. 440-445, & 468). 312p. 1966. text ed. 18.95 (*0-674-99486-8*) HUP.
— Works, 7 vols., 3. (Loeb Classical Library: No. 440-445, & 468). 426p. 1967. text ed. 18.95 (*0-674-99487-6*) HUP.
— Works, 7 vols., 4. (Loeb Classical Library: No. 440-445, & 468). 452p. 1967. text ed. 18.95 (*0-674-99488-4*) HUP.
— Works, 7 vols., 5. (Loeb Classical Library: No. 440-445, & 468). 332p. 1967. text ed. 18.95 (*0-674-99489-2*) HUP.
— Works, 7 vols., 6. (Loeb Classical Library: No. 440-445, & 468). 379p. 1988. text ed. 18.95 (*0-674-99490-6*) HUP.
— Works, 7 vols., 7. (Loeb Classical Library: No. 440-445, & 468). 352p. 1988. text ed. 18.95 (*0-674-99515-5*) HUP.
Plotke, A. J. Imperial Spies Invade Russia: The British Intelligence Interventions, 1918. LC 92-25731. (Contributions in Military Studies: No. 131). 304p. 1993. text ed. 57.95 (*0-313-28611-6*, PBI, Greenwood Pr) Greenwood.
***Plotke, David.** Building a Democratic Political Order: Reshaping American Liberalism in the 1930's & 1940's. (Illus.). 320p. (C). 1995. write for info. (*0-521-42059-8*) Cambridge U Pr.
Plotke, David, jt. ed. see Boggs, Carl.
Plotkin, Albert. The Ethics of World Religions. LC 93-35756. 192p. 1993. pap. 24.95 (*0-7734-1940-3*) E Mellen.
— Rabbi Plotkin: A Memoir. Sabine, Gordon A., ed. 160p. (Orig.). 1992. lib. bdg. write for info. (*1-879286-02-5*) AZ Bd Regents.
Plotkin, Allen, jt. auth. see Katz, Joseph.
Plotkin, B. Universal Algebra, Algebraic Logic, & Databases. LC 93-44246. 438p. 1994. lib. bdg. 189.00 (*0-7923-2665-2*) Kluwer Ac.
Plotkin, B. I., et al. Algebraic Structures in Automata & Database Theory. 300p. 1992. text ed. 61.00 (*981-02-0936-3*) World Scientific Pub.
Plotkin, Cary H. The Tenth Muse: Victorian Philology & the Genesis of the Poetic Language of Gerard Manley Hopkins. LC 88-39600. 214p. (C). 1989. 25.95 (*0-8093-1488-6*) S Ill U Pr.
Plotkin, D. Using Lotus Approach 3.0 for Windows. Date not set. pap. 29.99 (*1-56529-177-8*) Que.

***Plotkin, David N. Selling to Humans: A New Approach to Exchange. 268p. 1995. pap. 14.00 (*0-9643549-4-2*) Influence Trning.**
WE SHOULD SELL THE WAY WE'D LIKE TO BUY IF WE WERE BUYERS & KNEW NOTHING ABOUT SELLING. But the sales process that has been taught for the past 150 years has created deception, a feeling of powerlessness in the buyer & a total distrust of anyone who sells for a living. SELLING TO HUMANS provides an alternative by introducing Ten Principles which are steeped in a human-centered values ethic. It then redefines the entire process of selling, from the initial approach through the service after a sale. It THROWS AWAY THE CONCEPT OF "CLOSING" in favor of new techniques for agreeing on courses of action. In addition, it covers territory which no other business book has covered in this way, such as how to become a professional communicator, & why people really do what they do. SELLING TO HUMANS features time-tested techniques used in thousands of selling situations for a decade. It is motivational, inspiring & to quote one SELLING TO HUMANS seminar graduate, it shows that "success does not have to be difficult." Paperback, 272-pages. Call INFLUENCE TRAINING SYSTEMS. Retail $14 (volume pricing, wholesale & premium programs available). P.O. Box 900, Dept. FB1, Cotati, CA 94931, or phone (800) 792-1231. FAX 707-792-6969. Call for distributor name. ***Publisher Provided Annotation.***

Plotkin, Fred. The Authentic Pasta Book. 1989. pap. 14.00 (*0-671-68212-1*, Fireside) S&S Trade.
— Opera 101: A Complete Guide to Learning & Loving Opera. LC 94-9477. 512p. 1994. pap. 14.95 (*0-7868-8025-2*) Hyperion.
Plotkin, Fred & Cernea, Dana. The Nine Month Cookbook: Healthy Gourmet Eating for Pregnant Women. LC 93-6458. 1994. 14.00 (*0-517-88002-4*, Crown) Crown Pub Group.
Plotkin, Frederick. Milton's Inward Jerusalem: "Paradise Lost" & the Ways of Knowing. LC 76-159468. (Studies in English Literature: No. 72). 155p. 1971. text ed. 29.50 (*90-279-1818-X*) Mouton.
Plotkin, G., jt. ed. see Huet, G.
Plotkin, G., jt. ed. see Huet, Gerard.
Plotkin, Gary R., et al, eds. Behcet's Disease: A Contemporary Synopsis. (Illus.). 352p. 1988. 62.00 (*0-87993-313-5*) Futura Pub.
Plotkin, Gordon, jt. ed. see Dezani-Ciancaglini, Mariangiola.
Plotkin, Gordon, jt. ed. see Lassez, Jean-Louis.
Plotkin, Gregory & Plotkin, Rita. Cooking the Russian Way. (Easy Menu Ethnic Cookbooks Ser.). (Illus.). 48p. (J). (gr. 5 up). 1986. lib. bdg. 14.95 (*0-8225-0915-6*, Lerner Publctns) Lerner Group.
Plotkin, Henry. Darwin Machines & the Nature of Knowledge. 287p. (C). 1994. text ed. 27.95 (*0-674-19280-X*) HUP.
— The Nature of Knowledge: Concerning Adaptations, Instinct & the Evaluation of Intelligence. LC 93-39328. 1994. write for info. (*0-674-60482-2*) HUP.
Plotkin, Henry C., ed. Learning, Development, & Culture: Essays in Evolutionary Epistemology. LC 82-1947. 505p. reprint ed. pap. 144.00 (*0-685-15447-5*, 2026683) Bks Demand.
— The Role of Behavior in Evolution. 240p. 1988. 30.00 (*0-262-16107-9*) MIT Pr.
Plotkin, Ira L. Anarchism in Japan: A Study of the Great Treason Affair, 1910-1911. LC 90-24281. (Japanese Studies: Vol. 1). 180p. 1991. lib. bdg. 79.95 (*0-88946-729-3*) E Mellen.
Plotkin, Mark. Tales of a Shaman's Apprentice: An Ethnobotanist Searches for New Medicines in the Amazonian Rain Forest. LC 92-50768. 320p. 1993. 22.00 (*0-670-83137-9*, Viking) Viking Penguin.
Plotkin, Mark & Famolare, Lisa, eds. Sustainable Harvest & Marketing of Rain Forest Products. LC 91-43278. 325p. (Orig.). 1992. 40.00 (*1-55963-169-4*); pap. 20.00 (*1-55963-168-6*) Island Pr.
Plotkin, Mark J. Tales of a Shaman's Apprentice: An Ethnobotanist Searches for New Medicines in the Amazonian Rain Forest. (Illus.). 352p. 1994. 11.95 (*0-14-012991-X*, Penguin Bks) Viking Penguin.
Plotkin, Martha R. A Time for Dignity: Police & Domestic Abuse of the Elderly. LC 88-62067. 112p. (Orig.). (C). 1988. pap. text ed. 15.00 (*1-878734-05-9*) Police Exec Res.
Plotkin, R. The Intervention Handbook. 64p. pap. 8.95 (*0-318-41637-9*) Am Bartenders.
— Preventing Internal Theft. 81p. 14.95 (*0-318-41631-X*, 206) Am Bartenders.
Plotkin, Rita, jt. auth. see Plotkin, Gregory.
Plotkin, Robert, ed. The Bartender's Companion: A Complete Drink Recipe Guide. 2nd ed. LC 93-83097. (Illus.). (Orig.). 1993. pap. 10.95 (*0-945562-11-X*) PSD Pub.
Plotkin, Robert & Hermansen, Carol A. Professional Guide to Bartending: An Encyclopedia of American Mixology. 2nd ed. LC 91-60296. (Illus.). 183p. (C). 1991. pap. 39.95 (*0-945562-10-1*) PSD Pub.
Plotkin, Robert A. The Bartender's Companion: A Complete Drink Recipe Guide. LC 88-9089. (Illus.). 101p. (Orig.). (C). 1988. pap. 10.95 (*0-945562-05-5*) PSD Pub.
— Intervention Handbook: The Legal Aspects of Serving Alcohol. LC 88-9095. (Illus.). 65p. (Orig.). (C). 1988. pap. 9.95 (*0-945562-00-4*) PSD Pub.
— Preventing Internal Theft: A Bar Owner's Guide. LC 88-9076. 81p. (Orig.). (C). 1988. pap. 14.95 (*0-945562-04-7*) PSD Pub.
— The Professional Guide to Commercial Bartending. 216p. (Orig.). 1988. 27.95 (*0-318-41630-1*, 204) Am Bartenders.
— The Professional Guide to Commercial Bartending. LC 88-9077. (Illus.). 240p. (Orig.). (C). 1988. pap. 24.95 (*0-945562-01-2*) PSD Pub.
Plotkin, S. A., jt. ed. see Majer, M.
Plotkin, Sidney. Keep Out: The Struggle for Land Use Control. 350p. (C). 1987. pap. 13.00 (*0-520-06127-6*) U CA Pr.
Plotkin, Sidney, jt. auth. see Scheuerman, William E.
Plotkin, Stanley A. & Mortimer, Edward A., Jr. Vaccines. 2nd ed. LC 93-10761. (Illus.). 1024p. 1994. reprint ed. text ed. 165.00 (*0-7216-6584-5*) Saunders.
Plotkin, Stanley A., jt. ed. see Michelson, Susan.
Plotkin, V. Y. The Dynamics of the English Phonological Systems. (Janua Linguarum, Ser. Practica: No. 155). 98p. 1972. pap. text ed. 20.00 (*90-279-2324-8*) Mouton.
Plotnick, Alan R. Petroleum: Canadian Markets & United States Foreign Trade Policy. LC 64-25731. 175p. 1965. 25.00 (*0-295-73876-6*) U of Wash Pr.
Plotnick, Charles, jt. auth. see Consumer Reports Books Editors.
Plotnick, Charles K. & Leimberg, Stephan R. Keeping Your Money: How to Avoid Taxes & Probate Through Estate Planning. LC 87-6121. 352p. 1987. pap. text ed. 14.95 (*0-471-85948-6*) Wiley.
Plotnick, Gary D., intro. Unstable Angina: A Clinical Approach. (Illus.). 400p. 1985. 59.50 (*0-87993-231-7*) Futura Pub.
Plotnick, Harvey M. Notes of a Refugee: Poems. LC 92-14940. 64p. 1992. pap. 12.95 (*0-7734-0002-8*, Mellen Poetry Pr) E Mellen.
Plotnicov, Leonard. Strangers to the City: Urban Man in Jos, Nigeria. LC 67-13928. (Illus.). 333p. (C). 1967. pap. 14.95 (*0-8229-5135-5*) U of Pittsburgh Pr.
Plotnicov, Leonard, ed. American Culture: Essays on the Familiar & Unfamiliar. LC 89-16638. 320p. 1990. 49.95 (*0-8229-1157-4*); pap. 19.95 (*0-8229-6092-3*) U of Pittsburgh Pr.
Plotnicov, Leonard & Tuden, Arthur, eds. Essays in Comparative Social Stratification. LC 79-81666. 357p. reprint ed. pap. 101.80 (*0-317-28774-5*, 2020620) Bks Demand.
Plotnicov, Leonard, jt. ed. see Coy, Michael W., Jr.
Plotnik. Elements of Editing. 1982. 9.13 (*0-02-597700-8*) Macmillan.
Plotnik, Arthur. Elements of Editing. 176p. 1986. pap. 5.95 (*0-02-047430-X*, Pub. by Gebrueder Borntraeger GW) Macmillan.
Plotnik, Arthur, et al. The CLAST Review Book. 445p. 1993. text ed. write for info. (*0-15-500041-1*) HB Coll Pubs.
***Plotnik, Frank.** Explorations in Microeconomics. 1995. pap. text ed. write for info. (*1-56226-226-2*) CT Pub.
Plotnik, Gene. Sales Artillery: How to Arm the Sales Force for Successful Selling. 240p. 1989. pap. 16.95 (*0-13-786575-9*, Busn) P-H.
Plotnik, Rod. Introduction to Psychology. 3rd ed. 770p. (C). 1993. student ed, pap. 17.95 (*0-534-16448-X*) Brooks-Cole.
— Introduction to Psychology. 3rd ed. 770p. (C). 1993. text ed. 49.95 (*0-534-16446-3*) Brooks-Cole.
Plotnik, Rodney. Introduction to Psychology. 2nd ed. 688p. (C). 1989. text ed. 37.50 (*0-394-38336-2*); student ed write for info. (*0-394-38665-5*) Random.
Plotnik, Rodney & Mollenauer, Sandra. Psychology: An Introduction Study Guide. 160p. (C). 1986. text ed. 7.95 (*0-394-35262-9*) Random.
***Plotnikoff, Joyce & Woolfson, Richard.** Prosecuting Child Abuse: An Evaluation of the Government's Speedy Progress Policy. 109p. 1995. pap. 30.00 (*1-85431-404-1*, Pub. by Blackstone Pr UK) W W Gaunt.
Plotnikoff, Nicholas P., et al. Stress & Immunity. (Illus.). 528p. 1991. 104.95 (*0-8493-8845-7*, QP82) CRC Pr.
Plotnikoff, Nicholas P., et al, eds. Enkephalins & Endorphins: Stress & the Immune System. LC 85-23234. 458p. 1986. 95.00 (*0-306-42226-3*, Plenum Pr) Plenum.
Plotnikov, A. F., ed. Electron Processes in MIS-Structure Memories. Makinen, Paul, tr. (Proceedings of the Lebedev Physics Institute Ser.: Vol. 184). 227p. (C). 1989. text ed. 115.00 (*0-941743-53-5*) Nova Sci Pubs.
Plotnikov, L. M. Shear Structures of Layered Geological Bodies. Sychanthavong, S. P., ed. (Russian Translation Ser.: No. 104). (Illus.). 171p. (C). 1994. text ed. 55.00 (*90-5410-220-9*, Pub. by A A Balkema NE) Ashgate Pub Co.
Plotnikov, N. I. & Roginets, I. I. Hydrogeology of Ore Deposits. Viswanathan, S., tr. (Russian Translation Ser.: No. 72). (Illus.). 298p. (C). 1990. text ed. 95.00 (*90-6191-900-2*, Pub. by A A Balkema NE) Ashgate Pub Co.
Plotnikova, Julia, tr. see Sckolnick, Lewis B.
Plotnitsky, Arkady. Complementarity: Anti-Epistemology after Bohr & Derrida. LC 93-29583. 328p. 1994. lib. bdg. 49.95 (*0-8223-1433-9*); pap. text ed. 17.95 (*0-8223-1437-1*) Duke.
— In the Shadow of Hegel: Complementarity, History, & the Unconscious. LC 92-42561. 544p. 1993. lib. bdg. 49.95 (*0-8130-1202-3*); pap. text ed. 19.95 (*0-8130-1203-1*) U Press Fla.
— Reconfigurations: Critical Theory & General Economy. LC 92-22271. 440p. 1993. 49.95 (*0-8130-1172-8*); pap. 19.95 (*0-8130-1173-6*) U Press Fla.
Plotnitsky, Arkady, jt. ed. see Smith, Barbara H.
***Plotsky, Charlotte W.** Havens for Creatives. 8th ed. 128p. 1995. pap. text ed. 19.95 (*1-886527-00-8*) ACTS By C P.
Plott, Dave, ed. see Long, Evelyn.
Plott, John C. Global History of Philosophy, Vol. V. (C). 1989. 35.00 (*81-208-0552-6*, Pub. by Motilal Banarsidass II) S Asia.
Plott, Monte. Flashes of Fire: An American Anthology. 80p. (Orig.). 1985. pap. 10.00 (*0-932662-51-X*) St Andrews NC.
Plottel, Jeanine F., jt. ed. see Stanton, Domna C.
Plotts, J. N., ed. Poetical Tributes to the Memory of Abraham Lincoln. 1972. reprint ed. lib. bdg. 20.00 (*0-8422-8105-3*) Irvington.
Plotz, Helen. A Week of Lullabies. LC 86-18458. (Illus.). 32p. (J). (ps-3). 1988. 11.95 (*0-688-06652-6*); lib. bdg. 11.88 (*0-688-06653-4*) Greenwillow.
Plotz, Rob. Dingaling. 1983. pap. 1.75 (*0-912963-01-8*) Eldridge Pub.
Plouffe, Paul B., jt. auth. see Hatton, John.
Plouffe, Simon, jt. ed. see Sloane, Neil J.
Plouffe, W., jt. auth. see Bender, W.
Plough, Alonzo, jt. auth. see Krimsky, Sheldon.
Plough, Harold H. Sea Squirts of the Atlantic Continental Shelf from Maine to Texas. LC 76-47388. (Illus.). 128p. reprint ed. pap. 36.50 (*0-317-41676-6*, 2025851) Bks Demand.
Plough, M. & Ellis, V. The Molecular Basis of Plasminogen Activation. (Molecular Biology Intelligence Unit Ser.). write for info. (*1-57059-165-2*) R G Landes.
Plourde, Harvey S. The Compleat Taildragger Pilot. (Illus.). 263p. (Orig.). 1991. pap. 24.95 (*0-9639137-0-0*) H S Plourde.
Plous, Frederick K., Jr., tr. see Levine, Norman D., ed.
Plous, Frederick K., Jr., tr. see Naumov, N. P.
Plous, Phyllis. Bart Wasserman: North Wall Curving South. (Illus.). 24p. 1985. 10.00 (*0-942006-09-7*) U of CA Art.
— Howard Fenton: Recent Paintings. (Illus.). 20p. (Orig.). 1990. pap. 7.00 (*0-942006-19-4*) U of CA Art.
— Scapes. (Illus.). 59p. 1985. 10.00 (*0-942006-10-0*) U of CA Art.
Plous, Phyllis & Baker, Kenneth. Collaborations in Monotype: Garner Tullis Workshop. LC 87-35729. (Illus.). 1988. pap. 18.00 (*0-295-96694-7*) U of Wash Pr.
Plous, Phyllis & Colpitt, Frances. Abstract Options. (Illus.). 68p. 1989. pap. 14.95 (*0-295-96874-5*) U of Wash Pr.
Plous, Phyllis & Guggenheim, Eileen. A Heritage Renewed: Representational Drawing Today. (Illus.). 87p. (Orig.). 1983. 15.00 (*0-942006-03-8*) U of CA Art.
Plous, Phyllis & Klein, Michael R. Figuration. (Illus.). 56p. 1982. 9.00 (*0-942006-00-3*) U of CA Art.
Plous, Phyllis & Knight, Christopher. Terry Winters: Painting & Drawing. (Illus.). 88p. 1987. 18.00 (*0-942006-15-1*) U of CA Art.
Plous, Phyllis, jt. auth. see Colpitt, Frances.
Plous, Phyllis, et al. Neo York: Report on a Phenomenon. (Illus.). 72p. (Orig.). 1984. 15.00 (*0-942006-08-9*) U of CA Art.
— Pulse, No. 2: Report on a Phenomenon. (Illus.). 72p. 1990. 20.00 (*0-685-65611-X*) U of CA Art.
— PULSE Two: A Report on a Phenomenon. (Illus.). 160p. (Orig.). 1990. pap. 20.00 (*0-295-97036-7*) U of Wash Pr.
— Pulse Two: Report on a Phenomenon. (Illus.). 72p. (Orig.). 1990. pap. 20.00 (*0-942006-20-8*); vhs 20.00 (*0-317-02846-4*) U of CA Art.
Plous, Scott. Psychology of Judgement & Decision Making. (C). 1993. pap. text ed. write for info. (*0-07-050477-6*) McGraw.
— The Psychology of Judgment & Decision Making. LC 92-32752. (C). 1992. 39.95 (*0-87722-913-9*) Temple U Pr.
Plouwden, D. & Worthington, C. Techniques for Evaluation of Marginal Field Development. 1989. 125.00 (*90-6314-532-2*, Pub. by Lorne & MacLean Marine) St Mut.
Plovnick, Mark S., et al. Organization Development: Exercises, Cases, & Readings. (C). 1987. pap. text ed. 25.50 (*0-673-39033-0*) HarpCollege.
Plowden, Allison. The Elizabethan Secret Service. LC 91-4242. 176p. 1991. text ed. 49.95 (*0-312-06716-X*) St Martin.
Plowden, Celeste. Carousel Animals Cut & Use Stencils: 44 Full-Size Stencils Printed on Durable Stencil Paper. (Illus.). 64p. (Orig.). pap. 4.95 (*0-486-26889-6*) Dover.

An Asterisk (*) at the beginning of an entry indicates that the title is appearing in BIP for the first time.

— Carousel Animals Iron-on Transfer Patterns. (Transfer Patterns Ser.). (Illus.). 48p. (Orig.). 1991. pap. text ed. 2.95 (*0-486-26653-2*) Dover.

— Favorite Birds Charted Designs. LC 94-20405. (Illus.). 1994. pap. write for info. (*0-486-28220-1*) Dover.

— Horses Charted Designs. LC 93-18960. (Needlework Ser.). 1993. pap. 3.50 (*0-486-27578-7*) Dover.

Plowden, D. & Worthington, C., eds. Techniques for Evaluation of Marginal Field Development. (C). 1989. 125.00 (*0-89771-742-2*, Pub. by Lorne & MacLean Marine) St Mut.

Plowden, David. The End of an Era: The Last of the Great Lakes Steamboats. (Illus.). 160p. 1992. 50.00 (*0-393-03348-1*) Norton.

— The Hand of Man on America. LC 74-127823. (Illus.). 136p. 1973. reprint ed. pap. 14.95 (*0-85699-077-9*) Chatham Pr.

— A Sense of Place. 1988. 35.00 (*0-393-02618-3*) Norton.

Plowden, David, photos & text. Small Town America. LC 93-35961. (Illus.). 1994. 49.50 (*0-8109-3842-1*) Abrams.

Plowden, Gene. Singing Wheels & Circus Wagons. LC 75-21135. (Illus.). 1978. pap. 4.95 (*0-87004-256-4*) Caxton.

Plowden, Judith. Afterglow. 320p. 1986. reprint ed. pap. 3.50 (*0-8439-2353-9*) Dorchester Pub Co.

Plowden, Martha W. Famous Firsts of Black Women. (Illus.). 112p. (J). (gr. 4-8). 1993. 15.95 (*0-88289-973-2*) Pelican.

— Olympic Black Women. (Illus.). 160p. (J). (gr. 5-12). 1995. 16.95 (*1-56554-080-8*) Pelican.

Plowhead, Ruth G. Lucretia Ann on the Oregon Trail. LC 31-25267. 1993. reprint ed. pap. 8.95 (*0-87004-360-9*) Caxton.

Plowman, B. H. Plowman: A Register of Plowmans in America & Extr. from English & American Records. 90p. 1991. reprint ed. pap. 17.50 (*0-8328-1828-3*) Higginson Bk Co.

Plowman, Brian. Implementing Business Process Management: Implementing Business Process Management: Starting the Process of Corporate Transformation. (Financial Times Management Ser.). 240p. 1994. 105.00x (*0-273-60437-6*, Pub. by Pitman Pubng UK) St Mut.

Plowman, Brian, jt. ed. see Hand, Max.

Plowman, David H. Holding the Line: Compulsory Arbitration & National Employer Co-ordination in Australia. (Illus.). 272p. (C). 1989. 59.95 (*0-521-36085-4*) Cambridge U Pr.

Plowman, Edward E. Haunted Houses: Ghost Writing & Religious Publishing. 128p. 1994. reprint ed. pap. 5.99 (*0-8010-7130-5*) Baker Bk.

Plowman, Gillian. Cecily. 1992. pap. 2.75 (*0-87129-132-0*, C83) Dramatic Pub.

— The Janna Years. 1992. pap. 2.75 (*0-87129-130-4*, J22) Dramatic Pub.

— Me & My Friend. 1990. pap. 5.45 (*0-87129-140-1*, M78) Dramatic Pub.

— The Primrose Path. 1990. pap. 2.75 (*0-87129-129-0*, P70) Dramatic Pub.

— The Wooden Pear. 1992. pap. 2.75 (*0-87129-131-2*, W71) Dramatic Pub.

Plowman, Gillian, et al. Verity Bargate Award Plays, 1989. Keeffe, Barrie, ed. (Methuen New Theatrescripts Ser.). 110p. (Orig.). (C). 1988. pap. 12.95 (*0-413-62240-1*, A0408, Pub. by Methuen UK) Heinemann.

Plowman, Grant. Design CAD Inside & Out. 1992. pap. text ed. 39.95 (*0-07-881846-X*) McGraw.

Plowman, Kathryn J. Doctor's Letters: Interludes of War: 1944-45. 1983. pap. 8.50 (*0-9613217-0-9*) Augusta Pubs.

Plowman, Mary S. This Time. Goodfellow, Pamela R., ed. 384p. (Orig.). 1994. pap. 7.99 (*0-9639882-1-2*) Goodfellow Pr.

Plowman, P. N. Respiratory Medicine. LC 87-31999. (Illustrated Lecture Ser.). 236p. reprint ed. pap. 67.30 (*0-7837-4772-1*, 2044527) Bks Demand.

Plowman, P. N. & Pinkerton, C. R., eds. Paediatric Oncology: Clinical Practice & Controversies. (Illus.). 672p. 1992. 132.95 (*0-442-31595-3*) Chapman & Hall.

Plowman, P. N., et al, eds. Complications of Cancer Management. 528p. 1991. text ed. 295.00 (*0-7506-1341-6*) Buttrwrth-Heinemann.

Plowman, P. W. & Pinkerton, C. R. Paediatric Oncology: Clinical Practice & Controversies. (Illus.). 672p. 1991. 132.95 (*0-412-39780-3*) Chapman & Hall.

Plowman, Paul D. Teaching the Gifted & Talented in the Social Studies Classroom. 56p. 1980. 6.95 (*0-8106-0737-9*) NEA.

Plowman, Peter. The Wheels Still Turn: A History of Australian Paddleboats. (Illus.). 160p. 1993. 32.50 (*0-86417-428-4*, Pub. by Kangaroo Pr AT) Seven Hills Bk.

Plowman, Roscoe E. Twice Out of Sight. 122p. (Orig.). 1982. pap. 5.00 (*0-935680-11-X*) Kentucke Imprints.

Plowright, Poh-Sim. The Classical No Theatre of Japan. (C). 1991. lib. bdg. 105.00 (*0-85964-203-8*) Chadwyck-Healey.

Plowright, Richard. Himage. 48p. (Orig.). 1990. pap. 6.95 (*1-55583-160-5*) Alyson Pubns.

Plowright, Terrance. Stained Glass: Inspirations & Designs. (Illus.). 96p. 1993. 24.95 (*0-86417-495-0*, Pub. by Kangaroo Pr AT) Seven Hills Bk.

***Plowright, Terrence.** Stained Glass: Inspirations & Designs. (Illus.). 96p. (Orig.). 1995. pap. 16.95 (*0-86417-660-0*, Pub. by Kangaroo Pr AT) Seven Hills Bk.

***PLP Services Staff.** Crew List in Spanish (Official Foreign Documents) 1995. 9.95 (*0-9638470-3-1*) Pt Loma Pubng.

— 1996 Tide Tables for Pacific Mexico (Includes Baja, Sea of Cortez, & Gold Coast) 1995. 9.95 (*0-9638470-4-X*) Pt Loma Pubng.

Pluchino, F., jt. auth. see Morello, G.

Pluchinsky, Dennis A., jt. ed. see Alexander, Yonah.

Plucked String, Inc. Staff, ed. see Lind, Ekard.

Plucked String Staff, ed. see Wolki, Konrad.

Plucker, Lina S. & Roerick, Kaye L., eds. Brevet's Illinois Historical Markers & Sites. LC 75-253. (Historical Markers-Sites Ser.). (Illus.). 300p. (Orig.). 1976. pap. 9.95 (*0-88498-029-4*) Brevet Pr.

Pluckhan, Margaret. Human Communication: The Matrix of Nursing. (Illus.). 1977. text ed. 26.95 (*0-07-050352-4*) McGraw.

Plucknelt, D. L., ed. Detecting Mineral Nutrient Deficiences in Tropical & Temperate Crops. 563p. (C). 1990. text ed. 450.00 (*81-7089-133-7*, Pub. by Intl Bk Distr II) St Mut.

Plucknett, Donald, et al. Gene Banks & the World's Food. (Illus.). 248p. 1987. 45.00 (*0-691-08438-6*) Princeton U Pr.

Plucknett, Donald L., et al. International Agricultural Research: A Database of Networks. (Consultative Group on International Agricultural Research Study Paper Ser.: No. 26). 174p. 1990. 10.95 (*0-8213-1540-4*, 11540) World Bank.

— Networking in International Agriculture Research. LC 90-31276. (Illus.). 240p. 1990. 34.00 (*0-8014-2384-8*) Cornell U Pr.

Plucknett, Theodore F. A Concise History of the Common Law. 5th ed. 802p. 1912. 45.00 (*0-316-71083-0*) Little.

— Early English Legal Literature. LC 85-48155. (Cambridge Studies in English Legal History). 127p. 1986. reprint ed. 31.00 (*0-912004-35-5*) W W Gaunt.

— Statutes & Their Interpretation in the First Half of the 14th Century. LC 85-81796. (Cambridge Studies in English Legal History). 244p. 1986. reprint ed. 59.00 (*0-685-13258-7*) W W Gaunt.

— Studies in English Legal History. 350p. (C). 1983. text ed. 55.00 (*0-907628-11-7*) Hambledon Press.

Plucknett, Theodore F., ed. Readings on the History & System of the Common Law. 3rd ed. LC 93-78456. 756p. 1993. reprint ed. 110.00 (*1-56169-043-0*) W W Gaunt.

***Pluckrose, Henry.** Beginnings & Endings. LC 94-44515. (New Look Ser.). (Illus.). (J). 1995. write for info. (*0-516-08236-1*) Childrens.

— Book Craft. LC 91-40501. (Fresh Start Ser.). (Illus.). 48p. (J). (gr. 5-8). 1992. lib. bdg. 12.95 (*0-531-14169-1*) Watts.

— Changing Seasons. LC 93-44700. (Walkabout Ser.). 32p. (J). (ps-3). 1994. lib. bdg. 12.00 (*0-614-04457-X*) Childrens.

— Changing Seasons. LC 93-44700. (Walkabout Ser.). 32p. (J). (ps-3). 1994. pap. 4.95 (*0-516-40116-5*) Childrens.

— Exploring Our Senses: Complete Set, 5 vols., Set. (Illus.). 160p. 1995. lib. bdg. 86.35 (*0-8368-1286-7*) Gareth Stevens Inc.

— Exploring Our Senses: Hearing. (Exploring Our Senses Ser.). (Illus.). 32p. (J). 1995. lib. bdg. 17.27 (*0-8368-1287-5*) Gareth Stevens Inc.

— Exploring Our Senses: Seeing. (Exploring Our Senses Ser.). (Illus.). 32p. (J). 1995. lib. bdg. 17.27 (*0-8368-1288-3*) Gareth Stevens Inc.

— Exploring Our Senses: Smelling. (Exploring Our Senses Ser.). (Illus.). 32p. (J). 1995. lib. bdg. 17.27 (*0-8368-1289-1*) Gareth Stevens Inc.

— Exploring Our Senses: Tasting. (Exploring Our Senses Ser.). (Illus.). 32p. (J). 1995. lib. bdg. 17.27 (*0-8368-1290-5*) Gareth Stevens Inc.

— Exploring Our Senses: Touching. (Exploring Our Senses Ser.). (Illus.). 32p. (J). 1995. lib. bdg. 17.27 (*0-8368-1291-3*) Gareth Stevens Inc.

— Flowers. LC 93-45661. (Walkabout Ser.). (J). (ps-2). 1994. pap. 4.95 (*0-516-40117-3*) Childrens.

— Holes. LC 94-41102. (New Look Ser.). (Illus.). (J). 1995. write for info. (*0-516-08237-X*) Childrens.

— In the Air. LC 93-45662. (Walkabout Ser.). (J). (ps-2). 1994. pap. 4.95 (*0-516-40118-1*) Childrens.

— Inside & Outside. LC 94-41104. (New Look Ser.). (J). 1995. write for info. (*0-516-08238-8*) Childrens.

— KnowAbout Capacity. (J). 1995. write for info. (*0-516-05451-1*) Childrens.

— KnowAbout Counting. (J). 1995. write for info. (*0-516-05452-X*) Childrens.

— KnowAbout Length. (J). 1995. write for info. (*0-516-05453-8*) Childrens.

— KnowAbout Numbers. (J). 1995. write for info. (*0-516-05454-6*) Childrens.

— KnowAbout Shape. (J). 1995. write for info. (*0-516-05456-2*) Childrens.

— Knowabout Size. (J). 1995. write for info. (*0-516-05457-0*) Childrens.

— KnowAbout Sorting. (J). 1995. write for info. (*0-516-05458-9*) Childrens.

— KnowAbout Time. (J). 1995. write for info. (*0-516-05459-7*) Childrens.

— KnowAbout Weight. (J). 1995. write for info. (*0-516-05460-0*) Childrens.

— Minibeasts. LC 93-44697. (Walkabout Ser.). 32p. (J). (ps-3). 1994. lib. bdg. 12.00 (*0-614-04455-3*) Childrens.

— Minibeasts. LC 93-44697. (Walkabout Ser.). 32p. (J). (ps-3). 1994. pap. 4.95 (*0-516-40119-X*) Childrens.

— Pattern. (J). 1995. write for info. (*0-516-05455-4*) Childrens.

— Seashore. LC 93-44698. (Walkabout Ser.). 32p. (J). (ps-3). 1994. lib. bdg. 12.00 (*0-614-04456-1*) Childrens.

— Seashore. LC 93-44698. (Walkabout Ser.). 32p. (J). (ps-3). 1994. pap. 4.95 (*0-516-40120-3*) Childrens.

— Trees. LC 93-44699. (Walkabout Ser.). (J). 1994. lib. bdg. 12.00 (*0-516-08121-7*) Childrens.

— Trees. (Walkabout Ser.). (J). (ps-2). 1994. pap. 4.95 (*0-516-40121-1*) Childrens.

— Under the Ground. LC 93-45659. (Walkabout Ser.). (J). 1994. lib. bdg. 12.00 (*0-516-08122-5*) Childrens.

— Under the Ground. (Walkabout Ser.). (J). (ps-2). 1994. pap. 4.95 (*0-516-40122-X*) Childrens.

— Walls. LC 94-45584. (New Look Ser.). (Illus.). (J). 1995. write for info. (*0-516-08239-6*) Childrens.

— Weather. (Walkabout Ser.). (J). (ps-2). 1994. pap. 4.95 (*0-516-40123-8*) Childrens.

Pluckrose, Henry A. Flowers. LC 93-45661. (Walkabout Ser.). (Illus.). 32p. (J). (ps-3). 1994. lib. bdg. 12.00 (*0-516-08117-9*) Childrens.

— In the Air. LC 93-45662. (Walkabout Ser.). (Illus.). 32p. (J). (ps-3). 1994. lib. bdg. 12.00 (*0-516-08118-7*) Childrens.

— Weather. LC 93-45660. (Walkabout Ser.). (J). 1994. lib. bdg. 12.00 (*0-516-08123-3*) Childrens.

Pluckwell, George. John Constable's Essex. 1993. pap. 14.00 (*0-86025-413-5*, Pub. by Ian Henry Pubns UK) Empire Pub Srvs.

— Smuggling Villages of North East Essex. 1993. pap. 13.00 (*0-86025-403-8*, Pub. by Ian Henry Pubns UK) Empire Pub Srvs.

Plueckhahn, Vernon D. Ethics, Legal Medicine & Forensic Pathology. (Illus.). 287p. 1983. 44.95 (*0-522-84252-6*) Intl Spec Bk.

Plueddemann, Carol. Great Prayers of the Bible. (Fisherman Bible Studyguides Ser.). 64p. 1991. 4.99 (*0-87788-334-3*) Shaw Pubs.

Plueddemann, Carol, ed. Great Passages of the Bible. (Fisherman Bible Studyguide Ser.). 80p. (Orig.). 1987. 4.99 (*0-87788-332-7*) Shaw Pubs.

— Great People of the Bible. (Fisherman Bible Studyguide Ser.). 64p. (Orig.). 1988. 4.99 (*0-87788-333-5*) Shaw Pubs.

— Promises of Encouragement. (Pocketpac Bks.). 96p. 1991. pap. 2.99 (*0-87788-650-4*) Shaw Pubs.

— World Shapers: A Treasury of Quotes from Great Missionaries. 160p. 1991. per. 7.99 (*0-87788-946-5*) Shaw Pubs.

Plueddemann, Carol & Wright, Vinita H., comps. Family Prayers for All Occasions: Gift Edition. deluxe ed. 144p. 1995. 12.99 (*0-87788-645-8*) Shaw Pubs.

Plueddemann, Carol, jt. auth. see Plueddemann, Jim.

Plueddemann, Carol, jt. auth. see Wright, Vinita H.

Plueddemann, Edwin P. Silane Coupling Agents. 2nd ed. LC 90-21011. (Illus.). 245p. 1990. 59.50 (*0-306-43473-3*, Plenum Pr) Plenum.

Plueddemann, James E., jt. auth. see LeBar, Lois E.

Plueddemann, Jim. Keeping Cool in a Crazy World. (Bible Discovery Guide Ser.). (Illus.). 32p. (J). (gr. 4-6). 1988. student ed 1.50 (*0-87788-454-4*); teacher ed 3.50 (*0-87788-455-2*) Shaw Pubs.

— Ready! Get Set! Grow! (Bible Discovery Guide for Junior Campers Ser.). (Illus.). 48p. (J). 1987. Camper Ed. 1.50 (*0-87788-715-2*); Counselor Ed. 3.50 (*0-87788-716-0*) Shaw Pubs.

Plueddemann, Jim & Plueddemann, Carol. Meekness: Claiming Your Inheritance. (Beatitudes Ser.). 48p. 1993. Saddle stitch bdg. 4.99 (*0-310-59623-8*) Zondervan.

— Pilgrims in Progress: Growing Through Groups. 176p. (Orig.). 1990. pap. 8.99 (*0-87788-647-4*) Shaw Pubs.

— Spiritual Hunger: Filling Your Deepest Longings. (Beatitudes Ser.). 48p. 1993. Saddle stitch bdg. 4.99 (*0-310-59633-5*) Zondervan.

— Strengthened to Serve: 2 Corinthians. (Fisherman Bible Studyguide Ser.). 64p. 1991. pap. 4.99 (*0-87788-783-7*) Shaw Pubs.

***Plueddenmann, Carol.** Great Passages of the Bible. Wu, Jane C., tr. 82p. (CHI.). 1990. pap. 3.50 (*1-56582-002-9*) Christ Renew Min.

***Pluedemanns.** James: Growing in Mat. 64p. 1995. pap. 4.99 (*1-56476-366-8*, 6-3366, Victor Books) SP Pubns.

Plueger, Aaron L. Things to Come & Not to Come: Bible Prophecy & Modern Myths. 2nd rev. ed. LC 90-70068. (Illus.). 110p. 1990. pap. 8.95 (*0-9625719-0-3*) Truth & Error.

Plugge, Domis E. History of a Greek Play Production in American Colleges & Universities from 1881 to 1936. LC 75-177155. (Columbia University. Teachers College. Contributions to Education Ser.: No. 752). reprint ed. 37.50 (*0-404-55752-X*) AMS Pr.

Plugin, V. Frescoes of St. Demetrius' Cathedral. 44p. 1974. 40.00 (*0-569-08164-5*, Pub. by Collets UK) St Mut.

Plugin, Vladimir. Rublev, Andrei. (C). 1987. 45.00 (*0-569-09035-0*, Pub. by Collets UK) Pro-Am Music.

***Pluhar, Evelyn B.** Beyond Prejudice: The Moral Significance of Human & Nonhuman Animals. LC 95-865. 1995. write for info. (*0-8223-1634-X*); pap. write for info. (*0-8223-1664-8*) Duke.

Pluhar, Jennifer, jt. auth. see Hatch, Stephan L.

Pluhar, Werner S., tr. see Kant, Immanuel.

Plum, jt. auth. see Wayman.

Plum, Angela. Alternate Healing Methods: An Overview. LC 93-85295. (Illus.). 128p. (Orig.). 1993. pap. 8.50 (*1-56664-051-2*) WorldComm.

— An Interfaith Minister's Manual. (Illus.). 320p. 1993. 25.00 (*1-56664-026-1*, WrldComm Pr); text ed. 23.58 (*0-685-66305-1*, WrldComm Pr) WorldComm.

Plum, Carol T. The Butterfly Secret: I Am Special Childrens Story Books. 32p. (J). (ps-3). 1989. lib. bdg. 9.95 (*0-87973-017-X*, 17); pap. text ed. 5.95 (*0-87973-014-5*, 14) Our Sunday Visitor.

— Pandy's Rainbow. (I Am Special Story Bks.). (Illus.). 32p. (J). (gr. k-3). 1991. 9.95 (*0-87973-008-0*, 8); pap. 5.95 (*0-87973-009-9*, 9) Our Sunday Visitor.

— Peter Can't Wait. (I Am Special Story Bks.). (Illus.). 32p. (J). (gr. k-3). 1991. 9.95 (*0-87973-006-4*, 6); pap. 5.95 (*0-87973-007-2*, 7) Our Sunday Visitor.

— Peter's Angry Toys: I Am Special Childrens Story Books. 32p. (J). (ps-3). 1989. lib. bdg. 9.95 (*0-87973-015-3*, 15); pap. text ed. 5.95 (*0-87973-012-9*, 12) Our Sunday Visitor.

— The Swinging Tree: I Am Special Childrens Story Books. 32p. (J). (gr. 3-8). 1989. lib. bdg. 9.95 (*0-87973-016-1*, 16); pap. text ed. 5.95 (*0-87973-013-7*, 13) Our Sunday Visitor.

— Where the Big River Runs. (I Am Special Story Bks.). (Illus.). 32p. (J). (gr. k-3). 1991. 5.95 (*0-87973-011-0*, 11); pap. 9.95 (*0-87973-010-2*, 10) Our Sunday Visitor.

Plum, D. R. & Morris, L. J. Structural Steelwork Design. (Illus.). 208p. 1991. pap. 34.95 (*0-87683-615-5*) GP Pub.

Plum, Dorothy A., ed. Adirondack Bibliography. 1958. 10.00 (*0-910020-28-0*) Adirondack Mus.

— Adirondack Bibliography: Supplement 1956-65. 1973. 10.00 (*0-910020-29-9*, Adirondack Mus) Syracuse U Pr.

Plum, Fred, ed. Advances in Contemporary Neurology. LC 88-11826. (Contemporary Neurology Ser.: No. 29). (Illus.). 211p. (C). 1988. text ed. 45.00 (*0-8036-6971-2*) Davis Co.

— Brain Dysfunction in Metabolic Disorders. 1974. 33.50 (*0-7204-7521-X*, North Holland) Elsevier.

— Brain Dysfunction in Metabolic Disorders. fac. ed. LC 74-79190. (Association for Research in Nervous & Mental Disease Research Publications: No. 53). (Illus.). 336p. Date not set. pap. 95.80 (*0-7837-7296-3*, 2047010) Bks Demand.

— Handbook of Physiology: Section 1, The Nervous System, Vol. V, Pts. 1 & 2: Higher Functions of the Brain. (American Physiological Society Book). (Illus.). 964p. 1988. 325.00 (*0-19-520662-2*) OUP.

— Language, Communication, & the Brain. (Association for Research in Nervous & Mental Disease Research Publications: Vol. 66). 312p. 1988. text ed. 99.50 (*0-88167-365-X*) Raven.

Plum, Fred & Posner, Jerome. The Diagnosis of Stupor & Coma. 3rd ed. LC 80-10300. (Contemporary Neurology Ser.: No. 19). (Illus.). 377p. 1982. pap. text ed. 31.00 (*0-8036-6993-3*) Davis Co.

Plum, Fred, ed. see Research (Princeton-Williamsburg) Conference on Cerebrovascular Disease Staff.

Plum, Henry J. & Crisafi, Frank J. Wisconsin Juvenile Court Practice & Procedure in Protection of Children. 2nd ed. LC 93-25982. 425p. 1993. ring bd. 95.00 (*0-250-40708-6*) Michie Butterworth.

Plum, Joan. I Am Special Fun Book. 32p. (Orig.). (J). (ps-2). 1989. pap. 2.95 (*0-87973-055-2*, 55) Our Sunday Visitor.

Plum, K. D. Fly Away Home. LC 93-87021. (Illus.). 26p. (J). (ps). 1994. 10.95 (*0-8431-3687-1*) Price Stern.

Plum, Stephen H., jt. ed. see List, Charles J.

Plum, Sydney L., jt. ed. see Bain, David H.

Plum, Thomas. C Programming Guidelines. 2nd ed. 210p. 1989. pap. text ed. 29.95 (*0-911537-07-4*) Plum Hall.

— Learning to Program in C. (Illus.). 368p. (Orig.). (C). 1983. pap. text ed. 53.00 (*0-13-527847-3*) P-H.

— Learning to Program in C. 2nd ed. 320p. (Orig.). 1989. pap. text ed. 29.95 (*0-911537-08-2*) Plum Hall.

— Reliable Data Structures in C. 200p. 1985. pap. text ed. 29.95 (*0-911537-04-X*) Plum Hall.

Plum, Thomas & Brodie, Jim. Efficient C. 165p. 1985. pap. text ed. 29.95 (*0-911537-05-8*) Plum Hall.

Plum, Thomas & Saks, Dan. C Plus Plus Programming Guidelines. 274p. (C). 1991. pap. text ed. 34.95 (*0-911537-10-4*) Plum Hall.

Plum, William R. The Military Telegraph During the Civil War in the United States, 2 vols. LC 74-4690. (Telecommunications Ser.). 1566p. 1974. reprint ed. 60.95 (*0-405-06053-X*) Ayer.

Plumar, M., et al, eds. Correlations & Multiparticle Production. 480p. (C). 1991. text ed. 147.00 (*981-02-0331-4*) World Scientific Pub.

Plumb. Health Maintenance & Microbial Diseases of Culture Fish. 1994. 169.95 (*0-8493-4614-2*) CRC Pr.

Plumb, A., jt. auth. see Yeldham, R. F.

Plumb, A., jt. ed. see Yeldham, R. F.

Plumb, A. R. Birds of a Feather. (Further Adventures of Aladdin Ser.: No. 2). (Illus.). 64p. (Orig.). (J). (gr. k-3). 1994. 3.50 (*0-7868-4017-X*) Disney Pr.

— Iago's Promise. LC 94-72229. (Further Adventures of Aladdin Ser.: Bk. 4). (Illus.). 64p. (J). (gr. 1-4). 1995. pap. 3.50 (*0-7868-4024-2*) Disney Pr.

— Small Problem. LC 94-72228. (Further Adventures of Aladdin Ser.: Bk. 3). (Illus.). 64p. (J). (gr. 1-4). 1995. pap. 3.50 (*0-7868-4023-4*) Disney Pr.

— Thief in the Night. (Further Adventures of Aladdin Ser.: No. 1). (Illus.). 64p. (Orig.). (J). (gr. k-3). 1994. pap. 3.50 (*0-7868-4016-1*) Disney Pr.

Plumb, Alan R. Middle Atmosphere. 472p. 1989. 34.50 (*0-8176-2290-X*) Birkhauser.

Plumb, Barbara. Horst: Interiors. (Illus.). 240p. 1993. 75.00 (*0-8212-2046-2*) Bulfinch Pr.

Plumb, Barbara L., jt. auth. see Lewis, Janet T.

Plumb, Charlie. I'm No Hero: A POW Story. (Illus.). 287p. 1973. text ed. 16.95 (*1-881886-01-8*); pap. 9.95 (*1-881886-02-6*) J C Plumb.

Plumb, Cheryl J. Fancy's Craft: Art & Identity in the Early Works of Djuna Barnes. LC 85-62679. 120p. 1987. 32.50 (*0-941664-17-1*) Susquehanna U Pr.

Plumb, Cheryl J., ed. see Barnes, Djuna.

Plumb, D. Heating & Ventilating: A Handbook of Fitting Craft Practice. 220p. (C). 1987. 125.00 (*0-85950-051-9*, Pub. by S Thornes Pubs UK) St Mut.

Plumb, David. The Music Stopped & Your Monkey's on Fire. LC 78-73262. 1979. 7.50 (*0-930324-10-2*); pap. 4.50 (*0-930324-11-0*) Wings Pr.

Plumb, Donald C. Formulary of the Small Animal & Large Animal Pharmacies. 230p. (C). 1986. pap. text ed. 10.00 (*0-685-44316-7*) U MN-VTHPD.

— Veterinary Drug Handbook. LC 90-91729. 688p. (Orig.). 1991. pap. 39.95 (*0-9626619-0-2*) Pharmavet Pub.

— Veterinary Drug Handbook. 2nd ed. LC 94-38603. (Illus.). 732p. (Orig.). 1995. pap. 44.95 (*0-8138-2443-5*); pap. text ed. 44.95 (*0-8138-2352-8*) Iowa St U Pr.

Plumb, G. R., ed. Nuclear Waste Reprocessing. (Illus.). 72p. 1984. pap. 44.00 (*0-08-031509-7*, Pergamon Pr) Elsevier.
Plumb, Gordon B. & Lindley, Mary E. Humanizing Child Custody Disputes: The Family's Team. 156p. (C). 1990. text ed. 36.95x (*0-398-05663-3*) C C Thomas.
— Humanizing Child Custody Disputes: The Family's Team. 156p. 1990. pap. 19.95 (*0-398-06325-7*) C C Thomas.
Plumb, Gregory. The Waterfall Lover's Guide to the Pacific Northwest: Where to Find More Than 500 Scenic Waterfalls in WA, OR & ID. 2nd ed. LC 89-12959. (Illus.). 192p. 1989. pap. 12.95 (*0-89886-191-8*) Mountaineers.
Plumb, H. B. History of Hanover Township, PA, Including Sugar Notch, Ashley & Nanticoke Boroughs, & Also a History of Wyoming Valley in Luzerne Co., PA. 498p. 1990. reprint ed. lib. bdg. 51.00 (*0-8328-1633-7*) Higginson Bk Co.
Plumb, J. H. & Wheldon, Hew. Royal Heritage: The Story of Britain's Royal Builders & Collectors. (Illus.). 360p. 1981. pap. 16.95 (*0-563-17974-0*, Pub. by BBC UK) Parkwest Pubns.
Plumb, John H. The Collected Essays of J. H. Plumb, 2 vols., Vol. 1: The Making of an Historian. LC 88-17290. 416p. 1989. 35.00 (*0-8203-1095-6*) U of Ga Pr.
— The Collected Essays of J. H. Plumb, 2 vols., Vol. 2: The American Experience. LC 88-17290. 288p. 1989. 30.00 (*0-8203-1118-9*) U of Ga Pr.
— England in the Eighteenth Century. (Orig.). 1951. mass mkt. 5.95 (*0-14-020231-5*, Penguin Bks) Viking Penguin.
— Italian Renaissance. (American Heritage Library). 1986. pap. 12.95 (*0-8281-0485-9*) HM.
— Men & Centuries. LC 78-26300. 294p. 1979. reprint ed. text ed. 52.50 (*0-313-20868-9*, PLMC, Greenwood Pr) Greenwood.
— New Light on the Tyrant George III. (George Rogers Clark Lecture February 31, 1977 Ser.: No. 2). (Illus.). 46p. 1985. reprint ed. lib. bdg. 25.50 (*0-8191-4872-5*) U Pr of Amer.
Plumb, John H., ed. Studies in Social History. LC 71-80395. (Essay Index Reprint Ser.). 1977. 24.95 (*0-8369-1063-X*) Ayer.
Plumb, Joseph C. The Last Domino? A POW Looks Ahead. 96p. 1973. text ed. 7.95 (*1-881886-03-4*) J C Plumb.
Plumb, Lawrence. A Critique of the Human Potential Movement. LC 92-40360. (Cults & Nonconventional Religious Groups Ser.). 272p. 1993. 60.00 (*0-8153-0777-2*) Garland.
Plumb, Ron, jt. auth. see LaJoie, Jim.
***Plumb, Sally.** A Pika's Tail: A Children's Story about Mountain Wildlife. Milligan, Sharlene, ed. (Illus.). 40p. (J). (gr. k-5). 1994. 14.95 (*0-931895-26-X*) Grand Teton NHA.
Plumb, Steve. Monzano Trails: A Hiker's Guide to Appreciate the Nature of the Sandia-Monzano Mountains. Wilde, David, ed. (Sun Also Sets Ser.). (Illus.). 50p. (Orig.). 1992. pap. 13.95 (*0-9625472-7-1*) Wilde Pub.
Plumb, William T., Jr. Federal Tax Liens. 3rd ed. LC 72-89966. 397p. 1972. Incls. 1981 suppl. pap. 10.00 (*0-8318-0413-0*, B413) Am Law Inst.
Plumbe, Wilfred J. Tropical Librarianship. LC 87-19984. 334p. 1987. 35.00 (*0-8108-2057-9*) Scarecrow.
Plumbley, Philip, ed. Recruitment & Selection. 176p. (C). 1985. 90.00 (*0-85292-342-2*, Pub. by IPM Hse UK) St Mut.
— Recruitment & Selection. 176p. (C). 1991. pap. text ed. 59.00 (*0-85292-459-3*, Pub. by IPM Hse UK) St Mut.
Plume, Alice, tr. Salt: A Russian Folktale. LC 91-74007. (Illus.). 40p. (J). (gr. k-3). 1992. 14.95 (*1-56282-178-4*); lib. bdg. 14.89 (*1-56282-179-2*) Hyprn Child.
Plume, Ilse. The Bremen-Town Musicians. LC 86-42990. (Trophy Picture Bk.). (Illus.). 32p. (J). (ps-3). 1987. reprint ed. pap. 5.95 (*0-06-443141-X*, Trophy) HarpC Child Bks.
— Shoemaker & the Elves. 32p. (J). (ps-3). 1991. 14.95 (*0-15-274050-3*, HB Juv Bks) HarBrace.
Plume, Ilse, ed. & illus. Lullaby & Goodnight: Songs & Poems for Babies. LC 93-4425. 32p. (J). (ps-1). 1994. 12.00 (*0-06-023501-2*) HarpC Child Bks.
— Lullaby & Goodnight: Songs & Poems for Babies. LC 93-4425. 32p. (J). (ps-1). 1994. lib. bdg. 11.89 (*0-06-023502-0*) HarpC Child Bks.
Plume, Ilse, illus. & ret. The Christmas Witch. LC 91-71380. 32p. (J). (gr. k-3). 1991. 13.95 (*1-56282-077-X*); lib. bdg. 13.89 (*1-56282-078-8*) Hyprn Child.
— The Christmas Witch. LC 91-71380. 32p. (J). (gr. k-3). 1993. pap. 4.95 (*1-56282-524-0*) Hyprn Child.
***Plume, Ilse, illus.** The Farmer in the Dell. LC 94-44292. (J). 1995. write for info. (*0-7868-0179-4*); lib. bdg. write for info. (*0-7868-2151-5*) Hyprn Child.
***Plume, Russell W.** Hydrogeologic Framework of the Great Basin Region of Nevada, Utah, & Adjacent States. LC 94-45133. (U. S. Geological Survey Professional Papers: Vol. 1409-B). 1995. write for info. (*0-615-00440-7*) USGPO.
Plumely, S. Windows 3.1 Sure Steps. (Sure Steps Ser.). (Illus.). 300p. (Orig.). 1993. pap. 24.95 (*1-56529-240-5*) Que.
Plumer, Ada L. & Cosentino. Principles & Practice of Intravenous Therapy. 4th ed. (Illus.). 567p. (C). 1987. text ed. 31.50 (*0-673-39403-4*) Lippincott.
Plumer, Erwin H. When You Place A Child. . . (Illus.). 258p. (C). 1992. text ed. 47.95x (*0-398-05770-2*) C C Thomas.
— When You Place a Child... (Illus.). 258p. 1992. pap. 29.95 (*0-398-06326-5*) C C Thomas.
Plumer, James M., ed. see Warner, Langdon.
Plumer, L. Termination Proofs for Logic Programs. Siekmann, Joerg H., ed. (Lecture Notes in Artificial Intelligence Ser.: Vol. 446). viii, 142p. 1990. pap. 25.00 (*0-387-52837-7*) Spr-Verlag.
Plumer, Lutz, jt. ed. see Beierle, Christoph.
Plumer, W. S. Psalms. (Geneva Commentaries Ser.). 1978. 59.95 (*0-85151-209-7*) Banner of Truth.
Plumer, William, Jr. Life of William Plumer. LC 77-87384. (American History, Politics & Law Ser.). 1969. reprint ed. lib. bdg. 69.50 (*0-306-71608-9*) Da Capo.
— Missouri Compromises & Presidential Politics, 1820-1825: From the Letters of William Plumer. Jr. Brown, Everett S., ed. LC 76-103942. (American Constitutional & Legal History Ser). 1970. reprint ed. lib. bdg. 22.50 (*0-306-71869-3*) Da Capo.
Plumer, William S. Commentary on Romans. LC 73-155251. (Kregel Reprint Library). 646p. 1993. 25.99 (*0-8254-3501-3*); pap. 19.99 (*0-8254-3543-9*) Kregel.
Plumlee, Becky. Recreating Recipes: Nutritious & Delicious II. (Illus.). (Orig.). 1993. pap. 19.95 (*0-9637340-9-1*) Beckys Body.
***Plumley, Sue.** Easy Chicago. 1994. pap. 19.99 (*1-56529-989-2*) Que.
— Microsoft Office Quick Reference. 1994. pap. 14.99 (*1-56529-880-2*) Que.
Plumley, Sue, et al. Microsoft Office QuickStart. (Illus.). 450p. (Orig.). 1994. pap. 24.99 (*1-56529-840-3*) Que.
Plumley, Virginia. Orientation to Instructional Technology: A Workbook. 3rd ed. 116p. 1993. spiral bd. 9.95 (*0-8403-8460-2*) Kendall-Hunt.
Plumly, Stanley. Boy on the Step. 1989. 17.95 (*0-88001-228-5*) Ecco Pr.
— Boy on the Step. 1991. pap. 9.95 (*0-88001-229-3*) Ecco Pr.
— Out-of-the-Body Travel. LC 76-46174. (American Poetry Ser.: No. 10). 1978. pap. 4.95 (*0-912946-36-9*) Ecco Pr.
— Summer Celestial. (American Poetry Ser.: No. 27). 75p. (C). 1983. 13.50 (*0-88001-029-0*) Ecco Pr.
— Summer Celestial. (American Poetry Ser.: No. 27). 75p. (C). 1985. pap. 7.50 (*0-88001-084-3*) Ecco Pr.
Plummer, Aileen. Japan: The Silent Superpower? 1985. pap. 45.00 (*0-904404-50-1*, Pub. by P Norbury Pubns Ltd UK) St Mut.
***Plummer, Albert.** Civil War Infantry, the 48th Regiment, M. V. M., During the Civil War. (Illus.). 133p. 1995. reprint ed. lib. bdg. 29.50 (*0-8328-4636-8*) Higginson Bk Co.
Plummer, Alfred. Corinthians II: Critical & Exegetical Commentary. Driver, Samuel R. & Briggs, Charles A., eds. (International Critical Commentary Ser.). 462p. 1915. 36.95 (*0-567-05028-9*, Pub. by T & T Clark UK) Bks Intl VA.
— English Church History: From the Death of Archbishop Parker to the Death of King Charles I. 1977. lib. bdg. 59.95 (*0-8490-1772-6*) Gordon Pr.
— International Combines in Modern Industry. 2nd ed. LC 74-157354. (Select Bibliographies Reprint Ser.). 1977. reprint ed. 21.95 (*0-8369-5815-2*) Ayer.
— St. Luke: Critical & Exegetical Commentary. Driver, Samuel R. & Briggs, Charles A., eds. (International Critical Commentary Ser.). 688p. 1901. 39.95 (*0-567-05023-8*, Pub. by T & T Clark UK) Bks Intl VA.
Plummer, Alfred & Early, Richard E. Blanket Makers, Sixteen Sixty-Nine to Nineteen Sixty-Nine: A History of Charles Early & Marriott Whitney Ltd. LC 69-17112. (Illus.). 205p. 1969. 24.95 (*0-678-06508-X*) Kelley.
Plummer, Alfred, ed. see Charles, R. H.
Plummer, Alfred, ed. see Driver, Samuel R.
Plummer, Alfred, jt. auth. see Robertson, Archibald.
Plummer, Brenda G. Haiti & the Great Powers, 1902-1915. LC 87-33873. (Illus.). 280p. 1988. text ed. 35.00 (*0-8071-1409-X*) La State U Pr.
— Haiti & the United States: The Psychological Moment. LC 91-34105. (United States & the Americas Ser.). 320p. 1992. 45.00 (*0-8203-1422-6*); pap. 18.50 (*0-8203-1423-4*) U of Ga Pr.
Plummer, Brian & Shewan, Don, eds. City Gardens: A Survey of Open Spaces in the City of London. (Illus.). 256p. 1992. text ed. 65.00 (*1-85293-219-8*, Pub. by Pinter Pubs UK) St Martin.
Plummer, C. Life & Times of Alfred the Great. 1972. 250.00 (*0-8490-0523-X*) Gordon Pr.
— Life & Times of Alfred the Great. LC 68-25261. (English Biography Ser.: No. 31). 1969. reprint ed. lib. bdg. 75.00 (*0-8383-0230-0*) M S G Haskell Hse.
Plummer, Cameron, ed. see Walter, Eugene.
Plummer, Carlyle J. Ship Handling in Narrow Channels. 3rd enl. ed. LC 78-15384. 165p. reprint ed. pap. 47.10 (*0-317-55498-0*, 2029228) Bks Demand.
Plummer, Carol A. Preventing Sexual Abuse: Activities & Strategies for Those Working with Children & Adolescents. LC 83-82306. (Illus.). 166p. 1984. pap. text ed. 19.95 (*0-918452-52-X*) Learning Pubns.
Plummer, Charles. Life & Times of Alfred the Great. LC 72-131802. 1970. reprint ed. 49.00 (*0-403-00689-9*) Scholarly.
Plummer, Charles, ed. & tr. Irish Litanies. (Henry Bradshaw Society Ser.: Vol. LXII). 169p. (C). 1992. text ed. 59.00 (*1-870252-02-0*, Henry Bradshaw Soc) Boydell & Brewer.
Plummer, Charles C. & McGeary, David. Physical Geology. 5th ed. 560p. (C). 1990. pap. write for info. (*0-697-09827-3*) Wm C Brown Pubs.
— Physical Geology. 5th ed. 560p. (C). 1991. boxed write for info. (*0-697-09826-5*) Wm C Brown Pubs.
— Physical Geology. 6th ed. 560p. (C). 1993. text ed. 56.55 (*0-697-13806-2*); pap. text ed. write for info. (*0-697-13807-0*) Wm C Brown Pubs.
— Physical Geology. 6th ed. 560p. (C). 1994. Study guide. student ed write for info. (*0-697-13811-9*) Wm C Brown Pubs.
— Physical Geology with Interactive Plate Tectonics. (C). 1995. student ed write for info. (*0-697-26678-8*); student ed write for info. (*0-697-28732-7*) Wm C Brown Pubs.
— Physical Geology with Interactive Plate Tectonics. 7th ed. 560p. (C). 1995. cd-rom, pap. write for info. (*0-697-26676-1*) Wm C Brown Pubs.
— Physical Geology with Interactive Plate Tectonics. 7th ed. 560p. (C). 1995. boxed, cd-rom write for info. (*0-697-26675-3*) Wm C Brown Pubs.
Plummer, Charles C., jt. auth. see McGeary, David.
***Plummer, David, et al.** Sexually Transmitted Diseases. 120p. (Orig.). 1995. pap. 14.95 (*0-85572-249-5*) Seven Hills Bk.
Plummer, David T. Introduction to Practical Biochemistry. 3rd ed. 376p. 1987. text ed. write for info. (*0-07-084165-9*) McGraw.
Plummer, Ellen A. In Focus: Guercino's Esther. (Illus.). 16p. 1993. 6.00 (*0-912303-47-6*) Michigan Mus.
Plummer, F. B. & Sargent, E. C. Underground Waters & Subsurface Temperatures of the Woodbine Sand in Northeast Texas. (Bulletin Ser.: BULL 3138). (Illus.). 178p. 1931. 1.00 (*0-686-29351-7*) Bur Econ Geology.
Plummer, Gail. The Business of Show Business. LC 72-6180. (Illus.). 238p. 1973. reprint ed. text ed. 35.00 (*0-8371-6485-0*, PLSB, Greenwood Pr) Greenwood.
Plummer, George F. History of the Town of Wentworth, New Hampshire. (Illus.). 401p. 1994. reprint ed. lib. bdg. 45.00 (*0-8328-3635-4*) Higginson Bk Co.
Plummer, Henry. Poetics of Light. (Architecture & Urbanism Extra Edition Ser.). (Illus.). 196p. (Orig.). (ENG & JPN.). (C). pap. text ed. 68.00 (*4-900211-20-6*, Pub. by Japan Architect JA) Gingko Press.
— The Potential House. (Architecture & Urbanism Extra Edition Ser.). (Illus.). 280p. (Orig.). (ENG & JPN.). (C). pap. text ed. 82.50 (*4-900211-28-1*, Pub. by Japan Architect JA) Gingko Press.
Plummer, James L. QED Report on Venture Capital Financial Analysis. 217p. 1987. 295.00 (*0-9620093-0-X*) QED Research.
Plummer, James L., ed. Competition in Electricity: New Markets and New Structures. 1990. 65.00 (*0-910325-26-X*) Public Util.
Plummer, John, ed. In August Company: The Collections of the Pierpont Morgan Library. (Illus.). 192p. 1992. 49.50 (*0-8109-3863-4*) Abrams.
Plummer, John, ed. see Russell, John.
***Plummer, John F., ed.** Vox Feminae: Studies in Medieval Woman's Songs. (Studies in Medieval Culture: No. 25). 1989. pap. 10.95 (*0-918729-12-2*) Medieval Inst.
Plummer, Katherine. A Japanese Glimpse at the Outside World, 1839-1843: The Travels of Jirokichi in Hawaii, Siberia & Alaska. (Alaska History Ser.: No. 36). 1991. 28.00 (*0-919642-34-9*) Limestone Pr.
— Shogun's Reluctant Ambassadors: Japanese Sea Drifters in the North Pacific. (Illus.). 320p. 1991. pap. 19.95 (*0-87595-235-6*) Oregon Hist.
Plummer, Ken. Symbolic Interactionism: Vol. 1 - Foundations & History; Vol. 2 - Contemporary Issues, 2 vols. (Schools of Thought in Sociology Ser.). 976p. 1991. text ed. 289.95 (*1-85278-158-0*, Pub. by E Elgar Pub UK) Ashgate Pub Co.
— Telling Sexual Stories: Power, Change, & Social Worlds. LC 94-1215. 288p. 1995. 59.95 (*0-415-10295-2*, B4401); pap. 16.95 (*0-415-10296-0*, B4405) Routledge.
Plummer, Ken, ed. Modern Homosexualities: Fragments of Lesbian & Gay Experience. LC 92-6434. 272p. 1993. 49.95 (*0-415-06420-1*, A7748); pap. 15.95 (*0-415-06421-X*, A7752) Routledge.
Plummer, Kenneth, ed. The Making of the Modern Homosexual. 280p. 1981. 56.00 (*0-389-20159-6*, N6929) B&N Imports.
***Plummer, Kristin.** Where the Spirit Is Lord. 89p. (Orig.). 1995. pap. write for info. (*0-9645112-0-7*) Jeremiah.
Plummer, L. G. Mathematics of the Cosmic Mind. (Illus.). 240p. 19.00 (*0-913004-84-7*) Point Loma Pub.
Plummer, L. Gordon. By the Holy Tetraktys: Symbol & Reality in Man & Universe. (Study Ser.: No. 9). (Illus.). 96p. (Orig.). (C). 1982. pap. 6.50 (*0-913004-44-8*) Point Loma Pub.
— From Atom to Kosmos: Journey Without End. 2nd rev. ed. (Illus.). 136p. 1987. reprint ed. 5.95 (*0-913004-49-9*) Point Loma Pub.
— From Atom to Kosmos: Journey without End. 3rd ed. LC 88-40491. 142p. 1989. reprint ed. pap. 6.95 (*0-8356-0308-3*, Quest) Theos Pub Hse.
— Three Steps to Infinity. 1994. 7.50 (*0-913004-81-2*) Point Loma Pub.
— The Way to the Mysteries. 126p. 1992. pap. 7.50 (*0-913004-73-1*) Point Loma Pub.
Plummer, Louise. My Name Is Susan Smith, The 5 Is Silent. (YA). 1993. pap. 3.50 (*0-440-21451-3*) Dell.
— Thoughts of a Grasshopper. LC 91-42637. 134p. 1992. 10.95 (*0-87579-557-9*) Deseret Bk.
— The Unlikely Romance of Kate Bjorkman. LC 94-49614. (J). 1995. write for info. (*0-385-32049-3*) Delacorte.
Plummer, M. D., jt. auth. see Lovasz, L.
Plummer, Mark L., jt. auth. see Mann, Charles C.
Plummer, Mary A. Foods & Nutrition: Syllabus. 1976. pap. text ed. 5.75 (*0-89420-001-1*, 167070); audio 58.10 (*0-89420-147-6*, 167040) Natl Book.
Plummer, Michael V. & Shirer, Hampton W. Movement Patterns in a River Population of the Softshell Turtle, Trionyx Muticus. (Occasional Papers: No. 43). 26p. 1975. pap. 1.00 (*0-686-80377-9*) U of KS Mus Nat Hist.
***Plummer, Norman H.** Lambert Wickes: Pirate or Patriot? (Illus.). 1991. pap. 6.00 (*0-922249-03-2*) Ches Bay Mus.
— Maryland's Oyster Navy: The First Fifty Years. LC 93-26694. 1993. 19.95 (*0-922249-05-9*) Ches Bay Mus.
Plummer, Ralph W., et al. Minimizing Employee Exposure to Toxic Chemical Releases. LC 87-12213. (Pollution Technology Review Ser.: No. 145). (Illus.). 257p. 1988. 44.00 (*0-8155-1131-0*) Noyes.
Plummer, Stephen E., jt. ed. see Danson, F. Mark.
Plummer, Thomas G., et al, eds. Film & Politics in the Weimar Republic. (Germany in the Twenties Ser.). (Illus.). 98p. 1982. text ed. 24.50 (*0-8419-7502-7*); pap. text ed. 19.50 (*0-8419-7503-5*) Holmes & Meier.
Plummer, Tony. Forecasting Financial Markets: Technical Analysis & the Dynamics of Price. (Finance Editions Ser.). 259p. 1991. text ed. 55.00 (*0-471-53408-0*) Wiley.
— Psychology of Technical Analysis: Profiting from Crowd Behavior & the Dynamics of Price. 1993. 47.50 (*1-55738-543-2*) Probus Pub Co.
Plummer, Wilbur C. & Young, Ralph A. Sales Finance Companies & Their Credit Practices. (Financial Research Program II: Studies in Consumer Installment Financing: No. 2). 324p. 1940. reprint ed. 84.30 (*0-87014-461-8*); reprint ed. mic. film 42.20 (*0-685-61208-2*) Natl Bur Econ Res.
Plummer, William. Holy Goof. 1994. pap. 9.95 (*1-56924-925-3*) Marlowe & Co.
Plummeridge, Charles. Music Education in Theory & Practice. (Falmer Press Library on Aesthetic Education). 184p. 1991. 65.00 (*1-85000-765-9*, Falmer Pr); pap. 28.00 (*1-85000-766-7*, Falmer Pr) Taylor & Francis.
Plump, Sterling. Clinton. 1976. 2.00 (*0-910296-43-X*) Broadside Pr.
Plump, Wendy, jt. auth. see Gallup, George H., Jr.
Plumpe, jt. ed. see Quasten.
Plumpe, J., ed. see Augustine.
Plumpe, J., jt. ed. see Kuasten, J.
Plumpp, Sterling. Ballad of Harriet Tubman. (Illus.). (J). 1993. 18.95 (*0-88378-062-3*) Third World.
— Black Rituals. LC 72-80785. (Orig.). 1972. pap. 8.95 (*0-88378-024-0*) Third World.
— Blues: The Story Always Untold. LC 88-71680. 140p. (Orig.). 1989. pap. 9.50 (*0-9614644-8-8*) Another Chicago Pr.
— Johannesburg & Other Poems. LC 93-4508. 140p. (Orig.). 1993. pap. 11.95 (*0-929968-33-6*) Another Chicago Pr.
— Paul Robeson. (Illus.). (J). 1992. pap. 5.95 (*0-88378-065-8*) Third World.
Plumpton, A. J. International Symposium on the Production & Processing of Fine Particles: Proceedings of the Metallurgical Society of the Canadian Institute of Mining & Metallurgy, Vol. 7. 930p. 1988. 96.00 (*0-08-036449-7*, Pergamon Pr) Elsevier.
Plumpton, C. A. & Macilwaine, P. S. New Tertiary Mathematics. 1250p. 1981. text ed. 549.00 (*0-08-021646-3*) Franklin.
Plumpton, C. A. & MacIlwaine, P. S. New Tertiary Mathematics: Further Applied Mathematics, Vol. 2, Pt. 2. (Illus.). 1981. text ed. 101.00 (*0-08-025037-8*, Pub. by Pergamon Repr UK) Franklin.
— New Tertiary Mathematics: Further Pure Mathematics, Vol. 2, Pt. 1. LC 79-41454. (Illus.). 408p. 1980. text ed. 173.00 (*0-08-025033-5*, Pub. by Pergamon Repr UK) Franklin.
Plumpton, C. A. & Tomkys, W. H. Theoretical Mechanics in SI Units, 1. 2nd ed. (C). 1972. pap. 174.00 (*0-08-016268-1*, Pub. by Pergamon Repr UK) Franklin.
— Theoretical Mechanics in SI Units, 2. 2nd ed. (C). 1972. pap. 180.00 (*0-08-016591-5*, Pub. by Pergamon Repr UK) Franklin.
Plumpton, C. A., jt. auth. see Chirgwin, B. H.
Plumpton, C. A., jt. auth. see Kendall, P.
Plumpton, Edward. Plumpton Correspondence. Stapleton, Thomas, ed. (Camden Society, London. Publications, First Ser.: No. 4). reprint ed. 95.00 (*0-404-50104-4*) AMS Pr.
***Plumptre, George.** Edward VII. (Illus.). 256p. 1995. 35.00 (*1-85793-076-2*, Pub. by Pavilion UK) Trafalgar.
— The Garden Makers: The Great Tradition of Garden Design from 1600 to Present Day. LC 93-29405. 1994. 30.00 (*0-679-43014-8*) Random.
— Great Gardens' Great Designers. (Illus.). 160p. 1995. 35.00 (*0-7063-7203-4*, Pub. by Ward Lock UK) Sterling.
— The Water Garden: Styles, Designs & Visions. LC 92-82077. (Illus.). 208p. 1993. 45.00 (*0-500-01571-6*) Thames Hudson.
Plumptre, James. The Lakers. LC 90-40598. 88p. 1990. reprint ed. 40.00 (*1-85477-052-7*, Pub. by Woodstock Bks UK) Cassell.
— Observations on "Hamlet" LC 71-144672. reprint ed. 20.00 (*0-404-05066-2*) AMS Pr.
Plumptre, R. A. Some Wood Properties of Pinus Patula from Uganda & Techniques Developed. 1978. 59.00 (*0-85074-032-0*) St Mut.
Plumptre, Timothy W. Beyond the Bottom Line: Management in Government. 466p. 1988. pap. text ed. 23.95 (*0-88645-069-1*, Pub. by Inst Res Pub CN) Ashgate Pub Co.
Plumridge, Andrew & Meulenkamp, Wim. Brickwork: Architecture & Design. LC 92-24191. (Illus.). 224p. 1993. 39.95 (*0-8109-3123-0*) Abrams.
***Plumridge, Diane M., et al.** The Student with a Genetic Disorder: Educational Implications for Special Education Teachers & for Physical Therapists, Occupational Therapists, & Speech Pathologists. LC 92-39088. (Illus.). 382p. 1993. pap. 39.95 (*0-398-06327-3*) C C Thomas.
— The Student with a Genetic Disorder: Educational Implications for Special Education Teachers & for Physical Therapists, Occupational Therapists, & Speech Pathologists. LC 92-39088. (Illus.). 382p. 1993. text ed. 75.95x (*0-398-05839-3*) C C Thomas.
Plumridge, Jack. How to Propagate Plants. (Illus.). 214p. (Orig.). 1995. pap. 17.95 (*0-85091-243-1*, Pub. by Lothian Pub AT) Seven Hills Bk.
Plumstead, A. W., ed. The Wall & the Garden: Selected Massachusetts Election Sermons, 1670-1775. LC 68-19742. 398p. reprint ed. pap. 113.50 (*0-318-39689-0*, 2033284) Bks Demand.

Plumwood, Val. Feminism & the Mastery of Nature. LC 93-15995. (Opening Out Ser.). 1993. write for info. (*0-415-06809-6*); pap. write for info. (*0-415-50610-7*) Routledge.

Plung, D. L., jt. ed. see Harkins, C.

Plung, D. L., jt. ed. see Moore, L. K.

Plunka, Gene A. Peter Shaffer: Roles, Rites, & Rituals in the Theater. LC 87-46010. 256p. 1988. 37.50 (*0-8386-3329-3*) Fairleigh Dickinson.

— The Rites of Passage of Jean Genet: The Art & Aesthetics of Risk Taking. LC 91-55363. 360p. 1992. 45.00 (*0-8386-3461-3*) Fairleigh Dickinson.

Plunka, Gene A., ed. Antonin Artaud & the Modern Theater. LC 93-40087. 1994. write for info. (*0-8386-3550-4*) Fairleigh Dickinson.

— Micrographic Film Technology. 4th ed. (Illus.). 121p. 1992. pap. text ed. 30.00 (*0-89258-059-3*, R011) Assn Inform & Image Mgmt.

Plunket-Greene, Harry. Where the Bright Waters Meet. (Illus.). 221p. 1984. pap. 12.95 (*0-8329-0308-6*) Lyons & Burford.

Plunket, Ierne A. Isabel of Castille. LC 73-14464. (Illus.). reprint ed. 45.00 (*0-404-58282-6*) AMS Pr.

Plunket, Robert. Love Junkie: A Novel. LC 91-50451. 256p. 1993. reprint ed. pap. 10.00 (*0-06-092226-5*, PL) HarpC.

— My Search for Warren Harding. LC 91-50518. 224p. 1992. reprint ed. pap. 9.00 (*0-06-097390-0*, PL) HarpC.

***Plunkett, Bill.** Baseball. (The Summer Olympics Ser.). 32p. (J). (gr. 4-8). 1995. write for info. (*1-887068-05-8*) Smart Apple.

Plunkett, Dudley. Secular & Spiritual Values: Grounds for Hope in Education. 176p. 1990. 42.50 (*0-415-03508-2*, A4227) Routledge.

Plunkett, E. R. Folk Name & Trade Diseases. LC 78-72537. (Illus.). 1978. text ed. 17.95 (*0-932684-00-9*) Barrett Bk.

— Occupational Diseases: A Syllabus of Signs & Symptoms. 1977. text ed. 25.95 (*0-89185-128-3*) Barrett Bk.

Plunkett, E. R., ed. Handbook of Industrial Toxicology. 1987. 92.50 (*0-8206-0321-X*) Chem Pub.

Plunkett, George. Disappearing Norwich. 1994. pap. 18.00 (*0-86138-057-6*, Pub. by T Dalton UK) St Mut.

Plunkett, George A., ed. Rambles in Old Norwich. 136p. 1994. pap. 30.00 (*0-86138-078-9*) St Mut.

Plunkett, J. J., jt. auth. see Dale, B. G.

Plunkett, Jack W. The Almanac of American Employers, 1994-95. rev. ed. 1994. pap. 110.00 (*0-9638268-0-8*) Corp Jobs Outlk.

***Plunkett, Jack W. & Plunkett, Michelle L.** Plunkett's Health Care Industry Almanac. (Orig.). 1995. pap. 125.00 (*0-9638268-1-6*) Corp Jobs Outlk.

Plunkett, James. Boy on the Back Wall. 208p. 1987. pap. 8.95 (*0-905169-60-3*, Pub. by Poolbeg Pr IE) Dufour.

— The Trusting & the Maimed. 12.50 (*0-8159-6909-0*) Devin.

Plunkett, James R. AS-400 Disk Saving Tips & Techniques. (Quick Read Ser.). 74p. 1993. pap. text ed. 59.95 (*1-884322-01-8*) Comp Applicatns.

— Implementing an IS Help Desk. (Quick Read Ser.). 66p. 1993. pap. text ed. 39.95 (*1-884322-02-6*) Comp Applicatns.

— Understanding Bar Code. (Quick Read Ser.). (Illus.). 70p. (Orig.). 1993. pap. 39.95 (*1-884322-17-4*) Comp Applicatns.

Plunkett, Joseph M. The Poems of Joseph Mary Plunkett. LC 75-28839. reprint ed. 29.50 (*0-404-13828-4*) AMS Pr.

Plunkett, Linda M., et al. Using Accounting Information: An Interactive Learning Approach. Horan, ed. 200p. (C). 1993. pap. text ed. 19.00 (*0-314-02184-1*) West Pub.

Plunkett, Lorne & Fournier, Robert. Participative Management: Implementing Empowerment. 288p. 1991. text ed. 34.95 (*0-471-54374-8*) Wiley.

Plunkett, Mark W., ed. see Fine, W. Edward & Fine, Billy J.

Plunkett, Mark W., ed. see Jackson, Carol.

Plunkett, Michael. Afro-American Sources in Virginia: A Guide to Manuscripts. LC 89-16616. (Carter G. Woodson Institute Series in Black Studies). 323p. 1990. text ed. 35.00 (*0-8139-1251-2*) U Pr of Va.

Plunkett, Michelle L., jt. auth. see Plunkett, Jack W.

Plunkett, Oliver. Letters of St. Oliver Plunkett. Hanly, John, ed. 1979. 70.00 (*0-85105-344-0*, Pub. by Colin Smythe Ltd UK) Dufour.

Plunkett, P., jt. auth. see Dale, D.

***Plunkett, Paul M.** Shackspere of Stratford: A Monumental Design. 1995. 13.95 (*0-533-11068-8*) Vantage.

Plunkett-Powell, Karen. The Nancy Drew Scrapbook: Sixty Years of America's Favorite Teenage Sleuth. (Illus.). 192p. (Orig.). 1993. pap. 10.95 (*0-312-09881-2*) St Martin.

Plunkett, Richard J. & Gordon, John E. Epidemiology & Mental Illness. Grob, Gerald N., ed. LC 78-22581. (Historical Issues in Mental Health Ser.). 1980. reprint ed. lib. bdg. 17.95 (*0-405-11933-X*) Ayer.

Plunkett, Robert L. A California Dreamer in King Henry's Court. 213p. 1989. lib. bdg. 16.95 (*0-9623139-4-7*) Silver Dawn.

— A California Dreamer in King Henry's Court. 213p. 1991. reprint ed. pap. 8.95 (*0-9623139-3-9*) Silver Dawn.

Plunkett, Signe J. Standard Emergency Procedures for the Small Animal Veterinarian. LC 92-39992. 1993. pap. text ed. 27.95 (*0-7216-6781-3*) Saunders.

Plunkett, Stephanie H., ed. Kongi & Potgi: A Cinderella Story from Korea. LC 93-28426. (Illus.). (J). 1994. write for info. (*0-8037-1571-4*); lib. bdg. write for info. (*0-8037-1572-2*) Dial Bks Young.

— Sir Whong & the Golden Pig. LC 91-43389. (Illus.). 32p. (J). (ps-3). 1993. 13.99 (*0-8037-1344-4*); lib. bdg. 13.89 (*0-8037-1345-2*) Dial Bks Young.

Plunkett, T. J., jt. auth. see Brownstone, Meyer.

***Plunkett, Terence C., illus.** Cats' Meow! An Anthology of Cat Tales. LC 95-75502. 208p. (Orig.). 1995. pap. 12.95 (*0-9620600-1-1*) Maine Rhode Pubs.

Plunkett, W. Richard. Supervision: The Direction of People at Work. 7th ed. LC 93-33427. 602p. 1993. text ed. 46.00 (*0-205-15449-2*) Allyn.

Plunkett, Warren R. Supervision: The Direction of People at Work. 5th ed. 416p. 1989. teacher ed write for info. (*0-318-64394-4*, H17320) Allyn.

Plunkett, Warren R. & Attner, Raymond F. Introduction to Management. 4th ed. 679p. 1992. text ed. 55.95 (*0-534-92891-9*); student ed 18.95 (*0-534-93056-5*) Intl Thomson.

— Introduction to Management. 5th ed. 838p. 1994. text ed. 57.95 (*0-534-93321-1*) S-W Pub.

***Plunz, Richard, ed.** Keene & Kenne Valley Hamlets. LC 95-14701. 1995. write for info. (*0-925168-41-6*) North Country.

Plunz, Richard A. A History of Housing in New York City. (History of Urban Life Ser.). (Illus.). 480p. 1992. text ed. 45.00 (*0-231-06296-6*); pap. 18.95 (*0-231-06297-4*) Col U Pr.

Plunz, Richard A., ed. Housing Form & Public Policy in the United States. LC 77-22686. 264p. 1980. text ed. 59.95 (*0-275-90537-3*, C0537, Praeger Pubs) Greenwood.

Plunz, Richard A., jt. ed. see Chermayeff, Serge.

Plura, M., jt. auth. see Albrecht, R.

Pluskat, Thomas J. Real Estate to a Better Future & Financial Independence. 275p. (Orig.). (C). Date not set. pap. text ed. write for info. (*0-9618963-1-0*) Innovat Dynamics.

Plusquellec, Herve, jt. auth. see Safadi, Raed.

Plusquellec, Herve, et al. Modern Water Control in Irrigation: Concepts, Issues, & Applications. LC 94-3821. (World Bank Technical Paper Ser.: No. 246). 116p. 1994. write for info. (*0-8213-2819-0*) World Bank.

Pluszczewski, Stefan, tr. see Rozdzienski, Walenty.

***Pluta, Joseph, et al.** Explorations in Microeconomics. 1994. pap. text ed. 45.95 (*1-56226-173-8*) CT Pub.

Pluta, M. Advanced Light Microscopy: Specialized Methods, Vol. 2. 484p. 1989. 166.75 (*0-444-98918-8*) Elsevier.

— Advanced Light Microscopy, Vol. 1: Principles & Basic Properties. 460p. 1988. 146.25 (*0-444-98939-0*) Elsevier.

— Advanced Light Microscopy, Vol. 3: Measuring Techniques. 718p. 1993. 242.75 (*0-444-98819-X*, North Holland) Elsevier.

Pluta, Maksymilian, jt. ed. see Jaroszewicz, Zbigniew.

Pluta, Olaf. Kritker der Unsterblichkeitsdoktrin in Mittelalter und Renaissance. (B St. Ph. Ser.: 7). x, 137p. 1986. 35.00 (*90-6032-276-2*, Pub. by B R Gruener NE) Benjamins North Am.

— Die Philosophische Psychologie des Peter von Ailly. (Beitrag zur Geschichte der Philosophie des Spaten Mittelalters Bochumer Studien zur Philosophie: Vol. 6). (C). 1987. 56.00 (*90-6032-275-4*, Pub. by B R Gruener NE) Benjamins North Am.

Pluta, Olaf, ed. Die Philosophie im 14. und 15. Jahrhundert: In Memoriam Konstanty Michalski (1879-1947) (Bochumer Studien zur Philosophie Ser.: Vol. 10). lx, 613p. (GER.). (C). 1988. 80.00x (*90-6032-297-5*, Pub. by B R Gruener NE) Benjamins North Am.

Pluta, Olaf, jt. ed. see Mojsisch, Burkhard.

Pluta, Terry, jt. auth. see Ahbe, Dottie.

Plutarch. The Age of Alexander. Scott-Kilvert, Ian, tr. (Classics Ser.). 1973. pap. 10.95 (*0-14-044286-3*, Penguin Classics) Viking Penguin.

— The Education or Bringinge up of Children. Eliot, T., tr. LC 72-224. (English Experience Ser.: No. 184). 48p. 1969. reprint ed. 30.00 (*90-221-0184-3*) Walter J Johnson.

— Essays. Waterfield, Robin A., tr. 448p. 1993. 11.95 (*0-14-044564-1*, Penguin Classics) Viking Penguin.

— Fall of the Roman Republic (Six Roman Lives) Warner, Rex, tr. (Classics Ser.). 320p. 1954. pap. 10.95 (*0-14-044084-4*, Penguin Classics) Viking Penguin.

— The Governaunce of Good Helthe, Erasmus Beynge Interpretoure. LC 68-54657. (English Experience Ser.: No. 16). 32p. 1968. reprint ed. 7.00 (*90-221-0016-2*) Walter J Johnson.

— The Greek Question of Plutarch. Halliday, W. R., tr. & comment by. LC 75-10646. (Ancient Religion & Mythology Ser.). 1978. reprint ed. 25.95 (*0-405-07270-8*) Ayer.

— Life of Antony. Pelling, C. B., ed. (Illus.). 320p. 1988. 64.95 (*0-521-24066-2*); pap. 22.95 (*0-521-28418-X*) Cambridge U Pr.

— Life of Aratus. Connor, W. R., ed. LC 78-18593. (Greek Texts & Commentaries Ser.). (Illus.). 1979. reprint ed. lib. bdg. 19.95 (*0-405-11434-6*) Ayer.

— Life of Cicero. Moles, ed. (Classical Texts Ser.). 1989. 49.95 (*0-85668-360-4*, Pub. by Aris & Phillips UK); pap. 24.95 (*0-85668-361-2*, Pub. by Aris & Phillips UK) David Brown.

— Life of Dion. Connor, W. R., ed. LC 78-18594. (Greek Texts & Commentaries Ser.). (Illus.). 1979. reprint ed. lib. bdg. 21.95 (*0-405-11435-4*) Ayer.

— Lives of Aristeides & Cato. Sansone, ed. (Classical Texts Ser.). 1989. 49.95 (*0-85668-421-X*, Pub. by Aris & Phillips UK); pap. 24.95 (*0-85668-422-8*, Pub. by Aris & Phillips UK) David Brown.

— The Lives of the Noble Grecians & Romans, 2 vols., Vol. 1. Clough, Arthur H., ed. Dryden, John, tr. LC 92-50223. 800p. 1992. 19.00 (*0-679-60008-6*, Modern Lib) Random.

— The Lives of the Noble Grecians & Romans, 2 vols., Vol. 2. Clough, Arthur H., ed. Dryden, John, tr. LC 92-50223. 736p. 1992. 19.00 (*0-679-60009-4*, Modern Lib) Random.

— Makers of Rome: Nine Lives by Plutarch. 400p. 1985. 16.95 (*0-88029-045-5*) Dorset Pr.

— Makers of Rome: Nine Lives by Plutarch. Scott-Kilvert, Ian, tr. (Classics Ser.). 368p. 1965. pap. 9.95 (*0-14-044158-1*, Penguin Classics) Viking Penguin.

— Malice of Herodotus. 1992. 49.95 (*0-85668-568-2*, Pub. by Aris & Phillips UK); pap. 19.95 (*0-85668-569-0*, Pub. by Aris & Phillips UK) David Brown.

— Moralia. Incl. Vol. 1. 14.50 (*0-674-99217-2*); Vol. 2. 14.50 (*0-674-99245-8*); Vol. 3. 14.50 (*0-674-99270-9*); Vol. 4. 14.50 (*0-674-99336-5*); Vol. 5. 14.50 (*0-674-99337-3*); Vol. 6. 14.50 (*0-674-99371-3*); Vol. 7. 14.50 (*0-674-99446-9*); Vol. 8. 14.50 (*0-674-99466-3*); Vol. 9. 14.50 (*0-674-99467-1*); Vol. 10. 14.50 (*0-674-99354-3*); Vol. 11. 14.50 (*0-674-99469-8*); Vol. 12. 14.50 (*0-674-99447-7*); Vol. 14. 14.50 (*0-674-99472-8*); Vol. 15. 14.50 (*0-674-99473-6*); (Loeb Classical Library Nos. 197, 222, 245, 305, 306, 337, 405, 424, 425, 321, 426, 406, 427, 470, 428, 429). write for info. (*0-318-53118-6*) HUP.

— Parallel Lives, 11 vols. Incl. Vol. 1. 14.50 (*0-674-99052-8*); Vol. 2. 14.50 (*0-674-99053-6*); Vol. 3. 14.50 (*0-674-99072-2*); Vol. 4. 14.50 (*0-685-73341-6*); Vol. 5. 14.50 (*0-685-73342-4*); Vol. 6. 14.50 (*0-674-99109-5*); Vol. 7. 14.50 (*0-674-99110-9*); Vol. 8. 14.50 (*0-674-99111-7*); Vol. 9. 14.50 (*0-674-99112-5*); Vol. 10. 14.50 (*0-674-99113-3*); Vol. 11. 14.50 (*0-674-99114-1*); (Loeb Classical Library: Nos. 46-47, 65, 80, 87, 98-103). write for info. (*0-318-53133-X*) HUP.

— Plutarch, Moralia Vol. XIII, Pt. 1: Platonic Essays. 392p. 1957. text ed. 18.95 (*0-674-99470-1*) HUP.

— Plutarch on Sparta. 192p. 1988. pap. 9.95 (*0-14-044463-7*, Penguin Classics) Viking Penguin.

— Plutarch, the Parallel Lives Vol. IV: Alcibiades & Coriolanus, Lysander & Sulla. 1989. text ed. 18.95 (*0-674-99089-7*) HUP.

— Plutarch's Lives. White, John S., ed. LC 66-28487. (Illus.). 468p. (J). (gr. 7 up). 1900. 22.00 (*0-8196-0174-8*) Biblo.

— Plutarch's Lives. Dryden, John, tr. LC 32-17475. 1977. 20.00 (*0-394-60407-5*, Modern Lib) Random.

— Plutarch's Lives of the Noble Grecians & Romans, 6 Vols, Set. North, Thomas, tr. LC 70-158307. (Tudor Translations, First Ser.: Nos. 7-12). reprint ed. 345.00 (*0-404-51870-2*) AMS Pr.

— Plutarch's Rules of Health. (Longevity Ser.). 1991. lib. bdg. 75.00 (*0-8490-4183-X*) Gordon Pr.

— Rise & Fall of Athens: Nine Greek Lives. Scott-Kilvert, Ian, tr. (Classics Ser.). 320p. 1960. pap. 8.95 (*0-14-044102-6*, Penguin Classics) Viking Penguin.

— The Roman Questions of Plutarch. Rose, Herbert J., ed. LC 75-14267. (Ancient Religion & Mythology Ser.). 1976. reprint ed. 19.95 (*0-405-07272-4*) Ayer.

— Selected Essays & Dialogues. LC 92-18159. (World's Classics Ser.). 1993. 10.95 (*0-19-283094-5*) OUP.

— Les Vies des Hommes Illustres, Vol. 1. (FRE.). 1937. lib. bdg. 95.00 (*0-8288-3525-X*, F19161) Fr & Eur.

— Les Vies des Hommes Illustres, Vol. 2. (FRE.). 1937. lib. bdg. 95.00 (*0-8288-3526-8*, F19162) Fr & Eur.

Plutarchus. The Roman Questions of Plutarchus. Rose, H. J., tr. 1924. 25.00 (*0-8196-0284-1*) Biblo.

— Selected Lives from the Lives of the Noble Grecians & Romans, 1. Turner, Paul, ed. reprint ed. pap. 92.50 (*0-317-28721-4*, 2051320) Bks Demand.

— Selected Lives from the Lives of the Noble Grecians & Romans, 2. Turner, Paul, ed. reprint ed. pap. 70.30 (*0-317-28722-2*) Bks Demand.

Plutarchus, ed. see Skeat, Walter W.

Plutarco. Sobre el Amor. Guzman Guerra, Antonio, ed. & tr. by. (Nueva Austral Ser.: Vol. 127). (SPA.). 1991. pap. text ed. 24.95x (*84-239-1927-7*) Elliots Bks.

Plutarque. Les Vies des Homme Illustres, 2 vols., Ea. D'Amyot, tr. 37.50 (*0-318-52319-1*) Fr & Eur.

***Plutchak, Mary.** Circled in Red. 65p. 1995. pap. 8.00 (*0-9630322-1-6*) Carrousel Pr.

— So Small a Pocket. 68p. 1991. pap. 10.95 (*0-9630322-0-8*) Carrousel Pr.

Plutchik, Robert. The Emotions. rev. ed. 228p. (C). 1991. reprint ed. pap. text ed. 18.00 (*0-8191-8286-9*) U Pr of Amer.

— Psychology of Emotion. (C). 1993. text ed. 51.00 (*0-06-045236-6*) HarpCollege.

Plutchik, Robert & Kellerman, Henry, eds. Emotion: Theory, Research & Experience, Vol. 1. LC 79-51685. 1980. text ed. 97.00 (*0-12-558701-5*) Acad Pr.

— Emotion: Theory, Research & Experience, Vol. 2. 340p. 1983. text ed. 90.00 (*0-12-558702-3*) Acad Pr.

— Emotion: Theory, Research, & Experience, Vol. 3. 1985. text ed. 95.00 (*0-12-558703-1*); pap. text ed. 60.00 (*0-12-531953-3*) Acad Pr.

— Emotion: Theory, Research & Experience, Vol. 4: The Measurement of Emotions. 320p. 1989. text ed. 116.00 (*0-12-558704-X*) Acad Pr.

— Emotion: Theory, Research & Experience, Vol. 5: Emotion, Psychopathology, & Psychotherapy. 283p. 1990. text ed. 97.00 (*0-12-558705-8*) Acad Pr.

Plutchik, Robert, jt. ed. see Conte, Hope R.

Pluth, Alphonsus & Koch, Carl. The Catholic Church: Our Mission in History. (Illus.). 336p. (Orig.). 1985. pap. text ed. 11.50 (*0-88489-161-5*); teacher ed, spiral bd. 18.95 (*0-88489-162-3*) St Marys.

***Pluto Press Staff.** Breaking Point: A Guide to Preventing Occupational Overuse Syndrome. LC 95-1684. (International Labour Series, 1351-4530). (C). 1995. pap. text ed. 9.95 (*0-7453-1022-2*) Westview.

Pluto, Terry. The Curse of Rocky Colavito: A Loving Look at a Thirty-Year Slump. 1994. 22.50 (*0-671-86908-6*) S&S Trade.

— The Curse of Rocky Colavito: A Loving Look at a Thirty-Year Slump. 1995. pap. 12.00 (*0-684-80415-8*, Fireside) S&S Trade.

— Loose Balls: The Short, Wild Life of the American Basketball Association. (Illus.). 448p. 1991. pap. 12.00 (*0-671-74921-8*, Fireside) S&S Trade.

— Tall Tales. 1994. pap. 12.00 (*0-671-89937-6*, Fireside) S&S Trade.

— Tall Tales: The Glory Years of the NBA, in the Words of the Men Who Played, Coached, & Built Pro Basketball. (Illus.). 384p. 1992. 23.00 (*0-671-74279-5*) S&S Trade.

Pluto, Terry, jt. auth. see Kerr, Johnny.

Plutschov, H. & Fukuda, H., trs. Four Japanese Travel Diaries of the Middle Ages. LC 83-837366. (Cornell East Asia Ser.: No. 25). 136p. 1981. 9.00 (*0-939657-25-2*) Cornell East Asia Pgm.

Plutschow, H. E. Chaos & Cosmos: Ritual in Early & Medieval Japanese Literature. LC 89-9761. (Japanese Studies Library: Vol. 1). xii, 284p. 1990. 71.50 (*90-04-08628-5*) E J Brill.

Plutschow, Herbert. Introducing Kyoto. LC 79-51164. (Illus.). 1979. 28.00 (*0-87011-384-4*) Kodansha.

— Japan's Name Culture: The Significance of Names in a Religious, Political & Social Context. 256p. (C). 1995. text ed. 90.00 (*1-873410-42-5*, Pub. by Curzon Pr UK) Humanities.

Plutschow, Herbert E. Introducing Kyoto. LC 79-51164. (Illus.). 71p. 1989. pap. 18.00 (*0-87011-904-4*) Kodansha.

Plutt, Mary Jo & Food Editors of Prevention Magazine, eds. Prevention's Stop Dieting & Lose Weight Cookbook: Featuring the Seven-Step-Get-Slim Plan That Really Works. LC 94-8425. 448p. 1994. 27.95 (*0-87596-198-3*) Rodale Pr Inc.

Plutzik, Hyam. Hyam Plutzik: The Collected Poems. 1987. 30.00 (*0-918526-54-X*) BOA Edns.

— Hyam Plutzik: The Collected Poems. 1987. pap. 15.00 (*0-918526-55-8*) BOA Edns.

Plutzik, Roberta. Bargain Chic. 192p. pap. 7.95 (*0-8184-0383-7*) Carol Pub Group.

Pluyter-Wenting, Elly S., ed. see IMIA International Conference on Nursing Use of Computers & Information Science Staff.

Pluzhnikova, G., jt. auth. see Kalashnikova, N.

Plvar, William & Pivar, Bradley. Simplified Classifieds: 1001 Real Estate Ads That Sell. 352p. 1990. pap. 29.95 (*0-7931-0086-0*, 1926-02) Dearborn Finan.

Ply, Mary S. & Winchell, Donna H. Writer, Audience, Subject: Bridging the Communication Gap. (C). 1988. pap. text ed. 24.00 (*0-673-18325-4*) HarpCollege.

Plyatskii, V. M. Extrusion Casting. LC 65-29302. (Illus.). 316p. 1965. 39.50 (*0-911184-06-6*) Primary.

Plybon, Benjamin. An Introduction to Applied Numerical Analysis. 640p. 1992. text ed. 64.95 (*0-534-92284-8*) PWS Pubs.

Plymale, Steven F. The Prayer-Texts of Luke Acts. LC 91-18623. (American University Studies: Theology & Religion: Ser. VII, Vol. 118). 134p. (C). 1992. text ed. 35.95 (*0-8204-1658-4*) P Lang Pubs.

Plyman, Layton, ed. see Grayslake Historical Society Bk. Committee Staff, et al.

***Plymell, Charles.** The Last of the Moccasins. 1995. 20.00 (*0-9636829-8-9*); pap. 12.00 (*0-9636829-7-0*) Mother Road.

Plymen, Roger & Robinson, Paul. Spinors in Hilbert Space. (Tracts in Mathematics Ser.: No. 114). 150p. (C). 1995. 44.95 (*0-521-45022-5*) Cambridge U Pr.

Plymen, Roger J., jt. ed. see Baker, Andrew J.

Plympton, Bill. Tube Strips. 1976. pap. 50.00 (*0-918266-04-1*) Smyrna.

— Tube Strips. (Illus.). reprint ed. pap. 25.00 (*0-7837-9092-9*, 2049842) Bks Demand.

PMA, Ltd. Staff. Business Management. 160p. 1991. pap. text ed. 55.00 (*0-8403-6727-9*) Kendall-Hunt.

— Contracts & Agreements. 156p. 1991. pap. text ed. 65.00 (*0-8403-6728-7*) Kendall-Hunt.

— Cut Professional Liability Exposure Now. 60p. 1991. per. 40.00 (*0-8403-6530-6*) Kendall-Hunt.

— Fee Survey, 1990. 160p. 1991. pap. text ed. 145.00 (*0-8403-6725-2*) Kendall-Hunt.

— Financial Survey, 1990. 192p. 1991. pap. text ed. 145.00 (*0-8403-6724-4*) Kendall-Hunt.

— Human Resources Survey: Exclusively for Design Firms. 96p. 1991. pap. text ed. 145.00 (*0-8403-6812-7*) Kendall-Hunt.

— Key Financial Yardsticks. 128p. 1990. per. 40.00 (*0-8403-6473-3*) Kendall-Hunt.

— Proposal Strategies That Work. 128p. 1991. per. 40.00 (*0-8403-6536-5*) Kendall-Hunt.

— Salary Survey, 1990. 1991. pap. text ed. 145.00 (*0-8403-6726-0*) Kendall-Hunt.

PMA Staff. Executive Management Salary Survey, 1991. 208p. 1991. pap. text ed. 195.00 (*0-8403-7052-0*) Kendall-Hunt.

PMEF Staff. How to Value Oil Jobbership. 140p. 1992. 11.50 (*0-685-71208-7*) Kendall-Hunt.

P.M.E.F. Staff. Oil Heat Technician's Manual. 400p. 1992. 19.20 (*0-8403-7724-X*) Petro Mktg Ed Found.

***Pneuman, Roy W.** Building Small Church Coalitions: Learnings from the Northern Neck Project. 1993. pap. 8.75 (*1-56699-129-3*, OD104) Alban Inst.

Pnevmatikos, S. N., ed. Singularities & Dynamical Systems: Proceedings of the International Conference Held in Heraklion, Greece, 30 August-6 September 1983. (Mathematics Studies: Vol. 103). 460p. 1985. 87.25 (*0-444-87641-3*, North Holland) Elsevier.

Pnevmatikos, S. N., ed. see Abdullaev, Fatkhulla K., et al.

Pnevmatikos, S. N., et al. Singular Behaviour & Nonlinear Dynamics, 2 vols., Set. (C). 1989. 113.00 (*0-317-01710-1*) World Scientific Pub.

P'ng Chye Khim & Draeger, Donn F. Shaolin Lohan Kung-Fu. Orig. Title: Shaolin: An Introduction to Lohan Fighting Techniques. (Illus.). 170p. 1991. pap. 12.95 (*0-8048-1698-0*) C E Tuttle.

Pnueli, A., jt. auth. see Manna, Z.

Pnueli, Amir, jt. auth. see Manna, Zohar.

Pnueli, David & Gutfinger, Chaim. Fluid Mechanics. (Illus.). 470p. (C). 1992. 54.95 (0-521-41704-X) Cambridge U Pr.

Po-Chia Hsia, R. Social Discipline in the Reformation: Central Europe 1550-1750. 224p. 1990. 44.00 (0-415-01148-5, A3629) Routledge.

***Po-Chia Hsia, R. & Lehmann, Hartmut, eds.** In & Out of the Ghetto: Jewish-Gentile Relations in Late Medieval & Early Modern Germany. (Publications of the German Historical Insitute, Washington, D.C.). (Illus.). 336p. (C). 1995. 64.95 (0-521-47064-1) Cambridge U Pr.

Po-Fei Huang, Parker, jt. auth. see Stimson, Hugh M.

***Po-jen, Sung.** Guide to Capturing a Plum Blossom. Pine, Red, pseud., tr. (Illus.). 224p. (Orig.). 1995. pap. 14.95 (1-56279-077-3) Mercury Hse Inc.

Po, Li & Fu, Tu, eds. Li Po & Tu Fu. Cooper, Arthur, tr. (Classics Ser.). (Illus.). 256p. (Orig.). 1973. mass mkt. 8.95 (0-14-044272-3, Penguin Classics) Viking Penguin.

Po-Lung Yu. Multiple-Criteria Decision Making: Concepts, Techniques, & Extensions. LC 85-16723. (Mathematical Concepts & Methods in Science & Engineering Ser.: Vol. 30). 402p. 1985. 85.00 (0-306-41965-3, Plenum Pr) Plenum.

Po-Ta, Ch'En. Notes on Ten Years of Civil War, 1927-1936. LC 75-39023. (China Studies). 108p. 1976. reprint ed. 15.00 (0-88355-380-5) Hyperion Conn.

Poag, C. Wylie, ed. Geologic Evolution of the United States Atlantic Margin. (Illus.). 384p. 1985. text ed. 99.95 (0-442-27306-1) Chapman & Hall.

Poag, C. Wylie & De Graciansky, Pierre C. Geological Evolution of Atlantic Continental Rises. (Illus.). 368p. 1992. text ed. 99.95 (0-442-00498-2) Chapman & Hall.

Poag, James F. Wolfram von Eschenbach. LC 73-187627. (Twayne's World Authors Ser.). 136p. (C). 1972. lib. bdg. 17.95 (0-8290-1750-X) Irvington.

Poage, Bettyjane. The Guide to Psychic Awareness. 163p. (Orig.). 1989. pap. 12.50 (0-9625501-0-8) Parapsychology Pr.

Poage, Godfrey. In Garments All Red. 45p. 1971. 2.95 (0-911988-17-3) AMI Pr.

Poage, Greg A., jt. auth. see Moffat, Donald W.

Poage, James & Landis, Carolyn P. Contracting for Computing: A Checklist of Terms & Clauses for Use in Contracting with Vendors for Software Packages & Custom Software, Vol. II. 148p. 1975. 16.00 (0-318-14014-4); 9.00 (0-318-14015-2) EDUCOM.

Poage, Walter S. The Building Professional's Guide to Contract Documents. 375p. 1990. 59.95 (0-87629-210-4, 67261) R S Means.

***Poague, Leland.** Another Frank Capra. (Cambridge Studies in Film). (Illus.). 288p. (C). 1995. 54.95 (0-521-38066-9) Cambridge U Pr.

***Poague, Leland, ed.** Conversations with Susan Sontag. (Literary Conversations Ser.). 270p. 1995. text ed. 39.50 (0-87805-833-8); pap. 15.95 (0-87805-834-6) U Pr of Miss.

Poague, Leland, jt. ed. see Deutelbaum, Marshall.

Poague, William T. Gunner with Stonewall: Reminiscences of W. T. Poague. Cockrell, Monroe F., ed. (Illus.). 181p. 1989. reprint ed. 30.00 (0-916107-26-4); reprint ed. pap. 12.95 (0-916107-48-5) Broadfoot.

Poarch, John E. Limits: The Keystone of Emotional Growth. LC 90-82966. x, 118p. 1990. 17.95 (1-55959-020-3) Accel Devel.

Poate, C. D. & Daplyn, P. F. Data for Agrarian Development. LC 92-22831. (Wye Studies in Agricultural & Rural Development). (Illus.). 397p. (C). 1993. 84.95 (0-521-36566-X); pap. 32.95 (0-521-36758-1) Cambridge U Pr.

Poate, J. M., jt. ed. see Fan, J. C. C.

Poate, John M., ed. see Electrochemical Society, Thin Film Phenomena-Interfaces & Interactions Symposium Staff.

Poate, John M., ed. see Symposium on Thin Film Interfaces & Interactions.

Poate, John M., jt. ed. see Williams, James S.

Poatgieter, A. H., tr. see Lewis, Henry.

Poats, Susan V., jt. ed. see Feldstein, Hilary S.

Pobee, John S. Who Are the Poor? The Beatitudes As a Call to Community. (Risk Book Ser.: No. 32). 74p. (Orig.). 1987. pap. 5.50 (2-8254-0884-0) Wrld Coun Churches.

Pobee, John S. & Von Wartenberg-Potter, Barbel, eds. New Eyes for Reading: Biblical & Theological Reflections by Women from the Third World. LC 86-211225. 116p. (Orig.). reprint ed. pap. 33.10 (0-7837-6000-0, 2045810) Bks Demand.

Pobee, John S., jt. ed. see Amirtham, Samuel.

Pobell, F. Matter & Methods at Low Temperatures. 319p. 1992. 79.00 (0-387-53751-1) Spr-Verlag.

Poberezny, Paul, ed. Flying Manual, 1933. LC 21-14171. (Flying & Gliding Ser.). (Illus.). 75p. reprint ed. pap. 5.95 (0-940000-86-5) EAA Aviation.

Poberezny, Paul & Schmid, S. H., eds. Aircraft Welding. rev. ed. (How to Aircraft Building Ser.). (Illus.). 116p. 1991. pap. 11.95 (0-940000-49-0) EAA Aviation.

Poberezny, Paul H., ed. Flying & Glider Manual, 1931. (Flying & Gliding Ser.). (Illus.). 80p. reprint ed. pap. 6.95 (0-940000-84-9, 21-14169) EAA Aviation.

— Flying Manual, 1932. LC 21-14170. (Flying & Gliding Ser.). (Illus.). 75p. reprint ed. pap. 5.95 (0-940000-85-7) EAA Aviation.

Poberezny, Paul H., intro. Flying & Glider Manual, 1930. (Flying & Gliding Ser.). (Illus.). 80p. reprint ed. pap. 6.95 (0-940000-83-0, 21-14168) EAA Aviation.

Poberezny, Paul H. & Schmid, S. H., eds. Custom Built Sport Aircraft Handbook: A Guide to Construction Standards for the Amateur Aircraft Builder. rev. ed. (Illus.). 140p. 1991. pap. 14.95 (0-940000-43-1) EAA Aviation.

— Wood: Aircraft Building Techniques. rev. ed. (EAA How to Ser.). (Illus.). 136p. 1991. pap. 9.95 (0-940000-44-X) EAA Aviation.

Pobi-Asamani, Kwadwo O. W.E.B. Du Bois: His Contribution to Pan-Africanism. LC 93-4385. (Black Political Studies: No. 4). 136p. 1994. 27.00x (0-89370-351-6); pap. 17.00x (0-89370-451-2) Borgo Pr.

Pobo, Ken. Ferns on Fire. Zarucchi, Roy & Page, Carolyn, eds. (Chapbook Ser.). (Illus.). 28p. (Orig.). 1991. pap. text ed. 5.00 (1-879205-14-9) Nightshade Pr.

— Yes: Irises. 32p. (Orig.). 1992. pap. 4.00 (1-880286-08-4) Singular Speech Pr.

Pobst, Dick. Trout Stream Insects: An Orvis Streamside Guide. 1991. pap. 16.95 (1-55821-067-9) Lyons & Burford.

Pobst, Richard. Fish the Impossible Places. (Illus.). 1974. 9.95 (0-88395-025-1) Freshet Pr.

***Poccia, Dominic.** Molecular Aspects of Spermatogenesis. 155p. 1994. 89.95 (1-57059-204-7, LN9204) CRC Pr.

Pocek, Kenneth L., jt. auth. see Buell, Duncan A.

Poceski, A. Mixed Finite Element Method. (Lecture Notes in Engineering Ser.: Vol. 72). (Illus.). 352p. 1992. pap. 79.00 (0-387-54916-1) Spr-Verlag.

Poch. Simulation: Principles & Methods. 2nd ed. 1992. write for info. (0-318-69402-6, CRC Reprint) Franklin.

Poch, Gerald. Combined Effects of Drugs & Toxic Agents: Modern Evaluation in Theorie & Practice. LC 92-43470. 1993. 49.00 (0-387-82434-0); write for info. (3-211-82434-0) Spr-Verlag.

***Poch, M. Clementine.** Always & Forever: The Life & Times of Mother Franciska Lechner. 224p. (Orig.). 1994. pap. text ed. 12.95 (1-883520-04-5) Jeremiah Pr.

Poch, Pompeu F. Dictionary of the Catalan Language: Diccionari Manual de la Llengua Catalana. 9th ed. 1360p. (CAT.). 1991. 49.95 (0-7859-4960-7) Fr & Eur.

— General Dictionary of the Catalan Language: Diccionari General de la Llengua Catalana. 26th ed. 1826p. (CAT.). 1991. write for info. (0-7859-4959-3) Fr & Eur.

***Poch, Robert K.** Academic Freedom in American Higher Education: Rights, Responsibilities & Limitations. Fife, Jonathan D., ed. & frwd. by. (ASHE-ERIC Higher Education Report Ser.: No. 4). 85p. (Orig.). 1994. pap. 18.00x (1-878380-25-7) GWU Schl E&HD.

Pocha, J. J. An Introduction to Mission Design for Geostationary Satellites. (C). 1987. lib. bdg. 88.00 (90-277-2479-2) Kluwer Ac.

Pochat, Goetz. Figur und Landschaft. Historische Interpretation der Landschaftsmalerei von der Antike bis zur Renaissance. LC 72-87564. (Illus.). 560p. (C). 1973. 296.15 (3-11-004104-9) De Gruyter.

Poche, David J., jt. auth. see Fichter, Lynn.

Pochedley, Carl, ed. Non-Lymphoid Leukemias in Children. 256p. 1985. 45.00 (0-275-90009-6, C0009, Praeger Pubs) Greenwood.

Pochedly, et al. Disorders of the Spleen: Pathophysiology & Management. (Hematology Ser.: Vol. 10). 488p. 1988. 170.00 (0-8247-7933-9) Dekker.

Pochedly, C, ed. Acute Childhood Leukemia. (Modern Problems in Pediatrics Ser.: Vol. 16). (Illus.). viii, 214p. 1975. 75.25 (3-8055-2065-4) S Karger.

Pochedly, Carl, ed. Childhood Lymphoblastic Leukemia. LC 85-12102. 240p. 1985. text ed. 59.95 (0-275-90048-7, C0048, Praeger Pubs) Greenwood.

— Neuroblastoma: Tumor Biology & Therapy. 432p. 1990. 134.95 (0-8493-0157-2, RC280) CRC Pr.

— Reviews in Pediatric Hem-Oncology VI. LC 85-9547. 222p. 1985. text ed. 55.00 (0-275-91306-6, C1306, Praeger Pubs) Greenwood.

Pochedly, Carl, jt. ed. see Stockman, James A., III.

Pochedly, Carl, jt. ed. see Zeltzer, Paul M.

Pochedly, Carl, et al, eds. Neoplastic Diseases in Childhood, Set. LC 93-12664. 1994. text ed. 430.00 (3-7186-5340-0) Gordon & Breach.

Pochedly, Carl E., jt. auth. see Hilgartner, Margaret W.

Pochet, Michel. Sex Redeemed. 64p. 1991. pap. 5.95 (0-904287-31-9) New City.

Pochet, R., et al, eds. Calcium Binding Proteins in Normal & Transformed Cells. LC 90-6704. (Advances in Experimental Medicine & Biology Ser.: Vol. 269). (Illus.). 224p. 1990. 75.00 (0-306-43491-1, Plenum Pr) Plenum.

Pochi Yeh. Photorefractive Nonlinear Optics. 400p. 1995. text ed. 86.00 (981-02-1443-X) World Scientific Pub.

Pochiluk, William. Autofacts Yearbook, 1993, 2 vols., Set. 1993. text ed. 595.00 (0-9637549-0-4) AUTOFACTS Intl.

— Autofacts Yearbook, 1993, 2 vols., Vols. 1-2. 1993. Vol. 1, 523p. text ed. write for info. (0-9637549-1-2); Vol. 2, 480p. text ed. write for info. (0-9637549-2-0) AUTOFACTS Intl.

— Autofacts Yearbook, 1994, Set. Benko, Christopher, ed. 1125p. 1994. text ed. 1,190.00 (0-9637549-5-5) AUTOFACTS Intl.

— Autofacts Yearbook, 1994, Vol. 1. Benko, Christopher, ed. 525p. 1994. text ed. 595.00 (0-9637549-3-9) AUTOFACTS Intl.

— Autofacts Yearbook, 1994, Vol. 2. Benko, Christopher, ed. 600p. 1994. text ed. 595.00 (0-9637549-4-7) AUTOFACTS Intl.

— Autofacts 1995: Yearbook, Vol. 1. Ruhl, Mary, ed. 525p. 1995. text ed. 595.00 (0-9637549-7-1) AUTOFACTS Intl.

— Autofacts 1995: Yearbook, Vol. 2. Ruhl, Mary, ed. 490p. 1995. text ed. 595.00 (0-9637549-8-X) AUTOFACTS Intl.

— Autofacts 1995: Yearbook, 2 vols., Vols. 1-2. Ruhl, Mary, ed. 1115p. 1995. text ed. write for info. (0-9637549-6-3) AUTOFACTS Intl.

Pochiluk, William & Nash, David. Autofacts Yearbook, 1992, Vol. 1. 480p. 1992. text ed. 495.00 (1-879800-02-0) Autofacts.

Pochiluk, William R. Autofacts Yearbook, 1991, Vol. 1. Nash, David, ed. 625p. 1991. text ed. 495.00 (1-879800-00-4) Autofacts.

Pochiluk, William R. & Nash, David. Autofacts Yearbook, 1992. 1000p. 1992. text ed. 495.00 (1-879800-01-2) Autofacts.

Pochin, Edward. Nuclear Radiation: Risks & Benefits. (Monographs on Science, Technology & Society). (Illus.). 197p. 1985. pap. 16.95 (0-19-858337-0) OUP.

Pochin, Edward E. Why Be Quantitative about Radiation Risk Estimates? (Taylor Lecture Ser.: No. 2). 1978. 15.00 (0-913392-42-1) NCRP Pubns.

Pochin-Mould, Daphne. Irish Pilgrimage. 1957. 12.95 (0-8159-5816-1) Devin.

Pochin Mould, Daphne P. Discovering Cork. (Illus.). 320p. 1991. 59.95 (0-86322-129-7, Pub. by Brandon Bk Pubs IE) Irish Bks Media.

Pochis, Erica, ed. see Burke, Kay.

Pochman, Henry A. Washington Irving. 1988. reprint ed. lib. bdg. 75.00 (0-7812-0193-4) Rprt Serv.

Pochmann, Henry A. German Culture in America: Philosophical & Literary Influences 1600-1900. LC 78-5337. 865p. 1978. reprint ed. text ed. 93.50 (0-313-20378-4, POGC, Greenwood Pr) Greenwood.

— New England Transcendentalism & St. Louis Hegelianism. LC 68-55163. (Studies in Comparative Literature: No. 35). 1969. reprint ed. lib. bdg. 75.00 (0-8383-0610-1) M S G Haskell Hse.

Pochmann, Henry A., ed. see Irving, Washington.

Pochocki, Ethel. The Gypsies' Tale. LC 93-3320. (Illus.). (J). (gr. 4 up). 1994. pap. 15.00 (0-671-79934-7, S&S Bks Young Read) S&S Childrens.

— Mushroom Man. (J). 1993. 15.00 (0-671-75951-5, Green Tiger S&S) S&S Childrens.

— One-of-a-Kind Friends: Saints & Heroes for Kids. (Illus.). 232p. (J). 1994. 9.95 (0-86716-194-9) St Anthony Mess Pr.

— Wildflower Tea. LC 92-29872. (Illus.). (J). 1993. 14.00 (0-671-78115-4, Green Tiger S&S) S&S Childrens.

Pochop, L. O., jt. auth. see Burman, R. D.

Pocius, Gerald L. A Place to Belong: Community Order & Everyday Space in Calvert, Newfoundland. LC 91-7334. (Illus.). 384p. 1991. 45.00 (0-8203-1330-0) U of Ga Pr.

Pock, Max A. Consolidating Police Functions in Metropolitan Areas. LC 62-64274. (Michigan Legal Publications). v, 51p. 1985. reprint ed. lib. bdg. 34.00 (0-89941-384-6, 303540) W S Hein.

— Independent Special Districts: A Solution to the Metropolitan Area Problems. LC 62-63903. (Michigan Legal Publications). vii, 193p. 1985. reprint ed. lib. bdg. 36.00 (0-89941-385-4, 303550) W S Hein.

Pockell, ed. see Ariyoshi, Sawako.

Pockell, ed. see Dazai, Osamu.

Pockell, ed. see Hamill, Peter.

Pockell, ed. see Hoyt, Edwin.

Pockell, ed. see Kano, Jigoro.

Pockell, ed. see Kizaki, Satoko.

Pockell, ed. see Kodansha International Staff.

Pockell, ed. see Lifton, Betty J.

Pockell, ed. see McCarthy, Ralph F.

Pockell, ed. see Newton, Clyde.

Pockell, jt. ed. see Ogawa.

Pockell, ed. see Richie, Donald.

Pockell, ed. see Shiina, Makato.

Pockell, ed. see Tasker, Peter.

Pocket Pointers, Inc. Staff. Pocket Pointers: A Quick Reminder on Any Shot. Golf Gifts, Inc. Staff, ed. 1988. pap. 2.50 (1-878728-18-0) Golf Gifts.

Pockets, M. T. Beggar's Handbook. 39p. 1989. pap. text ed. 5.95 (1-55950-012-3) Loompanics.

Pockets Press Staff. Pocket Full of Christmas Memories. (J). 1993. pap. 19.95 (1-881511-01-4) Pockets Pr.

Pocklington, John. Sunday No Sabbath: A Sermon. LC 74-28881. (English Experience Ser.: No. 759). 1975. reprint ed. 20.00 (90-221-0759-0) Walter J Johnson.

Pocknell, ed. see Britton, Dorothy.

Pocknell, ed. see Dazai, Osamu.

Pocknell, ed. see Kanno, Eiji & O'Keefe, Constance.

Pocknell, ed. see Kodansha International Staff.

Pocknell, ed. see Richie, Donald.

Pockney, B. P. Soviet Statistics. 350p. 1992. text ed. 59.95 (0-312-04003-2) St Martin.

Pockrand, I. Surface Enhanced Raman Vibrational Studies at Solid-Gas Interfaces. (Tracts in Modern Physics Ser.: Vol. 104). (Illus.). 160p. 1984. 56.00 (0-387-13416-6) Spr-Verlag.

Pocock. Demanding Skill: Women & Technology. 1989. pap. text ed. 18.95 (0-04-332137-2, Pub. by Allen Unwin AT) Paul & Co Pubs.

Pocock, jt. auth. see Taylor.

Pocock, Charles. Quan Loi II. abr. ed. 625p. 1995. pap. 14.95 (1-56901-447-7) NW Pub.

Pocock, Chris. Dragon Lady: The Secret World of the Lockheed U-2. (Illus.). 224p. 1989. pap. 12.98 (0-87938-393-3) Motorbooks Intl.

Pocock, D. F., tr. see Durkheim, Emile.

***Pocock, David.** Build or Renovate Your Own Home. 1995. 23.95 (0-8062-5241-3) Carlton.

Pocock, Guy N. Little Room. LC 68-55854. (Essay Index Reprint Ser.). 1977. 20.95 (0-8369-0794-9) Ayer.

Pocock, J. G. The Ancient Constitution & the Feudal Law: A Study of English Historical Thought in the Seventeenth Century--A Reissue with a Retrospect. 2nd ed. 416p. 1987. 74.95 (0-521-30352-4) Cambridge U Pr.

— The Ancient Constitution & the Feudal Law: A Study of English Historical Thought in the Seventeenth Century--A Reissue with a Retrospect. 2nd ed. 416p. 1987. pap. 22.95 (0-521-31643-X) Cambridge U Pr.

— The Machiavellian Moment: Florentine Political Thought & the Atlantic Republican Tradition. LC 73-2490. 576p. 1975. pap. 27.95 (0-691-10029-2) Princeton U Pr.

— Politics, Language, & Time: Essays on Political Thought & History. viii, 292p. 1989. pap. text ed. 14.95 (0-226-67139-9) U Ch Pr.

— Virtue, Commerce & History: Essays on Political Thought & History, Chiefly in the Eighteenth Century. (Ideas in Context Ser.). 400p. 1985. 74.95 (0-521-25701-8); pap. 22.95 (0-521-27660-8) Cambridge U Pr.

Pocock, J. G., jt. ed. see Ball, Terence.

Pocock, J. G., ed. see Burke, Edmund.

Pocock, J. G., ed. see Harrington, James.

Pocock, J. G., et al. The Varieties of British Political Thought, 1500-1800. LC 92-37772. 320p. (C). 1994. 59.95 (0-521-44377-6) Cambridge U Pr.

Pocock, John W. Fund-Raising Leadership: A Guide for College & University Boards. (Illus.). (Orig.). 1989. 27.95 (0-318-41353-1) Assn Gov Bds.

Pocock, L. G. Sicilian Origin of the Odyssey. Scammacca, Nina & Scammacca, Nat, trs. 206p. 1986. pap. 15.00 (0-89304-568-3) Cross-Cultrl NY.

— Sicilian Origin of the Odyssey. Scammacca, Nina & Scammacca, Nat, trs. 206p. 1986. 36.00 (0-89304-593-4) Cross-Cultrl NY.

Pocock, L. G., ed. Cicero: In Vatinium. vi, 200p. 1967. reprint ed. 30.00 (0-685-54232-7, Pub. by A M Hakkert NE) Benjamins North Am.

Pocock, Leslie W. Comfort Ye My People. 128p. 1986. 30.00 (0-7223-2048-5, Pub. by A H S Ltd UK) St Mut.

Pocock, Nick. Did W. D. Custead Fly First? The Story of W. D. Custead of Elm Mott - Waco, Texas - Airship Builder Before the Wrights Flew. LC 74-83996. (Illus.). 1974. pap. 17.95 (0-915376-00-8); mic. film 20.00 (0-915376-01-6) Spec Aviation.

— Grumman-Schweizer AG-CAT. LC 94-69850. (Illus.). 1994. pap. 17.95 (0-915376-02-4) Spec Aviation.

Pocock, R. F. Nuclear Power, Its History. 280p. 1984. 60.00 (0-905418-15-8, Pub. by Gresham Bks UK) St Mut.

Pocock, R. I. Mammalia: Primates Carnivora Families Felidae & Viveridae, Vol. 1. (Fauna of British India Ser.). xxxiv, 464p. 1985. reprint ed. 50.00 (1-55528-038-2, Pub. by Today & Tomorrows P & P II) Scholarly Pubns.

Pocock, Rita. Annabelle & the Big Slide. 28p. (J). (ps-00). 1989. 10.95 (0-15-200407-6, Gulliver Bks) HarBrace.

Pocock, Stuart J. Clinical Trials: A Practical Approach. LC 83-1316. 266p. 1984. text ed. 82.00 (0-471-90155-5, A R Liss) Wiley.

***Pocock, Tom.** Horatio Nelson. (Pimlico Ser.). (Illus.). 364p. 1995. pap. 15.95 (0-7126-6123-9, Pub. by Pimlico) Trafalgar.

— Rider Haggard & the Lost Empire: A Biography. (Illus.). 258p. 1994. 45.00 (0-297-81308-0) Trafalgar.

— Sailer King: A Biography of William IV. (Illus.). 272p. 1992. 39.95 (1-85619-075-7, Sinclair-Stevenson) Trafalgar.

Pocs, Ollie. Our Intimate Relations: Marriage & the Family. 480p. (C). 1990. pap. text ed. 28.75 (0-06-045351-6) HarpCollege.

— Our Intimate Relationships: Marriage & the Family. 2nd ed. (Illus.). 577p. (C). 1994. pap. text ed. 28.95 (0-87563-465-6) Stipes.

***Pocs, T., et al, eds.** Proceedings of the Lab Conference of Bryoecology: Budapest-Vacratot, Hungary 5-10 August, 1985. (Symposia Biologica Hungarica Ser.: No. 35). 901p. (C). 1987. 267.00x (963-05-4633-7, Pub. by Akad Kiado HU) St Mut.

Pocsik, G., jt. auth. see Csikor, F.

Podach, E. The Madness of Nietzsche. 1973. 250.00 (0-87968-179-9) Gordon Pr.

Podack, Eckhard R. Cytolytic Lymphocytes & Complement: Effectors of the Immune System, Vol. I. 280p. 1988. 154.00 (0-8493-6968-1, QR185, CRC Reprint) Franklin.

— Cytolytic Lymphocytes & Complement: Effectors of the Immune System, Vol. II. 256p. 1988. 141.00 (0-8493-6969-X, 6969, CRC Reprint) Franklin.

Podanoffsky, Michael. Dissecting DOS. LC 93-42508. 1994. write for info. (0-201-62687-X) Addison-Wesley.

Podaras, C., tr. see Birolini, A.

Podbielkow. Slownik Roslin Uzytowych. 529p. (ENG, FRE, GER, LAT, POL & RUS.). 1980. write for info. (0-8288-0066-9, M 8482) Fr & Eur.

Podbielska, H. Holography, Interferometry, & Optical Pattern Recognition in Biomedicine, Vol. 1429. 1990. 53.00 (0-8194-0519-1) SPIE.

Podbielska, H., ed. Holography, Interferometry, & Optical Pattern Recognition in Biomedicine II. 1992. 62.00 (0-8194-0793-3, 1647) SPIE.

Podder, V. Technology in Paper Industry. 586p. 1990. 200.00 (81-209-0004-9, Pub. by Pitambar Pub II) St Mut.

***Podeh, Elie.** The Quest for Hegemony in the Arab World: The Struggle over the Baghdad Pact. LC 95-884. (Social, Economic & Political Studies of the Middle East: Vol. 52). 1995. 74.50 (90-04-10214-0) E J Brill.

Podell, Diane K. Thematic Atlases for Public, Academic, and High School Libraries. LC 94-4326. 208p. 1994. 27.50 (0-8108-2866-9) Scarecrow.

Podell, H. J., jt. auth. see Abrams, M. D.

Podell, Harold J., jt. ed. see Abrams, Marshall D.

Podell, Janet, ed. Annual Obituary 1981. 1982. 95.00 (0-912289-51-1) St James Pr.

— Annual Obituary 1982. 1983. 85.00 (0-912289-01-5) St James Pr.

Podell, Janet, jt. ed. see Anzovin, Steven.

Podell, Larry & Kaye, David. Audiotex Directory & Buyer's Guide. 1989. 40.00 (0-317-93152-0) ADBG Pub.

***Podell, Richard.** When Your Doctor Doesn't Know Best. 1995. 23.50 (0-671-87112-9) S&S Trade.

Podell, Richard N. Doctor: Why Am I So Tired? 1989. mass mkt. 4.99 (0-449-45320-0) Fawcett.

— Doctor: Why Am I So Tired? 1989. mass mkt. 4.99 (0-449-14578-6) Fawcett.

P Q

An Asterisk (*) at the beginning of an entry indicates that the title is appearing in BIP for the first time.

— Doctor, Why Am I So Tired? A Guide for Overcoming Chronic Fatigue. LC 87-60161. 256p. 1988. 17.95 (*0-88687-321-5*, Pharos) Wrld Almnc.

Podell, Richard N. & Proctor, William. The G-Index Diet: The Missing Link That Makes Permanent Weight Loss Possible. 336p. 1994. mass mkt. 5.99 (*0-446-36576-9*) Warner Bks.

Podell, Ronald M. Contagious Emotions. Zion, Claire, ed. 1993. reprint ed. pap. 10.00 (*0-671-70240-8*) PB.

Podell, Susan K. A Guide to Eating Right During Pregnancy. LC 92-42111. 1993. 2.99 (*0-385-46775-3*) Doubleday.

— The Pocket Guide to Carbohydrates. LC 95-3234. 1996. 2.99 (*0-385-47681-7*) Doubleday.

— The Pocket Guide to Vitamins. LC 93-2344. 1994. pap. 2.99 (*0-385-46823-7*) Doubleday.

— Vest Pocket Cholesterol Counter. 1991. pap. 2.99 (*0-385-41329-7*) Doubleday.

— Vest Pocket Fat Counter. 1992. pap. 2.99 (*0-385-42294-6*) Doubleday.

***Podelski, Andreas, ed.** Constraint Programming: Basics & Trends: 1994 Chatillon Spring School, Chantillon-sur-Seine, France, May 16-20, 1994: Selected Papers. LC 95-10074. (Lecture Notes in Computer Science: No. 910). 1995. write for info. (*0-387-59155-9*) Spr-Verlag.

Podelski, Andreas, jt. ed. see Nivat, Maurice.

Podemski, Richard S., et al. Comprehensive Administration of Special Education. 2nd ed. LC 94-11499. 336p. (C). 1994. write for info. (*0-02-395961-4*, Merrill Pub Co) Macmillan.

Podendorf, Illa. Animal Homes. LC 82-4466. (New True Bks.). (Illus.). 48p. (J). (gr. k-4). 1982. lib. bdg. 12.90 (*0-516-01666-0*) Childrens.

— Animals of Sea & Shore. LC 81-38453. (New True Bks.). (Illus.). 48p. (J). (gr. k-4). 1982. lib. bdg. 12.90 (*0-516-01615-6*); pap. 4.95 (*0-516-41615-4*) Childrens.

— Baby Animals. LC 81-9938. (New True Bks.). (Illus.). 48p. (J). (gr. k-4). 1981. lib. bdg. 12.90 (*0-516-01605-9*); pap. 4.95 (*0-516-41605-7*) Childrens.

— Energy. LC 81-12309. (New True Bks.). (Illus.). 48p. (J). (gr. k-4). 1982. lib. bdg. 12.90 (*0-516-01625-3*) Childrens.

— Insects. LC 81-7689. (New True Bks.). (Illus.). 48p. (J). (gr. k-4). 1981. lib. bdg. 12.90 (*0-516-01627-X*); pap. 4.95 (*0-516-41627-8*) Childrens.

— Jungles. LC 82-4454. (New True Bks.). (J). (gr. k-4). 1982. 12.90 (*0-516-01631-8*) Childrens.

— Pets. LC 81-7679. (New True Bks.). (Illus.). 48p. (J). (gr. k-4). 1981. lib. bdg. 12.90 (*0-516-01641-5*) Childrens.

— Rocks & Minerals. LC 81-38494. (New True Bks.). (Illus.). 48p. (J). (gr. k-4). 1982. lib. bdg. 12.90 (*0-516-01648-2*); pap. 4.95 (*0-516-41648-0*) Childrens.

— Seasons. LC 81-7751. (New True Bks.). (Illus.). 48p. (J). (gr. k-4). 1981. lib. bdg. 12.90 (*0-516-01647-4*); pap. 4.95 (*0-516-41647-2*) Childrens.

— Space. LC 82-4507. (New True Bks.). (J). (gr. k-4). 1982. 12.90 (*0-516-01650-4*) Childrens.

— Spiders. LC 81-38444. (New True Bks.). (Illus.). 48p. (J). (gr. k-4). 1982. lib. bdg. 12.90 (*0-516-01653-9*); pap. 4.95 (*0-516-41653-7*) Childrens.

— Trees. LC 81-12313. (New True Bks.). (Illus.). 48p. (J). (gr. k-4). 1982. lib. bdg. 12.90 (*0-516-01657-1*) Childrens.

Poderegin, Mike B. The Dawning. 365p. (C). 1990. 49.00 (*0-907855-05-9*, Pub. by Honeyglen Pub Ltd UK); pap. 39.00 (*0-907855-06-7*, Pub. by Honeyglen Pub Ltd UK) St Mut.

Poderegin, Nadja, tr. see Bajic-Poderegin, Milka.

Podeschi, John B. Books on the Horse & Horsemanship, Riding, Hunting, Breeding, & Racing, 1400-1941. (Illus.). 427p. 1981. 50.00 (*0-905005-53-8*) Yale Ctr Brit Art.

Podeschi, John B. Dickens & Dickensiana: A Catalogue of the Richard Gimbel Collection in the Yale University Library. LC 79-66938. 594p. 1981. text ed. 70.00 (*0-300-03574-8*) Yale U Pr.

Podesta, C., ed. Rapid Transport Systems: From Feasibility Studies to Operation. 348p. 1986. 120.50 (*0-444-87642-1*, North Holland) Elsevier.

Podesta, Connie. Self-Esteem & the Six-Second Secret. 96p. 1990. pap. 15.00 (*0-8039-6037-9*) Corwin Pr.

Podesta, Guido A. Desde Lutecia: Anacronismo y Modernidad en los Escritos Teatrales de Cesar Vallejo. 341p. (SPA.). 1995. pap. 18.00 (*0-9640795-0-X*) Latinoam Edit.

Podesta, Patti, intro. Resolution: A Critique of Video Art. (Illus.). 131p. (Orig.). (C). 1986. pap. 7.00 (*0-937335-01-0*) LA Contemp Exhib.

Podesta, Robert. Robert Podesta's One Million Dollar No Joke Italian's Success System. 10.00 (*0-686-23143-0*) Podesta Fishing.

Podesta, Ronald B., et al, eds. Membrane Physiology of Invertebrates. LC 81-17534. (Illus.). 678p. reprint ed. pap. 180.00 (*0-7837-0914-5*, 2041219) Bks Demand.

Podesta, Terry. Hockey for Men & Women. (EP Sports Ser.). (Illus.). 1978. 8.95 (*0-7158-0578-9*) Charles River Bks.

Podet, Allen H. The Success & Failure of the Anglo-American Committee of Inquiry, 1945-1946: Last Chance in Palestine. LC 87-1635. (Jewish Studies: Vol. 3). 384p. 1987. lib. bdg. 99.95 (*0-88946-255-0*) E Mellen.

Podgaetsky, V. V., jt. auth. see Pokhodnaya, I. K.

Podger, Christopher J., jt. auth. see Ioannides, Alexander C.

Podges, Hiram, Jr. A Practical Guide to Creative Senility. LC 88-9551. (Illus.). 176p. (Orig.). 1988. pap. 9.95 (*0-931892-16-3*) B Dolphin Pub.

Podgor, Ellen S. White Collar Crime in a Nutshell. (Nutshell Ser.). 303p. 1993. pap. text ed. 16.00 (*0-314-02349-6*) West Pub.

Podgorecki, Adam. Polish Society. LC 93-25056. 208p. 1993. text ed. 55.00 (*0-275-94728-9*, C4728, Praeger Pubs) Greenwood.

— Social Oppression. LC 93-7712. (Contributions in Sociology Ser.: No. 106). 152p. 1993. text ed. 47.95 (*0-313-29024-5*, GM9024, Greenwood Pr) Greenwood.

Podgurski, Walter B. Payroll Deduction: The Delivery System of the 90s. 2nd ed. 256p. 1991. pap. 28.50 (*0-87218-486-2*) Natl Underwriter.

Podgursky, Michael. Job Displacement & the Rural Worker. 20p. 1989. 10.00 (*0-944826-14-8*) Economic Policy Inst.

Podhajsky, Alois. Complete Training of Horse & Rider. 1982. pap. 10.00 (*0-87980-235-9*) Wilshire.

— The Riding Teacher: A Basic Guide to Correct Methods of Classical Instruction. (Illus.). 204p. 1993. 22.95 (*0-943955-84-X*, Trafalgar Sq Pub) Trafalgar.

Podhoretz, John. Hell of a Ride: Backstage at the White House Follies, 1989-1993. 320p. 1993. 21.00 (*0-671-79648-8*) S&S Trade.

Podhoretz, Norman. The Present Danger. 1980. pap. 3.95 (*0-671-41328-7*, Touchstone Bks) S&S Trade.

Podlecki, ed. Aeschylus-Eumenides. (Classical Texts Ser.). 1989. 49.95 (*0-85668-381-7*, Pub. by Aris & Phillips UK); pap. 24.95 (*0-85668-382-5*, Pub. by Aris & Phillips UK) David Brown.

Podlecki, A. Plutarch: Life of Pericles: A Companion to the Penguim Translation. 1987. write for info. (*0-86292-237-2*, Pub. by Brstl Class Pr UK) Focus Info Gr.

Podlecki, Anthony, tr. & intro. Euripides' Medea. 92p. 1991. 5.95 (*0-941051-10-2*) Focus Info Gr.

Podlecki, Anthony, jt. ed. see Gregory, T. E.

Podlecki, Anthony J. The Life of Themistocles: A Critical Survey of the Literary & Archaeological Evidence. LC 73-93001. 272p. reprint ed. pap. 77.60 (*0-7837-1027-5*, 2041338) Bks Demand.

Podmore, Frank. The Newer Spiritualism. LC 75-7392. (Perspectives in Psychical Research Ser.). 1975. reprint ed. 26.95 (*0-405-07041-1*) Ayer.

— Robert Owen, 2 vols. in 1. LC 68-9762. 1968. reprint ed. 57.50 (*0-678-00417-X*) Kelley.

— Robert Owen, 2 vols., Set. LC 78-156295. (World History Ser.: No. 48). 1971. lib. bdg. 79.95 (*0-8383-1265-9*) M S G Haskell Hse.

— Studies in Psychical Research. LC 75-7393. (Perspectives in Psychical Research Ser.). 1975. reprint ed. 39.95 (*0-405-07042-X*) Ayer.

Podmore, J., jt. auth. see Padley, F. B.

Podmore, P. C. The Slide Rule for Sea & Air Navigation. (C). 1987. 40.00 (*0-85174-213-0*, Pub. by Brwn Son Ferg) St Mut.

Podnecky-Spiegel, Janet, jt. auth. see Long, Lynellyn D.

Podobed, Vladimir V. Fundamental Astrometry: Determination of Stellar Coordinates. Vyssotsky, A. N., ed. LC 64-15810. 248p. reprint ed. pap. 70.70 (*0-317-08497-6*, 2020145) Bks Demand.

Podobedova, O., ed. Old Russian Art Problems & Authorships. 462p. 1972. 39.00 (*0-317-14268-2*, Pub. by Collets UK) Pro-Am Music.

Podoksik, Anatoly. Picasso. 1990. 39.95 (*0-8109-3705-0*) Abrams.

Podolefsky, Aaron & Brown, Peter J. Applying Anthropology: An Introductory Reader. 3rd ed. LC 93-9081. 352p. (C). 1994. pap. 18.95 (*1-55934-317-6*) Mayfield Pub.

— Applying Anthropology: An Introductory Reader. 3rd ed. LC 93-9081. (C). 1994. teacher ed, pap. write for info. (*1-55934-318-4*) Mayfield Pub.

— Applying Cultural Anthropology: An Introductory Reader. 2nd ed. LC 93-14433. (C). 1994. teacher ed, pap. write for info. (*1-55934-326-5*) Mayfield Pub.

Podoll, Brian A. Bound by Blood & Name: A History & Genealogies of the Podoll Families in Prussia & America. (Illus.). 600p. 1989. 40.00 (*0-9621809-0-4*) B A Podoll.

— Prussian Netzelanders & Other German Immigrants in Green Lake, Marquette, & Waushara Counties, Wisconsin. (Illus.). 241p. (Orig.). 1994. pap. text ed. 33.00 (*1-55613-954-3*) Heritage Bk.

Podoll, David. Small Scale Turkey Growing for the Beginner. (Shorey Lost Arts Ser.). 26p. 1975. reprint ed. pap. 2.95 (*0-8466-6044-X*, U44) Shorey.

Podolny, Walter & Scalzi, John B. Construction of Cable-Stayed Bridges. 2nd ed. LC 85-26622. 336p. 1986. text ed. 94.95 (*0-471-82655-3*) Wiley.

***Podolski, Alfred L., ed.** Massachusetts Family Law Journal. 1628p. 1985. 120.00 (*0-88063-029-9*) Michie Butterworth.

Podolski, W. F., et al. Pressurized Fluidized Bed Combustion Technology. LC 83-13215. (Energy Technology Review Series & Pollution Technology Review Ser.: Nos. 87 & 103). (Illus.). 429p. 1984. 45.00 (*0-8155-0960-X*) Noyes.

Podolsky, Baruch. A Greek-Tatar-English Dictionary. 51p. (ENG, GRE & TAR.). 1986. 49.95 (*0-8288-1648-4*, M 421) Fr & Eur.

Podolsky, Boris & Kunz, Kaiser S. Fundamentals of Electrodynamics. LC 78-78828. (Illus.). 508p. reprint ed. pap. 144.80 (*0-7837-0731-2*, 2041055) Bks Demand.

Podolsky, Edward. Red Miracle. LC 70-167402. (Essay Index Reprint Ser.). 1977. 24.95 (*0-8369-2818-0*) Ayer.

Podolsky, Joseph L. Computers & the Fortune One Thousand: Guidelines for Using PCs in the Corporate Environment. (Illus.). 304p. 1987. 19.95 (*0-13-162983-2*) P-H.

Podolsky, Kathleen M. World Point-World Line. LC 82-15164. (Illus.). 72p. (Orig.). 1982. pap. 14.95 (*0-942714-00-8*) LIM Press CA.

Podolsky, Leo, ed. Guild Repertoire: Elementary A & B. 48p. (gr. 3-12). 1960. pap. text ed. 7.95 (*0-87487-639-7*) Summy-Birchard.

— Guild Repertoire: Elementary C & D. 48p. (gr. 3-12). 1961. pap. text ed. 7.95 (*0-87487-640-0*) Summy-Birchard.

— Guild Repertoire: Intermediate A. 32p. (gr. 3-12). 1959. pap. text ed. 5.95 (*0-87487-641-9*) Summy-Birchard.

— Guild Repertoire: Intermediate B. 32p. (gr. 3-12). 1959. pap. text ed. 5.95 (*0-87487-642-7*) Summy-Birchard.

— Guild Repertoire: Intermediate C & D. 64p. (gr. 3-12). 1959. pap. text ed. 9.95 (*0-87487-643-5*) Summy-Birchard.

— Guild Repertoire: Prepatory A. (Guild Repertoire Ser.). 48p. (Orig.). (J). (gr. 6-12). 1960. pap. text ed. 7.95 (*0-87487-645-1*) Summy-Birchard.

Podolsky, Leo, ed. see Davison, June & Schaub, Ardelia.

***Podolsky, Stephen & Viswanathan, M., eds.** Secondary Diabetes: The Spectrum of the Diabetic Syndromes. fac. ed. LC 79-62976. (Illus.). 624p. Date not set. pap. 177.90 (*0-7837-7267-X*, 2047038) Bks Demand.

Podos, Batya. Ariadne. LC 80-70233. 52p. (Orig.). 1980. pap. 3.00 (*0-9603628-2-7*) Frog in Well.

Podraza, Eugene. The Memoirs of Ludwik Zychlinski: Reminiscences of the American Civil War, Siberia & Poland. LC 93-73796. (East European Monographs: No. CCCXCII). 111p. 1994. 18.00 (*0-88033-289-1*) East Eur Quarterly.

Podrazik, Walter, jt. auth. see Castleman, Harry.

Podrazik, Walter J., jt. auth. see Castleman, Harry.

Podrid, Philip J. & Kowey, Peter. Cardiac Arrhythmia: Mechanisms, Diagnosis, & Management. 1472p. 1994. 159.00 (*0-683-06905-5*) Williams & Wilkins.

Podrid, Philip J., jt. ed. see Falk, Rodney H.

Podro, Michael. The Critical Historians of Art. LC 82-4934. (Illus.). 260p. 1982. 45.00 (*0-300-02862-8*) Yale U Pr.

— The Critical Historians of Art. LC 82-4934. (Illus.). 260p. 1984. reprint ed. pap. 15.00 (*0-300-03240-4*, Y-499) Yale U Pr.

Podrug, Junius T. Frost of Heaven. 320p. 1992. 19.95 (*0-913165-70-0*) Dark Harvest.

Podulka, Ivan. Essentials: Messages in the Blood. Spelius, Carol, ed. 48p. (Orig.). 1989. pap. 7.95 (*0-941363-04-X*) Lake Shore Pub.

Poduska, Bernard. For Love & Money: A Guide to Finances & Relationships. 320p. (C). 1993. pap. 7.95 (*0-534-18852-4*) Brooks-Cole.

Podvesko, M. L., ed. English-Ukrainian Dictionary. 2nd ed. (ENG & UKR.). 42.50 (*0-685-04467-X*, 089-5) Saphrograph.

— Ukrainian-English Dictionary. 2nd ed. 42.50 (*0-87557-088-7*, 088-7) Saphrograph.

Podvesko, M. L. & Balla, M. J. English-Ukrainian Dictionary. 664p. (ENG & UKR.). 1980. 40.00 (*0-569-08127-0*, Pub. by Collets UK) St Mut.

Podwal, Mark. A Book of Hebrew Letters. LC 92-20241. 64p. 1992. 22.50 (*0-87668-317-0*) Aronson.

— The Book of Tens. LC 93-43871. (Illus.). 24p. (J). 1994. 15.00 (*0-688-12994-3*); lib. bdg. 14.93 (*0-688-12995-1*) Greenwillow.

— Golem: A Giant Made of Mud. (Illus.). 32p. (J). 1995. 15.00 (*0-688-13811-X*); lib. bdg. 14.93 (*0-688-13812-8*) Greenwillow.

— A Jewish Bestiary. (Illus.). 52p. 1984. 12.95 (*0-8276-0245-6*) JPS Phila.

Podziba, Susan L., jt. auth. see Susskind, Lawrence E.

Podzorski, A. C. An Illustrated & Annotated Check-list of Diatoms from the Black River Waterways, St. Elizabeth, Jamaica. (Bibliotheca Diatomologica Ser.: No. 7). (Illus.). 178p. 1985. lib. bdg. 39.00 (*3-7682-1422-2*) Lubrecht & Cramer.

Podzorski, A. C. & Hakansson, H. Freshwater & Marine Diatoms of Palawan (a Philippine Island) (Bibliotheca Diatomologica Ser.: Vol. 13). (Illus.). 134p. 1987. pap. text ed. 75.00 (*3-443-57004-6*) Lubrecht & Cramer.

Podzunas, Albert E., jt. auth. see Srikanth, Mokshagundam.

***Poe.** How to Profit from the Coming Russian Boom: The Insider's Guide to Business Opportunities. 1995. pap. text ed. 14.95 (*0-07-050455-5*) McGraw.

— Presenting Barbara Wersba. Date not set. 20.95 (*0-8057-4154-2*, Twayne) Macmillan.

Poe, Ann. Quilting School. LC 92-43792. (Learn-As-You-Go Guides Ser.). (Illus.). 176p. 1993. 22.00 (*0-89577-471-2*) RD Assn.

Poe, Arthur, jt. auth. see Lipschutz, Seymour.

Poe, Charles A., jt. auth. see Poe, Clarence.

Poe, Clarence & Poe, Charles A. Poe-Pourri: A North Carolina Cavalcade. LC 87-90549. (Illus.). 157p. 1987. 11.95 (*0-9618716-0-1*) Charles Poe.

***Poe, Clarence & Seymour, Betsy, eds.** True Tales of the South at War: How Soldiers Fought & Families Lived, 1861-1865. LC 94-34997. 224p. 1995. pap. text ed. 5.95 (*0-486-28451-4*) Dover.

Poe, E. Oeuvres en Prose. (FRE.). 1932. lib. bdg. 89.95 (*0-8288-3527-6*, M5172) Fr & Eur.

***Poe, Edgar A.** Poems. LC 95-15329. (Everyman's Library Pocket Poets). 1995. 10.95 (*0-679-44505-6*) Knopf.

— Tales of Mystery & Imagination. LC 94-45648. (Illus.). (J). 1995. write for info. (*1-56846-108-9*) Creative Ed.

Poe, Edgar Allan. Annabel Lee. 24p. 1987. 19.95 (*0-88776-200-X*); pap. 7.95 (*0-88776-230-1*) Tundra Bks.

— Aventures de Arthur Gordon Pym. (FRE.). 1975. pap. 11.95 (*0-7859-4040-5*) Fr & Eur.

— The Best of Poe. (Illustrated Classics Collection 3). 64p. 1994. pap. 3.60 (*1-56103-543-2*) Lake Pub Co.

— The Best of Poe. abr. ed. Farr, Naunerle, ed. (Now Age Illustrated III Ser.). (Illus.). (J). (gr. 4-12). 1977. pap. text ed. 2.95 (*0-88301-269-3*) Pendulum Pr.

— The Best of Poe Readalong. (Illustrated Classics Collection 3). 64p. 1994. audio, pap. 13.50 (*1-56103-545-9*) Lake Pub Co.

— The Black Cat. Redpath, Ann, ed. (Creative's Classic Short Stories Ser.). (Illus.). 32p. (YA). (gr. 9 up). 1985. lib. bdg. 13.95 (*0-88682-001-4*) Creative Ed.

— The Black Cat. (Illus.). 34p. 1994. pap. 7.95 (*1-55921-127-X*) Moyer Bell.

— The Black Cat. rev. ed. (Read-Along Radio Dramas Ser.). (YA). (gr. 6-12). 1985. reprint ed. boxed 35.00 (*0-685-31130-9*) Balance Pub.

— The Cask of Amontillado. LC 80-21466. (Creative's Classics Ser.). (Illus.). 32p. (YA). (gr. 9 up). 1980. lib. bdg. 13.95 (*0-87191-773-4*) Creative Ed.

— The Cask of Amontillado. LC 81-15997. (Illus.). 32p. (J). (gr. 5-10). 1982. lib. bdg. 10.79 (*0-89375-622-9*); pap. text ed. 2.95 (*0-89375-623-7*) Troll Assocs.

— Cask of Amontillado. rev. ed. (Read-along Radio Dramas Ser.). (YA). (gr. 6-12). Date not set. 35.00 (*1-878298-03-8*) Balance Pub.

— A Chapter on Autobiography. (Studies in Poe: No. 23). 1974. lib. bdg. 75.00 (*0-8383-2067-8*) M S G Haskell Hse.

— Classic Poe. (Poe Ser.). 1994. audio 16.95 (*1-883049-39-3*); audio, lib. bdg. 18.95 (*1-883049-45-8*) Commuters Lib.

— Collected Works of Edgar Allan Poe, Vol. 1: Poems. Mabbott, Thomas O., ed. LC 68-17627. (Illus.). 657p. 1969. 50.00 (*0-674-13935-6*) Belknap Pr.

— Comedies & Satires. 1987. pap. 8.95 (*0-14-039055-3*, 591, Penguin Classics) Viking Penguin.

— Complete Poems. 1992. reprint ed. lib. bdg. 21.95 (*0-89968-292-8*, Lghtyr Pr) Buccaneer Bks.

— Complete Poems of Edgar Allan Poe. 1992. 6.99 (*0-517-08245-4*) Random Hse Value.

— The Complete Stories. LC 92-52933. 944p. 1992. 20.00 (*0-679-41740-0*, Everymans Lib) Knopf.

— Complete Stories & Poems of Edgar Allan Poe. LC 66-24310. 1966. 19.95 (*0-385-07407-7*) Doubleday.

— Complete Tales & Poems (Giant) LC 75-9506. 1975. pap. 13.00 (*0-394-71678-7*, Vin) Random.

— Complete Tales & Poems of Edgar Allan Poe. LC 38-27279. 1977. 15.95 (*0-394-60408-3*, Modern Lib) Random.

— The Complete Tales & Poems of Edgar Allan Poe. LC 92-50231. 1992. 20.00 (*0-679-60007-8*, Modern Lib) Random.

— Complete Works of Edgar Allan Poe, 17 vols., Set. Harrison, James A., ed. LC 79-15593. reprint ed. 695.00 (*0-404-09400-7*) AMS Pr.

— Edgar Allan Poe. 1993. pap. 12.99 (*0-517-09290-5*) Random Hse Value.

— Edgar Allan Poe. Bagert, Brod, ed. LC 94-30774. (Poetry for Young People Ser.). (Illus.). 48p. (J). 1995. 14.95 (*0-8069-0820-3*) Sterling.

— Edgar Allan Poe. (BCL1-PS American Literature Ser.). 664p. 1993. reprint ed. lib. bdg. 109.00 (*0-7812-6999-7*) Rprt Serv.

— Edgar Allan Poe: A Collection of Stories. 352p. 1994. pap. 2.50 (*0-8125-0455-0*) Tor Bks.

— Edgar Allan Poe Letters until Now Unpublished. Stanard, Mary, ed. & intro. by. LC 72-11698. (Studies in Poe: No. 23). 1973. reprint ed. lib. bdg. 75.00 (*0-8383-1692-1*) M S G Haskell Hse.

— Edgar Allan Poe Reader. LC 92-54932. (Courage Literary Classics Ser.). 320p. 1993. 5.98 (*1-56138-277-9*) Courage Bks.

— Edgar Allan Poe Reader. write for info. (*0-318-58799-8*) S&S Trade.

— Edgar Allan Poe, Stories & Poems. (Airmont Classics Ser.). (J). (gr. 9 up). 1962. pap. 3.25 (*0-8049-0008-6*, CL-8) Airmont.

— Edgar Allan Poe's Tales of Terror. LC 90-52926. (Bullseye Chillers Ser.). (Illus.). 96p. (J). (gr. 2-6). 1991. pap. 3.50 (*0-679-81046-3*) Random Bks Yng Read.

— Eight Tales of Terror. 208p. (YA). (gr. 7-12). 1961. pap. 2.95 (*0-590-41136-5*) Scholastic Inc.

— Eighteen Best Stories of Edgar Allan Poe. Price, Vincent & Brossard, Chandler, eds. 288p. (Orig.). (gr. 7 up). 1965. mass mkt. 4.99 (*0-440-32227-8*, LE) Dell.

— Essays & Reviews. Thompson, G. R., ed. LC 83-19923. 1544p. 1984. 35.00 (*0-940450-19-4*) Library of America.

— Essential Poe. 1993. 6.98 (*0-88365-834-8*) Galahad Bks.

— Eureka. limited ed. (Illus.). 120p. 1991. 450.00 (*0-685-56698-6*) Arion Pr.

— The Fall of the House of Usher. (Illustrated Classics Ser.). 1987. lib. bdg. 13.95 (*0-88682-127-4*) Creative Ed.

— The Fall of the House of Usher. LC 81-15958. (Illus.). 32p. (J). (gr. 5-10). 1982. lib. bdg. 10.79 (*0-89375-624-5*); pap. text ed. 2.95 (*0-89375-625-3*) Troll Assocs.

— Fall of the House of Usher. 320p. 1983. reprint ed. lib. bdg. 17.95 (*0-89966-463-6*) Buccaneer Bks.

— Fall of the House of Usher & Other Tales. (J). (gr. 7). 1960. pap. 2.95 (*0-451-52174-9*, Sig Classics) NAL-Dutton.

— Fall of the House of Usher & Other Writings. Galloway, David, ed. 1986. mass mkt. 6.95 (*0-14-043291-4*, Penguin Classics) Viking Penguin.

— Forty-Two Tales. 33.95 (*0-685-10886-4*, Am Repr) Amereon Ltd.

— Ghostly Tales & Eerie Poems of Edgar Allan Poe. LC 92-30884. (Illustrated Junior Library). (Illus.). 256p. (J). 1993. 13.95 (*0-448-40533-4*, G&D) Putnam Pub Group.

— The Gold Bug. Harris, Raymond, ed. (Classics Ser.). (Illus.). 48p. (gr. 6-12). 1982. teacher ed 5.00 (*0-89061-269-2*, 481); pap. text ed. 4.00 (*0-89061-268-4*, 479); audio 13.00 (*0-89061-270-6*, 480) Jamestown Pubs.

— The Gold Bug. (Illustrated Classics Ser.). (Illus.). (gr. 7-12). 1987. pap. text ed. 3.75 (*0-13-357880-1*, 20482) Prentice ESL.

— The Gold-Bug. (Classic Short Stories Ser.). 80p. (J). (gr. 6). 1990. lib. bdg. 13.95 (*0-88682-303-X*) Creative Ed.

— The Gold-Bug & Other Tales. (Thrift Editions Ser.). 128p. (Orig.). 1991. pap. 1.00 (*0-486-26875-6*) Dover.

P Q

— Goldbug & Other Stories: The Black Cat, the Pit & the Pendulum. (Illus.). 1962. pap. 3.95 (0-8283-1437-3, 22, Intl Pocket Lib) Branden Pub Co.

— Great Short Works of Edgar Allan Poe. 1970. pap. 7.50 (0-06-083093-X, HarpT) HarpC.

— Letters & Documents in the Enoch Pratt Free Library. Bd. with Merlin & Recollections of Edgar A. Poe. LC 41-10640. LC 41-10640. 1978. 50.00 (0-8201-1199-6) Schol Facsimiles.

— Letters of Edgar Allan Poe, 2 vols., Set. Ostrom, John, ed. LC 66-20025. 731p. 1966. reprint ed. 75.00 (0-87752-085-2) Gordian.

— The Man of the Crowd. (Poe Ser.). 1994. audio 16.95 (1-883049-38-5); audio, lib. bdg. 18.95 (1-883049-44-X) Commuters Lib.

— Marginalia: With an Introduction by John Carl Miller. LC 80-22585. (Illus.). 255p. reprint ed. pap. 72.70 (0-8357-3133-2, 2039396) Bks Demand.

— The Masque of the Red Death. (Classic Short Stories Ser.). (J). 1991. lib. bdg. 13.95 (0-88682-477-X) Creative Ed.

— The Masque of the Red Death. LC 81-15959. (Illus.). 32p. (J). (gr. 5-10). 1982. lib. bdg. 10.79 (0-89375-620-2); pap. text ed. 2.95 (0-89375-621-0) Troll Assocs.

— Masque of the Red Death. Harris, Raymond, ed. (Classics Ser.). (Illus.). 48p. (Orig.). (gr. 6-12). 1982. teacher ed 5.00 (0-89061-272-2, 477); pap. text ed. 4.00 (0-89061-271-4, 475); audio 13.00 (0-89061-273-0, 476) Jamestown Pubs.

— The Narrative of Arthur Gordon Pym of Nantucket & Related Tales. LC 93-11717. (World's Classics Ser.). 280p. 1994. pap. 5.95 (0-19-282844-4) OUP.

— The Narrative of Arthur Gordon Pym of Nantucket & Related Tales. Beaver, Harold, ed. (English Library). 320p. 1976. mass mkt. 8.95 (0-14-043097-0) Viking Penguin.

— Oeuvres en Prose: Histoires Extraordinaires, Adventures d'Arthur Gordon Pym, Eureka, etc. Baudelaire, Charles P., tr. 1184p. 41.50 (0-686-56551-7) Fr & Eur.

— The Pit & the Pendulum. (Classic Short Stories on Tape Ser.). (YA). (gr. 8-12). 1993. 35.00 (1-878298-11-9) Balance Pub.

— The Pit & the Pendulum. (Creative's Classics Ser.). (Illus.). 48p. (YA). (gr. 9 up). 1980. lib. bdg. 13.95 (0-87191-771-8) Creative Ed.

— The Pit & the Pendulum. Harris, Raymond, ed. (Classics Ser.). (Illus.). 48p. (gr. 6-12). 1982. teacher ed 5.00 (0-89061-266-8, 473); pap. text ed. 4.00 (0-89061-265-X, 471); digital audio 13.00 (0-89061-267-6, 472) Jamestown Pubs.

— The Pit & the Pendulum. LC 81-16432. (Illus.). 32p. (J). (gr. 5-10). 1982. lib. bdg. 10.79 (0-89375-626-1); pap. text ed. 2.95 (0-89375-627-X) Troll Assocs.

— Les Poemes d'Edgar Poe. Mallarme, Stephane, tr. LC 77-11473. (Illus.). (FRE.). reprint ed. 57.50 (0-404-16335-1) AMS Pr.

— Poems. (BCL1-PS American Literature Ser.). 332p. 1992. reprint ed. lib. bdg. 89.00 (0-7812-6831-1) Rprt Serv.

— Poems of Edgar Allan Poe. LC 94-42278. 1995. pap. 8.99 (0-517-12285-5) Random Hse Value.

— The Poems of Edgar Allan Poe. Stovall, Floyd, ed. LC 65-23455. 400p. reprint ed. pap. 114.00 (0-7837-1246-4, 2041383) Bks Demand.

— The Poems of Edgar Allan Poe. Mabbott, Thomas O., ed. LC 79-28853. 511p. reprint ed. pap. 145.70 (0-7837-4168-5, 2059017) Bks Demand.

— Poetry & Tales. Quinn, Patrick F., ed. Incl. Eureka. LC 83-19931. 1984. (0-318-63077-X); LC 83-19931. 1408p. 1984. 35.00 (0-940450-18-6) Library of America.

— Politian: An Unfinished Tragedy. (BCL1-PS American Literature Ser.). 89p. 1992. reprint ed. lib. bdg. 59.00 (0-7812-6832-X) Rprt Serv.

— Portable Poe. Stern, Phillip V., ed. (Portable Library: No. 12). 1977. pap. 13.95 (0-14-015012-9, Penguin Bks) Viking Penguin.

— The Purloined Letter. LC 86-4156. (Creative's Classic Short Stories Ser.). 48p. (YA). (gr. 9 up). 1986. lib. bdg. 13.95 (0-88682-061-8) Creative Ed.

— The Raven. (Illus.). 32p. reprint ed. pap. 4.95 (0-9631135-3-4) Malan Class.

— Raven & Other Favorite Poems. 1991. pap. 1.00 (0-486-26685-0) Dover.

— The Raven & Other Poems. 80p. (YA). (gr. 7 up). 1992. pap. 2.95 (0-590-45260-6, Apple Classics) Scholastic Inc.

— The Raven & Three Tales of Terror. LC 89-42997. (Miniature Editions Ser.). 96p. 1989. 4.95 (0-89471-757-X) Running Pr.

— The Science Fiction of Edgar Allan Poe. Beaver, Harold, ed. (English Library). 1976. pap. 9.95 (0-14-043106-3, Penguin Classics) Viking Penguin.

— Selected Poems & Essays. Gray, Richard, ed. 320p. 1993. pap. 6.95 (0-460-87261-3, Everyman's Classic Lib) C E Tuttle.

— The Selected Poetry & Prose. Mabbott, Thomas O., ed. (Modern Library College Editions). 1951. pap. text ed. write for info. (0-07-553641-2) McGraw.

— Selected Stories of Poe. large type ed. (Large Print Ser.). 600p. 1993. reprint ed. lib. bdg. 22.00 (0-939495-47-3) North Bks.

— Selected Tales. Symons, Julian, ed. (World's Classics Paperback Ser.). 1980. pap. 4.95 (0-19-281522-9) OUP.

— Selected Tales of Edgar Allan Poe. LC 90-50620. 336p. 1991. pap. 11.50 (0-679-72524-5, Vin) Random.

— Selected Works of Edgar Allan Poe. (World's Great Bks.). 406p. 1991. 19.95 (1-879329-05-0) Time Warner Libraries.

— Selected Writings of Edgar Allan Poe. Davidson, E. H., ed. LC 56-13895. (C). 1956. pap. 9.96 (0-395-05110-X, Hill Stead Mus) HM.

— Tales of Edgar Allan Poe. (Classics - Bonded Leather Fibers Ser.). 850p. 1990. 18.95 (0-681-40999-1) Longmeadow Pr.

— Tales of Edgar Allan Poe. LC 80-14064. (Short Classics Ser.). (Illus.). 48p. (J). (gr. 4 up). 1980. lib. bdg. 22.80 (0-8172-1662-6) Raintree Steck-V.

— Tales of Mystery & Imagination. Clarke, Graham, ed. 576p. 1993. pap. 6.95 (0-460-87342-3, Everyman's Classic Lib) C E Tuttle.

— Tales of Mystery & Imagination. LC 94-45648. (Illus.). (J). 1995. write for info. (0-614-03644-5) Creative Ed.

— Tales of Mystery & Imagination. LC 88-40069. 304p. 1988. 25.00 (0-89296-350-6) Mysterious Pr.

— Tales of Mystery & Imagination. 1994. pap. 9.99 (0-517-11817-3) Random Hse Value.

— Tales of Mystery & Imagination. 1981. reprint ed. lib. bdg. 27.95 (0-89966-434-2) Buccaneer Bks.

— Tales of Mystery & Terror. 18.95 (0-8488-1127-5) Amereon Ltd.

— Tales of Terror & Detection. (Thrift Editions Ser.). 1995. pap. 1.00 (0-486-28744-0) Dover.

— The Tell-Tale Heart. (Creative's Classics Ser.). (Illus.). 32p. (YA). (gr. 9 up). 1980. lib. bdg. 13.95 (0-87191-772-6) Creative Ed.

— The Tell-Tale Heart. Harris, Raymond, ed. (Classics Ser.). (Illus.). 48p. (gr. 6-12). 1982. teacher ed 5.00 (0-89061-263-3, 469); pap. text ed. 4.00 (0-89061-262-5, 467); audio 13.00 (0-89061-264-1, 468) Jamestown Pubs.

— The Tell-Tale Heart. rev. ed. (Read-Along Radio Dramas Ser.). (YA). (gr. 6-12). 1993. reprint ed. boxed 35.00 (1-878298-04-6) Balance Pub.

— The Tell-Tale Heart & Other Writings. 432p. (gr. 7-12). 1983. pap. 4.95 (0-553-21228-1, Bantam Classics) Bantam.

— The Unabridged Edgar Allan Poe. LC 83-16023. (Illus.). 1280p. (Orig.). 1983. pap. 16.95 (0-89471-233-0) Running Pr.

— The Unknown Poe. Foye, Raymond, ed. LC 80-2431. 1980. pap. 7.95 (0-87286-110-4) City Lights.

— Works of Edgar Allan Poe. 1990. 15.99 (0-517-05358-6) Random Hse Value.

— Works of Edgar Allan Poe, 10 vols, Set. Stedman, Edmund C. & Woodberry, George E., eds. LC 71-169773. (Select Bibliographies Reprint Ser.). reprint ed. 250.00 (0-8369-5993-0) Ayer.

— The Works of Edgar Allan Poe: With a Study of His Life & Writings by Charles Baudelaire. Curwen, H., tr. LC 77-11472. reprint ed. 42.50 (0-404-16334-3) AMS Pr.

***Poe, Edgar Allan & Irving, Washington.** Poe & Irving. 1995. audio 18.95 (1-883049-62-8) Commuters Lib.

Poe, Edgar Allan & Wilson, Gahan. The Raven & Other Poems. (Classics Illustrated Ser.). (Illus.). 52p. (YA). Date not set. pap. 4.95 (1-57209-000-6) Classics Int Ent.

Poe, Edgar Allan, et al. The Fall of the House of Usher. (Classics Illustrated Ser.). (Illus.). 52p. (YA). Date not set. pap. 4.95 (1-57209-014-6) Classics Int Ent.

***Poe, Edgar Allen.** The Fall of the House of Usher. Date not set. 3.00 (0-87129-583-0, F56) Dramatic Pub.

Poe, Elizabeth A. Focus on Relationships. (Teenage Perspectives Ser.). 257p. 1993. lib. bdg. 39.50 (0-87436-672-0) ABC-CLIO.

— Focus on Sexuality. (Teenage Perspectives Ser.). 225p. (J). 1990. lib. bdg. 39.50 (0-87436-116-8) ABC-CLIO.

Poe, Elizabeth W. From Poetry to Prose in Old Provencal. LC 83-50518. 133p. (ENG & PRO.). 1984. 16.95 (0-917786-33-5) Summa Pubns.

Poe, Elmer, ed. Study Guide for the CET Test-Computer Option & Practice Test. 4th ed. 31p. 1993. pap. 10.00 (0-318-17467-7) Intl Soc Cert Elect.

Poe, Francis R. Teaching & Performing Renaissance Choral Music: A Guide for Conductors & Performers. LC 93-23597. 227p. 1994. 37.50 (0-8108-2778-6); pap. 25.00 (0-8108-2886-3) Scarecrow.

Poe, Jerry B. An Introduction to the American Business Enterprise. 7th ed. 608p. (C). 1989. text ed. 50.95 (0-256-07347-3) Irwin.

— An Introduction to the American Business Enterprise. 7th ed. (C). 1989. student ed 18.50 (0-256-07366-X) Irwin.

Poe, Jerry B., jt. auth. see Gallinger, George W.

Poe, Lenora M. Black Grandparents As Parents. (Orig.). 1992. pap. text ed. 13.95 (0-9633992-0-9) L M Poe.

Poe, Lori M. Dynamic Keys to Self-Healing. LC 91-92914. 233p. pap. 35.00 (0-9624804-5-2, Pub. by IPM Hse UK) St Mut.

— Journeys to Worlds Beyond. rev. ed. LC 91-92915. 136p. pap. 19.95 (0-9624804-3-6) Place Light.

— Milestones to God: Healing Mind & Emotions. LC 89-92799. (Orig.). 1990. pap. 17.45 (0-9624804-0-1) Place Light.

— Teach Me the Way. LC 91-92913. 131p. pap. 19.95 (0-9624804-7-9) Place Light.

Poe, Margie. The No-Cooking Cookbook for Kids. (Illus.). (J). (gr. k-6). 1985. pap. 4.95 (0-936985-75-5, 1096A) Kidsmart.

Poe, Marian M. A Family of Strangers. 320p. 1984. pap. 3.50 (0-8439-2156-0) Dorchester Pub Co.

Poe, Randy. Music Publishing: A Songwriter's Guide. 144p. 1990. pap. 18.95 (0-89879-415-3) Writers Digest.

Poe, Richard. How to Profit from the Coming Russian Boom: The Insider's Guide to Business Opportunities & Survival on the Frontiers of Capitalism. 320p. 1993. text ed. 24.95 (0-07-050450-4) McGraw.

— Wave Three: The New Era in Network Marketing. LC 94-9089. 1994. write for info. (1-55958-501-3) Prima Pub.

***Poe, Robert.** My Child Is Missing: How to Protect Your Child from Abduction & What to Do Should It Happen. Andres, Stephanie, ed. (Orig.). 1995. pap. 8.95 (0-9614914-4-2) Pax Pub.

Poe, Robert H. & Israel, Robert H., eds. Problems in Pulmonary Medicine for the Primary Physician. LC 82-8972. (Illus.). 426p. reprint ed. pap. 121.50 (0-7837-1494-7, 2057190) Bks Demand.

Poe, Roy W. Business Communications: A Problem-Solving Approach. 3rd ed. 416p. (C). 1984. teacher ed 12.10 (1-56118-316-4); student ed 8.25 (1-56118-314-8); pap. text ed. 27.95 (1-56118-315-6) Paradigm MN.

— The McGraw-Hill Handbook of Business Letters. 2nd ed. 320p. 1988. text ed. 49.50 (0-07-050369-9) McGraw.

— The McGraw-Hill Handbook of Business Letters. 3rd ed. LC 93-24986. 1993. text ed. 59.50 (0-07-050425-3) McGraw.

— The McGraw-Hill Handbook of Business Letters. 3rd ed. LC 93-24986. 1993. pap. text ed. 19.95 (0-07-050451-2) McGraw.

***Poe, Roy W. & Fruehling, Rosemary T.** Business Communication: A Case Method Approach. LC 94-21339. 1989. teacher ed, text ed. 8.00 (1-56118-338-5) Paradigm MN.

— Business Communication: A Case Method Approach. 5th ed. LC 94-21339. 425p. 1989. text ed. 25.95 (1-56118-337-7) Paradigm MN.

— Business Communication: A Problem-Solving Approach. 4th ed. 416p. (C). 1989. text ed. 29.95 (0-07-050443-1) McGraw.

— Business Communication: A Problem-Solving Approach. 4th ed. 406p. 1989. teacher ed 8.00 (1-56118-318-0); student ed 8.45 (1-56118-313-X); pap. text ed. 26.50 (1-56118-317-2) Paradigm MN.

Poe, Roy W., et al. Getting Invloved with Business. (Illus.). 576p. (gr. 9-10). 1981. text ed. 22.60 (0-07-050335-4) McGraw.

Poe, Shelly & Keys, Kevin. A Big Dream, a Little Luck: West Virginia Football 1994. 48p. 1994. 19.95 (1-885367-00-7) WVU Dept Intercollegiate.

Poe, Sidney. The Gospel According to Mark: A Commentary. LC 94-15350. 400p. (Orig.). 1994. pap. 10.99 (1-56722-024-X) Word Aflame.

Poe, W. Old Person in Your Home. 1986. pap. 2.45 (0-684-71871-5, Scribners) S&S Trade.

Poe, William A. Green W. Hartsfield, A Biography: Eighteen Eighty-Three to Eighteen Ninety-Six. LC 84-61196. (Illus.). 228p. 1984. 22.50 (0-917898-12-5) NSU Pr LA.

Poebel, Arno. Babylonian Legal & Business Documents: From the Time of the First Dynasty of Babylon; Chiefly from Nippur. (University of Pennsylvania, Babylonian Expedition, Series A: Cuneiform Texts: Vol. 6, Pt. 2). 251p. reprint ed. pap. 71.60 (0-8357-5940-7, 2052014) Bks Demand.

— Grammatical Texts. LC 15-2790. (University of Pennsylvania, the University Museum, Publications of the Babylonian Section: Vol. 6, No. 1). 122p. reprint ed. pap. 34.80 (0-317-28575-0, 2052025) Bks Demand.

— Historical & Grammatical Texts. LC 15-2790. (University of Pennsyvania, the University Museum, Publications of the Babylonian Section: Vol. 5). 136p. reprint ed. pap. 38.80 (0-317-28574-2, 2052024) Bks Demand.

— Historical Texts. LC 15-2790. (University of Pennsylvania, the University Museum, Publications of the Babylonian Section: Vol. 4, No. 1). 242p. reprint ed. pap. 69.00 (0-317-28573-4, 2052023) Bks Demand.

Poeck, Klaus. Diagnostic Decisions in Neurology. LC 85-18801. 145p. 1985. 39.00 (0-387-15779-4) Spr-Verlag.

Poeck, Klaus, et al, eds. New Trends in Diagnosis & Management of Stroke. (Illus.). 169p. 1988. pap. 33.10 (0-387-18369-8) Spr-Verlag.

Poedjosoedarmo, Soepomo, jt. auth. see Wolff, John U.

Poeg, Federico, jt. auth. see Hildebrand, Peter.

Poehling, Gary G., et al, eds. Arthroscopy of the Wrist & Elbow. LC 93-42821. 200p. 1995. 98.00 (0-7817-0194-5) Raven.

Poehlman, J. M. Mungbean. (C). 1991. text ed. 27.50 (81-204-0590-0, Pub. by Oxford IBH II) S Asia.

Poehlman, John M. Breeding Field Crops. 3rd ed. LC 93-44366. 740p. (C). 1994. 54.95 (0-8138-2426-5) Iowa St U Pr.

— The Mungbean. 375p. (C). 1991. text ed. 58.00 (0-8133-1378-3) Westview.

***Poehlman, John M. & Sleper, David A.** Breeding Field Crops. 4th ed. LC 94-36673. (Illus.). 432p. 1995. text ed. 62.95 (0-8138-2427-3) Iowa St U Pr.

— Breeding Field Crops. 4th ed. LC 94-36673. 1995. write for info. (0-8138-2437-0) Iowa St U Pr.

Poehlman, William R., tr. see Lohse, Eduard.

Poehlmann, JoAnna. Post Impressions: Cancelling Out. (Illus.). 148p. 1991. 10.95 (1-55859-233-4) Abbeville Pr.

— Post Impressions: Food for Thought. (Illus.). 148p. 1991. 10.95 (1-55859-232-6) Abbeville Pr.

— Post Impressions: Love Letters. (Illus.). 148p. 1991. 10.95 (1-55859-231-8) Abbeville Pr.

Poehlmann, William R., tr. see Lohfink, Gerhard.

Poekel, Wilhelm. Philologisches Schriftsteller Lexikon. 2nd ed. 1974. 95.00 (0-7859-0844-7, M-7582, Pub. by Wissenschaftliche Buchgesellschaft) Fr & Eur.

Poel, William. Shakespeare in the Theatre. LC 70-143343. reprint ed. 11.50 (0-404-05067-0) AMS Pr.

— Shakespeare in the Theatre. LC 67-31456. 1972. reprint ed. 19.95 (0-405-08859-0) Ayer.

Poeldinger, W., ed. Somatisierte Angst und Depressivitaet. (Illus.). vi, 136p. 1984. 32.00 (3-8055-3844-8) S Karger.

Poeldinger, W. & Taeuber, K., eds. Nomifensine-Clinical & Experimental Investigation. (Journal: International Pharmacopsychiatry: Vol. 17, Suppl. 1, 1982). iv, 148p. 1982. pap. 38.50 (3-8055-3585-6) S Karger.

Poeldinger, W., jt. ed. see Kielholz, P.

Poelker, Kathy. Amazing Musical Moments. (Illus.). 48p. 1985. teacher ed 7.95 (0-945405-06-5) LAM Co.

— At the Firehouse. Judge, Matt, ed. (Rhythms to Reading Ser.). (Illus.). 8p. (Orig.). (J). (ps-3). 1988. pap. text ed. 15.00 (0-929842-00-6) Hawthorne Pubs.

— Look at Me. (Illus.). 64p. 1987. teacher ed 7.95 (0-945405-00-6) LAM Co.

— Look at my World. (Illus.). 48p. 1983. teacher ed 7.95 (0-945405-04-9) LAM Co.

— Look at the Holidays. (Illus.). 64p. (J). (ps-4). 1988. reprint ed. teacher ed 7.95 (0-317-91200-3) LAM Co.

— One Little Drop of Sunshine. Judge, Matt, ed. (Rhythms to Reading Ser.). (Illus.). 8p. (Orig.). (J). (ps-3). 1988. pap. text ed. 15.00 (0-929842-01-4) Hawthorne Pubs.

Poellet, Luther, tr. see Quenstedt, J. A.

***Poellner, Peter.** Nietzsche & Metaphysics. (Oxford Philosophical Monographs). 352p. 1995. 56.00 (0-19-823517-8) OUP.

Poellot, Luther, tr. see Chemitz, Martin.

***Poelman, Anne O.** The Simeon Solution: One Woman's Spiritual Odyssey. 1995. 13.95 (0-87579-967-1) Deseret Bk.

Poelman, Cathrine. Since Stephen. abr. ed. 160p. 1995. pap. 7.95 (1-56901-438-8) NW Pub.

Poelsema, B. & Comsa, G. Scattering of Thermal Energy Atoms from Disordered Surfaces. (Tracts in Modern Physics Ser.: Vol. 115). (Illus.). 170p. 1989. 73.00 (0-387-50358-7) Spr-Verlag.

***Poelstra, Sharon R., ed.** Lifetime Memories, 1995-96: Summer Missions Handbook. rev. ed. 1995. pap. text ed. 5.00 (0-9621469-3-5) Biola Student Missionary.

Poelt, J. Bestimmungsschluessel Europaeischer Flechten. (Illus.). 1969. pap. 56.00 (3-7682-0159-7) Lubrecht & Cramer.

Poelt, J. & Hinteregger, Erika. Beitraege zur Kenntnis der Flechtenflora des Himalaya. VII Die Gattungen Caloplaca, Fulgensis, und Ioplaca: (Mit Englischem Bestimmungsschluessel) (Bibliotheca Lichenologica Ser.: Vol. 50). (Illus.). 247p. (GER.). 1993. pap. text ed. 78.50 (3-443-58029-7, Pub. by Cramer-Borntraeger GW) Lubrecht & Cramer.

Poelt, J. & Vezda, A. Bestimmungsschluessel Europaeischer Flechten. (Bibliotheca Lichenologica Ser.: No. 9, suppl. I). 1977. lib. bdg. 32.50 (3-7682-1162-2) Lubrecht & Cramer.

— Bestimmungsschluessel Europaeischer Flechten, Suppl. II. (Bibliotheca Lichenologica Ser.: No. 16). 390p. (GER.). 1981. text ed. 52.00 (3-7682-1312-9) Lubrecht & Cramer.

Poelt, J., jt. auth. see Mayrhofer, H.

Poem & the World Editorial Committee, jt. auth. see International Poets.

***Poems, C. K.** Selected Poems. 290p. Date not set. 211.00 (0-374-52455-6) FS&G.

Poenaru, Dorin N. & Ivascu, Marin S., eds. Particle Emission from Nuclei, 3 vols., Vol. I: Nuclear Deformation Energy. 256p. 1988. 152.00 (0-8493-4634-7, QC793, CRC Reprint) Franklin.

— Particle Emission from Nuclei, 3 vols., Vol. II: Alpha, Proton, & Heavy Ion Radioactives. 272p. 1988. 155.00 (0-8493-4635-5, QC793, CRC Reprint) Franklin.

— Particle Emission from Nuclei, 3 vols., Vol. III: Fission & Beta-Delayed Decay Modes. 224p. 1988. 147.00 (0-8493-4636-3, QC793, CRC Reprint) Franklin.

Poepoe, Karen, jt. auth. see Kahalewai, Marilyn.

Poeppig, E. & Endlicher, S. Nova Genera Ac Species Plantarum Quas in Regno Chilensi, Peruviano & in Terra Amazonica Annis 1827-32: 1835-45. 1968. 335.00 (3-7682-0549-5) Lubrecht & Cramer.

***Poerksen, Uwe.** Plastic Words: The Tyranny of Expertise. Mason, Jutta & Cayley, David, trs. LC 94-44589. 1995. 19.95 (0-271-01476-8) Pa St U Pr.

Poerschke, R., jt. ed. see Madelung, O.

Poertner, jt. auth. see Friesen, Barbara J.

Poertner, Dale F., ed. see Schmidt, Stan.

Poertner, John, jt. auth. see Rapp, Charles A.

Poeschel, E. & Unger, H., eds. Colloquium Uber Schaltkreis- und Schaltwerk Theorie: 1st Colloquim Bonn 1960. (International Series of Numerical Mathematics: No. 3). 198p. (GER.). 1980. 28.75 (0-8176-0187-2) Birkhauser.

Poeschke, Joachim. Donatello & His World: Italian Renaissance Sculpture. Stockman, Russell, tr. LC 92-38115. 1993. 95.00 (0-8109-3211-3) Abrams.

— Die Sieneser Domkanzel des Nicola Pisano. LC 72-81565. (Beitraege zur Kunstgeschichte Ser.: Vol. 9). (C). 1973. 62.35 (3-11-003961-3) De Gruyter.

Poeschl, Viktor. Die Dichtkunst Virgils. 3rd rev. ed. (C). 1977. 46.15 (3-11-006885-0) De Gruyter.

Poesnecker, G. E. Adrenal Syndrome. 186p. (Orig.). 1983. pap. 7.95 (0-916285-25-1) Humanitarian.

— Creative Sex. 62p. (Orig.). 1976. pap. 2.00 (0-916285-26-X) Humanitarian.

— It's Only Natural. 346p. (Orig.). pap. 6.95 (0-916285-30-8) Humanitarian.

Poesnecker, Gerald E. Chronic Fatigue Unmasked: What You & Your Doctor Should Know about the Adrenal Syndrome, Today's Most Misunderstood, Mistreated & Ignored Health Problem. 204p. 1994. pap. 12.00 (0-916285-39-1) Humanitarian.

— A Guide for the New Renaissance. LC 86-63004. 184p. 1986. 16.95 (0-318-23247-2); pap. 10.95 (0-318-23248-0) Randolph Pr.

Poesse, Walter. Internal-Line-Structure of Thirty Autography Plays of Lope De Vega. LC 72-6787. (Studies in Drama: No. 39). (C). 1972. reprint ed. lib. bdg. 42.95 (0-8383-1655-7) M S G Haskell Hse.

Poessehl, G. L. South Asian Archaeology Studies. 276p. (C). 1992. text ed. 49.00 (1-881570-17-7) Intl Sci Pub.

Poesy, SherryLynn. Book of Lives: Poetry by SherryLynn Poesy. LC 93-14296. 48p. 1993. pap. text ed. 12.00 (0-934172-26-9) WIM Pubns.

An Asterisk (*) at the beginning of an entry indicates that the title is appearing in BIP for the first time.

Poet of Pearl. Cleaness: An Alliterative Tripartite Poem on the Deluge, the Destruction of Sodom, & the Death of Belshazzar, 2 vols., Set. (BCL1-PR English Literature Ser.). 1992. reprint ed. lib. bdg. 150.00 (0-7812-7181-9) Rprt Serv.
— Patience, An Alliterative Version of Jonah. (BCL1-PR English Literature Ser.). 77p. 1992. reprint ed. lib. bdg. 59.00 (0-7812-7190-8) Rprt Serv.
Poet, Ron. The Programmers Guide to C Plus Plus. 208p. (C). 1990. pap. text ed. 90.00 (0-273-03162-7, Pub. by Pitman Pubng UK) St Mut.
Poethig, Eunice B., ed. Everybody, I Love You: A Philippine Folk Song Book. 1971. 3.50 (0-686-09444-1, Pub. by New Day Pub PH) Cellar.
Poethig, Eunice B., jt. auth. see Palm, James E.
Poeton, E., ed. see Bonham, Thomas.
***Poetry Harbor Staff, ed.** Poets Who Haven't Moved to St. Paul. 80p. (Orig.). 1991. pap. 7.95 (0-9641986-1-4) Poetry Harbor.
Poetry Society of Michigan. Golden Song. LC 84-82139. 160p. 1985. write for info. (0-8187-0056-4) Harlo Press.
Poets & Writers, Inc. Staff, et al. Writer's Guide to Copyright. 2nd ed. (Illus.). 64p. 1990. pap. 6.95 (0-913734-21-7) Poets & Writers.
Poets House Staff. Directory of American Poetry Books. LC 93-17778. 96p. (Orig.). 1993. pap. 8.95 (1-55921-099-0, Asphodel Pr) Moyer Bell.
— Directory of American Poetry Books. 2nd ed. LC 93-17778. 160p. (Orig.). 1994. pap. 9.95 (1-55921-122-9, Asphodel Pr) Moyer Bell.
Poets of Little Sister Publications Staff. Songs of Sacramento. Takseena, Ana, ed. (Illus.). 43p. (Orig.). 1987. pap. text ed. 4.00 (0-944667-01-5) Little Sister Pubns.
Poet's Workshop Staff. Be Somebody Be Yourself Poetry, Bk. 1. rev. ed. 11p. (YA). (gr. 7-12). 1994. pap. 4.50 (0-913597-98-8) Prosperity & Profits.
— Black American History: Rap & Rhyme. 8p. (YA). (gr. 6-12). 1989. pap. text ed. 2.50 (0-913597-53-8) Prosperity & Profits.
Poett, A. Dibblee. Rancho San Julian: The Story of a California Ranch & Its People. 2nd ed. (Illus.). 240p. 1993. reprint ed. pap. 14.95 (1-56474-080-3) Fithian Pr.
Poetzsch, Eleonore, jt. ed. see Lucke, Eva M.
Poewe, Karla, ed. Charismatic Christianity As a Global Culture. LC 94-6874. 290p. 1994. 34.95 (0-87249-996-0) U of SC Pr.
Poewe, Karla, jt. auth. see Hexham, Irving.
Poewe, Karla O. Childhood in Germany During World War II: The Story of a Little Girl. LC 88-8956. (Studies in German Thought & History: Vol. 4). 230p. 1989. lib. bdg. 89.95 (0-88946-354-9) E Mellen.
— The Namibian Herero: A History of Their Psychosocial Disintegration & Survival. LC 85-2991. (African Studies: Vol. 1). (Illus.). 364p. 1985. lib. bdg. 99.95 (0-88946-176-7) E Mellen.
— Religion, Kinship & Economy in Luapula, Zambia. LC 88-26643. (African Studies: Vol. 9). 253p. 1989. lib. bdg. 89.95 (0-88946-190-2) E Mellen.
Poey, Delia & Suarez, Virgil, eds. Iguana Dreams: New Latino Fiction. LC 92-52628. 1992. pap. 13.00 (0-06-096917-2, PL) HarpC.
— Iguana Dreams: New Latino Fiction. 400p. 1994. lib. bdg. 31.00x (0-8095-9142-1) Borgo Pr.
***Poeze, Harry A., comp.** Politiek-Politionelle Overzichten van Nederlandsch-Indie, Deel IV, 1935-41. (Illus.). 583p. (Orig.). 1995. pap. 38.50x (90-6718-051-3, Pub. by KLTV Pr NE) Cellar.
Poff, Frances, jt. ed. see Zimman, Jonathan F.
Poff, Ima, ed. see White, Carter.
Poff, Jan-Michael, ed. Addresses & Public Papers of James Grubbs Martin, Governor of North Carolina, 1985-1989 Vol. 1, 1985-1989, Vol. 1. (Illus.). 1089p. 1992. 3.00 (0-86526-250-0) NC Archives.
Poff, Martha G. I Speak What I Am: Memoirs of a Mountain Hillbilly. rev. ed. (Illus.). 315p. (C). 1989. 12.00 (0-685-28966-4) M G Poff.
Poffenbarger, jt. auth. see McCurnin, Dennis M.
Poffenberg, Nancy & Bane, Rosemary. Instant Recorder Package 2. (Illus.). 32p. (Orig.). (J). (gr. 3-6). 1989. pap. 11.95 (0-938293-17-6) Fun Pub OH.
Poffenberger, A. T., ed. James McKeen Cattell: Man of Science. LC 73-2984. (Classics in Psychology Ser.). 1976. reprint ed. 40.95 (0-405-05155-7) Ayer.
Poffenberger, Donald L., jt. auth. see Campagna, Daniel S.
Poffenberger, John D. How to Coach Winning Soccer: For the Mom or Dad Who Is Suddenly Coach. Poffenberger, Nancy, ed. 24p. (Orig.). 1987. pap. 5.95 (0-938293-50-8) Fun Pub OH.
***Poffenberger, Mark, ed.** Keepers of the Forest: Land Management Alternatives in Southeast Asia. fac. ed. LC 89-38879. (Kumarian Press Library of Management for Development). (Illus.). 319p. 1994. pap. 91.00 (0-7837-7577-6, 2047330) Bks Demand.
Poffenberger, Nancy. Instant Fun with Bells & Xylophones. 32p. 1986. pap. 3.95 (0-938293-00-1) Fun Pub OH.
— Instant Fun With Sacred Songs. 24p. (J). (gr. k up). reprint ed. pap. 5.95 (0-938293-27-3) Fun Pub OH.
— Instant Organ Fun for Christmas. 24p. pap. 5.95 (0-938293-29-X) Fun Pub OH.
— Instant Piano Fun, Bk. 2. 62p. 1975. pap. 10.95 (0-938293-26-5) Fun Pub OH.
— Instant Piano Fun: Book One. 34p. (J). (gr. 4). 1985. reprint ed. pap. 10.95 (0-938293-25-7) Fun Pub OH.
— Instant Piano Fun for Christmas. 24p. 1986. reprint ed. pap. text ed. 10.95 (0-938293-28-1) Fun Pub OH.
— Instant Recorder Fun: Book One. 32p. (J). (gr. 4). 1986. reprint ed. pap. 4.95 (0-938293-14-1) Fun Pub OH.
— Instant Recorder Fun Package 1 (recorder & book) 32p. (J). (ps-3). 1986. reprint ed. 11.95 (0-938293-15-X) Fun Pub OH.
— Now! Instant Keyboard Fun I. 32p. (J). (gr. 4 up). 1985. reprint ed. pap. 4.95 (0-938293-39-7) Fun Pub OH.
— Now! The Teacher Can Play. 32p. (Orig.). 1985. reprint ed. pap. text ed. 3.50 (0-938293-40-0) Fun Pub OH.
— Xylo-Fun I, Vol. 1. 24p. 1995. pap. 8.95 (0-938293-13-3) Fun Pub OH.
Poffenberger, Nancy & Bane, Rosemary C. Instant Recorder Fun Book, No. 2. 32p. (Orig.). 1988. pap. 5.95 (0-938293-16-8) Fun Pub OH.
Poffenberger, Nancy, ed. see Poffenberger, John D.
Poffenberger, Thomas. Fertility & Family Life in an Indian Village. LC 75-9025. (Michigan Papers on South & Southeast Asia: No. 10). (Illus.). xii, 114p. (Orig.). 1975. pap. 3.00 (0-89148-010-2) Ctr S&SE Asian.
Poffenberger, Thomas & Sebaly, Kim. The Socialization of Family Size Values: Youth & Family Planning in an Indian Village. LC 76-53996. (Michigan Papers on South & Southeast Asia: No. 12). (Illus.). xiv, 159p. (Orig.). 1976. pap. 3.00 (0-89148-012-9) Ctr S&SE Asian.
Poffo. Leaping Lanny Wrestling with Ryme. 1988. pap. 6.95 (0-9619169-0-7) Leilo Pub.
Poffo, Lanny. Leaping Lanny! Wrestling with Rhyme. LC 87-51044. (Illus.). 144p. 6.95 (0-318-23404-1) Leilo Pub.
Pogacar, Timothy, jt. auth. see Martin-Reynolds, Joanne.
Poganski, Donald J. Fifty Object Lessons. (J). (gr. 2-5). 1967. 5.99 (0-570-03172-9, 12-2282) Concordia.
— Forty Object Lessons. LC 72-86233. 160p. 1973. pap. 5.99 (0-570-03148-6, 12-2283) Concordia.
Pogany, Istvan, jt. auth. see Perrott, David L.
Pogany, Istvan S. The Arab League & Peacekeeper in the Lebanon. LC 87-12873. 224p. 1988. text ed. 45.00 (0-312-00782-5) St Martin.
— Nuclear Weapons & International Law. LC 86-31342. 226p. 1987. text ed. 39.95 (0-312-57986-1) St Martin.
Pogany, Willy. The Art of Drawing. (Quality Paperback Ser.: No. 257). (Illus.). 128p. 1976. reprint ed. pap. 9.95 (0-8226-0257-1) Littlefield.
Pogarell, Reiner. Minority Languages in Europe - Past & Present: A Classified Bibliography. viii, 208p. 1983. 62.70 (3-11-009783-4) Mouton.
Pogash, Carol. As Real As It Gets: The Life of a Hospital at the Center of the AIDS Epidemic. 272p. 1992. 18.95 (1-55972-127-8, Birch Ln Pr) Carol Pub Group.
— As Real As It Gets: The Life of a Hospital at the Center of the AIDS Epidemic. LC 93-6454. 272p. 1994. pap. 9.95 (0-452-27127-4, Plume) NAL-Dutton.
Pogel, Nancy. Woody Allen. (Twayne's Filmmakers Ser.). 240p. 1987. text ed. 23.95 (0-8057-9297-X, Pub. by Royal Botanic Garden UK) Macmillan.
— Woody Allen. (Filmmakers Ser.). 240p. 1988. pap. 13.95 (0-8057-9309-7, Pub. by Royal Botanic Garden UK) Macmillan.
Pogell, B. M., jt. ed. see McGilvery, R. W.
Pogge, Paul. Im Reiche des Muata Jamwo: Tagebuch Meiner im Auftrag der Deutschen Gesellschaft zur Erforschung Aequatorial-Afrikas in die Lunda- Staaten Unternommenen Reise. (B. E. Ser.: No. 159). (GER.). 1880. 26.00 (0-8115-3075-2) Periodicals Srv.
Pogge, Thomas W. Realizing Rawls. LC 89-42879. (Illus.). 320p. 1989. 41.95 (0-8014-2124-1); pap. 14.95 (0-8014-9685-3) Cornell U Pr.
Poggeler, Franz, jt. ed. see Jarvis, Peter.
Poggeler, Otto. Martin Heidegger's Path of Thinking. Magurshak, Dan & Barber, Sigmund, trs. LC 85-27152. (Contemporary Studies in Philosophy & the Human Sciences). 324p. (C). 1989. pap. 18.50 (0-391-03616-5) Humanities.
Poggenburg, Raymond P. Charles Baudelaire: Une Micro-Histoire. LC 87-6194. 739p. (Orig.). 1987. pap. 47.50 (0-8265-1224-0) Vanderbilt U Pr.
Poggenpohl, Sharon H., ed. Graphic Design: A Career Guide & Educational Directory. (Illus.). 160p. (Orig.). 1993. pap. 25.00 (1-884081-00-2) Am Inst Graphic Arts.
Poggi, Antonio, jt. ed. see Fabbrizzi, Luigi.
Poggi, Christine. In Defiance of Painting: Cubism, Futurism, & the Invention of Collage. (Publications in the History of Art). (Illus.). 320p. (C). 1993. text ed. 50.00 (0-300-05109-3) Yale U Pr.
Poggi, Gianfranco. Calvinism & the Capitalist Spirit: Max Weber's "Protestant Ethic" LC 83-40103. 136p. 1984. pap. 10.95 (0-87023-418-8) U of Mass Pr.
— Catholic Action in Italy: The Sociology of a Sponsored Organization. xv, 280p. 1967. 37.50 (0-8047-0292-6) Stanford U Pr.
— The Development of the Modern State: A Sociological Introduction. LC 77-76148. xii, 175p. 1978. 24.50 (0-8047-0959-9); pap. 10.95 (0-8047-1042-2) Stanford U Pr.
— Images of Society: Essays on the Sociological Theories of Tocqueville, Marx, & Durkheim. LC 79-183892. xvi, 268p. 1972. 37.50 (0-8047-0811-8) Stanford U Pr.
— Money & the Modern Mind: George Simmel's Philosophy of Money. LC 92-32231. 1993. 30.00 (0-520-07571-4) U CA Pr.
— The State: Its Nature, Development & Prospects. LC 90-70700. 222p. 1991. 32.50 (0-8047-1849-0); pap. 10.95 (0-8047-1877-6) Stanford U Pr.
Poggi, Gianfranco, ed. see Luhmann, Niklas.
Poggi, Isotta, jt. auth. see Melton, J. Gordon.
Poggi, Jack. The Monologue Workshop: From Search to Discovery in Audition & Performance. (Acting Ser.). 272p. (Orig.). 1990. pap. 10.95 (1-55783-031-2) Applause Theatre Bk Pubs.
Poggi, Jim, ed. see Ohsawa, George.
Poggi, Stefano, et al, eds. Romanticism in Science: Science in Europe, 1790-1840. LC 93-1728. (Boston Studies in the Philosophy of Science). 1994. lib. bdg. 107.00 (0-7923-2336-X) Kluwer Ac.
Poggie, John J., Jr. & Lynch, Robert N., eds. Rethinking Modernization. LC 72-826. 352p. 1974. text ed. 75.00 (0-8371-6394-3, POM/, Greenwood Pr) Greenwood.
Poggie, John J., et al, eds. Anthropological Research: Process & Application. LC 91-16528. (SUNY Series in Advances in Applied Anthropology). (Illus.). 334p. (C). 1992. 64.50 (0-7914-1001-3); pap. 21.95 (0-7914-1002-1) State U NY Pr.
Poggio, T. A. & Glaser, D. A. Exploring Brain Functions, Models in Neuroscience: Report of the Dahlem Workshop on Exploring Brain Functions, Models in Neuroscience, Berlin, 1991 September 29-October 4. LC 92-49367. (Life Sciences Research Report Ser.: No. 52). 340p. 1993. text ed. 169.95 (0-471-93602-2) Wiley.
Poggio, Tomaso, jt. ed. see Reichardt, Werner E.
Poggio, Tomaso, jt. auth. see Vaina, Lucia M.
Poggioli, Renato. The Spirit of the Letter: Essays in European Literature. LC 65-22064. 384p. reprint ed. pap. 109.50 (0-7837-4179-0, 2059028) Bks Demand.
— The Theory of the Avant-Garde. (Belknap Ser.). 256p. 1981. pap. 15.95 (0-674-88216-4) HUP.
Poggiolini, Duilio, ed. Technical Guidelines for Pharmaceuticals in the European Economic Community. LC 83-9580. 74p. 1983. 39.00 (0-89004-851-7) Raven.
Poglany-Balas, Edit. The Influence of Rome's Antique Monumental Sculptures on the Great Masters of the Renaissance. 116p. 1980. 135.00 (0-569-08643-4, Pub. by Collets UK) St Mut.
Poglazov, B. F. Morphogenesis of T-Even Bacteriophages. (Monographs in Developmental Biology: Vol. 7). 1973. 43.25 (3-8055-1645-2) S Karger.
Pogliani, Giuliano, jt. ed. see Vannini, Vanio.
Pogo, Beatriz G., jt. auth. see Dales, S.
***Pogodzinski, J. M., ed.** Readings in Public Policy. LC 94-26134. (Illus.). 350p. (C). 1995. pap. text ed. 24.95 (1-55786-521-3) Blackwell Pubs.
Pogoloff, Stephen M. Logos & Sophia: The Rhetorical Situation of First Corinthians. LC 92-34962. (Dissertation Ser.: No. 134). 313p. 1992. 29.95 (1-55540-784-6, 06 21 34); pap. 19.95 (1-55540-783-8) Scholars Pr GA.
Pogonowski, Iwo. Polish-English, English-Polish Concise Dictionary. 4th rev. ed. 424p. 1993. pap. 8.95 (0-7818-0133-8) Hippocrene Bks.
Pogonowski, Iwo C. English Conversations for Poles. 1990. pap. 8.95 (0-87052-873-4) Hippocrene Bks.
— Jews in Poland: a Documentary History: The Rise of Jews As a Nation from Congressus Judaicus in Poland to the Knesset in Israel. (Illus.). 384p. 1993. 22.50 (0-7818-0116-8) Hippocrene Bks.
— Poland: A Historical Atlas. deluxe limited ed. (Illus.). 320p. 1988. 50.00 (0-87052-502-2) Hippocrene Bks.
— Poland: A Historical Atlas. 2nd rev. ed. (Illus.). 320p. 1988. 27.50 (0-87052-282-5) Hippocrene Bks.
— Poland: An Historical Atlas. (Illus.). 320p. (Orig.). 1992. pap. 16.95 (0-7818-0117-6) Hippocrene Bks.
— Polish English, English Polish Standard Dictionary: With Business Terms. rev. ed. (Standard Dictionaries Ser.). 703p. 1994. pap. 18.95 (0-7818-0282-2) Hippocrene Bks.
— Polish Phrasebook & Dictionary. 2nd rev. ed. 240p. 1993. pap. 9.95 (0-7818-0134-6) Hippocrene Bks.
— Polish Practical Dictionary. 15th ed. (Practical Language Dictionaries Ser.). 340p. 1993. pap. 11.95 (0-7818-0085-4) Hippocrene Bks.
Pogony, G. E. Wing Beat: A Collection of Eagle Woodcuts. Graham, Douglas J., tr. LC 76-22176. (Illus.). 1976. 15.00 (0-933652-10-0) Domjan Studio.
Pogorel, Gerard, ed. Global Telecommunications Strategies & Technological Changes. LC 93-44144. 1994. write for info. (0-444-89960-X, North Holland) Elsevier.
Pogorel, Gerard, jt. auth. see Noam, Eli M.
Pogorel, Gerard, jt. ed. see Noam, Eli M.
Pogorelov, A. Bendings of Surfaces & Stability of Shells. LC 88-23511. (MMONO Ser.: No. 72). 77p. 1988. 47.00 (0-8218-4525-X, MMONO-72) Am Math.
— Geometry. 312p. (C). 1987. 60.00 (0-685-36903-X, Pub. by Collets) St Mut.
Pogorelov, A. V. Extrinsic Geometry of Convex Surfaces. LC 72-11851. (Translations of Mathematical Monographs: Vol. 35). 669p. 1973. 109.00 (0-8218-1585-7, MMONO-35) Am Math.
Pogorelov, A. V., ed. Topics in the Theory of Surfaces in Elliptic Space. (Russian Tracts on the Physical Sciences Ser.). (Illus.). 146p. 1962. text ed. 134.00 (0-677-20400-0) Gordon & Breach.
Pogorelsky, Antony. The Black Hen: or The Underground Inhabitants. LC 92-28599. (Illus.). 32p. (J). (gr. 2-5). 1994. 14.99 (0-525-65133-0, Cobblehill Bks) Dutton Child Bks.
Pogorzelski, H., ed. see Dedekind, Richard.
Pogorzelski, Henry A. & Ryan, William J. Foundations of Semiological Theory of Numbers, Vol. 1. LC 89-155354. 590p. (Orig.). 1982. pap. text ed. 31.50 (0-89101-053-X) U Maine Pr.
— Foundations of Semiological Theory of Numbers, Vol. 2. LC 89-155354. 746p. (Orig.). 1985. pap. text ed. 36.50 (0-89101-064-5) U Maine Pr.
— Foundations of Semiological Theory of Numbers, Vol. 3: Foundations of Computability. LC 89-155354. 530p. (Orig.). 1988. pap. text ed. 41.50 (0-89101-065-3) U Maine Pr.
Pogorzelski, W. & Sneddon, I. N. Integral Equations & Their Applications. LC 64-18247. (International Series Mono on Pure & Applied Mathematics: Vol. 1, Pts. 1-3). 1966. 292.00 (0-08-010662-5, Pub. by Pergamon Repr UK) Franklin.
Pogosian, Barbara. Experimental Exercises in General Microbiology: A Laboratory Manual. 2nd ed. Ardinger, Barbara, ed. (Illus.). 334p. (C). 1992. pap. text ed. 25.00 (0-938841-02-5) Biocomm.
Pogosov, V. S. & Antoniv, V. F. Malignant Tumors of the Ear, Nose, & Throat. (Illus.). 600p. 1984. text ed. 60.00 (0-8236-3082-X) Intl Univs Pr.
— Microscopy & Microsurgery of Larynx & the Laryngopharynx. 1987. 37.50 (0-8236-3363-2, BN#03363) Intl Univs Pr.
Pogossky, A. L., tr. see Ouspensky, P. D.
Pogosyan, K. P. The Air Envelope of the Earth. 240p. 1965. text ed. 61.50 (0-7065-0383-X, Pub. by Keter Pub IS) Coronet Bks.
Pogrebin, Bertrand B., jt. auth. see Getman, Julius G.
Pogrebin, Letty C. Deborah, Golda & Me: Being Female & Jewish in America. 400p. 1991. 22.00 (0-517-57517-5, Crown) Crown Pub Group.
— Deborah, Golda & Me: Being Female & Jewish in America. 1992. pap. 12.95 (0-385-42512-0, Anchor NY) Doubleday.
Pogrow, Stanley. Computer Decisions for Board Members: Getting the Most from What Your District Selects. LC 85-50953. 250p. (Orig.). 1985. pap. text ed. 18.95 (0-931028-70-1) Teach-em.
— Education in the Computer Age: Issues of Policy, Practice, & Reform. LC 83-11213. (Managing Information Ser.: No. 6). (Illus.). 231p. reprint ed. pap. 65.90 (0-8357-4869-3, 2037801) Bks Demand.
Pogrund, Benjamin. Nelson Mandela. LC 91-50541. (People Who Made a Difference Ser.). (Illus.). 68p. (J). (gr. 3-4). 1992. lib. bdg. 21.26 (0-8368-0621-2) Gareth Stevens Inc.
— Nelson Mandela: Strength & Spirit of a Free South Africa. LC 90-24026. (People Who Have Helped the World Ser.). (Illus.). 68p. (J). (gr. 5-6). 1992. lib. bdg. 21.26 (0-8368-0357-4) Gareth Stevens Inc.
— Sobukwe & Apartheid. 416p. (C). 1991. text ed. 45.00 (0-8135-1692-7); pap. 14.95 (0-8135-1693-5) Rutgers U Pr.
Pogrund, Rona, et al. Teaching Age-Appropriate Purposeful Skills: An Orientation & Mobility Curriculum for Students with Visual Impairments. LC 93-30831. 1993. pap. 40.00 (1-880366-10-X) Texas Schl BVI.
Pogrund, Rona L., et al, eds. Early Focus: Working with Young Blind & Visually Impaired Children & Their Families. LC 92-17874. 160p. 1992. 24.95 (0-89128-215-7) Am Foun Blind.
Pogson, Beryl. In the East My Pleasure Lies. LC 73-20439. (Studies in Shakespeare: No. 24). 1974. lib. bdg. 75.00 (0-8383-1760-X) M S G Haskell Hse.
— The Work Life: Based on the Teachings of G. I. Gurdjieff, P. D. Ouspensky & Maurice Nicoll. (Illus.). 304p. (Orig.). 1994. pap. 12.95 (0-87728-809-7) Weiser.
Pogson, Patricia. Before the Roadshow. (C). 1988. 25.00 (0-904524-47-7, Pub. by Rivelin Grapheme Pr) St Mut.
Pogson, Philip, jt. auth. see Tennant, Mark.
Pogue, Bill, jt. auth. see Bova, Ben.
Pogue, David. Hard-Drive. 304p. (Orig.). 1993. mass mkt. 4.99 (1-55773-884-X) Diamond.
— Hard Drive. 304p. 1993. pap. text ed. 4.99 (0-441-00255-2) Jove Pubns.
— Macs for Dummies. 2nd ed. 384p. 1993. pap. 19.95 (1-56884-051-9) IDG Bks.
— Macs for Dummies. 3rd ed. 1995. pap. 19.99 (1-56884-239-2) IDG Bks.
— Macs for Teachers. 1995. pap. 19.99 (1-56884-601-0) IDG Bks.
— Macworld MAC & Power MAC Secrets. 2nd ed. 1994. pap. 39.95 (1-56884-175-2) IDG Bks.
— Macworld Mac Faqs. 1995. pap. 19.99 (1-56884-480-8) IDG Bks.
— More MACs for Dummies. 1994. pap. 19.95 (1-56884-087-X) IDG Bks.
***Pogue, Dennis J.** King's Reach & 17th Century Plantation Life. (Occasional Papers: Studies in Archaeology: No. 1). (Illus.). 33p. 1990. pap. 4.95 (1-878399-05-5) Div Hist Cult Progs.
Pogue, Dennis J. & Smolek, Michael A. An Archaeological Resource Management Plan for the Southern Maryland Region. (Manuscript Ser.). 165p. 1985. reprint ed. spiral bd. 10.00 (1-878399-07-1, NO. 30) Div Hist Cult Progs.
Pogue, Dennis J., jt. ed. see Reinhart, Theodore R.
Pogue, Forrest C., ed. Access to Government Documents: Papers Presented to a Session of the American Historical Association, December, 1972. 53p. 1974. 17.95 (0-89126-008-0) MA-AH Pub.
Pogue, James T. The Worship Directory with Radio Callsigns & Frequencies, Vol. 1: U. S., Canada, Great Britain. 90p. 1990. 14.95 (0-936653-24-8) Tiare Pubns.
Pogue, Jerry H., ed. see Jones, Jeffery R.
Pogue, John F. Moolelo of Ancient Hawaii. Kenn, Charles W., tr. 1978. pap. 2.50 (0-914916-31-9) Ku Paa.
Pogue, John M., ed. see Pogue, Lloyd W.
Pogue, Joseph E., jt. auth. see Gilbert, Chester G.
Pogue, Julia A. & Jones, Eileen M. A Traveler's Journey Through Time & Space. 130p. (Orig.). 1989. pap. write for info. (0-9622814-1-7) Anonymous & Assocs.
Pogue, Julia R. & Jones, Eileen M. Commentaries by the Inner Christ Circle. 157p. (Orig.). 1989. pap. 7.95 (0-9622814-0-9) Anonymous & Assocs.
Pogue, Lloyd W. Pogue-Pollock-Polk Genealogy As Mirrored in History: From Scotland to Northern Ireland-Ulster, Ohio & Westward. Pogue, John M., ed. LC 84-73111. (Illus.). 720p. 1990. 35.00 (0-9622395-0-X) Gateway Balto.
Pogue, Pamela & Lee, Virginia. Public Access to the Rhode Island Coast. 1993. write for info. (0-938412-32-9) Sea Grant Pubns.
Pogue, Stephanie E., intro. Sources: Multicultural Influences on Contemporary African American Sculptors. 20p. (Orig.). (C). 1994. pap. 4.00 (0-937123-30-7) Art Gal U MD.
Pogue, Thomas F., ed. State Taxation of Business: Issues & Policy Options. LC 92-15767. 360p. 1992. text ed. 59.95 (0-275-94125-6, C4125, Praeger Pubs) Greenwood.
Pogue, William R. Astronaut Primer. (Illus.). (Orig.). 1986. pap. 5.50 (0-935291-00-8) Nat Space Soc.

P
Q

— How Do You Go to the Bathroom in Space? 160p. (Orig.). 1991. mass mkt. 5.99 (*0-8125-1728-8*) Tor Bks.
Poguntke, Thomas. Alternative Politics: The German Green Party. (Environment, Politics, & Society Ser.). 288p. 1993. text ed. 75.00 (*0-7486-0393-X*, Pub. by Edinburgh U Pr UK) Col U Pr.
Poguntke, Thomas, jt. ed. see Muller-Rommel, Ferdinand.
Pogzeba, Wolfgang & Overbeck, Joy. Ranchos De Taos: San Francisco De Asis Church. LC 81-82257. (Illus.). 68p. (Orig.). 1981. pap. 7.95 (*0-913504-66-1*) Lowell Pr.
Pohanish & Greene. Hazardous Substances Resource Guide. 1992. 175.00 (*0-8103-8494-9*, 101437) Gale.
Pohanka, Brian, ed. A Summer on the Plains, Eighteen Seventy: From the Diary of Annie Gibson Roberts. (Illus.). 27.50 (*0-8488-0003-6*, J M C & Co); pap. 19.95 (*0-8488-0028-1*, J M C & Co) Amereon Ltd.
Pohanka, Brian, ed. see Medford Historical Society Staff.
Pohanka, Brian C., ed. see Miles, Nelson A.
Pohanka, Brian C., ed. see Worthington, Glenn H.
Pohier, Jacques. God: In Fragments. 384p. 1986. 19.95 (*0-8245-0744-4*) Crossroad NY.
Pohjola, Erkki & Tuomisto, Matti. Tapiola Sound. 204p. 1993. pap. text ed. 24.95 (*1-884598-00-5*) Walton Music.
***Pohl, ed.** Hydrogen & Other Alternate Sources of Energy for Air & Ground Transportation. Date not set. text ed. 65.95 (*0-471-95336-9*) Wiley.
Pohl & Kornbluth. The Space Merchants. 1993. reprint ed. lib. bdg. 18.95 (*0-89968-359-2*, Lghtyr Pr) Buccaneer Bks.
Pohl, jt. auth. see Asimov.
Pohl, Alice N. Committees & Boards: How to Be an Effective Participant. 1990. pap. 9.95 (*0-8442-5635-8*, NTC Busn Bks) NTC Pub Grp.
— Formal Meeting: How to Prepare & Participate. 1990. pap. 9.95 (*0-8442-5633-1*, NTC Busn Bks) NTC Pub Grp.
— Meetings: Rules & Procedures. 1989. pap. 14.95 (*0-8442-5636-6*, NTC Busn Bks) NTC Pub Grp.
Pohl, C. F. Mozart & Haydn in London, 2 vols. in 1. LC 70-125059. (Music Ser.). 1970. reprint ed. lib. bdg. 55.00 (*0-306-70024-7*) Da Capo.
Pohl, Chris, jt. auth. see Guyomard, Irene.
Pohl, Constance & Harris, Kathleen K. Transracial Adoption: Children & Parents Speak. LC 92-10991. (Illus.). 144p. (YA). (gr. 9-12). 1992. lib. bdg. 15.05 (*0-531-11134-2*) Watts.
Pohl, Dieter W. & Courjon, Daniel, eds. Near Field Optics: Proceedings of the NATO Advanced Research Workshop at Arc-et-Senans, Oct. 26-28, 1992. LC 93-25336. (NATO Advanced Study Institutes Series E, Applied Sciences: No. 242). 1993. lib. bdg. 180.00 (*0-7923-2394-7*) Kluwer Ac.
Pohl, Frances K. Ben Shahn. LC 93-24781. (Illus.). 168p. 1993. 50.00 (*1-56640-313-8*); pap. 35.00 (*1-56640-312-X*) Pomegranate Calif.
— Ben Shahn: New Deal Artist in a Cold War Climate, 1947-1954. LC 88-39304. (American Studies Ser.). (Illus.). 250p. 1989. 24.95 (*0-292-75537-6*); pap. 14.95 (*0-292-75538-4*) U of Tex Pr.
Pohl, Frederick J. The New Columbus. (Illus.). 262p. 1986. 16.00 (*0-9611422-4-3*) Security Dupont.
— William Shakespeare: A Biography. Butterfield, Stephen & Burton, Bruce A., eds. 256p. 1983. 16.75 (*0-9611422-1-9*) Security Dupont.
Pohl, Frederik. The Annals of the Heechee. 1988. mass mkt. 5.99 (*0-345-32566-4*, Del Rey) Ballantine.
— Beyond the Blue Event Horizon, No. 2. 1987. mass mkt. 4.95 (*0-345-35046-4*, Del Rey) Ballantine.
— Day the Martians Came. 1989. pap. 3.95 (*0-312-91781-3*) St Martin.
— The Early Pohl. 17.95 (*0-89190-798-X*, Am Repr) Amereon Ltd.
— Gateway. 1987. mass mkt. 4.95 (*0-345-34690-4*, Del Rey) Ballantine.
— The Gateway Trip: Tales & Vignettes of the Heechee. 1991. mass mkt. 4.99 (*0-345-37544-0*, Del Rey) Ballantine.
— Heechee Rendezvous. (Heechee Saga Ser.: Bk. 3). 1985. mass mkt. 4.95 (*0-345-30055-6*, Del Rey) Ballantine.
— Homegoing. 288p. 1990. mass mkt. 4.95 (*0-345-36550-X*, Del Rey) Ballantine.
— Jem. 352p. 1994. mass mkt. 4.99 (*0-671-87625-2*) Baen Bks.
— Land's End. 1989. mass mkt. 4.95 (*0-8125-0024-5*) Tor Bks.
— Man Plus. 1994. mass mkt. 4.99 (*0-671-87618-X*) Baen Bks.
— The Merchants' War. 320p. 1986. pap. 3.50 (*0-312-90240-9*) St Martin.
— The Merchant's War. 1987. pap. 3.50 (*0-317-56928-7*) St Martin.
— Midas World. 320p. 1984. pap. 2.95 (*0-8125-4925-2*) Tor Bks.
— Mining the Oort. 1993. mass mkt. 5.99 (*0-345-37200-X*, Del Rey) Ballantine.
— Narabedla Ltd. 1989. mass mkt. 4.95 (*0-345-36026-5*, Del Rey) Ballantine.
— Starburst. 1986. pap. 5.99 (*0-345-33928-2*, Del Rey) Ballantine.
— Voices of Heaven. 352p. 1994. 21.95 (*0-312-85643-1*) Tor Bks.
— The Voices of Heaven. 1995. mass mkt. 5.99 (*0-8125-3518-9*) Tor Bks.
— The Way the Future Was: A Memoir. 1979. pap. 1.95 (*0-345-26059-7*, Del Rey) Ballantine.
— The World at the End of Time. 1991. mass mkt. 5.95 (*0-345-37197-6*, Del Rey) Ballantine.
— The Years of the City. 336p. 1995. mass mkt. 5.99 (*0-671-87639-2*) Baen Bks.
Pohl, Frederik & Asimov, Isaac. Our Angry Earth. 448p. 1993. mass mkt. 5.99 (*0-8125-2096-3*) Tor Bks.
Pohl, Frederik & Hull, Elizabeth A., eds. Tales from the Planet Earth. 1987. reprint ed. pap. 3.95 (*0-312-90779-6*) St Martin.
Pohl, Frederik & Kornbluth, C. M. The Space Merchants. 1987. pap. 3.50 (*0-312-90655-2*) St Martin.
Pohl, Frederik & Thomas, Thomas T. Mars Plus. 352p. 1994. 20.00 (*0-671-87605-8*) Baen Bks.
— Mars Plus. 352p. 1995. mass mkt. 5.99 (*0-671-87665-1*) Baen Bks.
Pohl, Frederik & Williamson, Jack. The Starchild Trilogy. 448p. 1986. reprint ed. mass mkt. 4.99 (*0-671-65558-2*) Baen Bks.
— Undersea Fleet. 1982. pap. write for info. (*0-345-27552-7*) Ballantine.
— The Undersea Trilogy. 512p. (Orig.). 1992. mass mkt. 5.99 (*0-671-72123-2*) Baen Bks.
***Pohl, Gayle.** Public Relations: Communication. 208p. (C). 1994. per., pap. text ed. 23.20 (*0-7872-0432-3*) Kendall-Hunt.
Pohl, Gerhard & Sorsa, Piritta. European Integration & Trade with the Developing World. LC 92-28788. (Policy & Research Ser.: Vol. 21). 100p. 1992. 7.95 (*0-8213-2204-4*, 12204) World Bank.
Pohl, Gladys L. The Key to the Universe. 64p. (Orig.). 1984. pap. 5.95 (*0-939332-10-8*) J Pohl Assocs.
Pohl, H. Taschen Lexikon Sicherheit der Informationstechnik. 184p. (ENG & GER.). 1989. pap. 95.00 (*0-8288-3883-6*, F120960) Fr & Eur.
Pohl, H. & Rudolph, B., eds. German Yearbook on Business History, 1987. 160p. 1989. 46.00 (*0-387-50074-X*) Spr-Verlag.
Pohl, H., jt. ed. see Engels, W.
Pohl, H., et al, eds. German Yearbook on Business History, 1981. (Illus.). 127p. 1982. 36.00 (*0-387-11230-8*) Spr-Verlag.
Pohl, Hans, ed. Innovation, Know How, Rationalization & Investment in the German & Japanese Economies 1868-1971 - 1930-1980: Proceedings of the German-Japanese Symposium, Berlin 1979. 295p. (Orig.). 1982. pap. text ed. 58.50 (*3-515-03685-7*) Coronet.
Pohl, Hartel. Roemische Politik & Piraterie im Oestlichen Mittelmeer: Vom 3. Bis 1, Jh. v. Chr. (Untersuchungen zur Antiken Literatur & Geschichte Ser.: Band 42). x, 310p. (GER.). (C). 1993. lib. bdg. 114.70 (*3-11-013890-5*) Mouton.
Pohl, Heinz. Kitab Al-Mirat: Das Buch der Erbschaft des Samaritaners Ibraham Abv Ishag: Kritische Edition mit Uebersetzung und Kommentar. LC 74-80633. (Studia Samaritana: Band 2). 328p. (GER.). (C). 1974. 115.00 (*3-11-002495-0*) De Gruyter.
Pohl, Ira. C Plus Plus for C Programmers. (Illus.). 300p. (Orig.). (C). 1989. pap. text ed. 36.75 (*0-8053-0910-1*) Benjamin-Cummings.
— C Plus Plus for C Programmers. 2nd ed. LC 93-30685. 370p. (Orig.). (C). 1994. pap. text ed. 38.75 (*0-8053-3159-X*) Benjamin-Cummings.
— C++ for Pascal Programmers. (C). 1991. pap. text ed. 34.50 (*0-8053-0911-X*) Benjamin-Cummings.
— C++ for Pascal Programmers. 2nd ed. (C). 1995. pap. text ed. 38.75 (*0-8053-3158-1*) Benjamin-Cummings.
— Easy Reference Guide to C Plus Plus. 430p. (C). 1995. pap. text ed. write for info. (*0-8053-3164-6*) Benjamin-Cummings.
— Object-Oriented Programming Using C Plus Plus. 425p. (C). 1993. pap. text ed. 38.75 (*0-8053-5382-8*) Benjamin-Cummings.
— Turbo C. (C). 1991. pap. text ed. 33.50 (*0-8053-6017-4*) Benjamin-Cummings.
Pohl, Ira, jt. auth. see Kelley, Al.
Pohl, James W. Battle of San Jacinto. 40p. 1989. pap. 5.95 (*0-87611-084-7*) Tex St Hist Assn.
Pohl, Jean, ed. Research in Terrestrial Impact Structures. (Earth Evolution Sciences Ser.). vi, 141p. 1987. 70.00 (*3-528-08940-7*, Pub. by Vieweg & Sohn GW) Ballen Bkslr.
Pohl, John M. The Politics of Symbolism in the Mixtec Codices. Spores, Ronald, ed. (Vanderbilt University Publications in Anthropology: No. 46). (Illus.). 157p. (Orig.). 1994. pap. 14.00 (*0-935462-37-6*) Vanderbilt Pubns.
Pohl, John M., jt. auth. see Byland, Bruce E.
Pohl, Karl O., jt. auth. see Gaidar, Yegor.
Pohl, Kathleen, adapt. Crabs. (Nature Close-Ups Ser.). (Illus.). 32p. (J). (gr. 3-7). 1986. lib. bdg. 10.95 (*0-8172-2716-4*) Raintree Steck-V.
— Crayfish. (Nature Close-Ups Ser.). (Illus.). 32p. (J). (gr. 3-7). 1986. pap. text ed. 10.95 (*0-8172-2718-0*) Raintree Steck-V.
— Dandelions. (Nature Close-Ups Ser.). (Illus.). 32p. (J). (gr. 3-7). 1986. pap. text ed. 10.95 (*0-8172-2708-3*) Raintree Steck-V.
— Giant Water Bugs. (Nature Close-Ups Ser.). (Illus.). 32p. (J). (gr. 3-7). 1986. pap. text ed. 10.95 (*0-8172-2714-8*) Raintree Steck-V.
— Gourds. (Nature Close-Ups Ser.). (Illus.). 32p. (J). (gr. 3-7). 1986. lib. bdg. 10.95 (*0-8172-2712-1*) Raintree Steck-V.
— Hermit Crabs. (Nature Close-Ups Ser.). (Illus.). 32p. (J). (gr. 3-7). 1986. lib. bdg. 10.95 (*0-8172-2721-0*) Raintree Steck-V.
— Killifish. (Nature Close-Ups Ser.). (Illus.). 32p. (J). (gr. 3-7). 1986. lib. bdg. 10.95 (*0-8172-2720-2*) Raintree Steck-V.
— Morning Glories. (Nature Close-Ups Ser.). (Illus.). 32p. (J). (gr. 3-7). 1986. lib. bdg. 10.95 (*0-8172-2711-3*) Raintree Steck-V.
— Potatoes. (Nature Close-Ups Ser.). (Illus.). 32p. (J). (gr. 3-7). 1986. lib. bdg. 10.95 (*0-8172-2723-7*) Raintree Steck-V.
— The Praying Mantis. (Nature Close-Ups Ser.). (Illus.). 32p. (J). (gr. 3-7). 1986. lib. bdg. 10.95 (*0-8172-2715-6*) Raintree Steck-V.
— Sparrows. (Nature Close-Ups Ser.). (Illus.). 32p. (J). (gr. 3-7). 1986. lib. bdg. 10.95 (*0-8172-2719-9*) Raintree Steck-V.
— Stickleback Fish. (Nature Close-Ups Ser.). (Illus.). 32p. (J). (gr. 3-7). 1986. lib. bdg. 10.95 (*0-8172-2722-9*) Raintree Steck-V.
— Sunflowers. (Nature Close-Ups Ser.). (Illus.). 32p. (J). (gr. 3-7). 1986. lib. bdg. 10.95 (*0-8172-2710-5*) Raintree Steck-V.
— Tulips. (Nature Close-Ups Ser.). (Illus.). 32p. (J). (gr. 3-7). 1986. lib. bdg. 10.95 (*0-8172-2709-1*) Raintree Steck-V.
Pohl, Kathleen, ed. see Oda, Hidetomo.
Pohl, Kathy, ed. see Endo, Kimio.
Pohl, Kathy, ed. see Hasegawa, Yo.
Pohl, Kathy, ed. see Nanao, Jun.
Pohl, Kathy, ed. see Oda, Hidetomo.
Pohl, Kathy, ed. see Ogawa, Hiroshi.
Pohl, Kathy, ed. see Otani, Takeshi.
Pohl, Kathy, ed. see Takeuchi, Hiroshi.
Pohl, Kathy, ed. see Yajima, Minoru.
Pohl, L., et al. Liquid Crystals. (Topics in Physical Chemistry Ser.: Vol. 3). 1994. 44.00 (*0-387-91421-8*) Spr-Verlag.
Pohl, Linda. The Ah-Chooo Book. (Illus.). 20p. (J). (ps-2). 1990. 3.95 (*0-9625453-0-9*) L P Pohl.
— The Wiggly Tooth Book. (Illus.). 16p. (J). (ps-2). 1991. 3.95 (*0-9625453-1-7*) L P Pohl.
Pohl, M. D. Aztec, Mixtex, & Zapotec Armies. (Men-at-Arms Ser.: No. 239). (Illus.). 48p. pap. 11.95 (*1-85532-159-9*, 9197, Pub. by Osprey UK) Stackpole.
Pohl, Manfred, ed. Handbook on the History of European Banks. 1328p. 1994. 299.95 (*1-85278-919-0*, Pub. by E Elgar Pub UK) Ashgate Pub Co.
Pohl, Margaret L. Teaching Function Nursing Practition. 4th ed. 176p. (C). 1981. pap. write for info. (*0-697-05546-9*) Wm C Brown Pubs.
Pohl, Mel, et al. The Caregivers' Journey: When You Love Someone with AIDS. LC 90-80390. 227p. (Orig.). 1991. pap. 10.00 (*0-89486-661-3*, 5115A) Hazelden.
Pohl, N., jt. auth. see Kazmier, Leonard J.
***Pohl, R.** German-English - English-German Dictionary of Hydrolic Engineering. (ENG & GER.). 1990. 38.00 (*0-7859-8961-7*) Fr & Eur.
Pohl, R., jt. ed. see Gershon, S.
Pohl, R. O., jt. ed. see Meissner, M.
Pohl, Reinhard. Wasserbau: Englisch - Deutsch Deutsch - Englisch. 1991. 49.95 (*0-685-40786-1*) Fr & Eur.
— Wasserbau: Englisch-Deutsch-Englisch. (DUT & ENG.). 49.95 (*0-8288-7936-2*, F58909) Fr & Eur.
Pohl, Richard W., et al. Grasses. 3rd ed. (Pictured Key Nature Ser.). 208p. (C). 1978. ring bd. write for info. (*0-697-04876-4*) Wm C Brown Pubs.
Pohl, Victoria. How to Enrich Geometry Using String Designs. LC 86-5189. (Illus.). 68p. 1986. pap. 11.50 (*0-87353-227-9*) NCTM.
Pohl, W., jt. ed. see Hobson, G. D.
Pohl, William, tr. see Husserl, Edmund.
Pohland, jt. auth. see Britz.
Pohland, A. E., et al, eds. Microbial Toxins in Foods & Feeds: Cellular & Molecular Modes of Action. LC 90-14343. (Illus.). 610p. 1990. 145.00 (*0-306-43716-3*, Plenum Pr) Plenum.
Pohland, Frederick G., jt. ed. see Malina, Joseph F., Jr.
Pohland, Frederick G., jt. ed. see Tedder, D. William.
Pohland, Vera, jt. ed. see Kaser, Rudolph.
Pohlandt, K. Materials Testing for the Metal Forming Industry. (Illus.). 240p. 1989. 79.00 (*0-387-50651-9*) Spr-Verlag.
Pohle, Joseph. Eschatology. LC 72-109823. 164p. 1971. reprint ed. text ed. 49.75 (*0-8371-4314-4*, POES, Greenwood Pr) Greenwood.
Pohle, Peter. Cut & Assemble a British Pub. (Illus.). (J). (gr. 4-7). 1993. pap. 3.95 (*0-486-27360-1*) Dover.
Pohle, Robert W., Jr. & Hart, Douglas C. The Films of Christopher Lee. LC 82-10424. (Illus.). 249p. 1983. 39.50 (*0-8108-1573-7*) Scarecrow.
Pohlen, Annelie, jt. auth. see Fonce, Jan.
Pohlenz, Max. Kleine Schriften, 2 vols., Set. xxxi, 1192p. 1965. Set. write for info. (*0-318-70819-1*, Pub. by Georg Olms GW) Lubrecht & Cramer.
Pohler, J. G. Foreign Participation in U. S. Academic Science & Engineering. (Illus.). 127p. (Orig.). (C). 1993. pap. text ed. 40.00 (*1-56806-420-9*) Diane Pub.
Pohlers, W. Proof Theory. (Lecture Notes in Mathematics Ser.: Vol. 1407). vi, 213p. 1989. pap. 24.00 (*0-387-51842-8*) Spr-Verlag.
Pohlman, Don, jt. auth. see Moe, Jerry.
Pohlman, H. L. Constitutional Debate in Action: Civil Rights & Liberties. LC 94-19167. 325p. (C). 1994. 23.00 (*0-06-500513-9*) HarpCollege.
— Constitutional Debate in Action: Criminal Justice. LC 94-19168. (C). 1994. 23.00 (*0-06-500512-0*) HarpCollege.
— Constitutional Debate in Action: Governmental Powers. LC 94-19166. 320p. (C). 1994. text ed. 23.00 (*0-06-500514-7*) HarpCollege.
— Justice Oliver Wendell Holmes: Free Speech & the Living Constitution. 312p. 1991. text ed. 50.00x (*0-8147-6614-5*); pap. text ed. 18.50 (*0-8147-6622-6*) NYU Pr.
Pohlman, H. L., ed. Political Thought & the American Judiciary. LC 92-30025. 344p. (C). 1993. lib. bdg. 45.00 (*0-87023-829-9*); pap. 17.95 (*0-87023-830-2*) U of Mass Pr.
Pohlman, Karl-Friedrich. Ezechielstudien: Zur Redaktionsgeschichte des Buches und zur Frage nach den Altesten Texten. (Beihefte zur Zeitschrift fuer die Alttestamentliche Wissenschaft Ser.: Bd. 202). ix, 262p. (C). 1992. lib. bdg. 98.60 (*3-11-012976-0*, 247-91) De Gruyter.
***Pohlman, Ken C.** Principles of Digital Audio. 3rd ed. LC 95-17259. 1995. write for info. (*0-07-050468-7*); pap. write for info. (*0-07-050469-5*) McGraw.
Pohlman, Neal. Pork Production. 176p. 1990. spiral bd. 21.95 (*0-8403-6092-4*) Kendall-Hunt.
Pohlman, Randolph. Understanding the Bottom Line: Finance for Non-Financial Managers & Supervisors. 1991. pap. 7.95 (*1-55852-057-0*) Natl Pr Pubns.
Pohlman, Richard W., jt. auth. see Morgan, Fred.
Pohlmann, Ken C. The Compact Disc Handbook. 2nd ed. LC 92-13287. (Computer Music & Digital Audio Ser.: Vol. 5). (Illus.). 349p. (C). 1992. 49.95 (*0-89579-301-6*); pap. 34.95 (*0-89579-300-8*) A-R Eds.
Pohlmann, Kenneth C. Advanced Digital Audio. (Illus.). 500p. (Orig.). 1991. pap. 39.95 (*0-672-22768-1*) Sams.
— Principles of Digital Audio. 2nd ed. 474p. 1989. pap. 29.95 (*0-672-22634-0*) Sams.
Pohlmann, Marcus D. Black Politics in Conservative America. 271p. (Orig.). (C). 1990. pap. text ed. 27.50 (*0-582-28684-0*, 71697) Longman.
— Governing the Post-Industrial City. 384p. (C). 1993. pap. text ed. 37.95 (*0-8013-0665-5*, 78642) Longman.
Pohlmann, S., jt. auth. see Weichselberger, K.
Pohorecky, Larissa A., et al, eds. Alcohol & Aggression: Proceedings of the Symposium on Alcohol & Aggression Held at the Center of Alcohol Studies, Rutgers University, October 1992. (Journal of Studies on Alcohol: Suppl. No. 11). 200p. 1993. pap. 26.95 (*0-911290-52-4*, AJS-106) Rutgers Ctr Alcohol.
Pohoryles, Ronald, et al, eds. European Transformations: Five Decisive Years at the Turn of the Century: An Innovative Reader 1988-1992. (Contemporary Trends in European Social Sciences Ser.). 421p. 1994. 63.95 (*1-85628-656-8*, Pub. by Avebury Pub UK) Ashgate Pub Co.
Pohost. New Concepts in Cardiac Imaging, 1990. 1991. write for info. (*0-8151-6741-5*, Yr Bk Med Pubs) Mosby Yr Bk.
— Principles & Practice of Cardiovascular Imaging. 1990. 135.00 (*0-316-71247-7*) Little.
Pohost, Gerald M., ed. Cardiovascular Applications of Magnetic Resonance. LC 92-48279. (American Heart Association Monograph Ser.). (Illus.). 480p. 1993. 86.00 (*0-87993-548-0*) Futura Pub.
Pohren, D. E. Adventures in Taste: The Wines & Folk Food of Spain. (Illus.). 302p. 1972. 19.95 (*0-933224-13-3*, Pub. by Soc Sp Studies SP) Bold Strummer Ltd.
— Art of Flamenco. 1985. lib. bdg. 250.00 (*0-8490-3248-2*) Gordon Pr.
— Lives & Legends of Flamenco: A Biographical History. rev. ed. (Society of Spanish Studies). (Illus.). 329p. 1988. reprint ed. pap. 29.95 (*0-933224-12-5*, Pub. by Soc Sp Studies SP) Bold Strummer Ltd.
— A Way of Life. (Illus.). 194p. (Orig.). 1988. reprint ed. 24.95 (*0-933224-02-8*, Pub. by Soc Sp Studies SP); reprint ed. pap. 15.95 (*0-933224-03-6*, Pub. by Soc Sp Studies SP) Bold Strummer Ltd.
Pohren, Don. The Art of Flamenco. rev. ed. (Illus.). 225p. 1990. text ed. 24.95 (*0-685-46241-2*, Pub. by Soc Sp Studies SP) Bold Strummer Ltd.
Pohribny, Arsen, jt. auth. see Elliott, David.
***Pohrt, Tom, illus. & ret.** Coyote Goes Walking. LC 94-24096. 32p. (J). 1995. 16.00 (*0-374-31628-7*) FS&G.
Pohs, Henry A. Metric Conversion Symbols: Pohs Shop. (Illus.). 24p. 1994. pap. 7.50 (*0-9641165-1-0*) Flame Pubng.
— The Miner's Flame Light Book. LC 92-97415. (Illus.). 833p. 1995. 89.50 (*0-9641165-0-2*) Flame Pubng.
Pohst, Michael E. Computational Algebraic Number Theory. LC 93-26028. (DMV Seminar Ser.: Bd. 21). 88p. 1993. pap. 26.50 (*0-8176-2913-0*, Pub. by Birkhauser Vlg SZ) Birkhauser.
Pohst, Michael E., ed. Algorithmic Methods in Algebra & Number Theory. 135p. 1988. text ed. 37.00 (*0-12-559190-X*) Acad Pr.
Pohst, Michael E. & Zassenhaus, H. Algorithmic Algebraic Number Theory. (Encyclopedia of Mathematics & Its Applications Ser.: No. 30). (Illus.). 450p. 1989. 115.00 (*0-521-33060-2*) Cambridge U Pr.
Poidevin, Raymond, jt. auth. see Spierenburg, Dirk.
Poidras, Henri. Critical & Documentary Dictionary of Violin Makers - Old & Modern, 2 vols. in 1. 1988. reprint ed. lib. bdg. 99.00 (*0-7812-0779-7*) Rprt Serv.
— Critical & Documentary Dictionary of Violin Makers Old & Modern, 2 vols. in 1. LC 70-166252. 1930. reprint ed. 59.00 (*0-403-01381-X*) Scholarly.
Poigford, D. V. & Baur, Gret. Expert Systems for Business: Concepts & Applications. 2nd ed. LC 93-4499. (C). 1995. pap. 35.95 (*0-87709-127-7*, BF1277) S-W Pub.
Poignant, Raymond. Education & Development in Western Europe, the United States, & the U. S. S. R. A Comparative Study. LC 72-77012. (Comparative Education Studies). 361p. reprint ed. pap. 102.90 (*0-317-41861-0*, 2026057) Bks Demand.
Poignard, Renee. Waxing Made Easy: A Step-by-Step Guide. LC 93-25343. 108p. 1994. pap. text ed. 9.95 (*1-56253-171-9*) Milady Pub.
Poikolainen, Kari. Alcohol Poisoning Mortality in Four Nordic Countries. (Finnish Foundation for Alcohol Studies: Vol. 28). 1977. 8.00 (*951-9191-47-X*) Rutgers Ctr Alcohol.
Poiky, Patrick D. How to Beat the New & Used Boat Salesman. 102p. (Orig.). 1994. pap. 12.95 (*0-9640800-0-1*) Peoples Interest.

Poiletman, Robert. How to Teach Your Child the Three R's: One Parent's Method. 153p. (Orig.). 1986. pap. text ed. 4.95 (0-937519-00-6) Poiletman Pub.

Poillon, Florence, ed. Dioxin Treatment Technologies. (Illus.). 68p. (Orig.). (C). 1994. pap. text ed. 45.00 (0-7881-0576-0) Diane Pub.

Poinar, George & Poinar, Roberta. The Quest for Life in Amber. (Illus.). 263p. 1994. write for info. (0-201-62660-8) Addison-Wesley.

Poinar, George O., Jr. Life in Amber. LC 91-5045. (Illus.). 374p. (C). 1992. 55.00 (0-8047-2001-0) Stanford U Pr.

Poinar, George O., Jr. & Jansson, Hans-Borje, eds. Diseases of Nematodes. 1988. write for info. (0-318-62929-1, SF997) CRC Pr.

— Diseases of Nematodes. 160p. 1988. Vol. I, 160 pgs. 95.00 (0-8493-4317-8, SF997, CRC Reprint); Vol. II, 160 pgs. 96.00 (0-8493-4318-6, SF997, CRC Reprint) Franklin.

Poinar, George O., Jr. & Thomas, Gerald M. Laboratory Guide to Insect Pathogens & Parasites. LC 84-9875. 408p. 1984. 89.50 (0-306-41680-8, Plenum Pr) Plenum.

Poinar, Roberta, jt. auth. see Poinar, George.

Poincare, H. Papers on Fuchsian Functions. Stillwell, John C., tr. (Illus.). iv, 483p. 1985. 59.00 (0-387-96215-8) Spr-Verlag.

Poincare, Henri. New Methods of Celestial Mechanics, 3 vols., Set. (History of Modern Physics & Astronomy Ser.: Vol. 13). 1600p. 1990. 195.00 (1-56396-117-2) Am Inst Physics.

— Science & Hypothesis. 1905. pap. 6.95 (0-486-60221-4) Dover.

Poincare, Raymond. The Memoirs of Raymond Poincare, 4 vols. Arthur, George, tr. reprint ed. write for info. (0-318-50656-4) AMS Pr.

— The Memoirs of Raymond Poincare, 4 vols, 1. Arthur, George, tr. LC 70-160452. reprint ed. 35.00 (0-404-09091-5) AMS Pr.

— The Memoirs of Raymond Poincare, 4 vols, 2. Arthur, George, tr. LC 70-160452. reprint ed. 35.00 (0-404-09092-3) AMS Pr.

— The Memoirs of Raymond Poincare, 4 vols, 3. Arthur, George, tr. LC 70-160452. reprint ed. 35.00 (0-404-09093-1) AMS Pr.

— The Memoirs of Raymond Poincare, 4 vols, 4. Arthur, George, tr. LC 70-160452. reprint ed. 35.00 (0-404-09094-X) AMS Pr.

— The Memoirs of Raymond Poincare, 4 vols, Set. Arthur, George, tr. LC 70-160452. reprint ed. 140.00 (0-404-09090-7) AMS Pr.

Poincelot, Raymond P. No-Dig No-Weed Gardening. LC 85-30012. (Illus.). 272p. 1986. pap. 14.95 (0-87857-612-6, 01-131-1) Rodale Pr Inc.

— Toward a More Sustainable Agriculture. (Illus.). (C). 1986. text ed. 43.95 (0-87055-518-9) AVI.

Poincelot, Raymond P. & Olson, Richard K., eds. Integrating Sustainable Agriculture, Ecology, & Environment Policy. LC 92-13752. (Journal of Sustainable Agriculture: Vol. 2, No. 3). (Illus.). 196p. 1992. 39.95 (1-56022-023-6); pap. 19.95 (1-56022-024-4) Haworth Jrnl Co-Edits.

Poindexter, Hildrus A. My World of Reality. LC 72-85752. (Illus.). 349p. 1973. 9.95 (0-913642-03-7) Balamp Pub.

Poindexter, Jeanne S. & Leadbetter, Edward R., eds. Bacteria in Nature, Vol. 2: Methods & Special Applications in Bacterial Ecology. LC 85-3433. 404p. 1986. 89.50 (0-306-42346-4, Plenum Pr) Plenum.

— Bacteria in Nature, Vol. 3: Structure, Physiology, & Genetic Adaptability. LC 85-3433. (Illus.). 406p. 1989. 89.50 (0-306-43173-4, Plenum Pr) Plenum.

Poindexter, Jeanne S., jt. ed. see Leadbetter, Edward R.

Poindexter, William T. From Me to You: A Book Designed to Bring Reality to the Hope That Is Within You. 1992. 10.95 (0-533-10188-3) Vantage.

Poiner, Gretchen. The Good Old Rule: Gender & Other Power Relationships in a Rural Community. (Sydney University Press Publication Ser.). 216p. 1991. pap. 29.95 (0-424-00160-8) OUP.

***Poinsatte, Charles.** Fort Wayne During the Canal Era, 1828-1855. 284p. 1993. pap. 10.00 (1-885323-23-9) IN Hist Bureau.

Poinsatte, Charles, jt. auth. see Norling, Bernard.

Poinsett, Alex. Black Power Gary Style: The Making of Mayor Richard Gordon Hatcher. LC 72-128545. 1970. 6.95 (0-87485-042-8) Johnson Chi.

***Poinsett, Norma & Burns, Vivian.** Rainbow Children: A Racial Justice & Diversity Program. 1995. pap. 25.00 (1-55896-292-1) Unitarian Univ.

Poinso, Yves. Diccionario Practico de Psicopatologia. 324p. (SPA.). 1976. 29.95 (0-8288-5618-4, S50194); pap. 29.95 (0-8288-5619-2, S50186) Fr & Eur.

Poinsot, Edmond-Antoinne, see Georges D'Heylli, pseud..

Poinsotte, J. P. Dictionary of Medical Siglas: Dictionnaire des Sigles Medicaux. 146p. (FRE.). 1982. pap. text ed. 24.95 (0-8288-4420-8, M9772) Fr & Eur.

Poinssot, Bernard. The Stinson Beach Salt Marsh: The Form of Its Growth. LC 77-70990. (Illus.). 1977. pap. 12.00 (0-918540-01-1) Stinson Beach.

Point of Purchase Advertising Institute Staff. Point of Purchase Design Annual No. 2: The 36th Merchandising Awards. (Illus.). 240p. 1994. 49.95 (0-934590-64-8) Retail Report.

Point Reyes Community Cookbook Committee Staff. Home on the Range: Favorite Recipes from the Point Reyes Community. (Illus.). 128p. (Orig.). 1988. pap. 12.00 (0-9620222-2-5) Chardon Pr.

Pointe de l'Eglise Genealogical & Historical Society Staff. Cemetery Listings of Acadia Parish, Louisiana: Tombstone Inscriptions from Rayne, La. & the Surrounding Area. Gremillion, Irma H., ed. 260p. 1994. pap. 18.00 (0-926764-91-8) LAcadie Pubng.

— Cemetery Listings of Acadia Parish, Louisiana, Vol. 1: Tombstone Inscriptions from Church Point, La. & the Surrounding Area. Gremillion, Irma H., ed. 210p. 1991. pap. 15.00 (0-926764-90-X) LAcadie Pubng.

Pointer, Bren. Movement Activities for Children with Learning Difficulties. 140p. 1993. pap. 32.50 (1-85302-167-9, Pub. by J Kingsley Pubs UK) Taylor & Francis.

***Pointer, Dennis D. & Ewell, Charles M.** Really Governing: How Health System & Hospital Boards Can Make More of a Difference. LC 94-25555. 240p. 1994. text ed. 59.95 (0-8273-5577-7) Delmar.

Pointer, Larry. In Search of Butch Cassidy. LC 77-14066. (Illus.). 312p. 1977. pap. 13.95 (0-8061-2143-2) U of Okla Pr.

Pointer, Lyle. Beginning Anew. (Christian Living Ser.). 27p. (Orig.). 1987. pap. 2.50 (0-8341-1189-6) Beacon Hill.

— Now That You Are Saved. (Christian Living Ser.). 40p. (Orig.). 1987. pap. 2.50 (0-8341-1157-8) Beacon Hill.

— Welcome Back to Jesus. (Christian Living Ser.). 32p. (Orig.). 1987. pap. 2.50 (0-8341-1190-X) Beacon Hill.

***Pointer, Michael.** Charles Dickens on the Screen: The Film, Television, & Video Adaptations. Slide, Anthony, ed. LC 94-49372. 1995. write for info. (0-8108-2960-6) Scarecrow.

Pointer, Richard W. Protestant Pluralism & the New York Experience: A Study of Eighteenth-Century Religious Diversity. LC 87-45371. (Illus.). 224p. 1988. 25.00 (0-253-34643-6) Ind U Pr.

Pointer, Steven R. Joseph Cook, Boston Lecturer & Evangelical Apologist: A Bridge Between Popular Culture & Academia in Late Nineteenth-Century America. LC 91-26362. (Studies in American Religion: Vol. 57). 268p. 1991. lib. bdg. 89.95 (0-7734-9702-1) E Mellen.

Pointing, John, jt. ed. see Maguire, Mike.

***Pointon.** Cartoon, Caricature, Animation. 1995. pap. (0-631-19487-8) Blackwell Pubs.

Pointon, A. J. & Howarth, H. M. AC & DC Network Theory. (Physics & Its Applications Ser.). 176p. 1991. pap. 29.95 (0-412-38310-1) Chapman & Hall.

— AC & DC Network Theory. 176p. 1991. pap. 30.95 (0-442-31376-4) Chapman & Hall.

Pointon, H. Carpet Surfaces. 254p. (C). 1975. pap. 85.00 (0-685-46411-3, Pub. by Textile Institue UK) St Mut.

Pointon, John. Issues in Business Taxation. 239p. 1994. 59.95 (1-85628-419-0, Pub. by Avebury Pub UK) Ashgate Pub Co.

Pointon, John & Spratley, Derek. Principles of Business Taxation. (Illus.). 352p. 1988. 69.00 (0-19-877257-2) OUP.

Pointon, John, jt. auth. see Davis, Edward.

Pointon, Leo D. Revenue Law in Singapore & Malaysia: Cases & Commentary. 308p. 1986. pap. 77.00 (0-409-99526-6) Butterworth Legal Pubs.

Pointon, Marcia. Hanging the Head: Portraiture & Social Formation in Eighteenth-Century England. LC 92-15841. (Illus.). 288p. (C). 1993. text ed. 65.00 (0-300-05738-5) Yale U Pr.

— History of Art: A Student's Handbook. 2nd ed. (Illus.). 96p. (C). 1986. pap. text ed. 12.95 (0-04-701016-9) Routledge Chapman & Hall.

— History of Art: A Students' Handbook. 3rd ed. LC 93-3534. 1993. write for info. (0-415-09036-9) Routledge.

Pointon, Marcia, ed. Art Apart: Art Institutions & Ideology Across England & North America. LC 93-44614. 1994. text ed. 79.95 (0-7190-3917-7, Pub. by Manchester Univ Pr UK); text ed. 24.95 (0-7190-3918-5, Pub. by Manchester Univ Pr UK) St Martin.

— Pre-Raphaelites Re-Viewed. (Cultural Politics Ser.). 192p. 1989. text ed. 22.95 (0-7190-2821-3, Pub. by Manchester Univ Pr UK) St Martin.

***Pointon, Marcia & Binski, Paul.** The Image in the Ancient & Early Christian Worlds. 160p. Date not set. pap. text ed. 19.95 (0-631-19474-6) Blackwell Pubs.

Pointon, Marcia, jt. ed. see Adler, Kathleen.

Pointon, R. C., ed. The Radiotherapy of Malignant Disease: Founded by Easson. 2nd ed. (Illus.). 496p. 1991. 198.00 (0-387-19622-6) Spr-Verlag.

Pointon, R. C., jt. ed. see Easson, E. C.

Points, ed. see Cota-Robles, Patricia D.

Points, Larry, jt. auth. see Jauck, Andrea.

Points, Maureen. The Adventures of Pepe the Poodle & Other Stories. (Illus.). (J). 1978. pap. 3.50 (0-9601594-1-X) Maureen Points.

Poirer, J., jt. ed. see Geiger, G. H.

Poirer, R., et al. Handbook of Gaussian Basis Sets: A Compendium for Ab-Initio Molecular Orbital Calculations. (Physical Sciences Data Ser.: No. 24). 674p. 1985. 218.00 (0-444-42493-8) Elsevier.

Poirer, Richard. Poetry & Pragmatism. 228p. 1993. pap. 13.95 (0-674-67991-1) HUP.

Poiret, Pierre. Oeuvres Diverses, No. Three: Petri Poireti Cogitationum Rationalium De Deo Anima et Malo. 1990. reprint ed. write for info. (3-487-09383-9, Pub. by Georg Olms GW) Lubrecht & Cramer.

Poirier, A. & Zaccour, G., eds. Maritime & Pipeline Transportation of Oil & Gas. (Illus.). 320p. (C). 1991. pap. text ed. 190.00 (2-7108-0606-1, Pub. by Edits Technip FR) St Mut.

Poirier-Brode, Karen. Adolescent Pregnancy & Prenatal Care. Head, J. J., ed. LC 84-71144. (Carolina Biology Readers Ser.: No. 148). (Illus.). 16p. (Orig.). (YA). (gr. 10 up). 1987. pap. text ed. 2.75 (0-89278-348-6, 45-9748) Carolina Biological.

***Poirier-Bures, Simone.** Candyman. 157p. 1994. 25.95 (0-88750-977-0, Pub. by Oberon Pr CN); pap. 12.95 (0-88750-978-9, Pub. by Oberon Pr CN) Pocahontas Pr.

Poirier, Charles C. & Houser, William F. Business Partnering for Continuous Improvement: How to Forge Enduring Alliances among Employees, Suppliers & Customers. LC 92-23473. 256p. 1994. pap. 19.95 (1-881052-39-7) Berrett-Koehler.

Poirier, Claude. Dictionary of Quebecois French: Dictionnaire du Francais Quebecois. 167p. (FRE.). 1985. pap. 29.95 (0-8288-1093-1, F780) Fr & Eur.

***Poirier, D. R. & Geiger, G. H.** Transport Phenomena in Materials Processing. LC 94-76335. 658p. 1994. 72.00 (0-87339-272-8) Minerals Metals.

Poirier, D. R., jt. auth. see Geiger, G. H.

***Poirier, Dale J.** Intermediate Statistics & Econometrics: A Comparative Approach. LC 94-28184. 1995. 65.00x (0-262-16149-4) MIT Pr.

Poirier, Dale J., ed. The Methodology of Econometrics. (International Library of Critical Writings in Business History: Vol. 6). 1008p. 1995. 309.95 (1-85278-844-5, Pub. by E Elgar Pub UK) Ashgate Pub Co.

Poirier, Frank E. In Search of Ourselves: An Introduction to Physical Anthropology. 3rd ed. 1981. pap. text ed. write for info. (0-8087-1666-2) Burgess MN Intl.

— An Introduction to Physical Anthropology & the Archeological Record. LC 81-70138. 480p. (Orig.). (C). 1982. pap. text ed. write for info. (0-8087-3329-X) Burgess MN Intl.

— Understanding Human Evolution. 3rd ed. LC 92-26288. 400p. 1993. pap. text ed. 20.00 (0-13-012477-X) P-H.

Poirier, Frank E. & Stini, William A. In Search of Ourselves. 4th ed. 448p. (C). 1990. pap. text ed. write for info. (0-13-455783-2) P-H.

Poirier, Frank E., jt. auth. see Wu, Xinzhi.

Poirier, Frank E., et al. In Search of Ourselves: An Introduction to Physical Anthropology. 5th ed. LC 93-16703. 1993. pap. text ed. write for info. (0-13-454463-3) P-H.

Poirier, G. & Moreau, P., eds. ADP - Ribosylation Reactions. (Illus.). 410p. 1992. 87.00 (0-387-97822-4) Spr-Verlag.

Poirier, J.

Poirier, J., ed. see Kirkwood, John G.

Poirier, J. P., jt. auth. see Nicolas, Adolphe.

Poirier, Jacques, et al. Manual of Basic Neuropathology. 3rd ed. 292p. 1990. pap. text ed. 33.95 (0-7216-3464-8) Saunders.

Poirier, Jean. Ethnologie Generale. (Methodique Ser.). 1932p. (FRE.). 1968. 95.00 (0-7859-5538-0) Fr & Eur.

— Ethnologie Regionale: Afrique, Oceanie, Vol. 1. 1632p. 1972. lib. bdg. 140.00 (0-7859-3925-3) Fr & Eur.

— Histoire des Moeurs, Vol. 1: Coordonnees de l'Homme et la Culture Materielle. (FRE.). 1989. lib. bdg. 190.00 (0-7859-3864-8) Fr & Eur.

— Histoire des Moeurs, Vol. 2: Modes et Modeles. (FRE.). 1991. lib. bdg. 190.00 (0-7859-3892-3) Fr & Eur.

— Histoire des Moeurs, Vol. 3: Themes et Systemes Culturels. (FRE.). 1991. lib. bdg. 190.00 (0-7859-3893-1) Fr & Eur.

Poirier, Jean, jt. auth. see Dorion, Henri.

Poirier, Jean-Paul. Creep of Crystals. (Cambridge Earth Science Ser.). (Illus.). 275p. 1985. 69.95 (0-521-26177-5); pap. 34.95 (0-521-27851-1) Cambridge U Pr.

— Introduction to the Physics of the Earth's Interior. (Topics in Mineral Physics & Chemistry Ser.: No. 3). (Illus.). 250p. (C). 1991. 74.95 (0-521-38097-9) Cambridge U Pr.

Poirier, Lionel A., et al, eds. Essential Nutrients in Carcinogenesis. LC 86-25356. (Advances in Experimental Medicine & Biology Ser.: Vol. 206). 572p. 1986. 95.00 (0-306-42471-1, Plenum Pr) Plenum.

Poirier, Maurice. Sean Scully. LC 90-80946. (Illus.). 208p. 1990. 75.00 (1-55595-040-X) Hudson Hills.

Poirier, Miriam C. & Beland, F. A., eds. Carcinogenesis & Adducts in Animals & Humans. (Progress in Experimental Tumor Research Ser.: Vol. 31). (Illus.). viii, 116p. 1987. 95.25 (3-8055-4457-X) S Karger.

Poirier, Philip P., jt. auth. see Adams, R. J.

Poirier, Richard. The Performing Self: Compositions & Decompositions in the Languages of Contemporary Life. LC 91-37410. 224p. (Orig.). (C). 1992. reprint ed. text ed. 40.00 (0-8135-1794-X); reprint ed. pap. text ed. 15.00 (0-8135-1795-8) Rutgers U Pr.

— Poetry & Pragmatism. 228p. (C). 1992. 25.00 (0-674-67990-3) HUP.

— The Renewal of Literature: Emersonian Reflections. LC 86-10232. 256p. 1987. 19.95 (0-394-50140-3) Random.

— Robert Frost: The Work of Knowing. LC 89-60362. 384p. 1990. 45.00 (0-8047-1741-9); pap. 13.95 (0-8047-1742-7) Stanford U Pr.

— A World Elsewhere: The Place of Style in American Literature. LC 85-40376. 272p. 1985. reprint ed. pap. 10.95 (0-299-09934-2) U of Wis Pr.

Poirier, Richard, ed. Raritan Reading. LC 89-36068. 400p. (Orig.). (C). 1990. text ed. 45.00 (0-8135-1504-1); pap. 14.95 (0-8135-1505-X) Rutgers U Pr.

Poirier, Richard, ed. see Emerson, Ralph Waldo.

Poirier, Suzanne. Chicago's War on Syphilis, 1937-40: The Times, The Trib & the Clap Doctor. LC 94-19357. 1995. write for info. (0-252-02147-9) U of Ill Pr.

Poirier, Suzanne, jt. ed. see Murphy, Timothy F.

Poirion, Daniel, ed. see Yale French Studies Staff.

Poirot-Delpech, Bertrand. L' Ete '36. (FRE.). 1986. pap. 11.95 (0-7859-4239-4) Fr & Eur.

— Le Grand Dadais. (FRE.). 1974. pap. 8.95 (0-7859-4032-4) Fr & Eur.

— Les Grands de Ce Monde. (FRE.). 1984. pap. 11.95 (0-7859-4211-4) Fr & Eur.

Poirot, Luis. Pablo Neruda. 1990. 39.95 (0-393-02770-8); pap. 22.50 (0-393-30643-7) Norton.

Poirot, Paul L., comp. The Farm Problem. (Freeman Library). 134p. 1986. pap. 9.95 (0-910614-72-5) Foun Econ Ed.

Poirot, Paul L., ed. see Foundation for Economic Education Staff, et al.

Pois, Robert A. Friedrich Meinecke & German Politics in the Twentieth Century. LC 70-157818. 174p. reprint ed. pap. 49.60 (0-685-23956-X, 2031510) Bks Demand.

Poisner, A. M. & Trifaro, J. M., eds. The Electrophysiology of the Secretory Cell: The Secretory Process, Vol. 2. 312p. 1985. 137.50 (0-444-80599-0) Elsevier.

— In Vitro Methods for Studying Secretion. (Secretory Process Ser.: Vol. 3). 356p. 1987. 146.75 (0-444-80834-5) Elsevier.

— Secretory Granule. (Secretory Process Ser.: Vol. 1). 416p. 1982. 187.75 (0-444-80383-1) Elsevier.

Poisot, Charles, ed. see Rameau, Jean-Philippe.

Poisson, Bette J. Life's Reflections: Dreams & Memories. 64p. (Orig.). 1992. pap. 9.95 (1-879260-03-4) Evanston Pub.

— Thoughts: Etcetera...Etcetera. (Illus.). 96p. (Orig.). 1994. pap. 12.95 (1-879260-21-2) Evanston Pub.

Poisson, Gretchen V., jt. auth. see Poisson, Leandre.

Poisson, Leandre & Poisson, Gretchen V. Solar Gardening: Growing Vegetables Year-Round the American-Intensive Way. (Illus.). 288p. (Orig.). 1994. pap. 24.95 (0-930031-69-5) Chelsea Green Pub.

Poisson, S. & DeGangi, G. Emotional & Sensory Processing Problems: Assessment & Treatment Approaches for Young Children & Their Families. 139p. 1991. pap. text ed. 20.00 (1-880341-00-X) R S Lourie Ctr.

Poissonet, P., ed. Vegetation Dynamics in Grasslands, Heathlands & Mediterranean Ligneous Formations. 1982. lib. bdg. 85.00 (0-686-36955-6) Kluwer Ac.

Poissons, Helen F. The Old Light Cord. (Illus.). 68p. (Orig.). 1991. pap. text ed. 9.00 (0-9621498-7-X, Robin Hood) R Hood Little.

Poister, John. New American Bartenders Guide. 1989. pap. 6.99 (0-451-15978-0, Sig) NAL-Dutton.

***Poister, John J.** The Pyromaniac's Cookbook: The Best in Flaming Food & Drink. LC 95-10157. (Illus.). 1996. write for info. (0-385-47958-1) Doubleday.

Poister, Theodore H. Public Program Analysis: Applied Research Methods. 625p. 1978. 44.00 (0-8391-1190-8) Aspen Pub.

Poitevin, G. & Rarirkar, H., eds. Indian Peasant Women Speak Up. 1993. text ed. 25.00 (0-86311-264-1, Pub. by Orient Longman Ltd II) Apt Bks.

Poitier, Sidney. This Life. 416p. 1981. pap. 2.95 (0-345-29407-6) Ballantine.

Poitras, Genell, tr. see Chong-hui, Choe.

Poizat, Michel. The Angel's Cry: Beyond the Pleasure Principle in Opera. Denner, Arthur, tr. LC 91-55532. 240p. 1992. 25.00 (0-8014-2388-0) Cornell U Pr.

Poizner, Howard, et al. What the Hands Reveal about the Brain. (Studies in the Biology of Language & Cognition). 264p. 1990. reprint ed. pap. 15.00 (0-262-66066-0) MIT Pr.

Pojam, Louis P. Ethics: Discovering Right & Wrong. 2nd ed. LC 94-5781. 283p. 1995. pap. 19.95 (0-534-17832-4) Intl Thomson.

— What Can We Know? An Introduction to the Theory of Knowledge. LC 94-30155. 340p. 1995. pap. 19.95 (0-534-24834-9) Intl Thomson.

Pojasek, Robert B. Toxic & Hazardous Waste Disposal, 4 vols., 1. 1187p. 1980. 19.95 (0-250-40251-3) Technomic.

— Toxic & Hazardous Waste Disposal, 4 vols., 2. 1187p. 1980. 19.95 (0-250-40252-1) Technomic.

— Toxic & Hazardous Waste Disposal, 4 vols., 4. 1187p. 1980. 19.95 (0-250-40265-3) Technomic.

— Toxic & Hazardous Waste Disposal, 4 vols., Set. 1187p. 1980. 39.00 (0-685-55169-5) Technomic.

Pojeta, J., Jr. & Pope, J. K., eds. Studies in Paleontology & Stratigraphy. (Illus.). 456p. 1975. 25.00 (0-87710-296-1) Paleo Res.

Pojman. Life & Death: A Reader in Moral Problems. (Philosophy Ser.). 536p. (C). 1992. boxed 33.75 (0-86720-342-0) Jones & Bartlett.

— Life & Death: Grappling with the Moral Dilemmas of Our Time. (Philosophy Ser.). 175p. (C). 1992. pap. text ed. 20.00 (0-86720-334-X) Jones & Bartlett.

Pojman, Louis, jt. auth. see Beckwith, Francis.

***Pojman, Louis P.** Ethical Theory: Classical & Contemporary Readings. 2nd ed. LC 94-22111. 727p. 1995. text ed. 44.95 (0-534-21636-6) Intl Thomson.

— Ethics: Discovering Right & Wrong. 210p. (C). 1990. pap. 19.95 (0-534-12378-3) Intl Thomson.

— Philosophy: The Pursuit of Wisdom. 395p. 1994. pap. 23.95 (0-534-17982-7) Intl Thomson.

— Philosophy of Religion: An Anthology. 2nd ed. 578p. (C). 1994. text ed. 43.95 (0-534-20532-1) Intl Thomson.

— Religious Belief & the Will. (Problems of Philosophy Ser.). 256p. (C). 1986. text ed. 44.00 (0-7102-0399-3, RKP) Routledge.

— The Theory of Knowledge: Classical & Contemporary Readings. 556p. (C). 1993. text ed. 39.95 (0-534-17826-X) Intl Thomson.

***Pojman, Louis P., comp.** Philosophy: The Quest for Truth. 3rd ed. LC 94-44144. 1995. write for info. (0-534-25453-5) Intl Thomson.

Pojman, Louis P., ed. Environmental Ethics: Readings in Theory & Application. LC 93-47678. (Philosophy Ser.). 537p. (C). 1994. pap. text ed. 35.00 (0-86720-951-8) Jones & Bartlett.

— Ethical Theory: Classical & Contemporary Readings. 665p. (C). 1989. text ed. 43.95 (0-534-09360-4) Intl Thomson.

— Introduction to Philosophy: Classical & Contemporary Readings. 644p. (C). 1991. text ed. 39.95 (0-534-14370-9) Intl Thomson.

P
Q

— Philosophy: The Quest for Truth. 2nd ed. 531p. (C). 1992. pap. 37.95 (*0-534-16530-3*) Intl Thomson.

— Philosophy of Religion: An Anthology. 537p. (C). 1987. text ed. 42.95 (*0-534-06672-0*) Intl Thomson.

Pojman, Louis P., intro. Moral Philosophy: A Reader. LC 93-8813. 288p. (Orig.). (C). 1993. lib. bdg. 31.95 (*0-87220-165-1*); pap. text ed. 12.95 (*0-87220-164-3*) Hackett Pub.

Pok, Attila, ed. A Selected Bibliography of Modern Historiography. LC 91-46699. (Bibliographies & Indexes in World History Ser.: No. 24). 304p. 1992. text ed. 59.95 (*0-313-27231-X*, PBM, Greenwood Pr) Greenwood.

***Pokarna, K. L.** Social Beliefs, Cultural Practices in Health & Disease. (C). 1994. 28.00x (*81-7033-254-0*, Pub. by Rawat II) S Asia.

Pokeberry, P. J. The Secret of Hilhouse: An Adult Book for Teens. LC 93-60940. (Illus.). 96p. (Orig.). (J). (gr. 4 up). 1993. pap. 8.95 (*0-943962-02-1*) Viewpoint Pr.

Poker, D. & Ortiz, C., eds. Optical Materials: Processing & Science: Materials Research Society Symposium Proceedings, Vol. 152. 1989. text ed. 44.00 (*1-55899-025-9*) Materials Res.

Poker, D. B., jt. auth. see Withrow, S. P.

Pokharel, B. Land Revenue Administration in Nepal. (C). 1991. text ed. 75.00 (*0-7855-0147-9*, Pub. by Ratna Pustak Bhandar) St Mut.

Pokhlebkin, William. History of Vodka. 1992. 34.95 (*0-86091-359-7*, Pub. by Verso UK) Routledge Chapman & Hall.

Pokhodnaya, I. K. & Podgaetsky, V. V. Welding & Surfacing Reviews: Metallurgy of Welding & Welding Materials. Paton, B. E., ed. (Soviet Technology Reviews Ser.: Vol. 1, Pt. 2). iv, 62p. 1989. pap. text ed. 42.00 (*3-7186-4947-0*) Gordon & Breach.

Pokhotelov, Oleg, tr. see Vanshtein, S. I., et al.

***Pokierser, Herbert & Lechner, G., eds.** European Scientific User Conference Somatom Plus. LC 94-3446. 1994. 93.00 (*0-387-58198-7*) Spr-Verlag.

Pokinski, Deborah F. The Development of the American Modern Style. LC 84-2565. (Studies in the Fine Arts - Architecture: No. 8). (Illus.). 165p. reprint ed. pap. 47.10 (*0-8357-1567-1*, 2070570) Bks Demand.

Pokoly, Judit, tr. see Lendvai, Erno.

***Pokorney, B. & Slaughter, P.** Journey Through the Baha'i World. 190p. 1995. 26.95 (*0-614-07224-7*) Onewrld Pubns.

— Journey Through the Baha'i World. (Mystical Classics of the World Ser.). 190p. 1995. reprint ed. pap. 19.95 (*1-85168-055-1*) Onewrld Pubns.

Pokorny, Cornel. Computer Graphics Using C Plus Plus. LC 94-2872. 1994. write for info. (*0-938661-55-8*) Franklin Beedle.

Pokorny, Cornel & Gerald, Curtis. Computer Graphics: The Principles Behind the Art & Science. LC 88-30719. (Computer Scientist Ser.). (Illus.). 752p. (C). 1989. text ed. 62.95 (*0-938661-08-6*) Franklin Beedle.

Pokorny, Dusan. Efficiency & Justice in the Industrial World, Vol. 1: The Failure of the Soviet Experiment. LC 92-41002. 310p. 1993. 73.95 (*1-56324-139-0*) M E Sharpe.

Pokorny, Elizabeth J. U. S. Government Documents: A Practical Guide for Library Assistants in Academic & Public Libraries. 175p. 1989. lib. bdg. 23.50 (*0-87287-507-5*) Libs Unl.

Pokorny, J., et al. Waterplants & Wetland Processes. (Advances in Limnology Ser.: Heft 27). (Illus.). 265p. 1988. pap. text ed. 78.00 (*3-510-47025-7*) Lubrecht & Cramer.

Pokorny, Julius. A Concise Old Irish Grammar & Reader, 2 vols., Set. LC 78-72643. (Celtic Language & Literature Ser.: Goidelic & Brythonic). 240p. reprint ed. 57.50 (*0-404-17576-7*) AMS Pr.

— Indogermanisches Etymologisches Woerterbuch, 2 vols., Set. 1648p. (GER.). 1969. 395.00 (*0-8288-6602-3*, M-7478) Fr & Eur.

Pokorny, Julius, ed. see Walde, Alois.

Pokorny, Michael. An Introduction to Econometrics. (Illus.). 384p. (C). 1987. pap. text ed. 32.95 (*0-631-15003-X*) Blackwell Pubs.

Pokorny, Michael, jt. auth. see Clarkson, Petruska.

Pokorny, Petr. Colossians: A Commentary. Schatzmann, Siegfried, tr. LC 91-2971. 224p. 1991. 19.95 (*0-943575-38-9*) Hendrickson MA.

Pokorny, V. & Allen, K. Principles of Zoological Micropalaeontology. LC 61-18668. (International Series of Monographs on Earth Sciences: Vol. 10, Pt. 1). 1963. 272.00 (*0-08-009866-5*, Pub. by Pergamon Repr UK) Franklin.

— Principles of Zoological Micropalaeontology, Vol. 2. LC 61-18668. (International Series of Monographs on Earth Sciences: No. 2). 1965. 198.00 (*0-08-013596-X*, Pub. by Pergamon Repr UK) Franklin.

— Principles of Zoological Micropalaeontology, Vol. 2. LC 61-18668. (International Series of Monographs on Earth Sciences: Vol. 20). 1965. 196.00 (*0-08-011211-0*, Pub. by Pergamon Repr UK) Franklin.

***Pokorski, Doug.** Death Rehearsal. LC 95-60159. 1995. pap. 12.95 (*0-87243-215-7*) Templegate.

Pokotilov, Dmitri & Loewenthal, Rudolf. History of the Eastern Mongols During the Ming Dynasty from 1368 to 1631. LC 75-32335. (Studies in Chinese History & Civilization). 148p. 1976. reprint ed. text ed. 55.00 (*0-313-26956-4*, U6956) Greenwood.

***Pokras, Judith.** Contexts in the College Curriculum: A Reading Skills Text to Build Your Information Base. LC 95-12562. 1996. pap. 22.95 (*0-534-24211-1*) Intl Thomson.

***Pokras, Sandy.** Rapid Team Deployment. Gerould, Philip, ed. (Fifty-Minute Ser.). (Illus.). 120p. (Orig.). 1995. pap. 9.95 (*1-56052-321-2*) Crisp Pubns.

— Team Problem Solving. rev. ed. Crisp, Michael, ed. LC 94-72611. (Fifty-Minute Ser.). (Illus.). 130p. 1994. pap. 9.95 (*1-56052-314-X*) Crisp Pubns.

Pokrass, David, jt. auth. see Bray, Gary.

Pokress, E. Advertising & Public Relations. 8.40 (*0-685-22752-9*) Aurea.

— Research & Technical Writing. 8.60 (*0-685-22754-5*) Aurea.

Pokress, E., jt. auth. see Sandri-White, Alex.

Pokriots, Will, jt. auth. see Cortright, Sandy.

Pokrovskii, A. V., jt. auth. see Krasnosel'Skii, M. A.

Pokrovskii, L. N., jt. auth. see Ivovich, V. A.

***Pokrovsky, Nikita E.** Ralph Waldo Emerson: An Intellectual Portrait. 320p. 1994. write for info. (*0-9642968-0-2*); pap. text ed. write for info. (*0-9642968-1-0*) Ctr Am Studies Concord.

Pokrovsky, V. L. & Talapov, A. L. Theory of Incommensurate Crystals. (Soviet Scientific Reviews, Section A, Physics Reviews Supplement Ser.: Vol. 1). 171p. 1984. text ed. 211.00 (*3-7186-0134-6*) Gordon & Breach.

Pokrovsky, V. L., et al, eds. Solitons. (Modern Problems in Condensed Matter Sciences Ser.: Vol. 17). 927p. 1987. 223.00 (*0-444-87002-4*, North Holland) Elsevier.

Pokrovsky, Valery, et al. Modulated Structures. (Modern Condensed Matter Physics Ser.: Vol. 3). 200p. (C). 1995. text ed. 51.00 (*981-02-0747-6*); pap. text ed. 28.00 (*981-02-0748-4*) World Scientific Pub.

Pokshishevsky, V. Geography of the Soviet Union: Economy, Geography, Population & Production Complexes. (Illus.). 280p. 1975. 22.95 (*0-8464-0448-6*) Beekman Pubs.

Pokshishevsky, V. V., ed. Evaluation of the Soviet Population Census, 1970. 100p. (C). 1975. pap. 23.00 (*0-08-019672-1*, Pergamon Pr) Elsevier.

Pol, L. G. & Thomas, R. K. The Demography of Health & Health Care. (Demographic Methods & Population Analysis Ser.). (Illus.). 380p. (C). 1991. 45.00 (*0-306-43981-6*, Plenum Pr) Plenum.

Pol, Louis G. Business Demography: A Guide & Reference for Business Planners & Marketers. LC 87-2494. 312p. 1987. text ed. 59.95 (*0-89930-218-1*, PDY/, Quorum Bks) Greenwood.

Pol, Louis G., jt. auth. see Guy, Rebecca F.

Pol, V. Optical-Laser Microlithography IV, Vol. 1463. 1991. 86.00 (*0-8194-0562-0*) SPIE.

Pol, V., ed. Optical - Laser Microlithography. 1990. 70.00 (*0-8194-0311-3*, VOL. 1264) SPIE.

Pola, Lee & Bozic, Patricia. Cutting Hair at Home: Step-by-Step Home Hair-Cutting for the Entire Family. (Illus.). 128p. (Orig.). 1986. pap. 9.95 (*0-452-25830-8*, Plume) NAL-Dutton.

***Polacco.** Babushka's Doll. (J). 1995. pap. 14.95 (*0-689-80255-2*, Aladdin Paperbacks) S&S Childrens.

Polacco, Patricia. Appelemando's Dreams. (Illus.). 32p. (J). (ps-3). 1991. 14.95 (*0-399-21800-9*, Philomel Bks) Putnam Pub Group.

— Appelemando's Dreams. (Illus.). (J). 1995. 5.95 (*0-399-22835-7*, Sandcastle Bks) Putnam Pub Group.

— Babushka Baba Yaga. LC 92-30361. (Illus.). 32p. (J). 1993. 14.95 (*0-399-22531-5*, Philomel Bks) Putnam Pub Group.

— Babushka's Doll. LC 89-6122. (Illus.). 40p. (J). (ps-1). 1990. pap. 15.00 (*0-671-68343-8*, S&S Bks Young Read) S&S Childrens.

— Babushka's Mother Goose. LC 94-32332. (J). 1995. write for info. (*0-399-22747-4*, Philomel Bks) Putnam Pub Group.

— The Bee Tree. LC 92-8660. (Illus.). 32p. (J). (ps up). 1993. lib. bdg. 14.95 (*0-399-21965-X*, Philomel Bks) Putnam Pub Group.

— Boatride with Lillian Two-Blossom. (Illus.). 32p. 1989. 14.95 (*0-399-21470-4*, Philomel Bks) Putnam Pub Group.

— Chicken Sunday. (Illus.). 32p. (J). (ps-3). 1992. lib. bdg. 14.95 (*0-399-22133-6*, Philomel Bks) Putnam Pub Group.

— Firetalking. LC 93-48162. (Meet the Author Ser.). (Illus.). 32p. (J). (gr. 2-5). 1994. 13.95 (*1-878450-55-7*) R Owen Pubs.

— The Forever Quilt. write for info. (*0-318-62789-2*) S&S Trade.

— The Great Triple Creek Dam Affair. LC 95-10112. (J). 1996. lib. bdg. write for info. (*0-399-22943-4*) Putnam Pub Group.

— Just Plain Fancy. (Illus.). (J). (ps-3). 1990. pap. 15.95 (*0-553-05884-3*, Little Rooster) Bantam.

— Just Plain Fancy. (J). (ps-3). 1994. mass mkt. 4.99 (*0-440-40937-3*) Dell.

— The Keeping Quilt. (Illus.). 32p. (J). (ps-3). 1988. pap. 15.00 (*0-671-64963-9*, S&S Bks Young Read) S&S Childrens.

— The Keeping Quilt. (One World Friends & Neighbors Ser.). (Illus.). (J). (gr. k-4). 1993. 14.95 (*0-685-64811-7*); audio 11.00 (*1-882869-82-6*) Varsity Read Servs.

— Meteor! (Illus.). 32p. (J). (gr. k-3). 1987. 14.95 (*0-399-21699-5*, Putnam) Putnam Pub Group.

— Meteor! (Illus.). 32p. (J). (ps-3). 1992. pap. 5.95 (*0-399-22407-6*, Sandcastle Bks) Putnam Pub Group.

— Mrs. Katz & Tush. (J). 1992. 15.00 (*0-553-08122-5*, Little Rooster) Bantam.

— Mrs. Katz & Tush. (J). (ps-3). 1994. mass mkt. 4.99 (*0-440-40936-5*) Dell.

— My Ol' Man. LC 94-15395. (J). (gr. k-3). 1995. 15.95 (*0-399-22822-5*, Philomel Bks) Putnam Pub Group.

— My Rotten, Redheaded, Older Brother. (J). (ps-2). 1994. pap. 15.00 (*0-671-72751-6*, S&S Bks Young Read) S&S Childrens.

— Picnic at Mudsock Meadow. (Illus.). 32p. (J). (ps-3). 1992. 14.95 (*0-399-21811-4*, Putnam) Putnam Pub Group.

— Pink & Say. LC 93-36340. (Illus.). 48p. (J). (ps-3). 1994. lib. bdg. 15.95 (*0-399-22671-0*, Philomel Bks) Putnam Pub Group.

— Rechenka's Eggs. (Illus.). 32p. (J). (ps-3). 1988. 14.95 (*0-399-21501-8*, Philomel Bks) Putnam Pub Group.

— Some Birthday! LC 90-10381. (Illus.). 40p. (J). (ps-2). 1991. pap. 14.95 (*0-671-72750-8*, S&S Bks Young Read) S&S Childrens.

— Some Birthday. (J). (ps-6). 1993. pap. 5.95 (*0-671-87170-6*, S&S Bks Young Read) S&S Childrens.

— Thunder Cake. (Illus.). 32p. (J). (ps-3). 1990. 14.95 (*0-399-22231-6*, Philomel Bks) Putnam Pub Group.

— Tikvah Means Hope. (J). (ps-3). 1994. 15.95 (*0-385-32059-0*) Doubleday.

— Uncle Vova's Tree. (Illus.). 32p. (J). (ps-3). 1989. 14.95 (*0-399-21617-0*, Philomel Bks) Putnam Pub Group.

Polacek, Karel. What Ownership's All About. Kussi, Peter, tr. & intro. by. LC 92-33558. 240p. 1993. 21.95 (*0-945774-19-2*, PG5038.P64D813) Catbird Pr.

Polach, Dilette, ed. Radiocarbon Dating Literature: The First 21 Years, 1947-1968 - An Annotated Bibliography. 370p. 1988. text ed. 80.00 (*0-12-559290-6*) Acad Pr.

Polacheck, Hilda S. I Came a Stranger: The Story of a Hull-House Girl. Epstein, Dena J., ed. (Women in American History Ser.). (Illus.). 288p. 1991. pap. 12.95 (*0-252-06218-3*) U of Ill Pr.

Polachek, James M. The Inner Opium War. (East Asian Monographs: No. 151). 400p. (C). 1992. 30.00 (*0-674-45446-4*) HUP.

Polachek, Solomon W. & Siebert, W. Stanley. The Economics of Earnings. (Illus.). 350p. (C). 1993. 64.95 (*0-521-36476-0*); pap. 19.95 (*0-521-36728-X*) Cambridge U Pr.

Polack, Frank M. Scanning Electron Microscopy: Atlas of Corneal Pathology. (Illus.). 168p. 1983. 74.50 (*0-89352-203-1*, Yr Bk Med Pubs) Mosby Yr Bk.

Polack, Joel S. Manners & Customs of the New Zealanders, 2 vols. LC 75-35263. reprint ed. 64.50 (*0-404-14435-7*) AMS Pr.

Polack, Michael, jt. auth. see McBurnie, Grant.

Polack, Philip, ed. see Jessurun, Reheul.

Polackova, Kaca, tr. see Vaculik, Ludvik.

Poladi, Hassan. The Hazaras. LC 88-92511. 430p. 1989. lib. bdg. 19.95 (*0-929824-00-8*) Mughal Pub.

Poladian, Vartapet T., tr. see Gulleserian, Papken.

Poladitmontri, Panurat & Lew, Judy. Thailand the Beautiful Cookbook. (Beautiful Cookbook Ser.). 256p. 1992. 45.00 (*0-00-255029-6*) Collins SF.

***Polak, A. Laurence.** Final Legal Fictions: A Series of Cases from Folk-Lore & Opera. (Illus.). 117p. 1995. reprint ed. 30.00 (*1-56169-106-2*) W W Gaunt.

— Legal Fictions: A Series of Cases from the Classics. (Illus.). 127p. 1995. reprint ed. 32.00 (*1-56169-105-4*) W W Gaunt.

— More Legal Fictions: A Series of Cases from Shakespeare. (Illus.). 134p. 1995. reprint ed. 35.00 (*1-56169-107-0*) W W Gaunt.

Polak, Ada, ed. see Charleston, R. J., et al.

Polak, Alfred L. More Legal Fictions: A Series of Cases from Shakespeare. LC 73-153344. reprint ed. 27.50 (*0-404-05068-9*) AMS Pr.

Polak, Craig A., ed. see Hale, Judith A.

Polak, E. Computational Methods in Optimization. (Mathematics in Science & Engineering Ser.: Vol. 77). 1971. text ed. 121.00 (*0-12-559350-3*) Acad Pr.

Polak, Emil J. Medieval & Renaissance Letter Treatises & Form Letters: A Census of Manuscripts Found in Eastern Europe & the Former U. S. S. R. LC 92-36557. (Davis Medieval Texts & Studies: Vol. 8). 1992. 91.50 (*90-04-09667-1*) E J Brill.

Polak, H. S., et al. Mahatma Gandhi: The Father of Modern India. 1986. 49.95 (*0-318-36651-7*) Asia Bk Corp.

Polak, J. Cyclic Plasticity & Low Cycle Fatigue Life of Metals. (Materials Science Monographs: No. 63). 316p. 1991. 128.75 (*0-444-98839-4*) Elsevier.

Polak, J., jt. ed. see Lukas, P.

Polak, Jacob, jt. ed. see Heertje, Arnold.

Polak, Jacob B. & Van Der Kamp, Jan B., eds. Changes in the Field of Transport Studies. (Developments in Transportation Studies: No. 1). 1979. lib. bdg. 87.50 (*90-247-2147-4*) Kluwer Ac.

Polak, Jacques. Financial Policies & Development. LC 89-77720. 41p. 1990. pap. 6.95 (*1-55815-100-1*) ICS Pr.

Polak, Jacques J. The Changing Nature of IMF Conditionality. LC 91-34812. (Essays in International Finance Ser.: No. 184). 1991. pap. text ed. 8.00 (*0-88165-091-9*) Princeton U Int Finan Econ.

— Economic Theory & Financial Policy: The Selected Essays of Jacques J. Polak, Set. LC 94-6263. (Economists of the Twentieth Century Ser.). 1994. 149.95 (*1-85278-936-0*, Pub. by E Elgar Pub UK) Ashgate Pub Co.

— Financial Policies & Development. OECD Staff, ed. (Development Centre Studies). 232p. 1989. pap. 29.50 (*92-64-13187-6*) OECD.

— The World Bank & the IMF. 100p. (C). 1994. pap. 9.95x (*0-8157-7149-5*) Brookings.

Polak, Jacques J., jt. ed. see Mundell, Robert A.

Polak, Jeanne. Food Service for Fitness. (Illus.). 88p. 1981. 7.95 (*0-8087-3418-0*) Plycon Pr.

Polak, Joseph F. Peripheral Vascular Sonography: A Practical Guide. (Illus.). 384p. 1992. 80.00 (*0-683-06914-4*) Williams & Wilkins.

Polak, Julia M. Regulatory Peptides. (BioSeries-EXS: No. 56). 400p. 1989. 163.50 (*0-8176-1976-3*) Birkhauser.

Polak, Julia M., ed. Diagnostic Histopathology of Neuroendocrine Tumours. LC 92-49111. 500p. 1993. 150.00 (*0-443-04480-5*) Churchill.

Polak, Julia M. & McGee, James O. In Situ Hybridization: Principles & Practice. (Illus.). 258p. 1990. 59.95 (*0-19-261906-3*) OUP.

Polak, Julia M. & Priestley, John V., eds. Electron Microscopic Immunocytochemistry. (Modern Methods in Pathology Ser.). (Illus.). 280p. 1992. 60.00 (*0-19-963248-0*) OUP.

Polak, Julia M. & Van Noorden, Susan. Immunocytochemistry: Practical Applications in Pathology & Biology. 2nd ed. (Illus.). 703p. 1986. 245.00 (*0-7236-0870-9*, Pub. by John Wright UK) Buttrwrth-Heinemann.

Polak, Julia M. & Van Noorden, Susan, eds. An Introduction to Immunocytochemistry: Current Techniques & Problems. 2nd ed. (Royal Microscopy Society Microscopy Handbooks Ser.: No. 11). (Illus.). 64p. 1987. 14.95 (*0-19-856415-5*) OUP.

Polak, Julia M. & Varndel, I. M. Immunolabelling for Electron Microscopy. 1984. 56.00 (*0-444-80563-X*, I-431-84) Elsevier.

Polak, Julia M., jt. ed. see Roberts, Gareth W.

Polak, Julia M., jt. ed. see Steward, Peter J.

Polak, Julia M., jt. ed. see Wharton, John.

Polak, L. Immunological Aspects of Contact Sensitivity. (Monographs in Allergy: Vol. 15). (Illus.). 1979. pap. 77.75 (*3-8055-3050-1*) S Karger.

Polak, M. V., jt. auth. see Van Rooy, R.

Polak, Michael. Bottles: Identification & Price Guide. viii, 400p. (Orig.). 1994. pap. 15.00 (*0-380-77218-3*, Confident Collect) Avon.

Polak, Peter. Designing for Strength. (Illus.). 315p. (C). 1983. pap. 28.50 (*0-333-32676-8*, Pub. by Macm Pr UK) NYU Pr.

— Designing for Strength. (Illus.). 315p. (C). 1983. 55.00 (*0-333-32674-1*, Pub. by Macmillan Ed UK) Players Pr.

Polak, R., jt. ed. see Zahradnik, R.

Polak, W. Compiler Specification & Verification. (Lecture Notes in Computer Science Ser.: Vol. 124). 269p. 1981. pap. 24.00 (*0-387-10886-6*) Spr-Verlag.

Polakiewicz, David M. & Mellen, Stephanie. The Teeny Tiny Voice. (Illus.). 52p. (Orig.). (J). (gr. k-12). 1992. pap. 5.95 (*1-878040-08-1*) Meltec.

Polakiewicz, Leonard A. Supplemental Materials for First Year Polish. (Illus.). lxii, 212p. (Orig.). (POL.). (C). 1991. pap. text ed. 16.95 (*0-89357-215-2*) Slavica.

Polakoff, Phillip L. Work & Health: Its Your Life, an Action Guide to Job Hazards. LC 84-61087. (Orig.). 1984. pap. 7.95 (*0-918763-00-2*) Pr Assocs.

Polakoff, Phillip L. & O'Rourke, Paul F. Healthy Worker - Healthy Workplace: The Productivity Connection. (Illus.). 65p. (Orig.). (C). 1994. pap. text ed. 35.00 (*0-7881-0348-2*) Diane Pub.

Polakoski, Kenneth, jt. ed. see Boyarsky, Saul.

Polakov, Lester. We Live to Paint Again. 216p. 1993. pap. 25.00 (*0-9639720-0-6*) Logbooks Pr.

***Polakova, Jolana.** The Possibilities of Transcendence: Human Destructiveness & the Universality of Constructive Relations. Valeska, Jan, tr. LC 95-8655. (Problems in Contemporary Philosophy Ser.). 104p. 1996. 59.95 (*0-7734-8896-0*) E Mellen.

***Polakow, Dia.** American Phrasebook for Poles. rev. ed. 1993. pap. 7.95 (*0-7818-0198-2*) Hippocrene Bks.

Polakow, Valerie. Lives on the Edge: Single Mothers & Their Children in the Other America. LC 92-21977. (Illus.). 232p. (C). 1993. 22.50 (*0-226-67183-6*) U Ch Pr.

— Lives on the Edge: Single Mothers & Their Children in the Other America. x, 222p. (C). 1994. pap. 10.95 (*0-226-67184-4*) U Ch Pr.

Polakowski, N. H. & Ripling, E. Strength & Structure of Engineering Materials. 1965. text ed. 54.00 (*0-13-851790-8*) P-H.

Polan, A. J. Lenin & the End of Politics. LC 84-2489. 240p. 1984. pap. 13.00 (*0-520-05316-8*) U CA Pr.

Polan, Dana. In a Lonely Place. (Illus.). 72p. 1994. pap. 9.95 (*0-85170-360-7*, Pub. by British Film Inst UK) Ind U Pr.

— Power & Paranoia: History, Narrative, & the American Cinema, 1940-1950. LC 86-4144. 352p. 1989. text ed. 41.00 (*0-231-06284-2*); pap. text ed. 16.00 (*0-231-06285-0*) Col U Pr.

Polan, Dana, tr. see De Duve, Thierry.

Polan, Dana, tr. see Deleuze, Gilles & Guattari, Felix.

Polan, Dana B. The Political Language of Film & the Avant-Garde. Kirkpatrick, Diane, ed. LC 84-24062. (Studies in Cinema: No. 30). 152p. reprint ed. pap. 43.10 (*0-8357-1604-X*, 2070751) Bks Demand.

Polanco, Bermudez Y., tr. see Judge, William Q.

Polanco, Rafael. El Misterioso Origen Del Cristianismo: Ensayo en Religion Comparativa. (Illus.). 423p. (Orig.). (SPA.). 1989. pap. write for info. (*0-318-65960-3*) R Polanco.

Polanco, Vincente. Valores de Puerto Rico: Spanish Text. LC 74-14242. (Puerto Rican Experience Ser.). 178p. 1975. reprint ed. 17.95 (*0-405-06229-X*) Ayer.

***Poland.** Getting to Know Your One-Year-Old. 1995. mass mkt. 4.99 (*0-312-95418-2*) St Martin.

Poland, A. Scott, jt. auth. see Pitcher, Gayle D.

Poland, Alan & Kimbrough, Renate D., eds. Biological Mechanisms of Dioxin Action. LC 84-22955. (Banbury Report Ser.: No. 18). 500p. 1985. 75.00 (*0-87969-218-9*) Cold Spring Harbor.

Poland, Elizabeth Y., jt. auth. see Martin, Robert A.

Poland, James M. Understanding Terrorism: Groups, Strategies, & Responses. (Illus.). 288p. (C). 1988. pap. text ed. 39.80 (*0-13-936113-8*) P-H.

Poland, Jeffrey. Physicalism: The Philosophical Foundations. 392p. 1994. 52.00 (*0-19-824980-2*) OUP.

Poland, Larry. Como-Prepararse-Persecucion Que Se Avecina (The Coming Persecution) (SPA.). 1990. 5.50 (*1-56063-439-1*, 494029) Editorial Unilit.

An Asterisk (*) at the beginning of an entry indicates that the title is appearing in BIP for the first time.

Poland, Lynn M. Literary Criticism & Biblical Hermeneutics. (American Academy of Religion Academy Ser.: No. 48). (C). 1985. pap. 15.95 (*0-89130-836-9*, 01-01-48) Scholars Pr GA.

Poland, Marguerite. The Wood-Ash Stars. (Illus.). 64p. (J). 1990. pap. 5.95 (*0-86486-089-7*, Pub. by D Philip SA) Interlink Pub.

Poland, Marilyn L., jt. ed. see Whiteford, Linda M.

Poland, Robert P. Processing Medical Documents Using WordPerfect. LC 94-12977. 1995. write for info. (*0-02-802536-9*) Glencoe.

Poland, Robert P., jt. auth. see Schrag, Adele F.

Poland, Scott. Suicide Intervention in the Schools. LC 88-36988. (Guilford School Practitioner Ser.). 214p. 1989. pap. 19.95 (*0-89862-232-8*); pap. text ed. 45.00 (*0-89862-353-7*) Guilford Pr.

Poland, Stephen R. Easy CorelDRAW! 1994. pap. 19.99 (*1-56529-780-6*) Que.

— Ten Minute Guide to the Mac. (Ten Minute Guide Ser.). (Illus.). 160p. (Orig.). 1991. pap. 9.95 (*0-672-30063-X*) Sams.

— Ten Minute Guide to the Mac: New Edition. 1994. pap. 10.95 (*1-56761-356-X*) Alpha Bks IN.

Polangin, Richard F. & Feigenbaum, Ernest. Florida Health Care Reference, 1994-95. Nelson-Morrill, Creston, ed. 320p. 1994. lib. bdg. 17.95 (*1-879919-95-8*); pap. 12.95 (*1-879919-88-5*) HealthTrac.

Polanski. Puntos de Vista en la Lectura. (Bridging the Gap Ser.). 1994. pap. 27.95 (*0-8384-4665-5*) Heinle & Heinle.

Polanski, Roman. Knife in the Water: With Repulsion & Cul-de-Sac. (Illus.). 214p. (Orig.). 1988. pap. 12.95 (*0-571-12590-5*) Faber & Faber.

— Polanski: Three Film Scripts, Knife in the Water, Repulsion, Cul-de-Sac. LC 74-24656. (Illus.). 214p. 1975. 24.95 (*0-06-438425-X*) Boulevard.

Polansky, Barbara F., jt. ed. see Weil, Ben H.

Polansky, Joseph. Your Personal Horoscope, 1994: Month-by-Month Forecasts for Every Sign. 1993. pap. 9.00 (*1-85538-281-4*, Pub. by Aquarian Pr UK) Thorsons SF.

— Your Personal Horoscope, 1995: Month-by-Month Forecast for Every Sign. 1994. pap. 9.00 (*1-85538-376-4*, Pub. by Aquarian Pr UK) Thorsons SF.

Polansky, Joseph, jt. auth. see Nielsen, Greg.

Polansky, Larry. New Instrumentation & Orchestration: An Outline for Study. (Illus.). 91p. (Orig.). (C). 1986. pap. text ed. 15.00 (*0-945996-01-2*) Frog Peak Music.

Polansky, Leslie, jt. auth. see Torrence, Susan.

Polansky, Norman, et al. Damaged Parents: An Anatomy of Child Neglect. LC 80-22793. (Illus.). xii, 272p. 1983. pap. 9.95 (*0-226-67222-0*) U Ch Pr.

Polansky, Norman A. Integrated Ego Psychology. (Modern Applications of Social Work Ser.). 387p. 1991. pap. text ed. 28.95 (*0-202-26100-X*) Aldine de Gruyter.

— Integrated Ego Psychology. 2nd ed. (Modern Applications of Social Work Ser.). 387p. 1991. lib. bdg. 54.95 (*0-202-26099-2*) Aldine de Gruyter.

— Treating Loneliness in Child Protection. 5.00 (*0-87868-239-2*, G-21) Child Welfare.

Polansky, Norman A., ed. Social Work Research: Methods for the Helping Professions. rev. ed. LC 74-26798. (Illus.). 352p. 1975. lib. bdg. 17.50 (*0-226-67219-0*) U Ch Pr.

Polansky, Norman A., et al. Child Neglect: Understanding & Reaching the Parent. LC 72-83496. 94p. (C). 1972. pap. 5.00 (*0-87868-097-7*) Child Welfare.

— Roots of Futility. LC 72-5894. (Jossey-Bass Behavioral Science Ser.). 286p. reprint ed. pap. 81.60 (*0-685-16139-0*, 2027766) Bks Demand.

Polansky, O. E., jt. auth. see Gutman, I.

Polansky, Paul J., ed. see Dvorak, Otakar.

Polansky, Ronald M. Philosophy & Knowledge: A Commentary on Plato's Theaetetus. LC 90-56167. 264p. 1992. 38.50 (*0-8387-5215-2*) Bucknell U Pr.

Polanskyi, Bohdan S. Ukrainian Churches in New Jersey. (Illus.). 107p. 1993. 85.00 (*0-9635415-0-1*) B S P Pub.

— Ukrainian Churches in New Jersey. deluxe ed. (Illus.). 107p. 1993. 125.00 (*0-9635415-1-X*) B S P Pub.

Polanyi, John C., jt. ed. see Griffiths, Franklyn.

Polanyi, Karl. Great Transformation: The Political & Economic Origins of Our Time. 1957. pap. 15.00 (*0-8070-5679-0*, BP45) Beacon Pr.

Polanyi, Livia. Telling the American Story: From the Structure of Linguistic Texts to the Grammar of a Culture. LC 84-24196. (Language & Being Ser.). 168p. 1985. 39.50 (*0-89391-041-4*) Ablex Pub.

Polanyi, M. Technical & Trade Dictionary of Textile Terms: German-American English--American English-German. LC 66-18387. 1967. 259.00 (*0-08-011561-6*, Pub. by Pergamon Repr UK) Franklin.

Polanyi, Michael. Atomic Reactions. 1980. lib. bdg. 49.95 (*0-8490-3138-9*) Gordon Pr.

— The Contempt of Freedom: The Russian Experiment & After. LC 74-29384. (History, Philosophy & Sociology of Science Ser.). 1979. reprint ed. 18.95 (*0-405-06643-0*) Ayer.

— Knowing & Being: Essays. Grene, Marjorie, ed. LC 76-77151. 264p. reprint ed. pap. 75.30 (*0-685-15534-X*, 2027214) Bks Demand.

— Personal Knowledge: Towards a Post-Critical Philosophy. LC 58-5162. xiv, 428p. 1974. reprint ed. pap. text ed. 14.95 (*0-226-67288-3*, P583) U Ch Pr.

— Science, Faith & Society. 1964. pap. text ed. 7.95 (*0-226-67290-5*, P155) U Ch Pr.

— Scientific Thought & Social Reality: Essays by Michael Polanyi. Schwartz, Fred, ed. LC 74-5420. (Psychological Issues Monograph: No. 32, Vol. 8, No. 4). 168p. (C). 1974. text ed. 26.00 (*0-8236-6005-2*) Intl Univs Pr.

— The Tacit Dimension. 1983. 16.00 (*0-8446-5999-1*) Peter Smith.

Polanyi, Michael & Prosch, Harry. Meaning. LC 75-5067. 1977. reprint ed. pap. text ed. 13.95 (*0-226-67295-6*, P740) U Ch Pr.

Polarization Phenomena in Nuclear Reactions Symposium Staff. Polarization Phenomena in Nuclear Reactions: Proceedings of the Symposium, 3rd, Madison, 1970. Barschall, Henry H. & Haeberli, Willy, eds. LC 71-143762. 960p. 1971. text ed. 60.00 (*0-299-05890-5*) U of Wis Pr.

Polasek, M., tr. see Schulz, Karl.

Polaski, Arlene & Warner, Judith P. Saunders Fundamentals for Nursing Assistants. (Illus.). 944p. 1994. pap. text ed. 25.00 (*0-7216-3608-X*) Saunders.

***Polasky, Janet.** The Democratic Socialism of Emile Vandervelde: Between Reform & Revolution. LC 94-46196. (Illus.). 288p. 1995. 45.95 (*0-85496-394-4*); pap. 19.95 (*1-85973-033-7*) Berg Pubs.

Polasky, Janet L. Revolution in Brussels, 1787-1793. LC 86-40130. (Illus.). 315p. 1987. pap. text ed. 35.00 (*0-87451-385-5*) U Pr of New Eng.

Polatin, Betsy. Macrobiotics in Motion: Yin & Yang in Moving Spirals. LC 87-80493. (Illus.). 192p. 1987. pap. 15.95 (*0-87040-687-6*) Japan Pubns USA.

Polatin, Paul F. Modeling & Inversion of the Radar Response of Vegetation Canopies. (University of Michigan Report Ser.: No. RL899). 240p. reprint ed. pap. 68.40 (*0-7837-6781-1*, 2046611) Bks Demand.

Polay, E., ed. Iniuria Types in Roman Law. 228p. (C). 1986. 168.00 (*0-569-08999-9*, Pub. by Collets UK) Pro-Am Music.

Polcari, Stephen. Abstract Expressionism & the Modern Experience. (Illus.). 400p. (C). 1991. 69.95 (*0-521-40453-3*) Cambridge U Pr.

— Abstract Expressionism & the Modern Experience. (Illus.). 432p. (C). 1993. pap. 29.95 (*0-521-44826-3*) Cambridge U Pr.

Polchinski, Joseph, ed. see Harvey, Jeffrey.

Polcovar, Jane. Harriet Tubman. (What Was It Like? Ser.). (Illus.). 48p. (J). (gr. 2-4). 1988. pap. 2.50 (*0-681-40357-8*) Longmeadow Pr.

Polczinski, Len C. Ginseng Culture in Marathon County, Wisconsin: Historical Growth, Distribution, & Soils Inventory. (Illus.). 143p. (Orig.). 1982. pap. text ed. 27.95 (*1-881417-03-4*) D F Curran Prods.

Poldauf, I. English-Czech-English Dictionary. 1223p. (CZE & ENG.). 1991. 69.95 (*0-8288-0536-9*, M14850) Fr & Eur.

Poldauf, I., ed. Czech-English, English-Czech Dictionary. 8th ed. 1223p. (CZE & ENG.). 1990. 39.50 (*80-04-25987-1*) IBD Ltd.

Poldauf, I., jt. auth. see Osicka, V.

Polden, Margie & Whiteford, Barbara. The Postnatal Exercise Book: A Program of Fitness & Well-Being for Mother & Baby. (Illus.). 128p. 1992. pap. 11.95 (*0-8120-4993-4*) Barron.

Polden, P. Guide to the Records of the Lord Chancellor's Department. 376p. 1988. pap. 80.00 (*0-11-380015-0*, HM3902, Pub. by HMSO UK) UNIPUB.

Polder, Jerome. Comprehensive Guide to United States Air Force Pocket-Shoulder Insignia Mottos. LC 85-60227. 258p. 1985. pap. 23.00 (*0-9615456-3-1*) Aeroemblem Pubns.

— The Comprehensive Illustrated Guide to United States Air Force Insignia of the Persian Gulf. (Illustrated Guide Series to Air Force Pocket-Shoulder Insignia). (Illus.). 68p. 1994. pap. 15.00 (*0-9615456-8-2*) Aeroemblem Pubns.

— Comprehensive Illustrated Guide to United States Air Force Pocket-Shoulder Insignia, Vol. 1. LC 85-72269. (Illus.). 235p. 1985. pap. 23.00 (*0-9615456-0-7*) Aeroemblem Pubns.

— Comprehensive Illustrated Guide to United States Air Force Pocket-Shoulder Insignia, Vol. 2. LC 85-72269. (Illus.). 235p. 1986. pap. 23.00 (*0-9615456-1-5*) Aeroemblem Pubns.

— The Comprehensive Illustrated Guide to United States Air Force Pocket-Shoulder Insignia, Vol. 3. LC 85-72269. (Illus.). 235p. 1986. pap. 23.00 (*0-9615456-2-3*) Aeroemblem Pubns.

— The Comprehensive Illustrated Guide to United States Air Force Pocket-Shoulder Insignia, Vol. 4. LC 85-72269. (Illus.). 235p. 1987. pap. 23.00 (*0-9615456-4-X*) Aeroemblem Pubns.

— Comprehensive Illustrated Guide to United States Air Force Pocket-Shoulder Insignia, Vol. 5. LC 85-72269. (Illus.). 238p. 1988. pap. 23.00 (*0-9615456-5-8*) Aeroemblem Pubns.

— Comprehensive Illustrated Guide to United State's Air Force Pocket Shoulder Insignia, Vol. 6. LC 85-72269. (Illus.). 169p. 1989. pap. 23.00 (*0-9615456-6-6*) Aeroemblem Pubns.

— The Comprehensive Illustrated Guide to USAF Pocket - Shoulder Insignia, Vol. 7. (Illus.). 240p. (Orig.). 1992. pap. 23.00 (*0-9615456-7-4*) Aeroemblem Pubns.

Polderman, A. M., jt. ed. see Kager, P. A.

Poldervaart, Arie W. Black-Robed Justice. Cortes, Carlos E., ed. LC 76-1472. (Chicano Heritage Ser.). 1977. reprint ed. lib. bdg. 18.95 (*0-405-09519-8*) Ayer.

Poldinger, Walter & Wider, Francois. Index Psychopharmacorum. 7th ed. 334p. 1992. text ed. 33.00 (*0-88937-072-9*) Hogrefe & Huber Pubs.

***Pole, Andy.** Applied Bayesian Forecasting & Time Series Analysis. 1994. 59.95 (*0-412-04401-3*, Blackie & Son-Chapman NY) Routledge Chapman & Hall.

Pole, Christopher J. Implementing Records of Achievement. LC 92-18995. 1993. 90.00 (*0-335-09961-0*, Open Univ Pr); pap. 32.50 (*0-335-09960-2*, Open Univ Pr) Taylor & Francis.

Pole, J. R. Equality, Status, & Power in Thomas Jefferson's Virginia. (Foundations of America Ser.). (Illus.). 40p. (Orig.). 1986. pap. 9.95 (*0-87935-114-4*) Colonial Williamsburg.

— The Pursuit of Equality in American History. 2nd enl. rev. ed. LC 92-12928. 1993. 18.00 (*0-520-07987-6*) U CA Pr.

Pole, J. R., ed. The Revolution in America, 1754-1788: Documents & Commentaries. LC 70-126037. xxxii, 616p. 1970. 67.50 (*0-8047-0761-8*) Stanford U Pr.

Pole, J. R., jt. ed. see Greene, Jack P.

Pole, Rupert, intro. Incest: From "A Journal of Love": The Unexpurgated Diary of Anais Nin, 1932-1934. LC 92-12441. 1992. 24.95 (*0-15-144366-1*) HarBrace.

Pole, Wellesley T. The Silent Road. 240p. (Orig.). Date not set. pap. 17.95 (*0-8464-4290-6*) Beekman Pubs.

Pole, Wellesley T. & Lehmann, Rosamond. A Man Seen Afar. 128p. (Orig.). Date not set. pap. 11.95 (*0-8464-4248-5*) Beekman Pubs.

Polednak, Anthony P. Racial & Ethnic Differences in Disease. (Illus.). 376p. 1989. 59.95 (*0-19-505970-0*) OUP.

Polek, David & Anderhub, Rita. Advent Begins at Home. 1979. pap. 2.95 (*0-89243-111-3*) Liguori Pubns.

Polelle, Michael J. & Ottley, Bruce L. Illinois Tort Law, 2 vols., Set. 2nd ed. LC 93-32151. 800p. 1994. ring bd. 165.00 (*1-56257-680-1*) Michie Butterworth.

Poleman, Charlotte M., jt. auth. see Peckenpaugh, Nancy J.

Poleman, Horace I. Census of Indic Manuscripts in the United States & Canada. (American Oriental Ser.: Vol. 12). 1938. 40.00 (*0-527-02686-7*) Periodicals Srv.

Poleman, John. All the Famous Battles That Have Been Fought in Our Age. LC 68-54658. (English Experience Ser.: No. 64). 337p. 1968. reprint ed. 55.00 (*90-221-0064-2*) Walter J Johnson.

Poleman, Thomas T. The Papaloapan Project: Agricultural Development in the Mexican Tropics. (Illus.). xi, 167p. 1964. 27.50 (*0-8047-0207-1*) Stanford U Pr.

Poleman, Thomas T., jt. auth. see Ewell, Peter T.

Poleman, Thomas T., jt. auth. see Sharma, Rita.

Polemis, Aphrodite. From a Traditional Greek Kitchen: Vegetarian Cuisine. LC 92-18500. 192p. 1992. pap. 9.95 (*0-913990-93-0*) Book Pub Co.

Polemon, John. The Second Part of the Booke of Battailes, Fought in Our Age. LC 78-38219. (English Experience Ser.: No. 483). 196p. 1972. reprint ed. 13.00 (*90-221-0483-4*) Walter J Johnson.

Polen, Dallas A., Jr. Choice Guide: A Workbook for Arrangements at the Time of a Death. 145p. (Orig.). 1992. pap. 9.95 (*0-9634285-0-0*) Alljoy Res.

— Funeral Arrangement Choice Guide: A Workbook for Arrangements at the Time of a Death. 144p. 1994. student ed, pap. 11.95 (*0-9634285-1-9*) Alljoy Res.

Polen, Lynn. Cubs Brain Twisters. (Illus.). 160p. 1990. pap. 12.00 (*1-879216-00-0*) Stny Brook Prods.

Polen, Nehemia. The Holy Fire: The Teachings of Rabbi Kalonymus Kalman Shapira, the Rebbe of the Warsaw Ghetto. LC 93-36791. 232p. 1994. 30.00 (*0-87668-842-3*) Aronson.

Polenberg, Richard. Fighting Faiths: The Abrams Case, the Supreme Court, & Free Speech. (Illus.). 464p. 1989. pap. 12.50 (*0-14-011736-9*, Penguin Bks) Viking Penguin.

— One Nation Divisible: Class, Race & Ethnicity in the U. S. Since 1938. (Pelican History of the United States Ser.). 1980. pap. 9.95 (*0-14-021246-9*, Penguin Bks) Viking Penguin.

— One Nation Divisible: Class, Race & Ethnicity in the United States since 1938. 1993. 19.75 (*0-8446-6676-9*) Peter Smith.

— War & Society: The United States 1941-1945. LC 76-155879. (Critical Periods of History Ser.). 286p. (C). 1990. pap. text ed. 13.00 (*0-397-47224-2*) HarpCollege.

— War & Society: The United States, 1941-1945. LC 80-10734. (Critical Periods of History Ser.). 298p. 1980. reprint ed. text ed. 55.00 (*0-313-22348-3*, POWS, Greenwood Pr) Greenwood.

Polenberg, Richard, jt. auth. see LaFeber, Walter.

Polenov, F. D. Polenovo: The Vasily Polenov Museum Estate. 178p. (ENG & RUS.). 1982. 80.00 (*0-317-57411-6*, Pub. by Collets UK) St Mut.

Polenske, Karen R. & Rose, Adam Z. Frontiers of Input-Output Analysis. Miller, Ronald E. et al, eds. (Illus.). 352p. 1989. 55.00 (*0-19-505758-9*) OUP.

Polenske, Karen R. & Xikang, Chen. Chinese Economic Planning & Input-Output Analysis. (Illus.). 368p. 1992. 65.00 (*0-19-585249-4*) OUP.

Polenton, Sicco. Sicconis Polentoni Scriptorum Illustrium Latinaelinguae Libri XVIII. Ullman, B. L., ed. LC 29-7429. (American Academy in Rome. Papers & Monographs: Vol. 6). 597p. reprint ed. pap. 170.20 (*0-685-15597-8*, 2026721) Bks Demand.

Polenz, Peter Von. Geschichte der Deutschen Sprache. 9th ed. (Sammlung Goeschen Ser.: Vol. 2206). (C). 1984. 13.20 (*3-11-007998-4*) De Gruyter.

Polese, Carolyn. Promise Not to Tell. LC 84-19767. (Illus.). 66p. (J). (gr. 3 up). 1985. 16.95 (*0-89885-239-0*) Human Sci Pr.

— Promise Not to Tell. LC 92-24599. (Illus.). 64p. (J). (gr. 4 up). 1993. reprint ed. pap. 3.95 (*0-688-12026-1*, Pub. by Beech Tree Bks) Morrow.

Polese, James. Tales from the Iron Triangle: Boyhood Days in the San Francisco Bay Area of the 1920's. Polese, Richard, ed. (Illus.). 96p. (Orig.). (J). (gr. 5-12). 1995. pap. 9.95 (*0-943734-12-6*) Ocean Tree Bks.

Polese, Richard, comp. Prayers of the World. 96p. 1995. pap. 8.00 (*0-943734-00-2*) Ocean Tree Bks.

Polese, Richard, ed. see Pinkerton, Elaine.

Polese, Richard, ed. see Polese, James.

Polese, Richard L. Discovering Dixie along the Magnolia Trail: The Day-by-Day Travel Guide to the Best of the Deep South. LC 91-15728. (Adventure Roads Ser.). (Illus.). 208p. (Orig.). 1991. pap. 11.95 (*0-943734-18-5*) Ocean Tree Bks.

Polese, Richard L., ed. see Coates, Ruth A.

Polesetsky, Matt, jt. ed. see Wekesser, Carol.

Polesetsky, Matthew & Cozic, Charles, eds. Energy Alternatives. LC 91-24387. (Current Controversies Ser.). 200p. (YA). (gr. 10 up). 1991. lib. bdg. 19.95 (*0-89908-577-6*); pap. text ed. 11.55 (*0-89908-583-0*) Greenhaven.

Polesetsky, Matthew & Dudley, William, eds. The New World Order: Opposing Viewpoints. LC 91-12374. (Opposing Viewpoints Ser.). (Illus.). 240p. (YA). (gr. 10 up). 1991. lib. bdg. 19.95 (*0-89908-183-5*); pap. 11.55 (*0-89908-158-4*) Greenhaven.

Polesetsky, Matthew, et al, eds. Global Resources: Opposing Viewpoints. LC 90-24088. (Opposing Viewpoints Ser.). (Illus.). 264p. (YA). (gr. 10 up). 1991. lib. bdg. 17.95 (*0-89908-177-0*); pap. 9.95 (*0-89908-152-5*) Greenhaven.

Polette, Doug & Landers, Jack. Construction Systems. (Illus.). 350p. 1995. 34.64 (*1-56637-041-8*) Goodheart.

Polette, Keith. Patterns for Reading, Writing & Thinking. (Illus.). 48p. 1990. pap. 5.95 (*0-913839-87-6*) Bk Lures.

— Read, Write, Now! (Illus.). 44p. (J). (gr. 5-9). 1993. pap. text ed. 5.95 (*1-879287-20-X*) Bk Lures.

Polette, Keith, jt. auth. see Mallett, Jerry.

Polette, Keith, jt. auth. see Polette, Nancy.

Polette, Nancy. The ABCs of Books & Thinking Skills. (Illus.). 144p. (YA). (gr. 1-8). 1987. pap. 14.95 (*0-913839-61-2*) Bk Lures.

— Amelia Bedelia Thinking Book. (Illus.). 48p. (J). (gr. k-3). 1994. pap. 5.95 (*1-879287-10-2*) Bk Lures.

— Apple Trees to Zinnias. (Illus.). 48p. (J). 1992. pap. 5.95 (*1-879287-14-5*) Bk Lures.

— Bartering with Books. (Illus.). 48p. (J). (gr. 4-7). 1992. pap. 5.95 (*1-879287-16-1*) Bk Lures.

— The Best Ever Writing Models. (Illus.). 124p. (J). (gr. 4-9). 1989. pap. 12.95 (*0-913839-78-7*) Bk Lures.

— Birds in Literature. (Illus.). 48p. (J). (gr. k-3). 1990. pap. 5.95 (*0-913839-86-8*) Bk Lures.

— The Book Bag. (Illus.). 64p. (J). 1986. pap. 7.95 (*0-913839-46-9*) Bk Lures.

— Books & Real Life: A Guide for Gifted Students & Teachers, Grades 1-9. LC 84-42607. 125p. (Orig.). 1984. pap. 17.50x (*0-89950-119-2*) McFarland & Co.

— Books to Begin On. (Illus.). 48p. (J). (ps-1). 1994. pap. 5.95 (*1-879287-28-5*) Bk Lures.

— Concert Reading. (Illus.). 48p. (J). (gr. k-3). 1992. pap. 5.95 (*1-879287-07-2*) Bk Lures.

— Developing Methods of Inquiry: A Source Book for Elementary Media Personnel. LC 72-11992. 200p. 1973. 16.50 (*0-8108-0575-8*) Scarecrow.

— E Is for Everybody: A Manual for Bringing Fine Picture Books into the Hands & Hearts of Children. 2nd ed. LC 82-10508. 194p. (J). (gr. 1-7). 1982. 20.00 (*0-8108-1579-6*) Scarecrow.

— Earthwatch. (Illus.). 48p. (J). (gr. 3-6). 1993. pap. 5.95 (*1-879287-26-9*) Bk Lures.

— Eight Cinderellas. (Illus.). 48p. (J). (gr. 3-6). 1994. pap. 5.95 (*1-879287-29-3*) Bk Lures.

— Enjoying Fairy Tales. (Illus.). 48p. 1991. pap. 5.95 (*0-913839-94-9*) Bk Lures.

— Expanded First Research Projects. 2nd ed. (Illus.). 48p. 1991. pap. 5.95 (*0-913839-92-2*) Bk Lures.

— Exploring Themes with Aesop's Fables & Picture Books. (Illus.). 48p. (J). (gr. 2-6). 1992. pap. 5.95 (*1-879287-12-9*) Bk Lures.

— Favorite Novel Animals. (Illus.). 48p. (J). (gr. 3-6). 1992. pap. 5.95 (*1-879287-15-3*) Bk Lures.

— Frog & Toad Thinking Book. (Illus.). 48p. (J). (gr. k-3). 1992. pap. 5.95 (*1-879287-09-9*) Bk Lures.

— Giants. (Illus.). 48p. 1990. pap. 5.95 (*0-913839-83-3*) Bk Lures.

— Hans Christian Andersen Couldn't Spell. (Illus.). 36p. 1987. pap. 3.95 (*0-913839-67-1*) Bk Lures.

— The Hole by the Apple Tree. LC 90-24646. 32p. (J). 1992. 14.00 (*0-688-10557-2*); lib. bdg. 13.93 (*0-688-10558-0*) Greenwillow.

— The How-To Book of Literature-Based Reading. (Illus.). 124p. 1990. pap. 12.95 (*0-913839-88-4*) Bk Lures.

— Literature-Based Spelling & Writing Activities for Primary Grades. (Illus.). 48p. (Orig.). (J). (gr. 1-4). 1993. pap. 5.95 (*1-879287-23-4*) Bk Lures.

— Little Old Woman & the Hungry Cat. LC 88-18788. (Illus.). 24p. (J). (ps up). 1989. 12.95 (*0-688-08314-5*); lib. bdg. 12.88 (*0-688-08315-3*) Greenwillow.

— The Little Old Woman & the Hungry Cat. Cohn, Amy, ed. LC 88-18778. (Illus.). 24p. (J). (ps up). 1994. reprint ed. pap. 4.95 (*0-688-13636-2*, Mulberry) Morrow.

— The Little Old Woman & the Hungry Cat: Big Book Edition. Cohn, Amy, ed. (Illus.). 24p. (J). (ps up). 1994. reprint ed. pap. 18.95 (*0-688-13631-1*, Mulberry) Morrow.

— Middle Ages: Learning Through Literature. (Illus.). 48p. (J). (gr. 3-6). 1994. pap. 5.95 (*1-879287-27-7*) Bk Lures.

— Mother Goose's Animals. (Illus.). 128p. (J). (gr. 1-4). 1992. pap. 12.95 (*1-879287-13-7*) Bk Lures.

— Multi-Cultural Literature: Books & Activities. (Illus.). 48p. (Orig.). (J). (gr. 3-6). 1993. pap. 5.95 (*1-879287-22-6*) Bk Lures.

— Multicultural Readers Theatre. 128p. 1994. pap. text ed. 12.95 (*1-879287-31-5*) Bk Lures.

— Novel Booktalks. 144p. (Orig.). (J). (gr. 4-8). 1992. pap. 9.95 (*1-879287-18-8*) Bk Lures.

— Novel Thinking. (Illus.). 128p. (YA). (gr. 6-12). 1987. pap. 12.95 (*0-913839-47-7*) Bk Lures.

— Pick a Pattern. 4th ed. (Illus.). 48p. (J). (gr. k-3). 1992. pap. 5.95 (*1-879287-05-6*) Bk Lures.

— Picture Books for Gifted Programs. LC 81-9113. 228p. 1981. 20.00 (0-8108-1461-7) Scarecrow.
— Picture Booktalks. 144p. (J). (gr. 1-3). 1992. pap. 9.95 (1-879287-17-X) Bk Lures.
— Reader's Almanac. (Illus.). 148p. (J). (gr. 4-8). 1985. pap. 14.95 (0-913839-44-2) Bk Lures.
— Reading the World with Folktales. (Illus.). 124p. (Orig.). (J). (gr. 2-4). 1993. pap. 12.95 (1-879287-19-6) Bk Lures.
— Reading with Music. (Illus.). 48p. (J). (gr. 4-7). 1992. pap. 5.95 (1-879287-04-8) Bk Lures.
— Research Book for Gifted Programs K-8. (Illus.). 176p. 1984. pap. 14.95 (0-913839-28-0) Bk Lures.
— Research Book of the Fifty States. (Illus.). 48p. 1991. pap. 5.95 (1-879287-03-X) Bk Lures.
— The Research Project Book. 2nd ed. (Illus.). 128p. (J). (gr. 4-9). 1992. pap. 12.95 (1-879287-06-4) Bk Lures.
— Research Without Copying. 2nd ed. (Illus.). 48p. 1991. pap. 5.95 (0-913839-91-4) Bk Lures.
— Survival. (Illus.). 48p. (Orig.). 1991. pap. 5.95 (0-913839-93-0) Bk Lures.
— Teaching Critical Reading with Children's Literature. (Illus.). 128p. (J). (gr. 4-9). 1988. pap. 12.95 (0-913839-73-6) Bk Lures.
— The Thinker's Mother Goose. (Illus.). 32p. (J). 1983. pap. 3.95 (0-913839-25-6) Bk Lures.
— U. S. Historical Fiction: A Whole Language Approach. (Illus.). 48p. (J). (gr. 5-8). 1990. pap. 5.95 (0-913839-85-X) Bk Lures.
— U. S. History Readers Theatre. 48p. 1994. pap. text ed. 5.95 (1-879287-30-7) Bk Lures.
— Ultimate Book Report Book. (Illus.). 48p. 1991. pap. 5.95 (0-913839-95-7) Bk Lures.
— Unforgettable Characters. (Illus.). 48p. (Orig.). 1991. pap. 5.95 (0-913839-97-3) Bk Lures.
— Whole Language in Action. (Illus.). 128p. 1990. pap. 12.95 (0-913839-80-9) Bk Lures.
— Whole Language Unit. (Illus.). 32p. 1989. pap. 4.95 (0-913839-79-5) Bk Lures.
— Write Your Own Fairy Tale. enl. ed. (Illus.). 48p. (J). (gr. 3-7). 1993. reprint ed. pap. 5.95 (1-879287-25-0) Bk Lures.
— Young Heroines. (Illus.). 48p. (Orig.). 1991. pap. 5.95 (0-913839-96-5) Bk Lures.

Polette, Nancy & Hamlin, Marjorie. Celebrating with Books. LC 77-3862. (Illus.). 184p. 1977. 20.00 (0-8108-1032-8) Scarecrow.
— Exploring Books with Gifted Children. LC 80-23721. 214p. 1980. lib. bdg. 19.00 (0-87287-216-5) Libs Unl.
— Reading Guidance in a Media Age. LC 75-26833. (Illus.). 275p. 1975. 22.50 (0-8108-0873-0) Scarecrow.

Polette, Nancy & Mealy, Virginia. Enjoying Tall Tales. (Illus.). 48p. (Orig.). 1991. 5.95 (0-913839-90-6) Bk Lures.

Polette, Nancy & O'Neal, Kathleen. The Crosby Bonsall Thinking Book. (Illus.). 32p. (J). 1987. pap. 4.95 (0-913839-65-5) Bk Lures.
— Easy Reader Thinking Book. (Illus.). 48p. (J). (gr. k-3). 1994. pap. 5.95 (1-879287-08-0) Bk Lures.

Polette, Nancy & Polette, Keith. Readers Theatre. (Illus.). 48p. (J). (gr. 4-8). 1986. pap. 5.95 (0-913839-56-6) Bk Lures.

Polette, Nancy, jt. auth. see Albert, Kristine.

Polette, Nancy, jt. intro. see Bernhardt, Edythe.

Polette, Nancy, jt. auth. see Levine, Gloria.

Polette, Nancy J. Brain Power Through Picture Books: Help Children Develop with Books That Stimulate Specific Parts of Their Minds. LC 91-50976. (Illus.). 144p. 1992. pap. text ed. 18.95x (0-89950-708-5) McFarland & Co.

Poletti, Jacques & Lillard, Louise. L' Hexagone, C'est la France. 302p. (FRE.). (C). 1984. pap. text ed. 22.75 (0-03-062021-X) HB Coll Pubs.

Polevoi, Boris N. Story about a Real Man. LC 79-98870. 558p. 1970. reprint ed. text ed. 65.00 (0-8371-3993-7, PORM, Greenwood Pr) Greenwood.

Polevoi, V. Popular Encyclopaedia of Art, Vol. 1. 447p. (RUS.). (C). 1986. 160.00 (0-685-46854-2, Pub. by Collets) St Mut.
— Popular Encyclopaedia of Art, Vol. 2. 432p. (RUS.). (C). 1986. 160.00 (0-685-46853-4, Pub. by Collets) St Mut.

Polevoy, Savely. Geothermal Energy in the U. S. S. R. A Survey of Resources, Methodology, Geology & Use. Jones, Steven, ed. 144p. (Orig.). 1985. pap. text ed. 75.00 (1-55831-034-7) Delphic Associates.

***Polevoy, Savely & Waltz, James P.** Concise Water Science & Engineering. LC 94-48014. 1995. 49.95 (0-412-05351-9); pap. 24.95 (0-412-05361-6) Chapman & Hall.

Polewczak, J., jt. ed. see Greenberg, W.

Poley, Franklin W. Contact Conditioning. (Illus.). 256p. 1991. text ed. 39.95 (0-89876-182-4) Gardner Pr.

Poley, Hans. Return to the Hiding Place. 1993. 16.99 (0-7814-0932-2, LifeJourney) Chariot Family.

Poley, Irvin C. & Poley, Ruth V. Quaker Anecdotes. (C). 1983. pap. 3.00 (0-87574-033-2) Pendle Hill.

***Poley, Michelle F.** Mastering the Art of Communication: Your Keys to Developing a More Effective Personal Style. Scanlon, Kelly, ed. 132p. (Orig.). 1995. pap. 15.95 (1-878542-34-6) SkillPath Pubns.
— A Winning Attitude: How to Develop Your Most Important Asset! (Illus.). x, 80p. 1992. pap. 10.95 (1-878542-28-1) SkillPath Pubns.

Poley Rowan, Janice & Master, Eileen. Works in Progress: Student Essays for Developing Writers. 96p. (C). 1993. per. 9.95 (0-8403-9010-6) Kendall-Hunt.

Poley, Ruth V., jt. auth. see Poley, Irvin C.

Poley, Wayne, et al. Alcoholism: A Treatment Manual. LC 78-13455. 1979. text ed. 25.00 (0-89876-063-1) Gardner Pr.

Polezhaev, L. V. Loss & Restoration of Regenerative Capacity in Tissues & Organs of Animals. Carlson, Bruce M., tr. LC 71-160029. 395p. 1972. 34.00 (0-674-53920-6) HUP.

Polfack, Robert L., et al. The Pain-Free Tryptophan Diet. 256p. 1987. 16.45 (0-446-51317-2) Warner Bks.

Polfen, M. N. A Practical Guide to European Travel. 200p. 1981. pap. 7.95 (0-934036-07-1) PMF Research.
— A Practical Guide to Grand Opera. 200p. (Orig.). 1981. pap. 7.95 (0-934036-08-X) PMF Research.

Polfer, Al, et al. A Practical Guide to Starting & Managing Your Central Florida Business. 236p. (Orig.). (C). 1989. pap. text ed. 24.95 (0-9623038-0-1) Busn Dev Assocs.

Polgar, Antoine, ed. see Reed, Dolores M.

Polgar, Laszlo. Mechanisms of Protease Action. 288p. 1989. 204.00 (0-8493-6901-0, QP609) CRC Pr.

Polgar, Stephen & Thomas, Shane A. Introduction to Research in the Health Sciences. 2nd ed. (Illus.). 357p. 1991. pap. text ed. 39.00 (0-443-04363-9) Churchill.
— Introduction to Research in the Health Sciences. 3rd ed. 1994. pap. 39.00 (0-443-05039-2) Churchill.

Polgar, Steven, ed. Population, Ecology, & Social Evolution. (World Anthropology Ser.). (Illus.). x, 354p. 1975. 30.70 (0-685-18668-7) Mouton.

Polgardy, Ed. From the Darkness. 114p. (Orig.). 1991. pap. 9.95 (0-944735-98-3) Malibu Graphics.

Polge, Coral & Hunter, Kay. The Living Image. 192p. 1984. 40.00 (0-7212-0634-4, Pub. by Regency Press) St Mut.

Polhamus, Jean B. Dinosaur Funny Bones. Rayburn, Cherie, ed. (Illus.). 27p. (J). (gr. k-6). 1994. pap. text ed. 14.25 (0-944943-53-5, 23846-0) Current Inc.

Polhamus, Jean B. & Funai, M. Dinosaur Funny Bones. (J). 1980. 4.95 (0-13-214536-7) P-H.

Polhemus, Allen V. Mohegan Indian Maps of Montville, Connecticut. (Illus.). 84p. 1993. 42.95 (1-883009-00-6) Nutmeg Pubs.

Polhemus, Robert M. Comic Faith: The Great Tradition from Austen to Joyce. LC 79-24856. x, 398p. (C). 1980. lib. bdg. 30.00 (0-226-67320-0) U Ch Pr.
— Comic Faith: The Great Tradition from Austen to Joyce. LC 79-24856. x, 398p. (C). 1982. pap. text ed. 9.95 (0-226-67321-9) U Ch Pr.
— Erotic Faith: Being in Love from Jane Austen to D. H. Lawrence. LC 89-20438. (Illus.). 396p. 1990. 29.95 (0-226-67322-7) U Ch Pr.
— Erotic Faith: Being in Love from Jane Austen to D. H. Lawrence. (Illus.). xii, 364p. 1994. pap. text ed. 17.95 (0-226-67323-5) U Ch Pr.

Polhemus, Robert M. & Henkle, Roger B., eds. Critical Reconstructions: The Relationship of Fiction & Life. 370p. (C). 1994. 42.50 (0-8047-2243-9) Stanford U Pr.

Polhemus, Ted. Streetstyle. LC 94-60281. (Illus.). 144p. 1994. pap. 19.95 (0-500-27794-X) Thames Hudson.

Polhill, Diana. Flora of Tropical East Africa: Index of Collecting Localities: Flora of Uganda, Kenya, Tanzania. (Illus.). 398p. 1988. pap. 30.00 (0-947643-09-5, Pub. by Royal Botanic Garden UK) Lubrecht & Cramer.

Polhill, John B. The New American Commentary, Vol. 26: Acts. 1992. 27.99 (0-8054-0126-1) Broadman.

Polhill, R. M. Crotalaria in Africa & Madagascar. 400p. (C). 1982. text ed. 140.00 (90-6191-090-0, Pub. by A A Balkema NE) Ashgate Pub Co.

Polhill, R. M., jt. ed. see Verdcourt, B.

Poli, jt. auth. see Boothroyd.

Poli, A. Applied Algebra, Algorithmics & Error-Correcting Codes. (Lecture Notes in Computer Science Ser.: Vol. 228). (Illus.). vi, 265p. 1986. pap. 36.00 (0-387-16767-6) Spr-Verlag.

Poli, Bernard J. Ford Madox Ford & the "Transatlantic Review" LC 67-15880. 1967. 39.95x (0-8156-2105-1) Syracuse U Pr.

Poli, Gianangelo, jt. auth. see Segatore, Luigi.

Poli, Guiseppe, et al, eds. Free Radicals: From Basic Science to Medicine. LC 93-16440. (Molecular & Cell Biology Updates Ser.). x, 528p. 1993. 117.00 (0-8176-2763-4) Birkhauser.

Poli, P. A., et al, eds. Free Radicals in the Pathogenesis of Liver Injury: Proceedings of the Second Congress on Free Radicals in Liver Injury, Turin, Italy, 9-11 June 1988. (Advances in the Biosciences Ser.: No. 76). (Illus.). 330p. 1989. 120.00 (0-08-037382-8, Pergamon Pr) Elsevier.

Poli, Roberto, ed. Consciousness, Knowledge, & Truth: Essays Presented to Jan Srzednicki for His 70th Birthday. LC 93-31426. 208p. (C). 1993. lib. bdg. 104.50 (0-7923-2497-8) Kluwer Ac.

Poliak, Gregory, ed. see Aksyonov, Vassily.

Poliak, Gregory, ed. see Chayanov, A.

Poliak, Gregory, ed. see Khodasevich, Vladislav.

Poliak, Gregory, ed. see Oleynikol, Nikolai.

Poliak, Gregory, ed. see Platonov, Andrei.

Poliak, Gregory, ed. see Venedict, Erofeev.

Poliak, Gregory, ed. see Yanovsky, Vasily.

Poliakin, Raymond I. What You Didn't Think to Ask Your Obstetrician: Answers to 1000 Questions about Your Pregnancy. 256p. 1994. pap. 11.95 (0-8092-3658-3) Contemp Bks.

Poliakoff, Gary A. Law of Condominium Operations, 2 vols. LC 88-8150. (Real Property-Zoning Ser.). 1988. ring bd. 250.00 (0-685-28164-7) Clark Boardman Callaghan.

Poliakoff, I. N., tr. see Fridman, A. M. & Polyachenko, V. I.

Poliakoff, I. N., tr. see Fridman, A. M. & Polyachenko, V. L.

Poliakoff, Stephen. Close My Eyes. 102p. (Orig.). 1991. pap. 11.95 (0-413-64920-2, AO581, Pub. by Methuen UK) Heinemann.
— Coming in to Land. 1988. pap. 8.95 (0-413-15430-0, A0059, Pub. by Methuen UK) Heinemann.
— Favourite Nights & Caught on a Train. 96p. 1988. pap. 8.95 (0-413-50100-0, A0088, Pub. by Methuen UK) Heinemann.
— Hitting Town & City Sugar. 134p. (C). 1988. pap. 8.95 (0-413-38880-8, A0126, Pub. by Methuen UK) Heinemann.
— Playing with Trains. (Methuen Modern Plays Ser.). 106p. (Orig.). 1989. pap. 9.95 (0-413-62510-9, A0433, Pub. by Methuen UK) Heinemann.
— Poliakoff: Plays One. (Methuen World Dramatists Ser.). 461p. (Orig.). 1989. pap. 13.95 (0-413-62460-9, A0414, Pub. by Methuen UK) Heinemann.
— Runners & Soft Targets. 112p. 1988. pap. 8.95 (0-413-54150-9, A0251, Pub. by Methuen UK) Heinemann.
— She's Been Away & Hidden City. (Methuen Screenplay Ser.). 189p. (Orig.). (C). 1989. pap. 13.95 (0-413-62210-X, A0399, Pub. by Methuen UK) Heinemann.
— Sienna Red. (Methuen Modern Plays Ser.). 1992. pap. 9.95 (0-413-66430-9, Pub. by Methuen UK) Heinemann.
— The Summer Party. (Methuen New Theatrescripts Ser.). 1988. pap. 6.95 (0-413-47600-6, A0279, Pub. by Methuen UK) Heinemann.

Poliakov, Leon. Harvest of Hate. LC 78-71294. 350p. 1979. pap. 12.95 (0-89604-006-2) Holocaust Pubns.
— Harvest of Hate: The Nazi Program for the Destruction of the Jews in Europe. rev. ed. 350p. reprint ed. pap. 5.95 (0-686-95066-6) ADL.
— Harvest of Hate: The Nazi Program for the Destruction of the Jews in Europe. rev. ed. LC 78-71294. 1987. reprint ed. pap. 12.95 (0-8052-5006-9) Schocken.
— Harvest of Hate: The Nazi Program for the Destruction of the Jews in Europe. LC 74-110836. 338p. 1971. reprint ed. text ed. 35.00 (0-8371-2635-5, POHH, Greenwood Pr) Greenwood.
— Jewish Bankers & the Holy See from the Thirteenth Century to the Seventeenth Century. Kochan, Miriam, tr. (Littman Library of Jewish Civilization). 288p. 1977. 29.00 (0-19-710028-7, Pub. by Littman Lib Jew UK) Bnai Brith Bk.

Poliakov, Leon & Sabille, Jacques. Jews under the Italian Occupation. LC 81-22202. 208p. (C). 1983. reprint ed. 35.00 (0-86527-344-8) Fertig.

Poliakov, Lev. Russia: A Portrait. (Illus.). 1991. 50.00 (0-374-25290-4) FS&G.

Poliakov, Sergei P. Everyday Islam: Religion & Tradition in Rural Central Asia. Olcott, Martha B., ed. LC 91-20989. 170p. 1992. 44.95 (0-87332-673-3); pap. 20.95 (0-87332-674-1) M E Sharpe.

Polian, A., et al, eds. Simple Molecular Systems at Very High Density. (NATO ASI Series B, Physics: Vol. 186). (Illus.). 449p. 1988. 125.00 (0-306-43028-2, Plenum Pr) Plenum.

Polic, Edward F. & Simon, George T., frwds. The Glenn Miller Army Air Force Band: Sustineo Alas - I Sustain the Wings, 2 vols., Set. LC 89-24047. (Studies in Jazz: No. 8). (Illus.). 1989. 127.50 (0-8108-2269-5) Scarecrow.

Policastro, Michael A. Understanding How to Build Guitar Chords & Arpeggios. LC 93-85006. (C). 1993. pap. text ed. 29.95 (0-9637292-0-9) Silvanus Pub.

Police, jt. auth. see Fletcher.

Police Conditions of Service Committee. Minutes of Evidence of the Committee Appointed to Consider & Report Whether Any & What Changes Should Be Made in the Method of Recruiting for, the Conditions of Service of, & the Rates of Pay, Pensions, & Allowances of the Police Forces of England, Wales & Scotland. LC 70-156282. (Police in Great Britain Ser.). 1971. reprint ed. 72.95 (0-405-03393-1) Ayer.
— Report of the Committee on Police Conditions of Service. LC 76-156281. (Police in Great Britain Ser.). 1971. reprint ed. 21.95 (0-405-03392-3) Ayer.

***Polich, Laurie.** Facing Your Future: Graduating Youth Group with a Faith That Lasts. 1994. 49.99 (0-310-49151-7) Zondervan.

Policoff, Ivan. Problem Sets on the Stellar System. 3rd ed. 88p. 1991. spiral bd. 10.95 (0-8403-6609-4) Kendall-Hunt.
— Solar System Astronomy: A Selected Study of Concepts. 3rd ed. 116p. 1992. ring bd. 10.95 (0-8403-7595-6) Kendall-Hunt.

Policoff, Stephen P. & Skinner, Jeffrey. Real Toads in Imaginary Gardens: Suggestions & Starting Points for Young Creative Writers. Teschner, Amy, ed. LC 91-26524. 200p. (Orig.). (YA). (gr. 5 up). 1991. pap. 11.95 (1-55652-137-5) Chicago Review.

Policy Development & Review Department Staff. Private Market Financing for Developing Countries. LC 92-38191. (World Economic & Financial Surveys Ser.). vii, 80p. 1992. pap. 20.00 (1-55775-318-0) Intl Monetary.

Policy Studies Associates, ed. Introduction to Statistics (PS-26) rev. ed. (Illus.). 57p. (Orig.). (C). 1987. pap. text ed. 9.50 (0-936826-24-X) PS Assocs Croton.

Policy Studies Organization Staff. Federal Lands Policy. Foss, Philip O., ed. LC 86-14983. (Contributions in Political Science Ser.: No. 162). 228p. 1987. text ed. 49.95 (0-313-25612-8, FFB/, Greenwood Pr) Greenwood.

***Polidora, Jim, rev. & sel.** Wellness Resources: An Annotated Guide to Essential Books, Periodicals, A-V Materials & Teaching Tools for Trainers, Consultants, Counselors, Educators, & Health Professionals. LC 94-42228. 1995. 34.95 (1-57025-065-0) Whole Person.

***Polidora, Jim, sel.** Stress Resources: An Annotated Guide to Essential Books, Periodicals, A-V Materials, & Teaching Tools for Trainers, Consultants, Counselors, Educators, & Health Professionals. LC 94-43752. 1995. 34.95 (1-57025-064-2) Whole Person.

Polidori. The Vampyre by Dr. Polidori. Adams, Donald K., ed. 1968. 12.50 (0-910330-14-X) Grant Dahlstrom.

Polidori, John. The Vampire. LC 88-34078. (Step-up Classic Chillers Ser.). (Illus.). 96p. (J). (gr. 2-6). 1994. lib. bdg. 5.99 (0-394-93844-5, Bullseye Bks); pap. 3.50 (0-394-83844-0, Bullseye Bks) Random Bks Yng Read.

Polidori, John W. The Vampyre & Ernestus Berchtold, or the Modern Oedipus. Macdonald, D. L. & Scherf, Kathleen, eds. (Illus.). 240p. 1993. 45.00 (0-8020-0506-3); pap. 17.95 (0-8020-7465-0) U of Toronto Pr.

Polier, Justine W. Everyone's Children, Nobody's Child: A Judge Looks at Underprivileged Children in the United States. LC 74-1698. (Children & Youth Ser.). 370p. 1974. reprint ed. 31.95 (0-405-05975-2) Ayer.
— Juvenile Justice in Double Jeopardy: The Distanced Community & Vengeful Retribution. 224p. 1989. 24.95 (0-8058-0462-5) L Erlbaum Assocs.
— The Rule of Law & the Role of Psychiatry. LC 68-12900. (Isaac Ray Award Lectures: No. 1966). 192p. reprint ed. pap. 54.80 (0-8357-8312-X, 2034124) Bks Demand.

Polifka, Janine, jt. auth. see Friedman, Jan M.

Polikanov, Sergei. Nuclear Physics in the Soviet Union: Current Status & Future Prospects. Jones, Steven, ed. 120p. (Orig.). 1984. pap. text ed. 75.00 (1-55831-035-5) Delphic Associates.

Polikarov, A. Methodological Problems of Science. 328p. 1983. 65.00 (0-317-46660-7, Pub. by Collets UK); 55.00 (0-317-89577-X, Pub. by Collets UK) Pro-Am Music.

Polikof, Barbara G. Herbert C. Hoover: Thirty-First President of the United States. Young, Richard G., ed. LC 89-39946. (Presidents of the United States Ser.). (Illus.). 128p. (J). (gr. 5-9). 1990. lib. bdg. 17.26 (0-944483-58-5) Garrett Ed Corp.
— James Madison: Fourth President of the United States. Young, Richard G., ed. LC 88-24537. (Presidents of the United States Ser.). (Illus.). (J). (gr. 5-9). 1989. lib. bdg. 17.26 (0-944483-22-4) Garrett Ed Corp.

Polikoff, Barbara. Life's a Funny Proposition, Horatio. LC 91-28010. 112p. (J). (gr. 4-7). 1992. 13.95 (0-8050-1972-3, Bks Young Read) H Holt & Co.

Polikoff, Barbara G. Life's a Funny Proposition, Horatio. 112p. (J). (gr. 3-7). 1994. pap. 3.99 (0-14-036644-X) Puffin Bks.
— Life's a Funny Proposition, Horatio. braille ed. 135p. 1994. text ed. 10.80 (1-56956-465-5, BR9328) W A T Braille.
— Riding the Wind. (J). 1995. 14.95 (0-8050-3492-7) H Holt & Co.

Polikov, Sheila, ed. see National Council of Jewish Women, Omaha Section Staff.

Polimeni, Albert & Straight, Joseph. Foundations of Discrete Mathematics. 2nd ed. LC 89-22147. 416p. (C). 1990. text ed. 60.95 (0-534-12402-X) Brooks-Cole.

Polimeni, Ralph S., et al. Cost Accounting: Concepts & Applications for Managerial Decision Making. 3rd ed. 1991. pap. text ed. write for info. (0-07-837443-X) McGraw.
— Cost Accounting: Concepts & Applications for Managerial Decision Making. 3rd ed. 1991. pap. text ed. write for info. (0-07-834990-7) McGraw.
— Cost Accounting: Concepts & Applications for Managerial Decision Making. 3rd ed. 1991. Microtest III Macintosh. pap. text ed. write for info. (0-07-836431-0) McGraw.

Polimeni, Ralph S. & Cashin, James A. Schaum's Outline of Cost Accounting I. 2nd ed. 272p. 1984. pap. text ed. 11.95 (0-07-010273-2) McGraw.

Polimeni, Ralph S., jt. auth. see Cashin, James A.

Polimeni, Ralph S., et al. Cost Accounting: Concepts & Applications for Managerial Decision Making. 3rd ed. 1991. Practice sets: Job Order Costing & Process Costing. pap. text ed. write for info. (0-07-010559-6) McGraw.
— Cost Accounting: Concepts & Applications for Managerial Decision Making. 3rd ed. 1991. text ed. write for info. (0-07-010553-7); Study guide. student ed, pap. text ed. write for info. (0-07-010554-5) McGraw.
— Schaum's Outline of Theory & Problems of Cost Accounting. 3rd ed. LC 93-23908. (Schaum's Outline Ser.). 1994. pap. text ed. 13.95 (0-07-011026-3) McGraw.

Polin, Bonnie S. & Giedt, Frances T. The Joslin Diabetes Gourmet Cookbook: Heart-Healthy, Everyday Recipes for Family & Friends. LC 93-25887. (Illus.). 1993. 24.95 (0-553-08760-6) Bantam.

Polin, Claire. The Ap Huw Manuscript. (Wissenschaftliche Abhandlungen-Musicological Studies: Vol. 34). 1982. lib. bdg. 80.00 (0-931902-13-4) Inst Mediaeval Mus.

Polin, Claire C. Music of the Ancient Near East. LC 73-20879. (Illus.). 138p. 1974. reprint ed. text ed. 45.00 (0-8371-5796-X, PONE, Greenwood Pr) Greenwood.

***Polin, Dan.** Let There Be Light, Words & Music. (Illus.). 160p. (Orig.). 1995. pap. 29.95 (0-9645795-0-2) Light Words & Music.

Polin, Gail K., ed. see American Institute of Certified Public Accountants Staff.

Polin, Richard A. & Ditmar, Mark F., eds. Pediatric Secrets: Questions You Will Be Asked on Rounds, in the Clinic, on Oral Exams. LC 88-82169. (Illus.). 447p. (Orig.). 1989. pap. text ed. 35.95 (0-932883-14-1) Hanley & Belfus.

Polin, Richard A. & Fox, William. Fetal & Neonatal Physiology. 1991. text ed. 365.00 (0-7216-2963-6) Saunders.

Polin, Richard A., et al, eds. Workbook in Practical Neonatology. 2nd ed. (Illus.). 496p. 1993. pap. text ed. 47.50 (0-7216-4292-6) Saunders.

An Asterisk (*) at the beginning of an entry indicates that the title is appearing in BIP for the first time.

Polinard, J. L., et al. Electoral Structure & Urban Policy: The Impact on Mexican American Communities. (Bureaucracies, Public Administration & Public Policy Ser.). (Illus.). 216p. 1994. text ed. 47.50 (*1-56324-348-2*); pap. text ed. 19.95 (*1-56324-349-0*) M E Sharpe.

Poling, Alan. A Primer of Human Behavioral Pharmacology. (Applied Clinical Psychology Ser.). 240p. 1986. 45.00 (*0-306-42186-0*, Plenum Pr) Plenum.

Poling, Alan & Fugua, R. Wayne, eds. Research Methods in Applied Behavior Analysis: Issues & Advances. (Applied Clinical Psychology Ser.). 352p. 1986. 54.50 (*0-306-42127-5*, Plenum Pr) Plenum.

Poling, Alan, et al. Drug Therapy for Behavior Disorders. (Practitioner Guidebook Ser.). (C). 1991. pap. 20.95 (*0-205-14453-5*, H4453, Longwood Div) Allyn.

— Psychology: A Behavioral Overview. (Applied Clinical Psychology Ser.). (Illus.). 411p. 1989. 34.50 (*0-306-43432-6*, Plenum Pr) Plenum.

Poling, Clark. Geometric Abstraction: A New Generation. (Illus.). 1981. 3.00 (*0-910663-27-0*) ICA Inc.

Poling, Clark V. Kandinsky: Russian & Bauhaus Years, 1915-1933. LC 83-50760. (Illus.). 360p. 1983. 19.50 (*0-89207-044-7*) S R Guggenheim.

Poling, David, jt. auth. see Marshall, George.

Poling, Evangeline K. Welcome Home to Deering, New Hampshire. LC 78-808. (Illus.). 1978. 12.00 (*0-914016-48-2*) Phoenix Pub.

Poling, James N. Abuse of Power: Theological Problem. 1991. pap. 15.95 (*0-687-00684-8*) Abingdon.

Poling, James N., jt. auth. see Fortune, Marie M.

Poling, Judson, jt. auth. see Cousins, Don.

Poling, Kempes. Harvey Girls. 1994. pap. 14.95 (*1-56924-926-1*) Marlowe & Co.

Poling-Kempes, Lesley. Far from Home: West by Rail with the Harvey Girls. (Illus.). 32p. (Orig.). 1994. pap. 7.95 (*0-89672-330-5*) Tex Tech Univ Pr.

Poling, Mitch. Building & Flying Electric-Powered Model Aircraft. Angle, Burr, ed. (Illus.). 76p. (Orig.). 1984. pap. 9.95 (*0-89024-050-7*) Kalmbach.

Poling, Nancy W. Most Ministers Wear Sneakers. LC 91-15116. (Illus.). 34p. (J). (gr. 4-8). 1991. 12.95 (*0-8298-0907-4*); pap. 7.95 (*0-8298-0901-5*, P-0901-5) Pilgrim OH.

Poling, Tommy H., jt. auth. see Kenny, J. Frank.

Polinger, V. Z., jt. auth. see Bersuker, I. B.

Polinski, Roth. Family Practice: A Medical Subject Analysis & Research Index with Bibliography. LC 83-70082. 154p. 1983. 39.50 (*0-88164-000-X*); pap. 34.50 (*0-88164-001-8*) ABBE Pubs Assn.

— Psychology & A.I.D.S. Index of Modern Information. LC 88-47613. 150p. 1990. 44.50 (*1-55914-232-4*); pap. 39.50 (*1-55914-233-2*) ABBE Pubs Assn.

— Psychology of Perceptions: Index of Modern Information. rev. ed. LC 88-47983. 150p. 1991. 44.50 (*1-55914-486-6*); pap. 39.50 (*1-55914-487-4*) ABBE Pubs Assn.

Polinsky. An Introduction to Law & Economics. 144p. 1983. pap. 8.95 (*0-316-71277-9*) Little.

— Law & Economics. 2nd ed. 1989. 15.95 (*0-316-71278-7*) Little.

Polinsky, Maria, jt. ed. see Comrie, Bernard.

Polinsky, Ronald J., et al. Autonomic Disorders - Disorders of the Spinal Cord & Cauda Equina - Neuropharmacology. (Current Opinion in Neurology & Neurosurgery, 1993 Ser.). (Illus.). 162p. (Orig.). 1993. pap. text ed. 49.95 (*1-85922-008-8*) Current Science.

Poliny, Valiant. A Public Policy Analysis of the Emerging Victims' Rights Movement. 600p. 1994. 94.95 (*1-880921-42-1*); pap. 74.95 (*1-880921-41-3*) Austin & Winfield.

Polioukhin, jt. auth. see Shevchuk.

Polioukhin, V., jt. ed. see Shevchuk, V.

Poliquin, Bud. Purely Poliquin: A Collection of 100 Writings. LC 94-21816. 1994. write for info. (*0-9629159-8-X*) Pine Tree NY.

***Polis, G. A. & Winemiller, K. O., eds.** Food Webs: Integration of Patterns & Dynamics. LC 94-43155. 1995. 68.00 (*0-412-04051-4*) Chapman & Hall.

Polis, Gary A., ed. The Biology of Scorpions. LC 84-40330. (Illus.). 614p. 1990. 89.50 (*0-8047-1249-2*) Stanford U Pr.

— The Ecology of Desert Communities. LC 90-20183. (Desert Ecology Ser.). (Illus.). 450p. 1991. 55.00 (*0-8165-1186-1*) U of Ariz Pr.

Polis, Lotty. Richer by Tomorrow: It's How You Save That Counts! 52p. (Orig.). 1989. pap. 4.95 (*0-9625247-0-0*) Davric Corp.

Polis, M., ed. see IFAC Symposium, 3rd, Montreal, PQ, Canada, Aug. 1980.

Polis, M., ed. see Joint Automatic Control Conference Staff.

***Polis, Tina B.** The Sun Is Always Shining above the Clouds. 77p. (Orig.). 1993. pap. 12.95 (*0-89716-471-7*) P B Pubng.

Polisar, Barry L. Captured Live & in the Act. (J). (gr. k-6). 1978. audio 9.95 (*0-9615696-9-7*) Rainbow Morn.

— Dinosaurs I Have Known. (Illus.). 48p. (Orig.). (J). (gr. 2-6). 1988. 9.95 (*0-938663-00-3*); pap. 7.95 (*0-938663-05-4*) Rainbow Morn.

— Don't Do That! A Child's Guide to Bad Manners, Ridiculous Rules & Inadequate Etiquette. (Illus.). 32p. (J). (gr. 2-6). 1995. reprint ed. write for info. (*0-938663-20-8*) Rainbow Morn.

— Family Concert. (J). (gr. k-6). 1990. audio 9.95 (*0-938663-12-7*) Rainbow Morn.

— The Haunted House Party: A Halloween Story. (Illus.). 40p. (J). (gr. 3-6). 1987. 9.95 (*0-938663-02-X*); pap. 7.95 (*0-938663-11-9*) Rainbow Morn.

— I Eat Kids & Other Songs for Rebellious Children. (J). (gr. k-6). 1987. reprint ed. 9.95 (*0-9615696-3-8*) Rainbow Morn.

— Juggling Babies. (J). (ps-6). 1989. digital audio 9.95 (*0-9615696-2-X*) Rainbow Morn.

— My Brother Thinks He's a Banana & Other Provocative Songs for Children. (J). (gr. k-6). 1987. reprint ed. audio 9.95 (*0-9615696-4-6*) Rainbow Morn.

— Naughty Songs for Boys & Girls. (J). (gr. k-6). 1987. reprint ed. audio 9.95 (*0-9615696-5-4*) Rainbow Morn.

— Noises from under the Rug: The Barry Louis Polisar Songbook. (Illus.). 208p. (J). (gr. k-6). 1985. 18.98 (*0-9615696-0-3*); pap. 13.95 (*0-9615696-1-1*) Rainbow Morn.

— Off Color Songs for Kids, Set. (J). (gr. k-6). 1983. audio 9.95 (*0-9615696-8-9*) Rainbow Morn.

— Peculiar Zoo. (Illus.). 32p. (J). (gr. k-6). 1993. 14.95 (*0-938663-14-3*) Rainbow Morn.

— The Snake Who Was Afraid of People. (Illus.). 32p. (J). (gr. k-4). 1993. reprint ed. 14.95 (*0-938663-16-X*) Rainbow Morn.

— Snakes & the Boy Who Was Afraid of Them. (Illus.). 32p. (J). (gr. 1-6). 1993. reprint ed. 14.95 (*0-938663-15-1*) Rainbow Morn.

— Stanley Stole My Shoelace & Rubbed It in His Armpit & Other Songs My Parents Won't Let Me Sing. (J). (gr. k-6). 1981. audio 9.95 (*0-9615696-7-0*) Rainbow Morn.

— The Trouble with Ben. (Illus.). 32p. (J). (gr. k-4). 1992. 14.95 (*0-938663-13-5*) Rainbow Morn.

***Polisar, Betty & Spina, Rita K.** Beyond the Traditional Family: New Choices, New Voices. 224p. 1995. write for info. (*0-8261-9030-8*) Springer Pub.

Polisar, Donna, et al. Where Do We Come From? What Are We? Where Are We Going? An Annotated Bibliography of Aging & the Humanities. LC 88-24578. (C). 1988. pap. 15.00 (*0-929596-01-3*) Gerontological Soc.

Polischuk, Pablo. Depresion y Su Tratamiento (Depression & Its Treatment) 154p. (Orig.). (SPA.). 1992. pap. 5.50 (*84-7645-566-6*, 223633, Pub. by Edit Clie SP) TSELF.

Polisensky, Josef V. Aristocrats & the Crowd in the Revolutionary Year 1848: A Contribution to the History of Revolution & Counter-Revolution. Snider, Frederick, tr. LC 79-14765. 245p. 1980. 64.50 (*0-87395-398-3*); pap. 21.95 (*0-87395-424-6*) State U NY Pr.

— War & Society in Europe, 1618-1648. LC 77-71423. (Illus.). 1978. 64.95 (*0-521-21659-1*) Cambridge U Pr.

Polisevski, Dan, jt. auth. see Ene, Horia I.

Polish Academy of Science Staff. Poetic Potentials in Information of Astronomy. 1976. pap. 1.95 (*0-934982-05-8*) Primary Pr.

Polish Book Fair, Inc. Staff, ed. see Kaluza, Jan & Kruppik, Blazej.

Polish Book Fair Staff, ed. see Choznacka, Dagmara.

Polish Book Fair Staff, ed. see Kaluza, Jan.

Polish, Daniel F., et al. Drugs, Sex, & Integrity: What Does Judaism Say? LC 90-28763. (Illus.). (YA). (gr. 7-9). 1991. pap. 10.00 (*0-8074-0459-4*, 168505) UAHC.

Polish, David. Give Us a King: Legal-Religious Sources of Jewish Sovereignty. 1989. 20.00 (*0-88125-309-X*) Ktav.

Polish, David, ed. Maaglei Zedek: Rabbi's Manual. 263p. 1988. 12.50 (*0-88123-004-9*) Central Conf.

Polish Institute of Arts & Sciences in America Staff. Studies in Polish Civilization: Selected Papers of the Polish Institute of Arts & Sciences in America, N. Y., 1966. Wandycz, Damian, ed. 1971. 9.00 (*0-940962-43-8*) Polish Inst Art & Sci.

Polish Wycinank Staff, et al. Folk Art Designs: From Polish Wycinanki, & Swiss & German Scherenschnitte. LC 78-13765. (International Design Library). (Illus.). 56p. 1978. pap. 5.95 (*0-916144-33-X*) Stemmer Hse.

Polishchuk, E. M. Continual Means & Boundary Value Problems in Function Spaces. (Operator Theory Ser.: No. 31). 180p. 1989. 64.00 (*0-8176-2217-9*) Birkhauser.

Polishook, Irwin H. Rhode Island & the Union, 1774-1795. LC 69-18021. (Studies in History Ser.: No. 5). 280p. reprint ed. pap. 79.80 (*0-8357-9469-5*, 2013681) Bks Demand.

Polishook, Irwin H., jt. ed. see Judd, Jacob.

Polisky, Mildred K. Solving Business Problems on the Electronic Calculator. 3rd ed. 256p. 1988. pap. text ed. 13.48 (*0-07-041283-9*) McGraw.

— Solving Business Problems on the Electronic Calculator. 4th ed. LC 92-31248. 1993. 16.95 (*0-02-800417-5*) Glencoe.

Polisky, Mildred K. & Meehan, James R. Solving Business Problems on the Electronic Calculator. 2nd ed. 256p. 1983. text ed. 16.56 (*0-07-041281-2*) McGraw.

Polit, Denise F. Essentials of Nursing Research. 3rd ed. 1993. text ed. 29.95 (*0-397-54922-9*) Lippincott.

— Study Guide to Essentials of Nursing Research. 3rd ed. 1993. text ed. 15.95 (*0-397-54923-7*) Lippincott.

Polit, Denise F. & Berman, Judith. Just the Right Size: A Guide to Family Size Planning. LC 83-24534. 242p. 1984. text ed. 49.95 (*0-275-91744-4*, C1744, Praeger Pubs) Greenwood.

Polit, Denise F. & Hungler, Bernadette. Nursing Research: Principles & Methods. 4th ed. (Illus.). 720p. 1991. text ed. 39.95 (*0-397-54820-6*) Lippincott.

— Study Guide to Accompany Nursing Research: Principles & Methods. 4th ed. 176p. 1991. text ed. 17.95 (*0-397-54821-4*) Lippincott.

***Polit, Denise F. & Hungler, Bernadette P.** Nursing Research: Principles & Methods. 5th ed. LC 94-30403. 1995. write for info. (*0-397-55138-X*) Lippincott.

***Polit Status ECC Staff.** Hale'Ta: I Manfayi Who's Who in Chamorro History. (Hale'-Ta Ser.). 250p. (J). (gr. 6-7). 1995. pap. text ed. write for info. (*0-9628367-1-4*)... Polit Status ECC.

Politakis, Peter. Empirical Analysis for Expert Systems. (Research Notes in Artificial Intelligence Ser.). 1985. 29. 95 (*0-273-08663-4*) Morgan Kaufmann.

Politano, Colleen. Lost in the Woods: Child Survival for Parents & Teachers. LC 93-25700. (Illus.). 64p. 1993. reprint ed. pap. 6.99 (*0-934802-83-1*) ICS Bks.

***Politano, Colleen & Davies, Anne.** Multi-Age & More. (Building Connections Ser.). 151p. (Orig.). 1994. teacher ed, pap. 17.95 (*1-895411-65-3*) Peguis Pubs Ltd.

Politano, Colleen, jt. auth. see Neudecker, Joan.

Politano, Frank L., jt. ed. see Epstein, Michael A.

Polite, Carlene H. The Flagellants. LC 86-47874. (Black Women Writers Ser.). 256p. 1988. reprint ed. pap. 7.95 (*0-8070-6321-5*, BP 752) Beacon Pr.

Polite, Craig K., jt. auth. see Edwards, Audrey.

Politella, Sue, ed. see Vivo, Pat.

Polites, George W. Precalculus Mathematics: A Study of Functions. (Illus.). 497p. (C). reprint ed. 35.00 (*1-878907-32-8*) TechBooks.

Politi, A., jt. ed. see Livi, R.

***Politi, Giancarlo.** Art Diary International 1995. 500p. 1995. pap. 25.00 (*88-7816-058-X*) Dist Art Pubs.

— Dictionary of Contemporary Artists 1995-1996. 400p. 1995. pap. 29.95 (*88-7816-067-9*) Dist Art Pubs.

Politi, Leo. Song of the Swallows. LC 49-8215. (Illus.). 32p. (J). (gr. 1-4). 1987. text ed. 14.95 (*0-684-18831-7*, C Scribner Sons Young) S&S Childrens.

— Song of the Swallows. (Illus.). 32p. (J). (gr. k-3). 1987. reprint ed. pap. 4.95 (*0-689-71140-9*, Aladdin Paperbacks) S&S Childrens.

— Three Stalks of Corn. 2nd ed. LC 75-35009. (Illus.). 32p. (J). (gr. k-3). 1993. lib. bdg. 14.95 (*0-684-19538-0*, C Scribner Sons Young) S&S Childrens.

— Three Stalks of Corn. LC 93-19737. (Illus.). 32p. (J). (gr. k-3). 1994. reprint ed. pap. 4.95 (*0-689-71782-2*, Aladdin Paperbacks) S&S Childrens.

Political & Economic Planning Staff. World Population & Resources: A Report. LC 78-14136. (Illus.). 1980. reprint ed. 30.25 (*0-88355-810-6*) Hyperion Conn.

Political Behavior Program, Survey Research Center Staff. American National Election Study, 1962. LC 76-5755. 1976. write for info. (*0-89138-000-0*) ICPSR.

— American National Election Study, 1966. 1977. write for info. (*0-89138-050-7*) ICPSR.

— American National Election Study, 1968. 1977. write for info. (*0-89138-061-2*) ICPSR.

Politiek, R. D. & Bakker, J. J., eds. Livestock Production in Europe: Perspectives & Prospects. (Developments in Animal & Veterinary Science Ser.: No. 8). 354p. 1982. 72.00 (*0-444-42105-X*) Elsevier.

Politino, Virginia, et al. Lifetime Fitness for Lifetime Activities. 96p. 1986. per. 14.95 (*0-8403-3911-9*) Kendall-Hunt.

— Lifetime Physical Fitness. 176p. (C). 1994. pap. text ed., spiral bd. 20.25 (*0-7872-0066-2*) Kendall-Hunt.

Politis, Vasilis, ed. see Kant, Immanuel.

Politis, Yael, tr. see Yossi, Ghinsberg.

***Polito, Robert.** Doubles. LC 95-2818. (Phoenix Poets Ser.). 1995. lib. bdg. 20.00 (*0-226-67337-5*); pap. 8.95 (*0-226-67338-3*) U Ch Pr.

— A Reader's Guide to James Merrill's the Changing Light at Sandover. 324p. 1994. text ed. 37.50 (*0-472-09524-2*); pap. text ed. 12.95 (*0-472-06524-6*) U of Mich Pr.

— Savage Art: A Biography of Jim Thompson. LC 94-48455. 1995. 28.00 (*0-394-58407-4*) Knopf.

Polito, Ronald, jt. auth. see Steele, Chris.

Polito, Serafin. Gdzie Jest Moj Dom Rodzinny? 70p. (Orig.). (POL.). 1987. pap. text ed. 6.00 (*0-930401-11-5*) Artex Pub.

Politoske, Daniel T. Music. 4th ed. (Illus.). 576p. (C). 1988. Cassette. audio write for info. (*0-318-62496-6*) P-H.

— Music with Cassette. 5th ed. 600p. 1992. text ed. 53.33 (*0-13-605460-9*) P-H.

Politt, Ronald & Wiltse, Virginia. Helen Steiner Rice: Ambassador of Sunshine. LC 93-36520. (Illus.). 288p. 1994. 17.99 (*0-8007-1701-5*) Revell.

Politycki, Matthias. Umwertung aller Werte? Deutsche Literatur im Urteil Nietzsches. (Monographien und Texte zur Nietzsche-Forschung Ser.: Vol. 21). x, 447p. (C). 1989. lib. bdg. 132.00 (*3-11-011709-6*) De Gruyter.

Politzer, Adam. History of Otology. Milstein, Stanley et al, trs. (Illus.). 324p. 1981. 115.00 (*0-9605972-0-4*) Columella Pr.

Politzer, Georges. Critique of the Foundations of Psychology: The Psychology of Psychoanalysis. Apprey, Maurice, tr. LC 94-4139. 250p. (C). 1994. pap. text ed. 22.50 (*0-8207-0257-9*) Duquesne.

— Critique of the Foundations of Psychology: The Psychology of Psychoanalysis. Apprey, Maurice, tr. LC 94-4139. 250p. (C). 1994. text ed. 54.00 (*0-8207-0256-0*) Duquesne.

Politzer, M. Mon Premier Dictionnaire L'Attrape-Mots-Hachette. 237p. (FRE.). 1980. 29.95 (*0-8288-1513-5*, M10420) Fr & Eur.

***Politzer, P. & Murray, J.S., eds.** Quantitative Treatments of Solute Solvent Interactions. LC 94-31159. (Theoretical & Computational Chemistry Ser.: 1). 1994. write for info. (*0-444-82054-X*) Elsevier.

Politzer, P., jt. ed. see Seminario, J. M.

Politzer, R. L. & Urrutibeheity, H. N. Peldanos. LC 72-75117. 191p. (C). student ed 54.50 (*0-685-07767-5*, 2016476) Bks Demand.

— Peldanos. LC 72-75117. 382p. (C). reprint ed. text ed. 108.90 (*0-8357-9949-2*, 2013629) Bks Demand.

Politzer, Robert, et al. La France: Une Tapisserie. 2nd ed. (Illus.). 496p. (C). 1972. text ed. 40.04 (*0-07-050384-2*) McGraw.

Politzer, Robert L. & Hagiwara, Michie P. Active Review of French: Selected Patterns, Vocabulary, & Pronunciation Problems for Speakers of English. LC 63-15633. 264p. reprint ed. pap. 75.30 (*0-8357-5088-4*, 2055978) Bks Demand.

Polivanov, E. D. Selected Works: Articles on General Linguistics. Armstrong, Daniel, tr. LC 73-83930. (Janua Linguarum, Ser. Major: No. 72). (Illus.). 386p. 1974. text ed. 109.25 (*90-279-2693-X*) Mouton.

Polivanov, Konstantin, ed. see Ivanov, V. V., et al.

Poliziano, Angelo. A Translation of the Orpheus of Angelo Politian & the Aminta of Torquato Tasso. LC 86-3172. 198p. 1986. reprint ed. text ed. 49.75 (*0-313-25211-4*, LOTR, Greenwood Pr) Greenwood.

— A Translation of the Orpheus of Angelo Politian & the Aminta of Torquato Tasso. Lord, Louis E., tr. LC 78-59036. 1985. reprint ed. 16.00 (*0-88355-708-8*) Hyperion Conn.

Poliziano, Angelo A. Angeli Politiani Opera, 3 vols. in 2. xviii, 1406p. reprint ed. write for info. (*0-318-71606-2*, Pub. by Georg Olms GW) Lubrecht & Cramer.

— Concordanza Delle 'Stanze' Di Poliziano. Rossi, Diego, ed. (Alpha-Omega, Series F, Italienische Autoren). xvi, 406p. 1983. write for info. (*3-487-06997-0*, Pub. by Georg Olms GW) Lubrecht & Cramer.

— Prose Volgari Inedite e Poesi Latine e Greche Edite e Inedite. (Illus.). xxxv, 568p. 1976. reprint ed. write for info. (*3-487-06101-5*, Pub. by Georg Olms GW) Lubrecht & Cramer.

Polizoides, G. Short Stories for Young & Old. (GRE.). 1977. pap. text ed. 3.00 (*0-685-81640-0*) Divry.

Polizzatti, Mark, tr. see Roche, Maurice.

***Polizzi, Bernadette C., ed.** WCCN Wireless Handbook-Leading RF Systems Integrators & Selected Applications. (Illus.). 192p. 1995. write for info. (*0-9638649-2-0*) WCCN Pubng.

Polizzi, D., et al. A Journey Together: A Program for the Newly Married. 1987. Couple's Wkbk. student ed 3.95 (*0-915388-28-6*, 161, Buckley Pubns); Leader's Guide. teacher ed 4.95 (*0-915388-29-4*, 162, Buckley Pubns); Training Kit. 2.95 (*0-915388-30-8*, 163, Buckley Pubns) ACTA Pubns.

***Polizzi, Rick.** Baby Boomer Games, Identification & Value Guide. 1995. 24.95 (*0-89145-631-7*, 3956) Collector Bks.

Polizzi, Rick & Schaefer, Fred. Spin Again: Games from the Fifties & Sixties. (Illus.). 120p. (Orig.). 1991. pap. 16.95 (*0-87701-830-8*) Chronicle Bks.

Polizzi, Tom. WCCN Wireless Handbook: RF Terminals & LANs. (WCCN Wireless Handbook Ser.). (Illus.). 96p. 1993. pap. text ed. 27.95 (*0-9638649-0-4*) WCCN Pubng.

— WCCN Wireless Handbook on Event-Time Data Processing. (Wireless Handbook Ser.). (Illus.). 100p. 1994. write for info. (*0-9638649-1-2*) WCCN Pubng.

Polizzotti, Mark. Revolution of the Mind: The Life of Andre Breton. LC 94-20166. 1995. 35.00 (*0-374-24982-2*) FS&G.

Polizzotti, Mark, tr. see Daumal, Rene.

Polizzotti, Mark, tr. see Echenoz, Jean.

Polizzotto, Lorenzo. The Elect Nation: The Savonarolan Movement in Florence, 1494-1545. LC 93-31942. (Oxford-Warburg Studies). 432p. 1995. 79.00 (*0-19-920600-7*, Clarendon Pr) OUP.

Poljakoff-Mayber, A., jt. auth. see Mayer, A. M.

Polk. Practice of Printing Nineteen Seventy-One. 1986. 19. 96 (*0-02-665410-5*) Macmillan.

Polk, Alvin L. Fragged. 1989. pap. 3.95 (*0-8217-2815-6*) Zebra.

Polk, Benjamin. Building for South Asia: An Architectural Autobiography. (C). 1993. 49.00 (*81-7017-300-0*, Pub. by Abhinav II) S Asia.

Polk, Benjamin & Polk, Emily. India Notebook: Two Americans in the South Asia of Nehru's Time. LC 86-7229. (Illus.). 182p. 1987. reprint ed. 12.95 (*0-931228-13-1*) Arts & Arch.

Polk, Benjamin, jt. auth. see Seneviratna, Anuradha.

Polk, Betty J., jt. auth. see Abbott, Marti.

Polk, Charles & Postow, Elliot. Handbook of Biological Effects of Electromagnetic Fields. 512p. 1986. 295.00 (*0-8493-3265-6*, QP82) CRC Pr.

***Polk, Charles & Postow, Elliot, eds.** Handbook of Biological Effects of Electromagnetic Fields. 600p. 1995. 125.00 (*0-8493-0641-8*, 641) CRC Pr.

Polk, David P. If Only I Had Known: Dramatic Monologues for Advent & Lent. 96p. (Orig.). 1994. pap. 9.99 (*0-8272-1611-4*) Chalice Pr.

— On the Way to God: An Exploration into the Theology of Wolfhart Pannenberg. LC 88-27871. 350p. (C). 1989. lib. bdg. 46.00 (*0-8191-7229-4*) U Pr of Amer.

Polk, David P., ed. Now What's a Christian to Do? 144p. (Orig.). 1993. pap. 10.99 (*0-8272-2510-5*) Chalice Pr.

***Polk, Dean.** Guide de Preparation a l'Examen Pour Fondements du Service a la Clientele. Duisit, Vivian, ed. (Associate, Customer Service Program Ser.). (FRE.). (C). 1994. pap. text ed. 22.00 (*0-939921-54-5*) LOMA.

***Polk, Dora B.** The Island of California: A History of the Myth. (Illus.). 400p. 1995. pap. 15.00 (*0-8032-8741-0*, Bison Books) U of Nebr Pr.

Polk, Emily, jt. auth. see Polk, Benjamin.

Polk, Hiram C., Jr., ed. see Gardner, Bernard & Stone, H. Harlan.

Polk, Hiram C., Jr., et al, eds. Basic Surgery. 4th ed. LC 92-49686. 1993. 40.00 (*0-942219-29-5*) Quality Med Pub.

Polk, Jacqueline K., jt. auth. see Pasch, Brian.

Polk, James K. Message of the President of the United States. 12p. 1972. reprint ed. pap. 1.00 (*0-87770-090-7*) Ye Galleon.

— Polk: The Diary of a Presidency, 1845-1849, Covering the Mexican War, the Acquisition of Oregon, & the Conquest of California & the Southwest. (American Biography Ser.). 412p. 1991. reprint ed. lib. bdg. 89.00 (*0-7812-8318-3*) Rprt Serv.

PQ

Polk, Judd. Sterling: Its Meaning in World Finance. Wilkins, Mira, ed. LC 78-3945. (International Finance Ser.). (Illus.). 1979. reprint ed. lib. bdg. 29.95 (*0-405-11245-9*) Ayer.

Polk, Keith. German Instrumental Music of the Late Middle Ages: Players, Patrons & Performance Practice. (Musical Texts & Monographs). (Illus.). 300p. (C). 1992. 74.95 (*0-521-38521-0*) Cambridge U Pr.

Polk, Kenneth. When Men Kill: Scenarios of Masculine Violence. LC 94-8969. (Illus.). 288p. (C). 1994. 59.95 (*0-521-46267-3*); pap. 17.95 (*0-521-46808-6*) Cambridge U Pr.

Polk, Kenneth, jt. auth. see Eaton, Joseph W.

Polk, L. Reed, jt. ed. see Wilson, Emery A.

Polk, Lee T. ERISA Practice & Litigation. 1993. 210.00 (*0-318-72272-0*) Clark Boardman Callaghan.

Polk, N. Go down, Moses: Nineteen Forty-Two, Typescript. Blotner, J. et al, eds. (William Faulkner Manuscripts). 692p. 1987. 115.00 (*0-8240-6823-8*) Garland.

Polk, Noel. Eudora Welty: A Bibliography of Her Work. (Illus.). 450p. 1993. 65.00 (*0-87805-566-5*) U Pr of Miss.

— Faulkner's Requiem for a Nun: A Critical Study. LC 80-8099. 286p. reprint ed. pap. 81.60 (*0-7837-1759-8*, 2057295) Bks Demand.

Polk, Noel, ed. Mississippi's Piney Woods: A Human Perspective. LC 85-22680. 208p. 1986. 29.50 (*0-87805-288-7*) U Pr of Miss.

— Natchez Before 1830. LC 88-28046. 232p. 1989. 27.50 (*0-87805-380-8*) U Pr of Miss.

— New Essays on "The Sound & the Fury" LC 93-568. (American Novel Ser.). 125p. (C). 1993. 34.95 (*0-521-45114-0*); pap. 12.95 (*0-521-45734-3*) Cambridge U Pr.

— Sanctuary I: The Holograph Manuscript & Miscellaneous Pages. LC 86-25622. (William Faulkner Manuscripts: Vol. 8). 312p. 1987. 50.00 (*0-8240-6810-6*) Garland.

Polk, Noel & Hart, John D., eds. Pylon: A Concordance to the Novel. LC 89-37165. 680p. reprint ed. lib. bdg. 180.00 (*0-8357-0880-2*, 2070619) Bks Demand.

Polk, Noel, jt. ed. see Blotner, Joseph.

Polk, Noel, ed. see Faulkner, William.

Polk, Noel, jt. ed. see Gresset, Michel.

Polk, Sam C. CORFA: Constitutional Rebirth for America. LC 88-71961. (Illus.). 240p. (Orig.). (C). 1989. pap. 10.95 (*0-9621836-0-1*) Corfa Bks.

Polk, Stella G. For All Those Pupils Whose Lives Touched Mine. LC 88-29359. (Wardlaw Bk.). 104p. 1989. 14.95 (*0-89096-405-X*) Tex A&M Univ Pr.

— Glory Girl. 144p. (J). (gr. 4-7). 1986. 9.95 (*0-89015-582-8*) Sunbelt Media.

Polk, Steven R. Medical Student's Survival Guide. 2nd ed. 409p. 1988. pap. 29.95 (*0-940401-63-0*) Trentland Pr.

— The Medical Student's Survival Guide: How to Succeed in Medicine Without Really Trying. 3rd ed. LC 92-10437. 405p. (C). 1992. pap. text ed. 29.95 (*0-940401-45-2*) Trentland Pr.

Polk, Timothy W. How to Outlive Your Lifetime! Preserving a Place in Your Family's Hearts & History. LC 94-8759. 1994. 10.95 (*0-9640587-0-7*) Fam Life Intl.

***Polk, W. Harrison.** Polk Family & Kinsmen. (Illus.). 742p. 1994. reprint ed. lib. bdg. 115.00 (*0-8328-4279-6*) Higginson Bk Co.

— Polk Family & Kinsmen. (Illus.). 742p. 1994. reprint ed. pap. 105.00 (*0-8328-4280-X*) Higginson Bk Co.

Polk, W. Timothy. Automated Tools for Testing Computer System Vulnerability. 51p. (Orig.). (C). 1993. pap. text ed. 40.00 (*0-7881-0043-2*) Diane Pub.

Polk, W. Timothy & Bassham, Lawrence E., III. A Guide to the Selection of Anti-Virus Tools & Techniques. 52p. (Orig.). (C). 1993. pap. text ed. 40.00 (*0-7881-0384-9*) Diane Pub.

***Polk, W. Timothy, et al.** Anti-Virus Tools & Techniques for Computer Systems. LC 94-31166. (Advanced Computing & Telecommunications Ser.). (Illus.). 79p. 1995. 24.00 (*0-8155-1364-X*) Noyes.

Polk, William H., et al. Polk Family & Kinsmen. 279p. 1993. 34.95 (*1-56869-036-3*); pap. 23.95 (*1-56869-037-1*) Oldbuck Pr.

Polk, William R. The Arab World Today. 538p. 1991. pap. text ed. 14.95 (*0-674-04320-0*, POLARY) HUP.

— The Opening of South Lebanon, 1788-1840: A Study of the Impact of the West on the Middle East. LC 63-13815. (Harvard Middle Eastern Studies: No. 8). 319p. reprint ed. pap. 91.00 (*0-317-08416-X*, 2006019) Bks Demand.

Polk, William R., ed. see Conference on the Beginnings of Modernization in the Middle East in the Nineteenth Century (1966: University of Chicago Staff).

Polka, Brayton. The Dialectic of Biblical Critique: Interpretation & Existence. LC 84-26216. 192p. 1986. text ed. 35.00 (*0-312-19874-4*) St Martin.

— Truth & Interpretation: An Essay in Thinking. 300p. 1990. text ed. 39.95 (*0-312-04218-3*) St Martin.

Polka, George E. Fort Custer (1877-1898) Then & Now. 80p. 1994. pap. 9.95 (*0-9641027-0-6*) G E Polka.

Polke, M., ed. see Epple, V. & Helm, M.

Polkey, C. E., jt. ed. see Schurr, Peter H.

Polking, Kirk. The Private Pilot's Dictionary & Handbook. write for info. (*0-318-59625-3*) S&S Trade.

— Writing Family Histories & Memoirs. 272p. 1995. 14.99 (*1-55870-394-2*) Betterway Bks.

Polking, Kirk, jt. auth. see Writer's Digest Staff.

Polkingharn, Anne T. & Toohey, Catherine. Creative Encounters: Activities to Expand Children's Responses to Literature. LC 83-8005. 138p. 1983. pap. text ed. 19.00 (*0-87287-371-4*) Libs Unl.

— More Creative Encounters: Activities to Expand Children's Responses to Literature. LC 88-8892. (Illus.). x, 116p. 1988. student ed 19.50 (*0-87287-663-2*) Libs Unl.

Polkinghorn, Philip K., jt. auth. see Tullis, Mark A.

Polkinghorn, Robert S. Micro-theory & Economic Choices. LC 78-70950. (Irwin Series in Economics). 420p. reprint ed. pap. 119.70 (*0-317-27995-5*, 2055810) Bks Demand.

Polkinghorne, Donald. Methodology for the Human Sciences: Systems of Inquiry. LC 82-5895. (SUNY Series in Transpersonal & Humanistic Psychology). 349p. (C). 1984. 49.50 (*0-87395-663-X*); pap. 16.95 (*0-87395-664-8*) State U NY Pr.

Polkinghorne, Donald E. Narrative Knowing & the Human Sciences. LC 87-17992. (SUNY Series in the Philosophy of the Social Sciences). 232p. 1988. 49.50 (*0-88706-622-4*); pap. 16.95 (*0-88706-623-2*) State U NY Pr.

Polkinghorne, J. C. Models of High Energy Processes. LC 79-296. (Monographs on Mathematical Physics). (Illus.). 1980. 49.95 (*0-521-22369-5*) Cambridge U Pr.

— Quantum World. LC 83-9411. (Illus.). 112p. 1984. text ed. 14.95 (*0-582-44682-1*) Longman.

— The Quantum World. LC 84-42953. 112p. 1985. pap. 9.95x (*0-691-02388-3*) Princeton U Pr.

Polkinghorne, John. The Faith of a Physicist: Reflections of a Bottom-Up Thinker - The Gifford Lectures for 1993-4. LC 93-41071. 1994. 24.95 (*0-691-03620-9*) Princeton U Pr.

— Reason & Reality: The Relationship Between Science & Theology. LC 91-23518. 128p. (C). 1991. pap. 13.95 (*1-56338-019-6*) TPI PA.

— Serious Talk: Science & Religion in Dialogue. LC 95-6976. 1995. pap. 13.50 (*1-56338-109-5*) TPI PA.

Polkinghorne, John C. The Way the World Is. LC 84-1527. 140p. reprint ed. 39.90 (*0-685-15952-3*, 2027549) Bks Demand.

Polkinhorn, Harry. Anesthesia. Walsh, Joy, ed. LC 84-72583. (Poetry Ser.). (Illus.). 50p. (Orig.). 1985. pap. text ed. 5.00 (*0-938838-14-8*) Textile Bridge.

— Bleeding. Winkler, Christ, ed. 38p. (Orig.). (YA). (gr. 10-12). 1989. pap. text ed. 4.00 (*0-929611-05-5*) Plutonium Pr.

— Summary Dissolution. (Illus.). 58p. (Orig.). 1988. pap. 3.00 (*0-926935-06-2*) Runaway Spoon.

— Travelling with Women. 56p. 1983. pap. 5.00 (*0-317-63763-0*) Atticus Pr.

Polkinhorn, Harry, ed. Border Literature. (Border Studies Ser.). 1989. 5.00 (*0-317-93038-9*) SDSU Inst Reg Studies.

Polkinhorn, Harry, jt. auth. see Beining, Guy.

Polkinhorn, Harry, tr. see Espinosa, Cesar, ed.

Polkinhorn, Harry, tr. see Gomez-Montero, Sergio.

Polkinhorn, Harry, tr. see Manuel Di Bella, Jose.

Polkinhorn, Harry, et al. El Libro de Calo. rev. ed. LC 86-4693. 95p. 1987. 17.95 (*0-915745-10-0*) Floricanto Pr.

— El Libro de Calo: The Dictionary of Chicano Slang. 2nd rev. ed. 100p. 1988. pap. 17.95 (*0-685-45617-X*) Floricanto Pr.

Polkinhorn, Harry, et al, eds. The Flight of the Eagle: Poetry on the U. S. - Mexico Border. (Binational Press Ser.: No. 5). 270p. (ENG & SPA.). 1993. pap. 17.50 (*1-879691-21-3*) SDSU Press.

— The Line: Essays on Mexican - American Border Literature. (Binational Press Ser.: No. 1). 192p. (ENG & SPA.). 1988. pap. 10.00 (*0-916304-92-2*) SDSU Press.

— The Line: Essays on Mexican-American Border Literature. 189p. (ENG & SPA.). 1988. pap. 10.00 (*0-317-02700-X*) Binatl Pr-Edit Binacional.

— Open Signs: Language & Society on the U. S. - Mexico Border. (Binational Press Ser.: No. 4). 310p. (ENG & SPA.). 1993. pap. 17.50 (*1-879691-20-5*) SDSU Press.

— U. S. Mexican Border Literature: Short Stories. 144p. (Orig.). 1989. pap. 10.00 (*0-685-45123-2*) Binatl Pr-Edit Binacional.

— Visual Arts on the U. S. - Mexico Border. (Binational Press Ser.: No. 3). 96p. (ENG & SPA.). 1991. pap. 12.50 (*0-916304-93-0*) SDSU Press.

Polko, Elise. Reminiscences of Felix Mendelssohn-Bartholdy. (Music Reprint Ser.). 1987. 35.00 (*0-306-76297-8*) Da Capo.

— Reminiscences of Felix Mendelssohn-Bartholdy. LC 87-81563. 222p. 1987. 24.95 (*0-944435-01-7*) Glenbridge Pub.

Poll, Gunther & Schneider, Friedrich. Returnable & Non-Returnable Packaging: The Management of Waste & Resources Towards an Eco-Social Market Economy. (Illus.). 160p. (Orig.). (C). 1993. 45.00 (*1-873936-25-7*, Pub. by J & J Sci Pubs UK) Bks Intl VA.

Poll, Ignacio R. Ethical Health Care Reform. 1993. 8.95 (*1-878901-53-2*) Hampton Roads Pub Co.

Poll, Morris. Roy Rogers King Cowboys LTD. Date not set. 75.00 (*0-685-69283-3*, HarpT) HarpC.

Poll, Richard D., et al, eds. Utah's History. rev. ed. (Illus.). 757p. (C). 1989. pap. text ed. 29.95 (*0-87421-142-5*) Utah St U Pr.

Poll, Roswitha. Literatur zu Umweltschutz und Umweltforschung. 3rd enl. ed. 380p. 1984. pap. text ed. 33.00 (*3-510-65119-7*) Lubrecht & Cramer.

Pollachek, Ellin R. Seasons. 352p. 1986. pap. 3.95 (*0-8217-1928-9*) Zebra.

Pollack. Clinical Urography: An Atlas & Textbook of Urological Imaging, 3 vols., 1. 3168p. 1989. text ed. 185.00 (*0-7216-1556-2*) Saunders.

— Clinical Urography: An Atlas & Textbook of Urological Imaging, 3 vols., 2. 3168p. 1989. text ed. 185.00 (*0-7216-1557-0*) Saunders.

— Clinical Urography: An Atlas & Textbook of Urological Imaging, 3 vols., 3. 3168p. 1989. text ed. 185.00 (*0-7216-1558-9*) Saunders.

— Clinical Urography: An Atlas & Textbook of Urological Imaging, 3 vols., Set. 3168p. 1989. 475.00 (*0-7216-1555-4*) Saunders.

— Shining Woman Tarot Cards. 1993. pap. 33.00 (*1-85538-098-6*) Thorsons SF.

Pollack, Abby, tr. see Tristan, Frederick.

Pollack, Aharon. Al Hasetumot Bamizmor: Commentary on the Book of Psalms. Nizri, Osnath, ed. 556p. (HEB.). 1991. text ed. 65.00 (*965-222-230-5*, Pub. by Nezer Pubng IS) Edit Orphee.

Pollack, Alan, jt. auth. see Guillemin, Victor.

Pollack, Barbara & Woodford, Charles. Dance Is a Moment: A Portrait of Jose Limon in Words & Pictures. (Illus.). 112p. 1993. pap. 19.95 (*0-87127-183-4*) Princeton Bk Co.

Pollack, Barbara, ed. see Humphrey, Doris.

Pollack, Barry. Popular Guitar Music. 256p. 1985. 16.95 (*0-13-685629-2*) P-H.

Pollack, Benny. The Paradox of Spanish Foreign Policy: Internal & External Political Structures. 240p. 1988. text ed. 39.95 (*0-312-59599-9*) St Martin.

Pollack, Benny & Roencranz, Herman. Revolutionary Social Democracy: The Chilean Socialist Party. LC 86-15507. 200p. 1986. text ed. 35.00 (*0-312-68031-7*) St Martin.

Pollack, Betsy, jt. auth. see Stern, Matthew H.

Pollack, Cecelia. Hip Reader Pack. rev. ed. 1979. pap. text ed. 39.95 (*0-87594-190-7*) Book-Lab.

— Hip Reader Program: Teachers Manual. rev. ed. 1979. pap. text ed. 5.95 (*0-87594-193-1*) Book-Lab.

— How Hip Are You, Bk. 2. (Hip Reader Program Ser.). (Illus.). (J). (gr. 5-12). 1978. student ed, pap. text ed. 5.95 (*0-87594-162-1*) Book-Lab.

— How Hip Are You?, Bk 3. (Hip Reader Program Ser.). (Illus.). (J). (gr. 5-12). 1978. student ed, pap. text ed. 5.95 (*0-87594-161-3*) Book-Lab.

— How Hip Are You, Bk. 4. (Hip Reader Program Ser.). (Illus.). (J). (gr. 5-12). 1978. student ed, pap. text ed. 5.95 (*0-87594-163-X*) Book-Lab.

Pollack, Cecelia & Lane, Patrick R. Hip Reader, 1. Ruchlis, Hy, ed. (Hip Reader Program Ser.). (Illus.). (Orig.). (gr. 5-12). 1970. pap. text ed. 5.95 (*0-87594-011-0*) Book-Lab.

— Hip Reader, 2. Ruchlis, Hy, ed. (Hip Reader Program Ser.). (Illus.). (Orig.). (gr. 5-12). 1970. 5.95 (*0-87594-045-5*) Book-Lab.

***Pollack, D. J.** The Austin Affair. 276p. 1994. 19.95 (*1-55793-041-4*) Guild Bindery Pr.

Pollack, D. S. The Algebra of Econometrics. LC 78-27237. (Wiley Series in Probability & Mathematical Statistics). 375p. reprint ed. pap. 106.90 (*0-8357-6709-4*, 2035340) Bks Demand.

Pollack, Daniel. Lair of the Fox. 1990. mass mkt. 4.95 (*0-06-100087-6*, Harp PBks) HarpC.

Pollack, David. The Fracture of Meaning: Japan's Synthesis of China from the Eighth Through the Eighteenth Centuries. LC 85-43305. 267p. reprint ed. pap. 76.10 (*0-8357-3424-2*, 2039682) Bks Demand.

— Reading against Culture: Ideology & Narrative in the Japanese Novel. LC 92-52769. 272p. 1992. 41.50 (*0-8014-2752-5*); pap. 14.95 (*0-8014-8035-3*) Cornell U Pr.

— Zen Poems of the Five Mountains. LC 84-13910. (American Academy of Religion, Studies in Religion). (C). 1985. 34.95 (*0-89130-776-1*, 01 00 37); pap. 16.95 (*0-89130-775-3*) Scholars Pr GA.

***Pollack, Doreen.** Educational Audiology for the Limited-Hearing Infant & Preschooler. 2nd ed. (Illus.). 414p. 1985. pap. 33.95 (*0-398-06328-1*) C C Thomas.

— Educational Audiology for the Limited-Hearing Infant & Preschooler. 2nd ed. (Illus.) 414p. 1985. 58.95 (*0-398-05053-8*) C C Thomas.

***Pollack, Dorothy B.** A Medley of Myths. (Illus.). 149p. (YA). (gr. 7-12). Date not set. spiral bd. 4.50 (*0-939507-46-3*, B206) Amer Classical.

Pollack, Eileen. The Rabbi in the Attic. 239p. 1991. 20.00 (*1-883285-08-9*) Delphinium.

— Whisper Whisper Jesse, Whisper Whisper Josh: A Story about AIDS. Templeman, Kristine, ed. LC 92-72471. (Illus.). 32p. (J). (ps up). 1992. lib. bdg. 16.95 (*0-9624828-4-6*); pap. 5.95 (*0-9624828-3-8*) Advantage-Aurora.

Pollack, Elisabeth. The Rowantree Crop. LC 89-39542. 280p. 1989. 16.95 (*0-945980-18-3*); pap. 9.95 (*0-945980-16-7*) Nrth Country Pr.

Pollack, Ervin H. Legal Research & Materials: Ohio Edition. LC 85-60265. (Legal Bibliographic & Research Reprint Ser.: Vol. 8). vii, 216p. 1985. reprint ed. lib. bdg. 42.00 (*0-89941-401-X*, 303680) W S Hein.

Pollack, Flora G. An Annotated Compilation of Cercospora Names. (Mycologia Memoirs Ser.: No. 12). 210p. 1987. lib. bdg. 55.50 (*3-443-76002-3*) Lubrecht & Cramer.

Pollack, Frederick. The Adventure. (Poetry Ser.). 182p. (Orig.). 1986. 15.00 (*0-934257-05-1*); pap. 8.00 (*0-934257-04-3*) Story Line.

Pollack, G. H., jt. ed. see Sugi, H.

Pollack, Gerald H. Muscles & Molecules: Uncovering the Principles of Biological Motion. 300p. (C). 1990. 55.00 (*0-9626895-0-5*) Ebner & Sons.

***Pollack, Gloria.** Eliezer Zweifel & the Intellectual Defenese of Hasidism. LC 94-42909. 1995. 39.50 (*0-88125-509-2*) Ktav.

Pollack, H. From Microbes to Microwaves: Autobiography of a Medical Man. (Illus.). 1992. 15.00 (*0-685-66038-9*) San Francisco Pr.

— Materials Science & Metallurgy. 4th ed. 1988. text ed. 82.00 (*0-8359-4287-2*) P-H.

Pollack, H., tr. see Honerkamp, Josef & Romer, Hartmann.

Pollack, H. N. & Murthy, V. Rama, eds. Structure & Evolution of the Continental Lithosphere. (Illus.). 210p. 1984. 83.00 (*0-08-030023-5*, Pergamon Pr) Elsevier.

Pollack, Harriet, jt. auth. see Smith, Alexander B.

Pollack, Herman W. Materials Science & Metallurgy. 4th ed. (Illus.). 560p. 1988. text ed. 24.00 (*0-13-560814-7*) P-H.

Pollack, Herman W., ed. Material Science & Metallurgy. 3rd ed. 1981. write for info. (*0-8359-4282-1*, Reston) P-H.

Pollack, Howard. Harvard Composers: Walter Piston & His Students, from Elliott Carter to Frederic Rzewski. LC 91-46438. (Illus.). 508p. 1992. 52.50 (*0-8108-2493-0*) Scarecrow.

— Skyscraper Lullaby: John Alden Carpenter & His Music. LC 93-46447. 1994. write for info. (*1-56098-400-7*) Smithsonian.

Pollack, Irv & Howland, George, Jr. Two Left Brains: Public Radio Commentaries from KCMU-Seattle, Washington. 40p. (Orig.). 1993. 6.00 (*0-940880-44-X*) Open Hand.

***Pollack, Jill S.** Lesbian & Gay Families: Redefining Parenting in America. (Changing Family Ser.). 128p. (YA). (gr. 9-12). 1995. lib. bdg. 14.49 (*0-531-11207-1*) Watts.

— Lesbian & Gay Families: Redefining Parenting in America. (Changing Family Ser.). (Illus.). 144p. (YA). (gr. 9 up). 1995. pap. 9.00 (*0-531-15749-0*) Watts.

— Shirley Chisholm. LC 93-31175. (First Bks.). (Illus.). 64p. (J). (gr. 5-8). 1994. lib. bdg. 13.93 (*0-531-20168-6*) Watts.

Pollack, Joe. Joe Pollack's Guide to St. Louis Restaurants. 2nd ed. LC 92-3382. 1992. pap. 9.95 (*1-55652-144-8*) Chicago Review.

Pollack, Joe, ed. see Zagat, Eugene H. & Zagat, Nina S.

Pollack, John, jt. ed. see Cummins, Robert.

Pollack, Jordan B., jt. auth. see Barnden, John A.

Pollack, Kenneth & Gergen, Michael J. Energy Storage: Four Major Alternatives: Heat Storage, Cool Storage, Compressed Air Energy Storage, & Underground Pumped Hydro Storage. LC 83-80664. 277p. reprint ed. pap. 79.00 (*0-7837-0329-5*, 2040648) Bks Demand.

Pollack, M. Noncrystalline Semiconductors, Vol. 1. LC 86-31045. 1987. reprint ed. 148.00 (*0-8493-5998-8*, CRC Reprint) Franklin.

— Noncrystalline Semiconductors, Vol. 2. LC 86-31045. 1987. reprint ed. 98.00 (*0-8493-5999-6*, CRC Reprint) Franklin.

— Noncrystalline Semiconductors, Vol. 3. LC 86-31045. 1987. reprint ed. 102.00 (*0-8493-6000-5*, CRC Reprint) Franklin.

Pollack, Michael, ed. Images of Primordial & Mystic Beauty: Paintings by Frithjof Schuon. (Illus.). 292p. 1992. 47.50 (*0-9629131-0-3*) Abodes IN.

Pollack, Minda, jt. auth. see Stock, Marc A.

Pollack, Norman. The Humane Economy: Populism, Capitalism, & Democracy. LC 90-31078. 224p. (C). 1990. text ed. 45.00 (*0-8135-1599-8*) Rutgers U Pr.

— The Just Polity: Populism, Law, & Human Welfare. LC 86-11433. 388p. 1987. reprint ed. pap. 110.60 (*0-7837-8084-2*, 2047837) Bks Demand.

— The Populist Response to Industrial America. 176p. 1976. pap. 12.50 (*0-674-69051-6*) HUP.

Pollack, Norman, ed. Populist Mind. (Orig.). (C). 1967. pap. write for info. (*0-672-60076-5*, AHS50, Bobbs) Macmillan.

Pollack, Oliver B. Empires in Collision: Anglo-Burmese Relations in the Mid-Nineteenth Century. LC 78-75239. (Contributions in Comparative Colonial Studies: No. 1). (Illus.). 214p. 1980. text ed. 59.95 (*0-313-20824-7*, PEC/, Greenwood Pr) Greenwood.

Pollack, R. L., jt. auth. see Morse, D. R.

Pollack, R. S. Tumor Surgery of the Head & Neck. (Illus.). x, 206p. 1975. 58.50 (*3-8055-2092-1*) S Karger.

Pollack, Rachel. Haindl Tarot. 24p. 1990. 15.00 (*0-88079-465-8*) US Games Syst.

— Haindl Tarot, II. 1990. 9.95 (*0-685-58856-4*) Newcastle Pub.

— Haindl Tarot, Vol. 1. 1990. 9.95 (*0-87877-155-7*) Newcastle Pub.

— The New Tarot. (Illus.). 176p. 1990. 22.50 (*0-87951-395-0*) Overlook Pr.

— The New Tarot: Modern Variations of Ancient Images. (Illus.). 176p. 1992. pap. 14.95 (*0-87951-475-2*) Overlook Pr.

— Tarot Readings & Meditations. (Illus.). 160p. 1991. pap. 9.95 (*1-85538-049-8*, Pub. by Aquarian Pr UK) Thorsons SF.

— Teach Yourself Fortune Telling: Palmistry, the Crystal Ball, Runes, Tea Leaves, the Tarot. rev. ed. 144p. 1993. pap. 12.95 (*0-8050-2681-9*) H Holt & Co.

— Temporary Agency. 202p. 1995. pap. 10.95 (*0-87951-602-X*) Overlook Pr.

— Temporary Agency. 202p. 1994. 18.95 (*0-312-11077-4*) St Martin.

— Unquenchable Fire. 390p. 1992. 23.95 (*0-87951-447-7*, Penguin Bks); pap. 13.95 (*0-87951-530-9*, Penguin Bks) Overlook Pr.

***Pollack, Rachel & Schwartz, Cheryl.** The Journey Out: A Book for & About Gay, Lesbian & Bisexual Teens. LC 95-14276. (Illus.). 176p. (YA). (gr. 7 up). 1995. pap. 5.99 (*0-14-037254-7*) Puffin Bks.

— The Journey Out: A Book for & About Gay, Lesbian & Bisexual Teens. LC 95-14276. (J). 1995. write for info. (*0-670-85845-5*, Viking) Viking Penguin.

Pollack, Randy B. In Search of Ourselves: Student Study Guide. 1981. pap. text ed. write for info. (*0-8087-3326-5*) Burgess MN Intl.

Pollack, Rhoda G. George S. Kaufman. (United States Authors Ser.: No. 525). 160p. 1988. text ed. 21.95 (*0-8057-7508-0*, Pub. by Royal Botanic Garden UK) Macmillan.

Pollack, Rhoda-Gale. A Sampler of Plays by Women. LC 89-13033. (American University Studies: English Language & Literature: Ser. IV, Vol. 52). 410p. (C). 1990. text ed. 64.50 (*0-8204-1172-8*) P Lang Pubs.

Pollack, Rhoda-Gale, ed. see Lokvam, Marian, et al.

Pollack, Robert. Laboratory Manual in Medical Microbiology. (Illus.). 200p. (C). 1992. pap. text ed. 16.00 (*1-878045-13-X*) Whittier Pubns.

An Asterisk (*) at the beginning of an entry indicates that the title is appearing in BIP for the first time.

— Signs of Life: The Language & Meanings of DNA. 224p. 1994. 19.95 (0-395-64498-4) HM.
— Signs of Life: The Language & Meanings of DNA. 1995. pap. 10.95 (0-395-73530-0) HM.
Pollack, Robert, et al. Laboratory Exercises in Medical Microbiology. (Illus.). 172p. (C). 1992. student ed 16.00 (0-685-75073-6) Whittier Pubns.
Pollack, Robert L. & Kravitz, Edward. Nutrition in Oral Health & Disease. LC 84-27804. 499p. reprint ed. pap. 142.30 (0-7837-2739-9, 2043119) Bks Demand.
Pollack, Robert L., jt. auth. see Morse, Donald R.
Pollack, Rosemary. White Hibiscus. large type ed. (Linford Romance Library). 295p. 1984. pap. 11.95 (0-7089-6020-0, Trailtree Bookshop) Ulverscroft.
Pollack, S. R., jt. ed. see Brighton, C. T.
Pollack, Sandra & Knight, Denise D., eds. Contemporary Lesbian Writers of the United States: A Bio-Bibliographical Critical Sourcebook. LC 92-39468. 688p. 1993. text ed. 99.50 (0-313-28215-3, PCL/) Greenwood.
Pollack, Sandra & Vaughn, Jeanne, eds. Politics of the Heart: A Lesbian Parenting Anthology. LC 87-27250. 360p. (Orig.). 1987. lib. bdg. 26.95 (0-932379-36-2); pap. 12.95 (0-932379-35-4) Firebrand Bks.
Pollack, Sandy. Alternative Careers for Teachers. rev. ed. LC 84-19727. 176p. 1984. pap. 9.95 (0-916782-60-3) Harvard Common Pr.
Pollack, Sara, jt. auth. see Gruenewold, Lee.
Pollack, Seymour, ed. Studies in Computer Science. LC 82-62390. (MAA Studies in Mathematics: No. 22). 408p. (C). 1983. 10.00 (0-88385-124-5) Math Assn.
Pollack, Seymour V. Effective Programming in Turbo Pascal. LC 90-2623. 864p. (C). 1991. pap. 47.95 (0-534-15294-5) PWS Pubs.
Pollack, Seymour V., jt. auth. see Ball, William E.
Pollack, Shalom. Jewish Destiny & Social Cycles. 1992. 16.95 (0-533-10005-4) Vantage.
Pollack, Sheldon V. Electrosurgery of the Skin. (Practical Manuals in Dermatologic Surgery Ser.). (Illus.). 93p. 1991. pap. text ed. 32.00 (0-443-08683-4) Churchill.
Pollack, Steve. Ecology. LC 93-10064. (Eyewitness Science Ser.). (Illus.). 64p. (J). (gr. 3-6). 1993. 15.95 (1-56458-326-0) Dorling Kindersley.
— Magic Lantern Guide to EOS Elan & EOS 100. (Magic Lantern Guide Ser.). (Illus.). 176p. (Orig.). (C). 1995. pap. 19.95 (1-883403-21-9, Silver Pixel Pr) Saunders Photo.
***Pollack, Suzanne.** Improving Environmental Performance. LC 94-43141. (Self-Development for Managers Ser.). 1995. write for info. (0-415-10237-5) Routledge.
Pollack, William, jt. ed. see Levant, Ronald.
Pollack, William S., jt. auth. see Betcher, R. W.
Pollack, William S., jt. auth. see Betcher, R. William.
Pollak, Andy, ed. A Citizen's Inquiry: The Opsahl Report on Northern Ireland. (Illus.). 464p. 1993. pap. 18.95 (1-874675-08-2, Pub. by Lilliput Pr Ltd IE) Irish Bks Media.
Pollak, Andy, jt. auth. see Moloney, Ed.
***Pollak, Emil & Pollak, Martyl.** A Guide to the Makers of American Wooden Planes. 3rd ed. (Illus.). 462p. 1994. pap. 35.00 (1-879335-51-4) Astragal Pr.
— Prices Realized on Rare Imprinted American Wooden Planes. (Illus.). 152p. 1993. pap. 16.95 (1-879335-36-0) Astragal Pr.
Pollak, Emil & Pollak, Martyl, eds. The Fascinating World of Early Tools & Trades: Selections from the Chronicle. (Illus.). 424p. 1991. 24.95 (1-879335-00-X) Astragal Pr.
Pollak, Emil, jt. auth. see Kean, Herbert.
Pollak, Emil S. The Stanley Catalog Collection. (Illus.). 400p. 1989. 29.50 (0-9618088-4-5) Astragal Pr.
Pollak, Emil S., jt. auth. see Kean, Herbert P.
Pollak, Erich W. Thoracic Outlet Syndrome. (Illus.). 248p. 1986. 39.50 (0-87993-246-5) Fairleigh Dickinson.
Pollak, F. Pump Users' Handbook. 3rd ed. 250p. 1988. 86.95 (0-85461-122-3, P7165) PennWell Bks.
Pollak, F., et al, eds. International Conference on Modulation Spectroscopy. 1990. 70.00 (0-8194-0337-7, VOL. 1286) SPIE.
Pollak, Felix. Benefits of Doubt. 200p. 1988. 15.95 (0-944024-04-1) Spoon Riv Poetry.
— The Castle & the Flaw. (J). 1963. pap. 4.00 (0-685-01010-4) Elizabeth Pr.
— Ginkgo. 1973. 16.00 (0-685-36869-6); pap. 8.00 (0-685-36870-X) Elizabeth Pr.
— Prose & Cons. (Juniper Bk. Ser.: No. 44). 1983. pap. 6.00 (1-55780-043-X) Juniper Pr WI.
Pollak, Felix, jt. auth. see Goldberger, Iefke.
Pollak, Fred H., jt. ed. see Brillson, Leonard J.
Pollak, G., ed. Algebraic Theory of Semigroups. (Colloquia Mathematica Societatis Janos Bolyai Ser.: Vol. 20). 754p. 1979. 146.25 (0-444-85282-4, North Holland) Elsevier.
Pollak, G., et al, eds. Semigroups: Structure & Universal Algebraic Problems. 502p. 1986. 128.25 (0-444-87553-0) Elsevier.
Pollak, Gabriel, ed. Transliterated Haggadah: Passover Haggadah. deluxe ed. 18.50 (0-87559-082-9) Shalom.
Pollak, Gustav. International Minds & the Search for the Restful. LC 73-107734. (Essay Index Reprint Ser.). 1977. 19.95 (0-8369-1532-1) Ayer.
Pollak, J. K. & Lee, J. W., eds. The Biochemistry of Gene Expression in Higher Organisms: Proceedings. LC 72-97960. 656p. 1973. lib. bdg. 145.50 (90-277-0289-6) Kluwer Ac.
Pollak, Karen, jt. auth. see Pollak, Oliver.
Pollak, Kurt. Knaurs Lexikon der Modernen Medizin: Knaurs Modern Lexicon of Medicine. (GER.). 1972. 19.95 (0-8288-6404-7, M-7519) Fr & Eur.
Pollak, M. & Fry, J. Commonsense Paediatrics. 1986. lib. bdg. 95.00 (0-85200-945-3) Kluwer Ac.
Pollak, M. & Shklovskii, B., eds. Hopping Transport in Solids. (Modern Problems in Condensed Matter Sciences Ser.: Vol. 28). 410p. 1991. 200.00 (0-444-88037-2, North Holland) Elsevier.
Pollak, M., jt. auth. see Efros, A. L.
Pollak, M., jt. ed. see Fritzsche, H.
Pollak, Margaret. Textbook of Developmental Paediatrics. LC 92-22842. (Illus.). 512p. 1993. text ed. 65.00 (0-443-04169-5) Churchill.
Pollak, Martha D. Military Architecture, Cartography, & the Representation of the Early Modern European City: A Checklist of Treatises on Fortification in the Newberry Library. (Illus.). 119p. 1991. pap. 15.00 (0-911028-45-5) Newberry.
— Turin 1564-1680: Urban Design, Military Culture, & the Creation of the Absolutist Capital. LC 90-44409. (Illus.). 312p. 1991. 49.95 (0-226-67342-1) U Ch Pr.
Pollak, Martyl, jt. auth. see Pollak, Emil.
Pollak, Martyl, jt. ed. see Pollak, Emil.
Pollak, Michael. The Jews of Dynastic China: A Critical Bibliography. (Bibliographica Judaica Ser.: No. 13). 225p. 1993. 24.95 (0-87820-911-5) Hebrew Union Coll Pr.
— The Second Plague of Europe: AIDS Prevention & Sexual Transmission among Men in Western Europe. LC 92-18354. 1993. pap. 9.95 (1-56023-020-7) Harrington Pk.
— The Second Plague of Europe: AIDS Prevention & Sexual Transmission among Men in Western Europe. LC 92-18354. (Illus.). 104p. 1993. 24.95 (1-56024-306-6) Haworth Pr.
Pollak, Michael, ed. Noncrystalline Semiconductors, 3 vols., Set. 1987. 348.00 (0-8493-5994-5, QC611, CRC Reprint) Franklin.
— Noncrystalline Semiconductors, 3 vols., Vol. I. 304p. 1987. write for info. (0-318-62343-9, CRC Reprint) Franklin.
— Noncrystalline Semiconductors, 3 vols., Vol. II. 192p. 1987. write for info. (0-318-62344-7, CRC Reprint) Franklin.
— Noncrystalline Semiconductors, 3 vols., Vol. III. 192p. 1987. write for info. (0-318-62345-5, CRC Reprint) Franklin.
Pollak, Michael, ed. see Loewenthal, Rudolf.
Pollak, Michael, jt. auth. see Nelkin, Dorothy.
Pollak, Michael, et al, eds. AIDS: A Problem for Sociological Research. (Special Issue of Current Sociology Ser.). (Illus.). 144p. (C). 1993. text ed. 55.00 (0-8039-8841-9); pap. text ed. 22.95 (0-8039-8840-0) Sage.
***Pollak, Nancy.** Mandelstam the Reader. (Parallax). 240p. 1994. text ed. 39.95x (0-8018-5006-1) Johns Hopkins.
Pollak, O. J. & Kritchevsky, D. Sitosterol. (Monographs on Atherosclerosis: Vol. 10). (Illus.). vii, 220p. 1981. pap. 118.50 (3-8055-0568-X) S Karger.
Pollak, Oliver & Pollak, Karen. Rhodesia-Zimbabwe. (World Bibliographical Ser.: No. 4). 195p. 1979. lib. bdg. 25.25 (0-903450-14-3) ABC-CLIO.
Pollak, Otto. The Criminality of Women. LC 77-13959. 180p. 1978. reprint ed. text ed. 65.00 (0-8371-9869-0, POCW, Greenwood Pr) Greenwood.
— Invitation to a Dialogue: Union & Separation in Family Life. LC 79-19154. 1983. pap. 16.50 (0-88331-154-2) Luce.
— Positive Experiences in Retirement. (C). 1957. 6.50 (0-256-00674-1) Irwin.
— Social Aspects of Retirement. (C). 1956. 5.50 (0-256-00675-X) Irwin.
Pollak, P. S. Halel Vzimrah: Commentary in Hebrew on the Passover Haggadah. 12.50 (0-87559-100-0); pap. 9.50 (0-87559-099-3) Shalom.
— Hermesh Bakomo: Commentary & Interpretation on Tractate Avoth. (HEB.). 9.50 (0-87559-092-6) Shalom.
— Marbin Besimho. 15.00 (0-87559-083-7); pap. 10.00 (0-87559-084-5) Shalom.
— Minhas Marheshes: Commentary on Genesis. 12.00 (0-87559-101-9) Shalom.
— Nefesh Hayah: Commentary & Interpretation on the Passover Haggadah with the Haggadah Text. (HEB.). 9.50 (0-87559-091-8) Shalom.
— Shaare Rahmin: Sermon Material for the High Holidays in Hebrew. 10.50 (0-87559-104-3) Shalom.
— Tal Hermon: Sermon Material for Yom Kippur & Eulogy in Hebrew. 12.00 (0-87559-086-1); pap. 7.50 (0-87559-085-3) Shalom.
Pollak, R., et al, eds. Electronic Packaging Materials Science Vol. 323, No. VII: Materials Research Society Symposium Proceedings. 1994. text ed. 71.00 (1-55899-222-7) Materials Res.
Pollak, Richard. Up Against Apartheid: The Role & the Plight of the Press in South Africa. LC 80-22363. (Science & International Affairs Ser.). 167p. 1981. 19.95 (0-8093-1013-9) S Ill U Pr.
Pollak, Richard A. Interactive Videodisc Training: A Series of Training Workshops for Educators: An Introduction. (Illus.). 50p. 1992. disk, ring bd. 270.00 (0-922649-06-5) ETC MN.
— K-12 Planning Guide for Videodisc Usage. rev. ed. 52p. 1994. 30.00 (0-922649-26-X) ETC MN.
Pollak, Richard A., ed. Explore Antarctica! (Illus.). 58p. (J). (gr. 5-9). 1991. ring bd. 295.00 (0-922649-14-6) ETC MN.
— Explore Antarctica! Barcode Guide. 188p. (J). (gr. 5-9). 1992. spiral bd. 125.00 (0-922649-15-4) ETC MN.
— Interactive Multimedia Training: Introduction to CD-ROMs: A Series of Training Workshops for Educators. (Illus.). 92p. 1994. cd-rom, ring bd. 395.00 (0-922649-22-7) ETC MN.
— Interactive Videodisc Training: A Series of Training Workshops for Educators: An Introduction. (Interactive Videodisc Training Ser.). (Illus.). 60p. 1989. disk, ring bd. 400.00 (0-922649-02-2) ETC MN.
— Interactive Videodisc Training: A Series of Training Workshops for Educators, Repurposing with HyperCard. (Interactive Videodisc Training Ser.). (Illus.). 60p. 1992. disk, ring bd. 325.00 (0-922649-04-9) ETC MN.
— Interactive Videodisc Training: A Series of Workshops for Educators: Evaluating Laserdiscs for Your Curriculum. (Illus.). 64p. 1992. disk, ring bd. 750.00 (0-922649-17-0) ETC MN.
— Interactive Videodisc Training: A Series of Workshops for Educators: LinkWay Applications. (Illus.). 80p. 1992. disk, ring bd. 270.00 (0-922649-11-1) ETC MN.
— Interactive Videodisc Training: Multimedia Access for Students with Disabilities: A Series of Training Workshops for Educators. (Illus.). 94p. 1994. ring bd., sl. 695.00 (0-922649-20-0) ETC MN.
— Interactive Videodisc Training Presenting & Authoring with HyperStudio: A Series of Training Workshops for Educators. (Interactive Videodisc Training Ser.). (Illus.). 50p. 1993. disk, ring bd. 325.00 (0-922649-21-9) ETC MN.
— Multimedia & Videodisc Compendium for Education & Training: 1995 Edition. 136p. 1994. per., pap. 45.00 (0-922649-24-3) ETC MN.
Pollak, Richard A., ed. see Holden, Steve & Doering, Ron.
Pollak, Robert A. The Theory of the Cost of Living Index. (Illus.). 224p. 1989. 48.00 (0-19-505870-4) OUP.
Pollak, Robert A. & Wales, Terence J. Demand System Specification & Estimation. (Illus.). 232p. 1992. 45.00 (0-19-506941-2) OUP.
— Demand System Specification & Estimation. (Illus.). 256p. 1995. reprint ed. pap. 19.95 (0-19-510121-9) OUP.
Pollak, Scott D., ed. Solutions & Strategies for Business Reengineering. 140p. 1993. 895.00 (0-945052-22-7) Computer Econ.
Pollak, Susan, jt. ed. see White, Merry I.
Pollak, Vivian R. Dickinson: The Anxiety of Gender. LC 83-45941. 260p. 1986. 36.50 (0-8014-1605-1); pap. 14.95 (0-8014-9370-6) Cornell U Pr.
Pollak, Vivian R., ed. New Essays on "Daisy Miller" & "The Turn of the Screw" LC 92-47280. (American Novel Ser.). 210p. 1993. 29.95 (0-521-41673-6) Cambridge U Pr.
— New Essays on "Daisy Miller" & "The Turn of the Screw" LC 92-47280. (American Novel Ser.). 210p. 1993. pap. 12.95 (0-521-42681-2) Cambridge U Pr.
— A Poet's Parents: The Courtship Letters of Emily Norcross & Edward Dickinson. LC 87-35868. (Illus.). xxxvii, 236p. (C). 1988. 32.50 (0-8078-1797-X) U of NC Pr.
Pollalis, Spiro N. Computer-Aided Project Management: A Visual Scheduling & Management System. xx, 242p. 1993. 56.00 (3-528-05347-X, Pub. by Vieweg & Sohn GW) Ballen Bkslr.
Pollan. Surviving the Squeeze. 320p. 1994. pap. 10.00 (0-02-081168-3, Collier S&S) S&S Trade.
Pollan, Corky. Shopping Manhattan: The Discriminating Buyer's Guide to Finding Almost Anything. 512p. (Orig.). 1989. pap. 12.95 (0-14-012401-2, Penguin Bks) Viking Penguin.
— Shopping Manhattan: The Discriminating Buyer's Guide to Finding Almost Anything. enl. rev. ed. 560p. (Orig.). 1992. reprint ed. pap. 15.00 (0-14-016950-4, Penguin Bks) Viking Penguin.
Pollan, Stephen M. Forget Starting a Business. 1990. pap. 10.95 (0-671-67505-2, Fireside) S&S Trade.
Pollan, Stephen M. & Levine, Mark. The Total Negotiator. 272p. 1994. pap. 10.00 (0-380-77019-9) Avon.
Pollan, Stephen M., et al. The Field Guide to Home Buying in America. 1988. pap. 10.00 (0-671-63961-7, Fireside) S&S Trade.
Polland, Alfred W., et al, eds. A Short-Title Catalogue of Books Printed in England, Scotland, & Ireland, & of English Books Printed Abroad, 1475-1640: Vol. III: Addenda, Corrigenda, & Indexes. 2nd ed. (Illus.). 430p. 1991. 275.00 (0-19-721791-5) OUP.
Polland, Barbara K. Feelings: Inside You & Outloud Too. LC 74-25835. (Illus.). 64p. (J). (ps-3). 1984. pap. 6.95 (0-89087-006-3) Celestial Arts.
— Grandma & Grandpa Are Special People. LC 80-66961. (Illus.). 80p. (J). (gr. k-3). 1984. pap. 7.95 (0-89087-343-7) Celestial Arts.
— The Parenting Challenge: Practical Answers to Childrearing Questions. rev. ed. LC 93-48937. 232p. (J). (gr. k-7). 1993. reprint ed. pap. 9.95 (1-883672-08-2) Tricycle Pr.
— The Sensible Book: A Celebration of Your Five Senses. rev. ed. (Illus.). 64p. (J). 1993. pap. write for info. (0-89087-707-6) Celestial Arts.
Polland, Jeffrey & Walker, John M., eds. Methods in Molecular Biology, Vol. 6: Plant Cell & Tissue Culture Techniques. LC 84-15696. (Illus.). 612p. 1990. 69.50 (0-89603-161-6) Humana.
Polland, Leon D., jt. auth. see Chapelle, Howard I.
***Polland, Madeleine.** The Pomegranate House. (Charnwood Large Print Ser.). 1994. 25.95 (0-7089-8794-X) Ulverscroft.
Polland, Madeleine A. All Their Kingdoms. large type ed. 592p. 1983. 21.95 (0-7089-0934-5) Ulverscroft.
— The Heart Speaks Many Ways. large type ed. (Romance Ser.). 580p. 1983. 21.95 (0-7089-1031-9) Ulverscroft.
— No Price Too High. large type ed. (Charnwood Romance Ser.). 576p. 1985. 23.95 (0-7089-8290-5, Charnwood) Ulverscroft.
— Rich Man's Flowers. large type ed. 576p. 1993. 23.95 (0-7089-8697-8, Trail West Pubs) Ulverscroft.
Pollar, Odette. Dynamics of Diversity. Gerould, W. Philip, ed. LC 93-73147. (Fifty-Minute Ser.). (Illus.). 100p. (Orig.). 1994. pap. 9.95 (1-56052-247-X) Crisp Pubns.
— Get Organised! A Guide to Personal Productivity. pap. text ed. write for info. (0-7494-0943-6, Pub. by Kogan Page Educ UK) Taylor & Francis.
— Organizing Your Workspace. Crisp, Michael G., ed. LC 91-76238. (Fifty-Minute Ser.). 90p. (Orig.). 1992. pap. 9.95 (1-56052-125-2) Crisp Pubns.
Pollard. Developments in Management Thought. 1986. 16.50 (0-8448-0069-4, Crane Russak) Taylor & Francis.
— The Social World of the Primary School. 1987. pap. text ed. 24.95 (0-304-31445-5) Cassell.
Pollard & Ross. European Community Law: Text & Mats. 1993. pap. write for info. (0-406-01621-6, UK) Butterworth Legal Pubs.
Pollard, jt. auth. see Carter, John.
Pollard, A. H., et al. Demographic Techniques. 2nd ed. (Illus.). 192p. 1981. pap. text ed. 25.00 (0-08-024817-9, Pergamon Pr) Elsevier.
— Demographic Techniques. 3rd ed. (Illus.). 185p. 1990. pap. text ed. 27.00 (0-08-040065-5, PPA) Elsevier.
Pollard, A. J. John Talbot & the War in France, 1427-1453. (Royal Historical Society Ser.: No. 35). 166p. 1983. 63.00 (0-901050-88-1) Boydell & Brewer.
— North-Eastern England During the Wars of the Roses: Lay Society, War, & Politics, 1450-1500. (Illus.). 464p. 1991. 105.00 (0-19-820087-0) OUP.
— Richard III & the Princes in the Tower. (Illus.). (Orig.). 1993. pap. 26.00 (0-7509-0354-6) A Sutton Pub.
— Richard III & the Princess in the Tower. 1991. text ed. 39.95 (0-312-06715-1) St Martin.
— The Wars of the Roses. (British History in Perspective Ser.). 140p. 1988. text ed. 15.95 (0-312-02466-5) St Martin.
***Pollard, A. J., ed.** The Wars of the Roses. LC 95-9735. 1995. write for info. (0-312-12697-2); pap. write for info. (0-312-12699-9) St Martin.
Pollard, A. W., et al, eds. A Short-Title Catalogue of Books Printed in England, Scotland, & Ireland & of English Books Printed Abroad, 3 vols., Set. 2nd rev. ed. 1992. 625.00 (0-19-721797-4) OUP.
Pollard, Alan P., ed. U. S. S. R. Facts & Figures Annual, Vol. 12-14: 1988-1990, Vol. 12-14. 1988. 95.00 (0-87569-103-X); 95.00 (0-685-44198-9) Academic Intl.
Pollard, Albert F. The History of England from the Accession of Edward Sixth to the Death of Elizabeth 1 (1547-1603) LC 75-5633. (Political History of England Ser.: No. 6). reprint ed. 45.00 (0-404-50776-X) AMS Pr.
— Thomas Cranmer & the English Reformation, 1849-1556. LC 83-45587. reprint ed. 42.50 (0-404-19905-4) AMS Pr.
Pollard, Albert F., ed. Reign of Henry Seventh from Contemporary Sources, 3 Vols, Set. LC 73-181970. reprint ed. 145.00 (0-404-05140-5) AMS Pr.
Pollard, Alfred, jt. auth. see Bartlett, Henrietta.
Pollard, Alfred F. Jesuits in Poland. LC 76-116799. (Studies in Philosophy: No. 40). 1970. reprint ed. lib. bdg. 49.95 (0-8383-1041-9) M S G Haskell Hse.
***Pollard, Alfred M.** Banking Law in the United States. LC 92-20020. 1994. 60.00 (0-250-40753-1) Michie Butterworth.
Pollard, Alfred M., et al. Banking Law in the United States, 2 vols. 2nd suppl. ed. LC 92-20020. 1993. 50.00 (0-685-74451-5) Butterworth Legal Pubs.
— Banking Law in the United States, 2 vols., Set. 2nd ed. LC 92-20020. 1160p. 1994. ring bd. 185.00 (0-88063-836-2) Michie Butterworth.
Pollard, Alfred W. Chaucer. LC 73-114911. (Select Bibliographies Reprint Ser.). 1977. 19.95 (0-8369-5316-9) Ayer.
— Chaucer. LC 76-174278. reprint ed. 21.50 (0-404-05069-7) AMS Pr.
— Chaucer. LC 69-14038. 136p. 1969. reprint ed. text ed. 45.00 (0-8371-1856-5, POCH, Greenwood Pr) Greenwood.
— Early Illustrated Books. LC 68-26366. (Bibliophile Ser.: No. 83). 1969. reprint ed. lib. bdg. 75.00 (0-8383-0278-5) M S G Haskell Hse.
— Fifteenth Century Prose & Verse. LC 64-16750. (Arber's an English Garner Ser.). reprint ed. 52.00 (0-8154-0178-7) Cooper Sq.
— Shakespeare's Fight with the Pirates & the Problems of the Transmission of His Text. (BCL1-PR English Literature Ser.). 110p. 1992. reprint ed. lib. bdg. 69.00 (0-7812-7310-2) Rprt Serv.
— Shakespeare's Fight with the Pirates & the Problems of the Transmission of the Text. LC 73-20426. (Studies in Shakespeare: No. 24). 1974. lib. bdg. 75.00 (0-8383-1754-5) M S G Haskell Hse.
— Shakespeare's Hand in the Play of Sir Thomas More: Papers. (BCL1-PR English Literature Ser.). 229p. 1992. reprint ed. lib. bdg. 79.00 (0-7812-7277-7) Rprt Serv.
Pollard, Alfred W. & Redgrave, G. R., eds. A Short-Title Catalogue of Books Printed in England, Scotland, & Ireland & of English Books Printed Abroad, 1475-1640, 2 vols., Vol. 1. 2nd ed. (Bibliographical Society Ser.). 1987. 275.00 (0-19-721789-3) OUP.
— A Short-Title Catalogue of Books Printed in England, Scotland, & Ireland & of English Books Printed Abroad, 1475-1640, 2 vols., Vol. 2. 2nd ed. (Bibliographical Society Ser.). 1976. 195.00 (0-19-721790-7) OUP.
Pollard, Alfred W., ed. see Chaucer, Geoffrey.
Pollard, Alton B., III. Mysticism & Social Change: The Social Witness of Howard Thurman. (Martin Luther King, Jr., Memorial Studies in Religion, Culture, & Social Development: Vol. 2). 219p. (Orig.). (C). 1992. text ed. 39.95 (0-8204-1612-6); pap. text ed. 29.95 (0-8204-1981-8) P Lang Pubs.
Pollard, Andrew. Learning in Primary Schools. Wragg, C. E., ed. (Education Matters Ser.). 160p. 1990. text ed. 50.00 (0-304-32250-4); pap. text ed. 17.95 (0-304-32251-2) Cassell.
Pollard, Andrew, ed. Children & Their Primary Schools: A New Perspective. 265p. 1987. 60.00 (1-85000-320-3, Falmer Pr); pap. 30.00 (1-85000-321-1, Falmer Pr) Taylor & Francis.

P Q

Pollard, Andrew & Bourne, Jill, eds. Teaching & Learning in the Primary School. LC 93-5056. 1994. write for info. (*0-415-10258-8*) Routledge.

Pollard, Andrew & Tann, Sarah. Reflective Teaching in the Primary School. 2nd ed. (Education Ser.). (Illus.). 224p. 1993. text ed. 70.00 (*0-304-32618-6*); pap. text ed. 24.95 (*0-304-32620-8*) Cassell.

Pollard, Andrew, jt. ed. see Woods, Peter.

Pollard, Andrew, et al. Changing English Primary Schools: The Impact of the Education Reform Act at Key Stage One. LC 93-40675. (Cassell Education Ser.). (Illus.). 224p. 1994. 60.00 (*0-304-32921-5*); pap. 17.95 (*0-304-32923-1*) Cassell.

Pollard, Andrew, et al, eds. Education, Training & the New Vocationalism: Experience & Policy. 192p. 1988. 90.00 (*0-335-15845-5*, Open Univ Pr); pap. 32.00 (*0-335-15844-7*, Open Univ Pr) Taylor & Francis.

Pollard, Arthur. Crabbe: The Critical Heritage. (Critical Heritage Ser.). 510p. 1975. 69.50 (*0-7100-7258-9*, RKP) Routledge.

Pollard, Arthur, ed. The Victorians. LC 87-47750. (New History of Literature Ser.). 500p. 1987. 39.50 (*0-87226-130-1*) P Bedrick Bks.

— The Victorians. 592p. 1994. pap. 13.00 (*0-14-017756-6*, Penguin Bks) Viking Penguin.

Pollard, Arthur, ed. see Crabbe, George.

Pollard, Arthur, ed. see Gaskell, Elizabeth C.

***Pollard, B. J., ed.** Applied Neuromuscular Pharmacology. (Illus.). 456p. 1994. text ed. 125.00 (*0-19-262148-3*) OUP.

Pollard, Bobbie J., et al. Access Information: Research in Business. 3rd ed. 292p. 1993. per. 26.95 (*0-8403-8943-4*) Kendall-Hunt.

Pollard, Carl & Sag, Ivan. Information-Based Syntax & Semantics. LC 87-71618. (Center for the Study of Language & Information-Lecture Notes Ser.: No. 13). 252p. 1987. 39.95 (*0-937073-23-7*); pap. 17.95 (*0-937073-24-5*) Ctr Study Language.

Pollard, Carl J. & Sag, Ivan A. Head-Driven Phrase Structure Grammar. LC 93-17533. (Studies in Contemporary Linguistics). (Illus.). 360p. 1994. lib. bdg. 80.00 (*0-226-67446-0*); pap. text ed. 34.95 (*0-226-67447-9*) U Ch Pr.

Pollard, Clarice F. Laugh, Cry & Remember: The Journal of a GI Lady! Westheimer, Mary, ed. LC 91-90262. (Illus.). 224p. (Orig.). 1992. pap. 14.95 (*0-9629334-0-6*) Journeys Pr.

Pollard, D. Convergence of Stochastic Processes. (Series in Statistics). (Illus.). 280p. 1984. 49.00 (*0-387-90990-7*) Spr-Verlag.

Pollard, D. E., jt. auth. see Tung, P. C.

Pollard, D. E., jt. auth. see T'ung, P. C.

Pollard, Dave & Porter. Improve & Modify Your MGB. 1989. 34.95 (*0-85429-668-9*, Pub. by G T Foulis Ltd) Haynes Pubns.

Pollard, Dave, jt. auth. see Porter, Lindsay.

Pollard, Dave, ed. see Porter, Lindsay.

Pollard, Dave, jt. auth. see Porter, Lindsay.

Pollard, David. Tolley's Employee & Pension Rights in Corporate Insolvency. 220p. 1993. 135.00 (*0-85459-737-9*, Pub. by Tolley Pubng UK) St Mut.

Pollard, David & Hughes, David J. Constitutional & Administrative Law - Text & Materials. 1990. U.K. pap. 44.00 (*0-406-50600-0*) Butterworth Legal Pubs.

Pollard, David E. A Chinese Look at Literature: The Literary Values of Chou Tso-Jen in Relation to the Tradition. LC 72-97732. 195p. reprint ed. pap. 55.60 (*0-685-44494-5*, 2031509) Bks Demand.

Pollard, David E., jt. ed. see Chan, Sin-wai.

Pollard, David W. & Burton, Joseph J. Guide to Effective Bankruptcy Litigation. 1294p. 1988. text ed. 90.00 (*0-07-050397-4*) Shepards-McGraw.

Pollard, Diane S., jt. ed. see Biklen, Sari K.

Pollard, E. & Yates, T. J. Monitoring Butterflies for Ecology & Conservation: The British Butterfly Monitoring Scheme. LC 93-12557. 1993. write for info. (*0-412-40220-3*) Chapman & Hall.

Pollard, E., jt. auth. see Setlow, R.

Pollard, E. A. Lost Cause. 1994. 12.99 (*0-517-10131-9*) Random Hse Value.

Pollard, Edward A. Life of Jefferson Davis, with a Secret History of the Southern Confederacy, Gathered Behind the Scenes in Richmond. LC 75-95074. (Select Bibliographies Reprint Ser.). 1977. 36.95 (*0-8369-5074-7*) Ayer.

— Lost Cause. LC 74-117888. (Select Bibliographies Reprint Ser.). 1977. 60.95 (*0-8369-5341-X*) Ayer.

— Lost Cause Regained. LC 78-117889. (Select Bibliographies Reprint Ser.). 1977. 20.95 (*0-8369-5342-8*) Ayer.

— Lost Cause Regained. LC 70-174279. reprint ed. 27.50 (*0-404-00097-5*) AMS Pr.

— Southern History of the War. 1990. 14.99 (*0-517-22899-8*) Random Hse Value.

***Pollard, Elaine, ed.** The Oxford English Minidictionary. 4th ed. 656p. 1995. 5.95 (*0-19-861324-5*) OUP.

***Pollard, Elaine & Liebeck, Helen, eds.** The Oxford Large Print Dictionary. 2nd ed. 960p. 1995. bds. 35.00 (*0-19-861322-9*) OUP.

— The Oxford Paperback Dictionary. 4th ed. LC 93-43215. (C). 1994. pap. 4.99 (*0-19-280012-4*) OUP.

Pollard, Elizabeth B. Visual Arts Research: A Handbook. LC 86-375. 180p. 1986. text ed. 49.95 (*0-313-24186-4*, PVA/, Greenwood Pr) Greenwood.

Pollard, Ernest C. The Cataclysm: Just the Facts. LC 88-63019. 264p. (Orig.). 1989. text ed. 16.00 (*0-9612798-2-6*) Woodburn Pr.

— Radiation: Cells & People. (Illus.). 133p. (Orig.). (C). 1991. pap. 12.00 (*0-9612798-3-4*) Woodburn Pr.

— Radiation: One Story of the M. I. T. Radiation Laboratory. (Illus.). 197p. (Orig.). 1982. pap. 12.95 (*0-9612798-1-8*) Woodburn Pr.

— Sermons in Stones: Science & People. LC 92-91167. (Illus.). 218p. (Orig.). 1993. pap. 10.00 (*0-9612798-6-9*) Woodburn Pr.

—Sermons in Stones: Science & People. 2nd ed. Giles, Marjorie B., ed. (Illus.). 215p. 1996. 21.95 (*0-9627680-3-0*) Inkwell CA.

A nuclear physicist's perceptions of the present conditions of living; covers such topics as reality, science, education, humility, tolerance, sex & the boundary of reality. REASONS FOR STUDYING SCIENCE. For FUTURE SCIENTISTS. Trained scientists understand the situation as it is explained by scientific knowledge. Science contains challenging problems which require the application of scientific principle. The problems often involve concealed information that the student must smoke out & supply. The ability to search & understand concealed information is essential & should be developed at an early age. Understanding THE CHARACTER OF NATURE illuminates knowledge of all kinds. Learning THE IMPACT OF SCIENTIFIC KNOWLEDGE ON PRESENT CONDITIONS OF LIVING provides reasons: for hygiene; how the car works; environmental preservation... "This book explains what I have always believed: That science, nature & mathematics are simple & are all closely related." Kurt Reaume. To order: 916/692-1581, INKWELL, P.O. Box 178, Dobbins, CA 95935, 2nd Edition:$21.95, S&H $2. ***Publisher Provided Annotation.***

***Pollard, Garland.** Pamunkey Indians of Virginia. (Bureau of American Ethnology Bulletins Ser.). 99p. 1995. lib. bdg. 89.00 (*0-7812-4017-4*) Rprt Serv.

— The Pamunkey Indians of Virginia. 1988. reprint ed. lib. bdg. 49.00 (*0-7812-0056-3*) Rprt Serv.

Pollard, George. Decision Acceptance among Radio Newsworkers. LC 89-6111. 214p. (Orig.). 1989. pap. 29.95 (*0-941216-46-2*) Cay-Bel.

Pollard, Graham, jt. auth. see Carter, John.

Pollard, H. B. & Barclay-Smith, Phyllis. British & American Game Birds. (Fifty Greatest Bks.). (Illus.). 48p. 1993. 50.00 (*1-56416-071-8*) Derrydale Pr.

Pollard, H. L., jt. ed. see Miller, P. R.

Pollard, Harry & Diamond, H. G. The Theory of Algebraic Numbers. 2nd ed. LC 75-27003. (Carus Mathematical Monograph: No. 9). xii, 162p. (C). 1975. 15.00 (*0-88385-018-4*) Math Assn.

Pollard, Harry, jt. auth. see Tenenbaum, Morris.

Pollard, Helen P. Tariacuri's Legacy: The Prehispanic Tarascan State. LC 92-37080. (Civilization of the American Indian Ser.: Vol. 209). 1993. 37.50 (*0-8061-2497-0*) U of Okla Pr.

Pollard, Helen P., jt. auth. see Gorenstein, Shirley.

Pollard, Hugh M. Pioneers of Popular Education: 1760-1850. LC 73-20922. 297p. 1975. reprint ed. text ed. 35.00 (*0-8371-5871-0*, POPP, Greenwood Pr) Greenwood.

Pollard, I. Financial Engineering. 1988. Australia. 68.00 (*0-409-49464-X*) Butterworth Legal Pubs.

Pollard, Irina. A Guide to Reproduction: Social Issues & Human Concerns. (Illus.). 348p. (C). 1994. 69.95 (*0-521-41862-3*); pap. 24.95 (*0-521-42925-0*) Cambridge U Pr.

Pollard, J. Graham, ed. Studies in the History of Art: Italian Medals. LC 72-600309. (Symposium Papers VIII: Vol. 21). (Illus.). 29p. 1987. pap. 20.00 (*0-89468-106-0*, U Pr of New Eng) Natl Gallery Art.

Pollard, J. H., jt. auth. see Benjamin, B.

Pollard, Jean A. The New Maine Cooking. (Illus.). 288p. (Orig.). 1987. pap. 12.95 (*0-912769-06-8*, 80-152-2) Yankee Bks.

Pollard, Jeffrey, ed. Evolutionary Theory: Paths into the Future. 294p. 1984. text ed. 140.00 (*0-471-90026-5*, Wiley-Interscience) Wiley.

Pollard, Jeffrey W., ed. Campus Violence: Kinds, Causes, & Cures. LC 93-35657. (Journal of College Student Psychotherapy). (Illus.). 314p. 1994. lib. bdg. 49.95 (*1-56024-568-9*) Haworth Pr.

Pollard, Jeffrey W. & Walker, John M., eds. Methods in Molecular Biology, Vol. 5: Animal Cell Culture. LC 84-15696. (Methods in Molecular Biology Ser.). (Illus.). 732p. 1989. 69.50 (*0-89603-150-0*) Humana.

Pollard, John F., jt. auth. see Kent, Peter C.

Pollard, John K., III. Self-Parenting: The Complete Guide to Your Inner Conversations. LC 86-83037. (Illus.). 250p. (Orig.). 1987. pap. 9.95 (*0-942055-25-X*) Generic Human Studies.

— Self-Parenting Primer. (Illus.). 20p. (Orig.). 1988. pap. 2.00 (*0-942055-30-6*) Generic Human Studies.

Pollard, John K. The Self Parenting Program: Core Guidelines for the Self-Parenting Practitioner. 172p. (Orig.). 1992. pap. 9.95 (*1-55874-214-X*) Health Comm.

***Pollard, John W.** The Physician Manager in Group Practice. 142p. 1994. pap. text ed. 35.00 (*1-56829-005-5*) Med Group Mgmt.

Pollard, Joseph K., jt. auth. see Chervin, Ronda D.

Pollard, Joseph P. Mister Justice Cardozo: A Liberal Mind in Action. LC 75-98790. 327p. 1970. reprint ed. text ed. 65.00 (*0-8371-2815-3*, POJD, Greenwood Pr) Greenwood.

Pollard, Lucille A. Women on College & University Faculities: A Historical Survey & a Study of Their Present Academic Status. Metzger, Walter P., ed. LC 76-55186. (Academic Profession Ser.). (Illus.). 1980. reprint ed. lib. bdg. 33.95 (*0-405-10019-1*) Ayer.

Pollard, M. Dublin's Trade in Books, Fifteen Fifty to Eighteen Hundred: Lyell Lectures, 1986-7. (Illus.). 296p. 1990. 72.00 (*0-19-818409-3*) OUP.

Pollard, Margaret, jt. auth. see Boyd, Jane.

Pollard, Mark, jt. ed. see Glimcher, Marc.

Pollard, Mark, jt. auth. see Morris, Georgia.

Pollard, Michael. Absolute Rulers. Stefoff, Rebecca, ed. LC 91-33297. (Pioneers in History Ser.). (Illus.). 48p. (J). (gr. 5-8). 1992. lib. bdg. 19.93 (*1-56074-034-5*) Garrett Ed Corp.

— Air, Water & Weather. (Discovering Science Ser.). (Illus.). 48p. (J). (gr. 1-4). 1987. 12.95 (*0-8160-1781-6*) Facts on File.

— Behind the Scenes. LC 94-6385. (Arts Library). (Illus.). 48p. (J). (gr. 2-6). 1994. lib. bdg. 14.40 (*1-56294-394-4*) Millbrook Pr.

— Beliefs & Believers. Stefoff, Rebecca, ed. LC 91-36503. (Pioneers in History Ser.). (Illus.). 48p. (J). (gr. 5-9). 1992. lib. bdg. 19.93 (*1-56074-037-X*) Garrett Ed Corp.

— The Clock & How It Changed the World. LC 94-15225. (History & Invention Ser.). 1995. write for info. (*0-8160-3142-8*) Facts on File.

— Discovering English Folksong. 1982. 4.50 (*0-913714-65-8*) Legacy Books.

— Discovering English Folksong. 1989. pap. 25.00 (*0-85263-609-1*, Pub. by Shire UK) St Mut.

— Empire Builders. Stefoff, Rebecca, ed. LC 91-36501. (Pioneers in History Ser.). (Illus.). 48p. (J). (gr. 5-8). 1992. lib. bdg. 19.93 (*1-56074-038-8*) Garrett Ed Corp.

— From Cycle to Spaceship: The Story of Transport. (Discovering Science Ser.). (Illus.). 48p. (J). (gr. 1-4). 1987. 12.95 (*0-8160-1779-4*) Facts on File.

— The House That Science Built. (Discovering Science Ser.). (Illus.). 48p. (J). (gr. 1-4). 1987. 12.95 (*0-8160-1780-8*) Facts on File.

— The Lightbulb & How It Changed the World. LC 94-15226. (History & Invention Ser.). 1995. write for info. (*0-8160-3145-2*) Facts on File.

— Maria Montessori. LC 89-49417. (People Who Have Helped the World Ser.). (Illus.). 64p. (J). (gr. 5-6). 1990. lib. bdg. 21.26 (*0-8368-0217-9*) Gareth Stevens Inc.

— Maria Montessori. LC 89-49417. (People Who Have Helped the World Ser.). (Illus.). 68p. (J). 1990. pap. 7.95 (*0-8192-1539-2*) Morehouse Pub.

— The Nineteenth Century. LC 92-19080. (Illustrated History of the World Ser.). (Illus.). 80p. (J). (gr. 2-6). 1993. 17.95 (*0-8160-2791-9*) Facts on File.

— North Sea Surge: The Story of the East Coast Floods of 1953. 136p. (C). 1988. 65.00 (*0-86138-021-5*, Pub. by T Dalton UK) St Mut.

— People Who Care. Stefoff, Rebecca, ed. LC 91-36502. (Pioneers in History Ser.). (Illus.). 48p. (J). (gr. 5-8). 1992. lib. bdg. 19.93 (*1-56074-035-3*) Garrett Ed Corp.

— The Red Cross & the Red Crescent. LC 93-26383. (Organizations That Help the World Ser.). 64p. (J). 1994. text ed. 13.95 (*0-02-774720-4*, New Dscvry Bks) Silver Burdett Pr.

— Revolutionary Power. Stefoff, Rebecca, ed. LC 91-36504. (Pioneers in History Ser.). (Illus.). 48p. (J). (gr. 5-8). 1992. lib. bdg. 19.93 (*1-56074-039-6*) Garrett Ed Corp.

— Theater Around the World. LC 94-6388. (Arts Library). (Illus.). 48p. (J). (gr. 2-6). 1994. 14.40 (*1-56294-396-0*) Millbrook Pr.

— Theater of Color & Spectacle. LC 94-6386. (Arts Library). (Illus.). 48p. (J). (gr. 2-6). 1994. lib. bdg. 14.40 (*1-56294-395-2*) Millbrook Pr.

— Theater Through the Ages. LC 94-6384. (Arts Library). (Illus.). 48p. (J). (gr. 2-6). 1994. lib. bdg. 14.40 (*1-56294-397-9*) Millbrook Pr.

— Thinkers. Stefoff, Rebecca, ed. LC 91-33296. (Pioneers in History Ser.). (Illus.). 48p. (J). (gr. 5-8). 1992. lib. bdg. 19.93 (*1-56074-036-1*) Garrett Ed Corp.

— United Nations. LC 93-24544. (Organizations That Help the World Ser.). (Illus.). 64p. (J). (gr. 7-9). 1994. text ed. 13.95 (*0-02-726333-9*, New Dscvry Bks) Silver Burdett Pr.

— United Nations: Organizations That Help the World. (YA). 1994. 13.95 (*0-02-720533-9*, New Dscvry Bks) Silver Burdett Pr.

Pollard, Michael, jt. auth. see Wilkinson, Philip.

Pollard, Miriam. The Laughter of God. LC 85-45545. 128p. 1986. 7.95 (*0-8146-5549-1*) Liturgical Pr.

***Pollard, Morris, ed.** Perspectives in Virology Vol 10: The Gustav Stern Symposium. fac. ed. LC 59-8415. (Illus.). 276p. Date not set. pap. 78.70 (*0-7837-7155-X*, 2047142) Bks Demand.

Pollard, Nan. Friends Together. (Real Mother Goose Library). (Illus.). 32p. (J). (ps-3). 1990. 4.95 (*1-56288-048-9*) Checkerboard.

Pollard, Nancy M. What's Love Got to Do with It? 180p. (Orig.). 1993. pap. 12.95 (*0-9637705-1-9*) Benchmark UT.

Pollard, Neil & McDonald, Mary. How Do You Measure Up? LC 93-20060. (J). 1994. pap. write for info. (*0-383-03697-6*) SRA Schl Grp.

Pollard, Nora L. The Book of LeBlanc. 1973. 30.00 (*0-87511-640-X*) Claitors.

Pollard, Patrick. Andre Gide: The Homosexual Moralist. (Illus.). 448p. (C). 1992. text ed. 47.50 (*0-300-04998-6*) Yale U Pr.

Pollard, R. J. The Roman Pottery of Kent. (Illus.). 296p. 1993. text ed. 66.00 (*0-906746-12-4*) A Sutton Pub.

Pollard, Richard, jt. auth. see Chan, Lois M.

Pollard, Richard, jt. ed. see Law, Clarence G., Jr.

Pollard, Rita, jt. auth. see Daniels, Lolee.

Pollard, Robert A. Economic Security & the Origins of the Cold War. 448p. 1985. text ed. 50.00 (*0-231-05830-6*) Col U Pr.

— Economic Security & the Origins of the Cold War, 1945-1950. LC 85-3786. (Political Economy of International Change Ser.). 378p. 1987. pap. text ed. 18.00 (*0-231-05831-4*) Col U Pr.

Pollard, Robert C., jt. auth. see Harper, William L.

Pollard, Robert D. Nazi Weapons & Munitions Code. 56p. (Orig.). 1983. pap. text ed. 2.00 (*0-86663-986-1*) Ide Hse.

Pollard, Robert T. China's Foreign Relations, Nineteen Seventeen to Nineteen Thirty-One. LC 70-111745. (American Imperialism: Viewpoints of United States Foreign Policy, 1898-1941 Ser.). 1970. reprint ed. 23.95 (*0-405-02046-5*) Ayer.

Pollard, Ruth M. The Official Price Guide to Collector Prints. 7th ed. 1986. pap. 12.95 (*0-87637-296-5*, House of Collect) Ballantine.

Pollard, S. Typology of Industrialization Processes in the Nineteenth Century. Lesourne, J. & Sonnenschein, H., eds. (Fundamentals of Pure & Applied Economics Ser.: 39). vi, 106p. 1990. pap. text ed. 36.00 (*3-7186-5007-X*) Gordon & Breach.

Pollard, Sidney. Britain's Prime & Britain's Decline: The British Economy, 1870-1914. 384p. 1989. 69.50 (*0-7131-6591-X*, Pub. by E Arnold UK) Routledge Chapman & Hall.

— Britain's Prime & Britain's Decline: The British Economy, 1870-1914. 352p. 1991. pap. 25.00 (*0-340-53913-5*, A5851, Pub. by E Arnold UK) Routledge Chapman & Hall.

— A History of Labour in Sheffield. (Modern Revivals in Economic & Social History Ser.). 392p. 1993. 69.95 (*0-7512-0215-0*, Pub. by Gregg Revivals UK) Ashgate Pub Co.

— Integration of the European Economy Since 1815. (Studies on Contemporary Europe: No. 4). 96p. (C). 1981. text ed. 24.95 (*0-04-336069-6*); pap. text ed. 8.95 (*0-04-336070-X*) Routledge Chapman & Hall.

— Peaceful Conquest: The Industrialization of Europe, 1760-1970. (Illus.). 1981. pap. 17.95 (*0-19-877095-2*) OUP.

Pollard, Sidney, ed. Wealth & Poverty: An Economic History of the Twentieth Century. (Illus.). 256p. 1990. 40.00 (*0-19-520821-8*) OUP.

Pollard, Sidney, intro. The Metal Fabrication & Engineering Industries. LC 93-43722. (Industrial Revolutions Ser.: No. 9). 1994. write for info. (*0-631-18121-0*) Blackwell Pubs.

Pollard, Sidney & Robertson, Paul. British Shipbuilding Industry Eighteen Seventy to Nineteen Fourteen. LC 78-12500. (Studies in Business History: No. 30). 336p. 1979. 34.50 (*0-674-08287-7*) HUP.

Pollard, Sidney & Salt, John, eds. Robert Owen: Prophet of the Poor. LC 70-156269. 318p. 1975. 40.00 (*0-8387-7952-2*) Bucknell U Pr.

Pollard, Sidney, jt. ed. see Feinstein, Charles H.

Pollard, Stephen. Philosophical Introduction to Set Theory. LC 89-40391. (C). 1990. text ed. 29.95 (*0-268-01584-8*); pap. text ed. 15.95 (*0-268-01585-6*) U of Notre Dame Pr.

Pollard, Stephen, tr. see Weyl, Hermann.

Pollard, Stephen F. Boatbuilding with Aluminium. 1993. text ed. 29.95 (*0-07-050426-1*) McGraw.

— Boatbuilding with Aluminum. 1993. 29.95 (*0-87742-377-6*) Intl Marine.

Pollard, Stewart M. Tied to Masonic Apron Strings. Cook, Lewis C., ed. vi, 121p. 1991. pap. 6.00 (*0-88053-059-6*, M-322) Macoy Pub.

Pollard, T. Dale. I Knew There Was More: One Person's Long Search for Spiritual Reality. 208p. (Orig.). 1989. pap. 6.95 (*0-9621960-1-0*) Compassion Ministries.

— Man of the Spirit: A Biblical Guide for a Balanced Personality. (Illus.). 192p. (Orig.). 1988. pap. 6.95 (*0-9621960-0-2*) Compassion Ministries.

Pollard, Ted. King of the Road: The Beginner's Guide to RV Travel. (Illus.). 221p. (Orig.). 1995. pap. 12.95 (*0-9637125-0-0*) Remington PA.

— King of the Road Diary & Trip Planner. 100p. 1993. pap. text ed. 10.95 (*0-9637125-1-9*) Remington PA.

Pollard, Velma. Considering Women. 100p. 1990. pap. 6.95 (*0-7043-4149-2*, Pub. by Womens Pr UK) Interlink Pub.

— Karl & Other Stories. LC 93-24169. (Caribbean Writers Ser.). (C). 1994. pap. text ed. 9.95 (*0-582-22726-7*) Longman.

Pollard, William, jt. auth. see Hull, Eugene.

Pollard, William C., Jr. Dark Friday: The Story of Quantrill's Lawrence Raid. (Illus.). 144p. 1990. 16.95 (*0-941974-13-8*) Baranski Pub Co.

Pollard, William L. A Study of Black Self Help. LC 78-62225. 1978. pap. 16.00 (*0-88247-532-0*) R & E Pubs.

Pollarine, Barbara. Great & Capital Changes: An Account of the Valley Forge Encampment. (Illus.). 64p. (C). 1993. pap. text ed. 5.95 (*0-939631-54-7*) Thomas Publications.

Pollastro, R. M., jt. ed. see Guven, N.

Pollatsek, Alexander, jt. auth. see Rayner, Keith.

Pollay, Richard W., ed. Information Sources in Advertising History. LC 78-75259. 330p. 1979. text ed. 59.95 (*0-313-21422-0*, PIA/, Greenwood Pr) Greenwood.

Polledri, Paolo, ed. Shin Takamatsu. LC 92-37714. 1993. write for info. (*0-918471-28-1*) San Fran MOMA.

PQ

— Shin Takamatsu, Architect. LC 92-37714. (Illus.). 144p. 1993. pap. 35.00 (*0-8478-1746-6*) Rizzoli Intl.

Pollen, Daniel A. Hannah's Heirs: The Quest for the Genetic Origins of Alzheimer's Disease. LC 93-66. (Illus.). 320p. 1993. pap. 25.00 (*0-19-506809-2*) OUP.

Pollen, Gerry, jt. auth. see Goodwin, Mary T.

Pollens, Stewart. The Early Pianoforte. (Cambridge Musical Texts & Monographs). (Illus.). 284p. (C). 1994. write for info. (*0-521-41729-5*) Cambridge U Pr.

Poller. Medical Block Buchenwald. 1987. pap. 7.95 (*0-8184-0448-5*) Carol Pub Group.

Poller, H. Leonard, jt. ed. see Jaffe, Hirshel.

Poller, L., ed. Recent Advances in Blood Coagulation, No. 5. (Illus.). 312p. 1991. text ed. 75.00 (*0-443-04343-4*) Churchill.

— Recent Advances in Blood Coagulation, No. 6. (Illus.). 228p. 1993. text ed. 65.95 (*0-443-04755-3*) Churchill.

Poller, Leon & Thomson, Jean M., eds. Thrombosis & Its Management. (Illus.). 272p. (Orig.). 1993. pap. text ed. write for info. (*0-443-04797-9*) Churchill.

Poller, Nidra, tr. see Kourouma, Ahmadou.

Poller, R. C., jt. auth. see Parkins, A. W.

Pollery, J. B. Soldier's Letters to Charming Nellie. 19.95 (*0-8488-1128-3*) Amereon Ltd.

Pollet, J. V. Julius Pflug (1499-1564) et la Crise Religieuse Dans l'Allemagne Du XVIe Siecle. (Studies in Medieval & Reformation Thought: No. 45). 446p. (FRE.). 1990. 111.50 (*90-04-09241-2*) E J Brill.

Pollet, Maurice. John Skelton: Poet of Tudor England. LC 73-124443. 302p. 1975. 38.50 (*0-8387-7737-6*) Bucknell U Pr.

Pollet, R. J. English-French Lexicon of Technical Terms: Lexique des Termes Techniques Anglais-Francais. 233p. (ENG & FRE.). 1981. pap. 24.95 (*0-8288-0618-7*, M6460) Fr & Eur.

— Lexicon of Amateur Photography: Lexique de la Photagraphie d'Amateur: Appareils et Accessoires. 127p. (FRE.). 1981. pap. 19.95 (*0-8288-2089-9*, M14196) Fr & Eur.

Pollett, Libby, jt. auth. see Head, Debby.

Polley, J. B. Hood's Texas Brigade. (Illus.). 357p. 1995. 30.00 (*0-89029-037-7*) Morningside Bkshop.

— Hood's Texas Brigade. 1993. reprint ed. lib. bdg. 75.00 (*0-7812-5893-6*) Rprt Serv.

— A Soldier's Letters to Charming Nellie. 350p. 1984. reprint ed. 32.50 (*0-942211-91-X*) Olde Soldier Bks.

Polley, L. & Pottinger, D. E., eds. Variational Calculations in Quantum Field Theory. 316p. (C). 1988. pap. 51.00 (*9971-5-0501-0*) World Scientific Pub.

Polley, Louis E. The History of the Mohawk Valley & Early Lumbering. Bailey, Sue, ed. LC 84-60964. (Illus.). 144p. (Orig.). 1984. pap. 19.50 (*0-916930-09-2*) Polley Pubs.

Polley, Max E. Amos & the Davidic Empire: A Socio-Historical Approach. (Illus.). 256p. 1989. 45.00 (*0-19-505478-4*) OUP.

Polley, Maxine. Dance Aerobics. LC 80-23906. (Illus.). 160p. (Orig.). 1980. pap. 5.95 (*0-89037-186-5*) Anderson World.

— Dance Aerobics: Two. 160p. 1983. pap. 6.95 (*0-89037-256-X*) Anderson World.

Polley, Michael. A Biography of George F. Kennan: The Education of a Realist. LC 89-27727. (Studies in Twentieth Century American History: Vol. 4). 256p. 1990. lib. bdg. 89.95 (*0-88946-693-9*) E Mellen.

Polley, Richard B., et al, eds. The Symlog Practitioner: Applications of Small Group Research. LC 87-37684. (Illus.). 427p. 1988. text ed. 69.50 (*0-275-92364-9*, C2364, Praeger Pubs) Greenwood.

Polli, E., ed. Neurochemistry of Hepatic Coma. (Experimental Biology & Medicine Ser.: Vol. 4). 1971. 28.00 (*3-8055-1187-6*) S Karger.

Polli, E. E., ed. Haematopoietic Growth Factors: Biology & Clinical Use - Journal: Acta Haematologica, Vol. 86, No. 3, 1991. (Illus.). 52p. 1992. pap. 53.00 (*3-8055-5557-1*) S Karger.

— Molecular Bases of Human Diseases: Proceedings of the International Meeting, Held in Milan, Italy, September 27-October 1, 1992. LC 93-13929. 1993. 137.25 (*0-444-81563-5*, Excerpta Medica) Elsevier.

Polliack, A. & Catovsky, D. Chronic Lymphocytic Leukemia. 400p. 1988. text ed. 149.00 (*3-7186-4802-4*) Gordon & Breach.

Polliack, Aaron. Human Leukemias. (Developments in Oncology Ser.). 1984. lib. bdg. 115.00 (*90-247-2338-8*) Kluwer Ac.

Polliack, Aaron, ed. Leukemia & Lymphoma Reviews 2. 1993. 78.00 (*3-7186-5374-5*) Kluwer Ac.

Polliack, Aaron, jt. ed. see Pangalis, Gerassimos A.

Polliack, Aaron, et al. A Scanning Electron Microscopy Atlas of Normal & Malignant Leukocytes. LC 92-49075. 1993. text ed. 80.00 (*3-7186-5362-1*) Gordon & Breach.

Pollice, L., ed. Hepatocellular Proliferative Process. (Journal: Applied Pathology: Vol. 6, No. 2, 1988). (Illus.). 88p. 1988. pap. 46.50 (*3-8055-4788-9*) S Karger.

Pollicini, A. A., ed. Using Toolpack Software Tools. (C). 1988. lib. bdg. 129.50 (*0-7923-0033-5*) Kluwer Ac.

***Pollick, Steve.** Starwalking with Sarah: And Other Essays. (Illus.). 144p. (Orig.). 1994. pap. 7.95 (*0-9614554-1-1*) Toledo Blade.

Pollicott, Mark. Lectures on Ergodic Theory & Pesin Theory on Compact Manifolds. (London Mathematical Society Lecture Note Ser.: No. 180). (Illus.). 180p. (C). 1993. pap. 37.95 (*0-521-43593-5*) Cambridge U Pr.

Pollin, Alice M., ed. see Lorca, Federico G.

Pollin, Burton. Music for Shelley's Poetry. LC 74-4446. (Music Reprint Ser.). 174p. 1974. lib. bdg. 29.50 (*0-306-70640-7*) Da Capo.

Pollin, Burton R. Dictionary of Names & Titles in Poe's Collected Works. LC 68-28982. (Paperback Ser.). 1968. pap. 32.50 (*0-306-71154-0*) Da Capo.

— Insights & Outlooks: Essays of Great Writers. LC 86-22955. 239p. 1986. 17.50 (*0-87752-237-5*) Gordian.

Pollin, Burton R., comp. Images of Poe's Works: An Analysis & Descriptive Catalogue. LC 89-17182. (Bibliographies & Indexes in American Literature Ser.: No. 9). 428p. 1989. text ed. 79.50 (*0-313-26582-8*, PPW/, Greenwood Pr) Greenwood.

Pollin, Burton R., ed. Collected Writings of Edgar Allan Poe: Poe's Nonfiction in the Broadway Journal, Set, Vols. 3 & 4. 760p. 1986. Set. 125.00 (*0-87752-232-4*) Gordian.

— Collected Writings of Edgar Allan Poe, Vol. 2: The Brevities. 640p. 1985. 75.00 (*0-87752-229-4*) Gordian.

— Collected Writings on Edgar Allan Poe Vol. 1: The Imaginary Voyages; The Narrative of Arthur Gordon Pym; The Unparalleled Adventure of One Hans Pfaall; The Journal of Julius Rodman. rev. ed. LC 81-2915. 667p. 1992. 70.00 (*0-87752-238-3*) Gordian.

— Word Index to Poe's Fiction. 512p. (C). 1982. 50.00 (*0-87752-225-1*) Gordian.

Pollin, Burton R. & Wilkes, John W., intros. Political Justice: A Poem in a Letter to the Right Hon. the Lord. LC 92-24282. (Augustan Reprints Ser.: No. 111 (1965)). reprint ed. 12.00 (*0-404-70111-6*) AMS Pr.

Pollin, Burton R., jt. auth. see Hansen, Thomas S.

Pollin, Irene & Golant, Susan K. Taking Charge: Mastering the Eight Fears of Chronic Illness. LC 93-29434. 1994. 22.00 (*0-8129-2258-1*, Times Bks) Random.

***Pollin, Irene & Kanaan, Susan B.** Medical Crisis Counseling: Short-Term Therapy for Long-Term Illness. 256p. (C). 1995. 30.00 (*0-393-70195-6*) Norton.

Pollin, Robert. Deeper in Debt: The Changing Financial Conditions of U. S. Households. LC 90-84862. (Illus.). 82p. (Orig.). 1990. pap. 12.00 (*0-944826-37-7*) Economic Policy Inst.

Pollin, Robert, jt. ed. see Dymski, Gary.

Pollinger, Eileen. Erica. LC 84-73384. 150p. (Orig.). 1985. pap. 3.99 (*0-87123-826-8*) Bethany Hse.

— Stacey. LC 87-71604. (Heartsong Bks.). 176p. (Orig.). (J). (gr. 9-12). 1987. pap. 3.99 (*0-87123-943-4*) Bethany Hse.

Pollinger, Gerald, jt. auth. see Green, William.

Pollington, Andrew & Moran, William, eds. Number Theory with an Emphasis on the Markoff Spectrum. LC 93-18075. (Lecture Notes in Pure & Applied Mathematics Ser.: Vol. 147). 352p. 1993. 140.00 (*0-8247-8902-4*) Dekker.

***Pollington, Stephen.** Rudiments of Runelore. 96p. 1995. pap. 12.95 (*1-898281-16-5*) Paul & Co Pubs.

Pollini, John, intro. Roman Portraiture: Images of Character & Virtue in the Late Republic & Early Principate. (Illus.). 44p. (Orig.). (C). 1990. pap. 15.00 (*0-945192-04-5*) USC Fisher Gallery.

Pollino, Emiliano. Microelectronic Reliability, Vol. II: Integrity Assessment & Assurance. (Materials Science Library). 551p. 1989. text ed. 78.00 (*0-89006-350-8*) Artech Hse.

Pollins, Donald. Church Sale. (Illus.). 50p. 1989. pap. 5.00 (*0-923621-00-8*) Infinity MD.

Pollins, Harold. Economic History of the Jews in England. (Littman Library of Jewish Civilization). 340p. 1984. 19.50 (*0-19-710048-1*, Pub. by Littman Lib Jew UK) Bnai Brith Bk.

Pollins, Harold, jt. auth. see Glass, Ruth.

Pollio, Gerald. Financial Innovation & Upstream Petroleum Development. 24p. 1991. pap. 10.00 (*0-918714-29-X*) Intl Res Ctr Energy.

— The U. S. Natural Gas Market in the 1990s. 20p. 1991. pap. 10.00 (*0-918714-27-3*) Intl Res Ctr Energy.

Pollio, Howard R., et al. Psychology & the Poetics of Growth: Figurative Language in Psychology, Psychotherapy, & Education. 272p. 1977. text ed. 49.95 (*0-89859-484-7*) L Erlbaum Assocs.

Pollio, Vitruvius. Vitruvius Teutsch (De Architectura Libri X, Deutsch) 641p. 1973. reprint ed. write for info. (*3-487-05010-2*, Pub. by Georg Olms GW) Lubrecht & Cramer.

Pollis, Adamantia, ed. Quality of Living: Environmental Viewpoints. (Make up Your Own Mind, Ser.: Bk. 3). 1973. 2.50 (*0-910092-03-6*) Am Inst Disc.

Pollis, Adamantia, ed. see American Institute of Discussion Staff.

Pollis, Adamantia, jt. ed. see Pinkele, Carl F.

Pollishuke, Mindy, jt. auth. see Schwartz, Susan.

Pollitt. Color Atlas of the Horse's Foot. Date not set. 95.00 (*0-8151-6743-1*, Yr Bk Med Pubs) Mosby Yr Bk.

— Reasonable Creatures. 1995. pap. write for info. (*0-679-76278-7*) Random Hse Value.

Pollitt, Christopher. Managerialism & the Public Services. 2nd ed. LC 92-26772. 1992. pap. 29.95 (*0-631-18837-1*) Blackwell Pubs.

***Pollitt, Christopher & Bouckaert, Geert.** Quality Improvement in European Public Services: Concepts, Cases, & Commentary. 256p. 1995. 69.95 (*0-8039-7464-7*); pap. 21.95 (*0-8039-7465-5*) Sage.

Pollitt, Christopher & Harrison, Stephen. Handbook of Public Services Management. 320p. 1994. pap. 39.95 (*0-631-19345-6*) Blackwell Pubs.

Pollitt, Christopher, jt. auth. see Harrison, Stephen.

Pollitt, Ernesto. Poverty & Malnutrition in Latin America: Early Childhood Intervention Programs. LC 80-18811. 150p. 1980. text ed. 45.00 (*0-275-90538-1*, C0538, Praeger Pubs) Greenwood.

Pollitt, Ernesto, et al. Early Supplementary Feeding & Cognition: Effect over Two Decades. (Monographs of the Society for Research on Child Development). 138p. 1993. pap. text ed. 14.00 (*0-226-67453-3*) U Ch Pr.

Pollitt, J. D., ed. Psychiatric Emergencies. (C). 1987. lib. bdg. 54.00 (*0-85200-676-4*) Kluwer Ac.

Pollitt, J. J. Art & Experience in Classical Greece. LC 74-160094. (Illus.). (C). 1972. pap. 17.95 (*0-521-09662-6*) Cambridge U Pr.

— Art in the Hellenistic Age. (Illus.). 352p. 1986. pap. 34.95 (*0-521-27672-1*) Cambridge U Pr.

— The Art of Ancient Greece: Sources & Documents. (Illus.). 296p. (C). 1990. pap. 24.95 (*0-521-27366-8*) Cambridge U Pr.

— The Art of Ancient Greece: Sources & Documents. (Illus.). 296p. (C). 1990. 74.95 (*0-521-25368-3*) Cambridge U Pr.

— The Art of Rome, Circa 753 B. C. - A. D. 337: Sources & Documents. LC 82-23439. 262p. 1983. 64.95 (*0-521-25367-5*); pap. 22.95 (*0-521-27365-X*) Cambridge U Pr.

Pollitt, Jerome J. The Ancient View of Greek Art: Criticism, History, & Terminology. LC 73-86915. (Yale Publications in the History of Art: No. 25). 480p. reprint ed. pap. 136.80 (*0-8357-5472-3*, 2022030) Bks Demand.

Pollitt, Josephine. Emily Dickinson: The Human Background of Her Poetry. LC 76-118052. (Illus.). 1970. reprint ed. lib. bdg. 58.50 (*0-8154-0335-6*) Cooper Sq.

Pollitt, Katha. Antarctic Traveller. LC 81-47521. 1982. pap. 9.95 (*0-394-74895-6*) Knopf.

— Reasonable Creatures: Feminism & Society in American Culture at the End of the Twentieth Century. LC 93-47492. 1994. 22.00 (*0-394-57060-X*) Knopf.

***Pollitt, Michael.** Ownership & Performance in Electric Utilities: The International Evidence on Privatization & Efficiency. (Oxford Institute for Energy Studies). (Illus.). 250p. 1995. 79.00 (*0-19-730015-4*) OUP.

Pollitt, R. J., et al, eds. Inborn Errors of Cellular Organelles: Peroxisomes & Mitochondria. (C). 1987. lib. bdg. 136.00 (*0-7462-0043-9*) Kluwer Ac.

— Studies in Inherited Metabolic Disease: Lipoproteins; Ethical Issues. (C). 1988. lib. bdg. 122.00 (*0-7462-0101-X*) Kluwer Ac.

Pollitt, Ronald & Curry, Herbert F. Portraits in British History. LC 74-24454. (Dorsey Series in History). 340p. reprint ed. pap. 96.90 (*0-317-29614-0*, 2021664) Bks Demand.

Pollitz, Linda, ed. Greater Boston Group Child Care Directory, 1992: Including Day Care, Nursery Schools & Preschool Facilities. 352p. 1991. pap. 15.95 (*0-9631108-0-2*) De Facto.

Pollitzer, R. Cholera. (Monograph Ser.: No. 43). (Illus.). 1019p. (FRE.). 1959. 26.80 (*92-4-140043-9*) World Health.

Pollnac, Richard B., ed. Small-Scale Fishery Development: Sociocultural Perspectives. (Illus.). 158p. 1991. pap. 11.00 (*1-882027-04-3*) URI ICMRD.

Pollnac, Richard B., intro. Monitoring & Evaluating the Impacts of Small-Scale Fishery Projects. 146p. 1989. pap. 4.00 (*1-882027-01-9*) URI ICMRD.

Pollnac, Richard B. & Weeks, Priscilla, eds. Coastal Aquaculture in Developing Countries: Problems & Perspectives. (Illus.). 183p. (Orig.). (C). 1992. pap. text ed. write for info. (*1-882027-06-X*) URI ICMRD.

Pollnac, Richard B., jt. ed. see Morrissey, Michael T.

Pollner, jt. auth. see Grusky.

Pollnitz, Christopher, ed. The International Terminal. 143p. (C). 1990. 50.00 (*0-7259-0620-0*, Pub. by Pascoe Pub AT) St Mut.

Pollnow, Jim. My God, Why? A Mastectomy from a Husbands Point of View. LC 79-55888. 127p. 1980. pap. 2.95 (*0-9603708-0-3*) J L Pollnow.

Pollock & Middleton. Elementary School Health Instruction. 2nd ed. 544p. (C). 1989. 36.95 (*0-8016-4039-3*) Mosby Yr Bk.

— Elementary School Health Instruction 3. 640p. 1993. 37.95 (*0-8016-6745-3*) Mosby Yr Bk.

Pollock, A. J. Office, Gift & Priesthood. 51p. pap. 3.95 (*0-88172-174-3*) Believers Bkshelf.

— The Savior-Sinless, Yet Tempted. 16p. pap. 0.50 (*0-88172-158-1*) Believers Bkshelf.

Pollock, A. V. Postoperative Complications in Surgery. (Illus.). 292p. 1991. 115.00 (*0-632-02735-5*) Blackwell Sci.

Pollock, Alan B. & Evans, Mary. Surgical Audit. 2nd ed. 192p. 1993. 75.00 (*0-7506-0774-2*) Buttrwrth-Heinemann.

Pollock, Algernon J. La Paz con Dios. 2nd ed. Mahecha, Alberto, ed. Bautista, SAra, tr. (Serie Diamante). (Illus.). 48p. (SPA.). 1982. pap. 0.85 (*0-942504-09-7*) Overcomer Pr.

Pollock, Algernon J. & Bennett, Gordon H. El Pecado Despues de la Conversion. 2nd ed. Bautista, Sara, tr. (Serie Diamante). (Illus.). 36p. (SPA.). 1982. pap. 0.85 (*0-942504-04-6*) Overcomer Pr.

Pollock, Allen, jt. auth. see Burkhalter, Howard J.

***Pollock, Andrew W., 3rd.** U. S. Patterns & Related Issues. (Illus.). 524p. 1994. text ed. 79.00 (*0-943161-58-4*) Bowers & Merena.

Pollock, Bruce. Hipper Than Our Kids: A Rock & Roll Journal of the Baby Boom Generation. 336p. 1993. text ed. 25.00 (*0-02-872063-6*) Schirmer Bks.

— Hipper Than Our Kids: A Rock & roll Journal of the Baby Boom Generation. 1995. pap. 15.00 (*0-02-872064-4*) Macmillan.

— Popular Music, Vol. 13, 1988. 1989. 66.00 (*0-8103-4945-0*) Gale.

— Popular Music, Nineteen Eighty-Seven, Vol. 12. annot. ed. Shapiro, Nat, ed. 350p. 1988. 66.00 (*0-8103-1810-5*) Gale.

— Popular Music 1991, Vol. 16. 1992. 66.00 (*0-8103-7485-4*) Gale.

— Popular Music 1993, Vol. 18. 93th ed. 1994. 66.00 (*0-8103-8498-1*, 007105) Gale.

— Rock Songs: A Comprehensive Index. 1996. text ed. 95.00 (*0-02-872068-7*) Macmillan.

— Soccer for Juniors. (J). 1980. 9.95 (*0-684-16487-6*, Scribners) S&S Trade.

***Pollock, Bruce, ed.** Popular Music Vol. 19, 1994: An Annotated Guide to American Popular Songs, Including Introductory Essays, Lyricists & Composer Index, Important Performances Index, Awards Index & List of Publishers, Vol. 19. 160p. 1995. text ed. 66.00 (*0-8103-9057-4*) Gale.

— Popular Music, Nineteen Twenty to Nineteen Seventy-Nine, 3 vols., Set. 2839p. 1985. 270.00 (*0-8103-0847-9*) Gale.

— Popular Music 1980-1989: A Revised Cumulation; An Annotated Guide to American Popular Songs, Including Introductory Essay, Lyricists & Composer Index, Important Performance Index, Chronological Index, Awards Index & List of Publishers. 911p. 1994. text ed. 132.00 (*0-7876-0205-1*) Gale.

— Popular Music 1989, Vol. 14: An Annotated Guide to American Popular Songs. LC 85-653754. 184p. 1990. lib. bdg. 66.00 (*0-8103-4946-9*, 06516) Gale.

— Popular Music 1990, Vol. 15. 177p. 1991. 66.00 (*0-8103-4947-7*, 007101-M99348) Gale.

Pollock, Bruce & Wilmore, D. W. Exercise in Health & Disease: Evaluation & Prescription for Prevention & Rehabilitation. 2nd ed. (Illus.). 736p. 1990. text ed. 52.50 (*0-7216-2948-2*) Saunders.

Pollock, Bruce, jt. ed. see Shapiro, Nat.

Pollock-Byrne, Jocelyn. Women, Prison, & Crime. LC 89-25164. 208p. (C). 1990. pap. 17.95 (*0-534-12888-2*) Intl Thomson.

Pollock-Byrne, Joycelyn M. Ethics in Crime & Justice: Dilemmas & Decisions. LC 88-21724. 169p. (C). 1989. pap. 16.95 (*0-534-09768-5*) Intl Thomson.

Pollock, C. J., jt. ed. see Farrar, J. F.

Pollock, C. J., et al, eds. Carbon Partitioning Within & Between Organisms. (Environmental Plant Biology Ser.). (Illus.). 258p. 1992. 147.50x (*1-872748-95-3*, Pub. by Bios Scientific UK) Coronet Bks.

Pollock, Carroll W. Communicate What You Mean: Grammar for High Level ESL. 224p. (C). 1982. pap. text ed. 20.75 (*0-13-153486-6*) P-H.

Pollock, Clifford R. Fundamentals of Optoelectronics. LC 94-13319. 592p. (C). 1994. text ed. 67.95 (*0-256-10104-3*) Irwin.

Pollock, Cynthia. Decommissioning: Nuclear Power's Missing Link. LC 86-50307. (Worldwatch Papers). 56p. 1986. pap. 5.00 (*0-916468-70-4*) Worldwatch Inst.

— Mining Urban Wastes: The Potential for Recycling. LC 87-50357. 52p. (Orig.). 1987. pap. 5.00 (*0-916468-77-1*) Worldwatch Inst.

Pollock, D. Physical Properties of Materials for Engineers. LC 81-839. 1982. 120.00 (*0-8493-6200-8*, CRC Reprint) Franklin.

Pollock, Dale. Skywalking: The Life & Films of George Lucas. rev. ed. LC 90-37372. (Illus.). 304p. 1990. reprint ed. pap. 14.95 (*0-573-60606-4*) S French Trade.

Pollock, Daniel. Duel of Assassins. Grose, Bill, ed. 352p. 1992. reprint ed. mass mkt. 5.50 (*0-671-70577-6*) PB.

— Lair of the Fox. 240p. 1989. 19.95 (*0-8027-1088-3*) Walker & Co.

— Pursuit into Darkness. Grose, Bill, ed. LC 93-10330. 384p. (Orig.). 1994. 22.00 (*0-671-70575-X*) PB.

Pollock, Daniel D. Thermocouples: Theory & Practice. 350p. 1991. 99.95 (*0-8493-4243-0*, QC274) CRC Pr.

Pollock, Daniel D., ed. Physical Properties of Materials for Engineers, Vol. I. 224p. 1981. 144.00 (*0-8493-6201-6*, QC176) CRC Pr.

— Physical Properties of Materials for Engineers, Vol. II. 1981. 124.95 (*0-8493-6202-4*, QC176, CRC Reprint) Franklin.

— Physical Properties of Materials for Engineers, Vol. III. 312p. 1982. 119.00 (*0-8493-6203-2*, QC176) CRC Pr.

Pollock, David. The "Arab" Street? Public Opinion in the Arab World. LC 92-44065. 1992. write for info. (*0-944029-21-3*) Wash Inst NEP.

— The Politics of Pressure: American Arms & Israeli Policy Since the Six Day War. LC 81-23720. (Contributions in Political Science Ser.: No. 79). 328p. 1982. text ed. 55.00 (*0-313-22113-8*, POP/, Greenwood Pr) Greenwood.

Pollock, David H., jt. ed. see Ritter, Archibald R.

Pollock, David R. Business Management in the Local Church. 1992. student ed 11.99 (*0-8024-0933-4*) Moody.

— Church Administration: The Dollars & Sense of It. (Christian Financial Concepts Ser.). 96p. (Orig.). 1991. pap. 5.00 (*1-56427-084-X*) Christian Fin Concepts.

Pollock, David W., jt. auth. see Reilly, Thomas E.

Pollock, Dean. Joseph: Chief of the Nez Perce. 5th ed. (Illus.). 64p. (J). (gr. 5 up). 1990. reprint ed. pap. 7.95 (*0-8323-0482-4*) Binford Mort.

Pollock, Edward. Sketch Book of Liberty VA: 1887 People & Trade. (Illus.). 144p. 1993. reprint ed. pap. 14.00 (*0-9608598-7-X*) Hamiltons.

Pollock, Eileen & Evans, Phil. Ireland for Beginners. 12.95 (*0-86316-016-6*); pap. 4.95 (*0-86316-017-4*) Writers & Readers.

Pollock, Ervin H. Human Rights: Amintaphil,, Vol. 1. LC 70-173834. xviii, 419p. 1971. lib. bdg. 45.00 (*0-930342-65-8*, 301190) W S Hein.

Pollock, Floyd A. A Navajo Crisis & Confrontation. LC 84-3483. 1984. 15.00 (*0-912586-55-9*) Navajo Coll Pr.

Pollock, Frank, tr. see Alfoldy, Geza.

Pollock, Frederick. A Digest of the Law of Partnership. xxxvi, 135p. 1988. reprint ed. lib. bdg. 25.00 (*0-8377-2514-3*) Rothman.

— Essays in Jurisprudence & Ethics. x, 383p. 1985. reprint ed. 35.00 (*0-8377-2508-9*) Rothman.

— Essays in the Law. LC 94-75659. 316p. 1994. reprint ed. 64.00 (*1-56169-088-0*) W W Gaunt.

— A First Book of Jurisprudence: For Students of the Common Law. 6th ed. LC 94-75658. 394p. 1994. reprint ed. 80.00 (*1-56169-089-9*) W W Gaunt.

— Genius of the Common Law. LC 12-6106. reprint ed. 27.50 (*0-404-05075-1*) AMS Pr.

P Q

An Asterisk (*) at the beginning of an entry indicates that the title is appearing in BIP for the first time.

— Jurisprudence & Legal Essays. LC 77-28352. xviii, 244p. 1978. reprint ed. text ed. 35.00 (*0-313-20249-4*, POJU, Greenwood Pr) Greenwood.
— The Land Laws. x, 233p. 1979. reprint ed. lib. bdg. 20.00 (*0-8377-1001-4*) Rothman.
— Oxford Lecture: And Other Discourses. LC 76-39718. (Essay Index Reprint Ser.). 1977. reprint ed. 20.95 (*0-8369-2780-X*) Ayer.
— Oxford Lectures. Mersky, Roy M. & Jacobstein, J. Myron, eds. LC 74-114033. (Classics in Legal History Reprint Ser.: Vol. 4). 303p. 1970. reprint ed. lib. bdg. 43.50 (*0-89941-003-0*, 301200) W S Hein.
— Principles of Contract at Law & in Equity: A Treatise on the General Principles Concerning the Validity of Agreements in the Law of England & America. cliv, 985p. 1988. reprint ed. lib. bdg. 95.00 (*0-8377-2516-X*) Rothman.
— Spinoza. 1972. 59.95 (*0-8490-1110-8*) Gordon Pr.
— Spinoza: His Life & Philosophy. (Reprints in Philosophy Ser.). (Illus.). reprint ed. lib. bdg. 47.00 (*0-697-00055-9*) Irvington.
Pollock, Frederick & Wright, Robert S. An Essay on Possession in the Common Law. xvi, 244p. 1985. reprint ed. lib. bdg. 27.50 (*0-8377-2507-0*) Rothman.
Pollock, George & Ross, John M., eds. The Oedipus Papers. (Classics in Psychoanalysis Monographs: No. 6). 550p. 1988. text ed. 62.50 (*0-8236-3730-1*) Intl Univs Pr.
Pollock, George H. Annual of Psychoanalysis, Vol. XV. (Chicago Institute for Psychoanalysis Ser.). 1987. lib. bdg. 60.00 (*0-8236-0375-X*) Intl Univs Pr.
— Mourning-Liberation Process, 2 vols., Vol. I. 315p. 1989. 55.00x (*0-8236-3485-X*) Intl Univs Pr.
— Mourning-Liberation Process, 2 vols., Vol. II. 325p. 1989. 45.00x (*0-8236-3486-8*) Intl Univs Pr.
Pollock, George H., ed. How Psychiatrists Look at Aging. 260p. (C). 1992. text ed. 32.50 (*0-8236-5722-1*) Intl Univs Pr.
— How Psychiatrists Look at Aging, Vol. II. (Mental Health Library Ser.: Monograph 3). 300p. 1994. text ed. 40.00 (*0-8236-2367-X*) Intl Univs Pr.
— Pivotal Papers on Identification. LC 93-9298. 508p. 1993. text ed. 60.00 (*0-8236-4130-9*) Intl Univs Pr.
Pollock, George H. & Greenspan, Stanley I., eds. The Course of Life, Vol. V: Early Adulthood. 430p. 1993. text ed. 55.00 (*0-8236-1127-2*) Intl Univs Pr.
— The Course of Life, Vol. VI: Late Adulthood. 550p. 1993. text ed. 65.00 (*0-8236-1128-0*) Intl Univs Pr.
Pollock, George H., jt. ed. see Gedo, John E.
Pollock, George H., jt. ed. see Greenspan, Stanley I.
Pollock, George H., jt. ed. see Moraitis, George.
Pollock, Geri, jt. auth. see Bennett, Cheryl.
Pollock, Gordon D. In Search of Security: The Mormons & the Kingdom of God on Earth, 1830-1844. (Nineteenth Century American Political & Social History Ser.). 392p. 1989. reprint ed. 25.00 (*0-8240-4071-6*) Garland.
Pollock, Griselda. Avant-Garde Gambits, Eighteen Eighty-Eight to Ninety-Three: Gender & the Color of Art History. LC 92-61579. (Walter Neurath Memorial Lecture Ser.). (Illus.). 64p. 1993. 14.95 (*0-500-55025-5*) Thames Hudson.
— Vision & Difference: Femininity, Feminism & the Histories of Art. 1988. pap. 14.95 (*0-415-00722-4*) Routledge.
— Vision & Difference: Femininity, Feminism & the Histories of Art. (Illus.). 272p. 1988. pap. text ed. 14.95 (*0-317-67353-X*) Routledge Chapman & Hall.
***Pollock, Griselda, pref.** Lictenberg Ettinger, Bracha. Matrix-Borderlines. 1993. pap. 28.00 (*0-905836-80-4*, Pub. by Museum Modern Art UK) St Mut.
Pollock, Harry E. Round Structures of Aboriginal Middle America. LC 77-11514. (Carnegie Institution of Washington. Publications: No. 471). reprint ed. 21.00 (*0-404-16274-6*) AMS Pr.
Pollock, Herman W. & Robinson, Terrance. Computer Numerical Control. 256p. 1990. text ed. 54.00 (*0-13-168378-0*) P-H.
Pollock, Horatio M. Family Care of Mental Patients: A Review of Systems of Family Care in America & Europe. LC 75-17236. (Social Problems & Social Policy Ser.). (Illus.). 1976. reprint ed. 21.95 (*0-405-07505-7*) Ayer.
— Mental Disease & Social Welfare. LC 75-17237. (Social Problems & Social Policy Ser.). (Illus.). 1976. reprint ed. 20.95 (*0-405-07506-5*) Ayer.
Pollock, J. B. Fringing & Fossil Reefs of Oahu. (BMB Ser.: No. 55). 1969. reprint ed. 15.00 (*0-527-02161-X*) Periodicals Srv.
Pollock, J. C. Centrifuge. 304p. 1992. mass mkt. 4.99 (*0-440-11156-0*) Dell.
— Crossfire. 1992. reprint ed. mass mkt. 4.99 (*0-440-11602-3*) Dell.
— The Dennecker Code. 224p. 1982. pap. 2.50 (*0-449-14454-2*, GM) Fawcett.
— Mission M. I. A. 320p. (Orig.). 1992. mass mkt. 4.99 (*0-440-15819-2*) Dell.
— Payback. 1992. reprint ed. mass mkt. 4.99 (*0-440-20518-2*) Dell.
— Threat Case. 1992. mass mkt. 5.99 (*0-440-21204-9*) Dell.
Pollock, J. G. Topical Reviews in Vascular Surgery, Vol. 1. (Illus.). 229p. 1982. text ed. 69.95 (*0-7236-0575-0*, Pub. by John Wright UK) Buttrwrth-Heinemann.
Pollock, J. L. Language & Thought. 1982. 45.00 (*0-691-07269-8*) Princeton U Pr.
Pollock, J. R., ed. Brewing Science, Vol. 1. (Food Science & Technology Ser.). 1979. text ed. 223.00 (*0-12-561001-7*) Acad Pr.
— Brewing Science, Vol. 3. (Food Science & Technology Ser.). 611p. 1987. text ed. 223.00 (*0-12-561003-3*) Acad Pr.
***Pollock, James K.** The Hitler Decrees. 1994. 10.00 (*1-884739-03-2*) Wahr.
— Making Michigan's Constitution. 1963. 10.00 (*0-911586-25-3*) Wahr.
— Money & Politics Abroad. LC 77-37909. (Select Bibliographies Reprint Ser.). 1977. reprint ed. 24.95 (*0-8369-6747-X*) Ayer.
— Source Materials on the Government & Politics of Germany. 1964. 25.00 (*0-911586-26-1*) Wahr.
Pollock, James K., et al. British Election Studies, 1950. 1951. 10.00 (*0-911586-27-X*) Wahr.
Pollock, Jean, jt. auth. see Pollock, Robert.
Pollock, Jocelyn M. Sex & Supervision: Guarding Male & Female Inmates. LC 86-9987. (Contributions in Criminology & Penology Ser.: No. 12). 175p. 1986. text ed. 49.95 (*0-313-25410-9*, PSS/, Greenwood Pr) Greenwood.
Pollock, John. Amazing Grace: The Dramatic Life Story of John Newton. LC 78-3142. 192p. 1983. pap. 5.72 (*0-06-066655-2*, RD-477) Harper SF.
— The Apostle. 312p. (Orig.). 1994. pap. 5.99 (*1-56476-242-4*, Victor Books) SP Pubns.
— El Apostol. 336p. (SPA.). 1990. pap. 9.95 (*0-8297-0467-1*) Life Pubs Intl.
— Cognitive Carpentry: A Blueprint for How to Build a Person. 354p. 1995. 34.95x (*0-262-16152-4*, Bradford Bks) MIT Pr.
— Contemporary Theories of Knowledge. LC 86-20221. (Texts in Philosophy Ser.). 224p. 1986. 60.50 (*0-8476-7452-5*); pap. 19.95 (*0-8476-7453-3*) Rowman.
— A Foreign Devil in China. 2nd ed. 1989. pap. 7.95 (*0-89066-141-3*) World Wide Pubs.
— How to Build a Person: A Prolegomenon. 250p. 1989. 27.50 (*0-262-16113-3*) MIT Pr.
— John Wesley. 260p. 1995. pap. 9.99 (*0-87788-424-2*) Shaw Pubs.
— El Maestro. 204p. (SPA.). 1990. pap. 6.95 (*0-8297-1463-4*) Life Pubs Intl.
— The Master. 240p. (Orig.). 1994. pap. 5.99 (*1-56476-241-6*, Victor Books) SP Pubns.
— The Master: A Life of Jesus. large type ed. (Large Print Inspirational Ser.). 1988. pap. 16.95 (*0-8027-2603-8*) Walker & Co.
— O Apostolo. 304p. (POR.). 1990. 11.95 (*0-8297-1621-1*) Life Pubs Intl.
— On Fire for God: Great Missionary Pioneers. 160p. (Orig.). reprint ed. pap. text ed. 4.99 (*1-884543-01-4*) O M Lit.
Pollock, John C. The Politics of Crisis Reporting: Learning to Be a Foreign Correspondent. LC 81-15350. (Praeger Special Studies). 240p. 1981. text ed. 55.00 (*0-275-90703-1*, C0703, Praeger Pubs) Greenwood.
Pollock, John C. & Finn, Peter, eds. The Connecticut Mutual Life Report on American Values in the '80s: The Impact of Belief. (Illus.). 346p. 1984. reprint ed. pap. text ed. 36.00 (*0-8191-4020-1*) U Pr of Amer.
Pollock, John C. & Heidt, Peter E. Transamerica Life Companies Report on Retirement Planning: Two Generations View Their Financial Future. (Orig.). 1989. pap. text ed. write for info. (*0-318-64800-8*) Transamerica.
Pollock, John L. The Foundations of Philosophical Semantics. LC 83-43088. (Illus.). 232p. 1984. 39.50 (*0-691-07283-3*) Princeton U Pr.
— The Foundations of Philosophical Semantics. LC 83-43088. Date not set. reprint ed. pap. 71.90 (*0-7837-9422-3*, 2060163) Bks Demand.
— Language & Thought. LC 82-414. Date not set. reprint ed. pap. 89.00 (*0-7837-9423-1*, 2060164) Bks Demand.
— Nomic Probability & the Foundations of Induction. 368p. 1990. 45.00 (*0-19-506013-X*) OUP.
— Subjective Reasoning. (Philosophical Studies in Philosophy Ser.: No. 8). 1976. lib. bdg. 84.00 (*90-277-0701-4*) Kluwer Ac.
— Technical Methods in Philosophy. 126p. (C). 1990. pap. text ed. 15.95 (*0-8133-7872-9*) Westview.
Pollock, Joy & Waller, Elisabeth. Day-to-Day Dyslexia in the Classroom. LC 93-46700. 192p. 1994. pap. 13.95 (*0-415-11132-3*, B3927, Routledge NY) Routledge.
Pollock, Joycelyn M. Ethics in Crime & Justice: Dilemmas & Decisions. 2nd ed. 236p. 1994. pap. 16.95 (*0-534-21456-8*) Intl Thomson.
Pollock, Judith, jt. auth. see Vierra, Andrea.
Pollock, K. H., et al. Angler Survey Methods & Their Applications in Fisheries Management. LC 94-70490. (Special Publication Ser.: No. 25). 371p. 1994. text ed. 88.00 (*0-913235-88-1*) Am Fisheries Soc.
Pollock, Linda. A Lasting Relationship: Parents & Children over Three Centuries. LC 87-6075. (Illus.). 319p. 1987. text ed. 40.00 (*0-87451-419-3*); pap. 15.95 (*0-87451-507-6*) U Pr of New Eng.
— With Faith & Physics: The Life of a Tudor Gentlewoman, Lady Grace Mildmay, 1552-1620. LC 94-24503. 179p. 1995. 39.95 (*0-312-12519-4*) St Martin.
Pollock, Linda, ed. see Mildmay, Grace.
Pollock, Linda A. Forgotten Children: Parent-Child Relations from 1500 to 1900. LC 83-5315. (Illus.). 360p. 1984. pap. 27.95 (*0-521-27133-9*) Cambridge U Pr.
Pollock, Marion, et al. Planning & Implementing Health Education in Schools. LC 86-62998. 408p. (C). 1987. text ed. 40.95 (*0-87484-563-7*) Mayfield Pub.
Pollock, Marvin E. Resale of Restricted Securities under SEC Rules 144 & 144A. 2nd ed. (Corporate Practice Ser.: Portfolio No. 46). 1990. ring bd. 92.00 (*1-55871-193-7*) BNA.
Pollock, Mary & Roth, Marcia, eds. The Educated Palate: Tasteful Recipes from A-Z. 240p. (Orig.). 1988. pap. 15.00 (*0-317-90973-8*) Calhoun Schl Parents Assn.
Pollock, Michael. Hostage to Fortune: Atlantic City & Casino Gambling. Sinding, Richard V., ed. 208p. (Orig.). 1987. 11.95 (*0-943136-01-6*) Ctr Analysis Public Issues.
Pollock, Michael L. & Schmidt, Donald H., eds. Heart Disease & Rehabilitation. 2nd ed. LC 85-12008. 752p. 1986. 57.50 (*0-471-09562-1*) Churchill.
— Heart Disease & Rehabilitation. 3rd ed. LC 94-12879. 488p. 1995. text ed. 59.00x (*0-87322-588-0*, BPOL0588) Human Kinetics.
Pollock, Mindy S. Computers in the Elementary Classroom. abr. ed. 130p. 1995. pap. 6.95 (*1-56901-336-5*) NW Pub.
Pollock, Norman, jt. auth. see Lemon, Anthony.
Pollock, Philip H., III, jt. auth. see Eismeier, Theodore J.
***Pollock, Polly.** Start a Craft: Basket Making. 1994. 7.98 (*0-7858-0060-3*) Bk Sales Inc.
Pollock, Ralph S., ed. Renewing the Dream: National Archives Bicentennial '87 Lectures on Contemporary Constitutional Issues. LC 86-19103. (Illus.). 194p. (Orig.). (C). 1987. 42.00 (*0-8191-5664-7*, National Archives & Recs); pap. text ed. 21.00 (*0-8191-5665-5*, National Archives & Recs) U Pr of Amer.
Pollock, Robert. Soccer for Juniors: A Guide for Players, Parents, & Coaches. (Illus.). 208p. 1985. pap. 9.95 (*0-684-18369-2*, Scribners) S&S Trade.
Pollock, Robert & Pollock, Jean. Common Campground Critters of the West. (J). (gr. 1-6). 1987. reprint ed. pap. 5.95 (*0-911797-77-7*) R Rinehart.
Pollock, Ross, jt. auth. see David, Paul T.
***Pollock, S. M., et al, eds.** Operations Research & the Public Sector. (Handbooks in Operations Research & Management Science: Vol. 6). 744p. 1994. 165.00 (*0-444-89204-4*, North Holland) Elsevier.
Pollock, Sean R., jt. ed. see Person, James E., Jr.
Pollock, Sheldon. Aspects of Versification in Sanskrit Lyric Poetry. (American Oriental Ser.: Vol. 61). 1977. 12.00 (*0-940490-61-7*) Am Orient Soc.
Pollock, Sheldon I., tr. see Goldman, Robert P., ed.
Pollock, Shirley. Sunday Morning Alive, Bk. I. (Orig.). 1987. pap. 6.85 (*0-89536-887-0*, 7873) CSS OH.
— Sunday Morning Alive!, Bk. II. (Orig.). 1988. pap. 7.30 (*1-55673-069-1*, 8866) CSS OH.
Pollock, Stephen. The Atlas of Endangered Animals. LC 92-20387. (Environmental Atlas Ser.). (Illus.). 64p. (J). (gr. 6-9). 1993. 16.95 (*0-8160-2856-7*) Facts on File.
***Pollock, Steve.** The Atlas of Endangered Peoples. LC 94-35296. 1995. 16.95 (*0-8160-3283-1*) Facts on File.
— The Atlas of Endangered Places. LC 92-20388. (Environmental Atlas Ser.). (Illus.). 64p. (YA). 1993. 16.95 (*0-8160-2857-5*) Facts on File.
— The Atlas of Endangered Resources. LC 94-32549. (J). 1995. 16.95 (*0-8160-3284-X*) Facts on File.
— Dinosaurs. (Illus.). 48p. (J). (gr. 7-9). 1992. 13.95 (*0-563-34753-8*, BBC-Parkwest); pap. 7.50 (*0-563-34607-8*, BBC-Parkwest) Parkwest Pubns.
— Wildlife Safari. (Illus.). 48p. (J). (gr. 7-9). 1992. 13.95 (*0-563-34354-0*, BBC-Parkwest); pap. 6.95 (*0-563-34162-9*, BBC-Parkwest) Parkwest Pubns.
Pollock, Steve & Marshall, Julian. Help Your Child with Science. (Illus.). 128p. (Orig.). 1993. pap. 9.95 (*0-563-36215-4*, BBC-Parkwest) Parkwest Pubns.
Pollock, T. & Mulla, B. Indian Contract & Specific Relief Act. (C). 1986. 200.00 (*0-685-25707-X*) St Mut.
Pollock, T. C. & Spaulding, J. G. General Semantics Monograph III: A Theory of Meaning Analyzed. 64p. 1942. pap. 6.95 (*0-910780-03-X*) Inst Gen Seman.
Pollock, T. M. Trials of Prophylactic Agents for the Control of Communicable Diseases: A Guide to Their Organization & Evaluation. (Monograph Ser.: No. 52). 92p. (ENG, FRE, RUS & SPA.). 1966. 4.80 (*0-686-09188-4*, 92-4-140052) World Health.
Pollock, Thomas C. Nature of Literature: Its Relation to Science, Language & Human Experiences. LC 65-25135. 218p. 1965. reprint ed. 45.00 (*0-87752-086-0*) Gordian.
Pollock, Thomas W. Meat & Health: Index of Modern Information with Bibliography. LC 88-47788. 150p. (Orig.). 1988. 44.50 (*0-88164-900-7*); pap. 39.50 (*0-88164-901-5*) ABBE Pubs Assn.
Pollock, Vivienne, jt. auth. see Hill, Myrtle.
Pollock, W. H. William Butler Yeats. LC 75-22355. (W. B. Yeats Ser.: No. 72). 1975. lib. bdg. 39.95 (*0-8383-2104-6*) M S G Haskell Hse.
Pollock, W. I. & Steely, C. N., eds. Corrosion under Wet Thermal Insulation. LC 90-62320. (Illus.). 104p. 1990. 43.00 (*1-877914-14-2*) NACE Intl.
Pollock, W. I., jt. ed. see Moniz, B. J.
Pollock, Walter. Jane Austen. LC 73-130248. (Studies in Fiction: No. 34). 1970. reprint ed. lib. bdg. 66.95 (*0-8383-1138-5*) M S G Haskell Hse.
Pollock, Warren I. & Barnhart, Jack M., eds. Corrosion of Metals under Thermal Insulation - STP 880. LC 85-1. (Illus.). 240p. 1985. text ed. 36.00 (*0-8031-0416-2*, PCN04-880000-27) ASTM.
Pollock, Warren I., ed. see American Society for Testing & Materials Staff.
Pollock, Wendy & McCormick, Susan, eds. Exhibits Report & Directory. (ASTC Science Center Survey Report Ser.). (Illus.). 220p. 1988. pap. 20.00 (*0-685-29591-5*) AST Ctrs.
Pollock, Yevonne. The Old Man's Mitten: A Ukrainian Tale. LC 94-30195. (Illus.). 24p. (Orig.). (J). (ps-3). 1994. pap. 4.95 (*1-879531-60-7*) Mondo Pubng.
***Pollock, Zailig.** A. M. Klein: The Story of the Poet. 324p. 1994. 60.00 (*0-8020-0446-6*); pap. 25.95 (*0-8020-7234-8*) U of Toronto Pr.
Pollock, Zailig, ed. see Klein, A. M.
Pollock, Zailig, et al. A. M. Klein: An Annotated Bibliography. 390p. (C). 1993. text ed. 65.00 (*1-55022-095-0*, Pub. by ECW Press CN) Genl Dist Srvs.
***Pollon, Earl K. & Matheson, Shirley S.** This Was Our Valley. (Illus.). 403p. (Orig.). 1989. pap. 17.95 (*0-920490-91-3*) Temeron Bks.
— This Was Our Valley. (Illus.). 1989. 26.95 (*0-920490-92-1*) Temeron Bks.
Pollon, Zelie, tr. see Gyatso, Tenzin.
Pollot, Mark. Grand Theft & Petit Larceny: Property Rights in America. LC 91-12545. 250p. (Orig.). 1992. pap. 21.95 (*0-936488-44-1*) PRIPP.
***Pollotta, Nick.** The 24 Hour War. LC 94-68158. (Endless Quest Ser.). (Orig.). Date not set. pap. 3.95 (*0-7869-0198-5*) TSR Inc.
Pollotta, Nick & Foglio, Phil. Illegal Aliens. LC 88-51727. (TSR Bks.). (Illus.). 320p. (Orig.). (J). 1989. pap. 3.95 (*0-88038-715-7*) TSR Inc.
Polloway, Edward A. & Patton, James R. Strategies for Teaching Learners with Special Needs. 5th ed. LC 92-29606. 560p. (C). 1992. pap. write for info. (*0-02-396021-3*, Merrill Pub Co) Macmillan.
Polloway, Edward A. & Smith, Tom E. Language Instruction for Students with Disabilities. 2nd ed. 1992. teacher ed 39.95 (*0-89108-221-2*, 9202) Love Pub Co.
Polloway, Edward A., jt. ed. see Patton, James R.
Polls, A., jt. ed. see Guardiola, R.
Polluck. Surgical Audit. 1989. 59.95 (*0-407-00823-3*) Buttrwrth-Heinemann.
***Pollution Engineering Staff.** Air Toxics. 186p. 1994. pap. 29.95 (*0-614-01881-1*) Gulf Pub.
— Answering NIMBY. 240p. 1994. 43.75 (*0-934165-44-0*) Gulf Pub.
— Bioremediation Desk Manual for the Environmental Professional Bioremediation. 97p. 1994. 24.95 (*0-934165-33-5*) Gulf Pub.
— Clean Air Regulation the Clean Air Act. 96p. 1994. 24.95 (*0-934165-49-1*) Gulf Pub.
— Dangerous Chemical Reactions. 94p. 1994. 34.95 (*0-934165-46-7*) Gulf Pub.
— Effective Environmental, Product Stewardship & Safety Management Practices. 84p. 1994. 31.25 (*0-934165-27-0*) Gulf Pub.
— Emerging On-Site & In Situ Hazardous Waste Treatment Technologies. 260p. 1994. 34.95 (*0-934165-32-7*) Gulf Pub.
— Environmental Acronyms & Glossary. 152p. 1994. 24.95 (*0-934165-42-4*) Gulf Pub.
— Environmental Assessments & Real Estate Transactions. 324p. 1994. 44.95 (*0-934165-50-5*) Gulf Pub.
— Environmental Crime Contents: Criminal Laws. 95p. Date not set. 24.95 (*0-934165-10-6*) Gulf Pub.
— Environmental Law Outline. 148p. 1994. 29.95 (*0-934165-41-6*) Gulf Pub.
— Environmental Rules of Thumb. 192p. 1994. 34.95 (*0-934165-35-1*) Gulf Pub.
— EPA's Handbook: Responding to Sinking Hazardous Substances. 312p. 1994. 34.95 (*0-934165-19-X*) Gulf Pub.
— The ESE National Precipitation Databook. 888p. 1994. 89.95 (*0-934165-37-8*) Gulf Pub.
— A Guide to Working with Hazardous Materials. 217p. 1994. 24.95 (*0-934165-06-8*) Gulf Pub.
— Hazardous Waste & Toxic Substances Laws & Regulations. 308p. 1994. 49.95 (*0-934165-52-1*) Gulf Pub.
— How to Review a Part B Permit. 160p. 1994. 24.95 (*0-934165-07-6*) Gulf Pub.
— Municipal Environmental Accident & Emergency Response Planning. 164p. 1994. 29.95 (*0-934165-47-5*) Gulf Pub.
— Pollution Control Engineers Handbook. 205p. 1994. 34.95 (*0-934165-02-5*) Gulf Pub.
— Pollution Engineering Flow Sheets: Hazardous Waste Treatment & Unit Operations. 225p. 1994. 34.95 (*0-934165-23-8*) Gulf Pub.
— Preacquisition Assessment of Commercial & Industrial Property. 96p. 1994. 31.25 (*0-934165-30-0*) Gulf Pub.
— Release Prevention Control & Counter. 66p. 1994. 24.95 (*0-934165-17-3*) Gulf Pub.
— Safety Deskbook. 269p. 1994. 34.95 (*0-934165-25-4*) Gulf Pub.
— Simplified Hazardous Materials Chemistry. 239p. 1994. 39.95 (*0-934165-39-4*) Gulf Pub.
— Site Histories Documenting Hazards for Environmental Site Assessments Contents: The Historical Imperative of Site Assessments. 128p. 1994. 29.95 (*0-934165-45-9*) Gulf Pub.
— Underground Storage Tanks Management. 136p. 1994. 29.95 (*0-934165-43-2*) Gulf Pub.
— VOC Calculation Manual. 238p. 1994. 39.95 (*0-934165-36-X*) Gulf Pub.
Polma, jt. auth. see DeSanto.
Polman, Bert, et al, eds. Amazing Grace: Hymn Texts for Devotional Use. 256p. (Orig.). 1994. pap. 14.99 (*0-664-25510-8*) Westminster John Knox.
***Polmar, N. & Allen, T. B.** World War II. 1994. pap. 14.99 (*0-517-13108-0*) Random.
Polmar, Norman. The Naval Institute Guide to the Ships & Aircraft of the U. S. Fleet. 15th ed. (Illus.). 639p. 1992. 72.50 (*1-55750-675-2*) Naval Inst Pr.
— The Naval Institute Guide to the Soviet Navy. 5th ed. LC 90-41568. (Illus.). 608p. 1991. 65.00 (*0-87021-241-9*) Naval Inst Pr.
— World War II: America at War 1941-1945. 1991. 35.00 (*0-394-58530-5*) Random.
Polmar, Norman & Bohn, John T. Strategic Air Command: People, Aircraft, & Missiles. 1980. 22.95 (*0-405-13275-1*) Ayer.
Polmar, Norman & Carpenter, Dorr B. Submarines of Imperial Japanese Navy. LC 85-31959. (Illus.). 177p. 1986. 37.95 (*0-87021-682-1*) Naval Inst Pr.
Polmar, Norman & Laur, Timothy. Strategic Air Command: People, Aircraft & Missiles. 2nd ed. LC 90-35105. (Illus.). 326p. 1990. 24.95 (*0-933852-77-0*) Nautical & Aviation.

An Asterisk (*) at the beginning of an entry indicates that the title is appearing in BIP for the first time.

Polmar, Norman & Noot, Jurrien. Submarines of the Russian & Soviet Navies, 1718-1990. LC 90-6687. (Illus.). 400p. 1991. 59.95 (*0-87021-570-1*) Naval Inst Pr.

Polmar, Norman, jt. auth. see Allen, Thomas B.

Polmar, Norman, jt. auth. see United States Navy, Office of Information Staff.

Polmar, Norman, et al. Dictionary of Military Abbreviations. LC 93-34566. 307p. 1994. 24.95 (*1-55750-680-9*) Naval Inst Pr.

Polmar, Stephen H. New Directions in the Clinical Use of Intravenous Immunoglobulin, Vol. IV. (Illus.). 60p. 1990. write for info. (*0-318-65782-1*) Health Dimensions.

Polmear, A., jt. auth. see Khot, A.

Polmear, I. J. Light Alloys: Metallurgy of the Light Metals. 2nd ed. (Metallurgy & Materials Science Ser.). (Illus.). 1989. 39.95 (*0-340-49175-2*, Pub. by E Arnold UK) Routledge Chapman & Hall.

— Light Alloys Metallurgy of the Light Metals. 224p. 1981. 110.00 (*0-685-05555-8*, Pub. by E Arnold UK) Routledge Chapman & Hall.

Polnac & Wilkerson. Aims & Modes in the Writing Process. 2nd ed. 208p. (C). 1992. pap. text ed. 13.95 (*0-8403-7811-4*) Kendall-Hunt.

Polnauer, Frederick & Marks, Morton. Senso-Motor Study & Its Application to Violin Playing. 15.95 (*0-318-18114-2*) Am String Tchrs.

Polnauer, Josef, ed. see Webern, Anton.

Polner, Jerry. Youth Enterprises: A How to Manual for Starting a Youth Business in Your Community. 41p. 1983. pap. 3.50 (*0-88156-020-0*) Comm Serv Soc NY.

Polner, Murray, jt. ed. see Goodman, Naomi.

Polner, Tikhon J., et al. Russian Local Government During the War & the Union of Zemstvos. (Economic & Social History of the World War Ser.). 1930. 100.00 (*0-317-27559-3*) Elliots Bks.

Polniaszek, Susan. Long Term Living: How to Live Independently As Long As You Can & Plan for the Time When You Can't. 1990. pap. 7.95 (*0-87491-969-X*) Acropolis.

Polo, Marco. The Book of Marco Polo, 2 vols. 1980. lib. bdg. 500.00 (*0-87968-332-5*) Krishna Pr.

— The Book of Sir Marco Polo, the Venetian, Concerning the Kingdoms & Marvels of the East, 3 vols., 1. 3rd ed. Yule, Henry, ed. & tr. by. LC 74-5240. reprint ed. write for info. (*0-404-11541-1*) AMS Pr.

— The Book of Sir Marco Polo, the Venetian, Concerning the Kingdoms & Marvels of the East, 3 vols., 2. 3rd ed. Yule, Henry, ed. & tr. by. LC 74-5240. reprint ed. write for info. (*0-404-11542-X*) AMS Pr.

— The Book of Sir Marco Polo, the Venetian, Concerning the Kingdoms & Marvels of the East, 3 vols., 3. 3rd ed. Yule, Henry, ed. & tr. by. LC 74-5240. reprint ed. write for info. (*0-404-11543-8*) AMS Pr.

— The Book of Sir Marco Polo, the Venetian, Concerning the Kingdoms & Marvels of the East, 3 vols., Set. 3rd ed. Yule, Henry, ed. & tr. by. LC 74-5240. reprint ed. write for info. (*0-404-11540-3*) AMS Pr.

— The Description of the World, 2 vols., Set. LC 74-5372. reprint ed. 225.00 (*0-404-11525-X*) AMS Pr.

— Travels. 24.95 (*0-8488-0187-3*) Amereon Ltd.

— Travels. Wright, T., ed. Marsden, tr. LC 68-57871. (Bohn's Antiquarian Library). reprint ed. 57.00 (*0-404-50023-4*) AMS Pr.

— Travels of Marco Polo. (Airmont Classics Ser.). (J). (gr. 9 up). 1968. pap. 1.50 (*0-8049-0186-4*, CL-186) Airmont.

— The Travels of Marco Polo. Latham, Ronald, tr. 318p. 1982. 35.00 (*0-89835-058-1*) Abaris Bks.

— The Travels of Marco Polo. 1982. reprint ed. lib. bdg. 18.95 (*0-89967-045-8*) Harmony Raine.

Polo, Marco, et al. The Travels of Marco Polo: The Complete Yule-Cordier Edition, 2 vols., 1. 3rd rev. ed. (Illus.). 1680p. 1993. reprint ed. pap. 17.95 (*0-486-27586-6*) Dover.

— The Travels of Marco Polo: The Complete Yule-Cordier Edition, 2 vols., 2. rev. ed. (Illus.). 1680p. 1993. reprint ed. pap. 17.95 (*0-486-27587-6*) Dover.

Pologruto, Donald, jt. auth. see Kemp, Carrie.

Poloma, Margaret M. The Assemblies of God at the Crossroads: Charisma & Institutional Dilemmas. LC 88-13761. 332p. 1989. text ed. 41.00x (*0-87049-604-2*); pap. 18.95 (*0-87049-607-7*) U of Tenn Pr.

— The Charismatic Movement: Is There a New Pentecost? (Social Movements Past & Present Ser.). 304p. 1987. pap. 11.95 (*0-8057-9721-1*, Twayne) Macmillan.

Poloma, Margaret M. & Gallup, George H., Jr. Varieties of Prayer: A Survey Report. LC 90-28578. 160p. (Orig.). (C). 1991. 24.95 (*1-56338-008-0*); pap. 14.95 (*1-56338-007-2*) TPI PA.

Poloma, Margaret M. & Pendleton, Brian F. Exploring Neglected Dimensions of Religion in Quality of Life Research. LC 91-27334. (Studies in the Psychology of Religion: Vol. 7). 236p. 1991. lib. bdg. 89.95 (*0-7734-9672-6*) E Mellen.

Polome, Edgar C. Essays on Germanic Religion. (Journal of Indo-European Studies Monograph: No. 6). (Illus.). (Orig.). (C). 1989. pap. text ed. 25.00 (*0-941694-34-8*) Inst Study Man.

— Language, Society, & Paleoculture: Essays by Edgar C. Polome. Dil, Anwar S., ed. LC 82-80925. (Language Science & National Development Ser.). 404p. 1982. 49.50 (*0-8047-1149-6*) Stanford U Pr.

— Research Guide on Language. (Trends in Linguistics, Studies & Monographs: No. 48). xii, 564p. (C). 1990. lib. bdg. 190.80 (*3-11-012046-1*) Mouton.

Polome, Edgar C., ed. Essays in Honor of Karl Kerenyi. (Journal of Indo-European Studies Monograph: No. 4). (Illus.). 144p. (Orig.). 1984. pap. 30.00 (*0-941694-20-8*) Inst Study Man.

— Homage to Georges Dumezil. (Journal of Indo-European Studies Monograph: No. 3). 172p. (Orig.). 1983. pap. 25.00 (*0-941694-28-3*) Inst Study Man.

Polome, Edgar C. & Hill, C. P., eds. Language in Tanzania. LC 81-147648. (Ford Foundation Language Surveys Ser.). 442p. reprint ed. pap. 126.00 (*0-8357-6964-X*, 2039024) Bks Demand.

Polome, Edgar C. & Winter, Werner, eds. Reconstructing Languages & Cultures. LC 91-45260. (Trends in Linguistics, Studies & Monographs: No. 58). ix, 550p. 1992. lib. bdg. 190.80 (*3-11-012671-0*) Mouton.

Polome, Edgar C., jt. ed. see Skomal, Susan S.

Polomka, Peter. Ocean Politics in Southeast Asia. 235p. (Orig.). 1978. pap. text ed. 19.00 (*0-566-04005-0*, Pub. by Inst SE Asian Studies SI) Ashgate Pub Co.

Polomski, Lothar, jt. comp. see Mackenzie, Harry.

Polon, Linda. Magic Story Starters: Grades One to Three. (Illus.). 44p. (Orig.). 1986. pap. 6.95 (*0-673-18561-3*) GdYrBks.

— Paragraph Production. (Study Skills Ser.). 48p. (J). (gr. 4-6). 1981. 5.95 (*0-88160-039-3*, LW 224) Learning Wks.

— Stir up a Story. (Learning Works Creative Writing Ser.). 48p. (J). (gr. 3-6). 1981. 5.95 (*0-88160-037-7*, LW 222) Learning Wks.

— Writing Whirlwind: Grades 2-4. (Illus.). 44p. (Orig.). 1986. pap. 6.95 (*0-673-18310-6*) GdYrBks.

Polon, Linda & Cantwell, Aileen. The Whole Earth Holiday Book: Grades 4-6. (Illus.). 218p. (Orig.). 1983. pap. 13.95 (*0-673-16585-X*) GdYrBks.

Polonnikov, D. & Inston, R. Electronic Amplifiers for Automatic Compensators. LC 93-21450. (International Series of Monographs on Automation & Automatic Control: No. 3). 1965. 142.00 (*0-08-010174-7*, Pub. by Pergamon Repr UK) Franklin.

Polonoff, David. Down the Yup Staircase: Decline & Fall of the Republican Empire. LC 92-91211. (Illus.). 184p. (Orig.). 1993. pap. text ed. write for info. (*0-9635664-4-X*) Pantagruel.

***Polonskaya, Ludmila & Malashenko, Alexei.** Islam in Central Asia. 172p. 1995. 55.00 (*0-86372-182-6*) Paul & Co Pubs.

Polonsky, Abraham. To Illuminate Our Time: The Blacklisted Teleplays of Abraham Polonsky. Schaubert, Mark, ed. LC 92-84081. 352p. (Orig.). 1993. pap. text ed. 12.95 (*0-9635823-0-5*) Sadanlaur Pubns.

Polonsky, Anthony, jt. auth. see Gomulka, Stanislaw.

Polonsky, Antony, ed. From Shtetl to Socialism: Studies from Polin. LC 93-29009. (Littman Library of Jewish Civilization). (Illus.). 608p. (Orig.). 1994. pap. 32.50 (*1-874774-14-5*, Pub. by Littman Lib Jew UK) Bnai Brith Bk.

— My Brother's Keeper? Recent Polish Debates on the Holocaust. LC 89-6208. 242p. 1990. 25.00 (*0-415-04232-1*) Routledge.

— Polin, Vol. 3. (Illus.). 458p. 1989. 50.00 (*0-631-16694-7*, Pub. by Littman Lib Jew UK) Bnai Brith Bk.

— Polin, Vol. 4. (Illus.). 502p. 1990. 50.00 (*0-631-17303-X*, Pub. by Littman Lib Jew UK) Bnai Brith Bk.

— Polin, Vol. 5. (Illus.). 512p. 1991. 58.00 (*0-631-17886-4*, Pub. by Littman Lib Jew UK) Bnai Brith Bk.

— Polin, Vol. 6. 512p. 1991. 58.00 (*0-631-18167-9*, Pub. by Littman Lib Jew UK) Bnai Brith Bk.

— Polin: A Journal of Polish Jewish Studies, Vol. 7. 350p. 1992. 64.95 (*0-631-18932-7*, Pub. by Littman Lib Jew UK) Bnai Brith Bk.

Polonsky, Antony & Davies, Norman, eds. Jews in Eastern Poland & the U.S.S.R., 1939-46. 440p. 1991. text ed. 65.00 (*0-312-06200-1*) St Martin.

Polonsky, Antony, jt. ed. see Gomulka, Stanislaw.

Polonsky, Antony, ed. see Lewin, Abraham.

Polonsky, Bruce. Hearing Music. (Illus.). 96p. (Orig.). 1981. pap. 14.95 (*0-9606112-0-7*) Private Bks.

Polonsky, Daniel L. The Letter Bandits. (Illus.). 72p. (J). (gr. 3 up). 1991. 14.95 (*0-931474-41-8*) TBW Bks.

Polonsky, Derek C., jt. ed. see Nadelson, Carol C.

Polonsky, Marc & Taylor, Russell. U. S. S. R. From an Idea by Karl Marx. 176p. (Orig.). 1986. pap. 8.95 (*0-571-13842-X*) Faber & Faber.

Polonsky, Michael J. & Mintu-Wimsatt, Alma T. Environmental Marketing: Strategies, Practice, Theory, & Research. LC 94-28993. (Illus.). 414p. 1995. lib. bdg. 79.95 (*1-56024-927-7*) Haworth Pr.

Polonsky, Michael J., jt. ed. see Lozada, Hector R.

Polonsky, Stanford I. The Truth about Tubby & Slim. LC 92-60812. 50p. (J). (gr. k-3). 1993. 7.95 (*1-55523-543-3*) Winston-Derek.

Polonyi, Michael J. Power & Process Control Systems. 1991. text ed. 44.00 (*0-07-050414-8*) McGraw.

Polopolus, L. C. & Alvarez, J., eds. Marketing Sugar & Other Sweeteners. (Developments in Agricultural Engineering Ser.: Vol. 9). 385p. 1991. 148.50 (*0-444-89150-1*) Elsevier.

Polopolus, Leo C., jt. ed. see Lopez, Rigoberto A.

***Polos, Laszlo & Masuch, Michael, eds.** Applied Logic: How, What & Why: Logical Approaches to Natural Language. LC 95-11570. (Synthese Library: Vol. 247). 400p. (C). 1995. lib. bdg. 115.00 (*0-7923-3432-9*) Kluwer Ac.

Polos, Laszlo, jt. ed. see Masuch, Michael.

***Poloskei, F.** Hungary after Two Revolutions. 148p. (C). 1980. 38.00x (*963-05-2481-3*, Pub. by Akad Kiado HU) St Mut.

— Istvan Tisza. (Studia Historica Academiae Scientiarum Hungaricae Ser.: No. 198). 164p. (GER.). 1994. 25.00 (*963-05-6761-X*, Pub. by A K HU) Intl Spec Bk.

Poloskei, Ference. Hungary After Two Revolutions: 1919-1922. 148p. 1980. 40.00 (*0-569-08679-5*, Pub. by Collets UK) Pro-Am Music.

Polotsky, H. J. Grundlagen des Koptischen Satzbaus. LC 86-21977. (American Studies in Papyrology). 133p. 1987. 37.95 (*1-55540-076-0*, 31-00-27) Scholars Pr GA.

Polotsky, J. H. Collected Papers. xi, 724p. 1971. text ed. 35.00 (*0-685-74253-9*, Pub. by Magnes Press IS) Eisenbrauns.

Polovets, Alexander. Beglyi Rachikhin (Figitibe Rachikhin) LC 87-82248. 208p. (RUS.). 1987. 15.50 (*0-911971-25-4*) Effect Pub.

Polovin, R. V. & Demutskii, V. P. Fundamentals of Magnetohydrodynamics. (Illus.). 352p. 1990. 95.00 (*0-306-11027-X*, Consultants) Plenum.

Polowetzky, Michael. A Bond Never Broken: The Relations Between Napoleon & the Authors of France. LC 92-58944. (Illus.). 192p. 1993. 32.50 (*0-8386-3482-6*) Fairleigh Dickinson.

— Jerusalem Recovered: Victorian Intellectuals & the Birth of Modern Zionism. LC 95-3355. 176p. 1995. text ed. 49.95 (*0-275-95213-4*, Praeger Pubs) Greenwood.

Polowinski. Template Polymerization & Copolymerization. 1994. write for info. (*0-8493-6778-6*) CRC Pr.

Polowniak, William. On Creating a Community: A Guide for Organizations, Personal Productivity & International Peace. 296p. 1994. 23.95 (*0-9639142-1-9*) Quantum Publications CA.

— On Creating a Community: A Guide for Organizations, Personal Productivity & International Peace. 296p. (C). 1994. pap. 14.95 (*0-9639142-0-0*) Quantum Publications CA.

Polowy, Barbara C., jt. auth. see Schweizer, Paul D.

Polowy, Teresa. The Novellas of Valentin Rasputin: Genre, Language & Style. (Middlebury Studies in Russian Language & Literature: Vol. 1). 262p. (C). 1989. text ed. 42.50 (*0-8204-0643-0*) P Lang Pubs.

Polozhii, G. & Tee, G. Method of Summary Representation for Numerical Solution of Problems of Mathematical Physics. LC 65-13073. (International Series Mono on Pure & Applied Mathematics: Vol. 79). 1965. 124.00 (*0-08-011017-7*, Pub. by Pergamon Repr UK) Franklin.

Polprasert, Chongrak. Organic Waste Recycling. 357p. 1989. text ed. 125.00 (*0-471-92098-3*) Wiley.

Pols, Cynthia M., jt. auth. see Cooper, Ronald S.

Pols, Edward. The Acts of Our Being: A Reflection on Agency & Responsibility. LC 81-16319. 248p. 1982. lib. bdg. 30.00x (*0-87023-354-8*) U of Mass Pr.

— Radical Realism: Direct Knowing in Science & Philosophy. LC 91-55531. 240p. 1992. 32.50 (*0-8014-2710-X*) Cornell U Pr.

Pols, Louis C., jt. ed. see Van Heuven, Vincent J.

Polsby, Nelson W. Consequences of Party Reform. (Illus.). 1983. pap. 9.95 (*0-19-503315-9*) OUP.

— Political Innovation in America. LC 83-14749. 200p. 1985. pap. 12.00 (*0-300-03428-8*, Y-538) Yale U Pr.

— Political Innovation in America: The Politics of Policy Initation. LC 83-14749. 200p. 1984. 32.00 (*0-300-03089-4*) Yale U Pr.

— The Renegotiation of the Social Contract. 1976. 1.00 (*1-55614-106-8*) U of SD Gov Res Bur.

Polsby, Nelson W., ed. The Modern Presidency. LC 81-40776. 250p. 1981. reprint ed. pap. text ed. 24.00 (*0-8191-1822-2*) U Pr of Amer.

Polsby, Nelson W. & Wildavsky, Aaron B. Presidential Elections. 6th ed. 361p. (C). 1984. pap. write for info. (*0-02-396260-7*, Scribners) S&S Trade.

— Presidential Elections: Contemporary Strategies of American Electoral Politics. 416p. 1991. pap. 14.95 (*0-02-922786-0*) Free Pr.

— Presidential Elections: Contemporary Strategies of American Electoral Politics. 7th ed. 350p. 1988. 24.95 (*0-02-925261-X*); pap. 14.95 (*0-02-925262-8*) Free Pr.

— Presidential Elections: Contemporary Strategies of American Electoral Politics. 8th ed. 416p. 1991. text ed. 24.95 (*0-02-922785-2*) Free Pr.

— Presidential Elections: Strategies of American Electoral Politics. 5th ed. LC 70-162761. 1900. 12.50 (*0-684-16415-9*, Scribners) S&S Trade.

Polsby, Nelson W., jt. ed. see Orren, Gary R.

Polsby, Nelson W., jt. ed. see Peabody, Robert L.

Polselli, Joseph. Drums of a Different War. LC 83-6443. 261p. 1984. 22.95 (*0-87949-241-4*) Ashley Bks.

***Polsgrove, Carol.** It Wasn't Pretty, Folks, But Didn't We Have Fun? Esquire in the Sixties. (Illus.). 300p. 1995. 27.50 (*0-393-03792-4*) Norton.

Polsgrove, Lewis. Reducing Undesirable Behaviors. 33p. 1991. 8.90 (*0-86586-201-X*, P342) Coun Exc Child.

Polshkov, Mikhail K., ed. Exploration Geophysics, Vol. 49. 174p. reprint ed. pap. 49.60 (*0-685-15858-6*, 2056112) Bks Demand.

Polsinelli, M., et al, eds. Nitrogen Fixation. (Developments in Plant & Soil Sciences Ser.). 704p. (C). 1991. lib. bdg. 241.50 (*0-7923-1410-7*) Kluwer Ac.

Polsky, Abe. Devour the Snow. 1979. pap. 4.75 (*0-8222-0304-9*) Dramatists Play.

Polsky, Andrew J. The Rise of the Therapeutic State. 296p. 1993. text ed. 42.50 (*0-691-07878-5*); pap. text ed. 16.95 (*0-691-00084-0*) Princeton U Pr.

Polsky, Carol, ed. see Los Angeles Children's Museum Staff.

Polsky, Howard W. Cottage Six: Social System of Delinquent Boys in Residential Treatment. LC 76-50144. (Illus.). 192p. 1977. reprint ed. pap. text ed. 10.50 (*0-88275-475-0*) Krieger.

Polsky, Howard W. & Wozner, Yaella. Everyday Miracles: The Healing Wisdom of Hasidic Stories. LC 88-21999. 512p. 1989. 40.00 (*0-87668-880-6*) Aronson.

Polsky, Jeffrey D., jt. auth. see McClain, Maureen E.

Polsky, Marion. First Latin, Bk. 2. 1987. student ed, pap. text ed. 5.85 (*0-582-99853-0*, 75278) Longman.

— First Latin, Set, Vols. I & II. 1990. Set. 22.60 (*0-8013-0570-5*, 78477) Longman.

— First Latin, Vol. I. 1987. teacher ed, pap. text ed. 31.96 (*0-582-90716-0*, 75230); student ed, pap. text ed. 5.85 (*0-582-90715-2*, 75229) Longman.

— First Latin, Vol. II. 1987. teacher ed, pap. text ed. 31.96 (*0-582-99854-9*, 75279) Longman.

Polsky, Michael. V Zashchitu Pravoslavnoj Vjeri ot Sektantov. 1950. pap. 1.00 (*0-317-30261-2*) Holy Trinity.

Polsky, Michael A. What Good Is Religion to Me. 1993. pap. 0.50 (*0-89981-140-X*) Eastern Orthodox.

Polsky, Milton, et al. The King of Escapes. (Orig.). (J). (gr. 3-12). 1985. pap. 6.00 (*0-88734-510-7*) Players Pr.

Polsky, Milton E. Let's Improvise: Becoming Creative, Expressive & Spontaneous Through Drama. LC 88-33699. (Illus.). 334p. (C). 1989. reprint ed. pap. text ed. 27.00 (*0-8191-7162-X*) U Pr of Amer.

***Polsky, Richard H.** User's Guide to the Scientific & Clinical Literature on Dog & Cat Behavior. 2nd ed. 97p. (C). 1995. pap. text ed. 49.95 (*0-614-04772-2*) Animal Behav.

Polsky, Walter P., ed. see Foxman, Loretta D.

Polsky, Yury. Soviet Research Institutes & the Formulation of Foreign Policy: The Institute of World Economy & International Relations (IMEMO) Michta, Andrew, ed. 120p. (Orig.). 1987. pap. text ed. 75.00 (*1-55831-036-3*) Delphic Associates.

Polson, Alan, ed. Periodontal Regeneration: Current Status & Directions. (Illus.). 200p. 1994. text ed. 72.00 (*0-86715-175-7*) Quint Pub Co.

Polson, Alfred, ed. Virus Separation & Purification Methods. LC 93-22933. 312p. 1993. 99.75 (*0-8247-9149-5*) Dekker.

Polson, Archer. Law & Lawyers: Sketches & Illustrations of Legal History & Biography, 2 Vols. (Illus.). 1982. reprint ed. lib. bdg. 57.50 (*0-8377-1013-8*) Rothman.

Polson, Beth & Newton, Miller. Not My Kid: A Parent's Guide to Kids & Drugs. 224p. 1985. mass mkt. 4.50 (*0-380-69997-4*) Avon.

Polson, Martha C., et al, eds. Foundations of Intelligent Tutoring Systems. 296p. 1988. pap. text ed. 27.50 (*0-8058-0054-9*) L Erlbaum Assocs.

***Polson, Nicholas G. & Tiao, George C., eds.** Bayesian Infern. (International Library of Critical Writings in Econometrics: Vol. 7). 800p. 1995. 239.95 (*1-85278-668-X*, Pub. by E Elgar Pub UK) Ashgate Pub Co.

Polster. Take Out Catering. 1993. text ed. write for info. (*0-442-01230-6*) Van Nos Reinhold.

***Polster, Erving.** A Population of Selves: A Therapeutic Exploration of Personal Diversity. LC 94-42595. (Social & Behavioral Sciences Ser.). 272p. 1995. 26.95 (*0-7879-0076-1*) Jossey-Bass.

Polster, Gary E. Inside Looking Out: The Cleveland Jewish Orphan Asylum, 1868-1924. LC 89-24414. 254p. 1990. 32.00 (*0-87338-406-7*) Kent St U Pr.

Polster, Irving & Polster, Miriam. Gestalt Therapy Integrated: Contours of Theory & Practice. LC 74-3424. 1974. pap. 9.00 (*0-394-71006-1*, V-6, Vin) Random.

Polster, J. & Lachmann, H., eds. Spectrometric Titrations: Analysis of Chemical Equilibria. LC 89-5544. 433p. 1989. lib. bdg. 170.00 (*0-89573-570-9*) VCH Pubs.

***Polster, James.** Brown: A Novel. 288p. 1995. 16.95 (*1-56352-195-4*) Longstreet Pr Inc.

***Polster, Leonard.** Pearls Before Swine. 1994. 15.95 (*0-533-10903-5*) Vantage.

Polster, Miriam, jt. auth. see Polster, Irving.

Polster, Miriam F. Eve's Daughters: The Forbidden Heroism of Women. LC 92-8806. (Social & Behavioral Science Ser.). 228p. 1992. 27.95 (*1-55542-464-3*) Jossey-Bass.

Polster, Richard A., jt. ed. see Dangel, Richard F.

Polston, Don. Living Without Losing: Finding the Secret of True Success. rev. ed. LC 75-27142. 176p. 1988. mass mkt. 3.99 (*0-89081-623-9*) Harvest Hse.

***Polt, John H.** Batilo: Estudios Sobre la Evolucion Estilistica de Melendez Valdes. LC 87-7056. (University of California Publications in Entomology: No. 119). 335p. (SPA.). 1987. pap. 95.50 (*0-7837-8421-X*, 2049223) Bks Demand.

— Gaspar Melchor de Jovellanos. LC 78-147263. (Twayne's World Authors Ser.). 163p. (C). 1971. lib. bdg. 17.95 (*0-8290-1740-2*) Irvington.

— Los Gramaticos; Historia Chinesca: Edicion Critica. LC 76-626070. (U. C. Publ. in Modern Philology Ser.: Vol. 95). 254p. reprint ed. 72.40 (*0-8357-9631-0*, 2013767) Bks Demand.

Polt, John H., tr. see Cela, Camilo J.

Polt, John H., jt. ed. see Herr, Richard.

Poltarnees, Welleran. Amy & Nathaniel. (Illus.). 32p. (J). 1991. 11.95 (*0-88138-118-7*, Green Tiger S&S) S&S Childrens.

— Children from the Golden Age. (Illus.). 128p. (J). 1991. pap. 14.95 (*0-88138-094-6*, Green Tiger S&S) S&S Childrens.

— Design in the Service of Beauty. (Illus.). 48p. 1994. 18.95 (*0-9621131-8-2*) Blue Lantern Studio.

— Friendly Book. (Illus.). 32p. 1995. 8.95 (*1-883211-05-0*) Blue Lantern Studio.

— A House Blessing. (Illus.). 48p. 1994. 18.95 (*1-883211-04-2*) Blue Lantern Studio.

— Most Memorable Birthday. (J). 1993. 15.00 (*0-671-77862-5*, Green Tiger S&S) S&S Childrens.

— Women & Flowers. (Illus.). 48p. 1994. 18.95 (*0-9621131-7-4*) Blue Lantern Studio.

Poltarnees, Welleran, et al, eds. A. B. C. of Fashionable Animals. (Illus.). 64p. (J). 1991. 12.95 (*0-88138-122-5*, Green Tiger S&S) S&S Childrens.

***Poltarness, Welleran.** Kindness Book. (Illus.). 32p. 1995. 8.95 (*0-614-07028-7*, Laugh Elephant) Blue Lantern Studio.

PQ

An Asterisk (*) at the beginning of an entry indicates that the title is appearing in BIP for the first time.

Poltawska, Wanda. And I Am Afraid of My Dreams. Craig, Mary, tr. 192p. 1989. 16.95 (*0-87052-745-2*) Hippocrene Bks.

Polte, W. & Hein, J. Clocks & Watches from the Landrock Collection. (Illus.). 296p. (C). 1988. 350.00 (*0-569-21424-6*) St Mut.

Polten, Eric P. Critique of the Psycho-Physical Identity Theory: A Refutation of Scientific Materialism & an Establishment of Mind-Matter Dualism by Means of Philosophy & Scientific Method. LC 72-94504. (Studies in the Social Sciences: No. 14). 290p. 1973. text ed. 44. 65 (*90-279-7224-9*) Mouton.

Polti, Georges. The Thirty-Six Dramatic Situations. 1988. pap. 8.95 (*0-87116-109-5*) Writer.

Poltimore, Mark, jt. auth. see Hook, Philip.

Polto, Pearl B. In America Is Bad Credit a Prison Term? LC 87-83736. 65p. (Orig.). 1988. pap. 4.95 (*0-916391-01-9*) Free & Easy Pubns.

— Pearl Polto's Easy Guide to Good Credit. 1990. pap. 7.95 (*0-425-12059-7*, Berkley Trade) Berkley Pub.

Polto, Pearl B. & Bell, Rick. We the People Have Credit Rights Too. 110p. (Orig.). 1993. pap. 5.95 (*0-9636397-0-6*) P B Polto.

Polton, D. J. Chemical Nomenclatures & the Computer. LC 93-6132. (Computers & Chemical Structure Information Ser.: Vol. 4). 264p. 1993. text ed. 91.95 (*0-471-94239-1*) Wiley.

Poltoratsky, Nikolai P. Ivan Aleksandrovich Il'in: Zhizn', Trudy, Mirovozzrenie. LC 89-7528. 320p. (Orig.). (RUS.). 1989. pap. 17.00 (*1-55779-016-7*) Hermitage.

Poltoratzky, Marianna, jt. auth. see Wolkonsky, Catherine.

Poltzer, P. & Martin, F. J., Jr., eds. Chemical Carcinogens: Activation Mechanisms, Structural & Elctronic Factors, & Reactivity. (Bioactive Molecules Ser.: No. 5). 366p. 1988. 143.75 (*0-444-43008-3*) Elsevier.

Polubarinova-Kochina, P. Theory of Ground Water Movement. De Wiest, Roger J., tr. 1962. 99.50x (*0-691-08048-8*) Princeton U Pr.

***Polubarinova-Kochina, P. Y.** Theory of Ground Water Movement. LC 62-12616. reprint ed. pap. 180.00 (*0-7837-9328-6*, 2060069) Bks Demand.

Poluchina, V., tr. see Chayanov, A.

Poluga, Charles, jt. auth. see Auvil, Daniel L.

Polugayevsky, Lyev. Grandmaster Performance. Neat, Kenneth P., tr. (Russian Chess Ser.). (Illus.). 220p. 1984. 29.90 (*0-08-026913-3*, Pergamon Pr); pap. 19.90 (*0-08-029749-8*, Pergamon Pr) Elsevier.

— Grandmaster Preparation. Neat, Kenneth P., tr. (Russian Chess Ser.). (Illus.). 240p. 1981. 29.95 (*0-08-024099-2*, Pergamon Pr); pap. 19.90 (*0-08-024098-4*, Pergamon Pr) Elsevier.

— The Sicilian Labyrinth, 2 vols., Set. (Russian Chess Ser.). 370p. 1991. pap. 45.00 (*0-08-037798-X*, P115) Macmillan.

— The Sicilian Labyrinth, Vol. I. (Russian Chess Ser.). 185p. 1991. pap. 24.95 (*0-08-032047-3*, Pub. by CHES UK) Macmillan.

— The Sicilian Labyrinth, Vol. 2. (Russian Chess Ser.). 185p. 1991. pap. 25.00 (*0-08-037796-3*) Macmillan.

Polugayevsky, Lyev & Damsky, I. Art of Defence in Chess: Defence & Counterattack Techniques in Chess. (Russian Chess Ser.). (Illus.). 270p. 1988. 29.95 (*0-08-032059-7*, Pergamon Pr); pap. 19.90 (*0-08-032058-9*, Pergamon Pr) Elsevier.

Polukhina, Valentina. Joseph Brodsky: A Poet for Our Time. (Cambridge Studies in Russian Literature). (Illus.). (C). 1989. 69.95 (*0-521-33484-5*) Cambridge U Pr.

Polukhina, Valentina, jt. ed. see Loseff, Lev.

Polumbaum, Nyna B., jt. auth. see Polumbaum, Ted.

Polumbaum, Ted & Polumbaum, Nyna B. Today Is Not Like Yesterday: A Chilean Journey. (Illus.). 132p. (Orig.). 1992. pap. 22.95 (*0-9633526-0-1*) Light & Shadow.

Polunin, Miriam. Whole-Grain Health Saver Cookbook. LC 81-84465. (Illus.). 1982. pap. 2.95 (*0-87983-270-3*) Keats.

Polunin, Miriam & Robbins, Christopher. The Natural Pharmacy. (Illus.). 144p. 1992. pap. 18.95 (*0-02-036041-X*, Collier S&S) S&S Trade.

Polunin, Nicholas & Burnett, John H., eds. Maintenance of the Biosphere: Proceedings of the Third International Conference on Environmental Future (3rd ICEF) LC 90-34387. 224p. 1990. text ed. 49.95 (*0-312-04825-4*) St Martin.

— Surviving with the Biosphere: Proceedings of the Fourth International Conference on Environmental Future. (Illus.). 561p. 1993. 79.00 (*0-7486-0314-X*, Pub. by Edinburgh U Pr UK) Col U Pr.

Polunin, Oleg. Flowers of Greece & the Balkans: A Field Guide. (Illus.). 676p. 1987. 26.95 (*0-19-281998-4*) OUP.

Polunin, Oleg & Huxley, Anthony. Flowers of the Mediterranean. (Illus.). 260p. 1990. pap. 29.95 (*0-7011-3695-2*, Pub. by Hogarth Pr UK) Trafalgar.

Polunin, Oleg & Smythies, B. E. Flowers of South-West Europe: A Field Guide. (Illus.). 584p. 1988. pap. 22.50 (*0-19-288178-7*) OUP.

Polunin, Oleg & Stainton, Adam. The Concise Flowers of the Himalaya. (Illus.). 426p. 1987. 39.95 (*0-19-561832-7*) OUP.

Polunin, Vladimir. The Continental Method of Scene Painting. Beaumont, Cyril W., ed. LC 77-19083. (Series in Dance). (Illus.). 1979. reprint ed. lib. bdg. 29.50 (*0-306-77578-6*) Da Capo.

— The Continental Method of Scene Painting. Beaumont, Cyril W., ed. (Illus.). xiii, 85p. (C). 1980. reprint ed. 29. 95 (*0-903102-57-9*, Pub. by Dance Bks UK) Princeton Bk Co.

Polushkin, Maria. The Dumpling Cookbook. LC 76-25437. (Illus.). 200p. 1976. pap. 7.95 (*0-911104-85-2*, 119) Workman Pub.

— Kitten in Trouble. LC 85-5753. (Illus.). 32p. (J). (ps-k). 1988. text ed. 13.95 (*0-02-774740-9*, Bradbury S&S) S&S Childrens.

— Mother, Mother, I Want Another. (Illus.). 32p. (J). (ps-1). 1988. pap. 5.99 (*0-517-55947-1*) Crown Bks Yng Read.

— Who Said Meow? LC 87-28073. (Illus.). 32p. (J). (ps). 1988. text ed. 13.95 (*0-02-774770-0*, Bradbury S&S) S&S Childrens.

Poluyan, Igor, tr. see Kosals, L.

***Poluyanov, L. V., et al.** Group Properties of the Acoustic Differential Equation: Separation of Variables, Exact Solution. 180p. 1995. 85.00x (*0-7484-0280-2*, Pub. by Tay Francis Ltd UK) Taylor & Francis.

Polvay. Slim & Healthy Italian Cooking. 1990. pap. 10.95 (*0-942084-33-0*) SeaSide Pub.

Polvay, Marina. All along the Danube: Recipes from Germany, Austria, Czechoslovakia, Yugoslavia, Hungary, Romania & Bulgaria. (International Cookbook Classics Ser.). (Illus.). 349p. 1992. pap. 11.95 (*0-7818-0098-6*) Hippocrene Bks.

Polvinen, Tuomo. Between East & West: Finland in International Politics, 1944-1947. Kirby, D. G. & Herring, Peter, eds. Herring, Peter, tr. LC 85-20863. (Nordic Ser.: Vol. 13). (Illus.). 374p. 1986. text ed. 44.95 (*0-8166-1459-8*) U of Minn Pr.

— Imperial Borderland: Bobrikov & the Attempted Russification of Finland, 1898-1904. Huxley, Steven, tr. LC 94-38507. (Illus.). 272p. 1995. 29.95 (*0-8223-1563-7*) Duke.

Polwhele, Richard. The English Orator: A Didactic Poem. (Anglistica & Americana Ser.: No. 16). 201p. 1968. reprint ed. 44.20 (*0-685-66504-6*, 05102037, Pub. by Georg Olms GW) Lubrecht & Cramer.

Poly, Jean-Pierre & Bournazel, Eric. The Feudal Transformation, 900-1200. LC 90-42094. (Europe Past & Present Ser.). x, 424p. 1991. 42.95 (*0-8419-1167-3*) Holmes & Meier.

Polya, D., jt. ed. see Pattrick, R. A.

Polya, George. George Polya - Collected Papers, 2 vols., Vol. 1: Singularities of Analytic Functions. Boas, Ralph, ed. 1974. Vol. 1, Singularities Of Analytic Functions. 70. 00 (*0-262-02104-8*) MIT Pr.

— George Polya - Collected Papers, 2 vols., Vol. 2: Location of Zeros. Boas, Ralph, ed. 1975. Vol. 2, 1975 Location Of Zeros. 60.00 (*0-262-02103-X*) MIT Pr.

— George Polya - Collected Papers: Analysis, Vol. III. Hersch, Joseph & Rota, Gian-Carlo, eds. (Mathematicians of Our Time Ser.: No. 22). 537p. 1984. 65.00 (*0-262-16096-X*) MIT Pr.

— Mathematical Discovery. LC 81-1063. 432p. (C). 1981. Net. pap. text ed. write for info. (*0-471-08975-3*) Wiley.

— Mathematical Methods in Science. Bowden, Leon, ed. LC 76-25863. (New Mathematical Library: No. 26). 234p. 1977. pap. 16.50 (*0-88385-626-3*) Math Assn.

— Mathematics & Plausible Reasoning, 1. (Illus.). 1990. pap. text ed. 14.95 (*0-691-02509-6*) Princeton U Pr.

— Mathematics & Plausible Reasoning, 2. (Illus.). 1990. pap. text ed. 14.95 (*0-691-02510-X*) Princeton U Pr.

— Mathematics & Plausible Reasoning, Vol. 1: Induction & Analogy in Mathematics. (Illus.). 296p. 1990. Vol. 1 Induction & Analogy in Mathematics; 296p. text ed. 39. 50 (*0-691-08005-4*) Princeton U Pr.

— Mathematics & Plausible Reasoning, Vol. 2: Patterns of Plausible Inference. (Illus.). 200p. 1990. Vol. 2 Patterns of Plausibile Inference; 200p. text ed. 39.50 (*0-691-08006-2*) Princeton U Pr.

— Mathematik und Plausibles Schliessen, 2 vols. Incl. Vol. 1. Induktion und Analogie in der Mathematik. 2nd ed. 404p. 1969. 43.95 (*0-8176-0295-X*); Vol. 2. Typen und Strukturen Plausibler Folgerung. 326p. 1980. 82.00 (*0-8176-0715-3*); (Science & Civilization Ser.: Nos. 14 & 15). write for info. (*0-318-51087-1*) Birkhauser.

— Vom Losen Mathematischer Aufgaben-Einsicht und Entdeckung, Lernen und Lehren, Vol. I. 2nd ed. (Science & Civilization Ser.: No. 20). (Illus.). 315p. (GER.). 1980. 71.00 (*0-8176-1101-0*) Birkhauser.

— Vom Losen Mathematischer Aufgaben-Einsicht und Entdeckung, Lernen und Lehren, Vol. II. (Science & Civilization Ser.: No. 21). (Illus.). 286p. 1980. 64.00 (*0-8176-0298-4*) Birkhauser.

Polya, George & Szego, G. Isoperimetric Inequalities in Mathematical Physics. (Annals of Mathematics Studies). 1951. 26.00 (*0-527-02743-X*) Periodicals Srv.

Polya, George & Szego, Gabor. Problems & Theorems in Analysis I: Series, Integral Calculus, Theory of Functions. (Illus.). 1989. reprint ed. pap. 39.00 (*0-387-90224-4*) Spr-Verlag.

— Problems & Theorems in Analysis II: Theory of Functions, Zeros, Polynomials, Determinants, Number Theory, Geometry. Billigheimer, C. E., tr. (Illus.). 1990. pap. text ed. 39.00 (*0-387-90291-0*) Spr-Verlag.

Polya, George & Szegoe, G. Problems & Theorems in Analysis I: Series, Integral Calculus, Theory of Functions. (Grundlehren der Mathematischen Wissenschaften Ser.: Vol. 193). 1978. 98.00 (*0-387-05672-6*) Spr-Verlag.

Polya, George, et al. Complex Variables. LC 73-14882. 343p. reprint ed. pap. 97.80 (*0-317-09340-1*, 2055266) Bks Demand.

— Notes on Introductory Combinatorics. (Progress in Computer Science Ser.: Vol. 4). 1990. 21.95 (*3-7643-3123-2*); pap. 29.50 (*0-8176-3170-4*) Birkhauser.

— The Stanford Mathematics Problem Book: With Hints & Solutions. LC 73-86270. 72p. reprint ed. pap. 25.00 (*0-317-09309-6*, 2019663) Bks Demand.

Polya, Gyorgy. How to Solve It. 1971. 37.50 (*0-691-08097-6*); pap. 9.95 (*0-691-02356-5*) Princeton U Pr.

Polyachenko, V. I., jt. auth. see Fridman, A. M.

Polyachenko, V. L., jt. auth. see Fridman, A. M.

***Polyaenus.** Polyaenus: Strategems of War, Vol. I. Krentz, Peter & Wheeler, Everett L., eds. Wheeler, Everett L., tr. (Orig.). 1994. pap. 22.50 (*0-614-00174-9*) Ares.

— Polyaenus: Strategems of War, 2 vols., Vol. I. rev. ed. Krentz, Peter & Wheeler, Everett L., eds. Wheeler, Everett L., tr. 400p. (Orig.). (GRE.). (C). 1994. pap. text ed. 45.00 (*0-89005-503-3*) Ares.

— Polyaenus: Strategems of War, Vol. II. Krentz, Peter & Wheeler, Everett L., eds. Wheeler, Everett L., tr. 400p. (Orig.). 1994. pap. 22.50 (*0-614-00176-5*) Ares.

— Stratagems of War. Krentz, Peter & Wheeler, Everett L., eds. Wheeler, Everett L., tr. (Orig.). (C). 1994. pap. text ed. 45.00 (*0-614-00203-6*) Ares.

— Stratagems of War II, 2 vols., Set. Krentz, Peter & Wheeler, Everett L., eds. Wheeler, Everett L., tr. iii, 542p. (Orig.). (C). 1994. pap. write for info. (*0-89005-504-1*) Ares.

Polyak, B. T. Introduction to Optimization. Balakrishnan, A. V., ed. LC 87-11290. (Translations Series in Mathematics & Engineering). 464p. 1987. text ed. 95.00 (*0-911575-14-6*) Optimization Soft.

Polyakov, A. F., ed. Thermo & Laser Anemometry. 186p. 1988. 58.00 (*0-89116-607-6*) Hemisp Pub.

Polyakov, A. F., jt. auth. see Pethukov, B. S.

Polyakov, A. M. Gauge Fields & Strings. (Contemporary Concepts in Physics Ser.: Vol. 3). 312p. 1987. text ed. 51.00 (*3-7186-0393-4*); pap. text ed. 19.00 (*3-7186-0392-6*) Gordon & Breach.

Polyakov, I. Y., jt. auth. see Gromov, I. M.

Polyakov, V. A., jt. auth. see Ferronsky, V. I.

Polyakova, A. A. & Khel'nitskii, R. A. Introduction to Mass Spectrometry of Organic Compounds. 160p. 1968. text ed. 43.00 (*0-7065-0605-7*, Pub. by Keter Pub IS) Coronet Bks.

Polyani, Karl & Rotsfein, Abraham. Dahomey & the Slave Trade: An Analysis of an Archaic Economy. LC 84-45535. (American Ethnological Society Monographs: No. 42). 1988. reprint ed. 30.00 (*0-404-62940-7*) AMS Pr.

Polyani, M. Jenseits des Nihilismus: Dreizehnte Vorlesung zum Gedaechtnis Von Arthur Stanley Eddington. Nitz, Irmela, tr. 45p. (GER.). 1961. pap. text ed. 26.50 (*90-277-0010-9*) Kluwer Ac.

Polyanin, A. D. & Dilman, V. V. Methods of Modeling Equations & Analogies in Chemical Engineering. 310p. 1993. 125.00 (*0-89116-769-2*) Begell Hse.

Polyanin, Andrei D. & Dilman, Victor V. Methods of Modeling Equations & Analogies in Chemical Engineering. Piterman, Mark A., tr. LC 93-2356. 1994. write for info. (*0-8493-9914-9*) CRC Pr.

***Polyanin, Andrei D. & Zaitsev, Valentin F.** Handbook of Exact Solutions for Ordinary Differential Equations. LC 95-1021. 720p. 1995. 95.00 (*0-8493-9438-4*, 9438) CRC Pr.

Polybe. Histoire. 1672p. 42.95 (*0-686-56553-3*) Fr & Eur.

Polybius. Histoire. (FRE.). 1989. lib. bdg. 105.00 (*0-8288-3528-4*, F22081) Fr & Eur.

— The Histories. Badian, E., ed. Chambers, Mortimer, tr. 340p. 1986. reprint ed. 29.50 (*0-8290-2014-4*) Irvington.

— Histories, 6 vols., 1. (Loeb Classical Library: No. 128, 137-138, 159-161). 442p. 1922. 18.95 (*0-674-99142-7*) HUP.

— Histories, 6 vols., 2. (Loeb Classical Library: No. 128, 137-138, 159-161). 528p. 1922. 18.95 (*0-674-99152-4*) HUP.

— Histories, 6 vols., 3. (Loeb Classical Library: No. 128, 137-138, 159-161). 560p. 1923. 18.95 (*0-674-99153-2*) HUP.

— Histories, 6 vols., 4. (Loeb Classical Library: No. 128, 137-138, 159-161). 570p. 1925. 18.95 (*0-674-99175-3*) HUP.

— Histories, 6 vols., 5. (Loeb Classical Library: No. 128, 137-138, 159-161). 542p. 1926. 18.95 (*0-674-99176-1*) HUP.

— Histories, 6 vols., 6. (Loeb Classical Library: No. 128, 137-138, 159-161). 574p. 1927. 18.95 (*0-674-99178-8*) HUP.

— The Histories of Polybius, Discoursing of the Warres Betwixt the Romanes & Carthaginenses. Watson, Christopher, tr. LC 75-25683. (English Experience Ser.: No. 132). 1969. reprint ed. 55.00 (*90-221-0132-0*) Walter J Johnson.

— Polybius on Roman Imperialism. Bernstein, Alvin H., ed. Shuckburgh, Evelyn S., tr. LC 79-66479. 540p. (Orig.). 1980. pap. text ed. 10.95 (*0-89526-902-3*) Regnery Pub.

— The Rise of the Roman Empire. Scott-Kilvert, Ian, tr. 1980. pap. 10.95 (*0-14-044362-2*, Penguin Classics) Viking Penguin.

Polycarpou, Susan, jt. auth. see Shoemaker, Connie.

Polychroniou, Chronis. Marxist Perspectives on Imperialism: A Theoretical Analysis. LC 90-45483. 200p. 1991. text ed. 45.00 (*0-275-93720-8*, C3720, Praeger Pubs) Greenwood.

Polychroniou, Chronis, ed. Perspectives & Issues in International Political Economy. LC 92-7496. 288p. 1992. text ed. 59.95 (*0-275-94016-0*, C4016, Praeger Pubs) Greenwood.

— Socialism: Crisis & Renewal. LC 92-36546. 272p. 1993. text ed. 57.95 (*0-275-94089-6*, C4089, Praeger Pubs) Greenwood.

***Polychroniou, Chronis & Targ, Harry R., eds.** Marxism Today: Essays on Capitalism, Socialism, & Strategies for Social Change. LC 95-14301. 1995. text ed. write for info. (*0-275-94604-5*, Praeger Pubs) Greenwood.

Polydoris, Nicholas, jt. auth. see Green, Orville C., III.

Polymetric Materials Division Staff. Particle Size Distribution: Assessment & Characterization: Symposium of the 190th Meeting, Chicago, IL, September 8-13, 1985. Provder, Theodore J., ed. LC 86-32185. (ACS Symposium Ser.: No. 332). (Illus.). x, 308p. 1987. 59.95 (*0-8412-1016-0*) Am Chemical.

Polytechnic Institute of New York Staff. Stress Relaxation in Copper-Base Alloys. 188p. 1974. 28.20 (*0-317-34549-4*, 207) Intl Copper.

Polyviou, Polyvios G. Cyprus: Conflict & Negotiation 1960-1980. LC 80-25942. 246p. 1981. 49.50 (*0-8419-0683-1*) Holmes & Meier.

Polywka, John & Gabrel, Stanley. Programming of Computer Numerical Controlled Machines. (Illus.). 256p. 1991. 34.95 (*0-8311-3035-0*) Indus Pr.

Polyzoides, G. Ancient Greek History. (Illus.). (GRE.). (J). (gr. 4-6). 4.00 (*0-686-79636-5*) Divry.

— History & Teachings of the Eastern Greek Orthodox Church. (Illus.). 96p. 5.00 (*0-686-83964-1*) Divry.

— History of Byzantine & Modern Greece. (Illus.). (GRE.). (J). (gr. 4-6). 4.00 (*0-686-79635-7*) Divry.

Polyzoides, G. Stories from the New Testament. (Illus.). 112p. (GRE.). 4.00 (*0-686-83966-8*) Divry.

Polyzoides, G. Stories from the Old Testament. (Illus.). 71p. (GRE.). (J). (gr. 5 up). 4.00 (*0-686-80434-1*) Divry.

— What We See & Hear in a Greek Eastern Orthodox Church. 92p. 5.00 (*0-686-83965-X*) Divry.

Polyzoides, M. Catechism of Eastern Greek Orthodox Church. 96p. 5.00 (*0-686-79625-X*) Divry.

Polyzoides, Stefanos, et al. Courtyard Housing in Los Angeles. LC 92-1072. (Illus.). 232p. 1992. reprint ed. pap. 24.95 (*0-910413-53-3*) Princeton Arch.

Polzer, Charles. Kino Guide II. LC 82-50218. (Illus.). 76p. 1982. pap. 7.00 (*0-915076-07-1*) SW Mission.

— Rules & Precepts of the Jesuit Missions of Northwestern New Spain. LC 75-8456. 141p. 1976. pap. 10.95 (*0-8165-0488-1*) U of Ariz Pr.

Polzer, Charles W., ed. see Cabat, Erni.

Polzer, Charles W., jt. auth. see Cabat, Erni.

Polzer, Charles W., jt. ed. see Naylor, Thomas H.

Polzer, Charles W., et al. Tucson: A Short History. LC 85-63503. (Illus.). 160p. (Orig.). 1986. pap. 8.95 (*0-915076-11-X*) SW Mission.

Polzer, Charles W., et al, eds. The Jesuit Missions of Northern Mexico. LC 91-25507. (Spanish Borderlands Sourcebooks Ser.: Vol. 19). 592p. 1991. 126.00 (*0-8240-2096-0*) Garland.

Polzer-Hoditz, Ludwig C. Memories of Rudolf Steiner. 1987. pap. 9.95 (*0-916786-93-5*, Saint George Pubns) R Steiner Col Pubns.

Polzin, Robert. David & the Deuteronomist: A Literary Study of the Deuteronomic History, Pt. 3: 2 Samuel. LC 93-22056. (Literary Study of the Deuteronomic History Ser.: Pt. 3). 1993. 39.95 (*0-253-34553-7*) Ind U Pr.

— Moses & the Deuteronomist: A Literary Study of the Deuteronomic History, Pt. 1. LC 93-7715. (Indiana Studies in Biblical Literature). 1993. reprint ed. 27.95 (*0-253-34554-5*); reprint ed. pap. 14.95 (*0-253-20848-3*) Ind U Pr.

— Samuel & the Deuteronomist: A Literary Study of the Deuteronomic History, Pt. 2: 1 Samuel. LC 92-43856. (Indiana Studies in Biblical Literature: Pt. 2). (C). 1993. 35.00 (*0-253-34552-9*); pap. 14.95 (*0-253-20849-1*) Ind U Pr.

Polzin, Robert & Rothman, Eugene, eds. The Biblical Mosaic. (Masoretic Studies). 1982. pap. 15.95 (*0-89130-692-7*, 06 06 10) Scholars Pr GA.

Polzin, Robert M. Biblical Structuralism: Method & Subjectivity in the Study of Ancient Texts. LC 76-15895. (Semeia Supplements Ser.). (Illus.). 224p. reprint ed. pap. 63.90 (*0-7837-5413-2*, 2045177) Bks Demand.

Polzin, T. & Stute, H. Intercomparison of Microhardness Measurements. 92p. 1992. pap. 12.00 (*92-826-3711-5*, CD-NA-13971-EN-, Pub. by Europ Com) UNIPUB.

Pom-son, Yi, jt. auth. see Sun-Won, Hwang.

Pomada, Elizabeth. Places to Go with Children in Northern California. LC 92-24736. 1993. pap. 9.95 (*0-8118-0261-2*) Chronicle Bks.

Pomada, Elizabeth & Larsen, Michael. America's Painted Ladies: The Ultimate Celebration of Our Victorians. LC 92-52872. (Illus.). 304p. 1992. 40.00 (*0-525-93440-5*, Dutton Studio) Studio Bks.

— America's Painted Ladies: The Ultimate Celebration of Our Victorians. LC 92-52872. (Illus.). 304p. 1994. 24.95 (*0-14-023857-3*, Viking Studio) Studio Bks.

— The Painted Ladies Guide to Victorian California. (Illus.). 128p. 1991. 29.95 (*0-525-93363-8*, Dutton Studio); pap. 18.95 (*0-525-48594-5*, Dutton Studio) Studio Bks.

— The Painted Ladies Revisited: San Francisco's Resplendent Victorians Inside & Out. (Illus.). 144p. 1989. pap. 22.95 (*0-525-48508-2*, Dutton) NAL-Dutton.

Pomada, Elizabeth, jt. auth. see Larsen, Michael.

Pomann, jt. auth. see Foley.

Pomann, Howard & Foley, Barbara. Lifelines, No. 2. (Lifelines Ser.). (Illus.). (gr. 9-12). 1987. pap. text ed. 7.00 (*0-13-535923-6*, 20026) Prentice ESL.

— Lifelines, No. 3. (Lifelines Ser.). (Illus.). 97p. (gr. 9-12). 1987. pap. text ed. 7.00 (*0-13-535931-7*, 20038) Prentice ESL.

— Lifelines, No.1. (Lifelines Ser.). (Illus.). 99p. (gr. 9-12). 1987. pap. text ed. 7.00 (*0-13-535915-5*, 20014) Prentice ESL.

— Lifelines, No.4. (Lifelines Ser.). (Illus.). (gr. 9-12). 1987. pap. text ed. 7.00 (*0-13-535949-X*, 20040) Prentice ESL.

Pomann, Howard, jt. auth. see Foley, Barbara.

Pomarantsev, A. A. Thermal Stresses in Solids of Revolution of Arbitrary Shape. 136p. 1970. text ed. 121.00 (*0-677-30460-9*) Gordon & Breach.

Pomare, Maui, et al. Legends of the Maori, 2 vols., Set. LC 75-35265. (Illus.). 1976. reprint ed. 125.00 (*0-404-14350-4*) AMS Pr.

***Pomares, Henry.** George Duncan Wickham. (Illus.). 1994. 15.00 (*0-9641486-0-9*) Goshen Chamber.

Pomares, Jose M., tr. see Thoele, Sue P.

Pomarnatsii, A. V., jt. auth. see Glinka, V. M.

Pomarska, Krystyna, jt. auth. see Jakobson, Roman.

An Asterisk (*) at the beginning of an entry indicates that the title is appearing in BIP for the first time.

***Pomaska, Ann.** Invisible ABC Magic Picture Book. (Invisible Magic Picture Books). (J). (ps). 1994. pap. text ed. 1.00 (0-486-28393-3) Dover.

— Invisible Circus Magic Picture Book. (Invisible Magic Picture Bks). (J). (ps). 1994. pap. text ed. 1.00 (0-486-28394-1) Dover.

Pomaska, Anna. Alphabet Hidden Picture Coloring Book. (Illus.). (J). (gr. k-3). 1992. pap. 2.50 (0-486-27261-3) Dover.

— Color Your Own Happy Birthday Postcards. (Illus.). (J). (gr. 4-7). 1993. pap. 1.00 (0-486-27837-9) Dover.

— Color Your Own Thank You Postcards. (Illus.). (J). (gr. 4-7). 1993. pap. 1.00 (0-486-27838-7) Dover.

— Create Your Own Pictures Coloring Book. (Illus.). (J). 1984. pap. 2.50 (0-486-24614-0) Dover.

— Cut & Assemble a Peter Rabbit. (J). 1984. pap. 4.95 (0-486-24713-9) Dover.

— Dinosaur Sticker Book. (Illus.). (J). (gr. k-3). 1989. pap. 1.00 (0-486-25907-2) Dover.

— Easy Animal Mazes. (Illus.). (J). (gr. k-3). 1990. pap. 1.00 (0-486-26282-0) Dover.

— Easy Mazes Activity Book. (Activity Bk.). (Illus.). (J). (ps up). 1988. pap. 1.00 (0-486-25531-X) Dover.

— Easy Search-a-Word Puzzles. 1991. pap. 1.00 (0-486-26672-9) Dover.

— Fairy Tale Hidden Coloring Book. (Illus.). (J). (gr. k-3). 1982. pap. 2.50 (0-486-24284-6) Dover.

— Follow-the-Dots Coloring Book. (Illus.). (J). 1983. pap. 2.50 (0-486-24543-8) Dover.

— Fun with Letters Coloring Book. (Illus.). (J). (gr. k-3). 1986. pap. 2.50 (0-486-25104-7) Dover.

— Fun with Numbers Coloring Book. (Illus.). (J). (gr. 4-7). 1984. pap. 2.50 (0-486-24707-4) Dover.

— Fun with Opposites Coloring Book. (Illus.). (J). (gr. 4-7). 1989. pap. 2.50 (0-486-25983-8) Dover.

— Hidden Picture Puzzle Coloring Book. (Illus.). (J). (gr. k-3). 1976. pap. 2.50 (0-486-23909-8) Dover.

— Little ABC Coloring Book. (Illus.). (J). (gr. k-3). 1989. pap. 1.00 (0-486-25156-X) Dover.

— The Little Alphabet Follow-the-Dots Book. (Activity Bk.). (J). (ps up). 1988. pap. 1.00 (0-486-25623-5) Dover.

— The Little Christmas Activity Book. (Activity Bk.). (J). (ps up). 1988. pap. 1.00 (0-486-25679-0) Dover.

— The Little Dinosaur Activity Book. (J). (ps up). 1987. pap. 1.00 (0-486-25344-9) Dover.

— The Little Follow the Dots Book. (J). 1986. pap. 1.00 (0-486-25157-8) Dover.

— Little Jemima Puddle Duck Stickers. (Illus.). (J). (gr. k-3). 1993. pap. 1.00 (0-486-27637-6) Dover.

— Little Mother Goose Coloring Book. (Illus.). (J). (gr. k-3). 1986. pap. 1.00 (0-486-25158-6) Dover.

— Little Numbers Coloring Book. (Illus.). (J). (gr. k-3). 1989. pap. 1.00 (0-486-25345-7) Dover.

— Little Old MacDonald's Farm Coloring Book. (Illus.). (J). (gr. k-3). 1986. pap. 1.00 (0-486-25159-4) Dover.

— The Little Seashore Activity Book. (Activity Bk.). (J). (ps up). 1988. pap. 1.00 (0-486-25608-1) Dover.

— Little Tom Kitten Stickers. (Illus.). (J). (gr. k-3). 1993. pap. 1.00 (0-486-27640-6) Dover.

— Make Your Own Calendar Coloring Book. (Illus.). (J). (gr. k-3). 1976. pap. 2.50 (0-486-24193-9) Dover.

— My Camp Book Diary. (J). (gr. k-3). 1991. pap. 1.00 (0-486-26641-9) Dover.

— My Diary. (J). (gr. 4-8). 1989. pap. 1.00 (0-486-26095-X) Dover.

— Peter Rabbit Bookmarks. (J). (ps up). 1989. pap. 3.50 (0-486-25444-5) Dover.

— Rainbow Sticker Book. (Illus.). (J). (gr. k-3). 1989. pap. 1.00 (0-486-25910-2) Dover.

— Six Hidden Picture Postcards. (Illus.). (J). (gr. k-3). 1994. pap. 1.00 (0-486-27926-X) Dover.

— What's Wrong with This Picture? Coloring Book. (Illus.). (J). (gr. k-3). 1983. pap. 2.50 (0-486-24485-7) Dover.

Pomaska, Anna, jt. auth. see Potter, Beatrix.

Pomazansky, Michael. The Old Testament in the New Testament Church. 40p. (Orig.). 1994. pap. 2.00 (0-317-30281-7) Holy Trinity.

— Orthodox Dogmatic Theology: A Concise Exposition. 2nd ed. Rose, Seraphim, tr. & pref. by. LC 84-51294. 430p. (Orig.). (C). 1994. pap. 19.95 (0-938635-69-7) St Herman AK.

Pombeiro, A. J. & McCleverty, J. A., eds. Molecular Electrochemistry of Inorganic, Bioinorganic & Organometallic Compounds: Proceedings of the NATO Advanced Research Workshop, Sintra, Portugal, March 25-29, 1992. LC 92-40897. (NATO Advanced Science Institutes Series C: Mathematical & Physical Sciences: Series C, Vol. 385). 692p. (C). 1992. lib. bdg. 250.00 (0-7923-2077-8) Kluwer Ac.

Pomberger, G. Software Engineering Tools for Professional Workstations: The Lilith Project. 1991. boxed 48.00 (0-13-823485-X) P-H.

Pomberger, G. & Bischofberger, W. Protyping-Oriented Software Development: Concepts & Tools. Gries, David, ed. LC 92-18009. (Texts & Monographs in Computer Science). (Illus.). xi, 215p. 1992. 49.00 (0-387-55448-3) Spr-Verlag.

Pombo, Fernando. Doing Business in Spain. 1987. write for info. (0-8205-1107-2) Bender.

Pombo, Fernando, jt. ed. see Campbell, Dennis.

Pomeau, Rene, jt. auth. see Beaumarchais, Pierre de.

Pomeau, Rene, ed. see Rousseau, Jean-Jacques.

Pomeau, Rene, ed. see Voltaire, Francois-Marie de.

Pomedli, Michael. Ethnophilosophical & Ethnolinguistic Perspectives on the Huron Indian Soul. LC 91-28521. 196p. 1991. lib. bdg. 79.95 (0-7734-9618-1) E Mellen.

— William Kurelek's Huronia Mission Paintings. LC 91-20048. (Canadian Studies: Vol. 14). (Illus.). 196p. 1991. lib. bdg. 79.95 (0-7734-9731-5) E Mellen.

Pomer, Marshall I. Intergenerational Occupational Mobility in the United States: A Segmentation Perspective. LC 80-20626. (University of Florida Monographs: Social Sciences: No. 66). 112p. (Orig.). reprint ed. pap. 32.00 (0-7837-5099-4, 2044798) Bks Demand.

Pomer, S. & Hull, W. E., eds. Magnetic Resonance in Nephrourology: Clinical & Experimental Applications. LC 93-9946. 1993. Alk. paper. 110.00 (0-387-56450-0) Spr-Verlag.

Pomer, S., jt. ed. see Staehler, G.

Pomerance. Cryptology & Computational Number Theory. LC 90-1248. (PSAPM Ser.: Vol. 42). 171p. 1990. 59.00 (0-8218-0155-4, PSAPM-42) Am Math.

Pomerance, Alan. Repeal of the Blues: How Black Entertainers Influenced Civil Rights. (Illus.). 288p. 1988. 17.95 (0-8065-1105-2, Citadel Pr) Carol Pub Group.

— Repeal of the Blues: How Black Entertainers Influenced Civil Rights. 1991. pap. 10.95 (0-8065-1244-X, Citadel Pr) Carol Pub Group.

Pomerance, Bernard. The Elephant Man. 72p. 1987. pap. 8.95 (0-8021-3041-0) Grove-Atltic.

Pomerance, H. H. & Bercu, B. B., eds. Topics in Pediatrics: A Festschrift for Lewis A. Barness. xxvi, 307p. 1990. 121.00 (0-387-96964-0) Spr-Verlag.

Pomerance, Jeffrey J. Neonatology for the Clinician. (Illus.). 464p. (C). 1993. text ed. 90.00 (0-8385-8027-0, A8027-3) Appleton & Lange.

Pomerance, Murray, ed. Ludwig Bemelmans: A Comprehensive Bibliography. (Illus.). 416p. 1995. 75.00 (0-87008-140-3) JAS Heineman.

Pomerance, Susan. For Women: Monologues They Haven't Heard. 64p. 1985. pap. 7.95 (0-9611792-6-0) Dramaline Pubns.

— Modern Scenes for Women. 50p. (Orig.). 1989. pap. 7.95 (0-940669-10-2) Dramaline Pubns.

— Woman: One Act Monologues for Women. 64p. 1988. pap. 8.95 (0-940669-07-2) Dramaline Pubns.

***Pomeraning, Denise O.** Operation Melody. LC 94-72210. (J). (gr. 4-7). 1994. pap. 3.99 (0-8066-2718-2, Augsburg) Augsburg Fortress.

Pomerans, A. J., tr. see Boehlich, Walter, ed.

Pomerans, A. J., tr. see Kiepenheuer, Karl O.

Pomerans, Arnold, tr. see Friedman, Carl.

Pomerans, Arnold, tr. see Presser, Jacob.

Pomerans, Arnold J., tr. see Claus, Hugo.

Pomerans, Arnold J., tr. see Frank, Anne.

Pomerans, Arnold J., tr. see Heisenberg, Werner.

Pomerans, Arnold J., tr. see Herrmann, Paul.

Pomerans, Arnold J., tr. see Molnar, Miklos.

Pomerans, Arnold J., tr. see Pahl, G. & Beitz, W.

Pomerans, Arnold J., tr. see Selvini, Matteo, ed.

Pomerans, Arnold J., tr. see Van Oostrom, Frits P.

Pomerans, Arnold J., tr. see Von Koenigswald, G. H.

Pomerans, Erica, tr. see Friedman, Carl.

Pomerantz, Barbara. Bubby, Me & Memories. LC 83-191743. (Illus.). 32p. (J). (ps up). 1983. 7.95 (0-8074-0253-2, 104025) UAHC.

— Who Will Lead Kiddush? (Illus.). 32p. (Orig.). (J). (gr. 1-3). 1985. pap. 6.00 (0-8074-0306-7, 102000) UAHC.

Pomerantz, Charlotte. The Chalk Doll. LC 88-872. (Illus.). 32p. (J). (gr. k-3). 1989. 15.00 (0-397-32318-2, Lipp Jr Bks); lib. bdg. 14.89 (0-397-32319-0, Lipp Jr Bks) HarpC Child Bks.

— Chalk Doll. LC 88-872. (Illus.). 32p. (J). (ps-3). 1993. pap. 4.95 (0-06-443333-1, Trophy) HarpC Child Bks.

— Flap Your Wings & Try. LC 88-18766. (Illus.). 24p. (J). (ps up). 1989. 12.95 (0-688-08019-7); lib. bdg. 12.88 (0-688-08020-0) Greenwillow.

— Halfway to Your House. LC 92-30083. (Illus.). 32p. (J). (ps up). 1993. 14.00 (0-688-11804-6); lib. bdg. 13.93 (0-688-11805-4) Greenwillow.

— Here Comes Henny. LC 93-5480. 24p. (J). 1994. 14.00 (0-688-12355-4); lib. bdg. 13.93 (0-688-12356-2) Greenwillow.

— How Many Trucks Can a Tow Truck Tow. LC 89-3657. (Tough Enough for Toddlers Ser.). (Illus.). 24p. (J). (ps-00). 1987. pap. 6.00 (0-394-88775-1) Random Bks Yng Read.

— If I Had a Paka. LC 81-6624. (Illus.). 32p. (J). (ps). 1993. 14.00 (0-688-11900-X); lib. bdg. 13.93 (0-688-11901-8) Greenwillow.

— If I Had a Paka: Poems in Eleven Languages. (Illus.). 32p. (J). 1982. 11.75 (0-688-00836-4); lib. bdg. 11.88 (0-688-00837-2) Greenwillow.

— If I Had a Paka: Poems in Eleven Languages. LC 92-33088. (Illus.). 32p. (J). (ps up). 1993. pap. 4.95 (0-688-12510-7, Mulberry) Morrow.

— One Duck, Another Duck. LC 83-20767. (Illus.). 24p. (J). (ps-1). 1984. 14.00 (0-688-03744-5); lib. bdg. 13.93 (0-688-03745-3) Greenwillow.

— The Outside Dog. LC 91-6351. (I Can Read Bk.). (Illus.). 64p. (J). (gr. k-3). 1993. 14.95 (0-06-024782-7); lib. bdg. 14.89 (0-06-024783-5) HarpC Child Bks.

— The Outside Dog. LC 91-6351. (I Can Read Bks.). (Illus.). 64p. (J). (gr. k-3). 1995. 3.50 (0-06-444187-3, Trophy) HarpC Child Bks.

— The Piggy in the Puddle. LC 73-6047. (Illus.). 32p. (J). (ps-1). 1974. text ed. 14.95 (0-02-774900-2, Mac Bks Young Read) S&S Childrens.

— The Piggy in the Puddle. LC 88-8368. (Illus.). 32p. (J). (ps-1). 1989. reprint ed. pap. 4.95 (0-689-71293-6, Aladdin Paperbacks) S&S Childrens.

— The Princess & the Admiral. (Illus.). 1992. 17.95 (1-55861-060-X); pap. 8.95 (1-55861-061-8) Feminist Pr.

— Serena Katz. LC 90-48672. (Illus.). 32p. (J). (gr. k-3). 1992. text ed. 13.95 (0-02-774901-0, Mac Bks Young Read) S&S Childrens.

— The Tamarindo Puppy. LC 79-16584. (Illus.). 32p. (J). (ps up). 1993. 14.00 (0-688-11902-6); lib. bdg. 13.93 (0-688-11903-4) Greenwillow.

— The Tamarindo Puppy & Other Poems. LC 79-16584. (Illus.). 32p. (J). (ps up). 1993. reprint ed. pap. 4.95 (0-688-11514-4, Mulberry) Morrow.

— Timothy Tall Feather. LC 85-24819. (Illus.). 32p. (J). (gr. k-3). 1986. 11.75 (0-688-04246-5); lib. bdg. 11.88 (0-688-04247-3) Greenwillow.

— Where's the Bear? LC 83-1697. (Illus.). 32p. (J). (ps-1). 1984. 15.00 (0-688-01752-5); lib. bdg. 14.93 (0-688-01753-3) Greenwillow.

— Where's the Bear. LC 83-1697. (Illus.). 32p. (J). (ps up). 1991. reprint ed. pap. 3.95 (0-688-10999-3, Mulberry) Morrow.

— Whiff, Sniff, Nibble, & Chew: The Gingerbread Boy Retold. LC 83-14179. (Illus.). 24p. (J). (gr. k-3). 1984. lib. bdg. 8.59 (0-688-02552-8) Greenwillow.

— You're Not My Best Friend Anymore. LC 93-42595. (J). 1995. write for info. (0-8037-1559-5); lib. bdg. write for info. (0-8037-1560-9) Dial Bks Young.

Pomerantz, Edward. Brisburial: A Feast. 1981. 14.95 (0-913660-13-2); pap. 7.95 (0-913660-14-0) Magic Cir Pr CT.

***Pomerantz, Ellene.** Aurora. 450p. Date not set. pap. 12.95 (0-7610-0382-7) NW Pub.

Pomerantz, James, jt. ed. see Lockhead, Gregory.

***Pomerantz, Kay.** Come for Anything but Cholent. 110p. 1995. pap. 9.95 (0-8197-0615-9) Bloch.

— Come for Cholent. LC 91-35294. 90p. 1992. pap. 7.95 (0-8197-0598-5) Bloch.

Pomerantz, Kay K. Come for Cholent Again: Cholent Stories & More Recipes. LC 93-30062. 1993. pap. 9.95 (0-8197-0602-7) Bloch.

Pomerantz, L. Know What You See: The Examination of Paintings by Photo-Optical Techniques. 1976. 1.25 (0-318-18695-0) Am Inst Conser Hist.

Pomerantz, Louis. Is Your Contemporary Painting More Temporary Than You Think? 2nd ed. LC 62-15290. (Illus.). 1962. pap. 5.00 (0-910790-00-0) Intl Bk Co IL.

Pomerantz, Rachel. Wildflower. (Illus.). 442p. (C). 1989. 18.95 (1-56062-020-X, Bristol Rhein) CIS Comm.

— Wings above the Flames. 400p. (C). 1991. 17.95 (1-56062-066-8) CIS Comm.

Pomerantz, Roger J., jt. ed. see Laughlin, Mark A.

Pomerantz, Susan, jt. auth. see Muench, Teri.

Pomerantz, Yitzchack. Clizek, Be Strong. LC 93-72594. (Illus.). 300p. 1993. 18.95 (1-56062-225-3) CIS Comm.

Pomerantz-Zhang, Linda. Wu Tingfang (1842-1922) Reform & Modernization in Modern Chinese History. 320p. (Orig.). 1992. pap. 67.50 (962-209-287-X, Pub. by Hong Kong Univ Pr HK) Coronet Bks.

Pomerantzev, B. I. Arachnida Ixodid Ticks (Ixodae) Elbl, A. & Anastos, G., trs. 1959. 17.95 (0-934454-08-6) Lubrecht & Cramer.

Pomeranz. Craniospinal Magnetic Resonance Imaging. 624p. 1989. text ed. 179.00 (0-7216-2428-6) Saunders.

Pomeranz, B., jt. auth. see Stux, G.

Pomeranz, Felix. Successful Audit: New Ways to Reduce Risk Exposure & Increase Efficiency. 512p. 1991. 65.00 (1-55623-391-4) Irwin Prof Pubng.

Pomeranz, Kenneth. The Making of a Hinterland: State, Society, & Economy in Inland North China, 1853-1937. LC 92-17008. 1993. 40.00 (0-520-08051-3) U CA Pr.

Pomeranz, Stephen J. Orthopaedic MRI: A Teaching File. (Illus.). 416p. 1991. text ed. 98.00 (0-397-51105-1) Lippincott.

Pomeranz, Virginia E. First Five Years. 1987. pap. 3.95 (0-317-65471-3) St Martin.

Pomeranz, Y. Modern Cereal Science & Technology. LC 87-13364. 468p. 1987. lib. bdg. 130.00 (0-89573-326-9) VCH Pubs.

Pomeranz, Y., ed. Advances in Cereal Science & Technology, Vol. II. LC 76-8695. 463p. 1978. pap. text ed. 80.00 (0-913250-08-2) Am Assn Cereal Chem.

— Advances in Cereal Science & Technology, Vol. III. LC 76-645872. 348p. 1980. pap. text ed. 80.00 (0-913250-16-3) Am Assn Cereal Chem.

— Advances in Cereal Science & Technology, Vol. IV. LC 76-645872. 342p. 1981. pap. text ed. 80.00 (0-913250-21-X) Am Assn Cereal Chem.

— Advances in Cereal Science & Technology, Vol. V. LC 76-645872. 294p. 1982. pap. text ed. 80.00 (0-913250-28-7) Am Assn Cereal Chem.

— Advances in Cereal Science & Technology, Vol. VI. LC 76-645872. 403p. 1984. pap. text ed. 80.00 (0-913250-33-3) Am Assn Cereal Chem.

— Advances in Cereal Science & Technology, Vol. VII. LC 76-645872. 362p. 1985. pap. text ed. 80.00 (0-913250-39-2) Am Assn Cereal Chem.

— Advances in Cereal Science & Technology, Vol. VIII. LC 76-645872. 364p. 1986. 80.00 (0-913250-45-7) Am Assn Cereal Chem.

— Advances in Cereal Science & Technology, Vol. IX. LC 76-645872. (Illus.). 345p. 1988. 80.00 (0-913250-51-1) Am Assn Cereal Chem.

— Advances in Cereal Science & Technology, Vol. X. LC 76-645872. (Illus.). 557p. 1990. 80.00 (0-913250-66-X) Am Assn Cereal Chem.

— Wheat: Chemistry & Technology, 2 vols., Set. 3rd ed. LC 88-71636. (Monograph Ser.). 1988. 145.00x (0-685-21698-5, 20000) Am Assn Cereal Chem.

— Wheat: Chemistry & Technology, 2 vols., Vol. I. 3rd ed. LC 88-71636. (Monograph Ser.). 514p. 1988. 90.00 (0-913250-65-1) Am Assn Cereal Chem.

— Wheat: Chemistry & Technology, 2 vols., Vol. II. 3rd ed. LC 88-71636. (Monograph Ser.). 562p. 1988. 90.00 (0-913250-73-2) Am Assn Cereal Chem.

— Wheat Is Unique: Structure, Composition, Processing, End-Use Properties, & Products. LC 89-84430. (Illus.). 715p. 1989. 89.00x (0-913250-68-6) Am Assn Cereal Chem.

Pomeranz, Y. & Munck, Lars, eds. Cereals: A Renewable Resource, Theory & Practice. LC 81-71369. 728p. 1981. 69.00x (0-913250-22-8) Am Assn Cereal Chem.

Pomeranz, Yeshajahu & Meloan, Clifton E. Food Analysis: Theory & Practice. 3rd ed. LC 94-12419. 778p. 1994. 64.95 (0-412-98551-9) Chapman & Hall.

— Food Analysis: Theory & Practice. 3rd ed. LC 94-12419. 778p. 1994. pap. 39.95 (0-412-06591-6) Chapman & Hall.

Pomeranz, Yeshajhu. Functional Properties of Food Components. 2nd ed. (Food Science & Technology Ser.). (Illus.). 569p. 1991. text ed. 121.00 (0-12-561281-8) Acad Pr.

Pomeray, J. K. Ireland. (Places & Peoples of the World Ser.). (Illus.). 128p. (J). (gr. 5 up). 1988. lib. bdg. 14.95 (1-55546-794-6) Chelsea Hse.

Pomeray, Sarah G., jt. auth. see Carr, John F.

Pomerening, jt. auth. see Mohr.

Pomerinke, June. The Young Years. LC 85-90524. (Illus.). 300p. (Orig.). 1986. pap. 8.50 (0-9616273-0-1) Young Pr Idaho.

Pomerinke, June L. Return to Whiskey Creek. (Illus.). 200p. (Orig.). 1994. pap. write for info. (0-318-72778-1) Young Pr Idaho.

Pomerleau, Cynthia S., jt. auth. see Pomerleau, Ovide F.

Pomerleau, Dean A. Neural Network Perception for Mobile Robot Guidance. LC 93-24616. (International Engineering & Computer Science Ser.: SECS 239). 1993. lib. bdg. 79.95 (0-7923-9373-2) Kluwer Ac.

Pomerleau, Ovide F. & Pomerleau, Cynthia S. Break the Smoking Habit: A Behavioral Program for Giving up Cigarettes. LC 84-70033. (Illus.). 136p. 1984. reprint ed. pap. 9.95 (0-9613198-0-1) Behavioral Med Pr.

— Break the Smoking Habit: A Behavioral Program for Giving up Cigarettes. (Illus.). 1984. reprint ed. pap. 9.95 (0-87822-136-0) Behavioral Med Pr.

Pomerleau, Wayne. Philosophical Perspectives on God & Religion: Descartes, Lock, Leibniz & Hume, Vol. 1. LC 92-19362. 325p. (C). 1995. text ed. 37.50 (0-89341-706-8) Hollowbrook.

— Philosophical Perspectives on God & Religion: Kant, Hegel, Kierkegaard & James, Vol. 2. LC 92-19362. 325p. (C). 1995. text ed. 37.50 (0-89341-713-0) Hollowbrook.

Pomerol, C. & Silva, I. Premoli, eds. Terminal Eocene Events. (Developments in Palaeontology & Stratigraphy Ser.: Vol. 9). 414p. 1986. 87.25 (0-444-42623-X) Elsevier.

Pomerol, Charles, ed. Wines & Winelands of France: Geological Journeys. (Illus.). 370p. 1990. text ed. 45.00 (1-85365-108-7, Pub. by McCarta UK) Seven Hills Bk.

Pomeroy. The Far West in the Twentieth Century. Date not set. 19.95 (0-06-016786-6, HarpT) HarpC.

***Pomeroy, A. A.** Pomeroy Pt. 3. (Illus.). 342p. 1994. reprint ed. lib. bdg. 63.00 (0-8328-4372-5); reprint ed. pap. 53.00 (0-8328-4373-3) Higginson Bk Co.

Pomeroy, Albert A. Pomeroy: Romance & History of Eltweed Pomeroy's Ancestors in Normandy & England. (Illus.). 81p. 1992. reprint ed. lib. bdg. 26.00 (0-8328-2612-X); reprint ed. pap. 16.00 (0-685-61607-X) Higginson Bk Co.

— Pomeroy, History & Genealogy of the Pomeroy Family: Collateral Lines in Family Groups, Nrmandy, Great Britain & America, Comprising the Ancestors & Descendants of Eltweed Pomeroy, from Beaminster, Co. Dorset, England, 1630. (Illus.). 962p. 1994. reprint ed. lib. bdg. 159.50 (0-8328-4271-0); reprint ed. pap. 149.00 (0-8328-4272-9) Higginson Bk Co.

Pomeroy, C., jt. auth. see Evans, I.

Pomeroy, Dana R., jt. auth. see Clausen, Barry.

Pomeroy, Dave. The Mything Link: A Study Guide on Gospel, Culture & Media. 1990. pap. 5.95 (0-377-00208-9) Friendship Pr.

— Video Violence & Values: A Guide to the Use of Video. 1990. pap. 5.95 (0-377-00213-5) Friendship Pr.

***Pomeroy, Diana.** One Potato: Potato Prints. LC 95-10986. (J). 1996. write for info. (0-15-200300-2) HarBrace.

Pomeroy, E. & Pomeroy, J. Textiles for You. (C). 1988. 65.00 (0-685-47486-0, Pub. by S Thornes Pubs UK) St Mut.

Pomeroy, Earl. In Search of the Golden West: The Tourist in Western America. LC 90-36467. (Illus.). xxii, 271p. 1990. reprint ed. pap. 9.95 (0-8032-8725-9, Bison Books) U of Nebr Pr.

Pomeroy, Elizabeth. The Heavenly Edible Diet. 150p. (Orig.). 1989. pap. text ed. 19.95 (0-685-28992-3) Rebel Pr.

— The Huntington. LC 83-50338. (Illus.). 144p. 1984. 25.00 (0-935748-56-3) Scala Books.

Pomeroy, J., jt. auth. see Pomeroy, E.

Pomeroy, James, ed. see Zerler, Kathryn S.

Pomeroy, James L. Advanced Photography. LC 89-92366. (Illus.). 140p. 1991. pap. text ed. 22.95 (0-9625017-2-7) Palms & Rhodes Pub.

— Basic Photography: Student Handbook. LC 89-92365. (Illus.). 144p. 1991. teacher ed 24.95 (0-9625017-1-9); pap. text ed. 19.95 (0-9625017-0-0) Palms & Rhodes Pub.

— Computer Graphics Fundamentals. (Illus.). 158p. 1993. pap. text ed. 48.00 (0-9625017-7-8) Palms & Rhodes Pub.

Pomeroy, Jane R. Alexander Anderson's Life & Engravings with a Checklist of Publications Drawn from His Diary. (Illus.). 75p. 1990. 8.00 (0-944026-25-7) Am Antiquarian.

Pomeroy, Janet. Among the Roses. 100p. 1993. pap. (0-9636130-0-6) Rec Ctr Handicapped.

Pomeroy, Johanna P. Content Area Reading Skills Electricity & Magnetism. (Illus.). (J). (gr. 4). 1987. pap. text ed. 3.25 (0-89525-859-5) Ed Activities.

— Content Area Reading Skills Geology: Detecting Sequence. (Illus.). (J). (gr. 4). 1987. pap. text ed. 3.25 (1-55737-085-0) Ed Activities.

P Q

— Content Area Reading Skills Light: Main Idea. (Illus.). (J). (gr. 3). 1989. pap. text ed. 3.25 (*1-55737-687-5*) Ed Activities.

— Content Area Reading Skills Machines: Detecting Sequence. (Illus.). (J). (gr. 3). 1989. pap. text ed. 3.25 (*1-55737-690-5*) Ed Activities.

— Content Area Reading Skills Matter: Locating Details. (Illus.). (J). (gr. 4). 1988. pap. text ed. 3.25 (*1-55737-086-9*) Ed Activities.

— Content Area Reading Skills Mechanics: Cause & Effect. (Illus.). (J). (gr. 4). 1988. pap. text ed. 3.25 (*1-55737-088-5*) Ed Activities.

— Content Area Reading Skills Oceans: Main Idea. (Illus.). (J). (gr. 4). 1987. pap. text ed. 3.25 (*0-89525-857-9*) Ed Activities.

— Content Area Reading Skills Our Earth: Locating Details. (Illus.). (J). (gr. 3). 1989. pap. text ed. 3.25 (*1-55737-688-3*) Ed Activities.

— Content Area Reading skills Reproduction & Heredity: Main Idea. (Illus.). (J). (gr. 4). 1988. pap. text ed. 3.25 (*1-55737-087-7*) Ed Activities.

— Content Area Reading Skills Solar System: Locating Details. (Illus.). (J). (gr. 4). 1987. pap. text ed. 3.25 (*0-89525-858-7*) Ed Activities.

— Content Area Reading Skills Sound & Hearing: Detecting Sequence. (Illus.). 1987. pap. text ed. 3.25 (*0-89525-860-9*) Ed Activities.

— Content Area Reading Skills Weather: Cause & Effect. (Illus.). (J). (gr. 3). 1989. pap. text ed. 3.25 (*1-55737-689-1*) Ed Activities.

Pomeroy, John, jt. auth. see Carr, Harold.

Pomeroy, John N. An Introduction to the Constitutional Law of the United States, 3 vols., Set. 1980. lib. bdg. 250.00 (*0-8490-3169-9*) Gordon Pr.

— A Treatise on Equity Jurisprudence: As Administered in the United States of America. Adapted for All the States, 5 vols., Set. Symons, Spencer W., ed. 4756p. Date not set. 450.00 (*1-886363-05-6*) Lawbk Exchange.

— A Treatise on Equity Jurisprudence: As Administered in the United States of America. Adapted for All the States, Vol. I. Symons, Spencer W., ed. ciii, 810p. Date not set. write for info. (*1-886363-00-5*) Lawbk Exchange.

— A Treatise on Equity Jurisprudence: As Administered in the United States of America. Adapted for All the States, Vol. II. Symons, Spencer W., ed. xxi, 1111p. Date not set. write for info. (*1-886363-01-3*) Lawbk Exchange.

— A Treatise on Equity Jurisprudence: As Administered in the United States of America. Adapted for All the States, Vol. III. Symons, Spencer W., ed. xvi, 1043p. Date not set. write for info. (*1-886363-02-1*) Lawbk Exchange.

— A Treatise on Equity Jurisprudence: As Administered in the United States of America. Adapted for All the States, Vol. IV. Symons, Spencer W., ed. xxiii, 1081p. Date not set. write for info. (*1-886363-03-X*) Lawbk Exchange.

— A Treatise on Equity Jurisprudence: As Administered in the United States of America. Adapted for All the States, Vol. V. Symons, Spencer W., ed. iii, 711p. Date not set. write for info. (*1-886363-04-8*) Lawbk Exchange.

Pomeroy, John N. & Mann, John C. Treatise on the Specific Performance of Contracts. 3rd ed. Hemholz, R. H. & Reams, Bernard D., Jr., eds. LC 86-62940. (Historical Writings in Law & Jurisprudence Ser.: No. 8). xl, 1045p. 1986. reprint ed. lib. bdg. 65.00 (*0-89941-523-7*, 304590) W S Hein.

Pomeroy, John N., ed. see Sedgwick, Theodore.

Pomeroy, L. R. & Alberts, J. J., eds. Concepts of Ecosystem Ecology. (Ecological Studies: Vol. 67). (Illus.). 345p. 1990. 97.00 (*0-387-96686-2*) Spr-Verlag.

Pomeroy, L. R. & Wiegert, R. G., eds. The Ecology of a Salt Marsh. (Ecological Studies Ser.: Vol. 38). (Illus.). 288p. 1981. 80.00 (*0-387-90555-3*) Spr-Verlag.

Pomeroy, Marcus M. Nonsense, or Hits & Criticisms on the Follies of the Day. LC 70-91091. (American Humorists Ser.). reprint ed. lib. bdg. 22.50 (*0-8398-1572-7*) Irvington.

Pomeroy, Marnie. Calendar for Dinah: Foundation Edition. 1966. 6.00 (*0-912156-03-1*); 20.00 (*0-912156-04-X*) Masterwork Pr.

Pomeroy, Olive G., ed. see Pomeroy, Richard M.

Pomeroy, Richard M. In Search of Meaning. McCoy, Charles S. & Pomeroy, Olive G., eds. 100p. 1991. pap. 12.95 (*0-9628719-0-7*) Glen-Berkeley.

Pomeroy, Robert W., III, jt. ed. see Trask, David F.

Pomeroy, Ruth. Redbook's Guide to Buying Your First Home. 1980. pap. 4.95 (*0-686-60934-4*, 24716, Fireside) S&S Trade.

Pomeroy, Sally & Tanner, Mary A., illus. Art Center of Corpus Christi Cookbook. 102p. (Orig.). 1991. spiral bd. 9.00 (*0-9629702-0-4*) Art Ctr Corpus Christi.

Pomeroy, Sarah B. Goddesses, Whores, Wives & Slaves: Women in Classical Antiquity. LC 74-8782. (Studies in the Life of Women). (Illus.). 280p. 1975. pap. 16.00 (*0-8052-0530-6*) Schocken.

— Goddesses, Whores, Wives, & Slaves: Women in Classical Antiquity. 1995. pap. 16.00 (*0-8052-1030-X*) Schocken.

— Women in Hellenistic Egypt: From Alexander to Cleopatra. LC 89-24894. (Illus.). 267p. (C). 1989. reprint ed. pap. text ed. 17.95 (*0-8143-2230-1*) Wayne St U Pr.

***Pomeroy, Sarah B., ed. & tr.** Oeconomicus: A Social & Historical Commentary, with a New English Translation. (Illus.). 400p. 1995. pap. 29.95 (*0-19-815025-3*) OUP.

Pomeroy, Sarah B., ed. Women's History & Ancient History. LC 90-24488. (Illus.). xviii, 318p. (C). 1991. 45.00 (*0-8078-1949-2*); pap. 14.95 (*0-8078-4310-5*) U of NC Pr.

Pomeroy, Sarah B., jt. ed. see Burstein, Stanley M.

Pomeroy, Sarah B., ed. see Xenophon.

Pomeroy, Trout. Oakland County: Making It Work. 1990. 32.95 (*0-89781-361-8*) Preferred Mktg.

Pomeroy, Wardell B. Boys & Sex. 3rd ed. (YA). 1991. pap. 3.95 (*0-440-20811-4*) Dell.

— Dr. Kinsey & the Institute for Sex Research. LC 82-4924. 496p. 1982. text ed. 52.00 (*0-300-02916-0*) Yale U Pr.

Pomeroy, Wardell B., jt. auth. see Steward, Samuel M.

Pomeroy, Wardell B., et al. Taking a Sex History: Interviewing & Recording. 353p. 1982. text ed. 19.95 (*0-02-925370-5*) Free Pr.

Pomeroy, William J. American Neo-Colonialism: Its Emergence in the Philippines & Asia. LC 71-108385. 255p. reprint ed. pap. 72.70 (*0-8357-5383-2*, 2020636) Bks Demand.

— Apartheid Axis: The United States & South Africa. LC 79-150661. 96p. reprint ed. pap. 27.40 (*0-8357-5652-1*, 2022868) Bks Demand.

— Apartheid, Imperialism & African Freedom. Smith, Betty, ed. LC 86-10488. 276p. (C). 1986. 14.00 (*0-7178-0640-5*); pap. 6.95 (*0-7178-0632-4*) Intl Pubs Co.

— The Philippines: Colonialism, Collaboration, & Resistance. Smith, Betty, ed. LC 92-35454. vi, 352p. (Orig.). 1993. pap. 9.95 (*0-7178-0692-8*) Intl Pubs Co.

Pomeroy, William J., ed. Guerrilla Warfare & Marxism. LC 65-55606. 336p. 1969. reprint ed. pap. 4.50 (*0-7178-0248-5*) Intl Pubs Co.

Pometta, D., jt. ed. see James, R. W.

Pomfret, John E. Colonial New Jersey: A History. LC 72-1228. (History of the American Colonies Ser.). 327p. 1973. lib. bdg. 35.00 (*0-527-18716-X*) Kraus Intl.

Pomfret, Richard. Diverse Paths of Economic Development. 256p. 1992. text ed. 63.00 (*0-13-220351-0*) P-H.

— International Trade: An Introduction to Theory & Policy. (Illus.). 288p. (Orig.). (C). 1991. text ed. 54.95 (*1-55786-104-8*); pap. text ed. 21.95 (*1-55786-105-6*) Blackwell Pubs.

— International Trade Policy with Imperfect Competition. LC 92-30715. (Special Papers in International Economics: No. 17). 1992. 11.00 (*0-88165-306-3*) Princeton U Int Finan Econ.

— Investing in China: Ten Years of the Open Door Policy. LC 90-22869. (Illus.). 168p. 1991. text ed. 22.95 (*0-8138-1206-2*) Iowa St U Pr.

— Mediterranean Policy of the European Community: A Study of Discrimination in Trade. LC 85-11882. 128p. 1986. text ed. 29.95 (*0-312-52817-5*) St Martin.

***Pomfret, Richard, ed.** Australia's Trade Policies. (Illus.). 256p. 1995. pap. 32.00 (*0-19-553536-7*) OUP.

***Pomfret, Richard W.** The Economies of Central Asia. LC 95-6829. 1995. write for info. (*0-691-04375-2*) Princeton U Pr.

— Trade Policies & Industralization in a Small Country: The Case of Israel. 220p. 1976. lib. bdg. 53.50 (*3-16-338831-0*, Pub. by J C B Mohr GW) Coronet Bks.

Pomian, Krzystof. Collectors & Curiosities: Paris & Venice, 1500-1800. 348p. 1991. 47.95 (*0-7456-0680-6*) Blackwell Pubs.

Pomichalek, Milan, tr. see Goetz-Stankiewicz, Marketa, ed.

***Pomidor, Bill.** Murder by Prescription. 288p. 1995. pap. 4.99 (*0-451-18416-5*, Sig) NAL-Dutton.

Pominov, I., jt. auth. see Kozlov, I.

Pommaret, J. Systems of Partial Differential Equations & Lie Pseudogroups. (Mathematics & Its Applications Ser.). 426p. 1978. text ed. 205.00 (*0-677-00270-X*) Gordon & Breach.

Pommaret, J. F. Differential Galois Theory. LC 81-6298. (Mathematics & Its Applications Ser.: Vol. 15). 775p. 1983. text ed. 432.00 (*0-677-05670-2*) Gordon & Breach.

— Lie Pseudogroups & Mechanics. (Mathematics & Its Applications Ser.: Vol. 16). 592p. 1988. text ed. 297.00 (*2-88124-213-8*) Gordon & Breach.

— Partial Differential Equations & Group Theory: New Perspectives for Applications. LC 94-19352. (Mathematics & Its Applications Ser.: Vol. 293). 484p. (C). 1994. lib. bdg. 204.00 (*0-7923-2966-X*) Kluwer Ac.

Pommer, Richard. Eighteenth Century Architecture in Piedmont: The Open Structures of Juvarra, Alfieri & Vittone. LC 67-10331. 399p. reprint ed. pap. 113.80 (*0-317-10753-4*, 2050320) Bks Demand.

Pommer, Richard & Otto, Christian F. Weissenhof 1927 & the Modern Movement in Architecture. LC 90-33628. (Illus.). 416p. 1991. 65.00 (*0-226-67515-7*) U Ch Pr.

Pommerantz, Inna, jt. ed. see Sussmann, Ayala.

Pommerencke, Peter, jt. auth. see Flemming, Monika.

Pommerenke, C. Boundary Behaviour of Conformal Maps. Berger, M. et al, eds. LC 92-10365. (Grundlehren der Mathematischen Wissenschaften Ser.: Vol. 299). (Illus.). 312p. 1992. 69.00 (*0-387-54751-7*) Spr-Verlag.

Pommeret, Francoise. Bhutan. LC 90-63329. (India Guides Ser.). (Illus.). 277p. 1993. reprint ed. pap. 14.95 (*0-8442-9924-3*, Passport Bks) NTC Pub Grp.

Pommerin, Reiner. American Impact on Postwar Germany, 1945-1965. LC 94-27019. 208p. (C). 1995. text ed. 32.00 (*1-57181-004-8*) Berghahn Bks.

Pommersheim, Frank. Braid of Feathers: American Indian Law & Contemporary Tribal Life. LC 94-4846. 1995. 30.00 (*0-520-08857-3*) U CA Pr.

— Snaps: Poetry & Prose from a Family Album. 125p. 1994. pap. 7.95 (*0-9636224-1-2*) Rose Hill Bks.

Pommert, John. Thirteen Lessons on Timothy & Titus. (Bible Student Study Guides Ser.). 92p. (C). 1978. 4.99 (*0-89900-162-9*) College Pr Pub.

Pommery, Jean. How Human the Animals. LC 78-24613. 224p. (C). 1981. pap. 6.95 (*0-8128-6086-1*, Scrbrough Hse) Madison Bks UPA.

Pommier. La Jeunesse Clericale d'Ernest Reman - Saint Sulpice. (Fac. Let. Strasbourg Ser.). 13.95 (*0-685-34961-6*) Fr & Eur.

Pommier, J., jt. auth. see De Balzac, Honore.

Pommier, Jean, ed. see Gautier, Theophile.

Pommier, Louis. Dictionary of Emergency Homeopathy (Dictionnaire Homeopathique d'Urgence) 13th ed. 765p. (FRE.). 1985. 75.00 (*0-7859-4836-8*, M6461) Fr & Eur.

— Dictionnaire Homeopathique. 1986. write for info. (*0-7859-7851-8*, 2-253-03815-6) Fr & Eur.

Pommy-Vega, Janine. Threading the Maze. LC 92-56590. 1992. pap. 6.95 (*1-880636-04-2*) Cloud Mtn.

Pomod, B. & Ballal, N. Murari. Sustainable Development of the Rural Poor. 1992. 27.50 (*81-7040-278-6*, Pub. by Himalaya II) Apt Bks.

Pomogailo, Anatoly D. & Savostyanov, Vladimir S. Synthesis & Polymerization of Metal-Containing Monomers. LC 93-49461. 192p. 1994. text ed. 89.95 (*0-8493-2863-2*, 2863) CRC Pr.

Pomorska, K. Themes & Variations in Pasternak's Poetics. 92p. 1975. pap. 21.00 (*0-685-53318-2*) Benjamins North Am.

Pomorska, Krystyna. Jakobsonian Poetics & Slavic Narrative: From Pushkin to Solzhenitsyn. Baran, Henryk, ed. LC 91-39157. (Sound & Meaning: The Roman Jakobson Series in Linguistics & Poetics). 352p. 1992. text ed. 45.00 (*0-8223-1233-6*) Duke.

— Russian Formalist Theory & Its Poetic Ambience. 1968. text ed. 55.40 (*3-10-800116-7*) Mouton.

Pomorska, Krystyna, ed. see Jakobson, Roman.

Pomorska, Krystyna, et al. Language, Poetry & Poetics: The Generation of the 1890's: Jakobson, Trubetzkoy, Majakovskj - Proceeding of the First Roman Jakobson Colloquim. (Illus.). 364p. 1987. lib. bdg. 119.25 (*0-89925-098-X*) Mouton.

Pomorski, Stanislaw. American Common Law & the Principle Nullum Crimen Sine Lege. 2nd rev. ed. Chodakowska, Elzbieta, tr. x, 219p. 1975. pap. 10.00 (*0-8377-1051-0*) Rothman.

Pompa, Delia, ed. see Gill, Lucia, et al.

Pompa, Leon. Human Nature & Historical Knowledge: Hume, Hegel & Vico. 256p. (C). 1990. 59.95 (*0-521-38137-1*) Cambridge U Pr.

— Vico's Theory of the Causes of Historical Change. 23p. 1971. pap. 6.00 (*0-9500029-2-5*, Pub. by Octagon Pr UK) ISHK Bk Service.

Pompa, Leon & Dray, Williams H., eds. Substance & Form in History. 198p. 1981. 22.50 (*0-85224-413-4*, Pub. by Edinburgh U Pr UK) Col U Pr.

Pompa, Leon, ed. see Giambattista, Vico.

Pompe, S., ed. Indonesian Law, 1949-1989: A Bibliography of Foreign-Language Materials with Brief Commentaries on the Law. LC 92-15181. 468p. (C). 1992. lib. bdg. 156.50 (*0-7923-1744-0*) Kluwer Ac.

Pompe, Wolfgang, jt. ed. see Kreher, Wolfgang.

***Pompeian, Helen N.** Gifts of Love & Life. 1995. 13.95 (*0-533-11454-3*) Vantage.

Pompeiano, O. & Allum, J. H., eds. Vestibulospinal Control of Posture & Locomotion. (Progress in Brain Research Ser.). 456p. 1988. 175.50 (*0-444-80976-7*) Elsevier.

Pompeiano, O., jt. ed. see Barnes, C. D.

Pompeiano, O., ed. see IBRO Symposium Staff.

Pompeiano, O., jt. ed. see Pirodda, E.

Pompella, Guiseppe, ed. Argonautica - Index in Orphei Argonautica. (Alpha-Omega, Reihe A Ser.: Bd. XXXIX). x, 156p. (GER.). 1979. write for info. (*3-487-06949-0*, Pub. by Georg Olms GW) Lubrecht & Cramer.

— Quintus Smyrnaeus - Index in Quintum Smyraneum. (Alpha-Omega, Reihe A Ser.: Bd. XLIX). v, 441p. 1982. write for info. (*3-487-07134-7*, Pub. by Georg Olms GW) Lubrecht & Cramer.

Pomper, Gerald, et al. The Election of Nineteen Eighty-Eight: Reports & Interpretations. LC 89-752. (Illus.). 224p. (Orig.). (C). 1989. 25.00 (*0-934540-77-2*); pap. text ed. 14.95 (*0-934540-76-4*) Chatham Hse Pubs.

— The Election of Nineteen Ninety-Two: Reports & Interpretations. LC 93-16269. 240p. (C). 1993. 25.00 (*1-56643-000-3*); pap. text ed. 19.95x (*1-56643-001-1*) Chatham Hse Pubs.

Pomper, Gerald M. The Election of 1980: Reports & Interpretations. Pomper, Marlene M., ed. LC 81-598. 208p. reprint ed. pap. 59.30 (*0-8357-4822-7*, 2037759) Bks Demand.

— The Election of 1984: Reports & Interpretations. Pomper, Marlene M., ed. LC 85-4223. 208p. reprint ed. pap. 59.30 (*0-8357-4823-5*, 2037760) Bks Demand.

— Passions & Interests: Political Party Concepts of American Democracy. LC 92-12328. (American Political Thought Ser.). xii, 180p. 1992. 27.50 (*0-7006-0551-7*); pap. 12.95 (*0-7006-0552-5*) U Pr of KS.

— Voters' Choice: Varieties of American Electoral Behavior. (Illus.). 276p. (C). 1983. reprint ed. pap. text ed. 22.00 (*0-8191-3188-1*) U Pr of Amer.

— Voters, Elections & Parties: The Practice of Democratic Theory. 320p. 1988. 39.95 (*0-88738-160-X*) Transaction Pubs.

— Voters, Elections, & Parties: The Practice of Democratic Theory. 424p. (C). 1992. pap. text ed. 22.95 (*1-56000-561-0*) Transaction Pubs.

Pomper, Gerald M., ed. Party Renewal in America: Theory & Practice. LC 79-25184. 220p. 1980. text ed. 36.95 (*0-275-90539-X*, C0539, Praeger Pubs) Greenwood.

— The Political State of New Jersey. 240p. (C). 1986. text ed. 40.00 (*0-8135-1150-X*); pap. text ed. 15.00 (*0-8135-1151-8*) Rutgers U Pr.

Pomper, Gerald M., ed. see Kleppner, Paul.

Pomper, Gerald M., ed. see Smith, Paul A.

Pomper, Gerald M., et al, eds. The Political Life of the American States: American Political Parties & Elections. LC 83-17756. 344p. 1984. pap. 14.95 (*0-275-91630-8*, B1630, Praeger Pubs) Greenwood.

Pomper, Marlene M., ed. see Pomper, Gerald M.

Pomper, Philip. Lenin, Trotsky, & Stalin. 1991. pap. text ed. 15.50 (*0-685-62749-7*) Col U Pr.

— Lenin, Trotsky, & Stalin: The Intelligentsia & Power. 456p. 1990. text ed. 47.50 (*0-231-06906-5*) Col U Pr.

— Lenin Trotsky Stalin. 1992. pap. 16.50 (*0-685-62548-6*) Col U Pr.

— The Russian Revolutionary Intelligentsia. 2nd ed. Eubank, Keith, ed. LC 92-5628. (European History Ser.). 256p. (C). 1993. pap. text ed. write for info. (*0-88295-895-X*) Harlan Davidson.

— The Structure of Mind in History: Five Major Figures in Psychohistory. LC 84-22988. 192p. 1985. text ed. 31.00 (*0-231-06064-5*) Col U Pr.

Pomper, Philip, tr. & anno. Trotsky's Notebooks, 1933-1935: Writings on Lenin, Dialectics, & Evolutionism. LC 85-29955. 160p. 1986. text ed. 39.50 (*0-231-06302-4*) Col U Pr.

Pompey, jt. auth. see Caesar.

***Pompili, Tony.** Lotus Notes Application: An Introduction for Programmer's & Power Users. 1995. disk, pap. 32.95 (*0-13-150723-0*) P-H.

***Pompino-Marschall, Bernd.** Einfuehrung in die Phoenetik. xiv, 310p. (C). 1995. lib. bdg. 90.75 (*3-11-013686-4*); pap. text ed. 36.95 (*3-11-014763-7*) De Gruyter.

Pompl, W. & Lavery, P., eds. Tourism in Europe: Structures & Developments. 363p. (Orig.). 1993. pap. text ed. 42.75 (*0-85198-852-0*) CAB Intl.

Pomponatius, Petrus, pseud. De Naturalium Effectuum Causis Sive De Incantationibus. 328p. 1970. reprint ed. write for info. (*0-318-71607-0*, Pub. by Georg Olms GW) Lubrecht & Cramer.

Pomponazzi, Pietro, see Petrus Pomponatius, pseud..

Pomponio, Alice. Seagulls Don't Fly into the Bush: Cultural Identity & Development in Melanesia. 242p. (C). 1992. pap. 17.95 (*0-534-16260-6*) Intl Thomson.

Pomraning, Dorothy E., jt. auth. see Clark, Virginia L.

Pomraning, G. C. Linear Kinetic Theory & Particle Transport in Stochastic Mixtures. (Series on Advances in Mathematics for Applied Sciences: Vol. 7). 250p. 1991. text ed. 61.00 (*981-02-0844-8*) World Scientific Pub.

— Radiation Hydrodynamics. 304p. (C). 1973. 120.00 (*0-08-016893-0*, Pub. by Pergamon Repr UK) Franklin.

Pomraning, G. C., et al. Theoretical & Computational Radiation Hydrodynamics, Vol. 1: Radiation-Hydrodynamics Theoretical Considerations. LC 70-135085. 228p. 1969. 20.00 (*0-403-04529-0*) Scholarly.

Pomrenke, G. S., et al, eds. Rare-Earth Doped Semiconductors. (Symposium Proceedings Ser.: Vol. 301). 1993. text ed. 65.00 (*1-55899-197-2*) Materials Res.

Poms, Lillian, jt. auth. see Dale, Paulette.

***Pomykala, Kenneth.** The Davidic Dynasty Tradition in Early Judaism: Its History & Significance for Messianism. LC 94-41342. (Early Judaism & Its Literature Ser.: No. 7). 1995. write for info. (*0-7885-0068-6*) Scholars Pr GA.

Pon, C. L., jt. ed. see Gualerzi, C. O.

Ponasse, Daniel. Mathematical Logic. LC 72-136738. (Notes on Mathematics & Its Applications Ser.). Orig. Title: Logique Mathematique. 136p. (C). 1973. text ed. 99.00 (*0-677-30390-4*) Gordon & Breach.

Ponath, Stegeman. Nonlinear Surface Electromagnetic Phenomena. 1991. 160.00 (*0-444-88359-2*) Elsevier.

Ponce, jt. ed. see Larson.

Ponce, Charles. The Archetype of the Unconscious & the Transfiguration of Therapy: Reflections On Jungian Psychology. 120p. (Orig.). 1990. pap. 9.95 (*1-55643-070-1*) North Atlantic.

— The Game of Wizards. 220p. 1991. pap. 10.95 (*0-8356-0669-4*, Quest) Theos Pub Hse.

— Kabbalah. LC 78-7385. (Illus.). 1978. reprint ed. pap. 12.00 (*0-8356-0510-8*, Quest) Theos Pub Hse.

— Papers Toward Radical Metaphysics: Alchemy. 160p. (Orig.). 1984. 20.00 (*0-938190-02-4*) North Atlantic.

— Working the Soul: Reflections on Jungian Psychology. (Illus.). 156p. 1987. pap. 12.95 (*1-55643-033-7*) North Atlantic.

***Ponce de Leon Paiva, Anton.** The Wisdom of the Ancient One: An Inca Initiation. LC 94-40696. 121p. 1995. pap. 9.95 (*1-885394-09-8*) Bluestar Commun.

Ponce, F. A. & Cardona, M., eds. Surface Science: Lectures on Basic Concepts & Applications - Proceedings of the Sixth Latin American Symposium on Surface Physics (SLAFS-6), Cusco, Peru, September 3-7, 1990. (Proceedings in Physics Ser.: Vol. 62). (Illus.). xiii, 525p. 1992. 128.00 (*0-387-53604-3*) Spr-Verlag.

Ponce, Manuel. Manuel Ponce: Some of My Poems. Miller, Yvette E., ed. Rodriguez-Lee, Maria L., tr. LC 87-3407. 128p. (C). 1987. pap. 11.50 (*0-935480-28-5*) Lat Am Lit Rev Pr.

Ponce, Mario. Waiting on America: A Food Server's Guide to Greater Income. Modesto, Robert, ed. (Illus.). 144p. (Orig.). (C). 1989. pap. 7.95 (*0-685-27820-4*) Amer Serv Pubns.

Ponce, Mary H. Hoyt Street: An Autobiography. LC 93-1346. 348p. 1993. 24.95 (*0-8263-1446-5*) U of NM Pr.

— Hoyt Street: Memories of a Chicana Childhood. LC 94-36505. 1995. 12.95 (*0-385-47547-0*, Anchor NY) Doubleday.

— Sp-Calle Hoyt. 1995. pap. 12.95 (*0-385-47551-9*, Anchor NY) Doubleday.

— Taking Control. LC 87-70272. 128p. (Orig.). 1987. 9.50 (*0-934770-70-0*) Arte Publico.

Ponce, Omar. Educate para una Mejor Condicion Fisica: Guia Basica para el Desarrollo de un Programa de Eficiencia Fisica. (Illus.). 75p. (Orig.). (SPA.). (YA). 1986. write for info. (*0-318-64880-6*) B Ponce.

Ponce, Victor M. Engineering Hydrology: Principles & Practices. 736p. 1989. text ed. 35.80 (*0-13-277831-9*) P-H.

P Q

An Asterisk (*) at the beginning of an entry indicates that the title is appearing in BIP for the first time.

Ponce, Wallace Y. Our Beginnings: The History of the Epworth United Methodist Church. (Orig.). 1988. 10.00 (0-9620308-3-X); text ed. 10.00 (0-9620308-2-1); lib. bdg. 10.00 (0-9620308-9-9); pap. 10.00 (0-9620308-8-0) Epworth United Methodist Church.

Ponce, Wallace Y., jt. auth. see Stewart, Paul W.

Poncela, E. Jardiel. Eloisa Esta Debajo de Almendro. 244p. (SPA.). 1974. 10.50 (0-8288-7042-X) Fr & Eur.

Poncela, Enrique J. Noche de Primavera sin Sueno: Comedia Humoristica en Tres Actos. Lacosta, Francisco C., ed. LC 67-25113. (SPA.). (YA). (gr. 9 up). 1967. pap. text ed. 6.95 (0-89197-320-6) Irvington.

Poncelet, G., et al, eds. Preparation of Catalysts III: Scientific Bases for the Preparation of Heterogeneous Catalysts; Proceedings of the International Symposium, Third, Louvain-la Neuve, Sept. 6-9, 1982. (Studies in Surface Science & Catalysis: Vol. 16). 854p. 1983. 231.00 (0-444-42184-X, I-192-83) Elsevier.

— Preparation of Catalysts, No. Five: Scientific Basis for the Preparation of Heterogeneous Catalysts: Proceedings of the 5th International Symposium, Louvain-la-Neuve, Sept. 3-6, 1990. (Studies in Surface Science & Catalysis: No. 63). 748p. 1991. 225.50 (0-444-88616-8) Elsevier.

— Preparation of Catalysts VI: Scientific Bases for the Preparation of Catalysts. (Studies in Surface Science & Catalysis: Vol. 91). 1194p. 1995. 350.00 (0-444-82078-7) Elsevier.

Poncelet, Thierry. Sit! The Dog Portraits of Thierry Poncelet. (Illus.). 96p. 1993. 19.95 (1-56305-380-2, 3380) Workman Pub.

Poncet, Sally. South Georgia. LC 94-13376. (J). (gr. 4 up). 1995. text ed. 17.95 (0-02-774905-3, Mac Bks Young Read) S&S Childrens.

Ponchard-Hyatte, Maryse, jt. auth. see Hyatte, Reginald.

Ponchie & Co. Staff, ed. see Ponchie, Jean-Pierre.

Ponchie, Jean P. French Periodical Index, 1989: Repertoriex. 400p. 1990. 36.00 (0-685-41119-2) Ponchie.

— French Periodical Index, 1991: Repertoriex. 400p. 1992. lib. bdg. 37.00 (1-878717-01-4) Ponchie.

— French Periodical Index, 1992: Repertoriex. 400p. 1993. lib. bdg. 37.00 (1-878717-02-2) Ponchie.

Ponchie, Jean-Pierre. French Periodical Index, 1973-1974. LC 75-28987. (Useful Reference Ser. of Library Bks.: Vol. 106). 1976. lib. bdg. 28.00 (0-87305-106-8) Faxon.

— French Periodical Index, 1976. LC 75-28987. (Useful Reference Ser. of Library Bks.: Vol. 113). 1977. lib. bdg. 24.00 (0-87305-117-3) Faxon.

— French Periodical Index, 1977: Repertoriex. LC 75-28987. (Usefule Reference Ser. of Library Bks.: No. 116). 1978. lib. bdg. 25.00 (0-87305-121-1) Faxon.

— French Periodical Index, 1978: Repertoriex. LC 75-28987. (Useful Reference Ser. of Library Bks.: No. 117). 1978. lib. bdg. 25.00 (0-87305-122-X) Faxon.

— French Periodical Index, 1985: Repertoriex. 474p. 1986. lib. bdg. 34.00 (0-9604418-6-7) Ponchie.

— French Periodical Index, 1986: Repertoriex. Ponchie & Co. Staff, ed. 529p. (FRE.). 1987. lib. bdg. 35.00 (0-9604418-7-5) Ponchie.

Ponchie, Jean-Pierre & Spleth, Janice. French Periodical Index, 1975, Vol. 115. LC 75-28987. (Useful Reference Ser. of Library Bks.). 1977. 24.00 (0-87305-115-7) Faxon.

Ponciano, Roberto. Canto Indispensable (Poesias) LC 87-81864. (Coleccion Espejo de Paciencia Ser.). 112p. (Orig.). (SPA.). 1987. pap. 9.00 (0-89729-446-7) Ediciones.

***Poncio, J. Steve, et al, eds.** Concrete: Surface Preparation, Coating & Lining, & Inspection. (Illus.). 124p. 1991. ring bd. 52.00 (1-877914-22-3) NACE Intl.

Pond, Barbara. A Sampler of Wayside Herbs: Rediscovering Old Uses for Familiar Wild Plants. LC 73-89773. (Illus.). 1974. 24.95 (0-85699-096-5) Chatham Pr.

***Pond, Clifford.** Beauty of Jesus. 1994. pap. 8.99 (0-85234-233-0, Pub. by Evangel Pr UK) Presby & Reformed.

— Only Servants. 1991. pap. 8.99 (0-946462-24-0, Pub. by Evangel Pr UK) Presby & Reformed.

***Pond, Dale & Baumgartner, Walter.** Nikola Tesla's Earthquake Machine: With Tesla's Original Patents Plus New Blueprints to Build Your Own Working Model. (Illus.). 184p. (Orig.). 1995. pap. 16.95 (1-57282-008-X, D2008X) Message NM.

***Pond, Dale, et al.** History of the American Constitutional or Common Law: With Commentary Concerning Equity & Merchant Law. LC 94-72953. (Illus.). 144p. 1995. pap. 11.95 (1-57282-010-1) Message NM.

— Universal Laws Never Before Revealed: Keely's Secrets: Understanding & Using the Science of Sympathetic Vibration. rev. ed. LC 94-77879. (Illus.). 288p. 1995. pap. 19.95 (1-57282-003-9) Message NM.

Pond, David & Pond, Lucy. The Metaphysical Handbook. LC 83-91290. (Illus.). 200p. 1984. pap. 11.00 (0-915395-18-5) Reflecting Pond.

Pond, David, et al. Crystals Stones & Chakras. 1988. 15.95 (0-915395-28-2); pap. text ed. 3.95 (0-915395-31-2) Reflecting Pond.

Pond, E. Leroy. Junius Smith: Biography of the Father of the Atlantic Liner. LC 75-179535. (Select Bibliographies Reprint Ser.). 1977. reprint ed. 23.95 (0-8369-6664-3) Ayer.

Pond, Elizabeth. After the Wall: American Policy Toward Germany - A Twentieth Century Fund Paper. 111p. (Orig.). (C). 1990. pap. 9.95 (0-87078-323-8) TCFP-PPP.

— Beyond the Wall: Germany's Road to Unification. 367p. (C). 1993. 28.95x (0-8157-7154-1); pap. 16.95x (0-8157-7155-X) Brookings.

Pond, George E. The Shenandoah Valley in Eighteen Sixty-Four. (Illus.). 287p. 1989. reprint ed. 25.00 (0-916107-54-X) Broadfoot.

Pond, Jane B., jt. ed. see Schaefer, Karen M.

Pond, Jesse E., Jr. The Square Peg: A Tight Fit in a Tin Can. Powell, Lilja B., ed. LC 92-85443. 208p. (Orig.). 1992. pap. 19.95 (0-9634347-0-5) Pearl Harbor Hist.

Pond, Jonathan. Jonathan Pond's Guide to Investment & Financial Planning: A Timely Reference for Improving Your Financial Life. 400p. 1991. pap. 24.95 (0-13-156324-6) NY Inst Finance.

— Personal Financial Planning Forms & Checklists. 352p. 1987. 100.00 (0-88712-914-5) Warren Gorham & Lamont.

— Personal Financial Planning Forms & Checklists. suppl. ed. 352p. 1991. Supplement, 1991-1. 49.75 (0-685-43910-0); Supplement, 1991-2. 51.25 (0-685-19482-5) Warren Gorham & Lamont.

— Personal Financial Planning Handbook. 800p. 1986. Supplemented semi-annually. 195.00 (0-7913-0900-2) Warren Gorham & Lamont.

— Personal Financial Planning Handbook. suppl. ed. 800p. 1991. Supplement, 1991-1. 49.75 (0-685-13265-X) Warren Gorham & Lamont.

— Personal Financial Planning Handbook. suppl. ed. 800p. 1992. Supplement, 1992. 58.00 (0-685-55799-5) Warren Gorham & Lamont.

Pond, Jonathan D. The ABCs of Managing Your Money. 250p. 1993. write for info. (1-884383-00-9) Natl Endowment.

— Jonathan Pond's Financial Management Guide: Retirement Planning for Asset-Rich Individuals. 1993. pap. 19.95 (0-13-031220-7) P-H.

— The New Century Family Money Book: Your Comprehensive Guide to a Lifetime of Financial Security. LC 92-33646. 1993. 29.95 (0-440-50478-3) Dell.

— New Century Family Money Book: Your Comprehensive Guide to a Lifetime of Financial Security. 1995. pap. 18.95 (0-440-50693-X) Dell.

— One Thousand & One Ways to Cut Your Expenses. 1992. mass mkt. 8.95 (0-440-50495-3) Dell.

— Prentice Hall's Personal Financial Planning Guide for People over Fifty. 1992. 69.95 (0-13-318692-X) P-H.

— Safe Money in Tough Times. 1990. mass mkt. 4.95 (0-440-21085-2) Dell.

Pond, Joyce. Lost in the Corn. (Illus.). 31p. (Orig.). (J). (gr. 6). 1992. pap. 6.95 (0-9635877-0-6) JBP Press.

Pond, Kathleen, tr. see Auclair, Marcelle.

Pond, Kathleen L. The Professional Guide. (Illus.). 250p. 1993. text ed. 39.95 (0-442-00148-7) Van Nos Reinhold.

Pond, Lily & Russo, Richard, eds. Yellow Silk: Erotic Arts & Letters. 320p. 1991. pap. 10.00 (0-517-58736-X, Harmony) Crown Pub Group.

***Pond, Lily & Russo, Richard A., eds.** The Books of Eros: Art & Letters from Yellow Silk. LC 94-33164. 1995. 22.00 (0-517-79962-6, Crown) Crown Pub Group.

Pond, Lucy, jt. auth. see Pond, David.

Pond, Marion. Shades of Yesteryear. LC 82-71114. (Illus.). 48p. (Orig.). 1982. pap. 7.50 (0-941284-13-1) J Shaw Studio.

Pond, Mike. How to Become a Credit Card Merchant Immediately Without Having to Apply at a Bank. 2nd ed. (Illus.). 96p. 1993. pap. write for info. (1-880199-49-1) Mindbuilders.

— How to Get, Keep & Use VISA, MasterCard & American Express Credit Card Merchant Status to Earn Millions: Even If You Work at Home, Operate a Mail Order Business or Just Starting a New Company. 295p. (Orig.). 1992. 69.95 (1-880199-99-8); pap. 49.95 (1-880199-95-5) Mindbuilders.

Pond, Mildred M. Mother Teresa: A Life of Charity. (Junior World Biographies Ser.). (Illus.). 80p. (J). (gr. 3-6). 1992. lib. bdg. 14.95 (0-7910-1755-9) Chelsea Hse.

Pond, Mimi. A Groom of One's Own: And Other Bridal Accessories. LC 92-31489. (Illus.). 176p. 1993. pap. 8.00 (0-452-26945-8, Plume) NAL-Dutton.

Pond, Oscar L. Municipal Control of Public Utilities: A Study of the Attitudes of Our Courts Toward an Increase of the Sphere of Municipal Activity. LC 79-76676. (Columbia University. Studies in the Social Sciences: No. 65). reprint ed. 27.50 (0-404-51065-5) AMS Pr.

Pond, Robert & Walker, Norval J. Prep High Tech. Dennison, Scott, ed. (Illus.). 262p. (Orig.). (C). 1986. pap. text ed. 12.00 (0-923231-03-X) Mohican Pub.

Pond, Robert A. & Kenny, Patrick B., eds. RETC Proceedings, 1989. LC 89-60829. (Illus.). 881p. 1989. 60.00 (0-87335-083-9, 083-9) SMM&E Inc.

Pond, Robert J. Fundamentals of Statistical Quality Control. LC 93-33889. (Illus.). 416p. (C). 1994. pap. write for info. (0-02-396034-5, Merrill Pub Co) Macmillan.

— Introduction to Engineering Technology. 2nd ed. LC 92-8682. (Illus.). 352p. (C). 1992. pap. write for info. (0-02-396031-0, Merrill Pub Co) Macmillan.

— Introduction to Engineering Technology. 3rd ed. LC 95-6172. 1995. pap. write for info. (0-02-396041-8, Merrill Pub Co) Macmillan.

Pond, Roger. It's Hard to Look Cool When Your Car's Full of Sheep: Tales from the Back Forty. LC 88-92371. (Illus.). 176p. (Orig.). 1989. pap. 11.95 (0-9617766-1-7) Pine Forest Pub.

— Livestock Showman's Handbook: A Guide for Raising Animals for Junior Livestock Shows. LC 86-63395. (Illus.). 216p. 1986. pap. 14.95 (0-9617766-0-9) Pine Forest Pub.

— Things That Go "Baa!" in the Night: Tales from a Country Kid. (Illus.). 176p. (Orig.). 1992. pap. 11.95 (0-9617766-2-5) Pine Forest Pub.

***Pond, Roy.** Mummy's Revenge. (J). (gr. 4-7). 1994. pap. 3.50 (0-590-48374-9) Scholastic Inc.

Pond, S., jt. auth. see Pickard, G. L.

Pond, Samuel W. The Dakota or Sioux in Minnesota As They Were in 1834. LC 85-31039. xxi, 192p. 1986. reprint ed. pap. 8.95 (0-87351-193-X, Borealis Book) Minn Hist.

Pond, Seymour G. History & Romance of Exploration, Told with Pictures. LC 65-17180. (Illus.). 126p. (Orig.). 1966. pap. 4.95 (0-8154-0182-5) Cooper Sq.

Pond, Thomas E., jt. auth. see Steila, Donald.

***Pond, W. G., et al.** Basic Animal Nutrition & Feeding. 4th ed. LC 94-39439. 1995. pap. text ed. write for info. (0-471-30864-1) Wiley.

Pond, Wilson G. & Maner, Jerome H. Swine Production & Nutrition. (Illus.). 733p. 1984. text ed. 76.95 (0-87055-450-6) AVI.

Pond, Wilson G., jt. auth. see Church, David C.

Pond, Wilson G., et al. Pork Production Systems: Effective Use of Swine & Feed Resources. LC 90-47270. (Illus.). 352p. 1991. text ed. 83.95 (0-442-00115-0) Chapman & Hall.

Ponder, B. A. & Waring, M. J., eds. The Science of Cancer Treatment. 224p. 1990. 77.50 (0-7923-8905-0) Kluwer Ac.

Ponder, B. A., jt. ed. see Waring, M. J.

Ponder, Catherine. Dare to Prosper. LC 82-74520. 80p. 1983. pap. 5.95 (0-87516-511-7) DeVorss.

— Dynamic Laws of Healing. 238p. 1972. pap. 12.95 (0-87516-156-1) DeVorss.

— The Dynamic Laws of Prayer. rev. ed. LC 86-72267. 353p. 1987. reprint ed. pap. 12.95 (0-87516-583-4) DeVorss.

— The Dynamic Laws of Prosperity. rev. ed. LC 62-18836. 448p. 1985. reprint ed. pap. 14.95 (0-87516-551-6) DeVorss.

— The Dynamic Laws of Prosperity. 253p. 1993. reprint ed. lib. bdg. 21.95 (0-89968-318-5, Lghtyr Pr) Buccaneer Bks.

— The Healing Secrets of the Ages. rev. ed. LC 67-26503. 278p. 1985. reprint ed. pap. 12.95 (0-87516-550-8) DeVorss.

— The Millionaire from Nazareth. (Millionaires of the Bible Ser.). 1979. pap. 10.95 (0-87516-370-X) DeVorss.

— The Millionaire Joshua. LC 77-86719. (Millionaires of the Bible Ser.). 1978. pap. 10.95 (0-87516-253-3) DeVorss.

— The Millionaire Moses. LC 77-71459. (Millionaires of the Bible Ser.). 1977. pap. 10.95 (0-87516-232-0) DeVorss.

— The Millionaires of Genesis. (Millionaires of the Bible Ser.). 224p. 1976. pap. 10.95 (0-87516-215-0, Pub. by White Eagl Pub Trust UK) DeVorss.

— Open Your Mind to Prosperity. rev. ed. LC 70-155720. 184p. 1984. reprint ed. pap. 9.95 (0-87516-531-1) DeVorss.

— Open Your Mind to Receive. LC 82-74283. 128p. 1983. pap. 9.95 (0-87516-507-9) DeVorss.

— The Prospering Power of Love. rev. ed. LC 66-25849. 126p. 1984. reprint ed. pap. 5.95 (0-87516-525-7) DeVorss.

— The Prospering Power of Prayer. 80p. 1983. pap. 5.95 (0-87516-516-8) DeVorss.

— The Prosperity Secrets of the Ages. rev. ed. LC 64-16436. 344p. 1986. reprint ed. pap. 12.95 (0-87516-567-2) DeVorss.

— The Secret of Unlimited Prosperity. 60p. 1981. pap. 5.95 (0-87516-419-6) DeVorss.

Ponder, Dorothy. The Civil War in Ripley County, Missouri. Prospect News Staff, ed. LC 92-82882. (Illus.). 102p. (Orig.). (C). 1992. pap. 5.00 (0-9623922-1-9) Ponder Bks.

***Ponder, Jerry.** The Battle of Chalk Bluff: An Account of General John S. Marmaduke's Second Missouri Raid. (Illus.). 202p. (C). 1995. pap. 13.95 (0-9623922-3-5) Ponder Bks.

— A History of the 15th Missouri Cavalry Regiment, C.S.A. (Illus.). 203p. (C). 1994. pap. 13.95 (0-9623922-2-7) Ponder Bks.

***Ponder, Jerry & Ponder, Victor.** Confederate Surrender & Parole, Jacksonport & Wittsburg, Arkansas, May & June, 1865. (Orig.). (C). Date not set. pap. text ed. 15.00 (0-9623922-4-3) Ponder Bks.

Ponder, Jerry & Vandiver, Eldon D. The Family of Abner Ponder. 400p. (C). 1989. 27.50 (0-685-27832-8) Ponder Bks.

***Ponder, Jim & Caudle, Brad.** Multiplication Country. (J). (gr. 3 up). 1993. audio 9.95 (1-878489-25-9) Rock & Learn Educ Prod.

Ponder, Melinda M. Hawthorne's Early Narrative Art. LC 89-13804. (Studies in American Literature: Vol. 9). 260p. 1990. lib. bdg. 89.95 (0-88946-117-1) E Mellen.

***Ponder, Pearlie.** Links to Ancestral Ties: George Primm, Sr., Family. 192p. 1995. text ed. write for info. (0-9644034-0-4) P Ponder.

Ponder, Purvis, jt. auth. see Hill, Everett.

Ponder, Suzanne. Guide to St. Louis Interior Design Professionals. (Design Registry Ser.: Vol. 1). (Illus.). 120p. 1989. 14.95 (0-9622567-3-0); pap. 7.95 (0-9622567-4-9) Design Registry.

— St. Louis Interior Design Resources. (Design Registry Ser.: Vol. 2). (Illus.). 200p. 1990. 17.95 (0-9622567-6-5); pap. 8.95 (0-9622567-7-3) Design Registry.

Ponder, Victor, jt. auth. see Ponder, Jerry.

***Ponder, William S.** Educational Apartheid in a Pluralistic Society. 88p. 1995. pap. 10.00 (1-57087-093-4) Prof Pr NC.

Ponder, Winifred. Clara Butt: Her Life Story. LC 77-16530. (Music Reprint Ser.: 1978). (Illus.). 1978. reprint ed. lib. bdg. 35.00 (0-306-77529-8) Da Capo.

Pondiscio, Robert, jt. auth. see Salzman, Marian.

Pondoey, Gravrill S. Notes of a Soviet Doctor. 2nd ed. Haigh, Basil, tr. LC 59-9232. 248p. reprint ed. pap. 70.70 (0-317-07736-8, 2020652) Bks Demand.

Pondrom, Cyrena N., jt. ed. see Dembo, L. S.

Pondrom, Lee G., jt. ed. see Durand, Loyal.

***Pondsmith, Michael.** Castle Falkenstein. (Illus.). 224p. (Orig.). 1994. 32.00 (0-937279-51-X, CF6002); pap. 27.00 (0-937279-43-9, CF6001) R Talsorian.

— Chromebook 2. (Cyberpunk Ser.). (Illus.). 112p. (Orig.). 1992. pap. 12.00 (0-614-02725-X, CP3181) R Talsorian.

***Pondsmith, Michael & Winn, Ross.** Listen up, You Primitive Screwheads!!! (Cyberpunk Ser.). (Illus.). 112p. (Orig.). 1994. pap. 10.00 (0-937279-45-5, CP3291) R Talsorian.

Pondsmith, Michael, et al. Cyberpunk 2020. 2nd ed. Quintanar, Derek, ed. (Cyberpunk Ser.). (Illus.). 260p. (C). 1990. pap. 20.00 (0-937279-13-7, CP3002) R Talsorian.

Pondsmith, Mike, et al. Solo of Fortune. (Cyberpunk Ser.). (Illus.). 80p. 1989. student ed 10.00 (0-937279-06-4, CP 3101) R Talsorian.

Pondy, L. R., jt. ed. see Bacharach, Samuel B.

Pondy, Louis R., jt. auth. see Leavitt, Harold J.

Pondy, Louis R., et al, eds. Managing Ambiguity & Change. LC 88-2437. 205p. 1988. text ed. 65.95 (0-471-91843-1) Wiley.

***Ponec, R.** Overlap Determinant Method in the Theory of Pericyclic Reactivity. LC 95-12985. (Lecture Notes in Chemistry Ser.: Vol. 65). 1995. write for info. (0-387-59189-3) Spr-Verlag.

Ponemon, L. A. & Gadhart, D. R., eds. Auditing: Advances in Behavioral Research. (Recent Research in Psychology Ser.). (Illus.). x, 166p. 1991. pap. 49.00 (0-387-97619-1) Spr-Verlag.

Ponente, Nello. Raphael. (Qui Etait Ser.). (Illus.). 150p. (FRE.). 1990. 65.00 (0-7859-5024-9) Fr & Eur.

Pong, David. A Critical Guide to the Kwangtung Provincial Archives Deposited at the Public Record Office, London. (East Asian Monographs: No. 63). 400p. 1975. pap. 14.00 (0-674-17722-3) HUP.

— Shen Pao-chen & China's Modernization in the Nineteenth Century. (Studies in Chinese History, Literature & Institutions). (Illus.). 325p. (C). 1994. 54.95 (0-521-44163-3) Cambridge U Pr.

Pong, David & Fung, Edmund S., eds. Ideal & Reality: Social & Political Change in Modern China 1860-1949. (Illus.). 400p. 1986. pap. text ed. 31.00 (0-8191-4919-5) U Pr of Amer.

Pong, Ted. Quilt. LC 81-90056. (Illus.). 87p. (Orig.). 1981. pap. 1.95 (0-939966-00-X) Pong.

Ponge, jt. auth. see Bly.

Ponge, et al. Quarterly Review of Literature: The 1970s, Poetry, Vol. XVII, Nos. 1-2. 1970. pap. 15.00 (0-317-05320-5) Quarterly Rev.

Ponge, Francis. L' Atelier Contemporain. 361p. (FRE.). 1977. pap. 59.95 (0-7859-1595-8, 207029630X) Fr & Eur.

— Comment une Figue de Paroles et Pourquoi. 213p. (FRE.). 1977. pap. 24.95 (0-7859-1440-4, 2082120023) Fr & Eur.

— La Fabrique du Pre. 272p. (FRE.). 1990. pap. 89.95 (0-7859-1606-7, 260500158X) Fr & Eur.

— Le Grand Recueil: Lyres, Vol. 1. 192p. (FRE.). 1987. pap. 18.95 (0-7859-1299-1, 2070251632) Fr & Eur.

— Lyres. (FRE.). 1980. pap. 11.95 (0-7859-2781-6) Fr & Eur.

— Lyres. (Poesie Ser.). 176p. (FRE.). 1980. pap. 9.95 (2-07-032188-6) Schoenhof.

— Methodes. 248p. (FRE.). 1988. pap. 16.95 (0-7859-1357-2, 2070324923) Fr & Eur.

— Methodes. (Folio Essais Ser.: No. 107). (FRE.). 1988. pap. 14.95 (2-07-032492-3) Schoenhof.

— Nouveau Recueil. 240p. (FRE.). 1992. pap. 24.95 (0-7859-1386-6, 2070722880) Fr & Eur.

— Le Parti Pris des Choses. (Poesie Ser.). 224p. (FRE.). 1966. pap. 9.95 (2-07-030223-7) Schoenhof.

— Le Parti Pris des Choses: Douze Petits Ecrits. (FRE.). 1966. pap. 11.95 (0-7859-2764-6) Fr & Eur.

— Pieces. (FRE.). 1971. pap. 11.95 (0-7859-2770-0) Fr & Eur.

— Pieces. (Poesie Ser.). 194p. 1971. 11.95 (2-07-031873-7) Schoenhof.

— La Rage de l'Expression. (FRE.). 1976. pap. 14.95 (0-7859-2780-8) Fr & Eur.

— La Rage de l'Expression. (Poesie Ser.). 214p. (FRE.). 1976. pap. 11.95 (2-07-032167-3) Schoenhof.

— Le Savon. 140p. (FRE.). 1992. pap. 10.95 (0-7859-1390-4, 2070725537) Fr & Eur.

— Selected Poems. LC 93-61394. 232p. 1994. 16.95 (0-916390-59-4); pap. 10.95 (0-916390-58-6) Wake Forest.

— Tome Premier. 620p. 1965. pap. 45.00 (0-7859-1300-9, 2070251675) Fr & Eur.

— Vegetation. Fahnestock, Lee, tr. 48p. 1987. pap. 4.00 (0-87376-058-1) Red Dust.

Ponghis, G., jt. auth. see Okun, D. A.

Pongpanich, B., et al, eds. Pediatric Cardiology: Proceedings of the 3rd World Conference, Bangkok, 26 November-1 December, 1989. (International Congress Ser.: No. 906). 524p. 1990. 180.00 (0-444-81143-5, Excerpta Medica) Elsevier.

Poniachek, Harvey A. Cases in International Finance. (Series in Finance). 639p. 1993. Net. pap. text ed. write for info. (0-471-53678-4) Wiley.

— Direct Foreign Investment in the United States. 272p. 1986. text ed. 45.00 (0-669-11076-0) Free Pr.

Poniachek, Harvey A., ed. International Corporate Finance. 400p. 1989. 80.00 (0-04-445394-9) Routledge Chapman & Hall.

Poniatowska, Elena. Massacre in Mexico. Lane, Helen R., tr. (Illus.). 352p. (C). 1991. pap. 16.95 (0-8262-0817-7) U of Mo Pr.

Poniatowska, Elena & Stellweg, Carla. Frida Kahlo: The Camera Seduced. (Illus.). 128p. 1992. 29.95 (0-8118-0238-8); pap. 18.95 (0-8118-0215-9) Chronicle Bks.

Poniatowska, Elena, jt. auth. see Conger, Amy.

Poniatowski, Martin. The HP-UX Systems Administrator's "How to" Book. LC 93-2011. (Hewlett Packard Professional Books Ser.). 1993. pap. text ed. 32.00 (0-13-099821-4) P-H.

***Ponichtera, Brenda J.** Quick & Healthy Vol. II: More Help for People Who Say They Don't Have Time to Cook Healthy Meals, 2. LC 91-90207. (Illus.). 262p. (Orig.). 1995. pap. 16.95 (0-9629160-1-3) ScaleDown.

— Quick & Healthy Recipes & Ideas: For People Who Say They Don't Have Time to Cook Healthy Meals. LC 91-90207. (Illus.). 262p. (Orig.). 1991. 16.95 (0-9629160-0-5) ScaleDown.

Ponick, Wes & Pugh, Frank. Experiments in Direct & Alternating Current Circuits. 176p. 1987. pap. text ed. 10.95 (0-07-050461-X) McGraw.

Ponick, Wes, jt. auth. see Pugh, Frank.

Poniewaz, Jeff. Dolphin Leaping in the Milky Way. (Illus.). 148p. 1986. reprint ed. pap. 12.95 (0-685-44851-7) Inland Ocean Bks.

Ponikvar, A. L., jt. ed. see Carr, D. S.

Ponjoan, Jose A. Mi Pecado Fue Quererte. LC 88-81863. (Coleccion Caniqui Ser.). 280p. (Orig.). (SPA.). 1989. pap. 15.00 (0-89729-499-8) Ediciones.

Ponka & Schulman. Iron Transport & Storage. 1990. 230.00 (0-8493-6677-1, QP535) CRC Pr.

Ponka, P., jt. auth. see Neuwirt, J.

Ponko, Vincent, Jr. Britain in the Middle East, Nineteen Twenty-One to Nineteen Fifty-Six: An Annotated Bibliography. LC 89-2325. (Themes in European Expansion Ser.: Vol. 9). 542p. 1990. 65.00 (0-8240-8551-5, 357) Garland.

Ponlisse, Nanda. The Use of Compensatory Strategies by Dutch Learners of English. (Studies on Language Acquisition). 1990. pap. 53.85 (3-11-013110-2) Mouton.

***Ponnamperuma, Cyril, ed.** Chemical Evolution: Structure & Model of the First Cell: Conference on the Structure & Model of the First Cell (ICTP) Held in Trieste, Italy on 29 August-2 September 1994. 392p. (C). 1995. lib. bdg. 228.00 (0-7923-3562-7) Kluwer Ac.

— Comets & the Origin of Life. 292p. 1981. lib. bdg. 80.00 (90-277-1318-9) Kluwer Ac.

— Cosmochemistry & the Origin of Life. 1983. lib. bdg. 136.50 (90-277-1544-0) Kluwer Ac.

Ponnamperuma, Cyril & Chela-Flores, Julian, eds. Chemical Evolution: Origin of Life. (Illus.). 336p. 1993. 50.00 (0-937194-31-X) A Deepak Pub.

Ponnamperuma, Cyril & Eirich, Frederick, eds. Prebiological Self Organization of Matter: The Eighth College Park Colloquium on Chemical Evolution. LC 90-3640. (Illus.). 305p. 1990. 50.00 (0-937194-18-2) A Deepak Pub.

Ponnamperuma, Cyril & Gehrke, Charles W., eds. A Lunar-Based Chemical Analysis Laboratory: Proceedings of the Ninth College Colloquium on Chemical Evolution. LC 91-40702. (Illus.). 281p. 1992. 50.00 (0-937194-25-5) A Deepak Pub.

Ponnamperuma, Cyril & Margulis, Lynn, eds. Limits of Life. 200p. 1980. lib. bdg. 60.00 (90-277-1155-0) Kluwer Ac.

***Ponnusamy, S.** Foundations of Complex Analysis. LC 95-9055. 1995. write for info. (0-471-13115-6) Wiley.

Ponomareff, Constantin V. On the Dark Side of Russian Literature, 1709-1910. (American University Studies: Slavic Languages & Literature: Ser. XII, Vol. 2). 261p. (C). 1987. text ed. 37.90 (0-8204-0503-5) P Lang Pubs.

Ponomarenko, S. V., tr. see Samchuk, A. I. & Pilipenko, A. T.

Ponomarev, Boris N. Communism in a Changing World. LC 82-25622. 266p. 1983. 17.95 (0-943071-01-7) Sphinx Pr.

— Winning for Peace: The Great Victory--Its World Impact. 136p. 1985. 40.00 (0-317-42824-1, Pub. by Collets UK) St Mut.

Ponomarev, L. I. & Kurchatov, I. V., eds. The Quantum Dice. (Illus.). 240p. 1993. 110.00 (0-7503-0251-8); pap. 35.00 (0-7503-0241-0) IOP Pub.

Ponomarev, V. I., jt. auth. see Arkangeliskii, A. V.

Ponomarev, Valerii N., jt. ed. see Ragsdale, Hugh.

Ponomarov, Sergius, tr. see Chekhov, Anton.

Ponomarov, Sergius, tr. see Chekov, Anton.

Ponomaryov, V. M., ed. Artificial Intelligence: Proceedings of the IFAC Symposium, Leningrad, U. S. S. R., 4-6 Oct., 1983. (IFAC Proceedings Ser.). 720p. 1984. 236.00 (0-08-031130-X, 11/2, Pub. by Pergamon Repr UK) Franklin.

Ponoroff, Lawrence, jt. auth. see Snyder, Stephen E.

Pons. Pons Fachwoerterbuch Marketing. (ENG & GER.). 1991. 75.00 (0-8288-7269-4, 3125179807) Fr & Eur.

— Pons Fachwoeterbuch Umwelt. (ENG & GER.). 1991. 75.00 (0-8288-7268-6, 3125179408) Fr & Eur.

***Pons, Bruno.** Architecture & Panelling: The James A. de Rothschild Collection at Waddersan Manors. (Illus.). 680p. 1996. 290.00 (0-302-00669-9) Scala Books.

***Pons, Frank M.** The Dominican Republic: A National History. 520p. 1994. 32.00 (1-885509-00-6); pap. 22.00 (1-885509-01-4) Hispaniola Bks.

Pons, Josh. Country Life Diary. (Illus.). 516p. (Orig.). 1992. pap. 19.95 (0-939049-49-X) Blood-Horse.

***Pons, Marie N., ed.** Bioprocess Monitoring & Control. 1993. text ed. 74.95 (0-471-03714-1) Wiley.

Pons, N. & Sutton, B. Mycological Papers, No. 160 - Cercospora & Similar Fungi on Yams: (Dioscorea Species) (Mycological Paper Ser.: No. 160). 78p. 1989. pap. 34.50 (0-85198-622-6) CAB Intl.

Pons, Pat & Goode, Elizabeth. Word of Mouth: Triangle Restaurant & Market Guide for 1990. (Illus.). (Orig.). 1989. pap. 8.95 (0-685-29455-2) Word Mouth NC.

Pons, Valdo. Stanleyville: An African Urban Community under Belgian Administration. LC 70-396468. 383p. reprint ed. pap. 109.20 (0-8357-3222-3, 2057116) Bks Demand.

***Pons, Xavier.** A Sheltered Land. 368p. 1995. pap. 29.95 (1-86373-639-5, Pub. by Allen Unwin AT) Paul & Co Pubs.

Ponse, A., ed. see British Computer Society Staff.

Ponse, A., ed. see First Workshop on the Algebra of Communicating Processes Staff.

Ponse, Barbara. Identities in the Lesbian World: The Social Construction of Self. LC 77-84763. (Contributions in Sociology Ser.: No. 28). 228p. 1978. text ed. 38.50 (0-8371-9889-5, PLW/, Greenwood Pr) Greenwood.

Ponsell, jt. auth. see Judd.

***Ponsett, B.** OT Survey Study Guide. 1994. pap. 7.99 (0-8054-1086-4) Broadman.

Ponsetto, Daniel. Praying Our Stories. Stamschror, Robert, ed. (Reflections for Youth Ministers Ser.). (Illus.). 104p. (Orig.). 1992. pap. 7.95 (0-88489-281-6) St Marys.

— Walking Together: Outreach & Evangelization for Youth. Stamschror, Robert, ed. (Illus.). (Orig.). 1995. pap. 15.95 (0-88489-293-X) St Marys.

Ponsky, Jeffrey L. Atlas of Surgical Endoscopy. (Illus.). 240p. 1991. 89.00 (0-8151-6742-3) Mosby Yr Bk.

— Techniques of Percutaneous Gastrostomy. LC 87-33929. (Illus.). 144p. 1988. 75.00 (0-89640-139-1) Igaku-Shoin.

Ponsky, Jeffrey L., jt. ed. see Greene, Frederick L.

Ponsonby, Arthur. English Diaries. LC 77-175708. (Select Bibliographies Reprint Ser.). 1977. reprint ed. 26.95 (0-8369-6623-6) Ayer.

— Falsehood in Wartime: Propaganda Lies of the First World War. 2nd ed. 192p. (C). 1991. reprint ed. pap. text ed. 6.95 (0-939484-39-0, 0339) Inst Hist Rev.

— Samuel Pepys. LC 71-160987. (Select Bibliographies Reprint Ser.). 1977. reprint ed. 24.95 (0-8369-5855-1) Ayer.

Ponsonby-Fane, Richard A. Fortunes of the Emperors: Studies in Revolution, Exile, Abdication, Usurpation, & Deposition in Ancient Japan. LC 79-52920. (Studies in Japanese History & Civilization). 332p. 1979. text ed. 65.00 (0-313-27025-2, U7025) Greenwood.

— Imperial Cities: The Capitals of Japan from the Oldest Times Until 1229. LC 79-52921. (Studies in Japanese History & Civilization). 243p. 1979. text ed. 55.00 (0-313-27032-5, U7032, Greenwood Pr) Greenwood.

Ponsonby, Laura. Marianne North at Kew Gardens. (Illus.). 128p. 1991. lib. bdg. 45.00 (0-86350-309-8, Pub. by Royal Botanic Garden UK) Lubrecht & Cramer.

Ponsor. Gawain & the Green Knights. 1979. 8.95 (0-02-598000-9) Macmillan.

Ponsot, Marie. The Green Dark. LC 87-46186. 80p. 1988. 16.95 (0-394-57054-5) Knopf.

Ponsot, Marie & Deen, Rosemary. Beat Not the Poor Desk: Writing: What to Teach, How to Teach It, & Why. LC 81-15519. 212p. (Orig.). 1981. pap. text ed. 18.50 (0-86709-009-X) Boynton Cook Pubs.

— The Common Sense: What to Write, How to Write it, & Why. LC 85-4126. 166p. (Orig.). (C). 1985. pap. text ed. 15.50 (0-86709-079-0) Boynton Cook Pubs.

Ponstein, J. Convexity & Duality in Optimization. (Lecture Notes in Economics & Mathematical Systems Ser.: Vol. 256). v, 142p. 1985. pap. 39.50 (0-387-15986-X) Spr-Verlag.

Ponstein, Jacob. Approaches to the Theory of Optimization. LC 79-41419. (Cambridge Tracts in Mathematics Ser.: No. 77). 217p. reprint ed. pap. 61.90 (0-8357-5697-1, 2031711) Bks Demand.

***Pont, Adrian C.** The Type-Material of Diptera (Insecta) Described by G. H. Verrall & J. E. Collin. (Illus.). 240p. 1995. 98.00 (0-19-854919-9) OUP.

Pont Quer, Pio. Diccionario de Botanica. 1244p. (SPA.). 1977. 59.95 (0-8288-5313-4, S50066) Fr & Eur.

— Diccionario de Botanica: Dictionary of Botany. 256p. (SPA.). 1973. 29.95 (0-7859-0888-9, S-50258) Fr & Eur.

Pont, Timothy. Topographical Account of the District of Cunningham, Ayrshire. LC 74-174280. (Maitland Club, Glasgow. Publications: No. 74). reprint ed. 27.50 (0-404-53112-1) AMS Pr.

Pont, Tony. Developing Effective Training Skills. 136p. 1991. pap. text ed. 24.95 (0-07-707383-5) McGraw.

— Investing in Training & Development: Turning Interest into Capital. 256p. 1995. text ed. 69.00 (0-89397-443-9) Nichols Pub.

Pontalis, J. B. Love of Beginnings. Greene, James & Reguis, Marie-Christine, trs. 192p. 1993. pap. 18.00 (1-85343-129-X) Col U Pr.

Pontalis, J. B., jt. auth. see Laplanche, J.

Pontalis, J-B., jt. auth. see Laplanche, Jean.

Pontalis, Jean-Baptiste. Vocabulaire de la Psychanalyse. 5th ed. Laplanche, Jean, ed. (FRE.). 1976. 85.00 (0-8288-5759-8, M6558) Fr & Eur.

Pontalis, Jean-Bertrand, jt. auth. see Laplanche, Jean.

Ponte, J. P., et al, eds. Mathematical Problem Solving & New Information Technologies: Research in Contexts of Practice. (NATO ASI Series F Computer & Systems Sciences, Special Programme AET: Vol. 89). xv, 346p. 1992. 94.00 (0-387-55735-0) Spr-Verlag.

***Ponte, T. G.** The Rainbow Princess & the Land of Black & White. LC 94-61590. (Illus.). 44p. (J). (gr. k-5). 1995. 7.95 (1-55523-730-4) Winston-Derek.

***Pontecorvo, Clotilde & Orsolini, Margherita, eds.** Children's Early Text Construction. 360p. 1995. text ed. 60.00 (0-8058-1504-X) L Erlbaum Assocs.

Pontecorvo, G. Trends in Genetic Analysis. LC 58-8805. (Columbia Biological Ser.: No. 18). 1958. text ed. 42.00 (0-231-02268-9) Col U Pr.

Pontecorvo, G. B., tr. see Ignatovich, V. K.

Pontecorvo, Giulio, ed. The Management of Food Policy. LC 75-33468. (Individual Publications). (Illus.). 1980. lib. bdg. 17.95 (0-405-06680-5) Ayer.

— The New Order of the Oceans: The Advent of a Managed Environment. LC 86-6804. 240p. 1986. text ed. 47.50 (0-231-05870-5) Col U Pr.

Pontecorvo, Giulio, jt. auth. see Crutchfield, James A.

Ponteilhet, Hubert. Les Paves du Diable. (FRE.). 1972. pap. 8.95 (0-7859-3991-1) Fr & Eur.

Pontell, Henry N., ed. Social Deviance: Readings in Theory & Research. LC 92-12825. 448p. (C). 1992. pap. text ed. 20.00 (0-13-815622-0) P-H.

— Social Deviance: Readings in Theory & Research. 2nd ed. LC 95-14296. 1995. pap. text ed. write for info. (0-13-148719-1) P-H.

Ponter, A. R., jt. ed. see Cocks, A. C.

Ponter, Anthony & Ponter, Laura. Spirits in Stone: The New Face of African Art. (Illus.). 204p. 1992. 95.00 (1-881407-07-1) Ukama Pr.

Ponter, Laura, jt. auth. see Ponter, Anthony.

Pontercorvo, G., tr. see Klimontovich, Yu. L.

***Ponterotto, Joseph G. & Casas, J. Manuel.** Handbook of Racial-Ethnic Minority Counseling Research. 208p. 1991. pap. 24.95 (0-398-06329-X) C C Thomas.

— Handbook of Racial-Ethnic Minority Counseling Research. 208p. (C). 1991. text ed. 39.95x (0-398-05716-8) C C Thomas.

Ponterotto, Joseph G. & Pedersen, Paul B. Preventing Prejudice: A Guide for Counselors & Educators. (Multicultural Aspects of Counseling Ser.: Vol. 2). (Illus.). 238p. 1993. 34.00 (0-8039-5284-8); pap. 15.95 (0-8039-5285-6) Sage.

***Ponterotto, Joseph G., et al.** Handbook of Multicultural Counseling. (Illus.). 688p. 1995. 85.00 (0-8039-5506-5); pap. 36.00 (0-8039-5507-3) Sage.

Ponterotto, Joseph G., et al, eds. Affirmative Action on Campus. LC 85-644751. (New Directions for Student Services Ser.: No. 52). 1990. 16.95 (1-55542-816-9) Jossey-Bass.

Pontes, Edison J. Operative Procedures in Genitourinary Cancer. 136p. 1993. text ed. 99.95 (0-471-58831-8) Wiley.

Pontes, J. E., jt. ed. see Kirk, D. N.

Ponteva, E., jt. auth. see Pesonen, Niilo.

Ponticelli, C. & De Vecchi, A., eds. Ciclosporin in Renal Transplantation. (Contributions to Nephrology Ser.: Vol. 51). (Illus.). viii, 168p. 1987. 107.25 (3-8055-4357-3) S Karger.

Ponticelli, C., et al, eds. Antiglobulins, Cryoglobulins & Glomerulonephritis. (Development in Nephrology Ser.). 1986. lib. bdg. 150.00 (0-89838-810-4) Kluwer Ac.

Ponticelli, Rick, jt. auth. see Slater, Jeffrey.

Pontiero, ed. see Garcia Marquez, Gabriel.

Pontiero, G. An Anthology of Brazilian Modernist Poetry. 1969. 110.00 (0-08-013327-4, Pub. by Pergamon Repr UK); pap. 110.00 (0-08-013326-6, Pub. by Pergamon Repr UK) Franklin.

Pontiero, Giovanni. Florencio Sanchez: La Gringa & Barranca Abajo. LC 72-6355. 150p. 1973. 28.50 (0-8386-1264-4) Fairleigh Dickinson.

Pontiero, Giovanni, ed. Duse on Tour: Guido Noccioli's Diaries, 1906-1907. LC 82-4751. (Illus.). 192p. 1982. lib. bdg. 32.00 (0-87023-369-6) U of Mass Pr.

Pontiero, Giovanni, tr. see Lispector, Clarice.

Pontiero, Giovanni, tr. see Nunes, Lygia B.

Pontiero, Giovanni, tr. see Saramago, Jose.

Pontifex, Zsuzsa. Teach Yourself Hungarian. (ENG & HUN.). 1993. pap. 18.95 (0-7859-1056-5, 0-340-562862); pap. 29.95 (0-7859-1057-3, 0-340-562889) Fr & Eur.

Pontifical Council for Interreligious Dialogue Staff & Bormans, Maurice. Guidelines for Dialogue Between Christians & Muslims. (Interreligious Documents Ser.: Vol. I). 1990. pap. 12.95 (0-8091-3181-1) Paulist Pr.

Pontifical Council for Social Communications Staff. New Era. 48p. 1992. pap. 4.95 (1-55586-504-6) US Catholic.

Pontifical Council for the Family Staff, ed. Marriage & Family: Experiencing the Church's Teaching in Married Life. LC 88-81273. 175p. (Orig.). 1989. pap. 9.95 (0-89870-218-6) Ignatius Pr.

Pontifical Institute of Medieval Studies, Ontario Staff. Dictionary Catalogue of the Library of the Pontifical Institute of Medieval Studies, 5 vols., Set. 1973. lib. bdg. 555.00 (0-8161-0970-2, Hall Library) G K Hall.

Pontifical Institute of Medieval Studies, Toronto Staff. Dictionary Catalog of the Library of the Pontifical Institute of Medieval Studies: First Supplement. 1979. lib. bdg. 145.00 (0-8161-1061-1, Hall Library) G K Hall.

Pontifical Justice & Peace Commission Staff. What Have You Done to Your Homeless Brother? The Church & the Housing Problem. 30p. (Orig.). 1987. pap. 1.95 (1-55586-203-9) US Catholic.

Pontiggia, Giuseppe. The Invisible Player. Cancogni, Annapaola, tr. LC 88-80809. 259p. 1989. 23.00 (0-941419-14-2, Eridanos Library); pap. 14.00 (0-941419-15-0, Eridanos Library) Marsilio Pubs.

Pontikis, Vassilis, jt. ed. see Meyer, Madeleine.

Pontin, Rosalind M. A Key to the Freshwater Planktonic & Semi-Planktonic Rotifera of the British Isles. 1978. 45.00 (0-900386-33-9) St Mut.

***Ponting, Clive.** Armageddon: The Second World War. LC 95-2995. 1995. 25.00 (0-679-43602-2) Random.

— A Green History of the World: Nature, Pollution & the Collapse of Societies. (Illus.). 448p. 1992. 24.95 (0-312-06987-1) St Martin.

— A Green History of the World: The Environment & the Collapse of Great Civilizations. 448p. 1993. pap. 12.95 (0-14-017660-8, Penguin Bks) Viking Penguin.

— Nineteen Forty: Myth & Reality. 272p. 1991. 24.95 (0-929587-68-5) I R Dee.

— Nineteen Forty: Myth & Reality. LC 93-11244. 276p. 1993. reprint ed. pap. 11.95 (1-56663-036-3) I R Dee.

— The Right to Know: The Inside Story of the Belgrano Affair. 1985. 25.00 (0-317-54919-7, Pub. by NCCL UK) St Mut.

— Secrecy in Britain. (Historical Association Studies). 96p. 1990. pap. text ed. 12.95 (0-631-16912-1) Blackwell Pubs.

Ponting, K. Wool Marketing. LC 66-23855. 1966. 51.00 (0-08-011675-2, Pub. by Pergamon Repr UK) Franklin.

Pontious, Alfred E. Feed My Sheep. 26p. pap. text ed. 1.95 (0-940227-01-0) Liberation FL.

Pontious, Vicki Jo. Baby Names (with Magic) 125p. (Orig.). 1984. pap. 3.95 (0-9615924-0-0) V J P Enter.

Pontis, Paul R. The Real Christmas Story. 1994. pap. 7.95 (1-55673-857-9) CSS OH.

***Pontius & Zaionchkovskaya.** Geodemography of the Former Soviet Union. Demko, ed. (C). 1995. text ed. 49.95 (0-8133-8939-9) Westview.

***Pontius, C. Birch.** Westward Women. 550p. 1995. pap. 12.95 (1-56901-887-1) NW Pub.

Pontius, John & Yakub, Yahya. Field Training Through Case Studies, No. 16. (Technical Notes Ser.). 21p. (Orig.). 1981. pap. 2.00 (0-932288-61-8) Ctr Intl Ed U of MA.

Ponton, Geoffrey. The Soviet Era: From Lenin to Yeltsin. LC 93-14804. 320p. 1993. 49.95 (0-631-18775-8); pap. 19.95 (0-631-18776-6) Blackwell Pubs.

Ponton, Geoffrey, jt. ed. see Bretherton, Charlotte.

Ponton, Geoffrey, et al. Introduction to Politics. 3rd ed. LC 92-39485. 1993. pap. 24.95 (0-631-18784-7) Blackwell Pubs.

Pontow, Regina. Proven Resumes & Confidence Builders. (Orig.). 1994. pap. 19.95 (1-884668-00-3) Abrams & Smith.

Pontrjagin, L. S. Learning Higher Mathematics. (Soviet Mathematics Ser.). (Illus.). 320p. 1984. pap. 58.00 (0-387-12351-2) Spr-Verlag.

Pontrjagin, L. S., ed. Theory of Functions & Its Applications. LC 77-10017. (Steklov Institute of Mathematics, Proceedings Ser.: No. 134). 458p. 1977. 112.00 (0-8218-3034-1, STEKLO 134) Am Math.

Pontryagin, L., ed. Optimal Control & Differential Games. (STEKLO Ser.: Vol. 185). 278p. 1990. pap. 138.00 (0-8218-3134-8) Am Math.

Pontryagin, L. & Boltyanskii, V. Mathematical Theory of Optimal Processes. LC 63-15354. 1964. 144.00 (0-08-010176-3, Pub. by Pergamon Repr UK) Franklin.

Pontryagin, L. & Kacinskas, L. Ordinary Differential Equations. LC 62-17075. 1962. 132.00 (0-08-009699-9, Pub. by Pergamon Repr UK) Franklin.

Pontryagin, L. S., jt. ed. see Ostianu, N. M.

Pontus. Life of St. Cyprian. pap. 1.50 (0-89981-046-2) Eastern Orthodox.

Pontuso, James F. Solzhenitsyn's Political Thought. 320p. 1990. 30.00 (0-8139-1283-0) U Pr of Va.

Pontusson, Jonas. The Limits of Social Democracy: Investment Politics in Sweden. LC 92-2694. (Cornell Studies in Political Economy). (Illus.). 272p. 1992. 31.50 (0-8014-2652-9) Cornell U Pr.

— The Limits of Social Democracy: Investment Politics in Sweden. LC 92-2694. (Studies in Political Economy). (Illus.). 272p. 1994. pap. 15.95 (0-8014-8235-6) Cornell U Pr.

Pontusson, Jonas, jt. ed. see Golden, Miriam.

Ponty, Marleau M. Texts & Dialogues. Silverman, Hugh & Barry, James, Jr., eds. LC 90-46082. (Contemporary Studies in Philosophy & the Human Sciences). 264p. (C). 1991. text ed. 49.95 (0-391-03702-1) Humanities.

Ponxin, jt. auth. see Jongrong, Wu.

Pony Club Staff. Correct Dress for Riding. (C). 1990. pap. 21.00 (0-900226-30-7, Pub. by J A Allen & Co UK) St Mut.

— The Foot & Showing. 71p. (C). 1990. 28.00 (0-900226-31-5, Pub. by J A Allen & Co UK) St Mut.

— The Instructor's Handbook. 140p. (C). 1990. 32.00 (0-900226-40-4, Pub. by J A Allen & Co UK) St Mut.

— Keeping a Pony at Grass. 96p. (C). 1990. 21.00 (0-900226-71-4, Pub. by J A Allen & Co UK) St Mut.

— The Pony Club Quiz Book. 112p. (C). 1990. pap. 21.00 (0-900226-29-3, Pub. by J A Allen & Co UK) St Mut.

Pony Club Training Committee Staff. Choosing & Buying a Pony. (Illus.). 96p. 1990. 18.95 (0-900226-38-2, Pub. by Brit Horse Soc & Pony Club UK) Half Halt Pr.

— Training Young Horses. (Illus.). 112p. 1990. 17.95 (0-900226-37-4, Pub. by Brit Horse Soc & Pony Club UK) Half Halt Pr.

Ponye, J., jt. auth. see Salanki, J.

Ponzetto, Pietro, jt. auth. see Bellin, Robert.

Ponzi, Maurizio. The Films of Gina Lollobrigida. Curto, Shula A., tr. (Illus.). 160p. (Orig.). 1989. pap. 14.95 (0-8065-1093-5, Citadel Pr) Carol Pub Group.

Ponzio, Augusto. Man as Sign: Essays on the Philosophy of Language. (Approaches to Semiotics Ser.: No. 89). xii, 412p. (C). 1990. lib. bdg. 129.25 (3-11-012167-0) Mouton.

— Signs, Dialogue & Ideology: Interdisciplinary Approaches to Language, Discourse & Ideology. LC 93-33214. (Critical Theory Ser.: No. 11). ix, 183p. 1992. 65.00 (1-55619-179-0) Benjamins North Am.

Poo, G. S., ed. Towards Network Globalization. 500p. (C). 1991. text ed. 118.00 (981-02-0796-4) World Scientific Pub.

***Poo, Mu-chou.** Wine & Wine Offering in the Religion of Ancient Egypt. LC 95-6571. (Studies in Egyptology). 1995. write for info. (0-7103-0501-X, Pub. by Kegan Paul Intl UK) Routledge Chapman & Hall.

Pooch. Handbook of Software Engineering. 1993. write for info. (0-8493-7175-9) CRC Pr.

Pooch, Heinz. Fachwoerterbuch des Nachrichtenwesens: Technical Dictionary of Communications. 2nd ed. 377p. (ENG & GER.). 1980. 75.00 (0-8288-0183-5, M7390) Fr & Eur.

Pooch, Udo W. Discrete Event Simulation: A Practical Approach. 1992. 59.95 (0-8493-7174-0, QA) CRC Pr.

Pooch, Udo W. & Chattergy, Rahul. Minicomputers: Hardware, Software, & Selection. (Illus.). 365p. 1980. text ed. 54.75 (0-8299-0055-1) West Pub.

An Asterisk (*) at the beginning of an entry indicates that the title is appearing in BIP for the first time.

Pooch, Udo W., et al. Telecommunications & Networking. (Illus.). 400p. 1991. 64.95 (*0-8493-7172-4*, T) CRC Pr.

Pook, P. L. The Role of Crack Growth in Metal Fatigue. 157p. (Orig.). 1983. pap. text ed. 31.50 (*0-904357-63-5*, Pub. by Inst Materials UK) Ashgate Pub Co.

Pookrum, Jewel. Vitamins & Minerals from A to Z. 138p. 1993. pap. text ed. write for info. (*1-881316-66-1*) A&B Bks.

Pool, Christopher A., jt. ed. see Bey, George J., III.

Pool, Clifford W. The California Homeowner's Guidebook: How to Deal with Home Alteration Contractors. F'Mayer, Keith L., ed. 106p. (Orig.). 1992. pap. 19.95 (*0-9635362-1-4*, TX3 401 617) Courier Pub.

Pool, Daniel. What Jane Austen Ate & Charles Dickens Knew. 1994. 14.00 (*0-671-88236-8*, Touchstone Bks) S&S Trade.

— What Jane Austen Ate & Charles Dickens Knew: From Fox Hunting to Whist - the Facts of Daily Life in 19th Century British Life. (Illus.). 480p. 1993. pap. 25.00 (*0-671-79337-3*) S&S Trade.

Pool, David. Hobbyist Guide to Successful Koi Keeping. (Aquarium Digest International - Collector's Edition Ser.). (Illus.). 1992. 12.95 (*3-89356-134-X*, 16583) Tetra Pr.

— Hobbyist Guide to Successful Pond Keeping. (Illus.). 144p. 1994. 12.95 (*3-89356-135-8*, 16584) Tetra Pr.

Pool, David, jt. auth. see Loiselle, P. V.

Pool, Elizabeth. The Unicorn Was There. LC 81-4747. (Illus.). 64p. 1981. reprint ed. pap. 5.95 (*0-87233-061-3*) Bauhan.

Pool, Ian. Te Iwi Maori: A New Zealand: Population Past, Present & Projected. (Illus.). 288p. 1991. 28.00 (*1-86940-049-6*) OUP.

Pool, Ithiel de Sola. Technologies of Freedom. 312p. 1984. pap. 15.95 (*0-674-87233-9*) Belknap Pr.

Pool, J. C., ed. see Society for Industrial & Applied Mathematics Staff & American Mathematical Society Staff.

***Pool, J. Charles & Frick, Robert L. The ABCs of Personal Finance. (Illus.). 125p. (Orig.). (YA). (gr. 9-12). 1995. pap. text ed. 9.95 (*1-882505-04-2*) Durell Inst MSASU.**
THE ABCs OF PERSONAL FINANCE provides to the layman, teacher or student the basics of personal financial planning--making plans & making choices. Times have changed & so has personal finance. This book attempts to address those issues in a simple, readable & understandable way. Here are the basics on how to plan for a prosperous & secure future for yourself & your family. Included are how to build a "safe" financial future, budgeting, thinking clearly about savings, credit, career planning & choices, inflation, taxes, home mortgages, retirement, how to buy a car & a house, planning for kids, college & life insurance, investing your money, the banking system, & how the economy works. Also available from the publisher are companion materials which make the book a complete teaching kit. These materials include workbook, homework exercises, transparency masters, wall chart & a 30-minute video that further explains the subject matter. All are available from The Durell Institute, Shenandoah University, 1460 University Drive, Winchester, VA 22601. (703) 665-5430. ***Publisher Provided Annotation.***

Pool, James C. & Stamos, Stephen C., Jr. The ABCs of International Finance: Understanding the Trade & Debt Crisis. 160p. 1987. pap. 17.95 (*0-669-14601-3*) Free Pr.

Pool, James M. Among These Hills: A Child's History of Harrison County. (Illus.). 240p. (J). 1985. 12.95 (*0-9615566-0-9*) Clarksburg-Harrison Bicent.

Pool, John C. The ABCs of Money & Banking. (Illus.). 71p. (Orig.). 1992. pap. text ed. 9.95 (*1-882505-01-8*) Durell Inst MSASU.
THE ABC's OF MONEY & BANKING provides an introduction to economics which will demystify the subject & provide the reader with the basics for life as a consumer. The detail approximates that found in most introductory economics textbooks, but avoids technical jargon & theoretical subtleties which make most economics texts difficult to read or teach at the secondary (high school) level. The subject matter includes: how our economy & the market system work, money & its history, the monetary system, the banking system, the Federal Reserve System, goals of monetary policy, need for economic growth, unemployment & its causes, scope of monetary policy/theory, problems & controversies, & recent developments. Also available from the publisher are companion materials that make the textbook a complete teaching kit. These materials include lesson plans, homework exercises, transparency masters, wall charts, answers to the discussion questions at the end of each chapter of the textbook, & a 20-minute video that explains how our monetary system evolved & how it functions today. ***Publisher Provided Annotation.***

Pool, John C. & Frick, Robert L. Demystifying the Stock Market. LC 93-72993. (Illus.). 126p. (Orig.). 1995. pap. 9.95 (*1-882505-02-6*) Durell Inst MSASU.
DEMYSTIFYING THE STOCK MARKET provides an introduction to the stock market: its function, its operations, its history. It helps the reader to overcome the mystique of Wall Street by explaining how the markets work, what the advantages & disadvantages might be of various types of investment & how the economy & basic economic principles affect investments & financial markets. Its premise is that knowledge about markets, investments & economics is key to confident & fear-free investing. The reader learns how to deal with a stockbroker, how to make a purchase of stock, how to decipher the stock tables, & how to keep track of investments. The book is a valuable tool for anyone seeking an understanding of this complex subject. Also available from the publisher are companion materials which make the book a complete teaching kit. These materials include workbook, homework exercises, transparency masters, wall charts, & a 30-minute video that explains how the stock market functions. All are available from The Durell Institute, Shenandoah University, 1460 University Drive, Winchester, VA 22601; (703) 665-5428. ***Publisher Provided Annotation.***

Pool, John C. & LaRoe, Ross M. Default! LC 87-60562. 139p. (C). 1987. pap. text ed. 10.00 (*0-312-00518-0*) St Martin.

— Instant Economist. 1985. pap. 10.58 (*0-201-16883-9*) Addison-Wesley.

Pool, John C. & Stamos, Stephen C., Jr. Exploring the Global Economy. (Illus.). 122p. (Orig.). (YA). (gr. 9-12). 1995. pap. 9.95 (*1-882505-03-4*) Durell Inst MSASU.
EXPLORING THE GLOBAL ECONOMY provides to the layman, teacher or student the basics of the international economy with focus on how the world economy is rapidly changing & becoming internationalized. The unique ability of the authors to communicate this complicated subject matter in uncomplicated language makes this volume easy to read. Accompanied by maps & charts which illustrate the subject, the book takes a broad look at international economic & trade issues, why international trade benefits everyone, the basic theory behind it & how it functions. It then examines the relationship between international trade & international finance & how & why international economic issues may dominate economic policy in the coming decade. Trade policy, the implications of NAFTA & GATT, European Integration & the competitive issues in the Pacific Basin are explored for the purpose of summary explanation, definition & related issues. Transition of modern economic systems from the fall of the Berlin Wall to the collapse of the Soviet economy are presented in factual detail. Prospects for world economies in the 21st century inform & prepare the reader for the challenges to come. Also available from the publisher are companion materials which make the book a complete teaching kit. These materials include workbook, homework exercises, transparency masters, wall charts & a 30-minute video that further explains the subject matter. All are available from The Durell Institute, Shenandoah University, 1460 University Drive, Winchester, VA 22601. (703) 665-5430. ***Publisher Provided Annotation.***

— International Economic Policy: Beyond the Trade & Debt Crisis. LC 87-45996. 160p. 1989. pap. 19.95 (*0-669-17110-7*) Free Pr.

— International Economics: Theory, Policy & Practice. 336p. 1990. pap. 32.95 (*0-669-17150-6*) Free Pr.

Pool, John C., et al. The ABCs of International Finance. 2nd ed. 224p. 1991. text ed. 27.95 (*0-669-27887-4*); pap. 16.95 (*0-669-24522-4*) Free Pr.

Pool, K. J. A History of Amateur Archaeology in the St. Louis Area: A History of Amateur Archaeology in the St. Louis Area. (Missouri Archaeologist Ser.: Vol. 50 (1989)). 1992. 7.50 (*0-943414-73-3*, 115000) MO Arch Soc.

Pool, Karen, et al. Getting What You Want in Life...Without Feeling Guilty. 1992. 9.95 (*1-55503-378-4*, 0111953) Covenant Comms.

Pool, Maria L. Widower & Some Spinsters: Short Stories. LC 78-101288. (Short Story Index Reprint Ser.). 1977. 21.95 (*0-8369-3225-0*) Ayer.

Pool, Mary J. Gardens of Florence. LC 91-32075. (Illus.). 224p. 1992. 45.00 (*0-8478-1488-2*) Rizzoli Intl.

Pool, Mary J., jt. auth. see Howard, Linn.

Pool, Phoebe. Impressionism. LC 84-51308. (World of Art Ser.). (Illus.). 288p. 1985. pap. 14.95 (*0-500-20056-4*) Thames Hudson.

Pool, Robert. Dialogue and the Interpretation of Illness: Conversations in a Cameroon Village. LC 93-4290. (Explorations in Anthropology Ser.). 250p. 1994. 49.95 (*0-85496-873-3*); pap. 19.95 (*1-85973-016-7*) Berg Pubs.

— Eve's Rib: Searching for the Biological Roots of Sex Differences. LC 93-39793. 1994. 22.00 (*0-517-59298-3*, Crown) Crown Pub Group.

— Yang-Mills Fields & Extension Theory. LC 86-28809. (Memoirs of the American Mathematical Society Ser.: Vol. 358). 63p. 1987. 15.00 (*0-8218-2422-8*, MEMO/65/358C) Am Math.

Pool, S. L. Orations of Mohammad. pap. 3.00 (*1-56744-175-0*) Kazi Pubns.

Pool, Thomas E. John Wesley the Soul Winner. pap. 4.99 (*0-88019-074-4*) Schmul Pub Co.

Pool, William C. Eugene C. Barker: Historian. LC 76-627820. (Illus.). 1971. 13.95 (*0-87611-025-1*) Tex St Hist Assn.

— The Historical Atlas of Texas. (Illus.). 216p. 1974. 25.00 (*0-88426-033-X*) Encino Pr.

Poole. Collectible Cars. 1991. 29.99 (*0-517-03594-4*) Random Hse Value.

— Frommer's Ireland on Forty-Five Dollars a Day, 94-95. (Illus.). 1994. pap. 17.00 (*0-671-86668-0*, P-H Travel) P-H Gen Ref & Trav.

Poole, ed. see Guthrie.

Poole, A. & Leslie, G. B. A Practical Approach to Toxicological Investigations. 144p. (C). 1990. 39.95 (*0-521-34118-3*) Cambridge U Pr.

Poole, Adrian. Coriolanus. LC 88-18051. 192p. 1988. text ed. 22.95 (*0-8057-8709-7*, Twayne); pap. 13.95 (*0-8057-8713-5*, Twayne) Macmillan.

***Poole, Adrian & Maule, Jeremy, eds.** The Oxford Book of Classical Verse in Translation. 620p. 1995. 29.95 (*0-19-214209-7*) OUP.

Poole, Adrian, ed. see James, Henry.

Poole, Arnold B. Echoes from the Mount. LC 91-62229. 71p. 1991. reprint ed. pap. 3.95 (*0-9624008-4-X*) Pulpit Rock.

— You Will Never Die Laughing. LC 91-62231. 78p. 1991. reprint ed. pap. 3.95 (*0-9624008-5-8*) Pulpit Rock.

Poole, Austin L. Domesday Book to Magna Carta, 1087-1216. 2nd ed. LC 92-32686. (Illus.). 560p. (C). 1993. pap. 17.95 (*0-19-285287-6*) OUP.

— From Domesday Book to Magna Carta, 1087-1216. 2nd ed. (Oxford History of England Ser.). 1956. 55.00 (*0-19-821707-2*) OUP.

— Henry the Lion: The Lothian Historical Essay for 1912. LC 80-2008. reprint ed. 22.00 (*0-404-18586-X*) AMS Pr.

— Obligations of Society in the Twelfth & Thirteenth Centuries: The Ford Lectures Delivered in the University of Oxford in Michaelmas Term. LC 80-2007. reprint ed. 22.00 (*0-404-18587-8*) AMS Pr.

Poole, Barbara. Introductory Algebra. 2nd ed. LC 93-41608. 1993. pap. text ed. write for info. (*0-13-503723-9*) P-H.

Poole, Barbara A. Basic Mathematics. LC 94-3089. 1994. pap. text ed. write for info. (*0-13-458019-2*) P-H Gen Ref & Trav.

— Intermediate Algebra. 2nd ed. LC 94-2931. 1994. pap. text ed. write for info. (*0-13-075326-2*) P-H.

Poole, Barbara C. Intermediate Algebra. 596p. (C). 1989. pap. text ed. write for info. (*0-13-470212-3*) P-H.

— Psychology & Medicine of Appetite Disorders: Research Subject Analysis with Reference Bibliography. rev. ed. LC 85-48101. 149p. 1994. 44.50 (*0-7883-0652-9*); pap. 39.50 (*0-7883-0653-7*) ABBE Pubs Assn.

Poole, Bernard J. Education for An Information Age: Teaching in the Computerized Classroom. 480p. (C). 1995. pap. text ed. write for info. (*0-697-15403-3*) Brown & Benchmark.

— Essential Microsoft Works: Tutorial for Teachers. 272p. 1994. spiral bd. write for info. (*0-697-21813-9*) Brown & Benchmark.

Poole, Bernard J., et al. The Resume Writer: Writing It Right. 128p. 1991. pap. text ed. 36.60 (*0-13-775388-8*) P-H.

***Poole, Bernice A.** The Listening Sky. 224p. 1995. 4.95 (*0-87067-864-7*) Holloway.

— Mary McLeod Bethune: (Educator) (Illus.). 208p. (Orig.). (YA). 1994. pap. 3.95 (*0-87067-783-7*, Melrose Sq) Holloway.

Poole-Burlingame, Mary, ed. see Burlingame, Burl & Kasher, Robert K.

Poole, C. F. & Schuette, S. A. Contemporary Practice of Chromatography. 708p. 1984. 95.00 (*0-444-42410-5*) Elsevier.

Poole, C. P. & Farach, H. A. Handbook of Electron Spin Resonance. LC 93-33834. (Illus.). 500p. 1994. text ed. 115.00 (*1-56396-044-3*) Am Inst Physics.

Poole-Carter, Rosemary. Mossy Cape. (Illus.). 27p. 1994. pap. 4.00 (*0-88680-396-9*) I E Clark.

Poole, Catherine & Parr, Elizabeth. Choosing a Nurse-Midwife: Your Guide to Safe, Sensitive Care During Pregnancy & the Birth of Your Child. LC 93-33105. 1994. pap. text ed. 12.95 (*0-471-58452-5*) Wiley.

Poole, Cecil A. Cares That Infest. AMORC Staff, ed. LC 77-91873. 120p. 1978. 15.95 (*0-912057-28-9*, 501730) AMORC.

— The Eternal Fruits of Knowledge. 3rd ed. LC 76-352583. 162p. 1978. 9.95 (*0-912057-27-0*, 501710) AMORC.

— In Search of Reality. LC 80-51705. 94p. 1980. pap. 9.95 (*0-912057-31-9*, 501880) AMORC.

— Mysticism - the Ultimate Experience. LC 81-86628. 166p. 1982. 16.95 (*0-912057-33-5*, 501900) AMORC.

Poole, Charle P., et al. Copper Oxide Superconductors. LC 88-18569. 289p. 1988. text ed. 79.95 (*0-471-62342-3*) Wiley.

Poole, Charles, ed. see Hemingway, Ernest.

Poole, Charles E. Don't Cry Past Tuesday: Hopeful Words for Difficult Days. 106p. (Orig.). 1991. pap. 9.95 (*0-9628455-7-4*) Smyth & Helwys.

Poole, Charles P. & Farach, Horacio A. Theory of Magnetic Resonance. 2nd ed. LC 86-11013. 359p. 1987. text ed. 126.00 (*0-471-81530-6*) Wiley.

***Poole, Charles P., Jr., et al.** Superconductivity. (Illus.). 504p. 1995. text ed. write for info. (*0-12-561455-1*) Acad Pr.

— Superconductivity. (Illus.). 528p. 1996. pap. text ed. write for info. (*0-12-561456-X*) Acad Pr.

Poole, Dave, ed. see Magon, Ricardo F.

Poole, David. The Rivers Bend. 74p. 1994. pap. 6.95 (*1-56901-259-8*) NW Pub.

Poole, David N. The History of the Covenant Concept from the Bible to Johannes Cloppenburg: De Foedere Dei. LC 92-11672. (Illus.). 316p. 1992. lib. bdg. 99.95 (*0-7734-9814-1*) E Mellen.

— Stages of Religious Faith in the Classical Reformation Tradition: The Covenant Approach to the Ordo Salutis. LC 95-7267. (Illus.). 336p. 1995. text ed. 99.95 (*0-7734-8890-1*) E Mellen.

Poole, Deborah & Renique, Gerardo. Peru: Time of Fear. (Latin America Bureau Ser.). 200p. (Orig.). (C). 1992. pap. 15.00 (*0-85345-869-3*, Pub. by Lat Am Bur UK) Monthly Rev.

Poole, Deborah A. Unruly Order: Violence, Power, & Identity in the Southern High Provinces of Peru. 256p. (C). 1994. text ed. 52.50 (*0-8133-8749-3*) Westview.

Poole, Dennis. Electrical Distribution in Buildings. 2nd rev. ed. LC 93-24612. 1993. write for info. (*0-632-03256-1*) Blackwell Sci.

Poole, Dennis L. Rural Social Welfare: An Annotated Bibliography for Educators & Practitioners. LC 80-28691. 334p. 1981. text ed. 55.00 (*0-275-90704-X*, C0704, Praeger Pubs) Greenwood.

Poole, Dennis L., jt. auth. see Coudroglou, Aliki.

Poole, E., jt. auth. see Newby, M.

Poole, Ernest. The Harbor. 1976. lib. bdg. 17.25 (*0-89968-099-2*, Lghtyr Pr) Buccaneer Bks.

— His Family. 1976. lib. bdg. 14.75 (*0-89968-100-X*, Lghtyr Pr) Buccaneer Bks.

— His Second Wife. 1976. lib. bdg. 14.25 (*0-89968-101-8*, Lghtyr Pr) Buccaneer Bks.

Poole, F. & Schuette, S. A. Contemporary Practice of Chromatography. 2nd ed. 1985. reprint ed. pap. 37.50 (*0-444-42506-3*) Elsevier.

Poole, Francis, jt. ed. see Brock, Van K.

Poole, Fred, jt. auth. see Nachwalter, Elliott.

Poole, Gary, jt. auth. see Donato, Vince.

Poole, Gary A., ed. High-Technology Editorial Stylebook. 64p. 1989. pap. 13.95 (*0-685-30787-5*) Renais CA.

Poole, Gray, jt. auth. see Poole, Lynn.

Poole, H. Edmund, ed. see Burney, Charles.

Poole, H. J. The Last Hundred Yards: The Infantry NCO's Contribution to Warfare. (Illus.). (Orig.). Date not set. pap. write for info. (*0-9638695-2-3*) Posterity Pr.

***Poole, Harry A.** The Buoy. 344p. 1995. 25.00 (*1-887189-02-5*); pap. text ed. 17.95 (*1-887189-03-3*) Symi Pub.

— Letters from Tarsus, 2 vols., Set. 1995. 85.00 (*1-887189-09-2*); pap. text ed. 55.00 (*1-887189-10-6*) Symi Pub.

— Letters from Tarsus: From Pythagoras to Paul, Vol. I. 324p. 1995. 45.00 (*1-887189-11-4*); pap. text ed. 29.50 (*1-887189-12-2*) Symi Pub.

— Letters from Tarsus: From Pythagoras to Paul, Vol. II. 296p. 1995. 45.00 (*1-887189-13-0*); pap. text ed. 29.50 (*1-887189-14-9*) Symi Pub.

— Poetic Flights: Poems on Assorted Subjects. 70p. 1995. 15.00 (*1-887189-06-8*); pap. 7.50 (*1-887189-15-7*) Symi Pub.

— The Pollenation Wand. 77p. (J). (gr. 6-7). 1995. 15.00 (*1-887189-04-1*); pap. 7.95 (*1-887189-05-X*) Symi Pub.

— The Puritan. 1185p. 1995. 35.00 (*1-887189-00-9*); pap. text ed. 20.00 (*1-887189-01-7*) Symi Pub.

P Q

Poole, Helen L. Hudson! (Whitewater Dynasty Ser.). 400p. (Orig.). 1980. pap. 2.50 (*0-89083-607-8*) Zebra.

— Ohio. (Whitewater Dynasty Ser.). (Orig.). 1981. pap. 2.75 (*0-89083-733-3*) Zebra.

— The Wabash. (Whitewater Dynasty Ser.: No. 4). 1983. pap. 3.50 (*0-8217-1293-4*) Zebra.

— Whitewater Dynasty, No. 3: The Cumberland. (Whitewater Dynasty Ser.). 1982. pap. 2.95 (*0-89083-979-4*) Zebra.

— Whitewater Dynasty, No. 5: The Mississippi. 448p. 1984. pap. 3.50 (*0-8217-1424-4*) Zebra.

Poole, Herbert. Theories of the Middle Range. LC 84-28402. (Libraries & Information Science). 172p. 1985. text ed. 39.50 (*0-89391-257-3*) Ablex Pub.

Poole, Islwyn. Earth! Test Planet or Test Tube? (Illus.). 464p. (Orig.). 1986. 4.50 (*0-9618329-0-8*) Islwyn Pub.

Poole, J. B. Independence & Interdependence. 305p. 1990. 63.00 (*0-08-036691-0*, Pub. by Brasseys UK) Brasseys Inc.

Poole, J. B., ed. Verification Report, 1991: Yearbook on Arms Control & Environmental Agreements. (Illus.). 288p. 1991. text ed. 35.00 (*0-945257-37-6*) Apex Pr.

Poole, J. B. & Guthrie, R., eds. Verification, 1994: Arms Control, Peacekeeping, & the Environment. (Illus.). 386p. 1994. 50.00 (*1-85753-110-8*) Macmillan.

Poole, James. Abraham. 16p. 1994. pap. 2.00 (*1-880573-16-4*) Grace WI.

— Badminton. 3rd ed. (Illus.). 162p. (C). 1991. reprint ed. pap. text ed. 8.95 (*0-88133-644-0*) Waveland Pr.

— Jacob. 16p. (Orig.). 1994. pap. text ed. 2.50 (*1-880573-09-1*) Grace WI.

Poole, Jill. Casebook on Contract. xxx, 499p. 1992. pap. 40.00 (*1-85431-198-0*, Pub. by Blackstone Pr UK) W W Gaunt.

Poole, John. Phineas Quiddy: Or, Sheer Industry, 3 vols. in 2, 1. LC 79-8190. reprint ed. write for info. (*0-404-62181-3*) AMS Pr.

— Phineas Quiddy: Or, Sheer Industry, 3 vols. in 2, 2. LC 79-8190. reprint ed. write for info. (*0-404-62182-1*) AMS Pr.

— Phineas Quiddy: Or, Sheer Industry, 3 vols. in 2, Set. LC 79-8190. reprint ed. 84.50 (*0-404-62180-5*) AMS Pr.

Poole, Josephine, ed. see Grimm, Jacob.

***Poole, Joyce.** Coming of Age with Elephants: A Memoir. (Illus.). 336p. 1996. 24.95 (*0-7868-6095-2*) Hyperion.

— The Harm We Do: A Catholic Doctor Confronts Church, Moral, & Medical Teaching. LC 92-82673. 168p. (Orig.). 1993. pap. 12.95 (*0-89622-543-7*) Twenty-Third.

***Poole, Julia E.** English Pottery. (Fitzwilliam Museum Publications). (Illus.). 150p. (C). 1995. pap. 15.95 (*0-521-47520-1*) Cambridge U Pr.

— English Pottery. (Fitzwilliam Museum Publications). (Illus.). 150p. (C). 1995. 44.95 (*0-521-47521-X*) Cambridge U Pr.

— Italian Maiolica & Incised Slipware in the Fitzwilliam Museum, Cambridge. (Fitzwilliam Museum Publications). (Illus.). 512p. (C). 1995. write for info. (*0-521-48275-5*) Cambridge U Pr.

***Poole, Karuna.** Letting Go of Suffering. (Orig.). 1994. pap. 12.95 (*0-9643629-0-2*) K Poole.

Poole, Kenneth. Entrepreneurial Development: Formalizing the Process. Murphy, Jenny, ed. 40p. (Orig.). 1987. pap. 17.00 (*0-317-04847-3*) Natl Coun Econ Dev.

— Financing Tools & Techniques: A Guide to Planning for Business Development. Murphy, Jenny, ed. 32p. (Orig.). 1987. pap. 17.00 (*0-317-04819-8*) Natl Coun Econ Dev.

— Marketing Strategies for Local Economic Development: From Design to Implementation. Murphy, Jenny & Kailo, Andrea, eds. 44p. (Orig.). 1986. pap. 17.50 (*0-317-04902-X*) Natl Coun Econ Dev.

— Non-Traditional Job Creation & Entrepreneurship. Murphy, Jenny, ed. 28p. (Orig.). 1988. pap. 18.00 (*0-317-04855-4*) Natl Coun Econ Dev.

— Self Emloyment Initiatives: How to Promote & Finance Micro-Enterprises. Murphy, Jenny, ed. 64p. (Orig.). 1988. pap. 20.00 (*0-317-04901-1*) Natl Coun Econ Dev.

— Telecommunications & Rural Economic Development. Murphy, Jenny, ed. 60p. (Orig.). 1991. pap. 22.50 (*0-317-04801-5*) Natl Coun Econ Dev.

— Trends in Economic Development Organizations: A Survey of Selected Metropolitan Areas. Murphy, Jenny, ed. 580p. (Orig.). 1991. pap. 225.00 (*0-317-04832-5*) Natl Coun Econ Dev.

— Working Capital for Small Business: Addressing the Need. Murphy, Jenny, ed. 32p. (Orig.). 1987. pap. 17.00 (*0-317-04818-X*) Natl Coun Econ Dev.

Poole, Kenneth, ed. see Murphy, Jenny & Welch, Wayne.

Poole, Kenyon E. German Financial Policies, Nineteen Thirty-Two to Nineteen Thirty-Nine. 1977. lib. bdg. 59.95 (*0-8490-1884-6*) Gordon Pr.

Poole, Laura. Shadow Songs: A Collection of Poems. Myers, M., ed. LC 91-75715. 55p. (Orig.). 1991. pap. text ed. 7.95 (*1-879183-11-0*) Bristol Banner.

— Statistical Concepts: A Basic Foundation for Social Science Research. (Illus.). Date not set. pap. 10.00 (*0-614-05599-7*) Vantage.

Poole, Lisa I. & Robinson, Dianne P. Torpedo Town, U. S. A. A History of the Naval Undersea Warfare Engineering Station, 1914-1989. LC 88-51503. (Illus.). 120p. (Orig.). 1989. pap. 8.00 (*0-9621829-0-7*) Diamond Anniversary.

Poole, Lon. Macworld Guia del Sistenia 7. 409p. 1992. pap. text ed. 27.95 (*968-18-4397-5*, Pub. by Limusa MX) Computer & Tech.

— Macworld Guide to System 7.1. 2nd ed. (Illus.). 480p. 1992. pap. 24.95 (*1-878058-65-7*) IDG Bks.

— Macworld System 7.5 Bible. 3rd ed. 1994. pap. 29.95 (*1-56884-098-5*) IDG Bks.

Poole, Lynn & Poole, Gray. Danger, Iceberg Ahead. (Illus.). (J). (gr. 1-4). 1961. lib. bdg. 4.39 (*0-394-90121-5*) Random Bks Yng Read.

— History of the Ancient Olympic Games. (Illus.). 1963. 11.95 (*0-8392-1049-3*) Astor-Honor.

— Weird & Wonderful Ants. (Illus.). (J). (gr. 5 up). 1961. 8.95 (*0-8392-3041-9*) Astor-Honor.

***Poole, M., et al.** Moving People - Transport Policy in the Cities of Brazil. 190p. 1994. pap. 24.95 (*0-88936-658-6*, IDRC6586, Pub. by IDRC CN) UNIPUB.

Poole, M. J., jt. auth. see Egelstaff, P. A.

Poole, Marie, ed. see De Paul, Vincent.

Poole, Marshall S., et al. Working Through Conflict: Strategies for Relationships, Groups, & Organizations. 2nd ed. LC 92-20474. (C). 1992. 30.00 (*0-06-500658-5*) HarpCollege.

Poole, Matthew. A Commentary on the Holy Bible, 3 vols. 1979. Vol.1, Genesis through Job. 56.95 (*0-85151-054-X*); Vol. 2, Psalms through Malachi. 56.95 (*0-85151-134-1*); Vol. 3, Matthew through Revelation. 56.95 (*0-85151-135-X*) Banner of Truth.

— A Commentary on the Holy Bible, 3 vols., Set. 1979. 159.95 (*0-85151-211-9*) Banner of Truth.

— Matthew Poole's Commentary on the Holy Bible, 3 vols. 3104p. 1985. 119.95 (*0-917006-28-3*) Hendrickson MA.

***Poole, Michael.** Beliefs & Values in Science Education. LC 94-41387. (Developing Science & Technology Education Ser.). 1995. write for info. (*0-335-15646-0*, Open Univ Pr); pap. write for info. (*0-335-15645-2*, Open Univ Pr) Taylor & Francis.

— Industrial Relations: The Origins & Patterns of National Diversity. (Illus.). 224p. 1986. text ed. 45.00 (*0-7100-9796-4*, RKP) Routledge.

— The Origins of Economic Democracy: Profit Sharing & Employee Shareholding Schemes. 176p. 1989. 49.50 (*0-415-02555-9*) Routledge.

Poole, Michael & Jenkins, Glenville. The Impact of Economic Democracy: Profit-Sharing & Employee Shareholding Schemes. 176p. (C). 1991. text ed. 74.00 (*0-415-03587-2*, A5121) Routledge.

Poole, Michael, jt. ed. see Jenkins, Glenville.

Poole, Michael, jt. auth. see Mansfield, Roger.

Poole, Millicent. Education & Work. (C). 1990. 80.00 (*0-86431-096-X*, Pub. by Aust Council Educ Res AT) St Mut.

Poole, Millicent E. & Langan-Fox, Janice. Women & Careers: Success & Orientations. 224p. 1993. 60.00 (*1-85000-849-3*, Falmer Pr); pap. 27.50 (*1-85000-850-7*, Falmer Pr) Taylor & Francis.

Poole, Millicent E., jt. auth. see Evans, Glen.

Poole, Monica. The Wood Engravings of John Farleigh. (Illus.). 128p. 1985. 125.00 (*0-946095-09-4*, Pub. by Gresham Bks UK); 500.00 (*0-946095-15-9*, Pub. by Gresham Bks UK) St Mut.

Poole, Peter A. The Expansion of the Vietnam War into Cambodia: Action & Response by the Governments of North Vietnam, South Vietnam, Cambodia, & the United States. LC 76-633329. (Papers in International Studies: Southeast Asia Ser.: No. 17). 137p. reprint ed. pap. 39.10 (*0-317-09472-6*, 2005119) Bks Demand.

Poole, Peter A., ed. Indochina: Perspectives for Reconciliation. LC 75-620006. (Papers in International Studies: Southeast Asia Ser.: No. 36). 100p. reprint ed. pap. 28.50 (*0-317-09583-8*, 2007454) Bks Demand.

Poole, R., jt. ed. see Hunt, W.

Poole, R. K. & Gadd, G. M., eds. Metal-Microbe Interactions. (Society for General Microbiology Special Publications: Vol. 26). 146p. 1989. 85.00 (*0-19-963024-0*, IRL Pr); pap. 50.00 (*0-19-963025-9*, IRL Pr) OUP.

Poole, R. K. & Trinci, A. P., eds. Spatial Organization in Eukaryotic Microbes. (Society for General Microbiology Special Publications: Vol. 23). 152p. (C). 1987. 64.00 (*1-85221-053-2*, IRL Pr); pap. text ed. 42.00 (*1-85221-052-4*, IRL Pr) OUP.

Poole, R. W. A Backwoodsman's Year. large type ed. 254p. 1991. 10.97 (*1-85089-885-5*, Pub. by ISIS UK) Transaction Pubs.

— Hunting: An Introductory Handbook. (Illus.). 192p. 1993. pap. 29.95 (*0-948253-67-3*, Pub. by Sportsmans Pr UK) Trafalgar.

Poole, Reginald L. Exchequer in the Twelfth Century. 196p. 1973. reprint ed. 32.50 (*0-7146-1510-2*, Pub. by F Cass Pubs UK) Intl Spec Bk.

— Lectures on Art. LC 77-39677. (Essay Index Reprint Ser.). 1977. reprint ed. 16.95 (*0-8369-2781-8*) Ayer.

— Medieval Reckonings of Time. 1977. lib. bdg. 59.95 (*0-8490-2220-7*) Gordon Pr.

— Wycliffe & Movements for Reform. LC 77-84729. reprint ed. 28.00 (*0-404-16129-4*) AMS Pr.

Poole, Reginald L. & Bateson, Mary, eds. Index Brittanie Scriptorum: John Bale's Index of British & Other Writers. 640p. 1990. 110.00 (*0-85991-297-3*) Boydell & Brewer.

Poole, Reginald L. & Davis, Henry W. Essays in History Presented to Reginald Lane Poole. LC 67-30186. (Essay Index Reprint Ser.). 1977. 30.95 (*0-8369-0424-9*) Ayer.

Poole, Reginald L., ed. see Bale, John.

Poole, Reginald L., jt. ed. see Hunt, William.

Poole, Richard. Inca Smiled: The Growing Pains of an Aid Worker in Ecuador. 1994. pap. 15.95 (*1-85168-078-0*) Onewrld Pubns.

— Richard Hughes: Novelist. LC 86-63545. 253p. 1987. 32.00 (*0-907476-52-X*, Pub. by Poetry Wales Pr UK) Dufour.

— Words Before Midnight. 60p. 1981. pap. 10.95 (*0-907476-03-1*) Dufour.

Poole, Richard, ed. see Hughes, Richard.

Poole, Richard L., jt. auth. see Glenn, George D.

***Poole, Robert K., ed.** Advances in Microbial Physiology, Vol. 37. (Illus.). 250p. 1995. text ed. write for info. (*0-12-027737-9*) Acad Pr.

Poole, Robert K. & Dow, Crawford S., eds. Microbial Gas Metabolism. (Society for General Microbiology Special Publications: Vol. 14). 1985. text ed. 138.00 (*0-12-561480-2*) Acad Pr.

Poole, Robert K., jt. auth. see Hughes, Martin N.

Poole, Robert K., et al, eds. Microbial Growth Dynamics. (Society for General Microbiology Special Publications: Vol. 28). (Illus.). 184p. 1990. 82.00 (*0-19-963118-2*, IRL Pr); pap. 52.00 (*0-19-963119-0*, IRL Pr) OUP.

Poole, Robert M., ed. Nature's Wonderlands: National Parks of the World. 304p. 1989. 29.95 (*0-87044-766-1*); 39.95 (*0-87044-767-X*) Natl Geog.

Poole, Robert M., ed. see National Geographic Society Staff.

Poole, Robert W. Lepidopterorum Catalogus, Fascicle 118, Noctuidae, Vol. 1, Vol. 1-3. (New Ser.). xii, 500p. 1988. Abablemma to Heraclia. 195.00 (*0-916846-45-8*) Sandhill Crane.

— Lepidopterorum Catalogus, Fascicle 118, Noctuidae, Vol. 3, Vols. 1-3. (New Ser.). 1988. Bibliography & Index. 195.00 (*0-916846-47-4*) Sandhill Crane.

— Lepidopterprum Catalogus, Fascicle 118, Noctuidae, Vol. 2, Vols. 1-3. (New Ser.). 1988. Heraclia (concl.) to Zutragum. 195.00 (*0-916846-46-6*) Sandhill Crane.

Poole, Robert W., Jr., ed. Defending a Free Society. LC 83-48627. 384p. 1984. text ed. 35.00 (*0-669-07240-0*) Free Pr.

Poole, Robert W., Jr. & Postrel, Virginia I., eds. Free Minds & Free Markets: Twenty-Five Years of Reason. LC 93-20435. (Illus.). 300p. (Orig.). 1993. pap. 24.95 (*0-936488-72-7*) PRIPP.

Poole, Roger. Kierkegaard: The Indirect Communication. LC 93-18805. 304p. (C). 1993. 39.50 (*0-8139-1460-4*) U Pr of Va.

Poole, Roger & Stangerup, Henrik. The Laughter Is on My Side: An Imaginative Introduction to Kierkegaard. 1989. 45.00 (*0-691-07361-9*); pap. 13.95 (*0-691-02058-2*) Princeton U Pr.

Poole, Rose M. Siren Sparks. 203p. 1984. 7.95 (*0-89697-173-2*) Intl Univ Pr.

Poole, Ross. Morality & Modernity. 224p. 1991. 49.95 (*0-415-03600-3*, A5259); pap. 14.95 (*0-415-03601-1*, A5263) Routledge.

Poole, Russell G. Viking Poems on War & Peace: A Study in Skaldic Narrative. (Medieval Texts & Translations Ser.: No. 8). 224p. 1991. text ed. 45.00 (*0-8020-5867-1*); pap. text ed. 14.95 (*0-8020-6789-1*) U of Toronto Pr.

Poole, Scott. New Finnish Architecture. LC 91-12431. (Illus.). 224p. 1992. 50.00 (*0-8478-1316-9*); pap. 35.00 (*0-8478-1317-7*) Rizzoli Intl.

***Poole, Stafford.** Our Lady of Guadalupe: The Origins & Sources of a Mexican National Symbol, 1531-1797. LC 94-18724. 320p. 1995. 40.00x (*0-8165-1526-3*) U of Ariz Pr.

Poole, Stafford & Slawson, Douglas J. Church & Slave in Perry County, Missouri, 1818-1865. LC 86-16374. (Studies in American Religion: Vol. 22). (Illus.). 252p. 1988. lib. bdg. 89.95 (*0-88946-666-1*) E Mellen.

Poole, Stafford, tr. see De Las Casas, Bartolome.

Poole, Stafford, ed. see Hanke, Lewis.

Poole, Stanley L. Aurangzib & the Decay of the Mughal Empire. 1990. reprint ed. 9.50 (*81-85418-10-1*, Pub. by Low Price II) S Asia.

— The Moors in Spain. (African Heritage Classical Research Studies). 290p. reprint ed. 16.00 (*0-938818-65-1*) ECA Assoc.

***Poole, Stephen.** Nova Scotia: A Color Guidebook. (Illus.). 192p. 1995. pap. 19.95 (*0-88780-268-0*) Formac Dist Ltd.

Poole, Stephen J. General Eujaryotic Genetics: Biology 130B Supplementary Material. 48p. (C). 1994. spiral bd. 5.00 (*0-8403-9254-0*) Kendall-Hunt.

Poole, Steven R., et al. Bibliographies of Behavioral Science Literature. 55p. 1983. 5.00 (*0-942295-01-3*, A) Soc Tchrs Fam Med.

Poole, Susan. Frommer's Dollarwise Guide to the Southeast & New Orleans. rev. ed. (Frommer's Dollarwise Guides Ser.). (Illus.). 1987. pap. 13.95 (*0-685-18518-4*) P-H.

Poole, Susan D. Chester A. Arthur: The President Who Reformed. LC 76-40379. 112p. (J). (gr. 7-9). 1977. text ed. 8.95 (*0-87881-056-0*) Mojave Bks.

Poole, William. Money & the Economy: A Monetarist View. LC 78-52499. (Perspectives on Economics Ser.). (Illus.). 1978. pap. write for info. (*0-201-08364-7*) Addison-Wesley.

Poole, William, jt. auth. see Henderson, J. Vernon.

Poole, William F. Anti-Slavery Opinions Before the Year 1800. LC 79-110001. reprint ed. 22.50 (*0-8371-4144-3*, POO&, Negro U Pr) Greenwood.

— The Tyler Davidson Fountain Given by Mr. Henry Probasco to the City of Cincinnati. deluxe ed. (Illus.). 117p. 1988. boxed 39.95 (*0-911497-06-4*) Cinc Hist Soc.

— The Tyler Davidson Fountain Given by Mr. Henry Probasco to the City of Cincinnati. (Illus.). 117p. 1988. reprint ed. pap. 19.95 (*0-911497-07-2*) Cinc Hist Soc.

Poole-Wilson, P. A., et al, eds. Mononitrates: International Symposium, Held at the Royal Society of Medicine, London , June 1986. (Journal: Cardiology: Vol. 74, Suppl. 1, 1987). (Illus.). viii, 80p. 1987. pap. 25.75 (*3-8055-4626-2*) S Karger.

Pooler, Victor H. Global Purchasing: Reaching for the World. (Materials Management & Logistics Ser.). (Illus.). 288p. 1992. text ed. 49.95 (*0-442-00711-6*) Chapman & Hall.

Pooley, A. M., ed. see Hayashi, Tadasu.

Pooley, Beverly J. The Evolution of British Planning Legislation. LC 60-63300. (Michigan Legal Publications). 100p. 1982. reprint ed. lib. bdg. 36.00 (*0-89941-173-8*, 302340) W S Hein.

— Planning & Zoning in the United States. LC 61-63301. (Michigan Legal Publications). 123p. 1982. reprint ed. lib. bdg. 37.50 (*0-89941-243-2*, 302330) W S Hein.

Pooley, Colin G. & Whyte, Ian D. Migrants, Emigrants & Immigrants: A Social History of Migration. (Social History Society Ser.). 240p. (C). 1991. text ed. 74.50 (*0-415-04976-8*, A5628) Routledge.

Pooley, Colin G., jt. auth. see Lawton, Richard.

Pooley, D., jt. auth. see Hughes, A. E.

Pooley, Fred, jt. auth. see Pooley, Lorraine.

Pooley, James. Trade Secrets: A Guide to Protecting Business Proprietary Information. LC 89-6872. 288p. 1989. pap. 16.95 (*0-8144-7724-0*) AMACOM.

Pooley, Lorraine & Pooley, Fred. The Cobbler's Guest. 1975. 4.25 (*0-8341-9147-4*, MC-246) Lillenas.

Pooley, Roger. English Prose of the Seventeenth Century, 1590-1700. LC 92-8343. (Literature in English Ser.). (C). 1992. text ed. 67.50 (*0-582-01658-4*) Longman.

— English Prose of the Seventeenth Century, 1590-1700. LC 92-8343. (Literature in English Ser.). (C). 1993. pap. text ed. 27.50 (*0-582-01659-2*, 79467) Longman.

Pooley, Sarah. A Night of Lullabies. (Illus.). 64p. (J). (ps-1). 1992. 16.95 (*0-370-31491-3*, Pub. by Bodley Head UK) Trafalgar.

Pooley, Sarah, illus. & comp. It's Raining, It's Pouring: A Book for Rainy Days. LC 92-16859. 80p. (J). (ps up). 1993. 18.00 (*0-688-11803-8*) Greenwillow.

Poolman, J. T., et al, eds. Gonococci & Meningococci. (C). 1988. lib. bdg. 359.00 (*90-247-3607-2*) Kluwer Ac.

Poolman, Kenneth. Allied Escort Carriers. LC 88-60817. (Illus.). 272p. 1988. 34.95 (*0-87021-005-X*) Naval Inst Pr.

Poolos, Jamie, jt. auth. see Addams, Shay.

Poom, Rilva, tr. see Manner, Eeva L.

Poom, Ritva, jt. ed. see Barkan, Stanley H.

Poom, Ritva, ed. see Pentikainen, Juha Y.

Poom, Ritva, tr. see Rummo, Paul-Eerik.

Poon, Auliana. Tourism, Technology & Competitive Strategies. 350p. 1993. text ed. 85.50 (*0-85198-751-6*) CAB Intl.

Poon, Leonard & Siegler, Ilene, eds. Aging Curriculum Content for Education in the Social-Behavioral Sciences. LC 89-11351. 368p. 1989. 44.95 (*0-8261-6070-0*) Springer Pub.

Poon, Leonard W. New Directions in Memory & Aging: Proceedings of the George A. Talland Memorial Conference. Fozard, James L. et al, eds. LC 79-27548. (Illus.). 572p. 1980. text ed. 115.00 (*0-89859-035-3*) L Erlbaum Assocs.

Poon, Leonard W., ed. The Georgia Centenarian Study. 91p. 1992. pap. text ed. 12.95 (*0-89503-094-2*) Baywood Pub.

Poon, Leonard W., et al, eds. Aging in the 1980s: Psychological Issues. LC 80-18515. 656p. reprint ed. pap. 180.00 (*0-7837-0482-8*, 2040806) Bks Demand.

— Everyday Cognition in Adulthood & Late Life. (Illus.). 708p. (C). 1992. pap. 29.95 (*0-521-42860-2*) Cambridge U Pr.

***Poon, Ron K.** Computer Circuits Electrical Design. LC 94-34252. 408p. 1995. text ed. 60.00 (*0-13-213471-3*) P-H.

***Poonai, Premsukh.** Origin of Civilization & Language. LC 94-65864. (Illus.). 239p. 1994. 29.00 (*1-883122-03-1*) Pearce Pub.

Poonam Sharma & Lata Gairala. Fundamentals of Child Development & Child Care. 1989. text ed. 27.50 (*81-207-1057-6*, Pub. by Sterling Pubs II) Apt Bks.

Poonawala, Ismail K., ed. & tr. The History of al-Tabari, Vol. 9: The Last Years of the Prophet: The Formation of the State, A.D. 630-632-A.H. 8-11. LC 87-7129. (SUNY Series in Near Eastern Studies). 250p. 1990. 59.50 (*0-88706-691-7*); pap. 19.95 (*0-88706-692-5*) State U NY Pr.

Poonja, H. W. Wake up & Roar, Vol. 1. Jaxon-Bear, Eli, ed. 200p. 1992. pap. 12.00 (*0-9632194-1-3*) Satsang Pr.

Poonja, H. W. L. Wake up & Roar, Vol. 2: Satsang with H. W. L. Poonja. 180p. (Orig.). 1993. pap. 12.00 (*0-9632194-2-1*) Satsang Pr.

Poonwassie, Deo H., jt. ed. see Ray, Douglas.

Poor, Agnes B., ed. Pan American Poems: An Anthology. 1977. lib. bdg. 59.95 (*0-8490-2400-5*) Gordon Pr.

Poor, Alfred. New Life for Old PCs: How to Keep Your Company's Computers from Becoming Obsolete. 256p. 1992. disk 32.00 (*1-55623-427-9*) Irwin Prof Pubng.

Poor, Alfred & Ridington, Richard W. Using Paradox. 1986. pap. 21.95 (*0-89303-927-6*) P-H.

Poor, Alfred E. Colonial Architecture of Cape Cod, Nantucket & Martha's Vineyard. (Illus.). 1970. reprint ed. pap. 5.95 (*0-486-22375-2*) Dover.

Poor Clares of New Orleans Staff. The New Orleans Monastery Cookbook: Recipes from St. Clare's Kitchen. Sister Olivia Wassmer, ed. 184p. 1992. 10.95 (*0-9634521-0-X*) St Clares Monastery.

Poor Clares of Rockford, ed. see Duboin, Alain-Marie.

Poor, Edith. Executive Writer: A Guide to Managing Words, Ideas, & People. 1992. pap. 10.95 (*0-8021-3290-1*) Grove-Atltic.

Poor, Gene W. The Illusion of Life: Lifelike Robotics. (Illus.). 96p. (Orig.). 1991. pap. 24.95 (*0-88157-000-1*) Creat Learn.

Poor, H. V. An Introduction to Signal Detection & Estimation. (Illus.). x, 549p. 1988. 65.00 (*0-387-96667-6*) Spr-Verlag.

Poor, H. V., jt. ed. see Blake, Ian F.

Poor, H. Vincent. Advances in Statistical Signal Processing, Vol. 1: Estimation. 73.25 (*0-89232-570-4*) Jai Pr.

— An Introduction to Signal Detection & Estimation. 2nd ed. LC 93-21312. (Texts in Electrical Engineering Ser.). 1994. 59.00 (*0-387-94173-8*) Spr-Verlag.

An Asterisk (*) at the beginning of an entry indicates that the title is appearing in BIP for the first time.

Poor, Henry V. History of the Railroads & Canals of the United States: Exhibiting Their Progress, Cost, Revenues, Expenditures & Present Condition. LC 68-56564. (Library of Early American Business & Industry: No. 34). 632p. 1970. reprint ed. 57.50 (*0-678-00665-2*) Kelley.
— Money & Its Laws. LC 69-19678. 623p. 1969. reprint ed. text ed. 125.00 (*0-8371-0618-4*, POML, Greenwood Pr) Greenwood.
Poor, Richard. She's That Universal Lady! More Information to Those Who Would Remove to America. 1994. 17.95 (*0-533-10910-8*) Vantage.
Poor, Robert J., et al. Ritual & Reverence: Chinese Art at the University of Chicago. Taylor, Sue, ed. LC 89-51202. (Illus.). 146p. (Orig.). 1989. pap. 20.00 (*0-935573-10-0*) D & A Smart Museum.
***Poorbaugh, Angela.** God First! Eyerly, Carey, ed. 82p. (Orig.). 1994. pap. write for info. (*1-885001-03-7*) Via Press.
Poore, A. A Memoir & Genealogy of John Poore: Ten Generations, 1615-1880. 333p. 1989. reprint ed. lib. bdg. 58.00 (*0-8328-0974-8*); reprint ed. pap. 50.00 (*0-8328-0975-6*) Higginson Bk Co.
Poore, Alfred. A Memoir & Genealogy of John Poore: Ten Generations: 1615-1880. 334p. 1990. reprint ed. pap. 22.50 (*1-55613-369-3*) Heritage Bk.
Poore, Benjamin P. Perley's Reminiscences of Sixty Years in the National Metropolis, 2 Vols, 1. LC 74-158970. reprint ed. write for info. (*0-404-05077-8*) AMS Pr.
— Perley's Reminiscences of Sixty Years in the National Metropolis, 2 Vols, 2. LC 74-158970. reprint ed. write for info. (*0-404-05078-6*) AMS Pr.
— Perley's Reminiscences of Sixty Years in the National Metropolis, 2 Vols, Set. LC 74-158970. reprint ed. 74.50 (*0-404-05076-X*) AMS Pr.
***Poore, Billy.** Rockabilly: A 40-Year Journey. (Illus.). 200p. (Orig.). 1995. pap. 19.95 (*0-7935-3706-1*, HL00330020) H Leonard.
Poore, Carol, ed. see Spies, August.
Poore, Clara. Weaving with Wheat: A Manual for Beginning Wheat Weavers, No. I. (Illus.). 16p. 1994. pap. 4.00 (*0-9613993-1-7*) Wheat N Flower.
Poore, Dawn. Bath Bramble. 1991. pap. 3.50 (*0-8217-3547-0*) Zebra.
Poore, Dawn A. The Brighton Burglar. 256p. 1993. mass mkt. 3.99 (*0-8217-4104-7*) Zebra.
— The Cairo Cats. 256p. 1994. mass mkt. 3.99 (*0-8217-4571-9*) Zebra.
— Miss Fortune's Folly. 256p. 1992. pap. 3.50 (*0-8217-3913-1*) Zebra.
— The Mummy's Mirror. 256p. 1995. pap. 3.99 (*0-8217-5050-X*) Zebra.
— The Secret Scroll. 256p. 1993. mass mkt. 3.99 (*0-8217-4337-6*) Zebra.
— Sweet Deceit. 1990. pap. 2.95 (*1-55817-415-X*, Pinnacle NY) Windsor NY.
Poore, Duncan, ed. Guidelines for Mountain Protected Areas. 56p. 1992. pap. 15.00 (*2-8317-0111-2*, Pub. by IUCN SZ) Island Pr.
Poore, Duncan & Sayer, Jeffrey. The Management of Tropical Moist Forest Lands: Ecological Guidelines. 2nd ed. (Illus.). 69p. 1991. pap. 17.00 (*2-8317-0071-X*, Pub. by IUCN SZ) Island Pr.
Poore, Henry R. Composition in Art. (Illus.). 1976. reprint ed. pap. 5.95 (*0-486-23358-8*) Dover.
— Pictorial Compositions & the Critical Judgment of Pictures. Sobieszek, Robert A. & Bunnell, Peter C., eds. LC 76-24676. (Sources of Modern Photography Ser.). (Illus.). 1979. reprint ed. lib. bdg. 20.95 (*0-405-09652-6*) Ayer.
Poore, J. H., jt. ed. see Kirkland, J. R.
***Poore, Jesse H. & Trammell, Carmen J., eds.** Readings in Cleanroom Software Engineering. (Illus.). 288p. (Orig.). 1995. pap. write for info. (*1-85554-654-X*) Blackwell Pubs.
Poore, Jonathan. Interior Color by Design. 160p. 1994. 29.99 (*1-56496-037-4*) Rockport Pubs.
***Poore, Linda.** Air: Hands on Elementary School Science. 18p. 1994. teacher ed 35.00 (*1-883410-18-5*) L Poore.
— Aquatic Habitats: Hands on Elementary School Science. 38p. 1994. teacher ed 35.00 (*1-883410-03-7*) L Poore.
— Chemistry: Hands on Elementary School Science. 40p. 1994. teacher ed 35.00 (*1-883410-15-0*); teacher ed 35.00 (*0-614-02583-4*) L Poore.
— Classification of Plants & Animals: Hands on Elementary School Science. 65p. 1994. teacher ed 35.00 (*1-883410-05-3*) L Poore.
— Earth's Resources: Hands on Elementary School Science. 50p. 1994. teacher ed 35.00 (*1-883410-08-8*) L Poore.
— Electricity: Hands on Elementary School Science. 25p. 1994. teacher ed 35.00 (*1-883410-13-4*) L Poore.
— Hands on Elementary School Science: Earth Science. 260p. 1994. teacher ed 130.00 (*1-883410-22-3*); 500.00 (*1-883410-23-1*) L Poore.
— Hands on Elementary School Science: Kindergarten. 100p. Date not set. teacher ed 100.00 (*1-883410-32-0*) L Poore.
— Hands on Elementary School Science: Life Science. 240p. 1994. teacher ed 130.00 (*1-883410-00-2*); teacher ed 500.00 (*1-883410-26-6*) L Poore.
— Hands on Elementary School Science: Physical Science. 290p. 1994. teacher ed 130.00 (*1-883410-24-X*); 500.00 (*1-883410-25-8*) L Poore.
— Hands on Middle School Science. 150p. Date not set. teacher ed 130.00 (*1-883410-33-9*) L Poore.
— Human Body: Hands on Elementary School Science. 58p. 1994. teacher ed 35.00 (*1-883410-21-5*) L Poore.
— Kindergarten Physical Science: Hands on Elementary School Science. 80p. 1994. teacher ed 100.00 (*1-883410-31-2*) L Poore.
— Life Cycles: Hands on Elementary School Science. 39p. 1994. teacher ed 35.00 (*1-883410-02-9*) L Poore.
— Light: Hands on Elementary School Science. 35p. 1994. teacher ed 35.00 (*1-883410-20-7*) L Poore.
— Machines: Hands on Elementary School Science. 36p. 1994. teacher ed 35.00 (*1-883410-16-9*) L Poore.
— Magnets: Hands on Elementary School Science. 29p. 1994. teacher ed 35.00 (*1-883410-12-6*) L Poore.
— Matter & Heat: Hands on Elementary School Science. 35p. 1994. teacher ed 35.00 (*1-883410-14-2*) L Poore.
— Motion & Energy: Hands on Elementary School Science. 20p. 1994. teacher ed 35.00 (*1-883410-17-7*) L Poore.
— Oceans: Hands on Elementary School Science. 57p. 1994. teacher ed 35.00 (*1-883410-10-X*) L Poore.
— Organisms: Hands on Elementary School Science. 33p. 1994. teacher ed 35.00 (*1-883410-01-0*) L Poore.
— Rocks & Soil: Hands on Elementary School Science. 28p. 1994. teacher ed 35.00 (*1-883410-06-1*) L Poore.
— Rocks, Erosion, & Weathering: Hands on Elementary School Science. 31p. 1994. teacher ed 35.00 (*1-883410-07-X*) L Poore.
— Sound: Hands on Elementary School Science. 29p. 1994. teacher ed 35.00 (*1-883410-19-3*) L Poore.
— Space: Hands on Elementary School Science. 58p. 1994. teacher ed 35.00 (*1-883410-09-6*) L Poore.
— Spanish Worksheets: Hands on Elementary School Science. 94p. 1994. teacher ed 75.00 (*1-883410-27-4*) L Poore.
— Spanish Worksheets - Physical Science: Hands on Elementary School Science. 30p. 1993. teacher ed 25.00 (*1-883410-28-2*) L Poore.
— Spanish Worksheets: Earth Science: Hands on Elementary School Science. 38p. 1994. teacher ed 25.00 (*1-883410-30-4*) L Poore.
— Spanish Worksheets: Life Science: Hands on Elementary School Science. 38p. 1994. teacher ed 25.00 (*1-883410-29-0*) L Poore.
— Terrariums: Animal & Plant Interactions: Hands on Elementary School Science. 38p. 1994. teacher ed 35.00 (*1-883410-04-5*) L Poore.
— Weather: Hands on Elementary School Science. 48p. 1994. teacher ed 35.00 (*1-883410-11-8*) L Poore.
Poore, Luz, ed. see Thomas, Mary A.
***Poore, Marge.** The Complete Chicken Breast Cookbook: Easy & Delicious Everyday Recipes for the Whole Family. LC 95-1605. 1995. write for info. (*0-7615-0005-7*) Prima Pub.
— Three Hundred & Sixty-Five Easy Mexican Recipes. LC 93-29183. (Three Hundred Sixty-Five Ways Ser.). 288p. 1994. 17.95 (*0-06-016963-X*, HarpT) HarpC.
Poore, Patricia, ed. The Old-House Journal Guide to Restoration. LC 92-52881. (Illus.). 576p. 1992. 39.95 (*0-525-93551-7*, Dutton) NAL-Dutton.
Poore, Patricia, jt. ed. see Labine, Clem.
Poore, Patricia, ed. see Old-House Journal Editors.
Poorman, Berta & Poorman, Sonja. Spread a Little Christmas Cheer. 1982. pap. 4.95 (*0-686-38388-5*) Eldridge Pub.
Poorman, Karen M., jt. auth. see Poorman, Ronald J.
Poorman, Mark L. Interactional Morality: A Foundation for Moral Discernment in Catholic Pastoral Ministry. 196p. (Orig.). 1993. pap. 21.00 (*0-87840-536-4*) Georgetown U Pr.
Poorman, Ronald J. & Poorman, Karen M. Everyone's Guide to Instrumental Music Lessons: For Less Than the Cost of One Private Lesson. (Illus.). 136p. (Orig.). 1990. pap. text ed. 5.00 (*0-9625874-0-0*) Univ Pub NJ.
Poorman, Sonja, jt. auth. see Poorman, Berta.
Poorman, Susan. Neal-Schuman Index to Performing & Creative Artists in Collective Biographies. 155p. 1991. pap. text ed. 35.00 (*1-55570-056-X*) Neal-Schuman.
Poort, John M. & Carlson, Rosean J. Historical Geology: Interpretations & Applications. 4th ed. (Illus.). 256p. (C). 1992. pap. write for info. (*0-02-395995-9*) Macmillan.
Poorten, Carolyn T. Can We See God. LC 91-68355. 42p. (J). (gr. k-3). 1992. 6.95 (*1-55523-507-7*) Winston-Derek.
Poortinga, Ype H., jt. ed. see Reyes Lagunes, I.
Poortmans, J., jt. ed. see Marconnet, P.
Poortmans, J. R., ed. Principles of Exercise Biochemistry. (Medicine & Sport Science Ser.: Vol. 27). (Illus.). viii, 260p. 1988. 179.25 (*3-8055-4790-0*) S Karger.
— Principles of Exercise Biochemistry. 2nd rev. ed. (Medicine & Sport Science Ser.: Vol. 38). (Illus.). viii, 304p. 1993. 125.00 (*3-8055-5778-7*) S Karger.
Poortsmans, J., jt. ed. see Di Prampero, P. E.
***Poortvliet.** Book of the Sandman. 1994. pap. 10.99 (*0-517-13401-2*) Random.
Poortvliet, H. M. C. Valerius Flaccus: Argonautica Book II. 357p. (Orig.). 1992. pap. text ed. 49.50 (*90-5383-022-7*, Pub. by VU Univ Pr NE) Paul & Co Pubs.
Poortvliet, Rien. The Book of the Sandman: And the Alphabet of Sleep. (Illus.). 122p. 1989. 17.95 (*0-685-27156-0*) Abrams.
— Daily Life in Holland in the Year 1566: And the Story of My Ancestor's Treasure Chest. (Illus.). 208p. 1992. 39.95 (*0-8109-3309-8*) Abrams.
— Dutch Treat, the Artist Life. 19.95 (*0-8488-1450-9*) Amereon Ltd.
— Farm Book. 1994. 29.95 (*0-8109-0817-4*) Abrams.
— Gnomes. 1979. pap. 19.95 (*0-553-34500-1*) Bantam.
— He Was One of Us. LC 77-16523. (Illus.). 132p. 1994. reprint ed. 24.99 (*0-8010-7135-6*) Baker Bk.
— In My Grandfather's House. 1988. 39.95 (*0-8109-1126-4*) Abrams.
— Journey to the Ice Age: Mammoths & Other Animals of the Wild. LC 94-1544. 1994. write for info. (*0-8109-3648-8*) Abrams.
— Noah's Ark. (Illus.). 240p. 1992. 49.50 (*0-8109-1371-2*) Abrams.
Poorvliet, Rien & Huygen, Wil. The Complete Book of the Gnomes. LC 94-4254. 1994. write for info. (*0-8109-3195-8*) Abrams.
Poorvu, William. Real Estate: Case Study Approach. 464p. 1992. pap. text ed. 33.33 (*0-13-763483-8*) P-H.
Poos, Larry. A Rural Society after the Black Death: Essex, 1350-1525. (Studies in Population, Economy & Society in Past Time: No. 18). (Illus.). 336p. (C). 1991. 64.95 (*0-521-38260-2*) Cambridge U Pr.
Pooser, Doris. Always in Style. Avedon, Phyllis, ed. LC 90-55625. (Fifty-Minute Ser.). (Illus.). 214p. 1989. pap. 14.95 (*0-931961-91-2*) Crisp Pubns.
— Secrets of Style: A Personal Profile, Just for You! Crisp, Michael G., ed. LC 92-10401. (Illus.). 120p. (Orig.). 1994. pap. 12.95 (*1-56052-152-X*) Crisp Pubns.
— Successful Style. Michael, Angie & Trupp, Phil, eds. LC 91-18338. (Illus.). 214p. 1990. reprint ed. 14.95 (*0-931961-92-0*) Crisp Pubns.
Poostchi, Iraj. Rural Development & the Developing Countries: An Interdisciplinary Introductory Approach. (Illus.). 690p. (Orig.). (C). 1986. reprint ed. text ed. 50.00 (*0-9692356-1-5*); reprint ed. pap. text ed. 40.00 (*0-9692356-0-7*) Am Overseas Bk Co.
Poot-yah, Eleuterio. Yuctec Maya Verbs (Hocaba Dialect) Ward, James H., tr. 35p. 1981. pap. 5.00 (*0-317-43427-6*) Tulane Lat Am Lib.
Pootaraksa, Kamolmal & Crawford, William. Thai Home Cooking. 1986. pap. 11.95 (*0-452-26133-3*, Plume) NAL-Dutton.
Pootaraksa, Kamolmal, jt. auth. see Crawford, William.
Pootler & Pillion. Take a Ride. LC 93-86728. (Illus.). 32p. (J). (ps-1). 1994. pap. 8.95 (*0-9638479-3-7*) Magnolia MA.
***Poovey, Mary.** Making a Social Body: British Cultural Formation, 1830-1864. LC 95-4153. 1995. lib. bdg. 34.00 (*0-226-67523-8*); pap. text ed. 12.95 (*0-226-67524-6*) U Ch Pr.
— Uneven Developments: The Ideological Work of Gender in Mid-Victorian England. (Women in Culture & Society Ser.). 224p. 1988. pap. text ed. 15.95 (*0-226-67530-0*) U Ch Pr.
Poovey, Mary, ed. see Nightingale, Florence.
***Pop, M. Scott.** Bubble Most Firm. 2p. 1995. 5.95 (*0-89815-661-0*) Ten Speed Pr.
***Pop, Snap C.** Yo' Mama. Kid Rank, ed. 128p. (Orig.). 1995. pap. 8.00 (*0-425-14861-0*, Berkley Trade) Berkley Pub.
Popa, Constantin M. The Paradoxist Literary Movement. Muiler, R. & Xiquan Publishing House Staff, eds. 60p. (Orig.). (RUM.). (C). 1992. pap. text ed. 6.99 (*1-879585-29-4*) Xiquan Pubng.
Popa, Constantin M., ed. see Smarandache, Florentin.
Popa, Opritsa D., ed. Ceausecu's Romania: An Annotated Bibliography. LC 94-13055. (Bibliographies & Indexes in World History Ser.: Vol. 36). 168p. 1994. text ed. 59.95 (*0-313-28939-5*, Greenwood Pr) Greenwood.
Popa, Vasco. Midnight Sun. Barkan, Stanley H., ed. Mikasinovich, Branko, tr. (Review Chapbook Ser.: No. 28). 48p. (ENG & SER.). 1992. 15.00 (*0-89304-963-8*); 15.00 (*0-89304-965-4*); pap. 5.00 (*0-89304-964-6*); pap. 5.00 (*0-89304-966-2*) Cross-Cultrl NY.
Popa, Vasko. Give Me Back My Rags. Simic, Charles, tr. (Poetry Ser.). (Illus.). (Orig.). 1985. ring bd. 9.95 (*0-317-39882-2*) Seluzicki Fine Bks.
— Homage to the Lame Wolf: Selected Poems. 2nd ed. Simic, Charles, tr. LC 87-60028. (Field Translation Ser.: No. 12). 125p. (Orig.). 1987. pap. 9.00 (*0-932440-22-3*) Oberlin Coll Pr.
— The Little Box. Simic, Charles, tr. LC 78-134539. 1973. 7.50 (*0-910350-09-4*) Charioteer.
Popay, Jennie, jt. ed. see Davey, Basiro.
Popay, Jenny, jt. ed. see Williams, Gareth.
***Popchock, Barry, ed.** Soldier Boy: The Civil War Letters of Charles O. Musser, 29th Iowa. (Illus.). 236p. 1995. 24.95 (*0-87745-523-6*) U of Iowa Pr.
Popcorn, Faith. The Popcorn Report: Faith Popcorn on the Future of Your Company, Your World, Your Life. LC 92-52682. 1992. pap. 13.00 (*0-88730-594-6*) Harper Busn.
***Popcorn, Faith & Marigold, Lys.** Clicking: The Author of the Popcorn Report Shows How to Position Yourself & Your Business for the Way Things Will Be. 224p. 1995. 22.00 (*0-88730-694-2*) Harper Busn.
Pope. Color Atlas of Inherited Connective Tissue Disease. 1994. 80.00 (*0-8151-6731-8*, Yr Bk Med Pubs) Mosby Yr Bk.
— Deadly Venom. (Curious Creatures Ser.). (Illus.). 48p. (J). (gr. 3-4). Date not set. lib. bdg. 22.80 (*0-8114-3154-1*) Raintree Steck-V.
— Musculoskeletal Imaging: A Teaching File. Date not set. 64.95 (*0-8151-6724-5*, Yr Bk Med Pubs) Mosby Yr Bk.
— On the Move. (Curious Creatures Ser.). (Illus.). 48p. (J). (gr. 3-4). 1992. lib. bdg. 22.80 (*0-8114-3156-8*) Raintree Steck-V.
— Selected Poetry & Prose. 2nd ed. 514p. (C). 1972. pap. text ed. 22.50 (*0-03-083262-4*) HB Coll Pubs.
— Self-Esteem Enhancement. (C). 1988. pap. 19.95 (*0-205-14455-1*, H4455) Allyn.
Pope, ed. see Post, et al.
Pope, et al. Occupational Low Back Pain: Assessment, Treatment, & Prevention. (Illus.). 348p. 1991. 79.00 (*0-8016-6252-4*) Mosby Yr Bk.
Pope, A., ed. see Institute of Medicine, Committee on the Health Effects of Indoor Allergens Staff.
Pope, Alan & Goin, Kenneth L. High-Speed Wind Tunnel Testing. LC 78-15823. 486p. 1978. reprint ed. lib. bdg. 52.50 (*0-88275-727-X*) Krieger.
Pope, Alan, Jr., jt. auth. see Rae, William H.
***Pope, Albert.** Ladders. LC 95-1240. (Architecture at Rice Ser.: No. 34). (Illus.). 208p. (Orig.). 1995. pap. 14.95 (*1-885232-01-2*) Rice U Sch Archit.
Pope, Alexander. Alexander Pope. Rogers, Pat, ed. (Oxford Poetry Library). 256p. 1994. pap. 7.95 (*0-19-282270-5*) OUP.
— The Best of Pope. (BCL1-PR English Literature Ser.). 467p. 1992. reprint ed. lib. bdg. 99.00 (*0-7812-7393-5*) Rprt Serv.
— Essay on Man. Brady, Frank, ed. 1965. pap. write for info. (*0-672-61159-7*, LLA103) Macmillan.
— Essay on Man & Other Poems. LC 93-42205. (Thrift Editions Ser.). 128p. (Orig.). 1994. pap. 1.00 (*0-486-28053-5*) Dover.
— Minor Poems. Ault, Norman, ed. (Twickenham Ser.). 514p. 1964. 97.50 (*0-416-47750-X*) Elliots Bks.
— Poems of Alexander Pope: A One-Vol. Ed. of the Twickenham Text with Selected Annotations. Butt, John, ed. (Illus.). 1966. pap. 19.00 (*0-300-00030-8*, Y163) Yale U Pr.
— Poetical Works. Davis, Herbert, ed. (Oxford Paperbacks Ser.). 1978. pap. 17.95 (*0-19-281246-7*) OUP.
— Poetry & Prose of Alexander Pope. Williams, Aubrey, ed. LC 76-4880. (C). 1969. pap. 9.96 (*0-395-05156-8*, RivEd) HM.
— The Poetry of Pope: A Selection. Abrams, M. H., ed. (Crofts Classics Ser.). 128p. 1954. pap. text ed. write for info. (*0-88295-067-3*) Harlan Davidson.
— Pope: Poems & Prose. (Poetry Library). 192p. 1985. mass mkt. 8.95 (*0-14-058508-7*, Penguin Bks) Viking Penguin.
— Rape of the Lock. Cunningham, J. S., ed. 1971. pap. 9.95 (*0-19-911012-3*) OUP.
— The Rape of the Lock. 3rd ed. Tillotson, G., ed. 1971. pap. 8.50 (*0-415-03999-1*, NO. 2389) Routledge.
— Selections, 1993: Alexander Pope. Rogers, Pat, ed. LC 92-23197. (Oxford Authors Ser.). 1993. 55.00 (*0-19-254182-X*); pap. 17.95 (*0-19-281346-3*) OUP.
— Works: New Edition, 10 vols., Set. (BCL1-PR English Literature Ser.). 1992. reprint ed. lib. bdg. 900.00 (*0-7812-7392-7*) Rprt Serv.
— Works of Alexander Pope, 10 Vols, Set. Croker, John W. et al, eds. LC 66-29708. 5462p. 1967. reprint ed. 450.00 (*0-87752-087-9*) Gordian.
Pope, Alexander, jt. auth. see Beardsley, Aubrey.
Pope, Alexander, tr. see Homer.
Pope, Alexander, ed. see Shakespeare, William.
Pope, Andrew M., ed. see Institute of Medicine Staff.
Pope, Arthur K. Barnum & Bailey in the Sky: A Collection of Soul Journeys. (Illus.). 30p. (Orig.). 1991. pap. write for info. (*0-9623500-3-6*) Ministry Two.
— Youth Experience in Travel & Service: A Program That Awakens Faith & Social Consciousness in Youth. LC 89-91777. 136p. (Orig.). 1989. lib. bdg. 18.95 (*0-9623500-1-X*); pap. 8.95 (*0-9623500-0-1*) Ministry Two.
Pope, Arthur U. Masterpieces of Persian Art. LC 76-97351. (Illus.). vi, 204p. 1970. reprint ed. text ed. 41.50 (*0-8371-3013-1*, POPA, Greenwood Pr) Greenwood.
— A Survey of Persian Art, Vol. XV: Pre-Islamic Bibliography. Ackerman, Phyllis, ed. lib. bdg. 85.00 (*4-89360-020-6*, Pub. by Prsnlly Oriented JA) Mazda Pubs.
— A Survey of Persian Art, Vol. XVI: Islamic Bibliography. Ackerman, Phyllis, ed. lib. bdg. 85.00 (*4-89360-021-4*, Pub. by Prsnlly Oriented JA) Mazda Pubs.
— A Survey of Persian Art, Vols. I-XVI: From Prehistoric Times to the Present, Set. Ackerman, Phyllis, ed. (Illus.). 3816p. lib. bdg. 1,295.00 (*4-89360-011-7*, Pub. by Prsnlly Oriented JA) Mazda Pubs.
— A Survey of Persian Art, Vols. IV & IX: Potery & Faience, Set. Ackerman, Phyllis, ed. 353p. lib. bdg. 145.00 (*4-89360-014-1*, Pub. by Prsnlly Oriented JA) Mazda Pubs.
— A Survey of Persian Art, Vols. V-a & X: Art of the Book, Set. Ackerman, Phyllis, ed. (Illus.). 186p. lib. bdg. 145.00 (*4-89360-015-X*, Pub. by Prsnlly Oriented JA) Mazda Pubs.
— A Survey of Persian Art, Vols. V-b & XI: Textiles, Set. Ackerman, Phyllis, ed. (Illus.). 262p. lib. bdg. 145.00 (*4-89360-016-8*, Pub. by Prsnlly Oriented JA) Mazda Pubs.
— A Survey of Persian Art, Vols. VI-a & XII: Carpets, Set. Ackerman, Phyllis, ed. (Illus.). 209p. lib. bdg. 170.00 (*4-89360-017-6*, Pub. by Prsnlly Oriented JA) Mazda Pubs.
Pope, B. C., ed. see Bierce, Ambrose.
Pope, Barbara. Workforce Management: How Today's Companies Are Meeting Business & Employee Needs. 225p. 1992. 27.50 (*1-55623-537-2*) Irwin Prof Pubng.
Pope, Barbara M., jt. ed. see Waggoner, Ellen A.
Pope, Bill, jt. auth. see Jeffs, Dan.
Pope, C., jt. auth. see Pettengell, J. M.
Pope, C. H. A History of the Dorchester Pope Family, 1634-1888: With Sketches of Other Popes in England & America. (Illus.). 340p. 1989. reprint ed. lib. bdg. 59.00 (*0-8328-0976-4*); reprint ed. pap. 51.00 (*0-8328-0977-2*) Higginson Bk Co.
— Merriam Genealogy in England & America. (Illus.). 515p. 1989. reprint ed. lib. bdg. 85.00 (*0-8328-0866-0*); reprint ed. pap. 77.00 (*0-317-92809-0*) Higginson Bk Co.
Pope, C. H. & Hooper, T. Hooper Genealogy. (Illus.). 321p. reprint ed. lib. bdg. 56.00 (*0-8328-0679-X*); reprint ed. pap. 48.00 (*0-8328-0680-3*) Higginson Bk Co.
Pope, C. H., ed. see Paine, S. C.
Pope, C. H., jt. auth. see Tobey, R.
Pope, Carol A., jt. ed. see Milner, Joseph O.
Pope, Charles H. Merriam Genealogy in England & America. rev. ed. LC 86-18882. (Illus.). xxxvi, 522p. 1986. pap. 40.00 (*0-9612610-1-3*) Bullbrier Pr.
— Pioneers of Maine & New Hampshire. 252p. 1985. reprint ed. pap. text ed. 5.50 (*0-935207-19-8*) Danbury Hse Bks.
— The Pioneers of Maine & New Hampshire, 1623-1660. 263p. 1989. reprint ed. 22.00 (*0-685-60332-6*, 4655) Clearfield Co.

P Q

— The Pioneers of Maine & New Hampshire, 1623-1660: A Descriptive List Drawn from Records of the Colonies, Towns, Churches, Courts, & Other Contemporary Sources. 264p. 1992. reprint ed. pap. 20.00 (1-55613-522-X) Heritage Bk.

— Pioneers of Massachusetts. 551p. 1985. reprint ed. pap. 15.00 (0-935207-36-8) Danbury Hse Bks.

— Pioneers of Massachusetts. 550p. 1991. reprint ed. pap. 27.50 (1-55613-398-7) Heritage Bk.

Pope, Charles H., jt. auth. see Farlow, Charles F.

Pope, Chris, jt. auth. see Palmer, Richard.

Pope, Clayne L. The Impact of the Ante-Bellum Tariff on Income Distribution. LC 75-2591. (Dissertations in American Economic History Ser.). (Illus.). 1975. 21.95 (0-405-07213-9) Ayer.

Pope, Clayne L., jt. auth. see Fox, Frank W.

Pope, Clyde R., jt. auth. see Freeborn, Donald K.

Pope, Colin. Working with the Unions. 216p. 1993. 60.00 (0-85292-529-8, Pub. by IPM Hse UK) St Mut.

Pope-Cordle, Jamie. Low-Fat Supermarket Shopper's Guide: Making Healthy Choices from Thousands of Brand-Name Items. 72p. 1993. pap. 2.99 (0-393-30923-1) Norton.

Pope-Cordle, Jamie & Katahn, Martin. The Low-Fat Fast Food Guide. 64p. 1993. pap. 2.99 (0-393-31007-8) Norton.

Pope-Cordle, Jamie & Katahn, Martin, eds. The T-Factor Fat Gram Counter. 1989. pap. 2.99 (0-393-30655-0) Norton.

Pope County Historical Society. History of Pope County, IL. LC 86-50883. 416p. 1986. 79.00 (0-938021-03-6) Turner Pub KY.

Pope County Historical Society Staff & Turner Publishing Co. Staff. History & Families of Pope County, Illinois, Vol. II. LC 88-51190. 384p. 1988. 49.95 (0-938021-70-2) Turner Pub KY.

***Pope, D. H., ed.** Development of Methods to Detect Sulfate-Reducing Bacteria: Agents of Microbiologically Influenced Corrosion, Pub. No. 37. (Illus.). 64p. 1990. 53.00 (1-877914-19-3) NACE Intl.

***Pope, Dan & Lynn, Mark.** Warbonnets: From Super Chief to Super Fleet. (Illus.). 104p. 1994. 49.95 (0-614-03236-9, B923) Pentrex.

***Pope, Dan & Moreau, Jeffrey.** Warbonnets. (Illus.). 104p. 1994. 49.95 (1-56342-004-X) Interurban.

Pope, Daniel C. Connecticut Actions & Remedies: Tort Law, 2 vols., Set. 700p. 1993. ring bd. 145.00 (0-88063-440-5) Michie Butterworth.

Pope, Daniel C. & Resmini, Ronald J. Rhode Island Actions & Remedies: Tort Law, 2 vols., Set. 1180p. 1992. ring bd. 145.00 (1-56257-270-9) Michie Butterworth.

Pope, Daniel C., jt. auth. see Hirsch, Jeffrey L.

Pope, Daniel C., jt. auth. see Murphy, Walter L.

Pope, Daniel H. Microbiologically Influenced Corrosion: A State-of-the-Art Review. LC 85-115610. (MTI Publication Ser.: No. 13). 88p. reprint ed. pap. 25.10 (0-7837-0120-9, 2040397) Bks Demand.

Pope, David & Alston, Lee. Australia's Greatest Asset. 336p. 1989. pap. 33.00 (1-86287-013-6, Pub. by Federation Pr AU) W W Gaunt.

Pope, Deborah. Fanatic Heart. Poems. LC 91-48332. 64p. 1992. text ed. 15.95 (0-8071-1747-1); pap. 8.95 (0-8071-1748-X) La State U Pr.

— Mortal World: Poems. LC 95-10354. 64p. (C). 1995. text ed. 15.95 (0-8071-1983-0); pap. 8.95 (0-8071-1984-9) La State U Pr.

— Separate Vision: Isolation in Contemporary Women's Poetry. LC 84-5735. 174p. 1984. text ed. 27.50 (0-8071-1159-7) La State U Pr.

Pope, Dudley. The Battle of the River Plate. 296p. 1990. mass mkt. 4.95 (0-380-71045-5) Avon.

— Convoy. 335p. 1987. 16.95 (0-8027-0960-5) Walker & Co.

— Decoy. large type ed. (Adventure Suspense Ser.). 560p. 1985. 15.95 (0-7089-1271-0) Ulverscroft.

— The Devil Himself: The Mutiny of 1800. 185p. 1988. 24.95 (0-436-37751-9, Pub. by Seck & Warburg UK) Trafalgar.

— Galleon. 1988. 17.95 (0-8027-0989-3) Walker & Co.

— Life in Nelson's Navy. LC 80-82726. 296p. 1981. 22.95 (0-87021-346-6) Naval Inst Pr.

— Ramage. 350p. 1991. reprint ed. lib. bdg. 26.95 (0-89966-840-2) Buccaneer Bks.

— Seventy-Three North. LC 88-61812. (Illus.). 320p. 1988. 28.95 (0-87021-660-0) Naval Inst Pr.

Pope, E., et al. Rules of Thumb: Mechanical Engineers. 400p. 1995. write for info. (0-318-72846-X) Gulf Pub.

Pope, Eddie M., jt. auth. see Wrobel, Leo A.

Pope, Edward J., jt. ed. see Lee, Burtrand I.

Pope, Elizabeth C. Opinions IV: Philatelic Expertizing. (Opinions Ser.). (Illus.). 250p. 1987. 21.00 (0-911989-18-8) Philatelic Found.

Pope, Elizabeth C., et al. Opinions-Philatelic Expertizing: An Inside View. LC 83-60036. (Illus.). 141p. 1983. 12.00 (0-911989-00-5) Philatelic Found.

Pope, Elizabeth M. The Perilous Gard. 288p. (J). (gr. 7 up). 1992. pap. 4.99 (0-14-034912-X) Puffin Bks.

— The Sherwood Ring. (J). (gr. 6 up). 19.00 (0-8446-6416-2) Peter Smith.

Pope, Ethel M. India in Portuguese Literature. 1989. reprint ed. 32.00 (81-206-0496-2, Pub. by Asian Educ Servs II) S Asia.

Pope, G. U. A Compendious Tamil English Dictionary. 100p. 1986. reprint ed. 12.50 (0-8364-1680-5, Pub. by Manohar II) S Asia.

— A Compendious Tamil-English Dictionary; a Handbook of the Tamil Language. 7th ed. 98p. (ENG & TAM.). 1992. 25.00 (0-8288-1724-3, M 14118) Fr & Eur.

— A Handbook of the Tamil Language. 208p. 1986. 24.00 (0-8364-1678-3, Pub. by Usha II) S Asia.

— Handbook of the Tamil Language. 205p. 1989. reprint ed. 19.00 (81-206-0016-9) IBD Ltd.

— The Sacred Kurral of Tiruvalluva Nayanar. 448p. 1986. reprint ed. 22.00 (0-8364-1681-3, Pub. by Abhinav II) S Asia.

— Tamil Prose Reader. 124p. 1982. 18.00 (0-88431-874-5) IBD Ltd.

— A Tamil Prose Reader. 132p. 1986. reprint ed. 12.50 (0-8364-1679-1, Pub. by Abhinav II) S Asia.

Pope, G. V., ed. Kurral of Tirruvalluvar. 1974. lib. bdg. 69.95 (0-8490-0478-0) Gordon Pr.

Pope, Gregory. Camelot World: Hot Machines. 128p. (Orig.). (J). 1990. pap. 2.95 (0-380-76039-8, Camelot) Avon.

Pope, Gustavus W. Journey to Mars. LC 73-13262. (Classics of Science Fiction Ser.). (Illus.). 551p. 1974. reprint ed. 31.00 (0-88355-116-0) Hyperion Conn.

Pope, Harrison, Jr., jt. auth. see Hudson, James I.

Pope, Hazel. The Machine Knitter's Design Book: A Practical Guide to Creating Beautiful Knitwearl. (Illus.). 128p. 1994. 24.95 (0-7153-9972-1, Pub. by D & C Pub UK) Sterling.

Pope-Hennessey, John. Fra Angelico. (Library of Great Masters). (Illus.). 80p. 1989. reprint ed. pap. 12.99 (1-878351-01-X) Riverside NY.

Pope-Hennessy, John. Cellini. LC 85-6111. (Illus.). 320p. 1985. 125.00 (0-89659-453-X) Abbeville Pr.

— Donatello Sculptor. 1993. 95.00 (1-55859-645-3) Abbeville Pr.

— Italian Paintings. (Robert Lehman Collection: Vol. 1). (Illus.). 352p. 1987. 95.00 (0-691-04045-1, Princeton U Pr) Metro Mus Art.

— The Piero della Francesca Trail. LC 91-66019. (Walter Neurath Memorial Lecture Ser.). (Illus.). 64p. 1993. pap. 10.95 (0-500-27703-6) Thames Hudson.

— Portrait in the Renaissance. (Bollingen Ser.: Vol. 35). (Illus.). 380p. 1990. 90.00 (0-691-09795-X) Princeton U Pr.

— The Portrait in the Renaissance: The A. W. Mellon Lectures in the Fine Arts, 1963. (Bollingen Ser.: Vol. XXXV, No. 12). (Illus.). 380p. (C). 1989. pap. text ed. 26.95 (0-691-01825-1) Princeton U Pr.

— The Study & Criticism of Italian Sculpture. LC 80-20651. (Illus.). 271p. 1981. 45.00 (0-87099-239-2) Metro Mus Art.

— The Study & Criticism of Italian Sculpture. LC 80-8589. (Illus.). 256p. (C). 1981. 85.00x (0-691-03967-4) Princeton U Pr.

Pope-Hennessy, John W. Paradiso: The Illuminations to Dante's Divine Comedy by Giovanni di Paolo. LC 93-16598. (Illus.). 1993. 75.00 (0-679-42739-2) Random.

Pope-Hennessy, Una B. Durham Company. LC 70-36167. (Essay Index Reprint Ser.). 1977. reprint ed. 21.95 (0-8369-2714-1) Ayer.

— Edgar Allan Poe. LC 77-92977. (Studies in Poe: No. 23). 1969. reprint ed. lib. bdg. 75.00 (0-8383-0998-4) M S G Haskell Hse.

Pope, Ingrid B. Musings. 96p. 1994. write for info. (1-56167-159-2) Noble Hse MD.

Pope, Isabel, tr. see Salazar, Adolfo.

***Pope, Ivan.** Internet UK. LC 94-31395. 1994. write for info. (0-13-190950-9) P-H.

Pope, J., ed. see Akers, Charles W. & Carter, John W.

Pope, J., ed. see Frick.

Pope, J. K., jt. ed. see Pojeta, J., Jr.

Pope, J. W. Marriage: For Better or for Verse. 1994. 8.95 (0-8062-4979-X) Carlton.

— Some Old Testament Characters in a Lighter Vein! (Illus.). 100p. (Orig.). 1995. pap. write for info. (1-885591-91-8) Morris Pubng.

Pope, Jack, et al. John Berry & His Children. 903p. 1988. 35.00 (0-317-91286-0); text ed. 35.00 (0-9621053-0-9) Jack Pope.

Pope, Jacqueline. Biting the Hand That Feeds Them: Organizing Women on Welfare at the Grass Roots Level. LC 88-27505. (Illus.). 170p. 1989. text ed. 47.95 (0-275-92922-1, C2922, Praeger Pubs) Greenwood.

Pope, James E., jt. auth. see McCombs, Barbara L.

***Pope, Jamie.** The Last Five Pounds: How to Lose Them & Leave Them Forever. Rubenstein, Julie, ed. 432p. 1995. 23.00 (0-671-88453-0) PB.

***Pope, Jamie & Katahn, Martin.** The Factor Fat Gram Counter. exp. rev. ed. 80p. 1995. pap. 5.95 (0-393-31331-X, Norton Paperbks) Norton.

Pope, Jeffrey L. Practical Marketing Research. 314p. 1993. 32.95 (0-8144-5086-5) AMACOM.

Pope, Jerome L., jt. ed. see Singer, Kenneth S.

Pope, John. The Hellions. LC 87-61721. 249p. 1988. 25.95 (0-87975-380-3) Prometheus Bks.

— Tour Through the Southern & Western Territories of the United States of North America, the Spanish Dominions on the River Mississippi & the Floridas, the Countries of the Creek Nations, & Many Uninhabited Parts. LC 70-146411. (First American Frontier Ser.). 1971. reprint ed. 13.95 (0-405-02875-X) Ayer.

Pope, John A. Fourteenth-Century Blue-&-White, a Group of Chinese Porcelains in Topkapu Sarayi Muzesi, Istanbul. rev. ed. (Occasional Papers Ser.: Vol. 2, No. 1). 1970. pap. 3.50 (0-934686-03-3) Freer.

Pope, John A., et al. The Freer Chinese Bronzes, Vol. 1. (Oriental Studies: No. 7). (Illus.). 1967. 45.00 (0-934686-10-6) Freer.

Pope, John C., ed. Seven Old English Poems. (Orig.). 1966. pap. 5.55 (0-672-60976-2, LL8, Bobbs) Macmillan.

— Seven Old English Poems. 240p. (Orig.). (C). 1981. reprint ed. pap. text ed. 9.95 (0-393-95174-X) Norton.

Pope John Center. Technological Powers & the Person: Nuclear Energy & Reproduction Technology: Proceedings of the 1983 Bishops' Workshop. Lossing, Larry D. et al, eds. (Illus.). 500p. (Orig.). 1983. pap. 15.95 (0-935372-12-1) Pope John Ctr.

Pope John Paul, II. And from That Hour... 1989. 0.50 (0-911988-77-7) AMI Pr.

— Angelus Meditations on the Litany of the Sacred Heart of Jesus. LC 91-66666. 108p. (Orig.). 1992. pap. 5.95 (0-87973-478-7, 478) Our Sunday Visitor.

— The Christian Family: In the Teachings of John Paul II. 1991. pap. 6.50 (0-949080-13-6) Alba.

— Familiaris Consortio. 1988. 1.50 (0-8198-6449-8, 508) Human Life Intl.

— I Will Give You Shepherds. 236p. 1992. pap. 8.95 (1-55586-519-4) US Catholic.

— Letters to My Brother Priests. rev. ed. 276p. 1994. pap. 9.95 (0-933932-61-8) Scepter Pubs.

Pope John Paul, II, pseud. Love & Responsibility. Willetts, H. T., tr. LC 92-75063. 310p. 1993. reprint ed. pap. 14.95 (0-89870-445-6) Ignatius Pr.

Pope John Paul, II. On the Dignity & Vocation of Women: Mulieris Dignitatem. 120p. 1988. pap. 4.95 (1-55586-244-6) US Catholic.

— On the Permanent Validity of the Church's Missionary Mandate: Redemptoris Missio. 160p. (Orig.). (C). 1990. pap. 6.95 (1-55586-424-4) US Catholic.

— PB: On the Occasion of the Marian Year. 25p. (Orig.). 1988. pap. 1.95 (1-55586-234-9) US Catholic.

— Reflections on Humanae Vitae. 1988. 2.75 (0-685-22241-1, 515); pap. write for info. (0-8198-6410-2) Human Life Intl.

— Sollicitudo Rei Socialis: On Social Concern. 104p. 1987. pap. 5.95 (1-55586-205-5) US Catholic.

***Pope John Paul II.** Conmigo Dia Tras Dia: Prayers & Devotions: 365 Daily Meditations. 1994. 15.95 (0-670-86199-5, Viking) Viking Penguin.

— Crossing the Threshold of Hope. 1994. 20.00 (0-679-44058-5); 22.00 (0-679-44084-4) Knopf.

— The Crossing Threshold of Hope. Date not set. pap. 12.00 (0-679-76119-5) Random.

— Cruzando el Embral de la Esperanza. 1994. 20.00 (0-679-44082-8) Knopf.

— Daily Meditations of John Paul II. 1988. pap. 8.00 (2-89039-066-7, EP0275) Pauline Bks.

— Lift up Your Hearts: The Pope John Paul II Reader. Orig. Title: Draw Near to God. 310p. 1995. pap. 9.99 (0-89283-923-6, Charis) Servant.

— Lord & Giver of Life. 120p. (Orig.). 1986. pap. 3.95 (1-55586-103-2) US Catholic.

— Mary - God's Yes to Man: Encyclical Letter of John Paul II. Von Balthasar, Hans U., ed. Krauth, Lothar, tr. LC 88-80726. 179p. (Orig.). 1988. pap. 9.95 (0-89870-219-4) Ignatius Pr.

— The Mother of the Redeemer: Redemptoris Mater. 120p. (Orig.). 1987. pap. 3.95 (1-55586-159-8) US Catholic.

— On Human Work. 62p. 1981. pap. 3.95 (1-55586-825-8) US Catholic.

— On Jews & Judaism, 1979-1986. (Orig.). 1987. pap. 3.95 (1-55586-151-2) US Catholic.

— On the Vocation & the Mission of the Lay Faithful in the Church & in the World: (Christifideles Laici) 196p. (Orig.). 1989. pap. 7.95 (1-55586-274-8) US Catholic.

— Place Within: The Poetry of Pope John Paul II. 1994. pap. 12.00 (0-679-76074-1) Knopf.

— Place Within: The Poetry of Pope John Paul II. 1994. 20.00 (0-679-44079-8) Random.

***Pope John Paul II, 2nd.** Place Within: The Poetry of Pope John Paul II. 1994. 10.00 (0-679-76064-4) Random.

Pope John Paul II. The Pope Speaks to the American Church: John Paul II's Homilies, Speeches & Letters to Catholics in America. LC 91-55298. 528p. 1992. pap. 18.00 (0-06-064211-4) Harper SF.

— Prayers & Devotions: Three Hundred Sixty-Five Daily Meditations. 1994. 17.95 (0-670-86179-0, Viking) Viking Penguin.

— Reflections on Humanae Vitae. LC 84-28625. 96p. 1984. pap. 3.50 (0-685-53930-X) Pauline Bks.

— The Splendor of Truth: (Latin Title: Veritatis Splendor) 154p. (Orig.). 1993. pap. 2.25 (0-8198-6964-3) Pauline Bks.

— Way to Christ. 1994. pap. 12.00 (0-06-064216-5) Harper SF.

— Word Made Flesh. 1994. pap. 11.00 (0-06-064215-7) Harper SF.

— Words of Certitude. large type ed. 266p. 1985. reprint ed. pap. 7.95 (0-8027-2477-9) Walker & Co.

Pope John Paul Second. Catechesis in Our Time. (C). 1988. 30.00 (0-85439-169-X, Pub. by St Paul Pubns UK) St Mut.

— Daily Meditations. (C). 1988. 39.00 (0-85439-246-7, Pub. by St Paul Pubns UK) St Mut.

— Fruitful & Responsible Love. (C). 1988. 39.00 (0-85439-159-2, Pub. by St Paul Pubns UK) St Mut.

— Sign of Contradiction. (C). 1988. 39.00 (0-85439-158-4, Pub. by St Paul Pubns UK) St Mut.

Pope John XXIII Medical-Moral Research & Education Center. Reproductive Technologies, Marriage & the Church: Proceedings of 1988 Bishops' Workshop. McCarthy, Donald G., ed. 318p. (Orig.). 1988. pap. 17.95 (0-935372-23-7) Pope John Ctr.

— Scarce Medical Resources & Justice: Proceedings of 1987 Bishops' Workshop. McCarthy, Donald G., ed. 308p. (Orig.). 1987. pap. 17.95 (0-935372-21-0) Pope John Ctr.

Pope, Joseph. Memoirs of the Right Honorable Sir John Alexander Macdonald, 2 Vols. LC 76-137271. reprint ed. 115.00 (0-404-05085-9) AMS Pr.

— Memoirs of the Right Honourable Sir John Alexander Macdonald, 2 vols., Set. (BCL1 - History - Canada Ser.). 1991. reprint ed. lib. bdg. 150.00 (0-7812-6364-6) Rprt Serv.

Pope, Joya. Upcoming Changes: The Next Twenty Years. (Michael Book Ser.). 228p. (Orig.). (C). 1992. pap. 12.95 (0-942531-33-7) Emerald Wave Pub.

— The World According to Michael. 1989. 8.95 (0-942663-04-7) Progress.

— The World According to Michael: An Old Soul's Guide to the Universe. (Orig.). 1987. pap. 8.95 (0-942531-00-0) Emerald Wave Pub.

— The World According to Michael: An Old Soul's Guide to the Universe. rev. ed. (Michael Book Ser.). 160p. (Orig.). (C). 1992. pap. 10.95 (0-942531-39-6, Focal) Buttrwrth-Heinemann.

Pope, Joyce. Animal Babies. LC 91-45381. (Nature Club Ser.). (Illus.). 32p. (J). (gr. 3-6). 1993. lib. bdg. 11.59 (0-8167-2773-2); pap. text ed. 3.95 (0-8167-2774-0) Troll Assocs.

— Animal Homes. LC 91-45380. (Nature Club Ser.). (Illus.). 32p. (J). (gr. 3-6). 1993. lib. bdg. 11.59 (0-8167-2775-9); pap. text ed. 3.95 (0-8167-2776-7) Troll Assocs.

— Animal Journeys. LC 91-45379. (Nature Club Ser.). (Illus.). 32p. (J). (gr. 3-6). 1993. lib. bdg. 11.59 (0-8167-2777-5); pap. text ed. 3.95 (0-8167-2778-3) Troll Assocs.

— The Children's Atlas of Natural Wonders. LC 95-11778. (Illus.). 96p. (J). (gr. 3-6). 1995. 18.90 (1-56294-564-5) Millbrook Pr.

— The Children's Atlas of Natural Wonders. (Illus.). 96p. (J). (gr. 2-6). 1995. pap. 12.95 (1-56294-886-5) Millbrook Pr.

— Deadly Venom. (Curious Creatures Ser.). (J). (gr. 4-7). 1993. pap. 4.95 (0-8114-6254-4) Raintree Steck-V.

— The Duck. (Animals in Towns Ser.). (Illus.). 24p. (J). (gr. 3-6). 1991. 8.95 (0-237-60249-0, Pub. by Evans Bros Ltd UK) Trafalgar.

— Fossil Detective. LC 91-45170. (Nature Club Ser.). (Illus.). 32p. (J). (gr. 3-6). 1993. lib. bdg. 11.59 (0-8167-2781-3); pap. text ed. 3.95 (0-8167-2782-1) Troll Assocs.

— Horses. (Finding Out about Ser.). (Illus.). 32p. (J). (gr. 4-6). 1991. 13.95 (0-237-60173-7, Pub. by Evans Bros Ltd UK) Trafalgar.

— Kenneth Lilly's Animals. LC 87-31147. (Illus.). 96p. (J). (gr. 3 up). 1988. 16.95 (0-688-07696-3) Lothrop.

— Life in the Dark. LC 91-18646. (Curious Creatures Ser.). (Illus.). 48p. (J). (gr. 4-8). 1992. lib. bdg. 22.80 (0-8114-3150-9); pap. 4.95 (0-8114-6252-8) Raintree Steck-V.

— Living Fossils. LC 91-13998. (Curious Creatures Ser.). (Illus.). 48p. (J). (gr. 4-8). 1992. lib. bdg. 22.80 (0-8114-3151-7); pap. 4.95 (0-8114-6256-0) Raintree Steck-V.

— Making Contact. (Curious Creatures Ser.). (J). (gr. 4-7). 1993. pap. 4.95 (0-8114-6258-7) Raintree Steck-V.

— Mistaken Identity. LC 91-17136. (Curious Creatures Ser.). (Illus.). 48p. (J). (gr. 4-8). 1992. lib. bdg. 22.80 (0-8114-3152-5); pap. 4.95 (0-8114-6253-6) Raintree Steck-V.

— Night Creatures. LC 91-45171. (Nature Club Ser.). (Illus.). 32p. (J). (gr. 3-6). 1993. lib. bdg. 11.59 (0-8167-2783-X); pap. text ed. 3.95 (0-8167-2784-8) Troll Assocs.

— On the Move. (Curious Creatures Ser.). (J). (gr. 4-7). 1993. pap. 4.95 (0-8114-6255-2) Raintree Steck-V.

— Plant Partnerships. LC 90-32395. (Plant Life Ser.). (Illus.). 62p. (YA). (gr. 6 up). 1991. lib. bdg. 15.95 (0-8160-2422-7) Facts on File.

— Plants & Flowers. LC 91-45378. (Nature Club Ser.). (Illus.). 32p. (J). (gr. 3-6). 1993. lib. bdg. 11.59 (0-8167-2779-1); pap. text ed. 3.95 (0-8167-2780-5) Troll Assocs.

— Plants of the Tropics. (Plant Life Ser.). 64p. (YA). 1990. 15.95 (0-8160-2423-5) Facts on File.

— Practical Plants. (Plant Life Ser.). 64p. (YA). 1990. 15.95 (0-8160-2424-3) Facts on File.

— Seashores. LC 89-20318. (Nature Club Ser.). (Illus.). 32p. (J). (gr. 3-6). 1990. lib. bdg. 11.59 (0-8167-1965-9); pap. text ed. 3.95 (0-8167-1966-7) Troll Assocs.

— Strange Nature. (Curious Creatures Ser.). (J). (gr. 4-7). 1993. pap. 4.95 (0-8114-6259-5) Raintree Steck-V.

— Two Lives. LC 91-17460. (Curious Creatures Ser.). (Illus.). 48p. (J). (gr. 4-8). 1992. lib. bdg. 22.80 (0-8114-3153-3); pap. 4.95 (0-8114-6257-9) Raintree Steck-V.

***Pope, Joyce & Lilly, Kenneth.** Kenneth Lilly's Animals. LC 94-5309. (J). 1995. write for info. (1-56402-513-6) Candlewick Pr.

Pope, Kenneth S., et al. Sexual Intimacy Between Therapists & Patients. LC 86-15165. (Sexual Medicine Ser.: No. 5). 197p. 1986. text ed. 49.95 (0-275-92253-7, B2953, Praeger Pubs) Greenwood.

— Sexual Intimacy Between Therapists & Patients. LC 86-15165. (Sexual Medicine Ser.: No. 5). 197p. 1988. pap. text ed. 17.95 (0-275-92953-1, Praeger Pubs) Greenwood.

Pope, Kenneth S. Sexual Involvement with Therapists: Patient Assessment, Subsequent Therapy, Forensics. LC 94-11534. 1994. pap. 24.95 (1-55798-248-1) Am Psychol.

Pope, Kenneth S. & Singer, Jerome L., eds. The Stream of Consciousness: Scientific Investigations into the Flow of Human Experience. LC 78-2003. (Emotions, Personality, & Psychotherapy Ser.). reprint ed. pap. 74.10 (0-317-08026-1, 2-17802) Bks Demand.

Pope, Kenneth S. & Vasquez, Melba J. Ethics in Psychotherapy & Counseling: A Practical Guide for Psychologists. LC 90-26036. (Social & Behavioral Sciences Ser.). 226p. 1991. 26.95 (1-55542-347-7) Jossey-Bass.

Pope, Kenneth S., jt. auth. see Caudill, O. Brant.

Pope, Kenneth S., et al. The MMPI, MMPI-2, & MMPI-A in Court: A Practical Guide for Expert Witnesses & Attorneys. 416p. 1993. 59.95 (1-55798-182-5); trans. 199.95 (1-55798-189-2) Am Psychol.

An Asterisk (*) at the beginning of an entry indicates that the title is appearing in BIP for the first time.

— On Love & Loving: Psychological Perspectives on the Nature & Experience of Romantic Love. LC 80-8012. (Jossey-Bass Social & Behavioral Science Ser.). 397p. reprint ed. pap. 113.20 (*0-7837-2548-5*, 2042707) Bks Demand.

— Sexual Feelings in Psychotherapy: Explorations for Therapists & Therapists-in-Training. 319p. (Orig.). 1993. pap. text ed. 24.95 (*1-55798-201-5*) Am Psychol.

Pope, Kevin. Dance of the Seven Veals: And Other Cartoons. 1991. pap. 7.95 (*0-312-05828-4*) St Martin.

Pope, L. E., et al, eds. New Materials Approaches to Tribology: Theory & Applications: Materials Research Society Symposium Proceedings, Vol. 140. 1989. text ed. 52.00 (*1-55899-013-5*) Materials Res.

Pope Leo XIII. Freemasonry-Humanum Genus. 32p. 1978. reprint ed. pap. 1.25 (*0-89555-171-3*) TAN Bks Pubs.

Pope-Levison, Priscilla & Levison, John R. Jesus in Global Contexts. 208p. (Orig.). 1992. pap. 17.99 (*0-664-25165-X*) Westminster John Knox.

Pope, Lillie. Guidelines for Teaching Children with Learning Problems. 333p. 1982. pap. 15.95 (*0-87594-201-6*) Book-Lab.

— Guidelines to Teaching Remedial Reading. LC 74-25232. (Illus.). 192p. 1975. pap. 15.95 (*0-87594-119-2*) Book-Lab.

— Learning Disabilities Glossary. 64p. 1976. pap. 3.95 (*0-87594-144-3*) Book-Lab.

Pope, Lillie, et al. Special Needs: Special Answers. (Illus.). (J). (gr. k-6). 1979. pap. 19.95 (*0-87594-181-8*) Book-Lab.

— Teacher's Sampler. (Illus.). 96p. (Orig.). 1973. pap. text ed. 9.95 (*0-87594-194-X*, 2565) Book-Lab.

***Pope, Liston, Jr.** Living Like the Saints: A Novel of Nicaragua (1996) 1996. write for info. (*0-9638900-1-8*) N A Gilbert.

Pope, Liston. Millhands & Preachers: A Study of Gastonia. (Studies in Religious Education: No. 15). (Illus.). (J). 1965. reprint ed. pap. 19.00 (*0-300-00182-7*) Yale U Pr.

Pope, Liston, Jr. Redemption: A Novel of War in Lebanon. LC 93-91788. 294p. 1994. 24.95 (*0-9638900-0-X*) N A Gilbert.

Pope, Liston. Religion & Class Structure. (Reprint Series in Social Sciences). (C). 1993. reprint ed. pap. text ed. 1.00 (*0-8290-3821-3*, S-225) Irvington.

Pope, Liston, ed. see Institute for Religious & Social Studies Staff.

Pope, Loren. Looking Beyond the Ivy League: Finding the College That's Right for You. 288p. 1990. pap. 11.95 (*0-14-012209-5*, Penguin Bks) Viking Penguin.

— Looking Beyond the Ivy League: Finding the College That's Right for You. LC 95-12252. 1995. pap. write for info. (*0-14-023952-9*, Penguin Bks) Viking Penguin.

Pope, M. H., jt. ed. see Krag, M. H.

Pope, M. T. Heteropoly & Isopoly Oxometalates. (Inorganic Chemistry Concepts Ser.: Vol. 8). (Illus.). 190p. 1983. 109.00 (*0-387-11889-6*) Spr-Verlag.

***Pope, Marcus.** Que's BBS Directory. 1994. pap. 24.99 (*0-7897-0018-2*) Que.

Pope, Margaret M. This Chosen Generation: Armed with the Gifts of God. 160p. 1994. 11.98 (*0-88290-483-3*, 1968) Horizon Utah.

***Pope, Markus W.** Building Internet Applications with Visual C Plus Plus. (Illus.). 608p. (Orig.). 1995. pap. 49. 99 (*0-7897-0213-4*) Que.

***Pope, Marvin H.** Probative Pontificating in Ugaritic & Biblical Literature: Collected Essays. Smith, Mark S., ed. (Ugaritische-Biblisch Literatur Ser.: Vol. 10). xv, 406p. 1994. text ed. 66.00x (*3-927120-15-4*, Pub. by UGARIT GW) Eisenbrauns.

Pope, Marvin H., ed. Job. rev. ed. (Anchor Bible Ser.: Vol. 15). 1965. 34.00 (*0-385-00894-5*, Anchor NY) Doubleday.

Pope, Marvin H., intro. Song of Songs. LC 72-79417. (Anchor Bible Ser.: Vol. 7C). (Illus.). 1977. 44.00 (*0-385-00569-5*, Anchor NY) Doubleday.

Pope, Nancy P. National History in the Heroic Poem. LC 90-42002. (Studies in Comparative Literature). 208p. 1990. reprint ed. 15.00 (*0-8240-5472-5*) Garland.

Pope, Nolan F., jt. auth. see Woods, Lawrence A.

Pope, Norris, Jr. Dickens & Charity. LC 78-3867. 303p. 1978. text ed. 42.00 (*0-231-04478-X*) Col U Pr.

Pope, P., jt. ed. see Loxton, R.

Pope, Pamela. Neither Angels Nor Demons. 416p. 1992. 24. 95 (*0-7126-3845-8*, Pub. by Century UK) Trafalgar.

— The Rich Pass By. 384p. 1991. 21.95 (*0-7126-2507-0*, Pub. by Century UK) Trafalgar.

Pope, Patricia. Seashore & Wading Birds of Florida. LC 75-2036. (Illus.). 48p. (Orig.). 1975. pap. 2.95 (*0-8200-0903-2*) Great Outdoors.

— Shellcraft Animals. LC 75-15906. (Short-Time Projects for Beginners Ser.). (Illus.). 32p. (Orig.). 1975. pap. 1.00 (*0-8200-0507-X*) Great Outdoors.

Pope, Patricia, ed. see Raymond, Dorothy.

Pope Paul II. Pope John Paul II & the Family & Text. LC 82-13308. 416p. 1983. 15.00 (*0-8199-0851-7*, Frncscn Herld) Franciscan Pr.

Pope Paul VI. The Credo of the People of God. 1989. 0.50 (*0-911988-93-9*) AMI Pr.

— Devotion to the Blessed Virgin Mary. 1974. pap. 0.75 (*0-8198-0295-6*) Pauline Bks.

— Humanae Vitae. 2nd rev. ed. Calegari, Marc, tr. 24p. 1983. pap. 1.95 (*0-89870-000-0*) Ignatius Pr.

— On Evangelization in the Modern World. 1976. pap. text ed. 1.25 (*0-8198-0409-6*) Pauline Bks.

— On Evangelization in the Modern World. 70p. 1975. pap. 4.95 (*1-55586-129-6*) US Catholic.

Pope Pius Eleventh. Essays in History, Written Between the Years 1896-1912. LC 67-26771. (Essay Index Reprint Ser.). 1977. 19.95 (*0-8369-0791-4*) Ayer.

Pope Pius V. The Traditional Latin Roman Catholic Mass. De Pauw, Gommar A., tr. (Illus.). 98p. (Orig.). 1989. ring bd. 10.00 (*0-685-25984-6*) CTM Pubns.

— The Traditional Latin Roman Catholic Mass for the Faithful Departed. De Pauw, Gommar A., tr. & illus. by. 78p. 1989. ring bd. 20.00 (*0-685-25985-4*) CTM Pubns.

Pope Pius X. On the Doctrine of the Modernists. 1973. pap. 0.95 (*0-8198-0248-4*) Pauline Bks.

***Pope Pius XII.** Pius XII: Selected Encyclicals & Addresses. vi, 387p. 1995. text ed. 21.95 (*0-912141-19-0*) Roman Cath Bks.

***Pope, Randolph.** Understanding Juan Goytisolo. LC 95-11606. (Understanding Modern European & Latin American Literature Ser.). 1995. write for info. (*1-57003-069-3*) U of SC Pr.

Pope, Randolph D., ed. The Analysis of Literary Texts: Current Trends in Methodology (Third & Fourth York College Colloquia) LC 79-54144. (Studies in Literary Analysis). 330p. 1980. lib. bdg. 26.00 (*0-916950-14-X*); pap. text ed. 18.00 (*0-916950-13-1*) Biling Rev-Pr.

Pope, Raymond P. Seventy Two Hours in Hell. 176p. (Orig.). 1989. pap. 10.00 (*0-944765-01-7*) Agape Bks.

Pope, Rex. Atlas of British Social & Economic History since 1700. 272p. 1989. text ed. 85.00 (*0-02-897341-0*) Macmillan.

Pope, Rex, et al, eds. Social Welfare in Britain, Eighteen Eighty-Five to Nineteen Eighty-Five. 192p. (Orig.). (C). 1986. 37.50 (*0-7099-4001-7*, Pub. by Croom Helm UK) Routledge Chapman & Hall.

Pope, Rob. Textual Intervention: Critical & Creative Strategies for Literary Studies. LC 94-4022. (Interface Ser.). 1994. 35.00 (*0-415-05436-2*); pap. 12.99 (*0-415-05437-0*) Routledge.

Pope, Robert. Jack's Universe: A Novel. LC 93-44122. 191p. 1994. pap. 10.95 (*0-929968-20-4*) Another Chicago Pr.

— North of North: Two Novellas. 298p. (Orig.). 1996. pap. 14.95 (*0-929968-42-5*) Another Chicago Pr.

— Private Acts. LC 90-80232. 240p. 1990. pap. 9.95 (*0-929968-10-7*) Another Chicago Pr.

Pope, Robert G. Half-Way Covenant: Church Membership in Puritan New England. 333p. reprint ed. 95.00 (*0-8357-9500-4*, 2011473) Bks Demand.

Pope, Robert G., ed. The Notebook of the Reverend John Fiske: 1644 to 1675. LC 74-81447. 256p. 1974. 17.50 (*0-88389-052-6*, Essx Institute) Peabody Essex Mus.

Pope, Rodney J. Andrews Field: First United States World War Two Airbase in Europe, with a Brief History of Great Saling. (Illus.). 80p. (Orig.). 1991. pap. 15.00 (*0-86025-428-3*, Pub. by Ian Henry Pubns UK) Empire Pub Srvs.

Pope, Rowena M. The Hungry Years: The Story of One Family's Struggle for Survival During the Great Depression. LC 82-71137. (Illus.). 176p. (Orig.). (gr. 11-12). 1982. pap. 5.95 (*0-9608182-0-0*) Bold Blue Jay Pubns.

— Speak the Truth in Love. 71p. (Orig.). 1988. pap. 4.00 (*0-9608182-2-7*) Bold Blue Jay Pubns.

Pope, Saxton. Adventurous Bowmen. 1991. 36.00 (*1-879356-06-6*) Wolfe Pub Co.

— Hunting with the Bow & Arrow. 1991. 36.00 (*1-879356-05-8*) Wolfe Pub Co.

— Hunting with the Bow & Arrow. (Legends of the Longbow Ser.: Vol. 12). (Illus.). 257p. 1993. reprint ed. 39.95 (*1-56416-098-X*) Derrydale Pr.

— A Study of Bows & Arrows. (Legends of the Longbow Ser.: Vol. 2). (Illus.). 160p. (YA). (gr. 10 up). 1992. reprint ed. 39.95 (*1-56416-088-2*) Derrydale Pr.

Pope-Selman, Linda, ed. see Ingold, Gerard.

Pope Staff. New Antoinette Pope School Cookbook. 1980. 22.95 (*0-02-598060-2*) Macmillan.

Pope, Stephen. The Evolution of Altruism & the Ordering of Love. LC 93-37489. (C). 1994. 40.00 (*0-87840-550-X*) Georgetown U Pr.

Pope, Stephen T., ed. The Well-Tempered Object: Musical Applications of Object Oriented Software Technology. (Illus.). 200p. 1991. 31.50 (*0-262-16126-5*) MIT Pr.

Pope, Thomas H. The History of Newberry County, South Carolina, 1749-1860, Vol. I. LC 72-14339. (Illus.). 406p. 1992. reprint ed. text ed. 39.95 (*0-87249-248-6*) U of SC Pr.

— The History of Newberry County, South Carolina, 1860-1990, Vol. II. LC 72-14339. (Illus.). 566p. 1992. text ed. 39.95 (*0-87249-777-1*) U of SC Pr.

Pope, Trey. Barbecue on My Mind. 70p. 1991. pap. 6.95 (*0-9632057-0-6*) Three Pubns.

— Barbecue on My Mind: The Thirty Best Barbecue Restaurants in Georgia. LC 92-15431. 80p. (Orig.). 1992. pap. 7.95 (*0-87797-240-0*) Cherokee.

Pope, Trey & Griffin, Carter. Atlanta's Best Bargains: The Quality Guide for Smart Shoppers. LC 92-18853. 80p. (Orig.). 1992. pap. 8.95 (*0-87797-243-5*) Cherokee.

Pope, Virginia, tr. see Papini, Giovanni.

Pope, Willard B., ed. see Barrett, Elizabeth B. & Haydon, Benjamin R.

Pope, Willard B., ed. see Haydon, Benjamin R.

Pope, William C. Managing for Performance Perfection: The Changing Emphasis, Vol. 1. (Illus.). 344p. (Orig.). (C). 1990. pap. text ed. 29.95 (*0-944453-00-7*) B Brae.

Pope, William L. Israel As a Nation. Hogg, Gayle, ed. 184p. 1983. pap. text ed. 13.50 (*0-311-72225-5*) Casa Bautista.

***Popeil, Ron & Graham, Jefferson.** As Seen on TV: RONCO's Ron Popeil, His Incredible Inventions & How to CAPITALize on the Home Shopping Revolution. LC 95-3043. 1995. write for info. (*0-385-31378-0*) Delacorte.

Popek, Gerald J. The Locus Distributed System Architecture. (MIT Press Series in Computer Systems). (Illus.). 150p. 1986. 30.00 (*0-262-16102-8*) MIT Pr.

Popel, A. S. & Johnson, P. C., eds. Microvascular Networks: Experimental & Theoretical Studies. (Illus.). x, 226p. 1986. 158.50 (*3-8055-4323-9*) S Karger.

Popel, Aleksander, jt. ed. see Gross, Joseph F.

Popelar, Carl H., jt. auth. see Kanninen, Melvin F.

Popelka, Eleanor, jt. auth. see Carlson, Ray.

Popelka, Gerald R., jt. auth. see Newby, Hayes A.

Popelka, Jan, jt. auth. see Lineman, Rose.

Popenoe, Cris. Japan for Westerners. (Bookshop Guides Ser.). (Illus.). 88p. (Orig.). 1986. pap. 5.95 (*0-936119-00-4*) Yes Inc.

Popenoe, David. Disturbing the Nest: Family Change & Decline in Modern Societies. (Social Institutions & Social Change Ser.). 407p. (Orig.). 1988. lib. bdg. 56.95 (*0-202-30350-0*); pap. text ed. 29.95 (*0-202-30351-9*) Aldine de Gruyter.

— Private Pleasure, Public Plight: American Metropolitan Community Life in Comparative Perspective. LC 84-16411. 192p. 1988. pap. 16.95 (*0-88738-766-7*) Transaction Pubs.

— Sociology. 8th ed. 640p. (C). 1990. pap. text ed. write for info. (*0-13-820465-9*) P-H.

— Sociology. 10th ed. LC 94-20359. 580p. 1994. pap. text ed. write for info. (*0-13-101163-4*) P-H.

— The Suburban Environment: Sweden & the United States. LC 76-8091. (Studies of Urban Society). 1977. lib. bdg. 24.00 (*0-226-67542-4*) U Ch Pr.

Popenoe, David, ed. The Urban-Industrial Frontier: Essays on Social Trends & Institutional Goals in Modern Communities. LC 73-75680. 191p. reprint ed. pap. 54.50 (*0-7837-5636-4*, 2050631) Bks Demand.

Popenoe, Paul, jt. auth. see Gosney, E. S.

Popescu, Adela. Between Us - Time. (Illus.). (Orig.). 1993. pap. 25.00 (*0-9619930-6-5*) Moonfall Pr VA.

Popescu, Bogdan M., ed. Hydrocarbon Exploration History in Eastern Central Europe. LC 93-26022. 1993. write for info. (*0-387-55014-3*) Spr-Verlag.

***Popescu, Calin & Charoenngam, Chotchai.** Project Planning, Scheduling & Control: Encyclopedia of Terms & Applications. LC 94-35464. 1995. text ed. 75.00 (*0-471-02858-4*) Wiley.

Popescu, Calin & Hamiani, Abdelwahab. Directory of Microcomputer Software for Cost Engineering. LC 85-12847. 199p. reprint ed. pap. 56.80 (*0-7837-3365-8*, 2043323) Bks Demand.

Popescu, Calin, jt. auth. see Spruill, Victor F.

Popescu, D., jt. ed. see Badescu, L.

Popescu, D. R. The Royal Hunt. Cottrell, J. E. & Bogdan, M., trs. LC 85-4985. Orig. Title: Vinatoarea Regala. 187p. 1985. 25.00 (*0-8142-0386-8*) Ohio St U Pr.

Popescu-Judetz, Eugenia, tr. see Neamtu, Cella.

Popescu, Julian. Bulgaria. (Let's Visit Places & Peoples of the World Ser.). (Illus.). 96p. (J). (gr. 5 up). 1988. 14.95 (*1-55546-177-8*) Chelsea Hse.

— Hungary. (Let's Visit Places & Peoples of the World Ser.). (Illus.). 96p. (J). (gr. 5 up). 1988. 14.95 (*0-222-00945-4*) Chelsea Hse.

Popescu, Ludmila. Select Scientific Developments in Romania: The Physical Chemistry of Molten Salts: A Case Study. Dawson, Melissa, ed. (Illus.). 109p. (Orig.). 1989. pap. text ed. 75.00 (*1-55831-097-5*) Delphic Associates.

Popescu, M., jt. auth. see Bunget, I.

Popescu, Petru. Amazon Beaming. (Illus.). 480p. 1992. pap. 14.00 (*0-14-012666-X*, Penguin Bks) Viking Penguin.

— In Hot Blood. 1988. pap. 3.95 (*0-449-14554-9*) Fawcett.

Popewiny, Stanton, ed. see ECRI Staff.

Pophal, Donald, jt. ed. see Blouke, Morley M.

Popham, A. E. The Drawings of Leonardo Da Vinci. (Pimlico Ser.). (Illus.). 528p. 1994. pap. 22.95 (*0-7126-6100-X*, Pub. by Pimlico) Trafalgar.

— Old Master Drawings at Holkham Hall. Lloyd, Christopher, ed. (Illus.). 128p. 1987. fiche, lib. bdg. 125. 00 (*0-226-69273-6*) U Ch Pr.

Popham, Estelle L., jt. auth. see Ettinger, Blanche.

Popham, Estelle L., jt. auth. see Grubbs, Robert L.

Popham, Estelle L., et al. A Teaching-Learning System for Business Education. 1975. text ed. 31.75 (*0-07-050504-7*) McGraw.

Popham, G. T. Government in Britain. 1969. text ed. 120.00 (*0-08-013418-1*, Pub. by Pergamon Repr UK) Franklin.

***Popham, James W.** Classroom Assessment: What Teachers Need to Know. LC 94-28527. 1994. pap. text ed. 34.00 (*0-205-15429-8*) Allyn.

Popham, Melinda W. Skywater. 256p. 1991. mass mkt. 4.95 (*0-345-37150-X*) Ballantine.

— Skywater. 208p. (C). 1990. 17.95 (*1-55597-127-X*) Graywolf.

Popham, Peter. Wooden Temples of Japan. (Travel to Landmarks Ser.). 1992. 24.95 (*1-85043-175-2*, Pub. by I B Tauris UK) St Martin.

Popham, Richard A. A Key to the Genera of the Compositales of Northeastern North America. (Bulletin Ser.: No. 38). 1941. 2.00 (*0-86727-037-3*) Ohio Bio Survey.

Popham, W. James. Criterion-Referenced Measurement. (Illus.). 1978. pap. 19.95 (*0-685-03817-3*) P-H.

— Educational Evaluation. 3rd ed. LC 92-13806. 1992. text ed. 49.00 (*0-205-14217-6*) Allyn.

— An Evaluation Guidebook - A Set of Practical Guidelines for the Educational Evaluator. 1972. pap. 5.95 (*0-932166-01-6*) IOX Amnt Assocs.

— Modern Education Measurement. 2nd ed. 464p. (C). 1989. Casebound. text ed. write for info. (*0-13-593898-8*) P-H.

Popham, W. James & Sirotnik, Kenneth A. Understanding Statistics in Education. LC 90-63795. 423p. (C). 1992. text ed. 47.00 (*0-87581-348-8*) Peacock Pubs.

Popic, R. English-Serbocroat Dictionary of Science & Technology. 1096p. (C). 1987. 275.00 (*0-685-46836-4*, Pub. by Collets) St Mut.

Popic, Relja. Russian-Serbocroatian Scientific-Technical Dictionary: Naucno - Tehnicki Recnik Rusko-Srpskohrvatski. 812p. (RUS & SER.). 1986. 75.00 (*0-8288-2129-1*, F28341) Fr & Eur.

Popic, Relja, et al. English-Serbocroatian Scientific & Technical Dictionary. 1140p. (ENG & SER.). 1988. 195. 00 (*0-8288-0658-6*, M 9688) Fr & Eur.

***Popiel, Paul A.** Financial Systems in Sub-Saharan Africa: A Comparative Study. LC 94-29423. (Discussion Papers Africa Technical Department: Vol. 260). 1994. write for info. (*0-8213-2996-0*) World Bank.

Popiel, Russell. Error-Handling Technique in RPG IV. (Programming Technique Ser.). (Illus.). 200p. (Orig.). 1995. pap. 119.00 (*1-884322-30-1*) Comp Applicatns.

Popielawski, J. & Gorecki, J., eds. Far from Equilibrium Dynamics of Chemical Systems. 440p. (C). 1991. text ed. 118.00 (*981-02-0528-7*) World Scientific Pub.

Popieluszko, Jerzy. The Way of My Cross: The Masses & Homilies of Father Jerzy Popieluszko. Wren, Michael, tr. LC 85-14469. 200p. 1986. reprint ed. pap. 9.95 (*0-89526-806-X*) Regnery Pub.

Popik, David S. Winning Blackjack Without Counting Cards. 216p. 1992. pap. 7.95 (*0-8216-2519-5*, Carol Paperbacks) Carol Pub Group.

Popio, Kathryn. Heart's Rest. 1992. pap. 7.95 (*1-55673-457-3*, 7912) CSS OH.

***Popken, Randall, et al.** Departures: A Reader for Developing Writers. LC 94-29358. 1994. pap. text ed. write for info. (*0-205-16249-5*) Allyn.

Popkes, Steve, jt. auth. see Anderson, Poul.

Popkewitz, Thomas S. Change & Stability in Schooling. 112p. (C). 1983. 45.00 (*0-7300-0002-8*, Pub. by Deakin Univ AT) St Mut.

— Paradigm & Ideology in Educational Research: The Social Function of the Intellectual. 208p. 1984. pap. 28.00 (*0-905273-97-4*, Falmer Pr) Taylor & Francis.

— A Political Sociology of Educational Reform: Power - Knowledge in Teaching, Teacher Education, & Research. 304p. (C). 1991. text ed. 48.95 (*0-8077-3091-2*); pap. text ed. 21.95 (*0-8077-3090-4*) Tchrs Coll.

Popkewitz, Thomas S., ed. Changing Patterns of Power: Social Regulation & Teacher Education Reform. (SUNY Series, Teacher Preparation & Development). 382p. (C). 1993. 59.50 (*0-7914-1447-7*); pap. 19.95 (*0-7914-1448-5*) State U NY Pr.

— Critical Studies in Teacher Education: Its Folklore, Theory & Practice. 250p. 1987. 65.00 (*1-85000-153-7*, Falmer Pr); pap. 33.00 (*1-85000-154-5*, Falmer Pr) Taylor & Francis.

— The Formation of School Subjects: The Struggle for Creating an American Institution. 250p. 1987. 65.00 (*1-85000-169-3*, Falmer Pr); pap. 35.00 (*1-85000-170-7*, Falmer Pr) Taylor & Francis.

Popkewitz, Thomas S. & Tabachnick, B. Robert. The Study of Schooling: Field-Based Methodologies in Educational Research & Evaluation. LC 81-1416. 316p. 1981. text ed. 55.00 (*0-275-90705-8*, C0705, Praeger Pubs) Greenwood.

Popkin. Introduction to Federal Income Taxation. 1987. write for info. (*0-8205-0291-X*, 524); teacher ed write for info. (*0-8205-0292-8*) Bender.

— Introduction to Federal Income Taxation. suppl. ed. 1990. Supplement 1990. write for info. (*0-8205-0293-6*) Bender.

— Women's Health Today: Perspectives on Current Research & Clinical Practice. LC 94-22810. (Illus.). 416p. (C). 1994. text ed. 75.00 (*1-85070-568-2*) Prthnon Pub.

Popkin, Arlene. My April Fool Book. (Illus.). (J). (ps-1). 1974. lib. bdg. 6.89 (*0-914844-04-0*) J Alden.

Popkin, Barney P., jt. ed. see Charbeneau, Randall J.

Popkin, Barry M., jt. auth. see McGuire, Judith S.

Popkin, Barry M., et al. The Infant-Feeding Triad: Infant, Mother, & Household. (Food & Nutrition in History & Anthropology Ser.: Vol. 5). 266p. 1986. text ed. 112.00 (*2-88124-142-5*) Gordon & Breach.

Popkin, Cathy. The Pragmatics of Insignificance: Chekhov, Zoshchenko, Gogol. LC 93-7021. (Illus.). 304p. (C). 1993. 39.50 (*0-8047-2209-9*) Stanford U Pr.

Popkin, David. Vocabulary Energizers: Stories of Word Origins. 143p. (Orig.). (C). 1988. pap. text ed. 9.95 (*0-929166-01-9*) Hada Pubns.

— Vocabulary Energizers II: Stories of Word Origins. 149p. (Orig.). (C). 1990. pap. text ed. 9.95 (*0-929166-02-7*) Hada Pubns.

Popkin, Gary S. Comprehensive Structured COBOL. 4th ed. LC 92-32568. 784p. 1993. pap. 52.95 (*0-534-93270-3*) PWS Pubs.

Popkin, Gary S. & Pike, Arthur M. Introduction to Data Processing, 2 Vols. 2nd ed. (Illus.). (C). 1980. teacher ed, pap. 3.16 (*0-395-29484-3*) HM.

Popkin, James M., jt. auth. see Scales, John K.

Popkin, Jeremy D. News & Politics in the Age of Revolution: Jean Luzac's "Gazette de Leyde" LC 89-31379. (Illus.). 304p. 1989. 38.50 (*0-8014-2301-5*) Cornell U Pr.

— Revolutionary News: The Press in France, 1789-1799. Baker, Keith M. & Kaplan, Steven L., eds. LC 89-28511. (Bicentennial Reflections on the French Revolution Ser.). 239p. (C). 1990. lib. bdg. 36.95 (*0-8223-0984-X*); pap. text ed. 11.95 (*0-8223-0997-1*) Duke.

— The Right-Wing Press in France, 1792-1800. LC 79-14067. 254p. reprint ed. pap. 72.40 (*0-7837-0310-4*, 2040632) Bks Demand.

— A Short History of the French Revolution. LC 94-35480. 240p. 1995. pap. text ed. write for info. (*0-13-288424-0*) P-H Gen Ref & Trav.

***Popkin, Jeremy D., ed.** Media & Revolution. LC 94-31808. (Illus.). 248p. 1995. text ed. 29.95 (*0-8131-1899-9*) U Pr of Ky.

P
Q

An Asterisk (*) at the beginning of an entry indicates that the title is appearing in BIP for the first time.

Popkin, Louise B. The Theatre of Rafael Alberti. (Serie A: Monagrafias, XLVII). 183p. (C). 1975. 45.00 (0-7293-0004-8, Pub. by Tamesis Bks Ltd UK) Boydell & Brewer.
Popkin, Louise B., jt. ed. see Sosnowski, Saul.
Popkin, Louise B., tr. see Sosnowski, Saul & Popkin, Louise B., eds.
Popkin, Mark & Glickman, Loren. Bassoon Reed Making. 1994. 15.00 (0-318-37569-9) Instrumental.
Popkin, Michael. Active Parenting: Teaching Courage, Cooperation & Responsibility. 1987. pap. 12.00 (0-06-254061-0, PL) HarpC.
Popkin, Michael, ed. Modern Black Writers. LC 76-15656. (Library of Literary Criticism). 400p. 1978. 65.00 (0-8044-3258-9, F Ungar Bks) Continuum.
Popkin, Michael, jt. auth. see Albert, Linda.
Popkin, Michael, jt. auth. see Hannaford, Mary J.
***Popkin, Michael H.** Active Parenting of Teens: Leader's Guide. (Illus.). 148p. 1990. ring bd. 25.95 (0-9618020-2-2) Active Parenting.
— Active Parenting of Teens: Parent's Guide. (Illus.). 192p. (Orig.). 1990. pap. text ed. 13.95 (0-9618020-3-0) Active Parenting.
— Active Parenting of Teens: The Basics, Parent's Guide. (Illus.). 144p. (Orig.). 1994. pap. text ed. 13.95 (1-880283-10-7) Active Parenting.
— Active Parenting Today: The Basics: A Guide for Parents of 2 to 12 Year Olds. (Illus.). 112p. (Orig.). 1993. pap. 13.95 (1-880283-06-9) Active Parenting.
— Active Parenting Today Leader's Guide: For Parents of 2-12 Year Olds. 168p. 1993. spiral bd. 24.95 (1-880283-04-2) Active Parenting.
— Active Parenting Today Parent's Guide: For Parents of 2-12 Year Olds. 168p. 1993. pap. 13.95 (1-880283-03-4) Active Parenting.
— Active Teaching Leader's Guide: Enhancing Discipline, Self-Esteem & Student Performance. (Illus.). 176p. (J). (gr. k-6). 1994. spiral bd. 39.95 (1-880283-07-7) Active Parenting.
— Active Teaching Teacher's Handbook: Enhancing Discipline, Self-Esteem & Student Performance. (Illus.). 191p. (Orig.). 1994. pap. 14.95 (1-880283-08-5) Active Parenting.
— Free the Horses: Storybook & Songbook. Greathead, Susan D. & Sardinas-Wyssling, Karen, eds. (Illus.). 80p. (J). (gr. 1-3). 1991. pap. 6.95 (0-9618020-7-3) Active Parenting.
Popkin, Michael H. & Greathead, Susan D. Free the Horses: A Self-Esteem Adventure. 234p. (J). (gr. 1-4). 1991. teacher ed 29.95 (0-9618020-6-5) Active Parenting.
***Popkin, Michael H., et al.** Helping Your Child Succeed in School: A Guide for Parents of 4 to 14 Year Olds. (Illus.). 215p. (Orig.). 1995. pap. text ed. 12.95 (1-880283-15-8) Active Parenting.
— Parents on Board: Building Academic Success Through Parent Involvement Leader's Guide: For Parents of 4 to 14 Year Olds. 111p. (Orig.). 1995. spiral bd. 24.95 (1-880283-14-X) Active Parenting.
Popkin, R. H. & Stroll, A. Philosophy. 3rd ed. (Made Simple Ser.). 408p. 1993. pap. write for info. (0-7506-0942-7) Buttrwrth-Heinemann.
Popkin, Richard, tr. see Bayle, Pierre.
Popkin, Richard A., jt. auth. see Surrey, Walter S.
Popkin, Richard H. The High Road to Pyrrhonism. Watson, Richard A. & Force, James E., eds. LC 93-35549. 1989. lib. bdg. 42.95 (0-87220-252-6); pap. text ed. 19.95 (0-87220-251-8) Hackett Pub.
— The History of Scepticism from Erasmus to Spinoza. LC 78-65469. 1979. pap. 15.00 (0-520-03876-2) U CA Pr.
— Philosophy of the Sixteenth & Seventeenth Centuries. LC 66-10365. (Orig.). 1966. pap. 15.95 (0-02-925490-6) Free Pr.
— Second Oswald. 17.95 (0-8488-0888-6) Amereon Ltd.
— The Third Force in Seventeenth-Century Thought. LC 91-10145. (Studies in Intellectual History: Vol. 22). vi, 377p. 1991. 88.75 (90-04-09324-9) E J Brill.
Popkin, Richard H., ed. Jewish Christians & Christian Jews: From the Renaissance to the Enlightenment. LC 93-28326. (Archives Internationales d'Histoire des Idees (International Archives of the History of Ideas) Ser.). 220p. (C). 1993. lib. bdg. 99.00 (0-7923-2452-8) Kluwer Ac.
Popkin, Richard H. & Stroll, Avrum. Philosophy Made Simple. 2nd rev. ed. LC 92-34537. 1993. 12.00 (0-385-42533-3) Doubleday.
Popkin, Richard H. & Vanderjagt, Arjo, eds. Scepticism & Irreligion in the 17th & 18th Centuries. LC 92-44598. (Brill's Studies in Intellectual History: Vol. 37). 1993. 91. 50 (90-04-09596-9) E J Brill.
Popkin, Richard H., tr. see Bayle, Pierre.
Popkin, Richard H., jt. auth. see Force, James E.
Popkin, Richard H., jt. ed. see Force, James E.
Popkin, Richard H., ed. see Hume, David.
Popkin, Richard H., jt. ed. see Kelley, Ronald R.
Popkin, Richard H., jt. auth. see Stroll, Avrum.
Popkin, Samuel L. The Rational Peasant: The Political Economy of Rural Society in Vietnam. LC 77-83105. 1979. pap. 15.00 (0-520-03954-8) U CA Pr.
— Reasoning Voter. (C). 1994. pap. 12.95 (0-226-67545-9) U Ch Pr.
— The Reasoning Voter: Communication & Persuasion in Presidential Campaigns. LC 91-7610. (Illus.). 272p. 1991. 19.95 (0-226-67544-0) U Ch Pr.
Popkin, Samuel L., jt. ed. see Kernell, Samuel.
Popkin, Susan A. & Allen, Roger B. Gone Fishing! A History of Fishing in River, Bay & Sea. (Illus.). 73p. 1987. pap. 2.00 (0-913346-14-4) Phila Maritime Mus.
Popkin, William D. Fundamentals of Federal Income Tax Laws. 2nd ed. LC 94-18174. (Cases & Materials Ser.). (C). 1994. 50.95 (0-256-16476-2) Irwin.
— Materials on Legislation: Political Language & the Political Process. (University Casebook Ser.). 718p. (C). 1993. text ed. 39.95 (1-56662-051-1) Foundation Pr.
— Materials on Legislation: Political Language & the Political Process, 1994 Supplement. (University Casebook Ser.). 129p. 1994. pap. text ed. 8.50 (1-56662-210-7) Foundation Pr.
— Teachers Manual for Materials on Legislation: Political Language & the Political Process. (University Casebook Ser.). 179p. 1993. pap. text ed. write for info. (1-56662-070-8) Foundation Pr.
Popkin, William D. & Oldman, Oliver. The Deduction for Business Expenses & Losses. LC 71-172245. (Tax Technique Handbook Ser.). (Illus.). 112p. (Orig.). 1973. pap. 5.00 (0-915506-14-9) Harvard Law Intl Tax.
Popkins, Jeremy D. A History of Modern France. LC 93-19241. 1993. pap. text ed. write for info. (0-13-389693-5) P-H.
Popkorn, Sally. First Steps in Modal Logic. (Illus.). 300p. (C). 1995. 39.95 (0-521-46482-X) Cambridge U Pr.
***Popkov, Yury S.** Macrosystems Theory & Its Applications: Equilibrium Methods. LC 95-15124. (Lecture Notes in Control & Information Sciences: Vol. 203). 1995. write for info. (3-540-19955-1) Spr-Verlag.
Popl, et al. Chromatographic Analysis of Alkaloids. (Chromatographic Science Ser.: Vol. 53). 664p. 1990. 195.00 (0-8247-8140-6) Dekker.
Poplack, D. G., et al, eds. The Role of Pharmacology in Pediatric Oncology. (Developments in Oncology Ser.). 1987. lib. bdg. 157.50 (0-89838-795-7) Kluwer Ac.
Poplack, Shana & Pousada, Alicia. A Comparative Study of Gender Assignment to Borrowed Nouns. (Illus.). 43p. Date not set. lib. bdg. 3.00 (1-878483-15-3) Hunter Coll CEP.
Poplasen, Ilija. The Analysis of the Present. (Illus.). 348p. 1987. 20.00 (0-935352-21-X) MIR PA.
— The Analysis of the Present. rev. ed. (Illus.). 370p. 1989. reprint ed. 20.00 (0-935352-23-6) MIR PA.
— The Authentic Existence. (Illus.). 454p. 1994. 20.00 (0-935352-26-0) MIR PA.
— The Authentic Rule of the World. (Illus.). 480p. (YA). (gr. 12-12). 1995. 20.00 (0-935352-35-X) MIR PA.
— Coming & Time. 220p. 1982. 20.00 (0-935352-07-4) MIR PA.
— Coming & Time. 3rd ed. (Illus.). 200p. reprint ed. 20.00 (0-935352-00-7) MIR PA.
— Computerized Two & Three Dimensional Finite Existents Analysis. 64p. 1982. 20.00 (0-935352-09-0) MIR PA.
— Computerized Two & Three Dimensional Finite Existents Analysis. 2nd ed. (Illus.). reprint ed. 20.00 (0-935352-01-5) MIR PA.
— The Final Battle for World Domination. (Illus.). 384p. 1985. 20.00 (0-935352-16-3) MIR PA.
— The Great Day of Judgment. (Illus.). 455p. 1989. 20.00 (0-935352-22-8) MIR PA.
— In Search for the Meaning of Existence in Cinematography. 34p. 1981. 20.00 (0-935352-06-6) MIR PA.
— The Medjugorje Apocalypse. (Illus.). 430p. 1991. 20.00 (0-935352-27-9) MIR PA.
— The Medjugorje Apocalypse. 2nd ed. (Illus.). 430p. 1992. reprint ed. 20.00 (0-935352-34-1) MIR PA.
— The New World Order. 301p. 1983. 20.00 (0-935352-12-0) MIR PA.
— The New World Order. (Illus.). 301p. 1984. 20.00 (0-935352-17-1) MIR PA.
— The Power & the Glory. (Illus.). 408p. 1990. 20.00 (0-935352-24-4) MIR PA.
— The Realism of the Coming. (Illus.). 540p. 1993. 20.00 (0-935352-25-2) MIR PA.
— Reference to the Present. 241p. 1982. 20.00 (0-935352-11-2) MIR PA.
— The Restoration of the State of Good in the World. (Illus.). 200p. (Orig.). 1980. 20.00 (0-935352-02-3) MIR PA.
— The Restoration of the State of Good in the World. 210p. (Orig.). 1982. 20.00 (0-935352-08-2) MIR PA.
— The Struggle for the Good, 2 pts., Pt. I. (Illus.). 61p. 1981. reprint ed. 20.00 (0-935352-03-1) MIR PA.
— The Struggle for the Good, 2 pts., Pt. II. (Illus.). 128p. 1981. reprint ed. 25.00 (0-935352-04-X) MIR PA.
— The Struggle for the Victory of Good, Pt. I. (Illus.). 61p. 1984. 20.00 (0-935352-18-X) MIR PA.
— The Struggle for the Victory of Good, Pt. II. (Illus.). 128p. 1984. 20.00 (0-935352-19-8) MIR PA.
— The Transfer of Power. (Illus.). 401p. 1984. 20.00 (0-935352-15-5) MIR PA.
— The Transition Time. (Illus.). 392p. 1984. 20.00 (0-935352-14-7) MIR PA.
— The Victorious Present. (Illus.). 372p. 1983. 20.00 (0-935352-13-9) MIR PA.
— The World History Made in the Present. (Illus.). 350p. 1986. 20.00 (0-935352-20-1) MIR PA.
— World History Made in the Present. (Illus.). 403p. 1991. 20.00 (0-935352-32-5) MIR PA.
Poplaski, Pete, ed. see Caniff, Milton.
Poplaski, Pete, ed. see Raymond, Alex.
Poplaski, Peter, ed. see Caniff, Milton.
Poplaski, Peter, ed. see Crumb, Robert.
Poplaski, Peter, ed. see Kane, Bob.
Poplaski, Peter, ed. see Raymond, Alex.
Poplavskii, Boris I. V Venke Iz Voska; Dirizhabl' Neizvestnogo Napravleniia. 2nd ed. Karlinsky, Simon, ed. (Modern Russian Litrature & Culture Studies & Texts: Vol. 9). (Illus.). 123p. (RUS.). 1981. pap. 7.50 (0-933884-19-2) Berkeley Slavic.
Poplawski, Paul. Promptings of Desire: Creativity & the Religious Impulse in the Works of D. H. Lawrence. LC 92-42429. (Contributions to the Study of World Literature Ser.: No. 49). 224p. 1993. text ed. 52.95 (0-313-28789-9, GM8789, Greenwood Pr) Greenwood.
***Poplawski, Wojciech A., intro.** Hydraulics in Civil Engineering, International Conference, 1994: Hydraulics Working with the Environment. (National Conference Publication Ser.: No. 94-1). (Illus.). 362p. (Orig.). 1994. pap. 72.00x (0-85825-597-9, Pub. by Inst Engrs Aust-EA Bks AT) Accents Pubns.
Pople, Anthony. Berg: "Violin Concerto" (Cambridge Music Handbooks Ser.). (Illus.). 150p. (C). 1991. pap. 10.95 (0-521-39976-9) Cambridge U Pr.
Pople, Anthony, ed. Theory, Analysis & Meaning in Music. (Illus.). 250p. (C). 1994. 49.95 (0-521-45236-8) Cambridge U Pr.
Pople, Anthony, jt. ed. see Marsden, Alan.
Popley, H. A. The Music of India. 1990. reprint ed. 8.00 (81-85418-06-3, Pub. by Low Price II) S Asia.
Popley, H. A., ed. & tr. The Sacred Kural. 2nd ed. Orig. Title: The Tamil Veda of Tiruvalluvar. 159p. pap. 2.80 (0-88253-386-X) Ind-US Inc.
Poplin, Cecil M. Discovery of Intracranial Ossicles in a Carboniferous North American Paleoniscid: Pisces: Actinopterygii. (Occasional Papers: No. 99). 17p. 1982. 1.00 (0-317-04811-2) U of KS Mus Nat Hist.
Poplin, Dick. A Yard of Poplin. (Illus.). 96p. (Orig.). 1991. pap. 9.95 (0-9624100-3-9) Bell Buckle.
Poploff, Michelle. Busy O'Brien & the Caterpillar Punch Bunch. (Illus.). 119p. (J). (gr. 2-5). 1992. 13.95 (0-8027-8151-9) Walker & Co.
— Busy O'Brien & the Great Bubble Gum Blowout. (Illus.). 96p. (J). (gr. 2-5). 1990. 12.95 (0-8027-6983-7); lib. bdg. 13.85 (0-8027-6984-5) Walker & Co.
— Busy O'Brien & the Great Bubblegum Blowout. MacDonald, Pat, ed. (Illus.). 96p. (J). 1992. reprint ed. pap. 2.99 (0-671-74082-2, Minstrel Bks) PB.
***Poploff, Michelle & Mitchell, Judith A.** Busy O'Brien & the Caterpillar Punch Bunch. (Illus.). (J). (gr. 2-6). 1995. reprint ed. pap. 3.50 (0-671-79407-8, Minstrel Bks) PB.
Poplstein, Maureen. Bringing Out the Best in Yourself & Others. Williams, Sally, ed. (Illus.). 184p. (Orig.). Date not set. pap. 29.95 (0-931571-11-1) Lifetime Pr.
Popma, Jeffrey J., et al. Atlas of Interventional Cardiology. LC 94-1694. (Illus.). 368p. 1994. text ed. 95.00 (0-7216-3569-5) Saunders.
***Popoff, B.** Accounting Essentials: An Introduction for Non-Accounting Majors. 161p. 1991. pap. 36.00 (0-409-30484-0, Austral); pap. 36.00 (0-614-05474-5, Austral) Butterworth Legal Pubs.
***Popoff, B. & Cowan, T.** Analysis & Interpretation of Financial Statements. 3rd ed. 464p. 1989. pap. 51.00 (0-614-05475-3, Austral) Butterworth Legal Pubs.
***Popoff, B. & Cowan, T. K.** Analysis & Interpretation of Financial Statements. 3rd ed. 451p. 1989. pap. 54.00 (0-409-49588-3, Austral) Butterworth Legal Pubs.
Popoff, Leo, jt. auth. see Prosor, Larry.
Popoff, Peter. America's Family Crisis. Tanner, Don, ed. LC 82-82843. 80p. 1982. pap. 2.00 (0-938544-15-2) Faith Messenger.
— Calamities, Catastrophies, & Chaos. Tanner, Don, ed. LC 80-69974. (Illus.). 108p. 1980. pap. 2.50 (0-938544-01-2) Faith Messenger.
— Demons At Your Doorstep. Tanner, Don, ed. LC 82-82842. (Illus.). 56p. 1982. pap. 1.50 (0-938544-13-6) Faith Messenger.
— A New Fire Is Blazing. Tanner, Don, ed. LC 80-67993. (Illus.). 194p. (Orig.). 1980. pap. 4.95 (0-938544-02-0) Faith Messenger.
— Set Free from Satan's Slavery. Tanner, Don, ed. LC 82-83455. 64p. 1982. pap. 2.00 (0-938544-17-9) Faith Messenger.
— Seven Delivery Systems for God's Healing Power. Tanner, Don, ed. LC 81-69730. (Illus.). 70p. 1981. pap. 1.50 (0-938544-07-1) Faith Messenger.
— Six Things Satan Uses to Rob You of God's Abundant Blessings. Tanner, Don, ed. LC 81-86521. (Illus.). 96p. 1982. pap. 2.00 (0-938544-11-X) Faith Messenger.
— Three Steps to Answered Prayer. Tanner, Don, ed. LC 81-70342. 92p. 1981. pap. 2.00 (0-938544-10-1) Faith Messenger.
— Twenty-Seven Things the Church Must Go Through Before the Great Tribulation. Tanner, Don, ed. LC 81-68675. (Illus.). 50p. 1981. pap. 1.00 (0-938544-08-X) Faith Messenger.
— Ye Shall Receive Power: The Amazing Miracle of Holy Spirit Baptism. Tanner, Don, ed. LC 82-71629. (Illus.). 96p. 1982. pap. 2.00 (0-938544-14-4) Faith Messenger.
Popolato, Alphonse, jt. ed. see Gibbs, Terry R.
Popousek, Dusan. Vibrational-Rotational Spectroscopy & Molecular Dynamics. (Advanced Series in Physical Chemistry). 1994. text ed. 95.00 (981-02-1635-1) World Scientific Pub.
Popouych. Tetraphenylborates. (IUPAC Solubility Data Ser.). 260p. 1981. 155.00 (0-08-023928-5, Pergamon Pr) Elsevier.
Popov & Hallenga. Modern NMR Techniques & Their Application in Chemistry. (Practical Spectroscopy Ser.: Vol. 11). 680p. 1990. 175.00 (0-8247-8332-8) Dekker.
Popov, A. A. Nganasan: The Material Culture of the Tavgi Samoyeds. Ristenen, Elaine K., tr. LC 66-63668. (Uralic & Altaic Ser.: Vol. 56). (Orig.). 1966. pap. text ed. 12.00 (0-87750-020-7) Res Inst Inner Asian Studies.
Popov, Alekdandr S., see Alexander Seravimovich, pseud..
Popov, Alexander, jt. auth. see Mamantov, Gleb.
Popov, Egor P. Engineering Mechanics of Solids. 800p. 1989. text ed. 76.00 (0-13-279258-3) P-H.
— Introduction to Mechanics of Solids. (C). 1968. text ed. 76.00 (0-13-487769-1) P-H.
Popov, Egor P. & Medwadowski, Stefan J., eds. Concrete Shell Buckling. LC 80-69968. (SP-67 Ser.). 240p. (Orig.). 1981. pap. 38.50 (0-686-95244-8) ACI.
Popov, Evgeny. The Soul of a Patriot: or Various Epistles to Ferfichkin. Porter, Robert, tr. LC 94-18887. (Writings from an Unbound Europe). 194p. 1994. reprint ed. 49.95 (0-8101-1203-5); reprint ed. pap. 14.95 (0-8101-1193-4) Northwestern U Pr.
Popov, G. A. Principles of Health Planning in the U. S. S. R. (Public Health Papers: No. 43). 1971. pap. 4.80 (92-4-130043-4) World Health.
Popov, Genrikh P., et al. Ten Plus Ten: Contemporary Soviet & American Painters. LC 89-80354. (Illus.). 176p. (Orig.). (ENG & RUS.). 1989. pap. write for info. (0-929865-03-0) Mod Art Mus Ft Worth.
Popov, Georgii K. City of the Red Plague, Soviet Rule in Baltic Town. LC 75-35059. (Russian Studies: Perspectives on the Revolution). (Illus.). 343p. 1986. reprint ed. lib. bdg. 29.15 (0-88355-439-9) Hyperion Conn.
Popov, Howard P. Mechanics of Materials. 2nd ed. 1976. text ed. 76.00 (0-13-571356-0) P-H.
Popov, Iu. Essays in Political Economy. 264p. (C). 1985. 42. 00 (0-685-31584-3, Pub. by Collets UK) Pro-Am Music.
Popov, Nicolai. Stravinsky. LC 92-40383. (J). 1993. 14.95 (0-88682-605-5) Creative Ed.
Popov, Nikolai P. The Russian People Speak: Democracy at the Crossroads. 144p. (C). 1994. 24.95 (0-8156-0300-2) Syracuse U Pr.
Popov, V. A., jt. auth. see Petrushev, P. P.
Popov, V. L. Gruppy, Obrazuiushchie, Sizigii i Orbity v Teoril Invariantov: English Groups, Generators, Syzygies & Orbits in Invariant Theory. LC 92-10604. (Translations of Mathematical Monographs: Vol. 100). 245p. 1992. 181.00 (0-8218-4557-8, MMONO-100) Am Math.
Popov, V. M. Hyperstability of Control Systems. Georgescu, R., tr. LC 73-83000. (Grundlehren der Mathematischen Wissenschaften Ser.: Vol. 204). 400p. 1973. 74.00 (0-387-06373-0) Spr-Verlag.
Popov, V. N. Functional Integrals & Collective Excitations. (Monographs on Mathematical Physics). 175p. 1988. 69. 95 (0-521-30777-5) Cambridge U Pr.
— Functional Integrals & Collective Excitations. (Monographs on Mathematical Physics). 224p. (C). 1991. pap. 32.95 (0-521-40787-7) Cambridge U Pr.
Popov, V. N., ed. Operator Theory with a Random Potential, & Some Questions of Statistical Physics. LC 91-24484. (Proceedings of the Steklov Institute of Mathematics Ser.: Vol. 184). 259p. 1991. reprint ed. 159.00 (0-8218-3139-9, STEKLO/184C) Am Math.
Popov, V. N. & Yarunin, V. S. Collective Effects in Quantum Statistics of Radiation & Matter. (C). 1988. lib. bdg. 100.50 (90-277-2735-X) Kluwer Ac.
Popov, V. N., jt. auth. see Konopleva, N. P.
Popov, Vasil A., jt. auth. see Sendov, Blagovest.
Popov, Yu. M., ed. Injection Lasers in Optical Communication & Information Processing Systems. Stewart, S., tr. (Proceedings of the Lebedev Physics Institute Ser.: Vol. 185). (Illus.). 326p. (C). 1989. text ed. 115.00 (0-941743-58-6) Nova Sci Pubs.
— Laser Cathode Ray Tubes: Proceedings of the Lebedev Physics Institute, Vol. 220. 287p. (C). 1994. lib. bdg. 98. 00 (1-56072-216-9) Nova Sci Pubs.
Popov, Yu M., ed. Stoichiometry in Crystal Compounds & Its Influence on Their Physical Properties. (Proceedings of the Lebedev Physics Institute Ser.: Vol. 177). 303p. 1988. text ed. 110.00 (0-941743-21-7) Nova Sci Pubs.
Popovac, Gwynn. Conversations with Bugs: A Journal with Words & Drawings. (Illus.). 128p. 1993. 17.95 (1-56640-681-1) Pomegranate Calif.
— Wet Paint. 1987. pap. 3.95 (0-345-34739-0) Ballantine.
Popovic & Bhatkar. Distributed Computer Control Systems in Industrial Automation. (Electrical Engineering & Electronics Ser.: Vol. 66). 712p. 1990. 160.00 (0-8247-8118-X) Dekker.
Popovic, B. D. CAD of Wire Antennas & Related Radiating Structures. (Electronic & Electrical Research Studies: Antenna Ser.: No. 1641). 324p. 1991. text ed. 145.00 (0-471-93067-9) Wiley.
***Popovic, B. D. & Kolundzija, B. M.** Analysis of Metallic Antennas & Scatterers. (Electromagnetic Waves Ser.: 38). 208p. 1994. 79.00 (0-85296-807-8) Inst Elect Eng.
Popovic, Branko D., et al. Analysis & Synthesis of Wire-Antennas. LC 82-11078. (Electronic & Electrical Engineering Research Ser.: No. 2). (Illus.). 320p. reprint ed. pap. 91.20 (0-8357-6011-1, 2034233) Bks Demand.
Popovic, Dejan B., ed. Advances in the Control of Human Extremities, Vol. 10. 616p. 1991. 84.95 (86-7621-001-2) Demos Vermande.
Popovic, Dobrivoje & Bhatkar, Vijay P. Methods & Tools for Applied Artificial Intelligence. LC 94-1715. (Computer Aided Engineering Ser.: Vol. 5). 528p. 1994. 150.00 (0-8247-9195-9) Dekker.
Popovic, Irena. Sarajevo's Home Cooking. 1991. pap. 10.00 (0-533-09303-1) Vantage.
Popovic, M. M., et al, eds. Physics of Ionized Gases: Proceeding of the XII International Symposium on the Physics of Ionized Gases (SPIG) 84 Yugoslavia, Sept. 1984. 1060p. 1985. 143.00 (9971-5-0001-9) World Scientific Pub.
Popovic, Nenad D. Yugoslavia: The New Class in Crisis. LC 68-26995. 256p. reprint ed. pap. 73.00 (0-317-52022-9, 2027416) Bks Demand.
Popovic, R. S. Hall Effect Devices: Magnetic Sensors & Characterization of Semiconductors. (Sensors Ser.). (Illus.). 320p. 1991. 127.00 (0-7503-0096-5) IOP Pub.
Popovic, Tatyana. Prince Marko: The Hero of South Slavic Epics. (Illus.). 280p. 1988. 45.00x (0-8156-2444-1) Syracuse U Pr.
Popovich, jt. auth. see Ansel, Howard C.
Popovich, Charles J. & Costello, M. Rita. Directory of Business & Financial Information Services. 9th ed. 471p. 1994. 75.00 (0-87111-420-8) SLA.

PQ

*Popovich, Christine. How to Play with Your Dog! For Children Ages 2-5 Years. (Illus.). 24p. (Orig.). (J). (ps). 1989. pap. 5.95 (1-886056-03-X) Super Puppy Pr.

*Popovich, Igor S. The Little Book of Awkward Questions. 160p. (Orig.). 1995. pap. 5.95 (0-86417-670-8, Pub. by Kangaroo Pr AT) Seven Hills Bk.

*Popovich, Justin, et al. Orthodox Faith & Life in Christ. LC 94-79270. (Illus.). 248p. 1994. pap. 17.50 (1-884729-02-9) Inst Byzantine.

Popovich, Mark. New Businesses, Entrepreneurship, & Rural Development: Building a State Strategy. (New Alliances for Rural America Ser.). (Orig.). 1988. pap. text ed. 6.00 (1-55877-016-X) Natl Governor.

Popovich, Richard E. The Measurement of Thought: A Heuristic Approach to This Development. 2nd ed. LC 81-90419. 180p. (C). 1982. 9.95 (0-9604876-0-3) REP Pubs.

Popovici, Neculai N., jt. ed. see Hodge, Charles A.

Popoviciu, L., ed. see European Congress on Sleep Research Staff.

Popovics, Sandor. Concrete Materials: Properties, Specifications & Testing. 2nd ed. LC 92-8953. (Illus.). 645p. 1992. 86.00 (0-8155-1308-9) Noyes.

Popovsky, J., et al. Suesswasserflora von Mitteleuropa, Vol. 6: Dinophyceae (Dinoflagellida) (Illus.). 272p. (GER.). 1990. lib. bdg. 75.00 (3-334-00247-0, Pub. by G Fischer Verlag GW) Lubrecht & Cramer.

Popovsky, Mark. Delo Akademika Vavilova. LC 83-16435. (Illus.). 280p. (Orig.). (RUS.). 1983. pap. 10.00 (0-938920-33-2) Hermitage.

Popovych, Erika & Levin-Stankevich, Brian. The Soviet Educational System. (C). 1991. pap. text ed. 40.00 (0-910054-97-5) Am Assn Coll Registrars.

Popowicz, Z., jt. ed. see Garbaczewski, P.

Popp, Adelheid D. The Autobiography of a Working Woman. Harvey, E. C., tr. LC 79-2950. (Illus.). 135p. 1986. reprint ed. 21.00 (0-8305-0113-4) Hyperion Conn.

Popp, Carol, jt. auth. see Wolfe, Gerald L.

Popp, Dennis J. Night Fighter's Handbook. (Illus.). 72p. 1986. pap. 12.00 (0-87364-361-3) Paladin Pr.

Popp, Dolores L., illus. The Confident Traveler: A Complete Travel Guide for the Business Woman. LC 88-60723. 128p. (Orig.). 1988. pap. 12.95 (0-945565-00-3) Shiro Pubs.

Popp, Edward E. The Great Cookie Jar: Taking the Mysteries Out of the Money System. LC 78-62961. 1978. pap. 1.95 (0-9600358-2-6) Wis Ed Fund.

— Money, Bona Fide or Non-Bona Fide. 1970. pap. 0.50 (0-9600358-1-8) Wis Ed Fund.

Popp, F. A., ed. Recent Advances in Biophoton Research & Its Applications. 300p. 1992. text ed. 98.00 (981-02-0855-3) World Scientific Pub.

Popp, Gwelda, ed. see Bay Village Women's Club Foundation Staff.

Popp, James A., ed. Mouse Liver Neoplasia: Current Perspectives. LC 84-3767. (Chemical Industry Institute of Toxicology Ser.). (Illus.). 400p. 1984. 105.00 (0-89116-300-X) Hemisp Pub.

Popp, John A., et al, eds. Neural Trauma. LC 78-24627. (Seminars in Neurological Surgery Ser.). 405p. 1979. text ed. 103.50 (0-89004-257-8) Raven.

*Popp, Marcia. Language & Literature in Elementary Classrooms: An Interactive Guide for Teachers. 432p. 1996. pap. 45.00 (0-8058-8021-6) L Erlbaum Assocs.

Popp, Richard L. The Presidents of the University of Chicago: A Centennial View. LC 92-28533. (Illus.). 57p. (C). 1992. pap. 7.00 (0-943056-18-7) Univ Chi Lib.

Popp, W., ed. see Soussmann, H.

Popp, Walter. History of Mathematics. 160p. 1978. pap. 21.00 (0-685-42572-X, Open Univ Pr) Taylor & Francis.

Poppe, Carol A & Van Matre, Nancy A. K-3 Science Activities Kit. 256p. (J). (gr. k-3). 1988. pap. 24.95 (0-87628-477-2) Ctr Appl Res.

— Language Arts Learning Centers for the Primary Grades. 240p. 1991. 24.95 (0-87628-505-1) P-H.

— Science Learning Centers for the Primary Grades. 1985. pap. 27.95 (0-87628-749-6) Ctr Appl Res.

— Social Studies Learning Centers for the Primary Grades. 248p. 1989. pap. 27.95 (0-87628-795-X) Ctr Appl Res.

Poppe, Erich, jt. ed. see Fife, James.

Poppe, Fred C. Fifty Rules to Keep a Client Happy. LC 87-45139. 112p. 1987. 8.95i (0-685-18544-3, PL 00-60-915218, HarpT) HarpC.

— One Hundred New Greatest Corporate Ads. LC 92-32665. 224p. 1993. text ed. 44.95 (0-471-57172-5) Wiley.

Poppe, Laszlo & Novak, Lajos. Selective Biocatalysis: A Synthetic Approach. LC 92-9284. 319p. 1993. 126.00 (1-56081-188-9) VCH Pubs.

Poppe, Nicholas N. Heroic Epic of the Khalkha Mongols. 2nd rev. ed. (Mongolia Society Occasional Papers: No. 11). 1979. pap. 12.00 (0-910980-51-9) Mongolia.

— Reminiscences. Schwarz, Henry G., ed. LC 82-4544. (Studies on East Asia: Vol. 16). (Illus.). vii, 330p. 1983. 25.00 (0-914584-16-2) WWUCEAS.

Poppe, Nicholas N., et al. Catalogue of the Manchu-Mongol Section of Toyo Bunko. LC 65-63112. (Publications on Asia of the School of International Studies: No. 12). 391p. 1964. 35.00 (0-295-73732-8) U of Wash Pr.

Poppel, Ernst. Mindworks: Time & Conscious Experience. 200p. 1988. 17.95 (0-15-152190-5) HarBrace.

Poppel, George. Battle of the Dinosaurs. 1988. 10.95 (0-915765-56-X) Natl Pr Bks.

— Planet of Trash. (Illus.). 32p. (J). (ps-3). 1987. 9.95 (0-915765-42-X, Panda Monium Bks) Natl Pr Bks.

Poppel, H. L. & Goldstein, B. Information Technology: The Trillion Dollar Opportunity. 224p. 1987. text ed. 29.95 (0-07-050511-X) McGraw.

Poppel, Hans & Bodden, Ilona. When the Moon Shines Brightly on the House. 24p. (J). (ps). 1985. 5.95 (0-8120-5669-8) Barron.

Poppel, Karl G. Unterrichten - Grundzuge und Gestaltungsformen Des Lehrens und Lernens. (Hildesheimer Beitrage Ser.: Bd. 27). 192p. (GER.). 1992. write for info. (3-487-09033-3, Pub. by Georg Olms GW) Lubrecht & Cramer.

Poppel, Martin. Heaven & Hell: The War Diary of a German Paratrooper. 256p. (C). 1991. 90.00 (0-946771-27-8, Pub. by Spellmount UK) St Mut.

Poppelbaum, W. J., jt. auth. see Mars, P.

Poppeliers, John, et al. What Style Is It? A Guide to American Architecture. 2nd ed. LC 83-19278. (Building Watchers Ser.). (Illus.). 112p. (C). 1984. pap. 8.95 (0-89133-116-6) Preservation Pr.

Poppelreuter, W. Disturbances of Lower & Higher Visual Capacities Caused by Occipital Damage: With Special Reference to the Psychopathological, Pedagogical, Industrial, & Social Implications. Zihl, J., tr. (History of Neuroscience Ser.: No. 2). (Illus.). 392p. 1991. 47.50 (0-19-852190-1) OUP.

Poppema, Sibrand, jt. ed. see Solez, Kim.

Poppen. Behavioral Relaxation Training. (Practitioner Guidebook Ser.). (C). 1988. pap. 25.95 (0-205-14457-8, H4457, Longwood Div) Allyn.

Poppen, Jerry D. Action Packet on Jumping Rope: Individual Rope Skills. LC 82-72160. 62p. (Orig.). 1989. pap. text ed. 6.50 (0-9608868-3-4) Action Prods.

— Action Packet on Physical Fitness Activities. LC 82-72160. 64p. (Orig.). 1989. pap. text ed. 6.50 (0-9608868-2-6) Action Prods.

— The BEST of Games That Come Alive! (Illus.). 235p. (Orig.). (C). 1990. pap. text ed. 15.00 (0-9608868-4-2) Action Prods.

— Dances That Come Alive! (Illus.). 213p. (Orig.). (C). 1993. pap. 21.50 (0-9608868-5-0) Action Prods.

Poppendieck, Hans-Helmut. Cochlospermaceae. LC 81-9456. (Flora Neotropica Monograph Ser.: No. 27). (Illus.). 34p. 1981. pap. 6.50 (0-89327-231-0) NY Botanical.

Popper, A. N. & Fay, R. R., eds. Comparative Studies of Hearing in Invertebrates. (Proceedings in Life Sciences Ser.). (Illus.). 512p. 1980. 119.00 (0-387-90460-3) Spr-Verlag.

Popper, A. N. & Schaffner, Fenton. Progress in Liver Diseases, Vol. 9. (Illus.). 736p. 1990. text ed. 205.00 (0-7216-2940-7) Saunders.

Popper, A. N., ed. see Fay, Jan, et al.

Popper, A. N., jt. ed. see Fay, R. R.

Popper, A. N., et al, eds. The Evolutionary Biology of Hearing. (Illus.). xlii, 859p. 1991. 139.00 (0-387-97588-8) Spr-Verlag.

Popper, Arthur N. & Fay, Richard R., eds. Comparative Hearing: Mammals. LC 93-43309. (Handbook of Auditory Research Ser.: Vol. 4). (Illus.). 280p. 1994. 79.00 (0-387-97841-0) Spr-Verlag.

— Hearing by Bats. LC 94-41860. (Handbook of Auditory Research: Vol. 5). 1994. write for info. (0-387-97844-5) Spr-Verlag.

Popper, Charles W., ed. Psychiatric Pharmacosciences of Children & Adolescents. LC 86-28826. (Progress in Psychiatry Ser.). 128p. 1987. text ed. 21.50 (0-88048-089-0, 48-089-0) Am Psychiatric.

Popper, Charles W., jt. auth. see Dulcan, Mina K.

Popper, Eva B. My Love, My Care, My Spouse: A Chronicle of Parkinson's Disease. LC 88-90551. 75p. (Orig.). 1988. pap. text ed. 6.95 (0-945520-09-3) PSGA.

Popper, Frank. Agam. 3rd ed. (Illus.). 474p. 1989. 95.00 (0-8109-1897-8) Abrams.

— Art of the Electronic Age. (Illus.). 192p. 1993. 45.00 (0-8109-1928-1) Abrams.

— The Politics of Land-Use Reform. 338p. 1981. 29.50 (0-299-08530-9); pap. text ed. 12.50 (0-299-08534-1) U of Wis Pr.

— President's Commissions. LC 73-12304. (Twentieth Century Fund Ser.). 74p. 1973. reprint ed. pap. 15.00 (0-527-71960-9) Periodicals Srv.

Popper, Frank J., jt. ed. see Geisler, Charles C.

Popper, Hans & Schaffner, Fenton, eds. Progress in Liver Diseases, Vol. 8. LC 79-3359. 675p. 1986. text ed. 132.50 (0-8089-1787-0, 793359, Grune) Saunders.

Popper, Hans, et al, eds. Structural Carbohydrates in the Liver: Falk Symposium, No 34. 600p. 1983. lib. bdg. 180.00 (0-85200-711-6) Kluwer Ac.

Popper, Hermine I., ed. see Stanislavski, Constantin.

Popper, Karl. Popper Selections. Miller, David, ed. LC 83-43084. 480p. 1985. pap. 65.00 (0-691-07287-6); pap. 16.95 (0-691-02031-0) Princeton U Pr.

— Unended Quest: An Intellectual Autobiography. rev. ed. LC 76-2155. 258p. 1982. 17.95 (0-87548-366-6) Open Court.

Popper, Karl, jt. auth. see Marcuse, Herbert.

Popper, Karl R. In Search of a Better World: Lectures & Essays of Thirty Years. LC 92-5394. 256p. 1992. 25.00 (0-415-08774-0, A9531) Routledge.

— Knowledge & the Body-Mind Problem: In Defence of Interaction. Notturno, M. A., ed. LC 94-14610. 128p. 1995. write for info. (0-415-11504-3, B4775) Routledge.

— The Myth of the Framework: In Defence of Science & Rationality. Notturno, M. A., tr. LC 94-13562. 176p. 1995. 22.95 (0-415-11320-2, B4639) Routledge.

— Objective Knowledge: An Evolutionary Approach. (C). 1972. pap. text ed. 19.95 (0-19-875024-2) OUP.

— The Open Society & Its Enemies: The High Tide of Prophecy, Vol. II. 1991. 18.95 (0-691-01972-X) Princeton U Pr.

— The Open Universe: An Argument for Indeterminism. Bartley, W. W., III, ed. LC 81-8706. (Postscript to the Logic of Scientific Discovery Ser.). (Illus.). 208p. (C). 1982. 48.25 (0-8476-7016-3); pap. 21.00 (0-8476-7388-X) Rowman.

— Quantum Theory & the Schism in Physics. LC 92-23685. (Postscript to the Logic of Scientific Discovery Ser.). 1992. pap. write for info. (0-415-09112-8, Routledge NY) Routledge.

— Quantum Theory & the Schism in Physics. Bartley, W. W., III, ed. LC 81-8706. (Postscript to the Logic of Scientific Discovery Ser.). 250p. 1984. 52.25 (0-8476-7018-X); pap. 23.00 (0-8476-7389-8) Rowman.

— Realism & the Aim of Science. Bartley, W. W., III, ed. LC 82-501. (Postscript to the Logic of Scientific Discovery Ser.). 464p. 1983. text ed. 55.50 (0-8476-7015-5) Rowman.

Popper, Karl R. & Eccles, John C. Self & Its Brain. rev. ed. (Illus.). 597p. 1985. 70.00 (0-387-08307-3) Spr-Verlag.

— The Self & Its Brain: An Argument for Interactionism. 616p. 1984. reprint ed. pap. 16.95 (0-7100-9584-8, RKP) Routledge.

*Popper-Lynkeus, Josef. The Individual & the Value of Human Life. Haber, Joram G., tr. LC 95-13950. (Studies in Social & Political Philosophy). 180p. (C). 1995. text ed. 54.00 (0-8476-8035-5); pap. text ed. 21.95 (0-8476-8036-3) Rowman.

Popper, Samuel H. Pathways to the Humanities in Educational Administration. 118p. (C). 1987. reprint ed. pap. text ed. 9.00 (0-922971-00-5, NT3) Univ Council Educ Admin.

— Pathways to the Humanities in School Administration. 231p. (Orig.). (C). 1990. pap. text ed. 13.95 (1-55996-144-9) Univ Council Educ Admin.

Popper, Virginia S., jt. ed. see Hastorf, Christine A.

Popper, William. The Cairo Nilometer: Studies in Ibn Iaghri Birdi's Chronicles of Egypt. LC 51-9495. (University of California Publications in Social Welfare: Vol. 12). 282p. reprint ed. pap. 80.40 (0-8357-7962-9, 2021491) Bks Demand.

— Egypt & Syria under the Circassian Sultans, 1382-1468 A. D. Systematic Notes to Ibn Taghri Birdi's Chronicles of Egypt, Pt. 1. (University of California Publications in Social Welfare: Vol. 15). 136p. reprint ed. pap. 38.80 (0-317-29576-4, 2021493) Bks Demand.

— Egypt & Syria under the Circassian Sultans, 1382-1468 A. D. Systematic Notes to Ibn Taghri Birdi's Chronicles of Egypt, Pt. 2. (University of California Publications in Social Welfare: Vol. 16). 134p. reprint ed. pap. 38.20 (0-317-29575-6, 2021494) Bks Demand.

— History of Egypt, 1382-1469 A. D. Translated from the Arabic Annals of Abu L-Mahasin Ibn Taghri Birdi. LC 54-4885. (University of California Publications in Social Welfare: Vol. 24). 116p. reprint ed. pap. 33.10 (0-317-29568-3, 2021500) Bks Demand.

— History of Egypt, 1382-1469 A. D. Translated from the Arabic Annals of Abu L-Mahasin Ibn Taghri Birdi, Pt. 1. LC 54-4885. (University of California Publications in Social Welfare: Vol. 13). 230p. reprint ed. pap. 65.60 (0-317-29577-2, 2021492) Bks Demand.

— History of Egypt, 1382-1469 A. D. Translated from the Arabic Annals of Abu L-Mahasin Ibn Taghri Birdi, Pt. 3. LC 54-4885. (University of California Publications in Social Welfare: Vol. 17). 188p. reprint ed. pap. 53.60 (0-317-29574-8, 2021495) Bks Demand.

— History of Egypt, 1382-1469 A. D. Translated from the Arabic Annals of Abu L-Mahasin Ibn Taghri Birdi, Pt. 4. LC 54-4885. (University of California Publications in Social Welfare: Vol. 18). 232p. reprint ed. pap. 66.20 (0-317-29573-X, 2021496) Bks Demand.

— History of Egypt, 1382-1469 A. D. Translated from the Arabic Annals of Abu L-Mahasin Ibn Taghri Birdi, Pt. 5. LC 54-4885. (University of California Publicaitons in Semitic Philology: Vol. 19). 270p. reprint ed. pap. 77.00 (0-317-29571-3, 2021497) Bks Demand.

— History of Egypt, 1382-1469 A. D. Translated from the Arabic Annals of Abu L-Mahasin Ibn Taghri Birdi, Pt. 6. LC 54-4885. (University of California Publications in Social Welfare: Vol. 22). 184p. reprint ed. pap. 52.50 (0-317-29570-5, 2021498) Bks Demand.

— History of Egypt, 1382-1469 A. D. Translated from the Arabic Annals of Abu L-Mahasin Ibn Taghri Birdi, Pt. 7. LC 54-4885. (University of California Publications in Social Welfare: Vol. 23). 187p. reprint ed. pap. 53.30 (0-317-29569-1, 2021499) Bks Demand.

Popper, William, tr. History of Egypt, an Extract from Abu l-Mahasin Ibn Taghri Birdi's Chronicle, Entitled Hawadith ad-Duhur fi Mada l'Ayyam wash-Shuhur (845-843 A.H.) (American Oriental Society Essays Ser.: 5). 1963. pap. 3.00 (0-940490-95-1) Am Orient Soc.

Popper, William, jt. auth. see Chen, Min.

Popper, William, tr. see Taghribirdi, Ibn & Al-Mahasin Yusuf, Abu.

Popperwell, Jeral. Human Body. (Science Crossword Puzzles Ser.). (Illus.). 48p. (Orig.). (J). (gr. 2-6). pap. 2.95 (0-8431-2291-9) Price Stern.

— Space. (Science Crossword Puzzles Ser.). (Illus.). 48p. (Orig.). (J). (gr. 2-6). pap. 2.95 (0-8431-2292-7) Price Stern.

Poppino, Mary A., jt. auth. see Cohen, Elaine L.

Poppiti. Practical Techniques for Laboratory Analysis. 1994. 59.95 (0-87371-361-3) Lewis Pubs.

*Popple, Keith. Analysing Community Work: Its Theory & Practice. LC 95-6959. 1995. write for info. (0-335-19409-5, Open Univ Pr); pap. write for info. (0-335-19408-7, Open Univ Pr) Taylor & Francis.

Popple, L. Advanced Ropeworking. (C). 1987. 60.00 (0-85174-137-1, Pub. by Brwn Son Ferg) St Mut.

— Marline Spike Seamanship: The Art of Handling, Splicing & Knotting Wire. (C). 1987. 40.00 (0-85174-138-X, Pub. by Brwn Son Ferg) St Mut.

Popple, Philip R. & Leighninger, Leslie. Social Work, Social Welfare & American Society. 600p. 1990. teacher ed write for info. (0-318-66411-9, H22726); text ed. 44.00 (0-205-12270-1, H22700) Allyn.

— Social Work, Social Welfare, & American Society. 2nd ed. LC 92-26068. 1992. text ed. write for info. (0-205-14070-X) Allyn.

Popple, Philip R., jt. ed. see Reid, P. Nelson.

Popple, William, jt. auth. see Hill, Aaron.

Popplestone, John & McPherson, Marion W. An Illustrated History of American Psychology. (Illus.). 240p. 1994. boxed write for info. (0-697-21127-4); sl. write for info. (0-697-22833-9) Brown & Benchmark.

Popplestone, John A. & McPherson, Marion W. Dictionary of Concepts in General Psychology. LC 88-3120. (Reference Sources for the Social Sciences & Humanities Ser.: No. 7). 391p. 1988. text ed. 79.50 (0-313-23190-7, PGP/, Greenwood Pr) Greenwood.

Poppleton, Gary, jt. auth. see Johnson, Steve.

Popplewell, Jack. Breakfast in Bed. 1963. pap. 4.75 (0-8222-0146-1) Dramatists Play.

— Dear Delinquent. 1958. pap. 4.75 (0-8222-0286-7) Dramatists Play.

— Hocus Pocus. 1963. pap. 4.75 (0-8222-0522-X) Dramatists Play.

Pops, Gerald M. & Pavlak, Thomas J. The Case for Justice: Strengthening Decision Making & Policy in Public Administration. LC 91-12793. (Public Administration Ser.). 221p. 1991. 29.95 (1-55542-375-2) Jossey-Bass.

Pops, Martin. Home Remedies. LC 84-2647. (Illus.). 160p. 1984. lib. bdg. 22.50 (0-87023-448-X); pap. 11.95 (0-87023-449-8) U of Mass Pr.

— Vermeer: Consciousness & the Chamber of Being. Kuspit, Donald, ed. LC 84-2564. (Studies in the Fine Arts: Criticism: No. 16). 132p. reprint ed. 37.70 (0-8357-1525-6, 2070460) Bks Demand.

Popst, Hans, jt. auth. see Haller, Klaus.

Popular Mechanics Co. Staff. How to Make Mission Style Lamps & Shades in Metal & Glass. rev. ed. (Illus.). 128p. 1982. reprint ed. pap. 4.95 (0-486-24244-7) Dover.

— Mission Furniture: How to Make It. (Illus.). vii, 342p. 1980. pap. 7.95 (0-486-23966-7) Dover.

Popular Mechanics Editors. Popular Mechanics Illustrated Guide to Basic Home Repairs. (Illus.). 224p. 1991. 23.00 (0-688-10854-7) Hearst Bks.

— Popular Mechanics Outdoor Gardener. LC 90-25333. 1994. 22.00 (0-688-12963-3) Hearst Bks.

Popular Mechanics Magazine Staff. Popular Mechanics Encyclopedia of Tools & Techniques. 1994. 30.00 (0-688-12460-7) Hearst Bks.

*Popular Staff. Plumbing & Heating. 1994. pap. 4.99 (0-517-13458-6) Random Hse Value.

— Weatherproof Insulation. 1994. pap. 4.99 (0-517-13460-8) Random Hse Value.

Population Council Editors. Catalogue of the Population Council Library. 1979. lib. bdg. 325.00 (0-8161-0278-3, Hall Library) G K Hall.

Population Institute Staff. The Nairobi Challenge: Global Directory of Women's Organizations Implementing Population Strategies. Harvyasi-Curtis, Lita, ed. (Illus.). 564p. (Orig.). (C). 1988. pap. text ed. 9.95 (0-9619165-3-2) Population Inst.

Population Reference Bureau Editors. World Population Growth & Response 1965-1975: A Decade of Global Action. (Illus.). 271p. (C). 1976. pap. text ed. 4.00 (0-917136-00-4) Population Ref.

Popushoi, I. S., ed. Biological & Chemical Methods of Plant Protection. Kothekar, V., tr. (Illus.). 64p. 1987. text ed. 55.00 (90-6191-492-2, Pub. by A A Balkema NE) Ashgate Pub Co.

Popv, Yuri. Essays in Political Economy Imperialism & Developing Countries. 294p. 1984. 35.00 (0-317-53752-0, Pub. by Collets) St Mut.

Popyk, Marilyn K. Up & Running: Microcomputer Applications. LC 86-26620. (C). 1987. pap. text ed. 35.50 (0-201-06274-7) Addison-Wesley.

— Word-Information Processing: Essentials Concepts. 2nd ed. 240p. 1986. text ed. 22.95 (0-07-050593-4) McGraw.

— Word Processing: Essential Concepts. LC 83-768. (Illus.). 240p. (C). 1983. text ed. 27.95 (0-07-048472-4) McGraw.

— Word Processing & Information Systems: A Practical Approach to Concepts. LC 82-25902. 352p. 1983. text ed. 34.75 (0-07-050574-8) McGraw.

— Word Processing & Information Systems: A Practical Approach to Concepts. 2nd ed. 372p. (C). 1986. text ed. 29.50 (0-07-050594-2) McGraw.

Popyk, Marilyn K., jt. auth. see Boyce, B. L.

Poquelin, Jean-Baptiste, see Moliere, pseud..

Poquelin, Jean-Baptiste, see Moliere, pseud..

Poquelin, Jean-Baptiste, see Moliere, pseud..

Poquelin, Jean-Baptiste, see Moliere, pseud..

Poquelin, Jean-Baptiste, see Moliere, pseud..

Poquelin, Jean-Baptiste, see Moliere, pseud..

Poquelin, Jean-Baptiste, see Moliere, pseud..

Poqueline, Jean-Baptiste, see Moliere, pseud..

Por, F. D. The Legacy of Tethys. (Monographiae Biologicae Ser.). (C). 1989. lib. bdg. 105.50 (0-7923-0189-7) Kluwer Ac.

— Sooretama: The Atlantic Forest of Brazil. (Illus.). x, 130p. 1992. pap. 35.00 (90-5103-077-0, Pub. by SPB Acad Pub NE) Koeltz Sci Bks.

Por, F. D. & Dor, I., eds. Hydrobiology of the Mangal. (Developments in Hydrobiology Ser.). 1984. lib. bdg. 152.50 (90-6193-771-X) Kluwer Ac.

Porac, C. & Coren, S. Lateral Preferences & Human Behavior. (Illus.). 288p. 1981. 65.00 (0-387-90596-0) Spr-Verlag.

*Porad, Francine. After Autumn Rain: Haiku, Senryu, Sketches. (Illus.). 28p. (Orig.). (C). 1987. pap. text ed. 5.00 (0-9618009-2-5) Vandina Pr.

— Blues on the Run: Haiku, Senryu, Sketches. (Illus.). 28p. (Orig.). (C). 1988. pap. text ed. 5.00 (0-9618009-3-3) Vandina Pr.

P Q

An Asterisk (*) at the beginning of an entry indicates that the title is appearing in BIP for the first time.

— Connections: Haiku, Senryu & Sketches. (Illus.). 32p. (Orig.). (C). 1986. pap. text ed. 5.00 (*0-9618009-0-9*) Vandina Pr.
— Free of Clouds: Haiku, Senryu, Sketches. (Illus.). 28p. (Orig.). (C). 1989. pap. text ed. 5.00 (*0-9618009-5-X*) Vandina Pr.
— Hundreds of Wishes: Haiku, Searyu, Sketches. (Illus.). 24p. (Orig.). (C). 1991. pap. text ed. 5.00 (*0-9618009-6-8*) Vandina Pr.
— Joy Is My Middle Name: Haiku, Scaryu, Tanka. (Illus.). 40p. (Orig.). (C). 1993. pap. text ed. 5.00 (*0-9618009-8-4*) Vandina Pr.
— Pen & Inklings: Haiku, Senryu & Sketches. (Illus.). 28p. (Orig.). (C). 1986. pap. text ed. 5.00 (*0-9618009-1-7*) Vandina Pr.
— Without Haste. (Amelia Chapbooks Ser.). 16p. (Orig.). 1990. pap. 4.50 (*0-936545-16-X*) Amelia.
***Porad, Francine, et al.** A Mural of Leaves: Haiku, Senryu, Renku. (Illus.). 48p. (Orig.). (C). 1991. pap. text ed. 5.00 (*0-9618009-7-6*) Vandina Pr.
— The Patchwork Quilt: Haiku, Senryu, Tanka, Renku, Artwork. (Illus.). 40p. (Orig.). (C). 1993. pap. text ed. 6.75 (*0-9618009-9-2*) Vandina Pr.
Porada, Edith. Ancient Art in Seals: Essays in Pierre Amiet, Nimet Ozguc, & John Boardman. LC 79-19462. (Franklin Jasper Walls Lectures). (Illus.). 153p. reprint ed. pap. 43.70 (*0-8357-4035-8*, 2036727) Bks Demand.
— Man & Images in the Ancient Near East. (Illus.). 144p. 1995. 19.95 (*1-55921-129-6*) Moyer Bell.
Poraikoshits, E. A., jt. ed. see Mazurin, Oleg V.
Poralla, P. Prosopographia Lacaedaemoniorum. 1985. reprint ed. 15.00 (*0-89005-521-1*) Ares.
Porat, Boaz. Digital Processing of Random Signals. 1993. text ed. 74.00 (*0-13-063751-3*) P-H.
Porat, Dan I. & Barna, Arpad. Introduction to Digital Techniques. 2nd ed. LC 85-29499. (Electronic Technology Ser.). 496p. 1987. text ed. 45.95 (*0-471-09187-1*) P-H.
Porat, Dan I., jt. auth. see Barna, Arpad.
Porat, Dina. The Blue & the Yellow Stars of David: The Zionist Leadership in Palestine & the Holocaust, 1939-1945. (Illus.). 334p. 1990. 36.00 (*0-674-07708-3*) HUP.
Porat, Freida & Will, Mimi. The Dynamic Secretary: A Practical Guide to Achieving Success as an Executive Assistant. (Illus.). 196p. 1983. pap. 7.95 (*0-685-06199-X*) P-H.
***Porat, Frieda.** Creative Life Management: Stress Reduction for an Enhanced Quality of Life. LC 94-69746. 185p. (Orig.). 1994. pap. 9.95 (*0-9643745-1-X*) NewLife CA.
— Creative Procrastination: Organizing Your Own Life. LC 80-7750. 192p. (Orig.). 1980. 8.95 (*0-06-250690-0*, BN3003) NewLife Bks.
— Creative Retirement: Shifting Gears from a Life of Work to a World of Options. LC 94-69745. 198p. (Orig.). 1994. pap. 9.95 (*0-9643745-0-1*) NewLife CA.
— How to be Your Own Marriage Counselor. 1978. write for info. (*0-89256-042-8*) NewLife Bks.
— Self Esteem: The Key to Success in Work & Love. LC 87-90732. 176p. (Orig.). 1988. 9.95 (*0-88247-778-1*) NewLife Bks.
Porat, Frieda & Carr, Jacqueyn. Equal Partners: The Art of Creative Marriage. Krebs, Estella, ed. 1987. 9.95 (*0-88247-761-7*) NewLife Bks.
Porat, Frieda & Myers, Karen. Changing Your Life Style. LC 73-76821. 1973. 6.95 (*0-8184-0020-X*) Carol Pub Group.
***Porat, Frieda & Quakenbush, Margaret.** Positive Selfishness. 1977. write for info. (*0-614-01667-3*) NewLife Bks.
***Porat, Frieda & Will, Mimi.** The Dynamic Secretary. 1978. pap. text ed. write for info. (*0-13-221846-1*) NewLife Bks.
***Porat, Frieda, et al.** Changing Your Lifestyle. 1973. write for info. (*0-614-01666-5*) NewLife Bks.
Porath, Ellen. Steel & Stone. (Dragonlance Meetings Sextet Ser.: Vol. 5). 320p. (Orig.). 1992. pap. 4.95 (*1-56076-339-6*) TSR Inc.
Porath, Jonathan D. Jews in Russia: The Last Four Centuries. 1973. pap. 3.75 (*0-8381-0220-4*) United Syn Bk.
***Porath, Sharon.** Dead File. 352p. 1995. mass mkt. 4.99 (*0-8217-4973-0*) Windsor NY.
— Secret Friend. 320p. 1992. mass mkt. 4.50 (*0-8217-3906-9*) Zebra.
Porath, Yehoshua. In Search of Arab Unity, 1930-1945. 384p. 1986. 40.00 (*0-7146-3264-3*, Pub. by F Cass Pubs UK); pap. 18.50 (*0-7146-4051-4*, Pub. by F Cass Pubs UK) Intl Spec Bk.
Porceddu, E. & Jenkins, G., eds. Seed Regeneration in Cross-Pollinated Species: Proceedings of the C. E. C. - Eucarpia Seminar, Nyborg, Denmark, 15-17 July 1981. 302p. (C). 1982. text ed. 85.00 (*90-6191-244-X*, Pub. by A A Balkema NE) Ashgate Pub Co.
***Porcel, Baltasar.** Horses into the Night. Getman, John L., tr. LC 94-41275. 1995. write for info. (*1-55728-332-X*); pap. write for info. (*1-55728-333-8*) U of Ark Pr.
***Porcella, Donald R., ed.** Mercury As a Global Pollutant: Proceedings of the Third International Conference Held in Whistler, British Columbia, July 10-14, 1994. 1312p. (C). 1995. lib. bdg. 349.00 (*0-7923-3544-9*) Kluwer Ac.
Porcella, Stephen F. California's Fourteeners: A Hiking & Climbing Guide. 1993. pap. 9.95 (*0-9630490-0-3*) Palisades.
***Porcella, Yvonne.** Colorful Book. Nadel, Harold, ed. LC 85-90510. 120p. 1994. pap. 24.95 (*0-914881-81-7*, 10091) C & T Pub.
— Colors Changing Hue. Nadel, Harold & Lytle, Joyce, eds. LC 94-13305. (Illus.). 96p. 1994. pap. 21.95 (*0-914881-86-8*, 10103) C & T Pub.
— Pieced Clothing. rev. ed. LC 86-90565. (Illus.). 60p. 1987. pap. 11.95 (*0-936589-01-9*) Porcella Studios.
— Pieced Clothing: Patterns for Simple Clothing Construction. LC 94-10962. 1994. pap. 11.95 (*0-914881-88-4*) C & T Pub.
— Yvonne Porcella: A Colorful Book. LC 85-90510. (Illus.). 120p. (Orig.). 1986. pap. 22.00 (*0-936589-00-0*) Porcella Studios.
Porcelli, illus. The Essential Poe. 19.95 (*0-8313-5001-6*) Lantern.
Porcelli, Joe. The Lampmaking Handbook. (Illus.). 1991. 24.95 (*0-9629053-6-4*) Glass Pr.
— The Photograph. Wyrick, Charles L., Jr., ed. 1995. 24.95 (*0-941711-30-7*) Wyrick & Co.
Porcelli, Joe, ed. see Radeschi, Loretta.
Porcelli, V. Lawrence. International Lighting Design. ID Magazine Staff, ed. (Illus.). 256p. 1991. 59.95 (*0-935603-49-2*, 30253) Rockport Pubs.
Porcellino, Michael R. Through the Telescope: A Guide for the Amateur Astronomer. 1989. pap. text ed. 19.95 (*0-07-156226-5*) McGraw.
— Through the Telescope: A Guide for the Amateur Astronomer. (Discovering Earth Science Ser.). (Illus.). 272p. 1989. 22.95 (*0-8306-1459-1*); pap. 19.95 (*0-8306-3159-3*) TAB Bks.
Porch, Adelle. Your First Ferret. (Illus.). 34p. (Orig.). 1991. pap. 1.95 (*0-86622-115-8*, YF-105) TFH Pubns.
Porch, Douglas. The Conquest of Morocco. LC 82-47804. 1983. 16.95 (*0-394-51158-1*) Knopf.
— The Conquest of the Sahara. LC 86-12092. 332p. 1986. reprint ed. pap. 11.95 (*0-88064-061-8*) Fromm Intl Pub.
— The French Foreign Legion: A Complete History of the Legendary Fighting Force. LC 90-55834. (Illus.). 752p. 1992. reprint ed. pap. 16.00 (*0-06-092308-3*, PL) HarpC.
— The French Secret Service: From the Dreyfus Affair to the Gulf War. LC 94-46833. 464p. 1995. 27.50 (*0-374-15853-3*) FS&G.
Porch, Ludlow. Beating a Dead Horse Is More Fun Than You Think: A Partisan's View of the Southland. LC 92-71794. 160p. 1992. 15.95 (*1-56352-049-4*) Longstreet Pr Inc.
— Can I Just Do It Till I Need Glasses? And Other Lies Grown-Ups Told You. LC 85-61976. 219p. 1985. 12.95 (*0-931948-81-9*) Peachtree Pubs.
— The Cornbread Chronicles. LC 83-61914. 208p. 1983. 12.95 (*0-931948-48-7*) Peachtree Pubs.
— Jonas Wilkerson Was a Gravy-Suckin' Pig. LC 88-81801. (Illus.). 176p. 1988. 11.95 (*0-929264-04-5*) Longstreet Pr Inc.
— There's Nothing Neat about Seeing Your Feet: The Life & Times of a Fat American. LC 84-60923. 157p. 1984. 12.95 (*0-931948-65-7*) Peachtree Pubs.
— A View from the Porch. LC 81-80383. 184p. 1981. 12.95 (*0-931948-17-7*) Peachtree Pubs.
— Weirdos, Winos & Defrocked Priests. 180p. 1986. 12.95 (*0-934601-05-4*) Peachtree Pubs.
— We're All in This Alone. LC 94-77591. 160p. 1994. 16.95 (*1-56352-171-7*) Longstreet Pr Inc.
— Who Cares about Apathy? LC 87-80972. 121p. 1987. 12.95 (*0-934601-30-5*) Peachtree Pubs.
Porcher, Francis. Resources of the Southern Fields & Forests, Medical, Economical, & Agricultural. (American Civil War Medical Ser.: No. 4). 601p. 1991. reprint ed. 75.00 (*0-930405-33-1*) Norman SF.
Porcher, Francis P. Resources of the Southern Fields & Forests. LC 74-125758. (American Environmental Studies). 1974. reprint ed. 46.95 (*0-405-02684-6*) Ayer.
***Porcher, Philip G., Jr.** What You Can Expect from an Interim Pastor & an Interim Consultant. Date not set. pap. 6.75 (*1-56699-101-3*, OD71) Alban Inst.
***Porcher, Richard D.** Wildflowers of the Carolina Lowcountry & Lower Pee Dee. LC 94-18771. 1995. pap. write for info. (*1-57003-027-8*) U of SC Pr.
Porchet, M., jt. ed. see Hoffmann, J.
Porchet, M., et al, eds. Advances in Invertebrate Reproduction 4: Proceedings of the Fourth International Society of Invertebrate Reproduction, Villeneuved'Ascq, France, September, 1986. 568p. 1987. 177.00 (*0-444-80857-4*) Elsevier.
Porcino, Jane. Growing Older, Getting Better: A Handbook for Women in the Second Half of Life. LC 82-24438. (Illus.). 366p. 1983. pap. 12.95 (*0-201-05592-9*) Addison-Wesley.
— Growing Older, Getting Bigger: A Handbook for Women in the Second Half of Life. (Illus.). 380p. 1991. pap. 16.95 (*0-8264-0544-4*) Crossroad NY.
— Living Longer, Living Better: Adventures in Community Housing for Those in the Second Half of Life. 240p. 1991. 26.95 (*0-8245-1323-1*); pap. 15.95 (*0-8245-1324-X*) Crossroad NY.
Porcioles, Lluis B. Diccionari Alemany-Catala. 2nd ed. 716p. (CAT & GER.). 1990. 41.95 (*0-7859-6336-7*, 8485194187) Fr & Eur.
Pordage, S., tr. see Willis, Thomas.
Pore, Renate. A Conflict of Interest: Women in German Social Democracy, 1919 to 1933. LC 80-27183. (Contributions in Women's Studies: No. 26). (Illus.). 152p. 1981. text ed. 45.00 (*0-313-22856-6*, PCW/, Greenwood Pr) Greenwood.
Pore, Renate, jt. ed. see Justice, Betty.
Poree, Guy. Moeurs et Coutumes des Khmers. LC 77-87069. (Illus.). reprint ed. 21.50 (*0-404-16850-7*) AMS Pr.
Porell, Frank W. Models of Intra-Urban Relocation. (Studies in Applied Regional Science). 1982. lib. bdg. 77.50 (*0-89838-089-8*) Kluwer Ac.
Poresky, Don, see Yankee Diablerie, pseud..
Poresky, Don, see Fresh Lemon, pseud..
Poresky, Don, see Red Pepper, pseud..
Poresky, Louise A. The Elusive Self: Psyche & Spirit in Virginia Woolf's Novels. LC 79-64503. 288p. 1981. 38.50 (*0-87413-170-7*, 170) U Delaware Pr.
Porete, Marguerite. Marguerite Porete: The Mirror of Simple Souls. LC 93-14479. (Classics of Western Spirituality Ser.). 288p. (Orig.). 1993. 24.95 (*0-8091-0464-4*); pap. 17.95 (*0-8091-3427-6*) Paulist Pr.
Porett, Jane. When I Was Little Like You. LC 93-13974. (Illus.). (J). 1993. 12.95 (*0-87868-530-8*) Child Welfare.
Poretz, Doraine. Scattered Light. 32p. (Orig.). 1987. pap. 3.95 (*0-941017-09-5*) Bombshelter Pr.
Poretz, Mel. What Would You Do? 112p. (Orig.). 1994. mass mkt. 5.99 (*0-449-90762-7*, ExPress) Fawcett.
Poretz, Mel & Sinrod, Barry. Do You Do It with the Lights On? 112p. 1991. pap. 8.00 (*0-449-90571-3*, Columbine) Fawcett.
Poretz, Mel, et al. Sam, the Ceiling Needs Painting. 32p. 1964. pap. 2.95 (*0-8431-0418-X*) Putnam Pub Group.
Porfyrio, Pomponius. Commentum in Horatium Flaccum. x, 599p. 1967. reprint ed. write for info. (*0-318-71203-2*, Pub. by Georg Olms GW) Lubrecht & Cramer.
Porges, F. Design of Electrical Services in Buildings. 3rd ed. 350p. 1989. 69.50 (*0-419-14580-X*, E & FN Spon) Routledge Chapman & Hall.
— HVAC Engineer's Handbook. 9th ed. (Illus.). 272p. 1991. 70.00 (*0-7506-1481-1*) Buttrwrth-Heinemann.
Porges, G. Applied Acoustics. 180p. 1987. reprint ed. 30.95 (*0-932146-18-X*) Peninsula CA.
Porges, L. Bibliographie Des Regions Du Senegal. 1977. 159.25 (*90-279-7544-2*) Mouton.
***Porges, Maria.** Forms of Address. (Illus.). 32p. (Orig.). 1994. pap. write for info. (*0-930495-24-1*) San Fran Art Inst.
Pories, Walter J. & Thomas, Francis T., eds. Office Surgery for the Family Physician. (Illus.). 352p. 1985. text ed. 80.00 (*0-409-95142-0*) Buttrwrth-Heinemann.
Pories, Walter J., jt. ed. see Dudley, Hugh.
Poris, Ruth F. Advanced Beadwork. (Illus.). 152p. (Orig.). 1990. per. 14.99 (*0-9616422-0-3*) Golden Hands Pr.
— Step-by-Step Bead Stringing: A Complete Illustrated Professional Approach. (Illus.). 45p. 1985. pap. 7.99 (*0-9616422-1-1*) Golden Hands Pr.
Poriss, Gerry H. & Poriss, Ralph G. While My Country Is in Danger: The Life & Letters of Lieutenant Colonel Richard S. Thompson, Twelfth New Jersey Volunteers. LC 94-11305. (Illus.). 251p. 1994. 21.95 (*0-9622393-6-4*) Edmonston Pub.
Poriss, Ralph G., jt. auth. see Poriss, Gerry H.
Poritsky, Bertrand. Minnesota Evidence Trialbook, 1987-1990. 210p. 1994. ring bd. 65.00 (*0-86678-279-6*) Michie Butterworth.
— Minnesota Evidence Trialbook, 1987-1990. suppl. ed. 210p. 1994. ring bd. 39.00 (*0-86678-004-1*) Butterworth Legal Pubs.
Poritsky, Ray. Anatomy to Color & Study. (Illus.). 544p. (Orig.). 1989. student ed 26.95 (*0-932883-18-4*) Hanley & Belfus.
— Neuroanatomy: A Functional Atlas of Parts & Pathways. (Illus.). 300p. 1992. student ed, pap. 31.95 (*1-56053-008-1*) Hanley & Belfus.
Poritzky-Lauvand, Rhona, tr. see Bilheux, Ronald & Escoffier, Alain.
Poritzky-Lauvand, Rhona, tr. see Thuries, Yves.
Porjtillo, Mariano N. Turbas Republicanas, 1900-1904. LC 90-81370. 218p. 1990. pap. 8.95 (*0-929157-07-9*) Ediciones Huracan.
Porkert, Manfred. The Essentials of Chinese Diagnostics. (Illus.). 292p. 1983. reprint ed. pap. 16.00 (*0-912379-00-6*) Ctr Traditional Acupuncture.
Porkert, Manfred & Ullmann, Christian. Chinese Medicine. 320p. 1990. pap. 12.95 (*0-8050-1277-X*, Owl) H Holt & Co.
Porkess, Roger. The HarperCollins Dictionary of Statistics. LC 90-56000. (Illus.). 288p. 1991. pap. 14.00 (*0-06-461020-9*, Harper Ref) HarpC.
***Porket, J. L.** Unemployment in Capitalist, Communist, & Post-Communist Economies. LC 94-34872. 1995. write for info. (*0-312-12484-8*) St Martin.
— Work, Employment & Unemployment in the Soviet Union. LC 88-37127. (Illus.). 304p. 1989. text ed. 59.95 (*0-312-03095-9*) St Martin.
Porkolab, Miklos, ed. Radio Frequency Power in Plasmas. (AIP Conference Proceedings Ser.: No. 289). (Illus.). 464p. 1993. text ed. 135.00 (*1-56396-264-0*, AIP Pr) Am Inst Physics.
Porlier, Linda, jt. auth. see Porlier, Terry.
Porlier, Linda K., jt. auth. see Porlier, Terry.
Porlier, Terry & Porlier, Linda. Living over the Limit: How to Get Out & Stay Out of the Credit Trap - the Credit Card Survival Kit. 130p. (Orig.). 1989. Incl. audio cassette tape. audio 49.95 (*0-9623584-2-8*) Emerald West.
Porlier, Terry & Porlier, Linda K. Living over the Limit: A Credit Card Survival Kit. 140p. 1989. student ed write for info. (*0-9623584-1-X*); pap. text ed. 29.95 (*0-9623584-0-1*) Emerald West.
Porn, Igmar. Action Theory & Social Science. (Synthese Library: No. 120). 1977. lib. bdg. 56.50 (*90-277-0846-0*) Kluwer Ac.
Pornbacher, Ulrike, comp. Migration & Intercultural Education in Europe. 180p. 1990. 49.00 (*1-85359-112-2*, Pub. by Multilingual Matters UK) Taylor & Francis.
Pornbacher, Ulrike, et al. Migration of Intercultural Education in Europe. 1990. 49.00 (*1-85359-094-0*, Pub. by Multilingual Matters UK) Taylor & Francis.
Pornschlegel, H., ed. Research & Development in Work & Technology. (Illus.). xiv, 413p. 1992. pap. 89.00 (*0-387-91427-7*) Spr-Verlag.
Poroner, Palmer. Twenty-First Century Art: Rene Robles Assertionism. (Illus.). 204p. 1994. 75.00 (*0-9638583-0-0*) P J Sweeney.
Poropat & Straka, Gene. MultiMate Advantage II for Office Professionals. 400p. 1988. pap. text ed. 31.00 (*0-13-605015-8*) P-H.
Poropat, jt. auth. see Straka, Gene.
Porosky, Peter. Beginning the Novel. LC 94-8397. 128p. (Orig.). 1994. lib. bdg. 39.50 (*0-8191-9501-4*); pap. text ed. 18.50 (*0-8191-9502-2*) U Pr of Amer.
— How to Find Your Own Voice: A Guide to Literary Style. LC 86-15895. 360p. 1986. 49.50 (*0-8191-5611-6*) U Pr of Amer.
Porot, Ann M., et al. S.F.B.J.-Captivating Character Children. (Illus.). 238p. 1986. 25.00 (*0-87588-279-X*, 3302) Hobby Hse.
Porot, Antoine. Diccionario de Psiquiatria, Vol. 1. 3rd ed. 650p. (SPA.). 1977. 59.95 (*0-7859-5924-6*, 8433566695) Fr & Eur.
— Diccionario de Psiquiatria, Vol. 2. 3rd ed. 650p. (SPA.). 1977. 59.95 (*0-7859-5925-4*, 8433566709) Fr & Eur.
— Diccionario de Psiquiatria: Dictionary of Psychiatry, 2 vols., Set. 3rd ed. 650p. (SPA.). 1977. 125.00 (*0-8288-5320-7*, S50071) Fr & Eur.
Porot, Antoine, ed. Manuel Alphabetique de Psychiatrie Clinique et Therapeutique. 6th ed. 768p. (FRE.). 1984. 135.00 (*0-7859-4832-5*, M6391) Fr & Eur.
***Porot, Daniel.** The Pie Method for Career Success: A New Job Search Strategy. (Illus.). 260p. (Orig.). 1995. pap. 14.95 (*1-56370-182-0*, J1820) JIST Works.
***Porozynski, Martin J.** Up-Front Sleeper: The Federal Witness "Protection" Program, True Involvement with Rapico Picnocrap. A "Letter" to Janet Reno. LC 94-74031. (Judicial Network Under Scrutiny Ser.). 200p. (Orig.). 1995. pap. 14.95 (*0-9644416-3-2*) Doublenight Pr.
Porphyrios, Demetri. Classical Architecture. LC 92-15369. 1992. text ed. 54.95 (*0-07-050478-4*) McGraw.
— Demetri Porphyrios Selected Buildings & Writings. (Architectural Monographs: No. 25). (Illus.). 144p. (Orig.). 1993. 55.00 (*1-85490-174-5*, Academy Edits) St Martin.
Porphyrios, Demetri, ed. Building & Rational Architecture. (Illus.). 88p. 1985. pap. 21.95 (*0-312-10770-6*) St Martin.
— Leon Krier: Houses, Palaces, Cities: An Architectural Design Profile. (Illus.). 128p. 1985. pap. 21.95 (*0-312-47990-5*) St Martin.
Porphyrios, Demetri, jt. ed. see Academy Edition Staff.
Porphyrius. De Philosophia Ex Oraculis Haurienda Librorum Reliquiae. Wolff, Gustav, ed. vi, 253p. 1984. reprint ed. write for info. (*3-487-00202-7*, Pub. by Georg Olms GW) Lubrecht & Cramer.
— Opuscula Selecta. xxiii, 320p. 1977. reprint ed. write for info. (*3-487-00421-6*, Pub. by Georg Olms GW) Lubrecht & Cramer.
Porphyry. Launching-Points to the Realm of Mind. Guthrie, Kenneth S., tr. LC 88-22517. 96p. (Orig.). 1988. 20.00 (*0-933999-58-5*); pap. 10.95 (*0-933999-59-3*) Phanes Pr.
— Life of Plotinus or Porphyry's Life of Plotinus. 1983. reprint ed. pap. 3.95 (*0-916411-12-5*, Pub. by Alexandrian Pr) Holmes Pub.
— On Abstinence from Animal Food. 250p. 1989. pap. 25.00 (*0-87556-238-8*) Saifer.
— On Aristotle's Categories. Strange, Steven K., tr. LC 92-14908. (Ancient Commentators on Aristotle Ser.). 1992. 47.95 (*0-8014-2816-5*) Cornell U Pr.
— On the Cave of the Nymphs. Taylor, Thomas, tr. LC 90-47421. (Illus.). (Orig.). 1991. 20.00 (*0-933999-60-7*); pap. 7.00 (*0-933999-61-5*) Phanes Pr.
— Porphyry's Letter to His Wife Marcella Concerning the Life of Philosophy & the Ascent to the Gods. Zimmern, Alice, tr. LC 85-29718. (Orig.). 1986. pap. 6.00 (*0-933999-27-5*) Phanes Pr.
Porphyry the Neo-Platonist. Neo-Platonic Letter to Marcella. Zimmern, Alice, tr. 1993. reprint ed. pap. 5.95 (*1-55818-202-0*, Pub. by Alexandrian Pr) Holmes Pub.
Porpora, Douglas V. The Concept of Social Structure. LC 87-12037. (Contributions in Sociology Ser.: No. 68). 192p. 1987. text ed. 49.95 (*0-313-25646-2*, PCS/, Greenwood Pr) Greenwood.
— How Holocausts Happen: The United States in Central America. 232p. 1990. 29.95 (*0-87722-750-0*) Temple U Pr.
— How Holocausts Happen: The United States in Central America. 1992. pap. 19.95 (*0-87722-923-6*) Temple U Pr.
Porporino, F., jt. auth. see Zamble, E.
Porqueras-Mayo, Albert, et al. The New Catalan Short Story: An Anthology. LC 82-21927. 278p. (Orig.). 1983. pap. text ed. 25.00 (*0-8191-2900-3*) U Pr of Amer.
Porras, Agustin. Desarrollo Agrario y Cambio Demografico en Tres Regiones de Mexico: (Agricultural Development & Demographic Change in Three Regions of Mexico) (Research Report Ser.: No. 18). 43p. (Orig.). (SPA.). (C). 1981. pap. 5.00 (*0-935391-17-7*, RR-18) UCSD Ctr US-Mex.
Porras Cruz, Jorge L. Estudios y Articulos. (UPREX, Estudios Literarios Ser.: No. 25). 274p. (C). 1974. pap. 1.50 (*0-8477-0025-9*) U of PR Pr.
Porras-Cruz, Jorge L. Vida y Obra De Luis G. Inclan. LC 76-1829. (Coleccion Mente y Palabra). 230p. (Orig.). (SPA.). 1976. 5.00 (*0-8477-0536-6*); pap. 4.00 (*0-8477-0537-4*) U of PR Pr.
Porras, Jerry I. Stream Analysis: Diagnosis & Planning for Managing Organization Development. LC 86-22183. (Organization Development Ser.). (Illus.). 180p. (C). 1987. pap. text ed. 26.95 (*0-201-05693-3*) Addison-Wesley.
Porras, Jerry I. & Kass, R. Stream Analysis. 2nd ed. (Organization Development Ser.). (Illus.). 163p. (C). 1995. pap. text ed. write for info. (*0-201-53971-3*) Addison-Wesley.
Porras, Jerry I., jt. auth. see Collins, James C.
Porras, Louis, jt. auth. see Wilson, Larry D.

PQ

An Asterisk (*) at the beginning of an entry indicates that the title is appearing in BIP for the first time.

Porrazzo, Ed & Odell, Karen. The Parents' Guide to Personal Computers. (Illus.). 1985. 19.95 (*0-13-649963-5*) P-H.

Porreco, Richard P., ed. Contemporary Obstetrics for Medical Students. (Illus.). 340p. 1991. pap. 22.50 (*0-916859-51-7*) Perinatology.

Porreco, Rocco, ed. The Georgetown Symposium on Ethics: Essays in Honor of Henry Babcock Veatch. 316p. (Orig.). 1984. pap. text ed. 29.00 (*0-8191-3777-4*) U Pr of Amer.

Porritt, Arthur, ed. Causes of War: Economic, Industrial, Racial, Religious, Scientific & Political. LC 70-99719. (Essay Index Reprint Ser.). 1977. 21.95 (*0-8369-1372-8*) Ayer.

Porritt, Edward. Evolution of the Dominion of Canada: Its Government & Its Politics. LC 72-33. (Select Bibliographies Reprint Ser.). 1977. reprint ed. 26.95 (*0-8369-9970-3*) Ayer.

— Unreformed House of Commons: Parliamentary Representation Before 1832, 2 vols., Set. LC 63-21104. 1963. reprint ed. 125.00 (*0-678-00012-3*) Kelley.

Porritt, Jonathon. Seeing Green: The Politics of Ecology Explained. 249p. 1985. pap. 17.95 (*0-631-13893-5*) Blackwell Pubs.

— Where on Earth Are We Going? (Illus.). 241p. 1992. pap. 17.95 (*0-563-20847-3*, BBC-Parkwest) Parkwest Pubns.

Porritt, Jonathon & Nadler, Ellis. Captain Eco & the Fate of the Earth. LC 91-60142. (Illus.). 48p. (J). (gr. 3 up). 1991. 13.95 (*1-879431-12-2*); lib. bdg. 14.99 (*1-879431-27-0*) Dorling Kindersley.

Porro, Jeffrey, ed. see WGBH Educational Foundation, Annenberg-CPB Project Staff.

Porro, Jeffrey D., jt. ed. see Kincade, William H.

Porrua Staff. Diccionario Castellano Ilustrado. (Illus.). (SPA.). pap. 17.95 (*0-7859-0429-8*, S31405) Fr & Eur.

— Diccionario de Sinonimos Espanoles. (SPA.). 9.95 (*0-7859-0422-0*, S12253) Fr & Eur.

— Diccionario Enciclopedico: Gran Omeba, 12 vols., Set. (SPA.). 450.00 (*0-7859-0430-1*, S33046) Fr & Eur.

— Diccionario Enciclopedico Ilustrado, 3 vols., Set. (illus.). (SPA.). 125.00 (*0-7859-0431-X*, S33077) Fr & Eur.

— Diccionario Oriente, 4 vols., Set. (SPA.). 350.00 (*0-7859-0432-8*, S33078) Fr & Eur.

Porrugues, Gladys & Vedral, Joyce L. The Hard Bodies Express Workout. (Orig.). 1988. pap. 14.95 (*0-440-53426-7*, Dell Trade Pbks) Dell.

Porsild, A. E. Rocky Mountain Wildflowers. 1987. pap. 9.95 (*0-226-56495-9*) U Ch Pr.

Porsild, A. Erling, jt. auth. see Cody, William J.

Porson, Richard. Adversaria, Notae et Emendationes in Poetas Graecos. xviii, 354p. 1982. reprint ed. write for info. (*3-487-07198-3*, Pub. by Georg Olms GW) Lubrecht & Cramer.

Porstendorfer, G. Principles of Magneto-Telluric Prospecting. (Geoexploration Monographs: Ser. 1, No. 5). (Illus.). 118p. 1975. lib. bdg. 44.80 (*3-443-13007-0*) Lubrecht & Cramer.

Port Authority of New York & New Jersey Staff, et al. The Arts As Industry: Their Economic Importance to the New York-New Jersey Metropolitan Region. (Illus.). 136p. (Orig.). 1983. pap. text ed. 12.00 (*0-912443-00-6*) Alliance Arts.

Port, Beverly. Antique Santa Post Cards, Vol. III. (Illus.). 12p. (Orig.). 1991. spiral bd. 4.95 (*0-87588-366-4*) Hobby Hse.

— Antique Santa Postcards, Vol. II. 12p. (Orig.). 1987. spiral bd. 4.95 (*0-87588-314-1*, 3596) Hobby Hse.

— Antique Teddy Bear Postcards, Vol. II. 12p. (Orig.). 1987. spiral bd. 4.95 (*0-87588-315-X*) Hobby Hse.

Port, C. Dictionnaire Historique, Geographique et Biographique de Maine et Loire, 3 vols., Set. 896p. (FRE.). 1978. 595.00 (*0-8288-5197-2*, M6463) Fr & Eur.

***Port, Kenneth.** Comparitive Law: The Role of Law & the Legal Process in Japan. LC 95-68701. 1996. write for info. (*0-89089-860-X*) Carolina Acad Pr.

Port, Len. Get to Know the Algarve: An Insider's Guide. (Illus.). 248p. (Orig.). 1994. pap. 18.95 (*972-804-401-1*, Pub. by Kuperard UK) Seven Hills Bk.

Port, M. H. Imperial London: Civil Government Building in London 1850-1915. LC 94-10254. (Illus.). 288p. 1995. 65.00 (*0-300-05977-9*) Yale U Pr.

***Port, Robert F. & Gelder, Timothy Van, eds.** Mind as Motion: Explorations in the Dynamics of Cognition. LC 94-23127. 668p. 1995. 55.00x (*0-262-16150-8*, Bradford Bks) MIT Pr.

Port, Sidney, jt. ed. see Ney, Peter.

Port, Sidney C. Theoretical Probability for Applications. LC 93-14725. (Hilbert Space Methods in Reliability & Statistical Inference). 928p. 1993. text ed. 95.00 (*0-471-63216-3*, Wiley-Interscience) Wiley.

Port, Sidney C. & Stone, Charles J. Brownian Motion & Classical Potential Theory. LC 78-6772. (Probability & Mathematical Statistics Ser.). 1978. text ed. 91.00 (*0-12-561850-6*) Acad Pr.

Port Sines Investigating Panel Staff. Failure of the Breakwater at Port Sines, Portugal. LC 82-70493. 290p. 1982. pap. 22.00 (*0-87262-298-3*) Am Soc Civil Eng.

Port, Stanley. The Management of CAD for Construction. (Illus.). 240p. 1989. text ed. 52.95 (*0-442-23698-0*) Chapman & Hall.

Porta, Antonio. As If It Were a Rhythm. Vangelisti, Paul, tr. 1978. 2.50 (*0-88031-051-0*) Invisible-Red Hill.

— Invasions & Other Poems. Vangelisti, Paul, ed. & tr. by. 1986. 10.00 (*0-88031-065-0*) Invisible-Red Hill.

— King of the Storeroom. LC 91-50819. 149p. (C). 1992. 19.95 (*0-8195-5247-X*, Wesleyan Univ Pr) U Pr of New Eng.

— Kisses from Another Dream. Molino, Anthony, tr. (Pocket Poets Ser.: No. 44). 128p. (Orig.). 1987. pap. 5.95 (*0-87286-206-2*) City Lights.

Porta, Carol B., jt. auth. see Griggs, James K.

Porta, E. A., ed. Lipofuscin & Ceroid Pigments. (Advances in Experimental Medicine & Biology Ser.: Vol. 266). (Illus.). 393p. 1989. 95.00 (*0-306-43519-5*, Plenum Pr) Plenum.

Porta, Pier L., ed. see Ricardo, David.

Portal, Christopher, ed. The History Curriculum for Teachers. LC 86-29305. 175p. 1987. 60.00 (*1-85000-165-0*, Falmer Pr); pap. 33.00 (*1-85000-166-9*, Falmer Pr) Taylor & Francis.

***Portalatin, Aida C.** Yania Tierra. Fenwick, M. J., tr. & intro. by. LC 94-79182. 196p. (Orig.). 1995. pap. 12.95 (*0-9632363-9-3*) Azul Edits.

Portales, Marco. Youth & Age in American Literature: The Rhetoric of Old Men in the Mathers, Franklin, Adams, Cooper, Hawthorne, Melville, & James. (American University Studies: American Literature: Ser. XXIV, Vol. 20). 169p. (C). 1990. text ed. 35.00 (*0-8204-1181-7*) P Lang Pubs.

Portalie, Eugene. A Guide to the Thought of Saint Augustine. Bastian, Ralph J., tr. LC 75-1182. 428p. 1975. reprint ed. text ed. 52.50 (*0-8371-7992-0*, POGS, Greenwood Pr) Greenwood.

Portaluppi, Francesco, jt. auth. see Luisada, Aldo A.

Portaro, Sam & Peluso, Gary. Inquiring & Discerning Hearts: Vocation & Ministry with Young Adults on Campus. LC 93-5720. 308p. 1993. 44.95 (*1-55540-892-3*, 000307); pap. 29.95 (*1-55540-893-1*) Scholars Pr GA.

Portch, Elizabeth, tr. see Jansson, Tove.

Portcullis Press, Ltd. Staff. Securitech. 300p. 1989. 400.00 (*0-317-54376-8*) St Mut.

Portcullis Press Ltd. Staff, ed. Glass Making Today. 1985. 210.00 (*0-685-43993-3*, Pub. by Portcullis Pr Ltd UK) St Mut.

***Porte, Barbara A.** A Black Elephant with a Brown Ear (in Alabama) & Other Tales. (Illus.). 32p. (J). 1996. write for info. (*0-688-14374-1*); lib. bdg. write for info. (*0-688-14375-X*) Greenwillow.

— Chickens! Chickens! LC 94-19552. (J). (ps-3). 1995. lib. bdg. 14.99 (*0-531-08727-1*) Orchard Bks Watts.

— Chickens! Chickens! LC 94-19552. (Illus.). 32p. (J). (ps-2). 1995. 14.95 (*0-531-06877-3*) Orchard Bks Watts.

— Fat Fanny, Beanpole Bertha, & the Boys. LC 90-7686. (Illus.). 112p. (J). (gr. 3-5). 1991. 14.95 (*0-531-05928-6*); lib. bdg. 14.99 (*0-531-08528-7*) Orchard Bks Watts.

— Harry Gets an Uncle. LC 90-39562. (Illus.). 48p. (J). (gr. k up). 1991. 13.95 (*0-688-09389-2*); lib. bdg. 13.88 (*0-688-09390-6*) Greenwillow.

— Harry in Trouble. LC 87-21253. (Illus.). 48p. (J). (gr. 1 up). 1989. 15.00 (*0-688-07633-5*); lib. bdg. 14.93 (*0-688-07722-6*) Greenwillow.

— Harry's Birthday. LC 93-18189. (Illus.). 48p. (J). (gr. k up). 1994. 14.00 (*0-688-12142-X*); lib. bdg. 13.93 (*0-688-12143-8*) Greenwillow.

— Harry's Dog. LC 83-14129. (Greenwillow Read-Alone Bks.). (Illus.). 48p. (J). (gr. 1-3). 1983. 13.95 (*0-688-02555-2*); lib. bdg. 13.88 (*0-688-02556-0*) Greenwillow.

— Harry's Mom. LC 84-25955. (Greenwillow Read-Alone Bks.). (Illus.). 48p. (J). (gr. 1-4). 1985. 10.25 (*0-688-04817-X*); lib. bdg. 10.88 (*0-688-04818-8*) Greenwillow.

— I Only Made up the Roses. LC 86-18307. 128p. (J). (gr. 7 up). 1987. 14.00 (*0-688-05216-9*) Greenwillow.

— Jesse's Ghost & Other Stories. LC 83-1451. 128p. (J). (gr. 7 up). 1983. 10.25 (*0-688-02301-0*) Greenwillow.

— Leave That Cricket Be, Alan Lee. LC 92-29401. (Illus.). 32p. (J). (ps up). 1993. 14.00 (*0-688-11793-7*); lib. bdg. 13.93 (*0-688-11794-5*) Greenwillow.

— Ruthann & Her Pig. LC 88-31452. (Illus.). 96p. (J). (gr. 2-5). 1989. 15.95 (*0-531-05825-5*); lib. bdg. 15.99 (*0-531-08425-6*) Orchard Bks Watts.

— Something Terrible Happened: A Novel. LC 94-6923. 224p. (J). (gr. 6-9). 1994. 16.95 (*0-531-06869-2*); lib. bdg. 16.99 (*0-531-08719-0*) Orchard Bks Watts.

— The Take-Along Dog. LC 88-18775. (Illus.). 40p. (J). (gr. 1 up). 1989. 11.95 (*0-688-08053-7*); lib. bdg. 11.88 (*0-688-08054-5*) Greenwillow.

— Taxicab Tales. LC 90-24609. 56p. (J). 1992. 13.00 (*0-688-09908-4*) Greenwillow.

— A Turkey Drive & Other Tales. LC 91-48032. (Illus.). 64p. (J). (gr. k up). 1993. 14.00 (*0-688-11336-2*) Greenwillow.

— When Aunt Lucy Rode a Mule & Other Stories. LC 93-4874. (Illus.). 32p. (J). (gr. k-2). 1994. 15.95 (*0-531-06816-1*); lib. bdg. 15.99 (*0-531-08666-6*) Orchard Bks Watts.

— When Grandma Almost Fell off the Mountain & Other Stories. LC 91-41174. (Illus.). 32p. (J). (ps-2). 1993. 14.95 (*0-531-05965-0*) Orchard Bks Watts.

— When Grandma Almost Fell off the Mountain & Other Stories. LC 91-41174. (Illus.). 32p. (J). (ps-2). 1993. lib. bdg. 14.99 (*0-531-08565-1*) Orchard Bks Watts.

Porte, J. F. Sir Charles V. Stanford. LC 76-12570. (Music Reprint Ser.). 1976. reprint ed. lib. bdg. 25.00 (*0-306-70790-X*) Da Capo.

Porte, Jacques. Encyclopedie des Musiques Sacrees: Encyclopedia of Sacred Music, 3 vols., Set. (FRE.). 1978. 295.00 (*0-8288-5233-2*, M6202) Fr & Eur.

Porte, Joel. Emerson: Prospect & Retrospect. (English Studies: No. 10). 208p. 1982. 18.50 (*0-674-24915-1*); pap. 7.95 (*0-674-24917-8*) HUP.

— Emerson & Thoreau: Transcendentalists in Conflict. LC 80-2512. (Thoreau Ser.). 240p. reprint ed. 31.50 (*0-404-19060-X*) AMS Pr.

— In Respect to Egotism: Studies in American Romantic Writing. (Cambridge Studies in American Literature & Culture: No. 53). 320p. (C). 1991. 49.95 (*0-521-36273-3*) Cambridge U Pr.

— New Essays on "The Portrait of a Lady" (American Novel Ser.). 160p. (C). 1990. 27.95 (*0-521-34508-1*); pap. 11.95 (*0-521-34753-X*) Cambridge U Pr.

— Representative Man: Ralph Waldo Emerson in His Time. (Illus.). 361p. 1988. text ed. 61.00 (*0-231-06740-2*); pap. text ed. 16.50 (*0-231-06741-0*) Col U Pr.

— The Romance in America: Studies in Cooper, Poe, Hawthorne, Melville, & James. LC 69-17795. 247p. reprint ed. pap. 70.40 (*0-685-23379-0*, 2032492) Bks Demand.

Porte, Joel, ed. see Emerson, Ralph Waldo.

Porte, John F. Chopin: The Composer & His Music. 1988. reprint ed. lib. bdg. 59.00 (*0-7812-0780-0*) Rprt Serv.

— Chopin the Composer & His Music. 1976. lib. bdg. 25.00 (*0-403-03791-3*) Scholarly.

— Edward MacDowell. 1972. 59.95 (*0-8490-0097-1*) Gordon Pr.

— Sir Edward Elgar. LC 75-107827. (Select Bibliographies Reprint Ser.). (Illus.). 1977. reprint ed. 21.95 (*0-8369-5194-8*) Ayer.

— Sir Edward Elgar. 214p. 1990. reprint ed. lib. bdg. 69.00 (*0-7812-9061-9*) Rprt Serv.

Porte, Michelle, jt. auth. see Duras, Marguerite.

Porte, Sanna, ed. see Wheat, Doug.

Porte, Sannat, ed. see Raup, Omar B., et al.

Portefaix, Lilian. Sisters Rejoice: Paul's Letter to the Philippians & Luke-Acts as Received by First Century Philippian Women. (Coniectanea Biblica. New Testament Ser.: No. 20). (Illus.). 260p. (Orig.). 1988. pap. 48.50x (*91-22-01201-X*, Pub. by Almqv & Wiksell SW) Coronet Bks.

Portela, A., et al. Crack Growth Analysis in Anistropic Materials. 1995. disk, ring bd. 440.00 (*1-56252-270-1*) Computational Mech MA.

— Crack Growth Analysis in Stiffened Sheets. 1994. disk, ring bd. 440.00 (*1-56252-271-X*) Computational Mech MA.

Portela, A. Dual Boundary Element Analysis of Crack Growth. LC 92-75028. (Topics in Engineering Ser.: Vol. 14). 192p. 1993. 108.00 (*1-56252-116-0*) Computational Mech MA.

Portela, A., et al. Thermoelastic Crack Growth Analysis. 1995. disk, ring bd. 440.00 (*1-56252-269-8*) Computational Mech MA.

Portela, A. & Aliabadi, M. H. Crack Growth Analysis Using Boundary Elements. LC 92-75034. 124p. 1993. disk, ring bd. 995.00 (*1-56252-115-2*) Computational Mech MA.

Portela, A., et al. Crack Growth Analysis Using Boundary Elements 3 Module Set. 1995. disk, ring bd. 1,030.00 (*1-56252-272-8*) Computational Mech MA.

***Portela, Jose I.** Don't Lose Your Unemployment Benefits: A Handbook for Workers & the Unemployed. LC 95-2020. 192p. (Orig.). 1995. pap. 12.95 (*0-945257-66-X*) Apex Pr.

Portell-Vila, Herminio. Los Otros Extranjeros En la Revolucion Norteamericana. LC 77-88537. (Coleccion de Estudios Hispanicos - Hispanic Studies Collection). 1978. pap. 8.00 (*0-89729-173-5*) Ediciones.

Portelli, Alessandra. Text & the Voice: Writing, Speaking, & Democracy in American Literature. 1994. 29.50 (*0-231-08498-6*) Col U Pr.

Portelli, Alessandro. The Death of Luigi Trastulli & Other Stories: Form & Meaning in Oral History. LC 89-26260. (SUNY Series in Oral & Public History). 341p. (C). 1991. 74.50 (*0-7914-0429-3*); pap. 24.95 (*0-7914-0430-7*) State U NY Pr.

— The Voice & the Text: Writing, Speaking, & Democracy in American Literature. 1994. write for info. (*0-318-72329-8*) Col U Pr.

***Portelli, John P., ed.** Philosophy of Education: Introductory Readings. 386p. (Orig.). (C). 1988. pap. text ed. 23.95x (*0-920490-84-0*) Temeron Bks.

***Portelli, John P. & Bailin, Sharon, eds.** Reason & Values: New Essays in Philosophy of Education. 228p. (Orig.). (C). 1993. pap. text ed. 20.95x (*1-55059-066-9*) Temeron Bks.

***Porten, Bezalel & Yardeni, Ada.** Textbook of Aramaic Documents from Ancient Egypt Vol. 1: Letters. ix, 143p. 1986. pap. text ed. 49.00x (*965-222-075-2*) Hebrew Union Coll Pr.

— Textbook of Aramaic Documents from Ancient Egypt Vol. 2: Contracts. liv, 191p. 1989. pap. text ed. 78.00x (*965-350-003-1*) Hebrew Union Coll Pr.

— Textbook of Aramaic Documents from Ancient Egypt Vol. 3: Literature, Accounts, Lists. xvi, 295p. 1993. pap. text ed. 79.00x (*965-350-014-7*) Hebrew Union Coll Pr.

***Portenier, Bob.** Take Control: You don't Have to be a Victim of Crime. Littlejohn, Shannon, ed. (Illus.). 128p. (Orig.). 1994. pap. 9.95 (*1-880652-38-2*) Wichita Eagle.

Portenier, C., jt. auth. see Anger, B.

Portenier, Lillian G. Pupils of Low Mentality in High School. LC 76-177158. (Columbia University. Teachers College. Contributions to Education Ser.: No. 568). reprint ed. 37.50 (*0-404-55568-3*) AMS Pr.

Portenko, L. A. Birds of the Chukchi Peninsula & Wrangel Island, Vol. 2. 1989. 39.50 (*81-205-0088-1*, Pub. by Oxford IBH II) S Asia.

Portenko, N. Generalized Diffusion Processes. LC 90-21198. (MMONO Ser.). 180p. 1990. 84.00 (*0-8218-4538-1*, MMONO-83) Am Math.

Porteous, A. Forest Folklore, Mythology & Romance. 1977. lib. bdg. 59.95 (*0-8490-1858-7*) Gordon Pr.

Porteous, A., ed. Developments in Environmental Control & Public Health, Vol. 1. (Illus.). 311p. 1979. 83.00 (*0-85334-834-0*, Pub. by Elsevier Applied Sci UK) Elsevier.

— Developments in Environmental Control & Public Health, Vol. 2. (Illus.). 311p. 1981. 83.00 (*0-85334-941-X*, Pub. by Elsevier Applied Sci UK) Elsevier.

Porteous, Andrew. Dictionary of Environmental Science & Technology. (Illus.). 416p. 1991. 75.00 (*0-335-09231-4*); pap. 33.00 (*0-335-09230-6*) Wiley.

— Dictionary of Environmental Science & Technology. rev. ed. 439p. 1992. pap. text ed. 37.95 (*0-471-93544-1*) Wiley.

Porteous, Andrew, ed. Desalination Technology: Developments & Practice. (Illus.). 271p. 1983. 74.00 (*0-85334-175-3*, I-453-82, Pub. by Elsevier Applied Sci UK) Elsevier.

***Porteous, Brenda.** Fun Dough: Over One Hundred Salt Dough Projects for All the Family. 1994. 18.95 (*1-870586-01-8*, Pub. by D Porteous Edits UK) Seven Hills Bk.

Porteous, Colin, jt. ed. see MacGregor, Kerr.

***Porteous, David J.** The Geography of Finance: Spatial Dimensions of Intermediary Behaviour. 240p. 1995. boxed, pap. 59.95 (*1-85972-046-3*, Pub. by Avebury Pub UK) Ashgate Pub Co.

***Porteous, I.** Clifford Algebras. (Studies in Advanced Mathematics: No. 50). 300p. Date not set. write for info. (*0-521-55177-3*) Cambridge U Pr.

Porteous, Ian. Geometric Differentiation: For the Intelligence of Curves & Surfaces. (Illus.). 200p. (C). 1994. 54.95 (*0-521-39063-X*) Cambridge U Pr.

Porteous, J. Douglas. Environment & Behavior: Planning & Everyday Urban Life. LC 76-1752. (C). 1977. text ed. write for info. (*0-201-05867-7*) Addison-Wesley.

— Landscapes of the Mind: Worlds of Sense & Metaphor. 228p. 1990. 40.00 (*0-8020-5857-4*) U of Toronto Pr.

— Planned to Death: The Annihilation of a Place Called Howdendyke. 254p. 1989. 47.50 (*0-8020-2661-3*) U of Toronto Pr.

***Porteous, J. R.** Introduction to Management Skills. 1995. 15.95 (*0-533-11060-2*) Vantage.

Porteous, Jeffrey. Taking Stock: A True Tale of Seattle's Investment Community. (Illus.). 1989. text ed. 17.95 (*0-685-29799-3*) NW Ctr Rsch Journalism.

Porteous, R. S. Cattleman. large type ed. 368p. 1982. 23.95 (*0-7089-8070-8*, Charnwood) Ulverscroft.

Porteous, Skipp. Jesus Doesn't Live Here Anymore: From Fundamentalist to Freedom Writer. 313p. 1991. 24.95 (*0-87975-689-6*) Prometheus Bks.

***Porter.** Addy, 6 vols., Set. 1994. 74.95 (*1-56247-088-4*) Pleasant Co.

— At Foot of Rainbow. 20.95 (*0-685-71942-1*) Amereon Ltd.

— Basic Technical Mathematics. 2nd ed. (C). 1995. student ed, text ed. 18.50 (*0-673-46376-1*) HarpCollege.

— Corrosion Resistance of Zinc & Zinc Alloys. (Corrosion Technology Ser.: Vol. 6). 528p. 1994. 185.00 (*0-8247-9213-0*) Dekker.

— Epilepsy: One Hundred Elementary Principles. 2nd ed. 200p. 1989. text ed. 54.50 (*0-7020-1365-X*, Bailliere-Tindall) Saunders.

— European Imperialism 1816-1914. (Studies in European History). (C). 1995. pap. 10.95 (*0-333-48104-6*) Humanities.

— Frommer's Portugal, 94-95. (Illus.). 1994. pap. 17.00 (*0-671-86797-0*, P-H Travel) P-H Gen Ref & Trav.

— Frommer's Switzerland & Leichten, 94-95. (Illus.). 1994. pap. 19.00 (*0-671-79769-7*, P-H Travel) P-H Gen Ref & Trav.

— Lower & Middle Egypt. (Topographical Bibliography of Ancient Egyptian Hieroglyphic Texts Ser.: Reliefs & Paintings, Vol. 4). reprint ed. fiche 35.00 (*0-900416-20-3*, Pub. by Aris & Phillips UK) David Brown.

— Management of Back Pain. 2nd ed. (Illus.). 368p. 1994. text ed. 95.00 (*0-443-04630-1*) Churchill.

— Memphis, Vol. 3, Pt. 1: Abu Rawash to Abusir. 2nd ed. (Topographical Bibliography of Ancient Egyptian Hieroglyphic Texts Ser.: Reliefs & Paintings, Vol. 3, Pt. 1). 1974. 65.00 (*0-900416-19-X*, Pub. by Aris & Phillips UK) David Brown.

— Memphis, Vol. 3, Pt. 2: Saqqara to Dahshur. (Topographical Bibliography of Ancient Egyptian Hieroglyphic Texts Ser.: Reliefs & Paintings, Vol. 3, Pt. 2). 1981. All Fascicles. 199.00 (*0-900416-23-8*, Pub. by Aris & Phillips UK) David Brown.

— Memphis, Vol. 3, Pt. 2, Fas. 1: Saqqara to Dahshur. (Topographical Bibliography of Ancient Egyptian Hieroglyphic Texts Ser.: Reliefs & Paintings, Vol. 3, Pt. 2). 1978. pap. 65.00 (*0-900416-13-0*, Pub. by Aris & Phillips UK) David Brown.

— Memphis, Vol. 3, Pt. 2, Fas. 2: Saqqara to Dahshur. (Topographical Bibliography of Ancient Egyptian Hieroglyphic Texts Ser.: Reliefs & Paintings, Vol. 3, Pt. 2). 1979. pap. 75.00 (*0-900416-14-9*, Pub. by Aris & Phillips UK) David Brown.

— Memphis, Vol. 3, Pt. 2, Fas. 3: Saqqara to Dahshur. (Topographical Bibliography of Ancient Egyptian Hieroglyphic Texts Ser.: Reliefs & Paintings, Vol. 3, Pt. 2). 1981. pap. 85.00 (*0-900416-24-6*, Pub. by Aris & Phillips UK) David Brown.

— Nubia Deserts & Outside Egypt. (Topographical Bibliography of Ancient Egyptian Hieroglyphic Texts Ser.: Reliefs & Paintings, Vol. 7). 1983. reprint ed. 70.00 (*0-900416-04-1*, Pub. by Aris & Phillips UK) David Brown.

— One Hundred Maxims in Neurology: Behavioral Neurology. 1993. 35.95 (*0-340-57720-7*) Mosby Yr Bk.

— One Hundred Maxims in Neurology: Stroke. 1993. 35.95 (*0-8016-7281-3*) Mosby Yr Bk.

— Parkinson's Disease. LC 92-49799. (One Hundred Maxims in Neurology Ser.). 169p. 1992. 35.95 (*0-8016-7279-1*) Mosby Yr Bk.

— Theban Necropolis, Vol. 01-1: Private Tombs. 2nd ed. (Topographical Bibliography of Ancient Egyptian Hieroglyphic Texts Ser.: Reliefs & Paintings, Vol. 1-1). 1985. reprint ed. 75.00 (*0-900416-10-6*, Pub. by Aris & Phillips UK) David Brown.

— Theban Necropolis, Vol. 01-2: Royal Tombs & Smaller Cemeteries. 2nd ed. (Topographical Bibliography of Ancient Egyptian Hieroglyphic Texts Ser.: Reliefs & Paintings, Vol. 1-2). 1973. reprint ed. 99.00 (*0-900416-15-7*, Pub. by Aris & Phillips UK) David Brown.

— Theban Temples. 2nd ed. (Topographical Bibliography of Ancient Egyptian Hieroglyphic Texts Ser.: Reliefs & Paintings, Vol. 2). 1972. 65.00 (*0-900416-18-1*, Pub. by Aris & Phillips UK) David Brown.

— Upper Egypt Chief Temples. (Topographical Bibliography of Ancient Egyptian Hieroglyphic Texts Ser.: Reliefs & Paintings, Vol. 6). 1970. reprint ed. 39.95 (*0-900416-30-0*, Pub. by Aris & Phillips UK) David Brown.

— Vietnam's Rural Transformation. Kerkvliet, ed. (Transitions: Asia & Asian America Ser.). (C). 1995. text ed. 54.95 (*0-8133-8950-X*) Westview.

— Year Book of Vascular Surgery, 1994. 400p. 1994. 63.95 (*0-8151-0683-1*, Yr Bk Med Pubs) Mosby Yr Bk.

— Year Book of Vascular Surgery, 1995. 400p. 1995. 65.95 (*0-8151-0684-X*, Yr Bk Med Pubs) Mosby Yr Bk.

— Year Book of Vascular Surgery, 1996. 400p. 1996. 67.95 (*0-8151-0685-8*, Yr Bk Med Pubs) Mosby Yr Bk.

— Year Book of Vascular Surgery, 1997. 400p. 1997. 64.95 (*0-8151-6800-4*, Yr Bk Med Pubs) Mosby Yr Bk.

— Yearbook of Vascular Surgery, 1993. 456p. 1993. 64.95 (*0-8151-0682-3*) Mosby Yr Bk.

Porter, ed. The Language of the Greek New Testament: Classic Essays. (JSNT Supplement Ser.: No. 60). 220p. (C). 1991. 22.50 (*1-85075-325-3*, Pub. by Sheffield Acad UK) CUP Services.

Porter & Carson, eds. Biblical Greek Language & Linguistics: Open Questions in Current Research. 280p. 1993. 35.00 (*1-85075-390-3*, Pub. by Sheffield Acad UK) CUP Services.

Porter & O'Grady. The Nurse Manager's Problem Solver. 360p. 1995. 26.95 (*0-8016-7945-1*) Mosby Yr Bk.

Porter, jt. auth. see Finston.

Porter, jt. auth. see Pollard, Dave.

Porter, jt. auth. see Skinner.

Porter, jt. auth. see Wortabet.

Porter, jt. auth. see Zachariades.

Porter, et al. Legal Writing & Oral Advocacy. 1989. write for info. (*0-8205-0406-8*, 676); write for info. (*0-8205-0407-6*) Bender.

— Literate Mind: Reading, Writing, Critical Thinking. 2nd ed. 384p. 1990. per. 24.95 (*0-8403-6175-0*) Kendall-Hunt.

Porter, A. & Holland, R., eds. Theory & Practice in the History of European Expansion Overseas: Essays in Honour of R. E. Robinson. (Illus.). 214p. 1988. text ed. 35.00 (*0-7146-3346-1*, Pub. by F Cass Pubs UK) Intl Spec Bk.

Porter, A. & Wood, T. Chemistry Tests for First Examinations. (C). 1987. text ed. 35.00 (*0-85950-754-8*, Pub. by S Thornes Pubs UK) St Mut.

— Further Chemistry Test for GCSE - Answer Books. (C). 1990. text ed. 50.00 (*0-7487-0488-4*, Pub. by S Thornes Pubs UK) St Mut.

— Further Chemistry Tests for GCSE. (C). 1990. text ed. 35.00 (*0-7487-0161-3*, Pub. by S Thornes Pubs UK) St Mut.

Porter, A. D., tr. see Borchert, Wolfgang.

Porter, A. Kingsley. Medieval Architecture, 2 vols. LC 67-4391. (Illus.). 1969. 100.00 (*0-87817-019-7*) Hacker.

Porter, A. N. The Atlas of British Overseas Expansion. (Illus.). 272p. 1991. 50.00 (*0-13-051988-X*) S&S Trade.

— European Imperialism 1860-1914: Studies in European History. 136p. (C). 1995. pap. 10.95 (*0-391-03723-4*) Humanities.

Porter, A. N. & Holland, R. F., eds. Money, Finance & Empire, 1790-1960. 192p. 1985. 34.00 (*0-7146-3273-2*, Pub. by F Cass Pubs UK) Intl Spec Bk.

Porter, A. P. Greg LeMond: Premier Cyclist. (Sports Achievers Ser.). (Illus.). 56p. (J). (gr. 4-9). 1990. lib. bdg. 13.50 (*0-8225-0476-6*, Lerner Publctns) Lerner Group.

— Greg Lemond: Premier Cyclist. LC 89-13700. (J). (gr. 4-7). 1991. pap. 4.95 (*0-8225-9584-2*, Lerner Publctns) Lerner Group.

— Jump at de Sun: The Story of Zora Neale Hurston. (Trailblazers Ser.). 88p. (J). (gr. 4-7). 1992. lib. bdg. 17.50 (*0-87614-667-1*, Carolrhoda) Lerner Group.

— Jump at de Sun: The Story of Zora Neale Hurston. (J). (gr. 4-7). 1992. pap. 6.95 (*0-87614-546-2*, Carolrhoda) Lerner Group.

— Kwanzaa. (Holiday on My Own Ser.). (Illus.). 48p. (J). (gr. k-4). 1991. lib. bdg. 14.95 (*0-87614-668-X*, Carolrhoda); pap. 5.95 (*0-87614-545-4*, Carolrhoda) Lerner Group.

— Kwanzaa. (Illus.). (J). (gr. 2-4). 1993. audio, pap. 14.95 (*0-87499-249-4*) Live Oak Media.

— Kwanzaa. (Illus.). (J). (gr. 2-4). 1993. audio 22.95 (*0-87499-250-8*) Live Oak Media.

— Kwanzaa, 4 bks., Set. (Illus.). (J). (gr. 2-4). 1993. audio, pap. 33.95 (*0-87499-251-6*) Live Oak Media.

— Minnesota. Lerner Geography Department Staff, ed. (Hello U. S. A. Ser.). (Illus.). 72p. (J). (gr. 3-6). 1992. lib. bdg. 17.50 (*0-8225-2718-9*, Lerner Publctns) Lerner Group.

— Nebraska. (Hello U. S. A. Ser.). (Illus.). 72p. (J). (gr. 3-6). 1991. lib. bdg. 17.50 (*0-8225-2708-1*, Lerner Publctns) Lerner Group.

— Zina Garrison. (Sports Achievers Ser.). 56p. (J). (gr. 4-9). 1991. lib. bdg. 13.50 (*0-8225-0499-5*, Lerner Publctns) Lerner Group.

— Zina Garrison: Ace. (Illus.). 64p. (J). (gr. 4-9). 1992. pap. 4.95 (*0-8225-9596-6*, Lerner Publctns) Lerner Group.

Porter, A. S. Lithographic Presswork. 316p. reprint ed. pap. 90.10 (*0-7837-0363-5*, 2040685) Bks Demand.

Porter, A. Toomer. Led on! Step by Step: Scenes from Clerical, Military, Educational & Plantation Life in the South. LC 75-89383. (Black Heritage Library Collection). 1977. 21.95 (*0-8369-8643-1*) Ayer.

Porter, Alan G. & Rezmer, Martin G. BASIC Business Subroutines for the Apple II & Apple IIe. 160p. 1983. pap. write for info. (*0-201-05663-1*) Addison-Wesley.

Porter, Alan L., jt. auth. see Becker, Henk A.

Porter, Alan L., jt. auth. see Kuehn, Thomas J.

Porter, Alan L., et al. Forecasting & Management of Technology. (Series in Engineering & Technology). 448p. 1991. text ed. 84.95 (*0-471-51223-0*) Wiley.

Porter, Albert O. County Government in Virginia: A Legislative History, 1607-1904. (Columbia University. Studies in the Social Sciences: No. 526). reprint ed. 26.00 (*0-404-51526-6*) AMS Pr.

Porter, Albert W. Expressive Watercolor Techniques. LC 81-70891. (Illus.). 128p. 1982. 23.00 (*0-87192-136-7*) Davis Mass.

— Pattern: Principles of Design. LC 75-21118. (Concepts of Design Ser.). (Illus.). 80p. (gr. 7-12). 1975. 10.95 (*0-87192-077-8*) Davis Mass.

***Porter, Alexandra B.** The Human Collision: The Internal Struggle to Merge with My Inner Self. LC 94-96226. (Illus.). 136p. (Orig.). 1994. pap. 7.95 (*1-886261-00-8*) LAVIE.

Porter, Alison I., jt. auth. see Rubin, Leona G.

Porter, Andrew. Musical Events. 1990. 16.95 (*0-671-69656-4*) S&S Trade.

— Victorian Shipping, Business & Imperial Policy: Donald Currie, the Castle Line & Southern Africa. LC 86-15619. (Royal Historical Society Studies in History). 352p. 1986. text ed. 39.95 (*0-312-84442-5*) St Martin.

Porter, Andrew & Von Rhein, John, eds. Bravi: Lyric Opera of Chicago. LC 94-6516. 1994. 50.00 (*1-55859-771-9*) Abbeville Pr.

Porter, Andrew, tr. see Verdi, Giuseppe.

Porter, Andrew, tr. see Wagner, Richard.

Porter, Andrew, et al. The New Grove Masters of Italian Opera. (New Grove Composer Biography Ser.). (Illus.). 1983. pap. 16.95 (*0-393-30089-7*) Norton.

Porter, Anna H., ed. Memories of Revolution: Russian Women Remember. LC 92-46113. (Illus.). 192p. 1993. 49.95 (*0-415-08806-2*, B2428); pap. 15.95 (*0-415-08807-0*, B2432) Routledge.

Porter, Anne. An Altogether Different Language: Poems 1934-1994. LC 94-14561. (Illus.). 128p. 1994. 16.95 (*0-944072-44-5*); pap. 10.95 (*0-944072-45-3*) Zoland Bks.

Porter, Anthony. The Best C Plus Plus Tips Ever. 1993. text ed. 29.95 (*0-07-881820-6*) Osborne-McGraw.

Porter, Arthur K. Crosses & Culture of Ireland. LC 68-56480. (Illus.). 1979. reprint ed. 36.95 (*0-405-08860-4*, Pub. by Blom Pubns UK) Ayer.

Porter, B. E. & Robinson, M. B. Protected Persons & Their Property in New South Wales. xvi, 176p. 1987. pap. 41.50 (*0-455-20719-4*, Pub. by Law Bk Co) W W Gaunt.

Porter, Barbara. All Kinds of Answers. LC 92-6976. (Illus.). 29p. (J). (gr. 1-3). 1992. 11.95 (*0-87579-538-2*) Deseret Bk.

Porter, Barbara A., ed. International Journal of Childbirth Education. 48p. 1985. 5.00 (*0-685-14722-3*) Intl Childbirth.

Porter, Barbara J. Grandpa & Me & the Wishing Star. LC 90-81831. (Illus.). 32p. (J). (ps). 1990. 10.95 (*0-87579-269-3*) Deseret Bk.

Porter, Barbara N. The Power of Symbols: Figurative Aspects of Esarhaddon's Babylonian Policy (681-669 B.C.) LC 92-85335. (Memoirs Ser.: Vol. 208). (Illus.). 420p. 1993. 30.00 (*0-87169-208-2*, M208-POB) Am Philos.

Porter, Barry. Dark Souls. 1989. pap. 3.95 (*0-8217-2651-X*) Zebra.

— Junkyard. 1989. pap. 3.95 (*0-8217-2816-4*) Zebra.

Porter, Basil & Seidelman, William E. The Politics of Reform in Medical Education & Health Services: The Negev Project. LC 91-4826. (Medical Education Ser.). 144p. (C). 1991. text ed. 29.95 (*0-8261-7730-1*) Springer Pub.

Porter, Benita. Colorstruck. 662p. (Orig.). 1991. pap. 19.95 (*0-9629199-0-X*) BQ Pub Co.

— Skindeep. 599p. 1991. pap. 19.95 (*0-9629199-1-8*) BQ Pub Co.

Porter, Benjamin F. Reminiscences of Men & Things in Alabama: Basic Historical Document (1829-1853) Walls, Sara, ed. (Illus.). 1983. 19.50 (*0-916620-56-5*) Portals Pr.

Porter, Bern. The Book of Do's. (Illus.). 400p. (Orig.). 1982. pap. 19.95 (*0-937966-11-8*) Tilbury Hse.

— Eighty-Nine Offenses. 1974. pap. 0.50 (*0-911856-11-0*) Abyss.

— Found Poems. (Illus.). 1972. 50.00 (*0-87110-079-7*); pap. 20.00 (*0-87110-080-0*) Ultramarine Pub.

— Gee-Whizzels. pap. 15.00 (*0-88448-070-4*) Tilbury Hse.

— Here Comes Everybody's Don't Book. (Illus.). 432p. (Orig.). 1984. pap. 19.95 (*0-937966-15-0*) Tilbury Hse.

— I've Left. 1971. 15.00 (*0-87110-076-2*); pap. 6.00 (*0-87110-077-0*) Ultramarine Pub.

— Less Than Overweight. 500p. 1993. 30.00 (*0-9638236-0-4*) Plaster Cramp.

— Neverends. (Illus.). 50p. (Orig.). 1988. pap. 3.00 (*0-926935-03-8*) Runaway Spoon.

— Numbers. (Illus.). 52p. (Orig.). 1989. pap. 3.00 (*0-926935-20-8*) Runaway Spoon.

— Sounds That Arouse Me: Selected Writings. LC 91-67868. 128p. (Orig.). 1992. pap. 9.95 (*0-88448-101-8*) Tilbury Hse.

— Sweet End. (Illus.). 400p. (Orig.). 1989. pap. 29.95 (*0-937966-27-4*) Tilbury Hse.

Porter, Bern & Malok. Vocrescends. 32p. (Orig.). 1991. pap. 3.00 (*0-926935-42-9*) Runaway Spoon.

Porter, Bern, jt. ed. see Leite, George.

Porter, Bernard. Britain, Europe & the World, 1850-1986: Illusions of Grandeur. 2nd ed. 184p. 1987. pap. text ed. 17.95 (*0-04-909040-2*) Routledge Chapman & Hall.

— Britannia's Burden: The Political Evolution of Modern Britain. 448p. 1994. 69.95 (*0-340-56196-3*, B4007, Pub. by E Arnold UK); pap. 24.95 (*0-340-56197-1*, B4011, Pub. by E Arnold UK) Routledge Chapman & Hall.

— The Lion's Share: A Short History of British Imperialism, 1850-1983. 2nd ed. 448p. (C). 1984. pap. text ed. 25.50 (*0-582-49387-0*, 73598) Longman.

— The Origins of the Vigilant State: The Metropolitan Police Special Branch before the First World War. (Illus.). 272p. 1991. reprint ed. 59.00 (*0-85115-283-X*) Boydell & Brewer.

— Plots & Paranoia: A History of Political Espionage in Britain, 1790-1988. 304p. 1989. 34.95 (*0-04-445258-6*) Routledge Chapman & Hall.

— The Refugee Question in Mid-Victorian Politics. LC 78-73947. 254p. reprint ed. pap. 72.40 (*0-317-55484-0*, 2029224) Bks Demand.

Porter, Bill. Road to Heaven: Encounters with Chinese Hermits. LC 92-42339. (Illus.). 256p. (Orig.). 1993. pap. 14.00 (*1-56279-041-2*) Mercury Hse Inc.

Porter, Brian. Mighty. 645p. (C). 1991. text ed. 34.95 (*1-881814-99-8*); pap. text ed. 24.95 (*0-685-62417-X*) Pace Pr MA.

Porter, Brian, ed. see Wight, Martin.

Porter, Bruce. Bill & the Burning Bush. (Illus.). 40p. (Orig.). (J). (gr. 1 up). 1987. pap. 3.95 (*0-939925-12-5*) R C Law & Co.

— Blow. 1994. mass mkt. 5.99 (*0-06-109164-2*) HarpC.

— Blow: How a Small Town Boy Made 100 Million Dollars with the Medellin Cartel & Lost it All. 1993. 20.00 (*0-06-179300-0*, HarpT) HarpC.

— Butch & the Bad Baloney. (Illus.). 40p. (Orig.). (J). (gr. 1 up). 1987. pap. 3.95 (*0-939925-15-X*) R C Law & Co.

— Jonah Gets the Jitters. (Illus.). 40p. (Orig.). (J). (gr. 3 up). 1987. pap. 3.95 (*0-939925-14-1*) R C Law & Co.

— The Parable of Pa Diggle's Son. (Illus.). 40p. (Orig.). (J). (gr. 3 up). 1987. pap. 3.95 (*0-939925-11-7*) R C Law & Co.

— Red Armies in Crisis. (Significant Issues Ser.: Vol. 13, No. 10). 128p. 1992. pap. text ed. 18.50 (*0-89206-175-8*) CSI Studies.

— Samuel & the Strange Sound. (Illus.). 40p. (Orig.). (J). (gr. 3 up). 1987. pap. 3.95 (*0-939925-13-3*) R C Law & Co.

— Squirt & the Super Soldier. (Illus.). 40p. (Orig.). (J). (gr. 3 up). 1987. pap. 3.95 (*0-939925-16-8*) R C Law & Co.

— War & the Rise of the State: The Military Foundations of Modern Politics. 350p. 1994. text ed. 27.95 (*0-02-925095-1*) Free Pr.

Porter, Bruce & Mooney, Raymond, eds. Machine Learning, 1990: Proceedings of the Seventh International Conference. 404p. 1990. 39.95 (*1-55860-141-4*) Morgan Kaufmann.

Porter, Bruce, jt. auth. see Curvin, Robert.

Porter, Bruce, et al. Art in California. (Illus.). 670p. (C). 1988. reprint ed. 65.00 (*0-9610520-2-3*) Westphal Pub.

Porter, Bruce D. The U. S. S. R. in Third World Conflicts: Soviet Arms & Diplomacy in Local Wars, 1945-1980. LC 83-26265. (Illus.). 256p. 1984. 49.95 (*0-521-26308-5*) Cambridge U Pr.

— The U. S. S. R. in Third World Conflicts: Soviet Arms & Diplomacy in Local Wars, 1945-1980. LC 83-26265. (Illus.). 256p. 1986. pap. 15.95 (*0-521-31064-4*) Cambridge U Pr.

Porter, Burton. The Good Life: Alterenatives in Ethics. 2nd ed. 301p. (C). 1995. text ed. 36.95 (*1-880157-15-2*) Ardsley.

Porter, Burton F. The Good Life: Alternatives in Ethics. 239p. (C). 1991. reprint ed. pap. text ed. 28.95x (*0-912675-99-3*) Ardsley.

— Philosophy: A Literary & Conceptual Approach. 2nd ed. 496p. (C). 1980. pap. text ed. 20.00 (*0-15-570553-9*) HB Coll Pubs.

— Reasons for Living: A Basic Ethics. 747p. (C). 1988. pap. write for info. (*0-02-396050-7*) Macmillan.

Porter, Burton F., ed. Religion & Reason: An Anthology. LC 92-50011. 576p. (C). 1992. pap. text ed. 34.00 (*0-312-04885-8*) St Martin.

Porter, Carlos W., ed. Made in Russia: The Holocaust. 415p. 1988. pap. 10.00 (*0-939484-30-7*) Inst Hist Rev.

Porter, Carol & Cleland, Janell. Portfolio As a Learning Strategy. LC 94-3522. 175p. 1994. pap. text ed. 17.50 (*0-86709-348-X*) Boynton Cook Pubs.

Porter, Carol & Hamel, Mike. Women's Ministry Handbook. 1992. 18.99 (*0-89693-885-9*) SP Pubns.

Porter, Carolyn, ed. see Anderson, Camille J. & Price, Don L.

Porter, Carolyn, ed. see Reid, T. J.

Porter, Caryl. Harvest from a Small Vineyard. 256p. (Orig.). 1992. pap. 9.99 (*0-87788-342-4*) Shaw Pubs.

Porter, Catherine & Minich, Elizabeth. English Connections, Bk. 3: Grammar for Education. LC 94-20479. 1994. pap. 9.66 (*0-8092-4207-9*) Contemp Bks.

Porter, Catherine, tr. see Borch-Jacobsen, Mikkel.

Porter, Catherine, tr. see David-Menard, Monique.

Porter, Catherine, tr. see Ducrot, Oswald & Todorov, Tzvetan.

Porter, Catherine, tr. see Felman, Shoshana.

Porter, Catherine, tr. see Genette, Gerard.

Porter, Catherine, tr. see Goux, Jean-Joseph.

Porter, Catherine, tr. see Irigaray, Luce.

Porter, Catherine, tr. see Kofman, Sarah.

Porter, Catherine, tr. see Latour, Bruno.

Porter, Catherine, tr. see Lipovetsky, Gilles.

Porter, Catherine, tr. see Robin, Regine.

Porter, Catherine, tr. see Todorov, Tzvetan.

Porter, Cathy. Women in Revolutionary Russia. (Women in History Ser.). (Illus.). 48p. (YA). (gr. 7-12). 1987. pap. 7.95 (*0-521-31969-2*) Cambridge U Pr.

Porter, Cathy, tr. see Grekova, I.

Porter, Cathy, tr. see Kollontai, Alexandra.

Porter, Cathy, tr. see Vasilieva, Larissa.

Porter, Cedric W., Jr., et al. Oral Contraceptives: A Guide for Programs & Clinics. 4th ed. 56p. (ENG, POR & SPA.). 1982. 3.50 (*0-933853-12-2*) Pathfinder Fund.

Porter, Charles. A Revision of the South American Species of Trachyphyrus -(Hymenoptera, Ichneumonidae) (Memoir Ser.: No. 10). (Illus.). 387p. 1967. 45.00 (*1-56665-008-9*) Assoc Pubs FL.

Porter, Charles A. Chateaubriand: Composition, Imagination & Poetry. (Stanford French & Italian Studies: No. 9). vi, 146p. 1978. pap. 46.50 (*0-915838-37-0*) Anma Libri.

Porter, Charles O., jt. auth. see Blaustein, Albert P.

Porter, Charles T. Engineering Reminiscences. 1985. reprint ed. pap. 14.95 (*0-917914-35-X*) Lindsay Pubns.

Porter, Charles W., III. Fort Raleigh & the First English Settlement in the New World. (National Park Service Handbook Ser.: No. 130). (Illus.). 56p. 1985. pap. 3.00 (*0-16-003508-2*, S/N 024-005-00959-1) USGPO.

Porter, Charlotte, ed. see Browning, Elizabeth Barrett.

Porter, Charlotte, tr. see D'Annunzio, Gabriele.

Porter, Charlotte M. The Eagle's Nest: Natural History & American Ideas, 1812-1842. LC 85-16465. (History of American Science & Technology Ser.). 272p. 1986. 29.50 (*0-8173-0280-8*) U of Ala Pr.

Porter-Chase, Mary. The Return of Sinta Claus: A Family Winter Solstice Tale. (Illus.). (Orig.). (J). (gr. 3-12). 1991. pap. 6.00 (*0-9630798-0-8*) Samary Pr.

***Porter, Cheryl.** Gross Grub: Retch-ed Recipes That Taste Heavenly but Look Like Heck. LC 94-3455. (Kidbacks Ser.). (Illus.). (J). 1995. 4.99 (*0-679-86693-0*) Random.

Porter, Cheryl A. Jessie's Outlaw. 368p. (Orig.). 1993. pap. 4.50 (*0-8439-3541-3*) Dorchester Pub Co.

— Kansas Wildlife. 400p. (Orig.). 1994. mass mkt., pap. text ed. 4.50 (*0-8439-3651-7*) Dorchester Pub Co.

— Sara's Bounty. 448p. (Orig.). 1995. mass mkt., pap. text ed. 4.99 (*0-8439-3785-8*) Dorchester Pub Co.

Porter, Claude L. Cuckoo over Vienna. LC 89-92105. (Illus.). 266p. 1989. 17.95 (*0-9624007-0-X*) C L Porter.

Porter, Clyde. Top Golf: Peak Performance Through Brain - Body Integration. (Illus.). 150p. (Orig.). 1993. pap. 14.95 (*0-9637669-4-5*) Life Enhance.

Porter, Cole. The Complete Lyrics of Cole Porter. Kimball, Robert, ed. (Illus.). 535p. 1992. reprint ed. pap. 19.95 (*0-306-80483-2*) Da Capo.

— Let's Do It. LC 93-1073. (Illus.). 32p. 1993. 9.95 (*0-8118-0448-8*) Chronicle Bks.

— Music & Lyrics by Cole Porter, Vol. 1. 1991. pap. 16.95 (*0-394-70794-X*) Random.

Porter, Connie. Addy Learns a Lesson. (American Girls Collection Ser.). (Illus.). 70p. (Orig.). (J). (gr. 2-5). 1993. lib. bdg. 12.95 (*1-56247-078-7*); pap. 5.95 (*1-56247-077-9*) Pleasant Co.

— Addy Save the Day. (American Girls Collection Ser.). (Illus.). 72p. (J). (gr. 2-5). 1994. lib. bdg. 12.95 (*1-56247-084-1*); pap. 5.95 (*1-56247-083-3*) Pleasant Co.

— Addy's Boxed Set. (American Girl Collection). 460p. (J). (gr. 2-5). Date not set. lib. bdg. 74.95 (*0-685-75412-X*); boxed, pap. 34.95 (*1-56247-087-6*) Pleasant Co.

— Addy's Surprise: A Christmas Story. LC 93-5162. (American Girls Collection Ser.). (Illus.). (J). 1993. 12.95 (*1-56247-080-9*); pap. 5.95 (*1-56247-079-5*) Pleasant Co.

— Changes for Addy. (American Girls Collection Ser.). (Illus.). 80p. (Orig.). (J). (gr. 2-5). 1994. lib. bdg. 12.95 (*1-56247-086-8*); pap. 5.95 (*1-56247-085-X*) Pleasant Co.

— Happy Birthday, Addy! A Springtime Story. LC 93-44184. (American Girls Collection Ser.). (Illus.). (J). (gr. 2-5). 1994. 12.95 (*1-56247-082-5*); pap. 5.95 (*1-56247-081-7*) Pleasant Co.

— Meet Addy. (American Girls Collection Ser.). (Illus.). 69p. (Orig.). (J). (gr. 2-5). 1993. lib. bdg. 12.95 (*1-56247-076-0*); pap. 5.95 (*1-56247-075-2*) Pleasant Co.

Porter, Curt. The Blue Mules. LC 92-61996. 136p. (Orig.). 1994. pap. 8.95 (*1-56002-211-6*, Univ Edtns) Aegina Pr.

Porter, Cynthia J., ed. see De Shazo, Jerry.

Porter, D. A. Phase Transformations in Metal. 1992. pap. 42.95 (*0-412-45030-5*, Blackie & Son-Chapman NY) Routledge Chapman & Hall.

Porter, D. A. & Easterling, K. E. Phase Transformations in Metals & Alloys. LC 92-13376. 1992. write for info. (*0-442-31638-0*) Chapman & Hall.

Porter, D. M., et al, eds. Compendium of Peanut Diseases. LC 84-70853. 93p. 1984. pap. 30.00 (*0-89054-055-1*) Am Phytopathol Soc.

Porter, Dan, jt. auth. see Coleman, Loren.

Porter, Dan, jt. ed. see Coleman, Loren.

Porter, Daniel J. Fifty Familiar Sayings from the Bible. LC 93-6012. (Illus.). 128p. (Orig.). 1993. pap. 6.95 (*0-8091-3422-5*) Paulist Pr.

Porter, Darwin. Scotland & Wales on Fifty Dollars a Day '92-'93. (Frommer's Budget Travel Guide Ser.). (Illus.). 672p. 1992. pap. 18.00 (*0-13-334814-8*, P-H Travel) P-H Gen Ref & Trav.

— Scotland & Wales on Twenty-Five Dollars a Day. 300p. 1986. pap. 10.95 (*0-685-11259-4*) S&S Trade.

Porter, David. The Big Steal: The Screenplay. 1991. pap. 12.95 (*0-7022-2372-7*, Pub. by Univ Queensland Pr AT) Intl Spec Bk.

— Dickinson: The Modern Idiom. LC 80-24322. 325p. 1981. 37.50 (*0-674-20444-1*) HUP.

— Group Interaction Modelling of Polymer Properties. LC 94-43930. 1995. write for info. (*0-8247-9599-7*) Dekker.

An Asterisk (*) at the beginning of an entry indicates that the title is appearing in BIP for the first time.

— Journal of a Cruise. LC 85-32024. (Classics of Naval Literature Ser.). 646p. 1986. 32.95 (0-87021-331-8) Naval Inst Pr.
— U. S. Economic Foreign Aid. LC 90-3612. (Foreign Economic Policy of the United States Ser.). 292p. 1990. reprint ed. 25.00 (0-8240-7466-1) Garland.
— The Vienna Passage. 288p. (Orig.). 1995. pap. 9.99 (0-89107-824-X) Crossway Bks.
Porter, David, ed. Between Men & Feminism. LC 92-10405. 208p. 1992. 49.95 (0-415-06987-4, A9844); pap. 15.95 (0-415-06988-2, A9848) Routledge.
— Vision on Fire: Emma Goldman on the Spanish Revolution. LC 82-74015. (Illus.). 383p. (Orig.). 1983. pap. 7.50 (0-9610348-2-3) Commonground Pr.
Porter, David & Stirling, David S. Integral Equations: A Practical Treatment, from Spectral Theory to Applications. (Texts in Applied Mathematics Ser.: No. 5). (Illus.). 384p. (C). 1990. pap. 29.95 (0-521-33742-9) Cambridge U Pr.
Porter, David H. Horace's Poetic Journey: A Reading of Odes 1-3. (Illus.). 300p. 1987. text ed. 45.00 (0-691-06702-3) Princeton U Pr.
— Horace's Poetic Journey: A Reading of Odes 1-3. LC 86-43136. Date not set. reprint ed. pap. 84.40 (0-7837-9424-X, 2060165) Bks Demand.
— Only Connect: Three Studies in Greek Tragedy. LC 86-28918. 128p. (Orig.). 1987. lib. bdg. 39.00 (0-8191-5950-6); pap. text ed. 16.00 (0-8191-5951-4) U Pr of Amer.
Porter, David L. Mixed Waste Treatment. 1995. write for info. (0-87371-477-6) Lewis Pubs.
— Seventy-Sixth Congress & World War II, 1939-1940. LC 79-4843. 248p. 1980. text ed. 27.00 (0-8262-0281-0) U of Mo Pr.
Porter, David L., comp. A Cumulative Index to the Biographical Dictionary of American Sports. LC 93-18030. 352p. 1993. text ed. 47.95 (0-313-28435-0, PBN/, Greenwood Pr) Greenwood.
***Porter, David L., ed.** African-American Sports Greats: A Biographical Dictionary. LC 95-7189. 1995. text ed. 59.95 (0-313-28987-5, Greenwood Pr) Greenwood.
— Biographical Dictionary of American Sports: Baseball. LC 86-12091. 730p. 1987. text ed. 75.00 (0-313-23771-9, PDS/, Greenwood Pr) Greenwood.
— Biographical Dictionary of American Sports: Basketball & Other Indoor Sports. LC 88-17776. 826p. 1989. text ed. 75.00 (0-313-26261-6, PID/, Greenwood Pr) Greenwood.
— Biographical Dictionary of American Sports: Football. LC 86-29386. 763p. 1987. text ed. 75.00 (0-313-25771-X, PFL/, Greenwood Pr) Greenwood.
— Biographical Dictionary of American Sports: Outdoor Sports. LC 87-317. 748p. 1988. text ed. 75.00 (0-313-26260-8, PRO/, Greenwood Pr) Greenwood.
— Biographical Dictionary of American Sports 1989-1992: Supplement for Baseball, Football, Basketball & Other Sports. LC 91-28742. 728p. 1992. text ed. 79.95 (0-313-26706-5, PAS/, Greenwood Pr) Greenwood.
Porter, David R. Hospital Architecture: Guidelines for Design & Renovation. LC 81-22906. (Illus.). 336p. 1982. pap. text ed. 43.00 (0-914904-53-1, 0644) Health Admin Pr.
Porter, David T. The Art of Emily Dickinson's Early Poetry. LC 66-13182. 222p. reprint ed. pap. 63.30 (0-7837-4125-1, 2057948) Bks Demand.
— Emerson & Literary Change. LC 78-6669. 245p. reprint ed. pap. 70.70 (0-7837-2314-8, 2057402) Bks Demand.
Porter, Dean A. Victor Higgins: An American Master. (Illus.). 320p. 1991. 49.50 (0-87905-362-3, Peregrine Smith) Gibbs Smith Pub.
Porter, Deirdre J. G., ed. see Alexander, Jason.
Porter, Dennis. Haunted Journeys: Desire & Transgression in European Travel Writing. 334p. (C). 1991. text ed. 39.50 (0-691-06850-X) Princeton U Pr.
— The Pursuit of Crime: Art & Ideology in Detective Fiction. LC 81-3399. 277p. reprint ed. pap. 79.00 (0-8357-3756-X, 2036482) Bks Demand.
— Rousseau's Legacy: Emergence & Eclipse of the Writer in France. (Illus.). 336p. 1995. 39.95 (0-19-509107-8) OUP.
Porter, Dennis, tr. see Miller, Jacques-Alain.
Porter, Diana, jt. auth. see Lee, Karen.
Porter, Dilwyn, jt. auth. see Newton, Scott.
Porter, Don, jt. ed. see Hughes, Arthur.
Porter, Donald. As If a Footnote to the Final Glory. 64p. 1974. 2.00 (0-915066-09-2) Assembling Pr.
Porter, Donald C. Ambush. large type ed. LC 93-26719. (White Indian Ser.: Bk. VIII). 1993. 21.95 (0-8161-5846-0, Large Print Bks) Hall.
— Seneca. large type ed. LC 93-27951. (White Indian Ser.). (Orig.). 1994. 21.95 (0-8161-5847-9, Large Print Bks) Hall.
— War Clouds. (WWI Ser.: No. 25). 1994. pap. 4.99 (0-553-56141-3, Bantam Domain) Bantam.
— White Indian. 1984. mass mkt. 4.99 (0-553-24650-X) Bantam.
— White Indian, Super Novel No. 1: Hawk's Journey. 1992. pap. 5.50 (0-553-29218-8) Bantam.
— The White Indians. (Red Stick Ser.: No. 26). 1994. mass mkt. 4.99 (0-553-56142-1) Bantam.
Porter, Donald J. The Cessna Citations. 1993. pap. 14.95 (0-07-050619-1) McGraw.
— The Cessna Citations. LC 93-18321. 1993. pap. 14.60 (0-8306-4147-5) TAB Bks.
— Learjets: The World's Executive Aircraft. 1990. pap. 11.95 (0-8306-2440-6) TAB Bks.
Porter, Donna V. & Earl, Robert O., eds. Food Labeling: Toward National Uniformity. 256p. 1992. pap. 27.00 (0-309-04737-4) Natl Acad Pr.
— Forestry Research: A Mandate for Change. 96p. 1990. pap. text ed. 14.95 (0-309-04248-8) Natl Acad Pr.
Porter, Dorothy. Driving Too Fast. 1989. pap. 11.95 (0-7022-2222-4, Pub. by Univ Queensland Pr AT) Intl Spec Bk.
— The Monkey's Mask. 272p. 1995. 19.95 (1-55970-304-0) Arcade Pub Inc.
— The Witch Number. (YA). 1993. pap. 10.95 (0-7022-2460-X, Pub. by Univ Queensland Pr AT) Intl Spec Bk.
Porter, Dorothy & Porter, Roy. Patient's Progress: Doctors & Doctoring in Eighteenth-Century England. LC 89-60692. (Illus.). 313p. 1989. 35.00 (0-8047-1744-3) Stanford U Pr.
Porter, Dorothy, jt. auth. see Porter, Roy.
Porter, Dorothy, et al, eds. Negro Protest Pamphlets: A Compendium. LC 79-75853. (American Negro: His History & Literature, Ser. No. 2). 1969. reprint ed. 11.95 (0-405-01888-6) Ayer.
Porter, Doug, et al. Development in Practice: Paved with Good Intentions. (Illus.). 288p. (C). 1991. text ed. 65.00 (0-415-03564-3, A5234) Routledge.
— Development in Practice: Paved with Good Intentions. 288p. 1991. pap. 25.00 (0-415-06626-3, A6425) Routledge.
***Porter, Douglas G.** How to Develop & Use the Gift of Administration: A Practical Guide for the Layperson. Spear, Cindy G., ed. LC 95-5503. 76p. (Orig.). 1995. pap. 5.95 (1-57052-030-5) Chrch Grwth VA.
— How to Develop & Use the Gift of Teaching: A Practical Guide for the Layperson. Spear, Cindy G., ed. LC 94-36192. 72p. (Orig.). 1995. pap. 5.95 (1-57052-021-6) Chrch Grwth VA.
Porter, Douglas J. Investing in the Harvest: Preparing for a Spiritual Harvest in Your Church & Community. Spear, Cindy G., ed. 56p. (Orig.). (C). 1991. pap. 59.95 (0-941005-37-2); pap. 1.99 (0-941005-38-0) Chrch Grwth VA.
***Porter, Douglas R.** Special Districts: A Useful Technique for Financing Infrastructure. 2nd ed. 90p. 1992. pap. text ed. 37.95 (0-87420-736-3, S38) Urban Land.
***Porter, Douglas R., ed.** State & Regional Initiatives for Managing Development: Policy Issues & Practical Concerns. 259p. 1992. pap. text ed. 45.95 (0-87420-727-4, S28) Urban Land.
Porter, Douglas R. & Cole, Susan. Affordable Housing: Twenty Examples from the Private Sector. LC 82-83409. (Illus.). 112p. reprint ed. pap. 32.00 (0-8357-3185-5, 2039455) Bks Demand.
Porter, Douglas R. & Marsh, Lindell L., eds. Development Agreements: Practice, Policy & Prospects. LC 89-51661. 160p. (Orig.). 1989. pap. text ed. 39.95 (0-87420-694-4, D59) Urban Land.
Porter, Douglas R. & Peiser, Richard B. Financing Infrastructure to Promote Community Growth. LC 83-51849. 1984. 13.95 (0-87420-626-X) Urban Land.
Porter, Douglas R. & Salveson, David A., eds. Collaborative Planning for Wetlands & Wildlife: Issues & Examples. LC 94-30143. 352p. (C). 1995. pap. text ed. 29.50 (1-55963-287-9) Island Pr.
Porter, Douglas R., et al. Covenants & Zoning for Research-Business Parks. 88p. 1986. pap. 43.95 (0-87420-648-0) Urban Land.
— Flexible Zoning: How It Works. LC 88-51229. 200p. (Orig.). 1988. pap. text ed. 45.95 (0-87420-686-3, F14) Urban Land.
— Working with the Community: A Developer's Guide. (Community Builders Handbook Supplement Ser.). 185p. 1985. pap. 56.95 (0-87420-646-4) Urban Land.
Porter, Duncan M. & Graham, Peter W., eds. The Portable Darwin. LC 93-17106. 640p. (Orig.). 1993. pap. 12.50 (0-14-015109-5, Penguin Bks) Viking Penguin.
Porter, Duncan M., jt. auth. see Wiggins, Ira L.
Porter, E. Buccaneer Bks. 1980. lib. bdg. 16.95 (0-89968-252-9, Lghtyr Pr) Buccaneer Bks.
— Pollyanna's Debt of Honor. 1980. lib. bdg. 16.95 (0-89968-253-7, Lghtyr Pr) Buccaneer Bks.
Porter, Ebenezer, et al. Letters on the Religious Revivals Which Prevailed about the Beginning of the Present Century: With Supplementary Material Compiled by Kurt R. Linde. xx, 316p. 1992. reprint ed. pap. 6.95 (0-9631745-0-9) Linde Pubns.
Porter, Edgar A. Foreign Teachers in China: Old Problems for a New Generation, 1979-1989. LC 89-78405. (Contributions to the Study of Education Ser.: No. 39). 216p. 1990. text ed. 49.95 (0-313-27386-3, PFT/, Greenwood Pr) Greenwood.
Porter, Edward A., jt. auth. see Fitch, Richard D.
Porter, Edwin H. The Fall River Tragedy: A History of the Borden Murders. LC 85-70910. (Illus.). 312p. 1985. reprint ed. 25.00 (0-9614811-0-2) King Philip Pub.
Porter, Eleanor. Pollyanna Grows Up. 1994. pap. 2.97 (1-55748-297-7) Barbour & Co.
Porter, Eleanor H. Dawn. 23.95 (0-8488-0309-4) Amereon Ltd.
— Hustler Joe, & Other Stories. LC 78-128750. (Short Story Index Reprint Ser.). 1977. 19.95 (0-8369-3641-8) Ayer.
— Just David. 1976. lib. bdg. 25.95 (0-89968-107-7, Lghtyr Pr) Buccaneer Bks.
— Little Pardner, & Other Stories. LC 70-142273. (Short Story Index Reprint Ser.). 1977. 20.95 (0-8369-3757-0) Ayer.
— Mary-Marie. 1976. lib. bdg. 14.25 (0-89968-102-6, Lghtyr Pr) Buccaneer Bks.
— Miss Billy-Married. 1976. lib. bdg. 16.75 (0-89968-104-2, Lghtyr Pr) Buccaneer Bks.
— Miss Billy's Decision. 1976. lib. bdg. 16.25 (0-89968-105-0, Lghtyr Pr) Buccaneer Bks.
— Oh Money! Money! 21.95 (0-8488-0305-1) Amereon Ltd.
— Pollyanna. (J). 19.95 (0-8488-1445-2) Amereon Ltd.
— Pollyanna. 1976. lib. bdg. 20.95 (0-89968-106-9, Lghtyr Pr) Buccaneer Bks.
— Pollyanna. (J). 1988. pap. 3.50 (0-14-035023-3, Puffin) Puffin Bks.
— Pollyanna. (J). 1994. 12.99 (0-517-11987-0) Random Hse Value.
— Pollyanna. (Illus.). (J). (gr. k-9). 1987. pap. 2.95 (0-590-44769-6) Scholastic Inc.
— Pollyanna Grows Up. (J). 19.95 (0-8488-1447-9) Amereon Ltd.
— Pollyanna Grows Up. 272p. (J). (gr. 5 up). 1989. pap. 3.50 (0-14-035024-1, Puffin) Puffin Bks.
— Pollyanna Grows Up. 308p. (J). (gr. 4 up). 1980. reprint ed. lib. bdg. 25.95 (0-89968-193-X, Lghtyr Pr) Buccaneer Bks.
— Pollyanna 'n Hollywood. (J). 15.95 (0-8488-1448-7) Amereon Ltd.
— Pollyanna's Debt of Honor. (J). 15.95 (0-8488-1446-0) Amereon Ltd.
— Road to Understanding. 21.95 (0-8488-0306-X) Amereon Ltd.
— Road to Understanding. 1976. lib. bdg. 16.75 (0-89968-108-5, Lghtyr Pr) Buccaneer Bks.
— Ship of Fools. 29.50 (0-8488-1129-1) Amereon Ltd.
Porter, Eleanor P. Miss Billy. 1976. lib. bdg. 16.25 (0-89968-103-4, Lghtyr Pr) Buccaneer Bks.
Porter, Eliot. Antarctica. (Illus.). 168p. 1988. 22.99 (0-517-66571-9) Random Hse Value.
— Appalachian Wilderness. 1988. 19.98 (0-88486-012-4) Arrowood Pr.
— Eliot Porter: Birds of North America. 1992. 19.98 (0-88486-070-1) Arrowood Pr.
— Eliot Porter's Southwest. (Illus.). 128p. 1991. pap. 29.95 (0-8050-1863-8, Owl) H Holt & Co.
— In Wildness Is the Preservation of the World: From Henry David Thoreau. 1989. pap. 24.95 (0-87156-610-9) Sierra.
— In Wildness Is the Preservation of the World: From Henry David Thoreau. LC 87-26592. (Exhibit Format Ser.). (Illus.). 168p. 1988. reprint ed. 35.00 (0-87156-793-8) Sierra.
— Maine. (Illus.). 160p. 1993. pap. 29.95 (0-8212-2018-7) Bulfinch Pr.
— Monuments of Egypt. LC 90-12871. (Illus.). 133p. 1990. 40.00 (0-8263-1232-2) U of NM Pr.
***Porter, Elisabeth.** Building Good Families in a Changing World. 224p. 1995. pap. 24.95 (0-522-84648-3) Paul & Co Pubs.
— Women & Moral Identity. 224p. 1991. pap. 22.95 (0-04-442332-2, Pub. by Allen & Unwin Aust Pty AT) Paul & Co Pubs.
Porter, Elizabeth. Classic Basket Quilts. 1991. pap. 16.95 (0-89145-973-1) Collector Bks.
Porter, Elliot & Auerbach, Ellen, photos. Mexican Celebrations. LC 90-12100. (Illus.). 115p. 1990. 40.00 (0-8263-1209-8) U of NM Pr.
— Mexican Churches. LC 87-13765. (Illus.). 109p. 1987. 27.50 (0-8263-1023-0) U of NM Pr.
Porter, Enid. Victorian Cambridge: Josiah Chater's Dieries, 1844-1883. (C). 1975. 40.00 (0-85033-213-3) St Mut.
Porter, Eric, jt. ed. see Schilling, Kyle E.
***Porter, Erika R.** All Visitors Welcome: Accessibility in State Park Interpretive Programs & Facilities. Helmich, Mary A. & Pozzi, Donna C., eds. (Illus.). 262p. (Orig.). (C). 1994. pap. 20.00 (0-941925-16-1) Cal Parks Rec.
Porter, Eugene. Treating the Young Male Victim of Sexual Assault: Issues & Intervention Strategies. LC 86-60720. (Safer Society Ser.: No. 2). (Illus.). 86p. 1994. reprint ed. pap. 12.50 (1-884444-08-3) Safer Soc.
Porter, Evan. Heal Your Mind, Heal Your Body: A Practical Guide to Wellness of Body, Mind, & Spirit. LC 94-65441. 290p. 1994. 19.95 (0-940683-20-2); pap. 9.95 (0-940683-21-0) Society Pubng.
— Syncreny: An Introduction. LC 86-62684. 220p. 1987. pap. 7.95 (0-940683-00-8) Society Pubng.
Porter, F., jt. auth. see Lake, E.
Porter, Fairfield. Art in Its Own Terms: Selected Criticism, 1935-1975. LC 92-38058. 288p. 1993. pap. 10.95 (0-944072-31-3) Zoland Bks.
Porter, Frank. Zinc Handbook: Properties, Processing & Use in Design. (Mechanical Engineering Ser.: Vol. 73). 648p. 1991. 190.00 (0-8247-8340-9) Dekker.
Porter, Frank, jt. auth. see Baird, W. David.
Porter, Frank W. The Bureau of Indian Affairs. (Know Your Government Ser.). (Illus.). 112p. (YA). (gr. 5 up). 1988. lib. bdg. 14.95 (0-87754-828-5) Chelsea Hse.
***Porter, Frank W., 3rd.** The Chippewa - Great Lakes. (Indians of North America Ser.). (Illus.). 144p. (YA). (gr. 5 up). 1995. 18.95 (0-7910-2650-7) Chelsea Hse.
Porter, Frank W. The Coast Salish Peoples. (Indians of North America Ser.). (Illus.). 104p. (J). (gr. 5 up). 1989. 17.95 (1-55546-701-6) Chelsea Hse.
Porter, Frank W., III. In Pursuit of the Past: An Anthropological & Bibliographic Guide to Maryland & Delaware. LC 85-10889. (Native American Bibliography Ser.: No. 8). 268p. 1986. 27.50 (0-8108-1825-6) Scarecrow.
***Porter, Frank W., 3rd.** Indians & Black Americans. (Indians of North America Ser.). (Illus.). 144p. (YA). (gr. 5 up). 1995. 18.95 (0-7910-2653-1) Chelsea Hse.
— Indians & Christianity. (Indians of North America Ser.). (Illus.). 144p. (YA). (gr. 5 up). 1995. 18.95 (0-7910-2651-5) Chelsea Hse.
— Indians & the Spanish. (Indians of North America Ser.). (Illus.). 144p. (YA). (gr. 5 up). 1995. 18.95 (0-7910-2654-X) Chelsea Hse.
Porter, Frank W., III. Maryland Indians Yesterday & Today. LC 83-60413. (Illus.). 1983. pap. 4.95 (0-938420-23-2) MD Hist.
— The Nanticoke. (Indians of North America Ser.). (Illus.). 96p. 1987. lib. bdg. 17.95 (1-55546-686-9) Chelsea Hse.
***Porter, Frank W., 3rd.** The Pawnee - Great Plains. (Indians of North America Ser.). (Illus.). 144p. (YA). (gr. 5 up). 1995. 18.95 (0-7910-1683-8) Chelsea Hse.
— The Santee Sioux - Great Plains. (Indians of North America Ser.). (Illus.). 144p. (YA). (gr. 5 up). 1995. 18.95 (0-7910-1685-4) Chelsea Hse.
— The Shoshone - Southwest. (Indians of North America Ser.). (Illus.). 144p. (YA). (gr. 5 up). 1995. 18.95 (0-7910-1687-0) Chelsea Hse.
Porter, Frank W., III, comp. Native American Basketry: An Annotated Bibliography. LC 87-37570. (Art Reference Collection: No. 10). 256p. 1988. text ed. 49.95 (0-313-25363-3, PBY/, Greenwood Pr) Greenwood.
Porter, Frank W., III, ed. The Art of Native American Basketry: A Living Legacy. LC 89-26008. (Contributions to the Study of Anthropology Ser.: No. 5). 368p. 1990. text ed. 69.50 (0-313-26716-2, PAH/, Greenwood Pr) Greenwood.
— Strategies for Survival: American Indians in the Eastern United States. LC 85-30189. (Contributions in Ethnic Studies: No. 15). 248p. 1986. text ed. 55.00 (0-313-25253-X, PST/, Greenwood Pr) Greenwood.
Porter, Frank W., 3rd & Aigner, Jean S. The Inuit (Eskimo) - Arctic. (Indians of North America Ser.). (Illus.). 144p. (YA). (gr. 5 up). 1995. 18.95 (1-55546-705-9) Chelsea Hse.
Porter, Frank W., III, ed. see Bonvillain, Nancy.
Porter, Frank W., III, jt. ed. see Bonvillain, Nancy.
Porter, Frank W., 3rd, ed. see Lacey, Theresa J.
Porter, Frank W., 3rd, et al. The Cahuilla - California. (Indians of North American Ser.). (Illus.). 144p. (YA). (gr. 5 up). 1989. 18.95 (1-55546-693-1) Chelsea Hse.
Porter, G. & Jennings, K. R. Progress in Reaction Kinetics, Vol. 2. LC 61-9784. 1964. 160.00 (0-08-010177-1, Pub. by Pergamon Repr UK) Franklin.
— Progress in Reaction Kinetics, Vol. 3. LC 61-9784. 1965. 216.00 (0-08-011030-4, Pub. by Pergamon Repr UK) Franklin.
— Progress in Reaction Kinetics, Vol. 4. LC 61-9784. 1967. 222.00 (0-08-012128-4, Pub. by Pergamon Repr UK) Franklin.
Porter, G. & Stevens, B. Progress in Reaction Kinetics, Vol. 1. LC 61-9784. 1961. 117.00 (0-08-009480-5, Pub. by Pergamon Repr UK) Franklin.
Porter, Gail, ed. Guide to NIST (National Institute of Standards & Technology) 116p. (Orig.). (C). 1994. pap. text ed. 50.00 (0-7881-0746-1) Diane Pub.
Porter, Gail & Layman, Sue. A Perfect Rose. Scoggan, Nita, ed. LC 86-61447. 100p. (Orig.). 1986. pap. 3.95 (0-910487-09-X) Royalty Pub.
Porter, Gareth. A Peace Denied: The United States, Vietnam, & the Paris Agreement. LC 75-3890. (Illus.). 371p. reprint ed. pap. 108.60 (0-685-20432-4, 2056434) Bks Demand.
— Vietnam: The Politics of Bureaucratic Socialism. LC 92-54976. (Politics & International Relations of Southeast Asia Ser.). 256p. 1993. 29.95 (0-8014-2168-3) Cornell U Pr.
Porter, Gareth & Brown, Janet W. Global Environmental Politics. 208p. (C). 1991. pap. text ed. 14.95 (0-8133-1035-0) Westview.
Porter, Gareth & Ganapin, Delfin J., Jr. Resources, Population, & the Philippines' Future: A Case Study. LC 88-51617. 78p. (Orig.). 1988. pap. text ed. 10.00 (0-915825-34-1) World Resources Inst.
Porter, Gareth, jt. auth. see Hildebrand, George C.
Porter, Garrett & Norris, Patricia. Why Me? Learning to Harness the Healing Power of the Human Spirit. LC 84-52877. 169p. (Orig.). 1985. pap. 10.95 (0-913299-19-7) Stillpoint.
Porter, Gary A., ed. Accounting Guide for Common Interest Realty Associations: An Analysis of the AICPA Guidelines. (C). 1991. pap. 12.95 (0-941301-18-4) CAI.
Porter, Gary A., et al. Homeowner's Association Tax Library. 1993. ring bd. 88.00 (1-56433-414-7) Prctnrs Pub Co.
— PPC's Homeowners' Association Tax Library. 1994. ring bd. 88.00 (1-56433-524-0) Prctnrs Pub Co.
Porter-Gaylord, Laurel. I Love My Daddy Because... LC 90-2865. (Illus.). 24p. (J). (ps). 1991. 6.99 (0-525-44624-9, DCB) Dutton Child Bks.
— I Love My Mommy Because... LC 90-2792. (Illus.). 24p. (J). (ps). 1991. 6.99 (0-525-44625-7, DCB) Dutton Child Bks.
Porter, Gene S. At the Foot of the Rainbow. 1990. reprint ed. lib. bdg. 18.95 (0-89968-543-9) Buccaneer Bks.
— Bird Woman. 27.95 (0-8488-1527-0) Amereon Ltd.
— Birds of the Bible. 50.95 (0-8488-0884-3) Amereon Ltd.
— Birds of the Bible. 1986. reprint ed. lib. bdg. 35.95 (0-89966-529-2) Buccaneer Bks.
— Birds of the Limberlost. 35.95 (0-8488-1526-2) Amereon Ltd.
— Firebird. 60.00 (0-8488-1528-9) Amereon Ltd.
— Freckles. 272p. (J). (gr. 5 up). 1992. pap. 3.99 (0-14-035144-2) Puffin Bks.
— Freckles. LC 93-42393. (J). 1994. 7.99 (0-517-10126-2, Pub. by Gramercy) Random Hse Value.
— A Girl of the Limberlost. 432p. (Orig.). (J). (gr. 5 up). 1992. pap. 3.99 (0-14-035143-4) Puffin Bks.
— A Girl of the Limberlost. (Orig.). 1991. pap. 9.99 (0-8423-1015-0) Tyndale.
— Girl of the Limberlost. (Illus.). 496p. (YA). 1992. 8.99 (0-517-07235-1, Pub. by Gramercy) Random Hse Value.
— Homing with the Birds. 34.95 (0-8488-1449-5) Amereon Ltd.
— Homing with the Birds. 1986. reprint ed. lib. bdg. 35.95 (0-89966-530-6) Buccaneer Bks.
— Jesus of the Emeralds. 80.00 (0-8488-1525-4) Amereon Ltd.
— Keeper of the Bees. 27.95 (0-89190-946-X) Amereon Ltd.
— Laddie. 1991. pap. 8.99 (0-8423-2664-2) Tyndale.

— Let Us Highly Resolve. 37.50 (*0-8488-1529-7*) Amereon Ltd.

— The Magic Garden. 1990. reprint ed. lib. bdg. 18.95 (*0-89968-544-7*) Buccaneer Bks.

— Morning Face. 18.95 (*0-8488-0872-X*) Amereon Ltd.

— Moths of the Limberlost. 40.95 (*0-8488-0699-9*) Amereon Ltd.

— Moths of the Limberlost. 1986. reprint ed. lib. bdg. 25.95 (*0-89966-512-8*) Buccaneer Bks.

— Music of Wild, Pt. 1. 17.95 (*0-8488-0611-5*) Amereon Ltd.

— Music of Wild, Pt. 2. 15.95 (*0-8488-0612-3*) Amereon Ltd.

— Music of Wild, Pt. 3. 15.95 (*0-8488-0613-1*) Amereon Ltd.

— The Song of the Cardinal. 1990. reprint ed. lib. bdg. 21.95 (*0-89968-545-5*) Buccaneer Bks.

— Tales You Won't Believe. 23.95 (*0-8488-0871-1*) Amereon Ltd.

— White Flag. 28.95 (*0-89190-943-5*) Amereon Ltd.

— Wings. 27.95 (*0-8488-0883-5*) Amereon Ltd.

— Wings. 1986. reprint ed. lib. bdg. 16.95 (*0-89966-531-4*) Buccaneer Bks.

Porter, George, ed. Nephrotoxic Mechanisms of Drugs & Environmental Toxins. LC 82-13156. 486p. 1982. 89.50 (*0-306-40977-1*, Plenum Med Bk) Plenum.

Porter, George, jt. ed. see Bragg, William L.

Porter, George A., ed. Acute Medical Problems in the Post-Operative Patient. (Illus.). 224p. 1987. pap. 32.00 (*0-443-08428-9*) Churchill.

Porter, George H. Ohio Politics During the Civil War Period. LC 76-76694. (Columbia University. Studies in the Social Sciences: No. 105). reprint ed. 21.00 (*0-404-51105-8*) AMS Pr.

Porter, George R. Progress of the Nation: In Its Various Social & Economic Relations from the Beginning of the 19th Century. LC 77-85189. (Reprints of Economic Classics Ser.). xvi, 735p. 1970. reprint ed. 57.50 (*0-678-00538-9*) Kelley.

Porter, Georgeanne B. Germany, Federal Republic Of. LC 86-14110. (World Education Ser.). (Illus.). 192p. (Orig.). (C). 1986. pap. text ed. 20.00 (*0-910054-84-3*) Am Assn Coll Registrars.

Porter, Gerald. The English Occupational Song. (Umea Studies in the Humanities: No. 105). 184p. (Orig.). 1992. pap. 55.00x (*91-7174-649-8*, Pub. by Almqv & Wiksell SW) Coronet Bks.

Porter, Gillian, jt. ed. see Handoussa, Heba.

Porter, Glenn. Encyclopedia of American Economic History, 3 vols., Set. LC 79-4946. 1232p. 1980. text ed. 295.00 (*0-684-16271-7*, Scribners) S&S Trade.

— Regional Economic History: The Mid-Alantic Area since 1700. 92p. 1976. pap. write for info. (*0-914650-13-0*) Hagley Museum.

— The Rise of Big Business, 1865-1920. 2nd ed. Franklin, John H. & Eisenstadt, A. S., eds. (American History Ser.). (Illus.). 120p. 1992. pap. text ed. write for info. (*0-88295-882-8*) Harlan Davidson.

— The Workers' World at Hagley. rev. ed. Hinsley, Jacqueline & Kaufmann, Joy, eds. LC 92-53198. 64p. reprint ed. pap. text ed. 9.95 (*0-914650-30-0*) Hagley Museum.

— The Workers' World at Hagley. rev. ed. 64p. 1992. reprint ed. pap. 7.50 (*0-914650-21-1*) Hagley Museum.

Porter, Glenn & Livesay, Harold C. Merchants & Manufacturers: Studies in the Changing Structure of Nineteenth-Century Marketing. LC 72-156071. 269p. reprint ed. pap. 76.70 (*0-8357-6706-X*, 2035268) Bks Demand.

— Merchants & Manufacturers: Studies in the Changing Structure of 19th-Century Marketing. 276p. 1989. reprint ed. pap. 8.95 (*0-929587-10-3*, Elephant Paperbacks) I R Dee.

Porter, Glenn, ed. see Blackford, Mansel G.

Porter, Glenn, ed. see Freyer, Tony A.

Porter, Glenn, ed. see Giebelhaus, August W.

Porter, Glenn, ed. see Pratt, Joseph.

Porter, Glenn, ed. see Tedlow, Richard S.

Porter, Glenn, ed. see Yeager, Mary.

Porter, Greg. Guns, Guns, Guns: Gun Design for Any RPG. 2nd ed. (Illus.). 56p. (C). 1989. 8.95 (*0-943891-04-3*) Blacksburg Tactical.

— SpaceTime: Science-Fiction Roleplaying in a Future That's Too Close for Comfort. (Illus.). 128p. (Orig.). 1988. pap. 14.95 (*0-943891-03-5*) Blacksburg Tactical.

— TimeLords. (Illus.). 124p. (Orig.). (C). 1987. pap. 12.95 (*0-943891-00-0*) Blacksburg Tactical.

Porter, H., jt. auth. see Wortabet, John.

Porter, H., jt. ed. see Wortabet, John.

Porter, H. Boone. Sunday: Day of Light. 104p. 1988. pap. 6.95 (*0-912405-40-6*) Pastoral Pr.

Porter, Hal. The Extra. 250p. (Orig.). 1987. pap. text ed. 14.95 (*0-7022-2052-3*, Pub. by Univ Queensland Pr AT) Intl Spec Bk.

— Hal Porter. Lord, Mary, ed. (Illus.). 408p. pap. 18.95 (*0-7022-1466-3*) Intl Spec Bk.

— The Paper Chase. 305p. (Orig.). 1980. reprint ed. pap. 14.95 (*0-7022-1504-X*, Pub. by Univ Queensland Pr AT) Intl Spec Bk.

— The Tilted Cross. 266p. 1989. reprint ed. pap. 14.95 (*0-7022-2183-X*, Pub. by Univ Queensland Pr AT) Intl Spec Bk.

— The Watcher on the Cast-Iron Balcony. (Orig.). 1993. pap. 14.95 (*0-7022-2558-4*, Pub. by Univ Queensland Pr AT) Intl Spec Bk.

Porter, Harvey, jt. auth. see Wortabet, John.

Porter, Hayden. Essentials of Lotus 1-2-3 for Macintosh. (Illus.). 368p. (C). 1992. teacher ed write for info. (*1-56527-025-8*); disk 49.95 (*1-56527-008-8*); disk 24.95 (*1-56527-009-6*) Course Tech.

Porter, Henry. Two Angry Women of Abingdon. LC 70-133722. (Tudor Facsimile Texts. Old English Plays Ser.: No. 87). reprint ed. 49.50 (*0-404-53387-6*) AMS Pr.

Porter, Horace. Campaigning with Grant. 632p. 1986. pap. 12.95 (*0-306-80277-5*) Da Capo.

— CWL: Campaigning with Grant. 558p. 1995. 12.98 (*0-8317-1333-X*) Smithmark.

Porter, Horace A. Stealing the Fire: The Art & Protest of James Baldwin. LC 88-27806. 240p. 1989. text ed. 35.00 (*0-8195-5197-X*, Wesleyan Univ Pr); pap. 15.95 (*0-8195-6239-4*, Wesleyan Univ Pr) U Pr of New Eng.

Porter, J., ed. Highway Research: Sharing the Benefits. 456p. 1991. text ed. 126.00 (*0-7277-1635-2*, Pub. by T Telford UK) Am Soc Civil Eng.

Porter, J. C. & Jezova, D., eds. Circulating Regulatory Factors & Neuroendocrine Function. LC 90-7365. (AEMB Candidate Ser.). (Illus.). 520p. 1990. 125.00 (*0-306-43609-4*, Plenum Pr) Plenum.

Porter, J. D., et al. Verification & Validation of Models, No. 14114: FAR Field Modelling of Radionuclide. 135p. 1992. pap. 19.00 (*92-826-3860-X*, CD-NA-14114-EN-C, Pub. by Europ Com) UNIPUB.

Porter, J. L., ed. Giant Cities of Bashan & Syria's Holy Places. 371p. (C). 1991. 125.00 (*1-85077-198-7*, Darf Pubs Ltd) St Mut.

Porter, J. M., ed. Sophia & Praxis: The Boundaries of Politics. LC 84-12154. 160p. (Orig.). reprint ed. pap. 45.60 (*0-7837-2599-X*, 2042763) Bks Demand.

Porter, J. M. & Vernon, Richard, eds. Unity, Plurality & Politics. LC 85-26262. 256p. 1986. text ed. 32.50 (*0-312-83331-8*) St Martin.

***Porter, J. R., ed.** The Illustrated Guide to the Bible. (Illus.). 288p. (YA). 1995. 35.00 (*0-19-521159-6*) OUP.

Porter, J. R. & Lawlor, David W., eds. Plant Growth: Interactions with Nutrition & Environment. (Society for Experimental Biology Symposia Ser.: No. 43). (Illus.). 220p. (C). 1991. 89.95 (*0-521-36133-8*) Cambridge U Pr.

Porter, J. R. & Woods, R. G. Extensions & Absolutes of Hausdorff Spaces. (Illus.). 860p. 1987. 109.00 (*0-387-96212-3*) Spr-Verlag.

Porter, J. R., jt. ed. see Armstrong, J. T.

Porter, J. R., jt. ed. see Janis, A. I.

Porter, J. R., tr. see Westermann, Claus.

Porter, J. W. A Genealogy of the Descendants of Richard Porter, Who Settled at Weymouth, Mass., 1635, & Allied Families; Also Some Account of the Descendants of John Porter, Who Settled at Hingham, Mass., 1635, & Salem (Danvers) Mass., 1644. 344p. 1989. reprint ed. lib. bdg. 59.50 (*0-8328-0978-0*); reprint ed. pap. 51.50 (*0-8328-0979-9*) Higginson Bk Co.

***Porter, Jack N.** The Agunah: A Sourcebook on the "Chained Wife" LC 95-9843. 1995. pap. write for info. (*1-56821-440-5*) Aronson.

— Handbook of Cults, Sects, & Self-Realization Groups. 95p. (Orig.). 1982. pap. 16.95 (*0-932270-03-4*) Spencer Pr.

— Notes of a Happy Sociologist. 30p. (Orig.). 1982. pap. 3.95 (*0-932270-04-2*) Spencer Pr.

— Sexual Politics in the Third Reich: The Persecution of Homosexuals During the Holocaust. rev. ed. (Holocaust Studies). (Illus.). 102p. 1995. reprint ed. pap. 24.95 (*0-932270-05-0*) Spencer Pr.

Porter, Jack N., comp. Jews & the Cults: Bibliography-Guide. LC 81-67448. 50p. 1981. pap. 4.00 (*0-9602036-4-8*) Biblio NY.

Porter, Jack N. & Doress, Irvin. Kids in Cults: Why They Join, Why They Stay, Why They Leave. rev. ed. 22p. (Orig.). 1982. pap. 14.95 (*0-932270-02-6*) Spencer Pr.

Porter, Jack N. & Taplin, Ruth. Conflict & Conflict Resolution: A Sociological Introduction with Updated Bibliography & Theory Section. LC 87-8215. 114p. (Orig.). (C). 1987. lib. bdg. 42.00 (*0-8191-6368-6*) U Pr of Amer.

Porter, Jack N., jt. auth. see Glazer, Gerald S.

Porter, Jack W. & Henrysson, Harald. A Jussi Bjoerling Discography. LC 82-81146. 192p. (Orig.). 1982. pap. 19.95 (*0-9608546-0-6*) J Bjoerling.

Porter, Jack W. & Stineman, William F. The Catholic Church in Greencastle, Putnam County, Indiana 1848-1978. LC 78-65724. (Illus.). 1979. 14.95 (*0-9602352-0-5*) St Paul the Apostle.

Porter, Jack W., jt. auth. see Stineman, William F.

Porter, Jadranka. Under Siege in Kuwait. 250p. 1991. 21.95 (*0-395-60909-7*) HM.

Porter, James. The Traditional Music of Britain & Ireland: A Research & Information Guide. (Music Research & Information Guides Ser.: Vol. 11). 440p. 1989. 58.00 (*0-8240-6623-5*, 807) Garland.

Porter, James, ed. Selected Reports in Ethnomusicology, Vol. 3, No. 1: The Traditional Music of Europeans in America. LC 76-640181. (Illus.). vii, 260p. 1978. pap. text ed. 11.95 (*0-88287-011-4*) UCLA Dept Ethnom.

Porter, James & Racy, A. Jihad, eds. Issues in the Conceptualization of Music. LC 76-640181. (Selected Reports in Ethnomusicology: Vol. 7). (Illus.). xi, 176p. (Orig.). 1988. audio 22.95 (*0-318-36431-X*) UCLA Dept Ethnom.

Porter, James A., Jr. Doctor, Matilda's in Labor. LC 85-23875. 200p. 1986. 17.95 (*0-8138-0463-9*) Iowa St U Pr.

Porter, James A. Modern Negro Art. LC 92-37421. (Moorland-Spingarn Ser.). (C). 1992. 24.95 (*0-88258-163-5*) Howard U Pr.

— Modern Negro Art. LC 69-18593. (American Negro: His History & Literature, Ser. No. 2). 1979. reprint ed. 15.95 (*0-405-01889-4*) Ayer.

Porter, James D. Tennessee. Evans, Clement A., ed. (Confederate Military History Extended Edition Ser.: Vol. X). (Illus.). 806p. 1988. reprint ed. 50.00 (*1-56837-029-6*) Broadfoot.

Porter, James E. Audience & Rhetoric: An Archaeological Composition of the Discourse Community. 204p. 1991. pap. text ed. 26.60 (*0-13-050675-3*, 640601) P-H.

Porter, James W., jt. ed. see Bareis, Charles J.

Porter, Jane. Parenting Alone. (NetWork Discussion Guides Ser.). 48p. (Orig.). 1992. 4.99 (*0-87788-639-3*) Shaw Pubs.

— Pastor's Fire-Side, 2 Vols. Nos. 18 & 19. reprint ed. write for info. (*0-318-50685-8*) AMS Pr.

— Pastor's Fire-Side, 2 Vols, 1. LC 75-162887. (Bentley's Standard Novels Ser.: Nos. 18 & 19). reprint ed. 13.00 (*0-404-54418-5*) AMS Pr.

— Pastor's Fire-Side, 2 Vols, 2. LC 75-162887. (Bentley's Standard Novels Ser.: Nos. 18 & 19). reprint ed. 13.00 (*0-404-54419-3*) AMS Pr.

— Pastor's Fire-Side, 2 Vols, Set. LC 75-162887. (Bentley's Standard Novels Ser.: Nos. 18 & 19). reprint ed. 25.00 (*0-404-54560-2*) AMS Pr.

— The Scottish Chiefs. LC 91-8521. (Scribner's Illustrated Classics Ser.). (Illus.). 528p. (YA). 1991. text ed. 26.95 (*0-684-19340-X*, C Scribner Sons Young) S&S Childrens.

— The Scottish Chiefs. limited ed. LC 91-8521. (Scribner's Illustrated Classics Ser.). (Illus.). 528p. (YA). 1991. text ed. 75.00 (*0-684-19339-6*, C Scribner Sons Young) S&S Childrens.

— The Scottish Chiefs. limited ed. Smith, Nora A. & Wiggin, Kate D., eds. (Illus.). 520p. 1982. 75.00 (*0-685-42432-4*, Scribners) S&S Trade.

— The Scottish Chiefs. (Illus.). 1994. reprint ed. lib. bdg. 49.95x (*1-56849-533-1*) Buccaneer Bks.

— Thaddeus of Warsaw. rev. ed. LC 70-162883. (Bentley's Standard Novels Ser.: No. 4). (Illus.). reprint ed. 17.50 (*0-404-54404-5*) AMS Pr.

Porter, Jane, ed. see Seaward, Edward.

Porter, Janice. Could I Have Your Recipe? (Illus.). 115p. (Orig.). 1981. pap. 5.95 (*0-9607670-0-2*) J Porter Bks.

***Porter, Jean.** Moral Action & Christian Ethics. (New Studies in Christian Ethics: No. 5). 288p. (C). 1995. 54.95 (*0-521-44329-6*) Cambridge U Pr.

— The Recovery of Virtue: The Relevance of Aquinas for Christian Ethics. 300p. (Orig.). 1990. text ed. 25.00 (*0-664-21924-1*) Westminster John Knox.

Porter, Jeanne C. Selected Works from the Collection of Samuel Gallu: Exhibition Catalogue. (Illus.). 68p. 1981. pap. 5.00 (*0-911209-21-2*) Palmer Mus Art.

Porter, Jessica. Unbridled Love. large type ed. (Linford Romance Library). 288p. 1992. pap. 14.95 (*0-7089-7289-6*, Trailtree Bookshop) Ulverscroft.

Porter, Jim, jt. auth. see Jimmerson, Michael.

Porter, Joe A. Eelgrass. LC 77-4996. 1977. pap. 4.95 (*0-8112-0655-6*, NDP438) New Directions.

— The Kentucky Stories. LC 82-49067. 144p. 1983. 17.95 (*0-8018-3008-7*) Johns Hopkins.

— Lithuania. LC 90-36785. (Poetry & Fiction Ser.). 144p. 1990. text ed. 26.00 (*0-8018-4091-0*); pap. 10.95 (*0-8018-4092-9*) Johns Hopkins.

Porter, John. AS-400 Information Engineering. (IBM Ser.). 352p. 1993. text ed. 45.00i (*0-07-050623-X*) McGraw.

— Creating Powerful Promotions with Non-Foods in Supermarkets. 128p. 1992. spiral bd. 19.95 (*0-9631297-5-9*) Agate MN.

— Synon Developer's Guide for the AS 400. 1995. text ed. 45.00 (*0-07-050667-1*) McGraw.

— Vertical Mosaic: An Analysis of Social Class & Power in Canada. LC 65-3947. 1965. pap. 21.95 (*0-8020-6055-2*) U of Toronto Pr.

***Porter, John, tr.** Anglo-Saxon Riddles. 112p. 1995. pap. 8.95 (*1-898281-13-0*) Paul & Co Pubs.

— Beowulf: Text & Translation. 192p. (Orig.). 1992. pap. text ed. 16.95 (*0-9516209-2-4*, Pub. by Anglo-Saxon Bks UK) Paul & Co Pubs.

Porter, John A. The Vertical Mosaic: An Analysis of Social Class & Power in Canada. LC 78-418980. (Studies in the Structure of Power: Decision-Making in Canada: No. 2). (Illus.). 646p. reprint ed. pap. 180.00 (*0-8357-6365-X*, 2035719) Bks Demand.

Porter, John D., Jr., jt. auth. see Veazey, Steve.

Porter, John M. & Taylor, Lloyd, eds. Basic Data Underlying Clinical Decision Making in Vascular Surgery. 1994. 75.00 (*0-942219-71-6*) Quality Med Pub.

Porter, John R. Studies in Euripides' Orestes. LC 94-16657. (Mnemosyne, Bibliotheca Classica Batava. Supplementum). 1994. 97.25 (*90-04-09662-0*) E J Brill.

Porter, John W. Biosynthesis of Isoprenoid Compounds, Vol. 1. Spurgeon, Sandra L., ed. LC 80-28511. 574p. reprint ed. pap. 163.60 (*0-8357-7256-X*, 2056302) Bks Demand.

***Porter, Johnathan, pseud.** Path to Wisdom. 208p. (Orig.). 1995. write for info. (*0-9644926-0-1*) Just Enlight.

Porter, Jonathan. Tseng Kuo-Fan's Private Bureaucracy. LC 72-619560. (China Research Monographs: No. 9). 148p. 1972. pap. 2.50 (*0-912966-10-6*) IEAS.

Porter, Joseph A. Shakespeare's Mercutio: His History & Drama. LC 88-17236. (Illus.). xiv, 282p. (C). 1989. 39.95 (*0-8078-1824-0*) U of NC Pr.

Porter, Joseph A., ed. see Southeastern Renaissance Conference Staff.

Porter, Joseph C. Paper Medicine Man: John Gregory Bourke & His American West. LC 85-40943. (Illus.). 352p. 1989. pap. 17.95 (*0-8061-2218-8*) U of Okla Pr.

Porter, Joseph C., jt. auth. see Goetzmann, William H.

Porter, Joseph W., ed. Maine Historical Magazine, 9 vols. in 4, Set. LC 93-84721. Orig. Title: Bangor Historical Magazine 1885-1895. 2624p. 1993. 195.00 (*0-89725-116-4*) Picton Pr.

Porter, Joyce. Dead Easy for Dover. (Inspector Dover of Scotland Yard Ser.). 176p. 1991. reprint ed. pap. 6.00 (*0-88150-212-X*, Foul Play) Countryman.

— Dover: The Collected Short Stories. (Chief Inspector Wilfred Dover Ser.). 160p. 1995. 19.00 (*0-88150-342-8*, Foul Play) Countryman.

— Dover & the Claret Tappers. (Chief Inspector Dover Mystery Ser.). 208p. 1992. pap. 6.00 (*0-88150-245-6*, Foul Play) Countryman.

— Dover & the Unkindest Cut of All. 188p. 1990. reprint ed. pap. 5.95 (*0-88150-174-3*, Foul Play) Countryman.

— Dover Beats the Band. (Dover Mysteries Ser.). 170p. 1993. pap. 6.00 (*0-88150-268-5*, Foul Play) Countryman.

— Dover Goes to Pott. 192p. 1990. reprint ed. pap. 5.95 (*0-88150-173-5*, Foul Play) Countryman.

— Dover One. 176p. 1989. reprint ed. pap. 6.00 (*0-88150-134-4*, Foul Play) Countryman.

— Dover Strikes Again. (Inspector Dover of Scotland Yard Ser.). 202p. 1991. reprint ed. pap. 5.95 (*0-88150-211-1*, Foul Play) Countryman.

— Dover Three. (Inspector Dover of Scotland Yard Ser.). 188p. 1989. reprint ed. pap. 6.00 (*0-88150-147-6*, Foul Play) Countryman.

— Dover Two. 192p. 1989. reprint ed. pap. 6.00 (*0-88150-135-2*, Foul Play) Countryman.

— Humanities on the Go! 80p. (C). 1992. pap. text ed. 9.95 (*0-8403-7848-3*) Kendall-Hunt.

— It's Murder with Dover. (Chief Inspector Dover Mystery Ser.). 192p. 1992. pap. 6.00 (*0-88150-233-2*, Foul Play) Countryman.

— A Meddler & Her Murder. 176p. 1992. pap. 5.95 (*0-89733-328-4*) Academy Chi Pubs.

Porter, Judith D. Black Child, White Child: The Development of Racial Attitudes. (Illus.). 278p. 1971. pap. 12.95 (*0-674-07611-7*) HUP.

Porter, Judy K. Cycle of Seasons: Spiral of Life. 68p. 1993. pap. write for info. (*0-9636230-0-1*) Transport Pub.

Porter, K., jt. auth. see Ellinwood, L.

Porter, K. R., et al. The Mortgage Debenture. xii, 108p. 1985. 34.50 (*0-455-20603-1*, Pub. by Law Bk Co) W W Gaunt.

Porter, Katherine, illus. Katherine Porter: Paintings - Drawings. LC 91-70220. (Orig.). 1991. pap. 15.00 (*0-916606-21-X*) Bowdoin Coll.

Porter, Katherine A. The Collected Stories of Katherine Anne Porter. LC 79-10398. 495p. 1979. pap. 11.95 (*0-15-618876-7*, Harvest Bks) HarBrace.

— Days Before. LC 77-117827. (Essay Index Reprint Ser.). 1977. 21.95 (*0-8369-2066-X*) Ayer.

— Flowering Judas: A Casebook. Carr, Virginia S., ed. LC 92-35362. (Woman Writers: Text & Contexts Ser.). 216p. (C). 1993. text ed. 30.00 (*0-8135-1978-0*); pap. text ed. 10.00 (*0-8135-1979-9*) Rutgers U Pr.

— Flowering Judas & Other Stories. 1990. 15.95 (*0-15-131811-5*) HarBrace.

— Letters of Katherine Anne Porter. 1981. pap. 16.95 (*0-87113-453-5*) Grove-Atltic.

— Mae Franking's "My Chinese Marriage" Franking, Holly, ed. LC 91-12698. (Illus.). 159p. 1991. 16.95 (*0-292-75132-X*) U of Tex Pr.

— The Old Order: Stories of the South from Flowering Judas, Pale Horse, Pale Rider & the Leaning Tower. LC 66-380. 182p. (Orig.). 1955. pap. 6.95 (*0-15-668519-1*, Harvest Bks) HarBrace.

— Pale Horse, Pale Rider. 1990. 15.95 (*0-15-170755-3*) HarBrace.

— Ship of Fools. 516p. 1984. reprint ed. pap. 13.95 (*0-316-71390-2*) Little.

— This Strange Old World & Other Book Reviews by Katherine Anne Porter. Unrue, Darlene H., ed. LC 90-20486. 192p. 1991. 25.00 (*0-8203-1331-9*) U of Ga Pr.

— Uncollected Early Prose of Katherine Anne Porter. Alvarez, Ruth M. & Walsh, Thomas F., eds. LC 93-3361. (Illus.). 288p. 1994. 35.00 (*0-292-76544-4*) U of Tex Pr.

Porter, Katherine A., intro. Selected Stories of Eudora Welty. LC 92-50232. 1992. 14.50 (*0-679-60002-7*, Modern Lib) Random.

Porter, Kay & Foster, Judy. The Mental Athlete: Inner Training for Peak Performance. 1987. pap. text ed. 4.95 (*0-345-34174-0*) Ballantine.

Porter, Keith. How Animals Behave. (Discovering Science Ser.). (Illus.). 48p. (J). (gr. 1-4). 1987. 12.95 (*0-8160-1785-9*) Facts on File.

— Looking at Animals. (Discovering Science Ser.). (Illus.). 48p. (J). (gr. 1-4). 1987. 12.95 (*0-8160-1784-0*) Facts on File.

Porter, Keith R., jt. ed. see Brinkley, B. R.

Porter, Kenneth W. The Negro on the American Frontier. LC 77-135872. 1973. reprint ed. 18.95 (*0-405-01983-1*) Ayer.

Porter, Kenneth W., jt. auth. see Clark, Malcolm, Jr.

Porter, Kenneth W., jt. auth. see Larson, Henrietta M.

Porter, Kent. The New American Computer Dictionary. 320p. 1983. pap. 4.50 (*0-451-13794-9*, Sig) NAL-Dutton.

Porter, Kevin & Weeks, Jeffrey, eds. Between the Acts: Lives of Homosexual Men, 1885-1967. 176p. 1990. pap. 16.95 (*0-415-00944-8*, A5058) Routledge.

Porter, Keyes, ed. see Historical Records Survey.

Porter, Kingsley A. Construction of Lombard & Gothic Vaults. limited ed. 1911. 100.00 (*0-685-69851-3*) Elliots Bks.

Porter, Kirk H. History of Suffrage in the United States. LC 70-137272. reprint ed. 21.00 (*0-404-00207-2*) AMS Pr.

— History of Suffrage in the United States. LC 18-22279. 260p. 1969. reprint ed. text ed. 38.50 (*0-8371-0620-6*, POHS, Greenwood Pr) Greenwood.

Porter, L., et al. The Law & the Treatment of Drug & Alcohol-Dependent Persons: A Comparative Study of Existing Legislation. 216p. 1986. pap. 20.40 (*92-4-156093-2*) World Health.

Porter-Lane, Esther. St. George & the Dragon. (Orig.). (J). (gr. 4 up). 1985. pap. 5.00 (*0-87602-249-2*) Anchorage.

Porter, Larry C. & Black, Susan E., eds. The Prophet Joseph: Essays on the Life & Mission of Joseph Smith. LC 88-22638. viii, 359p. 1988. 17.95 (*0-87579-177-8*) Deseret Bk.

Porter, Laurence M. The Crisis of French Symbolism. LC 89-45976. 288p. 1990. 35.95 (*0-8014-2418-6*) Cornell U Pr.

— The Renaissance of the Lyric in French Romanticism: Elegy, "Poeme," & Ode. LC 78-52832. (French Forum Monographs: No. 10). 143p. (Orig.). 1978. pap. 9.95 (*0-917058-09-7*) French Forum.

Porter, Laurence M., ed. Critical Essays on Gustave Flaubert. (Critical Essays on World Literature Ser.). 248p. 1986. lib. bdg. 40.00 (*0-8161-8831-9*) G K Hall.

***Porter, Laurence M. & Gray, Eugene F., eds.** Approaches to Teaching Flaubert's Madame Bovary. LC 95-13050. (Approaches to Teaching World Literature Ser.). 1995. write for info. (*0-87352-729-1*); pap. write for info. (*0-87352-730-5*) Modern Lang.

Porter, Laurin. The Banished Prince: Time, Memory, & Ritual in the Late Plays of Eugene O'Neill. LC 88-20820. (Theater & Dramatic Studies: No. 54). 142p. reprint ed. pap. 40.50 (*0-8357-1934-0*, 2070660) Bks Demand.

Porter, Lawrence & Mohr, Bernard, eds. Reading Book for Human Relations Training. 7th ed. 91p. 1984. per. 11.95 (*0-9610392-2-1*) NTL Inst.

Porter, Lawrence M. The Interpretation of Dreams: Freud's Theories Revisited. LC 87-11940. (Masterwork Studies: No. 9). 152p. 1987. text ed. 21.95 (*0-8057-7971-X*, Pub. by Royal Botanic Garden UK); pap. 7.95 (*0-8057-8009-2*, Twayne) Macmillan.

Porter, Lee. Faculty Perceptions of Continuing Education at Syracuse University. 1970. 2.25 (*0-87060-013-3*, OCP 20) Syracuse U Cont Ed.

Porter, Les, jt. auth. see Oakland, John S.

Porter, Leslie J., jt. auth. see Oakland, John S.

Porter, Lewis, ed. A Lester Young Reader. LC 90-24922. (Smithsonian Readers in American Music Ser.). (Illus.). 344p. 1991. 45.00 (*1-56098-064-8*); pap. 19.95 (*1-56098-065-6*) Smithsonian.

Porter, Lewis, et al. Jazz: From Its Origins to the Present. 512p. (C). 1992. text ed. 48.00 (*0-13-092776-7*); pap. text ed. write for info. (*0-13-512195-7*) P-H.

Porter, Lindsay. Classic Car Restoration Guide. (Illus.). 224p. 1994. 34.95 (*1-85010-890-0*, Pub. by J H Haynes & Co UK) Motorbooks Intl.

— Improve & Modify Peugeot 205. Pollard, Dave, ed. (Illus.). 240p. 1992. 35.95 (*0-85429-833-9*, Pub. by J H Haynes & Co UK) Motorbooks Intl.

— MG Midget & Austin Healey Sprite. (Illus.). 288p. 1995. 29.95 (*0-85429-969-6*, Pub. by J H Haynes & Co UK) Motorbooks Intl.

— MG Midget & Austin-Healey Sprite: Guide to Purchase & DIY Restoration. (Illus.). 254p. 29.95 (*0-85429-336-1*, F336, Pub. by G T Foulis Ltd) Haynes Pubns.

— MGB. 2nd ed. 1992. 29.95 (*0-85429-664-6*, Pub. by G T Foulis Ltd) Haynes Pubns.

— Mini: Guide to Purchase & DIY Restoration. (Illus.). 29.95 (*0-85429-379-5*, F379, Pub. by G T Foulis Ltd) Haynes Pubns.

— Morris Minor: Guide to Purchase & D. I. Y. Restoration. (Guide to Purchase DIY Restoration Ser.: No. 4). (Illus.). 224p. 1986. 29.95 (*0-85429-442-2*, F442, Pub. by G T Foulis Ltd) Haynes Pubns.

— Super Profile: Austin-Healey 'Frogeye' Sprite. (Illus.). 56p. 1983. 11.95 (*0-85429-343-4*, F343, Pub. by G T Foulis Ltd) Haynes Pubns.

— Triumph Spitfire Guide to Purchase & DIY Restoration. (Illus.). 29.95 (*0-85429-728-6*, F728, Pub. by G T Foulis Ltd) Haynes Pubns.

— VW Beetle & Transporter: Guide to Purchase & DIY Restoration. (Illus.). 270p. 1994. 34.95 (*0-85429-474-0*, Pub. by J H Haynes & Co UK) Motorbooks Intl.

Porter, Lindsay & Morgan, Peter. Porsche 911: Guide to Purchase & DIY Restoration. (Illus.). 275p. 1988. 29.95 (*0-85429-684-0*, F475, Pub. by G T Foulis Ltd) Haynes Pubns.

Porter, Lindsay & Pollard, Dave. Ford Fiesta: Improve & Modify. (Illus.). 240p. 1990. pap. 29.95 (*0-85429-785-5*, Pub. by G T Foulis Ltd) Haynes Pubns.

— Improve & Modify Capri. (Illus.). 240p. 1992. 35.95 (*0-85429-832-0*, Pub. by J H Haynes & Co UK) Motorbooks Intl.

— Improve & Modify Escort & Orion. (Improve & Modify Ser.). (Illus.). 240p. 1990. pap. 29.95 (*0-85429-784-7*, Pub. by G T Foulis Ltd) Haynes Pubns.

Porter, Linn B. A Black Adonis. LC 72-2028. (Black Heritage Library Collection). 1977. reprint ed. 30.95 (*0-8369-9060-9*) Ayer.

***Porter, Liz.** Quick Quilts from the Heart. 1995. pap. 19.95 (*0-8487-1442-3*) Oxmoor Hse.

Porter, Liz, jt. auth. see Fons, Mariane.

Porter, Liz, jt. auth. see Fons, Marianne.

***Porter, Lorle.** The Immigrant Cocoon Slavic Migration into the Cambridge, Ohio, Coalfield. (Illus.). 350p. 1994. write for info. (*0-9643184-4-X*) Locust Grove.

— Roscoe: Generations - Regeneration. (Illus.). 442p. 1991. 18.95 (*1-880443-05-8*) Roscoe Village.

Porter, Louise M. & Smith, Charles B. Territorial Giants: Florida's Founding Fathers. 136p. 1990. 18.00 (*0-9636228-1-1*) St Joseph Hist.

Porter, Luz. Child Health Nursing Review. 2nd ed. LC 79-14390. (Arco Nursing Review Ser.). 192p. pap. text ed. 10.95 (*0-668-04825-5*, Arco Test) P-H Gen Ref & Trav.

***Porter, Lyman W.** Human Relations. LC 94-42389. (History of Management Thought Ser.). (Illus.). 400p. 1995. text ed. 112.95 (*1-85521-435-0*, Pub. by Dartmth Pub UK) Ashgate Pub Co.

Porter, Lyman W. & McKibbin, Lawrence. The Future of Management Education & Development. 400p. 1988. pap. text ed. write for info. (*0-07-050521-7*) McGraw.

Porter, Lyman W. & Rosenzweig, Mark R., eds. Annual Review of Psychology, Vol. 44. (Illus.). 1993. text ed. 43.00 (*0-8243-0244-3*) Annual Reviews.

Porter, Lyman W., jt. ed. see Rosenzweig, Mark R.

Porter, Lyman W., et al, eds. Annual Review of Psychology, Vol. 45. (Illus.). 1994. text ed. 46.00 (*0-8243-0245-1*) Annual Reviews.

Porter, Lynnette R. & Coggin, William O. What It Takes to Write a Winning Grant Proposal. 175p. 1993. pap. write for info. (*1-883868-02-5*) Am Vision Pub.

Porter, Lynnette R., jt. auth. see Coggin, William O.

Porter, M., jt. auth. see Langfeldt, T.

Porter, M. E. Competitive Advantage. 557p. (C). 1986. 275.00 (*0-685-47811-4*, Inst Pur & Supply) St Mut.

— Mrs. Porter's New Southern Cookery Book, & Companion for Frugal & Economical Housekeepers. LC 72-9802. (Cookery Americana Ser.). 1973. reprint ed. 17.95 (*0-405-05053-4*) Ayer.

Porter, M. Erin, jt. auth. see Gabbard-Alley, Anne.

Porter, M. Gilbert. One Flew over the Cuckoo's Nest. (Twayne's Masterwork Studies: No. 22). 136p. 1988. text ed. 21.95 (*0-8057-7988-4*, Twayne); pap. 7.95 (*0-8057-8037-8*, Twayne) Macmillan.

Porter, M. R. Handbook of Surfactants. 256p. 1991. 99.50 (*0-412-02491-8*, A4215, Blackie & Son-Chapman NY) Routledge Chapman & Hall.

— Recent Developments in Analysis of Surfactants. 1991. 110.00 (*1-85166-581-1*) Elsevier.

Porter, M. R., ed. Recent Developments in the Technology of Surfactants. (Critical Reports on Applied Chemistry: Vol. 30). 210p. 1990. 81.00 (*1-85166-475-0*) Elsevier.

Porter, Malcolm, contrib. The Dillon Press Children's Atlas. LC 93-15593. (Illus.). 96p. (J). (gr. 5 up). 1993. text ed. 16.95 (*0-87518-606-8*, Dillon Silver Burdett) Silver Burdett Pr.

Porter, Marcia H. The Leg & I: A Rollicking Autobiography of an Amputee. Terra, Jean, ed. LC 89-64172. (Illus.). 192p. 1990. 11.95 (*0-9625040-0-9*) Legendary Pub.

Porter, Margaret E. Dangerous Diversions. (Signet Regency Romance Ser.). 224p. (Orig.). 1994. pap. 3.99 (*0-451-18069-0*) NAL-Dutton.

— Irish Autumn. 216p. 1990. 19.95 (*0-8027-1115-4*) Walker & Co.

— Irish Autumn. large type ed. LC 90-21574. 335p. 1991. reprint ed. bds. 17.95 (*1-56054-086-9*) Thorndike Pr.

— Jubilee Year. 224p. 1991. 18.95 (*0-8027-1167-7*) Walker & Co.

— Road to Ruin. (Signet Regency Romance Ser.). 224p. 1992. pap. 3.99 (*0-451-17508-5*, Sig) NAL-Dutton.

— Road to Ruin. 224p. 1991. 18.95 (*0-8027-1129-4*) Walker & Co.

— Sweet Lavender. 224p. 1993. pap. 3.99 (*0-451-17728-2*, Sig) NAL-Dutton.

— Sweet Lavender. (Regency Romance Ser.). 224p. 1992. 19.95 (*0-8027-1205-3*) Walker & Co.

***Porter, Marianna.** The Earth Game: Discovering the Cycle Inside Your Life & the Personal Adventure of Change. 240p. (Orig.). 1995. pap. 16.95 (*0-9643464-2-7*) Clary Pr.

Porter, Marilyn. Place & Persistence in the Lives of Newfoundland Women. 203p. 1993. 59.95 (*1-85628-444-1*, Pub. by Avebury Pub UK) Ashgate Pub Co.

Porter, Mark. Time of Your Life. 1988. pap. 7.00 (*0-937396-71-0*) Walterick Pubs.

— Wow, What a Week! (Wonders! Ser.). (Illus.). 24p. (Orig.). (J). (gr. 1-3). 1991. pap. text ed. 29.95 (*1-56334-051-8*); pap. text ed. 6.00 (*1-56334-057-7*) Hampton-Brown.

Porter, Mark C., ed. Handbook of Industrial Membrane Technology. LC 88-17876. (Illus.). 604p. 1990. 96.00 (*0-8155-1205-8*) Noyes.

Porter, Mark M. To Live, to Teach, to Learn, to Love. LC 91-90404. 113p. 1991. pap. 12.95 (*0-9629790-0-7*) Kenmark Ent.

Porter, Marsha, jt. auth. see Martin, Mick.

Porter, Martha & Bareiss, Peter. Off the Air: A Collection of Lively Voice-over Scripts for a Memorable Demo Reel. 58p. 1992. pap. 12.95 (*1-56850-006-8*) Chicago Plays.

Porter, Mary C., jt. auth. see Tarr, G. Alan.

Porter, Maurice M. The Embouchure. rev. ed. LC 67-20054. 1970. 26.00 (*0-913932-01-9*) Boosey & Hawkes.

Porter, McAdam. Tuberculosis: Back to the Future. LC 93-38817. 1994. text ed. 85.95 (*0-471-94121-2*) Wiley.

Porter, Melinda C. Art of Love: Love Poems & Paintings. 1993. pap. 14.00 (*0-86316-167-7*) Writers & Readers.

— Boat Child: A Comedy. LC 93-79300. 75p. 1994. pap. 9.95 (*0-9637552-0-X*) Blake Pr.

— Through Parisian Eyes: Reflections on Contemporary French Arts & Culture. (Illus.). 256p. 1993. reprint ed. pap. 13.95 (*0-306-80540-5*) Da Capo.

Porter, Melvin F. Linebacker: Overview of the First 120 Days. 79p. 1993. reprint ed. pap. 12.50 (*0-923135-68-5*) Dalley Bk Service.

***Porter, Michael A.** FEA Step by Step with Algor. (Illus.). 407p. (Orig.). 1993. pap. text ed. 99.50 (*0-9639253-0-X*) Dynamic Anal.

— FEA Step by Step with Algor. (Illus.). 305p. (Orig.). 1994. student ed, pap. text ed. 60.00 (*0-9639253-1-8*) Dynamic Anal.

Porter, Michael E. Cases in Competitive Strategy. (Illus.). 400p. 1983. text ed. 35.00 (*0-02-925410-8*) Free Pr.

— Competitive Advantage: Creating & Sustaining Superior Performance. LC 83-49518. (Illus.). 528p. 1985. 35.00 (*0-02-925090-0*) Free Pr.

— The Competitive Advantage of Nations & Their Firms. 352p. 1990. text ed. 37.50 (*0-02-925361-6*) Free Pr.

— Competitive Strategy: Techniques for Analyzing Industries & Competitors. LC 80-65200. (Illus.). 1980. 35.00 (*0-02-925360-8*) Free Pr.

— Interbrand Choice Strategy, & Bilateral Market Power. (Economic Studies: No. 146). 253p. 1976. 16.50 (*0-674-45820-6*) HUP.

Porter, Michael E., ed. Competition in Global Industries. 1986. text ed. 35.00 (*0-07-103262-2*) McGraw.

Porter, Michael E., jt. ed. see Montgomery, Cynthia A.

Porter, Michael P. Hawaii Corporation Law & Practice. (National Corporation Law Ser.). 1992. ring bd. 126.00 (*0-13-072456-4*) Aspen Law.

Porter, Milly H., ed. see Dorrance, Tom.

Porter, Monica. The Paper Bridge: A Return to Budapest. 256p. 1982. 17.95 (*0-7043-2296-X*, Pub. by Quartet UK) Charles River Bks.

Porter, N. E., ed. Cenus of India, 1931, Bengal & Sikkim. 1987. reprint ed. 160.00 (*0-8364-2071-3*, Pub. by Usha II) S Asia.

Porter, Natalie, jt. ed. see Lerman, Hannah.

Porter, Nina. His Lordship's Filly. 224p. 1993. mass mkt. 3.99 (*0-8217-4412-7*) Zebra.

— Lady Farrington's Folly. 224p. 1993. mass mkt. 3.99 (*0-8217-4202-7*) Zebra.

— A Matchmaker's Match. 1992. pap. 3.50 (*0-8217-3783-X*) Zebra.

Porter, Noah. American Colleges & the American Public. LC 78-89219. (American Education: Its Men, Institutions & Ideas, Ser.). 1978. reprint ed. 17.95 (*0-405-01458-9*) Ayer.

— The Human Intellect. 4th ed. LC 75-3319. reprint ed. 48.00 (*0-404-59299-6*) AMS Pr.

***Porter-O'Grady & Wilson.** Transformation & Transitions: Creating Leaders. 300p. 1995. 55.00 (*0-8342-0633-1*) Aspen Pub.

Porter-Ogrady, Tim. Implementing Shared Governance: Creating a Professional Organization. 292p. 1992. 39.95 (*0-8016-6318-0*) Mosby Yr Bk.

Porter-O'Grady, Tim. Reorganization of Nursing Practice: Creating the Corporate Venture. 258p. (C). 1989. 55.00 (*0-8342-0123-2*) Aspen Pub.

Porter-Ogrady, Tim. Shared Governance Implementation Manual. 208p. 1992. pap. 36.95 (*0-8016-6317-2*) Mosby Yr Bk.

Porter-O'Grady, Tim & Finnigan, Sharon. Shared Governance for Nursing: A Creative Approach to Professional Accountability. LC 84-16814. 256p. (C). 1984. text ed. 62.00 (*0-89443-874-3*) Aspen Pub.

Porter, Ona L. & Rand, Miriam. From Here to There! The Workbook for Families on the Move. 114p. (Orig.). 1992. pap. 15.00 (*0-9625747-5-9*) Niche OR.

Porter, Paige. Gender & Education. 144p. (C). 1986. 57.00 (*0-7300-0400-7*, Pub. by Deakin Univ AT) St Mut.

Porter, Pat & Sharp, Allen W. Active English: Understand, Practice, Communicate, Bk. 1. 224p. 1977. pap. text ed. 13.75 (*0-13-003400-2*) P-H.

— Active English: Understand, Practice, Communicate, Bk. 2. (Illus.). 272p. 1977. pap. text ed. 13.75 (*0-13-003418-5*) P-H.

Porter, Patricia A., et al. Communicating Effectively in English: Oral Communication for Non-Native Speakers. 2nd ed. 251p. (C). 1992. teacher ed write for info. (*0-534-17269-5*); pap. 22.95 (*0-534-17268-7*) Heinle & Heinle.

Porter, Patrick K. Awaken the Genius: Mind Technology for the 21st Century. De Shazo, Jerry, ed. (Illus.). 200p. (Orig.). 1994. pap. 14.98 (*0-9637611-8-8*) Pure Light.

— Awaken the Genius: Mind Technology for the 21st Century. Massengill, Paul K., ed. LC 93-86044. 200p. (Orig.). Date not set. reprint ed. pap. 12.95 (*1-887630-03-1*) Renaissnce Pub.

— The Power of Your Voice: Patterns of Psycho-Linguistics. De Shazo, Jerry, ed. 180p. (Orig.). 1993. pap. 19.98 (*0-9637611-5-3*) Pure Light.

— The Power of Your Voice: Patterns of Psycho-Linguistics. Massengill, Paul K., ed. LC 93-86046. 180p. (Orig.). (C). Date not set. reprint ed. pap. 19.98 (*1-887630-01-5*) Renaissnce Pub.

— Psycho-Linguistics: THe Language of the Mind. De Shazo, Jerry, ed. 240p. (Orig.). (C). 1993. pap. 19.98 (*0-9637611-7-X*) Pure Light.

— Psycho-Linguistics: The Language of the Mind. Massengill, Paul K., ed. LC 93-86045. 240p. (C). Date not set. reprint ed. pap. 19.98 (*1-887630-02-3*) Renaissnce Pub.

Porter, Paul R. & Sweet, David C., eds. Rebuilding America's Cities: Roads to Recovery. LC 84-4299. 270p. 1984. pap. text ed. 2.00x (*0-88285-099-7*) Ctr Urban Pol Res.

Porter, Penny. The Keymaker: Born to Steal. LC 94-14806. (Illus.). 144p. (Orig.). (YA). (gr. 7-12). 1994. pap. 10.95 (*0-943173-99-X*) Harbinger AZ.

Porter, Peter. The Automatic Oracle. (Oxford Poets Ser.). 80p. 1987. pap. 8.95 (*0-19-282088-5*) OUP.

— The Chair of Babel. 80p. 1992. pap. 11.95 (*0-19-282920-3*) OUP.

— Collected Poems. 352p. 1984. pap. 7.95 (*0-19-211965-6*) OUP.

— English Subtitles. 1981. pap. 9.95 (*0-19-211942-7*) OUP.

— Fast Forward. 1984. pap. 7.95 (*0-19-211967-2*) OUP.

— George Herbert: (T. S. Eliot) 1990. 40.00 (*0-7463-0741-1*, Pub. by Northcote House UK) St Mut.

— Millennial Fables. 96p. 1995. pap. 11.95 (*0-19-282391-4*) OUP.

— A Porter Selected: Poems, Nineteen Fifty-Nine to Nineteen Eighty-Nine. (Oxford Poets Ser.). 160p. 1989. pap. 11.95 (*0-19-282661-1*) OUP.

— Possible Worlds. 80p. 1989. pap. 10.95 (*0-19-282660-3*) OUP.

— William Butler Yeats. (Great Poets Ser.). 1990. 10.00 (*0-517-57379-2*, Crown) Crown Pub Group.

Porter, Peter, ed. Elizabeth Barrett Browning. (Great Poets Ser.). (Illus.). 64p. 1992. 10.00 (*0-517-58935-4*, C P Pubs) Crown Pub Group.

Porter, Peter, intro. & sel. Percy Bysshe Shelley. LC 93-5584. (Great English Poets Ser.). 1994. 10.00 (*0-517-59648-2*, C P Pubs) Crown Pub Group.

Porter, Peter, intro. William Shakespeare. (Great Poets Ser.). (Illus.). 64p. 1987. 10.00 (*0-517-56708-3*, Crown) Crown Pub Group.

Porter, Peter & Moore, Geoffrey, intros. Christina Rossetti. (Great Poets Ser.). (Illus.). 1986. 10.00 (*0-517-56288-X*, Crown) Crown Pub Group.

— Emily Dickinson. (Great Poets Ser.). (Illus.). 1986. 10.00 (*0-517-56290-1*, Crown) Crown Pub Group.

— Robert Frost. (Great Poets Ser.). (Illus.). 1988. 10.00 (*0-517-56289-8*, C P Pubs) Crown Pub Group.

— William Blake. (Great Poets Ser.). (Illus.). 1988. 10.00 (*0-517-56291-X*, Crown) Crown Pub Group.

Porter, Peter, jt. auth. see Boyd, Arthur.

Porter, Phil. Eagle at Mackinac: The Establishment of the United States Military & Civil Authority on Mackinac Island, 1796-1802. (Reports in Mackinac History & Archaeology: No. 11). (Illus.). 56p. (Orig.). 1991. pap. 9.95 (*0-911872-59-0*) Mackinac Island.

— View from the Veranda: The History & Architecture of the Summer Cottages on Mackinac Island. Armour, David A., ed. LC 83-198939. (Reports in Mackinac History & Archaeology: No. 8). (Illus.). 76p. (Orig.). 1981. pap. 8.50 (*0-911872-41-8*) Mackinac Island.

— Wonder of Mackinac: A Guide. (Illus.). 52p. (Orig.). 1984. pap. 7.00 (*0-911872-49-3*) Mackinac Island.

***Porter, Phil, ed.** A Boy at Fort Mackinac: The Diary of Harold Dunbar Corbusier 1883-1884, 1892. (Illus.). vi, 97p. (Orig.). 1994. pap. text ed. 7.00 (*0-911872-62-0*) Mackinac Island.

Porter, Phil, jt. auth. see Cameron, Robert.

Porter, Philip. Jag XJ 220. (Illus.). 288p. 1994. 120.00 (*1-85532-397-4*, Pub. by Osprey Pubng Ltd UK) Motorbooks Intl.

— Jaguar - The Complete Illustrated History. (Illus.). 275p. 1995. 39.95 (*0-85429-962-9*, Pub. by J H Haynes & Co UK) Motorbooks Intl.

— Jaguar E-Type: The Definitive History. LC 88-82502. (Illus.). 712p. 1990. 84.95 (*0-915038-71-4*, 3-AQ-0061) Auto Quarterly.

— Original Jaguar E Type. (Illus.). 96p. 1990. 29.95 (*1-870979-12-5*, Pub. by Bay View Bks UK) Motorbooks Intl.

Porter, Philip W. Cleveland: Confused City on a Seesaw. LC 76-21700. (Illus.). 332p. 1976. 36.50 (*0-8142-0264-0*) Ohio St U Pr.

— Food & Development in the Semi-Arid Zone of East Africa. LC 79-20312. (Foreign & Comparative Studies Program, African Ser.: No. 32). (Illus.). 114p. 1979. reprint ed. pap. text ed. 7.50 (*0-915984-54-7*) Syracuse U Foreign Comp.

***Porter, Phillip.** Jaguar Sports Racing Cars C-Type, D-Type. (Illus.). 160p. 1995. 39.95 (*1-870979-67-2*, Pub. by Bay View Bks UK) Motorbooks Intl.

Porter, Phillip & Andrew, Tim. Original Jaguar XK: The Restorer's Guide to Jaguar XK120, XK140 & XK150. (Illus.). 96p. 1988. 29.95 (*1-870979-05-2*, Pub. by Bay View Bks UK) Motorbooks Intl.

Porter, Phoebe A., jt. auth. see Medina, Hector.

Porter, R., ed. see CIBA Foundation Symposium Staff.

Porter, R., jt. ed. see Rousseau, G. S.

Porter, R. Bruce & Hammel, Eric. Ace! A Marine Night-Fighter Pilot in World War II. (Illus.). 300p. 1985. 25.00 (*0-935553-01-0*) Pacifica Pr.

— Ace: A Marine Night-Fighter Pilot in World War II. 304p. 1987. mass mkt. 4.99 (*0-515-09159-6*) Jove Pubns.

Porter, R. C., ed. Seven Soviet Poets. 128p. (C). 1988. pap. text ed. 14.95 (*0-631-15567-8*, Pub. by Duckworth UK) Focus Info Gr.

Porter, R. F., et al. Flight Identification of European Raptors. 3rd ed. (Illus.). 288p. 1990. text ed. 34.95 (*0-85661-027-5*, 784627, Pub. by Poyser UK) Acad Pr.

Porter, R. N., jt. auth. see Karplus, M.

Porter, R. S., jt. auth. see Bynum, William F.

Porter, R. S., jt. auth. see Griffin, A. C.

Porter, R. W., jt. ed. see Aspden, R. M.

Porter, Randy & Sorrells, Nancy. A Cyclist's Guide to the Shenandoah Valley: Exploring the Past & Present on Rural Routes. 250p. 1993. pap. 14.95 (*0-9637819-0-1*) Shenand Odys.

Porter, Richard, jt. auth. see Cozzens, Margaret B.

Porter, Richard, jt. auth. see Cozzens, Margaret.

Porter, Richard, et al. Henry Varnum Poor, Nineteen Eighty-Seven to Nineteen Seventy: A Retrospective Exhibition: Exhibition Catalogue. (Illus.). 168p. 1983. pap. 14.50 (*0-911209-29-8*) Palmer Mus Art.

Porter, Richard D. Introduction to Fibre Bundles. (Lecture Notes in Pure & Applied Mathematics Ser.: Vol. 31). 184p. 1977. 99.75 (*0-8247-6626-1*) Dekker.

Porter, Richard D., jt. auth. see Cozzens, Margaret B.

Porter, Richard E., jt. auth. see Samovar, Larry A.

Porter, Richard N., tr. see Cizevskij, Dmitrij.

Porter, Richard N., tr. see Tschizewskij, Dmitrij.

***Porter, Robert.** Paul Hasluck: A Political Biography. Date not set. 39.95 (*1-875560-20-3*, Pub. by Univ of West Aust Pr AT) Intl Spec Bk.

— Russia's Alternative Prose. 288p. 1994. 59.95 (*0-85496-935-7*) Berg Pubs.

Porter, Robert, ed. Emigrants at Worship: One Hundred & Twenty-Five Years of Chisago Lake Methodism. (Illus.). 85p. (Orig.). 1983. pap. 8.75 (*0-933565-02-X*) Porter Pub Co.

PO

An Asterisk (*) at the beginning of an entry indicates that the title is appearing in BIP for the first time.

— Guide to Corporate Giving in the Arts. 4th ed. LC 87-18738. 481p. (Orig.). 1987. 25.00 (*0-915400-56-1*, ACA Bks) Am Council Arts.

— Studies in Neurophysiology: Presented to A. K. McIntyre. LC 78-1695. (Illus.). 470p. reprint ed. pap. 134.00 (*0-685-20565-7*, 2030614) Bks Demand.

Porter, Robert & Lemon, Roger. Corticospinal Function & Voluntary Movement. (Monographs of the Physiological Society: No. 45). (Illus.). 440p. 1993. 90.00 (*0-19-857745-1*) OUP.

Porter, Robert, jt. auth. see Crouch, Martin.

Porter, Robert, tr. see Popov, Evgeny.

Porter, Robert B. How to Trace Your Minnesota Ancestors. rev. ed. 48p. 1985. reprint ed. pap. 4.95 (*0-933565-00-3*) Porter Pub Co.

— Nord-Enlid. (Illus.). 86p. (Orig.). 1980. pap. 6.50 (*0-933565-03-8*) Porter Pub Co.

— The Secrets of Glader: Minnesota's Oldest Swedish Cemetery. (Illus.). 230p. 1989. pap. 12.95 (*0-933565-06-2*) Porter Pub Co.

Porter, Robert C. Four Contemporary Russian Writers. LC 88-14816. 191p. 1989. 59.95 (*0-85496-246-8*) Berg Pubs.

Porter, Robert P. Industrial Cuba. 1976. lib. bdg. 59.95 (*0-8490-0405-5*) Gordon Pr.

— Industrial Cuba: Being a Study of Present Commercial & Industrial Conditions. Bruchey, Stuart & Bruchey, Eleanor, eds. LC 76-5029. (American Business Abroad Ser.). (Illus.). 1976. reprint ed. 51.95 (*0-405-09296-2*) Ayer.

Porter, Robert T., jt. ed. see Josephson, Martin M.

Porter, Robert W. & Swatton, Richard. Intermediate Bulk Containers. 55p. (C). 1979. 72.00 (*0-906297-03-6*, Pub. by ICHCA UK) St Mut.

Porter, Robin. Industrial Reformers in Republican China. LC 94-16058. (Studies on Contemporary China). 320p. 1994. text ed. 55.00 (*1-56324-393-8*, East Gate Bk) M E Sharpe.

Porter, Robin, jt. ed. see Brown, David H.

Porter, Roger, jt. ed. see Johnson, Julian.

Porter, Roger B. Presidential Decision Making: The Economic Policy Board. LC 80-10165. 272p. 1982. pap. 21.95 (*0-521-27112-6*) Cambridge U Pr.

Porter, Roger J. & Malone, Thomas E., eds. Biomedical Research: Collaboration & Conflict of Interest. 232p. 1992. text ed. 45.00 (*0-8018-4400-2*) Johns Hopkins.

Porter, Roger J. & Morselli, Paolo L. The Epilepsies. (BIMR Neurology Ser.: Vol. 5). 416p. 1985. text ed. 75.00 (*0-407-02298-8*) Buttrwrth-Heinemann.

Porter, Roger J. & Schoenberg, Bruce S., eds. Controlled Clinical Trials in Neurological Disease. 464p. 1990. lib. bdg. 156.00 (*0-7923-0613-9*) Kluwer Ac.

Porter, Roger J., et al, eds. Advances in Epileptology: The 15th Epilepsy International Symposium. (Advances in Epileptology Ser.). 710p. 1984. text ed. 175.50 (*0-89004-561-5*) Raven.

— Alcohol & Seizures: Basic Mechanisms & Clinical Concepts. LC 90-2712. (Illus.). 342p. (C). 1990. text ed. 75.00 (*0-8036-7008-7*) Davis Co.

Porter, Roger S., et al. High Modulus Polymers & Composites: Lectures at the Chinese University of Hong Kong. Choy, C. L., ed. 436p. 1985. pap. text ed. 69.50x (*962-201-331-7*, Pub. by Chinese Univ HK) Coronet Bks.

Porter-Roth, Bud. Proposal Development: How to Respond & Win the Bid. 2nd ed. 238p. 1993. pap. 19.95 (*1-55571-165-0*) Oasis Pr OR.

— Proposal Development: How to Respond & Win the Bid. 2nd rev. ed. (Successful Business Library). 238p. 1993. ring bd. 39.95 (*1-55571-067-0*) Oasis Pr OR.

Porter-Roth, Richard. Electronic Imaging Display Devices, Current Technologies in the Office Document Management Environment. Date not set. write for info. (*0-318-72179-1*, TR19) Assn Inform & Image Mgmt.

Porter, Roy. English Society in the Eighteenth Century. (Social History of Britain Ser.). 424p. 1983. mass mkt. 6.95 (*0-14-022099-2*, Penguin Bks) Viking Penguin.

— English Society in the Eighteenth Century. rev. ed. 496p. 1990. pap. 12.95 (*0-14-013819-6*, Penguin Bks) Viking Penguin.

— The Enlightenment. 2nd ed. LC 89-19897. (Studies in European History). 96p. (C). 1990. pap. 10.95 (*0-391-03636-X*) Humanities.

— Health for Sale: Quackery in England, 1660-1850. LC 88-35613. 240p. 1989. text ed. 39.95 (*0-7190-1903-6*, Pub. by Manchester Univ Pr UK) St Martin.

— London: A Social History. LC 94-33025. (Illus.). 447p. 1995. pap. text ed. 29.95 (*0-674-53838-2*, PORLON) HUP.

— The Making of Geology: Earth Science in Britain, 1660-1815. LC 76-56220. 300p. reprint ed. pap. 85.50 (*0-317-27575-5*, 2024515) Bks Demand.

— Mind-Forg'd Manacles: A History of Madness from the Restoration to the Regency. LC 87-8703. 424p. 1988. 47.50 (*0-674-57617-9*) HUP.

***Porter, Roy, ed.** The Biographical Dictionary of Scientists. 2nd ed. (Illus.). 960p. 1994. text ed. 85.00 (*0-19-521083-2*) OUP.

— The Faber Book of Madness. 480p. 1991. 24.95 (*0-571-14387-3*) Faber & Faber.

— The Faber Book of Madness. 480p. 1993. pap. 14.95 (*0-571-14388-1*) Faber & Faber.

— George Cheyne: The English Malady (1733) (Tavistock Classic Reprints in the History of Psychiatry Ser.). 440p. 1990. 85.00 (*0-415-01733-5*, A4900) Routledge.

— Man Masters Nature: Twenty-Five Centuries of Science. (Illus.). 234p. 1989. pap. 9.95 (*0-8076-1233-2*) Braziller.

— Myths of the English. LC 92-28892. 272p. 1993. pap. 24.95 (*0-7456-1306-3*) Blackwell Pubs.

— Patients & Practitioners: Lay Perceptions of Medicine in Pre-Industrial Society. (Cambridge History of Medicine Ser.). 352p. 1986. 69.95 (*0-521-30915-8*) Cambridge U Pr.

— The Popularization of Medicine 1650-1850. LC 91-32849. (Wellcome Institute Series in the History of Medicine). 297p. 1993. 87.50 (*0-415-07217-4*) Routledge.

Porter, Roy & Keller, David. There & Back: The Roy Porter Story. LC 91-18913. (Illus.). 216p. 1991. 24.95 (*0-8071-1689-0*) La State U Pr.

Porter, Roy & Porter, Dorothy. In Sickness & in Health. 324p. 1989. 29.95 (*1-55786-036-X*) Blackwell Pubs.

***Porter, Roy & Teich, Mikulas, eds.** Drugs & Narcotics in History. (Illus.). 240p. (C). 1995. 49.95 (*0-521-43163-8*) Cambridge U Pr.

— The Renaissance in National Context. 236p. (C). 1991. 49.95 (*0-521-36181-8*); pap. 17.95 (*0-521-36970-3*) Cambridge U Pr.

— Romanticism in National Context. 382p. 1988. 69.95 (*0-521-32605-2*); pap. 22.95 (*0-521-33913-8*) Cambridge U Pr.

— The Scientific Revolution in National Context. 400p. (C). 1992. 59.95 (*0-521-39510-0*); pap. 19.95 (*0-521-39699-9*) Cambridge U Pr.

— Sexual Science, Sexual Knowledge: The History of Attitudes to Sexuality. LC 93-28940. 290p. (C). 1994. pap. 19.95 (*0-521-44891-3*) Cambridge U Pr.

— Sexual Science, Sexual Knowledge: The History of Attitudes to Sexuality. LC 93-28940. 290p. (C). 1994. 69.95 (*0-521-44434-9*) Cambridge U Pr.

Porter, Roy & Tomaselli, Sylvana, eds. The Dialectics of Friendship. 178p. 1990. pap. 16.95 (*0-415-01751-3*, A3950) Routledge.

— Rape. LC 86-6148. (Illus.). 304p. 1986. pap. text ed. 14.95 (*0-631-16906-7*) Blackwell Pubs.

Porter, Roy & Wear, Andrew. Problems & Methods in the History of Medicine. (Welcome Institute Series in the History of Medicine). 256p. 1987. 67.50 (*0-7099-3687-7*, Pub. by Croom Helm UK) Routledge Chapman & Hall.

Porter, Roy, jt. ed. see Berrios, German.

Porter, Roy, ed. see Black, Jeremy.

Porter, Roy, ed. see Bowler, Peter J.

Porter, Roy, jt. ed. see Brewer, John.

Porter, Roy, jt. ed. see Brock, William H.

Porter, Roy, jt. ed. see Burke, Peter.

Porter, Roy, jt. ed. see Bynum, William F.

Porter, Roy, jt. ed. see Granshaw, Lindsay.

Porter, Roy, jt. auth. see Hall, Lesley.

Porter, Roy, ed. see Haslam, John.

Porter, Roy, ed. see Hobbs, William.

Porter, Roy, jt. ed. see Jones, Colins.

Porter, Roy, jt. ed. see Micale, Mark S.

Porter, Roy, jt. auth. see Porter, Dorothy.

Porter, Roy, jt. ed. see Roberts, Marie M.

Porter, Roy, jt. ed. see Rousseau, G. S.

Porter, Roy, jt. ed. see Teich, Mikulas.

Porter, Roy, ed. see Trotter, Thomas.

Porter, Roy, et al, eds. The Anatomy of Madness, 2 vols. 528p. 1985. Set. 87.50 (*0-422-60350-3*, 9688, Pub. by Tavistock UK) Routledge Chapman & Hall.

— The Anatomy of Madness, 3 vols. 352p. 1988. Set. text ed. 137.50 (*0-318-35451-9*); Vol. III, The Asylum & Its Psychiatry. text ed. 65.00 (*0-415-00859-X*) Routledge Chapman & Hall.

— The Anatomy of Madness, Vol. 1: People & Ideas. 264p. 1985. 47.50 (*0-422-79430-9*, 9617, Pub. by Tavistock UK) Routledge Chapman & Hall.

— The Anatomy of Madness, Vol. 2: Institutions & Society. 264p. 1985. 47.50 (*0-422-79440-6*, 9618, Pub. by Tavistock UK) Routledge Chapman & Hall.

Porter, Rufus. Yankee Inventor's Flying Ship. Gilman, Rhoda R., ed. LC 75-95571. (Illus.). 51p. 1969. 7.25 (*0-87351-052-6*) Minn Hist.

Porter, Russ. Chicago & North Western Milwaukee Road Pictorial. LC 94-75627. 76p. 1994. 29.95 (*0-911581-30-8*) Heimburger Hse Pub.

Porter, Russell W. The Arctic Diary of Russell Williams Porter. Friis, Herman, ed. LC 75-45375. 184p. reprint ed. pap. 52.50 (*0-8357-5726-9*, 2020271) Bks Demand.

Porter, Ruth B. The Story of Somerset. rev. ed. 70p. 1972. pap. 3.00 (*0-685-29128-6*) Niagara Cnty Hist Soc.

Porter, Ruth S. A Dialect Study in Dartmouth Massachusetts. (American Dialect Society Bks.: No. 43). 60p. 1965. pap. 4.95 (*0-8173-0643-9*) U of Ala Pr.

Porter, S. C., jt. auth. see Skinner, B. J.

Porter, Sarah H. The Life & Times of Anne Royall. LC 72-2619. (American Women Ser.: Images & Realities). 302p. 1974. reprint ed. 23.95 (*0-405-04472-0*) Ayer.

Porter Sargent Staff. Handbook of Private Schools. 75th ed. LC 15-12869. (Handbook Ser.). (Illus.). 1396p. 1994. 80.00 (*0-87558-132-3*) Porter Sargent.

Porter Sargent Staff, ed. Directory for Exceptional Children. 13th ed. LC 54-4975. (Special Education Ser.). (Illus.). 1312p. 1994. 60.00 (*0-87558-131-5*) Porter Sargent.

— Guide to Summer Camps & Summer Schools. 26th ed. LC 37-4715. (Handbook Ser.). (Illus.). 492p. 1990. 26.00 (*0-87558-123-4*) Porter Sargent.

— Schools Abroad of Interest to Americans. 8th ed. LC 67-18844. (Handbook Ser.). (Illus.). 552p. 1991. 35.00 (*0-87558-127-7*) Porter Sargent.

Porter, Shirley A. But You Can't Leave Shirley. LC 92-64097. 176p. (Orig.). 1992. pap. 9.95 (*0-936029-28-5*) Western Bk Journ.

Porter, Sindhu, ed. Transformation, Vol. 1: On Tour with Gurumayi Chidvilasananda. (Illus.). 176p. (Orig.). 1985. pap. 9.95 (*0-914602-92-6*) SYDA Found.

***Porter, Spencer K.** Remembering Galileo. LC 95-10747. 1995. write for info. (*0-8191-9962-1*); pap. write for info. (*0-8191-9963-X*) U Pr of Amer.

Porter, Stanley E. Idioms of the Greek New Testament. (Biblical Languages (Greek) Ser.). 320p. (C). 1992. 27.50 (*1-85075-357-1*, Pub. by Sheffield Acad UK); pap. 14.95 (*1-85075-379-2*, Pub. by Sheffield Acad UK) CUP Services.

***Porter, Stanley E., et al, eds.** Crossing the Boundaries: Essays in Biblical Interpretation in Honor of Michael D. Goulder. LC 94-26021. (Biblical Interpretation Ser.: 8). 1994. 83.00 (*90-04-10131-4*) E J Brill.

Porter, Stephen. Destruction in the English Civil Wars. 192p. 1994. 40.00 (*0-7509-0516-6*) A Sutton Pub.

— Exploring Urban History. 189p. 1991. 45.00 (*0-7134-5137-8*, Pub. by Batsford UK) Trafalgar.

Porter, Stephen C., jt. auth. see Skinner, Brian J.

Porter, Stephen C., jt. auth. see Skinner, Brian.

Porter, Stephen R. & Scully, Crispian, eds. Radiographic Interpretation in Orofacial Disease. (Illus.). 128p. 1991. pap. 41.95 (*0-19-261585-8*) OUP.

Porter, Stephen R., et al. Medicine & Surgery for Dentistry Trainees. Scully, ed. LC 92-48968. (Colour Guide Ser.). 144p. (Orig.). 1993. pap. 19.95 (*0-443-04613-1*) Churchill.

Porter, Steven. The American Musical Theatre: A Complete Musical Theatre Course. LC 87-14495. 152p. (Orig.). 1987. pap. 15.00 (*0-935016-97-X*, Barclay House) Excelsior Music Pub Co.

— The Ethics of a Democracy. LC 91-62678. 144p. (Orig.). (C). 1994. pap. text ed. 8.95 (*0-9625372-2-5*) Phantom Pubns.

— The Harmonization of the Chorale: A Comprehensive Workbook Course in Harmony & Counterpoint. 147p. (Orig.). 1995. spiral bd. 18.00 (*0-935016-80-5*) Excelsior Music Pub Co.

— Music: A Comprehensive Introduction. LC 85-16847. 336p. (Orig.). 1986. pap. 18.00 (*0-935016-81-3*) Excelsior Music Pub Co.

— Music: A Comprehensive Introduction, Workbook Number 1: Music Theory. 26p. 1986. pap. text ed. 5.95 (*0-935016-83-X*); pap. text ed. 5.95 (*0-935016-84-8*) Excelsior Music Pub Co.

— New Monologues for Reader's Theater. LC 94-46526. 74p. 1995. pap. 10.00 (*0-88734-651-0*) Players Pr.

— The Prairie Man. LC 89-92532. 62p. (Orig.). (YA). 1990. pap. text ed. 6.00 (*0-9625372-0-9*) Phantom Pubns.

— The Prairie Man. 2nd rev. ed. LC 92-80226. (Illus.). 80p. (Orig.). (C). 1992. pap. 9.95 (*0-9625372-3-3*) Phantom Pubns.

— The Senator's Son & Other Stories. LC 90-61762. 154p. (Orig.). 1994. pap. write for info. (*0-9625372-1-7*) Phantom Pubns.

— Wisdom's Passing. xii, 304p. 1991. pap. 16.95 (*0-935016-71-6*, Barclay House) Excelsior Music Pub Co.

Porter, Steven, comp. New Works for Readers' Theatre. LC 93-47112. 112p. (Orig.). 1994. pap. 10.00 (*0-88734-644-8*) Players Pr.

— Voices from Russia & America. LC 93-83376. (Illus.). 340p. (Orig.). 1994. pap. write for info. (*0-9625372-4-1*) Phantom Pubns.

***Porter, Steven, ed. & comp.** New Works for Reader's Theatre. 112p. 1994. pap. 10.00 (*81-87848-91-X*) Phantom Pubns.

Porter, Steven L. Save Your Home: How to Protect Your Home & Property from Foreclosure. 2nd ed. LC 90-30371. (Illus.). 160p. 1990. pap. 15.95 (*0-941599-14-0*) Piccadilly Bks.

Porter, Stuart R. Basic Technical Mathematics with Calculus. Ernst, John F., ed. LC 84-9168. 1985. teacher ed write for info. (*0-201-05591-0*); text ed. 35.16 (*0-201-05589-9*); Student sol. manual. student ed 13.56 (*0-201-05590-2*) Addison-Wesley.

Porter, Stuart R. & Ernst, John F. Basic Technical Mathematics. LC 84-8369. 1985. teacher ed write for info. (*0-201-05588-0*); teacher ed write for info. (*0-201-05598-8*); text ed. write for info. (*0-201-05586-4*); student ed write for info. (*0-201-05587-2*) Addison-Wesley.

— Basic Technical Mathematics. LC 94-12265. (C). 1995. 46.00 (*0-673-46177-7*) HarpCollege.

— Basic Technical Mathematics with Calculus. 2nd ed. LC 94-13873. (C). 1995. 49.00 (*0-673-46176-9*) HarpCollege.

Porter, Stuart R., jt. auth. see Angel, Allen R.

Porter, Sue. Little Wolf & the Giant. (J). (ps-1). 1990. pap. 13.95 (*0-671-70363-3*, S&S Bks Young Read) S&S Childrens.

— Little Wolf & the Giant. LC 89-21886. (Illus.). 32p. (J). (ps-6). 1993. pap. 7.95 (*0-671-79853-7*, S&S Bks Young Read) S&S Childrens.

— Moose Music. (Illus.). 32p. (J). 1994. 12.95 (*0-307-17511-1*, Artsts Writrs) Western Pub.

— My Little Rabbit Tale. LC 93-29765. (Illus.). 32p. (J). (ps-1). 1994. 13.95 (*1-56458-339-2*) Dorling Kindersley.

Porter, Susan L. With an Air Debonair: Musical Theatre in America, 1785-1815. LC 90-24921. (Illus.). 648p. (C). 1992. text ed. 55.00 (*1-56098-063-X*) Smithsonian.

Porter, Susan L., ed. British Opera in America: Children in the Wood, 1795 & Blue Beard, 1811. LC 93-49049. (Nineteenth-Century American Musical Theater Ser.). (Illus.). 314p. 1994. 70.00 (*0-8153-1368-3*) Garland.

— Women of the Commonwealth: Work, Family, & Social Change in Nineteenth-Century Massachusetts. (Illus.). 248p. (C). 1996. text ed. 45.00 (*1-55849-004-3*); pap. 15.95 (*1-55849-005-1*) U of Mass Pr.

Porter, Susan S., ed. Anesthesia for Surgery of the Spine. LC 94-8964. 350p. 1995. 65.00 (*0-07-050622-1*) Hlth Prof Div.

Porter, Sylvia. Sylvia Porter's a Home of Your Own. 176p. 1989. pap. 7.95 (*0-380-89755-5*) Avon.

— Sylvia Porter's Four Hundred & Forty-Two Tax Saving Tips, 1989. 256p. (Orig.). 1988. mass mkt. 6.95 (*0-380-89996-5*) Avon.

— Sylvia Porter's Four Hundred Ninety-Five Tax-Savings Tips: 1990 Edition. 288p. (Orig.). 1989. pap. 7.95 (*0-380-89997-3*) Avon.

— Sylvia Porter's Guide to Your Health Care: How You Can Have the Best Health Care for Less. 304p. 1990. pap. 9.95 (*0-380-89758-X*) Avon.

— Sylvia Porter's Love & Money. 256p. 1986. pap. 3.95 (*0-380-89753-9*) Avon.

— Sylvia Porter's New Money Book for the 80's. 1328p. 1980. pap. 10.95 (*0-380-51060-X*) Avon.

— Sylvia Porter's Planning Your Retirement. 304p. 1991. pap. 16.00 (*0-13-877812-4*, J K Lasser) P-H Gen Ref & Trav.

— Sylvia Porter's Your Financial Security: Making Your Money Work at Every Stage of Your Life. 240p. 1989. reprint ed. pap. 8.95 (*0-380-89754-7*) Avon.

Porter, T., jt. auth. see Gilbert, N. D.

Porter, T., jt. auth. see Kamps, K. H.

Porter, T. E. King's Day. LC 75-20728. (Haystack Ser). (Illus.). 64p. 1975. 6.00 (*0-913142-14-X*); pap. 3.50 (*0-913142-13-1*) Mulch Pr.

Porter, Theodore M. The Rise of Statistical Thinking, 1820-1900. 352p. 1988. reprint ed. pap. text ed. 15.95 (*0-691-02409-X*) Princeton U Pr.

— Trust in Numbers: The Pursuit of Objectivity in Science & Public Life. LC 94-21440. 1994. 24.95 (*0-691-03776-0*) Princeton U Pr.

Porter, Thomas E. Myth & Modern American Drama. LC 68-21543. (Waynebooks Ser.: No. 36). 286p. 1969. 34.95 (*0-8143-1360-4*); pap. text ed. 19.95 (*0-8143-1512-7*) Wayne St U Pr.

— The Zemstvo & the Emergence of Civil Society in Late Imperial Russia 1864-1917. LC 91-3067. (Distinguished Dissertations Ser.: Vol. 18). 324p. 1991. lib. bdg. 99.95 (*0-7734-9972-5*) E Mellen.

Porter, Tom. Animal Crackers. (Illus.). 64p. (Orig.). 1994. pap. 5.95 (*0-941711-09-9*) Wyrick & Co.

— Architectural Drawing. 1990. text ed. 19.95 (*0-442-30304-1*) Van Nos Reinhold.

— Architectural Drawing Masterclass: Graphic Techniques of the World's Leading Architecture. LC 93-13558. (Illus.). 160p. 1993. pap. 50.00 (*0-684-19521-6*, Scribners) S&S Trade.

Porter, Tom & Goodman, Sue. Design Drawing Techniques: A Reference Book for Architects, Graphic Designers & Artists. (Illus.). 144p. (Orig.). 1991. pap. 15.95 (*0-684-19045-1*, Scribners) S&S Trade.

— Design Drawing Techniques: For Architects, Graphic Designers & Artists. (Illus.). 144p. 1992. pap. 37.95 (*0-7506-0812-9*) Buttrwrth-Heinemann.

— Designer Primer. (Illus.). 144p. 1988. pap. 14.95 (*0-684-18457-5*, Scribners) S&S Trade.

— Manual of Graphic Techniques 2. 128p. 1982. pap. 16.00 (*0-684-17441-3*, Scribners) S&S Trade.

— Manual of Graphic Techniques 3: For Architects, Graphic Designers & Artists. (Illus.). 128p. 1983. pap. 12.95 (*0-684-18018-9*, Scribners) S&S Trade.

— Manual of Graphic Techniques 4: For Architects, Graphic Designers, & Artists. (Illus.). 128p. 1985. pap. 15.95 (*0-684-18216-5*, Scribners) S&S Trade.

— Treasury of Graphic Techniques: For Architects, Graphic Designers & Artists. (Illus.). 192p. 1992. pap. 20.00 (*0-684-19341-8*, Scribners) S&S Trade.

Porter, Tom & Greenstreet, Robert. Manual of Graphic Techniques 1. (Illus.). 112p. 1980. pap. 15.95 (*0-684-16504-X*, Scribners) S&S Trade.

Porter, Valerie. Cattle: A Handbook to the Breeds of the World. (Illus.). 400p. 1992. lib. bdg. 45.00 (*0-8160-2640-8*) Facts on File.

— Pigs: A Handbook to the Breeds of the World. (Comstock Book Ser.). (Illus.). 272p. 1993. 36.00 (*0-8014-2920-X*) Cornell U Pr.

***Porter, Venetia.** Islamic Tiles. LC 95-2034. 1995. 16.95 (*1-56656-191-4*) Interlink Pub.

Porter, Vicki & Thornes, Robin. A Guide to the Description of Architectural Drawings. LC 94-7769. 352p. 1994. text ed. 40.00 (*0-8161-0623-1*) G K Hall.

Porter, Vincent & Hasselbach, Suzanne. Pluralism, Politics & the Marketplace: The Regulation of West German Broadcasting in the 1980s. (Communication & Society Ser.). (Illus.). 240p. 1991. 74.50 (*0-415-05394-3*, A6007) Routledge.

Porter, Vondra C. Rednecks & Niggers. 64p. (Orig.). 1993. pap. 7.95 (*1-56167-150-9*) Am Literary Pr.

Porter, W. A. & Kak, S. C., eds. Advances in Communications & Signal Processing. (Illus.). 384p. 1989. pap. 63.00 (*0-387-51424-4*, 3308) Spr-Verlag.

Porter, W. A., jt. ed. see Bedrosian, S. D.

Porter, W. A., et al, eds. Advances in Computing & Control. (Illus.). 374p. 1989. pap. 63.00 (*0-387-51425-2*, 3309) Spr-Verlag.

Porter, Wes. The Garden Book & Greenhouse. LC 89-40372. (Illus.). 64p. (Orig.). (J). (gr. k-5). 1992. Packaged in greenhouse with seed packets & peat pellets. pap. 10.95 (*0-89480-346-8*, 1346) Workman Pub.

***Porter, Will.** Annals of Polk County, Iowa. (Illus.). 1064p. 1993. lib. bdg. 105.00 (*0-8328-3531-5*) Higginson Bk Co.

***Porter, William.** Porter's Pocket Guide to Critical Care. 4th ed. 1995. pap. 14.95 (*1-882740-06-8*) Porter & Assocs.

— Porter's Pocket Guide to Pediatrics. 1993. write for info. (*0-318-69779-3*) Porter & Assocs.

— Porter's Pocket Guide to Pediatrics. 1995. pap. 14.95 (*1-882740-04-1*) Porter & Assocs.

Porter, William E. Assault on the Media: The Nixon Years. LC 75-14898. 330p. reprint ed. pap. 94.10 (*0-7837-4720-9*, 2059072) Bks Demand.

An Asterisk (*) at the beginning of an entry indicates that the title is appearing in BIP for the first time.

— Virginia State Government: Fun, Frustrating, & Frightening. LC 92-44977. 1993. 37.50 (*0-8191-9031-4*); pap. 18.50 (*0-8191-9032-2*) U Pr of Amer.

Porter, William E., jt. auth. see Schramm, Wilbur L.

Porter, William M. Reading the Classics & Paradise Lost. LC 92-24241. xx, 222p. 1993. 30.00 (*0-8032-3706-5*) U of Nebr Pr.

Porter, William N. A Hundred Verses from Old Japan: Being a Translation of the "Hyaku-Nin-Isshu" LC 77-83039. (Illus.). 224p. 1979. pap. 12.95 (*0-8048-1256-X*) C E Tuttle.

Porter, William S. The Best of O. Henry. (Illustrated Classics Collection 3). 64p. 1994. pap. 3.60 (*1-56103-540-8*) Lake Pub Co.

— The Best of O. Henry. abr. ed. Fago, John N., ed. (Now Age Illustrated III Ser.). (Illus.). (J). (gr. 4-12). 1977. pap. 2.95 (*0-88301-268-5*) Pendulum Pr.

— The Best of O. Henry Readalong. (Illustrated Classics Collection 3). 64p. 1994. audio, pap. 13.50 (*1-56103-542-4*) Lake Pub Co.

— Rolling Stones. 1993. reprint ed. lib. bdg. 75.00 (*0-7812-5894-4*) Rprt Serv.

Porter, William T., ed. Big Bear of Arkansas, & Other Sketches. LC 75-144673. reprint ed. 29.50 (*0-404-05079-4*) AMS Pr.

— Quarter Race in Kentucky & Other Sketches Illustrative of Scenes, Characters & Incidents Throughout the Universal Yankee Nation. LC 78-174281. reprint ed. 32.50 (*0-404-05088-3*) AMS Pr.

Porter, Wright, Morris & Arthur Law Firm Staff. Wetlands & Real Estate Development Handbook. 2nd ed. 218p. 1991. pap. text ed. 75.00 (*0-86587-269-4*) Gov Insts.

Porter, Wright, Morris & Arthur Staff. Ohio Environmental Law Handbook. 2nd ed. 220p. 1992. pap. text ed. 74.00 (*0-86587-296-1*) Gov Insts.

***Porter, Yves.** Painters, Paintings & Books: An Essay on Indo-Persian Technical Literature 12-19th Centuries. (C). 1994. text ed. 28.00 (*81-85425-95-7*, Pub. by Manohar II) S Asia.

***Portera, Joe.** Grinning & Grinding: A Collection of America's Dental Humor. (Illus.). 264p. (Orig.). 1995. pap. 12.95 (*1-886049-02-5*) Best Times Inc.

Portera, Joseph J. Tribute to a Champion: A Fight for Life. LC 81-84291. (Illus.). 145p. (Orig.). 1981. 10.95 (*0-941602-00-1*); pap. 8.95 (*0-941602-01-X*) Iapetus Pr.

Porterfield & DeRosa. Mechanical Low Back Pain: Perspectives in Functional Anatomy. (Illus.). 224p. 1990. text ed. 43.50 (*0-7216-7297-3*) Saunders.

Porterfield, Allen W. Karl Lebrecht Immermann: A Study in German Romanticism. 1977. lib. bdg. 59.95 (*0-8490-2112-X*) Gordon Pr.

Porterfield, Amanda. Female Piety in Puritan New England: The Emergence of Religious Humanism. (Religion in America Ser.). 224p. 1991. 35.00 (*0-19-506821-1*) OUP.

Porterfield, Bill. A Loose Herd of Texans. LC 77-99277. 212p. 1978. 15.95 (*0-89096-044-5*) Tex A&M Univ Pr.

***Porterfield, Billy.** Diddy Waw Diddy: Passage of an American Son. (Southwest Life & Letters Ser.). (Illus.). 448p. 1995. pap. 12.95 (*0-87074-382-1*) SMU Press.

— Diddy Waw Diddy: The Passage of an American Son. LC 93-25301. (Illus.). 416p. 1994. 23.00 (*0-06-016999-0*, HarpT) HarpC.

Porterfield, Frank B. Porterfield: The Porterfields. 345p. 1993. reprint ed. lib. bdg. 64.00 (*0-8328-3386-X*); reprint ed. pap. 54.00 (*0-8328-3387-8*) Higginson Bk Co.

Porterfield, James. Dining by Rail: The History & Recipes of America's Golden Age of Railroad Cuisine. LC 92-34987. 1992. 35.00 (*0-312-08768-3*) St Martin.

Porterfield, James & St. Pierre, Richard. Wellness: Healthful Aging. 160p. 1992. 13.50 (*0-87967-866-6*) Dushkin Pub.

Porterfield, James A. & DeRosa, Carl. Mechanical Neck Pain: Perspectives in Functional Anatomy. (Illus.). 272p. 1994. text ed. 40.00 (*0-7216-6640-X*) Saunders.

Porterfield, Jim. Business Career Planning Guide. 1993. pap. 9.95 (*0-538-82039-X*) S-W Pub.

Porterfield, Kay. Violent Voices: Twelve Steps to Freedom from Emotional & Verbal Abuse. 1989. pap. 9.95 (*1-55874-028-7*) Health Comm.

Porterfield, Kay, ed. What's a Nice Girl Like You Doing in a Relationship Like This? Women in Abusive Relationships. 200p. (Orig.). 1992. pap. 9.95 (*0-89594-492-8*) Crossing Pr.

Porterfield, Kay M. Coping with an Alcoholic Parent. rev. ed. (Coping Ser.). (YA). (gr. 7-12). 1990. 15.95 (*0-8239-1143-8*) Rosen Group.

— Focus on Addictions: A Reference Handbook. LC 92-26623. (Teenage Perspectives Ser.). 1992. lib. bdg. 39.50 (*0-87436-674-7*) ABC-CLIO.

— Straight Talk about Cults. LC 94-37296. (J). 1995. 16.95 (*0-8160-3115-0*) Facts on File.

Porterfield, Kay M., comp. Sleeping with Dionysus: Women, Ecstacy, & Addiction. LC 93-23620. 1994. pap. 8.95 (*0-89594-652-1*) Crossing Pr.

Porterfield, Marjorie S. Involvement with Music. 250p. (C). 1989. pap. write for info. (*0-318-63664-6*) P-H.

— Involvement with Music. 250p. (C). 1989. pap. text ed. write for info. (*0-318-68001-7*) P-H.

Porterfield, Nolan. Jimmie Rodgers: The Life & Times of America's Blue Yodeler. rev. ed. (Music in American Life Ser.). (Illus.). 512p. (C). 1992. pap. 16.95 (*0-252-06268-X*) U of Ill Pr.

Porterfield, Richard L. The Insider's Guide to Winning Government Contracts. 256p. 1993. text ed. 60.00 (*0-471-57025-7*); pap. text ed. 19.95 (*0-471-57023-0*) Wiley.

Porterfield, Sally F. Jung's Advice to the Players: A Jungian Reading of Shakespeare's Problem Plays. LC 94-5150. (Contributions in Drama & Theatre Studies: No. 57). 136p. 1994. text ed. 39.95 (*0-313-29305-8*, Greenwood Pr) Greenwood.

Porterfield, Susan, ed. Zen, Poetry, the Art of Lucien Stryk. 360p. (C). 1993. text ed. 45.00 (*0-8040-0975-9*) Swallow.

Porterfield, William W. Inorganic Chemistry. LC 82-18485. (Illus.). 650p. 1984. text ed. write for info. (*0-201-05660-7*); teacher ed write for info. (*0-201-05661-5*) Addison-Wesley.

— Inorganic Chemistry: A Unified Approach. 2nd ed. (Illus.). 921p. 1993. text ed. 34.95 (*0-12-562980-X*) Acad Pr.

Porters, Eleanor H. Pollyanna. 176p. (YA). (gr. 6 up). 1993. pap. 5.95 (*1-55748-296-9*) Barbour & Co.

***Portes, Alejandro.** City on the Edge: The Transformation of Miami. 1994. pap. 15.00 (*0-520-08932-4*) U CA Pr.

— The New Second Generation. 224p. 1995. 29.95 (*0-87154-683-3*) Russell Sage.

Portes, Alejandro, ed. The Economic Sociology of Immigration: Essays on Networks, Ethnicity, & Entrepreneurship. 320p. 1995. 29.95 (*0-87154-682-5*) Russell Sage.

Portes, Alejandro & Bach, Robert L. Latin Journey: Cuban & Mexican Immigrants in the United States. LC 83-9292. 432p. 1985. 60.00 (*0-520-05003-7*); pap. 14.00 (*0-520-05004-5*) U CA Pr.

Portes, Alejandro & Rumbaut, Ruben G. Immigrant America: A Portrait. 1990. pap. 13.00 (*0-520-07038-0*) U CA Pr.

Portes, Alejandro & Stepick, Alex. City on the Edge: The Transformation of Miami. LC 92-39417. 1993. 25.00 (*0-520-08217-6*) U CA Pr.

Portes, Alejandro & Walton, John. Labor, Class, & the International System. LC 80-2772. 1981. text ed. 44.00 (*0-12-562020-9*) Acad Pr.

Portes, Alejandro, jt. ed. see Kincaid, A. Douglas.

Portes, Alejandro, et al, eds. The Informal Economy: Studies in Advanced & Less Developed Countries. LC 88-23004. 360p. 1989. pap. text ed. 16.95 (*0-8018-3736-7*) Johns Hopkins.

Portes Gil, Emilio. The Conflict Between the Civil Power & the Clergy: Historical & Legal Essay. 1976. lib. bdg. 59.95 (*0-87968-928-5*) Gordon Pr.

Portes, Richard. Deficits & Detente: Report of an International Conference on the Balance of Trade in the Comecon Countries. 92p. (Orig.). (C). 1983. pap. text ed. 6.00 (*0-87078-150-2*) TCFP-PPP.

Portes, Richard, ed. Economic Transformation in Central & Eastern Europe: A Progress Report. 312p. (C). Date not set. pap. 37.50 (*1-898128-00-6*) Brookings.

Portes, Richard, jt. auth. see Bryant, Ralph.

Portes, Richard, jt. ed. see Faini, Riccardo.

Portes, Richard, jt. ed. see Kaser, Michael.

Porteus, Elizabeth D., jt. auth. see Dole, Richard.

Porteus, H. Wyndham Lewis: A Discursive Explosion. 1972. 59.95 (*0-8490-1341-0*) Gordon Pr.

Porteus, Mark. The Gdansk Poetical Kit. 1982. 20.00 (*0-933466-03-X*); pap. 10.95 (*0-933466-02-1*) Bellevue Pr.

Porteus, Richard. Cat Owners Shape up Manual: Learn Aerobics from Your Cat. 1993. pap. 5.95 (*0-918259-51-7*) CCC Pubns.

Porteus, S. D. Ethnic Group Differences. 1984. lib. bdg. 79.95 (*0-87700-579-6*) Revisionist Pr.

Porteus, Stanley D. Century of Social Thinking in Hawaii. LC 62-21039. 1962. 24.95 (*0-87015-113-4*) Pacific Bks.

— Porteus Maze Test: Fifty Years' Application. LC 65-18125. (Illus.). 1965. 24.95 (*0-87015-139-8*) Pacific Bks.

— A Psychologist of Sorts: The Autobiography & Publications of the Inventor of the Porteus Maze Tests. LC 68-31287. (Illus.). 1969. 21.95x (*0-87015-174-6*) Pacific Bks.

— The Psychology of a Primitive People: Study of the Australian Aborigine. LC 71-37910. (Select Bibliographies Reprint Ser.). 1977. reprint ed. 41.95 (*0-8369-6748-8*) Ayer.

— Streamlined Elementary Education. LC 64-23745. (Illus.). 32p. (Orig.). 1964. pap. text ed. 3.95 (*0-87015-125-8*) Pacific Bks.

Porth, Carol M., et al. Pathophysiology: Concepts of Altered Health States. 4th ed. (Illus.). 1504p. (C). 1994. text ed. 57.95 (*0-397-54961-X*, Lippincott Nursing) Lippincott.

Porth, Richard H., jt. auth. see Maurer, John H.

Porthault, Marc, jt. auth. see De Bonneville, Francoise.

Portice, Jack, jt. auth. see Bass, Gene.

Portier, William L. Isaac Hecker & the First Vatican Council, Including Hecker's Notes in Italy: 1869-1870. LC 85-3034. (Studies in American Religion: Vol. 15). 360p. 1985. lib. bdg. 99.95 (*0-88946-653-X*) E Mellen.

— Tradition & Incarnation: Foundations of Christian Theology. LC 93-42702. 1994. 14.95 (*0-8091-3467-5*) Paulist Pr.

Portilla, Lorraine. He Brought Me out of a Horrible Pit. DeLellis, Leatrice, ed. & intro. by. (Orig.). pap. 5.00 (*0-9616892-0-X*) Your New Beginning.

Portillo, Carlos E. Eternal Security Is Conditional. LC 85-52117. 150p. (Orig.). 1987. pap. write for info. (*0-937365-03-3*) WCP Pubns.

— Evil Side of Good. LC 85-52117. 200p. (Orig.). pap. write for info. (*0-937365-04-1*) WCP Pubns.

— His Revelation from Apocalypses. LC 85-52117. 150p. (Orig.). 1987. pap. write for info. (*0-937365-02-5*) WCP Pubns.

— That Unknown Day. LC 85-52117. (Illus.). 400p. (Orig.). 1986. 14.95 (*0-937365-00-9*); pap. 9.95 (*0-937365-01-7*) WCP Pubns.

Portillo-Garcia, Rafael. Diccionario Ingles-Espanol, Espanol-Ingles de Terminoligia Teatral. 232p. 1986. pap. 29.95 (*0-7859-5773-1*) Fr & Eur.

Portillo, Jose A. De Campeon De Boxeo De Espana: From Boxing to Discipleship. (SPA.). 2.95 (*84-7228-818-8*, 220255, Pub. by Edit Clie SP) TSELF.

Portillo, Jose L. They Are Coming: The Conquest of Mexico. Berler, Beatrice, tr. LC 92-3142. (Illus.). 464p. (C). 1992. 34.50 (*0-929398-35-1*) UNTX Pr.

Portillo, Jose L. & Krashen, Stephen. Proceedings-Memoria Conference on Books in Spanish for Young Readers: Third Annual. Schon, Isabel, ed. 27p. (Orig.). (ENG & SPA.). (C). 1993. pap. 5.00 (*0-9639354-2-9*) CAU Ctr Study Bks.

Portillo, Peggy, tr. see Danner, David.

Portillo, Tina, ed. Dykescapes: Short Fiction by Lesbians. 176p. (Orig.). 1991. pap. 8.95 (*1-55583-195-8*) Alyson Pubns.

Portinara, Pierluigi. Cartography of North America. 1990. 24.99 (*0-517-03079-9*) Random Hse Value.

Portis, A. M. Electrodynamics of High Temperature Superconductors. (Lecture Notes in Physics Ser.). 1993. pap. text ed. 28.00 (*981-02-1248-8*) World Scientific Pub.

— Electrodynamics of High Temperature Superconductors. (Lecture Notes in Physics Ser.). 256p. 1993. text ed. 86.00 (*981-02-1215-1*) World Scientific Pub.

Portis, Charles. The Dog of the South. LC 78-65780. 1979. 13.95 (*0-394-50614-6*) Knopf.

— Masters of Atlantis. LC 85-40212. 256p. 1985. 15.95 (*0-394-54683-0*) Knopf.

— Norwood. 1994. lib. bdg. 24.95x (*1-56849-403-3*) Buccaneer Bks.

— True Grit. 304p. 1995. mass mkt. 5.50 (*0-451-18545-5*, Sig) NAL-Dutton.

Portis, Edward B. Reconstructing the Classics: Political Theory from Plato to Marx. LC 93-27199. (Chatham House Studies in Political Thinking). 192p. (Orig.). (C). 1994. pap. text ed. 19.95x (*1-56643-003-8*) Chatham Hse Pubs.

Portis, Edward B. & Levy, Michael B., eds. Handbook of Political Theory & Policy Science. LC 88-3119. 301p. 1988. text ed. 69.50 (*0-313-25598-9*, PHP/, Greenwood Pr) Greenwood.

Portis, Jonathan, jt. auth. see Allen, Charles F.

Portisch, Lajos & Sarkozy, Balazs. Six Hundred Endings. Eszenyi, Sandor et al, trs. (Chess Ser.). (Illus.). 198p. 1981. 21.90 (*0-08-024137-9*, Pergamon Pr) Elsevier.

Portland Art Museum Staff. Masterworks in Wood: The Christian Tradition. (Illus.). 108p. (Orig.). 1975. pap. 12.95 (*0-295-96134-1*, Portland Art Mus) U of Wash Pr.

***Portland Cement Association Staff.** Alternative Uses of Cement Kiln Dust. 18p. 1994. 17.00 (*0-89312-133-9*, RP327) Portland Cement.

— Cementitious Grouts & Grouting. (Illus.). 64p. (Orig.). (C). 1990. pap. text ed. 20.50 (*0-89312-088-X*, EB111) Portland Cement.

— Circular Concrete Tanks Without Prestressing. rev. ed. (Illus.). 55p. (C). 1993. 15.00 (*0-89312-125-8*, IS072D) Portland Cement.

— Concrete Construction & Estimating. Avery, Craig, ed. LC 80-12349. (Illus.). 576p. 1980. reprint ed. pap. 20.50 (*0-910460-75-2*) Craftsman.

— Connections for Tilt-Up Wall Construction. 43p. (Orig.). (C). 1987. pap. text ed. 10.00 (*0-89312-086-3*, EB110T) Portland Cement.

— Design & Control of Concrete Mixtures. 13th rev. ed. 212p. (Orig.). (C). 1992. reprint ed. pap. text ed. 33.00 (*0-89312-087-1*, EB001T) Portland Cement.

— Detailed Illustration of Contingent Management Practices for Cement Kiln Dust. (Illus.). 52p. 1993. 28.00 (*0-89312-126-6*, SP115.01T) Portland Cement.

— Effects on Cement of High Efficiency Separators. 42p. 1995. 29.00 (*0-89312-132-0*, RD110) Portland Cement.

— High-Strength Concrete. rev. ed. (Illus.). 56p. (C). 1994. 7.25 (*0-89312-127-4*, EB114) Portland Cement.

— Notes on ACI 318-89 Building Code Requirements for Reinforced Concrete with Design Applications. 5th rev. ed. Ghosh, S. K. & Rabbat, Basile G., eds. (Illus.). 890p. 1990. pap. 45.00 (*0-89312-090-1*, EB070) Portland Cement.

— Optimizing Surface Texture of Concrete Pavement. 108p. 1995. 25.00 (*0-89312-134-7*, RD111.01T) Portland Cement.

— Role of Minor Elements in Cement Manufacturing & Use. (Illus.). 46p. 1994. 25.00 (*0-89312-131-2*, RD109T) Portland Cement.

— Simplified Design: Reinforced Concrete Buildings of Moderate Size & Height. 2nd ed. (Illus.). 250p. (C). 1993. 30.00 (*0-89312-129-0*, EB104) Portland Cement.

Portlock, Carol S. Clinical Problems in Oncology. 1986. 10.95 (*0-316-71427-5*) Little.

— Manual Oncology, No. 2. 1986. 15.95 (*0-316-71426-7*) Little.

Portlock, Carol S. & Goffinet, Donald R. Manual of Clinical Problems in Oncology. 2nd ed. (Little, Brown Spiral Manual Ser.). 1986. 27.00 (*0-316-71425-9*) Little.

Portlock, Melinda J. Cooperative Education Student Journal. 48p. 1993. spiral bd. 12.95 (*0-8403-8790-3*) Kendall-Hunt.

Portlock, Rob. Buster the Biker Sheep. LC 93-19201. (Portlock Books for Kids). (Illus.). 32p. (Orig.). (J). (ps-2). 1993. pap. 4.99 (*0-8308-1904-5*, 1904) InterVarsity.

— Climbing the Church Walls. LC 91-17872. (Illus.). 104p. (Orig.). 1991. pap. 6.99 (*0-8308-1830-8*, 1830) InterVarsity.

— Families off the Wall. LC 94-18628. 104p. (Orig.). 1994. pap. 6.99 (*0-8308-1823-5*, 1823) InterVarsity.

— My Dad Ran over a Frog. LC 92-11584. (Portlock Kids Ser.). (Illus.). 32p. (Orig.). (J). (ps-1). 1992. pap. 4.99 (*0-8308-1901-0*, 1901) InterVarsity.

— Noon on the Moon. LC 93-19202. (Portlock Books for Kids). (Illus.). 32p. (Orig.). (J). (ps-2). 1993. pap. 4.99 (*0-8308-1903-7*, 1903) InterVarsity.

— Off the Church Wall. LC 87-2774. (Illus.). 108p. 1987. pap. 6.99 (*0-87784-753-3*, 753) InterVarsity.

— Someone's Trying to Cut off My Head. LC 92-12483. (Portlock Kids Ser.). (Illus.). 32p. (Orig.). (J). (ps-1). 1992. pap. 4.99 (*0-8308-1902-9*, 1902) InterVarsity.

— Way off the Church Wall. LC 89-11230. (Illus.). 108p. (Orig.). 1989. pap. 6.99 (*0-8308-1281-4*, 1281) InterVarsity.

Portman, Ian. Guide to Luxor. (Illus.). 120p. 1988. pap. 25.00 (*977-424-189-4*, Pub. by Am Univ Cairo Pr UA) Col U Pr.

***Portman, M. V.** A History of Our Relations with the Andamanese, Set. (C). 1995. 94.00x (*81-206-0608-6*, Pub. by Asian Educ Servs II) S Asia.

— History of Our Relations with the Andamanese, 2 vols., Set. (C). 1990. reprint ed. text ed. 100.00 (*0-685-39099-3*, Pub. by Asian Educ Servs II) S Asia.

Portman, V. T., jt. ed. see Reshetov, D. N.

Portmann. Ear & Temporal Bone. 1979. 103.50 (*0-89352-034-9*) Mosby Yr Bk.

Portmann, et al. Color Symbolism: Six Excerpts from the Eranos Yearbook 1972. Jennings et al, trs. LC 87-28764. 202p. 1983. pap. 18.00 (*0-88214-400-6*) Spring Pubns.

Portmann, Adolf. Essays in Philosophical Zoology by Adolf Portmann: The Living Form & the Seeing Eye. Carter, Richard B., tr. LC 90-5672. (Problems in Contemporary Philosophy Ser.: Vol. 20). 296p. 1991. lib. bdg. 89.95 (*0-88946-323-9*) E Mellen.

— A Zoologist Looks at Humankind. Schaefer, Judith, tr. 192p. 1990. text ed. 36.50 (*0-231-06194-3*) Col U Pr.

Portmann, Michael, et al. Rhino-Otological Microsurgery of the Skull Base. LC 93-33094. (Practice of Surgery Ser.). (Illus.). 320p. 1994. 185.00 (*0-443-04539-9*) Churchill.

Portnay, Linda. Wishing for the Worst. 40p. 1993. pap. 10.00 (*0-942292-12-X*) Warthog Pr.

Portner, Hal & Pauker, Robert. How to Study Less & Accomplish More: Time Management for Students. (Illus.). 44p. (Orig.). (C). (gr. 11 up). 1983. pap. 6.95 (*0-913149-00-4*) Portner.

Portney-Chase, Mildred. Improvisation: Music from the Inside Out. LC 87-30472. 120p. (Orig.). 1988. pap. 7.95 (*0-88739-058-7*) Creat Arts Bk.

Portney, Kent, jt. auth. see Danziger, Sheldon.

Portney, Kent E. Controversial Issues in Environmental Policy. (Controversial Issues In Public Policy Ser.: Vol. 1). (Illus.). 192p. (C). 1992. 38.00 (*0-8039-4221-4*); pap. 17.50 (*0-8039-4222-2*) Sage.

— Siting Hazardous Waste Treatment Facilities: The Nimby Syndrome. LC 90-1217. 192p. 1991. text ed. 45.00 (*0-86569-016-2*, T016, Auburn Hse) Greenwood.

Portney, Kent E., jt. ed. see Danziger, Sheldon H.

Portney, Leslie G. & Watkins, Mary P. Foundations of Clinical Research: Applications to Practice. (Illus.). 560p. (C). 1993. text ed. 47.95 (*0-8385-1065-5*, A1065-0) Appleton & Lange.

Portney, Paul R., ed. Economic Issues in Metropolitan Growth. LC 76-15906. (Resources for the Future Ser.). 160p. 1977. 15.00 (*0-8018-1885-0*) Johns Hopkins.

— Economic Issues in Metropolitan Growth: Papers Presented at a Forum Conducted by Resources for the Future, May 28-29, 1975 in Washington D. C. LC 76-15906. (Illus.). 157p. reprint ed. pap. 44.80 (*0-685-23705-2*, 2032161) Bks Demand.

— Natural Resources & the Environment: The Reagan Approach. (Illus.). 144p. (Orig.). 1984. pap. text ed. 18.50 (*0-87766-334-3*) Urban Inst.

— Public Policies for Environmental Protection. LC 89-24363. 328p. 1990. pap. 12.95 (*0-915707-53-5*) Resources Future.

Portney, Paul R. & Haas, Ruth B., eds. Current Issues in Natural Resource Policy. LC 87-47982. 300p. 1982. 20.00 (*0-8018-2916-X*); pap. 9.95 (*0-8018-2917-8*) Resources Future.

Portney, Paul R., jt. auth. see Probst, Katherine N.

Portney, Paul R., et al, eds. Current Issues in U. S. Environmental Policy. LC 78-4328. 207p. 1978. pap. 9.95 (*0-8018-2118-5*) Resources Future.

Portnoi, Henry. Creative Bass Technique. 12.00 (*0-318-18108-8*) Am String Tchrs.

***Portnoi, L. M. & Dibirov, M. P.** Radiodiagnosis of Endophytic Gastric Cancer. LC 95-12084. 1995. write for info. (*1-56700-028-2*) Begell Hse.

***Portnov, Anna, des.** Awakening: Articles & Stories about Jews & Yeshua (Jesus) 104p. (RUS.). 1991. write for info. (*1-880226-01-4*) Lederer Pubns.

— Awakening: Articles & Stories about Jews & Yeshua (Jesus) 104p. 1992. write for info. (*1-880226-09-X*) Lederer Pubns.

Portnov, Mikhail, jt. auth. see Sedov, Alexander.

Portnoy, Dina. Women: The Recruiter's Last Resort. 40p. 1974. 2.00 (*0-686-43095-6*) Recon Pubns.

Portnoy, J. Elias. Let the Seller Beware. 256p. (Orig.). 1991. pap. 9.95 (*0-02-036047-9*, Collier S&S) S&S Trade.

Portnoy-James, Jeanne. Write It Down. 160p. (C). 1987. pap. text ed. 18.00 (*0-03-000174-9*) HB Coll Pubs.

Portnoy, Joan, jt. auth. see Portnoy, Sanford.

Portnoy, Julius. Music in the Life of Man. LC 73-9265. (Illus.). 300p. 1973. reprint ed. text ed. 35.00 (*0-8371-7000-1*, POMU, Greenwood Pr) Greenwood.

— The Philosopher & Music. LC 79-28303. (Music Reprint Ser.). 1980. reprint ed. lib. bdg. 35.00 (*0-306-76006-1*) Da Capo.

Portnoy, Kathy L., jt. auth. see Callner, Bruce W.

Portnoy, Kenneth. Screen Adaptation: A Scriptwriting Handbook. 192p. 1991. pap. 21.95 (*0-240-80095-8*, Focal) Buttrwrth-Heinemann.

Portnoy, Linda & Farley, Eileen P. Washington Criminal Practice in Court of Limited Jurisdiction, 2 vols., Set. LC 92-42802. 1993. ring bd. 175.00 (*1-56257-834-0*) Michie Butterworth.

Portnoy, Mindy A. Matzah Ball. LC 93-39402. (Illus.). (J). (gr. 1-5). 1994. pap. 5.95 (*0-929371-69-0*) Kar Ben.

P Q

An Asterisk (*) at the beginning of an entry indicates that the title is appearing in BIP for the first time.

— Mommy Never Went to Hebrew School. LC 89-30874. (Illus.). 32p. (J). (gr. k-5). 1989. pap. 4.95 (*0-930494-97-0*) Kar Ben.

Portnoy, Samuel A., tr. Henryk Erlich & Victor Alter: Two Heroes & Martyrs for Jewish Socialism. rev. ed. 39.50 (*0-88125-357-X*) Ktav.

***Portnoy, Sanford & Portnoy, Joan.** How to Take Great Trips with Your Kids. rev. ed. Ziedrich, Linda, ed. 208p. 1995. 16.95 (*1-55832-073-3*) Harvard Common Pr.

— How to Take Great Trips with Your Kids. rev. ed. Ziedrich, Linda, ed. 208p. 1995. pap. 9.95 (*1-55832-074-1*) Harvard Common Pr.

Porto Editora Staff. Dicionario Alamao - Portugues - German - Portuguese Dictionary. 1991. 75.00 (*0-8288-8543-5*) Fr & Eur.

— Dicionario Da Lingua Portuguesa. 591p. 1992. 29.95 (*0-8288-8529-X*) Fr & Eur.

— Dicionario Espanhol - Portugues, Portugues - Espanhol - Portuguese - Spanish, Span ish - Portuguese Dictionary. 1195p. 1990. 49.95 (*0-8288-8533-8*) Fr & Eur.

— Dicionario Ingles - Portugues - English - Portuguese Dictionary. 1991. 75.00 (*0-8288-8542-7*) Fr & Eur.

— Dicionario Italiano - Portugues - Italian - Portuguese Dictionary. 1991. 75.00 (*0-8288-8547-8*) Fr & Eur.

— Dicionario Latim - Portugese - Latin - Portuguese Dictionary. 1991. 75.00 (*0-8288-8545-1*) Fr & Eur.

— Dicionario Portugues - Alemao - Portuguese - German Dictionary. 1991. 75.00 (*0-8288-8544-3*) Fr & Eur.

— Dicionario Portugues - Espanhol - Portuguese - Spanish Dictionary. 594p. 1989. 29.95 (*0-8288-8531-1*) Fr & Eur.

— Dicionario Portugues - Frances - Portuguese French Dictionary. 652p. 1991. 29.95 (*0-8288-8530-3*) Fr & Eur.

— Dicionario Portugues - Italiano - Portuguese - Italian Dictionary. 1991. 75.00 (*0-8288-8548-6*) Fr & Eur.

— Dicionario Portugues - Latim - Portuguese - Latin Dictionary. 1991. 75.00 (*0-8288-8546-X*) Fr & Eur.

— Dicionario Romeno - Portugues - Romanian - Portuguese Dictionary. 1991. 75.00 (*0-8288-8549-4*) Fr & Eur.

— Dictionario Frances - Portugues. 543p. 1992. 29.95 (*0-8288-8534-6*) Fr & Eur.

— Dictionario Frances - Portugues, Portugues - Frances. 1195p. 1992. 49.95 (*0-8288-8532-X*) Fr & Eur.

Porto, Manuel, jt. auth. see McGahan, John P.

Portocarero, Lucienne. Social Mobility in Industrial Societies: Women in France & Sweden. (Swedish Institute for Social Research Ser.: No. 3). 118p. (Orig.). 1987. pap. text ed. 36.00x (*91-7604-025-9*, Pub. by Almqv & Wiksell SW) Coronet Bks.

Portocarrero, Nestor de J., jt. auth. see Moncarz, Elisa S.

Portoghesi, Paolo, jt. auth. see Borsi, Franco.

Portolese, Domenick A. Pilots, Not Passengers. 1992. pap. 12.50 (*0-533-10340-1*) Vantage.

Porton, Gary G. Goyim: Gentiles & Israelites in Mishnah-Tosefta. LC 88-30827. (Brown Judaic Studies). 373p. 1989. 62.95 (*1-55540-278-X*, 14-01-55) Scholars Pr GA.

— The Stranger Within Your Gates: Converts & Conversion in Rabbinic Literature. 240p. 1994. 29.95 (*0-226-67586-6*) U Ch Pr.

— Understanding Rabbinic Midrash. 1985. 16.95 (*0-88125-056-2*) Ktav.

Portoraro, Arthur. Formal Logic. 1993. text ed. write for info. (*0-13-327628-7*) P-H.

Ports, Michael A., ed. Hydraulic Engineering. 1200p. 1989. pap. text ed. 107.00 (*0-87262-719-5*, 719) Am Soc Civil Eng.

Portsmouth Polytechnic Staff. Immobilization of Copper by Marine Fouling Micro-Organisms. 67p. 1984. write for info. (*0-318-60403-5*) Intl Copper.

Portsmouth, Wiulliam. Healing Prayer. (C). 1990. pap. 24.00 (*0-85305-230-1*, Pub. by J Arthur Ltd UK) St Mut.

Portugal, Ana M., ed. Mujeres e Iglesia: Sexualidad y Aborto en America Latina. (Illus.). 146p. (Orig.). (SPA.). 1989. pap. 10.00 (*0-915365-15-4*) Cath Free Choice.

Portugal, Armando S., photos. Luis Barragan: The Architecture of Light, Color, & Form. LC 92-15545. (Illus.). 168p. 1992. 45.00 (*0-8478-1482-3*) Rizzoli Intl.

Portugal, Jan. ABC Sillies. LC 83-10291. (Living on This Planet Ser.). (Illus.). 56p. (Orig.). (J). (ps-1). 1983. pap. 3.00 (*0-937148-13-X*) Wild Horses.

Portugal, Nancy & Main, Jody. Potted Plant Organic Care. 3rd ed. LC 79-22173. (Living on This Planet Ser.). (Illus.). 80p. 1978. pap. 4.50 (*0-9601088-7-4*) Wild Horses.

Portugal, Pam Rainbear. A Place for Human Beings. 2nd ed. (Living on This Planet Ser.). (Illus.). 160p. 1978. pap. 6.95 (*0-9601088-5-8*) Wild Horses.

Portugali. Distribution, Allocation, Social Structure & Spatial Form: Elements of Planning Theory. (Progress in Planning Ser.: Vol. 14, Part 3). (Illus.). 83p. 1980. pap. 16.25 (*0-08-026808-0*, Pergamon Pr) Elsevier.

Portugali, Juval. Implicate Relations: Society & Space in the Israeli-Palestinian Conflict. 1993. lib. bdg. 90.00 (*0-7923-1886-2*) Kluwer Ac.

Portuges, Catherine. Screen Memories: The Hungarian Cinema of Marta Meszaros. LC 92-2359. (International Women Filmmakers Ser.). 208p. 1993. 35.00 (*0-253-34558-8*); pap. 14.95 (*0-253-20782-7*) Ind U Pr.

Portuges, Paul. Paper Song. (Illus.). 160p. 1985. pap. 9.95 (*0-915520-80-X*) R-E CA.

— The Visionary Poetics of Allen Ginsberg. LC 78-6094. 1978. lib. bdg. 11.95 (*0-915520-17-6*); pap. 6.95 (*0-915520-12-5*) R-E CA.

Portugues, Gladys & Vedral, Joyce L. Hard Bodies. (Orig.). 1986. pap. 14.95 (*0-440-53424-0*, Dell Trade Pbks) Dell.

Portune, Robert. Changing Adolescent Attitudes Toward Police. LC 77-358331. (Criminal Justice Ser.: Vol. 4). 285p. reprint ed. pap. 81.30 (*0-8357-9036-3*, 2015227) Bks Demand.

Portuondo, Aleyda T. Vigencia Politica & Literaria De Martin Morua Delgado. (Coleccion Cuba y Sus Jueces Ser.). 1978. pap. 2.00 (*0-89729-205-7*) Ediciones.

Portuondo, Alicia E. & Singer, Greta L. Spanish for Social Workers. LC 80-53983. (Senda Didactica Ser.). 96p. (Orig.). (C). 1981. pap. 8.50 (*0-918454-25-5*) Senda Nueva.

Portuondo, Marie F. Ups & Downs of an Unaccompanied Minor Refugee. (Illus.). 31p. (Orig.). 1984. pap. 4.50 (*0-89729-352-5*) Ediciones.

***Portvliet, Rien.** Rien Portvliet's Horses. (Illus.). 248p. 1995. 60.00 (*1-55670-430-5*) Stewart Tabori & Chang.

***Portway, Patrick & Lane, Carla.** Guide to Teleconferencing & Distance Learning. 2nd ed. 420p. (C). Date not set. pap. text ed. 55.00 (*0-9643270-1-5*) Applied Busn.

Portwood, Doris. Commonsense Suicide: The Final Right. 142p. 1983. pap. 8.00 (*0-9606030-2-6*) Hemlock Soc.

Portwood, Pamela, et al, eds. Rebirth of Power: Overcoming the Effects of Sexual Abuse Through the Experiences of Others. LC 87-62737. 210p. 1988. pap. 9.95 (*0-941300-07-2*) Mother Courage.

***Portwood, Timothy.** Joint Ventures Under EEC Competition Law. (European Community Law Ser.). 192p. (C). 1996. text ed. 90.00 (*0-485-70012-3*, Pub. by Athlone Pr UK) Humanities.

— Mergers under EEC Competition Law. (European Community Law Ser.). 240p. (C). 1994. text ed. 90.00 (*0-485-70009-3*, Pub. by Athlone Pr UK) Humanities.

Portwood, Timothy, ed. Commercial Law, Vol. 2: International Trade. 252p. (C). 1991. 72.00 (*1-85352-383-6*, Pub. by HLT Pubns UK) St Mut.

— International Trade. 260p. (C). 1991. 120.00 (*1-85352-904-4*, Pub. by HLT Pubns UK) St Mut.

Portz, John. The Politics of Plant Closings. LC 90-32817. (Studies in Government & Public Policy). x, 214p. 1990. 29.95 (*0-7006-0472-3*); pap. 12.95 (*0-7006-0473-1*) U Pr of KS.

Portz, M. Susan. The Wedding Resource Directory: An Annual Directory of Wedding Services in the Denver-Boulder Area. 3rd ed. (Illus.). 110p. 1989. pap. 8.95 (*0-9617718-2-8*) Bascom Pr.

— The Wedding Resource Directory: An Annual Directory of Wedding Services in the Denver-Boulder Area. 4th ed. (Illus.). 104p. 1990. write for info. (*0-318-66813-0*); pap. 8.95 (*0-9617718-3-6*) Bascom Pr.

Poruchikov, V. B. Methods of the Classical Theory of Elastodynamics. Khokhryakov, V. A., tr. (Illus.). 336p. 1993. 89.00 (*0-387-54817-3*) Spr-Verlag.

***Porus, Marcus & Porus, Shirley.** Who Is Gribich. (Gribich & Friends Ser.). (Illus.). 32p. (J). (ps). 1995. 14.95 (*0-9646125-0-X*) Doog Pub Grp.

***Porus, Marcus, et al.** Trip to Planet Doog. (Gribich & Friends Ser.). (Illus.). 32p. (J). (ps). 1996. 14.95 (*0-9646125-1-8*) Doog Pub Grp.

Porus, Shirley, jt. auth. see Porus, Marcus.

Porush. Renal Disease in the Aged. 1991. 82.95 (*0-316-71401-1*) Little.

Porush, David. Rope Dances. LC 78-68135. 127p. 1979. 15. 95 (*0-914590-50-2*); pap. 6.95 (*0-914590-51-0*) Fiction Coll.

— A Short Guide to Writing about Science. LC 94-3119. (Short Guide Ser.). (C). 1995. 16.00 (*0-06-500754-9*) HarpCollege.

Porwit, K. & Stadler, J. Central Planning Evaluation of Variants. LC 66-17808. 1967. 83.00 (*0-08-011773-2*, Pub. by Pergamon Repr UK) Franklin.

Pory, John, tr. see Africanus, John L.

Pory, John, tr. see Leo, Johannes.

Porzak, Brian. The One. (Illus.). 395p. (Orig.). 1987. pap. 12.95 (*0-937983-00-4*) Copy Concepts.

Porzel, Michele. Resources for Early Childhood Training: An Annotated Bibliography. LC 87-62944. 72p. 1987. pap. text ed. 5.00 (*0-935989-12-9*, NAEYC #790) Natl Assn Child Ed.

Porzner, Konrad, et al, eds. Vierzig Jahre Deutscher Bundestag. 309p. 1991. pap. 38.50 (*3-7890-1962-3*, Pub. by Nomos Verlags GW) Intl Bk Import.

Posada, E. & Violini, G., eds. Search of Gravitational Waves: Proceedings of the Workshop Held in Bogota, Columbia, March 30-April 7, 1982. (CIF Ser.: Vol. 2). 244p. 1983. 47.00 (*9971-950-78-2*) World Scientific Pub.

Posada, J. G. Messenger of Mortality: Popular Prints of J. G. Posada. Rothenstein, Julian, ed. (Illus.). 196p. (Orig.). 1989. pap. 24.95 (*0-918825-79-2*) Moyer Bell.

Posada, Jose G. Posada's Popular Mexican Prints. Berdecio, Robert & Appelbaum, Stanley, eds. LC 77-178994. (Illus.). 192p. (Orig.). 1972. pap. 10.95 (*0-486-22854-1*) Dover.

Posadas, Barbara & McColley, Robert, eds. Refracting America: Gender, Ethnicity, Class, Race, & Environment. (American History to Eighteen Seventy-Seven Ser.: Vol. 1). 256p. (Orig.). (C). 1993. pap. text ed. 11.36 (*1-881089-16-9*) Brandywine Press.

Posadas, Barbara, jt. ed. see Guyette, Roland L.

Posadskaya, Anastasia, ed. Women in Russia: A New Era in Russian Feminism. Clarke, Kate, tr. LC 94-17273. 256p. 1994. 59.95 (*0-86091-487-9*, B3657, Pub. by Verso UK); pap. 18.95 (*0-86091-657-X*, B3661, Pub. by Verso UK) Routledge Chapman & Hall.

***Posamentier, Alfred S.** Teaching Secondary School Mathematics. 4th ed. 1995. pap. 47.00 (*0-02-396262-3*) Macmillan.

Posamentier, Alfred S. & Stepelman, Jay. Teaching Secondary School Mathematics: Techniques & Enrichment Units. 3rd ed. 496p. (C). 1990. pap. write for info. (*0-675-21209-X*, Merrill Pub Co) Macmillan.

Posamentier, Henry, jt. ed. see Weimer, Paul.

Posamentier, Henry W., et al, eds. Sequence Stratigraphy & Facies Associations. LC 92-34625. (International Association of Sedimentologists Special Publication Ser.: No. 18). 1994. write for info. (*0-632-03548-X*) Blackwell Sci.

Posavac, Emil J. & Carey, Raymond G. Program Evaluation: Methods & Case Studies. 4th ed. 352p. 1991. text ed. 62.00 (*0-13-678129-2*, 670802) P-H.

Posch, Robert J., Jr. The Complete Guide to Marketing & the Law. 848p. 1988. text ed. 79.95 (*0-13-160904-1*) P-H.

— The Complete Guide to Marketing & the Law, 1990 Cumulative Supplement. 240p. 1990. pap. 40.00 (*0-685-38167-6*) P-H.

Poschel, Jurgen & Trubowitz, Eugene. Inverse Spectral Theory. (Pure & Applied Mathematics Ser.). 200p. 1987. text ed. 53.00 (*0-12-563040-9*) Acad Pr.

Poschl, Viktor. The Art of Vergil: Image & Symbol in the "Aeneid" Seligson, Gerda, tr. LC 85-27077. 222p. 1986. reprint ed. text ed. 45.50 (*0-313-25053-7*, POAV, Greenwood Pr) Greenwood.

Poschlod, P. Vegetationsentwickelung in Abgetorften Hochmooren des Bayerischen Alpenvorlandes unter Besonderer Beruecksichtigung Standorts-Kundlicher und Populationsbiologischer Factoren. (Dissertationes Botanicae Ser.: Vol. 152). (Illus.). 332p. 1990. pap. 110. 00 (*3-443-64064-8*, Pub. by Cramer-Borntraeger GW) Lubrecht & Cramer.

Poscovsky, Aaron D. Football Cards Reference Guide. Orig. Title: Football Card Checklist. (Illus.). 200p. 1982. reprint ed. pap. 8.95 (*0-943110-50-5*) Vantage Printing.

Pose, K. S., jt. auth. see Smith, M. D.

Posel. Enjoy Investing on the Stock Exchange. 1990. pap. text ed. 36.95 (*0-409-10262-8*) Buttrwrth-Heinemann.

Posel, Deborah. The Making of Apartheid, 1948-1961: Conflict & Compromise. (Oxford Studies in African Affairs). 312p. 1992. 75.00 (*0-19-827334-7*) OUP.

***Posel, K.** Quantitative Methods for Tax Planning & Decision Making. 265p. 1991. pap. 74.00 (*0-409-10962-2*, SA) Butterworth Legal Pubs.

Posel, Norman S., tr. see Epstein, Simon.

Poseljanin, E. Russkije Podvizhniki Blagotchestija 19-20 vekev. 908p. reprint ed. 35.00 (*0-317-29250-1*) Holy Trinity.

Posell, Elsa. Cats. LC 82-23484. (New True Bks.). (Illus.). 48p. (J). (gr. k-4). 1983. lib. bdg. 12.90 (*0-516-01671-7*) Childrens.

— Deserts. LC 81-15548. (New True Bks.). (Illus.). 48p. (J). (gr. k-4). 1982. lib. bdg. 12.90 (*0-516-01613-X*); pap. 4.95 (*0-516-41613-8*) Childrens.

— Dogs. LC 81-7742. (New True Bks.). (Illus.). 48p. (J). (gr. k-4). 1981. lib. bdg. 12.90 (*0-516-01614-8*); pap. 4.95 (*0-516-41614-6*) Childrens.

— Elephants. LC 81-38470. (New True Bks.). (Illus.). 48p. (J). (gr. k-4). 1982. lib. bdg. 12.90 (*0-516-01621-0*) Childrens.

— Homecoming. 230p. (YA). (gr. 7 up). 1987. 14.95 (*0-15-235160-4*, HB Juv Bks) HarBrace.

— Horses. LC 81-7741. (New True Bks.). (Illus.). 48p. (J). (gr. k-4). 1981. lib. bdg. 12.90 (*0-516-01623-7*); pap. 4.95 (*0-516-41623-5*) Childrens.

— Whales & Other Sea Mammals. LC 82-4451. (New True Bks.). (J). (gr. k-4). 1982. 12.90 (*0-516-01663-6*); pap. 4.95 (*0-516-41663-4*) Childrens.

Posen, Barry R. Inadvertent Escalation: Conventional War & Nuclear Risks. LC 91-55055. (Cornell Studies in Security Affairs). 304p. 1992. 39.95 (*0-8014-2563-8*) Cornell U Pr.

— The Sources of Military Doctrine: France, Britain & Germany Between the World Wars. LC 84-7610. (Cornell Studies in Security Affairs). 288p. 1984. 39.95 (*0-8014-1633-7*); pap. 14.95 (*0-8014-9427-3*) Cornell U Pr.

Posen, I. Sheldon. For Singing & Dancing & All Sorts of Fun: The Story of the Ottawa Valley's Most Famous Song: The Chapeau Boys. (Illus.). xiv, 144p. (Orig.). 1992. pap. text ed. 10.95 (*0-88879-178-X*) Legacy Books.

— You Hear the Ice Talking: The Ways of People & Ice on Lake Champlain. LC 86-29914. (Illus.). 70p. (Orig.). 1986. pap. 11.00 (*0-9617701-1-2*) C E F Lib Syst.

Posener, Georges. Dictionnaire de la Civilisation Egytienne: Dictionary of the Egyptian Civilization. 326p. (FRE.). 1988. 79.95 (*0-8288-6512-4*, M-6462) Fr & Eur.

Posener, Julius, ed. Hans Poelzig: Reflections on His Life & Work. (Illus.). 348p. 1992. 55.00x (*0-262-16127-3*) MIT Pr.

Poser. International Securities Regulations. 1990. 175.00 (*0-316-71441-0*) Little.

Poser, jt. auth. see Oppenlander.

Poser, G., jt. auth. see Oppenlander, K. H.

Poser, Gunter, jt. auth. see Oppenlander, Karl H.

Poser, Gunter, jt. ed. see Oppenlander, Karl H.

Poser, Hans. Philosophie und Mythos. (C). 1979. text ed. 68.70 (*3-11-007601-2*) De Gruyter.

Poser, Hans, ed. see Wright, Georg H. Von.

Poser, Margaret, tr. see Baldacci, Paolo, et al.

Poser, William J., ed. Papers from the Second International Workshop on Japanese Syntax. LC 88-18763. 243p. 1988. 35.00 (*0-937073-39-3*); pap. 14.95 (*0-937073-38-5*) Ctr Study Language.

Poser, Yvonne, jt. auth. see Pfister, Guenter G.

Poses, Steven, et al. The Frog: Commissary Cookbook. LC 84-7089. (Illus.). 288p. 1985. pap. 17.50 (*0-385-18457-3*) Doubleday.

***Posewitz, Jim.** Beyond Fair Chase: The Ethic & Tradition of Hunting. 1994. 17.95 (*1-56044-302-2*) Falcon Pr MT.

— Beyond Fair Chase: The Ethic & Tradition of the Hunt. LC 94-10052. 128p. (Orig.). 1994. pap. 5.95 (*1-56044-283-2*) Falcon Pr MT.

Posey, Alexander. The Fus Fixico Letters. Littlefield, Daniel F., Jr. & Petty-Hunter, Carol A., eds. LC 92-46061. (Illus.). xviii, 330p. 1993. 37.50 (*0-8032-3704-9*) U of Nebr Pr.

Posey, Anita. Don't Look Back. LC 90-71364. 175p. 1991. 12.95 (*1-55523-389-9*) Winston-Derek.

***Posey, Carl.** Big Book of Weirdos. Taggart, B. C., ed. (Illus.). 224p. 1995. pap. 12.95 (*1-56389-180-8*, Paradox) DC Comics.

— Bushmaster Fall. 1992. 19.95 (*1-55611-245-9*) D I Fine.

Posey, Carl A. Kiev Footprint. 256p. 1987. mass mkt. 3.95 (*0-373-62103-5*) Harlequin Bks.

Posey, Carl A., Jr. The Living Earth Book of Wind & Weather. LC 94-16264. (Reader's Digest Living Earth Ser.). (Illus.). 224p. 1994. 30.00 (*0-89577-625-1*) RD Assn.

Posey, Carl S. The Wasted Seed. Van Treese, James B., ed. 280p. 1994. pap. 8.95 (*1-56901-122-2*) NW Pub.

Posey County, Indiana Historical Society Staff. Posey County, Indiana One Hundred Seventy-Fifth Anniversary 1814-1989. LC 89-51786. 208p. 1989. 49. 95 (*0-938021-72-9*) Turner Pub KY.

Posey, Darrell A. & Balee, William, eds. Resource Management in Amazonia: Indigenous & Folk Strategies. LC 89-9392. (Advances in Economic Botany Ser.: Vol. 7). (Illus.). 304p. 1989. pap. text ed. 59.00 (*0-89327-340-6*) NY Botanical.

Posey, Ellis. The Funny Side of Texas. LC 93-49648. (Illus.). 120p. 1994. pap. 7.95 (*1-55622-323-4*, Rep of TX Pr) Wordware Pub.

***Posey, Harry H., et al, eds.** Proceedings: Summitville Forum '95: Summitville Forum 95. (Special Publications: No. 38). (Illus.). 375p. 1995. text ed. 95.00 (*1-884216-51-X*) Colo Geol Survey.

Posey, Imogene A. Study Guide to Accompany Hanson-Hamre-Walgenbach, Principles of Accounting, Vol. II, Chapters 14-28. 6th ed. 642p. (C). 1993. student ed, pap. text ed. 18.50 (*0-03-097392-9*) Dryden Pr.

Posey, John T. General Thomas Posey: Son of the American Revolution. LC 92-50243. (C). 1992. 31.95 (*0-87013-316-0*) Mich St U Pr.

Posey, Josephine M. Against Great Odds: The History of Alcorn State University. LC 93-38375. (Illus.). 224p. 1994. 29.50 (*0-87805-681-5*) U Pr of Miss.

Posey, Michael. Reflections on the Wall. 1994. 9.95 (*1-881116-31-X*) Black Forrest Pr.

Posey, Pam, illus. Thomas the Tank Engine: Coming & Going -- A Book of Opposites. (Thomas the Tank Engine Toddler Board Bks.). 14p. (J). (ps). 1993. pap. 57.48 (*0-679-81645-3*) McKay.

— Thomas the Tank Engine - Colors. (Thomas the Tank Engine Toddler Board Bks.). 12p. (J). (ps). 1993. bds. 2.29 (*0-679-81646-1*) Random Bks Yng Read.

Posey, Rollin B. American Government. 11th ed. LC 82-24896. (Quality Paperback Ser.). (Illus.). 394p. (Orig.). 1983. pap. 17.95 (*0-8226-0372-1*) Littlefield.

Posey, Walter B. The Development of Methodism in the Old Southwest: 1783-1824. LC 73-18408. (Perspectives in American History Ser.: No. 19). (Illus.). 151p. 1974. reprint ed. lib. bdg. 29.50 (*0-87991-339-8*) Porcupine Pr.

Posey, Walter B., ed. Alabama in the 1830's. (Illus.). 5.95 (*0-317-68073-0*) Southern U Pr.

Posgay, Mike & Warner, Ian. The World of Head Vase Planters. (Illus.). 152p. (Orig.). 1992. pap. 34.95 (*0-915410-84-2*, 4015); write for info. (*0-318-69707-6*, 4017) Antique Pubns.

Posgay, Mike, jt. auth. see Warner, Ian.

Poshek, Lucy. Bed & Breakfast Guide - Southwest: Arizona, New Mexico, Texas. LC 92-24998. 1993. 16.00 (*0-671-84952-2*, P-H Travel) P-H Gen Ref & Trav.

Poshek, Lucy, comp. & intro. Inn Side Views: A Collection of Inn-Sights by B&B Guests. LC 87-91317. (Illus.). 81p. 1987. pap. 4.95 (*0-9619275-0-X*) Poshek Prodns.

Posher, Roland, tr. see Lewis, David K.

Poshyananda, Apinan. Modern Art in Thailand in the Nineteenth & Twentieth Centuries. (Illus.). 316p. 1992. 110.00 (*0-19-588562-7*) OUP.

Posidonius. The Fragments, Vol. 1. 2nd ed. Edelstein, L. & Kidd, I. G., eds. (Cambridge Classical Texts & Commentaries Ser.: No. 13). 390p. (C). 1989. 94.95 (*0-521-36298-9*) Cambridge U Pr.

Posin, Daniel Q. Corporate Tax Planning: Takeovers, Leveraged Buyouts, & Restructurings. 900p. 1989. 155. 00 (*0-316-71403-8*) Little.

— Corporation Tax Set. 1990. 155.00 (*0-316-71405-4*) Little.

— Federal Income Taxation Individuals & Basic Concepts in the Taxation of All Entities. 2nd ed. (Hornbook Ser.). 650p. 1993. pap. text ed. 29.00 (*0-314-01832-8*) West Pub.

Posin, E., et al. Coal Cutting by Winning Machines. Sarve, S. D., tr. (Russian Translation Ser.: No. 74). (Illus.). 288p. (C). 1990. text ed. 90.00 (*90-6191-909-6*, Pub. by A A Balkema NE) Ashgate Pub Co.

Positano, Nicholas J., jt. auth. see NYS Department of Motor Vehicles Staff.

Positive Parenting Inc. Staff. The Write Connection: Love a Child by Mail. (Illus.). 104p. 1989. student ed 24.95 (*0-9621840-0-4*) Positive Parenting.

— The Write Connection Program, Military Edition: Love a Child by Mail. (Illus.). 75p. 1989. student ed 24.95 (*0-9621840-1-2*) Positive Parenting.

— The Write Connection Program, Military Refill, No. 1: Love a Child by Mail, No. 1. (Illus.). 1989. 14.95 (*0-9621840-3-9*) Positive Parenting.

— The Write Connection Program, Military Trial Kit: Love a Child by Mail. (Illus.). 1989. 6.50 (*0-9621840-5-5*) Positive Parenting.

— The Write Connection Program, Standard Refill, No. 1: Love a Child by Mail. (Illus.). 1989. 19.95 (*0-9621840-2-0*) Positive Parenting.

An Asterisk (*) at the beginning of an entry indicates that the title is appearing in BIP for the first time.

— The Write Connection Program, Standard Trial Kit: Love a Child by Mail. (Illus.). 1989. 6.50 (*0-9621840-4-7*) Positive Parenting.

Poska, Valentine J. Miniature Horses. (Illus.). 48p. 1981. 20.00 (*0-88014-026-7*) Mosaic Pr OH.

***Poskanzer, Susan.** Riddles about Hannukah. Brook, Bonnie, ed. (What Can It Be? Ser.). (Illus.). 32p. (J). (ps-3). 1990. pap. 2.95 (*0-382-24384-6*) Silver Burdett Pr.

— Riddles about Hannukah. Brook, Bonnie, ed. (What Can It Be? Ser.). (Illus.). 32p. (J). (ps-3). 1990. 4.95 (*0-671-70555-5*); lib. bdg. 6.95 (*0-671-70553-9*) Silver Burdett Pr.

— Riddles about Passover. (What Can It Be? Ser.). (Illus.). 32p. (J). (ps-3). 1991. pap. 2.95 (*0-382-24381-1*) Silver Burdett Pr.

— Riddles about Passover. (What Can It Be? Ser.). (Illus.). 32p. (J). (ps-3). 1991. 4.95 (*0-671-72725-7*); lib. bdg. 6.95 (*0-671-72724-9*) Silver Burdett Pr.

Poskanzer, Susan C. Dairy Farmer. LC 88-10040. (What's It Like to Be a...Ser.). (Illus.). 32p. (J). (gr. k-3). 1989. lib. bdg. 10.89 (*0-8167-1426-6*); pap. text ed. 2.95 (*0-8167-1427-4*) Troll Assocs.

— The Great Soap-Bubble Ride. LC 85-14022. (Illus.). 48p. (Orig.). (J). (gr. 1-3). 1986. lib. bdg. 10.59 (*0-8167-0622-0*); pap. text ed. 3.50 (*0-8167-0623-9*) Troll Assocs.

— Little Raccoon Who Could. LC 85-14020. (Illus.). 48p. (Orig.). (J). (gr. 1-3). 1986. lib. bdg. 10.59 (*0-8167-0624-7*); pap. text ed. 3.50 (*0-8167-0625-5*) Troll Assocs.

— Puppeteer. LC 88-10042. (What's It Like to Be a...Ser.). (Illus.). 32p. (J). (gr. 1-3). 1989. lib. bdg. 10.89 (*0-8167-1432-0*); pap. text ed. 2.95 (*0-8167-1433-9*) Troll Assocs.

— Sanitation Worker. LC 88-10044. (What's It Like to Be a. ..Ser.). (Illus.). 32p. (J). (gr. k-3). 1989. lib. bdg. 10.89 (*0-8167-1436-3*); pap. text ed. 2.95 (*0-8167-1437-1*) Troll Assocs.

— The Superduper Collector. LC 85-14051. (Illus.). 48p. (Orig.). (J). (gr. 1-3). 1986. lib. bdg. 10.59 (*0-8167-0606-9*); pap. text ed. 3.50 (*0-8167-0607-7*) Troll Assocs.

— What's It Like to Be a Chef. LC 89-34390. (What's It Like to Be a...Ser.). (Illus.). 32p. (J). (gr. k-3). 1990. lib. bdg. 10.89 (*0-8167-1797-4*); pap. text ed. 2.95 (*0-8167-1798-2*) Troll Assocs.

— What's It Like to Be an Astronaut. LC 89-34393. (Illus.). 32p. (J). (gr. k-3). 1990. lib. bdg. 10.89 (*0-8167-1793-1*); pap. text ed. 2.95 (*0-8167-1794-X*) Troll Assocs.

Poskas, Peter & Smith, J. J. The Illuminated Landscape. (Illus.). 144p. 1992. pap. 18.95 (*0-8230-2531-4*, Watsn-Guptill) Watsn-Guptill.

Poskitt, J., jt. auth. see Oxley, R.

Poslusney, Venard. Attaining Spiritual Maturity for Contemplation (According to St. John of the Cross) 28p. (Orig.). 1973. pap. 4.95 (*0-914544-04-7*) Living Flame Pr.

— Prayer of Love: The Art of Aspiration. 128p. (Orig.). 1975. pap. 4.95 (*0-914544-06-3*) Living Flame Pr.

Posluszny, Patricia. Thomas Nashe's Summer's Last Will & Testament: A Critical Modern-Spelling Edition. LC 89-34168. (American University Studies: English Language & Literature: Ser. IV, Vol. 108). 214p. 1990. text ed. 36.95 (*0-8204-1110-8*) P Lang Pubs.

Posnansky, Merrick, jt. ed. see Ehret, Christopher.

Posner. Polypeptide Hormone Receptors. (Receptors & Ligands in Intercellular Communications Ser.: Vol. 4). 624p. 1985. 190.00 (*0-8247-7110-9*) Dekker.

Posner, Alan R. State Government Export Promotion: An Exporter's Guide. LC 84-1999. x, 192p. 1984. text ed. 49.95 (*0-89930-042-1*, PGE/, Quorum Bks) Greenwood.

Posner, Alice. Women in Engineering. 1981. 13.95 (*0-8442-6396-6*, VGM Career Bks) NTC Pub Grp.

Posner, Barry Z. & Randolph, Alan. Effective Project Planning & Management: Getting the Job Done. LC 87-11399. (Illus.). 128p. 1987. 22.50 (*0-13-244815-7*) P-H.

Posner, Barry Z., jt. auth. see Kouzes, James M.

Posner, Barry Z., jt. auth. see Kouzes, James S.

Posner, Barry Z., jt. auth. see Randolph, Alan.

Posner, Ben. Water Island Study: Summary Report & Fiscal Analysis. 64p. 1980. 10.00 (*0-318-14621-5*) Isl Resources.

Posner, David. Geographies. 1979. 20.00 (*0-933466-01-3*); pap. 12.95 (*0-933466-00-5*) Bellevue Pr.

Posner, Donald. Watteau. LC 83-45154. (Illus.). 288p. 1983. 88.50 (*0-8014-1571-3*) Cornell U Pr.

Posner, Donald, jt. auth. see Held, Julius.

Posner, Edward C., tr. see Inose, Hiroshi & Hamada, Takashi, eds.

Posner, Edward C., jt. auth. see Pierce, John R.

***Posner, Eileen, ed.** Mother of the Groom: A Collection of Women's Voices. 256p. 1995. pap. 12.95 (*0-942963-64-4*) Distinctive Pub.

Posner, Ernst. American State Archives. LC 64-23425. 414p. reprint ed. pap. 118.00 (*0-8357-5401-4*, 2025788) Bks Demand.

Posner, Gary H. An Introduction to Synthesis Using Organocopper Reagents. LC 85-4744. 160p. (C). 1988. reprint ed. lib. bdg. 24.50 (*0-89874-853-4*) Krieger.

Posner, George J. Analyzing the Curriculum. 1992. pap. text ed. write for info. (*0-07-050620-5*) McGraw.

— Analyzing the Curriculum. 2nd ed. LC 94-33750. 1995. pap. text ed. write for info. (*0-07-050705-8*) McGraw.

— Field Experience: A Guide to Reflective Teaching. 3rd ed. LC 92-30985. 208p. (C). 1993. pap. text ed. 22.95 (*0-8013-0764-3*, 78794) Longman.

Posner, George J. & Rudnitsky, Alan N. Course Design: A Guide to Curriculum Development for Teachers. 4th ed. LC 93-6513. 224p. (C). 1994. pap. text ed. 28.50 (*0-8013-0765-1*, 78795) Longman.

Posner, Gerald L. Case Closed: Lee Harvey Oswald & the Assassination of JFK. 1994. pap. 14.95 (*0-385-47446-6*, Anchor NY) Doubleday.

— Case Closed: Lee Harvey Oswald & the Assassination of JFK. LC 93-12821. 1993. 25.00 (*0-679-41825-3*) Random.

— Hitler's Children. 288p. (Orig.). 1992. mass mkt. 5.50 (*0-425-13509-8*) Berkley Pub.

— Hitler's Children: Sons & Daughters of Leaders of the Third Reich Talk about Themselves. 1991. 20.50 (*0-394-58299-3*) Random.

Posner, Grace. In My Sister's Eyes. 1983. pap. 2.25 (*0-449-70083-6*) Fawcett.

***Posner, Helaine.** Angela Grauerholz: Recent Photographs. LC 93-79813. (Illus.). 32p. (Orig.). 1993. pap. 8.00 (*0-938437-45-3*) MIT List Visual Arts.

— Per Kirkeby: Paintings & Drawings, 1982-1989. LC 91-50794. (Illus.). 48p. (Orig.). 1991. pap. 15.00 (*0-938437-39-9*) MIT List Visual Arts.

Posner, Helaine, jt. auth. see Kline, Katy.

Posner, Helaine, jt. ed. see Perchuk, Andrew.

***Posner, Holly & Jason, Katherine.** Explorations in American Culture: Readings for Critical Thinking, Writing, & Discussion. 240p. 1994. pap. 18.95 (*0-8384-4069-X*) Heinle & Heinle.

Posner, Jerome, jt. auth. see Plum, Fred.

***Posner, Jerome B.** Neurologic Complications of Cancer. (Contemporary Neurology Ser.: Vol. 45). (Illus.). 496p. (C). 1995. 99.00 (*0-8036-0006-2*) Davis Co.

Posner, Judith. The Feminine Mistake: Women, Work, & Identity. 256p. (Orig.). 1992. mass mkt. 4.99 (*0-446-36298-0*) Warner Bks.

Posner, Julia L. Adoption Resource Guide. 1990. pap. 29.95 (*0-87868-370-4*) Child Welfare.

Posner, Julie, jt. auth. see Fry, Macon.

Posner, M. V. & Woolf, Stuart J. Italian Public Enterprises. LC 67-4204. 171p. 1967. 20.00 (*0-674-46951-8*) HUP.

***Posner-Mayer, Joanne.** Swiss Ball Applications for Orthopedic & Sports Medicine: A Guide for Home Exercise Programs Utilizing the Swiss Ball. Hyer, Jauna et al, eds. (Illus.). 250p. (C). 1995. pap. text ed. 29.95 (*0-9645341-4-2*) Ball Dynam.

Posner, Michael, ed. Problems of International Money, 1972-85. ix, 191p. 1986. pap. 8.50 (*0-939934-58-2*) Intl Monetary.

— Problems of International Money, 1972-85: Papers Presented at a Seminar Organized by the IMF & the Overseas Development Institute in London in March 1985. LC 86-10480. (Illus.). 202p. reprint ed. pap. 57.60 (*0-685-23634-X*, 2029088) Bks Demand.

— Public Expenditure: Allocation Between Competing Ends. LC 76-53522. 278p. reprint ed. pap. 79.30 (*0-318-34837-3*, 2031712) Bks Demand.

Posner, Michael, ed. see Doggett, Martha.

Posner, Michael, ed. see Sherry, Virginia N.

Posner, Michael I. Chronometric Exploration of Mind. (Illus.). 288p. 1986. reprint ed. pap. 19.95 (*0-19-503999-8*) OUP.

Posner, Michael I., ed. The Foundations of Cognitive Science. 896p. 1989. 80.00 (*0-262-16112-5*) MIT Pr.

— The Foundations of Cognitive Science. (Illus.). 896p. 1993. pap. 37.50 (*0-262-66086-5*, Bradford Bks) MIT Pr.

Posner, Michael I. & Raichle, Marcus E. Images of Mind. LC 93-49413. 1995. text ed. 32.95 (*0-7167-5045-7*) W H Freeman.

Posner, Michael I., jt. auth. see Fitts, Paul M.

Posner, Michael J., ed. see Ross, James D.

Posner, Mitchell J. Executive Essentials: The Complete Sourcebook for Success. 204p. 1987. pap. 12.95 (*0-380-75376-6*) Avon.

***Posner, Nathan.** Call It Immortality. LC 94-94163. 260p. (Orig.). 1994. pap. 14.95 (*1-883335-12-4*) Botany Bay Pr.

Posner, Neil, ed. see Delson, Donn & Hurst, Walter E.

Posner, Neil, ed. see Delson, Donn & Michalove, Ed.

Posner, Prudence S., jt. ed. see Kling, Joseph M.

Posner, R. The Romance Languages: A Linguistic Introduction. 24.25 (*0-8446-0853-X*) Peter Smith.

Posner, Raphael. Junior Judaica: Encyclopedia Judaica for Youth, 6 vols. rev. ed. 1994. 125.00 (*0-8246-0366-4*) Jonathan David.

Posner, Raphael, tr. see Urbach, Ephraim E.

Posner, Raphael, et al, eds. Jewish Liturgy: Prayer & Synagogue Service Through the Ages. (Illus.). 1976. 25.00 (*0-8148-0596-5*) L Amiel Pub.

Posner, Rebecca & Green, John, eds. Trends in Romance Linguistics & Philology, Vol. 2. (Synchronic Romance Linguistics Ser.). 422p. 1981. 123.10 (*90-279-7896-4*) Mouton.

— Trends in Romance Linguistics & Philology, Vol. 5: Bilingualism & Linguistic Conflict in Romance. (Trends in Linguistics, Studies & Monographs: No. 71). x, 630p. (C). 1993. lib. bdg. 221.55 (*3-11-011724-X*) Mouton.

Posner, Rebecca, ed. see Green, John N.

Posner, Richard. Can You Hear Me Scream? MacDonald, Pat, ed. 256p. (Orig.). (J). 1994. pap. 3.50 (*0-671-88744-0*, Archway) PB.

— Goodnight, Cinderella. LC 89-17091. 242p. (YA). 1989. 13.95 (*0-87131-587-4*) M Evans.

— Someone to Die For. MacDonald, Pat, ed. 256p. (Orig.). (J). 1993. pap. 2.99 (*0-671-74940-4*, Archway) PB.

— Sweet Sixteen & Never Been Killed. MacDonald, Pat, ed. 256p. (Orig.). (J). (gr. 5 up). 1993. pap. 3.50 (*0-671-86506-4*, Archway) PB.

— Terror Runs Deep. MacDonald, Pat, ed. 240p. (Orig.). (J). 1995. pap. 3.50 (*0-671-88745-9*, Archway) PB.

***Posner, Richard A.** Aging & Old Age. 336p. 1995. 29.95 (*0-226-67566-1*) U Ch Pr.

— Antitrust Law: An Economic Perspective. LC 76-598. 1978. pap. text ed. 17.95 (*0-226-67558-0*, P760) U Ch Pr.

— Cardozo: A Study in Reputation. LC 90-35479. 176p. 1990. 18.95 (*0-226-67555-6*) U Ch Pr.

— Cardozo: A Study in Reputation. (Illus.). xii, 156p. 1993. pap. 10.95 (*0-226-67556-4*) U Ch Pr.

— The Economics of Justice. 428p. 1983. pap. 17.95 (*0-674-23526-6*) HUP.

— The Federal Courts: Crisis & Reform. LC 84-19126. 382p. 1985. pap. 108.90 (*0-7837-2315-6*, 2057403) Bks Demand.

— Law & Literature: A Misunderstood Relation. LC 88-11210. 384p. 1988. 38.00 (*0-674-51468-8*) HUP.

— Law & Literature: A Misunderstood Relation. 384p. 1990. pap. text ed. 13.95 (*0-674-51469-6*) HUP.

— Overcoming Law. LC 94-12753. 605p. 1995. text ed. 39.95 (*0-674-64925-7*, POSOVE) HUP.

— The Problems of Jurisprudence. 485p. 1990. 38.00 (*0-674-70875-X*) HUP.

— The Problems of Jurisprudence. 485p. (C). 1993. pap. 16.95 (*0-674-70876-8*) HUP.

— The Robinson-Patman Act: Federal Regulation of Price Differences. LC 76-383361. (AEI Studies: No. 131). 63p. reprint ed. pap. 25.00 (*0-8357-4528-7*, 2037405) Bks Demand.

— Sex & Reason. 458p. (C). 1992. text ed. 29.95 (*0-674-80279-9*) HUP.

— Sex & Reason. 458p. (C). 1994. pap. text ed. 15.95 (*0-674-80280-2*) HUP.

Posner, Richard A. & Easterbrook, Frank H. Antitrust-Cases, Economic Notes, & Other Materials. suppl. ed. LC 80-25590. (American Casebook Ser.). 168p. 1991. pap. text ed. 10.00 (*0-314-85073-2*) West Pub.

— Antitrust-Cases, Economic Notes, & Other Materials. 2nd ed. LC 80-25590. (American Casebook Ser.). 1077p. 1992. reprint ed. text ed. 48.00 (*0-8299-2115-X*) West Pub.

Posner, Richard A. & Scott, Kenneth E. Economics of Corporation Law & Securities Regulation. 1981. pap. 20.00 (*0-316-71435-6*) Little.

Posner, Richard A., jt. auth. see Casper, Gerhard.

Posner, Richard A., ed. see Holmes, Oliver W., Jr.

Posner, Richard A., jt. auth. see Kronman, Anthony T.

Posner, Richard A., jt. auth. see Landes, William M.

Posner, Richard A., jt. auth. see Philipson, Tomas J.

Posner, Roland. Rational Discourse & Poetic Communication: Methods of Linguistic, Literary, & Philosophical Analysis. LC 82-3502. (Janua Linguarum, Series Major: No. 103). xvi, 258p. 1982. 60.00 (*90-279-3419-3*) Mouton.

Posner, Roland, ed. & intro. Kategorialgrammatik. (Grundlagen der Kommunikation Ser.). (C). pap. text ed. write for info. (*3-11-004478-1*) De Gruyter.

Posner, Steve. Israel Undercover: Secret Warfare & Hidden Diplomacy in the Middle East. LC 87-18811. (Illus.). 367p. reprint ed. pap. 104.60 (*0-8357-8188-7*, 2034056) Bks Demand.

Posner, Susan F., jt. auth. see Solomon, Lewis D.

Posner, Susan F., jt. auth. see Solomon, Lewis.

Posner, Theodore R. Current French Security Policy: The Gaullist Legacy. LC 91-21195. (Contributions in Military Studies: No. 118). 184p. 1991. text ed. 49.95 (*0-313-27934-9*, PCK, Greenwood Pr) Greenwood.

Posner, Vladimir, jt. ed. see Keyssar, Helene.

Posner, Zalman I. Think Jewish: A Contemporary View of Judaism, a Jewish View of Today's World. LC 78-71323. 1979. 8.95 (*0-9602394-0-5*); pap. 4.95 (*0-9602394-1-3*) Kesher.

Posnock, Ross. The Trial of Curiosity: Henry James, William James, & the Challenge of Modernity. 382p. 1991. 52.00 (*0-19-506606-5*); pap. 22.00 (*0-19-507124-7*) OUP.

Pososhkov, Ivan. The Book of Poverty & Wealth. Vlasto, A. P. & Lewitter, L. R., eds. LC 86-61841. 450p. 1987. 55.00 (*0-8047-1361-8*) Stanford U Pr.

Pospesel, Howard. Introduction to Logic: Predicate Logic. (Illus.). 224p. 1976. pap. text ed. write for info. (*0-13-486225-2*) P-H.

— Introduction to Logic: Propositional Logic. 2nd ed. 256p. (C). 1983. pap. text ed. write for info. (*0-13-486167-1*) P-H.

Pospesel, Howard & Marans, David. Arguments: Deductive Logic Exercises. 2nd ed. (Illus.). 1978. pap. text ed. write for info. (*0-13-045880-5*) P-H.

Pospeshil, Bob. The Fires of God. 46p. 1987. pap. 2.95 (*0-88144-094-9*) Christian Pub.

Pospielovsky, Dimitry. The Russian Church under the Soviet Regime, Set. LC 84-5336. 533p. 1984. 25.95 (*0-88141-033-0*) St Vladimirs.

— The Russian Church under the Soviet Regime, Vol. I. LC 84-5336. 248p. 1984. 12.95 (*0-88141-015-2*) St Vladimirs.

— The Russian Church under the Soviet Regime, Vol. II. LC 84-5336. 285p. 1984. 12.95 (*0-88141-016-0*) St Vladimirs.

Pospielovsky, Dimitry V. A History of Marxist-Leninist Atheism & Soviet Antireligious Policies, Vol. 1. 200p. 1987. text ed. 39.95 (*0-312-38132-8*); pap. 14.95 (*0-312-38133-6*) St Martin.

— Soviet Antireligious Campaigns & Persecutions: A History of Soviet Atheism in Theory & Practice, & the Believer, Vol. 2. LC 87-4826. 256p. 1988. text ed. 39.95 (*0-312-00904-6*); pap. 14.95 (*0-312-00905-4*) St Martin.

— Soviet Studies on the Church & the Believer's Response to Atheism. 1988. text ed. 49.95 (*0-312-01291-8*); pap. 16.95 (*0-312-01292-6*) St Martin.

***Pospischil, Hans-Georg & Kreye, Andrian.** Vivir la Muerte: Rituals of Death in Latin America. 148p. Date not set. 39.95 (*3-905514-73-7*) Dist Art Pubs.

Pospishil, Victor J. Eastern Catholic Marriage Law According to the Code of Canons of the Eastern Churches. LC 90-64249. 536p. 1991. text ed. 42.00 (*0-9628727-0-9*) St Maron Pubns.

Pospisil, Jan & Klemchuk, Peter P., eds. Oxidation Inhibition in Organic Materials, Vol. I. 384p. 1989. 358.00 (*0-8493-4767-X*, TP156) CRC Pr.

— Oxidation Inhibition in Organic Materials, Vol. II. 400p. 1989. 358.00 (*0-8493-4768-8*, TP156) CRC Pr.

— Oxidation Inhibition in Organic Materials, Vols. I-II. 1989. 311.00 (*0-685-74180-X*) CRC Pr.

Pospisil, Leopold. Kapauku Papuan Economy. LC 78-188171. (Yale University Publications in Anthropology Reprints Ser.: No. 67). 502p. 1972. pap. 30.00x (*0-87536-526-4*) HRAFP.

— Kapauku Papuans & Their Law. LC 64-20560. (Yale University Publications in Anthropology Reprints Ser.: No. 54). 296p. 1964. pap. 20.00x (*0-87536-502-7*) HRAFP.

— Obernberg: A Quantitative Analysis of a Peasant Tirolean Economy. (Memoirs of the Connecticut Academy of Arts & Sciences Ser.: Vol. 24). (Illus.). 416p. 1995. text ed. 60.00 (*1-878508-09-1*) CT Acad Arts & Sciences.

Pospisilova, J. & Solarova, J., eds. Water in Plants Bibliography: 1979, Vol. 5. 1980. pap. text ed. 117.00 (*90-6193-905-4*) Kluwer Ac.

— Water in Plants Bibliography Vol. 9: 1983. 1984. pap. text ed. 114.50 (*90-6193-520-2*) Kluwer Ac.

***Poss, Joe & Schlesinger, Henry R.** Brooklyn Bounce. 240p. (Orig.). 1994. mass mkt. 4.99 (*0-380-77337-6*) Avon.

Poss, Robert, ed. Orthopaedic Knowledge Update 3: Home Study Syllabus. 3rd ed. LC 88-645327. (Illus.). 1990. pap. 60.00 (*0-89203-035-6*) Amer Acad Ortho Surg.

Posse, Abel. Daimon. 288p. 1992. text ed. 20.00 (*0-689-12123-7*, Atheneum S&S) S&S Trade.

— The Dogs of Paradise. Peden, Margaret S., tr. 196p. 1990. text ed. 9.95 (*0-689-12091-5*, Pub. by Ctrl Bur voor Schimmel NE) Macmillan.

Posse, Otto. Die Lehre von den Privaturkunden. (Illus.). viii, 242p. (GER.). (C). 1974. reprint ed. 337.00 (*3-11-002301-6*) De Gruyter.

Possee, R. D., jt. auth. see King, L. A.

Possehl. The Harappan Civilization. 1982. 39.95 (*0-85668-211-X*, Pub. by Aris & Phillips UK) David Brown.

Possehl, et al. Harappan Civilization & Rojdi. (C). 1989. 40.00 (*81-204-0404-1*, Pub. by Oxford IBH II) S Asia.

Possehl, G., ed. South Asian Archaeology Studies. (C). 1992. text ed. 45.00 (*81-204-0734-2*, Pub. by Oxford IBH II) S Asia.

Possehl, Gregory & Tosi, Maurizio, eds. Harappan Studies, Vol. 1. (Illus.). 79p. (C). 1993. text ed. 15.00 (*1-881570-18-5*) S Asia.

Possehl, Gregory L. Kulli: An Exploration of an Ancient Civilization in South Asia. LC 80-58074. (Centers of Civilization Ser.). (Illus.). 184p. 1986. lib. bdg. 29.75 (*0-89089-173-7*) Carolina Acad Pr.

Possehl, Gregory L. & Raval, M. H. Harappan Civilization & Rojdi. LC 89-9690. (Illus.). xv, 197p. 1990. 57.25 (*90-04-09157-2*) E J Brill.

Possehl, Suzanne, ed. Automation of Soviet Railroads: Selected Papers with Analysis. (Illus.). 218p. (Orig.). 1990. pap. 100.00 (*1-55831-116-5*) Delphic Associates.

Possehl, Suzanne, ed. see Litvak, Eugene.

Possehl, Suzanne R., ed. see Belkindas, Misha V.

Possemiers, Marc, jt. auth. see Brodie, Peter.

***Possevino, Antonio.** The Moscovia of Antonio Possevino, S. J. Graham, Hugh F., tr. & intro. by. LC 77-12648. (UCIS Series in Russian & East European Studies: No. 1). 214p. 1977. pap. 61.00 (*0-7837-8539-9*, 2049354) Bks Demand.

***Possidente, John.** 1942 Vol. 1: Pacific Air War; the Official Strategy Guide. 1994. pap. 19.95 (*1-55958-617-6*) Prima Pub.

Possidius. The Life of Saint Augustine. Rotelle, John E., ed. O'Connell, Matthew, tr. LC 88-71357. (Augustinian Ser.). (Illus.). 144p. 1988. pap. 7.95 (*0-941491-19-6*) Augustinian Pr.

Possolo, A., ed. Spatial Statistics & Imaging. LC 91-77910. (IMS Lecture Notes - Monograph Ser.: Vol. 20). vii, 426p. 1991. pap. 35.00 (*0-940600-27-7*) Inst Math.

Possolo, Antonio. Spatial Point Processes. 1990. 32.50 (*0-412-01221-9*, 9750, Chap & Hall NY) Chapman & Hall.

Possony, Stefan T., jt. auth. see Mick, Colin K.

Post. Omaha Orange: History of EMS in America. 1992. pap. 22.50 (*0-86720-187-8*) Jones & Bartlett.

— Radiographic Evaluation of the Spine. 1980. 169.00 (*0-89352-050-0*) Mosby Yr Bk.

Post, jt. auth. see Djinis.

Post, et al. Database Marketing. 1994. 44.95 (*0-7506-0036-5*) Buttrwrth-Heinemann.

— Use of Anticonvulsants in Psychiatry: Recent Advances. Pope, ed. LC 88-60779. 192p. 1988. 22.50 (*0-945986-00-9*) Health Care NJ.

Post, Alan, jt. ed. see Pacheco, Larry.

Post, Alexandra. Anatomy of a Merger: The Causes & Effects of Mergers & Acquisitions. LC 93-16695. 1993. text ed. 62.00 (*0-13-179243-1*); pap. text ed. 34.00 (*0-13-179235-0*) P-H Gen Ref & Trav.

Post, Alexandra M. Deep Sea Mining & the Law of the Sea. 1983. lib. bdg. 149.50 (*90-247-3049-X*) Kluwer Ac.

Post, Alfred B. Double Jeopardies: Twin Threats to Our Freedoms. LC 88-90638. 298p. (Orig.). 1988. pap. 14.95 (*0-9620117-0-3*) Roanoke Pubs.

Post Ambassador Staff. Faribault County, Minnesota. (Illus.). 343p. 1987. 62.50 (*0-88107-099-8*) Curtis Media.

Post-Baccalaureate Education of Teachers of Mathematics Task Force Staff. Guidelines for the Post-Baccalaureate Education of Teachers of Mathematics. 24p. 1989. pap. 5.00 (*0-87353-275-9*) NCTM.

Post, Barton L., et al. The Law of Medical Practice in Pennsylvania & New Jersey. LC 83-83245. 1984. 115.00 (*0-318-01198-0*) Lawyers Cooperative.

— The Law of Medical Practice in Pennsylvania & New Jersey. suppl. ed. LC 83-83245. 1992. Suppl. 1992. 62.50 (*0-317-03240-2*) Lawyers Cooperative.

Post, Beverly & Eads, Sandra. Logic, Anyone? One Hundred Sixty-Five Brain-Stretching Problems. (Makemaster Bk.). (J). (gr. 5-12). 1982. student ed 5.99 (*0-8224-4327-9*); pap. 13.99 (*0-8224-4326-0*) Fearon Teach Aids.

Post, Beverly, jt. auth. see Eads, Sandra.

Post, C. R. History of Spanish Painting, Nineteen Thirty to Nineteen Sixty-Six, Set, Vols. 1-14. LC 30-7776. 1969. reprint ed. Set. write for info. (*0-527-72000-3*) Periodicals Srv.

Post, Chandler R. Mediaeval Spanish Allegory. (Harvard Studies in Comparative Literature: No. 4). xii, 351p. 1971. reprint ed. 50.70 (*3-487-04058-1*, Pub. by Georg Olms GW) Lubrecht & Cramer.

— Medieval Spanish Allegory. 1977. lib. bdg. 59.95 (*0-8490-2221-5*) Gordon Pr.

— Medieval Spanish Allegory. 1984. lib. bdg. 90.00 (*0-8490-3235-0*) Gordon Pr.

Post, Charles G. The Supreme Court & Political Questions. LC 78-64164. (Johns Hopkins University. Studies in the Social Sciences. Thirtieth Ser. 1912: 4). reprint ed. 14.50 (*0-404-61274-1*) AMS Pr.

Post, Charles G., Jr. Supreme Court & Political Questions. LC 74-87386. (American History, Politics & Law Ser.). 1969. reprint ed. lib. bdg. 25.00 (*0-306-71610-0*) Da Capo.

Post, Constance J. Signs of the Times in Cotton Mather's "Paterna" A Study of Puritan Autobiography. LC 91-58798. (Studies in Religious Tradition: No. 2). 1992. 39.50 (*0-404-62532-0*) AMS Pr.

Post, D. E. & Behrisch, R., eds. Physics of Plasma-Wall Interactions in Controlled Fusion. (NATO ASI Series B, Physics: Vol. 131). 1196p. 1986. 155.00 (*0-306-42097-X*, Plenum Pr) Plenum.

Post, D. L., jt. ed. see Widdel, H.

Post, Dan R. Cord-Without Tribute to Tradition: The Front Drive Legend. LC 72-96734. (Illus.). 224p. 1974. 21.95 (*0-911160-50-7*) Post Group.

— Volkswagen: Nine Lives Later. 2nd ed. LC 82-173212. (Illus.). 320p. 1982. pap. 19.95 (*0-911160-42-6*) Post Group.

Post, Dan R., ed. Cord Model 810 & 812 Owner's Companion. 224p. 1975. 18.95 (*0-911160-54-X*) Post Group.

— Duesenberg Model J Owners Companion. 192p. 1974. 18.95 (*0-911160-53-1*) Post Group.

— Mills of the Forties Operator's Companion. LC 79-53627. (Slot Machines of Yesteryear Ser.). (Illus.). 1980. 21.95 (*0-911160-75-2*) Post Group.

— Mills of the Thirties Operator's Companion. LC 79-53627. (Slot Machines of Yesteryear Ser.). (Illus.). 1979. 21.95 (*0-911160-73-6*) Post Group.

— Watling Operator's Companion. LC 79-53627. (Slot Machines of Yesteryear Ser.). (Illus.). 1979. 21.95 (*0-911160-74-4*) Post Group.

Post, Dan R., ed. see American Bantam Car Company Staff.

Post, Dan R., ed. see Ford Motor Company, Airplane Division Staff.

Post, Dan R., ed. see Ford Motor Company Staff.

Post, Dan R., ed. see GMC, Chevrolet Division Staff.

Post, Dan R., ed. see Mills Novelty Company Staff.

Post, Dan R., jt. ed. see U. S. War Department Staff.

Post, Dan W. Porsche Owner's Companion: A Manual of Preservation & Theft Protection. LC 80-82464. (Illus.). 192p. 1981. 16.95 (*0-911160-64-7*) Post Group.

— Profit from the IBM PC: A Non-Technical Guide to Selling User Services. LC 83-82632. (Illus.). 192p. 1984. 14.95 (*0-911160-89-2*) Post Group.

Post, Daniel, et al. High Sensitivity Moire: Experimental Analysis for Mechanics & Materials. LC 93-29790. 1993. 69.00 (*0-387-94149-5*); write for info. (*3-540-94149-5*) Spr-Verlag.

Post, Deborah W., jt. auth. see Harmon, Louise.

Post, Donna C., jt. ed. see Aronson, Miriam K.

Post, Douglas. Earth & Sky. 1992. pap. 4.75 (*0-8222-0348-0*) Dramatists Play.

— Murder in Green Meadows. 1991. pap. 4.75 (*0-8222-0789-3*) Dramatists Play.

— Wind in the Willows: Musical. 87p. (Orig.). 1987. pap. 4.95 (*0-87129-172-X*, W05) Dramatic Pub.

Post, Elizabeth. The Emily Post Wedding Book. 1991. 27.50 (*0-06-270005-7*, HarpT) HarpC.

Post, Elizabeth L. Emily Post on Etiquette. rev. ed. (Illus.). 160p. (Orig.). 1994. mass mkt. 6.00 (*0-06-274007-5*, Harper Ref) HarpC.

— Emily Post on Etiquette. rev. ed. 1995. pap. 7.00 (*0-06-274011-3*, Harper Ref) HarpC.

— Emily Post on Guests & Hosts. 160p. (Orig.). 1994. mass mkt. 6.00 (*0-06-274009-1*, Harper Ref) HarpC.

— Emily Post on Second Weddings: Answers to All Your Questions about Getting Married Again. 160p. 1991. mass mkt. 5.50 (*0-06-274000-8*, Harper Ref) HarpC.

— Emily Post on Weddings. (Illus.). 135p. (Orig.). 1992. pap. 4.95 (*0-685-52545-7*, Harper Ref) HarpC.

— Emily Post on Weddings. rev. ed. (Illus.). 160p. (Orig.). 1994. mass mkt. 6.00 (*0-06-274008-3*, Harper Ref) HarpC.

— Emily Post Talks with Teens about Manners & Etiquette. (YA). 1991. pap. 9.00 (*0-06-273163-7*, Harp PBks) HarpC.

— Emily Post's Complete Book of Wedding Etiquette. rev. ed. LC 90-55548. (Illus.). 256p. 1991. 22.00 (*0-06-270006-5*, Harper Ref) HarpC.

— Emily Post's Etiquette. 14th ed. LC 83-48375. (Illus.). 922p. 1984. 18.45 (*0-685-42642-4*, HarpT) HarpC.

— Emily Post's Etiquette. 15th ed. 800p. 1992. 28.00 (*0-06-270047-2*, Harper Ref); 30.00 (*0-06-270028-6*, Harper Ref) HarpC.

— Emily Post's Table Manners for Today: Advice for Every Dining Occasion. LC 93-32393. 224p. 1994. 16.00 (*0-06-270099-5*, Harper Ref) HarpC.

— Emily Post's Wedding Planner. rev. ed. 96p. 1991. pap. 7.50 (*0-06-273018-5*, Harper Ref) HarpC.

***Post, Elizabeth L. & Coles, Joan M.** Emily Post's Teen Etiquette. rev. ed. 1995. pap. 11.00 (*0-06-273337-0*, Harper Ref) HarpC.

Post, Elizabeth L. & Staffieri, Anthony. The Complete Book of Entertaining From the Emily Post Institute. 1982. pap. 8.50 (*0-686-97246-5*, Fireside) S&S Trade.

Post, Emil L. Two-Valued Iterative Systems of Mathematical Logic. (Annals of Mathematics Studies). 1941. pap. 16.00 (*0-527-02721-9*) Periodicals Srv.

Post, F. Persistent Persecutory States Elderly. LC 66-25608. 1966. 45.00 (*0-08-013168-9*, Pub. by Pergamon Repr UK) Franklin.

Post, F., jt. ed. see Isaacs, Anthony D.

Post, Frederick J. Laboratory Manual for Food Microbiology & Biotechnology. 160p. (C). 1988. pap. text ed. 22.95 (*0-89863-127-0*) Star Pub CA.

Post, Frederick J., jt. auth. see Kelley, Susan G.

Post, G. C. Flora of Syria, Palestine & Sinai. 919p. (C). 1991. text ed. 375.00 (*0-89771-627-2*, Pub. by Intl Bk Distr II) St Mut.

— Flora of Syria, Palestine & Sinai. 919p. (C). 1980. reprint ed. 375.00 (*0-685-21860-0*, Pub. by Intl Bk Distr II) St Mut.

Post, Gaines, Jr. Dilemmas of Appeasement: British Deterrence & Defense, 1934-1937. LC 92-27606. (Cornell Studies in Security Affairs). 384p. 1993. 48.50 (*0-8014-2748-7*) Cornell U Pr.

Post, Gaines, Jr., ed. German Unification: Problems & Prospects. LC 92-42236. (Monograph Ser.: No. 3). 1992. write for info. (*0-930607-14-7*) Keck Ctr.

Post, George. Out of the Fast Lane. 160p. 1993. pap. 6.95 (*0-8059-3399-9*) Dorrance.

— Textbook of Fish Health. (Illus.). 256p. 1987. 29.95 (*0-86622-491-2*, H-1043) TFH Pubns.

Post, Glen D. Who Will Fill Our Shoes? Thirteen Dramatic Sketches for Missions Awareness. Howard, Gina, ed. 43p. (Orig.). 1991. pap. text ed. 4.95 (*1-56309-011-2*, New Hope AL) Womans Mission Union.

Post, Gregory & Turner, Charles. The Feast: Meditations on the Bread of Life. LC 91-59030. 1992. 15.00 (*0-06-066689-7*) Harper SF.

***Post, Harry H., ed.** International Economic Law & Armed Conflict. LC 94-38233. (Nova et Vetera Iuris Gentium, Series A, Modern Law). 1994. lib. bdg. 93.00 (*0-7923-3189-3*, Pub. by M Nijhoff) Kluwer Ac.

Post, Howard, jt. auth. see Emerson, Scott.

Post, J. E., jt. auth. see Bish, D. L.

Post, Jerrold M. & Robins, Robert S. When Illness Strikes the Leader: The Dilemma of the Captive King. LC 92-25302. 320p. (C). 1993. 25.00 (*0-300-05683-4*) Yale U Pr.

— When Illness Strikes the Leader: The Dilemma of the Captive King. 1995. 15.00 (*0-300-06314-8*) Yale U Pr.

Post, John D. Food Shortage, Climatic Variability, & Epidemic Disease in Preindustrial Europe: The Mortality Peak in the Early 1740s. LC 85-4684. 304p. (C). 1985. 38.95 (*0-8014-1773-2*) Cornell U Pr.

— The Last Great Subsistence Crisis in the Western World. LC 76-41239. (Illus.). 256p. 1977. 36.00 (*0-8018-1850-8*) Johns Hopkins.

Post, John F. The Faces of Existence: An Essay in Nonreductive Metaphysics. LC 86-19894. 392p. 1987. 37.95 (*0-8014-1968-9*) Cornell U Pr.

— Metaphysics: A Contemporary Introduction. (Issues in Philosophy Ser.). 213p. (C). 1991. pap. text ed. 16.95 (*1-55778-204-0*) Paragon Hse.

Post, Jonathan F. Henry Vaughan: The Unfolding Vision. LC 82-47609. 264p. 1983. 37.50 (*0-691-06527-6*) Princeton U Pr.

— Henry Vaughan: The Unfolding Vision. LC 82-47609. Date not set. reprint ed. pap. 75.90 (*0-7837-9425-8*, 2060166) Bks Demand.

— Sir Thomas Browne. (English Authors Ser.: No. 448). 1987. text ed. 26.95 (*0-8057-6948-X*, Pub. by Royal Botanic Garden UK) Macmillan.

***Post, Jory.** Family Relationships. (Comprehensive Health for Middle Grades Ser.). (J). (gr. 6-9). 1996. 24.00 (*1-56071-461-1*, H563) ETR Assocs.

— Violence. (Comprehensive Health for Middle Grades Ser.). (J). (gr. 6-9). 1996. 24.00 (*1-56071-472-7*, H574) ETR Assocs.

Post, Jory & Friedman, Alan. Communication for a Livable World: A Curriculum for Grades 4-8. 149p. 1988. pap. text ed. 19.95 (*0-941816-51-6*) ETR Assocs.

***Post, Jory & McPherson, Carole.** HIV & STD. (Comprehensive Health for Middle Grades Ser.). (J). (gr. 6-9). 1996. 24.00 (*1-56071-459-X*, H561) ETR Assocs.

— Into Adolescence: Learning about AIDS. Middleton, Kathleen, ed. (Contemporary Health Ser.). (Illus.). 231p. (Orig.). 1988. teacher ed, pap. 19.95 (*0-941816-62-1*) ETR Assocs.

Post, Joyce, comp. Special Libraries: A Cumulative Index, 1981-1986. 40p. 1987. pap. 25.00 (*0-87111-327-9*) SLA.

Post, Joyce A. Gerontology & Geriatrics Libraries & Collections in the United States & Canada: A History, Description, & Directory. LC 91-46862. 224p. 1992. text ed. 47.95 (*0-313-28443-1*, PGG, Greenwood Pr) Greenwood.

Post, Kalmon, jt. auth. see Goodrich, James T.

Post, Kalmon D., et al, eds. Post Operative Complications in Intracranial Neurosurgery. LC 92-49908. 1992. 79.00 (*0-86577-438-2*) Thieme Med Pubs.

Post, Ken. Revolution, Socialism & Nationalism in Viet Nam, 4 vols., Set. (C). 1989. text ed. write for info. (*0-534-11940-9*) Intl Thomson.

— Revolution, Socialism & Nationalism in Viet Nam, Vol. 1: An Interrupted Revolution. 366p. 1989. 39.95 (*1-85521-037-1*, Pub. by Dartmth Pub UK) Ashgate Pub Co.

— Revolution, Socialism & Nationalism in Viet Nam, Vol. 2: Viet Nam Divided. 1989. 39.95 (*1-85521-047-9*, Pub. by Dartmth Pub UK) Ashgate Pub Co.

— Revolution, Socialism & Nationalism in Viet Nam, Vol. 3: Socialism in Half a Country. 397p. 1989. 39.95 (*1-85521-056-8*, Pub. by Dartmth Pub UK) Ashgate Pub Co.

— Revolution, Socialism & Nationalism in Viet Nam, Vol. 4: The Failure of Counter-Insurgency in the South. 417p. 1989. 39.95 (*1-85521-091-6*, Pub. by Dartmth Pub UK) Ashgate Pub Co.

— Revolution, Socialism & Nationalism in Viet Nam, Vol. 5: Winning the War & Losing the Peace, 5 vols. LC 93-21341. 416p. (C). 1994. text ed. 59.95 (*1-85521-097-5*, Pub. by Dartmth Pub UK) Ashgate Pub Co.

Post, Ken & Wright, Philip. Socialism & under Development. 242p. 1989. 39.95 (*0-415-01627-4*); pap. 14.95 (*0-415-01628-2*) Routledge.

Post, Kenneth & Vickers, Michael. Structure & Conflict in Nigeria Nineteen Sixty to Nineteen Sixty-Five. 256p. 1974. 29.50 (*0-299-06470-0*) U of Wis Pr.

Post, Kenneth H., jt. auth. see Combs, Eugene.

Post, Lauren C. Cajun Sketches: From the Prairies of Southwest Louisiana. LC 90-31294. (Illus.). 215p. 1990. pap. 11.95 (*0-8071-1605-X*) La State U Pr.

***Post-Lauria, Sheila.** Correspondent Colorings: Melville in the Marketplace. (Illus.). 272p. (C). 1996. text ed. 50.00 (*1-55849-002-7*); pap. 17.95 (*1-55849-003-5*) U of Mass Pr.

Post, Libby, ed. Through the Eyes of Children: Liberty & Justice for All. (Illus.). 48p. (Orig.). (J). 1989. pap. write for info. (*0-318-65750-3*) NY State Alliance.

Post, Linda W. Stony Ground: One Teacher's Fight Against Juvenile Crime. LC 93-9095. 1994. 16.95 (*0-89015-918-1*) Sunbelt Media.

Post, Louis F. An Account of the George-Hewitt Mayoralty Campaign in the Municipal Election of 1886. LC 75-341. (Radical Tradition in America Ser.). 202p. 1975. reprint ed. 19.25 (*0-88355-244-2*) Hyperion Conn.

— Deportations Delirium of Nineteen-Twenty. LC 73-114343. (Civil Liberties in American History Ser.). 1970. reprint ed. lib. bdg. 42.50 (*0-306-71882-0*) Da Capo.

— Ethics of Democracy. 1976. lib. bdg. 59.95 (*0-8490-1790-4*) Gordon Pr.

— The Prophet of San Francisco Henry George. 1972. 59.95 (*0-8490-0901-4*) Gordon Pr.

Post, Louis F. & Leubuscher, Fred C. Henry George's Eighteen Hundred Eighty-Six Campaign. 193p. 1961. reprint ed. pap. 2.00 (*0-911312-21-8*) Schalkenbach.

Post, Melville D. The Bradmoor Murder. 297p. 1980. reprint ed. lib. bdg. 14.25 (*0-89968-197-2*, Lghtyr Pr) Buccaneer Bks.

— Corrector of Destinies: Vol. 3 of Randolph Mason Stories. LC 72-150559. (Short Story Index Reprint Ser.). 1977. reprint ed. 20.95 (*0-8369-3856-9*) Ayer.

— The Man of Last Resort. 284p. 1980. reprint ed. lib. bdg. 14.25 (*0-89968-198-0*, Lghtyr Pr) Buccaneer Bks.

— The Methods of Uncle Abner. Schantz, Tom & Schantz, Enid, eds. (Illus.). 96p. 1974. 6.95 (*0-915230-03-8*) Rue Morgue.

— The Mountain School Teacher. 196p. 1980. reprint ed. lib. bdg. 12.75 (*0-89968-199-9*, Lghtyr Pr) Buccaneer Bks.

— Strange Schemes of Randolph Mason. 13.95 (*0-8488-1451-7*) Amereon Ltd.

— The Strange Schemes of Randolph Mason. LC 75-32776. (Literature of Mystery & Detection Ser.). 1976. reprint ed. 24.95 (*0-405-07895-1*) Ayer.

— The Strange Schemes of Randolph Mason. 280p. 1980. reprint ed. lib. bdg. 14.25 (*0-89968-200-6*, Lghtyr Pr) Buccaneer Bks.

— The Strange Schemes of Randolph Mason. LC 74-10490. (Milestones of Mystery Ser.). 280p. 1975. reprint ed. 15.00 (*0-88355-204-3*) Hyperion Conn.

— Uncle Abner & the Devil's Tools. 15.95 (*0-89190-987-7*, Am Repr) Amereon Ltd.

— Uncle Abner & the Doomsdorf Mystery. 15.95 (*0-89190-988-5*, Am Repr) Amereon Ltd.

Post, Melvin, ed. Physical Examination of the Musculoskeletal System. (Illus.). 1986. 75.00 (*0-8151-6744-X*, QJZ-1, Yr Bk Med Pubs) Mosby Yr Bk.

Post, Richard & Schachtsiek, David. Security Manager's Desk Reference. 480p. 1986. text ed. 54.95 (*0-409-90014-1*) Buttrwrth-Heinemann.

Post, Richard, jt. auth. see Houk, Clifford C.

Post, Richard S., et al. Security Administration: An Introduction to the Protective Services. 4th ed. (Illus.). 256p. 1990. text ed. 34.95 (*0-409-90096-6*) Buttrwrth-Heinemann.

Post, Richard W., jt. auth. see Pivar, William H.

Post, Robert. Reading the Water: Adventures in Surf Fishing on Martha's Vineyard. LC 88-14071. 272p. 1989. pap. 13.95 (*0-87106-543-6*) Globe Pequot.

Post, Robert, ed. Law & the Order of Culture. LC 90-50927. (Representation Bks.: No. 4). 200p. 1991. 35.00 (*0-520-07500-5*); pap. 12.00 (*0-520-07337-1*) U CA Pr.

Post, Robert, et al. Clinical Use of Anticonvulsants in Psychiatric Disorders. LC 89-50472. (Illus.). 184p. 1989. 29.95 (*0-939957-20-5*) Demos Vermande.

***Post, Robert C.** Constitutional Domains: Democracy, Community, Management. LC 94-29882. 475p. 1995. text ed. 45.00x (*0-674-16545-4*, POSCON) HUP.

— High Performance: The Culture & Technology of Drag Racing, 1950-1990. LC 93-4845. (Studies in the History of Technology). 1994. 35.95 (*0-8018-4654-4*) Johns Hopkins.

— Street Railway & the Growth of Los Angeles. LC 89-23777. (Illus.). 188p. 1989. 48.95 (*0-87095-104-1*) Gldn West Bks.

— The Tancook Whalers: Origins, Rediscovery & Revival. LC 85-63457. (Illus.). 113p. (Orig.). 1986. pap. 15.00 (*0-937410-05-5*) ME Maritime Mus.

Post, Robert C., ed. Eighteen Seventy-Six: A Centennial Exhibition. (Illus.). 223p. (Orig.). 1976. pap. 6.95 (*0-685-21907-0*) Natl Mus Am.

Post, Robert C., jt. ed. see Mayr, Otto.

Post, Roy G. & Seale, Robert L., eds. Water Production Using Nuclear Energy. LC 66-24303. (Illus.). 392p. reprint ed. pap. 111.80 (*0-317-10713-5*, 2055358) Bks Demand.

Post, Stephen G. Inquiries in Bioethics. LC 93-17564. 208p. 1993. 35.00 (*0-87840-538-0*); pap. 17.95 (*0-87840-539-9*) Georgetown U Pr.

— The Moral Challenge of Alzheimer Disease. LC 95-13505. 160p. 1995. text ed. 29.95x (*0-8018-5174-2*) Johns Hopkins.

— Spheres of Love: Toward a New Ethics of the Family. 208p. 1994. text ed. 25.95 (*0-87074-370-8*); pap. 12.95 (*0-87074-371-6*) SMU Press.

Post, Stephen G., jt. ed. see Binstock, Robert H.

Post, Thomas R., ed. & contrib. Teaching Mathematics in Grades K-8: Research Based Methods. 2nd ed. 576p. (C). 1991. text ed. 48.00 (*0-205-13414-9*) Allyn.

Post, Tom. Teaching Elementary Mathematics: Research Based Material. 496p. (C). 1988. pap. text ed. 45.00 (*0-205-11076-2*, H10762) Allyn.

Post, W. Ellwood. Saints, Signs & Symbols. 2nd ed. LC 62-19257. (Illus.). 96p. 1974. pap. 6.95 (*0-8192-1171-0*) Morehouse Pub.

Post, Waldron K. Harvard Stories. LC 77-90589. (Short Story Index Reprint Ser.). 1977. 20.95 (*0-8369-3072-X*) Ayer.

Postacchini, F. Lumbar Spinal Stenosis. (Illus.). 230p. 1989. 101.00 (*0-387-82111-2*) Spr-Verlag.

Postal, Frederic. Finding Hidden Travel Bargains: How to Travel Farther & Better for Less Money. 190p. (Orig.). 1991. pap. 19.95 (*0-9629864-0-2*) MP Pub Co.

Postal, Paul M. Masked Inversion in French. (Illus.). 168p. 1989. 27.50 (*0-226-67569-6*) U Ch Pr.

— Studies of Passive Clauses. LC 84-26850. (Linguistics Ser.). 271p. 1985. 89.50 (*0-88706-083-8*); pap. 29.95 (*0-88706-084-6*) State U NY Pr.

Postal, Paul M. & Joseph, Brian D., eds. Studies in Relational Grammar, No. 3. LC 82-6945. (Illus.). 408p. 1990. pap. text ed. 32.50 (*0-226-67573-4*) U Ch Pr.

— Studies in Relational Grammar, No. 3. LC 82-6945. (Illus.). 408p. 1990. lib. bdg. 65.00 (*0-226-67572-6*) U Ch Pr.

Postal, Paul M., jt. auth. see Johnson, David E.

Postan, Cynthia, tr. see Bairoch, Paul.

Postan, Cynthia, tr. see Duby, Georges.

Postan, M. M. Medieval Trade & Finance. (Illus.). 350p. 1973. 74.95 (*0-521-08745-7*) Cambridge U Pr.

Postcard Collector Staff. Postcard Collector Annual: A Standard Reference for Today's Deltiologist. 80p. (Orig.). 1991. pap. 9.95 (*1-879825-00-7*) Jones Publish.

Poste, E., tr. Aristotle on the Constitution of Athens. 2nd ed. xiv, 172p. 1992. reprint ed. 27.50 (*0-8377-2520-8*) Rothman.

Poste, Edward, tr. see Gaius.

Poste, George & Crooke, Stanley T., eds. Cellular & Molecular Aspects of Inflammation. LC 87-37400. (New Horizons in Therapeutics Ser.). (Illus.). 460p. 1988. 110.00 (*0-306-42852-0*, Plenum Pr) Plenum.

— Dopamine Receptor Agonists. LC 84-8290. (New Horizons in Therapeutics Ser.). 414p. 1984. 89.50 (*0-306-41654-9*, Plenum Pr) Plenum.

— Mechanisms of Receptor Regulation. LC 85-28339. (New Horizons in Therapeutics Ser.). 392p. 1985. 110.00 (*0-306-42125-9*, Plenum Pr) Plenum.

— New Frontiers in the Study of Gene Functions. LC 86-30313. (New Horizons in Therapeutics Ser.). 218p. 1987. 59.50 (*0-306-42502-5*, Plenum Pr) Plenum.

— New Insights Into Cell & Membrane Transport Processes. LC 86-8175. (New Horizons in Therapeutics Ser.). 456p. 1986. 95.00 (*0-306-42183-6*, Plenum Pr) Plenum.

Poste, George & Nicholson, G. Cytoskeletal Elements. (Cell Surface Reviews Ser.: Vol. 7). 350p. 1982. 151.50 (*0-444-80335-1*) Elsevier.

— Membrane Reconstitution. (Cell Surface Reviews Ser.: Vol. 8). 274p. 1983. 127.75 (*0-444-80391-2*) Elsevier.

— The Synthesis, Assembly & Turnover of Cell Surface Components. (Cell Surface Reviews Ser.: Vol. 4). 884p. 1978. 218.50 (*0-444-00232-4*) Elsevier.

Poste, George & Nicholson, G., eds. The Cell Surface in Animal Embryogenesis & Development. (Cell Surface Reviews Ser.: Vol. 1). 766p. 1977. 236.50 (*0-7204-0597-1*) Elsevier.

— Virus Infection & the Cell Surface. (Cell Surface Reviews Ser.: Vol. 2). 342p. 1977. 153.50 (*0-7204-0598-X*) Elsevier.

Poste, George & Nicolson, G., eds. Dynamic Aspects of Cell Surface Organization. (Cell Surface Reviews Ser.: Vol. 3). 1977. 236.50 (*0-7204-0623-4*) Elsevier.

Poste, George, jt. ed. see Gregoriadis, Gregory.

Poste, George, jt. ed. see Hook, J. B.

Poste, George H., jt. ed. see Moyer, Mary P.

Postek, M. T., ed. Integrated Circuit Metrology, Inspection, & Process Control VI. 1992. 86.00 (*0-8194-0828-X*, 1673) SPIE.

***Postek, Michael T.** Critical Issues in Scanning Electron Microscope Metrology. (Illus.). 50p. (Orig.). (C). 1994. pap. text ed. 25.00x (*0-7881-1552-9*) Diane Pub.

Postel, A. Williams. Mineral Resources of Africa. (African Handbooks Ser.: Vol. 2). (Illus.). 105p. 1943. pap. 10.00 (*0-686-24091-X*) U PA Mus Pubns.

Postel, J., jt. auth. see Knowles, J. W.

An Asterisk (*) at the beginning of an entry indicates that the title is appearing in BIP for the first time.

***Postel, Jacques.** Larousse Dictionnaire de Psychiatrie et de Psychopathologie Clinique. 630p. (FRE.). 1993. pap. 29. 95 (*0-7859-7685-X*, 2037202210) Fr & Eur.

Postel, Michel. Antiquities of Himachal. (C). 1992. 100.00 (*0-8364-2869-2*, Pub. by Franco-Indian II) S Asia.

— Ear Ornaments of Ancient India. (Illus.). 323p. (C). 1991. 120.00 (*0-935681-02-7*) D J Content.

— Ear Ornaments of Ancient India. (C). 1992. 160.00 (*0-8364-2870-6*, Pub. by Franco-Indian II) S Asia.

***Postel, Mitchell P.** San Mateo: A Centennial History. (Illus.). 312p. 1994. 29.95 (*0-942087-08-9*) Scottwall Assocs.

— San Mateo County: Peninsula Portrait: An Illustrated History. 160p. (YA). (gr. 7 up). 1988. 29.95 (*0-89781-255-7*) Preferred Mktg.

— The University Club of San Francisco Centennial History 1890-1990: With an Appendix on the Clubhouse. (Illus.). 112p. 1990. 30.00 (*0-9627540-0-5*) Univ Club.

Postel, Sandra. Air Pollution, Acid Rain, & the Future of Forests. LC 84-50653. (Worldwatch Papers). 1984. pap. 5.00 (*0-916468-57-7*) Worldwatch Inst.

— Altering the Earth's Chemistry: Assessing the Risks. LC 86-61917. (Worldwatch Papers). 68p. (Orig.). 1986. pap. 5.00 (*0-916468-72-0*) Worldwatch Inst.

— Conserving Water: The Untapped Alternative. LC 85-51713. (Worldwatch Papers). 1985. pap. 5.00 (*0-916468-67-4*) Worldwatch Inst.

— Defusing the Toxics Threat: Controlling Pesticides & industrial Waste. (Worldwatch Papers). 70p. (Orig.). 1987. pap. 5.00 (*0-916468-80-1*) Worldwatch Inst.

— The Last Oasis: Facing Water Scarcity. (Worldwatch Environmental Alert Ser.). 128p. 1992. 21.95 (*0-393-03428-3*); pap. 9.95 (*0-393-30961-4*) Norton.

— Water: Rethinking Management in an Age of Scarcity. LC 84-52522. (Worldwatch Papers). 1984. pap. 4.00 (*0-916468-62-3*) Worldwatch Inst.

— Water for Agriculture: Facing the Limits. (Orig.). (C). 1989. pap. 5.00 (*0-916468-94-1*) Worldwatch Inst.

Postel, Sandra & Heise, Hori. Reforesting the Earth. (Papers). 64p. (Orig.). (C). 1988. pap. 5.00 (*0-916468-84-4*) Worldwatch Inst.

Postell, Alice E. Where Did the Reindeer Come From? Alaska Experience the First Fifty Years. York, Susan P., ed. LC 90-146. (Illus.). 144p. (YA). (gr. 9 up). 1990. write for info. (*0-9626090-0-5*) Amaknak Pr.

Postell, Catherine. On Toplecote Bayou. LC 72-1518. (Black Heritage Library Collection). 1977. reprint ed. 15. 95 (*0-8369-9048-X*) Ayer.

Postels, A. & Ruprecht, F. J. Illustrationes Algarum in Itinere Circa Orben...Collectarum. 1963. reprint ed. 120. 00 (*3-7682-0158-9*) Lubrecht & Cramer.

Postema, Donald H. Space for God: Leader's Guide. 120p. 1983. pap. 6.25 (*0-933140-47-9*) CRC Pubns.

— Space for God, Study & Practice of Spirituality & Prayer. LC 83-15504. 180p. 1983. pap. 13.50 (*0-933140-46-0*) CRC Pubns.

Postema, Gerald J. Bentham & the Common Law Tradition. LC 86-5274. (Clarendon Law Ser.). 512p. 1989. reprint ed. pap. 38.00 (*0-19-825651-5*) OUP.

***Postema, Maarten H.** C-Glycoside Synthesis. 400p. 1995. 99.50 (*0-8493-9150-4*, 9150) CRC Pr.

Poster, Amy G. From Indian Earth: Four Thousand Years of Terracotta Art. LC 85-30964. (Illus.). 208p. 1968. pap. 19.95 (*0-295-96456-1*) U of Wash Pr.

Poster, Amy G., et al. Indian Miniature Plqs in TBM. (Illus.). 352p. Date not set. pap. 45.00 (*0-87273-131-6*) Bklyn Mus.

— Japanese Paintings & Prints of the Shijo School. (Illus.). 48p. 1981. pap. 1.00 (*0-87273-085-9*) Bklyn Mus.

— Realms of Heroism: Indian Paintings in the Brooklyn Museum. (Illus.). 352p. Date not set. 75.00 (*1-55595-000-0*) Hudson Hills.

Poster, Carol. The Basic Essentials of Alpine Skiing. LC 93-29016. (Basic Essentials Ser.). (Illus.). 72p. (Orig.). 1993. pap. 5.99 (*0-934802-40-8*) ICS Bks.

— Skiing: Faceplants, Eggbeaters, & Snowsnakes. (Illus.). 1995. 11.95 (*1-57034-030-7*) ICS Bks.

Poster, Cyril & Kruger, Angelika, eds. Community Education & the Western World. 288p. 1990. 52.50 (*0-415-03140-0*, A4320); pap. 18.95 (*0-415-04715-3*, A4324) Routledge.

Poster, Cyril & Poster, Doreen. Teacher Appraisal: A Guide to Training. (Educational Management Ser.). 208p. 1991. 69.95 (*0-415-06167-9*, A5446); pap. 19.95 (*0-415-06168-7*, A5450) Routledge.

— Teacher Appraisal: A Guide to Training. 2nd ed. LC 93-16582. 256p. 1993. pap. 22.50 (*0-415-09577-8*, B2445) Routledge.

Poster, Cyril & Zimmer, Jurgen, eds. Community Education in the Third World. LC 92-4405. 256p. 1992. 69.95 (*0-415-04209-7*, A5928) Routledge.

Poster, Cyril, jt. auth. see Day, Chris.

Poster, Donna. The Quilter's Guide to Rotary Cutting. LC 90-55879. (Illus.). 240p. 1991. pap. 17.95 (*0-8019-8130-1*) Chilton.

— Speed-Cut Quilts. LC 88-43312. (Illus.). 232p. 1989. pap. 18.95 (*0-8019-7889-0*) Chilton.

Poster, Doreen, jt. auth. see Poster, Cyril.

Poster, Harry. The Illustrated Price Guide to Vintage TV's & Deco Radios. 80p. 1991. pap. 15.95 (*0-9630932-0-7*) H Poster.

— Radio & Television Price Guide: 1920-1990. 2nd ed. (Illus.). 264p. 1994. pap. 17.95 (*0-87069-687-4*, Wallace-Hmestead) Chilton.

Poster, Jem. The Thirties Poets. LC 92-45681. (Open Guides to Literature Ser.). 1993. 75.00 (*0-335-09664-6*, Open Univ Pr); pap. 18.00 (*0-335-09663-8*, Open Univ Pr) Taylor & Francis.

Poster, Mark. Critical Theory & Poststructuralism: In Search of a Context: Including 7 charts. LC 89-7262. (Illus.). 200p. 1989. pap. 12.95 (*0-8014-9588-1*) Cornell U Pr.

— Existential Marxism in Postwar France: From Sartre to Althusser. LC 75-3471. 428p. reprint ed. pap. 122.00 (*0-8357-8874-1*, 2033390) Bks Demand.

— Foucault, Marxism & History: Mode of Production Versus Mode of Information. 184p. 1985. pap. 17.95 (*0-7456-0018-2*) Blackwell Pubs.

— The Mode of Information: Poststructuralism & Social Context. LC 90-34770. 200p. 1990. lib. bdg. 39.95 (*0-226-67595-5*); pap. text ed. 18.95 (*0-226-67596-3*) U Ch Pr.

— Sartre's Marxism. LC 81-18146. 136p. 1982. 21.95 (*0-521-24559-1*) Cambridge U Pr.

— The Second Media Age. 192p. 1995. text ed. write for info. (*0-7456-1395-0*, Pub. by Polity Pr UK); pap. text ed. write for info. (*0-7456-1396-9*, Pub. by Polity Pr UK) Blackwell Pubs.

Poster, Mark, ed. Politics, Theory, & Contemporary Culture. LC 92-23573. 336p. (C). 1993. text ed. 55.00 (*0-231-08056-5*); pap. 17.50 (*0-231-08057-3*) Col U Pr.

Poster, Mark, ed. see Baudrillard, Jean.

Poster, Mark, tr. see Baudrillard, Jean.

Posterski, Donald C. Reinventing Evangelism. LC 89-15363. 202p. (Orig.). 1989. pap. 10.99 (*0-8308-1269-5*, 1269) InterVarsity.

Postgate. Fifty Neo-Assyrian Legal Documents. 1976. 39.95 (*0-85668-054-0*, Pub. by Aris & Phillips UK) David Brown.

Postgate, J. N. Early Mesopotamia: Society & Economy at the Dawn of History. LC 93-48475. 1994. write for info. (*0-415-11032-7*, Routledge NY) Routledge.

Postgate, J. N., jt. auth. see Fales, F. M.

Postgate, J. N., jt. auth. see Steinkeller, Piotr.

Postgate, J. P., ed. see Tibullus, et al.

Postgate, J. R. Nitrogen Fixation. 2nd ed. (New Studies in Biology). 80p. (C). 1992. pap. 13.95 (*0-521-42779-7*) Cambridge U Pr.

— The Outer Reaches of Life. LC 93-11579. (Illus.). 280p. (C). 1994. 22.95 (*0-521-44010-6*) Cambridge U Pr.

Postgate, J. R., jt. ed. see Bergersen, F. J.

***Postgate, John.** The Outer Reaches of Life. (Canto Bk.). (Illus.). 288p. (C). Date not set. pap. 10.95 (*0-521-55873-5*) Cambridge U Pr.

— The Sulfate-Reducing Bacteria. 2nd ed. LC 83-15307. 250p. 1984. 64.95 (*0-521-25791-3*) Cambridge U Pr.

Postgate, Nicholas, jt. auth. see Roaf, Michael.

Postgate, Oliver & Linnell, Naomi. Columbus: The Triumphant Failure. (Illus.). 44p. (J). (gr. 5-8). 1992. 14. 95 (*0-531-15240-5*) Watts.

Postgate, Raymond. Revolution from 1789 to 1906. 11.75 (*0-8446-0332-5*) Peter Smith.

— Verdict of Twelve. 208p. 1986. reprint ed. pap. 5.95 (*0-89733-198-2*) Academy Chi Pubs.

Postgate, Raymond, jt. auth. see Cole, G. D.

***Posthuma, Barbara W.** Small Groups in Counseling and Therapy: Process & Leadership. 2nd ed. 1995. pap. text ed. 32.95 (*0-205-16169-3*) Allyn.

Posthumus, Cyril, ed. see Monkhouse, George.

Posthumus, Meyjes & Guillaume, H. M. Hugo Grotius Meletius Sive de Lis Qua Inter Christianos Conveniunt Epistola. (Studies in the History of Christian Thought: Vol. XL). (Illus.). 1987. 48.75 (*90-04-08356-1*) E J Brill.

Postian, Charles W., jt. auth. see Pratt, Timothy.

Postiglione, Gerard A., ed. Education & Society in Hong Kong: Toward One Country & Two Systems. LC 90-24658. (Hong Kong Becoming China Ser.). 328p. (C). 1992. 46.95 (*0-87332-743-8*) M E Sharpe.

Postiglione, Gerard A. & Ming, Julian L., eds. Education & Society in Hong Kong: Toward One Country & Two Systems. 328p. (C). 1992. pap. text ed. 78.00 (*962-209-300-0*, Pub. by Hong Kong U Pr HK) St Mut.

Postiglione, Marianne, ed. The External Environment. (Illus.). 250p. (Orig.). 1991. pap. 12.95 (*0-9625431-3-6*) ITEST Faith.

— The Human Genome Project. (Illus.). iv, 286p. (Orig.). 1993. pap. 12.95 (*0-9625431-6-0*) ITEST Faith.

— Some Christian & Jewish Perspectives on the Creation. 260p. (Orig.). 1991. pap. 12.95 (*0-9625431-4-4*) ITEST Faith.

— Transfiguration: Elements of Science & Christian Faith. (Illus.). iii, 294p. (Orig.). 1993. pap. 12.95 (*0-9625431-7-9*) ITEST Faith.

***Postiglione, Marianne & Brungs, Robert, eds.** Secularism versus Biblical Secularity. 272p. (Orig.). (C). 1994. pap. 12.95 (*1-885583-00-1*) ITEST Faith.

Postiglione, Marianne, jt. auth. see Brungs, Robert.

Postiglione, Marianne, jt. ed. see Brungs, Robert.

Postill, Keith J. Gambling 101: An Introduction to Casino Gambling. 62p. 1992. pap. text ed. 7.00 (*0-9633998-0-2*) Rollem Pubns.

Postl, Karl, see Sealsfield, Charles, pseud..

Postle, Martin J. Sir Joshua Reynolds: The Subject Pictures. LC 93-28687. (Illus.). 328p. (C). 1995. 75.00 (*0-521-42066-0*) Cambridge U Pr.

Postlethwait, John H. & Hopson, Janet. The Nature of Life. 2nd ed. 1992. text ed. write for info. (*0-07-050633-7*) McGraw.

***Postlethwait, John H. & Hopson, Janet L.** The Nature of Life. LC 94-37994. 1995. pap. write for info. (*0-07-050751-1*) McGraw.

— The Nature of Life. 3rd ed. LC 94-37994. 1995. text ed. write for info. (*0-07-050750-3*) McGraw.

Postlethwait, John N., et al. Biology! Bringing Science to Life. 1991. text ed. write for info. (*0-07-050631-0*); Study guide. student ed, pap. text ed. write for info. (*0-07-050638-8*) McGraw.

Postlethwait, Virgil A. The Armstrong Report, ET's & UFO's - They Need Us, We Don't Need Them, No. 1. 150p. (Orig.). 1989. pap. 7.95 (*0-925390-33-X*) Armstrong Assocs.

Postlethwaite. Clinical Paediatric Nephrology. 495p. 1986. 90.00 (*0-7236-0784-2*, Pub. by John Wright UK) Buttrwrth-Heinemann.

Postlethwaite, jt. auth. see Skogestad.

Postlethwaite, Alan. The Last Days of Steam on the Southern: London, Brighton & South Coast Lines & the Isle of Wight. (Illus.). 160p. 1994. 30.00 (*0-7509-0413-5*) A Sutton Pub.

Postlethwaite, Diana. Making It Whole: A Victorian Circle & the Shape of Their World. LC 84-20677. 302p. 1984. pap. 22.50 (*0-8142-0401-5*) Ohio St U Pr.

Postlethwaite, Keith. Differentiated Science Teaching: Responding to Individual Differences & to Special Education Needs. LC 92-20523. 1992. 82.00 (*0-335-15707-6*, Open Univ Pr); pap. 27.50 (*0-335-15706-8*, Open Univ Pr) Taylor & Francis.

Postlethwaite, N. & Wiley, D. The IEA Study of Science II: Science Achievement in Twenty Three Countries. LC 91-26614. (International Studies in Educational Achievement). 1992. reprint ed. 107.00 (*0-08-041035-9*, CRC Reprint) Franklin.

Postlethwaite, R. J., ed. Clinical Paediatric Nephrology. 2nd ed. LC 93-44212. 1994. write for info. (*0-7506-1347-5*) Buttrwrth-Heinemann.

Postlethwaite, T. Neville, ed. The Encyclopedia of Comparative Education & National Systems of Education. LC 86-9346. (Illus.). 806p. 1988. 323.00 (*0-08-030853-8*, CRC Reprint) Franklin.

Postlethwaite, T. Neville & Thomas, R. Murray, eds. Schooling in the Asian Region: Primary & Secondary Education in Indonesia, Malaysia, the Philippines, Singapore & Thailand. LC 79-41357. (Illus.). 348p. 1980. 140.00 (*0-08-024289-8*, Pub. by Pergamon Repr UK) Franklin.

Postlethwaite, T. Neville, ed. see Choppin, B. H.

Postlethwaite, T. Neville, jt. ed. see Choppin, B. H.

Postlethwaite, T. Neville, jt. auth. see Husen, Torsten.

Postlethwaite, T. Neville, jt. ed. see Husen, Torsten.

Postlethwaite, T. Neville, jt. ed. see Thomas, R. Murray.

Postlethwaite, T. Neville, jt. auth. see Trijnman, Albert C.

Postlethwaite, T. Neville, jt. ed. see Walberg, Herbert J.

Postlethwaite, Virgil A. Citizens Alert! Alternatives for Low-Profile Survival. Clemens, Paul M., ed. 80p. (Orig.). 1981. pap. text ed. 7.95 (*0-931892-02-3*) B Dolphin Pub.

Postlethwayt, Malachy. Britain's Commercial Interest Explained & Improved, 2 vols., Set. LC 68-22376. (Reprints of Economic Classics Ser.). 1968. reprint ed. 87.50 (*0-678-00392-0*) Kelley.

— Great Britain's True System. LC 67-18579. (Reprints of Economic Classics Ser.). 363p. 1967. reprint ed. 50.00 (*0-678-00250-9*) Kelley.

Postlewait, Thomas. Prophet of the New Drama: William Archer & the Ibsen Campaign. LC 85-9878. (Contributions in Drama & Theatre Studies: No. 20). (Illus.). 210p. 1986. text ed. 55.00 (*0-313-24540-1*, POW/, Greenwood Pr) Greenwood.

Postlewait, Thomas, ed. William Archer on Ibsen: The Major Essays, 1889-1919. LC 84-15744. (Contributions in Drama & Theatre Studies: No. 13). (Illus.). 323p. 1984. text ed. 59.95 (*0-313-24499-5*, PWA/, Greenwood Pr) Greenwood.

***Postlewait, Thomas & Davis, Peter A., eds.** Directory of Doctoral Programs in Theatre Studies in the U. S. A. & Canada. 2nd ed. 1995. write for info. (*0-614-04176-7*) Am Soc Theatre Res.

Postlewait, Thomas & McConachie, Bruce A., eds. Interpreting the Theatrical Past: Essays in the Historiography of Performance. LC 88-35045. (Illus.). 339p. 1989. text ed. 37.95x (*0-87745-228-8*); pap. text ed. 16.00 (*0-87745-238-5*) U of Iowa Pr.

Postlewait, Thomas, jt. ed. see Paradis, James.

Postlewait, Thomas, jt. ed. see Williams, Simon.

Postlewaite, A., ed. see Palfrey, Thomas R. & Srivastava, Sanjay.

Postlewaite, Jack A. Wisconsin Corporations: Practice Systems Library Manual. LC 79-91166. ring bd. 120.00 (*0-317-00430-1*) Lawyers Cooperative.

— Wisconsin Corporations: Practice Systems Library Manual. suppl. ed. LC 79-91166. 1991. 67.50 (*0-317-03171-6*) Lawyers Cooperative.

Postlewaite, Pat. Bury Me with Balloons. 250p. 1991. pap. 9.95 (*0-938577-06-9*) St Johns Pub.

Postlewaite, Philip F. & Collins, Michael P. International Individual Taxation. LC 81-14468. (Tax & Estate Planning Ser.). 507p. 1982. text ed. 115.00 (*0-07-050544-6*) Shepards-McGraw.

***Postlewaite, Philip F. & Frantzen, Tamara L.** International Taxation: Corporate & Individual. 2nd ed. LC 94-24980. (Tax & Estate Planning Ser.). 1994. write for info. (*0-07-172569-5*) Shepards-McGraw.

— International Taxation: U. S. Tax Treaties. LC 93-44999. 1993. text ed. 195.00 (*0-07-172492-3*) Shepards-McGraw.

Postlewaite, Philip R., jt. auth. see Shepard's Citation, Inc. Staff.

Postlewate, Charles, jt. auth. see Viola, Al.

***Postley, John E.** Soul Medicine: Medical Challenges on Life's Uncertain Journey. 288p. (Orig.). 1995. pap. 14.95 (*0-944634-33-8*, Love & Logic Pr) Cline-Fay Inst.

Postma, D., jt. auth. see Appelo, C. A.

Postma, H., ed. Hydrography of the Wadden Sea: Movements & Properties of Water & Particulate Matter: Final Report on Hydrography of the Wadden Sea Working Group (Report 2) 76p. (C). 1982. text ed. 43. 00 (*90-6191-052-8*, Pub. by A A Balkema NE) Ashgate Pub Co.

Postma, H. & Stone, N. J., eds. Low Temperature Nuclear Orientation. 1100p. 1987. 341.00 (*0-444-86994-8*, North Holland) Elsevier.

Postma, H. & Zijlstra, J. J., eds. Continental Shelves. (Ecosystems of the World Ser.: No. 27). 406p. 1988. 228.00 (*0-444-42609-4*) Elsevier.

Postma, J. Tennyson As Seen by His Parodists. LC 68-748. (Studies in Tennyson: No. 27). 1969. reprint ed. lib. bdg. 75.00 (*0-8383-0674-8*) M S G Haskell Hse.

Postma, Johannes M. The Dutch in the Atlantic Slave Trade. (Illus.). (C). 1990. 74.95 (*0-521-36585-6*) Cambridge U Pr.

Postma, Patricia D. & Prescott, Susannah S., eds. Tennessee Statistical Abstract, 1980. (Illus.). 720p. (C). 1980. pap. text ed. 18.00 (*0-940191-04-0*) Univ TN Ctr Bus Econ.

***Postman, Andrew.** Now I Know Everything. LC 94-5410. 1995. 21.00 (*0-517-59940-6*) Crown Pub Group.

Postman, Leo J. & Rau, Lucy. Retention As a Function of the Method of Measurement. LC 57-9951. (California' University, University of California Publications in Psychology: Vol. 8, No. 3). 56p. reprint ed. pap. 25.00 (*0-317-08156-X*, 2021417) Bks Demand.

Postman, Neil. Amusing Ourselves to Death: Public Discourse in the Age of Show Business. 192p. 1986. pap. 11.95 (*0-14-009438-5*, Penguin Bks) Viking Penguin.

— Conscientious Objection. 1992. 10.00 (*0-679-73421-X*) McKay.

— The Disappearance of Childhood. LC 94-16385. 1994. write for info. (*0-679-75166-1*) Vintage NY.

— No Gods to Serve: The Quest for Meaning in Education. LC 94-46605. 1995. 23.00 (*0-679-43006-7*) Knopf.

— Technology. 1992. 21.00 (*0-685-51846-9*) Knopf.

— Technopoly. 1992. pap. 22.00 (*0-394-58272-1*) Knopf.

— Technopoly: The Surrender of Culture to Technology. LC 92-50584. 1993. pap. 11.00 (*0-679-74540-8*, Vin) Random.

Postman, Neil & Powers, Steve. How to Watch TV News. 160p. (Orig.). 1992. pap. 10.95 (*0-14-013231-7*, Penguin Bks) Viking Penguin.

Postman, Neil, et al, eds. Language in America: A Report on Our Deteriorating Semantic Environment. LC 73-77137. 1969. text ed. 26.50 (*0-672-53552-1*) Irvington.

— Language in America: A Report on Our Deteriorating Semantic Environment. LC 73-77137. 1969. pap. 10.83 (*0-672-63552-6*) Pegasus.

***Postman, Robert, comp.** How to Prepare for the PRAXIS: NTE, PPST, MSAT. LC 94-35579. 1995. write for info. (*0-8120-8225-7*) Barron.

Postmus, Bouwe, ed. George Gissing's American Notebook: Notes - G.R.G. - 1877. LC 92-45565. (Illus.). 108p. 1993. text ed. 59.95 (*0-7734-9227-5*) E Mellen.

— The Poetry of George Gissing. LC 94-5679. 204p. 1994. 69.95 (*0-7734-9148-1*) E Mellen.

Postmus, Simon, ed. Nutrition Bibliography of Indonesia. LC 55-10494. 146p. reprint ed. pap. 41.70 (*0-317-10441-1*, 2001357) Bks Demand.

Postner, jt. auth. see Rubin, Robert A.

Postnikov, A. G. Ergodic Problems in the Theory of Congruences & of Diophantine Approximations. LC 66-26640. (Proceedings of the Steklov Institute of Mathematics Ser.: Vol. 82). 128p. 1967. 45.00 (*0-8218-1882-1*, STEKLO-82) Am Math.

— Introduction to Analytic Number Theory. LC 87-33428. (MMONO Ser.: No. 68). 320p. 1988. 138.00 (*0-8218-4521-7*, MMONO-68) Am Math.

Postnikov, A. G., ed. Tauberian Theory & Its Applications. LC 80-23821. (Proceedings of the Steklov Institute of Mathematics Ser.: No. 144). 138p. 1980. 47.00 (*0-8218-3048-1*, STEKLO-144) Am Math.

Postnikov, M. & Swinfen, A. Foundations of Galois Theory. (International Series of Monographs on Pure & Applied Mathematics: Vol. 29). 1962. 53.00 (*0-08-009686-7*, Pub. by Pergamon Repr UK) Franklin.

Postnikov, M. M. Fundamentals of Galois Thoery. (Russian Tracts on the Physical Sciences Ser.). 196p. 1964. 79.00 (*0-677-20440-X*) Gordon & Breach.

Postnikov, M. M., jt. auth. see Boltyanskii, V. G.

Postnikov, Sergei P. Politika, Ideologia, Byt I Uchenye Trudy Russkoi Emigratsii, 1918-1945 Bibliografiia Iz Kataloga Biblioteki R.Z.I. Arkhiva, GG, Set. Blinov, Sergei, ed. xviii, 272p. 1993. write for info. (*0-88354-355-9*) N Ross.

— Politika, Ideologia, Byt I Uchenye Trudy Russkoi Emigratsii, 1918-1945 Bibliografiia Iz Kataloga Biblioteki R.Z.I. Arkhiva, GG, 2 vols., Vol. 1. Blinov, Sergei, ed. xviii, 324p. 1993. 225.00 (*0-318-71721-2*) N Ross.

— Politika, Ideologia, Byt I Uchenye Trudy Russkoi Emigratsii, 1918-1945 Bibliografiia Iz Kataloga Biblioteki R.Z.I. Arkhiva, GG, Vol. 2. Blinov, Sergei, ed. 272p. 1993. (*0-88354-354-0*) N Ross.

Postnikova-Loseva, Marina. The Historical Museum, Moscow. 168p. 1985. 67.00 (*0-317-61277-8*, Pub. by Collets UK) Pro-Am Music.

Postnikova-Loseva, N. G. Gold & Silver Work in Russian in Fifteenth to Twentieth Centuries. 376p. 1983. 135.00 (*0-317-61275-1*, Pub. by Collets UK) Pro-Am Music.

Postol, Lawrence. Legal Guide for Handling Toxic Substances in the Workplace, No. A79. 600p. 1990. ring bd. 125.00 (*0-929576-54-3*) Busn Laws Inc.

Poston, Carol. Tender Is the Night Notes. (Orig.). 1974. pap. 4.25 (*0-8220-1241-3*) Cliffs.

Poston, Carol & Lison, Karen C. Reclaiming Our Lives: Adult Survivors of Incest. 1989. 17.95 (*0-316-71472-0*) Little.

Poston, Carol H., ed. see Shelley, Mary Wollstonecraft.

Poston, David. The Blacksmith & the Farmer: Rural Manufacturing in Sub-Saharan Africa. 160p. (Orig.). 1994. pap. 28.50 (*1-85339-127-1*, Pub. by Intermed Tech UK) Women Ink.

P Q

Poston, Dudley L., Jr. & Yaukey, David, eds. The Population of Modern China. LC 92-15525. (Demographic Methods & Population Analysis Ser.). 1992. 79.50 (0-306-44235-3, Plenum Pr); pap. 44.50 (0-306-44138-1, Plenum Pr) Plenum.

Poston, Dudley L., jt. auth. see Bouvier, Leon F.

Poston, Graeme J. Aids to Operative Surgery. LC 86-8320. (Illus.). 224p. (Orig.). (C). 1987. pap. 28.00 (0-443-03566-0) Churchill.

Poston, Jeffrey. A Man Called Trouble. (Orig.). 1991. pap. 3.50 (0-87067-369-6) Holloway.

Poston, Larry. Islamic Da'wah in the West: Muslim Missionary Activity & the Dynamics of Conversion to Islam. (Illus.). 224p. 1992. 32.00 (0-19-507227-8) OUP.

Poston, M., jt. auth. see Power, Eileen E.

Poston, Richard W. Action Now! A Citizen's Guide to Better Communities. LC 76-949. 270p. 1976. 11.85 (0-8093-0760-X); pap. 7.95 (0-8093-0763-4) S Ill U Pr.

— Small Town Renaissance: A Story of the Montana Study. LC 76-109300. 231p. 1971. reprint ed. text ed. 55.00 (0-8371-3843-4, POST, Greenwood Pr) Greenwood.

Poston, Susan L. Nonformal Education in Latin America: An Annotated Bibliography. LC 75-620142. (Reference Ser.: Vol. 8). 268p. 1976. 16.95 (0-87903-108-5) UCLA Lat Am Ctr.

Poston, T., jt. auth. see Dodson, C. T.

Poston, Ted. The Dark Side of Hopkinsville: Stories by Ted Poston. Hauke, Kathleen A., ed. LC 90-11251. 144p. 1991. 25.00 (0-8203-1302-5); pap. 12.95 (0-8203-1303-3) U of Ga Pr.

Poston, Ted M. & Purdy, Rich, eds. Aquatic Toxicology & Environmental Fate, Vol. 9. LC 86-14648. (Special Technical Publication Ser.: No. 921). (Illus.). x, 535p. 1986. text ed. 64.00 (0-8031-0489-8, 04-921000-16) ASTM.

Poston, William K., Jr. Making Governance Work: TQE for School Boards. (Total Quality Education for the World's Best Schools Ser.: Vol. 8). 144p. 1994. pap. 17.00 (0-8039-6144-8) Corwin Pr.

Poston, William K., Jr., et al. Making Schools Work. 208p. 1992. pap. 21.95 (0-8039-6016-6) Corwin Pr.

Postone, Moishe. Time, Labor, & Social Domination: A Reinterpretation of Marx's Critical Theory. 500p. (C). 1993. 49.95 (0-521-39157-1) Cambridge U Pr.

Postow, Elliot, jt. auth. see Polk, Charles.

Postow, Elliot, jt. ed. see Polk, Charles.

***Postrel.** The Future & Its Enemies. Date not set. 25.00 (0-02-874108-0) Free Pr.

Postrel, Virginia I., jt. ed. see Poole, Robert W., Jr.

***Posts, Emily.** Complete Guide to Weddings: An Interactive Wedding Etiquette & Planning Guide. rev. ed. 1995. 49.95 (0-06-279018-8) HarpC.

***Posudievsky, Leonid.** Yulkina Skazka - Yuly's Tale. (Illus.). 50p. (Orig.). (RUS.). Date not set. write for info. (1-885563-03-5) Vestnik Info.

Poswillo, David & Alberman, Eva, eds. Effects of Smoking on the Fetus, Neonate & Child. LC 92-13005. (Illus.). 248p. (C). 1992. 83.00 (0-19-262260-9) OUP.

***Posy, Arnold.** Mystic Trends in Judaism. 1993. pap. 15.00 (0-8246-0368-0) Jonathan David.

Posy, Carl J., ed. Kant's Philosophy of Mathematics: Modern Essays. (Synthese Library). 384p. (C). 1992. lib. bdg. 122.00 (0-7923-1495-6) Kluwer Ac.

Posypaiko, V. I. & Alekseeva, E. A., eds. Phase Equilibria in Binary Halides. Indyk, B., tr. LC 87-29267. (Illus.). 496p. 1988. 125.00 (0-306-65211-0, IFI-Plenum) Plenum.

Posz, Joseph D. Military Heroes of New Mexico Military Institute. LC 94-65906. (Illus.). 108p. 1994. 21.67 (0-9641019-0-4) N Mex Military.

Poszar, Adam, jt. auth. see Harfield, Darvin P.

Potaman, Vladimir N., jt. auth. see Soyfer, Valery N.

Potamkin, Harry A. The Compound Cinema: The Film Writings of Harry Alan Potamkin. Jacobs, Lewis, ed. LC 76-55401. (Studies in Culture & Communication). 703p. reprint ed. pap. 180.00 (0-317-41931-5, 2026026) Bks Demand.

Potapchouck, V. S., tr. see Akulin, V. M. & Karlov, N. V.

Potapenko, J. Selected Writings of J. Potapenko, 3 vols., Set. 1976. lib. bdg. 350.00 (0-8490-2589-3) Gordon Pr.

Potapov, V., jt. auth. see Kovalishina, I.

Potapova, Nina. Russian Elementary Course, 2 Vols, Vol. 1. 3rd ed. 366p. (C). 1969. text ed. 106.00 (0-677-20890-1) Gordon & Breach.

— Russian Elementary Course, 2 Vols, Vol. 2. 3rd ed. 488p. (C). 1969. text ed. 128.00 (0-677-20900-2) Gordon & Breach.

Potapova, Nina F. Learn Russian, 2 Vols. 27.50 (0-318-57631-7, 070-4) Saphrograph.

— Learn Russian, 2 Vols., Set. 55.00 (0-87557-070-4, 0704X) Saphrograph.

— Learning Russian, 4 vols. 1985. pap. 11.00 (0-318-59484-6) Saphrograph.

— Learning Russian, 4 vols., Set. 1985. pap. 48.00 (0-87557-073-9) Saphrograph.

— Russian Elementary, Vol. 2. pap. 27.50 (0-317-02504-X, 070-4X) Saphrograph.

Potaracke, Rochelle. Nanny's Special Gift. LC 93-26093. (Illus.). 32p. (Orig.). (J). (gr. 1-4). 1994. pap. 4.95 (0-8091-6615-1) Paulist Pr.

Potash, Betty, ed. Widows in African Societies: Choices & Constraints. 336p. 1986. 39.50 (0-8047-1299-9) Stanford U Pr.

Potash, Dorothy. El Cuento de Ned y Su Nariz. (Illus.). 24p. (SPA.). (J). (ps-4). 1993. lib. bdg. 13.95 (1-879567-24-5, Valeria Bks) Wonder Well.

— The Tale of Ned & His Nose. (Illus.). 24p. (J). (gr. k-4). 1993. lib. bdg. 13.95 (1-879567-23-7, Valeria Bks) Wonder Well.

Potash, Herbert M. Inside Clinical Psychology: A Handbook for Graduate Students & Interns. LC 81-82640. 135p. 1981. text ed. 19.95 (0-940524-00-7); pap. text ed. 9.95 (0-940524-01-5) G Handwerk.

— Pragmatic-Existential Psychotherapy with Personality Disorders. 300p. (C). 1993. text ed. 35.00 (0-940524-05-8) G Handwerk.

Potash, Larry. X-Rated: Poems by Larry Potash. 75p. 1993. pap. 7.50 (0-9638688-0-2) L&M Press.

Potash, P. Jeffrey. Vermont's Burned-Over District: Patterns of Community Development & Religious Activity, 1761-1850. LC 91-28028. (Chicago Studies in the History of American Religion Ser.: Vol. 16). 330p. 1991. 60.00 (0-926019-52-X) Carlson Pub.

Potash, P. Jeffrey & Hand, Samuel B. Litigious Vermonters: Court Records to 1825. (Occasional Papers: No. 2). (Illus.). 30p. (Orig.). 1979. pap. text ed. 2.50 (0-944277-03-9, P67) U VT Ctr Rsch VT.

Potash, Robert A. The Army & Politics in Argentina, 1928-1945: Yrigoyen to Peron. LC 69-13182. (Illus.). xiv, 314p. 1969. 42.50 (0-8047-0683-2) Stanford U Pr.

— The Army & Politics in Argentina, 1945-1962: Peron to Frondizi. LC 79-64220. (Illus.). xiv, 418p. 1980. 49.50 (0-8047-1056-2) Stanford U Pr.

— The Army & Politics in Argentina, 1962-1973 Vol. 3: From Frondizi's Fall to the Peronist Restoration. (Illus.). 592p. Date not set. 55.00x (0-8047-2414-8) Stanford U Pr.

— Mexican Government & Industrial Development in the Early Republic: The Banco de Avio. rev. ed. LC 82-15969. 264p. 1983. lib. bdg. 30.00x (0-87023-382-3) U of Mass Pr.

***Potash, W.** Your Lower Back. 1994. pap. 3.99 (0-517-13383-0) Random.

Potash, Warren J., et al. Your Lower Back: A Patient & His Doctor Answer Questions & Present Exercises to Help You Manage Your Lower Back. Holt, Lenna, ed. (Illus.). 1993. pap. 9.95 (0-9636076-3-4) Paragon Comm.

— Your Lower Back: You Are Not Alone! 2nd rev. ed. Holt, Lenna, ed. (Illus.). 230p. 1994. pap. 9.95 (0-9636076-4-2) Paragon Comm.

Potchen, et al. MRI Angiography. 650p. 1992. 139.00 (1-55664-270-9) Mosby Yr Bk.

Potchen, James, et al, eds. Pulmonary Radiology: By Members of the Fleischner Society. LC 93-3835. 600p. 1993. text ed. 78.95 (0-7216-4821-5) Saunders.

Poteat, Hubert M. Practical Hymnology. LC 72-1693. reprint ed. 29.50 (0-404-09912-2) AMS Pr.

Poteat, Patricia Lewis. Walker Percy & the Old Modern Age: Reflections on Language, Argument, & the Telling of Stories. LC 84-10005. (Southern Literary Studies). 177p. 1985. text ed. 30.00 (0-8071-1187-2) La State U Pr.

Poteat, William H. A Philosophical Daybook: Post-Critical Investigations. LC 90-34577. 144p. 1990. text ed. 22.50 (0-8262-0748-0) U of Mo Pr.

— Polanyian Meditations: In Search of a Post-Critical Logic. LC 85-20429. x, 330p. 1985. 45.50 (0-8223-0542-9) Duke.

— The Primacy of Persons & the Language of Culture: Essays. Stines, James W., ed. LC 93-14356. 360p. 1993. text ed. 49.95 (0-8262-0919-X) U of Mo Pr.

— Recovering the Ground: Critical Exercises in Recollection. LC 93-45489. 257p. (C). 1994. 49.50x (0-7914-2131-7); pap. 16.95x (0-7914-2132-5) State U NY Pr.

Poteat, William H., jt. ed. see Langford, Thomas A.

Poteau-Tralie, Mary L. Voices of Authority: The Criminal Obsession in Guy de Maupassant's Short Works. LC 94-902. (Currents in Comparative Romance Languages & Literatures Ser.: Vol. 30). 146p. (C). 1995. text ed. 44.95 (0-8204-2479-X) P Lang Pubs.

Poteet, G. Howard. Starting up Your Own Small Business: Expert Advice from the Small Business Administration. 1991. pap. text ed. 19.95 (0-07-155565-X) McGraw.

— Starting up Your Own Small Business: Expert Advice from the Small Business Administration. 264p. 1990. pap. 19.95 (0-8306-3548-3, 3548) TAB Bks.

Poteet, G Howard & Santora, Joseph C. Death & Dying: Supplement 1974-1978. 556p. 1989. 38.50 (0-87875-351-6) Whitston Pub.

Poteet, G. Howard & Santora, Joseph C. Suicide: a Bibliography for Nineteen Fifty to Nineteen Seventy-Four: A Supplement to Death & Dying a Bibliography Nineteen Fifty to Nineteen Seventy-Four. LC 76-24093. 1978. 12.50 (0-87875-108-4) Whitston Pub.

Poteet, George H. Film Criticism in Popular American Periodicals, 1933-1967. (Cinema Ser.). 1976. lib. bdg. 250.00 (0-87700-240-1) Revisionist Pr.

Poteet, James A., jt. auth. see Hargrove, Linda J.

Potega, Patrick H. Basics of R-C Scale. 80p. pap. 11.95 (0-942794-00-1) Model Agency.

Potegal, Michael, ed. Spatial Abilities: Development & Physiological Foundations. rev. ed. (Developmental Psychology Ser.). 1982. text ed. 72.00 (0-12-563080-8) Acad Pr.

Potegal, Michael & Knutson, John. The Dynamics of Aggression: Biological & Social Processes in Dyads & Groups. 352p. 1994. text ed. 69.95 (0-8058-0729-2) L Erlbaum Assocs.

Potel, Mike, jt. auth. see Cotter, Sean.

Potemra, T., ed. Magnetospheric Substorms. (Geophysical Monograph Ser.: Vol. 64). 488p. 70.00 (0-87590-030-5, GM0640305) Am Geophysical.

Potemra, T. A., ed. Magnetospheric Currents. (Geophysical Monograph Ser.: Vol. 28). (Illus.). 357p. 1983. 33.00 (0-87590-055-0) Am Geophysical.

Potential Unlimited Staff. I Want to Be Happy. 1992. pap. 9.98 (0-87082-341-8) Potentials.

Poterba, James M. Tax Policy & the Economy, Vol. 6. (Illus.). 200p. 1992. 28.95 (0-262-16130-3); pap. 14.95 (0-262-66077-6) MIT Pr.

Poterba, James M., ed. International Comparisons of Household Saving. (Illus.). 272p. 1994. 42.50 (0-226-67621-8) U Ch Pr.

— Public Policies & Household Saving. LC 93-42088. (National Bureau of Economic Research Project Report Ser.). 1994. 36.00 (0-226-67618-8) U Ch Pr.

— Tax Policy & the Economy, Vol. 7. (Illus.). 200p. 1993. 28.95 (0-262-16135-4); pap. 14.95 (0-685-68793-7) MIT Pr.

— Tax Policy & the Economy, Vol. 8. (Illus.). 200p. 1994. 28.95 (0-262-16143-5); pap. 14.95 (0-262-66091-1) MIT Pr.

— Tax Policy & the Economy, Vol. 9. 350p. 1995. 28.95 (0-262-16153-2); pap. 14.95 (0-262-66095-4) MIT Pr.

Poterba, James M., jt. auth. see Dornbusch, Rudiger.

Poterba, James M., jt. ed. see Noguchi, Yukio.

Potgieter, J. M., jt. auth. see Visser, J.

Potgieter, J. M., jt. auth. see Visser, P. J.

Potgieter, Pieter. Victory: The Work of the Spirit. 42p. 1984. pap. 1.45 (0-85151-430-8) Banner of Truth.

***Poth, Dee.** The Goddess Speaks: Myths & Meditations. (Illus.). 120p. (Orig.). 1994. pap. 29.95 (0-9638327-2-7) Sibyl Pubns.

Poth, Jim, et al. Hidden Pacific Northwest: The Adventurer's Guide. 2nd ed. LC 94-60055. (Hidden Travel Guide Ser.). (Illus.). 552p. 1994. pap. 14.95 (1-56975-009-2) Ulysses Pr.

— Ultimate Washington. 2nd ed. LC 93-60066. (Ultimate Ser.). (Illus.). 320p. (Orig.). 1995. pap. 11.95 (1-56975-032-7) Ulysses Pr.

Poth, M. A. Is Mid-Life Easier in a Mink Coat? The Choices & Challenges of Today's Mature Women. 183p. 1989. 25.95 (0-87975-510-5) Prometheus Bks.

Pothen, K. P., jt. auth. see Singh, S. D.

Pothering, jt. auth. see Naps, Thomas L.

***Pothering, George J. & Naps, Thomas L.** Introduction to Data Structures & Algorithm Analysis with C Plus Plus. 600p. 1995. text ed. 52.00 (0-314-04574-0) West Pub.

Pothier, Dom J. Les Melodies Gregoriennes d'Apres la Tradition. vii, 306p. 1982. reprint ed. write for info. (3-487-07199-1, Pub. by Georg Olms GW) Lubrecht & Cramer.

***Pothier, Pat.** Float Tube Magic: A Fly Fishing Escape. (Illus.). 48p. 1995. pap. 15.95 (1-878175-91-2) F Amato Pubns.

Potholm, Christian P., et al. Just Do It: Political Participation in the 1990s. 176p. (Orig.). (C). 1993. lib. bdg. 48.50 (0-8191-9096-9); pap. text ed. 17.50 (0-8191-9097-7) U Pr of Amer.

Pothoven, K. Solutions Manual for College Algebra. 1988. pap. text ed. 18.50 (0-931541-09-3) Mancorp Pub.

— Solutions Manual for Precalculus Algebra & Trigonometry. 1988. pap. text ed. 18.50 (0-931541-08-5) Mancorp Pub.

Pothoven, K., jt. auth. see Mukherjea, A.

Poti, Walter M. Where River Waters Flow. 1992. 15.95 (0-533-10127-1) Vantage.

Poticha, Joseph & Southwood, Art. The Life-Long Guide to Sexual Fulfillment: Use It or You'll Lose It. 1983. pap. 3.25 (0-8217-1197-0) Zebra.

Potichnvj, Peter J. Soviet Agricultural Trade Unions, 1917-70. LC 70-163810. 288p. reprint ed. pap. 82.10 (0-317-09701-6, 2014344) Bks Demand.

***Potichnyj, Peter.** Ukraine in the Seventies. 360p. 1995. 27.00 (0-8095-4945-X) Borgo Pr.

Potichnyj, Peter, jt. auth. see Aster, Howard.

Potichnyj, Peter J., ed. Soviet Union: Party & Society. (Illus.). 264p. 1988. 59.95 (0-521-34460-3) Cambridge U Pr.

Potichnyj, Peter J., ed. see Mazlakh, Serhifi & Shakhrai, Vasyl.

Potichnyj, Peter J., et al, eds. Politics & Participation under Communist Rule. LC 82-15082. 304p. 1983. text ed. 55.00 (0-275-91060-1, C1060, Praeger Pubs) Greenwood.

***Potichnyj, Petery, et al, eds.** Soviet & Eastern European Studies: A Guide to Western Institutions. 90p. 1995. 33.00 (0-614-04378-6) Borgo Pr.

Potier, D., ed. Modelling Techniques & Tools for Performance Analysis. 1985. 107.75 (0-444-87696-0) Elsevier.

Potier, D., jt. ed. see Puigjaner, R.

Potier, Jean-Pierre. Piero Sraffa, Unorthodox Economist (1898-1983) A Biographical Essay. 160p. 1991. 49.95 (0-415-05959-3, A6286) Routledge.

Potier, Kenneth R. Cedar Bay: The Alternative. 1986. 23.00 (0-7223-2047-7, Pub. by A H S Ltd UK) St Mut.

Potier, R. & Roberts, T., eds. Energy Savings by Wastes Recycling. (Illus.). x, 243p. 1985. 72.00 (0-85334-353-5) Elsevier.

***Potiki, Grace & Grace, Patricia.** Potiki. LC 94-45651. (Talanoa Ser.). 192p. 1995. pap. 10.95 (0-8248-1706-0) UH Pr.

Potjes, J. C. Empirical Studies in Japanese Retailing. (Tinbergen Institute Ser.). 160p. 1992. pap. 25.00 (90-5170-185-3, Pub. by Thesis Pubs NE) IBD Ltd.

Potkay, Adam. The Fate of Eloquence in the Age of Hume. (Rhetoric & Society Ser.). 272p. 1994. 36.95x (0-8014-3014-3) Cornell U Pr.

***Potkay, Adam & Burr, Sandra, eds.** Black Atlantic Writers of the Eighteenth Century: Living the New Exodus in England & the Americas. LC 94-36117. 1995. text ed. 39.95 (0-312-12133-4) St Martin.

— Black Atlantic Writers of the Eighteenth Century: Living the New Exodus in England & the Americas. 288p. 1995. text ed. 16.95 (0-312-12518-6) St Martin.

Potkay, Charles R., jt. auth. see Allen, Bem P.

Potkonjak, V., jt. auth. see Vukobratovic, M.

Potmesil, Ina & Guillot, Katherine. Czech-Out Cajun Cooking. 2nd ed. (Illus.). 1991. pap. text ed. 15.95 (0-9627496-0-5) Czech Out Cajun.

***Potmesil, Milan & Pinedo, Herbert M.** Camptothecins: New Anticancer Agents. 160p. 1994. 129.95 (0-8493-4764-5, 4764) CRC Pr.

Potmesil, Milan, et al, eds. DNA Topoisomerases in Cancer. (Illus.). 354p. 1991. 75.00 (0-19-506106-3) OUP.

Potocka, Theodora G. Potocki: A Dorset Worthy? (Illus.). 48p. 1983. 75.00 (0-930126-13-0) Typographeum.

***Potocki.** Manuscript Found in Saragossa. 1995. (0-670-83428-9, Viking) Viking Penguin.

Potocki, Andrzej, tr. see Wojtyla, Karol.

Potocki, Comte J. Fragments Historiques et Geographiques sur la Scythie, la Sarmatie et les Slaves, 4 vols. 1497p. reprint ed. write for info. (0-318-71392-6, Pub. by Georg Olms GW) Lubrecht & Cramer.

Potocki, J., tr. see Heller, Michael.

Potocki, Jan. Tales from the Saragossa Manuscript or Ten Days in the Life of Alphonse Van Worden. (Dedalus European Classics Ser.). 192p. 1990. pap. 11.95 (0-87052-936-6) Hippocrene Bks.

Potocki, Jean. La Duchessa d'Avila (Manuscrit Trouve a Saragosse) 320p. (FRE.). 1972. pap. 10.95 (0-7859-3992-X, 2070362159) Fr & Eur.

Potocnik, Herman, jt. auth. see Noordung, Hermann.

***Potok.** Zebra & Other Stories. write for info. (0-679-95440-6) Random.

Potok, Adam. Horoskop i ty. 56p. (Orig.). (POL.). 1988. pap. 6.00 (0-930401-20-4) Artex Pub.

Potok, Chaim. The Book of Lights. LC 81-47505. 416p. 1981. 19.95 (0-394-52031-9) Knopf.

— The Book of Lights. 400p. 1982. mass mkt. 5.95 (0-449-24569-1, Crest) Fawcett.

— Chosen. 1987. mass mkt. 5.95 (0-449-21344-7) Fawcett.

— The Chosen. 1994. reprint ed. lib. bdg. 29.95 (1-56849-319-3) Buccaneer Bks.

— Davita's Harp. LC 84-48526. 336p. 1985. 16.95 (0-394-54290-8) Knopf.

— Davita's Harp. LC 85-17672. 448p. 1986. mass mkt. 5.95 (0-449-20775-7, Crest) Fawcett.

— The Gift of Asher Lev. 1990. 19.95 (0-394-57212-2) Knopf.

— The Gift of Asher Lev. 368p. 1991. mass mkt. 5.95 (0-449-21978-X, Crest) Fawcett.

— Gift of Asher Lev. braille ed. 728p. 1992. vinyl bd. 58.24 (1-56956-242-3, BR8354) W A T Braille.

— I Am the Clay. 1992. pap. 19.50 (0-679-41195-X) McKay.

— I Am the Clay. 1993. mass mkt. 5.99 (0-449-22138-5, Crest) Fawcett.

— I Am the Clay. Date not set. pap. 4.99 (0-517-11257-4) Random Hse Value.

— In the Beginning. 432p. 1986. mass mkt. 5.95 (0-449-20911-3, Crest) Fawcett.

— My Name Is Asher Lev. 1972. 25.00 (0-394-46137-1) Knopf.

— My Name Is Asher Lev. 352p. 1984. mass mkt. 5.95 (0-449-20714-5, Crest) Fawcett.

— The Promise. 384p. 1985. mass mkt. 5.95 (0-449-20910-5, Crest) Fawcett.

— The Tree of Here. LC 92-28412. (Illus.). (J). (gr. k-4). 1993. 13.00 (0-679-84010-9); lib. bdg. 13.99 (0-679-94010-3) Knopf Bks Yng Read.

— Wanderings: Chaim Potok's History of the Jews. LC 78-54915. 1978. 40.00 (0-394-50110-1) Knopf.

— Wanderings: Chaim Potok's History of the Jews. 1987. mass mkt. 5.95 (0-449-21582-2) Fawcett.

Potokar, Jure. Endurance. Biggins, Michael, tr. 16p. 1992. pap. text ed. 4.00 (1-881489-06-X) Poetry Miscellany.

Potokar, Stanley. Peregrine: Daring, Exciting, Canoeing Adventures. 128p. 1991. pap. 7.50 (0-9630056-0-X) Potokar Pub.

Potomac Corral of the Westerners Staff. Great Western Indian Fights. LC 60-15191. (Illus.). 352p. 1966. pap. 10.95 (0-8032-5186-6, Bison Books) U of Nebr Pr.

Potondi, Paul, tr. see Bertola, Carlo.

Potonniee, Georges. The History of the Discovery of Photography. LC 72-9222. (Literature of Photography Ser.). 1978. reprint ed. 21.95 (0-405-04929-3) Ayer.

Potonnier, B., jt. auth. see Potonnier, G.

Potonnier, G. & Potonnier, B. Commercial, Legal & Business Dictionary: Woerterbuch Fuer Wirtschaft, Recht und Handel, Vol. 1: Deutsch-Franzoesisch. 2nd ed. 1595p. (FRE & GER.). 1982. 175.00 (0-8288-0812-0, M6919) Fr & Eur.

Potonnier, Georges. Woerterbuch fuer Wirtschaft: Recht und Handel, Vol. 2. 2nd rev. ed. 1678p. (FRE & GER.). 1990. 350.00 (0-7859-4850-3) Fr & Eur.

Potosky, Alice. Promoting School Music: A Practical Guide. 48p. 1984. pap. 6.00 (0-940796-54-6, 1038) Music Ed Natl.

Potparic, O. & Gibson, J. A Dictionary of Clinical Tests. (Illus.). 250p. 1992. 48.00 (1-85070-416-3) Prthnon Pub.

— A Dictionary of Infections & Infectious Diseases. 140p. (C). 1995. 35.00 (1-85070-607-7) Prthnon Pub.

Potparic, O., jt. auth. see Gibson, J.

***Potparic, Olivera & Gibson, John.** A Dictionary of Congenital Malformations & Disorders. (Illus.). 193p. (C). 1995. text ed. 55.00 (1-85070-577-1) Prthnon Pub.

Potra, F. A., tr. see Deuflhard, Peter & Hohmann, Andreas.

Potrebenko. Sometimes They Sang. (NFS Canada Ser.). 1999. pap. 6.95 (0-88974-007-0, Pub. by Press Gang CN) InBook.

Potrebenko, Helen. Taxi: A Novel. 168p. 1975. pap. 4.00 (0-919888-02-X) Left Bank.

***Potrykus, I. & Spangenberg, G., eds.** Gene Transfer to Plants. LC 95-7854. (Lab Manuals Ser.). 1995. write for info. (3-540-58406-4) Spr-Verlag.

P Q

Potrykus, I, et al, eds. Protoplasts Poster Proceedings 1983. (Experientia Supplementa Ser.: Vol. 45). 388p. (C). 1983. pap. text ed. 93.95 (*3-7643-1513-X*) Birkhauser.
— Protoplasts Poster Proceedings 1983, Vol. 46. (Experientia Supplementa Ser.: Vol. 45). 388p. (C). 1983. 70.95 (*3-7643-1514-8*) Birkhauser.
***Potsch, Gerd & Michaeli, Walter.** Injection Molding: An Introduction. 176p. (C). 1995. pap. text ed. write for info. (*1-56990-193-7*) Hanser-Gardner.
Potscher, Walter. Aspekte und Probleme der Minoischen Religion. (Religionswissenschaftliche Texte und Studien Ser.: Bd. 4). viii, 288p. 1990. write for info. (*3-487-09359-6*, Pub. by Georg Olms GW) Lubrecht & Cramer.
— Hellas und Rom. (Collectanea Ser.: Bd. XXI). xiv, 670p. (GER.). 1988. write for info. (*3-487-07998-4*, Pub. by Georg Olms GW) Lubrecht & Cramer.
— Vergil und die Gottlichen Machte. (Spudasmata Ser.: Bd. XXXV). vi, 184p. (GER.). 1977. write for info. (*3-487-06410-3*, Pub. by Georg Olms GW) Lubrecht & Cramer.
***Potsic, William P., et al.** Primary Care Pediatric Otolaryngology. 244p. 1995. text ed. 35.00 (*1-887064-00-1*) J M Ryan.
Pott. ERCP Atlas. 236p. 1990. 83.00 (*1-55664-195-8*) Mosby Yr Bk.
***Pott, Alexander.** Finite Geometry & Character Theory. LC 95-4084. (Lecture Notes in Mathematics: Vol. 1601). 188p. 1995. 33.00 (*3-540-59065-X*); write for info. (*0-387-59065-X*) Spr-Verlag.
Pott, August F. Einleitung in die Allgemeine Sprachwissenschaft: Together with Zur Literatur der Sprachenkunde Europas. (Amsterdam Classics in Linguistics Ser.: No. 10). xlvi, 502p. 1974. pap. 97.00x (*90-272-0921-9*) Benjamins North Am.
Pott-Buter, Hettie A. Facts & Fairy Tales about Female Labor, Family & Fertility: A Seven-Country Comparison, 1850-1990. 370p. 1993. 59.00 (*90-5356-045-9*); pap. 39.50 (*90-5356-044-0*) IBD Ltd.
Pott, Constance M. Francis Bacon & His Secret Society. LC 71-174282. reprint ed. 52.50 (*0-404-05096-4*) AMS Pr.
Pott, Henry. Francis Bacon & His Secret Society. 421p. 1992. reprint ed. pap. 29.95 (*1-56459-111-5*) Kessinger Pub.
Pott, Jeronimo J. Estudio De la Biblia Libro Por Libro. (SPA.). 1976. 5.30 (*1-55955-069-4*) CITE MI.
Pott, John, tr. see Hebly, J. A.
***Pottage, Dave & Evans, Mike.** Workbased Stress: Prescription Is Not the Cure. 1992. pap. 35.00 (*0-902789-79-1*, Pub. by Natl Inst Soc Work) St Mut.
— Workbased Stress: Prescription Is Not the Cure. (C). 1992. 50.00 (*0-7855-0070-7*, Pub. by Natl Inst Soc Work) St Mut.
Pottage, Dave, jt. auth. see Evans, Mike.
Pottage, J. Geometrical Investigations: Illustrating the Art of Discovery in the Mathematical Field. 480p. 1983. text ed. 55.95 (*0-201-05733-6*) Addison-Wesley.
Pottage, Julian, jt. auth. see Reese, Terence.
Pottasch, Stuart R. Planetary Nebulae. 1983. lib. bdg. 107. 50 (*90-277-1672-2*) Kluwer Ac.
Pottasch, Stuart R., jt. ed. see Kwok, S.
Pottash, A. L., jt. ed. see Gold, Mark S.
Potte, R., ed. Technology of Stratified Media: Critical Reviews. 157p. 1983. 44.00 (*0-89252-422-7*, 387) SPIE.
Pottebaum, Gerard A. The Rites of People: Exploring the Ritual Character of Human Experience. rev. ed. (Orig.). 1992. pap. text ed. 7.95 (*0-912405-94-5*) Pastoral Pr.
Potten, C. S. Radiation & Skin. 226p. 1984. 77.00 (*0-85066-257-5*) Taylor & Francis.
Potten, C. S., ed. Perspectives on Mammalian Cell Death. (Illus.). 384p. 1987. 80.00 (*0-19-854184-8*) OUP.
Potten, I. A. Looking Back in Longing. 1985. 29.00 (*0-7223-1921-5*, Pub. by A H S Ltd UK) St Mut.
***Pottengen, Mark, ed.** Astrological Research Methods: An ISAR Anthology, Vol. 1. (Illus.). 428p. (C). 1995. pap. text ed. write for info. (*0-9646366-0-3*) ISAR MI.
Pottenger, Doris. UFO's, Aliens or Demons? Smith, Don, ed. 128p. (Orig.). 1990. pap. 5.50 (*0-927022-02-8*) CHJ Pub.
Pottenger, Francis M., Jr. Pottengers' Cats: A Study in Nutrition. LC 83-80360. (Illus.). 126p. 1983. 5.95 (*0-916764-06-0*) Price-Pottenger.
Pottenger, John R. The Political Theory of Liberation Theology: Toward a Reconvergence of Social Values & Social Sciences. LC 88-34838. 264p. 1989. 64.50 (*0-7914-0118-9*); pap. 21.95 (*0-7914-0119-7*) State U NY Pr.
Pottenger, Maritha. Astro Essentials: Planets in Signs, Houses & Aspects. 416p. (Orig.). 1991. pap. 19.95 (*0-935127-14-3*) ACS Pubns.
— Complete Horoscope Interpretation: Putting Together Your Plantary Profile. 568p. (Orig.). 1986. pap. 19.95 (*0-917086-81-3*) ACS Pubns.
— Encounter Astrology. (Illus.). 140p. (Orig.). 1978. pap. text ed. 7.50 (*0-685-28050-0*) TIA Pubns.
— Healing with the Horoscope: A Guide to Counseling. 256p. (Orig.). 1982. pap. 12.95 (*0-917086-45-7*) ACS Pubns.
Pottenger, Maritha & Pottenger, Rique. Your Starway to Love Easy Compatibility Analysis. 608p. 1994. pap. 19. 95 (*0-935127-22-4*) ACS Pubns.
Pottenger, Maritha, jt. auth. see Dobyns, Zipporah.
Pottenger, Mark & Vail, Scott G. Tables for Aspect Research. 128p. 1986. pap. 9.95 (*0-917086-90-2*) ACS Pubns.
***Pottenger, Milton A.** Symbolism: A Treatise on the Soul of Things; How the Natural World Is but a Symbol of the Real World; the Modern Church, with Its Spire & Cross, & the Bible Account of Noah's Ark Symbols of the Phallic Religion. (Illus.). 312p. Date not set. pap. 24.95 (*1-56459-464-5*) Kessinger Pub.
— Three Master Masons. 402p. 1972. reprint ed. spiral bd. 9.90 (*0-7873-0672-X*) Mokelumne.
Pottenger, Rique, jt. auth. see Pottenger, Maritha.
Potter. Basic Nursing Three: Theory & Practice. 1152p. 1994. 47.95 (*0-8016-7876-5*) Mosby Yr Bk.
— Comp Package for Fundamentals of Nursing. 3rd ed. 1993. write for info. (*0-8016-7299-6*) Mosby Yr Bk.
— Fundamentals of Nursing, No. 3. 1992. write for info. (*0-8016-6958-8*) Mosby Yr Bk.
— Fundamentals of Nursing, No. 3: And Performance Checklist. 128p. 1992. pap. 58.95 (*0-8016-7402-6*) Mosby Yr Bk.
— Our Baby's Book. 8.99 (*0-517-12421-1*) Random Hse Value.
— Performance Checklists T-A Fundamentals of Nursing. 3rd ed. 128p. 1992. pap. 12.95 (*0-8016-7297-X*) Mosby Yr Bk.
— Pocket Guide to Physical Assessment. 336p. 1990. spiral bd. 19.95 (*0-8016-3377-X*) Mosby Yr Bk.
— Pocket Nurse Guide to Physical Assessment, No. 3. 352p. 1994. spiral bd. 19.95 (*0-8016-7657-6*) Mosby Yr Bk.
— Resumes that Get Jobs. 1994. pap. 8.00 (*0-671-86404-1*) P-H Gen Ref & Trav.
— Roman Britain. 1983. pap. 9.95 (*0-674-77765-4*) HUP.
— Schaums Outline Thermodynamics for Engineers. 1994. pap. text ed. 38.95 (*0-07-842717-7*) McGraw.
— Student Learning Guide to Accompany Basic Nursing. 3rd ed. 224p. 1994. 12.95 (*0-8016-8024-7*) Mosby Yr Bk.
— Tools 9 & 12: Technology of Object Oriented Languages. (Illus.). 500p. (C). 1994. pap. text ed. 67.00 (*0-13-124512-0*) P-H.
***Potter, ed.** The Madonna Reader: A Decade of Debate over the Diva. 350p. 1996. pap. text ed. 19.95 (*0-8264-0855-9*) Continuum.
— Technologies for Optoelectronics. 1987. 45.00 (*0-89252-904-0*, 869) SPIE.
***Potter & Efron.** Letting Go of Anger: The Ten Most Common Anger Styles & What to Do about Them. LC 94-73923. (Orig.). 1995. pap. text ed. 12.95 (*1-57224-001-6*) New Harbinger.
— Letting Go of Anger: The Ten Most Common Anger Styles & What to Do about Them. LC 94-73923. 160p. (Orig.). 1995. 19.95 (*1-57224-002-4*) New Harbinger.
Potter & Perry. Basic Nursing Theory & Practice, No. 2. (Illus.). 1050p. 1990. teacher ed 46.95 (*0-8016-3950-6*) Mosby Yr Bk.
Potter & Tokoro. Tools Six Tech. 264p. 1992. pap. text ed. 74.00 (*0-13-926940-1*) P-H.
Potter, jt. ed. see Bryan.
Potter, jt. auth. see Perry.
Potter, A. E. & Wilson, T. L., eds. Physics & Astrophysics from a Lunar Base. LC 90-55073. (AIP Conference Proceedings Ser.: No. 202). (Illus.). 344p. 1990. 70.00 (*0-88318-646-2*) Am Inst Physics.
Potter, Adrienne. Parents Book for the Toddler Years. 336p. (Orig.). 1986. mass mkt. 5.99 (*0-345-31429-8*) Ballantine.
***Potter, Alice.** Lincoln County, Colorado War Book. (Illus.). 115p. 1993. 34.95 (*0-88107-230-3*) Curtis Media.
— The Positive Thinker: Self-Motivating Strategies for Personal Success. 240p. (Orig.). 1994. mass mkt. 4.99 (*0-425-14257-4*) Berkley Pub.
Potter, Alice H. How to Be a Lesbian with Class. LC 87-11343. (Illus.). 1989. pap. 8.95 (*0-87949-276-7*) Ashley Bks.
Potter, Ambrose G. A Bibliography of the "Rubaiyat" of Omar Khayyam. xvi, 314p. reprint ed. write for info. (*0-318-71553-8*, Pub. by Georg Olms GW) Lubrecht & Cramer.
***Potter, Ann E.** Inside Out: Rebuilding Self & Personality Through Inner Child Therapy. 150p. 1994. student ed, pap. 17.95x (*1-55959-062-9*); teacher ed, pap. 7.95x (*1-55959-063-7*); audio 9.95x (*1-55959-076-9*) Accel Devel.
Potter, Annie L. A Living Mystery: The International Art & History of Crochet. 160p. Date not set. write for info. (*1-879409-00-3*) A J Pub Intl.
Potter, Annie L., ed. see Elmore, William E.
Potter, Areon. From Darkness to Light: Demonic Oppression & the Christian. LC 93-73290. 368p. (Orig.). 1994. pap. 14.95 (*0-9638782-1-2*) Adonai Res.
Potter, B., et al. Water Island Study: Economic Development Options. 170p. 1980. 20.00 (*0-318-14620-7*) Isl Resources.
***Potter, Barry.** Macintosh OLE 2.0 Developer's Reference: Programmer's Reference. 871p. 1994. cd-rom, pap. 44.95 (*1-55851-420-1*) M&T Bks.
Potter, Beatrice. The Co-Operative Movement in Great Britain. 280p. 1987. text ed. 68.95 (*0-566-05143-5*, Pub. by Avebury Pub UK) Ashgate Pub Co.
Potter, Beatrix. The Adventures of Peter Rabbit (& His Friends) 1994. 4.95 (*0-87129-356-0*, A53) Dramatic Pub.
— Animal Homes. 12p. (J). 1991. bds. 3.50 (*0-7232-3782-4*) Warne.
— Appley Dapply's Nursery Rhymes. (Original Peter Rabbit Books: No. 22). (J). 1987. 5.95 (*0-7232-3481-7*); pap. 2.25 (*0-7232-3506-6*) Warne.
— Beatrix Potter & Peter Rabbit Classic Treasury. (J). 1988. 9.99 (*0-517-67150-6*) Random Hse Value.
— Beatrix Potter Collection, 3 vols. (Frederick Warne Picture Bks). (J). (ps-3). 1987. Collection #1. 24.00 (*0-7232-5163-0*); Collection #2. 21.00 (*0-7232-5164-9*); Collection #3. 21.00 (*0-7232-5165-7*) Warne.
— Beatrix Potter Collection, 3 vols., Set. (Frederick Warne Picture Bks). (J). (ps-3). 1987. write for info. (*0-317-52263-9*) Warne.
— The Beatrix Potter Sticker Book. (Illus.). 24p. (J). (ps-3). 1995. 6.99 (*0-7232-4087-6*) Warne.
— Beatrix Potter Tale of Baby Da. (J). (gr. k up). 1979. 17. 00 (*0-8378-8011-4*) Gibson.
— Beatrix Potter's Country World Postcard Collection. 1990. pap. 6.95 (*0-7232-3646-1*) Warne.
— Beatrix Potter's Farmhouse Box, Set. (Illus.). (J). (ps-3). 1989. 28.95 (*0-7232-5169-X*) Warne.
— Beatrix Potter's Nursery Rhyme Book. 56p. (J). (ps-4). 1984. 11.00 (*0-7232-3254-7*) Warne.
— Beatrix Potter's Nursery Rhyme Book. (Illus.). 48p. (J). 1995. 12.99 (*0-7232-4249-6*) Warne.
— Beatrix Potter's Peter Rabbit: A Lift-the-Flap Rebus Book. (J). (ps-3). 1991. 11.95 (*0-7232-3798-0*) Warne.
— Beatrix Potter's Peter Rabbit Tales. (Illus.). 80p. (J). (ps-3). 1995. 6.99 (*0-7232-3665-8*) Warne.
— Benjamin Bunny. (Illus.). 10p. (J). (ps). 1994. 3.99 (*0-7232-0018-1*) Warne.
— Benjamin Bunny. (Illus.). 10p. (J). (ps-5). 1995. 5.99 (*0-7232-4187-2*) Warne.
— Benjamin Bunny: Beatrix Potter Deluxe Pop Up. (Illus.). (J). 1992. 4.99 (*0-517-07001-4*) Random Hse Value.
— Benjamin Bunny Visits Peter Rabbit. 1988. 2.99 (*0-517-60594-5*) Random Hse Value.
— Benjamin Bunny's Colors. (Illus.). 24p. (J). (ps). 1994. bds. 2.99 (*0-7232-4118-X*) Warne.
— Big Big Book of Peter Rabbit & His Friends. LC 87-15671. 1988. 5.99 (*0-517-64374-X*) Random Hse Value.
— The Big Peter Rabbit Coloring Book. (Illus.). 64p. (J). (ps-3). 1995. pap. 4.99 (*0-7232-4263-1*) Warne.
— Birthday Book of Peter Rabbit. (Illus.). 256p. (J). (ps up). 1983. 5.99 (*0-517-40303-X*) Random Hse Value.
— Cecily Parsley's Nursery Rhymes. (Original Peter Rabbit Books: No. 23). (J). 1987. 5.95 (*0-7232-3482-5*); pap. 2.25 (*0-7232-3507-4*) Warne.
— A Child's Treasury of Beatrix Potter. (Illus.). 80p. (J). (gr. k-3). 1987. 6.98 (*0-681-40281-4*) Longmeadow Pr.
— The Complete Adventures of Peter Rabbit. (Illus.). 96p. (J). (ps-3). 1987. 13.00 (*0-7232-2951-1*) Warne.
— The Complete Adventures of Peter Rabbit. (Picture Puffins Ser.). 80p. (J). (ps-3). 1984. pap. 6.99 (*0-14-050444-3*, Puffin) Puffin Bks.
— Complete Adventures of Tom Kitten & His Friends. (Illus.). 80p. (J). (ps-3). 1985. 13.00 (*0-7232-3288-1*) Warne.
— The Complete Tales of Beatrix Potter. (Illus.). 384p. (J). (ps-6). 1989. 35.00 (*0-7232-3618-6*) Viking Child Bks.
— Complete Tales of Peter Rabbit: And Other Favorite Stories. LC 86-10116. (Illus.). 56p. (J). (gr. k up). 1986. 9.98 (*0-89471-460-0*) Courage Bks.
— El Cuento de la Oca Carlota. (Original Peter Rabbit Bks.). (Illus.). 64p. (SPA.). (J). 1988. 5.95 (*0-7232-3557-0*) Warne.
— El Cuento de los Dos Malvados Ratones. (Original Peter Rabbit Bks.). (Illus.). 64p. (SPA.). (J). 1988. 5.95 (*0-7232-3559-7*) Warne.
— El Cuento de Pedrito Conejo. Marcuse, Aida, tr. (Illus.). (SPA.). (J). (gr. k-4). 1993. pap. 2.95 (*0-590-46475-2*) Scholastic Inc.
— El Cuento de Pedro, el Conejo - The Tales of Peter Rabbit. (J). (ps-3). 1994. pap. 2.95 (*0-486-27995-2*) Dover.
— El Cuento De Pedro, El Conejo, y Otros Once Cuentos De Beatrix Potter: 11 Stories. DeZardain, Paul F. & Saludes, Esperanza G., trs. (Illus.). 96p. (SPA.). (J). 1995. pap. text ed. 1.00 (*0-486-28566-9*) Dover.
— El Cuento de Perico, el Conejo Travieso. (Original Peter Rabbit Bks.). (Illus.). 64p. (SPA.). (J). 1988. 5.95 (*0-7232-3556-2*) Warne.
— El Cuento De Perico El Conejo Travieso. (Illus.). (J). (gr. k-3). 1991. audio, bds. 14.95 (*0-87499-225-7*) Live Oak Media.
— El Cuento De Perico El Conejo Travieso, 4 bks., Set. (Illus.). (J). (gr. k-3). 1991. audio, bds. 33.95 (*0-87499-226-5*) Live Oak Media.
— El Cuento del Conejito Benjamin. (Original Peter Rabbit Bks.). (Illus.). 64p. (SPA.). (J). 1988. 5.95 (*0-7232-3558-9*) Warne.
— El Cuento Del Conejo Pedrin (The Tale of Peter Rabbit) (Pudgy Pal Board Bks.). (Illus.). 18p. (SPA.). (J). (ps). 1995. bds. 3.95 (*0-448-40847-3*, G&D) Putnam Pub Group.
— El Cuento del Gato Tomas. (Original Peter Rabbit Bks.). (Illus.). 64p. (SPA.). (J). 1988. 4.95 (*0-7232-3565-1*) Warne.
— Dear Peter Rabbit: A Beatrix Potter Mini Letters Book. (Illus.). 24p. (J). 1995. 10.99 (*0-7232-4139-2*) Warne.
— Deux Vilaines Souris. 59p. (FRE.). (J). 1990. 9.95 (*0-7859-3625-4*, 2070560708) Fr & Eur.
— Deux Vilaines Souris. (Gallimard Ser.). 59p. (FRE.). (J). 1990. 10.95 (*2-07-056070-8*) Schoenhof.
— Dinner Time. 12p. (J). 1991. bds. 3.50 (*0-7232-3781-6*) Warne.
— Farmyard Noises. 12p. (J). 1991. bds. 3.50 (*0-7232-3784-0*) Warne.
— Further Adventures of Peter Rabbit. 1989. 6.99 (*0-517-68371-7*) Random Hse Value.
— Die Geschichte von Peterchen Hase: Ein Buntes Marchenbuch. (Illus.). 32p. (GER.). (J). 1995. pap. text ed. 1.00 (*0-486-28557-X*) Dover.
— Giant Treasury of Beatrix Potter. (Illus.). 52p. (J). (gr. k-6). 1985. 6.99 (*0-517-43121-1*) Random Hse Value.
— A Giant Treasury of Mouse Stories: The Tales of Johnny Town-Mouse & Other Mice. LC 94-35476. (J). 1995. pap. 7.99 (*0-517-12261-8*) Random Hse Value.
— Giant Treasury of Peter Rabbit. (Illus.). 92p. (J). (gr. k-6). 1985. 6.99 (*0-517-31687-0*) Random Hse Value.
— Ginger & Pickles. LC 85-13641. (Illus.). 64p. (J). (gr. 2 up). 1985. reprint ed. pap. 1.75 (*0-486-24969-7*) Dover.
— The Great Big Treasury of Beatrix Potter. LC 92-12165. (J). 1992. 11.99 (*0-517-07246-7*, Derrydale Bks) Random Hse Value.
— Happy Families. 12p. (J). 1991. bds. 3.50 (*0-7232-3783-2*) Warne.
— Hill Top Tales. (Illus.). 128p. (J). (ps up). 1989. 8.95 (*0-7232-3548-1*) Warne.
— Jeannot Lapin. (Illus.). 58p. (FRE.). (J). 1990. 9.95 (*0-7859-3631-9*, 2070560945) Fr & Eur.
— Jeannot Lapin. (Gallimard Ser.). 58p. (FRE.). (J). 1990. 10.95 (*2-07-056094-5*) Schoenhof.
— Jemima Puddle-Duck. (Little Hide-&-Seek Bks.). (Illus.). 12p. (J). (ps-1). 1994. 3.50 (*0-7232-4107-4*) Warne.
— Jemima Puddle-Duck. (Illus.). 10p. (J). (ps-3). 1995. 5.99 (*0-7232-4185-6*) Warne.
— Jemima Puddle-Duck Bath Book. (Illus.). 8p. (J). (ps). 1988. pap. 3.99 (*0-7232-3512-0*) Warne.
— The Jemima Puddle-Duck Pop-up Book. (Illus.). 6p. (J). (ps-3). 1993. 12.95 (*0-7232-4122-8*) Viking Child Bks.
— Jemima Puddle-Duck's Numbers. (Illus.). 24p. (J). (ps). 1994. bds. 2.99 (*0-7232-4091-4*) Warne.
— Jemima Puddleduck. (J). 1988. 2.99 (*0-517-65275-7*) Random Hse Value.
— Jemima Puddleduck. (Classic Tales from Beatrix Potter Ser.). (Illus.). 24p. (J). (ps-1). 1992. 3.99 (*0-517-05077-3*) Random Hse Value.
— Jemima Puddleduck: Beatrix Potter Deluxe Pop Up. (Illus.). (J). 1992. 4.99 (*0-517-06999-7*) Random Hse Value.
— Jemima Puddleduck Pop-Up. (J). 1988. 3.99 (*0-517-67097-6*) Random Hse Value.
— Jeremie Peche-a-la-Ligne. (Illus.). 58p. (FRE.). (J). 1990. 9.95 (*0-7859-3628-9*, 2070560740) Fr & Eur.
— Jeremie Peche-a-la-Ligne. (Gallimard Ser.). 58p. (FRE.). (J). 1990. 10.95 (*2-07-056074-0*) Schoenhof.
— Jeremy Fisher. (Mini Pop-up Bk.). (Illus.). 10p. (J). (ps-5). 1992. 5.95 (*0-7232-3999-1*) Warne.
— Jeremy Fisher Bath Book. (Illus.). 8p. (J). (ps). 1989. 3.50 (*0-7232-3513-9*) Warne.
— Letters to Children. (Illus.). 48p. (J). (gr. 2 up). 1986. pap. 5.95 (*0-8027-7293-5*) Walker & Co.
— Little Nursery Rhymes, Vol. 4. (J). 1995. pap. 4.99 (*0-517-12256-1*) Random Hse Value.
— Little Tale of Jemima Puddle Duck Coloring Book. (Illus.). (J). (gr. k-3). 1993. pap. 1.00 (*0-486-27494-2*) Dover.
— Little Tale of Mr. Jeremy Fisher Coloring Book. (Illus.). (J). (gr. k-3). 1992. pap. 1.00 (*0-486-27291-5*) Dover.
— Little Tale of Two Bad Mice Coloring Book. (Illus.). (J). (gr. k-3). 1994. pap. 1.00 (*0-486-27868-9*) Dover.
— Little Treasury of Fairy Tales. (J). 1995. 4.99 (*0-517-12254-5*) Random Hse Value.
— Little Treasury of Mother Goose. (J). 1995. 4.99 (*0-517-12252-9*) Random Hse Value.
— Little Treasury of Peter Rabbit. 1995. 4.99 (*0-517-12255-3*) Random Hse Value.
— Little Treasury of Peter Rabbit & His Friends. (J). 1994. 5.95 (*0-517-10084-3*) Random Hse Value.
— Little Treasury of the Velveteen Rabbit. (J). 1995. 4.99 (*0-517-12257-X*) Random Hse Value.
— Madame Piquedru. (Illus.). 58p. (FRE.). (J). 1990. 9.95 (*0-7859-3623-8*, 2070560686) Fr & Eur.
— Madame Piquedru. (Gallimard Ser.). 58p. (FRE.). (J). 1990. 10.95 (*2-07-056068-6*) Schoenhof.
— Madame Trotte-Menu. (Illus.). 58p. (FRE.). (J). 1990. 9.95 (*0-7859-3634-3*, 2070561054) Fr & Eur.
— Madame Trotte-Menu. (Gallimard Ser.). 59p. (FRE.). (J). 1990. 10.95 (*2-07-056105-4*) Schoenhof.
— Mademoiselle Mitoufle. (Illus.). 58p. (FRE.). (J). 1990. 9.95 (*0-7859-3633-5*, 2070561046) Fr & Eur.
— Mademoiselle Mitoufle. (Gallimard Ser.). 37p. (FRE.). (J). 1990. 10.95 (*2-07-056104-6*) Schoenhof.
— Mechant Petit Lapin. (Illus.). 58p. (FRE.). (J). 1990. 9.95 (*0-7859-3627-0*, 2070560732) Fr & Eur.
— Mechant Petit Lapin. (Gallimard Ser.). (FRE.). (J). (gr. 5-10). 1990. 10.95 (*2-07-056073-2*) Schoenhof.
— Meet Benjamin Bunny. (Illus.). 12p. (J). (ps). 1987. bds. 2.95 (*0-7232-3451-5*) Warne.
— Meet Hunca Munca. (Board Bks.). (Illus.). 12p. (J). (ps). 1986. bds. 2.95 (*0-7232-3421-3*) Warne.
— Meet Jemima Puddle-Duck. (Board Bks.). (Illus.). 12p. (J). (ps). 1986. bds. 3.50 (*0-7232-3420-5*) Warne.
— Meet Peter Rabbit. (Board Bks.). (Illus.). 12p. (J). (ps). 1986. bds. 3.50 (*0-7232-3418-3*) Warne.
— Meet Peter Rabbit. 1988. 2.99 (*0-517-60595-3*) Random Hse Value.
— Meet Tom Kitten. (Board Bks.). (Illus.). 12p. (J). (ps). 1986. bds. 3.50 (*0-7232-3419-1*) Warne.
— Mini Peter Rabbit Bookshop, 23 bks., Set. (Illus.). (J). (ps-3). 1993. 35.00 (*0-7232-3989-4*) Warne.
— Mouse Tales. (Illus.). 128p. (J). 1989. 8.95 (*0-7232-3543-0*) Warne.
— Mrs. Tiggy-Winkle. (Illus.). 10p. (J). (ps). 1994. 3.99 (*0-7232-0019-X*) Warne.
— My First Peter Rabbit Book & Toy. (J). (ps-3). 1991. 16. 99 (*0-7232-4014-0*) Warne.
— My First Year: A Beatrix Potter Baby Book. (Illus.). 29p. (J). 1989. 10.00 (*0-7232-3157-5*) Warne.
— My First Year: My Peter Rabbit Keepsake. (Illus.). (J). 1999. boxed 19.99 (*0-7232-8921-2*) Warne.
— My Peter Rabbit Cloth Book. (Illus.). 10p. (J). (ps). 1994. 4.99 (*0-7232-0020-3*) Warne.
— My Peter Rabbit Learning Box: Peter Rabbit's 123 & Peter Rabbit's ABC, Set. (J). (ps-3). 1988. boxed 13.95 (*0-7232-5168-1*) Warne.
— My Peter Rabbit Play Box. (J). 1991. bds. 14.95 (*0-7232-3794-8*) Warne.
— My Tom Kitten. (J). 1994. 4.99 (*0-7232-4159-7*) Warne.
— My Tom Kitten Cloth Book. (Illus.). 10p. (J). (ps). 1994. 4.99 (*0-7232-0021-1*) Warne.
— Noisette l'Ecureuil. (Illus.). 58p. (FRE.). (J). 1990. 9.95 (*0-7859-3629-7*, 2070560759) Fr & Eur.
— Noisette l'Ecureuil. (Gallimard Ser.). 58p. (FRE.). (J). 1990. 10.95 (*2-07-056075-9*) Schoenhof.

— The One Hundredth Anniversary 1-12 Presentation Box: The World of Beatrix Potter, 12 bks., Set. (Illus.). (J). 1993. 70.00 (*0-7232-4113-9*) Warne.

— The One Hundredth Anniversary 1-23 Presentation Box: The World of Beatrix Potter, 23 bks., Set. (Illus.). (J). 1993. 135.00 (*0-7232-4112-0*) Warne.

— The One Hundredth Anniversary 13-23 Presentation Box: The World of Beatrix Potter, 11 bks., Set. (Illus.). (J). 1993. 65.00 (*0-7232-4114-7*) Warne.

— The Original Peter Rabbit Books, 23 bks., Set. 1986. Presentation Box, 23 bks. 135.00 (*0-7232-5162-2*) Warne.

— Original Peter Rabbit Books: 13-23 Presentation Box. (J). 1990. 65.00 (*0-7232-5178-9*) Warne.

— Original Peter Rabbit Miniature Collection. (Illus.). (J). 1989. Twelve-copy drawer. pap. 18.50 (*0-7232-5173-8*) Warne.

— The Original Peter Rabbit Miniature Collection, No. III. (Illus.). (J). (ps-3). 1989. boxed 4.95 (*0-7232-3984-3*) Warne.

— Original Peter Rabbit Miniature Collection, No. IV. (J). (ps-3). 1990. pap. 4.95 (*0-7232-5076-6*) Warne.

— The Original Peter Rabbit Miniature Collection II. (J). (ps-3). 1988. pap. 5.95 (*0-7232-3983-5*) Warne.

— The Original Peter Rabbit Miniature Collection, No. I. (Picture Bks.). (Illus.). (J). (ps-3). 1991. pap. 5.95 (*0-7232-3982-7*) Warne.

— Original Peter Rabbit Miniature Collection V. (J). (ps-3). 1990. pap. 4.95 (*0-7232-5078-2*) Warne.

— Panache Petitgris. (Illus.). 60p. (FRE.). (J). 1990. 9.95 (*0-7859-3713-7*) Fr & Eur.

— Panache Petitgris. (Gallimard Ser.). 59p. (FRE.). (J). 1990. 10.95 (*2-07-056102-X*) Schoenhof.

— Peter Rabbit. (Mini Pop-up Bk.). (Illus.). 10p. (J). (ps-5). 1992. 5.99 (*0-7232-3997-5*) Warne.

— Peter Rabbit. (Little Hide-&-Seek Bks.). (Illus.). 12p. (J). (ps-1). 1994. 3.50 (*0-7232-4105-8*) Warne.

— Peter Rabbit. (Classic Tales from Beatrix Potter Ser.). (Illus.). 24p. (J). (ps-1). 1992. 3.99 (*0-517-05079-X*) Random Hse Value.

— Peter Rabbit: Bath Book. 8p. (J). (ps). 1989. 3.99 (*0-7232-3584-8*) Warne.

— Peter Rabbit & Benjamin Bunny Coloring Book. (Illus.). (J). (gr. 1 up). 1987. pap. 1.49 (*0-671-62987-5*, Litl Simon S&S) S&S Childrens.

— Peter Rabbit & Eleven Other Favorite Tales. LC 93-14417. (Children's Thrift Classics Ser.). (Illus.). 96p. (J). 1994. reprint ed. pap. 1.00 (*0-486-27845-X*) Dover.

— Peter Rabbit & Friends: Three Complete Tales, 3 vols., Set. (Illus.). 178p. (J). (gr. 2 up). 1985. pap. 5.25 (*0-486-24772-4*) Dover.

— The Peter Rabbit & Friends Cookbook. (Illus.). 48p. (J). (ps-3). 1994. 6.99 (*0-7232-4146-5*) Warne.

— The Peter Rabbit & Friends Poster Activity Book. (Illus.). 32p. (J). (ps-3). 1995. 6.99 (*0-7232-4088-4*) Warne.

— Peter Rabbit & His Friends. (Illus.). 24p. (J). (ps). 1994. bds. 2.99 (*0-7232-4093-0*) Warne.

— Peter Rabbit & His Friends Word Book. (J). 1989. 4.99 (*0-517-64156-9*) Random Hse Value.

— Peter Rabbit & Other Stories. (J). 1993. 4.98 (*0-89009-187-0*) Bk Sales Inc.

— The Peter Rabbit Bedtime Box. (Illus.). 32p. (J). (gr. k-3). 1995. 25.00 (*0-7232-5453-2*) Warne.

— Peter Rabbit Birthday Book. (J). (ps-3). 1987. 6.95 (*0-7232-3523-6*) Warne.

— Peter Rabbit Comes Home. (J). 1988. 2.99 (*0-517-60596-1*) Random Hse Value.

— Peter Rabbit in Mr. McGregor's Garden. (J). 1988. 2.99 (*0-517-60597-X*) Random Hse Value.

— The Peter Rabbit Make-a-Mobile Book. 20p. (J). 1991. pap. 5.95 (*0-7232-3764-6*) Warne.

— The Peter Rabbit Nursery Frieze. (Illus.). (J). (ps-00). 1989. 5.00 (*0-7232-3583-X*) Warne.

— The Peter Rabbit Pop-Up Book. 12p. (J). 1983. 12.99 (*0-7232-2950-3*) Warne.

— The Peter Rabbit Spectacular: A Giant Pop-up-&-Play Book. (Illus.). 24p. (J). (ps-3). 1994. 18.99 (*0-7232-4161-9*) Warne.

— The Peter Rabbit Stencil Book. (Illus.). 28p. (J). (ps-3). 1994. pap. 6.99 (*0-7232-4046-9*) Warne.

— The Peter Rabbit Theatre. (Illus.). 16p. (J). (gr. 1). 1992. 6.95 (*0-7232-4006-X*) Warne.

— Peter Rabbit with Many Other Beloved Beatrix Potter Characters Coloring Book. (Illus.). (J). (gr. 1 up). 1987. pap. 1.49 (*0-671-62984-0*, Litl Simon S&S) S&S Childrens.

— Peter Rabbit's ABC. (Illus.). 48p. (J). (ps-2). 1987. 6.95 (*0-7232-3423-X*) Warne.

— Peter Rabbit's ABC 123. (Illus.). 48p. (J). (gr. k-1). 1995. 10.99 (*0-7232-4188-0*) Warne.

— Peter Rabbit's Christmas Book. (J). (ps-3). 1990. pap. 5.95 (*0-7232-3778-6*) Warne.

— Peter Rabbit's Colors. 48p. (J). (ps-00). 1988. 6.95 (*0-7232-3612-7*); 5.00 (*0-7232-3613-5*) Warne.

— Peter Rabbit's One Two Three. (J). (ps-00). 1988. 6.95 (*0-7232-3424-8*) Warne.

— The Pie & the Patty-Pan. (Illus.). 46p. (J). 1976. reprint ed. pap. 1.75 (*0-486-23383-9*) Dover.

— Pierre Lapin. (Illus.). 62p. (FRE.). (J). 1980. 9.95 (*0-7859-3624-6*, 2070560694) Fr & Eur.

— Pierre Lapin. (Gallimard Ser.). 62p. (FRE.). (J). 1980. 10.95 (*2-07-056069-4*) Schoenhof.

— Pierre Lapin: Peter Rabbit. (Illus.). (FRE.). (J). (gr. 3-7). 1973. 5.00 (*0-7232-0650-3*) Warne.

— The Roly-Poly Pudding. LC 93-34679. (Illus.). (Orig.). (J). 1994. 6.95 (*0-681-45606-X*) Longmeadow Pr.

— The Roly-Poly Pudding. 80p. (Orig.). (J). (gr. 1 up). 1986. reprint ed. pap. 2.75 (*0-486-25099-7*) Dover.

— Samuel Whiskers. (Little Hide-&-Seek Bks.). (Illus.). 12p. (J). (ps-1). 1994. 3.50 (*0-7232-4108-2*) Warne.

— Scenes from the Tale of Peter Rabbit. (Illus.). (J). 1989. 6.95 (*0-7232-3547-3*) Warne.

— Sophie Canetang: The Tale Jemima Puddle-Duck: French Edition. 58p. (FRE.). 1990. 9.95 (*0-7859-3622-X*, 2070569678) Fr & Eur.

— The Stories of Beatrix Potter, Vol. 1. (Audio Gift Pack Ser.). (Illus.). 96p. (J). (ps-2). 1991. audio 16.98 (*1-55886-063-0*) Smarty Pants.

— The Stories of Beatrix Potter, Vol. 2. (Audio Gift Pack Ser.). (Illus.). 96p. (J). (ps-2). 1992. audio 16.98 (*1-55886-067-3*) Smarty Pants.

— The Story of a Fierce Bad Rabbit. (Original Peter Rabbit Books: No. 20). (J). 1987. 5.95 (*0-7232-3479-5*); pap. 2.25 (*0-7232-3504-X*) Warne.

— The Story of Miss Moppet. (Original Peter Rabbit Books: No. 21). (J). 1987. 5.95 (*0-7232-3480-9*); pap. 2.25 (*0-7232-3505-8*) Warne.

— Tailleur de Gloucester. (Illus.). 58p. (FRE.). (J). 1991. 9.95 (*0-7859-3630-0*, 2070560767) Fr & Eur.

— Tailleur de Gloucester. (Gallimard Ser.). 58p. (FRE.). (J). 1991. 10.95 (*2-07-056076-7*) Schoenhof.

— The Tailor of Gloucester. (Original Peter Rabbit Bks.: No. 3). (J). 1987. 5.95 (*0-7232-3462-0*); pap. 2.25 (*0-7232-3487-6*) Warne.

— The Tailor of Gloucester. (World of Peter Rabbit & Friends Ser.). (Illus.). 60p. (J). 1993. 16.00 (*0-7232-4094-9*) Warne.

— The Tailor of Gloucester. LC 88-11510. (Illus.). 44p. (J). (ps up). 1991. pap. 14.95 (*0-88708-080-4*, Rabbit); audio 19.95 (*0-88708-085-5*, Rabbit) S&S Childrens.

— Tailor of Gloucester. (World of Peter Rabbit & Friends Ser.). (Illus.). 36p. (J). (ps-3). 1993. 4.99 (*0-7232-4137-6*) Warne.

— The Tailor of Gloucester. (Illus.). 57p. (J). (gr. k-3). 1973. reprint ed. pap. 1.75 (*0-486-20176-7*) Dover.

— The Tailor of Gloucester: Lift-the-Flap Book. (Illus.). 24p. (J). (ps-1). 1994. 11.99 (*0-7232-4147-3*) Warne.

— The Tailor or Gloucester Christmas Activity Book. (Illus.). 36p. (J). (ps-3). 1993. 4.99 (*0-7232-4136-8*) Warne.

— The Tale of Benjamin Bunny. (Original Peter Rabbit Bks.: No.4). (J). 1987. 5.95 (*0-7232-3463-9*); pap. 3.95 (*0-7232-3488-4*) Warne.

— The Tale of Benjamin Bunny. (Beatrix Potter Book & Storytape Collection). (Illus.). (J). (ps-3). 1989. pap. 6.95 (*0-7232-3628-3*) Warne.

— The Tale of Benjamin Bunny. (Illus.). 32p. (J). (ps-3). 1994. pap. 3.99 (*0-14-054300-7*) Puffin Bks.

— The Tale of Benjamin Bunny. (J). 1992. 3.99 (*0-517-07240-8*) Random Hse Value.

— The Tale of Benjamin Bunny. (Illus.). 64p. (J). (ps-3). 1986. 3.95 (*0-671-62925-5*, Litl Simon S&S) S&S Childrens.

— The Tale of Benjamin Bunny. LC 80-27468. (Illus.). 32p. (J). (gr. k-3). 1981. lib. bdg. 9.79 (*0-89375-484-6*); pap. text ed. 2.50 (*0-89375-485-4*) Troll Assocs.

— Tale of Benjamin Bunny. (J). 1988. 2.99 (*0-517-65277-3*) Random Hse Value.

— Tale of Benjamin Bunny. (J). 1995. 3.99 (*0-517-10236-6*) Random Hse Value.

— The Tale of Benjamin Bunny. LC 74-78812. (Illus.). 59p. (J). (gr. 2 up). 1974. reprint ed. pap. 1.75 (*0-486-21102-9*) Dover.

— Tale of Benjamin Bunny Coloring Book. (Illus.). (J). (gr. k-3). 1981. pap. 2.50 (*0-486-24114-9*) Dover.

— The Tale of Benjamin Bunny Paint with Water Book. (Illus.). (J). (gr. 1 up). 1987. pap. 1.49 (*0-671-62986-7*, Litl Simon S&S) S&S Childrens.

— Tale of Benjamin Bunny Pop Up. (J). 1988. 3.99 (*0-517-67096-8*) Random Hse Value.

— Tale of Benjamin Bunny-Sticker. (J). 1990. pap. 2.95 (*0-671-69254-2*, Litl Simon S&S) S&S Childrens.

— The Tale of Ginger & Pickles. (Original Peter Rabbit Books: No. 18). (J). 1987. 5.95 (*0-7232-3477-9*); pap. 2.25 (*0-7232-3502-3*) Warne.

— The Tale of Jemima Puddle-Duck. (Original Peter Rabbit Bks.: No. 9). (Illus.). (Orig.). (J). (ps-3). 1987. 5.95 (*0-7232-3468-X*); pap. 2.25 (*0-7232-3493-0*) Warne.

— The Tale of Jemima Puddle-Duck. (Beatrix Potter Book & Storytape Collection). (Illus.). (Orig.). (J). (ps-3). 1989. pap. 6.95 (*0-7232-3630-5*) Warne.

— The Tale of Jemima Puddle-Duck. (Illus.). 32p. (Orig.). (J). (ps-3). 1992. pap. 3.99 (*0-14-054498-4*) Puffin Bks.

— The Tale of Jemima Puddle-Duck. (Illus.). 64p. (Orig.). (J). (ps-3). 1987. 3.95 (*0-671-63236-1*, Litl Simon S&S) S&S Childrens.

— The Tale of Jemima Puddle-Duck. (Golden Deluxe Book & Cassette Ser.). (Illus.). 24p. (Orig.). (J). (ps-2). 1991. 5.98 (*1-55886-057-6*) Smarty Pants.

— Tale of Jemima Puddle-Duck. (J). 1995. 3.99 (*0-517-10238-2*) Random Hse Value.

— The Tale of Jemima Puddle-Duck. deluxe ed. (Illus.). 60p. (J). 1995. boxed 16.00 (*0-7232-4248-8*) Warne.

— The Tale of Jemima Puddle-duck. (Illus.). 64p. (J). 1984. reprint ed. pap. 1.75 (*0-486-24634-5*) Dover.

— The Tale of Jemima Puddle-Duck & Other Farmyard Tales. (Frederick Warne Picture Bks.). (Illus.). 80p. (J). (ps-3). 1987. 13.00 (*0-7232-3425-6*) Warne.

— Tale of Jeremy Fisher-Coloring Book. (J). 1985. pap. 2.50 (*0-486-24964-6*) Dover.

— The Tale of Johnny Town-Mouse. (Original Peter Rabbit Books: No. 13). (J). (ps-3). 1987. 5.95 (*0-7232-3472-8*); pap. 2.25 (*0-7232-3497-3*) Warne.

— The Tale of Little Pig Robinson. (Original Peter Rabbit Books: No. 19). (J). 1987. 5.95 (*0-7232-3478-7*); pap. 2.25 (*0-7232-3503-1*) Warne.

— The Tale of Mr. Jeremy Fisher. (Original Peter Rabbit Bks.: No. 7). (J). 1987. 5.95 (*0-7232-3466-3*); pap. 2.25 (*0-7232-3491-4*) Warne.

— The Tale of Mr. Jeremy Fisher. (Beatrix Potter Book & Storytape Collection). (J). (ps-3). 1989. pap. 6.95 (*0-7232-3669-0*) Warne.

— The Tale of Mr. Jeremy Fisher. (J). 1992. 3.99 (*0-517-07238-6*) Random Hse Value.

— The Tale of Mr. Jeremy Fisher. LC 88-34668. (Illus.). 32p. (J). (ps up). 1991. 19.95 (*0-88708-095-2*, Rabbit); pap. 14.95 (*0-88708-094-4*, Rabbit) S&S Childrens.

— The Tale of Mr. Jeremy Fisher. LC 74-75269. (Illus.). 59p. (J). (gr. 2-4). 1974. reprint ed. pap. 1.75 (*0-486-23066-X*) Dover.

— The Tale of Mr. Jeremy Fisher. LC 92-22584. (Illus.). 64p. (J). 1992. reprint ed. 5.95 (*0-88708-253-X*, Rabbit); reprint ed. Mini-bk. 9.95 (*0-88708-252-1*, Rabbit) S&S Childrens.

— The Tale of Mr. Tod. (Original Peter Rabbit Books: No. 14). (J). 1987. 5.95 (*0-7232-3473-6*); pap. 2.25 (*0-7232-3498-1*) Warne.

— The Tale of Mrs. Tiggy-Winkle. (Original Peter Rabbit Bks.: No. 6). (J). 1987. 5.95 (*0-7232-3465-5*); pap. 2.25 (*0-7232-3490-6*) Warne.

— The Tale of Mrs. Tiggy-Winkle. (Beatrix Potter Book & Storytape Collection). (Illus.). (J). (ps-3). 1989. pap. 6.95 (*0-7232-3629-1*) Warne.

— The Tale of Mrs. Tiggy-Winkle. (J). 1992. 3.99 (*0-517-07237-8*) Random Hse Value.

— The Tale of Mrs. Tiggy-Winkle. (Golden Deluxe Book & Cassette Ser.). (Illus.). 24p. (J). (ps-2). 1991. 5.98 (*1-55886-058-4*) Smarty Pants.

— The Tale of Mrs. Tiggy-winkle. (Illus.). 57p. (J). (gr. k-6). 1973. reprint ed. pap. 1.75 (*0-486-20546-0*) Dover.

— The Tale of Mrs. Tiggy-Winkle & Mr. Jeremy Fisher. (Illus.). 32p. (J). (ps-3). 1994. pap. 4.99 (*0-7232-4149-X*) Warne.

— The Tale of Mrs. Tittlemouse. (Original Peter Rabbit Books: No. 11). (J). 1987. 5.95 (*0-7232-3470-1*); pap. 2.25 (*0-7232-3495-7*) Warne.

— The Tale of Mrs. Tittlemouse. 64p. 1986. reprint ed. pap. 1.75 (*0-486-25230-2*) Dover.

— The Tale of Peter Rabbit. (J). (ps-3). 1987. 5.95 (*0-7232-3460-4*); pap. 2.25 (*0-7232-3485-X*) Warne.

— The Tale of Peter Rabbit. (Beatrix Potter Book & Storytape Collection). (Illus.). (J). (ps-3). 1989. pap. 6.95 (*0-7232-3627-5*) Warne.

— The Tale of Peter Rabbit. (Giant Bk. Ser.). (Illus.). 24p. (J). (ps-3). 1993. pap. 17.99 (*0-7232-4029-9*) Warne.

— The Tale of Peter Rabbit. LC 87-40282. (Illus.). 24p. (J). (ps up). 1990. 6.95 (*1-55782-015-5*, Warner Juvenile Bks) Little.

— The Tale of Peter Rabbit. (Illus.). 32p. (J). (ps-3). 1992. pap. 3.99 (*0-14-054497-6*, Puffin) Puffin Bks.

— The Tale of Peter Rabbit. LC 85-70809. (Pudgy Pal Board Bks.). (Illus.). 13p. (J). (ps). 1986. 3.95 (*0-448-10224-2*, G&D) Putnam Pub Group.

— The Tale of Peter Rabbit. (All Aboard Bks.). (Illus.). 32p. (J). 1991. pap. 2.25 (*0-448-40061-8*, Platt & Munk Pubs) Putnam Pub Group.

— The Tale of Peter Rabbit. (J). 1992. 3.99 (*0-517-07236-X*) Random Hse Value.

— The Tale of Peter Rabbit. (Easy to Read Folktales Ser.). (Illus.). 32p. (J). (gr. k-3). 1986. 5.95 (*0-590-63091-1*); pap. 2.50 (*0-590-41101-2*) Scholastic Inc.

— The Tale of Peter Rabbit. (Illus.). 64p. (J). (ps-3). 1986. 3.95 (*0-671-62924-7*, Litl Simon S&S) S&S Childrens.

— The Tale of Peter Rabbit. LC 88-11509. (Illus.). 36p. (J). (ps up). 1991. 14.95 (*0-317-89758-6*, Rabbit); audio 19.95 (*0-88708-084-7*, Rabbit) S&S Childrens.

— The Tale of Peter Rabbit. (Golden Deluxe Book & Cassette Ser.). (Illus.). 24p. (J). (ps-2). 1991. 5.98 (*1-55886-055-X*) Smarty Pants.

— The Tale of Peter Rabbit. (Big Golden Book Ser.). (Illus.). 24p. (J). (ps-3). 1993. 3.50 (*0-307-12349-9*, 12349, Golden Pr) Western Pub.

— Tale of Peter Rabbit. LC 78-18071. (J). 1988. 2.99 (*0-517-65276-5*) Random Hse Value.

— Tale of Peter Rabbit. LC 78-18071. (J). 1995. 3.99 (*0-517-10235-8*) Random Hse Value.

— Tale of Peter Rabbit. LC 78-18071. (Illus.). 32p. (J). (ps-k). 1995. bds. 4.95 (*0-590-20547-1*, Cartwheel) Scholastic Inc.

— Tale of Peter Rabbit. LC 78-18071. (J). 1991. pap. 14.95 (*0-88708-079-0*, Rabbit) S&S Childrens.

— Tale of Peter Rabbit. LC 78-18071. (Illus.). 32p. (J). (gr. k-3). 1979. lib. bdg. 9.79 (*0-89375-124-3*); pap. 2.50 (*0-89375-102-2*) Troll Assocs.

— A Tale of Peter Rabbit. (Children's Classics Ser.). (Illus.). (J). 1991. 6.95 (*0-8362-4908-9*) Andrews & McMeel.

— The Tale of Peter Rabbit. deluxe ed. (Illus.). 60p. (J). 1993. 16.00 (*0-7232-4026-4*) Warne.

— The Tale of Peter Rabbit. (Illus.). 60p. (J). (gr. 1-5). 1972. reprint ed. pap. 1.75 (*0-486-22827-4*) Dover.

— The Tale of Peter Rabbit. LC 92-36655. (Illus.). 64p. (J). 1993. reprint ed. 4.95 (*0-88708-296-3*, Rabbit); reprint ed. 9.95 (*0-88708-297-1*, Rabbit) S&S Childrens.

— The Tale of Peter Rabbit, Set. limited ed. (Illus.). 60p. (J). 1993. Cased set. boxed 150.00 (*0-7232-4045-0*) Warne.

— The Tale of Peter Rabbit: Die Geschichte Des Peterchen Hase. Werner, Meike, tr. (Illus.). 64p. (Orig.). (GER.). (J). 1992. pap. 2.75 (*0-486-27014-9*) Dover.

— The Tale of Peter Rabbit: La Storia Del Coniglietto Pietro. Vettori, Alessandro, tr. (Illus.). 64p. (Orig.). (ITA.). (J). 1992. pap. 2.75 (*0-486-27015-7*) Dover.

— The Tale of Peter Rabbit & Benjamin Bunny. (World of Peter Rabbit & Friends Ser.). (Illus.). 32p. (J). (ps-3). 1993. 4.99 (*0-7232-4124-4*) Warne.

— The Tale of Peter Rabbit & Other Favorite Stories, 7 vols., Set. 447p. (J). (gr. 2 up). boxed 12.25 (*0-486-23903-9*) Dover.

— Tale of Peter Rabbit Coloring Book. (Illus.). (J). (gr. k-3). 1976. pap. 2.50 (*0-486-21711-6*) Dover.

— Tale of Peter Rabbit Coloring Book. (Illus.). (J). (gr. k-3). 1986. pap. 1.00 (*0-486-25160-8*) Dover.

— The "Tale of Peter Rabbit" in French. Greenberg, Judith L., tr. 64p. (Orig.). (FRE.). 1987. pap. 2.50 (*0-486-25313-9*) Dover.

— The "Tale of Peter Rabbit" in Spanish. Saludes, Esperanza G., tr. 64p. (Orig.). (SPA.). 1987. pap. 2.75 (*0-486-25314-7*) Dover.

— Tale of Peter Rabbit Pop Up. (J). 1988. 3.99 (*0-517-67098-4*) Random Hse Value.

— The Tale of Peter Rabbit Sticker Book. (Illus.). (J). (gr. 1 up). 1986. pap. 1.49 (*0-671-62579-9*, Litl Simon S&S) S&S Childrens.

— Tale of Peter Rabbit Sticker Book. (J). 1990. pap. 2.95 (*0-671-69255-0*, Litl Simon S&S) S&S Childrens.

— The Tale of Pigling Bland. (Original Peter Rabbit Books: No. 15). (J). 1987. 5.95 (*0-7232-3474-4*); pap. 2.25 (*0-7232-3499-X*) Warne.

— The Tale of Pigling Bland. (Illus.). (J). (ps-3). 1994. pap. 4.99 (*0-7232-4150-3*) Warne.

— The Tale of Samuel Whiskers. (Original Peter Rabbit Books: No. 16). (J). 1987. 5.95 (*0-7232-3475-2*); pap. 2.25 (*0-7232-3500-7*) Warne.

— The Tale of Samuel Whiskers. (World of Peter Rabbit & Friends Ser.). (Illus.). 32p. (J). (ps-3). 1993. pap. 4.99 (*0-7232-4142-2*) Warne.

— Tale of Squirrel Nutkin. (J). 1992. 3.99 (*0-517-07239-4*) Random Hse Value.

— The Tale of Squirrel Nutkin. (Original Peter Rabbit Bks.: No. 2). (J). 1987. 5.95 (*0-7232-3461-2*); pap. 2.25 (*0-7232-3486-8*) Warne.

— The Tale of Squirrel Nutkin. (Illus.). 60p. (J). (gr. 1-5). 1972. reprint ed. pap. 1.75 (*0-486-22828-2*) Dover.

— The Tale of the Flopsy Bunnies. (Original Peter Rabbit Books: No. 10). (J). 1987. 5.95 (*0-7232-3469-8*); pap. 2.25 (*0-7232-3494-9*) Warne.

— The Tale of the Flopsy Bunnies. (Illus.). 64p. (J). (ps-3). 1987. 3.95 (*0-671-63237-X*, Litl Simon S&S) S&S Childrens.

— The Tale of the Flopsy Bunnies. (Juveniles Ser.). 64p. (J). (gr. 1 up). 1985. reprint ed. pap. 1.75 (*0-486-24806-2*) Dover.

— The Tale of the Flopsy Bunnies & Mrs. Tittlemouse. (Illus.). 24p. (J). (gr. k-3). 1995. pap. 4.99 (*0-7232-4268-2*) Warne.

— The Tale of the Pie & the Patty-Pan. (Original Peter Rabbit Books: No. 17). (J). 1987. 5.95 (*0-7232-3476-0*); pap. 2.25 (*0-7232-3501-5*) Warne.

— The Tale of Timmy Tiptoes. (Original Peter Rabbit Books: No. 12). (J). 1987. 5.95 (*0-7232-3471-X*); pap. 2.25 (*0-7232-3496-5*) Warne.

— The Tale of Timmy Tiptoes. (Illus.). 64p. (J). (gr. 3 up). 1987. reprint ed. pap. 1.75 (*0-486-25541-7*) Dover.

— Tale of Tom Kitten. (J). 1988. bds. 2.99 (*0-517-65278-1*) Random Hse Value.

— Tale of Tom Kitten. (J). 1995. 3.99 (*0-517-10237-4*) Random Hse Value.

— The Tale of Tom Kitten. (Original Peter Rabbit Bks.: No. 8). (Illus.). (J). (ps-3). 1987. 5.95 (*0-7232-3467-1*); pap. 2.25 (*0-7232-3492-2*) Warne.

— The Tale of Tom Kitten. (Beatrix Potter Book & Storytape Collection). (J). (ps-3). 1989. pap. 6.95 (*0-7232-3670-4*) Warne.

— The Tale of Tom Kitten. LC 87-40285. (Illus.). 24p. (J). (ps up). 1990. 6.95 (*1-55782-018-X*, Warner Juvenile Bks) Little.

— The Tale of Tom Kitten. (Illus.). 32p. (J). (ps-3). 1994. pap. 3.99 (*0-14-054296-5*) Puffin Bks.

— The Tale of Tom Kitten. (Classic Tales from Beatrix Potter Ser.). (Illus.). 24p. (J). (ps-1). 1992. 3.99 (*0-517-05076-5*) Random Hse Value.

— The Tale of Tom Kitten. (Illus.). 64p. (J). (ps-3). 1986. 3.95 (*0-671-62927-1*, Litl Simon S&S) S&S Childrens.

— The Tale of Tom Kitten. (Illus.). 58p. (J). (gr. k up). 1983. reprint ed. pap. 1.75 (*0-486-24502-0*) Dover.

— The Tale of Tom Kitten & Jemima Pubble-Duck. 1993. pap. 4.99 (*0-7232-4128-7*) Warne.

— Tale of Tom Kitten Pop-Up. (J). 1988. 3.99 (*0-517-67099-2*) Random Hse Value.

— The Tale of Two Bad Mice. (Original Peter Rabbit Bks.: No. 5). (Illus.). (J). (ps-3). 1987. 5.95 (*0-7232-3464-7*); pap. 2.25 (*0-7232-3489-2*) Warne.

— The Tale of Two Bad Mice. (J). 1992. 3.99 (*0-517-07241-6*) Random Hse Value.

— The Tale of Two Bad Mice. (Silver Elm Classic Ser.). (Illus.). 32p. (J). (gr. k-3). 1992. pap. 2.99 (*0-87406-620-4*) Willowisp Pr.

— The Tale of Two Bad Mice. LC 74-75268. (Illus.). 59p. (J). (gr. 2-4). 1974. reprint ed. pap. 1.75 (*0-486-23065-1*) Dover.

— Tales from Beatrix Potter. (Picture Bks.). (Illus.). 228p. (J). (ps-3). 1986. 8.95 (*0-7232-3971-1*) Warne.

— Tales of Peter Rabbit. LC 91-52695. (Miniature Editions Ser.). (Illus.). 128p. (J). 1991. 4.95 (*1-56138-039-3*) Running Pr.

— Tales of Peter Rabbit & His Friends, 2 vols. in 1. (J). 1988. 7.99 (*0-517-44901-3*) Random Hse Value.

— Tom Chaton. (Illus.). 58p. (FRE.). (J). 1980. 9.95 (*0-7859-3626-2*, 2070560715) Fr & Eur.

— Tom Chaton. (Gallimard Ser.). 58p. (FRE.). (J). 1980. 10.95 (*2-07-056071-6*) Schoenhof.

— Tom Kitten. (Little Hide-&-Seek Bks.). (Illus.). 12p. (J). (ps-1). 1994. 3.50 (*0-7232-4106-6*) Warne.

— Tom Kitten: Bath Book. (J). 1989. 3.50 (*0-7232-3585-6*) Warne.

— Tom Kitten's Playtime. (Illus.). 24p. (J). (ps). 1994. bds. 2.99 (*0-7232-4092-2*) Warne.

— A Treasury of Peter Rabbit & Other Stories. LC 94-35477. (Illus.). (J). (gr. k up). 1984. 7.99 (*0-517-23948-5*) Random Hse Value.

— The Two Bad Mice Pop-Up Book. (Illus.). (J). (ps-3). 1986. 11.95 (*0-7232-3360-8*) Warne.
— What Time Is It, Peter Rabbit? (Illus.). (J). (ps-00). 1989. 6.95 (*0-7232-3586-4*); pap. 5.00 (*0-7232-3624-0*) Warne.
— Where's Peter Rabbit? (Illus.). (J). (ps-3). 1988. 6.95 (*0-7232-3519-8*) Warne.
— Where's Tom Kitten? (Lift-the-Flap Book Ser.). 24p. (J). (ps-3). 1990. 6.95 (*0-7232-3597-X*) Warne.
— The World of Peter Rabbit & Friends Bedtime Storybook. (Illus.). 128p. (J). (ps-3). 1995. 12.99 (*0-7232-4182-1*) Warne.
— The World of Peter Rabbit Postcard Book. (Illus.). (J). 1990. pap. 6.95 (*0-7232-3647-X*) Warne.
— The World of Peter Rabbit Sticker Book. (Illus.). 32p. (J). (ps-3). 1990. pap. 6.95 (*0-7232-3645-3*) Warne.
Potter, Beatrix, illus. My Peter Rabbit Keepsake: A Photograph Album. 32p. (J). 1994. 9.95 (*0-7232-4121-X*) Warne.
— The Peter Rabbit Make-&-Play Book. 32p. (J). (ps-5). 1992. pap. 6.99 (*0-7232-3991-6*) Warne.
— The Peter Rabbit Sticker Book. rev. ed. 20p. (J). (ps-3). 1991. pap. 6.99 (*0-7232-3979-7*) Warne.
***Potter, Beatrix & Pomaska, Anna.** El Cuento De Pedro, El Conejo: Libro De Cuentos En Colores - Por Beatrix Potter, Ilustrato Por Anna Pomaska. LC 94-44061. (Little Activity Bks.). (Illus.). 32p. (SPA.). (J). 1995. pap. text ed. 1.00 (*0-486-28539-1*) Dover.
— El Cuento Del Conejito Benjamin: Libro De Cuentos En Colores - Por Beatrix Potter, Ilustrado Por Anna Pomaska. DeZardain, Paul F., tr. LC 94-43851. (Dover Little Activity Bks.). (Illus.). 32p. (SPA.). (J). 1995. pap. text ed. 1.00 (*0-486-28536-7*) Dover.
— L' Histoire De Pierre Lapin: Livre d'Histoires En Couleurs - Par Beatrix Potter, Illustre Par Anna Pomaska. (Illus.). 32p. (FRE.). (J). 1995. pap. text ed. 1.00 (*0-486-28540-5*) Dover.
— L' Histoire Du Lapereau Benjamin: Livre D'Histoires En Couleurs - Par Beatrix Potter, Illustre Par Anna Pomaska. Brodkey, Florence A., tr. (Illus.). 32p. (FRE.). (J). 1995. pap. text ed. 1.00 (*0-486-28537-5*) Dover.
— La Storia Del Coniglietto Pietro: Libro Di Racconti in Colore - Di Beatrix Potter, Con Disegni Di Anna Pomaska. Vettori, Alessandra, tr. (Illus.). 32p. (ITA.). (J). 1995. reprint ed. pap. text ed. 1.00 (*0-486-28558-8*) Dover.
— The Tale of Benjamin Bunny: Full-Color Storybook. LC 94-24672. (Little Activity Bks.). (Illus.). 32p. (Orig.). (J). 1995. pap. text ed. 1.00 (*0-486-28538-3*) Dover.
— The Tale of Peter Rabbit: Full-Color Storybook. LC 94-24671. (Little Activity Bks.). (Illus.). 32p. (Orig.). (J). 1995. pap. text ed. 1.00 (*0-486-28541-3*) Dover.
Potter, Beatrix & Stewart, Pat. The Little Tale of Mrs. Tiggy-Winkle Coloring Book. (Little Activity Bks.). (J). 1994. pap. 1.00 (*0-486-28068-3*) Dover.
Potter, Beatrix & Wynne, Patricia. The Tale of Jemima Puddle-Duck in Spanish Coloring Book. (Little Activity Bks.). (J). 1994. pap. 1.00 (*0-486-27914-6*) Dover.
— The Tales of Jemima Puddle-Duck in French Coloring Book. (Little Activity Bks.). (J). 1994. 1.00 (*0-486-27913-8*) Dover.
Potter, Beatrx. Petit-Jean des Villes. (Illus.). 58p. (FRE.). (J). 1990. 9.95 (*0-7859-3632-7*, 2070560953) Fr & Eur.
Potter, Ben, et al. Introduction to Formal Specification & Z. 300p. 1991. pap. 39.00 (*0-13-478561-4*) P-H.
— Introduction to Formal Specification & Z. 300p. 1991. pap. text ed. 44.95 (*0-13-478702-1*) P-H.
Potter, Betty, ed. see Grace, Kendra.
Potter, Betty M. Chocolate Mousse & Other Fabulous Chocolate Creations. 220p. (Orig.). 1986. spiral bd. 9.95 (*0-913703-11-7*) Branches.
— The Just for Kids Cookbook. (Illus.). 180p. (Orig.). (J). (gr. 1-6). 1985. spiral bd. 9.95 (*0-913703-06-0*) Branches.
Potter, Beverly. Beating Job Burnout: How to Transform Work Pressure into Productivity. rev. ed. (Illus.). 302p. 1994. pap. 12.95 (*0-914171-69-0*) Ronin Pub.
— Drug Testing at Work: A Guide for Employers & Employees. 2nd ed. 1995. pap. 14.95 (*0-914171-70-4*) Ronin Pub.
— Finding a Path with a Heart: How to Go from Burnout to Bliss. Orfali, Sebastian, ed. (Illus.). 356p. (Orig.). 1994. pap. 12.95 (*0-914171-74-7*) Ronin Pub.
— From Conflict to Cooperation: How to Mediate a Dispute. 156p. (Orig.). 1995. pap. 9.95 (*0-914171-79-8*) Ronin Pub.
Potter, Beverly & Orfali, J. Sebastian. Brain Boosters: Foods & Drugs That Make You Smarter. 257p. (Orig.). 1993. pap. 12.95 (*0-914171-65-8*) Ronin Pub.
Potter, Beverly A. Preventing Job Burnout. Crisp, Michael G., ed. LC 86-72077. (Fifty-Minute Ser.). (Illus.). 88p. (Orig.). 1987. pap. 9.95 (*0-931961-23-8*) Crisp Pubns.
— Turning Around: Keys to Motivation & Productivity. 292p. 1989. pap. 9.95 (*0-914171-16-X*) Ronin Pub.
— Turning Around: Keys to Motivation & Productivity. 2nd ed. (Illus.). 267p. (C). 1984. reprint ed. 19.95 (*0-914171-00-3*) Ronin Pub.
— The Way of the Ronin: Riding the Waves of Change at Work. (Illus.). 252p. 1989. reprint ed. pap. 9.95 (*0-914171-26-7*) Ronin Pub.
Potter, Beverly A. & Orfali, J. Sebastian. Drug Testing at Work. (Guide for Employers & Employees Working in the New Age Ser.). (Illus.). 252p. (Orig.). 1990. pap. 17.95 (*0-914171-32-1*) Ronin Pub.
Potter, Beverly A., jt. auth. see Bewicke, Dhyana.
***Potter, Bill.** The Mahogany Ship Relic or Legend? 130p. 1987. pap. 20.00 (*0-949759-09-0*, Pub. by Deakin Univ AT) St Mut.
***Potter, Bill, et al.** Visual Basic XX SuperBible: Ole, Database Controls & Object, Professional Programming, & Language Reference, Bk. 2. 1000p. Date not set. cd-rom, pap. text ed. 44.95 (*1-57169-007-7*) Waite Group Pr.
— Visual Basic XX SuperBible, Bk. 1. 1000p. Date not set. cd-rom, pap. text ed. 44.95 (*1-57169-006-9*) Waite Group Pr.
Potter, Bonnie D., jt. auth. see Barhydt, Rose M.
***Potter, Brian & Green, Wayne.** Another New Day. (Illus.). 24p. (J). (ps-6). 1995. 19.95 (*0-9645529-0-6*) Hear We Go.
— Fun Stuff Holiday. (Illus.). 24p. (J). (ps-6). 1995. 19.95 (*0-9645529-1-4*) Hear We Go.
Potter, Brian E. Nomads of the Nine Nations. Ruemmler, John D., ed. (Shadow World Ser.). (Illus.). 64p. (Orig.). (C). 1990. pap. 12.00 (*1-55806-098-7*, 6013) Iron Crown Ent Inc.
***Potter, C. E.** History of Manchester, NH, Formerly Derryfield, in New Hampshire, Including That of Ancient Amoskeag, or the Middle Merrimack Valley. (Illus.). 764p. 1995. reprint ed. lib. bdg. 77.50 (*0-8328-4473-X*) Higginson Bk Co.
Potter, C. W. Potter: Genealogy of the Potter Families & Their Descendants in America. (Illus.). 300p. 1990. reprint ed. lib. bdg. 55.00 (*0-8328-1520-9*); reprint ed. pap. 47.00 (*0-8328-1521-7*) Higginson Bk Co.
Potter, C. W., jt. ed. see Stuart-Harris, Charles.
Potter, Carol. Before We Were Born. LC 89-20069. 72p. 1990. pap. 9.95 (*0-914086-90-1*) Alicejamesbooks.
— Upside down in the Dark. (Orig.). 1995. pap. 9.95 (*1-882295-05-6*) Alicejamesbooks.
***Potter, Carole.** Encyclopedia of Superstition. (Illus.). 263p. 1994. pap. 17.95 (*1-85479-943-6*, Pub. by Picador UK) Trans-Atl Phila.
***Potter, Charles E.** Genealogies of Some Old Families of Concord, Massachusetts & Their Descendants in Part to the Present Generation. (Illus.). 143p. (Orig.). 1995. pap. text ed. 22.50 (*0-7884-0161-0*) Heritage Bk.
Potter, Charles F. Is That in the Bible? 272p. 1985. mass mkt. 4.99 (*0-345-32109-X*) Ballantine.
— The Lost Years of Jesus Revealed. 160p. 1985. mass mkt. 4.99 (*0-449-13039-8*, GM) Fawcett.
Potter, Charles H. Perennials in the Garden for Lasting Beauty. LC 59-6124. (Illus.). 1959. 29.95 (*0-87599-094-0*) S G Phillips.
Potter, Charles L., et al. Pennsylvania Tax Handbook. 464p. 1988. 17.50 (*0-13-655994-8*) P-H.
— Pennsylvania Tax Handbook 1985. write for info. (*0-318-58212-0*) P-H.
— Pennsylvania Tax Handbook, 1989. 430p. 1988. 18.95 (*0-13-655648-5*, Busn) P-H.
Potter, Cherry. Image, Sound & Story: The Art of Telling in Film. (Illus.). 256p. 1992. 45.00 (*0-436-38032-3*, Pub. by Seck & Warburg UK) Trafalgar.
Potter, Christine, illus. The Christmas Story. 32p. (J). 1994. write for info. (*0-307-16176-5*) Western Pub.
Potter, Christopher S., et al, eds. Perspectives on Biodiversity: Case Studies of Genetic Resource Conservation & Development, Vol. 93-01S. LC 93-10544. 1993. pap. 34.95 (*0-87168-512-4*) AAAS.
Potter, Clare, comp. The Lesbian Periodicals Index. LC 85-21798. 432p. 1986. pap. 29.95 (*0-930044-74-6*) Naiad Pr.
***Potter, Clarkson.** The Martha Stewart Cookbook: Collected Recipes for Every Day. 1995. 27.50 (*0-517-70335-1*) Random.
Potter, Clarkson N. Who Does What & Why in Book Publishing: Writers, Editors, & Money Men. 1990. 12.95 (*1-55972-056-5*, Birch Ln Pr) Carol Pub Group.
Potter, Clive, et al. The Diversion of Land: Conservation in a Period of Farming Contraction. (Natural Environment: Problems & Management Ser.). (Illus.). 260p. (C). 1991. text ed. 65.00 (*0-415-03627-5*, A5127) Routledge.
Potter, Cora V. My Recitations. LC 75-39380. (Granger Index Reprint Ser.). 1977. reprint ed. 20.95 (*0-8369-6347-4*) Ayer.
***Potter, David.** A History of France, 1460-1560: The Emergence of a Nation-State. 456p. 1995. 45.00 (*0-312-12479-1*) St Martin.
— A History of France, 1460-1560: The Emergence of a Nation-State. (New Studies in Medieval History). 438p. 1995. 17.95 (*0-312-12480-5*) St Martin.
— Operation: Crumb Weasel. 28p. 1995. pap. 3.50 (*0-9644300-0-2*) Trihawk Prods.
— Prophets & Emperors: Human & Divine Authority from Augustus to Theodosius. LC 94-25982. (Revealing Antiquity: 7). (Illus.). 291p. 1994. text ed. 45.00 (*0-674-71565-9*, POTPRO) HUP.
— Too Soon to Die. 1982. pap. 3.99 (*0-85234-169-5*, Pub. by Evangel Pr UK) Presby & Reformed.
— War & Government in Early Modern France: Picardy, 1470-1560. LC 92-11887. (Illus.). 384p. (C). 1993. 69.95 (*0-521-43189-1*) Cambridge U Pr.
Potter, David & Thomas, Gordon L., eds. Colonial Idiom. LC 71-83669. (Landmarks in Rhetoric & Public Address Ser.). 653p. 1970. 25.00 (*0-8093-0431-7*); pap. 7.00 (*0-8093-9100-7*) S Ill U Pr.
— Colonial Idiom. LC 71-83669. (Landmarks in Rhetoric & Public Address Ser.). 653p. 1970. pap. 7.00 (*0-8093-9700-5*) S Ill U Pr.
Potter, David C. India's Political Administrators, 1919-1983. (Illus.). 350p. 1987. 59.00 (*0-19-821574-6*) OUP.
Potter, David E. Computational Physics. LC 72-8613. (Wiley-Interscience Publication Ser.). 316p. reprint ed. pap. 90.10 (*0-317-26325-0*, 2025203) Bks Demand.
Potter, David E., jt. auth. see Lamberts, David W.
Potter, David F. Maya Architecture of the Central Yucatan Peninsula, Mexico. (Publication Ser.: No. 44). (Illus.). xi, 118p. 1977. 17.50 (*0-939238-49-7*) Tulane MARI.
Potter, David M. Freedom & Its Limitations in American Life. Fehrenbacher, Don E., ed. LC 76-17786. xiv, 90p. 1976. 17.50 (*0-8047-0933-5*); pap. 9.95 (*0-8047-1009-0*) Stanford U Pr.
— Impending Crises, 1848-1861. (New American Nation Ser.). 1977. reprint ed. pap. text ed. 16.00 (*0-06-131929-5*, TB1929, Torch) HarpC.
— Lincoln & His Party in the Secession Crisis. 440p. (C). 1995. reprint ed. pap. 16.95 (*0-8071-2027-8*) La State U Pr.
— People of Plenty: Economic Abundance & the American Character. LC 54-12797. 1958. pap. text ed. 11.95 (*0-226-67633-1*) U Ch Pr.
— Select Problems in Historical Interpretation, 2 vols., Set. (History - United States Ser.). 1993. reprint ed. lib. bdg. 150.00 (*0-7812-4840-X*) Rprt Serv.
— The South & the Sectional Conflict. LC 68-8941. 335p. Date not set. pap. 95.50 (*0-7837-8531-3*, 2049340) Bks Demand.
Potter, David S. Prophecy & History in the Crisis of the Roman Empire: A Historical Commentary on the Thirteenth Sibylline Oracle. (Oxford Classical Monographs). (Illus.). 464p. 1991. 115.00 (*0-19-814483-0*) OUP.
Potter, Dennis. Blackeyes. (Orig.). 1988. pap. 6.95 (*0-679-72047-2*, Vin) Random.
— Potter on Potter. Fuller, Graham, ed. (Illus.). 224p. 1993. 19.95 (*0-571-16367-X*) Faber & Faber.
— Potter on Potter. 1994. pap. 11.95 (*0-571-17046-3*) Faber & Faber.
— Seeing the Blossom: Two Interviews & a Lecture. 1994. pap. 11.95 (*0-571-17436-1*) Faber & Faber.
— The Singing Detective. 256p. 1994. 8.99 (*1-56865-113-9*, GuildAmerica) Dblday Bk Music.
— The Singing Detective. 1988. pap. 6.95 (*0-679-72046-4*, Vin) Random.
— Sufficient Carbohydrate. LC 83-20755. 80p. (Orig.). 1984. pap. 7.95 (*0-571-13261-8*) Faber & Faber.
— Ticket to Ride. 1989. pap. 6.95 (*0-679-72353-6*, Vin) Random.
— Waiting for the Boat. LC 83-25374. 256p. (Orig.). 1984. pap. 9.95 (*0-571-13081-X*) Faber & Faber.
Potter, Diana O. & Rose, Minnie B., eds. Assessment. LC 82-11760. (Nurse's Reference Library). (Illus.). 839p. 1982. text ed. 29.95 (*0-916730-39-5*) Springhouse Pub.
— Emergencies. LC 84-14122. (Nurse's Reference Library). (Illus.). 832p. 1985. text ed. 29.95 (*0-916730-85-9*) Springhouse Pub.
Potter, Diane L. & Brockmeyer, Gretchen A. Softball: Steps to Success. LC 88-34421. (Steps to Success Activity Ser.). (Illus.). 228p. (Orig.). 1989. pap. text ed. 14.95 (*0-88011-358-8*, PPOT0358) Human Kinetics.
— Teaching Softball: Steps to Success. LC 88-36782. (Steps to Success Activity Ser.). (Illus.). 256p. (Orig.). 1989. pap. text ed. 19.95 (*0-88011-359-6*, PPOT0359) Human Kinetics.
Potter, Dick, jt. auth. see Griffin, Jim.
Potter, Doreen, jt. auth. see Kaan, Fred.
***Potter, Dorothy W.** Passports of Southeastern Pioneers, 1770-1823: Indian, Spanish & Other Land Passports for Tennessee, Kentucky, Georgia, Mississippi, Virginia, North & South Carolina. (Illus.). 461p. 1994. 32.50 (*0-614-03822-7*, 4683) Genealog Pub.
Potter, Douglas A. Automated Accounting Systems & Procedures Handbook. 562p. 1991. text ed. 135.00 (*0-471-54466-3*) Wiley.
— Automated Accounting Systems & Procedures Handbook. 576p. 1992. pap. text ed. 65.00 (*0-471-55939-3*) Wiley.
Potter, E. B. Admiral Arleigh Burke: A Biography. 1990. 24.95 (*0-394-58424-4*) Random.
— Bull Halsey: A Biography. LC 85-15419. (Illus.). 421p. 1985. 34.95 (*0-87021-146-3*) Naval Inst Pr.
— Nimitz. LC 76-1056. (Illus.). 507p. 1976. 35.00 (*0-87021-492-6*) Naval Inst Pr.
Potter, E. B., ed. Sea Power: A Naval History. 2nd rev. ed. LC 81-81668. (Illus.). 419p. 1981. Avail. bulk rates. 25.95 (*0-87021-607-4*) Naval Inst Pr.
***Potter, Eddward E. & Reesman, Ann E.** Employment Tests Are Not Medical Examinations. 17p. 1992. pap. 8.00 (*0-614-06151-2*, 2042-PP-4040) EPF.
Potter, Edgar F. Cowboy Slang. LC 85-24930. (Illus.). 128p. (Orig.). 1986. pap. 5.95 (*0-914846-23-X*) Golden West Pub.
***Potter, Edgar R.** Cowboys Talk Right Burty! LC 94-40725. 1994. write for info. (*1-885590-00-8*) Golden West Pub.
— Whoa...Yuh Sonsabitches. (Illus.). 1977. pap. 6.95 (*0-918292-00-X*) Griggs Print.
Potter, Edith L. & Craig, John M. Pathology of the Fetus & the Infant. LC 75-16021. 711p. reprint ed. pap. 180.00 (*0-685-15284-7*, 2026505) Bks Demand.
***Potter, Edward E.** The Potential Impact of Proposed Civil Rights Legislation on Corporate Affirmative Action Practices. 32p. 1991. pap. 10.00 (*0-614-06156-3*, 2027-PP-4040) EPF.
— Quality at Risk: Are Employee Participation Programs in Jeopardy? 72p. 1991. pap. 10.00 (*0-614-06154-7*, 2034-PP-4040) EPF.
Potter, Edward E., ed. Employee Selection: Legal & Practical Alternatives to Compliance & Litigation. 2nd ed. LC 86-60481. (Monograph Ser.). 330p. 1986. pap. 19.75 (*0-916559-03-3*) EPF.
Potter, Edward E. & McGuiness, Kenneth C. Freedom of Association, the Right to Organize & Collective Bargaining: The Impact on U. S. Law & Practice of ILO Conventions No. 87 & No. 98. LC 84-80187. 118p. (Orig.). (C). 1984. pap. 15.00 (*0-916603-00-8*) Labor Pol.
***Potter, Edward E. & Reesman, Ann E.** The Americans with Disabilities Act: Testing & Other Employee Selection Procedures. 29p. 1990. pap. 10.00x (*0-614-06165-2*, 2023C-PP-4040) EPF.
— An Assessment of Remedies: The Impact of Compensatory & Punitive Damages on Title Vi. 110p. 1990. pap. 10.00 (*0-614-06160-1*, 2019-PP-4040) EPF.
— Comepnsatory & Punitive Damages under Title VII - a Foreign Perspective. 2nd ed. 11p. 1992. pap. 5.00x (*0-614-06149-0*) EPF.
***Potter, Edward E. & Youngman, Judith A.** Keeping America Competitive: Employment Policy for the Twenty-First Century. LC 94-77235. 434p. 1995. 27.95 (*0-944435-28-9*, 2053-MO-4035) Glenbridge Pub.
Potter-Efron, Patricia, ed. The Treatment of Shame & Guilt in Alcoholism Counseling. LC 87-29724. (Alcoholism Treatment Quarterly Ser.: Vol. 4, No. 2). (Illus.). 218p. 1989. text ed. 39.95 (*0-86656-718-6*); pap. 14.95 (*0-86656-941-3*) Haworth Pr.
Potter-Efron, Patricia, jt. ed. see Potter-Efron, Ronald T.
Potter-Efron, Patricia, jt. auth. see Potter-Efron, Ronald.
Potter-Efron, Patricia S., jt. auth. see Potter-Efron, Ronald T.
***Potter-Efron, Ron.** Angry All the Time: An Emergency Guide to Anger Control. LC 94-67046. 160p. (Orig.). Date not set. text ed. 19.95 (*1-879237-97-0*) New Harbinger.
— Angry All the Time: An Emergency Guide to Anger Control. LC 94-67046. (Orig.). Date not set. pap. 12.95 (*1-879237-98-9*) New Harbinger.
— How to Control Your Anger (Before it Controls You) A Guide for Teenagers. 32p. 1993. pap. 3.95 (*1-56246-025-0*, P277) Johnsn Inst.
Potter-Efron, Ronald & Potter-Efron, Patricia. Letting Go of Shame: Understanding How Shame Affects Your Life. 192p. (Orig.). 1989. pap. 11.00 (*0-89486-635-4*) Hazelden.
Potter-Efron, Ronald T. Shame, Guilt & Alcoholism: Treatment Issues in Clinical Practice. LC 88-32058. (Addictions Treatment Ser.: Vol. 2). 287p. 1989. pap. text ed. 17.95 (*0-86656-856-5*) Harrington Pk.
— Shame, Guilt & Alcoholism: Treatment Issues in Clinical Practice. LC 87-29724. (Addiction Treatment Ser.: Vol. 2). 287p. 1989. text ed. 49.95 (*0-86656-855-7*) Haworth Pr.
Potter-Efron, Ronald T. & Potter-Efron, Patricia, eds. Aggression, Family Violence & Chemical Dependency. LC 89-24737. (Journal of Chemical Dependency Treatment: Vol. 3, No. 1). (Illus.). 226p. 1989. text ed. 39.95 (*0-86656-964-2*); pap. text ed. 17.95 (*0-86656-977-4*) Haworth Pr.
Potter-Efron, Ronald T. & Potter-Efron, Patricia S. Anger, Alcoholism & Addiction: Treating Anger in a Chemical Dependency Setting. 304p. 1992. 32.95 (*0-393-70126-3*) Norton.
— Letting Go of Shame. 1990. pap. 12.00 (*0-06-255411-5*, Hazelden SF) Harper SF.
Potter, Eliza. A Hairdresser's Experience in High Life. (Schomburg Library of Nineteenth-Century Black Women Writers). (Illus.). 352p. 1991. 29.95 (*0-19-506198-5*) OUP.
— A Hairdresser's Experience in High Life. Baxter, Annette K., ed. LC 79-8805. (Signal Lives Ser.). 1980. reprint ed. lib. bdg. 33.95 (*0-405-12851-7*) Ayer.
Potter, Elizabeth, jt. ed. see Alcoff, Linda.
Potter, Elizabeth, tr. see Cipolla, Carlo M.
Potter, Eloise F. & Funderburg, John B. Native Americans: The People & How They Lived. LC 86-61434. (Illus.). 80p. (gr. 4-12). 1986. 18.95 (*0-917134-09-5*); lib. bdg. 14.95 (*0-917134-10-9*) NC Natl Sci.
Potter, Eloise F., ed. see Ross, Steve W., et al.
Potter, Eloise F., ed. see Simpson, Marcus B., Jr.
Potter, Eloise F., jt. auth. see Taylor, Tom.
Potter, Eloise F., et al. Birds of the Carolinas. LC 79-14201. (Illus.). viii, 408p. 1986. reprint ed. pap. 17.95 (*0-8078-4155-2*) U of NC Pr.
Potter, Eugenia C., ed. see Comras, Jay & Zerowin, Jeffrey.
Potter, Frank & Peck, Charles. Dynamic Models in Physics: A Workbook of Computer Simulations Using Electronic Spreadsheets. Barkley, David, ed. & illus. by. 400p. (C). 1989. pap. text ed. 19.95 (*0-9622556-1-0*) Simonson & Co.
— Dynamic Models in Physics, Vol. I Mechanics (Templates) Microsoft Excel Templates for MacIntosh Computers. Barkley, David S., ed. (Illus.). 6p. 1990. Incl. 6 diskettes. disk 28.95 (*0-9622556-5-3*) Simonson & Co.
Potter, G. Printed Bygones. 88p. 1986. pap. 25.00 (*0-7212-0742-1*, Pub. by Regency Press) St Mut.
Potter, Gabriel. Gauguin. 1993. 5.98 (*1-55521-825-3*) Bk Sales Inc.
— Munch. 1994. 5.98 (*0-7858-0206-1*) Bk Sales Inc.
— Picasso. 1992. 5.98 (*1-55521-764-8*) Bk Sales Inc.
Potter, Gary. After the Boston Heresy Case. 1993. pap. write for info. (*0-9620994-6-5*) Cath Treas.
Potter, Gary W. Criminal Organizations: Vice, Racketeering, & Politics in an American City. (Illus.). 213p. (Orig.). (C). 1993. pap. text ed. 12.95 (*0-88133-770-6*) Waveland Pr.
Potter, Gary W., jt. auth. see Lyman, Michael D.
Potter, Geoff. The Publisher's Guide to Binding & Finishing. (Illus.). 192p. 1991. 41.95 (*0-948905-18-2*) Chapman & Hall.
Potter, George. To the Golden Door. LC 73-3928. (Illus.). 631p. 1973. reprint ed. text ed. 35.00 (*0-8371-6862-7*, POGD, Greenwood Pr) Greenwood.
Potter, George A. Dialogue on Debt: Alternative Analyses & Solutions. 160p. (Orig.). (C). 1988. pap. text ed. 7.95 (*0-934255-06-7*) Center Concern.
Potter, George R., ed. see Donne, John.
Potter, Gillian, tr. see El-Gamasy, M., et al.
Potter, Gregory C., jt. auth. see Pritchard, Robert E.
Potter, Harold. The Quest of Justice. (Legal Reprint Ser.). ix, 88p. 1986. reprint ed. lib. bdg. 17.50 (*0-421-35510-7*) Rothman.
Potter, Harold W., Jr. & Troy, Paul E. A Practical Guide to Introducing Evidence: Basic Foundations & Objections. suppl. ed. LC 86-72608. 203p. 1987. ring bd. 50.00 (*0-944490-02-6*) Mass CLE.

P Q

An Asterisk (*) at the beginning of an entry indicates that the title is appearing in BIP for the first time.

Potter, Harold W., Jr. & Troy, Paul E., eds. Practical Guide to Introducing Evidence: Basic Foundations & Objections. suppl. ed. LC 86-72608. 1991. 19.50 (*0-944490-40-9*) Mass CLE.
Potter, Harry. Hanging in Judgment: Religion & the Death Penalty in England. 276p. 1993. 24.95 (*0-8264-0626-2*) Continuum.
Potter, Harry R., jt. auth. see Perrucci, Robert.
Potter, Henry C. The Scholar & the State: And Other Orations & Addresses. LC 72-4509. (Essay Index Reprint Ser.). 1977. reprint ed. 23.95 (*0-8369-2969-1*) Ayer.
Potter, I. C., jt. ed. see Hardisty, M. W.
Potter, I. G., jt. ed. see Hardisty, M. W.
Potter, I. N. The Sick Building Syndrome. (C). 1988. 220.00 (*0-86022-212-8*, Pub. by Build Servs Info Assn UK) St Mut.
— Ventilation Effectiveness in Mechanical Ventilation Systems. (C). 1988. 115.00 (*0-86022-189-X*, Pub. by Build Servs Info Assn UK) St Mut.
Potter, Irving. The Cause of Anti-Jewism in the United States. 1982. lib. bdg. 59.95 (*0-87700-394-7*) Revisionist Pr.
Potter, J. H. SI-Ten Asme Steam Charts, SI Metric & U. S. Customary Units. 128p. 1976. pap. text ed. 25.00 (*0-685-62575-3*, E00090) ASME.
Potter, J. H., ed. Steam Charts: S1-10. 128p. 1976. 25.00 (*0-317-33617-7*, E00090); 12.50 (*0-317-33618-5*) ASME.
Potter, J. L. Associative Computing: A Programming Paradigm for Massively Parallel Computers. (Frontiers of Computer Science Ser.). (Illus.). 336p. 1991. 59.50 (*0-306-43987-5*, Plenum Pr) Plenum.
Potter, J. L., ed. The Massively Parallel Processor. (Scientific Computation Ser.). (Illus.). 275p. 1985. 37.50 (*0-262-16100-1*) MIT Pr.
Potter, J. Leith, ed. Rarefied Gas Dynamics, 2 vols. LC 76-57748. (PAAS Ser.: Vol. 51). (Illus.). 1337p. 1977. 108.95 (*0-915928-15-9*) AIAA.
Potter, J. M., jt. ed. see Abelkis, P. R.
***Potter, J. N.** CO2 Controlled Ventilation Systems. 1994. 125.00 (*0-86033-376-0*, Pub. by Build Servs Info Assn UK) St Mut.
Potter, J. R., jt. auth. see Buckingham, M. J.
Potter, Jack M., jt. auth. see Potter, Sulamith H.
***Potter, James E.** Bridging the Internet Gap. 2nd ed. (C). 1994. pap. text ed. 17.50 (*0-9632069-9-0*) Bridge Lrn Systs.
— Bridging the Internet Gap. 4th ed. (C). 1995. student ed, pap. text ed. 12.00 (*1-885587-07-4*) Bridge Lrn Systs.
— DBASE III, III Plus & IV. Garrotto, Alfred J., ed. (FasTrak Jr. Ser.). 110p. 1993. spiral bd. 18.50 (*0-9632069-4-X*) Bridge Lrn Systs.
— FasTrak. 2nd ed. Garrotto, Alfred J., ed. 315p. 1993. pap. text ed. 24.95 (*0-9632069-3-1*) Bridge Lrn Systs.
— FasTrak: A Collection of Software Tutorials. 270p. (Orig.). (C). 1992. disk, pap. 24.95 (*0-9632069-1-5*) Bridge Lrn Systs.
— Lotus 1-2-3 (for DOS) Garrotto, Alfred J., ed. (FasTrak Jr. Ser.). 52p. 1993. spiral bd. 9.00 (*0-9632069-6-6*) Bridge Lrn Systs.
— MS-DOS. Garrotto, Alfred J., ed. (FasTrak Jr. Ser.). 56p. 1993. spiral bd. 21.50 (*0-9632069-5-8*) Bridge Lrn Systs.
— Quattro Pro. Garrotto, Alfred J., ed. (FasTrak Jr. Ser.). 21p. 1993. spiral bd. 6.00 (*0-9632069-7-4*) Bridge Lrn Systs.
— QuickStart. 1994. pap. text ed. 5.00 (*1-885587-00-7*) Bridge Lrn Systs.
— VM - CMS: A Survival Guide. (Orig.). (C). 1993. pap. text ed. 39.95 (*0-9632069-2-3*) Bridge Lrn Systs.
***Potter, James E. & Garrotto, Alfred J.** Jumpstart. 2nd ed. 200p. (C). 1995. student ed 20.95 (*1-885587-06-6*) Bridge Lrn Systs.
Potter, James L. Robert Frost Handbook. LC 79-9145. 1980. text ed. 30.00 (*0-271-00230-1*) Pa St U Pr.
Potter, James M. Middle Paleolithic Assemblage & Settlement Variability in West-Central Jordan. (Anthropological Research Papers: No. 45). (Illus.). v, 57p. 1993. 10.00 (*0-936249-08-0*) AZ Univ ARP.
Potter, Jamie & Powers, Janet. The Happy Garden. (Illus.). 52p. (Orig.). (J). (ps-4). 1985. pap. 5.95 (*0-936511-00-1*) Gopher.
Potter, Janice. The Liberty We Seek: Loyalist Ideology in Colonial New York & Massachusetts. 256p. 1983. 35.00 (*0-674-53026-8*) HUP.
Potter, Jean. The Flying North. (Illus.). 240p. 1977. pap. 6.95 (*0-89174-018-X*) Comstock Edns.
— Nature in a Nutshell: Over 100 Activities You Can Do in Ten Minutes or Less. LC 94-28953. (J). 1995. pap. text ed. 10.95 (*0-471-04444-X*) Wiley.
— Science in Seconds for Kids: Over 100 Experiments You Can Do in Ten Minutes or Less. LC 94-31443. 1995. pap. text ed. 10.95 (*0-471-04456-3*) Wiley.
Potter, Jean, jt. auth. see Kohl, MaryAnn.
Potter, Jeffrey. To a Violent Grave: An Oral Biography of Jackson Pollock. (Illus.). 1987. pap. 15.00 (*0-916366-47-2*) Pushcart Pr.
Potter, Jeremy. Good King Richard? (Reprints Ser.). 304p. 1989. 24.95 (*0-88029-309-8*) Dorset Pr.
— Good King Richard? Richard III, the Last English King of England. (Illus.). 304p. 1994. pap. 33.50x (*0-09-468840-0*, Pub. by Constable Pubs UK) Trans-Atl Phila.
Potter, Jerold C. Books of the Bible. Bowen & Bowen Type Setters Staff, ed. 36p. (J). 1988. pap. text ed. 1.50 (*0-925306-00-2*) WOFPPM.
Potter, Jerry A. & Bost, Fred. Fatal Justice: The Reinvestigation of the MacDonald Murders. 448p. 1995. 25.00 (*0-393-03000-8*) Norton.
Potter, Jerry O. The Sultana Tragedy: America's Greatest Maritime Disaster. LC 91-29521. (Illus.). 272p. 1992. 23.95 (*0-88289-861-2*) Pelican.

PQ

Potter, Joan & Claytor, Constance. African-American Firsts: Famous, Little-Known, & Unsung Triumphs of Blacks in America. LC 93-84716. (Illus.). 352p. (Orig.). (YA). (gr. 7 up). 1994. pap. 14.95 (*0-9632476-1-1*) Pinto Pr.
Potter, Joan, ed. see Cantin, Sadie, et al.
Potter, Joan, jt. auth. see Cross, David.
Potter, John. Archaeologica Graeca: Or, the Antiquities of Greece, 2 vols., Set. Feldman, Burton & Richardson, Robert, eds. LC 78-60893. (Myth & Romanticism Ser.: Vol. 19). (Illus.). 1979. lib. bdg. 15.00 (*0-8240-3568-2*) Garland.
— Improve Your Odds Against Cancer: What Everyone Should Know. 1992. pap. 4.50 (*1-56171-076-8*, S P I Bks) Sure Sellers.
Potter, John & Warn-Varnas, Alex, eds. Ocean Variability & Acoustic Propagation: Proceedings of the Workshop Held in La Spezia, Italy, June 4-8, 1990. (C). 1991. lib. bdg. 190.00 (*0-7923-1079-9*) Kluwer Ac.
Potter, John F. How To Improve Your Odds Against Cancer. Bartimole, John, ed. 1988. 15.95 (*0-8119-0702-3*) LIFETIME.
Potter, John M. Plots Against Presidents. 2nd ed. 1969. 14.95 (*0-8392-1178-3*) Astor-Honor.
— Thirteen Desperate Days. 1964. 12.95 (*0-8392-1114-7*) Astor-Honor.
Potter, John M., ed. Fatigue in Mechanically Fastened Composite & Metallic Joints. LC 86-22288. (Special Technical Publication Ser.: No. 927). (Illus.). 288p. 1986. text ed. 48.00 (*0-8031-0927-X*, 04-927000-30) ASTM.
Potter, John M. & Fosdal, Frederick. The Tangled Web: The Murder of Cad Bates; an Historic True Crime Mystery. Balousek, Marv, ed. (Illus.). 274p. 1993. 21.95 (*1-878569-12-0*); pap. 12.95 (*1-878569-13-9*) Waubesa Pr.
Potter, John M. & Watanabe, Roy T., eds. Development of Fatigue Loading Spectra. LC 88-35065. (Special Technical Publication Ser.: No. STP 1006). (Illus.). 252p. 1989. text ed. 54.00 (*0-8031-1185-1*) ASTM.
Potter, John M., jt. ed. see McHenry, Harry I.
Potter, John S. Treasure Diver's Guide. (Illus.). 590p. 1988. pap. 19.95 (*0-912451-22-X*) Florida Classics.
Potter, John W., et al. Binocular Indirect Ophthalmoscopy. (Illus.). 128p. 1988. 24.95 (*0-409-95169-2*) Buttrwrth-Heinemann.
Potter, Jonathan & Wetherell, Margaret. Discourse & Social Psychology: Beyond Attitudes & Behavior. 216p. (C). 1987. text ed. 39.95 (*0-8039-8055-8*); pap. text ed. 17.50 (*0-8039-8056-6*) Sage.
Potter, Jonathan, jt. auth. see Edwards, Derek.
Potter, Jonathan, jt. auth. see Wetherell, Margaret.
Potter, Joseph, jt. auth. see Miro, Carmen.
Potter, Joy H. Five Frames for the Decameron: Communication & Social Systems in the Cornice. LC 81-47942. 241p. reprint ed. pap. 68.70 (*0-8357-3305-X*, 2039528) Bks Demand.
Potter, Karl H. Presuppositions of India's Philosophies. (C). 1991. 16.00 (*81-208-0779-0*, Pub. by Motilal Banarsidass II) S Asia.
Potter, Karl H., ed. Encyclopedia of Indian Philosophies: Bibliography. 2nd rev. ed. (C). 1983. 65.00 (*0-8364-2193-0*, Pub. by Motilal Banarsidass II) S Asia.
Potter, Karl H. & Bhattacharyya, Sibajiban, eds. Encyclopedia of Indian Philosophies: Nyaya-Vaisesika from Gangesa to Raghunatha Siromani. (Indian Philosophical Analysis Ser.: Vol. VI). 633p. 1992. text ed. 65.00 (*0-691-07384-8*) Princeton U Pr.
Potter, Karl H., ed. see Coward, Harold C. & Raja, K. Kunjunni.
Potter, Kasdon & Hazama. Hawaii: Our Island State. rev. ed. 1979. 29.95 (*0-935848-73-8*) Bess Pr.
Potter, Katherine. My Mother the Cat. LC 92-17864. (J). 1993. pap. 14.00 (*0-671-79632-1*, S&S Bks Young Read) S&S Childrens.
— Spike. LC 93-11476. (J). 1994. 15.00 (*0-671-86733-4*, S&S Bks Young Read) S&S Childrens.
Potter, Kim. Portrait of an American Town - Chesterfield, Missouri. 128p. 1992. 44.95 (*0-9631787-0-9*) W Countian.
— Portrait of an American Town - Chesterfield, Missouri. deluxe limited ed. 128p. 1992. 79.95 (*0-9631787-1-7*) W Countian.
Potter, L. J., ed. see Milton, John.
***Potter, L. N.** CO: Controlled Ventilation System. (C). 1994. 115.00x (*0-86022-376-0*, Pub. by Build Servs Info Assn UK) St Mut.
Potter, Lois. A Preface to Milton. 2nd ed. (Preface Bks.). 184p. (C). 1986. pap. text ed. 21.95 (*0-582-35479-X*, 72231) Longman.
— Secret Rites & Secret Writing: Royalist Literature, 1641-1660. (Illus.). 264p. (C). 1989. 64.95 (*0-521-25512-0*) Cambridge U Pr.
Potter, Louis, Jr. The Art of Cello Playing. (Illus.). 236p. (Orig.). (C). 1980. pap. text ed. 24.95 (*0-87487-071-2*) Summy-Birchard.
Potter, Louise & Cole, Jerryne. Wild Flowers: Along Mt. McKinley Park Road. LC 79-52424. (Illus.). (Orig.). 1979. pap. 5.95 (*0-9602792-0-2*) Camp Denali.
Potter, M. & Melchers, F., eds. Mechanisms in B-Cell Neoplasia, 1988. (Current Topics in Microbiology & Immunology Ser.: Vol. 141). (Illus.). 340p. 1988. 107.00 (*0-387-50212-2*) Spr-Verlag.
— Mechanisms in B-Cell Neoplasia 1994. (Currents Topics in Microbiology & Immunology Ser.: Vol. 194). 480p. 1994. 156.00 (*3-540-58447-1*) Spr-Verlag.
Potter, M., jt. ed. see Melchers, F.
Potter, M., jt. ed. see Obrams, G. I.

Potter, M., et al, eds. Mechanisms in B-Cell Neoplasia, 1992: Workshop at the National Cancer Institute, National Institutes of Health, Bethesda, MD, U. S. A., April 21-23, 1992. (Current Topics in Microbiology & Immunology Ser.: Vol. 182). (Illus.). 528p. 1992. 145.00 (*0-387-55658-3*) Spr-Verlag.
Potter, M. E. A Cumulated Index to the Books of 1898, 1899 & 1901, 2 vols. 1972. 250.00 (*0-87968-974-9*) Gordon Pr.
Potter-MacKinnon, Janice. While the Women Only Wept: Loyalist Refugee Women in Eastern Ontario. 216p. 1993. 39.95 (*0-7735-0962-3*, Pub. by McGill CN) U of Toronto Pr.
— While the Women Only Wept: Loyalist Refugee Women in Eastern Ontario. 216p. 1995. pap. 17.95 (*0-7735-1317-5*) U of Toronto Pr.
Potter, Margaret H. Istar of Babylon: A Phantasy. Reginald, R. & Melville, Douglas, eds. LC 77-84263. (Lost Race & Adult Fantasy Ser.). 1978. reprint ed. lib. bdg. 44.95 (*0-405-11004-9*) Ayer.
Potter, Martha, jt. auth. see Baby, Raymond.
Potter, Martha, et al. Exploratory Survey of the James Chase Hambleton Mound. (Illus.). 13p. 1967. pap. 1.75 (*0-318-00845-9*) Ohio Hist Soc.
Potter, Mary. Devotion for the Dying: Mary's Call to Her Loving Children. LC 91-65351. 224p. 1991. reprint ed. pap. 8.00 (*0-89555-442-9*) TAN Bks Pubs.
Potter, Maureen. Theatre Cat. 64p. (J). 1986. 11.95 (*0-86278-085-3*, Pub. by OBrien Pr IE) Dufour.
— Tommy the Theatre Cat. 1989. pap. 7.95 (*0-86278-130-2*, Pub. by OBrien Pr IE) Dufour.
Potter, Merle C. Schaum's Outline of Mechanical Engineering Thermodynamics: Including Hundreds of Solved Problems. 1992. pap. text ed. 12.95 (*0-07-050616-7*) McGraw.
Potter, Merle C., intro. Fundamentals of Engineering, Vol. 3. rev. ed. 70p. 1990. Incl. practice exam, 70p. pap. 37.00 (*0-685-31309-3*) Grt Lks Pr.
— Fundamentals of Engineering, Vol. 3. 3rd rev. ed. 70p. 1990. Incl. practice exam, 70p. 37.00 (*0-9614760-5-2*) Grt Lks Pr.
Potter, Merle C., et al. Fundamentals of Engineering: An Efficient Review for the Fundamentals of Engineering (FE-EIT) Exam & Excellent General Engineering Reference. 4th ed. (Illus.). 412p. (C). 1993. 42.00 (*1-881018-05-9*) Grt Lks Pr.
— GMAT Time-Saver: An Efficient Guide to the GMAT Exam. (Time-Saver Ser.). (Illus.). 416p. (C). 1993. 17.95 (*1-881018-04-0*) Grt Lks Pr.
— GRE Engineering Review: A Complete Review for the GRE Engineering Exam. (Illus.). 320p. 1992. 17.95 (*0-9614760-6-0*) Grt Lks Pr.
— GRE Time-Saver: An Efficient Guide to the General Test. (Time-Saver Ser.). (Illus.). 620p. (C). 1992. 15.95 (*0-9614760-9-5*) Grt Lks Pr.
— GRE Time-Saver: An Efficient Guide to the GRE Exam. 2nd ed. (Illus.). 496p. 1994. 17.95 (*1-881018-06-7*) Grt Lks Pr.
— Mechanics of Fluids. 768p. 1991. text ed. 77.00 (*0-13-572793-6*) P-H.
— Professional Civil Engineering Review: An Efficient Review for the Principles & Practice of Engineering (PE) Civil Exam & Excellent Engineering Reference. (Illus.). 688p. 1994. 69.00 (*1-881018-08-3*) Grt Lks Pr.
— SAT Time-Saver: An Efficient Guide to the SAT Exam. (Illus.). 416p. 1994. 17.95 (*1-881018-07-5*) Grt Lks Pr.
Potter, Michael, jt. auth. see Azar, Henry A.
Potter, Michael C. Electronic Greyhounds: The Spruance-Class Destroyers. (Illus.). 320p. 1995. 49.95 (*1-55750-682-5*) Naval Inst Pr.
Potter, Miles. Oregon's Golden Years. LC 75-12292. 185p. 1976. pap. 12.95 (*0-87004-254-8*) Caxton.
Potter, Murray A. Four Essays. (Harvard Studies in Romance Languages: Vol. 3). 1917. 15.00 (*0-527-01101-0*) Periodicals Srv.
— Sohrab & Rustem, the Epic Theme of a Combat Between Father & Son: A Study of Its Genesis & Use in Literature & Popular Tradition. LC 75-144527. (Grimm Library: No. 14). reprint ed. 27.50 (*0-404-53557-7*) AMS Pr.
Potter, N. I. & Jones, T. J. Ventilation Heat Loss in Factories & Warehouses. (C). 1992. 110.00x (*0-86022-296-9*, Pub. by Build Servs Info Assn UK) St Mut.
Potter, Nancy. Legacies. Stories. LC 86-30851. (Illinois Short Fiction Ser.). 144p. 1987. 14.95 (*0-252-01428-6*) U of Ill Pr.
Potter, Neal & Christy, Francis T. Trends in Natural Resource Commodities: Statistics of Prices, Output, Consumption, Foreign Trade, & Employment in the United States, 1870-1957. Manning, Pauline, ed. LC 62-11711. 580p. reprint ed. pap. 165.30 (*0-317-26474-5*, 2023809) Bks Demand.
Potter, Nelson & Timmons, Mark, eds. Morality & Universality. 1985. lib. bdg. 110.00 (*90-277-1909-8*) Kluwer Ac.
Potter, Norman N. Food Science. 4th ed. (Illus.). (C). 1986. text ed. 65.00 (*0-87055-496-4*) AVI.
***Potter, Norman N. & Hotchkiss, Joseph H.** Food Science. 5th ed. LC 95-16000. 1995. write for info. (*0-412-06451-0*, Chap & Hall NY) Chapman & Hall.
Potter, Norris, et al. The Hawaiian Monarchy. LC 82-74176. (Illus.). 256p. (J). (gr. 5-8). 1983. 29.95 (*0-935848-17-7*); student ed 7.95 (*0-935848-31-2*); pap. 19.95 (*0-935848-16-9*) Bess Pr.
Potter, Norris W. Punahou Story. LC 68-31288. (Illus.). 1969. 17.95 (*0-87015-176-2*) Pacific Bks.
Potter, O. E. & Nicklin, D. J., eds. Fluidization, No. VII. 1000p. 1992. write for info. (*0-939204-47-9*) Eng Found.
Potter, O. M. The Color of Rome, Historic, Personal & Local. 1977. lib. bdg. 59.95 (*0-8490-1645-2*) Gordon Pr.

Potter, P., jt. auth. see Newson, T.
Potter, P. E. & Pettijohn, F. J. Paleocurrents & Basin Analysis. 2nd ed. LC 76-30293. (Illus.). 1977. 94.00 (*0-387-07952-1*) Spr-Verlag.
Potter, P. E., et al. Sedimentology of Shale: Study Guide & Reference Source. (Illus.). 316p. 1984. pap. 72.00 (*0-387-90430-1*) Spr-Verlag.
Potter, Parker B., Jr. Public Archaeology in Annapolis: A Critical Approach to History in Maryland's Ancient City. LC 93-20779. (Illus.). 288p. (C). 1994. text ed. 45.00 (*1-56098-318-3*); pap. text ed. 19.95 (*1-56098-410-4*) Smithsonian.
Potter, Parker B., jt. ed. see Leone, Mark P.
Potter, Parker B., Jr.
Potter, Pat & Wiseman, Vanessa. Improving Residential Practice: Promoting Choice in Homes for Elderly People. (C). 1989. 45.00 (*0-685-28586-3*, Pub. by Natl Inst Soc Work); 52.00 (*0-685-40331-9*, Pub. by Natl Inst Soc Work); 45.00 (*0-902789-55-4*, Pub. by Natl Inst Soc Work) St Mut.
Potter, Patricia. Dragonfire. (Historical Ser.: No. 48). 1990. mass mkt. 3.25 (*0-373-28648-1*) Harlequin Bks.
— Island of Dreams. 1991. mass mkt. 5.50 (*0-06-100149-X*, Harp PBks) HarpC.
— Island of Dreams. 1991. 19.95 (*0-7278-4281-1*) Severn Hse.
— Lawless. (Fanfare Ser.). 1992. mass mkt. 4.99 (*0-553-29071-1*) Bantam.
— Lightning. 1992. 4.99 (*0-553-29070-3*) Bantam.
— Notorious. 1993. pap. 5.50 (*0-553-56225-8*, Fanfare) Bantam.
— Rainbow. 432p. 1991. mass mkt. 5.50 (*0-553-29069-X*) Bantam.
— Relentless. 1994. 5.50 (*0-553-56226-6*) Bantam.
— Renegade. 1993. pap. 5.50 (*0-553-56199-5*) Bantam.
— Swamp Fire. 1995. mass mkt. 4.99 (*1-55166-078-4*, 1-66078-6, Mira Bks) Harlequin Bks.
— Wanted. 1994. pap. 5.50 (*0-553-56600-8*) Bantam.
— Wanted. large type ed. LC 95-5403. (Large Print Book Ser.). 1995. pap. 21.95 (*1-56895-125-6*) Wheeler Pub.
Potter, Patricia A. Fundamentals of Nursing: Concepts, Process, & Practice. 3rd ed. LC 92-49926. 1808p. 1992. 53.95 (*0-8016-6667-8*) Mosby Yr Bk.
***Potter, Paul, ed. & tr.** Hippocrates. (Loeb Classical Library: Vol. 482). (Illus.). 432p. (C). 1995. text ed. 18.95 (*0-674-99531-7*) HUP.
Potter, Paul, tr. see Hippocrates.
Potter, Philip J. Power Plant Theory & Design. 2nd ed. LC 87-17348. 722p. 1988. reprint ed. 72.50 (*0-89464-236-7*) Krieger.
Potter, Phillip. Life in All Its Fullness. LC 82-5079. 183p. reprint ed. pap. 52.20 (*0-317-30158-6*, 2025340) Bks Demand.
Potter, Pitman B. The Economic Contract Law of China: Legitimation & Contract Autonomy in the PRC. LC 91-36749. (Asian Law Ser.: No. 10). 246p. 1992. text ed. 50.00 (*0-295-97127-4*) U of Wash Pr.
Potter, Pitman B., ed. Domestic Law Reforms in Post-Mao China. LC 93-23228. (Studies on Contemporary China). 326p. (C). 1994. 55.00 (*1-56324-107-2*, East Gate Bk) M E Sharpe.
Potter, R. B., ed. Urbanization, Planning & Development in the Caribbean. 336p. 1989. text ed. 90.00 (*0-7201-2012-8*, Mansell Pub) Cassell.
***Potter, R. Charles.** The "Tab-Slide-Guide" for All Major Keys of the Ten-Hole Diatonic Harmonica, No. 1. Date not set. 6.95 (*0-9646765-1-6*) Charles Publns.
— The "Tab-Slide-Guide" for All Major Keys of the Lee Oskar Melody Maker Ten-Hole Diatonic Harmonica, No. 3. Date not set. 6.95 (*0-9646765-3-2*) Charles Publns.
— The "Tab-Slide-Guide" for All Natural Minor Keys of the Ten-Hole Diatonic Harmonica, No. 2. Date not set. 6.95 (*0-9646765-2-4*) Charles Publns.
— This Harmonica Is for "You", No. 1. 54p. Date not set. pap. 16.95 (*0-9646765-0-8*) Charles Publns.
Potter, R. F. Modern Technologies Applied to Medical Practice (Nov 1989, Berlin), Vol. 1321. 1990. 42.00 (*0-8194-0382-2*) SPIE.
Potter, R. William. Issues for the Eighties: Energy, 1981. 1981. 4.00 (*0-943136-06-7*) Ctr Analysis Public Issues.
Potter, Reuben. The Fall of the Alamo. Grosvenor, Charles, ed. LC 77-75152. (Illus.). 1977. reprint ed. 10.00 (*0-918868-01-7*) Otterden.
Potter, Rick D. Dumped! The Broken Relationship Survival Manual. (Illus.). 112p. 1983. pap. 6.95 (*0-317-01200-2*) Laylah Pubns.
Potter, Robert B. St. Vincent & the Grenadines. (World Bibliographical Ser.). 1992. lib. bdg. 79.00 (*1-85109-183-1*) ABC-CLIO.
— Urbanization & Planning in the Third World: Spatial Perspectives & Public Participation. LC 85-10924. 284p. 1985. text ed. 39.95 (*0-312-83497-7*) St Martin.
Potter, Robert B. & Dann, Graham M. Barbados. (World Bibliographical Ser.: No. 76). 356p. 1987. lib. bdg. 70.00 (*1-85109-022-3*) ABC-CLIO.
Potter, Robert B. & Salau, Ademola T., eds. Cities & Development in the Third World. (Illus.). 208p. 1990. text ed. 80.00 (*0-7201-2066-7*, Mansell Pub) Cassell.
Potter, Robert B. & Unwin, Timothy. The Geography of Urban-Rural Interaction in Developing Countries. 288p. (C). 1989. lib. bdg. 62.50 (*0-415-00444-6*) Routledge.
Potter, Robert G., jt. ed. see Bongaarts, John.
Potter, Robert R. Benjamin Franklin. (Pioneers in Change Ser.). (Illus.). 144p. (J). (gr. 5-9). 1992. lib. bdg. 13.95 (*0-382-24173-8*); pap. 6.95 (*0-382-24178-9*) Silver Burdett Pr.
— Buckminster Fuller. Gallin, Richard, ed. (Pioneers in Change Ser.). (Illus.). 144p. (J). (gr. 5-9). 1990. lib. bdg. 13.95 (*0-382-09967-2*); pap. 6.95 (*0-382-09972-9*) Silver Burdett Pr.

An Asterisk (*) at the beginning of an entry indicates that the title is appearing in BIP for the first time.

— Jefferson Davis. LC 92-16914. (American Troublemakers Ser.). (Illus.). 128p. (J). (gr. 7-10). 1992. lib. bdg. 24.26 (*0-8114-2330-1*) Raintree Steck-V.

— John Brown: Militant Abolitionist. LC 94-17020. (American Troublemakers Ser.). (Illus.). (J). 1994. lib. bdg. 24.26 (*0-8114-2378-6*) Raintree Steck-V.

Potter, Roderick. Garsh. 8p. (Orig.). 1991. pap. 2.00 (*0-9627192-2-6*) We Pr.

Potter, Rosanne G., ed. Literary Computing & Literary Criticism: Theoretical & Practical Essays on Theme & Rhetoric. LC 88-38159. (Illus.). 320p. (C). 1989. text ed. 39.95 (*0-8122-8156-X*) U of Pa Pr.

Potter, Rosemary L. The Positive Use of Commercial Television with Children. LC 81-9646. (Analysis & Action Ser.). (Illus.). 136p. reprint ed. pap. 38.80 (*0-8357-6414-1*, 2035778) Bks Demand.

— Using Microcomputers for Teaching Reading in the Middle School. LC 89-61967. (Fastback Ser.: No. 296). 40p. (Orig.). (C). 1989. pap. 1.25 (*0-87367-296-8*) Phi Delta Kappa.

— Using Television in the Curriculum. LC 83-83090. (Fastback Ser.: No. 208). 50p. (Orig.). 1984. pap. 1.25 (*0-87367-208-9*) Phi Delta Kappa.

***Potter, Russell A.** Spectacular Vernaculars: Hip-Hop & the Politics of Postmodernism. (SUNY Series in Postmodern Culture). 160p. 1995. text ed. 44.50x (*0-7914-2625-4*); pap. 14.95x (*0-7914-2626-2*) State U NY Pr.

Potter, S. B. Fundamentals of Music. 2nd ed. (Illus.). 140p. (Orig.). 1990. pap. text ed. 10.95 (*0-910648-04-2*) Gamut Music.

— A Survey of Western Music to 1750. (Illus.). 445p. (C). 1993. pap. text ed. 17.95 (*0-910648-05-0*) Gamut Music.

Potter, Sally. Orlando. 96p. (Orig.). 1994. pap. 8.95 (*0-571-17295-4*) Faber & Faber.

Potter, Simeon. Language in the Modern World. LC 83-8248. 205p. 1983. reprint ed. text ed. 55.00 (*0-313-24009-4*, POLA, Greenwood Pr) Greenwood.

Potter, Simon M., jt. ed. see Pesaran, M. Hashem.

Potter, Stephen. D. H. Lawrence. LC 78-64051. (Des Imagistes: Literature of the Imagist Movement Ser.). 168p. reprint ed. 32.50 (*0-404-17091-9*) AMS Pr.

— Lifemanship. 1993. reprint ed. lib. bdg. 18.95 (*1-56849-093-3*) Buccaneer Bks.

— On the Right Lines? The Limits of Technological Innovation. LC 86-27894. 200p. 1987. text ed. 39.95 (*0-312-00488-5*) St Martin.

— One-Upmanship. 1993. reprint ed. lib. bdg. 18.95 (*1-56849-092-5*) Buccaneer Bks.

— The Theory & Practice of Gamesmanship. 1993. reprint ed. lib. bdg. 18.95 (*1-56849-094-1*) Buccaneer Bks.

Potter, Stephen, ed. see Coleridge, Sara.

Potter, Stephen J., jt. auth. see Llewellyn, John.

Potter, Stephen R. Commoners, Tribute, & Chiefs: The Development of Algonquian Culture in the Potomac Valley. LC 92-28417. (Illus.). 288p. 1993. 29.95 (*0-8139-1422-1*); pap. 12.95 (*0-8139-1540-6*) U Pr of Va.

Potter, Sulamith H. Family Life in a Northern Thai Village: A Study in the Structural Significance of Women. LC 76-52035. 1978. pap. 14.00 (*0-520-04044-9*) U CA Pr.

Potter, Sulamith H. & Potter, Jack M. China's Peasants: The Anthropology of a Revolution. (Illus.). (C). 1990. 74.95 (*0-521-35521-4*); pap. 17.95 (*0-521-35787-X*) Cambridge U Pr.

Potter, Sylvia, comp. Directory of Caribbeanists. 82p. (Orig.). 1989. pap. 8.00 (*0-317-93928-9*) Editorial Academica.

Potter, T. Car Travel Games. (Travel Games Ser.). (Illus.). 32p. (J). (gr. 2 up). 1986. pap. 4.95 (*0-86020-926-1*) EDC.

— Pottery. (Practical Guides Ser.). (Illus.). 48p. (J). (gr. 6 up). 1986. lib. bdg. 14.96 (*0-88110-319-5*); pap. 7.95 (*0-86020-944-X*) EDC.

Potter, T. & Butterfield, M. Travel Games. (Illus.). 64p. (J). (gr. 2 up). 1986. pap. 7.95 (*0-86020-999-7*, Usborne) EDC.

Potter, T., jt. auth. see Rac, G.

Potter, T., et al. Robotics. (Introductions Ser.). (Illus.). 48p. (J). (gr. 6 up). 1983. lib. bdg. 13.96 (*0-88110-661-5*); pap. 6.95 (*0-7460-1466-X*) EDC.

Potter, T. W. Roman Britain. (Illus.). 72p. 1983. pap. 11.95 (*0-674-77766-2*) HUP.

— Roman Italy. (Exploring the Roman World Ser.: Vol. 1). 240p. 1987. 35.00 (*0-520-06065-2*); pap. 16.00 (*0-520-06975-7*) U CA Pr.

Potter, T. W. & Johns, Catherine. Roman Britain. LC 92-25283. (Exploring the Roman World Ser.). (C). 1993. 35.00 (*0-520-08168-4*) U CA Pr.

Potter, T. W. & Trow, S. D. Puckeridge-Braughing: The Late Iron Age & Early Roman Settlement. (Illus.). 208p. 1993. pap. text ed. 33.00 (*0-901194-40-9*) A Sutton Pub.

Potter, Tessa. Cows. LC 89-26080. (Animal World Ser.). (Illus.). 32p. (J). (gr. 1-4). 1990. lib. bdg. 19.97 (*0-8114-2626-2*); pap. 3.95 (*0-8114-4610-7*) Raintree Steck-V.

— Donkeys. LC 89-26079. (Animal World Ser.). (Illus.). 32p. (J). (gr. 1-4). 1990. lib. bdg. 19.97 (*0-8114-2631-9*) Raintree Steck-V.

— Ducks & Geese. LC 89-22013. (Animal World Ser.). (Illus.). 32p. (J). (gr. 1-4). 1990. lib. bdg. 19.97 (*0-8114-2628-9*) Raintree Steck-V.

— Goats. LC 89-22021. (Animal World Ser.). (Illus.). 32p. (J). (gr. 1-4). 1990. lib. bdg. 19.97 (*0-8114-2629-7*); pap. 3.95 (*0-8114-4617-4*) Raintree Steck-V.

— Hens. LC 89-22020. (Animal World Ser.). (Illus.). 32p. (J). (gr. 1-4). 1990. lib. bdg. 19.97 (*0-8114-2627-0*) Raintree Steck-V.

— Sheep. LC 89-22022. (Animal World Ser.). (Illus.). 32p. (J). (gr. 1-4). 1990. lib. bdg. 19.97 (*0-8114-2630-0*) Raintree Steck-V.

Potter, Thelma M. An Analysis of the Work of General Clerical Employees. LC 78-177161. (Columbia University. Teachers College. Contributions to Education Ser.: No. 903). reprint ed. 37.50 (*0-404-55903-4*) AMS Pr.

Potter, Theodore E. The Autobiography of Theodore Edgar Potter. (Michigan Heritage Library: Vol. 1). 1978. reprint ed. 9.95 (*0-915056-08-9*) Hardscrabble Bks.

Potter, Thomas A., jt. auth. see Nelson, Theron R.

***Potter, Tom & Parnes, Beatrice.** Parenting Playfully: Dancing the Developmental Ladder, Birth to Three. 112p. (Orig.). 1995. pap. 12.95 (*0-9646045-0-7*) Parent Educ.

Potter, Tony. How Television Works. (Illus.). 48p. (J). (gr. 7-9). 1992. 13.95 (*0-563-34579-9*, BBC-Parkwest); pap. 6.95 (*0-563-34578-0*, BBC-Parkwest) Parkwest Pubns.

— See How It Works: Cars. (Illus.). 28p. (J). (ps-3). 1989. pap. 7.95 (*0-689-71303-7*, Aladdin Paperbacks) S&S Childrens.

— See How It Works: Earth Movers. (Illus.). 28p. (J). (ps-3). 1989. pap. 7.95 (*0-689-71302-9*, Aladdin Paperbacks) S&S Childrens.

— See How It Works: Planes. (Illus.). 28p. (J). (ps-3). 1989. pap. 7.95 (*0-689-71304-5*, Aladdin Paperbacks) S&S Childrens.

— See How It Works: Trucks. (Illus.). 28p. (J). (ps-3). 1989. pap. 7.95 (*0-689-71301-0*, Aladdin Paperbacks) S&S Childrens.

— Weather. (Illus.). 48p. (J). (gr. 7-9). 1992. 13.95 (*0-563-21428-7*, BBC-Parkwest); pap. 6.95 (*0-563-21427-9*, BBC-Parkwest) Parkwest Pubns.

Potter, Tony & Wright, Nicola. The Macmillan First Atlas. LC 91-31257. (Macmillan Children's Reference Ser.). (Illus.). 40p. (J). (ps-2). 1992. text ed. 12.95 (*0-02-774920-7*, Mac Bks Young Read) S&S Childrens.

Potter, Van R. Global Bioethics: Building on the Leopold Legacy. LC 88-42901. 203p. (C). 1988. pap. 13.00 (*0-87013-264-4*) Mich St U Pr.

Potter, Velma M. God Flies Benny's Flag. Russell, Jervis F., ed. (Illus.). 235p. (J). (gr. 4 up). 1989. pap. 12.95 (*0-939116-20-0*) Frontier OR.

Potter, Vilma. A Reference Guide to Afro-American Publications & Editors, 1827-1946. LC 91-17167. 104p. 1993. text ed. 21.95 (*0-8138-0677-1*) Iowa St U Pr.

Potter, Vincent. On Understanding Understanding: A Philosophy of Knowledge. 2nd rev. ed. LC 93-7931. (Illus.). xvi, 249p. (C). 1994. pap. 15.50 (*0-8232-1486-9*) Fordham.

Potter, Vincent, tr. John Pecham's "On the Eternity of the World" 96p. (C). 1993. 25.00 (*0-8232-1488-5*) Fordham.

***Potter, Vincent G.** Peirce's Philosophical Perspective. Colapietro, Vincent, ed. (American Philosophy Ser.: No. 2). 1995. 30.00 (*0-8232-1615-2*) Fordham.

Potter, Vincent G., ed. Doctrine & Experience: Essays in American Philosophy. LC 88-82221. x, 273p. 1988. 40.00 (*0-8232-1210-6*) Fordham.

Potter, Vincent G., et al. Readings in Epistemology: From Aquinas, Bacon, Galileo, Descartes, Locke, Hume, Kant. 2nd ed. LC 92-45079. xvi, 235p. (C). 1993. 25.00 (*0-8232-1493-1*); pap. 14.50 (*0-8232-1492-3*) Fordham.

Potter, W. C., jt. ed. see Valenta, Jiri.

***Potter, W. James.** An Analysis of Thinking & Research about Qualitative Methods. (LEA's Communication Ser.). 400p. 1996. text ed. 80.00 (*0-8058-1750-6*); pap. 40.00 (*0-8058-1751-4*) L Erlbaum Assocs.

Potter, William, et al. Visual BASIC Superbible. 2nd ed. (Illus.). 1600p. 1993. pap. 44.95 (*1-878739-50-6*) Waite Group Pr.

Potter, William C. Creating a Database on International Nuclear Commerce. (CISA Working Paper Ser.: No. 59). 27p. (Orig.). Date not set. pap. 10.00 (*0-86682-076-0*) Ctr Intl Relations.

— A Guide to Simulating U. S.-Soviet Arms Control Negotiations. (CISA Working Paper Ser.: No. 62). 40p. (Orig.). Date not set. pap. 10.00 (*0-86682-079-5*) Ctr Intl Relations.

Potter, William C., ed. International Missile Bazaar: The New Suppliers' Network. 341p. (C). 1993. text ed. 62.00 (*0-8133-8796-5*) Westview.

— International Nuclear Trade & Nonproliferation. 448p. 1990. text ed. 55.00 (*0-669-21120-6*) Free Pr.

Potter, William C., et al. Nuclear Profiles of the Soviet Successor States. (Orig.). 1993. 9.95 (*0-9633859-5-X*) Ctr Rus & Eura Stud.

Potter, William G., intro. Leadership in Academic Libraries: Proceedings of the W. Porter Kellam Conference, the University of Georgia, May 7, 1991. LC 92-36461. (Journal of Library Administration: Vol. 17, No.4). 122p. 1993. 29.95 (*1-56024-400-3*) Haworth Pr.

Potter, William G., ed. see American Library Association Staff.

Potterbaum, Charlene. Thanks Lord, I Needed That! LC 77-86470. 155p. 1979. 3.95 (*0-88270-411-7*) Bridge Pub.

Potterfield, Peter & Nelson, Jim. Selected Climbs in the Cascades. (Illus.). 240p. 1993. 22.95 (*0-89886-368-6*) Mountaineers.

***Potterson, David.** Herbal Remedies: Irritable Bowel Syndromes. 1993. pap. 7.95 (*0-572-01818-5*, Pub. by W Foulsham UK) Trans-Atl Phila.

Potterton, Homan. National Gallery - London. LC 88-51948. (Illus.). 216p. 1989. pap. 11.95 (*0-500-20161-7*) Thames Hudson.

Pottharst, Karl, intro. Research Explorations in Adult Attachments. (American University Studies: Psychology: Ser. VIII, Vol. 14). 353p. (C). 1989. text ed. 53.95 (*0-8204-1050-0*) P Lang Pubs.

Pottie, Charles. A More Profound Alleluia. 1984. 5.95 (*0-912405-12-0*) Pastoral Pr.

***Pottie, Kaye & Ellis, Vernon.** Folksongs of the Maritimes. (Illus.). 192p. 1995. 29.95 (*0-88780-201-X*); pap. 16.95 (*0-88780-200-1*) Formac Dist Ltd.

Pottier, Bernard, jt. ed. see Gill, Harjeet S.

Pottier, Edmond. Douris & the Painters of Greek Vases. Kahnweiler, Bettina, tr. (Illus.). 115p. reprint ed. text ed. 30.00 (*0-89241-431-6*) Caratzas.

Pottier, Johan. Migrants No More: Settlement & Survival in Mambwe Villages, Zambia. LC 88-9373. (International African Library). (Illus.). 224p. 1988. 35.00 (*0-253-33894-8*) Ind U Pr.

Pottier, Johan, ed. Practising Development: Social Science Perspectives. LC 92-13084. (European Inter-University Development Opportunity Study Group Ser.). 240p. 1993. 65.00 (*0-415-08910-7*, A9868); pap. 18.95 (*0-415-08911-5*, A9872) Routledge.

Pottiez, Jean-Marc, ed. see Van der Post, Laurens.

Pottiglio, Denise H. & Powers, Lawerence W. Clinical Hematology for Blood Bankers: A Case History Approach to Hemolytic Anemia. Ciesla, Betty et al, eds. (S.U.C.C.E.S.S. Program Ser.: No. 1). (Illus.). 64p. (Orig.). 1987. student ed 19.95 (*0-943903-00-9*) DH Pub PA.

Pottinger, D. E., jt. ed. see Polley, L.

Pottinger, David. Printers & Printing. LC 70-175709. (Select Bibliographies Reprint Ser.). 1977. reprint ed. 12.95 (*0-8369-6624-4*) Ayer.

— Quilts from the Indiana Amish: A Regional Collection. (Illus.). 87p. 1983. pap. 15.95 (*0-525-48043-9*, Dutton) NAL-Dutton.

Pottinger, Don, jt. auth. see Norman, A. V.

Pottinger, Evelyn A. Napoleon Third & the German Crisis, 1865-1866. LC 66-18253. (Historical Studies: No. 75). 248p. 1966. 20.00 (*0-674-60050-9*) HUP.

Pottinger, Marion G. & Yager, Thomas J., eds. The Tire Pavement Interface, STP 929. LC 86-20565. (Special Technical Publication (STP) Ser.). (Illus.). 330p. 1986. text ed. 54.00 (*0-8031-0497-9*, 04-929000-27) ASTM.

***Pottinger, Stanley.** The Fourth Procedure. LC 94-34282. 560p. 1995. 23.95 (*0-345-38400-8*) Ballantine.

Pottker, Jan. Born to Power: Heirs to America's Leading Companies. 1992. pap. 12.95 (*0-8120-1456-1*) Barron.

Pottker, Janice & Fishel, Andrew, eds. Sex Bias in the Schools: The Research Evidence. LC 74-200. 571p. 1976. 50.00 (*0-8386-1464-7*) Fairleigh Dickinson.

Pottkotter, Louis. The Natural Nursery: The Parent's Guide to Ecologically Sound, Nontoxic, Safe & Healthy Baby Care. 400p. 1994. pap. 14.95 (*0-8092-3766-0*) Contemp Bks.

Pottle, Frederick A., ed. see Boswell, James.

Pottle, Marion S., et al, eds. Catalogue of the Papers of James Boswell at Yale University, 3 vols., Set. 1400p. (C). 1993. text ed. 275.00 (*0-300-05410-6*) Yale U Pr.

***Pottleer, Jan.** Crisis in Candyland: Melting the Chocolate Shell of the Mars Family Empire. (Illus.). 256p. 1995. 23.95 (*1-882605-20-9*) Natl Pr Bks.

***Pottor, Dennis.** Waiting for the Boat. 192p. 1994. 11.99 (*1-56865-114-7*, GuildAmerica) Dblday Bk Music.

Pottorff, Susan. Demonstration Techniques. (C). 1993. 15.52 (*1-56870-093-8*) RonJon Pub.

***Potts.** Little Book of Creative Dried & Silk Flowers. 1995. (*0-7858-0239-8*) Bk Sales Inc.

— Little Book of Creative Flower Arranging. 1995. (*0-7858-0345-9*) Bk Sales Inc.

Potts, et al. Alien Legion: A Grey Day to Die. 64p. 1986. 5.95 (*0-87135-207-9*) Marvel Entmnt.

— Last of the Dragons. 64p. 1988. 6.95 (*0-87135-335-0*) Marvel Entmnt.

— Shadowmasters, No. 2. 48p. 1989. 3.95 (*0-87135-547-7*) Marvel Entmnt.

— Shadowmasters, No. 3. 48p. 1989. 3.95 (*0-87135-548-5*) Marvel Entmnt.

— Shadowmasters, No. 4. 48p. 1989. 3.95 (*0-87135-549-3*) Marvel Entmnt.

***Potts, Adeline J.** Walk by the Spirit. 128p. 1994. pap. 9.00 (*0-936204-81-8*) Jelm Mtn.

Potts, Albert M. The World's Eye. LC 79-4009. (Illus.). 104p. 1982. 22.00 (*0-8131-1387-3*) U Pr of Ky.

Potts, Alex. Flesh & the Ideal: Winckelmann & the Origins of Art History. (Illus.). 312p. 1994. 30.00 (*0-300-05813-6*) Yale U Pr.

Potts, Billie. Witches Heal. 2nd ed. (Illus.). 200p. 1988. reprint ed. pap. 12.50 (*0-929784-00-6*) DuReve Pubns.

Potts, Carl & Anderson, Brent. Punisher Movie Adaptation. 64p. 1990. 5.95 (*0-87135-672-4*) Marvel Entmnt.

Potts, Carl & Lee, Jim. Punisher: Eye for an Eye. (Illus.). 80p. 1991. pap. 9.95 (*0-87135-777-1*) Marvel Entmnt.

Potts, Carl, et al. Wolverine vs. the Punisher: African Saga - Rep., Nos. 6 & 7. 48p. 1990. 5.95 (*0-87135-611-2*) Marvel Entmnt.

***Potts, Charles.** Charlie Kiot. 1976. per. 10.00 (*0-914656-01-5*) Current.

—How the South Finally Won the Civil War: And Controls the Political Future of the United States. LC 96-61861. (Illus.). 440p. 1995. 29.00 (*0-9644440-0-3*) Tsunami. This book turns the world upside down. It will change the way you read American history. Conservative & aristocratic economic ideals motivated the founders of the British Empire who transplanted their plantation economics from Barbados to South Carolina in 1670. By 1771, 9 of the 10 richest men in the American Colonies were Charlestonians. South Carolina, birthplace of Andrew Jackson & John Calhoun, "The Marx of the Master Class," is the pituitary gland of the American political system & "dissolved" the union in 1860, leading to the Civil War. Unreconstructed Southerners finally regained power with the Truman Doctrine & the Cold War's state of siege at the end of WWII. Along the way they Texified the west, subducted California into a southern state, while the Fraud of 1876 restored state rights & white supremacy in the South. The Roosevelt imperialists in the Spanish-American War revived the empire & put colonies into the pre-Civil War "Southern Dreams of a Caribbean Empire." Goldwater reconnected the Neo-Confederate Republican west with South Carolina. Five of the 6 things the South fought for are public policy. It's been 130 years since Lee surrendered to Grant at Appomattox. It is time to declare a Confederate victory. To order by credit card: 1-800-285-4929. Ext. 20. Tsunami Inc., P.O. Box 1773, Walla Walla, WA 99362-0033. FAX: 1-509-527-3691; Phone 1-509-529-0813. ***Publisher Provided Annotation.***

— Loading Las Vegas. (Cybersatires Ser.). 192p. (Orig.). 1991. pap. 10.00 (*0-915214-20-2*) Current.

— Railroad Transportation in Texas. 1993. reprint ed. lib. bdg. 75.00 (*0-7812-5895-2*) Rprt Serv.

— Rocky Mountain Man. LC 77-82730. 148p. 1978. pap. 6.00 (*0-912292-47-4*) The Smith.

Potts, Cheryl. Poetry Galore & More with Shel Silverstein. 64p. (J). (gr. 2-5). 1993. pap. 12.95 (*0-913853-35-6*, 32554, Alleyside) Highsmith Pr.

Potts, D. Gordon, jt. auth. see Newton, Thomas H.

Potts, D. T. The Arabian Gulf in Antiquity, Vol. 1: From Prehistory to the Fall of the Achamenid Empire. (Illus.). 460p. 1991. 110.00 (*0-19-814390-7*) OUP.

— The Arabian Gulf in Antiquity, Vol. 2: Alexander the Great to the Coming of Islam. (Illus.). 408p. 1991. 98.00 (*0-19-814391-5*) OUP.

— Supplement to the Pre-Islamic Coinage of Eastern Arabia. (Carsten Niebuhr Institute Publications (CNI): No. 16). (Illus.). 100p. 1994. 65.00 (*87-7289-272-2*, Pub. by Mus Tusculanum DK) Paul & Co Pubs.

Potts, Daniel L. & Gensure, John G. International Metallic Materials Cross- Reference. 3rd ed. 704p. 1988. 179.00 (*0-931690-23-4*) Genium Pub.

Potts, David B. Wesleyan University, 1831-1910: Collegiate Enterprise in New England. (Illus.). 368p. (C). 1992. text ed. 35.00 (*0-300-05160-3*) Yale U Pr.

Potts, Donald F. & Spangenberg, N. Earl, eds. Changing Roles in Water Resources Management & Policy: Water Resources Education: A Lifetime of Learning. LC 93-71755. (Technical Publication Ser.: No. 93-2). (Illus.). 716p. (Orig.). 1993. pap. 55.00 (*1-882132-25-4*) Am Water Resources.

Potts, Donald F., ed. see Symposium on Headwaters Hydrology Staff.

Potts, Donna L. Howard Nemerov & Objective Idealism: The Influence of Owen Barfield. LC 94-5650. 128p. 1994. 27.50 (*0-8262-0962-9*) U of Mo Pr.

Potts, Evangela, jt. auth. see Potts, Leanna K.

Potts, Eve & Morra, Marion. Understanding Your Immune System. 224p. 1986. pap. 3.95 (*0-380-89728-8*) Avon.

Potts, Eve, jt. auth. see Morra, Marion.

Potts, F. E. F. Potts' Guide to Bush Flying. (Illus.). 278p. (Orig.). 1993. pap. 34.95 (*0-9635210-1-2*) ACS Pub AZ.

Potts, George, jt. auth. see Gress, Bob.

Potts, J. F., tr. see Swedenborg, Emanuel.

Potts, Jackie. Computer-Aided Drafting & Design Using Autocad. 412p. (C). 1988. pap. text ed. 37.25 (*0-15-512629-6*) SCP.

Potts, Jean. Go, Lovely Rose. (Black Dagger Crime Ser.). 192p. 16.50 (*0-86220-728-2*, Black Dagger) Chivers N Amer.

— Go, Lovely Rose. large type ed. 1994. 18.95 (*0-7451-6453-6*, Scarlet Dagger Lrg Print) Chivers N Amer.

— Home Is the Prisoner. (Black Dagger Crime Ser.). 176p. 1989. reprint ed. text ed. 16.50 (*0-86220-763-0*, Black Dagger) Chivers N Amer.

Potts, Jim. The House That Makes Shapes. LC 92-5847. (Illus.). 32p. (J). (gr. k-3). 1992. 14.95 (*0-943173-74-4*) Harbinger AZ.

Potts, John. Radio in Australia. (Illus.). 189p. 1989. pap. 19.95 (*0-86840-331-8*, Pub. by New South Wales Univ Pr AT) Intl Spec Bk.

Potts, Judith B. The Home Buyer's Workbook. (Illus.). 230p. (C). 1988. text ed. 19.95 (*1-882107-00-4*) Real Property Advisor.

— The Home Finance Workbook: A Complete Guide to Home Finance. 63p. (Orig.). 1990. pap. text ed. 11.95 (*1-882107-01-2*) Real Property Advisor.

Potts, Kathryn H. & Machell, Keith. The Manual Screw Press for Small-Scale Oil Extraction. 64p. (Orig.). 1994. pap. 15.50 (*1-85339-198-0*, Pub. by Intermed Tech UK) Women Ink.

Potts, Ken & Moody, John, eds. Make Room for Science: A Manual of Hands-on Activities for the Elementary Classroom. (Illus.). 224p. 1990. teacher ed 13.95 (*0-944584-85-3*) Sopris.

Potts, Kenneth C., jt. auth. see Jones, Jeffrey D.

P Q

Potts, L. C. Weimer: Biographical Sketches & Family Records of the Gabriel Weimer & David Weimer Families. (Illus.). 270p. 1992. reprint ed. lib. bdg. 52.50 (*0-8328-2333-3*); reprint ed. pap. 42.50 (*0-8328-2334-1*) Higginson Bk Co.

***Potts, Laura.** Little Book of Chocolate. 1994. 4.98 (*0-7858-0139-1*) Bk Sales Inc.

Potts, Lawrence W. Quantitative Analysis. (C). 1990. text ed. 48.25 (*0-06-045269-2*) HarpCollege.

Potts, Leanna K. From Seed to Serve: A Beginners Guide to Growing & Using Herbs. (Illus.). 153p. 1990. pap. 10.95 (*0-935069-19-4*) White Oak Pr.

Potts, Leanna K. & Potts, Evangela. Thyme for Kids. (Illus.). 84p. (J). (ps-8). 1990. pap. 7.95 (*0-935069-24-0*) White Oak Pr.

***Potts, Lee W.** Responsible Police Administration: Issues & Approaches. LC 82-16059. 195p. 1983. pap. 55.60 (*0-7837-8398-1*, 2059209) Bks Demand.

Potts, Lydia. The World Labour Market: A History of Migration. Bond, Terry, tr. LC 89-25041. (Illus.). 304p. (C). 1990. text ed. 55.00 (*0-86232-882-9*, Pub. by Zed Books UK); pap. 17.50 (*0-86232-883-7*, Pub. by Zed Books UK) Humanities.

Potts, M., jt. auth. see Senanayake, P.

Potts, Malcolm. Birth Control. Head, J. J., ed. LC 84-45839. (Carolina Biology Readers Ser.: No. 178). (Illus.). 16p. (gr. 10 up). 1987. pap. 2.75 (*0-89278-104-1*, 45-9778) Carolina Biological.

Potts, Malcolm, jt. auth. see Clarke, Loren K.

Potts, Malcolm, et al, eds. Breast-Feeding & Fertility. (Journal of Biological Science, Supplement Ser.: No. 9). 170p. 1985. pap. 25.00 (*0-907232-04-3*) Portland NC.

Potts, Marie. The Northern Maidu. LC 77-10739. (Illus.). 48p. 1977. pap. 5.95 (*0-87961-070-0*) Naturegraph.

Potts, Marion, et al. Structure & Development in Child Language: The Preschool Years. LC 78-10968. 224p. 1979. 34.95 (*0-8014-1184-X*) Cornell U Pr.

Potts, Mark, et al. Dirty Money: BCCI - The Inside Story of the World's Sleaziest Bank. 1992. 21.95 (*0-915765-99-3*) Natl Pr Bks.

Potts, Maureen A. The Three-Edged Sword: Being Ill in America. 128p. (C). 1992. lib. bdg. 34.50 (*0-8191-8669-4*) U Pr of Amer.

Potts, Merlin K., ed. Campfire Tales of Jackson Hole. rev. ed. (Illus.). 95p. reprint ed. pap. 6.95 (*0-931895-12-X*) Grand Teton NHA.

Potts, Michael. The Independent Home: Living Well with Power from the Sun, Wind, & Water. (Real Goods Independent Living Bks.). (Illus.). 300p. (Orig.). 1993. pap. 19.95 (*0-930031-65-2*) Chelsea Green Pub.

***Potts, Nancy D.** As the Spirit Moves: Stories of the Spiritual Quest. 200p. 1994. pap. text ed. 14.95 (*0-9640010-2-0*) Peace Pubng.

— The Spiritual Quest. Bridgewater, Shirlene, ed. 65p. (Orig.). 1995. pap. text ed. 7.00 (*0-9640010-3-9*) Peace Pubng.

— Women of Vision, Women of Peace. 225p. 1994. pap. text ed. 15.95 (*0-9640010-0-4*) Peace Pubng.

Potts, P. & Fido, F. A Fit Person to Be Removed. 1990. pap. 30.00 (*0-7463-0580-X*, Pub. by Northcote UK) St Mut.

Potts, P., tr. see Barth, E. M.

Potts, P. J., et al. Geochemical Reference Material Compositions: Rocks, Minerals, Sediments, Soils, Carbonates, Refractories, & Ores Used in Research & Industry. 1992. 130.95 (*0-8493-7757-9*, QE438) CRC Pr.

Potts, Patricia, et al, eds. Equality & Diversity in Education 1: Learning, Teaching & Managing in Schools. LC 94-20720. (Open University Set Book Ser.). (Illus.). 256p. 1995. pap. 22.95x (*0-415-11997-9*, C0397) Routledge.

— Equality & Diversity in Education 2: National & International Contexts. LC 94-26653. (Illus.). 256p. 1995. pap. 22.95x (*0-415-11998-7*, C0398) Routledge.

Potts, Phyllis L. Going Against the Grain: Wheat-Free Cookery. (Illus.). 230p. (Orig.). 1992. pap. 14.95 (*0-9630479-0-6*) Central Pt.

— Still Going Against the Grain: Wheat-Free Cookery. LC 94-94308. (Illus.). 260p. (Orig.). 1994. pap. 14.95 (*0-9630479-1-4*) Central Pt.

***Potts, Randall.** Collision Center. LC 94-65731. 68p. 1994. 9.00 (*1-882022-19-X*) O Bks.

Potts, Renfrey B. & Oliver, Robert M. Flows in Transportation Networks. (Mathematics in Science & Engineering Ser.). 1972. text ed. 105.00 (*0-12-563650-4*) Acad Pr.

Potts, Richard B. Early Hominid Activities at Olduvai. (Foundations of Human Behavior Ser.). (Illus.). 407p. (C). 1988. lib. bdg. 57.95 (*0-202-01176-3*) Aldine de Gruyter.

Potts, Robert A., ed. see Shelley, Percy Bysshe.

Potts, Sandra. There's a Blue Bear in the Bathtub & My Mother Is Mad. LC 93-93801. (Illus.). 64p. (Orig.). (J). 1994. pap. 5.00 (*1-56002-327-9*, Univ Edtns) Aegina Pr.

Potts, Stephen W. Catch-Twenty-Two: Antiheroic Antinovel. (Masterwork Studies). 160p. 1989. text ed. 21.95 (*0-8057-7992-2*, Twayne); pap. 12.95 (*0-8057-8041-6*, Twayne) Macmillan.

— From Here to Absurdity: The Moral Battlefields of Joseph Heller. rev. ed. (Milford Series: Popular Writers of Today: Vol. 36). 144p. 1995. pap. write for info. (*0-89370-418-0*) Borgo Pr.

— From Here to Absurdity: The Moral Battlefields of Joseph Heller. 2nd rev. ed. (Milford Series: Popular Writers of Today: Vol. 36). 144p. 1995. lib. bdg. write for info. (*0-89370-318-4*) Borgo Pr.

— Price of Paradise: The Magazine Career of F. Scott Fitzgerald. LC 93-344. (Milford Ser.: Popular Writers of Today: Vol. 58). 136p. 1993. lib. bdg. 27.00x (*0-89370-187-4*); pap. 17.00x (*0-89370-287-0*) Borgo Pr.

— The Second Marxian Invasion: The Fiction of the Strugatsky Brothers. LC 84-309. (Milford Series: Popular Writers of Today: Vol. 50). 104p. (C). 1991. lib. bdg. 25.00x (*0-89370-179-3*); pap. text ed. 15.00x (*0-89370-279-X*) Borgo Pr.

Potts, Steve. All-Star Game. (Great Moments in Sports Ser.). (YA). (gr. 5 up). 1992. lib. bdg. 14.95 (*0-88682-537-7*) Creative Ed.

— Buffalo Bills. (NFL Today Ser.). (J). (gr. 4 up). 1991. lib. bdg. 14.95 (*0-88682-360-9*) Creative Ed.

— Denver Broncos. (NFL Today Ser.). (J). (gr. 4 up). 1991. lib. bdg. 14.95 (*0-88682-365-X*) Creative Ed.

— Houston Oilers. (NFL Today Ser.). (J). (gr. 4 up). 1991. lib. bdg. 14.95 (*0-88682-368-4*) Creative Ed.

— Minnesota Vikings. (NFL Today Ser.). (J). (gr. 4 up). 1991. lib. bdg. 14.95 (*0-88682-374-9*) Creative Ed.

— New Orleans Saints. (NFL Today Ser.). (J). (gr. 4 up). 1991. lib. bdg. 14.95 (*0-88682-376-5*) Creative Ed.

— San Francisco Forty Niners. (NFL Today Ser.). (J). (gr. 4 up). 1991. lib. bdg. 14.95 (*0-88682-383-8*) Creative Ed.

— Track & Field Championship. (Great Moments in Sports Ser.). (J). (gr. 5 up). 1992. lib. bdg. 14.95 (*0-88682-533-4*) Creative Ed.

Potts, Steve, jt. auth. see Bhugra, Dinesh.

Potts, T. M. Bi-Centenary Memorial of Jeremiah Carter Who Came to the Provence of Pennsylvania in 1682, a Historic-Genealogy of His Descendents down to the Present. (Illus.). 304p. 1989. reprint ed. lib. bdg. 59.00 (*0-8328-0372-3*); reprint ed. pap. 49.00 (*0-8328-0373-1*) Higginson Bk Co.

— Potts: Historical Collection Relating to the Potts Family in Great Britain & America. (Illus.). 735p. 1990. reprint ed. lib. bdg. 112.50 (*0-8328-1522-5*); reprint ed. pap. 104.50 (*0-8328-1523-3*) Higginson Bk Co.

***Potts, Timothy.** Mesopotamia & the East: An Archaeological & Historical Study of Foreign Relations 3400-2000 BC. (Oxford University Committee for Archaeology Monograph Ser.: No. 37). (Illus.). 340p. 1995. 49.50 (*0-947816-37-2*, Pub. by Oxbow Bks UK) David Brown.

Potts, Timothy C. Structures & Categories for the Representation of Meaning. (Illus.). 314p. (C). 1994. 59.95 (*0-521-43481-5*) Cambridge U Pr.

***Potts, Tom.** 98 Wise Rules for Grandpa. (Fingertip Books). 96p. (Orig.). 1995. mass mkt. 4.99 (*0-8010-7131-3*) Baker Bk.

Potts, Tom & Sykes, Arnold. Executive Talent: How to Identify & Develop the Best. LC 92-16741. 247p. 1992. 32.50 (*1-55623-754-5*) Irwin Prof Pubng.

Potts, W. & Parry, G. Osmotic & Ionic Regulation in Animals. LC 62-11560. 1964. 182.00 (*0-08-013598-6*, Pub. by Pergamon Repr UK) Franklin.

Potts, Willard, ed. Portraits of the Artist in Exile: Recollections of James Joyce by Europeans. (Illus.). 320p. 1986. pap. 7.95 (*0-15-672980-6*, Harvest Bks) HarBrace.

— Portraits of the Artist in Exile: Recollections of James Joyce by Europeans. LC 78-4367. (Illus.). 320p. 1979. 30.00 (*0-295-95614-3*) U of Wash Pr.

Potts, William F. McGraw-Hill Data Communications Dictionary. 1992. text ed. 34.50 (*0-07-003154-1*) McGraw.

Potty, S. N., ed. Placrosym VI. 476p. (C). 1987. 34.00 (*81-204-0239-1*, Pub. by Oxford IBH II) S Asia.

Potuto, Josephine. Prisoner Collateral Attacks. LC 91-60701. 1991. 98.00 (*0-685-59842-X*) Clark Boardman Callaghan.

Potuto, Josephine R., et al. Federal Criminal Jury Instructions, 3 vols., Set. 2nd suppl. ed. 1993. 240.00 (*0-87473-820-2*) Michie Butterworth.

***Potvin.** White Lies: For My Mother. Date not set. per. 14.95 (*0-920897-13-4*, Pub. by NeWest Pr CN) InBook.

Potvin, Alfred R. & Tourtellotte, Wallace W., eds. Quantitative Examination of Neurologic Functions, 2 vols., Vol. I. 272p. 1985. 168.00 (*0-8493-5926-0*, RC348, CRC Reprint) Franklin.

— Quantitative Examination of Neurologic Functions, 2 vols., Vol. II. 224p. 1985. 168.00 (*0-8493-5927-9*, CRC Reprint) Franklin.

Potvin, Charles, jt. auth. see Chretien de Troyes.

Potvin, J., ed. Computational Physics: Proceedings of the 2nd IMACS Conference. 272p. 1994. text ed. 99.00 (*981-02-1747-1*) World Scientific Pub.

Potvin, Raymond H. Seminarians of the Eighties: A National Survey. 64p. 1986. 5.65 (*0-318-20579-3*) Natl Cath Educ.

Potvin, Raymond H., jt. auth. see Westoff, Charles F.

Poty, Bernard, jt. ed. see Roth, Etienne.

Potzl, Otto, et al. Preconscious Stimulation in Dreams, Associations & Images: Classical Studies. (Psychological Issues Monograph: No. 7, Vol. 2, No. 3). 156p. (Orig.). 1961. text ed. 26.00 (*0-8236-4260-7*) Intl Univs Pr.

Pou, P. J., et al, eds. La Edicion De Textos: Actas Del I Congreso Internacional De Hispanistas De Siglo De Oro. (Series A: Monagrafias: No. CXXXIX). 256p. (C). 1990. 53.00 (*0-7293-0305-5*, Pub. by Tamesis Bks Ltd UK) Boydell & Brewer.

Pouba, Z. & Stemprok, M., eds. Problems of Hydrothermal Ore Deposition: Origin, Evolution & Control of Oreforming Fluids. (Illus.). 396p. 1970. text ed. 46.95 (*3-510-56002-7*, Pub. by Schweitzerbart'sche GW) Lubrecht & Cramer.

Pouch, J. J. & Alterovitz, S. A., eds. Plasma Properties, Deposition & Etching. (Materials Science Forum Ser.: Vol. 140-142). (Illus.). 749p. (C). 1993. text ed. 210.00 (*0-87849-670-X*, Pub. by Trans Tech SZ) LPS Dist Ctr.

— Properties & Characterization of Amorphous Carbon Films. 714p. (C). 1990. text ed. 152.00 (*0-87849-604-1*, Pub. by Trans Tech GW) LPS Dist Ctr.

Pouch, J. J., et al, eds. Advances in High-Tc Superconductors. (Materials Science Forum Ser.: Vol. 137-139). (Illus.). 802p. (C). 1993. text ed. 210.00 (*0-87849-667-X*, Pub. by Trans Tech SZ) LPS Dist Ctr.

— Synthesis & Characterization of High-Temperature Superconductors. 710p. (C). 1993. text ed. 210.00 (*0-87849-658-0*, Pub. by Trans Tech SZ) LPS Dist Ctr.

Pouchelle, Marie-Christien. The Body & Surgery in the Middle Ages. Morris, Rosemary, tr. LC 90-8126. 300p. (C). 1990. text ed. 40.00 (*0-8135-1605-6*) Rutgers U Pr.

***Poucher, W. A.** The Production, Manufacture & Application of Perfumes. LC 94-111088. (Perfumes, Cosmetics & Soaps Ser.: Vol. 2). 379p. 1994. 110.00 (*0-412-27350-0*) Chapman & Hall.

Pouchkine, Alexandre. La Dame de Pique, Recist de Feu Ivan Petrovich, Bielkine, Doubrovski. 288p. (FRE.). 1974. pap. 10.95 (*0-7859-4027-8*) Fr & Eur.

***Pouchot, Pierre.** Memoirs on the Late War in North America Between France & England. Dunnigan, Brian L., ed. Cardy, Michael, tr. (Illus.). 568p. 1994. 24.95 (*0-941967-14-X*) Old Fort Niagara Assn.

Poudel, Madan R. Tribuhaven University & Its educational Activities. 210p. 1989. pap. 18.00 (*0-317-04776-0*) Am-Nepal Ed.

Poudyal, Madhab. Aspects of Public Administration in Nepal. 1986. 24.00 (*0-8364-1800-X*, Pub. by Somaiya) S Asia.

Poudyal, Madhab P. Administrative Reform in Nepal. 1989. 42.50 (*81-85135-41-X*, Pub. by Natl Bk Org II) S Asia.

Pouget, Emile. Sabotage. (Illus.). 120p. 1991. reprint ed. lib. bdg. 22.95 (*0-88286-184-0*); reprint ed. pap. 9.95 (*0-88286-183-2*) C H Kerr.

***Pouget, Jean-Henri-Prosper & Prosper-Pouget, Jean-Henri.** Five Hundred Fifty Authentic Rococo Designs & Motifs for Artists & Craftspeople. LC 94-25929. (Pictorial Archive Ser.). Orig. Title: Traites des Pierres Precieuses et de la Maniere de le Employer en Parure. 1994. write for info. (*0-486-28193-0*) Dover.

Pough, F. Harvey, et al. Vertebrate Life. 3rd ed. 962p. (C). 1989. text ed. write for info. (*0-02-396360-3*) Macmillan.

— Vertebrate Life. 4th ed. LC 95-14458. 1995. text ed. 64.00 (*0-02-396370-0*) P-H.

Pough, Frederick H. A Field Guide to Rocks & Minerals. (Peterson Field Guide Ser.). (Illus.). 336p. 1976. pap. 15.95 (*0-395-24049-2*) HM.

— A Field Guide to Rocks & Minerals. 4th ed. (Peterson Field Guide Ser.). (Illus.). 336p. 1976. 21.95 (*0-395-24047-6*) HM.

— Peterson First Guide to Rocks & Minerals. (Peterson Field Guide Ser.). (Illus.). 128p. 1991. pap. 4.95 (*0-395-56275-9*) HM.

***Pough, Frederick H. & Peterson, Roger T.** A Field Guide to Rocks & Minerals. 5th ed. Peterson, Roger T., ed. LC 94-49005. (Peterson Field Guides Ser.: Vol. 7). (Illus.). 480p. 1995. 26.95 (*0-395-72778-2*); pap. 16.95 (*0-395-72777-4*) HM.

Pough, J. C., jt. auth. see Buchanan, Keith.

***Pougin, Arthur.** Dictionnaire Historique et Pittoresque du Theatre et des Art. 1985. write for info. (*0-7859-7980-8*, 2-7307-0280-6) Fr & Eur.

— The Life & Music of Pierre Rode: Containing an Account of Rode, French Violinist. (Illus.). 81p. 1994. 25.00 (*0-9641631-0-1*) Lyre of Orpheus.

Pougin, Arthur, ed. see Rameau, Jean-Philippe.

Pougin, Artur. Les Vrais Createurs De l'Opera Francais: Perrin et Cambert. LC 80-2296. reprint ed. 33.50 (*0-404-18862-1*) AMS Pr.

Pouilliard, James, jt. ed. see Miller, David C.

Pouillon, Fernand. The Stones of the Abbey. Gillot, Edward, tr. LC 84-22440. 228p. 1985. pap. 7.95 (*0-15-685100-8*, Harvest Bks) HarBrace.

Pouillon, Jean & Maranda, Pierre, eds. Echanges & Communications, Melanges Offerts a Claude Levi-Strauss, a l'Occasion de Son 60'eme Anniversaire: 2 Vols, Set. LC 78-91207. (Studies in General Anthropology: No. 5). 1970. 284.65 (*90-279-0540-1*) Mouton.

Poujol, J. Echography in Ophthalmology. 1986. 34.00 (*0-89352-228-7*, MA228, Yr Bk Med Pubs) Mosby Yr Bk.

Poulain, D. A., jt. ed. see Vincent, J. D.

Poulain, S. J., et al. The Graces of Interior Prayer. 637p. 1970. reprint ed. spiral bd. 22.00 (*0-7873-0674-6*) Mokelumne.

Poulakos, John. Sophistical Rhetoric in Classical Greece. (Studies in Rhetoric-Communication). 1994. write for info. (*0-87249-899-9*) U of SC Pr.

Poulakos, Takis. Rethinking the History of Rhetoric: Multidisciplinary Essays on the Rhetorical Tradition. (Polemics Ser.). 292p. (C). 1993. pap. text ed. 24.50 (*0-8133-1801-7*) Westview.

Poulakos, Takis, ed. Rethinking the History of Rhetoric: Multidisciplinary Essays on the Rhetorical Tradition. LC 93-8535. (Polemics Ser.). 292p. 1993. text ed. 61.00 (*0-8133-1800-9*) Westview.

Poulantzas, Nicos. Fascism & Dictatorship: The Third International & the Problem of Fascism. White, Judith, tr. 366p. 1979. pap. text ed. 16.95 (*0-86091-716-9*, Pub. by Verso UK) Routledge Chapman & Hall.

— Political Power & Social Classes. O'Hagan, Timothy, tr. 368p. 1987. pap. text ed. 16.95 (*0-86091-705-3*, Pub. by Verso UK) Routledge Chapman & Hall.

Poulard, Othello W. The Expanding Role of Community-Based Organizations: Implications for Vocational Education. 13p. 1983. 2.25 (*0-318-22102-0*, OC90) Ctr Educ Trng Employ.

Poularikas & Seely. Elements of Signals & Systems. 512p. (C). 1988. text ed. 72.95 (*0-534-91440-3*) PWS Pubs.

***Poularikas, Alexander D., ed.** The Transforms & Applications Handbook. LC 95-2513. (Electrical Engineering Handbook Ser.). 1,288p. 1995. 89.95 (*0-8493-8342-0*, 8342) CRC Pr.

Poularikas, Alexander D. & Seely, Samuel. Signals & Systems. 2nd ed. LC 93-48738. 1038p. 1994. reprint ed. 99.50 (*0-89464-875-6*) Krieger.

Poulenc, Ceser. Jean Laffite Gentleman Pirate. (Illus.). 50p. (Orig.). 1987. pap. 4.95 (*0-944939-00-7*) Privateer Pr.

Poulenc, Francis. Album of Six Pieces. Date not set. pap. 13.95 (*0-685-68971-9*, Chester Music) Music Sales.

— Sonata for Recorder Quartet: For Recorder Quartet. (Contemporary Consort Ser.: No. 11). i, 40p. 1990. 12.00 (*1-56571-013-4*) PRB Prods.

***Pouler.** BPR Machine Trades - IG. 32p. 1995. teacher ed 14.00 (*0-8273-6652-3*) Delmar.

***Pouler, Wilfred B.** Blueprint for Reading the Machine Trades. 2nd ed. LC 94-25405. (Illus.). 416p. 1995. 24.95 (*0-8273-6651-5*) Delmar.

Poulet, Denise, jt. auth. see Carton, Fernand.

Poulet, Georges. Exploding Poetry: Baudelaire-Rimbaud. Meltzer, Francoise, tr. LC 83-18062. 160p. 1984. 16.95 (*0-226-67650-1*) U Ch Pr.

— The Metamorphoses of the Circle. Dawson, Carley & Coleman, Elliott, trs. LC 66-24406. 431p. reprint ed. pap. 122.90 (*0-317-20606-0*, 2024147) Bks Demand.

— Proustian Space. Coleman, Elliott, tr. LC 76-47390. 120p. reprint ed. pap. 34.20 (*0-317-41757-6*, 2025864) Bks Demand.

— Studies in Human Time. Coleman, Elliot, tr. LC 78-13572. 363p. 1979. reprint ed. text ed. 65.00 (*0-8371-9348-6*, POSH, Greenwood Pr) Greenwood.

Poulet, H. & Mathieu, J. P. Spectres De Vibration et Symetrie des Cristaux. 452p. (FRE.). 1970. text ed. 260.00 (*0-677-50180-3*) Gordon & Breach.

— Vibration Spectra & Symmetry of Crystals. 586p. 1976. text ed. 342.00 (*0-677-30180-4*) Gordon & Breach.

Poulet, Virginia. Azulin Visita a Mexico (Blue Bug Visits Mexico) LC 89-25420. (Blue Bug Bks.). (Illus.). 32p. (SPA.). (J). (ps-3). 1990. lib. bdg. 11.85 (*0-516-33429-8*); pap. 3.95 (*0-516-53429-7*) Childrens.

— Blue Bug Goes to School. LC 84-23161. (Blue Bug Bks.). (Illus.). 32p. (J). (ps-3). 1985. lib. bdg. 11.85 (*0-516-03416-2*); pap. 3.95 (*0-516-43416-0*) Childrens.

— Blue Bug Goes to the Library. LC 79-15219. (Blue Bug Bks.). (Illus.). 32p. (J). (ps-3). 1979. lib. bdg. 11.85 (*0-516-03430-8*) Childrens.

— Blue Bug Visits Mexico. LC 89-25420. (Blue Bug Bks.). (Illus.). 32p. (J). (ps-2). 1990. lib. bdg. 11.85 (*0-516-03429-4*); pap. 3.95 (*0-516-43429-2*) Childrens.

— Blue Bug's Beach Party. LC 74-31224. (Blue Bug Bks.). (Illus.). 32p. (J). (gr. k-3). 1975. lib. bdg. 11.85 (*0-516-03423-5*) Childrens.

— Blue Bug's Book of Colors. LC 80-23229. (Blue Bug Bks.). (Illus.). 32p. (J). (ps-3). 1981. lib. bdg. 11.85 (*0-516-03442-1*); pap. 3.95 (*0-516-43442-X*) Childrens.

— Blue Bug's Christmas. LC 87-15793. (Blue Bug Bks.). (Illus.). 32p. (J). (ps-3). 1987. lib. bdg. 11.85 (*0-516-03483-9*) Childrens.

— Blue Bug's Safety Book. LC 72-8348. (Blue Bug Bks.). (Illus.). 32p. (J). (gr. k-3). 1973. lib. bdg. 11.85 (*0-516-03419-7*) Childrens.

— El Libro de Colores de Azulin: Blue Bug's Book of Colors. (Spanish Blue Bug Bks.). 32p. (J). (ps-3). 1989. lib. bdg. 11.85 (*0-516-33442-5*); pap. 3.95 (*0-516-53442-4*) Childrens.

— El Libro de Seguridad de Azulin: Blue Bug's Safety Book. LC 72-8348. (Blue Bug Bks.). (Illus.). 32p. (SPA.). (J). (ps-3). 1992. lib. bdg. 11.85 (*0-516-33419-0*); pap. 3.95 (*0-516-53419-X*) Childrens.

— El Tesoro de Azulin (Blue Bug's Treasure) LC 75-40352. (Blue Bug Bks.). (Illus.). 32p. (SPA.). (J). (ps-2). 1988. pap. 3.95 (*0-516-53424-6*) Childrens.

Poulett, G. J., jt. auth. see Scrope, George J.

***Poulette, Jim.** Into the Adirondacks. LC 94-45453. 1994. pap. 10.00 (*0-925168-35-1*) North Country.

Pouletti, J. Dictionnaire Pratique de Droit Medicale. 424p. (FRE.). 1982. 110.00 (*0-8288-4421-6*, M9773) Fr & Eur.

Pouliezos, A. D. & Stavrakakis, G. S. Real Time Fault Monitoring of Industrial Processes. LC 94-2137. (International Series on Microprocessor-Based & Intelligent Systems Engineering: Vol. 12). 576p. (C). 1994. lib. bdg. 225.00 (*0-7923-2737-3*) Kluwer Ac.

Poulik, M. D., ed. Beta Two-Microglobulin: Its Significance in Clinical Medicine. (Journal: Vox Sanguinis: Vol. 38, No. 6). (Illus.). 1980. pap. 26.50 (*3-8055-1560-X*) S Karger.

Poulikakos, Dimos. Conduction Heat Transfer. LC 93-1504. 1993. text ed. 77.00 (*0-13-175845-4*) P-H.

Poulin, tr. see Hebert, Anne.

Poulin, A., Jr. Cave Dwellers. (Poetry Ser.). 160p. (C). 1991. 18.95 (*1-55597-139-3*) Graywolf.

— Contemporary American Poetry. 5th ed. (C). 1991. write for info. (*0-395-43231-6*) HM Soft Schl Col Div.

— A Momentary Order. LC 87-80009. 160p. (Orig.). 1987. pap. 9.00 (*0-915308-92-4*) Graywolf.

Poulin, A., Jr., tr. see Hebert, Anne.

Poulin, A., Jr., ed. see Logan, John.

Poulin, A., Jr., jt. auth. see Rilke, Rainer M.

Poulin, A., Jr., tr. see Rilke, Rainer Maria.

Poulin, Bernard. Colored Pencil Drawing Techniques Workbook: Basic Skills. 48p. 1989. pap. 10.95 (*0-89134-280-X*, 30117) North Light Bks.

— Colored Pencil Drawing Techniques Workbook: Creative Illustration. 48p. 1989. pap. 10.95 (*0-89134-283-4*, 30120) North Light Bks.

— The Complete Colored Pencil Book. 185p. 1992. 27.99 (*0-89134-418-7*, 30363) North Light Bks.

Poulin, J. D. Predators of the Night. 1993. 17.95 (*0-533-10556-0*) Vantage.

An Asterisk (*) at the beginning of an entry indicates that the title is appearing in BIP for the first time.

Poulin, Jacques. Spring Tides. Fischman, Sheila, tr. 166p. (Orig.). 1986. reprint ed. pap. 9.95 (*0-88784-149-X*, Pub. by Hse of Anansi Pr CN) Genl Dist Srvs.

Poulin, James E. Hysteria & Other Cases: A Maine Doctor Looks Back. 88p. 1993. pap. 7.95 (*0-9635457-0-1*) Mtn Greenery.

Poulin, Joseph R. Pauline in Catalepsy & Psycho Therapeutics. 78p. 1973. reprint ed. spiral bd. 5.50 (*0-7873-1263-0*) Mokelumne.

Poulin, Mary. New Strategies for Innovations in Medical Information Systems. 50p. 1984. 7.50 (*0-318-19205-5*, R-61) Inst Future.

Poulin, Pamela L., tr. see Bach, Johann S.

Poulin, Pamela L., tr. see Niedt, Friederich E.

Poulin, Stephane. As-Tu Vu Josephine? LC 86-51044. (Illus.). 24p. (FRE.). (J). (gr. k-4). 1988. 12.95 (*0-88776-188-7*); pap. 6.95 (*0-88776-224-7*) Tundra Bks.

— Benjamin & the Pillow Saga. (Illus.). (J). 1990. 14.95 (*1-55037-069-3*, Pub. by Annick CN); pap. 5.95 (*1-55037-068-5*, Pub. by Annick CN) Firefly Bks Ltd.

— Can You Catch Josephine? LC 87-50374. (Illus.). 24p. (J). (gr. k-4). 1988. 12.95 (*0-88776-198-4*); pap. 6.95 (*0-88776-214-X*) Tundra Bks.

— Could You Stop Josephine? LC 88-50260. (Josephine Ser.). (Illus.). 24p. (J). (ps-3). 1988. 12.95 (*0-88776-216-6*); pap. 6.95 (*0-88776-227-1*) Tundra Bks.

— Have You Seen Josephine? LC 86-51043. (Illus.). 24p. (J). (gr. k-4). 1988. 12.95 (*0-88776-180-1*); pap. 6.95 (*0-88776-215-8*) Tundra Bks.

— My Mother's Love. (Illus.). 32p. (J). (ps-1). 1990. 15.95 (*1-55037-149-5*, Pub. by Annick CN); pap. 5.95 (*1-55037-148-7*, Pub. by Annick CN) Firefly Bks Ltd.

— Peux-tu Attraper Josephine? LC 87-50375. (Illus.). 24p. (Orig.). (FRE.). (J). (gr. k-4). 1988. 12.95 (*0-88776-199-2*); pap. 6.95 (*0-88776-225-5*) Tundra Bks.

— Pourrais-Tu Arreter Josephine? LC 88-50261. (Illus.). 24p. (FRE.). (J). (ps-3). 1989. 12.95 (*0-88776-217-4*); pap. 6.95 (*0-88776-228-X*) Tundra Bks.

— Travels for Two: Stories & Lies from My Childhood. (Illus.). 32p. (J). (ps-2). 1991. lib. bdg. 15.95 (*1-55037-205-X*, Pub. by Annick CN); pap. 5.95 (*1-55037-204-1*, Pub. by Annick CN) Firefly Bks Ltd.

Poulin, Thomas G., ed. Avoiding Contract Disputes. 151p. 1985. 19.00 (*0-87262-484-6*) Am Soc Civil Eng.

Pouliot, Julie J., jt. auth. see Pouliot, Richard A.

Pouliot, Richard A. & Pouliot, Julie J. Shipwrecks on the Virginia Coast & the Men of the United States Life Saving Service. LC 85-41004. (Illus.). 240p. 1986. 18.95 (*0-87033-352-6*, Tidewtr Pubs) Cornell Maritime.

Pouliquen, Louis Y. Risk Analysis in Project Appraisal. LC 79-120709. (World Bank Staff Occasional Papers: No. 11). 95p. (Orig.). reprint ed. pap. 27.10 (*0-7837-0342-2*, 2040661) Bks Demand.

Poullada, Leila D., jt. auth. see Poullada, Leon B.

Poullada, Leon B. & Poullada, Leila D. The Kingdom of Afghanistan & the United States: 1828-1973. LC 93-73121. 280p. (C). 1995. pap. 14.95 (*0-9637515-0-6*) Dageforde Pub.

Poullaos, Chris. Making the Australian Chartered Accountant. LC 94-2646. (New Works in Accounting History). 368p. 1994. reprint ed. 63.00 (*0-8153-1717-4*) Garland.

Poullet, Hector. Dictionnaire Creole-Francais. 480p. (CRE & FRE.). 1991. pap. write for info. (*0-7859-0505-7*, 2868770061) Fr & Eur.

***Poullet, Hector, et al.** Dictionnaire Creole Francais. 1991. write for info. (*0-7859-8164-0*, 2-86877-006-1) Fr & Eur.

Poullet, Y. & Vandenberghe, G. P., eds. Telebanking, Teleshopping & the Law. (Computer - Law Ser.: Vol. 1). 402p. 1988. pap. 104.00 (*90-6544-349-5*) Kluwer Law Tax Pubs.

Poullet, Y., jt. ed. see Vandenberghe, G. P.

Poulos. Anatomy of Criminal Justice. 1976. text ed. 34.00 (*0-88277-364-X*) Foundation Pr.

— Biography of Homicide. 1976. pap. text ed. 19.25 (*0-88277-421-2*) Foundation Pr.

— Dynamics of Criminal Corrections. 1976. pap. text ed. 16. 95 (*0-88277-422-0*) Foundation Pr.

— Pile Foundation Analysis & Design. 410p. 1990. 72.50 (*0-89464-449-1*) Krieger.

Poulos, George. A Breath of God - Portrait of a Prelate: A Biography of Archbishop Iakovos. 177p. 1984. pap. 12. 95 (*0-916586-98-7*) Holy Cross Orthodox.

— Pomfret the Golden Decade. (Illus.). xii, 320p. (Orig.). 1988. pap. 24.95 (*0-917651-50-2*) Holy Cross Orthodox.

Poulos, H. G. Marine Geotechnics. (Illus.). 448p. 1988. 155. 00 (*0-04-620024-X*) Routledge Chapman & Hall.

Poulos, Kathleen, jt. ed. see Boydston, Jo Ann.

Poulos, Nellie. Life's Story & Healings. 160p. pap. 2.00 (*0-686-29128-X*) Faith Pub Hse.

Poulos, Steve J., jt. ed. see Hirschfeld, Ronald C.

Poulsen, E. & Lawesson, J. E., eds. Dryland Degradation: Causes & Consequences. (Illus.). 134p. (Orig.). 1991. pap. 29.50 (*87-7288-346-4*, Pub. by Aarhus Univ Pr DK) Coronet Bks.

Poulsen, F., jt. ed. see Lindahl, Lars-Ake.

Poulsen, Frederik. Delphi. 38.95 (*0-405-19034-4*) Ayer.

Poulsen, Hemming, jt. auth. see Dallenbach-Hellweg, Gisela.

Poulsen, Hemming, jt. ed. see Dallenbach-Hellweg, Gisela.

Poulsen, Henrik. Conations: On Striving, Willing & Wishing & Their Relationships with Cognition, Emotions, & Motives. 151p. (Orig.). 1991. pap. 37.50 (*87-7288-358-8*, Pub. by Aarhus Univ Pr DK) Coronet Bks.

Poulsen, O. Danish-German Correspondence Dictionary: Dansk-Tysk Ordbog for Correspondenter. 415p. (DAN & GER.). 1980. 59.95 (*0-8288-0832-5*, M1273) Fr & Eur.

Poulsen, Peter. Scandinavian Revenue Stamps: Denmark. Nelson, Paul A., ed. (Illus.). 96p. (Orig.). (C). 1989. pap. text ed. 14.00 (*0-929850-00-9*) SPLOSC.

***Poulsen, Richard C.** The Body As Text: In a Perpetual Age of Non-Reason. LC 94-22607. (Revisioning Philosophy Ser.: 18). 1995. write for info. (*0-8204-2507-9*) P Lang Pubs.

— The Landscape of the Mind: Cultural Transformations of the American West. LC 92-2950. (American University Studies: American Literature: Ser. XXIV, Vol. 23). 136p. (C). 1992. text ed. 33.95 (*0-8204-1375-5*) P Lang Pubs.

— Misbegotten Muses: History & Anti-History. (American University Studies: History: Ser. IX, Vol. 32). 219p. (C). 1988. text ed. 36.50 (*0-8204-0535-3*) P Lang Pubs.

— The Mountain Man Vernacular: Its Historical Roots, Its Linguistic Nature, & Its Literary Uses. (American University Studies: English Language & Literature: Ser. IV, Vol. 22). 330p. (C). 1985. text ed. 36.00 (*0-8204-0197-8*) P Lang Pubs.

Poulsen, Thomas M. Nations & States: A Geographic Background to World Affairs. LC 94-13925. 1994. text ed. 60.00 (*0-13-678913-7*) P-H.

Poulson, Barry W. Economic Development: Private & Public Choice. Horan, ed. LC 93-27985. 700p. (C). 1994. text ed. 57.00 (*0-314-02750-5*) West Pub.

— Value Added in Manufacturing, Mining, & Agriculture in the American Economy from 1809 to 1839. LC 75-2592. (Dissertations in American Economic History Ser.). (Illus.). 1975. 20.95 (*0-405-07214-7*) Ayer.

Poulson, Clair. Samuel: Moroni's Young Warrior. LC 92-70859. 1993. pap. 8.95 (*1-55503-553-1*, 29004799) Covenant Comms.

— Samuel Gadianton's Foe. LC 94-10385. 1994. pap. 9.95 (*1-55503-658-9*, 01111574) Covenant Comms.

Poulson, Lynn H. Uncommon Common Sense: A Guide for Engaged & Married Couples. LC 92-46167. (Illus.). 336p. 1993. pap. 15.95 (*0-935834-98-2*) Rainbow Books.

Poulson, Thomas L. & Wells, Bethany J., eds. Cave Research Foundation Annual Report, 1979. (Illus.). 74p. (Orig.). 1981. pap. 5.00 (*0-939748-14-2*) Cave Bks MO.

***Poulson, Twila R.** Pollywogs & Penny Candy. 260p. 1996. pap. 8.95 (*0-7610-0511-0*) NW Pub.

***Poulsson, Emilie.** Baby's Breakfast. LC 95-12785. (Lift-the-Flaps Bks.). (Illus.). (J). 1996. write for info. (*0-8050-3868-X*) H Holt & Co.

— Finger Plays for Nursery & Kindergarten. LC 74-165397. (Illus.). (J). (ps-00). 1971. reprint ed. pap. 2.25 (*0-486-22588-7*) Dover.

Poulter, Christine. Playing the Game. LC 90-53168. (Illus.). 150p. (Orig.). 1991. pap. 16.00 (*0-88734-611-1*) Players Pr.

Poulter, G. C. Corbould Genealogy, in England. 165p. 1994. reprint ed. lib. bdg. 35.00 (*0-8328-4143-9*); reprint ed. pap. 25.00 (*0-8328-4144-7*) Higginson Bk Co.

Poulter, J. D. Early History of Electricity Supply: The Story of the Electric Light in Victorian Leeds. Bowers, B., ed. (IEE History of Technology Ser.). 222p. 1986. boxed 79. 00 (*0-86341-060-X*, HT005) Inst Elect Eng.

***Poulter, Neil, et al, eds.** Cardiovascular Disease: Risk Factors & Intervention. 1993. 99.00 (*1-870905-54-7*) Scovill Paterson.

Poulter, Ron, jt. auth. see Fletcher, Ian.

Poulter, Ron, jt. ed. see Fletcher, Ian.

Poulter, Virgil, ed. see Hall, William C.

Poulter, Virgil L. An Introduction to Old Spanish: A Guide to the Study of the History of Spanish with Selected Readings. (American University Studies: Romance Languages & Literature: Ser. II, Vol. 130). 190p. (C). 1990. text ed. 41.80 (*0-8204-1170-1*) P Lang Pubs.

Poultney, David. Dictionary of Western Church Music. LC 91-12325. (Illus.). 272p. 1991. 45.00 (*0-8389-0569-2*) ALA.

— Studying Music History: Learning, Reasoning & Writing about Music History & Literature. 256p. 1983. pap. text ed. write for info. (*0-13-858860-0*) P-H.

— Studying Music History: Learning, Reasoning & Writing about Music History & Literature. 2nd ed. LC 95-13540. 1995. pap. text ed. write for info. (*0-13-190224-5*) P-H.

Poultney, James W., ed. see Mittenthal, Suzanne M.

Poulton, Adrian S. Microcomputer Speech Synthesis & Recognition. (Illus.). 194p. 1983. 15.95 (*0-905104-39-0*, Pub. by Sigma Pr UK) Bk Clearing Hse.

Poulton, Diana. John Dowland. 2nd ed. (Illus.). 550p. 1982. pap. 15.00 (*0-520-04649-8*) U CA Pr.

Poulton, E. C. Bias in Quantifying Judgments. 328p. 1989. 69.95 (*0-86377-105-X*) L Erlbaum Assocs.

— Fallacies in Dealing with Probabilities. LC 93-26636. (Illus.). 445p. (C). 1994. 59.95 (*0-521-44368-7*) Cambridge U Pr.

Poulton, Gail, ed. see Pfeifer, Diane.

Poulton, Helen. Index to History of Nevada, 1881: Thompson & West. (Illus.). 1981. 10.00 (*0-913814-43-1*) Nevada Pubns.

Poulton, Helen J. & Howland, Marguerite S. The Historian's Handbook: A Descriptive Guide to Reference Works. LC 71-165774. 300p. 1972. pap. 19.95 (*0-8061-1009-0*) U of Okla Pr.

Poulton, Hugh. The Balkans: Minorities & States in Conflict. 2nd ed. 250p. 1993. 49.95 (*1-873194-45-5*, Pub. by Minority Rts Pubns UK); pap. 19.95 (*1-873194-40-4*, Pub. by Minority Rts Pubns UK) Paul & Co Pubs.

— Who Are the Macedonians? LC 94-10136. 1994. 29.95 (*0-253-34598-7*) Ind U Pr.

Poulton, J. E., et al, eds. Plant Nitrogen Metabolism. (Recent Advances in Phytochemistry Ser.: Vol. 23). (Illus.). 492p. 1989. 110.00 (*0-306-43322-2*, Plenum Insight) Plenum.

Poulton, Jane W., ed. A Better Legend: From the World War II Letters of Jack & Jane Poulton. 350p. (C). 1993. text ed. 29.95 (*0-8139-1425-6*) U Pr of Va.

Poulton, M. L., ed. Alternative Engines for Road Vehicles. LC 94-70408. 192p. 1994. text ed. 89.00 (*1-56252-224-8*) Computational Mech MA.

— Alternative Fuels for Road Vehicles. LC 94-70407. 232p. 1994. text ed. 89.00 (*1-56252-225-6*) Computational Mech MA.

Poulton, Michael. Augustus & the Ancient Romans. LC 92-5824. (Life in the Time of Ser.). (Illus.). 63p. (J). (gr. 6-7). 1992. lib. bdg. 24.26 (*0-8114-3350-1*) Raintree Steck-V.

— Life in the Time of Pericles & the Ancient Greeks. LC 92-5817. (Life in the Time of Ser.). (Illus.). 63p. (J). (gr. 6-7). 1992. lib. bdg. 24.26 (*0-8114-3352-8*) Raintree Steck-V.

Poulton, Michael S., et al, eds. The Constitution of the Socialist Federal Republic of Yugoslavia. LC 76-13392. (Constitutions of the World Ser.: Vol. 1). 1976. 30.00 (*0-89304-020-7*, CCC104); pap. 15.00 (*0-89304-006-1*) Cross-Cultrl NY.

Poulton, Pauline, ed. see Wangchen, Geshe N.

Poulton, Simon. Packet Switching & X.25 Networks. 272p. (C). 1989. pap. text ed. 210.00 (*0-685-40849-3*, Pub. by Pitman Pubng UK) St Mut.

Pouncey, Peter R. The Necessities of War: A Study of Thucydides' Pessimism. LC 80-16887. 213p. reprint ed. pap. 60.80 (*0-8357-8965-9*, 2033595) Bks Demand.

Pouncy, Carolyn J., ed. & tr. The Domostroi: Rules for Russian Households in the Time of Ivan the Terrible. (Illus.). 280p. 1994. 29.95 (*0-8014-2410-0*) Cornell U Pr.

Pound & Michaux. Signs in Action. LC 87-42539. 48p. 1987. pap. 4.00 (*0-87376-057-3*) Red Dust.

Pound, A. Johnson of the Mohawks. 1977. lib. bdg. 59.95 (*0-8490-2107-3*) Gordon Pr.

***Pound, Andrea.** Newpin - a Befriending & Therapeutic Network for Carers of Young Children. 54p. 1994. pap. 8.00 (*0-11-321661-0*, HM16610, Pub. by HMSO UK) UNIPUB.

Pound, Arthur. The Golden Earth: The Story of Manhattan's Landed Wealth. LC 75-1865. (Leisure Class in America Ser.). (Illus.). 1975. reprint ed. 25.95 (*0-405-06931-6*) Ayer.

— Johnson of the Mohawks. 568p. 1993. reprint ed. lib. bdg. 99.00 (*0-7812-5195-8*) Rprt Serv.

— Native Stock. LC 70-90674. (Essay Index Reprint Ser.). 1977. 23.95 (*0-8369-1373-6*) Ayer.

— Penns of Pennsylvania & England. 1993. reprint ed. lib. bdg. 89.00 (*0-7812-5819-7*) Rprt Serv.

Pound, Arthur & Day, Richard E. Johnson of the Mohawks. LC 75-164621. (Select Bibliographies Reprint Ser.). 1977. reprint ed. 48.95 (*0-8369-5904-3*) Ayer.

Pound, Arthur, ed. see Barron, Clarence W.

Pound, Daniel. Political Economy & Ideology in the Managerial - Technological Society. 144p. 1990. per. 22. 95 (*0-8403-5697-8*) Kendall-Hunt.

Pound, E. Quarterly Review of Literature: The 1940s, Special Issue, Vol. V, No. 2. 1940. pap. 10.00 (*0-317-05287-X*) Quarterly Rev.

Pound, Ezra. ABC of Reading. LC 60-30304. 1960. pap. 9.95 (*0-8112-0151-1*, NDP89) New Directions.

— America, Roosevelt & the Causes of the Present War. 1983. lib. bdg. 250.00 (*0-87700-462-5*) Revisionist Pr.

— Antheil & the Treatise on Harmony. 2nd ed. LC 68-27463. (Music Ser.). (gr. 9 up). 1968. reprint ed. lib. bdg. 25.00 (*0-306-70981-3*) Da Capo.

— Cantos of Ezra Pound: No. 1-117. LC 70-117217. 1970. 31.95 (*0-8112-0350-6*) New Directions.

— The Cantos (121-150) Andre, Michael, ed. LeWitt, Sol, tr. 120p. Date not set. 69.95 (*0-934450-56-0*) Unmuzzled Ox.

— Classic Noh Theatre of Japan. LC 59-9488. Orig. Title: Noh, or Accomplishment, a Study of the Classical Stage of Japan. (C). 1959. pap. 10.95 (*0-8112-0152-X*, NDP79) New Directions.

— The Collected Early Poems of Ezra Pound. King, Michael et al, eds. LC 76-7086. (Illus.). 352p. 1982. reprint ed. pap. 12.95 (*0-8112-0843-5*, NDP540) New Directions.

— Diptych Rome-London. (Bibelot Ser.). 64p. 1994. pap. 5.00 (*0-8112-1268-8*, NDP783) New Directions.

— A Draft of XXX Cantos. LC 74-6379. (Studies in Pound: No. 103). 1974. lib. bdg. 75.00 (*0-8383-1997-1*) M S G Haskell Hse.

— A Draft of XXX Cantos. LC 89-13432. 160p. 1990. reprint ed. pap. 9.95 (*0-8112-1128-2*, NDP690) New Directions.

— Early Poems. (Thirft Editions Ser.). 1995. pap. 1.00 (*0-486-28745-9*) Dover.

— Exultations. LC 72-10016. (Studies in Poetry: No. 38). 1973. reprint ed. lib. bdg. 75.00 (*0-8383-1683-2*) M S G Haskell Hse.

— Ezra Pound & the Visual Arts. Zinnes, Harriet, ed. LC 80-36720. 352p. 1980. 25.95 (*0-8112-0772-2*) New Directions.

— Gaudier-Brzeska: A Memoir. LC 78-107490. 1970. pap. 7.95 (*0-8112-0527-4*, NDP372) New Directions.

— Gold & Work. 1983. lib. bdg. 250.00 (*0-87700-461-7*) Revisionist Pr.

— Guide to Kulchur. LC 52-12142. 1968. reprint ed. pap. 12.95 (*0-8112-0156-2*, NDP257) New Directions.

— How to Read. 1972. 200.00 (*0-87968-021-0*) Gordon Pr.

— How to Read. LC 79-169105. (American Literature Ser.: No. 49). 1971. lib. bdg. 75.00 (*0-8383-1315-9*) M S G Haskell Hse.

— An Introduction to the Economic Nature of the United States. 1983. lib. bdg. 79.95 (*0-87700-460-9*) Revisionist Pr.

— Letters of Ezra Pound. LC 74-11145. (Studies in Pound: No. 103). 1974. lib. bdg. 75.00 (*0-8383-1991-2*) M S G Haskell Hse.

— The Letters of Ezra Pound to Alice Corbin Henderson. Nadel, Ira B., ed. LC 93-9162. (Illus.). 296p. (C). 1993. 34.95 (*0-292-71134-4*) U of Tex Pr.

— Letters to Ibbotson. LC 78-55724. (Ezra Pound Scholarship Ser.). 145p. 1979. 15.00 (*0-915032-10-4*) Natl Poet Foun.

— Letters to John Theobald. Pearce, Donald & Schneidau, Herbert, eds. (Literary Ser.). (Illus.). 170p. 1984. 30.00 (*0-933806-02-7*) Black Swan CT.

— Letters to Tom Carter. Martz, Louis, ed. (Literary Ser.). (Illus.). 200p. 1997. 35.00 (*0-933806-25-6*) Black Swan CT.

— Literary Essays. Eliot, T. S., ed. LC 54-7905. 1968. reprint ed. pap. 13.95 (*0-8112-0157-0*, NDP250) New Directions.

— Lustra. LC 72-11762. (Studies in Poetry: No. 38). 1973. reprint ed. lib. bdg. 75.00 (*0-8383-1688-3*) M S G Haskell Hse.

— Make It New: Essays. 1988. reprint ed. lib. bdg. 79.00 (*0-7812-0195-0*) Rprt Serv.

— Make It New: Essays. LC 71-145243. 1971. reprint ed. 59.00 (*0-403-01158-2*) Scholarly.

— Pavannes & Divagations. LC 58-9510. 256p. 1975. reprint ed. pap. 9.95 (*0-8112-0575-4*, NDP397) New Directions.

— Personae: The Shorter Poems of Ezra Pound. LC 89-14036. 304p. 1990. reprint ed. 23.95 (*0-8112-1120-7*); reprint ed. pap. 14.95 (*0-8112-1138-X*, NDP697) New Directions.

— Plays Modelled on the Noh (1916) Gallup, Donald C., ed. LC 87-124514. (Illus.). 38p. 1987. pap. 17.00 (*0-918160-02-2*) Friends Univ Toledo.

— Pound - Joyce: Letters & Essays. LC 66-27616. (Correspondence of Ezra Pound Ser.). 1970. pap. 10.95 (*0-8112-0159-7*, NDP296) New Directions.

— A Quinzaine for This Yule. 1973. 200.00 (*0-87968-087-3*) Gordon Pr.

— A Quinzaine for This Yule. 32p. 1984. 10.00 (*0-8139-1045-5*) U Pr of Va.

— Selected Cantos. LC 75-11446. 1970. pap. text ed. 7.95 (*0-8112-0160-0*, NDP304) New Directions.

— Selected Letters of Ezra Pound, 1907-1941. Paige, D. D., ed. LC 71-145933. 1971. reprint ed. pap. 6.95 (*0-8112-0161-9*, NDP317) New Directions.

— Selected Poems. LC 57-8603. 1957. pap. 8.95 (*0-8112-0162-7*, NDP66) New Directions.

— Selected Prose Nineteen Nine to Nineteen Sixty-Five. Cookson, William, ed. LC 72-93978. 480p. 1975. pap. 12.95 (*0-8112-0574-6*, NDP396) New Directions.

— Social Credit: An Impact. 1983. lib. bdg. 79.95 (*0-87700-457-9*) Revisionist Pr.

— Spirit of Romance. LC 53-5860. 1968. reprint ed. pap. 12. 95 (*0-8112-0163-5*, NDP266) New Directions.

— Translations. rev. ed. LC 53-11965. 1953. pap. 12.95 (*0-8112-0164-3*, NDP145) New Directions.

— A Visiting Card: Ancient & Modern History of Script & Money. 1983. lib. bdg. 79.95 (*0-87700-458-7*) Revisionist Pr.

— A Walking Tour in Southern France: Ezra Pound among the Troubadours. LC 92-19890. (Illus.). 160p. 1992. 22. 95 (*0-8112-1223-8*) New Directions.

— What Is Money for? 1983. lib. bdg. 79.95 (*0-87700-459-5*) Revisionist Pr.

— What Is Money For? A Sane Man's Guide to Economics. 1982. lib. bdg. 59.95 (*0-87700-408-0*) Revisionist Pr.

Pound, Ezra, tr. Confucius: The Great Digest, the Unwobbling Pivot, the Analects. LC 74-87911. 1969. pap. 11.95 (*0-8112-0154-6*, NDP285) New Directions.

Pound, Ezra & Anderson, Margaret. Pound the Little Review: The Letters of Ezra Pound to Margaret Anderson. Scott, Thomas L. et al, eds. LC 88-3410. (Correspondence of Ezra Pound Ser.: Vol. 6). 384p. 1988. 37.50 (*0-8112-1059-6*) New Directions.

Pound, Ezra & Ford, Ford Madox. Pound-Ford: The Story of a Literary Friendship. Seyersted, Brita L., ed. LC 82-2255. (Correspondence of Ezra Pound Ser.). 384p. (C). 1982. 22.95 (*0-8112-0833-8*) New Directions.

Pound, Ezra & Lewis, Wyndham. Pound-Lewis: The Letters of Ezra Pound & Wyndham Lewis. Materer, Timothy, ed. LC 85-3007. (Correspondence of Ezra Pound Ser.). 384p. 1985. 37.50 (*0-8112-0932-6*) New Directions.

Pound, Ezra & Shakespear, Dorothy. Ezra Pound & Dorothy Shakespear: Their Letters 1909-1914. Pound, Omar & Litz, A. Walton, eds. LC 84-11545. (Correspondence of Ezra Pound Ser.). (Illus.). 288p. 1984. 40.00 (*0-8112-0900-8*) New Directions.

Pound, Ezra & Spann, Marcella, eds. Confucius to Cummings: An Anthology of Poetry. LC 62-17274. (C). 1964. 14.95 (*0-8112-0352-2*); pap. 12.95 (*0-8112-0155-4*, NDP126) New Directions.

***Pound, Ezra & Williams, William C.** Selected Correspondence of Ezra Pound & William Carlos Williams. Witemeyer, Hugh, ed. 480p. 1995. 39.95 (*0-8112-1301-3*) New Directions.

Pound, Ezra & Zukofsky, Louis. Pound - Zukofsky. LC 86-19181. (Correspondence of Ezra Pound Ser.). 384p. 1987. 38.50 (*0-8112-1013-8*) New Directions.

Pound, Ezra, tr. see Cavalcanti, Guido.

Pound, Ezra, tr. see Morand, Paul.

Pound, Ezra, tr. see Sophokles.

Pound, Ezra, et al. What Thou Lovest Well Remains: 100 Years of Ezra Pound. limited ed. Ardinger, Richard, ed. 1986. pap. 9.95 (*0-931659-01-9*) Limberlost Pr.

Pound, Ezra L. Confucion Analects. 136p. 1980. 30.00 (*0-7206-1850-9*, Pub. by P Owen Ltd UK) Dufour.

— Ezra Pound Translations. enl. ed. LC 78-13153. 1978. reprint ed. text ed. 69.50 (*0-313-21169-8*, POTO, Greenwood Pr) Greenwood.

— Instigations. LC 67-23261. (Essay Index Reprint Ser.). 1977. 23.95 (*0-8369-0795-7*) Ayer.

— Literary Essays. LC 78-131133. 464p. 1978. reprint ed. text ed. 75.00 (*0-313-21167-1*, POLE, Greenwood Pr) Greenwood.

— Polite Essays. LC 67-22111. (Essay Index Reprint Ser.). 1977. 23.95 (*0-8369-0796-5*) Ayer.

Pound, Ezra L., tr. Shih-Ching: The Classic Anthology Defined by Confucius. 335p. 1976. pap. text ed. 7.95 (*0-674-13397-8*) HUP.

P Q

Pound, Ezra L., jt. auth. see Fenollosa, Ernest F.

Pound, G., jt. auth. see Hirth, J.

Pound House Staff. Dylife. (C). 1985. text ed. 25.00 (*0-906885-04-3*, Pub. by Pound Hse UK) St Mut.

— Frongoch Lead & Zinc Mine. (C). 1985. text ed. 35.00 (*0-685-50528-6*, Pub. by Pound Hse UK) St Mut.

— The Hereford & Gloucester Canal. 80p. (C). 1985. text ed. 39.00 (*0-906874-05-X*, Pub. by Pound Hse UK) St Mut.

— The Mines of Newent & Ross. (C). 1985. text ed. 40.00 (*0-906885-06-X*, Pub. by Pound Hse UK) St Mut.

— The Old Copper Mines of Snowdonia. 128p. (C). 1985. pap. text ed. 40.00 (*0-906885-03-5*, Pub. by Pound Hse UK) St Mut.

— The Old Industries of Dean. (C). 1985. pap. text ed. 45. 00 (*0-685-50527-8*, Pub. by Pound Hse UK) St Mut.

Pound, John. Are Takeover Targets Undervalued? An Empirical Examination of the Financial Characteristics of Target Companies. 39p. 1986. pap. 35.00 (*0-931035-54-6*) IRRC Inc DC.

— The Effects of Institutional Investors on Takeover Activity: A Quantitative Analysis. 21p. 1985. 35.00 (*0-931035-59-7*) IRRC Inc DC.

— The Impact of Antitakeover Charter Amendments on Contests for Corporate Control. 23p. 1985. 35.00 (*0-931035-61-9*) IRRC Inc DC.

— The Long Trick of Pennywise. (C). 1990. pap. 25.00 (*0-7223-2457-X*, Pub. by A H S Ltd UK) St Mut.

Pound, John F. The Military Survey of Fifteen Twenty-Two for Babergh Hundred. (Suffolk Records Society-Suffolk Charters Ser.: No. XXVII). 128p. 1986. 30.00 (*0-85115-438-7*) Boydell & Brewer.

Pound, L. The American Dialect Society: A Historical Sketch. Bd. with Press As an Ally in Collecting Folk Speech. (Publications of the American Dialect Society: No. 17). 44p. 1952. Set pap. 1.65 (*0-8173-0617-X*) U of Ala Pr.

Pound, Louise. American Ballads & Songs. (BCL1-PS American Literature Ser.). 266p. 1992. reprint ed. lib. bdg. 79.00 (*0-7812-6647-5*) Rprt Serv.

— Nebraska Folklore. LC 89-32799. xii, 243p. 1989. reprint ed. pap. 8.95 (*0-8032-8724-0*, Bison Books) U of Nebr Pr.

Pound, Omar. Arabic & Persian Poems in English. 124p. (Orig.). 1986. 12.95 (*0-915032-09-0*) Natl Poet Foun.

— Pissle & the Holy Grail. LC 86-62329. 64p. 1987. 12.95 (*0-913506-18-4*) Woolmer-Brotherson.

Pound, Omar, ed. Arabic & Persian Poems in English. LC 85-50527. 123p. (Orig.). 1986. boxed 22.00 (*0-89410-466-7*) Three Continents.

Pound, Omar, tr. Arabic & Persian Poems. LC 72-122106. (Orig.). 1970. 7.50 (*0-8112-0358-1*) New Directions.

Pound, Omar & Spoo, Robert, eds. Ezra Pound & Margaret Cravens: A Tragic Friendship, 1910-1912. LC 88-7156. (Illus.). 168p. 1988. lib. bdg. 29.95 (*0-8223-0862-2*) Duke.

Pound, Omar, tr. see Obeyd-i-Zakani.

Pound, Omar, ed. see Pound, Ezra & Shakespear, Dorothy.

Pound, Richard. A Book of Five Rings. LC 94-543. 1994. 27.95 (*0-316-71507-7*) Little.

Pound, Ron, jt. auth. see Pritchett, Price.

Pound, Roscoe. Administrative Law: Its Growth Procedure & Significance. x, 138p. 1981. reprint ed. lib. bdg. 18.50 (*0-8377-1009-X*) Rothman.

— Contemporary Juristic Theory. viii, 83p. 1981. reprint ed. lib. bdg. 15.00 (*0-8377-1008-1*) Rothman.

— Criminal Justice in America. LC 79-37841. (American Constitutional & Legal History Ser). 224p. 1972. reprint ed. lib. bdg. 27.50 (*0-306-70435-8*) Da Capo.

— Criminal Justice in America. LC 74-22045. (Quality Paperbacks Ser.). xiv, 226p. 1975. reprint ed. pap. 7.95 (*0-306-80007-1*) Da Capo.

— The Development of Constitutional Guarantees of Liberty. LC 75-14600. 207p. 1975. reprint ed. text ed. 38.50 (*0-8371-8225-5*, PODC, Greenwood Pr) Greenwood.

— The Future of the Common Law. 11.25 (*0-8446-1361-4*) Peter Smith.

— Interpretations of Legal History. 11.25 (*0-8446-1360-6*) Peter Smith.

— Interpretations of Legal History. LC 85-81797. (Cambridge Studies in English Legal History). 198p. 1986. reprint ed. 55.00 (*0-912004-50-9*) W W Gaunt.

— Introduction to the Philosophy of Law. rev. ed. (Storrs Lecture Ser.). (C). 1959. pap. 12.00 (*0-300-00188-6*, Y10) Yale U Pr.

— An Introduction to the Philosophy of Law. LC 94-75666. 308p. 1994. reprint ed. 65.00 (*1-56169-090-2*) W W Gaunt.

— Law & Morals. ix, 144p. 1987. reprint ed. text ed. 17.50 (*0-8377-2501-1*) Rothman.

— Masonic Jurisprudence. 120p. 1992. reprint ed. pap. 12.95 (*1-56459-048-8*) Kessinger Pub.

— Organization of Courts. LC 79-12700. (Judicial Administration Ser.). xiii, 322p. 1980. reprint ed. text ed. 35.00 (*0-313-21998-2*, POOC, Greenwood Pr) Greenwood.

Pound, Roscoe, ed. National Law Library, 6 vols., Set. LC 39-8999. 1980. reprint ed. lib. bdg. 265.00 (*0-89941-262-9*, 200730) W S Hein.

Pound, Roscoe & Clements, Frederic E. The Phytogeography of Nebraska: General Survey. rev. ed. Egerton, Frank N., 3rd, ed. LC 77-74248. (History of Ecology Ser.). (Illus.). 1978. reprint ed. lib. bdg. 39.95 (*0-405-10417-0*) Ayer.

Pound, Roscoe, ed. see Cleveland Foundation Staff.

Pound, Roscoe, et al. Federalism As a Democratic Process. LC 78-23818. reprint ed. 15.00 (*0-89201-031-2*) Zenger Pub.

Pounder. Color Atlas of the Digestive System. 1989. 75.95 (*0-8151-6789-X*, Yr Bk Med Pubs) Mosby Yr Bk.

Pounder, Chris. Managing Personal Information. 320p. 1991. write for info. (*0-434-91524-6*) Buttrwrth-Heinemann.

Pounder, Chris N. & Kosten, Freddie. Managing Data Protection. 2nd ed. 320p. 1992. 80.00 (*0-7506-0355-0*) Buttrwrth-Heinemann.

Pounder, E. Physics of Ice. LC 65-21141. 1965. 73.00 (*0-08-011148-3*, Pub. by Pergamon Repr UK) Franklin.

Pounder, Roy, ed. Recent Advances in Gastroenterology, No. 8. (Illus.). 280p. 1990. text ed. 75.00 (*0-443-04324-8*) Churchill.

— Recent Advances in Gastroenterology - Nine. (Illus.). 258p. 1993. text ed. 79.95 (*0-443-04674-3*) Churchill.

Pounders, Donnie. Celebrity Wedding Ceremonies: Complete Ceremonies & Signed Marriage Certificates from Famous People. 192p. (Orig.). 1994. pap. 19.95 (*0-9642144-9-0*) Lucky Duck.

Pounds, Bette G., jt. ed. see Baum, Laurie A.

***Pounds, Dwight R.** The American Viola Society: A History & Reference. 2nd ed. 293p. 1994. write for info. (*1-886601-00-3*) Am Viola Soc.

Pounds, F. Sims. Seventy-Five Windows. LC 78-56418. 120p. 1978. 8.00 (*0-86690-143-4*, P1377-014) Am Fed Astrologers.

Pounds, K., jt. ed. see Beer, P.

Pounds, N. J. The Culture of the English People: Iron Age to the Industrial Revolution. (Illus.). 512p. (C). 1994. 69. 95 (*0-521-45099-3*); pap. 22.95 (*0-521-46671-7*) Cambridge U Pr.

— An Historical Geography of Europe. (Illus.). 448p. (C). 1990. pap. 21.95 (*0-521-31109-8*) Cambridge U Pr.

— An Historical Geography of Europe. (Illus.). 448p. (C). 1990. 69.95 (*0-521-32217-0*) Cambridge U Pr.

Pounds, Norman J. An Economic History of Medieval Europe. 2nd ed. LC 93-27069. (C). 1995. pap. text ed. 31.50 (*0-582-21599-4*, 76669) Longman.

— Hearth & Home: A History of Material Culture. LC 87-46367. (Illus.). 450p. 1989. 57.50 (*0-253-32712-1*); pap. 17.95 (*0-253-20839-4*) Ind U Pr.

— An Historical Geography of Europe, 1500-1840. LC 78-18102. (Illus.). 1980. 89.95 (*0-521-22379-2*) Cambridge U Pr.

— The Medieval Castle in England & Wales: A Political & Social History. (Illus.). 384p. (C). 1991. 49.95 (*0-521-38349-8*) Cambridge U Pr.

— The Medieval Castle in England & Wales: A Political & Social History. (Illus.). 384p. (C). 1993. pap. 27.95 (*0-521-45828-5*) Cambridge U Pr.

Pounds, V. H. & Rant, Lilian V. Staffordshire Bull Terriers: An Owner's Companion. (Illus.). 240p. 1995. 39.95 (*1-85223-365-6*, Pub. by Crowood Pr UK) Trafalgar.

***Pounds, Walter C., Jr.** The Family History of a Lot of Pounds & Their Travels, 2 vols., Set. 681p. (Orig.). 1995. pap. text ed. 43.50 (*0-7884-0128-9*) Heritage Bk.

Pounds, Wayne. Proletarian Tales. (Illus.). 59p. (Orig.). 1987. 10.95 (*0-941720-50-0*); pap. 4.95 (*0-941720-51-9*) Slough Pr TX.

Poundstone, William. Big Secrets: The Uncensored Truth about All Sorts of Stuff You Are Never Supposed to Know. LC 85-3603. (Illus.). 256p. 1985. reprint ed. pap. 10.00 (*0-688-04830-7*, Quill) Morrow.

— Bigger Secrets: More Than One Hundred Twenty-Five Things They Prayed You'd Never Find Out. 320p. 1989. pap. 10.95 (*0-395-53008-3*) HM.

— Biggest Secrets: More Uncensored Truth about All Sorts of Stuff You Are Never Supposed to Know. LC 92-33948. 1993. 20.00 (*0-688-11529-2*) Morrow.

— Biggest Secrets: More Uncensored Truth about All Sorts of Stuff You Are Never Supposed to Know. 1994. pap. 10.00 (*0-688-13792-X*, Quill) Morrow.

— The Labyrinths of Reason: Paradox, Puzzles, & the Frailty of Knowledge. 288p. 1990. mass mkt. 9.95 (*0-385-24271-9*, Anchor NY) Doubleday.

— Prisoner's Dilemma: John Von Neumann, Game Theory, & the Puzzle of the Bomb. 1992. 22.50 (*0-385-41567-2*) Doubleday.

— Prisoner's Dilemma: John von Neumann, Game Theory, & the Puzzle of the Bomb. LC 92-29903. 1993. pap. 12. 95 (*0-385-41580-X*, Anchor NY) Doubleday.

— The Recursive Universe: Cosmic Complexity & the Limits of Scientific Knowledge. Date not set. pap. write for info. (*0-688-07290-9*, Quill) Morrow.

Pountain, C. J., jt. auth. see Batchelor, R. E.

Pountain, Christopher J. Structures & Transformations: The Romance Verb. LC 83-12287. (Illus.). 272p. 1983. 44.00 (*0-389-20436-6*, N7322) B&N Imports.

Pountain, Christopher J., jt. auth. see De Bruyne, Jacques.

Pountain, Dick. Object-Oriented Forth. 119p. (Orig.). 1987. text ed. 35.00 (*0-12-563570-2*) Acad Pr.

Pountney, David C., jt. auth. see Townend, M. Stewart.

Pountney, Ernie. For the Socialist Course. 80p. 1973. pap. 12.00 (*0-8464-1465-1*) Beekman Pubs.

Pountney, W. J. Old Bristol Potteries. 1976. reprint ed. 20. 00 (*0-85409-923-9*) Charles River Bks.

Poupard, Dennis. Twentieth-Century Literary Criticism, Vol. 26. LC 76-46132. 600p. 1987. 122.00 (*0-8103-2408-3*) Gale.

— Twentieth Century Literary Criticism, Vol. 29, Vol. 29. 600p. 1988. 122.00 (*0-8103-2411-3*) Gale.

Poupard, Dennis, ed. Twentieth-Century Literary Criticism, Vol. 27. LC 76-46132. 600p. 1988. 122.00 (*0-8103-2409-1*) Gale.

— Twentieth Century Literary Criticism, Vol. 28, Vol. 28. 600p. 1988. 122.00 (*0-8103-2410-5*) Gale.

Poupard, Dennis & Kepos, Paula, eds. Twentieth-Century Literary Criticism, Vol. 32. 1989. 122.00 (*0-8103-2414-8*) Gale.

Poupard, Dennis & Kronick, Jelena. Classical & Medieval Literary Criticism, Vol. 1. 1987. 114.00 (*0-8103-2350-8*) Gale.

Poupard, Dennis, jt. ed. see Kepos, Paula.

Poupard, J. A., et al, eds. Antimicrobial Susceptibility Testing: Critical Issues for the 90s. (Advances in Experimental Medicine & Biology Ser.: Vol. 349). (Illus.). 200p. 1994. 69.50 (*0-306-44673-1*) Plenum.

Poupard, Paul. Dictionnaire des Religions. 2nd ed. 1856p. (FRE.). 1985. 225.00 (*0-8288-9471-X*) Fr & Eur.

— Dictionnaire des Religions, 2 vols. 3rd ed. 2248p. (FRE.). 1993. 495.00 (*0-7859-7749-X*, 2130451128) Fr & Eur.

— Vatican Treasures: Two Hundred Years of Art & Culture in the Vatican & Italy. (Illus.). 304p. 1993. 55.00 (*1-55859-298-9*) Abbeville Pr.

Poupard, Paul, ed. Galileo Galilei: Toward a Resolution of 350 Years of Debate, 1633-1983. Campbell, Ian, tr. LC 86-24125. 208p. 1986. text ed. 28.00x (*0-8207-0193-9*) Duquesne.

***Poupard, Paul C.** The Church & Culture: Challenge & Confrontation: Inculturation & Evangelization. Miller, John H., tr. 160p. 1994. pap. 15.00 (*0-9626257-7-9*) CBCCU Amer.

Pouquelin, Jean-Baptiste, see Moliere, pseud..

Pouquet, J. Earth's Science in the Age of the Satellite. LC 73-94454. Orig. Title: Les Sciences de la Terre a l'Heure des Satellites. 190p. 1974. lib. bdg. 70.00 (*90-277-0437-6*) Kluwer Ac.

Pour-El, Akiva, ed. Functionality & Protein Structure. LC 78-31964. (ACS Symposium Ser.: No. 92). 1979. 32.95 (*0-8412-0478-0*) Am Chemical.

Pour-El, M. B. & Richards, J. L. Computability in Analysis & Physics. (Perspectives in Mathematical Logic Ser.). (Illus.). 220p. 1989. 69.00 (*0-387-50035-9*, 2028) Spr-Verlag.

Pour, P. M., et al, eds. Atlas of Pancreatic Exocrine Tumors: Morphology, Biology, & Diagnosis, with an International Guide for Tumor Classification. LC 94-9950. 1994. write for info. (*0-387-70129-X*) Spr-Verlag.

Pourade, Richard, ed. see Linsenmeyer, Helen.

Pourchot, Mary E. When the Land Calls. LC 91-77561. (Illus.). 272p. 1992. pap. 8.95 (*0-87341-195-1*) Krause Pubns.

Pourciau, Pam, jt. auth. see Townsend, Nancy.

Pourdeyhimi, B., ed. Vacular Grafts: Textile Structures & Their Performance, Vol. 15, No. 3. (C). 1986. pap. text ed. 70.00 (*0-900739-90-8*, Pub. by Textile Institue UK) St Mut.

Pourdum, Jack. C Programmer's Toolkit. 2nd ed. 700p. 1991. pap. 39.95 (*0-88022-788-5*) Que.

***Poure, Ken.** God's Gusto for the Family. 176p. 1994. pap. 8.95 (*0-939497-36-0*) Promise Pub.

Pourgerami, Abbas. Development & Democracy in the Third World. 210p. (C). 1991. pap. text ed. 33.50 (*0-8133-8005-7*) Westview.

Pouring, A. A., ed. see Joint Applied Mechanics, Fluids Engineering & Bioengineering Conference Staff.

Pourjavady, Nasrollah, tr. see Ghazzali, Ahmad.

Pourjavady, Nasrollah, jt. tr. see Wilson, Peter L.

Pournelle, Jerry. Birth of Fire. 256p. (Orig.). 1987. mass mkt. 4.99 (*0-671-65649-X*) Baen Bks.

— Blood Feuds. (War World Ser.: No. 4). 1993. mass mkt. 5.99 (*0-671-72150-X*) Baen Bks.

— Exiles to Glory. 224p. 1993. mass mkt. 4.99 (*0-671-72199-2*) Baen Bks.

— Falkenberg's Legion. 448p. (Orig.). 1990. mass mkt. 4.99 (*0-671-72018-X*) Baen Bks.

— High Justice. 288p. (Orig.). 1989. mass mkt. 4.99 (*0-671-69877-X*) Baen Bks.

— Imperial Star: Stars at War, Vol. I. pap. 3.95 (*0-685-18046-8*) PB.

— Jerry Pournelle Windows with an Attitude. 1993. pap. 26. 95 (*1-56686-101-2*) Brady Compu Bks.

— Jerry Pournelle's Guide to DOS & Easy Computing DOS Over Easy! 500p. 1989. pap. 21.95 (*0-13-126129-0*) P-H.

— King David's Spaceship. 384p. (Orig.). 1991. mass mkt. 4.95 (*0-671-72068-6*) Baen Bks.

— Prince of Mercenaries. 352p. (Orig.). 1989. mass mkt. 5.99 (*0-671-69811-7*) Baen Bks.

— That Buck Rogers Stuff. Claypool, Gavin, ed. (Illus.). 101p. 1977. 9.00 (*0-935892-01-X*) Extequer.

— Twenty-Twenty Vision. 1976. pap. 0.95 (*0-380-01632-X*) Avon.

— Twenty-Twenty Vision. 256p. 1980. pap. 2.25 (*0-449-24302-8*, Crest) Fawcett.

Pournelle, Jerry, creator. Blood Vengeance. 1994. mass mkt. 5.99 (*0-671-72201-8*) Baen Bks.

— CoDominium: Revolt on War World. 480p. (Orig.). 1992. mass mkt. 5.99 (*0-671-72126-7*) Baen Bks.

— Invasion. (War World Ser.: Vol. IV). (Orig.). 1994. mass mkt. 5.99 (*0-671-87616-3*) Baen Bks.

— War World III: Sauron Dominion. 368p. 1991. mass mkt. 4.95 (*0-671-72072-4*) Baen Bks.

Pournelle, Jerry, ed. Day of the Tyrant: There Will be War, No. 4. 352p. 1988. pap. 3.95 (*0-8125-0066-0*) Tor Bks.

— There Will Be War. 352p. 1990. pap. 3.95 (*0-8125-0900-5*) Tor Bks.

— There Will Be War: After Armageddon, Vol. IX. 1990. pap. 3.95 (*0-8125-4967-8*) Tor Bks.

— There Will Be War: Armageddon, Vol. VIII. 1989. pap. 3.95 (*0-8125-4965-1*) Tor Bks.

— There Will Be War: Blood & Iron, Vol. III. 384p. (Orig.). 1984. pap. 2.95 (*0-8125-4955-4*) Tor Bks.

— There Will Be War: Call to Battle, Vol. VII. 384p. 1988. pap. 3.95 (*0-8125-4963-5*) Tor Bks.

— There Will Be War: Men of War, Vol. II. 320p. (Orig.). 1990. pap. 3.95 (*0-8125-0902-1*) Tor Bks.

— War World I: The Burning Eye. 384p. (Orig.). 1988. mass mkt. 4.99 (*0-671-65420-9*) Baen Bks.

Pournelle, Jerry & Baen, Jim. Far Frontier, Vol. VII. pap. 2.95 (*0-685-18048-4*) PB.

Pournelle, Jerry & Carr, John F., eds. The Survival of Freedom. 384p. 1981. pap. 2.95 (*0-449-24435-0*) Fawcett.

Pournelle, Jerry & Stirling, S. M. The Children's Hour. 1991. mass mkt. 4.99 (*0-671-72089-9*) Baen Bks.

— Go Tell the Spartans. 352p. 1991. mass mkt. 5.99 (*0-671-72061-9*) Baen Bks.

— Prince of Sparta. 416p. (Orig.). 1993. mass mkt. 4.99 (*0-671-72158-5*) Baen Bks.

Pournelle, Jerry, jt. auth. see Niven, Larry.

Pournelle, Jerry, et al. War World II: Death's Head Rebellion. (Orig.). 1990. mass mkt. 4.99 (*0-671-72027-9*) Baen Bks.

Pournelle, Jerry, et al, eds. The Science Fiction Yearbook. 344p. 1985. 15.95 (*0-317-27055-9*, Baen Bks) PB.

Pournelle, Larry, jt. auth. see Niven, Larry.

Pourrain, Alexis, tr. see Hildebrand, Peter & Poeg, Federico.

Pourrat, Henri. French Folktales. (Fairy Tale & Folklore Library). 1994. reprint ed. pap. 17.00 (*0-679-74833-4*) Pantheon.

— Le Mauvais Garcon. (FRE.). 1979. pap. 10.95 (*0-7859-4113-4*) Fr & Eur.

***Pourroy, Janine.** The Making of Waterworld. 160p. (Orig.). 1995. pap. 15.00 (*1-57297-005-7*) Blvd Books.

Pourroy, Janine, jt. auth. see Duncan, Jody.

Pourzanjani, M. M. & Roberts, G. N., eds. Modeling & Control of Marine Craft: Proceedings of the International Conference, Held at Exeter, U. K., 18-20 April 1990. 432p. 1991. 130.00 (*1-85166-592-7*) Elsevier.

Pousada, Alicia. Puerto Rican Community Participation in East Harlem Bilingual Programs. 66p. 1987. lib. bdg. 5.00 (*1-878483-14-5*) Hunter Coll CEP.

Pousada, Alicia, jt. auth. see Poplack, Shana.

Pousada, Lidia, et al. Case Studies in Emergency Medicine for the House Officer. LC 92-48917. (Illus.). 244p. 1993. 20.00 (*0-683-06966-7*) Williams & Wilkins.

— Emergency Medicine. 2nd ed. (House Officer Ser.). (Illus.). 600p. 1994. 20.00 (*0-683-06963-2*) Williams & Wilkins.

Pousard, Melanie. The LDS Bride's Guide. LC 88-25739. vii, 116p. 1988. pap. 10.95 (*0-87579-140-9*) Deseret Bk.

Poussaint, Alvin F., jt. auth. see Comer, James P.

Pousset, Edouard. Life in Faith & Freedom: An Essay Presenting Gaston Fessard's Analysis of the Dialectic of the Spiritual Exercises of St. Ignatius. Donahue, E. L., tr. LC 79-84200. (Modern Scholarly Studies about the Jesuits, in English Translations Series II: No. 4). xxviii, 240p. 1980. 9.00 (*0-912422-41-6*); pap. 7.00 (*0-912422-39-4*) Inst Jesuit.

Poussin, Charles D., jt. auth. see Bernstein, Serge.

Poussin, Nicolas. Drawings of Poussin. Longstreet, Stephen, ed. (Master Draughtsman Ser.). (Illus.). (Orig.). 1963. 10.95 (*0-87505-027-1*); pap. 4.95 (*0-87505-180-4*) Borden.

***Pousson, Jeanie B.** Foundations & Funding Sources of Louisiana 1994-1995: Resource Guide to Private Grants & Scholarships. 176p. (Orig.). (C). 1994. per. 53.00 (*0-9643379-0-8*) Res Review.

— Foundations of Mississippi: Resource Guide to Private Grants & Scholarships. 160p. (Orig.). (YA). 1995. per. 37.00 (*0-9643379-1-6*) Res Review.

Poust. Business Law Text. 1991. pap. text ed. 22.75 (*0-314-70828-6*) West Pub.

Poustie, Mark, jt. auth. see Robson, Peter.

Poutiatine, Olga. War & Revolution: Excerpts from the Letters & Diaries of the Countess Olga Poutiatine. Lensen, George A., ed. & tr. by. LC 74-164854. (Illus.). 111p. 1971. 12.50 (*0-910512-12-4*) Diplomatic IN.

Poutney, David, tr. see Wagner, Richard.

Pouts-Lajus, Serge. Robots y Ordenadores (Robots & Computers) Villanueva, Marciano, tr. (Explorer Ser.). (Illus.). 96p. (SPA.). (J). (gr. 4 up). 1992. lib. bdg. 15.90 (*1-56294-178-X*) Millbrook Pr.

Poutsma, E., et al, eds. Process Innovation & Automation in Small & Medium Sized Business. 146p. (Orig.). 1987. pap. 33.50 (*90-6275-365-5*, Pub. by Delft U Pr NE) Coronet Bks.

Pouwels, Randall L. Horn & Crescent: Cultural Change & Traditional Islam on the East African Coast, 800-1900. (African Studies: No. 53). (Illus.). 288p. 1987. 74.95 (*0-521-32308-8*) Cambridge U Pr.

Pouwels, Randall L., ed. see Farsy, Shaikh A.

Pouyanne. Hare, Reading Level 3-4. (World Animal Library). (Illus.). 28p. (J). (gr. 2-5). 1983. 12.50 (*0-685-58818-1*); lib. bdg. 16.67 (*0-86592-853-3*) Rourke Corp.

— Hippo, Reading Level 3-4. (World Animal Library). (Illus.). 28p. (J). (gr. 2-5). 1983. 12.50 (*0-685-58819-X*); lib. bdg. 16.66 (*0-86592-855-X*) Rourke Corp.

— Ladybug, Reading Level 3-4. (World Animal Library). (Illus.). 28p. (J). (gr. 2-5). 1983. 12.50 (*0-685-58821-1*); lib. bdg. 16.67 (*0-86592-863-0*) Rourke Corp.

Pouzar, Jay, jt. auth. see Illman, Paul E.

Pouzet, M. & Richard, D. Orders: Descriptions & Roles. (Mathematical Studies, No. 99; Annals of Discrete Mathematics: No. 23). 1984. 113.00 (*0-444-87601-4*, North Holland) Elsevier.

Pouzin. The Cyclades Computer Network: Toward Layered Network Architectures. (International Council for Computer Communications Ser.: Vol. 2). 388p. 1982. 72. 00 (*0-444-86482-2*, North Holland) Elsevier.

***Povah, Nigel.** Chess Training. 1995. 17.95 (*1-85744-170-2*) Macmillan.

Povah, Nigel, jt. auth. see Ballantyne, Iain.

Povanda, Albert J. Meet Me at the Mountain Top. (Illus.). 40p. (Orig.). 1992. pap. text ed. 6.95 (*1-56315-054-9*) Sterling Hse.

Povar, Gail, jt. auth. see Riegelman, Richard K.

***Povar, Lotte B.** I Married Veterinary Medicine: Veterinary Vignettes. (Illus.). 24p. 1995. pap. 7.00 (*0-8059-3727-7*) Dorrance.

Poveda, Tony G. Lawlessness & Reform: The FBI in Transition. 224p. (C). 1990. pap. 19.95 (*0-534-12882-3*) Intl Thomson.
— Rethinking White Collar Crime. LC 94-1143. (Criminology & Crime Control Policy Ser.). 184p. 1994. text ed. 55.00 (*0-275-94586-3*, Praeger Pubs) Greenwood.
Povelikhina, A., jt. auth. see Kovtun, E.
Poverman, C. E. The Black Velvet Girl: The 1976 Iowa Short Fiction Award. LC 76-23408. (Iowa Short Fiction Award Ser.). 272p. 1976. 19.95 (*0-87745-068-4*); pap. 12.95 (*0-87745-069-2*) U of Iowa Pr.
— Skin. LC 92-9249. 279p. 1992. 19.95 (*0-86538-076-7*) Ontario Rev NJ.
Poveromo, George, jt. auth. see Sosin, Mark.
Povey, John. Roy Campbell. LC 77-1358. (Twayne's World Authors Ser.). 233p. (C). 1977. lib. bdg. 17.95 (*0-8057-6277-9*) Irvington.
Povey, John, jt. ed. see Angoff, Charles.
Povey, John F. Literature for Discussion. LC 83-18627. 179p. (C). 1984. pap. text ed. 19.50 (*0-03-063868-2*) HB Coll Pubs.
Povey, P., tr. see Mailer, F.
Povey, S. & Abbott, C. Cell Hybrids: The Basics. (Basics Ser.). (Illus.). 100p. 1995. pap. 17.95 (*0-19-963443-2*, IRL Pr) OUP.
Povilus, Judith. United in His Name: Jesus in Our Midst in the Writings of Chiara Lubich. Hearne, Jerry, tr. 160p. (Orig.). 1992. pap. 8.95 (*1-56548-003-1*) New City.
Povinec, P., ed. Rare Nuclear Processes. 350p. (C). 1992. text ed. 98.00 (*981-02-0802-2*) World Scientific Pub.
Povinelli, Elizabeth A. Labor's Lot: The Power, History, & Culture of Aboriginal Action. LC 93-2511. (Illus.). 312p. 1994. lib. bdg. 57.95 (*0-226-67673-0*); pap. text ed. 19. 95 (*0-226-67674-9*) U Ch Pr.
***Povlik, Gregory P., ed.** Forgotten Lessons: Selected Essays by John T. Flynn. 208p. (Orig.). 1995. pap. 14.95 (*1-57246-015-6*) Foun Econ Ed.
Povolayev, Valeri. Man at the Limit. (Dramatised Eyewitness Reports Ser.). 272p. 1984. 22.00 (*0-317-53791-1*, Pub. by Collets) St Mut.
Povondra, Pavel, jt. auth. see Sulcek, Zdenek.
Povsic, Frances F. Eastern Europe in Children's Literature: An Annotated Bibliography of English-Language Books. LC 86-3104. (Bibliographies & Indexes in World Literature Ser.: No. 8). 226p. 1986. text ed. 65.00 (*0-313-23777-8*, PVE/) Greenwood.
Povsic, Frances F., comp. The Soviet Union in Literature for Children & Young Adults: An Annotated Bibliography of English-Language Books. LC 91-25095. (Bibliographies & Indexes in World Literature Ser.: No. 31). 320p. 1991. text ed. 55.00 (*0-313-25175-4*, PSU/, Greenwood Pr) Greenwood.
Povzner, A. Y., jt. auth. see Bogaevski, V. N.
Powaga, Wiesiek, ed. & tr. Dedalus Book of Polish Fantasy. (Dedalus European Fantasy Anthologies Ser.). 320p. (Orig.). 1995. pap. 14.95 (*0-7818-0292-X*) Hippocrene Bks.
Powanda, Michael C. & Canonico, P. G., eds. Infection: The Physiologic & Metabolic Responses of the Host. 450p. 1982. 172.00 (*0-444-80336-X*) Elsevier.
Powar, C. B. & Sahasrabuddhe, J. D. Development of the Frog. 1992. 22.50 (*81-7040-447-9*, Pub. by Himalaya II) Apt Bks.
Powaski, Ronald E. The Entangling Alliance: The United States & European Security, 1950-1993. LC 93-20830. (Contributions to the Study of World History Ser.: No. 42). 288p. 1994. text ed. 59.95 (*0-313-27275-1*, Greenwood Pr) Greenwood.
— March to Armageddon: The United States & the Nuclear Arms Race, 1939 to the Present. 318p. 1987. reprint ed. 27.95 (*0-19-503878-9*) OUP.
— March to Armageddon: The United States & the Nuclear Arms Race, 1939 to the Present. 318p. 1989. reprint ed. pap. 9.95 (*0-19-504411-8*) OUP.
— Thomas Merton on Nuclear Weapons. LC 87-31108. 187p. (C). 1988. pap. 7.25 (*0-8294-0586-0*) Loyola Univ Pr.
— Toward an Entangling Alliance: American Isolationism & Europe, 1901-1950. LC 90-45604. (Contributions to the Study of World History Ser.: No. 22). 312p. 1991. text ed. 55.00 (*0-313-27274-3*, PEH, Greenwood Pr) Greenwood.
Powden, Margaret & Mantle, Jill. Physiotherapy in Obstetrics & Gynecology. 441p. 1991. 59.95 (*0-7506-0016-0*) Buttrwrth-Heinemann.
Powder & Bulk Solids Conference - Exhibition Staff. Powder & Bulk Solids Conference - Exhibition: Fifteenth Annual Proceedings of the Technical Program, June 4-7, 1990, O'Hare Exposition Center, Rosemont, IL. 676p. reprint ed. pap. 180.00 (*0-7837-2610-4*, 2042774) Bks Demand.
— Powder & Bulk Solids Conference - Exhibition: Proceedings of the 1991 Technical Program, May 6-9, 1991, Rosemont O'Hare Exposition Center, Rosemont, IL. 584p. pap. 166.50 (*0-7837-0354-6*, 2040673) Bks Demand.
— Powder & Bulk Solids Conference - Exhibition: Proceedings of the 1993 Technical Program, May 3- 6, 1993, Rosemont Convention Center, Rosemont, IL. (Illus.). 708p. reprint ed. pap. 180.00 (*0-7837-7033-2*, 2046848) Bks Demand.
Powder & Bulk Solids Conference-Exhibition Staff. Powder & Bulk Solids Conference-Exhibition, 13th: Proceedings of the Technical Program, May 9-12, 1988, O'Hare Exposition Center, Rosemont, IL. 800p. reprint ed. pap. 180.00 (*0-685-23806-7*, 2032973) Bks Demand.
Powder & Bulk Solids Handling & Processing Staff. Powder & Bulk Solids Handling & Processing: Proceedings of the Technical Program, 10th, May 7-9, 1985, Rosemont, IL. 929p. reprint ed. pap. 180.00 (*0-317-26157-6*, 2025192) Bks Demand.
Powder & Bulk Solids Handling & Processing (12th: 1987: Rosemont, IL) Staff. Powder & Bulk Solids Handling & Processing: Proceedings of the Technical Program: May 12-14, 1987. (Illus.). 716p. pap. 180.00 (*0-685-20416-2*, 2030234) Bks Demand.
Powder & Bulk Solids Handlings & Processing. Powder & Bulk Solids Handling & Processing: Proceedings of the Technical Program: 11th, O'Hare Exposition Center, Rosemont, IL, May 13-15, 1986. 786p. reprint ed. pap. 180.00 (*0-317-55767-X*, 2029367) Bks Demand.
Powder Metallurgy Conference Staff. Powder Metallurgy Conference: Proceedings of the Twenty-Second Annual Conference Presented at the 1966 Design Engineering Conference, Chicago, Illinois, May 9-12. (Progress in Powder Metallurgy Ser.: No. 22). 150p. reprint ed. pap. 42.80 (*0-8357-6987-9*, 2057071) Bks Demand.
Powder Metallurgy Equipment Association Staff. Powder Metallurgy Equipment Manual. 2nd ed. LC 76-52333. 174p. reprint ed. pap. 49.60 (*0-8357-7858-4*, 2036254) Bks Demand.
Powder Metallurgy Technical Conference Staff. Progress in Powder Metallurgy, 1962: Proceedings of the Eighteenth Annual Powder Metallurgy Technical Conference & Magnetic Inductance Core Conference Held at the Hotel Sheraton, Philadelphia, PA, April 23-25, 1962. (Progress in Powder Metallurgy Ser.: Vol. 18). (Illus.). 243p. reprint ed. pap. 69.30 (*0-7837-1553-6*, 2041846) Bks Demand.
— Progress in Powder Metallurgy, 1963: Proceedings of the Nineteenth Annual Powder Metallurgy Technical Conference Held at the Hotel Sheraton-Cadillac, Detroit, MI, April 29-May 1, 1963. (Progress in Powder Metallurgy Ser.: Vol. 19). (Illus.). 204p. reprint ed. pap. 58.20 (*0-7837-1554-4*, 2041847) Bks Demand.
— Progress in Powder Metallurgy, 1964: Proceedings of the Twentieth Annual Powder Metallurgy Technical Conference Magnetic Inductance Core Conference Held at the Drake Hotel, Chicago, IL, April 27-29, 1964. (Progress in Powder Metallurgy Ser.: Vol. 20). (Illus.). 333p. reprint ed. pap. 95.00 (*0-7837-1555-2*, 2041848) Bks Demand.
— Progress in Powder Metallurgy, 1969: Proceedings of the Twenty-Fifth Annual Powder Metallurgy Conference Sponsored by the Metal Powder Industries Federation & Presented at the New York Park Sheraton Hotel, May 5-7, 1969, New York, NY. (Progress in Powder Metallurgy Ser.: No. 25). 147p. reprint ed. pap. 41.90 (*0-7837-3166-3*, 2042812) Bks Demand.
Powder Metallurgy World Congress Staff. Characterization of Powder & Compacts: Preprint of a Seminar Held at the 1992 Powder Metallurgy World Congress, San Francisco, California, June 22-23, 1992. 212p. reprint ed. pap. 60.50 (*0-7837-6977-6*, 2046788) Bks Demand.
— Spray Forming: Science, Technology & Applications: Preprint of a Seminar Held at the 1992 Powder Metallurgy World Congress, San Francisco, California, June 23-24, 1992. (Illus.). 178p. reprint ed. pap. 50.80 (*0-7837-6978-4*, 2046789) Bks Demand.
Powderly, Terence V. Path I Trod. LC 77-181971. reprint ed. 31.50 (*0-404-05098-0*) AMS Pr.
— Thirty Years of Life & Labor, 1859-1889. rev. ed. LC 66-21692. (Reprints of Economic Classics Ser.). 372p. 1967. reprint ed. 49.50 (*0-678-00249-5*) Kelley.
Powdermaker, Florence B. & Frank, Jerome D. Group Psychotherapy, Studies in Methodology of Research & Therapy. LC 72-6188. (Illus.). 615p. 1973. reprint ed. text ed. 89.50 (*0-8371-6450-8*, POGP, Greenwood Pr) Greenwood.
Powdermaker, Hortense. After Freedom: A Cultural Study in the Deep South. LC 92-56923. (New Directions in Anthropological Writing Ser.). 462p. (C). 1993. reprint ed. lib. bdg. 42.50 (*0-299-13780-5*); reprint ed. pap. 17. 95 (*0-299-13784-8*) U of Wis Pr.
— Hollywood: The Dream Factory; an Anthropologist Looks at the Movie-Makers. Coser, Lewis A. & Powell, Walter W., eds. LC 79-7013. (Perennial Works in Sociology Ser.). 1980. reprint ed. lib. bdg. 31.95 (*0-405-12112-1*) Ayer.
— Life in Lesu: The Study of a Melanesian Society in New Ireland. LC 76-44778. reprint ed. 40.00 (*0-404-15877-3*) AMS Pr.
— Stranger & Friend. 1967. pap. 11.95 (*0-393-00410-4*) Norton.
Powders, Donna. Twisted Concepts. Van Treese, James B., ed. 192p. 1994. pap. 8.95 (*1-56901-008-0*) NW Pub.
***Powe.** Outage: A Journey into the Electric City. rev. ed. LC 94-42171. 1995. 21.00 (*0-88001-418-0*) Ecco Pr.
Powe, James E. FoxPro 2.5 for Windows Developer's Library. Leventhal, Lance A., ed. LC 93-18966. (Lance A. Leventhal Microtrend Ser.). 400p. (Orig.). 1993. pap. 44.95 (*0-915391-81-3*, Microtrend) Slawson Comm.
Powe, Lucas A., Jr., jt. auth. see Krattenmaker, Thomas G.
Powe, Lucas A., Jr.
Powe, Marc B. The Emergence of the War Department Intelligence Agency: 1885-1918. 161p. 1974. pap. text ed. 24.00 (*0-89126-013-7*) MA-AH Pub.
Powel, Harford., Jr. Walter Camp, the Father of American Football. LC 70-126246. (Select Bibliographies Reprint Ser.). (Illus.). 1977. 20.95 (*0-8369-5473-4*) Ayer.
Powel, Kevin, jt. auth. see Blankson, Irene.
Powel, Nick, ed. Friend at Court Nineteen Ninety-One. rev. ed. (Illus.). 128p. 1991. 3.00 (*0-938822-83-7*) USTA.
***Powell.** Casual Body. 1995. 16.95 (*971-616-002-X*) Atrium Pubs.
— Considering Computer Contracting. 1990. pap. 30.95 (*1-85384-022-X*) Buttrwrth-Heinemann.
— Getting by in Italian. (Getting by Ser.). 1982. pap. 3.95 (*0-8120-2576-8*); pap. 18.95 (*0-8120-7106-9*) Barron.
— Japans Modern Theatre: A Century of Change & Continuity. 1995. text ed. 90.00 (*1-873410-30-1*, Pub. by Curzon Pr UK) Humanities.
— O, How the Wheel Becomes It! 1995. pap. text ed. 10.95 (*1-55713-221-6*) Sun & Moon CA.
— Senior Rights Movement. 1995. 26.95 (*0-8057-9710-6*, Twayne); pap. 14.95 (*0-8057-9746-7*, Twayne) Macmillan.
— The Solar System. 371p. reprint ed. spiral bd. 27.50 (*0-7873-1153-7*) Mokelumne.
— Testing Active & Passive Electronic Components. (Electrical Engineering & Electronics Ser.: Vol. 8). 232p. 1987. 110.00 (*0-8247-7705-0*) Dekker.
— Tickets to the Devil. Date not set. 5.95 (*0-910791-41-4*, 0670) Devyn Pr.
Powell & Stelling. Diagnosis & Detection of Breast Diseases. 544p. 1992. 85.00 (*0-8016-7487-5*) Mosby Yr Bk.
Powell & Treadgold. Sidereal Zodiac. 52p. 1979. 8.00 (*0-86690-276-7*, P2533-014) Am Fed Astrologers.
Powell & Tsinakis. Ordered Algebraic Structures. (Lecture Notes in Pure & Applied Mathematics Ser.: Vol. 99). 216p. (C). 1985. 99.75 (*0-8247-7342-X*) Dekker.
Powell & Van Dyke. Minnesota & Manitoba One Hundred Years Ago. (Historical Ser.). (Illus.). 1977. pap. 3.50 (*0-89540-056-1*, SB-056) Sun Pub.
Powell, jt. auth. see Andomus.
Powell, ed. see Cicero.
Powell, A. E. The Solar System. 1991. lib. bdg. 79.95 (*0-87700-997-X*) Revisionist Pr.
Powell, A. J., ed. A Stratigraphic Index of Dinoflagellate Cysts. (British Micropalaeontological Society Publication Ser.). (Illus.). 296p. (C). 1992. text ed. 165.00 (*0-412-36280-5*, A6924) Chapman & Hall.
Powell, A. Michael. Grasses of the Trans-Pecos & Adjacent Areas. LC 93-47656. (Illus.). 440p. (C). 1994. text ed. 75.00 (*0-292-76553-3*); pap. 29.95 (*0-292-76556-8*) U of Tex Pr.
— Trees & Shrubs of Trans Pecos, Texas. (Illus.). 533p. (Orig.). 1987. pap. 19.95 (*0-912001-14-3*) Big Bend.
Powell, Aaron M. The National Purity Congress, Its Papers, Addresses, Portraits. LC 75-17238. (Social Problems & Social Policy Ser.). (Illus.). 1976. reprint ed. 39.95 (*0-405-07507-3*) Ayer.
Powell, Adam C., Jr. Adam on Adam: The Autobiography of Adam Clayton Powell, Jr. LC 94-20247. Orig. Title: Adam by Adam. 1994. reprint ed. 12.95 (*0-8065-1538-4*, Citadel Pr) Carol Pub Group.
Powell, Adam C., Sr. Against the Tide: An Autobiography. Gaustad, Edwin S., ed. LC 79-52603. (Baptist Tradition Ser.). 1980. reprint ed. 33.95 (*0-405-12468-6*) Ayer.
— Palestine & Saints in Caesar's Household. 215p. Date not set. reprint ed. 35.95 (*0-933121-91-1*) Black Classic.
Powell, Adriana, tr. see Decker, Ed & Hunt, Dave.
Powell, Adriana, tr. see Swindoll, Charles R.
Powell, Alan. Far Country: A Short History of the Northern Territory. 2nd ed. 1988. pap. 24.95 (*0-522-84377-8*) Intl Spec Bk.
— Patrician Democrat: The Political Life of Charles Cowper 1843-1870. (Illus.). 1978. 29.95 (*0-522-84132-5*) Intl Spec Bk.
Powell, Alice & McAroy, Hazel, eds. A Taste of the Valley. (Illus.). 300p. 1988. write for info. (*0-318-64734-6*) St John Don Bosco Ch.
Powell, Allan. Fort Cumberland. 1989. pap. 5.00 (*0-9619995-2-7*) A R Powell.
Powell, Allan K. Splinters of a Nation: German Prisoners of War in Utah. LC 89-4787. (Utah Centennial Ser.). (Illus.). 350p. (C). 1990. text ed. 25.00 (*0-87480-330-6*) U of Utah Pr.
— The Utah Guide. (Travel Ser.). (Illus.). 656p. 1995. pap. 18.95 (*1-55591-130-7*) Fulcrum Pub.
— Utah Remembers World War Two. (Illus.). 280p. 1991. 29.95 (*0-87421-152-2*) Utah St U Pr.
Powell, Allan K., ed. Utah History Encyclopedia. LC 94-18977. (Illus.). 605p. 1994. text ed. 50.00 (*0-87480-425-6*) U of Utah Pr.
Powell, Allan K., ed. see Horner, Helmut.
Powell, Allan R. From Seminary to Skepticism. 1989. write for info. (*0-318-66923-4*) R B Clarkson.
Powell, Allen Kent. The Next Time We Strike: Labor in Utah's Coal Fields, 1900-1933. (Illus.). 272p. 1985. pap. text ed. 17.95 (*0-87421-161-1*) Utah St U Pr.
Powell, Alton C. Wedgwood International Seminar: An Index to the Published Proceedings, 1956-1992. LC 94-66653. 56p. 1994. pap. text ed. 17.00 (*0-9641682-0-0*) A C Powell.
Powell, Amanda, tr. see De la Cruz, Sor J.
***Powell, Andrew.** Living Buddhism. (Illus.). 200p. 1995. 24. 95 (*0-520-20410-7*) U CA Pr.
Powell, Anne, jt. auth. see Markova, Dawna.
***Powell, Anthony.** A Dance to the Music of Time: All Four Movements, 4 vols. Incl. Second Movement. 724p. 1995. pap. 17.95 (*0-226-67716-8*); Third Movement. 734p. 1995. pap. 17.95 (*0-226-67717-6*); Fourth Movement. 792p. 1995. pap. 18.95 (*0-226-67718-4*); First Movement. LC 94-47228. 728p. 1995. pap. 17.95 (*0-226-67714-1*); 1995. Set pap. 72.80 (*0-226-67719-2*) U Ch Pr.
— A Dance to the Music of Time: First Movement. Incl. Question of Upbringing. 1962. (*0-318-54087-8*); Buyer's Market. 1962. (*0-318-54088-6*); Acceptance World. 1962. (*0-318-54089-4*); 1962. 24.95 (*0-316-71535-2*) Little.
— A Dance to the Music of Time: Third Movement. Incl. Valley of Bones. 1971. (*0-318-54093-2*); Soldier's Art. 1971. (*0-318-54094-0*); Military Philosophers. 1971. (*0-318-54095-9*); 1971. 24.95 (*0-316-71546-8*) Little.
— Fisher King. large type ed. (Mainstream Ser.). 1988. 9.47 (*1-85089-188-5*, Pub. by ISIS UK) Transaction Pubs.
— Miscellaneous Verdicts. 1992. 34.95 (*0-226-67710-9*) U Ch Pr.
— O, How the Wheel Becomes It! (Classics Ser.: No. 76). 142p. 1995. pap. 10.95 (*1-55713-208-9*) Sun & Moon CA.
— O, How the Wheel Becomes It! (Classics Ser.: No. 76). 142p. 1995. pap. 10.95 (*1-55713-223-2*) Sun & Moon CA.
— Under Review: Further Writings on Writers, 1946-1990. LC 93-41020. 1994. 34.95 (*0-226-67712-5*) U Ch Pr.
— What Fools These Mortals Be: A Mediatation on Love Taken from the Works of Shakespeare. 19p. (Orig.). (YA). (gr. 6 up). 1995. pap. 3.00 (*1-57514-130-2*, 1111) Encore Perform Pub.
Powell, Antoinette P. The Landscape Architecture Book Catalog: A Bibliography of Holdings on the University of Kentucky Campus Through 1977. (University of Kentucky Libraries Occasional Papers: No. 3). 335p. 1982. pap. 10.00 (*0-317-27432-5*) U of KY Libs.
Powell, Anton. Ancient Greece. (Cultural Atlas for Young People Ser.). (Illus.). 96p. (YA). 1989. 17.95 (*0-8160-1972-X*) Facts on File.
— Athens & Sparta: Constructing Greek Political & Social History from 478 B.C. (Illus.). 448p. 1991. pap. 16.95 (*0-415-00338-5*, A5756) Routledge.
— Athens & Sparta: Constructing Greek Political & Social History, 478-371 B.C. 288p. 1988. text ed. 29.95 (*0-918400-09-0*) Areopagitica.
— Londonwalks. (Orig.). 1991. pap. 12.95 (*0-8050-1300-8*, Owl) H Holt & Co.
Powell, Anton, ed. Classical Sparta: Techniques Behind Her Success. LC 88-20748. (Oklahoma Series in Classical Culture: Vol. 1). 210p. 1989. 38.95 (*0-8061-2177-7*) U of Okla Pr.
— Euripides, Women & Sexuality. 208p. 1990. 35.00 (*0-415-01025-X*, A4044) Routledge.
— The Greek World. LC 94-41576. (Illus.). 600p. 1995. 99. 95 (*0-415-06031-1*, B4181) Routledge.
Powell, Anton & Hodkinson, Stephen, eds. The Shadow of Sparta. LC 93-43480. 1993. write for info. (*0-415-10413-0*, Routledge NY) Routledge.
Powell, Ardal, ed. see Tromlitz, Johann G.
Powell, Arthur E. The Astral Body. LC 73-4775. (Classics Ser.). 280p. 1973. reprint ed. pap. 12.00 (*0-8356-0438-1*, Quest) Theos Pub Hse.
— Etheric Double. (Illus.). 1969. pap. 10.00 (*0-8356-0075-0*, Quest) Theos Pub Hse.
— Mental Body. 1975. pap. 17.95 (*0-8356-5504-0*) Theos Pub Hse.
Powell, Arthur G. I Can Go Home Again. LC 84-6935. (Illus.). 308p. 1984. reprint ed. 18.50 (*0-87152-398-1*) Reprint.
— The Uncertain Profession: Harvard & the Search for Educational Authority. LC 79-26096. 349p. reprint ed. pap. 99.50 (*0-7837-4180-4*, 2059029) Bks Demand.
Powell, Arthur G., et al. The Shopping Mall High School: Winners & Losers in the Educational Marketplace. 1986. pap. 11.95 (*0-395-42638-3*) HM.
Powell, Avril A. Muslims & Missionaries in Pre-Mutiny India. (London Studies in South Asia (Centre of South Asian Studies, School of Oriental & African Studies, University of London): No. 7). 280p. (C). 1993. text ed. 70.00 (*0-7007-0210-5*, Pub. by Curzon Pr UK) Humanities.
Powell, B. Athenian Mythology: Erechthonius & the Three Daughters of Cecrops. (Illus.). 90p. 1976. 15.00 (*0-89005-121-6*) Ares.
***Powell, Barbara.** A Guide to Hindu Scriptures. (Illus.). 480p. (C). 1995. text ed. 75.00 (*0-87573-071-X*, Asian Human Pr) Jain Pub Co.
***Powell, Barry B.** Classical Myth. Howe, Herbert M., ed. LC 94-27441. 736p. 1994. pap. text ed. write for info. (*0-13-143470-5*) P-H.
— Homer & the Origin of the Greek Alphabet. (Illus.). 312p. (C). 1991. 89.95 (*0-521-37157-0*) Cambridge U Pr.
Powell, Benjamin W. Man of Labrador. 234p. 1993. pap. write for info. (*1-883704-00-6*) Cleaveland.
Powell, Betty B. & Park, Jeff. I Was That Woman at the Well. (Illus.). 176p. (Orig.). 1986. pap. 5.95 (*0-939241-00-5*) Faith Print.
Powell, Bill, jt. auth. see Waters, Rick.
***Powell, Bob.** Scottish Agricultural Implements. 1989. pap. 25.00 (*0-85263-925-2*, Pub. by Shire UK) St Mut.
Powell, Brenda J. The Metaphysical Quality of the Tragic: A Study of Sophocles, Giraudoux, & Sartre. (American University Studies: Comparative Literature: Ser. III, Vol. 27). 213p. (C). 1989. text ed. 40.50 (*0-8204-1068-3*) P Lang Pubs.
Powell, Brian. Kabuki in Modern Japan: Mayama Seika & His Plays. LC 89-70288. 254p. 1990. text ed. 45.00 (*0-312-04505-0*) St Martin.
Powell, C. & Fowler, P. Study of Elementary Particles by the Photographic Method: Account of Principle Technology & Discovery by Atlas Photomicrography. LC 59-10527. 1959. 277.00 (*0-08-009309-4*, Pub. by Pergamon Repr UK) Franklin.
Powell, C. E., jt. auth. see Brummitt, R. K.
Powell, C. M., jt. ed. see Veevers, J. J.
***Powell, Caleb.** This Seething Ocean, That Damned Eagle. LC 93-807018. 127p. (Orig.). 1993. pap. text ed. 9.95 (*1-878815-04-0*) Reflected Images.
Powell, Carl, III. Network Your Mac (& Live to Tell about It!) The REAL Beginner's Guide. (Illus.). 140p. (C). 1994. pap. text ed. 19.00 (*1-878956-41-8*) CBM Bks.
Powell, Carroll F., et al, eds. Vapor Deposition. LC 66-13515. (Electrochemical Society Ser.). (Illus.). 741p. reprint ed. pap. 180.00 (*0-317-11088-8*, 2051258) Bks Demand.

Powell, Cecilia. Turner in the South. LC 86-26673. 216p. 1987. 45.00 (*0-300-03870-4*) Yale U Pr.
— Turner's Rivers of Europe: The Rhine, Meuse & Mosel. (Illus.). 236p. 1992. pap. 35.00 (*1-85437-079-0*) U of Wash Pr.
Powell, Cedric J., jt. ed. see Casper, Lawrence A.
***Powell, Charles.** Juan Carlos of Spain: Self-Made Monarch. LC 95-15318. (St. Antony's-Macmillan Ser.). 1995. write for info. (*0-312-12752-9*) St Martin.
Powell, Charles & Rossetti, Rosemarie. The Healthy Indoor Plant: A Guide to Successful Indoor Gardening. LC 92-90698. 304p. 1992. pap. 27.00 (*0-9631767-0-6*) Rosewell Pub.
Powell, Charles, jt. auth. see Benjamin, Charles.
Powell, Charles, jt. auth. see London, Bill.
Powell, Charles A. Servants of Power. LC 90-91860. 314p. 1990. 18.95 (*0-9627161-9-7*) QLP Phila PA.
***Powell, Charles C., et al.** El Manejo Integrado de los Insectos, Acaros, y Enfermedades en los Cultivos Ornamentales. LC 94-28537. (Illus.). 126p. (Orig.). (SPA.). 1994. pap. text ed. 36.00 (*1-883052-06-8*) Ball Pub.
Powell, Charles C. & Lindquist, Richard K. Ball Pest & Disease Manual. LC 91-35855. (Illus.). 332p. (C). 1992. text ed. 58.00 (*0-9626796-4-X*) Ball Pub.
Powell, Charles C., jt. auth. see Hodges, Larry.
Powell, Chris & Paton, George E., eds. Humour in Society: Resistance & Control. LC 87-23261. 220p. 1988. text ed. 39.95 (*0-312-00933-X*) St Martin.
Powell, Christopher. Discovering Cottage Architecture. 1989. pap. 25.00 (*0-85263-673-3*, Pub. by Shire UK) St Mut.
— Stables & Stable Blocks. 1989. pap. 25.00 (*0-7478-0105-3*, Pub. by Shire UK) St Mut.
***Powell, Claire.** Murder at White House Farm: The Story of Jeremy Bamber. (Illus.). 320p. 1995. pap. 9.95 (*0-7472-4366-2*, Pub. by Headline UK) Trafalgar.
***Powell, Clarence A.** Acoustics. 1966. pap. 6.00 (*0-615-00360-5*) Atlantis Edns.
Powell, Claud, ed. see Powell, Dora.
Powell, Colin. Autobiography. 1995. 27.50 (*0-679-43296-5*) Random.
Powell, Colin L., ed. see Stilwell, Paul.
***Powell, Consie.** A Bold Carnivore: An Alphabet of Predators. (Illus.). 32p. (J). (gr. k-6). 1995. 14.95 (*1-57098-023-3*) R Rinehart.
Powell, Conway L. & Bagaraj, D. Joseph. VA Mycorrhiza. 240p. 1984. 156.00 (*0-8493-5694-6*, QK604) CRC Pr.
Powell-Cope, Gail M., jt. auth. see Brown, Marie A.
Powell-Cotton, P. H. In Unknown Africa: A Narrative of Twenty Months Travel & Sport in Unknown Lands & among New Tribes. (B. E. Ser.: No. 163). 1904. 60.00 (*0-8115-3078-7*) Periodicals Srv.
***Powell, Craig.** The Ocean Remembers It Is Visible: Poems 1966-1989. (QRL Poetry Book Ser.: Vols. XXVIII-XXIX). 20.00 (*0-614-06430-9*); pap. 10.00 (*0-614-06431-7*) Quarterly Rev.
Powell, Cynthia. The Bear Affair. 1993. 13.95 (*0-8034-9031-3*) Bouregy.
— Collector's Guide to Miniature Teddy Bears. 1993. pap. 17.95 (*0-89145-567-1*) Collector Bks.
— The Teddy Bear Bandit. 1994. 17.95 (*0-8034-9086-0*, 094524) Bouregy.
Powell, D., et al, eds. Delta Four: A Generic Architecture for Dependable Distributed Computing. (Research Reports ESPRIT, Project 818, 2252 Delta- 4: Vol. 1). x, 484p. 1991. pap. 55.00 (*0-387-54985-4*) Spr-Verlag.
Powell, D. Arnold, jt. auth. see Royce, Joseph R.
Powell, Dannye R. At Every Wedding Someone Stays Home: Poems. LC 93-38795. 96p. 1994. 18.00 (*1-55728-315-X*); pap. 10.00 (*1-55728-316-8*) U of Ark Pr.
— Parting the Curtains: Interviews with Southern Writers. LC 94-24853. (Illus.). 1994. 25.95 (*0-89587-116-5*) Blair.
***Powell, Dannye R., told to.** Parting the Curtains: Voices of the Great Southern Writers. LC 95-13122. 1995. pap. write for info. (*0-385-47853-4*, Anchor NY) Doubleday.
Powell, David. British Politics & the Labour Questions, 1868-1990. LC 92-18697. (British History in Perspective Ser.). 1993. text ed. 39.95 (*0-312-08374-2*) St Martin.
— Letters from America Pt. 1: September 1860-January 1863. 135p. 1995. pap. 14.95 (*1-85756-246-1*) Paul & Co Pubs.
Powell, David, tr. see Schaeffer, Edith.
Powell, David, tr. see Sisson, Richard, et al.
Powell, David A. George Sand. (Twayne's World Authors Ser.: No. 761). 176p. 1990. text ed. 26.95 (*0-8057-8260-5*, Twayne) Macmillan.
— George Sand Today: Proceedings of the Eighth International George Sand Conference - Tours, 1989. 310p. 1992. lib. bdg. 42.50 (*0-8191-8522-1*) U Pr of Amer.
***Powell, David E.** The Russian Health Care Crisis: History, Evaluation, & Recommendations. 120p. (C). 1995. pap. 9.95x (*0-87078-373-4*) TCFP-PPP.
Powell, David E., jt. ed. see Jones, Anthony.
Powell, David G., ed. Equine Infectious Diseases, No. 5: Proceedings of the Fifth International Conference. LC 88-27670. 312p. 1989. text ed. 70.00 (*0-8131-1676-7*) U Pr of Ky.
Powell, David J. Clinical Supervision: Skills for Substance Abuse Counselors. LC 79-20586. 1980. student ed 20.95 (*0-87705-407-X*); student ed, pap. 30.95 (*0-89885-442-3*) Human Sci Pr.
Powell, David J., ed. Alcoholism & Sexual Dysfunction: Issues in Clinical Management. LC 89-1998. (Alcoholism Treatment Quarterly Ser.: Vol. 1, No. 3). 145p. 1984. text ed. 32.95 (*0-86656-365-2*) Haworth Pr.
Powell, David J. & Brodsky, Archie. Clinical Supervision in Alcohol & Drug Abuse Counseling: Principles, Models, Methods. LC 93-14505. 1993. text ed. 45.00 (*0-02-925055-2*) Free Pr.
Powell, Dawn. The Bridge's House. 1990. pap. 8.95 (*0-679-72685-3*, Vin) Random.
— Dawn Powell at Her Best: Including the Novels "Dance Night" & "Turn Magic Wheel" & Selected Stories. 452p. 1994. 28.00 (*1-883642-16-7*) Steerforth Pr.
— The Diaries of Dawn Powell 1920-1967. Page, Tim, ed. & intro. by. 475p. 1995. 30.00 (*1-883642-08-6*) Steerforth Pr.
— Golden Spur. 1990. pap. 8.95 (*0-679-72687-X*, Vin) Random.
— My Home is Far Away: An Autobiographical Novel. 220p. 1995. pap. 12.00 (*1-883642-43-4*) Steerforth Pr.
— A Time to Be Born. LC 83-45842. reprint ed. 30.00 (*0-404-20206-3*, PS3531) AMS Pr.
— A Time to Be Born. LC 90-24900. 352p. 1991. reprint ed. pap. 9.95 (*1-878274-06-6*) Yarrow Pr.
— Wicked Pavilion. 1990. pap. 8.95 (*0-685-29464-1*, Vin) Random.
Powell, Deborah. Houston Town. (Hollis Carpenter Mystery Ser.). 224p. 1992. pap. 8.95 (*1-56280-006-X*) Naiad Pr.
Powell, Derek. Interpretation of Geological Structure Through Maps: An Introductory Practice Manual. (Illus.). 176p. 1992. pap. text ed. 37.95 (*0-470-21822-3*) Halsted Pr.
Powell, Dilys. Descent from Parnassus. LC 75-99720. (Essay Index Reprint Ser.). 1977. 21.95 (*0-8369-1374-4*) Ayer.
— The Dilys Powell Film Reader. Cook, Christopher, ed. (Film Reader Ser.). 468p. 1995. 39.95 (*1-55783-206-4*) Applause Theatre Bk Pubs.
— The Dilys Powell Film Reader. Cook, Christopher, ed. LC 92-12538. 480p. 1993. pap. 17.95 (*0-19-283082-1*) OUP.
Powell, Don L. Literary Perspectives, Vol. 1. 432p. 1992. pap. text ed. 49.95 (*0-8403-7832-7*) Kendall-Hunt.
— Literary Perspectives, Vol. II. 448p. 1992. pap. text ed. 49.95 (*0-8403-7871-8*) Kendall-Hunt.
Powell, Don R. A Year of Health Hints. large type ed. 664p. 1992. reprint ed. lib. bdg. 21.95 (*1-56054-291-8*) Thorndike Pr.
— A Year of Health Hints. large type ed. 664p. 1992. pap. 13.95 (*1-56054-943-2*) Thorndike Pr.
— A Year of Health Hints: Three Hundred Sixty-Five Practical Ways to Feel Better & Live Longer. rev. ed. 374p. (CHI, POR & SPA.). (C). reprint ed. 23.95 (*0-9635612-1-9*) Am Inst Prevent.
Powell, Don R., jt. auth. see American Institute for Preventive Medicine Staff.
Powell, Donald B. & Powell, Mary J. The Fightin' Texas Aggie Band. LC 93-33734. (Centennial Series of the Association of Former Students: No. 53). (Illus.). 192p. 1994. 29.95 (*0-89096-595-1*) Tex A&M Univ Pr.
— The Fightin' Texas Aggie Band. limited ed. (Centennial Series of the Association of Former Students: No. 53). (Illus.). 192p. 1994. 75.00 (*0-89096-631-1*) Tex A&M Univ Pr.
Powell, Donald M. Arizona Gathering Two, 1950-1969: An Annotated Bibliography. LC 72-82946. 214p. reprint ed. pap. 61.00 (*0-8357-4764-6*, 2037691) Bks Demand.
Powell, Donalyn. A Reason to Live. 160p. (Orig.). (YA). (gr. 9 up). 1989. pap. 6.99 (*1-55661-076-9*) Bethany Hse.
Powell, Dora. Edward Elgar: Memories of a Variation. Powell, Claud, ed. (Illus.). 144p. 1994. 42.95 (*0-85967-996-9*, Pub. by Scolar Pr UK) Ashgate Pub Co.
Powell, Doris. Dust Storm. (Illus.). 52p. 1987. pap. text ed. 4.00 (*0-9618256-0-X*) D Powell Pub.
— Last Bouquet. (Illus.). 52p. 1987. pap. text ed. 4.00 (*0-9618256-1-8*) D Powell Pub.
— Walk by Faith. (Illus.). 274p. (Orig.). 1992. pap. 9.95 (*0-9618256-2-6*) D Powell Pub.
Powell, Dorothy. Defiant Enchantress. (Hologram Romances Ser.). 512p. 1988. pap. 3.95 (*0-8217-2252-2*) Zebra.
Powell, Douglas. Explosions & Small Geometries. Mycue, Edward, ed. (Took Modern Poetry in English Ser.: No. 15). (Illus.). 28p. (Orig.). 1991. pap. 4.00 (*1-879457-14-8*) Norton Coker Pr.
Powell, Douglas A., et al. Consequences. Mycue, Edward, ed. (Took Modern Poetry in English Ser.: No. 35). (Illus.). 32p. (Orig.). 1993. pap. 4.50 (*1-879457-37-7*) Norton Coker Pr.
Powell, Douglas H. & Whitla, Dean K. Profiles in Cognitive Aging. LC 94-18126. (Illus.). 270p. 1994. text ed. 42.50 (*0-674-71331-1*, POWPRO) HUP.
Powell, Douglas R. Families & Early Childhood Programs. LC 89-61025. 141p. 1989. pap. text ed. 6.00 (*0-935989-22-6*, NAEYC#142) Natl Assn Child Ed.
— Parent Education As Early Childhood Intervention: Emerging Directions in Theory, Research & Practice. Sigel, Irving, ed. (Advances in Applied Developmental Psychology Ser.: Vol. 3). 256p. (C). 1988. text ed. 55.00 (*0-89391-502-5*) Ablex Pub.
Powell, Douglas R., jt. ed. see Unger, Donald G.
Powell, Dwane. The Reagan Chronicles: A Cartoon Carnival. 146p. 1987. pap. 6.95 (*0-912697-72-5*) Algonquin Bks.
— Surely Someone Can Still Sing. 1981. 9.95 (*0-935400-05-2*) News & Observer.
Powell, E. A. Adventures in Nepal - The Last Home of Mystery. (C). 1991. text ed. 90.00 (*0-7855-0127-4*, Pub. by Ratna Pustak Bhandar) St Mut.
Powell, E. Alexander. The Last Frontier: The White Man's War for Civilization in Africa. 1976. lib. bdg. 59.95 (*0-8490-2129-4*) Gordon Pr.
— Long Roll on the Rhine: A Study of Hitler's Germany. 1976. 250.00 (*0-8490-2183-9*) Gordon Pr.
— Thunder over Europe. 1972. 250.00 (*0-8490-1213-9*) Gordon Pr.
Powell, E. S. Washington. LC 92-13366. (Hello U. S. A. Ser.). (J). (gr. 3-6). 1993. lib. bdg. 17.50 (*0-8225-2726-X*, Lerner Publctns) Lerner Group.
Powell, E. Sandy. Chance to Grow. (J). (gr. 1-4). 1992. 14.95 (*0-87614-741-4*, Carolrhoda) Lerner Group.
— Chance to Grow. (J). (gr. 1-4). 1992. pap. 4.95 (*0-87614-580-2*, Carolrhoda) Lerner Group.
— Daisy. (Contemporary Concerns Ser.). (Illus.). 40p. (J). (gr. 1-4). 1991. lib. bdg. 14.95 (*0-87614-449-0*, Carolrhoda) Lerner Group.
— Daisy: A Book about Child Abuse. (J). (gr. 1-4). 1991. pap. 4.95 (*0-87614-543-8*, Carolrhoda) Lerner Group.
— Geranium Morning. (Contemporary Concerns Ser.). 40p. (J). (gr. 1-4). 1990. lib. bdg. 14.95 (*0-87614-380-X*, Carolrhoda) Lerner Group.
— Geranium Morning: A Book about Grief. (J). (gr. 1-4). 1991. pap. 4.95 (*0-87614-542-X*, Carolrhoda) Lerner Group.
— Heart to Heart Caregiving: A Sourcebook of Family Day Care Activities, Projects & Practical Provider Support. LC 89-20496. (Illus.). 125p. (Orig.). 1990. pap. 12.95 (*0-934140-59-6*) Redleaf Pr.
— Rats. LC 93-40925. (Early Bird Nature Bks.). 48p. (J). (gr. 2-3). 1994. lib. bdg. 18.95 (*0-8225-3003-1*, Lerner Publctns) Lerner Group.
Powell, Earl A., III. Thomas Cole. (Illus.). 144p. 1990. 49.50 (*0-8109-3158-3*) Abrams.
Powell, Earl A., III, ed. The James A. Michener Collection, Twentieth Century American Paintings. LC 77-89177. (Illus.). 354p. 1977. text ed. 15.00 (*0-935213-03-1*); pap. 12.00 (*0-935213-11-2*) A M Huntington Art.
Powell, Earl A., frwd. Treasures of Impressionism & Post-Impressionism from the National Gallery of Art. LC 93-10768. (Tiny Folios Ser.). 1993. pap. 11.95 (*1-55859-561-9*) Abbeville Pr.
Powell, Earl A., III, intro. Masterpieces from the Los Angeles County Museum of Art Collection. LC 87-36685. (Illus.). 154p. (Orig.). 1988. pap. 9.95 (*0-87587-146-1*) LA Co Art Mus.
Powell, Earl A., III, et al. The Robert O. Anderson Building. LC 86-20862. (Illus.). 96p. (Orig.). 1986. pap. 14.95 (*0-87587-132-1*) LA Co Art Mus.
Powell, Earl N., ed. Designing for Product Success: Essays & Case Studies from the Triad Design Project Exhibit. (Illus.). 46p. (Orig.). 1989. pap. 20.00 (*0-9624445-0-2*) Design Mgmt Inst.
Powell, Edgar & Trevelyan, G. M., eds. The Peasants' Rising & the Lollards. LC 78-63202. (Heresies of the Early Christian & Medieval Era Ser.: Second Ser.). reprint ed. 34.50 (*0-404-16238-X*) AMS Pr.
Powell, Edward. Kingship, Law & Society: Criminal Justice in the Reign of Henry V. 332p. 1990. 72.00 (*0-19-820082-X*) OUP.
Powell, Edward A. The Army Behind the Army. LC 74-75242. (United States in World War I Ser.). (Illus.). xiii, 470p. 1974. reprint ed. lib. bdg. 48.95 (*0-89198-107-1*) Ozer.
***Powell, Eileen.** From Seed to Bloom: How to Grow over 500 Annuals, Perennials & Herbs. LC 94-35380. 304p. 1995. pap. 18.95 (*0-88266-259-7*, Garden Way Pub) Storey Comm Inc.
Powell, Elfreda, tr. see Lescourret, Marie-Anne.
Powell, Elizabeth A. Pennsylvania Butter: Tools & Processes, Vol. I. (Illus.). 27p. 1974. pap. 3.00 (*0-910302-09-X*) Bucks Co Hist.
— Pennsylvania Pottery: Tools & Processes. (Tools of the Nation Maker Ser.: Vol. II). (Illus.). 20p. 1972. pap. 3.00 (*0-910302-10-3*) Bucks Co Hist.
Powell, Ella M. Clio: A Child of Fate. LC 74-137730. (American Fiction Reprint Ser.). 1977. 16.95 (*0-8369-7029-2*) Ayer.
Powell, Ellis T. Evolution of the Money Market. 732p. 1966. reprint ed. 37.50 (*0-7146-1243-X*, Pub. by F Cass Pubs UK) Intl Spec Bk.
Powell, Elwin H. The Design of Discord: Studies of Anomie: Suicide, Urban Society, War. 2nd ed. 288p. 1987. pap. 21.95 (*0-88738-704-7*) Transaction Pubs.
Powell, Emily. Soul Flight. LC 86-62447. 72p. 1986. pap. 3.95 (*0-938875-02-7*) Pittenbrauch Pr.
***Powell, Ena K.** When Mountains Touch Heaven. 1995. pap. 17.95 (*0-88839-365-2*) Hancock House.
Powell, Eric. Kelp, the Health Giver. 1982. pap. 2.95 (*0-87904-041-6*) Lust.
Powell, Eric F. Health from the Kitchen. 64p. 1969. pap. 6.95 (*0-8464-1018-4*) Beekman Pubs.
— A Home Course in Nutrition. 110p. Date not set. pap. 7.95 (*0-8464-4226-4*) Beekman Pubs.
— The Natural Home Physician. 288p. Date not set. 17.95 (*0-8464-4316-3*) Beekman Pubs.
Powell, Erica. Private Secretary (Female)--Gold Coast. LC 83-40285. 240p. 1984. text ed. 24.95 (*0-312-64719-0*) St Martin.
Powell, Ester W. Early Ohio Tax Records: Reprinted with "The Index to Early Ohio Tax Records", 2 vols. in 1. 632p. 1993. reprint ed. 40.00 (*0-8063-1129-0*, 4695) Genealog Pub.
Powell, Esther W. Tombstone Inscriptions & Other Records of Delaware, Ohio. 1972. 17.00 (*0-935057-50-1*) OH Genealogical.
Powell, Esther W., ed. Ohio Records & Pioneer Families, Vol. 12. 1971. 5.00 (*0-935057-11-0*) OH Genealogical.
— Ohio Records & Pioneer Families, Vol. 13. 1972. 2.50 (*0-935057-12-9*) OH Genealogical.
— Ohio Records & Pioneer Families, Vol. 14. 1973. 5.00 (*0-935057-13-7*) OH Genealogical.
— Ohio Records & Pioneer Families, Vol. 15. 1974. 5.00 (*0-935057-14-5*) OH Genealogical.
— Ohio Records & Pioneer Families, Vol. 16. 1975. 5.00 (*0-935057-15-3*) OH Genealogical.
— Ohio Records & Pioneer Families, Vol. 17. 1976. 5.00 (*0-935057-16-1*) OH Genealogical.
— Ohio Records & Pioneer Families, Vol. 18. 1977. 5.00 (*0-935057-17-X*) OH Genealogical.
— Ohio Records & Pioneer Families, Vol. 19. 1978. 5.00 (*0-935057-18-8*) OH Genealogical.
Powell, Etha E. The Depression. LC 90-70220. 195p. 1990. pap. 8.95 (*1-55523-330-9*) Winston-Derek.
Powell, Evan. The Unfinished Gospel: Notes on the Quest for the Historical Jesus. 347p. (C). 1994. 23.95 (*0-9639650-6-9*) Symposium Bks.
Powell, Evan & Hern, Ernest V. Popular Science Book of Home Heating & Cooling. (Illus.). 380p. 1983. 28.95 (*0-8359-5564-8*, Reston) P-H.
Powell, F. C. Statistical Tables for the Social, Biological & Physical Sciences. LC 80-42241. (Illus.). 96p. 1982. pap. 7.95 (*0-521-28473-2*) Cambridge U Pr.
Powell, F. E. Windmill Construction & Generating Power. (Illus.). 80p. 1991. reprint ed. 20.00 (*1-877767-52-2*); reprint ed. pap. 10.00 (*1-877767-51-4*) Univ Publng Hse.
— Windmills & Wind Motors. 1985. reprint ed. pap. 4.95 (*0-917914-27-9*) Lindsay Pubns.
Powell, Francis D. Theory of Coping Systems: Change in Supportive Health Organizations. 244p. 1975. boxed 32.95x (*0-87073-029-0*) Transaction Pubs.
Powell, Frank J. & Matthews, Stanley L., eds. Thermal Insulation: Materials & Systems. LC 87-27045. (Special Technical Publication Ser.: No. 922). (Illus.). 728p. 1987. text ed. 87.00 (*0-8031-0493-6*, 04-922000-10) ASTM.
Powell, Fred. Bartenders Standard Manual. 1988. 5.99 (*0-517-29305-6*) Random Hse Value.
Powell, Fred W. The Bureau of Mines: Its History, Activities & Organization. LC 72-3016. (Brookings Institution. Institute for Government Research. Service Monographs of the U. S. Government: No. 3). reprint ed. 25.00 (*0-404-57103-4*) AMS Pr.
— The Bureau of Plant Industry: Its History, Activities & Organization. LC 72-3064. (Brookings Institution. Institute for Government Research. Service Monographs of the U. S. Government: No. 47). reprint ed. 21.50 (*0-404-57147-6*) AMS Pr.
Powell, Fred W., ed. Hall J. Kelley on Oregon. LC 79-87635. (American Scene Ser.). (Illus.). 412p. 1972. reprint ed. lib. bdg. 49.50 (*0-306-71796-4*) Da Capo.
Powell, Fred W., jt. auth. see Cleveland, Frederick A.
Powell, Fred W., jt. auth. see Smith, Darrell H.
Powell, Frederick W. The Politics of Irish Social Policy 1600-1990. LC 91-48166. 384p. 1992. lib. bdg. 99.95 (*0-7734-9463-4*) E Mellen.
Powell-Froissard, Lily. The Spanish-English, English-Spanish Crossword Puzzle Book. (ENG & SPA.). 1979. pap. 2.95 (*0-8065-0676-8*, Citadel Pr) Carol Pub Group.
Powell, G. Bingham, Jr. Contemporary Democracies: Participation, Stability & Violence. 296p. 1984. pap. 14.95 (*0-674-16687-6*) HUP.
— Social Fragmentation & Political Hostility: An Austrian Case Study. LC 74-83119. xvi, 208p. 1970. 32.50 (*0-8047-0715-4*) Stanford U Pr.
Powell, G. Bingham, Jr., jt. auth. see Almond, Gabriel A.
Powell, G. Bingham, jt. auth. see Almond, Gabriel A., Jr.
Powell, G. E., tr. see Arnason, J.
Powell, G. E., jt. auth. see Lindsay, S. J.
Powell, Gabriel. The Catholikes Supplication Unto the King's Majestie, for Toleration of Catholike Religion in England. LC 76-57406. (English Experience Ser.: No. 822). 1977. lib. bdg. 6.00 (*90-221-0822-8*) Walter J Johnson.
Powell, Gary N. Gender & Diversity in the Workplace: Learning Activities & Exercises. 120p. (C). 1994. pap. text ed. 16.95 (*0-8039-4486-1*) Sage.
— Women & Men in Management. 2nd ed. (Illus.). 304p. (C). 1993. text ed. 45.00 (*0-8039-5223-6*); pap. text ed. 21.95 (*0-8039-5224-4*) Sage.
Powell, Geoffrey. The Kandyan Wars, the British Army in Ceylon. (C). 1984. reprint ed. 21.00 (*0-8364-2366-6*, Pub. by Navrang) S Asia.
— Notes on the Logics of Human Life. 109p. 1987. text ed. 39.95 (*0-566-05477-9*, Pub. by Avebury Pub UK) Ashgate Pub Co.
— The Order of Knowledge. (Philosophy Ser.). 162p. 1993. 58.95 (*1-85628-555-3*, Pub. by Avebury Pub UK) Ashgate Pub Co.
Powell, Geoffrey S. Buller: the Scapecoat? A History of General Sir Redvers Buller, V. C. (Illus.). 256p. 1994. 42.50 (*0-85052-279-X*, Pub. by L Cooper Bks UK) Trans-Atl Phila.
Powell, Gloria J., jt. ed. see Wyatt, Gail E.
Powell, Gordon W., et al. A Fractography Atlas of Casting Alloys. LC 92-5859. (Illus.). 192p. 1992. per. 87.50 (*0-935470-67-0*) Battelle.
Powell, Graham. Brain & Personality. LC 79-87638. 122p. 1979. text ed. 45.00 (*0-275-90408-3*, C0408, Praeger Pubs) Greenwood.
Powell, Graham, jt. auth. see Lindsay, Stan.
Powell, Graham, jt. ed. see Lindsay, Stan.
***Powell, Grosvenor.** Language As Being in the Poetry of Yvor Winters. fac. ed. LC 79-14975. 196p. 1980. reprint ed. pap. 55.90 (*0-7837-7815-5*, 2047571) Bks Demand.
— Yvor Winters: An Annotated Bibliography 1919-1982. LC 83-14466. (Author Bibliographies Ser.: No. 66). 214p. 1983. 22.50 (*0-8108-1653-9*) Scarecrow.
Powell, H. Benjamin. Philadelphia's First Fuel Crisis: Jacob Cist & the Developing Market for Pennsylvania Anthracite. LC 77-88471. (Illus.). 1978. 30.00 (*0-271-00533-5*) Pa St U Pr.
Powell, H. Jefferson. The Moral Tradition of American Constitutionalism: A Theological Interpretation. LC 92-42290. 309p. 1993. text ed. 39.00 (*0-8223-1314-6*) Duke.
Powell, H. M. Santa Fe Trail to California, 1849-1852. Watson, Douglas S., ed. LC 79-174284. (Illus.). reprint ed. lib. bdg. 125.00 (*0-404-05099-9*) AMS Pr.

Powell, Harriet, comp. Game-Songs with Prof Dogg's Troupe. (Illus.). 64p. (J). (ps-3). 1991. pap. 13.95 (*0-7136-2306-3*, Pub. by A&C Black UK) Talman.

Powell, Herbert. The Life & Death of Colonel Blimp: Powell & Pressburger. (Illus.). 304p. (Orig.). 1994. pap. 12.95 (*0-571-14355-5*) Faber & Faber.

Powell, Hickman. The Last Paradise. (Oxford Asia Paperbacks Ser.). (Illus.). 332p. 1986. pap. 9.95 (*0-19-582537-3*) OUP.

— Ninety Times Guilty. LC 73-11909. (Metropolitan America Ser.). 356p. 1974. reprint ed. 23.95 (*0-405-05411-4*) Ayer.

Powell, Hugh. Louise von Gail: Her World & Work. (Studies in German Literature, Linguistics & Culture). 1993. 59.00 (*1-879751-55-0*) Camden Hse.

***Powell, Ivor.** The Amazing Acts. LC 87-3627. 478p. 1987. pap. 16.99 (*0-8254-3545-5*) Kregel.

— The Amazing Acts. LC 87-3627. 478p. 1987. 19.99 (*0-8254-3526-9*) Kregel.

— Bible Cameos. LC 84-23535. 192p. 1985. reprint ed. pap. 8.99 (*0-8254-3515-3*) Kregel.

— Bible Highways. LC 85-8097. 176p. 1985. pap. 8.99 (*0-8254-3521-8*) Kregel.

— Bible Names of Christ. LC 87-29722. 176p. 1988. pap. 8.99 (*0-8254-3530-7*) Kregel.

— Bible Nuggets. LC 91-24340. 190p. 1991. pap. 8.99 (*0-8254-3512-9*) Kregel.

— Bible Oasis. 192p. 1994. pap. 8.99 (*0-8254-3520-X*) Kregel.

— Bible Pinnacles. LC 84-26136. 192p. 1985. reprint ed. pap. 8.99 (*0-8254-3516-1*) Kregel.

— Bible Promises. LC 93-1921. 192p. 1993. pap. 8.99 (*0-8254-3542-0*) Kregel.

— Bible Windows. LC 85-8103. 180p. 1985. pap. 8.99 (*0-8254-3522-6*) Kregel.

— The Exciting Epistle to the Ephesians. LC 88-12841. 304p. (C). 17.99 (*0-8254-3537-4*) Kregel.

— Heaven - My Father's Country. 144p. 1995. pap. 8.99 (*0-8254-3517-X*, 95-028) Kregel.

— John's Wonderful Gospel. LC 83-16192. 446p. (C). 1983. 19.99 (*0-8254-3514-5*) Kregel.

— Luke's Thrilling Gospel. LC 84-9637. 508p. 1984. lib. bdg. 19.99 (*0-8254-3513-7*) Kregel.

— Matthew's Majestic Gospel. LC 86-10401. 526p. 1993. pap. 17.99 (*0-8254-3544-7*) Kregel.

Powell, Ivor, tr. see Maxwell, Joseph.

Powell, Ivor C. Bible Gems. LC 86-27525. 176p. 1987. pap. 8.99 (*0-8254-3527-7*) Kregel.

— David: His Life & Times. LC 90-36487. 368p. 1990. pap. 12.99 (*0-8254-3532-3*) Kregel.

— Mark's Superb Gospel. LC 85-25615. 432p. 1986. pap. 16.99 (*0-8254-3510-2*) Kregel.

— What in the World Will Happen Next? LC 85-7579. 176p. 1985. pap. 6.99 (*0-8254-3524-2*) Kregel.

Powell, J. C. American Siberia: Or, Fourteen Years Experience in a Southern Convict Camp. LC 70-90188. (Mass Violence in America Ser.). 1969. reprint ed. 15.95 (*0-405-01333-7*) Ayer.

— American Siberia, or Fourteen Years' Experience in a Southern Convict Camp. LC 79-108222. (Criminology, Law Enforcement, & Social Problems Ser.: No. 105). (Illus.). 1970. reprint ed. 12.00 (*0-87585-105-3*) Patterson Smith.

— The American Siberia, or Fourteen Years' Experience in a Southern Convict Camp. LC 76-44514. (Floridiana Facsimile & Reprint Ser.). 1976. reprint ed. 22.95 (*0-8130-0372-5*) U Press Fla.

Powell, J. David, jt. auth. see Franklin, Gene F.

Powell, J. Enoch. The Evolution of the Gospel: A Commentary on the First Gospel, with Translation & Introductory Essay. LC 93-35985. 224p. 1994. 27.50 (*0-300-05421-1*) Yale U Pr.

— The History of Herodotus. 103p. reprint ed. lib. bdg. 25.00 (*0-685-13362-1*, Pub. by A M Hakkert SP) Coronet Bks.

— A Lexicon to Herodotus. (Olms Paperbacks Ser.: Vol. 26). x, 392p. 1977. reprint ed. lib. bdg. 63.50 (*3-487-00036-9*, Pub. by Georg Olms GW); reprint ed. pap. write for info. (*3-487-01149-2*, Pub. by Georg Olms GW) Lubrecht & Cramer.

Powell, J. G. An Historical Geography of Modern Australia. (Studies in Historical Geography: No. 11). (Illus.). 410p. 1988. 74.95 (*0-521-25619-4*) Cambridge U Pr.

— An Historical Geography of Modern Australia. (Studies in Historical Geography: No. 11). (Illus.). 420p. (C). 1991. pap. 29.95 (*0-521-40829-6*) Cambridge U Pr.

Powell, J. G., ed. see Cicero, Marcus T.

Powell, J. H. Bring Out Your Dead: The Great Plague of Yellow Fever in Philadelphia in 1793. (Studies in Health, Illness, & Caregiving). 334p. (C). 1993. reprint ed. text ed. 31.95 (*0-8122-3210-0*); reprint ed. pap. text ed. 13.95 (*0-8122-1423-4*) U of Pa Pr.

— Dartmoor Themes: A Walker's Guide. (Illus.). 224p. 1995. pap. 22.95 (*1-85223-915-8*, Pub. by Crowood Pr UK) Trafalgar.

Powell, J. L., jt. auth. see Faure, G.

Powell, J. Lewis. Executive Speaking: An Acquired Skill. 2nd ed. LC 80-395. 173p. reprint ed. pap. 49.40 (*0-685-15884-5*, 2026791) Bks Demand.

Powell, J. Robin. Working Women's Guide to Managing Stress. 1994. pap. text ed. 14.95 (*0-13-969213-4*) P-H.

Powell, J. Robin & George-Warren, Holly. The Working Woman's Guide to Managing Stress. LC 94-11400. 1994. text ed. 27.95 (*0-13-969205-3*) P-H.

— The Working Woman's Guide to Managing Stress. LC 94-11400. 1994. pap. 14.95 (*0-13-969212-6*) P-H.

Powell, J. U. Collectanea Alexandrina. 263p. 1981. reprint ed. 25.00 (*0-89005-373-1*) Ares.

Powell, J. U. & Barber, E. A., eds. New Chapters in the History of Greek Literature. 1921. 25.00 (*0-8196-0286-8*) Biblo.

— New Chapters in the History of Greek Literature. (Second Ser.). 1929. 25.00 (*0-8196-0287-6*) Biblo.

Powell, J. W. Introduction to the Study of Indian Languages with Words, Phrases & Sentences to Be Collected. 1977. lib. bdg. 69.95 (*0-8490-2074-3*) Gordon Pr.

Powell, J. W., ed. see Boas, Franz.

Powell, Jacie & Lovelock, Robin. Changing Patterns of Mental Health Care: A Case Study in the Development of Local Services. 190p. 1992. 59.95 (*1-85628-333-X*, Pub. by Avebury Pub UK) Ashgate Pub Co.

Powell, Jackie, jt. auth. see Lovelock, Robin.

Powell, James. Aircraft Radio Systems. LC 92-46754. (Illus.). 255p. 1990. reprint ed. pap. text ed. 24.95 (*0-89100-356-8*, EA-356) IAP.

— Mastering Approach 3 for Windows. LC 94-68435. 841p. 1994. pap. 29.99 (*0-7821-1306-0*) Sybex.

— Microsoft Access 2 Instant Reference. LC 93-87700. 297p. 1994. pap. 9.99 (*0-7821-1469-5*) Sybex.

— The Mule Thieves. LC 86-1622. 192p. 1986. 14.95 (*0-8027-4058-8*) Walker & Co.

Powell, James B. Super Investment Trends: Cashing in on the Dynamic '90s. 300p. 1992. text ed. 32.00 (*1-55623-500-3*) Irwin Prof Pubng.

Powell, James E. FoxPro 2 Developer's Library. Leventhal, Lance A., ed. (Lance A. Leventhal Microtrend Ser.). 400p. (Orig.). 1992. pap. 44.95 (*0-915391-61-9*, Microtrend) Slawson Comm.

— Windows NT Instant Reference. LC 93-84946. 377p. 1993. pap. 12.95 (*0-7821-1219-6*) Sybex.

Powell, James H., jt. auth. see McCright, Grady E.

***Powell, James L.** Pathways to Leadership: How to Achieve & Sustain Success. LC 94-43956. (Nonprofit Sector Ser.). 288p. 1995. 27.95 (*0-7879-0094-X*) Jossey-Bass.

Powell, James M. Albertanus of Brescia: The Pursuit of Happiness in the Early Thirteenth Century. LC 91-29777. (Middle Ages Ser.). 168p. (C). 1992. text ed. 24.95 (*0-8122-3138-4*) U of Pa Pr.

— Anatomy of a Crusade, 1213-1221. LC 86-11403. (Middle Ages Ser.). (Illus.). 310p. (C). 1986. pap. text ed. 17.95 (*0-8122-1323-8*) U of Pa Pr.

Powell, James M., ed. Innocent III: Vicar of Christ or Lord of the World? LC 93-12609. (C). 1994. pap. 14.95 (*0-8132-0783-5*) Cath U Pr.

— The Liber Augustalis; or, Constitutions of Melfi Promulgated by the Emperor Frederick the Second for the Kingdom of Sicily in 1231. LC 76-150107. 201p. reprint ed. pap. 57.30 (*0-685-20511-8*, 2029970) Bks Demand.

— Medieval Studies: An Introduction. rev. ed. LC 91-31160. (Illus.). 500p. (C). 1992. pap. text ed. 19.95 (*0-8156-2556-1*) Syracuse U Pr.

— Medieval Studies: An Introduction. 2nd rev. ed. LC 91-31160. (Illus.). 500p. (C). 1992. text ed. 45.00 (*0-8156-2555-3*) Syracuse U Pr.

— Muslims under Latin Rule, 1100-1300. 228p. (C). 1990. text ed. 35.00 (*0-691-05586-6*) Princeton U Pr.

Powell, James M., jt. ed. see Iggers, Georg G.

Powell, James N. The Tao of Symbols. LC 82-5383. 1982. pap. 13.45 (*0-688-01354-6*, Quill) Morrow.

Powell, James R., Jr. The Audiophile's Technical Guide to 78 rpm, Transcription, & Microgroove Recordings. viii, 86p. 1992. pap. 50.00 (*0-9634921-2-8*) Gramophone.

Powell, James R., Jr. & Powell, Russell H. Core List of Books & Journals in Science & Technology. 2nd ed. 176p. Date not set. 45.00 (*0-89774-730-5*) Oryx Pr.

Powell, James R., Jr. & Stehle, Randall G. Playback Equalizer Settings for 78 rpm Recordings. (Illus.). v, 89p. (Orig.). 1993. pap. 50.00 (*0-9634921-3-6*, 1003) Gramophone.

Powell, James R., Jr., jt. ed. see Powell, Russell H.

Powell, James T. Two Hundred Thousand: A Proven Program You Can Use to Get 200,000 Miles of Reliable Transportation from Your Automobile. 200p. (Orig.). 1989. pap. 8.95 (*0-911168-85-0*) Prakken.

Powell, Jan, jt. auth. see Simms, Willard.

Powell, Janet C., jt. auth. see Norris, Rosalie N.

***Powell, Jeanne.** February Voices: First Poems. (Orig.). 1995. pap. 8.00 (*0-932693-08-3*) Jukebox Press.

Powell, Jeanne & Foley, Carol. Pattern Making. (Illus.). 430p. (C). 1987. pap. text ed. 38.00 (*0-13-654211-5*) P-H.

Powell, Jeff, jt. auth. see Impey, Ken.

Powell, Jefferson. Languages of Power: A Source Book of Early Constitutional History. LC 90-85342. 352p. 1991. 39.95 (*0-89089-379-9*); pap. 19.95 (*0-89089-380-2*) Carolina Acad Pr.

Powell, Jehu Z. History of Cass County, Indiana, Set, Vols. I & II. (Illus.). 1197p. 1992. reprint ed. Set. lib. bdg. 109.00 (*0-8328-2539-5*) Higginson Bk Co.

Powell, Jerry A. & Hogue, Charles L. California Insects. LC 78-62876. (California Natural History Guides Ser.: No. 44). (Illus.). 1980. pap. 15.00 (*0-520-03782-0*) U CA Pr.

— California Insects. LC 78-62876. (California Natural History Guides Ser.: No. 44). (Illus.). 398p. reprint ed. pap. 113.50 (*0-7837-4692-X*, 2044439) Bks Demand.

Powell, Jerry A., jt. auth. see Brown, John W.

Powell, Jesse J. A Study of Problem Material in High School Algebra. LC 71-177162. (Columbia University. Teachers College. Contributions to Education Ser.: No. 405). reprint ed. 37.50 (*0-404-55405-9*) AMS Pr.

Powell, Jillian. Ancient Art. LC 94-6079. (Arts & Artists Ser.). (Illus.). 48p. (J). (gr. 6-10). 1994. 16.95 (*1-56847-216-1*) Thomson Lrning.

— Art in the Nineteenth Century: Art & Artists. (Art & Artists Ser.). (Illus.). 48p. (J). (gr. 6-10). 1994. 16.95 (*1-56847-219-6*) Thomson Lrning.

— Body Decoration. (Traditions Around the World Ser.). (Illus.). 48p. (J). (gr. 5-7). 1995. 16.95 (*1-56847-276-5*) Thomson Lrning.

— Climbers. (J). (ps-2). 1992. 15.95 (*0-87614-700-7*, Carolrhoda) Lerner Group.

— Flyers. (J). (ps-2). 1992. 15.95 (*0-87614-701-5*, Carolrhoda) Lerner Group.

— Food. (Traditions Around the World Ser.). (Illus.). 48p. (J). (gr. 5-7). 1995. 16.95 (*1-56847-346-X*) Thomson Lrning.

— A History of France Through Art. (History Through Art Ser.). (Illus.). 48p. (J). (gr. 4-6). 1996. 15.95 (*1-56847-441-5*) Thomson Lrning.

— Jumpers. (J). (ps-2). 1992. 15.95 (*0-87614-702-3*, Carolrhoda) Lerner Group.

— Painting & Sculpture. LC 89-21863. (Arts Ser.). (Illus.). 48p. (J). (gr. 6-11). 1990. lib. bdg. 11.95 (*0-8114-2361-1*) Raintree Steck-V.

— Swimmers. (J). (ps-2). 1992. 15.95 (*0-87614-703-1*, Carolrhoda) Lerner Group.

Powell, Jim. Designing User Interfaces. Leventhal, Lance A., ed. LC 90-61738. (Lance A. Leventhal Data Based Advisor Ser.). 500p. (Orig.). 1990. pap. 27.95 (*0-915391-40-6*, Microtrend) Slawson Comm.

— It Was Fever That Made the World. LC 88-20720. 88p. 1989. lib. bdg. 20.00 (*0-226-67706-0*); pap. 8.95 (*0-226-67707-9*) U Ch Pr.

— Sappho: A Garland. 1994. pap. 9.00 (*0-374-52421-1*, Noonday) FS&G.

Powell, Joanna, comp. Things I Should Have Said to My Father. 144p. (Orig.). 1994. pap. 10.00 (*0-380-77348-1*) Avon.

Powell, Joel. Memory Management in a Multimedia World. LC 93-49871. 1994. pap. 18.95 (*1-878739-65-4*) Waite Group Pr.

Powell, Joel & Basham, Tom. Falcon Three: The Complete Handbook. (Illus.). 652p. (Orig.). 1992. disk, pap. 34.95 (*1-878739-29-8*) Waite Group Pr.

Powell, John. Abortion: The Silent Holocaust. LC 81-69697. 190p. (Orig.). 1981. pap. 9.50 (*0-89505-063-3*, 21056) Tabor Pub.

— The Arts - Jack London. LC 92-46766. (Biographies Ser.). (J). 1993. 19.93 (*0-86625-486-2*); 14.95 (*0-685-66540-2*) Rourke Pubns.

— CO B2 S Laser Cutting. LC 92-36190. 1993. 129.00 (*0-387-19786-9*) Spr-Verlag.

— The Fully Alive Experience Personal Notebook. (Illus.). 64p. 1980. pap. 4.95 (*0-89505-406-X*) Tabor Pub.

— Fully Human, Fully Alive: A New Life Through a New Vision. rev. ed. (John Powell, S. J., Library). 152p. 1989. pap. 8.95 (*1-55924-281-7*, 22034) Tabor Pub.

— Happiness Is an Inside Job. (John Powell, S. J., Library). 128p. 1989. pap. 8.95 (*1-55924-005-9*, 22030) Tabor Pub.

— He Touched Me: My Pilgrimage of Prayer. 1974. pap. 5.50 (*0-913592-47-1*, 20945) Tabor Pub.

— The John Powell, S. J., Library, 7 bks., Set. 1990. boxed, pap. 49.95 (*1-55924-292-2*, 21047) Tabor Pub.

— A Life-Giving Vision: How to Be a Christian in Today's World. (Illus.). 352p. (Orig.). 1995. pap. 17.95 (*0-88347-294-5*) Thomas More.

— Path Through Christian Living. Cheney, Michael H., ed. 208p. (YA). 1995. student ed 27.50 (*0-7829-0452-1*) Tabor Pub.

— The Secret of Staying in Love. (Illus.). 168p. 1995. reprint ed. pap. 8.95 (*0-88347-299-6*) Thomas More.

— The Secret of Staying in Love: Loving Relationships Through Communication. rev. ed. (Illus.). 176p. 1990. pap. 8.95 (*1-55924-280-9*, 22032) Tabor Pub.

— Solving the Riddle of Self: The Search for Self-Discovery. (Illus.). 96p. (Orig.). 1995. pap. 9.95 (*0-88347-300-3*) Thomas More.

— Through Seasons of the Heart. (Illus.). 384p. 1989. pap. 14.95 (*1-55924-197-7*, 21109) Tabor Pub.

— Through the Eyes of Faith. 156p. 1992. 8.95 (*0-7829-0114-X*, 22044) Tabor Pub.

— Unconditional Love. (Illus.). 124p. 1995. reprint ed. pap. 8.95 (*0-88347-312-7*) Thomas More.

— Unconditional Love: Love Without Limits. rev. ed. (Illus.). 128p. 1989. pap. 8.95 (*1-55924-282-5*, 22035) Tabor Pub.

— Why Am I Afraid to Love? Overcoming Rejection & Indifference. rev. ed. (John Powell, S. J., Library). 112p. 1990. pap. 8.95 (*1-55924-278-7*, 22031) Tabor Pub.

— Why Am I Afraid to Tell You Who I Am? rev. ed. (John Powell, S. J., Library). 1990. pap. 8.95 (*1-55924-279-5*, 22033) Tabor Pub.

— Will the Real Me Please Stand Up? (Illus.). 215p. 1995. reprint ed. write for info. (*0-614-06511-9*) Thomas More.

— Will the Real Me Please Stand Up? Twenty-Five Guidelines for Good Communication. rev. ed. (John Powell, S. J., Library). 224p. 1990. pap. 9.95 (*1-55924-283-3*, 22036) Tabor Pub.

***Powell, John & Cheney, Michael H.** Path Through Christian Living. (Illus.). 338p. (YA). (gr. 9-12). 1994. pap. text ed. 14.50 (*0-7829-0451-3*) Tabor Pub.

Powell, John, jt. auth. see Woods, Frank.

Powell, John A., jt. auth. see McDonald, Laughlin.

Powell, John B. My Twenty-Five Years in China. LC 76-27721. (China in the 20th Century Ser.). 1976. reprint ed. lib. bdg. 45.00 (*0-306-70761-6*) Da Capo.

Powell, John D. Political Mobilization of the Venezuelan Peasant. LC 70-134947. (Center for International Affairs Ser.). (Illus.). 275p. 1971. 29.95 (*0-674-68626-8*) HUP.

Powell, John H. Bring Out Your Dead: The Great Plague of Yellow Fever in Philadelphia in 1793. LC 77-112567. (Rise of Urban America Ser.). (Illus.). 1976. reprint ed. 23.95 (*0-405-02471-1*) Ayer.

Powell, John J. Golden State & Its Resources. LC 78-125759. (American Environmental Studies). 1974. reprint ed. 17.95 (*0-405-02685-4*) Ayer.

Powell, John L. & Crasemann, Bernd. Quantum Mechanics. (Illus.). 1961. write for info. (*0-201-05920-7*) Addison-Wesley.

Powell, John S. The Christian Vision: The Truth That Sets Us Free. LC 83-73231. (Illus.). 155p. 1984. pap. 9.95 (*0-89505-183-4*, 21082) Tabor Pub.

Powell, John S., ed. see De Saint Lambert.

Powell, John T. Origins & Aspects of Olympism. 239p. (Orig.). (C). 1994. pap. text ed. 17.20 (*0-87563-502-4*) Stipes.

— Track & Field Fundamentals for Teacher & Coach. 4th ed. (Illus.). 1987. spiral bd. 17.80 (*0-87563-294-7*) Stipes.

Powell, John W. Exploration of the Colorado River & Its Canyons. (Illus.). 400p. 1895. pap. 7.95 (*0-486-20094-9*) Dover.

— The Exploration of the Colorado River & Its Canyons. (Nature Library). 448p. 1987. pap. 10.95 (*0-14-017000-6*, Penguin Bks) Viking Penguin.

— The Hopi Villages (the Ancient Province of Tusayan) LC 75-25049. (Wild & Woolly West Ser.). Orig. Title: Ancient Province of Tusayan. (Illus.). 48p. 1972. pap. 3.00 (*0-910584-73-7*) Filter.

— Learning & Change, the Problems of Evaulation in Liberal Adult Education. 1960. 2.50 (*0-87060-084-2*, PUC 12) Syracuse U Cont Ed.

— An Overland Trip to the Grand Canyon: Northern Arizona As Powell Saw It in 1870. LC 77-29657. (Wild & Woolly West Ser.: No. 28). (Illus.). 40p. 1974. pap. 3.00 (*0-910584-84-2*) Filter.

— Powell & the Anthropology of Canyon Country. (Illus.). 30p. 1977. reprint ed. pap. 4.95 (*0-938216-26-0*) GCNHA.

— Truth & Error: Or, the Science of Intellection. LC 75-3322. reprint ed. 31.50 (*0-404-59318-6*) AMS Pr.

Powell, John W. & Jones, William R. The Canons of the Colorado. (Illus.). 1980. reprint ed. pap. 5.95 (*0-89646-059-2*) Vistabooks.

Powell, John W., et al. Campus Security & Law Enforcement. 2nd ed. LC 93-21319. 272p. 1994. 44.95 (*0-7506-9441-6*) Buttrwrth-Heinemann.

Powell, Jon T. Direct Broadcast by Satellite: Issues of Regulations, Barriers to Communication. LC 85-6342. xviii, 300p. 1985. text ed. 65.00 (*0-89930-067-7*, PDP/, Quorum Bks) Greenwood.

Powell, Jon T. & Gair, Wally, eds. Public Interest & the Business of Broadcasting: The Broadcast Industry Looks at Itself. LC 88-3098. 203p. 1988. text ed. 59.95 (*0-89930-198-3*, PLI/, Quorum Bks) Greenwood.

***Powell, Jonathan, ed. & intro.** Cicero the Philosopher. 376p. 1995. 65.00 (*0-19-814751-1*) OUP.

Powell, Jonathan, jt. auth. see Champion, Bob.

Powell, Jonathan, jt. ed. see Woodman, Tony.

Powell-Jones, Mark. Impressionism. (Color Library Ser.). (Illus.). 128p. (C). 1994. reprint ed. pap. 14.99 (*0-7148-3053-4*, Pub. by Phaidon Press UK) Chronicle Bks.

— Impressionism. (Color Library). (Illus.). 128p. (C). 1994. reprint ed. 19.95 (*0-7148-3219-7*, Pub. by Phaidon Press UK) Chronicle Bks.

Powell, Jordan, jt. auth. see Adams, Pat.

***Powell, Joseph.** Counting the Change. (QRL Poetry Book Ser.: Vol. XXVI). 20.00 (*0-614-06417-1*) Quarterly Rev.

— Winter Insomnia. 1993. 19.95 (*0-934847-15-0*); pap. 9.95 (*0-934847-16-9*) Arrowood Bks.

Powell, Jouett L. Three Uses of Christian Discourse in John Henry Newman: An Example of Nonreductive Reflection on the Christian Faith. LC 75-29423. (American Academy of Religion. Dissertation Ser.: No. 10). 242p. reprint ed. pap. 69.00 (*0-7837-5487-6*, 2045252) Bks Demand.

Powell, Joyce, jt. auth. see Hatfield, Gene.

***Powell, Judith.** Discover Your Perfect Soul Mate. 1995. audio, pap. text ed. 12.95 (*1-56087-078-8*) Top Mtn Pub.

Powell, Judith, ed. see Allen, James & Powell, Tag.

Powell, Judith, ed. see Davis, Samantha A.

Powell, Judith, ed. see Elliott, Virginia B.

Powell, Judith, ed. see Kelly, Dorothy V.

Powell, Judith, ed. see Ollivier, John J.

Powell, Judith, ed. see Powell, Tag & Mills, Carol H.

Powell, Judith, jt. auth. see Powell, Tag.

Powell, Judith, ed. see Powell, Tag.

Powell, Judith, jt. auth. see Wattles, Wallace D.

Powell, Judith A. Wonder, Liberty & Love: Huxley's Analogical Uses of Shakespeare. 120p. (C). 1992. text ed. 24.95 (*0-9628916-4-9*) Vande Vere.

Powell, Judith A., ed. see Murray, Raymond L.

Powell, Judith L., ed. see Allen, James & Powell, Tag.

Powell, Judith L., ed. see Hadsell, Helen.

Powell, Judith L., ed. see Suggs, Jackie.

Powell, K., et al. Scale-Chord Synopticon. 634p. (Orig.). (C). 1987. pap. 29.95 (*0-926954-00-8*) Synopticon Pub.

Powell, K. A., et al, eds. The Genius Aspergillus: From Taxonomy & Genetics to Industrial Application. (FEMS Symposium Ser.: No. 69). (Illus.). 374p. (C). 1994. 105.00 (*0-306-44701-0*) Plenum.

Powell, Karen H. How to Form a Catechumenate Team. (Font & Table Ser.). 72p. 1986. pap. 4.75 (*0-930467-53-1*) Liturgy Tr Pubns.

Powell, Karen H. & Sinwell, Joseph P., eds. Breaking Open the Word of God: Resources for Using the Lectionary for Catechists in the RCIA (Cycle C) 192p. (Orig.). 1988. pap. 12.95 (*0-8091-2973-6*) Paulist Pr.

Powell, Karla, ed. see Rau, Bob.

Powell, Kay, jt. ed. see Boseman, Glenn.

Powell, Kay E., ed. The Country Kitchen Stoneware Cookbook. (Illus.). 100p. (Orig.). 1983. pap. 6.00 (*0-930528-05-0*) Sassafras Pr.

Powell, Ken. Fight Stress & Win! 176p. (C). 1989. reprint ed. lib. bdg. 29.00x (*0-8095-7113-7*) Borgo Pr.

— Stansted: Norman Foster & the Architecture of Flight. (Illus.). 112p. 1992. 29.95 (*1-872180-99-X*, Pub. by Fourth Estate UK) Trafalgar.

Powell, Ken, jt. auth. see Wilford, Michael.

P Q

Powell, Ken L. The Shadows of America. Lewis, Rosemary P., ed. 47p. (Orig.). 1993. pap. 9.95 (0-9635327-0-7) Undergrnd Pubns.

***Powell, Kenneth.** Graves Residence: Princeton 1986-93: Michael Grave. (Architecture in Detail Ser.). (Illus.). 60p. (Orig.). (C). 1995. pap. 29.95 (0-7148-3292-8, Pub. by Phaidon Press UK) Chronicle Bks.

— Lloyd's Building: London 1986, Richard Rogers Partnership. (Architecture in Detail Ser.). (Illus.). 60p. (C). 1994. pap. 29.95 (0-7148-3006-2, Pub. by Phaidon Press UK) Chronicle Bks.

Powell, Kenneth G. Vortical Solutions of the Conical Euler Equations. (Notes on Numerical Fluid Mechanics Ser.: Vol. 28). x, 285p. (C). 1990. 80.00 (3-528-07627-5, Pub. by Vieweg & Sohn GW) Ballen Bkslr.

Powell, Kerry. Oscar Wilde & the Theatre of the 1890s. (Illus.). 224p. (C). 1990. 47.95 (0-521-38008-1) Cambridge U Pr.

Powell, Kevin. In the Tradition: An Anthology of Young Black Writers. (Orig.). 1993. pap. 14.00 (0-86316-316-5) Writers & Readers.

— Recognize. 128p. 1995. pap. 11.00 (0-86316-324-6) Writers & Readers.

Powell, Kevin, et al, eds. In the Tradition: An Anthology of Young Black Writers. 200p. (Orig.). 1993. 28.00 (0-86316-315-7); pap. 14.00 (0-685-53678-5) Writers & Readers.

Powell, Kirsten H. & Childs, Elizabeth. Femmes d'Esprit: Women & Satire in Daumier's Caricature. LC 89-13898. (Illus.). 156p. 1990. pap. 19.95 (0-9625262-0-7) Middlebury Coll Mus.

Powell, L. C. An Introduction to Robinson Jeffers. 1992. reprint ed. lib. bdg. 75.00 (0-7812-5075-7) Rprt Serv.

— Manuscripts of D. H. Lawrence. 1972. 200.00 (0-87968-020-2) Gordon Pr.

Powell, Lane, ed. see Loverseed, Helga.

Powell, Larry. I Hear the Rolling Thunder. 1986. 9.70 (0-89536-803-X, 6821) CSS OH.

Powell, Larry D. Blow the Silver Trumpets. 1991. pap. 8.50 (1-55673-314-3, 9135) CSS OH.

Powell, Laura. Video 101: A Primer for the Hospitality & Travel Industry. Benedict, Ruth C., ed. (Illus.). 56p. (Orig.). 1989. pap. 34.95 (0-912150-11-4) Magna Pubns.

Powell, Lawrence, ed. see Olmsted, Frederick L.

Powell, Lawrence C. Bookman's Progress: Selected Writings. Targ, William & Ritchie, Ward, eds. 246p. 1968. 15.00 (0-910740-25-9) Holmes.

— Books Are Basic: The Essential Lawrence Clark Powell. Marshall, John D., ed. LC 85-14099. 95p. 1985. 14.95 (0-8165-0952-2) U of Ariz Pr.

— Books in My Baggage: Adventures in Reading & Collecting. LC 73-726. 255p. 1973. reprint ed. text ed. 65.00 (0-8371-6784-1, POBB, Greenwood Pr) Greenwood.

— Books West Southwest. 137p. 1994. pap. 12.95 (0-614-05596-2) Bks West SW.

— California Classics. LC 82-12759. (Illus.). 416p. (C). 1989. reprint ed. pap. 11.95 (0-88496-184-2) Capra Pr.

— Eucalyptus Fair. 271p. 1992. 20.00 (0-9632966-0-4) Bks West SW.

— Eucalyptus Fair. deluxe ed. 271p. 1992. boxed 100.00 (0-9632966-1-2) Bks West SW.

— Fay. 64p. 1993. 100.00 (0-9625610-1-0) L C Powell.

— A Good Place to Begin. 12p. 1987. pap. 2.95 (0-929722-14-0) CA State Library Fndtn.

— The Holly & the Fleece. 136p. 1995. 20.00 (0-88496-402-7) Capra Pr.

— Land of Fact. LC 92-72094. 60p. 1992. 30.00 (0-914421-07-7) Hist Soc So CA.

— The Little Package: Pages on Literature & Landscape from a Traveling Bookman's Life. LC 73-156705. (Essay Index Reprint Ser.). 1977. reprint ed. 20.95 (0-8369-2422-3) Ayer.

— Manuscripts of D. H. Lawrence. (Studies in D. H. Lawrence: No. 20). 1970. reprint ed. pap. 27.95 (0-8383-0099-5) M S G Haskell Hse.

— Mysterious Transformation: or When Does History Become Literature. 276p. 1993. 32.50 (0-9632966-2-0) Bks West SW.

— Mysterious Transformation: or When Does History Become Literature. deluxe ed. 276p. 1993. boxed 100.00 (0-9632966-3-9) Bks West SW.

— A Passion for Books. LC 73-727. 249p. 1973. reprint ed. text ed. 55.00 (0-8371-6783-3, POPB, Greenwood Pr) Greenwood.

— Robinson Jeffers: The Man & His Work. 1973. lib. bdg. 59.95 (0-8490-0966-9) Gordon Pr.

— Robinson Jeffers: The Man & His Work. LC 68-54176. (American Biography Ser.: No. 32). (Illus.). 1969. reprint ed. lib. bdg. 75.00 (0-8383-0675-6) M S G Haskell Hse.

— Southwest Classics: The Creative Literature of the Arid Lands: Essays on the Books & Their Writers. LC 82-20314. 378p. reprint ed. pap. 107.80 (0-7837-5053-6, 2044731) Bks Demand.

Powell, Lawrence C., contrib. The Drawings of Maynard Dixon. (Illus.). 64p. 1989. pap. 14.95 (0-295-96649-1) U of Wash Pr.

— Next to Mother's Milk ... An Engelhard Lecture on the Book, Presented at the Library of Congress on Tuesday, April 8, 1986. LC 87-4160. 25p. 1989. reprint ed. 3.95 (0-8444-0551-5) Lib Congress.

Powell, Lawrence C., jt. auth. see Everson, William.

Powell, Lawrence C., jt. auth. see Sanchez, Thomas.

***Powell, Lawrence N.** Louisiana's Capitols: The Power & the Beauty. (Illus.). 144p. 1995. 35.00 (0-917541-03-0) Galerie Pr.

— New Masters: Northern Planters During the Civil War & Reconstruction. LC 79-64226. 1980. 35.00 (0-300-02217-4) Yale U Pr.

Powell, Lawrie W., ed. Metals & the Liver. LC 78-11947. (Liver, Normal Function & Disease Ser.: No. 1). (Illus.). 464p. reprint ed. pap. 132.30 (0-7837-0822-X, 2041136) Bks Demand.

***Powell, Lawrie W. & Piper, Douglas W.** Fundamentals of Gastroenterology. 6th ed. (Illus.). 292p. 1995. pap. text ed. 39.00 (0-07-470192-4) Hlth Prof Div.

Powell, Lee. J. William Fulbright & America's Lost Crusade: Fulbright's Opposition to the Vietnam War. (Illus.). 264p. 1984. pap. 16.45 (0-914546-51-1) Rose Pub.

***Powell, Len.** A Guide to the Overhead Projector. (C). 1974. pap. 30.00x (0-85171-077-8, Pub. by IPM Hse UK) St Mut.

— Lecturing to Large Groups. (C). 1979. pap. 30.00x (0-85171-017-4, Pub. by IPM Hse UK) St Mut.

Powell, Lenore S. & Courtice, Katie. Alzheimer's Disease: A Guide for Families. LC 83-3887. 288p. 1983. pap. 10.53 (0-201-06099-X) Addison-Wesley.

Powell, Leroy. Out of My Head: Coon Dogs That Lie to You, Killer Pancakes, & Other Lunacies. LC 89-28418. (Illus.). 240p. (YA). 1990. 15.95 (0-934601-95-X) Peachtree Pubs.

Powell, Lew. Lew Powell's Carolina Follies: A Nose-Tweaking Look at Life in Our Two Great & Goofy States. Bledsoe, Jerry, ed. LC 90-60346. (Illus.). 96p. (Orig.). 1990. pap. 6.95 (0-9624255-1-6) Down Home NC.

Powell, Lilja B., ed. see Pond, Jesse E., Jr.

Powell, Lillian L., et al. Grave Markers in Burke County, Georgia, with Thirty-nine Cemeteries in Four Adjoining Counties. 384p. 1988. reprint ed. 32.50 (0-685-54355-2, GA 83) Southern Hist Pr.

Powell, Linton. A History of Spanish Piano Music. LC 79-3761. 223p. reprint ed. pap. 63.60 (0-7837-3723-8, 2057901) Bks Demand.

Powell, Lucas A., Jr. The Fourth Estate & the Constitution: Freedom of the Press in America. (C). 1992. 14.00 (0-520-08038-6) U CA Pr.

Powell, Lyman P. Mary Baker Eddy: A Life Size Portrait. LC 91-72519. (Twentieth-Century Biographers Ser.). (Illus.). 408p. 1992. 17.95 (0-87510-260-3) Christian Sci.

Powell, Lynn S. Residential Mortgage Banking Basics. 40p. 1990. pap. 20.00 (0-945359-95-0) Mortgage Bankers.

— Secondary Mortgage Market Basics. 40p. (Orig.). (C). 1990. pap. text ed. 20.00 (0-945359-96-9) Mortgage Bankers.

Powell, Lynn S., ed. see Healy, Tom & Briggs, Jeff.

Powell, Lynn S., ed. see MBA Staff.

Powell, Lynn S., ed. see Taylor, Jeffrey & Austin, Kenneth, Jr.

***Powell, M. Anne.** Child Maltreatment & the Family: Background Briefing Report with Seminar Presentations. 94p. 1994. pap. 10.00 (0-929722-80-9) CA State Library Fndtn.

***Powell, M. Anne, ed.** Teen Pregnancy in California: Effective Prevention Strategies: Background Briefing Report with Seminar Presentations. 168p. 1994. pap. 15.00 (0-929722-82-5) CA State Library Fndtn.

Powell, M. J. Approximation Theory & Methods. (Illus.). 300p. 1981. 80.00 (0-521-22472-1); pap. 42.95 (0-521-29514-9) Cambridge U Pr.

Powell, M. J., jt. ed. see Iserles, A.

Powell, M. John. Salt Water Fishing for Fun & Food. (Illus.). 1982. pap. 8.95 (0-941238-03-2) Penobscot Bay.

Powell, Marcia, jt. auth. see Fishman, Diane.

Powell, Margaret J., ed. Bible, N. T. Epistles of Paul: The Pauline Epistles Contained in Ms. (EETS, ES Ser.: No. 116). 1972. reprint ed. 45.00 (0-527-00320-4) Periodicals Srv.

Powell, Marian. One Thousand-Plus Patterns in Four, Six & Eight Harness Shadow Weaves. 1976. reprint ed. pap. 12.95 (1-56659-016-7) Robin & Russ.

Powell, Marianne & Preisler, Bent, eds. English Past & Present: A Selection of Essays by Knud Serensen. 240p. (Orig.). 1988. pap. 58.00x (87-7288-168-2, Pub. by Almqv & Wiksell SW) Coronet Bks.

Powell, Marie. White Wings: And Other Stories. 176p. (Orig.). 1993. pap. 9.95 (1-56474-055-2) Fithian Pr.

Powell, Marie B. Expressions in Poetry. (Illus.). 60p. 1990. boxed 10.95 (0-923568-17-4) Wilderness Adventure Bks.

Powell, Mark & Svensson, John. In-Line Skating. LC 92-16686. (Illus.). 152p. 1993. pap. 13.95 (0-87322-399-3, PPOW0399) Human Kinetics.

***Powell, Mark A.** God with Us: A Pastoral Theology of Matthew's Gospel. LC 95-3448. 1995. write for info. (0-8006-2881-0, Fortress Pr) Augsburg Fortress.

— What Are They Saying about Acts? LC 91-27685. (What Are They Saying about...Ser.). 160p. 1992. pap. 6.95 (0-8091-3279-6) Paulist Pr.

— What Are They Saying about Luke. (What Are They Saying about...Ser.). 1989. pap. 7.95 (0-8091-3111-0) Paulist Pr.

— What Is Narrative Criticism? LC 90-13863. (Guides to Biblical Scholarship Ser.). 144p. (Orig.). 1991. pap. 10.00 (0-8006-0473-3, 1-473, Fortress Pr) Augsburg Fortress.

Powell, Mark A., comp. The Bible & Modern Literary Criticism: A Critical Assessment & Annotated Bibliography. LC 91-38128. (Bibliographies & Indexes in Religious Studies: No. 22). 512p. 1992. text ed. 75.00 (0-313-27546-7, PBD, Greenwood Pr) Greenwood.

Powell, Martin. Frankenstein Graphic Album. (Illus.). 86p. 1990. pap. 9.95 (0-944735-39-8) Malibu Graphics.

— Robin Hood. 114p. (Orig.). 1991. pap. 9.95 (0-944735-94-0) Malibu Graphics.

— Sherlock Holmes: A Case of Blind Fear. (Illus.). 113p. 1990. pap. 9.95 (0-944735-50-9) Malibu Graphics.

Powell, Martin & Smith, Wayne R. Sherlock Holmes: Scarlet in Gaslight, An Adventure in Terror. 2nd ed. (Illus.). 120p. 1988. pap. 7.95 (0-944735-09-6) Malibu Graphics.

Powell, Martin & Solity, Jonathan. Teachers in Control: Cracking the Code. 183p. 1990. 65.00 (0-415-04885-0, A4650); pap. 19.95 (0-415-03668-2, A4654) Routledge.

Powell, Martin, et al. In His Steps. 96p. 1994. 9.99 (0-685-75213-5) Marvel Entmnt.

Powell, Martin C., et al. Magnetic Resonance Imaging in Obstetrics & Gynaecology. (Illus.). 168p. 1993. 150.00 (0-7506-1321-1) Buttrwrth-Heinemann.

Powell, Marvin. Psychology of Adolescence. 2nd ed. 678p. 1971. text ed. 13.15 (0-672-60782-4, Bobbs) Macmillan.

Powell, Marvin, et al. Individual Progression. LC 74-88052. 1976. pap. 2.30 (0-685-93230-3, Bobbs) Macmillan.

Powell, Marvin A., ed. Labor in the Ancient Near East. (American Oriental Ser.). (Illus.). 289p. (C). 1987. 32.00 (0-940490-68-4, #HD8656: L33) Am Orient Soc.

Powell, Marvin A., ed. see Dandamaev, Muhammad A.

Powell, Mary. Orthopaedic Nursing & Rehabilitation. 9th ed. (Illus.). 640p. 1986. 53.00 (0-443-03238-6) Churchill.

Powell, Mary, ed. Wolf Tales: Native American Children's Stories. LC 92-29690. (Illus.). 70p. (Orig.). (J). (gr. 3 up). 1993. pap. 8.95 (0-941270-73-4) Ancient City Pr.

Powell, Mary C. Focus on Suzuki Piano. 76p. 1994. pap. text ed. 12.95 (0-87487-582-X) Summy-Birchard.

— Queen of the Air: The Story of Katherine Stinson. Petrick, Thomas W., ed. (Southwesterners Ser.). (Illus.). 124p. (Orig.). (J). (gr. 4-7). 1994. per. 8.95 (1-880384-07-8) Coldwater Pr.

Powell, Mary J., jt. auth. see Powell, Donald B.

Powell, Mary L. Status & Health in Prehistory: A Case Study of the Moundville Chiefdom. LC 87-23318. (Archaeological Inquiry Ser.). (Illus.). 352p. (C). 1988. 35.00 (0-87474-756-2) Smithsonian.

Powell, Mary L., et al, eds. What Mean These Bones? Studies in Southeastern Bioarchaeology. 248p. 1991. pap. 19.95 (0-8173-0484-3) U of Ala Pr.

Powell, Meris, jt. ed. see Atkins, Dale.

Powell, Michael. Edge of the World: The Making of a Film. (Illus.). 352p. (Orig.). 1990. pap. 11.95 (0-571-15306-2) Faber & Faber.

— Getting Computer Jobs Overseas. 160p. 1991. pap. text ed. 32.95 (0-85384-016-4) Buttrwrth-Heinemann.

— A Life in Movies: An Autobiography. 700p. 24.95 (0-685-18173-1) Knopf.

— Million-Dollar Movie. LC 94-14495. 1995. 30.00 (0-679-43443-7) Random.

— Million Dollar Movie. (Illus.). 626p. 1995. 30.00 (0-615-00708-2) Random.

***Powell, Michael F. & Newman, Mark J., eds.** Vaccine Design: The Subunit & Adjuvant Approach. (Pharmaceutical Biotechnology Ser.: Vol. 6). 930p. 1995. 145.00 (0-306-44867-X) Plenum.

Powell, Michael H. Compactly Covered Reflections, Extension of Uniform Dualities & Generalized Almost Periodicity. (Memoirs Ser.: No. 1/105). 235p. 1970. pap. 17.00 (0-8218-1805-8, MEMO 1/105) Am Math.

Powell, Michael J. From Patrician to Professional Elite: The Transformation of the New York City Bar Association. LC 88-32476. 256p. 1989. 42.50 (0-87154-686-8) Russell Sage.

Powell, Montagu. Studies in the Lesser Mysteries. 124p. 1971. reprint ed. spiral bd. 5.50 (0-7873-0675-4) Mokelumne.

Powell, Neil. Carpenters of Light: Some Contemporary English Poets. LC 79-54320. 154p. 1980. text ed. 38.00 (0-06-495665-2, N6785) B&N Imports.

Powell, Nelson & Humphreys, Brian. Proportions of the Aesthetic Face. (American Academy of Facial Plastic & Reconstructive Surgery Monograph). (Illus.). 96p. 1983. 65.00 (0-86577-117-0) Thieme Med Pubs.

Powell, Nicholas, jt. auth. see Webster, Paul.

Powell, Oliver. Carrying My Chalice. LC 88-29988. 156p. (Orig.). 1988. pap. 8.95 (0-8298-0799-3) Pilgrim OH.

Powell, Orrin E. Educational Returns at Varying Expenditure Levels: A Basis for Relating Expenditures to Outcomes in Education. LC 75-177163. (Columbia University. Teachers College. Contributions to Education Ser.: No. 573). reprint ed. 37.50 (0-404-55573-X) AMS Pr.

Powell, Padgett. Edisto. LC 83-25334. 192p. (C). 1984. 11.95 (0-374-14651-9) FS&G.

— Edisto. LC 84-15871. 192p. 1985. pap. 9.95 (0-8050-1370-9, Owl) H Holt & Co.

— Typical: Short Stories. 176p. 1991. 19.00 (0-374-28022-3) FS&G.

— Typical Stories. 192p. 1992. pap. 9.95 (0-8050-2111-6, Owl) H Holt & Co.

— A Woman Named Drown. 1988. pap. 7.95 (0-8050-0750-4, Owl) H Holt & Co.

Powell, Pamela. The Turtle Watchers. 128p. (J). (gr. 3-7). 1994. pap. 3.99 (0-14-037077-3) Puffin Bks.

— The Turtle Watchers. LC 92-5822. 160p. (J). (gr. 3-7). 1992. 13.00 (0-670-84294-X) Viking Child Bks.

Powell, Pamela C. Reflected Light: A Century of Photography in Chester County. (Illus.). 80p. 1988. 30.25 (0-929706-01-3); pap. 24.25 (0-929706-02-1) Chester Co Hist Soc.

Powell, Patricia. Diddle Diddle Red Hot Fiddle. (Illus.). 32p. (J). (gr. 1-8). 1990. pap. text ed. 6.95 (0-944512-01-1) Radiant LA.

— Me Dying Trial. (Caribbean Writers Ser.). 192p. 1993. pap. 9.95 (0-435-98935-9) Heinemann.

— Small Gathering of Bones. 144p. 1994. pap. 9.95 (0-435-98936-7) Heinemann.

Powell, Patricia, ed. American Color Woodcuts: Bounty from the Block, 1890s-1990s. LC 92-90494. (Illus.). 135p. 1993. pap. 29.95 (0-932900-32-1) Elvejhem Mus.

Powell, Patricia, ed. see Louise Lone Dog.

Powell, Patsy K. Dulac, Dat Cajun Cat: Dulac, Dat Cajun Party Animal. LC 87-91307. (Illus.). 32p. (J). (gr. k up). 1988. pap. 6.95 (0-944512-00-3) Radiant LA.

Powell, Paul W. Basic Bible Sermons on Handling Conflict. 1992. pap. 5.99 (0-8054-2279-X) Broadman.

Powell, Peter C. Engineering with Fibre-Polymer Laminates. LC 93-16825. 1993. write for info. (0-412-49610-0) Chapman & Hall.

— Engineering with Polymers. LC 83-7180. 1983. 69.50 (0-412-24160-9, NO. 6825); pap. 36.00 (0-412-24170-6, NO. 6826) Chapman & Hall.

Powell, Peter J. Sweet Medicine: The Continuing Role of the Sacred Arrows, The Sun Dance, & The Sacred Buffalo Hat in Northern Cheyenne History, 2 vols. (Civilization of the American Indian Ser.: Vol. 100). (Illus.). 986p. 1969. 75.00 (0-8061-0885-1) U of Okla Pr.

Powell, Peter W. Confederate States of America, Markings & Postal History of Richmond, Virginia. Hartmann, Leonard H., ed. LC 87-32110. (Illus.). 188p. 1987. 50.00 (0-917528-09-3) L H Hartmann.

Powell, Philip A., jt. auth. see Bailey, Edward P.

Powell, Phillip W. Mexico's Miguel Caldera: The Taming of America's First Frontier, 1548-1597. LC 76-62551. 334p. reprint ed. pap. 95.20 (0-8357-8585-8, 2034956) Bks Demand.

***Powell, Polly.** Just Dessert. LC 94-48360. (J). 1996. write for info. (0-15-200383-5) HarBrace.

Powell, R. A., ed. Dry Etching for Microelectronics. (Materials Processing Theory & Practice Ser.: Vol. 4). 298p. 1985. 105.25 (0-444-86905-0, North Holland) Elsevier.

Powell, R. C., ed. Selected Papers on Solid State Lasers, MS31. 1991. pap. 109.00 (0-8194-0629-5) SPIE.

— Selected Papers on Solid State Lasers, MS31/HC. 1991. 124.00 (0-8194-0628-7) SPIE.

Powell, R. E., jt. auth. see Daugherty, J. S.

Powell, R. E., et al, eds. San Andreas Fault System: Displacement, Palinspastic Reconstruction, & Geologic Evolution. (Memoir Ser.: No. 178). (Illus.). 1993. 115.00 (0-8137-1178-9) Geol Soc.

Powell, R. F. & Forrest, M. R. Noise in the Military Environment. (Battlefield Weapons Systems & Technology Ser.: Vol. 3). 200p. 1988. 40.00 (0-08-035830-6, Pub. by Brasseys UK); 25.00 (0-08-035831-4, Pub. by Brasseys UK) Brasseys Inc.

Powell, Rachel. Powell: Family Records of the Powell & Griffiths, with Poetry of John Powell. 119p. 1994. reprint ed. lib. bdg. 29.50 (0-8328-4110-2); reprint ed. pap. 19.50 (0-8328-4111-0) Higginson Bk Co.

Powell, Ralph L. The Rise of Chinese Military Power, 1895-1912. LC 55-6247. 393p. reprint ed. pap. 112.10 (0-317-08480-1, 2000276) Bks Demand.

Powell, Randall. Career Planning Today. 528p. (C). 1994. per., pap. text ed. 24.95 (0-8403-8469-6) Kendall-Hunt.

***Powell, Randy.** Dean Duffy. LC 94-29037. 176p. 1995. 15.00 (0-374-31754-2) FS&G.

— Is Kissing a Girl Who Smokes Like Licking an Ashtray? 192p. (YA). 1992. 15.00 (0-374-33632-6) FS&G.

— Is Kissing a Girl Who Smokes Like Licking an Ashtray? (YA). 1994. pap. 3.95 (0-374-43627-4) FS&G.

— My Underrated Year. 184p. (J). (gr. 6 up). 1988. 12.95 (0-374-35109-0) FS&G.

— My Underrated Year. 184p. (J). (gr. 6 up). 1991. pap. 3.95 (0-374-45453-1, Sunburst Bks) FS&G.

Powell, Raymond P., jt. auth. see Moorsteen, Richard H.

Powell, Richard. All over but the Shooting. (Black Dagger Crime Ser.). 192p. 1989. reprint ed. text ed. 16.50 (0-86220-764-9, Black Dagger) Chivers N Amer.

— How to Deal with Babies. LC 91-3461. (Child's Practical Guide Ser.). (Illus.). 24p. (J). (gr. k-3). 1992. lib. bdg. 9.59 (0-8167-2420-2); pap. text ed. 2.95 (0-8167-2421-0) Troll Assocs.

— How to Deal with Friends. LC 91-15164. (Illus.). 24p. (J). (gr. k-3). 1992. lib. bdg. 9.59 (0-8167-2422-9); pap. text ed. 2.95 (0-8167-2423-7) Troll Assocs.

— How to Deal with Monsters. LC 91-14975. (Child's Practical Guide Ser.). (Illus.). 24p. (J). (gr. k-3). 1992. lib. bdg. 9.59 (0-8167-2424-5); pap. text ed. 2.95 (0-8167-2425-3) Troll Assocs.

— How to Deal with Parents. LC 91-14997. (Child's Practical Guide Ser.). (Illus.). 24p. (J). (gr. k-3). 1992. lib. bdg. 9.59 (0-8167-2418-0); pap. text ed. 2.95 (0-8167-2419-9) Troll Assocs.

— In the Garden. (Illus.). 20p. (J). (ps). 1994. 6.50 (1-881445-28-3) Sandvik Pub.

— On the Farm. (Illus.). 20p. (J). (ps). 1994. 6.50 (1-881445-27-5) Sandvik Pub.

Powell, Richard, jt. auth. see Robinson, Jontyle T.

Powell, Richard C., jt. auth. see Di Bartolo, Baldassare.

Powell, Richard J. Homecoming: The Art & Life of William H. Johnson. LC 91-5267. (Illus.). 288p. 1991. 45.00 (0-8478-1421-1) Rizzoli Intl.

— Homecoming: The Art & Life of William H. Johnson. 1993. pap. 32.50 (0-393-31127-9) Norton.

— Jacob Lawrence. Broude, Norma, ed. (Rizzoli Art Ser.). (Illus.). 24p. (Orig.). 1992. pap. 7.95 (0-8478-1515-3); pap. 47.70 (0-685-74405-1) Rizzoli Intl.

Powell, Richard R. The Law of Future Interests in California. 91p. 1980. pap. write for info. (0-318-57529-9) West Pub.

Powell, Richard R. & Rohan, Patrick J. Powell on Real Property, 16 vols. 1949. Updates. ring bd. write for info. (0-8205-1550-7) Bender.

***Powell, Richard R., et al.** Classrooms under the Influence: Addicted Families-Addicted Students. (Illus.). 184p. 1994. 38.95 (0-8039-6101-4) Corwin Pr.

— Classrooms under the Influence: Addicted Families-Addicted Students. (Illus.). 184p. 1994. pap. 18.95 (0-8039-6102-2) Corwin Pr.

***Powell, Robert.** The Asian House: Contemporary Houses of Southeast Asia. (Illus.). 176p. 1995. 55.00 (981-00-3496-2, Pub. by Select Bks SI) Weatherhill.

— Crisis in Consciousness: The Source of All Conflict. 208p. 1988. pap. 12.00 (0-89540-167-3, SB-167) Sun Pub.

PQ

— Depopulation Arranged, Convicted & Condemned by the Lawes of God & Man. LC 76-57407. (English Experience Ser.: No. 823). 1977. reprint ed. lib. bdg. 16.00 (*90-221-0823-6*) Walter J Johnson.

— The Free Mind: The Inward Path to Liberation. 200p. 1987. pap. 12.00 (*0-89540-168-1*, SB-168) Sun Pub.

— The Great Awakening. Nicholson, Shirley, ed. LC 83-70688. Orig. Title: Zen & Reality. 179p. 1983. pap. 7.95 (*0-8356-0577-9*, Quest) Theos Pub Hse.

— Innovative Architecture of Singapore. (Illus.). 160p. 1995. 45.00 (*981-00-0683-7*, Pub. by Select Bks SI) Weatherhill.

— Nuclear Deterrence Theory: The Search for Credibility. (Illus.). 240p. (C). 1990. 59.95 (*0-521-37527-4*) Cambridge U Pr.

— Why Does God Allow Suffering? And Other Essays on the Spiritual Quest. LC 88-83535. 158p. reprint ed. pap. 45.10 (*0-7837-5211-3*, 2044942) Bks Demand.

Powell, Robert, tr. Meditations on the Tarot. (Wellspring Bks.). (Illus.). 704p. 1986. 44.95 (*0-916349-02-0*); pap. 19.95 (*0-685-13296-X*) Amity Hse Inc.

Powell, Robert, ed. see Sri Nisargadatta Maharaj.

Powell, Robert L., jt. auth. see Jackman, Alan P.

Powell, Robert M. Recollections of a Texas Colonel at Gettysburg. Coco, Gregory A., ed. (Illus.). 62p. (YA). 1990. pap. text ed. 4.95 (*0-939631-26-1*) Thomas Publications.

Powell, Robin, jt. auth. see Herzfeld, Gerald.

Powell, Roger. Equilibrium Thermodynamics in Petrology: An Introduction. 300p. (C). 1978. 38.00 (*0-06-318073-1*, Pub. by P Chapman Pub UK) St Mut.

Powell, Roger A. The Fisher: Life History, Ecology, & Behavior. 2nd ed. LC 93-3716. 256p. 1993. text ed. 39.95 (*0-8166-2265-5*); pap. 16.95 (*0-8166-2266-3*) U of Minn Pr.

— The Fisher: Life History, Ecology, & Behavior. LC 81-14775. (Illus.). 235p. reprint ed. pap. 67.00 (*0-8357-7667-0*, 2056995) Bks Demand.

Powell, Ronald. Basic Research Methods for Librarians. 2nd ed. McClure, Charles & Hernon, Peter, eds. (Information Management, Policies & Services Ser.: Vol. 10). 208p. (C). 1991. text ed. 45.00 (*0-89391-688-9*) Ablex Pub.

Powell, Ronald J., jt. auth. see Glazier, Jack D.

Powell, Ronald R. The Relationship of Library User Studies to Performance Measures: A Review of the Literature. (Occasional Papers: No. 181). (Orig.). 1988. pap. 2.50 (*0-685-34544-0*) U of Ill Lib Info Sci.

— The Relationship of Library User Studies to Performance Measures: A Review of the Literature. (Occasional Papers: No. 181). (Orig.). (C). 1988. pap. text ed. 5.00 (*0-318-33039-3*) U IL Bd Trustees.

Powell, Ronald R., jt. auth. see Benham, Frances.

Powell, Ronald R., jt. auth. see Taylor, Margaret T.

Powell, Rosemarie A. Communicating Effectively with Teenagers: A Home Study Course. (Home Study Ser.). 28p. 1981. audio, pap. text ed. 30.00 (*0-939926-08-3*) Fruition Pubns.

***Powell, Roxanne D.** Cat, Mouse & Moon. (Illus.). (J). 1994. 14.95 (*0-395-59348-4*) HM.

Powell, Russell H. Handbooks & Tables in Science & Technology. 3rd ed. LC 94-16149. 384p. 1994. 95.00 (*0-89774-534-5*) Oryx Pr.

Powell, Russell H. & Powell, James R., Jr., eds. Core List of Books & Journals in Science & Technology. LC 87-10970. 144p. 1987. 38.50 (*0-89774-275-3*) Oryx Pr.

Powell, Russell H., jt. auth. see Powell, James R., Jr.

Powell, S., jt. auth. see Land, Ailsa H.

Powell, S. R., Jr., jt. ed. see Mecholsky, J. J.

Powell, S. Steven. Covert Cadre. LC 87-6095. (Illus.). 550p. 1987. 29.95 (*0-915463-39-3*) Green Hill.

Powell, Sarah, jt. auth. see Furniss, Kim.

Powell, Scott. History of Marshall County, West Virginia. 334p. 1993. reprint ed. lib. bdg. write for info. (*0-8328-2929-3*) Higginson Bk Co.

Powell, Shirley. Mobility & Adaptation: The Anasazi of Black Mesa, Arizona. LC 83-626. (Publications in Archaeology). 304p. 1983. 29.95 (*0-8093-1107-0*) S Ill U Pr.

Powell, Shirley, ed. Excavations on Black Mesa, 1971-1976: A Descriptive Report. LC 82-72189. (Center for Archaeological Investigations Research Paper Ser.: No. 48). xxvi, 316p. 1984. pap. 15.00 (*0-88104-020-7*) Center Archaeo.

Powell, Shirley & Gummerman, George J. People of the Mesa: The Archaeology of Black Mesa, Arizona. LC 87-4490. (Illus.). 192p. 1987. 24.95 (*0-8093-1400-2*) S Ill U Pr.

Powell, Shirley, jt. ed. see Klesert, Anthony L.

Powell, Shirley, jt. ed. see Plog, Stephen.

Powell, Shirley, et al, eds. Excavation on Black Mesa, 1979: A Descriptive Report. (Center for Archaeological Investigations Research Paper Ser.: No. 18). (Illus.). xii, 516p. 1980. pap. 20.00 (*0-88104-028-2*) Center Archaeo.

Powell, Shirley S. Discovering the Magic of Museums: Especially Children's Museums. 32p. 1991. pap. write for info. (*0-9628995-0-X*) S Powell.

Powell, Simon G. Agricultural Reform in China. (Studies on East Asia). 256p. 1992. text ed. 79.95 (*0-7190-3382-9*, Pub. by Manchester Univ Pr UK) St Martin.

Powell-Smith. Malaysian Standard Form of Building Contract. 1990. 54.00 (*0-409-99592-4*) Butterworth Legal Pubs.

Powell-Smith, jt. auth. see Houghton-Brown.

Powell-Smith, V. & Billington, M. J. Building Regulations. 9th ed. (Illus.). 664p. 1993. pap. write for info. (*0-632-03378-9*) Blackwell Sci.

Powell-Smith, V., jt. ed. see Furmston, M. P.

***Powell-Smith, Vincent, ed.** The Asia-Pacific Construction Law Reports, 1991. 575p. 1994. write for info. (*0-409-99705-6*) Butterworth Legal Pubs.

***Powell-Smith, Vincent, ed. & intro.** The Asia-Pacific Construction Law Reports 1992. 548p. 1994. write for info. (*0-409-99653-X*) Butterworth Legal Pubs.

***Powell-Smith, Vincent & Billington, M. J.** The Building Regulations: Explained & Illustrated. 10th ed. LC 95-3605. (Illus.). 1995. write for info. (*0-632-03933-7*, Pub. by Blckwell Sci Pubns UK) Blackwell Sci.

Powell-Smith, Vincent & Chappell, David. Building Contract Dictionary. 464p. 1985. 94.95 (*0-85139-758-1*, Butterwrth Archit) Buttrwrth-Heinemann.

***Powell-Smith, Vincent & Hashim, Tan.** The Annotated Statutes of Malaysia. 1100p. 1994. write for info. (*0-409-99718-8*) Butterworth Legal Pubs.

Powell-Smith, Vincent, jt. auth. see Brown, Jeremy H.

Powell-Smith, Vincent, jt. auth. see Chappell, David.

***Powell, Staccato & Proctor, Dennis V. Christians under Construction: A Guide to Spiritual Growth. (Illus.). 130p. 1995. pap. 10.00 (*0-9646729-0-1*) Kairos Pr. Have you ever thought you "had it all together" - only to discover you were not as "together" as you thought? You are not alone. If you are serious about delving into the realm of spirituality & becoming more intimate in your relationship with God. This work explores the challenges encountered in faith formation. It presents the dimensions of spiritual development in a very inspiring & illuminating fashion. Provides strategies for overcoming the obstacles to spiritual growth faced in everyday life. It reveals practical approaches & emphasizes the dynamic nature of spiritual maturation. CHRISTIANS UNDER CONSTRUCTION is a guide to help you pass inspection & hear those coveted words. "Well done, thou good & faithful servant." Order from: Kairos Press, P.O. Box 21237, Baltimore, MD 21228; 410-728-7416 or 314-533-0316.**

Publisher Provided Annotation.

***Powell, Stephanie.** Hit Me with Music: How to Start, Manage, Record, & Perform with Your Own Rock Band. LC 95-1965. (Illus.). 128p. (YA). (gr. 7-12). 1995. 14.90 (*1-56294-653-6*) Millbrook Pr.

Powell, Stuart, jt. auth. see Jordan, Rita.

Powell, Sumner C. Puritan Village: The Formation of a New England Town. LC 63-8862. (Illus.). 235p. (C). 1970. pap. 13.95 (*0-8195-6014-6*, Wesleyan Univ Pr) U Pr of New Eng.

Powell, Susan. When You Can't Have a Child: Personal Stories of Living Through Infertility & Childlessness. 1993. pap. 11.95 (*1-86373-295-0*, Pub. by Allen & Unwin Aust Pty AT) IPG Chicago.

Powell, Susan, jt. ed. see Pickering, O. S.

***Powell, Susan A.** Stolen Memories. 1995. 10.95 (*0-533-11360-1*) Vantage.

***Powell, Sutter.** Executive Priviledges. (Orig.). Date not set. mass mkt., pap. 5.95 (*1-56333-383-X*) Masquerade.

Powell, Suzanne. The Pueblos. LC 93-18368. (First Bks.). (Illus.). 64p. (J). (gr. 4-6). 1993. lib. bdg. 13.93 (*0-531-20068-X*) Watts.

— The Pueblos. (First Bks.). (Illus.). 64p. (J). (gr. 5-8). 1994. pap. 5.95 (*0-685-70386-X*) Watts.

Powell, T., jt. ed. see Nobel, D.

Powell, T. G. The Celts. LC 79-63879. (Ancient Peoples & Places Ser.). (Illus.). 1983. reprint ed. pap. 15.95 (*0-500-27275-1*) Thames Hudson.

Powell, Tag. Slash Your Mortgage in Half. Fawcett, Yvonne & Powell, Judith, eds. LC 91-2643. (Illus.). 104p. 1991. pap. text ed. 10.00 (*0-914295-91-8*) Top Mtn Pub.

— Taming the Wild Pendulum. Fawcett, Yvonne & Powell, Judith, eds. LC 94-11030. (Illus.). 192p. (Orig.). 1995. pap. 19.95 (*1-56087-057-5*) Top Mtn Pub.

— Think Wealth...Put Your Money Where Your Mind Is! Powell, Judith & Fawcett, Yvonne, eds. LC 91-11420. 160p. 1991. pap. 8.95 (*1-56087-011-7*) Top Mtn Pub.

Powell, Tag & Mills, Carol H. ESP for Kids: How to Develop Your Child's Psychic Ability. Powell, Judith & Fawcett, Yvonne, eds. LC 92-40253. 192p. 1993. pap. 12.95 (*0-914295-98-5*) Top Mtn Pub.

***Powell, Tag & Powell, Judith.** Silva Mind Mastery for the Nineties. Van Horn, Carol & Fawcett, Yvonne, eds. LC 91-10758. (Illus.). 256p. 1995. reprint ed. pap. 17.95x (*1-56087-116-4*) Top Mtn Pub.

Powell, Tag, jt. auth. see Allen, James.

Powell, Terry, jt. auth. see Collins, Brian.

Powell, Thelma & Stein, Eva. Crossword Puzzle Dictionary. 192p. 1993. 7.95 (*0-8059-3309-3*) Dorrance.

Powell, Theodore. The School Bus Law: A Case Study in Education, Religion & Politics. LC 60-13155. 1960. 28.95 (*0-89197-392-3*); pap. text ed. 6.95 (*0-8290-2016-0*) Irvington.

Powell, Thomas. The Attorneys Academy, or the Manner of Proceeding upon Any Suite. LC 74-80209. (English Experience Ser.: No. 684). 1974. reprint ed. 30.00 (*90-221-0684-5*) Walter J Johnson.

— Direction for Search of Records. LC 74-80208. (English Experience Ser.: No. 685). 1974. reprint ed. 9.50 (*90-221-0685-3*) Walter J Johnson.

— The Persistence of Racism in America. 344p. (Orig.). (C). 1993. pap. 16.95 (*0-8226-3022-2*) Littlefield.

— The Persistence of Racism in America. 344p. (Orig.). (C). 1993. lib. bdg. 47.50 (*0-8191-8587-6*); pap. text ed. 19.75 (*0-8191-8588-4*) U Pr of Amer.

Powell, Thomas G. Mexico & the Spanish Civil War. LC 80-52280. 224p. reprint ed. pap. 63.90 (*0-317-55695-9*, 2029317) Bks Demand.

Powell, Thomas H. & Gallagher, Peggy A. Brothers & Sisters - a Special Part of Exceptional Families. 2nd ed. LC 92-14205. 320p. (C). 1992. pap. text ed. 23.00 (*1-55766-110-3*) P H Brookes.

Powell, Thomas H., et al. Supported Employment: Providing Integrated Employment Opportunities for Persons with Disabilities. 304p. (Orig.). (C). 1991. pap. text ed. 30.95 (*0-8013-0504-7*, 78375) Longman.

Powell, Thomas J. Self-Help Organizations & Professional Practice. LC 86-21761. 367p. 1987. 22.95 (*0-87101-133-6*) Natl Assn Soc Wkrs.

Powell, Thomas J., ed. Understanding the Self-Help Organization: Frameworks & Findings. 336p. 1994. 52.00 (*0-8039-5487-5*); pap. 24.95 (*0-8039-5488-3*) Sage.

— Working with Self-Help. LC 89-14031. 355p. 1990. 26.95 (*0-87101-174-3*) Natl Assn Soc Wkrs.

***Powell, Thomas M.** Ecological Time Series. 1994. pap. 35.00 (*0-412-05201-6*, Blackie & Son-Chapman NY) Routledge Chapman & Hall.

Powell, Thomas M., jt. ed. see Steele, John H.

Powell, Thomas R. The Logic & Rhetoric of Constitutional Law. (Reprint Series in Social Sciences). (C). 1993. reprint ed. pap. text ed. 1.00 (*0-8290-3097-2*, PS-230) Irvington.

— Vagaries & Varieties in Constitutional Interpretation. LC 74-181973. reprint ed. 16.50 (*0-404-05118-9*) AMS Pr.

Powell, Timothy M. You've Gotta Hand It to God! LC 84-73557. (Radiant Life Ser.). 128p. 1985. 2.95 (*0-88243-859-X*, 02-0859); teacher ed 4.50 (*0-88243-199-4*, 32-0199) Gospel Pub.

Powell, Timothy W. The HighTech Marketing Machine: Applying the Power of Computers to Out-Smart the Competition. 225p. 1993. 24.95 (*1-55738-439-8*) Probus Pub Co.

Powell, Trevor & Enright, Simon. Anxiety & Stress Management. 176p. 1990. pap. 17.95 (*0-415-01069-1*, A3368) Routledge.

Powell, Victor. Improving Public Enterprise Performance: Concepts & Techniques. (Management Development Ser.: No. 22). v, 226p. (Orig.). 1987. pap. 24.00 (*92-2-105563-9*) Intl Labour Office.

Powell, Victoria A., tr. see Dandamaev, Muhammad A.

Powell, W. Conrad, jt. auth. see Blackburn, Jack E.

***Powell, W. H.** And God Said, Let There Be Light! Vol. I. 84p. (Orig.). Date not set. pap. text ed. 9.95 (*0-9643370-0-2*) W H R Powell.

— List of Officers of the Army of the U. S. Seventeen Seventy-Nine to Nineteen Hundred. 1972. 75.00 (*0-8490-0542-6*) Gordon Pr.

Powell, Walter L., intro. To Gettysburg by Train. (Illus.). 68p. (C). 1989. pap. text ed. 4.95 (*0-939631-17-2*) Thomas Publications.

Powell, Walter L., ed. see Hamblen, Charles P.

Powell, Walter W. Getting into Print: The Decision-Making Process in Scholarly Publishing. LC 84-23962. (Illus.). xxxii, 296p. 1985. 19.95 (*0-226-67704-4*) U Ch Pr.

— Getting into Print: The Decision-Making Process in Scholarly Publishing. LC 84-23962. (Illus.). xxxii, 296p. 1988. pap. 9.95 (*0-226-67705-2*) U Ch Pr.

— Non-Profit Sector. LC 86-15984. 464p. (C). 1989. reprint ed. pap. 25.00 (*0-300-04497-6*) Yale U Pr.

— The Nonprofit Sector. LC 86-15984. 464p. 1987. text ed. 60.00 (*0-300-03702-3*) Yale U Pr.

— Organizations in a World Economy. 128p. 1994. pap. 15.95 (*0-8039-9020-0*) Pine Forge.

Powell, Walter W. & DiMaggio, Paul, eds. The New Institutionalism in Organizational Analysis. LC 91-9999. (Illus.). 528p. 1991. pap. text ed. 24.95 (*0-226-67709-5*) U Ch Pr.

Powell, Walter W. & Robbins, Richard, eds. Conflict & Consensus: A Festchrift in Honor of Lewis A. Coser. LC 83-48642. 464p. (C). 1984. text ed. 35.00 (*0-02-925400-0*) Free Pr.

Powell, Walter W., ed. see Abegglen, James C.

Powell, Walter W., ed. see Aron, Raymond.

Powell, Walter W., ed. see Bernard, Luther L.

Powell, Walter W., ed. see Chapin, Francis S.

Powell, Walter W., jt. ed. see Coser, Lewis A.

Powell, Walter W., ed. see DeGre, Gerard.

Powell, Walter W., ed. see Granick, David.

Powell, Walter W., ed. see Hughes, Everett C.

Powell, Walter W., ed. see Keller, Suzanne I.

Powell, Walter W., ed. see Lazarsfeld, Paul F. & Kendall, Patricia L.

Powell, Walter W., ed. see Levy-Bruhl, Lucien.

Powell, Walter W., ed. see Pareto, Vilfredo.

Powell, Walter W., ed. see Powdermaker, Hortense.

Powell, Walter W., ed. see President's Research Committee on Social Trends.

Powell, Walter W., ed. see Rainwater, Lee, et al.

Powell, Walter W., ed. see Riesman, David & Glazer, Nathan.

Powell, Walter W., ed. see Rogoff, Natalie.

Powell, Walter W., ed. see Rosenberg, Bernard & Fliegel, Norris.

Powell, Walter W., ed. see Roth, Guenther.

Powell, Walter W., ed. see Selznick, Philip.

Powell, Walter W., ed. see Simmel, Georg.

Powell, Walter W., ed. see Sorokin, Pitirim A.

Powell, Walter W., ed. see Sumner, William G.

Powell, Walter W., ed. see Svalastoga, Kaare.

Powell, Walter W., ed. see Tiryakian, Edward A.

Powell, Walter W., ed. see United States Office of Education Staff, et al.

Powell, Walter W., ed. see Walker, Charles R. & Guest, Robert H.

Powell, Walter W., ed. see Warner, W. Lloyd & Abegglen, James C.

Powell, Walter W., ed. see Wood, Robert C.

Powell, Wanda, ed. Recipes from Hope, Arkansas: Birthplace of Bill Clinton. 178p. 1992. pap. text ed. 12.95 (*0-9636174-0-0*) Legacy Pubs.

Powell, Wayne. Divorce Guide for British Columbia. 15th ed. (Legal Ser.). 112p. 1992. 14.95 (*0-88908-444-0*); 14.95 (*0-88908-466-1*) Self-Counsel Pr.

— Divorce Guide for British Columbia. 16th ed. (Legal Ser.). 128p. 1994. pap. text ed. 11.95 (*0-88908-473-4*) Self-Counsel Pr.

Powell, Weldon, jt. auth. see Wildman, John R.

Powell, William. Anarchist Cookbook. 19.95 (*0-8488-1130-5*) Amereon Ltd.

— The Anarchist Cookbook. LC 71-127797. (Illus.). 160p. 1990. reprint ed. pap. 25.00 (*0-9623032-0-8*) Barricade Bks.

— Clouds & Skyscapes. (How to Draw & Paint Ser.). (Illus.). 32p. (Orig.). 1989. pap. 5.95 (*0-929261-48-8*, HT206) W Foster Pub.

— Color Thick & Thin. (How to Draw & Paint Ser.). (Illus.). 32p. (Orig.). 1989. pap. 5.95 (*1-56010-048-6*, HT182) W Foster Pub.

— Cooke County, Texas. (Illus.). 681p. 1992. 61.00 (*0-88107-212-5*) Curtis Media.

— Evaluative Criteria for a Middle School. Romano, Louis G., ed. 91p. 1988. pap. text ed. 6.50 (*0-918449-10-3*) MI Middle Educ.

— The First Casualty. 1979. 10.00 (*0-8184-0291-1*) Carol Pub Group.

— Perspective. (Artist's Library). (Illus.). 64p. (Orig.). 1989. pap. 6.95 (*0-929261-13-5*, AL13) W Foster Pub.

— Saudi Arabia & Its Royal Family. 384p. 1982. 14.95 (*0-8184-0326-8*) Carol Pub Group.

— Understanding Color. rev. ed. (How to Draw & Paint Ser.). (Illus.). 32p. (Orig.). 1993. pap. 5.95 (*1-56010-167-9*, HT154) W Foster Pub.

— Watercolor & Acrylic Painting Materials & Their Uses. (Artist's Library). (Illus.). 64p. (Orig.). 1990. pap. 6.95 (*1-56010-060-5*, AL18) W Foster Pub.

Powell, William F. Color & How to Use It. (Artist's Library). (Illus.). 64p. (Orig.). 1989. pap. 6.95 (*0-929261-05-4*, AL05) W Foster Pub.

— Knife Painting. (Artist's Library). (Illus.). 64p. (Orig.). 1995. pap. 6.95 (*1-56010-126-1*, AL23) W Foster Pub.

— Oil Painting Materials & Their Uses. (Artist's Library). (Illus.). 64p. (Orig.). 1990. pap. 6.95 (*1-56010-056-7*, AL17) W Foster Pub.

— The Record of Tung Shan. LC 86-4305. (Classics in East Asian Buddhism Ser.). 112p. 1986. pap. text ed. 8.50 (*0-8248-1070-8*) UH Pr.

Powell, William H. Fifth Army Corps. 1993. 60.00 (*0-89029-076-8*) Morningside Bkshop.

Powell, William S. Annals of Progress: The Story of Lenoir County & Kinston, North Carolina. (Illus.). x, 107p. 1963. pap. 5.00 (*0-86526-124-5*) NC Archives.

— The First State University: A Pictorial History of the University of North Carolina. 3rd enl. rev. ed. LC 91-47718. (Illus.). x, 382p. (C). 1992. 29.95 (*0-8078-2049-0*) U of NC Pr.

— Higher Education in North Carolina. rev. ed. (Illus.). viii, 84p. 1970. pap. 2.00 (*0-86526-080-X*) NC Archives.

— John Pory, 1572-1636 Vol. 1, Text: The Life & Letters of a Man of Many Parts; Letters & Other Minor Writings. LC 75-45074. (Illus.). 205p. reprint ed. pap. 58.50 (*0-7837-9022-8*, 2049774) Bks Demand.

— John Pory, 1572-1636 Vol. 2, Supplement: The Life & Letters of a Man of Many Parts; Letters & Other Minor Writings. LC 75-45074. (Illus.). 399p. reprint ed. pap. 58.50 (*0-7837-9023-6*, 2049774) Bks Demand.

— North Carolina: A History. LC 88-40142. xvi, 232p. 1988. reprint ed. pap. 10.95 (*0-8078-4219-2*) U of NC Pr.

— The North Carolina Gazetteer. LC 68-25916. xviii, 561p. 1976. pap. 16.95 (*0-8078-1247-1*) U of NC Pr.

— North Carolina Through Four Centuries. LC 88-7691. (Illus.). xviii, 652p. (C). 1989. 32.50 (*0-8078-1846-1*); text ed. 29.95 (*0-8078-1850-X*) U of NC Pr.

— Proprietors of Carolina. (Illus.). vi, 70p. 1968. reprint ed. pap. 3.00 (*0-86526-101-6*) NC Archives.

— The War of the Regulation & the Battle of Alamance, May 16, 1771. (Illus.). 32p. 1976. reprint ed. pap. 3.00 (*0-86526-102-4*) NC Archives.

Powell, William S., ed. The Correspondence of William Tryon & Other Selected Papers: Vol. I, 1758-1767. (Illus.). lvi, 664p. 1980. 25.00 (*0-86526-141-5*) NC Archives.

— Correspondence of William Tryon & Other Selected Papers: Vol. II, 1768-1818. (Illus.). xxxiii, 958p. 1981. 28.00 (*0-86526-147-4*) NC Archives.

— Dictionary of North Carolina Biography, Vol. 2, D-G. LC 79-10106. vii, 389p. 1986. 49.95 (*0-8078-1656-6*) U of NC Pr.

— Dictionary of North Carolina Biography, Vol. 3, H-K. LC 79-10106. vii, 384p. (C). 1988. 49.95 (*0-8078-1806-2*) U of NC Pr.

— Dictionary of North Carolina Biography, Vol. 5, P-S. LC 79-10106. 530p. (C). 1994. 49.95 (*0-8078-2100-4*) U of NC Pr.

— Dictionary of North Carolina Biography, Vol. 1: A-C, Vol. 1, A-C. LC 79-10106. ix, 477p. 1979. 49.95 (*0-8078-1329-X*) U of NC Pr.

— Dictionary of North Carolina Biography, Vol. 4: L-O, Vol. 4, L-O. LC 79-10106. viii, 416p. (C). 1991. 49.95 (*0-8078-1918-2*) U of NC Pr.

Powell, William S., jt. auth. see Lefler, Hugh T.

Powell, Wm. F., et al. How to Draw & Paint in Watercolor. (Collector's Ser.). (Illus.). 144p. 1991. pap. 19.95 (*1-56010-187-3*, CS02-S) W Foster Pub.
Powelll, Douglas, jt. auth. see Shreiner, Curt.
***Powells, Anita.** Taming the Tongue. 60p. 1994. pap. 5.95 (*1-882185-18-8*) Crnrstone Pub.
Powellson, Jack. Holistic Economics & Social Protest. LC 83-62745. (C). 1983. pap. 3.00 (*0-87574-252-1*) Pendle Hill.
Powels, Sylvia. Der Kalender der Samaritaner anhand des Kitab Hisab As-Sinin und Anderer Handschriften. (Studia Samaritana). (Illus.). (C). 1976. 111.00 (*3-11-004763-2*) De Gruyter.
Powelson, David R. & Powelson, Melinda A. The Recycler's Manual for Business, Government, & Environmentalists. LC 92-10099. 1992. text ed. 64.95 (*0-442-01190-3*) Van Nos Reinhold.
Powelson, Jack. Facing Social Revolution: The Personal Journey of a Quaker Economist. 2nd rev. ed. 146p. (Orig.). 1987. pap. 6.95 (*0-9618242-0-4*) Horizon Soc Pubns.
Powelson, John P. Centuries of Economic Endeavor: Parallel Paths in Japan & Europe, & their Contrast with the Third World. LC 94-17693. 576p. 1994. 45.00 (*0-472-10547-7*) U of Mich Pr.
— Economic Accounting. LC 70-100172. 500p. 1970. reprint ed. text ed. 65.00 (*0-8371-3998-8*, POEA, Greenwood Pr) Greenwood.
— The Story of Land: A World History of Land Tenure & Agrarian Reform. LC 87-11247. 347p. (C). 1988. text ed. 30.00 (*0-89946-218-9*) Lincoln Inst Land.
Powelson, John P. & Stock, Richard. The Peasant Betrayed. rev. ed. 400p. 1990. reprint ed. pap. 20.00 (*0-932790-74-7*) Cato Inst.
— The Peasant Betrayed: Agriculture & Land Reform in the Third World. LC 86-21770. (Lincoln Institute of Land Policy Book Ser.). 322p. reprint ed. pap. 91.80 (*0-7837-5769-7*, 2045434) Bks Demand.
Powelson, John P., jt. auth. see Loehr, William.
Powelson, Melinda A., jt. auth. see Powelson, David R.
Powelstock, David, tr. see Pekarkova, Iva.
Power. Angel of Midnight. 1995. mass mkt. 5.99 (*0-671-89705-5*) PB.
— Guide to Buying & Selling Businesses. 1991. pap. 29.95 (*0-409-10014-5*) Buttrwrth-Heinemann.
— Health & Class. 1991. 97.50 (*1-56593-004-5*, 0245) Singular Publishing.
Power, et al. Lawrence Kohlberg's Approach to Moral Education. 1991. pap. text ed. 18.00 (*0-231-05977-9*) Col U Pr.
Power, Anne. Hovels to Highrise: State Housing in Europe Since 1850. LC 92-35541. 400p. 1993. 65.00 (*0-415-08935-2*, B0149); pap. write for info. (*0-415-08936-0*) Routledge.
Power, Brenda M. & Hubbard, Ruth, eds. Literacy in Process: The Heinemann Reader. 352p. 1990. teacher ed, text ed. 5.00 (*0-435-08533-6*, 08533); pap. text ed. 20.00 (*0-435-08532-8*, 08532) Heinemann.
Power, Brenda M., jt. auth. see Hubbard, Ruth S.
Power, Charlene. Leapin Lena. (Illus.). 59p. 1984. pap. 2.95 (*0-88498-051-0*) Brevet Pr.
— Uff-Da. LC 77-9240. (Illus.). 62p. 1978. 2.95 (*0-88498-048-0*) Brevet Pr.
— Ya, Sure, Ya Betcha! (Illus.). 63p. 1981. 2.95 (*0-88498-050-2*) Brevet Pr.
Power, Christine, jt. ed. see Pigott, Rod.
Power, Crawford. The Encounter. LC 83-42918. 320p. 1983. 22.50 (*0-87951-199-0*); Tusk. pap. 9.95 (*0-87951-191-5*) Overlook Pr.
Power, D. M., ed. Current Ornithology, Vol. 6. LC 84-640616. (Illus.). 344p. 1989. 85.00 (*0-306-43056-8*, Plenum Pr) Plenum.
— Current Ornithology, Vol. 7. LC 84-640616. (Illus.). 402p. 1990. 85.00 (*0-306-43307-9*, Plenum Pr) Plenum.
— Current Ornithology, Vol. 8. LC 84-640616. (Illus.). 305p. 1990. 85.00 (*0-306-43640-X*, Plenum Pr) Plenum.
— Current Ornithology, Vol. 9. (Illus.). 250p. 1991. 69.50 (*0-306-43990-5*, Plenum Pr) Plenum.
— Current Ornithology, Vol. 10. (Illus.). 390p. (C). 1992. 85.00 (*0-306-44282-5*, Plenum Pr) Plenum.
— Current Ornithology, Vol. 11. 1994. 79.50 (*0-306-44550-6*, Plenum Pr) Plenum.
***Power, Dale.** Bears to Carve with Dale Power: With Dale Power. LC 94-23248. (Illus.). 64p. (Orig.). 1995. pap. 12.95 (*0-88740-719-6*) Schiffer.
— Carving Realistic Faces with Power. (Illus.). 64p. (Orig.). 1993. pap. 12.95 (*0-88740-486-3*) Schiffer.
Power, Dale & Snyder, Jeff. Carving the Cheetah. (Illus.). 64p. (Orig.). 1994. pap. 12.95 (*0-88740-696-3*) Schiffer.
***Power, Dale & Snyder, Jeffrey B.** Carving the Coyote. (Illus.). 64p. (Orig.). 1994. pap. 12.95 (*0-88740-567-3*) Schiffer.
— Carving the Elk. (Illus.). 64p. (Orig.). 1994. pap. 12.95 (*0-88740-566-5*) Schiffer.
Power, Dale L. Carving Dolphins & Whales. LC 94-65851. (Illus.). 64p. (Orig.). 1994. pap. text ed. 12.95 (*0-88740-620-3*) Schiffer.
Power, Daniel J., et al. Strategic Management Skills. 300p. (C). 1986. pap. text ed. 31.25 (*0-201-13978-2*) Addison-Wesley.
Power, D'Arcy. Medicine in the British Isles. LC 75-23651. (Clio Medica Ser.: No. 2). reprint ed. 20.00 (*0-404-58902-2*) AMS Pr.
— Selected Writings Eighteen Seventy-Seven to Nineteen Thirty. LC 78-95632. (Illus.). x, 368p. 1970. reprint ed. 45.00 (*0-678-03750-7*) Kelley.
— A Short History of Surgery. LC 75-23751. reprint ed. 20.00 (*0-404-13357-6*) AMS Pr.
Power, D'Arcy, ed. British Masters of Medicine. LC 79-99721. (Essay Index Reprint Ser.). 1977. 26.95 (*0-8369-1375-2*) Ayer.
— John Arderne's Treatises of Fistula in Ano, Etc. (EETS, OS Ser.: Vol. 139). 1969. reprint ed. 18.00 (*0-685-09919-9*) Periodicals Srv.
Power, David. David Lindsay's Vision. 40p. 1991. reprint ed. lib. bdg. 23.00x (*0-8095-6764-4*) Borgo Pr.
— David Lindsay's Vision. 40p. 1991. reprint ed. pap. 13.00x (*0-946650-30-6*) Borgo Pr.
— Gifts That Differ. 205p. 1992. pap. 12.95 (*0-8146-6043-6*, Pueblo Bks) Liturgical Pr.
Power, David N. The Eucharistic Mystery: Revitalizing the Tradition. 352p. 1993. 29.95 (*0-8245-1220-0*) Crossroad NY.
— The Sacrifice We Offer: Tridentine Dogma & Its Reinterpretation. 240p. 1987. 16.95x (*0-8245-0743-6*) Crossroad NY.
— Unsearchable Riches: The Symbolic Nature of Liturgy. 240p. 1992. pap. 14.95 (*0-8146-6062-2*, Pueblo Bks) Liturgical Pr.
— Worship: Culture & Theology. 284p. (Orig.). (C). 1991. pap. 11.95 (*0-912405-77-5*) Pastoral Pr.
Power, David N., jt. ed. see Lumbala, Kabasele.
Power, David W. The Eucharistic Mystery: Revitalizing the Tradition. 384p. 1994. reprint ed. pap. 19.95 (*0-8245-1426-2*) Crossroad NY.
***Power, Dennis M., ed.** Current Ornithology, Vol. 12. 280p. 1995. 79.50 (*0-306-44978-1*) Plenum.
Power, Edward J. A Legacy of Learning: A History of Western Education. LC 90-37218. (SUNY Series, the Philosophy of Education). 400p. (C). 1991. 64.50 (*0-7914-0610-5*); pap. 21.95 (*0-7914-0611-3*) State U NY Pr.
— Philosophy of Education: Studies in Philosophies, Schooling, & Educational Policies. 385p. (C). 1990. reprint ed. pap. text ed. 21.95x (*0-88133-523-1*) Waveland Pr.
Power, Effie. Bag O'Tales: A Sourcebook for Story-Tellers. LC 89-62654. 340p. 1990. reprint ed. lib. bdg. 44.00 (*1-55888-834-9*) Omnigraphics Inc.
Power, Eileen. Medieval English Nunneries. 1988. 22.00 (*0-8196-0140-3*) Biblo.
— Medieval People. 1993. 20.50 (*0-8446-6685-8*) Peter Smith.
Power, Eileen E. The Goodman of Paris. 1977. 25.95 (*0-8369-6986-3*, 7863) Ayer.
— Medieval People. LC 91-58523. 240p. 1992. reprint ed. pap. 12.00 (*0-06-092275-3*, PL) HarpC.
— The Wool Trade in English Medieval History. LC 86-29442. 136p. 1987. reprint ed. text ed. 55.00 (*0-313-25656-X*, POWT, Greenwood Pr) Greenwood.
Power, Eileen E. & Poston, M. Medieval Women. LC 75-7212. (Illus.). 144p. 1976. pap. 14.95 (*0-521-09946-3*) Cambridge U Pr.
Power, Eileen E., tr. see Boissonnade, Prosper.
***Power, Eileen L.** Lasher Lincage: With Supplement. 545p. 1994. reprint ed. lib. bdg. 75.00 (*1-56012-131-9*, 129) Kinship Rhinebeck.
Power, Elizabeth. Host of Riches. large type ed. 1993. 17.95 (*0-263-13424-5*, Pub. by Mills & Boon Ltd UK) Chivers N Amer.
— If Change Is All There Is, Choice Is All You've Got: A Collection of Personal Vignettes about Change & Choice. 86p. 1993. reprint ed. pap. 12.95 (*1-883307-00-7*) E Power & Assocs.
— Managing Our Selves: Building a Community of Caring. 115p. 1992. student ed 17.95 (*1-883307-01-5*) E Power & Assocs.
— Managing Our Selves: God in Our Midst. 63p. 1993. reprint ed. student ed 12.95 (*1-883307-02-3*) E Power & Assocs.
— Straw on the Wind. 1995. mass mkt. 3.25 (*0-373-11768-X*, 1-11768-8) Harlequin Bks.
— Le Vent de la Passion. (Azur Ser.). (FRE.). 1994. pap. 3.50 (*0-373-34434-1*, 1-34434-0) Harlequin Bks.
Power, Eugene B. Edition of One: The Autobiography of Eugene B. Power, Founder of University Microfilms. LC 90-10808. 456p. 1990. pap. text ed. 9.95 (*0-8357-0899-3*) UMI Res Collect.
Power, F. Clark & Lapsley, Daniel K., eds. The Challenge of Pluralism: Education, Politics, & Values. LC 91-50571. (C). 1993. pap. text ed. 16.95 (*0-268-00788-8*) U of Notre Dame Pr.
Power, F. Clark, jt. ed. see Lapsley, D. K.
***Power, Gene & Stratton, Shawn.** Resistance Training with Machines. (Illus.). 116p. 1994. pap. text ed. 10.95x (*0-87563-531-8*) Stipes.
Power, H., ed. Bio-Fluid Mechanics. LC 94-69712. (Advances in Fluid Mechanics Ser.: Vol. 3). 336p. 1995. 150.00 (*1-56252-210-8*) Computational Mech MA.
— Boundary Element Applications in Fluid Mechanics. (Advances in Fluid Mechanics Ser.: Vol. 4). 376p. 1995. 157.00 (*1-56252-212-4*) Computational Mech MA.
— Urban Air Pollution Vol. 2, Vol. 2. 330p. 1995. 145.00 (*1-56252-296-5*) Computational Mech MA.
***Power, H. & Brebbia, C. A., eds.** High-Performance Computing in Engineering Vol. 2: Applications to Partial Differential Equations. LC 94-69714. 336p. 1995. 119.00 (*1-56252-304-X*) Computational Mech MA.
Power, H. & Wrobel, L. C., eds. Boundary Integral Methods in Fluid Mechanics. LC 94-70411. (Computational Engineering Ser.). 344p. 1995. 99.00 (*1-56252-176-4*) Computational Mech MA.
Power, H., jt. ed. see Brebbia, C. A.
Power, Harry W. Foraging Behavior of Mountain Bluebirds with Emphasis on Sexual Foraging Differences. 72p. 1980. 8.50 (*0-943610-28-1*) Am Ornithologists.
Power, Hugh. Battleship Texas. LC 92-7432. (Centennial Series of the Association of Former Students: No. 45). (Illus.). 166p. 1993. 29.50 (*0-89096-516-1*); pap. 9.95 (*0-89096-519-6*) Tex A&M Univ Pr.
Power, J. M., jt. auth. see Low, N. P.
Power, J. Tracy. I Will Not Be Silent & I Will Be Heard: Martin Luther King, Jr., & the Southern Christian Leadership Conference. Brimelow, Judith M., ed. 28p. 1993. pap. write for info. (*1-880067-16-1*) SC Dept of Arch & Hist.
Power, Jo-Ann. The Last Duchess of Wolff's Lair. 352p. 1993. mass mkt. 3.99 (*0-8217-4266-3*) Zebra.
— The Mark of the Chadwicks. 288p. 1993. mass mkt. 3.99 (*0-8217-4072-5*) Zebra.
— Rememberance. 400p. 1995. pap. 4.99 (*0-8217-0101-0*) Zebra.
— Remembrance. 1995. pap. 4.99 (*0-7860-0101-1*, Pinnacle NY) Windsor NY.
— You & No Other. Tolley, Caroline, ed. 352p. (Orig.). 1994. mass mkt. 5.50 (*0-671-89704-7*) PB.
Power, Jo-Ann, jt. auth. see Cummings, Barbara.
Power, John. History of Salvation. 200p. 1989. pap. 6.95 (*0-8189-0566-2*) Alba.
Power, John, jt. auth. see Chamberlain, Nancy.
Power, John, tr. see Oedo, Yusuke, ed.
Power, John H. Review of the Lectures of Wm. A. Smith DD, on the Philosophy & Practice of Slavery. 1977. 22.95 (*0-8369-9172-9*, 9046) Ayer.
Power, Jonathan. Amnesty International: Human Rights Story. (Illus.). 128p. 1981. 64.00 (*0-08-028902-9*, Pub. by Pergamon Repr UK) Franklin.
Power, Jonathan & Holenstein, Anne-Marie. World of Hunger: A Strategy for Survival. 1977. 24.00 (*0-85117-097-8*) Transatl Arts.
Power, Jonathan, et al. Migrant Workers in Western Europe & the United States. LC 78-41199. 1979. 79.00 (*0-08-023385-6*, Pub. by Pergamon Repr UK) Franklin.
***Power, Joseph F.** Francis de Sales: Finding God Wherever You Are. 160p. (Orig.). 1993. pap. 8.95 (*1-56548-074-0*) New City.
Power, Joseph F., ed. Francis de Sales: Finding God Wherever You Are. 160p. (Orig.). 1993. pap. 8.95 (*1-56548-021-X*) New City.
Power, Julia. Shelley in America in the Nineteenth Century. LC 70-90370. 233p. (C). 1969. reprint ed. 50.00 (*0-87752-088-7*) Gordian.
— Shelley in America in the Nineteenth Century. LC 65-15892. (Studies in Shelley: No. 25). 1969. reprint ed. lib. bdg. 75.00 (*0-8383-0611-X*) M S G Haskell Hse.
Power, Kenneth. Power Baking: A Contemporary American Baking Manual. LC 91-66742. 512p. (Orig.). 1991. pap. 149.95 (*1-880650-14-2*) YCart Pub.
Power, Kenneth, jt. auth. see Power, Lyndal.
Power, Kenneth J. Case Presentations in Anaesthesia & Intensive Care. (Illus.). 1992. pap. 30.00 (*0-7506-0497-2*) Buttrwrth-Heinemann.
Power, Kevin & Baselitz, Georg. Georg Baselitz: Hammergreen' (Illus.). 68p. 1992. 35.00 (*0-947564-39-X*, Pub. by A D'Offay Gallery UK) Dist Art Pubs.
Power, Lawrence. Winning the Wellness Game: Your Play by Play Guide to Full Health & Peak Performance. LC 91-60284. (Illus.). 348p. (Orig.). 1991. pap. 19.95 (*1-879963-04-3*) Ntl Health Syst.
Power, Lyndal & Power, Kenneth. Baking Solutions: Helpful Hints for Home Baking. LC 92-64417. 320p. (Orig.). 1993. pap. 12.95 (*1-880650-12-6*) YCart Pub.
Power, M. S., jt. auth. see Williams, Philip.
Power, M. Susan. Before the Convention: Religion & the Founders. LC 84-12004. 268p. (Orig.). 1984. pap. text ed. 23.00 (*0-8191-4134-8*) U Pr of Amer.
— Jacques-Maritain, (1882-1973), Christian Democrat: And the Quest for a New Commonwealth. LC 92-43733. 196p. 1993. text ed. 79.95 (*0-7734-9219-4*) E Mellen.
Power, Margaret. The Egalitarians, Human & Chimpanzee: An Anthropological View of Social Organization. (Illus.). 300p. (C). 1991. 54.95 (*0-521-40016-3*) Cambridge U Pr.
Power, Marjorie. Living with It. 60p. 1983. 5.95 (*0-931694-24-8*) Wampeter Pr.
Power, Marjory W., jt. auth. see Haviland, William A.
Power, Mary J. In the Name of the Bee: The Significance of Emily Dickinson. LC 74-115690. (Illus.). 1970. reprint ed. 22.00 (*0-8196-0266-3*) Biblo.
— Poets at Prayer. LC 68-29239. (Essay Index Reprint Ser.). 1977. 20.95 (*0-8369-0797-3*) Ayer.
Power, Matthew. Demons of the Burning Night. Amthor, Terry K. & Ruemmler, John D., eds. (Shadow World Ser.). (Illus.). 64p. (Orig.). (C). 1989. pap. 12.00 (*1-55806-071-5*, 6003) Iron Crown Ent Inc.
Power, Michael. Religion in the Reich. LC 78-63706. (Studies in Fascism: Ideology & Practice). 1979. reprint ed. 41.50 (*0-404-16976-7*) AMS Pr.
***Power, Michael, ed.** Accounting & Science: Natural Inquiry & Commercial Reason. (Environmental Chemistry Ser.). 285p. (C). Date not set. write for info. (*0-521-55325-3*) Cambridge U Pr.
— Accounting & Science: Natural Inquiry & Commercial Reason. 285p. (C). 1995. pap. write for info. (*0-521-55699-6*) Cambridge U Pr.
Power, Michael, jt. ed. see Freedman, Judith.
Power, Michael A., jt. auth. see Jacobs, George M.
Power, Michael J. & Champion, Lorna A., eds. Adult Psychological Problems: An Introduction. 224p. 1992. 75.00 (*0-7507-0037-8*, Falmer Pr); pap. 27.00 (*0-7507-0038-6*, Falmer Pr) Taylor & Francis.
Power, Nancy G. The Gardens of California. LC 93-43789. (Illus.). 1995. 50.00 (*0-517-58381-X*, C P Pubs) Crown Pub Group.
Power, Nick. The Code. (Illus.). 16p. 1985. 0.75 (*0-938822-44-6*) USTA.
Power, P. B. A Book of Comfort. 1974. pap. 4.95 (*0-85151-203-8*) Banner of Truth.
— The I Wills of Christ. 382p. 1984. reprint ed. pap. 9.95 (*0-85151-429-4*) Banner of Truth.
— The I Wills of the Psalms. 395p. 1985. reprint ed. pap. 9.95 (*0-85151-445-6*) Banner of Truth.
Power, Patrick C. The Book of Irish Curses. 1975. pap. 5.95 (*0-87243-060-X*) Templegate.
— History of South Tipperary. 1989. 100.00 (*0-85342-885-9*) Dufour.
— History of Waterford City & County. 1990. 100.00 (*0-85342-945-6*) Dufour.
— Sex & Marriage in Ancient Ireland. 89p. 1993. pap. 9.95 (*1-85635-062-2*, Pub. by Mercier Pr IE) Dufour.
Power, Paul, et al, eds. Family Interventions Throughout Chronic Illness & Disability. (Series on Rehabilitation: No. 7). 336p. 1988. 33.95 (*0-8261-5580-4*) Springer Pub.
Power, Paul F., ed. The Meaning of Gandhi. LC 72-170180. 205p. reprint ed. pap. 58.50 (*0-685-17129-9*, 2027032) Bks Demand.
Power, Paul W., jt. auth. see Dell Orto, Arthur E.
Power, R. J., ed. Cooperation among Organizations: The Potential of Computer Supported Cooperative Work. (Research Reports ESPRIT, Project 688, AMICE: Vol. 1). vii, 140p. 1993. pap. 29.00 (*0-387-56263-X*) Spr-Verlag.
Power, Ray, et al. Discover Sociology. 300p. (Orig.). (C). 1986. pap. text ed. 26.50 (*0-273-02282-2*) Trans-Atl Phila.
Power, Richard. Don Juan in Tulsa: First Volume of Trilogy, To Be Followed by Faust in Space City & Merlin Druid City. 1985. 12.50 (*0-916620-54-9*) Portals Pr.
— Hungry Grass. 1988. pap. 8.95 (*1-85371-009-1*, Pub. by Poolbeg Pr IE) Dufour.
Power, Richard L. Planting Corn Belt Culture: The Impress of the Upland Southerner & Yankee in the Old Northwest. LC 83-8491. (Indiana Historical Society Publications Ser.). xvi, 196p. 1983. reprint ed. text ed. 49.75 (*0-313-24060-4*, POPC) Greenwood.
***Power, Robert.** Evolution of the Bill of Rights. (Orig.). 1995. pap. 12.95 (*0-8062-5198-0*) Carlton.
Power, Robert B. Steam Jet Ejectors for the Process Industries. 400p. 1994. text ed. 85.00 (*0-07-050618-3*) McGraw.
Power, Robert D. & Fung, Frederick Y. Workers' Compensation Handbook: A Guide to Job-Related Health Problems. LC 93-79792. (Illus.). 116p. (Orig.). 1994. pap. 10.95 (*0-929894-07-3*) K-W Pubns.
Power, Roderick P., et al. Workshops in Perception. 244p. 1981. pap. 9.95 (*0-7100-0931-3*, RKP) Routledge.
Power, S. C., ed. Operators & Function Theory. 1985. lib. bdg. 117.00 (*90-277-2008-8*) Kluwer Ac.
***Power Scheduling Staff.** Power Scheduling. 96p. 1994. per., pap. text ed. 14.95 (*0-7872-0516-8*) Kendall-Hunt.
***Power, Scott E.** Cooking the Sourdough Way: Tips, Stores & Recipes. LC 94-41249. (Illus.). 1995. 9.99 (*1-57034-008-0*) ICS Bks.
Power, Stephen C. Limit Algebras: An Introduction to Subalgebras of C Algebras. (Pitman Research Notes in Mathematics Ser.). 201p. 1993. pap. text ed. 57.95 (*0-470-22080-5*) Halsted Pr.
***Power, Susan.** The Grass Dancer. 352p. Date not set. pap. text ed. 5.99 (*0-425-14962-5*) Berkley Pub.
— The Grass Dancer. 288p. 1994. 22.95 (*0-399-13911-7*, Putnam) Putnam Pub Group.
— The Grass Dancer. large type ed. LC 95-15714. 1995. 23.95 (*1-56895-215-5*) Wheeler Pub.
Power, T. & Whelan, K., eds. Emergence & Endurance: Catholics in Ireland in the Eighteenth Century. 216p. 1989. 39.50 (*0-7165-2420-1*, I2420, Pub. by Irish Acad Pr IE) Intl Spec Bk.
Power, T. W. The Price of an Apple. 249p. (Orig.). (YA). 1992. lib. bdg. write for info. (*0-9634105-0-4*) A J Pub CA.
Power, Thomas A. Family Matters: A Layman's Guide to Family Functioning. (Illus.). 205p. (Orig.). 1989. pap. 6.95 (*0-934080-17-8*) Elan Pub Co.
Power, Thomas C. Electronics Mathematics. LC 84-7828. 416p. (C). 1985. teacher ed 10.00 (*0-8273-2411-1*) Delmar.
— Practical Shop Mathematics. (Illus.). 1979. text ed. 30.95 (*0-07-050591-8*) McGraw.
Power, Thomas M. Economic Pursuit of Quality. LC 87-12128. 224p. (C). 1988. pap. text ed. 25.95 (*0-87332-449-8*) M E Sharpe.
Power, Thomas P. Land, Politics, & Society in Eighteenth-Century Tipperary. LC 93-22481. (C). 1993. 59.00 (*0-19-820316-0*, Clarendon Pr) OUP.
Power, Vicki. Medicine & Health. LC 91-39578. (New Directions Ser.). (Illus.). 32p. (J). (gr. 5-8). 1992. lib. bdg. 12.60 (*0-531-14198-5*) Watts.
***Power, Vincent J.** Competition Law in Ireland. 1995. boxed write for info. (*1-85475-065-8*, IE) Butterworth Legal Pubs.
Power, Wja. Once upon a Time: A Humorous Retelling of the Genesis Story. 1992. pap. 5.95 (*0-687-28849-5*) Abingdon.
Powers. Diagnostic Hematology Clinical & Technical Principles. (Illus.). 576p. 1989. text ed. 41.95 (*0-8016-4042-3*) Mosby Yr Bk.
— Handbook of Dibetes Nutritional Management. 2nd ed. 544p. 1995. 74.00 (*0-8342-0631-5*) Aspen Pub.
— Life's Little Inspiration Book. 1995. pap. 7.00 (*0-00-638038-7*) Harper SF.
— Public Speak the Lively Art. pap. 22.95 (*0-8087-7432-8*) Burgess MN Intl.
— Public Speaking: The Lively Art. (C). 1994. text ed. 24.00 (*0-06-501654-8*) HarpCollege.
Powers, jt. auth. see Sowers.
Powers, et al. Structured Systems Development: Analysis, Design, Implementation. 800p. 1990. 39.50 (*0-87835-550-2*) Boyd & Fraser.
Powers, Alex. Painting People in Watercolor. (Illus.). 144p. 1989. 27.50 (*0-8230-3816-5*, Watsn-Guptill) Watsn-Guptill.

P
Q

An Asterisk (*) at the beginning of an entry indicates that the title is appearing in BIP for the first time.

Powers, Alice & Wyatt, Andrea, eds. The Brooklyn Reader. LC 93-14527. 1994. 22.50 (0-517-59134-0, Harmony) Crown Pub Group.

Powers, Analine M. Silva Mind Control: An Anthropological Inquiry. LC 91-39376. (Cults & Nonconventional Religious Groups Ser.). 336p. 1992. 78.00 (0-8153-0770-5) Garland.

Powers, Ann, jt. comp. see McDonnell, Evelyn.

Powers, Anne. Eleanor: The Passionate Queen. 288p. 1987. reprint ed. pap. 3.50 (0-8439-2505-1) Dorchester Pub Co.

— Heart's Journey. 336p. 1986. reprint ed. pap. 3.75 (0-8439-2406-3) Dorchester Pub Co.

— Queen's Ransom. 400p. 1986. reprint ed. pap. 3.95 (0-8439-2352-0) Dorchester Pub Co.

Powers, Bernard E., Jr. Black Charlestonians: A Social History, 1822-1885. LC 94-7861. (Illus.). 384p. 1994. 36.00 (1-55728-364-8) U of Ark Pr.

Powers, Bethel A. & Knapp, Thomas R. A Dictionary of Nursing Theory & Research. (Illus.). 184p. (C). 1990. text ed. 48.00 (0-8039-3411-4); pap. text ed. 22.95 (0-8039-3412-2) Sage.

— A Dictionary of Nursing Theory & Research. 2nd ed. 224p. 1995. text ed. 46.00 (0-8039-5625-8); pap. text ed. 22.95 (0-8039-5626-6) Sage.

Powers, Betty & Mall, E. Jane. Church Office Handbook for Ministers. 80p. 1983. pap. 6.00 (0-8170-1011-4) Judson.

Powers, Bob. Instructor Excellence: Mastering the Delivery of Training. LC 91-38692. (Management Ser.). 254p. 1992. 29.95 (1-55542-429-5) Jossey-Bass.

Powers, Brian, jt. auth. see Wachtel, Betsy.

Powers, Bruce P. Church Administration Handbook. LC 84-29249. 1992. pap. 12.99 (0-8054-3112-8) Broadman.

Powers, Bruce P., ed. Christian Education Handbook. LC 80-69522. 1991. pap. 12.99 (0-8054-3229-9) Broadman.

Powers, Bruce R., jt. auth. see McLuhan, Marshall.

Powers, C. Martin. Europe: All in One Guidebook. LC 86-61916. (Illus.). 320p. pap. 11.95 (0-933448-01-5) Outstanding VA.

Powers, Carolyn D., ed. The Hagley Cookbook: Recipes with a Brandywine Tradition. LC 83-80986. (Illus.). 189p. 1983. pap. 10.95 (0-9610990-0-3) Hagley Vol Ckbk.

Powers, Charles. Vilfredo Pareto. Turner, Jonathan, ed. (Matters of Social Theory Ser.: Vol. 5). (Illus.). 160p. (C). 1987. 44.00 (0-8039-2284-1); pap. text ed. 18.95 (0-8039-2285-X) Sage.

Powers, Charles, ed. see Pareto, Vilfredo.

Powers, Charles W., jt. auth. see Simon, John G.

Powers, D. B. Dictionary of Russian Verb Forms. 353p. 1985. pap. 9.95 (0-87501-010-5) Ardis Pubs.

Powers, D. M. Legal Street Smarts: How to Survive in a World of Lawyers. (Illus.). 364p. 1994. pap. 19.95 (0-306-44760-6, Plenum Insight) Plenum.

— Machine Learning of Natural Language. (Illus.). x, 358p. 1989. pap. 49.00 (0-387-19557-2) Spr-Verlag.

Powers, D. W., Jr., jt. auth. see Howarth, R. J.

Powers, D. W., jt. auth. see Jerald, J. P.

***Powers, David.** Nuclear Countdown. 1995. pap. 5.99 (1-56171-369-4, S P I Bks) Sure Sellers.

Powers, David L. Boundary Value Problems. 3rd ed. 351p. (C). 1987. text ed. 60.00 (0-15-505535-6) SCP.

Powers, David R. & Powers, Mary F. Making Participatory Management Work. LC 82-49282. (Jossey-Bass Higher Education Ser.). 267p. reprint ed. pap. 76.10 (0-8357-4916-9, 2037846) Bks Demand.

Powers, David R., et al. Higher Education in Partnership with Industry: Opportunities & Strategies for Training, Research, & Economic Development. LC 87-46348. (Higher & Adult Education Ser.). 392p. 1988. 43.95x (1-55542-071-0) Jossey-Bass.

Powers, David S., tr. History of al-Tabari, Vol. 24: The Empire in Transition: The Caliphates of Sulayman, Cumar, & Yazid, A.D. 715-724-A.H. 96-105. LC 88-39752. (SUNY Series in Near Eastern Studies). 218p. 1989. 44.50 (0-7914-0072-7); pap. 16.95 (0-7914-0073-5) State U NY Pr.

Powers, Deborah D. The Court of Appeals at Austin: 1892-1992. LC 92-28116. (Illus.). 86p. 1992. 24.95 (0-938349-92-9) State House Pr.

***Powers, Dennis.** Legal Expense Defense: How to Control Your Business' Legal Costs & Problems. Pinkham, Linda, ed. (Successful Business Library Ser.). 275p. (Orig.). 1995. pap. 19.95 (1-55571-348-3); ring bd. 39.95 (1-55571-349-1) Oasis Pr OR.

***Powers, Dennis M.** Beating the Tough Times: How to Win Your Financial & Personal Battles. 250p. 1995. pap. 18.95 (0-306-45082-8, Plenum Pr) Plenum.

Powers, Doris C. English Formal Satire: Elizabethan to Augustan. (De Proprietatibus Litterarum, Ser. Practica: No. 19). 214p. (Orig.). 1971. pap. text ed. 33.85 (90-279-1905-4) Mouton.

Powers, Dorothy R. Dorothy: Powers to the People. LC 88-62872. 320p. 1988. 19.95 (0-923910-00-X); pap. 13.95 (0-923910-01-8) Cowles Pub Co.

Powers, Douglas, ed. Adoption for Troubled Children: Prevention & Repair of Adoptive Failures Through Residential Treatment. LC 83-26424. (Residential Group Care & Treatment Ser.: Vol. 2, Nos. 1-2). 201p. 1984. text ed. 39.95 (0-86656-245-1) Haworth Pr.

Powers, Douglas C., et al, eds. Aging, Immunity, & Infection. LC 93-42177. 328p. 1993. 47.95 (0-8261-8180-5) Springer Pub.

***Powers, Edna & Kriegel, Gaye.** Affordable Heirlooms. LC 95-10550. (Creative Machine Arts Ser.). 128p. 1995. pap. 15.95 (0-8019-8647-8) Chilton.

Powers, Edward A. Later Life Transitions: Older Males in Rural America. 1985. lib. bdg. 52.50 (0-89838-137-1) Kluwer Ac.

Powers, Edwin & Witmer, Helen. Experiment in the Prevention of Delinquency: The Cambridge - Somerville Youth Study. LC 70-172573. (Criminology, Law Enforcement, & Social Problems Ser.: No. 159). 1972. reprint ed. 25.00 (0-87585-159-2) Patterson Smith.

Powers, Elizabeth. Nero. (World Leaders - Past & Present Ser.). (Illus.). 112p. (J). (gr. 5 up). 1988. lib. bdg. 17.95 (0-87754-544-8) Chelsea Hse.

Powers, Elvin M. Building a Caring-Sharing Community of Believers. 128p. 1983. pap. 3.95 (0-8341-0822-4) Beacon Hill.

Powers, Gene R. Cleft Palate. LC 72-86554. (Studies in Communicative Disorders). 37p. 1973. pap. text ed. 4.50 (0-672-61288-7, Bobbs) Macmillan.

— Cleft Palate. Halpern, Harvey, ed. LC 86-3062. (PRO-ED Studies in Communicative Disorders). (Illus.). 52p. 1986. pap. text ed. 9.00 (0-89079-094-9, 1384) PRO-ED.

Powers, George. Cradle of Steel Unionism: Monogahela, PA. 163p. 1972. lib. bdg. 25.95 (0-88286-098-4) C H Kerr.

***Powers, Georgia D.** I Shared the Dream: The Pride Passion & Politics of the First Black Woman Senator from Kentucky. LC 94-66756. 320p. 1995. 25.95 (0-88282-127-X) New Horizon NJ.

Powers, Grant. Historical Sketches of the Discovery, Settlement, & Progress of Events in the Coos Country & Vicinity Principally Included Between the Years 1754 & 1785. 246p. 1987. reprint ed. pap. 16.00 (1-55613-022-8) Heritage Bk.

Powers, Harold, ed. Studies in Music History: Essays for Oliver Strunk. LC 80-14086. (Illus.). x, 527p. 1980. reprint ed. text ed. 85.00 (0-313-22501-X, POSM, Greenwood Pr) Greenwood.

Powers, Harold, jt. auth. see Ashbrook, William.

Powers, Helen W., jt. auth. see DiAntonio, Robert.

Powers, Hiram C. The Hiram C. Powers Story, 1905: An Autobiography, on Pioneer Life, Travels in the Wild West, & a Legendary Feud of Western Kentucky. LC 92-37914. 1993. write for info. (0-941677-73-7); pap. write for info. (0-941677-72-9) White Cliffs Media.

Powers, Isaias. Father Ike's Stories for Children: Teaching Christian Values Through Animal Stories. LC 88-50332. (Illus.). 64p. (Orig.). (J). 1988. pap. 4.95 (0-89622-370-1) Twenty-Third.

— Letters from an Understanding Friend: Jesus on the Way to Jerusalem. LC 84-50409. 96p. (Orig.). 1985. pap. 5.95 (0-89622-413-9) Twenty-Third.

— Quiet Places with Jesus. LC 78-64452. 128p. 1978. pap. 5.95 (0-89622-086-9) Twenty-Third.

— Quiet Places with Mary. LC 86-50123. 160p. (Orig.). 1986. pap. 5.95 (0-89622-297-7) Twenty-Third.

— Women of the Gospel: Sharing God's Compassion. LC 92-81796. (Illus.). 160p. (Orig.). 1993. pap. 5.95 (0-89622-521-6) Twenty-Third.

Powers, J. Quality Assurance Procedures: For Department of Defense & Industry. (Illus.). 154p. 1983. pap. 45.00 (0-912702-18-4, QAP) Global Eng Doc.

Powers, J. F. The Old Bird, A Love Story. (Winter Book Ser.: No. 4). (Illus.). 32p. 1991. 155.00 (1-879832-25-9); pap. 65.00 (1-879832-26-7) MN Ctr Book Arts.

— Wheat That Springeth Green. LC 87-46104. 352p. 1988. 18.95 (0-394-49609-4) Knopf.

Powers, J. H. Computer Automated Manufacturing. 368p. 1987. pap. text ed. 29.95 (0-07-050601-9) McGraw.

— Historical Reminiscences of Chickasaw County, Iowa. (Illus.). 332p. 1992. reprint ed. lib. bdg. 36.00 (0-8328-2585-9) Higginson Bk Co.

Powers, J. P., ed. Dewatring-Avoiding Its Unwanted Side Effects. (C). 1987. text ed. 55.00 (0-685-61675-4, Pub. by Scientific Pubs II) St Mut.

Powers, J. Patrick. Construction Dewatering: New Methods & Applications. 2nd ed. (Series of Practical Construction Guides: No. 1344). 528p. 1992. text ed. 74.95 (0-471-60185-3) Wiley.

— Dewatering: Avoiding Its Unwanted Side Effects. (C). 1986. 115.00 (0-685-54221-1, Scientific) St Mut.

Powers, J. Patrick, ed. Dewatering-Avoiding Its Unwanted Side Effects. (C). 1987. reprint ed. text ed. 100.00 (0-685-22082-6, Scientific) St Mut.

Powers, J. Patrick, ed. see American Society of Civil Engineers Staff.

Powers, Jack. Dental Office Plans, Vol. 2. 116p. 1985. 31.95 (0-87814-287-8, D4242) PennWell Bks.

Powers, Jack & Layman, George. Dental Office Plans, Vol. 1. 112p. 1982. 31.95 (0-87814-193-6, D4216) PennWell Bks.

Powers, Jack, jt. auth. see Layman, George.

Powers, James F. Presence of Grace. LC 77-85694. (Short Story Index Reprint Ser.). 1977. 19.95 (0-8369-3037-1) Ayer.

***Powers, Jamilla & Gibbs, Tyson.** Afro-Centric Guide to: Reflections, Affirmations, Meditations & Prayers. 130p. (Orig.). 1994. pap. 10.95 (0-9638548-0-1) Jamilla Powers.

***Powers, Jan.** Word Wizardry: A Book of Poems. 64p. 1995. 12.95 (0-8233-0501-5) Golden Quill.

Powers, Jane B. The Girl Question in Education: Vocational Training for Young Women in the Progressive Era. (Studies in Curriculum History Ser.). 224p. 1992. 60.00 (1-85000-847-7, Falmer Pr) Taylor & Francis.

Powers, Jane L. & Jaklitsch, Barbara W. Understanding Survivors of Abuse: Stories of Homeless & Runaway Adolescents. 160p. 1989. text ed. 27.95 (0-669-20902-3) Free Pr.

Powers, Janet, jt. auth. see Potter, Jamie.

Powers, Jeffrey, jt. auth. see Klotz, Suzanne.

Powers, Jennifer, jt. ed. see Campbell, Dennis.

Powers, Jo M. Farmers' Market Cookbook. (Illus.). 238p. 1984. pap. 12.95 (0-7737-5005-3, Pub. by Stoddart Pubng CN) Genl Dist Srvs.

Powers, Jo M., jt. auth. see Powers, Thomas F.

***Powers, John.** And Grace Will Lead Me Home: A Spiritual Journey. LC 94-31498. 208p. 1994. 9.95 (1-56977-635-0) McCracken Pr.

— Introduction to Tibetan Buddhism. 501p. (Orig.). 1995. text ed. 34.95 (1-55939-028-X) Snow Lion Pubns.

— Introduction to Tibetan Buddhism. 501p. (Orig.). (C). 1995. pap. 18.95 (1-55939-026-3) Snow Lion Pubns.

Powers, John, Jr. Megabit Data Communications: A Guide for Professionals. 1989. text ed. 71.00 (0-13-573569-6) P-H.

Powers, John. The Yogacara School of Buddhism: A Bibliography. LC 91-37139. (American Theological Library Association Monograph: No. 27). 267p. 1991. 29.50 (0-8108-2502-3) Scarecrow.

Powers, John, tr. Wisdom of Buddha: The Samdhiriro Mocana Sutra. 1994. pap. 25.00 (0-89800-246-X) Dharma Pub.

— Wisdom of Buddha: The Samdhiriro Mocana Sutra. 1994. 40.00 (0-89800-247-8) Dharma Pub.

Powers, John, tr. see Asanga & Jnanagarbha.

Powers, John, jt. auth. see Gowdy, Curt.

Powers, John A., jt. auth. see Easton, Edward J., Jr.

Powers, John D. Holy & Human: Mystics for Our Time. LC 89-50565. 128p. 1989. pap. 7.95 (0-89622-398-1) Twenty-Third.

— If They Could Speak: Ten Witnesses to the Passion of Jesus. Brauch, Judy, tr. LC 89-51902. (Illus.). 64p. (Orig.). 1990. pap. 4.95 (0-89622-421-X) Twenty-Third.

— Mirror, Mirror, on the Wall: The Art of Talking with Yourself. LC 87-50839. 112p. (Orig.). 1987. pap. 5.95 (0-89622-344-2) Twenty-Third.

Powers, John P. An Introduction to Fiber Optic Systems. LC 92-31650. (Aksen Associates Series in Electrical & Computer Engineering). 500p. (C). 1993. text ed. 64.95 (0-256-12996-7) Irwin.

***Powers, John R.** The Junk-Drawer Corner-Store Front-Porch Blues. braille ed. 324p. 1994. text ed. 25.92 (1-56956-506-6, BR9344) W A T Braille.

— The Junk-Drawer Corner-Store Front Porch Blues. 256p. 1993. reprint ed. pap. 5.99 (0-451-17602-2, Sig) NAL-Dutton.

— Last Catholic in America. 1993. pap. 4.99 (0-451-17614-6, Sig) NAL-Dutton.

— The Last Catholic in America. LC 79-24431. 1981. reprint ed. lib. bdg. 18.00 (0-8376-0439-7) Bentley.

Powers, Jonathan. Philosophy & the New Physics. (Methuens Ideas Ser.). (Illus.). 150p. 1982. pap. 12.95 (0-416-73480-4, NO. 3795) Routledge Chapman & Hall.

Powers, Judith, ed. Norfolk to Jacksonville Chart Book. 1993. pap. 79.95 (0-915962-76-4) Argus GA.

— Waterway Guide: Great Lakes, 1994. (Illus.). 1993. pap. 33.95 (0-915962-77-2) Argus GA.

— Waterway Guide: Mid-Atlantic Edition, 1994. (Illus.). 1993. pap. 33.95 (0-915962-79-9) Argus GA.

— Waterway Guide: Northern Edition, 1994. (Illus.). 1994. pap. 33.95 (0-915962-80-2) Argus GA.

Powers, Judith, jt. auth. see Maloney, Elberrt S.

Powers, Judy. Cooking with Honey. 64p. 1984. pap. 3.49 (0-942320-12-3) Am Cooking.

Powers, Judy, jt. auth. see Hahn, Joan.

Powers, Katherine R. The Influence of William Godwin on the Novels of Mary Shelley. Varma, Devendra P., ed. LC 79-7469. (Gothic Studies & Dissertations). 1980. lib. bdg. 23.95 (0-405-12657-3) Ayer.

Powers, Laurie E., jt. ed. see Singer, George H.

Powers, Lawerence W., jt. auth. see Pottiglio, Denise H.

Powers, Lyall H. Faulkner's Yoknapatawpha Comedy. LC 79-23140. 295p. 1980. reprint ed. pap. 84.10 (0-7837-5652-6, 2059077) Bks Demand.

— Henry James & Edith Wharton: Letters: 1900-1915. 352p. 1990. text ed. 29.95 (0-684-19146-6, Scribners) S&S Trade.

— Leon Edel & Literary Art. Litz, A. Walton, ed. LC 87-19211. (Studies in Modern Literature: No. 84). 206p. reprint ed. 58.80 (0-8357-1839-5, 2070753) Bks Demand.

— The Portrait of a Lady: Maiden, Woman & Heroine. (Twayne's Masterwork Studies: No. 78). 128p. 1991. text ed. 21.95 (0-8057-8066-1, Twayne); pap. 12.95 (0-8057-8550-7, Twayne) Macmillan.

Powers, Lyall H., ed. see James, Henry.

Powers, Lynn & Van-Si, Laurie. Helping Children Heal from Loss: A Keepsake Book of Special Memories. 35p. (Orig.). 1994. pap. 12.95 (0-87678-102-4) PSU CE Pr.

Powers, Mala, ed. see Chekhov, Michael.

Powers Management Consultants Staff. Configuration Management Procedures. Leiblich, J. H., ed. 121p. 1984. pap. 35.00 (0-912702-25-7) Global Eng Doc.

— Quality Assurance Procedures Manual. Leiblich, J. H., ed. 81p. 1983. pap. 45.00 (0-912702-21-4) Global Eng Doc.

Powers, Margaret A. & Johnson, Byron P. Defensive Sites of Dinetah: Bureau of Land Management New Mexico State Office. (Cultural Resources Ser.: No. 2). (Illus.). 142p. (Orig.). 1991. reprint ed. pap. 8.00 (1-878178-02-4) Bureau of Land Mgmt NM.

Powers, Margaret A., ed. see American Diabetes Association Staff.

Powers, Margaret F. Footprints: The True Story Behind the Poem That Inspired Millions. 1993. pap. 8.00 (0-00-647425-X, PL) HarpC.

Powers, Marian. Lecture Outlines for Accounting 110. 3rd ed. 80p. 1991. spiral bd. 9.65 (0-8403-7198-5) Kendall-Hunt.

Powers, Marion D. The Legal Citation Directory. LC 75-25703. 302p. 1971. lib. bdg. 42.00 (0-9600482-0-0) Franas Pr.

Powers, Mark. Getting Started in Commodity Futures Trading. (Illus.). 1983. pap. 12.95 (0-914230-01-8) Investor Pubns.

Powers, Mark J. Starting Out in Futures Trading. 5th ed. 1993. pap. 24.95 (1-55738-506-8) Probus Pub Co.

Powers, Mark J. & Castelino, Mark G. Inside the Financial Futures Markets. 3rd ed. 400p. 1991. text ed. 55.00 (0-471-53674-1) Wiley.

Powers, Marla N. Oglala Women: Myth, Ritual, & Reality. (Women in Culture & Society Ser.). (Illus.). xvi, 242p. 1988. pap. 12.95 (0-226-67749-4) U Ch Pr.

Powers, Martha. Double Masquerade. large type ed. LC 90-28491. 370p. 1991. reprint ed. lib. bdg. 18.95 (1-56054-146-6) Thorndike Pr.

Powers, Martin J. Art & Political Expression in Early China. (Illus.). 352p. 1992. text ed. 50.00 (0-300-04767-3) Yale U Pr.

Powers, Mary E. Our Teacher's in a Wheelchair. Tucker, Kathleen, ed. LC 86-1623. (Albert Whitman Concept Bks.). (Illus.). 32p. (J). (ps-3). 1986. 11.95 (0-8075-6240-8) A Whitman.

Powers, Mary F., jt. auth. see Powers, David R.

Powers, Mary G. & Macisco, John J., Jr. Los Puertorriquenos en Nueva York: Un Analisis de su Participacion Laboral y Experiencia Migratoria, 1970. vi, 201p. 1982. pap. 5.00 (0-8477-2468-9) U of PR Pr.

***Powers, Mary G. & Macisco, John J., Jr., eds.** International Migration Conference. LC 94-22724. 1994. 14.50 (0-934733-84-8) Ctr Migration.

Powers, Mary G., jt. auth. see Nam, Charles B.

Powers, Mary R. A Woman's Overland Journal to California. (Illus.). 75p. 1985. reprint ed. 12.00 (0-87770-349-3) Ye Galleon.

Powers, Melvin. Dynamic Thinking. 1980. pap. 5.00 (0-87980-031-3) Wilshire.

— How to Get Rich in Mail Order. 1980. pap. 20.00 (0-87980-373-8) Wilshire.

— How to Self-Publish Your Book & Have the Fun Excitement of Being a Best-Selling Author. 1984. pap. 20.00 (0-87980-406-8) Wilshire.

— Hypnotism Revealed. 1970. pap. 3.00 (0-87980-080-1) Wilshire.

— Making Money with Classified Ads. 1995. pap. 20.00 (0-87980-435-1) Wilshire.

— Mental Power Thru Sleep Suggestion. 1971. pap. 3.00 (0-87980-097-6) Wilshire.

— Practical Guide to Better Concentration. (Orig.). 1980. pap. 5.00 (0-87980-120-4) Wilshire.

— Practical Guide to Self-Hypnosis. (Orig.). 1960. pap. 5.00 (0-87980-122-0) Wilshire.

— Self-Hypnosis: Its Theory, Technique & Application. 1975. pap. 7.00 (0-87980-138-7) Wilshire.

Powers, Meredith A. The Heroine in Western Literature: The Archetype & Her Reemergence in Modern Prose. LC 91-52597. 240p. 1991. lib. bdg. 32.50 (0-89950-615-1) McFarland & Co.

Powers, Michael, ed. Children with Autism: A Parents' Guide. LC 87-51322. (Illus.). 368p. (Orig.). 1989. pap. 14.95 (0-933149-16-6) Woodbine House.

Powers, Michael, et al. Medical Negligence. 1990. U.K. 270.00 (0-406-13001-9, U.K.) Butterworth Legal Pubs.

Powers, Michael D. Educating Children with Autism: A Guide to Selecting an Appropriate Program. (Topics in Autism Ser.). 200p. (Orig.). 1995. pap. 12.95 (0-933149-70-0) Woodbine House.

Powers, Michael D., ed. see Harris, Sandra L.

Powers, N. Thompson. Employment Discrimination Law, 1987-89 Supplement. 200p. 1991. pap. text ed. 45.00 (0-87179-675-9, 0675) BNA.

Powers, Nancy. Cooking for One Hundred. (Illus.). 256p. 1992. pap. 14.95 (0-941684-04-0) Powers Pub.

Powers, Nora. Woman of the West. braille ed. 233p. 1992. vinyl bd. 18.64 (1-56956-333-0, BR7955) W A T Braille.

Powers, Paul. A Guide to Vocational Assessment. 2nd ed. LC 90-15579. 321p. (C). 1991. pap. text ed. 31.00 (0-89079-426-X, 1946) PRO-ED.

Powers, Paul & Russell, Deborah. Love Your Job! Loving the Job You Have...Finding a Job You Love. (Illus.). 210p. (Orig.). 1993. pap. 12.95 (1-56592-036-8) OReilly & Assocs.

Powers, Paul A. They That Go down to the Sea: A Bicentennial Pictorial History of the United States Coast Guard. LC 90-61231. (Illus.). vii, 208p. 1990. 35.00 (0-9626717-0-3); 75.00 (0-9626717-1-1) USCG CPO Assn.

Powers, Pauline S. & Fernandez, R. C., eds. Current Treatment of Anorexia Nervosa & Bulimia. (Biobehavioral Medicine Ser.: Vol. 4). xvi, 348p. 1984. 78.50 (3-8055-3879-0) S Karger.

Powers, Peggy. The Activity Gourmet. LC 91-66393. (Illus.). 135p. (Orig.). 1991. spiral bd. 15.95 (0-910251-51-7) Venture Pub PA.

Powers, Peter. Touring California's Wine Country by Bicycle: Cycling in the Wine Growing Regions of North & Central California. 174p. 1990. pap. 10.95 (0-944376-06-1) Terragraphics.

— Touring New England by Bicycle: Cycling in Vermont, Maine & the Cape Islands. 174p. (Orig.). 1991. pap. 10.95 (0-944376-08-8) Terragraphics.

— Touring Seattle by Bicycle: Cycling in Seattle & the Lower Puget Sound Area. 174p. (Orig.). 1991. pap. 10.95 (0-944376-02-9) Terragraphics.

— Touring the Los Angeles Area by Bicycle: Cycling in Santa Barbara, Ventura, Los Angeles, Riverside & Orange Counties. 174p. (Orig.). 1992. pap. 12.95 (0-944376-09-6) Terragraphics.

— Touring the Pennsylvania Countryside by Bicycle: Cycling in Southeastern Pennsylvania & Western New Jersey. 174p. (Orig.). 1992. pap. 12.95 (0-944376-12-6) Terragraphics.

— Touring the San Francisco Bay Area by Bicycle: Cycling in Marin, Contra Costa, San Mateo, Alameda, Santa Clara & Santa Cruz Counties. 174p. (Orig.). 1990. pap. 11.95 (0-944376-05-3) Terragraphics.

— Touring the Washington D.C. Area by Bicycle: Cycling in Maryland, Virginia & D.C. 1991. pap. 10.95 (*0-944376-07-X*) Terragraphics.

Powers, Peter & Travis, Renee. Touring the Islands: Bicycling in the San Juan, Gulf, & Vancouver Islands. 174p. (Orig.). 1988. pap. 12.95 (*0-944376-01-0*) Terragraphics.

Powers, Phil. NOLS Wilderness Mountaineering. LC 93-6856. (Illus.). 224p. 1993. pap. 14.95 (*0-8117-3086-7*) Stackpole.

Powers, Rachell C. Kaleidoscope of Poetry. (Illus.). 36p. 1988. 10.00 (*0-9621323-0-6*) R Powers.

Powers, Remus. Kansas City BBQ Pocket Guide. 128p. (Orig.). 1992. pap. 7.95 (*0-925175-08-0*) Pig Out Pubns.

Powers, Rhea & Bantle, Gawain. Riding the Dragon: The Power of Committed Relationship. 240p. 1995. pap. 14.95 (*1-880823-09-8*) N Star Pubns.

***Powers, Richard.** Galatea 2.2. LC 94-44319. 320p. 1995. 22.00 (*0-374-19948-5*) FS&G.

— The Gold Bug Variations. LC 92-52616. 1992. pap. 13.00 (*0-06-097500-8*, PL) HarpC.

— Operation Wandering Soul. 352p. 1994. reprint ed. pap. 12.00 (*0-06-097611-X*, PL) HarpC.

— Operation Wandering Soul: A Novel. LC 92-43860. 1993. 23.00 (*0-688-11548-9*) Morrow.

— Pathways to Spiritual Understanding: An Exciting Introduction to the Basics of the Christian Life. 245p. 1988. pap. text ed. 14.99 (*1-56322-023-7*) V Hensley.

— Prisoner's Dilemma. 348p. 1989. pap. 9.95 (*0-02-036055-X*, Collier S&S) S&S Trade.

— Three Farmers on Their Way to a Dance. LC 92-52617. 1992. pap. 12.00 (*0-06-097509-1*, PL) HarpC.

Powers, Richard, jt. auth. see Madden, David.

Powers, Richard G. Not Without Honor: The History of American Anti-Communism. 400p. 1995. text ed. 30.00 (*0-02-925301-2*) Free Pr.

— Secrecy & Power: The Life of J. Edgar Hoover. (Illus.). 656p. 1987. text ed. 32.95 (*0-02-925060-9*) Free Pr.

— Secrecy & Power: The Life of J. Edgar Hoover. (Illus.). 656p. 1988. pap. 16.95 (*0-02-925061-7*) Free Pr.

Powers, Richard G. & Kato, Hidetoshi, eds. Handbook of Japanese Popular Culture. LC 87-7586. 368p. 1989. text ed. 79.50 (*0-313-23922-3*, PJC/, Greenwood Pr) Greenwood.

Powers, Robert. Three Farmers on the Way to a Dance. 1987. pap. 4.95 (*0-317-56921-X*) McGraw.

***Powers, Robert L. & Griffith, Jane.** The Individual Psychology Client Workbook with Supplements. 45p. (Orig.). 1995. student ed, pap. text ed. 17.50x (*0-918287-08-1*) AIAS.

— Understanding Life-Style: The Psycho-Clarity Process. LC 87-13146. 336p. 1987. text ed. 32.50 (*0-918287-02-2*); pap. text ed. 22.50 (*0-918287-03-0*) AIAS.

Powers, Robert L., jt. auth. see Griffith, Jane.

Powers, Robert L., jt. auth. see Wedge, Thomas W.

Powers, Rodney G., jt. auth. see Sagues, Alberto A.

Powers, Rohn. The Newscasters. 1980. pap. 2.50 (*0-8439-0806-8*) Dorchester Pub Co.

Powers, Ron. The Beast, the Eunuch & the Glass-Eyed Child: Television in the 80's. 1990. 24.95 (*0-15-111251-7*) HarBrace.

— The Cruel Radiance: Notes of a Prosewriter in a Visual Age. LC 94-20541. 288p. 1994. 25.00 (*0-87451-690-0*) U Pr of New Eng.

— Far from Home: Life & Loss in Two American Towns. 1991. 21.50 (*0-394-57034-0*) Random.

Powers, Sally I., jt. auth. see Cobb, Stephen.

Powers, Samuel R. A Diagnostic Study of the Subject Matter of High School Chemistry. LC 79-177164. (Columbia University. Teachers College. Contributions to Education Ser.: No. 149). reprint ed. 37.50 (*0-404-55149-1*) AMS Pr.

Powers, Scott K. & Howley, Edward T. Exercise Physiology: Theory & Application to Fitness & Performance. 2nd ed. 624p. 1994. boxed 47.85 (*0-697-12657-9*) Brown & Benchmark.

Powers, Stanley P., et al, eds. Developing the Municipal Organization. LC 74-79125. (Municipal Management Ser.). 1974. text ed. 30.00 (*0-87326-001-5*) Intl City-Cnty Mgt.

Powers, Stephen. Tribes of California. LC 74-7994. reprint ed. 67.50 (*0-404-11881-X*) AMS Pr.

— Tribes of California. LC 75-13150. 1977. reprint ed. pap. 15.00 (*0-520-03172-5*) U CA Pr.

Powers, Stephen T., jt. auth. see Bookman, John T.

Powers, Steve, jt. auth. see Postman, Neil.

Powers, Susan, jt. ed. see Brown, Brisbane.

***Powers, Susan J.** Pocket Mentor: How to Get Every Promotion You Want from Now On! 390p. 1995. 29.95 (*1-886573-02-6*); pap. 19.95 (*1-886573-01-8*) Change Pubns.

Powers, Terry A., ed. El Calculo de los Precios de Cuenta en la Evaluacion de Proyectos: Estudios de Casos con Base en el Metodo Little-Mirrlees - Squire van der Tak. 482p. 1981. write for info. (*0-940602-01-6*) IADB.

— Estimating Accounting Prices for Project Appraisal: Case Studies in the Little-Mirrlees - Squire-van der Tak Method. 430p. 1981. write for info. (*0-940602-00-8*) IADB.

Powers, Thomas. Heisenberg's War: The Secret History of the German Bomb. LC 92-14910. 1993. 27.00 (*0-394-51411-4*) Knopf.

— Heisenberg's War: The Secret History of the German Bomb. 1994. pap. 16.95 (*0-316-71623-5*) Little.

Powers, Thomas & Tremain, Ruthven. Total War: What It Is, How It Got That Way. LC 87-29951. 224p. 1988. 16.95 (*0-688-06919-3*) Morrow.

***Powers, Thomas E.** Invitation to a Great Experiment: Exploring the Possibility That God Can Be Known. rev. ed. (Illus.). 352p. Date not set. pap. 16.95 (*0-914896-42-3*) East Ridge Pr.

Powers, Thomas F. & Powers, Jo M. Food Service Operations: Planning & Control. LC 83-10364. (Service Management Ser.). 384p. (C). 1991. reprint ed. 44.50 (*0-89464-600-1*) Krieger.

Powers, Thomas L. Modern Business Marketing: A Strategic Planning Approach to Business & Industrial Markets. Fenton, ed. 642p. (C). 1991. text ed. 66.50 (*0-314-66808-X*) West Pub.

Powers, Thomas R. Integrated Circuit Hobbyist's Handbook. 1994. pap. 19.95 (*1-878707-12-4*) HighText.

— The Master Handbook of IC Circuits. pap. 18.60 (*0-8306-1370-6*) TAB Bks.

Powers, Tim. The Anubis Gates. 416p. 1984. pap. 4.95 (*0-441-02382-7*) Ace Bks.

— Anubis Gates. limited ed. (Illus.). 396p. 1990. reprint ed. 65.00 (*0-929480-11-2*) Mark Ziesing.

— Anubis Gates. (Illus.). 396p. 1990. reprint ed. 25.00 (*0-929480-10-4*) Mark Ziesing.

— The Drawing of the Dark. 1987. mass mkt. 3.99 (*0-345-35008-1*, Del Rey) Ballantine.

— Expiration Date. 1996. write for info. (*0-614-05499-0*) Tor Bks.

— Last Call. 544p. 1993. mass mkt. 4.99 (*0-380-71557-0*) Avon.

— Last Call. (Illus.). 576p. 1992. 150.00 (*0-927389-05-3*) Charnel Hse.

— Last Call. braille ed. 1061p. 1994. text ed., vinyl bd. 84.88 (*1-56956-553-8*, BR9436) W A T Braille.

— Last Call. limited ed. (Illus.). 576p. 1992. 650.00 (*0-927389-04-5*) Charnel Hse.

— Last Call: A Novel. 420p. 1992. 23.00 (*0-688-10732-X*) Morrow.

— On Stranger Tides. 1988. pap. 3.95 (*0-441-62686-6*) Ace Bks.

— Stress of Her Regard. 1991. pap. 4.95 (*0-441-79097-6*) Ace Bks.

— The Stress of Her Regard. limited ed. (Illus.). 544p. 1989. 125.00 (*0-927389-01-0*); 400.00 (*0-927389-00-2*) Charnel Hse.

Powers, Tim, jt. auth. see Isaacs, Richard B.

Powers, Tom. Horror Movies. (Silver Screen Ser.). (Illus.). 80p. (J). (gr. 5 up). 1989. 18.95 (*0-8225-1636-5*, Lerner Publctns) Lerner Group.

— Horror Movies. (Illus.). 80p. (J). (gr. 5 up). reprint ed. pap. 7.95 (*0-8225-9570-2*, Lerner Publctns) Lerner Group.

— Introduction to Hospitality. 3rd ed. LC 94-31663. 1995. pap. text ed. write for info. (*0-471-31036-0*) Wiley.

— Introduction to Management in the Hospitality Industry. 4th ed. (Service Management Ser.). 656p. 1992. Net. text ed. write for info. (*0-471-53055-7*) Wiley.

— Introduction to Management in the Hospitality Industry 94-022961. 5th ed. LC 94-22961. (Service Management Ser.). 1995. text ed. 29.00 (*0-471-31035-2*) Wiley.

— Introduction to the Hospitality Industry. 2nd ed. (Service Management Ser.). 528p. 1992. Net. pap. text ed. write for info. (*0-471-53054-9*) Wiley.

— Marketing Hospitality. 434p. 1990. Net. text ed. write for info. (*0-471-63846-3*); Net. student ed, pap. text ed. write for info. (*0-471-62298-2*) Wiley.

— Michigan in Quotes. (Illus.). 176p. (Orig.). 1994. pap. 12.95 (*0-923756-08-6*) Friede Pubns.

— Michigan State & National Parks: A Complete Guide. rev. ed. (Illus.). 240p. (Orig.). 1993. pap. 14.95 (*0-9608588-9-X*) Friede Pubns.

— Movie Monsters. (Silver Screen Ser.). (Illus.). 80p. (J). (gr. 5 up). 1989. 18.95 (*0-8225-1637-3*, Lerner Publctns) Lerner Group.

— Movie Monsters. (Illus.). 80p. (J). (gr. 5 up). reprint ed. 7.95 (*0-8225-9571-0*, Lerner Publctns) Lerner Group.

— Natural Michigan: A Guide to 288 Natural Attractions. expanded rev. ed. (Illus.). 260p. 1995. pap. 14.95 (*0-923756-13-2*) Friede Pubns.

— Special Effects in the Movies. LC 89-12703. (Overview Ser.). (Illus.). 96p. (J). (gr. 5-8). 1989. lib. bdg. 16.95 (*1-56006-102-2*) Lucent Bks.

***Powers, Treval C. Leakage: the Bleeding of the American Economy: A Quantitative Analysis of the Economic Progress of the United States from 1898-1988. (Illus.). 375p. 1995. pap. write for info. (*0-9647121-1-3*) Benchmark CT.**
LEAKAGE: THE BLEEDING OF THE AMERICAN ECONOMY is a long overdue, unbiased look at how the economy really works, what causes fluctuations, & how it can be repaired. Written by a research scientist with a lifelong discipline in the scientific method, this scholarly work presents incontrovertible evidence that the conventional Economics wisdom is based on false assumptions--that what is basically a simple system has been distorted by the application of popular, but erroneous, theories. The author rejects the apparent notion that somehow the economy can be stopped long enough to measure it. Instead, he offers the Composite Producer & the Composite Consumer--inconstant motion--a continuum of human activity. To measure this moving target, the author selects a slice of time, always shown in the context of the prevailing economic influences, & applies basic research techniques for the statistical analysis of multiple variables. This is startling breakthrough, revealing what's been called Empirical Macroeconomics: economic REALITY as opposed to economic THEORY. LEAKAGE: THE BLEEDING OF THE AMERICAN ECONOMY is amply illustrated with graphs & tables. To order, call Benchmark Publications at 203-966-6653, FAX 203-972-7129 or write to 76 Elm St., P.O. Box 1594, New Canaan, CT 06840-1594. *Publisher Provided Annotation.*

Powers, W. Robert. Electrical Fires in New York City - 1976. 1977. 2.50 (*0-686-22739-5*, TR 77-3) Society Fire Protect.

— Sprinkler Experience in High-Rise Buildings. 1979. 3.25 (*0-686-26148-8*, TR 79-1) Society Fire Protect.

Powers, Will & Strickland, Bob. Bowling Tough: Three Simple Methods to Improve Your Performance under Pressure. 112p. 1993. pap. text ed. 9.95 (*0-9635919-0-8*) R H Strickland.

Powers, William, Jr. Texas Products Liability Law. 380p. 1994. ring bd. 115.00 (*1-56257-955-X*) Michie Butterworth.

— Texas Products Liability Law. suppl. ed. 380p. 1993. 55.00 (*0-685-46138-6*) Butterworth Legal Pubs.

Powers, William, Jr., jt. auth. see Fischer, David A.

Powers, William C., Jr., jt. auth. see Fischer, David A.

Powers, William C., Jr., ed. see Fischer, David A.

Powers, William D. Uncle Isaac. LC 74-170703. (Black Heritage Library Collection). 1977. reprint ed. 22.95 (*0-8369-8893-0*) Ayer.

Powers, William F. Free Priests: The Movement for Ministerial Reform in the American Catholic Church. LC 92-8492. (Orig.). 1992. pap. 13.50 (*0-8294-0729-4*) Loyola Univ Pr.

Powers, William F., et al, eds. Astrodynamics, 1975. (Advances in the Astronautical Sciences Ser.: Vol. 33). (Illus.). 1976. lib. bdg. 35.00 (*0-87703-079-0*, Pub. by Am Astro Soc); fiche 40.00 (*0-87703-142-8*, Pub. by Am Astro Soc) Univelt Inc.

Powers, William H. Guide to Milwaukee Taverns. rev. ed. McCaig, Barbara, ed. (Illus.). 200p. 1987. pap. 4.95 (*0-935201-24-6*) Affordable Adven.

Powers, William J. & Raichle, Marcus E., eds. Cerebrovascular Diseases: Fifteenth Research (Princeton) Conference on Cerebrovascular Diseases. (Illus.). 396p. 1987. text ed. 142.50 (*0-88167-289-0*) Raven.

Powers, William K. Beyond the Vision: Essays on American Indian Culture. LC 87-40218. (Civilization of the American Indian Ser.: Vol. 184). (Illus.). 256p. 1987. 35.00 (*0-8061-2091-6*) U of Okla Pr.

— Oglala Religion. LC 76-30614. (Illus.). xxii, 237p. 1977. pap. 9.95 (*0-8032-8706-2*, Bison Books) U of Nebr Pr.

— Sacred Language: The Nature of Supernatural Discourse in Lakota. LC 86-40079. (Civilization of the American Indian Ser.: Vol. 179). (Illus.). 264p. 1992. pap. 14.95 (*0-8061-2458-X*) U of Okla Pr.

— War Dance: Plains Indian Musical Performance. LC 90-32421. (Illus.). 199p. 1990. 27.50 (*0-8165-1170-5*) U of Ariz Pr.

— War Dance: Plains Indian Musical Performance. LC 90-32421. (Illus.). 199p. 1993. reprint ed. pap. 10.95 (*0-8165-1365-1*) U of Ariz Pr.

— Yuwipi: Vision & Experience in Oglala Ritual. LC 81-10501. (Illus.). xiv, 113p. 1982. reprint ed. pap. 5.95 (*0-8032-8710-0*, Bison Books) U of Nebr Pr.

Powers, William T. Behavior: The Control of Perception. LC 73-75697. 309p. 1973. lib. bdg. 41.95 (*0-202-25113-6*) Aldine de Gruyter.

— Living Control Systems: Selected Papers of William T. Powers. LC 89-62634. (Illus.). xx, 300p. (Orig.). (C). 1989. pap. 16.50 (*0-9624154-0-5*) Control Systs Group.

— Living Control Systems II. (Selected Papers of William T. Powers). (Illus.). 277p. (Orig.). (C). 1992. pap. text ed. 22.00 (*0-9624154-2-1*) Control Systs Group.

Powers, William T., jt. ed. see Robertson, Richard J.

Powhida, Elizabeth C. Anthony Mouse Goes Swimming. (Illus.). 40p. (J). (ps-5). 1995. pap. write for info. (*0-9625842-1-5*, TXU538146) Kinderhook Pubs.

Powicke, Frederick J. The Cambridge Platonists. viii, 219p. (GER.). 1970. reprint ed. write for info. (*0-318-70503-6*, Pub. by Georg Olms GW); reprint ed. write for info. (*0-318-71273-3*, Pub. by Georg Olms GW) Lubrecht & Cramer.

— The Cambridge Platonists: A Study. (Illus.). viii, 219p. 1970. reprint ed. 32.37 (*0-685-66505-4*, 05102832, Pub. by Georg Olms GW) Lubrecht & Cramer.

Powicke, Frederick M. Modern Historians & the Study of History: Essays & Papers. LC 75-25496. 256p. 1976. reprint ed. text ed. 35.00 (*0-8371-8428-2*, POMH, Greenwood Pr) Greenwood.

— Thirteenth Century, 1216-1307. 2nd ed. (Illus.). 1962. 59.00 (*0-19-821708-0*) OUP.

— Ways of Medieval Life & Thought. LC 64-13394. (Illus.). 1949. 24.00 (*0-8196-0137-3*) Biblo.

Powicke, Frederick M. & Fryde, E. B., eds. Handbook of British Chronology. (Royal Historical Society Guides & Handbooks Ser.: No. 2). 600p. 1986. 50.00 (*0-86193-106-8*) Boydell & Brewer.

Powicke, J. C. Government in the Economy. 1977. pap. text ed. 2.40 (*0-08-018120-1*, Pergamon Pr) Elsevier.

Powicke, Maurice. The Thirteenth Century, 1216-1307. 2nd ed. (Oxford History of England Ser.: Vol. 4). (Illus.). 848p. 1991. reprint ed. pap. 22.00 (*0-19-285249-3*) OUP.

Powicke, Maurice, ed. see Daniel, Walter.

Powills, Leo I. Dyslexia: Subject, Reference & Research Guidebook. LC 87-47651. 160p. 1987. 39.50 (*0-88164-602-4*); pap. 34.50 (*0-88164-603-2*) ABBE Pubs Assn.

Powis, David. The Signs of Crime: A Field of Manual for Police. LC 77-30173. (Illus.). 1978. pap. text ed. 5.95 (*0-89444-007-1*) John Jay Pr.

***Powis, David A. & Bunn, Stephen J., eds.** Neurotransmitter Release & Its Modulation: Biochemical Mechanisms, Physiological Function & Clinical Relevance. (Illus.). 350p. (C). 1992. write for info. (*0-521-44068-8*); pap. write for info. (*0-521-44616-3*) Cambridge U Pr.

Powis, Garth, ed. Anticancer Drugs: Antmetabolite Metabolism & Natural Anticancer Agents. 500p. 1994. 195.00 (*0-08-042334-5*, Pergamon Pr) Elsevier.

— Anticancer Drugs: Reactive Metabolism & Drug Interactions. 500p. 1994. 195.00 (*0-08-042335-3*, Pergamon Pr) Elsevier.

Powis, Garth & Hackar, M. The Toxicity of Anticancer Drugs: A Study in Human Toxicity. 240p. 1991. text ed. 55.00 (*0-07-105305-0*) Hlth Prof Div.

Powis, Garth & Hacker, Miles. Mechanisms of Toxicity of Anticancer Drugs. 256p. 1991. 49.50 (*0-08-040302-6*, Pub. by PPI UK) McGraw.

Powis, Garth & Prough, R. A., eds. Metabolism & Action of Anti-Cancer Drugs. LC 86-23179. 336p. 1987. 125.00 (*0-85066-369-5*) Taylor & Francis.

***Powis, Ivan, et al, eds.** High Resolution Laser Photoionization & Photoelectron Studies. LC 94-35538. (Series in Ion Chemistry & Physics). 1995. text ed. 144.00 (*0-471-94158-1*) Wiley.

Powis, Raymond L. & Powis, Wendy J. A Thinker's Guide to Ultrasonic Imaging. LC 83-21704. (Illus.). 430p. 1984. 55.00 (*0-683-06961-6*) Williams & Wilkins.

Powis, Raymond L. & Schwartz, Robert A. Practical Doppler Ultrasound for the Clinician. (Illus.). 208p. 1991. 60.00 (*0-683-06958-6*) Williams & Wilkins.

***Powis, Robert E.** Complying with the Bank Secrecy Act. rev. ed. 22p. 1994. 22.00 (*1-55738-399-5*) Probus Pub Co.

— The Money Launderers: Lessons from the Drug Wars - How Billions of Illegal Dollars Are Washed Through Banks & Businesses. 300p. 1992. 21.95 (*1-55738-262-X*) Probus Pub Co.

Powis, Wendy J., jt. auth. see Powis, Raymond L.

Powitt, A. H. Hair Structure & Chemistry Simplified. (Illus.). 320p. 1977. text ed. 31.50 (*0-87350-080-6*) Milady Pub.

— Lectures in Hair Structure & Chemistry for Cosmetology Teachers. (Illus.). 1983. 27.50 (*0-87350-354-6*) Milady Pub.

Powlas, Joe. The Church with the Golden Roof. 1988p. 12.00 (*0-8187-0103-X*) Harlo Press.

— To Walk in Heaven. 176p. 1991. 15.00 (*0-8187-0144-7*) Harlo Press.

Powledge, F. Something to Eat. Date not set. 25.00 (*0-06-016970-2*, HarpT) HarpC.

Powledge, Fred. Free at Last? The Civil Rights Movement & the People Who Made It. LC 91-55515. 720p. 1992. reprint ed. pap. 15.00 (*0-06-097463-X*, PL) HarpC.

— So You're Adopted. LC 81-23278. 112p. (YA). (gr. 5 up). 1982. text ed. 13.95 (*0-684-17347-6*, C Scribner Sons Young) S&S Childrens.

— To Change a Child: A Report on the Institute for Developmental Studies. (Illus.). 110p. reprint ed. pap. 2.45 (*0-686-95040-2*) ADL.

— Water: The Nature, Uses, & Future of Our Most Precious & Abused Resource. 384p. 1983. pap. 7.95 (*0-374-51798-3*) FS&G.

— We Shall Overcome: Heroes of the Civil Rights Movement. LC 92-25184. (Illus.). 224p. (YA). (gr. 7 up). 1993. text ed. 16.95 (*0-684-19362-0*, C Scribner Sons Young) S&S Childrens.

— Working River. LC 94-33363. 128p. (YA). (gr. 4 up). 1995. 16.00 (*0-374-38527-0*) FS&G.

— You'll Survive! Late Blooming, Early Blooming, Loneliness, Klutziness, & Other Problems of Adolescence, & How to Live Through Them. LC 85-43351. 96p. (J). (gr. 6-8). 1986. text ed. 13.95 (*0-684-18632-2*, C Scribner Sons Young) S&S Childrens.

Powledge, Tabitha M. Your Brain: How You Got It & How It Works. LC 94-14273. (J). 1994. text ed. 14.95 (*0-684-19659-X*, Scribners) S&S Trade.

Powles & Smith. Medical Management of Breast Cancer. (Illus.). 359p. 1991. text ed. 120.00 (*0-397-58329-X*) Lippincott.

Powles, David G. Powles: The Mareva Injunction & Associated Orders. 1985. 48.00 (*0-86205-069-3*) Butterworth Legal Pubs.

Powles, Stephen & Holtum, Joseph, eds. Herbicide Resistance in Plants: Biology & Biochemistry. LC 93-44552. 1994. write for info. (*0-87371-713-9*) Lewis Pubs.

Powles, William E. Human Development & Homeostasis: The Science of Psychiatry. LC 90-15604. 600p. (C). 1992. text ed. 65.00 (*0-8236-2363-7*) Intl Univs Pr.

Powley, Terry L., jt. ed. see Capaldi, Elizabeth D.

Powlinson, David A. Power Encounters: Reclaiming Spiritual Warfare. 128p. (Orig.). 1994. pap. 7.99 (*0-8010-7138-0*) Baker Bk.

Powlison, Esther & Powlison, Paul. La Fiesta Yagua, Jina: Una Rica Herencia Cultural, 2 fiche, Set. (Comunidades y Culturas Peruanas Ser.: No. 8). 102p. 1976. fiche 8.00x (*0-88312-530-7*) Summer Instit Ling.

P Q

An Asterisk (*) at the beginning of an entry indicates that the title is appearing in BIP for the first time.

Powlison, Keith. Profits of the National Banks. Bruchey, Stuart, ed. LC 80-1166. (Rise of Commercial Banking Ser.). (Illus.). 1981. reprint ed. lib. bdg. 15.95 (*0-405-13676-5*) Ayer.

Powlison, Paul, jt. auth. see Powlison, Esther.

Powlison, Paul S. Yagua Mythology: Epic Tendencies in a New World Mythology. Merrifield, William R., ed. LC 84-63152. (International Museum of Cultures Publications: No. 16). (Illus.). 132p. (Orig.). 1985. fiche 8.00 (*0-88312-254-5*) Summer Instit Ling.

Pownall, David. The Gardener. 256p. 1991. 23.95 (*0-575-04724-0*, Pub. by V Gollancz UK) Trafalgar.

Pownall, David E., comp. Articles on Twentieth Century Literature: An Annotated Bibliography, 1954-1970, 7 vols., Set. LC 73-6588. lib. bdg. 630.00 (*0-527-72150-6*) Kraus Intl.

***Pownall, Henry J. & Spector, Arthur A., eds.** Proceedings from the Scientific Conference on Omega-3 Fatty Acids in Nutrition, Vascular Biology, & Medicine. (Illus.). 275p. Date not set. write for info. (*0-614-04637-8*); pap. text ed. write for info. (*0-87493-007-3*) Am Heart.

Pownall, Malcolm. Functions & Graphs: Calculus Preparatory Mathematics. (Illus.). 592p. (C). 1983. text ed. write for info. (*0-13-332304-8*) P-H.

Pownall, Malcolm W. Real Analysis: A First Course with Foundations. 496p. (C). 1993. text ed. write for info. (*0-697-12908-X*) Wm C Brown Pubs.

Pownall, Mark. Heroin. LC 91-27815. (Drugs The Complete Story Ser.). (Illus.). 64p. (YA). (gr. 6-12). 1991. lib. bdg. 24.26 (*0-8114-3201-7*) Raintree Steck-V.

Pownall, Peter. Fisheries of Australia. 1978. 40.00 (*0-685-63414-0*) St Mut.

Pownall, Thomas. Administration of the Colonies. LC 79-146155. (Era of the American Revolution Ser.). 1971. reprint ed. lib. bdg. 49.50 (*0-306-70123-5*) Da Capo.

— The Administration of the Colonies: 1668. LC 93-36377. 1993. 75.00 (*0-8201-1487-1*) Schol Facsimiles.

— Letter from Governor Pownall to Adam Smith: Being an Examination of Several Points of Doctrine Laid down in His Inquiry. LC 66-15563. (Reprints of Economic Classics Ser.). 1967. reprint ed. 15.00 (*0-678-00258-4*) Kelley.

— A Topographical Description of the Dominions of the United States of America. Mulkearn, Lois, ed. LC 75-22835. (America in Two Centuries Ser.). 1976. reprint ed. 23.95 (*0-405-07706-8*) Ayer.

Pownall, Tim, tr. see Caron, Jean.

Pownall, Tim, tr. see Gombert, Jean E.

Pownall, Tim, tr. see Hauptmann, Peter.

Pownall, Tim, tr. see Jodelet, Denise.

Pownall, Tim, tr. see Streri, Arlette.

Powne, Michael. Ethiopian Music, an Introduction: A Survey of Ecclesiastical & Secular Ethiopian Music & Instruments. LC 80-14087. (Illus.). xix, 160p. 1980. reprint ed. text ed. 35.00 (*0-313-22161-8*, POEM, Greenwood Pr) Greenwood.

Powrie, P., jt. ed. see Atack, M.

Powszechna, W. Large French-Polish Dictionary: Grand Dictionnaire Francais-Polonais. 2220p. (FRE & POL.). 1984. 95.00 (*0-8288-0481-8*, F 53100) Fr & Eur.

Powszechna, Wiedza, et al. Wiedza Powszechna Compact Polish & English Dictionary. 712p. 1993. 16.95 (*0-8442-8366-5*, 8366-5, Natl Textbk); pap. 12.95 (*0-8442-8367-3*, Natl Textbk) NTC Pub Grp.

***Powter, Susan.** Alto a la Enfermedad! Coma Bien y Viva Mejor. (ENG & SPA.). 1995. pap. 11.00 (*0-684-81327-0*) S&S Trade.

— Food. (Illus.). 1995. 24.00 (*0-671-89225-8*) S&S Trade.

— Portable Powter. 1994. pap. 6.99 (*0-671-89456-0*, Fireside) S&S Trade.

— Stop the Insanity! (Illus.). 320p. 1993. 22.00 (*0-671-79598-8*) S&S Trade.

— Stop the Insanity. Grose, Bill, ed. 384p. 1995. mass mkt. 6.99 (*0-671-52292-2*) PB.

— Susan Powter's Food Catalogue. 1995. pap. 12.00 (*0-684-81317-3*, Fireside) S&S Trade.

Powton, Betty. A Penny for Them. 84p. (C). 1989. 50.00 (*0-7223-2365-4*, Pub. by A H S Ltd UK) St Mut.

Powys, Albert R. From the Ground Up: Collected Papers. LC 77-156706. (Essay Index Reprint Ser.). 1977. reprint ed. 12.95 (*0-8369-2292-1*) Ayer.

Powys, John C. Autobiography. 652p. 1994. pap. 22.95 (*0-912568-17-8*) Colgate U Pr.

— The Brazen Head. 348p. text ed. 26.95 (*0-912568-11-9*) Colgate U Pr.

— Dostoievsky. LC 72-8975. (Studies in European Literature: No. 56). 1973. reprint ed. lib. bdg. 75.00 (*0-8383-1677-8*) M S G Haskell Hse.

— A Glastonbury Romance. 1120p. text ed. 38.00 (*0-912568-10-0*) Colgate U Pr.

— A Glastonbury Romance. LC 87-5762. 1120p. 1987. reprint ed. 30.00 (*0-87951-282-2*) Overlook Pr.

— Homer & the Aether. 298p. text ed. 25.95 (*0-912568-12-7*) Colgate U Pr.

— Letters to His Brother Llewelyn, Vol. I: 1902-1925. Elwin, Malcolm, ed. 367p. 1975. pap. text ed. 9.95 (*0-912568-06-2*) Colgate U Pr.

— Letters to His Brother Llewlyn, Vol. II: 1925-1939. Elvin, Malcolm, ed. 284p. 1975. pap. text ed. 9.95 (*0-912568-07-0*) Colgate U Pr.

— Maiden Castle. Hughes, Ian, ed. xx, 484p. 1990. 70.00 (*0-7083-1061-3*, Pub. by U of Wales UK) Bks Intl VA.

— Maiden Castle. 1966. 19.95 (*0-912568-01-1*) Colgate U Pr.

— Maiden Castle. 496p. 1994. pap. 19.95 (*0-912568-18-6*) Colgate U Pr.

— Morwyn: Or, the Vengeance of God. Reginald, R. & Menville, Douglas, eds. LC 75-46301. (Supernatural & Occult Fiction Ser.). 1976. reprint ed. lib. bdg. 26.95 (*0-405-08161-8*) Ayer.

— Poems: A Selection. Hopkins, Kenneth, ed. 224p. 1964. text ed. 26.95 (*0-912568-00-3*) Colgate U Pr.

— Porius: A Romance of the Dark Ages. Albrecht, Wilbur, ed. 900p. 1994. text ed. 48.95 (*0-912568-16-X*) Colgate U Pr.

— Rodmoor. LC 73-77361. 1973. 33.95 (*0-912568-05-4*) Colgate U Pr.

— Visions & Revisions. 221p. text ed. 24.95 (*0-912568-13-5*) Colgate U Pr.

— Visions & Revisions: A Book of Literary Devotions. LC 78-58263. (Essay Index in Reprint Ser.). 1978. reprint ed. 23.75 (*0-8486-3025-4*) Roth Pub Inc.

— Wolf Solent. 614p. text ed. 35.95 (*0-912568-09-7*) Colgate U Pr.

— Wolf Solent: A Novel, 2 vols., Set. 1971. reprint ed. 79.00 (*0-403-01159-0*) Scholarly.

Powys, John C. & Powys, Lewellyn. Confessions of Two Brothers. LC 70-131804. 1971. reprint ed. 29.00 (*0-403-00691-0*) Scholarly.

Powys, Lewellyn, jt. auth. see Powys, John C.

Powys, Littleton C. The Powys Family. LC 74-7023. (English Biography Ser.: No. 31). 1974. lib. bdg. 29.95 (*0-8383-1995-5*) M S G Haskell Hse.

Powys, Llewelyn. Baker's Dozen. LC 79-86776. (Essay Index Reprint Ser.). 1977. 19.95 (*0-8369-1153-9*) Ayer.

— Earth Memories. LC 73-90675. (Essay Index Reprint Ser.). 1977. 21.95 (*0-8369-1376-0*) Ayer.

— Earth Memories. 144p. 1983. 39.00 (*0-317-20308-8*, Pub. by Redcliffe Pr Ltd) St Mut.

— Ebony & Ivory. 1988. 29.00 (*0-317-38804-5*, Pub. by Redcliffe Pr Ltd) St Mut.

— Ebony & Ivory. LC 75-144168. (Short Story Index Reprint Ser.). 1977. reprint ed. 24.95 (*0-8369-3783-X*) Ayer.

— Rats in the Sacristy. LC 67-30226. (Essay Index Reprint Ser.). 1977. 19.95 (*0-8369-0798-1*) Ayer.

— Thirteen Worthies. LC 67-22112. (Essay Index Reprint Ser.). 1977. 18.95 (*0-8369-0799-X*) Ayer.

— Thirteen Worthies. 1985. 35.00 (*0-317-38814-2*, Pub. by Redcliffe Pr Ltd) St Mut.

— The Twelve Months. 96p. (C). 1987. 42.00 (*0-948265-90-6*, Pub. by Redcliffe Pr Ltd) St Mut.

Powys, Marian. Lace & Lace Making. (Illus.). 1981. reprint ed. 50.00 (*1-55888-179-4*) Omnigraphics Inc.

Powys, T. F. Father Adam. (C). 1990. 75.00 (*0-907839-47-9*, Pub. by Brynmill Pr Ltd UK) St Mut.

— Mark Only. (Literature Ser.). 270p. 1972. reprint ed. 25.00 (*0-403-00692-9*) Scholarly.

Powys, Theodore F. Fables. 1971. reprint ed. 29.00 (*0-403-01160-4*) Scholarly.

— Left Leg. LC 72-140337. (Short Story Index Reprint Ser.). 1977. 18.95 (*0-8369-3729-5*) Ayer.

— Mr. Tasker's Gods. LC 72-145246. 320p. 1972. reprint ed. 39.00 (*0-403-01161-2*) Scholarly.

— Two Thieves. LC 79-167466. (Short Story Index Reprint Ser.). 1977. reprint ed. 20.95 (*0-8369-3992-1*) Ayer.

— Unclay. (Literature Ser.). 328p. 1972. reprint ed. 39.00 (*0-403-01162-0*) Scholarly.

— White Paternoster, & Other Stories. LC 70-178455. (Short Story Index Reprint Ser.). 1977. reprint ed. 18.95 (*0-8369-4056-3*) Ayer.

Powzyk, Joyce. Animal Camouflage: A Closer Look. LC 89-9848. (Illus.). 40p. (J). (gr. 2-9). 1990. text ed. 15.95 (*0-02-774980-0*, Bradbury S&S) S&S Childrens.

— Madagascar Journey. LC 94-21053. (YA). (gr. 9-12). 1995. write for info. (*0-688-09487-2*); pap. write for info. (*0-688-13964-7*) Lothrop.

— Tasmania: A Wildlife Journey. LC 86-7288. (Illus.). 32p. (J). (gr. 3-6). 1987. 12.95 (*0-688-06459-0*) Lothrop.

— Tracking Wild Chimpanzees. LC 87-16099. (Illus.). 32p. (J). (gr. 1-4). 1988. 13.95 (*0-688-06733-6*); lib. bdg. 13.88 (*0-688-06734-4*) Lothrop.

— Wallaby Creek. LC 84-29757. (Illus.). 32p. (J). (gr. 1-4). 1985. lib. bdg. 12.88 (*0-688-05693-8*) Lothrop.

Poxon, Nancy J., jt. auth. see Farrand, Scott.

Poxton, I. R., jt. ed. see Hancock, Ian.

Poy-Wing, Celina. All Women's Health in the 90s Series. Date not set. write for info. (*0-9638783-4-4*) All Womens Hlth. A series of books dealing with women's health & sexuality by Celina Poy-Wing, MD, a practicing gynecologist. Just out, CLIMAXX!! ORGASMIC SEX (9.95, ISBN 0-9638783-1-X), deals with sexual joy & potency. From the essential facts to exotic, erotic tips, Dr. Celina Poy-Wing covers the wide territory of orgasmic sex. Can a woman ejaculate (& how?) Giving oral sex, responding to petit mort, & getting sexual energy flowing with aphrodisiacs & fantasies are just a few of the topics covered. CLIMAXX!! is the second book in Dr. Poy-Wing's series on All Women's Health in the 90s. Her first book, TAME THE YEAST BEAST! (4.95, ISBN 0-9638783-0-1), is a comprehensive & easily read "must" for any woman who suffers from recurring yeast infections. An upcoming book called SEX-ED MANUAL (6.95, ISBN 0-9638783-2-8), answers questions that address the concerns & expectations of teenagers ages 12-17. HAZARDOUS LOVE: STDs (5.95, ISBN 0-9638783-3-6), a clinically-based exploration of sexually-transmitted diseases, is scheduled for release in October 1995. To order Dr. Poy-Wing's books, write: All Women's Health Publishers Corporation (AWHP Corp.), 817 S. University Dr., Suite 101, Plantation, FL 33324 or call 910-656-3700.** ***Publisher Provided Annotation.

— Climaxx!! Orgasmic Sex. 220p. 1995. pap. 9.95 (*0-9638783-1-X*) All Womens Hlth.

— Tame the Yeast Beast! Self-Help for Yeast Infections. (All Women's Health in the 90s Ser.). (Illus.). 80p. (Orig.). 1994. pap. 4.95 (*0-9638783-0-1*) All Womens Hlth.

Poyatos, F. Cross-Cultural Perspectives in Nonverbal Communication. LC 87-7485. 354p. (C). 1988. 56.00 (*0-88937-018-4*) Hogrefe & Huber Pubs.

Poyatos, Fernando. Paralanguage: A Linguistic & Interdisciplinary Approach to Interactive Speech & Sound. LC 92-42014. (Current Issues in Linguistic Theory Ser.: Vol. 92). xiv, 478p. 1993. 125.00 (*1-55619-149-9*) Benjamins North Am.

Poyatos, Fernando, ed. Advances in Non-Verbal Communication: Sociocultural, Clinical, Esthetic & Literary Perspectives. LC 92-599. xxiv, 412p. 1992. 118.00 (*1-55619-121-9*); pap. 29.95 (*1-55619-491-9*) Benjamins North Am.

— Literary Anthropology: A New Interdisciplinary Approach to People, Signs & Literature. LC 87-21820. xxiii, 342p. (C). 1988. 97.00x (*90-272-2041-7*); pap. 27.95 (*90-272-2059-X*) Benjamins North Am.

Poyen, Charles. Progress of Animal Magnetism. (Hypnosis & Altered States of Consciousness Ser.). 1982. reprint ed. lib. bdg. 25.00 (*0-306-76163-7*) Da Capo.

Poyer, David. Louisiana Blue. 304p. 1994. 22.00 (*0-312-10494-4*) St Martin.

— The Only Thing to Fear. 432p. 1995. 22.95 (*0-312-85709-8*) Forge NYC.

— The Only Thing to Fear. 480p. 1996. mass mkt. write for info. (*0-614-05527-X*) Forge NYC.

— The Passage. 1994. 22.95 (*0-312-11874-0*) St Martin.

— Winter in the Heart. 416p. 1994. mass mkt. 5.99 (*0-8125-2298-2*) Tor Bks.

Poyer, David C. Bahamas Blue. 1992. mass mkt. 4.99 (*0-312-92846-7*) St Martin.

— Circle. 1993. mass mkt. 5.99 (*0-312-92964-1*) St Martin.

— The Gulf. 1991. mass mkt. 5.95 (*0-312-92577-8*) St Martin.

— Med. 1991. mass mkt. 5.99 (*0-312-92722-3*) St Martin.

— Winter in the Heart. 352p. 1993. 21.95 (*0-312-85421-8*) Tor Bks.

***Poyer, Joe.** The Colt Single Action: Three Generations. (For Collectors Only Ser.). (Illus.). 150p. 1995. pap. 16.95 (*1-882391-06-3*) N Cape Pubns.

— U. S. Winchester Trench & Riot Guns & Other U. S. Combat Shotguns: And Other U. S. Combat Shot Guns. (For Collectors Only Ser.). (Illus.). 122p. (Orig.). 1992. pap. 15.95 (*1-882391-02-0*) N Cape Pubns.

Poyer, Joe & Riesch, Craig. The 45-70 Springfield. (For Collectors Only Ser.). (Illus.). 102p. (Orig.). 1991. pap. 14.95 (*1-882391-01-2*) N Cape Pubns.

— The Mi Garaud 1936-1957. (For Collectors Only Ser.). (Illus.). 130p. 1995. pap. 15.95 (*1-882391-08-X*) N Cape Pubns.

Poyer, Joe, jt. auth. see Lightbody, Andy.

Poyer, Lin. The Ngatik Massacre: History & Identity on a Micronesian Atoll. LC 92-37911. (Ethnographic Inquiry Ser.). (Illus.). 336p. (C). 1993. text ed. 49.00 (*1-56098-261-6*); pap. text ed. 17.95 (*1-56098-262-4*) Smithsonian.

Poyer, Lin, jt. ed. see Linnekin, Jocelyn.

Poynder, Michael. Price Guide to Jewellery: 3000 BC-1950 AD. (Price Guide Ser.). (Illus.). 388p. 1976. 69.50 (*0-902028-50-2*) Antique Collect.

Poyner, Alice. East into Yesterday. 178p. (Orig.). (YA). (gr. 7-12). 1990. pap. 4.95 (*9971-972-94-8*) OMF Bks.

— From the Campus to the World. LC 86-3024. 157p. (Orig.). 1986. pap. 8.99 (*0-87784-947-1*, 947) InterVarsity.

Poyner, Barry & Webb, Barry. Crime Free Housing. (Illus.). 128p. 1991. 52.95 (*0-7506-1273-8*, Butterwrth Archit) Buttrwrth-Heinemann.

Poyner, J. Electroplating. (Workshop Practice Ser.: No. 11). (Illus.). 64p. (Orig.). 1987. pap. 18.50x (*0-85242-862-6*, Pub. by Argus Books UK) Trans-Atl Phila.

Poyner, Rick, ed. Typography Now: The Next Wave. 1994. pap. 34.95 (*0-89134-621-X*) North Light Bks.

Poyner, Robin. Power Concealed, Power Revealed: The Arts of Africa. Libby, Gary R. & Miller, Sandra L., eds. (Illus.). 50p. (C). 1988. pap. 5.00 (*0-933053-01-0*) Museum Art Sciences.

Poynet, John, comp. A Shorte Treatise of Politike Power. LC 72-38220. (English Experience Ser.: No. 484). 184p. 1972. reprint ed. 35.00 (*90-221-0484-2*) Walter J Johnson.

Poynor, Alice. East of the Misty Mountains. 1991. 4.95 (*981-3009-12-8*) OMF Bks.

— East to the Shifting Sands. (Jeff Anderson Ser.: Bk. 3). 190p. (Orig.). (J). (gr. 6-9). 1992. pap. 4.95 (*981-3009-05-5*) OMF Bks.

— Spice Islands Mystery. 1989. pap. 3.95 (*9971-972-82-4*) OMF Bks.

Poynor, Rick. The Graphic Edge. (Illus.). 208p. 1994. 49.95 (*0-89134-587-6*, 30598) North Light Bks.

***Poynor, Robin.** African Art at the Harn Museum: Spirit Eyes, Human Hands. LC 94-25648. (Illus.). 256p. 1995. lib. bdg. 49.95 (*0-8130-1325-9*) U Press Fla.

Poynter, Dan. Book Fulfillment: Order Entry, Picking, Packing & Shipping. 3rd ed. (Book Publishing Consultation with Dan Poynter Ser.). (Illus.). 86p. 1992. pap. 19.95 (*0-915516-64-0*) Para Pub.

— Book Marketing: A New Approach. 5th ed. (Book Publishing Consultation with Dan Poynter Ser.) (Illus.). 70p. 1994. student ed, pap. 14.95 (*0-568-60009-6*) Para Pub.

— Book Production: Composition, Layout, Editing & Design - Getting It Ready for Printing. 3rd ed. (Book Publishing Consultation with Dan Poynter Ser.). (Illus.). 42p. 1992. 19.95 (*0-915516-62-4*) Para Pub.

— Book Reviews. 4th ed. (Book Publishing Consultation with Dan Poynter Ser.). 46p. 1994. student ed, pap. 19.95 (*0-568-60012-6*) Para Pub.

— Brochures for Book Publishers. 3rd ed. (Book Publishing Consultation with Dan Poynter Ser.). (Illus.). 50p. 1992. student ed 19.95 (*0-915516-48-9*) Para Pub.

— Business Letters for Publishers: Creative Correspondence Outlines. 2nd rev. ed. 82p. 1985. disk 29.95 (*0-915516-47-0*) Para Pub.

— Buying Book Printing. 4th ed. (Book Publishing Consultation with Dan Poynter Ser.). (Illus.). 35p. 1994. student ed 14.95 (*0-568-60013-4*) Para Pub.

— Direct Mail for Book Publishers. 3rd ed. (Book Publishing Consultation with Dan Poynter Ser.). (Illus.). 55p. 1990. student ed 19.95 (*0-915516-59-4*) Para Pub.

— Expert Witness Handbook: Tips & Techniques for the Litigation Consultant. LC 87-2279. (Illus.). 248p. (Orig.). 1987. 29.95 (*0-915516-45-4*) Para Pub.

— Exports-Foreign Rights: Selling U. S. Books Abroad. 3rd ed. (Book Publishing Consultation with Dan Poynter Ser.). (Illus.). 57p. 1992. student ed 19.95 (*0-915516-57-8*) Para Pub.

— Hang Gliding Manual with Log. rev. ed. LC 76-14105. (Illus.). 24p. 1982. pap. 3.95 (*0-685-03950-1*) Para Pub.

— Hang Gliding Manual with Log. 7th rev. ed. LC 76-14105. (Illus.). 24p. 1982. pap. 1.50 (*0-915516-12-8*) Para Pub.

— Hang Gliding Syllabus & Exam. 2nd rev. ed. 6p. 1980. pap. 9.95 (*0-915516-39-X*, 12-D) Para Pub.

— News Releases & Book Publicity. 3rd ed. (Book Publishing Consultation with Dan Poynter Ser.). (Illus.). 47p. 1992. 19.95 (*0-915516-52-7*) Para Pub.

— The Parachute Manual, Vol. 1: A Technical Treatise on Aerodynamic Decelerators. 3rd ed. LC 83-13350. (Illus.). 592p. 1984. student ed 49.95 (*0-915516-35-7*) Para Pub.

— The Parachute Manual, Vol. 2: A Technical Treatise on Aerodynamic Decelerators. 4th ed. LC 91-8828. 416p. 1991. student ed, pap. 49.95 (*0-915516-80-2*) Para Pub.

— Parachuting: The Skydivers' Handbook. 6th ed. LC 88-32405. (Illus.). 400p. 1992. pap. 19.95 (*0-915516-86-1*); Spanish Edition. pap. 13.95 (*0-685-62377-7*) Para Pub.

— Parachuting I-E Course. 5th rev. ed. (Illus.). 70p. 1994. pap. 14.95 (*1-56860-004-6*) Para Pub.

— Parachuting Manual with Log for Round Canopies. rev. ed. LC 76-14106. (Illus.). 26p. 1984. pap. 2.50 (*84-400-3931-X*) Para Pub.

— Parachuting Manual with Log for Round Canopies. 7th rev. ed. LC 76-14106. (Illus.). 24p. 1984. pap. 1.50 (*0-915516-11-X*) Para Pub.

— Parachuting Manual with Log for the Static Line Course. 7th rev. ed. (Illus.). 24p. 1993. pap. 2.50 (*0-915516-84-5*) Para Pub.

— Publishing Forms: A Collection of Applications & Information for the Beginning Publisher. 4th rev. ed. (Orig.). 1992. pap. 14.95 (*0-685-62378-5*) Para Pub.

— Publishing Short-Run Books: How to Paste up & Reproduce Books Instantly Using Your Quick Print Shop. 5th rev. ed. LC 80-13614. (Illus.). 144p. 1988. pap. 5.95 (*0-915516-61-6*) Para Pub.

— Self-Publishing Manual: How to Write, Print & Sell Your Own Book. 8th rev. ed. (Illus.). 464p. 1994. pap. 19.95 (*0-568-60003-7*) Para Pub.

— The Self-Publishing Manual: How to Write, Print, & Sell Your Own Book. 8th rev. ed. LC 94-33200. (Illus.). 464p. 1995. pap. 19.95 (*1-56860-003-8*) Para Pub.

— Selling Books in the United States: A Marketing Plan for Foreign Publishers. 3rd ed. 1992. student ed 9.95 (*0-915516-60-8*) Para Pub.

— Toobee Players' Handbook: The Amazing Flying Cylinder. LC 80-20529. (Illus.). 52p. (Orig.). 1981. pap. 4.95 (*0-915516-25-X*) Para Pub.

Poynter, Dan, ed. Book Fairs: An Exhibiting Guide for Publishers. 4th ed. LC 85-16733. (Illus.). 96p. 1986. reprint ed. pap. 7.95 (*0-915516-43-8*) Para Pub.

Poynter, Dan & Bingham, Mindy. Is There a Book Inside You? A Step-by-Step Plan for Writing Your Book. rev. ed. Stryker, Sandy, ed. LC 90-46852. (Illus.). 236p. 1992. digital audio 69.95 (*0-915516-73-X*) Para Pub.

— Is There a Book Inside You? A Step-by-Step Plan for Writing Your Book. 4th rev. ed. Stryker, Sandy, ed. LC 90-46852. (Illus.). 236p. 1992. pap. 14.95 (*0-915516-68-3*) Para Pub.

Poynter, Dan & Blackmon, Deborah. Parachute Rigger Study Guide: Questions, Answers, Explanations & References. 2nd rev. ed. LC 94-4951. 66p. 1994. pap. 19.95 (*1-56860-006-2*) Para Pub.

Poynter, Dan & Danna, Mark. Frisbee Players' Handbook. rev. ed. LC 77-79101. (Illus.). 180p. 1980. pap. 9.95 (*0-685-03949-8*); disk 9.95 (*0-915516-15-2*); disk 6.95 (*0-915516-19-5*) Para Pub.

Poynter, Dan & Kent, Charles. Publishing Contracts: Sample Agreements for Book Publishers on Disk. LC 87-6872. (Orig.). 1987. disk 29.95 (*0-915516-46-2*) Para Pub.

Poynter, Dan & Schlatter, Mark. Parachute Rigging Course: A Course of Study for the FAA Senior Rigging Certificate. 3rd rev. ed. LC 94-4950. 92p. 1994. pap. 19.95 (*1-56860-005-4*) Para Pub.

Poynter, Dan, jt. auth. see Blackmon, Deborah.

P Q

Poynter, Edward J. Ten Lectures on Art. 1977. 17.95 (*0-8369-7325-9*, 8118) Ayer.

Poynter, J. R. Russell Grimwade. 1967. 29.95 (*0-522-83827-8*) Intl Spec Bk.

***Poynter, James.** Multicultural Multinational. 208p. (C). 1995. pap. text ed. 55.20 (*0-7872-1069-2*) Kendall-Hunt.

— Travel Agency Accounting Procedures. 320p. 1991. teacher ed 10.00 (*0-8273-3390-0*); text ed. 31.95 (*0-8273-3389-7*) Delmar.

Poynter, James M. Corporate Travel Management. (Illus.). 384p. 1990. text ed. 60.00 (*0-13-176140-4*) P-H.

— How to Research & Write a Thesis in Hospitality & Tourism: A Step-by-Step Guide for College Students. 224p. 1993. Net. pap. text ed. write for info. (*0-471-55240-2*) Wiley.

— Tour Design, Marketing, & Management. LC 92-15906. 400p. 1992. text ed. 53.00 (*0-13-205345-4*) P-H.

Poynter, Margaret. Frisbee Fun. (J). (gr. 3-6). 1978. pap. 7.29 (*0-685-00479-1*, Archway) PB.

— Killer Asteroids. LC 94-49124. (Weird & Wacky Science Ser.). (J). 1996. lib. bdg. write for info. (*0-89490-616-X*) Enslow Pubs.

— Marie Curie: Discoverer of Radium. LC 93-21224. (Great Minds of Science Ser.). (Illus.). 128p. (J). (gr. 4-10). 1994. lib. bdg. 17.95 (*0-89490-477-9*) Enslow Pubs.

Poynter, William L. The Preferred Provider's Handbook: Building a Successful Private Therapy Practice in the Managed Care Marketplace. LC 93-38869. 184p. 1994. pap. 21.95 (*0-87630-708-X*) Brunner-Mazel.

Poynting, Jeremy. Resource Guide to Travel in the Caribbean. 250p. 1995. 125.00 (*0-905450-62-0*, Pub. by H Zell Pubs UK) Bowker-Saur.

Poynton. Metering Pumps: Selection & Application. (Chemical Industries Ser.: Vol. 9). 216p. 1983. 125.00 (*0-8247-1759-7*) Dekker.

Poynton, Cate. Language & Gender Making the Difference. 104p. (C). 1985. pap. 45.00x (*0-7300-0347-7*, ECS806, Pub. by Deakin Univ AT) St Mut.

Poyo, Gerald E. With All & for the Good of All: The Emergence of Popular Nationalism in the Cuban Communities of the United States, 1848-1898. LC 88-21129. (Illus.). xvii, 182p. (C). 1989. lib. bdg. 30.95 (*0-8223-0881-9*) Duke.

Poyo, Gerald E. & Hinojosa, Gilberto M., eds. Tejano Origins in Eighteenth-Century San Antonio. (Illus.). 222p. 1991. 19.95 (*0-292-71138-7*) U of Tex Pr.

Poyser, J., ed. see GP-Info Symposium Staff.

Poyser, Norman L. Prostaglandins in Reproduction. LC 81-181787. (Prostaglandins Research Studies Ser.: No. 2). (Illus.). 272p. reprint ed. pap. 77.60 (*0-8357-8996-9*, 2033348) Bks Demand.

Poyss. S.M. to Clinical Pharmacology & Nursing. 2nd ed. 1991. 14.95 (*0-87434-401-8*) Springhouse Pub.

***Poyssick, Gary.** FreeHand Production Techniques. (Illus.). 320p. (Orig.). 1995. pap. text ed. 30.00 (*1-56830-175-8*) Alpha Bks IN.

— Illustrator Production Techniques. (Illus.). 300p. (Orig.). 1995. pap. text ed. 25.00 (*1-56830-133-2*) Alpha Bks IN.

— PageMaker Production Techniques. (Illus.). 320p. (Orig.). 1995. pap. text ed. 30.00 (*1-56830-170-7*) Alpha Bks IN.

— Photoshop Production Techniques. (Illus.). 300p. (Orig.). 1995. pap. text ed. 25.00 (*1-56830-132-4*) Alpha Bks IN.

— QuarkXPress Production Techniques. (Illus.). 300p. (Orig.). 1995. pap. text ed. 25.00 (*1-56830-134-0*) Alpha Bks IN.

Poythress, Vern S. Science & Hermeneutics. 1988. 17.99 (*0-310-40971-3*) Zondervan.

— The Shadow of Christ in the Law of Moses. 440p. (C). 1995. pap. 14.99 (*0-87552-375-7*) Presby & Reformed.

— Understanding Dispensationalists. 2nd ed. LC 93-39295. 1993. 7.99 (*0-87552-374-9*) Presby & Reformed.

Poza, Ernesto J. Smart Growth: Critical Choices for Business Continuity & Prosperity. LC 89-8191. (Management Ser.). 233p. 1989. 25.95 (*1-55542-170-9*) Jossey-Bass.

Pozar, David M. Antenna Design Using Personal Computers. LC 85-47745. (Artech House Microwave Library). (Illus.). 153p. reprint ed. pap. 43.70 (*0-8357-3934-1*, 2036669) Bks Demand.

— Microwave Engineering. (Electrical & Computer Engineering Ser.). (Illus.). (C). 1990. text ed. 73.25 (*0-201-50418-9*) Addison-Wesley.

***Pozar, David M. & Schaubert, Daniel H., eds.** Microstrip Antennas: The Analysis & Design of Microstrip Antennas & Arrays. LC 95-1229. 1995. reprint ed. write for info. (*0-7803-1078-0*) Inst Electrical.

Pozas, Ricardo. Juan the Chamula: An Ethnological Recreation of the Life of a Mexican Indian. Kemp, Lysander, tr. (Illus.). 123p. 1962. pap. 13.00 (*0-520-01027-2*) U CA Pr.

Pozdena, Randall J. The Modern Economics of Housing: A Guide to Theory & Policy for Finance & Real Estate Professionals. LC 87-32593. 224p. 1988. text ed. 55.00 (*0-89930-231-9*, Quorum Bks) Greenwood.

Pozdeyev, A., jt. auth. see Tarnovskii, Y.

***Pozel, Lynda A.** Lynda's Low-Fat Kitchen: Meatless Meals for Every Day. Joachim, David, ed. (Illus.). 124p. (Orig.). 1995. pap. 11.95 (*1-885588-02-X*) Chitra Pubns.

Pozela, J., ed. Physics of High-Speed Transistors. (Microdevices: Physics & Fabrication Technologies Ser.). (Illus.). 355p. 1994. 85.00 (*0-306-44619-7*, Plenum Pr) Plenum.

Pozgar, George D. Legal Aspects of Health Care Administration. 5th ed. (Health Care Administration Ser.). 602p. 1993. 49.00 (*0-8342-0360-X*, 20360) Aspen Pub.

Pozgar, George D., et al. Long-Term Care & the Law: A Legal Guide for Health Care Professionals. 510p. 1992. 53.00 (*0-8342-0289-1*, 20289) Aspen Pub.

Pozharskaya, Militsa & Volodina, Tatiana. The Art of the Ballets Russes: The Russian Seasons in Paris, 1908-1929. (Illus.). 288p. 1991. 49.95 (*1-55859-151-6*) Abbeville Pr.

Pozhela, J. Plasma & Current Instabilities in Semiconductors. Germogenova, O. A., tr. (International Series in the Science of the Solid State: Vol. 18). (Illus.). 314p. 1981. 129.00 (*0-08-025048-3*, Pub. by Pergamon Repr UK) Franklin.

Pozin, Mikhail, comp. Russian-English, English-Russian Dictionary of Free Market Era Economics. LC 92-56681. 327p. 1993. lib. bdg. 45.00 (*0-89950-876-6*) McFarland & Co.

Poznanski, Andrew K. Practical Approaches to Pediatric Radiology. LC 75-16022. 478p. reprint ed. pap. 136.30 (*0-317-28230-1*, 2022728) Bks Demand.

***Poznanski, Kazimierz, ed.** Evolutionary Transition to Capitalism. (C). 1995. pap. text ed. 18.95 (*0-8133-2271-5*) Westview.

— Evolutionary Transition to Capitalism. 1995. text ed. 49.95 (*0-8133-2270-7*) Westview.

Poznanski, Kazimierz A. Stabilization & Privatization in Poland: An Economic Evaluation of the Shock Therapy Program. LC 93-885. 1993. lib. bdg. 89.00 (*0-7923-9341-4*) Kluwer Ac.

Poznanski, Kazimierz A., ed. Constructing Capitalism: The Reemergence of Civil Society & Liberal Economy in the Post-Communist World. 230p. (C). 1992. pap. text ed. 19.95 (*0-8133-1482-8*) Westview.

Poznanski, Kazimierz Z. Technology, Competition, & the Soviet Bloc in the World Market. LC 87-35050. (Research Ser.: No. 70). (Illus.). x, 226p. 1987. pap. 13.95 (*0-87725-170-3*) U of Cal IAS.

Poznansky, Alexander. Tchaikovsky: Quest for the Inner Man. 680p. 1991. text ed. 39.95 (*0-02-871885-2*) Schirmer Bks.

— Tchaikovsky: The Quest for the Inner Man. 680p. 1993. pap. 18.00 (*0-02-871886-0*) Schirmer Bks.

***Pozner, Larry S. & Dodd, Roger J.** Cross-Examination: Science & Techniques. 763p. 1993. 105.00 (*1-55834-071-8*) Michie Butterworth.

Pozner, Vladimir. Parting with Illusions. 352p. 1991. pap. 9.95 (*0-380-71349-7*) Avon.

Pozniak, A., jt. auth. see Johnson, N. I.

Pozniak, G. Russian-English Dictionary of Helminthology & Plant Nematology. 108p. (Orig.). (C). 1979. 125.00 (*0-89771-926-3*, Pub. by Collets) St Mut.

Pozniak, G. I. Russian-English Dictionary of Helminthology & Plant Nematology. 108p. (Orig.). (ENG & RUS.). 1979. 30.50 (*0-685-72326-7*) CAB Intl.

Pozniak, G. I., ed. Dictionary of Helminthology & Plant Nematology. 108p. (ENG & RUS.). 1979. 35.00 (*0-8288-4786-X*) Fr & Eur.

— Russian-English Dictionary of Helminthology & Plant Nematology. 108p. (Orig.). (ENG & RUS.). 1979. pap. text ed. 30.50x (*0-85198-447-9*) CAB Intl.

Poznyak, Alexandr S., jt. auth. see Najim, Kaddour.

Poznyak, E. G., jt. auth. see Ilyin, V. A.

Pozo, Susan, ed. Essays on Legal & Illegal Immigration. LC 86-24605. 128p. 1986. 19.00 (*0-88099-041-4*); pap. 9.00 (*0-88099-040-6*) W E Upjohn.

Pozorski, Shelia & Pozorski, Thomas. Early Settlement & Subsistence in the Casma Valley, Peru. LC 87-25517. (Illus.). 160p. 1987. text ed. 24.95 (*0-87745-183-4*) U of Iowa Pr.

Pozorski, Thomas, jt. auth. see Pozorski, Shelia.

Pozovich, Gregory J. Productive Personnel: California Employment, Training, & Management. 200p. 1994. pap. 14.95 (*0-9640592-0-7*) Pacific St Pubng.

Pozrikidis, C. Boundary Integral & Singularity Methods for Linearized Viscous Flow. (Texts in Applied Mathematics Ser.: No. 8). (Illus.). 250p. (C). 1992. 79.95 (*0-521-40502-5*); pap. 29.95 (*0-521-40693-5*) Cambridge U Pr.

***Pozsgai, Frank.** The Scroll Saw Book. LC 95-1944. (Illus.). 64p. (Orig.). 1995. pap. 12.95 (*0-88740-774-9*) Schiffer.

— A Scroll Saw Christmas with Frank Pozsgai: Step-by-Step to a 3-D Sleigh & Reindeer. (Illus.). 64p. (Orig.). 1995. pap. 12.95 (*0-88740-786-2*) Schiffer.

— Scroll Saw Pictures. LC 95-4998. (Illus.). 64p. (Orig.). 1995. pap. 12.95 (*0-88740-775-7*) Schiffer.

***Pozsonyi, G.** Film Production & Cinematography Vol. 26. 220p. 1975. 30.00x (*963-05-0592-4*, Pub. by Akad Kiado HU) St Mut.

Pozza, D., jt. ed. see Colpi, Giovanni M.

Pozza, Guido, et al, eds. Diet, Diabetes & Atherosclerosis. 296p. 1984. text ed. 86.00 (*0-88167-017-0*) Raven.

***Pozzessere.** Eyes of Fire. 1995. mass mkt. 4.99 (*1-55166-89X-8*, Mira Bks) Harlequin Bks.

Pozzessere, et al. Forbidden Fire. (Harlequin Historical Ser.: No. 66). 1991. mass mkt. 3.95 (*0-373-28666-X*) Harlequin Bks.

***Pozzessere, Heather G.** All in the Family. (Men Made in America Ser.). 1995. mass mkt. 3.99 (*0-373-45198-9*, 1-45198-8) Harlequin Bks.

— Angel of Mercy. 1995. 4.99 (*1-55166-069-5*, 1-66069-5, Mira Bks) Harlequin Bks.

— Eyes of Fire. 1995. pap. 5.99 (*1-55166-089-X*, 1-66089-3, Mira Bks) Harlequin Bks.

— For All of Her Life: To Love Again. 512p. 1995. mass mkt. 5.99 (*0-8217-4950-1*) Zebra.

— The Game of Love. 1994. mass mkt. 4.50 (*0-373-48280-9*, 5-48280-7) Silhouette.

— Hatfield & McCoy. (Silhouette Intimate Moments Ser.: No. 416). 1992. mass mkt. 3.29 (*0-373-07416-6*) Silhouette.

— Hatfield & Mccoy. large type ed. (Silhouette Romance Ser.). 1995. 18.95 (*0-373-59419-4*) Thorndike Pr.

— The Last Cavalier. (Shadows Ser.: No. 1). 1993. mass mkt. 3.50 (*0-373-27001-1*) Silhouette.

— Lonesome Rider. (Historical Short Stories Ser.). 1993. mass mkt. 4.99 (*0-373-83259-1*, 1-83259-1) Silhouette.

— A Matter of Circumstance. 1994. mass mkt. 4.99 (*1-55166-005-9*, 1-66005-9, Mira Bks) Harlequin Bks.

— A Matter of Circumstance. 1994. mass mkt. 4.50 (*0-373-48281-7*, 5-48281-5) Silhouette.

— Slow Burn. 1994. pap. 5.99 (*1-55166-000-8*, 1-66000-0, Mira Bks) Harlequin Bks.

— Snowfire. (Silhouette Intimate Moments Ser.: No. 386). 1991. mass mkt. 3.25 (*0-373-07386-0*) Silhouette.

— Strangers in Paradise. 1995. mass mkt. 4.99 (*1-55166-038-5*, 1-66038-0, Mira Bks) Harlequin Bks.

— The Trouble with Andrew. (Silhouette Intimate Moments Ser.). 1993. mass mkt. 3.50 (*0-373-07525-1*, 5-07525-4) Silhouette.

Pozzetta, George. Americanization, Social Control, & Philanthropy. LC 90-49267. (Immigration & Ethnicity Ser.: Vol. 14). 360p. 1991. reprint ed. 60.00 (*0-8240-7414-9*) Garland.

— Assimilation Acculturation, & Social Mobility. (Immigration & Ethnicity Ser.: Vol. 13). 368p. 1991. reprint ed. 61.00 (*0-8240-7413-0*) Garland.

— Contemporary Immigration. (Immigration & Ethnicity Ser.: Vol. 20). 424p. 1991. reprint ed. 65.00 (*0-8240-7420-3*) Garland.

— Education & the Immigrant. (Immigration & Ethnicity Ser.: Vol. 10). 424p. 1991. reprint ed. 65.00 (*0-8240-7410-6*) Garland.

— Emigration & Immigration: The Old World Confronts the New. (Immigration & Ethnicity Ser.: Vol. 2). 736p. 1991. reprint ed. 95.00 (*0-8240-7402-5*) Garland.

— Ethnic Communities. LC 90-49261. (Immigration & Ethnicity Ser.: Vol. 3). 250p. 1991. reprint ed. 75.00 (*0-8240-7403-3*) Garland.

— Ethnicity & Gender Immigrant Woman. (Immigration & Ethnicity Ser.: Vol. 12). 344p. 1991. reprint ed. 60.00 (*0-8240-7412-2*) Garland.

— Ethnicity, Ethnic Identity. LC 90-49269. (Immigration & Ethnicity Ser.: Vol. 16). 464p. 1991. reprint ed. 70.00 (*0-8240-7416-5*) Garland.

— Folklore, Culture, & the Immigrant Mind. (Immigration & Ethnicity Ser.: Vol. 18). 376p. 1991. reprint ed. 60.00 (*0-8240-7418-1*) Garland.

— Immigrant Family Patterns. (Immigration & Ethnicity Ser.: Vol. 11). 400p. 1991. reprint ed. 65.00 (*0-8240-7411-4*) Garland.

— Immigrant Institutions. LC 90-48319. (Immigration & Ethnicity Ser.: Vol. 5). 352p. 1991. reprint ed. 60.00 (*0-8240-7405-X*) Garland.

— Immigrant Radicals. (Immigration & Ethnicity Ser.: Vol. 9). 256p. 1991. reprint ed. 70.00 (*0-8240-7409-2*) Garland.

— Immigrants on the Land. LC 90-49262. (Immigration & Ethnicity Ser.: Vol. 4). 416p. 1991. reprint ed. 65.00 (*0-8240-7404-1*) Garland.

— Law, Crime, & Justice: Naturalization & Citizenship. (Immigration & Ethnicity Ser.: Vol. 17). 1991. reprint ed. 70.00 (*0-8240-7417-3*) Garland.

— Nativism, Prejudice, & Discrimination. (Immigration & Ethnicity Ser.: Vol. 15). 480p. 1991. reprint ed. 75.00 (*0-8240-7415-7*) Garland.

— Politics & the Immigrant. (Immigration & Ethnicity Ser.: Vol. 8). 480p. 1991. reprint ed. 75.00 (*0-8240-7408-4*) Garland.

— Themes in Immigration History. (Immigration & Ethnicity Ser.: Vol. 1). 368p. 1991. reprint ed. 60.00 (*0-8240-7401-7*) Garland.

— Unions & Immigrants. (Immigration & Ethnicity Ser.: Vol. 7). 368p. 1991. reprint ed. 62.00 (*0-8240-7407-6*) Garland.

— The Work Experience. (Immigration & Ethnicity Ser.: Vol. 6). 528p. 1991. reprint ed. 77.00 (*0-8240-7406-8*) Garland.

Pozzetta, George E., ed. American Immigration & Ethnicity, 20 vols. Set. 1,365.00 (*0-8240-7400-9*) Garland.

Pozzetta, George E., jt. ed. see Colburn, David R.

Pozzetta, George E., jt. ed. see Miller, Randall M.

Pozzetta, George E., jt. auth. see Mormino, Gary R.

Pozzi, A. Application of Pade's Approximation Theory in Fluid: Advances in Mathematics for Applied Sciences Ser. 252p. 1994. text ed. 61.00 (*981-02-1414-6*) World Scientific Pub.

Pozzi, Donna C., ed. see Porter, Erika R.

Pozzi, Dora C. & Wickersham, John M., eds. Myth & the Polis. LC 90-55716. (Myth & Poetics Ser.). 248p. 1991. 31.95 (*0-8014-2473-9*); pap. 10.95 (*0-8014-9734-5*) Cornell U Pr.

Pozzi, Lucio. Hender. (Illus.). 1980. 6.00 (*0-935694-01-3*) St Edns.

— Hender. deluxe ed. (Illus.). 1980. 12.00 (*0-686-34459-6*) St Edns.

Pozzo, Andrea. Rules & Examples of Perspective. LC 69-13450. (Illus.). 1972. reprint ed. 38.95 (*0-405-08861-2*, Pub. by Blom Pubns UK) Ayer.

Pozzo, Laura, jt. auth. see Hillman, James.

PPI Staff. Nine One One: Communication Manual. 2nd ed. 512p. 1993. per., pap. text ed. 42.95 (*0-8403-8551-X*) Kendall-Hunt.

PPI Staff & Pivetta. The How to Book: 9-1-1 Trainer Guide. 142p. 1993. per. 14.95 (*0-8403-8767-9*) Kendall-Hunt.

— The Nine-One-One Classroom Training Manual: College & Agency Guide to Implementing & Enhancing Classroom Training. 2nd ed. 352p. 1993. per., pap. text ed. 69.95 (*0-8403-8702-4*) Kendall-Hunt.

PPU Staff. Diccionario de Psicologia Para Educadores. 374p. 1989. pap. 39.95 (*0-7859-6252-2*, 8476653476) Fr & Eur.

PQ Systems, Inc. Staff. Total Quality Transformation Improvement Tools. 338p. 1991. spiral bd. 85.00 (*1-882683-00-5*) PQ Systs.

— Total Quality Transformation Improvement Tools - Educational. 300p. (Orig.). 1995. spiral bd., pap. 39.95 (*1-882683-01-3*) PQ Systs.

— Total Quality Transformation Improvement Tools-Commercial. 300p. (Orig.). 1995. spiral bd., pap. 39.95 (*1-882683-02-1*) PQ Systs.

***PR Japan Staff, tr.** Polynesian Cultural Center - Japanese. (Illus.). 50p. (JPN.). 1995. pap. write for info. (*0-9644640-1-2*) Polynesian Cult.

Praaning, Rio D. & Perry, Charles M., eds. East-West Relations in the 1990's: Politics & Technology: Proceedings of the Third International Roundtable Conference. (C). 1988. lib. bdg. 79.00 (*90-247-3766-4*) Kluwer Ac.

Prabhakar, Eric. Madiera at Sundown: A Raj Trilogy. (C). 1990. 23.00 (*81-7001-071-3*, Pub. by Chanakya II) S Asia.

Prabhakar, L. R. In a Lighter Vein. 116p. 1986. text ed. 18.95 (*81-207-0117-8*, Pub. by Sterling Pubs II) Apt Bks.

Prabhakar, Vishnu. Awara Messiah: A Biography of Sarat Chandra Chatterjee. (New World Literature Ser.). 1989. 19.50 (*81-7018-564-5*, Pub. by BR Pub II) S Asia.

— Story of Swarajya: Part I. (Nehru Library for Children). (Illus.). (J). (gr. 1-10). 1979. pap. 2.50 (*0-89744-185-0*) Auromere.

***Prabhakara, F. S.** Industrial & Commercial Power System Handbook. 1995. text ed. 69.50 (*0-07-050624-8*) McGraw.

Prabhakara, N. R. & Usha, M. N. Population Growth & Umemployment in India. 1986. 15.00 (*81-7024-041-7*, Pub. by Ashish II) S Asia.

***Prabhakaran, V. T.** Statistical Techniques for Studying Genotype-Environment Interactions. (C). 1994. 24.00x (*81-7003-168-0*, Pub. by S Asia Pubs II) S Asia.

Prabhat Rainjan Sarkar. Baba's Grace: Discourses of P. R. Sarkar. (Illus.). 197p. (Orig.). 1987. reprint ed. pap. 6.95 (*0-88476-001-4*) Ananda Marga.

— Human Society, Pt. I. 3rd rev. ed. Avadhuta, Acarya V. & Kumar, Jayanta, trs. 185p. 1989. pap. 5.95 (*0-685-33561-5*) Ananda Marga.

— Human Society, Pt. II. 3rd rev. ed. Acarya Vijayananda Avadhuta & Kumar, Jayanta, trs. 105p. (C). 1987. pap. text ed. 5.95 (*0-88476-015-4*) Ananda Marga.

— The Liberation of Intellect: Neo-Humanism. Avadhutika Anamda Mitra Acarya & Acarya Vijayananda Avadhuta, trs. 102p. (Orig.). (C). 1982. pap. 4.95 (*0-88476-011-1*) Ananda Marga.

— Light Comes. 248p. (Orig.). 1989. 4.95 (*0-88476-017-0*) Ananda Marga.

— Neo-Humanism in a Nutshell, Pt. I. Avadhuta, Acarya V. & Avadhuta, Acarya M., trs. 67p. (Orig.). (C). 1987. pap. 3.95 (*0-88476-027-8*) Ananda Marga.

— Neo-Humanism in a Nutshell, Pt. II. Acarya Mantreshwarananda Avadhuta, tr. (Orig.). (C). 1987. pap. text ed. 3.95 (*0-88476-028-6*) Ananda Marga.

— Problem of the Day. 64p. 1968. pap. 3.95 (*0-686-95454-8*) Ananda Marga.

— Prout in a Nutshell, Pt. 1. Acarya Vijayananda Avadhuta & Kumar, Jayanta, trs. 62p. (Orig.). (C). 1987. pap. 3.95 (*0-88476-050-2*) Ananda Marga.

An Asterisk (*) at the beginning of an entry indicates that the title is appearing in BIP for the first time.

— Prout in a Nutshell, Pt. 2. Acarya Vijayananda Avadhuta & Kumar, Jayanta, trs. 68p. (Orig.). (C). 1987. pap. text ed. 3.95 (*0-88476-051-0*) Ananda Marga.
— Prout in a Nutshell, Pt. 3. Acarya Vijayananda Avadhuta & Kumar, Jayanta, trs. 64p. (Orig.). (C). 1987. pap. text ed. 3.95 (*0-88476-052-9*) Ananda Marga.
— Prout in a Nutshell, Pt. 4. 3rd ed. Acarya Vijayananda Avadhuta & Kumar, Jayanta, trs. 53p. (Orig.). (C). 1987. pap. text ed. 3.95 (*0-88476-053-7*) Ananda Marga.
— Prout in a Nutshell, Pt. 5. Acarya Vijayananda Avadhuta & Kumar, Jayanta, trs. 89p. (Orig.). (C). 1987. pap. 3.95 (*0-88476-054-5*) Ananda Marga.
— Prout in a Nutshell, Pt. 6. Acarya Vijayananda Avadhuta & Kumar, Jayanta, trs. 62p. (Orig.). (C). 1987. pap. 3.95 (*0-88476-055-3*) Ananda Marga.
— Prout in a Nutshell, Pt. 7. Acarya Vijayananda Avadhuta & Kumar, Jayanta, trs. 67p. (Orig.). (C). 1987. pap. 3.95 (*0-88476-056-1*) Ananda Marga.
— Prout in a Nutshell, Pt. 8. Acarya Vijayananda Avadhuta & Kumar, Jayanta, trs. 67p. (Orig.). (C). 1987. pap. 3.95 (*0-88476-057-X*) Ananda Marga.
— Prout in a Nutshell, Pt. 9. Acarya Vijayananda Avadhuta & Kumar, Jayanta, trs. 69p. (Orig.). (C). 1987. pap. 3.95 (*0-88476-058-8*) Ananda Marga.
— Prout in a Nutshell, Pt. 10. Acarya Vijayananda Avadhuta & Kumar, Jayanta, trs. 82p. (Orig.). (C). 1987. pap. 3.95 (*0-88476-059-6*) Ananda Marga.
— Prout in a Nutshell, Pt. 11. Acarya Vijayananda Avadhuta & Kumar, Jayanta, trs. 62p. (Orig.). (C). 1987. pap. 3.95 (*0-88476-060-X*) Ananda Marga.
— Prout in a Nutshell, Pt. 12. Acarya Vijayananda Avadhuta & Kumar, Jayanta, trs. 60p. (Orig.). (C). 1987. pap. 3.95 (*0-88476-061-8*) Ananda Marga.
— Prout in a Nutshell, Pt. 13. Acarya Vijayananda Avadhuta & Kumar, Jayanta, trs. 64p. (Orig.). (C). 1988. pap. 3.95 (*0-88476-062-6*) Ananda Marga.
— Prout in a Nutshell, Pt. 14. Acarya Vijayananda Avadhuta & Kumar, Jayanta, trs. 60p. (Orig.). (C). 1988. pap. 3.95 (*0-88476-063-4*) Ananda Marga.
— Prout in a Nutshell, Pt. 15. Acarya Vijayananda Avadhuta & Kumar, Jayanta, trs. 64p. (Orig.). (C). 1988. pap. 3.95 (*0-88476-064-2*) Ananda Marga.
— The Thoughts of P. R. Sarkar. Avadhutika Anandamtra Acarya, ed. 214p. (Orig.). (C). 1981. pap. text ed. 4.95 (*0-88476-016-2*) Ananda Marga.
— Universal Humanism: Selected Social Writings of P. R. Sarkar. Anderson, Tim & Coyle, Gary, eds. 108p. (Orig.). (C). 1983. pap. 4.95 (*0-9591792-0-8*) Proutist Universal.
— Yogic Treatments & Natural Remedies. 100p. (Orig.). 1989. text ed. 5.95 (*0-88476-029-4*) Ananda Marga.

Prabhavananda. Sermon on the Mount According to Vedanta. 1991. pap. 8.95 (*0-87481-050-7*) Vedanta Pr.

Prabhavananda, Swami. Bhagavatam, Srimad: The Wisdom of God. 1978. reprint ed. 5.95 (*0-87481-483-9*) Vedanta Pr.
— Eternal Companion: Brahmananda, His Life & Teachings. 3rd ed. LC 72-113256. 1960. pap. 7.95 (*0-87481-024-8*) Vedanta Pr.
— Religion in Practice. 1960. 8.95 (*0-87481-016-7*) Vedanta Pr.
— The Sermon on the Mount According to Vedanta. 1972. pap. 4.50 (*0-451-62679-6*, Ment); pap. 4.95 (*0-451-62829-2*, Ment) NAL-Dutton.
— Sermon on the Mount According to Vedanta. LC 64-8660. 1963. 12.95 (*0-87481-002-7*) Vedanta Pr.
— Spiritual Heritage of India. LC 63-10517. (C). 1979. reprint ed. pap. 9.95 (*0-87481-035-3*) Vedanta Pr.
— Vedic Religion & Philosophy. 4.50 (*0-87481-411-1*) Vedanta Pr.
— Yoga & Mysticism: An Introduction to Vedanta. 53p. 1984. reprint ed. pap. 3.95 (*0-87481-020-5*) Vedanta Pr.

Prabhavananda, Swami, tr. Memories of a Loving Soul. (Orig.). 1968. pap. 3.50 (*0-87481-015-9*, Pub. by Advaita Ashrama II) Vedanta Pr.

Prabhavananda, Swami, et al, trs. Upanishads: Breath of the Eternal. LC 48-5935. (C). 1947. 9.95 (*0-87481-007-8*); pap. 7.95 (*0-87481-040-X*) Vedanta Pr.

Prabhavananda, Swami & Isherwood, Christopher. How to Know God: The Yoga Aphorisms of Patanjali. 1969. pap. 3.95 (*0-451-62590-0*, Ment) NAL-Dutton.

Prabhavananda, Swami & Isherwood, Christopher, trs. How to Know God: The Yoga Aphorisms of Patanjali. 224p. 1983. pap. 7.95 (*0-87481-041-8*) Vedanta Pr.

Prabhavananda, Swami & Manchester, Frederick, trs. The Upanishads: Breath of the Eternal. 128p. 1957. pap. 4.99 (*0-451-62607-9*, MJ2298, Ment) NAL-Dutton.

Prabhavananda, Swami, tr. see Bhagavad-Gita.

Prabhavananda, Swami, tr. see Narada.

Prabhavananda, Swami. The Song of God: Bagavad-Gita. Isherwood, Christopher, tr. 1989. pap. 3.50 (*0-451-62671-0*) NAL-Dutton.

Prabhavathi, V. Perceptions, Motivations, & Performance of Women Legislators. (C). 1991. 27.50 (*81-7054-145-X*, Pub. by Classical Pub II) S Asia.

Prabhu, Barbara W., ed. Spotlight on New Jersey Government. 6th ed. LC 91-45493. 400p. (C). 1992. text ed. 42.00 (*0-8135-1843-1*); pap. text ed. 15.95 (*0-8135-1844-X*) Rutgers U Pr.

Prabhu, C. S. Semantic Database Systems: A Functional Introduction. 1993. text ed. 25.00 (*0-86311-346-X*, Pub. by Universities Pr II) Apt Bks.

Prabhu, G. & Wright, Charles. Assembly Language & Architecture for the MC 68000. (Orig.). 1994. pap. 38.00 (*1-881991-34-2*) Scott Jones Inc.

Prabhu, Krishna, ed. see Osho.

Prabhu, Krishna, ed. see Rajneesh, Osho.

Prabhu, Manjiri. Symphony of Hearts. (C). 1994. text ed. 7.00 (*81-7167-183-7*, Pub. by Rupa II) S Asia.

Prabhu, N., ed. Statistical Inference from Stochastic Processes. LC 88-31369. (CONM Ser.: No. 80). 386p. 1988. pap. 44.00 (*0-8218-5087-3*, CONM-80) Am Math.

Prabhu, N. D. Excellence Through People: The Canbank Way. ix, 190p. (C). 1991. text ed. 25.00 (*81-220-0248-X*) Advent Bks Div.

Prabhu, N. U. Stochastic Storage Processes: Queues, Insurance Risk & Dams. (Applications of Mathematics Ser.: Vol. 15). 140p. 1980. 52.00 (*0-387-90522-7*) Spr-Verlag.

Prabhu, N. U. & Basawa, I. V., eds. Statistical Inference in Stochastic Processes. (Probability Ser.: Vol. 6). 288p. 1991. 120.00 (*0-8247-8417-0*) Dekker.

Prabhu, Pandharinath. Hindu Social Organization. 400p. 1986. reprint ed. pap. 11.50 (*0-8364-1836-0*, Pub. by Popular Prakashan II) S Asia.

Prabhu, R. K., ed. see Gandhi, M. K.

Prabhu, R. K., ed. see Gandhi, M. K. & Tagore, Rabindranath.

Prabhu, S. R., et al, eds. Oral Diseases in the Tropics. (Illus.). 824p. 1992. 165.00 (*0-19-262008-8*) OUP.

Prabhu, Sw K., ed. see Osho.

Prabhu, Swami K., ed. see Osho.

Prabhu, Swami Krishna, ed. see Rajneesh, Osho.

Prabhupada, A. C. Bhagavad-Gita As It Is. 904p. 1988. 19.95 (*0-318-37155-3*) Asia Bk Corp.
— Dialectic Spiritualism: A Vedic View of Western Philosophy. LC 85-90424. 566p. 1985. 14.95 (*0-932215-10-6*); pap. 7.95 (*0-932215-02-5*) Palace Pub.

Prabhupada, Bhaktivedanta S. The Nector of Instruction. 130p. 1990. pap. 2.95 (*0-912776-85-4*) Bhaktivedanta.
— Teachings of Lord Cartanya. 1990. 17.95 (*0-912776-07-2*) Bhaktivedanta.

Prabhupada, Srila. Journey to Self-Discovery. 283p. 1991. pap. 7.95 (*0-685-66066-4*) Bhaktivedanta.
— Journey to Self-Discovery. 283p. 1991. 9.95 (*0-89213-270-1*) Bhaktivedanta.
— Message of Godhead. 68p. 1991. pap. 2.95 (*0-89213-299-X*) Bhaktivedanta.
— Topmost Yoga. 108p. 1991. 2.95 (*0-912776-11-0*) Bhaktivedanta.

Prabhupada, Swami, jt. auth. see Bhaktivedanta, A. C.

Prabir Basu & Fraser, Scott. Circulating Fluidized Bed Boilers Design & Applications. 408p. 1991. 69.95 (*0-7506-9226-X*) Buttrwrth-Heinemann.

Prabodhanandadasarasvati. Srila Prabodhananda Sarasvati's Sri Caitanya-candramrta: The Nectar Moon of Sri Caitanya. Kusakrathadasa, tr. (Krsna Library: Vol. 2). 156p. (C). 1987. pap. text ed. 10.00 (*0-944833-07-1*) Krsna Inst.

Prabodhanandasarasvati. Srila Prabodhananda Sarasvatis: Sri Vrndavana Mahimamrta Sataka Seventeen. Kusakrathadasa, tr. (Krsna Library: Vol. 186). 78p. (C). 1993. pap. text ed. 6.00 (*1-56130-106-X*) Krsna Inst.
— Srila Prabodhananda Sarasvati's Sri Radha-Rasa-Sudha-Nidhi: The Nectar Moon of Sri Radha's Sweetness. Kusakrathadasa, tr. (Krsna Library: Vol. 204). 180p. (C). 1993. pap. text ed. 10.00 (*1-56130-129-9*) Krsna Inst.
— Srila Prabodhananda Sarasvati's Sri Vrndavana-Mahimamrta: The Nectar Glory of Sri Vrndavana, Vol. 1. Kusakrathadasa, tr. (Krsna Library: Vol. 17). 166p. (Orig.). (C). 1988. pap. text ed. 6.00 (*0-944833-16-0*) Krsna Inst.
— Srila Prabodhananda Sarasvati's Sri Vrndavana-Mahimamrta: The Nectar Glory of Sri Vrndavana, Vol. 2. Kusakrathadasa, tr. (Krsna Library: Vol. 18). 166p. (Orig.). (C). 1988. pap. text ed. 6.00 (*0-944833-17-9*) Krsna Inst.
— Srila Prabodhananda Sarasvati's Sri Vrndavana-Mahimamrta: The Nectar of Glory Sri Vrndavana, Vol. 3. Kusakrathadasa, tr. (Krsna Library: Vol. 19). 150p. (Orig.). (C). 1988. pap. text ed. 6.00 (*0-944833-18-7*) Krsna Inst.
— Srila Prabodhananda Sarasvati's Sri Vrndavana-Mahimamrta, Vol. 10: The Nectar Glory of Sri Vrndavana. Kusakrathadasa, tr. (Krsna Library: Vol. 31). 80p. (Orig.). (C). 1988. pap. text ed. 6.00 (*0-944833-40-3*) Krsna Inst.
— Srila Prabodhananda Sarasvati's Sri Vrndavana-Mahimamrta, Vol. 11: The Nectar Glory of Sri Vrndavana. Kusakrathadasa, tr. (Krsna Library: Vol. 32). 72p. (Orig.). (C). 1988. pap. text ed. 6.00 (*0-944833-41-1*) Krsna Inst.
— Srila Prabodhananda Sarasvati's Sri Vrndavana-Mahimamrta, Vol. 12: The Nectar Glory of Sri Vrndavana. Kusakrathadasa, tr. (Krsna Library: Vol. 36). (Orig.). (C). 1988. pap. text ed. 6.00 (*0-944833-42-X*) Krsna Inst.
— Srila Prabodhananda Sarasvati's Sri Vrndavana-Mahimamrta, Vol. 13: The Nectar Glory of Sri Vrndavana. Kusakrathadasa, tr. (Krsna Library: Vol. 37). (Orig.). (C). 1988. pap. text ed. 6.00 (*0-944833-43-8*) Krsna Inst.
— Srila Prabodhananda Sarasvati's Sri Vrndavana-Mahimamrta, Vol. 14: The Nectar Glory of Sri Vrndavana. Kusakrathadasa, tr. (Krsna Library: Vol. 38). (Orig.). (C). 1988. pap. text ed. 6.00 (*0-944833-44-6*) Krsna Inst.
— Srila Prabodhananda Sarasvati's Sri Vrndavana-Mahimamrta, Vol. 4: The Nectar Glory of Sri Vrndavana. Kusakrathadasa, tr. (Krsna Library: Vol. 25). 80p. (Orig.). (C). 1988. pap. text ed. 6.00 (*0-944833-19-5*) Krsna Inst.
— Srila Prabodhananda Sarasvati's Sri Vrndavana-Mahimamrta, Vol. 5: The Nectar Glory of Sri Vrndavana. Kusakrathadasa, tr. (Krsna Library: Vol. 26). 72p. (Orig.). (C). 1988. pap. text ed. 6.00 (*0-944833-20-9*) Krsna Inst.
— Srila Prabodhananda Sarasvati's Sri Vrndavana-Mahimamrta, Vol. 6: The Nectar Glory of Sri Vrndavana. Kusakrathadasa, tr. (Krsna Library: Vol. 27). 72p. (Orig.). (C). 1988. pap. text ed. 6.00 (*0-944833-21-7*) Krsna Inst.
— Srila Prabodhananda Sarasvati's Sri Vrndavana-Mahimamrta, Vol. 7: The Nectar Glory of Sri Vrndavana. Kusakrathadasa, tr. (Krsna Library: Vol. 28). 64p. (Orig.). (C). 1988. pap. text ed. 6.00 (*0-944833-22-5*) Krsna Inst.
— Srila Prabodhananda Sarasvati's Sri Vrndavana-Mahimamrta, Vol. 8: The Nectar Glory of Sri Vrndavana. Kusakrathadasa, tr. (Krsna Library: Vol. 29). 72p. (Orig.). (C). 1988. pap. text ed. 6.00 (*0-944833-23-3*) Krsna Inst.
— Srila Prabodhananda Sarasvati's Sri Vrndavana-Mahimamrta, Vol. 9: The Nectar Glory of Sri Vrndavana. Kusakrathadasa, tr. (Krsna Library: Vol. 30). 80p. (Orig.). (C). 1988. pap. text ed. 6.00 (*0-944833-24-1*) Krsna Inst.

Prachand, S. L. Mob Violence in India. 144p. 1979. 12.95 (*0-318-37211-8*) Asia Bk Corp.

Prachowny, Martin. Money in the Macroeconomy. (Illus.). 336p. 1986. pap. 29.95 (*0-521-31594-8*) Cambridge U Pr.

Prachowny, Martin F. The Goals of Macroeconomic Policy. LC 93-43158. (Illus.). 240p. 1994. 59.95x (*0-415-10763-6*, B3794, Routledge NY); pap. 19.95 (*0-415-10764-4*, B3798, Routledge NY) Routledge.

Pracht-Fitzell, Ilse. Blendung und Wandlung: Lessings Dramen in Psychologischer Sicht. LC 90-36425. (Enlightenment: German & Interdisciplinary Studies: Vol. 3). 361p. (C). 1991. text ed. 59.95 (*0-8204-1374-7*) P Lang Pubs.

Pracht, Klaus. Making & Repairing Furniture: A Visual Guide. (Illus.). 128p. 1994. pap. 29.95 (*0-7134-7501-3*, Pub. by Batsford UK) Trafalgar.
— Woodturning. 1989. pap. 22.95 (*0-486-25887-4*) Dover.

Practer, Trudi. Screen Kisses. 1991. mass mkt. 4.95 (*0-06-100186-4*, Harp PBks) HarpC.

Practical Sailor Editors. Practical Boat Buying. 3rd ed. 608p. (Orig.). 1994. 29.95 (*1-879620-20-0*) Belvoir Pubns.

Practices National Conference of Catholic Bishops, jt. auth. see Bishops' Committee for Pastoral Research Staff.

Practices National Conference of Catholic Bishops Staff

Practising Law Institute Staff. Non-Profit Organizations, 1990. (Tax Law & Estate Planning Ser.). 231p. 1990. 70.00 (*0-685-38047-5*) PLI.

Prada, Manuel Gonzalez. Grafitos. 254p. 1.00 (*0-318-14270-8*) Hispanic Inst.

Pradas, Jorge. Congregados Para Darle Gloria: Gathered to Worship. (SPA.). 4.95 (*84-7645-100-8*, 222994, Pub. by Edit Clie SP) TSELF.
— Tiempo de Cancion (Poesias) Time for Singing: Poems. (SPA.). 3.25 (*84-7645-232-2*, 223256, Pub. by Edit Clie SP) TSELF.

Prade, Henri, jt. auth. see Dubois, Didier.

Pradeau, Alberto. Numismatic History of Mexico. LC 77-93447. (Illus.). 1978. reprint ed. lib. bdg. 25.00 (*0-915262-20-7*) S J Durst.

Pradeau, Alberto F., tr. see Nentvig, Juan.

Pradel, J., jt. auth. see Hureau, J.

***Pradell, Steven.** Winning the War Against Life-Threatening Diseases. LC 94-66759. 256p. 1994. pap. 13.95 (*0-88282-125-3*) New Horizon NJ.

Prader, A., jt. ed. see Cacciari, E.

Pradera, Victor. The New State. Malley, B., tr. LC 79-180421. reprint ed. 36.00 (*0-404-56196-9*) AMS Pr.

Pradere, Alexandre. French Furniture Makers. LC 89-60462. (Illus.). 444p. 1990. 140.00 (*0-89236-183-2*) J P Getty Trust.

Praderie, Francoise, jt. auth. see Schatzman, Evry L.

Pradervand, Pierre. Listening to Africa: Developing Africa from the Grassroots. LC 89-35347. 250p. 1989. text ed. 59.95 (*0-275-93389-X*, C3389, Praeger Pubs) Greenwood.
— Listening to Africa: Developing Africa from the Grassroots. 1990. pap. text ed. 14.95 (*0-275-93692-9*, B3692, Praeger Pubs) Greenwood.

Prades, Juana de Jose, jt. auth. see Diaz, Jose Simon.

Pradesh, Andhra & Prasad, Rajendra. Art of South India. (C). 1980. 35.00 (*0-8364-2466-2*, Pub. by Sundeep II) S Asia.

Pradham, Dhiraj. Tolerant Systems. 1995. text ed. 51.00 (*0-13-057887-8*) P-H.

Pradham, U. C. Indian Orchids, Vols. I & II: Guide to Identification & Culture, I. (C). 1988. 50.00 (*0-685-22331-0*, Scientific) St Mut.
— Indian Orchids, Vols. I & II: Guide to Identification & Culture, II. (C). 1988. 70.00 (*0-685-22332-9*, Scientific) St Mut.

Pradhan, Ayoda P. The Buddha's System of Meditation: Phase (I-VIII), 4 vols., Set. 1986. text ed. 150.00 (*81-207-0140-2*, Pub. by Sterling Pubs II) Apt Bks.

Pradhan, Babulall. English Nepali Dictionary. 696p. (C). 1990. 55.50 (*0-89771-072-X*, Pub. by Ratna Pustak Bhandar) St Mut.
— English-Nepali Dictionary. 1991. 35.00 (*0-7855-0269-6*, Pub. by Ratna Pustak Bhandar) St Mut.

Pradhan, Dhiraj, jt. ed. see Avresky, Dimiter.

Pradhan, Dhiraj K. Fault Tolerant Computing, Vol. I. 2nd ed. 1993. boxed 45.00 (*0-13-300963-7*) P-H.
— Fault-Tolerant Computing: Theory & Technique, Vol. I. (Illus.). 432p. (C). 1986. text ed. 89.00 (*0-13-308230-X*) P-H.

Pradhan, G. P. India's Freedom Struggle. 1990. 22.50 (*0-86132-216-9*, Pub. by Popular Prakashan II) S Asia.

Pradhan, G. P., jt. auth. see Duncan, H. C.

Pradhan, Kumar. The Gorkha Conquests: The Process & Consequences of the Unification of Nepal, with Particular Reference to Eastern Nepal. 302p. 1991. 28.00 (*0-19-562723-7*) OUP.

Pradhan, Mahmood, jt. auth. see Haldane, Andrew G.

Pradhan, Mahmood, jt. ed. see Phylaktis, Kate.

***Pradhan, Menno.** Sector Participation Decisions in Labor Supply Models. LC 94-41478. (LSMS Working Papers: No. 113). 1994. write for info. (*0-8213-3124-8*) World Bank.

Pradhan, Prabha, jt. auth. see Banerji, M. L.

Pradhan, Prachanda P. Local Institutions & People's Participation in Rural Public Works in Nepal. (Special Series on Rural Local Organization: No. 4). 103p. (Orig.). (C). 1980. pap. text ed. 5.80 (*0-86731-031-6*) Cornell CIS RDC.

Pradhan, R., ed. Metallurgy of Vacuum-Degassed Steel Products. (Illus.). 510p. 1989. 20.00 (*0-87339-115-2*, 368) Minerals Metals.

Pradhan, R. & Gupta, I., eds. Developments in the Annealing of Sheet Steels. (Illus.). 510p. 1992. 115.00 (*0-87339-181-0*, 440) Minerals Metals.

Pradhan, R., ed. see Metallurgical Society of AIME Staff.

Pradhan, R., ed. see Metallurgical Society Staff.

Pradhan, R., ed. see Minerals, Metals & Materials Society Staff.

Pradhan, Radhe S. Public Corporations of Nepal: A Study of Financial Ratios. 1986. 19.00 (*0-8364-1943-X*, Pub. by Natl Bk Org II) S Asia.

Pradhan, Rajendra B. Parental Reasons for Not Sending Children to School. 56p. 1981. pap. 9.00 (*0-318-03450-6*) Am-Nepal Ed.

Pradhan, S. D. Indian Army in East Africa. (C). 1991. 27.00 (*81-85135-53-3*, Pub. by Natl Bk Org II) S Asia.

Pradhan, S. D., jt. auth. see Ellinwood, DeWitt C.

Pradhan, Sachin N., et al, eds. Pharmacology in Medicine: Principles & Practice. 1100p. (C). 1986. text ed. 55.00 (*0-9617129-0-2*) SP Press Intl.

Pradhan, Shubhangi S. Word-Index of Abhidharmakosa. (Bibliotheca Indo-Buddhica Ser.: No. 121). (C). 1993. text ed. 28.00 (*81-7030-369-9*) S Asia.

Pradhan, Suresh B. International Pharmaceutical Marketing. LC 82-15022. xxv, 281p. 1983. text ed. 59.95 (*0-89930-009-X*, PPH/, Quorum Bks) Greenwood.

Pradhan, T., ed. Superstrings & Grand Unification: Proceedings of the Winter School on High Energy Physics. 148p. (C). 1989. pap. 36.00 (*9971-5-0528-2*) World Scientific Pub.

Pradier, Claire-Marie, jt. ed. see Paul, Jan.

***Pradissis, A. G.** Dragon Sleep. 1995. pap. 7.00 (*0-533-11327-X*) Vantage.

Pradl, Gordon M., ed. see Britton, James N.

***Prado.** Genealogy & Truth: An Introduction. 1995. text ed. 39.95 (*0-8133-1790-8*) Westview.
— Genealogy & Truth: An Introduction. (C). 1995. pap. text ed. 15.95 (*0-8133-1791-6*) Westview.

Prado, Adelia. The Alphabet in the Park. Watson, Ellen, tr. LC 89-38463. (Wesleyan Poetry in Translation Ser.). 80p. 1990. 22.50 (*0-8195-2175-2*, Wesleyan Univ Pr); pap. 10.95 (*0-8195-1177-3*, Wesleyan Univ Pr) U Pr of New Eng.
— The Headlong Heart. Watson, Ellen, tr. 1988. pap. 7.95 (*0-942979-03-6*) Livingston U Pr.

Prado, C. G. Descartes & Foucault: A Contrastive Introduction to Philosophy. 171p. 1992. pap. 17.00 (*0-7766-0275-6*, Pub. by Univ Ottawa Pr CN) Paul & Co Pubs.
— The Last Choice: Preemptive Suicide in Advanced Age. LC 89-25735. (Contributions in Philosophy Ser.: No. 41). 224p. 1990. text ed. 49.95 (*0-313-27301-4*, PLA/, Greenwood Pr) Greenwood.
— Making Believe: Philosophical Reflections on Fiction. LC 83-5693. (Contributions in Philosophy Ser.: No. 25). 192p. 1984. text ed. 45.00 (*0-313-24013-2*, PMB/, Greenwood Pr) Greenwood.
— Rethinking How We Age: A New View of the Aging Mind. LC 85-9862. (Contributions in Philosophy Ser.: No. 28). 185p. 1986. text ed. 49.95 (*0-313-24785-4*, PRA/, Greenwood Pr) Greenwood.

Prado-Flores, Jose, jt. auth. see Tardif, Emiliano.

Prado, G., jt. ed. see Lahaye, Jacques.

Prado, Holly. Nothing Breaks Off at the Edge. 1976. pap. 2.50 (*0-89823-081-0*) New Rivers Pr.
— Specific Mysteries. 60p. 1990. pap. 8.00 (*0-685-56992-6*) SPD-Small Pr Dist.

Prado, J. Fisherman's Handbook. (Illus.). 192p. 1990. pap. 39.95 (*0-85238-163-8*) Blackwell Sci.

Prado, Marcial. More Practical Spanish Grammar. LC 82-21785. (Self Teaching Guides Ser.). 384p. (C). 1984. pap. text ed. 16.95 (*0-471-89893-7*, 1-581) Wiley.
— National Textbook Company's Dictionary of Spanish False Cognates. 240p. 1993. pap. 16.95 (*0-8442-7978-1*, Natl Textbk) NTC Pub Grp.
— Practical Spanish Grammar. (Self-Teaching Ser.). 360p. 1983. pap. text ed. 14.95 (*0-471-89894-5*, 1-581) Wiley.

Prado, Marcial, tr. see Frazee, Charles A. & Yopp, Hallie K.

Prado, Miguelanxo. Streak of Chalk. 88p. 1994. pap. 15.95 (*1-56163-108-6*, Comics Lit) NBM.

Prado, Pedro. Alsino Vol. 21: Pedro Prado. Castillo-Feliu, Guillermo I., tr. LC 93-22219. (American University Studies: No. XXII). 191p. (SPA.). (C). 1994. text ed. 39.95 (*0-8204-2148-0*) P Lang Pubs.

Prado Velazquez, Ernesto, jt. auth. see Ocampo de Gomez, Aurora.

Prados, John. Combined Fleet Decoded: American Intelligence & the Japanese Navy in World War II. LC 94-20784. 1995. 37.50 (*0-679-43701-0*) Random.
— The Hidden History of the Vietnam War. LC 94-46662. 1995. write for info. (*1-56663-079-7*) I R Dee.

— Keepers of the Keys: A History of the National Security Council from Truman to Bush. 894p. 1991. 24.95 (*0-688-07397-2*) Morrow.
— Keepers of the Keys: A History of the National Security Council from Truman to Bush. 1992. pap. 15.00 (*0-688-11605-1*, Quill) Morrow.
— The Soviet Estimate: U. S. Intelligence Analysis & Soviet Strategic Forces. LC 85-43379. 384p. 1986. text ed. 49. 50x (*0-691-07685-5*); pap. 15.95x (*0-691-02235-6*) Princeton U Pr.
— Valley of Decision: The Seige of Khe Sahn. 1993. mass mkt. 5.99 (*0-440-21345-2*) Dell.
Prados, John & Stubbe, Ray W. Valley of Decision: The Siege of Khe Sanh. (Illus.). 512p. 1991. 29.95 (*0-395-55003-3*) HM.
***Pradt, Mary A.** You Must Remember This 1956: Milestones, Memories, Trivia & Facts, News Events, Prominent Personalities & Sports Highlights of the Year. 24p. 1995. 4.95 (*0-446-91032-5*) Warner Bks.
***Pradt, Mary A., comp.** You Must Remember This 1950: Milestones, Memories, Trivia & Facts, News Events, Prominent Personalities & Sports Highlights of the Year. 24p. 1995. 4.95 (*0-446-91025-2*) Warner Bks.
— You Must Remember This 1951: Milestones, Memories, Trivia & Facts, News Events, Prominent Personalities & Sports Highlights of the Year. 24p. 1995. 4.95 (*0-446-91026-0*) Warner Bks.
— You Must Remember This 1952: Milestones, Memories, Trivia & Facts, News Events, Prominent Personalities & Sports Highlights of the Year. 24p. 1995. 4.95 (*0-446-91028-7*) Warner Bks.
— You Must Remember This 1953: Milestones, Memories, Trivia & Facts, News Events, Prominent Personalities & Sports Highlights of the Year. 24p. 1995. 4.95 (*0-446-91029-5*) Warner Bks.
— You Must Remember This 1954: Milestones, Memories, Trivia & Facts, News Events, Prominent Personalities & Sports Highlights of the Year. 24p. 1995. 4.95 (*0-446-91030-9*) Warner Bks.
— You Must Remember This 1955: Milestones, Memories, Trivia & Facts, News Events, Prominent Personalities & Sports Highlights of the Year. 24p. 1995. write for info. (*0-446-51919-7*) Warner Bks.
— You Must Remember This 1955: Milestones, Memories, Trivia & Facts, News Events, Prominent Personalities & Sports Highlights of the Year. 24p. 1995. 4.95 (*0-446-91031-7*) Warner Bks.
— You Must Remember This 1957: Milestones, Memories, Trivia & Facts, News Events, Prominent Personalities & Sports Highlights of the Year. 24p. 1995. 4.95 (*0-446-91033-3*) Warner Bks.
— You Must Remember This 1958: Milestones, Memories, Trivia & Facts, News Events, Prominent Personalities & Sports Highlights of the Year. 24p. 1995. 4.95 (*0-446-91034-1*) Warner Bks.
— You Must Remember This 1959: Milestones, Memories, Trivia & Facts, News Events, Prominent Personalities & Sports Highlights of the Year. 24p. 1995. 4.95 (*0-446-91035-X*) Warner Bks.
— You Must Remember This 1960: Milestones, Memories, Trivia & Facts, News Events, Prominent Personalities & Sports Highlights of the Year. 24p. 1995. 4.95 (*0-446-91036-8*) Warner Bks.
— You Must Remember This 1961: Milestones, Memories, Trivia & Facts, News Events, Prominent Personalities & Sports Highlights of the Year. 24p. 1995. 4.95 (*0-446-91037-6*) Warner Bks.
— You Must Remember This 1962: Milestones, Memories, Trivia & Facts, News Events, Prominent Personalities & Sports Highlights of the Year. 24p. 1995. 4.95 (*0-446-91038-4*) Warner Bks.
— You Must Remember This 1963: Milestones, Memories, Trivia & Facts, News Events, Prominent Personalities & Sports Highlights of the Year. 24p. 1995. 4.95 (*0-446-91039-2*) Warner Bks.
— You Must Remember This 1964: Milestones, Memories, Trivia & Facts, News Events, Prominent Personalities & Sports Highlights of the Year. 24p. 1995. 4.95 (*0-446-91041-4*) Warner Bks.
— You Must Remember This 1965: Milestones, Memories, Trivia & Facts, News Events, Prominent Personalities & Sports Highlights of the Year. 24p. 1995. 4.95 (*0-446-91042-2*) Warner Bks.
— You Must Remember This 1966: Milestones, Memories, Trivia & Facts, News Events, Prominent Personalities & Sports Highlights of the Year. 24p. 1995. 4.95 (*0-446-91043-0*) Warner Bks.
— You Must Remember This 1967: Milestones, Memories, Trivia & Facts, News Events, Prominent Personalities & Sports Highlights of the Year. 24p. 1995. 4.95 (*0-446-91044-9*) Warner Bks.
— You Must Remember This 1968: Milestones, Memories, Trivia & Facts, News Events, Prominent Personalities & Sports Highlights of the Year. 24p. 1995. write for info. (*0-446-51931-6*) Warner Bks.
— You Must Remember This 1968: Milestones, Memories, Trivia & Facts, News Events, Prominent Personalities & Sports Highlights of the Year. 24p. 1995. 4.95 (*0-446-91045-7*) Warner Bks.
— You Must Remember This 1969: Milestones, Memories, Trivia & Facts, News Events, Prominent Personalities & Sports Highlights of the Year. 24p. 1995. 4.95 (*0-446-91046-5*) Warner Bks.
— You Must Remember This 1970: Milestones, Memories, Trivia & Facts, News Events, Prominent Personalities & Sports Highlights of the Year. 24p. 1995. 4.95 (*0-446-91047-3*) Warner Bks.
— You Must Remember This 1975: Milestones, Memories, Trivia & Facts, News Events, Prominent Personalities & Sports Highlights of the Year. 24p. 1995. write for info. (*0-446-51937-5*) Warner Bks.
— You Must Remember This 1975: Milestones, Memories, Trivia & Facts, News Events, Prominent Personalities & Sports Highlights of the Year. 24p. 1995. 4.95 (*0-446-91052-X*) Warner Bks.
Prady, Bill. Muppet Babies & the Time Machine. (Muppet Magic Ser.). (Illus.). 26p. (J). (ps up). 1987. 12.95 (*1-55578-605-7*) Worlds Wonder.
Praechter, Karl. Kleine Schriften. (Collectanea Ser.: Vol. VII). xxiii, 474p. 1973. write for info. (*3-487-04672-5*, Pub. by Georg Olms GW) Lubrecht & Cramer.
Praeder, Susan M. The Word in Women's Worlds: Four Parables. (Zacchaeus Studies). 120p. (Orig.). 1988. pap. 7.95 (*0-8146-5667-6*) Liturgical Pr.
Praeger, Betzabe M. & Praeger, Frank C. Places & Occasions: Poems. LC 91-60318. 64p. (Orig.). 1991. pap. 8.00 (*0-9628816-0-0*) Keweenaw Pr.
Praeger, D. K., jt. auth. see Littlebury, F. E.
Praeger, Frank C., jt. auth. see Praeger, Betzabe M.
Praeger, Michele & Robbe-Grillet, Alain. Les Romans de Robert Pinget: Une Ecriture des Possibles. LC 86-80313. (French Forum Monographs: No. 65). 165p. 1986. pap. 12.95 (*0-917058-66-6*) French Forum.
Praeger, R. L. An Account of the Genus Sedum As Found in Cultivation. (Illus.). 1967. pap. 27.60 (*3-7682-0446-4*) Lubrecht & Cramer.
Praeger, Rosamond. The Young Stamp-Collectors. (Illus.). 56p. 1985. 15.95 (*0-9508551-1-1*, Pub. by Portmoon Pr UK) R Clark.
Prael, Charles E., jt. auth. see Tymes, Elna.
Praem, O., jt. auth. see McBride, Alfred.
Praem, O., jt. auth. see Van Straaten, Werenfried.
Praeter, Jeffrey L., tr. see Eggebrecht, Hans H.
Praetorius, Henry. An Immigrant Settler. LC 88-70298. (Illus.). 136p. 1988. pap. 7.50 (*0-8323-0460-3*) Binford Mort.
Praetorius, Michael. Syntagma Musicum: Tomus Secundus se Organographie. Eitner, Robert, ed. (Publikation aelterer praktischer und theoretischer Musikwerke Ser.: Vol. 13). (Illus.). (GER.). 1966. reprint ed. lib. bdg. 75. 00 (*0-8450-1713-6*) Broude.
— The Syntagma Musicum of Michael Praetorius, Vol. 2: De Organographica. Blumenfeld, Harold, tr. LC 79-20847. (Music Reprint Ser.). (Illus.). 1980. reprint ed. 29.50 (*0-306-70563-X*) Da Capo.
— Syntagma Musicum Two: (Translated from the Edition of 1619) - De Organographia, Pts. I & II. Crookes, David Z., ed. & tr. by. (Early Music Ser.: No. 7). (Illus.). 174p. 1991. reprint ed. pap. 32.50 (*0-19-816260-X*) OUP.
Praetorius, Pete & Culhane, Alys. Alaska Bicycle Touring Guide: Including Parts of the Yukon Territory & Northwest Territories. 2nd ed. (Illus.). 320p. 1992. pap. 17.50 (*0-938737-27-9*) Denali Press.
Praetz, Helen. Building a School System. 178p. 1980. 32.50 (*0-522-84213-5*) Intl Spec Bk.
Praff, Giora. Glimmers of Light in a Betraying Land. Schreiber, Mordecai, tr. LC 92-82824. 122p. 1992. 18.95 (*0-88400-159-8*) Shengold.
Prag. Archaeological Reports for 1977-1978, Vol. 24. 1991. pap. write for info. (*0-318-68517-5*, Pub. by Aris & Phillips UK) David Brown.
— Archaeological Reports for 1978-1979, Vol. 25. 1991. pap. write for info. (*0-318-68518-3*, Pub. by Aris & Phillips UK) David Brown.
— Archaeological Reports for 1979-1980, Vol. 26. 1991. pap. write for info. (*0-318-68516-7*, Pub. by Aris & Phillips UK) David Brown.
— Archaeological Reports for 1980-1981, Vol. 27. 1991. pap. write for info. (*0-318-68519-1*, Pub. by Aris & Phillips UK) David Brown.
Prag, K., ed. see Eshel, Itzak.
Prag, Kay. Jerusalem. (Blue Guides Ser.). (Illus.). 1989. pap. 19.95 (*0-393-30480-9*) Norton.
Prager, Annabelle. The Baseball Birthday Party. LC 93-25258. (Illus.). (J). 1995. 3.99 (*0-679-84171-7*) Random Bks Yng Read.
— The Baseball Birthday Party. LC 93-25258. (Illus.). (J). 1995. lib. bdg. 9.99 (*0-679-94171-1*) Random Bks Yng Read.
— The Spooky Halloween Party. LC 81-1945. (I Am Reading Bks.). (Illus.). 48p. (J). (gr. 1-4). 1981. 6.95 (*0-394-84370-3*); lib. bdg. 7.99 (*0-394-94370-8*) Pantheon.
— The Spooky Halloween Party. (Step into Reading Book & Cassette Library). (Illus.). 48p. (J). (gr. k-4). 1992. audio 6.99 (*0-679-83056-1*) Random Bks Yng Read.
— The Spooky Halloween Party: A Step 2 Book. LC 88-37571. (Step into Reading Bks.). (Illus.). 48p. (J). (gr. 1-3). 1989. lib. bdg. 7.99 (*0-394-94961-7*); pap. 3.50 (*0-394-84961-2*) Random Bks Yng Read.
— The Surprise Party. LC 87-20649. (Step into Reading Bks.). (Illus.). 48p. (J). (gr. 1-3). 1988. 3.50 (*0-394-89596-7*); lib. bdg. 7.99 (*0-394-99596-1*) Random Bks Yng Read.
Prager, Audrey & Gettleman, Barry. Job Creation in the Community: An Evaluation of Locally Initiated Employment Projects in Massachusetts. 186p. 1977. 32. 95 (*0-89011-506-0*, EMT 114) Transaction Pubs.
***Prager, Carolyn, ed.** Accreditation of the Two-Year College. LC 85-644753. (New Directions for Community Colleges Ser.: No. 83). 110p. (Orig.). 1993. pap. 16.95 (*1-55542-718-9*) Jossey-Bass.
***Prager, Dennis.** Think a Second Time. 1995. 23.00 (*0-06-039157-X*, HarpT) HarpC.
Prager, Dennis & Telushkin, Joseph. The Nine Questions People Ask about Judaism. 1986. pap. 8.95 (*0-671-62261-7*, Touchstone Bks) S&S Trade.
— Why the Jews? 1985. pap. 11.00 (*0-671-55624-X*, Touchstone Bks) S&S Trade.
Prager, Emily. Clea & Zeus Divorce. LC 87-10456. (Vintage Contemporaries Ser.). 256p. 1987. pap. 10.00 (*0-394-75591-X*, Vin) Random.
— Eve's Tattoo. LC 91-52663. 194p. 1991. 19.00 (*0-394-57490-7*) Random.
— Eve's Tattoo. 1992. 10.00 (*0-679-74053-8*, Vin) Random.
— A Visit from the Footbinder. LC 87-40110. (Contemporaries Ser.). 208p. 1987. pap. 10.00 (*0-394-75592-8*, Vin) Random.
Prager, Herman. Global Marine Environment: Does the Water Planet Have a Future? LC 92-44141. (C). 1993. 42.50 (*0-8191-9016-0*); pap. 18.50 (*0-8191-9017-9*) U Pr of Amer.
***Prager, Jan.** Environmental Contaminant Reference Handbook Vol. 1. (Illus.). 1100p. 1995. text ed. 129.95 (*0-442-01918-1*) Van Nos Reinhold.
Prager, Janice & LePoff, Arlene. Why Be Different: A Look into Judasim. 118p. (J). (gr. 6-8). 1986. pap. text ed. 8.50 (*0-87441-427-X*) Behrman.
Prager, Jeffrey & Rustin, Michael, eds. Psychoanalytic Sociology, 2 vols. in 1. (Schools of Thought in Sociology Ser.: Vol. 10). (Illus.). 816p. 1993. 224.95 (*1-85278-336-2*, Pub. by E Elgar Pub UK) Ashgate Pub Co.
Prager, Jeffrey, et al, eds. School Desegregation Research: New Directions in Situational Analysis. (Critical Issues in Social Justice Ser.). 284p. 1986. 45.00 (*0-306-42151-8*, Plenum Pr) Plenum.
Prager, Jonas. Intermediate Microeconomics. 608p. (C). 1992. text ed. 62.95 (*0-256-05780-X*) Irwin.
Prager, Kate. Infant Mortality by Birthweight & Other Characteristics: United States, 1985 Birth Control. LC 94-10819. (Vital & Health Statistics. Series 20, Data from the National Vital Statistics System: No. 24). 1994. write for info. (*0-8406-0489-0*) Natl Ctr Health Stats.
Prager, Leonard, ed. see Jewish Language Review Staff.
Prager, Martin, ed. Factors Influencing the Time-Dependent Properties of Carbon Steels for Elevated Temperature Pressure Vessels, Vol. 19. 102p. 1983. pap. text ed. 24.00 (*0-317-02616-X*, H00265) ASME.
Prager, Moshe. Rabbi Yisroel Baal Shem Tov. (Illus.). (HEB.). 2.00 (*0-914131-51-6*, D500) Torah Umesorah.
— Rabbi Yisroel Baal Shem Tov. (Illus.). 1987. 2.00 (*0-914131-50-8*, D510) Torah Umesorah.
— Sparks of Glory: Inspiring Episodes of Jewish Spiritual Resistance. (ArtScroll History Ser.). (Illus.). 208p. 1985. 16.95 (*0-89906-456-6*) Mesorah Pubns.
Prager, Susan W., jt. intro. see Carroll, William A.
Prager, W., ed. see International Symposium on Stress Waves in Anelastic Solids Staff.
Prager, W., jt. ed. see Save, M.
Pragnell. Machine-God Laughs. 3.50 (*0-686-05843-7*); pap. 1.50 (*0-686-05844-5*) Fantasy Pub Co.
Prago, Albert, jt. ed. see Bessie, Alvah.
Pragoff, Fiona. Alphabet. LC 87-635. (Illus.). (J). (ps-00). 1987. mass mkt. 6.95 (*0-385-24171-2*) Doubleday.
— Autumn. (Illus.). 20p. (J). (ps). 1993. spiral bd. 5.95 (*0-689-71705-9*, Aladdin Paperbacks) S&S Childrens.
— Fiona Pragoff's Board Books: Baby Days. (Illus.). (J). 1995. 3.95 (*0-671-89911-2*, Litl Simon S&S) S&S Childrens.
— Fiona Pragoff's Board Books: Baby Plays. (Illus.). (J). 1995. 3.95 (*0-671-89913-9*, Litl Simon S&S) S&S Childrens.
— Fiona Pragoff's Board Books: Baby Says. (Illus.). (J). 1995. 3.95 (*0-671-89914-7*, Litl Simon S&S) S&S Childrens.
— Fiona Pragoff's Board Books: Baby Ways. (Illus.). (J). 1995. 3.95 (*0-671-89912-0*, Litl Simon S&S) S&S Childrens.
— It's Fun to Be One. (Illus.). 24p. (J). (ps). 1994. pap. 6.95 (*0-689-71813-6*, Aladdin Paperbacks) S&S Childrens.
— It's Great to Be Two. (Illus.). 24p. (J). (ps). 1994. bds. 6.95 (*0-689-71814-4*, Mac Bks Young Read) S&S Childrens.
— Let's Find Teddy. LC 92-2765. (Illus.). 32p. (J). (ps). 1992. 10.00 (*0-679-83501-6*) Random Bks Yng Read.
— Spring. (Illus.). 20p. (J). (ps). 1993. spiral bd. 5.95 (*0-689-71707-5*, Aladdin Paperbacks) S&S Childrens.
— Summer. (Illus.). 20p. (J). (ps). 1993. spiral bd. 5.95 (*0-689-71706-7*, Aladdin Paperbacks) S&S Childrens.
— Winter. (Illus.). 20p. (J). (ps). 1993. spiral bd. 5.95 (*0-689-71704-0*, Aladdin Paperbacks) S&S Childrens.
Prague, Cary. DBASE for Windows Handbook. 1994. pap. 30.00 (*0-679-79131-0*) Random.
Prague, Cary N. The DBase IV Programming. 1990. pap. 32. 95 (*0-8306-3569-6*) TAB Bks.
— The DBase IV Programming. 1991. 5.25 hd 24.95 (*0-8306-6687-7*); 3.5 hd 24.95 (*0-8306-6688-5*) TAB Bks.
— DBase IV 2.0 Programming. 1993. pap. text ed. 34.95 (*0-8306-4578-0*, Windcrest) TAB Bks.
— PC World Microsoft Access 2 Bible. 2nd ed. 1994. pap. 39.95 (*1-56884-086-1*) IDG Bks.
— XBASE Programming. (Illus.). 944p. 1993. pap. 36.95 (*0-8306-4051-7*, 4188, Windcrest) TAB Bks.
Prague, Cary N. & Hammitt, James E. Advanced dBASE IV Programming. 1989. pap. 22.95 (*0-8306-9376-9*, 3076P) TAB Bks.
— Advanced Programming with dBASE IV. 1991. 24.95 (*0-8306-6647-8*) TAB Bks.
— The DBase III Programming Handbook. (Illus.). 240p. 1986. pap. 16.95 (*0-8306-2676-X*, 2676P) TAB Bks.
— The dBASE III Programming Handbook. 1986. pap. text ed. 16.95 (*0-07-155669-9*) McGraw.
— DBase IV Programming. 1989. 29.95 (*0-8306-9466-8*, 3066); pap. 26.95 (*0-8306-9366-1*, 3066P) TAB Bks.
— The dBASE IV Programming: Tips & Techniques. 350p. 1989. pap. 24.95 (*0-13-199050-0*) P-H.
— The DBase IV 1.1 Program. 2nd ed. 1991. 29.95 (*0-8306-6757-1*); 29.95 (*0-8306-8758-0*) TAB Bks.
— DBASE IV 1.5 Programming. 1000p. 1992. pap. 36.95 (*0-8306-4050-9*, 4187, Windcrest) TAB Bks.
— DBASE IV 1.5 Programming. 3rd ed. 1992. pap. 36.95 (*0-07-050693-0*) McGraw.
— Programming with dBASE II. (Illus.). 288p. (Orig.). 1984. 26.95 (*0-8306-0776-5*, 1776); pap. 16.60 (*0-8306-1776-0*, 1776P) TAB Bks.
— Programming with dBASE III Plus. (Illus.). 384p. 1986. pap. 19.95 (*0-8306-2726-X*) TAB Bks.
— Programming with dBASE III Plus. 1991. 24.95 (*0-8306-6632-X*) TAB Bks.
— Programming with R: Base 5000. (Illus.). 304p. 1986. 28. 95 (*0-8306-0366-2*, 2666) TAB Bks.
Prague, Cary N. & Kasevich, Lawrence S. Framework Three. (Illus.). 500p. 1988. pap. 24.95 (*0-8306-9386-6*, 3086) TAB Bks.
Prague, Cary N., jt. auth. see Byers, Robert A.
Prague, Cary N., jt. auth. see Hammitt, James E.
Prague, Cary N., jt. auth. see Hartman, Patricia A.
Prague, Cary N., et al. Programming with R: BASE for DOS. 1991. 24.95 (*0-8306-6676-1*); 24.95 (*0-8306-9575-3*) TAB Bks.
Prague, Gary N. DBASE IV 2.0 Programming. 1993. pap. text ed. 36.95 (*0-07-050699-X*) McGraw.
Prague, Ken, jt. auth. see Dobbins, Bill.
Prague Symposium on Asymptatic Statistics Staff. Proceedings: Second Prague Symposium on Asymptoic Statistics, 2nd. Mandl, P. & Huskova, M., eds. 340p. 1979. 92.50 (*0-444-85375-8*, North Holland) Elsevier.
Prah, Kwesi K. Capitein: A Critical Study of an 18th Century African. LC 91-78314. 175p. 1992. 29.95 (*0-86543-331-3*); pap. 8.95 (*0-86543-332-1*) Africa World.
Prahalad, C. K. & Doz, Yves L. The Multinational Mission: Balancing Local Demands & Global Vision. 256p. 1987. text ed. 35.00 (*0-02-925050-1*) Free Pr.
Prahalad, C. K., jt. auth. see Hamel, Gary.
Prahl, Earl J. & Branster, Mark. Archaeological Investigations on Mackinac Island 1983: The Watermain & Sewer Project. LC 85-622249. (Archaeological Completion Report Ser.: No. 8). (Illus.). 125p. (Orig.). 1984. pap. 10.00 (*0-911872-50-7*) Mackinac Island.
Prahlow, Lois, jt. auth. see Rathert, Donna.
Prahrit & Apabhramasa. International Encyclopedia of Indian Literature: Sanskrit, Pali, Vol. 1, Pt. 1. 1987. 98. 00 (*0-8364-2316-X*, Pub. by Mittal II) S Asia.
Prain, D. Flora of Sundaribans. 370p. (C). 1979. reprint ed. 150.00 (*0-685-21859-7*, Pub. by Intl Bk Distr II) St Mut.
— Flora of Sunderbuns. 370p. (C). 1979. text ed. 150.00 (*0-89771-629-9*, Pub. by Intl Bk Distr II) St Mut.
— Some Additional Leguminosae Proceedings of the Third World Orchid Conference, London. (C). 1960. 250.00 (*0-685-22330-2*, Scientific) St Mut.
— The Species of Dalbergia of South-Eastern Asia: Annals of the Royal Botanic Garden, Calcutta, Vol. 10, Pt. 1. 114p. (C). 1983. 170.00 (*0-685-22301-9*, Scientific) St Mut.
Prain, D., ed. Index Kewensis: Supplement (from 1911 to 1915), Vol. 5. 277p. 1978. reprint ed. text ed. 100.00 (*0-685-26520-X*) Lubrecht & Cramer.
Prain, D., jt. auth. see Royal Botanic Garden, Calcutta Staff.
***Prain, E. M.** Live Hands: A Key to Better Golf. 1995. text ed. 14.95 (*1-886346-50-X*) Warde Pubs.
— Live Hands: A Key to Better Golf. (Illus.). 128p. 1994. 16.95 (*1-885198-02-7*) Sports Log Pubs.
Prainatis. The Talmud Unmasked. 1979. lib. bdg. 300.00 (*0-8490-3010-2*) Gordon Pr.
***Prairie, Michel, ed.** Nouvelle Internationale, No. 5. 366p. (FRE.). 1995. pap. 15.00 (*0-87348-803-2*) Pathfinder NY.
Prairie-Plains Resource Institute Staff & Whitney, William S. Microcosm of the Platte: A Guide to Bader Memorial Park Natural Area. Whitney, Jan & Twedt, Curt, eds. (Illus.). 140p. (Orig.). (YA). (gr. 10-12). 1988. pap. text ed. 10.00 (*0-945614-00-4*) Prairie Plains Res Inst.
Prairie Rambler Staff. Whimsey 'N' Whizdum. LC 83-60209. 116p. (Orig.). 1983. pap. write for info. (*0-912279-00-1*) Prairie Ramb.
Prais, S. J. The Evolution of Giant Firms in Britain: A Study in the Growth of Concentration in Manufacturing Industry in Britain, 1909-1970. LC 76-18410. (National Institute of Economic & Social Research Occasional Papers: No. 30). (Illus.). 321p. 1981. pap. 21.95 (*0-521-28273-X*) Cambridge U Pr.
— Productivity, Education & Training: Facts & Policies in International Perspective. (National Institute of Economic & Social Research Occasional Papers). (Illus.). 120p. (C). 1995. write for info. (*0-521-48305-0*) Cambridge U Pr.
Praizler, Nancy C., jt. auth. see Guinta, Lawrence R.
Prajna, Yogadhi. The Story of Ho' Autobiography of the Spiritual Journey of Yogadhi Prajna. Champion, Judith & Shankar, Sri Sri R., eds. 285p. (Orig.). 1994. 21.00 (*1-885289-00-6*); pap. 14.95 (*1-885289-01-4*) Art of Living.
Prajnakarmiti. Santideva's Bodhicharyavatara, 2 vols., Set. (C). 1990. 72.00 (*81-85179-13-1*, Pub. by Aditya Prakashan II) S Asia.
Prajnanananda, Swami. Christ the Savior & Christ Myth. rev. ed. 1961. 7.95 (*0-87481-652-1*, Pub. by Advaita Ashrama II) Vedanta Pr.
— A History of Indian Music. 1963. pap. 7.95 (*0-87481-626-2*) Vedanta Pr.
Prajnananda, pref. The Nectar of Self-Awareness. 104p. 1979. pap. text ed. 7.95 (*0-914602-49-7*) SYDA Found.
Prajnananda, Swami. The Philosophical Ideas of Swami Abhenananda: A Critical Study (A Guide to the Complete Works of Swami Abhedananda) (Illus.). 7.95 (*0-87481-623-8*) Vedanta Pr.
Prajzner, Nancy. Natural Wonders of Massachusetts. LC 94-18860. (Natural Wonders Ser.). 140p. 1994. pap. 9.95 (*1-56626-108-2*) Country Rds.

P Q

An Asterisk (*) at the beginning of an entry indicates that the title is appearing in BIP for the first time.

Prakasa Rao, B. L. Identifiability in Stochastic Models: Characterization of Probability Distributions. (Probability & Mathematical Statistics Ser.). 272p. 1992. text ed. 59.95 (*0-12-564015-3*) Acad Pr.

Prakasan, K. P. Space - Gagarin & After. 1987. text ed. 25. 00 (*81-207-0584-X*, Pub. by Sterling Pubs II) Apt Bks.

Prakash. Pulmonary Manifestations of Systemic Diseases. 1990. 34.95 (*0-8151-6830-6*, Yr Bk Med Pubs) Mosby Yr Bk.

Prakash, jt. auth. see Swaminathan.

Prakash, et al. Tenth National ACCP Pulmonary Board Review Course Syllabus, 2 vols. American College of Chest Physicians Staff, ed. (Illus.). 350p. 1994. pap. text ed. 65.00 (*0-615-00229-3*) Am Chest Phys.

Prakash, Anand. Botanical Pesticides in Agriculture. 1995. write for info. (*0-87371-825-9*) Lewis Pubs.

Prakash, Arun J., et al. Financial, Commercial, & Mortgage Mathematics & Their Applications. LC 86-30579. 255p. 1987. text ed. 49.95 (*0-275-92119-0*, C2119, Praeger Pubs) Greenwood.

***Prakash, B. A.** Kerala's Economy: Performance, Problems, Prospects. 420p. 1994. 38.95 (*0-8039-9161-4*) Sage.

Prakash, Gyan. Bonded Histories: Genealogies of Labor Servitude in Colonial India. (Cambridge South Asian Studies: No. 44). (Illus.). 272p. (C). 1990. 59.95 (*0-521-36278-4*) Cambridge U Pr.

— The World of the Rural Labourer in Colonial India. (Themes in Indian History Ser.). 276p. 1992. 19.95 (*0-19-562832-2*) OUP.

***Prakash, Gyan, ed.** After Colonialism: Imperial Histories & Postcolonial Displacements. LC 94-21310. 1994. 16.95 (*0-691-03742-6*) Princeton U Pr.

— The World of the Rural Labourer in Colonial India. (Oxford in India Readings: Themes in Indian History, Oxford India Paperbacks Ser.). 320p. 1994. reprint ed. pap. 7.95 (*0-19-563440-3*) OUP.

Prakash, Gyan, jt. ed. see Haynes, Douglas.

Prakash, I. & Ghosh, P. K. Rodents in Indian Agriculture, 2 vols., 1. (C). 1992. text ed. 325.00 (*0-685-61679-7*, Pub. by Scientific Pubs II); text ed. 450.00 (*0-685-63524-4*, Pub. by Scientific Pubs II) St Mut.

— Rodents in Indian Agriculture, 2 vols., 2. (C). 1992. text ed. 100.00 (*0-685-61680-0*, Pub. by Scientific Pubs II); text ed. 150.00 (*0-685-63525-2*, Pub. by Scientific Pubs II) St Mut.

— Rodents in Indian Agriculture, 2 vols., Set. (C). 1992. text ed. 415.00 (*0-685-61678-9*, Pub. by Scientific Pubs II) St Mut.

Prakash, Ishwar, ed. Desert Ecology. (C). 1988. text ed. 125.00 (*0-685-22070-2*, Scientific) St Mut.

— Rodent Pest Management, 2 vols. 1988. 298.00 (*0-8493-6726-3*, SB994) CRC Pr.

Prakash, Iswar, jt. ed. see Ghosh, P. K.

Prakash, J. & Pierik, T. Plant Biotechnology: Commercial Prospects & Problems. 300p. 1993. text ed. 69.00 (*1-881570-31-2*) Intl Sci Pub.

Prakash, J., jt. ed. see Pierik, R. L.

Prakash, Jagdish, ed. Privatization of Public Enterprises in India. 1992. 30.00 (*81-7040-401-0*, Pub. by Himalaya II) Apt Bks.

Prakash, K. Paisleys & Other Textile Designs from India. LC 93-39105. 1994. pap. write for info. (*0-486-27959-6*) Dover.

Prakash, N., et al, eds. Information System Development Process: Proceedings of the IFIP WG8.1 Working Conference on Information Development Process. LC 93-11376. (IFIP Transactions Ser.: Vol. 30). 1993. write for info. (*0-444-81594-5*, North Holland) Elsevier.

Prakash, Nirupama. Scheduled Castes: Socio-Economic Changes. (C). 1988. 44.00 (*81-85076-58-8*, Pub. by Chugh Pubns II) S Asia.

Prakash, O. Applied Physiology in Clinical Respiratory Care. 1982. lib. bdg. 164.50 (*90-247-2662-X*) Kluwer Ac.

Prakash, O., ed. Critical Care of the Child. (Developments in Critical Care, Medicine, & Anesthesiology Ser.). 1984. lib. bdg. 85.50 (*0-89838-661-6*) Kluwer Ac.

Prakash, Om. The Dutch East India Company & the Economy of Bengal, 1630-1720. LC 84-26484. 320p. 1985. text ed. 49.50x (*0-691-05447-9*) Princeton U Pr.

— The Dutch East India Company & the Economy of Bengal, 1630-1720. LC 84-26484. (Illus.). Date not set. reprint ed. pap. 86.70 (*0-7837-9426-6*, 2060167) Bks Demand.

— Precious Metals & Commerce. (Collected Studies: No. CS 443). 312p. 1994. 89.95 (*0-86078-434-7*, Pub. by Variorum UK) Ashgate Pub Co.

Prakash, Om & Srivastava, K. C. Mango Diseases & Their Management: A World Review. 180p. 1987. 59.00 (*1-55528-101-X*, Pub. by Today & Tomorrows P & P II) Scholarly Pubns.

Prakash, Omar, jt. ed. see Rahn, Herman.

Prakash, Ram. Advances in Forestry Research in India, Vols. 1-8. 265p. (C). 1988. text ed. 295.00 (*0-685-74393-4*, Pub. by Intl Bk Distr II) St Mut.

— Forest Surveying. 371p. (C). 1982. 125.00 (*81-7089-001-2*, Pub. by Intl Bk Distr II) St Mut.

— Some Favourite Trees for Fuel & Fodder. 187p. (C). 1986. 150.00 (*81-7089-039-X*, Pub. by Intl Bk Distr II) St Mut.

Prakash, S. S. Bonded Labour & Social Justice. 1990. 17.00 (*81-7100-197-1*, Pub. by Deep) S Asia.

— Bonded Labour & Social Justice. (C). 1990. 60.00 (*0-89771-316-8*) St Mut.

***Prakash, Shamsher, et al.** Displacement Based Aseismic Design Charts for Rigid Walls. (Illus.). vi, 120p. (C). 1995. write for info. (*0-9641737-2-7*) S Prakash Fnd.

***Prakash, Shamsher.** Fundamentals of Soil Mechanics. (Illus.). xx, 452p. 1995. write for info. (*0-9641737-1-9*) S Prakash Fnd.

— Introduction to Prevention & Yoga. (Illus.). (Orig.). (YA). Date not set. pap. text ed. write for info. (*0-9641737-0-0*) S Prakash Fnd.

Prakash, Shamsher, ed. Piles under Dynamic Loads: Proceedings of Sessions Sponsored by the Geotechnical Engineering Division of the American Society of Civil Engineers in Conjunction with the ASCE National Convention, New York, New York, September 13-17, 1992. LC 92-27783. (Geotechnical Special Publication Ser.: No. 34). 264p. 1992. 26.00 (*0-87262-905-8*) Am Soc Civil Eng.

Prakash, Shamsher & Pathak, K. N. Advances in Statistical Physics of Solids & Liquids. 422p. 1991. text ed. 63.95 (*0-470-21710-3*) Halsted Pr.

Prakash, Shamsher & Puri, Vijay. Foundations for Machines. LC 87-21678. 656p. 1988. text ed. 115.00 (*0-471-84686-4*, Wiley-Interscience) Wiley.

Prakash, Shamsher & Sharma, Hart D. Pile Foundations in Engineering Practice. 734p. 1990. text ed. 89.95 (*0-471-61653-2*) Wiley.

Prakash, Shamsher, ed. see American Society of Civil Engineers Geotechnical Engineering Division Staff.

Prakash, Shyam, jt. ed. see Chopra, V. L.

Prakash, Sumangal. Story of Swarajya: Part II. (Nehru Library for Children). (Illus.). (J). (gr. 1-10). 1979. pap. 2.50 (*0-89744-186-9*) Auromere.

Prakash, Swami S. & Vidyalankar, Pandit S. Rigveda Samhita, 10 vols. 1986. 40.00 (*0-685-73822-1*, Pub. by S Chand II) St Mut.

Prakash, Udaya B., ed. Bronchoscopy: A Text Atlas. LC 93-7652. 560p. 1994. 190.00 (*0-7817-0095-7*); sl. write for info. (*0-7817-0221-6*) Raven.

— Mayo Internal Medicine Board Review 1994-1995. 1000p. 1994. text ed. 89.95 (*0-9627865-1-9*) Mayo Fndtn Med Ed & Res.

— Mayo Internal Medicine Board Review 1996-97. 1000p. 1996. text ed. 89.95 (*0-9627865-2-7*) Mayo Fndtn Med Ed & Res.

Prakash, V. Leafy Spices. 144p. 1990. 121.00 (*0-8493-6723-9*, SB351) CRC Pr.

Prakash, Vidya. Khajuraho: A Study of the Cultural Conditions of Chandella Society. (Illus.). 319p. 1983. reprint ed. text ed. 60.00 (*0-86590-192-9*, Pub. by Taraporevala II) Apt Bks.

Prakashan, V., ed. Semantic Theories & Language Teaching. (C). 1986. 17.50 (*81-7023-080-2*, Pub. by Allied II) S Asia.

Prakesh, Ved. Financing Urban Development in Developing Countries. (Working Papers Ser.: No. 82-6). 56p. 1982. pap. 5.00 (*0-686-43294-0*, CRD141) UNIPUB.

Prakhar, Gulab M. Indo Pakistan Relations. 476p. (C). 1987. 66.00 (*81-7024-084-0*, Pub. by Ashish II) S Asia.

Prakke, Hendricus J. Drenthe in Michigan. LC 84-115348. 96p. reprint ed. pap. 27.40 (*0-317-30159-4*, 2025341) Bks Demand.

Prakken, Lawrence, et al, eds. Technician Education Directory, 1986. 12th ed. LC 63-22652. 1986. 20.00 (*0-911168-61-3*) Prakken.

Praktikos. Evagrius Ponticus. Bamberger, John E., tr. LC 76-152483. (Cistercian Studies: No. 4). xciv, 88p. 1970. pap. 4.00 (*0-87907-804-9*) Cistercian Pubns.

Prall, D. Aesthetic Judgment. 1972. 59.95 (*0-87968-583-2*) Gordon Pr.

Prall, Richard D. The Prall Family. LC 89-64217. (Illus.). 546p. 1990. 50.00 (*0-9625633-0-7*) R D Prall.

Prall, S. E. Puritan Revolution: A Documentary History. 12. 50 (*0-8446-2756-9*) Peter Smith.

Prall, Stuart E. The Bloodless Revolution: England, Sixteen Eighty-Eight. LC 79-175415. 368p. 1985. reprint ed. pap. 13.95 (*0-299-10294-7*) U of Wis Pr.

— Church & State in Tudor & Stuart England. Eubank, Keith, ed. LC 92-35135. (European History Ser.). 190p. (C). 1993. pap. text ed. write for info. (*0-88295-904-2*) Harlan Davidson.

— The Puritan Revolution & the English Civil War. (Orig.). 1997. pap. write for info. (*0-89464-889-6*) Krieger.

Prall, Stuart E. & Willson, David H. A History of England, Vol. I. 4th ed. (Illus.). 520p. (C). 1991. pap. text ed. 32. 00 (*0-03-033424-1*) HB Coll Pubs.

— A History of England, Vol. II. 4th ed. (Illus.). 416p. (C). 1991. pap. text ed. 32.00 (*0-03-033427-6*) HB Coll Pubs.

Pramamick, P., jt. auth. see Bhartia, P.

***Pramanich, S. K.** Sociology of G. S. Ghurye. (C). 1995. 34. 00x (*81-7033-261-3*, Pub. by Rawat II) S Asia.

Pramanik, M. A. Impacts of Disasters on Environment & Development: International Cooperation. 53p. (Orig.). (C). 1993. pap. text ed. 40.00 (*0-7881-0097-1*) Diane Pub.

***Pramanik, S. K.** Fishermen Community of Coastal Villages in West Bengal. (C). 1993. 17.50x (*81-7033-186-2*, Pub. by Rawat II) S Asia.

Pramik-Holdaway, Mary J., ed. see Nara, Andrew R., et al.

Pramik, Janice, ed. see Matherly, Sandra & Hodges, Shannon.

Pramik, Janice, ed. see Zimmerman, David.

Pramling, I. Learning to Learn. (Recent Research in Psychology Ser.). 144p. 1989. pap. 35.00 (*0-387-97122-X*) Spr-Verlag.

Pran, Dith, jt. auth. see Hall, Kari R.

Pranavananda, Yogi. Pure Yoga: A Translation from the Sanskrit into English of the Tantric Work, the Gherandasamhita, with a Guiding Commentary. (C). 1992. text ed. 20.00 (*81-208-0922-X*, Pub. by Motilal Banarsidass II) S Asia.

Prance, Anne E. Bark: The Formation, Characteristics, & Uses of Bark Around the World. LC 92-19569. (Illus.). 176p. 1993. 49.95 (*0-88192-262-5*) Timber.

Prance, Claude A. The Characters in the Novels of Thomas Love Peacock (1785-1866) LC 92-5982. 312p. 1992. 99. 95 (*0-7734-9510-X*) E Mellen.

— E. V. Lucas & His Books. LC 88-15728. 243p. 1988. lib. bdg. 35.00 (*0-933951-19-1*) Locust Hill Pr.

— Essays of a Book Collector: Reminiscences on Some Old Books & Their Authors. LC 89-12734. (Locust Hill Literary Studies: No. 3). 209p. (C). 1989. lib. bdg. 30.00 (*0-933951-30-2*) Locust Hill Pr.

Prance, G. T. Flora of the Guianas: Series A: Phanerogams: Chrysobalanaceae, incl. Wood & Timber, No. 85. Gorts Van Rijn, A. R., ed. (Illus.). 148p. 1986. pap. text ed. 89. 00 (*3-87429-266-5*) Koeltz Sci Bks.

— Tropical Rain Forests & the World Atmosphere. 105p. 1988. 100.00 (*81-7089-057-8*, Pub. by Intl Bk Distr II) St Mut.

Prance, G. T. & Kallunki, J. A., eds. Ethnobotany in the Neotropics. LC 84-16517. (Advances in Economic Botany Ser.: Vol. 1). (Illus.). 156p. 1984. 28.00 (*0-89327-253-1*) NY Botanical.

Prance, G. T., jt. auth. see Cunningham, S.

Prance, G. T., jt. auth. see Mori, S. A.

Prance, G. T., jt. ed. see Whitmore, T. C.

***Prance, G. T., et al.** Ethnobotany & the Search for New Drugs. LC 94-28300. (Ciba Foundation Symposium Ser.: 185). 1994. text ed. 76.00 (*0-471-95024-6*) Wiley.

Prance, Ghillean, jt. auth. see Mori, Scott A.

Prance, Ghillean T. Chrysobalanaceae. LC 70-180014. (Flora Neotropica Monograph Ser.: No. 9). (Illus.). 410p. (Orig.). 1972. pap. 27.95 (*0-89327-292-2*) NY Botanical.

— Chrysobalanaceae. (Flora Neotropica Monographs: No. 9S). (Illus.). 268p. (Orig.). 1989. pap. text ed. 50.00 (*0-89327-338-4*) NY Botanical.

— Dichapetalaceae & Rhabdodendraceae. LC 73-180015. (Flora Neotropica Monograph Ser.: No. 10-11). (Illus.). 106p. (Orig.). 1972. pap. 13.95 (*0-89327-293-0*) NY Botanical.

Prance, Ghillean T., ed. Biological Diversification in the Tropics: Proceedings of the Fifth International Symposium of the Association for Tropical Biology, Held at Macuto Beach, Caracas, Venezuela, February 8-13, 1979. LC 81-367. 730p. reprint ed. pap. 180.00 (*0-7837-0419-4*, 2040742) Bks Demand.

— Reproductive Biology & Evolution of Tropical Woody Angiosperms: A Symposium from the XIVth International Botanical Congress, Berlin, 1987. LC 89-13542. (Memoirs Ser.: No. 55). (Illus.). 195p. 1990. pap. 40.50 (*0-89327-348-1*) NY Botanical.

Prance, Ghillean T. & Balick, Michael J., eds. New Directions in the Study of Plants & Peoples: Research Contributions from the Institute of Economic Botany. LC 89-13336. (Advances in Economic Botany Ser.: Vol. 8). (Illus.). 292p. 1990. pap. text ed. 55.00 (*0-89327-347-3*) NY Botanical.

Prance, Ghillean T. & Da Silva, Marlene F. Caryocaraceae. LC 72-88119. (Flora Neotropica Monograph Ser.: No. 12). (Illus.). 75p. (Orig.). 1973. pap. 9.95 (*0-89327-294-9*) NY Botanical.

Prance, Ghillean T. & Mori, Scott A. Lecythidaceae-Part One the Actinomorphic-Flowered New World Lecythidaceae: Asteranthos, Gustavia, Grias, Allantoma & Cariniana. LC 79-4659. (Flora Neotropica Monograph Ser.: No. 21). (Illus.). 270p. 1979. pap. 28.00 (*0-89327-193-4*) NY Botanical.

Prance, Ghillean T., jt. ed. see DeWitt, Calvin B.

Prance, Ghillean T., ed. see Yungjohann, John C.

Prandi, Julie D. Dare to Be Happy! A Study of Goethe's Ethics. LC 92-37746. 238p. 1993. lib. bdg. 39.50 (*0-8191-8991-X*) U Pr of Amer.

— Spirited Women Heroes of the Goethezeit. LC 83-48708. (American University Studies: Germanic Languages & Literature: Ser. I, Vol. 22). 151p. 1983. pap. text ed. 15. 25 (*0-8204-0033-5*) P Lang Pubs.

Prandtl, Ludwig & Tietjens, O. G. Applied Hydro- & Aeromechanics. Den Hartog, Jacob P., ed. (Illus.). 1934. pap. text ed. 8.95 (*0-486-60375-X*) Dover.

— Fundamentals of Hydro- & Aeromechanics. Rosenhead, L., tr. (Illus.). pap. text ed. 5.95 (*0-486-60374-1*) Dover.

Prandy, Ken, ed. see Stewart, Alexander, et al.

Pranevicius, L. Coating Technology: Ion Beam Deposition. 458p. 1993. text ed. 79.00 (*0-9637993-0-4*) Satas & Assocs.

***Prange.** Respiratory Physiology, Understanding Gas Exchange. 1995. pap. (*0-412-05211-3*) Chapman & Hall.

Prange, Bette & Kelly, Maureen. Wood & Technology. LC 93-28503. (C). 1994. pap. 12.95 (*0-521-43822-5*) Cambridge U Pr.

Prange, Gordon W. At Dawn We Slept: The Untold Story of Pearl Harbor. 892p. 1982. pap. 15.95 (*0-14-006455-9*, Penguin Bks) Viking Penguin.

Prange, Gordon W., ed. December 7, 1941: The Day the Japanese Attacked Pearl Harbor. (Illus.). 512p. 1991. reprint ed. 9.99 (*0-517-06658-0*) Random Hse Value.

Prange, Gordon W., et al. At Dawn We Slept: The Untold Story of Pearl Harbor. enl. rev. ed. LC 91-50176. (Illus.). 944p. 1991. pap. 18.95 (*0-14-015734-4*, Penguin Bks) Viking Penguin.

— God's Samurai: Lead Pilot at Pearl Harbor. (Brassey's WWII Commemorative Ser.). 368p. 1990. 16.95 (*0-08-037440-9*) Brasseys Inc.

— God's Samurai: Lead Pilot at Pearl Harbor. (Brassey's WWII Commemorative Ser.). 368p. 1991. pap. 11.95 (*0-08-037441-7*) Brasseys Inc.

— Miracle at Midway. 512p. 1983. pap. 15.00 (*0-14-006814-7*, Penguin Bks) Viking Penguin.

Prange, Janet L. & Zufelt, David L. Reading Success for Each Child Every Day. (Illus.). 184p. 1980. pap. text ed. 10.95x (*0-89641-037-4*) American Pr.

Prange, Kathy. Muffin Mania. 1984. spiral bd. 7.95 (*0-89709-187-6*) Liberty Pub.

***Prange, Marnie.** Dangerous Neighborhoods. LC 93-71913. 57p. (Orig.). 1994. pap. 10.00 (*1-880834-70-7*) Cleveland St Univ Poetry Ctr.

Prange, R. E. & Girvin, S. M., eds. The Quantum Hall Effect. (Graduate Texts in Contemporary Physics Ser.). (Illus.). 440p. 1986. 32.00 (*0-387-96286-7*) Spr-Verlag.

— The Quantum Hall Effect. 2nd ed. (Graduate Texts in Contemporary Physics Ser.). (Illus.). 488p. 1989. pap. 49.00 (*0-387-97177-7*) Spr-Verlag.

Prange, Shari, jt. auth. see Brown, Michael.

Prange, Victor. Luke. (People's Bible Commentary Ser.). 266p. (Orig.). 1992. pap. 9.99 (*0-570-04586-X*) Concordia.

Prange, Victor H. Why So Many Churches. 1985. pap. 3.99 (*0-8100-0188-8*, 15N0413) Northwest Pub.

***Pranger, M. B.** Bernard of Clairvaux & the Shape of Monastic Thought: Broken Dreams. LC 94-3716. (Studies in Intellectual History Ser.: 56). 1994. 85.75 (*90-04-10055-5*) E J Brill.

Pranger, Robert J. Action, Symbolism & Order: The Existential Dimensions of Politics in Modern Citizenship. LC 68-20548. 1968. 17.50 (*0-8265-1115-5*) Vanderbilt U Pr.

— American Policy for Peace in the Middle East, 1969-1971: Problems of Principle, Maneuver & Time. LC 70-188039. (Foreign Affairs Study Ser.: No. 1). 74p. reprint ed. pap. 25.00 (*0-8357-5389-1*, 2017131) Bks Demand.

— Detente & Defense: A Reader. LC 76-44607. (Foreign Affairs Study Ser.: No. 40). 456p. reprint ed. pap. 130.00 (*0-8357-4464-7*, 2037308) Bks Demand.

Pranger, Robert J. & Labrie, Roger P., eds. Nuclear Strategy & National Security: Points of View. LC 77-15624. (AEI Studies: No. 175). 526p. reprint ed. pap. 150.00 (*0-8357-4517-1*, 2037375) Bks Demand.

Pranger, Robert J., jt. ed. see Chelkowski, Peter J.

Pranger, Robert J., et al. Toward a Realistic Military Assistance Program. LC 74-29150. (Foreign Affairs Study Ser.: No. 15). 56p. reprint ed. pap. 25.00 (*0-317-08189-6*, 2017151) Bks Demand.

Prangwatthanakun, Songsak & Cheesman, Patricia. Lan Na Textiles. (Illus.). (ENG & THA.). 1987. text ed. 25.00 (*0-8248-1216-6*, Pub. by Chiang Mai CPAC TH) UH Pr.

Pranis, Eve & Cohen, Joy. GrowLab: Activities for Growing Minds. 307p. (Orig.). (J). (ps-8). 1990. 24.95 (*0-915873-33-8*) Natl Gardening Assn.

— GrowLab: Activities for Growing Minds. (Illus.). 307p. (Orig.). 1990. pap. text ed. write for info. (*0-915873-32-X*) Natl Gardening Assn.

Pranjpe, Nalina. Social Welfare in India. 1990. text ed. 18. 95 (*81-7045-051-9*, Pub. by Associated Pub Hse II) Advent Bks Div.

Pransky, George S. Divorce Is Not the Answer: A Change of Heart Will Save Your Marriage. 1991. pap. text ed. 10.95 (*0-07-156015-7*) McGraw.

— Divorce Is Not the Answer: You Can Save Your Marriage. 192p. 1990. pap. 9.95 (*0-8306-3583-1*, 3583, TAB-Human Servs Inst) TAB Bks.

— Life Without Stress. 154p. 1992. pap. 8.95 (*0-8306-3867-9*, 4136, TAB-Human Servs Inst) TAB Bks.

— The Relationships Handbook. 1991. 9.95 (*0-8306-3834-2*) TAB Bks.

Pransky, Jack. Prevention: The Critical Need. (Illus.). 384p. (Orig.). 1991. pap. 24.95 (*0-943741-02-5*) Paradigm VT.

***Pransky, Judith M., ed.** A Marmac Guide to Philadelphia. 3rd ed. (Illus.). 288p. Date not set. pap. 10.95 (*1-56554-083-2*) Pelican.

Prantzos, Nikos, jt. ed. see Durouchoux, Philippe.

Prantzos, Nikos, et al, eds. Origin & Evolution of the Elements. (Illus.). 562p. (C). 1993. 69.95 (*0-521-43428-9*) Cambridge U Pr.

Pranzo, Donard. Academic Sportfolio: Excuse Notes Are No Excuse. rev. ed. Gallup, Beth, ed. (Easy Reader Ser.). (Illus.). (J). 1985. 249.00 (*0-924086-28-9*); Group 1, 400 photo masters incl. write for info. (*0-924086-29-7*); Group 2, 400 photo masters incl. write for info. (*0-924086-30-0*) Acad Sportfolio.

Pranzo, Donard, ed. see Matovcik, Gerard.

Pranzo, Donard, ed. see Norberg, Jon.

Prarie, Arleen, jt. auth. see Olenick, Rhoda.

Prasad. Invertebrate Zoology. 14th ed. (C). 1989. pap. 14.00 (*0-85226-929-3*, Pub. by Wiley Eastern II) S Asia.

Prasad, A. Zinc in Human Nutrition. LC 79-15272. 1979. 57.00 (*0-8493-0145-9*, CRC Reprint) Franklin.

Prasad, A. S., ed. Biochemistry of Zinc. (Biochemistry of the Elements Ser.: Vol. 11). (Illus.). 328p. (C). 1994. 79.50 (*0-306-44399-6*, Plenum Pr) Plenum.

Prasad, Ananda S. Trace Elements & Iron in Human Metabolism. LC 78-13446. (Topics in Hematology Ser.). 408p. reprint ed. pap. 116.30 (*0-317-26186-X*, 2052077) Bks Demand.

Prasad, Ananda S., ed. Essential & Toxic Trace Elements in Human Health & Disease. 704p. 1988. text ed. 150.00 (*0-471-61449-1*) Wiley.

— Essential & Toxic Trace Elements in Human Health & Disease. LC 92-48662. (Progress in Clinical & Biological Research Ser.: Vol. 380). 402p. 1992. text ed. 185.00 (*0-471-59109-2*, Wiley-Liss) Wiley.

Prasad, Anirudh. Centre & State Powers under Indian Federalism. (C). 1989. 175.00 (*0-685-36529-8*) St Mut.

— Reservation Policy & Practice in India. (C). 1991. 67.50 (*81-7100-297-8*, Pub. by Deep) S Asia.

Prasad, Anubhuti K. Coal Industry of India. 515p. 1986. 58. 50 (*81-7024-055-7*, Pub. by Ashish II) S Asia.

Prasad, Anuradha. Entrepreneurship Development under Trysem. (C). 1988. 21.00 (*81-7022-167-6*, Pub. by Mittal II) S Asia.

Prasad, Ashoka J., ed. Biological Basis & Therapy of Neuroses. 208p. 1988. 119.00 (*0-8493-4899-4*, RC530, CRC Reprint) Franklin.

Prasad, B., ed. Robotics & Factories of the Future, 3 vols., Set. 1180p. 1989. 207.00 (*0-387-51135-0*) Spr-Verlag.

— Robotics & Factories of the Future, Vol. I. (Illus.). 468p. 1989. 97.00 (*0-387-51132-6*) Spr-Verlag.

P Q

An Asterisk (*) at the beginning of an entry indicates that the title is appearing in BIP for the first time.

— Robotics & Factories of the Future, Vol. 2. (Illus.). 312p. 1989. 66.00 (*0-387-51133-4*) Spr-Verlag.

— Robotics & Factories of the Future, Vol. 3. (Illus.). 400p. 1989. 87.00 (*0-387-51134-2*) Spr-Verlag.

Prasad, B., jt. ed. see Bocks, P.

Prasad, B., jt. ed. see Zaremba, M. B.

Prasad, B. K. Staining Techniqiue in Botany. 107p. (C). 1986. 95.00 (*0-685-21858-9*, Pub. by Intl Bk Distr II) St Mut.

— Staining Technique in Botany. 107p. 1986. 45.00 (*81-7089-081-0*, Pub. by Intl Bk Distr II) St Mut.

Prasad, Bandreddi E., jt. ed. see Gupta, Amar.

Prasad, Bimal. Gandhi, Nehru & JP: Studies in Leadership. 1985. 25.00 (*0-8364-1366-0*, Pub. by Chanakya II) S Asia.

Prasad, Bimal, ed. Regional Cooperation in South Asia. viii, 221p. 1989. text ed. 27.95 (*0-7069-4264-7*, Pub. by Vikas II) S Asia.

— A Revolutionary's Quest. 406p. 1980. 29.95 (*0-318-37198-7*) Asia Bk Corp.

— Swami Vivekananda: Selected Speeches & Writings. (Orig.). (C). 1994. 12.00x (*0-7069-7552-9*, Pub. by Vikas II) S Asia.

Prasad, C. V., jt. auth. see Khan, M. E.

Prasad, D. N. Food for Peace. 172p. 1980. 12.95 (*0-210-40627-5*) Asia Bk Corp.

Prasad, D. Ravindra, ed. Urban Renewal: The Indian Experience. 304p. 1989. text ed. 30.00 (*81-207-0950-0*, Pub. by Sterling Pubs II) Apt Bks.

Prasad, D. Ravindra, et al, eds. Administrative Thinkers. 300p. 1989. text ed. 35.00 (*81-207-0954-3*, Pub. by Sterling Pubs II) Apt Bks.

Prasad, Deo K., jt. ed. see Samuels, Robert.

Prasad, Devki N. Food for Peace: U. S. Food Assistance to India. xviii, 172p. (C). 1982. pap. text ed. 8.95 (*0-86590-011-6*) Apt Bks.

Prasad, H. S. The Uttaratantra of Maitreya. (Bibliotheca Indo-Buddhica Ser.: No. 79). 436p. (C). 1991. text ed. 30.00 (*81-7030-263-3*) S Asia.

Prasad, Hari M. The Dramatic Art of Eugene O'Neill. 113p. 1987. text ed. 18.95 (*81-7045-003-9*, Pub. by Associated Pub Hse II) Advent Bks Div.

Prasad, Hari S., ed. Time in Indian Philosophy: A Collection of Essays. (C). 1992. 58.00 (*81-7030-267-6*) S Asia.

Prasad, Indira. Philosophy & Common Sense: A Study in the Philosphy of C. S. Peirce. 1983. text ed. 24.00 (*0-685-14090-3*) Coronet Bks.

Prasad, Joshi & Prasad, Kharbanda, eds. Supreme Court Labour Judgements, 1950-83, 13 vols. (C). 1990. 100.00 (*0-89771-303-6*) St Mut.

Prasad, Jwala, ed. History of Indian Epistemology. 1988. 32.00 (*81-215-0072-9*, Pub. by Munshiram Manoharial II) S Asia.

Prasad, Jyoti N. Impact of the Foreign Corrupt Practices Act of 1977 on U. S. Export. LC 92-39946. (Foreign Economic Policy of the United States Ser.). 224p. 1993. 53.00 (*0-8153-1107-9*) Garland.

Prasad, K. N. Foundations of Modern Economics. 1986. text ed. 60.00 (*81-207-0147-X*, Pub. by Sterling Pubs II) Apt Bks.

— An Outline of Growth, Development & Planning. 1992. 40.00 (*81-7040-407-X*, Pub. by Himalaya II) Apt Bks.

— Poverty, Inequality & Unemployment in India: (Incorporating Their Regional - Inter-State Dimensions) 1993. 44.00 (*81-7022-459-4*, Pub. by Concept II) S Asia.

Prasad, K. N., ed. Vitamins, Nutrition & Cancer. (Illus.). xii, 320p. 1984. 158.50 (*3-8055-3846-4*) S Karger.

Prasad, K. N., jt. ed. see Meyskens, F. L.

Prasad, K. Siva. Technological Breakthrough in Agriculture. (C). 1987. 17.50 (*81-85076-15-4*, Pub. by Chugh Pubns II) S Asia.

Prasad, Kamta. Planning at the Grassroots. xii, 200p. 1988. text ed. 27.50 (*81-207-0782-6*, Pub. by Sterling Pubs II) Apt Bks.

Prasad, Kamta & Sinha, R. K., eds. Perspectives on Economic Development & Thought. 1986. 24.00 (*0-8364-1659-7*, Pub. by Somaiya) S Asia.

Prasad, Kedar, jt. ed. see Meyskens, Frank L., Jr.

***Prasad, Kedar, et al, eds.** Nutrients in Cancer Prevention & Treatment. LC 95-15205. (Experimental Biology & Medicine Ser.). (Illus.). 408p. 1995. text ed. 140.00 (*0-89603-318-X*) Humana.

Prasad, Kedar N. Handbook of Radiobiology. 304p. 1984. 110.00 (*0-8493-2938-8*, QP82) CRC Pr.

— Handbook of Radiology. 2nd ed. LC 94-30433. (Illus.). 1995. write for info. (*0-8493-2501-3*) CRC Pr.

— Vitamins in Cancer Prevention & Treatment: A Practical Guide. rev. ed. 128p. 1993. pap. 9.95 (*0-89281-483-7*, Heal Arts VT) Inner Tradit.

Prasad, Kedar N. & Meyskens, Frank L., Jr., eds. Nutrients & Cancer Prevention. LC 90-4677. (Experimental Biology & Medicine Ser.). (Illus.). 368p. 1990. 89.50 (*0-89603-171-3*) Humana.

Prasad, Kedar N. & Vernadakis, Antonia, eds. Mechanisms of Actions of Neurotoxic Substances. 236p. 1982. text ed. 70.00 (*0-89004-638-7*) Raven.

Prasad, Kharbanda, jt. ed. see Prasad, Joshi.

Prasad, Kunwar. Taxation in Ancient India. 1987. 21.00 (*0-317-89531-1*, Pub. by Mittal II) S Asia.

Prasad, L. C. Religion, Mortality & Politics According to Mahatma Gandhi. (C). 1991. 27.50 (*81-7054-128-X*, Pub. by Classics India Pubns II) S Asia.

Prasad, Lallan & Bannerjee, A. M. Management of Human Resources. 1986. text ed. 30.00 (*81-207-0045-7*, Pub. by Sterling Pubs II) Apt Bks.

Prasad, M. S. Study in Law of Evidence. 292p. 1982. 45.00 (*0-317-54676-7*) St Mut.

Prasad, Madhusudan, ed. Contemporary Indian-English Stories. 120p. 1988. text ed. 18.95 (*81-207-0903-9*, Pub. by Sterling Pubs II) Apt Bks.

— Indian-English Novelists: An Anthology of Critical Essays. 240p. 1982. 24.95 (*0-940500-48-5*, Pub. by Sterling II) Asia Bk Corp.

— Living Indian - English Poets: An Anthology of Critical Essays. xvi, 271p. 1989. text ed. 35.00 (*81-207-0852-0*, Pub. by Sterling Pubs II) Apt Bks.

— The Poetry of Jayanta Mahapatra. 312p. 1986. text ed. 40.00 (*0-685-14271-X*, Pub. by Sterling Pubs II) Apt Bks.

Prasad, Maheshwari. Social Aspects of Mining Towns of the Tribal Regions, Pt. I. 196p. 1986. 21.00 (*1-55528-082-X*, Pub. by Today & Tomorrows P & P II) Scholarly Pubns.

— Social Aspects of Mining Towns of the Tribal Regions, Pt. II. (Illus.). 60p. 1986. 12.00 (*1-55528-083-8*, Pub. by Today & Tomorrows P & P II) Scholarly Pubns.

Prasad, Marehalli G., jt. ed. see Quinlan, Daniel A.

Prasad, N. Lakshmi. Conversations with J. Krishnamurti: The Message & the Man. LC 90-50202. (Illus.). 124p. (Orig.). 1990. pap. 7.95 (*0-8356-0661-9*, Quest) Theos Pub Hse.

Prasad, N. S. IBM Mainframes: Architecture & Design. 420p. 1989. text ed. 48.00 (*0-07-050686-8*) McGraw.

Prasad, Nageshwar. Ideology & Organization in Indian Politics. 304p. 1980. 29.95 (*0-940500-77-9*, Pub. by Allied Pubs II) Asia Bk Corp.

Prasad, Nageshwar, ed. Gandhi & the Contemporary World. 194p. 1992. 25.00 (*81-7027-187-8*, Pub. by Radiant Pubs II) S Asia.

— Gandhi Today. 175p. 1992. text ed. 30.00 (*0-685-47337-6*, Pub. by Radiant Pubs II) S Asia.

— JP & Social Change in India. 200p. 1991. text ed. 27.95 (*0-685-47338-4*, Pub. by Radiant Pubs II) S Asia.

Prasad, Nallur. IBM Mainframes: Architecture & Design. 2nd ed. 1994. text ed. 45.00 (*0-07-050691-4*) McGraw.

***Prasad, Nandini, ed.** Vision Unveiled: Women on Television. (C). 1994. 28.00 (*81-241-0243-0*, Pub. by Har-Anand Pubns II) S Asia.

Prasad, Naresh, ed. Radiotherapy & Cancer Immunology. 216p. 1981. 98.95 (*0-8493-5901-5*, RC268) CRC Pr.

Prasad, Narmadeshwar. Iconography of Time. (Redbird Ser.). 1976. 4.80 (*0-89253-093-6*) Ind-US Inc.

Prasad, Om P. Decay & Revival of Urban Centres in Medieval South India C.A.D. 600-1200. 1989. 14.00 (*81-7169-006-8*, Pub. by Commonwealth II) S Asia.

Prasad, P. N., ed. Frontiers of Polymers & Advanced Materials. (Illus.). 696p. (C). 1994. text ed. 149.50 (*0-306-44716-9*, Plenum Pr) Plenum.

Prasad, P. S. S., jt. auth. see Munshi, M. Z. A.

Prasad, Paras N. & Nigam, J. K., eds. Frontiers of Polymer Research. (Illus.). 622p. 1992. 129.50 (*0-306-44096-2*, Plenum Pr) Plenum.

Prasad, Paras N. & Ulrich, D. R., eds. Nonlinear Optical & Electroactive Polymers. 448p. 1987. 105.00 (*0-306-42768-0*, Plenum Pr) Plenum.

Prasad, Paras N. & Williams, David J. Introduction to Nonlinear Optical Effects in Molecules & Polymers. 307p. 1991. text ed. 69.95 (*0-471-51562-0*) Wiley.

Prasad, Phoolan. Propagation of a Curved Shock & Nonlinear Ray Theory. 124p. 1993. pap. text ed. 54.95 (*0-470-20007-3*) Halsted Pr.

***Prasad, Prem.** Padmavati. (Illus.). 28p. (Orig.). (C). 1994. pap. text ed. 5.00 (*1-878173-37-5*) Birnham Wood.

Prasad, Pushpa. Sanskrit Inscriptions of Delhi Sultanate 1191-1526. (Illus.). 292p. 1991. 24.95 (*0-19-562123-9*) OUP.

Prasad, R., ed. Candida Albicans: Cellular & Molecular Biology. (Illus.). 296p. 1991. 149.00 (*0-387-51926-2*) Spr-Verlag.

Prasad, R. C. Ambedkarism. (C). 1993. text ed. 18.50 (*81-208-1070-8*, Pub. by Motilal Banarsidass II) S Asia.

— Preface to Ambedkarism. (C). 1993. 21.00 (*81-208-1088-0*, Pub. by Motilal Banarsidass II) S Asia.

***Prasad, R. C., ed.** Maha Calisa Samgraha: An Anthology of Calisas & Aratis Forming Part of the Hindu Religious Poetry & Public Worship Text in Nagari & Roman Scripts with Hindi & English Translation. Sharma, Atma R., tr. (C). 1994. 14.00x (*81-208-1199-2*, Pub. by Motilal Banarsidass II) S Asia.

— Tulidasa's Shriramacharitamanasa. (C). 1990. 42.00 (*0-685-39090-X*, Pub. by Motilal Banarsidass II) S Asia.

Prasad, R. C., tr. Vivaha: The Hindu Marriage Samskaras. (C). 1993. pap. 11.50 (*81-208-1132-1*, Pub. by Motilal Banarsidass II) S Asia.

Prasad, R. C., ed. see Growse, F. S.

Prasad, R. C., ed. see Tulsidasa.

Prasad, R. C., ed. see Udupa, K. N.

***Prasad, R. N.** Autonomy Movements in Mizoram. (C). 1994. text ed. 20.00 (*0-614-04136-8*, Pub. by Vikas II) S Asia.

Prasad, R. R. Pastoral Nomadism in Arid Zones of India: Socio-Demographic & Ecological Aspects. (C). 1994. text ed. 24.00 (*81-7141-237-8*, Pub. by Discovery Pub Hse II) S Asia.

— Tribal Situation in Forest Villages: Changing Subsistence Strategies & Adaptation. (C). 1993. 27.50 (*81-7141-234-3*, Pub. by Discovery Pub Hse II) S Asia.

***Prasad, R. R. & Chandra, K. Suman.** Bonded Labourers: A Study of Rehabilitation & Organisational Dynamics. (C). 1994. text ed. 22.00 (*81-241-0211-2*, Pub. by Har-Anand Pubns II) S Asia.

Prasad, R. R. & Jahagirdar, M. P. Social Factors in Social Forestry. (C). 1992. 21.50 (*81-85613-64-8*, Pub. by Chugh Pubns II) S Asia.

Prasad, Rai G. Chronology of the North Indian Kings. 1990. 46.00 (*81-7186-003-6*, Pub. by Agam II) S Asia.

Prasad, Raj. A Digest of Selected California Laws Related to Certified Personnel, 1994. 100p. 1994. pap. text ed. 25.00 (*0-943397-25-1*, 115) Assn Calif Sch Admin.

Prasad, Rajendra. At the Feet of Mahatma Gandhi. LC 79-156204. 1971. reprint ed. text ed. 69.50 (*0-8371-6154-1*, PRMG, Greenwood Pr) Greenwood.

— Karma Causation & Retributive Morality: Conceptual Essays in Ethics & Metaethics. 1989. 36.00 (*0-685-37835-7*, Pub. by Munshiram Manoharial II) S Asia.

— Karma, Causation & Retributive Morality: Conceptual Essays in Ethics & Metaethics. 460p. 1989. reprint ed. 33.00 (*81-215-0481-3*, Pub. by M Manoharial II) Coronet Bks.

— Politico-geographical Analysis of the Arthasastra. (C). 1989. 30.00 (*81-210-0224-9*, Pub. by Inter-India Pubns) S Asia.

Prasad, Rajendra, jt. auth. see Pradesh, Andhra.

Prasad, Ram. Mahua: The Tree of the Poor. 175p. 1993. 88. 00 (*81-7089-168-X*, Pub. by Intl Bk Distr II) St Mut.

Prasad, Ram C. Rajneesh: The Mystic of Feeling. 239p. 1978. 16.95 (*0-318-36385-2*) Asia Bk Corp.

Prasad, Rama. Generation Gap. (C). 1992. 25.00 (*81-7099-351-2*, Pub. by Mittal II) S Asia.

— Nature's Finer Forces. 251p. 1969. reprint ed. spiral bd. 13.75 (*0-7873-1031-X*) Mokelumne.

— The Science of Breath & the Philosophy of the Tattvas. 2nd rev. ed. 251p. 1969. reprint ed. spiral bd. 14.85 (*0-7873-0676-2*) Mokelumne.

Prasad, Ramanand, tr. The Bhagavadgita: The Song of God. LC 88-72192. 144p. (Orig.). 1988. pap. 4.95 (*0-9621099-1-6*) Gita Pr W.

Prasad, Ranga N., jt. auth. see Levitsky, Jacob.

Prasad, Ray. Surface Mount Technology: Principles & Practice. (Illus.). 416p. 1989. text ed. 74.95 (*0-442-20527-9*) Van Nos Reinhold.

***Prasad, Rayasam.** Socialism in India. 350p. (Orig.). Date not set. pap. 9.95 (*0-7610-0189-1*) NW Pub.

Prasad, S. A., jt. auth. see Hussey, J.

Prasad, S. Benjamin, ed. Management in International Perspective. LC 67-10930. (Orig.). 1967. pap. text ed. 9.95 (*0-89197-289-7*) Irvington.

Prasad, S. N. Survey of Work Done in the Military History of India. 1976. 6.50 (*0-88386-939-X*) S Asia.

Prasad, S. N. & Kashyap, Vasantika. A Textbook of Vertebrate Zoology. 14th ed. (C). 1989. pap. 17.50 (*0-85226-928-5*, Pub. by Wiley Eastern II) S Asia.

Prasad, Saffa A. Studies in Sinological Sex: Religion, Racism, & Nationalism, Vol. I: The Patriotism Thesis & Argument in Tokugawa, Japan. 71p. 1975. pap. text ed. 17.95 (*0-685-54937-2*) Transaction Pubs.

Prasad, Saroj, jt. auth. see Chanchreek, K. L.

Prasad, Saroj, jt. ed. see Chanchreek, K. L.

Prasad, Sushama S. Tribal Woman Labourers: Aspects of Economic & Physical Exploitation. 1988. 36.00 (*81-212-0193-4*, Pub. by Gian Publng Hse II) S Asia.

***Prasad, Swami M.** Karma & Reincarnation. (C). 1994. 7. 00x (*81-246-0022-8*, Pub. by DK Pubs Dist II) S Asia.

***Prasad, Swami Muni Narayana.** Taittiriya Upanisad. (C). 1994. 14.00x (*81-246-0014-7*, Pub. by DK Pubs Dist II) S Asia.

Prasad, V. & Arimilli, R. V., eds. Advanced Computations in Materials Processing. (HTD Ser.: Vol. 241). 92p. 1993. 35.00 (*0-7918-1154-9*, G00798) ASME.

Prasad, V. R., ed. T. S. Eliot & Eugene O'Neill: The Dream & the Nightmare. (C). 1991. 20.00 (*81-202-0313-5*, Pub. by Ajanta II) S Asia.

Prasad, V. V. Five Indian Novelists: The Self, the Family & Society. 172p. 1991. text ed. 27.50 (*81-85218-27-7*, Pub. by Prestige II) Advent Bks Div.

Prasad, Vs, jt. auth. see Rvr Chandrasekhara Rao.

Prasada, Ajit, ed. see Amritacandra.

Prasada, Rama, tr. see Patanjali.

Prasada Rao, D. S., jt. auth. see Selvanathan, E. A.

Prasadd, V. N. Principles & Practices in Socialcum-Community Forestry Pub. 118p. (C). 1985. 110.00 (*81-7089-032-2*, Pub. by Intl Bk Distr II) St Mut.

Prasado Rao, D. S., jt. ed. see Salazar-Carrillo, Jorge.

Prasanna, A. R., et al, eds. Gravitation & Relativistic Astrophysics: Proceedings of the Workshop held in Ahmedabad, India, Jan. 18-20, 1982. 149p. 1984. 46.00 (*9971-966-67-0*) World Scientific Pub.

Prasanna Kumar, V. K., ed. Parallel Architectures & Algorithms for Image Understanding. (Illus.). 565p. 1991. text ed. 69.95 (*0-12-564040-4*) Acad Pr.

Prasansuk, S., et al, eds. Aspects of Modern Otolaryngological Practice: First Congress of the Asian Otorhinolaryngological Federation, Pattaya, 1981. (Advances in Oto-Rhino-Laryngology Ser.: Vol. 29). (Illus.). xii, 236p. 1983. 131.25 (*3-8055-3592-9*) S Karger.

Prasch, John. How to Organize for School-based Management. LC 90-43061. 59p. 1990. pap. 6.95 (*0-87120-174-7*, 611-90093) Assn Supervision.

Prasek, Edward D. The Beginner's Guide to Micro & Mini Reef Systems. Thiel, Albert J., ed. 72p. (Orig.). Date not set. pap. write for info. (*0-945777-09-4*) Aardvark Pr.

— The Beginner's Guide to Micro & Mini Reef Systems. rev. ed. Thiel, Albert J., ed. 144p. (Orig.). reprint ed. pap. write for info. (*0-945777-12-4*) Aardvark Pr.

Prashad, Baini, ed. Tabaqat-i-Akbari of Khwajah Nizamuddin Ahmad: (A History of India from the Early Musabhman Invasions to the Thirty-Eighth Year of the Reign of Akbar), 3 vols., Set. Brajendranath, tr. (C). 1992. reprint ed. 28.00 (*81-85418-90-X*, Pub. by Low Price II) S Asia.

Prashananda, Swami. More about Ramakrishna. 276p. (Orig.). 1994. pap. 4.95 (*0-87481-242-9*, Pub. by Advaita Ashrama II) Vedanta Pr.

Prashant Bhushan. Bofors: The Selling of a Nation. 1990. 27.50 (*81-7094-066-4*, Pub. by Vision) S Asia.

Prashant, Saroj. Drug Abuse & Society: The Indian Scenario. (Illus.). xii, 219p. 1993. 17.95 (*1-881338-34-7*) Nataraj Bks.

Prasher, C. L. Crushing & Grinding Process Handbook. LC 85-26434. 474p. 1987. text ed. 315.00 (*0-471-10535-X*) Wiley.

Prasher, R. G. Indian Library Literature: An Annotated Bibliography. 544p. 1971. 8.00 (*0-88065-176-8*, Messers Today & Tomorrow) Scholarly Pubns.

— Managing University Libraries. (Illus.). 350p. 1991. 45.00 (*1-55528-250-4*, Pub. by Today & Tomorrows P & P II) Scholarly Pubns.

Prashkov, L. Wall Painting in Bulgaria: 9th to 19th Centuries. (C). 1981. 95.00 (*0-685-34406-1*) Collets.

Prasifka, David W. Water Supply Planning. LC 93-28392. 282p. 1994. 42.50 (*0-89464-838-1*) Krieger.

Prasifka, Karol, jt. auth. see Knox, William A.

Prask, H. J., et al. Cold Neutron Research in the U. S. Government. (Illus.). 145p. (Orig.). (C). 1993. pap. text ed. 50.00 (*0-7881-0046-7*) Diane Pub.

***Praskiewicz, Szczepan T.** Saint Raphael Kalinowski: An Introduction to His Life & Spirituality. Coonan, Thomas & Griffin, Michael, trs. LC 94-29713. Date not set. pap. write for info. (*0-935216-53-7*) ICS Pubns.

Praslov, N. D., jt. ed. see Soffer, Olga.

Prasnikar, Janez. Workers' Participation & Self-Management in Developing Countries. 156p. (C). 1991. pap. text ed. 33.50 (*0-8133-8172-X*) Westview.

***Prasolov, V. V.** Intuitive Topology. Sossinsky, A., tr. LC 94-23133. (Mathematical World Ser.: 4). (ENG.). 1994. pap. 25.00 (*0-8218-0356-5*) Am Math.

— Problems & Theorems in Liner Algebra. Ivanov, Simeon, ed. Leites, D. A., tr. LC 94-13332. (Translations of Mathematical Monographs: Vol. 136). 1994. write for info. (*0-8218-0236-4*) Am Math.

Prassas, John N. Royal Family: Finding Your Identity & Purpose in the Kingdom of God. LC 93-90361. (Orig.). 1993. pap. 11.95 (*0-9636999-0-3*) ABBA Pr.

***Prasse, Karl G.** The Tuaregs: The Blue People. (Illus.). 136p. 1995. 34.00 (*87-7289-313-3*, Pub. by Mus Tusculanum DK) Paul & Co Pubs.

Prasse, Keith W., jt. auth. see Duncan, J. Robert.

Prassel, Frank R. The Great American Outlaw: A Legacy of Fact & Fiction. LC 93-14675. 1993. 29.95 (*0-8061-2534-9*) U of Okla Pr.

— The Western Peace Officer: The Legacy of Law & Order. LC 71-39627. 304p. 1980. pap. 14.95 (*0-8061-1694-3*) U of Okla Pr.

Prasser, Scott, et al, eds. Corruption & Reform: The Fitzgerald Vision. 1990. pap. 29.95 (*0-7022-2234-8*, Pub. by Univ Queensland Pr AT) Intl Spec Bk.

Prassides, Kosmas, ed. Mixed Valency Systems: Applications in Chemistry Physics & Biology. 464p. (C). 1991. lib. bdg. 154.50 (*0-7923-1381-X*) Kluwer Ac.

— Physics & Chemistry of the Fullerenes: Proceedings of the NATO Advanced Research Workshop, Aghia Pelaghia, Greece, June 7-13, 1993. (NATO Advanced Science Institutes Series C: 444). 352p. (C). 1994. lib. bdg. 149. 00 (*0-7923-3109-5*) Kluwer Ac.

Prastaro, A., ed. Geometrodynamics Proceedings 1985. 466p. 1985. 66.00 (*9971-978-63-6*) World Scientific Pub.

Prastaro, A. & Rassias, T. M. Geometry in Partial Differential Equations. 500p. 1994. text ed. 121.00 (*981-02-1407-3*) World Scientific Pub.

Prasuhn, Alan L. Fundamentals of Hydraulic Engineering. 600p. (C). 1987. text ed. 63.00 (*0-03-003948-7*) SCP.

Prat, H., jt. auth. see Calvet, E.

Prat Turu, Clara. Diccionari Portugues-Catala, Catala-Portugues. 512p. 1982. 31.95 (*0-7859-6216-6*, 8473061829) Fr & Eur.

Prat, William. Description of Aphrique. 1972. 59.95 (*0-8490-0019-X*) Gordon Pr.

Prata, Giuliana. A Systemic Harpoon into Family Games: Preventive Interventions in Therapy. LC 90-2157. 192p. 1991. 26.95 (*0-87630-591-5*) Brunner-Mazel.

Prata, Stephen. Artificial Life Playhouse: Evolution at Your Fingertips. (Illus.). 190p. (Orig.). 1993. disk, pap. 23.95 (*1-878739-32-8*) Waite Group Pr.

— C Plus Plus Primer Plus: Teach Yourself Object Oriented Programming. (Illus.). 720p. (Orig.). 1991. pap. 26.95 (*1-878739-02-6*) Waite Group Pr.

— C++ Primer Plus: Teach Yourself Object-Oriented Programming. 2nd ed. 844p. 1995. disk, pap. 32.95 (*1-878739-74-3*) Waite Group Pr.

— Certified Course in Visual Basic X.0: Earn Your Certificate Through Self-Paced Instruction. 500p. 1995. cd-rom, pap. 32.95 (*1-57169-056-5*) Waite Group Pr.

— EMF Handbook: Understanding & Controlling Electromagnetic Fields in Your Life. (Illus.). 116p. (Orig.). 1993. pap. 12.95 (*1-878739-55-7*) Waite Group Pr.

Prata, Stephen W. & Martin, Donald. Waite Group's UNIX System V Bible. 528p. 1987. pap. 29.95 (*0-672-22562-X*) Sams.

Prata, Stephen W., jt. auth. see Waite, Mitchell.

Pratap, Vijayendra. A Teacher's Guide for Beginning Yoga. 2nd ed. LC 87-91956. (Illus.). 122p. 1987. 9.95 (*0-944731-00-7*) Sky Fnd.

Pratchett. Lords & Ladies. Date not set. 20.00 (*0-06-017751-9*, HarpT) HarpC.

Pratchett, Terry. Colour of Magic. 1990. 25.00 (*0-86140-324-X*, Pub. by Colin Smythe Ltd UK) Dufour.

— The Colour of Magic. 256p. 1985. pap. 4.99 (*0-451-45112-0*, ROC) NAL-Dutton.

— Equal Rites: A Novel of Discworld. 256p. 1988. pap. 4.99 (*0-451-45092-2*, ROC) NAL-Dutton.

— ERIC. 224p. 1995. pap. 4.99 (*0-451-45357-3*, Sig) NAL-Dutton.

— Guards! Guards! A Novel of Discworld. (Illus.). 352p. 1991. pap. 4.99 (*0-451-45089-2*, ROC) NAL-Dutton.

— The Light Fantastic. LC 86-60218. 218p. 1987. 27.00 (*0-86140-203-0*, Pub. by Colin Smythe Ltd UK) Dufour.

— The Light Fantastic. 256p. 1988. pap. 4.99 (*0-451-16241-2*, ROC) NAL-Dutton.

— The Light Fantastic. 256p. 1988. pap. 3.50 (*0-451-15297-2*, Sig) NAL-Dutton.

P
Q

An Asterisk (*) at the beginning of an entry indicates that the title is appearing in BIP for the first time.

— Mort. 240p. 1989. pap. 5.50 (*0-451-45113-9*, ROC) NAL-Dutton.
— Moving Pictures. (Discworld Ser.). 352p. 1992. pap. 4.99 (*0-451-45131-7*, ROC) NAL-Dutton.
— Pyramids: A Novel of Discworld. 304p. (Orig.). 1989. pap. 4.99 (*0-451-45044-2*, ROC) NAL-Dutton.
— Reaper Man. 352p. (Orig.). 1992. pap. 4.99 (*0-451-45168-6*, ROC) NAL-Dutton.
— Small Gods: A Discworld Novel. LC 93-25127. 272p. 1994. 20.00 (*0-06-017750-0*, HarpT) HarpC.
— Small Gods: A Novel of Discworld. 1994. pap. 4.99 (*0-06-109217-7*, Harp PBks) HarpC.
— Soul Music: A Novel of Discworld. LC 94-29450. 1995. 20.00 (*0-06-105203-5*) P-H.
— Sourcery. 256p. 1989. pap. 4.99 (*0-451-16233-1*, ROC) NAL-Dutton.
— Strata. 224p. 1983. reprint ed. pap. 4.99 (*0-451-45111-2*, ROC) NAL-Dutton.
— Wings. large type ed. (J). 1993. 16.95 (*0-7451-1805-4*, Galaxy Child Lrg Print) Chivers N Amer.
— Witches Abroad: A Fantasy Novel. (Discworld Ser.). 320p. (Orig.). 1993. pap. 4.99 (*0-451-45225-9*, ROC) NAL-Dutton.
— Wyrd Sisters. 320p. 1990. pap. 4.99 (*0-451-45012-4*, ROC) NAL-Dutton.

Prate, Kit. Greenhorn Stampede. large type ed. (Linford Western Library). 352p. (Orig.). 1992. pap. 14.95 (*0-7089-7172-5*, Trailtree Bookshop) Ulverscroft.
— Wild Texas Winds. 480p. 1988. pap. 3.95 (*1-55817-082-0*, Pinnacle NY) Windsor NY.

Pratelli, M., jt. ed. see Letta, G.

Prater, A. J. Estuary Birds of Britain & Ireland. (Illus.). 456p. 1991. text ed. 39.95 (*0-85661-029-1*, 784629, Pub. by Poyser UK) Acad Pr.

Prater, Bacon & Tucker. Employee Benefits Guide, Vol. 1. 1991. write for info. (*0-8205-1574-4*) Bender.

Prater, Bayliss & McNeal, Kathleen. Full Circle: Restoring Your Habitat to Wilderness. (Illus.). 127p. (Orig.). 1993. pap. 15.00 (*0-9635867-1-8*) Last Resort.

Prater, Burt. Family Masonic Education Workbook: Using Masonic Symbolism in Daily Life. (Illus.). 192p. (Orig.). 1993. pap. 14.95 (*0-9635766-0-7*) Source.

Prater, Donald. A Ringing Glass: The Life of Rainer Maria Rilke. (Illus.). 472p. 1994. reprint ed. pap. 19.95 (*0-19-815891-2*) OUP.

***Prater, Donald A.** Thomas Mann: A Life. (Illus.). 480p. 1995. 35.00 (*0-19-815861-0*) OUP.

Prater, Eugene G. Essays on Drama & Theatre. LC 90-91773. 330p. (Orig.). 1994. pap. 12.95 (*0-9636125-1-4*) E G Prater.
— An Existential View of John Osborne. LC 90-91772. 270p. 1993. pap. 11.95 (*0-9636125-0-6*) E G Prater.

Prater, Gene. Snowshoeing. 3rd ed. LC 88-24452. (Illus.). 184p. (Orig.). 1988. pap. 10.95 (*0-89886-178-0*) Mountaineers.

Prater, Jeffrey. The Study of Harmony: An Historical Perspective. 384p. (C). 1991. boxed write for info. (*0-697-11966-1*) Brown & Benchmark.

Prater, John. The Gift. LC 86-43071. (Illus.). 32p. (J). (gr. 3-8). 1987. pap. 3.95 (*0-317-63653-7*, Puffin) Puffin Bks.
— The Greatest Show on Earth. LC 94-24991. (J). 1995. write for info. (*1-56402-563-2*) Candlewick Pr.
— Once Upon a Time. LC 92-53139. 1995. pap. 5.99 (*1-56402-456-3*) Candlewick Pr.
— Tim & the Blanket Thief. LC 93-6563. (Illus.). 32p. (J). (ps-1). 1993. lib. bdg. 14.95 (*0-689-31881-2*, Atheneum Bks Young) S&S Childrens.

Prater, Rex J. & Swift, Roger W. Manual of Voice Therapy. LC 90-50380. 288p. (C). 1984. spiral bd. 29.00 (*0-89079-279-8*, 1773) PRO-ED.
— Manual of Voice Therapy. LC 90-50380. 288p. 1984. 44.00 (*0-316-71729-0*, 1713) PRO-ED.

Prater, Tony, jt. auth. see Marchant, John.

Prater, Yvonne & Mendenhall, Ruth D. Gorp, Glop, & Glue Stew: Favorite Foods from 165 Outdoor Experts. LC 81-18836. (Illus.). 204p. (Orig.). 1981. pap. 10.95 (*0-89886-017-2*) Mountaineers.

Pratesi, P., jt. auth. see Franconi, Cafiero.

Pratesi, R., ed. Optronic Techniques in Diagnostic & Therapeutic Medicine. (Illus.). 302p. 1991. 89.50 (*0-306-43938-7*, Plenum Pr) Plenum.

Prathap, G. The Finite Element Method in Structural Engineering. LC 93-30133. (Solid Mechanics & Its Applications Ser.). 424p. (C). 1993. lib. bdg. 139.00 (*0-7923-2492-7*) Kluwer Ac.

Prather, Alfred G., jt. auth. see Prather, Gloria A.

Prather, Alfred G., jt. auth. see Prather, Gloria M.

Prather, Angela, ed. see Prather, Dewitt G.

Prather, Arden C., ed. see Prather, Gloria A. & Prather, Alfred G.

Prather, Arden C., ed. see Prather, Gloria M. & Prather, Alfred G.

Prather, Charlotte. A Generous Openness: Praying the Spiritual Exercises of St. Ignatius. (Orig.). 1992. pap. 7.95 (*0-932506-85-2*) St Bedes Pubns.

Prather, Dewitt G. United States National Bank Notes & Their Seals. Prather, J. S. & Prather, Angela, eds. (Illus.). 200p. 1986. 40.00 (*0-9616836-0-0*); 60.00 (*0-317-58449-9*) D G Prather.

Prather, Elizabeth M., et al. Screening Test of Adolescent Language (STAL) rev. ed. 1987. Additional test forms, pkg. of 100. 17.50 (*0-295-77003-1*) U of Wash Pr.

Prather, Gayle, jt. auth. see Prather, Hugh.

Prather, Gloria A. & Prather, Alfred G. My First Reader & Skills Book: One Hundred Words Plus. Prather, Arden C., ed. (Illus.). 36p. (Orig.). (J). (gr. 1-3). 1988. pap. write for info. (*0-9619655-2-5*) Academic Parks Co.

Prather, Gloria M. & Prather, Alfred G. Especially for Special Children: The A-B-C's of Super Stars. Prather, Arden C., ed. 30p. (Orig.). (J). 1988. Picture bk. lib. bdg. write for info. (*0-9619655-3-3*) Academic Parks Co.
— The Way to Go: Academic Travel Pack. Prather, Arden C. & Smith, Ellen, eds. (Illus.). 48p. (J). (gr. k-2). 1987. student ed write for info. (*0-9619655-0-9*) Academic Parks Co.

Prather, H. Leon, Sr. Resurgent Politics & Educational Progressivism in the New South: North Carolina, 1890-1913. LC 77-74394. (Illus.). 186p. 1979. 40.00 (*0-8386-2071-X*) Fairleigh Dickinson.

Prather, Hugh. I Touch the Earth, the Earth Touches Me. LC 72-79420. 160p. 1972. mass mkt. 8.95 (*0-385-05063-1*, Dolp) Doubleday.
— Notes on How to Live in the World (And Still Be Happy) LC 85-16167. 288p. 1986. mass mkt. 9.95 (*0-385-18261-9*, Dolp) Doubleday.
— Notes on Love & Courage. LC 77-75873. 1977. mass mkt. 8.95 (*0-385-12772-3*, Dolp) Doubleday.
— Notes to Each Other. 1991. pap. 10.00 (*0-553-35282-2*) Bantam.
— Notes to Myself. 160p. 1983. mass mkt. 5.50 (*0-553-27382-5*, Bantam Classics) Bantam.
— Quiet Answer. LC 80-2979. 176p. 1982. mass mkt. 8.95 (*0-385-17605-8*, Dolp) Doubleday.
— There Is a Place Where You Are Not Alone. LC 80-912. 224p. 1980. mass mkt. 7.95 (*0-385-14778-3*, Dolp) Doubleday.

Prather, Hugh & Prather, Gayle. A Book for Couples. LC 83-45343. 224p. 1988. mass mkt. 9.95 (*0-385-18785-8*) Doubleday.
— I Will Never Leave You: How Couples Can Achieve the Power of Lasting Love. LC 94-31397. 1995. 19.95 (*0-553-09533-1*) Bantam.

Prather, Hugh E., Jr. Circle of a Thought. 2nd rev. ed. Helberg, Bob, ed. LC 87-73314. 80p. (YA). (gr. 9-12). 1987. reprint ed. pap. 7.95 (*0-944944-00-0*) Amethyst Aura.

Prather, J. S., ed. see Prather, Dewitt G.

Prather, James E., jt. auth. see Gibson, Frank K.

Prather, Jeff, jt. auth. see Gregutt, Paul.

Prather, Jo Beecher. Mississippi Beau. LC 93-50614. (J). 1995. pap. 7.95 (*0-89015-961-0*) Sunbelt Media.

Prather, John W., Jr. Praters in Wiltshire, 1480-1670, Vol. I. (Prater-Prather Family History & Genealogy). (Illus.). 215p. 1987. write for info. (*0-9619434-1-6*) J W Prather.
— Praters in Wiltshire, 1480-1670, Vol. I, Set. (Prater-Prather Family History & Genealogy). (Illus.). 215p. 1987. 30.00 (*0-9619434-0-8*) J W Prather.

***Prather, Marilyn.** A Light in the Darkness. 1995. 17.95 (*0-8034-9098-4*, 094632) Bouregy.

Prather, Marla. Gaugin: A Retrospective. 1989. 34.99 (*0-517-68612-0*) Random Hse Value.

Prather-Moses, Alice I. The International Dictionary of Women Workers in the Decorative Arts: A Historical Survey from the Distant Past to the Early Decades of the Twentieth Century. LC 81-8947. 218p. 1981. 25.00 (*0-8108-1450-1*) Scarecrow.

Prather, Patricia S. & Monday, Jane C. From Slave to Statesman: The Legacy of Joshua Houston, Servant to Sam Houston. LC 93-25464. (Illus.). 276p. 1993. 32.50 (*0-929398-47-5*) UNTX Pr.
— From Slave to Statesman: The Legacy of Joshua Houston, Servant to Sam Houston. 292p. 1995. pap. 14.95 (*0-929398-87-4*) UNTX Pr.

Prather, Richard. Hot Rock Rumble & The Double Take. (Gryphon Double Novel Ser.: No. 5). 100p. 1994. per. 9.95 (*0-936071-31-1*) Gryphon Pubns.

Prather, Richard S. Shellshock. 352p. 1988. pap. 3.95 (*0-8125-0783-5*) Tor Bks.

Prather, Ronald, jt. auth. see Demsey, David.

Prather, Ronald E. Problem-Solving Principles: Programming with PASCAL. (Illus.). 352p. 1982. pap. text ed. write for info. (*0-13-721308-5*) P-H.
— Ronald Prather: Laboratory Manual for Data Structures: To Accompany Horowitz & Sahni Fundamentals of Data Structure. 3rd ed. (Illus.). (C). 1995. write for info. (*0-7167-8236-7*) W H Freeman.

***Prather, Stephen, et al.** Behavioral Types & the Art of Patient Management. Rogers, Gregg, ed. 212p. 1995. text ed. 39.95 (*1-57066-031-X*) Practice Mgmt Info.

Prather, Stephen E., et al. Medical Risk Management. (Practice & Financial Management Ser.). 208p. 1990. text ed. 45.00 (*0-87489-581-2*) Med Economics.

Prati, G., ed. Coherent Optical Communications & Photonic Switching: Proc. of the 4th Internat. Workshop on Digital Communications, Tirrenia, Italy, 19-23 Sept. 1989. 364p. 1990. 107.75 (*0-444-88412-2*) Elsevier.

Prati, G., jt. ed. see Biglieri, E.

Prati, G. L., jt. ed. see Faienza, C.

***Pratico, Gary D.** Egypt-Sinai-Negev: With Slides. Shanks, Hershel, ed. 43p. (Orig.). 1987. pap. text ed. 119.50 (*1-880317-34-6*, 5092-AC) Biblical Arch Soc.
— Nelson Glueck's 1938-1940 Excavations at Tell el-Kheleifeh: A Reappraisal. (ASOR Archaeological Reports). 223p. 1993. 74.95 (*1-55540-883-4*, 85003) Scholars Pr GA.

Pratkanis, Anthony, jt. ed. see Aronson, Elliot.

Pratkanis, Anthony R., et al, eds. Attitude Structure & Function. 472p. 1989. text ed. 89.95 (*0-89859-991-1*); pap. text ed. 39.95 (*0-8058-0323-8*) L Erlbaum Assocs.

Pratley, Gerald. Torn Sprockets: The Uncertain Projection of the Canadian Film. LC 83-40110. (Illus.). 336p. 1987. 65.00 (*0-87413-194-4*) U Delaware Pr.

Pratley, J. E., ed. Principles of Field Crop Production. 3rd ed. (Sydney University Press Publication). 483p. 1994. pap. 55.00 (*0-424-00200-0*) OUP.

Pratley, J. E., jt. ed. see Cornish, P. S.

***Pratley, Peter.** The Essence of Business Ethics. LC 95-6669. (Essence of Management Ser.). 1995. pap. 19.95 (*0-13-356544-0*) P-H.

Pratley, Rhiannedd. Spelling It Out. 128p. 1988. pap. 7.95 (*0-563-21437-6*, Pub. by BBC UK) Parkwest Pubns.

Pratney, Winkey. El Joven y Su Dios. (Joven y Sus Inquietudes Ser.). 1982. 3.50 (*0-88113-163-6*) Edit Betania.
— El Joven y Su Mundo. (Joven y Sus Inquietudes Ser.). 1982. 3.50 (*0-88113-164-4*) Edit Betania.
— El Joven y Sus Amigos. (Joven y Sus Inquietudes Ser). 1982. 3.50 (*0-88113-162-8*) Edit Betania.
— El Joven y Sus Dilemas. (Joven y Sus Inquietudes Ser.). 1982. 3.50 (*0-88113-165-2*) Edit Betania.
— Nature & Character of God. LC 88-19451. 450p. (C). 1988. text ed. 14.99 (*1-55661-041-6*) Bethany Hse.
— Revival: Its Principles & Personalities. LC 93-61365. 240p. 1993. pap. 10.99 (*1-56384-058-8*) Huntington Hse.

Pratney, Winkie. Devil Take the Youngest. LC 85-90017. 271p. (Orig.). 1985. pap. 8.99 (*0-910311-29-3*) Huntington Hse.
— Doorways to Discipleship. LC 77-80008. 272p. 1977. pap. 7.99 (*0-87123-106-9*) Bethany Hse.
— Guia para el Discipulado, Tomo I. 144p. (Orig.). (SPA.). 1988. pap. text ed. 3.95 (*0-88113-167-9*) Edit Betania.
— Guia para el Discipulado, Tomo II. 160p. (Orig.). (SPA.). 1988. pap. 3.95 (*0-88113-168-7*) Edit Betania.
— Guia para el Discipulado, Tomo III. 128p. (Orig.). (SPA.). 1988. pap. 3.95 (*0-88113-169-5*) Edit Betania.
— A Handbook for Followers of Jesus. LC 76-44385. 336p. 1976. pap. 8.99 (*0-87123-378-9*) Bethany Hse.
— Healing the Land: A Supernatural View of Ecology. LC 93-25494. 240p. (Orig.). 1993. pap. 11.99 (*0-8007-9210-6*) Chosen Bks.
— The Thomas Factor: Key to Believing When You Cannot Find an Answer. LC 89-37259. 160p. 1989. pap. 7.99 (*0-8007-9154-1*) Chosen Bks.
— Youth Aflame. LC 82-74507. 448p. (Orig.). 1983. pap. 9.99 (*0-87123-659-1*) Bethany Hse.

Prato, Lou. Covering the Environmental Beat: An Overview for Radio & TV Journalists. Media Institute Staff, ed. LC 91-66458. 113p. (Orig.). (C). 1991. pap. 9.95 (*0-937790-47-8*, 4390) Media Institute.

Pratolini, Vasco. Family Chronicle. LC 87-82245. Orig. Title: Cronaca Familiare. 136p. (Orig.). 1988. pap. 9.50 (*0-934977-07-0*) Italica Pr.
— A Tale of Poor Lovers. (Voices of Resistance Ser.). 368p. 1988. reprint ed. pap. 7.50 (*0-85345-723-9*) Monthly Rev.

Prator, Clifford H., Jr. & Robinett, Betty W. Manual of American English Pronounciation. 4th ed. LC 84-25222. 244p. (C). 1985. pap. text ed. 20.50 (*0-03-000703-8*) HB Coll Pubs.

Prats, A. J. The Autonomous Image: Cinematic Narration & Humanism. LC 81-50182. 192p. (C). 1981. 21.00 (*0-8131-1406-3*) U Pr of Ky.

Prats, Michael. Thermal Recovery. 174p. 1982. 35.00 (*0-89520-314-6*) Soc Petrol Engineers.

Pratsinak, George & Alexander, Robert, eds. Understanding Substance Abuse & Treatment. 212p. (Orig.). 1992. pap. text ed. 26.25 (*0-929310-73-X*, 449) Am Correctional.

***Pratson, Frederick.** Guide to Cape Cod: Everything You Need to Know to Enjoy One of New England's Perfect Vacation Destinations. 3rd ed. Morris, Jerry, ed. LC 94-24044. (Illus.). 256p. 1995. pap. 10.95 (*1-56440-629-6*) Globe Pequot.
— Guide to Eastern Canada. 4th ed. (Voyager Book Ser.). (Illus.). 416p. 1992. pap. 15.95 (*0-87106-191-0*) Globe Pequot.
— Guide to Eastern Canada. 5th ed. Loverseed, Helga, ed. (Illus.). 416p. 1995. pap. 17.95 (*1-56440-635-0*) Globe Pequot.

Pratson, Frederick & Chatelin, Raymond. Guide to Western Canada. 3rd ed. LC 93-28551. (Voyager Book Ser.). (Illus.). 352p. 1993. pap. 16.95 (*1-56440-279-7*) Globe Pequot.

Pratson, Frederick J. A Guide to Atlantic Canada. LC 72-93258. (Illus.). (Orig.). 1973. pap. 6.95 (*0-85699-073-6*) Chatham Pr.

Pratt. Barefoot Mailman. 220p. 1993. pap. 7.95 (*0-912451-32-7*) Florida Classics.
— Big Bubble. 220p. 1995. pap. write for info. (*0-912451-34-3*) Florida Classics.
— Botany. (Applied Science Review Ser.). 1993. 11.95 (*0-87434-570-7*) Springhouse Pub.
— Cases in Financial Analysis. 1994. text ed. 16.95 (*0-538-83676-8*) S-W Pub.
— Construction Estimating IG. 56p. 1995. teacher ed 14.00 (*0-8273-6137-8*) Delmar.
— Flame Tree. 250p. 1994. pap. 11.95 (*0-912451-33-5*) Florida Classics.
— A Guide to SQL. 2nd ed. 176p. 1991. 15.50 (*0-87835-669-X*) Boyd & Fraser.
— HIV & AIDS: A Strategy for Nursing Care. 486p. 1992. pap. 35.25 (*1-56593-544-6*, 0516) Singular Publishing.
— Learning to Use dBASE IV Version 1.1. (Shelly Cashman Ser.). (Illus.). 320p. (C). 1992. teacher ed, per. 19.00 (*0-87835-766-1*) Boyd & Fraser.
— Microcomputer Database Management. 1988. pap. 30.00 (*0-87835-303-8*) Boyd & Fraser.
— Microcomputer Database Management Using dBASE III PLUS. 2nd ed. 464p. 1991. 32.00 (*0-87835-684-3*) Boyd & Fraser.
— Using dBASE III PLUS. 324p. 1991. 15.50 (*0-685-47883-1*) Boyd & Fraser.
— Vascular Surgery: Guide & Handbook. LC 75-27628. (Illus.). 416p. 1976. 27.60 (*0-87527-138-3*) Green.

Pratt & Allen. Occupational Therapy for Children. 2nd ed. (Illus.). 672p. 1988. 51.95 (*0-8016-2466-5*) Mosby Yr Bk.

***Pratt & Garton, eds.** Systems of Representation in Young Children: Development & Use. (Developmental Psychology Ser.). Date not set. pap. text ed. 29.95 (*0-471-95585-X*) Wiley.

Pratt & Last. MCDMU Paradox for Windows. (C). 1994. text ed. write for info. (*0-318-70354-8*, BF4012) S-W Pub.
— Using Paradox for Windows. (C). 1994. text ed. write for info. (*0-318-70355-6*, BF3962) S-W Pub.

Pratt & Leidig. Microcomputer Database Management Using Access. (C). 1994. text ed. write for info. (*0-318-70356-4*, BF3911) S-W Pub.

Pratt, jt. auth. see Hill.

Pratt, jt. auth. see Norris.

Pratt, jt. auth. see Wray.

Pratt, et al. Aural Awareness. 1990. 90.00 (*0-335-09418-X*, Open Univ Pr); pap. 29.00 (*0-335-09417-1*, Open Univ Pr) Taylor & Francis.

Pratt, A. E. Tibet Through China. (C). 1987. 28.50 (*0-8364-2348-8*, Pub. by Mittal II) S Asia.

Pratt, A. W. Heat Transmission in Buildings. LC 80-42021. 320p. reprint ed. pap. 91.20 (*0-318-34897-7*, 2031294) Bks Demand.

Pratt, Alan R. The Dark Side: Thoughts on the Futility of Life from Ancient Greeks to the Present. LC 93-45556. 1994. 10.95 (*0-8065-1481-7*) Carol Pub Group.

Pratt, Alan R., ed. Black Humor: Critical Essays. LC 92-7387. (Studies in Humor: Vol. 2). 408p. 1992. 60.00 (*0-8153-0619-9*, H1503) Garland.

Pratt, Alice D. Homesteader's Portfolio. (Northwest Reprints Ser.). 256p. (C). 1993. reprint ed. text ed. 24.95 (*0-87071-516-X*); reprint ed. pap. 13.95 (*0-87071-517-8*) Oreg St U Pr.

Pratt, Alice E. Use of Color in the Verse of English Romantic Poets from Langland to Keats. (English Literature Ser.: No. 33). 1970. reprint ed. pap. 39.95 (*0-8383-0061-8*) M S G Haskell Hse.

Pratt, Allan D. The Information of the Image. LC 81-15075. (Libraries & Information Science). 118p. 1981. 25.00 (*0-89391-055-4*) Ablex Pub.

Pratt, Ambrose. The Living Mummy. LC 87-60464. (Illus.). 313p. 1988. reprint ed. pap. 15.95 (*0-915431-02-5*) N American Archives.

Pratt, Andrew. Uneven Reproduction: Industry, Space & Society. (Policy, Planning, & Critical Theory Ser.). 270p. 1994. text ed. 93.00 (*0-08-040487-1*, Pergamon Pr); pap. text ed. 40.00 (*0-08-040486-3*, Pergamon Pr) Elsevier.

Pratt, Ann B. The Emlen Physick House Museum. (Cape May Ser.). (Illus.). 60p. (Orig.). 1990. pap. 6.50 (*0-925436-07-0*) Cam-Tech Pub.

Pratt, Anne, tr. see Taupin, Rene.

Pratt, Anne H. Junior Missionary Handbook. 64p. (Orig.). (J). (gr. 3-6). 1987. pap. 5.98 (*0-88290-318-7*) Horizon Utah.

Pratt, Annis. Dancing with Goddesses: Archetypes, Poetry, & Empowerment. LC 93-28442. 1994. 39.95 (*0-253-34586-3*); pap. 17.95 (*0-253-20865-3*) Ind U Pr.

Pratt, Annis, jt. ed. see Dembo, L. S.

Pratt, Annis, et al. Archetypal Patterns in Women's Fiction. LC 81-47167. 221p. reprint ed. pap. 63.00 (*0-8357-5719-6*, 2056716) Bks Demand.

Pratt, Antoinette M. The Attitude of the Catholic Church Toward Witchcraft & the Allied Practices of Sorcery & Magic. LC 79-8116. 144p. reprint ed. 32.50 (*0-404-18429-4*) AMS Pr.

Pratt, Arden L., jt. auth. see Gillie, Angelo C.

Pratt, Arthur. How to Help & Understand the Alcoholic or Drug Addict. LC 80-82964. 127p. 1981. pap. 4.95 (*0-915216-63-9*) Marathon Intl Bk.
— The Party's over. (Orig.). 1977. pap. 2.95 (*0-685-78487-8*) Fountain Pr.

Pratt, Brian & Boyden, Jo. The Field Directors Handbook: An Oxfam Guide for Development Workers. 512p. (C). 1988. pap. text ed. 60.00 (*0-85598-073-7*, Pub. by Oxfam Pubns UK) St Mut.

Pratt, Brian & Boyden, Jo, eds. The Field Directors' Handbook: An Oxfam Manual for Development Workers. (Illus.). 512p. 1986. pap. 49.95 (*0-19-920153-6*) OUP.

Pratt, Brian & Lizos, Peter. Choosing Research Methods: Data Collection for Development Workers. 80p. (C). 1980. text ed. 80.00 (*0-85598-176-8*, Pub. by Oxfam Pubns UK); pap. text ed. 24.00 (*0-85598-177-6*, Pub. by Oxfam Pubns UK) St Mut.

Pratt, Carl R. Ecology. LC 94-10645. (Applied Science Review). 1994. write for info. (*0-87434-689-4*) Springhouse Pub.

Pratt Center Staff. Cooking in the Litchfield Hills. 224p. 1994. 15.95 (*0-9639175-0-1*) Pratt Center.

Pratt, Charles W. Fables in Two Languages & Similar Diversions: Fables en Deux Langues et Divertissements de Ce Genre. LC 94-65599. (Illus.). 48p. (Orig.). (ENG & FRE.). 1994. pap. 13.95 (*0-9641028-0-3*) Pomme Pr.
— In the Orchard. LC 94-67304. (Illus.). 51p. 1994. reprint ed. pap. 12.95 (*0-9641028-1-1*) Pomme Pr.

Pratt, Chris & Garton, Alison F., eds. Systems of Representation in Children: Development & Use. LC 92-25523. (Developmental Psychology & Its Applications Ser.). 283p. 1993. text ed. 77.95 (*0-471-92501-2*) Wiley.

Pratt, Chris, jt. auth. see Garton, Alison F.

Pratt, Chris, et al, eds. Research Issues in Child Development. 208p. (C). 1986. pap. text ed. 29.95 (*0-86861-414-9*) Routledge Chapman & Hall.

Pratt, Cranford. The Critical Phase in Tanzania, 1945-1968: Nyerere & the Emergence of a Socialist Strategy. LC 75-22979. 327p. reprint ed. pap. 93.20 (*0-317-27579-8*, 2024516) Bks Demand.

Pratt, Cranford, ed. Canadian International Development Assistance Policies: An Appraisal. 432p. 1994. 39.95 (*0-7735-1180-6*, Pub. by McGill CN) U of Toronto Pr.
— Internationalism under Strain: The North-South Policies of Canada, the Netherlands, Norway, & Sweden. 1989. 37.50 (*0-8020-2695-8*) U of Toronto Pr.

— Middle Power Internationalism: The North-South Dimension. 176p. (C). 1990. pap. 44.95 (0-7735-0725-6, Pub. by McGill CN) U of Toronto Pr.
Pratt, Cranford, jt. ed. see Matthews, Robert O.
Pratt, Cranford, jt. ed. see Mwansasu, Bismarck U.
Pratt, Cranford, jt. ed. see Mwansasu, Bismarck.
Pratt, D. T., jt. ed. see Smoot, L. Douglas.
Pratt, Dallas. Animal Films for Humane Education. LC 86-70683. 284p. 1986. pap. 7.95 (0-916858-07-3) Argus Archives.
***Pratt, Daniel D., ed.** Five Perspectives on Teaching Adults. 1996. write for info. (0-89464-937-X) Krieger.
Pratt, Darnell D., jt. auth. see Pratt, L. H.
Pratt, David. Curriculum: Design & Development. 503p. (C). 1980. text ed. 37.25 (0-15-516735-9) HB Coll Pubs.
— Curriculum Planning: A Handbook for Professionals. 480p. 1993. write for info. (0-15-501098-0) HB Coll Pubs.
— Fundamentals of Construction Estimating. LC 94-21788. 448p. 1995. 42.95 (0-8273-6135-1) Delmar.
— How to Find & Measure Bias in Textbooks. LC 76-168615. 64p. 1972. pap. 14.95 (0-87778-031-5) Educ Tech Pubns.
Pratt, David, jt. auth. see Gork, Mardi.
Pratt, David B., ed. see Feagins, Jim D., et al.
Pratt, David H. Researching British Probates, 1354-1858: A Guide to the Microfilm Collection of the Family History Library, Northern England, Province of York. LC 92-18338. (Illus.). 240p. 1992. 75.00 (0-8420-2420-4) Scholarly Res Inc.
Pratt, David T., jt. auth. see Heiser, William H.
***Pratt, Debora C.** Celebrating Me & My World: A Unitarian Universalist Preschool Curriculum. Hoertdoerfer, Patricia, ed. 1995. pap. 30.00 (1-55896-328-6) Unitarian Univ.
Pratt, Derek. Discovering London's Canals. 1989. pap. 25.00 (0-85263-901-5, Pub. by Shire UK) St Mut.
Pratt-Dewey, Beth. One Hundred Twenty-Eight Ways to Say I Love You to Your Cat. LC 92-21919. 1993. 10.00 (0-688-11643-4) Morrow.
Pratt-Dewey, Beth, jt. auth. see Adler, Bill, Jr.
Pratt, Diana V. Legal Writing: A Systematic Approach. 2nd ed. LC 93-9682. (American Casebook Ser.). 414p. 1993. pap. text ed. 19.50 (0-314-01843-3) West Pub.
— Legal Writing: A Systematic Approach, Teacher's Manual to Accompany. 2nd ed. (American Casebook Ser.). 138p. (C). 1993. pap. text ed. 20.00 (0-314-02394-1) West Pub.
Pratt, Doug. Basics of Model Rocketry. 2nd ed. Spohn, Terry, ed. LC 92-46672. (RC Performance Ser.: No. 16). (Illus.). 64p. (Orig.). 1993. pap. 8.95 (0-89024-142-2) Kalmbach.
Pratt, Doug, ed. see Radio Control Car Action Editors.
Pratt, Douglas. How to Choose R-C Model Engines: How to Make the Right Choice for Your Plane, Boat, or Buggy. (Illus.). 128p. 1987. pap. 12.95 (0-87938-276-7) Motorbooks Intl.
— The Laser Video Disc Companion: A Guide to the High End Delivery System for Home Video. 2nd ed. LC 91-67114. 472p. 1992. pap. 24.95 (0-685-55372-8) Baseline Bks.
Pratt, Douglas H., et al. A Field Guide to the Birds of Hawaii & the Tropical Pacific. (Illus.). 640p. 1986. text ed. 75.00 (0-691-08402-5); pap. 32.50 (0-691-02399-9) Princeton U Pr.
Pratt, Douglas R. Advanced Guide to Radio Control Sport Flying. (Illus.). 128p. 1988. pap. 9.95 (0-8306-9360-2, 3060P) TAB Bks.
— The Beginner's Guide to Radio Control Sport Flying. (Illus.). 144p. 1988. pap. 9.95 (0-8306-9320-3, 3020P) TAB Bks.
Pratt, Edward E. Industrial Causes of Congestion of Population in New York City. LC 68-56682. (Columbia University. Studies in the Social Sciences: No. 109). reprint ed. 37.50 (0-404-51109-0) AMS Pr.
Pratt, Edwin A. History of Inland Transport & Communication in England. LC 68-58857. xii, 532p. 1970. reprint ed. 49.50 (0-678-05560-2) Kelley.
Pratt, Edwin J. E. J. Pratt on His Life & Poetry. Gingell, Susan, ed. LC 83-208681. (Collected Works of E. J. Pratt). 268p. reprint ed. pap. 76.40 (0-685-16057-2, 2056129) Bks Demand.
Pratt, Erik K. Selling Strategic Defense: Interests, Ideologies & the Arms Race. LC 89-24351. 180p. 1990. lib. bdg. 32.00 (1-55587-190-9) Lynne Rienner.
Pratt, Fevrel, jt. auth. see Sheets, Lucille.
Pratt, Fletcher. The Blue Star. 1981. pap. 2.50 (0-345-29852-7, Del Rey) Ballantine.
Pratt, Fletcher, jt. auth. see De Camp, L. Sprague.
Pratt, Frances H. La Belle Zoa; Or, the Insurrection of Haiti. LC 72-1820. (Black Heritage Library Collection). 1977. reprint ed. 15.95 (0-8369-9049-8) Ayer.
Pratt, Frank G., ed. see Forselles, Charles A.
Pratt, Frank G., ed. see Pratt, Verna E.
Pratt, Frank G., jt. auth. see Pratt, Verna E.
Pratt, Frank G., ed. see Pratt, Verna E. & Pratt, Frank G.
Pratt, Frank G., ed. see Pratt, Verna E.
Pratt, Frantz, comp. Haiti: Guide to the Periodical Literature in English, 1800-1990. LC 91-7572. (Bibliographies & Indexes in Latin American & Caribbean Studies: No. 1). 328p. 1991. text ed. 55.00 (0-313-27855-5, PHI, Greenwood Pr) Greenwood.
Pratt, G. E. & Brooks, G. T., eds. Juvenile Hormone Biochemistry. (Developments in Endocrinology Ser.: Vol. 15). 456p. 1982. 121.00 (0-444-80390-4) Elsevier.
Pratt, Geoff, jt. auth. see Pratt, Jean.
Pratt, George. The Dynamics of Harmony: Principles & Practice. 1984. 29.00 (0-335-10595-5, Open Univ Pr) Taylor & Francis.
— Enemy Ace: War Idyll. Helfer, Andrew, ed. (Illus.). 128p. (Orig.). 1991. pap. 14.95 (0-930289-78-1) DC Comics.
— Enemy Ace: War Idyll. (Illus.). 128p. (Orig.). 1992. reprint ed. pap. 14.99 (0-446-39365-7) Warner Bks.
— No Man's Land. Baisden, Greg, ed. (Illus.). 112p. 1992. text ed. 50.00 (1-879450-98-4); pap. text ed. 14.95 (1-879450-64-X) Tundra MA.
Pratt, George J., et al. A Clinical Hypnosis Primer. LC 79-92665. (C). 1984. 36.00 (0-930626-07-9) Psych & Consul Assocs.
— Clinical Hypnosis Primer. enl. rev. ed. LC 88-5566. 407p. 1988. text ed. 74.95 (0-471-61384-3) Wiley.
Pratt, Geraldine, jt. auth. see Hanson, Susan.
Pratt, Geraldine, jt. ed. see Harris, Richard.
Pratt, H. Douglas. Enjoying Birds in Hawaii. 208p. 1993. pap. 18.95 (0-935180-00-1) Mutual Pub HI.
Pratt, Helen G. China & Her Unfinished Revolution. LC 75-32327. (Studies in Chinese History & Civilization). 173p. 1977. reprint ed. text ed. 55.00 (0-313-26970-X, U6970, Greenwood Pr) Greenwood.
— The Hawaiians: An Island People. (Illus.). 214p. (YA). (gr. 6 up). 1991. reprint ed. pap. 9.95 (0-8048-1709-X) C E Tuttle.
Pratt, Henry J. Gray Agendas: Interest Groups & Public Pensions in Canada, Britain, & the United States. 300p. (C). 1993. text ed. 39.50 (0-472-10430-6) U of Mich Pr.
— The Gray Lobby. LC 75-43232. 1977. reprint ed. lib. bdg. 21.00 (0-226-67917-9, P876) U Ch Pr.
— The Liberalization of American Protestantism: A Case Study in Complex Organizations. LC 74-38837. 304p. reprint ed. pap. 86.70 (0-7837-3618-5, 2043484) Bks Demand.
***Pratt, Horace R.** Caring for the Poor: A Strategy for Self-Empowerment. 124p. (Orig.). (C). 1994. pap. write for info. (1-885591-10-1) Morris Pubng.
Pratt-Howe, Diana, jt. auth. see Garcia, Nicholas.
Pratt, Hugo. Banana Conga. Nantier, Terry, tr. (Corto Maltese Ser.). 96p. 1986. pap. 8.95 (0-918348-19-6, Comics Lit) NBM.
— The Early Years: 1904-1905. Gilbert, Erick, tr. (Corto Maltese Ser.). 48p. 1988. pap. 8.95 (0-918348-48-X, Comics Lit) NBM.
— Fable of Venice. Bell, Elizabeth, tr. (Corto Maltese Ser.: No. 8). 80p. 1990. pap. 10.95 (0-918348-96-X, Comics Lit) NBM.
— In Africa. Gilbert, Erick, tr. (Corto Maltese Ser.). 96p. 1987. pap. 8.95 (0-918348-38-2, Comics Lit) NBM.
— In Siberia. Bell, Elisabeth, tr. (Corto Maltese Ser.). 128p. (Orig.). 1988. pap. 10.95 (0-918348-57-9, Comics Lit) NBM.
— A Mid-Winter Morning's Dream. Nantier, T., tr. (Corto Maltese Ser.). 112p. 1987. pap. 8.95 (0-918348-29-3, Comics Lit) NBM.
— Voodoo for the President. Nantier, Terry, tr. (Corto Maltese Ser.). 96p. 1986. pap. 8.95 (0-918348-25-0, Comics Lit) NBM.
Pratt, Hugo, jt. auth. see Manara, Milo.
***Pratt, Ian.** Artificial Intelligence. (Macmillan Computer Science Ser.). (Illus.). 280p. (C). 1994. pap. text ed. 35.00 (0-333-59755-9, Pub. by Macmill Press UK) Scholium Intl.
Pratt, J. & Gibbons, J. D. Concepts of Nonparametric Theory. (Series in Statistics). (Illus.). 462p. 1981. 59.50 (0-387-90582-0) Spr-Verlag.
Pratt, J., jt. auth. see Fuchs, N.
Pratt, J. G. On the Evaluation of Verbal Material in Parapsychology. LC 70-94866. (Parapsychological Monograph Ser.: No. 10). 1969. pap. 5.00 (0-912328-14-2) Parapsych Foun.
Pratt, J. H. Life on the Ridge. (Illus.). 170p. 1987. pap. 9.95 (1-55787-021-7, NY76064, Empire State Bks) Hrt of the Lakes.
— Saga of the Ridge. 224p. 1983. pap. 9.50 (1-55787-023-3, NY76001) Hrt of the Lakes.
Pratt, J. N. Electrotransport in Metals & Alloys. 1973. 36.00 (0-87849-502-9, Pub. by Trans Tech GW) LPS Dist Ctr.
Pratt, J. R., jt. ed. see Cairns, John, Jr.
***Pratt, James & Kulsrud, William.** Corporate Partnership Estate & Gift Taxation, 1994. 7th ed. (C). 1993. text ed. 62.95 (0-256-10940-0) Irwin.
— Federal Taxation 1994. 7th ed. (C). 1993. text ed. 64.95 (0-256-10938-9) Irwin.
— Individual Taxation, 1994. 7th ed. (C). 1993. text ed. 61.95 (0-256-10939-7) Irwin.
***Pratt, James & Kulsrud, William N.** Individual Taxation. 8th ed. 1248p. (C). 1994. text ed. 66.95 (0-256-12724-7) Irwin.
Pratt, James B. Adventures in Philosophy & Religion. LC 75-3323. reprint ed. 16.00 (0-404-59319-4) AMS Pr.
— The Pilgrimage of Buddhism & a Buddhist Pilgrimage. LC 75-3325. (Philosophy America Ser.). reprint ed. 94.50 (0-404-59320-8) AMS Pr.
— Pilgrimage of Buddhism & a Buddhist Pilgrimage, 2 vols., Set. (C). 1993. reprint ed. 60.00 (81-85326-47-9, Pub. by Vintage II) S Asia.
— The Psychology of Religious Belief. LC 75-3326. (Philosophy America Ser.). reprint ed. 54.00 (0-404-59321-6) AMS Pr.
— What Is Pragmatism? LC 75-3327. reprint ed. 36.00 (0-404-59322-4) AMS Pr.
Pratt, James N. Tea Lover's Treasury. rev. ed. (One Hundred One Production Ser.). 238p. 1995. reprint ed. pap. 12.95 (1-56426-565-X) Cole Group.
Pratt, James W. & Kulsrud, William. Corporate, Partnership, Estate & Gift Taxation, 1993. 1120p. 1992. text ed. 61.95 (0-256-10842-0) Irwin.
***Pratt, James W. & Kulsrud, William N.** Corporate, Partnership, Estate, & Gift Taxation. 8th ed. 1088p. (C). 1994. text ed. 67.95 (0-256-12739-5) Irwin Prof Pubng.
— Federal Taxation, 1995 Edition. 8th ed. 1616p. (C). 1994. text ed. 68.95 (0-256-12712-3) Irwin Prof Pubng.
Pratt, James W., et al. Individual Taxation, 1988. 213p. (C). 1987. 13.50 (0-256-06469-5) Irwin.
Pratt, James W., et al, eds. Corporate, Partnership, Estate & Gift Taxation, 1992. (C). 1991. text ed. 61.95 (0-256-10043-8) Irwin.
Pratt, Jamie. Financial Accounting. 2nd ed. LC 93-13807. (C). 1994. text ed. 62.95 (0-538-82894-3, AO79BA) S-W Pub.
— Financial Accounting. LC 89-29574. 1071p. reprint ed. pap. 180.00 (0-7837-4741-1, 2044550) Bks Demand.
***Pratt, Jane & Pryor, Kelli.** For Real: The Uncensored Truth about America's Teenagers. 256p. 1995. pap. 9.95 (0-7868-8064-3) Hyperion.
Pratt, Jean & Pratt, Geoff. Suffolk Rambles. 64p. 1987. 50.00 (0-905392-85-X) St Mut.
***Pratt, Jeremy M.** Cessna 150. LC 95-16303. (Pilot's Guide Ser.). 1995. write for info. (1-56027-213-9) Av Suppl & Acad.
— Cessna 152. LC 95-16302. (Pilot's Guide Ser.). 1995. write for info. (1-56027-212-0) Av Suppl & Acad.
— Cessna 172. LC 95-16301. (Pilot's Guide Ser.). 1995. write for info. (1-56027-211-2) Av Suppl & Acad.
— PA-28 Warrior. (Pilot's Guide Ser.). 1995. write for info. (1-56027-214-7) Av Suppl & Acad.
— PA-28 Cherokee. LC 95-15210. (Pilot's Guide Ser.). 1995. write for info. (1-56027-215-5) Av Suppl & Acad.
— PA-38 Tomahawk. LC 95-15209. (Pilot's Guide Ser.). 1995. write for info. (1-56027-216-3) Av Suppl & Acad.
***Pratt, Joanne & West, Gill.** Pressure Garments: A Manual on Their Design & Fabrication. LC 94-33550. (Illus.). 1995. pap. 19.95 (0-7506-2064-1) Buttrwrth-Heinemann.
Pratt, Joanne H., et al. Environmental Encounter: Experiences in Decision-Making for the Built & the Natural Environment. (Illus.). 1979. pap. 14.95 (0-9601902-0-1) Reverchon Pr.
Pratt, John & Silverman, Susanne. Responding to Constraint: Policy & Management in Higher Education. 160p. 1988. 95.00 (0-335-09500-3, Open Univ Pr) Taylor & Francis.
Pratt, John, et al. Introduction to Statistical Decision Theory. (Illus.). 500p. 1994. 65.00x (0-262-16144-3) MIT Pr.
Pratt, John C. The Laotian Fragments. (Vietnam Ser.). 240p. 1985. pap. 3.50 (0-380-69841-2) Avon.
— The Royal Laotian Air Force, 1954-1970. 184p. 1993. reprint ed. pap. 20.00 (0-923135-50-2) Dalley Bk Service.
— Writing from Scratch: The Essay. 144p. 1991. pap. text ed. 10.95 (0-8226-3009-5) Littlefield.
Pratt, John C., ed. see Kesey, Ken.
Pratt, John T. War & Politics in China. LC 78-146869. (Select Bibliographies Reprint Ser.). 1977. reprint ed. 24.95 (0-8369-5636-2) Ayer.
Pratt, John W. & Zeckhauser, Richard J. Principals & Agents: The Structure of Business. 250p. 1991. pap. 16.95 (0-87584-256-9) Harvard Busn.
Pratt, John W. & Zeckhauser, Richard J., eds. Principals & Agents: The Structure of Business. 1991. pap. text ed. 16.95 (0-07-103308-4) McGraw.
Pratt, John W., ed. see Satellite Symposium on Statistical Aspects of Pollution Problems (1971: Harvard Business School) Staff.
Pratt-Johnson, Betty. One Hundred Forty-One Dives: In the Protected Waters of Washington & British Columbia. 2nd ed. (Illus.). 394p. (Orig.). 1976. write for info. (0-318-59867-1) Gordon Soules Bk.
— One Hundred Forty-One Dives in the Protected Waters of Washington & B. C. (Illus.). 394p. (Orig.). 1991. pap. 24.95 (0-919574-20-3) Gordon Soules Bk.
— Whitewater Trips & Hot Springs in the Kootenays of British Columbia: For Kayakers, Canoeists & Rafters. (Illus.). 185p. (Orig.). 1989. pap. 16.95 (0-921009-18-6) Adventure WA.
— Whitewater Trips for Kayakers, Canoeists & Rafters in British Columbia: Greater Vancouver Through Whistler, Okanagan & Thompson River Regions. (Illus.). 215p. (Orig.). 1986. pap. 16.95 (0-931397-08-1) Adventure WA.
— Whitewater Trips for Kayakers, Canoeists & Rafters on Vancouver Island. LC 83-26190. (Illus.). 127p. (Orig.). 1984. pap. 8.95 (0-914718-90-8) Adventure WA.
Pratt-Johnson, John A. & Tillson, Geraldine. Management of Strabismus & Amblyopia. LC 93-28854. 1993. 49.00 (0-86577-499-4) Thieme Med Pubs.
Pratt, Jon, jt. ed. see Davies, Norah.
Pratt, Jon, et al. Minnesota Philanthropic Support for Disadvantaged People 1984. 45p. (Orig.). 1985. pap. 6.00 (0-317-90474-4) MN Council Nonprofits.
— Minnesota Philanthropy & Disadvantaged People. 56p. (Orig.). 1986. pap. 10.00 (0-317-90473-6) MN Council Nonprofits.
Pratt, Joseph. The Growth of a Refining Region, Vol. 4. Porter, Glenn, ed. LC 77-7797. (Industrial Development & the Social Fabric Ser.). 313p. (Orig.). 1980. 73.25 (0-89232-090-7) Jai Pr.
Pratt, Joseph, jt. auth. see Galambos, Louis.
Pratt, Joseph A., jt. auth. see Buenger, Walter L.
Pratt, Joseph A., jt. auth. see Castaneda, Christopher J.
Pratt, Joseph A., jt. auth. see Lipartito, Kenneth J.
Pratt, Josiah, ed. Thought of the Evangelical Leaders: John Newton, Thomas Scott, Charles Simeon, Etc. 1978. 29.95 (0-85151-270-4) Banner of Truth.
Pratt, Judith, ed. The Biological Bases of Drug Tolerance & Dependence. (Neuroscience Perspectives Ser.). (Illus.). 301p. 1992. text ed. 69.95 (0-12-564250-4) Acad Pr.
Pratt, K. J. & Bennett, S. G. Elements of Personnel Management. 2nd ed. 384p. 1990. pap. 32.50 (0-412-02721-6, A4468, Chap & Hall NY) Chapman & Hall.
***Pratt, Karen, ed.** Shifts & Transpositions in Medieval Narrative: A Festschrift for Dr. Elspeth Kennedy. (Illus.). 256p. (C). 1994. text ed. 53.00 (0-85991-421-6, DS Brewer) Boydell & Brewer.
***Pratt, Keith.** Korean Painting. (Images of Asia Ser.). (Illus.). 96p. 1995. text ed. 16.95 (0-19-585885-9) OUP.
Pratt, Kerry C., jt. auth. see Anderson, John R.
Pratt, Kristen J. Walk in the Rainforest. (Illus.). 32p. (J). 1992. 16.95 (1-878265-99-7); pap. 7.95 (1-878265-53-9) Dawn CA.
Pratt, Kristin. Un Paseo Por el Bosque Lluvioso: A Walk in the Rainforest. Kohen, Clara, tr. (Illus.). 32p. (ENG & SPA.). (J). (ps-5). 1993. pap. 7.95 (1-883220-02-5) Dawn CA.
***Pratt, Kristin J.** Bajo Las Olas. Ada, Alma F., tr. (Illus.). 44p. (Orig.). (J). (ps-7). 1995. pap. 7.95 (1-883220-30-0) Dawn CA.
— A Swim Through the Sea. (Illus.). 44p. (Orig.). (J). (ps-5). 1994. 16.95 (1-883220-03-3); pap. 7.95 (1-883220-04-1) Dawn CA.
Pratt, L. H. & Pratt, Darnell D. Alice Malsenior Walker: An Annotated Bibliography. 162p. 1988. text ed. 49.95 (0-313-27705-2, PMW/, Greenwood Pr) Greenwood.
Pratt, L. J., ed. The Physical Oceanography of Sea Straits. (C). 1990. lib. bdg. 197.50 (0-7923-0905-7) Kluwer Ac.
Pratt, Lauren, ed. see Tenney, James.
Pratt, Laurence. Saga of a Paper Mill. LC 35-4692. 77p. reprint ed. pap. 25.00 (0-317-41725-8, 2052050) Bks Demand.
Pratt, Lee. Directory of Health, Education & Research Journals. LC 83-49214. 144p. 1984. 29.50 (0-8386-3213-0) Fairleigh Dickinson.
Pratt, Leonard, tr. see Shen Fu.
Pratt, Lester A. Bank Frauds: Their Detection & Prevention. 2nd ed. LC 65-21814. 282p. reprint ed. pap. 80.40 (0-8357-5960-1, 2055178) Bks Demand.
Pratt, Linda W., jt. auth. see Stone, Charles P.
Pratt, Lindsay L. & Quinn, Dominic. Now Hear This: A Consumer's Guide to Testing for Hearing Loss, & the Selection & Purchase of a Suitable Hearing Aid. LC 91-76438. 100p. (Orig.). 1991. pap. 9.95 (0-9630765-0-7) Forum.
Pratt, Lisa M., jt. ed. see Katz, Barry J.
Pratt, Lisa M., et al, eds. Geochemistry of Organic Matter in Sediments & Sedimentary Rocks. 100p. 1992. pap. text ed. 37.80 (1-56576-000-X) SEPM.
Pratt, Louis. Sing Praises to His Name. Sherer, Michael L., ed. (Orig.). 1986. pap. 7.10 (0-89536-831-5, 6845) CSS OH.
Pratt, Louis H. James Baldwin. (United States Authors Ser.). 160p. 1978. text ed. 20.95 (0-8057-7193-X, Pub. by Royal Botanic Garden UK) Macmillan.
Pratt, Louis H., jt. ed. see Standley, Fred L.
Pratt, Louise. Lying & Poetry from Homer to Pindar: Falsehood & Deception in Archaic Poetics. LC 92-45214. (Monographs in Classical Antiquities). 180p. 1993. text ed. 37.50 (0-472-10417-9) U of Mich Pr.
Pratt, Mara L. American History Stories: You Never Read in School, but Should Have. 150p. 1993. pap. text ed. 7.95 (0-9640546-0-4) Randall UT.
Pratt, Mary L. Imperial Eyes: Studies in Travel Writing & Transculturization. LC 91-21435. (Illus.). 304p. (Orig.). 1992. 55.00 (0-415-02675-X, A3111); pap. 16.95 (0-415-06095-8, A3115) Routledge.
— Toward a Speech Act Theory of Literary Discourse. LC 76-26424. 255p. reprint ed. pap. 72.70 (0-685-44461-9, 2056732) Bks Demand.
Pratt, Mary L., jt. auth. see Millones, Luis.
Pratt, Mary L., jt. auth. see Traugott, Elizabeth C.
Pratt, Michael. Great Houses of Central Europe: Czechoslovakia, Hungary & Poland. (Illus.). 380p. 1991. 95.00 (0-89659-942-6) Abbeville Pr.
Pratt, Michael C. Meditations for Mother. rev. ed. Mouton, Boyce, ed. 50p. 1975. pap. 1.99 (0-89900-651-5) College Pr Pub.
Pratt, Michael W. & Norris, Joan E. The Social Psychology of Aging: A Cognitive Perspective. (Understanding Aging Ser.). (Illus.). 272p. 1994. 54.95 (1-55786-491-8); pap. 24.95 (1-55786-492-6) Blackwell Pubs.
Pratt, Minnie B. Crime Against Nature. LC 90-2778. 128p. (Orig.). 1990. 18.95 (0-932379-73-7); pap. 8.95 (0-932379-72-9) Firebrand Bks.
— Rebellion: Essays 1980-1991. LC 91-35238. 248p. (Orig.). 1991. lib. bdg. 22.95 (1-56341-007-9); pap. 10.95 (1-56341-006-0) Firebrand Bks.
— S-HE. LC 95-3894. 1995. write for info. (1-56341-060-5); pap. write for info. (1-56341-059-1) Firebrand Bks.
— We Say We Love Each Other. LC 92-24947. 102p. (Orig.). 1992. reprint ed. lib. bdg. 18.95 (1-56341-024-9); reprint ed. pap. 8.95 (1-56341-023-0) Firebrand Bks.
Pratt, Neal E. Clinical Musculoskeletal Anatomy. (Illus.). 333p. 1991. text ed. 39.95 (0-397-54825-7, Lippincott Medical) Lippincott.
Pratt, Noel. Homeopathic Prescribing. LC 82-84324. 1983. reprint ed. pap. 8.95 (0-87983-325-4) Keats.
Pratt, Norma F. Morris Hillquit: A Political History of an American Jewish Socialist. LC 78-55349. (Illus.). 272p. 1979. text ed. 55.00 (0-313-20526-4, PMH/, Greenwood Pr) Greenwood.
Pratt, Norman T. Seneca's Drama. LC 82-23791. viii, 230p. 1983. 34.95 (0-8078-1555-1) U of NC Pr.
***Pratt, Orson.** The Seer. 320p. (C). 1994. 24.95 (0-910523-18-5) Grandin Bk Co.
Pratt, Orson, ed. see Smith, Joseph.
Pratt, P. W., ed. Laboratory Procedures for Veterinary Technicians. 2nd ed. LC 92-81927. (Illus.). 600p. 1992. 29.00 (0-939674-38-6) Am Vet Pubns.
— Medical, Surgical & Anesthetic Nursing for Veterinary Technicians. LC 94-70822. 621p. 1994. 29.00 (0-939674-49-1) Am Vet Pubns.

P Q

— Review Questions & Answers for Veterinary Boards: Ancillary Topics. LC 93-70151. 311p. 1993. 33.00 (*0-939674-43-2*) Am Vet Pubns.
— Review Questions & Answers for Veterinary Boards: Basic Sciences. LC 93-70147. 271p. 1993. 33.00 (*0-939674-39-4*) Am Vet Pubns.
— Review Questions & Answers for Veterinary Boards: Clinical Sciences. LC 93-70148. 287p. 1993. 33.00 (*0-939674-40-8*) Am Vet Pubns.
— Review Questions & Answers for Veterinary Boards: Large Animal Medicine & Surgery. LC 93-70150. 313p. 1993. 33.00 (*0-939674-42-4*) Am Vet Pubns.
— Review Questions & Answers for Veterinary Boards: Small Animal Medicine & Surgery. LC 93-70149. 363p. 1993. 33.00 (*0-939674-41-6*) Am Vet Pubns.
— Review Questions & Answers for Veterinary Technicians. LC 93-70152. 409p. 1993. 29.00 (*0-939674-44-0*) Am Vet Pubns.

Pratt, P. W., ed. see Pedersen, Niels C.

Pratt, Pamela, ed. Woman in the Window. LC 91-62409. 160p. (Orig.). 1993. pap. 9.95 (*1-877978-32-9*, STARbks Pr) Woldt.

Pratt, Parley P. Autobiography of Parley P. Pratt. LC 85-10264. (Illus.). 447p. 1994. pap. 13.95 (*0-87579-841-1*) Deseret Bk.

***Pratt, Paul.** Attitude Awareness: Creating Your Own Healthy Outlook. LC 94-69092. 160p. (Orig.). 1995. pap. 12.95 (*0-9643578-0-1*) C O R E Ent.

***Pratt, Paula B.** Architecture. LC 94-23499. (World History Ser.). (J). 1995. 16.95 (*1-56006-286-X*) Lucent Bks.
— The End of Apartheid in South Africa. LC 94-37202. (Overview Ser.). (YA). 1995. 16.95 (*1-56006-170-7*) Lucent Bks.
— Maps: Plotting Places on the Globe. (Encyclopedia of Discovery & Invention Ser.). (Illus.). 112p. (J). (gr. 5-9). 1995. lib. bdg. 17.95 (*1-56006-255-X*, 255X) Lucent Bks.
— Martha Graham. LC 94-10883. (Importance of... Biographies Ser.). (Illus.). 112p. (J). (gr. 5-8). 1995. 16.95 (*1-56006-056-5*) Lucent Bks.

Pratt, Peter, ed. History of Japan: Compiled from the Records of the English East India Company at the Instance of the Court of Directors, 2 vols., I. LC 79-65369. (Studies in Japanese History & Civilization). 518p. 1979. reprint ed. text ed. 75.00 (*0-313-26914-9*, U6914) Greenwood.
— History of Japan: Compiled from the Records of the English East India Company at the Instance of the Court of Directors, 2 vols., Vol. 2. LC 79-65369. (Studies in Japanese History & Civilization). 518p. 1979. reprint ed. text ed. 65.00 (*0-313-26915-7*, U6915) Greenwood.

Pratt, Peter P. Archaeology of the Oneida Iroquois. (Occasional Publications in Northeastern Anthropology: No. 1). 1976. 5.50 (*0-686-30586-8*) Fund Anthrop.
— Archaeology of the Oneida Iroquois, Vol. 1. (Occasional Publications in Northeastern Anthropology: No. 1). (Illus.). xii, 303p. 5.50 (*0-318-22319-8*) F Pierce College.

Pratt, Phil. A Guide to SQL. (C). 1989. pap. text ed. write for info. (*0-318-65187-4*, BF3364) S-W Pub.
— Microcomputer Database Management Using dBASE IV Version 1.1. 576p. (C). 1992. 5.25 hd, pap. text ed. 39.95 (*0-87835-786-6*); 3.5 hd, pap. text ed. 39.95 (*0-87835-825-0*) Boyd & Fraser.

Pratt, Phil & Adamski, Joseph. Database Systems: Management & Design. 2nd ed. 848p. 1991. 38.00 (*0-87835-579-0*) Boyd & Fraser.

Pratt, Philip. The Concepts of Database Management. LC 94-10049. 1994. write for info. (*0-87709-779-8*) Boyd & Fraser.

***Pratt, Philip & Timmer, Marybeth.** His Grandfather's Cap. LC 94-24032. (Illus.). 80p. (Orig.). (J). (gr. 4-6). 1995. pap. 6.95 (*0-942963-62-8*) Distinctive Pub.

***Pratt, Philip J.** A Guide to SQL. 3rd ed. LC 94-10491. 191p. 1995. pap. 18.95 (*0-87709-520-5*) Boyd & Fraser.
— Microcomputer Database Management Using dBASE IV, Version 2.0. LC 94-1014. 1994. write for info. (*0-87709-513-2*) Boyd & Fraser.
— Microcomputer Database Management Using dBASE IV, Version 2.0. LC 94-1014. 539p. 1994. pap. 44.75 (*0-87709-539-6*) Boyd & Fraser.
— Microcomputer Database Management Using Microsoft Access. 1994. 40.95 (*0-87709-386-5*) Boyd & Fraser.
— Microcomputer Database Management Using Paradox for Windows. 1994. pap. 40.95 (*0-87709-401-2*) Boyd & Fraser.
— Microcomputer Database Management Using Paradox 4.0. LC 92-29991. 1993. write for info. (*0-87835-962-1*) Boyd & Fraser.
— Using dBase IV, Version 1.1. 1992. pap. 22.95 (*0-87835-824-2*) Boyd & Fraser.
— Using dBASE IV, Version 2.0. LC 94-1006. 1994. write for info. (*0-87709-514-0*) Boyd & Fraser.
— Using dBase IV, Version 2.0. 1994. pap. 24.95 (*0-87709-540-X*) Boyd & Fraser.
— Using Microsoft Access. 1994. 24.95 (*0-87709-391-1*) Boyd & Fraser.
— Using Paradox for Windows. 1994. 24.95 (*0-87709-396-2*) Boyd & Fraser.
— Using Paradox 4.0. LC 92-27539. (C). 1994. pap. 25.95 (*0-87835-960-5*, BF9605) S-W Pub.

Pratt, Philip J. & Adamski, Joseph J. Database Systems: Management & Design. 3rd ed. LC 93-1901. (C). 1994. text ed. 53.95 (*0-87709-115-3*, BF1153) S-W Pub.

Pratt, Philip J. & Last, Mary Z. Advanced dBASE IV Programming. LC 92-35336. 554p. 1992. pap. 39.25 (*0-87835-958-3*) Boyd & Fraser.
— Microcomputer Database Management Using Paradox for Windows. 1994. write for info. (*0-318-72549-5*) Boyd & Fraser.

***Pratt, Phillip.** Using Microsoft Access, 2.0. 1994. pap. 22.95 (*0-87709-565-5*) Boyd & Fraser.

Pratt, Pierre. Follow that Hat! (Illus.). 32p. (J). (ps-2). 1992. lib. bdg. 15.95 (*1-55037-261-0*, Pub. by Annick CN); pap. 5.95 (*1-55037-259-9*, Pub. by Annick CN) Firefly Bks Ltd.
— Leon sans Son Chapeau: Follow That Hat! (Illus.). 32p. (FRE.). (J). (ps-2). 1992. 15.95 (*1-55037-263-7*, Pub. by Annick CN); pap. 6.95 (*1-55037-262-9*, Pub. by Annick CN) Firefly Bks Ltd.

Pratt, R. K. & Tell. Ora Con los Ojos Abiegtos. 198p. 1994. 8.00 (*0-939125-67-6*) Evangelical Lit.

Pratt, Ray. Rhythm & Resistance: Explorations in the Political Uses of Popular Music. LC 89-16197. (Media & Society Ser.). 248p. 1990. text ed. 55.00 (*0-275-92624-9*, C2624, Praeger Pubs) Greenwood.
— Rhythm & Resistance: Political Uses of American Popular Music. LC 93-30228. 256p. 1994. pap. 16.95 (*1-56098-351-5*) Smithsonian.

***Pratt, Richard.** El Ingles de Los Negocios. Anton, Francisco J., tr. (Illus.). 427p. 1984. 19.95 (*2-7005-0111-X*, Pub. by ASSIMIL FR) Distribks Inc.
— El Ingles de Los Negocios, Incl. 3 60-min. cassettes. Anton, Francisco J., tr. 1984. audio write for info. (*2-7005-1307-X*, Pub. by ASSIMIL FR) Distribks Inc.

Pratt, Richard, jt. ed. see Smith, Zachary.

Pratt, Richard H. Battlefield & Classroom: Four Decades with the American Indian, 1867-1904. Utley, Robert M., ed. LC 64-20931. (Yale Western Americana Ser.: Vol. 6). 412p. reprint ed. pap. 117.50 (*0-8357-5997-0*, 2051681) Bks Demand.
— Battlefield & Classroom: Four Decades with the American Indian, 1876-1904. Utley, Robert M., ed. LC 86-25019. (Landmark Edition Ser.). xx, 390p. 1987. reprint ed. 35.00 (*0-8032-3679-4*) U of Nebr Pr.

Pratt, Richard L., Jr. Designed for Dignity: What God Has Made It Possible For You to Be. 224p. 1993. 14.99 (*0-87552-380-3*) Presby & Reformed.
— Every Thought Captive. 1979. pap. 6.99 (*0-87552-352-8*) Presby & Reformed.
— He Gave Us Stories: The Bible Student's Guide to Interpreting Old Testament Narratives. 494p. 1993. reprint ed. pap. 12.99 (*0-87552-379-X*) Presby & Reformed.
— Pray with Your Eyes Open. LC 87-2762. 1987. pap. 7.99 (*0-87552-378-1*) Presby & Reformed.

Pratt, Richard T., jt. auth. see Johnson, Ramon E.

Pratt, Robert A. The Color of Their Skin: A History of School Desegregation in Richmond, Virginia, 1954-89. (Carter G. Woodson Institute Series in Black Studies). (C). 1992. text ed. 24.95 (*0-8139-1372-1*) U Pr of Va.
— The Color of Their Skin: Education & Race in Richmond, Virginia, 1954-89. 151p. (C). 1994. pap. text ed. 10.95 (*0-8139-1481-7*) U Pr of Va.

***Pratt, Robert J.** HIV & AIDS: A Strategy for Nursing Care. 4th ed. 320p. 1995. pap. text ed. 45.95 (*1-56593-398-2*, 0820) Singular Publishing.

Pratt, Roger. The Architecture of Sir Roger Pratt. Gunther, R. T., ed. LC 72-177516. (Illus.). 1979. reprint ed. 23.95 (*0-405-08862-0*, Pub. by Blom Pubns UK) Ayer.

Pratt, Rosalie, jt. ed. see Gray, Genevieve.

Pratt, Rosalie R., ed. Fourth International Symposium on Justice in Rehabilitation & Human Well-Being. (Illus.). 214p. (Orig.). 1987. lib. bdg. 47.50 (*0-8191-5969-7*, Music Education for the Handicapped Inc); pap. text ed. 25.50 (*0-8191-5970-0*, Music Education for the Handicapped Inc) U Pr of Amer.
— Music Therapy & Music Education of the Handicapped - Developments & Limitations in Practice & Research: Proceedings of the Fifth International Congress, Leeuwenhorst Congress Center, Noordwijkerhout, The Netherlands, August 23-27, 1989. LC 92-12557. 190p. 1993. 14.95 (*0-918812-73-9*) MMB Music.

Pratt, Rosalie R., pref. Music Therapy & Music in Special Education, Vol. Two: The International State of the Art. (ISME Edition Ser.: No. 4). 176p. (Orig.). 1989. pap. 11.95 (*0-918812-62-3*, ST 191) MMB Music.

Pratt, Rosalie R. & Moog, Helmut, eds. First Research Seminar of the ISME Commission on Music Therapy & Music in Special Education. (Illus.). 172p. 1989. pap. 11.95 (*0-918812-60-7*, ST 192) MMB Music.

Pratt, Sally R., jt. auth. see Dressel, Paul L.

Pratt, Sarah. Russian Metaphysical Romanticism: The Poetry of Tiutchev & Boratynskii. LC 82-42863. 272p. 1984. 37.50 (*0-8047-1188-7*) Stanford U Pr.

Pratt, Sereno S. The Work of Wall Street: An Account of the Functions, Methods & History of the New York Money & Stock Markets. (Third Edition, Revised & Enlarged) LC 75-2661. (Wall Street & the Security Market Ser.). 1975. reprint ed. 41.95 (*0-405-06985-5*) Ayer.

Pratt, Shannon. Valuing a Business: The Analysis & Appraisal of Closely Held Companies. 2nd ed. 737p. 1988. text ed. 92.50 (*1-55623-127-X*) Irwin Prof Pubng.
— Valuing Small Businesses & Professional Practices. 2nd ed. 720p. 1993. 92.50 (*1-55623-551-8*) Irwin Prof Pubng.

Pratt, Shannon P. Valuing a Property Management Company. 69p. 1988. pap. 32.00 (*0-944298-20-6*) Inst Real Estate.
— Valuing Small Businesses & Professional Practices. 1985. 90.00 (*0-87094-598-X*) Irwin Prof Pubng.

***Pratt, Shannon P., et al.** Valuing a Business: Analysis & Appraisal of Closely Held Companies. 3rd ed. 785p. 1995. text ed. 95.00 (*1-55623-971-8*) Irwin Prof Pubng.

Pratt, Sherman W. Decisive Battles of the Korean War. 1992. 24.95 (*0-533-09584-0*) Vantage.

Pratt, Shirley. Don't Wait to Be Rescued: Transcending the Death Experience. LC 91-90036. 179p. (Orig.). 1991. pap. 8.50 (*0-9628951-0-5*) S Pratt.

Pratt, Stanley E., et al, eds. Pratt's Guide to Venture Capital Sources, 1993. 17th ed. 746p. 1993. 195.00 (*0-914470-65-5*) SDC Pubng.

Pratt, T. K. Dictionary of Prince Edward Island English. 224p. (C). 1988. 30.00 (*0-8020-5781-0*) U of Toronto Pr.

Pratt, Terrence W. Pascal: A New Introduction to Computer Science. 672p. 1989. pap. text ed. 61.00 (*0-13-654286-7*) P-H.
— Programming Languages: Design & Implementation. 2nd ed. (Illus.). 624p. 1983. text ed. 71.00 (*0-13-730580-X*) P-H.

Pratt, Theodore. The Barefoot Mailman. large type ed. 1970. 15.95 (*0-85456-010-6*) Ulverscroft.

Pratt, Timothy. Satellite Communications: Self Study Course Package. (Illus.). 1989. student ed, teacher ed 299.00 (*0-87942-459-1*, HL0410-1) Inst Electrical.

Pratt, Timothy & Postian, Charles W. Satellite Communications. 472p. 1986. Net. text ed. write for info. (*0-471-87837-5*) Wiley.

***Pratt, Verna E.** Alaska's Wild Berries: And Berry-Like Fruit. Pratt, Frank G., ed. (Illus.). 128p. (Orig.). 1995. pap. 9.95 (*0-9623192-4-4*) Alaskakrafts Pub.
— Field Guide to Alaskan Wildflowers: Commonly Seen along Highways & Byways. Pratt, Frank G., ed. LC 89-84536. (Illus.). 144p. (Orig.). 1990. pap. 13.95 (*0-9623192-0-1*) Alaskakrafts Pub.
— Wildflowers along the Alaska Highway: From Dawson Creek, BC - to Delta Jct., AK & on to Fairbanks, AK. Pratt, Frank G., ed. LC 91-77654. (Illus.). 224p. (Orig.). 1991. pap. 19.95 (*0-9623192-1-X*) Alaskakrafts Pub.

***Pratt, Verna E. & Pratt, Frank G.** Wildflowers of Denali National Park. Pratt, Frank G., ed. LC 92-75672. (Illus.). 176p. (Orig.). 1993. pap. 16.95 (*0-9623192-2-8*) Alaskakrafts Pub.

Pratt, Vernon. The Philosophy of the Social Sciences. 1978. pap. 14.95 (*0-415-04288-7*, NO. 2392) Routledge Chapman & Hall.

Pratt, Virginia A. Coming Alive: How Mates Help Each Other Solve Problems & Find Freedom & Intimacy. LC 88-83618. 171p. (Orig.). 1989. pap. 9.50 (*0-9622749-3-3*) Green Twig Pr.
— Coming Alive: How Mates Help Each Other Solve Problems & Find Freedom & Intimacy. Best, Walter, ed. 171p. (Orig.). 1989. pap. text ed. write for info. (*0-9622749-0-9*) Green Twig Pr.

Pratt, W. K. Digital Image Processing. 2nd ed. 698p. 1991. text ed. 98.00 (*0-471-85766-1*) Wiley.

Pratt, W. K., jt. ed. see Arps, R. B.

Pratt, Waldo S. The Music of the Pilgrims: A Description of the Psalm-Book Brought to Plymouth in Sixteen Twenty. 1980. lib. bdg. 59.00 (*0-8490-3180-X*) Gordon Pr.
— Musical Ministries in the Church. LC 74-24193. reprint ed. 36.00 (*0-404-13095-X*) AMS Pr.
— The New Encyclopedia of Music & Musicians. 969p. 1990. reprint ed. lib. bdg. 129.00 (*0-7812-9009-0*) Rprt Serv.

Pratt, Walter F. Privacy in Britain. LC 76-50289. 266p. 1979. 36.50 (*0-8387-2030-7*) Bucknell U Pr.

Pratt, Wendy B., jt. auth. see Schwartz, Seymour.

Pratt, William. The Fugitive Poets: Modern Southern Poetry in Perspective. rev. ed. (Southern Classics Ser.). 159p. (C). 1991. pap. 10.95 (*1-879941-00-7*) J S Sanders.
— Piks Foundation. 300p. 1995. 55.00 (*1-884777-03-1*) Manning Pubns.
— Piks Foundation: A C Programmer's Guide. 1995. text ed. 55.00 (*0-13-172339-1*) P-H.

Pratt, William & Richardson, Robert, eds. Homage to Imagism. LC 91-11028. (Studies in Modern Literature: No. 20). 1992. 37.50 (*0-404-61590-2*) AMS Pr.

Pratt, William, ed. see Hibbett, T. C.

Pratt, William, ed. see MacKaye, Percy & Torrence, Ridgely.

Pratt, William B. & Fekety, Robert. The Antimicrobial Drugs. LC 84-29603. (Illus.). 640p. 1986. text ed. 49.95 (*0-19-503560-7*); pap. text ed. 35.00 (*0-19-503561-5*) OUP.

Pratt, William B. & Taylor, Palmer, eds. Principles of Drug Action. 3rd ed. (Illus.). 834p. 1990. text ed. 63.50 (*0-443-08676-1*) Churchill.

Pratt, William B., et al. The Anticancer Drugs. 2nd ed. (Illus.). 360p. 1994. 69.95 (*0-19-506738-X*); pap. 39.95 (*0-19-506739-8*) OUP.

Pratt, William K. & Marton, L. L., eds. Advances in Electronics & Electron Physics: Supplement No. 12 Image Transmission Techniques. LC 63-12814. 1979. text ed. 121.00 (*0-12-014572-3*) Acad Pr.

Pratt, Willis S. Lord Byron & His Circle. (Studies in Byron: No. 5). 1970. pap. 39.95 (*0-8383-0062-6*) M S G Haskell Hse.

Pratt, Willis W. Byron at Southwell. LC 72-6745. (Studies in Byron: No. 5). 1972. reprint ed. lib. bdg. 51.95 (*0-8383-1646-8*) M S G Haskell Hse.

Pratte, Francois. Awa En el Desierto. (Coleccion Rosa Ser.). (Illus.). 60p. (SPA.). (J). (gr. 5 up). 1994. pap. 5.95 (*958-07-0066-4*) Firefly Bks Ltd.
— El Blabla de los Gemelos. (Coleccion Rosa Ser.). (Illus.). 60p. (SPA.). (J). (gr. 5 up). 1994. pap. 5.95 (*958-07-0068-0*) Firefly Bks Ltd.
— El Ejercito Rosado de Awa. (Coleccion Rosa Ser.). (Illus.). 60p. (SPA.). (J). (gr. 5 up). 1994. pap. 5.95 (*958-07-0064-8*) Firefly Bks Ltd.
— El Secreto de Awa. (Coleccion Rosa Ser.). (Illus.). 60p. (SPA.). (J). (gr. 5 up). 1994. pap. 5.95 (*958-07-0069-9*) Firefly Bks Ltd.

***Pratte, Paul Alfred.** Gods Within the Machine: A History of the American Society of Newspaper Editors, 1923-1993. LC 94-24624. 248p. 1995. text ed. 55.00 (*0-275-94976-1*, Praeger Pubs) Greenwood.

Pratte, Richard. The Civic Imperative: Examining the Need for Civic Education. (Advances in Contemporary Educational Thought Ser.). 224p. (C). 1988. text ed. 23.95 (*0-8077-2922-1*) Tchrs Coll.
— Philosophy of Education: Two Traditions. 358p. 1992. pap. 34.95 (*0-398-06330-3*) C C Thomas.
— Philosophy of Education: Two Traditions. 358p. (C). 1992. text ed. 59.95x (*0-398-05778-8*) C C Thomas.

Pratte, Richard N. Multicultural Education: The Need for Philosophical Perspective. (TWEC World Education Monographs). 16p. 1980. 2.00 (*0-918158-99-0*) I N Thut World Educ Ctr.

Pratten, C. F. Applied Macroeconomics. 2nd ed. (Illus.). 320p. 1990. 55.00 (*0-19-828331-8*) OUP.

Pratten, Cliff. Overseas Investments, Capital Gains & the Balance of Payments. 121p. (C). 1992. text ed. 75.00 (*0-255-36303-6*, Pub. by Inst Economic Affairs UK) St Mut.

Pratten, Clifford F. The Competitiveness of Small Firms & the Economies of Scale. (Department of Applied Economics, Occasional Papers). (Illus.). 300p. (C). 1991. 54.95 (*0-521-40035-X*) Cambridge U Pr.
— The Stock Market. LC 93-2761. (Department of Applied Economics, Occasional Papers: No. 59). (Illus.). 220p. (C). 1993. 42.95 (*0-521-44065-3*) Cambridge U Pr.

Prattis, J. Iain, ed. Reflections: The Anthropological Muse. (Special Publication). 1985. pap. 24.00 (*0-913167-10-X*) Am Anthro Assn.

Pratton, Norah, jt. auth. see Henifin, Karen.

Pratzel, Alan D., jt. auth. see Mooney, Margaret M.

Pratzner, Frank C. & Russell, Jill F. The Changing Workplace: Implications of Quality of Work Life for Vocational Education. 89p. 1984. 7.25 (*0-318-22062-8*, RD249) Ctr Educ Trng Employ.

Pratzner, Frank C., jt. ed. see Lewis, Morgan V.

Prausnitz, John M., et al. Molecular Thermodynamics of Fluid-Phase Equilibria. 2nd ed. (Illus.). 720p. (C). 1985. text ed. 84.00 (*0-13-599564-7*) P-H.

Prauss, Gerold. Erscheinung bei Kant: Ein Problem der Kritik der reinen Vernunft. (Quellen und Studien zur Philosophie Ser.: Vol. 1). (C). 1971. 94.10 (*3-11-006427-8*) De Gruyter.

Prautzsch, Hartmut, jt. auth. see Boehm, Wolfgang.

Praval. Indian Army after Independence. 623p. 1987. 50.00 (*81-7062-014-7*, Pub. by Lancer II) S Asia.

Pravda, Alex. The End of the Other Empire: Soviet Union - East European Relations in Transition. (Illus.). 256p. (C). 1992. 65.00 (*0-8039-8723-4*) Sage.

Pravda, Alex, ed. The Tauris Soviet Directory: The Elite of the U. S. S. R. Today. 700p. 1990. text ed. 185.00 (*1-85043-090-X*) St Martin.
— Yearbook of Soviet Foreign Relations, 1991. 400p. 1991. text ed. 110.00 (*1-85043-242-2*, Pub. by I B Tauris UK) St Martin.

Pravda, Alex & Duncan, Peter J., eds. Soviet-British Relations Since the 1970s. (Illus.). 228p. (C). 1990. 69.95 (*0-521-37494-4*) Cambridge U Pr.

Pravda, Alex & Ruble, Blair A. Trade Unions in Communist States. LC 85-30717. 250p. (C). 1986. text ed. 49.95 (*0-04-331108-3*) Routledge Chapman & Hall.

Pravda, Alex, jt. ed. see Hasegawa, Tsuyoshi.

Pravda, Alex, jt. ed. see White, Stephen.

Pravda, Myra & Weiland, Jeanne. Off to Camp! LC 89-80301. (Illus.). 72p. (Orig.). (J). (gr. 2-7). 1989. per., pap. 4.95 (*0-9622328-0-7*) JSP Pub.

Pravdin, L. F. Scots Pine: Variation, Intraspecific Taxonomy, & Selection. 216p. 1964. text ed. 64.00 (*0-7065-0717-7*, Pub. by Keter Pub IS) Coronet Bks.

Prave, P., et al, eds. Basic Biotechnology: A Student's Guide. LC 87-10606. 344p. 1989. pap. text ed. 45.00 (*0-89573-646-2*) VCH Pubs.
— Fundamentals of Biotechnology. LC 87-10604. (Illus.). 792p. 1987. lib. bdg. 265.00 (*0-89573-224-6*) VCH Pubs.

Prawat, Carolyn M. Gourd Craft: Growing, Designing, & Decorating Ornamental & Hardshell Gourds. 2nd rev. ed. (Illus.). 212p. 1989. reprint ed. write for info. (*0-9623516-0-1*) Am Gourd Soc.

Prawer, Joshua. The History of the Jews in the Latin Kingdom of Jerusalem. (Illus.). 328p. 1988. 78.00 (*0-19-822557-1*) OUP.

Prawer, S. S. Israel at Vanity Fair: Jews & Judaism in the Writings of W. M. Thackery. LC 91-25465. (Series in Jewish Studies: Vol. 2). (Illus.). 439p. 1992. 123.00 (*90-04-09403-2*) E J Brill.

Prawer, Seigbert S. Caligari's Children: The Film As Tale of Terror. (Quality Paperbacks Ser.). (Illus.). 334p. 1989. reprint ed. pap. 11.95 (*0-306-80347-X*) Da Capo.
— Heine: The Tragic Satirist: A Study of the Later Poetry, 1827-1856. LC 61-4707. 327p. reprint ed. pap. 93.20 (*0-317-27564-X*, 2024511) Bks Demand.

Prawitz, Dag & Westerstahl, Dag, eds. Logic & Philosophy of Science in Uppsala: Papers from the 9th International Congress of Logic, Methodology & Philosophy of Science. LC 93-50753. (Synthese Library: Vol. 236). 620p. (C). 1994. lib. bdg. 168.50 (*0-7923-2702-0*) Kluwer Ac.

***Prawitz, Dag, et al, eds.** Logic, Methodology & Philosophy of Science IX: Proceedings of the Ninth International Congress of Logic, Methodology, & Philosophy of Science, Uppsala, Sweden, August 7-14, 1991. LC 94-39279. (Studies in Logic & the Foundations of Mathematics: Vol. 134). 1004p. 1994. 242.75 (*0-444-89341-5*) Elsevier.

Pray, Barbara. Path to the Spirit. Talkington, Sandra, ed. (Grandmother Ser.). (Illus.). 77p. (Orig.). (C). 1994. pap. 12.95 (*0-922863-05-9*) Dream Wvrs Pub Co.
— Spirit Vision of a Grandmother. Talkington, S., ed. (Illus.). 42p. (Orig.). (C). 1991. pap. 10.95 (*0-922863-02-4*) Dream Wvrs Pub Co.

Pray, Bobbie & Holt, Marilyn J. Kansas History: A Journal of the Central Plains, a Ten-Year Cumulative Index. LC 88-82171. 315p. 1988. pap. 15.95 (*0-87726-034-6*) Kansas St Hist.

Pray, Bobbie A. & Mann, Glennis A. Let's Go Eat: The Kansas Guide to Good Dining. LC 91-66141. 200p. (Orig.). 1991. pap. 18.00 (*0-9627361-1-2*) Turn Century Pr.

Pray, Francis C., ed. Handbook for Educational Fund Raising. LC 81-81964. (Jossey-Bass Series in Higher Education). 474p. reprint ed. pap. 135.10 (*0-8357-4917-7*, 2037847) Bks Demand.

Pray, Isaac C. Memoirs of James Gordon Bennett & His Times. LC 73-125712. (American Journalists Ser.). 1977. reprint ed. 35.95 (*0-405-01693-X*) Ayer.

Pray, Lloyd C. & Murray, Raymond C., eds. Dolomitization & Limestone Diagenesis: A Symposium. LC 73-15328. (Society of Economic Paleontologists & Mineralogists, Special Publication Ser.: No. 13). 190p. reprint ed. pap. 54.20 (*0-317-27156-3*, 2024739) Bks Demand.

Pray, Thomas & Strang, Daniel. Decide: A Computer-Based Decision Game Student Manual. (Business Division Ser.). 120p. (C). 1984. pap. text ed. write for info. (*0-07-554259-5*) McGraw.

Pray, Toni. Lessons for the Library Student Staff. (Professional Growth Ser.). 234p. 1992. 29.95 (*0-938865-11-0*) Linworth Pub.

Prayson, Alex. A Love-Hate Anthology: Releasing the Bitch Within... (Illus.). 52p. (Orig.). 1993. pap. 10.00 (*0-9639301-0-9*) A Prayson.

Praytor, Phyllis, jt. auth. see Craig, Linda.

Praz, Manrio. Studies in Seventeenth Century Imagery, 2 vols. in 1. LC 40-3654. reprint ed. 79.00 (*0-403-07208-5*) Somerset Pub.

Praz, Mario. Conversation Pieces: A Survey of the Informal Group Portrait in Europe & America. LC 76-127380. (Illus.). 285p. 1971. Individually boxed. 70.00 (*0-271-00132-1*) A Wofsy Fine Arts.

— The Flaming Heart. 400p. (C). 1973. reprint ed. pap. text ed. 3.95 (*0-393-00669-7*) Norton.

— The Flaming Heart: Essays on Crashaw, Machiavelli & Other Studies from Chaucer to T. S. Eliot. 1958. 11.75 (*0-8446-1365-7*) Peter Smith.

— An Illustrated History of Interior Decoration: From Pompeii to Art Nouveau. LC 94-61063. (Illus.). 398p. 1995. pap. 27.50 (*0-500-27815-6*) Thames Hudson.

— An Illustrated History of Interior Decoration: From Pompeii to Art Nouveau. LC 81-85473. (Illus.). 1987. reprint ed. 75.00 (*0-500-23358-6*) Thames Hudson.

Prazak, Ludwig J., tr. see Huckstadt, Jurgen.

Prazak, Ludwig J., tr. see Mollmann, Gerd.

***Prazmowska, Anita J.** Britain & Poland, 1939-1943: The Betrayed Ally. (Cambridge Russian, Soviet & Post-Soviet Studies: 97). 270p. (C). 1995. 64.95 (*0-521-40309-X*); pap. 29.95 (*0-521-48385-9*) Cambridge U Pr.

— Britain, Poland & the Eastern Front, 1939. LC 86-31015. (Cambridge Russian, Soviet & Post-Soviet Studies: No. 53). 240p. 1987. 59.95 (*0-521-33148-X*) Cambridge U Pr.

PRC Environmental Management, Inc. Staff. Hazardous Waste Reduction in the Metal Finishing Industry. LC 89-22922. (Pollution Technology Review Ser.: No. 176). (Illus.). 205p. 1990. 42.00 (*0-8155-1223-6*) Noyes.

PRC, Inc. Staff, ed. see Daniels, William R.

PRC Publishing, Inc. Staff, ed. see Hawkins, Jerald D.

***Prcela, John.** Operation Slaughterhouse. (Illus.). 608p. 1995. text ed. 14.00 (*0-8059-3737-4*) Dorrance.

Pre-Hospital Trauma Life Support Committee of the National Association of Emergency Medical Technicians. National Association of Emergency Medical Technicians - Pre-Hospital Trauma Life Support. 3rd ed. McSwain, Norman E., Jr. et al, eds. LC 94-6964. 1994. write for info. (*0-8151-6333-9*, Yr Bk Med Pubs) Mosby Yr Bk.

Preacher, James W., jt. auth. see Westbrooks, Randy G.

Preacher, Stephen. Anasazi Sunrise: The Mystery of Sacrifice Rock. LC 92-90872. (Illus.). 108p. (Orig.). 1992. pap. 6.95 (*1-881553-01-9*) Rugged Indiv.

Preacher's Homiletic Commentary Staff. The Preacher's Homiletic Commentary, 31 vols., Set. 19256p. 1974. 595.00 (*0-8010-6962-9*) Baker Bk.

Preas, Bryan & Lorenzetti, Michael, eds. Physical Design Automation of VLSI Systems. (Illus.). 510p. (C). 1988. text ed. 59.25 (*0-8053-0142-9*) Benjamin-Cummings.

Preat, V., jt. ed. see Roberfroid, M. B.

Preato, Robert R. New York: Empire City in the Age of Urbanism, 1875-1945. (Illus.). 160p. 1989. 35.00 (*0-942750-00-4*) Grand Crtl Art Gal.

***Preaud, Maxime.** Dictionnaire des Editeurs d'Estampes a Paris Sous l'Ancien Regime. 334p. (FRE.). 1987. pap. 145.00 (*0-7859-8214-0*, 2903181608) Fr & Eur.

Preaux, Claire. L' Economie Royale des Lagides. Finley, Moses, ed. LC 79-4999. (Ancient Economic History Ser.). (FRE.). 1979. reprint ed. lib. bdg. 56.95 (*0-405-12388-4*) Ayer.

Prebal, Bernard. A Practical Guide to Molecular Cloning. 2nd ed. 811p. 1988. text ed. 206.95 (*0-471-85071-3*); pap. text ed. 110.95 (*0-471-85070-5*) Wiley.

Prebble, J. N. Mitochondria, Chloroplasts & Bacterial Membranes. LC 80-40777. (Illus.). 392p. reprint ed. pap. 111.80 (*0-8357-6216-5*, 2034506) Bks Demand.

***Prebble, John.** Dimensions in Banking Law & Foreign Exchange. 361p. 1992. pap. 54.00 (*0-409-79045-1*, NZ) Butterworth Legal Pubs.

— Dimensions in Business Finance Law. 296p. 1992. pap. 54.00 (*0-409-79011-7*, Austral) Butterworth Legal Pubs.

— The High Girders. large type ed. 1980. 12.00 (*0-7089-0430-0*) Ulverscroft.

— The Taxation of Companies & Corporate Investors. 64p. 1984. pap. 29.00 (*0-409-70142-4*, NZ) Butterworth Legal Pubs.

Prebenna, David, illus. A Car Trip for Mole & Mouse. 32p. (J). (ps-3). 1991. pap. 3.50 (*0-14-054392-9*, Puffin) Puffin Bks.

Prebisch, Raul, pref. Terms of Trade & the Optimum Tariff in Latin America. write for info. (*0-318-69857-9*) IADB.

Prebish, Charles S. Buddhist Ethics: A Cross Cultural Approach. 248p. 1992. per. 21.95 (*0-8403-7424-0*) Kendall-Hunt.

— Historical Dictionary of Buddhism. LC 93-4247. (Historical Dictionaries of Religions, Philosophies, & Movements Ser.: No. 1). (Illus.). 425p. 1993. 42.50 (*0-8108-2698-4*) Scarecrow.

— Religion & Sport: The Meeting of Sacred & Profane. LC 92-30020. (Contributions to the Study of Popular Culture Ser.: No. 36). 264p. 1992. text ed. 47.95 (*0-313-28729-5*, GM8729, Greenwood Pr) Greenwood.

Prebish, Charles S., ed. Buddhism: A Modern Perspective. LC 74-300085. 346p. 1975. pap. 14.95 (*0-271-01195-5*) Pa St U Pr.

***Preble.** Artforms. 5th ed. 1994. pap. text ed. (*0-8230-4959-0*) Watsn-Guptill.

Preble, Dave. Sport Fishing for Yellowfin Tuna. Rhodes, Bob, ed. (Fisherman Library). (Illus.). 136p. (Orig.). 1988. pap. text ed. 9.95 (*0-923155-07-4*) Fisherman Lib.

Preble, Duane & Preble, Sarah. Artforms: An Introduction to the Visual Arts. 5th ed. LC 93-4725. (C). 1993. text ed. 50.00 (*0-06-500834-0*, Harper Ref) HarpC.

Preble, G. H. Genealogical Sketch of the First Three Generations in America; with an Account of Abraham Preble the Emigrant, & of Brig. General Jedediah Preble & His Descendants. (Illus.). 340p. 1989. reprint ed. lib. bdg. 59.00 (*0-8328-0986-1*); reprint ed. pap. 51.00 (*0-8328-0987-X*) Higginson Bk Co.

Preble, George H. Opening of Japan, a Diary of Discovery in the Far East 1853-1856. Szczesniak, Boleslaw, ed. LC 62-16484. (Illus.). 492p. reprint ed. 140.30 (*0-8357-9737-6*, 2010998) Bks Demand.

Preble, George H., ed. see Green, Ezra.

Preble, Jack. Land of Canaan. 4th ed. 1981. reprint ed. pap. 8.00 (*0-87012-012-3*) McClain.

Preble, Linda M., jt. auth. see Sevarino, Ferne B.

Preble, Sarah, jt. auth. see Preble, Duane.

Precek, Katharine W. Penny in the Road. LC 88-13331. (Illus.). 32p. (J). (gr. k-3). 1989. text ed. 14.95 (*0-02-774970-3*, Mac Bks Young Read) S&S Childrens.

Precek, Katherine W. The Keepsake Chest. LC 91-14808. 160p. (J). (gr. 3-7). 1992. text ed. 13.95 (*0-02-775045-0*, Mac Bks Young Read) S&S Childrens.

***Prechal, Sacha.** Directives in European Community Law: A Study of Directives & Their Enforcement in National Courts. (Oxford European Community Law Ser.). 300p. 1995. 65.00 (*0-19-826016-4*) OUP.

Prechal, Sacha & Burrows, Noreen. Gender Discrimination Law. 414p. 1990. text ed. 59.95 (*1-85521-058-4*, Pub. by Dartmth Pub UK) Ashgate Pub Co.

Precht, Dave, jt. auth. see Dalrymple, Byron.

Precht, Fred L., jt. ed. see Brauer, James L.

Precht, H., et al. Temperature & Life. LC 73-13495. (Illus.). 779p. 1973. 98.00 (*0-387-06441-9*) Spr-Verlag.

Prechtel, jt. auth. see Barth.

Prechtel, Martin. Grandmother Sweat Bath: A Story of the Tzutujil Mana. Rodney, Janet, ed. (Illus.). 39p. (Orig.). (YA). (gr. 6 up). 1990. write for info. (*1-878460-00-5*) Weaselsleeves Pr.

***Prechter, Robert R., Jr.** At the Crest of the Tidal Wave: A Forecast for the Great Bear Market. LC 95-68295. (Illus.). 1995. 49.00 (*0-932750-39-7*) New Classics Lib.

— The Complete Elliott Wave Writings of A. Hamilton Bolton. (Illus.). 412p. 1994. 39.00 (*0-932750-22-2*) New Classics Lib.

— The Elliott Wave Educational Series, Set. (Illus.). 1990. student ed, vhs 1,349.00 (*0-932750-25-7*) New Classics Lib.

— Precision Ratio Compass Utility Manual. 3rd ed. (Illus.). 70p. 1987. pap. 99.00 (*0-932750-13-3*) New Classics Lib.

— R. N. Elliott's Market Letters (1938-1946) (Illus.). 234p. 1993. 55.00 (*0-932750-20-6*) New Classics Lib.

— Special Report Collection, Nineteen Seventy-Nine to Date. 98p. 1987. pap. 39.00 (*0-932750-09-5*) New Classics Lib.

— A Turn in the Tidal Wave, Pts. I & II. (Illus.). 108p. 1989. pap. 19.00 (*0-932750-12-5*) New Classics Lib.

Prechter, Robert R., Jr., ed. Popular Culture & the Stock Market: A Collection, 1983-1991. rev. ed. (Illus.). 70p. 1991. reprint ed. pap. 55.00 (*0-932750-19-2*) New Classics Lib.

Prechter, Robert R., Jr., ed. see Elliott, R. N.

Prechter, Robert R., Jr., jt. auth. see Frost, A. J.

Prechtl, Heinz F., ed. Continuity of Neural Functions from Prenatal to Postnatal Life. LC 65-80476. (Clinics in Developmental Medicine Ser.: No. 94). (Illus.). 255p. (C). 1991. 54.95 (*0-521-41214-5*, Pub. by Mc Keith Pr UK) Cambridge U Pr.

Prechtl, Heinz F. & Beintema, David. The Neurological Examination of the Full-Term Newborn Infant. 2nd ed. (Clinics in Developmental Medicine Ser.: No. 63). (Illus.). 76p. (C). 1991. reprint ed. 27.95 (*0-521-41199-8*, Pub. by Mc Keith Pr UK) Cambridge U Pr.

Preciado, Kathleen, ed. see Rappaport, Susan.

***Precious, B. B.** The Byrant Series: My New Home. Williams, Dewilda M., ed. (Byrant Ser.). (Illus.). 12p. (J). (gr. k-2). 1995. 10.95 (*1-886493-01-4*) NBC Study Pub.

— What Makes Me Happy. Williams, Dewilda M., ed. (Byrant Series). (Illus.). 10p. (J). (gr. k-2). 1995. 6.95 (*1-886493-03-0*) NBC Study Pub.

Precious, Lloyd, et al. Classroom TOEFL. 1993. teacher ed 14.95 (*0-8120-1517-7*); teacher ed 12.95 (*0-8120-1800-1*); teacher ed 79.95 (*0-8120-8027-0*) Barron.

— Classroom TOEFL, 4 cass., Set. 1993. audio 40.00 (*0-8120-1516-9*) Barron.

Precious Moments Staff. Precious Moments Library, 3 vols., Set. (Illus.). 832p. 1990. 45.99 (*0-8010-7114-3*) Baker Bk.

Precision Indexing Staff. Georgia Census Index, 1870, 3 vols., Set. Steuart, Bradley W., ed. 3344p. 1991. lib. bdg. 350.00 (*1-877677-11-6*) Precision Indexing.

— Indianapolis (Marion County), Indiana Mortality Records, September 1872-December 1881. 651p. 1989. lib. bdg. 49.95 (*1-877677-08-6*) Precision Indexing.

— Ohio Census Index, 1880, 3 vols., Set. 3252p. 1991. lib. bdg. 395.00 (*1-877677-14-0*) Precision Indexing.

— The Soundex Reference Guide. Steuart, Bradley W., ed. 253p. 1990. lib. bdg. 29.95 (*1-877677-12-4*); pap. 19.96 (*1-877677-09-4*) Precision Indexing.

— South Carolina Census Index, 1870, 2 vols., Set. Steuart, Bradley W., ed. 1983p. 1989. lib. bdg. 195.00 (*1-877677-10-8*) Precision Indexing.

Preconference Institute on Library Automation Staff. Library Automation: A State of the Art Review: Papers of the Preconference Institute on Library Automation, San Francisco, 1967. Salmon, Stephen R., ed. LC 73-77283. 186p. reprint ed. pap. 53.10 (*0-317-29366-4*, 2024208) Bks Demand.

Precosky, Don. W. W. E. Ross & His Works. (Canadian Author Studies). 26p. (C). 1987. pap. text ed. 9.95 (*0-920763-20-0*, Pub. by ECW Press CN) Genl Dist Srvs.

***Pred, Allan.** Recognizing European Modernities: A Montage of the Present. LC 94-46281. (Illus.). 304p. 1995. 65.00 (*0-415-11904-9*, C0002); pap. 19.95 (*0-415-12136-1*, C0003) Routledge.

Pred, Allan & Watts, Michael J. Reworking Modernity: Capitalisms & Symbolic Discontent. LC 91-42894. (Hegemony & Experience Ser.). (Illus.). 265p. (C). 1992. text ed. 45.00 (*0-8135-1831-8*); pap. text ed. 17.00 (*0-8135-1832-6*) Rutgers U Pr.

Pred, Allan R. Lost Words & Lost Worlds: Modernity & the Language of Everyday Life in Nineteenth-Century Stockholm. (Cambridge Human Geography Ser.). (Illus.). 336p. (C). 1990. 69.95 (*0-521-37531-2*) Cambridge U Pr.

— Place, Practice & Structure: Social & Spatial Transformation in Southern Sweden, 1750-1850. LC 85-30652. 300p. 1986. 56.00 (*0-389-20615-6*, N8173) B&N Imports.

— Urban Growth & City-Systems in the United States, 1840-1860. LC 80-12098. (Studies in Urban History). (Illus.). 297p. 1980. text ed. 38.50 (*0-674-93091-6*) HUP.

— Urban Growth & the Circulation of Information: The United States System of Cities, 1790-1840. LC 73-76384. (Studies in Urban History). 384p. (C). 1973. text ed. 39.95 (*0-674-93090-8*) HUP.

Pred, Deborah R., jt. auth. see Fiedler, Donald B.

Preda, Eugen, jt. auth. see Bogdan, Corneliu.

Preda, S., ed. Funds & Portfolio Management Institutions: An International Survey. 420p. 1991. 69.50 (*0-444-88895-0*, North Holland) Elsevier.

Predazzi, E., jt. auth. see Anselmino, Isi.

Predazzi, Enrico, jt. auth. see Leader, Elliot.

Predel, B. Lanolt-Boernstein Numerical Data & Functional Relationships in Science & Technology: Macroscopic Properties of Matter; Phase Equilibria, Crystallographic Data, & Values of Thermodynamic Properties of Binary Alloys; Ca-Cd...Co-Zr, Group IV; Vol. 5; Subvol. C. Madelung, O. & Schafer, K., eds. 480p. 1993. 1,111.00 (*0-387-56072-6*) Spr-Verlag.

— Phase Equilibria, Crystallographic & Thermodynamic Data of Binary Alloys, Vol. 5, Subvol. b: B-Ba - C-Zr. (Illus.). xxviii, 403p. 1992. 970.00 (*0-387-55115-8*) Spr-Verlag.

Predeleanu, M., ed. Computational Methods for Predicting Material Processing Defects. 366p. 1987. 105.25 (*0-444-42859-3*) Elsevier.

Predeleanu, M., jt. ed. see Ghosh, S. K.

Predeteanu, Constantin. The ABCs of Cosmetics. 377p. 1987. text ed. 48.00 (*0-9619278-0-1*) Inst Predete Pub.

Predika, Bryon & Dehart, Jon, eds. Cooking with Pride. (Illus.). 104p. (Orig.). 1989. pap. text ed. 8.25 (*0-9623939-0-8*) Act One.

Predika, Jerry. The Sausage-Making Cookbook. LC 82-19679. (Illus.). 192p. 1983. 16.95 (*0-8117-1693-7*) Stackpole.

Predmore, Helen, et al, eds. Cemeteries of Chester, New York. LC 77-12179. (Orange County, New York Cemeteries Ser.: No. 1). 142p. (Orig.). 1977. pap. 7.00 (*0-685-03716-9*) Orange County Genealog.

Predmore, Richard L. The World of Don Quixote. LC 67-20879. 147p. reprint ed. pap. 41.90 (*0-317-29791-0*, 2017010) Bks Demand.

Predmore, Richard L., tr. see Machado y Ruiz, Antonio.

***Predock, Antoine.** Architectural Journeys. (Illus.). 144p. 1995. 35.00 (*0-8478-1904-3*) Rizzoli Intl.

Predvoditelev, A. S. High-Temperature Properties of Gases. 216p. 1969. text ed. 57.00 (*0-7065-0702-9*, Pub. by Keter Pub IS) Coronet Bks.

Pree, Bernice W. Quiet Time. Hyman, Mark, ed. 82p. (Orig.). (YA). Date not set. pap. write for info. (*0-915515-03-2*) Way Pub.

***Pree, Wolfgang.** Design Patterns for Object-Oriented Software Development. (C). 1995. text ed. 39.75 (*0-201-42294-8*) Addison-Wesley.

Preece & Light. Cell Electrophoresis in Cancer & Other Clinical Research. (Developments in Cancer Research Ser.: Vol. 6). 314p. 1981. 67.75 (*0-444-80374-2*) Elsevier.

Preece, et al. Cancer of the Bile Ducts & Pancreas. 320p. 1989. text ed. 115.00 (*0-7216-2631-9*) Saunders.

Preece, Alison & Cowden, Diane. Young Writers in the Making: Sharing the Process with Parents. LC 93-24636. 144p. (YA). 1993. pap. text ed. 15.00 (*0-435-08778-9*, 08778) Heinemann.

***Preece, Alun, ed.** Validation & Verification of Knowledge-Based Systems. (Technical Reports). (Illus.). 149p. (Orig.). 1994. pap. 25.00x (*0-929280-65-2*) Amer Artificial.

Preece, C. M., ed. see Metallurgical Society of AIME Staff.

Preece, Carolyn M., ed. see Metallurgical Society of AIME Staff.

Preece, Charles O. Edward Willis & Ellen Browning Scripps: An Unmatched Pair. LC 89-90125. (Illus.). 232p. (Orig.). 1990. text ed. 16.95 (*0-9619349-4-8*) C O Preece.

— Teaching Without Tears: The Classroom Teachers Survival Book. rev. ed. LC 88-80829. 124p. (C). 1988. pap. 12.95 (*0-9619349-3-X*) C O Preece.

***Preece, David.** Organizations & Technical Change: Strategy, Objectives, & Involvement. rev. ed. LC 94-34917. (The Routledge Series in the Management of Technology). 272p. 1995. 59.95 (*0-415-12514-6*, B4890); 22.95 (*0-415-10186-7*, C0296) Routledge.

Preece, David A. Managing the Adoption of New Technology. 256p. 1989. lib. bdg. 79.50 (*0-415-01273-2*) Routledge.

***Preece, Debbie. From Combat Zone to Love at Home. (Illus.). 100p. 1995. pap. 19.95 (*0-9647070-0-4*) DKP.**
What mother hasn't felt like she is living in a "Combat Zone" at some time or other? Who hasn't wondered how to get the children to help around the house when asked the first time & to cheerfully empty the garbage & set the table? Only in your dreams you say? Not True! This book is a How-To guide to escape the combat & replace it with happy faces & children willing to help on the first request. This book contains revolutionary concepts that will produce Love at home even by the most difficult child. Included in this book are many color pages, charts & graphs & how to use them instructions. There are also complete worksheets for most any room in the house that details children's assignments for the month with a check off column for the child to complete. This method has been tried & tested for over 13 years. It is truly inspired & will help every mother in combat go FROM COMBAT ZONE TO LOVE AT HOME. To order DKP Inc., 5632 Bayside Dr., Orlando, FL 32819. Phone: (407) 876-0829 or FAX (407) 876-6568. ***Publisher Provided Annotation.***

Preece, Gordon, jt. auth. see Banks, Rob.

Preece, Jenny. Guide to Usability: Human Factors in Computing. (C). 1992. pap. text ed. 26.95 (*0-201-62768-X*) Addison-Wesley.

— Human-Computer Interaction. (C). 1994. text ed. 45.25 (*0-201-62769-8*) Addison-Wesley.

Preece, John E. & Read, Paul. The Biology of Horticulture: An Introductory Textbook. 720p. 1993. Net. text ed. write for info. (*0-471-05989-7*) Wiley.

Preece, John F. The Use of Computers in General Practice. 2nd ed. (Illus.). 256p. 1989. pap. text ed. 48.00 (*0-443-04258-6*) Churchill.

Preece, M. A., jt. ed. see Tanner, James M.

Preece, Paul E., et al, eds. Cancer of the Stomach. 320p. 1986. text ed. 70.50 (*0-8089-1835-4*, 793380, Grune) Saunders.

Preece, R. A. Designs on the Landscape: Everyday Landscapes, Values & Practice. 283p. 1991. text ed. 73. 95 (*0-470-21830-4*) Halsted Pr.

— An Evaluation of the General Public of Scenic Quality in the Cotswolds Area of Outstanding Natural Beauty: A Basis for Monitoring Future Change. (C). 1980. 35.00 (*0-685-30295-4*, Pub. by Oxford Polytechnic UK) St Mut.

***Preece, R.A.** Designs of the Landscape: Everyday Landscapes, Values & Practice. 1993. text ed. 79.95 (*0-471-94752-0*) Wiley.

Preece, Rod & Chamberlain, Lorna. Animal Welfare & Human Values. 280p. (C). 1993. text ed. 45.00 (*0-88920-227-3*, Pub. by Wilfrid Laurier CN) Humanities.

— Animal Welfare & Human Values. 334p. 1995. pap. 19.95 (*0-88920-256-7*, Pub. by Wilfrid Laurier CN) Humanities.

Preece, Roy. Starting Research: A New Guide to Researching & Writing Up. 192p. 1994. 48.00 (*1-85567-090-9*, Pub. by Pinter Pubs UK); pap. 16.00 (*1-85567-091-7*, Pub. by Pinter Pubs UK) St Martin.

***Preece-Sandoval, Pam & Reese, Bob.** Noodles. (Ten Word Book Ser.). (Illus.). (J). (gr. k-3). 1994. lib. bdg. 9.25 (*0-89868-253-3*, Read Res) ARO Pub.

— Noodles. (Ten Word Book Ser.). (Illus.). (J). (gr. k-3). 1994. pap. 3.50 (*0-89868-254-1*, Read Res) ARO Pub.

An Asterisk (*) at the beginning of an entry indicates that the title is appearing in BIP for the first time.

— Noodles. Schaffer-Melendez, Gloria, tr. (Libro de Diaz Palabras Ser.). (Illus.). (SPA.). (J). (gr. k-3). 1994. lib. bdg. 9.25 (0-89868-261-4, Read Res) ARO Pub.

— Noodles. Schaffer-Melendez, Gloria, tr. (Un Libro de Diaz Palabras Ser.). (Illus.). (SPA.). (J). (gr. k-3). 1994. pap. 3.50 (0-89868-262-2, Read Res) ARO Pub.

Preece-Sandoval, Pam, jt. auth. see Reese, Bob.

Preedy, Margaret, ed. Approaches to Curriculum Management. (Management in Education Ser.). 192p. 1989. 85.00 (0-335-09249-7, Open Univ Pr); pap. 27.00 (0-335-09248-9, Open Univ Pr) Taylor & Francis.

***Preedy, Victor R. & Watson, Ronald R.** Alcohol & the Gastrointestinal Tract. 336p. 1995. 159.95 (0-8493-2480-7, 2480) CRC Pr.

Preeg, Ernest H. The American Challenge in World Trade: U. S. Interests in the GATT Multilateral Trading System. LC 89-9987. (Significant Issues Ser.: Vol. 11, No. 7). 116p. reprint ed. pap. 33.10 (0-7837-6714-5, 2046341) Bks Demand.

— The Evolution of a Revolution: Peru & Its Relations with the United States, 1968-1980. LC 81-85655. (Committee on Changing International Realities Ser.). 76p. 1981. pap. 7.00 (0-686-36871-1) Natl Planning.

— Neither Fish Nor Fowl: U. S. Economic Assistance for Non-Economic Objectives in the Philippines. (Significant Issues Ser.). (Orig.). 1991. pap. 1.00 (0-89206-169-3) CSI Studies.

— Trade Policy Ahead: Three Tracks & One Question. (Significant Issues Ser.: vol. 17, no. 1). 96p. (C). 1995. pap. 11.95 (0-89206-309-2) CSI Studies.

— Traders in a Brave New World: The Urugay Round & the Future of the International Trading System. 820p. 1995. 33.95 (0-226-67959-4) U Ch Pr.

Preeg, Ernest H. & Levine, Jonathan D. Cuba & the New Caribbean Economic Order. LC 93-2780. (Significant Issues Ser.: Vol. 15). 94p. (gr. 13). 1993. pap. text ed. 10.50 (0-89206-209-6) CSI Studies.

Preeg, Ernest H. & Maingot, Anthony P. The Haitian Crisis - Two Perspectives: Haiti & the C.B.I., a Time of Change & Opportunity; Haiti, Problems of Transition to Democracy in an Authoritarian Soft State. rev. ed. 74p. (C). 1988. 8.95 (0-685-63343-8, LA216) U Miami N-S Ctr.

Preeg, Ernest H., ed. see Krueger, Anne O., et al.

Preer, James R., et al. Integrated Sciences. 1988. spiral bd. 10.50 (0-88252-147-0) Paladin Hse.

Preer, Jean L. Competence, Admissions, & Articulation: Returning to the Basics in Higher Education. Fife, Jonathan D., ed. LC 84-160913. (ASHE-ERIC Higher Education Report Ser.: No. 6, 1983). 115p. (Orig.). 1983. pap. 7.50 (0-913317-05-5) GWU Schl E&HD.

— Lawyers vs. Educators: Black Colleges & Desegregation in Public Higher Education. LC 81-22567. (Contributions in American Studies: No. 61). vii, 278p. 1982. text ed. 55.00 (0-313-23094-3, PLE/, Greenwood Pr) Greenwood.

Preer, Robert W. The Emergence of Technopolis: Knowledge-Intensive Technologies & Regional Development. LC 91-30616. 200p. 1992. text ed. 47.95 (0-275-94090-X, C4090, Praeger Pubs) Greenwood.

***Prefer.** MacArthur's New Guinea Campaign. 1995. 24.95 (0-938289-51-9) Combined Bks.

Preferred Hotels Worldwide Staff. Chef Prefers: Favorite Recipes by the Chef of Preferred Hotels. 1989. 19.98 (0-8241-4010-9) Allan Pubs.

***Prefontaine, Yves.** This Desert Now. Cowan, Judith, tr. (Essential Poets Ser.: No. 52). 64p. 1994. pap. 8.00 (0-920717-66-7) Guernica Editions.

Pregeant, Russell. Christology Beyond Dogma: Matthew's Christ in Process Hermeneutic. LC 77-78638. (Society of Biblical Literature. Semeia Supplements Ser.: No. 7). 176p. (Orig.). reprint ed. pap. 50.20 (0-7837-5439-6, 2045204) Bks Demand.

— Engaging the New Testament: An Interdisciplinary Approach. LC 95-5018. 1995. write for info. (0-8006-2803-9, Fortress Pr) Augsburg Fortress.

— Mystery Without Magic. LC 87-23961. 192p. (Orig.). 1988. pap. 12.95 (0-940989-19-0) Meyer Stone Bks.

Pregel, Boris, et al, eds. World Priorities. LC 75-29389. 277p. 1977. reprint ed. pap. text ed. 17.95x (0-87855-633-8) Transaction Pubs.

Pregent, Carol. When a Child Dies. LC 92-72923. 120p. (Orig.). 1992. pap. 6.95 (0-87793-487-8) Ave Maria.

Pregent, Richard. Charting Your Course: How to Prepare to Teach More Effectively. 1994. 21.50 (0-912150-30-0) Magna Pubns.

Preger, L. Iatrogenic Diseases. LC 85-24300. 1986. 94.00 (0-8493-5888-4, CRC Reprint) Franklin.

— Iatrogenic Diseases, Vol. 2. LC 85-24300. 1986. 203.00 (0-8493-5889-2) CRC Pr.

Preger, Leslie, ed. Iatrogenic Diseases: Ultrasound of Iatrogenic Disease. 208p. 1986. 298.00 (0-8493-5879-5, RC90) CRC Pr.

Preger, Th., ed. Inscriptiones Graecae Metricae: Ex Scriptoribus Praeter Anthologiam Collectae. xxvii, 215p. 1977. reprint ed. 30.00 (0-89005-214-X) Ares.

Preger, Theodorus, ed. Scriptores Originum Constantino-Politanarum. LC 75-7335. (Roman History Ser.). (GRE.). 1975. reprint ed. 35.95 (0-405-07054-3) Ayer.

Pregill, Gregory. Late Pleistocene Herpetofaunas from Puerto Rico. (Miscellaneous Publications: No. 71). 72p. 1981. 4.25 (0-317-04884-8) U of KS Mus Nat Hist.

Pregill, Gregory, jt. ed. see Estes, Richard.

Pregill, P. Landscapes in History. 1993. text ed. 69.95 (0-442-31804-9) Van Nos Reinhold.

Pregosin, P. S. Transition Metal Nuclear Magnetic Resonance. (Studies in Inorganic Chemistry: Vol. 13). 1991. 169.25 (0-444-88176-X, SIC 13) Elsevier.

Preheim, Beth, ed. see Cleaver, Richard G.

Prehistoric Fenland Centre Staff & Pryor, Francis T. English Heritage Book of Flag Fen. (Illus.). 144p. 1991. 60.00 (0-7134-6752-5, Pub. by Batsford UK); pap. 34.95 (0-7134-6753-3, Pub. by Batsford UK) Trafalgar.

Prehistoric Society of East Anglia Staff. Report on the Excavations at Grime's Graves: Weeting, Norfolk, March - May, 1914. Clarke, W. G., ed. LC 77-86437. reprint ed. 28.00 (0-404-16676-8) AMS Pr.

Prehm, Herbert J. & Altman, Reuben. Improving Instruction Through Classroom Research. 1976. pap. 6.95 (0-89108-056-2, 7601) Love Pub Co.

Prehn, Alyene E. Prehn: Journal of a Genealogist, with Ancestral Wills, Includes Anderson, Bass, Elder, Gaddy, Griggs, Ingersoll, Kelsey, Lewis, Westall, Wright Families. (Illus.). 864p. 1994. reprint ed. lib. bdg. 125.00 (0-8328-4098-X); reprint ed. pap. 115.00 (0-8328-4099-8) Higginson Bk Co.

Prehn, John W. On the Edge. 150p. (Orig.). 1993. pap. text ed. 16.00 (1-878045-16-4) Whittier Pubns.

— On the Edge: Strip Tease in a Small Town Setting. 150p. (C). 1993. pap. text ed. 17.00 (1-878045-15-6) Whittier Pubns.

Prehn, S. & Toetenel, W. J., eds. VDM '91 Formal Software Development Methods, 4th International Symposium of VDM Europe, Noorwijkerhout, the Netherlands, October 21-25, 1991 Proceedings, Vol. 1: Conference Contributions. (Lecture Notes in Computer Science Ser.: Vol. 551). xiii, 699p. 1991. pap. 66.00 (0-387-54834-3) Spr-Verlag.

— VDM '91 Formal Software Development Methods, 4th International Symposium of VDM Europe, Noorwijkerhout, the Netherlands, October 21-25, 1991 Proceedings, Vol. 2: Tutorials. (Lecture Notes in Computer Science Ser.: Vol. 552). xiv, 430p. 1991. pap. 41.00 (0-387-54868-8) Spr-Verlag.

Preibisch, P. Two Studies on the Roman Pontifices. LC 75-10647. (Ancient Religion & Mythology Ser.). 1976. 23.95 (0-405-07271-6) Ayer.

Preibisz, J. Polish Dissident Publications. LC 82-7677. 382p. 1982. text ed. 65.00 (0-275-90878-X, C0878, Praeger Pubs) Greenwood.

***Preik, Brooks.** Haunted Wilmington: And the Cape Fear Coast. LC 95-79611. (Illus.). 156p. (Orig.). 1995. pap. 9.95 (0-9635967-3-X) Banks Channel.

Preikschat, W., jt. auth. see Plohn, H.

Preil, Gabriel. To Be Recorded. Barkan, Stanley H., ed. Gilson, Estelle, tr. (Review Jewish Writers Chapbook Ser.: No. 6). 48p. 1991. 15.00 (0-89304-306-0); 15.00 (0-89304-308-7); pap. 5.00 (0-89304-307-9); pap. 5.00 (0-89304-309-5); audio 10.00 (0-89304-310-9); vhs 50.00 (0-89304-311-7) Cross-Cultrl NY.

Prein, J., et al, eds. Atlas of Tumors of the Facial Skeleton. (Illus.). 180p. 1986. 246.00 (0-387-16167-8) Spr-Verlag.

Prein, M., et al, eds. Multivariate Methods in Aquaculture Research: Case Studies of Tilapias in Experimental & Commercial Systems. 200p. pap. 15.00 (971-10-2285-0, Pub. by ICLARM PH) Intl Spec Bk.

Preinreich, Gabriel A. The Nature of Dividends. Brief, Richard P., ed. LC 77-87286. (Development of Contemporary Accounting Thought Ser.). 1978. reprint ed. lib. bdg. 24.95 (0-405-10914-8) Ayer.

Preis, Art. Labor's Giant Step: The First Twenty Years of the CIO: 1936-55. LC 72-79771. 538p. 1994. reprint ed. lib. bdg. 65.00 (0-87348-371-5); reprint ed. pap. 26.95 (0-87348-263-8) Pathfinder NY.

Preis, Donna, jt. photos see Siede, George.

Preisendorfer, R. & Sneddon, I. N. Radiative Transfer on Discrete Spaces. LC 64-12663. (International Series Mono on Pure & Applied Mathematics: Vol. 74). 1965. 192.00 (0-08-010592-0, Pub. by Pergamon Repr UK) Franklin.

Preiser, Gerd. Allgemeine Krankheitsbezeichnungen im Corpus Hippocraticum: Bedeutung und Gebrauch von Nousos und Nosema. (Ars Medica, Abt. 2, Griechisch Lateinische Medizin Ser.). (C). 1976. text ed. 97.75 (3-11-001830-6) De Gruyter.

Preiser, Jerry. How to Shoot a Gun. 96p. (Orig.). 1993. pap. 3.99 (0-425-13844-5) Berkley Pub.

Preiser, Stanley E., et al. Handling Soft Tissue Injury Cases, 2 vols. suppl. ed. 1991. 35.00 (0-87473-634-X) Michie Butterworth.

— Handling Soft Tissue Injury Cases, 2 vols. suppl. ed. 1992. 35.00 (0-930273-52-4) Michie Butterworth.

— Handling Soft Tissue Injury Cases. suppl. ed. 1992. write for info. (0-614-05830-9) Michie Butterworth.

— Handling Soft Tissue Injury Cases, 3 vols., Set. 1985. 240.00 (0-930273-13-3) Michie Butterworth.

— Preparing & Winning Medical Negligence Cases, 2 vols. 1989. 170.00 (0-87473-438-X) Michie Butterworth.

— Preparing & Winning Medical Negligence Cases, 3 vols., Set. 2nd ed. 1989. 240.00 (1-55834-132-3) Michie Butterworth.

— Preparing & Winning Medical Negligence Cases, 2 vols., Vol. 2. suppl. ed. 1991. 40.00 (0-87473-788-5) Michie Butterworth.

Preiser, Wolfgang F. Design Intervention. 1991. text ed. 59.95 (0-442-27333-9) Van Nos Reinhold.

Preiser, Wolfgang F., ed. Building Evaluation. (Illus.). 344p. 1989. 89.50 (0-306-43337-0, Plenum Pr) Plenum.

— Professional Practice in Facility Programming. LC 92-16174. 1993. pap. 49.95 (0-442-00936-4) Van Nos Reinhold.

Preiser, Wolfgang F. E., jt. auth. see Scheer, Brenda C.

Preisigke, Friedrich. Fachworter Des Offentlichen Verwaltungsdienstes Agyptens in Den Griechischen Papyrusurkunden der Ptolemaisch-Romischen Zeit. x, 186p. 1975. reprint ed. write for info. (3-487-05896-0, Pub. by Georg Olms GW) Lubrecht & Cramer.

— Girowesen Im Griechischen Agypten, Enthaltend Korngiro, Geldgiro, Girobanknotariat Mit Einschlub Des Archivwesens. xvi, 575p. 1971. reprint ed. write for info. (0-318-71002-1, Pub. by Georg Olms GW) Lubrecht & Cramer.

— Sammelbuch griechischer Urkunden aus Aegypten, 3 vols. 1530p. 1974. reprint ed. 481.00 (3-11-004756-X) De Gruyter.

Preisler, Bent. A Handbook of English Grammar on Functional Principles. 288p. 1992. 62.50x (87-7288-405-3, Pub. by Aarhus Univ Pr DK) Coronet Bks.

— Linguistic Sex Roles in Conversation. (Contributions to the Sociology of Language Ser.: No. 45). (Illus.). xviii, 350p. 1986. lib. bdg. 115.40 (0-89925-225-7) Mouton.

Preisler, Bent, jt. ed. see Powell, Marianne.

Preisler, Jerome. The Pact. 368p. pap. 3.95 (0-8439-2784-4) Dorchester Pub Co.

Preisler, Jerome, jt. auth. see Alexander, David.

Preisner, Olga K. Chinese Export Porcelains from the Collection of Dr. & Mrs. Harold L. Tonkin: Exhibition Catalogue. (Illus.). 48p. 1980. pap. 4.50 (0-911209-17-4) Palmer Mus Art.

— French Drawings from European Collections: The Former Armand Gobiet Collection. Landman, Hedy, ed. (Illus.). 64p. 1979. pap. 5.00 (0-911209-16-6) Palmer Mus Art.

— Hemline, Neckline, Streamline: Women's Fashions 1890-1940 from the Collection of Beverley Birks. (Illus.). 44p. 1981. pap. 7.50 (0-911209-23-9) Palmer Mus Art.

— Paintings & Sculpture from Central Pennsylvania Collectors: Exhibition Catalogue. (Illus.). 80p. 1984. pap. 4.50 (0-911209-30-1) Palmer Mus Art.

Preisner, Olga K., ed. Bellefonte Collects: Exhibition Catalogue. (Illus.). 54p. 1989. pap. 10.00 (0-911209-40-9) Palmer Mus Art.

— Gods of the Greeks: Greek Coins from a Private Collection: Exhibition Catalogue. (Illus.). 24p. (Orig.). 1984. pap. 1.00 (0-911209-31-X) Palmer Mus Art.

— The Numismatic History of Ireland: History of Irish Coinage 1000 A. D. to the Present - Coins from a Private Collection: Exhibition Catalogue. (Illus.). 28p. (Orig.). 1984. 2.50 (0-911209-32-8) Palmer Mus Art.

Preisner, Olga K. & Landman, Hedy B. The England of William Penn: 1644-1718. (Illus.). 92p. 1982. 12.50 (0-911209-26-3) Palmer Mus Art.

Preiss, Byron. Where's Lulu? (J). (ps-3). 1991. 3.50 (0-553-35211-3) Bantam.

Preiss, Byron, ed. The Ultimate Witch. 1993. pap. 11.95 (0-440-50531-3, Dell Trade Pbks) Dell.

— The Ultimate Zombie. 1993. pap. 11.95 (0-440-50534-8, Dell Trade Pbks) Dell.

Preiss, Byron, ed. see Bradbury.

Preiss, Jack. Camp William James. (Illus.). 1978. 15.00 (0-912148-07-1); pap. 9.50 (0-912148-08-X) Argo Bks.

Preiss, Jack, jt. ed. see Heath, Robert L.

Preiss, Jack, jt. auth. see Tolbert, N. Edward.

Preiss, Jack, et al, eds. The Biochemistry of Plants, Carbohydrates Vol. 14: A Comprehensive Treatise. 529p. 1988. text ed. 163.00 (0-12-675414-4) Acad Pr.

Preiss, Jack J. & Ehrlich, Howard J. An Examination of Role Theory: The Case of the State Police. LC 66-10874. 296p. reprint ed. pap. 84.40 (0-8357-2943-5, 2039199) Bks Demand.

Preiss, Kenneth, ed. Agile Customer-Supplier Relations. (Report Ser. in Agility). 75p. (Orig.). 1994. pap. 25.00 (1-885166-00-1) Agile Manufact.

Preiss, Kenneth, ed. see Twenty-First Century Manufacturing Enterprise Strategy Staff.

***Preiss, Kenneth, et al.** Agile Competitors & Virtual Organizations: Strategies for Enriching the Customer. (Industrial Engineering Ser.). 250p. 1994. text ed. 29.95 (0-442-01903-3) Van Nos Reinhold.

Preiss, Leah P. The Pig's Alphabet. LC 88-45808. (Illus.). 36p. (J). 1989. 9.95 (0-87923-781-3) Godine.

Preiss, Linda, ed. see Baoudndi, M. Salah, et al.

Preissinger, Adrian. From Sachsenhausen to Buchenwald: Death Camps of the Soviets, 1945-1950. Clary-Smith, Heather, tr. (Illus.). 317p. (C). 1994. 29.95 (1-880881-11-X) Landpost Pr.

Preissle, Judith, jt. auth. see LeCompte, Margaret D.

Preissner, Klaus T., et al, eds. Biology of Vitronectins & Their Receptors: Proceedings of the First International Vitronectin Workshop. LC 93-33787. (International Congress Ser.: Vol. 1042). 1993. 203.25 (0-444-81680-1, Excerpta Medica) Elsevier.

Preister, Steven, ed. see Schervish, Paul, et al.

Preiswerk, Roy, ed. see Kapp, K. William.

Preiswork, Roy & Perrot, Dominique. Ethnocentrism & History. LC 74-81856. 1978. 21.50 (0-88357-071-8); pap. 8.95 (0-88357-072-6) NOK Pubs.

Prejean, Blanche G. & Danielson, Wayne A. Programmed News Style. (Basic Skills in Journalism Ser.). 1978. pap. text ed. write for info. (0-13-730655-5) P-H.

— Programmed News Style. 2nd ed. (Basic Skills in Journalism Ser.). 144p. 1987. pap. text ed. write for info. (0-13-729070-5) P-H.

Prejean, Helen. Dead Man Walking: An Eyewitness Account of the Death Penalty in the United States. LC 92-56839. 192p. 1993. 21.00 (0-679-40358-2) Random.

— Dead Man Walking: An Eyewitness Account of the Death Penalty in the United States. 1994. pap. 12.00 (0-679-75131-9, Vin) Random.

Prejevalsky, N. Mongolia: The Tangut Country & the Solitudes of Northern Tibet. (C). 1991. reprint ed. text ed. 74.00 (81-206-0680-9, Pub. by Asian Educ Servs II) S Asia.

Prejovich, S, ed. Socialism: Institutional, Philosophical & Economic Issues. (C). 1987. lib. bdg. 80.50 (90-247-3487-8) Kluwer Ac.

***Prekopa, A.** Stochastic Programming. 600p. 1995. 85.00 (963-05-6872-1, Pub. by A K HU) Intl Spec Bk.

— Studies on Mathematical Programming. 200p. 1980. 74.00 (0-569-08626-4, Pub. by Collets UK) Pro-Am Music.

— Studies on Mathematical Programming. (Mathematical Methods of Operations Research Ser.: No. 1). 200p. (C). 1980. 53.00x (963-05-1854-6, Pub. by Akad Kiado HU) St Mut.

Prekopa, A., ed. Survey of Mathematical Programming: Proceedings of the 9th Math Programming Symposium, Budapest, 1976, 3 vols., Set. 1554p. 1980. 266.75 (0-444-85033-3, North Holland) Elsevier.

Prekopa, A., jt. ed. see Wets, Roger J.

Prekopa, A., et al, eds. System Modelling & Optimization. (Lecture Notes in Control & Information Sciences Ser.: Vol. 84). (Illus.). 1060p. 1986. pap. 153.00 (0-387-16854-0) Spr-Verlag.

***Prekopa, Andras.** Stochastic Programming. LC 95-10779. (Mathematics & Its Applications Ser.). 1995. write for info. (0-7923-3482-5) Kluwer Ac.

***Prelas, Mark A., et al, eds.** Wide Band Gap Electronic Materials: Proceedings of the NATO Advanced Research Workshop on "Wide Band Gap Electronic Materials-Diamond, Aluminum Nitride & Boron Nitride", Minsk, Belarus, May 4-6, 1994. LC 95-7367. (NATO Advanced Science Institutes - Partnership Sub Series 3: Vol. 1). 552p. (C). 1995. lib. bdg. 247.00 (0-7923-3405-1) Kluwer Ac.

Prelec, Krsto, ed. Production & Neutralization of Negative Ions & Beams: International Symposium, Brookhaven, 1983. 3rd ed. LC 84-70379. (AIP Conference Proceedings Ser.: No. 111). 778p. 1984. lib. bdg. 53.75 (0-88318-310-2) Am Inst Physics.

Prelinger, Catherine M. Charity, Challenge, & Change: Religious Dimensions of the Mid-Nineteenth Century Women's Movement in Germany. LC 86-19432. (Contributions in Women's Studies: No. 75). 225p. 1987. text ed. 55.00 (0-313-25401-X, PCY/) Greenwood.

Prelinger, Catherine M., ed. Episcopal Women: Gender, Spirituality, & Commitment in an American Mainline Denomination. (Religion in America Ser.). (Illus.). 384p. 1992. 29.95 (0-19-507433-5) OUP.

Prelinger, Elizabeth. Edvard Munch: Master Printmaker. LC 83-42651. (Illus.). 158p. 1995. pap. 14.95 (0-393-01797-4, 797-4) A Schwartz & Co.

— Kathe Kollwitz. LC 91-46307. (Illus.). 192p. 1992. pap. 27.50 (0-89468-170-2) Natl Gallery Art.

— Kathe Kollwitz. (Illus.). 272p. 1994. pap. 27.50 (0-300-06168-4) Yale U Pr.

Prelinger, Richard, ed. Monitor America. (Frequency Guide Ser.: No. 8). (Illus.). 608p. 1985. 14.95 (0-939430-07-X) Scanner Master.

Prelinger, Richard & Hoffnar, Celeste R., eds. Footage Eighty-Nine: North American Film & Video Sources. LC 88-90769. (Orig.). 1989. pap. 95.00 (0-927347-01-6) Prelinger Assocs.

Prell, Frank. Balloon Pins, Vol. 1. LC 85-71996. (Illus.). 112p. (Orig.). 1985. per. 12.95 (0-9615189-0-1) Oxford Promot.

Prell, Jan R., jt. auth. see Orcutt, Ted L.

Prell, Riv-Ellen. Interdisciplinary Writing Through Multidisciplinary Writing. Bridwell-Bowles, Lillian et al, eds. (Technical Report Ser.: No. 3). 26p. (Orig.). 1993. pap. 3.00 (1-881221-06-7) U Minn Ctr Interdis.

— Prayer & Community: The Havurah Movement in American Judaism. LC 88-25107. (Illus.). 336p. 1989. 39.95 (0-8143-1934-3); pap. 19.95 (0-8143-1935-1) Wayne St U Pr.

Preller, James. Wake Me in Spring. (Hello Reader! Ser.). (Illus.). (J). (gr. 2). 1994. pap. 2.95 (0-590-48189-4, Cartwheel) Scholastic Inc.

— Wake Me in the Spring. LC 93-16787. (Hello Reader! Ser.). (Illus.). (J). 1994. pap. 2.95 (0-590-47500-2, Cartwheel) Scholastic Inc.

Preller, Ludwig. Griechische Mythologie, Bd. I: Theogonie und Gotter. xviii, 964p. 1964. write for info. (3-296-15101-X, Pub. by Georg Olms GW) Lubrecht & Cramer.

— Griechische Mythologie, Bd. II: Die Griechische Heldensage: Landschaftliche Sagen, Buch 1. xii, 420p. 1966. write for info. (3-296-15102-8, Pub. by Georg Olms GW) Lubrecht & Cramer.

— Griechische Mythologie, Bd. II, Buch 3: Die Groben Heldenepen. Date not set. write for info. (3-296-15104-4, Pub. by Georg Olms GW) Lubrecht & Cramer.

— Griechische Mythology. Bolle, Kees W., ed. LC 77-79153. (Mythology Ser.). (GER.). 1978. lib. bdg. 68.95 (0-405-10562-2) Ayer.

— Griechiscshe Mythologie, Bd. II, Buch 2: Die Nationalheroen. viii, 156p. 1966. write for info. (3-296-15103-6, Pub. by Georg Olms GW) Lubrecht & Cramer.

— Romische Mythologie: Roman Mythology. Bolle, Kees W., ed. LC 77-79154. (Mythology Ser.). (GER.). 1978. reprint ed. lib. bdg. 58.95 (0-405-10563-0) Ayer.

— Romisscshe Mythologie, Bd. 1. xii, 455p. 1978. write for info. (3-296-15111-7, Pub. by Georg Olms GW) Lubrecht & Cramer.

— Romisscshe Mythologie, Bd. 2. xi, 490p. 1978. write for info. (3-296-15112-5, Pub. by Georg Olms GW) Lubrecht & Cramer.

Preller, Victor. Divine Science & the Science of God: A Reformulation of Thomas Aquinas. LC 66-21838. 291p. reprint ed. pap. 83.00 (0-317-08468-2, 2010543) Bks Demand.

Prelli, Lawrence. A Rhetoric of Science: Inventing Scientific Discourse. Arnold, Carroll C., ed. (Studies in Rhetoric-Communication). 331p. (C). 1989. text ed. 34.95 (0-87249-645-7) U of SC Pr.

Prelock, Patricia & Prendeville, Jo-Anne. Communication Science Resource Manual. 2nd ed. 76p. (C). 1993. spiral bd. 14.95 (0-8403-9100-5) Kendall-Hunt.

P Q

Prels, M. Kino: A Study of the German Film 1915-1919. 1976. lib. bdg. 70.00 (*0-8490-2118-9*) Gordon Pr.

***Prelutsky, Burt.** Interviews with Everyday Angels. (Illus.). 1995. 9.95 (*0-8431-3899-8*) Price Stern.

Prelutsky, Jack. A. Nonny Mouse Writes Again! LC 92-5214. (Illus.). 40p. (J). (ps-5). 1993. 13.00 (*0-679-83715-9*); lib. bdg. 13.99 (*0-679-93715-3*) Knopf Bks Yng Read.

— The Baby Uggs Are Hatching. LC 81-7266. (Illus.). 32p. (J). (ps up). 1989. pap. 3.95 (*0-688-09239-X*, Mulberry) Morrow.

— The Baby Uggs Are Hatching! LC 81-7266. (Illus.). 32p. (J). (gr. k-3). 1982. 15.00 (*0-688-00922-0*); lib. bdg. 14.93 (*0-688-00923-9*) Greenwillow.

— Beneath a Blue Umbrella. LC 86-19406. (Illus.). 64p. (J). (ps up). 1990. 15.95 (*0-688-06429-9*) Greenwillow.

— Circus! 2nd ed. (Illus.). 32p. (J). (ps-2). 1989. reprint ed. pap. 4.95 (*0-689-70806-8*, Aladdin Paperbacks) S&S Childrens.

— The Dragons Are Singing Tonight. LC 92-29013. (Illus.). 40p. (J). (ps up). 1993. 16.00 (*0-688-09645-X*); lib. bdg. 15.93 (*0-688-12511-5*) Greenwillow.

— The Headless Horseman Rides Tonight. LC 80-10372. (Illus.). 40p. (J). (gr. 1-4). 1980. 13.95 (*0-688-80273-7*); lib. bdg. 13.88 (*0-688-84273-9*) Greenwillow.

— The Headless Horseman Rides Tonight. ALC Staff, ed. LC 80-10372. (Illus.). 40p. (J). (gr. 1 up). 1992. pap. 4.95 (*0-688-11705-8*, Mulberry) Morrow.

— It's Christmas. LC 81-1100. (Greenwillow Read-Alone Bks.). (Illus.). 48p. (J). (gr. 1-3). 1981. 15.00 (*0-688-00439-3*); lib. bdg. 14.93 (*0-688-00440-7*) Greenwillow.

— It's Christmas. (Illus.). 48p. (J). (gr. k-3). 1986. 2.75 (*0-590-44048-9*) Scholastic Inc.

— It's Christmas. (Illus.). 48p. (J). (gr. k-3). 1987. audio 5.95 (*0-590-63171-3*) Scholastic Inc.

— It's Halloween. LC 77-2141. (Greenwillow Read-Alone Bks.). (Illus.). 56p. (J). (gr. 1-4). 1977. 13.95 (*0-688-80102-1*); lib. bdg. 13.88 (*0-688-84102-3*) Greenwillow.

— It's Halloween. (Illus.). 48p. (J). (ps-3). 1987. Books & Cassette. audio 5.95 (*0-590-63252-3*) Scholastic Inc.

— It's Halloween. (Illus.). 48p. (J). (ps-3). 1994. pap. 2.50 (*0-590-41536-0*) Scholastic Inc.

— It's Snowing! It's Snowing! LC 83-16583. (Illus.). 48p. (J). (gr. 1-3). 1984. 12.95 (*0-688-01512-3*); lib. bdg. 14.93 (*0-688-01513-1*) Greenwillow.

— It's Thanksgiving. LC 81-1929. (Greenwillow Read-Alone Bks.). (Illus.). 48p. (J). (gr. 1-3). 1982. 14.00 (*0-688-00441-5*); lib. bdg. 13.93 (*0-688-00442-3*) Greenwillow.

— It's Thanksgiving. (Illus.). 48p. (J). (gr. k-3). 1987. reprint ed. Bk.-Cassette prepack. audio 5.95 (*0-590-63169-1*) Scholastic Inc.

— It's Thanksgiving. (Illus.). 48p. (J). (gr. k-3). 1994. reprint ed. pap. 2.50 (*0-590-41571-9*) Scholastic Inc.

— It's Valentine's Day. LC 83-1449. (Greenwillow Read-Alone Bks.). (Illus.). 48p. (J). (gr. 1-3). 1983. 15.00 (*0-688-02311-8*); lib. bdg. 14.93 (*0-688-02312-6*) Greenwillow.

— It's Valentine's Day. (Illus.). 48p. (J). (gr. k-3). 1985. reprint ed. pap. 2.50 (*0-590-40979-4*) Scholastic Inc.

— It's Valentine's Day. (Book Cassette Ser.). (Illus.). 48p. (J). (gr. k-3). 1988. reprint ed. digital audio 5.95 (*0-590-63172-1*) Scholastic Inc.

— Kermit's Garden of Verses. LC 82-480. (Muppet Press Bks.). (Illus.). 64p. (J). (gr. 4-6). 1982. lib. bdg. 5.99 (*0-394-95410-6*) Random Bks Yng Read.

— The Mean Old Mean Hyena. LC 78-2300. (Illus.). 32p. (J). (gr. k-3). 1978. lib. bdg. 11.88 (*0-688-84163-5*) Greenwillow.

— My Parents Think I'm Sleeping. LC 84-13640. (Illus.). 48p. (J). (gr. 2-4). 1985. 16.00 (*0-688-04018-7*); lib. bdg. 15.93 (*0-688-04019-5*) Greenwillow.

— My Parents Think I'm Sleeping. Cohn, Amy, ed. LC 84-13640. (Illus.). 48p. (J). (gr. k up). 1995. reprint ed. pap. 4.95 (*0-688-14028-9*, Mulberry) Morrow.

— New Kid on Block. 1994. pap. 29.50 (*1-57135-072-1*) Living Bks.

— The New Kid on the Block. LC 83-20621. (Illus.). 160p. (J). (gr. 1 up). 1984. 17.95 (*0-688-02271-5*); lib. bdg. 15.88 (*0-688-02272-3*) Greenwillow.

— Nightmares: Poems to Trouble Your Sleep. LC 76-4820. (Illus.). 40p. (J). (gr. 3 up). 1976. 14.00 (*0-688-80053-X*); lib. bdg. 13.93 (*0-688-84053-1*) Greenwillow.

— Nightmares: Poems to Trouble Your Sleep. LC 92-43780. (Illus.). 40p. (J). 1993. pap. 4.95 (*0-688-04589-8*, Mulberry) Morrow.

— The Queen of Eene. LC 77-17311. (Illus.). 32p. (J). (gr. k-3). 1978. lib. bdg. 14.88 (*0-688-84144-9*) Greenwillow.

— Rainy, Rainy Saturday. LC 79-22217. (Greenwillow Read-Alone Bks.). (Illus.). 48p. (J). (gr. 1-3). 1980. lib. bdg. 14.93 (*0-688-84252-6*) Greenwillow.

— Rainy, Rainy Saturday. LC 79-22217. (Greenwillow Read-Alone Bks.). (Illus.). 48p. (J). (gr. 1-3). 1980. 15.00 (*0-688-80252-4*) Greenwillow.

— The Random House Book of Poetry for Children. LC 81-85940. (Illus.). 248p. (J). (gr. 1-5). 1983. 19.00 (*0-394-85010-6*); lib. bdg. 17.99 (*0-394-95010-0*) Random Bks Yng Read.

— Ride a Purple Pelican. LC 84-6024. (Illus.). 64p. (J). (ps up). 1986. 17.95 (*0-688-04031-4*) Greenwillow.

— Rolling Harvey Down the Hill. LC 79-18236. (Illus.). 32p. (J). (gr. k-3). 1980. 14.95 (*0-688-80258-3*); lib. bdg. 12.88 (*0-688-84258-5*) Greenwillow.

— Rolling Harvey Down the Hill. LC 92-24606. (Illus.). 40p. (J). (gr. 2 up). 1993. reprint ed. pap. 4.95 (*0-688-12270-1*, Mulberry) Morrow.

— The Sheriff of Rottenshot. LC 81-6420. (Illus.). 32p. (J). (gr. k-3). 1982. 12.95 (*0-688-00205-6*); lib. bdg. 14.93 (*0-688-00198-X*) Greenwillow.

— The Sheriff of Rottenshot. Cohn, Amy, ed. LC 81-6420. (Illus.). 48p. (J). (gr. k up). 1994. reprint ed. pap. 4.95 (*0-688-13635-4*, Mulberry) Morrow.

— The Snopp on the Sidewalk & Other Poems. LC 76-46323. (Illus.). 32p. (J). (gr. 3 up). 1977. lib. bdg. 15.93 (*0-688-84084-1*) Greenwillow.

— Something Big Has Been Here. LC 89-34773. (Illus.). 160p. (J). (gr. k up). 1990. 17.95 (*0-688-06434-5*) Greenwillow.

— Sweet & Silly Muppet Poems. (First Little Golden Bks.). 24p. (J). (ps). 1992. 1.09 (*0-307-10249-1*, Golden Pr) Western Pub.

— The Terrible Tiger. LC 88-7901. (Illus.). 32p. (J). (ps-2). 1989. reprint ed. pap. 3.95 (*0-689-71300-2*, Aladdin Paperbacks) S&S Childrens.

— Tyrannosaurus Was a Beast. LC 87-25131. (Illus.). 32p. (J). (ps-6). 1988. 13.95 (*0-688-06442-6*); lib. bdg. 13.88 (*0-688-06443-4*) Greenwillow.

— Tyrannosaurus Was a Beast. LC 87-25131. (Illus.). 32p. (J). (ps up). 1992. pap. 4.95 (*0-688-11569-1*, Mulberry) Morrow.

— Tyrannosaurus Was a Beast: Big Book Edition. (Illus.). 32p. (J). (ps up). 1993. reprint ed. pap. 18.95 (*0-688-12613-8*, Mulberry) Morrow.

— Wednesday's Troll. LC 95-7085. (Illus.). 32p. (J). 1996. write for info. (*0-688-09644-1*); lib. bdg. write for info. (*0-688-14373-3*) Greenwillow.

— What I Did Last Summer. LC 83-11561. (Greenwillow Read-Alone Bks.). (Illus.). 48p. (J). (gr. 1-3). 1984. 13.95 (*0-688-01754-1*) Greenwillow.

— Zoo Doings: Animal Poems. LC 82-11996. (Illus.). 80p. (J). (gr. 1-3). 1983. 13.00 (*0-688-01782-7*); lib. bdg. 12.93 (*0-688-01784-3*) Greenwillow.

Prelutsky, Jack, ed. Read Aloud Rhymes for the Very Young. LC 86-7147. (Illus.). 112p. (J). (ps-3). 1986. 19.00 (*0-394-87218-5*); lib. bdg. 17.99 (*0-394-97218-X*) Knopf Bks Yng Read.

Prelutsky, Jack, tr. see Lindgren, Barbro.

Prem, Anand, ed. see Osho.

Prem, Ananda, ed. see Osho.

Prem, Daulat R. Criminal Practice, Eighteen Sixty-Four to Nineteen Eighty. 7th ed. (C). 1983. 130.00 (*0-685-36518-2*) St Mut.

Prem, Krishna, ed. see Rajneesh, Osho.

Prem, Sri K. & Ashish, Sri Madhava. Man: The Measure of All Things. LC 74-87256. 1969. 16.95 (*0-8356-0006-8*, Quest) Theos Pub Hse.

Prem, Sri-Krishma. The Yoga of the Bhagavad Gita. 256p. 1988. pap. 13.95 (*1-85230-023-X*) Element MA.

Prem, T. Criminal Practice, 7 vols. (C). 1988. 1,000.00 (*0-685-25687-1*) St Mut.

Premack, Ann J., jt. auth. see Premack, David.

Premack, David & Premack, Ann J. The Mind of an Ape. (Illus.). 176p. 1984. reprint ed. pap. 6.95 (*0-393-30160-5*) Norton.

Premazzi, Guido & Volterra, Laura. Microphyte Toxins: A Manual for Toxin Detection, Environmental Monitoring. 338p. 1994. pap. 50.00 (*92-826-2731-4*, Pub. by Europ Com) UNIPUB.

Premchand, A. Godan. Lal, P., tr. 1972. pap. 5.50 (*0-88253-069-0*) Ind-US Inc.

— Government Budgeting & Expenditure Controls: Theory & Practice. xii, 540p. 1983. 24.00 (*0-939934-24-8*); pap. 18.00 (*0-939934-25-6*) Intl Monetary.

— Nirmala. Rubin, David, tr. (C). 1988. 17.50 (*81-7094-030-3*, Pub. by Vision Books II) Asia Bk Corp.

— Public Expenditure Management. LC 92-44308. x, 282p. 1993. pap. 20.00 (*1-55775-323-7*) Intl Monetary.

Premchand, A., ed. Government Financial Management: Issues & Country Studies. LC 90-41275. x, 374p. 1990. pap. 21.50 (*1-55775-149-8*) Intl Monetary.

Premchand, A. & Antonaya, A. L., eds. Aspectos del Presupuesto Publico. x, 285p. 1988. pap. 12.50 (*1-55775-014-9*) Intl Monetary.

Premchand, A. & Burkhead, Jesse. Comparative International Budgeting & Finance. 319p. 1984. pap. 21.95x (*0-87855-966-3*) Transaction Pubs.

Premeaux, Shane R., jt. auth. see Mondy, R. Wayne.

Premfors, R. Higher Education Organization: Conditions for Policy Implementation. 180p. (Orig.). 1984. pap. text ed. 45.50x (*91-22-00688-5*, Pub. by Almqv & Wiksell SW) Coronet Bks.

Premi, Kusum K. Scheduled Castes & Scheduled Tribes in Industrial Training Institutes. 150p. 1988. text ed. 25.00 (*0-7069-4263-9*, Pub. by Vikas II) S Asia.

Premi, Mahendra K. The Demographic Situation in India. LC 82-1509. (Papers of the East-West Population Institute: No. 80). ix, 152p. (Orig.). 1982. pap. text ed. 2.50 (*0-86638-011-6*) EW Ctr HI.

Premi, Mahendra K. & Tom, Judith A. City Characteristics, Migration, & Urban Development Policies in India. LC 85-13102. (Papers of the East-West Population Institute: No. 92). vii, 127p. 1985. pap. 3.00 (*0-86638-061-2*) EW Ctr HI.

Preminger, Alex & Brogan, T. V., eds. Princeton Encyclopedia of Poetry & Poetics. 3rd ed. text ed. 125.00 (*0-691-03271-8*); pap. text ed. 29.95 (*0-691-02123-6*) Princeton U Pr.

Preminger, Alex, jt. ed. see Greenstein, Edward L.

Preminger, Alex, et al, eds. The Princeton Handbook of Poetic Terms. LC 85-43380. 250p. 1986. text ed. 44.50 (*0-691-06659-0*); pap. 12.95 (*0-691-01425-6*) Princeton U Pr.

Preminger, Glenn M., jt. auth. see Sagalowsky, Arthur I.

Premm, Mattias. Dogmatic Theology for the Laity. 1977. pap. 18.00 (*0-89555-022-9*) TAN Bks Pubs.

Premo, Kent F., ed. see Virts, William B.

Premo, Terri L. Winter Friends: Women Growing Old in the New Republic, 1785-1835. LC 89-4980. (Women in American History Ser.). (Illus.). 216p. 1990. 24.95 (*0-252-01656-4*) U of Ill Pr.

Premoe, David, ed. Zion, the Growing Symbol. 1980. pap. 8.50 (*0-8309-0301-1*) Herald Hse.

Premoe, David, jt. auth. see Premoe, Deborah.

Premoe, Deborah & Premoe, David. Multiple Faith Relationships. (Pastoral Care Office Pamphlet Ser.). 84p. 1984. pap. text ed. 6.50 (*0-8309-0390-9*) Herald Hse.

Premoli, Orazio M. Contemporary Church History. 1977. lib. bdg. 59.95 (*0-8490-1669-X*) Gordon Pr.

Premoli, P. Flessoni, Rime, Anagrammi: L'Italiano in Scatola di Montaggio. 1991. 85.00 (*0-8288-3920-4*, F127300) Fr & Eur.

— Italiano - Ortografia. 1991. 24.95 (*0-8288-3921-2*, F18320) Fr & Eur.

— Vocabolario Nomenclatorio. 1991. 250.00 (*0-8288-3919-0*, F83910) Fr & Eur.

Premuzic, Eugene T. & Woodhead, Avril D., eds. Microbial Enhancement of Oil Recovery: Recent Advances. LC 93-22897. (Developments in Petroleum Science: Vol. 39). 1993. write for info. (*0-444-89690-2*) Elsevier.

Prendergast, jt. auth. see Caws.

Prendergast, jt. ed. see Caws.

Prendergast, Alan. The Poison Tree: A True Story of Family Terror. 336p. 1987. mass mkt. 4.95 (*0-380-70346-7*) Avon.

Prendergast, Alice. Medical Terminology. 2nd ed. 1983. teacher ed write for info. (*0-201-05956-8*) Addison-Wesley.

— Medical Terminology: A Text-Workbook. 3rd ed. McCormick, Mark, ed. 384p. (C). 1991. pap. text ed. 29.25 (*0-201-52258-6*) Addison-Wesley.

Prendergast, Christine, jt. auth. see Rosenberg, Helane S.

Prendergast, Christopher. Balzac: Fiction & Melodrama. LC 78-11267. 205p. 1979. text ed. 32.50 (*0-8419-0457-X*) Holmes & Meier.

— The Order of Mimesis: Balzac, Stendhal, Nerval & Flaubert. (Cambridge Studies in French: No. 12). (Illus.). 288p. 1986. 64.95 (*0-521-23789-0*) Cambridge U Pr.

— The Order of Mimesis: Balzac, Stendhal, Nerval & Flaubert. (Cambridge Studies in French: No. 12). (Illus.). 288p. 1988. pap. 24.95 (*0-521-36977-0*) Cambridge U Pr.

— Paris & the Nineteenth Century. (Writing the City Ser.). (Illus.). 296p. 1995. pap. text ed. 21.95 (*0-631-19694-3*) Blackwell Pubs.

— Paris & the Nineteenth Century. (Writing the City Ser.). (Illus.). 296p. 1995. reprint ed. text ed. 24.95 (*0-631-15788-3*) Blackwell Pubs.

***Prendergast, Christopher, ed.** Cultural Materialism: On Raymond Williams. LC 94-36190. (Cultural Politics: Vol. 9). 1995. text ed. 49.95 (*0-8166-2280-9*); pap. text ed. 21.95 (*0-8166-2281-7*) U of Minn Pr.

— Nineteenth-Century French Poetry: Introductions to Close Reading. 1990. 59.95 (*0-521-34541-3*); pap. 17.95 (*0-521-34774-2*) Cambridge U Pr.

Prendergast, Christopher, jt. auth. see Caws, Mary A.

Prendergast, Christopher, jt. auth. see Cohen, Margaret.

Prendergast, Curtis, ed. Productivity: The Link to Social & Economic Progress. LC 76-19833. (Swedish-American Exchange of Views Ser.). 55p. 1976. pap. text ed. 3.50 (*0-89361-000-3*) Work in Amer.

Prendergast, Dorothy. The Wolf Hybrid. 2nd rev. ed. (Illus.). (Orig.). 1989. pap. 17.00 (*0-9623640-0-2*) Rudelhaus Enter.

***Prendergast, Dorothy, ed.** Across the Years. (Illus.). 1995. pap. write for info. (*0-614-04961-X*) Rudelhaus Enter.

Prendergast, Guy L. A Complete Concordance to the Iliad of Homer. enl. rev. ed. vii, 427p. 1983. reprint ed. 128.70 (*3-487-04161-8*, Pub. by Georg Olms GW) Lubrecht & Cramer.

***Prendergast, James C.** Red Flags. 1994. write for info. (*0-7931-1203-6*, Real Estate Ed) Dearborn Finan.

Prendergast, James H., jt. auth. see Chiarito, Marian D.

Prendergast, James J., jt. auth. see Franklin, David A.

***Prendergast, John.** Jump. (First Novel Ser.). 256p. (Orig.). 1995. pap. 14.00 (*0-922811-23-7*) Mid-List.

— The Road to India: Guide to the Overland Routes to India. (Illus.). 1978. 19.50 (*0-7195-3396-1*) Transatl Arts.

***Prendergast, John & Miller, Terence.** A Guide for Activists: Handbook on African Hunger. 28p. (Orig.). 1993. pap. text ed. write for info. (*0-934255-13-X*) Center Concern.

Prendergast, John & Pauling, Sharon. Peace, Development & People of the Horn of Africa. (Hunger Policy Occasional Papers: No. 1). (Orig.). (C). 1992. pap. text ed. 5.00 (*0-685-48887-X*) Bread for the World.

Prendergast, John, jt. auth. see Duffield, Mark.

Prendergast, Lesley J. Secretary to Paralegal: A Career Manual & Guide. LC 84-6641. 272p. 1984. 24.95 (*0-87624-510-6*, Inst Busn Plan) P-H.

Prendergast, Maurice. Beechmont. (Fine Art Jigsaw Puzzles Ser.). 1989. 9.95 (*0-934967-48-2*) Battle Rd Pr.

Prendergast, Renee & Singer, H. W., eds. Development Perspectives for the 1990s. LC 91-24054. 350p. 1991. text ed. 69.95 (*0-312-06803-4*) St Martin.

***Prendergast, Richard A.** Learn PROCOMM Plus 2.0 for Windows in a Day. (Popular Applications Ser.). 144p. (Orig.). 1995. pap. 15.95 (*1-55622-443-5*) Wordware Pub.

Prendergast, Roy M. Film Music: A Neglected Art. 2nd ed. 352p. 1992. 24.95 (*0-393-02988-3*); pap. 12.95 (*0-393-30874-X*) Norton.

Prendergast, Thomas F. Forgotten Pioneers: Irish Leaders in Early California. LC 72-1248. (Essay Index Reprint Ser.). 1977. reprint ed. 22.95 (*0-8369-2854-7*) Ayer.

Prendergast, William E. The Merry-Go-Round of Sexual Abuse: Identifying & Treating Survivors. LC 93-17364. (Illus.). 282p. 1994. lib. bdg. 39.95 (*1-56024-387-2*); pap. 19.95 (*1-56024-388-0*) Haworth Pr.

***Prendergrast, Dorothy, et al.** Above Reproach: A Guide for Wolf Hybrid Owners. (Illus.). 200p. (Orig.). 1995. pap. 23.00 (*0-9623640-1-0*) Rudelhaus Enter.

Prendes, J. M., ed. see Menendez Pidal, Ramon.

Prendeville, Dennis E. Common Stock Price Histories: 1910-1987. 2nd ed. (Illus.). 253p. 1988. pap. 39.95 (*0-9618454-1-4*) WIT Financial Pubs.

— Common Stock Price Histories: 1910-1987. 2nd suppl. ed. (Illus.). 253p. 1988. 14.95 (*0-685-19812-X*) WIT Financial Pubs.

— Common Stock Price Histories 1910-1986. (Illus.). 208p. (Orig.). 1987. pap. 39.95 (*0-9618454-0-6*) WIT Financial Pubs.

Prendeville, Jo-Anne, jt. auth. see Prelock, Patricia.

Prendiville, Brendan. Environmental Politics in France. 190p. (C). 1994. text ed. 49.95 (*0-8133-8822-8*) Westview.

Prendiville, Walter, ed. Large Loop Excision of the Transformation Zone: A Practical Guide to LLETZ. LC 92-49021. 1992. write for info. (*0-412-46240-0*); write for info. (*0-442-31708-5*) Chapman & Hall.

Preneel, Bart, et al, eds. Computer Security & Industrial Cryptography: State of the Art & Evolution: ESAT Course, Leuven, Belgium, May 21-23, 1991. LC 93-32467. (Lecture Notes in Computer Science Ser.: Vol. 741). 1993. 44.00 (*0-387-57341-0*) Spr-Verlag.

***Prenelau, Sheryl.** B. Y. Times Kid Sisters No. 10: Giant Steps. (Illus.). 108p. (Orig.). (J). (gr. 3-7). 1994. pap. 6.95 (*1-56871-063-1*) Targum Pr.

Prengaman, jt. auth. see Little.

Prengaman, R. D., jt. ed. see Mackey, T. S.

Prenis, John. The Windowsill Herb Garden. LC 90-52739. (Illus.). 96p. (Orig.). 1990. pap. 8.95 (*0-89471-890-8*); 12.98 (*0-89471-886-X*) Running Pr.

Prenn, U. L. Graham Joke Book. (Illus.). 74p. (Orig.). 1990. pap. 12.00x (*0-937041-71-8*) Systems Co.

— Introduction to Ball Lightning: Rare Events. (Illus.). 100p. (Orig.). 1991. 70.00 (*0-937041-95-5*); pap. 40.00 (*0-937041-96-3*) Systems Co.

— Introduction to Biological Radiation Effects. 2nd ed. (Illus.). 120p. 1994. 110.00 (*1-56216-205-5*); pap. 80.00 (*1-56216-206-3*) Systems Co.

— Introduction to Biological Radiation Effects: An Overview of Terrestrial & Space Radiation Effects on Humans. (Illus.). 103p. (Orig.). (C). 1992. text ed. 100.00 (*1-56216-100-8*); pap. 70.00 (*1-56216-101-6*) Systems Co.

— Know These Facts. (Illus.). 100p. (Orig.). 1994. 65.00x (*1-56216-157-1*); pap. 35.00x (*1-56216-158-X*) Systems Co.

— Learn Successful Investment Techniques. (Illus.). 74p. (Orig.). 1990. pap. 12.00 (*0-937041-94-7*) Systems Co.

— Learn Successful Investment Techniques. 2nd ed. (Illus.). 74p. (Orig.). 1992. pap. 12.00 (*1-56216-159-8*) Systems Co.

— True Life Stories. (Illus.). 80p. (Orig.). 1991. 35.00x (*0-937041-97-1*); pap. 15.00x (*0-937041-98-X*) Systems Co.

— True Life Stories. 2nd ed. (Illus.). 80p. (Orig.). 1993. 55.00x (*1-56216-215-2*); pap. 35.00x (*1-56216-216-0*) Systems Co.

Prenowitz, W. & Jantosciak, J. The Theory of Join Spaces: A Contemporary Approach to Convex Sets & Linear Geometry. (Undergraduate Texts in Mathematics Ser.). (Illus.). 1979. 49.90 (*0-387-90340-2*) Spr-Verlag.

Prenowitz, Walter & Jordan, Meyer. Basic Concepts of Geometry. (Illus.). 350p. 1989. pap. text ed. 37.95 (*0-912675-48-9*) Ardsley.

Prenshaw, Peggy W., ed. Conversations with Elizabeth Spencer. LC 91-19455. (Literary Conversations Ser.). 1991. 37.50 (*0-87805-527-4*); pap. 15.95 (*0-87805-528-2*) U Pr of Miss.

— Conversations with Eudora Welty. LC 83-21668. (Literary Conversations Ser.). 367p. 1984. pap. 15.95 (*0-87805-206-2*) U Pr of Miss.

— Eudora Welty, Thirteen Essays: Selected from Eudora Welty, Critical Essays. LC 83-6945. 272p. reprint ed. pap. 77.60 (*0-7837-1065-8*, 2041587) Bks Demand.

Prenshaw, Peggy W. & McKee, Jesse O., eds. Sense of Place, Mississippi. LC 79-26098. (Illus.). 235p. reprint ed. pap. 67.00 (*0-7837-1074-7*, 2041598) Bks Demand.

Prensky, Arthur L. & Palkes, Helen. Care of the Neurologically Handicapped Child. (Illus.). 1982. 32.95 (*0-19-502917-8*) OUP.

Prenslau, Sheryl. Missing! (Kid Sisters Ser.: No. 9). (Illus.). 115p. (Orig.). (J). (gr. 3-6). 1994. pap. 6.95 (*1-56871-059-3*) Targum Pr.

Prenter, P. M. Splines & Variational Methods. 323p. 1989. pap. text ed. 49.95 (*0-471-50402-5*) Wiley.

Prentice. Fitness for College & Life. 3rd ed. 352p. (C). 1990. pap. 18.95 (*0-8016-3688-4*) Mosby Yr Bk.

— Fitness for College & Life. 4th ed. 352p. 1993. pap. 18.95 (*0-8016-7854-4*) Mosby Yr Bk.

— Rehabilitation Techniques in Sports Medicine. (Illus.). 400p. (C). 1990. 44.95 (*0-8016-6147-1*) Mosby Yr Bk.

— Rehabilitation Techniques in Sports Medicine. 1993. pap. 49.95 (*0-8016-7819-6*); pap. 49.95 (*0-8016-7820-X*) Mosby Yr Bk.

— Therapeutic Modalities in Sports Medicine. (SPA.). 1992. 40.90 (*0-8016-6714-3*) Mosby Yr Bk.

— Therapeutic Modalities in Sports Medicine. 1994. 44.95 (*0-8016-7922-2*) Mosby Yr Bk.

— Therapeutic Modalities in Sports Medicine. 2nd ed. (Illus.). 336p. (C). 1989. 44.95 (*0-8016-3358-3*) Mosby Yr Bk.

— Webster's New World Dictionary. 1995. pap. 11.00 (*0-671-8944X-4*) PB.

An Asterisk (*) at the beginning of an entry indicates that the title is appearing in BIP for the first time.

Prentice, Alison & Theobald, Marjorie R., eds. Women Who Taught: Perspectives on the History of Women & Teaching. 304p. 1991. 45.00 (*0-8020-2745-8*); pap. 17.95 (*0-8020-6785-9*) U of Toronto Pr.

Prentice, Alison, jt. auth. see Houston, Susan E.

Prentice, Ann, jt. ed. see Pemberton, J. Michael.

Prentice, Ann E. Financial Planning for Libraries. LC 82-7330. 236p. 1983. 20.00 (*0-8108-1565-6*) Scarecrow.

— Financial Planning for Libraries. 2nd ed. LC 94-42908. (Library Administration: No. 12). 1995. write for info. (*0-8108-2974-6*) Scarecrow.

Prentice, Ann E. & Shaw, Debra, eds. Public Library Networking & Interlibrary Co-Operation. (Public Library Quarterly: Vol. 2, Nos. 3-4). 113p. 1982. pap. text ed. 24.95 (*0-86656-116-1*) Haworth Pr.

Prentice, Ann E., jt. auth. see Lindsey, Jonathan A.

Prentice, Archibald. Historical Sketches & Personal Recollections of Manchester: Intended to Illustrate Progress of Public Opinion from 1792-1832. 3rd rev. ed. 432p. 1970. reprint ed. 35.00 (*0-7146-1353-3*, BHA-01353, Pub. by F Cass Pubs UK) Intl Spec Bk.

— History of the Anti-Corn Law League, 2 vols., Set. 2nd ed. 1968. reprint ed. 65.00 (*0-7146-1352-5*, Pub. by F Cass Pubs UK) Intl Spec Bk.

Prentice, Beatriz G. Beatriz: A Manual for Peace. LC 83-51579. (Illus.). 414p. (Orig.). 1984. pap. 9.95 (*0-915485-10-9*) World Purpose Found.

Prentice, D. D. EEC Directives on Company Law & Financial Markets. 336p. 1991. pap. 59.00 (*0-19-825259-5*) OUP.

Prentice, D. D. & Stokes, Mary, eds. Butterworths Company Law Cases. 1988. U.K. 1,260.00 (*0-406-07650-2*) Butterworth Legal Pubs.

Prentice, Diana & Payne, James. More Than Talking. 2nd ed. 246p. (gr. 10-12). 1989. pap. 15.33 (*0-931054-20-6*) Clark Pub.

Prentice, E. Parmalee & Egan, John G. The Commerce Clause of the Federal Constitution. lxxv, 386p. 1981. reprint ed. lib. bdg. 37.50 (*0-8377-2505-4*) Rothman.

***Prentice, Ernest, et al, eds.** Current Issues & New Frontiers in Animal Research. 1995. pap. write for info. (*0-614-06555-0*) Scientists Ctr.

Prentice, Geoffrey & Smyrl, William, eds. Perspectives on Corrosion. (AIChE Symposium Ser.: Vol. 86, No. 278). 1990. pap. 44.00 (*0-8169-0495-2*) Am Inst Chem Eng.

Prentice, Geoffrey A. Electrochemical Engineering Principles. 320p. 1990. text ed. 78.00 (*0-13-249038-2*) P-H.

Prentice-Hall Editorial Staff. All States Tax Handbook. 320p. 1987. 17.50 (*0-13-022799-4*) P-H.

— All States Tax Handbook 1989. 300p. 1988. 18.95 (*0-13-023219-X*, Busn) P-H.

— Almanac of the Federal Judiciary, 2 Vols. 1994. Vol. 1. ring bd. 295.00 (*0-13-288854-8*) Aspen Law.

— The Business of Law: A Handbook on How to Manage Law Firms. 2nd ed. 1138p. 1990. ring bd. 95.00 (*0-13-292625-3*) Aspen Law.

— California Income Tax Laws. 1100p. 1989. pap. text ed. 41.50 (*0-13-112285-1*, Busn) P-H.

— California Tax Handbook. 1,987th ed. 1986. pap. 17.00 (*0-13-112046-8*) P-H.

— Client Development Series. 1984. write for info. (*0-318-58012-8*) P-H.

— Common Secretarial Mistakes & How to Avoid Them. (Illus.). 1986. 5.95 (*0-13-152744-4*, Reward) P-H.

— A Complete Guide to the Tax Reform Act of 1986. LC 87-110898. write for info. (*0-13-160649-2*) P-H.

— Corporation, Partnership & Fiduciary Federal Income Tax Specimen Returns. 72p. 1989. pap. text ed. 8.00 (*0-13-308651-8*, Busn) P-H.

— Corporations: Tax Choices for Business Planning-Explanation, Law & Regulations, Legislative History, Cases & Rulings, Indexes. (Illus.). ring bd. write for info. (*0-318-57847-6*) P-H.

— D. C. Federal Courts Handbook. 2nd ed. 1544p. 1993. ring bd. 116.00 (*0-13-297664-1*) Aspen Law.

— Directory of Corporate Counsel, 1994-95, 2 vols., Set. 15th ed. 2850p. 1994. 375.00 (*0-13-165664-3*) Aspen Law.

— Directory of Environmental Attorneys, 1995. 1756p. 1994. 195.00 (*0-13-169269-0*) Aspen Law.

— Employee Benefit Plans under ERISA: Federal Regulations. 1492p. 1989. pap. text ed. 41.50 (*0-13-275299-9*, Busn) P-H.

— Encyclopedia of Accounting Systems, 3 vols., Set. Pescow, Jerome, ed. 1975. text ed. 125.00 (*0-13-275214-X*, Busn) P-H.

— Estate & Gift Taxes: Complete. 1984. write for info. (*0-318-58010-1*) P-H.

— Estate Planning, Wills, Trusts. 1964. write for info. (*0-318-58305-4*) P-H.

— FDIC Enforcement Decisions, 2 vols. write for info. (*0-318-65472-5*, 115) P-H.

— Federal Income Tax Regulations. 1984. write for info. (*0-318-58009-8*) P-H.

— Federal Income Tax Regulations: 1990 Edition. 1990. pap. 52.50 (*0-13-313537-3*) P-H.

— Federal Tax Handbook. 750p. 1988. 19.50 (*0-13-313164-5*, Busn) P-H.

— Federal Tax Handbook, 1985. 1985. write for info. (*0-318-58198-1*) P-H.

— Federal Tax Handbook 1988. 750p. 1987. 19.00 (*0-13-313099-1*) P-H.

Prentice Hall Editorial Staff. Federal Tax Handbook 1990. 1989. pap. 21.50 (*0-13-308883-9*) P-H.

Prentice-Hall Editorial Staff. Federal Withholding Tax Tables. 48p. 1989. pap. 8.00 (*0-13-313768-6*, Busn) P-H.

— Handbook on Experimental Mechanics. rev. ed. Kobayashi, Albert S., ed. & intro. by. (Illus.). 1024p. 1986. 104.00 (*0-912053-07-0*) P-H.

— How to Save Time & Money in Filing Your 1981 Personal Tax Return: Individual Federal Income Tax Specimen Returns for Filing in 1982. LC 82-243692. (Illus.). 64p. 1982. 3.95 (*0-13-308619-4*) P-H.

— How to Save Time & Money in Filing Your 1988 Personal Tax Returns. 78p. 1988. 8.00 (*0-13-431214-7*, Busn) P-H.

— Internal Revenue Code. 1984. write for info. (*0-318-58008-X*) P-H.

— The Lawyer's Almanac, 1995. 1300p. 1995. 116.00 (*0-13-126597-0*) Aspen Law.

— Lawyers Desk Book. 9th ed. 752p. 1989. text ed. 69.95 (*0-13-526773-0*) P-H.

***Prentice Hall Editorial Staff.** Lawyer's Desk Book. 10th ed. LC 95-13736. 1995. write for info. (*0-13-206749-8*) P-H.

Prentice-Hall Editorial Staff. Nineteen Eighty-Five Federal Tax Course. 1984. write for info. (*0-318-58023-3*) P-H.

— Nineteen Eighty-Four SEC Guidelines, Rules & Regulations. 650p. 1984. 15.75 (*0-317-07502-0*, 79723-3) P-H.

— Partnership Tax Handbook. 176p. 1988. 19.50 (*0-13-697104-0*) P-H.

— Partnership Tax Handbook. 200p. 1989. 21.50 (*0-13-705873-X*, Busn) P-H.

— Pension Provisions of the Tax Equity & Fiscal Responsibility Act of 1982. LC 83-179605. 28p. 2.00 (*0-13-655753-8*) P-H.

— Personnel Management: Communications. 1984. write for info. (*0-318-58014-4*) P-H.

— Personnel Management: Compensation. 1984. write for info. (*0-318-58015-2*) P-H.

— Personnel Management: Policies & Practices. 1984. write for info. (*0-318-58013-6*) P-H.

— Prentice-Hall Federal Tax Course. Rubin, Alan, ed. 1981. student ed 21.00 (*0-685-03902-1*); student ed, pap. 7.95 (*0-685-03903-X*) P-H.

— Prentice-Hall Federal Tax Treaties, 2 vols., Set. ring bd. write for info. (*0-318-57895-6*) P-H.

— Prentice-Hall Inheritance Taxes. (Illus.). write for info. (*0-318-58375-5*) P-H.

Prentice Hall Editorial Staff. Prentice Hall 1040 Handbook 1990: For Filing 1989 Individual Income Tax Returns. 1989. pap. 49.50 (*0-13-903634-2*) P-H.

Prentice-Hall Editorial Staff. Prentice-Hall's Guide to Sales & Use Taxes. 720p. 1988. 37.95 (*0-13-705881-0*, Busn) P-H.

— Prentice-Hall's Social Security Deskbook, 1988. Hillman, Marvin, ed. 450p. 1988. pap. 30.00 (*0-13-703035-5*, Busn) P-H.

— Primary Teacher's Ready-to-Use Activities Program. 112p. 1988. text ed. 11.95 (*0-87628-651-1*, Busn) P-H.

— Professional Corporate Guide: Organization, Administration, Termination, Employee Benefits, Forms & Laws. 1983. write for info. (*0-318-57211-7*) P-H.

— Real Estate Guide. 1966. 131.50 (*0-13-762740-8*) P-H.

— S Corporations: Tax Choices for Business Planning. 1984. write for info. (*0-318-58011-X*) P-H.

— SEC Guidelines, Rules & Regulations. 590p. 1989. pap. text ed. 22.95 (*0-685-21947-X*, Busn) P-H.

— Secretary's Desktop Library, Set. 1989. pap. 24.95 (*0-13-798497-9*) P-H.

— State & Local Tax Service. write for info. (*0-318-62096-0*) P-H.

— Structuring Committees for a Board of Directors. 22p. 1984. 2.75 (*0-317-07503-9*, 85526-2) P-H.

— Tax Tips for Professionals. LC 85-154863. 4.25 (*0-13-884973-0*) P-H.

— Tax-Wise Ways to Sell Your House. 30p. 1984. 2.75 (*0-685-08926-6*, 88679-6) P-H.

Prentice-Hall Editorial Staff, jt. auth. see Faber, Peter L.

Prentice-Hall Editorial Staff, jt. auth. see Wilkie, Robert C.

***Prentice-Hall Editors.** Professional Secretary's Encyclopedic Dictionary. 5th ed. LC 94-28490. 1994. text ed. 29.95 (*0-13-030453-0*) P-H.

Prentice Hall International Staff, jt. auth. see Institute of Personnel Management Staff.

Prentice Hall Japan Staff, tr. see Adobe Systems Staff, et al.

Prentice Hall Japan Staff, tr. see Cohen, Luanne.

Prentice-Hall Muncher Staff, jt. auth. see Adobe Systems Staff.

Prentice Hall PTR Staff, ed. Excel 4.0 for Windows: Simplified & in Full Color. (MaranGraphics Simplified Computer Guide Ser.). (Illus.). 1992. pap. 12.95 (*0-13-001017-0*) P-H.

— Lotus One-Two-Three for DOS: Release 2.3. (MaranGraphics Simplified Computer Guide Ser.). (Illus.). 1992. pap. 12.95 (*0-13-000878-8*) P-H.

— MS-DOS 5.0: Simplified User Guide for Microsoft. (MaranGraphics Simplified Computer Guide Ser.). (Illus.). 1991. pap. 12.95 (*0-13-000044-2*) P-H.

— Windows 3.1: Simplified. (MaranGraphics Simplified Computer Guide Ser.). (Illus.). 1992. pap. 12.95 (*0-13-001074-X*) P-H.

— Word for Windows 2: Simplified & in Full Color. (MaranGraphics Simplified Computer Guide Ser.). (Illus.). 1992. pap. 12.95 (*0-13-001067-7*) P-H.

— WordPerfect 5.1 for Windows. (MaranGraphics Simplified Computer Guide Ser.). (Illus.). 1992. pap. 12.95 (*0-13-000746-3*) P-H.

Prentice Hall Staff. ESL 1994 Catalog. (Regents Prep Series for the TOEFL Test). 1993. pap. write for info. (*0-13-102138-9*) P-H.

— 1995 Prentice Hall Regents ESL Catalog. (Illus.). 1994. pap. write for info. (*0-13-188087-X*) P-H.

— PH Grade Manager 5.25 IBM (Generic) Date not set. write for info. (*0-13-008426-3*) P-H.

Prentice Hall Staff, tr. see Adobe Systems Staff.

Prentice Hall Staff, tr. see Adobe Systems Staff, et al.

Prentice, Helaine K., et al. Rehab Right. LC 86-5945. (Illus.). 144p. (Orig.). 1986. pap. 11.95 (*0-89815-172-4*) Ten Speed Pr.

Prentice, I. C. & Van Der Maarel, Eddy, eds. Theory & Models in Vegetation Science. (Advances in Vegetation Science Ser.). (C). 1987. lib. bdg. 184.00 (*90-6193-646-2*) Kluwer Ac.

Prentice, J. H. Dairy Rheology: A Concise Guide. LC 92-34877. (Food Science & Technology Ser.). 165p. 1992. 95.00 (*1-56081-505-1*) VCH Pubs.

Prentice, J. H., ed. Measurements in the Rheology of Foodstuffs. (Illus.). 200p. 1984. 63.00 (*0-85334-248-2*, I-221-84, Pub. by Elsevier Applied Sci UK) Elsevier.

Prentice, Jeff & Bennett, Bronwen. Guide to Australian Children's Literature. 324p. 1992. pap. 39.50 (*1-875589-11-2*) D W Thorpe.

Prentice, Lee, jt. auth. see Wyman, Walker D.

Prentice, Lloyd. Words, Pictures, Media: Communication in Educational Politics. 91p. 1979. pap. text ed. 4.00 (*0-917754-01-8*) Inst Responsive.

***Prentice, Mary.** Catch Them Learning: A Handbook of Classroom Strategies - Grades K-12. LC 94-78534. 120p. 1994. pap. 17.95 (*0-932935-79-6*) IRI-Skylght.

Prentice, Penelope. The Pinter Ethic: The Erotic Aesthetic. LC 93-7620. (Studies in Modern Drama: Vol. 3). (Illus.). 480p. 1993. 65.00 (*0-8153-1385-3*) Garland.

Prentice, R. L., jt. auth. see Kalbfleisch, J. D.

***Prentice, Richard.** Change & Policy in Wales in the Era of Privatism. 305p. 1993. pap. 39.00 (*0-86383-978-9*, Pub. by Gomer Pr UK) St Mut.

— Tourism & Heritage Attractions. (Issues in Tourism Ser.). 240p. 1993. 69.95 (*0-415-08525-X*, A7681) Routledge.

Prentice, Richard, jt. auth. see Roberts, Arthur.

Prentice, Richard, jt. auth. see Ryan, Michael.

Prentice, Robert A. Law of Business Organizations & Securities Organization. 2nd ed. LC 93-34759. 1993. text ed. write for info. (*0-13-530189-0*) P-H.

Prentice, Robert A., jt. auth. see Allison, John R.

Prentice, Robert P. Psychology of Love According to St. Bonaventure. (Philosophy Ser.). 1957. 8.00 (*0-686-11536-8*) Franciscan Inst.

Prentice, Ross L. & Thompson, Donovan J., eds. Atomic Bomb Survivor Data: Utilization & Analysis. LC 84-50378. (SIAM-SIMS Conference Ser.: No. 10). ix, 289p. 1984. pap. text ed. 35.00 (*0-89871-194-0*) Soc Indus-Appl Math.

Prentice, Ross L., jt. ed. see Moolgavkar, Suresh H.

Prentice, Simon, tr. see Togawa, Masako.

Prentice, Tom. The Climbing Guide to Scotland. (Illus.). 205p. 1992. pap. 34.95 (*1-85223-527-6*, Pub. by Crowood Pr UK) Trafalgar.

Prentice, W. P. Police Powers Arising under the Law of Overruling Necessity. xli, 516p. 1993. reprint ed. lib. bdg. 52.50 (*0-8377-2523-2*) Rothman.

***Prentice, William E.** Getting Fit: Basics for Life. LC 95-16131. 1995. write for info. (*0-8151-6843-8*) Mosby Yr Bk.

Prentice, William E., ed. Rehabilitation Techniques in Sports Medicine. 2nd ed. LC 93-35546. 448p. 1993. 44.95 (*0-8016-7675-4*) Mosby Yr Bk.

Prentis, Barbara. The Bronte Sisters & George Eliot: A Unity of Difference. 208p. 1987. 57.50 (*0-389-20756-X*, N8315) B&N Imports.

Prentis, Joseph. The Garden Book & Monthly Kalendar of Joseph Prentis. Crotz, D. Keith, ed. (American Horticultural Ser.: No. 3). (Illus.). 85p. 1990. 29.95 (*0-929332-02-4*) Amer Botanist.

Prentis, Noble L. Southern Letters. 1977. text ed. 16.95 (*0-8369-9232-6*, 9086) Ayer.

Prentis, Richard S. Passages of Retirement: Personal Histories of Struggle & Success. LC 92-1131. (Contributions to the Study of Aging Ser.: No. 23). 240p. 1992. text ed. 45.00 (*0-313-28493-8*, PPN/, Greenwood Pr) Greenwood.

Prentis, S. J., jt. ed. see Bradshaw, Ralph A.

Prentis, Steve. Biotechnology. LC 83-26571. (Illus.). 192p. 1984. 18.50 (*0-8076-1094-1*) Braziller.

Prentiss, Charlotte. Children of the Ice. 496p. (Orig.). 1993. pap. 5.50 (*0-451-17792-4*, Onyx) NAL-Dutton.

— People of the Mesa. 416p. (Orig.). 1995. pap. 5.50 (*0-451-17850-5*, Onyx) NAL-Dutton.

Prentiss, Chris. For Once in Your Life: Be Who You Want, Have What You Want. LC 87-60641. 331p. 1987. 9.95 (*0-943015-00-6*) Power Press.

Prentiss County Historical Association Staff, ed. The History of Prentiss County, Mississippi: Vol. I. (Illus.). 472p. 1984. 57.00 (*0-88107-019-X*) Curtis Media.

Prentiss, Elizabeth. Stepping Heavenward. pap. 10.99 (*0-87377-078-1*) GAM Pubns.

— Stepping Heavenward. rev. ed. 288p. 1992. pap. 10.95 (*1-879737-06-X*) Calvary Press.

***Prentiss, George L.** More Love to Thee: The Life & Letters of Elizabeth Prentiss. 605p. (Orig.). 1994. pap. 18.95 (*1-879737-14-0*) Calvary Press.

Prentiss, Hervey Putnam. Timothy Pickering As the Leader of New England Federalism, 1800-1815. LC 71-124882. (American Scene Ser.). (Illus.). 118p. 1972. reprint ed. lib. bdg. 22.50 (*0-306-71052-8*) Da Capo.

***Prentiss, Lee.** Explosive & Contraband Detection. Berkel, Bob, ed. (CCS SecuritySource Library: Vol. VII). (Illus.). 720p. 1995. 300.00 (*1-884674-07-0*) CCS Security.

Prentiss, Stan. The Complete Book of Oscilloscopes. 1992. pap. 16.95 (*0-07-157781-5*) McGraw.

— The Complete Book of Oscilloscopes. 2nd ed. 320p. 1991. 26.95 (*0-8306-3909-8*); pap. 16.95 (*0-8306-3908-X*) TAB Bks.

— Electronic Signals. (Illus.). 272p. 1991. 29.95 (*0-8306-8557-X*, 3557); pap. 19.95 (*0-8306-3557-2*) TAB Bks.

— Electronic Signals: Television, Stereo, Satellite TV & Automotive. 1991. pap. 19.95 (*0-07-050767-8*) McGraw.

— HDTV: High Definition Television. 1993. pap. text ed. 16.95 (*0-07-050769-4*) McGraw.

— HDTV: High-Definition Television. 2nd ed. LC 92-43819. 1993. 29.95 (*0-8306-4296-X*); pap. 16.95 (*0-8306-4295-1*) TAB Bks.

— HDTV: High Definition Television. 2nd ed. 1993. 29.95 (*0-07-050768-6*) McGraw.

— Troubleshooting & Repairing TVRO Systems. (Illus.). 224p. 1988. 24.95 (*0-8306-0592-4*); pap. 16.95 (*0-8306-2992-0*) TAB Bks.

Prentiss, Stanton R. Modern Television: Service & Repair. 304p. 1989. text ed. 65.00 (*0-13-586975-7*) P-H.

Prentki, Tim, jt. ed. see Bushrui, S. B.

Prentky, Robert A. Creativity & Psychopathology: A Neurocognitive Perspective. LC 80-15856. 282p. 1980. text ed. 41.95 (*0-275-90540-3*, C0540, Praeger Pubs) Greenwood.

Prentout, Henri. Essai sur les Origines et la Fondation Du Duche De Normandie. LC 80-2214. reprint ed. 42.50 (*0-404-18776-5*) AMS Pr.

— Histoire de Guillaume le Conquerant: Le Duc de Normandie, Vol. 1. LC 80-2252. reprint ed. 42.50 (*0-404-18777-3*) AMS Pr.

Prentzas, G. S. The Hopi Indians. LC 93-47541. (Junior Library of American Indians). (Illus.). 80p. (J). (gr. 3-7). 1994. lib. bdg. 14.95 (*0-7910-1662-5*, Am Art Analog); pap. 6.95 (*0-7910-2487-3*, Am Art Analog) Chelsea Hse.

— Jim Brown. LC 94-1349. (Football Legends Ser.). (Illus.). 64p. (J). (gr. 3 up). 1994. lib. bdg. 14.95 (*0-7910-2452-0*) Chelsea Hse.

— Joe Montana. LC 94-1350. (Football Legends Ser.). (Illus.). 64p. (J). (gr. 3 up). 1994. lib. bdg. 14.95 (*0-7910-2453-9*) Chelsea Hse.

— Joe Namath. LC 94-1351. (Football Legends Ser.). (Illus.). 64p. (J). (gr. 3 up). 1994. lib. bdg. 14.95 (*0-7910-2454-7*) Chelsea Hse.

— Mario Andretti. LC 95-8238. (Race Car Legends Ser.). (J). 1996. write for info. (*0-7910-3176-4*); pap. write for info. (*0-7910-3177-2*) Chelsea Hse.

— Terry Bradshaw. LC 94-5780. (Football Legends Ser.). (Illus.). 64p. (J). (gr. 3 up). 1994. lib. bdg. 14.95 (*0-7910-2451-2*) Chelsea Hse.

Prentzas, Scott. The Kwakiutl Indians. (Junior Library of American Indians). (Illus.). 80p. (J). (gr. 3-7). 1993. lib. bdg. 14.95 (*0-7910-1664-1*) Chelsea Hse.

— Tribal Law. LC 94-5531. (Native American Culture Ser.). (J). 1994. write for info. (*0-86625-536-2*) Rourke Corp.

Prentzes, G. S. Thurgood Marshall: Champion of Justice. LC 92-34222. (Junior Black Americans of Achievement Ser.). (Illus.). 80p. (J). (gr. 3-6). 1993. lib. bdg. 14.95 (*0-7910-1769-9*, Am Art Analog); pap. 4.95 (*0-7910-1969-1*, Am Art Analog) Chelsea Hse.

Prenzlau, Sheryl. B. Y. Times Kid Sisters: Running Away, No. 5. (Illus.). 120p. (Orig.). (J). (gr. 2-6). 1993. pap. 5.95 (*1-56871-018-6*) Targum Pr.

— B. Y. Times Kid Sisters No. 6: Teacher's Pet. (Illus.). 115p. (Orig.). (J). (gr. 3-7). 1993. pap. 6.95 (*1-56871-025-9*) Targum Pr.

— Changing Places. (Kid Sisters Ser.: No. 8). (Illus.). 112p. (J). (gr. 3-5). 1994. pap. 6.95 (*1-56871-044-5*) Targum Pr.

Prenzlau, Sheryl, ed. Everything under the Sun: An Anthology for Young Teens. 448p. (J). (gr. 5 up). 1993. 17.95 (*1-56871-020-8*); pap. 14.95 (*1-56871-021-6*) Targum Pr.

Preobrazhensky, A. Russian Orthodox Church: Tenth to Twentieth Centuries. (Illus.). 464p. (C). 1988. 60.00 (*0-685-31573-8*, Pub. by Collets UK) Pro-Am Music.

Preobrazhensky, B. V. Contemporary Reefs. Chakravarty, R., tr. (Russian Translation Ser.: No. 100). (Illus.). 326p. (ENG.). 1993. text ed. 110.00 (*90-6191-945-2*, Pub. by A A Balkema NE) Ashgate Pub Co.

Preobrazhensky, Evgeny, jt. auth. see Bukharin, Nikolai.

***Preobrazhensky, Yevgeny.** Ot NEPa K Sotsializmu: (Russian Original of "From the NEP to Socialism") 1995. pap. 10.00 (*1-883468-06-X*) Iskra Res.

Preparata, Franco. Advances in Computing Research: The Theory of Databases, Vol. 3. 1986. 73.25 (*0-89232-611-5*) Jai Pr.

Preparata, Franco P. Introduction to Computer Engineering. 1984. Net. text ed. write for info. (*0-471-60374-0*) Wiley.

Preparata, Franco P., ed. Advances in Computing Research, Vol. 1. 1983. 73.25 (*0-89232-356-6*) Jai Pr.

— Advances in Computing Research: Parallel & Distributed Computing, Vol. 4. 1987. 73.25 (*0-89232-682-4*) Jai Pr.

— VLSI Theory. (Advances in Computing Research Ser.: Vol. 2). 275p. 1985. 73.25 (*0-89232-461-9*) Jai Pr.

Preparata, Franco P. & Micali, Silvio, eds. Advances in Computing Research, Vol. 5. 505p. 1989. 68.50 (*0-89232-896-7*) Jai Pr.

Preparata, Franco P. & Shamos, M. I. Computational Geometry: An Introduction. (Texts & Monographs in Computer Science). (Illus.). xii, 390p. 1993. 49.50 (*0-387-96131-3*) Spr-Verlag.

***Preparata, Giuliano.** QED Coherence in Matter. LC 95-13463. 252p. 1995. text ed. 67.00 (*981-02-2249-1*) World Scientific Pub.

Prerau, David S. Developing & Managing Expert Systems. (Illus.). 384p. (C). 1990. text ed. 35.50 (*0-201-13659-7*) Addison-Wesley.

Prereau, D., jt. auth. see Liebowitz, J.

Presas, Remy A. Modern Arnis: Filipino Art of Stick Fighting. LC 83-60128. (Specialties Ser.). (Illus.). 1983. pap. 12.95 (*0-89750-089-X*, 426) Ohara Pubns.

***Presbey, Gail M., et al, eds.** The Philosophical Quest: A Cross Cultural Reader. LC 94-33149. 1994. 32.81 (*0-07-062547-6*) McGraw.

P Q

Presbyterian Church Historical Society of Campbell Hall, N.Y. Staff. Cemeteries of the Town of Hamptonburgh, Orange County, New York. LC 80-81240. (Orange County, New York Cemeteries Ser.: No. 2). 88p. (Orig.). 1980. pap. 5.00 (*0-9604116-2-3*) Orange County Genealog.

Presbyterian Church in the United States of America Staff. Records of the Presbyterian Church in the United States of America, 1706-1788. LC 75-83434. (Religion in America, Ser. 1). 1975. reprint ed. 33.95 (*0-405-00259-9*) Ayer.

Presbyterian Church, Theology & Worship Ministry Unit Staff & Cumberland Presbyterian Church Staff. The Book of Common Worship. 1008p. 1993. text ed. 30.00 (*0-664-21991-8*) Westminster John Knox.

Presbyterian Church (U. S. A.), Theology & Worship Ministry Unit Staff & Cumberland Presbyterian Church Staff. Book of Common Worship, Pastoral Edition. deluxe ed. LC 93-4538. 368p. 1993. 25.00 (*0-664-22033-9*) Westminster John Knox.

Presbyterian Eco-Justice Task Force Staff. Keeping & Healing the Creation. 128p. (Orig.). 1989. pap. text ed. 3.00 (*0-317-93816-9*) PC USA CSWP.

***Presbyterian Women's Missionary Union Staff.** The New P.W.M.U. Cookbook. (Illus.). 287p. (Orig.). 1995. spiral bd., pap. 10.95 (*0-85091-388-8*, Pub. by Lothian Pub AT) Seven Hills Bk.

Presbyter's Peartree Staff, tr. see Corrales, Jose.

Presbyter's Peartree Staff, tr. see Cruz, Migdalia.

Presbyter's Peartree Staff, tr. see de Cardenas, Raul.

Presch, William, jt. auth. see Weichert, Charles K.

***Prescher, Ray E.** National Plumbing & HVAC Estimator, 1995. (Illus.). 352p. (Orig.). 1994. pap. 32.50 (*1-57218-003-X*) Craftsman.

Prescience Corp. Staff. Theorist, Student Edition. LC 93-6707. 1993. 69.95 (*0-534-20340-X*) PWS Pubs.

Prescott-Allen, Christine & Prescott-Allen, Robert. The First Resource: Wild Species in the North American Economy. LC 86-1657. 560p. 1986. text ed. 75.00 (*0-300-03228-5*) Yale U Pr.

Prescott-Allen, Robert, jt. auth. see Prescott-Allen, Christine.

Prescott, Anne L. French Poets & the English Renaissance: Studies in Fame & Transformation. LC 77-5482. 304p. reprint ed. pap. 86.70 (*0-8357-8139-9*, 2033860) Bks Demand.

Prescott, Anne L., ed. see Spenser, Hugh.

Prescott, Arthur T., ed. Drafting the Federal Constitution: A Rearrangement of Madison's Notes, Giving Consecutive Developments of Provisions in the Constitution of the United States. LC 68-54433. (Illus.). 838p. 1969. reprint ed. text ed. 105.00 (*0-8371-0196-4*, PRFC) Greenwood.

Prescott, Carolyn A., jt. auth. see Hull, Daniel M.

***Prescott-Clarke, P., et al.** Routes into Local Authority Housing - a Study of Local Authority Waiting Lists & New. 118p. 1994. pap. 25.00 (*0-11-752920-6*, HM29206, Pub. by HMSO UK) UNIPUB.

— Tenant Feedback: A Step-by-Step Guide to Tenant Satisfaction Surveys. 178p. 1993. pap. 35.00 (*0-11-752792-0*, HM27920, Pub. by HMSO UK) UNIPUB.

Prescott, Dana E. Maine Family Law Forms: Discovery, Trial & Settlement, 2 vols., Set. LC 93-23910. 750p. 1994. disk, ring bd. 195.00 (*0-250-40712-4*) Michie Butterworth.

Prescott, David. Cells: Principles of Molecular Structure & Function. 640p. (C). 1988. teacher ed 435.00 (*0-86720-102-9*); Intl student ed. pap. 5.65 (*0-534-98266-2*); student ed 13.75 (*0-86720-098-7*); trans. 195.00 (*0-86720-100-2*); boxed 46.25 (*0-86720-092-8*); sl. 195.00 (*0-86720-099-5*); 45.00 (*0-86720-101-0*) Jones & Bartlett.

Prescott, David M. & Flexer, Abraham S. Cancer: The Misguided Cell. 2nd rev. ed. LC 85-27714. (Illus.). 349p. 1986. pap. text ed. 29.95 (*0-87893-708-0*) Sinauer Assocs.

Prescott, David M. & Hand, Arthur, eds. Methods in Cell Biology: Basic Mechanisms of Cellular Secretion, Vol. 23. LC 64-14220. (Serial Publication Ser.). 1981. text ed. 143.00 (*0-12-564123-0*) Acad Pr.

Prescott, David M. & Harris, Curtis, eds. Methods in Cell Biology: Methods to Culture Normal Human Tissues & Cells: Respiratory, Cardiovascular, & Intgumentary Systems, Vol. 21. (Serial Publication Ser.: Pt. A). 1980. text ed. 143.00 (*0-12-564121-4*) Acad Pr.

— Methods in Cell Biology: Methods to Culture Normal Human Tissues & Cells: Respiratory, Cardiovascular, & Intgumentary Systems, Vol. 21. (Serial Publication Ser.: Pt. B). 1980. text ed. 143.00 (*0-12-564140-0*) Acad Pr.

Prescott, David M. & Turner, James, eds. Methods in Cell Biology: Three-Dimensional Ultrastructure in Biology, Vol. 22. 1981. text ed. 143.00 (*0-12-564122-2*) Acad Pr.

Prescott, David M. & Wilson, Leslie, eds. Methods in Cell Biology: The Cytoskeleton: Biological Systems & in-Vitro Models, Vol. 25B. 448p. 1982. text ed. 143.00 (*0-12-564125-7*) Acad Pr.

— Methods in Cell Biology: The Cytoskeleton: Cytoskeletal Proteins, Isolation & Characterization, Vol. 24A. 464p. 1982. text ed. 143.00 (*0-12-564124-9*) Acad Pr.

Prescott, David M., jt. ed. see Goldstein, L.

Prescott, David M., et al, eds. Methods in Cell Biology, 17. 1978. text ed. 143.00 (*0-12-564117-6*) Acad Pr.

— Methods in Cell Biology, 18. 1978. text ed. 143.00 (*0-12-564118-4*) Acad Pr.

— Methods in Cell Biology, 19. 1978. text ed. 143.00 (*0-12-564119-2*) Acad Pr.

— Methods in Cell Biology, 20. 1978. text ed. 143.00 (*0-12-564120-6*) Acad Pr.

Prescott, Edgar. Before the Bulldozers Came. (Orig.). 1985. pap. 3.00 (*0-936563-05-2*) Signpost.

Prescott, Edward C. & Wallace, Neil, eds. Contractual Arrangements for Intertemporal Trade. (Minnesota Studies in Microeconomics Ser.). 169p. 1987. text ed. 49.95 (*0-8166-1533-0*); pap. text ed. 10.95 (*0-8166-1534-9*) U of Minn Pr.

Prescott, Elizabeth. The English Medieval Hospital. (Illus.). 288p. 1992. 45.00 (*1-85264-054-5*, Pub. by Seaby UK) Trafalgar.

Prescott, Elizabeth, ed. Parajudges: Their Role in Today's Court Systems. 78p. 1976. pap. write for info. (*0-89656-010-4*, R-027) Natl Ctr St Courts.

Prescott, Elizabeth, ed. see National Center for State Courts Staff.

Prescott, Frederick C. The Poetic Mind. LC 83-1547. xx, 308p. 1983. reprint ed. text ed. 65.00 (*0-313-23925-8*, PRPO, Greenwood Pr) Greenwood.

Prescott, Frederick C., ed. Selections from the Critical Writings of Edgar Allan Poe. 425p. (C). 1981. reprint ed. 50.00 (*0-87752-182-4*) Gordian.

Prescott, G. W., et al. Aquatic Plants. 2nd ed. (Pictured Key Nature Ser.). 176p. (C). 1979. spiral bd. write for info. (*0-697-04775-X*) Wm C Brown Pubs.

— Freshwater Algae. 3rd ed. (Pictured Key Nature Ser.). 304p. (C). 1978. spiral bd. write for info. (*0-697-04754-7*) Wm C Brown Pubs.

Prescott, Gary R., ed. see Rowe, James G., Jr.

Prescott, George B. Bell's Electric Speaking Telephone: Its Invention, Construction, Application, Modification & History. LC 72-5069. (Technology & Society Ser.). (Illus.). 536p. 1977. reprint ed. 42.95 (*0-405-04718-5*) Ayer.

Prescott, Gerald W. The Algae: A Review. (Illus.). xi, 436p. 1984. reprint ed. ring bd. 85.00 (*3-87429-244-4*) Koeltz Sci Bks.

— Algae of the Western Great Lakes Area: With Illustrated Key to the Genera of Desmids on Freshwater Diatoms. (Illus.). 977p. 1983. pap. text ed. 89.00 (*3-87429-205-3*) Koeltz Sci Bks.

— Bibliographia Desmidiacearum Universalis: A Contribution to a Bibliography of Desmid Systematics, Biology & Ecology from 1744 to 1982. 704p. 1985. lib. bdg. 185.00 (*3-87429-215-0*) Koeltz Sci Bks.

— A Contribution to a Bibliography of Antarctic & Subantarctic Algae Together with a Checklist of Freshwater Taxa Reported to 1977. (Bibliotheca Phycologica Ser.: No. 45). 1979. lib. bdg. 48.00 (*3-7682-1216-5*) Lubrecht & Cramer.

Prescott, Gerald W., et al. A Synopsis of North American Desmids Pt. 2: Desmidiaceae: Placodermae, 5 Sections, Sect. 1. LC 70-183418. (Illus.). 285p. reprint ed. Section 1, 285p. pap. 81.30 (*0-8357-3791-8*, 2036522) Bks Demand.

— A Synopsis of North American Desmids Pt. 2: Desmidiaceae: Placodermae, 5 Sections, Sect. 2. LC 70-183418. (Illus.). 423p. reprint ed. Section 2, 423. pap. 120.60 (*0-8357-3792-6*, 2036522) Bks Demand.

— A Synopsis of North American Desmids Pt. 2: Desmidiaceae: Placodermae, 5 Sections, Sect. 3. LC 70-183418. (Illus.). 730p. reprint ed. Section 3, 730p. pap. 180.00 (*0-8357-3793-4*, 2036522) Bks Demand.

— A Synopsis of North American Desmids Pt. 2: Desmidiaceae: Placodermae, 5 Sections, Sect. 4. LC 70-183418. (Illus.). 710p. reprint ed. Section 4, 710p. pap. 180.00 (*0-8357-3794-2*, 2036522) Bks Demand.

— A Synopsis of North American Desmids Pt. 2: Desmidiaceae: Placodermae, 5 Sections, Sect. 5. LC 70-183418. (Illus.). 127p. reprint ed. Section 5, 127p. pap. 36.20 (*0-8357-3795-0*, 2036522) Bks Demand.

Prescott, J. R. The Map of Mainland Asia by Treaties. 1975. 39.95 (*0-522-84083-3*) Intl Spec Bk.

— The Maritime Political Boundaries of the World. 550p. (C). 1986. text ed. 55.00 (*0-416-41750-7*, 6424) Routledge Chapman & Hall.

— Political Frontiers & Boundaries. 320p. 1987. text ed. 49.95 (*0-04-341030-8*) Routledge Chapman & Hall.

Prescott, J. R., et al. Frontiers of Asia & Southeast Asia. (Illus.). 1977. pap. 19.95 (*0-522-84116-3*) Intl Spec Bk.

Prescott, James. Le Viandier de Taillevent: Fourteenth Century Cookery. 2nd ed. LC 89-80811. (Illus.). 129p. 1989. 15.00 (*0-9623719-0-4*); pap. 8.00 (*0-9623719-1-2*) Alfarhaugr Pub Soc.

Prescott, James R., et al, eds. Urban-Regional Aconomics, Social Systems Accounts, & Eco-Behavioral Science. LC 94-8239. 1994. 49.95 (*0-8138-2338-2*) Iowa St U Pr.

Prescott, James R. & Abu-Kishk, Bakir. Regional Economic Development in the Middle East: A Survey. (Studies in Technology & Social Change: No. 3). 61p. (Orig.). (C). 1988. pap. 6.00 (*0-945271-03-4*) ISU-TSCP.

***Prescott, Jerome.** America at the Crossroads. (Illus.). 128p. 1995. 15.98 (*0-8317-0739-9*) Smithmark.

— Unspoiled West: The Western Landscape As Seen by Its Greatest Photographers. (Illus.). 128p. 1995. 15.98 (*0-8317-9058-X*) Smithmark.

Prescott, John. In Flanders Fields: The Story of John McCrae. (Illus.). 144p. (Orig.). pap. 10.95 (*0-317-05877-0*, Pub. by Boston Mills Pr CN) Genl Dist Srvs.

Prescott, John & Bagget, Desmond. Antimicrobial Therapy in Veterinary Medicine. LC 93-13907. (Illus.). 528p. (C). 1993. text ed. 64.95 (*0-8138-0889-8*) Iowa St U Pr.

Prescott, John E., ed. Advances in Competitive Intelligence. 228p. (Orig.). 1989. pap. 24.95 (*0-9621241-0-9*) SCIP.

Prescott, John E. & Gibbons, Patrick T., eds. Global Perspectives on Competitive Intelligence. LC 93-24750. 24.95 (*0-9621241-1-7*) SCIP.

Prescott, Joseph. Aphorisms & Other Observations. 1985. 7.95 (*0-318-18396-X*) J Prescott.

Prescott, Julian K. A History of the Modern Age. 10.00 (*0-8446-4798-5*) Peter Smith.

Prescott, Kate, jt. auth. see Welford, Richard.

Prescott, Kelvyn. Annotated Summary Offences Act: (South Australia) 157p. 1992. pap. 93.00 (*0-455-21156-6*, Pub. by Law Bk Co) W W Gaunt.

Prescott, Lansing, et al. Microbiology. 1016p. (C). 1989. write for info. (*0-697-03005-9*) Wm C Brown Pubs.

— Microbiology. 1016p. (C). 1990. write for info. (*0-697-00246-2*) Wm C Brown Pubs.

Prescott, Michael K. & Brossman, Douglas. The Environmental Liability Handbook for Property Transfer & Financing. (Illus.). 1990. 69.95 (*0-87371-360-5*, KF1298) Lewis Pubs.

Prescott, N. J., ed. see Welding Institute Staff.

Prescott, Orville. In My Opinion. LC 73-111857. (Essay Index Reprint Ser.). 1977. 23.95 (*0-8369-2014-7*) Ayer.

Prescott, Peter, ed. The Norton Book of American Short Stories. 1988. 25.00 (*0-393-02619-1*) Norton.

— The Norton Book of American Short Stories. (Books of... Ser.). (C). 1990. pap. text ed. write for info. (*0-393-96092-7*) Norton.

Prescott, Peter S. Child Savers. 1990. 3.98 (*0-394-50235-3*) Random.

Prescott, Ralph P. The Simplistic Poet. Hagar, Fern, ed. LC 87-71726. (Illus.). 77p. (Orig.). 1988. pap. 10.80 (*0-9618378-0-2*) Parishs Poetry.

Prescott, Roger. Hello, My Friend. 1981. 7.10 (*0-89536-474-3*, 0800) CSS OH.

— The Second Mile. 1985. 5.20 (*0-89536-739-4*, 5823) CSS OH.

Prescott, S. C. & Goldblith, S. A. Pioneers in Food Science, Vol. 1. 194p. 1993. pap. 25.00 (*0-917678-33-8*) Food & Nut Pr.

***Prescott, Stephen H.** Cowtown Carving: Tips & Techniques from the Texas Whittling Champion. 2nd rev. ed. (Illus.). 96p. 1994. pap. 14.95 (*1-56523-049-3*) Fox Chapel Pub.

Prescott, Susan, jt. auth. see Muncaster, Barbara.

Prescott, Susannah S., jt. ed. see Postma, Patricia D.

Prescott, Thomas, ed. Clinical Aphasiology, Vol. 20. 369p. 1992. text ed. 49.00 (*0-89079-466-9*, 1803) PRO-ED.

Prescott, Thomas E., ed. Clinical Aphasiology, Vol. 18. 531p. (C). 1989. pap. text ed. 49.00 (*0-89079-322-0*, 1774) PRO-ED.

— Clinical Aphasiology, Vol. 19. (Illus.). 331p. 1991. pap. text ed. 45.00 (*0-89079-407-3*, 1587) PRO-ED.

Prescott, V. P. Prescott: A History of the McCaffree & Prescott Family, in Three Parts. 1993. write for info. (*0-318-70234-7*) P E Randall Pub.

Prescott, Victor, jt. auth. see Davis, Stephen.

Prescott, Victor, jt. auth. see Lovering, John F.

Prescott, W. The Prescott Memorial: A Genealogical Memoir of the Prescott Family in America. (Illus.). 667p. 1989. reprint ed. lib. bdg. 108.00 (*0-8328-0990-X*); reprint ed. pap. 100.00 (*0-8328-0991-8*) Higginson Bk Co.

Prescott, W. H. Correspondence of William Hickling Prescott, 1833-1847. Wolcott, Roger, ed. LC 76-112312. (American Public Figures Ser.). 1970. reprint ed. lib. bdg. 49.50 (*0-306-71912-6*) Da Capo.

***Prescott, William H.** The Art of War in Spain: The Conquest of Granada, 1481-1492. McJoynt, Albert D., ed. & intro. by. (Illus.). 288p. 1995. 40.00 (*1-85367-193-2*, Pub. by Greenhill Bks UK) Stackpole.

— The Conquest of Mexico. Bd. with Conquest of Peru. LC 36-27495. LC 36-27495. 1979. 22.00 (*0-394-60471-7*, Modern Lib) Random.

— History of Conquest of Mexico & History of the Conquest of Peru. LC 36-27495. 1288p. 1979. 15.95 (*0-685-19921-5*, Modern Lib) Random.

— Prescott's Histories: Rise & Decline of the Spanish Empire. (Illus.). 568p. 1990. 19.95 (*0-88029-476-0*) Dorset Pr.

— Works, 22 vols., Set. Munro, Wilfred H. et al, eds. LC 69-16761. reprint ed. 1,250.00 (*0-404-05150-2*) AMS Pr.

Prescott, William M. History of the Conquest of Mexico & History of the Conquest of Peru. LC 36-27495. 1288p. 1989. 16.95 (*0-685-28566-9*) Random.

***Prescott, William P.** Business, Legal, & Tax Planning for Dental Practices. LC 94-30140. 1994. write for info. (*0-87814-424-2*) PennWell Bks.

Present, Thelma. Dear Margaret: Letters from Oak Ridge to Margaret Mead. (Illus.). 205p. 1985. 14.95 (*0-941199-07-X*) ETHS.

Presents, Elizabeth P. Malice Domestic One. Chelius, Jane, ed. 288p. (Orig.). 1992. mass mkt. 4.99 (*0-671-73826-7*) PB.

Preservation League NYS Staff. How to Care for Religious Properties. (Illus.). 40p. 1982. pap. 2.00 (*0-942000-03-X*) Pres League NYS.

Preservation Society of Asheville & Buncombe County. Color Me Asheville. (Coloring Book for Adults & Children Ser.). (Illus.). 40p. (J). (gr. 4-8). 1987. pap. 4.00 (*0-937481-01-7*) Pres Soc Asheville.

Preservation Society of Charleston Staff. The Churches of Charleston & the Lowcountry. Jacoby, Mary M., ed. LC 93-10057. 136p. (C). 1993. 39.95 (*0-87249-888-3*) U of SC Pr.

Preshaw, G. O. Banking Under Difficulties: Life on the Goldfields of Victoria, New South Wales & New Zealand, Vol. 8. LC 74-357. (Gold Ser.). 179p. 1974. reprint ed. 23.95 (*0-405-05918-3*) Ayer.

Presidential Commission on the Assignment of Women in the Armed Forces. Women in Combat: Report to the President. (Association of the U. S. Army Book Ser.). 413p. 1994. 38.95x (*0-02-881097-X*); pap. 20.00 (*0-02-881091-0*) Brasseys Inc.

President's Commission. Warren Commission Report: The Official Report of the President's Commission on the Assassination. 1992. 12.98 (*0-681-41586-X*) Longmeadow Pr.

President's Commission on Campus Unrest. The Kent State Tragedy: Special Report, Including Pictures. (Mass Violence in America Ser.). (Illus.). 1989. pap. 12.95 (*0-88143-103-6*) Ayer.

President's Commission On Immigration & Naturalization. Whom We Shall Welcome. LC 73-146270. (Civil Liberties in American History Ser.). 1971. reprint ed. lib. bdg. 45.00 (*0-306-70145-6*) Da Capo.

President's Commission on Law Enforcement & Administration of Justice. Task Force Report: The Police. LC 73-154585. (Police in America Ser.). 1979. reprint ed. 29.95 (*0-405-03383-4*) Ayer.

President's Commission on National Goals. Goals for Americans. LC 60-53566. 1960. pap. 1.00 (*0-936904-09-7*) Am Assembly.

President's Commission on the Health Needs of the Nation. Building America's Health: A Report, 5 vols. in 2, 1-3. LC 75-17239. (Social Problems & Social Policy Ser.). (Illus.). 1976. reprint ed. 66.95 (*0-405-07509-X*) Ayer.

— Building America's Health: A Report, 5 vols. in 2, Set. LC 75-17239. (Social Problems & Social Policy Ser.). (Illus.). 1976. reprint ed. 134.95 (*0-405-07508-1*) Ayer.

— Building America's Health: A Report, 5 vols. in 2, Vols. 4-5. LC 75-17239. (Social Problems & Social Policy Ser.). (Illus.). 1976. reprint ed. 66.95 (*0-405-07510-3*) Ayer.

President's Commission Staff. A National Agenda for the Eighties. (Illus.). 225p. 1982. pap. 5.95 (*0-13-609529-1*) P-H.

President's Conference on Home Building & Home Ownership Staff. Negro Housing. Gries, John M. & Ford, James, eds. LC 79-89053. 282p. 1970. reprint ed. text ed. 45.00 (*0-8371-1921-9*, NEH&, Negro U Pr) Greenwood.

President's Conference on Unemployment Committee. Business Cycles & Unemployment: Proceedings. LC 75-19697. (National Bureau of Economic Research Ser.). (Illus.). 1975. reprint ed. 36.95 (*0-405-07577-4*) Ayer.

President's Research Committee on Social Trends. Recent Social Trends in the United States, 2 vols., 1. Coser, Lewis A. & Powell, Walter W., eds. LC 79-7010. (Perennial Works in Sociology Ser.). (Illus.). 1980. reprint ed. lib. bdg. 61.95 (*0-405-12108-3*) Ayer.

— Recent Social Trends in the United States, 2 vols., 2. Coser, Lewis A. & Powell, Walter W., eds. LC 79-7010. (Perennial Works in Sociology Ser.). (Illus.). 1980. reprint ed. lib. bdg. 61.95 (*0-405-12109-1*) Ayer.

— Recent Social Trends in the United States, 2 vols., Set. Coser, Lewis A. & Powell, Walter W., eds. LC 79-7010. (Perennial Works in Sociology Ser.). (Illus.). 1979. reprint ed. lib. bdg. 122.95 (*0-405-12107-5*) Ayer.

President's Scientific Research Board Staff & Steelman, John R. Science & Public Policy: A Report to the President, 5 vols. in 1. Cohen, I. Bernard, ed. LC 79-7998. (Three Centuries of Science in America Ser.). (Illus.). 1980. reprint ed. lib. bdg. 94.95 (*0-405-12586-0*) Ayer.

***Presidio Press Staff.** Quest: Searching for the Truth of Germany's Nazi Past. 1994. pap. 12.95 (*0-89141-552-1*) Presidio Pr.

Presilla, Maricel. Feliz Nochebuena Feliz Navidad: Christmas Feasts of the Hispanic Caribbean. (J). 1994. 15.95 (*0-8050-2512-X*) H Holt & Co.

Preskill, Hallie, jt. ed. see Larson, Colleen L.

Preskitt, Steve & Walker, Dan. E! Update for the Yamaha DX711. Alexander, Peter L., ed. (Yamaha DX Support Ser.). (Illus.). 193p. (C). 1989. pap. text ed. 24.95 (*0-939067-65-X*) Alexander Pub.

***Preskorn, Sheldon H.** Outpatient Management of Depression. 159p. 1994. pap. 17.95 (*0-9632400-4-8*) Prof Comms.

Presler, Franklin A. Religion under Bureaucracy: Policy & Administration for Hindu Temples in South India. (Cambridge South Asian Studies: No. 38). (Illus.). 220p. 1988. 59.95 (*0-521-32177-8*) Cambridge U Pr.

***Presley & Brown.** Introduction to Computing Using Microsoft Works: Version Three for Windows. 525p. 1995. text ed. 40.67 (*1-879233-43-6*) Lawrenceville Pr.

— Introduction to Computing Using Microsoft Works, Version 3 for Windows. 1995. student ed, disk 20.00 (*1-879233-45-2*) Lawrenceville Pr.

— Introduction to Computing Using Microsoft Works, Version 3 for Windows. 360p. 1995. teacher ed, ring bd. 34.95 (*1-879233-44-4*) Lawrenceville Pr.

Presley, et al. An Introduction to Business Using Works. 1992. text ed. 40.67 (*1-879233-12-6*); pap. text ed. 33.27 (*1-879233-11-8*) Lawrenceville Pr.

— An Introduction to Business Using Works. 1992. teacher ed, ring bd. 34.95 (*1-879233-15-0*); write for info. (*1-879233-14-2*) Lawrenceville Pr.

— Introduction to Computing Using Microsoft Works, Version 4 for Macintosh. Date not set. student ed, disk 20.00 (*1-879233-56-8*); teacher ed, ring bd. 34.95 (*1-879233-53-3*) Lawrenceville Pr.

— Introduction to Computing Using Microsoft Works, Version 4 for Macintosh: Version Four for Macintosh, Presley, Freitas, Brown. 512p. Date not set. 40.67 (*1-879233-52-5*); pap. text ed. 33.27 (*1-879233-51-7*) Lawrenceville Pr.

***Presley & Brown Staff.** Introduction to Computing Using Microsoft Works: Version Three for Windows. 525p. 1995. pap. text ed. 33.27 (*1-879233-42-8*) Lawrenceville Pr.

Presley, Bruce. A Guide to Programming in BASIC-Plus. 324p. 1983. pap. 18.95 (*0-685-47521-2*) Inst Meeting Con Mgmt.

— A Guide to Structured Programming in BASIC, for IBM PC & Compatibles. 3rd ed. 404p. 1991. text ed. 40.67 (*0-931717-89-2*); pap. text ed. 33.27 (*0-931717-58-2*) Lawrenceville Pr.

An Asterisk (*) at the beginning of an entry indicates that the title is appearing in BIP for the first time.

— A Guide to Structured Programming in BASIC, for IBM PC & Compatibles. 3rd ed. 404p. 1992. teacher ed, ring bd. 34.95 (*0-931717-59-0*) Lawrenceville Pr.

Presley, Bruce & Corica, Tim. Teacher's Resource Package for the Advanced Placement Computer Science A Examination. 1988. ring bd. 39.95 (*0-931717-20-5*) Lawrenceville Pr.

Presley, Bruce & Freitas, William. An Introduction to Computing Using Microsoft Works, for IBM PC & Compatibles, 2.0 version. (Illus.). 404p. (Orig.). 1990. text ed. 40.67 (*0-931717-91-4*); pap. 33.27 (*0-931717-90-6*); teacher ed, ring bd. 34.95 (*0-931717-95-7*) Lawrenceville Pr.

— Introduction to Computing Using Microsoft Works 3.0, Mac Version. 496p. 1993. text ed. 40.67 (*1-879233-01-0*); pap. 33.27 (*1-879233-00-2*) Lawrenceville Pr.

— Introduction to Computing Using Microsoft Works 3.0, Mac Version, 10 disks. 1993. student ed, disk 20.00 (*1-879233-34-7*) Lawrenceville Pr.

— Introduction to Computing Using Microsoft Works 3.0, Mac Version. 360p. 1993. teacher ed, ring bd. 34.95 (*1-879233-02-9*) Lawrenceville Pr.

— Introduction to Desktop Publishing Using PageMaker, MAC Version. 416p. 1994. text ed. 40.67 (*1-879233-04-5*); pap. 33.27 (*1-879233-03-7*) Lawrenceville Pr.

— Introduction to Desktop Publishing Using PageMaker, MAC Version, 10 disks. 1994. student ed, disk 20.00 (*1-879233-37-1*) Lawrenceville Pr.

— Introduction to Desktop Publishing Using PageMaker, MAC Version. 1994. teacher ed, ring bd. 34.95 (*1-879233-05-3*) Lawrenceville Pr.

— Introduction to Desktop Publishing Using PageMaker, Windows Version. 1994. text ed. 40.67 (*1-879233-18-5*); pap. 33.27 (*1-879233-17-7*) Lawrenceville Pr.

— Introduction to Desktop Publishing Using PageMaker, Windows Version, 10 disks. 1994. student ed, disk 20.00 (*1-879233-39-8*) Lawrenceville Pr.

— Introduction to Desktop Publishing Using PageMaker, Windows Version. 1994. teacher ed, ring bd. 34.95 (*1-879233-19-3*) Lawrenceville Pr.

Presley, Bruce, jt. auth. see Freitas, William.

Presley, Bruce, et al. A Guide to Programming in Turbo Pascal Version 4.0-6.0. 2nd ed. (Illus.). 410p. 1991. text ed. 46.60 (*0-931717-73-6*); pap. text ed. 39.34 (*0-931717-72-8*) Lawrenceville Pr.

— A Guide to Programming in Turbo Pascal Version 4.0-6.0. 2nd ed. (Illus.). 410p. 1991. teacher ed 34.95 (*0-931717-78-7*) Lawrenceville Pr.

— An Introduction to Computing Using Claris Works 2.0, Mac Version. (Illus.). 512p. (Orig.). 1994. 40.67 (*1-879233-26-6*); pap. 33.27 (*1-879233-25-8*) Lawrenceville Pr.

— An Introduction to Computing Using Claris Works 2.0, Mac Version, 10 disks. (Orig.). 1994. student ed, disk 20.00 (*1-879233-36-3*) Lawrenceville Pr.

— An Introduction to Computing Using Claris Works 2.0, Mac Version. (Illus.). 464p. (Orig.). 1994. teacher ed, ring bd. 34.95 (*1-879233-29-0*) Lawrenceville Pr.

Presley, Cora A. Kikuyu Women, the Mau Mau Rebellion & Social Change in Kenya. 213p. (C). 1992. pap. text ed. 39.50 (*0-8133-7887-7*) Westview.

Presley, Delma E. Glass Menagerie: An American Memory. 1990. text ed. 21.95 (*0-8057-8058-0*, Twayne); pap. 12.95 (*0-8057-8127-7*, Pub. by Royal Botanic Garden UK) Macmillan.

Presley, Delma E., jt. auth. see Harper, Francis.

Presley, Deni. Sites & Insights: The Special Event Location & Resource Directory for Southern California. Berry, Kathryn E., ed. (Illus.). 208p. (Orig.). 1994. pap. text ed. 24.95 (*0-9640791-0-0*) Site Network.

Presley, Frances, jt. auth. see Taylor, Marilyn.

Presley, Horton. Principles of Music & Visual Arts. LC 86-1525. (Illus.). 144p. (Orig.). 1986. pap. text ed. 14.00 (*0-8191-5258-7*) U Pr of Amer.

— Restoring & Collecting Antique Reed Organs. 2nd ed. LC 92-15651. (Illus.). 313p. 1987. reprint ed. pap. 16.95 (*0-911572-56-2*) Vestal.

Presley, Jennifer B., ed. Organizing Effective Institutional Research Offices. LC 85-645339. (New Directions for Institutional Research Ser.: No. 66). 1990. 16.95 (*1-55542-829-0*) Jossey-Bass.

Presley, John & Dodd, William. Essential Reading Skills. (C). 1982. pap. text ed. 22.00 (*0-03-058001-3*) HB Coll Pubs.

Presley, John R. A Directory of Islamic Banking & Financial Institutions. 384p. 1988. lib. bdg. 120.00 (*0-7099-1347-8*) Routledge Chapman & Hall.

— A Guide to the Saudi Arabian Economy. LC 83-13781. 256p. 1984. text ed. 35.00 (*0-312-35304-9*) St Martin.

— Robertsonian Economics: An Examination of the Work of Sir D. H. Robertson on Industry Fluctuation. LC 78-25958. 320p. 1979. 45.00 (*0-8419-0471-5*) Holmes & Meier.

Presley, John R., ed. Essays on Robertsonian Economics. LC 91-38713. 160p. 1992. text ed. 69.95 (*0-312-06826-3*) St Martin.

Presley, John R., jt. ed. see Greenaway, David.

Presley, John R., jt. ed. see O'Brien, D. P.

Presley, John R., ed. see Robertson, Dennis H.

Presley, John W. The Robert Graves Manuscripts & Letters at Southern Illinois University: An Inventory. LC 75-8383. vii, 261p. 1976. 18.00 (*0-87875-075-4*) Whitston Pub.

Presley, M. & Levin, J. R., eds. Cognitive Strategy Research 1: Psychological Foundations. (Cognitive Development Ser.). (Illus.). 350p. 1983. 73.00 (*0-387-90818-8*) Spr-Verlag.

Presley, M. W. & McGillis, K. A. Coastal Evaporite & Tidal-Flat Sediments of the Upper Clear Fork & Glorieta Formations, Texas Panhandle. (Report of Investigations Ser.: RI 115). (Illus.). 50p. 1982. 2.00 (*0-318-03248-1*) Bur Econ Geology.

Presley, Priscilla B. Selected from Elvis & Me. abr. ed. (Writers' Voices Ser.). 64p. (Orig.). 1991. pap. text ed. 3.50 (*0-929631-27-7*, Signal Hill) New Readers.

Presley, Priscilla B. & Harmon, Sandra. Elvis & Me. 1986. mass mkt. 5.99 (*0-425-09103-1*) Berkley Pub.

Presley-Rippingale, Sally & Ballow, John E. The Secret Word Is Groucho! (Illus.). 208p. 1992. 13.95 (*0-8059-3272-0*) Dorrance.

Presley, William, jt. auth. see Freitas, Bruce.

Presley, William, jt. auth. see Freitas.

Preslo, L. M., et al. Remedial Technologies for Leaking Underground Storage Tanks. (Illus.). 220p. 1988. 74.95 (*0-87371-125-4*, TP692) Lewis Pubs.

Presman, E. L. & Sonon, I. N. Sequential Control with Incomplete Information. (Economic Theory, Econometrics & Mathematical Economics Ser.). 266p. 1990. text ed. 113.00 (*0-12-564435-3*) Acad Pr.

***Presnall, Judith J.** Animal Skeletons. (Illus.). 64p. (J). (gr. 5-7). 1995. lib. bdg. 15.33 (*0-531-11160-1*) Watts.

— Animals That Glow. LC 92-25529. (First Bks.). (J). 1993. lib. bdg. 13.93 (*0-531-20071-X*) Watts.

— Animals That Glow. (First Bks.). (Illus.). 64p. (J). (gr. 5-8). 1993. pap. 5.95 (*0-531-15672-9*) Watts.

— Rachel Carson. LC 93-49487. (Importance of... Biographies Ser.). (Illus.). 112p. (J). (gr. 5-8). 1995. 16.95 (*1-56006-052-2*) Lucent Bks.

***Presnell, Barbara.** Snakedreams. Zarucchi, L. D., ed. (Illus.). 36p. (Orig.). 1994. pap. 6.95 (*1-879205-54-8*) Nightshade Pr.

Presnell, Mick, jt. ed. see Carter, Kathryn.

Presner, Lewis A. The International Business Dictionary & Reference. 504p. 1991. text ed. 49.95 (*0-471-54594-5*) Wiley.

Presniakov, A. E. Tsardom of Muscovy. Price, R. F., ed. & tr. by. 1978. pap. 15.00 (*0-87569-090-4*) Academic Intl.

Presniakov, Alexander E. Emperor Nicholas the First of Russia: The Apogee of Autocracy, 1825-1855. Zacek, Judith C., tr. Bd. with Nicholas the First & the Course of Russian History, Vol. 23. LC 73-90779. LC 73-90779. (Russian Ser.: No. 23). (Illus.). 1974. 35.00 (*0-87569-053-X*) Academic Intl.

Presno, C., jt. auth. see Presno, V.

Presno, V. & Presno, C. The Value Realms: Activities for Helping Students Develop Values. LC 80-13051. 1980. pap. text ed. 11.95 (*0-8077-2584-6*) Tchrs Coll.

Presno, V., jt. auth. see Fournier, Robert.

***Preson, Richard.** The Hot Zone. LC 95-5751. 1995. 6.99 (*0-385-47956-5*, Anchor NY) Doubleday.

Press. State & Community Government Federal System. (C). 1990. text ed. 50.00 (*0-06-045366-4*) HarpCollege.

Press & Siever. Understanding Earth. (C). 1995. Instr.'s Manual. teacher ed, text ed. write for info. (*0-7167-2521-5*); Student Guide. student ed, text ed. write for info. (*0-7167-2522-3*) W H Freeman.

***Press, et al.** Functional Rehabilitation of Sports & Musculoskeletal Injuries. 300p. 1996. 65.00 (*0-8342-0612-9*) Aspen Pub.

Press, Allan N., jt. auth. see Osterkamp, Lynn.

Press, Andrea L. Women Watching Television: Gender, Class, & Generation in the American Television Experience. LC 90-21274. 258p. (C). 1991. pap. text ed. 17.95x (*0-8122-1286-X*) U of Pa Pr.

Press Association Staff & Jenkins, John. John Major: Prime Minister. (Illus.). 224p. 1991. 24.95 (*0-7475-0942-5*, Pub. by Bloomsbury Pub Ltd UK) Trafalgar.

Press, Bill. Eyewitness: A California Perspective. 192p. (Orig.). 1988. pap. text ed. 7.95 (*0-939061-01-5*) Redwood Press.

Press, Charles. Primer for Board of Review Members. 4th ed. LC 87-620000. 65p. 1987. 4.50 (*0-941872-53-X*) MSU Dept Res Dev.

Press, Daniel. Democratic Dilemmas in the Age of Ecology: Trees & Toxics in the American West. LC 94-7247. 176p. 1994. lib. bdg. 34.95 (*0-8223-1503-3*); pap. text ed. 15.95 (*0-8223-1514-9*) Duke.

Press, David P. A Multicultural Portrait of America's Music. LC 93-48847. (Perspectives Ser.). (J). 1994. 18.95 (*1-85435-666-6*) Marshall Cavendish.

— A Multicultural Portrait of Professional Sports. LC 93-10316. (Perspectives Ser.). (J). 1993. 18.95 (*1-85435-661-5*) Marshall Cavendish.

***Press, David P. & Kaplan, Elizabeth.** Jewish Americans. (Cultures of America Ser.). 80p. (J). (gr. 3-5). 1995. lib. bdg. 19.95 (*0-7614-0153-9*) Marshall Cavendish.

Press, Frank, frwd. Headline News, Science Views. 180p. 1991. 24.95 (*0-309-04480-4*) Natl Acad Pr.

Press, Frank & Siever, Raymond. Earth. 4th ed. LC 85-20581. (Illus.). 656p. (C). 1995. text ed. write for info. (*0-7167-1743-3*) W H Freeman.

— Understanding the Earth. LC 93-4967. (C). 1995. pap. text ed. write for info. (*0-7167-2239-9*) W H Freeman.

Press, Gerald A. The Development of the Idea of History in Antiquity. LC 84-239837. (McGill-Queen's Studies in the History of Religion: No. 2). 191p. reprint ed. pap. 54.50 (*0-7837-1028-3*, 2041339) Bks Demand.

Press, Gerald A., ed. Plato's Dialogues: New Studies & Interpretations. 288p. (Orig.). (C). 1993. lib. bdg. 58.50 (*0-8476-7835-0*); pap. text ed. 23.50 (*0-8476-7836-9*) Rowman.

Press, Ian & Pugh, Stefan. Colloquial Ukrainian. LC 93-38897. 1994. write for info. (*0-415-09202-7*); audio write for info. (*0-415-09204-3*) Routledge.

Press, Irwin. Tradition & Adaptation: Life in a Modern Yucatan Maya Village. LC 75-71. (Illus.). 288p. 1975. text ed. 55.00 (*0-8371-7954-8*, PYM/, Greenwood Pr) Greenwood.

Press, J. Ian. A Grammar of Modern Breton. (Mouton Grammar Library: No. 2). (Illus.). x, 406p. 1986. lib. bdg. 89.25 (*0-89925-135-8*) Mouton.

Press, James S. Bayesian Statistics: Principles, Models & Applications. LC 88-5407. (Probability & Mathematical Statistics Ser.). 237p. 1989. text ed. 69.95 (*0-471-63729-7*) Wiley.

Press, John, jt. ed. see Palgrave, Francis T.

Press, Jon. The Footwear Industry in Ireland, 1922-1973. (Illus.). 224p. 1988. 39.50 (*0-7165-2439-2*, Pub. by Irish Acad Pr IE) Intl Spec Bk.

Press, Jon, jt. auth. see Harvey, Charles.

Press, Jon, jt. ed. see Harvey, Charles.

Press, Jonathan. Professional Publishing with Ventura. (Orig.). 1989. 29.95 (*0-317-93951-3*); pap. 19.95 (*0-317-93952-1*) Jonathan Pr.

Press, Joy, jt. auth. see Reynolds, Simon.

Press, Judy. The Little Hands Art Book: Exploring Arts & Crafts with 2-to-6 Year Olds. LC 94-1391. (J). (ps-1). 1994. pap. 12.95 (*0-913589-86-1*) Williamson Pub Co.

Press, Leonard J. & Moore, Bruce D. Clinical Pediatric Optometry. (Illus.). 400p. 1992. 65.00 (*0-7506-9080-1*) Buttrwrth-Heinemann.

Press, Leonard J., et al. Computers & Vision Therapy Programs. Corngold, Sally M., ed. (Introduction to Behavioral Optometry Ser.). (Illus.). 82p. (Orig.). lib. bdg. 15.00 (*0-943599-57-1*) OEPF.

Press, Margaret L. Chemehuevi, a Grammar & Lexicon. LC 78-62874. (University of California Publications in Social Welfare: No. 92). 211p. reprint ed. pap. 60.20 (*0-685-44444-9*, 2032901) Bks Demand.

Press, Mike & Thomson, Don, eds. Solidarity for Survival: The Don Thomson Reader on Trade Union Internationalism. 161p. 1989. 49.50 (*0-85124-510-2*, Pub. by Spokesman Bks UK) Coronet Bks.

Press, Mike, jt. auth. see Cooper, Rachel.

***Press, Petra.** Mexican Americans. (Cultures of America Ser.). 80p. (J). (gr. 3-5). 1995. lib. bdg. 19.95 (*0-7614-0152-0*) Marshall Cavendish.

— A Multicultural Portrait of Immigration. (Perspectives Ser.). 80p. (J). (gr. 5-9). 1995. lib. bdg. write for info. (*0-7614-0055-9*, Benchmark NY) Marshall Cavendish.

— A Multicultural Portrait of Learning in America. LC 93-48769. (J). 1994. 18.95 (*1-85435-665-8*) Marshall Cavendish.

— Puerto Rican Americans. (Cultures of America Ser.). 80p. (J). (gr. 3-5). 1995. lib. bdg. write for info. (*0-7614-0160-1*, Benchmark NY) Marshall Cavendish.

Press Research Center Staff, et al, eds. Who's Who in Mass Communication Research. 2nd ed. 191p. 1990. lib. bdg. 135.00 (*3-598-10884-2*) K G Saur.

Press, Skip. Awesome Almanacs - California. 1994. pap. 14.95 (*1-880190-21-4*) B&B Pub.

— Candice & Edgar Bergen. LC 94-20395. (Star Families Ser.). (J). 1995. lib. bdg. 13.95 (*0-89686-878-8*, Crstwood Hse) Silver Burdett Pr.

— Candice & Edgar Bergen. (Star Families Ser.). (Illus.). (YA). (gr. 5 up). 1995. pap. 7.95 (*0-382-24940-2*, Crstwood Hse) Silver Burdett Pr.

— Charlie Sheen, Emilio Estevez & Martin Sheen. LC 95-11619. (Star Families Ser.). (J). 1995. write for info. (*0-89686-884-2*, Crstwood Hse); pap. write for info. (*0-382-39180-2*, Crstwood Hse) Silver Burdett Pr.

— Cliffhanger. Parker, Liz, ed. (Take Ten Bks.). (Illus.). 45p. (Orig.). (J). (gr. 6-12). 1993. pap. text ed. 2.95 (*1-56254-055-6*) Saddleback Pubns.

— How to Write What You Want & Sell What You Write. 192p. (Orig.). 1995. pap. 10.99 (*1-56414-152-7*) Career Pr Inc.

— Ken Griffey, Jr. & Ken Griffey, Sr. LC 95-11815. (Star Families Ser.). (J). 1995. pap. write for info. (*0-382-39189-6*, Crstwood Hse) Silver Burdett Pr.

— Ken Griffey, Jr. & Ken Griffey, Sr. deluxe ed. LC 95-11815. (Star Families Ser.). (J). 1995. write for info. (*0-89686-881-8*, Crstwood Hse) Silver Burdett Pr.

— Knucklehead. Parker, Liz, ed. (Take Ten Bks.). (Illus.). 50p. (Orig.). (YA). (gr. 6-12). 1993. pap. text ed. 2.95 (*1-56254-095-5*) Saddleback Pubns.

— The Kuwaiti Oil Fires. Parker, Liz, ed. (Take Ten Bks.). 46p. (Orig.). (YA). (gr. 6-12). 1993. pap. text ed. 2.95 (*1-56254-097-1*) Saddleback Pubns.

— Mark Twain. LC 93-1827. (Importance of Ser.). (J). (gr. 5-8). 1994. 16.95 (*1-56006-043-3*) Lucent Bks.

— Melissa & Joan Rivers. LC 95-13087. (Star Families Ser.). (J). 1995. lib. bdg. write for info. (*0-89686-883-4*, Crstwood Hse); pap. write for info. (*0-382-39178-0*, Crstwood Hse) Silver Burdett Pr.

— Michael & Kirk Douglas. LC 94-28650. (Star Families Ser.). (J). 1995. 13.95 (*0-89686-880-X*, Crstwood Hse) Silver Burdett Pr.

— Michael & Kirk Douglas. (Star Families Ser.). (Illus.). (YA). (gr. 5 up). 1995. pap. 7.95 (*0-382-24941-0*, Crstwood Hse) Silver Burdett Pr.

— Natalie & Nat King Cole. LC 94-22429. (J). 1995. text ed. 13.95 (*0-89686-879-6*, Crstwood Hse) Silver Burdett Pr.

— Natalie & Nat "King" Cole. (Star Families Ser.). (Illus.). (YA). (gr. 5 up). 1995. pap. 7.95 (*0-382-24942-9*, Crstwood Hse) Silver Burdett Pr.

— A Rave of Snakes. (You-Solve-It Mysteries Ser.: No. 1). 224p. 1994. pap. 3.50 (*0-8217-4546-8*) Zebra.

— A Shift of Coyotes. (You-Solve-It Mysteries Ser.: No. 6). 224p. 1994. pap. 3.50 (*0-8217-4706-1*) Zebra.

— Tori & Aaron Spelling. LC 95-11600. (Star Families Ser.). (J). 1995. write for info. (*0-89686-885-0*, Crstwood Hse); pap. write for info. (*0-382-39179-9*, Crstwood Hse) Silver Burdett Pr.

— A Web of Ya Yas. (You-Solve-It Mysteries Ser.: No. 4). 224p. 1994. pap. 3.50 (*0-8217-4643-X*) Zebra.

— Wynonna & Naomi Judd. LC 94-28465. (Star Families Ser.). (Illus.). (YA). (gr. 5 up). 1995. pap. 7.95 (*0-382-24943-7*, Crstwood Hse) Silver Burdett Pr.

***Press, Skip, contrib.** Wynonna & Naomi Judd. LC 94-28465. (Star Families Ser.). (Illus.). (J). (gr. 5). 1995. 13.95 (*0-89686-882-6*, Crstwood Hse) Silver Burdett Pr.

Press, T. D. Manitou's Dream. LC 83-51837. 184p. (Orig.). 1984. pap. 2.95 (*0-916597-00-8*) Tunnel Pr FL.

Press, William H., et al. Numerical Recipes for the Macintosh. 1988. Fortran Disk. pap. 34.95 (*0-521-35469-2*) Cambridge U Pr.

— Numerical Recipes in C: The Art of Scientific Computing. 2nd ed. 1035p. (C). 1992. 49.95 (*0-521-43108-5*) Cambridge U Pr.

— Numerical Recipes in C: The Art of Scientific Computing. 2nd ed. 1035p. (C). 1992. pap. 29.95 (*0-521-43720-2*); IBM, 3 1/2 inch, 720K. pap. 39.95 (*0-521-43724-5*) Cambridge U Pr.

— Numerical Recipes in C: The Art of Scientific Computing. 2nd ed. 1035p. (C). 1993. Macintosh. pap. 39.95 (*0-521-43715-6*) Cambridge U Pr.

— Numerical Recipes in FORTRAN: The Art of Scientific Computing. 2nd ed. 92p. (C). 1992. 49.95 (*0-521-43064-X*) Cambridge U Pr.

— Numerical Recipes in FORTRAN: The Art of Scientific Computing. 2nd ed. 92p. (C). 1992. pap. 29.95 (*0-521-43721-0*); IBM, 3 1/2 inch, 720K. pap. 39.95 (*0-521-43719-9*); IBM, 5 1/4 inch, 1.2M. pap. 39.95 (*0-521-43717-2*) Cambridge U Pr.

— Numerical Recipes in FORTRAN: The Art of Scientific Computing. 2nd ed. 92p. (C). 1993. Macintosh. pap. 39.95 (*0-521-43716-4*); 90.00 (*0-685-70863-2*) Cambridge U Pr.

— Numerical Recipes in Pascal: The Art of Scientific Computing. rev. ed. (Illus.). (C). 1989. 49.95 (*0-521-37516-9*) Cambridge U Pr.

— Numerical Recipes in Pascal: The Art of Scientific Computing. rev. ed. (Illus.). (C). 1989. pap. 27.95 (*0-521-37675-0*); pap. 34.95 (*0-521-37532-0*); pap. 29.95 (*0-521-37533-9*) Cambridge U Pr.

Pressat, Roland. Dictionnaire de Demographie. 304p. (FRE.). 1979. 75.00 (*0-8288-9468-X*, F70763) Fr & Eur.

— Statistical Demography. Courtney, Damien A., tr. LC 78-19251. 1978. text ed. 25.00 (*0-312-76134-1*) St Martin.

***Pressburger, Giorgio.** Law of White Spacers. 1994. pap. 3.99 (*0-517-13101-3*) Random.

— The Law of White Spaces. Spence, Piers, tr. LC 92-50470. 176p. 1993. 19.00 (*0-679-42048-7*) Pantheon.

— Law of White Spaces. 1994. pap. 10.00 (*0-679-75246-3*, Vin) Random.

Pressburger, Giorgio & Pressburger, Nicola. Homage to the Eighth District: Tales from Budapest. Moore, Gerald, tr. 150p. (Orig.). 1990. 17.95 (*0-930523-75-X*); pap. 9.95 (*0-930523-76-8*) Readers Intl.

Pressburger, Nicola, jt. auth. see Pressburger, Giorgio.

Presse Commerciale Staff. Lexique de la Geographie en Cinq Langues. 2248p. (FRE.). 1993. 75.00 (*0-7859-5674-3*, 7100008379) Fr & Eur.

Presseisen, Barbara. Learning & Thinking Styles: Classroom Interaction. 160p. 1990. 15.95 (*0-8106-1841-9*) NEA.

Presseisen, Barbara, ed. see Langrehr, John.

Presseisen, Barbara Z. Critical Thinking & Thinking Skills: State-of-the-Art Definitions & Practice in Public Schools. 57p. 1986. pap. 13.95 (*1-56602-011-5*) Research Better.

— Thinking Skills: Research & Practice. (What Research Says to the Teacher Ser.). 1986. 3.95 (*0-8106-1073-6*) NEA.

— Thinking Skills Throughout the Curriculum: A Conceptual Design. (Illus.). 109p. (Orig.). (C). pap. 8.95 (*0-9618056-0-9*) Pi Lambda Theta.

— Understanding Adolescence: Issues & Implications for Effective Schools. 60p. 1990. reprint ed. pap. 16.95 (*1-56602-002-6*) Research Better.

— The Unlearned Lessons: Current & Past Reforms for School Improvement. LC 85-29659. 258p. 1985. 55.00 (*1-85000-079-4*, Falmer Pr); pap. 28.00 (*1-85000-080-8*, Falmer Pr) Taylor & Francis.

Presseisen, Barbara Z., ed. At-Risk Students & Thinking: Perspectives from Research. 160p. 1988. 14.95 (*0-8106-1483-9*) NEA.

Presseisen, Barbara Z., jt. auth. see Kruse, Janice.

Presseisen, Ernst L. Amiens & Munich. (Comparisons in Appeasement Ser.). 1978. lib. bdg. 62.00 (*90-247-2067-2*) Kluwer Ac.

— Before Aggression: Europeans Prepare the Japanese Army. LC 65-20235. (Association for Asian Studies, Monographs & Papers: No. 21). 173p. reprint ed. pap. 49.40 (*0-8357-7089-3*, 2002932) Bks Demand.

Pressel, Lloyd & Gardner, Robert H. Supervision for Empowered Workers: View Leadership Styles for Self-Managing Teams. 210p. 1992. 24.95 (*0-9634821-0-6*) Loma Linda Pub.

Pressel, Ralph, jt. auth. see Field, John.

***Presser, ArLynn.** Getting Out: Emily. (Loop Ser.). 1995. pap. 3.50 (*0-373-20207-5*, 1-20207-6) Harlequin Bks.

— The Romantics. (Voices Romance Ser.: No. 4). 224p. 1994. mass mkt. 3.50 (*0-8217-4705-3*) Zebra.

— Second to None. 224p. 1994. pap. 3.50 (*0-8217-4514-X*) Zebra.

Presser, Beat, photos. Coming Attractions. 64p. 1984. pap. 10.95 (*0-912810-42-4*) Lustrum Pr.

Presser, Carole. Protection Mutual Insurance Company: The First Hundred Years. LC 87-61723. (Illus.). 72p. (Orig.). 1987. pap. write for info. (*0-916371-07-7*) Mobium Pr.

Presser, Jacob. Ashes in the Wind: The Destruction of Dutch Jewry. Pomerans, Arnold, tr. LC 88-225. (Illus.). 571p. 1988. reprint ed. 49.95 (*0-8143-2036-8*); reprint ed. pap. 19.95 (*0-8143-2037-6*) Wayne St U Pr.

Presser, Jaques. Night of the Girondists. 80p. (Orig.). 1992. pap. 10.00 (*0-00-271209-1*, Pub. by HarpC UK) HarpC.

P Q

An Asterisk (*) at the beginning of an entry indicates that the title is appearing in BIP for the first time.

Presser, Stanley, jt. auth. see Converse, Jean M.
Presser, Stanley, jt. auth. see Schuman, Howard.
Presser, Stanley, jt. ed. see Singer, Eleanor.
Presser, Stephen B. The Original Misunderstanding: The English, the Americans, & the Dialectic of Federalist Jurisprudence. LC 90-85344. 284p. 1991. lib. bdg. 34.95 (*0-89089-425-6*) Carolina Acad Pr.
— Recapturing the Constitution. 416p. 1994. 24.95 (*0-89526-492-7*) Regnery Pub.
Presser, Stephen B. & Zainaldin, Jamil S. Jurisprudence in American. 2nd ed. (American Casebook Ser.). 1092p. 1991. reprint ed. text ed. 51.00 (*0-314-53540-3*) West Pub.
— Law & Jurisprudence in American History, Cases & Materials On. 3rd ed. (American Casebook Ser.). 1092p. (C). 1995. text ed. write for info. (*0-314-06359-5*) West Pub.
— Law & Jurisprudence in American History, Teacher's Manual to Accompany Cases & Materials On. 2nd ed. (American Casebook Ser.). 126p. 1989. pap. text ed. write for info. (*0-314-69306-8*) West Pub.
Presser, William. Song for Three Viols. (Contemporary Consort Ser.: No. 20). 7p. 1992. 6.00 (*1-56571-057-6*, CC020) PRB Prods.
***Presses de l'Universite Laval Staff.** Dictionnaire Biographique du Canada. 1982. write for info. (*0-7859-8456-9*, 2-7637-6950-0) Fr & Eur.
— Dictionnaire Biographique du Canada 1701-1740. 1969. write for info. (*0-7859-8028-8*, 2-7637-0007-1) Fr & Eur.
— Dictionnaire Biographique du Canada 1741-1770. 1974. write for info. (*0-7859-8031-8*, 2-7637-6736-2) Fr & Eur.
— Dictionnaire Biographique du Canada 1771-1800. 1980. write for info. (*0-7859-8033-4*, 2-7637-6900-4) Fr & Eur.
— Dictionnaire Biographique du Canada 1821-1835. 1987. write for info. (*0-7859-8034-2*, 2-7637-7099-1) Fr & Eur.
— Dictionnaire Biographique du Canada 1861-1870. 1977. write for info. (*0-7859-8032-6*, 2-7637-6812-1); write for info. (*0-7859-8592-1*, 0774668113) Fr & Eur.
— Dictionnaire Biographique du Canada 1871-1880. 1972. write for info. (*0-7859-8029-6*, 2-7637-0010-1) Fr & Eur.
Pressey, Benfield, jt. auth. see Watson, Bradlee E.
Pressey, Benfield, jt. ed. see Watson, Bradlee E.
***Pressfield, Steven.** The Legend of Bagger Vance: A Novel. LC 94-32223. 1995. 16.00 (*0-688-14048-3*) Morrow.
Pressing, Jeff. Synthesizer Performance & Real-Time Techniques. LC 91-39700. (Computer Music & Digital Audio Ser.: Vol. 8). (Illus.). 462p. (C). 1992. 49.95 (*0-89579-257-5*) A-R Eds.
Pressler, Carolyn. The View of Women Found in the Deuteronomic Family Laws. LC 93-27800. (Beiheft zur Zeitschrift fuer die Alttestamentliche Wissenschaft Ser.: Vol. 216). ix, 127p. (C). 1993. lib. bdg. 83.10 (*3-11-013743-7*) De Gruyter.
Pressler, David E. The Theory of Unity: The Final Theory. (Illus.). 162p. 1994. 39.95 (*0-9638572-0-7*) Primary Nuclear.
Pressler, Larry. Star Wars: The Strategic Defense Initiative Debates in Congress. LC 86-809. 193p. 1986. text ed. 55.00 (*0-275-92052-6*, C2052, Praeger Pubs) Greenwood.
***Pressley & McCormick.** Cognition, Teaching & Assessment. (C). 1995. text ed. 34.00 (*0-673-99400-7*) HarpCollege.
Pressley, Andrew & Segal, Graeme. Loop Groups. (Oxford Mathematical Monographs). 328p. 1988. pap. 35.00 (*0-19-853561-9*) OUP.
Pressley, Andrew, jt. auth. see Chari, Vyjayanthi.
Pressley, Andrew N., jt. auth. see Chari, Vyjayanthi.
Pressley, M. & Brainerd, Charles J., eds. Cognitive Learning & Memory in Children. (Cognitive Development Ser.). (Illus.). 290p. 1985. 69.00 (*0-387-96076-7*) Spr-Verlag.
Pressley, M., jt. ed. see Brainerd, Charles J.
Pressley, M., jt. ed. see McDaniel, M. A.
Pressley, M., jt. auth. see Schneider, W.
Pressley, Michael & Afflerbach, Peter. Verbal Protocols of Reading: The Nature of Constructively Responsive Reading. 168p. 1995. text ed. 39.95 (*0-8058-1537-6*); pap. 17.50 (*0-8058-1764-6*) L Erlbaum Assocs.
Pressley, Michael & McCormick, Christine. Advances Educational Psychology for Educators, Researchers, & Policymakers. LC 93-49883. 722p. (C). 1995. 45.00 (*0-673-46914-X*) HarpCollege.
***Pressley, Michael & Woloshyn, Vera.** Cognitive Strategy Instruction That Really Improves Children's Academic Performance. 2nd ed. LC 95-2310. (Cognitive Strategy Training Ser.). 1995. pap. text ed. 27.95 (*1-57129-005-2*) Brookline Bks.
Pressley, Michael, ed. see Harris, Karen R. & Graham, Steven.
Pressley, Michael, ed. see Scruggs, Thomas & Mastropieri, Margo.
Pressley, Michael, et al. Cognitive Strategy Instruction That Really Improves Children's Academic Performances. (Illus.). 200p. 1990. text ed. 24.95 (*0-914797-66-2*) Brookline Bks.
— Promoting Academic Competence & Literacy in School. (Illus.). 506p. 1992. text ed. 49.95 (*0-12-564438-8*) Acad Pr.
Pressley, Patsy, jt. auth. see Brophy, Maureen.
Pressling, Robert. My Magnet. LC 94-7110. (First Step Science Ser.). (Illus.). 32p. (J). (gr. 1 up). 1994. lib. bdg. 17.27 (*0-8368-1117-8*) Gareth Stevens Inc.
Pressly, Thomas J., jt. auth. see Linden, Glenn M.
Pressly, William L. A Catalogue of Paintings in the Folger Shakespeare Library: "As Imagination Bodies Forth" (Illus.). 416p. (C). 1993. text ed. 50.00 (*0-300-05214-6*) Yale U Pr.
— The Formative Years at Atlanta's Westminster Schools. 212p. 1991. text ed. write for info. (*0-9628381-0-1*) McGuire Pub.
— The Life & Art of James Barry. LC 80-29665. (Paul Mellon Centre for Studies in British Art). (Illus.). 320p. 1981. 80.00 (*0-300-02466-5*) Yale U Pr.
Pressman, jt. auth. see Dublin.
Pressman, Abraham I. Switching Power Supply Design. 1991. text ed. 58.00 (*0-07-050806-2*) McGraw.
Pressman, Alan H. & Adams, Alan H. Clinical Assessment of Nutritional Status. 2nd ed. 220p. 1990. 40.00 (*0-683-06970-5*) Williams & Wilkins.
Pressman, Andy. Architecture 101: A Guide to the Design Studio. 179p. 1993. pap. text ed. 29.95 (*0-471-57318-3*) Wiley.
— The Fountainheadache: The Politics of Architect-Client Relations. 1995. pap. text ed. 29.95 (*0-471-30992-3*) Wiley.
Pressman, Barbara, et al, eds. Intervening with Assaulted Women: Current Theory, Research & Practice. 196p. (C). 1989. text ed. 29.95 (*0-8058-0456-0*) L Erlbaum Assocs.
***Pressman, David.** Patent It Yourself. 4th ed. Elias, Stephan, ed. LC 95-13318. (Illus.). 464p. 1995. pap. 39.95 (*0-87337-291-3*) Nolo Pr.
Pressman, David, jt. auth. see EDS Staff.
Pressman, David, jt. auth. see Grissom, Fred.
Pressman, Harvey, ed. Making an Exceptional Difference: Enhancing the Impact of Microcomputer Technology on Children with Disabilities. 320p. (Orig.). 1987. pap. text ed. 24.95 (*0-930958-03-9*) Excptnl Parent.
Pressman, Harvey, jt. ed. see Dublin, Peter.
Pressman, Hope H. A New Resource for Welfare Reform: The Poor Themselves. LC 75-2399. 140p. reprint ed. pap. 39.90 (*0-7837-2138-2*, 2042424) Bks Demand.
Pressman, Jeffrey L. House vs. Senate: Conflict in the Appropriations Process. LC 66-21532. (Yale College Ser.: No. 5). 151p. reprint ed. pap. 43.10 (*0-8357-8171-2*, 2033861) Bks Demand.
Pressman, Jeffrey L. & Wildavsky, Aaron B. Implementation: How Great Expectations in Washington Are Dashed in Oakland; Or, Why It's Amazing That Federal Programs Work at All, This Being a Saga of the Economic Development Administration As Told by Two Sympathetic Observers Who Seek to Build Morals on a Foundation of Ruined Hopes. 3rd ed. LC 83-17987. (Oakland Project Ser.). 304p. (C). 1984. pap. 13.00 (*0-520-05331-1*) U CA Pr.
Pressman, Kati. The Big Picture Book: Gift Edition, A Primer of Spiritual Qualities for Adults. 62p. 1992. pap. 5.95 (*1-881422-01-1*) Jester Pr CO.
Pressman, Michael. FORTRAN for Today & Tomorrow. 512p. (C). 1992. pap. text ed. write for info. (*0-697-04483-1*) Wm C Brown Pubs.
Pressman, Paul S. Residential Treatment: Past Policies, Present Issues, Future Priorities. 61p. 1983. pap. 14.95 (*0-89885-165-3*) Human Sci Pr.
***Pressman, Robert & Weinstein, Susan.** Procedural Due Process Rights in Student Discipline. 193p. 1990. pap. 20.00 (*0-912585-05-6*) Ctr Law & Ed.
Pressman, Robert M. & Siegler, Rodie. The Independent Practitioner: Practice Management for the Allied Health Professional. LC 82-73633. (Professional Bks.). 266p. (C). 1983. text ed. 37.95 (*0-534-11281-1*) Brooks-Cole.
Pressman, Robert M., jt. auth. see Donaldson-Pressman, Stephanie.
Pressman, Roger S. A Manager's Guide to Software Engineering. LC 92-13456. (Systems Design & Implementation Ser.). 1992. text ed. 55.00 (*0-07-050820-8*) McGraw.
— Software Engineering. LC 87-35396. 1988. pap. text ed. write for info. (*0-07-050790-2*) McGraw.
— Software Engineering: A Practitioner's Approach. 3rd ed. 1992. text ed. write for info. (*0-07-050814-3*) McGraw.
— Software Engineering Principles. 256p. 1988. pap. write for info. (*0-318-62548-2*) McGraw.
— Software Engineering Strategies: A Guide for Instituting Technology for the 1990s. (Illus.). 288p. 1988. text ed. 38.00 (*0-13-823030-7*) P-H.
Pressman, Roger S. & Herron, S. Russell. Software Shock: The Danger & the Opportunity. LC 91-20988. (Illus.). 240p. (Orig.). 1991. pap. 18.95 (*0-932633-20-X*) Dorset Hse Pub Co.
Pressman, Steven. Outrageous Betrayal: The Real Story of Werner Erhard, Est & the Forum. 320p. 1993. 22.95 (*0-312-09296-2*) St Martin.
— Poverty in America. 313p. 1994. 40.00 (*0-8108-2833-2*) Scarecrow.
— Quesnay's "Tableau Economique" A Critique & Reassessment. x, 198p. 1994. lib. bdg. 35.00x (*0-678-01471-X*) Kelley.
Pressman, Thelma. Three Hundred & Sixty-Five Quick & Easy Microwave Recipes. LC 89-45057. (Three Hundred Sixty-Five Ways Ser.). (Illus.). 224p. 1989. 17.95 (*0-06-016026-8*, HarpT) HarpC.
Pressnell, Jon. Great Cars of the World. 216p. 1994. 14.98 (*0-8317-4043-4*) Smithmark.
— Touring Caravans. 1989. pap. 25.00 (*0-7478-0119-3*, Pub. by Shire UK) St Mut.
Pressnell, L. S. & Orbell, John. A Guide to the Historical Records of British Banking. LC 85-2002. 130p. 1985. text ed. 35.00 (*0-312-35303-0*) St Martin.
Pressouyre, G. M., ed. see International Conference on Current Solutions to Hydrogen Problems in Steels Staff.
Pressure Vessels & Piping Conference Staff. Aspects of Fracture Mechanics in Pressure Vessels & Piping. Palusamy, S. S. & Sampath, S. G., eds. LC 82-71607. (Illus.). 329p. reprint ed. pap. 93.80 (*0-8357-6028-6*, 2056814) Bks Demand.
— Component Support Snubbers: Design, Application, & Testing: Presented at the Pressure Vessels & Piping Conference, ASME Century 2--Emerging Technology Conferences, San Francisco, California, August 12-15, 1980. Reiff, D. D., ed. LC 80-66043. (PVP Ser.: No. 42). (Illus.). 75p. reprint ed. pap. 25.00 (*0-8357-2818-8*, 2039057) Bks Demand.
Prest, A. R. Public Finance in Developing Countries. 3rd ed. LC 85-1955. 256p. 1985. text ed. 39.95 (*0-312-65462-6*) St Martin.
Prest, A. R. & Coppock, D. J., eds. The U. K. Economy: Manual of Applied Economics. 6th ed. 1977. 24.95 (*0-8464-0942-9*) Beekman Pubs.
Prest, A. R., ed. see British Association for the Advancement of Science, Section F, Economics Staff.
Prest, Arthur. Illustrated History of the Nigerian People. LC 73-92798. (J). (gr. 4 up). 1974. write for info. (*0-89388-138-4*) Okpaku Communications.
Prest, C. B. Interlocutory Interdicts. xxxvi, 236p. 1994. pap. 60.00 (*0-7021-3078-8*, Pub. by Juta SA) W W Gaunt.
Prest, D., jt. auth. see Breckon, A.
Prest, John. The Garden of Eden: The Botanic Garden & the Re-Creation of Paradise. 127p. (C). 1988. reprint ed. 17.00 (*0-300-04370-8*) Yale U Pr.
— Liberty & Locality: Parliament, Permissive Legislation & Ratepayers' Democracies in the Mid-Nineteenth Century. 248p. 1990. 59.00 (*0-19-820175-3*) OUP.
Prest, John, ed. The Illustrated History of Oxford University. LC 92-35199. (Illus.). 452p. 1993. 45.00 (*0-19-820158-3*) OUP.
Prest, M. Y. Model Theory & Modules. (London Mathematical Society Lecture Note Ser.: No. 130). 350p. 1988. pap. 54.95 (*0-521-34833-1*) Cambridge U Pr.
Prest, M. Y., jt. auth. see Humphreys, J. F.
Prest, Thomas P. Varney, the Vampire, or, The Feast of Blood, 3 vols, Set. Varma, Devendra P., ed. LC 70-120557. (Gothic Novels). 933p. 1972. reprint ed. boxed 51.95 (*0-405-00801-5*) Ayer.
Prest, Wilfrid, ed. Lawyers in Early Modern Europe & America. LC 80-22574. 224p. 1981. 37.95 (*0-8419-0679-3*) Holmes & Meier.
Prest, Wilfrid R. The Rise of the Barristers: A Social History of the English Bar, 1590-1640. (Oxford Studies in Social History). 440p. 1987. 79.00 (*0-19-821764-1*) OUP.
— The Rise of the Barristers: A Social History of the English Bar, 1590-1640. (Oxford Studies in Social History). 464p. 1991. reprint ed. pap. 29.95 (*0-19-820258-X*) OUP.
Prestage, Edgar. Chivalry: A Series of Studies to Illustrate Its Historical Significance & Civilizing Influence, by Members of King's College, London. LC 72-11293. (Illus.). reprint ed. 37.50 (*0-404-57491-2*) AMS Pr.
— D. Francisco Manuel De Mello. 98p. (Orig.). 1992. pap. text ed. 10.00 (*0-87535-012-7*) Hispanic Soc.
Prestage, Edgar, ed. Chapters in Anglo-Portuguese Relations. LC 73-109826. (Illus.). 198p. 1971. reprint ed. text ed. 49.75 (*0-8371-4317-9*, PRCA, Greenwood Pr) Greenwood.
Prestbo, John, jt. auth. see Sease, Douglas.
Prestedge, Margie, jt. auth. see Bird, Madeline.
Prestel, A. Lectures on Formally Real Fields. (Lecture Notes in Mathematics Ser.: Vol. 1093). xi, 125p. 1984. reprint ed. pap. 28.10 (*0-387-13885-4*) Spr-Verlag.
Prestel, A. & Roquette, P. Formally P Adic Fields. (Lecture Notes in Mathematics Ser.: Vol. 1050). v, 167p. 1984. pap. 29.60 (*0-387-12890-5*) Spr-Verlag.
Prestel, Alexander. Einfuhrung in die Mathematische Logik und Modelltheorie. (Vieweg Studium: Aufbaukurs Mathematik Ser.: Vol. 60). xiv, 286p. (GER.). (C). 1986. pap. 34.00 (*3-528-07260-1*, Pub. by Vieweg & Sohn GW) Ballen Bkslr.
Prestera, Hector, jt. auth. see Kurtz, Ron.
Presthus, Robert V. Elites in the Policy Process. LC 73-94135. 539p. reprint ed. pap. 153.70 (*0-318-34838-1*, 2031713) Bks Demand.
Presti, Michael, jt. auth. see Whalen, Tom.
***Presti, Patricia.** Love Search. 320p. (Orig.). Date not set. pap. 9.95 (*0-7610-0364-9*) NW Pub.
Presti, Santo M. IRS in Action: Straight Talk from a Former Treasury Agent. (Illus.). 155p. 1983. pap. 9.95 (*0-914877-00-3*) Sherwood Comns.
Prestia, Kenneth L. Chocolates for the Pillows, Nightmares for the Guests: The Failure of the Hotel Industry to Protect the Traveling Public from Violent Crime. LC 93-5928. 1993. pap. 12.95 (*0-910155-25-9*) Bartleby Pr.
Prestia, Phyllis S. Slicing Eggplant. 32p. 1984. pap. 3.50 (*0-913719-72-2*) High-Coo Pr.
Prestiano, Robert. The Inland Architect: Chicago's Major Architectural Journal, 1883-1908. LC 85-1178. (Architecture & Urban Design Ser.: No. 9). (Illus.). 265p. reprint ed. pap. 75.60 (*0-8357-1680-5*, 2070518) Bks Demand.
Prestige, George L. St. Basil the Great & Apollinaris of Laodicea. LC 82-45832. (Orhtodoxies & Heresies in the Early Church Ser.). reprint ed. 17.50 (*0-404-62399-9*) AMS Pr.
Prestine, Joan. Family Day Care Activities A to Z. 1989. pap. 9.99 (*0-8224-3073-8*) Fearon Teach Aids.
Prestine, Joan S. Someone Special Died, Picturebook. (J). (ps-3). 1993. pap. 8.99 (*0-86653-929-8*) Fearon Teach Aids.
— Someone Special Died, Resource. (J). (ps-3). 1993. pap. 8.99 (*0-86653-928-X*) Fearon Teach Aids.
— Sometimes I Feel Awful, Picturebook. (J). (ps-3). 1993. pap. 8.99 (*0-86653-927-1*) Fearon Teach Aids.
— Sometimes I Feel Awful, Resource. (J). (ps-3). 1993. pap. 8.99 (*0-86653-926-3*) Fearon Teach Aids.
***Presto, Fay.** Making Magic. (Illus.). (J). 1995. write for info. (*0-8120-9182-5*) Barron.
Preston. Frommer's Delaware & Maryland. (Illus.). 1994. pap. 15.00 (*0-671-87117-X*, P-H Travel) P-H Gen Ref & Trav.
— Lady Beware. (Loveswept Ser.: No. 742). 1995. mass mkt. (*0-553-44512-X*, Loveswept) Bantam.
— Perspectives in Dental Ceramics. 1988. text ed. 156.00 (*0-86715-136-6*, 1366) Quint Pub Co.
— Spain, EEC & NATO. 1985. pap. 10.95 (*0-7100-9559-7*, RKP) Routledge.
Preston & Crawford. CAD-CAM Dictionary. 224p. 1985. 99.75 (*0-8247-7524-4*) Dekker.
Preston, jt. auth. see Lewin.
Preston, et al. Natural Resource Damages. 234p. 1993. pap. 75.00 (*0-86587-340-2*) Gov Insts.
Preston, A. J. & Pagan, A. R. The Theory of Economic Policy: Statics & Dynamics. LC 81-10196. 400p. 1982. 69.95 (*0-521-23366-6*) Cambridge U Pr.
Preston, Adrian, ed. In Relief of Gordon: Lord Wolseley's Campaign Journal of the Khartoum Relief Expedition, 1884-1885. LC 79-92562. 267p. 1975. 22.50 (*0-8386-7572-7*) Fairleigh Dickinson.
Preston, Anthony. Aircraft Carriers. LC 84-9669. (Modern Military Techniques Ser.). (Illus.). 48p. (J). (gr. 5 up). 1985. pap. 4.95 (*0-8225-9504-4*, Lerner Publctns) Lerner Group.
— Aircraft Carriers. LC 84-9669. (Modern Military Techniques Ser.). (Illus.). 48p. (YA). (gr. 5 up). 1985. lib. bdg. 14.95 (*0-8225-1377-3*, Lerner Publctns) Lerner Group.
Preston, Anthony, ed. Warship, Vol. I. LC 78-55455. (Illus.). 256p. 1978. 39.95 (*0-87021-975-8*) Naval Inst Pr.
Preston, Antony. The Destroyers. LC 77-82132. (Illus.). 1977. 14.95 (*0-685-03827-0*) P-H.
— Pictorial History of South Africa. (Illus.). 128p. 1995. 14.98 (*0-8317-7081-3*) Smithmark.
Preston, Antony, tr. see Jentschura, Hansgeorg, et al.
Preston, B. Bassett - Preston Ancestors: History of Ancestors in America of the Children of Edward M. & Annie Preston Bassett. 359p. 1991. reprint ed. 59.00 (*0-8328-1853-4*); reprint ed. pap. 49.00 (*0-8328-1854-2*) Higginson Bk Co.
***Preston, Brenda B.** Andrew Davidson Firebaugh & Susan Burgess Firebaugh: California Pioneers. LC 95-68049. (Illus.). 300p. 1995. 27.95 (*0-9645475-4-6*) Rio Del Mar Pr.
Preston, Brian J. Environmental Litigation. xxxix, 415p. 1989. 87.50 (*0-455-20898-0*, Pub. by Law Bk Co) W W Gaunt.
Preston, C. H. Preston: Descendants of Roger Preston. (Illus.). 355p. 1991. reprint ed. lib. bdg. 66.00 (*0-8328-2080-6*); reprint ed. pap. 56.00 (*0-8328-2081-4*) Higginson Bk Co.
Preston, Cathy L. A Concordance to the Child Ballads. 1000p. Date not set. 158.00 (*0-8240-8983-9*, H484) Garland.
— A KWIC Concordance to Thomas Hardy's Tess of the D'Urbervilles. LC 89-1507. 986p. 1989. 75.00 (*0-8240-9076-4*, 749) Garland.
***Preston, Cathy L., ed.** Folklore, Literature, & Cultural Theory. LC 95-13920. (New Perspectives in Folklore Ser.: Vol. 2). (Illus.). 280p. 1995. 42.00 (*0-8240-7271-5*, H1395) Garland.
***Preston, Charles.** Charles Preston's Giant Crossword Puzzle Treasury No. 11. 128p. (Orig.). 1994. pap. 8.95 (*0-399-52147-X*) Berkley Pub.
— Charles Preston's Giant Crossword Treasury, No. 10. 1993. pap. 8.95 (*0-399-52114-3*) Putnam Pub Group.
— Crossword for the Connoisseur, No. 49. 1993. pap. 6.95 (*0-399-52113-5*) Putnam Pub Group.
— Crossword Puzzles, No. 18. large type ed. 96p. 1994. pap. 6.95 (*0-399-52119-4*, Perigree Bks) Berkley Pub.
— Crossword Puzzles No. 19. large type ed. 96p. 1995. pap. 6.95 (*0-399-51912-2*, Perigree Bks) Berkley Pub.
— Crossword Puzzles No. 19, No. 13. 1989. pap. 6.95 (*0-399-52085-6*, Perigree Bks) Berkley Pub.
— Crossword Puzzles No. 19, No. 15. large type ed. 96p. 1991. pap. 6.95 (*0-399-52101-1*) Putnam Pub Group.
— Crossword Puzzles in Large Print, No. 17. large type ed. 1993. pap. 6.95 (*0-399-52112-7*) Putnam Pub Group.
— Crossword Puzzles in Large Type Omnibus No. 6. 176p. (Orig.). 1994. pap. 8.95 (*0-399-52143-7*, Perigree Bks) Berkley Pub.
— Crosswords for the Connoisseur, No. 43. 80p. 1990. pap. 6.95 (*0-399-52089-9*, Perigree Bks) Berkley Pub.
— Crosswords for the Connoisseur, No. 46. 80p. 1991. pap. 6.95 (*0-399-52102-X*, Perigree Bks) Berkley Pub.
— Crosswords for the Connoisseur, No. 50. LC 93-30008. 80p. 1994. pap. 6.95 (*0-399-52116-X*, Perigree Bks) Berkley Pub.
— Crosswords for the Connoisseur No. 51. 80p. (Orig.). 1994. pap. 6.95 (*0-399-52140-2*, Perigree Bks) Berkley Pub.
— Crosswords for the Connoisseur, No. 52, No. 52. 80p. (Orig.). 1995. pap. 6.95 (*0-399-51951-3*, Perigree Bks) Berkley Pub.
— Crosswords for the Connoisseur Omnibus, No. 6. 128p. 1994. pap. 8.95 (*0-399-52118-6*, Perigree Bks) Berkley Pub.
— Crosswords for the Connoisseur Omnibus No. 47. 128p. (Orig.). 1995. pap. 8.95 (*0-399-51945-9*, Perigree Bks) Berkley Pub.
— Dow Jones Crosswords for the Serious, Bk. 32. (Crosswords Ser.). 48p. 1985. pap. 5.00 (*0-87094-699-4*) Irwin Prof Pubng.
— U. S. A. Today Crossword Book, No. 3. 1987. pap. 6.95 (*0-399-52063-5*) Putnam Pub Group.
— The U. S. A. Today Crossword Puzzle Book No. 17. 80p. 1995. pap. 6.95 (*0-399-51907-6*, Perigree Bks) Berkley Pub.

An Asterisk (*) at the beginning of an entry indicates that the title is appearing in BIP for the first time.

— The U. S. A. Today Crossword Puzzle Book No. 17, No. 5. 80p. 1988. pap. 6.95 (*0-399-52075-9*, Perigree Bks) Berkley Pub.
— The U. S. A. Today Crossword Puzzle Book No. 17, No. 10. 80p. 1991. pap. 6.95 (*0-399-52100-3*) Berkley Pub.
— The U. S. A. Today Crossword Puzzle Book No. 17, No. 15. 80p. 1994. pap. 6.95 (*0-399-52117-8*) Berkley Pub.
— The U. S. A. Today Crossword Puzzle Book No. 17, No. 16. 80p. 1994. pap. 6.95 (*0-399-52133-X*, Perigree Bks) Berkley Pub.
— USA Crosswords, No. 18. 80p. (Orig.). 1995. pap. 6.95 (*0-399-51963-7*, Perigree Bks) Berkley Pub.
— USA Today Crossword Puzzle Book, No. 14. 1993. pap. 6.95 (*0-399-52115-1*) Putnam Pub Group.
Preston, Charles, ed. Crossword Puzzles No. 19. large type ed. (Perigee Crossword Puzzles Ser.: No. 16). 96p. 1992. pap. 6.95 (*0-399-52108-9*) Putnam Pub Group.
— Crossword Puzzles No. 19, No. 14. large type ed. (Perigee Crossword Puzzles Ser.). 96p. 1990. pap. 6.95 (*0-399-52094-5*) Putnam Pub Group.
— Crossword Puzzles in Large Type Omnibus. (Perigee Crossword Puzzle Ser.: No. 5). 176p. 1993. pap. 8.95 (*0-399-52109-7*, Perigree Bks) Berkley Pub.
— Crossword Puzzles in Large Type Omnibus, No. 4. large type ed. (Perigee Crossword Puzzle Ser.). 176p. 1991. pap. 8.95 (*0-399-52099-6*) Putnam Pub Group.
— Crosswords for the Connoisseur. (Perigee Crossword Puzzles Ser.: No. 47). 80p. 1992. pap. 6.95 (*0-399-52107-0*, Perigree Bks) Berkley Pub.
— Crosswords for the Connoisseur. (Perigee Crossword Puzzles Ser.: No. 48). 80p. 1993. pap. 6.95 (*0-399-52110-0*, Perigree Bks) Berkley Pub.
— Crosswords for the Connoisseur, No. 36. 96p. 1986. pap. 4.95 (*0-399-52052-X*, Perigree Bks) Berkley Pub.
— Crosswords for the Connoisseur, No. 44. (Perigee Crossword Puzzles Ser.). 80p. 1990. pap. 6.95 (*0-399-52093-7*, Perigree Bks) Berkley Pub.
— Crosswords for the Connoisseur Omnibus. (Perigree Crossword Puzzles Ser.: No. 5). 128p. 1992. pap. 8.95 (*0-399-52104-6*, Perigree Bks) Berkley Pub.
— Crosswords from the National Observe. (Perigee Crossword Puzzles Ser.: No. 13). 64p. (Orig.). 1992. pap. 7.95 (*0-399-52105-4*, Perigree Bks) Berkley Pub.
— U. S. A. Today Crossword Puzzle Book. (Perigee Crossword Puzzles Ser.: No. 13). 80p. (Orig.). 1993. pap. 6.95 (*0-399-52111-9*, Perigree Bks) Berkley Pub.
— The U. S. A. Today Crossword Puzzle Book No. 17. 80p. 1986. pap. 6.95 (*0-399-52053-8*, Perigree Bks) Berkley Pub.
— The U. S. A. Today Crossword Puzzle Book No. 17. (Perigee Crossword Puzzles Ser.: No. 11). 80p. 1992. pap. 6.95 (*0-399-52103-8*, Perigree Bks) Berkley Pub.
— The U. S. A. Today Crossword Puzzle Book No. 17. (Perigee Crossword Puzzles Ser.: No. 12). 80p. 1992. pap. 6.95 (*0-399-52106-2*, Perigree Bks) Berkley Pub.
— The U. S. A. Today Crossword Puzzle Book No. 17, No. 7. 80p. 1989. pap. 6.95 (*0-399-52083-X*, Perigree Bks) Berkley Pub.
— The U. S. A. Today Crossword Puzzle Book No. 17, No. 9. (Perigee Crossword Puzzles Ser.). 80p. 1990. pap. 6.95 (*0-399-52092-9*, Perigree Bks) Berkley Pub.
***Preston, Charles & Kipfer, Barbara A.** The U. S. A. Today Crossword Puzzle Dictionary: The Newest, Most Comprehensive & Authoritative Crossword Reference Book. 768p. 1995. pap. 12.95 (*0-7868-8060-0*) Hyperion.
Preston, Charles F., jt. ed. see Shoenberg, Mark B.
Preston, Charlotte, jt. auth. see Winterowd, W. Ross.
Preston, Cheryl, jt. auth. see Preston, Robert.
***Preston, Claire, ed.** Sir Thomas Browne: Selected Poems. 192p. 1995. pap. 18.95 (*1-85754-052-2*) Paul & Co Pubs.
Preston, Daniel. The Era of A. J. Tomlinson. 206p. (Orig.). 1984. pap. 6.95 (*0-934942-41-2*, 1925) White Wing Pub.
— Twentieth Century United States History. LC 91-55400. (College Outline Ser.). 224p. (Orig.). 1992. pap. 13.00 (*0-06-467132-1*, Harper Ref) HarpC.
Preston, Daniel, jt. ed. see Harris, C. M.
Preston, Daryl W. Experiments in Physics: A Labratory Manual for Scientists & Engineers. 312p. (C). 1985. Net. pap. text ed. write for info. (*0-471-80571-8*) Wiley.
Preston, David A., ed. Environment, Society & Rural Change in Latin America: The Past, Present & Future in the Countryside. LC 79-41481. 256p. 1980. text ed. 124. 90 (*0-471-27713-4*, Wiley-Interscience) Wiley.
— Environment, Society, & Rural Change in Latin America: The Past, Present, & Future in the Countryside. LC 79-41481. (Illus.). 278p. reprint ed. pap. 79.30 (*0-685-20603-3*, 2030537) Bks Demand.
— Latin American Development: Geographical Perspectives. 1987. pap. text ed. 46.95 (*0-470-20783-3*) Halsted Pr.
Preston, David A., jt. auth. see Odell, Peter R.
Preston, David G., tr. see Blocher, Henri.
Preston, David L. Exploring Sociology: A Reading & Writing Workbook. (C). 1990. pap. text ed. 3.95 (*0-942587-03-0*) Papyrus Bks.
— The Social Organization of Zen Practice: Constructing Transcultural Reality. (Illus.). 240p. 1988. 64.95 (*0-521-35000-X*) Cambridge U Pr.
Preston, Deborah, ed. see Drill, Alma.
Preston, Dennis R. Bituminous Coal Mining Vocabulary of the Eastern United States. (Publications of the American Dialect Society: No. 59). (Illus.). 128p. (Orig.). 1973. pap. 8.50 (*0-8173-0659-5*) U of Ala Pr.
— Perceptual Dialectology: Nonlinguists' Views of Areal Linguistics. (Topics in Sociolinguistics Ser.: No. 7). xvi, 141p. 1989. 67.70 (*90-6765-392-6*); pap. 44.65 (*90-6765-393-4*) Mouton.
— Sociolinguistics & Second Language Acquisition. (Illus.). 320p. 1989. pap. text ed. 21.95 (*0-631-15247-4*) Blackwell Pubs.
Preston, Dennis R., ed. American Dialect Research: Celebrating the 100th Anniversary of the American Dialect Society, 1888-1989. LC 93-18385. xv, 460p. 1993. 89.00 (*1-55619-488-9*); pap. 29.95 (*1-55619-489-7*) Benjamins North Am.
***Preston, Dickson J.** Newspapers of Maryland's Eastern Shore. LC 85-40533. (Illus.). reprint ed. pap. 82.70 (*0-7837-9082-1*, 2049832) Bks Demand.
— Talbot County: A History. Harrington, Norman, ed. LC 83-40048. (Illus.). reprint ed. pap. 112.90 (*0-7837-9091-0*, 2049841) Bks Demand.
— Young Frederick Douglass: The Maryland Years. LC 80-7992. (Maryland Paperback Bookshelf Ser.). 264p. (C). 1985. reprint ed. pap. 9.95 (*0-8018-2739-6*) Johns Hopkins.
Preston, Dietz. The Art of Experimental Physics. 432p. 1991. Net. pap. text ed. write for info. (*0-471-84748-8*) Wiley.
Preston, Doris, jt. auth. see Lipsey, Robert E.
Preston, Doris C. Needle-Made Laces & Net Embroideries: Reticella Work, Carrickmacross Lace, Princess Lace & Other Traditional Techniques. 160p. 1984. reprint ed. pap. 3.95 (*0-486-24708-2*) Dover.
Preston, Douglas. Cities of Gold: A Journey Across the American Southwest in Pursuit of Coronado. LC 92-10081. 1992. 25.00 (*0-671-73759-7*) S&S Trade.
— Jennie. 336p. 1994. 21.95 (*0-312-11294-7*) St Martin.
— Red & the Colonel. 1993. pap. 14.00 (*0-671-86990-6*, Touchstone Bks) S&S Trade.
— Talking to the Ground: Bone Family's Journey on Horseback Across the Sacred Land of the Navajo. LC 94-46362. 288p. 1995. 24.00 (*0-684-80391-7*) S&S Trade.
Preston, Douglas & Child, Lincoln. Relic. 384p. 1995. 22.95 (*0-312-85630-X*) Forge NYC.
— Relic. 384p. 1996. mass mkt. write for info. (*0-614-05542-3*) Tor Bks.
Preston, Douglas J. Dinosaurs in the Attic: An Excursion into the American Museum of Natural History. (Illus.). 256p. 1993. pap. 13.95 (*0-312-10456-1*) St Martin.
Preston-Dunlop, Valerie. Modern Educational Dance. LC 90-36091. (Illus.). 238p. (C). 1990. pap. text ed. 12.95 (*0-8238-0292-2*) Plays.
Preston-Dunlop, Valerie & Lahusen, Suzanne, eds. Schrifttanz: A View of German Dance in the Weimar Republic. (Illus.). 136p. 1990. pap. text ed. 24.95 (*1-85273-016-1*, Dance Horizons) Princeton Bk Co.
Preston, E., ed. How to Buy Land Cheap. 1986. lib. bdg. 79. 95 (*0-8490-3657-7*) Gordon Pr.
Preston, E. M., jt. ed. see Lauenroth, W. K.
Preston, Edna M. Squawk to the Moon, Little Goose. LC 84-22296. (Illus.). 32p. (J). (ps-1). 1985. pap. 3.95 (*0-14-050546-6*, Puffin) Puffin Bks.
Preston, Edna M. & Bennett, Rainey. The Temper Tantrum Book. (Picture Puffins Ser.). (Illus.). (J). (ps-3). 1976. pap. 4.99 (*0-14-050181-9*, Puffin) Puffin Bks.
Preston, Edward. How to Buy Land Cheap. 4th rev. ed. (Illus.). 152p. 1991. reprint ed. pap. 14.95 (*1-55950-064-6*, 17054) Loompanics.
Preston, Effa E. Popular Commencement Book. 1995. reprint ed. 45.00 (*1-55888-209-X*) Omnigraphics Inc.
Preston, Elaine. Look for a Field to Land: Poems. LC 94-7129. 74p. (Orig.). 1994. pap. 8.95 (*1-882593-06-5*) Bridge Wrks.
Preston, Elizabeth. Preparing your Manuscript. rev. ed. LC 93-43417. 114p. 1994. pap. 12.00 (*0-87116-172-9*) Writer.
Preston, Elizabeth, ed. The Double Eagle Guide to Western Public Campgrounds: Far West. (Double Eagle Guides Ser.: Vol. III). (Illus.). 336p. (Orig.). 1988. pap. 8.95 (*0-929760-03-4*) Discovery MT.
— The Double Eagle Guide to Western Public Campgrounds: Pacific Northwest. (Double Eagle Guides Ser.: Vol. I). (Illus.). 336p. (Orig.). 1988. pap. 8.95 (*0-929760-01-8*) Discovery MT.
— The Double Eagle Guide to Western Public Campgrounds: Rocky Mountains. (Double Eagle Guides Ser.: Vol. II). (Illus.). 304p. (Orig.). 1988. pap. 8.95 (*0-929760-02-6*) Discovery MT.
— The Double Eagle Guide to Western Public Campgrounds: Southwest. (Double Eagle Guides Ser.: Vol. IV). (Illus.). 304p. (Orig.). 1988. pap. 8.95 (*0-929760-04-2*) Discovery MT.
Preston, Elizabeth, ed. see Blavatsky, Helena P.
Preston, Elizabeth, jt. auth. see Preston, Thomas.
Preston, Elizabeth, jt. intro. see Preston, Thomas.
Preston, Fayrene. A Baby for Daisy. (Loveswept Ser.: No. 701). 1994. pap. 3.50 (*0-553-44416-6*, Loveswept) Bantam.
— Just in Time. 1994. mass mkt. 4.99 (*0-553-56928-7*) Bantam.
— One Enchanted Autumn. (Loveswept Ser.: No. 710). 1994. pap. 3.50 (*0-553-44417-4*, Loveswept) Bantam.
— Satin & Steele. 1993. mass mkt. 4.50 (*0-553-56457-9*) Bantam.
— The Shamrock Trinity: Burke, the Kingpin. large type ed. LC 92-27538. (Nightingale Ser.). 240p. (Orig.). 1993. pap. 14.95 (*0-8161-5629-8*, Nightingale) Hall.
— What Emily Wants. (Loveswept Ser.: No. 620). 1993. pap. 3.50 (*0-553-44173-6*, Loveswept) Bantam.
— The Witching Time. large type ed. (Nightingale Ser.). 230p. 1991. pap. 14.95 (*0-8161-5265-9*) G K Hall.
Preston-Foster, Mary. Fun With Fiction. (J). (gr. 2-5). 1988. pap. 9.99 (*0-8224-3173-4*) Fearon Teach Aids.
Preston Foster, Mary. Looking It Up. (J). (gr. 2-5). 1988. pap. 8.99 (*0-8224-4345-7*) Fearon Teach Aids.
Preston, Frederick W. & Beal, John M. Basic Surgical Physiology. LC 69-13375. (Illus.). 508p. reprint ed. pap. 144.80 (*0-8357-9598-5*, 2013103) Bks Demand.
Preston, Frederick W. & Smith, Ronald W. Sociology: A Contemporary Approach. 668p. (Orig.). (C). 1988. student ed 18.00 (*0-685-18769-1*, H13857) Allyn.
— Sociology: A Contemporary Approach. rev. ed. 668p. (Orig.). (C). 1988. write for info. (*0-318-62209-2*, H13865); write for info. (*0-318-62210-6*, H17007) Allyn.
Preston, Fredrica. Memory Bank for Chemotherapy. 256p. 1987. spiral bd. 19.95 (*0-683-06972-1*) Jones & Bartlett.
Preston, Fredrica A. & Wilfinger, Cecila. Chemotherapy Memory Bank. 2nd ed. (Nursing-Health Science Ser.). 234p. (C). 1992. pap. text ed., spiral bd. 29.95 (*0-86720-629-2*) Jones & Bartlett.
Preston, G. B., jt. auth. see Clifford, A. H.
Preston, George N. African Art Masterpieces. (Illus.). 120p. 1991. 35.00 (*0-88363-801-0*) H L Levin.
***Preston, Georgette.** Songs of Cities. 30p. (Orig.). (C). 1992. pap. text ed. 5.00 (*1-878173-27-8*) Birnham Wood.
Preston-Gomez, Cheryl & Reisfeld, Randi. When No Means No: A Guide to Sexual Harassment by a Woman Who Won a Million Dollar Verdict. 224p. 1992. 17.95 (*1-55972-143-X*, Birch Ln Pr) Carol Pub Group.
Preston, H. B. Mollusca: Vol. 4: Freshwater Gastropoda & Pelycypoda. (Fauna of British India Ser.). xx, 246p. 1978. reprint ed. 30.00 (*0-88065-177-6*, Messers Today & Tomorrow) Scholarly Pubns.
Preston, Hap. Three Seas: A Christopher Columbus Counting Book. LC 92-80784. (Illus.). 44p. (J). (ps-3). 1992. pap. 5.95 (*1-55523-529-8*) Winston-Derek.
Preston, Harriet W., tr. see Sainte-Beuve, Charles A.
Preston, Howard H. History of Banking in Iowa. Bruchey, Stuart, ed. LC 80-1167. (Rise of Commercial Banking Ser.). (Illus.). 1981. reprint ed. lib. bdg. 42.95 (*0-405-13677-3*) Ayer.
Preston, Howard L. Dirt Roads to Dixie: Accessibility & Modernization in the South. LC 90-37726. (Illus.). 220p. 1991. text ed. 38.50 (*0-87049-676-X*); pap. 18.95 (*0-87049-677-8*) U of Tenn Pr.
Preston, Howard L., jt. ed. see Dunn, Joe P.
Preston, Irene F. & Seltman, Arthur J. Coinage of the Crusader States, 1098-1291. (Illus.). 1994. write for info. (*0-915018-39-X*) Attic Bks.
Preston, Ivan L. The Great American Blow-Up: Puffery in Advertising & Selling. LC 74-27313. 384p. 1975. 32.50 (*0-299-06730-0*) U of Wis Pr.
— Great American Blow-Up: Puffery in Advertising & Selling. LC 74-27313. 384p. 1977. pap. 14.95 (*0-299-06734-3*) U of Wis Pr.
— The Tangled Web They Weave: Truth, Falsity, & Advertisers. LC 93-39166. 236p. 1994. 22.50 (*0-299-14190-X*) U of Wis Pr.
Preston, Ivy. The Blue Remembered Hills. large type ed. (Linford Romance Library). 304p. 1988. pap. 10.95 (*0-7089-6594-6*, Linford) Ulverscroft.
— A Fleeting Breath. large type ed. (Romance Ser.). 1991. 21.95 (*0-7089-2556-1*) Ulverscroft.
— Interlude in Greece. large type ed. (Linford Romance Library). 256p. 1994. pap. 14.95 (*0-7089-7516-X*, Linford) Ulverscroft.
— Interrupted Journey. large type ed. (Linford Romance Library). 1989. pap. 11.95 (*0-7089-6790-6*, Trailtree Bookshop) Ulverscroft.
— Love in Las Vegas. (Rainbow Romances Ser.). 160p. 1993. 14.95 (*0-7090-4830-0*, Hale-Parkwest) Parkwest Pubns.
— Love in Las Vegas. large type ed. (Romance Ser.). 1994. pap. 14.95 (*0-7089-7622-0*, Linford) Ulverscroft.
— Moonlight on the Lake. large type ed. (Linford Romance Library). 1990. pap. 12.95 (*0-7089-6886-4*, Linford) Ulverscroft.
— Mountain Magic. large type ed. (Romance Ser.). 288p. 1992. 21.95 (*0-7089-2683-5*) Ulverscroft.
— Nicolette. large type ed. (Linford Romance Library). 304p. 1988. pap. 11.95 (*0-7089-6542-3*, Linford) Ulverscroft.
— None So Blind. large type ed. (Linford Romance Library). 336p. 1989. pap. 11.95 (*0-7089-6706-X*, Linford) Ulverscroft.
— Pacific Magic. large type ed. (Romance Ser.). 320p. 1987. 16.95 (*0-7089-1690-2*) Ulverscroft.
— Petals in the Wind. large type ed. (Linford Romance Library). 320p. 1992. pap. 14.95 (*0-7089-7207-1*, Linford) Ulverscroft.
— Portrait of Pierre. large type ed. (Linford Romance Library). 320p. 1992. pap. 14.95 (*0-7089-7136-9*, Linford) Ulverscroft.
— Release the Past. large type ed. (Romance Ser.). 1989. 17. 95 (*0-7089-2078-0*) Ulverscroft.
— Romance in Glenmore Street. large type ed. (Romance Ser.). 1991. 21.95 (*0-7089-2467-0*) Ulverscroft.
— Rosemary for Remembrance. large type ed. (Romance Ser.). 304p. 1985. 15.95 (*0-7089-1368-7*) Ulverscroft.
— The Secret Love of Nurse Wilson. large type ed. (Linford Romance Library). 1988. pap. 10.95 (*0-7089-6480-X*, Linford) Ulverscroft.
— Stranger from the Sea. large type ed. (Linford Romance Library). 240p. 1992. pap. 14.95 (*0-7089-7294-2*, Trailtree Bookshop) Ulverscroft.
— Summer at Willowbank. large type ed. (Romance Ser.). 1994. pap. 14.95 (*0-7089-7611-5*, Linford) Ulverscroft.
— Sunlit Seas. large type ed. (Linford Romance Library). 304p. 1994. pap. 14.95 (*0-7089-7535-6*, Linford) Ulverscroft.
— Tamarisk in Bloom. large type ed. (Linford Romance Library). 336p. 1989. pap. 11.95 (*0-7089-6666-7*, Linford) Ulverscroft.
— Voyage of Destiny. large type ed. (Linford Romance Library). 1990. pap. 12.95 (*0-7089-6827-9*, Trailtree Bookshop) Ulverscroft.
— Where Ratas Twine. large type ed. (Linford Romance Library). 336p. 1993. pap. 14.95 (*0-7089-7326-4*, Linford) Ulverscroft.
— Where Stars May Lead. large type ed. (Romance Library). 304p. 1995. pap. 14.95 (*0-7089-7668-9*, Linford) Ulverscroft.
Preston, Izola. Arkansas Black Heritage: A Tour of Historical Sites. LC 93-77484. (Illus.). 71p. (Orig.). 1993. pap. 15.00 (*0-938041-13-4*) Arc Pr AR.
Preston, Izola, jt. auth. see Morgan, Gordon D.
Preston, Izola, jt. auth. see Morgan, Marian.
Preston, J., jt. ed. see Black, W. Bruce.
Preston, J., jt. auth. see Lewin, M.
Preston, J. B., ed. see Battle, James.
Preston, Jack D., ed. Computer in Clinical Dentistry: Proceedings of the First International Conference, Houston, Texas, September 26-29, 1991. LC 92-49188. 1993. pap. text ed. 48.00 (*0-86715-229-X*) Quint Pub Co.
Preston, Jacqueline N., ed. see Bellucci, Elio C.
Preston, James. Bushfire. 1993. 17.00 (*0-86025-258-2*, Pub. by Ian Henry Pubns UK) Empire Pub Srvs.
Preston, James, jt. ed. see Misra, Bhabagrahi.
Preston, James F. Air Conditioning & Refrigeration Technician's EPA Certification Guide: Getting Certified, Understanding the Rules, & Preparation for EPA Inspections. Damp, Dennis V., ed. (Illus.). 192p. (Orig.). 1994. pap. 29.95 (*0-943641-10-1*) Bookhaven Pr.
Preston, James J. Cult of the Goddess: Social & Religious Change in a Hindu Temple. (Illus.). 109p. (C). 1985. reprint ed. pap. text ed. 8.50 (*0-88133-135-X*) Waveland Pr.
Preston, James J., ed. Mother Worship: Theme & Variations. LC 81-3336. (Studies in Religion). xxiv, 360p. 1983. pap. 17.95 (*0-8078-4114-5*) U of NC Pr.
Preston, Jean F. & Stoneman, William P., eds. A Summary Guide to Western Medieval & Renaissance Manuscripts at Princeton University. 75p. 1991. 7.00 (*0-87811-034-8*) Princeton Lib.
Preston, Jean F. & Yeandle, Laetitia. English Handwriting, 1400-1650: An Introductory Manual. (Pegasus Paperbooks Ser.). 116p. 1991. pap. 12.00 (*0-86698-086-5*, P6) MRTS.
Preston, Jean F., jt. auth. see Krochalis, Jeanne E.
Preston, Jill. Cases in European Business. 256p. (Orig.). 1992. pap. 47.50 (*0-273-03740-4*, Pub. by Pitman Pub Ltd UK) Trans-Atl Phila.
— International Business: Text & Cases. 352p. (Orig.). 1993. pap. 47.50 (*0-273-60148-2*, Pub. by Pitman Pub Ltd UK) Trans-Atl Phila.
***Preston, Jill, ed.** Regional Policy. (Spicers European Union Policy Briefings Ser.). 228p. 1994. 150.00 (*1-56159-083-5*, Stockton Pr) Groves Dictionaries.
Preston, John. The Arena. (Orig.). 1993. pap. 4.95 (*1-56333-083-0*) Masquerade.
— The Big Gay Book: A Man's Survival Guide for the Nineties. (Illus.). 416p. (Orig.). 1991. pap. 14.95 (*0-452-26621-1*, Plume) NAL-Dutton.
— Breastplate of Faith & Love. 241p. 1979. reprint ed. 35.95 (*0-85151-289-5*) Banner of Truth.
— Deadly Lies. (Mission of Alex Kane Ser.: No. 3). 1993. reprint ed. pap. 4.95 (*1-56333-076-8*) Masquerade.
— Entertainment for a Master. 160p. (Orig.). 1986. pap. 7.95 (*0-932870-94-5*) Alyson Pubns.
— Fanny the Queen of Provincetown. 1995. 15.95 (*0-312-11792-2*) St Martin.
— The Golden Sceptre. 220p. 1990. reprint ed. 14.95 (*1-877611-17-4*) Soli Deo Gloria.
— Golden Years. (Mission of Alex Kane Ser.: No. 2). (Orig.). 1992. reprint ed. pap. 4.95 (*1-56333-069-5*) Masquerade.
— Growing Beyond Emotional Pain: Action Plans for Healing. LC 93-3212. 288p. 1993. pap. 12.95 (*0-915166-78-X*) Impact Pubs CA.
— The Heir - the King. (Orig.). 1992. pap. 4.95 (*1-56333-048-2*) Masquerade.
— Hustling: A Gentleman's Guide to the Fine Art of Homosexual Prostitution. (Orig.). 1994. pap. 12.95 (*1-56333-137-3*) Masquerade.
— I Once Had a Master: & Other Tales of Erotic Love. 120p. (Orig.). 1984. pap. 8.95 (*0-932870-51-1*) Alyson Pubns.
— In Search of a Master. 1989. pap. 7.95 (*0-8216-2005-3*, Univ Books) Carol Pub Group.
— Lethal Silence. rev. ed. (Mission of Alex Kane Ser.). (Orig.). 1993. pap. text ed. 4.95 (*1-56333-125-X*) Masquerade.
— Love of a Master. 155p. (Orig.). 1987. pap. 7.95 (*0-932870-95-3*) Alyson Pubns.
— Mr. Benson. 1992. reprint ed. pap. 4.95 (*1-56333-041-5*) Masquerade.
— My Life As a Pornographer & Other Indecent Acts. (Orig.). 1993. pap. 12.95 (*1-56333-135-7*) Masquerade.
— The Saints Daily Exercise. LC 76-57409. (English Experience Ser.: No. 824). 1977. reprint ed. lib. bdg. 53. 00 (*90-221-0824-4*) Walter J Johnson.
— Secret Danger. rev. ed. (Mission of Alex Kane Ser.). (Orig.). 1993. pap. text ed. 4.95 (*1-56333-111-X*) Masquerade.
— Stolen Moments. (Mission of Alex Kane Ser.). (Orig.). 1993. reprint ed. pap. text ed. 4.95 (*1-56333-098-9*) Masquerade.
— Sweet Dreams. rev. ed. (Mission of Alex Kane Ser.). 1992. reprint ed. pap. 4.95 (*1-56333-062-8*) Masquerade.
— Tales from the Dark Lord. (Orig.). 1992. pap. 4.95 (*1-56333-053-9*) Masquerade.
— Tales from the Dark Lord. 2nd ed. (Orig.). 1995. pap. text ed. 5.95 (*1-56333-323-6*) Masquerade.
— Tales from the Dark Lord II. (Orig.). 1994. pap. text ed. 4.95 (*1-56333-176-4*) Masquerade.
— Winter's Light: Reflections of a Yankee Queer. Lowenthal, Michael, ed. & intro. by. LC 94-48734. 1995. write for info. (*0-87451-674-9*) U Pr of New Eng.

PQ

— You Can Beat Depression: A Guide to Recovery. LC 89-7543. 160p. (Orig.). 1989. pap. 9.95 (*0-915166-64-X*) Impact Pubs CA.

Preston, John, ed. Flesh & the Word: An Anthology of Erotic Writing. 320p. 1994. pap. 13.95 (*0-452-26775-7*, Plume) NAL-Dutton.

***Preston, John, ed. & intro.** Friends & Lovers: Gay Men Write about the Families They Create. 320p. 1995. 22.95 (*0-525-93858-3*, Dutton) NAL-Dutton.

Preston, John, ed. Hometowns: Gay Men Write about Where They Belong. 336p. 1991. 21.95 (*0-525-93353-0*, Dutton) NAL-Dutton.

— Hot Living: Erotic Stories about Safer Sex. 200p. (Orig.). 1985. pap. 8.95 (*0-932870-85-6*) Alyson Pubns.

— A Member of the Family: Gay Men Write about Their Closest Relations. LC 92-52867. 384p. 1992. 22.00 (*0-525-93549-5*, Dutton) NAL-Dutton.

— Personal Dispatches: Writers Confront AIDS. 208p. 1990. pap. 8.95 (*0-312-05141-7*) St Martin.

Preston, John, intro. The Flesh & the Word 2. 336p. (Orig.). 1993. pap. 13.00 (*0-452-27087-1*, Plume) NAL-Dutton.

— Hometowns: Gay Men Write about Where They Belong. LC 92-53554. 384p. 1992. pap. 12.00 (*0-452-26855-9*, Plume) NAL-Dutton.

— A Member of the Family: Gay Men Write about Their Families. LC 93-30305. 352p. 1994. pap. 10.95 (*0-452-27032-4*, Plume) NAL-Dutton.

Preston, John & Ferrett, Robert. Database Management Using Micrsoft Access. 128p. 1994. pap. write for info. (*0-697-22283-7*) Bus & Educ Tech.

— Word 6.0 for Windows with Style Manual References. 160p. (C). 1995. spiral bd. write for info. (*0-697-26016-X*) Bus & Educ Tech.

***Preston, John & Johnson, James.** Clinical Psychopharmacology Made Ridiculously Simple. 2nd ed. (Illus.). 62p. 1995. pap. text ed. 10.95 (*0-940780-23-2*) MedMaster.

***Preston, John & Lowenthal, Michael, eds.** Flesh & the Word 3: An Anthology of Gay Erotic Writing. LC 94-42651. 1995. 13.95 (*0-452-27252-1*, Plume) NAL-Dutton.

Preston, John, jt. auth. see Nestle, Joan.

***Preston, John, et al.** Every Session Counts: Making the Most of Your Brief Therapy. 96p. (Orig.). 1995. pap. 9.95 (*0-915166-88-7*) Impact Pubs CA.

— The Puritans on Prayer. Kistler, Don, ed. (Puritans on... Ser.). 300p. 1995. 24.95 (*1-877611-77-8*) Soli Deo Gloria.

— Understanding Psychiatric Medications in the Treatment of Chemical Dependency & Dual Diagnoses. (Illus.). 134p. (C). 1995. text ed. 37.95x (*0-398-05963-2*); pap. text ed. 22.95x (*0-398-05964-0*) C C Thomas.

Preston, John H. The Liberals. LC 74-22803. (Labor Movement in Fiction & Non-Fiction Ser.). reprint ed. 45.00 (*0-404-58460-8*) AMS Pr.

Preston, Joseph H. Arundel: A History of the Town & the Castle. LC 91-51134. (Illus.). 296p. 1993. 48.50 (*0-945636-39-3*) Susquehanna.

Preston, Judy J. The Outer Banks Story. (Illus.). 117p. (Orig.). (J). (gr. 5 up). 1985. pap. 3.49 (*0-9613824-0-6*) Seabright.

Preston, K. Blake & Rossetti. LC 73-117999. (Studies in Comparative Literature: No. 35). 1970. reprint ed. lib. bdg. 59.95 (*0-8383-1054-0*) M S G Haskell Hse.

Preston, Karl, jt. auth. see Hullana, Lisa.

Preston, Katherine. Scott Joplin. (Orig.). 1990. pap. 3.95 (*0-87067-557-5*, Melrose Sq) Holloway.

Preston, Katherine K. Music for Hire: A Study of Professional Musicians in Washington, 1877-1900. LC 85-28399. (Sociology of Music Ser.: No. 6). (Illus.). 280p. 1992. lib. bdg. 47.00 (*0-918728-66-5*) Pendragon NY.

— Opera on the Road: Traveling Opera Troupes in the United States, 1825-60. LC 92-20644. (Music in American Life Ser.). (Illus.). 496p. (C). 1993. 39.95 (*0-252-01974-1*) U of Ill Pr.

***Preston, Katherine K., ed.** Irish American Theater: The Mulligan Guard Ball (1879) & Reilly & the Four Hundred (1891), Scripts by Edward Harrigan, Music by David Braham. fac. ed. LC 94-584. (Nineteenth-Century American Musical Theater Ser.: No. 10). (Illus.). 452p. 1994. 111.00 (*0-8153-1376-4*) Garland.

Preston, Ken R., jt. ed. see Rasper, Vladimir F.

Preston, Kendall, Jr. & Duff, Michael J. Modern Cellular Automata: Theory & Applications. LC 84-11672. (Advanced Applications in Pattern Recognition Ser.). 368p. 1984. 89.50 (*0-306-41737-5*, Plenum Pr) Plenum.

Preston, Kendall, Jr. & Uhr, Leonard, eds. Multicomputers & Image Processing: Algorithms & Programs; Based on a Symposium held in Madison, Wisc., May 26-29, 1981. LC 82-1623. (Notes & Reports in Computer Science & Applied Mathematics Ser.). 1982. text ed. 97.00 (*0-12-564480-9*) Acad Pr.

Preston, Kitty. Scott Joplin. (Black Americans of Achievement Ser.). (Illus.). 112p. (Orig.). (YA). (gr. 5 up). 1988. 17.95 (*1-55546-598-6*); pap. 9.95 (*0-7910-0205-5*) Chelsea Hse.

Preston, Larry M. Freedom & the Organizational Republic. LC 92-14093. (Studies on North America: No. 6). xi, 235p. (C). 1992. lib. bdg. 105.75 (*3-11-013418-7*, 101-92) De Gruyter.

Preston, Laurence W. The Devs of Cincvad: A Lineage & State in Maharashtra. 300p. 1989. 64.95 (*0-521-34633-9*) Cambridge U Pr.

Preston, Lee E., ed. Research in Corporate Social Performance & Policy, Vol. 1. 291p. 1978. 73.25 (*0-89232-069-9*) Jai Pr.

— Research in Corporate Social Performance & Policy, Vol. 2. 1980. lib. bdg. 73.25 (*0-89232-133-4*) Jai Pr.

— Research in Corporate Social Performance & Policy, Vol. 3. 325p. 1981. 73.25 (*0-89232-184-9*) Jai Pr.

— Research in Corporate Social Performance & Policy, Vol. 5. 256p. 1983. 73.25 (*0-89232-412-0*) Jai Pr.

— Research in Corporate Social Performance & Policy, Vol. 7. 1985. 73.25 (*0-89232-585-2*) Jai Pr.

Preston, Lee E. & Frederick, William C., eds. Research in Corporate Social Performance & Policy, Vol. 9. 1987. 73.25 (*0-89232-742-1*) Jai Pr.

Preston-Mafham, Ken. Cacti & Succulents in Habitat. (Illus.). 160p. 1994. 24.95 (*0-304-34294-7*, Pub. by Cassell UK) Sterling.

— Cacti & Succulents in Habitat. (Illus.). 160p. 1995. pap. 19.95 (*0-304-34551-2*, Pub. by Cassell UK) Sterling.

— Grasshoppers & Mantids of the World. (Illus.). 192p. 1991. 25.95 (*0-8160-2298-4*) Facts on File.

— Madagascar: A Natural History. (Illus.). 224p. 1991. 45.00 (*0-8160-2403-0*) Facts on File.

Preston-Mafham, Ken, jt. auth. see Preston-Mafham, Rod.

Preston-Mafham, Rod & Preston-Mafham, Ken. Butterflies of the World. (Of the World Ser.). (Illus.). 192p. 1988. 25.95 (*0-8160-1601-1*) Facts on File.

— Cacti: The Illustrated Dictionary. (Illus.). 224p. 1995. pap. 19.95 (*0-304-34616-0*, Pub. by Cassell UK) Sterling.

— The Encyclopedia of Land Invertebrate Behavior. (Illus.). 300p. 1993. 47.50x (*0-262-16137-0*) MIT Pr.

— Primates of the World. (Of the World Ser.). (Illus.). 192p. 1992. lib. bdg. 25.95 (*0-8160-2745-5*) Facts on File.

— Spiders of the World. 192p. 1984. 25.95 (*0-87196-996-3*) Facts on File.

Preston, Margaret J. Aunt Dorothy: An Old Virginia Plantation Story. LC 72-1508. (Black Heritage Library Collection). (Illus.). 1977. reprint ed. 15.95 (*0-8369-9050-1*) Ayer.

Preston, Marianne & Morton, Jane. Fresh Herb Companion. LC 93-74031. (Traditional Country Life Recipe Ser.). (Illus.). 96p. (Orig.). 1994. pap. 9.95 (*1-883283-04-3*) Brick Tower.

Preston, Mary. Spear-it Land. (Illus.). 152p. (Orig.). Date not set. pap. 12.95 (*0-9636819-0-7*) Kairos Books.

Preston, Michael, jt. ed. see Palley, Marian.

Preston, Michael B., jt. ed. see Jackson, Bryan O.

Preston, Mike. Mathematics in Primary Education. (Contemporary Analysis in Education Ser.: Vol.15). 200p. 1987. 55.00 (*1-85000-196-0*, Falmer Pr); pap. 29.00 (*1-85000-197-9*, Falmer Pr) Taylor & Francis.

Preston, Nathaniel S., jt. auth. see Abeles, Charles C.

***Preston, Noel, ed.** Ethics for the Public Sector: Education & Training. 277p. (Orig.). 1994. text ed. 49.00 (*1-86287-145-0*, Pub. by Federation Pr AU) W W Gaunt.

Preston, P. W. Making Sense of Development: An Introduction to Classical & Contemporary Theories of Development & Their Application to Southeast Asia. 304p. 1987. text ed. 49.95 (*0-7102-0813-8*, RKP) Routledge.

— Rethinking Development. 256p. 1987. lib. bdg. 69.50 (*0-7102-1263-1*, RKP) Routledge.

— Theories of Development. (International Library of Sociology). 300p. 1982. 29.50 (*0-7100-9055-2*, RKP) Routledge.

Preston, Paschal, jt. ed. see Corcoran, Farrel.

Preston, Patricia. Reflections of Ireland. 1991. 19.98 (*0-8317-4984-9*) Smithmark.

Preston, Paul. The Coming of the Spanish Civil War: Reform, Reaction & Revolution in the Second Republic. LC 93-40967. 1994. pap. 19.95 (*0-415-06355-8*, A7864) Routledge.

— The Coming of the Spanish Civil War: Reform, Reaction & Revolution in the Second Republic. 1983. pap. 14.95 (*0-416-35720-2*, NO. 3948) Routledge Chapman & Hall.

— The Coming of the Spanish Civil War: Reform, Reaction & Revolution in the Second Republic. 2nd ed. LC 93-40967. 360p. 1994. 69.95x (*0-415-06354-X*, A7860) Routledge.

— Franco: A Biography. LC 94-28636. (Illus.). 1,002p. 1994. 37.50 (*0-465-02515-3*) Basic.

— Mother Father Deaf: Living Between Sound & Silence. LC 93-44895. 288p. (Orig.). (C). 1994. text ed. 24.95 (*0-674-58747-2*) HUP.

— Mother Father Deaf: Living Between Sound & Silence. 288p. (Orig.). (C). 1995. pap. 14.95 (*0-674-58748-0*) HUP.

— The Politics of Revenge: Fascism & the Military in Twentieth Century Spain. 240p. 1995. pap. 16.95 (*0-415-12000-4*, C0394) Routledge.

— The Spanish Civil War: 1936-1939. 161p. (C). 1986. pap. 15.95 (*0-534-10771-0*) Intl Thomson.

— Strategies for Productive Motor Carrier Sales Management. 237p. 1987. pap. 10.80 (*0-88711-108-4*) Am Trucking Assns.

— The Triumph of Democracy in Spain. 263p. 1986. 35.00 (*0-416-36350-4*, 9880) Routledge Chapman & Hall.

— The Triumph of Democracy in Spain. 288p. 1987. pap. text ed. 14.95 (*0-416-90010-0*) Routledge Chapman & Hall.

Preston, Paul, ed. Revolution & War in Spain, Nineteen Thirty-One to Nineteen Thirty-Nine. 320p. (Orig.). 1984. pap. 15.95 (*0-416-34970-6*, 9074) Routledge Chapman & Hall.

Preston, Paul & Nelson, Ralph. Salesmanship: A Contemporary Approach. (C). 1981. teacher ed write for info. (*0-318-55522-0*, Reston) P-H.

Preston, Paul, jt. auth. see American Trucking Associations, Sales.

Preston, Paul, jt. ed. see Graham, Helen.

Preston, Paul, jt. ed. see Lanon, Frances.

Preston, Percy. A Dictionary of Pictorial Subjects from Classical Literature: A Guide to Their Identification in Works of Art. LC 83-4470. (Illus.). 336p. 1983. 39.95 (*0-684-17913-X*, Scribners) S&S Trade.

Preston, Peter. A D. H. Lawrence Chronology. LC 93-43707. 1994. 45.00 (*0-312-12114-8*) St Martin.

Preston, Peter, ed. Literature in the Adult Class: Tradition & Challenge. 200p. 1994. 24.95 (*1-85041-072-0*, Pub. by U Nottingham UK) Paul & Co Pubs.

Preston, Peter & Hoare, Peter, eds. D. H. Lawrence in the Modern World. 192p. (C). 1989. 42.95 (*0-521-37169-4*) Cambridge U Pr.

Preston, Peter & Simpson-Housley, Paul. Writing the City: Literature & the Urban Experience. LC 93-44177. (Illus.). 300p. 1994. 65.00x (*0-415-10667-2*, B3896, Routledge NY) Routledge.

Preston, Peter, jt. ed. see Morgan, W. John.

***Preston, Peter W.** Discourses of Development: State, Market & Polity in the Analysis of Complex Change. 256p. 1994. pap. 63.95 (*1-85972-026-9*, Pub. by Ashgate UK) Ashgate Pub Co.

— Europe, Democracy & the Dissolution of Britain: An Essay on the Issue of Europe in U. K. Public Discourse. 232p. 1994. 57.95 (*1-85521-519-5*, Pub. by Dartmth Pub UK) Ashgate Pub Co.

Preston, Philip & Kannair, Jonathan A. White Mountains-West. LC 79-66098. (Illus.). (Orig.). 1979. pap. 7.50 (*0-9603106-0-6*) Waumbek.

Preston, Praschal, jt. auth. see Hall, Peter.

Preston, R. A., ed. Advances in Botanical Research, Vol. 13. (Serial Publication Ser.). 224p. 1987. text ed. 107.00 (*0-12-005913-4*) Acad Pr.

Preston, R. C, ed. Output Measurements for Medical Ultrasound. (Illus.). xvi, 180p. 1991. 105.00 (*0-387-19692-7*) Spr-Verlag.

Preston, R. D. & Woolhouse, W. H., eds. Advances in Botanical Research, Vol. 5. (Serial Publication Ser.). 1978. text ed. 174.00 (*0-12-005905-3*) Acad Pr.

Preston, Ralph N. Early California Atlas: Northern Edition. 2nd ed. LC 83-72442. (Illus.). 1983. pap. 12.95 (*0-8323-0313-5*) Binford Mort.

— Early California Atlas: Southern Edition. 2nd ed. LC 78-57008. (Illus.). 1988. pap. 12.95 (*0-8323-0314-3*) Binford Mort.

— Early Idaho Atlas. 2nd ed. LC 78-57018. (Illus.). 1978. pap. 12.95 (*0-8323-0312-7*) Binford Mort.

— Early Oregon Atlas. 2nd ed. LC 78-57019. (Illus.). 1991. pap. 12.95 (*0-8323-0304-6*) Binford Mort.

— Early Washington Atlas. 2nd ed. LC 78-57006. (Illus.). 1981. pap. 12.95 (*0-8323-0311-9*) Binford Mort.

Preston, Ralph N., comp. Oregon Gold & Gems Maps. rev. ed. (Illus.). 1991. pap. 7.95 (*0-8323-0309-7*) Binford Mort.

Preston, Raymond. Four Quartets Rehearsed. LC 74-100779. (Studies in T. S. Eliot: No. 11). 1970. reprint ed. lib. bdg. 75.00 (*0-8383-0337-4*, 0-8383-0337-4) M S G Haskell Hse.

Preston, Richard. American Steel. 288p. 1992. pap. 10.00 (*0-380-71822-7*) Avon.

— First Light: The Search for the Edge of the Universe. LC 95-12925. 1995. write for info. (*0-385-48009-1*, Anchor NY) Doubleday.

— The Hot Zone. LC 94-13415. 1994. 23.00 (*0-679-43094-6*) Random.

— The Hot Zone. large type ed. LC 95-3710. (Large Print Book Ser.). 1995. write for info. (*1-56895-205-8*) Wheeler Pub.

Preston, Richard, ed. see Serle, Geoffrey, et al.

Preston, Richard A. Canada & Imperial Defense: A Study of the Origins of the British Commonwealth's Defense Organization, 1867-1919. LC 66-29550. (Duke University, Commonwealth-Studies Center, Publication Ser.: No. 29). reprint ed. pap. 149.50 (*0-8357-7987-4*, 2023435) Bks Demand.

— Canada's RMC: A History of the Royal Military College. LC 77-413015. (Illus.). 467p. reprint ed. pap. 133.10 (*0-8357-4027-7*, 2036719) Bks Demand.

— The Defence of the Undefended Border: Planning for War in North America, 1867-1939. LC 78-313309. 312p. reprint ed. pap. 89.00 (*0-7837-1149-2*, 2041678) Bks Demand.

— Royal Fort Frontenac. LC 58-3089. (Champlain Society Publications, Ontario Ser.: No. 2). 547p. reprint ed. pap. 155.90 (*0-7837-2050-5*, 2042325) Bks Demand.

— To Serve Canada: A History of the Royal Military College Since the Second World War. 250p. 1991. 34.95 (*0-7766-0327-2*, Pub. by Univ Ottawa Pr CN) Paul & Co Pubs.

Preston, Richard A., ed. see Abella, Irving M., et al.

Preston, Richard A., et al. Men in Arms: A History of Warfare & Its Interrelationships with Western Society. 5th ed. (C). 1991. pap. text ed. 22.75 (*0-03-033428-4*) HB Coll Pubs.

Preston, Richard J., Jr. North American Trees: Exclusive of Mexico & Tropical Florida. 4th ed. LC 89-1944. (Illus.). 436p. (C). 1989. 41.95 (*0-8138-1171-6*); pap. 20.95 (*0-8138-1172-4*) Iowa St U Pr.

Preston, Robert & Preston, Cheryl. Believe in Yourself: Be Your Own Best Friend. 70p. (Orig.). 1991. pap. write for info. (*0-939759-04-7*, BIY-S) Ctr Dynamic Living.

— Divorce Without Guilt. (Illus.). 360p. 1991. 12.95 (*0-939759-00-4*, DWG-H); pap. 8.95 (*0-939759-01-2*, DWG-P) Ctr Dynamic Living.

— Lover's Checklist for Compatibility. 185p. 1991. write for info. (*0-939759-02-0*, CG-600) Ctr Dynamic Living.

Preston, Robert L. Building Your Fortune with Silver. 112p. 1973. pap. 1.00 (*0-89036-024-3*) Hawkes Pub Inc.

— How to Prepare for the Coming Crash. 128p. 1971. pap. 2.95 (*0-89036-025-1*) Hawkes Pub Inc.

Preston, Rod. Book of Spiders & Scorpions. 1991. 14.99 (*0-517-06092-2*) Random Hse Value.

Preston, Rohan. Dreams in Soy Sauce. 66p. (Orig.). 1991. pap. 6.95 (*0-9624287-7-9*) Tia Chucha Pr.

***Preston, Ronald H.** Confusions in Christian Social Ethics: Problems for Geneva & Rome. 202p. 1995. pap. 16.99 (*0-8028-4125-2*) Eerdmans.

— Religion & the Ambiguities of Capitalism. LC 92-43014. 192p. (C). 1993. reprint ed. pap. 14.95 (*0-8298-0946-5*) Pilgrim OH.

Preston, S. J. A Whimsical Look at Kids. (C). 1989. 25.00 (*0-7223-2255-0*, Pub. by A H S Ltd UK) St Mut.

Preston, Samuel H. Mortality Patterns in National Populations: With Special Reference to Recorded Causes of Death. (Studies in Population). 1976. text ed. 43.00 (*0-12-564450-7*) Acad Pr.

— Older Male Mortality & Cigarette Smoking, Vol. 6. LC 76-4875. (Population Monograph Ser.: No. 7). (Illus.). 150p. 1976. reprint ed. text ed. 24.75 (*0-8371-8830-X*, PROM, Greenwood Pr) Greenwood.

Preston, Samuel H. & Haines, Michael R. Fatal Years: Child Mortality in Late Nineteenth-Century America. 272p. 1991. text ed. 39.50 (*0-691-04268-3*) Princeton U Pr.

Preston, Samuel H., jt. ed. see Gribble, James N.

Preston, Samuel H., ed. see National Research Council, Population Committee.

Preston, Sarah, ed. see Jacob, Alice.

Preston, Scott. Thought Crimes Against Old Glory. 12p. 1991. pap. 3.00 (*0-915214-22-9*) Current.

Preston, Seaton T., Jr. & Pandratz, Ronald. A Guide to the Analysis of Alcohols by Gas Chromatography. 3rd ed. 190p. 1984. pap. 35.00 (*0-913106-25-9*) PolyScience.

Preston, Seaton T., Jr. & Pankratz, Ronald. A Guide to Selected Liquid Phases & Absorbents Used in Gas Chromatography. 194p. 1969. spiral bd. 25.00 (*0-913106-19-4*) PolyScience.

— A Guide to the Analysis of Amines by Gas Chromatography. 3rd rev. ed. 176p. 1981. spiral bd. 35.00 (*0-913106-20-8*) PolyScience.

— Guide to the Analysis of Fatty Acids & Their Esters by Gas Chromatography. 2nd ed. 250p. 1985. spiral bd. 35.00 (*0-318-41822-3*) PolyScience.

— Guide to the Analysis of Hydrocarbons by Gas Chromatography. 3rd ed. 349p. 1983. spiral bd. 45.00 (*0-913106-21-6*) PolyScience.

— A Guide to the Analysis of Pesticides by Gas Chromatography. 473p. 1981. spiral bd. 45.00 (*0-913106-15-1*) PolyScience.

— A Guide to the Analysis of Thioalcohols & Thioethers: (Mercaptans & Alkyl Sulfides) by Gas Chromatography. rev. ed. 193p. 1980. spiral bd. 35.00 (*0-913106-16-X*) PolyScience.

Preston, Seaton T., Jr. & Pankratz, Ronald E. Guide to the Analysis of Ketones & Aldehydes by Gas Chromatography. 3rd ed. 230p. 1985. 35.00 (*0-318-41823-1*) PolyScience.

— A Guide to the Analysis of Phenols by Gas Chromatography. 3rd rev. ed. 160p. 1985. pap. 35.00 (*0-913106-26-7*) PolyScience.

Preston, Seaton T., Jr., et al. Qualitative Analysis by Gas Chromatography. 30p. 1982. write for info. (*0-913106-18-6*) PolyScience.

Preston-Shoot, Michael, jt. auth. see Braye, Suzy.

Preston-Shoot, Michael, jt. auth. see Corden, John.

Preston, Stuart. Vuillard. (Masters of Art Ser.). (Illus.). 128p. 1985. 22.95 (*0-8109-1706-8*) Abrams.

Preston, T. M., et al. Cytoskeleton & Cell Motility. (Tertiary Level Biology Ser.). (Illus.). 200p. 1990. text ed. 69.95 (*0-412-02041-6*, A3603, Chap & Hall NY); pap. text ed. 32.00 (*0-412-02051-3*, A3607, Chap & Hall NY) Chapman & Hall.

Preston, T. R. & Willis, M. B. Intensive Beef Production. 2nd ed. LC 74-5276. (Pergamon International Library Science Technology Engineering & Social Studies). 1974. text ed. 239.00 (*0-08-017788-3*, Pub. by Pergamon Repr UK) Franklin.

Preston, Thomas. Cambises. LC 74-133723. (Tudor Facsimile Texts. Old English Plays Ser.: No. 44). reprint ed. 49.50 (*0-404-53344-2*) AMS Pr.

— The Clay Pedestal: A Re-examination of the Doctor-Patient Relationship. LC 81-11742. 228p. 1981. 12.95 (*0-914842-68-4*) Madrona Pubs.

Preston, Thomas, intro. The Double Eagle Guide to Western State Parks Vol. 1: Pacific Northwest. (Double Eagle Guides Ser.). (Illus.). 304p. (Orig.). 1991. pap. 11.95 (*0-929760-11-5*) Discovery MT.

— The Double Eagle Guide to Western State Parks Vol. 3: Far West. (Double Eagle Guides Ser.). (Illus.). 320p. (Orig.). 1991. pap. 12.95 (*0-929760-13-1*) Discovery MT.

— The Double Eagle Guide to Western State Parks Vol. 4: Desert Southwest. (Double Eagle Guides Ser.). (Illus.). 224p. (Orig.). 1991. pap. 9.95 (*0-929760-14-X*) Discovery MT.

***Preston, Thomas & Preston, Elizabeth.** The Double Eagle Guide to Camping in Wesern Parks & Forests: Washington. large type ed. (Double Eagle Guides Ser.). (Illus.). 188p. 1995. 17.95 (*0-929760-41-7*) Discovery MT.

— The Double Eagle Guide to Camping in Western Parks & Forests: Arizona. large type ed. (Double Eagle Guides Ser.). (Illus.). 128p. 1995. 16.95 (*0-929760-49-2*) Discovery MT.

— The Double Eagle Guide to Camping in Western Parks & Forests: Colorado. large type ed. (Double Eagle Guides Ser.). 190p. 1995. 17.95 (*0-929760-44-1*) Discovery MT.

— The Double Eagle Guide to Camping in Western Parks & Forests: Idaho. large type ed. (Double Eagle Guides Ser.). (Illus.). 120p. 1995. 15.95 (*0-929760-43-3*) Discovery MT.

— The Double Eagle Guide to Camping in Western Parks & Forests: Montana. large type ed. (Double Eagle Guides Ser.). (Illus.). 128p. 1995. 16.95 (*0-929760-45-X*) Discovery MT.

An Asterisk (*) at the beginning of an entry indicates that the title is appearing in BIP for the first time.

— The Double Eagle Guide to Camping in Western Parks & Forests: Nebraska & Kansas. large type ed. (Double Eagle Guides Ser.). (Illus.). 162p. 1995. 17.95 (*0-929760-53-0*) Discovery MT.

— The Double Eagle Guide to Camping in Western Parks & Forests: Nevada-Utah. large type ed. (Double Eagle Guides Ser.). (Illus.). 188p. 1995. 17.95 (*0-929760-51-4*) Discovery MT.

— The Double Eagle Guide to Camping in Western Parks & Forests: New Mexico. large type ed. (Double Eagles Guides Ser.). (Illus.). 118p. 1995. 15.95 (*0-929760-50-6*) Discovery MT.

— The Double Eagle Guide to Camping in Western Parks & Forests: North Dakota-South Dakota. large type ed. (Double Eagle Guides Ser.). (Illus.). 138p. 1995. 16.95 (*0-929760-52-2*) Discovery MT.

— The Double Eagle Guide to Camping in Western Parks & Forests: Northern California. large type ed. (Double Eagle Guide Ser.). (Illus.). 230p. 1995. 18.95 (*0-929760-47-6*) Discovery MT.

— The Double Eagle Guide to Camping in Western Parks & Forests: Oklahoma. large type ed. (Double Eagle Guides Ser.). (Illus.). 150p. 1995. 16.95 (*0-929760-54-9*) Discovery MT.

— The Double Eagle Guide to Camping in Western Parks & Forests: Oregon. large type ed. (Double Eagle Guides Ser.). (Illus.). 168p. 1995. 16.95 (*0-929760-42-5*) Discovery MT.

— The Double Eagle Guide to Camping in Western Parks & Forests: Southern California. large type ed. (Double Eagle Guides Ser.). (Illus.). 220p. 1995. 18.95 (*0-929760-48-4*) Discovery MT.

— The Double Eagle Guide to Camping in Western Parks & Forests: Texas. large type ed. (Double Eagle Guides Ser.). (Illus.). 210p. 1995. 17.95 (*0-929760-55-7*) Discovery MT.

— The Double Eagle Guide to Camping in Western Parks & Forests: Wyoming. large type ed. (Double Eagle Guides Ser.). (Illus.). 116p. 1995. 15.95 (*0-929760-46-8*) Discovery MT.

— The Double Eagle Guide to Camping in Western Parks & Forests Vol. I: Pacific Northwest. (Double Eagle Guides). (Illus.). 448p. (Orig.). 1992. pap. 12.95 (*0-929760-21-2*) Discovery MT.

— The Double Eagle Guide to Camping in Western Parks & Forests Vol. I: Pacific Northwest. (Double Eagle Guides). (Illus.). 238p. 1994. 18.95 (*0-929760-27-1*) Discovery MT.

— The Double Eagle Guide to Camping in Western Parks & Forests Vol. II: Far West. (Double Eagle Guides). (Illus.). 240p. 1994. 18.95 (*0-929760-23-9*) Discovery MT.

— The Double Eagle Guide to Camping in Western Parks & Forests Vol. II: Rocky Mountains. (Double Eagle Guides). (Illus.). 214p. 1994. 17.95 (*0-929760-22-0*) Discovery MT.

— The Double Eagle Guide to Camping in Western Parks & Forests Vol. IV: Desert Southwest. (Double Eagle Guides). (Illus.). 384p. (Orig.). 1992. pap. 12.95 (*0-929760-24-7*) Discovery MT.

— The Double Eagle Guide to Camping in Western Parks & Forests Vol. IV: Desert Southwest. (Double Eagle Guides). (Illus.). 212p. 1994. 17.95 (*0-929760-29-8*) Discovery MT.

— The Double Eagle Guide to Camping in Western Parks & Forests Vol. V: Northern Plains. (Double Eagle Guides). (Illus.). 170p. 1994. 16.95 (*0-929760-25-5*) Discovery MT.

— The Double Eagle Guide to Camping in Western Parks & Forests Vol. VI: Southwest Plains. (Double Eagle Guides). (Illus.). 192p. 1994. 17.95 (*0-929760-26-3*) Discovery MT.

— The Double Eagle Guide to Western State Parks Vol. 5: Northern Plains. (Double Eagle Guides Ser.). (Illus.). 150p. 1994. 16.95 (*0-929760-15-8*) Discovery MT.

— The Double Eagle Guide to Working in Western Parks & Forests. (Double Eagle Guides Ser.). (Illus.). 224p. 1995. 19.95 (*0-929760-57-3*) Discovery MT.

Preston, Thomas & Preston, Elizabeth, intros. The Double Eagle Guide to Western Public Campgrounds: Northern Great Plains. (Double Eagle Guides Ser.: Vol. V). (Illus.). 304p. (Orig.). 1989. pap. 8.95 (*0-929760-05-0*) Discovery MT.

— The Double Eagle Guide to Western Public Campgrounds: Southwest Plains. (Double Eagle Guides Ser.: Vol. VI). (Illus.). 336p. (Orig.). 1990. pap. 8.95 (*0-929760-06-9*) Discovery MT.

Preston, Thomas A. Coronary Artery Surgery: A Critical Review. LC 76-51977. 278p. reprint ed. pap. 79.30 (*0-7837-7117-7*, 2046946) Bks Demand.

Preston, Thomas R., ed. see Smollett, Tobias G.

Preston, Thomas R., ed. see Smollett, Tobias.

Preston, Thorgrimson, Shidler, Gates & Ellis Staff. Oregon Environmental Law Handbook. 214p. (Orig.). 1992. pap. text ed. 69.00 (*0-86587-285-6*) Gov Insts.

— Washington Environmental Law Handbook. 2nd ed. (State Environmental Law Ser.). 380p. 1992. pap. text ed. 79.00 (*0-86587-317-8*) Gov Insts.

Preston, Trevor S., tr. see Klant, Johannes J.

Preston, W. B., jt. ed. see Wilson, L. A.

Preston, Walter W. History of Harford County, Maryland. 379p. 1990. reprint ed. 20.00 (*0-685-60387-3*, 4700) Clearfield Co.

Preston, Ward. What an Art Director Does: An Introduction to Motion Picture Production Design. LC 94-30605. (Illus.). 190p. (Orig.). 1994. pap. 18.95 (*1-879505-18-5*) Silman James Pr.

Preston-Whyte, Eleanor. Speaking with Beads: Zulu Arts from Southern Africa. LC 94-60280. (Illus.). 96p. (Orig.). 1994. pap. 19.95 (*0-500-27757-5*) Thames Hudson.

Preston-Whyte, R. A. & Tyson, P. D. The Atmosphere & Weather of Southern Africa. (Illus.). 386p. 1989. pap. 27.95 (*0-19-570496-7*) OUP.

***Preston, William, Jr.** Aliens & Dissenters: Federal Suppression of Radicals, 1903-1933. 2nd ed. LC 94-27501. 1994. pap. text ed. write for info. (*0-252-06452-6*) U of Ill Pr.

Preston, William, Jr., et al. Hope & Folly: The United States & UNESCO, 1945-1985. 392p. 1989. text ed. 49.95 (*0-8166-1788-0*); pap. text ed. 16.95 (*0-8166-1789-9*) U of Minn Pr.

Prestopino, Chris J. Estate Planning & Taxation, 1994. 5th ed. 896p. (C). 1993. per. 59.95 (*0-8403-8791-1*) Kendall-Hunt.

— Estate Planning & Taxation, 1995. 944p. (C). 1994. per. 59.95 (*0-8403-9388-1*) Kendall-Hunt.

— Estate Planning & Taxation, 1995. abr. ed. 1048p. (C). 1994. 65.95 (*0-8403-9533-7*) Kendall-Hunt.

— Introduction to Estate Planning. 512p. 1988. text ed. 40.00 (*1-55623-132-6*) Irwin Prof Pubng.

Prestopnik, Richard J. Digital Electronics: Concepts & Applications for Digital Design. 735p. (C). 1990. text ed. 56.00 (*0-03-026757-9*); Instr.'s manual with transparency masters. teacher ed, pap. text ed. 28.50 (*0-03-030867-4*); Laboratory manual. student ed, pap. text ed. 22.75 (*0-03-026758-7*); Instr.'s lab manual. teacher ed, pap. text ed. 28.50 (*0-03-032017-8*) SCP.

— Microprocessor Peripheral IC Reference Manual. 320p. 1989. text ed. 34.00 (*0-13-580705-0*, Busn) P-H.

Prestowitz, Clyde V. Powernomics: Economics & Strategy after the Cold War. 1991. pap. 16.95 (*0-8191-8039-4*) Madison Bks UPA.

Prestowitz, Clyde V., Jr. Trading Places: How We Are Giving Our Future to Japan & How to Reclaim It. LC 87-47775. 592p. 1990. reprint ed. pap. 12.95 (*0-465-08679-9*) Basic.

Prestowitz, Clyde V., Jr., et al. The New North American Order: A Win-Win Strategy for U. S.-Mexico Trade. 134p. (C). 1991. lib. bdg. 42.00 (*0-8191-8437-3*); pap. text ed. 15.50 (*0-8191-8438-1*) U Pr of Amer.

Prestressed Concrete Institute Staff. Approaches to Standardization of Architectural Precast Concrete Panels. (PCI Journal Reprints Ser.). 20p. 1985. pap. 6.00 (*0-318-19769-3*, JR200) P-PCI.

— The Baton Rouge Hilton Tower: An All Precast Prestressed Systems Building. (PCI Journal Reprints Ser.). 16p. 1976. pap. 6.00 (*0-318-19851-7*, JR185) P-PCI.

— Behavior & Design of Prestressed Concrete Beams with Large Web Openings. (PCI Journal Reprints Ser.). 32p. 1985. pap. 7.00 (*0-318-19855-X*, JR193) P-PCI.

— Considerations for the Design of Precast Concrete Bearing Wall Buildings to Withstand Abnormal Loads. (PCI Journal Reprints Ser.). 36p. 1985. pap. 7.00 (*0-318-19752-9*, JR170) P-PCI.

— Criteria for Design of Bearing Pads. 118p. 1985. ring bd. 35.00 (*0-318-19829-0*, TR-4-85) P-PCI.

— Design & Behavior of Dapped-End Beams. (PCI Journal Reprints Ser.). 18p. 1985. pap. 7.00 (*0-318-19861-4*, JR212) P-PCI.

— Design of Elastomer Bearings. (PCI Journal Reprints Ser.). 17p. 1964. pap. 6.00 (*0-318-19834-7*, JR24) P-PCI.

— Design of Partially Prestressed Flexural Members. (PCI Journal Reprints Ser.). 20p. 1977. pap. 6.00 (*0-318-19854-1*, JR189) P-PCI.

— Design Supplement to SSB-1-81. 80p. pap. 20.00 (*0-318-19822-3*, SSB-Z) P-PCI.

— Fire Resistance of Architectural Precast Concrete. 13p. 1974. pap. 6.00 (*0-318-19812-6*, JR-150) P-PCI.

— Guide Specification for Architectural Precast Concrete. 12p. 1985. 4.00 (*0-318-19827-4*, SPC-119-85) P-PCI.

— High-Range Water-Reducing Admixtures in Prestressed Concrete Operations. (PCI Journal Reprints Ser.). 18p. 1978. pap. 7.00 (*0-318-19860-6*, JR208) P-PCI.

— The Pasco-Kennewick Intercity Bridge & Geometry Control for the Intercity Bridge. (PCI Journal Reprints Ser.). 36p. 1979. pap. 8.00 (*0-318-19859-2*, JR205) P-PCI.

— Precast Trapezoidal Girders Spliced with Post-Tensioning for Highway Underpass. (PCI Journal Reprints Ser.). 4p. 1980. pap. 4.00 (*0-318-19863-0*, JR219) P-PCI.

— Recommendations for Estimating Prestress Losses. (PCI Journal Reprints Ser.). 36p. 1975. pap. 6.00 (*0-318-19842-8*, JR162) P-PCI.

— Recommended Practice for Grouting of Post-Tensioned Prestressed Concrete. (PCI Journal Reprints Ser.: No. 119). 8p. 1972. pap. 5.00 (*0-318-19838-X*, JR119) P-PCI.

— Research, Application, & Experience with Precast Prestressed Bridge Deck Panels. (PCI Journal Reprints Ser.). 24p. 1975. pap. 6.00 (*0-318-19843-6*, JR167) P-PCI.

— Stretched Out AASHO-PCI Beams Types III & IV for Longer Span Highway Bridges. (PCI Journal Reprints Ser.). 19p. 1973. pap. 6.00 (*0-318-19840-1*, JR134) P-PCI.

— A Utility's Development & Use of Prestressed Concrete Poles. (PCI Journal Reprints Ser.). 8p. 1972. pap. 5.00 (*0-318-19837-1*, JR114) P-PCI.

Prestwich, Glenn D. & Blomquist, Gary J., eds. Pheromone Biochemistry. 565p. 1987. text ed. 140.00 (*0-12-564485-X*) Acad Pr.

Prestwich, Ken. Introduction to Biology. (C). 1993. student ed 17.24 (*1-56870-103-9*) RonJon Pub.

Prestwich, Michael. English Politics in the Thirteenth Century. Black, Jeremy, ed. LC 89-78230. (British History in Perspective Ser.). 160p. 1990. text ed. 45.00 (*0-312-04527-1*) St Martin.

— The Three Edwards: War & State in England, 1272-1377. LC 92-19386. 352p. 1992. pap. 17.95 (*0-415-05133-9*, A9854) Routledge.

— War, Politics & Finance under Edward the First. (Modern Revivals in History Ser.). 318p. 1992. 59.95 (*0-7512-0000-X*, Pub. by Gregg Revivals UK) Ashgate Pub Co.

Prestwich, Michael, ed. Crisis of 1297-98 in England. (Royal Historical Society: Camden Fourth Ser.: Vol. 24). 216p. 1980. 30.00 (*0-901050-56-3*, BAB 03307) Boydell & Brewer.

Prestwich, Patricia. Drink & the Politics of Social Reform: Antialcoholism in France since 1870. LC 88-11576. 365p. 1988. 36.00 (*0-930664-08-6*) SPOSS.

Prestwood, Brian, jt. auth. see Mann, William P.

Prestwood, Edward. The Creative Writer's Phrase-Finder. LC 83-5617. 384p. 1984. 23.95 (*0-88280-104-X*) ETC Pubns.

Prestwood, Mike. What Every Paradox for Windows Programmer Should Know. 1200p. 1993. pap. 44.95 (*0-672-30368-X*) Sams.

— What Every Paradox for Windows Programmer Should Know. 2nd ed. (Illus.). 1100p. 1994. pap. 44.95 (*0-614-06064-8*) Sams.

Prestwood, Mike, jt. auth. see Atkinson, Lee.

Prete, Barbara & Strong, Gary E., eds. Literate America Emerging. 130p. 1991. pap. 11.95 (*0-929722-45-0*) CA State Library Fndtn.

Prete, R. & Ion, A. Hamish, eds. Armies of Occupation. 160p. (C). 1984. text ed. 25.00 (*0-88920-156-0*, Pub. by Wilfrid Laurier CN) Humanities.

Preteceille, E., jt. auth. see Pickvance, C. G.

Preteceille, Edmond. Jeux, Modeles et Simulations: Critique des Jeux Urbains. (Recherche Urbaine Ser.: No. 9). (Illus.). 208p. (FRE.). 1975. pap. text ed. 21.55 (*90-279-7793-3*) Mouton.

Preterm Institute Staff. Exploring Human Sexuality. 115p. 1975. pap. 13.95 (*0-87073-786-4*) Schenkman Bks Inc.

PreTest Services, Inc. Staff. PreTest for Physicians Preparing for the Federation Licensing Examination: FLEX. 4th ed. 104p. 1982. 34.00 (*0-685-05737-2*) McGraw.

Pretiz, Paul, jt. auth. see Berg, Mike.

Pretlove, A. J. BASIC Mechanical Vibrations. (Basic Ser.). (Illus.). 128p. 1985. pap. text ed. 24.95 (*0-408-01554-3*) Buttrwrth-Heinemann.

Pretlove, John, ed. see Carey, William.

Pretlow, Theresa P., jt. auth. see Pretlow, Thomas G., II.

Pretlow, Theresa P., jt. ed. see Pretlow, Thomas G., II.

Pretlow, Thomas G., II & Pretlow, Theresa P. Cell Separation: Methods & Selected Applications, Vol. 1. 1982. text ed. 90.00 (*0-12-564501-5*) Acad Pr.

Pretlow, Thomas G., II & Pretlow, Theresa P., eds. Biochemical & Molecular Aspects of Selected Cancers, Vol. 1. (Illus.). 444p. 1991. text ed. 121.00 (*0-12-564498-1*) Acad Pr.

— Biochemical & Molecular Aspects of Selected Cancers, Vol. 2. (Illus.). 542p. 1994. text ed. 120.00 (*0-12-564499-X*) Acad Pr.

— Cell Separation: Methods & Selected Applications, Vol. 2. 1983. text ed. 93.00 (*0-12-564502-3*) Acad Pr.

— Cell Separation: Methods & Selected Applications, Vol. 3. 1984. text ed. 103.00 (*0-12-564503-1*) Acad Pr.

— Cell Separation: Methods & Selected Applications, Vol. 4. 1987. text ed. 97.00 (*0-12-564504-X*) Acad Pr.

— Cell Separation: Methods & Selected Applications, Vol. 5. 374p. 1987. text ed. 115.00 (*0-12-564505-8*) Acad Pr.

Pretner, Janko. Russian-Slovene Dictionary: Rusko-Slovenski Slovar. 995p. (RUS & SLV.). 1986. 59.95 (*0-8288-1139-3*, F114898) Fr & Eur.

Preto-Rodas, Richard A. Negritude as a Theme in the Poetry of the Portuguese-Speaking World. LC 79-107879. (University of Florida Humanities Monographs: No. 31). 98p. reprint ed. pap. 28.00 (*0-7837-5082-X*, 2044780) Bks Demand.

Preto-Rodas, Richard A. & Hower, Alfred, eds. Carlos Drummond de Andrade-Quarenta Historinhas (e Cinco Poemas) LC 84-27151. xvi, 268p. (Orig.). (ENG & POR.). (C). 1985. pap. text ed. 22.95 (*0-8130-0789-5*) U Press Fla.

Preto-Rodas, Richard A., jt. ed. see Hower, Alfred.

Preto-Rodas, Richard A., et al, eds. Cronicas Brasileiras: Nova Fase. (Center for Latin American Studies, University of Florida). (Illus.). 352p. (C). 1994. pap. text ed. 24.95 (*0-8130-1246-5*) U Press Fla.

Pretolani, S., ed. see Fourth Workshop of the Helicobacter Pylori Study Group Staff.

Pretorius, Anika. Gifts from the Home. 96p. (C). 1989. 90.00 (*1-85368-081-8*, Pub. by New Holland Pubs UK) St Mut.

***Pretorius, Deiderika.** Surrogate Motherhood: A Worldwide View of the Issues. (American Series in Behavioral Sciences & Law: No. 1085). (Illus.). 262p. 1994. pap. 34.95 (*0-614-02345-9*) C C Thomas.

— Surrogate Motherhood: A Worldwide View of the Issues. (American Series in Behavioral Sciences & Law: No. 1085). (Illus.). 262p. (C). 1994. text ed. 56.95x (*0-398-05787-7*) C C Thomas.

***Pretorius, H. L.** Historiography & Historical Sources Regarding African Indigenous Churches in South Africa: Writing Indigenous Church History. LC 94-40519. (African Studies: Vol. 40). 160p. 1995. text ed. 69.95 (*0-7734-9149-X*) E Mellen.

Pretorius, J., jt. auth. see Delport, H. J.

Pretorius, J. Companies Act 61 of 1973 & Close Corporations Act 69 of 1984. 2nd ed. 634p. 1993. pap. 30.00 (*0-7021-2917-8*, Pub. by Juta SA) W W Gaunt.

— Maatskappywet 61 van 1973 en Wet op Beslote Korporasies 69 van 1984. 2nd ed. 634p. 1993. pap. write for info. (*0-7021-2918-6*, Pub. by Juta SA) W W Gaunt.

***Pretorius, J. T., ed.** Student Case Book on Business Entities. 256p. 1994. pap. 20.00 (*0-7021-3337-X*, Pub. by Juta SA) W W Gaunt.

Pretorius, J. T., jt. auth. see Forsyth, C. F.

Pretorius, Paul. Dispute Resolutions. 1993. pap. write for info. (*0-7021-2833-3*, Pub. by Juta SA) W W Gaunt.

Pretsch, E., et al. Tables of Spectral Data for Structure Determination of Organic Compounds. 2nd ed. (Chemical Laboratory Practice Ser.). xiii, 415p. 1994. pap. 49.50 (*0-387-51202-0*) Spr-Verlag.

Pretschner, D. P. Personal Computing in Nuclear Medicine. (Lecture Notes in Medical Informatics Ser.: Vol. 18). 133p. 1982. pap. 27.00 (*0-387-11598-6*) Spr-Verlag.

Pretsell, James, intro. National Engineering Management Conference, 1991: Managing in a Changing Future. (Illus.). 202p. (Orig.). 1991. pap. 57.75 (*0-85825-541-3*, Pub. by Inst Engrs Aust-EA Bks AT) Accents Pubns.

Prett, David M. & Garcia, Carlos E. Fundamental Process Control. (Illus.). 264p. 1988. text ed. 52.95 (*0-7506-9205-7*) Buttrwrth-Heinemann.

Prett, David M. & Morari, Manfred. Shell Process Control Workshop. (Illus.). 392p. 1987. text ed. 79.95 (*0-409-90136-9*) Buttrwrth-Heinemann.

Prett, David M., et al. Second Shell Process Control Workshop: Solutions to the Shell Standard Problem. 696p. 1989. text ed. 89.95 (*0-409-90186-5*) Buttrwrth-Heinemann.

Prettre, M. & Claudel, B. Elements de Cinetique Chimique. 208p. 1969. text ed. 169.00 (*0-677-50080-7*); pap. text ed. 125.00 (*0-677-50085-8*) Gordon & Breach.

— Elements of Chemical Kinetics. (Documents in Chemistry Ser.). 200p. 1970. text ed. 169.00 (*0-677-30080-8*) Gordon & Breach.

Pretty, David A. The Rural Revolt That Failed: Farm Workers' Trade Unions in Wales, 1889-1950. xiv, 291p. 1989. 50.00 (*0-7083-1024-9*, Pub. by U of Wales UK) Bks Intl VA.

***Pretty, Joan.** Chappy Goes to the Beach. LC 94-90155. (Illus.). 64p. (Orig.). (J). 1994. pap. 7.00 (*1-56002-456-9*) Aegina Pr.

Pretty, Lida. Life's Journey. 56p. 1990. 9.95 (*0-910147-90-6*) World Poetry Pr.

Pretty, Ron. The Habit of Balance. 64p. (C). 1989. 29.00 (*0-9587972-0-X*, Pub. by Five Islands Pr AT) St Mut.

Pretz, Bernhard. Dictionary of Military & Technological Abbreviations & Acronyms. 450p. 1983. 45.00 (*0-7100-9274-1*, RKP) Routledge.

Pretzel, O. Error-Correcting Codes & Finite Fields. (Oxford Applied Mathematics & Computing Science Ser.). (Illus.). 416p. 1992. 92.00 (*0-19-859678-2*) OUP.

Pretzer, William S., intro. Working at Inventing: Thomas Edison & the Menlo Park Experience. (Illus.). 144p. 1989. 24.95 (*0-933728-33-6*, Ford Mus); pap. 12.95 (*0-933728-34-4*, Ford Mus) Edison Inst.

Pretzsch, Karl. Verzeichnis der Breslauer Universitatsschriften, 1811-1885. xv, 387p. 1975. reprint ed. write for info. (*3-487-05573-2*, Pub. by Georg Olms GW) Lubrecht & Cramer.

Preu, James. The Dean & the Anarchist. LC 72-888. (Studies in Anarchy & Anarchism Ser.: No. 99). 124p. (C). 1972. reprint ed. lib. bdg. 42.95 (*0-8383-1419-8*) M S G Haskell Hse.

Preucel, Robert W., Jr. Seasonal Circulation & Dual Residence in Pueblo Southwest: A Prehistoric Example from the Pajarito Plateau, New Mexico. LC 90-21476. (Evolution of North American Indians Ser.: Vol. 16). 261p. 1991. reprint ed. 20.00 (*0-8240-2511-3*) Garland.

Preucel, Robert W., ed. Processual & Postprocessual Archaeologies: Multiple Ways of Knowing the Past. LC 90-84175. (Center for Archaeological Investigations Research Paper Ser.: No. 10). (Illus.). xii, 324p. (Orig.). 1991. pap. 25.00 (*0-88104-074-6*) Center Archaeo.

Preucil, Doris. Suzuki Viola School: Piano Accompaniments, Vol. 3. Suzuki, Shinichi, ed. 32p. (J). (gr. k-12). 1983. pap. text ed. 6.50 (*0-87487-246-4*, Suzuki Method) Summy-Birchard.

— Suzuki Viola School, Viola Part, Vol. 1. Suzuki, Shinichi, ed. (Suzuki Viola School Ser.). 32p. (J). (gr. k-12). 1981. pap. text ed. 6.50 (*0-87487-241-3*) Summy-Birchard.

— Suzuki Viola School, Viola Part, Vol. 2. Suzuki, Shinichi, ed. (Suzuki Viola School Ser.). 32p. (J). (gr. k-12). 1982. pap. text ed. 6.50 (*0-87487-242-1*) Summy-Birchard.

Preucil, Doris & Suzuki, Shinichi, eds. Suzuki Viola School, Vol. A. (Piano Accompaniment Ser.). 64p. (J). (gr. k-12). 1982. pap. text ed. 10.95 (*0-87487-245-6*, Suzuki Method) Summy-Birchard.

Preucil, Doris, ed. see Suzuki, Shinichi.

Preumont, A., et al. Application of the Random Vibration Approach in the Seismic Analysis. 89p. 1992. pap. 15.00 (*92-826-4287-9*, CD-NA-14153-EN-C, Pub. by Europ Com) UNIPUB.

***Preumont, Andre.** Random Vibration & Spectral Analysis. (Solid Mechanics & Its Applications Ser.). 288p. (C). 1994. lib. bdg. 122.00 (*0-7923-3036-6*) Kluwer Ac.

Preus, Anthony. Aristotle & Michael of Ephesus: On the Movement & Progression of Animals. (Studien und Materialien Zur Geschichte der Philosophie Ser.: Vol. XXII). 209p. 1981. 50.70 (*3-487-07073-1*, Pub. by Georg Olms GW) Lubrecht & Cramer.

— Science & Philosophy in Aristotle's Biological Works. (Studien und Materialien Zur Geschichte der Philosophie Ser.: No. 1). ix, 404p. 1975. 83.20 (*3-487-05832-4*, Pub. by Georg Olms GW) Lubrecht & Cramer.

Preus, Anthony & Anton, John P., eds. Essays in Ancient Greek Philosophy V: Aristotle's Ontology. LC 69-14648. 352p. (C). 1992. 59.50 (*0-7914-1027-7*); pap. 19.95 (*0-7914-1028-5*) State U NY Pr.

Preus, Anthony, jt. ed. see Anton, John P.

Preus, Herman A. Vivacious Daughter: Seven Lectures on the Religious Situation among Norwegians in the United States. Nichol, Todd W., ed. LC 90-212645. (Publications of the Norwegian-American Historical Association: No. 11). 246p. reprint ed. pap. 70.20 (*0-7837-0109-8*, 2040386) Bks Demand.

P Q

An Asterisk (*) at the beginning of an entry indicates that the title is appearing in BIP for the first time.

Preus, J. A., tr. see Chemnitz, Martin.

Preus, J. A. O. The Second Martin: The Life & Theology of Martin Chemnitz. LC 94-15925. 336p. (Orig.). (C). 1994. pap. 34.95 (*0-570-04645-9*) Concordia.

Preus, J. Samuel. Explaining Religion. LC 86-32418. 234p. 1987. 32.00 (*0-300-03822-4*) Yale U Pr.

— Explaining Religion: Criticism & Theory from Bodin to Freud. 234p. (C). 1991. reprint ed. pap. text ed. 15.00 (*0-300-05134-4*) Yale U Pr.

Preus, James S. From Shadow to Promise: Old Testament Interpretation from Augustine to the Young Luther. LC 69-12732. 308p. reprint ed. pap. 89.30 (*0-7837-2316-4*, 2057404) Bks Demand.

Preus, Mary. Eloquence & Ignorance in Augustine's "On the Nature & Origin of the Soul" (American Academy of Religion Academy Ser.). (C). 1986. 30.95 (*0-89130-927-6*, 01-01-51); pap. 21.95 (*0-89130-928-4*) Scholars Pr GA.

— Growing Herbs. (Cascadia Gardening Ser.). (Illus.). 104p. (Orig.). 1994. pap. 9.95 (*0-912365-98-6*) Sasquatch Bks.

Preus, R. & Rosin, W., eds. A Contemporary Look at the Formula of Concord. 304p. 1987. 15.95 (*0-570-03271-7*, 15HH2716) Concordia.

Preus, Robert, ed. see Marquart, Kurt.

Preus, Robert D., ed. see Scaer, David P.

Preusch, Deb, jt. auth. see Barry, Tom.

Preuschoft, H. & Chivers, D. J., eds. Hands of Primates. ix, 421p. 1993. 136.00 (*0-387-82385-9*) Spr-Verlag.

Preuse, Claus J., jt. ed. see Piper, Hans M.

Preuss, Arthur, ed. see Grisar, Hartmann.

Preuss, Emil, jt. auth. see Engelmann, Wilhelm.

Preuss, Evelyn, jt. auth. see Preuss, Gunter.

Preuss, Gehard. Theory of Topological Structures: An Approach to Categorical Topology. (C). 1987. lib. bdg. 109.50 (*90-277-2627-2*) Kluwer Ac.

***Preuss, Gunter & Preuss, Evelyn.** The Broussard's Restaurant Cookbook. (Illus.). 256p. 1995. 22.95 (*1-56554-139-1*) Pelican.

Preuss, Julius. Biblical & Talmudic Medicine. Rosner, Fred, ed. & tr. by. LC 93-33952. 688p. 1994. pap. 35.00 (*1-56821-134-1*) Aronson.

— Biblisch-Talmudische Medizin: Beitraege zur Geschichte der Heilkunde und der Kultur Ueberhaupt. viii, 736p. 1990. reprint ed. 160.00 (*3-8055-4976-8*) S Karger.

Preuss, L., jt. auth. see International Organization of Vacuum Sicence.

Preuss, Mary H. Gods of the Popol Vuh: Xmukane', K'ucumatz, Tojil, & Jurakan. LC 87-81583. (Illus.). 118p. 1988. pap. 23.00 (*0-911437-25-8*) Labyrinthos.

Preuss, Mary H., ed. Past, Present, & Future: Selected Papers on Latin American Indian Literature. LC 91-75066. (Illus.). 160p. (C). 1991. pap. text ed. 32.00 (*0-911437-45-2*) Labyrinthos.

Preuss, Mary M., ed. LAIL Speaks: Selected Papers from the 7th International Symposium on Latin American Indian Literatures. LC 90-60870. (Illus.). 160p. (Orig.). (C). 1990. pap. 32.00 (*0-911437-44-4*) Labyrinthos.

Preuss, Mary M., intro. In Love & War: Hummingbird Lore & Other Selected Papers from Laila - Alila's 1988 Symposium. LC 89-84020. (Illus.). 120p. (Orig.). (C). 1990. pap. 25.00 (*0-911437-42-8*) Labyrinthos.

Preuss, Paul. Arthur C. Clarke's Venus Prime, Vol. 6: The Shining Ones. 272p. (Orig.). 1991. pap. 3.95 (*0-380-75350-2*) Avon.

— Breaking Strain. (Arthur C. Clarke's Venus Prime Ser.: Vol. 1). 272p. 1987. mass mkt. 4.99 (*0-380-75344-8*) Avon.

— Broken Symmetries. LC 83-4809. 333p. 1983. 25.00 (*0-89366-151-1*) Ultramarine Pub.

— Core. 400p. 1994. mass mkt. 5.99 (*0-380-71182-6*, AvoNova) Avon.

— Core: A Novel. LC 93-12167. 1993. 23.00 (*0-688-09662-X*) Morrow.

— The Diamond Man. (Arthur C. Clarke's Venus Prime Ser.: Vol. 5). 1990. pap. 3.95 (*0-380-75349-9*) Avon.

— Hide & Seek. (Arthur C. Clarke's Venus Prime Ser.: Vol. 3). 288p. (Orig.). 1989. pap. 3.95 (*0-380-75346-4*) Avon.

— Maelstrom. (Arthur C. Clarke's Venus Prime Ser.: Vol. 2). 1988. mass mkt. 4.50 (*0-380-75345-6*) Avon.

— The Medusa Encounter. (Arthur C. Clarke's Venus Prime Ser.: Vol. 4). 304p. 1990. pap. 3.95 (*0-380-75348-0*) Avon.

Preuss, Peter. Epicurean Ethics: Katastematic Hedonism. LC 93-48974. (Studies in the History of Philosophy: Vol. 35). 288p. 1994. 89.95 (*0-7734-9124-4*) E Mellen.

— Reincarnation: An Inquiry into Its Possibility & Significance. LC 88-32604. (Problems in Contemporary Philosophy Ser.: Vol. 14). 266p. 1989. lib. bdg. 89.95 (*0-88946-342-5*) E Mellen.

Preuss, Peter, tr. see Fichte, Johann G.

Preuss, Peter, tr. see Nietzsche, Friedrich.

Preuss, S., jt. auth. see Menge, R.

Preuss, Siegmund. Index Demosthenicus. 330p. 1975. reprint ed. write for info. (*3-487-00542-5*, Pub. by Georg Olms GW) Lubrecht & Cramer.

— Index Isocrateus. 208p. 1974. reprint ed. write for info. (*3-487-04169-3*, Pub. by Georg Olms GW) Lubrecht & Cramer.

— Vollstandiges Lexikon Zu Den Pseudo-Casarianischen. 433p. 1964. reprint ed. write for info. (*0-318-71204-0*, Pub. by Georg Olms GW) Lubrecht & Cramer.

— Vollstandiges Lexikon Zu Den Pseudo-Casarianischen Schriftwerkern. 433p. 1964. reprint ed. write for info. (*0-318-72068-X*, Pub. by Georg Olms GW) Lubrecht & Cramer.

***Preuss, Ulrich K.** Constitutional Revolution: The Link Between Constitutionalism & Progress. Schneider, Deborah L., tr. LC 94-37939. 136p. (C). 1995. text ed. 45.00 (*0-391-03853-2*); pap. 15.00 (*0-391-03854-0*) Humanities.

Preussische Akademie der Wissenschaften Staff, ed. see Humboldt, Wilhelm Von.

Preussische Akademie der Wissenschaften Staff, ed. see Kant, Immanuel.

Preussler, Otfried. The Satanic Mill. (J). (gr. 5-9). 19.00 (*0-8446-6196-1*) Peter Smith.

— The Tale of the Unicorn. LC 88-7141. (Illus.). 32p. (J). (ps up). 1989. 12.95 (*0-8037-0583-2*) Dial Bks Young.

— The Tale of the Unicorn. (Illus.). 32p. (J). (ps up). 1992. pap. 4.99 (*0-14-054568-9*, Puff Pied Piper) Puffin Bks.

Preussmann, R., et al, eds. Environmental Carcinogens-Selected Methods of Analysis, Vol. 6: N-Nitroso Compounds. (Scientific Publications: No. 45). (Illus.). 1981. 73.50 (*0-19-723045-8*) OUP.

Prevallet, Elaine M. Interconnections. LC 85-61134. 32p. (Orig.). 1985. pap. 3.00 (*0-87574-261-0*) Pendle Hill.

— Reflections on Simplicity. LC 82-80439. 31p. 1982. pap. 3.00 (*0-87574-244-0*) Pendle Hill.

Prevedouros, P. D., jt. auth. see Papacostas, C. S.

***Prevel, Anne.** Dictionnaire de la Cuisine de Normandie. 160p. (FRE.). 1993. 39.95 (*0-7859-8120-9*, 2862531480) Fr & Eur.

Prevelakis, Pandelis. The Cretan. Rick, Abbott & Mackridge, Peter, trs. LC 91-62529. xvii, 480p. 1991. 35.00 (*0-932963-06-4*) Nostos Bks.

Prevenier, Walter & Blockmans, W. M. The Burgundian Netherlands. (Illus.). 420p. 1986. 125.00 (*0-521-30611-6*) Cambridge U Pr.

Prevention Editors. Hands-on Healing. Date not set. 14.99 (*0-517-09306-5*) Random Hse Value.

Prevention Magazine Editors. Doctor's Book of Home Remedies. 1991. pap. 6.99 (*0-553-29156-4*) Bantam.

— Doctors Book of Home Remedies for Children. 1995. mass mkt. 6.99 (*0-553-56985-6*) Bantam.

— Fighting Disease. LC 84-6971. (Prevention Total Health System Ser.). (Illus.). 176p. 1984. 17.95 (*0-87857-487-5*, 051760) Rodale Pr Inc.

— Foolproof Planting. 1994. 9.98 (*1-56731-040-0*, MJF Bks) Fine Comms.

— The Healing Foods Cookbook. (Illus.). 1994. 15.98 (*1-56731-037-0*, MJF Bks) Fine Comms.

— High Energy Living. LC 85-19606. 176p. 1986. 17.95 (*0-87857-554-5*, 05-184-0) Rodale Pr Inc.

— High Speed Healing: The Fastest, Safest & Most Effective Shortcuts to Lasting Relief. LC 91-7127. (Illus.). 576p. 1991. 29.95 (*0-87857-971-0*, 05-797-0) Rodale Pr Inc.

— Lifespan - Plus. 1994. 8.98 (*1-56731-025-7*, MJF Bks) Fine Comms.

— Lifespan-Plus: Nine Hundred Techniques to Live Longer. LC 90-35849. 432p. 1990. 23.95 (*0-87857-908-7*, 05-814-0) Rodale Pr Inc.

— Prevention Magazine's Nutrition Advisor. 1995. reprint ed. 12.98 (*1-56731-039-7*, MJF Bks) Fine Comms.

— Prevention Magazine's Nutrition Advisor: The Ultimate Guide to the Health-Boosting & Health-Harming Factors in Your Diet. Bricklin, Mark, ed. (Illus.). 596p. 1994. pap. 15.95 (*0-87596-225-4*) Rodale Pr Inc.

— Prevention Magazine's Quick & Healthy Low-Fat Cooking: Light Ways with Poultry. 128p. 1995. 21.95 (*0-87596-277-7*); pap. 15.95 (*0-87596-245-9*) Rodale Pr Inc.

— Prevention's Super Foods Cookbook: Two Hundred Fifty Delicious Recipes Using Nature's Healthiest Foods. LC 92-37485. (Illus.). 320p. 1993. 24.95 (*0-87596-167-3*) St Martin.

Prevention Magazine Editors & Bechtel, Stefan. The Practical Encyclopedia of Sex & Health: From Aphrodisiacs & Hormones to Potency, Stress, & Vasectomy. LC 92-35043. 352p. 1993. 26.95 (*0-87596-163-0*) Rodale Pr Inc.

— The Sex Encyclopedia. (Illus.). 352p. 1993. pap. 14.00 (*0-671-74324-4*, Fireside) S&S Trade.

Prevention Magazine Editors & Brenton, Myron. Aging Slowly. LC 83-13975. (Prevention Total Health System Ser.). (Illus.). 176p. 1984. 17.95 (*0-87857-465-4*, 05-129-0) Rodale Pr Inc.

Prevention Magazine Editors & Bricklin, Mark. Prevention Magazine's Nutrition Advisor. LC 91-46322. 608p. 1992. 29.95 (*0-87596-172-X*, 05-053-0) Rodale Pr Inc.

***Prevention Magazine Editors & Davis, Julie.** Young Skin for Life: Your Guide to Smoother, Clearer, More Beautiful Skin At Any Age, Vol. 1. 304p. 1995. pap. text ed. 14.95 (*0-87596-241-6*) Rodale Pr Inc.

Prevention Magazine Editors & Faelten, Sharon. The Allergy Self-Help Book: A Complete Guide to Nondrug Relief of Asthma, Hay Fever, Headaches, Fatigue, Digestive Problems & over 50 Other Allergy-Related Problems. LC 83-11197. 384p. 1983. 21.95 (*0-87857-458-1*, 05-121-0) Rodale Pr Inc.

Prevention Magazine Editors & Nugent, Nancy. Food & Nutrition. LC 83-10963. (Prevention Total Health System Ser.). (Illus.). 176p. 1984. 17.95 (*0-87857-464-6*, 05-128-0) Rodale Pr Inc.

Prevention Magazine Editors, jt. auth. see Davis, Julie.

Prevention Magazine Editors, jt. auth. see Rosensweig, Linda.

Prevention Magazine Editors, et al. Boost Your Brainpower: A Total Program to Sharpen Your Thinking & Age-Proof Your Mind. LC 91-3914. 480p. 1991. 26.95 (*0-87857-975-3*, 05-317-0) Rodale Pr Inc.

— Listen to Your Body. 1994. 9.98 (*1-56731-038-9*, MJF Bks) Fine Comms.

— The Thirty-Day Immune Power Program. 256p. (Orig.). 1992. pap. 14.95 (*0-87596-120-7*, 05-042-0) Rodale Pr Inc.

— Women's Encyclopedia of Health & Emotional Healing: Top Women Doctors Share Their Unique Self-Help Advice on Your Body, Your Feelings & Your Life. LC 92-23361. 1992. 27.95 (*0-87596-151-7*, 05-059-0) Rodale Pr Inc.

Prevention Magazine Editors Staff. Prevention Pain-Relief System: A Total Program for Relieving Any Pain in Your Body. 1994. pap. 6.99 (*0-553-56491-9*) Bantam.

***Prevention Magazine Food Editors.** Healthy Hometown Favorites: The Best-Loved Recipes from America's Community Cookbooks. (Illus.). 320p. 1995. 23.95 (*0-87596-251-3*) Rodale Pr Inc.

***Prevention Magazine Health Book Editors.** Healthy Home Cooking: Family Favorites Old & New for Today's Health-Conscious Cooks. LC 94-44421. (Prevention Magazine's Quick & Healthy Low-Fat Cooking Ser.). 128p. 1995. 25.95 (*0-87596-276-9*); pap. 15.95 (*0-87596-244-0*) Rodale Pr Inc.

— Prevention Magazine's Quick & Healthy Low-Fat Cooking: Pastas & Sauces. 128p. 1995. 21.95 (*0-87596-275-0*); pap. 15.95 (*0-87596-236-X*) Rodale Pr Inc.

— Prevention's System of Health & Natural Healing: Healing Yourself with Food. (Illus.). 176p. 1995. 19.95 (*0-87596-242-4*) Rodale Pr Inc.

— Your Family Will Love It: Quick & Healthy Weekday Meals for the Hard to Please. LC 94-23899. (Illus.). 368p. 1995. 26.95 (*0-87596-256-4*) Rodale Pr Inc.

Prevention Magazine Health Book Editors, ed. The Complete Book of Natural & Medicinal Cures: How to Choose the Most Potent Healing Agents for over 200 Conditions & Diseases. LC 94-4888. 1994. 29.95 (*0-87596-190-8*) Rodale Pr Inc.

Prevention Magazine Health Books Editors. The Doctor's Book of Home Remedies. LC 89-38656. 688p. 1990. 27.95 (*0-87857-873-0*, 05-627-0) Rodale Pr Inc.

— The Doctors' Book of Home Remedies for Children. (Illus.). 450p. (SPA.). 1995. 27.95 (*0-87596-266-1*) Rodale Pr Inc.

— The Prevention How-To Dictionary of Healing Remedies & Techniques: From Acupressure & Aspirin to Yoga & Yogurt, Over 350 Curative Options. LC 92-9053. (Illus.). 496p. 1992. 27.95 (*0-87596-114-2*, 05-041-0) Rodale Pr Inc.

— The Prevention Pain-Relief System: A Total Program for Relieving Any Pain in Your Body. LC 91-39791. (Illus.). 512p. 1992. 27.95 (*0-87596-104-5*, 05-213-0) Rodale Pr Inc.

— Prevention's Food & Nutrition: The Most Complete Book Ever Written on Using Food & Vitamins to Feel Healthy & Cure Disease. LC 92-39974. 544p. 1993. 27.95 (*0-87596-166-5*) Rodale Pr Inc.

Prevention Magazine Health Books Editors & Kirchheimer, Sid. The Doctors' Book of Home Remedies Two: Over 1,000 New Doctor-Tested Tops & Techniques Anyone Can Use to Heal Hundreds of Everyday Health Problems. LC 93-7754. 640p. 1993. 27.95 (*0-87596-158-4*) Rodale Pr Inc.

Prevention Magazine Health Books Editors & Monte, Tom. Staying Young: How to Prevent, Slow or Reverse More than 60 Signs of Aging. LC 93-39905. (Illus.). 352p. 1994. 24.95 (*0-87596-209-2*) Rodale Pr Inc.

Prevention Magazine Health Books Editors, et al. Disease Free: How to Prevent, Treat, & Cure More Than 150 Illnesses & Conditions. LC 92-23249. 600p. 1993. 27.95 (*0-87596-149-5*, 05-412-0) Rodale Pr Inc.

— The Doctors Book of Home Remedies for Children: From Allergies & Animal Bites to Toothache & TV Addiction: Hundreds of Doctor-Proven Techniques & Tips to Care for Your Kid. LC 93-5854. 1993. write for info. (*0-87596-183-5*) Rodale Pr Inc.

Prevention Magazine Health Books Staff. Age Erasers for Women: Actions You Can Take Right Now to Look Younger & Feel Great. (Illus.). 500p. 1994. 27.95 (*0-87596-214-9*) Rodale Pr Inc.

— Hands-On Healing: Massage Remedies for Hundreds of Health Problems. LC 88-32241. (Illus.). 448p. 1991. pap. 17.95 (*0-87857-966-4*, 05-725-1) Rodale Pr Inc.

— High Speed Healing: The Fastest, Safest, & Most Effective Shortcuts to Lasting Relief. 1993. mass mkt. 6.99 (*0-553-56476-5*) Bantam.

— Training the Body to Cure Itself: How to Use Exercise to Heal. (Illus.). 528p. 1992. 27.95 (*0-87596-131-2*, 05-692-0) Rodale Pr Inc.

***Prevention Magazine Health Books Staff, ed.** Curing Common Complaints: From Bad Breath & Blemishes to Fatigue, Heartburn, & Tooth Stains: the Best Doctor-Tested Tips to Relieve Everyday Health Concerns. (Family Home Remedies Collection). 1995. write for info. (*0-87596-262-9*) Rodale Pr Inc.

— Fighting Disease: Hundreds of Strategies for Preventing, Treating, & Curing Common Illnesses & Conditions. LC 94-24202. (Family Home Remedies Collection). 1995. write for info. (*0-87596-263-7*) Rodale Pr Inc.

— Keeping Kids Healthy: Cures & Remedies for Childhood Illnesses & Conditions. LC 94-24200. (Family Home Remedies Collection). 1995. write for info. (*0-87596-264-5*) Rodale Pr Inc.

— Self-Healing for Women: Let America's Top Doctors, Therapists, & Health Experts Solve Women's Unique Health Problems. LC 94-24203. (Family Home Remedies Collection). 1995. write for info. (*0-87596-265-3*) Rodale Pr Inc.

Prevention Magazine Health Books Staff, jt. ed. see Rogers, Jean.

Prevention Magazine Staff. Complete Book of Vitamins & Minerals. 1992. 14.99 (*0-517-08132-6*) Random Hse Value.

— Listen to Your Body. Date not set. 14.99 (*0-517-08129-6*) Random Hse Value.

— Prevention Magazine Everyday Health Tips. 1993. 14.99 (*0-517-08922-X*) Random Hse Value.

— Prevention's Giant Book of Health Facts. 1992. 14.99 (*0-517-08130-X*) Random Hse Value.

Prevention Magazine Staff, ed. All About Vitamins & Minerals: Key Nutrients for Optimum Health. (No Nonsense Health Guide Ser.). (Illus.). 88p. 1989. pap. 4.95 (*0-681-40715-8*) Longmeadow Pr.

— The Healing Foods Cookbook: Four Hundred Delicious Recipes with Curative Power. large type ed. (General Ser.). 855p. 1992. text ed. 23.95 (*0-8161-5520-8*, Large Print Bks); pap. 17.95 (*0-8161-5521-6*, Large Print Bks) Hall.

— Lower Your Blood Pressure: Controlling Your Blood Pressure without Drugs. (No Nonsense Health Guide Ser.). (Illus.). 88p. 1991. pap. 4.95 (*0-681-41022-1*) Longmeadow Pr.

— Permanent Weight Loss: An Easy, Sensible Program for a Slimmer You. (No Nonsense Health Guide Ser.). (Illus.). 88p. 1989. pap. 4.95 (*0-681-40716-6*) Longmeadow Pr.

— Unstress Your Life: How to Reduce Tension & Feel Great. (No Nonsense Health Guide Ser.). 86p. 1986. pap. 4.95 (*0-681-40135-4*) Longmeadow Pr.

— Walk for Health: How to Start a Personal Fitness Program. (No Nonsense Health Guide Ser.). (Illus.). 88p. 1991. pap. 4.95 (*0-681-41020-5*) Longmeadow Pr.

— Your Emotional Health & Well-Being: How to Cope with Stress & Feel Better Fast. (No Nonsense Health Guide Ser.). (Illus.). 88p. 1989. pap. 4.50 (*0-681-40717-4*) Longmeadow Pr.

Prevention Magazine Staff & Cooper, Kenneth, eds. Reducing Cholesterol: A Heart-Smart Guide to Low-Fat Eating. (No Nonsense Health Guide Ser.). (Illus.). 88p. 1989. pap. 4.95 (*0-681-40718-2*) Longmeadow Pr.

Prevention Magazine Staff, et al, eds. Symptoms: Their Causes & Cures - How to Understand & Treat 265 Health Concerns. LC 93-23014. 660p. 1994. 25.00 (*0-87596-179-7*) Rodale Pr Inc.

Prevert, Jacques. Arbres. (Illus.). 69p. (FRE.). 1976. pap. 17.95 (*0-7859-1348-3*, 2070295222) Fr & Eur.

— Blood & Feathers: Selected Poems of Jacques Prevert. Zinnes, Harriet, tr. 144p. 1993. reprint ed. pap. 11.95 (*1-55921-056-7*) Moyer Bell.

— Choses et Autres. 264p. (FRE.). 1975. pap. 10.95 (*0-7859-2355-1*, 2070366464) Fr & Eur.

— Choses et Autres. (Folio Ser.: No. 646). (FRE.). 1975. pap. 8.95 (*2-07-036646-4*) Schoenhof.

— Contes pour Enfants pas Sages. 89p. (FRE.). 1977. pap. 10.95 (*0-7859-1360-2*, 2070330214) Fr & Eur.

— Contes pour Enfants pas Sages. (Folio - Cadet Bleu Ser.: No. 181). (Illus.). 88p. (FRE.). (J). (gr. 1-5). 1990. pap. 12.95 (*2-07-031181-3*) Schoenhof.

— Fatras & Cinquante-Sept Images Composees par l'Auteur. (Folio Ser.: No. 877). 285p. (FRE.). 1977. 8.95 (*2-07-036877-7*) Schoenhof.

— Grand Bal du Printemps & Charmes de Londres. (Folio Ser.: No. 1075). 168p. (FRE.). 1976. 6.95 (*2-07-037075-5*) Schoenhof.

— Grand Bal du Printemps suivi de Charmes de Londres. 154p. (FRE.). 1979. pap. 10.95 (*0-7859-2410-8*, 2070370755) Fr & Eur.

— Hebdromadaires. 192p. (FRE.). 1974. pap. 10.95 (*0-7859-2332-2*, 2070365220) Fr & Eur.

— Histoires. 256p. (FRE.). 1972. pap. 10.95 (*0-7859-2266-0*, 2070361195) Fr & Eur.

— Histoires. (Folio Ser.: No. 119). 256p. (FRE.). 1972. 8.95 (*2-07-036119-5*) Schoenhof.

— Imaginaires. (Coll. Les Sentiers de la Creation). 25.00 (*0-685-37050-X*) Fr & Eur.

— Lettre des Iles Baladar. (Illus.). 93p. (FRE.). 1977. pap. 10.95 (*0-7859-1361-0*, 2070330257) Fr & Eur.

— Lettres des Iles Baladar. pap. 3.40 (*0-685-37051-8*) Fr & Eur.

— Oeuvres Completes. deluxe ed. 1536p. (FRE.). 1993. 150.00 (*0-7859-0965-6*, 2070112306) Fr & Eur.

— L' Opera de la Lune. (Illus.). 48p. (FRE.). 1986. pap. 10.95 (*0-7859-1381-5*, 2070391418) Fr & Eur.

— Paroles. 251p. (FRE.). 1976. pap. 10.95 (*0-7859-2400-0*, 2070367622) Fr & Eur.

— Paroles. (Folio Ser.: No. 762). (FRE.). 1957. pap. 8.95 (*2-07-036762-2*) Schoenhof.

— Paroles: Selected Poems. rev. ed. Ferlinghetti, Lawrence, tr. (Pocket Poets Ser.: No. 9). 176p. 1990. pap. 8.95 (*0-87286-249-6*) City Lights.

— La Pluie et le Beau Temps. (FRE.). 1972. pap. 10.95 (*0-7859-2264-4*, 2070360903) Fr & Eur.

— La Pluie et le Beau Temps. (Folio Ser.: No. 90). 256p. 1955. 8.95 (*2-07-036090-3*) Schoenhof.

— Soleil de Nuit. 310p. (FRE.). 1989. pap. 11.95 (*0-7859-2574-0*, 2070381757) Fr & Eur.

— Soleil de Nuit. (Folio Ser.). (FRE.). pap. 9.95 (*2-07-038175-7*) Schoenhof.

— Spectacle. (FRE.). 1972. pap. 11.95 (*0-7859-1628-8*, 2070361047) Fr & Eur.

— Spectacle. (Folio Ser.: No. 104). (FRE.). 1972. 9.95 (*2-07-036104-7*) Schoenhof.

— Tentatives de Description d'un Diner de Tetes a Paris-France. 9.65 (*0-685-37053-4*) Fr & Eur.

Prevert, Jacques & Carne, Marcel. Le Jour se Leve. 9.95 (*0-686-54911-2*) Fr & Eur.

— Les Visiteurs du Soir. (Illus.). 256p. 1974. 25.00 (*0-686-54920-1*) Fr & Eur.

Prevert, Jacques & Guilbaud, P. Les Primitifs du XIIIe. 5.95 (*0-686-54917-1*) Fr & Eur.

Prevert, Jacques & Lamorisse, Albert. Bim le Petit Ane. (Illus.). 48p. (FRE.). 1976. pap. 10.95 (*0-7859-1445-5*, 2211040659) Fr & Eur.

Prevert, Jacques & Prevert, P. Paris la Belle. 5.95 (*0-686-54914-7*) Fr & Eur.

Prevert, Joseph. Fatras. 285p. (FRE.). 1977. pap. 10.95 (*0-7859-2383-7*, 2070368777) Fr & Eur.

Prevert, P., jt. auth. see Prevert, Jacques.

Prevezer, Martha, jt. ed. see Dimsdale, Nicholas.

Previdi, Taimi. Art of Finnish Cooking. 290p. 1994. 19.95 (*0-7818-0284-9*) Hippocrene Bks.

P Q

An Asterisk (*) at the beginning of an entry indicates that the title is appearing in BIP for the first time.

Previn, Andre. Matthew's Piano Book. Date not set. pap. 9.95 (0-685-69091-1, Chester Music) Music Sales.

***Previtali, David R.** Raymond's Two Crowns. (Illus.). 48p. (YA). (gr. 6-12). 1994. pap. text ed. 3.95 (0-9625953-3-0) Immaculata Pr.

— Saints for Young Christians. (Orig.). 1996. pap. 9.95 (0-8189-0666-9) Alba.

Previte, Mary T. Hungry Ghosts: One Woman's Mission to Save America's Empty Souls. 224p. 1994. 15.99 (0-310-59420-0) Zondervan.

Previte-Orton, C. W. Political Satire in English Poetry. 244p. (C). 1966. text ed. 75.00 (0-8383-0676-4) M S G Haskell Hse.

Previte-Orton, Charles W. Outlines of Medieval History. 2nd ed. LC 64-25837. 1916. 25.00 (0-8196-0147-0) Biblo.

— The Shorter Cambridge Medieval History: The Twelfth Century to the Renaissance, Vol. 2. LC 75-31398. 579p. reprint ed. pap. 165.10 (0-318-34767-9, 2031627) Bks Demand.

Previts, Gary J. A Critical Evaluation of Comparative Financial Accounting Thought in America: 1900-1920. Brief, Richard P., ed. LC 80-1517. (Dimensions of Accounting Theory & Practice Ser.). 1980. lib. bdg. 28.95 (0-405-13496-7) Ayer.

Previts, Gary J., ed. Research in Accounting Regulation, Vol. 4. 1991. 73.25 (1-55938-084-5) Jai Pr.

Previts, Gary J., frwd. Accountics: April 1897 to August 1900, 3 vols., Set. LC 10-601228. (New Works in Accounting History). 1128p. 1992. 270.00 (0-8153-0683-0) Garland.

Previts, Gary J. & Taylor, Richard F. Lest We Forget...John Raymond Wildman, 1878-1938. (Monograph Series of the Academy of Accounting Historians: Monograph 2). 84p. 1978. pap. 5.00 (1-879750-00-7) Acad Acct Hist.

Previts, Gary J., jt. ed. see Brief, Richard P.

Previts, Gary J., ed. see Symposium on Financial Reporting & Standard Setting Staff.

Previtts, Gary J., jt. auth. see Magill, Harry T.

Prevo, Helen R. English That We Need. 64p. 1986. teacher ed 1.25 (0-88323-221-9, 203); pap. 4.50 (0-88323-212-X, 109) Pendergrass Pub.

— More English That We Need. 64p. 1984. teacher ed 1.25 (0-88323-237-5, 261); pap. 4.50 (0-88323-198-0, 155) Pendergrass Pub.

Prevos, Andre J., tr. see Springer, Robert.

Prevost, Abbe. Manon Lescaut. (Folio Ser.: No. 757). 249p. (FRE.). 1988. pap. 8.95 (2-07-036757-6) Schoenhof.

Prevost, Abbe F. Histoire du Chevalier Des Grieux et de Manon Lescaut. Deloffre & Picard, eds. (Class. Garnier Ser.). 27.95 (0-685-34051-1); pap. 14.95 (0-685-34050-3) Fr & Eur.

— Histoire du Chevalier Des Grieux et de Manon Lescaut. 1976. pap. 10.95 (0-7859-2883-9) Fr & Eur.

— Histoire d'un Grecque Moderne. (FRE.). 1990. pap. 16.95 (0-7859-3000-0) Fr & Eur.

— Manon Lescaut. (FRE.). 1976. pap. 8.95 (0-7859-3078-7) Fr & Eur.

— Manon Lescaut. 1983. pap. 3.50 (0-452-00654-6, Mer) NAL-Dutton.

— Manon Lescaut. Tancock, Leonard W., tr. 192p. 1988. mass mkt. 4.95 (0-14-044498-X, Penguin Classics) Viking Penguin.

— Manon Lescaut. Sgard, Jean, ed. Tancock, Leonard W., tr. 192p. 1992. 9.95 (0-14-044559-5, Penguin Classics) Viking Penguin.

Prevost, Abbe F., jt. auth. see Honegger, M.

Prevost, Antoine F. Manon Lescaut. Waddell, Helen, tr. LC 76-48453. (Library of World Literature Ser.). 1992. reprint ed. 30.00 (0-88355-600-6) Hyperion Conn.

Prevost, Antoine-Francois. Manon. Waddell, Helen, tr. LC 88-60594. 262p. 1988. reprint ed. pap. 14.95 (0-948166-15-0, Pub. by Soho Bk Co UK) Dufour.

— The Story of a Fair Greek of Yesteryear: A Translation from the French of Antoine-Francois Prevost's "L'Histoire D'Une Grecque Moderne" Jones, James F., Jr., tr. 294p. 1984. 30.00 (0-916379-08-6) Scripta.

Prevost, Bernard. God's Dream: His Plan for Us. (C). 1988. 39.00 (0-85439-262-9, Pub. by St Paul Pubns UK) St Mut.

Prevost, Dale. Update Map Co. 102p. reprint ed. spiral bd. 18.00 (0-685-29952-X) Update Map.

Prevost, Gary, jt. ed. see Castro, Vanessa.

Prevost, Gary, jt. ed. see Chaffee, Wilbur R., Jr.

Prevost, Gary, jt. ed. see Lancaster, Thomas D.

Prevost, Gary, jt. auth. see Vanden, Harry E.

Prevost, Jean-Pierre. How to Read the Apocalypse. (Illus.). 160p. 1993. reprint ed. pap. 15.95 (0-8245-1280-4) Crossroad NY.

***Prevost, John F.** Beluga Whales. LC 95-6374. (J). 1995. lib. bdg. 9.95 (1-56239-477-0) Abdo & Dghtrs.

— Blue Whales. LC 95-9676. (J). 1995. lib. bdg. 9.95 (1-56239-475-4) Abdo & Dghtrs.

— Bottlenose Dolphins. LC 95-3316. (Dolphins Ser.). (J). 1995. lib. bdg. 9.95 (1-56239-493-2) Abdo & Dghtrs.

— Common Dolphin. LC 95-12363. (Dolphins Ser.). (J). 1995. write for info. (1-56239-496-7) Abdo & Dghtrs.

— Freshwater Dolphins. LC 95-3315. (Dolphins Ser.). (J). 1995. lib. bdg. 9.95 (1-56239-492-4) Abdo & Dghtrs.

— Gray Whales. LC 95-9677. (J). 1995. lib. bdg. 9.95 (1-56239-476-2) Abdo & Dghtrs.

— Great White Sharks. LC 95-1511. (Sharks Ser.). (J). 1995. lib. bdg. 9.95 (1-56239-469-X) Abdo & Dghtrs.

— Hammerhead Sharks. LC 95-1171. (Sharks Ser.). (J). 1995. lib. bdg. 9.95 (1-56239-471-1) Abdo & Dghtrs.

— The Humpback Whale. LC 95-12367. (Whales Ser.). (J). 1995. write for info. (1-56239-479-7) Abdo & Dghtrs.

— Killer Whales. LC 95-2750. (Whales Ser.). (J). 1995. lib. bdg. 9.95 (1-56239-474-6) Abdo & Dghtrs.

— Sand Sharks. LC 95-3314. (Sharks Ser.). (J). 1995. lib. bdg. 9.95 (1-56239-470-3) Abdo & Dghtrs.

— Sperm Whale. LC 95-12364. (J). 1995. write for info. (1-56239-478-9) Abdo & Dghtrs.

— Tiger Sharks. LC 95-2749. (Sharks Ser.). (J). 1995. lib. bdg. 9.95 (1-56239-468-1) Abdo & Dghtrs.

— Whale Sharks. LC 95-6375. (J). 1995. lib. bdg. 9.95 (1-56239-473-8) Abdo & Dghtrs.

— White-Sided Dolphin. LC 95-8121. (J). 1995. write for info. (1-56239-494-0) Abdo & Dghtrs.

Prevost, Marie-Laure, ed. see Rolland, Romain.

Prevost, Michel & Roman-D'Amat, Jean-Claude. Dictionnaire de Biographie Francaise: French Biographical Dictionary, 16 vols., Set. 8040p. (FRE.). 1972. 2,495.00 (0-8288-6370-9, M-6466) Fr & Eur.

Prevost, Nancy M. Paradise in the Palouse. 36p. (Orig.). 1985. pap. 4.95 (0-87770-365-5) Ye Galleon.

Prevost, P., jt. auth. see Honegger, M.

Prevost, Robert. Montreal: A History. 1993. 29.95 (0-7710-7034-9, Pub. by McClelland & Stewart CN) Firefly Bks Ltd.

— Probability & Theistic Explanation. (Oxford Theological Monographs). 208p. 1990. 59.00 (0-19-826735-5) OUP.

Prevost, Robert W., jt. ed. see Abraham, William J.

***Prevost, Ruffin.** Internet Insider. 1995. pap. text ed. 14.95 (0-07-882084-7) Osborne-McGraw.

Prevost, Ruffin & Terrell, Rob. The Mac Shareware 500: The Last Word on the Best, Virus-Free Mac Shareware. 2nd ed. (Illus.). 504p. 1994. disk, pap. 34.95 (1-56604-076-0) Ventana Pr.

— The Mac Shareware 500: The Last Word on the Best, Virus-Free, System 7 Savvy Macintosh Shareware. (Illus.). 475p. disk, pap. 39.95 (0-940087-89-8) Ventana Pr.

Prevost, S. Vertex Algebras & Integral Bases for the Enveloping Algebras of Affine Lie Algebras. LC 91-44874. 97p. 1992. 25.00 (0-8218-2527-5, MEMO 96/466) Am Math.

Prevost, Toni J. The Delaware & Shawnee Admitted to Cherokee Citizenship & the Related Wyandotte & Moravian Delaware. viii, 123p. (Orig.). 1993. pap. text ed. 21.50 (1-55613-761-3) Heritage Bk.

— Indians from New York in Wisconsin & Elsewhere: A Genealogy Reference. 228p. (Orig.). 1995. pap. text ed. 27.00 (0-7884-0209-9) Heritage Bk.

Prevot, Andre. Love, Peace & Joy: Devotion to the Sacred Heart of Jesus According to St. Gertrude. LC 84-51822. 224p. 1985. reprint ed. pap. 5.00 (0-89555-255-8) TAN Bks Pubs.

Prevot, Floriane. Dictionnaire de la Beaute Feminine. 268p. (FRE.). 1972. pap. 10.95 (0-7859-1444-7, 2203221011) Fr & Eur.

Prevot, Floriane & Roman-D'Amat, Jean-Claude. Dictionnaire de Biographie Francaise, Fasc. 1018 & 31-60. 230.00 (0-685-35951-4) Fr & Eur.

Prevots, Naima. American Pageantry: A Movement for Art & Democracy. LC 89-29255. (Theatre & Dramatic Studies: No. 61). 266p. (C). reprint ed. 73.30 (0-8357-1991-X, 2070682) Bks Demand.

— Dancing in the Sun: Hollywood Choreographers, 1915-1937. Brockett, Oscar, ed. LC 87-13859. (Theater & Dramatic Studies: No. 44). (Illus.). 292p. reprint ed. pap. 82.70 (0-8357-1825-5, 2070754) Bks Demand.

Prewett, P. D. & Mair, G. L. Focused Ion Beams from Liquid Metal Ion Sources. (Electronic & Electrical Engineering Research Ser.). 332p. 1991. text ed. 155.00 (0-471-93088-1) Wiley.

Prewit, John. The Lucky Bastard. (Illus.). 285p. 1983. pap. 15.00 (0-910303-05-3) Writers Pub Serv.

Prewit-Parker, Jolene. Bahama Rapture. (Orig.). 1982. pap. 3.50 (0-8217-1018-4) Zebra.

— Homecoming. 1990. mass mkt. 4.50 (0-8217-2923-3) Zebra.

— Lovers & Deceivers. 1989. pap. 3.95 (0-8217-2705-2) Zebra.

— Reckless Abandon. 448p. (Orig.). 1988. pap. 3.95 (0-8439-2566-3) Dorchester Pub Co.

— Sweet Paradise. 448p. (Orig.). 1988. pap. 3.95 (0-8439-2639-2) Dorchester Pub Co.

— Sweet Stolen Passion. 448p. 1993. mass mkt. 4.50 (0-8217-4218-3) Zebra.

Prewitt, Bobby W. & Butler, Kathleen A. Learning Styles & Performance Assessment: A Model Teaching Guide. 208p. (Orig.). 1993. pap. text ed. 22.95 (0-945852-04-5) Learners Dimension.

Prewitt, C. T., ed. Pyroxenes. (Reviews in Mineralogy Ser.: Vol. 7). 525p. 1980. per. 10.00 (0-939950-07-3) Mineralogical Soc.

Prewitt, Kenneth. Introduction American Government. 6th ed. (C). 1991. pap. text ed. 34.50 (0-06-045279-X) HarpCollege.

— The Recruitment of Political Leaders: A Study of Citizen-Politicians. LC 81-6344. (Urban Government Ser.). (Illus.). 234p. 1981. reprint ed. text ed. 59.75 (0-313-22744-6, PRRP, Greenwood Pr) Greenwood.

Prewitt, Kenneth & Verba. Introduction American Government: Study Guide. 6th ed. (C). 1991. 16.00 (0-06-500077-3) HarpCollege.

Prewitt, Kenneth, jt. auth. see Eulau, Heinz.

Prewitt, Roger W. & Fardo, Stephen W. Electronic Instrumentation: A Lab Text. 2nd ed. (Illus.). 220p. (C). 1983. reprint ed. pap. text ed. 16.95 (0-89917-387-X) Tichenor Pub.

Prewitt, Roger W., jt. auth. see Fardo, Stephen W.

Prewitt, Terry, jt. ed. see Deely, John.

Prewitt, Terry, et al, eds. Semiotics, 1988. LC 84-640162. (Illus.). 612p. (C). 1989. lib. bdg. 103.00 (0-8191-7478-5, Semiotic Society of America) U Pr of Amer.

Prewitt, Terry J. The Elusive Covenant: A Structural-Semiotic Reading of Genesis. (Illus.). 160p. 1990. 20.00 (0-253-34599-5) Ind U Pr.

— German-American Settlement in an Oklahoma Town: Ecologic, Ethnic & Cultural Change. LC 89-84003. (Immigrant Communities & Ethnic Minorities in the U. S. & Canada Ser.: No. 56). 1989. 52.50 (0-404-19466-4) AMS Pr.

Prewitt, Terry J., jt. auth. see Blanchard, Dallas A.

Prewitt, Vana, ed. Productivity Management. (ACCRUE Ser.: Level II). 175p. 1991. ring bd. 63.00 (1-879907-01-1) Am Soc Hlth-Syst.

Prey, Hermann. First Night Fever. Shackelton, Andrew, tr. LC 86-6491. (Illus.). 1991. 24.95 (0-7145-3998-8) Riverrun NY.

— First Night Fever. Shackelton, Andrew, tr. LC 86-6491. (Illus.). 288p. 1996. pap. 14.95 (0-7145-4102-8) Riverrun NY.

***Preyde, James & Preyde, Susan.** A Century of Gold: (Yukon Gold: High Hopes & Dashed Dreams) 1995. pap. 15.95 (0-88839-362-8) Hancock House.

— Steeple Chase: Ontario's Historic Churches. (Illus.). 72p. 20.00 (1-55046-030-7, Pub. by Boston Mills Pr CN) Genl Dist Srvs.

Preyde, Susan, jt. auth. see Preyde, James.

Preyer, Gerhard, et al, eds. Language, Mind, & Epistomology: On Don Davidson's Philosophy. LC 94-7208. (Synthese Library). 464p. (C). 1994. lib. bdg. 149.00 (0-7923-2811-6) Kluwer Ac.

Preyer, William. Embryonic Motility & Sensitivity. (SRCD Ser.: Vol. 2, No. 6). 1937. 12.00 (0-527-01499-0) Periodicals Srv.

— Mental Development in the Child. Brown, H. W., tr. LC 78-72818. (Brainedness, Handedness, & Mental Abilities Ser.). reprint ed. 18.50 (0-404-60887-6) AMS Pr.

— The Mind of the Child, 2 vols. in 1. LC 73-2985. (Classics in Psychology Ser.). 1977. reprint ed. 47.95 (0-405-05156-5) Ayer.

Preyma, Nadia, et al. Management Tools. Schulz, William, ed. (Options Ser.). 129p. (Orig.). (gr. 1-8). 1989. teacher ed, pap. 8.95 (0-920541-59-3) Peguis Pubs Ltd.

Prez, Cecilio. Addimu: Ofrendas a Los Orichas. LC 88-82519. (Illus.). 201p. (SPA.). (C). 1988. pap. 24.95 (0-918901-51-0) Obaecun Bks.

Prezbindowski. A Study Guide to Accompany Anthony Textbook. 11th ed. 370p. 1993. pap. 15.95 (0-8016-4011-3) Mosby Yr Bk.

Prezbindowski, Kathleen S. & Tortora, Gerard J. Learning Guide for Tortora & Grabowski Principles of Anatomy & Physiology. 7th rev. ed. LC 92-48208. (C). 1990. 14.00 (0-06-045374-5) HarpCollege.

Prezeau, Jael, ed. see Lynde, Stan.

Prezelin, Bernard, ed. Naval Institute Guide to Combat Fleets of the World, 1995: Their Ships, Aircraft, & Armament. (Illus.). 1088p. 1995. 145.00 (1-55750-109-2) Naval Inst Pr.

Prezelski, Carmen V., tr. see Cabat, Erni.

Prezelski, Carmen V., tr. see Cabat, Erni & Polzer, Charles W.

Preziosi, Donald. Architecture, Language & Meaning. (Approaches to Semiotics Ser.: No. 49). 1979. pap. text ed. 35.00 (90-279-7828-X) Mouton.

— Minoan Architectural Design: Formation & Signification. LC 82-22415. (Approaches to Semiotics Ser.: No. 63). xxxi, 522p. 1983. 133.85 (90-279-3409-6) Mouton.

— Rethinking Art History: Meditations on a Coy Science. (Illus.). 296p. (C). 1991. reprint ed. pap. text ed. 14.00 (0-300-04983-8) Yale U Pr.

— The Semiotics of the Built Environment: An Introduction to Architectonic Analysis. LC 78-20404. (Advances in Semiotics Ser.). 126p. pap. 36.50 (0-8357-3956-2, 2057052) Bks Demand.

Preziosi, Giochi, tr. see Perego, Maria.

Preziosi, L., jt. auth. see Monaco, R.

Prezwalski, Jim. The Kiss of the Whip: Explorations in SM. 256p. (Orig.). 1994. pap. 15.95 (0-943595-51-7) Leyland Pubns.

Prezzolini, Giuseppe. The Case of the Casa Italiana. LC 76-9908. 63p. 1976. 3.00 (0-916322-14-9) Am Inst Ital Stud.

— Fascism. Macmillan, Kathleen, tr. LC 78-63707. (Studies in Fascism: Ideology & Practice). 1977. reprint ed. 37.50 (0-404-16977-5) AMS Pr.

Prezzolini, Giuseppe, jt. auth. see Marchione, Margherita.

P.R.G. Holland Staff, jt. auth. see D.D. Prentice Staff.

***Pri, Michael.** Cupid & the King. 1995. 20.00 (0-00-223911-6, Pub. by HarpC UK) HarpC.

***Prial, Frank.** Companion to Wine. 1994. pap. 34.98 (0-8317-4237-2) Smithmark.

— Wine Talk. LC 78-58165. 1978. write for info. (0-8129-0793-0, Times Bks) Random.

Priamos, James S., jt. auth. see Hughes, Joseph H., Jr.

Prianishnikoff, Boris. Novopokolenstsy. (Illus.). 320p. 1986. write for info. (0-9616413-1-2) Multilingual.

Pribble, L. W., Jr. Planning & Construction of Remote Communities. LC 84-2323. 248p. 1984. 39.95 (0-471-88784-6) Wiley.

Pribble, Wayne I., jt. ed. see Buckleitner, Eric.

Pribble, Wayne I., jt. auth. see DuBois, J. Harry.

Pribic, Rado, ed. Nobel Laureates in Literature: A Biographical Dictionary. LC 89-11803. 497p. 1990. 95.00 (0-8240-5741-4, H849) Garland.

Pribic, Rado, jt. ed. see Wollenberg, Jorg.

Pribic, Rado, tr. see Wollenberg, Jorg & Pribic, Rado, eds.

Pribicevic-Zoric, Christina, tr. see Pavic, Milorad.

Pribichevich, Stoyan. Macedonia: Its People & History. LC 82-80455. (Illus.). 304p. 1982. 32.50 (0-271-00315-4) Pa St U Pr.

Pribil, F. Analytical Application of EDTA & Related Compounds. 368p. (C). 1972. 160.00 (0-08-016363-7, Pub. by Pergamon Repr UK) Franklin.

Pribil, R. Applied Complexometry, Vol.5. Stulikova, M. et al, trs. (Analytical Chemistry Ser.). (Illus.). 425p. 1982. 176.00 (0-08-026277-5, Pub. by Pergamon Repr UK) Franklin.

Pribor, Hugo C. The Laboratory Consultant. (Illus.). 792p. 1991. pap. 63.50 (0-8121-1387-X) Williams & Wilkins.

Pribor, Hugo C., et al. Drug Monitoring & Pharmacokinetic Data. LC 79-90657. 190p. 29.50 (0-930376-10-2) Chem-Orbital.

Pribram, Alfred F. Austria-Hungary & Great Britain, 1908-1914. LC 70-138174. 328p. 1972. reprint ed. text ed. 59.75 (0-8371-5631-9, PRAG, Greenwood Pr) Greenwood.

Pribram, E. Deidre, ed. Female Spectators: Looking at Film & Television. (Questions for Feminism Ser.). 224p. 1988. text ed. 39.95 (0-86091-204-3, Pub. by Verso UK); pap. text ed. 14.95 (0-86091-922-6, Pub. by Verso UK) Routledge Chapman & Hall.

Pribram, John G. Horizons of Hope: An Autobiography. LC 91-76307. 115p. 1991. 12.95 (1-880488-08-6); pap. 6.95 (1-880488-09-4) HP Print.

Pribram, Karl. Cartel Problems: An Analysis of Collective Monopolies in Europe with American Application: The Institute of Economics of the Brookings Institution, No. 69. (Business Enterprises Reprint Ser.). x, 287p. 1986. reprint ed. lib. bdg. 40.00 (0-89941-479-6, 304060) W S Hein.

— A History of Economic Reasoning. LC 82-13042. 832p. (C). 1983. text ed. 75.00 (0-8018-2291-2) Johns Hopkins.

***Pribram, Karl, ed.** Origins: Brain & Self Organization. (INNS Ser.). 728p. 1994. text ed. 110.00 (0-8058-1786-7) L Erlbaum Assocs.

— Rethinking Neural Networks: Quantum Fields & Biological Data. 568p. 1993. pap. 95.00 (0-8058-1466-3) L Erlbaum Assocs.

Pribram, Karl H. Brain & Perception: Holonomy & Structure in Figural Processing. (John M. MacEachran Lectures Ser.). 400p. 1991. 79.95 (0-89859-995-4) L Erlbaum Assocs.

— Languages of the Brain: Experimental Paradoxes & Principles in Neuropsychology. 5th ed. 432p. 1982. reprint ed. text ed. 35.00 (0-913412-22-8) Brandon Hse.

Pribram, Karl H., jt. ed. see Isaacson, Robert L.

Pribula. Lab Manual Experiments to General Chemistry by P. W. Atkins. (C). 1995. write for info. (0-7167-2042-6) W H Freeman.

— Lab Manual for General Chemistry by P. W. Atkins. (C). 1995. pap. text ed. write for info. (0-7167-2022-1) W H Freeman.

Pribus, Marilyn, ed. see Williamson, Bonnie.

Pribyl, Virginia M. Recipes for Living. (Illus.). 160p. (Orig.). 1988. pap. 9.95 (0-9621089-0-1) VMP Servs.

Pribylovskii, Vladimir. Dictionary of Political Parties & Organizations in Russia. Sloan, Dauphine & Helmstadter, Sarah, eds. (Significant Issues Ser.). 1992. pap. text ed. 21.00 (0-89206-180-4) CSI Studies.

Pribytkov, Victor, ed. Soviet U. S. Relations: The Selected Speeches & Writings of Chernenko. LC 84-23789. 218p. 1984. text ed. 45.00 (0-275-91243-4, C1243, Praeger Pubs) Greenwood.

Pric, Wilson. First Look at dBASE IV, Version 1.5-2.0 for DOS. 1993. pap. text ed. write for info. (0-07-051075-X) McGraw.

Pricard, B. Serbian-Croation-English Maritime Dictionary. 285p. 1989. 32.00 (86-03-99208-8) IBD Ltd.

— Serbo-Croatian-English Dictionary of Maritime Terms. 285p. (CRO, ENG & SER.). 1989. 29.95 (0-8288-7251-1, 8603992088) Fr & Eur.

***Price.** Antinuclear Movement. 1995. text ed. 40.00 (0-8161-7268-4) G K Hall.

— Corporate Venturing in Health Care. (Orig.). 1989. pap. write for info. (0-8273-4332-9) Delmar.

— An Introduction to Multicomplex Spaces & Functions. (Pure & Applied Mathematics Ser.: Vol. 140). 424p. 1991. 125.00 (0-8247-8345-X) Dekker.

— Mountain Research in Europe: An Overview of MAB Research from the Pyreness to Siberia. LC 94-27565. 1994. 65.00 (1-85070-570-4) Prthnon Pub.

— On the Wall: Presenting Maroon Tradition-Bearers at the 1992 Festival of American Folklife. 1995. pap. text ed. 12.00 (1-879407-06-X) IN Univ Folk Inst.

— Pathophysiology: Clinical Concepts of Disease Processes. (Illus.). 1137p. 1991. 55.95 (0-8016-6051-3) Mosby Yr Bk.

— Regulatory Reporting Compliance Handbook: 1994 Edition. 1994. pap. text ed. 60.00 (1-55738-704-4) Probus Pub Co.

— Relational Database. 1988. text ed. write for info. (0-07-556424-6) McGraw.

— Right Every Time: Using the Deming Approach. 216p. 1990. 69.75 (0-8247-8328-X) Dekker.

— Securities Compliance Handbook: 1994 Edition. 1994. pap. text ed. 60.00 (1-55738-706-0) Probus Pub Co.

— Trust Compliance Handbook: 1994 Edition. 1994. pap. text ed. 60.00 (1-55738-707-9) Probus Pub Co.

— Workbook for Affective Legal Research. 5th ed. 1979. 9.95 (0-316-71855-6) Little.

Price, ed. see Cervantes.

Price, jt. auth. see Grossman.

Price, jt. auth. see Turner.

Price, et al. Modern Agriculture: Science, Finance, Production & Economics. (Illus.). 361p. 1989. teacher ed 27.95 (0-9606246-7-8); student ed 14.95 (0-9606246-8-6); lib. bdg. 34.50 (0-9606246-6-X) SWI.

Price, A., jt. ed. see Ball, J.

Price, A. F. & Mou-Lam, Wong, trs. The Diamond Sutra & the Sutra of Hui-Neng. 1974. pap. 9.95 (0-394-73019-4) Shambhala Pubns.

— The Diamond Sutra & the Sutra of Hui Neng. LC 78-237407. 192p. 1974. reprint ed. pap. 14.00 (0-87773-005-9) Shambhala Pubns.

PQ

Price, A. Grenfell, ed. see Cook, James.

Price, A. Lindsay. Swans of the World: In Nature, History, Myth & Art. (Illus.). 220p. 1994. 26.95 (0-933031-81-5) Coun Oak Bks.

Price, A. St. J. Buying a Shop. 128p. (Orig.). 1990. pap. text ed. 20.95 (0-8464-1373-6) Beekman Pubs.

Price, A. W. Mental Conflict. LC 94-3935. (Issues in Ancient Philosophy Ser.). 208p. 1994. 49.95x (0-415-04151-1, B4613); pap. 15.95 (0-415-11557-4, B4617) Routledge.

Price, Alan, jt. ed. see Joslin, Katherine.

Price, Alfred. Air Battle Central Europe. 200p. 1987. text ed. 22.95 (0-02-925451-5) Free Pr.

— The Last Year of the Luftwaffe: May 1944 - May 1945. (Illus.). 192p. 1995. pap. 14.95 (1-85409-189-1) Sterling.

— The Last Year of the Luftwaffee. (Illus.). 224p. 1991. 24.95 (0-87938-555-3) Motorbooks Intl.

— Pictorial History of the Luftwaffe. (Illus.). 160p. 1992. 29.95 (0-87938-640-1) Motorbooks Intl.

— Sky Battles: Dramatic Air Warfare Actions. (Illus.). 176p. 1994. 24.95 (1-85409-191-3) Sterling.

Price, Alfred, jt. auth. see Ethell, Jeffrey L.

Price, Alfred, jt. auth. see Ethell, Jeffrey.

Price, Alice L., ed. see Baron, Enid.

Price, Alvin & Parry, Jay A. Discipline: One Hundred One Alternatives to Nagging, Yelling & Spanking. (Illus.). 172p. (C). 1983. pap. 7.95 (0-944803-68-7) Brite Music.

Price, Andrew & Humphrey, Sarah, eds. Application of the Biosphere Reserve Concept to Coastal Marine Areas: Papers Presented at the UNESCO-IUCN San Francisco Workshop, 14-20 August 1989. 114p. (C). 1993. pap. text ed. 10.00 (2-8317-0135-X, Pub. by IUCN SZ) Island Pr.

Price, Ann & Palmer, Pati. The Serger Idea Book. 2nd ed. (Illus.). 160p. 1991. pap. 19.95 (0-935278-18-4) Palmer-Pletsch.

Price, Ann, ed. see Hickey, Mary.

Price, Anne & Dana, Nancy B. The Working Woman's Guide to Breastfeeding. 146p. 1987. pap. 7.00 (0-671-63624-3) S&S Trade.

Price, Anne, jt. auth. see Dana, Nancy.

Price, Anne J., jt. auth. see Morton, Herbert C.

Price, Annie, jt. auth. see Davis, Dee.

Price, Anthony. The Alamut Ambush. large type ed. (Adventure Suspense Ser.). 406p. 1988. 15.95 (0-7089-1854-9) Ulverscroft.

— The Eyes of the Fleet: A Popular History of Frigates & Frigate Captains 1793-1815. (Illus.). 304p. 1996. 25.00 (0-393-03846-7) Norton.

— The Forty-Four Vintage. large type ed. 1979. 12.00 (0-7089-0287-1) Ulverscroft.

— Gunner Kelly. large type ed. (Adventure Suspense Ser.). 416p. 1988. 15.95 (0-7089-1918-9) Ulverscroft.

— Here Be Monsters. 256p. 1986. 15.95 (0-89296-154-6) Mysterious Pr.

— The Labyrinth Makers. large type ed. 369p. 1981. 12.00 (0-7089-0711-3) Ulverscroft.

— The Memory Trap. LC 91-7305. 224p. 1991. 18.95 (0-922890-87-0); 25.00 (0-922890-88-9) Armchair Detective.

— The Memory Trap. limited ed. LC 91-7305. 224p. 1991. 75.00 (0-922890-89-7) Armchair Detective.

— A Prospect of Vengeance. LC 90-39385. 256p. 1990. 18.95 (0-922890-51-X); 25.00 (0-922890-52-8) Armchair Detective.

— A Prospect of Vengeance. limited ed. LC 90-39385. 256p. 1990. 75.00 (0-922890-53-6) Armchair Detective.

— War Game. large type ed. (Adventure Suspense Ser.). 512p. 1988. 15.95 (0-7089-1870-0) Ulverscroft.

Price, Archibald G. The Western Invasions of the Pacific & Its Continents: A Study of Moving Frontiers & Changing Landscapes, 1513-1958. LC 80-14037. (Illus.). xi, 236p. 1980. reprint ed. text ed. 38.50 (0-313-22433-1, PRWE, Greenwood Pr) Greenwood.

— White Settlers & Native Peoples: An Historical Study of Racial Contacts Between English-Speaking Whites & Aboriginal Peoples in the United States, Canada, Australia, & New Zealand. LC 71-142320. (Illus.). 232p. 1972. reprint ed. text ed. 59.75 (0-8371-5923-7, PRWH) Greenwood.

— White Settlers in the Tropics. LC 75-41217. reprint ed. 72.50 (0-404-14731-3) AMS Pr.

Price, Ardin C. & Leszczyc, Trishna. The Dracula Cookbook of Blood. 160p. (Orig.). Date not set. pap. 14.95 (1-883281-42-3) Mugwort Soup.

Price, Arlen. Five Hundred Things Your Sunday School Teacher Tried to Tell You. 1992. pap. 5.99 (1-56233-038-1) Star Song TN.

Price, Arnold H., ed. Missionary to the Malagasy: The Madagascar Diary of the Rev. Charles T. Price, 1875-1877. (American University Studies: History: Ser. IX, Vol. 60). 273p. (C). 1989. text ed. 48.00 (0-8204-1083-7) P Lang Pubs.

Price, Arthur & Cohen, Allen C. Fabric Science. 5th ed. (Illus.). 450p. 1987. 25.00 (0-87005-571-2) Fairchild.

— Fabric Science Swatch Kit & Binder, 1990. 1990. pap. 20.00 (0-87005-735-9) Fairchild.

Price, Ashland. Autumn Angel. 1990. mass mkt. 4.25 (0-8217-2933-0) Zebra.

— Cajun Caress. 1990. mass mkt. 4.25 (0-8217-3109-2) Zebra.

— Viking Flame. 448p. 1993. mass mkt. 4.50 (0-8217-4323-6) Zebra.

— Viking Rose. 480p. 1993. mass mkt. 4.50 (0-8217-4030-X) Zebra.

— Viking Tempest. 448p. 1994. mass mkt. 4.50 (0-8217-4716-9) Zebra.

— Wild Irish Heather. 384p. 1991. mass mkt. 4.25 (0-8217-3326-5) Zebra.

Price, B. B. Medieval Thought: An Introduction. 256p. (C). 1991. pap. text ed. 21.95 (0-631-17509-1) Blackwell Pubs.

Price, B. B., jt. auth. see Hamouda, O. F.

Price, B. Byron. Lougheed. (Illus.). 148p. 1991. 65.00 (0-9620327-2-7) Nygard Pub.

Price, B. J., jt. ed. see Roberts, S. M.

***Price, Barrie.** The Big Bugattis Types 46 & 50. (Illus.). 128p. 1995. 59.95 (1-874105-43-X, Pub. by Veloce Pub UK) Motorbooks Intl.

Price, Ben, jt. auth. see Dooley, Kirk.

Price, Benton, ed. Water Reclamation: Here, Now... & How. LC 89-52216. 140p. 1990. pap. 19.50 (0-87762-719-3) Technomic.

Price, Bernard L. Do-It-Yourself Projects from Attic to Basement. LC 85-29023. (Illus.). 328p. 1986. 24.95 (0-937558-15-X) Scharff Ltd.

Price, Bernie. Outdoor Projects in Wood. Roundtable Press Editors, ed. LC 84-17438. (Illus.). 160p. (Orig.). 1985. pap. 9.95 (0-932944-73-6) Creative Homeowner.

Price, Bertram, jt. auth. see Chatterjee, Samprit.

Price, Bessie D. Sum Phun with Phobias. 1977. 3.00 (0-87012-282-7) McClain.

Price, Betty J. One Hundred One Ways to Fix Broccoli. 1993. 10.95 (0-8062-4707-X) Carlton.

Price, Bill. Close Calls: Two Tours with the 35th SQ, 353rd Fighter Group WWII. Frisque, Tom, ed. (Illus.). 128p. (Orig.). 1992. pap. 14.95 (0-9623080-3-X) Aviation Usk.

***Price, Billie.** Letters to Bill. 1995. 18.95 (0-533-11158-7) Vantage.

***Price, Bob.** Family Memories: A Guide to Reminiscing. (Illus.). 1995. reprint ed. pap. text ed. 13.95 (0-943873-20-7) Elder Bks.

Price, Bobby G. Visualize. 58p. (Orig.). 1986. pap. 10.00 (0-932662-60-9) St Andrews NC.

Price, Bren T. Basic Composition Activities Kit. 232p. 1982. spiral bd. 29.95 (0-87628-169-2) Ctr Appl Res.

Price, Brena. Giving, Christian Stewardship: Teaching Bks. (Illus.). 14p. (J). (gr. 1-8). 1971. pap. text ed. 4.50 (0-86508-154-9) BCM Pubn.

— Our Bodies: Learning to Use Them to Please God. (BMC Teaching Bks.). (Illus.). 20p. (J). (gr. 1-8). 1983. pap. 4.50 (0-86508-157-3) BCM Pubn.

Price, Bronte. School Industry Links. (C). 1990. 59.00 (0-86431-100-1, Pub. by Aust Council Educ Res AT) St Mut.

Price, Bruce. American Dreams. LC 83-63241. 266p. 1985. 22.00 (0-932966-37-3); pap. 16.00 (0-932966-62-4) Permanent Pr.

Price, Bruce D. Too Easy. 1994. 21.00 (0-671-88673-8) S&S Trade.

Price, Byron. The National Cowboy Hall of Fame Chuckwagon Cookbook: Authentic Recipes from the Ranch & the Range. LC 94-18568. 1995. write for info. (0-688-12989-7) Morrow.

Price, Byron B., intro. Tales of the Wild West: An Illustrated Collection of Adventure Stories. LC 93-20148. (Illus.). 144p. 1993. 24.95 (0-8478-1748-2) Rizzoli Intl.

Price, C. & Newman, D. Principles & Practice of Immunoassay. 650p. 1991. 99.00 (1-56159-020-7, Stockton Pr) Groves Dictionaries.

Price, C. E., jt. auth. see McNeil, J. A.

Price, C. Houston, ed. see Hibben, Gil.

***Price, C. J., ed.** Manual of Parrots, Budgerigars, & Other Psittacine Birds. (Illus.). 208p. 1995. pap. 41.95 (0-905214-07-2) Iowa St U Pr.

Price, C. J., ed. see Sheridan, Richard B.

Price, Carl & Horton, J. Local Liposome Drug Delivery. (Medical Intelligence Unit Ser.). 100p. 1992. 89.95 (1-879702-12-6) R G Landes.

Price, Carol, jt. auth. see Stull, Elizabeth C.

***Price, Carol S.** Mystic Rhythms: The Philosophical Vision of Rush. LC 95-2218. (Woodstock Ser. : Popular Music of Today: Vol. 2). 1995. lib. bdg. write for info. (0-8095-0800-1); pap. write for info. (0-8095-1800-7) Borgo Pr.

Price, Catherine, jt. ed. see Jackson, Peter.

Price, Cecil, ed. see Sheridan, Richard B.

Price, Charles, ed. The American Golfer. rev. ed. 1988. 28.00 (0-940889-15-3) Classics Golf.

Price, Charles, jt. auth. see Hoeber, Thomas R.

Price, Charles, jt. ed. see Hoeber, Thomas R.

Price, Charles A. Malta & the Maltese: A Study in Nineteenth Century Migration. LC 77-87724. reprint ed. 22.50 (0-404-16516-8) AMS Pr.

Price, Charles E. The Day They Hung the Elephant. (Illus.). 64p. 1992. pap. 5.95 (0-932807-75-5) Overmountain Pr.

— Demon in the Woods: Tall Tales & True from East Tennessee. 74p. 1992. pap. 7.95 (0-932807-82-8) Overmountain Pr.

— Haints, Witches & Boogers: Tales from Upper East Tennessee. LC 92-12664. 104p. 1992. 10.95 (0-89587-093-2) Blair.

— Haunted Jonesborough. 79p. 1993. pap. 7.95 (0-932807-93-3) Overmountain Pr.

— I'd Rather Have a Talking Frog. 96p. 1993. pap. 7.95 (0-932807-98-4) Overmountain Pr.

— The Infamous Bell Witch of Tennessee. (Illus.). 142p. (Orig.). 1994. 14.95 (1-57072-015-0); pap. 9.95 (1-57072-008-8); audio 14.95 (1-57072-014-2) Overmountain Pr.

— The Mystery of Ghostly Vera & Other Haunting Tales of Southwest Virginia. 128p. 1993. 12.95 (0-932807-88-7) Overmountain Pr.

***Price, Charles M. & Bell, Charles G.** California Government Today: Politics of Reform. 5th ed. LC 95-13452. 1996. pap. 25.95 (0-534-25998-7) Intl Thomson.

Price, Charles M., jt. auth. see Bell, Charles G.

Price, Charles P. & Weil, Louis. Liturgy for Living. (Church's Teaching Ser.: Vol. 5). 1984. pap. 4.95 (0-8164-2218-4) Harper SF.

Price, Charles S. The Creative Word. LC 93-72394. 110p. 1994. reprint ed. pap. 5.95 (0-88270-676-4) Bridge Pub.

— Real Faith: One of the Classic Faith-Builders. 125p. 1972. pap. 6.95 (0-88270-000-6) Bridge Pub.

***Price, Charles W.** Alive in Christ: How to Find Renewed Spiritual Power. LC 94-37821. 160p. 1995. pap. 5.99 (0-8254-3551-X) Kregel.

— Christ for Real: How to Grow into God's Likeness. 192p. 1995. pap. 4.99 (0-8254-3550-1) Kregel.

— Life after Bankruptcy: The Complete Do-It-Yourself Guide to Surviving & Prospering after Personal Bankruptcy. LC 93-83404. (Illus.). 352p. (Orig.). 1993. pap. 19.95 (1-882784-13-8) Pract Pubns.

Price, Cheryl. Bible Learning Centers. (Teacher Helper Ser.). 96p. (J). (gr. 2-6). 1989. 10.95 (0-86653-498-9, SS1817, Shining Star Pubns) Good Apple.

— Memory Verse Motivators. (Teacher Helper Ser.). 96p. (J). (ps-5). 1990. 10.95 (0-86653-550-0, SS1823, Shining Star Pubns) Good Apple.

Price, Christopher P. & Spencer, Kevin C., eds. Centrifugal Analysers in Clinical Chemistry. LC 80-81330. (Illus.). 520p. 1980. text ed. 115.00 (0-275-91339-2, C1339, Praeger Pubs) Greenwood.

Price, Clement A. Many Voices, Many Opportunities: Cultural Pluralism & American Arts Policy. LC 93-34290. (Illus.). 96p. (Orig.). 1993. pap. 9.95 (1-879903-16-4, ACA Bks) Am Council Arts.

Price-Cohen, Cynthia. Human Rights of Indigenous Peoples. 1995. lib. bdg. 115.00 (0-941320-93-6) Transnatl Pubs.

Price, Colin. The Theory & Application of Forest Economics. (Illus.). 320p. 1989. pap. 22.95 (0-631-15366-7) Blackwell Pubs.

— Time, Discounting, & Value. LC 92-36108. 1993. 54.95 (0-631-17985-2); pap. 24.95 (0-631-17986-0) Blackwell Pubs.

***Price, Con.** Memories of Old Montana. (American Autobiography Ser.). 154p. 1995. reprint ed. lib. bdg. 69.00 (0-7812-8620-4) Rprt Serv.

— Trails I Rode. (American Autobiography Ser.). 262p. 1995. reprint ed. lib. bdg. 79.00 (0-7812-8621-2) Rprt Serv.

Price, Courtney. Courtney Price Answers the Most Asked Questions from Entrepreneurs. 1994. pap. text ed. 15.95 (0-07-050831-3) McGraw.

— The Group Practice Personnel Policies Manual. 500p. 1990. 109.00 (0-933948-25-5) Med Group Mgmt.

— Health Care Innovations & Venture Trends. 1992. text ed. 38.95 (0-8273-4964-5) Delmar.

— Waltzing with a Moose: Following the Wizard's Path to Corporate Creativity. 70p. pap. 8.95 (0-944303-08-0) Creat Mgmt Unltd.

Price, Courtney & Baker, Dianne. Creatively Designing Your Future. 124p. pap. 14.95 (0-944303-05-6) Creat Mgmt Unltd.

Price, Courtney & Novak, Alys. The Medical Practice Performance Management Manual: How to Evaluate Employees. (Employee Performance Management Ser.). 234p. (Orig.). 1993. pap. 85.00 (1-56829-027-6) Med Group Mgmt.

Price, Courtney, et al. The Entrepreneur's Resource Handbook. 178p. pap. 19.95 (0-944303-00-5) Creat Mgmt Unltd.

Price, Courtney M., ed. Asbestos in Buildings, Facilities & Industry. 296p. 1987. pap. text ed. 69.00 (0-86587-727-0) Gov Insts.

Price, Craig G. & Dennie, Ronald W. Impairment & Disability Ratings: A Guide to the Guides. 186p. 1992. write for info. (1-882678-00-1) Meriah-Morgan.

***Price, Curtis, ed.** Purcell Studies. (Illus.). 360p. (C). 1995. write for info. (0-521-44174-9) Cambridge U Pr.

Price, Curtis, ed. see Purcell, Henry.

Price, Curtis, et al. Italian Opera in Late Eighteenth-Century London, Vol. 1: The King's Theatre, Haymarket, 1778-1791. (Illus.). 350p. 1995. 85.00 (0-19-816166-2) OUP.

Price, D. & Todd, J. F., eds. Dynamic Mass Spectrometry, Vol. 6. LC 80-641839. 338p. reprint ed. 96.40 (0-685-15428-9, 2026679) Bks Demand.

Price, D. & Williams, J. E. Time of Flight Mass Spectrometer. 1969. 128.00 (0-08-013444-0, Pub. by Pergamon Repr UK) Franklin.

Price, D., ed. see European Symposium on the Time-of-Flight Mass Spectrometer (2nd: 1969: University of Salford) Staff.

Price, D., ed. see European Symposium on the Time-of-Flight Mass Spectrometer (3rd: 1971: Salford, Eng.) Staff.

Price, D., ed. see International Dynamic Mass Spectrometry Symposium (1974: University of Salford).

Price, D., et al, eds. Bromine Compounds: Chemistry & Applications. 422p. 1988. 146.25 (0-444-42982-4) Elsevier.

Price, D. G., ed. Proceedings: Sixth International Congress International Association of Engineering Geology, Amsterdam, 6-10 August 1990, 6 vols., Set. (Illus.). 2500p. (C). 1990. text ed. 695.00 (90-6191-130-3, Pub. by A A Balkema NE) Ashgate Pub Co.

Price, D. L., et al. Neurodegenerative Disorders: Mechanisms & Prospects for Therapy. (Dahlem Workshop Reports - Life Sciences). 301p. 1991. 121.00 (0-685-70063-1, Wiley-Liss) Wiley.

Price, D. P. Real World Answers to Cattle Management Problems. (Illus.). 250p. (Orig.). 1991. pap. 37.50 (0-685-50311-9) SWI.

— Real World Answers to Cattle Management Problems. LC 91-66767. (Illus.). 228p. (Orig.). 1992. pap. text ed. 37.50 (0-685-59458-0) SWI.

Price, D. Porter. Beef Production, Science & Economics, Application & Reality. LC 81-51944. (Illus.). 358p. 1985. 32.00 (0-9606246-0-0); pap. text ed. 24.95 (0-9606246-3-5) SWI.

— Cattle Nutrition Primer. 1986. write for info. (0-9606246-4-3) SWI.

— Cattle Reproduction Primer. 1986. write for info. (0-9606246-5-1) SWI.

— Intelligent Dieting for Weight Loss & Prevention of Disease. LC 82-61578. (Illus.). 200p. (Orig.). 1982. lib. bdg. 17.95 (0-9606246-1-9); pap. 13.95 (0-9606246-2-7) SWI.

Price, D. T. A History of Saint David's University College, Lampeter, Vol. 1: To 1898. xv, 222p. 1977. 17.50 (0-7083-0606-3, Pub. by U of Wales UK) Bks Intl VA.

Price, Danny, tr. see French Ramblers Association Staff.

Price, Darryl, jt. auth. see Welch, Jennifer.

Price, David. Appeals. 439p. 1982. 104.00 (0-906840-42-2, Pub. by Fourmat Pub UK) St Mut.

— Appeals Procedure. 1981. 100.00 (0-686-97087-X, Pub. by Fourmat Pub UK) St Mut.

— Before the Bulldozer: The Nambiquara Indians & the World Bank. LC 89-6065. 212p. 1989. 18.95 (0-932020-67-4) Seven Locks Pr.

— Introduction to Ada. 1984. 26.95 (0-13-477646-1) P-H.

— Janus Secundus Writing Love in the Renaissance. (Illus.). 152p. 1995. write for info. (0-86698-180-2, MR142) MRTS.

— The Political Dramaturgy of Nicodemus Frischlin: Essays on Humanist Drama in Germany. LC 89-16733. (Germanic Languages & Literatures Ser.: No. 111). xii, 156p. (C). 1990. 30.00 (0-8078-8111-2) U of NC Pr.

Price, David, illus. Birds & Beasts. 80p. (J). (gr. 1-6). 12.95 (0-7136-5653-0, Pub. by A&C Black UK) Talman.

— Charles Dickens, Eighteen Hundred Twelve to Eighteen Seventy. 1970. pap. 8.00 (0-87959-009-2) U of Tex H Ransom Ctr.

— An Exhibition of Judaica & Hebraica. 26p. 1973. pap. 7.00 (0-87959-034-3) U of Tex H Ransom Ctr.

— Johannes Kepler, Fifteen Seventy-One to Sixteen Thirty: An Exhibit of Books, Manuscripts, & Related Materials. LC 70-180652. 1971. pap. 10.00 (0-87959-014-9) U of Tex H Ransom Ctr.

— John Herschel & Victorian Science. (Orig.). 1966. pap. 8.00 (0-87959-005-X) U of Tex H Ransom Ctr.

Price, David, illus. & comp. Katherine Mansfield: An Exhibition. LC 75-620027. 1975. pap. 10.00 (0-87959-018-1) U of Tex H Ransom Ctr.

Price, David, illus. Siegfried Sassoon: A Memorial Exhibition. LC 77-628295. 1969. pap. 8.00 (0-87959-007-6) U of Tex H Ransom Ctr.

— The Stanley Marcus Collection of Christmas Books. (Orig.). 1968. pap. 10.00 (0-87959-029-7) U of Tex H Ransom Ctr.

Price, David, jt. auth. see Hacker, Jonathan.

Price, David E. The Congressional Experience: A View from the Hill. LC 92-13949. (Transforming American Politics Ser.). 194p. (C). 1992. pap. text ed. 17.95 (0-8133-1156-X) Westview.

— The Congressional Experience: A View from the Hill. LC 92-13949. (Transforming American Politics Ser.). 194p. 1992. text ed. 61.00 (0-8133-1157-8) Westview.

— Who Makes the Laws? Creativity & Power in Senate Committees. 380p. 1972. boxed, ring bd. 34.95 (0-87073-298-6) Transaction Pubs.

Price, David H. Atlas of World Cultures: A Geographical Guide to Ethnographic Literature. 160p. (C). 1990. text ed. 49.95 (0-8039-3240-5); pap. text ed. 22.50 (0-8039-4075-0) Sage.

Price, David L. The Grimmetts of Virginia of the Revolutionary War Era & Their Descendants. LC 80-81609. 250p. 1980. pap. 15.00 (0-9604482-0-9) D L Price.

— Magic: A Pictoral History of Conjurers in the Theater. LC 81-68623. 544p. 1985. 60.00 (0-8453-4738-1, Cornwall Bks) Assoc Univ Prs.

Price, David T., jt. auth. see Kruse, Robert L.

***Price, Deb & Murdoch, Joyce.** And Say Hi to Joyce: America's First Gay Column Comes Out. LC 94-24067. 368p. 1995. 22.50 (0-385-47365-6) Doubleday.

Price, Dennis, ed. Dynamic Mass Spectrometry: Invited Papers & Specially Commissioned Reviews Embracing the Whole Field of Dynamic Mass Spectrometry, Vol. 2. LC 73-107612. 282p. reprint ed. pap. 80.40 (0-317-12997-X, 2022544) Bks Demand.

Price, Derek D. Little Science Big Science & Beyond. 1986. text ed. 51.50 (0-231-04956-0) Col U Pr.

— Science since Babylon. enl. ed. 1975. pap. 13.00 (0-300-01798-7) Yale U Pr.

Price, Derek J., ed. The Equatorie of the Planetis. LC 55-1173. (Illus.). 232p. reprint ed. pap. 66.20 (0-317-07953-0, 2050724) Bks Demand.

Price, Dianne. Proud Captive. 496p. 1986. pap. 3.95 (0-8217-1925-4) Zebra.

— The Savage Spirits of Seahedge Manor. (Orig.). 1982. pap. 2.95 (0-89083-940-9) Zebra.

***Price, Don.** Secrets of Personal Marketing Power: Strategies for Achieving Greater Personal & Business Success. 208p. 1994. per., pap. text ed. 19.95 (0-8403-9392-X) Kendall-Hunt.

Price, Don C. Russia & the Roots of the Chinese Revolution, 1896-1911. LC 74-80443. (Harvard East Asian Ser.: No. 79). 318p. reprint ed. pap. 90.70 (0-7837-3858-7, 2043680) Bks Demand.

***Price, Don K.** America's Unwritten Constitution: Science, Religion, & Political Responsibility. LC 83-5439. (Miller Center Series on the American Presidency). 220p. 1983. pap. 62.70 (0-7837-8468-6, 2049273) Bks Demand.

— America's Unwritten Constitution: Science, Religion & Political Responsibility. 224p. 1985. pap. 13.50 (0-674-03142-3) HUP.

An Asterisk (*) at the beginning of an entry indicates that the title is appearing in BIP for the first time.

— Government & Science: Their Dynamic Relation in American Democracy. LC 81-6584. ix, 203p. 1981. reprint ed. text ed. 59.75 (0-313-23108-7, PRGS, Greenwood Pr) Greenwood.

— The Parliamentary & Presidential Systems. (Reprint Series in Social Sciences). (C). 1993. reprint ed. pap. text ed. 1.00 (0-8290-3375-0, PS-232) Irvington.

— The Scientific Estate. LC 65-22047. 343p. 1965. 37.00 (0-674-79485-0) Belknap Pr.

Price, Don K., ed. Secretary of State. LC 60-53378. 1960. 3.50 (0-317-02964-9, 79749-C) Am Assembly.

Price, Don K. & Evans, Robert H. Political Transitions & Foreign Affairs in Britain & France: Their Relevance for the United States. Mosher, Frederick C., ed. & intro. by. (Papers on Presidential Transitions & Foreign Policy: Vol. III). 100p. (Orig.). (C). 1986. lib. bdg. 34.50 (0-8191-5313-3, Pub. by White Miller Center); pap. text ed. 15.00 (0-8191-5314-1) U Pr of Amer.

Price, Don L., jt. auth. see Anderson, Camille J.

Price, Donald D. Psychological & Neural Mechanisms of Pain. (Illus.). 254p. 1988. text ed. 88.50 (0-88167-383-8) Raven.

Price, Donald L. Procedure Manual for the Diagnosis of Intestinal Parasites. LC 93-7450. 368p. 1993. 89.95 (0-8493-8654-3, RC862) CRC Pr.

Price, Donna. Greenberg's LGB Coloring Book. (Illus.). 32p. (Orig.). (J). (gr. k-5). 1987. pap. 3.50 (0-89778-093-0, 10-7020) Greenberg Bks.

Price, Doug & Gebauer, Gette. Adventures in Fugawiland: A Computer Simulation in Archeology. 106p. (C). 1990. disk, pap. text ed. 19.95 (0-87484-948-9) Mayfield Pub.

Price, E., et al. Language Roundup. large type ed. Incl. Mustang Book. (gr. 5). 1983. 42.20 (0-317-02363-2, 4-1211); Mustang Book. (gr. 5). 1983. 4.75 (0-317-04455-9, 4-1212); Cowboy Book. (gr. 4). 1983. 42.20 (0-317-02365-9, 4-1213); Cowboy Book. (gr. 4). 1983. 3.55 (0-317-03503-7, 4-1214); Lariat Book. (gr. 3). 1983. 21.10 (0-317-02367-5, 4-1215); Lariat Book. (gr. 3). 1983. 3.55 (0-317-03504-5, 4-1216); Ranch Book. (gr. 6). 1983. 42.20 (0-317-02369-1, 4-1217); Ranch Book. (gr. 6). 1983. 3.55 (0-317-03505-3, 4-1218); (J). (gr. 3-6). 1983. reprint ed. write for info. (0-318-66153-5) Am Printing Hse.

Price, E. A., jt. auth. see Godfrey, Charles.

Price, E. Hoffman. Grubstake. (Orig.). 1980. pap. 1.95 (0-89083-577-2) Zebra.

Price, E. Hoffmann. Far Lands Other Days. (Illus.). 587p. 1975. 15.00 (0-913796-01-8) Carcosa.

Price, E. W. Acts in Prayer. LC 74-15278. 1974. pap. 0.99 (0-8054-9209-7) Broadman.

— The Character Connection. 196p. (Orig.). 1992. pap. 7.99 (1-56043-066-4) Destiny Image.

— Podoconiosis: Non-Filarial Elephantiasis. (Illus.). 144p. 1991. 47.50 (0-19-262002-9) OUP.

Price, Edna C. Burro Bill & Me. 2nd ed. (Illus.). 300p. (C). 1993. reprint ed. pap. 9.95 (1-878900-28-5) DVNH Assn.

Price, Edward R., ed. see Denny, Hugh W.

Price, Edward R., ed. see Georgopoulos, Chris J.

Price, Edward R., ed. see Mardiguian, Michael.

Price, Edward R., ed. see White, Donald R.

***Price, Edward T.** Dividing the Land: Early American Beginnings of Our Private Property Mosaic. (Geography Research Paper: Vol. 238). 1995. pap. text ed. 26.00 (0-226-68065-7) U Ch Pr.

Price, Elisabeth. Looking for Paradise: A Fable. 1992. 10.95 (0-533-10142-5) Vantage.

Price, Enoch S., tr. see Swedenborg, Emanuel.

Price, Esther & Lipsett, Linda O. Chocolate Covered Cherries: Esther Price's Memories. (Illus.). 112p. 1992. pap. 11.99 (0-9629399-1-9) Halstead Meadows.

Price, Eugenia. At Home on St. Simons. LC 81-1412. (Illus.). 92p. 1981. 12.95 (0-931948-16-9) Peachtree Pubs.

— Beauty from Ashes. LC 94-38912. 1995. 23.50 (0-385-26703-7) Doubleday.

— Beauty from Ashes. large type ed. LC 94-38912. 1995. pap. 27.50 (0-385-42314-4) Doubleday.

— Before the Darkness Falls. LC 87-556. 480p. 1987. 17.95 (0-385-23068-0) Doubleday.

— Before the Darkness Falls. 1980. pap. 6.99 (0-515-10538-4) Jove Pubns.

— The Beloved Invader. 1977. mass mkt. 4.99 (0-553-26909-7) Bantam.

— The Beloved Invader. large type ed. LC 91-15592. 456p. 1991. reprint ed. lib. bdg. 20.95 (1-56054-182-2) Thorndike Pr.

— Beloved World. 1991. mass mkt. 10.00 (0-385-41716-0) Doubleday.

— Bright Captivity. 1992. mass mkt. 6.50 (0-553-29523-3) Bantam.

— Bright Captivity. 1991. 20.00 (0-385-26701-0) Doubleday.

— Bright Captivity. braille ed. 1162p. 1992. vinyl bd. 92.96 (1-56956-200-8, BR8538) W A T Braille.

— Bright Captivity. large type ed. 1991. 25.00 (0-385-41823-X, Doubleday LT) BDD LT Grp.

— The Burden Is Light. large type ed. (Large Print Inspirational Ser.). 1985. pap. 11.95 (0-8027-2514-7) Walker & Co.

— Descubrelo Tu Mismo: Find Out for Yourself. (SPA.). 4.95 (84-7228-199-X, 220259, Pub. by Edit Clie SP) TSELF.

— Descubrimientos: Discoveries. (SPA.). 4.25 (84-7228-337-2, 220267, Pub. by Edit Clie SP) TSELF.

— Don Juan McQueen. large type ed. LC 92-18881. 626p. 1993. reprint ed. lib. bdg. 20.95 (1-56054-466-X) Thorndike Pr.

— Este O Sus Padres? No Pat Answers. (SPA.). 3.25 (84-7228-207-4, 220740, Pub. by Edit Clie SP) TSELF.

— Getting Through the Night: Finding Your Way after the Loss of a Loved One. large type ed. 168p. 1985. pap. 7.95 (0-8027-2482-5) Walker & Co.

— Getting Through the Night: Finding Your Way Through Grief. LC 91-70317. (Illus.). 128p. 1991. reprint ed. 12.95 (0-06-066509-2) Harper SF.

— God Speaks to Women Today. 1994. pap. 5.99 (0-06-104329-X, Harp PBks) HarpC.

— Inside One Author's Heart. 1992. 15.00 (0-385-42321-7) Doubleday.

— Lighthouse. 352p. 1972. mass mkt. 5.99 (0-553-26910-0) Bantam.

— Lighthouse. large type ed. LC 91-30413. 546p. 1992. reprint ed. bds. 20.95 (1-56054-185-7) Thorndike Pr.

— Make Love Your Aim. 1989. pap. 3.95 (0-515-10039-0) Jove Pubns.

— Margaret's Story. 432p. 1984. mass mkt. 5.50 (0-553-26559-8) Bantam.

— Margaret's Story. large type ed. LC 92-18864. 723p. 1993. bds. 20.95 (1-56054-468-6) Thorndike Pr.

— Maria. 1984. mass mkt. 5.99 (0-553-26362-5) Bantam.

— Maria. large type ed. LC 92-20070. 701p. 1993. bds. 20.95 (1-56054-467-8) Thorndike Pr.

— New Moon Rising. large type ed. LC 91-18383. 483p. 1991. reprint ed. lib. bdg. 19.95 (1-56054-184-9) Thorndike Pr.

— No Dudes un Momento: Never a Dull Moment. (SPA.). 3.95 (84-7228-197-3, 220628, Pub. by Edit Clie SP) TSELF.

— Savannah. 1984. pap. 6.99 (0-515-10486-8) Jove Pubns.

— St. Simons Memoir. 1987. mass mkt. 4.99 (0-515-09264-9) Jove Pubns.

— Stranger in Savannah. 1990. pap. 6.99 (0-515-10344-6) Jove Pubns.

— To See Your Face Again. 1986. pap. 6.99 (0-515-10564-3) Jove Pubns.

— The Unique World of Women. large type ed. 1995. 20.95 (0-7838-1194-2, Large Print Bks) Hall.

— Where Shadows Go. LC 92-38400. 1994. mass mkt. 6.50 (0-553-56503-6) Bantam.

— Where Shadows Go. large type ed. LC 92-38400. 1993. 26.00 (0-385-42313-6, Doubleday LT) BDD LT Grp.

— Woman to Woman. 256p. 1994. pap. 5.50 (0-06-104310-9) Zondervan.

— Woman to Woman. large type ed. (Large Print Inspirational Ser.). 396p. 1986. pap. 16.95 (0-8027-2562-7) Walker & Co.

Price, Eva J. China Journal 1889-1900: An American Missionary Family During the Boxer Rebellion. 320p. 1990. pap. 9.95 (0-02-036065-7, Collier S&S) S&S Trade.

Price Evans, David A. Genetic Factors in Drug Therapy: Clinical & Molecular Pharmacogenetics. (Illus.). 500p. (C). 1994. 180.00 (0-521-41296-X) Cambridge U Pr.

Price, F. Right Every Time. 182p. (C). 1990. 270.00 (0-685-39879-X, Inst Pur & Supply) St Mut.

***Price, Frances.** Healthy Cooking for Two (or Just You) Low-Fat Recipes with Half the Fuss & Double the Taste. 1995. 27.95 (0-87596-274-2) Rodale Pr Inc.

Price, Francis, tr. see Ousmane, Sembene.

***Price, Frank.** Loving Work. 200p. 1995. 50.95 (0-566-07634-9, Pub. by Gower UK) Ashgate Pub Co.

— Right Every Time. 200p. 1993. pap. 18.95 (0-566-07419-2, Pub. by Gower UK) Ashgate Pub Co.

— Right First Time: Using Quality Control for Profit. 296p. 1984. text ed. 67.95 (0-566-02467-5); pap. 19.95 (0-7045-0522-3) Ashgate Pub Co.

Price, Frank W., tr. see Sun Yat-sen.

Price, Fred W. The Moon Observer's Handbook. (Illus.). 300p. 1989. 39.95 (0-521-33500-0) Cambridge U Pr.

— The Planet Observer's Handbook. (Illus.). 512p. (C). 1994. 34.95 (0-521-44257-5) Cambridge U Pr.

Price, Frederick. Como Obra la Fe. 111p. 1980. pap. 2.95 (0-89274-157-0) Harrison Hse.

Price, Frederick K. Faith, Foolishness, or Presumption. 160p. (Orig.). 1979. pap. 6.95 (0-89274-103-1) Harrison Hse.

— The Faithfulness of God. 53p. (Orig.). 1993. pap. 3.99 (1-883798-02-7) Faith One.

— High Finance. 180p. (Orig.). 1984. pap. 6.95 (0-89274-326-3) Harrison Hse.

— The Holy Spirit the Missing Ingredient. 1978. pap. text ed. 1.95 (0-89274-081-7) Harrison Hse.

— Homosexuality. 56p. (Orig.). 1993. pap. 2.99 (1-883798-04-3) Faith One.

— Homosexuality: State of Birth or a State of Mind. 60p. (Orig.). 1989. pap. 2.95 (0-89274-574-6, HH574) Harrison Hse.

— How Faith Works. 128p. (Orig.). 1979. pap. 5.95 (0-89274-001-9) Harrison Hse.

— How to Believe God for a Mate. (Orig.). pap. 0.98 (0-89274-453-7) Harrison Hse.

— How to Obtain Strong Faith: Six Principles. 184p. pap. 6.95 (0-89274-042-6) Harrison Hse.

— Is Healing for All? 127p. (Orig.). 1979. pap. 5.95 (0-89274-005-1) Harrison Hse.

— Living in the Realm of the Spirit. 41p. (Orig.). 1995. pap. 2.99 (1-883798-07-8) Faith One.

— A New Law for a New People. 92p. (Orig.). 1993. pap. 6.99 (1-883798-01-9) Faith One.

— Now Faith Is. 32p. 1984. pap. 0.98 (0-89274-302-6) Harrison Hse.

— Practical Suggestions for Successful Ministry. 112p. (Orig.). 1991. pap. 5.95 (0-89274-880-X, HH880) Harrison Hse.

— The Promise Land. 27p. (Orig.). 1993. pap. 1.99 (1-883798-03-5) Faith One.

— Prosperity on God's Terms. 112p. (Orig.). 1989. pap. 4.95 (0-89274-670-X, HH670) Harrison Hse.

— The Realm of the Spirit. 50p. 1989. 2.95 (0-89274-569-X) Harrison Hse.

— Thank God for Everything. 31p. pap. 0.98 (0-89274-056-6) Harrison Hse.

— Three Keys to Positive Confession. 71p. (Orig.). 1994. pap. 5.99 (1-883798-05-1) Faith One.

— Victorious Overcoming Life. 159p. (Orig.). 1993. pap. 7.99 (1-883798-00-0) Faith One.

— The Way, the Walk, the Warfare of the Believer. 403p. (Orig.). 1994. pap. 10.99 (1-883798-06-X) Faith One.

Price, G. & Ross, N., eds. The Stability of Minerals. (Mineralogical Society Ser.: No. 3). (Illus.). 352p. 1992. 150.00 (0-412-44150-0, A9494) Chapman & Hall.

Price, G. B. Multivariable Analysis. (Illus.). 995p. 1984. 59.00 (0-387-90934-6) Spr-Verlag.

Price, George G., see Achad, Frater, pseud..

Price, George M. Modern Factory: Safety, Sanitation & Welfare. LC 74-89758. (American Labor, from Conspiracy to Collective Bargaining Ser., No. 1). 574p. 1975. reprint ed. 51.95 (0-405-02144-5) Ayer.

Price, George R. Thomas Dekker. LC 68-17241. (Twayne's English Authors Ser.). 1969. lib. bdg. 17.95 (0-8057-1148-1); pap. text ed. 5.95 (0-8290-2006-3) Irvington.

Price, George R., ed. see Middleton, Thomas & Rowley, William.

Price, Gerry, illus. Fun Math Flip Book Series, 4 bks., No. 4: I Can Divide! (J). (ps-3). 1994. 7.99 (0-553-09567-6) Bantam.

Price, Gillel. Sunday Times Self Help Directory. 300p. 1980. 15.95 (0-8464-1241-1) Beekman Pubs.

Price, Glanville. A Comprehensive French Grammar. 4th ed. 608p. 1993. pap. 22.95 (0-631-18165-2) Blackwell Pubs.

— An Introduction to French Pronunciation. 116p. 1991. pap. 15.95 (0-631-15476-0) Blackwell Pubs.

— Ireland & the Celtic Connection. (Princess Grace Irish Library Lecture Ser.: Vol. 4). 47p. 1987. pap. 7.95 (0-86140-269-3, Pub. by Colin Smythe Ltd UK) Dufour.

***Price, Glanville, ed.** The Celtic Connection. 361p. (C). 1994. lib. bdg. 76.50 (0-86140-248-0, Pub. by C Smythe Ltd UK) B&N Imports.

Price, Glanville, ed. see Manoliu-Manea, Maria.

Price-Gresty, David. The Hymnal. (Amelia Chapbooks Ser.). 48p. (Orig.). 1989. pap. 10.95 (0-936545-08-9) Amelia.

Price, H. H. Blackberry Season: A Time to Mourn, a Time to Heal. Geiger, Lura J., ed. LC 92-44882. 176p. (Orig.). 1993. pap. 14.95 (0-931055-93-8) LuraMedia.

— Thinking & Representation. (Studies in Philosophy: No. 40). (C). 1977. lib. bdg. 24.95 (0-8383-0117-7) M S G Haskell Hse.

Price, H. Marcus, III. Disputing the Dead: U. S. Law on Aboriginal Remains & Grave Goods. 152p. 1991. text ed. 37.50 (0-8262-0779-0) U of Mo Pr.

Price, Harry. Confessions of a Ghost-Hunter. LC 93-7302. (Collector's Library of the Unknown). (Illus.). 385p. 1993. reprint ed. 18.99 (0-8094-8133-2) Time-Life.

— Fifty Years of Psychical Research: A Critical Survey. LC 75-7394. (Perspectives in Psychical Research Ser.). (Illus.). 1975. reprint ed. 34.95 (0-405-07043-8) Ayer.

— The Most Haunted House in England. rev. ed. (Collector's Library of the Unknown). 260p. 1990. reprint ed. write for info. (0-8094-8058-1); reprint ed. lib. bdg. write for info. (0-8094-8059-X) Time-Life.

— Short Title Catalogue of Works on Psychical Research. (Hypnosis & Altered States of Consciousness Ser.). 468p. 1982. lib. bdg. 49.50 (0-306-76166-1) Da Capo.

Price, Harry & Dingwall, Eric J. Revelations of a Spirit Medium. LC 75-7395. (Perspectives in Psychical Research Ser.). 1975. reprint ed. 31.95 (0-405-07044-6) Ayer.

***Price, Haydn & Fisher, Rod.** Shoeing for Performance: In the Sound & Lame Horse. (Illus.). 144p. 1995. pap. 16.95 (1-57076-033-0, Trafalgar Sq Pub) Trafalgar.

Price, Helen M. Poems from the Hearth. 133p. 1992. pap. 14.95 (0-9635029-0-5) W Price & Assocs.

Price, Henry H. Belief: The Gifford Lectures Delivered at the University of Aberdeen in 1960. LC 76-390002. (Muirhead Library of Philosophy, The Gifford Lectures: 1960). 493p. reprint ed. pap. 140.60 (0-8357-7120-2, 2012171) Bks Demand.

— Hume's Theory of the External World. LC 80-25734. 231p. 1981. reprint ed. text ed. 35.00 (0-313-22707-1, PRTE, Greenwood Pr) Greenwood.

— Perception. LC 81-13236. ix, 332p. 1982. reprint ed. text ed. 59.50 (0-313-23153-2, PRPT, Greenwood Pr) Greenwood.

Price, Hickman, jt. auth. see Ford, Franklin.

***Price, Hope.** Angels. 240p. (Orig.). 1994. mass mkt. 4.99 (0-380-72331-X) Avon.

Price, J. C. Interpretation of Thermal Infrared Data: The Heat Capacity Mapping Mission. (Remote Sensing Reviews Ser.: Vol. 1, Pt. 2). 198p. 1986. pap. text ed. 121.00 (3-7186-0289-X) Gordon & Breach.

Price, J. D., tr. see Ouvaroff, M.

Price, J. G., et al. Annotated Bibliography of Mineral Deposits in Trans-Pecos Texas. (Mineral Resource Circular Ser.: MRC 73). (Illus.). 108p. 1983. 5.00 (0-318-17363-8) Bur Econ Geology.

Price, J. H., et al, eds. The Shore Environment, Vol. 2: Ecosystems. (Systematics Association Special Ser.: No. 17). 1981. text ed. 248.00 (0-12-564702-6) Acad Pr.

Price, J. L. Holland & the Dutch Republic in the Seventeenth Century: The Politics of Particularism. 320p. 1994. 52.00 (0-19-820383-7) OUP.

Price, J. M. & Estudio, Guias de. Guia de Estudios Sobre Jesus el Maestro. 50p. 1982. reprint ed. pap. 2.95 (0-311-43501-7) Casa Bautista.

Price, J. R., et al. Plants for Medicines: A Chemical & Pharmacological Survey of Australian Plants. 1990. 90.00 (0-643-04992-4, Pub. by CSIRO AT) Intl Spec Bk.

Price, J. R., et al, eds. The Shore Environment, Vol. 1: Methods. (Systematics Association Special Ser.: No.17). 1981. text ed. 174.00 (0-12-564701-8) Acad Pr.

Price, J. W. Tin & Tin-Alloy Plating. 1982. 240.00 (0-686-81702-8) St Mut.

Price, J. W. & Smith, R. Tin. (Handbook of Analytical Chemistry Ser.: Vol. 4, Pt. 3, Section A, Y). (Illus.). 1978. 105.00 (0-387-08234-4) Spr-Verlag.

Price, Jacob M. Capital & Credit in British Overseas Trade: The View from the Chesapeake 1770-1776. LC 80-13815. 233p. 1980. 32.00 (0-674-09480-8) HUP.

— Perry of London: A Family & a Firm on the Seaborne Frontier, 1615-1753. (Historical Studies: Vol. No. III). (Illus.). 208p. 1992. text ed. 30.00 (0-674-66306-3) HUP.

Price, James D. The Syntax of Masoretic Accents in the Hebrew Bible. LC 90-20265. (Studies in the Bible & Early Christianity: Vol. 27). 344p. 1990. lib. bdg. 99.95 (0-88946-510-X) E Mellen.

Price, James E. Analysis of a Middle Mississippian House in Butler County, Missouri. LC 70-628940. (Museum Briefs Ser.: No. 1). (Illus.). iv, 31p. 1969. pap. 1.70 (0-913134-00-7) Mus Anthro MO.

Price, James E. & Griffin, James B. The Snodgrass Site of the Powers Phase of Southeast Missouri. (Anthropological Papers: No. 66). (Illus.). (Orig.). 1979. pap. 3.00 (0-932206-77-8) U Mich Mus Anthro.

Price, James E. & Krakker, James J. Dalton, Occupation of the Ozark Border. Feldman, L. H., ed. LC 75-327206. (Museum Briefs Ser.: No. 20). (Illus.). vii, 41p. 1975. pap. 3.00 (0-913134-20-1) Mus Anthro MO.

Price, James E., et al. Recent Investigations at Towosahgy State Historic Site & Its Physical Environment: Recent Investigations at Towosahgy State Historic Site & Its Physical Environment. Wood, W. Raymond, ed. (Missouri Archaeologist Ser.: Vol. 51). (Illus.). 91p. (Orig.). 1993. pap. 6.50 (0-943414-74-1) MO Arch Soc.

Price, James F. & Schweigert, Bernard S., eds. Science of Meat & Meat Products. 3rd ed. 639p. 1987. 98.00 (0-917678-21-4) Food & Nut Pr.

Price, James H., jt. auth. see Steen, Edwin B.

Price, James L. The New Testament. 544p. (C). 1987. lib. bdg. write for info. (0-02-396610-6) Macmillan.

Price, James L. & Mueller, Charles W. Absenteeism & Turnover of Hospital Employee. LC 85-23779. (Monographs in Organizational Behavior & Industrial Relations: Vol. 5). 282p. 1986. 73.25 (0-89232-441-4) Jai Pr.

— Handbook of Organizational Measurement. LC 85-8136. 304p. 1986. text ed. 28.00 (0-685-10496-6) Harper Busn.

— Professional Turnover: The Case of Nurses. (Health Systems Management Ser.). 218p. (C). 1980. 25.00 (0-88331-184-4) Luce.

Price, Janet R., et al. The Rights of Students: The Basic ACLU Guide to a Student's Rights. LC 87-9890. (American Civil Liberties Union Handbook Ser.). 195p. 1988. 7.95 (0-8093-1423-1) S Ill U Pr.

Price, Jeanie. Bedtime Thoughts for Pleasant Dreams. 1993. pap. 4.95 (1-56233-089-6, Mustard Seed Bks) Star Song TN.

— Five Hundred Things Your Minister Tried to Tell You but the Guy Sitting Next to You Was Snoring. 1993. pap. 4.95 (1-56233-087-X, Mustard Seed Bks) Star Song TN.

— Gift of Love. 1993. 19.99 (1-56233-050-0) Star Song TN.

— Joy in the Morning, Joy in the Evening, Joy in the Afternoon: The Top 100 Reasons Why Christians. 1993. pap. 4.95 (1-56233-086-1, Mustard Seed Bks) Star Song TN.

— Questions to Ask Yourself Today in Case Jesus Comes Back Tomorrow. 1993. pap. 4.95 (1-56233-085-3, Mustard Seed Bks) Star Song TN.

— Teenagers with the Courage to Serve the Lord Have the Power to Influence Their Family. 1993. pap. 4.95 (1-56233-090-X, Mustard Seed Bks) Star Song TN.

— Things the Media, Talk Show Host, & Liberals Never Tell You about Dan Quayle. 1992. pap. 6.99 (1-56233-040-3) Star Song TN.

Price, Jeanne & Zamkoff, Bernard. Grading Techniques for Modern Design. LC 73-8403. (Illus.). 150p. (C). 1973. 23.50 (0-87005-102-4) Fairchild.

Price, Jeanne, jt. auth. see Zamkoff, Bernard.

***Price, Jeff, et al, eds.** The Summer Atlas of North American Birds. (Illus.). 320p. 1995. text ed. 47.95 (0-12-564660-7) Acad Pr.

***Price, Jeffrey.** Taxation of Land Transactions. 4th ed. 482p. 1994. pap. text ed. 110.00 (0-406-62410-0, UK) Butterworth Legal Pubs.

— Yellow Pages Advertising: How to Get the Greatest Return on Your Investment. (Illus.). 115p. 1991. write for info. (0-945909-01-2) Idlewood Pub.

— The Yellow Pages Handbook of Objections & Responses. (Illus.). 132p. (Orig.). 1988. pap. 13.95 (0-945909-00-4) Idlewood Pub.

Price, Jeffrey, jt. auth. see Delson, Rod.

Price, Jeffrey T. Language & Being in Wittgenstein's "Philosophical Investigations" 1973. pap. text ed. 26.95 (90-279-2443-0) Mouton.

Price, Jeffrey W. The Songs of Vittorio Giannini on Poems by Karl Flaster. 112p. 1994. per. 16.95 (0-8403-9398-9) Kendall-Hunt.

Price, Jerome B. The Antinuclear Movement. (Social Movements Past & Present Ser.). 224p. 1982. lib. bdg. 20.95 (0-8057-9705-X, Twayne) Macmillan.

— The Antinuclear Movement. (Social Movements Past & Present Ser.). 224p. 1987. pap. 12.95 (0-8057-9720-3, Twayne) Macmillan.

— The Antinuclear Movement. rev. ed. (Social Movements Past & Present Ser.). 240p. 1989. text ed. 14.95 (0-8057-9735-1, Twayne) Macmillan.

— The Antinuclear Movement. rev. ed. (Social Movements Past & Present Ser.). 240p. 1990. pap. 14.95 (0-8057-9736-X, Twayne) Macmillan.

Price, Joan. The Honest Truth about Losing Weight & Keeping It Off. (Illus.). (Orig.). 1991. pap. text ed. 9.95 (0-9627708-1-7) NordicPress.

— Truth Is a Bright Star. LC 82-1345. (J). 1982. pap. 8.95 (0-89087-333-X) Celestial Arts.

Price, Joanne K. Applied Math for Wastewater Plant Operators. LC 90-71881. 488p. 1991. student ed 38.50 (0-87762-809-2); write for info. (0-87762-810-6) Technomic.

— Applied Math for Water Plant Operators. LC 91-65983. 535p. 1991. 38.50 (0-87762-874-2); write for info. (0-87762-875-0) Technomic.

— Basic Math Concepts for Water & Wastewater Plant Operators. LC 90-71880. 368p. 1991. 32.50 (0-87762-808-4) Technomic.

***Price, Jody.** A Map with Utopia: Oscar Wilde's Theory for Social Transformation. LC 94-22374. (American University Studies, Series IV, English Language & Literature: Vol. 162). 1995. write for info. (0-8204-2069-7) P Lang Pubs.

Price, John. Pub Walks Around Portsmouth & the South Downs. (C). 1989. 39.00 (1-85455-070-5, Pub. by Ensign Pubns & Print UK) St Mut.

Price, John, jt. auth. see Rees, John.

Price, John A. Indians of Canada: Cultural Dynamics. 262p. 1988. reprint ed. pap. text ed. 11.95 (0-88133-307-7) Sheffield WI.

— Pursuit of the Phoenix. 1990. mass mkt. 4.50 (0-8217-2962-4) Zebra.

Price, John A., jt. auth. see Henderson, Schuyler K.

Price, John-Allen. Doomsday Ship. 1982. pap. 3.25 (0-8217-1107-5) Zebra.

— Eagle's Revenge. 432p. 1993. mass mkt. 4.50 (0-8217-4404-6) Zebra.

— Extinction Cruise. 528p. 1987. pap. 3.95 (0-8217-2039-2) Zebra.

— A Mission for Eagles. 352p. 1988. pap. 3.95 (0-8217-2487-8) Zebra.

— Phoenix Caged. 448p. 1993. mass mkt. 4.50 (0-8217-4192-6) Zebra.

— Siege of Ocean Valkyrie. 1992. mass mkt. 4.50 (0-8217-3662-0) Zebra.

Price, John E., jt. auth. see Copeland, Benny R.

Price, John E., et al. College Accounting. 7th ed. LC 93-19084. 1993. write for info. (0-02-801441-3) Glencoe.

Price, John R. The Abundance Book. 90p. (Orig.). 1987. pap. 7.00 (0-942082-08-7) Quartus Bks.

— Angel Energy: How to Harness the Power of Angels in Your Everyday Life. 240p. 1995. pap. 12.00 (0-449-90983-2) Fawcett.

— The Angels Within Us. 336p. (Orig.). 1994. pap. 12.00 (0-449-90784-8, Columbine) Fawcett.

— Empowerment. LC 92-61916. 152p. (Orig.). 1992. pap. 10.95 (0-942082-12-5) Quartus Bks.

— The Planetary Commission. LC 84-61264. 176p. (Orig.). 1984. pap. 12.00 (0-942082-05-2) Quartus Bks.

— Practical Spirituality. LC 85-62275. 160p. (Orig.). 1985. pap. 10.95 (0-942082-06-0) Quartus Bks.

— Price on Contemporary Estate Planning. 1360p. 1992. 145.00 (0-316-71859-9) Little.

— A Spiritual Philosophy for the New World. LC 90-61586. 160p. (Orig.). 1990. pap. 10.95 (0-942082-11-7) Quartus Bks.

— The Superbeings. 160p. (Orig.). 1987. reprint ed. pap. 3.95 (0-449-21543-1) Fawcett.

— With Wings As Eagles. LC 87-60003. 112p. (Orig.). 1987. pap. 11.00 (0-942082-07-9) Quartus Bks.

Price, John R., jt. auth. see Stein, Robert A.

Price, John V. David Hume. (Twayne's English Authors Ser.: TEAS No. 77). 160p. 1991. text ed. 24.95 (0-8057-7004-6, Twayne) Macmillan.

Price, John W. Focus Keysheet: Quick Reference Guide. 2nd ed. LC 92-74256. 250p. 1992. pap. 59.95 (0-9627237-0-3) L M Joy & Assocs.

— Food Habits of Some Lake Erie Fishes. 1962. 3.00 (0-86727-048-9) Ohio Bio Survey.

Price, Jonathan. LOGO for the Apple IIc: The Magic Turtle. write for info. (0-318-58181-7) P-H.

— The Trial Guide to America Online. LC 94-13867. 1995. pap. 12.95 (0-201-40833-3) Addison-Wesley.

Price, Jonathan, ed. Critics on Robert Lowell. LC 78-161435. (Readings in Literary Criticism Ser.: No. 17). 1972. 10.95 (0-87024-210-5) U of Miami Pr.

Price, Jonathan & Korman, Henry. How to Communicate Technical Information: A Handbook of Software & Hardware Documentation. 2nd ed. 325p. (C). 1993. pap. text ed. 37.75 (0-8053-6829-9) Benjamin-Cummings.

Price, Jonathan, jt. auth. see Coulombre, Rich.

Price, Jonathan J. Jerusalem under Siege: The Collapse of the Jewish State, 66-77 C.E. LC 91-40266. (Brill's Series in Jewish Studies: Vol. 3). 372p. 1992. 91.50 (90-04-09471-7) E J Brill.

Price, Jonathan L., jt. auth. see Campanelli, Jeanne F.

Price, Joseph G., ed. The Triple Bond: Audience, Actors & Renaissance Playwrights. LC 74-15140. 256p. 1975. 35.00 (0-271-01177-7) Pa St U Pr.

Price, Joseph L., ed. see Murse.

Price, Joseph L., jt. ed. see Musser, Donald W.

Price, Joseph M. Coronaries, Cholesterol & Chlorine. 100p. 1984. pap. 3.95 (0-515-09461-7) Jove Pubns.

— Lives Never Lived. 1994. 7.95 (0-8062-4852-1) Carlton.

Price, Joseph P. Park, Recreation, Leisure Film Bibliography: Annotated & Cross Indexed Bibliography of Audiovisual Materials Relating to Parks, Recreation & Leisure. 119p. reprint ed. pap. 34.00 (0-7837-1545-5, 2041830) Bks Demand.

Price, Joy. Rum-Tum-Tum: Mississippi Recipes for a Festive Southern Christmas. (Illus.). 48p. (Orig.). 1985. reprint ed. pap. 5.00 (0-945301-01-4) Druid Pr.

Price, Joyce. A Banged up Angel. Jones, M. L., ed. 192p. (Orig.) (YA). 1993. pap. text ed. 6.95 (1-882270-07-X) Old Rugged Cross.

Price, Joyce, jt. auth. see Schmitt, Lois.

Price, Juanita. Interviews That Get Jobs: A Step-by-Step Approach in the Job Hunt. 144p. 1989. per. 21.95 (0-8403-5550-5) Kendall-Hunt.

***Price, Juanita B., comp.** Child's World: Children's: A Bibliography of 275 Oregon Authors & 50 Illustrators of Children's Book in the 20th Century. 4th ed. 60p. 1995. pap. 19.95 (0-9621683-3-5) Price Prodns.

— Child's World: Children's Books: A Bibliography of 220 Oregon Authors & 30 Illustrators of Children's Books in the 20th Century. 3rd ed. 45p. 1991. pap. 19.95 (0-9621683-2-7) Price Prodns.

Price, Julia, ed. see Carlut, Charles & Meiden, Walter.

Price, Julia, ed. see Copeland, John G., et al.

Price, Julia, ed. see Mendez-Faith, Kienzle.

Price, Julia, ed. see Speroni, Charles & Golino, Carlo L.

Price, Justin J., jt. auth. see Flanders, Harley.

Price, K. F., jt. ed. see Niehaus, R. J.

Price, Karen. A Tiny Taste of the Southwest. 128p. 1993. pap. write for info. (0-9637591-0-8) KAP Ent.

Price, Kathleen M. The Lady & the Unicorn. LC 94-75989. 32p. 1994. 14.95 (1-880851-16-4) Greene Bark Pr.

***Price, Kathy A.** Letting Go: the Zen of Bowel Movements: A Book of Spiritual Encouragement for Constipated People. 112p. 1994. pap. 15.00 (0-9642906-8-5) Rock Rose Pubng.

Price, Kenneth. The Eagle Christian. (Illus.). (Orig.). 1984. 8.95 (0-685-22527-5); pap. 7.95 (0-685-22528-3) Old Faithful.

— The Eagle Christian. rev. ed. LC 88-92413. (Illus.). (Orig.). 1989. reprint ed. 8.95 (0-9621224-0-8); reprint ed. pap. 7.95 (0-9621224-1-6) Old Faithful.

Price, Kenneth M. Whitman & Tradition: The Poet in His Century. LC 89-27380. 208p. (C). 1990. text ed. 20.00x (0-300-04683-9) Yale U Pr.

Price, Kenneth M. & Leitz, Robert C., III. Critical Essays on George Santayana. (Critical Essays on American Literature Ser.). 288p. 1991. text ed. 45.00 (0-8161-7303-6, Hall Reference) Macmillan.

***Price, Kenneth M. & Smith, Susan B., eds.** Periodical Literature in Nineteenth-Century America. (Illus.). 352p. (C). 1995. text ed. 45.00 (0-8139-1629-1); pap. text ed. 17.50 (0-8139-1630-5) U Pr of Va.

Price, Kenneth M., ed. see Whitman, Thomas J.

Price, Kent A., ed. The Dilemmas of Choice. LC 86-195396. 270p. reprint ed. pap. 77.00 (0-7837-0116-0, 2040393) Bks Demand.

— Regional Conflict & National Policy. LC 82-47983. xviii, 142p. 1982. pap. 12.95 (0-8018-2919-4) Resources Future.

Price, Kent A., jt. ed. see Castle, Emery N.

Price, Kevin S. Leadership: An Exploration. LC 93-85063. 132p. (Orig.). (C). 1993. pap. text ed. 9.95 (0-9637452-0-4) Proactive Pubs.

Price, Kingsley, ed. On Criticizing Music: Five Philosophical Perspectives. LC 81-47597. 127p. reprint ed. pap. 36.20 (0-317-55534-0, 2029241) Bks Demand.

Price, L. Greer. Grand Canyon: The Story Behind the Scenery. 4th rev. ed. LC 91-60043. (Illus.). 64p. 1991. pap. 6.95 (0-88714-060-2) KC Pubns.

Price, Larkin B., ed. Marcel Proust: A Critical Panorama. LC 72-83033. 302p. reprint ed. pap. 86.10 (0-317-29081-9, 2020226) Bks Demand.

Price, Larry W. Mountains & Man: A Study of Process & Environment. LC 76-14294. (Illus.). 496p. 1981. pap. 20.00 (0-520-05886-0, CAL 833) U CA Pr.

Price, Laurence W. Starting & Operating a Landscape Maintenance Business. (Illus.). 133p. (Orig.). (C). 1989. pap. text ed. 7.95 (0-9611966-1-0) Botany Bks.

Price, Laurie. Except for Memory. (Orig.). Date not set. pap. 8.95 (1-880766-06-X) Pantograph Pr.

Price, Lawrence M. Reception of English Literature in Germany. LC 68-21223. 1972. reprint ed. 36.95 (0-405-08863-9) Ayer.

Price, Leland. Parted on Her Wedding Morn. 1942. pap. 2.75 (0-8222-0873-3) Dramatists Play.

Price, Leo. Hoover Wants to Help. LC 88-19188. (Illus.). 35p. (Orig.). (J). (gr. 2-3). 1988. pap. 1.95 (0-8198-3313-4); write for info. (0-8198-3312-6) Pauline Bks.

***Price, Leon C.** Beyond Survival to Victory: A Practical Guide for Victorious Christian Living. 96p. 1993. pap. 6.00 (0-9637311-0-6) Evergreen AL.

Price, Les. Rottweilers: An Owner's Companion. (Illus.). 224p. 1991. 25.95 (0-87605-297-9) Howell Bk.

Price, Leslie. African Journal. 156p. (Orig.). 1990. pap. text ed. 3.95 (0-936625-73-2, New Hope AL) Womans Mission Union.

Price, Leslie A. & Kindersley, Dorling. Kids' Knits. 1986. pap. 9.95 (0-345-34467-7, Ballantine Trade) Ballantine.

Price, Lew P. Aquarian Anastasis. LC 65-9503. 1975. pap. 15.00 (0-917578-01-5) L Paxton Price.

— Astrology: The Music of Life. 1984. pap. 25.00 (0-917578-05-8) L Paxton Price.

— Creating & Using the Native American Love Flute. (Illus.). 1994. pap. 8.00 (0-917578-09-0) L Paxton Price.

— Dimensions in Astrology. 1986. pap. 12.00 (0-317-55795-5) L Paxton Price.

— Native North American Flutes. (Illus.). 1990. pap. 4.50 (0-917578-07-4) L Paxton Price.

— The Oldest Magic. (Illus.). 200p. 1995. pap. 24.00 (0-917578-10-4) L Paxton Price.

— Secrets of the Flute: The Physics, Math, & Design of Non-Mechanical Folk Flutes. (Illus.). 80p. (Orig.). (C). 1991. pap. 12.00 (0-917578-08-2) L Paxton Price.

Price, Linda. Dare to Dream. 416p. (Orig.). 1989. mass mkt. 4.50 (0-380-75361-8) Avon.

Price, Lindy H. Sports & New Exercise Research: Index of Current Information. 150p. 1994. 44.50 (0-7883-0068-7); pap. 39.50 (0-7883-0069-5) ABBE Pubs Assn.

Price, Llewellyn I., jt. auth. see Romer, Alfred S.

Price, Lorna. The Plan of St. Gall in Brief: An Overview Based on the Three-Volume Work by Walter Horn & Ernest Born. LC 82-70215. (Illus.). 120p. 1982. pap. 48.00 (0-520-04334-0) U CA Pr.

Price, Lorna, ed. Fourth Newport Biennial: Southern California 1993. LC 93-35628. (Illus.). 56p. (Orig.). 1993. pap. text ed. 12.95 (0-917493-20-6) Newport Harbor.

Price, Lorna, ed. see Guenther, Bruce.

Price, Louise. Creative Group Work on the Campus: A Developmental Study of Certain Aspects of Student Life. LC 76-177166. (Columbia University. Teachers College. Contributions to Education Ser.: No. 830). reprint ed. 37.50 (0-404-55830-5) AMS Pr.

Price, Lucy K., jt. auth. see Salam, Debera J.

Price, Lucy M. Sydney: Sydney-Smith & Clagett-Price Genealogy, with the Lewis, Montgomery, Harrison, Hawley, Moorhead, Rixey, et al. (Illus.). 324p. 1992. reprint ed. lib. bdg. 59.50 (0-8328-2740-1); reprint ed. pap. 49.50 (0-8328-2741-X) Higginson Bk Co.

***Price, Lynn F.** Every Person in the Book of Mormon: A Chronological Reference & Synopsis. 1995. pap. 16.98 (0-88290-533-3) Horizon Utah.

Price, M. & Le Cain, Errol. Have You Seen My Sister? (J). (ps-2). 1991. 12.95 (0-15-200467-X, HB Juv Bks) HarBrace.

Price, M. Philip. Economic Problems of Europe, Pre-War & After. (Business Enterprises Reprint Ser.). 218p. 1986. reprint ed. lib. bdg. 42.00 (0-89941-503-2, 304360) W S Hein.

Price, Marean J. For the Things He Has Done. (Illus.). 98p. (Orig.). Date not set. pap. text ed. 9.95 (1-883372-01-1) Rondelle Pub.

— Lord, Why Not Me? A Mother's Story of an Autistic Child. (Illus.). 104p. (Orig.). Date not set. pap. text ed. 14.95 (1-883372-00-3) Rondelle Pub.

Price, Margaret. I Can Read at Last. Carlin, Chip, ed. 42p. 1988. 60.00 (0-685-23147-X) Lit Vol Am.

Price, Margaret, et al. Management Handbook for Volunteer Programs. McKallip, Jonathan & Lawson, V. K., eds. 1984. pap. text ed. 6.50 (0-930713-37-0) Lit Vol Am.

Price, Margaret M. Emerging Stock Markets: A Complete Investment Guide to New Markets Around the World. 1994. text ed. 39.95 (0-07-051049-0) McGraw.

Price, Marian. Reader-Response Criticism: A Test of Its Usefulness in a First-Year College Course in Writing about Literature. LC 89-2444. (American University Studies: English Language & Literature: Ser. IV, Vol. 109). 161p. 1990. text ed. 34.95 (0-8204-1115-9) P Lang Pubs.

Price, Marjorie. Emerald Embrace. 1989. mass mkt. 4.25 (0-8217-2855-5) Zebra.

— Renegade Heart. 448p. 1987. pap. 3.75 (0-8217-2244-1) Zebra.

Price, Marjorie, jt. auth. see Franck, Phyllis.

Price, Mark R. Animal Reintroductions: The Arabian Oryx in Oman. (Cambridge Studies in Applied Ecology & Resource Management). (Illus.). 250p. (C). 1989. 42.95 (0-521-34411-5) Cambridge U Pr.

Price, Marla. David Bates: Forty Paintings. Sweeney, Jane, ed. LC 88-62325. (Illus.). 100p. (Orig.). 1988. pap. 20.00 (0-929865-00-6) Mod Art Mus Ft Worth.

— George Segal: Still Lifes & Related Works. LC 89-64288. (Illus.). 64p. (Orig.). 1990. pap. 19.95 (0-929865-04-9) Mod Art Mus Ft Worth.

— Milton Avery: Works from the Nineteen Fifties. LC 90-61490. (Illus.). 48p. (Orig.). 1990. 19.95 (0-929865-05-7) Mod Art Mus Ft Worth.

***Price, Marla, frwd.** Drawing Rooms: Jonathan Borofsky, Sol Le-Witt, Richard Serra. LC 94-73343. 124p. (Orig.). 1994. pap. 29.95 (0-929865-10-3) Mod Art Mus Ft Worth.

— History & Memory: Paintings by Christopher Brown. (Illus.) 104p. (Orig.). Date not set. pap. 25.00 (0-929865-11-1) Mod Art Mus Ft Worth.

— Metal & Stone: Six Young Sculptors. (Illus.). 76p. (Orig.). 1992. pap. 11.95 (0-929865-08-1) Mod Art Mus Ft Worth.

Price-Mars, Jean. So Spoke the Uncle. 2nd ed. Shannon, Magdaline W., tr. LC 82-74251. (Illus.). xxviii, 252p. 1990. 32.00 (0-89410-389-X); pap. 15.00 (0-89410-390-3) Three Continents.

Price, Martin. Forms of Life: Character & Moral Imagination in the Novel. LC 82-16064. 400p. 1983. text ed. 42.00 (0-300-02867-9) Yale U Pr.

Price, Martin, ed. Restoration & the Eighteenth Century. (Illus.). 1973. pap. text ed. 22.00 (0-19-501614-9) OUP.

Price, Martin & Heywood, Ian, eds. GIS & Mountain Environments. 300p. 1994. 95.00 (0-7484-0088-5, Pub. by Tay Francis Ltd UK) Taylor & Francis.

Price, Martin, jt. ed. see Brady, Frank.

Price, Martin, jt. ed. see Casson, Lionel.

Price, Martin, jt. ed. see Clayton, Peter.

Price, Martin, ed. see Morcom, John.

Price, Martin J. & Trell, Bluma L. Coins & Their Cities: Architecture on the Ancient Coins of Greece, Rome, & Palestine. LC 78-321015. (Illus.). 300p. reprint ed. pap. 85.50 (0-7837-3593-6, 2043457) Bks Demand.

Price, Martin J., jt. auth. see Carradice, Ian.

Price, Mary. The Photograph - a Strange Confined Space. LC 93-31698. 1994. 35.00 (0-8047-2308-7) Stanford U Pr.

Price, Mary, jt. auth. see Price, Vincent.

Price, Mary C., jt. auth. see Price, Tim.

Price, Mary E. Love Me to Sleep Tonight. Van Treese, James B., ed. 182p. 1994. pap. 7.95 (1-56901-124-9) NW Pub.

Price, Mary K. & Axtmann, Margaret M., eds. Setting the Legal Information Agenda for the Year 2000: Based on a Workshop of the American Association of Law Libraries National Legal Resources Committee Washington, D. C. October 23-26, 1988, 3 vols. LC 91-21935. (American Association of Law Libraries Publications Ser.: No. 42). 1994. 240.00 (0-8377-0142-2) Rothman.

Price, Mary R. Integration Plan Using "Calculate with Care", 2 pts. (Diskovery: Computer-Assisted Learning Ser.). 1960. 36.95 (0-685-74178-8) DCAHE.

— Integration Plan Using "Calculate with Care", Pt. I: Basic Math Skills. (Diskovery: Computer-Assisted Learning Ser.). 100p. 1960. write for info. (0-9622253-4-7) DCAHE.

— Integration Plan Using "Calculate with Care", Pt. II: Problem-Solving & Dosage Calculation. (Diskovery: Computer-Assisted Learning Ser.). 100p. 1960. write for info. (0-9622253-5-5) DCAHE.

— Integration Plan Using "Eliminating Medication Errors" (Diskovery: Computer-Assisted Learning Ser.). 56p. 1990. teacher ed 36.95 (0-9622253-9-8) DCAHE.

— Integration Plan Using "Intravenous Therapy" (Diskovery: Computer-Assisted Learning Ser.). 70p. 1990. teacher ed 36.95 (1-878275-03-8) DCAHE.

Price, Mary S., ed. see Apfel, Iris B.

Price, Mary S., ed. see Reynolds, Valrae.

Price, Mathew. Peekaboo! (Illus.). 24p. (J). (ps). 1993. 5.99 (0-679-84031-1) Knopf Bks Yng Read.

Price, Max B. Comprendamos al Escolar de Hoy. Bedford, Nancy A., tr. 160p. (Orig.). (SPA.). 1992. pap. 5.70 (0-311-11902-6) Casa Bautista.

Price, Michael. The Account Book for the Borough of Swansea, Wales 1640-1660: A Study in Local Administration During the Civil War & Interregnum. LC 90-5645. (Welsh Studies: Vol. 1). (Illus.). 340p. 1990. lib. bdg. 99.95 (0-88946-480-4) E Mellen.

— Introducing Groundwater. (Special Topics in Geology Ser: No. 2). (Illus.). 176p. 1985. text ed. 60.00 (0-04-553005-X); pap. text ed. 19.95 (0-04-553006-8) Routledge Chapman & Hall.

Price, Michael F. Power Bankers: Sales Culture Secrets of High Performance Banks. 224p. 1992. text ed. 59.00 (0-471-55555-X) Wiley.

Price, Michael H. Carnival of Souls: Herk Harvey's Classic Chiller. (Illus.). 56p. 1991. pap. 4.95 (1-56398-019-3) Malibu Graphics.

Price, Michael H. & Camp, Todd. Holiday for Screams. 56p. 1992. pap. 4.95 (1-56398-038-X) Malibu Graphics.

Price, Mike, jt. auth. see Williams, Marsha P.

Price, Milburn, jt. auth. see Reynolds, William J.

Price, Moe. Reindeer Christmas. (J). (ps-3). 1993. 15.95 (0-15-266199-9, HB Juv Bks) HarBrace.

Price, Molly. The Iris Book. (Illus.). 224p. 1973. reprint ed. pap. 5.95 (0-486-21522-9) Dover.

Price, Monroe E. Shattered Mirrors: Our Search for Identity & Community in the AIDS Era. LC 89-33265. 160p. 1989. text ed. 27.00 (0-674-80590-9) HUP.

— Television, the Public Sphere, & National Identity. 272p. 1995. 49.95 (0-19-818362-3); pap. 21.00 (0-19-818338-0) OUP.

Price, Morgan P. America after Sixty Years: Diaries of Two Generations of Englishmen. LC 73-13146. (Foreign Travelers in America, 1810-1935 Ser.). (Illus.). 242p. 1974. reprint ed. 23.95 (0-405-05470-X) Ayer.

— My Reminiscences of the Russian Revolution. LC 79-2922. (Illus.). 402p. 1983. reprint ed. 33.25 (0-8305-0091-X) Hyperion Conn.

***Price, Munro.** Preserving the Monarchy: The Comte de Vergennes, 1774-1787. 272p. (C). 1995. 59.95 (0-521-46566-4) Cambridge U Pr.

Price, Nancy. Night Woman. 352p. 1993. mass mkt. 5.99 (0-671-74994-3, Pocket Star Bks) PB.

— Night Woman. large type ed. LC 92-33705. 550p. 1993. reprint ed. lib. bdg. 18.95 (1-56054-583-6) Thorndike Pr.

— Sleeping with the Enemy. 1991. mass mkt. 5.99 (0-425-12792-3) Berkley Pub.

Price, Nancy W., jt. auth. see Van der Meulen, Jan.

Price, Neil D. On the Edge: The Love-Hate World of the Borderline Personality. 144p. (Orig.). 1989. pap. 7.95 (0-929162-10-2) PIA Pr.

Price, Nelson. New Age, the Occult & Lion Country. LC 89-3667. 1989. pap. 7.99 (0-8007-5300-3) Revell.

Price, Nelson L. Only the Beginning. LC 79-55662. (J). (gr. 10 up). 1980. 7.99 (0-8054-5331-8, 4253-31) Broadman.

Price, Neville J. & Cosgrove, John W. Analysis of Geological Structures. (Illus.). 560p. 1990. pap. 49.95 (0-521-31958-7) Cambridge U Pr.

Price, Nicholas C. & Dwek, Raymond A. Principles & Problems in Physical Chemistry for Biochemists. 2nd ed. (Illus.). 1980. pap. 18.95 (0-19-855512-1) OUP.

Price, Nicholas C. & Stevens, Lewis. Fundamentals of Enzymology. 2nd ed. (Illus.). 544p. (C). 1989. pap. text ed. 33.95 (0-19-855296-3) OUP.

Price, Norman. Notes on Mada Phonology. Merrifield, William R., ed. LC 88-63673. (Language Data, African Ser.: No. 23). 51p. 1989. pap. text ed. 4.15 (0-88312-600-1); fiche 4.00 (0-88312-733-4) Summer Instit Ling.

Price, Oliver R. High Leverage Real Estate Investments: Inside Secrets of Using OPM. 1978. pap. 5.95 (0-685-03912-9, Busn) P-H.

Price, P. J. Competency in English: A Life Skills Approach. (Orig.). 1990. pap. text ed. write for info. (0-07-556988-4) McGraw.

Price, Pamela V. France for the Gourmet Traveler. 1991. pap. 16.95 (0-8442-9934-0, Passport Bks) NTC Pub Grp.

An Asterisk (*) at the beginning of an entry indicates that the title is appearing in BIP for the first time.

— The Wines of the Graves. LC 88-60435. (Illus.). 388p. 1988. 45.00 (0-85667-334-X, Pub. by P Wilson Pubs) Sothebys Pubns.

Price, Pamela V. & Fielden, Christopher. Alsace Wines & Spirits. LC 84-50547. (Illus.). 216p. 1984. 29.95 (0-85667-183-5, Pub. by P Wilson Pubs) Sothebys Pubns.

Price, Pat, ed. see Manuscriptors Guild Members.

Price, Pat L. & Ouvry, Philip. Ocean Yachtmaster Exercises. (Illus.). 128p. 1986. pap. 24.50 (0-229-11792-9) Sheridan.

— Yachtmaster: An Examination Handbook with Exercises. 2nd ed. (Illus.). 288p. 1993. 29.95 (0-7136-3772-2) Sheridan.

— Yachtmaster Exercises. 2nd ed. (Illus.). 128p. 1993. pap. 23.50 (0-7136-3810-9, Adlard Coles) Sheridan.

Price, Patricia. Transformational Breathwork: The Basics of Renewal & Rebirth. 100p. (Orig.). 1989. pap. text ed. 6.50 (0-926625-88-8) Trilogy Pubns.

Price, Paul, jt. ed. see Slavkin, Harold.

***Price, Paxton P.** Pioneers of the Mesilla Valley. (Illus.). 450p. (Orig.). 1995. pap. 19.95 (1-881325-12-1) Yucca Tree Pr.

Price, Peter W. Evolutionary Biology of Parasites. LC 79-3227. (Monographs in Population Biology: No. 15). 1980. pap. 16.95 (0-691-08257-X) Princeton U Pr.

— Insect Ecology. 2nd ed. LC 83-23385. 607p. 1984. text ed. 84.95 (0-471-07892-1, Wiley-Interscience) Wiley.

Price, Peter W., jt. ed. see Cappuccino, Naomi.

Price, Peter W., et al. A New Ecology: Novel Approaches to Interactive Systems. 515p. 1984. text ed. 99.95 (0-471-89670-5) Wiley.

Price, Peter W., et al, eds. Plant-Animal Interactions: Evolutionary Ecology in Tropical & Temperate Regions. 639p. 1991. text ed. 150.00 (0-471-50937-X) Wiley.

Price, Philip, jt. auth. see Carter, Ray.

Price, Planaria J. Competency in English: A Life Skills Approach. 208p. (Orig.). (C). 1988. pap. text ed. write for info. (0-318-62869-4) Random.

— Now That You're Here, What Do You Say? 208p. (C). 1988. pap. text ed. 8.50 (0-394-35393-5) Random.

Price, Polly S. Sand in Our Shoes: A Guide Book to Pharaonic Egypt. (Illus.). 307p. 1979. pap. text ed. 8.50 (0-9604012-0-2) P S Price.

Price, R. Douglas & Brown, James A., eds. Prehistoric Hunters - Gatherers: The Emergence of Cultural Complexity. (Studies in Archaeology). 450p. 1988. reprint ed. pap. text ed. 66.00 (0-12-564751-4) Acad Pr.

Price, R. F. Marx & Education in Late Capitalism. LC 86-3541. 318p. 1986. 53.00 (0-389-20617-2, N8175) B&N Imports.

— Reference Book of English Words & Phrases for Foreign Science Students. 1966. 84.00 (0-08-011750-3, Pub. by Pergamon Repr UK) Franklin.

Price, R. F., ed. see Presniakov, A. E.

Price, R. M. Firearms Self-Defense: An Introductory Guide for the Layman on How to Use Firearms as a Last Resort Safely & Legally. (Weaponry Ser.). 1986. lib. bdg. 79.95 (0-8490-3709-3) Gordon Pr.

Price, R. M., tr. see Cyril of Scythopolis.

Price, R. M., tr. see Theodoret.

Price, Randall. In Search of Temple Treasures: The Lost Ark of the Covenant & the Last Days. 1994. pap. 9.99 (1-56507-127-1) Harvest Hse.

Price, Randall, jt. auth. see Ice, Thomas.

Price, Ray B. & Cox, Gale R. How to Acquire Wealth: One Man's Odyssey. LC 90-61189. 87p. (Orig.). (YA). 1990. pap. text ed. 8.95 (0-9626318-0-9) Price Pub SC.

Price, Raymond A. & Douglas, R. J., eds. Variations in Tectonic Styles in Canada. LC 73-331222. (Geological Association of Canada. Special Paper Ser.: No. 11). 698p. reprint ed. pap. 180.00 (0-685-17104-3, 2027842) Bks Demand.

Price, Realto E. History of Clayton County, Iowa, 2 vols., Set. (Illus.). 953p. 1992. reprint ed. lib. bdg. 94.00 (0-8328-2552-2) Higginson Bk Co.

Price, Realto E., ed. History of Lee County, Iowa: A History of the County, Its Cities, Towns; A Biographical Directory of Its Citizens. (Illus.). 887p. 1992. reprint ed. lib. bdg. 87.50 (0-8328-2586-7) Higginson Bk Co.

Price, Reese E., jt. ed. see Gilligan, Stephen.

Price, Reynolds. August Snow. 1991. pap. 4.75 (0-8222-0075-9) Dramatists Play.

— Back Before Day. LC 89-62735. 64p. 1989. 25.00 (0-933598-16-5) NC Wesleyan Pr.

— Better Days. 1991. pap. 4.75 (0-8222-0111-9) Dramatists Play.

— Blue Calhoun. 1994. mass mkt. 5.99 (0-345-37722-2) Ballantine.

— Blue Calhoun. 416p. 1992. text ed. 23.00 (0-689-12146-6, Atheneum S&S) S&S Trade.

— Blue Calhoun Ltd. 2nd ed. 373p. 1992. text ed. 100.00 (0-689-12171-7, Atheneum S&S) S&S Trade.

— Clear Pictures: First Loves, First Guides. 288p. 1989. text ed. 19.95 (0-689-12075-3, Atheneum S&S) S&S Trade.

— The Collected Stories. 640p. 1994. pap. 12.95 (0-452-27218-1, Plume) NAL-Dutton.

— The Collected Stories of Reynolds Price. 672p. 1993. text ed. 25.00 (0-689-12147-4, Atheneum S&S) S&S Trade.

— A Common Room. 416p. 1989. pap. 11.95 (0-689-70817-3, Atheneum S&S) S&S Trade.

— A Common Room: New & Selected Essays. 352p. 1987. text ed. 24.95 (0-689-11948-8, Atheneum S&S) S&S Trade.

— The Foreseeable Future. 288p. 1991. text ed. 21.95 (0-689-12110-5, Pub. by Ctrl Bur voor Schimmel NE) Macmillan.

— Foreseeable Future. 1992. mass mkt. 5.99 (0-345-37721-4) Ballantine.

— Full Moon & Other Plays. LC 92-44383. 312p. 1993. pap. 13.95 (1-55936-064-X) Theatre Comm.

— Good Hearts. large type ed. 454p. 1988. reprint ed. lib. bdg. 7.95 (0-89621-192-4) Thorndike Pr.

— Home Made. deluxe ed. LC 90-63100. (Illus.). 64p. 1990. 55.00 (0-933598-23-8) NC Wesleyan Pr.

— The Honest Account of a Memorable Life: An Apocryphal Gospel. 1994. 25.00 (0-933598-52-1) NC Wesleyan Pr.

— The Honest Account of a Memorable Life: An Apocryphal Gospel. deluxe limited ed. 1994. 50.00 (0-933598-53-X) NC Wesleyan Pr.

— House Snake. 24p. 1986. 50.00 (0-935716-38-6) Lord John.

— Kate Vaiden. 1987. mass mkt. 5.99 (0-345-34358-1) Ballantine.

— The Laws of Ice. LC 86-47698. 112p. (Orig.). 1986. pap. 12.95 (0-689-11861-9) Macmillan.

— A Long & Happy Life. LC 61-12790. 208p. 1987. text ed. 17.95 (0-689-11947-X, Atheneum S&S); pap. 4.95 (0-689-10224-0, Atheneum S&S) S&S Trade.

— Love & Work. 1987. pap. 3.50 (0-345-34995-4) Ballantine.

— Love & Work. LC 68-22422. (C). 1975. reprint ed. pap. 7.95 (0-689-70520-4, 210, Atheneum S&S) S&S Trade.

— Mustian: Two Novels & a Story. 384p. 1987. mass mkt. 4.95 (0-345-34521-5) Ballantine.

— The Names & Faces of Heroes. 176p. 1989. mass mkt. 4.95 (0-345-36182-2) Ballantine.

— New Music: A Trilogy. LC 90-48090. 240p. 1990. 22.95 (1-55936-015-1); pap. 10.95 (1-55936-016-X) Theatre Comm.

— Night Dance. 1991. pap. 4.75 (0-8222-0819-9) Dramatists Play.

— Presence & Absence: Versions from the Bible. limited ed. 1976. 45.00 (0-89723-007-8) Bruccoli.

— The Promise of Rest. LC 94-48086. (Great Circle Ser.). 353p. 1995. 24.00 (0-684-80149-3, Scribners) S&S Trade.

— Real Copies. LC 88-62140. (Orig.). 1988. pap. 10.00 (0-933598-08-4) NC Wesleyan Pr.

— The Source of Light. 1995. pap. 12.00 (0-684-81338-6, Scribners) S&S Trade.

— Surface of Earth. 1989. mass mkt. 4.95 (0-345-34994-6) Ballantine.

— The Surface of Earth. 1995. pap. 14.00 (0-684-81339-4, Scribners) S&S Trade.

— The Tongues of Angels. 1991. mass mkt. 5.99 (0-345-37102-X) Ballantine.

— The Tongues of Angels. 176p. 1990. 17.95 (0-689-12093-1, Atheneum S&S) S&S Trade.

— The Tongues of Angels. large type ed. LC 90-41188. 264p. 1990. reprint ed. lib. bdg. 19.95 (1-56054-048-6) Thorndike Pr.

— The Use of Fire. 160p. 1990. text ed. 19.95 (0-689-12109-1, Pub. by Ctrl Bur voor Schimmel NE) Macmillan.

— A Whole New Life. 224p. 1994. text ed. 20.00 (0-689-12197-0, Pub. by Ctrl Bur voor Schimmel NE) Macmillan.

— A Whole New Life. large type ed. LC 94-48471. 1995. 10.95 (0-452-27473-7, Plume) NAL-Dutton.

— A Whole New Life: An Illness & a Healing. large type ed. LC 94-27310. 261p. 1994. 20.95 (0-8161-7478-4) Hall.

Price, Richard. Alabi's World. LC 89-15488. (Illus.). 480p. 1990. text ed. 65.00x (0-8018-3862-2); pap. 19.95 (0-8018-3956-4) Johns Hopkins.

— Bloodbrothers. 288p. 1993. pap. 9.00 (0-380-77476-3) Avon.

— The Breaks. (Contemporary American Fiction Ser.). 448p. 1984. pap. 11.00 (0-14-007037-0, Penguin Bks) Viking Penguin.

— Clockers. 640p. 1993. mass mkt. 5.99 (0-380-72081-7) Avon.

— Clockers. 592p. 1992. 22.95 (0-395-53761-4) HM.

— Discourse on the Love of Our Country. 104p. 1992. reprint ed. 40.00 (1-85477-108-6, Pub. by Woodstock Bks UK) Cassell.

— Equatoria. 1994. pap. 16.95 (0-415-90895-7, Pub. by Tavistock UK) Routledge Chapman & Hall.

— First-Time: The Historical Vision of an Afro-American People. LC 83-29. (Studies in Atlantic History & Culture). 224p. 1983. pap. text ed. 14.95 (0-8018-2985-2) Johns Hopkins.

— The Guiana Maroons: A Historical & Bibliographical Introduction. LC 76-8498. (Johns Hopkins Studies in Atlantic History & Culture Ser.). 196p. reprint ed. pap. 55.90 (0-7837-2649-X, 2043003) Bks Demand.

— Labour in British Society: An Interpretive History. 272p. 1990. pap. 16.95 (0-415-04453-7, A4049) Routledge.

— Labour in British Society: An Interpretive History. 288p. 1986. 49.95 (0-85664-736-5, Pub. by Croom Helm UK) Routledge Chapman & Hall.

— Ladies' Man. 272p. 1993. pap. 9.00 (0-380-77475-5) Avon.

— Neil Gunn. 1991. text ed. 35.00 (0-7486-0259-3, Pub. by Edinburgh U Pr UK) Col U Pr.

— Observations on the Importance of the American Revolution & the Means of Making It a Benefit to the World. LC 75-31129. reprint ed. 15.00 (0-404-13607-9) AMS Pr.

— Political Writings. Thomas, D. O., ed. (Cambridge Texts in the History of Political Thought Ser.). 232p. (C). 1992. 59.95 (0-521-40162-3); pap. 18.95 (0-521-40969-1) Cambridge U Pr.

— A Review of the Principle Questions in Morals. (C). 1986. reprint ed. lib. bdg. 21.95 (0-935005-25-0); reprint ed. pap. text ed. 11.95 (0-935005-26-9) Lincoln-Rembrandt.

— Three Screenplays: The Color of Money, Sea of Love, Night & the City. LC 93-12236. 352p. 1993. pap. 10.95 (0-395-66923-5) HM.

— Two Tracts on Civil Liberties. LC 74-169641. (Era of the American Revolution Ser.). 1972. reprint ed. lib. bdg. 42.50 (0-306-70233-9) Da Capo.

— The Wanderers. 256p. 1993. pap. 9.00 (0-380-77474-7) Avon.

Price, Richard, ed. Maroon Societies: Rebel Slave Communities in the Americas. LC 73-83603. 1979. pap. 15.95x (0-8018-2247-5) Johns Hopkins.

***Price, Richard & Price, Sally.** Enigma Variations. LC 95-1362. (Illus.). 176p. (C). 1995. pap. 18.95 (0-674-25726-X) HUP.

— Equatoria. (Illus.). 240p. 1992. 25.00 (0-415-90610-5, A7342, Routledge NY) Routledge.

— On the Mall: Presenting Maroon Tradition-Bearers at the 1992 Festival of American Folklore. (Illus.). 122p. 1995. text ed. 25.00 (0-87940-707-7); pap. 12.00 (0-87940-706-9) Ind U Pr.

— Two Evenings in Saramaka: Afro-American Tale-Telling in the Suriname Rain Forest. LC 90-35941. (Illus.). 288p. 1991. pap. text ed. 19.95 (0-226-68062-2) U Ch Pr.

— Two Evenings in Saramaka: Afro-American Tale-Telling in the Suriname Rain Forest. LC 90-35941. (Illus.). 288p. 1991. lib. bdg. 55.00 (0-226-68061-4) U Ch Pr.

Price, Richard, jt. ed. see Belchem, John.

Price, Richard, jt. auth. see Mintz, Sidney W.

Price, Richard, ed. see Stedman, John G.

Price, Richard H. Contemporary Secrets to Finding Love. 172p. 1994. pap. 12.95 (1-885280-09-2) Golf Supplies.

Price, Richard H., et al, eds. Fourteen Ounces of Prevention: A Casebook for Practitioners. LC 88-14471. 198p. 1988. pap. 30.00 (1-55798-036-5) Am Psychol.

— Prevention in Mental Health: Research, Policy & Practice. LC 80-14676. (Sage Annual Reviews of Community Mental Health Ser.: No. 1). 320p. reprint ed. pap. 91.20 (0-8357-4846-4, 2037777) Bks Demand.

Price, Richard L., jt. auth. see Murvin, Harry J.

Price, Richard W. & Perry, Samuel W., III, eds. HIV, AIDS, & the Brain. LC 93-36006. (Association for Research in Nervous & Mental Disease Research Publications: Vol. 72). 352p. 1994. 99.00 (0-7817-0063-9) Raven.

Price, Richard W., jt. ed. see Martin, John H.

Price, Richard W., jt. ed. see Whitehouse, David B.

Price, Rini, ed. see Seed, Sally.

Price, Robert. Johnny Appleseed: Man & Myth. (Illus.). 1954. 18.50 (0-8446-1366-5) Peter Smith.

— Scotland's Golf Courses: An Extraordinary Variety of Experience. (Illus.). 254p. 1989. 25.00 (0-08-036591-4, Pub. by Aberdeen U Pr) Macmillan.

Price, Robert, ed. UFOs over Hampshire & the Low. (C). 1989. 39.00 (1-85455-037-3, Pub. by Ensign Pubns & Print UK) St Mut.

Price, Robert, jt. auth. see Finley, Eddy.

Price, Robert C., jt. auth. see Mead, Tray C.

***Price, Robert E.** Blues Blood: New & Selected Poems. LC 94-72477. 83p. (Orig.). 1994. pap. 12.00 (0-9642183-0-5) CAC Press.

Price, Robert F. Mixail Soloxov in Yugoslavia: Reception & Literary Impact. (East European Monographs: No. 4). 180p. 1973. text ed. 54.00 (0-231-03748-1) East Eur Quarterly.

Price, Robert F., jt. auth. see Sljivic-Simsic, Biljana.

Price, Robert G. & Hudson, Billy G., eds. Renal Basement Membranes in Health & Disease. 456p. 1987. text ed. 93.00 (0-12-564725-5) Acad Pr.

Price, Robert J. Glacial & Fluvioglacial Landforms. (Geomorphology Texts Ser.: No. 5). 250p. reprint ed. pap. 71.30 (0-317-28356-1, 2022533) Bks Demand.

— Highland Landforms. (Illus.). 110p. 1991. pap. 13.95 (0-08-041196-7, Pub. by Aberdeen U Pr) Macmillan.

***Price, Robert M.** The Crisis of Biblical Authority: The Setting & Range of the Current Evangelical Controversy. LC 95-3865. (Studies in Philosophy & Religion: No. 3). 1995. lib. bdg. write for info. (0-912134-16-X, St Willibrords Pr); pap. write for info. (0-912134-17-8, St Willibrords Pr) Borgo Pr.

— H. P. Lovecraft & the Cthulhu Mythos: Essays on America's Classic Writer of Horror Fiction. 2nd exp. rev. ed. LC 95-2764. (I. O. Evans Studies in the Philosophy & Criticism of Literature: No. 25). 1995. lib. bdg. write for info. (1-55742-233-8) Borgo Pr.

— H. P. Lovecraft & the Cthulhu Mythos: Essays on America's Classic Writer of Horror Fiction. 2nd expanded rev. ed. LC 95-2764. (I. O. Evans Studies in the Philosophy & Criticism of Literature: No. 25). 1995. pap. write for info. (1-55742-234-6) Borgo Pr.

— Lin Carter: A Look Behind His Imaginary Worlds. LC 93-242547. (Starmont Studies in Literary Criticism: No. 36). vi, 172p. 1991. lib. bdg. 29.00x (1-55742-230-3); pap. 19.00x (1-55742-229-X) Borgo Pr.

— South Africa: The Process of Political Transformation. (Illus.). 336p. (C). 1991. 55.00 (0-19-506749-5); pap. 18.95 (0-19-506750-9) OUP.

— U. S. Foreign Policy in Sub-Saharan Africa: National Interest & Global Strategy. LC 78-65499. (Policy Papers in International Affairs Ser.: No. 8). 1978. pap. 4.50 (0-87725-508-3) U of Cal IAS.

Price, Robert M., ed. Black Forbidden Things: Cryptical Secrets from the Crypt of Cthulhu. LC 93-201926. (Starmont Studies in Literary Criticism: No. 44). iv, 200p. 1992. lib. bdg. 31.00x (1-55742-249-4); pap. 21.00x (1-55742-248-6) Borgo Pr.

— Horror of It All: Encrusted Gems from "The Crypt of Cthulhu" 2nd ed. (I. O. Evans Studies in the Philosophy & Criticism of Literature). 1995. write for info. (1-55742-187-0) Borgo Pr.

— Horror of It All: Encrusted Gems from "The Crypt of Cthulhu" 2nd ed. (I. O. Evans Studies in the Philosophy & Criticism of Literature). 1995. pap. write for info. (1-55742-188-9) Borgo Pr.

Price, Robert M., intro. Tales of the Lovecraft Mythos. (C). 1991. 25.00 (1-878252-02-X) Fedogan & Bremer.

Price, Robert M. & Rosberg, Carl G., eds. The Apartheid Regime: Political Power & Racial Domination. LC 79-27269. (Research Ser.: No. 43). (Illus.). 1980. pap. 12.50 (0-87725-143-6) U of Cal IAS.

Price, Robert M., ed. see Bierce, et al.

Price, Robert M., ed. see Bloch, Robert.

Price, Robert R., jt. auth. see Finley, Eddy.

Price, Robert S. ABCs of Industrial Development Bonds. rev. ed. 248p. (Orig.). 1989. pap. text ed. 25.00 (0-936093-13-7) Packard Pr Fin.

Price, Robert S. & Magnotta, George. ABCs of Industrial Development Bonds. 5th ed. 336p. (Orig.). 30.00 (0-685-71083-1) Packard Pr Fin.

Price, Robert V. Computer-Aided Instruction: A Guide for Authors. 464p. (C). 1991. pap. 38.95 (0-534-13710-5) Boyd & Fraser.

***Price, Robin.** Healing Within; Medicine, Health & Wholeness. 19p. 1986. pap. 4.00 (0-904674-11-8, Pub. by Octagon Pr UK) ISHK Bk Service.

Price, Roger. A Concise History of France. (Cambridge Concise Histories Ser.). (Illus.). 375p. (C). 1993. 44.95 (0-521-36239-3); pap. 14.95 (0-521-36809-X) Cambridge U Pr.

— The Revolutions of Eighteen Forty-Eight. LC 88-13059. (Studies in European History). 98p. (C). 1989. pap. 10.95 (0-391-03595-9) Humanities.

— A Social History of Nineteenth-Century France. LC 87-22684. (Illus.). 370p. (C). 1988. 49.50 (0-8419-1165-7); pap. 29.95 (0-8419-1166-5) Holmes & Meier.

Price, Roger & Stern, Leonard. Camp Daze Mad Libs: World's Greatest Part Game. (Illus.). 48p. (J). (gr. 4 up). 1988. pap. 2.95 (0-8431-2239-0) Price Stern.

— Christmas Fun Mad Libs. (Mad Libs Ser.). 48p. (Orig.). (J). (gr. 3 up). 1985. bds. 2.95 (0-8431-1238-7) Price Stern.

— Goofy Mad Libs, No. 5. (Mad Libs Ser.). 48p. (Orig.). (J). (gr. 2 up). 1968. bds. 2.95 (0-8431-0059-1) Price Stern.

— Kid Libs. (Mad Libs Ser.). 48p. (Orig.). (J). (gr. 2 up). 1990. bds. 2.95 (0-8431-2827-5) Price Stern.

— Monster Mad Libs, No. 4. (Mad Libs Ser.). 48p. (Orig.). (J). (gr. 2 up). 1965. bds. 2.95 (0-8431-0058-3) Price Stern.

— Night of the Living Mad Libs: World's Greatest Word Game. (Mad Libs Ser.). (Illus.). 48p. (J). (gr. 3 up). 1994. pap. 2.95 (0-8431-3735-5) Price Stern.

— Off the Wall Mad Libs, No. 6. (Mad Libs Ser). 48p. (Orig.). (J). (gr. 2 up). 1970. bds. 2.95 (0-8431-0108-3) Price Stern.

— Original No. One Mad Libs. (Mad Libs Ser.). 48p. (J). (gr. 2 up). 1958. bds. 2.95 (0-8431-0055-9) Price Stern.

— Slam Dunk Mad Libs. (Mad Libs Ser.). 48p. (Orig.). (J). (gr. 2 up). 1994. bds. 2.95 (0-8431-3722-3) Price Stern.

— Son of Mad Libs, No. 2. (Mad Libs Ser.). 48p. (Orig.). (J). (gr. 2 up). 1959. bds. 2.95 (0-8431-0056-7) Price Stern.

— Sooper Dooper Mad Libs, No. 3. (Mad Libs Ser.). 48p. (Orig.). (J). (gr. 2 up). 1974. bds. 2.95 (0-8431-0057-5) Price Stern.

— Vacation Fun Mad Libs. 48p. (Orig.). (J). (gr. 3 up). bds. 2.95 (0-8431-1921-7) Price Stern.

***Price, Roger & Stern, Leonard, adapts.** Casper Mad Libs. (Mad Libs Ser.). 48p. (J). (gr. 1 up). 1995. pap. 2.95 (0-8431-3855-6) Price Stern.

Price, Roger, jt. auth. see Stern, Leonard.

Price, Ron, ed. & intro. B & B Our Guests for Comfort & Cuisine. (Illus.). 300p. 1992. spiral bd. 16.95 (0-9632838-0-4) OH Bed & Brkfst.

***Price, Rumi K., et al, eds.** Social Psychiatry Across Cultures: Studies from North America, Asia, Europe, & Africa. (Topics in Social Psychiatry Ser.). (Illus.). 210p. 1995. 42.50 (0-306-44971-4) Plenum.

Price, Russell, ed. see Machiavelli, Niccolo.

Price, Ruth. Rebel: A Biography of Agnes Smedley. 400p. 1994. text ed. 24.95 (0-02-925452-3) Free Pr.

Price, S. R. Rituals & Power: The Roman Imperial Cult in Asia Minor. (Illus.). 316p. 1985. pap. 24.95 (0-521-31268-X) Cambridge U Pr.

Price, Sabra, jt. auth. see Hein, George E.

Price, Sally. Co-Wives & Calabashes. 2nd ed. LC 92-43700. (Women & Culture Ser.). (Illus.). 248p. 1993. pap. text ed. 14.95 (0-472-08218-3) U of Mich Pr.

— Primitive Art in Civilized Places. LC 89-4932. (Illus.). xii, 148p. 1991. pap. 10.95 (0-226-68064-9) U Ch Pr.

Price, Sally, jt. auth. see Price, Richard.

Price, Sally, ed. see Stedman, John G.

Price, Seymour G. A Guide to Monitoring & Controlling Utility Costs. LC 73-88887. (BNA Operations Manual Ser.). 121p. reprint ed. pap. 34.50 (0-317-26779-5, 2024338) Bks Demand.

Price, Sharon. My All Sufficient One. 159p. (Orig.). 1985. pap. 5.95 (0-917595-08-4) Kingdom Pubs.

Price, Sharon & Elliott, Barbara, eds. Vision 2010, Vol. 1, No. 1: Families & Health Care. 40p. (Orig.). (C). 1993. pap. 14.95 (0-916174-39-5) Natl Coun Family.

Price, Sharon J., et al, eds. Vision Two Thousand Ten: Families & Adolescents, Vol. 2 No. 1. 44p. (Orig.). (C). 1994. pap. 14.95 (0-916174-43-3) Natl Coun Family.

Price, Sharon J. & Mckenry, Patrick C. Divorce. (Family Studies Text Ser.: Vol. 9). 160p. (C). 1988. text ed. 37.00 (0-8039-2356-2); pap. text ed. 16.95 (0-8039-2357-0) Sage.

Price, Sharon J., jt. auth. see McKenry, Patrick C.

Price, Shirley. Aromatherapy for Common Ailments. 1991. pap. 11.95 (0-671-73134-3, Fireside) S&S Trade.

— Aromatherapy Workbook: Understanding Essential Oils from Plant to Bottle. (Illus.). 176p. 1994. pap. 14.00 (0-7225-2645-8) Thorsons SF.

— Practical Aromatherapy: How to Use Essential Oils to Restore Health & Vitality. 1994. pap. 10.00 (0-7225-2850-7) Thorsons SF.

Price, Simon, jt. ed. see Cannadine, David.

Price, Simon, jt. ed. see Murray, Oswyn.

Price, Stan. Managing Computer Projects. 183p. 1986. text ed. 87.95 (0-471-91113-5) Wiley.

Price, Stanley E. The Antediluvian Giants & the Prophecy of Noah. 150p. (Orig.). 1992. pap. 6.95 (1-879366-24-X) Hearthstone OK.

Price Stern Editors. World's Worst Jokes. (J). 1969. pap. 2.95 (0-8431-0068-0) Putnam Pub Group.

Price Stern Sloan Staff. Super Christmas Puzzles & Mazes Activity Book. (Super Activity Bks.). (Illus.). 48p. (Orig.). (J). (gr. k-7). 1993. pap. 2.95 (0-8431-3609-X) Price Stern.

Price, Steve. Bare. 200p. 1994. pap. 7.00 (0-9642048-0-0) Garlic Hills.

Price, Steve, jt. auth. see Gibson, Eva.

Price, Steven. Whole Horse Catalogue. (Illus.). 1993. pap. 18.00 (0-671-86681-8, Fireside) S&S Trade.

Price, Steven D. The Beautiful Baby Naming Book. (Illus.). 96p. (Orig.). 1984. pap. 5.95 (0-671-43171-4) S&S Trade.

Price, Steven D., et al, eds. The Whole Horse Catalog. (Illus.). 288p. 1985. pap. 16.00 (0-671-54196-X, Fireside) S&S Trade.

Price, Stuart. The U. K. Fast Food Industry, 1993: A Market Analysis. (Illus.). 96p. 1994. spiral bd. 390.00 (0-304-32728-X) Cassell.

Price, Susan. Comparative Constructions in Spanish & French Syntax. 272p. 1990. 75.00 (0-415-01024-1, A4910) Routledge.

— Ghost Dance. LC 94-9841. (J). (gr. 4-7). 1995. 16.00 (0-374-32537-5) FS&G.

— The Ghost Drum. 176p. (J). (gr. 3 up). 1989. pap. 3.50 (0-374-42547-7, Sunburst Bks) FS&G.

— The Ghost Drum: A Cat's Tale. LC 86-46032. 176p. (J). (gr. 5 up). 1987. 12.95 (0-374-32538-3) FS&G.

— Ghost Song. (YA). 1992. 15.00 (0-374-32544-8) FS&G.

Price, Susan, tr. The Law of God, for Study at Home & School. (Illus.). 650p. (J). (gr. 1-7). 1993. 50.00 (0-88465-044-8) Holy Trinity.

***Price, Susan & Horse, Harry, comps.** Horror Stories. LC 95-7088. (Story Library). (YA). 1995. write for info. (1-85697-592-4, Kingfisher LKC) LKC.

Price, Susan C. & Price, Tom. The Working Parents Help Book: Practical Advice for Dealing with the Day-to-Day Challenges of Kids. 288p. 1994. pap. 15.95 (1-56079-333-3) Petersons Guides.

Price, Susan C., jt. auth. see Binder, David A.

Price, Sylvia & Wilson, Lorraine. Pathophysiology. 2nd ed. (Illus.). 1024p. (C). 1982. text ed. 45.95 (0-07-050863-1) McGraw.

— Pathophysiology. 3rd ed. 1200p. 1986. text ed. 49.95 (0-07-050864-X) McGraw.

Price, T. D., jt. ed. see Kroll, E. M.

Price, T. Douglas, ed. The Chemistry of Prehistoric Human Bone. (School of American Research Advanced Seminar Ser.). (Illus.). 280p. (C). 1989. 74.95 (0-521-36216-4) Cambridge U Pr.

Price, T. Douglas & Feinman, Gary M. Images of the Past. LC 92-15785. (Illus.). 529p. (C). 1993. pap. text ed. 38. 95x (0-87484-814-8) Mayfield Pub.

***Price, T. Douglas & Feinman, Gary M., eds.** Foundations of Social Inequality. (Fundamental Issues in Archaeology Ser.). 280p. 1995. 45.00 (0-306-44979-X) Plenum.

***Price, T. Douglas & Gebauer, Anne B., eds.** Last Hunters - First Farmers: New Perspectives on the Prehistory Transition to Agriculture. (School of American Research Advanced Seminar Ser.). (Illus.). 250p. 1995. 40.00 (0-933452-90-X); pap. 18.00 (0-933452-91-8) Schol Am Res.

Price, T. Douglas, jt. ed. see Gebauer, Anne B.

Price, T. E. Introduction to VLSI Technology. LC 93-29795. 340p. 1994. pap. text ed. 60.00 (0-13-500422-5) P-H.

Price, Taff. Fly Patterns. (Illus.). 192p. 1992. pap. 17.95 (0-7063-6898-3, Pub. by Ward Lock UK) Sterling.

Price, Terence. Political Electricity: What Future for Nuclear Energy? 432p. 1990. 45.00 (0-19-217780-X) OUP.

Price, Theodore. Hitchcock & Homosexuality: His Fifty-Year Obsession with Jack the Ripper & the Superbitch Prostitute - A Psychoanalytic View. LC 91-38865. 434p. 1992. 49.50 (0-8108-2471-X) Scarecrow.

Price, Theron D. Revelation & Faith: Theological Reflections on the Knowing & Doing of Truth. LC 86-33224. 192p. 1987. pap. 14.95 (0-86554-261-9, MUP P-45) Mercer Univ Pr.

Price, Thomas. Dramatic Structure & Meaning in Theatrical Productions. LC 92-21128. 364p. 1992. pap. text ed. 34. 95 (0-7734-9897-4) E Mellen.

— English-Nyanja Dictionary. (ENG & NYA.). 24.50 (0-87559-114-0) Shalom.

— Slavery in America. LC 71-92449. 1837. 15.00 (0-403-00170-6) Scholarly.

Price, Thomas, jt. auth. see Shepperson, George.

Price, Thomas J. Standoff at the Border: A Failure of Microdiplomacy. (Southwestern Studies: No. 87). (Orig.). 1989. pap. 10.00 (0-87404-173-2) Tex Western.

Price, Thomas R. Construction & Types of Shakespeare's Verse As Seen in the Othello. LC 78-168837. (Shakespeare Society of New York. Publications: No. 8). reprint ed. 27.50 (0-404-54208-5) AMS Pr.

***Price, Thomas R. & Nelson, Erland, eds.** Cerebrovascular Diseases: Eleventh Princeton Conference. fac. ed. LC 75-25125. (Illus.). 424p. Date not set. pap. 120.90 (0-7837-7191-6, 2047108) Bks Demand.

Price, Tim. Favorite Hymns Arranged for Piano Solo. 1993. 4.95 (0-87166-728-2, 93421); audio 9.98 (0-87166-050-4, 93421); audio 13.95 (0-87166-222-1, 93421) Mel Bay.

— Fun with the Piano. (Fun Bks.). 1993. 3.95 (0-87166-456-9, 93343) Mel Bay.

— Wedding Music for Piano. 1993. 6.95 (0-87166-273-6, 94308); audio 9.98 (0-87166-306-6, 94308); audio 15.95 (0-87166-902-1, 94308) Mel Bay.

Price, Tim & Price, Mary C. Developing Left & Right Hand Technique for the Young Pianist: Level 1. (Building Excellence Ser.). 1993. 4.95 (0-685-64650-5, 94602) Mel Bay.

— An Introduction to Musical Phrasing for the Young Pianist: Level 1. (Building Excellence Ser.). 1993. 4.95 (0-685-64649-1, 94600) Mel Bay.

— An Introduction to Variations in Style for the Young Pianist: Level 1. (Building Excellence Ser.). 1993. 4.95 (0-685-64648-3, 94601) Mel Bay.

Price, Tim R., jt. auth. see Reynolds, Kevin.

Price, Todd M. Freedom from Pain. 61p. 1992. pap. 4.00 (0-9633584-0-5) T M Price.

Price, Tom, jt. auth. see Price, Susan C.

Price, Tom, jt. auth. see Stumpf, Charles.

Price, Tony, ed. see Ball, John.

Price, V. B. Chaco Body. (Illus.). 88p. 1990. 40.00 (0-8263-1277-2); pap. 19.95 (0-8263-1278-0) U of NM Pr.

— A City at the End of the World. LC 92-9028. (Illus.). 210p. 1992. 24.95 (0-8263-1371-X) U of NM Pr.

Price, Victor, tr. see Buchner, Georg.

Price, Victoria H. Christian Allusions in the Novels of Thomas Pynchon. (American University Studies: English Language & Literature: Ser. IV, Vol. 89). 264p. (C). 1989. text ed. 37.95 (0-8204-0859-X) P Lang Pubs.

***Price, Vincent.** I Want a Woman: Nine Poems by Vincent Price. 22p. 1993. pap. text ed. 4.00 (1-885902-00-X) Printable Arts.

— Public Opinion. (Communication Concepts Ser.: Vol. 4). 112p. (C). 1992. text ed. 24.00 (0-8039-4022-X); pap. text ed. 10.95 (0-8039-4023-8) Sage.

***Price, Vincent & Price, Mary.** A Treasury of Great Recipes. (Illus.). 1995. reprint ed. lib. bdg. 75.00x (1-56849-540-4) Buccaneer Bks.

Price, Vincent, ed. see Delacroix, Ferdinand V.

Price, Vincent, ed. see Poe, Edgar Allan.

Price, Vincent B. Semblances (1962-1971) 1976. pap. 4.95 (0-913270-64-4) Sunstone Pr.

Price, Virginia A. The Type A Behavior Pattern: A Model for Research & Practice. 1983. text ed. 55.00 (0-12-564680-1) Acad Pr.

Price, W. A., jt. ed. see Abbott, M. B.

Price, W. C., ed. see International Organization of Citrus Virologists Conference Staff.

Price, W. C., ed. see International Organization of Citrus Virologists Staff.

Price, W. F., jt. auth. see Bamforth, P. B.

***Price, W. G. & Keane, A. J., eds.** Statistical Energy Analysis: An Overview, with Applications in Structural Dynamics. (Illus.). 150p. (C). 1995. write for info. (0-521-55175-7) Cambridge U Pr.

Price, W. G., jt. auth. see Bishop, R. E.

Price, W. L., jt. ed. see Chaum, D.

Price, W. L., jt. auth. see Davies, D. W.

Price, W. L., jt. auth. see Lindsay, D. T.

Price, W. V., jt. auth. see Van Slyke, L. L.

***Price, W. Wayne.** Confessions of a Perfect Parent. 176p. (Orig.). 1994. 9.95 (1-56865-111-2, GuildAmerica) Dblday Bk Music.

— Confessions of a Perfect Parent. 166p. (Orig.). 1993. pap. 10.99 (0-8028-0676-7) Eerdmans.

Price, Walter, ed. see Carreras, Jose.

Price, Warren C. Eugene Register-Guard. LC 76-15203. (Illus.). 384p. 1977. 15.00 (0-8323-0271-6) Binford Mort.

— The Literature of Journalism: An Annotated Bibliography. LC 59-13522. 507p. reprint ed. pap. 144.50 (0-317-10434-9, 2001006) Bks Demand.

***Price Waterhouse Change Interg. Staff.** Better Change: Best Practices for Transforming Your Organization. 208p. 1994. 30.00 (0-7863-0342-5) Irwin Prof Pubng.

***Price Waterhouse LLP Staff.** The Price Waterhouse Personal Financial Adviser. 320p. 1995. text ed. 15.00 (0-7863-0461-8) Irwin Prof Pubng.

***Price Waterhouse Mayernel Staff.** The Standard Trust Income Tax Guide 1992-93. 230p. 1993. pap. 28.00 (0-409-07654-6, SA) Butterworth Legal Pubs.

Price Waterhouse Staff. Canada Business Corporations Act. 3rd ed. 136p. 1987. pap. 25.00 (0-409-80656-0) Butterworth Legal Pubs.

— Consumer Compliance Handbook: 1995 Edition. 225p. 1995. 60.00 (1-55738-762-1) Probus Pub Co.

— Corporate Tax Strategy, 1994-95. 128p. 1994. pap. 30.00 (0-409-91614-5) Butterworth Legal Pubs.

— Financial Statement Presentation 1988-89. 268p. 1988. pap. 32.00 (0-409-88950-4); pap. 37.00 (0-409-88951-2) Butterworth Legal Pubs.

— A Guide to TIN Compliance: Interest, Dividend, Backup Withholding & Related IRS Reporting Issues. 6th ed. 225p. 1994. 75.00 (1-55738-387-1) Probus Pub Co.

— Hospital Financial Reports: A Survey. 150p. (C). 1987. pap. 35.00 (0-930228-52-9) Hlthcare Fin Mgmt.

— Price Waterhouse Investors Tax Advisor. 1993. pap. 12. 00 (0-671-87525-6) P-H Gen Ref & Trav.

— Price Waterhouse Personal Tax Adviser, 1994-1995 Edition. 368p. 1994. pap. 15.00 (0-7863-0357-3) Irwin Prof Pubng.

— Price Waterhouse Personal Tax Advisor. 1993. pap. 12.00 (0-671-87524-8) P-H Gen Ref & Trav.

— Regulatory Reporting Compliance Handbook: 1995 Edition. 124p. 1995. 60.00 (1-55738-765-6) Probus Pub Co.

— Safety & Soundness Compliance Handbook: 1995 Edition. 180p. 1995. 60.00 (1-55738-763-X) Probus Pub Co.

— Securities Compliance Handbook: 1995 Edition. 136p. 1995. 60.00 (1-55738-766-4) Probus Pub Co.

— Tolley's Estate Planning 1993-94. 450p. 1993. 90.00 (0-85459-785-9, Pub. by Tolley Pubng UK) St Mut.

— Trust Compliance Handbook: 1995 Edition. 158p. 1995. 60.00 (1-55738-764-8) Probus Pub Co.

— VAT in the Single Market: The Price Waterhouse Guide Through the Maze. 128p. (C). 1993. lib. bdg. 53.00 (1-85333-944-X, Pub. by Graham & Trotman UK) Kluwer Ac.

Price Waterhouse Staff, ed. The Complete Computer Virus Handbook. 192p. (C). 1989. text ed. 170.00 (0-273-03255-0, Pub. by Pitman Pubng UK) St Mut.

— The Price Waterhouse A-Z of Vat, 1989-1990. 160p. 1990. lib. bdg. 37.50 (1-85333-308-5, Pub. by Graham & Trotman UK) Kluwer Ac.

— VAT in the Single Market: The Price Waterhouse Guide Through the Maze. LC 93-39924. 128p. (C). 1993. lib. bdg. 53.00 (1-85333-923-7) G & T Inc.

Price Waterhouse Staff, jt. auth. see IBC - Donoghue, Inc. Staff.

Price Waterhouse, Staff, jt. auth. see Reynolds, Bob.

Price Waterhouse Staff, et al. Accounting for Income Taxes: Analysis & Commentary. 1990. 39.50 (0-7913-0115-X) Warren Gorham & Lamont.

Price, Weston A. Nutrition & Physical Degeneration. 1989. 39.95 (0-87983-502-8) Keats.

— Nutrition & Physical Degeneration. 9th ed. (Illus.). 560p. 1977. 34.95 (0-916764-00-1) Price-Pottenger.

Price, Will. Relational Database: Using dBASE III Plus. 1988. Incl. 5.25" diskette. write for info. (0-07-556416-5); pap. text ed. write for info. (0-07-555426-7) McGraw.

Price, William, jt. ed. see Claiborne, Jack.

Price, William B. Tales & Lores of the Mountaineers. 1986. reprint ed. 10.00 (0-685-53558-4) McClain.

Price, William C. & Chissick, Seymour S., eds. The Uncertainty Principle & Foundations of Quantum Mechanics: A Fifty Years' Survey. LC 76-18213. 590p. reprint ed. pap. 168.20 (0-685-20688-2, 2030478) Bks Demand.

Price, William H. Civil War Handbook: A Civil War Research Associates Series. (Illus.). 72p. reprint ed. pap. 2.95 (1-879295-00-8) L B Prince.

— The English Patents of Monopoly. LC 75-41218. reprint ed. 37.50 (0-404-14759-3) AMS Pr.

Price, William J. Spectrochemical Analysis by Atomic Absorption. 404p. reprint ed. pap. 105.10 (0-8357-7033-8, 2033347) Bks Demand.

Price, William L. A Manual of Photographic Manipulation Treating of the Practice of the Art; & Its Various Applications to Nature. 2nd ed. LC 72-9223. (Literature of Photography Ser.). 1973. reprint ed. 24.95 (0-405-04930-7) Ayer.

Price, William S., Jr. Not a Conquered People: Two Carolinians View Parliamentary Taxation. (Illus.). 49p. 1975. pap. 3.00 (0-86526-111-3) NC Archives.

— There Ought to Be a Bill of Rights: North Carolina Enters a New Nation. (Illus.). 19p. (Orig.). (YA). (gr. 8-12). 1991. pap. 4.00 (0-86526-254-3) NC Archives.

Price, William T. Historical Sketches of Pocahontas County, West Virginia. (Illus.). 670p. 1990. reprint ed. pap. 36.50 (1-55613-347-2) Heritage Bk.

Price-Williams, Douglas, jt. ed. see Goldschmidt, Walter.

Price-Williams, Douglass R. Explorations in Cross-Cultural Psychology. LC 74-28740. (Publications in Anthropology). 144p. 1975. 7.50 (0-88316-515-5) Chandler & Sharp.

Price, Wilson & Olson, Jack. Modern COBOL Programming. 480p. 1987. pap. text ed. 32.00 (0-317-54024-6) Mitchell Pub.

Price, Wilson T. Microcomputer Applications. (Illus.). 736p. (C). 1989. pap. text ed. 43.00 (0-03-026403-0) Dryden Pr.

Price, Wilson T. & Miller, M. Elements of Data Processing Mathematics. 3rd ed. (C). 1987. pap. text ed. 43.00 (0-03-000178-1) Dryden Pr.

Price, Wilson T. & Spitzer, Richard. Structured VAX BASIC: A GOTO-less Approach. 581p. (C). 1988. pap. write for info. (0-02-396620-3) Macmillan.

Price, W.V., jt. auth. see Van Slyke, L. L.

Price, Wyn, jt. auth. see Hawkes, Peter.

Priceman, Marjorie. How to Make an Apple Pie & See The World. LC 93-12341. (Illus.). 40p. (J). (ps-3). 1994. 16. 00 (0-679-83705-1); lib. bdg. 16.99 (0-679-93705-6) Knopf Bks Yng Read.

Priceman, Marjorie, illus. For Laughing Out Loud: Poems to Tickle Your Funnybone. LC 90-33010. 96p. (J). (gr. 2-7). 1991. 14.95 (0-394-82144-0); lib. bdg. 15.99 (0-394-92144-5) Knopf Bks Yng Read.

— For Laughing Out Louder: More Poems to Tickle Your Funnybone. LC 94-40655. (J). 1995. 14.00 (0-679-87063-6) Knopf.

Pricer, Robert W., jt. auth. see Filley, Alan C.

***Pricew, Alfred.** Late Marque Spitfire Aces 1942-1945. (Aircraft of the Aces Ser.: Vol. 5). (Illus.). 96p. 1995. pap. 14.95 (1-85532-487-3, Pub. by Osprey Pubng Ltd UK) Motorbooks Intl.

Prichard, A. M. Read: Allied Families of Read, Corbin, Luttrell, & Bywaters of Culpepper Co., Va. (Illus.). 292p. 1991. reprint ed. lib. bdg. 56.00 (0-8328-1875-5); reprint ed. pap. 46.00 (0-8328-1876-3) Higginson Bk Co.

Prichard, Allyn. Questions Smart Kids Ask. 1987. 7.95 (0-88047-076-3, 8617) DOK Pubs.

Prichard, Allyn & Taylor, Jean. Accelerating Learning: The Use of Suggestion in the Classroom. 144p. 1980. pap. text ed. 10.00 (0-87879-249-X) Acad Therapy.

Prichard, Arthur C. An Appalachian Legacy: Mannington Life & Spirit. (Illus.). 330p. 1983. 18.00 (0-9612788-0-3) McClain.

Prichard, B. N. & Messerli, Franz H., eds. Imidazolines & Blood Pressure Control. LC 94-12346. 1994. pap. text ed. write for info. (0-7923-2896-5) Kluwer Ac.

Prichard Committee for Academic Excellence Staff. The Path to a Larger Life: Creating Kentucky's Education Future. 2nd ed. LC 89-78107. 176p. 1990. pap. text ed. 12.00 (0-8131-0199-9) U Pr of Ky.

Prichard, Doris, jt. comp. see Sicignano, Robert.

Prichard, E. F., Jr., ed. see Frankfurter, Felix.

Prichard, Ed. Wholesome Example. 172p. 1993. 9.95 (0-917851-71-4) Bristol Hse.

Prichard, Elizabeth R., et al. Geriatrics & Thanatology. LC 84-3286. 224p. 1984. text ed. 55.00 (0-275-91447-X, C1447, Praeger Pubs) Greenwood.

Prichard, Elizabeth R., et al, eds. Home Care: Living with Dying. LC 78-21983. (Foundation of Thanatology Ser.). 1979. text ed. 50.00 (0-231-04258-2) Col U Pr.

— Social Work with the Dying Patient & the Family. Lefkowitz, Irene et al, trs. LC 77-8679. (Foundation of Thanatology Ser.). (Illus.). 350p. 1980. text ed. 52.00 (0-231-04021-0) Col U Pr.

Prichard, F. E., jt. auth. see James, Arthur M.

Prichard, F. Elizabeth, ed. see Day, John A.

Prichard, F. Elizabeth, jt. auth. see Metcalfe, Ed.

Prichard, F. Elizabeth, ed. see Whiston, Clive.

***Prichard, H. Hesketh.** Sniping in France: How the British Army Won the Sniping War in the Trenches. 211p. 1993. 25.00 (1-884849-08-3) R&R Bks.

Prichard, H. M., et al, eds. Magmatic Processes & Plate Tectonics. (Geological Society Special Publications: No. 76). (Illus.). 536p. (C). 1993. 108.00 (0-903317-94-X, Pub. by Geol Soc Pub Hse UK) AAPG.

Prichard, Harold A. Moral Obligation & Duty & Interest: Essays & Lectures. (Orig.). 1969. pap. 8.95 (0-19-881151-9) OUP.

Prichard, Hesketh. Where Black Rules White. LC 70-161272. (Black Heritage Library Collection). 1977. reprint ed. 27.95 (0-8369-8831-0) Ayer.

Prichard, James C. Eastern Origin of the Celtic Nations. 1977. lib. bdg. 59.95 (0-8490-1744-0) Gordon Pr.

— On the Different Forms of Insanity in Relation to Jurisprudence. Bd. with Suggestions for the Future Provision of Criminal Lunatics.; Statistics of Insanity. (Contributions to the History of Psychology Ser.: Vol. III, Pt. F). 1983. reprint ed. (0-89093-328-6) U Pubns Amer.

— Researches into the Physical History of Man. Stocking, George W., Jr., ed. LC 75-190425. (Classics in Anthropology Ser.). 928p. 1973. lib. bdg. 25.00 (0-226-68120-3) U Ch Pr.

— A Treatise on Insanity & Other Disorders Affecting the Mind. LC 73-2412. (Mental Illness & Social Policy; the American Experience Ser.). 1973. reprint ed. 26.95 (0-405-05222-7) Ayer.

Prichard Jones, K. V., jt. auth. see Adams, John.

Prichard, Katharine S. Tribute: Selected Stories of Katharine Susannah Prichard. Throssell, Ric, ed. (Orig.). 1989. pap. 16.95 (0-7022-2166-X, Pub. by Univ Queensland Pr AT) Intl Spec Bk.

Prichard, Keith W. & Sawyer, R. McLaran, eds. Handbook of College Teaching: Theory & Applications. LC 93-30982. (Educators' Reference Collection Ser.). 488p. 1994. text ed. 75.00 (0-313-28142-4, Greenwood Pr) Greenwood.

***Prichard, Lillian & Key, Alexander.** Stormy, the Brave Sponge Diver. 1955. pap. 0.75 (0-614-05558-X) Dietz.

Prichard, Lillian & Venos, Fannie. Can the Greeks Cook. 1950. pap. 8.75 (0-87517-002-1) Dietz.

Prichard, Mari, jt. auth. see Carpenter, Humphrey.

Prichard, Michael, ed. Sea Angling. (Know the Game Ser.). (Illus.). 1976. pap. 2.50 (0-7158-0521-5) Charles River Bks.

***Prichard, Nancy.** The I Hate to Train Performance Guide for Climbers. (How to Rock Climb Ser.). (Illus.). 48p. 1995. pap. 5.95 (0-934641-65-X) Chockstone Pr.

Prichard, Peter. The Making of McPaper: The Inside Story of U. S. A. Today. 1989. pap. 5.95 (0-318-42582-3) St Martin.

— Making of McPaper: The Inside Story of U.S.A. Today. 1989. mass mkt. 5.95 (0-312-91168-8) St Martin.

Prichard, Robert W. The Bat & the Bishop. LC 89-32719. (Illus.). 128p. (Orig.). 1988. reprint ed. pap. 7.95 (0-8192-1508-2) Morehouse Pub.

— History of the Episcopal Church. LC 90-46763. 1993. pap. 19.95 (0-8192-1613-5) Morehouse Pub.

Prichard, Robert W., ed. Readings from the History of the Episcopal Church. LC 86-12741. 192p. (Orig.). 1986. pap. 14.95 (0-8192-1383-7) Morehouse Pub.

Prichard, Robert W. & Robinson, Robert E. Twenty Thousand Medical Words. 288p. 1972. pap. text ed. 19. 95 (0-07-050874-7) Mosby Yr Bk.

Prichard, Susan P. Film Costume: An Annotated Bibliography. LC 81-5274. 577p. 1981. 49.50 (0-8108-1437-4) Scarecrow.

Prichett, Gordon D. & Saber, John C. Mathematics with Applications in Management & Economics. 7th rev. ed. LC 92-36042. 1088p. (C). 1993. text ed. 67.95 (0-256-09237-0) Irwin.

Prick, L. G., jt. ed. see Voorbach, J. T.

Prickel, Donald, jt. auth. see Mitchell, Robert.

Pricken, Marie-Luise L., jt. auth. see Lemke, Stefan.

Prickett, Hugh T., ed. Advocacy for Deaf Children. (Illus.). 114p. (C). 1989. text ed. 32.95x (0-398-05610-2) C C Thomas.

— Advocacy for Deaf Children. (Illus.). 114p. 1989. pap. 18. 95 (0-398-06332-X) C C Thomas.

An Asterisk (*) at the beginning of an entry indicates that the title is appearing in BIP for the first time.

Prickett, Hugh T. & Duncan, Earlene, eds. Coping with the Multi-Handicapped Hearing Impaired: A Practical Approach. 90p. (C). 1988. text ed. 28.95x (*0-398-05412-6*) C C Thomas.
— Coping with the Multi-Handicapped Hearing Impaired: A Practical Approach. 90p. 1988. pap. 15.95 (*0-398-06333-8*) C C Thomas.
***Prickett, Jeanne G., ed.** Hand in Hand: An Annotated Bibliography on Working with Students Who Are Deaf-Blind. LC 94-32260. 1994. pap. write for info. (*0-89128-939-9*) Am Foun Blind.
***Prickett, Jeanne G., et al.** Hand in Hand: Essentials of Communication & Orientation & Mobility for Your Students Who Are Deaf-Blind. LC 95-8265. 1995. teacher ed, pap. write for info. (*0-89128-940-2*) Am Foun Blind.
Prickett, Robert, jt. auth. see Richardson, Michael.
Prickett, S. England & the French Revolution. (Context & Commentary Ser.). 184p. (C). 1989. pap. 15.00 (*0-333-38706-6*, Pub. by Macmillan UK) Humanities.
Prickett, Stephen. Romanticism & Religion. LC 75-2254. 320p. 1976. 79.95 (*0-521-21072-0*) Cambridge U Pr.
— Words & the Word: Language Poetics, & Biblical Interpretation. 288p. 1986. 69.95 (*0-521-32248-0*) Cambridge U Pr.
— Words & the Word: Language Poetics, & Biblical Interpretation. 288p. 1988. pap. 22.95 (*0-521-36838-3*) Cambridge U Pr.
Prickett, Stephen, ed. Reading the Text: Biblical Criticism & Literary Theory. (C). 1991. text ed. 54.95 (*0-631-16012-4*) Blackwell Pubs.
Prickett, Stephen & Barnes, Robert. The Bible. (Landmarks of World Literature Ser.). (Illus.). 192p. (C). 1991. 29.95 (*0-521-36569-4*); pap. 10.95 (*0-521-36759-X*) Cambridge U Pr.
Prida, Dolores. Beautiful Senoritas & Other Plays. Weiss, Judith, ed. LC 90-1239. 180p. (Orig.). 1994. pap. 11.00 (*1-55885-026-0*) Arte Publico.
Pridantsev, M. V., ed. Structure & Properties of Heat-Resistant Metals. 380p. 1970. text ed. 99.00 (*0-7065-0703-7*, Pub. by Keter Pub IS) Coronet Bks.
Priddis, Ronald L., jt. auth. see Bergera, Gary J.
Priddle, J. & Fryxell, G. Handbook of the Common Plankton Diatoms of the Southern Ocean: Centrales Except the Genus Thalassiosira. (Illus.). 155p. 1985. lib. bdg. 36.00 (*0-85665-115-X*) Lubrecht & Cramer.
Priddle, L. G., jt. auth. see Dixon, J.
Priddy, A. Paul, jt. auth. see Li, Kam W.
Priddy, Bob. Across Our Wide Missouri, 2 vols., Vol. 1. 1982. pap. 20.00 (*0-8309-0331-3*) Ind Pr MO.
— Across Our Wide Missouri, 2 vols., Vol. 2. 1984. pap. 20.00 (*0-8309-0397-6*) Ind Pr MO.
— Across Our Wide Missouri Vol. III: More Stories. 1994. pap. text ed. 20.00 (*0-8309-0657-6*) Herald Hse.
— Only the Rivers Are Peaceful. 1989. 28.00 (*0-8309-0540-5*); pap. 23.00 (*0-8309-0534-0*) Herald Hse.
Priddy, James R. Kahlua on the Rocks. LC 89-52185. 245p. 1990. pap. 9.95 (*1-55523-317-1*) Winston-Derek.
***Priddy, Laurance L.** A Son of Durango. 160p. (Orig.). 1996. pap. 14.95 (*0-86534-242-3*) Sunstone Pr.
— Winning Passion. LC 93-13982. 288p. (Orig.). 1994. pap. 14.95 (*0-86534-200-8*) Sunstone Pr.
Priddy, S., jt. auth. see Mahowald, M.
Priddy, Wayne, jt. auth. see Summers, B. J.
Pride, Anne, ed. see Ippolito, Donna.
Pride, Bill & Pride, Mary. Prides' Guide to Educational Software. (Illus.). 408p. (Orig.). 1992. pap. 25.00 (*0-89107-665-4*) Crossway Bks.
Pride, Charley & Henderson, Jim. Pride: The Charley Pride Story. LC 93-34360. 1994. 20.00 (*0-688-12638-3*) Morrow.
***Pride, Charlie.** Pride: The Charley Pride Story. 1995. 9.75 (*0-688-14232-X*, Quill) Morrow.
Pride, Emrys. Pride in Britain's High Tech Progress. 72p. (C). 1989. 59.00 (*0-905928-47-4*, Pub. by D Brown & Sons Ltd UK) St Mut.
***Pride, Glen L.** The Kingdom of Fife: An Illustrated Architectural Guide. (Illus.). 208p. (C). 1990. pap. 35.00x (*1-85158-256-8*, Pub. by Rutland Pr UK) St Mut.
Pride in America Company Staff. Big Ideas. LC 78-58760. 96p. 1978. 3.00 (*0-9614917-0-1*) Pride in Am.
Pride, Kitty. Current Trends & Issues in Hispanic Linguistics. (Publications in Linguistics: No. 80). 136p. 1987. pap. 22.00 (*0-88312-012-7*); fiche 8.00 (*0-88312-419-X*) Summer Instit Ling.
Pride, Mary. Afterschooling & Enrichment. LC 89-81254. (Big Book of Home Learning Ser.: Vol. 4). 320p. 1991. pap. 20.00 (*0-89107-551-8*) Crossway Bks.
— All the Way Home. LC 87-71897. 284p. 1989. pap. 13.99 (*0-89107-465-1*) Crossway Bks.
— The Big Book of Home Learning, Vols. 1-4. LC 89-81254. 1991. pap. 82.50 (*0-89107-567-4*) Crossway Bks.
— Getting Started. LC 89-81254. (Big Book of Home Learning Ser.: Vol. 1). 288p. 1990. pap. 17.50 (*0-89107-548-8*) Crossway Bks.
— Preschool & Elementary. LC 89-81254. (Big Book of Home Learning Ser.: Vol. 2). 480p. 1991. pap. 22.50 (*0-89107-549-6*) Crossway Bks.
— Schoolproof: How to Help Your Family Beat the System & Learn to Love Learning the Easy, Natural Way. LC 87-72953. 1988. pap. 8.99 (*0-89107-480-5*) Crossway Bks.
— Teen & Adult. LC 89-81254. (Big Book of Home Learning Ser.: Vol. 3). 288p. 1991. pap. 22.50 (*0-89107-550-X*) Crossway Bks.
— The Way Home; Beyond Feminism, Back to Reality. LC 84-73078. 240p. (Orig.). 1985. pap. 9.99 (*0-89107-345-0*) Crossway Bks.
Pride, Mary, jt. auth. see DeParrie, Paul.
Pride, Mary, jt. auth. see Pride, Bill.
***Pride, Richard A.** The Confession of Dorothy Danner: Telling a Life Story. (Illus.). 1995. write for info. (*0-8265-1270-4*) Vanderbilt U Pr.
Pride, Richard A. & Woodard, J. David. The Burden of Busing: The Politics of Desegregation in Nashville, Tennessee. LC 85-5302. (Illus.). 317p. reprint ed. pap. 90.40 (*0-7837-7081-2*, 2046893) Bks Demand.
Pride, William & Ferrell, O. C. Marketing: Concepts & Strategies. 7th ed. (C). 1991. write for info. (*0-395-43358-4*) HM Soft Schl Col Div.
Pride, William, et al. Business. 3rd ed. (C). 1991. write for info. (*0-395-47308-X*) HM Soft Schl Col Div.
Pride, William M. & Ferrell, O. C. Marketing: Basic Concepts & Decisions. LC 83-83389. 768p. (C). 1984. disk 45.00 (*0-395-36498-1*) HM.
— Marketing: Basic Concepts & Decisions. 6th ed. 1988. write for info. (*0-318-63331-0*); trans., vhs write for info. (*0-318-63332-9*) HM.
Prideau, Marquette. The Glamour Is Gone. 64p. 1992. pap. text ed. 9.95 (*0-9633368-0-0*) Brandcarr.
Prideaux, Gary D. Syntax of Japanese Honorifics. (Janua Linguarum, Series Practica: No. 102). 1970. pap. text ed. 50.00 (*90-279-0741-2*) Mouton.
Prideaux, Gary D., ed. Perspectives in Experimental Linguistics: Papers from the University of Alberta Conference on Experimental Linguistics, Edmonton, 13-14 Oct. 1978. (Current Issues in Linguistic Theory Ser.: No. 10). xi, 176p. 1979. 46.00x (*90-272-3503-1*) Benjamins North Am.
Prideaux, Gary D. & Baker, William J. Strategies & Structures: The Processing of Relative Clauses. LC 86-26863. (Current Issues in Linguistic Theory Ser.: Vol. 46). vii, 195p. 1987. 52.00x (*90-272-3540-6*) Benjamins North Am.
Prideaux, James. The Housekeeper. 1984. pap. 4.75 (*0-8222-0537-8*) Dramatists Play.
— The Last of Mrs. Lincoln. 1973. pap. 4.75 (*0-8222-0638-2*) Dramatists Play.
— Lemonade, & the Autograph Hound: Two Short Plays. 1969. pap. 4.75 (*0-8222-0081-3*) Dramatists Play.
— Mixed Couples. 1981. pap. 4.75 (*0-8222-0766-4*) Dramatists Play.
— The Orphans: A Play in Two Acts. 1980. pap. 4.75 (*0-8222-0864-4*) Dramatists Play.
— Postcards. 1970. pap. 2.75 (*0-8222-0907-1*) Dramatists Play.
— Stuffings: And an American Sunset. 1973. pap. 4.75 (*0-8222-0037-6*) Dramatists Play.
Prideaux, P. From Spear to Pearl-Shell-Somerset, Cape York Peninsula, 1864-1877. 206p. (C). 1990. 75.00 (*0-9589799-1-X*, Pub. by Boolarong Pubns AT) St Mut.
Prideaux, Sally. Art at Auction - 90-91. 33th ed. (Illus.). 70.00 (*0-685-39050-0*) Edns Publisol.
Prideaux, Sarah. An Historical Sketch of Bookbinding, Vol. 11. Huttner, Sidney F., ed. (History of Bookbinding & Design Ser.). 300p. 1989. 69.00 (*0-8240-4024-4*) Garland.
Prideaux, Tom. Love or Nothing: The Life & Times of Ellen Terry. LC 87-20345. (Illus.). 288p. 1988. pap. 9.95 (*0-87910-105-9*) Limelight Edns.
Pridgen, Dee. Consumer Credit & the Law. LC 90-37060. 1990. ring bd. 135.00 (*0-87632-742-0*) Clark Boardman Callaghan.
— Consumer Protection & the Law. LC 86-6825. 1987. ring bd. 135.00 (*0-87632-501-0*) Clark Boardman Callaghan.
Pridgeon, Alec, ed. The Illustrated Encyclopedia of Orchids. (Illus.). 304p. 1992. 39.95 (*0-88192-267-6*) Timber.
Pridham, Arthur. Notes on Romans. 461p. 1977. 15.99 (*0-8254-3519-6*) Kregel.
Pridham, Brian R., ed. The Arab Gulf & the West. LC 85-18298. 251p. 1985. text ed. 39.95 (*0-312-04703-7*) St Martin.
— Oman: Economic, Social & Strategic Developments. 59.95 (*0-7099-4056-4*, Pub. by Croom Helm UK) Routledge Chapman & Hall.
Pridham, G. J. Electronic Devices & Circuits, Vol. 1. LC 67-26692. 1968. 150.00 (*0-08-012549-2*, Pub. by Pergamon Repr UK) Franklin.
— Electronic Devices & Circuits, Vol. 3. LC 67-26692. 1972. 154.00 (*0-08-016626-1*, Pub. by Pergamon Repr UK) Franklin.
— Solid State Circuits. 196p. (C). 1973. 86.00 (*0-08-016932-5*, Pub. by Pergamon Repr UK) Franklin.
Pridham, G. J., jt. auth. see Abrahams, J. R.
Pridham, Geoffrey. The Nature of the Italian Party System. 1981. text ed. 18.95 (*0-312-56194-6*) St Martin.
— Political Parties & Coalitional Behavior in Italy: An Interpretive Study. 256p. 1987. lib. bdg. 57.50 (*0-415-00503-5*) Routledge.
Pridham, Geoffrey, ed. Coalitional Behaviour in Theory & Practice: An Inductive Model for Western Europe. (Illus.). 320p. 1986. 69.95 (*0-521-30537-3*) Cambridge U Pr.
— Encouraging Democracy: The International Context of Regime Transition in Southern Europe. LC 91-15987. 240p. 1991. text ed. 55.00 (*0-312-06708-9*) St Martin.
— Securing Democracy: Political Parties & Democratic Consolidation in Southern Europe. 256p. 1990. 65.00 (*0-415-02326-2*, A4201) Routledge.
— Transitions to Democracy: Comparative Perspectives from Southern Europe, Latin America & Eastern Europe. LC 94-47359. (International Library of Politics & Comparative Government). 1995. write for info. (*1-85521-424-5*) Ashgate Pub Co.
Pridham, Geoffrey & Vanhanen, Tatu. Democratization in Eastern Europe: Domestic & International Perspectives. LC 94-7513. 272p. 1994. 65.00x (*0-415-11063-7*, B4709); pap. 18.95 (*0-415-11064-5*, B4713) Routledge.
Pridham, Geoffrey, jt. ed. see Muller-Rommel, Ferdinand.
Pridham, Geoffrey, et al, eds. Building Democracy? The International Dimension of Democratisation in Eastern Europe. LC 94-10228. 1994. text ed. 45.00 (*0-312-12231-4*) St Martin.
Pridham, J. Enzyme Chemistry of Phenolic Compounds: Proceedings of the Plant Phenolic Group Symposium, Liverpool, April, 1962. LC 63-12795. 1963. 66.00 (*0-08-009946-7*, Pub. by Pergamon Repr UK) Franklin.
— Methods in Polyphenol Chem: Proceedings of Plant Phenolic Group Symposium, Oxford, April 1963. LC 64-25365. 1964. 64.00 (*0-08-010887-3*, Pub. by Pergamon Repr UK) Franklin.
Pridham, M. Proceedings of Tenth International Conference & Production Research. 1991. 220.00 (*0-85066-752-6*) Taylor & Francis.
Pridmore, F. Coins & Coinages of the Straits Settlements & British Malaya, 1786-1951. 1968. 35.00 (*0-685-51510-9*) S J Durst.
Pridmore, Jay. A Garden for All Seasons. (Illus.). 136p. 1990. 29.95 (*0-939914-06-9*); pap. 14.95 (*0-685-31711-0*) Chi Horticult.
— John Gunther: Inside Journalism. (Illus.). 64p. (Orig.). 1990. 6.00 (*0-943056-13-6*) Univ Chi Lib.
— Many Hearts & Many Hands: The History of Ferry Hall & Lake Forest Academy. Gendler, Anne, ed. 264p. 1994. 50.00 (*0-9643350-0-X*) Lke Forest Acad.
Pridmore, Jay, jt. auth. see Larson, George A.
Pridmore, Saxby & McGrath, Mary. Julia, Mungo, & the Earthquake: A Story for Young People about Epilepsy. LC 91-7232. (Illus.). 48p. (J). (gr. 3-6). 1992. pap. 8.95 (*0-945354-31-2*) Magination Pr.
Prieb, Wesley, ed. Peter C. Hiebert: He Gave Them Bread. (Illus.). 149p. (Orig.). 1990. pap. 10.00 (*1-877941-02-6*) Ctr Mennonite Brethren Studies.
Priebe, Duane A., tr. see Ebeling, Gerhard.
Priebe, Duane A., tr. see Pannenberg, Wolfhart.
Priebe, Richard & Hale, Thomas, eds. Artist & Audience: African Literature As a Shared Experience. LC 79-89930. (Annual Selected Papers of the African Literature Association). 203p. (Orig.). 1979. pap. 14.00 (*0-89410-123-4*) Three Continents.
Priebe, Richard, jt. ed. see Hale, Thomas.
Priebe, Richard K. Myth, Realism & the African Writer. Arnold, Stephen H. & Lang, George, eds. LC 88-71174. (Comparative Studies in African-Caribbean Literature Ser.). 200p. (C). 1988. 35.00 (*0-86543-097-7*); pap. 11.95 (*0-86543-098-5*) Africa World.
Priebe, Richard K., ed. Ghanaian Literatures. LC 88-16110. (Contributions in Afro-American & African Studies: No. 120). 320p. 1988. text ed. 59.95 (*0-313-26438-4*, PGL/, Greenwood Pr) Greenwood.
Priebe, Vel. Wendy's Gift. (Kinderbook Ser.). (Illus.). 24p. (Orig.). (J). (ps-2). 1988. pap. 1.50 (*0-919797-67-9*) Kindred Prods.
Priebe, Waldemar, ed. see American Chemical Society Division of Carbohydrate Chemistry Staff.
Prieberg, Fred K. Trial of Strength: Wilhelm Furtwangler in the Third Reich. Dolan, Christopher, tr. 394p. 1994. text ed. 32.50 (*1-55553-196-2*) NE U Pr.
Priede, Imants G. & Swift, Susan M. Wildlife Telemetry: Remote Monitoring & Tracking Animals. LC 92-20704. (Ellis Horwood Series in Environmental Management, Science & Technology). 500p. 1992. text ed. 162.00 (*0-13-957994-X*, Tavistock-E Horwood) Routledge Chapman & Hall.
Prieditis, Armand, ed. Analogica: Proceedings of the First Workshop on Analogical Reasoning. 160p. (C). 1988. pap. text ed. 180.00 (*0-273-08780-0*, Pub. by Pitman Pubng UK) St Mut.
Prieditis, Armand E. Analogica. LC 86-33749. (Research Notes in Artificial Intelligence Ser.). (Illus.). 176p. (Orig.). 1988. pap. text ed. 29.95 (*0-934613-37-0*) Morgan Kaufmann.
Prieels, Ann-Marie. Development of an Environmental Bio-Industry: European Perceptions. 131p. 1993. pap. 17.00 (*92-826-4691-2*, SY-76-92-051-EN, Pub. by Europ Com) UNIPUB.
Priehs, T. J., ed. see Arnberger, Leslie P. & Dodson, Carolyn.
Priehs, T. J., ed. see Barey, Pat.
Priehs, T. J., ed. see Bleser, Nicholas J.
Priehs, T. J., ed. see Bogard, Travis.
Priehs, T. J., ed. see Bowers, Janice E.
Priehs, T. J., ed. see Brown, Joseph E.
Priehs, T. J., ed. see Cunningham, Richard L.
Priehs, T. J., ed. see Dodge, Natt N.
Priehs, T. J., ed. see Dowty, Robert R.
Priehs, T. J., ed. see Evans, Doris.
Priehs, T. J., ed. see Fisher, Pierre C.
Priehs, T. J., ed. see Gardner, Mark.
Priehs, T. J., ed. see Gnesios, Gregory.
Priehs, T. J., ed. see Hansen, Wallace.
Priehs, T. J., ed. see Hodge, Carle.
Priehs, T. J., ed. see Houk, Rose.
Priehs, T. J., ed. see Jorgen, Randolph.
Priehs, T. J., ed. see Keith, Sandra.
Priehs, T. J., ed. see Lamb, Susan.
Priehs, T. J., ed. see Lister, Robert H. & Lister, Florence C.
Priehs, T. J., ed. see Mabery, Marilyne V.
Priehs, T. J., ed. see Murphy, Daniel O.
Priehs, T. J., ed. see Nabhan, Gary P.
Priehs, T. J., ed. see Parent, Laurence E.
Priehs, T. J., ed. see Phillips, Arthur M., 3rd.
Priehs, T. J., ed. see Rubissow, Ariel.
Priehs, T. J., ed. see Sperry, T. J.
Priehs, T. J., ed. see Threlkeld, Kay.
Priehs, T. J., ed. see Thybony, Scott.
Priehs, T. J., ed. see Torres, Luis.
Priehs, T. J., ed. see Trimble, Stephen.
Priehs, T. J., ed. see Udall, Stewart L. & Haury, Emil W.
Priehs, T. J., ed. see Utley, Robert.
Priel, P. Systematic Maintenance Organisation. 1990. 32.00 (*0-7121-1926-4*, Pub. by Northcote UK) St Mut.
Priel, V. Multi-Coordinate Data Presentation. 1977. 35.00 (*0-8464-0657-8*) Beekman Pubs.
Prielipp, Bob, jt. auth. see Kuenzi, N. J.
Priemer, August B. Effective Media Planning: A Guide to Help Advertisers & Agencies Develop Plans That Work. 288p. 1989. text ed. 45.00 (*0-669-20808-6*) Free Pr.
Priemer, R., ed. Introductory Signal Processing. (Advanced Series in Electrical & Computer Engineering: Vol. 6). 752p. (C). 1990. text ed. 90.00 (*9971-5-0919-9*); pap. text ed. 55.00 (*9971-5-0920-2*) World Scientific Pub.
Prien, Jochen & Rodeike, Peter. Messerschmitt Bf 109 F, G & K: An Illustrated Study. LC 92-81713. (Illus.). 208p. 1992. 35.00 (*0-88740-424-3*) Schiffer.
Prien, Robert F. & Robinson, Donald S., eds. Clinical Evaluation of Psychotropic Drugs: Principles & Guidelines. LC 94-12397. 752p. 1994. 85.00 (*0-7817-0143-0*) Raven.
***Priencen.** Intermediaries in International Conflict. 1995. pap. (*0-691-00163-4*) Princeton U Pr.
Prier, Raymond A. Countercurrents: On the Primacy of Texts in Literary Criticism. LC 91-13268. (SUNY Series, The Margins of Literature). 302p. 1992. 59.50 (*0-7914-0941-4*); pap. 19.95 (*0-7914-0942-2*) State U NY Pr.
— Thauma Idesthai: The Phenomenology of Sight & Appearance in Archaic Greek. 312p. 1989. lib. bdg. 34.95 (*0-8130-0919-7*) U Press Fla.
Pries, Mitchell P. A Physician Looks at the Crucifixion: An Extraordinary Account of Jesus' Last Days on Earth. LC 94-75400. 64p. (Orig.). 1994. pap. 5.95 (*1-879560-24-0*) Harbor Hse West.
— A Physician Looks at the Resurrection: A Brilliant New View of the Act of the Resurrection. LC 94-75401. 48p. (Orig.). 1994. pap. 5.95 (*1-879560-25-9*) Harbor Hse West.
— Why Nutrition: The Nutritional Path to a Vigorus & Healthy Life. LC 92-72195. 125p. (Orig.). 1992. pap. 14.95 (*1-879560-13-5*) Harbor Hse West.
***Priesack & Tomscha.** One World: American English Speaking Book, Level 2. (Illus.). 128p. 1994. pap. text ed. 12.75 (*0-13-185992-7*) P-H.
Priesack, Tim & Tomscha, Terry. One World: Coursebook 1. LC 94-16067. 128p. 1995. write for info. (*0-13-157132-X*) Prentice ESL.
— One World: Coursebook 4. LC 94-26090. (English Language Teaching Ser.). 1994. 10.50 (*0-13-635616-8*) P-H.
Priese, Karl-Heinz. The Gold of Meroe. LC 93-23009. (Illus.). 49p. 1993. pap. 16.95 (*0-87099-684-3*) Metro Mus Art.
Priesing, Dorothy, jt. auth. see Zimmerman, Marian.
Priesmeyer, H. Richard. Organization & Chaos: Defining the Methods of Nonlinear Management. LC 92-7486. 272p. 1992. text ed. 55.00 (*0-89930-630-6*, PMM, Quorum Bks) Greenwood.
— Strategy: A Business Unit Simulation. 2nd ed. (C). 1992. text ed. write for info. (*0-538-80776-8*, GH72B8H81) S-W Pub.
Priesner, H. Die Thysanopteren Europas. 1963. reprint ed. 77.00 (*90-6123-121-3*) Lubrecht & Cramer.
Priesnitz, Wendy. Markham: Canada's Community of the Future. 1990. 34.95 (*0-89781-327-8*) Preferred Mktg.
Priessnitz, Vincent. The Cold Water Cure. 48p. 1976. reprint ed. spiral bd. 8.80 (*0-7873-0677-0*) Mokelumne.
Priest. Engineering Design for Producibility & Reliability. (Quality & Reliability Ser.: Vol. 14). 328p. 1988. 110.00 (*0-8247-7708-5*) Dekker.
— Handbook: Psychiatry. 8th ed. (Illus.). 211p. 1986. pap. text ed. 29.95 (*0-433-26206-0*) Buttrwrth-Heinemann.
Priest & Vyver. Trace Metals & Fluoride in Bones & Teeth. 1990. 240.00 (*0-8493-6190-7*, QP88) CRC Pr.
Priest, Alan. Costumes from the Forbidden City. LC 74-168427. (Metropolitan Museum of Art Publications in Reprint). (Illus.). 72p. 1974. reprint ed. 23.95 (*0-405-02265-4*) Ayer.
Priest, Alan, jt. auth. see Metropolitan Museum of Art Staff.
Priest, Ames. Governmental & Judicial Ethics in the Bible & Rabbinic Literature. 1980. 20.00 (*0-87068-697-6*) Ktav.
***Priest, Barbara R.** Accompaniments to Murder. 145p. (Orig.). Date not set. pap. 7.95 (*0-7610-0360-6*) NW Pub.
Priest, Christine, jt. auth. see Rimm, Sylvia B.
Priest, Christopher. Indoctrinaire. LC 76-123984. 1970. 25.00 (*0-06-013406-2*) Ultramarine Pub.
Priest, Denis. Problems in Play: First Book of Bridge Problems. LC 81-19815. 167p. (Orig.). 1982. 9.95 (*0-7022-1675-5*, Pub. by Univ Queensland Pr AT) Intl Spec Bk.
Priest, Donald E., et al. Joint Development: Making the Real Estate-Transit Connection. LC 79-66189. (Illus.). 216p. 1979. pap. 40.95 (*0-87420-588-3*, L57) Urban Land.
***Priest, Doug, Jr., ed.** The Gospel Unhindered: Modern Missions & the Book of Acts. 225p. (Orig.). 1994. pap. 7.95 (*0-87808-256-5*, WCL256-5) William Carey Lib.
Priest, E. Louise, ed. see Council for National Cooperation in Aquatics Staff.
Priest, E. R. Solar Flare Magnetohydrodynamics. (Fluid Mechanics of Astrophysics & Geophysics Ser.). 576p. 1981. text ed. 310.00 (*0-677-05530-7*) Gordon & Breach.
— Solar Magnetohydrodynamics. 1982. lib. bdg. 219.00 (*90-277-1374-X*) Kluwer Ac.
— Solar Magnetohydrodynamics. 1984. pap. text ed. 89.00 (*90-277-1833-4*) Kluwer Ac.

Priest, E. R., ed. Dynamics & Structure of Quiescent Solar Prominences. (C). 1988. lib. bdg. 104.00 (*90-277-2833-X*); pap. text ed. 56.50 (*90-277-2834-8*) Kluwer Ac.

— Solar System Magnetic Fields. 1985. lib. bdg. 87.50 (*90-277-2137-8*) Kluwer Ac.

Priest, E. R. & Krishan, V., eds. Basic Plasma Processes on the Sun. (C). 1990. lib. bdg. 144.00 (*0-7923-0879-4*); pap. text ed. 61.50 (*0-7923-0880-8*) Kluwer Ac.

Priest, Eric R. & Hood, Alan W., eds. Advances in Solar System Magnetohydrodynamics. (Illus.). 452p. (C). 1991. 59.95 (*0-521-40325-1*) Cambridge U Pr.

Priest, F. G. & Campbell, I., eds. Brewing Microbiology. 278p. 1987. 84.75 (*1-85166-062-3*, Pub. by Elsevier Applied Sci UK) Elsevier.

***Priest, F. G., et al, eds.** Bacterial Diversity & Systematics. (F. E. M. S. Symposium Ser.: 75). (Illus.). 340p. (C). 1994. 95.00 (*0-306-44832-7*, Plenum Pr) Plenum.

Priest, Fergus & Austin, Brian. Modern Bacterial Taxonomy. 2nd ed. LC 93-31642. 1993. pap. 34.50 (*0-412-46120-X*, Chap & Hall NY) Chapman & Hall.

Priest, George E. Life in the Middle Lane. 1989. pap. 23.00 (*0-89258-145-X*, C120) Assn Inform & Image Mgmt.

Priest, George E. & Wallace, Lynn. Voice Mail: Much More Than an Answering Machine. 1989. pap. 23.00 (*0-89258-147-6*, C121) Assn Inform & Image Mgmt.

***Priest, Graham.** Beyond the Limits of Thought. 287p. (C). 1995. 54.95 (*0-521-45420-4*) Cambridge U Pr.

Priest, Graham, et al, eds. Paraconsistent Logic: Essays on the Inconsistent. (Analytica Ser.). 704p. 1989. 265.00 (*3-88405-058-3*) Philosophia Pr.

Priest, Harold M. Divine Comedy, No. 2: Purgatorio Notes. 1971. pap. 4.25 (*0-8220-0394-5*) Cliffs.

— Divine Comedy, No. 3: Paradiso Notes. 1972. pap. 4.50 (*0-8220-0396-1*) Cliffs.

— Faerie Queene Notes. 1968. pap. 4.25 (*0-8220-0452-6*) Cliffs.

— Utopia & Utopian Literature Notes. 64p. (Orig.). 1975. pap. text ed. 3.50 (*0-8220-1318-5*) Cliffs.

Priest, James D. Kirins: The Flight of the Ain. LC 91-91110. (Kirins, A Trilogy Ser.: Bk. 2). (Illus.). 336p. (Orig.). (YA). (gr. 6-12). 1992. pap. 11.95 (*0-9626225-5-9*) Yellow Pr MN.

— Kirins: The Spell of No'an. LC 90-90174. (Illus.). 470p. (Orig.). (YA). 1990. pap. 11.95 (*0-9626225-4-0*) Yellow Pr MN.

Priest, Jean H. Medical Cytogenetics & Cell Culture. 2nd ed. LC 76-7402. 364p. reprint ed. pap. 103.80 (*0-317-55563-4*, 2052213) Bks Demand.

***Priest, Joan.** Sir Harry Gibbs: Without Fear Or Favour. 207p. 1995. 43.00 (*0-646-23693-8*); pap. 32.00 (*0-614-07153-4*) W W Gaunt.

— Sir Harry Gibbs: Without Fear or Favour. 1995. pap. 32.00 (*0-614-07438-X*) W W Gaunt.

Priest, John. Scholars & Gentlemen. 336p. (C). 1990. 78.00 (*0-86439-013-0*, Pub. by Boolarong Pubns AT) St Mut.

Priest, John M. Antietam: The Soldiers Battle. LC 89-5557. (Illus.). 463p. (C). 1989. 34.95 (*0-942597-09-5*) White Mane Pub.

— Antietam: The Soldiers' Battle. LC 92-46293. 424p. 1994. 15.95 (*0-19-508466-7*) OUP.

— Before Antietam: The Battle of South Mountain. LC 92-189217. (Illus.). 350p. (C). 1993. 34.95 (*0-942597-37-0*) White Mane Pub.

— No Where to Run: The Wilderness, 1864, Vol. I. (Illus.). 350p. (C). 1995. text ed. 29.95 (*0-942597-74-5*) White Mane Pub.

— A Self-Guided Mini-Tour of Antietam. LC 94-10648. (Illus.). 40p. (Orig.). 1994. pap. 6.95 (*0-942597-67-2*) White Mane Pub.

— Stephen Elliott Welch of the Hampton Legion. LC 94-10652. (Civil War Heritage Ser.: Vol. III). (Illus.). 107p. (Orig.). (C). 1994. pap. 12.00 (*0-942597-66-4*, Burd St Pr) White Mane Pub.

Priest, John M., ed. John T. McMahon's Diary of the 136th New York, 1861-1864. LC 92-37207. (Illus.). 200p. (C). 1993. 24.95 (*0-942597-46-X*) White Mane Pub.

Priest, John M., ed. see Wren, James.

Priest, Joseph. Energy: Principles Problems Alternatives. 4th ed. (Illus.). 328p. (C). 1991. text ed. 41.95 (*0-201-50356-5*) Addison-Wesley.

Priest, Joseph, jt. auth. see Snider, John.

Priest, Josiah. Slavery As It Relates to the Negro or African Race: The Light of Circumstances History & the Holy Scriptures. Grob, Gerald, ed. LC 76-46096. (Anti-Movements in America Ser.). (Illus.). 1977. reprint ed. lib. bdg. 29.95 (*0-405-09969-X*) Ayer.

Priest, Josiah & Brown, W. S. Bible Defence of Slavery. LC 74-92439. 1851. 95.00 (*0-403-00171-4*) Scholarly.

Priest, Josiah, jt. auth. see Brown, W. S.

Priest, Judy & Schott, Judith. Leading Antenatal Classes. (Illus.). 216p. 1991. pap. 24.95 (*0-7506-0050-0*) Buttrwrth-Heinemann.

Priest, Keith, jt. auth. see Royal, Lyssa.

Priest, Lisa. Women Who Killed: Stories of Canadian Female Murderers. (Illus.). 272p. 1992. pap. 5.99 (*0-7710-7153-1*, Pub. by McClelland & Stewart CN) Firefly Bks Ltd.

Priest, Louise, ed. see Council for National Cooperation in Aquatics Staff.

Priest, Lyman W. The Penick Family: Descendants of Edward Penick-Penix-Pinix of St. Peter's Parish, New Kent County, Virginia. LC 82-82022. 344p. reprint ed. pap. 98.10 (*0-8357-4711-5*, AU00407) Bks Demand.

Priest, Mary W. Diary of Courage: Coping with Life-Threatening Illness. 176p. (Orig.). 1990. pap. 9.95 (*0-89407-099-1*) Strawberry Hill.

Priest, Nancy, ed. see Silverstein, Stuart.

Priest, Nicholas D., ed. Metals in Bone. 1985. lib. bdg. 148.00 (*0-85200-909-7*) Kluwer Ac.

Priest Nikolai Deputatov. Revnitel' Blagotchestija 19-go vjeka, Episkop Theofan Zatvornik. 71p. 1971. pap. 3.00 (*0-317-29261-7*) Holy Trinity.

***Priest, Patricia J.** Public Intimacies: Talk Show Participants & Tell All TV. Dervin, Brenda, ed. (Communication Series). 192p. (C). 1995. text ed. 42.50 (*1-57273-002-1*) Hampton Pr NJ.

— Public Intimacies: Talk Show Participants & Tell All TV. Dervin, Brenda, ed. (Communication Series). 192p. 1995. pap. text ed. 17.95 (*1-57273-003-X*) Hampton Pr NJ.

Priest, Prudence, ed. see Taylor, Joseph.

Priest, R., ed. see Annual Conference for Psychosomatic Research Staff.

Priest, Robert. Ten Big Babies. 1989. pap. 4.95 (*0-88753-196-2*, Pub. by Black Moss Pr CN) Firefly Bks Ltd.

— The Town that Got Out of Town. LC 88-46108. (Illus.). 32p. (J). 1989. 14.95 (*0-87923-786-4*) Godine.

Priest, Simon. Preparing Effective Outdoor Pursuit Leaders (People) 122p. 1987. pap. write for info. (*0-943272-18-1*) Inst Recreation Res.

Priest, Simon, jt. auth. see Miles, John C.

Priest, Stephen. Theories of the Mind. 256p. 1992. pap. 9.95 (*0-395-62338-3*) HM.

Priest, Stephen, ed. Hegel's Critique of Kant. (Modern Revivals in Philosophy Ser.). 241p. 1992. 59.95 (*0-7512-0064-6*, Pub. by Gregg Revivals UK) Ashgate Pub Co.

Priest, Stephen D. Discontinuity Analysis for Rock Engineering. LC 92-27172. 1992. write for info. (*0-412-47600-2*) Chapman & Hall.

— Hemispherical Projection Methods in Rock Mechanics. (Illus.). 128p. (C). 1984. pap. text ed. 24.95 (*0-04-622007-0*) Routledge Chapman & Hall.

***Priester, Gary.** CorelDraw F-X. 300p. 1995. cd-rom 39.95 (*1-56604-274-7*) Ventana Pr.

— Looking Good in Color: The Desktop Publisher's Design Guide. (Illus.). 1995. 29.95 (*1-56604-219-4*) Ventana Pr.

Priester, Michael & Hentschel, Thomas. Small-Scale Gold Mining: Processing Techniques in Developing Countries. Deutsches Zentrum fur Entwicklungstechnologien GATE In: Deutsche Gesellschaft fur Technische Zusammenarbeit (GTZ) GmbH Staff, ed. (Illus.). 96p. (C). 1992. pap. text ed. 14.00 (*3-528-02066-0*) Ballen Bkslr.

Priestland, Gerald. The Unquiet Suitcase. large type ed. 224p. 1991. 9.97 (*1-85089-306-3*, Pub. by ISIS UK) Transaction Pubs.

Priestland, R. Radcliffe on Trent, 1710-1837. (C). 1985. text ed. 40.00 (*0-685-22173-3*, Pub. by Univ Nottingham UK) St Mut.

Priestley. Salt Is Leaving. (Black Dagger Crime Ser.). 16.50 (*0-86220-806-8*, BD012, Black Dagger) Chivers N Amer.

Priestley, Brian. Mingus: A Critical Biography. LC 83-26155. (Quality Paperbacks Ser.). (Illus.). 320p. 1984. pap. 11.95 (*0-306-80217-1*) Da Capo.

Priestley, Charles H. Turbulent Transfer in the Lower Atmosphere. LC 59-10427. 138p. reprint ed. pap. 39.40 (*0-317-08496-8*, 2011234) Bks Demand.

Priestley, Dinah. Hector the Bully. (Carolrhoda Picture Bks.). (Illus.). 24p. (J). (ps-3). 1989. lib. bdg. 17.50 (*0-87614-356-7*, Carolrhoda) Lerner Group.

Priestley, Eric. Abracadabra. Peditto, C. Natale, ed. LC 94-12721. (Open Mouth Poetry Ser.). 118p. (Orig.). 1994. pap. 9.95 (*1-884773-02-8*) Heat Press.

Priestley, H. I. The Mexican Nation, a History. 1972. 250.00 (*0-8490-0617-1*) Gordon Pr.

Priestley, Herbert I. Jose de Galvez, Visitor General of New Spain 1765-1771. LC 78-10953. (Perspectives in Latin American History Ser.: No. 1). (Illus.). xiii, 449p. 1980. reprint ed. lib. bdg. 49.50 (*0-87991-605-2*) Porcupine Pr.

— Tristan de Luna, Conquistador of the Old South: A Study of Spanish Imperial Strategy. LC 80-21168. (Perspectives in American History Ser.: No. 49). (Illus.). 215p. 1981. reprint ed. lib. bdg. 35.00 (*0-87991-375-4*) Porcupine Pr.

Priestley, Herbert I., ed. The Luna Papers, 2 vols, Set. LC 75-165803. (Select Bibliographies Reprint Ser.). 1977. reprint ed. 49.95 (*0-8369-5959-0*) Ayer.

Priestley, Hilary A. Introduction to Complex Analysis. rev. ed. (Illus.). 232p. 1990. pap. 24.00 (*0-19-853428-0*) OUP.

Priestley, J. B. Balconinny. LC 70-99645. (Essay Index Reprint Ser.). 1977. 23.95 (*0-8369-1426-0*) Ayer.

— Delight. LC 70-117828. (Essay Index Reprint Ser.). 1977. 20.95 (*0-8369-2015-5*) Ayer.

— English Comic Characters. LC 75-159118. 255p. (C). 1972. reprint ed. 30.00 (*0-87753-052-1*) Phaeton.

— English Journey: Jubilee Edition. LC 83-40619. (Illus.). 320p. 1984. 24.95 (*0-226-68212-9*) U Ch Pr.

— English Novel. Hawke, Edward G., ed. LC 75-158906. 1971. reprint ed. 14.00 (*0-403-01311-9*) Scholarly.

— Figures in Modern Literature. LC 70-93372. (Essay Index Reprint Ser.). 1977. 19.95 (*0-8369-1772-3*) Ayer.

— The Good Companions. 1980. lib. bdg. 21.95 (*0-89967-044-X*) Harmony Raine.

— I for One. LC 67-23262. (Essay Index Reprint Ser.). 1977. reprint ed. 19.95 (*0-8369-0800-7*) Ayer.

— An Inspector Calls. 1948. pap. 4.75 (*0-8222-0572-6*) Dramatists Play.

— The Magicians. LC 90-43613. 160p. 1995. 17.95 (*0-913720-73-9*) Beil.

— The Other Place: & Other Stories of the Same Sort. LC 72-167467. (Short Story Index Reprint Ser.). 1977. reprint ed. 20.95 (*0-8369-3993-X*) Ayer.

— Salt Is Leaving. 224p. 1986. reprint ed. pap. 3.95 (*0-88184-227-3*) Carroll & Graf.

— Self-Selected Essays. (Essay Index Reprint Ser.). 1977. 20.95 (*0-8369-0801-5*) Ayer.

— The Shapes of Sleep. large type ed. 266p. 1990. 19.95 (*1-85089-299-7*, Pub. by ISIS UK) Transaction Pubs.

— Too Many People & Other Reflections. LC 71-128289. (Essay Index Reprint Ser.). 1977. 21.95 (*0-8369-2016-3*) Ayer.

Priestley, J. B. & Brett, R. L. William Hazlitt. (Writers & Their Work Ser.). 96p. (Orig.). 1994. pap. text ed. 11.50 (*0-7463-0745-4*, Pub. by Northcote House UK) Trans-Atl Phila.

Priestley, J. B., ed. see Moore, Thomas.

Priestley, John., ed. Essayists Past & Present. LC 67-30227. (Essay Index Reprint Ser.). 1977. 20.95 (*0-8369-0802-3*) Ayer.

Priestley, John B. The English Comic Characters. (BCL1-PR English Literature Ser.). 276p. 1992. reprint ed. lib. bdg. 79.00 (*0-7812-7126-6*) Rprt Serv.

— The English Novel. (BCL1-PR English Literature Ser.). 79p. 1992. reprint ed. lib. bdg. 59.00 (*0-7812-7115-0*) Rprt Serv.

— Figures in Modern Literature. (BCL1-PR English Literature Ser.). 215p. 1992. reprint ed. lib. bdg. 79.00 (*0-7812-7066-9*) Rprt Serv.

— George Meredith. (BCL1-PR English Literature Ser.). 204p. 1992. reprint ed. lib. bdg. 79.00 (*0-7812-7597-0*) Rprt Serv.

— George Meredith. LC 70-131807. 1970. reprint ed. 25.00 (*0-403-00694-5*) Scholarly.

— Thomas Love Peacock. (BCL1-PR English Literature Ser.). 215p. 1992. reprint ed. lib. bdg. 79.00 (*0-7812-7617-9*) Rprt Serv.

Priestley, John V., jt. ed. see Polak, Julia M.

Priestley, Joseph. Autobiography of Joseph Priestley. 159p. 1990. 25.00 (*0-685-37308-8*) Fairleigh Dickinson.

— Disquisitions Relating Matter & Spirit, 2 vols. in 1. Wellek, Rene, ed. Bd. with Doctrine of Philosophical Necessity Illustrated: Being an Appendix to the Disquestions Relating to Matter & Spirit. LC 75-11248. LC 75-11248. (British Philosophers & Theologians of the 17th & 18th Centuries Ser.: Vol. 47). 1976. reprint ed. Set lib. bdg. 51.00 (*0-8240-1799-4*) Garland.

— Disquisitions Relating to Matter & Spirit. LC 74-26285. (History, Philosophy & Sociology of Science Ser.). 1975. reprint ed. 29.95 (*0-405-06612-0*) Ayer.

— A Farewell Sermon. LC 90-119278. 176p. 1989. reprint ed. 40.00 (*1-85477-007-1*, Pub. by Woodstock Bks UK) Cassell.

— Historical Account of the Navigable Rivers, Canals & Railways Throughout Great Britain. (Illus.). 776p. 1967. reprint ed. 60.00 (*0-7146-1067-4*, Pub. by F Cass Pubs UK) Intl Spec Bk.

— History & Present State of Discoveries Relating to Vision, Light, & Colours. Cohen, I. Bernard, ed. LC 80-2142. (Development of Science Ser.). (Illus.). 1981. lib. bdg. 77.95 (*0-405-13897-0*) Ayer.

— Jesus & Socrates Compared. 64p. 1994. pap. 9.95 (*1-56459-454-8*) Kessinger Pub.

— Political Writings. Miller, Peter, ed. LC 92-27753. (Cambridge Texts in the History of Political Thought Ser.). 288p. (C). 1993. 49.95 (*0-521-41540-3*); pap. 14.95 (*0-521-42561-1*) Cambridge U Pr.

— The Theological & Miscellaneous Works, 25 vols. in 26, Set. 1974. reprint ed. pap. 1,560.00 (*0-527-72751-2*) Periodicals Srv.

Priestley, K. E. & Wright, Beryl R. Mental Health & Education in Hong Kong. LC 58-4702. (Hong Kong University Extra-Mural Lecture Ser.). 104p. reprint ed. pap. 29.70 (*0-317-09368-1*, 2017711) Bks Demand.

Priestley, Lee. Journeys of Faith: The Story of Preacher & Edith Lewis. (Illus.). 212p. (Orig.). 1992. pap. 14.95 (*0-9623682-2-9*) Arroyo Pr.

— Shalam: Utopia on the Rio Grande. (Southwestern Studies: No. 84). (Orig.). 1990. reprint ed. pap. 10.00 (*0-87404-167-8*) Tex Western.

Priestley, Lee & Peterson, Marquita. Billy the Kid: The Good Side of a Bad Man. rev. ed. LC 93-61580. (Illus.). 72p. 1993. pap. 7.95 (*1-881325-10-5*) Yucca Tree Pr.

Priestley, M. B., ed. Spectral Analysis & the Time Series, 2 Vols. in 1, Vol. 1 & Vol.2. (Probability & Mathematical Statistics Ser.). 1983. pap. text ed. 69.00 (*0-12-564922-3*) Acad Pr.

***Priestley, M. J. & Calvi, Gian M.** Seismic Design & Retrofit of Bridges. Date not set. text ed. 74.95 (*0-471-57998-X*) Wiley.

Priestley, M. J., jt. auth. see Paulay, Tom.

***Priestley, Mary.** Essays on Analytical Music Therapy. 335p. (C). 1994. pap. 30.00 (*0-9624080-2-6*) Barcelona Pubs.

Priestley, Philip. Jail Journeys: The English Prison Experience, 1918-1986. 256p. 1989. lib. bdg. 39.95 (*0-415-03458-2*) Routledge.

Priestley, Philip, jt. auth. see McGuire, James.

Priestley, W. M. Calculus: An Historical Approach. (Undergraduate Texts in Mathematics Ser.). (Illus.). 1984. 39.00 (*0-387-90349-6*) Spr-Verlag.

Priestly, Brian. Jazz on Record: A History. (Illus.). 240p. 1991. pap. 14.95 (*0-8230-7562-1*, Billboard Bks) Watsn-Guptill.

Priestly, David A. Seed Aging: Implications for Seed Storage & Persistence in the Soil. LC 85-21334. (Comstock Book Ser.). (Illus.). 304p. (C). 1986. 43.50 (*0-8014-1865-8*) Cornell U Pr.

Priestly, E. B., et al. Introduction to Liquid Crystals. LC 75-34195. 356p. 1975. 69.50 (*0-306-30858-4*, Plenum Pr) Plenum.

Priestly, Eric. Raw Dog. (Orig.). 1985. pap. 3.25 (*0-87067-809-4*, BH809) Holloway.

Priestly, G. C. Molecular Aspects of Dermatology. LC 93-2652. (Molecular Medical Science Ser.). 226p. 1993. text ed. 79.95 (*0-471-93639-1*) Wiley.

Priestly, Gail F., jt. auth. see Traver, Gayle A.

Priestly, H. A. & Davey, B. A. Introduction to Lattices & Order. (Illus.). 150p. (C). 1990. pap. 22.95 (*0-521-36766-2*) Cambridge U Pr.

Priestly, H. E. English Home. 1971. 20.00 (*0-584-10076-0*) Transatl Arts.

Priestly, J. B. Man & Time. 1989. 17.99 (*0-517-69042-X*) Random Hse Value.

— Tom Moore's Diary. 1988. reprint ed. lib. bdg. 75.00 (*0-7812-0039-3*) Rprt Serv.

Priestly, John B. Thomas Love Peacock. LC 74-131808. 1970. reprint ed. 49.00 (*0-403-00695-3*) Scholarly.

Priestly, Joseph. Disquisitions Relating to Matter & Spirit. 356p. 1993. pap. 21.00 (*1-56459-314-2*) Kessinger Pub.

— The Doctrines of Heathen Philosophy. 1987. 50.00 (*0-8201-1426-X*) Schol Facsimiles.

Priestly, Michael. Performance Assessment in Education & Training: Alternative Techniques. LC 81-19598. (Illus.). 280p. 1982. 34.95 (*0-87778-181-8*) Educ Tech Pubns.

Priestly, Philip. Victorian Prison Lives. (Illus.). 250p. 1985. 27.50 (*0-416-34770-3*, 9594) Routledge Chapman & Hall.

Priestly, R. J., ed. Effects of Heating on Foodstuffs. (Illus.). 410p. 1979. 106.25 (*0-85334-797-2*, Pub. by Elsevier Applied Sci UK) Elsevier.

Priestman, Barbara. Frobel Education Today. 1972. 59.95 (*0-8490-0202-8*) Gordon Pr.

Priestman, Martin. Cowper's Task: Structure & Influence. LC 82-22049. 250p. 1983. 64.95 (*0-521-23643-6*) Cambridge U Pr.

Priestman, T. J. Cancer Chemotherapy. 3rd ed. 225p. 1989. pap. 44.00 (*0-387-19551-3*) Spr-Verlag.

***Priests for Equality Staff. The Inclusive New Testament. 470p. (Orig.). (C). 1994. pap. 19.95 (*0-9644279-0-7*) Priests for Equality.**
THE INCLUSIVE NEW TESTAMENT uses non-sexist & non-classist language in this powerful new translation. It underwent a four-year grassroots field testing by over three hundred individuals, faith groups & intentional communities; it reflects the scholarship of contemporary feminist biblical hermeneutics & a faithful reliance on the original KOINE Greek. THE INCLUSIVE NEW TESTAMENT emphasizes the poetic beauty of the ancient texts, while gently & creatively recasting it in inclusive language. It is designed to be READ--by individuals, for private reflection & devotional study; & read ALOUD--by lectors, from the pulpit. The unique & attractive format has no columns or artificial section breaks, giving greater attention to the storyline of each book & de-emphasizing its "bibleness," while retaining the traditional chapter & verse numbering for quick reference & ease of study. The large & clear typeface makes it an extremely readable text for old & young alike. The "sew-&-cover" binding gives the book the flexibility to lie flat without breaking the spine. THE INCLUSIVE NEW TESTAMENT is an essential addition to the bookshelf of anyone interested in biblical, feminist or contemporary language studies. Generous volume & trade discounts. Call 301-699-0042 (voice) or FAX: 301-864-2182 or write to Priests for Equality, P.O. Box 5243, Hyattsville, MD 20782-0243. ***Publisher Provided Annotation.***

Prieto. Pablo's Petunias. LC 72-190269. (Illus.). 32p. (J). (gr. 3-5). 1972. lib. bdg. 9.95 (*0-87783-058-4*) Oddo.

— Pablo's Petunias. deluxe ed. LC 72-190269. (Illus.). 32p. (J). (gr. 3-5). 1972. pap. 3.94 (*0-87783-102-5*) Oddo.

Prieto, A., et al, eds. Artificial Neural Networks: International Workshop IWANN '91 Granada, Spain, September 17-19, 1991 Proceedings. (Lecture Notes in Computer Science Ser.: Vol. 540). xiii, 476p. 1991. pap. 44.00 (*0-387-54537-9*) Spr-Verlag.

Prieto, Diaz, jt. auth. see Shafer, Wilhelm.

Prieto-Diaz, R. & Arango, G. Domain Analysis & Software Systems Modeling. LC 91-11714. 312p. 1991. 50.00 (*0-8186-8996-X*, 1996) IEEE Comp Soc.

Prieto, F. English-Spanish Dictionary of Media Terms. 387p. (ENG & SPA.). 1991. pap. 50.00 (*84-86168-62-7*) IBD Ltd.

Prieto, Florencio. Diccionario Terminologico De Medios De Communicacion: Ingles-Espanol. 400p. 1991. pap. 55.00 (*0-7859-6392-8*, 8486168627) Fr & Eur.

Prieto, J., et al, eds. Hepatobiliary Diseases. LC 91-5205. (Illus.). xxv, 1128p. 1992. 166.00 (*0-387-54326-0*) Spr-Verlag.

Prieto, Jorge. Harvest of Hope: The Pilgrimage of a Mexican-American Physician. LC 89-40024. 168p. (C). 1989. text ed. 20.95 (*0-268-01087-0*) U of Notre Dame Pr.

— Harvest of Hope: The Pilgrimage of a Mexican-American Physician. LC 89-40024. 168p. (C). 1990. pap. text ed. 8.95 (*0-268-01092-7*) U of Notre Dame Pr.

P Q

— The Quarterback Who Almost Wasn't. LC 93-29314. 128p. 1994. pap. 9.95 (*1-55885-109-7*) Arte Publico.

Prieto, Muriel H. Vocabulary Made Easy for Spanish Speakers: Teacher's Guide. LC 76-3732. 49p. 1978. pap. text ed. 2.50 (*0-8477-2635-5*) U of PR Pr.

Prieto, Raymond. Waldenlake. 170p. 1994. pap. 7.95 (*1-56901-239-3*) NW Pub.

Prieto, Rene. Miguel Angel Asturias's Archaeology of Return. LC 92-24500. (Studies in Latin American & Iberian Literature: Vol. 7). 275p. (C). 1993. 54.95 (*0-521-43412-2*) Cambridge U Pr.

Prieto, Rene, jt. auth. see Perry, Ted.

Prieto, Ulises. Los Mascarones De Oliva. LC 78-55925. (Coleccion Espejo de Paciencia Ser.). 1978. pap. 5.00 (*0-89729-195-6*) Ediciones.

Prietula, Michael J., jt. ed. see Carley, Kathleen M.

***Prietula, Mike, ed.** AI & Theories of Groups & Organizations: Conceptual & Empirical Research: Papers from the 1993 Workshop. (Technical Reports). (Illus.). 102p. (Orig.). 1994. pap. 25.00x (*0-929280-55-5*) Amer Artificial.

Prietz, G. Huf und Klauenkunde mit Hufbeschlaglehre. (Illus.). 166p. (GER.). 1985. 40.00 (*3-8055-4003-5*) S Karger.

Prieur, Benoit, jt. auth. see Couture, Pascale.

Prieve, E. Arthur. Guide to Arts Administration Training, 1993-1994. LC 91-12452. 1993. pap. 11.95 (*1-879903-10-5*) Am Council Arts.

Prieve, E. Arthur, ed. Survey of Arts Administration Training: 1991-1992. rev. ed. LC 91-12452. 96p. (Orig.). 1991. pap. 11.95 (*0-915400-90-1*, ACA Bks) Am Council Arts.

Priezzhev, V. B., jt. auth. see Shirkov, D. V.

Prifti, Peter R. Socialist Albania since Nineteen Forty-Four: Domestic & Foreign Developments. LC 78-1728. (Studies in Communism, Revisionism, & Revolution: No. 22). 1978. 40.00 (*0-262-16070-6*) MIT Pr.

Prifti, William. Securities: Public & Private Offerings, 2 vols. LC 82-24495. (Securities Law Ser.). 1983. ring bd. 250.00 (*0-317-11924-9*) Clark Boardman Callaghan.

Prifti, William M. Securities: Public & Private Offerings. write for info. (*0-318-57517-5*) West Pub.

— Securities: Public & Private Offerings, 2 vols., Set. 2nd ed. (Securities Ser.). 1995. ring bd. write for info. (*0-614-06274-8*) Clark Boardman Callaghan.

Prigal, Alan. Federal Tax Guidebook. 2nd ed. 1986. Updates. ring bd. write for info. (*0-8205-1589-2*) Bender.

Prigatano, George P. & Schacter, Daniel L., eds. Awareness of Deficit after Brain Injury: Clinical & Theoretical Issues. (Illus.). 290p. 1991. 49.95 (*0-19-505941-7*) OUP.

***Prigen, P. M.** Communication in Successful Total Quality Management. (C). 1994. 150.00x (*0-946655-61-8*, Pub. by S Thornes Pubs UK) St Mut.

Priggee, Milt. Some Priggee Good Stuff. 112p. 1992. pap. text ed. 12.95 (*0-8403-7748-7*) Kendall-Hunt.

Prigmore, Charles S., jt. auth. see Atherton, Charles R.

Prignitz, Earl J. One Man's Life. (Illus.). 90p. (Orig.). 1988. pap. 4.95 (*0-932970-51-6*) Prinit Pr.

Prigoff, James, jt. auth. see Chalfant, Henry.

Prigogine. Being to Becomming 2. 1995. pap. text ed. write for info. (*0-7167-1855-3*) W H Freeman.

***Prigogine & Rice, eds.** Advances in Chemical Physics Vol. 91, Vol. 91. Date not set. text ed. 145.00 (*0-471-12002-2*) Wiley.

***Prigogine, I. & Rice, Stuart A., eds.** Advances in Chemical Physics, Vol. 89. (Progress in Clinical & Biological Research Ser.: Vol. 89). 422p. 1994. text ed. 145.00 (*0-471-05157-8*) Wiley.

***Prigogine, I. & Rice, Stuart S., eds.** Advances in Chemical Physics, Vol. 90. Date not set. text ed. 130.00 (*0-471-04234-X*) Wiley.

Prigogine, I., jt. auth. see Defay, Raymond.

Prigogine, I., et al. Chaotic Dynamics & Transport in Fluids & Plasmas. (Research Trends in Physics Ser.). 256p. 1992. 120.00 (*0-88318-923-2*) Am Inst Physics.

Prigogine, Ilya & Nocolis, G. Exploring Complexity. LC 88-33555. 384p. 1995. text ed. write for info. (*0-7167-1859-6*); pap. text ed. write for info. (*0-7167-1860-X*) W H Freeman.

Prigogine, Ilya & Rice, Staurt A., eds. Advances in Chemical Physics, Vol. 77. 645p. 1990. text ed. 175.00 (*0-471-51609-0*) Wiley.

Prigogine, Ilya & Rice, Stuart A., eds. Advances in Chemical Physics, Vol. 68. 416p. 1987. text ed. 199.00 (*0-471-84901-4*) Wiley.

— Advances in Chemical Physics, Vol. 72. 345p. 1988. text ed. 163.00 (*0-471-63626-6*) Wiley.

— Advances in Chemical Physics, Vol. 74. LC 87-37248. 401p. 1988. text ed. 174.00 (*0-471-61212-X*) Wiley.

— Advances in Chemical Physics, Vol. 75. 588p. 1989. text ed. 185.00 (*0-471-62219-2*) Wiley.

— Advances in Chemical Physics, Vol. 78. 299p. 1990. text ed. 129.00 (*0-471-52666-5*) Wiley.

— Advances in Chemical Physics, Vol. 79. 322p. 1990. text ed. 136.00 (*0-471-52768-8*) Wiley.

— Advances in Chemical Physics, Vol. 80. 489p. 1991. text ed. 174.00 (*0-471-53281-9*) Wiley.

— Advances in Chemical Physics, Vol. 81. 832p. 1992. text ed. 227.00 (*0-471-54570-8*) Wiley.

— Advances in Chemical Physics, Vol. 83. 752p. 1992. text ed. 265.00 (*0-471-54018-8*) Wiley.

— Advances in Chemical Physics, Vol. 84. 560p. 1993. text ed. 190.00 (*0-471-58726-5*) Wiley.

— Advances in Chemical Physics, Vol. 86. LC 58-9935. 433p. 1993. text ed. 140.00 (*0-471-59845-3*) Wiley.

— Evolution of Size Effect in Chemical Dynamics, Vol. 70. (Advances in Chemical Physics Ser.). 556p. 1988. text ed. 199.00 (*0-471-62784-4*) Wiley.

— Evolution of Size Effects in Chemical Dynamics, Vol. 70. (Advances in Chemical Physics Ser.). 594p. 1988. text ed. 199.00 (*0-471-62951-0*) Wiley.

Prigogine, Ilya & Stengers, Isabelle. Order Out of Chaos: Man's New Dialogue with Nature. (Illus.). 448p. (Orig.). 1984. pap. 13.95 (*0-553-34363-7*) Bantam.

Prigogine, Ilya, jt. auth. see Nicolis, G.

Prigogine, Ilya, et al. Chaos: The New Science. Holte, John, ed. LC 92-34498. (Nobel Conference Ser.). (Illus.). 144p. (Orig.). 1993. lib. bdg. 44.00 (*0-8191-8933-2*); pap. 17.50 (*0-8191-8934-0*) U Pr of Amer.

Prijatelj, Kruno. Dalmatian Painting of the Fifteenth & Sixteenth Centuries. 125p. 1983. 30.00 (*0-918660-44-0*) Ragusan Pr.

Prijs, B. Chymia Basiliensis. (Illus.). x, 126p. 1983. 16.00 (*3-8055-3786-7*) S Karger.

Prik, J., et al. Safety Evaluation of Geological Disposal Concepts for Low & Medium Level Wastes, No. EUR 13178. 573p. 1991. pap. 65.00 (*92-826-0351-2*, CD-NA-13178-EN-C, Pub. by Europ Com) UNIPUB.

Priklonsky, Alexander. Blessed Athanasia & the Desert Ideal. 2nd ed. St. Herman of Alaska Brotherhood Staff, ed. & tr. by. LC 89-62427. (Modern Matericon Ser.). (Illus.). 169p. 1994. pap. 5.00 (*0-938635-40-9*) St Herman AK.

Prikry, K., jt. auth. see Jech, T.

Prikrylova. Mathematical Modeling of the Immune Response. 1992. 110.00 (*0-8493-6753-0*, QR186) CRC Pr.

Prilesky, C., jt. auth. see Erdo, J.

Prilik, Pearl. The Art of Stepmothering. 256p. 1994. 19.95 (*1-56796-042-1*) WRS Group.

***Prill, Clarence E.** Radionics - Psionics Phenomena: The Prill Method of Monitoring. Templar, Thor, ed. 75p. (Orig.). Date not set. 20.00 (*1-57179-047-0*) Intern Guild ASRS.

Prill, D., tr. see Ahiezer, N. I. & Krein, M. G.

***Prill, David.** Unnatural. 1995. 21.00 (*0-312-11910-0*) St Martin.

Prill, H. J. & Stauber, M., eds. Advances in Psychosomatic Obstetrics & Gynecology, Berlin 1980: Proceedings. (Illus.). 560p. 1982. pap. 59.00 (*0-387-11710-5*) Spr-Verlag.

Prillaman, A. Renee, et al, eds. The Tapestry of Caring: Education as Nurturance. LC 93-46343. 1994. 39.50 (*0-89391-971-3*); pap. 24.95 (*1-56750-075-7*) Ablex Pub.

Prilleltensky, Isaac. The Morals & Politics of Psychology: Psychological Discourse & the Status Quo. LC 93-37494. (SUNY Series, Alternatives in Psychology). 283p. 1994. 64.50x (*0-7914-2037-X*); pap. 21.95x (*0-7914-2038-8*) State U NY Pr.

Prillwitz, Siegmund & Vollhaber, Tomas, eds. Current Trends in European Sign Language Research. (International Studies on Sign Language & the Communication of the Deaf: Vol. 9). 406p. 1993. pap. 37.95 (*3-927731-03-X*, Pub. by Signum-Verlag GW) Gallaudet Univ Pr.

— Sign Language Research & Application. (International Studies on Sign Language & the Communication of the Deaf: Vol. 13). 304p. 1993. 39.95 (*3-927731-12-9*, Pub. by Signum-Verlag GW) Gallaudet Univ Pr.

***Prima.** Fast Attack the Official Strategy Guide. 1995. pap. (*0-7615-0070-7*) Prima Pub.

— Rise of the Robots the Official CD-ROM Strategy Guide. 1995. pap. (*0-7615-0037-5*) Prima Pub.

***Prima Staff.** Cyberia: The Official Strategy Guide. 1995. pap. 19.95 (*1-55958-795-4*) Prima Pub.

— Malcom's Revenge. (Legend of Kyrandia Ser.: No. 3). 1994. pap. 19.95 (*1-55958-782-2*) Prima Pub.

— Mortal Kombat II Official Power Play Guide. 1994. pap. 9.95 (*1-55958-681-8*) Prima Pub.

Primack, jt. auth. see Willis.

Primack, Alice L. Journal Literature of the Physical Sciences: A Manual. LC 92-29762. (Illus.). 220p. 1992. 29.50 (*0-8108-2592-9*) Scarecrow.

Primack, Marshall P., jt. auth. see Henley, Arthur.

Primack, Martin, jt. auth. see Willis, James F.

Primack, Martin, jt. auth. see Willis, James.

Primack, Martin L. Farm Formed Capital in American Agriculture, 1850-1910. Bruchey, Stuart, ed. LC 76-45108. (Nineteen Seventy-Seven Dissertations Ser.). 1977. lib. bdg. 30.95 (*0-405-09920-7*) Ayer.

Primack, Martin L., jt. auth. see Willis, James F.

Primack, Richard B. Essentials of Conservation Biology. LC 93-6933. (Illus.). 555p. 1993. 39.95 (*0-87893-722-6*) Sinauer Assocs.

— A Primer of Conservation Biology. LC 95-13972. (Illus.). 230p. (Orig.). (C). 1995. pap. text ed. 18.95 (*0-87893-730-7*) Sinauer Assocs.

***Primack, Richard B. & Lovejoy, Thomas E., eds.** Ecology, Conservation, & Management of Southeast Asia Rainforests. LC 94-45878. 1995. write for info. (*0-300-06234-6*) Yale U Pr.

Primak, W. The Compacted States of Vitreous Silica. (Studies in Radiation Effects in Solids: Vol. 4). 202p. 1975. text ed. 145.00 (*0-677-03340-0*) Gordon & Breach.

Primary Comm. Research Centre Staff, ed. Scholary Publishers Guide: Financial & Legal Aspects. 1979. 40.00 (*0-906083-08-7*) St Mut.

***Primary Research Staff.** The Law Library Budget & Expenditure Report. 110p. 1993. ring bd. 75.00x (*0-9626749-4-X*) Primary Research.

— The Medical Library Budget & Expenditure Report. 110p. 1994. 82.50 (*0-9626749-6-6*) Primary Research.

— The Report on Corporate Library Spending. 112p. 1995. pap. 80.00 (*1-57440-000-2*) Primary Research.

— The Scientific & Technical Library Budget & Expenditure Report. 120p. 1993. ring bd. 65.00 (*0-9626749-5-8*) Primary Research.

***Primatesta, Fulvio.** TUXEDO: An Open Approach to OLTP. LC 95-8367. 1995. pap. text ed. 40.00 (*0-13-101833-7*) P-H.

Primavera, Elise. Plantpet. LC 93-36526. (Illus.). 32p. (J). (ps-3). 1994. lib. bdg. 15.95 (*0-399-22627-3*, Putnam) Putnam Pub Group.

— Ralph's Frozen Tale. LC 90-35521. 32p. (J). 1991. 14.95 (*0-399-22252-9*, Putnam) Putnam Pub Group.

— The Three Dots. LC 92-12979. (Illus.). 40p. (J). (ps-3). 1993. 14.95 (*0-399-22429-7*, Putnam) Putnam Pub Group.

***Primavera Systems, Inc. Staff.** Expedition: Construction Contract Control Software User Guide. abr. rev. ed. (Illus.). 786p. 1992. disk write for info. (*0-926282-60-3*) Primavera Syst.

— Expedition: Perspectives. (Illus.). 287p. 1992. disk write for info. (*0-926282-61-1*) Primavera Syst.

— Monte Carlo: Project Risk Analysis & Simulation Software. (Illus.). 262p. 1993. disk write for info. (*0-926282-75-1*) Primavera Syst.

— Parade: Cost Control & Performance Measurement Software. (Illus.). 492p. 1993. disk write for info. (*0-926282-73-5*) Primavera Syst.

— Primavera Project Planner for Windows: Planning & Control Guide. 330p. 1994. disk write for info. (*0-926282-79-4*) Primavera Syst.

— Primavera Project Planner for Windows: Reference. (Illus.). 797p. 1994. disk write for info. (*0-926282-78-6*) Primavera Syst.

— SureTrak Project Manager for Windows: User Manual. (Illus.). 663p. 1994. disk write for info. (*0-926282-84-0*) Primavera Syst.

Primavesi, Anne. From Apocalypse to Genesis: Ecology, Feminism & Christianity. LC 09-14229. 336p. 1991. pap. 17.00 (*0-8006-2522-6*, 1-2522) Augsburg Fortress.

Primavesi, Anne & Henderson, Jennifer. Our God Has No Favorites: A Liberation Theology of the Eucharist. 120p. (C). 1989. pap. 8.95 (*0-89390-165-2*) Resource Pubns.

Primc, M., jt. auth. see Lepowsky, James.

***Prime.** Multilingual Dictionary of Automatic Cont Technology. (IFAC Ser.). 1994. 88.00 (*0-08-041913-5*, Pergamon Pr) Elsevier.

Prime, Alfred C., ed. Arts & Crafts in Philadelphia, Maryland, & South Carolina, 1721-1785, 2 Vols, Set. LC 79-75356. (Architecture & Decorative Art Ser.). 1969. reprint ed. lib. bdg. 79.50 (*0-306-71320-9*) Da Capo.

Prime, Daniel N. Prime: The Autobiography of an Octogenarian, with the Genealogy of His Ancestors & Sketches of Their History. 293p. 1992. reprint ed. lib. bdg. 54.00 (*0-8328-2396-1*); reprint ed. pap. 44.00 (*0-8328-2397-X*) Higginson Bk Co.

Prime, E. D. Prime: Notes - Genealogical, Biographical & Bibliographical - of the Prime Family. 118p. 1992. reprint ed. lib. bdg. 29.50 (*0-8328-2708-8*); reprint ed. pap. 19.50 (*0-8328-2709-6*) Higginson Bk Co.

***Prime, H. A. & Work, Ants, eds.** Multilingual Dictionary of Automatic Control Technology: English-French, German, Spanish, Italian, Japanese, Chinese & Russian. (IFAC Workshop Ser.). 280p. 1995. 128.00 (*0-08-037192-2*, Pergamon Pr) Elsevier.

Prime, Samuel. The Power of Prayer. 320p. 1991. text ed. 18.95 (*0-85151-602-5*) Banner of Truth.

Prime, Samuel I. The Life of Samuel F. B. Morse, L. L. D: Inventor of the Electro-Magnetic Recording Telegraph. LC 74-4691. (Telecommunications Ser.). (Illus.). 816p. 1974. reprint ed. 60.95 (*0-405-06054-8*) Ayer.

Prime, Temple. Some Account of the Temple Family. 2nd ed. (Illus.). 111p. 1990. reprint ed. lib. bdg. 27.50 (*0-8328-1542-X*); reprint ed. pap. 19.50 (*0-8328-1543-8*) Higginson Bk Co.

— Some Account of the Temple Family. 3rd ed. (Illus.). 146p. 1990. reprint ed. lib. bdg. 30.00 (*0-8328-1544-6*); reprint ed. pap. 22.00 (*0-8328-1545-4*) Higginson Bk Co.

— Some Account of the Temple Family. 4th ed. (Illus.). 77p. 1990. reprint ed. lib. bdg. 24.00 (*0-8328-1546-2*); reprint ed. pap. 16.00 (*0-8328-1547-0*) Higginson Bk Co.

— Some Account of the Temple Family. (Illus.). 100p. 1990. reprint ed. lib. bdg. 26.00 (*0-8328-1540-3*); reprint ed. pap. 18.00 (*0-8328-1541-1*) Higginson Bk Co.

Prime, Terence. Commercial Law. (C). 1990. 110.00 (*1-85431-087-9*, Pub. by Blackstone Pr UK) St Mut.

— Contract & Tort. (Student Statutes Ser.). 192p. 1993. pap. text ed. 20.00 (*0-406-02300-X*, UK) Butterworth Legal Pubs.

— The Law of Copyright. 337p. 1992. 104.00 (*1-85190-180-9*, Pub. by Tolley Pubng UK) St Mut.

— Prime: International Bonds & Certificates of Deposit. 1990. 160.00 (*0-406-11460-9*) Butterworth Legal Pubs.

***Prime, Terence & Scanlan, Gary.** The Law of Partnership. 1995. pap. text ed. write for info. (*0-406-02512-6*, UK) Butterworth Legal Pubs.

— Prime & Scanlan: The Law of Limitations. 336p. 1993. pap. 75.00 (*0-406-00598-2*, U.K.) Butterworth Legal Pubs.

Prime, William C. Tent Life in the Holy Land. Davis, Moshe, ed. LC 77-70734. (America & the Holy Land Ser.). (Illus.). 1977. reprint ed. lib. bdg. 42.95 (*0-405-10278-X*) Ayer.

Primeau, John K., jt. auth. see Sickinger, Raymond L.

Primeau, Ronald. Beyond Spoon River: The Legacy of Edgar Lee Masters. 230p. (C). 1981. text ed. 22.50 (*0-292-70731-2*) U of Tex Pr.

— Beyond Spoon River: The Legacy of Edgar Lee Masters. LC 80-25825. (Dan Danciger Publication Ser.). 231p. reprint ed. pap. 65.90 (*0-7837-5193-1*, 2044927) Bks Demand.

Primeaux, Martha, jt. auth. see Henderson, George.

Primeaux, Patrick. Richard R. Niebuhr on Christ & Religion: The Four-Stage Development of His Theology. LC 81-38369. (Toronto Studies in Theology: Vol. 4). (Illus.). xiv, 288p. 1981. lib. bdg. 89.95 (*0-88946-973-3*) E Mellen.

Primeaux, Walter J. Direct Electric Utility Competition: The Natural Monopoly Myth. LC 85-20487. 316p. 1985. text ed. 59.95 (*0-275-90032-0*, C0032, Praeger Pubs) Greenwood.

Primer. Mandeville Studies. (International Archives of the History of Ideas Ser.: No. 81). 1975. lib. bdg. 84.00 (*90-247-1686-1*) Kluwer Ac.

Primi, John. Charging System Explained. LC 80-730673. 1980. student ed 7.00 (*0-8064-0137-0*, 436); audio 419.00 (*0-8064-0138-9*) Bergwall.

— Troubleshooting with the Vat Forty. LC 80-730756. (Orig.). 1980. student ed 5.00 (*0-8064-0147-8*, 441); audio 359.00 (*0-8064-0148-6*) Bergwall.

Primiani, Rose, jt. auth. see Crane, Stephen.

Primicerio, M., jt. ed. see Fasano, A.

Primm, Clyde, ed. The Musical! Where to Find It. 219p. 1984. pap. 24.95 (*0-918933-00-5*) Magnetic Inds.

— The Musical! Where to Find It. 371p. (Orig.). 1985. pap. 29.95 (*0-918933-01-3*) Magnetic Inds.

Primm, Ronald G., jt. auth. see Lewis, John S.

Primmer, Brian. The Berlioz Style. LC 83-18920. (Music Reprint Ser.). 202p. 1983. reprint ed. lib. bdg. 29.50 (*0-306-76223-4*) Da Capo.

Primo, Pauline. Vida Saludable. (SPA). 84p. 1990. pap. 9.95 (*0-685-51944-9*) Woodland UT.

***Primorac, Karen & Adorni, Sergio.** English Grammar for Students of Italian. 2nd ed. Morton, Jacqueline, ed. 208p. Date not set. pap. 9.95x (*0-934034-20-6*) Olivia & Hill.

Primoratz, Igor. Justifying Legal Punishment. LC 88-9198. (Studies in Applied Philosophy). 200p. (C). 1989. text ed. 45.00 (*0-391-03574-6*) Humanities.

***Primozic.** Strategic Choices: Supremacy, Survival, or Sayonara. 1995. pap. text ed. 14.95 (*0-07-051926-9*) McGraw.

Primozic, Edward, et al. Strategic Choices: Supremacy, Survival or Sayonara. 256p. 1991. text ed. 24.95 (*0-07-051036-9*) McGraw.

***Primozich, Jean & Strandness, D. E.** Techniques of Cerebrovascular Sonography. Date not set. text ed. write for info. (*0-941022-30-7*); vhs write for info. (*0-941022-33-1*) Appleton Davies.

Primrose, E., tr. see Burago, Yu D., et al, eds.

Primrose, E., tr. see Resehtnyak, Y. G.

Primrose, Jan, ed. see Aitkenhead, Donna I.

Primrose, P. Investment in Manufacturing Technology. 256p. 1991. 89.95 (*0-412-40920-8*, A6260) Chapman & Hall.

Primrose, S., jt. auth. see Dimmock, N.

Primrose, S. B. Molecular Biotechnology. 2nd ed. (Illus.). 208p. 1991. 75.00 (*0-632-03233-2*); pap. 49.95 (*0-632-03053-4*) Blackwell Sci.

— Principles of Genome Analysis: A Guide to Mapping & Sequencing DNA from Different Organisms. LC 95-6173. 1995. write for info. (*0-86542-946-4*) Blackwell Sci.

Primrose, S. B., jt. auth. see Old, R. W.

***Primus, Ginger & Westlake, Barbara.** Shape It Up. 112p. (C). 1994. 23.95 (*0-8403-9936-7*) Kendall-Hunt.

Prin, John, ed. see Miller, Dennis & Hunt, Amelia.

Prina, Stephen & Tillman, Lynn. Stephen Prina: "It Was the Best He Could Do at the Moment" (Illus.). 104p. (Orig.). 1992. pap. 35.00 (*90-6918-094-4*, Pub. by Museum Boymans-van NE) Dist Art Pubs.

Prince. Anne Frank, Lev. 4. (International Reader's Library). 1985. pap. 7.95 (*0-8384-3418-5*) Heinle & Heinle.

— John Lennon, Level 5. (International Reader's Library). 1992. pap. 7.95 (*0-8384-3812-1*) Heinle & Heinle.

— Write Soon! 1990. pap. 18.95 (*0-8384-3389-8*) Heinle & Heinle.

— Write Soon! 1991. pap. 7.95 (*0-8384-3445-2*) Heinle & Heinle.

***Prince Aage of Denmark.** My Life in the Foreign Legion. (European War Ser.: No. 1). (Illus.). 204p. 1994. reprint ed. 34.95 (*0-89839-196-2*) Battery Pr.

Prince, Alan, jt. ed. see Savitsky, Evgeny M.

***Prince, Alison.** On Arran. 112p. (C). 1994. pap. 32.00 (*1-874640-80-7*, Pub. by Argyll Pubng UK) St Mut.

Prince, Amy, tr. see Winter, Jonah.

Prince, Amy D., tr. see Galeana, Benita.

***Prince, Anne.** Excel 5 for Windows: How to Work with Lists, Pivot Tables & External Databases. LC 95-7064. (Illus.). 60p. 1995. pap. 11.95 (*0-911625-87-9*) M Murach & Assoc.

— Excel 5.0 for Windows. LC 94-49320. (Essential Guide Ser.). (Illus.). 497p. 1994. pap. 25.00 (*0-911625-79-8*) M Murach & Assoc.

— 1-2-3 for Windows Release 4. LC 93-40584. (Essential Guide Ser.). (Illus.). 477p. 1994. pap. 20.00 (*0-911625-75-5*) M Murach & Assoc.

— VS COBOL II: A Guide for Programmers & Managers. 2nd ed. LC 89-13671. 271p. 1991. pap. 27.50 (*0-911625-54-2*) M Murach & Assoc.

— Work Like a Pro with Excel 5 for Windows. 200p. 1995. pap. 20.00 (*0-911625-89-5*) M Murach & Assoc.

Prince, Anne & Murach, Mike. How to Design & Develop COBOL Programs: Case Studies. LC 85-61543. 56p. 1985. pap. 6.00 (*0-911625-22-4*) M Murach & Assoc.

— How to Design & Develop COBOL Programs: Instructor's Guide. LC 84-62207. 320p. 1985. ring bd. 75.00 (*0-911625-23-2*) M Murach & Assoc.

Prince, Anne, jt. auth. see McQuillen, Kevin.

Prince, Anthony, jt. auth. see Collins, Trish.

Prince, Arnold. Carving Wood Stone. 1994. pap. 15.95 (*1-57101-004-1*) MasterMedia Ltd.

Prince, Barbara. Talking with Your Child about AIDS. LC 92-42452. (Growing Together Ser.). 1993. pap. 1.95 (*0-8298-0865-5*) Pilgrim OH.

Prince, Beth. Christmas Collectibles. 1993. 12.98 (*1-55521-910-1*) Bk Sales Inc.

Prince, Betty. Semiconductor Memories. 2nd ed. 500p. 1992. text ed. 98.00 (0-471-92465-2) Wiley.

Prince, Beverley, jt. auth. see Prince, Bobby.

Prince, Bobby & Prince, Beverley. How to Find Your Perfect Mate & Cure Loneliness. 96p. (Orig.). 1992. pap. text ed. 8.95 (0-9634483-8-2) Y H W H.

Prince Carl. Texas, 1844-45. 1993. reprint ed. lib. bdg. 75.00 (0-7812-5962-2) Rprt Serv.

Prince, Carl E. The Federalists & the Origins of the U. S. Civil Service. LC 76-53708. (Illus.). 1978. 55.00 (0-8147-6570-X) NYU Pr.

— New Jersey's Jeffersonian Republicans: The Genesis of an Early Party Machine, 1789-1817. LC 67-15103. 282p. reprint ed. pap. 80.40 (0-8357-3919-8, 2036654) Bks Demand.

Prince, Carl E., ed. The Papers of William Livingston, Vol. III. 576p. (C). 1986. text ed. 50.00 (0-8135-1144-5) Rutgers U Pr.

Prince, Carl E. & Keller, Mollie. The U. S. Customs Service: A Bicentennial History. LC 89-600730. (Illus.). 320p. (C). 1989. pap. text ed. 12.00 (0-317-93799-5) DT US Customs.

— The U. S. Customs Service; A Bicentennial History. (Illus.). 320p. 1989. pap. 12.00 (0-16-004612-2, 048-002-00106-1) USGPO.

Prince, Carl E. & Lustig, Mary L., eds. The Papers of William Livingston, Vol. IV. (Illus.). 590p. 1987. text ed. 50.00 (0-8135-1213-1) Rutgers U Pr.

Prince, Carl E., et al, eds. The Papers of William Livingston: April 1783-1790, Vol. V. (Illus.). 683p. 1988. 75.00 (0-8135-1297-2) Rutgers U Pr.

Prince, Clive, jt. auth. see Pickett, Lynn.

***Prince, Dan.** Passing in the Outsider Lane. LC 95-14926. 1995. write for info. (1-885203-17-9) Jrny Editions.

Prince, David & Gage, Julia. Put Your English to Work. (Illus.). 160p. (C). 1986. pap. text ed. 9.95 (0-13-744350-1) P-H.

Prince, Dawn, ed. Text & Concordance of the Aragonese Translation of Brunetto Latini's Li Livres dou Tresor, Garona Cathedral, MS20-2-5. (Dialect Ser.: No. 11). 16p. (SPA.). 1990. 10.00 (0-940639-46-7) Hispanic Seminary.

Prince, Derek. Baptism in the Holy Spirit. 1966. pap. 2.95 (0-934920-07-9, B-19) Derek Prince.

— Blessing or Curse: You Can Choose. LC 90-38671. 1990. pap. 8.99 (0-8007-9166-5) Chosen Bks.

— Chords from David's Harp. LC 83-7372. (Illus.). 219p. 1983. pap. 8.99 (0-8007-9117-7) Chosen Bks.

— Cita En Jerusalen: Appointment in Jerusalem. (SPA.). 5.95 (84-7228-360-7, 360091, Pub. by Edit Clie SP) TSELF.

— Does Your Tongue Need Healing. 112p. 1992. pap. 3.99 (0-88368-239-7) Whitaker Hse.

— Expelling Demons. 1969. pap. 0.25 (0-934920-18-4, B70) Derek Prince.

— Faith to Live by. 1977. pap. 5.95 (0-89283-042-5, B-29) Derek Prince.

— Fasting. 64p. 1993. pap. 3.99 (0-88368-258-3) Whitaker Hse.

— Fe Por la Cual Vivir: Faith to Live By. (SPA.). 4.95 (84-7228-704-1, 220408, Pub. by Edit Clie SP) TSELF.

— God's Plan for Your Money. 96p. 1993. pap. 3.99 (0-88368-287-7) Whitaker Hse.

— The Grace of Yielding. 1977. pap. 2.95 (0-934920-20-6, B-30) Derek Prince.

— Holy Spirit in You. 112p. 1993. pap. 3.99 (0-88368-238-9) Whitaker Hse.

— How to Fast Successfully. 1976. pap. 2.95 (0-934920-19-2, B-28) Derek Prince.

— Last Word on the Middle East. 1982. pap. 5.95 (0-934920-40-0) Derek Prince.

— The Marriage Covenant. 1978. 4.95 (0-934920-16-8, B-31) Derek Prince.

— The Marriage Covenant. 128p. Date not set. pap. 4.99 (0-88368-333-4) Whitaker Hse.

— Philosophy, the Bible & the Supernatural. 1969. pap. 0.10 (0-934920-22-2, B71) Derek Prince.

— Praying for the Government. 1970. pap. 1.95 (0-934920-11-7, B-20) Derek Prince.

— Prophetic Destinies. LC 92-73202. 126p. pap. 7.99 (0-88419-323-3, Creation Hse) Strang Comms Co.

— Self Study Bible Course. 1969. pap. 5.95 (0-934920-08-7, B-90) Derek Prince.

— Shaping History Through Prayer & Fasting. 1973. pap. 5.95 (0-686-12766-8) Derek Prince.

— Shaping History Through Prayer & Fasting. 224p. 1994. pap. 4.99 (0-88368-339-3) Whitaker Hse.

— Spirit Filled Believers Handbook. 1993. 19.99 (0-88419-329-2, Creation Hse) Strang Comms Co.

— Spiritual Warfare. 144p. 1993. pap. 4.99 (0-88368-256-7) Whitaker Hse.

Prince, Derek & Prince, Ruth. God Is a Matchmaker. LC 85-2989. (Orig.). 1986. pap. 8.99 (0-8007-9058-8) Chosen Bks.

Prince, E. Mathematical Techniques in Crystallography & Materials Sciences. (Illus.). 192p. 1982. 54.00 (0-387-90627-4) Spr-Verlag.

Prince, E. M., tr. see Bordewijk, F.

Prince, Edward. Mathematical Techniques in Crystallography & Materials Science. 2nd ed. LC 94-17913. 1994. 79.00 (0-387-58115-4) Spr-Verlag.

Prince, Eileen. Write More! An Intermediate Text for ESL Writers. LC 93-27959. 1993. pap. 18.95 (0-8384-3405-3) Heinle & Heinle.

Prince, Eleanor F. & Collier, Gaydell M. Basic Horse Care. 1989. pap. 14.95 (0-385-26199-3) Doubleday.

— Basic Training for Horses: English & Western. 1989. pap. 17.50 (0-385-26238-8) Doubleday.

Prince, Ezra M., ed. Convention of May Twenty-Ninth Eighteen Fifty-Six: That Organized the Republican Party in the State of Illinois. (Transactions of the Mclean County Historical Society Ser.: Vol. III). (Illus.). 184p. 1900. 25.00 (0-943788-03-X) McLean County.

Prince, F. T. Collected Poems, 1935-1992. LC 92-33032. 275p. (C). 1993. 13.95 (1-878818-16-3) Sheep Meadow.

— Walks in Rome. 32p. 1987. pap. 7.95 (0-935296-72-7) Sheep Meadow.

Prince, F. T., ed. see Milton, John.

Prince, F. T., ed. see Shakespeare, William.

***Prince, Francine.** The Diabetic Gourmet. 320p. 1994. write for info. (0-9631701-3-9) R A Rapaport.

— Francine Prince's New Jewish Cuisine. 224p. 1992. pap. 11.00 (0-399-51755-3, Perigree Bks) Berkley Pub.

Prince, Frank A. C & the Box: A Paradigm Parable. Padgett, JoAnn & Pechtimaldjian, Katharine, eds. LC 92-51021. (Illus.). 112p. 1993. 12.95 (0-88390-364-4); pap. 7.95 (0-89384-226-5) Pfeiffer & Co.

Prince George's County Genealogical Society Records Committee Staff, ed. Index to the Probate Records of Prince George's County, Maryland, 1696-1900. LC 88-63482. (Illus.). 264p. 1989. 18.00 (0-916805-05-0) Prince Georges County Gen Soc.

Prince, Gerald. A Dictionary of Narratology. LC 87-4998. x, 118p. 1987. pap. 11.00 (0-8032-8714-3) U of Nebr Pr.

— A Grammar of Stories: An Introduction. LC 73-85691. (De Proprietatibus Litterarum, Ser. Minor: No. 13). 106p. 1974. pap. text ed. 20.80 (90-279-2535-6) Mouton.

— Narrative As Theme: Studies in French Fiction. LC 91-22481. x, 161p. 1992. 27.50 (0-8032-3699-9) U of Nebr Pr.

Prince, Gerald, jt. ed. see Motte, Warren.

Prince, Gregory A. Having Authority: The Origins & Development of Priesthood During the Ministry of Joseph Smith. LC 93-10136. (John Whitmer Historical Association Monograph). 93p. 1993. pap. text ed. 6.00 (0-8309-0635-5) Herald Hse.

— Power from on High: The Development of Mormon Priesthood. 1995. 24.95 (1-56085-071-X) Signature Bks.

Prince, Harold B., comp. A Presbyterian Bibliography. LC 83-10116. (American Theological Library Association Monograph: No. 8). 466p. 1983. pap. 39.50 (0-8108-1639-3) Scarecrow.

Prince, J. D. & Budge, E. A. Assyrian Primer & Assyrian Texts. 104p. 1978. pap. 15.00 (0-89005-226-3) Ares.

Prince, J. Dyneley. Assyrian Primer: An Inductive Method of Learning the Cuneiform Characters. LC 17-31948. (Columbia University. Contributions to Oriental History & Philology Ser.: No. 3). reprint ed. 20.00 (0-404-50533-3) AMS Pr.

***Prince, Jan & Chamberlaine, Sally.** From the Inside Out: Leading Your Clients Out of Codependence. (Illus.). 1992. pap. 21.95 (0-9644385-0-X) Chamberlaine & Prince.

Prince, John D. Fragments from Babel. LC 39-13100. reprint ed. 12.50 (0-404-05136-7) AMS Pr.

— Passamaquoddy Texts. LC 73-3545. (American Ethnological Society Publications: No. 10). reprint ed. 19.00 (0-404-58160-9) AMS Pr.

Prince, John L., jt. auth. see Senthinathan, Ramesh.

Prince, Judith S., jt. auth. see Miller, Theodore K.

Prince, K., tr. see Ibach, Harald & Luth, Hans.

Prince, Keith R. & Johnson, A. Ivan, eds. Aquifers of the Far West: Regional Aquifer Systems of the United States. (Monograph Ser.: No. 16). (Illus.). 127p. (Orig.). 1992. pap. 11.00 (1-882132-21-1) Am Water Resources.

Prince, Keith R., ed. see American Water Resouces Association Staff.

Prince, L. Bradford. Spanish Mission Churches of New Mexico. LC 77-1749. (Beautiful Rio Grande Classics Ser.). (Illus.). 535p. 1983. reprint ed. lib. bdg. 50.00 (0-87380-126-1) Rio Grande.

Prince, Leslie. The Farrier & His Craft. 280p. 1990. 60.00 (0-85131-353-1, Pub. by J A Allen & Co UK) St Mut.

Prince, Lydia. Appointment in Jerusalem. LC 75-19469. 189p. reprint ed. pap. 8.99 (0-8007-9090-1) Chosen Bks.

Prince, Mary, et al. Six Women's Slave Narratives, 1831-1909. (Schomburg Library of Nineteenth-Century Black Women Writers). 384p. 1988. 29.95 (0-19-505262-5) OUP.

Prince, Mary M. Bieber's Dictionary of Legal Abbreviations: Reference Guide for Attorneys, Legal Secretaries, Paralegals & Law Students. 4th ed. LC 93-13817. 792p. 1993. 45.00 (0-89941-847-3, 307830) W S Hein.

— Bieber's Dictionary of Legal Citations: Reference Guide for Attorneys, Legal Secretaries, Paralegals & Law Students. 4th ed. LC 92-27176. 372p. 1992. 29.00 (0-89941-824-4, 307710) W S Hein.

Prince, Mary M., ed. World Dictionary of Legal Abbreviations. 278p. 1991. 95.00 (0-89941-781-7, 307320) W S Hein.

Prince, Matthew S. & New Life Inc. Staff. Building Your Relationship with Christ. 1988. pap. text ed. 3.00 (0-942026-02-0) ATAP Corp.

Prince, Michael. Oscar the Otter. (J). 1992. 10.95 (0-533-10235-9) Vantage.

— The Pigs of Lake Hood. 64p. 1994. pap. 6.95 (0-9642662-0-2) Sundog Pubng.

— The Totems of Seldovia. 160p. (J). (gr. 5-6). 1994. pap. 8.95 (0-9642662-1-0) Sundog Pubng.

Prince, Michael B. New Guide to Washington D. C. 8 Tours with 80 Photos - City Maps. (Illus.). 82p. 1990. pap. 5.95 (1-879295-03-2) L B Prince.

Prince Michael of Greece. Nicholas & Alexandra: The Family Albums. (Illus.). 240p. 1992. 49.50 (1-85043-494-8, Pub. by I B Tauris UK) St Martin.

Prince Michael of Russia. Imperial Palaces of Russia. (Illus.). 1994. 59.50 (1-85043-231-7, Pub. by I B Tauris UK) St Martin.

Prince, Michele. Mandatory Celibacy in the Catholic Church: A Handbook for the Laity. LC 92-16145. 114p. (C). 1992. lib. bdg. 14.95 (0-932727-61-1, N Paradigm Bks); pap. 9.95 (0-932727-60-3, N Paradigm Bks) Hope Pub Hse.

Prince, Morton. Clinical & Experimental Studies in Personality. rev. ed. LC 72-100197. (Illus.). 671p. 1970. reprint ed. text ed. 85.00 (0-8371-3995-3, PRPE, Greenwood Pr) Greenwood.

— Dissociation of a Personality: A Biographical Study in Abnormal Psychology. LC 69-10148. 575p. 1969. reprint ed. text ed. 35.00 (0-8371-1988-X, PRAP, Greenwood Pr) Greenwood.

— Psychotheraphy & Multiple Personality: Selected Essays. Hale, Nathan G., Jr., ed. LC 74-82574. 336p. 1975. 35.50 (0-674-72225-6) HUP.

— The Unconscious: The Fundamentals of Human Personality Normal & Abnormal. 2nd ed. LC 73-2411. (Mental Illness & Social Policy; the American Experience Ser.). 1973. reprint ed. 44.95 (0-405-05221-9) Ayer.

Prince, Morton, et al. Psychotherapeutics: A Symposium. LC 75-16728. (Classics in Psychiatry Ser.). 1976. reprint ed. 18.95 (0-405-07451-4) Ayer.

Prince, Nancy. A Black Woman's Odyssey Through Russia & Jamaica: The Narrative of Nancy Prince. LC 89-24945. (Topics in World History Ser.). (Illus.). 164p. (Orig.). (C). 1990. reprint ed. 19.95 (1-55876-028-8); reprint ed. pap. text ed. 8.95 (1-55876-019-9) Wiener Pubs Inc.

Prince of Wales. Highgrove: Portrait of an Estate. 1993. 50.00 (0-671-79177-X) S&S Trade.

***Prince, Pamela.** Best of Friends. 1994. pap. 5.99 (0-517-13137-4) Random.

— C Is for Cat. 1994. pap. 5.99 (0-517-13139-0) Random.

— Day with Josephine & Her Friends: The Art of Honor C. Appleton. 1992. 14.00 (0-517-58303-8, Harmony) Crown Pub Group.

— Once upon a Time. LC 87-33359. (Illus.). 48p. (J). (ps up). 1988. 12.95 (0-517-56832-2, Harmony) Crown Pub Group.

Prince, Pamela & Pease, Bessie. Sweet Dreams: The Art of Bessie Pease Gutman. 1985. 14.95 (0-517-55672-3, Harmony) Crown Pub Group.

Prince, Patricia. Chapter for a Married Woman. LC 93-93770. 96p. (Orig.). 1994. pap. 7.00 (1-56002-305-8, Univ Edtns) Aegina Pr.

— The Contreras Clinic Laetrile Cookbook. LC 79-89609. (Illus.). 248p. 1979. pap. 12.00 (0-8159-5221-X) Devin.

Prince Philip. The Environmental Revolution. 156p. 1990. 19.00 (0-8464-1453-8) Beekman Pubs.

***Prince, Richard.** Adult Comedy Action Drama. 1995. 60.00 (1-881616-36-3, Pub. by Scalo Pubs) Dist Art Pubs.

— Inside World. (Illus.). 88p. 1989. pap. 30.00 (1-878607-09-X) Kent Gallery.

— Spiritual America. (Illus.). 128p. (Orig.). 1989. pap. 25.00 (0-89381-395-8) Aperture.

Prince, Richard A. From Bondage to Freedom. LC 92-75259. (Illus.). 153p. (Orig.). (C). 1992. pap. text ed. 7.95 (1-879667-12-6) Dove Pr TX.

Prince, Robert. Dallas from a Different Perspective. 15.95 (0-89015-930-0) Sunbelt Media.

Prince, Robert H. Apostolic Ceremony of Marriage: Victory Collection. Koger, Dorothy, ed. 1992. pap. text ed. write for info. (1-882821-10-6) DPK Pubns.

— Why a Woman Should Not Preach: Victory Collection. Randolph, Jean, ed. 20p. 1993. reprint ed. pap. 3.50 (1-882821-02-5) DPK Pubns.

Prince, Robert M. The Legacy of the Holocaust: Psychohistorical Themes in the Second Generation. LC 84-24036. (Research in Clinical Psychology Ser.: No. 12). 239p. reprint ed. pap. 68.20 (0-8357-1627-9, 2070411) Bks Demand.

Prince, Russ A. & File, Karen F. The Seven Faces of Philanthropy: A New Approach to Cultivating Major Donors. LC 94-8095. (Nonprofit Sector Ser.). 216p. 1994. 27.95 (0-7879-0008-7) Jossey-Bass.

Prince, Ruth, jt. auth. see Prince, Derek.

Prince, Simon, jt. auth. see Chrystal, Alec.

Prince, Soledad G., tr. see Garbee, Ed & Van Dyke, Henry.

Prince, Stephen. Visions of Empire: Political Imagery in Contemporary American Film. LC 91-44449. (Political Communication Ser.). 232p. 1992. text ed. 55.00 (0-275-93661-9, C3661, Praeger Pubs); pap. text ed. 15.95 (0-275-93662-7, B3662, Praeger Pubs) Greenwood.

— The Warrior's Camera: The Cinema of Akira Kurosawa. (Illus.). 370p. 1991. pap. text ed. 15.95 (0-691-00859-0) Princeton U Pr.

Prince, Steve. The Skylight Cave Mystery. LC 93-79312. 187p. (Orig.). (YA). (gr. 9 up). 1993. pap. 9.95 (0-939116-36-7) Frontier OR.

Prince, Sue A., ed. The Old Guard & the Avant-Garde: Modernism in Chicago, 1910-1940. LC 90-35236. (Illus.). 280p. 1990. 35.00 (0-226-68284-6) U Ch Pr.

Prince, Thane. Quick Cook. (Illus.). 192p. 1992. pap. 19.95 (0-7011-3704-5, Pub. by Chatto & Windus UK) Trafalgar.

Prince-Tharp, Barbara. Thrice Blessed. (Illus.). 250p. 1981. 25.00 (0-87012-399-8) McClain.

Prince, Thelma F. Our Southern Ancestors: Cain, Cash, Cooper, Hughes, Martin, Moore, Prince, Sanders, Sorrells, Still, Williams, Wright Families. LC 84-82188. xii, 484p. 1985. 30.00 (0-9614020-0-8) T F Prince.

Prince, Thomas. A Chronological History of New England in the Form of Annals. LC 75-31100. reprint ed. 35.00 (0-404-13517-X) AMS Pr.

Prince, Thomas R. Financial Reporting & Cost Control for Health Care Entities. LC 92-1450. 612p. (C). 1992. text ed. 65.00 (0-910701-50-4, 0915) Health Admin Pr.

Prince, Tony, jt. tr. see Buzo, Adrian.

Prince, W. Bartlett. Pilot - Take Charge. (C). 1987. 42.00 (0-85174-139-8, Pub. by Brwn Son Ferg) St Mut.

Prince, Walter F. The Enchanted Boundary: Being a Survey of Negative Reactions to Claims of Psychic Phenomena, 1820-1930. LC 75-7396. (Perspectives in Psychical Research Ser.). 1975. reprint ed. 29.95 (0-405-07045-4) Ayer.

— Noted Witnesses for Psychic Occurrences. 1963. 10.00 (0-8216-0127-X, Univ Bks) Carol Pub Group.

Prince, William R. Prince's Manual of Roses. (Old Roses Ser.). 1979. reprint ed. text ed. 19.50 (0-930576-18-7) E M Coleman Ent.

Prince, William S. Crusade & Pilgrimage: A Soldier's Death, a Mother's Journey, & a Grandson's Quest. (Illus.). 128p. (Orig.). 1986. pap. 14.95 (0-87595-160-0) Oregon Hist.

Prince, Wilson. Relational Database: Using dBASE III Plus. 2nd ed. 1990. pap. text ed. write for info. (0-07-051043-1) McGraw.

***Prince, Yvonne M.** Price-Cost Margins in Dutch Manufacturing: With An Emphasis on Cyclical & Firm-Size Effects. (Tinbergen Institute Research Ser.: No. 86). 167p. 1994. pap. 25.00 (90-5170-316-3, Pub. by Thesis Pubs NE) IBD Ltd.

Princen, Finger. Environmental NGOs in World Politics: Linking the Global & the Local. LC 94-7512. 272p. 1994. pap. 16.95 (0-415-11510-8, B4797) Routledge.

Princen, Thomas. Beagle Channel Negotiations. (Pew Case Studies in International Affairs). 50p. (C). 1988. pap. text ed. 2.50 (1-56927-401-0) Geo U Inst Dplmcy.

— Intermediaries in International Conflict. (Illus.). 264p. 1992. text ed. 32.50 (0-691-07897-1) Princeton U Pr.

Princen, Thomas & Finger, Matthias. Environmental NGOs in World Politics: Linking the Global & the Local. LC 94-7512. 272p. 1994. 59.95 (0-415-11509-4, B4793) Routledge.

Princenthal, Nancy. Mary Miss: Photo - Drawings. (Illus.). 68p. (C). 1991. pap. text ed. 25.00 (0-941972-12-7) Freedman.

Princess Alice. Memories of Ninety Years. (Illus.). 160p. 1992. 39.95 (1-85585-048-6) Trafalgar.

Princess Anne. What Is Punishment for & How Does It Relate to the Concept of Community? (C). 1991. pap. 7.95 (0-521-42416-X) Cambridge U Pr.

Princess Elizabeth of Toro. African Princess. large type ed. 464p. 1985. 15.95 (0-7089-1336-9) Ulverscroft.

Princess Grace Irish Library Staff. Irishness in a Changing Society. LC 88-7828. 280p. 1988. lib. bdg. 53.00 (0-389-20857-4, N8415) B&N Imports.

***Princeton.** Twenty-First Century Guide to Improving Your Writing. 1995. mass mkt. (0-440-21727-X) Dell.

— Twenty-First Century Manual of Style. 1995. mass mkt. (0-440-22074-2) Dell.

Princeton Language Institute. Twenty-First Century Dictionary of Computer Terms. 1994. mass mkt. 6.99 (0-440-21557-9) Dell.

Princeton Language Institute Staff. Roget's Twenty-First Century Thesaurus in Dictionary Form. 1993. mass mkt. 5.99 (0-440-21555-2) Dell.

— Twenty-First Century Dictionary of Acronyms & Abbreviations. 1993. mass mkt. 5.99 (0-440-21548-X) Dell.

— Twenty-First Century Dictionary of Quotations. 1993. mass mkt. 5.99 (0-440-21447-5) Dell.

— Twenty-First Century Dictionary of Slang. 1994. mass mkt. 5.99 (0-440-21551-X) Dell.

— Twenty-First Century Guide to Increasing Your Reading Speed. 1995. pap. 5.99 (0-440-21724-5) Dell.

— Twenty-First Century Guide to Pronunciation. 1994. mass mkt. 5.99 (0-440-21554-4) Dell.

***Princeton Multimedia Group, Staff, ed.** CD-Rom Review. (Illus.). 688p. (Orig.). 1995. pap. 18.00 (0-06-273382-6) HarpC.

Princeton Review Editors. GMAT Computer Diagnostics 1995 Edition: IBM Version. 1994. 34.95 (1-884536-16-6, Villard Bks) Random.

— GMAT Computer Diagnostics 1995 Edition: MAC Version. 1994. 34.95 (1-884536-17-4, Villard Bks) Random.

— GRE Computer Diagnostics 1995 Edition: MAC Version. 1994. 34.95 (1-884536-15-8, Villard Bks) Random.

— LSAT Computer Diagnostics 1995 Edition: Mac Version. 1995. 16.78 (1-884536-12-3, Villard Bks) Random.

— The Princeton Review: LSAT V2.0 Disk for Windows. 1995. 3.5 hd, pap. text ed. 16.78 (1-884536-13-1, Villard Bks) Random.

— Princeton Review GRE V2.0 Disk for Windows. 1995. 3.5 hd, pap. text ed. 16.78 (1-884536-11-5, Villard Bks) Random.

— SAT &PSAT Computer Diagnostics 1995 Edition: Mac Version. 1995. 16.78 (1-884536-10-7, Villard Bks) Random.

Princeton Review Editors & Robinson, Adam. The Princeton Review-Cracking the System: The LSAT, 1991 Edition. 1990. pap. 11.95 (0-679-73139-3, Villard Bks) Random.

***Princeton Review Staff.** The Princeton Review Access Guide to Law Schools. 1995. pap. 14.00 (0-679-76150-0) Random.

— The Princeton Review Word Smart Junior: How to Build a Straight "A" Vocabulary. 1995. pap. 12.00 (0-679-75936-0, Villard Bks) Random.

— The Princeton Review: Writing Smart Junior: An Introduction to the Art of Writing. 1995. pap. 12.00 (0-679-76131-4, Villard Bks) Random.

***Princeton Review Staff & Custard, Edward.** The Princeton Review Student Access 1995 Guide: The Big Book of Colleges '96. 1995. pap. 22.00 (0-679-76152-7, Villard Bks) Random.

An Asterisk (*) at the beginning of an entry indicates that the title is appearing in BIP for the first time.

*Princeton Review Staff & Lerner, Marcia. The Princeton Review Math Smart Junior: Grade School Math Made Easy. 1995. pap. 12.00 (0-679-75935-2, Villard Bks) Random.

*Princeton Review Staff & Silver, Theodore. Cracking the MCAT '96. (Princeton Review Ser.). 1995. pap. 20.00 (0-679-76272-8, Villard Bks) Random.

— Cracking the MCAT '96: With Sample Tests on Computer Disk (MAC) (Princeton Review Ser.). 1995. disk, pap. 34.95 (0-679-76073-3, Villard Bks) Random.

— Cracking the MCAT '96: With Sample Tests on Computer Disk (WIN) (Princeton Review Ser.). 1995. disk, pap. 29.95 (0-679-76072-5, Villard Bks) Random.

Princeton Review Staff, jt. auth. see Gilbert, Nedda.

Princeton Review Staff, jt. auth. see Halpern, Emma.

Princeton Review Staff, jt. auth. see Nagy, Andrea.

Princeton Review Staff, jt. auth. see Robinson, Adam.

Princeton University, Office of Population Research Staff. Population Index Bibliography: Cumulated 1969 to 1981. 1700p. 1984. lib. bdg. 370.00 (0-8161-0906-0, Hall Library) G K Hall.

Princeton University Office of Population Research Staff. Population Index Bibliography Cumulated 1935-1968 by Authors & Geographical Areas, 9 vols. 1971. By author. lib. bdg. 480.00 (0-8161-0231-7, Hall Library); By geographical area. lib. bdg. 500.00 (0-8161-0116-7, Hall Library) G K Hall.

— Population Index Bibliography Cumulated 1935-1968 by Authors & Geographical Areas, 9 vols., Set. 1971. lib. bdg. 980.00 (0-8161-0880-3, Hall Library) G K Hall.

Princeton University Staff. Dictionary Catalog of the Princeton University Plasma Physics Laboratory Library, 4 vols, Set. 1970. lib. bdg. 435.00 (0-8161-0881-1, Hall Library) G K Hall.

— Dictionary Catalog of the Princeton University Plasma Physics Laboratory Library, First Supplement. 1973. lib. bdg. 175.00 (0-8161-1032-8, Hall Library) G K Hall.

— Princeton Manuscripts: A Guide to Modern Manuscripts in the Princeton University Library. (Library Catalogs). 2000p. 1989. lib. bdg. 250.00 (0-8161-0469-7) G K Hall.

Princeton/Masters Press Staff, ed. see Gerberg, Bob.

Principe, Angelo A. World War II War Birds: Solid Wood Airplane Modeling. (Illus.). 200p. 1993. spiral bd. 19.95 (0-9634736-0-3) Hist In Wood.

Principe, Jacob. El Otro Lado de la Biblia - The Other Side of the Bible: Lo Que la Teologia No Ha Revalado - What Theology Has Not Revealed - un Amanecev a la Realidad - a Dawn to Reality. 250p. (Orig.). (SPA.). Date not set. pap. write for info. (0-9641776-0-9) El Otro Lado.

Principe, Walter H. Faith, History & Cultures: Stability & Change in Church Teachings. LC 90-64240. (Pere Marquette Lectures). 1991. 10.00 (0-87462-546-7) Marquette.

***Princzes, Elinor.** Arctic Fives Arrive. LC 95-3693. (Illus.). (J). 1996. write for info. (0-395-73577-7) HM.

Prindle, Andreas R. & Prodhan, Bimal, eds. The ACT Guide to Ethical Conflicts in Finance. 144p. 1994. pap. 34.95 (0-631-19264-6) Blackwell Pubs.

Prindle, Anthony. Mathematics the Easy Way. 2nd ed. (Easy Way Ser.). 240p. 1988. pap. 10.95 (0-8120-4079-1) Barron.

Prindle, David F. Petroleum Politics & the Texas Railroad Commission. LC 81-7535. (Elma Dill Russell Spencer Foundation Ser.: No. 12). (Illus.). 240p. (C). 1981. pap. 10.95 (0-292-76489-8) U of Tex Pr.

— The Politics of Glamour: Ideology & Democracy in the Screen Actors Guild. LC 88-40194. (Illus.). 240p. (C). 1988. 24.50 (0-299-11810-X) U of Wis Pr.

— Risky Business: The Political Economy of Hollywood. LC 93-2975. 189p. 1993. text ed. 52.50 (0-8133-1770-3) Westview.

— Texas Monthly's Political Reader. 3rd ed. LC 84-24067. 256p. 1985. pap. text ed. 11.95 (0-87719-003-8, Lone Star Bks) Gulf Pub.

Prindle, Dennis, jt. auth. see Kent, Conrad.

Prindle, F. C. Prindle Genealogy, Embracing the Descendants of William Pringle, the First Settler, & Also the Ancestors & Descendants of Zalmon Prindle, 1654-1906. 352p. 1989. reprint ed. lib. bdg. 60.75 (0-8328-0994-2); reprint ed. pap. 52.75 (0-8328-0995-0) Higginson Bk Co.

Prindle, Peter H. Tinglatar: Socio-Economic Relationship of a Brahmin Village in Eastern Nepal. 1983. 75.00 (0-7855-0237-8, Pub. by Ratna Pustak Bhandar); 60.00 (0-7855-0322-6, Pub. by Ratna Pustak Bhandar) St Mut.

Prindle, Peter H., ed. Tinglatar: Socio-Economic Relationship of a Brahmin Village in Eastern Nepal. 157p. (C). 1989. 125.00 (0-89771-126-2, Pub. by Ratna Pustak Bhandar) St Mut.

Prindle, Tamae, ed. see Watanabe, Kazuo.

***Prindle, Tamae K.** Kinjo the Corporate Bouncer: And Other Stories from Japanese Business. 1992. pap. write for info. (0-8348-0254-6) Weatherhill.

Prindle, Tamae K., ed. & tr. Made in Japan & Other Japanese "Business Novels" LC 89-4218. 200p. 1990. 36. 95 (0-87332-529-X); pap. text ed. 18.95 (0-87332-772-1) M E Sharpe.

Prindle, Tamae K., ed. see Shimizu, Ikko.

Prindle, Wilford. I Hear You Talking Job. 96p. (Orig.). 1988. pap. 4.95 (0-8341-1257-4) Beacon Hill.

Prine, Mary, jt. auth. see Rosenbaum, Jean.

Prinetti, Emanuela S. Salads. Wertz, Laurie, ed. LC 92-18191. (Williams-Sonoma Kitchen Library). (Illus.). 108p. 1993. 17.95 (0-7835-0237-0); pap. write for info. (0-7835-0238-9) Time-Life.

Pring, Adele. Women of the Centre. 192p. (C). 1990. 51.00 (0-947087-23-0, Pub. by Pascoe Pub AT) St Mut.

Pring, David, jt. auth. see Bradshaw, Kenneth.

Pring, J. T., ed. The Oxford Dictionary of Modern Greek. rev. ed. 640p. 1995. pap. 15.95 (0-19-864197-4) OUP.

Pring, Julian T., ed. The Oxford Dictionary of Modern Greek: Greek-English, English-Greek. (ENG & GRE.). 1986. pap. 13.95 (0-19-864148-6) OUP.

Pring, Martin J. All-Season Investor: Successful Strategies for Every Stage in the Business Cycle. 352p. 1992. text ed. 29.95 (0-471-54977-0) Wiley.

— Investment Psychology Explained: Classic Strategies To Beat the Markets. LC 92-15914. 288p. 1992. text ed. 27. 95 (0-471-55721-8) Wiley.

— Martin Pring on Market Momentum. 250p. 1993. 49.95 (1-55738-508-4) Probus Pub Co.

— Technical Analysis Explained: The Successful Investor's Guide to Spotting Investment Trends & Turning Points. 3rd ed. 544p. 1991. text ed. 49.95 (0-07-051042-3) McGraw.

Pring-Mill, Robert, ed. see Cardenal, Ernesto.

Pring, Richard. The New Curriculum. 2nd ed. Wragg, C. E., ed. (Education Matters Ser.). 144p. 1994. text ed. 60.00 (0-304-32749-2); pap. text ed. 18.95 (0-304-32741-7) Cassell.

Pring, S. W., tr. see Lourie, Arthur.

Pring, S. W., tr. see Sabaneev, Leonid L.

Pringeheim, Fritz. Der Kauf mit Frimdem Geld. Vlastos, Gregory, ed. (Morals & Law in Ancient Greece Ser.). (GER, GRE & LAT.). 1979. reprint ed. lib. bdg. 17.95 (0-405-11568-7) Ayer.

Pringle. Batman: Exploring the World of Bats. (J). 1993. pap. 2.95 (0-590-46128-1) Scholastic Inc.

Pringle, A., jt. auth. see Burtt, E. T.

Pringle, Allan R., et al. Drugs of Abuse Digest: A Prevention Guide for the Family, School & Workplace. 9th ed. (Illus.). 72p. 1994. pap. 6.95 (0-935847-09-X) Inst Subs Abuse Res.

Pringle, Bruce D. Colorado Law Annotated, 2 vols., Set. 2nd ed. LC 84-71934. 1991. 230.00 (0-317-04259-9) Lawyers Cooperative.

Pringle, C. R. Respiratory Syncytial Virus. (Perspectives in Medical Virology Ser.: Vol. 1). write for info. (0-317-15191-6) Elsevier.

Pringle, Catherine M., jt. ed. see Almeda, Frank.

Pringle, Charles D., jt. auth. see Longenecker, Justin G.

Pringle, Charles D., et al. Managing Organizations. 608p. (C). 1988. write for info. (0-675-20813-0, Merrill Pub Co); pap. write for info. (0-675-20814-9, Merrill Pub Co) Macmillan.

Pringle, Cyrus. Civil War Diary of Cyrus Pringle: Record of Quaker Conscience. LC 62-18328. Orig. Title: Record of a Quaker Conscience. (Orig.). 1962. pap. 3.00 (0-87574-122-3) Pendle Hill.

Pringle, David. Earth Is the Alien Planet: J. G. Ballard's Four-Dimensional Nightmare. LC 79-13065. (Milford Ser.: Popular Writers of Today: Vol. 26). 63p. 1979. lib. bdg. 20.00 (0-89370-138-6); pap. 10.00 (0-89370-238-2) Borgo Pr.

— Science Fiction: The One Hundred Best Novels. 1987. pap. 7.95 (0-88184-346-6) Carroll & Graf.

— Science Fiction: The 100 Best Novels; An English-Language Selection, 1949-1984. 220p. 1986. 15.95 (0-88184-259-1) Carroll & Graf.

— The Ultimate Guide to Science Fiction: An A-Z of Science Fiction Books by Title. 2nd ed. 480p. 1995. 59. 95 (1-85928-071-4, Pub. by Scolar Pr UK) Ashgate Pub Co.

Pringle, Denys. Churches of the Crusader Kingdom of Jerusalem: A Corpus, Vol. 1: A-K (Excluding Acre & Jerusalem) (Illus.). 352p. (C). 1993. 125.00 (0-521-39036-2) Cambridge U Pr.

Pringle, Denys, jt. auth. see Fojut, Noel.

Pringle, Elizabeth A. Rab & Dab. limited ed. Blythe, Anne, ed. & intro. by. 1985. 27.50 (0-685-13973-5) Seajay Society.

Pringle, Elizabeth A., see Patience Pennington, pseud..

Pringle, Froncine R. Tiny Bops: Wee Bop out Alone. (J). 1995. 7.95 (0-8062-4974-9) Carlton.

Pringle, Henry F. Alfred E. Smith: A Critical Study. LC 75-101271. reprint ed. 20.00 (0-404-00627-2) AMS Pr.

— Alfred E. Smith: A Critical Study. (History - United States Ser.). 402p. 1992. reprint ed. lib. bdg. 99.00 (0-7812-6217-8) Rprt Serv.

— Mod Bio: T. Roosevelt. 448p. 1995. 12.98 (0-8317-5715-9) Smithmark.

— Theodore Roosevelt: A Biography. LC 56-13739. 435p. 1956. pap. 14.00 (0-15-688943-9, HB15, Harvest Bks) HarBrace.

Pringle, J. E., jt. ed. see Eggleton, P. P.

Pringle, J. M. China Struggles for Unity. 1976. lib. bdg. 59. 95 (0-8490-1609-6) Gordon Pr.

***Pringle, Janice, et al.** Treatment of the Pregnant Addict. 135p. 1994. pap. 49.50 (1-884937-16-0) Manisses Communs.

Pringle, John J. & Harris, Robert. Essentials of Managerial Finance. 2nd ed. (C). 1987. text ed. 41.75 (0-673-18331-9) HarpCollege.

Pringle, John J. & Harris, Robert S. Essentials of Managerial Finance. 2nd ed. LC 86-31333. (Illus.). 945p. reprint ed. pap. 180.00 (0-7837-4747-0, 2044556) Bks Demand.

Pringle, Kenneth. Waters of the West. 1976. lib. bdg. 59.95 (0-8490-2809-4) Gordon Pr.

Pringle, Laurence. Animal Rights Controversy. 1989. 16.95 (0-15-203559-1) HarBrace.

— Antarctica. 64p. (J). 1992. pap. 16.00 (0-671-73850-X, S&S Bks Young Read) S&S Childrens.

— Batman: Exploring the World of Bats. LC 90-8679. (Illus.). 48p. (J). (gr. 4-6). 1991. text ed. 14.95 (0-684-19232-2, C Scribner Sons Young) S&S Childrens.

— Bearman: Exploring the World of Black Bears. LC 89-5890. (Illus.). 48p. (J). (gr. 5-7). 1989. text ed. 13.95 (0-684-19094-X, C Scribner Sons Young) S&S Childrens.

— Bearman: Exploring the World of Black Bears. braille ed. (Illus.). 49p. (J). 1992. Braille. vinyl bd. 3.92 (1-56956-351-9, BR8735) W A T Braille.

— Chemical & Biological Warfare: The Cruelest Weapons. LC 92-16641. (Issues in Focus Ser.). (Illus.). 104p. (J). 1993. lib. bdg. 17.95 (0-89490-280-6) Enslow Pubs.

— Death Is Natural. LC 90-46402. (Illus.). 64p. (J). (gr. 1 up). 1991. reprint ed. lib. bdg. 12.88 (0-688-10467-3) Morrow Jr Bks.

— Death Is Natural. LC 90-46402. (Illus.). 64p. (J). (gr. 1 up). 1991. reprint ed. pap. 5.95 (0-688-10528-9, Pub. by Beech Tree Bks) Morrow.

— Dinosaurs! Strange & Wonderful. (Illus.). 32p. (J). (ps-2). 1995. 14.95 (1-878093-16-9) Boyds Mills Pr.

— Dolphin Man: Exploring The World of Dolphins. LC 95-5290. 1995. write for info. (0-689-80299-4, Atheneum S&S) S&S Trade.

— The Earth Is Flat & Other Great Mistakes. LC 83-7966. (Illus.). 96p. (J). (gr. 3-7). 1983. lib. bdg. 12.88 (0-688-02467-X) Morrow Jr Bks.

— The Earth Is Flat & Other Great Mistakes. (Illus.). 80p. (J). 1995. pap. 3.99 (0-380-72319-0, Camelot) Avon.

— Fire in the Forest. LC 92-32257. (Illus.). 32p. (J). (gr. 2 up). 1994. text ed. 15.95 (0-02-775215-1, Mac Bks Young Read) S&S Childrens.

— Jackal Woman: Exploring the World of Jackals. LC 92-28207. (Illus.). 48p. (J). (gr. 4-6). 1993. text ed. 14.95 (0-684-19435-X, C Scribner Sons Young) S&S Childrens.

— Living in a Risky World. LC 88-31686. (Illus.). 112p. (J). (gr. 5 up). 1989. 12.95 (0-688-04326-7) Morrow Jr Bks.

— Living Treasure: Saving Earth's Threatened Biodiversity. LC 90-21463. 64p. (J). (gr. 3 up). 1991. 13.95 (0-688-07709-9); lib. bdg. 13.88 (0-688-07710-2) Morrow Jr Bks.

— Nuclear Energy: Troubled Past, Uncertain Future. LC 88-28664. (Science for Survival Ser.). (Illus.). 128p. (YA). (gr. 7 up). 1989. text ed. 14.95 (0-02-775391-3, Mac Bks Young Read) S&S Childrens.

— Octopus Hug. (Illus.). 32p. (J). (ps-3). 1993. 14.95 (1-56397-034-1) Boyds Mills Pr.

— Oil Spills. LC 92-30348. (Save-the-Earth Ser.). (Illus.). 64p. (J). (gr. 3 up). 1993. 15.00 (0-688-09860-6); lib. bdg. 14.93 (0-688-09861-4) Morrow Jr Bks.

— Rain of Troubles: The Science & Politics of Acid Rain. LC 87-34950. (Science for Survival Ser.). (Illus.). 128p. (YA). (gr. 7 up). 1988. text ed. 14.95 (0-02-775370-0, Mac Bks Young Read) S&S Childrens.

— Restoring Our Earth. LC 87-615. (Illus.). 64p. (YA). (gr. 6 up). 1985. lib. bdg. 15.95 (0-89490-143-5) Enslow Pubs.

— Scorpion Man: Exploring the World of Scorpions. LC 93-34936. (Illus.). (YA). (gr. 5 up). 1994. 15.95 (0-684-19560-7, Scribners) S&S Trade.

— Smoking. (Save the Earth Ser.). (Illus.). (J). 1996. write for info. (0-688-13039-9) Morrow Jr Bks.

— Smoking. (Save the Earth Ser.). (Illus.). (J). 1996. lib. bdg. write for info. (0-688-13040-2) Morrow Jr Bks.

— Vanishing Ozone. LC 94-25928. (Save the Earth Ser.). (Illus.). 64p. (YA). (gr. 3 up). 1995. 16.00 (0-688-04157-4); lib. bdg. 15.93 (0-688-04158-2) Morrow Jr Bks.

— Water: The Next Great Resource Battle. LC 81-23694. (Science for Survival Ser.). (Illus.). 144p. (YA). (gr. 6 up). 1982. lib. bdg. 14.95 (0-02-775400-6, Mac Bks Young Read) S&S Childrens.

Pringle, Lawrence. Coral Reefs. LC 94-5875. (J). (gr. 3 up). 1995. write for info. (0-671-79166-4, S&S Bks Young Read) S&S Childrens.

Pringle, Lillie. Methodological Perception of Imagery Literature. (Orig.). 1990. pap. 12.50 (0-913412-30-9) Brandon Hse.

Pringle, M. & Naidoo, S. Early Child Care in Britain. LC 74-80075. (International Monographs on Early Child Care). (Illus.). 188p. 1975. text ed. 64.00 (0-677-05200-6) Gordon & Breach.

Pringle, M. A. Journey in East Africa: Towards the Mountains of the Moon. LC 72-3957. (Black Heritage Library Collection). 1977. reprint ed. 35.95 (0-8369-9105-2) Ayer.

Pringle, Malcolm S., et al, eds. The Mesozoic Pacific: Geology, Tectonics, & Volcanism. LC 93-33017. (Geophysical Monograph Ser.: No. 77). 435p. 1993. 54. 00 (0-87590-036-4) Am Geophysical.

Pringle, Marian J., jt. auth. see Brock, Susan.

Pringle, Mary L. & Ellis, Joseph. Sis & Chris & the Knowbots in "We Don't Need Drugs to Be O. K." Educational Coloring Book. (J). (gr. k-5). 1987. reprint ed. pap. 1.95 (0-935847-03-0) Inst Subs Abuse Res.

Pringle, Patrick. Hue & Cry: The Birth of the British Police. (Criminology Ser.). 1992. lib. bdg. 300.00 (0-8490-5300-5) Gordon Pr.

— Stand & Deliver: Highwaymen from Robin Hood to Dick Turpin. 1992. 19.95 (0-88029-698-4) Marboro Bks.

Pringle, Peter K. & Clinton, Helen E. Radio & Television: A Selected, Annotated Bibliography; Supplement Two: 1982-1986. LC 88-23968. 249p. 1989. 27.50 (0-8108-2158-3) Scarecrow.

Pringle, Peter K., et al. Electronic Media Management. 2nd ed. 416p. 1991. pap. 34.95 (0-240-80050-8, Focal) Buttrwrth-Heinemann.

— Electronic Media Management. 3rd ed. (Illus.). 416p. 1994. pap. 36.95 (0-240-80199-7, Focal) Buttrwrth-Heinemann.

Pringle, Robert. Indonesia & the Philippines. 1980. text ed. 56.50 (0-231-05008-9) Col U Pr.

Pringle, Robert, ed. A Color Atlas of Transthoracic Repair of Hiatus Hernia. (Illus.). 64p. 1987. 40.00 (0-8151-6842-X, CAW-1, Yr Bk Med Pubs) Mosby Yr Bk.

Pringle, Robert, jt. auth. see Deane, Marjorie.

Pringle, Rosemary. Secretaries Talk: Sexuality, Power & Work. (Questions for Feminism Ser.). 200p. 1989. 42.50 (0-86091-234-5, Pub. by Verso UK); pap. 14.95 (0-86091-950-1, Pub. by Verso UK) Routledge Chapman & Hall.

Pringle, Rosemary, jt. ed. see Caine, Barbara.

Pringle, Rosemary, jt. auth. see Game, Ann.

Pringle, Terry. A Fine Time to Leave Me. LC 88-7670. 340p. 1989. 14.95 (0-945575-16-5) Algonquin Bks.

— The Preacher's Boy. LC 87-28948. 280p. 1988. 15.95 (0-912697-77-6) Algonquin Bks.

— This Is the Child. LC 91-52776. 208p. 1992. reprint ed. text ed. 19.95 (0-87074-335-X); reprint ed. pap. 10.95 (0-87074-332-5) SMU Press.

— Tycoon. 300p. 1990. lib. bdg. 18.95 (0-945575-30-0) Algonquin Bks.

Pringsheim, E. G. Farblose Algen. Ein Beitrag zur Evolutionsforschung. (Illus.). 471p. (GER.). 1963. lib. bdg. 66.00 (3-437-30046-6) Lubrecht & Cramer.

— Die Gattungen Chlorogonium und Hyalogonium: Volvocales. (Nova Hedwigia Ser.: No. 18). (Illus.). 38p. 1969. pap. text ed. 10.00 (3-7682-0662-9) Lubrecht & Cramer.

***Pringsheim, Klaus.** Neighbours Across the Pacific: Canadian-Japanese Relations 1870-1982. 242p. 1995. lib. bdg. 37.00 (0-8095-4867-4) Borgo Pr.

Pringsheim, Klaus H. Neighbors Across the Pacific: The Development of Economic & Political Relations Between Canada & Japan. LC 82-11713. (Contributions in Political Science Ser.: No. 90). xvi, 241p. 1983. text ed. 55.00 (0-313-23507-4, PRN/) Greenwood.

***Pringsheim, Klaus H. & Bosen, Victor.** Man of the World: Memoirs of Europe, Asia, & North America, 1930s-1980s. (Illus.). 180p. 1995. lib. bdg. 45.00 (0-8095-4888-7) Borgo Pr.

Prinn, R. G., jt. auth. see Bras, R. L.

***Prinn, Ronald G., ed.** Global Atmospheric-Biospheric Chemistry. LC 94-22508. (Environmental Science Research Ser.: Vol. 48). 261p. 1994. 79.50 (0-306-44884-X, Plenum Pr) Plenum.

Prins, Adriann H. The Swahili-Speaking Peoples of Zanzibar & the East African Coast: Arabs, Shirazi & Swahili. LC 68-5550. (Ethnographic Survey of Africa: East Central Africa Ser.: Pt. 12). 157p. reprint ed. pap. 44.80 (0-8357-6965-8, 2039025) Bks Demand.

Prins, Corien, jt. ed. see Meijboom, Alfred P.

Prins, Eliezer, jt. auth. see Lehmann, Marcus.

Prins, Gwyn. Threats Without Enemies: Facing Environmental Insecurity. 192p. (Orig.). 1992. 19.95 (1-85383-157-3, Pub. by Erthscan Pubns UK) Island Pr.

Prins, Gwyn, ed. Spring in Winter: The Nineteen Eighty-Nine Revolutions. 160p. 1991. 29.95 (0-685-38699-6, Pub. by Manchester Univ Pr UK); text ed. 12.95 (0-7190-3445-0, Pub. by Manchester Univ Pr UK) St Martin.

Prins, H. A. & Whyte, M. B. Social Work & Medical Practice. LC 71-184453. 94p. 1972. 45.00 (0-08-016847-7, Pub. by Pergamon Repr UK) Franklin.

Prins, Herschel. Bizarre Behaviours. (Tavistock Bk.). 128p. 1990. 57.00 (0-415-01835-8, A4677); pap. 17.95 (0-415-01836-6, A4681) Routledge.

— Dangerous Behaviour, the Law & Mental Disorder. 240p. 1986. pap. 18.95 (0-422-79220-9, 9931, Pub. by Tavistock UK) Routledge Chapman & Hall.

— Fire-Raising: Its Motivation & Management. LC 93-7385. 224p. 1994. 59.95 (0-415-05984-4, B0870); pap. 19.95 (0-415-05985-2, B0874) Routledge.

— Offenders, Deviants or Patients? 2nd ed. LC 94-34150. (Illus.). 272p. 1995. 59.95x (0-415-10220-0, C0116) Routledge.

***Prins, Herschel A.** Offenders, Deviants or Patients? 2nd ed. LC 94-34150. (Illus.). 272p. 1995. pap. 18.95 (0-415-10221-9, C0117) Routledge.

Prins, J. Egbert, jt. ed. see Wunderlich, W. O.

Prins, Jack. Six Sigma Quality Control Charts. LC 92-37808. (Six Sigma Research Institute Ser.). 1993. write for info. (0-201-63403-1) Addison-Wesley.

Prins, Jack & Harry, Mikel J. Six Sigma Metrics. LC 92-37809. (Six Sigma Research Institute Ser.). 1993. write for info. (0-201-63405-8) Addison-Wesley.

Prins, Jack, et al. Basic Statistics. LC 92-41299. (Six Sigma Research Institute Ser.). 1993. write for info. (0-201-63406-6) Addison-Wesley.

Prins, Jan. The Illustrated Swimmer. LC 82-23390. (Illus.). 102p. (Orig.). 1983. pap. 10.95 (0-9612452-0-4) Swim HI.

Prins, Johanna H., tr. see Pelgrom, Els.

Prins, Johanna W., tr. see Pelgrom, Els.

Prins, R., jt. ed. see Koningsberger, D. C.

Prinsley, Derek M. & Standstead, Harold H., eds. Nutrition & Aging. (Progress in Clinical & Biological Research Ser.). 408p. 1989. text ed. 140.00 (0-471-56680-2) Wiley.

Prinsley, Roslyn T., ed. The Role of Trees in Sustainable Agriculture: Review Papers Presented at the Australian Conference, Albury, Victoria, Australia, October 1991. LC 92-36592. (Forestry Sciences Ser.: Vol. 43). 192p. (C). 1992. lib. bdg. 84.00 (0-7923-2030-1) Kluwer Ac.

Prinsloo, Willem S. The Theology of the Book of Joel. (Beiheft zur Zeitschrift fuer die Alttestamentliche Wissenschaft Ser.: Vol. 163). viii, 136p. 1985. 64.45 (0-89925-131-5) De Gruyter.

***Print Project, Staff.** The Wholesale-by-Mail Catalog 1996: How Consumers Can Shop by Mail, Phone or Online Service and Save 30% to 90% Off List Price. 640p. 1995. pap. 16.00 (0-06-273311-7) HarpC.

Printen, jt. auth. see Griffen.

Printer, Les. Microsoft FoxPro 2.5 Applications Programming. 1993. pap. text ed. 24.95 (0-8306-4568-3, Windcrest) TAB Bks.

Prints India Staff. Great Books on Indian Education, 18 vols., Set. (C). 1988. 995.00 (*0-7855-0041-3*, Pub. by Print Hse II) St Mut.
— Indian Art Collection, 22 vols., Set. (C). 1988. 4,000.00 (*0-7855-0049-9*, Pub. by Print Hse II) St Mut.
— Indian Historical Researches, 78 vols., Set. (C). 1988. 5,000.00 (*0-7855-0045-6*, Pub. by Print Hse II) St Mut.
— Landmarks in Indian Anthropology, 74 vols., Set. (C). 1988. 5,000.00 (*0-7855-0046-4*, Pub. by Print Hse II) St Mut.
— Loudon's Encyclopaedia of Plants, 3 vols., Set. (C). 1988. 500.00 (*0-7855-0053-7*, Pub. by Print Hse II) St Mut.
— Max Muller's Encyclopaedia of Languages, 2 vols., Set. (C). 1988. 395.00 (*0-7855-0060-X*, Pub. by Print Hse II) St Mut.
— The New Gesham World Encyclopaedia, 12 vols., Set. (C). 1988. 990.00 (*0-7855-0043-X*, Pub. by Print Hse II) St Mut.
— Rediscovering India-Indian Philosophy Library, 71 vols., Set. (C). 1988. 1,600.00 (*0-7855-0047-2*, Pub. by Print Hse II) St Mut.
— Sir Aurel Stein's Central Asia, 12 vols., Set. (C). 1988. 4,000.00 (*0-7855-0048-0*, Pub. by Print Hse II) St Mut.
— Story of the Civilisation, 15 vols., Set. (C). 1988. 1,500.00 (*0-7855-0042-1*, Pub. by Print Hse II) St Mut.
— The William Shakespeare Encyclopaedia, 8 vols., Set. (C). 1988. 1,000.00 (*0-7855-0044-8*, Pub. by Print Hse II) St Mut.
Printup, A. D., II. History of New York Indians & the Printup Family. LC 83-72027. (Illus.). 89p. 1985. 66.66 (*0-685-09879-6*) DeWitt & Sheppard.
Printup, A. D., II, et al. How I Lost Weight. LC 84-71480. 84p. 1985. pap. 5.25 (*0-932365-00-0*) DeWitt & Sheppard.
Printup, A. D., II. N. Y. Indians & the Printup Family. Harder, Arvid, ed. LC 83-72027. (Illus.). 99p. 1983. 66.66 (*0-685-07429-3*); pap. 33.33 (*0-685-07430-7*) Clark Inc.
— The Scatterings (Based upon a True Story) LC 85-71343. 192p. 1986. pap. 6.95 (*0-685-10438-9*, TS-027) DeWitt & Sheppard.
***Printz, Charles T.** The Printz-Prince Family. LC 94-80149. 450p. 1995. 29.95 (*0-9636320-2-7*) Nuggets Wisdom.
Printz, Neil, jt. auth. see Hopps, Walter.
Printz, Neil, jt. auth. see Hopps, Walter.
Printz, Neil, et al. Texas Art. LC 88-60136. 25p. 1988. pap. 5.00 (*0-939594-09-9*) Menil Collect.
Prinz. Endocrine Surgery. 1995. write for info. (*0-8493-4534-0*) CRC Pr.
Prinz, G., jt. ed. see Hadjipanayis, G. C.
Prinz, Jessica. Art Discourse - Discourse in Art. LC 90-19388. (Illus.). 225p. (C). 1991. text ed. 35.00 (*0-8135-1673-0*); pap. text ed. 15.00 (*0-8135-1734-6*) Rutgers U Pr.
Prinz, Johannes. John Wilmot, Earl of Rochester: His Life & Writings. 1988. reprint ed. lib. bdg. 59.00 (*0-7812-0228-0*) Rprt Serv.
— John Wilmot, Earl of Rochester: His Life & Writings. reprint ed. 59.00 (*0-403-04129-5*) Somerset Pub.
— John Wilmot, Earl of Rochester, His Life & Writings. 1971. reprint ed. 69.00 (*0-403-01165-5*) Scholarly.
Prinz, Karl E., ed. see Abraham, Nicholas A.
Prinz, Noelle, jt. auth. see Montagne, Anne.
Prinz, Phyllis & Saia, Stephanie. Private Moments in Public Places. LC 79-64330. (Illus.). 72p. 1979. pap. 16.00 (*0-932966-04-7*) Permanent Pr.
Prinz, Richard, jt. ed. see Boswell, Richard A.
Prinz, Ronald J., ed. Advances in the Behavioral Assessment of Children & Families, Vol. 5. 320p. 1991. 85.00 (*1-85302-069-9*, Pub. by J Kingsley Pubs UK) Taylor & Francis.
Prinz, Ronald J., jt. ed. see Ollendick, Thomas H.
Prinz, Tom. Dragon Slaying for Parents. 336p. 1992. pap. 9.95 (*0-914984-35-7*) Starburst.
Prinz, W. & Sanders, A. F., eds. Cognition & Motor Processes. (Illus.). 385p. 1984. 80.00 (*0-387-12855-7*) Spr-Verlag.
***Prinzhorn, Hans.** Artistry of the Mentally Ill: A Contribution to the Psychology & Psychopathology of Configuration. Von Brockdorff, Eric, tr. LC 95-18. (ENG & GER.). 1995. 35.00 (*3-211-82639-4*) Spr-Verlag.
Prinzhorn, M., jt. ed. see Haider, H.
Prinzing, Anita, jt. auth. see Prinzing, Fred.
Prinzing, Fred & Prinzing, Anita. Mixed Messages; Responding to Interracial Marriage. 1991. pap. 7.99 (*0-8024-5245-0*) Moody.
Prinzing, Fred W. Handling Church Tensions Creatively. LC 86-80687. 216p. (Orig.). 1986. pap. 5.95 (*0-935797-23-8*) Harvest IL.
Prinzing, Friedrich. Epidemics Resulting from Wars. Westergaard, Harold, ed. 1977. lib. bdg. 59.95 (*0-8490-1781-5*) Gordon Pr.
Prioh, John G., jt. ed. see Clive, Williams S.
Prioleau, Elizabeth S. The Circle of Eros: Sexuality in the Work of William Dean Howells. LC 82-14788. xvii, 227p. (C). 1983. text ed. 30.75 (*0-8223-0492-9*) Duke.
Prioli, Carmine A., ed. see Patton, George S., Jr.
Priolo, Lou. As for Me & My House. 228p. 1992. pap. 2.99 (*0-88368-245-1*) Whitaker Hse.
Prior, Andrew, jt. auth. see Thompson, Leonard.
Prior, Arthur N. The Doctrine of Propositions & Terms. Geach, P. T. & Kenny, A. J., eds. LC 76-9375. 148p. 1976. 22.50 (*0-87023-214-2*) U of Mass Pr.
— Papers in Logic & Ethics. Geach, P. T. & Kenny, A. J., eds. LC 76-9376. 238p. 1976. 27.50 (*0-87023-213-4*) U of Mass Pr.
— Time & Modality. LC 78-26696. (Illus.). 148p. 1979. reprint ed. text ed. 35.00 (*0-313-20911-1*, PRTI, Greenwood Pr) Greenwood.
Prior, Arthur N. & Fine, Kit. Worlds, Times & Selves. LC 76-45042. 176p. 1977. 25.00 (*0-87023-227-4*) U of Mass Pr.
Prior, Billy. Flight to Glory. Shaw, Thelma, ed. LC 85-60792. (Illus.). 241p. 1985. pap. 12.50 (*0-933829-02-7*) Ponce Pr.
Prior, C. & Lomer, C. J., eds. Biological Control of Locusts & Grasshoppers. 394p. 1992. pap. 64.50 (*0-85198-779-6*) CAB Intl.
Prior, C., jt. auth. see Keane, P. J.
Prior, David. Creating Christian Community. LC 92-85283. 240p. (Orig.). 1993. pap. 12.00 (*0-89109-713-9*) NavPress.
— The Message of First Corinthians. Stott, John R. & Motyer, J. A., eds. LC 85-239. (Bible Speaks Today Ser.). 270p. (C). 1985. pap. 12.99 (*0-87784-297-3*, 297) InterVarsity.
Prior, David B., jt. ed. see Brunsden, Denys.
Prior, E., ed. Dispositions. (Scots Philosophical Monographs: No. 7). 176p. 1985. text ed. 31.95 (*0-08-032418-5*, Pub. by Aberdeen U Pr) Macmillan.
Prior, Edward S. History of Gothic Art in England. (Illus.). 1977. reprint ed. 25.00 (*0-7158-1022-7*) Charles River Bks.
Prior, James L. The Divine Moment. (Salamander Ser.: No. 4). 19p. 1993. pap. 2.95 (*1-56640-594-7*) Pomegranate Calif.
Prior, Jean C. Landforms of Iowa. LC 91-16136. (Bur Oak Original Ser.). (Illus.). 168p. 1991. 34.95x (*0-87745-350-0*); pap. 15.95 (*0-87745-347-0*) U of Iowa Pr.
Prior, Jennifer. The Games of Africa. (Illus.). 48p. (J). (gr. 2 up). 1994. 17.95 (*0-694-00597-5*, Festival) HarpC Child Bks.
Prior, John. Gower Handbook of Training & Development. 2nd ed. 750p. 1994. 93.95 (*0-566-07446-X*, Pub. by Gower UK) Ashgate Pub Co.
Prior-Jonson, Elizabeth. AIDS: Myths, Facts & Ethics. 165p. 1989. pap. text ed. 17.00 (*0-08-034434-8*, Pergamon Pr) Elsevier.
Prior, Julian. Pastoral Development Planning. 144p. (C). 1993. text ed. 100.00 (*0-85598-203-9*, Pub. by Oxfam Pubns UK); pap. text ed. 36.00 (*0-85598-204-7*, Pub. by Oxfam Pubns UK) St Mut.
Prior, Katherine. Initiation Customs. LC 93-516. (Comparing Religions Ser.). 32p. (J). (gr. 4-8). 1993. 13.95 (*1-56847-035-5*) Thomson Lrning.
— Pilgrimages & Journeys. LC 93-16318. (Comparing Religions Ser.). (Illus.). 32p. (J). (gr. 4-8). 1993. 13.95 (*1-56847-032-0*) Thomson Lrning.
Prior, Lindsay. The Social Organisation of Death: Medical Discourse & Social Practices in Belfast. LC 88-15868. 240p. 1989. text ed. 45.00 (*0-312-02374-X*) St Martin.
— The Social Organization of Mental Illness. (Illus.). 240p. (C). 1993. text ed. 55.00 (*0-8039-8499-5*); pap. text ed. 19.95 (*0-8039-8500-2*) Sage.
Prior, Mary. Women in English Society Fifteen Hundred to Eighteen Hundred. 304p. 1985. pap. 13.95 (*0-416-35710-5*, 9177) Routledge Chapman & Hall.
Prior, Matthew. The Shorter Poems of Matthew Prior. 1977. 16.95 (*0-8369-7120-5*, 7954) Ayer.
Prior, Mike & Purdy, Dave. Out of the Ghetto: A Path to Socialist Rewards. 193p. 1979. pap. 19.95 (*0-85124-260-X*, Pub. by Spokesman Bks UK) Coronet Bks.
Prior, Moody E. Science & the Humanities. LC 62-13293. 136p. reprint ed. 38.80 (*0-8357-9470-9*, 2015306) Bks Demand.
Prior, Moorly E. The Language of Tragedy. 12.00 (*0-8446-1367-3*) Peter Smith.
Prior, Natalie J. Amabel Abroad: More Amazing Adventures. (Illus.). (Orig.). (J). (gr. 6 up). 1993. pap. 7.95 (*1-86373-130-X*, Pub. by Allen & Unwin Aust Pty AT) IPG Chicago.
— The Amazing Adventures of Amabel. (Illus.). 112p. (Orig.). (YA). (gr. 6 up). 1993. pap. 7.95 (*0-04-442163-X*, Pub. by Allen & Unwin Aust Pty AT) IPG Chicago.
— The Paw. (Illus.). (J). (gr. 1-5). 1995. pap. 6.95 (*1-86373-411-2*) IPG Chicago.
— Tasha's Witch. (Storybridge Ser.). 96p. (J). (gr. 4-7). 1995. pap. 9.95 (*0-7022-2793-5*, Pub. by Univ Queensland Pr AT) Intl Spec Bk.
— Yesterday's Heroes. (YA). 1995. pap. 12.95 (*0-7022-2808-7*, Pub. by Univ Queensland Pr AT) Intl Spec Bk.
Prior, O. H., ed. Caxton's Mirrour of the World: With All the Woodcuts. (EETS, ES Ser.: Vol. 110). 1972. reprint ed. 25.00 (*0-8115-3410-3*) Periodicals Srv.
Prior, P. & Maynard, D., eds. Monitoring Cerebral Function: Long-Term Monitoring of EEG & Evoked Potentials. 2nd rev. ed. 442p. 1987. 173.50 (*0-444-80742-X*) Elsevier.
Prior, Paul, jt. ed. see Bridwell-Bowles, Lillian.
Prior, Paul, ed. see Fang, Irving.
Prior, Pauline. Mental Health & Politics: A History of the Mental Health Services in Northern Ireland. 206p. 1993. 59.95 (*1-85628-540-5*, Pub. by Avebury Pub UK) Ashgate Pub Co.
Prior, R. W. The Great Monarch Butterfly Chase. LC 92-7423. (Illus.). 32p. (J). (ps-3). 1993. text ed. 14.95 (*0-02-775145-7*, Bradbury S&S) S&S Childrens.
Prior, Richard. Trees & Deer. (Illus.). 216p. 1994. 40.00 (*1-85310-432-9*) Voyageur Pr.
***Prior, Robert E.** Road Talk. 24p. 1993. spiral bd. write for info. (*0-9643523-0-3*) Road Talk.
Prior, Robin & Wilson, Trevor. Command on the Western Front: The Military Career of Sir Henry Rawlinson, 1914-1918. 384p. (C). 1991. text ed. 44.95 (*0-631-16683-1*) Blackwell Pubs.
Prior, Robin, jt. auth. see O'Connor, Joseph.
Prior, Roger, jt. auth. see Lasocki, David.
***Prior, Sandra P.** The Fayre Formez of the Pearl Poet. (Medieval Texts & Studies: No. 18). 1995. 36.00 (*0-614-07113-5*) Colleagues Pr Inc.
— The Pearl Poet Revisited. (Twayne's English Author Ser.: No. 512). 176p. 1994. lib. bdg. 22.95x (*0-8057-4516-5*, Twayne) Macmillan.
Prior, William J. Unity & Development in Plato's Metaphysics. LC 85-5073. 202p. (C). 1985. 24.95 (*0-8126-9000-1*) Open Court.
— Virtue & Knowledge: An Introduction to Ancient Greek Ethics. 240p. 1991. 59.95 (*0-415-02470-6*, A4687); pap. 15.95 (*0-415-05324-2*, A4691) Routledge.
Prior, Yehiam, et al, eds. Methods of Laser Spectroscopy. LC 86-12304. (Fritz Haber International Symposium Ser.). 510p. 1986. 110.00 (*0-306-42285-9*, Plenum Pr) Plenum.
***Priore, Domenic.** Look! Listen! Vibrate! SMILE! 300p. 1995. 19.95 (*0-86719-417-0*) Last Gasp.
Priore, Domenic, ed. The Dumb Angel Gazette, No. 3: Potpourri. 145p. (Orig.). 1989. pap. 6.00 (*0-9621744-1-6*) Surfin Colours.
Priore, Frank W. Holiday Play, Vol. 2. 1985. pap. 4.25 (*0-687-17259-4*) Abingdon.
Prioreschi, Plinio. A History of Human Responses to Death: Mythologies, Rituals & Ethics. LC 89-38896. (Studies in Health & Human Services: Vol. 17). 504p. 1990. lib. bdg. 119.95 (*0-88946-142-2*) E Mellen.
— A History of Medicine Vol. 2: Greek Medicine. LC 91-29934. 765p. 1994. text ed. 139.95 (*0-7734-9663-7*) E Mellen.
— The History of Medicine, Vol. 1: Primitive & Ancient Medicine. LC 91-29934. 672p. 1991. lib. bdg. 129.95 (*0-7734-9661-0*) E Mellen.
Priou, A. Dielectric Properties of Heterogeneous Materials, Vol. 6: Progress in Electromagnetic Research. 1991. 82.00 (*0-444-01646-5*) Elsevier.
Priovolos, Theophilos & Duncan, Ronald C., eds. Commodity Risk Management & Finance. (World Bank Publication). (Illus.). 186p. 1991. 24.95 (*0-19-520867-6*, 60867) OUP.
Priozzolo, F., jt. ed. see Johnston, C. W.
Prip-Moller, Johannes. Chinese Buddhist Monasteries: Their Plan & Function As a Setting for Buddhist Monastic Life. (Illus.). 410p. 1982. 127.50 (*962-209-067-2*, Pub. by Hong Kong Univ Pr HK) Coronet Bks.
***Pripps, Robert.** Illustrated International Harvestor Buyers Guide. (Ills. Tractor Buyers Guide Ser.). (Illus.). 160p. 1995. pap. 16.95 (*0-7603-0011-9*) Motorbooks Intl.
— Illustrated John Deere: Two Cycle Tractor Buyers Guide. (MBI Illustrated Buyer's Guide Ser.). (Illus.). 160p. 1992. pap. 16.95 (*0-87938-659-2*) Motorbooks Intl.
Pripps, Robert & Morlands, Andrew. Oliver Tractors: Oliver, Hart-Parr & Cockshutt. (Tractor Color Histories Ser.). (Illus.). 128p. 1994. pap. text ed. 19.95 (*0-87938-853-6*) Motorbooks Intl.
Pripps, Robert, jt. auth. see Morland, Andrew.
Pripps, Robert N. How to Restore Your Farm Tractor. (Illus.). 192p. 1992. pap. 21.95 (*0-87938-593-6*) Motorbooks Intl.
— Illustrated Ford & Fordson Tractors Buyer's Guide. (MBI Illustrated Buyer's Guide Ser.). (Illus.). 160p. 1994. pap. 16.95 (*0-87938-890-0*) Motorbooks Intl.
— John Deere Model B Restoration Guide. (Illus.). 224p. 1995. pap. 26.95 (*0-87938-974-5*) Motorbooks Intl.
— John Deere Photographic History. (Illus.). 240p. 1995. pap. 24.95 (*0-7603-0058-5*) Motorbooks Intl.
Pripps, Robert N. & Morland, Andrew. Farm Crawlers. (Farm Tractor Color History Ser.). (Illus.). 128p. 1994. pap. 19.95 (*0-87938-912-5*) Motorbooks Intl.
— Farmall Tractors. LC 93-13162. (Farm Tractor Color History Ser.). 1993. pap. 19.95 (*0-87938-763-7*) Motorbooks Intl.
— Ford Tractors - N-Series, Fordson, Ford & Ferguson: 1914-1954. (Illus.). 128p. 1990. pap. 19.95 (*0-87938-471-9*) Motorbooks Intl.
— John Deere General Purpose Tractors. (Farm Tractor Color History Ser.). (Illus.). 128p. 1994. pap. 19.95 (*0-87938-937-0*) Motorbooks Intl.
Pris, Claude. Une Grande Entreprise Francaise sous l'Ancien-Regime: La Manufacture Royale des Glaces des Saint-Gobain, 1665-1830, 2 Vols., Set. Bruchey, Stuart, ed. LC 80-2824. (Dissertations in European Economic History Ser.: II). (Illus.). 1981. lib. bdg. 72.95 (*0-405-14008-8*, 12919) Ayer.
***Prisciandaro, Joseph.** Letters from Fair Oaks: Selected Poems 1974-1994. 1995. 14.95 (*0-533-11394-6*) Vantage.
Priscilla Publishing Company Staff. Irish Crochet: Techniques & Projects. 48p. 1984. reprint ed. pap. 2.95 (*0-486-24705-8*) Dover.
— Old-Fashioned Monogramming for Needle-Workers. (Embroidery, Needlepoint, Charted Designs Ser.). 48p. 1985. reprint ed. pap. 3.50 (*0-486-24786-4*) Dover.
Priscilla Publishing Company Staff, ed. Traditional Hardanger Embroidery. 32p. 1985. reprint ed. pap. 2.95 (*0-486-24906-9*) Dover.
Priscu, Radu, et al. Earthquake Engineering for Large Dams. LC 84-3730. 407p. reprint ed. pap. 116.00 (*0-7837-4013-1*, 2043843) Bks Demand.
Prishvin, Mikhail. The Lake & the Woods: Or, Nature's Calendar. Goodman, W. L., tr. LC 75-27685. (Illus.). 258p. 1975. reprint ed. text ed. 55.00 (*0-8371-8465-7*, PRLW, Greenwood Pr) Greenwood.
Prishvin, Mikhail M. Jen Sheng: The Root of Life. Walton, George & Gibbons, Philip, trs. LC 72-90307. (Soviet Literature in English Translation Ser.). (Illus.). 177p. 1973. reprint ed. 19.00 (*0-88355-018-0*) Hyperion Conn.
Prisk, Berneice. Stage Costume Handbook. LC 78-27695. 198p. 1979. reprint ed. text ed. 62.50 (*0-313-20912-X*, PRSC, Greenwood Pr) Greenwood.
Prisk, Court, jt. ed. see Manwaring, Max G.
Prisk, Courtney E., ed. The Comandante Speaks: Memoirs of an El Salvadoran Guerrilla Leader. 145p. (C). 1991. pap. text ed. 35.50 (*0-8133-1066-0*) Westview.
***Prisma, Bokforlaget R.** Prisma's Abridged English-Swedish & Swedish-English Dictionary. abr. ed. LC 94-49413. (ENG & SWE.). 1995. text ed. 24.95 (*0-8166-2734-7*) U of Minn Pr.
Prisma International Staff, ed. see Kissinger, Katie.
Prisma Staff. English-Swedish-English Dictionary. 275p. (ENG & SWE.). 1981. pap. 29.95 (*0-7859-0913-3*, M9449) Fr & Eur.
— Finnish-Swedish-Finnish Dictionary. 272p. (FIN & SWE.). 1981. pap. 29.95 (*0-8288-4659-6*, M9444) Fr & Eur.
— French-Swedish-French Dictionary. 370p. (FRE & SWE.). 1980. pap. 19.95 (*0-8288-4702-9*, M9445) Fr & Eur.
— Italian-Swedish-Italian Dictionary. 279p. (ITA & SWE.). 1978. pap. 19.95 (*0-8288-5248-0*, M9446) Fr & Eur.
— Prisma's Lilla Modern French-Swedish, Swedish-French Dictionary: Prismas Lilla Moderna Fransk-Svensk Och Svensk-Franska Ordbok. 585p. (FRE & SWE.). 1983. 75.00 (*0-8288-1680-8*, F31845) Fr & Eur.
Prison Discipline Society Staff. Reports of the Prison Discipline Society, Boston: Reports 1-29, 1826-1854 (With Intro. essay & Analytical Index Added), 6 vols., Set. LC 71-129322. (Criminology, Law Enforcement, & Social Problems Ser.: No. 155). (Illus.). 1972. 175.00 (*0-87585-155-X*) Patterson Smith.
Prison Fellowship Staff & Spring, Beth. Staying Safe: The Prison Fellowship Guide to Crime Prevention. 160p. 1994. pap. 4.99 (*0-310-40681-1*) Zondervan.
Prisse, D'Avennes. Arabic Designs in Color. (Pictorial Archive Ser.). (Illus.). 1978. pap. 7.95 (*0-486-23658-7*) Dover.
Prisse d'Avennes, E. Atlas of Egyptian Art. (Illus.). 426p. 1991. 270.00 (*977-5170-00-1*) U of Wash Pr.
Prisse d'Avennes, Emile. L' Atlas de l'Art Egyptien: Atlas of Egyptian Art. rev. ed. 405p. (FRE.). 1993. reprint ed. lib. bdg. 495.00 (*0-7859-3710-2*, 9775170001) Fr & Eur.
Prista, Alexander R. Essential Portuguese Grammar. 114p. (Orig.). 1966. pap. 3.95 (*0-486-21650-0*) Dover.
— Say It in Portuguese (European Usage) LC 77-73311. 1979. pap. 3.95 (*0-486-23676-5*) Dover.
Priszter, J., ed. see Javorka, S. & Csapody, V.
Priszter, S. Trees & Shrubs of Europe. 300p. (ENG, FRE, GER, HUN, ITA, RUS & SPA.). 1983. 95.00 (*0-8288-0070-7*, M15341) Fr & Eur.
— Trees & Shrubs of Europe: Dictionary in Eight Languages. 300p. (ENG, FRE, GER, HUN, ITA, LAT, RUS & SPA.). 1983. 125.00 (*0-569-08756-2*, Pub. by Collets UK) Pro-Am Music.
Priszter, S. Z., ed. Dictionary of Trees & Shrubs of Europe: A Dictionary in Eight Languages. 300p. 1983. 59.00 (*963-05-2946-7*, Pub. by Akade Kiado HU) IBD Ltd.
Pritam, Amrita. Forty-Nine Days. 1981. 11.00 (*0-8364-0798-9*, Pub. by Chanakya II) S Asia.
— The Haunted House & the Thirteenth Sun: Two Novels. 155p. 1993. text ed. 15.95 (*0-685-66338-8*, Pub. by Vikas II) S Asia.
— Life & Poetry of Sara Shagufta. (Orig.). (C). 1994. 8.50x (*81-7018-771-0*, Pub. by BR Pub II) S Asia.
— The Skeleton & That Man. 2nd rev. ed. Singh, Khushwant, tr. 97p. 1992. pap. 5.95 (*81-207-0243-3*, Pub. by Sterling Pubs II) Apt Bks.
***Pritchard.** Chaos Cookbook. 2nd ed. 1995. pap. write for info. (*0-7506-1777-2*, Focal) Buttrwrth-Heinemann.
— Using the Magnetic Forces of Your Mind. 1957. pap. 4.95 (*0-87505-094-8*) Borden.
Pritchard & Trebbau. Turtles of Venezuela. LC 83-51450. 1984. Regular ed. write for info. (*0-916984-11-7*); Patron's ed. write for info. (*0-916984-12-5*) SSAR.
Pritchard, A. J., ed. see IFAC Symposium Staff.
Pritchard, A. P. & Mallett, Jane. The Royal Marsden Hospital Manual of Clinical Nursing Procedures. 3rd ed. (Illus.). 560p. 1992. pap. 34.95 (*0-632-03387-8*) Blackwell Sci.
Pritchard, A. Phylip, ed. Cancer Nursing: A Revolution in Care. 192p. 1989. pap. 36.95 (*0-8261-7220-2*) Springer Pub.
***Pritchard, Andrea, et al, eds.** Alien Discussions: Proceedings of the Abduction Study Conference Held at M. I. T. Cambridge, MA. (Illus.). 684p. 1994. 69.95 (*0-9644917-0-2*) N Cambridge Pr.
Pritchard, Andrew. The Microscope Cabinet. (History of Microscopy Ser.). 256p. 1987. reprint ed. 62.40 (*0-940095-02-5*) Sci Heritage Ltd.
Pritchard, Angela E., comp. Eleventh Symposium on Nucleic Acids Chemistry. (Nucleic Acids Symposium Ser.: No. 12). 232p. 1983. pap. 40.00 (*0-904147-53-3*, IRL Pr) OUP.
— Tenth Symposium on Nucleic Acids Chemistry. (Nucleic Acids Symposium Ser.: No. 11). 296p. 1982. pap. 40.00 (*0-904147-48-7*, IRL Pr) OUP.
Pritchard, Anthony. Grand Prix Racing - The Enthusiast's Companion. (Illus.). 255p. 1992. text ed. 29.95 (*0-946627-79-7*, Pub. by Aston Pubns UK) Motorbooks Intl.
— Marlboro McLaren: The Tag & Honda Powered Grand Prix Cars, 1983-90. (Illus.). 144p. 1990. 24.95 (*0-946627-59-2*, Pub. by Aston Pubns UK) Motorbooks Intl.
***Pritchard, Anthony J.** Lending by the World Bank for Agricultural Research: A Review of the Years 1981 Through 1987. (Technical Paper Ser.: No. 118). 46p. 1990. 6.95 (*0-614-02817-5*, 11516) World Bank.
Pritchard, Arnold. Catholic Loyalism in Elizabethan England. LC 78-10208. 255p. reprint ed. pap. 72.70 (*0-7837-6851-6*, 2046680) Bks Demand.

An Asterisk (*) at the beginning of an entry indicates that the title is appearing in BIP for the first time.

***Pritchard, B., ed.** Bridge Modification: Proceedings of the Conference Bridge Modification Organized by the Institution of Civil Engineers, London, March 23-24, 1994. 302p. 1994. 67.20 (*0-7277-2028-7*) Am Soc Civil Eng.

Pritchard, B., tr. see Ferrero, Guglielmo.

Pritchard, Brian. Bridge Design for Economy & Durability: Concepts for New, Strengthened & Replacement Bridges. (Illus.). 172p. 1992. 79.00 (*0-7277-1671-9*, Pub. by T Telford UK) Am Soc Civil Eng.

Pritchard, Brian, ed. Antonio Caladara Sixteen Seventy to Seventeen Thirty-Six. 400p. 1987. text ed. 93.95 (*0-85967-720-6*, Pub. by Scolar Pr UK) Ashgate Pub Co.

Pritchard, Carol. Avoiding Rape on & off Campus. 2nd ed. 68p. (Orig.). 1988. pap. 8.00 (*1-877858-24-2*, AROOC2) Amer Focus Pub.

***Pritchard, Colin.** Suicide: The Ultimate Rejection : a Psycho-Social Study. LC 94-43417. 1995. write for info. (*0-335-19033-2*); pap. text ed. write for info. (*0-335-19032-4*, Open Univ Pr) Taylor & Francis.

Pritchard, Colin, jt. auth. see Taylor, Richard.

Pritchard, Colin W., jt. auth. see Carr-Hill, Roy A.

Pritchard, D. C., jt. ed. see Lynes, J. A.

Pritchard, D. J., ed. Foundations of Developmental Genetics. LC 86-5884. 350p. 1986. 110.00 (*0-85066-356-3*); pap. 55.00 (*0-85066-287-7*) Taylor & Francis.

Pritchard, D. J. & Scott, C. J., eds. Applications of Transputers Two: Proceedings of the 2nd International Conference on Applications of Transputers, Southampton, U. K. July 11-13, 1990. (Transputer & Occam Engineering Ser.). 587p. 1990. 110.00 (*90-5199-035-9*, Pub. by IOS Pr NE) IOS Press.

Pritchard, Dale. The Bible in a Nutshell. LC 94-11993. 80p. (Orig.). 1995. 7.00 (*0-87573-029-9*) Jain Pub Co.

Pritchard, David A. Tests of Neuropsychological Malingering. 1992. disk 175.00 (*1-878205-55-2*) GR Press.

Pritchard, David A., jt. auth. see Hall, Harold V.

Pritchard, David B. Begin Chess. 160p. 1987. pap. 2.95 (*0-451-14723-5*, Sig) NAL-Dutton.

— Begin Chess. 2nd ed. 168p. 1992. pap. 4.99 (*0-451-17438-0*, Sig) NAL-Dutton.

Pritchard, David W., jt. auth. see Foy, Chester L.

Pritchard, Donna L., ed. see Colorado Assoc. of Legal Secretaries Staff.

Pritchard, Donna L., jt. auth. see Colorado Assoc. of Legal Secretaries Staff.

Pritchard, Donna L., ed. see Colorado Association of Legal Secretaries Staff.

Pritchard, Doris. Monmouth Court. LC 81-3589. (Illus.). 1981. 10.00 (*0-87233-064-8*) Bauhan.

Pritchard, E. B., ed. Mars: Past, Present, & Future. (PAAS Ser.: Vol. 145). 324p. 1992. 69.95 (*1-56347-043-8*) AIAA.

Pritchard, Eileen & Scott, Paula R. Literature Searching in Science, Technology, & Agriculture. LC 83-18471. x, 174p. 1984. text ed. 49.95 (*0-313-23710-7*, PLR/, Greenwood Pr) Greenwood.

Pritchard, Evan T. From the Temple Within: The Fourth Book of Light. 160p. (Orig.). 1993. pap. 8.95 (*0-9637990-0-2*) Resonance Comm.

— The Secrets of Whole-Hearted Thinking: 100 Sayings, Ideas, & Paradoxes That Can Make Your Life Fuller, Happier, & Less Complicated. LC 93-33283. 1993. 8.95 (*0-88268-160-5*) Station Hill Pr.

Pritchard, Florence F. Teaching Writing As Thinking. 395p. (C). 1994. pap. text ed. 34.95 (*0-9636011-4-8*) Shore Educ.

— Teaching-Writing-As-Thinking Strategy Masters: Reproducible Handouts to Guide the Thinking - Writing Process in Grades 4-14. 68p. (Orig.). (C). 1994. student ed 19.95 (*0-9636011-1-3*) Shore Educ.

— Teaching Writing Mechanics with Concept Attainment: A Guide for Teaching Grammar, Punctuation, Spelling & Capitalization. 101p. (Orig.). (C). 1994. pap. text ed. 19. 95 (*0-9636011-2-1*) Shore Educ.

Pritchard, G., ed. Developments in Reinforced Plastics, Vol. 1. (Illus.). 283p. 1980. 93.75 (*0-85334-919-3*, Pub. by Elsevier Applied Sci UK) Elsevier.

— Developments in Reinforced Plastics, Vol. 2. (Illus.). 196p. 1982. 61.25 (*0-85334-125-7*, Pub. by Elsevier Applied Sci UK) Elsevier.

— Developments in Reinforced Plastics, Vol. 3. (Illus.). 202p. 1984. 63.00 (*0-85334-266-0*, I-169-84, Pub. by Elsevier Applied Sci UK) Elsevier.

— Developments in Reinforced Plastics, Vol. 4. (Illus.). 272p. 1985. 88.25 (*0-85334-305-5*, Pub. by Elsevier Applied Sci UK) Elsevier.

— Developments in Reinforced Plastics, No. 5. 284p. 1986. 84.75 (*0-85334-400-0*, Pub. by Elsevier Applied Sci UK) Elsevier.

Pritchard, Gerylin, ed. see Dunn, Edith B.

Pritchard, Gretchen W. Offering the Gospel to Children. LC 92-23900. 219p. 1992. pap. 13.95 (*1-56101-065-0*) Cowley Pubns.

Pritchard, H. Baden. About Photography & Photographers. LC 72-9225. (Literature of Photography Ser.). 1973. reprint ed. 19.95 (*0-405-04931-5*) Ayer.

— The Photographic Studios of Europe. LC 72-9226. (Literature of Photography Ser.). 1973. reprint ed. 23.95 (*0-405-04932-3*) Ayer.

Pritchard, H. M., et al, eds. Geo-Platinum Eighty-Seven: Proceedings of a Symposium Held at the Open University, Milton Keynes, U. K., 22-23 April, 1987. 424p. 1988. 126.00 (*1-85166-197-2*) Elsevier.

Pritchard, H. W., ed. Modern Methods in Orchid Conservation. (C). 1990. 54.95 (*0-521-37294-1*) Cambridge U Pr.

Pritchard, J. M. Africa: Geography of a Changing Continent. LC 71-145838. 248p. 1971. 39.50 (*0-8419-0071-X*, Africana) Holmes & Meier.

Pritchard, Jacki. The Abuse of Elderly People: A Handbook for Professionals. 160p. 1992. pap. 39.00 (*1-85302-122-9*, Pub. by J Kingsley Pubs UK) Taylor & Francis.

— The Abuse of Older People: A Training Manual for Detection & Prevention. 2nd rev. ed. LC 95-11795. Orig. Title: The Abuse of Elderly People. 1995. pap. write for info. (*1-85302-305-1*, Pub. by J Kingsley Pubs UK) Taylor & Francis.

***Pritchard, Jacki, ed.** Good Practice in Supervision: Statutory & Voluntary Organisations. 190p. 1994. pap. 29.95x (*1-85302-279-9*, Pub. by J Kingsley Pubs UK) Taylor & Francis.

Pritchard, Jacki, jt. ed. see Owen, Hilary.

Pritchard, James, ed. Proceedings of the Eighteenth Meeting of the French Colonial Historical Society, Montreal, May 1992: (Actes du Dix-Huitieme Colloque de la Societe d'Histoire Coloniale Francaise. Montreal. Mai 1992) v, 116p. 1993. text ed. 30.00 (*1-884679-00-5*) Fr Colonial Hist.

— Proceedings of the Nineteenth Meeting of the French Colonial Historical Society, Providence, R. I., May, 1993. (Illus.). v, 228p. (ENG & FRE.). (C). 1994. text ed. 30.00 (*1-884679-01-3*) Fr Colonial Hist.

Pritchard, James, jt. auth. see Pritchard, Peter.

Pritchard, James B. Archaeology & the Old Testament. LC 58-10053. 279p. reprint ed. pap. 79.60 (*0-8357-5716-1*, 2016011) Bks Demand.

— The Bronze Age Cemetery at Gibeon. (University Museum Monographs: No. 25). (Illus.). x, 123p. 1963. pap. 20.00 (*0-934718-17-2*) U PA Mus Pubns.

— The Cemetery at Tell es-Sa'idiyeh, Jordan. (University Museum Monographs: No. 41). (Illus.). xii, 103p. (Orig.). (C). 1980. pap. 25.00 (*0-934718-32-6*) U PA Mus Pubns.

— Gibeon, Where the Sun Stood Still: The Discovery of a Biblical City. 1962. pap. 14.95x (*0-691-00210-X*) Princeton U Pr.

— Gibeon, Where the Sun Stood Still: The Discovery of the Biblical City. LC 62-11963. (Illus.). 244p. reprint ed. pap. 69.60 (*0-7837-6765-X*, 2046595) Bks Demand.

— Recovering Sarepta, a Phoenician City. LC 77-28304. (Illus.). 1978. 45.00 (*0-691-09378-4*); pap. 12.95 (*0-691-00213-4*) Princeton U Pr.

— Tell Es-Sa'Idiyeh: Excavations on the Tell, 1964-1966. (University Museum Monographs: No. 60). (Illus.). 216p. (ARA & ENG.). 1985. text ed. 75.00 (*0-934718-60-1*) U PA Mus Pubns.

— The Water System of Gibeon. (University Museum Monographs: No. 22). viii, 34p. 1961. pap. 15.00 (*0-934718-14-8*) U PA Mus Pubns.

— Winery, Defenses, & Soundings at Gibeon. (University Museum Monographs: No. 26). (Illus.). viii, 85p. 1964. pap. 15.00 (*0-934718-18-0*) U PA Mus Pubns.

Pritchard, James B., ed. Ancient Near East in Pictures. 2nd ed. Incl. , 2 vols. 1969. Set. 99.50 (*0-691-03502-4*); An Anthology of Texts & Pictures1969. pap. 14.95 (*0-691-00209-6*); An Anthology of Texts & Pictures1969. pap. 16.95 (*0-691-00200-2*); Pictures1969. (*0-691-03610-1*); 1969. Set pap. write for info. (*0-318-70291-6*) Princeton U Pr.

— Ancient Near Eastern Texts: Relating to the Old Testament. 3rd ed. LC 78-76499. 734p. reprint ed. pap. 180.00 (*0-8357-8801-6*, 2052276) Bks Demand.

— Ancient Near Eastern Texts Relating to the Old Testament, Set. 3rd ed. 1969. 89.50 (*0-691-03503-2*) Princeton U Pr.

— The Harper Concise Atlas of the Bible. LC 21-9. (Illus.). 152p. 1991. 30.00 (*0-06-270029-4*, Harper Ref) HarpC.

Pritchard, James B., et al. Sarepta: A Preliminary Report on the Iron Age. (University Museum Monographs: No. 35). (Illus.). ix, 114p. 1975. pap. 30.00 (*0-934718-24-5*) U PA Mus Pubns.

Pritchard, James S. Louis XV's Navy, Seventeen Forty-Eight to Seventeen Sixty-Two: A Study of Organization & Administration. 320p. 1987. 49.95 (*0-7735-0570-9*, Pub. by McGill CN) U of Toronto Pr.

Pritchard, Jeff. Heads You Win, Tails You Win: The Inside of Rare Coin Investing. 1983. 24.95 (*0-8359-2808-X*, Reston) P-H.

Pritchard, Joe. The Chaos Cookbook: A Practical Programming Guide. (Illus.). 240p. 1992. 39.95 (*0-7506-0304-6*) Buttrwrth-Heinemann.

— Newnes Amateur Radio Computing Handbook. (Illus.). 363p. 1990. pap. 36.95 (*0-434-91516-5*) Buttrwrth-Heinemann.

— PC Telecommunications: A Practical Guide. (Illus.). 400p. 1993. pap. write for info. (*0-7506-1725-X*) Buttrwrth-Heinemann.

Pritchard, John. Respiratory Protection Program for Industry. 250p. 1992. pap. 64.95 (*0-442-00802-3*) Van Nos Reinhold.

Pritchard, John, ed. see Dixon, Donnie.

Pritchard, John, ed. see Dunn, Edith B.

Pritchard, John, ed. see Voorhees, Russell.

Pritchard, John, ed. see Walker, Jim.

Pritchard, John G. Poly(Vinyl Alcohol) (Polymer Monographs). (Illus.). 152p. 1970. text ed. 117.00 (*0-677-01670-0*) Gordon & Breach.

Pritchard, John P. A Literary Approach to the New Testament. LC 72-1793. 1972. pap. 16.95 (*0-8061-1710-9*) U of Okla Pr.

Pritchard, L., jt. ed. see Lawrence, M.

Pritchard, M. L. Psychological Aspects of Rheumatoid Arthritis. (Recent Research in Psychology Ser.). (Illus.). xv, 208p. 1989. pap. 40.00 (*0-387-97116-5*) Spr-Verlag.

Pritchard, Margaret B. & Sites, Virginia L. William Byrd the Second & His Lost History: Engravings of the Americas. LC 92-31382. (Illus.). 224p. 1993. 26.99 (*0-87935-088-1*) Colonial Williamsburg.

Pritchard, Mary H. & Kruse, Gunther O. The Collection & Preservation of Animal Parasites. LC 81-19869. (Harold W. Manter Laboratory Technical Bulletin Ser.: No. 1). 147p. (Orig.). reprint ed. pap. 41.90 (*0-7837-1465-3*, 2057160) Bks Demand.

***Pritchard, Melissa.** The Instinct for Bliss: Short Stories. LC 94-35507. 192p. 1995. 20.95 (*0-944072-49-6*) Zoland Bks.

— Phoenix. LC 91-71514. 133p. (Orig.). (C). 1991. pap. text ed. 8.95 (*0-943433-08-8*) Cane Hill Pr.

— Spirit Seizures. LC 87-5932. (Flannery O'Connor Award for Short Fiction Ser.). 186p. 1987. 19.95 (*0-8203-0959-1*) U of Ga Pr.

Pritchard, Michael S. On Becoming Responsible. LC 90-41613. x, 278p. 1991. 29.95 (*0-7006-0444-8*) U Pr of KS.

— Philosophical Adventures with Children. LC 85-15795. 166p. (Orig.). 1985. pap. text ed. 19.50 (*0-8191-4897-0*) U Pr of Amer.

Pritchard, Michael S., jt. auth. see Jaksa, James A.

Pritchard, Michael S., jt. ed. see Robison, Wade L.

Pritchard, Pat. The Candy Dad. 224p. (Orig.). 1993. pap. 2.95 (*1-56597-102-7*, Kismet) Meteor Pub.

— Rough Edges. 224p. (Orig.). 1993. pap. 2.95 (*1-56597-069-1*, Kismet) Meteor Pub.

Pritchard, Paul. An Introduction to Programming with Macintosh Pascal. (Illus.). 608p. (C). 1988. pap. text ed. 33.50 (*0-201-17539-8*) Addison-Wesley.

— Managing Environmental Risks & Liabilities. (Business & the Environment Practitioner Ser.). (C). 1994. 150.00x (*0-946655-91-X*, Pub. by S Thornes Pubs UK) St Mut.

Pritchard, Paul C., ed. Views of the Green: Presentations from New Directions for the Conservation of Parks; An International Working Conference. 154p. 1985. 14.95 (*0-940091-14-3*); pap. 9.95 (*0-940091-13-5*) Natl Parks & Cons.

***Pritchard, Peter & Pritchard, James.** Teamwork for Primary & Shared Care. 2nd ed. (Practical Guides for General Practice Ser.). (Illus.). 136p. 1994. pap. text ed. 26.95 (*0-19-262527-6*) OUP.

Pritchard, Peter C. The Alligator Snapping Turtle: Biology & Conservation. LC 89-13935. (Illus.). 104p. 1989. pap. text ed. 29.95 (*0-89326-124-6*) Milwaukee Pub Mus.

— Encyclopedia of Turtles. (Illus.). 1979. 59.95 (*0-87666-918-6*, H-1011) TFH Pubns.

Pritchard, R. E., ed. Poetry by English Women: Elizabethan to Victorian. 272p. (Orig.). (C). 1993. pap. text ed. 14.95 (*0-8264-0599-1*) Continuum.

***Pritchard, Ray.** The Road Best Traveled: Knowing God's Will for Your Life. 224p. (Orig.). 1995. pap. 10.99 (*0-89107-851-7*) Crossway Bks.

Pritchard, Robert, jt. ed. see Spangenberg-Urbschat, Karen.

Pritchard, Robert D. Measuring & Improving Organizational Productivity: A Practical Guide. LC 90-34680. 264p. 1990. text ed. 59.95 (*0-275-93668-6*, C3668, Praeger Pubs) Greenwood.

***Pritchard, Robert D., ed.** Productivity Measurement & Improvement: Organizational Case Studies. LC 94-32932. 400p. 1995. text ed. 75.00 (*0-275-93907-3*) Greenwood.

Pritchard, Robert E. & Hindelang, Thomas J. The Strategic Evaluation & Management of Capital Expenditures. LC 80-69702. 336p. reprint ed. pap. 95.80 (*0-317-27193-8*, 2023925) Bks Demand.

Pritchard, Robert E. & Potter, Gregory C. Fitness Inc: A Guide to Corporate Health & Wellness Programs. 200p. 1989. text ed. 30.00 (*1-55623-274-8*) Irwin Prof Pubng.

Pritchard, Roger M. Housing & the Spatial Structure of the City: Residential Mobility & the Housing Market in an English City since the Industrial Revolution. LC 75-3859. (Cambridge Geographical Studies: No. 7). 244p. reprint ed. pap. 69.60 (*0-685-20566-5*, 2030615) Bks Demand.

Pritchard, Rosalind M. The End of Elitism? The Democratisation of the West German University System. LC 89-39611. 256p. 1991. 59.95 (*0-85496-661-7*) Berg Pubs.

Pritchard, Samuel. Jachin & Boaz: An Authentic Key to the Door of Freemasonry Calculated Not Only for the Instruction of Every New-Made Mason but Also for the Information of All Who Intend to Become Brethren As Practiced in 1762. 60p. 1992. reprint ed. pap. 7.00 (*1-56459-246-4*) Kessinger Pub.

— The Three Distinct Knocks: On the Door of the Most Ancient Freemasonry; Being a Universal Description of All Its Branches from Its First Rite to This Present Time. 73p. 1992. reprint ed. pap. 9.00 (*1-56459-247-2*) Kessinger Pub.

***Pritchard, Sara, ed.** 1995 AACE International Transactions. (Illus.). 450p. (Orig.). 1995. pap. text ed. 94.95 (*1-885517-01-7*) AACE Intl.

Pritchard, Sarah M., ed. The Women's Annual, No. 4: 1983-1984. 248p. 1984. pap. 20.00 (*0-8161-8725-8*, Hall Reference) Macmillan.

Pritchard, Sonia Z. Oil Pollution Control. 240p. 1987. 59.95 (*0-7099-2094-6*, Pub. by Croom Helm UK) Routledge Chapman & Hall.

Pritchard, Syd. A Golfer's Guide to Shakespeare. 114p. (C). 1988. pap. 35.00 (*0-7212-0799-5*, Pub. by Regency Press) St Mut.

Pritchard, Thomas J. Representative Bodies. 213p. (C). 1988. 39.00x (*0-86383-403-5*, Pub. by Gomer Pr UK) St Mut.

***Pritchard, Tom.** Madderlake's Natural Christmas. Date not set. write for info. (*0-517-70132-4*) Random.

— Madderlake's Trade Secrets: Finding & Arranging Flowers Naturally. 1994. 27.50 (*0-517-88158-6*, Crown) Crown Pub Group.

Pritchard, W. E. Tolley's Tax Planning for New Businesses. 150p. 1993. 90.00 (*0-85459-565-1*, Pub. by Tolley Pubng UK) St Mut.

Pritchard, Wendy, jt. auth. see Beckhard, Richard.

Pritchard, Wilbur L. & Harford, James J., eds. China Space Report. (Illus.). 200p. 25.00 (*0-317-32131-5*) AIAA.

Pritchard, Wilbur L. & Sciulli, Joseph A. Communications Satellite Systems Engineering. (Illus.). 352p. (C). 1986. text ed. 42.95 (*0-685-10916-X*) P-H.

Pritchard, Wilbur L., et al. Satellite Communication Systems Engineering. 2nd ed. LC 92-2361. 544p. 1993. text ed. 82.00 (*0-13-791468-7*) P-H Gen Ref & Trav.

***Pritchard, William H.** English Papers: A Teaching Life. 176p. 1995. 22.95 (*1-55597-234-9*) Graywolf.

— Frost: A Literary Life Reconsidered. 2nd ed. LC 92-36872. (Illus.). 312p. (C). 1993. pap. 16.95 (*0-87023-838-8*) U of Mass Pr.

— Playing It by Ear: Literary Essays & Reviews. LC 94-12255. 288p. (C). 1994. lib. bdg. 45.00 (*0-87023-947-3*); pap. 16.95 (*0-87023-948-1*) U of Mass Pr.

— Randall Jarrell: A Literary Life. 1990. 25.00 (*0-374-24677-7*) FS&G.

— Randall Jarrell: A Literary Life. 1992. pap. 14.95 (*0-374-52277-4*, Noonday) FS&G.

Pritchard, William H., ed. see Jarrell, Randall.

Pritchet, Christopher J. The Extragalactic Distance Scale. Van Den Bergh, Sidney, ed. (ASP Conference Series Publications: Vol. 4). (Illus.). 397p. 1988. 25.00 (*0-937707-21-X*) Astron Soc Pacific.

Pritchett, B. Michael. Financing Growth: A Financial History of American Life Insurance Through 1900. LC 84-62400. (S. S. Huebner Foundation Monographs: No. 13). 90p. (Orig.). 1985. pap. 17.95 (*0-918930-13-8*) Huebner Foun Insur.

Pritchett, Bradley L. Grammatical Competence & Parsing Performance. LC 91-43480. (Illus.). 208p. 1992. lib. bdg. 55.00 (*0-226-68441-5*); pap. text ed. 19.95 (*0-226-68442-3*) U Ch Pr.

Pritchett, Bruce M. A Study of Capital Mobilization: The Life Insurance Industry of the 19th Century. Bruchey, Stuart, ed. LC 76-45109. (Nineteen Seventy-Seven Dissertations Ser.). (Illus.). 1977. lib. bdg. 41.95 (*0-405-09921-5*) Ayer.

Pritchett, C. Herman. Congress Versus the Supreme Court, Nineteen Fifty-Seven to Nineteen Sixty. LC 73-249. (American Constitutional & Legal History Ser). 182p. 1973. reprint ed. lib. bdg. 25.00 (*0-306-70568-0*) Da Capo.

Pritchett, Charles H., jt. auth. see Murphy, Walter F.

Pritchett, Davis W. Man & the Living World Laboratory. 128p. 1993. spiral bd. 16.50 (*0-8403-8681-8*) Kendall-Hunt.

Pritchett, Doug. Immortality. 1993. pap. 7.95 (*0-533-10536-6*) Vantage.

Pritchett, Frances W. Nets of Awareness: Urdu Poetry & Its Critics. LC 92-43826. 1994. 42.00 (*0-520-08194-3*); pap. 17.00 (*0-520-08386-5*) U CA Pr.

— The Romance Tradition in Urdu. 1991. text ed. 35.00 (*0-231-07164-7*) Col U Pr.

— The Romance Tradition in Urdu: Adventures from the Dastan of Amir Hamzah. 1990. 35.00 (*0-685-45923-3*) Col U Pr.

— Urdu Literature: A Bibliography of English Language Sources. 1979. 15.00 (*0-8364-0534-X*) S Asia.

Pritchett, Harry H., Jr. Morning Run: Sabbatical Reflections on the Church & the City. LC 89-28745. (Illus.). 120p. (Orig.). 1989. pap. 8.95 (*0-932419-26-7*) Cherokee.

***Pritchett, James.** Aaron's Solution. Daniels, Sharon et al, eds. 140p. (Orig.). 1994. pap. 8.95 (*0-9643232-0-6*) Pandamonium.

— The Music of John Cage. LC 92-44525. (Music in the Twentieth Century Ser.: No. 5). (Illus.). 275p. (C). 1993. 44.95 (*0-521-41621-3*) Cambridge U Pr.

Pritchett, James W. Practical Bone Growth. 1993. 35.00 (*0-89716-455-5*) P B Pubng.

Pritchett, Jennifer. Providing Reference Service in Church & Synagogue Libraries. LC 87-15776. (Guide Ser.: No. 15). 60p. 1987. pap. 8.25 (*0-915324-26-1*); pap. 6.50 (*0-318-32514-4*) CSLA.

Pritchett, John P. Black Robe & Buckskin. 1960. 12.95 (*0-8084-0063-0*); pap. 8.95 (*0-685-01124-0*) NCUP.

Pritchett, Kay, tr. Four Post-Modern Poets of Spain: A Critical Introduction & Translation. LC 90-33978. 247p. 1991. 29.95 (*1-55728-173-4*); pap. 19.95 (*1-55728-174-2*) U of Ark Pr.

Pritchett, Kay, tr. see Urzagasti, Jesus.

Pritchett, Kay, tr. see Vannuci, Jose W.

Pritchett, Kendrick W. Studies in Ancient Greek Topography, Pt. VI. (UC Publications in Classical Studies: Vol. 33). 1989. 45.00 (*0-520-09746-7*) U CA Pr.

***Pritchett, Lou.** Stop Paddling & Start Rocking the Boat: Business Lessons from the School of Hard Knocks. 1995. 25.00 (*0-88730-731-0*, PL) HarpC.

Pritchett, Michael. The Venus Tree. LC 88-21795. (John Simmons Short Fiction Award Ser.). 138p. 1988. 19.95 (*0-87745-220-2*) U of Iowa Pr.

Pritchett, Morgan H., ed. see Enoch Pratt Free Library.

Pritchett, Nash L. One Flower While I Live: Elvis As I Remember Him. LC 87-32391. (Illus.). 154p. 1987. pap. 10.95 (*0-942179-05-6*) Shelby Hse.

***Pritchett, Norman M. & Richardson, William G.** Cooks in Cadence. LC 94-74894. (Illus.). 220p. (Orig.). 1995. pap. 15.00x (*0-943335-04-3*) Marblehead Pub.

Pritchett, Price. After the Merger: Managing the Shockwaves. LC 84-73046. 140p. 1985. text ed. 45.00 (*0-87094-627-7*) Irwin Prof Pubng.

— Culture Shift: The Employee Handbook for Changing Corporate Culture. 35p. 1993. pap. 5.95 (0-944002-12-9) Pritchett Assocs.

— The Employee Handbook of New Work Habits for a Radically Changing World: Thirteen Ground Rules for Job Success in the Information Age. 42p. (Orig.). 1994. pap. 5.95 (0-944002-15-3) Pritchett Assocs.

— The Employee Survival Guide to Mergers & Acquisitions. 94p. (Orig.). 1988. pap. write for info. (0-944002-00-5) Pritchett Assocs.

— The Ethics of Excellence. 25p. (Orig.). 1991. pap. 5.95 (0-944002-09-9) Pritchett Assocs.

— Firing up High Commitment During Organizational Change. 42p. (Orig.). 1994. pap. 5.95 (0-944002-14-5) Pritchett Assocs.

— Making Mergers Work: A Guide to Managing Mergers & Acquisitions. 160p. 1987. text ed. 45.00 (0-87094-980-2) Irwin Prof Pubng.

— The Quantum Leap Strategy. 90p. (Orig.). 1991. pap. 5.95 (0-944002-08-0) Pritchett Assocs.

— Service Excellence! 31p. (Orig.). 1989. pap. 5.95 (0-944002-02-1) Pritchett Assocs.

— The Team Member Handbook for Teamwork. 60p. (Orig.). 1992. pap. 5.95 (0-944002-11-0) Pritchett Assocs.

***Pritchett, Price & Pound, Ron.** Business As Unusual: The Handbook for Managing & Supervising Organizational Change. 27p. 1988. pap. 5.95 (0-944002-01-3) Pritchett Assocs.

— The Employee Handbook for Organizational Change. 1990. pap. 5.95 (0-944002-07-2) Pritchett Assocs.

— High-Velocity Culture Change: A Handbook for Managers. 44p. (Orig.). 1993. pap. 5.95 (0-944002-13-7) Pritchett Assocs.

— Smart Moves: A Crash Course on Merger Integration Management. (Orig.). 1989. pap. 5.95 (0-944002-03-X) Pritchett Assocs.

— A Survival Guide to the Stress of Organizational Change. 30p. (Orig.). 1995. pap. 5.95 (0-944002-16-1) Pritchett Assocs.

— Team ReConstruction: High Velocity Moves for Repairing Work Groups Rocked by Change. 24p. (Orig.). 1992. pap. 5.95 (0-944002-10-2) Pritchett Assocs.

Pritchett, Ron. Cougar City. large type ed. (Linford Western Library). 256p. 1992. pap. 14.95 (0-7089-7150-4, Trailtree Bookshop) Ulverscroft.

Pritchett, S. Travis & Wilder, Ronald P. Stock Life Insurance Company Profitability & Workable Competition. LC 85-61668. (S. S. Huebner Foundation Monographs: No. 14). (Illus.). 1986. pap. 20.95 (0-918930-14-6) Huebner Foun Insur.

Pritchett, Sue, ed. see Harlan, Timothy S.

Pritchett, Sue, ed. see Spicer, Myrna R.

Pritchett, V. S. At Home & Abroad. braille ed. 719p. 1991. vinyl bd. 57.52 (1-56956-188-5, BR8318) W A T Braille.

— Cab at the Door & Midnight Oil. 1994. 16.00 (0-679-60103-1, Modern Lib) Random.

— The Gentle Barbarian: The Life & Work of Ivan Turgenev. 243p. (C). 1986. reprint ed. pap. 9.50 (0-88001-120-3) Ecco Pr.

— Marching Spain. 236p. 1991. pap. 15.95 (0-7012-0824-4, Pub. by Hogarth Pr UK) Trafalgar.

— The Spanish Temper. (Travels Ser.). 224p. 1989. reprint ed. pap. 8.95 (0-88001-182-3) Ecco Pr.

Pritchett, Victor S. Books in General. LC 70-110378. 258p. 1970. reprint ed. text ed. 38.50 (0-8371-4582-1, PRBG, Greenwood Pr) Greenwood.

— Camberwell Beauty & Other Stories. LC 74-5215. 1974. 9.95 (0-394-49222-6) Random.

— Careless Widow & Other Stories. 172p. 1989. 16.95 (0-394-57612-8) Random.

— Chekhov: A Spirit Set Free. LC 87-43213. 224p. 1988. 17.95 (0-394-54650-4) Random.

— Chekhov: A Spirit Set Free. 1989. pap. 8.95 (0-679-72546-6, Vin) Random.

— Collected Stories. 1982. pap. 20.00 (0-394-52417-9) Random.

— Comp Coll Stories. 1991. 35.00 (0-679-40215-2) McKay.

— Complete Collected Essays. 1992. 34.50 (0-679-41112-7) Random.

— Complete Collected Stories. LC 91-5806. 1992. pap. 20.00 (0-679-73892-4, Vin) Random.

— Complete Collected Stories. LC 91-58068. 1992. pap. 20.00 (0-06-797389-2, Vin) Random.

— Dead Man Leading. (Twentieth-Century Classics Ser.). 1984. pap. 6.95 (0-19-281469-9) OUP.

— Lasting Impressions: Essays 1961-1987. 224p. 1990. 19.95 (0-394-58720-0) Random.

— London Perceived. LC 62-14471. 185p. 1966. pap. 3.95 (0-15-652970-X, HB103, Harvest Bks) HarBrace.

— More Collected Stories. 290p. 1983. 17.95 (0-394-53128-0) Random.

— Myth Makers: Essays on European Novelists, Including Russian, Spanish, & French. 1979. 11.95 (0-394-50472-0) Random.

— On the Edge of the Cliff & Other Stories. LC 79-4805. 1979. 11.95 (0-394-50485-2) Random.

— Selected Stories of V. S. Pritchett. 1978. 11.95 (0-394-50128-4) Random.

Pritchett, Victor S., sel. The Oxford Book of Short Stories. 576p. 1981. 29.95 (0-19-214116-3) OUP.

— The Oxford Book of Short Stories. 576p. 1988. pap. 12.95 (0-19-282113-X) OUP.

***Pritchett, W. Kendrick.** Essays in Greek History. (Illus.). x, 294p. 1994. lib. bdg. 63.00x (90-5063-316-1, Pub. by Egbert Forsten NE) Benjamins North Am.

— The Greek State at War, Pt. III. 1980. 50.00 (0-520-03781-2) U CA Pr.

— The Greek State at War, Pt. IV. LC 75-312653. 1985. 50.00 (0-520-05379-6) U CA Pr.

— The Greek State at War, Pt. V. LC 75-312653. 545p. 1991. 60.00 (0-520-07374-6) U CA Pr.

— The Liar School of Herodotus. v, 359p. 1993. 63.00 (90-5063-088-X, Pub. by Gieben NE) Benjamins North Am.

— Studies in Ancient Greek Topography, Pt. VII. x, 224p. 1991. pap. 83.00 (90-5063-071-5, Pub. by Gieben NE) Benjamins North Am.

— Studies in Ancient Greek Topography, Pt. VIII. (Illus.). xxi, 159p. 1993. pap. 83.00 (90-5063-087-1, Pub. by Gieben NE) Benjamins North Am.

Pritchett, William Kendrick. Ancient Greek Military Practices, Part 1. LC 71-633960. (University of California Publications: Classical Studies: Vol. 7). 177p. reprint ed. pap. 50.50 (0-8357-5465-0, 2011037) Bks Demand.

— Studies in Ancient Greek Topography, Pt. V. (UC Publications in Classical Studies: Vol. 31). 1986. pap. 48.00 (0-520-09698-3) U CA Pr.

— Studies in Ancient Greek Topography: Battlefields, Part 2. LC 65-65210. (University of California Publications: Classical Studies: Vol. 4). 292p. reprint ed. pap. 83.30 (0-317-29555-1, 2021261) Bks Demand.

— Studies in Ancient Greek Topography: Part III (Roads) (UC Publications in Classical Studies: Vol. 22). 436p. 1981. pap. 45.00 (0-520-09635-5) U CA Pr.

— Studies in Ancient Greek Topography, Pt. 4: Passes. LC 65-65210. (University of California Publications, Classical Studies: No. 28). (Illus.). 374p. reprint ed. pap. 106.60 (0-8357-6855-4, 2035553) Bks Demand.

Pritchett, William L. & Fisher, Richard F. Properties & Management of Forest Soils. 2nd ed. LC 86-22421. 494p. 1987. Net. text ed. write for info. (0-471-89572-5) Wiley.

Prithvi Ram Mudiam. India & the Middle East. 192p. 1994. text ed. 59.50 (1-85043-703-3, Pub. by I B Tauris UK) St Martin.

Pritikin, Enid & Reece, Trudy. Parentcare Survival Guide: Helping Your Folks Through the Not-So-Golden Years. 256p. 1993. pap. 8.95 (0-8120-4975-6) Barron.

Pritikin, Ilene, jt. auth. see Pritikin, Nathan.

Pritikin, Nathan. The Pritikin Promise. 1991. mass mkt. 5.99 (0-671-73267-6) PB.

Pritikin, Nathan & McGrady, Patrick. The Pritikin Program for Diet & Exercise. 1984. mass mkt. 5.95 (0-553-27192-X) Bantam.

Pritikin, Nathan & Pritikin, Ilene. The Official Pritikin Guide to Dining Out. LC 83-3853. 224p. 1984. write for info. (0-672-52773-1) Macmillan.

Pritikin, Renny. Fourth Gear City Limits. 1976. pap. 6.00 (0-685-73664-4) Twowindows Pr.

Pritikin, Robert C. The New Pritikin Program. Rubenstein, Julie, ed. 464p. 1991. reprint ed. pap. 6.50 (0-671-73194-7) PB.

— Pritikin's Testament: Miracle Ads for Big & Small Advertisers, Retailers & Entrepreneurs. 1991. pap. 14.95 (0-13-585191-2) P-H.

Pritikin Staff. Off Pritikin Guide. rev. ed. 1985. 11.95 (0-02-599200-7) Macmillan.

Pritsak, Omeljan, jt. intro. see Subtelny, Orest.

***Pritsak, Omeljan.** On the Writing of History in Kievan Rus' 40p. 1994. write for info. (0-9609822-9-9) Ukrainian Studies Fund.

— The Origin of Russia, Vol. I. (Series in Ukrainian Studies). 850p. (C). 1982. 50.00 (0-674-64465-4) HUP.

— The Origins of the Old Rus' Weights & Monetary Systems: Two Studies in Western Eurasian Metrology & Numismatics in the Seventh to Eleventh Centuries. (Harvard Series in Ukrainian Studies). (Illus.). 100p. (C). 1992. text ed. 29.00 (0-916458-48-2) Harvard Ukrainian.

— Studies in Medieval Eurasian History. (Collected Studies: No. CS132). 376p. (C). 1981. reprint ed. lib. bdg. 115.00 (0-86078-078-3, Pub. by Variorum UK) Ashgate Pub Co.

— When & Where Was Ol'ga Baptized? 24p. 1994. write for info. (0-940465-01-9) Ukrainian Studies Fund.

Pritsak, Omeljan & Subtelny, Orest, intros. The Diariusz Podrozny of Pylyp Orlyk: (1727-1730) LC 88-84116. (Library of Early Ukrainian Literature: Vol. 6). xxviii, 868p. (C). 1989. text ed. 35.00 (0-916458-26-1) Harvard Ukrainian.

— The Diariusz Podrozny of Pylyp Orlyk: (1731-1733) (Library of Early Ukrainian Literature: Vol. 7). (C). Date not set. text ed. write for info. (0-916458-34-2) Harvard Ukrainian.

***Pritsker, A. Alan.** Introduction to Simulation & SLAM II. 4th ed. (Illus.). 860p. 1995. 60.00 (0-470-23457-1) Systems Pub.

Pritsker, A. Alan, et al. Introduction to Simulation & SLAM II, Solutions Manual. (Illus.). 305p. 1986. 50.00 (0-938974-01-7) Systems Pub.

Pritsker, Alan B. Papers, Experiences, Perspectives. 250p. 1990. 30.00 (0-938974-03-3, PR-1) Soc Computer Sim.

— Slam II-Network Models for Decision Support. 704p. 1989. text ed. 50.00 (0-13-812819-7) P-H.

Pritsker, Alan B. & Young, Robert E. Simulation with GASP-PL-I: A PL-I Based Continuous-Discrete Simulation Language. LC 75-23182. 351p. reprint ed. pap. 100.10 (0-317-11035-7, 2022490) Bks Demand.

Pritt, Donald S. & Walker, Morton. The Complete Foot Book: First Aid for Your Feet. LC 91-33326. (Illus.). 176p. (Orig.). 1992. pap. 12.95 (0-89529-434-6) Avery Pub.

Prittie, Jodie. Better Homes & Gardens Seasons of Giving. 1994. pap. 14.95 (0-696-20294-8) Meredith Bks.

Prittie, Joni. The Best of Iron-on Transfers. (Illus.). 87p. 1990. 9.95 (0-937769-53-3) Mark Inc CA.

— The Best of Victorian Christmas Crafts. (Illus.). 76p. 1991. write for info. (0-937769-84-3) Mark Inc CA.

— Better Homes & Gardens Seasons of Giving. 168p. 1993. 22.95 (0-696-02391-1) Meredith Bks.

— Crafter's Garden. 1994. pap. 14.95 (0-696-20295-6) Meredith Bks.

— Crafter's Garden: At a Glance. 1993. 24.95 (0-696-02382-2) Meredith Bks.

— The Victorian Home. (Illus.). 76p. 1990. 11.95 (0-937769-81-9) Mark Inc CA.

Prittie, Terence. The Velvet Chancellors: A History of Post-War Germany. (Illus.). 286p. 1981. 24.50 (0-8419-6750-4) Holmes & Meier.

***Pritts, Kim D.** Ginseng: How to Find, Grow, & Use America's Forest Gold. LC 95-7210. (Illus.). 160p. 1995. pap. 16.95 (0-8117-2477-8) Stackpole.

— The Mystery of Sadler Marsh. (Illus.). 112p. (Orig.). (J). (gr. 3-7). 1993. pap. 4.95 (0-8361-3618-7) Herald Pr.

Prittwitz, Karl L. von. Berlin 1848: Das Erinnerungswerk des Generalleutnants Karl Ludwig von Prittwitz und Andere Quellen zur Berliner Maerzrevolution und zur Geschichte Preussens um die Mitte des 19 Jahrunderts. (Veroeffentlichungen der Historischen Kommission zu Berlin, Band 67, Beitraege zu Inflation und Wiederaufbau in Deutschland und Europa 1914-1924: Vol. 60, Quellenwerke Band 7). (Illus.). lxvi, 518p. (GER.). 1985. 106.00 (3-11-008326-4) De Gruyter.

Pritzlaff, John A., ed. International Safety Standard Guidelines for the Operation of Tourist Submersibles. 311p. 1993. 76.00 (0-939773-14-7, R-39) Soc Naval Arch.

— International Safety Standard Guidelines for the Operation of Tourist Submersibles. 311p. 1993. 76.00 (0-614-06720-0) Soc Naval Arch.

Prival, Jody & Stadolsky, Daniel, eds. Guide to Living in Pittsburgh: A Narrative for New Pittsburghers. 1994. pap. 7.95 (0-9642186-8-2) Dec Five.

Privalko, V. P. & Novikov, V. V. The Science of Heterogeneous Polymers: Structure & Thermophysical Properties. LC 94-19288. 1995. text ed. 95.00 (0-471-94167-0) Wiley.

Privalko, V. P., jt. ed. see Godovsky, Y. K.

***Privara, I., et al, eds.** Mathematical Foundations of Computer Science 1994, 841. (Lecture Notes in Computer Science Ser.: Vol. 841). 628p. 1994. pap. text ed. 82.00 (0-387-58338-6) Spr-Verlag.

Privarova, V., jt. auth. see Blazej, Anton.

Private Philanthropy & Public Need Commission. Research Papers, 5 vols. in 6 bks., Set. 1986. reprint ed. lib. bdg. 312.00 (0-89941-446-X, 303990) W S Hein.

***Private Sector Conference.** The Academic Health Center & Health Care Reform: Proceedings of the Duke Private Sector Conference, 1994. Snyderman, Ralph et al, eds. LC 95-7174. 1995. pap. write for info. (0-7817-0326-3) Raven.

Privateer, Paul M. Romantic Voices: Identity & Ideology in British Poetry, 1789-1850. LC 90-33568. 272p. 1991. 40.00 (0-8203-1251-7) U of Ga Pr.

Priven, Judith S. Terminos Utiles. Arribel, Luis, tr. 40p. (Orig.). (SPA.). 1993. pap. 4.95 (0-9635633-1-9) Hello America.

Priven, Judy. Easy Writer: Basics to GED. (Cambridge Writing Ser.). 160p. (C). 1991. pap. text ed. 6.50 (0-13-971136-8, 640304) P-H.

— Hello! Washington: A Handbook on Everyday Living for International Residents. 250p. 1993. pap. 12.95 (0-9635633-0-0) Hello America.

Privensen, Alice. Shaker Lane. (J). 1990. pap. 4.95 (0-14-050713-2, Puffin) Puffin Bks.

Priver, David, jt. auth. see Leveen, Louis.

Priver, John & Foxall, Gordon R. Advertising: Policy & Practice. LC 84-40336. 172p. 1984. text ed. 39.95 (0-312-00731-0) St Martin.

Privett, Judy & Privett, Tony. What America's Teachers Wish Parents Knew. LC 93-79657. 144p. 1993. pap. 5.95 (1-56352-104-0) Longstreet Pr Inc.

Privett, Katherine H. The Dreams of Exiles. LC 82-2886. (Kestrel Chapbks.). 24p. 1982. pap. 3.00 (0-914974-34-3) Holmgangers.

Privett, Stephen A. The U. S. Catholic Church & Its Hispanic Members: The Pastoral Vision of Archbishop Robert E. Lucey. 229p. pap. 17.00 (0-939980-22-3) Trinity U Pr.

Privett, Tony, jt. auth. see Privett, Judy.

Privette, Eleanor T. The Living Christmas Card. 32p. 1990. pap. 3.25 (0-687-22288-5) Abingdon.

Privitera, Walter. Problems of Style: Michel Focault's Epistomology. Keller, Jean, tr. LC 94-10398. (SUNY Series in Social & Political Thought). 184p. (C). 1995. text ed. 49.50 (0-7914-2333-6); pap. text ed. 16.95 (0-7914-2334-4) State U NY Pr.

Privman, V. & Svrakie, N. M. Directed Models of Polymers, Interfaces & Clusters: Scaling & Finite-Size Properties. (Lecture Notes in Physics Ser.: Vol. 338). vi, 120p. 1989. 31.00 (0-387-51429-5, 3454) Spr-Verlag.

Priya. Birth Traditions & Modern Obstetrics. 1992. pap. 10.95 (1-85230-321-2) Element MA.

***Priz, Edward J.** CompControl: Secrets of Reducing Workers' Compensation Costs. Akin, Camille, ed. LC 95-17314. (Successful Business Library Ser.). 150p. (Orig.). 1995. pap. 19.95 (1-55571-355-6); ring bd. 39.95 (1-55571-356-4) Oasis Pr OR.

Prizel, Ilya. Latin America Through Soviet Eyes: The Evolution of Soviet Perceptions During the Brezhnev Era 1964-1982. (Cambridge Russian, Soviet & Post-Soviet Studies: No. 72). 288p. (C). 1990. 59.95 (0-521-37303-4) Cambridge U Pr.

***Prizel, Ilya & Michta, Andrew A., eds.** Polish Foreign Policy Reconsidered: Challenges of Independence. LC 94-35327. 1995. text ed. 39.95 (0-312-12293-4) St Martin.

Prizel, Ilya, ed. see Michta, Andrew A.

Prizio, Diana. Beyond Granola: An Evolutionary Approach to Natural Foods. 63p. (Orig.). 1990. pap. text ed. 4.00 (0-9621498-1-0, Robin Hood) R Hood Little.

Prizzi, Elaine & Hoffman, Jeanne. Reading Around the World. (J). (gr. 4-6). 1985. pap. 7.99 (0-8224-3182-3) Fearon Teach Aids.

— Reading Around Town. (J). (gr. 4-6). 1985. pap. 7.99 (0-8224-3181-5) Fearon Teach Aids.

— Reading Everyday Stuff. (J). (gr. 4-6). 1985. pap. 7.99 (0-8224-3180-7) Fearon Teach Aids.

— Teaching off the Wall. LC 80-81836. (J). (gr. 2-5). 1981. pap. 10.99 (0-8224-6830-1) Fearon Teach Aids.

Prizzi, Elaine & Hoffmann, Jeanne. Beginning Book Reporting. LC 83-63175. (J). (gr. 2-5). 1984. pap. 12.99 (0-8224-2175-5) Fearon Teach Aids.

— Interactive Bulletin Boards. LC 82-63176. (J). (gr. 1-4). 1984. pap. 11.99 (0-8224-6256-7) Fearon Teach Aids.

Prizzi, Elaine, jt. auth. see Hoffman, Jeanne.

Prizzia, Ross. Thailand in Transition: The Role of Oppositional Forces. LC 85-1059. (Asian Studies at Hawaii: No. 32). 136p. 1985. pap. text ed. 9.00 (0-8248-0977-7) UH Pr.

***Prlando, Louise.** Multicultural Game Book: More Than 70 Traditional Games from 30 Countries. 1999. pap. 12.95 (0-590-49409-0) Scholastic Inc.

Proakis, John G. Digital Communications. 2nd ed. (Electrical Engineering Ser.). 928p. (C). 1989. text ed. write for info. (0-07-050937-9) McGraw.

— Digital Communications. 3rd ed. LC 94-41620. (Electrical & Computer Engineering Ser.). 1995. text ed. write for info. (0-07-051726-6) McGraw.

Proakis, John G. & Manolakis, Dimitris G. Introduction to Digital Signal Processing: Principles, Algorithms, & Applications. 2nd ed. (Illus.). 992p. (C). 1992. Other materials avail. text ed. write for info. (0-02-396815-X) Macmillan.

Proakis, John G. & Salehi, Masoud. Communications Systems Engineering. LC 93-23109. 1993. text ed. 76.00 (0-13-158932-6) P-H.

Proakis, John G., et al. Advanced Topics in Digital Signal Processing. (Illus.). 624p. (C). 1992. text ed. write for info. (0-02-396841-9) Macmillan.

***Proal, Jean.** Farandole. deluxe limited ed. (Ediciones Especiales y de Bibliofilo Ser.). (Illus.). (FRE.). 1993. 7,500.00 (84-343-0108-3) Elliots Bks.

Proal, Louis. Political Crime. LC 70-172565. (Criminology, Law Enforcement, & Social Problems Ser.: No. 146). 1973. reprint ed. 24.00 (0-87585-146-0) Patterson Smith.

Proano, Franklin. La Poesia Femenina Actual De Sudamerica. Date not set. 59.50 (1-882528-04-2) Scripta.

Proano, Mario, tr. see Twitchell, Paul.

Proaps, Linda. Capitol Punishment. (Illus.). 295p. 1991. 24.95 (1-879563-03-7) Lexicon CA.

Probabilistic Conference Staff. Probabilistic Methods in Differential Equations: Proceedings of the Probabilistic Conference, University of Victoria, August 1974. (Lecture Notes in Mathematics Ser.: Vol. 451). 190p. (Orig.). 1975. pap. 16.00 (0-387-07153-9) Spr-Verlag.

Probart, M. E., et al. The Properties & Management of Vertisols. 36p. (Orig.). 1987. pap. text ed. 31.00 (0-85198-601-3) CAB Intl.

Probasco, Jim. A Parent's Guide to Band & Orchestra. (Illus.). 136p. (Orig.). 1991. pap. 7.95 (1-55870-183-4) Betterway Bks.

— A Parent's Guide to Teaching Music. (Illus.). 136p. (Orig.). 1992. pap. 7.95 (1-55870-240-7) Betterway Bks.

***Probasco, Steve.** Yakima River. (River Journal Ser.: No. 6). (Illus.). 48p. 1994. pap. 14.95 (1-878175-75-0) F Amato Pubns.

Probasco, Teri. Blue Jean Gum. 35p. (J). (ps-4). Date not set. pap. 5.90 (0-932970-95-8) Prinit Pr.

— Imprints. 177p. (J). (gr. 3-8). 1994. pap. 10.95 (0-932970-99-0) Prinit Pr.

— Simple Things. 36p. (J). (ps-6). 1994. pap. 5.90 (0-932970-98-2) Prinit Pr.

Probdorf, Siegfried & Silbermann, Bernd. Numerical Analysis for Integral & Related Operator Equations. (Mathematische Lehrbucher und Monographien: Abt. II, Band 84). 540p. 1991. text ed. 106.00 (3-05-500696-8, Pub. by Akademie GW) VCH Pubs.

Probert, Belinda & Wilson, Bruce, eds. Pink Collar Blues: Work Gender & Technology. (Orig.). 1993. pap. 19.95 (0-522-84520-7) Intl Spec Bk.

Probert, Chris. Pearls in the Landscape: The Conservation & Management of Ponds. (Illus.). 240p. 1989. 29.95 (0-85236-198-X, Pub. by Farming Pr UK) Diamond Farm Bk.

Probert, Christina & Lee-Potter, Charlie. Fashion in Vogue since 1910: Lingerie. LC 81-14926. (Accessories in Vogue Ser.). (Illus.). 96p. (Orig.). 1982. pap. 12.95 (0-89659-268-5); 59.70 (0-89659-276-6) Abbeville Pr.

— Fashion in Vogue since 1910: Sportswear. LC 83-26574. (Accessories in Vogue Ser.). (Illus.). 96p. 1984. pap. 12.95 (0-89659-499-8) Abbeville Pr.

— Fashion in Vogue since 1910: Swimwear. LC 81-67879. (Accessories in Vogue Ser.). (Illus.). 96p. 1981. pap. 12.95 (0-89659-242-1) Abbeville Pr.

Probert, D. Cloze Clues. (Learning Works Reading Ser.). (J). (gr. 4-6). 1988. 5.95 (0-88160-166-7, LW 276) Learning Wks.

Probert, Ellen, jt. auth. see Schueler, Sally H.

Probert, Henry. High Commanders of the RAF. 245p. 1991. 39.95 (0-11-772635-4, HM5634) UNIPUB.

Probert, M. E. A Search for Strategies for Sustainable Dryland Cropping in Semi-Arid Eastern Kenya. 134p. (C). 1992. text ed. 104.00 (1-86320-068-1, Pub. by ACIAR) St Mut.

Probert, P., jt. auth. see Cameron, S.

Probert, Randall. Katrina's Valley. 226p. 1991. pap. 14.95 (0-87949-350-X) Ashley Bks.

Probert, Richard E. Fishing Hot Spots (of the Upper Fraser Valley) 96p. 1992. pap. 8.95 (0-88839-307-5) Hancock House.

An Asterisk (*) at the beginning of an entry indicates that the title is appearing in BIP for the first time.

Probert, Sidney, ed. see Schueler, Sally H. & Probert, Ellen.

Probleme der Sprachwissenschaft Staff. Beitrage zur Linguistik. (Janua Linguarum, Ser. Minor: No. 118). 1971. pap. text ed. 64.60 (*90-279-1797-3*) Mouton.

Probosz, Kathilyn S. Martha Graham. LC 94-8992. (People in Focus Ser.). (Illus.). 128p. (YA). (gr. 5 up). 1995. text ed. 13.95 (*0-87518-568-1*, Dillon Silver Burdett) Silver Burdett Pr.

Probst, Charles. Bosch Fuel Injection & Engine Management. (Orig.). 29.95 (*0-8376-0300-5*) Bentley.

Probst, Charles O. Ford Fuel Injection & Electronic Engine Control: How to Understand, Service, & Modify, 1988-1993. LC 93-7168. 1993. pap. 29.95 (*0-8376-0301-3*) Bentley.

Probst, D. K., jt. ed. see Bochmann, G. V.

Probst, G. J., jt. ed. see Ulrich, H.

Probst, Gary K. Learning Skills for Success. 384p. 1992. spiral bd. 37.95 (*0-8403-7567-0*) Kendall-Hunt.

Probst, George E., intro. The Happy Republic: A Reader in Tocqueville's America. 11.75 (*0-8446-1368-1*) Peter Smith.

*__Probst, George T. & Reichmann, Eberhard.__ The Germans in Indianapolis, Vol. 1. (Illus.). xii, 200p. 1989. 16.00 (*0-614-04948-2*) MKGAC & IGHS.

Probst, Gerhard F. Erwin Piscator & the American Theatre. LC 90-28359. (American University Studies: Theatre Arts: Ser. XXVI, Vol. 6). 220p. (C). 1991. text ed. 45.95 (*0-8204-1591-X*) P Lang Pubs.

Probst, Gerhard F. & Bodine, Jay F., eds. Perspectives on Max Frisch. LC 80-5181. 232p. 1982. 25.00 (*0-8131-1438-1*) U Pr of Ky.

Probst, Katherine N. & Portney, Paul R. Assigning Liability for Superfund Cleanups: An Analysis of Policy Options. 62p. 1992. pap. text ed. 15.00 (*0-915707-64-0*) Resources Future.

Probst, Raymond R. Good Offices in the Light of Swiss International Practice & Experience. (C). 1989. lib. bdg. 88.00 (*0-7923-0141-2*) Kluwer Ac.

Probst, Robert E. Response & Analysis: Teaching Literature in Junior & Senior High School. LC 87-24509. viii, 279p. (Orig.). 1987. pap. text ed. 18.50 (*0-86709-203-3*) Boynton Cook Pubs.

*__Probst, Volker G.__ Arno Breker, das Bildnis des Menschen. (Illus.). 160p. (Orig.). 1981. pap. 15.00 (*0-914301-26-8*, Pub. by Marco GW) West-Art.

— Der Bildhauer Arno Breker. (Illus.). 168p. (Orig.). 1978. pap. 15.00 (*0-914301-25-X*, Pub. by Marco GW) West-Art.

— Schriften: Collected Writings of Arno Breker. (Illus.). 192p. 1983. text ed. 20.00 (*0-914301-28-4*, Pub. by Marco GW) West-Art.

Probst, Volker G., ed. see Breker, Arno.

Probstein, Bobbie. Healing Now: A Personal Guide Through Challenging Times. (Illus.). 64p. (Orig.). 1992. pap. 9.95 (*1-880823-00-4*) N Star Pubns.

— Living Now: A Personal Guide to Meeting the Challenges of Cancer. (Illus.). 96p. 1991. pap. 17.95 (*1-880823-03-9*) N Star Pubns.

— Return to Center. LC 85-70723. (Illus.). 256p. (Orig.). 1985. pap. 10.95 (*0-87516-554-0*) DeVorss.

Probstein, Ian E., ed. see Murphy, Remington.

Probstein, Ian E., ed. see Ogniedou, Altan.

Probstein, Jan. A Passage to the World (Doroga v Mir) 112p. 1992. pap. 8.00 (*1-882725-00-X*) Arch-Arcada.

— Vita Nuoja: A Book of Poems Written in English & Translated from Russian by the Author. Graves, Michael, ed. 64p. (Orig.). 1993. pap. 4.00 (*0-9635200-3-2*) R E M Pr.

*__Probstein, Jan E.__ Requiem: A Book of Poems. (Illus.). 92p. (Orig.). (RUS.). 1994. pap. text ed. 8.00 (*0-911971-86-6*) Effect Pub.

— Vremion Naskvozniake: A Book of Poems. (Illus.). 112p. (Orig.). (RUS.). 1993. pap. text ed. 8.00 (*0-911971-85-8*) Effect Pub.

— Zhemchuzhina - A Pearl: A Book of Poems. Kazakova, Natalia, ed. 104p. (RUS.). 1994. pap. text ed. 8.00 (*1-882725-09-3*) Arch-Arcada.

Probstein, Ronald F. Physiochemical Hydrodynamics. 2nd ed. LC 93-49459. 1994. text ed. 69.95 (*0-471-01011-1*) Wiley.

Probstein, Ronald F. & Hicks, R. Edwin. Synthetic Fuels. LC 81-8274. (Illus.). 504p. (C). 1990. reprint ed. text ed. 39.00 (*0-9628070-0-1*) pH Press.

Proby, Kathryn H. Audubon in Florida: With Selections from the Writings of John James Audubon. LC 72-85114. (Illus.). 384p. 1974. pap. 15.95 (*0-87024-301-2*) U of Miami Pr.

— Mario Sanchez-Painter of Key West Memories. LC 81-50557. (Illus.). 64p. 1981. pap. 14.95 (*0-916224-70-8*) Banyan Bks.

Probyn, Clive T. English Fiction in the Eighteenth Century, 1700-1789. (Literature in English Ser.). 288p. (Orig.). (C). 1987. pap. text ed. 25.50 (*0-582-49369-2*, 73587) Longman.

— The Sociable Humanist: Life & Work of James Harris, 1709-1740: Provincial & Metropolitan Culture in Eighteenth-Century England. (Illus.). 392p. 1991. 89.00 (*0-19-818563-4*) OUP.

Probyn, Clive T., ed. see Fielding, Henry & Fielding, Sarah.

Probyn, Elspeth. Sexing the Self: Gendered Positions in Cultural Studies. LC 92-22143. 226p. 1993. 49.95 (*0-415-07355-3*, B0131, Routledge NY); pap. 15.95 (*0-415-07356-1*, B0135, Routledge NY) Routledge.

Probyn, Elspeth, jt. ed. see Grosz, Elizabeth A.

Probyn, John W., ed. Systems of Land Tenure in Various Countries. LC 75-153000. (Select Bibliographies Reprint Ser.). 1977. reprint ed. 30.95 (*0-8369-5752-0*) Ayer.

Procaccini, Alfonso. Francesco Jovine: The Quest for Realism. (American University Studies: Romance Languages & Literature: Ser. II, Vol. 37). 223p. 1987. text ed. 37.50 (*0-8204-0267-2*) P Lang Pubs.

*__Procassini, Andrew A.__ Competitors in Alliance: Industry Associations, Global Rivalries & Business. LC 94-39659. 360p. 1995. text ed. 59.95 (*0-89930-962-3*, Quorum Bks) Greenwood.

Proceedings Magazine Staff, ed. Naval Review 1991. (Illus.). 271p. 1991. 25.00 (*1-55750-603-5*) Naval Inst Pr.

— Naval Review 1992. (Illus.). 240p. 1992. 25.00 (*1-55750-605-1*) Naval Inst Pr.

Proceedings of the International Conference, Los Angeles, 1972, et al. Few Particle Problems in the Nuclear Interaction. Moszkowski, Steven A. et al, eds. 1973. 102.75 (*0-444-10439-9*, North Holland) Elsevier.

Proceedings of the 2nd European Conference on Advanced Materials & Processes Staff. Euromat 91: Proc. 2nd European Conf. of Advanced Materials & Processes, 3 vols., Set. 1800p. 1992. 330.00 (*0-901716-14-6*, Pub. by Inst Materials UK) Ashgate Pub Co.

Proceedings of the 2nd Int'l Conference on the Behavior of Materials in Machining Staff. Advanced Machining for Quality & Productivity: Proc. 2nd Int'l Conf. on the Behaviorial Materials in Machining. 176p. 1991. pap. 80.00 (*0-901716-24-3*, Pub. by Inst Materials UK) Ashgate Pub Co.

Procesi, Claudio, ed. Geometry Today: Giornate Di Geometria, Roma, 1984. (Progress in Mathematics Ser.: Vol. 60). 1985. 43.95 (*0-8176-3290-5*) Birkhauser.

Process Management Inst. Inc. Staff & Gitlow, Howard S. Planning for Quality, Productivity, & Competitive Position. 250p. 1990. text ed. 42.00 (*1-55623-357-4*) Irwin Prof Pubng.

Process Measurement & Control Division & New Orleans Section of ISA Staff, ed. see ISA Final Control Elements Symposium Staff.

Process Technology Conference Staff. New Ironmaking & Steelmaking Processes: Proceedings of the 7th Process Technology Conference, April 17-20, 1988, Toronto, Ontario. LC 82-197229. (Illus.). 307p. reprint ed. pap. 87.50 (*0-8357-5552-5*, 2035181) Bks Demand.

Proch, D., jt. auth. see Gower, M.

Proch, Kathleen, jt. auth. see Saltzman, Andrea.

Prochak, Michael, jt. auth. see Pilling, Elaine.

Prochaska, Bernadette. The Myth of the Fall & Walker Percy's Last Gentleman. LC 91-42105. (American University Studies: American Literature: Ser. XXIV, Vol. 32). 148p. 1993. pap. 29.95 (*0-8204-1806-4*) P Lang Pubs.

Prochaska, David. Making Algeria French. (Illus.). 320p. (C). 1990. 64.95 (*0-521-34303-8*) Cambridge U Pr.

Prochaska, F. K. Philanthropy & the Hospitals of London: The King's Fund, 1897-1990. 320p. 1992. 65.00 (*0-19-820266-0*) OUP.

*__Prochaska, Frank.__ The Rise of the Welfare Monarchy. LC 95-12271. 1995. write for info. (*0-300-06453-5*) Yale U Pr.

Prochaska, Georg. A Dissertation on the Functions of the Nervous System. Laycock, T., tr. LC 78-72819. (Brainedness, Handedness, & Mental Abilities Ser.). reprint ed. 34.50 (*0-404-60888-4*) AMS Pr.

— Dissertation on the Functions of the Nervous System. Laycock, T., tr. Bd. with On the Study of Character. (Contributions to the History of Psychology Ser.: Vol. XIV, Pt. A). 1983. reprint ed. (*0-89093-316-2*) U Pubns Amer.

Prochaska, James, et al. Changing for Good. LC 93-44897. 1994. 22.00 (*0-688-11263-3*) Morrow.

Prochaska, James O. Systems of Psychotherapy: A Transtheoretical Analysis. 2nd ed. 442p. (C). 1984. boxed 48.95 (*0-534-10708-7*) Brooks-Cole.

Prochaska, James O. & DiClemente, Carlo C. The Transtheoretical Approach: Crossing Traditional Boundaries of Therapy. 204p. (C). 1994. reprint ed. lib. bdg. 25.00 (*0-89464-848-9*) Krieger.

Prochaska, James O. & Norcross, John C. Systems of Psychotherapy: A Transtheoretical Analysis. 3rd ed. LC 93-41023. 1994. text ed. 49.95 (*0-534-22290-0*) Brooks-Cole.

*__Prochaska, James O., et al.__ Changing for Good. 304p. 1995. reprint ed. pap. 11.00 (*0-380-72572-X*) Avon.

Prochazka, Theodore, Jr. Saudi Arabian Dialects. 400p. 1987. text ed. 82.50 (*0-7103-0204-5*, Pub. by Kegan Paul Intl UK) Routledge Chapman & Hall.

Prochazka, V., ed. Narodni Divadlo, Slovnik Umelcu Divadel Vlastenskeho, Stavovskeho, Prozatimniho a Narodniho. 624p. (CZE.). 1990. 70.00 (*0-317-03839-7*) Szwede Slavic.

Prochazkova, Iva. The Season of Secret Wishes. Crawford, Elizabeth D., tr. LC 89-45291. 208p. (J). (gr. 4-8). 1989. 12.95 (*0-688-08735-3*) Lothrop.

Prochelo, Barbara B. Draw from Within: A Workbook for Self-Expression & Self-Discovery. (Illus.). 66p. (Orig.). 1990. pap. 9.95 (*0-9626838-0-9*) Sun Dance Creat.

Prochiantz, Alain. How the Brain Evolved. Gladstone, William J., tr. (Horizons of Science Ser.). 1992. pap. text ed. 11.95 (*0-07-050929-8*) McGraw.

*__Prochnau, William.__ Once upon a Distant War. LC 95-7327. 1995. 27.50 (*0-8129-2633-1*, Times Bks) Random.

Prochnicky, Jerry, jt. auth. see Riordan, James.

Prochnov, Dave. Superconductivity: The Threshold of a New Technology. 1988. pap. text ed. 12.95 (*0-07-157168-X*) McGraw.

*__Prochnow.__ Toastmaster's Quips & Stories & How to Use Them. Date not set. (*0-8069-0238-8*) Sterling.

Prochnow, Dave. Experiments in CMOS Technology. (Advanced Technology Ser.). (Illus.). 304p. 1988. 24.95 (*0-8306-9262-2*, 3062); pap. 16.95 (*0-8306-9362-9*, 3062) TAB Bks.

— Experiments with E-PROMs. 1988. pap. text ed. 18.95 (*0-07-156490-X*) McGraw.

— Experiments with EPROMs. (Advanced Technology Ser.). (Illus.). 208p. 1988. 24.95 (*0-8306-0362-X*); pap. 17.95 (*0-8306-2962-9*) TAB Bks.

— Flight Simulator & Flight Simulator II. 1987. pap. 12.95 (*0-07-155250-2*) McGraw.

— One Thousand & One Things to Do with Your IBM. 1989. pap. 17.95 (*0-8306-3232-8*, Windcrest) TAB Bks.

— One Thousand One Things to Do. 1991. 24.95 (*0-8306-6249-9*) TAB Bks.

— Superconductivity: Experiments in a New Technology. (Advanced Technology Ser.). (Illus.). 208p. 1988. pap. 14.95 (*0-8306-3132-1*, 3132) TAB Bks.

Prochnow, Dave & Banning, D. J. Experiments in Gallium Arsenide Technology. 1988. text ed. 24.95 (*0-07-157459-X*); pap. text ed. 16.95 (*0-07-157470-0*) McGraw.

Prochnow, Dave & Branning, D. J. Experiments in CMOS Technology. 1988. text ed. 24.95 (*0-07-155026-7*); pap. text ed. 16.95 (*0-07-155039-9*) McGraw.

Prochnow, Dave & Knott. One Thousand One Things to Do with Your Amiga. 1991. 24.95 (*0-8306-6427-0*) TAB Bks.

Prochnow, Dave & Prochnow, Kathy. How? More Experiments for the Young Scientist. 1993. 16.95 (*0-07-051051-2*); pap. text ed. 10.95 (*0-07-051052-0*) McGraw.

— How? More Experiments for the Young Scientist. (Illus.). 160p. (J). 1992. 16.95 (*0-8306-4024-X*, 4177); pap. 9.95 (*0-8306-4025-8*, 4177) TAB Bks.

— Why? Experiments for the Young Scientist. (Illus.). 160p. (J). (gr. 4-7). 1992. 16.95 (*0-8306-4015-0*, 4176); pap. 9.95 (*0-8306-4023-1*, 4176) TAB Bks.

Prochnow, Dave & Sawusch, Mark R. One Thousand One Things to Do with Your IBM PS-2. 1991. 24.95 (*0-8306-8686-X*) TAB Bks.

Prochnow, Dave, jt. auth. see Prochnow, Kathy.

Prochnow, Dave, et al. Why? Experiments for the Young Scientist. 1992. 16.95 (*0-07-051059-8*); pap. text ed. 10.95 (*0-07-051058-X*) McGraw.

Prochnow, David. Flight Simulator & Flight Simulator II: 82 Challenging New Adventures. 1987. 19.95 (*0-8306-0462-6*, 2862); pap. 12.95 (*0-8306-2862-2*) TAB Bks.

— Jet: Eighty-Two Challenging New Adventures. 1987. pap. 12.95 (*0-8306-2872-X*) TAB Bks.

Prochnow, Herbert V. American Financial Institutions. LC 76-128290. (Essay Index Reprint Ser.). 1977. 47.95 (*0-8369-2017-1*) Ayer.

— Eighteen Hundred Quips & Illustrations for All Occasions. (Prochnow Speaker's Library). 320p. 1995. reprint ed. pap. 11.99 (*0-8010-7146-1*) Baker Bk.

— Four Hundred Illustrations for Ministers & Teachers. (Prochnow Speaker's Library). 144p. 1995. pap. 8.99 (*0-8010-7148-8*) Baker Bk.

— Fourteen Hundred Ideas for Speakers & Toastmasters. (Prochnow Speaker's Library). 160p. 1995. reprint ed. pap. 8.99 (*0-8010-7143-7*) Baker Bk.

— Inspirational Thoughts on the Beatitudes. (Herbert V. Prochnow Inspirational Library). 76p. 1995. reprint ed. mass mkt. 5.99 (*0-8010-7149-6*) Baker Bk.

— Inspirational Thoughts on the Lord's Prayer. (Herbert V. Prochnow Inspirational Library). 74p. 1995. reprint ed. mass mkt. 5.99 (*0-8010-7151-8*) Baker Bk.

— Inspirational Thoughts on the Ten Commandments. (Herbert V. Prochnow Inspirational Library). 88p. 1995. reprint ed. mass mkt. 5.99 (*0-8010-7152-6*) Baker Bk.

— One Thousand Stories & Illustrations for All Occasions. (Prochnow Speaker's Library). 224p. 1995. reprint ed. pap. 9.99 (*0-8010-7144-5*) Baker Bk.

— One Thousand Tips & Quips for Speakers & Toastmasters. LC 62-19654. (Speakers & Toastmasters Library). 144p. 1991. reprint ed. pap. 6.99 (*0-8010-6895-9*) Baker Bk.

— Seven Hundred Illustrations & Ideas for Speakers. (Prochnow Speaker's Library). 168p. 1995. reprint ed. pap. 8.99 (*0-8010-7145-3*) Baker Bk.

— Speaker's & Toastmaster's Handbook. 352p. 1992. pap. 14.95 (*1-55958-146-8*) Prima Pub.

— The Speaker's Treasury of Stories for All Occasions. 344p. 1982. 16.95 (*0-685-05562-0*) P-H.

— A Treasury of Inspiration: Illustrations, Quotations, Poems, & Selections. LC 58-12417. (Speakers & Toastmasters Library). (Illus.). 120p. 1991. reprint ed. pap. 6.99 (*0-8010-6868-1*) Baker Bk.

Prochnow, Herbert V., ed. Great Stories from Great Lives. LC 77-111858. (Essay Index Reprint Ser.). 1977. 29.95 (*0-8369-2018-X*) Ayer.

Prochnow, Herbert V. & Prochnow, Herbert V., Jr. Five Thousand One Hundred Quotations for Speakers & Writers. 640p. 1992. reprint ed. pap. 24.99 (*0-8010-7121-6*) Baker Bk.

Prochnow, Herbert V., Jr., jt. auth. see Prochnow, Herbert V.

Prochnow, Kathy & Prochnow, Dave. The Art of Fine Furniture Building: A Guide to Designing, Constructing, & Finishing High Quality Furniture. (Illus.). 176p. (Orig.). 1993. pap. 16.95 (*1-55870-282-2*) Betterway Bks.

Prochnow, Kathy, jt. auth. see Prochnow, Dave.

Prochnow, Peter-Michael. Staat Im Wachstum Versucheiner Finanzwirthschaftlichen Analyse der Preussischen Haushaltsrechnungen, 1871-1913, 2 vols. Bruchey, Stuart, ed. LC 80-2825. (Dissertations in European Economic History Ser.). (Illus.). 1981. lib. bdg. 35.95 (*0-405-14009-6*) Ayer.

Prochorov, A. M. Dictionary of Micro-Electronics. (DUT, ENG, FRE, GER & RUS.). 150.00 (*0-8288-9438-8*) Fr & Eur.

— Encyclopedia Dictionary of Physics. 928p. (RUS.). 1983. 85.00 (*0-8288-2240-9*, M15362) Fr & Eur.

Procidano, Mary & Fisher, Celia B. Contemporary Families: A Handbook for School Professionals. 336p. (C). 1992. text ed. 26.00 (*0-8077-3166-8*) Tchrs Coll.

Proclus. Elements of Theology, or Divine Arithmetic. Holmes, J. D., ed. Ionides, A., tr. 1993. 45.00 (*1-55818-204-7*, Pub. by Alexandrian Pr) Holmes Pub.

— Fragments of the Lost Writings of Proclus. 2nd ed. Robb, R. I., ed. Taylor, Thomas, tr. 128p. 1988. reprint ed. 13.00 (*0-913510-58-0*) Wizards.

— Proclus: A Commentary on the First Book of Euclid's "Elements" Morrow, Glenn R., tr. 402p. 1992. pap. text ed. 19.95 (*0-691-02090-6*) Princeton U Pr.

— Proclus' Commentary on Plato's "Parmenides" Morrow, Glenn R. & Dillon, John M., trs. 664p. 1992. pap. 24.95 (*0-691-02089-2*) Princeton U Pr.

Procope, J. F., ed. see Seneca.

Procopio, Richard, photos. Maine Scenes & Seasons. LC 92-81160. (Illus.). 72p. (Orig.). 1992. pap. 14.95 (*0-933050-95-X*) New Eng Pr VT.

Procopiow, Norma. Robert Lowell, the Poet & His Critics. LC 84-467. (Poet & His Critics Ser.). 352p. reprint ed. pap. 100.40 (*0-685-16242-7*, 2027726) Bks Demand.

Procopius. History of the Wars. Secret History, 7 vols. Incl. Vol. 1, Bks. 1 & 2. Persian War. 600p. 1914. 18.95 (*0-674-99054-4*); Vol. 2, Bks. 3 & 4. Vandalic War. 494p. 1916. 18.95 (*0-674-99090-0*); Vol. 3. Gothic War. 458p. 1919. 18.95 (*0-674-99119-2*); Vol. 4. Gothic War. 496p. 1924. 18.95 (*0-674-99191-5*); Vol. 5. Gothic War. 448p. 1928. 18.95 (*0-674-99239-3*); Vol. 6. Anecdota or Secret History. 406p. 1935. 18.95 (*0-674-99320-9*); Vol. 7. On Buildings; General Index. 562p. 1940. 18.95 (*0-674-99378-0*); (Loeb Classical Library: Nos. 48, 81, 107, 173, 217, 290, 343). write for info. (*0-318-53074-0*) HUP.

— Secret History. Atwater, Richard, tr. 1961. pap. 8.95 (*0-472-08728-2*, Ann Arbor Bks) U of Mich Pr.

Procopius, Serge, ed. The Bible for Americans. 103p. (Orig.). 1991. pap. 11.81 (*0-685-48278-2*) Dayspring Pr.

*__Procter.__ Nurses, Computers & Information Technology. 118p. 1992. pap. 34.95 (*1-56593-019-3*, 0262) Singular Publishing.

Procter & Gamble Educational Services Staff. The How to Clean Handbook. LC 86-61512. 233p. (Orig.). 1986. pap. 5.95 (*0-938973-00-2*) Procter Gamble Educ.

Procter, Ben. Just One Riot: Episodes of Texas Rangers in the Twentieth Century. (Illus.). 192p. 1991. 18.95 (*0-89015-806-1*) Sunbelt Media.

Procter, Ben & McDonald, Archie P., eds. The Texas Heritage. 2nd ed. 366p. 1992. pap. text ed. write for info. (*0-88295-880-1*) Harlan Davidson.

Procter, Ben H. The Battle of the Alamo. LC 86-50749. (Illus.). 37p. 1986. pap. 5.95 (*0-87611-081-2*) Tex St Hist Assn.

Procter, Bryan W. Life of Edmund Kean, 2 Vols. in 1. LC 70-82840. 1972. reprint ed. 31.95 (*0-405-08864-7*, Pub. by Blom Pubns UK) Ayer.

Procter, David E. Enacting Political Culture: Rhetorical Transformations of Liberty Weekend 1986. LC 90-7462. (Praeger Series in Political Communication). 144p. 1990. text ed. 42.95 (*0-275-93489-6*, C3489, Praeger Pubs) Greenwood.

Procter, Evelyn S. Alfonso X of Castile, Patron of Literature & Learning. LC 80-10508. (Norman Macoll Lectures Ser.: 1949). vi, 149p. 1980. reprint ed. text ed. 35.00 (*0-313-22347-5*, PRAL, Greenwood Pr) Greenwood.

— Curia & Cortes in Leon & Castile, 1072-1295. LC 79-51750. (Cambridge Iberian & Latin American Studies). 336p. reprint ed. pap. 95.80 (*0-685-16165-X*, 2027259) Bks Demand.

Procter, Everett. Christian Controversy in Alexandria: Clement's Polemic Against the Basilideans & Valentinians. LC 93-37342. (AUS VII: Vol. 172). 136p. (C). 1995. text ed. 37.95 (*0-8204-2378-5*) P Lang Pubs.

Procter, George H. The Fisherman's Memorial & Record Book. (Illus.). 192p. 1989. reprint ed. lib. bdg. 39.00 (*0-8328-1397-4*) Higginson Bk Co.

Procter, Johanna, ed. see Jonson, Ben.

Procter, Margaret, jt. auth. see Cook, Michael.

Procter, Maurice. The Devil Was Handsome. large type ed. (Mystery Ser.). 1979. 15.95 (*0-7089-0259-6*) Ulverscroft.

— Devil's Due. large type ed. 1972. 12.00 (*0-85456-133-1*) Ulverscroft.

— The Dog Man. large type ed. 1972. 12.00 (*0-85456-091-2*) Ulverscroft.

Procter, Pam, jt. auth. see Schoen, Allen M.

Procter-Smith, Marjorie. In Her Own Rite: Constructing Feminist Liturgical Tradition. 160p. 1990. pap. 11.95 (*0-687-18790-7*) Abingdon.

— Shakerism & Feminism: Reflections on Women's Religion & the Early Shakers. (Illus.). 24p. 1991. pap. text ed. 4.95 (*0-937942-16-2*) Shaker Mus.

— Women in Shaker Community & Worship: A Feminist Analysis of Religious Symbolism. LC 85-13776. (Studies in Women & Religion: Vol. 16). 253p. 1985. lib. bdg. 89.95 (*0-88946-533-9*) E Mellen.

Procter, Sue, jt. ed. see Reed, Jan.

Procter, Thomas. Of the Knowledge & Conduct of Warres. LC 79-25921. (English Experience Ser.: No. 268). 96p. 1970. reprint ed. 13.00 (*90-221-0268-8*) Walter J Johnson.

— A Profitable Worke to This Whole Kingdome Concerning the Mending of All Highways, As Also for Waters & Iron Workes. LC 77-7425. (English Experience Ser.: No. 885). 1977. reprint ed. lib. bdg. 15.00 (*90-221-0885-6*) Walter J Johnson.

Proctor. Experience of Thucydides. 1980. pap. 39.95 (*0-85668-206-3*, Pub. by Aris & Phillips UK) David Brown.

PQ

An Asterisk (*) at the beginning of an entry indicates that the title is appearing in BIP for the first time.

Proctor, Alan. A Doreset Downs Walk. (C). 1988. pap. text ed. 29.00 (*0-904110-96-6*, Pub. by Thornhill Pr UK) St Mut.

— A Severn to Solent Walk. (C). 1988. pap. 35.00 (*0-904110-91-5*, Pub. by Thornhill Pr UK) St Mut.

— The Tyrol. (Visitor's Guides Ser.). (Illus.). 144p. (Orig.). 1986. pap. 8.95 (*0-935161-42-2*) Hunter NJ.

— The Wessex Way. (C). 1988. pap. 29.00 (*0-904110-83-4*, Pub. by Thornhill Pr UK) St Mut.

Proctor, Alexander P. Alexander Phimister Proctor, Sculptor in Buckskin: An Autobiography. Proctor, Hester E., ed. LC 77-108803. (Illus.). 281p. reprint ed. 80.10 (*0-8357-9716-3*, 2016251) Bks Demand.

***Proctor, Anne, et al.** Learning to Teach in the Primary Classroom. LC 94-25720. (Illus.). 208p. 1995. pap. 22.95 (*0-415-11065-3*, B4208, Routledge NY) Routledge.

Proctor, Arthur M. Safeguarding the School Board's Purchase of Architects' Working Drawings. LC 73-177168. (Columbia University. Teachers College. Contributions to Education Ser.: No. 474). reprint ed. 37.50 (*0-404-55474-1*) AMS Pr.

Proctor, Astrid, jt. auth. see Livesey, Rupert.

Proctor, Bruce. Chronic Progressive Deafness: Resume of World-Wide Publications 1952-1959. LC 63-19171. 758p. pap. 180.00 (*0-685-15701-6*, 2027661) Bks Demand.

— Surgical Anatomy of the Ear & Temporal Bone. (Illus.). 240p. 1989. text ed. 75.00 (*0-86577-295-9*) Thieme Med Pubs.

Proctor, C. R., ed. see Materials Handling Conference Staff.

Proctor, Candice E. Women, Equality & the French Revolution. LC 90-2963. (Contributions in Women's Studies: No. 115). 224p. 1990. text ed. 49.95 (*0-313-27245-X*, PWE, Greenwood Pr) Greenwood.

Proctor, Carol. The Dangerous Dandy. (Regency Romance Ser.). 224p. (Orig.). 1993. pap. 3.99 (*0-451-17359-7*, Sig) NAL-Dutton.

— A Dashing Widow. (Regency Romance Ser.). 224p. (Orig.). 1991. pap. 3.99 (*0-451-17042-3*, Sig) NAL-Dutton.

— Theodora's Dreadful Mistake. (Regency Romance Ser.). 224p. (Orig.). 1992. pap. 3.99 (*0-451-17351-1*, Sig) NAL-Dutton.

Proctor, Claude O. NTC's Multilingual Dictionary of American Sign Language. 1994. 49.95 (*0-8442-0731-4*) NTC Pub Grp.

Proctor, David. Music of the Sea. 140p. 1992. pap. 24.95 (*0-11-290520-X*, HM0520X, Pub. by HMSO UK) UNIPUB.

Proctor, Deborah M., jt. auth. see Turnbow, Gloria N.

Proctor, Dennis V., jt. auth. see Powell, Staccato.

***Proctor, Dorothy & Rosen, Fred.** Chameleon: The Lives of Dorothy Proctor from Street Criminal to International Special Agent. LC 94-66762. 304p. 1994. 22.95 (*0-88282-099-0*) New Horizon NJ.

Proctor, Elizabeth M. Front Street: A Journey into the Past. 2nd ed. Lane, Mary H., ed. (Illus.). 230p. 1986. 22.95 (*0-943104-07-6*) Serrell-Simons.

Proctor, Enola, jt. auth. see Davis, Larry.

Proctor, Frank. Growing Through an Effective Church School. 160p. (Orig.). 1990. pap. 9.99 (*0-8272-1235-6*) Chalice Pr.

Proctor, George A. Canadian Music of the Twentieth Century. LC 81-143054. (Illus.). 323p. reprint ed. pap. 92.10 (*0-7837-0531-X*, 2040859) Bks Demand.

Proctor, George R. Ferns of Puerto Rico & the Virgin Islands. LC 89-13193. (Memoirs Ser.: No. 53). (Illus.). 389p. 1989. text ed. 79.50 (*0-89327-341-4*) NY Botanical.

***Proctor, George W.** Enemies. 1994. mass mkt. 4.99 (*0-553-56912-0*) Bantam.

— Shadowman. 256p. 1980. pap. 1.95 (*0-449-14350-3*, GM) Fawcett.

Proctor, Henry. Perpetual Youth: An Occult & Historical Romance. 115p. 1993. reprint ed. spiral bd. 7.15 (*0-7873-0678-9*) Mokelumne.

Proctor, Henry H. Between Black & White. LC 79-173611. (Black Heritage Library Collection). 1977. reprint ed. 20.95 (*0-8369-8903-1*) Ayer.

Proctor, Hester E., ed. see Proctor, Alexander P.

Proctor, J. The Ecology of Areas with Serpentinized Rocks: A World Review. Roberts, B. A., ed. 440p. 1992. lib. bdg. 229.00 (*0-7923-0922-7*) Kluwer Ac.

— Mineral Nutrients in Tropical Forests & Savannah Ecosystems. 1990. 115.00 (*0-632-02559-X*) Blackwell Sci.

Proctor, Jesse H., ed. Islam & International Relations. LC 80-1914. 1981. reprint ed. 27.50 (*0-404-18969-5*) AMS Pr.

***Proctor, John M.** Viktor, Vodka, & Raw Fish: The Last Crossing of the U. S. S. R. LC 94-60891. (Illus.). 300p. (Orig.). 1994. pap. 19.95 (*0-9639519-4-7*) Whitewing Pr.

Proctor, Kate. Bittersweet Yesterdays. (Presents Ser.). 1994. mass mkt. 2.99 (*0-373-11710-8*, 1-11710-0) Harlequin Bks.

— Bittersweet Yesterdays. large type ed. (Romance Ser.). 1993. 17.95 (*0-263-13425-3*, Pub. by Mills & Boon Ltd UK) Chivers N Amer.

— Contract to Love. 1994. mass mkt. 2.99 (*0-373-11661-6*, 1-11661-5) Harlequin Bks.

— Prince of Darkness. 1995. mass mkt. 3.25 (*0-373-11767-1*, 1-11767-0) Harlequin Bks.

— A Temporary Affair. large type ed. 1994. 17.95 (*0-263-13654-X*, Pub. by Mills & Boon Ltd UK) Chivers N Amer.

***Proctor, M. R. & Gilbert, A. D., eds.** Lectures on Solar & Planetary Dynamos. (Publications of the Newton Institute: No. 2). (Illus.). 384p. (C). 1995. 69.95 (*0-521-46142-1*) Cambridge U Pr.

— Lectures on Solar & Planetary Dynamos. (Publications of the Newton Institute: No. 2). (Illus.). 384p. (C). 1995. pap. 29.95 (*0-521-46704-7*) Cambridge U Pr.

Proctor, M. R., jt. ed. see Fearn, D. R.

Proctor, M. R., et al, eds. Solar & Planetary Dynamos. (Publications of the Newton Institute). (Illus.). 366p. (C). 1994. 49.95 (*0-521-45470-0*) Cambridge U Pr.

Proctor, Maurine & Proctor, Scot. Light from the Dust. LC 93-72676. (Illus.). 208p. 1993. 25.99 (*0-87579-680-X*) Deseret Bk.

Proctor, Maurine J. & Proctor, Scot F. Source of the Light: A Witness & Testimony of Jesus Christ, the Savior & Redeemer of All. LC 92-27973. (Illus.). 208p. 1992. 39.95 (*0-87579-648-6*) Deseret Bk.

***Proctor, Mel.** Official Fan's Guide to the Fugitive. 1994. pap. 12.95 (*0-681-00754-0*) Longmeadow Pr.

Proctor, Mortimer R. The English University Novel: University of California Publications, No. 15, 1977. Metzger, Walter P., ed. LC 76-55197. (Academic Profession Ser.). 1977. reprint ed. lib. bdg. 20.95 (*0-405-10030-2*) Ayer.

Proctor, N. The U. K. Economy: An Integrated Approach. 150p. 1986. 39.00 (*1-85313-004-4*, Pub. by Checkmate Pubns UK) St Mut.

Proctor, Nigel, ed. The Aims of Primary Education & the National Curriculum. (Contemporary Analysis in Education Ser.). 220p. 1990. 70.00 (*1-85000-559-1*); pap. 33.00 (*1-85000-560-5*) Taylor & Francis.

Proctor, Noble. Garden Birds: How to Attract Birds to Your Garden. LC 85-24464. (Illus.). 160p. 1986. 21.95 (*0-87857-592-8*, 01-335-0) Rodale Pr Inc.

Proctor, Noble S. & Lynch, Patrick J. Bird Anatomy, No. 2: Avian Structure & Function. mac hd 75.00 (*0-300-05403-3*) Yale U Pr.

— Manual of Ornithology: Avian Structure & Function. LC 92-17066. (Illus.). 40p. (C). 1993. text ed. 40.00 (*0-300-05746-6*) Yale U Pr.

Proctor, Pam, jt. auth. see Raphael, Sally J.

***Proctor, Paul, ed.** The Cambridge International Dictionary of English. (Illus.). 1792p. (C). 1995. 24.95 (*0-521-48236-4*) Cambridge U Pr.

— The Cambridge International Dictionary of English. 1995. pap. 22.95 (*0-521-48469-3*) Cambridge U Pr.

— The Cambridge International Dictionary of English. (Illus.). 1792p. (C). 1995. pap. 19.95 (*0-521-48421-9*) Cambridge U Pr.

— Longman Dictionary of Contemporary English. (Illus.). 1229p. (C). 1987. 25.95 (*0-582-84223-9*, 75140); pap. text ed. 38.44 (*0-582-84222-0*, 75139) Longman.

Proctor, Paul D. & Shirts, Morris A. Silver Sinners & Saints: A History of Old Silver Reef, Utah. (Illus.). 225p. (Orig.). 1991. text ed. 19.95 (*0-9625042-1-1*); pap. text ed. 17.95 (*0-9625042-2-X*) Paulmar.

Proctor, Paul D., et al. Mineral-Rock Handbook. LC 89-205367. (Illus.). 272p. (Orig.). 1989. lib. bdg. 14.95 (*0-9625042-0-3*) Paulmar.

Proctor, R. W. & Reeve, T. G., eds. Stimulus-Response Compatibility: An Integrated Perspective. (Advances in Psychology Ser.: No. 65). 508p. 1990. 125.75 (*0-444-88092-5*, North Holland) Elsevier.

Proctor, R. W. & Weeks, D. J. The Goal of B. F. Skinner & Behavior Analysis. (Recent Research in Psychology Ser.). (Illus.). ix, 223p. 1991. pap. 33.00 (*0-387-97236-6*) Spr-Verlag.

Proctor, Raymond L. Hitler's Luftwaffe in the Spanish Civil War. LC 83-5526. (Contributions in Military History Ser.: No. 35). (Illus.). x, 289p. 1983. text ed. 37.50 (*0-313-22246-0*, PCC/, Greenwood Pr) Greenwood.

Proctor, Richard, jt. auth. see Hirschman, Robert.

Proctor, Richard, jt. ed. see Pipkin, Bernard.

Proctor, Richard A. Chance & Luck. 263p. 1974. reprint ed. spiral bd. 9.35 (*0-7873-0679-7*) Mokelumne.

— Wages & Wants of Science-Workers. 270p. 1970. reprint ed. 38.00 (*0-7146-1627-3*, Pub. by F Cass Pubs UK) Intl Spec Bk.

Proctor, Richard M. Principles of Pattern Design. 1990. pap. 8.95 (*0-486-26349-5*) Dover.

Proctor, Richard M. & Lew, Jennifer F. Surface Design for Fabric. LC 81-7420. (Illus.). 192p. 1984. pap. 24.95 (*0-295-96087-6*) U of Wash Pr.

— Surface Design for Fabric. rev. ed. (Illus.). 192p. 1995. pap. 24.95 (*0-295-97446-X*) U of Wash Pr.

Proctor, Rob. The Indoor Potted Bulb. LC 93-6663. (Illus.). 1993. write for info. (*0-671-87033-5*) S&S Trade.

— Indoor Potted Bulb: Decorative Container Gardening with Flowering Bulbs. (Illus.). 128p. 1993. 20.00 (*0-671-77951-6*) S&S Trade.

— The Outdoor Potted Bulb. LC 93-6664. (Illus.). 128p. 1993. 20.00 (*0-671-87034-3*) S&S Trade.

***Proctor, Rob, text.** Annuals & Bulbs. LC 95-13796. (Successful Organic Gardening Ser.). 1995. write for info. (*0-87596-669-1*) Rodale Pr Inc.

— Annuals & Bulbs. LC 95-13796. (Successful Organic Gardening Ser.). 1995. pap. write for info. (*0-87596-670-5*) Rodale Pr Inc.

Proctor, Robert. The Printing of Greek in the Fifteenth Century. (Monographs: No. 8). (Illus.). 222p. 1966. reprint ed. 50.70 (*0-685-66506-2*, 05101254, Pub. by Georg Olms GW) Lubrecht & Cramer.

Proctor, Robert E. Education's Great Amnesia: Reconsidering the Humanities from Petrarch to Freud with a Curriculum for Today's Students. LC 87-46002. 252p. 1988. 25.00 (*0-253-34925-7*) Ind U Pr.

Proctor, Robert N. Cancer Wars: How Politics Shapes What We Know & Don't Know about Cancer. 288p. 1995. 25.00 (*0-465-02756-3*) Basic.

— Racial Hygiene: Medicine under the Nazis. (Illus.). 496p. 1990. pap. text ed. 18.95 (*0-674-74578-7*) HUP.

— Value-Free Science? Purity & Power in Modern Knowledge. 331p. (C). 1991. 39.95 (*0-674-93170-X*) HUP.

***Proctor, Robert W. & Dutta, Addie.** Skill Acquisition & Human Performance. (Advanced Psychology Texts Ser.: Vol. 1). 400p. 1994. 48.00 (*0-8039-5010-1*) Sage.

Proctor, Robert W. & Van Zandt, Trisha. Human Factors in Simple & Complex Systems. LC 93-10148. 1993. text ed. write for info. (*0-205-13999-X*) Allyn.

Proctor, Roscoe. Black Workers & the Class Struggle. 40p. 1972. pap. 0.45 (*0-87898-078-4*) New Outlook.

Proctor, S., jt. auth. see Reed, J.

Proctor, Samuel. Eighteenth Century Florida & Its Borderlands. LC 74-31385. (Illus.). 173p. reprint ed. pap. 49.40 (*0-8357-6731-0*, 2035373) Bks Demand.

— Napoleon Bonaparte Broward: Florida's Fighting Democrat. 2nd ed. LC 92-39694. (Florida Sand Dollar Book Ser.). (Illus.). 416p. 1993. pap. 16.95 (*0-8130-1191-4*) U Press Fla.

Proctor, Samuel, ed. Eighteenth Century Florida & the Revolutionary South. LC 77-23576. (Papers of the Annual Bicentennial Symposium: No. 4). 1978. 15.95 (*0-8130-0584-1*) U Press Fla.

Proctor, Samuel, ed. see Bicentennial Symposium Staff.

Proctor, Samuel, ed. see Florida Technological University, Bicentennial Symposium Staff.

Proctor, Samuel, jt. ed. see Milanich, Jerald T.

Proctor, Samuel, et al, eds. Jews of the South: Selected Essays. LC 83-25060. viii, 131p. 1984. 12.95 (*0-86554-102-7*, H94) Mercer Univ Pr.

Proctor, Samuel D. Certain Sound of the Trumpet: Crafting a Sermon of Authority. 152p. 1994. pap. 12.00 (*0-8170-1202-8*) Judson.

— How Shall They Hear? Effective Preaching for Vital Faith. 112p. 1992. pap. 9.00 (*0-8170-1172-2*) Judson.

— Preaching about Crises in the Community. LC 87-17195. (Preaching about...Ser.). 132p. (Orig.). 1988. pap. 10.99 (*0-664-24084-4*, Westminster) Westminster John Knox.

— Samuel Proctor: My Moral Odyssey. 176p. 1989. pap. 12.00 (*0-8170-1151-X*) Judson.

Proctor, Samuel D. & Watley, William D. Sermons from the Black Pulpit. 128p. 1984. pap. 9.95 (*0-8170-1034-3*) Judson.

Proctor, Scot. Witness of the Light: A Photographic Journey in the Footsteps of the American Prophet, Joseph Smith. LC 91-71335. (Illus.). 208p. 1991. 39.95 (*0-87579-389-4*) Deseret Bk.

Proctor, Scot, jt. auth. see Proctor, Maurine.

Proctor, Scot F., jt. auth. see Proctor, Maurine J.

Proctor-Smith, Marjorie & Walton, Janet R., eds. Women at Worship: Interpretations of North American Diversity. 272p. (Orig.). 1993. pap. 18.99 (*0-664-25253-2*) Westminster John Knox.

Proctor, T. & LaTorre, D. R. Calculator Enhancement for Differential Equations. (Clemson Calculator Enhancement Ser.). 140p. (C). 1992. pap. text ed. 12.00 (*0-03-092730-7*) SCP.

Proctor, T. G. Calculator Enhancement for Differential Equations. 105p. (C). 1990. pap. text ed. 8.00 (*0-15-505673-5*) HB Coll Pubs.

Proctor, Thomas E. & Gosse, J. F. Printreading for Welders. (Illus.). 348p. 1992. 21.96 (*0-8269-3025-5*) Am Technical.

Proctor, Thomas E. & Mazur, G. A. Troubleshooting Electric Motors. (Illus.). 299p. 1993. 22.96 (*0-8269-1762-3*) Am Technical.

Proctor, Thomas E., jt. auth. see Mazur, Glen A.

Proctor, Thomas E., jt. auth. see Sundberg, E. W.

Proctor, Thomas H. The Banker's Dream: A Fiction - an Argument for the Free Coinage of Silver. LC 74-30648. (American Farmers & the Rise of Agribusiness Ser.). 1975. reprint ed. 24.95 (*0-405-06820-4*) Ayer.

***Proctor, Tony.** The Essence of Management Creativity. LC 95-12260. 1995. write for info. (*0-13-356536-X*) P-H.

Proctor, W. L. A Genealogy of the Descendants of Robert Proctor of Concord & Chelmsford, Mass., with Notes of Some Connected Families. (Illus.). 315p. 1989. reprint ed. lib. bdg. 56.50 (*0-8328-0996-9*); reprint ed. pap. 48.50 (*0-8328-0997-7*) Higginson Bk Co.

Proctor, Wesley, tr. see Meredith, Howard & Milan, Virginia E.

Proctor, William. The Terrible Speller. LC 93-21946. 1993. 15.00 (*0-688-09981-5*) Morrow.

Proctor, William, jt. auth. see Bellar, Sam.

Proctor, William, jt. auth. see Benna, R. Theodore.

Proctor, William, jt. auth. see Benson, Herbert.

Proctor, William, jt. auth. see Burkett, Larry.

Proctor, William, jt. auth. see Minear, Ralph E.

Proctor, William, jt. auth. see Minear, Ralph.

Proctor, William, jt. auth. see Podell, Richard N.

Proctor, William, jt. auth. see Robertson, Arthur K.

Proctor, William, jt. auth. see Seibert, Donald V.

Proctor, William, jt. auth. see Yoder, Jean.

Procyk, Oksana, et al. Famine in the Soviet Ukraine Nineteen Thirty-Two to Nineteen Thirty-Three. (College Library). (Illus.). 116p. 1986. pap. 12.95 (*0-674-29426-2*) HUP.

Prodan, M. & Gardiner, S. Forest Biometrics. LC 67-27489. 1968. 186.00 (*0-08-012441-0*, Pub. by Pergamon Repr UK) Franklin.

Prodano, Sylvio. Pension Funds: Investment & Performance. 180p. 1986. text ed. 56.95 (*0-566-00817-3*, Pub. by Avebury Pub UK) Ashgate Pub Co.

— Pension Funds: Investment & Performance. (C). 1987. 260.00 (*0-685-32702-7*, Pub. by Witherby & Co UK) St Mut.

Prodanov, Vasil & Stoyanova, Maria, eds. Morality & Public Life in a Time of Change: Bulgarian Philosophical Studies, I. LC 93-11927. (Cultural Heritage & Contemporary Change Series VI: Foundations of Moral Education,: Vol. IVA,6). 200p. (Orig.). 1994. 45.00 (*1-56518-054-2*); pap. 15.00 (*1-56518-055-0*) Coun Res Values.

Proddow, Penny, et al. Hollywood Jewels: Movies - Jewelry - Stars. (Illus.). 192p. 1992. 49.50 (*0-8109-3412-4*) Abrams.

Proden, Robert, jt. auth. see Honek, Walter.

Prodgers, Jeanette. The Only Good Bear Is a Dead Bear. LC 86-90513. 224p. 1986. pap. 9.95 (*0-934318-96-4*) Falcon Pr MT.

Prodhan, Bimal. Multinational Accounting: Segment Disclosure & Risk. (International Accounting Ser.). 320p. 1986. 55.00 (*0-7099-4010-6*, Pub. by Croom Helm UK) Routledge Chapman & Hall.

Prodhan, Bimal, jt. ed. see Prindle, Andreas R.

Prod'homme, J. G. Les Symphonies De Beethoven. 13th ed. LC 76-52485. (Music Reprint Ser.). (Illus.). (FRE.). 1977. reprint ed. lib. bdg. 55.00 (*0-306-70859-0*) Da Capo.

Prod'homme, J. G., ed. Ecrits de Musiciens. (Music Reprint Ser.). 455p. (FRE.). 1984. reprint ed. lib. bdg. 49.50 (*0-306-76246-3*) Da Capo.

Prod'Homme, Jacques G. Gluck. LC 76-43934. (Music & Theatre in France in the 17th & 18th Centuries Ser.). (FRE.). reprint ed. 49.50 (*0-404-60185-5*) AMS Pr.

— Nicolo Paganini. LC 74-24195. reprint ed. 29.50 (*0-404-13096-8*) AMS Pr.

Prodi, G., et al, eds. Cancer Metastasis: Biological & Biochemical Mechanisms & Clinical Aspects. (Advances in Experimental Medicine & Biology Ser.: Vol. 233). (Illus.). 504p. 1988. 125.00 (*0-306-42907-1*, Plenum Pr) Plenum.

Prodi, Giovanni, jt. auth. see Ambrosetti, Antonio.

Prodi, Paolo. The Papal Prince: One Body & Two Souls: The Papal Monarchy in Early Modern Europe. Haskins, Susan, tr. 320p. 1988. 69.95 (*0-521-32259-6*) Cambridge U Pr.

Prodsky, Joseph, ed. see Khodasevich, Vladislav.

Production Consulting & Construction Staff. Americans with Disabilities Act Compliance Evaluation Survey: A Do-It-Yourself Assessment. 237p. 1992. pap. 85.00 (*1-883337-29-1*) Ctr Energy Envir.

Products Finishing Staff. Electrocoat Conference Proceedings, 1992. 246p. (C). 1992. pap. text ed. 45.00 (*1-56990-074-4*) Hanser-Gardner.

— Electroless Nickel Conference Proceedings, 1993. 700p. (C). 1993. pap. text ed. 65.00 (*1-56990-075-2*) Hanser-Gardner.

— Electroless Nickel Conference Proceedings '91. 302p. (C). 1991. pap. text ed. 45.00 (*0-685-67268-9*) Hanser-Gardner.

— Pretreat Conference Proceedings, 1990. 347p. (C). 1990. pap. text ed. 45.00 (*1-56990-076-0*) Hanser-Gardner.

— Pretreat Conference Proceedings, 1993. 360p. (C). 1993. pap. text ed. 45.00 (*1-56990-077-9*) Hanser-Gardner.

— Qualifinish Conference Proceedings, 1993. 405p. (C). 1993. pap. text ed. 45.00 (*1-56990-078-7*) Hanser-Gardner.

— SprayPaint Conference Proceedings, 1993. 316p. (C). 1993. pap. text ed. 45.00 (*1-56990-079-5*) Hanser-Gardner.

Proefriedt, William A. How Teachers Learn: Toward a More Liberal Teacher Education. LC 94-8960. 168p. (C). 1994. text ed. 37.00 (*0-8077-3359-8*); pap. text ed. 16.95 (*0-8077-3358-X*) Tchrs Coll.

Proehl, Carl W. The Fourth Marine Division in World War II. (Elite Unit Ser.). (Illus.). 238p. 1988. reprint ed. 35.00 (*0-89839-116-4*) Battery Pr.

Proehl, Jean A. Adult Emergency Nursing Procedures. (Nursing-Health Science Ser.). 619p. (C). 1993. text ed. 49.95 (*0-86720-328-5*) Jones & Bartlett.

Proehl, Karl H. & Shupe, Barbara. Long Island Gazetteer. 300p. 1984. 34.95 (*0-935912-15-0*) LDA Pubs.

Proell, Wayne. High Efficiency Internal Combustion Engines. LC 92-75671. (Illus.). 512p. 1993. text ed. 200.00 (*0-9635505-1-9*) Cloud Hill.

— SuperCarnot Heat Engines. 439p. 1994. text ed. 200.00 (*0-9635505-0-0*) Cloud Hill.

Proes & Serena. Children of the Sun: The Great Aton Family. 240p. 1987. pap. 8.99 (*0-9639066-1-5*) Crystal Star.

— Eden Isles: A Journey Through Time & Space with Spirit Teachers & Guides. 130p. 1986. pap. 3.95 (*0-9639066-0-7*) Crystal Star.

***Proescholdt, Kevin & Rapson, Rip.** Boundary Waters: The Fight for the Boundary Waters Canoe Area. (Illus.). 160p. (Orig.). 1995. 12.95 (*0-87839-100-2*) North Star.

Proescholdt, Ludwig. On the Sources of Shakespeare's Midsummer Night's Dream. LC 72-977. reprint ed. 5.00 (*0-404-05137-5*) AMS Pr.

Proescholdt, Ludwig, jt. ed. see Warnke, Karl.

***Proethero, Walt.** The Hunting Adventures of Me & Joe. (Illus.). 220p. 1995. 22.50 (*1-57157-015-2*) Safari Pr.

Prof. Jones. The Basics of Lotto - Lottery. LC 91-70330. (Basics of Gambling Ser.). (Illus.). 48p. (Orig.). 1991. pap. 2.95 (*0-940685-18-3*, Gambling Res) Cardoza Pub.

— Winning Lotto for Everyday Players. LC 91-77143. (Illus.). 80p. (Orig.). 1992. pap. 6.95 (*0-940685-22-1*) Cardoza Pub.

Proface, Dom. College Men: Their Making & Unmaking. LC 67-26772. (Essay Index Reprint Ser.). 1977. 20.95 (*0-8369-0803-1*) Ayer.

Profatt, John. A Treatise on Trial by Jury: Including Questions of Law & Fact. With an Introductory Chapter on the Origin & History of Jury Trial. viii, 608p. 1986. reprint ed. lib. bdg. 47.50 (*0-8377-2506-2*) Rothman.

Profesonal Responsibility & Ethics Committee, Los Angeles County Bar Association Staff, ed. see Lamport, Stanley W.

Professional Builder & Remodeler Magazine Staff. Custom Creations Inc. 152p. Date not set. pap. 29.95 (*1-56056-004-5*) Cahners Pub.

Professional Builder Magazine. Luxury Homes Collection. 1994. pap. 24.95 (*1-55701-118-4*) P-H.

An Asterisk (*) at the beginning of an entry indicates that the title is appearing in BIP for the first time.

— Sunlight Designs. 1994. pap. 19.95 (1-55701-119-2) P-H.

Professional Concerns Committee NPM Director of Music Ministries Division Staff. Hiring a Director of Music: A Handbook & Guide. 34p. (Orig.). 1991. pap. 5.00 (0-912405-83-X) Pastoral Pr.

Professional Engineering Associates Inc. Staff, comp. Handbook of Underground Storage Tank Safety & Correction Technology. (Science Information Research Center Ser.). 196p. 1988. 67.00 (0-89116-824-9) Hemisp Pub.

Professional Golf Association Staff. The PGA Tour 1994: Official Media Guide of the PGA Tour. (Illus.). 384p. 1994. lib. bdg. 34.95 (1-880141-52-3); pap. 12.95 (1-880141-41-8) Triumph Bks.

Professional Instrument Courses, Inc. Staff, jt. auth. see Dogan, Peter.

***Professional Management & Marketing Staff.** Medical Practice Forms. 330p. (Orig.). 1995. disk, pap. 39.95 (0-07-600760-X); disk, pap. 39.95 (0-07-810163-8) Hlthcare Mgmt Grp.

Professional Picture Framers Association Staff. Art Print & Graphics Glossary. LC 85-155639. (Orig.). 1985. pap. 10.00 (0-88445-017-1) Prof Picture Frame.

***Professional Pub. Staff.** Engineer-in-Training Reference Manual. 8th ed. (Illus.). 1048p. 1992. 49.00 (0-912045-38-8) NACE Intl.

— Engineering Law, Design Liability, & Professional Ethics. 120p. 1983. 15.00 (0-932276-37-7) NACE Intl.

— Engineering Unit Conversions. 2nd ed. 160p. (C). 1991. 22.00 (0-912045-29-9) NACE Intl.

— Mini-Exams for the Engineer-in-Training Exam. 88p. 1990. 15.00 (0-922276-39-0) NACE Intl.

— Solutions Manual for the Engineer-in-Training Reference Manual: English Units. 8th ed. (Engineering Reference Manual Ser.). 256p. 1992. 18.00 (0-912045-39-6) NACE Intl.

***Professional Publications Editors & Davis, Michael W.** Engineering Your Job Search: A Job-Finding Resource for Engineering Professionals. LC 94-23515. 128p. (Orig.). 1995. pap. 12.95 (0-912045-81-7) Prof Pubns CA.

***Professional Publications Staff.** Engineering Law, Design Liability, & Professional Ethics. 1983. pap. 15.95 (0-912045-80-9) Prof Pubns CA.

Professional Report Editors & Kirk, John. Incorporating Your Business: The Complete Guide That Tells All You Should Know about Establishing & Operating a Small Corporation. 192p. 1986. reprint ed. pap. 12.95 (0-8092-5902-8) Contemp Bks.

***Professional Resources, Inc. Staff.** Preventing Sexual Harassment in the Workplace. 1994. ring bd. 99.95 (0-87425-979-7) Human Res Dev Pr.

Professional Ski Instructors of America, Inc. Staff. The American Teaching System: Alpine Skiing. 2nd ed. LC 92-61778. (Illus.). 1992. pap. 49.90 (1-882409-00-0); pap. 24.95 (0-685-61451-4) Prof Ski Instructors.

— The American Teaching System: Snowboard Skiing. LC 92-61802. (Illus.). (Orig.). 1992. pap. 35.90 (1-882409-01-9); pap. 17.95 (0-685-61452-2) Prof Ski Instructors.

Professional Symposium on Human Services & Professional Responsibility (2nd: 1968: San Francisco). Human Services & Social Work Responsibility: Papers. Richan, Willard C., ed. LC 72-108195. 382p. reprint ed. pap. 108.90 (0-317-55744-0, 2029276) Bks Demand.

Professional Translating Services, Inc. Staff, tr. see Lipcon, Charles R.

Professional Truck Driving Institute of America (PTDIA) Staff. Trucking: Tractor-Trailer Driver Handbook-Workbook. Martin, Marilyn, ed. 800p. 1993. teacher ed 99.95 (0-89262-428-0); pap. text ed. 39.95 (0-89262-426-4); 149.95 (0-89262-453-1) Career Pub.

Professor Emeritus. The Evolution of Culture Elements: A Small Step in Defense of Western Culture. 351p. 1991. 34.50 (0-685-49039-4) KABEL Pubs.

Professor You & Edgar. Video Recorders: Principles & Operation. 300p. 1992. pap. text ed. 55.00 (0-13-945890-5) P-H.

***Profet, Margie.** Protecting Your Baby-To Be: Preventing Birth Defects in the First Three Months of Pregnancy. 168p. 1995. write for info. (0-201-40768-X) Addison-Wesley.

Proffatt, John. Curiosities & Law of Wills. LC 89-85976. 236p. 1989. reprint ed. lib. bdg. 40.00 (0-89941-707-8, 306060) W S Hein.

Proffer, Carl & Proffer, Ellendea, eds. The Barsukov Triangle, the Two-Toned Blonde & Other Stories. LC 84-387. 360p. 1984. 29.50 (0-88233-805-6) Ardis Pubs.

Proffer, Carl, tr. see Akhmatova, Anna.

Proffer, Carl, tr. see Sokolov, Sasha.

Proffer, Carl, et al, eds. Russian Literature of the Twenties: An Anthology. 480p. 1987. 39.50 (0-88233-820-X); pap. 22.95 (0-88233-821-8) Ardis Pubs.

Proffer, Carl R. Widows of Russia. 1992. pap. 12.00 (0-679-74262-X, Vin) Random.

Proffer, Carl R., comp. Nineteenth-Century Russian Literature in English: A Bibliography of Criticism & Translations. (Illus.). 260p. 1990. 49.50 (0-88233-943-5) Ardis Pubs.

Proffer, Carl R., ed. From Karamzin to Bunin: An Anthology of Russian Short Stories. LC 79-85097. 480p. 1969. pap. 13.95 (0-253-32506-4) Ind U Pr.

— Russian Romantic Prose: An Anthology. (Illus.). 1979. 17.50 (0-931556-00-7) Translation Pr.

Proffer, Carl R., tr. see Bulgakov, Mikhail.

Proffer, Ellendea, ed. A Pictorial Biography of M. Bulgakov - Fotobiografiia M. Bulgakova. 140p. 1984. pap. 15.00 (0-88233-813-7) Ardis Pubs.

— Vladimir Nabokov: A Pictorial Biography. (Illus.). 1991. 39.95 (0-87501-078-4) Ardis Pubs.

Proffer, Ellendea, ed. see Bulgakov, Mikhail.

Proffer, Ellendea, tr. see Bulgakov, Mikhail.

Proffer, Ellendea, ed. see Bulgakov, Mikhail.

Proffer, Ellendea, jt. ed. see Proffer, Carl.

Proffer, Ellendea C., ed. Marina Tsvetaeva: A Pictorial Biography. (Illus.). 1980. pap. 15.95 (0-88233-359-3) Ardis Pubs.

Proffit & White. Surgical-Orthodontic Treatment: A Contemporary Synthesis. (Illus.). 752p. 1990. 189.00 (0-8016-5291-X) Mosby Yr Bk.

***Proffit, Brian.** OS 2.2 Workplace Shell Survival Kit, Set. 1995. disk 19.95 (0-201-40915-1) Addison-Wesley.

Proffit, William R., et al. Contemporary Orthodontics. 2nd ed. LC 92-22056. 668p. 1992. 63.95 (0-8016-6393-8) Mosby Yr Bk.

Proffitt, Bettina, tr. see Hutchinson, Hanna.

Proffitt, Dennis. General Psychology Reader. 256p. (C). 1993. per. 28.75 (0-8403-8859-4) Kendall-Hunt.

Proffitt, Edward. Instructor's Manual for The Organized Writer: A Brief Rhetoric. 191p. (C). 1992. teacher ed, pap. text ed. write for info. (1-55934-129-7) Mayfield Pub.

— The Organized Writer: A Brief Rhetoric. LC 91-36782. 191p. (C). 1992. pap. text ed. 20.95 (1-55934-118-1) Mayfield Pub.

— Prose in Brief: Reading & Writing Essays. 512p. (C). 1990. pap. text ed. 20.00 (0-15-572262-X) HB Coll Pubs.

— Reading & Writing about Literature: Fiction, Poetry, Drama, & the Essay. 1030p. (C). 1990. pap. text ed. 28. 00 (0-15-575526-9); pap. text ed. 2.00 (0-15-575527-7) HB Coll Pubs.

— Reading & Writing about Short Fiction. 605p. (C). 1988. pap. text ed. 18.75 (0-15-575520-X); pap. text ed. 2.75 (0-15-575521-8) HB Coll Pubs.

***Proffitt, Mark A. & Yang, Chen-Jui.** A Story of Innovation: The Alexian Village Health Center, Milwaukee. (Illus.). xi, 75p. (C). 1995. 15.00 (0-938744-86-0, R94-5) U of Wis Ctr Arch-Urban.

Proffitt, Nicholas. Gardens of Stone. rev. ed. 446p. 1987. pap. 4.50 (0-88184-312-1) Carroll & Graf.

Proffitt, Ray, jt. ed. see Glennon, Eric.

Proffitt, T. D., III. Tijuana: The History of a Mexican Metropolis. abr. ed. 426p. (C). 1993. lib. bdg. 66.00 (1-879691-01-9); pap. text ed. 29.50 (0-916304-90-6) SDSU Press.

Profile Corporation Staff. Buckle down! on Ohio Writing: Student Workbook. 88p. 1994. 30.00 (0-7836-1313-X, BD21) Profiles Corp.

Profiles Corporation. Buckle down! on Ohio Reading: Workbook & Diagnostic Tests. (Illus.). 168p. 1994. 35. 00 (0-7836-1316-4, BD15) Profiles Corp.

Profiles Corporation Staff. Buckle down! on American Citizenship: Student Text. 2nd ed. (Illus.). 73p. (YA). (gr. 7-12). 1992. pap. text ed. 30.00 (0-7836-1302-4, ST BD01) Profiles Corp.

— Buckle down! on American Citizenship: Teacher's Guide. 2nd ed. (Illus.). 73p. (YA). (gr. 7-12). 1992. Grades 7-12. 14.00 (0-7836-1303-2, ST BD02) Profiles Corp.

— Buckle down on Ohio Mathematics: Student Workbook. (Illus.). 120p. (Orig.). (YA). (gr. 7-12). 1992. 30.00 (0-7836-1246-X, ST BD51) Profiles Corp.

— Buckle down on Ohio Mathematics: Teacher's Guide. (Illus.). 120p. (Orig.). (YA). (gr. 7-12). 1992. 40.00 (0-7836-1248-6, ST BD52) Profiles Corp.

— Inside the SAT. (Illus.). 80p. (YA). (gr. 11-12). 1992. student ed 15.95 (0-7836-1306-7, 2103) Profiles Corp.

Profilet, Cynthia. Kamal's Quest. (Illus.). 40p. (J). (gr. 5-6). 1993. 15.95 (0-9637735-0-X) Sterling Pr MS.

***Profillidis, Vassilios.** Railway Engineering. 304p. 1995. boxed, pap. 59.95 (0-291-39828-6) Avebury Technical UK.

Profio, A. Edward. Biomedical Engineering. LC 92-27830. 296p. 1993. text ed. 79.95 (0-471-57768-5) Wiley.

— Radiation Shielding & Dosimetry. LC 78-15649. (Illus.). 557p. reprint ed. pap. 159.40 (0-685-23828-8, 2056609) Bks Demand.

Profit, Vera B. Ein Portrat Meiner Selbst: Karl Krolow's Autobiographical Poems (1945-1958) & Their French Sources. LC 90-22033. (American University Studies: Germanic Languages & Literature: Ser. I, Vol. 74). 214p. (C). 1991. text ed. 37.95 (0-8204-0851-4) P Lang Pubs.

Profor. Initiation to Building & Public Works Vocabulary: Initiation au Vocabulaire du Batiment et des Travaux Publics. 176p. (FRE.). 1979. 65.50 (0-8288-4812-2, M6467) Fr & Eur.

Profos, P. Dictionary - Lexicon of Industrial Measurement. 417p. (GER.). 1986. spiral bd. 95.00 (0-8288-7941-9) Fr & Eur.

***Proft, R. J., ed.** United States of America's Congressional Medal of Honor Recipients: And Their Official Citations. rev. ed. (Illus.). 3p. 1994. 29.95 (0-9644590-0-0) Highland House.

Proga, Rosanne. Arithmetic & Algebra. 3rd ed. 688p. 1992. pap. 49.95 (0-534-92997-4) PWS Pubs.

— Basic Mathematics. 4th ed. LC 94-25641. 560p. 1995. text ed. 48.95 (0-534-94548-1) PWS Pubs.

Progelhof, R. C. & Throne, James L. Polymer Engineering Principles: Properties, Processes, & Tests for Designs. LC 92-26915. 1993. write for info. (0-19-520977-X) OUP.

Progelhof, Richard C. & Throne, James L. Polymer Engineering Principles. 720p. (C). 1992. text ed. 149.00 (1-56990-081-7); pap. text ed. 68.00 (1-56990-080-9) Hanser-Gardner.

Progelhoff, Richard C. & Throne, James L. Polymer Engineering Principles: Properties, Processes, & Tests for Design. LC 93-34614. 720p. (C). 1993. text ed. 68.00 (1-56990-150-3); pap. text ed. write for info. (1-56990-151-1) Hanser-Gardner.

Progoff, Ira. At a Journal Workshop: The Basic Text & Guide for Using the Intensive Journal Process. LC 75-13932. 320p. 1975. pap. 15.95 (0-87941-006-X) Dialogue Hse.

— At a Journal Workshop: Writing to Access the Power of the Unconscious & Evoke Creative Ability. rev. ed. 432p. (Orig.). 1992. pap. 15.95 (0-87477-638-4) J P Tarcher.

— Dynamics of Hope: Perspectives of Process in Anxiety & Creativity, Imagery & Dreams. LC 85-16236. 265p. (Orig.). 1985. pap. 9.95 (0-87941-013-2) Dialogue Hse.

— Jung's Psychology & Its Social Meaning: A Comprehensive Statement of C. G. Jung's Psychological Theories & an Interpretation of Their Significance for the Social Sciences. 3rd ed. LC 85-25406. 300p. 1985. 8.95 (0-87941-014-0) Dialogue Hse.

— Life-Study: Experiencing Creative Lives by the Intensive Journal Method. LC 83-72877. 302p. (Orig.). 1983. pap. text ed. 9.95 (0-87941-012-4) Dialogue Hse.

— The Practice of Process Meditation: The Intensive Journal Way to Spiritual Experience. LC 80-68847. 343p. 1980. pap. 15.95 (0-87941-008-6) Dialogue Hse.

— The Star-Cross. enl. ed. LC 70-176111. (Entrance Meditation Ser.). 125p. 1983. audio 12.50 (0-685-01459-2) Dialogue Hse.

— The Star-Cross. 3rd enl. ed. LC 70-176111. (Entrance Meditation Ser.). 125p. 1983. pap. 3.95 (0-87941-001-9) Dialogue Hse.

— Well & the Cathedral. 5th ed. LC 76-20823. (Entrance Meditation Ser.). 166p. 1983. 4.95 (0-685-10571-7); pap. 12.50 (0-87941-005-1) Dialogue Hse.

— The White Robed Monk. enl. rev. ed. LC 79-1553. (Entrance Meditation Ser.). 111p. 1983. pap. 12.50 (0-685-01460-6) Dialogue Hse.

— The White Robed Monk. 3rd enl. rev. ed. LC 79-1553. (Entrance Meditation Ser.). 111p. 1983. pap. 3.95 (0-87941-007-8) Dialogue Hse.

Progovac, Ljiljana. Negative & Positive Polarity: A Binding Approach. (Cambridge Studies in Linguistics: No. 68). 232p. (C). 1994. 44.95 (0-521-44480-2) Cambridge U Pr.

***Program Committee for the Comittee for Economic Development.** Prescription for Progress: The Uruguay Round in the New Global Economy: Version of July 7, 1994. LC 94-34588. 1994. 10.00 (0-87186-118-6) Comm Econ Dev.

Program for Art on Film Joint Venture Staff. Art on Screen: A Directory of Films & Videos on the Visual Arts. (Illus.). 350p. (C). 1992. text ed. 65.00 (0-8161-7294-3); pap. text ed. 35.00 (0-8161-0538-3) G K Hall.

***Programming Staff & Marchuk.** Building Internet Applications with Visual Basic. (Illus.). 480p. (Orig.). 1995. pap. 39.99 (0-7897-0214-2) Que.

Progress in Mathematics. Progress in Mathematics, Vol. 2. Gamkrelidze, R. V., ed. LC 67-27902. 169p. (RUS.). reprint ed. pap. 48.20 (0-685-15818-7, 2026305) Bks Demand.

***Progress in Pesticide Biochemistry & Toxicology Staff.** Progress in Pesticide Biochemistry & Toxicology Vol. 2. fac. ed. LC 80-41419. (Wiley-Interscience Publication Ser.). (Illus.). 238p. Date not set. pap. 67.90 (0-7837-7379-X, 2043295) Bks Demand.

Progress in Powder Metallurgy Staff. Progress in Powder Metallurgy: Proceedings of the Twenty-Fourth Annual Powder Metallurgy Conference, Chicago, IL, April 22-25, 1968, Vol. 24. LC 79-18458. (Illus.). 96p. reprint ed. pap. 27.40 (0-7837-1559-5, 2041851) Bks Demand.

— Progress in Powder Metallurgy, 1960: Proceedings of the 16th Annual Meeting of the Metal Powder Industries Federation. LC 79-18458. (Progress in Powder Metallurgy Ser.: Vol. 16). (Illus.). 215p. reprint ed. pap. 61.30 (0-7837-1552-8, 2041845) Bks Demand.

Progress Publishers, Moscow Staff, ed. Fundamentals of Soviet Legislation of the U. S. S. R. & the Union Republics. 385p. (C). 1975. 27.00 (0-8464-0439-7) Beekman Pubs.

Progressive Education Association Staff. Social Frontier, Nineteen Thirty-Four to Nineteen Forty-Three: A Journal of Educational Criticism & Reconstruction, 5 Vols. LC 70-168564. 1971. reprint ed. 198.00 (0-405-03723-6) Ayer.

Progressive Media, Inc. Staff. Financial Aid Report with the Directory of Private Scholarships & Grants. 2nd ed. (Illus.). 333p. (Orig.). (C). 1993. pap. 24.95 (1-881199-25-8, Perpetual Pr) Progress Media.

— Now Hiring! The American Job Opportunity in Asia. 2nd ed. (Illus.). 140p. (Orig.). (C). 1993. pap. text ed. write for info. (1-881199-00-2) Progress Media.

Progressive Staff. Progressive Bengali English Dictionary. 1992. reprint ed. 29.95 (0-8288-8474-9) Fr & Eur.

— Progressive English - Bengali Dictionary. 1992. reprint ed. 29.95 (0-8288-8475-7) Fr & Eur.

Progris. Baroque with That Jazz Feeling. 1990. 5.95 (0-685-32165-7, K742) Hansen Ed Mus.

— Go Baroque with That Jazz Feeling. 1990. 5.95 (0-685-47128-4, K743) Hansen Ed Mus.

— The Heart of Dixieland: Tenor Saxophone. 1990. 4.95 (0-685-32215-7, B083) Hansen Ed Mus.

— The Heart of Jazz. 1990. 4.95 (0-685-32173-8, B137) Hansen Ed Mus.

— The Heart of Jazz: Alto Saxophone. 1990. 4.95 (0-685-32209-2, B139) Hansen Ed Mus.

— The Heart of Jazz: Tenor Saxophone. 1990. 4.95 (0-685-32214-9, B140) Hansen Ed Mus.

Progris, jt. auth. see Dentato.

Progris, jt. auth. see Lee.

Prohaska, Elizabeth. Trivial Pursuit - Science (Primary) (Illus.). 64p. (J). (gr. 1-3). 1992. 12.95 (0-86653-647-7, GA1385) Good Apple.

Prohaska, Mark, jt. auth. see Scogin, Forrest.

Prohaska, S. Cultural Heritage Tourism. 1992. text ed. write for info. (0-442-00721-3) Van Nos Reinhold.

Prohle, Wilhelm. Vergleichende Syntax der Uralaltaischen (Turanischen) Sprachen. (Bibliotheca Nostratica Ser.: Vol. 4). 229p. 1978. pap. 26.00 (0-685-57925-5) Eurolingua.

— Vergleichende Syntax der Uralaltaischen (Turanischen) Sprachen. (Bibliotheca Nostratica Ser.: Vol. 4). 229p. 1978. 66.00 (3-447-02003-2) Eurolingua.

***Prohofsky, Earl.** Statistical Mechanics & Stability of Macromolecules: Application to Bond Disruption, Base Pair Separation, Melting, & Drug Dissociation of the DNA Double Helix. (Illus.). 275p. (C). 1994. write for info. (0-521-45184-1) Cambridge U Pr.

Prohorov, Yu. V. & Rozanov, J. A. Probability Theory: Basic Concepts, Limit Theorems, Random Processes. Krickeberg, K. & Urmitzer, H., trs. (Grundlehren der Mathematischen Wissenschaften Ser.: Vol. 157). (Illus.). 1969. 75.00 (0-387-04508-2) Spr-Verlag.

Prohorov, Yu. V. & Sazonov, V. V., eds. Bernoulli Society, U. S. S. R. Proceedings of the First World Congress, 1986, 2 vols., Set. 1690p. 1987. lib. bdg. 400.00 (90-6764-103-0, Pub. by VSP NE) Coronet Bks.

Prohorov, Yu. V., et al, eds. Probability Theory & Mathematical Statistics: Proceedings of the 4th Vilnius Conference, U. S. S. R., 1985, 2 Vols., Set. 1298p. 1986. lib. bdg. 317.50 (90-6764-069-7, Pub. by VSP NE) Coronet Bks.

Proietti, Gerald. Xenophon's Sparta: An Introduction. (Mnemosyne, Bibliotheca Classica Batava Ser.: Vol. 98). (Orig.). 1987. pap. 26.50 (90-04-08338-3) E J Brill.

Proimos, Jim. As a Cat Thinketh. (Illus.). 168p. (Orig.). 1994. pap. 5.95 (1-56245-089-1) Great Quotations.

Prois, Karyn, jt. auth. see Brown, James I.

Prois, Karyn S., jt. auth. see Brown, James I.

Project Adventure Inc Staff. Adventure Based Counseling Workshop Manual. 96p. 1994. spiral bd. 4.18 (0-8403-8511-0) Kendall-Hunt.

***Project Adventure Staff.** A-B Counseling Workshop. 144p. 1995. pap. text ed., spiral bd. 4.39 (0-614-06048-6) Kendall-Hunt.

— Adapted Adventure Activities: A Rehabilitation Model for Adventure Programming & Group Initiatives. 192p. (C). 1994. per., pap. text ed. 19.50 (0-8403-9812-3) Kendall-Hunt.

— Bridges to Accessibility. 144p. 1992. per. 12.00 (0-8403-7891-2) Kendall-Hunt.

Project Adventure Staff, jt. auth. see Fortier.

Project Air Force Desert Shield Assessment Team Staff. Project Air Force Assessment of Operation Desert Shield: The Buildup of Combat Power. LC 94-7952. 1994. 13.00 (0-8330-1521-4, MR-356) Rand Corp.

Project Care for Children Staff. Childhood Emergencies - What to Do: A Quick Reference Guide. (Illus.). 44p. (Orig.). 1989. pap. 13.95 (0-915950-93-6) Bull Pub.

Project Censored Staff, jt. auth. see Jensen, Carl.

Project for Public Spaces, Inc. Staff. Managing Downtown Public Spaces. LC 84-60857. (Illus.). 76p. (Orig.). 1984. pap. 24.95 (0-918286-33-6) Planners Pr.

Project Gen Staff, tr. see Nakazawa, Keiji.

Project Impact Staff. Child Sexual Abuse: Impact & Aftershocks. Freese, Sue, ed. 272p. (Orig.). 1989. pap. 19.95 (0-9622478-0-4) Project Impact.

***Project on Disney Staff.** Inside the Mouse: Work & Play at Disney World. LC 94-40192. (Post-Contemporary Interventions Ser.). (Illus.). 288p. 1995. lib. bdg. 47.95 (0-8223-1607-2); pap. 15.95 (0-8223-1624-2) Duke.

***Project Open Hand Staff.** Comforting Foods. LC 95-11422. 1995. write for info. (0-02-566401-8) Macmillan.

Project Scoresheet Staff & James, Bill. Bill James Presents the Great American Baseball Stat Book. LC 87-40610. 600p. 1988. pap. 14.95 (0-394-75925-7, Villard Bks) Random.

Project Squid Workshop on Combustion Measurement in Jet Propulsion System Staff. Combustion Measurements: Modern Techniques & Instrumentation Proceedings. Goulard, Robert J., ed. LC 76-25999. 495p. reprint ed. pap. 141.10 (0-317-08914-5, 2055326) Bks Demand.

***Projects Group Staff.** Prince & CA-Super Project. Date not set. pap. text ed. 100.00 (1-85554-380-X) Blackwell Pubs.

Prokasy, William F., ed. Classical Conditioning. LC 65-16466. (Century Psychology Ser.). (Illus.). 1965. 29.50 (0-89197-082-7) Irvington.

Prokes, Jaroslav, ed. see Zyvotko, Arkadii.

Prokes, M. Timothy. Women's Challenge: Ministry in the Flesh. 1969. pap. 4.95 (0-87193-006-4) Dimension Bks.

Prokes, Mary T. Mutuality: The Human Image of Trinitarian Love. 176p. (Orig.). 1994. pap. 12.95 (0-8091-3443-8) Paulist Pr.

Prokesch-Osten, Anton F. Denkwurdigkeiten und Erinnerungen Aus Dem Orient, 3 vols. lvi, 2080p. reprint ed. write for info. (0-318-71554-6, Pub. by Georg Olms GW) Lubrecht & Cramer.

Prokh, L. Z. Dictionary of Winds. 312p. (RUS.). 1983. 19. 95 (0-8288-1402-3, M15586) Fr & Eur.

Prokhorenko, V. Ya. & Fortov, V. E. Thermophysical Properties & Structure of Molten Metals under Extreme Conditions, Vol. 2. (Thermal Physics Ser.: Vol. 2, Pt. 2). 68p. 1989. pap. text ed. 46.00 (3-7186-4908-X) Gordon & Breach.

***Prokhoris, Sabine.** The Witch's Kitchen: Freud, "Faust" & the Transference. Goshgarian, G. M., tr. 200p. 1995. 39. 95x (0-8014-3043-7); pap. 16.95 (0-8014-8315-8) Cornell U Pr.

Prokhorov, A. Soviet Encyclopaedic Dictionary. 1600p. (RUS.). (C). 1981. 160.00 (0-685-46852-6, Pub. by Collets) St Mut.

PQ

Prokhorov, A., et al. Coherent Radiation Generation & Particle Accelerators. (Research Trends in Physics Ser.). 528p. 1992. 120.00 (0-88318-926-7) Am Inst Physics.

Prokhorov, A. M. Dictionary of Microelectronics: English, Russian, German, French, Dutch. 544p. (DUT, ENG, FRE, GER & RUS.). 1991. 95.00 (0-7859-1084-0, 5200006376) Fr & Eur.

— Encyclopedia of Physics. 1000p. 1990. 300.00 (0-89116-422-7) Begell Hse.

Prokhorov, A. M. & Kuz'minov, Yu S. Ferroelectric Crystals for Laser Radiation Control. (Optics & Optoelectronics Ser.). (Illus.). 468p. 1990. 191.00 (0-7503-0047-7) IOP Pub.

— Physics & Chemistry of Crystalline Lithium Niobate. (Optics & Optoelectronics Ser.). (Illus.). 392p. 1990. 166.00 (0-85274-002-6) IOP Pub.

Prokhorov, A. M. & Prokhorov, A. S. Problems in Solid-State Physics. 366p. 1984. 45.00 (0-317-46693-3, Pub. by Collets UK) Pro-Am Music.

Prokhorov, A. M. & Ursu, I., eds. Trends in Quantum Electronics: (September 1988, Bucharest, Romania) 569p. 1989. 84.00 (0-8194-0068-8, 1033) SPIE.

Prokhorov, A. M., et al. Laser Heating of Metals. (Optics & Optoelectronics Ser.). (Illus.). 260p. 1990. 114.00 (0-7503-0040-X) IOP Pub.

Prokhorov, A. S., jt. auth. see Prokhorov, A. M.

Prokhorov, B. Frunze, a Guide. (Illus.). 124p. (C). 1984. 40.00 (0-685-37527-7, Pub. by Collets) St Mut.

Prokhorov, Iu. Russian for Everybody: Background Reader. 176p. (C). 1983. 30.00 (0-317-92472-9, Pub. by Collets UK) Pro-Am Music.

Prokhorov, Yu V. & Skorohod, A. V. Probability Theory IV: Markov Processes. LC 92-27610. (Encyclopaedia of Mathematical Sciences Ser.: Vol. 46). 1993. write for info. (0-387-54688-X) Spr-Verlag.

Prokhorov, Yu V., jt. ed. see Watanabe, S.

Prokhovnik, Raia. Rhetoric & Philosophy in Hobbes's Leviathan. rev. ed. LC 91-10709. (Political Theory & Political Philosophy Ser.). 268p. 1991. 20.00 (0-8153-0142-1) Garland.

Prokhovnik, S. J. Light in Einstein's Universe: The Role of Energy in Cosmology & Relativity. LC 85-14183. 1985. lib. bdg. 91.50 (90-277-2093-2) Kluwer Ac.

Prokhovnik, S J. The Logic of Special Relativity. LC 67-13854. 142p. reprint ed. pap. 40.50 (0-317-08631-6, 2050785) Bks Demand.

Prokofieff, Sergei. Peter & the Wolf. (Tell Me a Story Ser.). (Illus.). 26p. (J). (ps). 1988. audio 9.95 (0-317-89541-9) Worlds Wonder.

Prokofiev, Oleg, ed. see Prokofiev, Sergei.

Prokofiev, Sergei. Four Orchestral Works. Roth, Lewis, ed. LC 73-87515. 448p. (Orig.). 1974. pap. 17.95 (0-486-20279-8) Dover.

— Peter & the Wolf. Carlson, Maria, tr. (Illus.). (J). (gr. 2-5). 1987. audio, pap. 14.95 (0-87499-073-4) Live Oak Media.

— Peter & the Wolf. Carlson, Maria, tr. (Picture Puffins Ser.). (Illus.). 32p. (J). (ps-3). 1986. pap. 4.99 (0-14-050633-0, Puffin) Puffin Bks.

— Peter & the Wolf. Crampton, Patricia, tr. LC 87-13915. (Illus.). (J). (ps up). 1991. pap. 13.95 (0-88708-049-9, Picture Book Studio) S&S Childrens.

— Peter & the Wolf. Crampton, Patricia, tr. LC 91-40185. (Pixies Miniature Reprint Ser.). (Illus.). 28p. (J). (gr. k up). 1992. reprint ed. pap. 4.95 (0-88708-226-2, Picture Book Studio) S&S Childrens.

— Peter & the Wolf, 4 bks., Set. Carlson, Maria, tr. (Illus.). (J). (gr. 2-5). 1987. student ed, audio 31.95 (0-87499-075-0) Live Oak Media.

— Peter & the Wolf Book Case. 1994. 19.95 (0-679-86156-4) Random.

— Peter & the Wolf Pop-up-Book. (Illus.). (J). (gr. k-12). 1986. pap. 17.00 (0-670-80849-0) Viking Child Bks.

— Soviet Diary 1927 & Other Writings. Prokofiev, Oleg & Palmer, Christopher, eds. 290p. 1992. text ed. 29.95 (1-55553-120-2) NE U Pr.

Prokofieva, Rose, tr. see Vigdorova, F.

Prokop, Ales & Bajpai, Rakesh K., eds. Recombinant DNA Technology I. LC 92-5973. (Annals Ser.: Vol. 646). 386p. 1992. pap. 115.00 (0-89766-674-7, TP248) NY Acad Sci.

Prokop, Ales, jt. ed. see Bajpai, Rakesh.

Prokop, Alexander D., jt. auth. see Volkwein, Jon C.

Prokop, Charles K. & Bradley, Laurence A., eds. Medical Psychology: Contributions to Behavioral Medicine. LC 80-1676. 1981. text ed. 66.00 (0-12-565960-1) Acad Pr.

Prokop, Dave, ed. The Dart Book. LC 77-85322. (Illus.). 109p. 1978. pap. 4.95 (0-89037-124-5) Anderson World.

Prokop, Friedrich W. Future Economic Significance of Large Lowgrade Copper & Nickel Deposits. (Mineral Deposits on Monograph Ser.: No. 13). (Illus.). 75p. 1975. text ed. 30.00 (3-443-12013-X, Pub. by Gebruder Borntraeger GW) Lubrecht & Cramer.

***Prokop, Irene.** 50 Best Places to Take Your Kids in New York. 1995. pap. 7.50 (1-885492-19-7) City & Co.

Prokop, M. S. Concentration, Relaxation & Academic Success: A Guide for Students. 1990. 9.95 (0-933879-35-0) Alegra Hse Pubs.

— Divorce, Confidence & Relaxation: A Guide for Kids. 1986. 9.95 (0-933879-31-8) Alegra Hse Pubs.

— The Divorce Group Counseling Program. 1987. 164.95 (0-933879-34-2) Alegra Hse Pubs.

— Kids' Confidence & Creativity Kit. 1988. 8.95 (0-933879-33-4) Alegra Hse Pubs.

— Prokop Divorce Adjustment Inventory. 1986. 8.40 (0-933879-30-X) Alegra Hse Pubs.

— Weight Loss Through Hypnosis. 1990. 9.95 (0-685-35655-8) Alegra Hse Pubs.

Prokop, Manfred. Learning Strategies for Second Language Users: An Analytical Appraisal with Case Studies. LC 88-39605. (Studies in Education: Vol. 2). 250p. 1989. lib. bdg. 89.95 (0-88946-937-7) E Mellen.

Prokop, Marian K. Managing to Be Green: An Environmental Primer. LC 92-30807. 86p. 1993. pap. 9.95 (0-88390-348-2) Pfeiffer & Co.

— Managing to Be Green: Help Your Organization Protect the Environment & Improve Profitability. rev. ed. Padgett, JoAnn, ed. LC 92-51086. 125p. 1993. pap. 9.95 (0-89384-203-6) Pfeiffer & Co.

Prokop, Michael S. Divorce Happens to the Nicest Kids: A Self-Help Book For Kids (3-15) & Adults. Peters, Robert C., ed. LC 85-72180. (Illus.). 224p. (Orig.). (J). (gr. k up). 1986. 18.95 (0-933879-25-3); 6.45 (0-933879-27-X); pap. 6.45 (0-933879-26-1) Alegra Hse Pubs.

Prokop, Phyllis S. Two Birds Flying. Goodman, Frances B., ed. (Illus.). 1984. 12.95 (0-89896-150-5) Larksdale.

Prokopchak, Mary, jt. auth. see Prokopchak, Steve.

Prokopchak, Steve & Prokopchak, Mary. Called Together: Building a Foundation for a Christian Marriage. 160p. 1992. pap. text ed. write for info. (0-9634951-0-0) S&M Prokopchak.

Prokopczyk, Czeslaw. Truth & Reality in Marx & Hegel: A Reassessment. LC 80-7976. 144p. 1980. lib. bdg. 22.50x (0-87023-306-7) U of Mass Pr.

Prokopenko, Joseph. Productivity Management: A Practical Handbook. xiv, 287p. (Orig.). 1992. pap. 32.00 (92-2-105901-4) Intl Labour Office.

Prokopenko, Joseph & Pavlin, Igor, eds. Entrepreneurship Development in Public Enterprises. (Management Development Ser.: No. 29). vi, 208p. 1991. pap. 22.00 (92-2-107286-X) Intl Labour Office.

— Entrepreneurship Development in Public Enterprises. (Illus.). 208p. 1991. 20.00 (92-9038-004-7, Pub. by Intl Ctr Pub Ent XV) Kumarian Pr.

Prokopenko, Joseph, jt. auth. see Kubr, Milan.

***Prokopetz, Andrew T.** Safety in the Chemistry & Biochemistry Laboratory. Picot, Andre et al, eds. Dodd, Robert H., tr. 1994. 9.95 (1-56081-040-8) VCH Pubs.

Prokopiw, Orysia, ed. see Teliha, Olena.

Prokopoff, Stephen. Marilyn Levine: A Decade of Ceramic Sculpture. (Illus.). 1981. 4.00 (0-910663-29-7) ICA Inc.

— Nathan Lerner: A Photographic Retrospective, 1932-1979. (Illus.). 1979. 3.00 (0-910663-21-1) ICA Inc.

— Northwest Visionaries. (Illus.). 1981. 3.00 (0-910663-31-9) ICA Inc.

Prokopoff, Stephen, frwd. Boston Now: Abstract Painting. (Illus.). 1981. 3.50 (0-910663-32-7) ICA Inc.

Prokopoff, Stephen, et al. Dream Vision: The Work of Arthur B. Davies. (Illus.). 1981. pap. 5.00 (0-910663-30-0) ICA Inc.

Prokopovich, N. N. Noun & Verb Government in Modern Russian. 188p. (C). 1981. 30.00 (0-317-92404-4, Pub. by Collets UK) Pro-Am Music.

Prokopp, Maria. Italian Trecento Influence on Murals in East Central Europe, Particularly Hungary. 200p. (C). 1983. text ed. 300.00 (0-569-08765-1, Pub. by Collets) St Mut.

Prokosch, Frederic. The Asiatics: A Novel. LC 70-138620. (Illus.). 371p. 1972. reprint ed. text ed. 62.50 (0-8371-5732-3, PRAS, Greenwood Pr) Greenwood.

— A Ballad of Love. LC 74-178787. 311p. 1972. reprint ed. text ed. 38.50 (0-8371-6287-4, PRBL, Greenwood Pr) Greenwood.

— The Idols of the Cave. LC 78-178788. 373p. 1973. reprint ed. text ed. 38.50 (0-8371-6289-0, PRIC, Greenwood Pr) Greenwood.

— Night of the Poor. LC 71-178789. 359p. 1972. reprint ed. text ed. 52.50 (0-8371-6288-2, PRNP, Greenwood Pr) Greenwood.

— A Tale for Midnight. LC 76-178790. 354p. 1973. reprint ed. text ed. 38.50 (0-8371-6281-5, PRTM, Greenwood Pr) Greenwood.

***Prokosh, Eric.** The Technology of Killing: A Military & Political History of Anti-Personnel Weapons. 256p. (C). 1995. text ed. 69.95 (1-85649-357-1, Pub. by Zed Books UK); pap. 29.95 (1-85649-358-X, Pub. by Zed Books UK) Humanities.

Prokoshin, D. A. & Vasil'eva, E. V. Alloys of Niobium. 352p. 1965. text ed. 88.50 (0-7065-0578-6, Pub. by Keter Pub IS) Coronet Bks.

Proksch, B., jt. auth. see Kaulbach, B.

Proksch, Reinhard, jt. ed. see Campbell, Dennis.

Prokunin, A. N., jt. auth. see Leonov, A. I.

Prokurat, Michael, tr. see Leskov, Nikolai.

Prolla, J. B. Approximation Theory & Functional Analysis. (Mathematical Studies: Vol. 35). 450p. 1979. 102.75 (0-444-85264-6, North Holland) Elsevier.

— Topics in Functional Analysis over Valued Decision Rings. (Mathematical Studies: Vol. 77). 302p. 1983. 72.00 (0-444-86535-7, I-466-82, North Holland) Elsevier.

***Prolman, Marilyn.** The Constitution. LC 94-35657. (Cornerstones of Freedom Ser.). (Illus.). 32p. (J). (gr. 3-6). 1995. lib. bdg. 12.30 (0-516-06692-7) Childrens.

— The Story of the Constitution. LC 69-14680. (Cornerstones of Freedom Bks.). (Illus.). 32p. (J). (gr. 3-6). 1969. lib. bdg. 12.30 (0-516-04605-5); pap. 3.95 (0-516-44605-3) Childrens.

Promack, Jennie. Seasons of the Moose. (Illus.). 128p. (Orig.). 1992. pap. 17.95 (0-87905-455-7, Peregrine Smith) Gibbs Smith Pub.

Prombaum, Ephraim H., tr. The Drama of Slavuta by Saul Moiseyevich Ginsburg. 172p. (C). 1991. lib. bdg. 34.00 (0-8191-8297-4) U Pr of Amer.

Promersberger, William J., et al. Modern Farm Power. 3rd ed. 1979. teacher ed write for info. (0-8359-4561-8, Reston) P-H.

Prometheus Research Library Staff, ed. Guidelines on the Organizational Structure of Communist Parties, on the Methods & Content of Their Work: Prometheus Research Ser., No. 1. 93p. 1993. 5.00 (0-9633828-3-7) Spartacist Pub.

Prometheus Research Library Staff, ed. see Norden, Jan.

***Prometric, Drake.** The Drake Guide to Technical Certification. LC 95-9204. 1995. pap. 24.95 (0-07-017949-2) McGraw.

— The Drake Guide to Technical Certification. LC 95-9204. 1995. write for info. (0-07-017948-4) McGraw.

Promey, Sally M. Spiritual Spectacles: Vision & Image in Mid-Nineteenth-Century Shakerism. LC 92-19337. (Religion in North America Ser.). 320p. (C). 1993. 35.00 (0-253-34614-2) Ind U Pr.

Promis, Jose. The Identity of Hispanoamerica: An Interpretation of Colonial Literature. Kelley, Alita & Kelley, Alec E., trs. LC 91-9979. 137p. 1991. 26.95 (0-8165-1251-5) U of Ariz Pr.

Promis, Jose & Roman-Lagunas, Jorge, eds. La Prosa Hispanoamericana: Evolucion y Antologia. LC 88-18742. 502p. (Orig.). (C). 1988. lib. bdg. 58.50 (0-8191-7098-4); pap. text ed. 35.75 (0-8191-7099-2) U Pr of Amer.

Promisel, N., jt. auth. see Jaffe, R. I.

Promotion Marketing Assn of America Staff. Winning with Promotion Power: 100 Best of the Best Promotions. 250p. 1994. 59.95 (0-85013-230-4, TE7609) Dartnell Corp.

***Promotional Reprint Company Staff.** The World Between the Wars. 1938p. 1995. write for info. (1-57215-090-4) World Pubns.

Pronath, Eleanor C. College Prep Reading II: Supplement. 144p. (C). 1990. per., pap. text ed. 12.95 (0-8403-6046-0) Kendall-Hunt.

Pronay, Nicholas & Cox, John, eds. The Crowland Chronicle Continuations 1459-1486. (Illus.). 2072p. 1993. text ed. 55.00 (0-948993-00-6) A Sutton Pub.

Prone, Terry. Irish Murders: The Shocking True Stories. (Illus.). 227p. 1993. pap. 11.95 (1-85371-139-X, Pub. by Wolfhound Pr IE) Dufour.

— Just a Few Words. 182p. 1989. pap. 9.95 (1-85371-031-8, Pub. by Poolbeg Pr IE) Dufour.

— Just a Few Words: Ways of Making You Talk. 140p. 1985. pap. 8.95 (0-7145-2844-7) M Boyars Pubs.

— Write & Get Paid for It. 198p. 1989. pap. 9.95 (1-85371-030-X, Pub. by Poolbeg Pr IE) Dufour.

Pronek, Neal. Land Hermit Crabs. (Illus.). 96p. 1989. 9.95 (0-86622-967-1, KW-098) TFH Pubns.

— Oscars. 1972. 9.95 (0-87666-765-5, PS-687) TFH Pubns.

Pronger, Brian. The Arena of Masculinity: Sports, Homosexuality, & the Meaning of Sex. (Stonewall Inn Editions Ser.). (Illus.). 320p. 1992. pap. 14.95 (0-312-06293-1) St Martin.

— Arena of Masculinity; Sports: Sports, Homosexuality, & the Meaning of Sex. 1990. 22.95 (0-312-05053-4) St Martin.

Pronin, Alex. Russian Vocabulary Builder, Seven Verbs a Day. (RUS.). 1971. 8.00 (0-87505-314-9) Borden.

Pronin, Barbara. Substitute Teaching: A Handbook for Hassle-Free Subbing. (Illus.). 241p. 1983. pap. 9.95 (0-312-77484-2) St Martin.

— Thicker Than Water. 1995. pap. 4.99 (0-440-21671-0) Dell.

— West Covina: Fulfilling the Promise. 1989. 29.95 (0-89781-291-3) Preferred Mktg.

Pronin, P. I. & Obukhov, Yu N., eds. Modern Problems of Theoretical Physics. 360p. (C). 1991. text ed. 101.00 (981-02-0259-8) World Scientific Pub.

Pronina, I. A. Decorative Art in the Academy of Arts. 312p. (RUS.). 1983. 60.00 (0-317-57303-9, Pub. by Collets UK) St Mut.

Pronk & Gorman. Soccer Everyone. 160p. 1991. pap. text ed. 12.95 (0-88725-137-4) Hunter Textbks.

Pronk, Cornelis, tr. see Bakker, Frans.

Pronk, Fredrika, tr. see Bakker, Frans.

Pronk, Mary, ed. see Pawczuk, Eugene.

***Pronk, Ron.** Power Mac Book! 1995. pap. 34.95 (1-883577-09-8) Coriolis Grp.

Pronk, Ron & Duntemann, Jeff. Inside the Power PC Revolution. 400p. (Orig.). 1994. pap. 24.95 (1-883577-04-7) Coriolis Grp.

Pronk, Ron & Weiskamp, Keith. DOS 6 Insider. 544p. 1993. pap. text ed. 26.95 (0-471-59394-X) Wiley.

Pronko, Leonard, jt. ed. see Fujita, Minoru.

Pronko, Leonard C. Avant Garde: The Experimental Theater in France. LC 77-26017. (Illus.). 225p. 1978. reprint ed. text ed. 38.50 (0-313-20096-3, PRAV, Greenwood Pr) Greenwood.

— Eugene Ionesco. LC 65-16380. (Columbia Essays on Modern Writers Ser.: No. 7). (Orig.). (C). 1965. pap. text ed. 7.50 (0-231-02681-1) Col U Pr.

Pronko, N. H. From AI to Zeitgeist: A Philosophical Guide for the Skeptical Psychologist. LC 87-14921. (Contributions in Psychology Ser.: No. 11). 288p. 1988. text ed. 55.00 (0-313-25888-0, PPT/, Greenwood Pr) Greenwood.

Pronsky, Zaneta M. Food-Medication Interactions. 8th ed. Epstein, Solomon et al, eds. LC 93-93999. 256p. (C). 1993. pap. text ed. 13.95 (0-9606164-4-6) FMI.

— Food-Medication Interactions. 9th ed. Epstein, Solomon et al, eds. 310p. (C). Date not set. pap. text ed. 16.45x (0-9606164-5-4) FMI.

Pronych, Peter M., jt. auth. see Christen, Arden G.

Pronzato, Allessandro. Meditations on the Sand. (C). 1988. 39.00 (0-85439-218-1, Pub. by St Paul Pubns UK) St Mut.

Pronzini, B., et al, eds. Manhattan Mysteries. 8.98 (0-517-63179-2) Random Hse Value.

Pronzini, Bill. Best Western Stories of Bill Pronzini. Greenberg, Martin M., ed. LC 89-21778. (Best Western Stories Ser.). 200p. 1990. 24.95 (0-8040-0932-5) Swallow.

— Best Western Stories of Bill Pronzini. LC 89-21778. (Best Western Stories of...Ser.). 200p. 1991. pap. 14.95 (0-8040-0933-3) Swallow.

— The Best Western Stories of Bill Pronzini. large type ed. Greenberg, Martin H., ed. (Nightingale Ser.). 287p. 1991. pap. 14.95 (0-8161-5115-6, Nightingale) Hall.

— Blue Lonesome. LC 95-13049. 1995. write for info. (0-8027-3268-2) Walker & Co.

— Blue Lonesome: An Evan Horne Mystery. LC 95-13048. 1995. write for info. (0-8027-3269-0) Walker & Co.

— Cattlemen. 1987. pap. 2.50 (0-449-13145-9) Fawcett.

— Child's Ploy. 1984. 16.95 (0-02-599250-3) Macmillan.

— Dead Run. (Mystery Scene Book Ser.). 194p. 1992. pap. 3.95 (0-88184-838-7) Carroll & Graf.

— Demons: A "Nameless Detective" Mystery. LC 92-40280. 1993. 19.95 (0-385-30505-2) Delacorte.

— Demons: A "Nameless Detective" Mystery. 1994. pap. 4.99 (0-440-21118-2) Dell.

— Epitaphs. large type ed. 372p. 1993. reprint ed. lib. bdg. 19.95 (1-56054-593-3) Thorndike Pr.

— Firewind. LC 88-33578. (Novel of the West Ser.). 180p. 1989. 14.95 (0-87131-555-6) M Evans.

— Great Tales of Horror & the Supernatural. 1988. 9.98 (0-88365-699-X) Galahad Bks.

— The Hangings. 192p. 1989. 17.95 (0-8027-4082-0) Walker & Co.

— Jackpot. large type ed. (General Ser.). 342p. 1991. lib. bdg. 19.95 (0-8161-5037-0, Large Print Bks) Hall.

— The Jade Figurine. 208p. 1991. pap. 3.95 (0-88184-773-9) Carroll & Graf.

— Masques. LC 86-72531. 272p. 1988. reprint ed. pap. 4.95 (0-88739-075-7, Blk Lizard) Creat Arts Bk.

— Snowbound. 256p. 1994. pap. 4.95 (0-7867-0108-0) Carroll & Graf.

— Son of Gun in Cheek. LC 87-7872. 192p. 1988. pap. 9.95 (0-89296-952-0) Mysterious Pr.

— Starvation Camp. LC 93-8123. (Mystery Scene Bks.). 192p. 1994. 25.00x (0-913960-24-1); pap. 8.95 (0-913960-25-X) Borgo Pr.

— With an Extreme Burning. 304p. 1994. 19.95 (0-7867-0139-0) Carroll & Graf.

— With an Extreme Burning. large type ed. LC 95-7489. 536p. 1995. 22.95 (0-7862-0460-5) Thorndike Pr.

Pronzini, Bill, ed. Great Tales of Mystery & Suspense. 1994. 9.98 (0-88365-700-7) Galahad Bks.

— Great Tales of the West. 1994. 10.98 (0-88365-702-3) Galahad Bks.

— More Wild Westerns. 192p. (J). 1989. 19.95 (0-8027-4097-9) Walker & Co.

— Wild Westerns. 192p. 1986. 14.95 (0-8027-4066-9) Walker & Co.

Pronzini, Bill & Greenberg, M. H. Mammoth Book of Private Eye Stories. 660p. 1988. pap. 9.95 (0-88184-430-6) Carroll & Graf.

Pronzini, Bill & Greenberg, Martin, eds. The Best Western Stories of Lewis B. Patten. large type ed. 336p. 1989. pap. 13.95 (0-8161-4781-7, Large Print Bks) Hall.

Pronzini, Bill & Greenberg, Martin H., eds. The Arizonans: The Best of the West, Vol. 3. large type ed. (General Ser.). 384p. 1990. 18.95 (0-8161-5049-4, Large Print Bks) G K Hall.

— The Best of the West II: More Stories That Inspired Classic Western Films. 224p. 1990. pap. 3.95 (0-317-02737-9, Sig) NAL-Dutton.

— The Best Western Stores of Ed Gorman. large type ed. 205p. 1995. 17.95 (0-7838-1283-3) Hall.

— The Best Western Stories of Ryerson Johnson. large type ed. 283p. 1995. reprint ed. pap. 18.95 (0-7838-1381-3) Hall.

— The Californians: The Best of the West. large type ed. 1990. 19.50 (0-8161-4975-5, Large Print Bks) Hall.

— Great Modern Police Stories. 192p. 1986. 15.95 (0-8027-0881-1); pap. 11.95 (0-8027-7291-9) Walker & Co.

— The Gunfighters: The Best of the West. large type ed. 400p. 1991. text ed. 19.95 (0-8161-5273-X) G K Hall.

— Uncollected Crimes. 224p. 1987. 15.95 (0-8027-0967-2); pap. 9.95 (0-8027-7304-4) Walker & Co.

Pronzini, Bill & Malzberg, Barry. The Running of Beasts. LC 86-72530. 320p. 1988. reprint ed. pap. 4.95 (0-88739-076-5, Blk Lizard) Creat Arts Bk.

Pronzini, Bill & Malzberg, Barry N. Acts of Mercy. 256p. 1985. reprint ed. pap. 2.95 (0-8439-2219-2) Dorchester Pub Co.

Pronzini, Bill & Wallmann, Jeffrey. Day of the Moon. 192p. 1993. pap. 3.95 (0-88184-976-6) Carroll & Graf.

Pronzini, Bill & Wilcox, Collin. Twospot. 272p. 1993. 4.95 (0-7867-0042-4) Carroll & Graf.

Pronzini, Bill, jt. ed. see Adrian, Jack C.

Pronzini, Bill, ed. see Bonham, Frank.

Pronzini, Bill, ed. see Estleman, Loren D.

Pronzini, Bill, ed. see Frazee, Steve.

Pronzini, Bill, ed. see Gorman, Ed.

Pronzini, Bill, ed. see Greenberg, Martin H.

Pronzini, Bill, jt. ed. see Greenberg, Martin H.

Pronzini, Bill, jt. ed. see Greenberg, Martin.

Pronzini, Bill, jt. ed. see Greenburg, Martin H.

Pronzini, Bill, ed. see Jakes, John.

Pronzini, Bill, ed. see Johnson, Ryerson.

Pronzini, Bill, jt. auth. see Muller, Marcia.

Pronzini, Bill, ed. see Overholser, Wayne D.

Pronzini, Bill, ed. see Patten, Lewis.

Pronzini, Bill, ed. see Savage, Les, Jr.

Proof Theory Symposium Staff. Proof Theory Symposium, Keil 1974: Proceedings. Muller, G. H. & Diller, J., eds. (Lecture Notes in Mathematics Ser.: Vol. 500). 1976. pap. 21.00 (0-387-07533-X) Spr-Verlag.

An Asterisk (*) at the beginning of an entry indicates that the title is appearing in BIP for the first time.

Proops, John L., jt. auth. see Faber, Malte.
Proops, John L., et al. Reducing CO B2 S Emissions: A Comparative Input-Output Study for Germany & the U. K. LC 92-34932. 1993. 98.00 (*0-387-55947-7*) Spr-Verlag.
Prop, G., jt. ed. see Parnham, Michael J.
***Proper.** Pheasants of the Mind. 1994. 25.00 (*1-885106-07-6*) Wild Adven Pr.
Proper, C. B. A. Social Elements in English Prose Fiction Between 1700 & 1832. LC 68-1013. 1970. reprint ed. 75.00 (*0-8383-0612-8*) M S G Haskell Hse.
***Proper, Datus.** Pheasants of the Mind: A Hunter's Search for a Mythic Bird. deluxe limited ed. (Illus.). 166p. 1995. 90.00 (*1-885106-08-4*) Wild Adven Pr.
— What the Trout Said. rev. ed. (Illus.). 280p. 1989. reprint ed. pap. 16.95 (*1-55821-187-X*) Lyons & Burford.
Proper, Datus C. The Last Old Place: A Search Through Portugal. LC 92-22628. 1993. 22.00 (*0-671-78226-6*) S&S Trade.
Proper, Emberson E. Colonial Immigration Laws. LC 04-2636. (Columbia University. Studies in the Social Sciences: No. 31). reprint ed. 31.50 (*0-404-51031-0*) AMS Pr.
Proper, Stan. And Justice for All. 24p. (Orig.). (C). 1988. pap. 2.00 (*0-9619992-1-7*) Walden Sudbury.
— And This Is What They Said. (Illus.). 24p. (Orig.). (C). 1988. pap. 2.00 (*0-9619992-0-9*) Walden Sudbury.
— Views of Spaceship Earth. 1985. 3.00 (*0-932593-02-X*) Black Bear.
Propert, W. A. Russian Ballet in Western Europe, 1909-1920. LC 72-86601. (Illus.). 1972. reprint ed. 36.95 (*0-405-08865-5*, Pub. by Blom Pubns UK) Ayer.
Propertius. Carmina. 2nd ed. Barber, E. A., ed. (Oxford Classical Texts Ser.). 1954. 18.95 (*0-19-814630-2*) OUP.
— Elegies, 3 bks. Camps, W. A., ed. 1977. pap. 18.95 (*0-521-29210-7*) Cambridge U Pr.
— The Poems. Shepherd, W. G., tr. (Classics Ser.). 240p. 1986. mass mkt. 9.95 (*0-14-044464-5*, Penguin Classics) Viking Penguin.
— Propertius: Elegies. Goold, G. P., ed. (Loeb Classical Library). 528p. 1990. text ed. 15.50 (*0-674-99020-X*) HUP.
— Propertius Elegies: Book IV. Connor, W. R. & Camps, W. A., eds. LC 78-67126. (Latin Texts & Commentaries Ser.). (ENG & LAT.). 1979. reprint ed. lib. bdg. 20.95 (*0-405-11597-0*) Ayer.
***Propertius, Sextus.** Charm. Katz, Vincent, tr. & intro. by. (Sun & Moon Classics Ser.: No. 89). 61p. (Orig.). 1995. pap. 11.95 (*1-55713-224-0*) Sun & Moon CA.
— The Poems: Translated with Explanatory Notes. Lee, Guy, tr. LC 93-42190. 256p. (C). 1994. 42.00 (*0-19-814497-0*, Clarendon Pr) OUP.
— Poems of Propertius. Watts, A. E., tr. 25.00 (*0-87556-244-2*) Saifer.
Propertius, Sextus A. Carmina. xxviii, 413p. 1973. reprint ed. write for info. (*3-487-04626-1*, Pub. by Georg Olms GW) Lubrecht & Cramer.
— Die Elegien, Bd. 1: Buch 1 & 2. Rothstein, Max, ed. vi, 500p. 1966. Bd. 1: Buch 1 und 2, vi, 500p. write for info. (*3-296-15151-6*, Pub. by Georg Olms GW) Lubrecht & Cramer.
— Die Elegien, Bd. 2: Buch 3 & 4. Rothstein, Max, ed. 418p. 1966. Bd. 2: Buch 3 und 4, 418p. write for info. (*3-296-15152-4*, Pub. by Georg Olms GW) Lubrecht & Cramer.
Propes, Steve & Gart, Galen. Recorded in Hollywood: The Glory Years of L.A. Doo-Wop. 200p. 1995. pap. write for info. (*0-936433-18-3*) Big Nickel.
Propes, Steve, jt. auth. see Dawson, Jim.
Propes, Steve, jt. auth. see Marsh, Dave.
Propher, John. The Councillor. (C). 1987. pap. 50.00 (*0-7219-0851-9*, Scientific) St Mut.
Prophet, Elizabeth C. Astrology of the Four Horsemen: How You Can Heal Yourself & Planet Earth. (Pocketbook Ser.). 640p. 1990. pap. 5.95 (*0-922729-06-9*) Summit Univ.
— La Ciencia de la Palabra Hablada. 262p. 1991. pap. write for info. (*0-318-71307-1*) Edic Gran Dir.
— La Ciencia de la Palabra Hablada. Garces, Soledad, tr. 262p. (SPA.). 1991. pap. write for info. (*1-883482-00-3*) Edic Gran Dir.
— Las Ensenanzas Perdidas de Jesus, 4 vols. Garces, Soledad, tr. (SPA.). pap. write for info. (*1-883482-01-1*) Edic Gran Dir.
— Ensenanzas Perdidas de Jesus, No. 2. 404p. 1990. pap. write for info. (*0-318-71309-8*) Edic Gran Dir.
— Ensenanzas Perdidas de Jesus, No.3. 446p. 1991. pap. write for info. (*0-318-71308-X*) Edic Gran Dir.
— Las Ensenanzas Perdidas de Jesus, Vol. I. Garces, Soledad, tr. 404p. (SPA.). 1990. pap. write for info. (*1-883482-02-X*) Edic Gran Dir.
— Las Ensenanzas Perdidas de Jesus, Vol. II. Garces, Soledad, tr. 404p. (SPA.). 1990. pap. write for info. (*1-883482-03-8*) Edic Gran Dir.
— Las Ensenanzas Perdidas de Jesus, Vol. III. Garces, Soledad, tr. 446p. (SPA.). 1991. pap. write for info. (*1-883482-04-6*) Edic Gran Dir.
— Ensenanzas Perdidas de Jesus One. 1988. pap. 8.95 (*0-922729-10-7*) Summit Univ.
— Ensenanzas Perdidas de Jesus Three. 1988. pap. 8.95 (*0-922729-12-3*) Summit Univ.
— Ensenanzas Perdidas de Jesus Two. 1988. pap. 8.95 (*0-685-65911-9*) Summit Univ.
— Ensenanzas Perdidas de Jseus, No. 1. 404p. 1990. pap. write for info. (*0-318-71310-1*) Edic Gran Dir.
— Forbidden Mysteries of Enoch: Fallen Angels & the Origins of Evil. LC 82-62445. (Illus.). 516p. 1983. pap. 14.95 (*0-916766-60-8*) Summit Univ.
— Great White Brotherhood in the Culture, History & Religion of America. LC 76-7635. (Illus.). 448p. (Orig.). 1976. pap. 10.95 (*0-916766-16-0*) Summit Univ.
— Handwriting on the Wall Bks I & II, Bk. I. 396p. 1986. 19.95 (*0-916766-83-7*) Summit Univ.
— Handwriting on the Wall Bks I & II, Bk. II. 392p. 1986. 19.95 (*0-916766-84-5*) Summit Univ.
— The Lost Years of Jesus. (Pocketbook Ser.). (Illus.). 480p. 1984. pap. 5.95 (*0-916766-87-X*) Summit Univ.
— The Lost Years of Jesus. (Illus.). 418p. 1984. pap. 14.95 (*0-916766-61-6*) Summit Univ.
— The Lost Years of Jesus. LC 81-52784. (Illus.). 418p. 1986. 19.95 (*0-916766-79-9*) Summit Univ.
— Saint Germain: Prophecy to the Nations, Bk. I. 594p. 1988. 24.95 (*0-922729-00-X*) Summit Univ.
— Saint Germain: Prophecy to the Nations, Bk. II. 680p. 1988. 24.95 (*0-922729-01-8*) Summit Univ.
— Sanat Kumara on the Path of the Ruby Ray: The Opening of the Seventh Seal. 316p. 1987. 19.95 (*0-916766-97-7*) Summit Univ.
Prophet, Elizabeth C., ed. Ich Dien. LC 74-20377. (Illus.). 254p. (Orig.). 1975. pap. 3.95 (*0-916766-11-X*) Summit Univ.
Prophet, Elizabeth C., pref. The Martyrdom of an Empress. LC 81-85401. (Illus.). 316p. 1981. 9.95 (*0-916766-50-0*) Summit Univ.
Prophet, Elizabeth C., ed. see Djwal Kul.
Prophet, Elizabeth C., ed. see El Morya.
Prophet, Elizabeth C., ed. see Germain, Saint.
Prophet, Elizabeth C., ed. see Jesus & Kuthumi.
Prophet, Elizabeth C., ed. see Morya, El.
Prophet, Elizabeth C., jt. auth. see Prophet, Mark L.
Prophet, Elizabeth C., jt. ed. see Prophet, Mark L.
Prophet, Elizabeth C., ed. see Saint Germain.
Prophet, Elizabeth C., ed. see St. Germain.
Prophet, John, ed. Fair Rents. (C). 1985. pap. 100.00 (*0-7219-0702-4*, Scientific) St Mut.
Prophet, Mark L. The Soulless One. LC 81-52501. (Pocketbook Ser.). 224p. 1981. pap. 1.95 (*0-916766-43-8*) Summit Univ.
— Understanding Yourself. LC 76-28089. (Pocketbook Ser.). 192p. 1979. pap. 4.99 (*0-916766-46-2*) Summit Univ.
Prophet, Mark L. & Prophet, Elizabeth C. Ascended Masters on Soul Mates & Twin Flames Bks I & II. 418p. (J). 1985. 19.95 (*0-916766-85-3*); 19.95 (*0-916766-86-1*) Summit Univ.
— Ciencia de la Palabra Hablada. 1965. pap. 9.95 (*0-922729-13-1*) Summit Univ.
— Climb the Highest Mountain. LC 72-175101. (Illus.). 700p. 1978. pap. 16.95 (*0-916766-26-8*) Summit Univ.
— Climb the Highest Mountain. 2nd ed. LC 72-175101. (Illus.). 700p. 1973. 21.95 (*0-916766-02-0*) Summit Univ.
— Cosmic Consciousness One Man's Search for God. LC 74-24023. (Illus.). 346p. (Orig.). 1976. pap. 9.95 (*0-916766-17-9*) Summit Univ.
— Lords of the Seven Rays. LC 86-63284. (Pocketbook Ser.). (Illus.). 608p. (Orig.). 1986. pap. text ed. 5.95 (*0-916766-75-6*) Summit Univ.
— The Lost Teachings of Jesus, Vol. 1. LC 81-52784. (Illus.). 520p. (Orig.). 1986. 19.95 (*0-916766-45-4*); pap. 14.95 (*0-916766-71-3*) Summit Univ.
— The Lost Teachings of Jesus, Vol. 2. LC 81-52784. (Illus.). 644p. (Orig.). 1986. 21.95 (*0-916766-72-1*); pap. 16.95 (*0-916766-73-X*) Summit Univ.
— The Lost Teachings of Jesus, Pt. 1: Missing Texts-Karma & Reincarnation. (Pocketbook Ser.). 384p. 1986. pap. 4.95 (*0-916766-90-X*) Summit Univ.
— The Lost Teachings of Jesus, Vol. 2: Mysteries of the Higher Self. (Pocketbook Ser.). 352p. 1986. pap. 4.95 (*0-916766-91-8*) Summit Univ.
— The Lost Teachings of Jesus, Vol. 3: Masters & Disciples on the Path. (Pocketbook Ser.). 352p. 1986. pap. 4.95 (*0-916766-92-6*) Summit Univ.
— The Lost Teachings of Jesus, Vol. 4: Good & Evil-Atlantis Revisited. (Pocketbook Ser.). 368p. 1986. pap. 5.99 (*0-916766-93-4*) Summit Univ.
— My Soul Doth Magnify the Lord! rev. ed. (Illus.). 400p. 1974. pap. 7.95 (*0-916766-35-7*) Summit Univ.
Prophet, Mark L. & Prophet, Elizabeth C., eds. Pearls of Wisdom 1973: On the Path of the Ascension, Vol. 16. LC 75-196014. 262p. 1973. 14.95 (*0-916766-28-4*) Summit Univ.
— The Science of the Spoken Word. LC 74-82293. (Illus.). 218p. 1965. reprint ed. pap. 9.95 (*0-916766-07-1*) Summit Univ.
Prophet, Mark L., ed. see Jesus & Kuthumi.
Prophet, Mark L., ed. see Saint Germain.
Prophet of Islam. Letters of the Holy Prophet. Qureshi, Ahmed, tr. 125p. (Orig.). 1985. pap. 10.50 (*1-56744-323-0*) Kazi Pubns.
Prophit, jt. auth. see Long.
Prophit, Penny, jt. auth. see Long, Lynette.
Propp, Jonathan. Neighborhood Open-Space Amenity Strategies. 67p. 1985. pap. 2.50 (*0-317-66253-8*) Partners Livable.
Propp, V. Morphology of the Folktale. 2nd ed. Wagner, Louis A., ed. Scott, Laurence, tr. (American Folklore Society Bibliographical & Special Ser.: No. 9). 184p. 1968. pap. 8.95 (*0-292-78376-0*) U of Tex Pr.
Propp, Vladimir. Theory & History of Folklore. Liberman, Anatoly, ed. Martin, Ariadna Y. & Martin, Richard P., trs. LC 83-14840. (Theory & History of Literature Ser.: Vol. 5). (Illus.). 288p. (RUS.). 1984. pap. text ed. 15.95 (*0-8166-1182-3*) U of Minn Pr.
Propp, William H. Water in the Wilderness: A Biblical Motif & Its Mythological Background. LC 87-16314. (Harvard Semitic Monographs). 152p. 1987. 16.95 (*1-55540-157-0*, 04-00-40) Scholars Pr GA.
Propp, William H., et al, eds. The Hebrew Bible & Its Interpreters. LC 89-23372. (Biblical & Judaic Studies from the University of California, San Diego: No. 1). vi, 225p. 1990. text ed. 25.00 (*0-931464-52-8*) Eisenbrauns.
Proppe, Karl H., jt. auth. see Suit, Herman D.
Propper. Bear, Reading Level 3-4. (World Animal Library). (Illus.). 28p. (J). (gr. 2-5). 1983. lib. bdg. 16.67 (*0-86592-865-7*) Rourke Corp.
— Dolphin, Reading Level 3-4. (World Animal Library). (Illus.). 28p. (J). (gr. 2-5). 1983. 12.50 (*0-685-58815-7*); lib. bdg. 16.67 (*0-86592-861-4*) Rourke Corp.
— Giraffe, Reading Level 3-4. (World Animal Library). (Illus.). 28p. (J). (gr. 2-5). 1983. 12.50 (*0-685-58817-3*); lib. bdg. 16.67 (*0-86592-860-6*) Rourke Corp.
— Panda, Reading Level 3-4. (World Animal Library). (Illus.). 28p. (J). (gr. 2-5). 1983. 12.50 (*0-685-58822-X*); lib. bdg. 16.67 (*0-86592-851-7*) Rourke Corp.
— Turtle, Reading Level 3-4. (World Animal Library). (Illus.). 28p. (J). (gr. 2-5). 1983. lib. bdg. 16.67 (*0-86592-856-8*); lib. bdg. 12.50 (*0-685-58828-9*) Rourke Corp.
Propper, et al. World Animal Library, 17 bks., Reading Level 3-4. (Illus.). 476p. (J). (gr. 2-5). 1983. lib. bdg. 212.50 (*0-685-58814-9*) Rourke Corp.
— World Animal Library, 17 bks., Set. (Illus.). 476p. (J). (gr. 2-5). 1983. lib. bdg. 283.39 (*0-86592-850-9*) Rourke Corp.
Propping, Peter, jt. ed. see Bouchard, Thomas J., Jr.
***Propps, Robert & Morland, Andrew.** Fordson Tractors. LC 95-14007. (Farm Tractor Color History Ser.). 1995. pap. write for info. (*0-7603-0065-8*) Motorbooks Intl.
Propst, jt. auth. see Perun.
Propst, C. & Perun, Thomas, eds. Nucleic Acid Targeted Drug Design. LC 92-17585. 644p. 1992. 180.00 (*0-8247-8662-9*) Dekker.
Propst, H. Dean, ed. see Winthrop, Theodore.
Propst, Nell B. Those Strenuous Dames of the Colorado Prairie. (Illus.). 310p. 1994. reprint ed. pap. 15.95 (*0-9634839-6-X*) Tamarack Bks.
— Uncommon Men & the Colorado Prairie. LC 92-10825. 1992. pap. 17.95 (*0-87004-347-1*) Caxton.
Propst, Rebecca L. Psychotherapy in a Religious Framework: Spirituality in the Emotional Healing Process. LC 86-27582. 209p. 1987. 38.95 (*0-89885-350-8*) Human Sci Pr.
Propst, Robert. The Office: A Facility Based on Change. 71p. 1986. 8.50 (*0-936658-01-0*) H Miller Res.
Prorok, P. C. & Miller, A. B., eds. Screening for Cancer: General Principles on Evaluation of Screening for Cancer & Screening for Lung, Bladder & Oral Cancer. (UICC Technical Report Ser.: Vol. 78). 186p. 1984. pap. text ed. 18.00 (*0-685-11815-0*) Hogrefe & Huber Pubs.
Prorok, Paul, ed. see Murphy, Bill.
Prorokova, Elena, illus. A Midsummer Night's Dream. LC 92-14522. (Shakespeare: The Animated Tales Ser.). 48p. (J). (gr. 5 up). 1993. pap. 6.99 (*0-679-83870-8*) Knopf Bks Yng Read.
Pros-Hymna. Geographical Analogues. 1992. 10.00 (*0-533-09445-3*) Vantage.
Pros, Jorge S. Diccionario de Axiomas, Juicios y Reflexiones. 1040p. (SPA.). 1991. 95.00 (*0-7859-5883-5*, 8430206132) Fr & Eur.
— Diccionario de la Felicidad. 2nd ed. 1046p. (SPA.). 1988. pap. 75.00 (*0-7859-4897-X*) Fr & Eur.
— Diccionario de Maximas Pensamientos y Sentacias. 9th ed. 744p. 1989. write for info. (*0-7859-5026-5*) Fr & Eur.
— Diccionario Humoristico. 3rd ed. 552p. (SPA.). 1982. pap. write for info. (*0-7859-4898-8*) Fr & Eur.
— Dictionary of Celebrated Phrases: Diccionario de Frases Celabres. 6th ed. 1000p. 1988. 89.95 (*0-7859-5025-7*) Fr & Eur.
Prosch, Charles. Reminiscences of Washington Territory. enl. ed. 128p. 1969. 14.95 (*0-87770-022-2*) Ye Galleon.
Prosch, Harry. Michael Polanyi: A Critical Exposition. LC 85-27849. (SUNY Series in Cultural Perspectives). 354p. 1986. 64.50 (*0-88706-277-6*); pap. 21.95 (*0-88706-276-8*) State U NY Pr.
Prosch, Harry, jt. auth. see Polanyi, Michael.
Proschan, jt. auth. see Hollander.
Proschan, Frank & Serfling, R. J., eds. Reliability & Biometry: Statistical Analysis of Lifelength. (Proceedings in Applied Mathematics Ser.: No. 5). x, 815p. 1974. 53.00 (*0-89871-159-2*) Soc Indus-Appl Math.
Proschek, L., jt. ed. see Gaetan, Jasmin.
Prosdocimo de' Beldomandi. Contrapunctus. Herlinger, Jan, tr. LC 83-23367. (Greek & Latin Music Theory Ser.). xii, 109p. 1984. 25.00 (*0-8032-3669-7*) U of Nebr Pr.
Prosdocimo de'Beldomandi. Brief Treatise on Ratios That Pertain to Music & A Little Treatise on the Method of Dividing the Monochord. Herlinger, Jan, ed. & tr. by. LC 87-10818. (Greek & Latin Music Theory Ser.). x, 182p. 1987. 25.00 (*0-8032-3677-8*) U of Nebr Pr.
Prose, Francine. Household Saints. 1993. mass mkt. 4.99 (*0-8041-1165-0*) Ivy Books.
— Hunters & Gatherers. 256p. 1995. 20.00 (*0-374-17371-0*) FS&G.
— A Peaceable Kingdom. LC 93-10080. 1993. 20.00 (*0-374-23042-0*) FS&G.
— Primitive People. 250p. 1992. 20.00 (*0-374-23722-0*) FS&G.
— Primitive People. 1993. mass mkt. 4.99 (*0-8041-1110-3*) Ivy Books.
— Stories from Our Living Past. Harlow, Jules, ed. LC 74-8514. (Illus.). 128p. (J). (gr. 3-4). 1974. pap. 8.95 (*0-87441-081-9*); teacher ed. pap. 14.95 (*0-87441-082-7*) Behrman.
— Stories from Our Living Past, No. 1. Harlow, Jules, ed. LC 74-8514. (Illus.). 128p. (J). (gr. 3-4). 1974. student ed 3.50 (*0-87441-083-5*) Behrman.
— Stories from Our Living Past, No. 2. Harlow, Jules, ed. LC 74-8514. (Illus.). 128p. (J). (gr. 3-4). 1974. student ed 3.50 (*0-87441-084-3*) Behrman.
Prose, Francine, tr. see Fink, Ida.
Prose, Neil S., jt. auth. see Weinberg, Samuel.
Prosen, jt. auth. see Chan.
Proser, Maria, ed. see Lara, Jesus.
Proser, Maria A., tr. see Jesus, Teresa De.
***Proser, Matthew N.** The Gift of Fire: Aggression & the Plays of Christopher Marlowe. LC 94-21588. (Renaissance & Baroque Studies & Texts: 12). 1995. write for info. (*0-8204-2276-2*) P Lang Pubs.
— The Heroic Image in Five Shakespearian Tragedies. LC 78-17428. 259p. 1978. reprint ed. 50.00 (*0-87752-200-6*) Gordian.
Proser, Phillip A. & Miles, John J. Antitrust Aspects of Mergers & Acquisitions. (Corporate Practice Ser.: No. 56). 1990. ring bd. 92.00 (*1-55871-103-1*) BNA.
Proshansky, Harold M., ed. Genetic Destiny: Scientific Controversy & Social Conflict, No. 11. LC 76-5964. (Studies in Modern Society: Political & Social Issues). 32.50 (*0-404-10130-5*) AMS Pr.
Proshchakov, Vitold. In the Friendly Family of Fraternal Peoples. 120p. 1983. 22.00 (*0-317-53781-4*, Pub. by Collets) St Mut.
Prosise, Jeff. How Computer Graphics Work. (Orig.). 1994. pap. 24.95 (*1-56276-242-7*) Ziff-Davis.
— PC Magazine DOS 5 Memory Management with Utilities. (Techniques & Utilities Ser.). (Illus.). 244p. (Orig.). 1992. disk 34.95 (*1-56276-050-5*) Ziff-Davis.
— PC Magazine DOS 5 Techniques & Utilities. (Techniques & Utilities Ser.). (Illus.). 1012p. (Orig.). 1991. disk 39.95 (*1-56276-007-6*) Ziff-Davis.
— PC Magazine DOS 6 Techniques & Utilities. 1993. disk 39.95 (*1-56276-095-5*) Ziff-Davis.
— PC Magazine Guide to DOS 6 Memory Management with Utilities. 1993. disk 29.95 (*1-56276-097-1*) Ziff-Davis.
— Programming Windows 95 with MFC. 1995. pap. 39.95 (*1-55615-902-1*) Microsoft.
— Windows Desktop Utilities. 1994. disk, pap. 34.95 (*1-56276-098-X*) Ziff-Davis.
Prosise, Michael, jt. auth. see Ramirez, Ron.
Proskauer, et al. New York Employment Discrimination Handbook: With Federal Statutory Appendix & Forms. LC 92-41658. 1993. write for info. (*0-8205-1965-0*) Bender.
— New York Employment Law, 3 vols., Set. 1992. write for info. (*0-8205-1796-8*) Bender.
Proskauer, Heinrich O. The Rediscovery of Color. (Illus.). 180p. 1990. pap. 16.95 (*0-88010-088-5*, 1055) Anthroposophic.
Proske, Beatrice G. Archer Milton Huntington. (Illus.). 1965. 5.00 (*0-87535-098-4*) Hispanic Soc.
— Brookgreen Gardens Sculpture. rev. ed. (Illus.). 574p. (C). 1968. text ed. 15.00 (*0-9638206-0-5*) Brookgreen.
— Castilian Sculpture. (Illus.). 525p. 1951. 15.00 (*0-317-00617-7*, Hispanic Soc) Interbk Inc.
— Castilian Sculpture: Gothic to Renaissance. (Illus.). 1988. reprint ed. 15.00 (*0-87535-069-0*) Hispanic Soc.
— Catalogue of Sculpture (13th to 15th Centuries) in the Collection. (Illus.). 360p. 1932. 10.00 (*0-87535-030-5*) Hispanic Soc.
— Catalogue of Sculpture (16th to 18th Centuries) in the Collection. (Illus.). 1930. 10.00 (*0-87535-027-5*) Hispanic Soc.
— Juan Martinez Montanes, Sevillian Sculptor. (Illus.). 199p. 1967. 35.00 (*0-87535-107-7*) Hispanic Soc.
— Martinez Montanes: Sevillian Sculptor. (Illus.). 412p. 1967. 35.00 (*0-317-00603-7*, Hispanic Soc) Interbk Inc.
— Pompeo Leoni: Work in Marble & Alabaster in Relation to Spanish Sculpture. (Illus.). 1956. 5.00 (*0-87535-088-7*) Hispanic Soc.
— Pompeo Leoni: Work in Marble & Alabaster in Relation to Spanish Sculpture. (Illus.). 80p. 1956. pap. 1.50 (*0-317-00614-2*, Hispanic Soc) Interbk Inc.
— Sculpture by Anna Hyatt Huntington. (Illus.). 24p. 1957. pap. text ed. 0.50 (*0-87535-093-3*) Hispanic Soc.
***Proske, Beatrice G. & Salmon, Robin R.** Brookgreen Gardens Sculpture & Brookgreen Gardens Sculpture Vol. II. (Illus.). 885p. (C). 1993. text ed. 30.00 (*0-9638206-2-1*) Brookgreen.
Proske, Uwe, jt. ed. see Ferrell, William R.
Proskine, Alec. Adirondack Canoe Waters: South & West Flow. 2nd rev. ed. LC 88-34398. (Canoe Guide Ser.: Vol. 2). 176p. 1994. reprint ed. pap. 12.95 (*0-935272-50-X*) ADK Mtn Club.
***Proskine, Alec C.** No Two Rivers Alike: Fifty-Six Canoeable Rivers in New York State. LC 95-12495. (Illus.). 232p. 1995. pap. 17.50 (*0-935796-51-7*) Purple Mnt Pr.
Proskouriakoff, Tatiana. An Album of Maya Architecture. LC 63-17166. 1976. reprint ed. pap. 18.95 (*0-8061-1351-0*) U of Okla Pr.
— Maya History. Joyce, Rosemary A., ed. LC 92-9387. (Illus.). 240p. 1993. text ed. 50.00x (*0-292-75085-4*) U of Tex Pr.
Proskouriakoff, Tatiana, jt. ed. see Knorozov, Yuri V.
Proskouriakoff, Tatiana A. A Study of Classic Maya Sculpture. LC 77-11515. (Carnegie Institution of Washington. Publications: No. 593). reprint ed. 62.50 (*0-404-16275-4*) AMS Pr.
Proskurin, Alexander, ed. The Stalin Phenomenon. 1990. text ed. 22.50 (*81-207-1141-6*, Pub. by Sterling Pubs II) Apt Bks.
Proskurovsky, D. I., jt. auth. see Mesyats, G. A.
Prosky, Ida. You Don't Need Four Women to Play Shakespeare: Bias in Contemporary American Theater. LC 92-54091. 172p. 1992. lib. bdg. 27.50x (*0-89950-729-8*) McFarland & Co.
Prosky, Leon & DeVries, Jonathan. Controlling Dietary Fibers in Food Products. (Illus.). 152p. 1991. text ed. 52.95 (*0-442-00239-4*) Chapman & Hall.
Prosnitz, D., ed. Free-Electron Lasers & Applications. 1990. 53.00 (*0-8194-0268-0*, VOL. 1227) SPIE.

P Q

***Prosor, Larry & Moreno, Richard.** Nevada: Desert Lows & Mountain Highs. Lippert, Laurel H., ed. (Illus.). 174p. 1994. 39.95 (1-885515-00-6) Fineline Productions.

Prosor, Larry & Popoff, Leo. Lake Tahoe: A Photo Essay of the Lake Tahoe Region. Lippert, Laurel H., ed. (Illus.). 150p. (Orig.). (C). 1992. pap. 19.95 (0-9620148-0-X) Fineline Productions.

— Lake Tahoe: A Photo Essay of the Lake Tahoe Region. 2nd ed. Lippert, Laurel H., ed. (Illus.). 135p. (Orig.). 1993. 34.95 (0-9620148-2-6) Fineline Productions.

Prosorova, L. P. & Kreizer, V. L. English-Russian Television Dictionary. 429p. (ENG & RUS.). 1960. 24.95 (0-8288-6837-9, M-9065) Fr & Eur.

Prospect News Staff, ed. see Ponder, Dorothy.

Prosper, Charles. How to Become a Balloon Artist & Make up to One Hundred Thousand Dollars a Year: An Expert's Step-by-Step Guide. LC 87-81325. (Illus.). 165p. (Orig.). 1987. pap. 35.00 (0-943845-77-7) Global Pub CA.

Prosper, Peter A., Jr. Concentration & the Rate of Change of Wages in the United States, 1950-1962. Bruchey, Stuart, ed. LC 76-4511. (Nineteen Seventy-Seven Dissertations Ser.). (Illus.). 1977. lib. bdg. 23.95 (0-405-09922-3) Ayer.

Prosper-Pouget, Jean-Henri, jt. auth. see Pouget, Jean-Henri-Prosper.

Prospere, Susan. Sub Rosa. 88p. 1992. 18.95 (0-393-03095-4) Norton.

— Sub Rosa: Poems. 96p. 1993. pap. 8.95 (0-393-31003-5) Norton.

Prosperetti, A., jt. ed. see Arndt, R. E.

***Prosperi, G. M. & Brambilla, N.** Quark Confinement & the Hadron Spectrum: Proceeding of the International Conference. 396p. 1995. text ed. 112.00 (981-02-2085-5) World Scientific Pub.

Prosperity & Profits Unlimited Staff. Party Plan Sales: A Reference & Workbook. rev. ed. 1992. pap. text ed. 18. 95 (0-317-04782-5) Prosperity & Profits.

***Prosperoso, Rico.** Silhouette Designs for Artists & Craftspeople. LC 94-37319. (Illus.). 1995. pap. write for info. (0-486-28452-2) Dover.

***Pross.** Basic Principles of Organic Reactivity. Date not set. text ed. 54.95 (0-471-55599-1) Wiley.

Pross, Paul & Yungclas, Jack H. The Sound of Sleigh Bells: A Christmas Story for All Seasons. rev. ed. 70p. 1993. 13.95 (0-9630307-2-8) Vertex Pr.

Pross, Paul E. Winter Songs & Final Dreams: Memoirs of a Wayward Cherub. 120p. 1995. write for info. (0-9630307-1-X) Vertex Pr.

Pross, Paul E. & Yungclas, Jack H. The Sound of Sleigh Bells: A Christmas Story for all Seasons. 70p. 1991. 13. 95 (0-9630307-0-1) Vertex Pr.

Prossdorf, S. Some Classes of Singular Equations. (Mathematical Library: Vol. 17). 418p. 1978. 107.75 (0-7204-0501-7, North Holland) Elsevier.

Prossdorf, S. & Silbermann, B. Numerical Analysis for Integral & Related Operator Equations. (Operator Theory Ser.: Vol. 52). 560p. 1991. 198.00 (0-8176-2620-4) Birkhauser.

Prossdorf, S., tr. see Maz'ya, V. G. & Nikol'skij, S. M.

Prossdorf, S., jt. auth. see Michlin, S. G.

Prosser, Albert L. Nasson: The Seventy Years. D'Abate, Richard, ed. LC 93-25217. (Illus.). 376p. 1993. 30.00 (0-914659-63-4) Phoenix Pub.

Prosser, Alex & Meredith, Carol. The Font Directory, Version 1.0 for Windows. 90p. (Orig.). 1992. spiral bd. 11.95 (0-9696751-0-0, Pub. by Beaver Pnd CN) DIMI Pr.

Prosser, B. Gathered Together. (C). 1984. text ed. 75.00 (0-7175-1191-X, Pub. by S Thornes Pubs UK) St Mut.

Prosser, C., jt. auth. see Troshin, A.

Prosser, C. Ladd. Adaptational Biology: Molecules to Organisms. LC 86-1563. (Environmental Science & Technology: A Wiley-Interscience Series of Texts & Monographs). 784p. 1986. pap. text ed. 79.95 (0-471-89486-9) Wiley.

— Comparative Animal Physiology, Pt. A. 4th ed. 590p. 1991. text ed. 69.95 (0-471-85767-X) Wiley.

Prosser, C. Ladd, ed. Comparative Animal Physiology, 2 vols., Set. 4th ed. 1376p. 1991. text ed. 97.90 (0-471-56093-6) Wiley.

— Comparative Animal Physiology: Neural & Integrative Animal Physiology, Vol. 2. 4th ed. 786p. 1991. text ed. 59.95 (0-471-56071-5) Wiley.

Prosser, D. J., jt. ed. see North, C. P.

Prosser, Eleanor. Drama & Religion in the English Mystery Plays: A Re-evaluation. vi, 229p. 1961. 32.50 (0-8047-0060-5) Stanford U Pr.

— Hamlet & Revenge. 2nd ed. LC 71-120745. xvi, 302p. 1971. 39.50 (0-8047-0316-7); pap. 14.95 (0-8047-0317-5) Stanford U Pr.

— Shakespeare's Anonymous Editors: Scribe & Compositor in the Folio Text of "2 Henry IV" LC 79-66179. (Illus.). xiv, 219p. 1981. 32.50 (0-8047-1033-3) Stanford U Pr.

Prosser, Franklin P. & Winkel, David E. The Art of Digital Design: An Introduction to Top-Down Design. 2nd ed. (Illus.). 560p. 1986. text ed. 78.00 (0-13-046780-4) P-H.

Prosser, H. J., jt. ed. see Wilson, A. D.

***Prosser, H. Lee.** Running from The Hunter: The Life & Works of Charles Beaumont. LC 95-5346. (Milford Ser.: Popular Writers of Today: No. 68). 1995. write for info. (0-89370-191-2); pap. write for info. (0-89370-291-9) Borgo Pr.

Prosser, J. I., ed. Nitrification. (Society for General Microbiology Special Publications: Vol. 20). 228p. (C). 1987. 70.00 (1-85221-013-3, IRL Pr) OUP.

Prosser, James I., jt. ed. see Bazin, Michael J.

***Prosser, Jerry.** Aliens: Hive. 2nd ed. (Illus.). 112p. 1995. pap. 14.95 (1-56971-122-4) Dark Horse Comics.

Prosser, Jerry & Jones, Kelley. Aliens: Hive Collection. Kesel, Barbara, ed. (Illus.). 112p. 1993. pap. 13.95 (1-878574-47-7) Dark Horse Comics.

Prosser, Jerry, ed. see Arcudi, John.

Prosser, Jerry, ed. see Barker, Clive, et al.

Prosser, Jerry, see Stanislaw Mayakovsky, pseud..

Prosser, Jerry, ed. see McCheever, Ted.

Prosser, Jerry, ed. see Miller, Frank & Darrow, Geof.

Prosser, Jerry, ed. see Miller, Frank.

Prosser, Jerry, ed. see Moench, Doug & Gulacy, Paul.

Prosser, Jerry, ed. see Robinson, James.

Prosser, Jerry, ed. see Stradley, Randy.

Prosser, Jerry, ed. see Verheiden, Mark, et al.

Prosser, Jerry, ed. see Vess, Charles.

Prosser, Larry. For Rent by Owner: Hassle-Free Landlording from A to Z. 2nd ed. 180p. 1993. pap. 8.95 (1-55850-251-3) Adams Pubng.

Prosser, Michael H., jt. ed. see Benson, Thomas W.

Prosser, R. T. On the Ideal Structure of Operator Algebras. (Memoirs of the American Mathematical Society Ser.: Vol. 45). 28p. 1974. reprint ed. 17.00 (0-8218-1245-9, MEMO/1/45C) Am Math.

Prosser, Reese T. A New Formulation of Particle Mechanics. LC 52-42839. (Memoirs Ser.: No. 1/61). 57p. 1980. reprint ed. pap. 17.00 (0-8218-1261-0, MEMO 1/61) Am Math.

Prosser, Sharon S. Spanish on the Job: Quick, Easy Word Guide. 107p. (Orig.). 1990. pap. 6.95 (0-923176-09-8) SW Pr.

Prosser, Tony, jt. auth. see Graham, Cosmo.

Prosser, Tony, jt. ed. see Graham, Cosmo.

Prosser, Tony, jt. ed. see Moran, Michael.

Prosser, William L. Torts: Adaptable to Courses Utilizing Materials by Prosser. 3rd ed. LC 87-116625. (Legalines Ser.). 362p. 13.95 (0-685-18533-8) HarBrace.

Prosser, William L., ed. The Judicial Humorist: A Collection of Judicial Opinions & Other Frivolities. xvii, 284p. 1989. reprint ed. lib. bdg. 32.50 (0-8377-2518-6) Rothman.

Prosser, William L. & Keeton, Page. Prosser & Keeton on Torts: Lawyers Edition. 5th ed. LC 83-19714. (Hornbook Ser.). 1456p. 1985. reprint ed. text ed. write for info. (0-314-74442-8) West Pub.

Prosser, William L., et al. Torts, Cases & Materials On. 8th ed. (University Casebook Ser.). 1266p. 1991. reprint ed. text ed. 39.75 (0-88277-641-X) Foundation Pr.

Prost, Alain & Hill, Damon, prefs. The Williams-Renault Formula 1 Motor Racing Book. LC 93-40596. (Illus.). 64p. 1994. 15.95 (1-56458-627-8) Dorling Kindersley.

Prost, Andre, jt. auth. see Le Bris, Pierre.

Prost, Antoine. In the Wake of War: Les Anciens Combattants & French Society. McPhail, Helen, tr. LC 92-13236. (Legacy of the Great War Ser.). 160p. 1992. 49.95 (0-85496-672-2); pap. 16.50 (0-85496-337-5) Berg Pubs.

***Prost, Antoine & Vincent, Gerard, eds.** A History of Private Life Vol. 5: Riddles of Identity in Modern Times, Vol. 2. (Illus.). 640p. 1994. pap. text ed. 19.95 (0-674-40004-6, PROHIX) Belknap Pr.

***Prost, Charles, photos.** The Garden of Claude Monet: The Four Seasons of Giverny. LC 95-5289. (Illus.). 1995. write for info. (0-8120-6512-3) Barron.

Prost, Gary L. Remote Sensing for Geologists: A Guide to Image Interpretation. LC 93-50702. 1994. text ed. 115. 00 (2-88449-101-5) Gordon & Breach.

Prost, Helen, jt. auth. see Young, Blanche.

Prost, J., jt. auth. see De Gennes, P. G.

Prostano, Emanuel T. & Prostano, Joyce S. School Library Media Center. 4th ed. 250p. 1987. lib. bdg. 35.00 (0-87287-568-7); pap. text ed. 27.50 (0-87287-569-5) Libs Unl.

Prostano, Joyce S., jt. auth. see Prostano, Emanuel T.

Prosterman, Leslie. The Aspect of the Fair: Aesthetics & Festival in Midwestern County Fairs. LC 93-49385. 1994. write for info. (1-56098-408-2) Smithsonian.

Prosterman, Roy L. & Riedinger, Jeffrey M. Land Reform & Democratic Development. LC 87-4188. (Studies in Development). 336p. 1987. text ed. 47.50x (0-8018-3482-1) Johns Hopkins.

Prosterman, Roy L., et al, eds. Agrarian Reform & Grassroots Development: Ten Case Studies. LC 90-8493. 342p. 1990. lib. bdg. 40.00 (1-55587-231-X) Lynne Rienner.

Prosyniok, Joann R., ed. Modern Arts Criticism, Vol. 1. (Illus.). 575p. 1990. 99.00 (0-8103-7689-X) Gale.

Prosyniuk. Modern Arts Criticism, Vol. 2. 1991. 99.00 (0-8103-7874-4) Gale.

— Modern Arts Criticism, Vol. 3. 1992. 99.00 (0-8103-8310-1) Gale.

— Modern Arts Criticism, Vol. 4. 1993. 99.00 (0-8103-8311-X) Gale.

— Modern Arts Criticism, Vol. 5. 1994. 75.00 (0-8103-8478-7) Gale.

Prot, Viviane A. The Story of Birth. Bogard, Vicki, tr. LC 90-50777. (Young Discovery Library). (Illus.). 38p. (J). (gr. k-5). 1991. 5.95 (0-944589-34-0, 340) Young Discovery Lib.

Prota, Guiseppe. Melanins & Melanogenesis. (Illus.). 290p. 1992. text ed. 59.95 (0-12-565970-9) Acad Pr.

Protase, E. Woodford, et al. Bridges to English, Bk. 1. (Bridges to English). (Illus.). 1981. text ed. 6.67 (0-07-034481-7); Wkbk. student ed 4.60 (0-07-034483-3); Tchr's. ed. teacher ed 4.60 (0-07-034482-5); Cassettes. audio 115.00 (0-07-034484-1); Cue cards. 74.75 (0-07-034485-X); Tests. 40.25 (0-07-034486-8) McGraw.

Protase, E. Woodford & Kernan, Doris. Bridges to English, Bk. 2. Rebrisz, J., ed. (Bridges to English). (Illus.). 1981. text ed. 6.67 (0-07-034487-6); Wkbk. student ed 4.05 (0-07-034489-2); Tchr's. ed. teacher ed 2.88 (0-07-034488-4); Cue cards. 74.75 (0-07-034491-4); Tests. 40.25 (0-07-034492-2) McGraw.

— Bridges to English, Bk. 3. Rebrisz, J., ed. (Bridges to English). (Illus.). 1981. text ed. 6.67 (0-07-034493-0); Wkbk. student ed 4.60 (0-07-034495-7); Tchr's. ed. teacher ed 2.88 (0-07-034494-9); Cassettes. audio 140.30 (0-07-034496-5); Cue cards. 74.75 (0-07-034497-3); Tests. 40.25 (0-07-034498-1) McGraw.

— Bridges to English, Bk. 4. Rebrisz, J., ed. (Bridges to English). (Illus.). 1981. text ed. 6.67 (0-07-034499-X); Tests. 40.25 (0-07-034504-X) McGraw.

— Bridges to English, Bk. 5. Rebrisz, J., ed. (Bridges to English). (Illus.). 1981. Wkbk. student ed 4.60 (0-07-034507-4); Tchr's. ed. teacher ed 2.88 (0-07-034506-6); Cassettes. audio 140.30 (0-07-034508-2); Cue cards. 74.75 (0-07-034509-0); Tests. 40.25 (0-07-034510-4) McGraw.

— Bridges to English, Bk. 6. Rebrisz, J., ed. (Bridges to English). (Illus.). 1981. text ed. 6.67 (0-07-034511-2); Wkbk. student ed 4.60 (0-07-034513-9); Tchr's. ed. teacher ed 2.88 (0-07-034512-0); Cassettes. audio 123.65 (0-07-034514-7); Cue cards. 74.75 (0-07-034515-5); Tests. 40.25 (0-07-034516-3) McGraw.

Protasi, M., jt. ed. see Ausiello, G.

Protasio, John. To the Bottom of the Sea: True Accounts of Major Ship Disasters. 1990. 18.95 (0-8184-0530-9) Carol Pub Group.

— The World's Worst Disasters at Sea. 212p. 1993. reprint ed. pap. 5.50 (1-56171-196-9, S P I Bks) Sure Sellers.

Protasov, V. R. Vision & Near Orientation of Fish. 180p. 1970. text ed. 54.50 (0-7065-1041-0, Pub. by Keter Pub IS) Coronet Bks.

Protasov, Yu S., jt. ed. see U. S. S. R., National Standard Reference Data Service Staff.

Protected Areas Data Unit of the Conservation Monitoring Center Staff & IUCN Commission on National Parks & Protected Areas. The IUCN Directory of Afro-Tropical Protected Areas. (International Union for the Conservation of Nature & Natural Resources: A Belhaven Press Book Ser.). (Illus.). 1054p. 1986. 60.00 (2-88032-804-7, Pub. by IUCN SZ) Island Pr.

Protein-Ligand Interactions Symposium Staff. Proceedings of the Protein-Ligand Interactions Symposium, University of Konstanz, Germany, Sept. 1974. Blauer, Gideon & Sund, Horst, eds. (C). 1975. 174.00 (3-11-004881-7) De Gruyter.

Protello, Watson. Inferno: Uncensored Horror for Adults. (Illus.). 87p. 1991. pap. 9.95 (0-944735-99-1) Malibu Graphics.

Protess, D. & McCombs, M., eds. Agenda Setting: Readings on Media, Public Opinion & Policymaking. (Communication Textbook (Journalism) Ser.). 328p. (C). 1991. pap. 29.95 (0-8058-0841-8) L Erlbaum Assocs.

Protess, David. Gone in the Night. 1994. mass mkt. 5.99 (0-440-21243-X) Dell.

Protess, David L., et al. The Journalism of Outrage: Investigative Reporting & Agenda Building in America. LC 91-8932. (Communication Ser.). 301p. 1991. lib. bdg. 35.00 (0-89862-314-6) Guilford Pr.

— The Journalism of Outrage: Investigative Reporting & Agenda Building in America. (Communication Ser.). 301p. 1992. pap. 17.95 (0-89862-591-2) Guilford Pr.

Protestant Episcopal Church Staff. The Hymnal Nineteen Forty Companion. 741p. 1993. reprint ed. lib. bdg. 109. 00 (0-7812-9680-3) Rprt Serv.

Protevi, John. Time & Exteriority: Aristotle, Heidegger, Derrida. LC 93-49860. 1994. write for info. (0-8387-5229-2) Bucknell U Pr.

Proth, J. M. & Hillion, H. P. Mathematical Tools in Production Management. (Competitive Methods in Operations Research & Data Analysis Ser.). (Illus.). 400p. 1990. 89.50 (0-306-43358-3, Plenum Pr) Plenum.

Prothero & Berggren. Eocene-Oligocene Climatic & Biotic Evolution. (Geology & Paleontology Ser.). 568p. 1992. text ed. 110.00 (0-691-08738-5); pap. text ed. 49.95 (0-691-02542-8) Princeton U Pr.

Prothero, Donald R. The Eocene-Oligocene Transition: Paradise Lost. (Illus.). 208p. 1993. 65.00 (0-231-08090-5); pap. 24.00 (0-231-08091-3) Col U Pr.

— Interpreting the Stratigraphic Record. (C). 1995. text ed. write for info. (0-7167-1854-5) W H Freeman.

Prothero, Donald R. & Schoch, Robert M. Horns, Tusks, Hooves, & Flippers: The Evolution of Hoofed Mammals & Their Relatives. LC 92-41539. 1993. 49.50 (0-691-08776-8) Princeton U Pr.

Prothero, Donald R. & Schoch, Robert M., eds. The Evolution of Perissodactyls. (Oxford Monographs on Geology & Geophysics: No. 15). (Illus.). 560p. 1989. 75. 00 (0-19-506039-3) OUP.

Prothero, Donald R., jt. auth. see Dott, Robert H., Jr.

Prothero, George W., ed. Select Statutes & Other Constitutional Documents Illustrative of the Reigns of Elizabeth & James I. 4th ed. LC 83-1740. cxxv, 490p. 1983. reprint ed. text ed. 150.00 (0-313-23973-8, PRSE, Greenwood Pr) Greenwood.

Prothero, Jon C. Driving & Surviving. LC 80-82627. (Illus.). 73p. (Orig.). (gr. 10-12). 1980. pap. 5.00 (0-938026-01-1) Instruct Res.

Prothero, Joyce, jt. ed. see Montgomery, Rhonda J.

Prothero, Joyce, jt. ed. see O'Conner, Kathleen.

Prothero, Rowland E. English Farming Past & Present. LC 72-83276. 519p. 1972. reprint ed. 30.95 (0-405-08866-3, Pub. by Blom Pubns UK) Ayer.

Prothero, Rowland E., ed. see Gibbon, Edward.

Prothero, Walt. Stalking Big Game. LC 92-754. (Illus.). 224p. 1992. 19.95 (0-8117-0282-0) Stackpole.

Prothero, Walter. Stalking Trophy Mule Deer. 240p. 1993. 18.98 (0-88290-476-0, 1240) Horizon Utah.

Protheroe, et al. Exploring the Universe. 4th ed. 768p. (C). 1989. pap. write for info. (0-675-20898-X, Merrill Pub Co) Macmillan.

Protheroe, Nancy J., jt. auth. see Robinson, Glen E.

Protherough, Robert. Developing Response to Fiction. 192p. 1983. pap. 27.00 (0-335-10405-3, Open Univ Pr) Taylor & Francis.

— Students of English. 200p. 1989. 59.95 (0-415-01637-1) Routledge.

— Teaching Literature for Examinations. LC 86-754. (English, Language & Education Ser.). 160p. 1986. pap. 27.00 (0-335-15076-4, Open Univ Pr) Taylor & Francis.

Protherough, Robert & Atkinson, Judith. The Making of English Teachers. (English, Language & Education Ser.). 176p. 1991. pap. 27.00 (0-335-09374-4, Open Univ Pr) Taylor & Francis.

***Protherough, Robert & King, Peter, eds.** The Challenge of English in the National Curriculum. LC 94-45380. 1995. write for info. (0-415-09061-X) Routledge.

Prothro, Edwin T. Child Rearing in the Lebanon. LC 61-18039. (Middle Eastern Monographs: No. 8). (Illus.). 194p. 1961. pap. 4.50 (0-674-11500-7) HUP.

Prothro, Edwin T. & Diab, Lutfy N. Changing Family Patterns in the Arab East. 1974. 29.95 (0-8156-6039-1, Am U Beirut) Syracuse U Pr.

Prothro, James W. Dollar Decade: Business Ideas in the 1920s. LC 70-88923. 256p. 1970. reprint ed. text ed. 59. 75 (0-8371-2299-6, PRDD, Greenwood Pr) Greenwood.

Prothro, James W., jt. auth. see Matthews, Donald R.

Prothrow-Stith, Deborah. Deadly Consequences. LC 90-55938. 288p. 1993. pap. 13.00 (0-06-092402-0, PL) HarpC.

— Violence Prevention Curriculum for Adolescents. (Illus.). 80p. (Orig.). 1987. pap. 15.00 (0-89292-093-9) Educ Dev Ctr.

Proto, A. N., ed. Nonlinear Phenomena in Complex Systems: Proceedings of the First International Workshop on Nonlinear Phenomena, Mar de Plata, Argentina, Nov. 1-18, 1988. (Delta Ser.). 252p. 1989. 105.25 (0-444-88035-6, North Holland) Elsevier.

Proto, A. N. & Aliaga, J. L., eds. Condensed Matter Theories, Vol. 7. (Illus.). 432p. (C). 1992. 125.00 (0-306-44201-9, Plenum Pr) Plenum.

Proto, Anthony V., et al. Chest Disease (Fourth Series) Test & Syllabus. (Professional Self-Evaluation & Continuing Education Program Ser.: Vol. 27). (Illus.). 814p. 1989. 150.00 (1-55903-027-5) Am Coll Radiology.

Proto, Louis. Be Your Own Best Friend: How to Achieve Greater Self-Esteem, Health, & Happiness. 176p. 1994. reprint ed. pap. text ed. 4.99 (0-425-14296-5) Berkley Pub.

— Increase Your Energy: The Science of Smart Living. 144p. (Orig.). 1992. pap. 8.95 (0-87728-755-4) Weiser.

— Self-Healing: Use Your Mind to Heal Your Body. (Illus.). 207p. (Orig.). 1991. pap. 10.95 (0-87728-732-5) Weiser.

Protopappas, John J. & McNeal, Alvin R., eds. Washington on Foot: Twenty-Three Walking Tours of Washington, D. C., & Old Town Alexandria. rev. ed. LC 83-12880. (Illus.). 224p. 1992. pap. 6.95 (1-56098-176-8) Smithsonian.

Protopopescu, Orel O. The Perilous Pit. LC 92-290. (Illus.). 40p. (J). (ps-1). 1993. 14.00 (0-671-76910-3, Green Tiger S&S) S&S Childrens.

— Since Lulu Learned the Cancan. LC 90-85014. (Illus.). (J). (ps). 1991. 13.95 (0-671-74791-6, Green Tiger S&S) S&S Childrens.

Protopopova, I., ed. see Viatiutnev, M. & Sosenko, E.

Protopresbyter Michael Pomazansky. Bog Nash na Njbesi i na zjemli. 140p. 1985. pap. 5.00 (0-317-29087-8) Holy Trinity.

— O Zhizni o Vjere o Tzerkvje, 2 vols. 650p. 1976. pap. 23. 00 (0-317-29072-X) Holy Trinity.

Prott, Lyndel V., jt. auth. see O'Keefe, P. J.

Prottas, Jeffrey. The Most Useful Gift: Altruism & the Public Policy of Organ Transplants. LC 93-38239. (Health-Management Ser.). 211p. 1994. 29.95 (1-55542-644-1) Jossey-Bass.

Protter. Calculus. 4th ed. 1000p. (C). 1988. boxed 30.00 (0-86720-093-6); 12.50 (0-86720-174-6); 13.75 (0-86720-115-0) Jones & Bartlett.

— Calculus, 1. 4th ed. 1000p. (C). 1988. 12.50 (0-86720-111-8) Jones & Bartlett.

Protter, B., jt. auth. see Travin, S.

Protter, M. & Weinberger, H. Maximum Principles in Differential Equations. (Illus.). 1984. 49.90 (0-387-96068-6) Spr-Verlag.

Protter, Murray H., intro. Reviews in Partial Differential Equations, 1980-1986, 5 vols. LC 88-6681. 3998p. 1988. pap. 355.00 (0-8218-0103-1, REVPDE-86) Am Math.

Protter, Murray H. & Morrey, Charles B., Jr. Calculus with Analytic Geometry: A First Course. 3rd ed. LC 76-12801. (Mathematics Ser.). (C). 1977. teacher ed write for info. (0-201-06031-0); text ed. 34.36 (0-201-06037-X); student ed write for info. (0-318-50136-8) Addison-Wesley.

— College Calculus with Analytic Geometry. 3rd ed. LC 76-12800. (Mathematics Ser.). (C). 1977. student ed write for info. (0-201-06036-1); text ed. write for info. (0-201-06030-2) Addison-Wesley.

— A First Course in Real Analysis. LC 76-43978. (Undergraduate Texts in Mathematics Ser.). 1987. 39.80 (0-387-90215-5) Spr-Verlag.

— A First Course in Real Analysis. 2nd ed. Ewing, J. H. et al, eds. (Undergraduate Texts in Mathematics-Readings in Mathematics Ser.). (Illus.). xviii, 534p. 1994. 44.95 (0-387-97437-7) Spr-Verlag.

— Intermediate Calculus. 2nd ed. (Undergraduate Texts in Mathematics Ser.). (Illus.). 600p. 1986. 45.00 (0-387-96058-9) Spr-Verlag.

— Modern Mathematical Analysis. 1964. text ed. 68.95 (0-201-05995-9) Addison-Wesley.

Protter, P. Stochastic Integration & Differential Equations. (Applications of Mathematics Ser.: Vol. 21). x, 302p. 1992. 59.00 (0-387-50996-8) Spr-Verlag.

Protti, Maria E., ed. Webster v. Reproductive Health Services: Briefs & Related Documents. LC 90-83331. 818p. 1990. lib. bdg. 195.00 (0-89941-741-8, 306660) W S Hein.

Protz, Roger. Beer, Bed & Breakfast. 4th ed. (Illus.). 260p. 1993. pap. 10.95 (0-86051-785-3, Robson-Parkwest) Parkwest Pubns.

— English Village Pubs. 160p. 1992. 27.50 (1-55859-409-4) Abbeville Pr.

— The European Beer Almanac. (Illus.). 168p. 1991. per. 16.99 (0-948403-28-4, Pub. by Camra Bks UK) Info Devels.

— The Great British Beer Book. (Illus.). 156p. 1987. pap. 12.99 (0-245-54599-9, Pub. by Camra Bks UK) Info Devels.

— The Real Ale Drinkers Almanac. 3rd ed. (Illus.). 320p. 1993. per. 14.99 (1-897784-17-1, Pub. by Camra Bks UK) Info Devels.

Protz, Roger & Wheeler, Graham. Brew Your Own Real Ale at Home. (Illus.). 187p. (Orig.). 1993. per., pap. 14.99 (1-85249-113-2, Pub. by Camra Bks UK) Info Devels.

Protzen, Jean-Pierre. Inca Architecture & Construction at Ollantaytambo. (Illus.). 320p. 1993. 75.00 (0-19-507069-0) OUP.

Protzman, John M. Confounded Interest. (Illus.). 44p. (Orig.). 1982. pap. 11.95 (0-9608898-0-9, 2-EJD) JMP Mfg.

Prou, Jean. Le Chant Gregorien et la Sanctification des Fideles. 24p. (FRE.). (C). 1985. pap. 5.95 (1-55725-128-2, 4080, Pub. by Abbey St Peter Solesmes FR) Paraclete MA.

***Proud-Bailey Co. Ltd., Staff.** British Post Office in the Far East. (C). 1989. 175.00x (1-872465-09-9, Pub. by Proud Bailey UK) St Mut.

***Proud Bailey Co. Ltd., Staff.** History of the Australian Military Postal Service 1914 - 1950. 1989. 175.00 (1-872465-60-9, Pub. by Proud Bailey UK) St Mut.

— History of the South African Postal Service. 1989. 175.00 (1-872465-76-5, Pub. by Proud Bailey UK) St Mut.

***Proud-Bailey Co. Ltd., Staff.** The Postal History of British Airmails. (C). 1989. 175.00x (1-872465-72-2, Pub. by Proud Bailey UK) St Mut.

***Proud Bailey Co., Ltd., Staff.** The Postal History of Hong Kong. 1989. 175.00 (1-872465-07-2, Pub. by Proud Bailey UK) St Mut.

***Proud Bailey Co. Ltd., Staff.** The Postal History of Kenya. 1989. 175.00 (0-614-01353-4, Pub. by Proud Bailey UK) St Mut.

***Proud-Bailey Co. Ltd., Staff.** The Postal History of Tanganyika. 1989. 175.00 (1-872465-06-4, Pub. by Proud Bailey UK) St Mut.

***Proud Bailey Co. Ltd., Staff.** The Postal History of the Naval & R. A. F. Postal Services. (C). 1989. 175.00x (1-872465-62-5, Pub. by Proud Bailey UK) St Mut.

***Proud Bailey Co., Ltd., Staff.** The Postal History of the Occupation of Malaya & British Borne. (C). 1989. 175.00x (1-872465-73-0, Pub. by Proud Bailey UK) St Mut.

***Proud-Bailey Co. Ltd., Staff.** The Postal History of Uganda & Zanzibar. 1989. 175.00 (1-872465-08-0, Pub. by Proud Bailey UK) St Mut.

Proud, John. Master Production Scheduling: The Practical Guide for Managing World Class MPS. LC 93-60667. 400p. 1994. 150.00 (0-939246-36-8, TM7638) Oliver Wight.

Proud, Joseph M. & Luessen, Lawrence H., eds. Radiative Processes in Discharge Plasmas. (NATO ASI Series B, Physical Sciences: Vol. 149). 600p. 1987. 115.00 (0-306-42550-5, Plenum Pr) Plenum.

Proud, Richard F. Portrait of a Legislature. 413p. 1989. 15.95 (0-9621473-0-3) Duorp Pr.

Proudfit, Charles L., ed. see Landor, Walter S.

Proudfoot, A. J., jt. auth. see Giles, T. E.

Proudfoot, A. T. Acute Poisoning: Diagnosis & Management. 2nd ed. 253p. 1993. pap. 45.00 (0-7506-1445-5) Buttrwrth-Heinemann.

***Proudfoot, Alex J. & Hutchings, Lawrence.** Teacher Beware: A Legal Primer for the Classroom Teacher. 391p. (Orig.). (C). 1988. pap. text ed. 23.95x (0-920490-82-4) Temeron Bks.

Proudfoot, Anna. Teach Yourself Italian Grammar. (Teach Yourself Ser.). 1992. 15.95 (0-8288-8360-2) Fr & Eur.

Proudfoot, Clementa R. Sunday Afternoons. 128p. 1988. write for info. (0-9621357-0-4) C R Proudfoot.

Proudfoot, G. R., ed. Tom a Lincoln. (Malone Society Ser.: No. 153). 120p. 1992. 39.00 (0-19-729030-2) OUP.

Proudfoot, L. J., jt. ed. see Graham, B. J.

***Proudfoot, Lindsay J.** Urban Patronage & Social Authority: The Management of the Duke of Devonshire's Towns in Ireland, 1764-1891. LC 94-22416. 1995. 69.95 (0-8132-0819-X) Cath U Pr.

Proudfoot, Madge. Wickenden Hall. 1992. 18.95 (0-533-09676-6) Vantage.

Proudfoot, Malcolm J. Population Movements in the Caribbean. LC 75-109359. 187p. 1970. reprint ed. text ed. 35.00 (0-8371-3634-2, PCA&, Greenwood Pr) Greenwood.

Proudfoot, Mary M. Britain & the U. S. in the Caribbean. 1976. lib. bdg. 69.95 (0-8490-1555-3) Gordon Pr.

Proudfoot, Mary M. & Perham, Margery F. Britain & the United States in the Caribbean: A Comparative Study in Methods of Development. LC 74-385. (Illus.). 434p. 1977. reprint ed. text ed. 35.00 (0-8371-7382-5, PRBR, Greenwood Pr) Greenwood.

Proudfoot, Merrill. Diary of a Sit-in. 2nd ed. (Blacks in the New World Ser.). (Illus.). 272p. 1990. 11.95 (0-252-06062-8) U of Ill Pr.

Proudfoot, Peter. The Secret Plan of Canberra. 160p. 29.95 (0-86840-030-0, Pub. by New South Wales Univ Pr AT) Intl Spec Bk.

Proudfoot, Robert. Even the Birds Don't Sound the Same Here: The Laotian Refugees Search for Heart in American Culture. (American University Studies Anthropology & Sociology: Ser. XI, Vol. 28). 276p. (C). 1989. text ed. 52.95 (0-8204-0841-7) P Lang Pubs.

Proudfoot, Wayne. God & the Self: Three Types of Philosophy of Religion. LC 75-28983. 241p. 1976. 34.50 (0-8387-1769-1) Bucknell U Pr.

— Religious Experience. LC 84-23928. 1985. pap. 13.00 (0-520-06128-4) U CA Pr.

Proudhon, P. J. Proudhon's Solution of the Social Problem. Cohen, Henry E., ed. (Men & Movements in the History & Philosophy of Anarchism Ser.). 1980. lib. bdg. 69.95 (0-87700-044-1) Revisionist Pr.

— What Is Property. 1972. 300.00 (0-8490-1287-2) Gordon Pr.

Proudhon, Pierre J. System of Economic Contradictions; Or, the Philosophy of Misery. Tucker, Benjamin R., tr. LC 75-38261. (Evolution of Capitalism Ser.). 482p. 1978. reprint ed. 30.95 (0-405-04134-9) Ayer.

Proudhon, Pierre-Joseph. General Idea of Revolution in the Nineteenth Century. 301p. (C). 1989. pap. text ed. 23.00 (0-85305-067-8, Pub. by Pluto Pr UK) Westview.

— General Idea of the Revolution in the Nineteenth Century. Robinson, John B., ed. (Studies in Individualist Anarchism & Mutualism). 1992. lib. bdg. 250.00 (0-87968-009-1) Gordon Pr.

— General Idea of the Revolution in the Nineteenth Century. LC 70-92978. (World History Ser.: No. 48). 1970. reprint ed. lib. bdg. 75.00 (0-8383-1005-2) M S G Haskell Hse.

— The Principle of Federation. Vernon, Richard, tr. & intro. by. LC 79-4192. 136p. reprint ed. pap. 38.80 (0-8357-3504-4, 2034035) Bks Demand.

Proudhon, Pierre-Joseph, et al. What Is Property? LC 93-16214. (Cambridge Texts in the History of Political Thought Ser.). 260p. (C). 1994. 54.95 (0-521-40555-6); pap. 16.95 (0-521-40556-4) Cambridge U Pr.

Proudlove, A., jt. auth. see Lichfield, N.

Proudman, Robert & Birchard, William, Jr. Trail Design, Construction & Maintenance. (Illus.). 176p. 1981. pap. 5.80 (0-917953-07-X) Appalachian Trail.

Proudman, Robert D. & Rajala, Reuben. Trail Building & Maintenance. 2nd ed. LC 82-121206. (Illus.). 288p. 1981. 12.95 (0-910146-30-6) AMC Books.

Proudman, Robert D., jt. auth. see Birchard, William, Jr.

Prough. Common Problems in Critical Care, Vol. 1: Pulmonary. 1991. write for info. (0-8151-6783-0, Yr Bk Med Pubs) Mosby Yr Bk.

Prough, et al. Decision Making in Critical Care. 2nd ed. 320p. Date not set. 59.00 (1-55664-376-4) Mosby Yr Bk.

Prough, R. A., jt. ed. see Powis, Garth.

Proulx, E. Annie. Heart Songs & Other Stories. LC 93-34060. 160p. 1995. pap. 10.00 (0-02-036075-4) Macmillan.

— Postcards. 352p. 1992. text ed. 22.95 (0-684-18718-3, Scribners) S&S Trade.

— Postcards: A Novel. 320p. 1993. pap. 11.00 (0-02-081185-3, Collier S&S) S&S Trade.

— The Shipping News. 1994. pap. 12.00 (0-671-51005-3, Touchstone Bks) S&S Trade.

— The Shipping News. 352p. 1994. pap. 10.00 (0-02-036078-9, Collier S&S) S&S Trade.

— The Shipping News. LC 94-8057. 1994. 24.95 (1-56895-069-1) Wheeler Pub.

— The Shipping News: A Novel. Grossman, B., ed. 352p. 1993. text ed. 20.00 (0-684-19337-X, Scribners) S&S Trade.

Proulx, Earl, jt. auth. see Yankee Magazine Editors.

Proulx, Ernest I., jt. auth. see Monks, Robert L.

Proulx, Jean-Pierre. Basque Whaling in Labrador in the 16th Century. (Illus.). 108p. (Orig.). Date not set. pap. 10.70 (0-660-14819-6, Pub. by Canada Commun Grp CN) Accents Pubns.

Proulx, Kevin E. Fear to the World: Eleven Voices in a Chorus of Horror. LC 93-242564. (Starmont Studies in Literary Criticism: No. 35). x, 243p. 1992. lib. bdg. 33.00x (1-55742-174-9); pap. 23.00x (1-55742-173-0) Borgo Pr.

Proulx, L., jt. auth. see Labrie, F.

Proum, Im, jt. auth. see Huffman, Franklin E.

Proum, Im, jt. ed. see Huffman, Franklin E.

Prouse, Derek, tr. see Ionesco, Eugene.

Prousis, Theophilus C. Russian Society & the Greek Revolution. LC 94-7870. 269p. 1994. lib. bdg. 30.00 (0-87580-193-5) N Ill U Pr.

Proussis, Costas M., jt. ed. see Arnakis, George G.

Proust, Joelle. Questions of Form: Logic & the Analytic Proposition from Kant to Carnap. Brenner, Anastasios A., tr. Orig. Title: Questions de Forme. 327p. (Orig.). 1989. text ed. 39.95 (0-8166-1760-0) U of Minn Pr.

Proust, L., jt. auth. see Pitard, J.

Proust, Marcel. A la Recherche du Temps Perdu, 4 vols., Vol. 1. Tadie, Jacques, ed. 1987. lib. bdg. 145.00 (0-7859-3879-6) Fr & Eur.

— A la Recherche du Temps Perdu, Vol. 1. deluxe ed. (Pleiade Ser.). 400p. (FRE.). 1969. 89.95 (2-07-011126-1) Schoenhof.

— A la Recherche du Temps Perdu, Vol. 2. Tadie, Jean-Yves, ed. (FRE.). 1988. lib. bdg. 145.00 (0-7859-3882-6) Fr & Eur.

— A la Recherche du Temps Perdu, Vol. 2. deluxe ed. (Pleiade Ser.). 376p. (FRE.). 1969. 89.95 (2-07-011136-9) Schoenhof.

— A la Recherche du Temps Perdu, Vol. 3. Tadie, Jean-Yves, ed. (FRE.). 1988. lib. bdg. 150.00 (0-7859-3884-2) Fr & Eur.

— A la Recherche du Temps Perdu, Vol. 3. deluxe ed. (Pleiade Ser.). 488p. (FRE.). 1969. 89.95 (2-07-011143-1) Schoenhof.

— A la Recherche du Temps Perdu, Vol. 4. Tadie, Jean-Yves, ed. (FRE.). 1989. lib. bdg. 155.00 (0-7859-3886-9) Fr & Eur.

— A la Recherche du Temps Perdu, Vol. 4. deluxe ed. (Pleiade Ser.). 504p. (FRE.). 1989. 89.95 (2-07-011164-4) Schoenhof.

— A l'Ombre des Jeunes Filles en Fleurs. 492p. (FRE.). 1992. pap. 24.95 (0-7859-1639-3, 2070724913) Fr & Eur.

— A l'Ombre des Jeunes Filles en Fleurs. (Folio Ser.: No. 1946). 568p. (FRE.). 1988. pap. 12.95 (2-07-038051-3, 1428) Schoenhof.

— A l'Ombre des Jeunes Filles en Fleurs, Vol. 9. 1965. 12.95 (0-685-74005-6, F52240) Fr & Eur.

— A l'Ombre des Jeunes Filles en Fleurs, Bk. 2: A la Recherche du Temps Perdu. (FRE.). 1972. pap. 13.95 (0-8288-3758-9, F119540) Fr & Eur.

— Albertine Disparu La Fugitive, Bk. 7: A la Recherche du Temps Perdu. (FRE.). 1990. pap. 15.95 (0-8288-3759-7, F119550) Fr & Eur.

— Albertine Disparue: (La Fugitive) (Folio Ser.: No. 2139). 374p. (FRE.). 1984. pap. 9.95 (2-07-038233-8, 2127) Schoenhof.

— Un Amour de Swann. (FRE.). 1976. pap. 10.95 (0-8288-3760-0, F119603) Fr & Eur.

— Un Amour de Swann. Sonnenfeld, Albert, ed. 278p. (ENG & FRE.). 1986. 3.95 (0-88332-466-0) Schoenhof.

— Un Amour de Swann. (Folio Ser.: No. 780). 254p. (FRE.). 1987. 8.95 (2-07-036780-0) Schoenhof.

— Autour de la Recherche: Lettres. (FRE.). 1988. pap. 24.95 (0-7859-3311-5, 2870272650) Fr & Eur.

— The Captive. 1987. reprint ed. lib. bdg. 22.95 (0-89966-582-9) Buccaneer Bks.

— The Captive - The Fugitive, Vol. 5. 1993. 19.50 (0-679-42477-6, Modern Lib) H Leonard.

— Captive the Fugitive Time, Vol. III. 1982. pap. 22.00 (0-394-71184-X, Vin) Random.

— Cities of the Plain. 1988. reprint ed. lib. bdg. 23.95 (0-89966-583-7) Buccaneer Bks.

— Combray. Bree, Germaine & Lynes, Carlos, Jr., eds. (Orig.). (FRE.). 1952. pap. text ed. write for info. (0-13-152439-9) P-H.

— Contre Sainte-Beuve. write for info. (0-318-63466-X) Fr & Eur.

— Contre Sainte-Beuve. (Folio Ser.: No. 68). (FRE.). pap. 11.95 (2-07-032428-1) Schoenhof.

— Contre Sainte-Beuve, Etc. (FRE.). 1971. lib. bdg. 99.50 (0-8288-3529-2, F119354) Fr & Eur.

— Contre Sainte-Beuve; Pastiches et Melanges; Essais et Articles. deluxe ed. (Pleiade Ser.). 1022p. (FRE.). 1971. 64.95 (2-07-010651-9) Schoenhof.

— Correspondance Avec Gaston Gallimard. (Gallimard Ser.). (FRE.). pap. 49.95 (2-07-071629-5) Schoenhof.

— Correspondance avec Sa Mere. (FRE.). 1992. pap. 16.95 (0-7859-3205-4, 2264017929) Fr & Eur.

— Cote de Guermantes, 2 tomes, Set. 354p. (FRE.). 1988. pap. 12.95 (0-7859-1377-7, 2070381900) Fr & Eur.

— Cote de Guermantes, Tome 1. (Folio Ser.: No. 2005). (FRE.). pap. 9.95 (2-07-038094-7) Schoenhof.

— Cote de Guermantes, Tome 2. (Folio Ser.: No. 2006). (FRE.). pap. 9.95 (2-07-038190-0) Schoenhof.

— Cote de Guermantes: A la Recherche du Temps Perdu: Avec: Sodome et Gomorrhe, Vol. 4. 504p. (FRE.). 1992. pap. 29.95 (0-685-74008-0, 207072638X) Fr & Eur.

— La Cote de Guermantes, Vol. 1, Bks. 3-4: A la Recherche du Temps Perdu. (FRE.). 1988. pap. 11.95 (0-8288-3761-9, FC1509) Fr & Eur.

— La Cote de Guermantes, Vol. 2, Bks. 3-4: A la Recherche du Temps Perdu. (FRE.). 1988. pap. 11.95 (0-8288-3762-7, FC1510) Fr & Eur.

— Du Cote de Chez Swann. (Folio Ser.: No. 1924). (FRE.). 1965. pap. 13.95 (2-07-037924-8) Schoenhof.

— Du Cote de Chez Swann, Bk. 1: A la Recher che du Temps Perdu. 527p. (FRE.). 1989. pap. 16.95 (0-7859-4618-7, F119560) Fr & Eur.

— La Fugitive. (FRE.). 1986. pap. 16.95 (0-7859-3399-9) Fr & Eur.

— Guermantes Way. 1993. 18.50 (0-679-60028-0, Modern Lib) Random.

— Guermantes Way. (In Search of Lost Time Ser.: Vol. 3). 1993. 18.50 (0-685-62549-4, Modern Lib) Random.

— The Guermantes Way. rev. ed. Moncrieff, C. K. & Kilmartin, Terence, trs. 1993. write for info. (0-318-69701-7, Modern Lib) Random.

— L' Indifferent: Nouvelle. (FRE.). 1978. pap. 10.95 (0-7859-1351-3, 2070297713) Fr & Eur.

— Jean Santeuil. (FRE.). 1971. lib. bdg. 89.95 (0-8288-3530-6, F119353) Fr & Eur.

— Jean Santeuil; Les Plaisirs et les Jours. deluxe ed. (Pleiade Ser.). 1123p. (FRE.). 1987. 63.95 (2-07-010650-0) Schoenhof.

— Lettres a Bibesco. 11.95 (0-685-37066-6) Fr & Eur.

— Lettres a Reynaldo Hahn. pap. 6.50 (0-685-37068-2) Fr & Eur.

— Lettres Retrouvees. 6.95 (0-685-37069-0) Fr & Eur.

— Marcel Proust: Selected Letters, Vol. II: 1904-1909. Kolb, Philip, ed. Kilmartin, Terence, tr. (Illus.). 512p. 1989. 35.00 (0-19-505961-1) OUP.

— On Reading. Sturrock, John, tr. & pref. by. (Syrens Ser.). 1995. mass mkt. 3.95 (0-14-038903-2, Penguin Bks) Viking Penguin.

— On Reading Ruskin. LC 86-22467. (Illus.). 192p. 1987. 25.00 (0-300-03513-6) Yale U Pr.

— Par les Yeux de Marcel Proust. Muhlstein, ed. 16.50 (0-685-37070-4) Fr & Eur.

— Past Recaptured. Mayor, Andreas, tr. Date not set. Date Not Set. pap. write for info. (0-394-50649-9) Random.

— Les Pastiches de Proust. Milly, ed. 48.25 (0-685-37071-2) Fr & Eur.

— Pastiches et Melanges. 1970. pap. 8.95 (0-7859-2836-7) Fr & Eur.

— Plaisirs Et Les Jours. (Imaginaire Ser.). (FRE.). 1924. pap. 13.95 (2-07-028613-4) Schoenhof.

— Les Plaisirs et les Jours. (FRE.). 1979. pap. 17.95 (0-7859-2743-3) Fr & Eur.

— Pleasures & Days: & Other Writings. Varese, L. et al, trs. LC 78-2432. 1978. reprint ed. 45.00 (0-86527-293-X) Fertig.

— Pleasures & Regrets. 236p. 1986. reprint ed. 26.00 (0-7206-0655-1) Dufour.

— Pleasures & Regrets. Varese, Louise, tr. LC 84-6120. (Neglected Books of the 20th Century Ser.). 221p. 1984. reprint ed. pap. 7.50 (0-88001-063-0) Ecco Pr.

— La Prisonniere. (Folio Ser.: No. 785). 499p. (FRE.). 1987. pap. 12.95 (2-07-038177-3) Schoenhof.

— La Prisonniere, Bk. 6: A la Recherche du Temps Perdu. (FRE.). 1989. pap. 15.95 (0-8288-3764-3, F119580) Fr & Eur.

— Proust on Art & Literature. 250p. 1984. pap. 8.95 (0-88184-114-5) Carroll & Graf.

— Remembrance of Things Past. 1982. pap. 22.00 (0-394-71183-1, Vin) Random.

— Remembrance of Things Past, 1. 1981. 25.00 (0-394-50644-8) Random.

— Remembrance of Things Past, 2. 1981. 25.00 (0-394-50645-6) Random.

— Remembrance of Things Past, 3. 1981. 25.00 (0-394-50646-4) Random.

— Remembrance of Things Past, Set. 1981. 75.00 (0-394-50643-X) Random.

— Remembrance of Things Past, 3 vols., Set. Scott-Moncrieff, C. K. et al, trs. LC 82-40052. (C). 1982. pap. 62.95 (0-394-71243-9, Vin) Random.

— Selected Letters, Eighteen Eighty to Nineteen Hundred Three. Kolb, Philip, ed. Manheim, Ralph, tr. (Illus.). xxviii, 376p. 1988. pap. text ed. 16.95 (0-226-68459-8) U Ch Pr.

— Sodome et Gomorrhe. 1966. write for info. (0-318-63599-2, 1641) Fr & Eur.

— Sodome et Gomorrhe. (Folio Ser.: No. 2047). 599p. (FRE.). 1985. pap. 15.95 (2-07-038135-8, 1641) Schoenhof.

— Sodome et Gomorrhe, Bk. 5: A la Recherche du Temps Perdu. (FRE.). 1972. pap. 18.95 (0-8288-3765-1, F119590) Fr & Eur.

— Sur Baudelaire, Flaubert et Morand. (FRE.). 1987. pap. 24.95 (0-7859-3309-3, 2870271980) Fr & Eur.

— Swann's Way. Scott-Moncrieff, C. K., tr. 1965. pap. text ed. write for info. (0-07-553647-1, T67) McGraw.

— Swann's Way. Moncrieff, C. K. & Kilmartin, Terence, trs. LC 92-25657. (In Search of Lost Time Ser.: Vol. 1). 1992. 17.50 (0-679-60005-1, Modern Lib) Random.

— Swann's Way. 1986. reprint ed. lib. bdg. 21.95 (0-89966-581-0) Buccaneer Bks.

— Swanns Way, Vol. 1. 1982. pap. 20.00 (0-394-71182-3) Random.

— Swann's Way: Remembrance of Things Past. Scott-Moncrieff, C. K. & Kilmartin, Terence, trs. (International Ser.). 1989. pap. 13.00 (0-679-72009-X, Vin) Random.

— Le Temps Retrouve. (Folio Ser.: No. 2203). 442p. (FRE.). 1987. pap. 10.95 (2-07-038293-1) Schoenhof.

— Le Temps Retrouve, Bk. 8: A la Recherche du Temps Perdu. (FRE.). 1990. pap. 16.95 (0-8288-3766-X, F128080) Fr & Eur.

— Time Regained - Guide to Proust, Vol. 6. 1993. 18.50 (0-679-42476-8, Modern Lib) Random.

— Within a Budding Grove. Moncrieff, C. K. & Kilmartin, Terence, trs. LC 92-25656. (In Search of Lost Time Ser.: Vol. 2). 1992. 18.50 (0-679-60006-X, Modern Lib) Random.

Proust, Marcel & Riviere, Jacques. Correspondance 1914-1922. Kolb, Phillip, ed. 353p. (FRE.). 1976. pap. 18.95 (0-7859-1594-X, 207029420X) Fr & Eur.

Prout, Alan, jt. ed. see James, Allison.

Prout, B. J. & Cooper, J. G. An Outline of Clinical Diagnosis. 2nd ed. (Illus.). 264p. 1987. pap. 24.95 (0-7236-0928-4, Pub. by John Wright UK) Buttrwrth-Heinemann.

— Outline of Clinical Diagnosis. 2nd ed. (Illus.). 280p. 1987. pap. 18.00 (0-318-35047-5, Yr Bk Med Pubs) Mosby Yr Bk.

Prout, Christopher. Market Socialism in Yugoslavia. (Economies of the World Ser.). 1986. pap. 21.00 (0-19-828287-7) OUP.

Prout, Curtis & Ross, Robert N. Care & Punishment: The Dilemmas of Prison Medicine. LC 87-35331. (Contemporary Community Health Ser.). (Illus.). 272p. (Orig.). 1988. 49.95 (0-8229-3581-3); pap. 14.95 (0-8229-5403-6) U of Pittsburgh Pr.

Prout, E. Double Counterpoint & Canon. LC 68-25300. (Studies in Music: No. 42). 1969. reprint ed. lib. bdg. 75.00 (0-8383-0312-9) M S G Haskell Hse.

Prout, Ebenezar. Instrumentation. LC 68-25302. (Studies in Music: No. 42). (Illus.). 1969. reprint ed. lib. bdg. 55.95 (0-8383-0314-5) M S G Haskell Hse.

Prout, Ebenezer. Applied Forms: A Sequel to Musical Form. 3rd ed. LC 71-155615. reprint ed. 34.50 (0-404-05138-3) AMS Pr.

— Applied Forms: A Sequel to Musical Form. LC 77-10853. 1971. reprint ed. 7.00 (0-403-00329-6) Scholarly.

— Applied Forms: A Sequel to "Musical Form" 307p. 1990. reprint ed. lib. bdg. 79.00 (0-7812-0784-3) Rprt Serv.

— Counterpoint: Strict & Free. LC 73-108530. 1970. 7.00 (0-403-00325-3) Scholarly.

— Counterpoint: Strict & Free. 2nd ed. LC 70-149692. reprint ed. 45.00 (0-404-05139-1) AMS Pr.

— Counterpoint: Strict & Free. 249p. 1990. reprint ed. lib. bdg. 69.00 (*0-7812-9141-0*) Rprt Serv.
— Double Counterpoint & Canon. 273p. 1990. reprint ed. lib. bdg. 69.00 (*0-7812-9142-9*) Rprt Serv.
— Fugal Analysis. 1973. lib. bdg. 59.95 (*0-8490-0206-0*) Gordon Pr.
— Fugue. 4th ed. LC 69-14043. 258p. 1970. reprint ed. text ed. 59.75 (*0-8371-1872-7*, PRFU, Greenwood Pr) Greenwood.
— Fugue. LC 68-25301. (Studies in Music: No. 42). 1969. reprint ed. lib. bdg. 48.95 (*0-8383-0313-7*) M S G Haskell Hse.
— Fugue. 258p. 1990. reprint ed. lib. bdg. 69.00 (*0-7812-9134-8*) Rprt Serv.
— Fugue. LC 71-108527. 1970. reprint ed. 14.00 (*0-403-00328-8*) Scholarly.
— Harmony: Its Theory & Practice. 342p. 1990. reprint ed. lib. bdg. 79.00 (*0-7812-9137-2*) Rprt Serv.
— Harmony, Its Theory & Practice. rev. ed. LC 79-151598. reprint ed. 34.50 (*0-404-05144-8*) AMS Pr.
— Instrumentation. 144p. 1990. reprint ed. lib. bdg. 59.00 (*0-7812-9150-X*) Rprt Serv.
— Musical Form. 257p. 1990. reprint ed. lib. bdg. 69.00 (*0-7812-9147-X*) Rprt Serv.
— Musical Form. LC 78-108526. 1970. reprint ed. 6.50 (*0-403-00327-X*) Scholarly.
— The Orchestra. 1990. reprint ed. lib. bdg. 140.00 (*0-7812-9151-8*) Rprt Serv.
— The Orchestra, 2 vols. (Illus.). 577p. reprint ed. 59.00 (*0-403-00322-9*) Scholarly.
— The Orchestra: The Works of Ebenezer Prout, 2 vols. reprint ed. lib. bdg. 99.00 (*0-7812-0781-9*) Rprt Serv.
Prout, G. Motor Boating for Beginners. (C). 1987. 25.00 (*0-85174-142-8*, Pub. by Brwn Son Ferg) St Mut.
— Simple Boat Building. (C). 1987. 36.00 (*0-85174-143-6*, Pub. by Brwn Son Ferg) St Mut.
Prout, H. Thompson, jt. auth. see Brown, Douglas T.
Prout, H. Thompson, jt. auth. see Knoff, Howard M.
Prout, H. Thompson, jt. ed. see Strohmer, Douglas C.
Prout, Henry G. A Life of George Westinghouse. LC 72-5068. (Technology & Society Ser.). (Illus.). 406p. 1977. reprint ed. 34.95 (*0-405-04719-3*) Ayer.
Prout, James H. & Bienvenue, Gordon R. Acoustics for You. LC 88-7699. 276p. (C). 1990. lib. bdg. 29.50 (*0-89464-328-2*) Krieger.
Prout, N. M. & Moorhouse, J. S., eds. Modern Chlor-Alkali Technology, Vol. 4. 380p. 1990. 99.00 (*1-85166-392-4*) Elsevier.
Prout, T. P. Industrial Market Research Workbook. 240p. 1973. 35.00 (*0-8464-0509-1*) Beekman Pubs.
Prouty, Charles T. Contention & Shakespeare's 2 Henry V. 1954. 59.50 (*0-685-69852-1*) Elliots Bks.
— George Gascoigne. LC 65-19620. 1972. 23.95 (*0-405-08867-1*, Pub. by Blom Pubns UK) Ayer.
— The Sources of Much Ado About Nothing. Bd. with Ariodanto & Ieneura. LC 76-128893. LC 76-128893. (Select Bibliographies Reprint Ser.). 1977. reprint ed. 19.95 (*0-8369-5513-7*) Ayer.
Prouty, Charles T., ed. Shakespeare: Of an Age & for All Time. LC 72-960. reprint ed. 21.50 (*0-404-05146-4*) AMS Pr.
Prouty, Charles T., ed. see Kyd, Thomas.
Prouty, Charles T., ed. see Shakespeare, William.
Prouty, Chris. Empress Taytu & Menilek II: Ethiopia 1883-1910. 430p. 1987. 29.95 (*0-932415-10-5*); pap. 11.95 (*0-932415-11-3*) Red Sea Pr.
Prouty, Chris & Rosenfeld, Eugene. Historical Dictionary of Ethiopia & Eritrea. 2nd ed. LC 93-29501. (African Historical Dictionaries Ser.: No. 56). (Illus.). 644p. 1994. 69.50 (*0-8108-2663-1*) Scarecrow.
Prouty, David F. In Spite of Us: My Education in the Big & Little Games of Amateur & Olympic Sports in the U. S. George, Barbara, ed. LC 88-51231. 288p. 1988. 19.95 (*0-941950-16-6*); pap. 12.95 (*0-941950-18-2*) Vitesse Pr.
Prouty, Dick, jt. auth. see Shelton, David C.
Prouty, Garry. Theoretical Evolutions in Person-Centered - Experiential Therapy: Applications to Schizophrenic & Retarded Psychoses. LC 93-42143. 144p. 1994. text ed. 49.95 (*0-275-94543-X*, Praeger Pubs) Greenwood.
Prouty, Graciela P., tr. see Rubio, Pedro.
Prouty, Howard H. Variety TV Reviews, Index 1923-1990. LC 89-17088. (Variety Television Reviews Ser.: Vol. 15). 640p. 1991. reprint ed. 375.00 (*0-8240-3794-4*) Garland.
Prouty, Howard H., ed. Variety Television Reviews, 1923-1950. LC 89-17088. (Variety Television Reviews Ser.: Vol. 3). 528p. 1989. 165.00 (*0-8240-2589-X*) Garland.
— Variety Television Reviews, 1923-1990, 16 vols., Ea. 1992. 165.00 (*0-318-69656-8*) Garland.
— Variety Television Reviews, 1923-1990, 16 vols., Set. 1992. 3,015.00 (*0-8153-0363-7*) Garland.
— Variety Television Reviews, 1946-56. LC 89-17088. (Variety Television Reviews Ser.: Vol. 1). 776p. 1990. 165.00 (*0-8240-2587-3*) Garland.
— Variety Television Reviews, 1951-1953. LC 89-17088. (Variety Television Reviews Ser.: Vol. 4). 528p. 1989. 165.00 (*0-8240-2590-3*) Garland.
— Variety Television Reviews, 1957-1959. LC 89-17088. (Variety Television Reviews Ser.: Vol. 6). 536p. 1989. 165.00 (*0-8240-2592-X*) Garland.
— Variety Television Reviews, 1957-60. LC 88-17088. (Variety Television Reviews Ser.: Vol. 2). 496p. 1990. 165.00 (*0-8240-2588-1*) Garland.
— Variety Television Reviews, 1960-1962. LC 89-17088. (Variety Television Reviews Ser.: Vol. 7). 496p. 1989. 165.00 (*0-8240-2593-8*) Garland.
— Variety Television Reviews, 1963-1965. LC 89-17088. (Variety Television Reviews Ser.: Vol. 8). 520p. 1989. 165.00 (*0-8240-2594-6*) Garland.
— Variety Television Reviews, 1966-1969. LC 89-17088. (Variety Television Reviews Ser.: Vol. 9). 560p. 1989. 165.00 (*0-8240-2595-4*) Garland.
— Variety Television Reviews, 1970-1973. LC 89-17088. (Variety Television Reviews Ser.: Vol. 10). 472p. 1989. 165.00 (*0-8240-2596-2*) Garland.
— Variety Television Reviews, 1974-1977. LC 89-17088. (Variety Television Reviews Ser.: Vol. 11). 464p. 1989. 165.00 (*0-8240-2597-0*) Garland.
— Variety Television Reviews, 1978-1982. LC 89-17088. (Variety Television Reviews Ser.: Vol. 12). 424p. 1989. 165.00 (*0-8240-2598-9*) Garland.
— Variety Television Reviews, 1983-1986. LC 89-17088. (Variety Television Reviews Ser.: Vol. 13). 544p. 1989. 165.00 (*0-8240-3792-8*) Garland.
— Variety Television Reviews, 1987-1988. LC 89-17088. (Variety Television Reviews Ser.: Vol. 14). 328p. 1990. 165.00 (*0-8240-3793-6*) Garland.
— Variety Television Reviews, 1989-1990. LC 89-17088. (Variety Television Reviews Ser.: Vol. 16). 592p. 1992. 165.00 (*0-8240-3795-2*) Garland.
Prouty, John C., et al. The ACC Basketball Stat Book. 362p. 1993. pap. 11.95 (*0-9640369-0-8*) Willow Oak.
Prouty, L. Fletcher. JFK: The CIA, Vietnam & the Plot to Assassinate John F. Kennedy. 352p. 1992. 22.00 (*1-55972-130-8*, Birch Ln Pr) Carol Pub Group.
— The Secret Team: The CIA & Its Allies in Control of the United States & the World. 496p. reprint ed. pap. 14.95 (*0-939484-35-8*) Inst Hist Rev.
Prouty, Olive H. Now, Voyager. 340p. 1991. reprint ed. lib. bdg. 25.95 (*0-89966-791-0*) Buccaneer Bks.
***Prouty, Raymond W.** Helicopter Performance, Stability & Control. 746p. 1995. 86.50 (*0-89464-929-9*) Krieger.
— Helicopter Performance, Stability, & Control. LC 90-4119. 746p. 1990. reprint ed. 86.50 (*0-89464-457-2*) Krieger.
Prouty, Tim, jt. auth. see Bird, Annette.
Provan, C. The Bible & Birth Control. 1989. 6.00 (*0-685-59738-5*, X601) Human Life Intl.
***Provan, Iain.** First & Second Kings. expanded rev. ed. Alexander, Patrick H., ed. (New International Biblical Commentary Ser.). 380p. 1995. pap. 9.95 (*1-56563-053-X*) Hendrickson MA.
— Lamentations. Clements, Ronald E. & Black, Matthew, eds. (New Century Bible Commentary Ser.). 160p. (Orig.). 1991. pap. 14.99 (*0-8028-0547-7*) Eerdmans.
Provan, Iain W. Hezekiah & the Books of Kings: A Contribution to the Debate about the Composition of the Deuteronomistic History. (Beiheft zur Zeitschrift fuer die Alttestamentliche Wissenschaft Ser.: Vol. 172). 218p. (C). 1988. lib. bdg. 60.00 (*0-89925-461-6*) De Gruyter.
Provan, James W., jt. ed. see Sih, G. C.
Provan, Jill & Glogowski, Maryruth P., eds. Management Media Directory: An Annotated Guide of Commercially Available Audiovisual Programs for Business & Management Schools, in-House Training & Development Programs, Management Consultants, & Human Resource Managers. (Neal Schuman Bk.). 512p. 1982. 200.00 (*0-8103-0170-9*) Gale.
Provan, Jill E. & Hunter, Joy W., eds. Health Media Review Index. LC 84-14079. 844p. 1985. 59.50 (*0-8108-1739-X*) Scarecrow.
Provan, John. Count Zeppelin - A System Builder: The Zeppelin Company & Its Subsidiaries. (Illus.). 128p. (Orig.). 1988. pap. 11.75 (*0-945794-07-X*) Luftschiff-Zeppelin.
Provder, Theodore, ed. Chromotography of Polymers: Characterization by SEC & FFF. LC 93-186. (Symposium Ser.: Vol. 521). (Illus.). 338p. 1993. 94.95 (*0-8412-2625-3*) Am Chemical.
— Computer Applications in Applied Polymer Science. LC 82-13735. (ACS Symposium Ser.: No. 197). 469p. 1982. lib. bdg. 54.95 (*0-8412-0733-X*) Am Chemical.
— Computer Applications in Applied Polymer Science, No. 2: Automation, Modeling, & Simulation. LC 89-17602. (Symposium Ser.: No. 404). (Illus.). 551p. 1989. 109.95 (*0-8412-1662-2*) Am Chemical.
— Computer Applications in the Polymer Laboratory. LC 86-10831. (ACS Symposium Ser.: No. 313). (Illus.). 321p. 1986. 76.95 (*0-8412-0977-4*) Am Chemical.
— Detection & Data Analysis in Size Exclusion Chromatography. LC 87-19480. (Symposium Ser.: No. 352). (Illus.). ix, 370p. 1987. 76.95 (*0-8412-1429-8*) Am Chemical.
— Particle Size Distribution Two: Assessment & Characterization. LC 91-25166. (ACS Symposium Ser.: No. 472). (Illus.). 408p. 1991. 89.95 (*0-685-50550-2*) Am Chemical.
— Size Exclusion Chromatography: Methodology & Characterization of Polymers & Related Materials. LC 83-27515. (ACS Symposium Ser.: No. 245). 391p. 1984. lib. bdg. 72.95 (*0-8412-0826-3*) Am Chemical.
— Size Exclusion Chromatography (GPC) LC 80-22015. (ACS Symposium Ser.: No. 138). 1980. 41.95 (*0-8412-0586-8*) Am Chemical.
Provder, Theodore, ed. see American Chemical Society Division of Polymeric Materials, Science & Engineering Staff, et al.
Provder, Theodore J., ed. see Polymetric Materials Division Staff.
Provence, Sally. Guide for the Care of Infants in Groups. LC 67-26025. 104p. (C). 1967. pap. 12.95 (*0-87868-061-0*) Child Welfare.
Provence, Sally, ed. Infants & Parents: Clinical Case Reports. LC 83-18441. (Clinical Infant Reports: No. 2). xix, 306p. (C). 1983. text ed. 45.00x (*0-8236-2636-9*) Intl Univs Pr.
Provence, Sally & Lipton, Rose C. Infants in Institutions: A Comparison of Their Development During the First Year of Life with Family-Reared Infants. LC 62-21560. 191p. 1967. text ed. 30.00 (*0-8236-2648-2*) Intl Univs Pr.
Provence, Sally, jt. ed. see Fenichel, Emily.
Provence, Sally, et al. The Challenge of Daycare. LC 75-43331. 313p. 1977. reprint ed. pap. 89.20 (*0-7837-3307-0*, 2057709) Bks Demand.
Provencher, Jean. Quebec. (Discover Canada Ser.). (Illus.). 144p. (J). (gr. 4 up). 1992. lib. bdg. 20.55 (*0-516-06617-X*) Childrens.
Provencher, R. G. Arson 1976. 1976. 3.25 (*0-686-17605-7*, TR 76-3) Society Fire Protect.
***Provensen, A.** Owl & Three Pussycats. 1981. 8.99 (*0-224-01821-3*) Random.
***Provensen, Alice.** My Fellow Americans: A Family Album. LC 95-15527. (Illus.). (J). 1995. write for info. (*0-15-276642-1*, Browndeer Pr) HarBrace.
— Punch in New York. (J). (ps-3). 1991. pap. 14.95 (*0-670-82790-8*) Viking Child Bks.
Provensen, Alice & Provensen, Martin. The Glorious Flight. (J). (gr. 3-5). 1987. audio 22.95 (*0-87499-062-9*); audio, pap. 14.95 (*0-87499-061-0*) Live Oak Media.
— The Glorious Flight. (J). (gr. 4-6). 1987. pap. 5.99 (*0-14-050729-9*, Puffin) Puffin Bks.
— The Glorious Flight, 4 bks., Set. (J). (gr. 3-5). 1987. audio, pap. 31.95 (*0-87499-063-7*) Live Oak Media.
— The Glorious Flight: Across the Channel with Louis Bleriot. (Illus.). 40p. (J). (gr. 3-8). 1987. pap. 4.95 (*0-317-63651-0*, Puffin) Puffin Bks.
— The Glorious Flight Across the Channel with Louis Bleriot. LC 82-7034. (Illus.). 40p. (J). (gr. 5-8). 1983. pap. 16.99 (*0-670-34259-9*) Viking Child Bks.
— Leonardo da Vinci: The Artist, Inventor, Scientist in Three-Dimensional Movable Pictures. LC 83-26005. (Illus.). 12p. (J). 1984. pap. 19.95 (*0-670-42384-X*) Viking Child Bks.
— El Libro de las Estaciones. Cuenca, Pilar de & Alvarez, Ines, trs. LC 81-13821. (Bilingual Picturebacks Ser.). Orig. Title: A Book of Seasons. (Illus.). 32p. (SPA.). (J). (ps-3). 1982. reprint ed. pap. 2.25 (*0-394-85143-9*) Random Bks Yng Read.
— The Mother Goose Book. LC 76-8548. (Illus.). 64p. (J). (gr. 1 up). 1976. 10.00 (*0-394-82122-X*) Random Bks Yng Read.
— Our Animal Friends at Maple Hill Farm. LC 74-828. (Illus.). 64p. (J). (ps-3). 1992. 10.00 (*0-394-82123-8*) Random Bks Yng Read.
— An Owl & Three Pussycats. LC 93-44747. (J). 1994. 16.95 (*0-15-200183-2*, Browndeer Pr) HarBrace.
— Shaker Lane. (J). (ps up). 1987. 14.95 (*0-670-81568-3*) Viking Child Bks.
— Town & Country. LC 93-44749. (J). 1994. 16.95 (*0-15-200182-4*, Browndeer Pr) HarBrace.
— The Year at Maple Hill Farm. LC 88-10367. (Illus.). 32p. (J). (ps-2). 1988. pap. 4.95 (*0-689-71270-7*, Aladdin Paperbacks) S&S Childrens.
Provensen, Alice & Provensen, Martin, illus. A Peaceable Kingdom: The Shaker Abecedarius. (Picture Puffins Ser.). (J). (gr. k-3). 1981. pap. 5.99 (*0-14-050370-6*, Puffin) Puffin Bks.
Provensen, Martin, jt. auth. see Provensen, Alice.
Provensen, Martin, jt. illus. see Provensen, Alice.
Provenza, Dominic V. Oral Histology: Inheritance & Development. 2nd ed. LC 84-20140. 497p. reprint ed. pap. 141.70 (*0-7837-2740-2*, 2043120) Bks Demand.
Provenzale, James M. & Taveras, Juan M. Clinical Cases in Neuroradiology. LC 93-629. (Illus.). 400p. 1993. 125.00 (*0-8121-1590-2*) Williams & Wilkins.
Provenzano, Anthony J., jt. auth. see Bliss, Dorothy E.
Provenzano, J., jt. ed. see Bliss, Dorothy E.
Provenzano, Joe. The Philosophy of Conscious Energy. 182p. 1992. pap. 8.95 (*1-55523-493-3*) Winston-Derek.
Provenzano, Johanna Z., comp. Promising Practices: A Teacher Resource (Grades K-3) LC 85-61129. 104p. 1985. pap. 6.00 (*0-89763-108-0*) Natl Clearinghse Bilingual Ed.
Provenzano, Paul. Pedro the Kid. 240p. 1994. pap. 8.95 (*1-56901-269-5*) NW Pub.
***Provenzano, Paul & D'Amico, Nash, Jr.** Italian Food, Family & Foolishness: Cooking Italian Style. 200p. 1995. pap. 14.95 (*0-9634839-9-4*) Tamarack Bks.
Provenzano, Steven. The Guide to Basic Cover Letter Writing. 1995. pap. 7.95 (*0-8442-8196-4*, VGM Career Bks) NTC Pub Grp.
— Top Secret Resumes & Cover Letters. 208p. 1995. pap. 12.95 (*0-7931-1359-8*, 5614-3401) Dearborn Finan.
Provenzano, Steven A. Slam Dunk Resumes. Kennedy, Sarah, ed. LC 93-45862. (Orig.). 1994. pap. 7.95 (*0-8442-8191-3*, VGM Career Bks) NTC Pub Grp.
— TOP SECRET Resumes for the '90s: Discover What Really Works, & the Secrets "Professional" Resume Writers Won't Tell You. rev. ed. Desktop Publishing Inc. Staff, ed. LC 93-70858. (Careers-Resume Writing Ser.). 214p. (Orig.). 1994. reprint ed. pap. 10.95 (*0-9633558-1-3*) DeskTop IL.
Provenzano, Tobi E. Medjugorje Coloring Book: A Coloring Book with Messages for All Ages! (Illus.). 24p. (Orig.). 1993. pap. 1.98 (*0-685-72756-4*) Riehle Found.
Provenzo, Asterie B. Favorite Board Games You Can Make & Play. 1990. pap. 7.95 (*0-486-26410-6*) Dover.
Provenzo, Eugene. Forty-Seven Easy to Do Classic Science Experiments. 1990. pap. 3.95 (*0-486-25856-4*) Dover.
Provenzo, Eugene E., Jr. An Introduction to Education in American Society. 320p. (C). 1986. write for info. (*0-675-20242-6*, Merrill Pub Co) Macmillan.
Provenzo, Eugene E., Jr., jt. auth. see Button, H. Warren.
Provenzo, Eugene F. Beyond the Gutenberg Galaxy: Microcomputers & the Emergence of Post-Typographic Culture. LC 86-1938. 128p. (Orig.). reprint ed. pap. 36.50 (*0-7837-4629-6*, 2044352) Bks Demand.
Provenzo, Eugene F., Jr. Religious Fundamentalism & American Education: The Battle for the Public Schools. LC 89-4456. (Philosophy of Education Ser.). 134p. 1990. 59.50 (*0-7914-0217-7*); pap. 19.95 (*0-7914-0218-5*) State U NY Pr.
— Video Kids: Making Sense of Nintendo. 192p. 1991. pap. text ed. 10.95 (*0-674-93709-0*) HUP.
Provenzo, Eugene F., Jr. & Brett, Arlene. The Complete Block Book. (Illus.). 182p. 1983. text ed. 34.95 (*0-8156-2300-3*); pap. 14.95 (*0-8156-0188-3*) Syracuse U Pr.
Provenzo, Eugene F. & Carlebach, Michael, Jr. Farm Security Administration Photographs of Florida. LC 93-2846. (Illus.). 144p. (C). 1993. lib. bdg. 34.95 (*0-8130-1212-0*); pap. 19.95 (*0-8130-1213-9*) U Press Fla.
***Provenzo, Eugene F., Jr. & Fradd, Sandra H.** Hurricane Andrew, the Public Schools & the Rebuilding of Community. (SUNY Series, Education & Culture). 160p. 1995. text ed. 44.50x (*0-7914-2481-2*); pap. 14.95x (*0-7914-2482-0*) State U NY Pr.
Provenzo, Eugene F., Jr., jt. auth. see Brett, Arlene.
Provenzo, Eugene F., Jr., ed. see Lewis, Mary H.
Provenzo, Therese M., ed. see Lewis, Mary H.
***Prover, Jorja.** No One Knows Their Names. LC 94-70377. 176p. (C). 1994. 37.95 (*0-87972-657-1*); pap. text ed. 17.95 (*0-87972-658-X*) Bowling Green Univ.
Providence Record Commissioners Staff. The Early Records of the Town of Providence, Vol. 1: Being the First Book of the Town of Providence Called the Long Old Book with Parchment Cover. x, 139p. 1993. reprint ed. pap. text ed. 14.00 (*1-55613-794-X*) Heritage Bk.
Providence Records Commissioners Staff. The Early Records of the Town of Providence, Vol. 2. (Illus.). 244p. 1993. reprint ed. pap. 18.00 (*1-55613-826-1*) Heritage Bk.
Provin, Robert, jt. auth. see Willis, Brad.
Province, C. M. The Unknown Patton. (Illus.). 272p. 1988. 5.99 (*0-517-45595-1*) Random Hse Value.
***Province, Charles M.** Patton's One-Minute Messages: Tactical Leadership Skills for Business Management. LC 95-11869. 104p. 1995. pap. 8.95 (*0-89141-546-7*) Presidio Pr.
— Patton's Third Army: A Chronology of Third Army Advance August 1944-May 1945. 336p. 1994. reprint ed. pap. 11.95 (*0-7818-0239-3*) Hippocrene Bks.
Provincial Archives Staff & Victoria, British Columbia. Dictionary Catalogue of the Library of the Provincial Archives of British Columbia, 8 vols., Set. 1971. lib. bdg. 870.00 (*0-8161-0912-5*, Hall Library) G K Hall.
Provincial Congress of Massachusetts Colony, 1775 Staff. Narrative of the Excursions & Ravages of the King's Troops Under Command of General Gage. LC 67-29008. (Eyewitness Accounts of the American Revolution Ser., No. 1). 1968. reprint ed. 14.95 (*0-405-01119-9*) Ayer.
Provine, Doris M. Case Selection in the United States Supreme Court. LC 79-25967. 1980. lib. bdg. 21.00 (*0-226-68468-7*) U Ch Pr.
— Judging Credentials: Nonlawyer Judges & the Politics of Professionalism. LC 85-16516. xviii, 248p. 1986. pap. text ed. 13.95 (*0-226-68471-7*) U Ch Pr.
Provine, Dorothy S. Index to District of Columbia Wills, 1801-1920. 218p. 1992. 25.00 (*0-8063-1354-4*, 4705) Genealog Pub.
Provine, Dorothy S., comp. Alexandria County, Virginia, Free Negro Registers, 1797-1861. 358p. (Orig.). 1991. pap. 35.00 (*1-55613-416-9*) Heritage Bk.
Provine, Harriet T., jt. auth. see Gardner, Pierce.
Provine, William B. The Origins of Theoretical Population Genetics. LC 73-153711. (Chicago History of Science & Medicine Ser.). xii, 202p. 1987. pap. text ed. 16.95 (*0-226-68466-0*) U Ch Pr.
— Sewall Wright & Evolutionary Biology. LC 85-24651. (Illus.). xvi, 546p. 1986. 30.00 (*0-226-68474-1*) U Ch Pr.
— Sewall Wright & Evolutionary Biology. LC 85-24651. (Illus.). xvi, 546p. 1989. pap. text ed. 18.95 (*0-226-68473-3*) U Ch Pr.
Provine, William B., jt. auth. see Mayr, Ernst.
Provine, Williams B., ed. see Wright, Sewall.
Provisional Government of Ireland Staff. The Irish Proclamation, 1916. McCormick, Malachi, ed. 16p. 1982. pap. text ed. 4.00 (*0-943984-04-1*) Stone St Pr.
Provisor, Janis. Bada Shanren & Me. (Illus.). 16p. 1991. pap. 5.00 (*0-930495-11-X*) San Fran Art Inst.
Provizer, Norman W., ed. Analyzing the Third World: Essays from "Comparative Politics" 510p. 1978. pap. 21.95 (*0-87073-943-3*) Transaction Pubs.
— Analyzing the Third World: Essays from Comparative Politics. LC 77-13286. 509p. reprint ed. pap. 145.10 (*0-8357-5430-8*, 2056583) Bks Demand.
Provo, Diane & Bott, Diane. Kids Are Great...When You Know How They Work: An Owners Manual. 2nd ed. (Illus.). 72p. 1992. pap. 11.95 (*0-9631607-2-9*) Starting Blocks.
Provo, Diane, jt. auth. see Bott, Diane.
Provo, Patti. Inspiration Tarot. (Illus.). 24p. 1992. 12.00 (*0-88079-524-7*) US Games Syst.
Provo, Patti, jt. auth. see Fairfield, Gail.
Provonsha, Jack W. A Remnant in Crisis. LC 92-41459. 1992. write for info. (*0-8280-0698-9*) Review & Herald.
Provoost, jt. ed. see Wolff.
Provost. Advanced Indoor Exercise. (Runner's World Ser.). 1981. pap. 16.95 (*0-02-499470-7*) Macmillan.
Provost, jt. auth. see Hyink.
Provost, C. Antonio. Modern Renaissance Poetry & Philosophy. Kroll, William, ed. LC 92-96848. (Illus.). 148p. (YA). (gr. 9-12). 1992. 14.00 (*0-317-05253-5*); pap. 10.00 (*0-317-05254-3*) Provost.
— Opening of the American Mind. LC 89-64102. 1990. 15.95 (*0-87212-246-8*); pap. 9.95 (*0-87212-235-2*) Libra.
— The Reformation of Society Through Adequate Education. LC 94-69192. 1995. 15.95 (*0-8158-0511-X*) Chris Mass.

P Q

An Asterisk (*) at the beginning of an entry indicates that the title is appearing in BIP for the first time.

— The Sexual Revolution: Its Impact on Society & a Challenge against the Makers with a Plea for Reforms & Some Recommendations. write for info. (*0-318-23066-6*) Provost.

Provost, C. Antonio & Blaney, Worth. The Senior Olympics, Preventive Medicine, & Findings Pertaining to Health & Longevity. 1981. 6.00 (*0-686-32025-5*) Provost.

Provost, Foster. Columbus: An Annotated Guide to the Scholarship on His Life & Writings, 1750-1988. (Illus.). 225p. 1991. lib. bdg. 54.00 (*1-55888-157-3*) Omnigraphics Inc.

— Columbus: Dream & Act. 70p. 1986. 15.00 (*0-916617-23-8*) J C Brown.

— A Columbus Dictionary. 142p. 1991. lib. bdg. 54.00 (*1-55888-158-1*) Omnigraphics Inc.

Provost, Gary. Across the Border: The True Story of the Satanic Cult Killings in Matamoros, Mexico. 256p. 1989. mass mkt. 4.50 (*0-671-69319-0*) PB.

— Good If It Goes. LC 89-18339. 160p. (J). (gr. 4-7). 1990. pap. 3.95 (*0-689-71381-9*, Aladdin Paperbacks) S&S Childrens.

— High Stakes: Inside Today's Las Vegas. LC 93-24040. (Illus.). 320p. 1994. 22.95 (*0-525-93650-5*, Dutton-Truman Talley) NAL-Dutton.

— How to Write & Sell True Crime. 192p. 1989. 17.95 (*0-89879-446-3*) Writers Digest.

— Into Their Own Hands. 1994. 5.99 (*0-553-56117-0*) Bantam.

— Make Your Words Work. 304p. 1994. pap. 14.95 (*0-89879-636-9*) Writers Digest.

— One Hundred Ways to Improve Your Writing. 1985. pap. 4.99 (*0-451-62721-0*, Ment) NAL-Dutton.

— Perfect Husband. Zion, Claire, ed. 264p. 1992. reprint ed. mass mkt. 5.50 (*0-671-72494-0*) PB.

— Without Mercy: Obsession & Murder under the Influence. Zion, Claire, ed. 328p. 1990. reprint ed. mass mkt. 5.99 (*0-671-66997-4*) PB.

Provost, Gary & Levine-Provost, Gail. David & Max. 196p. (J). (gr. 5-9). 1991. pap. 9.95 (*0-8276-0392-4*) JPS Phila.

Provost, J. C. Obedient to God's Word. LC 92-75258. 200p. (Orig.). 1992. pap. 7.95 (*1-879667-11-8*) Dove Pr TX.

Provost, James & Walf, Knut, eds. Catholic Identity. (Concilium Ser.). 125p. (Orig.). 1994. pap. 15.00 (*0-88344-880-7*) Orbis Bks.

***Provost, John F.** Nurse Shark. LC 95-1173. (Sharks Ser.). (J). 1995. write for info. (*1-56239-472-X*) Abdo & Dghtrs.

Provost, Judith A. A Casebook: Applications of the Myers-Briggs Type Indicator in Counseling. 2nd ed. LC 93-41360. 124p. 1993. pap. 10.00 (*0-935652-17-5*) Ctr Applications Psych.

— Procrastination: Using Psychological Type Concepts to Help Students. 11p. 1988. 5.00 (*0-935652-14-0*) Ctr Applications Psych.

— Strategies for Success: Using Type to Do Better in High School & College. 13p. 1992. 4.50 (*0-935652-15-9*) Ctr Applications Psych.

— Work, Play, & Type: Achieving Balance in Your Life. 128p. 1990. pap. 11.95 (*0-89106-040-5*) Consulting Psychol.

Provost, Judith A. & Anchors, Scott, eds. Applications of the MBTI in Higher Education. 296p. 1987. pap. 21.95 (*0-89106-032-4*, 6869) Consulting Psychol.

Provost, Louis. Honore Daumier: A Thematic Guide to His Oeuvre. 300p. 1989. 135.00 (*0-8240-9302-X*) Garland.

Provost, Rene, tr. see Conforti, Benedetto.

Provost, Rhoda, jt. auth. see Benyo, Rich.

Provost, Rhonda, jt. auth. see Benyo, Rich.

***Provost, Richard.** The Art & Technique of Performance. 62p. (Orig.). (C). 1995. pap. text ed. 14.95 (*0-9627832-4-2*, DK 10020) Guitar Solo.

— The Art & Technique of Practice. 53p. (Orig.). (C). 1992. pap. text ed. 14.95 (*0-9627832-0-X*) Guitar Solo.

Provost, Ronnie, jt. auth. see Reed, James E.

Provost, Sarah. Inland, Thinking of Waves. LC 90-83468. (CSU Poetry Ser.: No. XXX). 70p. (Orig.). 1991. 12.00 (*0-914946-80-3*); pap. 8.00 (*0-914946-81-1*) Cleveland St Univ Poetry Ctr.

Provost, Thomas T. & Weston, William L., eds. Bullous Diseases. LC 92-49760. 279p. 1992. 70.00 (*0-8016-6532-9*) Mosby Yr Bk.

Provost, Thomas T., jt. ed. see Sontheimer, Richard D.

Prowe, Diethelm. Weltstadt in Krisen: Berlin, 1949-1958. (Veroeffentlichungen der Historischen Kommission zu Berlin, Band 67, Beitraege zu Inflation und Wiederaufbau in Deutschland und Europa 1914-1924: Vol. 42). x, 359p. (C). 1973. 103.00 (*3-11-003876-5*) De Gruyter.

Prowe, Gunhild & Schneider, Jill, comps. The Oxford German Minidictionary. 720p. 1993. pap. 5.95 (*0-19-864150-8*) OUP.

***Prowe, Gunhild & Schneider, Jill, eds.** Oxford Colour German Dictionary. 576p. (GER.). 1995. 8.95 (*0-19-864541-4*) OUP.

— The Oxford Paperback German Dictionary. LC 93-28761. (Oxford Paperback Reference Ser.). 576p. 1994. pap. 5.95 (*0-19-280011-6*) OUP.

***Prowell.** By Evil Means. 1995. mass mkt. 5.99 (*0-553-56966-X*) Bantam.

Prowell, George R. History of Camden County, New Jersey. (Illus.). 769p. 1992. reprint ed. lib. bdg. 77.50 (*0-8328-2442-9*) Higginson Bk Co.

— History of Camden County, N.J. (Illus.). 769p. 1993. reprint ed. lib. bdg. 77.00 (*0-8328-2876-9*) Higginson Bk Co.

— History of York County, PA, Vol. I. (Illus.). 1118p. 1993. reprint ed. lib. bdg. 109.00 (*0-8328-2861-0*) Higginson Bk Co.

— History of York County, PA, Vol. II. (Illus.). 1058p. 1993. reprint ed. lib. bdg. 99.00 (*0-8328-2862-9*) Higginson Bk Co.

— History of York County, Pa. with Modern Subject Index Vols. I & II. (Illus.). 474p. 1994. reprint ed. lib. bdg. 47.50 (*0-8328-4431-4*) Higginson Bk Co.

— History of York County, Pa. with Modern Subject Index Vols. I & II, 2 Vols., Vols. I & II. (Illus.). 2650p. 1994. lib. bdg. 195.00 (*0-8328-4430-6*) Higginson Bk Co.

Prowell, Sandra W. By Evil Means. 216p. 1993. 19.95 (*0-8027-1248-7*) Walker & Co.

— The Killing of Monday Brown: A Phoebe Siegel Mystery. 240p. 1994. 19.95 (*0-8027-3184-8*) Walker & Co.

Prowense, Mary J. Pamela & the Revolution. Schatz, Molly, ed. (Illus.). 130p. (J). (gr. 7 up). 1993. 12.95 (*0-9635107-2-X*) Marc Anthony.

Prowler, David. A Telegram from Marcel Duchamp. LC 90-91685. (Illus.). (Orig.). 1990. pap. 15.00 (*0-9628062-1-8*) Ready Made Pr.

Prowler, Don, ed. see National Passive Solar Conference Staff.

Prown, Jules D. John Singleton Copley, 2 vols. Incl. Vol. 1. In America, 1738 to 1774. LC 66-13183. (Illus.). 1966. (*0-318-53084-8*); Vol. 2. In England, 1774 to 1815. LC 66-13183. (Illus.). 1966. (*0-318-53085-6*); LC 66-13183. (Aisla Mellon Bruce Studies in American Art). 1966. Set. 40.00 (*0-674-48000-7*) HUP.

Prown, Jules D., et al. Discovered Lands, Invented Pasts: Transforming Visions of the American West. LC 92-53537. 217p. (C). 1992. pap. 30.00 (*0-89467-061-1*) Yale Art Gallery.

— Discovered Lands, Invented Pasts: Transforming Visions of the American West. (Illus.). 256p. (C). 1992. pap. text ed. 40.00 (*0-300-05722-9*) Yale U Pr.

— Discovered Lands, Invented Pasts: Transforming Visions of the American West. (Illus.). 232p. 1994. pap. 25.00 (*0-300-05731-8*) Yale U Pr.

***Prown, Pete.** Van Halen: Riff by Riff. 83p. (YA). 1995. pap. 17.95 (*0-89524-900-6*) Cherry Lane.

***Prown, Pete & Newquist, H. P.** Electric Warriors: The History of Rock Guitar. (Illus.). 300p. (Orig.). 1995. pap. text ed. 19.95 (*0-7935-4042-9*, HL00330019) H Leonard.

Prowse, C., et al, eds. Hepatitis: A Virus Transmission by Blood Products. (Journal: Vox Sanguinis Ser.: Vol. 67, Supplement 1, 1994). (Illus.). iv, 86p. 1994. pap. 36.00 (*3-8055-6006-0*) S Karger.

Prowse, Christopher V. Plasma & Recombinant Blood Products in Medical Therapy. 227p. 1992. text ed. 59.95 (*0-471-93200-0*, Wiley-Liss) Wiley.

Proxmire, Bill. Your Joy Ride to Health. LC 93-93538. 318p. 1994. 24.95 (*0-9637988-2-0*) B Proxmire.

Proxmire, William. Can Small Business Survive? Bruchey, Stuart & Carosso, Vincent P., eds. LC 78-18974. (Small Business Enterprise in America Ser.). 1979. reprint ed. lib. bdg. 21.95 (*0-405-11477-X*) Ayer.

Proysen, Alf. Little Old Mrs. Pepperpot. (J). (gr. 1-4). 1960. 12.95 (*0-8392-3021-4*) Astor-Honor.

— Mrs. Pepperpot Again. (Illus.). (J). (gr. 1-4). 1961. 12.95 (*0-8392-3023-0*) Astor-Honor.

— Mrs. Pepperpot to the Rescue. (J). (gr. 1-4). 1988. pap. 3.50 (*0-317-69648-3*, Puffin) Puffin Bks.

Prozan, Charlotte. Feminist Psychoanalytic Psychotherapy. LC 91-47122. 384p. 1992. 50.00 (*0-87668-456-8*) Aronson.

— The Technique of Feminist Psychoanalytic Psychotherapy. LC 93-20278. 584p. 1993. 50.00 (*0-87668-268-9*) Aronson.

Prozesky, Martin. New Guide to the Debate about God. 192p. (Orig.). 1992. pap. 18.00 (*0-334-01123-X*, SCM Pr) TPI PA.

— Religion & Ultimate Well-Being: An Explanatory Theory. LC 84-3340. 224p. 1984. text ed. 29.95 (*0-312-67057-5*) St Martin.

Prozesky, Martin, ed. Christianity Amidst Apartheid: Selected Perspectives on the Church in South Africa. LC 89-34299. 256p. 1990. text ed. 39.95 (*0-312-03529-2*) St Martin.

***Prozesky, Martin & De Gruchy, John, eds.** Living Faiths in South Africa. LC 95-16661. 1995. write for info. (*0-312-12776-6*) St Martin.

Prozier, Norman W., jt. ed. see Pederson, William D.

***Prozini, Bill.** Hardcase: A "Nameless Detective" Mystery. LC 95-5723. 1995. write for info. (*0-385-30506-0*) Delacorte.

Prozini, Bill, jt. auth. see Muller, Marcia.

Prozorova, L. A., jt. auth. see Kotyuzhanskii, B. Y.

Prpic, George J. Croatia & the Croatians: An Annotated Bibliography. LC 80-66277. (Illus.). 315p. 1982. 16.95 (*0-910164-05-3*); pap. 9.95 (*0-910164-02-9*) Assoc Bk Pubs.

— Croatian & the Croatians: An English-Language Bibliography & Resource Guide. rev. ed. Kapetanovic, Ruzica, ed. (Illus.). 450p. 1993. pap. 17.95 (*0-910164-24-X*) Assoc Bk Pubs.

— Croatian & the Croatians: An English-Language Bibliography & Resource Guide. 2nd rev. ed. Kapetanovic, Ruzica, ed. (Illus.). 450p. 1993. 24.95 (*0-910164-23-1*) Assoc Bk Pubs.

— The Croatian Immigrants in America. (Illus.). 1971. 12.00 (*0-686-61038-5*) Ragusan Pr.

Prpic, K. J & Davey, B. R., eds. The Genus Yersinia: Epidemiology, Molecular Biology & Pathogenesis. (Contributions to Microbiology & Immunology Ser.: Vol. 9). (Illus.). x, 346p. 1987. 224.00 (*3-8055-4482-0*) S Karger.

Prssat, Roland. Diccionario de Demografia. 248p. (SPA.). 1987. 75.00 (*0-7859-5853-3*, 8428105979) Fr & Eur.

Prstojevic, Miroslav. Sarajevo: Survival Guide. 1994. pap. 10.00 (*1-56305-688-7*) Workman Pub.

Prubhupada, A. C., tr. see Wilson, Karen.

Pruce, Dale. The Golf Trekker: Courses of Southern California. 272p. (Orig.). 1992. pap. text ed. 9.95 (*0-9628144-2-3*) Butler Pubns.

— The Golf Trekker Courses of San Diego. rev. ed. 136p. 1991. pap. 5.95 (*0-9628144-1-5*) Butler Pubns.

Pruce, Earl. Synagogues, Temples & Congregations of Maryland, 1830-1990. 255p. 1993. pap. 15.00 (*1-883312-00-0*) Jew Hist Soc MD.

Prucha, David J., tr. see Paulus, Trina.

Prucha, Francis P. American Indian Treaties: The History of a Political Anomaly. LC 93-36297. (C). 1994. 45.00 (*0-520-08531-0*) U CA Pr.

— Atlas of American Indian Affairs. LC 90-675000. (Illus.). x, 191p. 1990. 50.00 (*0-8032-3689-1*) U of Nebr Pr.

— Broadax & Bayonet: The Role of the United States Army in the Development of the Northwest, 1815-1860. LC 94-44363. 1995. write for info. (*0-8032-8738-0*) U of Nebr Pr.

— Broadaxe & Bayonet: The Role of the U. S. Army in the Development of the Northwest, 1815-1860. (Illus.). 304p. 1995. pap. 12.00 (*0-8032-5151-3*, Bison Books) U of Nebr Pr.

— Churches & the Indian Schools, 1888-1912. LC 79-12220. (Illus.). xiv, 278p. 1979. 30.00 (*0-8032-3657-3*) U of Nebr Pr.

— The Great Father: The United States Government & the American Indians. abr. ed. LC 85-5875. (Illus.). xii, 426p. 1986. 40.00 (*0-8032-3675-1*); pap. 13.95 (*0-8032-8712-7*) U of Nebr Pr.

— The Great Father: The United States Government & the American Indians, 2 vols., Set. (Illus.). 1405p. 1995. pap. text ed. 50.00 (*0-8032-8734-8*) U of Nebr Pr.

— The Great Father: The United States Government & the American Indians, Vol. II. (Illus.). xviii, 649p. 1984. write for info. (*0-318-57804-2*) U of Nebr Pr.

— Handbook for Research in American History: A Guide to Bibliographies & Other Reference Works. LC 86-30871. xiv, 289p. 1987. pap. 10.95 (*0-8032-8719-4*) U of Nebr Pr.

— Handbook for Research in American History: A Guide to Bibliographies & Other Reference Works. rev. ed. LC 93-4240. xiv, 214p. (C). 1994. pap. 9.95 (*0-8032-8731-3*) U of Nebr Pr.

— Handbook for Research in American History: A Guide to Bibliographies & Other Reference Works. 2nd rev. ed. LC 93-4240. xii, 214p. (C). 1994. 25.00 (*0-8032-3701-4*) U of Nebr Pr.

— Indian Peace Medals in American History. LC 95-8353. 1995. pap. write for info. (*0-9630731-4-1*) Rivilo Bks.

— Indian Policy in the United States: Historical Essays. LC 81-1667. (Illus.). 282p. reprint ed. pap. 80.40 (*0-7837-1895-0*, 2042099) Bks Demand.

— Indian-White Relations in the United States: A Bibliography of Works Published 1975-1980. LC 81-14722. viii, 179p. 1982. 20.00 (*0-8032-3665-4*); pap. 10.00 (*0-8032-8705-4*) U of Nebr Pr.

— The Indians in American Society: From the Revolutionary War to the Present. LC 85-1023. (Quantum Bks.: No. 29). 1985. 35.00 (*0-520-05503-9*); pap. 12.00 (*0-520-06344-9*) U CA Pr.

— The Sword of the Republic: The United States Army on the Frontier, 1783-1846. LC 86-6951. (Illus.). xviii, 458p. 1986. pap. 13.95 (*0-8032-8713-5*) U of Nebr Pr.

— U. S. Indian Policy: A Critical Bibliography. LC 77-6920. (Bibliographical Ser.). 64p. reprint ed. pap. 25.00 (*0-685-44453-8*, 2056714) Bks Demand.

Prucha, Francis P., ed. Documents of United States Indian Policy. LC 89-16408. (Illus.). xiv, 338p. 1990. pap. 15.00 (*0-8032-8726-7*) U of Nebr Pr.

— Documents of United States Indian Policy. 2nd ed. LC 89-16408. (Illus.). xiv, 338p. 1990. 40.00 (*0-8032-3688-3*) U of Nebr Pr.

Prucha, Francis P., ed. see Croghan, George.

Prucha, Isabel D. Your Library: A Friend. Duy, Hoang Chu, tr. (Illus.). 77p. (Orig.). (ENG & VIE.). 1986. pap. 10.95 (*0-937319-00-7*) Golden Palm Pr.

Prucha, Jan. Information Sources in Psycholinguistics: Biographical Handbook. 1972. pap. text ed. 19.25 (*90-279-2362-0*) Mouton.

— Pragmalinguistics: East European Approaches. (Pragmatics & Beyond: An Interdisciplinary of Language Studies: Vol. IV, No. 5). v, 103p. (Orig.). 1983. pap. 38.00x (*0-915027-28-3*) Benjamins North Am.

— Soviet Psycholinguistics. (Janua Linguarum, Ser. Minor: No. 143). 117p. (Orig.). 1972. pap. text ed. 53.10 (*90-279-2317-5*) Mouton.

Prucha, Jan, ed. Soviet Studies in Language & Language Behavior. (Linguistic Ser.: Vol. 24). 240p. 1976. pap. 59.00 (*0-444-10990-0*, North Holland) Elsevier.

Prucha, Lynette. Smokescreen: A Mystery. 296p. (Orig.). 1993. pap. 10.95 (*1-878533-01-0*) Clothespin Fever Pr.

***Pruchansky, Lisa.** 1995 Marketing Guidebook. 1994. 320.00 (*0-911790-26-8*) Trade Dimensns.

Pruchnik, F. P. Organometallic Chemistry of Transition Elements. Duraj, S. A., tr. (Modern Inorganic Chemistry Ser.). (Illus.). 774p. 1990. 150.00 (*0-306-43192-0*, Plenum Pr) Plenum.

Prudden. Fit for Life. 1986. pap. 12.95 (*0-02-599400-X*) Macmillan.

Prudden, Bonnie. Exer-Sex. (Illus.). 1980. pap. 6.50 (*0-553-10698-8*) Bonnie Prudden.

— How to Keep Your Family Fit & Healthy. (Illus.). 1975. 10.00 (*0-88349-041-2*) Bonnie Prudden.

— Myotherapy: Bonnie Prudden's Guide to Pain-Free Living. 1985. pap. 12.50 (*0-345-32688-1*, Ballantine Trade) Ballantine.

— Pain Erasure: The Bonnie Prudden Way. 1985. pap. 12.00 (*0-345-33102-8*, Ballantine Trade) Ballantine.

— Teach Your Baby to Swim. LC 73-79534. (Illus.). 1978. pap. text ed. 12.95 (*0-9602146-0-7*) Bonnie Prudden.

Prudden, P. M. Further Study of Prehistoric Small House-Ruins in the San Juan Watershed. LC 18-15717. (American Anthropological Association Memoirs Ser.: No. 21). 1918. pap. 15.00 (*0-527-00520-7*) Periodicals Srv.

Prudden, Suzy. Myotherapy. 1999. pap. write for info. (*0-385-27762-8*) Doubleday.

— Suzy Prudden's Exercise Program for Young Children. LC 82-40506. (Illus.). 192p. 1983. pap. 6.95 (*0-89480-371-9*, 371) Workman Pub.

Prudden, Suzy & Sussman, Jeffrey. Suzy Prudden's Pregnancy & Back-to-Shape Exercise Program. LC 80-51614. (Illus.). 224p. 1980. pap. 9.95 (*0-89480-129-5*, 430) Workman Pub.

— Suzy Prudden's Spot Reducing Program. LC 79-64784. (Illus.). 224p. 1979. 7.95 (*0-89480-114-7*, 288) Workman Pub.

Prude, Jonathan. The Coming of Industrial Order: Town & Factory Life in Rural Massachusetts, 1810-1860. (Illus.). 372p. 1985. pap. 19.95 (*0-521-31396-1*) Cambridge U Pr.

Prude, Jonathan, jt. ed. see Hahn, Steven.

Pruden, Donald. Around Town Cycling. LC 75-20739. (Illus.). 112p. 1975. pap. 2.95 (*0-89037-066-4*) Anderson World.

Pruden, Durward. A Sociological Study of a Texas Lynching. (Reprint Series in Sociology). (C). 1993. reprint ed. pap. text ed. 1.00 (*0-8290-2939-7*, S-479) Irvington.

Pruden, Leo M., tr. see De la Vallee Poussin, Louis.

Pruden, Vic. A Conceptual Approach to Basketball. LC 87-2671. (Illus.). 120p. 1987. text ed. 19.95 (*0-88011-287-5*, PPRU0287) Human Kinetics.

Prudentius. Poems, Vol. 1. LC 63-5499. (Fathers of the Church Ser.: Vol. 43). 280p. 1962. 29.95 (*0-8132-0043-1*) Cath U Pr.

— Poems, Vol. 2. LC 63-5499. (Fathers of the Church Ser.: Vol. 52). 224p. 1965. 29.95 (*0-8132-0052-0*) Cath U Pr.

— Works, 2 vols. No. 387, 398. write for info. (*0-318-53222-0*) HUP.

— Works, 2 vols., 1. (Loeb Classical Library: No. 387, 398). 15.50 (*0-674-99426-4*) HUP.

— Works, 2 vols., 2. (Loeb Classical Library: No. 387, 398). 15.50 (*0-674-99438-8*) HUP.

***Prudenziati, M., ed.** Thick Film Sensors. LC 94-29429. (Handbook of Sensors & Actuators Ser.: 1). 471p. 1994. 148.50 (*0-444-89723-2*) Elsevier.

Prudhoe, J., tr. see Goethe, Johann Wolfgang Von.

Prudhoe, John. The Theatre of Goethe & Schiller. (Drama & Theatre Studies). (Illus.). 218p. 1973. 29.00 (*0-8464-1191-1*) Beekman Pubs.

Prudhoe, Stephen. A Monograph on Polyclad Turbellaria. (Illus.). 264p. 1986. 65.00 (*0-19-858518-7*) OUP.

***Prud'homme.** Foams. (Surfactant Science Ser.). 690p. 1995. write for info. (*0-8247-9395-1*) Dekker.

Prudhomme, Enola. Enola Prudhomme's Low-Calorie Cajun Cooking. LC 90-5244. (Illus.). 224p. 1991. spiral bd. 17.95 (*0-688-09255-1*) Hearst Bks.

— Enola Prudhomme's Low-Fat Favorites: Enjoy Low-Fat Versions of Your Favorite Southern Dishes. LC 94-6973. 1994. 17.95 (*0-688-11894-1*) Hearst Bks.

Prudhomme, Frances & Sternberg, Susan T. The Gift of the Greeks: Art & Civilization of Ancient Greece. 24p. (Orig.). (J). (gr. 4-7). 1982. pap. 8.95 (*0-935213-04-X*) A M Huntington Art.

Prudhomme, Paul. Chef Paul Prudhomme's Fork in the Road. 1993. 23.00 (*0-688-12165-9*) Morrow.

— Chef Paul Prudhomme's Louisiana Cajun Magic Cookbook. 96p. 1989. 6.99 (*0-517-68642-2*) Random Hse Value.

— Chef Paul Prudhomme's Louisiana Kitchen. LC 83-63236. (Cookbook Library). (Illus.). 344p. 1984. 23.00 (*0-688-02847-0*) Morrow.

— Chef Paul Prudhomme's Pure Magic: Great Recipes Featuring Chef Paul's Magic Seasoning Blends. LC 94-46213. (Illus.). 1995. write for info. (*0-688-14202-8*) Morrow.

— Chef Paul Prudhomme's Seasoned America. (Illus.). 384p. 1991. 23.00 (*0-688-05282-7*) Morrow.

— The Prudhomme Family Cookbook: Old Time Louisiana Recipes. LC 87-18345. (Cookbook Library). (Illus.). 384p. 1987. 19.95 (*0-688-07549-5*) Morrow.

Prud'homme, Paul, tr. see Walling, Regis M. & Rupp, N. Daniel, eds.

Prud'homme, Robert K., jt. ed. see Harland, Ronald S.

Prud'homme, Robert K., jt. ed. see Herb, Craig A.

Prudhommeaux, Jules. Icarie et Son Fondateur, Etienne Cabet: Contribution a l'Etude Du Socialisme Experimental. LC 72-187458. (American Utopian Adventure Ser.). 688p. 1973. reprint ed. lib. bdg. 57.50 (*0-87991-005-4*) Porcupine Pr.

***Prudlo, Ester H.** The Butterfly Bandit. LC 95-78162. (Illus.). (J). (gr. 1-4). 1995. 14.95 (*1-880851-19-9*) Greene Bark Pr.

Prudnikov, A., jt. auth. see Ditkin, V.

Prudnikov, A. P., jt. auth. see Brychkov, Yu.

Prudnikov, A. P., et al. Direct Laplace Transforms, Vol. 4. (Integrals & Ser.). 1992. text ed. 190.00 (*2-88124-837-3*) Gordon & Breach.

— Integrals & Series, 2 vols., Set. Queen, N. M., tr. 1560p. 1986. text ed. 382.00 (*2-88124-089-5*) Gordon & Breach.

— Integrals & Series, 2 vols., Vol. 2. Queen, N. M., tr. 1560p. 1986. text ed. 382.00 (*2-88124-097-6*) Gordon & Breach.

— Integrals & Series: More Special Functions, Vol. 3. Gould, G. G., tr. 820p. 1990. text ed. 182.00 (*2-88124-682-6*) Gordon & Breach.

Prue, J. E. Ionic Equilibria. 1966. 60.00 (*0-08-011344-3*, Pub. by Pergamon Repr UK) Franklin.

Prue, Lucinda K. Atlas of Mammographic Positioning. LC 92-49800. (Illus.). 176p. 1993. text ed. 36.95 (*0-7216-3683-7*) Saunders.

Prueher, Terry. The Art of Discipline, Thought & Control. Nemetz, Jennifer, ed. 112p. (C). 1993. pap. 9.95 (*0-936417-35-8*) Axelrod Pub.

Prueitt, Melvin L. Computer Graphics: 118 Computer-Generated Designs. LC 74-18611. (Pictorial Archive Ser.). (Illus.). 80p. 1975. pap. 4.95 (*0-486-23178-X*) Dover.

Pruen, S. Tristram. The Arab & the African. 368p. 1986. 250.00 (*1-85077-136-7*, Darf Pubs Ltd) St Mut.

Pruett, Barbara J. Marty Robbins: Fast Cars & Country Music. LC 90-8709. (Illus.). 621p. 1990. 59.50 (*0-8108-2325-X*) Scarecrow.

— Popular Entertainment Research: How to Do It & How to Use It. LC 92-3800. 593p. 1992. 62.50 (*0-8108-2501-5*) Scarecrow.

Pruett, David J., jt. auth. see Gump, Barry H.

Pruett, David J., jt. ed. see Gump, Barry H.

Pruett, Gordon, intro. Life & Exploits of S. Glenn Young: A Reprint of the 1925 Biography of S. Glenn Young, Southern Illinois' Most Infamous Law Officer. (Illus.). 253p. 1989. reprint ed. 16.95 (*0-685-28059-4*); reprint ed. pap. 12.95 (*0-685-28060-8*) Crossfire Pr.

Pruett, Gordon E. As a Father Loves His Children: The Image of God As Loving Father in Judaism, Christianity, & Islam. LC 94-12974. (Catholic Scholars Press). 1994. 34.95 (*1-883255-68-6*); 54.95 (*1-883255-69-4*) Intl Scholars.

Pruett, Harold L. & Brown, Vivian B., eds. Crisis Intervention & Prevention. LC 85-644751. (New Directions for Student Services Ser.: No. 49). 1990. 16.95 (*1-55542-836-3*) Jossey-Bass.

Pruett, Jakie L. & Cole, Everett B. As We Lived - Stories Told by Black Story Tellers. 1982. 9.95 (*0-89015-309-4*) Sunbelt Media.

Pruett, James & Rigsby, Lee. Selective Music Bibliography from the Period 1663-1763. (Illus.). vii, 53p. 1962. pap. 2.00 (*0-86526-109-1*) NC Archives.

***Pruett, James M.** Fundamentals of Programming with FORTRAN 77. LC 86-21331. (Independent Learning Module from the Instrument Society of America Ser.). (Illus.). reprint ed. pap. 88.10 (*0-7837-9048-1*, 2049799) Bks Demand.

Pruett, James M. & Schneider, Helmut. Essentials of SPC in the Process Industries. LC 92-29678. (Independent Learning Module from the Instrument Society of America Ser.). 425p. 1993. 70.00 (*1-55617-391-1*) Instru Soc.

Pruett, James W., comp. Studies in Musicology: Essays in History, Style & Bibliography of Music in Memory of Glenn Haydon. LC 76-7574. (Illus.). 286p. 1976. reprint ed. text ed. 59.75 (*0-8371-8883-0*, PRSM, Greenwood Pr) Greenwood.

***Pruett, James W. & Slavens, Thomas P.** Research Guide to Musicology. fac. ed. LC 84-24379. (Sources of Information in the Humanities Ser.: No. 4). 178p. 1994. pap. 50.80 (*0-7837-7314-5*, 2047241) Bks Demand.

***Pruett, Joe, ed.** Negative Burn: Best of Year One. (Illus.). 128p. 1995. 9.95 (*0-941613-68-2*) Stabur Pr.

***Pruett, John H.** The Parish Clergy under the Later Stuarts: The Leicesterhire Experience. LC 78-8174. (Illus.). 213p. 1978. reprint ed. pap. 60.80 (*0-7837-8085-0*, 2047838) Bks Demand.

Pruett, Nancy J. Scientific & Technical Libraries, Vol. 1. (Library & Information Science Ser.). 1986. text ed. 75.00 (*0-12-566041-3*) Acad Pr.

— Scientific & Technical Libraries, Vol. 2. (Library & Information Science Ser.). 1986. text ed. 75.00 (*0-12-566042-1*) Acad Pr.

Pruett, Nancy J., ed. see Geoscience Information Society Staff.

Pruett, Robert H., ed. see Chewning, Alpheus J.

Pruett, Robert H., ed. see Williams, Jane S.

Pruett, Sarah C., tr. see Tarango, Yolanda, et al.

Pruett, Sven. How-to Build & Modify Ford V-6 60 Degree Engines. (PowerPro Ser.). (Illus.). 160p. 1994. pap. 17.95 (*0-87938-914-1*) Motorbooks Intl.

Pruette, Lorine. G. Stanley Hall. LC 73-126247. (Select Bibliographies Reprint Ser.). 1977. 20.95 (*0-8369-5474-2*) Ayer.

— Women & Leisure: A Study of Social Waste. LC 72-2620. (American Women Ser.: Images & Realities). 230p. 1974. reprint ed. 17.95 (*0-405-04473-9*) Ayer.

Pruetz, Rick. Putting Transfer of Development Rights to Work in California. 232p. (Orig.). 1993. pap. 25.00 (*0-923956-29-8*) Solano Pr.

Prufer, Olaf H. Raven Rocks: A Specialized Late Woodland Rockshelter Occupation in Belmont County, Ohio. LC 80-28085. (Kent State Research Papers in Archaeology: No. 1). 103p. reprint ed. pap. 29.40 (*0-7837-1343-6*, 2041491) Bks Demand.

Prufer, Olaf H. & Long, Dana A. The Archaic of Northeastern Ohio. LC 86-33. (Kent State Research Papers in Archaeology: No. 6). 95p. reprint ed. pap. 27.10 (*0-7837-1344-4*, 2041492) Bks Demand.

Prufer, Olaf H. & McKenzie, Douglas H., eds. Studies in Ohio Archaeology. rev. ed. LC 75-45380. 400p. reprint ed. pap. 114.00 (*0-317-28372-3*, 2025452) Bks Demand.

Prufer, Olaf H. & Shane, Orrin C. Blain Village & the Fort Ancient Tradition in Ohio. LC 79-99082. (Kent Studies in Anthropology & Archaeology: No. 1). 295p. reprint ed. pap. 84.10 (*0-7837-0300-7*, 2040621) Bks Demand.

Prufer, Olaf H., et al. Krill Cave: A Stratified Rockshelter in Summit County, Ohio. LC 88-30600. (Research Papers in Archaeology: No. 8). (Illus.). 109p. 1989. pap. 12.50 (*0-87338-379-6*) Kent St U Pr.

Prufer, Thomas. Recapitulations: Essays in Philosophy. LC 91-44978. (Studies in Philosophy & the History of Philosophy: Vol. 26). 112p. 1993. 34.95 (*0-8132-0764-9*) Cath U Pr.

Pruger, Robert. Efficiency & the Social Services. (Administration in Social Work Ser.: Vol. 15, Nos. 1 & 2). (Illus.). 187p. 1991. text ed. 39.95 (*1-56024-113-6*) Haworth Pr.

Pruger, Robert, jt. auth. see Gambrill, Eileen.

Prugh, Charles C. How to Jumpstart a Stalled Career. LC 93-3897. (Illus.). 1994. pap. write for info. (*0-8442-4171-7*, VGM Career Bks) NTC Pub Grp.

Prugh, Dane G. The Psychosocial Aspects of Pediatrics. LC 81-8289. 700p. reprint ed. pap. 180.00 (*0-7837-2741-0*, 2043121) Bks Demand.

Prugh, Dane G., jt. ed. see Stuart, Harold C.

Prugh, Jeff. The Herschel Walker Story. 1983. pap. 2.95 (*0-449-12622-6*) Fawcett.

Prugh, Richard W. Guidelines for Vapor Release Mitigation. LC 87-26987. 148p. 1988. 65.00 (*0-8169-0401-4*, G-4) Am Inst Chem Eng.

***Prugh, Thomas, et al.** Natural Capital & Human Economic Survival. 200p. 1995. 24.95 (*0-614-07417-7*) Chelsea Green Pub.

Prugl, Elisabeth, jt. ed. see Boris, Eileen.

Prugovecki, Eduard. Quantum Geometry: A Framework for Quantum General Relativity. (Fundamental Theories of Physics Ser.). 544p. (C). 1992. lib. bdg. 162.50 (*0-7923-1640-1*) Kluwer Ac.

— Quantum Mechanics in Hilbert Space. 2nd ed. LC 80-534. (Pure & Applied Mathematics Ser.). 1981. text ed. 97.00 (*0-12-566060-X*) Acad Pr.

— Stochastic Quantum Mechanics & Quantum Spacetime. 1984. lib. bdg. 48.50 (*0-318-00434-8*) Kluwer Ac.

***Prugovecki, Edward.** Principles of Quantum General Relativity. LC 94-41518. 376p. 1995. text ed. 74.00 (*981-02-2077-4*) World Scientific Pub.

Pruissen, Catherine. Start & Run a Profitable Home Daycare: Your Step-by-Step Business Plan. (Business Ser.). 1993. pap. 14.95 (*0-88908-294-4*) Self-Counsel Pr.

Pruit, A. R., ed. see Blazer, Almer N.

Pruit, jt. auth. see Goodwin.

Pruitt, jt. auth. see Tenovuov.

Pruitt, A. B. Abstracts of Land Entries: Gates, Chowan, Perquimans, Pasquotank, Camden, & Currituck Cos, NC. (Illus.). 198p. (Orig.). (YA). (gr. 12). 1992. pap. 18.75 (*0-944992-44-7*) ABP Abstracts.

— Abstracts of Lincoln Co, NC, Deeds (1786-1793) Books 3, 4, & 16. (Illus.). 159p. (Orig.). 1988. pap. 14.50 (*0-944992-12-9*) ABP Abstracts.

— Abstracts of Sales of Confiscated Land & Property in North Carolina. (Illus.). 249p. (Orig.). (YA). (gr. 12). 1990. pap. 23.00 (*0-944992-26-9*) ABP Abstracts.

— Colonial Petitions for Land Resurveys, Land Warrants, & Caveats. 142p. (YA). (gr. 12). 1993. pap. 14.50 (*0-944992-47-1*) ABP Abstracts.

— Glasgow Land Fraud Papers Seventeen Eighty-Three - Eighteen Hundred: North Carolina Revolutionary War Bounty Land in Tennessee. (Illus.). xxviii, 541p. (Orig.). 1988. pap. text ed. 47.30 (*0-944992-14-5*) ABP Abstracts.

— Petitions for Land Grant Suspensions in North Carolina. (Illus.). 402p. (Orig.). (YA). (gr. 12). 1993. pap. 39.00 (*0-944992-48-X*) ABP Abstracts.

Pruitt, Albert B. Spartanburg County - District, South Carolina, Deed Abstracts, Book A-T, 1785-1827. 872p. 1988. 55.00 (*0-89308-553-7*, SC 86) Southern Hist Pr.

Pruitt, Anne S., ed. In Pursuit of Equality in Higher Education. LC 86-80125. 236p. 1987. text ed. 28.95 (*0-930390-68-7*) Gen Hall.

***Pruitt, Bernadette.** Indian Summer. 1994. 17.95 (*0-8034-9071-2*, 094411) Bouregy.

— Salt of the Earth. LC 87-83381. 71p. 1988. 12.00 (*0-934188-27-0*) Evans Pubns.

Pruitt, Betty H. The Making of Harcourt General: A History of Growth Through Diversification, 1922-1992. 1994. text ed. 35.99 (*0-07-103589-3*) McGraw.

Pruitt, Bettye, ed. The Massachusetts Tax Valuation List of, 1171. 1978. lib. bdg. 105.00 (*0-8161-0245-7*, Hall Library) G K Hall.

Pruitt, Bettye H. The Making of Harcourt General: A History of Growth Through Diversification, 1922-1992. LC 93-50567. 320p. 1994. 35.00 (*0-87584-509-6*) Harvard Busn.

Pruitt, Bettye H., jt. auth. see Graham, Margaret B.

Pruitt, Dean G. & Carnevale, Peter J. Negotiation in Social Conflict. LC 93-16972. (Mapping Social Psychology Ser.). 1993. pap. 18.95 (*0-534-20689-1*) Brooks-Cole.

Pruitt, Deborah. Employee Participation Programs in Employee Ownership Companies. Young, Karen M., ed. (Illus.). 72p. (Orig.). (C). 1988. pap. 25.00 (*0-926902-03-2*) NCEO.

Pruitt, Elisabeth A., ed. see MacLane, Mary.

Pruitt, Fred. The New Testament Church & Its Symbols. 131p. 1.50 (*0-686-29157-3*) Faith Pub Hse.

— Past, Present & Future of the Church. 72p. pap. 0.60 (*0-686-29133-6*) Faith Pub Hse.

Pruitt, Fred & Pruitt, Lawrence. God's Gracious Dealings. (Illus.). 496p. 5.50 (*0-686-29110-7*) Faith Pub Hse.

Pruitt, G. R., jt. auth. see Melugin, R. K.

Pruitt, Gerald R., ed. Selected Papers on Cryogenic Optical Systems. LC 94-11392. (Milestone Ser.: Vol. MS 98). 1994. write for info. (*0-8194-1633-9*); pap. write for info. (*0-8194-1632-0*) SPIE.

Pruitt, Ida. Old Madam Yin: A Memoir of Peking Life. LC 78-68782. xii, 129p. 1979. 22.50 (*0-8047-1038-4*); pap. 9.95 (*0-8047-1099-6*) Stanford U Pr.

Pruitt, Ida, ed. see T'ai-t'ai, Ning L.

Pruitt, Ida, ed. see Wu, Yung.

***Pruitt, James.** Angels Beside You. 224p. (Orig.). 1994. mass mkt. 4.99 (*0-380-77766-5*) Avon.

— The Complete Angel: Angels Through the Ages-All You Need to Know. 256p. (Orig.). 1995. mass mkt. 5.50 (*0-380-78045-3*) Avon.

Pruitt, James B. Telecommunication Project Management. LC 86-51046. 1987. 50.00 (*0-917845-05-6*) Intertec IL.

Pruitt, James N. Fire Force. 192p. (Orig.). 1992. mass mkt. 3.99 (*0-380-76617-5*) Avon.

— Lobo One. 240p. (Orig.). 1992. mass mkt. 4.50 (*0-380-76616-7*) Avon.

Pruitt, Jim. Coaching Beginning Basketball. (Coaching Ser.). (Illus.). 138p. 1980. 12.95 (*0-8092-7089-7*); pap. 11.95 (*0-8092-7088-9*) Contemp Bks.

— Play Better Basketball. (Illus.). 128p. (Orig.). 1982. pap. 10.95 (*0-8092-5799-8*) Contemp Bks.

Pruitt, K. Wayne, jt. auth. see Lee, Jackson F., Jr.

Pruitt, Lawrence, jt. auth. see Pruitt, Fred.

Pruitt, Pamela, jt. auth. see Johnston, Brenda A.

Pruitt, Pamela, et al. Henry Box Brown; Struggle for Freedom; Wildfire. 2nd ed. McCluskey, John A., ed. (Stories from Black History Series II: Vol. 1). (Illus.). (Orig.). (J). (gr. 4-7). 1993. pap. 3.00 (*0-913678-25-2*) New Day Pr.

Pruitt, Patricia. Construction Work. 36p. 1991. 6.00 (*0-9630045-0-6*) Longwood MA.

Pruitt, Raymond M. Fundamentals of the Faith. 1981. 16.95 (*0-934942-21-8*) White Wing Pub.

Pruitt, Rhonda R. Flames of Fire: Biographical Accounts of Pentecost Through the Centuries. (Orig.). pap. text ed. write for info. (*0-318-59338-6*) Faith Print.

Pruitt, Robert J. And Then Shall the End Come. 1979. pap. 2.25 (*0-934942-20-X*) White Wing Pub.

— The Death of the Third Nature. 1975. pap. 2.50 (*0-934942-04-8*) White Wing Pub.

— The Kingdom of God & the Church of God. 1977. pap. 2.25 (*0-934942-09-9*) White Wing Pub.

Pruitt, Sharon. Art of the Cameroon: Selections from the Spelman College Collection of African Art. (Illus.). 40p. 1990. 7.50 (*0-915977-05-2*) Georgia Museum of Art.

Pruitt, Sheryl K., jt. auth. see Dornbush, Marilyn P.

Pruitt, Stephen. The Microsoft Multimedia Viewer How-To: Create Exciting Ultimedia with Video, Animation, Music, & Speech for Windows. LC 93-47367. 450p. 1994. cd-rom, pap. 39.95 (*1-878739-60-3*) Waite Group Pr.

— Windows 95 Help: A Developer's Guide. 1995. 34.99 (*0-7821-1707-4*) Sybex.

Pruitt, Virginia D., jt. auth. see Faulkner, Howard J.

Pruitt, Virginia D., jt. ed. see Faulkner, Howard J.

Prum, Bernard & Fort, Jean C. Stochastic Processes on a Lattice & Gibbs Measures. (Mathematical Physics Studies). (C). 1991. lib. bdg. 105.50 (*0-7923-1069-1*) Kluwer Ac.

Prumm, Hans-Joachim. Film-Script - William Shakespeare: Eine Untersuchung der Film-Bearbeitungen von Shakespeares Dramen am Beispiel ausgewahlter Tragodien-Verfilmungen von 1945-1985. (Munchner Studien zur Neueren Englischen Literatur: Band 3). 439p. (GER.). 1987. 50.00 (*90-6032-287-8*, Pub. by B R Gruener NE) Benjamins North Am.

Prunckun, Henry W., Jr. Shadow of Death: An Analytical Bibliography on Political Violence, Terrorism, & Low-Intensity Conflict. LC 93-32400. (Illus.). 423p. 1993. 47.50 (*0-8108-2773-5*) Scarecrow.

— Special Access Required: A Practitioner's Guide to Law Enforcement Intelligence Literature. LC 90-46292. (Illus.). 212p. 1990. 27.50 (*0-8108-2371-3*) Scarecrow.

Prundnikov, A. P., et al. Inverse Laplace Transforms, Vol. 5. (Integrals & Ser.). 1992. text ed. 190.00 (*0-685-75217-8*) Gordon & Breach.

Pruner, Leonora. Love's Secret Storm. LC 81-2459. 262p. (Orig.). 1981. pap. 6.99 (*0-87123-347-9*) Bethany Hse.

Prunet, Antoine. Ferrari Legend: The Road Cars. 2nd ed. LC 87-81363. (Illus.). 494p. 1988. 45.00 (*0-393-01475-4*, F613, Pub. by G T Foulis Ltd) Haynes Pubns.

Prunet, Antoine & Vann, Peter. Fantastic Ferrari. (Illus.). 203p. 1988. 29.98 (*0-87938-327-5*) Motorbooks Intl.

Prunet, Jean-Francois, jt. ed. see Paradis, Carole.

***Prungel, Elizabeth & Spyer, Heather.** Top Ramen Noodle Cookbook: Over 175 Delicious, Inexpensive, Quick, & Easy Recipes Using America's Favorite Noodle. LC 94-21450. 1994. pap. 10.95 (*1-55958-565-X*) Prima Pub.

Prunhuber, Carol, jt. auth. see Mervin, Sabrina.

Prunier, J. & Galeron, H., illus. Dinosaure. (Gallimard - Mes Premieres Decouvertes Ser.: No. 30). (FRE.). (J). (ps-1). 1991. 17.95 (*2-07-056642-0*) Schoenhof.

Prunier, James. Livre des As et des Heros: Histoire de l'Aviation, No. 2. (Gallimard - Decouverte Cadet Ser.: No. 48). 77p. (FRE.). (J). (gr. 4-9). 1988. 13.95 (*2-07-039548-0*) Schoenhof.

— Livre des Trains. (Gallimard - Decouverte Cadet Ser.: No. 27). 93p. (FRE.). (J). (gr. 4-9). 1986. 15.95 (*2-07-039527-8*) Schoenhof.

Prunier, James, jt. auth. see Delafosse, Claude.

Prunier, Michael L., jt. ed. see Scaros, Michael.

Prunieras, M., ed. Epidermal Keratinocyte Differentiation & Fibrillogenesis. (Frontiers of Matrix Biology Ser.: Vol. 9). (Illus.). viii, 192p. 1981. 96.00 (*3-8055-0893-X*) S Karger.

Prunieres, Henry. Monteverdi: His Life & Work. MacKie, Marie D., tr. LC 70-100830. (Illus.). 293p. 1973. reprint ed. text ed. 55.00 (*0-8371-3996-1*, PRMO, Greenwood Pr) Greenwood.

— Monteverdi: His Life & Work. 293p. 1990. reprint ed. lib. bdg. 69.00 (*0-7812-9075-9*) Rprt Serv.

— New History of Music: Middle Ages to Mozart. (Music Book Index Ser.). 413p. 1992. reprint ed. lib. bdg. 99.00 (*0-7812-9465-7*) Rprt Serv.

— La Vie Illustre et Libertine de Jean-Baptiste Lully. LC 76-43934. (Music & Theatre in France in the 17th & 18th Centuries Ser.). reprint ed. 26.00 (*0-685-83142-6*) AMS Pr.

— La Vie Illustre et Libertine de Jean-Baptiste Lully. LC 76-43934. (Music & Theatre in France in the 17th & 18th Centuries Ser.). Date not set. reprint ed. 52.50 (*0-404-60186-3*) AMS Pr.

Prunieres, Henry, ed. see Lully, Jean-Baptiste.

Prunkl, Peter R. & Berry, Rebecca L. Death Week: Exploring the Dying Process. (Death Education, Aging & Health Care Ser.). 240p. 1988. 68.00 (*0-89116-784-6*); pap. 28.00 (*0-89116-112-0*) Hemisp Pub.

Prunster, Nicole, jt. ed. see Cicioni, Mirna.

Prunty, F. & McSwiney, R. Laboratory Manual of Chemical Pathology. 1959. 116.00 (*0-08-009144-X*, Pub. by Pergamon Repr UK) Franklin.

Prunty, John J. A Critical Reformulation of Educational Policy Analysis. 113p. (C). 1984. 56.00 (*0-7300-0113-X*, Pub. by Deakin Univ AT) St Mut.

Prunty, Wyatt. Balance As Belief. LC 89-33038. (Johns Hopkins Poetry & Fiction Ser.). 88p. 1989. pap. 9.95 (*0-8018-3894-0*) Johns Hopkins.

— Fallen from the Symboled World: Precedents for the New Formalism. 326p. 1990. 38.00 (*0-19-505786-4*) OUP.

— The Run of the House: Poems. LC 92-43034. (Poetry & Fiction Ser.). 68p. 1993. text ed. 30.00 (*0-8018-4625-0*); pap. 12.95 (*0-8018-4626-9*) Johns Hopkins.

— The Times Between. LC 81-13724. (Poetry & Fiction Ser.). 80p. 1982. text ed. 14.95 (*0-8018-2403-6*); pap. 9.95 (*0-8018-2407-9*) Johns Hopkins.

— What Women Know, What Men Believe. LC 85-24095. (Poetry & Fiction Ser.). 80p. 1986. text ed. 14.95 (*0-8018-3327-2*) Johns Hopkins.

Pruppacher, Hans R. & Klett, James D. Microphysics of Clouds & Precipitation. 730p. 1980. pap. text ed. 44.50 (*90-277-1106-2*) Kluwer Ac.

Prus, Boleslaw. Pharaoh. (Illus.). 400p. 1992. 25.00 (*0-87052-152-7*) Hippocrene Bks.

Prus, Joseph S., et al. Handbook of Certification & Licensure Requirements for School Psychologists. 219p. 1987. pap. text ed. 17.00 (*0-932955-06-1*) Natl Assn Psych.

***Prus, Robert.** Symbolic Interaction & Ethnographic Research: Intersubjectivity & the Study of Human Lived Experience. LC 94-49571. 1995. write for info. (*0-7914-2701-3*); pap. write for info. (*0-7914-2702-1*) State U NY Pr.

Prus, Robert & Irini, Styllianos. Hookers, Rounders, & Desk Clerks: The Social Organization of the Hotel Community. 279p. 1988. reprint ed. pap. text ed. 13.50 (*0-88133-337-9*) Sheffield WI.

Prusa, Thomas. International Trade Policies & Incentives. LC 90-3526. (Foreign Economic Policy of the United States Ser.). 165p. 1990. reprint ed. 20.00 (*0-8240-7473-4*) Garland.

— Shining South. (Advanced Dungeons & Dragons, Second Edition; Al-Qadim Ser.). (Illus.). 1993. pap. 10.95 (*1-56076-595-X*) TSR Inc.

Prusaczyk, J. E., et al. Fire Performance Characteristics in Rooms as the Result of Increased Insulation. 1978. 4.00 (*0-686-12079-5*, TR 78-2) Society Fire Protect.

Prusaensis, Dio. Quae Exstant Omnia, Vol. I. Von Arnim, Hans F., ed. xl, 338p. 1962. write for info. (*3-296-12301-6*, Pub. by Georg Olms GW) Lubrecht & Cramer.

— Quae Exstant Omnia, Vol. II. Von Arnim, Hans F., ed. xiv, 380p. 1962. write for info. (*3-296-12302-4*, Pub. by Georg Olms GW) Lubrecht & Cramer.

Prusak, Bernard P., ed. Raising the Torch of Good News: Catholic Authority & Dialogue with the World. LC 87-31695. (College Theology Society Annual Publications Ser.: Vol. 32). 342p. (Orig.). (C). 1988. lib. bdg. 51.00 (*0-8191-6699-5*); pap. text ed. 27.00 (*0-8191-6700-2*) U Pr of Amer.

Prusak, Larry & Matarazzo, Jim. Information Management & Japanese Success. 15p. 1992. 12.50 (*0-87111-383-X*) SLA.

Prusak, Laurence, jt. auth. see McGee, James.

Prusan, Peretz. Guide to Hebrew Lettering. (Illus.). 64p. 1982. pap. 5.95 (*0-8074-0155-2*, 282800) UAHC.

Prusek, Jaroslav. Chinese History & Literature: Collection of Studies. LC 77-733129. 586p. 1970. lib. bdg. 112.50 (*90-277-0175-X*) Kluwer Ac.

— Chinese Statelets & the Northern Barbarians in the Period 1400-300 B. C. LC 70-154745. 312p. 1971. lib. bdg. 80.00 (*90-277-0225-X*) Kluwer Ac.

— The Literatures of Liberated China & Its Popular Traditions. 1976. lib. bdg. 59.95 (*0-8490-2172-3*) Gordon Pr.

Prusiner, Stanley B., ed. Prions: Novel Infectious Pathogens Causing Scrapie & Greutzfeldt - Jakob Disease. 540p. 1987. text ed. 114.00 (*0-12-566300-5*) Acad Pr.

Prusiner, Stanley B., et al, eds. Prion Diseases of Humans & Animals. LC 92-1704. (Ellis Horwood Series in Neuroscience). 500p. 1993. 76.00 (*0-13-720327-6*, Tavistock-E Horwood) Routledge Chapman & Hall.

Prusinkiewicz, P. & Hanan, J. Lindenmayer Systems, Fractals, & Plants. (Lecture Notes in Biomathematics Ser.: Vol. 79). viii, 120p. 1992. pap. 28.00 (*0-387-97092-4*) Spr-Verlag.

Prusinkiewicz, P. & Lindenmayer, A. The Algorithmic Beauty of Plants. Cutter, M., ed. (Virtual Laboratory Ser.). (Illus.). xii, 228p. 1991. text ed. 39.95 (*0-387-97297-8*) Spr-Verlag.

Prusmack, Florence. Khan. 412p. 1992. pap. 4.00 (*0-9633903-0-9*) Ashby-Ferguson.

Pruss, Adrian, jt. auth. see Spencer, John.

Pruss, Boleslaw. The Doll. 700p. 1993. pap. 16.95 (*0-7818-0158-3*) Hippocrene Bks.

Pruss, Jan. Evolutionary Integral Equations & Applications. LC 93-20736. (Monographs in Mathematics: Vol. 87). 366p. 1993. 139.00 (*0-8176-2876-2*) Birkhauser.

Prussen, Ronald W. John Foster Dulles: The Road to Power. LC 81-69264. 1982. 27.95 (*0-02-925460-4*) Free Pr.

An Asterisk (*) at the beginning of an entry indicates that the title is appearing in BIP for the first time.

Prussia. War in South Africa. Du Cane, Hubert, tr. LC 69-19361. 374p. 1970. reprint ed. text ed. 59.75 (*0-8371-5089-2*, PRW&, Greenwood Pr) Greenwood.

Prussia Kriegsministerium Staff. Regulations for the Prussian Infantry: To Which Is Added the Prussian Tactick. LC 68-54803. 444p. 1969. reprint ed. text ed. 38.50 (*0-8371-0625-7*, PRPI, Greenwood Pr) Greenwood.

Prussia, Stanley E., jt. ed. see Shewfelt, Robert L.

Prussian, Claire, jt. ed. see Frantz, Claire W.

***Prussian General Staff.** The Campaign of 1866 in Germany. (European War Ser.: No. 2). (Illus.). 672p. 1994. write for info. (*0-89839-201-2*) Battery Pr.

***Prussin, Labelle.** African Nomadic Architecture: Space, Place, & Gender. LC 94-43109. 1995. write for info. (*1-56098-358-2*); pap. write for info. (*1-56098-366-3*) Smithsonian.

— Hatumere: Islamic Design in West Africa. LC 75-7202. 1985. 105.00 (*0-520-03004-4*) U CA Pr.

Prussing, John E. & Conway, Bruce A. Orbital Mechanics. LC 92-41505. (Illus.). 208p. (C). 1993. 35.00 (*0-19-507834-9*) OUP.

Prusski, Jeffrey. Bring Back the Deer. (Illus.). 32p. (J). (ps-3). 1988. 13.95 (*0-15-200418-1*, Gulliver Bks) HarBrace.

Prussner, Frederick, jt. auth. see Hayes, John H.

Prust, Jim, et al. The Czech & Slovak Federal Republic: An Economy in Transition. LC 90-47707. (Occasional Paper Ser.: No. 72). vii, 70p. 1990. pap. 10.00 (*1-55775-169-2*) Intl Monetary.

Prust, Z. A. Photo-Offset Lithography. LC 77-21607. (Illus.). 160p. (YA). 1977. text ed. 20.00 (*0-87006-240-9*) Goodheart.

Prust, Zeke. Graphic Communications: The Printed Image. LC 93-26404. 544p. 1994. 38.60 (*0-87006-080-5*) Goodheart.

Pruter, A. T. & Alverson, Dayton L., eds. The Columbia River Estuary & Adjacent Ocean Waters: Bioenvironmental Studies. LC 79-178705. (Illus.). 882p. 1972. 40.00 (*0-295-95177-X*) U of Wash Pr.

Pruter, Bishop K. The Strange Partnership of George Alexander McGuire & Marcus Garvey. LC 86-17628. 50p. 1986. lib. bdg. 20.00x (*0-89370-529-2*); pap. 10.00x (*0-912134-08-9*) Borgo Pr.

Pruter, Karl. Bishops Extraordinary. LC 86-2284. 58p. 1985. reprint ed. lib. bdg. 20.00x (*0-89370-544-6*); reprint ed. pap. 10.00x (*0-912134-04-6*) Borgo Pr.

— The Catholic Priest: A Guide to Holy Orders. LC 92-45059. (St. Willibrord Studies in Philosophy & Religion: No. 2). 88p. 1993. lib. bdg. 23.00x (*0-912134-14-3*, 27181559); pap. 13.00x (*0-912134-15-1*, 27181559) Borgo Pr.

— The Directory of Autocephalous Bishops of the Churches of the Apostolic Succession. 6th ed. LC 92-24123. (Autocephalous Orthodox Churches Ser.: No. 1). 96p. 1993. lib. bdg. 23.00 (*0-912134-12-7*, 26217486) Borgo Pr.

— A Directory of Autocephalous Bishops of the Churches of the Apostolic Succession. 7th expanded rev. ed. LC 95-5114. (Autocephalous Orthodox Churches Ser.: No. 1). 1995. pap. write for info. (*0-912134-25-9*) Borgo Pr.

— A Directory of Autocephalous Bishops of the Churches of the Apostolic Succession. 7th expanded rev. ed. LC 95-5114. (Autocephalous Orthodox Churches Ser.: Vol. 1). 1995. lib. bdg. write for info. (*0-912134-24-0*) Borgo Pr.

— Neo-Congregationalism. LC 85-13416. 90p. 1985. reprint ed. lib. bdg. 25.00x (*0-89370-598-5*); reprint ed. pap. 15.00 (*0-912134-02-X*) Borgo Pr.

— The Old Catholic Church: A History & Chronology. expanded rev. ed. LC 95-3866. (Autocephalous Orthodox Churches Ser.: No. 3). 1995. pap. write for info. (*0-912134-19-4*, St Willibrords Pr) Borgo Pr.

— The Old Catholic Church: A History & Chronology. 2nd expanded rev. ed. LC 95-3866. (Autocephalous Orthodox Churches Ser.: No. 3). 1995. lib. bdg. write for info. (*0-912134-18-6*, St Willibrords Pr) Borgo Pr.

— One Day with God: A Guide to Retreats & the Contemplative Life. rev. ed. LC 91-35733. (St. Willibrord Studies in Philosophy & Religion: No. 1). 56p. 1991. 20.00x (*0-912134-10-0*); pap. 10.00x (*0-912134-11-9*) Borgo Pr.

— The People of God. LC 85-13417. v, 162p. 1985. reprint ed. lib. bdg. 29.00x (*0-89370-596-9*); reprint ed. pap. 19.00x (*0-912134-03-8*) Borgo Pr.

— The Priest's Handbook. vi, 43p. (C). 1991. reprint ed. lib. bdg. 20.00x (*0-8095-6600-1*); reprint ed. pap. 10.00x (*0-912134-07-0*) Borgo Pr.

— Rufus. 42p. 1994. 20.00x (*0-8095-6605-2*) Borgo Pr.

— The Teachings of the Great Mystics. LC 85-13306. 118p. 1985. reprint ed. lib. bdg. 25.00x (*0-89370-595-0*); reprint ed. pap. 15.00x (*0-912134-00-3*) Borgo Pr.

— The Theology of Congregationalism. LC 85-12844. 100p. 1985. reprint ed. lib. bdg. 25.00x (*0-89370-597-7*); reprint ed. pap. 15.00x (*0-912134-09-7*) Borgo Pr.

Pruter, Karl & Melton, J. Gordon. The Old Catholic Sourcebook. LC 83-47610. 254p. 1983. 51.00 (*0-8240-9111-6*) Garland.

Pruter, Karl, ed. see Barriger, Lawrence.

Pruter, Robert. Chicago Soul. (Music in American Life Ser.). (Illus.). 464p. 1992. pap. 21.95 (*0-252-06259-0*) U of Ill Pr.

Pruter, Robert, ed. The Blackwell Guide to Soul Recordings. LC 93-12312. (Reference Bks.). 496p. 1993. 24.95 (*0-631-18595-X*) Blackwell Pubs.

Prutkovsky, Alexander. Phosphorus Research & Production in the U. S. S. R. Michta, Andrew, ed. 118p. (Orig.). 1987. pap. text ed. 75.00 (*1-55831-037-1*) Delphic Associates.

Prutton, M. Electronic Properties of Surfaces. (Illus.). 202p. 1984. 32.00 (*0-85274-773-X*) IOP Pub.

— Introduction to Surface Physics. LC 93-31100. (Illus.). 204p. (C). 1994. text ed. 49.95 (*0-19-853475-2*, Clarendon Pr); pap. text ed. 24.95 (*0-19-853476-0*, Clarendon Pr) OUP.

Prutzman, Deborah S. A Banker's Guide to Loan Participations. 2nd ed. 77p. (C). 1994. 75.00 (*0-89982-376-9*) Am Bankers.

Pruyn, John V. L. Catalogue of Books Relating to the Literature of the Law. 300p. 1982. reprint ed. lib. bdg. 32.50 (*0-8377-1015-4*) Rothman.

Pruyser, Paul W. The Minister As Diagnostician: Personal Problems in Pastoral Perspective. LC 76-8922. 144p. 1976. pap. 10.99 (*0-664-24123-9*, Westminster) Westminster John Knox.

— The Psychological Examination: A Guide for Clinicians. LC 78-70234. 311p. 1979. text ed. 42.50x (*0-8236-5605-5*) Intl Univs Pr.

Pruyser, Paul W., ed. Changing Views of the Human Condition. LC 86-31067. 256p. 1987. pap. 13.95 (*0-86554-230-9*, P32) Mercer Univ Pr.

Pruyt, Hans. Database Management with DBASE & SQL: A Practical Introduction. Lewis, Mike, tr. LC 92-38822. (DUT & ENG.). 1992. write for info. (*0-412-47750-5*) Chapman & Hall.

Pruzan, Elliot R. The Concept of Justice in Marx. (American University Studies: Political Science: Ser. X, Vol. 13). 238p. (C). 1989. text ed. 37.00 (*0-8204-0665-1*) P Lang Pubs.

Pruzan, P., jt. ed. see Bogetoft, P.

Pruzanski, W. & Seligmann, M., eds. Clinical Immunology: Proceedings of the 1st IUIS Conf. on Clinical Immunology, Toronto, 6-11 July 1986. 472p. 1987. 160.50 (*0-444-80885-X*, Excerpta Medica) Elsevier.

***Pruzanski, W. & Vadas, P., eds.** Novel Molecular Approaches to Anti-Inflammatory Therapy. LC 95-1382. (Agents & Actions Supplements Ser.: Vol. 46). 1995. 61.00 (*0-8176-5096-2*) Birkhauser.

Pruzham, I. & Kniazeva, V. The Russian Portrait of the Late Nineteenth-Early Twentieth Centuries. 294p. 1980. 90.00 (*0-686-97600-2*, Pub. by Collets UK) Pro-Am Music.

Pruzhan, V. Bakst - Set & Costume Designs, Book Illustrations, Paintings & Graphic Works. (C). 1990. pap. 130.00 (*0-685-34375-8*, Pub. by Collets) St Mut.

Pruzinsky, Thomas, jt. ed. see Cash, Thomas F.

Pruzzo, C., jt. ed. see Cabello, F. C.

Pry, Peter V. The Strategic Nuclear Balance, Vol. 1: And Why It Matters. 340p. (C). 1990. text ed. 63.00 (*0-8448-1642-6*, Crane Russak); pap. text ed. 36.00 (*0-8448-1643-4*, Crane Russak) Taylor & Francis.

— The Strategic Nuclear Balance, Vol. 2: Nuclear War: Exchanges & Outcomes. 450p. (C). 1990. text ed. 70.00 (*0-8448-1644-2*, Crane Russak); pap. text ed. 47.00 (*0-8448-1645-0*, Crane Russak) Taylor & Francis.

Pryakhin, Vladimir, jt. auth. see Sevstyanov, Vitali.

Prybyla, Jan. Reform in China & Other Socialist Economies. 372p. 1990. lib. bdg. 37.75 (*0-8447-3717-8*, AEI Pr) Am Enterprise.

Prybyla, Jan S. Issues in Socialist Economic Modernization. LC 80-18647. 140p. 1981. text ed. 49.95 (*0-275-90706-6*, C0706, Praeger Pubs) Greenwood.

— Market & Plan under Socialism: The Bird in the Cage. 400p. (C). 1987. text ed. 39.95 (*0-8179-8351-1*); pap. text ed. 18.95 (*0-8179-8352-X*) Hoover Inst Pr.

Prybyla, Jan S., ed. Comparative Economic Systems. LC 69-17707. (C). 1969. 44.50 (*0-89197-097-5*); pap. text ed. 24.50 (*0-89197-707-4*) Irvington.

Prybylowski, Douglas. Comex ASVAB-AFCT. (Illus.). 360p. 1989. pap. text ed. 14.95x (*1-56030-022-1*) Comex Systs.

***Pryce, C. R., et al, eds.** Motherhood in Human & Nonhuman Primates: Biological & Social Determinants. (Illus.). x, 176p. 1995. 130.50 (*3-8055-6109-1*) S Karger.

Pryce, Huw. Native Law & the Church in Medieval Wales. LC 92-25903. (Oxford Historical Monographs). (Illus.). 312p. 1993. 62.00 (*0-19-820362-4*, Clarendon Pr) OUP.

Pryce, John D. Numerical Solution of Sturm-Liouville Problems. (Monographs on Numerical Analysis). (Illus.). 336p. 1994. 56.50 (*0-19-853415-9*) OUP.

Pryce-Jones, David. You Can't Be Too Careful. LC 92-50291. (Illus.). 80p. 1992. pap. 4.95 (*1-56305-156-7*, 3156) Workman Pub.

Pryce, Melinda. Last Lord. 208p. (Orig.). 1993. pap. 3.99 (*1-55773-849-1*) Diamond.

— Loving Spirits. 208p. 1994. pap. text ed. 4.50 (*0-515-11474-X*) Jove Pubns.

— Rose for Lady Edwina. 1990. pap. 3.95 (*1-55817-368-4*, Pinnacle NY) Windsor NY.

***Pryce-Phillips, William.** Companion to Clinical Neurology. LC 94-19605. 1994. 99.95 (*0-316-72041-0*) Little.

Pryce, Roy, ed. The Dynamics of European Union. LC 87-592. 288p. 1986. 55.00 (*0-7099-4327-X*, Pub. by Croom Helm UK) Routledge Chapman & Hall.

Pryce, Roy, ed. see Duff, Andrew, et al.

Pryce, W. T., ed. From Family History to Community History. (Studying Family & Community History Ser.: No. 2). 224p. (C). 1994. 59.95 (*0-521-46002-6*); pap. 19.95 (*0-521-46578-8*) Cambridge U Pr.

***Prychitko, David, ed.** Individuals, Institutions, Interpretatons: Hermeneutics Applied to Economics. 186p. 1995. boxed, pap. 59.95 (*1-85628-968-0*, Pub. by Avebury Pub UK) Ashgate Pub Co.

Prychitko, David L. Marxism & Workers' Self-Management: The Essential Tension. LC 91-9152. (Contributions in Economics & Economic History Ser.: No. 123). 176p. 1991. text ed. 49.95 (*0-313-27854-7*, PPY, Greenwood Pr) Greenwood.

Prychitko, David L., jt. ed. see Boettke, Peter J.

Pryde, Duncan. Nunaga: Ten Years among the Eskimos. large type ed. 592p. 1988. 15.95 (*0-7089-1791-7*) Ulverscroft.

Pryde, Everett H., ed. Fatty Acids. 644p. (C). 1979. 40.00 (*0-935315-04-7*) AOCS Pr.

Pryde, George S., ed. Treaty of Union of Scotland & England. LC 78-24202. 120p. 1979. reprint ed. text ed. 45.00 (*0-313-20829-8*, SCTR, Greenwood Pr) Greenwood.

Pryde, Marion J., jt. auth. see Fleming, Beatrice J.

Pryde, Paul, jt. auth. see Green, Shelley.

***Pryde, Philip R.** Environmental Resources & Constraints in the Former Soviet Republics. LC 94-33120. 1995. text ed. 59.85 (*0-8133-1742-8*) Westview.

Pryde, Philip R., ed. San Diego: An Introduction to the Region. 3rd ed. (Illus.). 320p. 1992. per. 18.95 (*0-8403-7094-6*) Kendall-Hunt.

Prydz, H., ed. The Cell Biology of Triggers in Coagulation. (Journal: Haemostasis: Vol. 14, No. 5). (Illus.). 68p. 1985. pap. 45.00 (*3-8055-4046-9*) S Karger.

Pryer, Jane & Crook, Nigel. Cities of Hunger: Urban Malnutrition in Developing Countries. 120p. (C). 1990. text ed. 90.00 (*0-85598-154-7*, Pub. by Oxfam Pubns UK); pap. text ed. 28.00 (*0-85598-155-5*, Pub. by Oxfam Pubns UK) St Mut.

Pryer, Peter. Jottings: Historical & Political. (C). 1990. text ed. 35.00 (*0-7223-2519-3*, Pub. by A H S Ltd UK) St Mut.

— The New Communism. 108p. 1988. 40.00 (*0-7223-2044-2*, Pub. by A H S Ltd UK) St Mut.

Pryer, Richard R., tr. see Detrie, Philippe.

Pryke, E. J. Redactional Style in the Marcan Gospel: A Study of Syntax & Vocabulary as Guides to Redaction in Mark. LC 76-52184. (Society for New Testament Studies, Monograph: No. 33). 206p. reprint ed. pap. 58.80 (*0-318-34839-X*, 2031714) Bks Demand.

Pryke, Kenneth G. Nova Scotia & Confederation, 1864-74. LC 79-322022. (Canadian Studies in History & Government: No. 15). 252p. reprint ed. pap. 71.90 (*0-317-55719-X*, 2029345) Bks Demand.

Pryke, Martin. A Quest for Perfection: The Story of the Making of the Stained-Glass Windows in the Bryn Athyn Cathedral & Glencairn. 40p. (Orig.). 1990. pap. 2.75 (*0-910557-24-1*) Acad New Church.

— You & the Opposite Sex. 90p. (Orig.). 1986. pap. 3.80 (*0-910557-14-4*) Acad New Church.

***Pryke, Paula.** Flair with Flowers. LC 95-7852. Orig. Title: Flower Variations. (Illus.). 192p. 1995. 37.50 (*0-8478-1892-6*) Rizzoli Intl.

— Flowers, Flowers! Inspired Arrangements for All Occasions. LC 93-862. (Illus.). 192p. 1993. 37.50 (*0-8478-1679-6*) Rizzoli Intl.

Pryke, Susan. Explore Muskoka Lakes. (Illus.). 144p. 24.95 (*1-55046-010-2*, Pub. by Boston Mills Pr CN) Genl Dist Srvs.

Pryles, M. C., jt. auth. see Sykes, E. I.

Pryles, Michael C., jt. auth. see Sykes, Edward I.

Pryluck, Calvin. Sources of Meaning in Motion Pictures & Television. Lowett, Garth S., ed. LC 75-21434. (Dissertations on Film Ser.). 1976. lib. bdg. 23.95 (*0-405-07535-9*) Ayer.

***Prymak, Gregory.** Authority in the RLDS Theological Tradition: Two Views. Brown, Richard, ed. (Graceland-Park Press Theological Monograph Ser.). 144p. (Orig.). 1995. pap. text ed. 15.00 (*0-8309-0698-3*) Herald Hse.

Prymak, Thomas. Mykhailo Hrushevsky: The Politics of National Culture. 432p. 1987. 40.00 (*0-8020-5737-3*) U of Toronto Pr.

***Prymak, Thomas M.** Mykola Kostomarov: A Biography. 312p. (C). 1995. 60.00 (*0-8020-0758-9*) U of Toronto Pr.

Pryne, Abram, jt. auth. see Brownlow, William G.

***Pryne, Jane, et al.** Literature Unit: The Incredible Journey. (Literature Units Ser.). 1995. pap. text ed. 6.95 (*1-55734-521-X*) Tchr Create Mat.

Prynne, J. H. Poems. (Agneau 2 Paperbook Ser.: 1). 320p. (Orig.). 1982. pap. 18.00 (*0-907954-01-4*, Pub. by Allardyce Barnett UK) SPD-Small Pr Dist.

Prynne, William. Mount-Orgueil. LC 83-20361. 1984. reprint ed. 50.00 (*0-8201-1392-1*) Schol Facsimiles.

— The Unlovelinesse of Love-Lockes. LC 76-57410. (English Experience Ser.: No. 825). 1977. reprint ed. lib. bdg. 25.00 (*90-221-0825-2*) Walter J Johnson.

***Pryor.** Debt-Free Investing. 1995. pap. 3.99 (*0-8024-3994-2*) Moody.

— Investing Lessons I Learned the Hard Way. 1995. pap. 3.99 (*0-8024-3996-9*) Moody.

— Investments That Fit. 1995. pap. 3.99 (*0-8024-3995-0*) Moody.

Pryor, ed. Clinical Applications of the Limulus Amoebocyte Lysate Test. 1990. 121.00 (*0-8493-6209-1*, RC116) CRC Pr.

Pryor, Ainslie. The Baby Blue Cat & the Whole Batch of Cookies. (Illus.). 32p. (J). (ps-1). 1991. pap. 3.95 (*0-14-050770-1*, Puffin) Puffin Bks.

— The Baby Blue Cat Who Said No. (Illus.). 32p. (J). (ps-1). 1990. pap. 3.95 (*0-14-050768-X*, Puffin) Puffin Bks.

— The Baby Blue Cat Who Said No. LC 87-21026. (Illus.). 32p. (J). (ps-00). 1988. 14.99 (*0-670-81780-5*) Viking Child Bks.

Pryor, Andrew J. Browns Ferry Nuclear Plant Fire. 1977. 4.25 (*0-686-22684-4*, TR 77-2) Society Fire Protect.

Pryor, Anthony. The City of Lankhmar. (Advanced Dungeons & Dragons, Second Edition; Al-Qadim Ser.). (Illus.). 1992. pap. 18.00 (*1-56076-658-1*) TSR Inc.

— Patriots of Ulek. (Advanced Dungeons & Dragons, Second Edition; Al-Qadim Ser.). (Illus.). 1992. pap. 6.95 (*1-56076-449-X*) TSR Inc.

Pryor, Anthony, jt. auth. see Pearson, Charles S.

Pryor, Anthony, et al. The Compleat Alchemist. 2nd ed. (Illus.). 72p. 1993. pap. 10.95 (*1-880992-09-4*) Wizards Coast.

Pryor, Austin. IRAs & Annuities. (Sound Mind Investment Ser.). 80p. 1994. pap. 3.99 (*0-8024-3993-4*) Moody.

— Money Markets & Bonds. (Sound Mind Investing Ser.). 80p. 1994. pap. 3.99 (*0-8024-3992-6*) Moody.

— Mutual Funds. (Sound Mind Investment Ser.). 80p. 1994. pap. 3.99 (*0-8024-3991-8*) Moody.

— Sound Mind Investing: A Step-by-Step Guide to Financial Stability & Growth. 1992. pap. 19.99 (*0-8024-7927-8*) Moody.

— Stocks. (Sound Mind Investment Ser.). 80p. 1994. pap. 3.99 (*0-8024-3990-X*) Moody.

***Pryor, Betsy & Holst, Sanford.** Kombucha Phenomenon: The Health Drink Sweeping America: The Tea Mushroom Handbook. LC 95-68803. (Illus.). 120p. (Orig.). 1995. pap. 11.95 (*1-887263-10-1*) Sierra Sunrise Pub.

Pryor, Bonnie. Amanda & April. LC 85-15308. (Illus.). 32p. (J). (ps-1). 1986. 17.00 (*0-688-05869-8*); lib. bdg. 16.93 (*0-688-05870-1*) Morrow Jr Bks.

— The Beaver Boys. LC 90-38515. (Illus.). 40p. (J). (ps up). 1992. 15.00 (*0-688-08702-7*); lib. bdg. 14.93 (*0-688-08703-5*) Morrow Jr Bks.

— Birthday Blizzard. LC 92-1713. (Illus.). 32p. (J). (gr. k up). 1993. 15.00 (*0-688-09423-6*); lib. bdg. 14.93 (*0-688-09424-4*) Morrow Jr Bks.

— The Dream Jar. (Illus.). 1996. write for info. (*0-688-13061-5*); lib. bdg. write for info. (*0-688-13062-3*) Morrow Jr Bks.

— Grandpa Bear. LC 84-25545. (Illus.). 32p. (J). (ps-1). 1985. 16.00 (*0-688-04551-0*) Morrow Jr Bks.

— Grandpa Bear's Christmas. LC 85-29707. (Illus.). 32p. (J). (ps-1). 1986. 15.00 (*0-688-06063-3*); lib. bdg. 14.93 (*0-688-06064-1*) Morrow Jr Bks.

— Greenbrook Farm. LC 89-11573. 40p. (J). (gr. k-3). 1991. pap. 15.00 (*0-671-69205-4*, Litl Simon S&S) S&S Childrens.

— Greenbrook Farm. LC 89-11573. (Illus.). 40p. (J). (ps-2). 1993. pap. 4.95 (*0-671-79606-2*, S&S Bks Young Read) S&S Childrens.

— Horses in the Garage. LC 92-7287. 160p. (J). (gr. 4 up). 1992. 14.00 (*0-688-10567-X*) Morrow Jr Bks.

— The House on Maple Street. LC 86-12648. (Illus.). 32p. (J). (gr. k-3). 1987. 15.95 (*0-688-06380-2*); lib. bdg. 15.88 (*0-688-06381-0*) Morrow Jr Bks.

— The House on Maple Street. ALC Staff, ed. LC 86-12648. (Illus.). 32p. (J). (gr. k-3). 1987. pap. 4.95 (*0-688-12031-8*) Morrow Jr Bks.

— Jumping Jenny. (Illus.). 192p. (J). (gr. 2 up). 1992. 14.00 (*0-688-09684-0*) Morrow Jr Bks.

— Lottie's Dream. LC 91-3965. (J). (ps-3). 1992. pap. 14.00 (*0-671-74774-6*, S&S Bks Young Read) S&S Childrens.

— Marvelous Marvin & the Pioneer Ghost. LC 94-33237. (Illus.). 144p. 1995. 15.00 (*0-688-13886-1*) Morrow Jr Bks.

— Marvelous Marvin & the Wolfman Mystery. (Illus.). 128p. (YA). (gr. 7 up). 1994. 14.00 (*0-688-12866-1*) Morrow Jr Bks.

— Merry Christmas, Amanda & April. LC 89-39723. (Illus.). 32p. (J). (ps up). 1990. 13.95 (*0-688-07544-4*); lib. bdg. 13.88 (*0-688-07545-2*) Morrow Jr Bks.

— Mr. Munday & Space Creatures. (J). (gr. k-3). 1991. pap. 4.95 (*0-671-73620-5*, S&S Bks Young Read) S&S Childrens.

— Perfect Percy. 1990. pap. 2.50 (*0-671-69442-1*) S&S Trade.

— The Plum Tree War. LC 88-32426. (Illus.). 128p. (J). (gr. 3-6). 1989. 11.95 (*0-688-08142-8*) Morrow Jr Bks.

— Poison Ivy & Eyebrow Wigs. LC 92-38881. (Illus.). 176p. (J). (gr. 3 up). 1993. 14.00 (*0-688-11200-5*) Morrow Jr Bks.

— Poison Ivy & Eyebrow Wigs. Cohn, Amy, ed. LC 92-38881. 176p. (J). 1995. reprint ed. pap. 4.95 (*0-688-13562-5*, Pub. by Beech Tree Bks) Morrow.

— The Porcupine Mouse. LC 87-12305. (Illus.). 32p. (J). (ps-2). 1988. 15.00 (*0-688-07153-8*); lib. bdg. 14.93 (*0-688-07154-6*) Morrow Jr Bks.

— Rats, Spiders & Love. LC 85-25831. (Illus.). 128p. (J). (gr. 4-6). 1986. 15.00 (*0-688-05867-1*) Morrow Jr Bks.

— Seth of the Lion People. LC 88-18747. 128p. (J). (gr. 3-6). 1988. 11.95 (*0-688-07327-1*) Morrow Jr Bks.

— Seth of the Lion People. Cohn, Amy, ed. LC 88-18747. 128p. (J). (gr. 3-6). 1988. reprint ed. pap. 4.95 (*0-688-13624-9*) Morrow Jr Bks.

— The Twenty-Four Hour Lipstick Mystery. LC 89-34483. (Illus.). 128p. (J). (gr. 3 up). 1989. 15.00 (*0-688-08198-3*) Morrow Jr Bks.

— Vinegar Pancakes & Vanishing Cream. LC 86-31085. (Illus.). 128p. (J). (gr. 2-5). 1987. 15.00 (*0-688-06728-X*) Morrow Jr Bks.

Pryor, Burt, jt. auth. see Andersen, Sue.

***Pryor, Cheryl.** Legacy: A Story of Your Family History to Pass down from Generation to Generation & Keep the History Alive. (Illus.). 200p. (Orig.). 1995. pap. 18.00 (*1-886541-09-4*) Higher Priority.

Pryor, Chris. Small Business Marketing. rev. ed. (Network Workbooks Ser.). 83p. (C). 1990. student ed 14.95 (*1-878475-01-0*) Oregon Small Busn Dev Ctr.

— Your Marketing Plan. (Oregon SBDC Network Workbooks Ser.). 84p. (C). 1994. student ed 20.00 (*1-878475-11-8*) Oregon Small Busn Dev Ctr.

— Your Marketing Plan. rev. ed. (Network Workbooks Ser.). 83p. (C). 1991. student ed 14.95 (*1-878475-04-5*) Oregon Small Busn Dev Ctr.

— Your Marketing Plan. rev. ed. (Network Workbooks Ser.). 84p. (C). 1993. 20.00 (*1-878475-09-6*) Oregon Small Busn Dev Ctr.

Pryor, David. Arkansas: A Photographic Celebration. (Illus.). 96p. (Orig.). 1991. pap. 13.95 (*0-938314-97-1*) Am Wrld Geog.

Pryor, Deborah. The Love Talker. 1992. pap. 4.75 (*0-8222-1384-2*) Dramatists Play.

Pryor, E. J. Mineral Processing. 3rd ed. (Illus.). 844p. 1965. reprint ed. 124.25 (*0-444-20010-X*, Pub. by Elsevier Applied Sci UK) Elsevier.

P Q

Pryor, Elizabeth B. Clara Barton, Professional Angel. LC 87-13868. (Studies in Health, Illness, & Caregiving). (Illus.). 450p. 1987. pap. text ed. 25.95 (0-8122-1273-8) U of Pa Pr.

***Pryor, Eric.** Escape from the Dark Side: The Eric Pryor Story. St. Clair, A. Wendell, ed. 155p. (Orig.). 1994. pap. write for info. (1-884920-01-2) Jubilee Christian Ctr.

Pryor, Felix, ed. The Faber Book of Letters. 292p. 1989. pap. 12.95 (0-571-14395-4) Faber & Faber.

Pryor, Francis & Collison, David. Now Then: Digging up the Past. (Illus.). 48p. (YA). (gr. 7-10). 1994. 24.95 (0-7134-7290-1, Pub. by Batsford UK) Trafalgar.

Pryor, Francis T., jt. auth. see Prehistoric Fenland Centre Staff.

***Pryor, Frederic L.** Political Economy of Poverty, Equity, & Growth: Malawi & Madagascar. 484p. 1990. 39.95 (0-614-02829-9, 60823) World Bank.

— Poverty, Equity, & Growth in Malawi & Madagscar. (World Bank Publication Ser.). (Illus.). 464p. 1991. 37.95 (0-19-520823-4) OUP.

— Public Expenditures in Communist & Capitalist Nations. LC 68-14872. 550p. reprint ed. pap. 156.80 (0-8357-8292-1, 2033862) Bks Demand.

— The Red & the Green: The Rise & Fall of Collectivized Agriculture in Marxist Regimes. (Illus.). 483p. 1992. text ed. 65.00 (0-691-04299-3) Princeton U Pr.

— Revolutionary Grenada: A Study in Political Economy. LC 86-8109. 415p. 1986. text ed. 65.00 (0-275-92155-7, C2155, Praeger Pubs) Greenwood.

Pryor, Frederick L. The Energetic Manager: Fred Pryor's System for Unleashing the Power in Yourself & Your Organization. 228p. 1987. 21.95 (0-13-277203-5); 9.95 (0-13-277179-9) P-H.

— A Guidebook to the Comparative Study of Economic Systems. (Illus.). 368p. (C). 1985. pap. text ed. write for info. (0-13-368853-4) P-H.

Pryor, George L. Neither Bond nor Free. LC 79-144674. reprint ed. 36.00 (0-404-00208-0) AMS Pr.

Pryor, Glyn, jt. auth. see Parker, Martyn J.

Pryor, Harold, ed. see Armstrong, Emma P.

Pryor, Hugh C. Graded Units in Student-Teaching. LC 71-177170. (Columbia University. Teachers College. Contributions to Education Ser.: No. 202). reprint ed. 37.50 (0-404-55202-1) AMS Pr.

Pryor, J. B. & Day, J. D., eds. The Development of Social Cognition. (Illus.). 268p. 1985. 58.00 (0-387-96138-0) Spr-Verlag.

Pryor, J. P. & Chisholm, G. D., eds. Urological Prostheses, Appliances & Catheters. (Clinical Practice in Urology Ser.). (Illus.). xii, 288p. 1992. 163.00 (0-387-17490-7) Spr-Verlag.

Pryor, J. P., jt. ed. see Kelami, A.

Pryor, Jeff & Carroccio, Jean. The Ultimate Fundraising Workbook. Cronin, Jerry, ed. (Illus.). 200p. 1992. student ed 35.00 (0-916721-10-8) Ind Comm Con.

Pryor, Jennifer A., ed. Respiratory Care. (International Perspectives in Physical Therapy Ser.: Vol. 7). (Illus.). 244p. 1991. pap. text ed. 39.95 (0-443-03611-X) Churchill.

Pryor, John. John, Evangelist of the Covenant People: The Narrative & Themes of the Fourth Gospel. LC 91-38204. 244p. (Orig.). 1992. pap. text ed. 19.99 (0-8308-1762-X, 1762) InterVarsity.

Pryor, John & Reeder, Glenn, eds. The Social Psychology of HIV Infection. 376p. 1993. text ed. 69.95 (0-8058-0991-0) L Erlbaum Assocs.

Pryor, John H. Commerce, Shipping & Naval Warfare in the Medieval Mediterranean. (Collected Studies: No. CS259). (Illus.). 348p. (C). 1987. reprint ed. lib. bdg. 95.95 (0-86078-207-7, Pub. by Variorum UK) Ashgate Pub Co.

— Geography, Technology & War: Studies in the Maritime History of the Mediterranean, 649-1571. (Past & Present Publications). (Illus.). 256p. (C). 1992. pap. 18.95 (0-521-42892-0) Cambridge U Pr.

Pryor, John J., jt. ed. see Gregoire, Alain.

Pryor, Judith, jt. auth. see Murin, William J.

Pryor, Karen. Don't Shoot the Dog! How to Improve Yourself & Others Through Behavioral Training. 192p. 1985. mass mkt. 5.99 (0-553-25388-3) Bantam.

— Lads Before the Wind: Diary of a Dolphin Trainer. (Illus.). 240p. 1975. pap. 14.95 (0-9624017-3-0) Sunshine WA.

— Lads Before the Wind: Diary of a Dolphin Trainer. LC 89-92102. (Illus.). 278p. 1990. reprint ed. pap. 14.95 (0-9624017-0-6) Sunshine WA.

— Nursing Your Baby. 1991. mass mkt. 5.99 (0-671-74548-4) PB.

— On Behavior: Essays & Research. (Illus.). 432p. (Orig.). 1995. pap. 24.95 (0-9624017-1-4) Sunshine WA.

Pryor, Karen & Norris, Kenneth S., eds. Dolphin Societies: Discoveries & Puzzles. (Illus.). 400p. 1990. 35.00 (0-520-06717-7) U CA Pr.

Pryor, Kelli, jt. auth. see Pratt, Jane.

***Pryor, Lynn H.** Get with God. LC 94-39205. (Christian Life Ser.). (J). 1995. 8.99 (0-8054-6161-2) Broadman.

***Pryor, Mary.** On Occasion: Selected Poems, 1968-92. 1992. per. 5.00 (0-941127-12-5) Dacotah Terr Pr.

Pryor, Neale. You Can Trust Your Bible. 1980. 4.95 (0-89137-524-4); student ed 1.50 (0-89137-568-6) Quality Pubns.

Pryor, Nick. Putting on a Play. LC 93-50765. (Illus.). 48p. (J). (gr. 4-6). 1994. 15.95 (1-56847-104-1) Thomson Lrning.

Pryor, R. W., et al, eds. Disorder & Order in the Solid State: Concepts & Devices. LC 88-12574. (Institute for Amorphous Studies Ser.). (Illus.). 272p. 1988. 75.00 (0-306-42926-8, Plenum Pr) Plenum.

Pryor, Ray V., Jr. A Tough Row to Hoe. LC 88-70099. 184p. (Orig.). 1988. pap. 5.95 (0-916383-49-0) Aegina Pr.

***Pryor, Richard.** Pryor Convictions: And Other Life Sentences. (Illus.). 256p. 1995. 23.00 (0-679-43250-7) Pantheon.

***Pryor, Richard C.** Playback. LC 95-10561. 1995. write for info. (0-292-76567-3) U of Tex Pr.

Pryor, Roger A. Reminiscences of Peace & War. LC 77-126248. (Select Bibliographies Reprint Ser.). 1977. 25.95 (0-8369-5475-0) Ayer.

Pryor, S. N. An Economic Analysis of Silvicultural Options for Broadleaved Woodlands, Vol. I. 1982. 42.00 (0-85074-041-X) St Mut.

***Pryor, Sally.** Getting Back on Your Feet: How to Recover Mobility & Fitness after Injury to Your Leg, Foot, or Ankle. Date not set. reprint ed. pap. 16.95 (0-9624017-5-7) Sunshine WA.

Pryor, Sally R. Getting Back on Your Feet: How to Recover Mobility & Fitness after Injury or Surgery to Your Foot, Leg, Hip, or Knee. LC 90-28242. (Illus.). 215p. (Orig.). 1991. pap. 16.95 (0-930031-38-5) Chelsea Green Pub.

***Pryor, T. M.** Wealth Building Lessons of Booker T. Washington for a New Black America: Rebuilding Black America Using the Philosophy of Booker T. Washington. LC 95-67017. (Illus.). 152p. 1995. 15.95 (1-878647-21-0) Duncan & Duncan.

Pryor, Timothy R. & North, Walter, eds. Applying Automated Inspection. LC 85-61377. (Manufacturing Update Ser.). (Illus.). 287p. reprint ed. pap. 81.80 (0-8357-6495-8, 2035866) Bks Demand.

Pryor, William A. Free Radicals. LC 64-8731. (McGraw-Hill Series in Advanced Chemistry). 366p. reprint ed. pap. 104.40 (0-317-08742-8, 2003757) Bks Demand.

— Free Radicals in Biology, Vol. 5. LC 75-13080. 1982. text ed. 116.00 (0-12-566505-9) Acad Pr.

— Free Radicals in Biology, Vol. 6. 1984. text ed. 158.00 (0-12-566506-7) Acad Pr.

Pryor, William A., ed. Free Radicals in Biology, 3 vols., Vol. 1. 1976. text ed. 138.00 (0-12-566501-6) Acad Pr.

— Free Radicals in Biology, 3 vols., Vol. 3. 1977. text ed. 145.00 (0-12-566503-2) Acad Pr.

— Free Radicals in Biology, Vol. 4. 1980. text ed. 127.00 (0-12-566504-0) Acad Pr.

Pryor, William A., jt. ed. see Diana, John N.

Pryputniewicz, ed. Industrial Laser Interferometry. 224p. 1987. 57.00 (0-89252-781-1, 746) SPIE.

Pryputniewicz, R., jt. ed. see Hung, M. Y.

Pryputniewicz, R. J. Laser Interferometry Four: Computer-Aided Interferometry. 1992. 100.00 (0-8194-0681-3, 1553) SPIE.

Pryputniewicz, R. J., ed. Laser Interferometry III: Quantitative Analysis of Interferograms. 1990. 70.00 (0-8194-0198-6, VOL. 1162) SPIE.

Prys, Elined, jt. ed. see Kotsching, Walter M.

Prys-Jones, A. G. Collected Poems of A. G. Prys-Jones. (C). 1989. pap. 21.00x (0-86383-419-1, Pub. by Gomer Pr UK) St Mut.

— The Fountain of Life: Prose & Verse from the Bible. large type ed. 1979. 12.00 (0-7089-0311-8) Ulverscroft.

Prysby, Charles & Scavo, Carmine. Voting Behavior: The Nineteen Eighty-Eight Election. (SETUPS Ser. - Supplementary Empirical Teaching Units in Political Science). 70p. (Orig.). (C). 1989. pap. text ed. 8.00 (0-915654-87-3) Am Political.

Prysby, Charles L., jt. auth. see Books, John W.

Pryse, tr. see Morgan, James.

Pryse, J. M. The Sermon on the Mount: An Occult View. 1991. lib. bdg. 66.95 (0-8490-4548-7) Gordon Pr.

Pryse, James M. The Adorers of Dionysos. (Illus.). 166p. 1993. pap. 16.95 (1-56459-413-0) Kessinger Pub.

— The Apocalypse Unsealed: Being an Esoteric Interpretation of the Initiation of Ioannes Commonly Called the Revelation of St. John. 232p. 1993. pap. 24.95 (1-56459-336-3) Kessinger Pub.

— The Magical Message According to Ioannes. 230p. 1967. reprint ed. spiral bd. 9.35 (0-7873-0685-1) Mokelumne.

— The Magical Message According to Ioannes (St. John) 240p. 1993. pap. 24.95 (1-56459-337-1) Kessinger Pub.

— Prometheus Bound of Aischylos: A New Presentation. 207p. 1967. reprint ed. spiral bd. 9.35 (0-7873-0681-9) Mokelumne.

— Reincarnation in the New Testament. 92p. 1994. reprint ed. pap. 14.95 (1-56459-451-3) Kessinger Pub.

— Reincarnation in the New Testament. 92p. 1965. reprint ed. spiral bd. 6.05 (0-7873-0682-7) Mokelumne.

— The Restored New Testament, 2 vols., Set. 3rd ed. 1971. reprint ed. spiral bd. 27.50 (0-7873-0683-5) Mokelumne.

— The Restored New Testament: The Hellenic Fragments, Freed from the Pseudo-Jewish Interpolations, Harmonized, & Done Into English Verse & Prose (1925): With Introductory Analyses, & Commentaries, Giving an Interpretation According to Ancient Philosophy & Psychology & a New Literal Translation of the Synoptic Gospels, with Commentaries & Illustrations. (Illus.). 840p. 1994. pap. 49.95 (1-56459-433-5) Kessinger Pub.

— The Sermon on the Mount & Other Extracts from the New Testament. 80p. 1984. reprint ed. spiral bd. 10.45 (0-7873-0684-3) Mokelumne.

***Pryse, James M., comment.** The Sermon on the Mount & Other Selections from the New Testament. 1994. pap. write for info. (0-913004-92-8) Point Loma Pub.

Pryse, James M., tr. Apocalypse Unsealed. 222p. 1965. reprint ed. spiral bd. 11.00 (0-7873-0680-0) Mokelumne.

Pryse, John M. Spiritual Light: New Scripture by Many Authors & Translations from Ancient Manuscripts, Previously Unpublished. 193p. 1994. pap. 17.95 (1-56459-440-8) Kessinger Pub.

Pryse, Majorie, jt. ed. see Feterley, Judith.

Pryse, Marjorie. The Mark & the Knowledge: Social Stigma in Classic American Fiction. LC 78-23229. 190p. 1979. 37.50 (0-8142-0296-9) Ohio St U Pr.

— Teaching with the Norton Anthology of American Literature: A Guide for Instructors. 4th ed. LC 93-48016. (C). 1994. pap. text ed. write for info. (0-393-96463-9) Norton.

Pryse, Marjorie & Spillers, Hortense J., eds. Conjuring: Black Women, Fiction, & Literary Tradition. LC 84-43171. (Illus.). 274p. 1985. 29.95 (0-253-31407-0); pap. 10.95 (0-253-20360-0, MB-360) Ind U Pr.

Pryse, Marjorie, ed. see Austin, Mary.

Pryse, Marjorie, jt. ed. see Fetterley, Judith.

Prystowsky, Eric N. & Klein, George. Cardiac Arrhythmias: An Integrated Approach for the Clinician. (Illus.). 452p. 1994. text ed. 60.00 (0-07-050984-0) Hlth Prof Div.

Prystowsky, Eric N., jt. ed. see DiMarco, John P.

***Prystowsky, Richard J.** Careful Reading, Thoughtful Writing: A Guide with Models for College Writers. LC 95-2757. (C). 1995. pap. write for info. (0-06-501412-X) HarpCollege.

Prytherch, Ray. Handbook of Library Training Practice. 400p. (Orig.). 1986. text ed. 79.95 (0-566-03543-X, Pub. by Gower UK) Ashgate Pub Co.

— Handbook of Library Training Practice, Vol. 2. 288p. (Orig.). 1991. text ed. 69.95 (0-566-03633-9, Pub. by Gower UK) Ashgate Pub Co.

— Harrod's Librarians' Glossary: Nine Thousand Two Hundred Terms Used in Information Management, Library Science, Publishing, the Book Trades & Archive Management. 8th ed. 1995. 127.95 (0-566-07533-4, Pub. by Gower UK) Ashgate Pub Co.

— Sources of Information in Librarianship & Information Science. 2nd ed. 190p. 1987. text ed. 49.95 (0-566-05509-0, Pub. by Gower UK) Ashgate Pub Co.

— Sports & Fitness: An Information Guide. 200p. 1988. text ed. 21.95 (0-566-03569-3, Pub. by Gower UK) Ashgate Pub Co.

Prytherch, Ray, jt. auth. see Hicken, Mandy.

Prytherch, Ray, jt. auth. see MacDougall, Alan F.

Prytherch, Ray, jt. auth. see MacDougall, Alan.

***Prytherch, Raymond J.** The Basics of Reader's Advisory Work. LC 87-48257. reprint ed. pap. 32.00 (0-7837-9258-1, 2049998) Bks Demand.

Prytkova, Ksenia, illus. Twelfth Night. LC 92-14524. (Shakespeare: The Animated Tales Ser.). 48p. (J). (gr. 5 up). 1993. pap. 6.99 (0-679-83872-4) Knopf Bks Yng Read.

Prytz, Ulla, jt. auth. see Von Bornstedt, Marianne.

Prywes, Moshe & Klein, Maury. Unfinished Business: The Railroad in American Life. LC 93-8112. (Tauber Institute for the Study of European Jewry Ser.). (Illus.). 384p. (C). 1995. 39.95 (0-87451-653-6) U Pr of New Eng.

Pryzbilla, Carrie, jt. auth. see Krane, Susan.

Pryzbyla, D. Souls of Summer. LC 91-66857. 429p. 1992. pap. 9.95 (1-55523-476-3) Winston-Derek.

***Przbylski, R. & McDonald, B., eds.** Development of Vegetable Oils in Human Nutrition. 1995. write for info. (0-935315-66-7) AOCS Pr.

Przebienda, Edward, ed. Cumulative Personal Author Indexes for the Monthly Catalog of U. S. Government Publications, 1941-1975, 5 vols., Set. Incl. Decennial Cumulative Personal Author Index, 1941-50. LC 04-18088. 1971. 49.50 (0-87650-007-6); Decennial Cumulative Personal Author Index, 1951-60. LC 04-18088. 1971. 49.50 (0-87650-008-4); Quinquennial Cumulative Personal Author Index, 1961-65. LC 04-18088. 1971. 49.50 (0-87650-009-2); Quinquennial Cumulative Personal Author Index, 1966-70. LC 04-18088. 1971. 49.50 (0-87650-016-5); Quinquennial Cumulative Personal Author Index, 1971-75. LC 04-18088. 1979. 49.50 (0-87650-097-1); LC 04-18088. (Cumulative Author Index Ser.: No. 2). 1979. 225.00 (0-686-76934-1) Pierian.

Przebinda, T. The Oscillator Duality Correspondence for the Pair 0(2,2), SP(2,R) LC 89-6540. (MEMO Ser.: Vol. 79/403). 105p. 1989. pap. 20.00 (0-8218-2464-3, MEMO 79/403) Am Math.

Przecha, Donna & Lowrey, Joan. Guide to Genealogy Software. (Illus.). 206p. 1993. pap. 24.95 (0-8063-1382-X, 4707) Genealog Pub.

***Przedwojski, B., et al.** River Training Techniques: Fundamentals, Techniques & Applications. 650p. 9950. 145.00 (90-5410-196-2, Pub. by A A Balkema NE) Ashgate Pub Co.

Przelecki, Marian, et al, eds. Formal Methods in the Methodology of Empirical Sciences. (Synthese Library: No. 103). 1977. lib. bdg. 117.00 (90-277-0698-0) Kluwer Ac.

Przemieniecki, J. S. Defense Analyses Software. (Educ Ser.). 131p. 1991. student ed, 3.5 hd 29.95 (0-930403-91-6) AIAA.

— Introduction to Mathematical Methods in Defense Analysis. (Educ Ser.). 1990. 61.95 (0-930403-71-1) AIAA.

— Mathematical Methods in Defense Analyses. 2nd ed. LC 94-25921. (Illus.). 425p. 1994. 74.95 (1-56347-092-6, 92-6(89)) AIAA.

— Theory of Matrix Structural Analysis. 480p. 1985. reprint ed. pap. 10.00 (0-486-64948-2) Dover.

Przemieniecki, J. S., ed. Acquisition of Defense Systems. LC 93-27833. (Education Ser.). 358p. 1993. 61.95 (1-56347-069-1) AIAA.

— Critical Technologies for National Defense. (Educ Ser.). (Illus.). 318p. 1991. 46.95 (1-56347-009-8) AIAA.

***Przepiorka, Donna & Sollinger, Hans, eds.** Recent Developments in Transplantation Medicine: New Immunosuppressive Drugs. LC 94-65128. (Illus.). 208p. 1994. 42.95x (0-614-05152-5) Phys Sci Pub.

Przesmicki, Ben. Break Away from the Greatest Cons. LC 82-50672. 140p. (Orig.). 1982. pap. 9.00 (0-9608908-0-7) Singles World.

Przetacznik, Franciszek. Protection of Officials of Foreign States According to International Law. 1983. lib. bdg. 149.50 (90-247-2721-9) Kluwer Ac.

Przetacznik, Frank. The Catholic Concept of Genuine & Just Peace As a Basic Collective Human Right. LC 90-44321. (Roman Catholic Studies: Vol. 2). 352p. 1990. lib. bdg. 99.95 (0-88946-239-9) E Mellen.

— The Philosophical & Legal Concept of War. LC 93-16073. 680p. 1994. text ed. 129.95 (0-7734-9256-9) E Mellen.

Przeworska-Rolewicz, Dauta. Algebraic Analysis. (C). 1988. lib. bdg. 229.50 (90-277-2443-1) Kluwer Ac.

Przeworski, Adam. Capitalism & Social Democracy. (Studies in Marxism & Social Theory). 277p. 1986. pap. 19.95 (0-521-33656-2) Cambridge U Pr.

— Democracia y Mercado (Democracy & the Market) Reformas Politicas y Economicas en la Europa Del Este y America Latina (Political & Economic Reforms in Eastern Europe & Latin America) Abello, Mireia B., tr. (Illus.). 356p. (SPA.). (C). Date not set. pap. write for info. (0-521-47645-3) Cambridge U Pr.

— Democracy & the Market: Political & Economic Reforms in Eastern Europe & Latin America. (Studies in Rationality & Social Change). (Illus.). 200p. (C). 1991. 47.95 (0-521-41225-0); pap. 15.95 (0-521-42335-X) Cambridge U Pr.

— Sustainable Democracy. 160p. (C). 1995. write for info. (0-521-48261-5); pap. write for info. (0-521-48375-1) Cambridge U Pr.

Przeworski, Adam & Sprague, John. Paper Stones: A History of Electoral Socialism. LC 86-6984. (Illus.). vi, 224p. (C). 1986. 24.95 (0-226-68497-0) U Ch Pr.

Przeworski, Adam & Teune, Henry. Logic of Comparative Social Inquiry. LC 81-19332. 168p. 1982. reprint ed. lib. bdg. 21.50 (0-89874-462-8) Krieger.

Przeworski, Joanne F. The Decline of the Copper Industry in Chile & the Entrance of North American Capital, 1870 to 1916. Bruchey, Stuart, ed. LC 80-609. (Multinational Corporations Ser.). 1981. lib. bdg. 36.95 (0-405-13379-0) Ayer.

Przewoznik, J. & Pein, M. The Blumenfeld Gambit. (PECH Pergamon Chess Ser.). 128p. 1991. write for info. (0-08-037132-9, 6201, Pub. by CHES UK); pap. 15.95 (0-08-037133-7, 6201, Pub. by CHES UK) Macmillan.

Przexecki, Marian & Wojcicki, Ryszard, eds. Twenty-Five Years of Logical Methodology in Poland. LC 76-7064. (Synthese Library: No. 87). 1977. lib. bdg. 145.50 (90-277-0601-8) Kluwer Ac.

Przuntek, H., jt. ed. see Riederer, P.

Przybilla, B., jt. ed. see Ring, J.

Przybilla, Carrie. Art at the Edge: Elisa D'Arrigo. LC 90-84884. (Illus.). 16p. 1990. 4.00 (0-939802-66-X) High Mus Art.

— Art at the Edge: Jorge Tacla. LC 91-75674. (Illus.). 24p. 1991. pap. 6.00 (0-939802-71-6) High Mus Art.

***Przybylowicz, Donna.** Desire & Repression: The Dialectic of Self & Other in the Late Works of Henry James. LC 84-24068. 367p. 1986. pap. 104.60 (0-7837-8399-X, 2059210) Bks Demand.

Przybylski, Roberta, jt. auth. see Filson, Yolande.

Przybylski, Steven. Cache & Memory Hierarchy: A Performance Directed Approach. 223p. 1990. 49.95 (1-55860-136-8) Morgan Kaufmann.

— New DRAM Technologies: A Comprehensive Analysis of the New Architecture. (Illus.). 500p. 1994. spiral bd. 2,695.00 (1-885330-00-6) MicroDes Res.

Przybyszewska, Stanislawa. The Danton Case & Thermidor. 297p. 1989. pap. 14.95 (0-8101-0806-2) Northwestern U Pr.

Przybyszewski, Stanislaw. Homo Sapiens. Seltzer, Thomas, tr. reprint ed. 49.50 (0-404-05147-2) AMS Pr.

Przyklenk, Karin, ed. Ischemic "Preconditioning" The Concept of Endogenous Cardioprotection. LC 93-21904. (Developments in Cardiovascular Medicine Ser.). 224p. (C). 1993. lib. bdg. 95.00 (0-7923-2410-2) Kluwer Ac.

Przyklenk, Karin, jt. ed. see Kloner, Robert A.

Przyluski, J. & Roth, S., eds. Conducting Polymers-Transport Phenomena. 280p. (C). 1993. text ed. 80.00 (0-87849-659-9, Pub. by Trans Tech SZ) LPS Dist Ctr.

Przyluski, Jan & Roth, Siegmar, eds. Electrochemistry of Conducting Polymers. (Materials Science Forum Ser.: Vol. 21). 220p. 1987. text ed. 60.00 (0-87849-562-2, Pub. by Trans Tech GW) LPS Dist Ctr.

Przytula, K. Wojtek, jt. auth. see Kumar, V. K.

Przytulski, Karen, jt. auth. see Lutz, Carroll A.

Przytycki, Jozef H., jt. auth. see Murasugi, Kunio.

P.S., Inc. Staff, et al. Managing Your TIAA-CREF Retirement Accounts: Investment Strategies to Maximize Retirement Income. 160p. 1989. per., pap. text ed. 20.95 (0-8403-5631-5) Kendall-Hunt.

***Psacharopoulos, George.** Why Educational Policies Can Fail: An Overview of Selected African Experiences. (Discussion Paper Ser.: No. 82). 34p. 1990. 6.95 (0-614-02880-9, 11549) World Bank.

Psacharopoulos, George, ed. Economics of Education: Research & Studies. 500p. 1987. 205.00 (0-08-033379-6, Pub. by Pergamon Repr UK) Franklin.

Psacharopoulos, George & Tzannatos, P. Zafiris, eds. Case Studies on Women's Employment & Pay in Latin America. LC 92-40880. 490p. 1992. 29.95 (0-8213-2308-3, 12308) World Bank.

Psacharopoulos, George & Tzannatos, Zafiris. Women's Employment & Pay in Latin America: Overview & Methodology. LC 92-35611. 264p. 1992. 15.95 (0-8213-2270-2, 12270) World Bank.

***Psacharopoulos, George & Woodhall, Maureen.** Education for Development: An Analysis of Investment Choices. 360p. 1985. 12.95 (0-614-02775-6, 60478) World Bank.

An Asterisk (*) at the beginning of an entry indicates that the title is appearing in BIP for the first time.

— Education for Development: Analysis of Investment Choices. 352p. 1986. text ed. 29.95 (0-19-520477-8); pap. text ed. 10.95 (0-19-520478-6) OUP.

***Psacharopoulous, George & Patrinos, Harry A.** Indigenous People & Poverty in Latin America: An Empirical Analysis. LC 94-26584. 1994. write for info. (0-8213-2958-8) World Bank.

Psaedaens, J., et al. The Structure of the Relational Database Model. (EATCS Monographs on Theoretical Computer Science: Vol. 17). (Illus.). 231p. 1989. 49.00 (0-387-13714-9) Spr-Verlag.

Psakhis, Lev. The Complete French. (Batsford Chess Library). 256p. 1993. pap. 22.95 (0-8050-2641-X, Owl) H Holt & Co.

Psaki, Regina. Heldris De Cornuaille: Roman De Silence. LC 90-19393. (GLML Ser.: Vol. 63B). 240p. 1991. 35.00 (0-8240-4112-7) Garland.

***Psathas, George.** Conversation Analysis: The Study of Talk-in-Interaction. (Qualitative Research Methods: Vol. 35). 96p. 1994. 21.50 (0-8039-5746-7); pap. 9.50 (0-8039-5747-5) Sage.

— Phenomenological Sociology: Issues & Applications. LC 73-2805. 384p. reprint ed. pap. 109.50 (0-317-29298-6, 2055515) Bks Demand.

Psathas, George, ed. Everyday Language. 302p. (C). 1979. text ed. 29.50 (0-8290-0872-1) Irvington.

— Everyday Language. 302p. 1989. pap. text ed. 16.95 (0-8290-1042-4) Irvington.

— Interaction Competence. 300p. (C). 1989. text ed. 29.95 (0-8290-1459-4) Irvington.

— Interaction Competence. LC 89-27546. (Studies in Ethnomethodology & Conversation Analysis: No. 1). 324p. (C). 1990. lib. bdg. 46.00 (0-8191-7635-4) U Pr of Amer.

Psathas, George, jt. ed. see Ten Have, Paul.

Pschorr, Elizabeth. A Priviledged Marriage: The Autobiography of Elizabeth Pschorr. LC 94-15618. 1994. 25.00 (0-915269-13-9) Windgate Pr.

***Pschyrembel.** Klinisches Woerterbuch Data Disk. (GER.). 1994. write for info. (0-614-00371-7, 357011001X) Fr & Eur.

Pschyrembel, W. & Dudenhausen, J. W. Grundriss der Perinatalmedizin. (Illus.). 336p. (C). 1972. 25.50 (3-11-003694-0) De Gruyter.

Pschyrembel, Willibald. Clinical Dictionary: Klinisches Woerterbuch. 1876p. (GER.). 1993. 95.00 (0-8288-1839-8, 3110126923) Fr & Eur.

— Woerterbuch Radioaktivitat, Strahlenwirkung, Strahlenschutz. 2nd ed. 108p. (GER.). 1987. 39.95 (0-7859-8270-1, 3110113430) Fr & Eur.

PSECC Staff. Hale'-Ta: Governing Guam: Before & After the Wars. (Hale'-Ta Ser.). 300p. (YA). (gr. 8). 1994. 40.00 (1-883488-02-8) Polit Status ECC.

— Hale'-Ta: Hestorian Taotao Tano' History of the Chamorro People. (Hale'-Ta Ser.). 100p. (J). (gr. 5). 1993. 30.00 (1-883488-00-1) Polit Status ECC.

— Hale'-Ta: Issues in Guam's Political Development: The Chamorro Perspective. (Hale'-Ta Ser.). 100p. (YA). (gr. 9). 1994. 25.00 (1-883488-03-6) Polit Status ECC.

— Hale'Ta: Insights: The Chamorro Identity. (Hale'-Ta Ser.). 200p. (YA). (gr. 12). 1993. 25.00 (1-883488-01-X) Polit Status ECC.

Psellus, Michael. Fourteen Byzantine Rulers. Sewter, E. R., tr. 1979. pap. 10.95 (0-14-044169-7, Penguin Classics) Viking Penguin.

— The History (Chronographia) Sachas, Constantine, ed. x, 385p. Date not set. write for info. (0-318-71003-X, Pub. by Georg Olms GW) Lubrecht & Cramer.

— The History of Psellus. LC 76-24929. (Byzantine Texts: No. 1). reprint ed. 55.00 (0-404-60001-8) AMS Pr.

Psenner, R. & Gunatilaka, A., eds. The First International Workshop on Sediment Phosphorus: Proceedings. (Advances in Limnology Ser.: No. 30). (Illus.). 115p. 1988. pap. text ed. 37.95 (3-510-47028-1) Lubrecht & Cramer.

Pseud, see Armalinsky, Mikhail, pseud..

Pshenichny, Boris N. The Linearization Method for Constraint Optimization. Wilson, Steven S., tr. LC 94-1938. (Computational Mathematics Ser.: Vol. 22). viii, 147p. 1994. 88.00 (0-387-57037-3) Spr-Verlag.

Pshenichnyi, B. N. Necessary Conditions for An Extremum. (Pure & Applied Mathematics Ser.: Vol. 4). 248p. 1971. 110.00 (0-8247-1556-X) Dekker.

***PSI Research Staff.** Start Your Business: A Beginner's Guide. 2nd ed. Reierson, Vickie, ed. (Successful Business Library). 198p. 1995. pap. 9.95 (1-55571-363-7) Oasis Pr OR.

PSI Research Staff & Jenkins, Michael D. Starting & Operating a Business in Wyoming. 2nd ed. LC 80-83053. (Successful Business Library). 278p. 1994. pap. 24.95 (1-55571-152-9); ring bd. 29.95 (1-55571-016-6) Oasis Pr OR.

PSI Research Staff, jt. auth. see Jenkins, Michael D.

Psichari, ed. see Renan, Ernest.

Psihoyas, Louie & Knoebber, John. Hunting Dinosaurs. LC 94-10010. 1994. 40.00 (0-679-43124-1) Random.

***Psillakis, Jorge, ed.** Deep Face Lifting Techniques. (Illus.). 232p. 1994. 119.00 (0-86577-530-3) Thieme Med Pubs.

Psillakis, Jorge, et al. Color Atlas of Aesthetic Surgery of the Abdomen. (Illus.). 96p. 1991. text ed. 105.00 (0-86577-343-2) Thieme Med Pubs.

***Psillas, Benjamin S.** Washington Job Source: Everything You Need to Land the Internship, Entry-Level or Middle Management Job of Your Choice. 3rd ed. 436p. 1995. pap. 15.95 (0-9635651-2-5) Metcom.

— The Washington Job Source: Over 5,000 Actual Personnel Contacts to Washington's Top Organizations. 2nd ed. 367p. 1994. pap. 14.95 (0-9635651-1-7) Metcom.

— The Washington Job Source, 1993: The Most Comprehensive & Up-to-Date Guide to Finding Internships & Entry Level Jobs in Washington, D.C. (Illus.). 275p. (Orig.). (C). 1993. pap. 14.95 (0-9635651-0-9) Metcom.

PSM Port Regis Staff. PSM 0 Disk 10. (C). 1987. 135.00 (0-685-47495-X, Pub. by S Thornes Pubs UK) St Mut.

— PSM 0 Disk 9. (C). 1987. 135.00 (0-85950-682-7, Pub. by S Thornes Pubs UK) St Mut.

— PSM 1 Disk 2. (C). 1986. 135.00 (0-85950-609-6, Pub. by S Thornes Pubs UK) St Mut.

— PSM 1,2 Disk 5. (C). 1986. 135.00 (0-85950-612-6, Pub. by S Thornes Pubs UK) St Mut.

— PSM 1,2 Disk 6. (C). 1987. 135.00 (0-85950-678-9, Pub. by S Thornes Pubs UK) St Mut.

— PSM 2 Disk 3. (C). 1986. 135.00 (0-85950-610-X, Pub. by S Thornes Pubs UK) St Mut.

— PSM 2 Disk 4. (C). 1986. 135.00 (0-85950-611-8, Pub. by S Thornes Pubs UK) St Mut.

— PSM 3 Disk 7. (C). 1987. 135.00 (0-85950-679-7, Pub. by S Thornes Pubs UK) St Mut.

PSM Port Regis Staff, ed. PSM Port Regis. (C). 1987. 135.00 (0-85950-681-9, Pub. by S Thornes Pubs UK) St Mut.

— PSM 1 Disk 1. (C). 1986. 135.00 (0-85950-608-8, Pub. by S Thornes Pubs UK) St Mut.

Psotka, Joseph, jt. ed. see Farr, Marshall J.

Psotka, Joseph, et al, eds. Intelligent Tutoring Systems: Lessons Learned. 576p. 1988. text ed. 99.95 (0-8058-0023-9); pap. text ed. 49.95 (0-8058-0192-8) L Erlbaum Assocs.

***P.S.R.F. Mathijsen Staff.** Guide to European Union Law Vol. 1. 6th ed. 1994. pap. text ed. 42.00 (0-421-51230-X, Pub. by Sweet & Maxwll) W W Gaunt.

***Psuik, Karrie.** Love Letters, Lust Letters. 45p. (Orig.). 1994. pap. 7.95 (0-9645010-1-5, Karrie Angel) Prem Raja Baba.

Psv, N., tr. see Tsereteli, O. D., ed.

Psv, N., tr. see Vinogradov, I. M.

Psychiatry & Child Psychiatry Department, The Institute of Psychiatry & the Maudsley Hospital, London. Psychiatric Examination: Notes on Eliciting & Recording Clinical Information in Psychiatric Patients. 2nd ed. 88p. 1987. pap. 18.95 (0-19-261670-6) OUP.

Psychiatry in Industry Committee, Group for the Advancement of Psychiatry Staff. Introduction to Occupational Psychiatry, Report 138. LC 93-11640. 91p. 1993. 23.00 (0-87318-206-5) Am Psychiatric.

Psychology Staff, ed. see Fallowfield, Lesley & Clark, Andrew.

Psychos. The New Guide to Palmistry: The Mystery of Your Palm & How It Affects Your Life. 200p. 1995. pap. 6.95 (0-572-01378-7, Pub. by Foulsham UK) Atrium Pubs.

Psychosomatic Medicine, Editorial Committee. Psychosomatic Classics: Selected Papers from Psychosomatic Medicine, 1939-1958. 1972. pap. 28.50 (3-8055-1232-5) S Karger.

***Psychotherapy Letter Editors.** A Legal Primer for Psychotherapists & Counselors. 67p. 1993. 40.00 (1-884937-05-5) Manisses Communs.

Psyhogeos, Matina. Greek Anthology: An Advanced Modern Greek Reader. (Illus.). 130p. (GRE.). (C). 1981. pap. 11.95 (0-916586-85-5) Hellenic Coll Pr.

— A Greek Family Helps You Learn Greek. 118p. 1979. pap. 6.95 (0-916586-75-8) Holy Cross Orthodox.

— Learn to Read & Write Greek: The Basics of the Greek Language. 122p. (GRE.). (C). 1984. pap. 9.95 (0-318-35072-6) Hellenic Coll Pr.

Ptacek, Greg & Anderson, Lydia M. Champion for Children's Health: A Story about Dr. S. Josephine Baker. LC 93-10482. (Illus.). (J). (gr. 3-6). 1994. 15.95 (0-87614-806-2, Carolrhoda) Lerner Group.

Ptacek, Greg, jt. auth. see Vare, Ethlie A.

Ptacek, Greg, jt. auth. see Woodruff, Cheryl.

Ptacek, Kathryn. The Hunted. 272p. 1994. mass mkt. 4.99 (1-55773-982-X) Diamond.

— The Hunted. 205p. 1993. 19.95 (0-8027-1227-4) Walker & Co.

Ptacek, Kathryn, ed. Women of Darkness II. 1994. pap. write for info. (0-8125-0837-8) Tor Bks.

Ptacnik, Donald J. The EMT Review Manual: Self-Assessment Practice Tests for Basic Life Support Skills. 4th ed. 326p. 1993. pap. text ed. 22.50 (0-7216-5043-0) Saunders.

Ptacnik, Donald J., jt. auth. see Childs, B. J.

***Ptak, Diane S.** The American Loyalists: Origin & Nominal Lists. suppl. ed. 15p. 1995. pap. 14.00 (1-886905-07-X) D S Ptak.

— The American Loyalists: Origins & Nominal Lists. 40p. 1993. pap. 16.00 (1-886905-05-3) D S Ptak.

— Cast in Stone: Selected Albany, Rensselaer & Saratoga County, New York Burials. (Illus.). 168p. 1990. 35.00 (1-56012-108-4) Kinship Rhinebeck.

— Civil War Soldiers from New York: Origins & Nominal Lists. 25p. 1995. pap. 14.00 (1-886905-11-8) D S Ptak.

— A Compilation of American & Canadian Passenger - Emigration Registers. 25p. 1993. pap. 15.00 (1-886905-02-9) D S Ptak.

— A Compilation of American & Canadian Passenger/ Emigration Registers: Supplement. (Illus.). 15p. (Orig.). 1995. pap. 10.00 (1-886905-09-6) D S Ptak.

— Lost & Found: Albany (NY) Area Church & Synagogue Vital Record Compendium. 30p. 1993. pap. 14.00 (1-886905-03-7) D S Ptak.

— Lost & Found: Albany, NY Area Church & Synagogue Vital Record Compendium, 1654-1925 - Supplement. (Illus.). 15p. (Orig.). 1995. pap. 9.00 (1-886905-10-X) D S Ptak.

— A Passage in Time: The Ships That Brought Our Ancestors. 30p. 1992. pap. 15.00 (1-886905-01-0) D S Ptak.

— Surnames: Determining Origins with Biographical & Ethnic References. 30p. 1995. pap. 14.00 (1-886905-06-1) D S Ptak.

— Surnames: Their Meanings & Origins. 30p. 1993. pap. 14.00 (1-886905-04-5) D S Ptak.

Ptak, Pavel & Pulmannova, Sylvia. Orthomodular Structures As Quantum Logics: Intrinsic Properties, State Space & Probabilistic Topics. (C). 1991. lib. bdg. 114.00 (0-7923-1207-4) Kluwer Ac.

Ptak, Roderich & Rothermund, Dietmar, eds. Emporia, Commodities & Entrepreneurs in Asian Maritime Trade, C. 1400-1750. 517p. (Orig.). 1991. pap. 77.50 (3-515-05962-8) Coronet Bks.

Ptashne, M. A Genetic Switch. 2nd ed. (Illus.). (Orig.). 1992. pap. 29.95 (0-86542-209-5) Blackwell Sci.

Ptolemaeus, Claudius. Geographia, 3 vols. in 1. Nobbe, C. F., ed. xxxvi, 760p. (GER.). 1990. reprint ed. write for info. (3-487-01236-7, Pub. by Georg Olms GW) Lubrecht & Cramer.

— Die Harmonielehre Des Claudios Ptolemaios. During, Ingemar, ed. cvi, 147p. 1982. reprint ed. write for info. (3-487-07263-7, Pub. by Georg Olms GW) Lubrecht & Cramer.

Ptolemy, Claudius. The Geography. Orig. Title: Geography of Claudius Ptolemy. (Illus.). 304p. reprint ed. pap. 19.95 (0-486-26896-9) Dover.

— Geography of Claudius Ptolemy. Stevenson, Edward L., ed. LC 70-174287. reprint ed. 245.00 (0-404-05148-0) AMS Pr.

— Tetrabiblos. (Loeb Classical Library: No. 435). 502p. (C). 1980. text ed. 18.95 (0-674-99479-5) HUP.

Ptolomaeus, Claudius. Harmonicorum Libri Tres. Wallis, John, ed. & tr. by. (Monuments of Music & Music Literature in Facsimile: Series II, Vol. 60). (Illus.). 1977. reprint ed. lib. bdg. 55.00 (0-8450-2260-1) Broude.

Pu, S. C. & McCoy-Thompson, Steven, eds. Technology in the Pacific Century: Trade, Security & Competitiveness. (US-Asia Institute National Leadership Conference Ser.: No. 6). (Illus.). 224p. (C). 1989. pap. 35.00 (0-9621762-0-6) US-Asia Inst.

Pu, Songling. Strange Tales from Make-Do Studio. Mair, Denis C. & Mair, Victor H., trs. 446p. (Orig.). 1989. pap. 9.95 (0-8351-2256-5) China Bks.

Pu, Yushu. The Cosmos: A Book of Poetry. (Illus.). 24p. (Orig.). 1989. pap. 2.95 (0-9612480-0-9) Mount Pr DE.

Pubal, Z. Theory & Calculation of Frame Structures with Stiffening Walls. (Developments in Civil Engineering Ser.: No. 22). 1988. 95.00 (0-444-98923-4) Elsevier.

Pubey, ed. Cryptosporidiosis in Man & Animals. 1990. 144.00 (0-8493-6401-9, RC136) CRC Pr.

Publassist, Inc. Staff. Out of This Kitchen: A History of the Ethnic Groups & Their Foods in the Steel Valley. 2nd ed. (Illus.). 186p. 1993. 15.00 (0-9638745-0-0, TX-3-619-596) Publassist.

***Public.** The Night Before Christmas. (Classic Christmas Sticker Storybook Ser.). (J). 1995. 2.95 (0-689-80256-0, Aladdin Paperbacks) S&S Childrens.

— The Nutcracker. (Classic Christmas Sticker Storybook Ser.). (J). 1995. 2.95 (0-689-80257-9, Aladdin Paperbacks) S&S Childrens.

— Old McDonald's Farm. (J). 1995. 3.95 (0-689-80259-5, Mac Bks Young Read) S&S Childrens.

Public Agenda Foundation. The Four Trillion Dollar Debt: Tough Choices about Soaring Federal Deficits. 1993. pap. text ed. write for info. (0-07-051549-2) McGraw.

Public Agenda Foundation Staff. Criminal Violence: What Direction Now for the War on Crime? 1992. pap. text ed. write for info. (0-07-051081-4) McGraw.

— The Health Care Cost Explosion: Why It's So Serious, What Should Be Done. 1994. pap. text ed. write for info. (0-07-051547-6) McGraw.

— The Health Care Crisis: Containing Costs, Expanding Coverage. 1992. pap. text ed. write for info. (0-07-051083-0) McGraw.

— The Poverty Puzzle: What Should Be Done to Help the Poor. 1993. pap. text ed. write for info. (0-07-051548-4) McGraw.

— Prescription for Prosperity: Four Paths to Economic Renewal. 1992. pap. text ed. write for info. (0-07-051082-2) McGraw.

Public Archives Staff of Canada Ottawa. Catalogue of the National Map Collection, 16 vols., Set. 1976. lib. bdg. 1,640.00 (0-8161-1215-0, Hall Library) G K Hall.

— Catalogue of the Public Archives Library of Canada: Collection of Published Material with a Chronological List of Pamphlets. 1979. lib. bdg. 1,375.00 (0-8161-0316-X, Hall Library) G K Hall.

Public Citizen Buyers Up Group Staff. Fueling the Public: A Public Citizen Investigative Report on the Selling of Gasoline. (Illus.). 54p. (Orig.). (C). 1992. pap. 10.00 (0-937188-98-0) Pub Citizen Inc.

Public Citizen Environmental Working Group Staff, et al. Trading Away U. S. Food Safety. 100p. (C). 1994. pap. text ed. 20.00 (0-937188-54-9) Pub Citizen Inc.

Public Citizen Health Research Group Staff & Wolfe, Sidney. Worst Pills, Best Pills II. rev. ed. (Illus.). 690p. (C). 1993. pap. text ed. 17.00 (0-937188-52-2) Pub Citizen Inc.

Public Citizen's Congress Watch Staff. Take the Money & Run: How the Justice System Is Letting S&L Crooks off the Hook. 20p. (Orig.). (C). 1992. pap. text ed. 10.00 (0-937188-96-4) Pub Citizen Inc.

***Public Citizen's Critical Mass Energy Project Staff.** Renewable Source: A National Directory of Resources, Contacts, & Companies. 240p. (C). 1994. pap. text ed. 40.00 (0-937188-93-X) Pub Citizen Inc.

Public Citizen's Health Research Group Staff. Medical Records: Getting Yours. rev. ed. (Illus.). 75p. (C). 1992. pap. text ed. 10.00 (0-937188-99-9) Pub Citizen Inc.

Public Citizen's Health Research Group Staff, jt. auth. see National Alliance for the Mentally Ill Staff.

Public Domain Research Staff. The Public Domain Software on File Collection - Apple. 1989. Incl. 22 diskettes, 32 p. booklet, 16 p. handbook. 195.00 (0-8160-1251-2) Facts on File.

— The Public Domain Software on File Collection - IBM. 1989. Incl. 32 p. program description, 16 p. user's guide, 16 p. librarian's guide, 12 diskette basic set. 195.00 (0-8160-1664-X); 50.00 (0-8160-1786-7) Facts on File.

Public Employee Retirement Administration Staff. Retirement Sample, Vol. 1. 113p. 1973. 7.00 (0-317-34952-X) Municipal.

Public Health Institute Staff & Labor Institute Staff. Jobs & the Environment. 4th ed. (Illus.). 208p. 1994. pap. 22.50 (0-945257-62-7) Apex Pr.

Public Health Service Staff, et al. Health Characteristics of Large Metropolitan Statistical Areas: United States, 1988-1989. LC 93-7390. (Vital & Health Statistics Ser. 10: Data from the National Health Interview Survey: No. 187). 1993. write for info. (0-8406-0479-3) Natl Ctr Health Stats.

Public Library Association. The Library Connection: Essays Written in Praise of Public Libraries. LC 77-24687. 96p. reprint ed. pap. 27.40 (0-685-16416-0, 2027356) Bks Demand.

Public Library Association, Job & Career Information Committee Staff. PLA Guide to Basic Resume Writing. LC 90-50722. 96p. (YA). (gr. 9 up). 1991. pap. 7.95 (0-8442-8123-9, VGM Career Bks) NTC Pub Grp.

Public Management Institute, Research & Development Staff & Conrad, Daniel L. The New Grants Planner. rev. ed. LC 80-84395. 1980. ring bd. 49.00 (0-916664-31-7) Datarex Corp.

— Successful Fund Raising Techniques. 2nd ed. LC 76-49799. 1985. ring bd. 39.00 (0-916664-03-1) Datarex Corp.

Public Management Institute Staff. Board Member-Trustee Handbook. LC 80-80201. 464p. 1980. ring bd. 49.00 (0-916664-20-1) Datarex Corp.

— Bookkeeping for Nonprofits. LC 79-90010. 1979. ring bd. 49.00 (0-916664-14-7) Datarex Corp.

— Direct Mail Fund Raising. LC 80-80195. 400p. 1980. ring bd. 49.00 (0-916664-26-0) Datarex Corp.

— Evaluation Handbook. LC 80-80196. 400p. 1980. ring bd. 49.00 (0-916664-25-2) Datarex Corp.

— Grants Administration: A Systems Approach to Project Management. LC 80-81280. 1980. ring bd. 49.00 (0-916664-28-7) Datarex Corp.

— How to Build a Big Endowment. 3rd ed. LC 80-65011. 400p. 1985. ring bd. 95.00 (0-916664-17-1) Datarex Corp.

— How to Get Corporate Grants. LC 81-84590. 1981. ring bd. 49.00 (0-916664-37-6) Datarex Corp.

— Managing Staff for Results. LC 80-65012. 400p. 1980. ring bd. 49.00 (0-916664-16-3) Datarex Corp.

— Needs Assessment Handbook. LC 80-80197. 1980. ring bd. 49.00 (0-916664-24-4) Datarex Corp.

— Successful Meetings. LC 80-80198. 1980. ring bd. 39.00 (0-916664-23-6) Datarex Corp.

— Successful Public Relations Techniques. LC 79-93010. 400p. 1979. ring bd. 59.00 (0-916664-15-5) Datarex Corp.

— Successful Seminars, Conferences & Workshops. LC 80-65013. 400p. 1980. ring bd. 59.00 (0-916664-19-8) Datarex Corp.

Public Management Institute Staff & Gilman, Kenneth. Computers for Nonprofits. LC 81-80946. 1981. ring bd. 49.00 (0-916664-32-5) Datarex Corp.

Public Management Staff. Corporate Five Hundred: Directory of Corporate Philanthropy. 10th ed. Zuver, Debbie & Fetters, Tracy, eds. 1350p. 1991. pap. 355.00 (0-916664-55-4) Datarex Corp.

— Corporate Five Hundred: Directory of Corporate Philanthropy. 12th ed. Conrad, D. L., ed. 1400p. pap. 375.00 (0-916664-57-0) Datarex Corp.

— Corporate Five Hundred 1993: Directory of Corporate Philanthropy. 11th ed. Berriault, Julie, ed. 1350p. 1992. pap. 365.00 (0-916664-56-2, 071056) Datarex Corp.

Public Securities Association Staff. Fundamentals of Municipal Bonds. 3rd ed. LC 85-31982. (Illus.). 235p. 1987. 23.95 (0-9605198-1-5) Pub Securities.

— Fundamentals of Municipal Bonds: A Basic, Definitive Text on the Municipal Securities Market. 4th rev. ed. LC 89-39361. (Illus.). 236p. 1990. 23.95 (0-9605198-2-3) Pub Securities.

Public Technology, Inc., ed. Solutions for Technology-Sharing Networks, 1987. 400p. (Orig.). 1987. pap. 10.00 (0-317-60094-X) Pub Tech Inc.

Public Technology, Inc Staff, ed. Solutions for Technology-Sharing Networks 1986. (Annual Ser.). 436p. (Orig.). 1986. pap. 10.00 (1-55657-001-5) Pub Tech Inc.

Public Utilities Reports. Public Utilities Reports (Fourth Series) Containing Decisions of the Regulatory Commissions & of State & Federal Courts. Vols. 1 to 74, 1974-1986. pap. write for info. (0-318-61737-4, 2029598) Bks Demand.

Public Utilities Reports Editors. The P. U. R. Glossary for Utility Management. 170p. (Orig.). 1992. pap. 20.00 (0-910325-39-1) Public Util.

***Public Utilities Reports Staff.** Purview 1993. (Orig.). 1993. student ed. audio 159.00 (0-910325-44-8) Public Util.

Public Works Committee, jt. auth. see United States National Resources Committee.

Publican Staff. The Ark of Apocolypse. 260p. 1990. pap. 9.00 (0-941427-02-1) JMJ Pub.

— Born Again Christians & Our Lady of Guadalupe. 30p. 1990. pap. 0.50 (0-941427-09-9) JMJ Pub.

— The Greatest Prayer of the Bible. 120p. 1990. pap. 2.00 (0-941427-08-0) JMJ Pub.

— The Miracle of Damascus. (Illus.). 260p. (Orig.). 1989. pap. text ed. 9.00 (0-941427-04-8); 0.25 (0-941427-05-6) JMJ Pub.

P Q

An Asterisk (*) at the beginning of an entry indicates that the title is appearing in BIP for the first time.

— The Miracle of Nicaragua. 30p. 1990. pap. text ed. 0.50 (0-941427-10-2) JMJ Pub.
— The Tongues of Satan. Salbato, Richard P., ed. LC 86-83119. 224p. (Orig.). 1986. pap. text ed. 6.00 (0-941427-01-3) JMJ Pub.
— The Unforgive Able Sin. 60p. 1990. pap. text ed. 1.00 (0-941427-07-2) JMJ Pub.
Publican Staff, jt. auth. see Dwight, Joe.
Publications Committee of the XII ICSMFE Staff, ed. Proceedings of the 12th International Conference on Soil Mechanics & Foundation Engineering, Rio de Janeiro, 13-18 August 1989, 5 vols. 2500p. (C). 1989. text ed. 995.00 (90-6191-890-1, Pub. by A A Balkema NE) Ashgate Pub Co.
Publications Committee XIII ICSMFE Ser. Proceedings of the Thirteenth Annual International Conference on Soil Mechanics & Foundations Engineering, New Dehli, January 1994. (Illus.). 3500p. (C). 1994. text ed. 750.00 (90-5410-370-1, Pub. by A A Balkema NE) Ashgate Pub Co.
Publications Department of the American TFP Staff, ed. see Del Campo, Carlos P.
Publications International, Ltd. Editors, et al. Country Music Stars: The Legends & the New Breed. (Illus.). 192p. 1992. 19.95 (1-56173-697-X) Pubns Intl Ltd.
— Players of Cooperstown: Baseball's Hall of Fame. (Illus.). 256p. 1992. 29.95 (0-7853-0336-7) Pubns Intl Ltd.
— Southwest Expressions. (Illus.). 256p. 1992. 29.95 (1-56173-585-X) Pubns Intl Ltd.
Publications International, Ltd. Staff. Fascinating Bible Facts: People, Places & Events. (Illus.). 384p. (Orig.). 1993. pap. 5.99 (0-451-17787-8, Sig) NAL-Dutton.
— Golf Almanac, 1993. 672p. (Orig.). 1993. pap. 5.99 (0-451-17785-1, Sig) NAL-Dutton.
— Mortal Kombat Action Strategies: An Unauthorized Player's Guide. 1993. pap. 5.99 (0-451-82290-0, Sig) NAL-Dutton.
— Ross Perot: What Does He Stand For? 1992. pap. 4.99 (0-451-17598-0, Sig) NAL-Dutton.
Publications International Staff. Meet Shaquille O'Neal. 1993. pap. 3.99 (0-451-17899-8, Sig) NAL-Dutton.
— Treasury of Christmas Recipes. 1989. 5.99 (0-517-69242-2) Random Hse Value.
Publicola. New Vade Mecum: Or A Pocket Companion for Lawyers, Deputy Sheriffs & Constables; Suggesting Many Grievous Abuses & Alarming Evils, Which Attend. 155p. 1994. reprint ed. lib. bdg. 42.50 (0-8377-2551-8) Rothman.
Publicover, Robert J. My Unicorn Has Gone Away. 112p. 1993. 14.00 (0-9634759-0-8) Powder Hse Pub.
Publishers Association Staff, jt. auth. see Cassell Staff.
Publisher's Editorial Staff. District of Columbia Court Rules, 2 vols. 1992. 55.00 (0-87473-856-3) Michie Butterworth.
Publisher's Editorial Staff, ed. Ballentine's Law Dictionary with Pronunciations. 3rd ed. LC 68-30931. 1429p. 1969. 25.00 (0-686-14540-2) Lawyers Cooperative.
— Nichols Cyclopedia of Legal Forms: 1925-1990, 31 vols. LC 73-165177. 1,320.00 (0-685-09239-9) Clark Boardman Callaghan.
Publishers Group West Staff, jt. ed. see Reference Press, Inc. Staff.
Publisher's Staff & Michie Company. Colorado Court Rules. 1140p. 1989. ring bd. 70.00 (0-685-07733-0) Michie Butterworth.
Publishing Group Staff, ed. see Lowry, Linda.
Puc, Krystyna. Poland's Commitment to Its Past: A Report on Two Study Tours. LC 85-21716. (Illus.). 48p. (Orig.). 1985. pap. 7.00 (0-941182-16-9) Partners Livable.
Puccetti, A., ed. The Programming & Proof System ATES: Advanced Techniques Integration into Efficient Scientific Software. (Research Reports ESPRIT, Project 1158: Vol. 1). viii, 341p. 1991. pap. 39.00 (0-387-54188-8) Spr-Verlag.
Puccetti, Frederick, jt. auth. see Camara, Jose.
***Pucci, Idanna.** Crime of Passion. 1995. 18.95 (1-56858-034-7) FWEW.
Pucci, Pietro. Hesiod & the Language of Poetry. LC 76-234. 160p. reprint ed. pap. 45.60 (0-7837-1109-3, 2041639) Bks Demand.
— Language & the Tragic Hero: Essays on Greek & Tragedy in Honor of Gordon M. Kirkwood. LC 88-29710. (Homage Ser.). 207p. 1988. 34.95 (1-55540-268-2, 00 16 11) Scholars Pr GA.
— Odysseus Polutropos: Intertextual Readings in the Odyssey & the Iliad. LC 86-16798. (Cornell Studies in Classical Philology). 272p. 1987. 31.50 (0-8014-1888-7) Cornell U Pr.
— Odysseus Polutropos: Intertextual Readings in the "Odyssey" & the "Iliad" (Studies in Classical Philology). 264p. 1995. pap. 16.95x (0-8014-8270-4) Cornell U Pr.
— Oedipus & the Fabrication of the Father: The Oedipus Tyrannus in Modern Criticism & Philosophy. 240p. 1992. text ed. 35.00x (0-8018-4341-3) Johns Hopkins.
— The Violence of Pity in Euripides' Medea. LC 79-52501. (Cornell Studies in Classical Philology: No. 41). (Illus.). 239p. reprint ed. pap. 68.20 (0-685-44035-4, 2030231) Bks Demand.
Pucci, R. & Piccitto, G., eds. Molecular Systems under High Pressure: Proceedings of the II Archimedes Workshop, Catania, Italy, 28-31 May, 1990. 386p. 1991. 145.50 (0-444-88772-5, North Holland) Elsevier.
Puccia, Charles J. & Levins, Richard. Qualitative Modeling of Complex Systems: An Introduction to Loop Analysis & Time Averaging. (Illus.). 256p. 1986. 46.00 (0-674-74110-2) HUP.
Pucciani, jt. auth. see Cottino-Jones.
Pucciani, Oresta F., ed. The French Theater since Nineteen Thirty: Six Contemporary Full-Length Plays. 406p. reprint ed. pap. 115.80 (0-317-10075-0, 2055116) Bks Demand.
Pucciani, Oreste & Hamel, Jacqueline. Langue et Language: Le Francais par Le Francais. 5th ed. 608p. (C). 1987. text ed. 45.25 (0-03-004037-X) HB Coll Pubs.
Puccinelli, Patricia M. Yardsticks: Retarded Characters & Their Roles in Fiction. LC 92-43532. (AUS IV: Vol. 155). 104p. (C). 1995. text ed. 32.95 (0-8204-2001-8) P Lang Pubs.
Puccini, Giacomo. La Boheme. John, Nicholas, ed. Pinkerton, P. & Grist, W., trs. (English National Opera Guide Series: Bilingual Libretto, Articles: No. 14). (Illus.). 128p. (Orig.). 1983. pap. 9.95 (0-7145-3938-4) Riverrun NY.
— Letters of Giacomo Puccini. Makin, Ena, ed. LC 71-140038. reprint ed. 24.50 (0-404-05149-9) AMS Pr.
— Madam Butterfly. John, Nicholas, ed. Ellcin, R. H., tr. (English National Opera Guide Series: Bilingual Libretto, Articles: No. 26). (Illus.). (Orig.). 1984. pap. 9.95 (0-7145-4038-2) Riverrun NY.
— Madama Butterfly in Full Score. 1990. pap. 17.95 (0-486-26345-2) Dover.
— Puccini's La Boheme. (Music (General) Ser.). 75p. 1984. pap. 2.95 (0-486-24607-8) Dover.
— Puccini's Madama Butterfly. (Opera Libretto Ser.). 64p. (Orig.). 1983. pap. 2.95 (0-486-24465-2) Dover.
— Tosca. John, Nicholas, ed. & tr. by. (English National Opera Guide Series: Bilingual Libretto, Articles: No. 16). (Illus.). 128p. (Orig.). 1982. pap. 9.95 (0-7145-3772-1) Riverrun NY.
— Turandot. John, Nicholas, ed. (English National Opera - Royal Opera House Guide Series: Libretto, Articles: No. 27). (Illus.). 1984. pap. 9.95 (0-7145-4039-0) Riverrun NY.
Puccio, Joseph A. Serials Reference Work. 250p. 1989. lib. bdg. 34.50 (0-87287-757-4) Libs Unl.
***Puccio, Thomas & Collins, Dan.** In the Name of the Law: From the French Connection Prosecution to the Defense of Claus von Bulow, an Insider's Account of How American Justice Really Works. LC 94-41706. (Illus.). 288p. 1995. 25.00 (0-393-03728-2) Norton.
Pucel, D. J. Performance-Based Instructional Design. 1989. 24.95 (0-07-050911-5) McGraw.
Pucel, David J. Performance-Based Instructional Design. (C). 1989. student ed. 29.00 (0-943919-01-0) Perf Trning Systs.
Pucel, R. A., ed. see Todd, Alexandra D.
Pucelick, R. Frank, jt. auth. see Lewis, Byron A.
Pucelik, Frank, jt. auth. see Lewis, Byron A.
Puchala. Fiscal Harmonization in the European Communities. 1992. text ed. 45.00 (0-86187-465-X, Pub. by Pinter Pubs UK) St Martin.
Puchala, Donald, ed. see Kegley, Charles W., Jr. & Raymond, Gregory A.
Puchala, Donald, ed. see Onuf, Nicholas G.
Puchala, Donald, jt. ed. see Paolucci, Anne.
Puchala, Donald J., ed. see Ferguson, Yale H. & Mansbach, Richard W.
Puchala, Donald J., jt. auth. see Hopkins, Raymond F.
Puchala, Donald J., jt. ed. see Hopkins, Raymond F.
Puchala, Donald J., ed. see Jensen, Lloyd.
Puchala, Donald J., ed. see Most, Benjamin A. & Starr, Harvey.
Puchala, Donald J., Jr., ed. see Thompson, William.
Puchelle, E., jt. ed. see Koch, Ch.
Puchkov, V. P. Political Development of Bangladesh. (C). 1989. 32.00 (81-7050-084-2) S Asia.
Puchkovskaya, N. Corneal Transplantation in Complicated Leucomas. (Illus.). 303p. 1969. 26.95 (0-8464-1083-4) Beekman Pubs.
Puchta, H. & Schratz, M. Teaching Teenagers: Model Activity Sequences for Humanistic Language Learning. (Pilgrims Resource Bks.). 135p. 1993. pap. text ed. 17.95 (0-582-03763-8, 79897) Longman.
Puchta, H., jt. auth. see Gerngross, G.
Puchta, Herbert & Gerngross, Gunter. Pictures in Action. 160p. 1992. pap. 13.95 (0-13-675182-2) P-H.
***Puchtel, Glenn T.** Dynamtic Data Exchange for OS-2 Programmers. LC 94-31803. 200p. 1994. pap. 39.95 (0-442-01949-1) Van Nos Reinhold.
Pucik, Vladimir, et al, eds. Globalizing Management: Creating & Leading the Competitive Organization. 368p. 1992. text ed. 45.00 (0-471-50821-7) Wiley.
— Globalizing Management: Creating & Leading the Competitive Organization. 368p. 1993. pap. text ed. 17.95 (0-471-30491-3) Wiley.
Pucillo, Gladys, comp. God, Grant Me Serenity. 1982. 6.50 (0-8378-2030-8) Gibson.
— A Little Book about Baby. 1981. 5.95 (0-8378-1932-6) Gibson.
— A Little Book of Friendship. 1981. 5.95 (0-8378-1931-8) Gibson.
Puck, Theodore T. The Mammalian Cell As a Microorganism: Genetic & Biochemical Studies in Vitro. LC 73-188127. 219p. (C). 1972. 28.95 (0-8162-6980-7); pap. text ed. 26.95 (0-8162-6970-X) Holden-Day.
Puck, Theodore T., et al. Rhythmic & Synthetic Processes in Growth. Rudnick, Dorothea, ed. LC 55-10678. (Society for the Study of Development & Growth, Symposium Ser.: 15th). 233p. reprint ed. pap. 66.50 (0-7837-0245-0, 2040554) Bks Demand.
Puck, Wolfgang. Adventures in the Kitchen. (Illus.). 320p. 1991. 30.00 (0-394-55895-2) Random.
— Wolfgang Puck Checkbook. 1995. write for info. (0-679-76125-X) Random.
— The Wolfgang Puck Cookbook. LC 86-10155. (Illus.). 320p. 1986. 23.00 (0-394-53366-6) Random.
— Wolfgang Puck's Modern French Cooking. 1986. pap. 15.95 (0-395-41067-3) HM.
Puckahtikom, Chanpen, jt. auth. see Brau, Eduard H.
Pucke, Lawrence, jt. auth. see Stark, Thomas.
***Pucker, Bernard H. & St. Florian, Ilaria L., eds.** A Tribute to Sandra A. Wadsworth, A. I. A. (Illus.). (Orig.). 1995. pap. write for info. (0-9635318-1-6) Pucker Art Pubn.
Puckering, R. D. & Brough, S. Electronics for Electrical Installation Engineers. (Illus.). 224p. 1992. pap. 24.95 (0-632-03266-9) Blackwell Sci.
Pucket, Ann, jt. auth. see Kelly, Elizabeth S.
***Pucket, Thomas.** Mt. Vernon: A Pictorial History. (Illinois Pictorial History Ser.). (Illus.). 1992. write for info. (0-943963-21-4) G Bradley.
Puckett. Batman: The Collected Adventures, Vol. 2. Kahan, B., ed. (Illus.). 144p. 1994. pap. 5.95 (1-56389-124-7) DC Comics.
Puckett, Andrew. Blood-Hound. large type ed. (Dales Mystery Ser.). 317p. 1993. pap. 16.95 (1-85389-410-9, Dales) Ulverscroft.
— The Ladies of the Vale. LC 95-16055. 1995. 20.95 (0-312-13106-2) St Martin.
Puckett, Andrews A. Terminus. large type ed. 368p. 1992. 21.95 (0-7089-2751-3) Ulverscroft.
Puckett, Barry & Henderson, Helene, eds. Holidays & Festivals Index. 1100p. 1995. lib. bdg. 65.00x (0-7808-0012-5) Omnigraphics Inc.
Puckett, Barry, jt. ed. see Henderson, Helene.
Puckett, Christine S. & Barnes, Joe. A Panorama of Northeast Alabama & Etowah County: Lookout Mountain Meets the Coosa. 2nd ed. (Illus.). 136p. (Orig.). (J). (gr. 4 up). 1992. reprint ed. pap. 8.95 (0-9633116-0-3) Starr Pub AL.
Puckett, Dale & Dibble, Peter. The Complete Rainbow Guide to OS-9. Falk, Lawrence C. & Noe, Courtney, eds. (Illus.). 420p. (Orig.). (C). 1985. pap. 19.95 (0-932471-00-5) Falsoft.
— The Complete Rainbow Guide to OS-9 Level II. Arnott, JoAnne, ed. (Illus.). (Orig.). 1987. pap. 19.95 (0-932471-09-9) Falsoft.
***Puckett, David L.** John Calvin's Exegesis of the Old Testament. LC 94-31595. (Columbia Series in Reformed Theology). 192p. 1995. 17.00 (0-664-22044-4) Westminster John Knox.
Puckett, Doug. Coldwater Indian Artifacts Price Guide. 1994. pap. 20.00 (0-9637157-2-0) D Puckett Ent.
Puckett, G. Douglas, ed. see Sprunt, Hugh H., et al.
Puckett, Hugh W. Germany's Women Go Forward. LC 30-8154. reprint ed. 19.50 (0-404-05173-1) AMS Pr.
Puckett, James M. & Reese, Hayne W., eds. Mechanisms of Everyday Cognition. (West Virginia Series on Lifespan Developmental Psychology). 256p. 1993. text ed. 59.95 (0-8058-0976-7) L Erlbaum Assocs.
Puckett, John L. Foxfire Reconsidered: A Twenty-Year Experiment in Progressive Education. LC 88-17106. (Illus.). 376p. 1989. 29.95 (0-252-01574-6) U of Ill Pr.
Puckett, John R. Five Photo-Textual Documentaries from the Great Depression. LC 84-8536. (Studies in Photography: No. 6). (Illus.). 183p. reprint ed. pap. 52.20 (0-8357-1582-5, 2070571) Bks Demand.
Puckett, K. I Love This Game. 1994. mass mkt. 5.99 (0-06-109210-X, Harp PBks) HarpC.
— I Love This Game. 1994. pap. 4.99 (0-517-13207-9) Random Hse Value.
Puckett, Katharyn E. & Laughlin, Sara, eds. Directory of Indiana Children's Authors & Illustrators. 2nd rev. ed. 48p. 1991. pap. 6.95 (0-9624180-1-3) Stone Hills Area Lib Servs.
Puckett, Kelly & Pasko. Batman: The Collected Adventures, Vol. 1. Kahan, Bob, ed. (Illus.). 144p. (YA). 1993. pap. 5.95 (1-56389-098-4) DC Comics.
Puckett, Kirby. Be the Best You Can Be. (Illus.). 40p. (J). Date not set. 14.95 (0-931674-20-4) Waldman Hse Pr.
Puckett, Linda J. Cast a Long Shadow. 228p. 1986. 25.00 (0-317-69301-8) Jay Banks.
Puckett, Margaret B. & Black, Janet K. Authentic Assessment of the Young Child: Celebrating Development & Learning. (Illus.). 230p. (Orig.). (C). 1994. pap. write for info. (0-02-310261-6) Macmillan.
Puckett, Margaret B., jt. auth. see Black, Janet K.
Puckett, Newbell N. Folk Beliefs of the Southern Negro. LC 68-55780. (Criminology, Law Enforcement, & Social Problems Ser.: No. 22). (Illus.). 1968. reprint ed. 28.00 (0-87585-022-7) Patterson Smith.
Puckett, Robert, ed. The United States & Northeast Asia. 280p. 1993. pap. text ed. 18.95 (0-8304-1279-4) Nelson-Hall.
***Puckett, Ruby P. & Norton, L. Charkette.** HACCP the Future Challenge: Practical Application for the Foodservice Administrator. 127p. 1994. student ed. pap. text ed. 75.00 (0-9644447-0-4) Norton Grp.
Puckett, Sam B., jt. auth. see Emery, Alan R.
Puckett, Sandy. Fragile Beauty: The Victorian Art of Pressed Flowers. 96p. 1992. 19.95 (0-446-51673-2) Warner Bks.
Puckett, Susan. A Cook's Tour of Iowa. LC 87-35751. (Bur Oak Original Ser.). (Illus.). 310p. 1988. pap. 13.95 (0-87745-289-X) U of Iowa Pr.
— Dips. (Illus.). 96p. 1995. 14.95 (1-56352-241-1) Longstreet Pr Inc.
Puckett, Susan, jt. auth. see Auchmutey, Jim.
Puckle, Bertram S. Funeral Customs: Their Origin & Development. LC 89-63010. (Illus.). xiv, 399p. 1990. reprint ed. lib. bdg. 48.00 (1-55888-750-4) Omnigraphics Inc.
Puckler, Furst, jt. auth. see Kameke, Rochus.
Pucknell, Doug & Eshraghian, Kamram. Basic VLSI Design: Systems & Circuits. 3rd ed. 1994. pap. text ed. 50.00 (0-13-079153-9) P-H.
Pudaite, Rochunga. Horizons Never End. (Illus.). 20p. (J). (gr. k-6). 1988. pap. text ed. 4.25 (1-55976-144-X) CEF Press.
Pudaite, Rochunga & Hefley, James C. The Greatest Book Ever Written. 206p. (Orig.). 1989. pap. 9.95 (0-929292-03-0) Hannibal Bks.
Puddephatt, Noel. Homeopathic Correspondence Course: Advanced Level. 92p. reprint ed. spiral bd. 9.90 (0-7873-1076-X) Mokelumne.
— Puddephatt's Primers. 66p. (Orig.). Date not set. pap. 4.95 (0-8464-4276-0) Beekman Pubs.
Puddephatt, Richard J. The Chemistry of Gold. (Topics in Inorganic & General Chemistry: Vol. 16). 274p. 1978. 100.00 (0-444-41624-2) Elsevier.
Puddephatt, Richard J. & Monaghan, P. K. The Periodic Table of Elements. 2nd ed. (Chemistry Ser.: No. 32). (Illus.). 100p. 1986. pap. 17.95 (0-19-855516-4) OUP.
***Puddester, R. P.** Catalogue of British Historical Medals. 245p. 1987. 150.00 (0-9511308-2-X, Pub. by R C Senior UK) St Mut.
Puddington, Arch. Failed Utopias: Methods of Coercion in Communist Regimes. LC 88-28400. 300p. 1988. 19.95 (1-55815-010-2) ICS Pr.
Pudlak, Pavel, jt. auth. see Hajek, Petr.
Pudlow, Jan, jt. auth. see Myers, Howard.
Pudney, Stephen. Modelling Individual Choice: The Econometrics of Corners, Kinks & Holes. (Illus.). 352p. 1989. pap. 21.95 (1-55786-297-4) Blackwell Pubs.
PUDOC Staff. P.R.O.S.E.A., Vol. I: (Pulses) Van Maesen, L. J., ed. 108p. (C). 1991. text ed. 250.00 (0-89771-632-9, Pub. by Intl Bk Distr II) St Mut.
— P.R.O.S.E.A., Vol. II: (A Selection) Westphal, E. & Jansen, P. C., eds. 324p. (C). 1991. text ed. 650.00 (0-89771-634-5, Pub. by Intl Bk Distr II) St Mut.
— P.R.O.S.E.A., Vol. III: (Plant Resources of South-East Asia) Siemonsma, J. S. & Wolijarni-SoetJipto, N., eds. 337p. (C). 1991. text ed. 695.00 (0-89771-635-3, Pub. by Intl Bk Distr II) St Mut.
PUDOC Staff, ed. see Mannetje, L. T. & Jones, R. M.
PUDOC Staff, et al. Advances in Research & Technology of Seeds, Pts. I & II. (C). 1991. text ed. 2,500.00 (0-89771-631-0, Pub. by Intl Bk Distr II) St Mut.
Pudovik. Chemistry of Organophosphorus Compounds. 1990. 64.95 (0-8493-7124-4, QD) CRC Pr.
Pudritz, Ralph E. & Fich, Michel, eds. Galactic & Extragalactic Star Formation. (C). 1988. lib. bdg. 212.00 (90-277-2725-2) Kluwer Ac.
***Pudup, Mary B., et al, eds.** Mountain Life & Work. LC 94-47135. 1995. write for info. (0-8078-2229-9); pap. write for info. (0-8078-4534-5) U of NC Pr.
Puebla, Luis M., tr. see LeLoeuff, Jean.
Puech, jt. ed. see Ostrowsky.
Puech, Alain. The Use of Anchors in Offshore Petroleum Operations. LC 84-71684. (Illus.). 112p. 1984. 39.00 (0-87201-042-2) Gulf Pub.
— The Use of Anchors in Offshore Petroleum Operations. (Illus.). 160p. (C). 1984. text ed. 56.00 (2-7108-0453-0) Technip.
Puech, Claude, jt. auth. see Sillion, Francois X.
Puech, Henri C. Le Manicheisme: Son fondateur, sa doctrine.(Musee Guimet. Bibliotheque de diffusion, t. 56) LC 82-45821. (Orthodoxies & Heresies in the Early Church Ser.). reprint ed. 27.50 (0-404-62391-3) AMS Pr.
Puech, Henri-Charles. Histoire des Religions, 3 vols. 1520p. (FRE.). 1970. 125.00 (0-7859-4552-0) Fr & Eur.
— Histoire des Religions, 3 vols., Vols. 1 & 2. (Historique Ser.). 59.95 (0-686-56461-8) Fr & Eur.
— Histoires des Religions, Vol. 2. (FRE.). 1973. lib. bdg. 130.00 (0-7859-3820-6) Fr & Eur.
— Histoires des Religions, Vol. 3. (FRE.). 1976. lib. bdg. 135.00 (0-7859-3826-5) Fr & Eur.
Puech, Henri-Charles, et al. Gospel According to Thomas. 1959. 9.95 (0-06-066710-9) Harper SF.
Puel, Gaston. The Song Between Two Stars. 6.75 (0-89253-770-1); 4.80 (0-89253-771-X) Ind-US Inc.
***Puello, Andres D.** Brevisima Historia de Fray Bartolome de las Casas, Obispo de Chiapas. (Cuadernos Panamericanos Ser.). 44p. 1994. spiral bd. 11.95 (0-9631210-2-2) DPA Intl.
— Jose Marti en el Exilio. (Illus.). 44p. (SPA.). 1991. 9.95 (0-9631210-0-6) DPA Intl.
— Public Holidays in Latin America. (International Business Reports). 45p. 1993. spiral bd. 14.95 (0-9631210-1-4) DPA Intl.
Puente, A. E. & McCaffrey, R. J., eds. Handbook of Neuropsychological Assessment: A Biopsychosocial Perspective. (Critical Issues in Neuropsychology Ser.). (Illus.). 520p. 1991. 80.00 (0-306-43940-9, Plenum Pr) Plenum.
Puente, Antonio E., et al, eds. Teaching Psychology in America: A History. 598p. 1992. text ed. 59.95 (1-55798-181-7); pap. text ed. 36.95 (1-55798-183-3) Am Psychol.
Puente-Duany, N. Aventuras de Amor del Doctor Fonda (la Sombra de Helena) LC 78-73151. (Coleccion Caniqui Ser.). (Illus.). 1979. pap. 5.95 (0-89729-215-4) Ediciones.
Puente, E. A. & Nemes, L., eds. Information Control Problems in Manufacturing Technology 1989: Selected Papers from the Sixth IFAC-IFORS-IMACS Symposium, Madrid, Spain, 26-29 September 1989, 2 vols., Set. LC 90-7005. (IFAC Proceedings Ser.: No. IFPS 9013). 694p. 1990. 335.00 (0-08-037023-3, Pergamon Pr) Elsevier.
Puente, E. A., jt. auth. see IFAC-IFIP Symposium Staff.
Puente, Julius I. The Foreign Consul. His Juridical Status in the United States. xv, 157p. 1987. reprint ed. lib. bdg. 27.50 (0-8377-2513-5) Rothman.
— International Law as Applied to Foreign States: Being an Analysis of the Juridical Status of Foreign States in American Jurisprudence. xxiii, 299p. 1983. reprint ed. lib. bdg. 30.00 (0-8377-1017-0) Rothman.
Puentes, Nancy O., jt. auth. see Bresenhan, Karoline P.
Puerta, Mauricio, jt. auth. see Chaves, Alvaro.

P
Q

An Asterisk (*) at the beginning of an entry indicates that the title is appearing in BIP for the first time.

Puerto Rican Forum Staff. The Puerto Rican Community Development Project. LC 74-14243. (Puerto Rican Experience Ser.). (Illus.). 162p. 1975. reprint ed. 13.95 (*0-405-06230-3*) Ayer.

Puerto Rico. Universidad. Facultad de Humanidades. Programa Graduado de Traduccion Staff, ed. Problemas de la Traduccion: Problems in Translation. LC 77-12171. 187p. 1982. pap. 5.00 (*0-8477-3187-1*) U of PR Pr.

Puerto Rico, Universidad. Facultad de Humanidades, Centro de Investigaciones Historicas Staff, ed. Despachos de los Consules Norteamericanos en Puerto Rico: 1818-1868, Tomo I. LC 77-12721. 1395p. 1982. 25.00 (*0-8477-0845-4*) U of PR Pr.

Puertolas, Julio R., ed. see Santos, Francisco.

Puertorriqueno, Ateneo. Problemas de la Cultura en Puerto Rico (Foro Auspiciado por el Ateneo Puertorriqueno En 1940) LC 76-10701. 272p. (Orig.). (SPA.). 1976. 8.00 (*0-8477-2430-1*) U of PR Pr.

Pues, Sylvester. I've Got Style! You've Got Style! Understanding & Teaching to Learning Styles. 65p. (Orig.). (C). 1994. teacher ed 15.00 (*1-880830-49-3*) AEON-Hierophant.

Pueschel & Rynders. Down's Syndrome: Advances in Biomedicine & the Behavioral Sciences. 1982. 65.00 (*0-938552-50-3*) Acad Guild.

Pueschel & Steinberg. Down's Syndrome: A Comprehensive Bibliography. 1980. 50.00 (*0-685-42735-8*) Acad Guild.

Pueschel, Jeanette & Pueschel, Siegfried M. Sindrome De Down: Problematica Biomedica. 352p. (SPA.). 1994. pap. 55.00 (*84-458-0202-X*, Pub. by Ediciones Cientificas SP) P H Brookes.

Pueschel, Jeanette K., jt. ed. see Pueschel, Siegfried M.

Pueschel, Siegfried. An Overview of Down Syndrome. rev. ed. 26p. 1986. pap. 3.50 (*0-318-22870-X*, 10-6) Arc of the US.

Pueschel, Siegfried & Mulick, James, eds. Prevention of Developmental Disabilities: Strategies for the 80's. text ed. 34.95 (*0-938550-28-4*) Acad Guild.

Pueschel, Siegfried M. Sindrome De Down: Hacia un Futuro Mejor Guia Para los Padres. 286p. (SPA.). 1992. pap. 25.00 (*84-345-2429-5*, Pub. by Ediciones Cientificas SP) P H Brookes.

— The Young Child with Down Syndrome. 371p. 1984. 45. 95 (*0-89885-120-3*) Human Sci Pr.

Pueschel, Siegfried M., ed. A Parent's Guide to Down Syndrome: Toward a Brighter Future. (Illus.). 336p. (Orig.). (C). 1990. pap. text ed. 20.00 (*1-55766-060-3*, 0603) P H Brookes.

— Prevention of Developmental Disabilities. LC 90-1622. (Illus.). 384p. (C). 1990. text ed. 37.00 (*1-55766-052-2*, 0522) P H Brookes.

Pueschel, Siegfried M. & Pueschel, Jeanette K., eds. Biomedical Concerns in Persons with Down Syndrome. 336p. (Orig.). (C). 1992. text ed. 45.00 (*1-55766-089-1*) P H Brookes.

Pueschel, Siegfried M., jt. auth. see Pueschel, Jeanette.

Pueschel, Siegfried M., et al. The Special Child: A Source Book for Parents of Children with Developmental Disabilities. 2nd ed. LC 94-1018. 464p. (Orig.). 1994. pap. 26.00 (*1-55766-167-7*) P H Brookes.

Puett, Barbara & Apfelbaum, Jim. Golf Etiquette. (Illus.). 176p. 1992. 12.95 (*0-312-07686-X*) St Martin.

Puett, D., et al. Advances in Gene Technology: Molecular Biology of the Endocrine System: Proceedings of the 18th Miami Winter Symposium. (ICSU Short Reports: No. 4). 402p. 1986. 69.95 (*0-521-32658-3*) Cambridge U Pr.

Puett, J. F., jt. auth. see Roman, D. D.

Puette, William J. Tale of Genji: A Reader's Guide. 196p. 1993. pap. 9.95 (*0-8048-1879-7*) C E Tuttle.

— Through Jaundiced Eyes: How the Media View Organized Labor. 240p. (Orig.). 1992. 38.00 (*0-87546-184-0*); pap. 16.95 (*0-87546-185-9*) ILR Pr.

Puetz, Belinda E. & Flanagan, Lyndia. Survival Skills in the Workplace: An Independent Study Module. 174p. (Orig.). (C). 1991. pap. 39.95 (*1-55810-064-4*, COE-15) Am Nurses Pub.

Puetz, C. J., ed. Arkansas County Maps. (Illus.). 152p. (Orig.). 1987. pap. 14.85 (*0-916514-07-2*) Cnty Maps.

— Florida County Maps. rev. ed. (Illus.). 160p. 1988. pap. 14.85 (*0-916514-08-0*) Cnty Maps.

— Indiana County Maps. rev. ed. (Illus.). 128p. 1991. pap. 14.85 (*0-916514-09-9*) Cnty Maps.

— Kentucky County Maps. rev. ed. (Illus.). 136p. 1992. pap. 14.85 (*0-916514-10-2*) Cnty Maps.

— Ohio County Maps & Recreational Guide. rev. ed. (Illus.). 136p. 1992. pap. 14.85 (*0-916514-12-9*) Cnty Maps.

— Pennsylvania County Maps. rev. ed. (Illus.). 144p. 1988. pap. 14.85 (*0-916514-13-7*) Cnty Maps.

— South Carolina County Maps. rev. ed. (Illus.). 128p. 1989. pap. 14.85 (*0-916514-14-5*) Cnty Maps.

— Tennessee County Maps. rev. ed. (Illus.). 144p. 1992. pap. 14.85 (*0-916514-15-3*) Cnty Maps.

— West Virginia County Maps. rev. ed. (Illus.). 144p. (Orig.). 1990. pap. 14.85 (*0-916514-16-1*) Cnty Maps.

Puetz, Cy, ed. North Carolina County Maps. rev. ed. (Illus.). 156p. 1990. pap. 14.85 (*0-916514-11-0*) Cnty Maps.

Puetz, Detlev, jt. ed. see Von Braun, Joachim.

***Puetz, Manfred, ed.** Nietzsche in American Literature & Thought. (Studies in German Literature, Linguistics, & Culture). 390p. 1995. 59.95 (*1-57113-028-4*) Camden Hse.

Pufall, Peter, jt. ed. see Beilin, Harry.

Pufall, Peter, jt. ed. see Forman, George.

Pufendorf, Samuel. On the Duty of Man & Citizen According to Natural Law. Tully, James, ed. Silverthorne, Michael, tr. (Cambridge Texts in the History of Political Thought Ser.). 200p. (C). 1991. 59. 95 (*0-521-35195-2*); pap. 18.95 (*0-521-35980-5*) Cambridge U Pr.

— On the Natural State of Men. Seidler, Michael, tr. LC 89-77198. (Studies in History of Philosophy: Vol. 13). 152p. (ENG & LAT.). 1990. lib. bdg. 69.95 (*0-88946-299-2*) E Mellen.

— The Political Writings of Samuel Pufendorf. Carr, Craig L., ed. Seidler, Michael J., tr. 304p. 1994. 49.95 (*0-19-506560-3*) OUP.

Pufendorf, Samuel & Freiherr, Von. Les Devoirs De l'Homme et Du Citoyen, 2 vols in 1. lii, 523p. 1992. reprint ed. write for info. (*3-487-09562-9*, Pub. by Georg Olms GW) Lubrecht & Cramer.

***Puffenbarger, Charles E.** Dictionary of Computer Terms. 1993. pap. 9.95 (*1-882912-00-4*) Sunrise TN.

Puffer, Andrew, jt. ed. see Laska, Shirley.

Puffer, Darrick J. I'm Not Your Angel. LC 92-60490. 241p. (YA). (gr. 7 up). 1993. pap. 8.95 (*1-55523-533-6*) Winston-Derek.

Puffer, J. H. & Ragland, P. C., eds. Eastern North American Mesozoic Magmatism. (Special Paper Ser.: No. 268). 1992. pap. 78.00 (*0-8137-2268-3*) Geol Soc.

Puffer, John H., jt. auth. see Volkert, Richard A.

Puffer, Lela, jt. auth. see Fox, George.

Puffer, Sheila, jt. auth. see Marcic, Dorothy.

Puffer, Sheila M. Managerial Insights from Literature. 334p. (C). 1992. pap. 29.95 (*0-534-92481-6*) Intl Thomson.

Puffer, Sheila M., ed. & intro. The Russian Management Revolution: Preparing Managers for the Market Economy. LC 92-9034. 320p. 1992. 67.95 (*1-56324-042-4*); pap. text ed. 25.95 (*1-56324-043-2*) M E Sharpe.

Puffett, Derrick, ed. Richard Strauss: "Salome" (Cambridge Opera Handbooks Ser.). 1989. pap. 19.95 (*0-521-35970-8*) Cambridge U Pr.

Puffett, Derrick, tr. see Dahlhaus, Carl.

Puffett, Derrick, tr. see Nattiez, Jean-Jacques.

Puffr & Kubanek. Lactam Based Polyamides, Vol. II. 1991. 190.00 (*0-8493-4966-4*, QD383) CRC Pr.

Puffr, jt. auth. see Kubanek.

Pugach, Marleen C. & Johnson, Lawrence J. Collaborative Practitioners, Collaborative Schools. LC 94-75177. 224p. (Orig.). (C). 1994. pap. text ed. 24.95 (*0-89108-234-4*) Love Pub Co.

Pugachenkova, G. A. A Museum in the Open: The Architectural Treasures of Uzbekistan. 236p. 1981. 275. 00 (*0-569-08712-0*, Pub. by Collets UK) St Mut.

Pugachev. Probability Theory & Mathematical Statistics. Eykhoff, P., ed. Sinitsyna, I. V., tr. 450p. 1984. 196.00 (*0-08-029148-1*, Pub. by Pergamon Repr UK) Franklin.

Pugachev, V. S. & Sinitsyn, I. N. Stochastic Differential Systems: Analysis & Filtering. LC 86-15952. 549p. 1987. text ed. 330.00 (*0-471-91243-3*) Wiley.

Pugeat, M., jt. auth. see Forest, M. G.

Pugel, Thomas A. & Hawkins, Robert G., eds. The Fragile Interdependence: Economic Issues in U. S. -Japanese Trade & Investment. LC 85-45760. (Illus.). 288p. 1986. text ed. 37.95 (*0-669-12263-7*) Free Pr.

Pugh & Bergstrom, eds. Surface & Colloid Chemistry in Advanced Ceramics Processing. (Surfactant Science Ser.: Vol. 51). 376p. 1994. 145.00 (*0-8247-9098-7*) Dekker.

Pugh & Woodward-Smith. Nurse Manager: A Practical Guide to Better Employee Relations. 84p. 1989. pap. text ed. 14.95 (*0-7216-2863-X*) Saunders.

Pugh, A., ed. Assembly Automation. (Illus.). 450p. 1988. 153.00 (*0-387-19324-3*) Spr-Verlag.

— Robot Sensors: Tactile & Non-Vision, Vol. 2. (International Trends in Manufacturing Technology Ser.). 350p. 1986. 99.00 (*0-387-16126-0*) Spr-Verlag.

— Robot Sensors: Vision, Vol. 1. (International Trends in Manufacturing Technology Ser.). 300p. 1986. 93.00 (*0-387-16125-2*) Spr-Verlag.

— Robot Vision & Sensory Controls IV: Proceedings of the 4th International Conference, London, U. K., October 9-11, 1984. 540p. 1985. 154.00 (*0-444-87626-X*, North Holland) Elsevier.

— Robotic Technology. (Control Engineering Ser.: No. 23). 168p. 1983. boxed 79.00 (*0-86341-004-9*, CE 023) Inst Elect Eng.

Pugh, A., jt. auth. see Wong, A. K.

Pugh, A. K., jt. ed. see Mayor, Barbara.

Pugh, Alexander I., III, jt. ed. see Richardson, George P.

***Pugh, Alexander L., III.** Dynamo Users Manual. 6th ed. LC 83-43024. (Illus.). 310p. 1983. pap. text ed. 25.00 (*0-262-66029-6*) Prod Press.

Pugh, Ann. Across-the-Curriculum Guide, Diggy Armadillo Goes to Fort Worth Stock Show & Rodeo, Bk. 1: 140 Creative Activites. 60p. (Orig.). 1992. 10.00 (*1-879465-01-9*) Diggy & Assocs.

— Across-the-Curriculum Guide, Diggy Armadillo Goes to Fort Worth Stock Show & Rodeo, Bk. 1: 140 Creative Activites. 60p. (Orig.). (J). (gr. k-5). 1992. Eng. & Spa. audio 6.00 (*0-685-60626-0*) Diggy & Assocs.

Pugh, Ann & Utter, Betty. Heidi. LC 79-53859. (Illus.). 68p. (J). (gr. k up). 1962. pap. 4.50 (*0-88680-082-X*); Piano-Vocal Score, Music & Lyrics. pap. 15.00 (*0-88680-083-8*) I E Clark.

— It Happened in Hamelin. (Illus.). 56p. (J). (gr. k up). 1973. pap. 4.00 (*0-88680-095-1*); Piano-Vocal Score, Music & Lyrics. pap. 15.00 (*0-88680-096-X*) I E Clark.

Pugh, Ann, et al. Diggy Armadillo Goes to Fort Worth Stock Show & Rodeo, Bk. 2: Further Adventures: "Finding Rosita" LC 93-73103. (Illus.). 54p. (J). (gr. 3-6). 1993. 7.95 (*1-879465-02-7*) Diggy & Assocs.

***Pugh, Ann B.** Westy the Hare Goes to the National Western Stock Show & Rodeo. (Illus.). (SPA.). (J). 1995. 5.00 (*0-9643660-0-2*) Diggy & Assocs.

Pugh, Anthony. The Birth of a la Recherche du Temps Perdu. LC 87-80816. (French Forum Monographs: No. 68). 147p. (Orig.). 1987. pap. 13.95 (*0-917058-69-0*) French Forum.

Pugh, Anthony R. Balzac's Recurrring Characters. LC 72-190348. (University of Toronto Romance Ser.: No. 24). 544p. reprint ed. pap. 155.10 (*0-8357-5955-5*, 2029344) Bks Demand.

— The Composition of Pascal's Apologia. (Romance Ser.: No.49). 656p. 1984. 75.00 (*0-8020-5611-3*) U of Toronto Pr.

Pugh, Burton. Mastering Cotton. (Illus.). 27p. (C). 1976. pap. 20.00 (*0-939093-14-6*) Lambert Gann Pub.

Pugh, Burton H. A Better Way to Make Money. (Illus.). 1987. 25.00 (*0-939093-09-X*) Lambert Gann Pub.

— Science & Secrets of Wheat Trading, Vol. 6. 234p. 1980. pap. text ed. 60.00 (*0-939093-10-3*) Lambert Gann Pub.

— Traders Instruction Book. (Illus.). 1980. pap. 25.00 (*0-939093-08-1*) Lambert Gann Pub.

Pugh, Cedric. Housing & Urbanization: A Study of India. (Illus.). 298p. (C). 1990. text ed. 32.00 (*0-8039-9655-1*) Sage.

Pugh, Cedric, jt. auth. see Dean, Peter N.

Pugh, Charles. The Griot. (YA). (ps-12). 1993. pap. 3.95 (*0-87067-697-0*) Holloway.

— The Hospital Plot. Young, Billie, ed. LC 78-54163. 1979. 22.95 (*0-87949-116-7*) Ashley Bks.

Pugh, Charles W., jt. auth. see Pugh, Doris.

Pugh, Clifford A., ed. see American Society of Civil Engineers, Hydraulics Division.

***Pugh, Corky.** Family & Friends. 112p. 1994. pap. 8.95 (*0-9642888-0-X*) Longbeard Pub.

Pugh, D. S. Organization Theory: Selected Reading. rev. ed. 1990. pap. 12.00 (*0-14-012423-3*, Penguin Bks) Viking Penguin.

Pugh, D. S., ed. Organization Theory. 1985. pap. 7.95 (*0-14-022602-8*, Penguin Bks) Viking Penguin.

Pugh, D. S. & Hickson, D. J. Writers on Organizations. 4th ed. 240p. (C). 1989. text ed. 46.00 (*0-8039-3507-2*); pap. text ed. 21.95 (*0-8039-3508-0*) Sage.

Pugh, D. S., jt. auth. see Phillips, Estelle M.

Pugh, Darrell. Looking Back...Moving Forward. 140p. 1988. 27.95 (*0-936678-10-0*); pap. 17.95 (*0-685-25268-X*) Am Soc Pub Admin.

Pugh, David & Geeson, Linda. The Book of Baltimore Orioles Lists. (Illus.). 144p. (Orig.). 1993. pap. 9.95 (*1-56167-120-7*) Am Literary Pr.

Pugh, David, jt. auth. see Bowen-Simpkins, Peter.

Pugh, David G. Sons of Liberty: The Masculine Mind in Nineteenth Century America. LC 83-10755. (Contributions in American Studies: No. 68). xxii, 186p. 1983. text ed. 45.00 (*0-313-23934-7*, PSL/, Greenwood Pr) Greenwood.

Pugh, Derek S. & Hickson, David J., eds. Great Writers on Organisations: The Omnibus Edition. 4th ed. 396p. 1993. 39.95 (*1-85521-383-4*, Pub. by Dartmth Pub UK) Ashgate Pub Co.

Pugh, Dianne G. Cold Call. Isaacson, Dana, ed. LC 92-40549. 288p. 1993. 20.00 (*0-671-77841-2*) PB.

— Cold Call. Issacson, Dana, ed. 288p. 1994. mass mkt. 5.50 (*0-671-77842-0*) PB.

— Slow Squeeze. Isaacson, Dana, ed. 272p. 1994. 20.00 (*0-671-77843-9*) PB.

Pugh, Donna J., et al. Judicial Rulemaking: A Compendium. LC 83-73160. 307p. 1984. text ed. 55.00 (*0-313-27057-0*, U7057, Greenwood Pr) Greenwood.

Pugh, Doris & Pugh, Charles W. Country Woodcraft Patterns. LC 90-39880. (Illus.). 168p. (Orig.). (YA). (gr. 10-12). 1990. pap. 12.95 (*0-8069-7360-9*) Sterling.

Pugh, Edwin W. Charles Dickens: Apostle of the People. LC 75-176497. (Studies in Dickens: No. 52). 1971. reprint ed. lib. bdg. 52.95 (*0-8383-1364-7*) M S G Haskell Hse.

— Charles Dickens: The Apostle of the People. LC 78-148287. reprint ed. 19.50 (*0-404-08894-5*) AMS Pr.

— The Charles Dickens Originals. LC 71-148288. (Illus.). reprint ed. 37.50 (*0-404-08895-3*) AMS Pr.

***Pugh, Emerson W.** Building IBM: Shaping an Industry & Its Technology. LC 94-21609. 432p. 1995. 30.00x (*0-262-16147-8*) MIT Pr.

— Memories That Shaped an Industry: Decisions Leading to IBM System 360. (History of Computing Ser.). (Illus.). 336p. 1984. 29.95 (*0-262-16094-3*) MIT Pr.

Pugh, Emerson W., et al. IBM's 360 & Early 370 Systems. 848p. 1991. 42.50 (*0-262-16123-0*) MIT Pr.

Pugh, Frank & Ponick, Wes. Experiments in Basic Electronics. 2nd ed. 296p. 1989. pap. text ed. 12.00 (*0-07-050987-5*) McGraw.

— Experiments in Basic Electronics. 5th ed. 240p. 1987. 9.95 (*0-07-050855-0*) McGraw.

Pugh, Frank, jt. auth. see Ponick, Wes.

Pugh, Fred. Days along the Buckwheat & Dandelion. 142p. 1984. pap. 20.00 (*0-914821-04-0*) Worden Pr.

Pugh, G. Allen. Industrial Experiments Without Statistical Pain. LC 94-6301. 56p. 1994. pap. 14.95 (*0-87389-278-X*) ASQC Qual Pr.

Pugh, Geoff, jt. auth. see Cook, Chris.

Pugh, George, et al. Handbook on Louisiana Evidence Law. 670p. 1993. pap. text ed. write for info. (*0-314-01933-2*) West Pub.

***Pugh, George W., et al.** Handbook on Louisiana Evidence Law: 1995 Edition. 694p. (C). 1995. pap. text ed. write for info. (*0-614-03889-8*) West Pub.

Pugh, Gillian, ed. Contemporary Issues in the Early Years: Working Collaboratively for Children. 176p. 1992. pap. 27.00 (*1-85396-173-6*, Pub. by Paul Chapman UK) Taylor & Francis.

Pugh, Gillian & Hollows, Anne, eds. Child Protection in Early Childhood Services. 108p. 1995. 22.50 (*1-874579-19-9*, Pub. by Natl Childrens Bur UK) Paul & Co Pubs.

***Pugh, Gillian, et al.** Confident Parents, Confident Children: Policy & Practice in Parent Education & Support. 288p. 1995. 25.50 (*1-874579-37-7*, Pub. by Natl Childrens Bur UK) Paul & Co Pubs.

Pugh, Harry. U. S. Special Forces Shoulder & Pocket Insignia. LC 93-72379. (Elite Insignia Guides Ser.). (Illus.). 320p. (Orig.). 1993. pap. 24.00 (*0-9633231-2-1*) C&D Ent.

***Pugh, Harry & Bragg, Robert.** Portugal Elite Forces Insignia, 1951-Present. LC 95-67552. (Elite Insignia Guides Ser.). (Illus.). 140p. (Orig.). 1995. pap. 16.00 (*0-9633231-4-8*) C&D Ent.

***Pugh, Harry & Clark, Thomas.** Canadian Airborne Insignia, 1942-Present. LC 94-70190. (Elite Insignia Guides Ser.). (Illus.). 160p. (Orig.). 1994. pap. 16.00 (*0-9633231-3-X*) C&D Ent.

Pugh, Harry & Piotti, Vittorio. Italian Airborne Insignia, 1938-Present. LC 92-7891. (Elite Insignia Guides Ser.). (Illus.). 224p. (Orig.). 1993. pap. 20.00 (*0-9633231-1-3*) C&D Ent.

Pugh, Harry F. German Airborne Insignia 1956-1992. LC 92-81930. (Elite Insignia Guides Ser.). (Illus.). 128p. (Orig.). 1992. pap. 16.00 (*0-9633231-0-5*) C&D Ent.

Pugh, J. T. For Preachers Only. LC 86-10976. 192p. (Orig.). 1971. pap. 5.99 (*0-912315-35-0*) Word Aflame.

— How to Receive the Holy Ghost. 63p. (Orig.). 1969. pap. 2.99 (*0-912315-45-8*) Word Aflame.

Pugh, Jeffrey C. The Anselmic Shift: Christology & Method in Karl Barth's Theology. LC 90-34802. (American University Studies: Theology & Religion: Ser. VII, Vol. 68). 179p. (C). 1990. text ed. 42.95 (*0-8204-1121-3*) P Lang Pubs.

Pugh, John R. & LaLonde, Wilf R. Inside Smalltalk. 500p. 1990. text ed. 62.00 (*0-13-468414-1*) P-H.

Pugh, John R., jt. auth. see Lalonde, Wilf R.

Pugh, Ken. All on C. (C). 1989. pap. text ed. 35.50 (*0-673-18603-2*) HarpCollege.

Pugh, Kenneth. Learn C & Save Your Job: C for COBOL Programmers. 360p. 1993. pap. 29.95 (*0-89435-431-0*) Wiley.

— UNIX for the MS-DOS User. LC 93-46801. 240p. 1994. pap. 22.95 (*0-13-146077-3*) P-H.

Pugh, Kenneth, jt. auth. see Killeen, Leslie.

Pugh, Kenneth, jt. ed. see Killeen, Leslie.

Pugh, Lisa & Pugh, Virginia. Lisa's Story: A Young Girl's Life of Courage. LC 91-65722. 128p. (YA). (gr. 9-12). 1991. pap. 8.95 (*0-8358-0648-0*) Upper Room Bks.

Pugh, Lisa & Pugh, Virginia Y. Keep Your Finger on the Boat. LC 89-84931. 104p. (Orig.). 1990. pap. 8.95 (*0-942419-01-4*) Ana Pub.

Pugh, Luise R., tr. see Gruen, Anselm.

Pugh, Martin. Lloyd George: Profile in Power. (Illus.). 206p. (C). 1988. pap. text ed. 21.95 (*0-582-55268-0*, 79762) Longman.

— The Making of Modern British Politics, 1867-1939. 2nd ed. LC 92-22093. 344p. 1993. pap. 24.95 (*0-631-17928-3*) Blackwell Pubs.

— State & Society: British Political & Social History, 1870-1992. 384p. 1994. 74.95 (*0-340-50711-X*, B2315, Pub. by E Arnold UK); pap. 19.95 (*0-340-50710-1*, B2319, Pub. by E Arnold UK) Routledge Chapman & Hall.

— Women & the Women's Movement in Britain. 249p. (C). 1994. 49.95 (*1-56924-855-9*) Marlowe & Co.

Pugh, Mary J. Providing Reference Services for Archives & Manuscripts. (Archival Fundamentals Ser.). 124p. 1992. pap. 25.00 (*0-931828-82-1*) Soc Am Archivists.

Pugh, Meredith, jt. auth. see Perry, Joseph B., Jr.

Pugh, Michael. The Anzus Crisis, Nuclear Visiting & Deterrence. (Cambridge Studies in International Relations: No. 4). (Illus.). (C). 1989. 64.95 (*0-521-34355-0*) Cambridge U Pr.

— Maritime Security & Peacekeeping. LC 94-28597. 1995. text ed. 69.95 (*0-7190-4368-9*, Pub. by Manchester Univ Pr UK) St Martin.

***Pugh, Michael, ed.** Maritime Security & Peacekeeping. LC 94-28597. 1995. text ed. 24.95 (*0-7190-4563-0*, Pub. by Manchester Univ Pr UK) St Martin.

Pugh, Michael C., ed. European Security - Towards Two Thousand. LC 91-4025. 200p. 1992. text ed. 69.95 (*0-7190-3576-7*, Pub. by Manchester Univ Pr UK) St Martin.

Pugh, Nelda. Machine Transcription: A Simulation - Module 1. 160p. (C). 1989. pap. text ed. write for info. (*0-13-542051-2*) P-H.

Pugh, Olin S. & Ingram, Gerald. Credit Union Management: Past, Present & Future. LC 84-186431. (C). 1984. 43.50 (*0-8359-1173-X*) P-H.

Pugh, Olin S., jt. auth. see Kreps, Clifton H.

Pugh, P. D. Staffordshire Portrait Figures of the Victorian Era. (Illus.). 1987. 99.50 (*1-85149-010-8*) Antique Collect.

Pugh, Pat'rick N. Calif of Fornia. LC 93-92578. 216p. 1993. pap. 9.95 (*1-883184-08-8*) PNP.

— Cuisine Is Poetry. LC 93-92597. 1995. pap. 7.95 (*1-883184-12-6*) PNP.

— Paris on the March Thru the Heartland of California at 65 MPH. (Illus.). (Orig.). Date not set. pap. 7.95 (*1-883184-17-7*) PNP.

— Poet Tree Proof! LC 93-92580. 1995. pap. 9.95 (*1-883184-11-8*) PNP.

— Poet Tree Proof! 1995. 18.00 (*1-883184-15-0*) PNP.

— Recollections of Regret. (Illus.). (Orig.). Date not set. pap. 7.95 (*1-883184-16-9*) PNP.

— Sword Dance of the Generalissimos. 1995. pap. 7.95 (*1-883184-14-2*) PNP.

Pugh, S., jt. auth. see Hollins, W. J.

Pugh, S. F. An Introduction to Grain Boundary Fracture in Metals. 238p. 1991. 63.00 (*0-901462-59-4*, Pub. by Inst Materials UK) Ashgate Pub Co.

Pugh, Sharon, et al. Bridging: A Teacher's Guide to Metaphorical Thinking. (Illus.). 150p. (Orig.). 1992. pap. 11.95 (*0-8141-0384-7*) NCTE.

Pugh, Sharon L., jt. auth. see Pace, David.

P Q

An Asterisk (*) at the beginning of an entry indicates that the title is appearing in BIP for the first time.

Pugh, Sheenagh. Beware Falling Tortoises. LC 87-60981. 64p. 1987. pap. 10.95 (*0-907476-70-8*, Pub. by Poetry Wales Pr UK) Dufour.

— Selected Poems. 148p. 1990. pap. 15.95 (*1-85411-029-2*, Pub. by Seren Bks UK) Dufour.

— Sing for the Taxman. 63p. 1993. pap. 13.95 (*1-85411-085-3*, Pub. by Seren Bks UK) Dufour.

Pugh, Sheenagh, ed. Prisoners of Transience. LC 85-71578. 100p. 1985. pap. 13.95 (*0-907476-46-5*, Pub. by Poetry Wales Pr UK) Dufour.

Pugh, Shirley. In One Basket. (J). 1972. 5.00 (*0-87602-140-2*) Anchorage.

Pugh, Stefan, jt. auth. see Press, Ian.

Pugh, Stuart. Total Design. (C). 1991. text ed. 31.25 (*0-201-41639-5*) Addison-Wesley.

Pugh, T. B., ed. The Middle Ages. (Glamorgan County History Ser.: Vol. 3). 704p. 1971. 85.00 (*0-904730-00-X*, Pub. by U of Wales UK) Bks Intl VA.

Pugh, Ted. C User Interface Library. 356p. (Orig.). 1993. pap. 49.50 (*1-85058-295-5*, Pub. by Sigma Press UK) Coronet Bks.

Pugh, Virginia, jt. auth. see Pugh, Lisa.

Pugh, Virginia Y., jt. auth. see Pugh, Lisa.

Pugh, W., jt. ed. see Huth, H.

Pugh, W. C., jt. ed. see Katz, R. L.

Pughe, Thomas. Comic Sense: Reading Robert Couver, Stanley Elkin, Philip Roth. LC 94-6568. (International Cooper Series in English Language & Literature). 1994. 29.50 (*0-8176-5023-7*) Birkhauser.

Pugin, Augustus C. Pugin's Gothic Ornament: The Classic Sourcebook of Decorative Motifs-with 100 Plates. (Pictorial Archive Ser.). (Illus.). 112p. 1987. reprint ed. pap. 7.95 (*0-486-25500-X*) Dover.

Pugliese, Gina, et al, eds. Universal Precautions: Policies, Procedures, & Resources. LC 90-1111. 414p. (Orig.). 1991. 69.95 (*1-55648-055-5*, 094119) AHPI.

Pugliese, M. Dicionario de Expressoes Idiomaticas; Locucoes Mas Usuais da Lingua Portuguesa. 309p. (POR.). 1981. pap. 14.95 (*0-8288-1996-3*, M14432) Fr & Eur.

***Pugliese, Michael A.** The Ultimate SKS Full Auto Plans. (Illus.). 28p. (Orig.). Date not set. pap. text ed. write for info. (*1-886774-01-3*) M & M Engr.

— The Ultimate 7.62 X 39 mm SKS-AK-47-MAX 90 Muffler Pipe Silencer Plans. (Illus.). 28p. (Orig.). Date not set. pap. text ed. write for info. (*1-886774-00-5*) M & M Engr.

— The Ultimmate Do It Yourself Survival Shelters Construction Manual. rev. ed. (Illus.). 126p. 1994. pap. text ed. 19.95 (*1-886774-02-1*) M & M Engr.

Pugliese, Olga, jt. ed. see Eisenbichler, K.

Pugliese, Olga Z., tr. Lorenzo Valla: The Profession of the Religious & The Donation of Constantine. (Medieval & Renaissance Texts & Studies: Vol. CRR2). 74p. 1989. pap. 10.00 (*0-7727-2004-5*, CRR2, Centre Reform Renaiss Stu) MRTS.

Pugliese, Peter T. Advanced Professional Skin Care. Pugliese, Susan et al, eds. (Illus.). 428p. (C). 1991. text ed. 119.95 (*0-9630211-0-9*) P T Pugliese.

Pugliese, R. M. Matrimonio Bendecido Por Dios (The Marriage Blessed by God) (SPA.). Date not set. 2.49 (*1-56063-011-6*, 498053) Editorial Unilit.

Pugliese, Susan, ed. see Pugliese, Peter T.

Puglisi-Allegra, Stefan, ed. Psychobiology of Stress: Proceedings of the NATO Advanced Research Workshop Held in Sorrento, Italy, August 28 - September 2, 1988. (C). 1990. lib. bdg. 129.50 (*0-7923-0682-1*) Kluwer Ac.

***Puglisi, Gary.** Angel Crafts. 1995. 15.00 (*0-517-70093-X*) Random.

***Puglisi, James.** Process of Admission to Ordained Ministry, Vol. 1. Driscoll, Michael, tr. 400p. (Orig.). 1995. pap. text ed. 29.95 (*0-8146-6128-9*, Pueblo Bks) Liturgical Pr.

Puglisi, M., et al, eds. New Techniques for Future Accelerators. LC 87-20248. (Ettore Majorana International Science Series, Life Sciences: Vol. 29). (Illus.). 292p. 1987. 69.50 (*0-306-42608-0*, Plenum Pr) Plenum.

— New Techniques for Future Accelerators II: RF & Microwave Systems. (Ettore Majorana International Science Series, Life Sciences: Vol. 36). (Illus.). 322p. 1989. 85.00 (*0-306-43090-8*, Plenum Pr) Plenum.

Puglisi, Michael J. Puritans Beseiged: The Legacies of King Philip's War in the Massachusetts Bay Colony. 256p. (Orig.). 1991. lib. bdg. 47.50 (*0-8191-8278-8*); pap. text ed. 27.00 (*0-8191-8291-5*) U Pr of Amer.

Puglisi, Steven E. First Lights. 64p. (Orig.). 1990. pap. 8.00 (*0-937179-06-X*) Blue Scarab.

Pugmire-Stoy, M. C. Spontaneous Play in Early Childhood. 128p. 1991. teacher ed 10.00 (*0-8273-3661-6*); pap. text ed. 19.95 (*0-8273-3660-8*) Delmar.

Pugne, Melina S. The Communication Planning Process in the Philippine Commission on Population. (East-West Communication Institute Case Studies: No. 6). xii, 136p. (Orig.). 1983. pap. 5.00 (*0-86638-005-1*) EW Ctr HI.

Pugnetti. Simon & Schuster's Guide to Cats. Siegal, Mordecai, ed. (Illus.). 256p. 1983. pap. 13.00 (*0-671-49170-9*) S&S Trade.

Pugnetti, Gino. Mozart: Portraits of Greatness. Lawrence, Helen, tr. (Illus.). 75p. 1989. reprint ed. 17.50 (*0-918367-35-2*); reprint ed. pap. 12.50 (*0-918367-29-8*) Elite.

Pugsley, Anthony. Protein Targeting. 325p. 1989. text ed. 65.00 (*0-12-566770-1*) Acad Pr.

Pugsley, Betty C., jt. auth. see Pugsley, Richard.

Pugsley, Clement. In Sorrow's Lone Hour. (C). 1990. pap. 24.00 (*0-85305-104-6*, Pub. by J Arthur Ltd UK) St Mut.

***Pugsley, John A.** Reinventing Retirement: Life Without Boundaries. 200p. 1994. pap. 13.95 (*0-9639629-3-0*) Shot Tower.

Pugsley, Keith. Enquiries of Local Authorities: A Practical Guide. 192p. 1991. 60.00 (*1-85190-133-7*) St Mut.

— Enquiries of Local Authorities: A Practical Guide. 3rd ed. 192p. (C). 1994. 105.00x (*0-85459-947-9*, Pub. by Tolley Pubng UK) St Mut.

Pugsley, Richard & Pugsley, Betty C. The Sound Eternal, 2 vols., 1. LC 87-61191. 92p. (Orig.). 1987. pap. 9.95 (*0-941478-50-5*) Paraclete MA.

— The Sound Eternal, 2 vols., 2. LC 87-61191. 64p. (Orig.). 1987. pap. 9.95 (*0-941478-91-2*) Paraclete MA.

— The Sound Eternal, 2 vols., Set. LC 87-61191. (Orig.). 1987. pap. 18.95 (*0-941478-92-0*) Paraclete MA.

Pugsley, Richard K., ed. see Hourlier, Jacques.

Pugsley, Steven, ed. Devon Gardens: An Historical Survey. (Illus.). 192p. 1994. 40.00 (*0-7509-0055-5*) A Sutton Pub.

Puhakka, J., et al, eds. Forest Industry Wastewaters: Proceedings of the 3rd IAWPRC Symposium on Forest Industry Wastewaters, held in Tampere, Finland, 5-8 June 1990. (Water Science & Technology Ser.). (Illus.). 462p. 1991. pap. 155.00 (*0-08-041150-9*, Pergamon Pr) Elsevier.

***Puhakka, Kaisa.** Knowledge & Reality: A Comparative. (C). 1994. text ed. 8.00 (*81-208-1174-7*, Pub. by Motilal Banarsidass II) S Asia.

— Knowledge & Reality: A Comparative Study of Quine & Some Buddhist Logicians. 1975. 8.50 (*0-685-48701-6*, Pub. by Motilal Banarsidass II) S Asia.

***Puhala, Bob.** 52 Illinois Weekends. (Fifty-Two Weekends Ser.). (Illus.). 180p. (Orig.). 1995. pap. 9.95 (*1-56626-083-3*) Country Rds.

— 52 Michigan Weekends. LC 94-20740. (52 Weekends Ser.). 200p. 1994. pap. 9.95 (*1-56626-113-9*) Country Rds.

— 52 Wisconsin Weekends. LC 93-30998. (52 Weekends Ser.). (Illus.). 148p. (Orig.). 1993. pap. 9.95 (*1-56626-057-4*) Country Rds.

— Recommended Country Inns: The Midwest-IA, IL, IN, MI, MN, MO, NE, OH, WI. 5th ed. LC 92-25078. (Recommended Country Inns Ser.). (Illus.). 480p. 1994. pap. 14.95 (*1-56440-509-5*) Globe Pequot.

***Puhallo, Mike, et al.** Rhymes of the Range. 1995. pap. 7.95 (*0-88839-368-7*) Hancock House.

Puhalo, L. Lives of the Saints, Vol. 1. (J). (gr. 4-6). 1977. pap. 2.50 (*0-913026-75-1*) St Nectarios.

— Lives of the Saints, Vol. 2. (J). (gr. 4-6). 1977. pap. 2.50 (*0-685-73441-2*) St Nectarios.

Puhalo, Lazar. Creation & Fall. 36p. (Orig.). 1986. pap. text ed. 4.00 (*0-913026-97-2*) Synaxis Pr.

— Innokenty of Alaska. 86p. (Orig.). (J). (gr. 8 up). 1986. pap. 5.00 (*0-913026-86-7*) Synaxis Pr.

— Missionary Handbook. 49p. (Orig.). 1985. pap. text ed. 3.00 (*0-911523-00-6*) Synaxis Pr.

— The Soul, the Body & Death. 2nd ed. 1989. pap. 8.00 (*0-911523-03-0*) Synaxis Pr.

Puhalo, Lazar, tr. see Khrapovitsky, Antony.

Puhalo, Lev. Lives of Saints for Young People, Vol. 1. (J). (gr. 4-6). 1975. pap. 2.50 (*0-913026-11-5*) St Nectarios.

Puhl, Jacqueline, et al, eds. Sport Science Perspectives for Women. LC 87-4023. 248p. 1988. text ed. 35.00x (*0-87322-110-9*, BPUH0110) Human Kinetics.

Puhl, Jacqueline L. & Brown, C. Harmon, eds. The Menstrual Cycle & Physical Activity. LC 85-22427. 180p. (C). 1986. text ed. 32.00 (*0-87322-026-9*, BPUH0026) Human Kinetics.

Puhl, Klaus, ed. Meaning Scepticism. (Foundations of Communication & Cognition Ser.). ix, 258p. (C). 1991. lib. bdg. 101.45 (*3-11-011833-5*) De Gruyter.

Puhl, Louis J. The Spiritual Exercises of St. Ignatius: Based on Studies in the Language of the Autograph. (Request Reprint Ser.). 216p. 1968. pap. 5.95 (*0-8294-0065-6*) Loyola Univ Pr.

***Puhl, Wolfhart & Brandt, Kenneth D., eds.** Epidemiology of Osteoarthritis: International Workshop. LC 94-35368. 1994. write for info. (*0-86577-565-6*) Thieme Med Pubs.

Puhler, A., ed. see Timmis, K. N.

Puhler, A., jt. ed. see Timmis, K. N.

Puhler, S., jt. ed. see Broughton, W. J.

Puhn, Fred. Brake Handbook. LC 84-62610. 176p. 1985. pap. 14.95 (*0-89586-232-8*) Price Stern.

— How to Make Your Car Handle. LC 80-85270. 1976. pap. 14.95 (*0-912656-46-8*) Price Stern.

Puhvel, Jaan. Comparative Mythology. LC 86-20882. (Illus.). 320p. 1989. reprint ed. pap. text ed. 14.95 (*0-8018-3938-6*) Johns Hopkins.

— Hittite Etymological Dictionary, Vol. 3: Words Beginning with H. (Trends in Linguistics, Documentation Ser.: No. 5). x, 462p. (C). 1991. lib. bdg. 183.10 (*0-89925-431-4*) Mouton.

Puhvel, Jaan, ed. see Dumezil, Georges, et al.

Puhvel, Martin. The Crossroads in Folklore & Myth. (American University Studies: English Language & Literature: Ser. IV, Vol. 88). 131p. (C). 1989. text ed. 31.75 (*0-8204-0839-5*) P Lang Pubs.

Puhvel, Martin, et al. Arthurian Literature, Vol. V. Barber, Richard, ed. 192p. 1985. 63.00 (*0-85991-191-8*) Boydell & Brewer.

Pui-Lan, Kwok. Chinese Women & Christianity, 1860-1927. (American Academy of Religion Academy Ser.). 229p. (C). 1992. 29.95 (*1-55540-669-6*, 010175); pap. 19.95 (*1-55540-670-X*) Scholars Pr GA.

— Discovering the Bible in the Non-Biblical World. LC 95-10028. (Bible & Liberation Ser.). 160p. (Orig.). 1995. pap. 16.95 (*0-88344-997-8*) Orbis Bks.

Puig, Enric. Lord, I Am One of Your Little Ones. 93p. (J). (gr. 3-6). 1987. 8.95 (*0-8294-0545-3*) Loyola Univ Pr.

Puig, Evelyn. Chico the Street Boy. (Illus.). 85p. (J). (gr. 4-8). 1991. 3.95 (*0-901269-79-4*) Grosvenor USA.

Puig, J. J., jt. auth. see Parramon, J. M.

Puig, Manual. Kiss of the Spider Woman. Orig. Title: El Beso De la Mujer Arana. 21.95 (*0-8488-0614-X*) Amereon Ltd.

Puig, Manuel. El Beso de la Mujer Arana. (SPA.). 1994. pap. 11.00 (*0-679-75545-4*, Vin) Random.

— El Beso de la Mujer Arana. 12th ed. 287p. (SPA.). 1992. pap. 14.95 (*0-7859-0562-6*, 843223026X) Fr & Eur.

— Betrayed by Rita Hayworth. 224p. 1996. pap. 11.00 (*0-393-31384-0*, Norton Paperbks) Norton.

— Kiss of the Spider Woman. Colchie, Thomas, tr. LC 90-50626. Orig. Title: El Beso De la Mujer Arana. 288p. 1991. 11.00 (*0-679-72449-4*, Vin) Random.

— Tropical Night Falling. Levine, Suzanne J., tr. 192p. 1993. pap. 8.95 (*0-393-30908-8*) Norton.

— Under a Mantle of Stars. rev. ed. Christ, Ronald, tr. (Orig.). 1993. pap. 10.00 (*0-930829-32-8*) Lumen Inc.

Puig, Manuel, et al. DramaContemporary: Latin America. Woodyard, G. W., ed. 224p. 1986. pap. 14.95x (*1-55554-005-8*) PAJ Pubns.

— Kiss of the Spider Woman & Two Other Plays. LC 94-6549. 1994. pap. 10.95 (*0-393-31148-1*) Norton.

Puig-Pey, J. Computer Aided Engineering Systems Handbook. (Illus.). 650p. 1987. 231.00 (*0-387-17936-4*) Spr-Verlag.

Puig-Pey, J. & Brebbia, C. A., eds. Computer Aided Engineering Handbook, 1. LC 87-70842. 350p. 1987. 87.00 (*0-931215-25-0*) Computational Mech MA.

— Computer Aided Engineering Handbook, 2. LC 87-70842. 350p. 1987. 75.00 (*0-685-67616-1*) Computational Mech MA.

Puig Torne, Juan. Computers Dictionary: Diccionario de Informatica. 2nd ed. 208p. (SPA.). 1986. pap. write for info. (*0-7859-4926-7*) Fr & Eur.

Puigdefabergas, C., jt. ed. see Marzo, M.

Puigdomenech, Pedro, jt. ed. see Coruzzi, Gloria.

Puigjaner, L. & Espuna, A. Computer-Oriented Process Engineering. (Process Technology Proceedings Ser.: Vol. 10). 1991. 166.75 (*0-444-88786-5*, PTY 10) Elsevier.

Puigjaner, R. & Potier, D., eds. Modeling Techniques & Tools for Computer Performance Evaluation. (Illus.). 466p. 1989. 95.00 (*0-306-43368-0*, Plenum Pr) Plenum.

Puigjaner, R., jt. ed. see Pujolle, G.

Puigjaner, Ramon, jt. ed. see Cosnard, Michel.

Puiia, Nicholas. Rules for the Traditional Family. 114p. (Orig.). 1988. pap. 5.50 (*0-8294-0604-2*) Loyola Univ Pr.

Puippe, Jean-Claude & Leaman, Frank. Theory & Practice of Pulse Plating. (Illus.). 250p. 1986. 57.00 (*0-936569-02-6*); pap. 47.00 (*0-936569-01-8*) Am Electro Surface.

Pujado, Lynda. Mary of Nazareth. 1994. pap. write for info. (*0-318-72861-3*) CSS OH.

— Mary of Nazareth: A Dramatic Monologue for Lent or Easter. 20p. (Orig.). 1995. pap. 3.95 (*0-7880-0332-1*) CSS OH.

— Mothers of the Bible: A Worship Service for Mother's Day or Other Special Occasions. 52p. (Orig.). 1995. pap. 5.95 (*0-7880-0370-4*) CSS OH.

***Pujals, E.** Historia de la Literatura Inglesa. 830p. (SPA.). 1993. 150.00 (*84-249-0952-6*) Elliots Bks.

Pujals, Enrique J. La Obra Narrativa de Carlos Montenegro. LC 79-52537. (Coleccion Polymita Ser.). (Illus.). 153p. (Orig.). (SPA.). 1980. pap. 9.95 (*0-89729-231-6*) Ediciones.

— Vida y Memorias de Carlos Montenegro. LC 88-80535. (Coleccion Polymita Ser.). (Illus.). 81p. (Orig.). (SPA.). 1988. pap. 9.00 (*0-89729-469-6*) Ediciones.

Pujals, Estella, tr. see Bartnett, Beatrice.

Pujals, Josefina A. El Bosque Indomado...Donde Chilla el Obsceno Pajaro de la Noche. LC 81-69533. 134p. (Orig.). (SPA.). 1982. pap. 15.95 (*0-89729-304-5*) Ediciones.

Pujante, Angel-Luis, ed. see Shakespeare, William.

Pujol, Emilio. Guitar School: A Theoretical-Practical Method for the Guitar, Based on the Principles of Francisco Tarrega, Bks. 1 & 2. Ophee, Matanya, ed. Jeffery, Brian, tr. LC 82-84565. xxii, 192p. 1983. pap. 19.75 (*0-936186-07-0*) Edit Orphee.

— Guitar School, Bk. III: A Theoretical-Practical Method for the Guitar, Based on the Principles of Francisco Tarrega. Segal, Peter, ed. & tr. by. LC 82-64565. 144p. (Orig.). (C). 1991. pap. 17.95 (*0-936186-57-7*, RTFT-2) Edit Orphee.

Pujol, Louis. Tres Visiones Del Amor en la Obra de Jose Marti. LC 88-83427. (Coleccion Polymita Ser.). 87p. (SPA.). 1989. pap. 9.95 (*0-89729-517-X*) Ediciones.

Pujol, Michele A. Feminism & Anti-Feminism in Early Economic Thought. 256p. 1992. text ed. 52.95 (*1-85278-456-3*, Pub. by E Elgar Pub UK) Ashgate Pub Co.

Pujolle, G., et al. Integrated Digital Communications Networks, 2 vols., Vol. 1. LC 88-10647. (Communication & Distributed Systems Ser.). 288p. 1988. text ed. 98.00 (*0-471-91422-3*) Wiley.

Pujolle, G., ed. High-Capacity Local & Metropolitan Area Networks: Architecture & Performance Issues. (NATO ASI Series F: Computer & Systems Sciences, Special Programme AET: Vol. 72). x, 536p. 1991. 124.00 (*0-387-53767-8*) Spr-Verlag.

Pujolle, G. & Puigjaner, R., eds. Data Communication Systems & Their Performance: Proceedings of the IFIP TC6 Fourth International Conference, Barcelona, Spain, 20-22 June 1990. 500p. 1991. 131.50 (*0-444-88756-3*, North Holland) Elsevier.

Pujolle, G., jt. ed. see Fdida, S.

Pujolle, G., jt. auth. see Gelenbe, Erol.

Pujolle, G., et al. Integrated Digital Communications Networks, 2 vols., 1. LC 88-10647. (Communication & Distributed Systems Ser.). 1988. text ed. 98.00 (*0-471-91421-5*) Wiley.

— Integrated Digital Communications Networks, 2 vols., Vol. 2. LC 88-10647. (Communication & Distributed Systems Ser.). 299p. 1988. text ed. 90.00 (*0-685-73974-0*) Wiley.

Pujolle, Jean. Lexique-Guide D'Acoustique Architecturale. 152p. (FRE.). 1971. 59.95 (*0-8288-6470-5*, M-6470) Fr & Eur.

Puka, Bill. Towards Moral Perfectionism. (Harvard Dissertations in Philosophy Ser.). 500p. 1990. reprint ed. 30.00 (*0-8240-3208-X*) Garland.

Puka, Bill, ed. Caring Voices & Women's Moral Frames: Gilligan's View. LC 94-462. (Moral Development: a Compendium Ser.: No. 6). (Illus.). 544p. 1994. reprint ed. 79.00 (*0-8153-1553-8*) Garland.

— Defining Perspectives in Moral Development. LC 94-462. (Moral Development: a Compendium Ser.: No. 1). (Illus.). 264p. 1994. reprint ed. 47.00 (*0-8153-1548-1*) Garland.

— Fundamental Research in Moral Development. LC 94-462. (Moral Development: a Compendium Ser.: No. 2). (Illus.). 416p. 1994. reprint ed. 65.00 (*0-8153-1549-X*) Garland.

— The Great Justice Debate: Kohlberg Criticism. LC 94-462. (Moral Development: a Compendium Ser.: No. 4). (Illus.). 352p. 1994. reprint ed. 58.00 (*0-8153-1551-1*) Garland.

— Kohlberg's Original Study of Moral Development. LC 94-462. (Moral Development: a Compendium Ser.: No. 3). 520p. 1994. reprint ed. 78.00 (*0-8153-1550-3*) Garland.

— New Research in Moral Development. LC 94-462. (Moral Development: a Compendium Ser.: No. 5). (Illus.). 448p. 1994. reprint ed. 69.00 (*0-8153-1552-X*) Garland.

Puka, Bill, ed. & intro. Reaching Out: Caring Altruism, & Prosocial Behavior, Vol. 7. LC 94-462. 360p. 1994. Vol.7. 58.00 (*0-8153-1554-6*) Garland.

Pukelsheim, Friedrich. Optimal Experimental Design. (Probability & Mathematical Statistics: Applied Probability & Statistics Section Ser.). 480p. 1993. text ed. 79.95 (*0-471-61971-X*) Wiley.

***Pukite, Paul.** Markov Modeling for Reliability Analysis. (Illus.). 250p. (C). 1995. pap. text ed. 45.00 (*0-9644741-0-7*) Daina.

***Pukkala, Eero.** Cancer Risk by Social Class & Occupational: A Survey of 109,000 Cancer Cases among Finns of Working Age. LC 95-1186. (Contributions to Epidemiology & Biostatistics Ser.: Vol. 7). (Illus.). x, 278p. 1995. 96.00 (*3-8055-6152-0*) S Karger.

***Pukui, Mary K. & Curtis, Caroline.** Pikoi: And Other Legends of the Isladof Hawaii. 252p. (YA). (gr. 7-12). 1995. pap. text ed. 11.95 (*0-87336-032-X*) Kamehameha Schools.

— Pikoi: And Other Legends of the Island of Hawaii. (Illus.). 282p. (Orig.). (YA). (gr. 7-12). 1983. pap. 6.95 (*0-87336-042-7*) Kamehameha Schools.

— Tales of the Menehune. rev. ed. (Illus.). 130p. (YA). (gr. 7-12). 1994. pap. 8.95 (*0-87336-010-9*) Kamehameha Schools.

— The Water of Kane: And Other Legends of the Hawaiian Islands. rev. ed. (Illus.). 221p. (YA). (gr. 7-12). 1994. pap. 9.95 (*0-87336-020-6*) Kamehameha Schools.

Pukui, Mary K. & Elbert, Samuel H. Hawaiian Dictionary: Hawaiian-English, English-Hawaiian. enl. rev. ed. LC 85-24583. 600p. 1986. text ed. 29.95 (*0-8248-0703-0*) UH Pr.

— New Pocket Hawaiian Dictionary. rev. ed. LC 91-25854. 272p. 1992. pap. 4.95 (*0-8248-1392-8*) UH Pr.

Pukui, Mary K. & Korn, Alfons L., trs. The Echo of Our Song: Chants & Poems of the Hawaiians. LC 72-91620. 250p. 1979. pap. 7.95 (*0-8248-0668-9*) UH Pr.

Pukui, Mary K., jt. auth. see Elbert, Samuel H.

Pukui, Mary K., jt. auth. see Handy, E. S.

Pukui, Mary K., tr. see Kamakau, S. M.

Pukui, Mary K., tr. see Kamakau, Samuel M.

Pukui, Mary K., tr. see Papa, John.

Pukui, Mary K., et al. Nana I Ke Kumu, Vol. 1. LC 72-93779. 1972. pap. 12.00 (*0-9616738-0-X*) Hui Hanai.

— Nana I Ke Kumu, Vol. 2. LC 72-93779. 1980. pap. 12.00 (*0-9616738-2-6*) Hui Hanai.

— Place Names of Hawaii. 2nd ed. LC 73-85582. 310p. 1974. pap. 9.95 (*0-8248-0524-0*) UH Pr.

— Pocket Place Names of Hawai'i. LC 88-27747. (Illus.). 96p. (Orig.). 1989. pap. 3.95 (*0-8248-1187-9*) UH Pr.

Pula, Faafouina I., jt. auth. see Copp, John D.

Pula, James S. For Liberty & Justice. 288p. 1978. 20.00 (*0-942211-45-6*) Olde Soldier Bks.

Pula, James S. The Polish Americans. LC 94-20514. (Twayne's Immigrant Heritage of America Ser.). 1995. lib. bdg. 26.95x (*0-8057-8427-6*, Twayne); pap. 15.95 (*0-8057-8438-1*, Twayne) Macmillan.

Pula, James S. & Biskupski, M. B., eds. Polish Democratic Thought from the Renaissance to the Great Emigration: Essays & Documents. (East European Monographs: No. 289). 224p. 1990. 27.50 (*0-685-38713-5*) Col U Pr.

— Selected Essays from the Fiftieth Anniversary Congress of the Polish Institute of Arts & Sciences in America. 240p. 1994. 99.00 (*0-88033-287-5*) East Eur Quarterly.

Pula, James S. & Dziedzic, Eugene E. United We Stand: The Role of Polish Workers in the New York Mills Textile Strikes, 1912 & 1916. (East European Monographs: No. 286). 320p. 1990. 35.00 (*0-685-38712-7*) Col U Pr.

Pula, James S., jt. auth. see Biskupski, M. B.

Pula, James S., ed. see Kruszka, Waclaw.

Pulaski, Charles A. Criminal Pretrial & Trial Procedure: Cases & Materials. (Contemporary Legal Education Ser.). 886p. 1982. 28.00 (*0-87215-546-3*) Michie Butterworth.

Pulaski County Board of Commissioners. Pulaski County Illinois, 1819-1987. LC 87-71197. 408p. 1988. 49.95 (*0-938021-21-4*) Turner Pub KY.

P Q

An Asterisk (*) at the beginning of an entry indicates that the title is appearing in BIP for the first time.

Pulaski High School Drama Club Staff & Mueller, Tobin J. I Want to Know! A Musical Time Line about the History of Science & Invention. (Classroom Musicals Ser.). (Illus.). 55p. (J). (gr. 4-12). 1991. 14.95 (*1-56213-059-5*) Ctr Stage Prodns.

Pulaski, Jack. The St. Veronica Gig Stories. LC 86-50657. 178p. (Orig.). 1986. 15.95 (*0-939010-10-0*); pap. 8.95 (*0-939010-09-7*) Zephyr Pr.

— The St. Veronica Gig Stories. deluxe ed. LC 86-50657. 178p. (Orig.). 1986. 25.00 (*0-685-13535-7*) Zephyr Pr.

Pulat, B. Mustafa. Fundamentals of Industrial Ergonomics. 544p. 1991. text ed. 78.00 (*0-13-345364-2*) P-H.

Pulat, B. Mustafa & Alexander, David C., eds. Industrial Ergonomics: Case Studies. 1991. 34.95 (*0-89806-099-0*) Ind Eng Mgmt Pr.

Pulat, B. Mustafa, jt. ed. see Alexander, David C.

Pulat, P. Simin, jt. auth. see Badiru, Adedeji B.

Pulawski, Wojciech J. Revision of North American Tachysphex Wasps Including Central American & Caribbean Species (Hymenoptera: Sphecidae) LC 88-70114. (Memoirs of the California Academy of Sciences Ser.: No. 10). (Illus.). 1988. pap. 30.00 (*0-940228-16-5*) Calif Acad Sci.

Pulawski, Wojciech J., jt. auth. see Krombein, Karl V.

Puledda, Salvatore. The Tokarev Report. 140p. (Orig.). 1992. 15.00 (*1-878977-17-2*) Latitude Pr.

Puleo, Alicia H. Como Leer a Julio Cortazar. Date not set. 42.50 (*0-685-69533-6*) Scripta.

Puleo, Mev. The Struggle Is One: Voices & Visions of Liberation. LC 93-37873. 251p. (C). 1994. 59.50x (*0-7914-2013-2*); pap. 19.95 (*0-7914-2014-0*) State U NY Pr.

Puleo, Mev, jt. auth. see Kavanaugh, John F.

Puleo, Nancy F., jt. auth. see Weber, James M.

Pulermo, D. S., jt. ed. see Hoffman, R. R.

Puleston, Dennis. A Nature Journal: A Naturalist's Year on Long Island. (Illus.). 128p. 1992. 25.00 (*0-393-03429-1*) Norton.

Puleston, Dennis E. Tikal Report, No. 13: The Settlement Survey of Tikal. (University Museum Monographs: No. 48). (Illus.). 136p. 1983. text ed. 30.00 (*0-934718-47-4*) U PA Mus Pubns.

Puleston, William D. Influence of Sea Power in World War II. LC 71-104248. 310p. 1971. reprint ed. text ed. 38.50 (*0-8371-3997-X*, PUSP, Greenwood Pr) Greenwood.

Pulfer, Laura, ed. see Hair, Deidra.

Pulford, Florence. Morning Star Quilts. (Illus.). 80p. 1989. 34.95 (*0-942786-00-9*); pap. 24.95 (*0-685-57980-8*) Leone Pubns.

Pulfrey, David L. & Tarr, Garry N. Introduction to Microelectronic Devices. 416p. 1989. text ed. 75.33 (*0-13-488107-9*) P-H.

Pulgar, jt. auth. see Timms.

Pulgram, Ernst. Syllable, Word, Nexus, Cursus. (Janua Linguarum, Ser.: No. 81). 1970. pap. text ed. 40.80 (*90-279-0706-4*) Mouton.

Pulgram, Ernst, ed. Romanitas: Studies in Romance Linguistics. LC 81-50963. (Michigan Romance Studies: Vol. 4). 262p. (Orig.). 1984. pap. 8.00 (*0-939730-03-0*) Mich Romance.

Pulgram, Eva, tr. see Boltzius, John M. & Gronau, Christian I.

Pulham, Grace, jt. auth. see Eder, Enelle G.

Puli, Ali. The Center of Nature Concentrated: Or, The Regenerated Salt of Nature. 1988. pap. 4.95 (*1-55818-110-5*) Holmes Pub.

Puliafito, C. A. Ophthalmic Technologies, Vol. 1423. 1991. 53.00 (*0-8194-0513-2*) SPIE.

Puliafito, Carmen A., jt. auth. see Steinert, Roger F.

Pulich, Warren M. The Birds of North Central Texas. LC 87-9143. (W. L. Moody, Jr. Natural History Ser.: No. 9). (Illus.). 472p. 1988. 45.00 (*0-89096-319-3*); pap. 16. 95 (*0-89096-322-3*) Tex A&M Univ Pr.

Puliciano, Gina. Simply Italian: More Than Sixty Quick & Easy Recipes from Italy. Piade, Lynne, ed. (Illus.). 64p. 1993. 9.98 (*0-681-41736-6*) Longmeadow Pr.

Pulickal, Joseph, jt. comp. see Brys, Aurel.

Puligandla, R. Fundamentals of Indian Philosophy. LC 74-30009. reprint ed. pap. 90.50 (*0-317-08822-X*, 2016359) Bks Demand.

Puligandla, R., jt. auth. see Rama Rao Pappu.

Puligandla, R. Fact & Fiction in B. F. Skinner's Science & Utopia. LC 73-21001. 114p. 1974. 10.00 (*0-87527-130-8*) Green.

Puligandla, R., jt. auth. see Trundle, Robert C.

***Puligandla, Ramakrishma & Miller, David L., eds.** Buddhism & the Emerging World Civilization: Essays in Honor of Nolan Pliny Jacobson. LC 93-3267. 256p. (C). 1995. 29.95 (*0-8093-1842-3*) S Ill U Pr.

Pulin, Carol, ed. see Mason, Tim & Mason, Lynn.

Pulin, Carol, jt. auth. see Okeefe-Gravalos, Mary E.

***Pulippani, U. S., ed.** Biorhythms of Natal Moon: Mysteries of Pancha Pakshi. (C). 1994. 16.00 (*0-8364-2900-1*, Pub. by Ranjan Pubs II) S Asia.

Pulitzer, Copey, pseud. How to Manage Your Parents. (Illus.). 144p. (Orig.). 1992. pap. 7.95 (*0-9633496-0-0*) S C Pulitzer.

***Pulitzer, Lisa B.** Crossing the Line: The Joel Rifkin Serial Murder Case. Swirsky, Joan, ed. (Orig.). 1994. pap. text ed. 5.99 (*0-425-14441-0*) Berkley Pub.

Pulitzer, Ralph. New York Society on Parade. LC 75-1866. (Leisure Class in America Ser.). (Illus.). 1975. reprint ed. 15.95 (*0-405-06932-4*) Ayer.

Pulitzer, Roxanne. Prize Pulitzer. 1989. mass mkt. 5.95 (*0-345-35930-5*) Ballantine.

— The Prize Pulitzer: The Scandal That Rocked Palm Beach - The Real Story. 241p. 1991. 4.99 (*0-517-05098-6*) Random Hse Value.

— Twins. 320p. 1991. mass mkt. 5.95 (*0-345-36245-4*) Ballantine.

— Twins. 304p. 1990. 18.95 (*0-394-57919-4*, Villard Bks) Random.

Pulitzer, Roxanne & Maxa, Kathleen. The Prize Pulitzer: The Scandal That Rocked Palm Beach - The Real Story. 1988. 19.95 (*0-317-66206-6*, Villard Bks) Random.

Pulitzer, Roxanne & Maxa, Kathy. Prize Pulitzer. LC 87-40191. 320p. 1987. 17.95 (*0-394-55761-1*, Villard Bks) Random.

Pulitzer, Sidney C., see Copey Pulitzer, pseud..

Pulker, H. K. Coatings on Glass. (Thin Films Science & Technology Ser.: Vol. 6). 484p. 1984. 133.50 (*0-444-42360-5*, I-230-84) Elsevier.

— Coatings on Glass. 484p. 1987. pap. 79.00 (*0-444-42834-8*) Elsevier.

Pulker, H. K., jt. ed. see Guenther, K. H.

Pulkina, I. Russian: A Practical Grammar with Exercises. 582p. (C). 1992. 17.95 (*0-8285-4993-1*) Firebird NY.

Pulkina, I. & Zakhlava-Nekrasova, E., eds. Russian: A Practical Grammar with Exercises. 584p. (C). 1988. 80. 00 (*0-569-09174-8*, Pub. by Collets) St Mut.

Pulkina, I. M. A Short Russian Grammar. 352p. 1984. 50.00 (*0-317-42778-4*, Pub. by Collets UK) St Mut.

— Short Russian Reference Grammar. 352p. (C). 1987. 50. 00 (*0-569-00044-0*, Pub. by Collets UK) Pro-Am Music.

— A Short Russian Reference Grammar. 2nd ed. Kuznetsov, P. S., ed. 354p. 1969. text ed. 54.00 (*0-677-20820-0*) Gordon & Breach.

Pullaiah, T. Embryology of Compositae. (International Bioscience Monographs: No. 13). 192p. 1984. 19.00 (*1-55528-029-3*, Messers Today & Tomorrow) Scholarly Pubns.

***Pullam, A., et al, eds.** Modelling of Biomolecular Structures & Mechanisms: Proceedings of the Twenty-Seventh Jerusalem Symposium on Quantum Chemistry and Biochemistry Held in Jerusalem, Israel, May 23-26, 1994, 27. LC 94-32858. (The Jerusalem Symposia on Quantum Chemistry & Biochemistry Ser.). 1995. lib. bdg. write for info. (*0-7923-3102-8*) Kluwer Ac.

Pullan, jt. auth. see McGladrey.

Pullan, Brian. Poverty & Charity: Europe, Italy, Venice, 1400-1700. LC 94-5846. (Collected Studies). 1994. 89.95 (*0-86078-446-0*, Pub. by Variorum UK) Ashgate Pub Co.

Pullapilly, Cyriac K., ed. see Gualtieri, Antonio R.

Pullar, G. C. A Shifting Town: Glass Plate Images of Clermont & Its People. LC 86-16070. (Illus.). 232p. 1987. text ed. 49.95 (*0-7022-2012-4*, Pub. by Univ Queensland Pr AT) Intl Spec Bk.

Pullar, Laurence, jt. auth. see Murray, John.

Pullar, Philippa, jt. auth. see Bek, Lilla.

Pullar-Strecker, Peter. Corrosion Damaged Concrete: Assessment & Control. (Illus.). 99p. 1987. text ed. 36.95 (*0-408-02556-5*) Buttrwrth-Heinemann.

Pullein-Thompson, Christine. The Long Search. LC 92-40349. 160p. (J). (gr. 5-9). 1993. lib. bdg. 13.95 (*0-02-775445-6*, Bradbury S&S) S&S Childrens.

Pullein-Thompson, Diana. This Pony Is Dangerous. 174p. (C). 1990. pap. 21.00 (*0-85131-520-8*, Pub. by J A Allen & Co UK) St Mut.

Pullein-Thompson, J. Gin & Murder. large type ed. (Linford Mystery Library). 1990. pap. 12.95 (*0-7089-6848-1*, Trailtree Bookshop) Ulverscroft.

— Murder Strikes Pink. large type ed. (Linford Mystery Library). 1990. pap. 12.95 (*0-7089-6839-2*, Linford) Ulverscroft.

— They Died in the Spring. large type ed. (Linford Mystery Library). 1990. pap. 12.95 (*0-7089-6897-X*, Trailtree Bookshop) Ulverscroft.

Pullein-Thompson, Joseph. The Hidden Horse. 197p. (C). 1990. pap. 21.00 (*0-85131-490-2*, Pub. by J A Allen & Co UK) St Mut.

Pullein-Thompson, Josephin. Star Riders. 127p. (C). 1990. pap. 21.00 (*0-85131-519-4*, Pub. by J A Allen & Co UK) St Mut.

Pullen, jt. auth. see McGladrey.

Pullen, jt. auth. see Norton.

Pullen-Burry, Bessie. Ethiopia in Exile: Jamaica Revisited. LC 76-157376. (Black Heritage Library Collection). 1977. 21.95 (*0-8369-8814-0*) Ayer.

Pullen-Burry, Henry B. Qabalism. 167p. 1972. reprint ed. 12.00 (*0-911662-45-6*) Yoga.

Pullen, Charles H. Miss Columbia's Public School. LC 70-85687. (American Fiction Reprint Ser.). 1977. 17.95 (*0-8369-7016-0*) Ayer.

***Pullen, Dorothy.** The Happy House. 1995. 10.95 (*0-8062-5323-1*) Carlton.

Pullen, Gerald, jt. auth. see Grubbs, Bill.

Pullen, Ian, jt. ed. see Emery, Alan E.

Pullen, Ian, jt. auth. see Hume, Clephane A.

Pullen, Ian, jt. auth. see Hume, Clephane.

Pullen, Jo A., jt. auth. see Faiola, Theodora.

Pullen, John. The Twentieth Maine. 1980. 24.95 (*0-89029-055-5*); pap. 14.95 (*0-89029-755-X*) Morningside Bkshop.

Pullen, John, ed. see Malthus, Thomas R.

Pullen, John J., ed. see Judson, Amos.

Pullen, Martha C. Antique Clothing, French Sewing by Machine. LC 90-91872. (Illus.). 352p. (Orig.). 1990. 29. 00 (*1-878048-00-7*) M Pullen.

— Martha's Sewing Room: Program Guide for Public. Johnson, Kathy M., ed. (Illus.). 360p. 1995. 19.95 (*1-878048-04-X*) M Pullen.

— Martha's Sewing Room: Program Guide for Public T. V. Series-100. (Illus.). 274p. 1994. 19.95 (*1-878048-03-1*) M Pullen.

Pullen, Martha C., et al. Heirloom Sewing for Women: French Sewing by Machine. (Illus.). 350p. 1993. 39.95 (*1-878048-02-3*) M Pullen.

Pullen, Max. Business Cash Books Made Easy. (Business Basics Ser.). pap. text ed. write for info. (*0-7494-0735-2*, Pub. by Kogan Page Educ UK) Taylor & Francis.

Pullen, Rick, jt. auth. see Overbeck, Wayne.

***Pullen, Robert & Taylor, Stephen.** Montserrat Caballe: Casta Diva. LC 94-36295. 1995. text ed. 29.95 (*1-55553-228-4*) NE U Pr.

Pullen, Virginia A. They Chose This Valley. Mills, Charlotte, ed. LC 89-71479. (Illus.). 168p. (Orig.). 1991. pap. 8.95 (*0-9625483-0-8*) Dewey Pr.

Puller, Lewis B. Fortunate Son: The Autobiography of Lewis B. Puller. 1993. mass mkt. 5.99 (*0-553-56076-X*) Bantam.

Puller, Lewis B., Jr. Fortunate Son: An Autobiography. LC 91-4463. 389p. 1991. 21.95 (*0-8021-1218-8*) Grove-Atltic.

Pullerits, Albert. Estonia: Population, Cultural & Economic Life. LC 77-87536. reprint ed. 37.50 (*0-404-16604-0*) AMS Pr.

Pulles, Gregory, et al. FDICIA: A Legislative History & Section-by-Section Analysis. LC 92-35522. 3000p. 1992. ring bd. 190.00 (*0-07-172453-2*) Shepards-McGraw.

— FIRREA: A Legislative History & Section-by-Section Analysis, 2 vols., Set. (Corporate Ser.). 3080p. 1992. text ed., ring bd. 255.00 (*0-07-172402-8*) Shepards-McGraw.

Pulley. Patricia Wright. (J). 1993. lib. bdg. 13.98 (*0-8050-2212-0*) H Holt & Co.

Pulley, Andrew. How I Became a Socialist. 45p. 1981. reprint ed. 2.50 (*0-87348-548-3*) Pathfinder NY.

Pulley, Dennis, jt. auth. see Clark, Laurie K.

Pulley, Leland E. The Parent-Child Development Program. 500p. (Orig.). 1996. 29.95 (*0-9611282-2-4*); pap. 23.95 (*0-9611282-3-2*) Stewardship Enters.

— Reaching Up, Reaching Out. LC 85-90071. (Orig.). 1985. pap. 5.95 (*0-9611282-1-6*) Stewardship Enters.

Pulley, Mary L., jt. auth. see Horowitz, Leonard G.

Pulley, Nancy. Tremolo of Light. (Indiana Poetry Chapbook Contest Ser.: No. 2). 40p. 1992. pap. 3.95 (*1-880649-28-4*) Writ Ctr Pr.

Pulley, R., jt. auth. see Mantin, Peter.

Pulley, Richard, jt. auth. see Mantin, Peter.

Pulley, Robert V. Making the Poor Creditworthy: A Case Study of the Integrated Rural Development Program in India. (Discussion Paper Ser.: No. 58). 104p. 1989. 7.95 (*0-8213-1267-7*, 11267) World Bank.

Pulleyblank, Douglas. Tone Lexical Phonology. 1986. lib. bdg. 95.50 (*90-277-2123-8*); pap. text ed. 47.50 (*90-277-2124-6*) Kluwer Ac.

Pulleyblank, Douglas, jt. auth. see Archangeli, Diana.

Pulleyblank, Edwin G. The Background of the Rebellion of An Lu-Shan. LC 82-6200. (London Oriental Ser.). (Illus.). x, 264p. 1982. reprint ed. text ed. 55.00 (*0-313-23549-X*, PUBA, Greenwood Pr) Greenwood.

***Pulleyn, Micah & Bracken, Sarah.** Kids in the Kitchen: Delicious, Fun, & Healthy Recipes to Cook & Bake. (Illus.). 112p. 1995. pap. 12.95 (*0-8069-0446-1*) Sterling.

— Kids in the Kitchen: Delicious, Fun, & Healthy Recipes to Cook & Bake. LC 93-39111. 112p. (J). (gr. 4 up). 1993. reprint ed. 21.95 (*0-8069-0447-X*, Sterling-Main St) Sterling.

Pulleyn, Rob. The Basketmaker's Art: Contemporary Baskets & Their Makers. (Illus.). 164p. (C). 1991. reprint ed. lib. bdg. 47.00x (*0-8095-7594-9*) Borgo Pr.

— The Wreath Book. LC 87-51523. (Illus.). 144p. 1988. 21. 95 (*0-8069-6842-7*) Sterling.

— The Wreath Kit. (Illus.). 144p. 1991. 35.00 (*0-8069-8202-0*) Sterling.

Pulleyn, Rob, ed. Basketmaker's Art: Contemporary Baskets & Their Makers. LC 86-82336. (Illus.). 164p. 1992. pap. 19.95 (*0-937274-63-1*) Lark Books.

Pulleyn, Rob & Mautor, Claudette. Everlasting Floral Gifts. LC 89-21909. (Illus.). 144p. 1990. 24.95 (*0-8069-5826-X*) Sterling.

— Everlasting Floral Gifts. LC 89-21909. (Illus.). 144p. 1991. pap. 14.95 (*0-8069-5827-8*) Sterling.

Pulleyn, Rob, jt. auth. see Cusick, Dawn.

Pulleysblank, Edward G., et al. Studies in Language Origins, Vol. 1. Wind, Jan et al, eds. LC 88-7542. xxii, 332p. (C). 1989. 94.00x (*1-55619-054-9*) Benjamins North Am.

Pulliam, et al. Collier Labor Law & the Bankruptcy Code. 1989. Updates. ring bd. write for info. (*0-8205-1132-3*) Bender.

Pulliam, H. Ronald & Dunford, Christopher. Programmed to Learn: An Essay on the Evolution of Culture. LC 79-17941. (Illus.). 1980. text ed. 31.00 (*0-231-04838-6*) Col U Pr.

Pulliam, John & Van Pattern, James. History of Education in America. 6th ed. 320p. (C). 1994. pap. write for info. (*0-02-396818-4*) Macmillan.

Pulliam, John D. History of Education in America. 5th ed. 336p. (C). 1990. pap. write for info. (*0-675-21222-7*, Merrill Pub Co) Macmillan.

Pulliam, Kimberly A., jt. auth. see Bonds, Roger G.

Pulliam, Mark S., jt. auth. see Haggard, Thomas R.

Pulliam, Russell. Publisher Gene Pulliam: Last of the Newspaper Titans. LC 85-149654. 250p. 1984. 16.95 (*0-915463-02-4*) Green Hill.

***Pulliam, Tom & Grundman, Claire.** The New York Times Crossword Puzzle Dictionary. 3rd ed. LC 95-11416. 1995. 27.50 (*0-8129-2606-4*, Times Bks) Random.

Pulliam, Tom & Grundman, Clare. The New York Times Crossword Puzzle Dictionary. 2nd ed. LC 84-40108. 1984. 21.00 (*0-8129-1131-8*, Times Bks) Random.

— The New York Times Crossword Puzzle Dictionary. 2nd ed. 624p. 1989. pap. 14.95 (*0-446-38265-5*) Warner Bks.

Pulliam, Tom, et al, eds. New York Times Concise Crossword Puzzle Dictionary. 2nd ed. 704p. 1988. mass mkt. 5.99 (*0-446-35750-2*) Warner Bks.

Pullias, Earl & Young, James D. A Teacher Is Many Things. LC 68-14612. 314p. reprint ed. pap. 89.50 (*0-8357-6671-3*, 2056849) Bks Demand.

Pullicino, Patrick M., et al, eds. Cerebral Small Artery Disease. LC 92-48462. (Advances in Neurology Ser.: Vol. 62). 256p. 1993. 103.00 (*0-7817-0051-5*) Raven.

Pullin, Anne G. Glass Signatures, Trademarks & Trade Names. LC 85-51345. (Illus.). 368p. (Orig.). 1986. pap. 16.95 (*0-87069-462-6*, Wallace-Hmestead) Chilton.

Pullin, R. S., ed. Tilapia Genetic Resources for Aquaculture. (Conference Proceedings Ser.: No. 16). 1988. pap. 7.40 (*971-10-2244-3*, Pub. by ICLARM PH) Intl Spec Bk.

Pullin, R. S., jt. ed. see Moriarty, D. J.

Pullin, R. S., et al, eds. Second International Symposium on Tilapia in Aquaculture. 1990. 58.00 (*971-10-2260-5*, Pub. by ICLARM PH); pap. text ed. 45.00 (*971-10-2258-3*, Pub. by ICLARM PH) Intl Spec Bk.

Pulling, Alexander. Order of the Coif. Mersky, Roy M. & Jacobstein, J. Myron, eds. LC 75-15318. (Classics in Legal History Reprint Ser.: Vol. 28). 288p. 1975. reprint ed. lib. bdg. 43.50 (*0-89941-027-8*, 301220) W S Hein.

Pulling, Pat & Cawthon, Kathy. The Devil's Web. LC 89-84752. (Illus.). 206p. (Orig.). 1989. pap. 9.99 (*0-910311-59-5*) Huntington Hse.

— Devil's Web. LC 89-84752. (Illus.). 206p. (Orig.). 1989. pap. 16.99 (*0-910311-63-3*) Huntington Hse.

Pulling, Pierre. Canoeing the Indian Way: Straight Talk for Modern Paddlers from the Dean of American Canoeists. LC 88-19206. (Illus.). 128p. 1989. reprint ed. pap. 8.95 (*0-8117-2241-4*) Stackpole.

Pullinger, Jackie. Chasing the Dragon. 1980. pap. 5.99 (*0-89283-151-0*) Servant.

Pullinger, Kate. Border Lines: Stories of Exile & Home. 1993. pap. 13.99 (*1-85242-311-0*) Serpents Tail.

Pullinger, Kate, ed. A Gambling Box. LC 92-50339. (Redstone Editions Ser.). (Illus.). 144p. 1992. 25.00 (*0-87773-876-9*) Shambhala Pubns.

Pullinger, Kate, jt. auth. see Campion, Jane.

Pullinger, Kate, ed. see Gellner, David N.

Pullins, ed. see Baker, David & Engel, Robert.

Pullins, ed. see Bloomfield, Derek I.

Pullins, ed. see Brisk, Marion & Bosworth, Stefan.

Pullins, ed. see Goodman, Arthur & Hirsch, Lewis R.

Pullins, ed. see Hirsch, Lewis R. & Goodman, Arthur.

Pullins, ed. see Lissner, David.

Pullins, ed. see Malone, Katherine & Schneider, Jane.

Pullins, ed. see Myers, Nancy.

Pullins, ed. see Piascik, Chester.

Pullins, ed. see Pinet, Paul.

Pullins, ed. see Plascik, Chester.

Pullins, ed. see Radel, Stanley R. & Navidi, Marjorie.

Pullins, ed. see Renton, John.

Pullins, ed. see Spence, Alexander P. & Mason, Elliott B.

Pullins, ed. see Stevens, David E.

Pullins, ed. see Walsh, Eileen, et al.

Pullins, ed. see Wiedman, Lawrence A.

Pullis, Cheryl. Principles of Speedwriting Sho. 1985. pap. 9.52 (*0-02-679840-9*) Macmillan.

— Speedwriting Principles Regen. 1984. pap. 19.96 (*0-02-679810-7*) Macmillan.

— Speedwriting Regency SW PP 98503. 1984. pap. 9.92 (*0-02-679430-6*) Macmillan.

Pullis, Cheryl, jt. auth. see Pullis, Joe M.

Pullis, Joe M. Speedwriting for Notetaking & Study Skills. 1990. 18.70 (*0-02-685155-5*) Macmillan.

Pullis, Joe M. & Bippen, Linda. Principles of Speedwriting Shorthand: Regency Edition. (Speedwriting Shorthand Ser.). 304p. (gr. 10-12). 1984. teacher ed write for info. (*0-672-98502-0*); text ed. write for info. (*0-672-98501-2*); student ed write for info. (*0-672-98503-9*) Macmillan.

Pullis, Joe M. & Pullis, Cheryl. Speedwriting Shorthand Abridged Dictionary: Regency Edition. (Speedwriting Shorthand Ser.). 192p. (gr. 10-12). 1984. text ed. write for info. (*0-672-98504-7*) Macmillan.

Pullis, Joe M., et al. Speedwriting Shorthand Dictation & Transcription: Regency Edition. (Speedwriting Shorthand Ser.). 352p. (gr. 10-12). 1984. teacher ed write for info. (*0-317-00348-8*); text ed. write for info. (*0-672-98506-3*) Macmillan.

***Pullman.** Tin Princess. (J). write for info. (*0-679-87615-4*) Random.

Pullman, Alberte & Dordrecht, Joshua, eds. Membrane Proteins: Structures, Interactions & Models: Proceedings of the Twenty-Fifth Jerusalem Symposium on Quantum Chemistry & Biochemistry Held in Jerusalem, Israel, May 18-21, 1992. LC 92-26604. (Jerusalem Symposia on Quantum Chemistry & Biochemistry Ser.: Vol. 25). 516p. (C). 1992. lib. bdg. 200.00 (*0-7923-1951-6*) Kluwer Ac.

Pullman, Alberte, et al, eds. Transport Through Membranes: Carriers, Channels & Pumps. (C). 1988. lib. bdg. 201.50 (*90-277-2831-3*) Kluwer Ac.

Pullman, Bernard, ed. Catalysis in Chemistry & Biochemistry: Theory & Experiment. (Jerusalem Symposia on Quantum Chemistry & Biochemistry Ser.: No. 12). 1979. lib. bdg. 94.00 (*90-277-1039-2*) Kluwer Ac.

— Intermolecular Forces. 576p. 1981. lib. bdg. 164.50 (*90-277-1326-X*) Kluwer Ac.

— Intermolecular Interactions: From Diatomics to Biopolymers. LC 77-24278. (Perspectives in Quantum Chemistry & Biochemistry Ser.: Vol. 2). 457p. reprint ed. pap. 130.30 (*0-685-20634-3*, 2030419) Bks Demand.

— Quantum Mechanics of Molecular Conformations. LC 75-43927. (Perspectives in Quantum Chemistry & Biochemistry Ser.). 422p. reprint ed. pap. 120.30 (*0-7837-0195-0*, 2040491) Bks Demand.

— Specificity in Biological Interactions. 1984. lib. bdg. 179. 00 (*90-277-1813-X*) Kluwer Ac.

Pullman, Bernard & Goldblum, Nathan, eds. Excited States in Organic Chemistry & Biochemistry. (Jerusalem Symposia on Quantum Chemistry & Biochemistry Ser.: No. 10). 1977. lib. bdg. 112.50 (*90-277-0853-3*) Kluwer Ac.

Pullman, Bernard & Jortner, Joshua, eds. Molecular Basis of Specificity in Nucleic Acid-Drug Interactions. (C). 1990. lib. bdg. 226.00 (*0-7923-0897-2*) Kluwer Ac.

P Q

Pullman, Bernard, jt. ed. see Bergmann, Ernst.

Pullman, Bernard, jt. ed. see Daudel, Raymond.

Pullman, Bernard, ed. see International Congress of Quantum Chemistry Staff.

Pullman, Bernard, ed. see Jerusalem Symposium on Quantum Chemistry & Biochemistry Staff.

Pullman, Bernard, jt. ed. see Jortner, Joshua.

Pullman, Bernard, jt. ed. see Lowdin, Per-Olov.

Pullman, Bernard, jt. ed. see Yagi, Kunio.

Pullman, Bernard, et al, eds. Carcinogenesis: Fundamental Mechanisms & Environmental Effects. (Jerusalem Symposia on Quantum Chemistry & Biochemistry Ser.: No. 13). 560p. 1980. lib. bdg. 126.50 (*90-277-1171-2*) Kluwer Ac.

— Dynamics on Surfaces. 1984. lib. bdg. 152.50 (*90-277-1830-X*) Kluwer Ac.

— Interrelationship among Aging, Cancer & Differentiation. 1985. lib. bdg. 117.00 (*90-277-2117-3*) Kluwer Ac.

Pullman, Edward E. & Anema, Durlynn C. Diapers, Deadlines & Decisions: Careers & Children. 168p. 1988. spiral bd. 21.95 (*0-8403-4725-1*) Kendall-Hunt.

Pullman, Geoffrey K., jt. ed. see Derbyshire, Desmond C.

Pullman, N. J. Matrix Theory & Its Applications: Selected Topics. LC 75-40845. (Pure & Applied Mathematics Ser.: Vol. 35). 252p. reprint ed. pap. 71.90 (*0-685-15860-8*, 2027816) Bks Demand.

Pullman, Philip. The Broken Bridge. LC 91-15893. 256p. (YA). (gr. 7 up). 1992. lib. bdg. 15.99 (*0-679-91972-4*) Knopf Bks Yng Read.

— The Broken Bridge. 224p. (YA). (gr. 7 up). 1994. pap. 4.99 (*0-679-84715-4*, Bullseye Bks) Random Bks Yng Read.

— The Ruby in the Smoke. LC 86-20983. 208p. (YA). (gr. 7 up). 1987. lib. bdg. 11.99 (*0-394-98826-4*) Knopf Bks Yng Read.

— The Ruby in the Smoke. LC 86-20983. 240p. (YA). (gr. 7 up). 1988. reprint ed. pap. 4.99 (*0-394-89589-4*) Knopf Bks Yng Read.

— The Tin Princess. LC 93-38305. 304p. (YA). (gr. 9-12). 1994. 16.00 (*0-679-84757-X*); pap. write for info. (*0-679-84756-1*) Knopf Bks Yng Read.

Pullman, Phillip. White Mercedes. LC 92-11072. 160p. (J). (gr. 7 up). 1993. 16.00 (*0-679-83198-3*) Knopf Bks Yng Read.

— White Mercedes. 1992. pap. write for info. (*0-679-93198-8*) McKay.

Pullmann, B., jt. ed. see Bergmann, E. D.

Pullum, jt. ed. see Derbyshire.

Pullum, Geoffrey K. The Great Eskimo Vocabulary Hoax: And Other Irreverent Essays on the Study of Language. LC 90-11286. 200p. 1991. pap. 14.95 (*0-226-68534-9*) U Ch Pr.

Pullum, Geoffrey K. & Ladusaw, William A. Phonetic Symbol Guide. LC 86-7036. xxx, 266p. (C). 1987. pap. text ed. 13.95 (*0-226-68532-2*) U Ch Pr.

Pullum, Geoffrey K., jt. auth. see Jacobson, Pauline.

Pulman. Let Us Have Music for Violin, Vol. 2. (Illus.). 80p. 1944. pap. 9.95 (*0-8258-0247-4*, 0-3207) Fischer Inc NY.

Pulman, Jack. Collision. 256p. 1981. pap. 2.25 (*0-449-24362-1*, Crest) Fawcett.

Pulman, S. G. Word Meaning & Belief. LC 83-2622. 172p. 1983. text ed. 32.50 (*0-89391-201-8*) Ablex Pub.

Pulmannova, Sylvia, jt. auth. see Ptak, Pavel.

Pulmano, V. A. & Murti, V., eds. Impact of Computational Mechanics on Engineering Problems: Proceedings, Sydney, Australia, August 1993. (Illus.). 198p. 1993. text ed. 60.00 (*90-5410-324-8*, Pub. by A A Balkema NE) Ashgate Pub Co.

Pulmonary Circulation Symposium Staff. Pulmonary Circulation: Proceedings of the Symposium, Prague, 1969. Widimsky, J. et al, eds. (Progress in Respiration Research Ser.: Vol. 5). 1970. 115.25 (*3-8055-1152-3*) S Karger.

Pulos, Arthur J. The American Design Adventure. (Illus.). 450p. 1990. reprint ed. pap. 30.00x (*0-262-66068-7*) MIT Pr.

Pulp & Paper Manufacture Staff. Pulp & Paper Manufacture, Vol. 1: Pulping of Wood. 2nd ed. 1968. text ed. 79.95 (*0-07-050924-7*) McGraw.

— Pulp & Paper Manufacture, Vol. 2: Control, Secondary Fiber, Structural Board, Coating. 2nd ed. 1969. text ed. 79.95 (*0-07-050925-5*) McGraw.

Puls, Barbara, et al. Breaking New Ground: Community-Based Development Organizations. (Capitols & Communities Ser.). 21p. 1991. pap. text ed. 15.00 (*1-55516-804-3*, 3908) Natl Conf State Legis.

***Puls, Barbara.** Working Together for a Competitive Workforce: A Policy Handbook. 40p. 1994. 15.00 (*1-55516-330-0*, 3127) Natl Conf State Legis.

Puls, Herta. Art of Cutwork & Applique: Historic, Modern & Kuna Indian. (Illus.). 240p. 1978. 19.50 (*0-8231-4256-6*) Branford.

— Textiles of the Kuna Indians of Panama. 1989. pap. 25.00 (*0-85263-942-2*, Pub. by Shire UK) St Mut.

Puls, Joan. Every Bush Is Burning: A Spirituality for Today. 2nd ed. LC 85-51476. 120p. 1985. reprint ed. pap. 5.95 (*0-89622-280-2*) Twenty-Third.

— Hearts Set on the Pilgrimage: The Challenge of Discipleship in the World Church. LC 89-51385. 128p. (Orig.). 1989. pap. 7.95 (*0-89622-403-1*) Twenty-Third.

— Seek Treasures in Small Fields: Everyday Holiness. LC 91-68559. 160p. (Orig.). 1992. pap. 7.95 (*0-89622-509-7*) Twenty-Third.

— A Spirituality of Compassion. LC 87-51633. 144p. 1988. pap. 7.95 (*0-89622-352-3*) Twenty-Third.

Pulsiano, Phillip. An Annotated Bibliography of North American Doctoral Dissertations on Old English Language & Literature. LC 87-51125. (Medieval Texts & Studies: No. 3). 332p. 1988. 48.00 (*0-937191-06-X*) Colleagues Pr Inc.

***Pulsiano, Phillip, ed.** Anglo-Saxon Manuscripts in Microfiche Facsimile Vol. 2: Psalters I. 68p. 1994. mic. film, pap. 90.00 (*0-86698-146-2*, MR137) MRTS.

Pulsiano, Phillip & Skaptason, Jon. Barthar Saga. Nelson, Lowry, Jr. & Wilhelm, James J., eds. LC 83-48240. (Library of Medieval Literature). 178p. 1984. lib. bdg. 20.00 (*0-8240-9424-7*) Garland.

Pulsiano, Phillip & Wolf, Kirsten, eds. Medieval Scandinavia: An Encyclopedia, Vol. 1. LC 92-19300. (Illus.). 792p. 1993. 95.00 (*0-8240-4787-7*, H934) Garland.

Pulsifer, David, jt. ed. see Shurtleff, Nathaniel B.

Pulsifer, Gary, ed. Paul Bowles by His Friends. (Illus.). 160p. 1993. pap. 24.00 (*0-7206-0866-X*, Pub. by P Owen Ltd UK) Dufour.

Pulsinelli, Linda & Hooper, Patricia. Essential Mathematics: An Interactive Approach. 800p. (C). 1991. pap. write for info. (*0-02-357170-5*) Macmillan.

— Introductory Algebra: An Interactive Approach. 3rd ed. 720p. (C). 1990. pap. write for info. (*0-02-396984-9*) Macmillan.

Pulsinelli, Robert, jt. auth. see Miller, Roger L.

Pulsinelli, Robert W., jt. auth. see Miller, Roger L.

Pulsinelli, William A., ed. see Research (Princeton-Williamsburg) Conference on Cerebrovascular Disease Staff.

Pulszky, Agost. The Theory of Law & Civil Society. LC 79-1616. 1980. reprint ed. 35.00 (*0-88355-919-6*) Hyperion Conn.

Pultorak, Edward G. Customizing Your Resume for Teaching Positions. LC 92-34092. 52p. (Orig.). (C). 1993. pap. text ed. 16.50 (*0-8191-8938-3*) U Pr of Amer.

Pultz, Jane W., ed. see Rappolt, Miriam E.

***Pultz, John.** The Body & the Lens: Photography 1839 to the Present. LC 94-37844. (Perspectives Ser.). 1995. write for info. (*0-8109-2703-9*) Abrams.

Pultz, Mary Anne, ed. see Meyen, Franz J.

***Pulver.** Mrs. Toggle & the Dinosaur. (J). 1995. pap. 3.95 (*0-689-80341-9*, Aladdin Paperbacks) S&S Childrens.

Pulver, Carol, jt. auth. see Haigh, Rosemary.

Pulver, Dale. Linn's Introduction to the Stamps of Mexico. 112p. 1992. 30.00 (*0-940403-49-8*) Linns Stamp News.

— Linn's Introduction to the Stamps of Mexico. (Illus.). 112p. 1992. pap. 14.95 (*0-940403-48-X*) Linns Stamp News.

Pulver, David. Complete Druid's Handbook. (Advanced Dungeons & Dragons 2nd Ed. Accessory Ser.). 1994. pap. 18.00 (*1-56076-886-X*) TSR Inc.

— Ghost Rider & the Midnight Sons. (Marvel Super Heros Accessory Ser.: MHR4). Date not set. pap. 15.00 (*1-56076-578-X*) TSR Inc.

— Glory of Rome Campaign Sourcebook. (Advanced Dungeons & Dragons, Second Edition; Al-Qadim Ser.). (Illus.). 1993. pap. 18.00 (*1-56076-673-5*) TSR Inc.

Pulver, Glen. New Alliances for Community Education & Technical Assistance in Rural Areas. (New Alliances for Rural America Ser.). (Orig.). 1988. pap. text ed. 6.00 (*1-55877-020-8*) Natl Governor.

Pulver, Jeffrey. A Biographical Dictionary of Old English Music. LC 69-16666. (Music Ser.). 538p. 1973. reprint ed. lib. bdg. 59.50 (*0-306-71103-6*) Da Capo.

— A Biographical Dictionary of Old English Music. 537p. 1990. reprint ed. lib. bdg. 99.00 (*0-7812-9008-2*) Rprt Serv.

— A Dictionary of Old English Music & Musical Instruments. 1972. 75.00 (*0-8490-0042-4*) Gordon Pr.

— Paganini: The Romantic Virtuoso. LC 69-11669. (Music Ser.). 1970. reprint ed. lib. bdg. 37.50 (*0-306-71199-0*) Da Capo.

— Paganini, the Romantic Virtuoso. (Music Book Index Ser.). 328p. 1992. reprint ed. lib. bdg. 89.00 (*0-7812-9470-3*) Rprt Serv.

***Pulver, Kathryn.** Is That So? 300p. 1996. pap. 9.95 (*0-7610-0514-5*) NW Pub.

Pulver, Mary M. Original Sin. 256p. 1993. pap. 4.50 (*1-55773-846-7*) Diamond.

— Original Sin. 192p. 1991. 18.95 (*0-8027-5770-7*) Walker & Co.

— Show Stopper. 240p. (Orig.). 1993. pap. 4.50 (*1-55773-925-0*) Diamond.

— Show Stopper: A Kori & Peter Brichter Mystery. 204p. 1992. 19.95 (*0-8027-3210-0*) Walker & Co.

— The Unforgiving Minutes. 1992. pap. 4.50 (*1-55773-686-3*) Diamond.

Pulver, Robin. The Holiday Handwriting School. LC 89-77085. (Illus.). 32p. (J). (gr. k-3). 1991. text ed. 13.95 (*0-02-775455-3*, Four Winds Pr) S&S Childrens.

— Homer & the House Next Door. LC 93-4377. (Illus.). 32p. (J). (ps-2). 1994. text ed. 14.95 (*0-02-775457-X*, Four Winds Pr) S&S Childrens.

— Mrs. Toggle & the Dinosaur, Vol. 9. LC 90-35771. (Illus.). 32p. (J). (ps-2). 1991. text ed. 13.95 (*0-02-775452-9*, Four Winds Pr) S&S Childrens.

— Mrs. Toggle's Beautiful Blue Shoe. LC 92-40824. (Illus.). 32p. (J). (ps-2). 1994. text ed. 13.95 (*0-02-775456-1*, Four Winds Pr) S&S Childrens.

— Mrs. Toggle's Zipper. LC 88-37251. (Illus.). 32p. (J). (ps-2). 1990. text ed. 13.95 (*0-02-775451-0*, Four Winds Pr) S&S Childrens.

— Mrs. Toggle's Zipper. LC 92-39355. (Illus.). 32p. (J). (ps-2). 1993. reprint ed. pap. 3.95 (*0-689-71689-3*, Aladdin Paperbacks) S&S Childrens.

— Nobody's Mother Is in Second Grade. LC 91-16395. (Illus.). 32p. (J). (gr. k-3). 1992. 13.99 (*0-8037-1210-3*); lib. bdg. 13.89 (*0-8037-1211-1*) Dial Bks Young.

Pulverer, Gerhard, et al, eds. Pathogenicity & Clinical Significance of Coagulase-Negative Staphylococci. (Zentralblatt fur Bakteriologie Ser.: Vol. 16). 290p. 1987. lib. bdg. 140.00 (*0-89574-242-X*, Pub. by Gustav Fischer Verlag) VCH Pubs.

Pulvers, M., jt. auth. see Rumpf, K.

Pulvino, Charles J., jt. auth. see Lee, James L.

Pulvirenti, M., jt. ed. see Cercignani, C.

Pulvirenti, Mario, jt. auth. see Marchioro, Carlo.

Pulyer, Y. M. Electromagnetic Devices for Motion Control & Signal Processing. (Illus.). 472p. 1992. 69.00 (*0-387-97827-5*) Spr-Verlag.

***Pulzer, Peter.** German Politics, 1945-1995. 140p. 1995. 39.95 (*0-19-878110-5*); pap. 12.95 (*0-19-878111-3*) OUP.

— Jews & the German State: The Political History of a Minority, 1848-1933. 356p. 1992. 49.95 (*0-631-17282-3*) Blackwell Pubs.

— The Rise of Political Anti-Semitism in Germany & Austria. rev. ed. LC 88-15062. 384p. 1988. pap. 17.95 (*0-674-77166-4*) HUP.

Pume, N. D. Agricultural Dictionary in Eight Languages, 2 vols., Set. 1721p. (BUL, CZE, ENG, GER, HUN, POL, RUM & RUS.). 1970. 72.00 (*0-88431-080-9*) IBD Ltd.

Pume, N. D. & Magnyckij, A. V. Agricultural Dictionary in Eight Languages, 2 vols., Set. 1720p. (BUL, CZE, ENG, GER, HUN, POL, RUM & RUS.). 1970. write for info. (*0-8288-7191-4*) Fr & Eur.

Pumfrey, P. D., jt. ed. see Verma, G. K.

Pumfrey, Peter, jt. ed. see Owen, Pamela.

Pumfrey, Peter D. Improving Children's Reading in the Junior School: Challenges & Responses. 400p. 1991. pap. text ed. 24.95 (*0-304-31723-3*) Cassell.

Pumfrey, Peter D. & Elliot, Colin D., eds. Children's Difficulties in Reading, Spelling & Writing: Challenges & Responses. 260p. 1990. pap. 35.00 (*1-85000-691-1*) Taylor & Francis.

Pumfrey, Peter D. & Reason, Rea, eds. Specific Learning Difficulties (Dyslexia) Challenges & Responses. (Illus.). 352p. 1992. 69.95 (*0-7005-1268-3*, A7715) Routledge.

Pumfrey, Peter D. & Verma, Gajendra K., eds. The Foundation Subjects & Religious Education in Primary Schools. LC 93-27228. (Cultural Diversity & the Curriculum Ser.: Vol. 3). 216p. 1993. 85.00 (*0-7507-0143-9*, Falmer Pr); pap. 32.50 (*0-7507-0144-7*, Falmer Pr) Taylor & Francis.

Pumfrey, Peter D. & Verman, Gajendra K., eds. The Foundation Subjects & Religious Education in Secondary Schools. LC 92-39723. (Cultural Diversity & the Curriculum Ser.: Vol. 1). 256p. 1993. 90.00 (*0-7507-0139-0*, Falmer Pr); pap. 35.00 (*0-7507-0140-4*, Falmer Pr) Taylor & Francis.

Pumfrey, Peter D., jt. auth. see Verma, Gajendra K.

Pumfrey, Peter D., jt. ed. see Verma, Gajendra K.

Pumfrey, Stephen, et al, eds. Science, Culture & Popular Belief in Renaissance Europe. 240p. 1991. text ed. 79.95 (*0-7190-2925-2*, Pub. by Manchester Univ Pr UK) St Martin.

— Science, Culture & Popular Belief in Renaissance Europe. 352p. 1994. text ed. 24.95 (*0-7190-4322-0*, Pub. by Manchester Univ Pr UK) St Martin.

Pummer, K., ed. Biological Modulation of Solid Tumours by Interferons. LC 94-5664. (European School of Oncology Monographs). (Illus.). viii, 75p. 1994. 55.00 (*0-387-57764-5*) Spr-Verlag.

Pummer, Reinhard. The Samaritans. (Iconography of Religions Ser.: Vol. XXIII-5). (Illus.). xiv, 46p. 1987. pap. 41.25 (*90-04-07891-6*) E J Brill.

Pump, Anna. Loaves & Fishes Cookbook. 1985. 18.95 (*0-02-599450-6*) Macmillan.

— Loaves & Fishes Cookbook. 1987. 10.95 (*0-685-46249-8*, Collier S&S) S&S Trade.

Pump, Anna & Leroy, Gen. Loaves & Fishes. 272p. 1987. pap. 12.00 (*0-02-010080-9*) Macmillan.

Pumpel-Mader, Maria, et al. Deutsche Wortbildung: Typen und Tendenzen der Gegenwartssprache. Institut fur Deutsche Sprache Staff, ed. (Sprache der Gegenwart Ser.: No. 80). xx, 340p. (GER.). (C). 1992. lib. bdg. 127.15 (*3-11-012445-9*) De Gruyter.

Pumpelly, Raphael. Census of the United States: U. S. Decennial Census Reports, Tenth Census: 1880, Vol. 38, No. 123: Report on the Mining Industries of the United States (Exclusive of Precious Metals), with Special Investigation into the Iron Resources of the Republic & into the Cretaceous Coals of the Northwest. Allison, Peter, ed. LC 07-18862. (Illus.). 1064p. reprint ed. lib. bdg. 300.00 (*0-88354-438-5*) N Ross.

Pumphrey, Caroline. Charlbury of our Childhood. (C). 1989. pap. 21.00 (*1-85072-050-9*, Pub. by W Sessions UK) St Mut.

Pumphrey, Jane, jt. ed. see Ansley, Norman.

Pumphrey, Muriel W., jt. ed. see Pumphrey, Ralph E.

Pumphrey, Ralph E. & Pumphrey, Muriel W., eds. The Heritage of American Social Work: Readings in Its Philosophical & Institutional Development. LC 61-8989. 452p. 1964. text ed. 57.00 (*0-231-02486-X*); pap. text ed. 24.50 (*0-231-08619-9*) Col U Pr.

***Pumphrey, Richard.** Elements of Art. LC 94-36346. 1995. pap. text ed. 41.75 (*0-13-720376-4*) P-H.

Pumpian-Mindlin, Eugene, ed. Psychoanalysis As Science: The Hixon Lectures on the Scientific Status of Psychoanalysis. LC 70-106692. 174p. 1970. reprint ed. text ed. 52.50 (*0-8371-3365-3*, PUMP, Greenwood Pr) Greenwood.

Pumpin, Cuno. Corporate Dynamism: How World Class Companies Became World Class. 230p. 1991. text ed. 59.95 (*0-566-07277-7*, Pub. by Gower UK) Ashgate Pub Co.

— The Essence of Corporate Strategy. 160p. 1987. text ed. 65.95 (*0-566-02565-5*, Pub. by Gower UK) Ashgate Pub Co.

— Essence of Corporate Strategy. (Business Enterprise Ser.). 196p. 1989. pap. text ed. 29.95 (*0-7045-0638-6*, Pub. by Gower UK) Ashgate Pub Co.

— How World Class Companies Become World Class: Studies in Corporate Dynamism. 218p. 1993. pap. 19.95 (*0-566-07478-8*, Pub. by Gower UK) Ashgate Pub Co.

Pumroy, Eric & Brockman, Paul. A Guide to the Manuscript Collections of the Indiana Historical Society & Indiana State Library. LC 86-18593. 513p. 1986. 20.00 (*0-87195-006-5*) Ind Hist Soc.

***Pumtree, Anne.** Something New. McLeod, Deborah, ed. 250p. 1995. pap. 12.95 (*1-55111-079-2*) Broadview Pr.

Pun, K. K. Osteoporosis: Prevention & Treatment. (C). 1993. pap. text ed. 35.00 (*962-209-278-0*, Pub. by Hong Kong U Pr HK); pap. text ed. 35.00 (*962-209-223-3*, Pub. by Hong Kong U Pr HK) St Mut.

Pun, Lucas. Integrated Discrete Production Control: Analysis & Synthesis: A View Based on GRAI-Nets. LC 92-26789. (Manufacturing Research & Technology Ser.: Vol. 15). 1992. write for info. (*0-444-89629-5*) Elsevier.

Pun, Lucas, et al. Integrated Automation Practice. LC 74-81330. 368p. 1976. 41.00 (*0-444-10709-6*, North Holland) Elsevier.

***Pun, Pattle.** Evolution: Nature & Scripture in Conflict? 311p. (CHI.). 1992. pap. 8.00 (*1-56582-014-2*) Christ Renew Min.

***Puncel, Maria.** El Amigo Nuevo. (Illus.). 32p. (Orig.). (J). (gr. 3-5). Date not set. pap. text ed. 7.50 (*1-56492-108-5*) Laredo.

— El Premio. (Illus.). 32p. (Orig.). (J). (gr. 3-5). Date not set. pap. text ed. 7.50 (*1-56492-107-7*) Laredo.

Puncel, Maria, ed. Animales - Animals. Del Carmen Blazquez, Maria, tr. (Diccionarios Visuales Altea Ser. - Visual Dictionary Ser.). (Illus.). 64p. (SPA.). (YA). (gr. 5-12). 1992. write for info. (*84-372-4525-7*) Santillana.

— Las Cosas de Cada Dia - Everyday Things. Aixela, Javier F., tr. (Diccionarios Visuales Altea Ser. - Visual Dictionary Ser.). (Illus.). 64p. (SPA.). (YA). (gr. 5-12). 1992. write for info. (*84-372-4527-3*) Santillana.

Puncel, Maria & Basquez, Juan J., eds. Cuerpo Humano - The Human Body. Secanell, Jose M., tr. (Diccionarios Visuales Altea Ser. - Visual Dictionary Ser.). (Illus.). 63p. (SPA.). (YA). (gr. 5-12). 1992. write for info. (*84-372-4528-1*) Santillana.

Puncel, Maria, tr. see Ahlberg, Janet & Ahlberg, Allan.

Puncel, Maria, tr. see Hayes, Sarah.

Puncel, Maria, ed. see Henrietta.

Punch, Maurice. The Politics & Ethics of Fieldwork. (Qualitative Research Methods Ser.: No. 3). 96p. 1985. text ed. 21.50 (*0-8039-2562-X*); pap. text ed. 9.50 (*0-8039-2517-4*) Sage.

Punch, Maurice, ed. Control in the Police Organization. (Organization Studies: No. 4). 368p. 1983. 40.00 (*0-262-16090-0*) MIT Pr.

Punch, Terrence M., ed. Genealogist's Handbook for Atlantic Canada Research. 150p. 1989. 10.00 (*0-685-45722-2*, S2-85150) New Eng Hist.

Punch, Walter T., ed. see Massachusetts Horticultural Society Staff.

Punches, Lauri. How to Simply Cut Hair. (Orig.). 8.95 (*0-685-41159-1*) Hungerford & Holland.

Punches, Laurie. How to Simply Cut Children's Hair: A Step by Step Guide to the Six Basic Haircuts for Children. Rogers, Debbie & Martinez, Carla, eds. (Illus.). 1015p. 1989. pap. text ed. 7.95 (*0-685-25294-9*) Punches Prodns.

Punches, Laurie C. How to Simply Cut Children's Hair. Martinez, Carla, ed. LC 89-90694. (How to Simply Ser.: Vol. 2). (Illus.). 103p. (Orig.). 1989. pap. 7.95 (*0-929883-10-1*); VHS & Beta. bmax, vhs 29.95 (*0-685-24966-2*) Punches Prodns.

— How to Simply Cut Hair. Martinez, Carla et al, eds. LC 88-92443. (How to Simply Ser.: Vol. 1). (Illus.). 109p. (Orig.). (YA). (gr. 11 up). 1989. pap. 8.95 (*0-929883-06-3*); VHS & Beta. bmax, vhs 29.95 (*0-929883-07-1*) Punches Prodns.

— How to Simply Cut Hair Even Better: Advanced Haircutting. LC 88-92468. (How to Simply Ser.: Vol. 5). (Illus.). 129p. (Orig.). (YA). (gr. 11 up). 1989. pap. 9.95 (*0-929883-08-X*) Punches Prodns.

— How to Simply Highlight Hair. LC 88-92469. (How to Simply Ser.: Vol. 4). (Illus.). 79p. (Orig.). (YA). (gr. 11 up). 1989. pap. 6.95 (*0-929883-02-0*); VHS & Beta. bmax, vhs 19.95 (*0-929883-03-9*) Punches Prodns.

— How to Simply Perm Hair. LC 88-92467. (How to Simply Ser.: Vol. 3). (Illus.). 74p. (Orig.). (YA). (gr. 11 up). 1989. pap. 6.95 (*0-929883-04-7*); VHS & Beta. bmax, vhs 19.95 (*0-929883-05-5*) Punches Prodns.

Puncochar, Daniel E. Interpretation of Geometric Dimensioning & Tolerancing. (Illus.). 180p. 1990. 19.95 (*0-8311-3010-5*) Indus Pr.

***Pundeff, Marin.** Bulgaria in American Perspective: Political & Cultural Issues. 350p. 1994. 49.00 (*0-88033-295-6*) East Eur Quarterly.

Pundeff, Marin V. Bulgaria: A Bibliographic Guide. LC 65-60006. (Bibliographic Guides Ser.). 1968. reprint ed. 12.95 (*0-405-00059-6*) Ayer.

Pundik, Ron. The Struggle for Sovereignty: Relations Between Great Britain & Jordan, 1946-1951. 384p. 1994. 64.95 (*0-631-19295-6*) Blackwell Pubs.

Pundt, Helen M. AHEA: A History of Excellence. 1980. write for info. (*0-8461-5042-5*) Am Home Eco.

Pundt, Hermann G. Schinkel's Berlin: A Study in Environmental Planning. LC 75-172325. (Illus.). 283p. reprint ed. pap. 80.70 (*0-7837-4181-2*, 2059030) Bks Demand.

Puner, Helen W. Sigmund Freud: His Life & Mind. 295p. (C). 1992. pap. 19.95 (*1-56000-611-0*) Transaction Pubs.

Puner, Morton, jt. ed. see Melby, Ernest O.

***Punga, Inara, ed.** Guide to Latvia. LC 95-13700. (Bradt Guides Ser.). 1995. write for info. (*1-56440-812-4*) Globe Pequot.

Punga, Inara, ed. see Hough, Bill.

***Pungitore, Verna L.** Innovation & the Library: The Adoption of New Ideas in Public Libraries. LC 95-3808. 208p. 1995. text ed. 49.95 (*0-313-28673-6*, Greenwood Pr) Greenwood.

P
Q

An Asterisk (*) at the beginning of an entry indicates that the title is appearing in BIP for the first time.

— Public Librarianship: An Issues-Oriented Approach. LC 89-2189. (Contributions in Librarianship & Information Science Ser.: No. 63). 240p. 1989. text ed. 49.95 (*0-313-26072-9*, PPB/, Greenwood Pr) Greenwood.

Pungor, E. Coulometric Analysis. 302p. 1979. 175.00 (*0-569-08551-9*, Pub. by Collets) St Mut.

— Ion-Selective Electrodes. 264p. 1977. 110.00 (*0-569-08470-9*, Pub. by Collets) St Mut.

Pungor, E., ed. Bioelectroanalysis No. 2: Second Symposium Held at Matrafured, Hungary 11-15 October, 1992. (Illus.). 450p. 1993. 75.00 (*963-05-6529-3*, Pub. by A K HU) Intl Spec Bk.

— Ion-Selective Electrodes: Proceedings of the Fourth Symposium on Ion-Selective Electrodes Matrafured, Hungary, October 8-12, 1984, Vol. 4. (Analytical Chemistry Symposia Ser.: No. 22). 758p. 1985. 238.50 (*0-444-99553-6*) Elsevier.

***Pungor, E. & Buzas, I.** Coulometric Analysis: Conference Held at Matrafured, Hungary 17-19 October, 1978. 301p. (C). 1979. 81.00x (*963-05-2021-4*, Pub. by Akad Kiado HU) St Mut.

***Pungor, E. & Buzas, I., eds.** Bioelectroanalysis I: 1st Symposium Held at Matrafured, Hungary 6-8 October, 1986. 433p. (C). 1987. 147.00x (*963-05-4641-8*, Pub. by Akad Kiado HU) St Mut.

— Ion-Selective Electrodes: Proceedings of the 3rd Symposium in 1981. (Analytical Chemistry Symposia Ser.: Vol. 8). 428p. 1982. 123.00 (*0-444-99714-8*) Elsevier.

Pungor, E. & Damokos, T. Oscillometry & Conductometry. LC 63-17803. (International Series Mono on Analytical Chemistry: Vol. 21). 1965. 111.00 (*0-08-010539-4*, Pub. by Pergamon Repr UK) Franklin.

Pungor, E., et al. Modern Trends in Analytical Chemistry. (Analytical Chemistry Symposia Ser.: Vol. 18). 1984. 195.00 (*0-444-99631-1*, I-044-84) Elsevier.

***Pungor, Erno.** Ion-Selective Electrodes 5: Proceedings of the Fifth Symposium Held at Matrafured, Hungary 9-13, October, 1988. 674p. (C). 1989. 150.00x (*963-05-5623-5*, Pub. by Akad Kiado HU) St Mut.

— Practical Guide to Instrumental Analysis. 384p. 1994. 59.95 (*0-8493-8681-0*) CRC Pr.

Pungor, Erno, et al, eds. Dynamic Characteristics of Ion-Selective Electrodes. 192p. 1988. 89.00 (*0-8493-6493-0*, QD571, CRC Reprint) Franklin.

Pungur, Joseph. Theology Interpreted: A Guide to Christian Doctrine - God, the World & Mankind, Vol. I. LC 87-8250. (Christian Doctrine of God, Revelation, Creation, Providence, Man & Sin Ser.). 246p. (Orig.). (C). 1987. lib. bdg. 43.00 (*0-8191-6354-6*); pap. text ed. 24.00 (*0-8191-6355-4*) U Pr of Amer.

— Theology Interpreted, Vol. 2: A Guide to Christian Doctrine. 226p. (Orig.). (C). 1992. lib. bdg. 52.00 (*0-8191-8891-3*); pap. text ed. 24.50 (*0-8191-8892-1*) U Pr of Amer.

***Punia, Deep.** Social Values in Folklore. (C). 1993. 19.50x (*81-7033-193-5*, Pub. by Rawat II) S Asia.

Punia, R. K., jt. ed. see Sharma, M. L.

***Punica, George.** Messerschmitt ME 210-410 in Action. (Aircraft in Action Ser.). (Illus.). 50p. 1994. pap. 8.95 (*0-89747-320-5*) Squad Sig Pubns.

Punithalingam, E. Mycological Papers, No. 159: Ascochyta II. Species on Monocotyledons (excluding grasses), Cryptogams & Gymnosperms. 235p. (C). 1987. pap. text ed. 39.00 (*0-85198-592-0*) CAB Intl.

Punja, Shobita. Museums of India: India's Greatest Treasures. 1991. pap. 15.95 (*0-8442-9910-3*, Passport Bks) NTC Pub Grp.

Punjab Law Agency Staff, ed. Cases & Material on Arbitration Act, (1940-1988) 2nd ed. (C). 1989. 160.00 (*0-685-36487-9*) St Mut.

Punjaba, Tomas J. Medical Aspects of Food Handling: Medical Subject Research Analysis with Bibliography. LC 84-45737. 150p. 1986. 44.50 (*0-88164-252-5*); pap. 39.50 (*0-88164-253-3*) ABBE Pubs Assn.

***Punka, George.** FW-189 in Action. (Aircraft in Action Ser.). (Illus.). 50p. 1994. pap. 8.95 (*0-89747-310-8*) Squad Sig Pubns.

— Hungarian Air Force. (Foreign Air Forces Ser.). (Illus.). 64p. 1995. pap. 11.95 (*0-89747-349-3*) Squad Sig Pubns.

Punkus, Sue, jt. auth. see Robertson, Sue.

Punley, Randolph J., ed. see Frazier, Gregory W.

Punnett, Betty J. Experiencing International Business & Management. 2nd ed. 321p. 1994. pap. 32.95 (*0-534-21462-2*) S-W Pub.

— Experiencing International Management. 293p. (C). 1989. pap. 30.95 (*0-534-91699-6*) Intl Thomson.

Punnett, Betty J. & Ricks, David A. International Business. 672p. 1992. text ed. 58.95 (*0-534-92247-3*) Intl Thomson.

***Punnett, Betty J. & Shenkar, Oded, eds.** Handbook for International Management Research. LC 95-1581. 1995. 45.95 (*1-55786-500-0*) Blackwell Pubs.

Punnett, Dick & Punnett, Yvonne. Thrills, Chills & Spills: A Photographic History of Early Aviation on the World's Most Bizarre Airport - The Beach at Daytona Beach, Florida - 1906-1929. LC 90-42545. (Illus.). 120p. (Orig.). 1990. write for info. (*1-877633-10-0*); pap. text ed. 17.95 (*1-877633-09-7*) Luthers.

Punnett, R. M. British Government & Politics. 5th ed. 572p. (C). 1990. reprint ed. pap. text ed. 19.95 (*0-88133-560-6*) Waveland Pr.

— British Government & Politics. 6th ed. (Illus.). 608p. (C). 1994. text ed. 57.95 (*1-85521-497-0*, Pub. by Dartmth Pub UK); pap. text ed. 21.95 (*1-85521-508-X*, Pub. by Dartmth Pub UK) Ashgate Pub Co.

Punnett, Yvonne, jt. auth. see Punnett, Dick.

Punola, John A. Catskill Trout. 4th ed. (Illus.). 96p. 1993. pap. 7.95 (*0-939888-14-9*) Outdoors USA.

— Fishing & Canoeing the Upper Delaware River. rev. ed. (Illus.). 112p. (Orig.). 1981. pap. 5.95 (*0-939888-07-6*) Outdoors USA.

— Fishing Delaware River. (Illus.). 108p. 1993. pap. 8.75 (*0-939888-17-3*) Outdoors USA.

— Guide to New Jersey Lakes. (Illus.). 124p. (Orig.). 1993. pap. 8.75 (*0-939888-16-5*) Outdoors USA.

— Guide to New Jersey Saltwater Fishing. (Illus.). 120p. (Orig.). 1991. pap. 8.95 (*0-939888-13-0*) Outdoors USA.

— Guide to New Jersey Trout. (Illus.). 92p. (Orig.). 1985. pap. 5.95 (*0-939888-06-8*) Outdoors USA.

— Guide to Pennsylvania Trout. 2nd ed. (Illus.). 104p. (Orig.). 1990. reprint ed. pap. 7.95 (*0-939888-09-2*) Outdoors USA.

— New Jersey Trout. (Illus.). 124p. (Orig.). 1994. pap. 8.95 (*0-939888-18-1*) Outdoors USA.

Punola, John A., illus. Guide to Catskill Trout. 72p. (Orig.). 1984. pap. 5.95 (*0-939888-08-4*) Outdoors USA.

Punsalan, Victoria J., jt. comp. see Miller, A. Carolyn.

Punset, Eduardo & Sweeney, Gerry P. Information Resources & Corporate Development. 280p. 1992. 54.00 (*0-86187-720-9*, Pub. by Pinter Pubs UK) St Martin.

Punshon, John. Alternative Christianity. LC 81-85560. (C). 1982. pap. 3.00 (*0-87574-245-9*) Pendle Hill.

— Encounter with Silence: Reflections from the Quaker Tradition. LC 87-181. 156p. (Orig.). 1987. pap. 9.50 (*0-913408-96-4*) Friends United.

— Letter to a Universalist. LC 89-60789. (Orig.). 1989. pap. 3.00 (*0-87574-285-8*) Pendle Hill.

Punt, Barbara. Doing It Right: A Guide to Improving Exhibit Labels. (Illus.). 72p. 1989. pap. 15.95 (*0-685-29595-8*, Brooklyn Children s Museum) AST Ctrs.

***Punt, Capelle.** International Dictionary of Law, Commerce, & Finance: German-English-French-Spanish. 600p. (ENG, FRE & GER.). 1992. 105.00 (*0-7859-8341-4*, 3409199438) Fr & Eur.

Punt, H. Bernard Siegfried Albinus (1697-1770) on Human Nature: Anatomical & Physiological Ideas in 18th Century Leiden. (Illus.). 226p. 1983. lib. bdg. 97.50 (*90-6078-088-4*, Pub. by B M Israel NE) Coronet Bks.

Punt, Neal. Baker's Textual & Topical Filing System. deluxe ed. LC 60-53376. 628p. 1989. reprint ed. 54.95 (*0-945315-15-5*) Northland Bks.

— Unconditional Good News: Toward an Understanding of Biblical Universalism. LC 80-10458. 179p. reprint ed. pap. 51.10 (*0-317-39671-4*, 2023222) Bks Demand.

— What's Good About the Good News? The Plan of Salvation in a New Light. LC 87-63576. 156p. (Orig.). 1988. pap. 8.95 (*0-945315-07-4*) Northland Bks.

Punt, Norman A. The Singer's & Actor's Throat: The Vocal Mechanism of the Professional Voice User & Its Care in Health & Disease. 3rd ed. (Illus.). 100p. 1979. reprint ed. pap. text ed. 29.95 (*0-433-26451-9*) Buttrwrth-Heinemann.

Punt, W., ed. The Northwest European Pollen Flora, Vol. 1. 416p. 1976. 74.50 (*0-444-41421-5*) Elsevier.

Punt, W. & Blackmore, Stephen. Northwest European Pollen Flora VI. 1991. 123.00 (*0-444-89164-1*) Elsevier.

Punt, W. & Clarke, G. C. Northwest European Pollen Flora IV. 1984. 110.25 (*0-444-42405-9*) Elsevier.

Punt, W. & Clarke, G. C., eds. The Northwest European Pollen Flora, Vol. 2. 266p. 1980. reprint ed. 100.00 (*0-444-41880-6*) Elsevier.

— Northwest European Pollen Flora, Vol. 3. 138p. 1981. 79.50 (*0-444-41996-9*) Elsevier.

Punt, W., et al, eds. The Northwest European Pollen Flora, Vol. 5. 154p. 1988. 82.00 (*0-444-87268-X*) Elsevier.

***Puntch, Julie.** The Legend of the Christmas Spider. Dumelle, Grace, ed. (Illus.). 24p. (J). 1993. 19.95 (*0-937739-21-9*) Roman IL.

Puntel, Lorenz B. Grundlagen Einer Theorie der Wahrheit. (Grundlagen der Kommunikation & Kognition (Foundations of Communication & Cognition) Ser.). xiii, 408p. (C). 1990. lib. bdg. 132.00 (*3-11-012079-8*) De Gruyter.

***Puntenney, Pamela J., ed.** Global Ecosystems: Creating Options Through Anthropological Perspectives. LC 95-1455. (NAPA Bulletin Ser.: Vol. 15). 1995. write for info. (*0-913167-70-3*) Am Anthro Assn.

Punter, David, ed. William Blake: Selected Poetry & Prose. (English Texts Ser.). 256p. 1988. pap. 9.95 (*0-415-00666-X*) Routledge.

Puntillo, Kathleen A. Pain in the Critically Ill: Assessment & Management. 250p. 1991. text ed. 43.00 (*0-8342-0222-0*) Aspen Pub.

Punwar, Alice J. Occupational Therapy: Principles & Practice. 2nd ed. LC 92-48838. (Illus.). 304p. 1994. 34.00 (*0-683-06975-6*) Williams & Wilkins.

***Punzi, Henry A. & Flamenbaum, Walter, eds.** Hypertension. (Illus.). 416p. 1989. 49.00 (*0-87993-372-0*) Futura Pub.

Punzo, L. F., jt. ed. see Bohm, B.

Puolanne, E. & Demeyer, D. I., eds. Pork Quality: Genetic & Metabolic Factors. 335p. 1993. text ed. 73.00 (*0-85198-836-9*) CAB Intl.

Puopolo, Vito. Music Fundamentals. LC 75-4316. (Illus.). 256p. (C). 1976. pap. 16.00 (*0-02-871890-9*) Schirmer Bks.

Puotinen, Arthur E. Finnish Radicals & Religion in Midwestern Mining Towns: 1865-1914. Scott, Franklyn D., ed. LC 78-15851. (Scandinavians in America Ser.). (Illus.). 1979. lib. bdg. 30.95 (*0-405-11657-8*) Ayer.

Puotinen, C. J. Computing Horoscopes with Your Electronic Calculator. (Illus.). 1978. pap. 4.95 (*0-930840-07-0*) Ninth Sign.

— The Retrograde Mercury Workbook. 64p. 1982. pap. 4.95 (*0-930840-11-9*) Ninth Sign.

Pupil, A. The Serene Life. 1981. pap. 2.00 (*0-911794-47-6*) Aqua Educ.

Pupils of Farr Secondary School & Temperley, Alan. Tales of the North Coast. 251p. (C). 1989. 45.00 (*0-946487-18-9*, Pub. by Luath Pr UK) St Mut.

Pupin, Michael. From Immigrant to Inventor. Cohen, I. Bernard, ed. LC 79-7983. (Three Centuries of Science in America Ser.). (Illus.). 1980. reprint ed. lib. bdg. 37.95 (*0-405-12565-8*) Ayer.

Pupkiewicz, Chris. Colleges & Universities to Avoid: From Case Western Reserve University to University of Waterloo. 97p. 1992. pap. text ed. 88.59 (*1-895583-97-7*) MAYA Pubs.

— The Economics Profession: A Den of Backstabbers & Quislings. 71p. 1992. pap. text ed. 57.95 (*1-895583-96-9*) MAYA Pubs.

Pupo-Walker, Enrique, ed. Castaways - Alvar Nunez Cabeza de Vaca: The Narrative of Alvar Nunez Cabeza de Vaca. Lopez-Morillas, Frances M., tr. LC 92-25645. (C). 1993. 30.00 (*0-520-07062-3*); pap. 12.00 (*0-520-07063-1*) U CA Pr.

Pupo-Walker, Enrique, jt. ed. see Echevarria, Roberto G.

Puppe, C. Distorted Probabilities & Choice under Risk. Beckmann, Martin J. & Krelle, W., eds. (Lecture Notes in Economics & Mathematical Systems Ser.: Vol. 363). (Illus.). viii, 100p. 1991. pap. 27.00 (*0-387-54247-7*) Spr-Verlag.

Puppe, Frank. Systematic Introduction to Expert Systems: Knowledge Representations & Problem Solving Methods. LC 93-14650. 1993. 59.00 (*0-387-56255-9*) Spr-Verlag.

Puppe, Volker, jt. auth. see Allday, Christopher.

Puppel, Stanislaw, jt. ed. see Fisiak, Jacek.

***Puppel, Stanislaw, et al, eds.** The Biology of Language. LC 94-49701. x, 276p. 1995. lib. bdg. 84.00x (*1-55619-480-3*) Benjamins North Am.

Puppi, Lionello. Torment in Art: Pain, Violence & Martyrdom. LC 91-52772. (Illus.). 180p. 1991. 75.00 (*0-8478-1406-8*) Rizzoli Intl.

Puppo, P., jt. ed. see Giuliani, L.

***PUR, Inc. Staff, et al.** The Electric Industry in Transition. 305p. (Orig.). 1994. pap. 69.00 (*0-910325-58-8*) Public Util.

Puranas. Brahma-Vaivarta Puranam, 2 vols., Set. LC 73-3817. reprint ed. 74.50 (*0-404-57824-1*) AMS Pr.

— The Matsya Puranam, 2 vols., Set. LC 73-3808. reprint ed. 74.50 (*0-404-57817-9*) AMS Pr.

Puranas, Bhagavatapurana. The Bhakti-Ratnavali: With the Commentary of Visnu Puri. LC 73-3794. (Sacred Books of the Hindus: No. 7 Pt.3). reprint ed. 25.00 (*0-404-57835-7*) AMS Pr.

Puranas, Brahmandapurana. The Adhyatma Ramayana. Nath, Lala B., tr. LC 73-3828. (Sacred Books of the Hindus: Extra Vol. 1). reprint ed. 25.00 (*0-404-57846-2*) AMS Pr.

Purani, A. B. The Life of Sri Aurobindo. (Illus.). 440p. 1987. 15.00 (*81-7058-080-3*) Aurobindo Assn.

Puravs, Grace, ed. see University Microfilms International Staff.

Puravs, Grace, et al, eds. Accessing English Literary Periodicals: A Guide to the Microfilm Collection with Title, Subject, Editor, & Reel Number Indexes. LC 81-16124. 1981. 30.00 (*0-8357-0231-6*) Univ Microfilms.

Purba, Sanjiv. Developing Client-Server Systems Using Sybase SQL Server System 10. LC 94-12670. 1995. pap. text ed. 39.95 (*0-471-06249-9*) Wiley.

***Purba, Sanjiv & Shah, Bharat.** How to Manage a Successful Software Project: Methodologies, Techniques, Tools. 1995. pap. text ed. 39.95 (*0-471-04401-6*) Wiley.

Purce, Jill. The Mystic Spiral: Journey of the Soul. (Art & Imagination Ser.). (Illus.). 128p. 1980. reprint ed. pap. 15.95 (*0-500-81005-2*) Thames Hudson.

Purce, Jill, ed. see Zolla, Elemire.

Purcell, Ann & Purcell, Carl. A Guide to Travel Writing & Photography. 144p. 1991. pap. 22.95 (*0-89879-466-8*) Writers Digest.

— Stock Photography: The Complete Guide. 144p. 1993. pap. 19.95 (*0-89879-552-4*) Writers Digest.

Purcell, Anne, jt. auth. see Purcell, Ben.

Purcell, Ben & Purcell, Anne. Love & Duty. large type ed. 377p. 1992. reprint ed. lib. bdg. 17.95 (*1-56054-440-6*) Thorndike Pr.

— Love & Duty. (Illus.). 1992. reprint ed. mass mkt. 4.99 (*0-312-92890-4*) St Martin.

Purcell, Betty. Light After Darkness: An Experience of Nicaragua. 144p. (Orig.). (C). 1989. pap. 9.95 (*0-946211-76-0*, Pub. by Attic IE) InBook.

Purcell, Carl, jt. auth. see Purcell, Ann.

Purcell, Catherine. Checklist of Professional Schools in Canada. 300p. (C). 1993. pap. text ed. 28.00 (*1-55022-194-9*, Pub. by ECW Press CN) Genl Dist Srvs.

— Guide to Law Schools in Canada. 266p. (C). 1992. pap. text ed. 14.95 (*1-55022-160-4*, Pub. by ECW Press CN) Genl Dist Srvs.

— Guide to MBA Schools in Canada. 200p. (C). 1991. pap. text ed. 14.95 (*1-55022-131-0*, Pub. by ECW Press CN) Genl Dist Srvs.

Purcell, Deidre. On Lough Derg. 122p. 1989. 39.00 (*1-85390-095-8*, Pub. by Veritas IE) St Mut.

Purcell, Deirdre. Ashes of Roses. 528p. 1994. pap. 5.99 (*0-451-18246-4*, Sig) NAL-Dutton.

— On Lough Derg. (Illus.). 117p. 1988. 11.95 (*1-85390-012-5*, Pub. by Veritas Pubns IE) Irish Bks Media.

— A Place of Stones. 448p. (Orig.). 1993. pap. 5.99 (*0-451-17329-5*, Sig) NAL-Dutton.

— That Childhood Country. 528p. 1994. pap. 5.99 (*0-451-17871-8*, Sig) NAL-Dutton.

Purcell, E. M. Berkeley Physics Course: Electricity & Magnetism, Vol. 2. 2nd ed. 1985. text ed. write for info. (*0-07-004908-4*) McGraw.

Purcell, Edmund S. Life of Cardinal Manning, Archbishop of Westminster, 2 vols, Set. LC 70-126605. (Europe 1815-1945 Ser.). 1534p. 1973. reprint ed. lib. bdg. 115.00 (*0-306-70050-6*) Da Capo.

Purcell, Edward, jt. rev. see Purcell, Mary.

Purcell, Edward A., Jr. The Crisis of Democratic Theory: Scientific Naturalism & the Problem of Value. LC 72-91669. 344p. 1973. reprint ed. pap. 14.00 (*0-8131-0141-7*) U Pr of Ky.

Purcell, Edward A. Litigation & Inequality: Federal Diversity Jurisdiction in Industrial America, 1870-1958. 480p. 1992. 59.00 (*0-19-507329-0*) OUP.

Purcell, Edwin J. Calculus with Analytic Geometry. 3rd ed. (Illus.). 1978. 36.95 (*0-13-112052-2*); Solutions manual. pap. 6.95 (*0-13-112037-9*); Linear algebra supp. pap. text ed. write for info. (*0-13-112029-8*) P-H.

Purcell, Edwin J., jt. auth. see Varberg, Dale E.

Purcell, Elizabeth, ed. World Trends in Medical Education: Faculty, Students, & Curriculum. LC 79-144335. (Josiah Macy Foundation Ser.). 248p. reprint ed. 70.70 (*0-8357-9292-7*, 2015693) Bks Demand.

Purcell, Elizabeth F., ed. The Role of the University Teaching Hospital: An International Perspective: Report of a Conference. LC 82-83988. 266p. reprint ed. pap. 75.90 (*0-685-15485-8*, 2026696) Bks Demand.

Purcell, Elizabeth F., jt. ed. see Bowers, John Z.

Purcell, Elizabeth F., jt. ed. see Bradley, Stanley.

Purcell, Elizabeth F., jt. ed. see Friedman, Charles P.

Purcell, Elizabeth F., jt. ed. see Warren, Kenneth S.

Purcell, Francis P., jt. ed. see Brager, George A.

***Purcell-Gates, Victoria.** Other People's Words: The Cycle of Low Literacy. LC 94-31073. (Illus.). 256p. 1995. text ed. 29.95 (*0-674-64497-2*, PUROTH) HUP.

Purcell, Gervais. Japan Journal: The Private Notes of Gervais Purcell 1874-1900. Purcell, Hugh D., ed. (Illus.). 64p. 1975. 50.00 (*0-317-06150-X*) Rare Oriental Bk Co.

Purcell, H. J., ed. see Society for the Environmental Therapy, Inaugural Conference, 1981: Oxford, Oxfordshire.

Purcell, Henry. Choice Collection of Lessons for the Harpsichord or Spinnet. (Monuments of Music Literature in Facsimile: Ser. I, Vol. 26). (Illus.). 1978. reprint ed. lib. bdg. 40.00 (*0-8450-2026-9*) Broude.

— Dido & Aeneas, an Opera. Price, Curtis, ed. (Critical Scores Ser.). 1986. 27.50 (*0-393-02407-5*) Norton.

— Dido & Aeneas, an Opera. Price, Curtis, ed. (Critical Scores Ser.). (C). 1986. pap. text ed. 9.95 (*0-393-95528-1*) Norton.

— Harpsichord Works, Bk. 1. Date not set. pap. 13.95 (*0-685-69071-7*, Chester Music) Music Sales.

Purcell, Henry, jt. auth. see Playford, John.

Purcell, Hugh D., ed. see Purcell, Gervais.

Purcell, John, ed. Register of Research, 1987. 96p. (C). 1987. 60.00 (*0-85292-399-6*) St Mut.

Purcell, John & Ahlstrand, Bruce. Human Resource Management in the Multi-Divisional Company. LC 93-42896. 240p. 1994. 45.00 (*0-19-878021-4*) OUP.

— Human Resource Management in the Multi-Divisional Company. LC 93-42896. 248p. 1995. pap. 21.00 (*0-19-878020-6*) OUP.

Purcell, John, jt. ed. see Schmeal, W. R.

Purcell, John F. Trade Conflicts & U. S. - Mexican Relations. (Research Report Ser.: No. 38). 49p. (Orig.). (C). 1982. pap. 5.00 (*0-935391-37-1*, RR-38) UCSD Ctr US-Mex.

Purcell, John W. African Animals. LC 82-9541. (New True Bks.). (Illus.). 48p. (J). (gr. k-4). 1982. 12.90 (*0-516-01665-2*); pap. 4.95 (*0-516-41665-0*) Childrens.

Purcell, Juanita. Be Patient - I'm Not Perfect Yet. (Women's Ser.). 120p. (Orig.). 1993. pap. 5.95 (*0-87227-178-1*) Reg Baptist.

— How Can I Love Those Prickly People? Selected "One Anothers" in the Bible. (RBP Women's Ser.). 120p. (Orig.). 1995. per., pap. text ed. 5.95 (*0-87227-187-0*) Reg Baptist.

— Stretch My Faith, Lord. (Women's Ser.). 103p. (Orig.). 1992. pap. text ed. 5.95 (*0-87227-174-9*, RBP5207) Reg Baptist.

— Trials - Don't Resent Them As Intruders. (Women's Ser.). 96p. (Orig.). 1991. pap. text ed. 5.95 (*0-87227-161-7*) Reg Baptist.

Purcell, Julia A. Angioplasty. Hoffman, Faye W., ed. LC 86-25378. (Illus.). 24p. (Orig.). 1986. pap. text ed. 3.60 (*0-939838-22-2*) Pritchett & Hull.

— Cardiac Catheterization. rev. ed. Hull, Nancy R., ed. LC 82-10133. (Illus.). 36p. 1987. 3.75 (*0-939838-10-9*) Pritchett & Hull.

— Off the Beat: A Book about Abnormal Heart Rhythms. Hull, Nancy R., ed. LC 91-33673. (Illus.). 24p. (Orig.). 1992. pap. text ed. 3.85 (*0-939838-32-X*) Pritchett & Hull.

Purcell, Julia A. & Fletcher, Barbara J. A Stronger Pump. rev. ed. Hull, Nancy R., ed. LC 80-10191. (Illus.). 40p. (Orig.). 1994. pap. text ed. 4.00 (*0-939838-05-2*) Pritchett & Hull.

Purcell, Julia A., jt. auth. see Fletcher, Barbara J.

Purcell, Julia A., et al. Angina Pectoris. rev. ed. Hoffman, Faye, ed. LC 84-26382. (Illus.). 24p. 1994. pap. text ed. 3.50 (*0-939838-17-6*) Pritchett & Hull.

— Despues De Un Ataque Cardiaco: Que Sigue? Hull, Nancy R., ed. De la Vega, Olimpia, tr. LC 90-27143. (Illus.). 68p. (Orig.). 1991. pap. text ed. 4.90 (*0-939838-30-3*) Pritchett & Hull.

— Heart Attack: What's Ahead? rev. ed. Hull, Nancy R., ed. LC 80-25793. (Illus.). 64p. (Orig.). 1993. reprint ed. pap. text ed. 4.15 (*0-939838-02-8*) Pritchett & Hull.

Purcell, Kate & Pearson, Patti. Insiders' Guide to Sarasota - Bradenton. 1994. pap. 12.95 (*0-912367-55-5*) Insiders Guide.

Purcell, Kate, jt. auth. see Elias, Peter.

P Q

Purcell, Keith F. & Kotz, John C. An Introduction to Inorganic Chemistry. 600p. (C). 1980. text ed. 69.25 (*0-03-056768-8*) SCP.

Purcell, Keith F., jt. auth. see Kotz, John C.

Purcell, L. E., ed. Suggested State Legislation 1986, Vol. 45. 220p. (Orig.). 1986. pap. 15.00 (*0-87292-060-7*) Coun State Govts.

Purcell, L. Edward. Immigration. LC 94-38677. (Social Issues in American History Ser.). (Illus.). 192p. 1994. 29.95 (*0-89774-873-5*) Oryx Pr.

— Shakers. 1991. 10.99 (*0-517-64457-6*) Random Hse Value.

— Who Was Who in the American Revolution. 608p. 1993. lib. bdg. 65.00 (*0-8160-2107-4*) Facts on File.

Purcell, L. Edward & Garraty, John A., intros. The World Almanac of the American Revolution. (Illus.). 408p. 1992. 35.00 (*0-88687-574-9*); pap. 16.95 (*0-88687-665-6*) Wrld Almnc.

Purcell, Laurie. Secondary Progressions in Eidetic Analysis. 121p. 1993. pap. 11.00 (*0-913412-69-4*) Brandon Hse.

Purcell, Lawrie. Main Progressions in Eidetic Analysis. (Orig.). 1990. pap. 11.00 (*0-913412-29-5*) Brandon Hse.

***Purcell, Lee.** Super CD-ROM Madness! 1994. cd-rom, pap. 39.99 (*0-672-30638-7*) Sams.

Purcell, Lee, jt. auth. see Jost, Martin.

Purcell, Mary. The First Jesuit. rev. ed. 294p. 1981. 12.95 (*0-8294-0371-X*) Loyola Univ Pr.

— Matt Talbot: His Life & Times. 250p. 1977. 8.95 (*0-8199-0657-3*, Frncscn Herld) Franciscan Pr.

— The Quiet Companion: Peter Favre S. J., 1506-1546. vi, 198p. 1981. 1.95 (*0-8294-0377-9*) Loyola Univ Pr.

— Remembering Matt Talbot. 142p. (Orig.). 1990. pap. 10.95 (*1-85390-185-7*, Pub. by Veritas Publns IE) Ignatius Pr.

— The World of Monsieur Vincent. 256p. 1989. pap. 22.00 (*1-85390-019-2*, Pub. by Veritas IE) St Mut.

— The World of Monsieur Vincent: The Life St. Vincent de Paul. 250p. 1988. 12.95 (*0-8294-0606-9*); pap. 9.95 (*0-8294-0607-7*) Loyola Univ Pr.

***Purcell, Mary & Purcell, Edward, revs.** Pastor's Complete Book of Model Speeches. 1995. text ed. 39.95 (*0-13-653387-6*) P-H.

Purcell, Mia. The Industrial Incubator. Murphy, Jenny & Kailo, Andrea, eds. 20p. (Orig.). 1984. pap. 15.00 (*0-317-04906-2*) Natl Coun Econ Dev.

— Marketing & Managing Local Enterprise Zones. Kailo, Andrea, ed. 32p. (Orig.). 1985. pap. 16.00 (*0-317-04905-4*) Natl Coun Econ Dev.

— Revolving Loan Funds. Young, Laurie B., ed. 40p. (Orig.). 1983. pap. 13.00 (*0-317-04848-1*) Natl Coun Econ Dev.

— SBA's Section Five Hundred Three Program. Sampson, Stephanie, ed. 24p. (Orig.). 1983. pap. 11.00 (*0-317-04826-0*) Natl Coun Econ Dev.

Purcell, Nadine H., jt. ed. see Moore, Richard E.

Purcell, Norah, tr. see Saint-Exupery, Antoine de.

Purcell, Paul E. The Complete Guide to Homemade Income. 128p. (Orig.). 1987. pap. 7.95 (*0-942369-00-9*) P & P Pubns GA.

Purcell, Randall B., ed. Newly Industrializing Countries in the World Economy: Challenges for U. S. Policy. LC 89-30730. 250p. 1989. lib. bdg. 37.00 (*1-55587-154-2*) Lynne Rienner.

Purcell, Randall B. & Morrison, Elizabeth, eds. U. S. Agriculture & Third World Development: The Critical Linkage. LC 86-29860. 240p. 1987. lib. bdg. 36.50 (*1-55587-011-2*) Lynne Rienner.

Purcell, Robert Y. & Sharif, Gunseli S., eds. Handbook of Control Technologies for Hazardous Air Pollutants. (Science Information Research Center Ser.). 176p. 1988. 55.00 (*0-89116-825-7*) Hemisp Pub.

Purcell, Ronald. Anthology of Beloved Hymns for Guitar. 1993. 7.95 (*0-685-64339-5*, 94065) Mel Bay.

Purcell, Rosamond W., photos. Finders, Keepers: Eight Collectors. (Illus.). 128p. 1992. 50.00 (*0-393-03054-7*) Norton.

— Illuminations: A Bestiary. (Illus.). 1987. pap. 19.95 (*0-393-30436-1*) Norton.

Purcell, Royal. The Concept of Being Human. 173p. (Orig.). 1985. pap. 9.95 (*0-933189-00-1*) Purcell Pub.

— Ethics, Morality, & Mores. 177p. (Orig.). 1986. pap. 9.95 (*0-933189-01-X*) Purcell Pub.

— Purcell's Thesaurus of Knowledge. (Illus.). 301p. 1993. ring bd. 19.95 (*0-933189-04-4*) Purcell Pub.

Purcell, Sally. Gaspara Stampa. (C). 1990. 35.00 (*0-906887-15-1*, Pub. by Greville Pr UK) St Mut.

***Purcell, Steve.** Sam & Max: Surf the Highway. (Illus.). 170p. 1995. 22.50 (*1-56924-812-5*); pap. 12.95 (*1-56924-814-1*) Marlowe & Co.

— Sam & Max: Surf the Highway. limited ed. (Illus.). 1995. 50.00 (*1-56924-837-0*) Marlowe & Co.

— Sam & Max Color Collection. 64p. 1992. 4.95 (*0-87135-938-3*) Marvel Entmnt.

Purcell, Susan K. Cuba's Cloudy Future. 1990. 3.00 (*0-685-37920-5*) Cuban Amer Natl Fndtn.

— Debt & the Restructuring of Mexico. (Critical Issues Ser.: No. 5). 1988. 3.95 (*0-87609-044-7*) Coun Foreign.

— Is Cuba Changing? 1989. 3.00 (*0-685-47389-9*) Cuban Amer Natl Fndtn.

Purcell, Susan K., ed. Mexico in Transition: Implications for U. S. Policy. 168p. 1988. pap. 9.95 (*0-87609-028-5*) Coun Foreign.

— Mexico-United States Relations. No. 6. LC 80-70867. 224p. 1981. text ed. 49.95 (*0-275-90707-4*, C0707, Praeger Pubs) Greenwood.

Purcell, Susan K. & Immerman, Robert M., eds. Japan & Latin America in the New Global Order. LC 92-4865. (America's Society Ser.). 164p. 1992. pap. text ed. 10.95 (*1-55587-316-2*) Lynne Rienner.

Purcell, Susan K. & Simon, Francoise, eds. Europe & Latin America in the World Economy. LC 94-14624. 218p. 1995. pap. text ed. 14.95 (*1-55587-498-3*) Lynne Rienner.

Purcell, T. Robert. Doors to the Future: Steps to English Proficiency. rev. ed. (Illus.). 154p. (C). 1989. pap. text ed. write for info. (*1-878251-00-7*) English Tutors.

— Doors to the Future, Vol. 2: Steps to English Proficiency. rev. ed. (Illus.). 120p. (C). 1990. text ed. write for info. (*0-318-65773-2*) English Tutors.

— Keys to the Future, Vol. 1: Steps to English Proficiency. rev. ed. (Illus.). 140p. (C). 1990. text ed. write for info. (*0-318-65771-6*) English Tutors.

— Roads to the Future: Steps to English Proficiency, Vol. 3. (Illus.). 114p. (C). 1989. text ed. write for info. (*0-318-65772-4*) English Tutors.

Purcell, Theodore & Cavanagh, Gerald. Blacks in the Industrial World: Issues for the Manager. LC 74-184530. 1973. 22.95 (*0-02-925520-1*) Free Pr.

Purcell, Theodore F. Blue Collar Man: Patterns of Dual Allegiance in Industry. Stein, Leon, ed. LC 77-70524. (Work Ser.). (Illus.). 1977. reprint ed. lib. bdg. 34.95 (*0-405-10192-9*) Ayer.

Purcell, Theresa. Teaching Children Dance: Becoming a Master Teacher. LC 94-2170. (Illus.). 136p. 1994. pap. text ed. 14.00x (*0-87322-479-5*, BPUR0479) Human Kinetics.

Purcell, Trevor W. Banana Fallout: Class, Color, & Culture among West Indians in Costa Rica. (Afro-American Culture & Society Monograph Ser.: Vol. 12). 198p. (Orig.). (C). 1993. pap. text ed. 15.95 (*0-934934-37-1*) UCLA CAAS.

Purcell, Victor W. Malaya: Communist or Free? LC 75-30076. (Institute of Pacific Relations Ser.). reprint ed. 23.00 (*0-404-59553-7*) AMS Pr.

Purcell, W. R., Jr. Decision Graphs for Profit & Cash Flow Planning with an IBM PC. 256p. 1986. pap. text ed. write for info. (*0-07-050951-4*) McGraw.

— Understanding a Company's Finances: A Graphic Approach. 160p. 1993. pap. 9.95 (*0-395-65667-2*) HM.

Purcell, Wayne. Agricultural Futures & Options. 384p. (C). 1991. write for info. (*0-02-397011-1*) Macmillan.

— Agriculture Marketing: Systems, Coordination, Cash & Future Prices. (Illus.). 1979. teacher ed write for info. (*0-8359-0196-3*, Reston) P-H.

—Marketing Agricultural Commodities. Reynold, Ralph & Drummond, H. Evan, eds. (Farm Business Management Ser.). (Illus.). (Orig.). 1995. student ed, pap. text ed. write for info. (*0-86691-219-3*, FBM14601W) Deere & Co. Why Marketing is Important; Price Movement Over Time; The Deadly Micro-Macro Trap in Production Agriculture; Trace in Futures & Options; Basics in Managing Price Risk; Forward Pricing & Marketing Strategies for Crops; Forward Pricing & Marketing Strategies for Livestock; Analyzing the Markets; A Changing Marketplace; Marketing Skills are Critical. *Publisher Provided Annotation.*

—Marketing Agricultural Commodities. Reynold, Ralph & Drummond, H. Evan, eds. (Farm Business Management Ser.). (Illus.). 200p. (Orig.). (C). 1995. pap. text ed. 24.95 (*0-86691-217-7*, FBM14101B); teacher ed, pap. text ed. write for info. (*0-86691-218-5*, FBM14501T) Deere & Co. Why Marketing is Important; Price Movement Over Time; The Deadly Micro-Macro Trap in Production Agriculture; Trace in Futures & Options; Basics in Managing Price Risk; Forward Pricing & Marketing Strategies for Crops; Forward Pricing & Marketing Strategies for Livestock; Analyzing the Markets; A Changing Marketplace; Marketing Skills are Critical. *Publisher Provided Annotation.*

Purcell, William L. An Introduction to Asian Music Nineteen Sixty Six: Asia Society Guides. 44.00 (*0-685-43152-5*, 10753) Ayer.

Purcell, William P., et al. Strategy of Drug Design: A Guide to Biological Activity. LC 72-13240. 200p. reprint ed. pap. 57.00 (*0-8357-9983-2*, 2055156) Bks Demand.

Purchas, John. Death on the Isles of Scilly: The Grave in California Field. (C). 1989. 35.00 (*0-907566-79-0*, Pub. by Dyllansow Truran UK) St Mut.

Purchas, Samuel. Hakluytus Posthumus; or Purchas His Pilgrimes, 20 Vols, Set. LC 07-23966. reprint ed. 1,530.00 (*0-404-05180-4*) AMS Pr.

Purchase, Alan. The Office Technologies: Tomorrow's Tools for Automation Success. 94p. (Orig.). 1985. 21.95 (*0-916875-05-9*); pap. 14.95 (*0-916875-04-0*) Admin Mgmt.

Purchase, Edna, jt. auth. see Skinner, Joyce.

Purchase, Graham. Anarchism & Environmental Survival. 160p. (Orig.). 1994. reprint ed. pap. 9.95 (*0-9613289-8-3*) See Sharp Pr.

— My Journey with Aristotle to the Anarchrist Utopia. 128p. (Orig.). 1994. pap. 7.00 (*0-9622937-6-8*) III Pub.

Purchase, Rupert, ed. The Laboratory Environment. 270p. 1994. 89.95 (*0-85186-605-0*, R6605) CRC Pr.

— The Laboratory Environment. 270p. 1994. 89.95 (*0-85186-050-8*, R6605) CRC Pr.

Purchasing & Supply Research Committee Staff, prod. Cooperative Purchasing Guidelines. 46p. 1979. 6.00 (*0-910170-09-6*) Assn Sch Busn.

Purchon, R. D. & Kerkut, G. The Biology of the Mollusca. 2nd ed. LC 76-10804. (International Series of Monographs on Pure & Applied Mathematics: No. 57). 1977. 236.00 (*0-08-021028-7*, Pub. by Pergamon Repr UK) Franklin.

Purday, Richard, ed. Document Sets for the South in U. S. History. 256p. (C). 1991. write for info. (*0-669-27108-X*) Heath.

Purdie, ed. Hebbel: Herodes und Mariamne. (Bristol German Texts Ser.). (GER.). 12.95 (*0-631-01330-X*, Pub. by Brstl Class Pr UK) Focus Info Gr.

Purdie, Bob. Politics in the Street. 352p. 1990. pap. 19.95 (*0-85640-437-3*, Pub. by Blackstaff Pr IE) Dufour.

Purdie, Erica M., ed. Response to Love. (C). 1988. 35.00 (*0-7212-0825-8*, Pub. by Regency Press) St Mut.

Purdie, N., ed. see Brittain, H. G.

Purdie, P. W. & Noble, I. R., eds. Mountain Ecology in the Australian Region. 178p. (C). 1983. text ed. 75.00 (*0-909436-05-3*, Pub. by Surrey Beatty & Sons AT) St Mut.

Purdie, Susan. Comedy: The Mastery of Discourse. LC 92-95214. 186p. 1993. 45.00 (*0-8020-2980-9*); pap. 17.95 (*0-8020-7437-5*) U of Toronto Pr.

Purdom, C. B. The God-Man: The Life, Journeys & Work of Meher Baba with an Interpretation of His Silence & Spiritual Teaching. LC 72-175960. (Illus.). 464p. 1971. 20.00 (*0-913078-03-4*) Sheriar Pr.

— The Perfect Master. (Illus.). 330p. 1976. pap. 6.95 (*0-913078-24-7*) Sheriar Pr.

Purdom, Charles, jt. auth. see Schloss, Malcolm.

Purdom, Colin E. Genetics & Fish Breeding. LC 92-31147. 1992. write for info. (*0-442-31642-9*) Chapman & Hall.

Purdom, P. Walton, ed. Environmental Health. 2nd ed. LC 79-51672. 1980. text ed. 79.00 (*0-12-567860-6*) Acad Pr.

Purdom, Paul S. & Brown, Cynthia A. Analysis of Algorithms. 448p. (C). 1985. text ed. 52.00 (*0-03-072044-3*) SCP.

Purdon, Liam O. & Vitto, Cindy L., eds. The Rusted Hauberk: Feudal Ideals of Order & Their Decline. (Illus.). 352p. (C). 1994. lib. bdg. 44.95 (*0-8130-1281-3*); pap. text ed. 19.95 (*0-8130-1282-1*) U Press Fla.

Purdon, Nadina, jt. auth. see Hempstead, Andrew.

Purdue, Elizabeth, jt. auth. see Purdue, Howell.

Purdue, Howell & Purdue, Elizabeth. Patrick Cleburne. 499p. 1973. reprint ed. 35.00 (*0-942211-03-0*) Olde Soldier Bks.

Purdue, James R. & Styles, Bonnie W. Dynamics of Mammalian Distribution in the Holocene of Illinois. (Reports of Investigations Ser.: No. 41). 63p. (Orig.). 1986. pap. 5.00 (*0-89792-107-0*) Ill St Museum.

Purdue, James R., et al, eds. Beamers, Bobwhites, & Blue-Points: Tributes to the Career of Paul W. Parmalee. 436p. 1991. pap. 19.50 (*0-89792-134-8*) Ill St Museum.

Purdue, Joretta, ed. see Maynard, Edwin H.

Purdue, Michael. Planning Appeals: A Critique. (Studies in Law & Politics Ser.). 72p. 1991. pap. 20.00 (*0-335-09630-1*, Open Univ Pr) Taylor & Francis.

Purdue University, Thermophysical Properties Research Center Staff. Thermophysical Properties of High Temperature Solid Materials, Vols. 1-6. reprint ed. pap. write for info. (*0-318-63108-3*, 2056565) Bks Demand.

— Thermophysical Properties of Matter: Specific Heat - Metallic Elements & Alloys. LC 73-129616. (TPRC Data Ser.: Vol. 4). 814p. reprint ed. pap. 180.00 (*0-317-26282-3*, 2055697) Bks Demand.

— Thermophysical Properties of Matter: Specific Heat Nonmetallic Liquids & Gases, Vol. 6. LC 73-129616. 383p. reprint ed. pap. 109.20 (*0-317-27798-7*, 2055953) Bks Demand.

— Thermophysical Properties of Matter: The TPRC Data Series, Vol. 1: Thermal Conductivity; Metallic Elements & LC 73-129616. 1597p. reprint ed. pap. 180.00 (*0-317-28047-3*, 2055777) Bks Demand.

— Thermophysical Properties of Matter: The TPRC Data Series, Vol. 6 Supplement: Specific Heat: Nonmetallic Liqu. LC 73-129616. 169p. reprint ed. pap. 48.20 (*0-317-28042-2*, 2055778) Bks Demand.

— Thermophysical Properties of Matter: The TPRC Data Series, Vol 12: Thermal Expansion: Metallic Elements & Alloys. LC 73-129616. 1443p. reprint ed. pap. 180.00 (*0-317-07898-4*, 2022726) Bks Demand.

— Thermophysical Properties of Matter: Thermal Conductivity - Nonmetallic Liquids & Gases. LC 73-129616. (TPRC Data Ser.: Vol. 3). 707p. reprint ed. pap. 180.00 (*0-317-26375-7*, 2055696) Bks Demand.

— Thermophysical Properties Research Literature Retrieval Guide, Bk. 1. 2nd ed. Touloukian, Y. S. et al, eds. LC 60-14226. reprint ed. pap. 160.00 (*0-317-10668-6*, 2022724) Bks Demand.

— Thermophysical Properties Research Literature Retrieval Guide, Bk. 2. 2nd ed. Touloukian, Y. S. et al, eds. LC 60-14226. reprint ed. pap. 158.00 (*0-317-10669-4*) Bks Demand.

— Thermophysical Properties Research Literature Retrieval Guide, Bk. 3. 2nd ed. Touloukian, Y. S. et al, eds. LC 60-14226. reprint ed. pap. 160.00 (*0-317-10670-8*) Bks Demand.

Purdue University, Thermophysical Properties Research Center Staff & Touloukian, Y. S. Thermophysical Properties of Matter: Thermal Expansion-Nonmetallic Solids. LC 73-129616. (TPRC Data Ser.: Vol. 13). 1786p. reprint ed. pap. 180.00 (*0-317-26280-7*, 2055698) Bks Demand.

Purdue Workshop on Standardization of Industrial-Computer Languages, Glossary Committee. Dictionary of Industrial Digital Computer Terminology. LC 72-81778. 96p. reprint ed. pap. 27.40 (*0-317-08566-2*, 2051117) Bks Demand.

Purdum, Elizabeth, jt. ed. see Fernald, Edward A.

Purdum, Elizabeth D., ed. see Winsberg, Morton D.

***Purdum, Jack.** Accounting & Finance Developer's Guide with Visual BASIC. 1995. disk, pap. 39.99 (*0-672-30616-6*) Sams.

— First Book of Harvard Graphics. 1990. pap. 16.95 (*0-672-27310-1*, Bobbs) Macmillan.

— PC Magazine Guide to C Programming. (Programming Ser.). (Illus.). 498p. (Orig.). 1992. pap. 29.95 (*1-56276-069-6*) Ziff-Davis.

— Quick C Programming. 1990. pap. 29.95 (*0-672-22721-5*, Bobbs) Macmillan.

Purdum, Stan, ed. see Peacock, Larry J., et al.

***Purdy.** Eustace Chisholm & the Works. Date not set. per. 7.95 (*0-907040-33-0*, Pub. by Gay Mens Pr UK) InBook.

Purdy, A. C., jt. auth. see MacGregor, G. H.

Purdy, A. Jane. He Will Never Remember: Caring for the Victims of Child Abuse. Mueller, Phyllis, ed. LC 89-31362. 180p. (Orig.). 1989. pap. 9.95 (*0-932419-22-4*) Cherokee.

Purdy, A. T. Developments in Nonwoven Fabrics, Vol. 12, No. 4. 97p. (C). 1983. pap. text ed. 110.00 (*0-900739-62-2*, Pub. by Textile Institue UK) St Mut.

— Needle-Punching. 1986. 69.00 (*0-686-63775-5*) St Mut.

— Needle Punching. 63p. (C). 1980. pap. text ed. 70.00 (*0-900739-32-0*, Pub. by Textile Institue UK) St Mut.

Purdy, Alexander. The Reality of God: Thoughts on the Death of God Controversy. LC 67-23314. (Orig.). 1967. pap. 3.00 (*0-87574-154-1*) Pendle Hill.

Purdy, Andrew J. Master of the Courts. limited ed. LC 72-96446. (Illus.). 44p. 1973. 20.00 (*0-912292-31-8*) The Smith.

Purdy, Anthony. A Certain Difficulty of Being: Essays on the Quebec Novel. 200p. (C). 1990. text ed. 44.95 (*0-7735-0770-1*, Pub. by McGill CN) U of Toronto Pr.

Purdy, Barbara A. Florida's Prehistoric Stone Technology: A Study of the Flintworking Techniques of Early Florida Stone Implement Makers. LC 80-24726. (Illus.). xvi, 165p. 1981. 32.95 (*0-8130-0697-X*) U Press Fla.

Purdy, Barbara A., ed. Wet Site Archaeology. (Illus.). 450p. 1990. text ed. 49.95 (*0-936923-07-5*, Q); pap. text ed. 43.95 (*0-936923-08-3*) CRC Pr.

Purdy, Carol. Iva Dunnit & the Big Wind. LC 84-17441. (Pied Piper Bks.). 32p. (J). (ps-3). 1988. pap. 4.99 (*0-8037-0493-3*) Dial Bks Young.

— Iva Dunnit & the Big Wind. (J). (ps-3). 1994. pap. 4.99 (*0-14-054651-0*) Dial Bks Young.

— Least of All. LC 86-12613. (Illus.). 32p. (J). (gr. 1-4). 1987. text ed. 12.95 (*0-689-50404-7*, McElderry) S&S Childrens.

— Least of All. LC 92-19964. (Illus.). 32p. (J). (gr. k-3). 1993. pap. 3.95 (*0-689-71681-8*, Aladdin Paperbacks) S&S Childrens.

— Mrs. Merriwether's Musical Cat. LC 92-43934. (Illus.). 32p. (J). (ps-3). 1994. lib. bdg. 15.95 (*0-399-22543-9*, Putnam) Putnam Pub Group.

Purdy, D. L., jt. ed. see Laidler, D.

Purdy, Dave, jt. auth. see Prior, Mike.

Purdy, David. The Political Economy of Basic Income. (Illus.). 200p. 1996. write for info. (*0-12-567870-3*) Acad Pr.

***Purdy, Derek.** Advanced Mountain Biking. (Illus.). 160p. 1995. pap. 17.95 (*1-85688-046-X*) Lyons & Burford.

***Purdy, Don.** AeroCrafter: Homebuilt Aircraft Sourcebook. 3rd ed. 400p. 1995. pap. 25.00 (*0-9636409-2-5*) BAI Pub.

Purdy, Don, ed. Aerocrafter: Homebuilt Aircraft Sourcebook. 200p. 1993. pap. 12.95 (*0-9636409-0-9*) BAI Pub.

— AeroCrafter: Homebuilt Aircraft Sourcebook. 2nd ed. (Illus.). 300p. 1994. pap. 20.00 (*0-9636409-1-7*) BAI Pub.

Purdy, Dwight H. Biblical Echo & Allusion in the Poetry of W. B. Yeats: Poetics & the Art of God. LC 93-9005. Date not set. write for info. (*0-8387-5254-3*) Bucknell U Pr.

— Joseph Conrad's Bible. LC 83-40331. 160p. 1984. 26.95 (*0-8061-1876-8*) U of Okla Pr.

Purdy, Edward G. & Bertram, George T. Carbonate Concepts from the Maldives, Indian Ocean. (Studies in Geology: No. 34). (Illus.). 56p. (Orig.). 1993. pap. 27.00 (*0-89181-042-0*) AAPG.

Purdy, J. David. Little People, Big Choices. LC 90-86212. 218p. 1991. 7.99 (*0-87509-442-2*) Chr Pubns.

Purdy, J. M., jt. auth. see Edwards, R. G.

Purdy, James. Brooklyn Branding Parlors. limited ed. Gosciak, Josh & Kenny, Maurice, eds. LC 85-18994. (Illus.). 24p. (Orig.). (C). 1986. pap. 10.00 (*0-936556-13-7*) Contact Two.

— Cabot Wright Begins. 228p. 1986. pap. 4.50 (*0-88184-196-X*) Carroll & Graf.

— The Candles of Your Eyes. 160p. (Orig.). 1991. pap. 7.95 (*0-87286-256-9*) City Lights.

— Color of Darkness. LC 74-26739. 175p. 1975. reprint ed. text ed. 49.75 (*0-8371-7874-6*, PUCD, Greenwood Pr) Greenwood.

— Garments the Living Wear. 160p. (Orig.). 1989. 16.95 (*0-87286-240-2*); pap. 7.95 (*0-87286-239-9*) City Lights.

— House of the Solitary Maggot. 360p. 1986. 26.00 (*0-7206-0662-4*, Pub. by P Owen Ltd UK) Dufour.

An Asterisk (*) at the beginning of an entry indicates that the title is appearing in BIP for the first time.

— In a Shallow Grave. 160p. 1988. reprint ed. pap. 8.95 (*0-87286-234-8*) City Lights.
— Malcolm. LC 94-28945. 1995. 12.99 (*1-85242-368-4*) Serpents Tail.
— Malcolm. adapted ed. 1966. pap. 4.75 (*0-8222-0719-2*) Dramatists Play.
— Mourners Below. 295p. 1984. 28.00 (*0-7206-0621-7*, Pub. by P Owen Ltd UK) Dufour.
— Out with the Stars. 192p. 1993. pap. 9.95 (*0-87286-284-4*) City Lights.
— Out with the Stars. 192p. 1993. 30.00 (*0-7206-0861-9*, Pub. by P Owen Ltd UK) Dufour.
— Sixty-Three: Dream Palace, Selected Stories, 1956-1987. LC 91-27119. 356p. (Orig.). 1991. pap. 15.00 (*0-87685-844-2*) Black Sparrow.
***Purdy, James & Emami, Bahman, eds.** 3D Radiation Treatment Planning & Conformal Therapy. (C). Date not set. pap. text ed. write for info. (*0-944838-51-0*) Med Physics Pub.
— 3D Radiation Treatment Planning & Conformal Therapy. 1995. write for info. (*0-614-03714-X*) Med Physics Pub.
Purdy, James A., ed. Advances in Radiation Oncology Physics: Dosimetry, Treatment Planning, & Brachytherapy. LC 92-81653. (American Association of Physicists in Medicine Symposium Ser.: No. 19). 1099p. 1993. 75.00 (*1-56396-054-0*) Am Inst Physics.
Purdy, James A., jt. ed. see Smith, Alfred R.
Purdy, Jim, jt. auth. see Roffman, Peter.
Purdy, John C. God with a Human Face. LC 92-27788. 128p. (Orig.). 1993. pap. 9.99 (*0-664-25173-0*) Westminster John Knox.
— Parables at Work. LC 84-17323. 132p. 1986. pap. 8.99 (*0-664-24640-0*, Westminster) Westminster John Knox.
Purdy, John L. Word Ways: The Novels of D'Arcy McNickle. LC 89-27106. 167p. 1990. 27.95 (*0-8165-1157-8*) U of Ariz Pr.
Purdy, Laura M. In Their Best Interest? The Case Against Equal Rights for Children. LC 91-55550. 272p. 1992. 34.95 (*0-8014-2662-6*); pap. 13.95 (*0-8014-9956-9*) Cornell U Pr.
Purdy, Laura M., jt. ed. see Holmes, Helen B.
Purdy, Linda, jt. auth. see Woodard, James.
Purdy, Martin. Churches & Chapels: A Design & Development Guide. (Illus.). 128p. 1991. 54.95 (*0-7506-1222-3*) Buttrwrth-Heinemann.
Purdy, Michael, jt. ed. see Borisoff, Deborah.
***Purdy, Ralph E. & Boucek, Mark Jr.** Handbook of Cardiac Drugs. 2nd ed. LC 94-22278. 1994. 29.95 (*0-316-72246-4*, Little Med Div) Little.
Purdy, Rich, jt. ed. see Poston, Ted M.
Purdy, Richard L., ed. see Hardy, Thomas.
Purdy, Rob R. Fugitives' Reunion: Conversations at Vanderbilt, May 3-5, 1956. LC 59-9772. (Vanderbilt Studies in the Humanities: No. 3). 226p. reprint ed. pap. 64.50 (*0-8357-3267-3*, 2039488) Bks Demand.
Purdy, Scott. Time Management for Teachers: Essential Tips & Techniques. (Orig.). (C). Date not set. pap. 10.00 (*0-9641366-3-5*) Write Time.
Purdy, Susan G. As Easy As Pie. (Illus.). 448p. 1990. reprint ed. pap. 14.95 (*0-02-036080-0*, Collier S&S) S&S Trade.
— Have Your Cake & Eat It, Too: Two Hundred Luscious, Low-Fat Cakes, Pies, Cookies, Puddings, & Other Desserts You Thought You Could Never Eat Again. LC 93-1507. 1993. 25.00 (*0-688-11110-6*) Morrow.
— A Piece of Cake. LC 93-16077. (Illus.). 512p. 1993. pap. 15.00 (*0-02-036085-1*) Macmillan.
— A Piece of Cake. 512p. 1989. text ed. 24.95 (*0-689-11766-3*, Atheneum S&S) S&S Trade.
Purdy, Tim I. Honey Lake Justice: The Never Sweats of the 1860s. (Illus.). 112p. 1993. pap. 9.95 (*0-938373-08-0*) Lahontan Images.
— Purdy's Eagle Lake. (Illus.). 136p. 1988. 12.95 (*0-938373-04-8*) Lahontan Images.
— Sacred Heart Parish. (Illus.). 128p. 1995. pap. 10.00 (*0-938373-16-1*) Lahontan Images.
Purdy, Virginia C. Portrait of a Know-Nothing Legislature: The Massachusetts General Court of 1855. (Nineteenth Century American Political & Social History Ser.). 298p. 1989. reprint ed. 20.00 (*0-8240-4073-2*) Garland.
Purdy, William M. An Outline of the History of the Flaming Gorge Area. (Upper Colorado Ser.: No. 1). reprint ed. 20.00 (*0-404-60637-7*) AMS Pr.
Pure Mathematics Staff. Applications of Categorical Algebra. Heller, A., ed. LC 72-89866. (Proceedings of Symposia in Pure Mathematics Ser., Humboldt State University, Arcata, CA, July 29-August 16, 1974: Vol. 17). 231p. 1970. 45.00 (*0-8218-1417-6*, PSPUM-17) Am Math.
Pure Mathematics Symposium Staff. Algebraic Geometry - Arcata 1974. Hartshorne, Robin, ed. LC 75-9530. (Proceedings of Symposia in Pure Mathematics Ser., Humboldt State University, Arcata, CA, July 29-August 16, 1974: Vol. 29). 642p. 1982. 62.00 (*0-8218-1429-X*, PSPUM-29) Am Math.
— Algebraic Groups & Discontinous Subgroups: Proceedings. Borel, A. & Mostow, G. D., eds. LC 66-18581. (Proceedings of Symposia in Pure Mathematics Ser., Humboldt State University, Arcata, CA, July 29-August 16, 1974: Vol. 9). 426p. 1986. reprint ed. pap. 49.00 (*0-8218-1409-5*, PSPUM-9) Am Math.
— Algebraic Topology, Vol. 22. Liulevicius, Arunas, ed. LC 72-167684. (Proceedings of Symposia in Pure Mathematics Ser., Humboldt State University, Arcata, CA, July 29-August 16, 1974). 294p. 1971. text ed. 55.00 (*0-8218-1422-2*, PSPUM-22) Am Math.
— Analytic Number Theory. Diamond, H. G., ed. LC 72-10198. (Proceedings of Symposia in Pure Mathematics Ser., Humboldt State University, Arcata, CA, July 29-August 16, 1974: Vol. 24). 344p. 1990. 67.00 (*0-8218-1424-9*, PSPUM-24) Am Math.
— Axiomatic Set Theory, 2 Vols, Set. LC 78-125172. (Proceedings of the Symposia in Pure Mathematics Ser.: Vol. 13). 696p. 114.00 (*0-8218-1413-3*, PSPUM-13) Am Math.
— Axiomatic Set Theory, 2 Vols, Vol. 1. LC 78-125172. (Proceedings of the Symposia in Pure Mathematics Ser.: Vol. 13). 474p. 1967. 52.00 (*0-8218-0245-3*, PSPUM-13.1) Am Math.
— Axiomatic Set Theory, 2 Vols, Vol. 2. LC 78-125172. (Proceedings of the Symposia in Pure Mathematics Ser.: Vol. 13). 222p. 1974. 73.00 (*0-8218-0246-1*, PSPUM-13.2) Am Math.
— Combinatorics. Motzkin, T. S., ed. LC 74-153879. (Proceedings of Symposia in Pure Mathematics Ser., Humboldt State University, Arcata, CA, July 29-August 16, 1974: Vol. 19). 255p. 1971. 59.00 (*0-8218-1419-2*, PSPUM-19) Am Math.
— Differential Geometry, 2 pts. Chern, S. S. & Osserman, R., eds. LC 75-6593. (Proceedings of Symposia in Pure Mathematics Ser., Humboldt State University, Arcata, CA, July 29-August 16, 1974: Vol. 27). 451p. 1982. reprint ed. Pt. 1, 451 p. pap. 66.00 (*0-8218-0247-X*, PSPUM-27.1); reprint ed. Pt. 2, 443 p. pap. 73.00 (*0-8218-0248-8*, PSPUM-27.2) Am Math.
— Differential Geometry. Allendoerfer, C. B., ed. LC 50-1183. (Proceedings of Symposia in Pure Mathematics Ser., Humboldt State University, Arcata, CA, July 29-August 16, 1974: Vol. 3). 200p. 1983. reprint ed. 36.00 (*0-8218-1403-6*, PSPUM-3) Am Math.
— Differential Geometry, 2 pts., Set. Chern, S. S. & Osserman, R., eds. LC 75-6593. (Proceedings of Symposia in Pure Mathematics Ser., Humboldt State University, Arcata, CA, July 29-August 16, 1974: Vol. 27). 894p. 1982. reprint ed. pap. 113.00 (*0-8218-1427-3*, PSPUM-27) Am Math.
— Entire Functions & Related Parts of Analysis. Chern, S. S. et al, eds. LC 68-10458. (Proceedings of Symposia in Pure Mathematics Ser., Humboldt State University, Arcata, CA, July 29-August 16, 1974: Vol. 11). 554p. 1987. reprint ed. 52.00 (*0-8218-1411-7*, PSPUM-11) Am Math.
— Finite Groups. Albert, A. A. & Kaplansky, I., eds. LC 50-1183. (Proceedings of Symposia in Pure Mathematics Ser., Humboldt State University, Arcata, CA, July 29-August 16, 1974: Vol. 1). 110p. 1979. reprint ed. pap. 32.00 (*0-8218-1401-X*, PSPUM-1) Am Math.
— Harmonic Analysis on Homogeneous Spaces: Proceedings. Moore, Calvin C., ed. LC 73-10456. (Proceedings of Symposia in Pure Mathematics Ser., Humboldt State University, Arcata, CA, July 29-August 16, 1974: Vol. 26). 467p. 1978. reprint ed. pap. 58.00 (*0-8218-1426-5*, PSPUM-26) Am Math.
— Institute on Finite Groups, 1960. Hall, M., Jr., ed. LC 62-10812. (Proceedings of Symposia in Pure Mathematics Ser., Humboldt State University, Arcata, CA, July 29-August 16, 1974: Vol. 6). 114p. 1979. reprint ed. pap. 31.00 (*0-8218-1406-0*, PSPUM-6) Am Math.
— Lattice Theory. Dilworth, R. P., ed. LC 50-1183. (Proceedings of Symposia in Pure Mathematics Ser., Humboldt State University, Arcata, CA, July 29-August 16, 1974: Vol. 2). 208p. 1961. 33.00 (*0-8218-1402-8*, PSPUM-2) Am Math.
— Mathematical Developments Arising from the Hilbert Problems: Proceedings, 2 pts, Set. LC 76-20437. (Proceedings of Symposia in Pure Mathematics Ser., Humboldt State University, Arcata, CA, July 29-August 16, 1974: Vol. 28). 628p. 1979. reprint ed. pap. 45.00 (*0-8218-1428-1*, PSPUM-28) Am Math.
— Number Theory. LeVeque, W. J. & Straus, E. G., eds. LC 70-78057. (Proceedings of Symposia in Pure Mathematics Ser., Humboldt State University, Arcata, CA, July 29-August 16, 1974). 98p. 1989. reprint ed. pap. 34.00 (*0-8218-1412-5*, PSPUM-12) Am Math.
— Number Theory Institute, 1969: Proceedings of Symposia in Pure Mathematics, 20th, Stony Brook, N. Y., 1969, Vol. 20. Lewis, Donald J., ed. LC 76-125938. 451p. 1971. 60.00 (*0-8218-1420-6*, PSPUM-20) Am Math.
— Partial Differential Equations. Spencer, D. C., ed. LC 72-4071. (Proceedings of Symposia in Pure Mathematics Ser., Humboldt State University, Arcata, CA, July 29-August 16, 1974: Vol. 23). 505p. 1977. reprint ed. pap. 61.00 (*0-8218-1423-0*, PSPUM-23) Am Math.
— Partial Differential Equations. Morrey, C. B., Jr., ed. LC 50-1183. (Proceedings of Symposia in Pure Mathematics Ser., Humboldt State University, Arcata, CA, July 29-August 16, 1974: Vol.4). 169p. 1992. reprint ed. pap. 38.00 (*0-8218-1404-4*, PSPUM-4) Am Math.
— Probability: Proceedings, Vol. 31. Doob, J. L., ed. LC 77-2017. 169p. 1981. reprint ed. pap. 45.00 (*0-8218-1431-1*, PSPUM 31) Am Math.
— Recursive Function Theory. Dekker, J., ed. LC 50-1183. (Proceedings of Symposia in Pure Mathematics Ser., Humboldt State University, Arcata, CA, July 29-August 16, 1974: Vol. 5). 247p. 1979. reprint ed. pap. 42.00 (*0-8218-1405-2*, PSPUM-5) Am Math.
— Singular Integrals: Proceedings. Calderon, A. P., ed. LC 67-16553. (Proceedings of Symposia in Pure Mathematics Ser., Humboldt State University, Arcata, CA, July 29-August 16, 1974: Vol. 10). 375p. 1982. reprint ed. pap. 51.00 (*0-8218-1410-9*, PSPUM-10) Am Math.
— Tarski Symposium: Proceedings of the Symposium in Pure Mathematics, University of California, Berkeley, June 1971. Henkin, L., ed. LC 74-8666. (Proceedings of Symposia in Pure Mathematics Ser., Humboldt State University, Arcata, CA, July 29-August 16, 1974: Vol. 25). 498p. 1979. reprint ed. pap. 61.00 (*0-8218-1425-7*, PSPUM-25) Am Math.
— Theory of Numbers. Whiteman, A. L., ed. LC 65-17382. (Proceedings of Symposia in Pure Mathematics Ser., Humboldt State University, Arcata, CA, July 29-August 16, 1974: Vol. 8). 216p. 1979. reprint ed. pap. 38.00 (*0-8218-1408-7*, PSPUM-8) Am Math.
Purefoy, George W. History of the Sandy Creek Baptist Association, from Its Organization in A. D. 1758 to 1858. Gaustad, Edwin S., ed. LC 79-52604. (Baptist Tradition Ser.). (Illus.). 1980. reprint ed. lib. bdg. 29.95 (*0-405-12469-4*) Ayer.
Puregger, Marjorie. Mr. Chairman: A Guide to Meeting Procedure & Forms of Address. 5th ed. 1989. pap. text ed. 14.95 (*0-7022-1769-7*, Pub. by Univ Queensland Pr AT) Intl Spec Bk.
Puretz, Susan L., jt. auth. see Haas, Adelaide.
Purgathofer, W. & Schonhut, J., eds. Advances in Computer Graphics 5. (Eurographic Seminars Ser.). (Illus.). viii, 221p. 1989. 89.00 (*0-387-51420-1*, 3290) Spr-Verlag.
Purgraski. Sorting Life Out. 36p. 1978. student ed write for info. (*0-318-51257-2*); 24.00 (*0-930004-00-0*) C E M Comp.
Purgraski, Carolyn B., et al. Sorting Out Money Values & Student Packet of Ready-to-Be-Duplicated Worksheets. LC 59-4503. (Sorting Life Out Ser.). 292p. (C). 1981. teacher ed 25.00 (*0-930004-02-7*); P. 68. student ed write for info. (*0-318-51258-0*) C E M Comp.
Puri, A, ed. see Allbouy, Serge.
Puri, Asha, tr. see Sorman, Guy.
***Puri, B. B.** Mass Scale Housing for Hot Climate. (C). 1993. 18.00x (*81-204-0797-0*, Pub. by Oxford IBH II) S Asia.
Puri, B. N. Buddhism in Central Asia. (C). 1993. 25.00x (*81-208-0372-8*, Pub. by Motilal Banarsidass II) S Asia.
— The Changing Horizon. 249p. (C). 1986. 125.00 (*81-85009-19-8*, Pub. by Print Hse II) St Mut.
— The Gupta Administration. 1990. 18.50 (*81-7018-598-X*, Pub. by BR Pub II) S Asia.
— India in the Time of Patanjali. 1990. 34.00 (*0-685-40066-2*, Pub. by Munshiram Manoharial II) S Asia.
Puri, Balraj. Jammu & Kasmir: Triumph & Tragedy of Indian Federalisation. 280p. 1981. 33.95 (*0-940500-47-7*, Pub. by Sterling II) Asia Bk Corp.
Puri, Basant & Tyrer, Peter. Sciences Basic to Psychiatry. (Illus.). 334p. (Orig.). 1992. pap. text ed. 45.00 (*0-443-04478-3*) Churchill.
Puri, Basant K. & Sklar, John. Revision for MRCPsych, Pt. 1. 232p. 1990. pap. text ed. 28.00 (*0-443-04331-0*) Churchill.
Puri, Bhaskar, jt. auth. see Mathias, Chuck.
Puri, G. S., et al. Forest Ecology, Vol. 1. (C). 1985. 31.00 (*0-8364-2433-6*, Pub. by Oxford IBH II) S Asia.
— Forest Ecology, Vol. 2. (C). 1988. 50.00 (*81-204-0364-9*, Pub. by Oxford IBH II) S Asia.
Puri, Geeta. Bharatiya Jana Sangh: Organization & Ideology. 292p. 1980. 24.95 (*0-940500-26-4*) Asia Bk Corp.
Puri, Harish. Ghadar Movement: Ideology, Organisation & Strategy. 1984. 18.50 (*0-8364-1113-7*, Pub. by Nanak Dev Univ IA) S Asia.
Puri, Ishwar C. Beyond Logic & Reason. Ingram, Leonard, ed. 59p. 1983. pap. 3.00 (*0-937067-00-8*) Insti Study Aware.
— Go Within. Scott, Edward D., ed. 177p. (Orig.). 1986. pap. 6.00 (*0-937067-07-5*) Insti Study Aware.
— The Healing Arts. Crothers, Marta, ed. 37p. (Orig.). 1988. pap. 3.00 (*0-937067-10-5*) Insti Study Aware.
— Human Consciousness: The Key to Higher Knowledge. Ingram, Leonard, ed. 84p. (Orig.). 1983. pap. 5.00 (*0-937067-02-4*) Insti Study Aware.
— Journey to Totality. Scott, Edward D., ed. 121p. (Orig.). 1985. pap. 6.00 (*0-937067-05-9*) Insti Study Aware.
— Know Thyself. Ingram, Leonard, ed. 66p. 1983. pap. 3.00 (*0-937067-01-6*) Insti Study Aware.
— New Age-Old Path. Scott, Edward D., ed. 54p. (Orig.). 1985. pap. 3.00 (*0-937067-04-0*) Insti Study Aware.
— On Love. Scott, Edward D., ed. 28p. (Orig.). 1984. pap. 2.00 (*0-937067-03-2*) Insti Study Aware.
— Spirituality & Total Health. Scott, Edward D., ed. 29p. (Orig.). 1986. pap. 2.00 (*0-937067-08-3*) Insti Study Aware.
Puri, Ishwar K. Environmental Implications of Combustion Processes. 1993. 79.95 (*0-8493-4423-9*) CRC Pr.
Puri, M. L., jt. ed. see Vilaplana, J. P.
Puri, Madan L. & Sen, Pranab K. Nonparametric Methods in Multivariate Analysis. LC 90-19772. 456p. (C). 1993. reprint ed. lib. bdg. 74.50 (*0-89464-551-X*) Krieger.
Puri, Madan L., et al, eds. Mathematical Statistics & Probability Theory: Theoretical Aspects, Vol. A. (C). 1987. lib. bdg. 123.00 (*90-277-2580-2*) Kluwer Ac.
— New Perspectives in Theoretical & Applied Statistics. 544p. 1987. text ed. 133.00 (*0-471-84800-X*) Wiley.
Puri, Madan Lal, ed. see International Symposium on Nonparametric Techniques in Statistical Inference (1969: Indiana University) Staff.
Puri, Mohinder, ed. see Singer, Hans W.
Puri, P., ed. Congenital Diaphragmatic Hernia. (Modern Problems in Pediatrics Ser.: Vol. 24). (Illus.). 164p. 1989. 96.00 (*3-8055-4807-9*) S Karger.
— Surgery & Support of the Premature Infant. (Modern Problems in Pediatrics Ser.: Vol. 23). (Illus.). x, 210p. 1985. 130.50 (*3-8055-4073-6*) S Karger.
Puri, P., jt. ed. see Hoey, H.
***Puri, Prem, ed.** Operative Newborn Surgery. LC 94-49188. 700p. 1995. write for info. (*0-7506-1595-8*, Focal) Buttrwrth-Heinemann.
Puri, R., jt. auth. see Aggarwal, B. B.
Puri, Rakshat. Nineteen Poems. (Writers Workshop Redbird Ser.). (C). 1975. 8.00 (*0-89253-521-0*); pap. text ed. 4.80 (*0-88253-724-5*) Ind-US Inc.
— Poems. 8.00 (*0-89253-718-3*); 4.80 (*0-89253-719-1*) Ind-US Inc.
— Year Like a Fuse. (Writers Workshop Redbird Ser.). 28p. 1978. 8.00 (*0-86578-273-3*); 4.00 (*0-86578-274-1*) Ind-US Inc.
Puri, Rashmi-Sudha. Gandhi on War & Peace. LC 86-20489. 259p. 1986. text ed. 59.95 (*0-275-92303-7*, C2303, Praeger Pubs) Greenwood.
Puri, S. & Khosla, P. K. Nursery Technology for Agroforestry: Applications in Arid & Semi-arid Regions. (Winrock Ser.). 392p. (C). 1993. text ed. 62.00 (*1-881570-11-8*) Intl Sci Pub.
Puri, Sunita. Advent of Sikh Religion: A Socio-Political Perspective. 271p. 1993. 38.50 (*81-215-0572-0*, Pub. by Munshiram Manoharial II) S Asia.
Puri, Vijay, jt. auth. see Prakash, Shamsher.
Puri, Vishnu. Bhakti Ratnavali: An Anthology from the Bhagavata. Bhagavatam, tr. 256p. 1980. 5.95 (*0-87481-499-5*, Pub. by Ramakrishna Math II) Vedanta Pr.
Puri, Yogesh. Party Politics in the Nehru Era: (A Study of Congress in Delhi) (C). 1993. 28.50 (*81-85135-72-X*, National Bk Ctr) S Asia.
Puricelli, Luigi, jt. auth. see Cristini, Ermanno.
Purich, Daniel L., ed. Contemporary Enzyme Kinetics & Mechanisms. LC 82-16265. 1983. text ed. 80.00 (*0-12-568050-3*) Acad Pr.
***Purich, Daniel L., et al, eds.** Methods in Enzymology Vol. 249, Pt. D: Enzyme Kinetics & Mechanism, Pt. D. (Illus.). 662p. 1995. boxed 89.00 (*0-12-182150-1*) Acad Pr.
Purificacion Zabia Lasala, Maria, ed. Text & Concordance of MS1-17: Biblioteca Colombina, Tesoro de los Remedios. (Medieval Spanish Medical Texts Ser.: No. 22). 6p. (SPA.). 1987. 10.00 (*0-940639-20-3*) Hispanic Seminary.
Purificacion Zabia, Maria, ed. Regimiento Contra la Peste, Fernando Alvarez, I-51: Biblioteca Nacional de Madrid. (Medieval Spanish Medical Texts Ser.: No. 18). 6p. (SPA.). 1987. fiche 10.00 (*0-940639-14-9*) Hispanic Seminary.
— Tratado Nuevo, I-51: Alvarez Chanca, Biblioteca Nacional, Madrid. (Medieval Spanish Medical Texts Ser.: No. 19). 6p. (SPA.). 1987. 10.00 (*0-940639-15-7*) Hispanic Seminary.
— Tratado Util. Licenciado Fores, I-51: Biblioteca Nacional de Madrid. (Medieval Spanish Medical Texts Ser.: No. 17). 6p. (SPA.). 1987. 10.00 (*0-940639-13-0*) Hispanic Seminary.
Purificacion Zabia, Maria, ed. see De Taranto, Vasco.
Purinton, Edward. Philosophy of Fasting. 140p. 1984. reprint ed. pap. text ed. 15.00 (*0-87556-382-1*) Saifer.
Purinton, Edward E. The Philosophy of Fasting. 130p. 1906. reprint ed. spiral bd. 6.60 (*0-7873-0686-X*) Mokelumne.
Purinton, Edward E. & Day, Chet. Twenty Rules for Fasting: An Excerpt from the Philosophy of Fasting. 26p. 1993. pap. 8.50 (*1-885194-02-1*) Hlth & Beyond.
Purinton, Marjean D. Romantic Ideology Unmasked: The Mentally Constructed Tyranies in Dramas of William Wordsworth, Lord Byron, Percy Shelley, & Joanna Baillie. LC 93-41730. 1994. write for info. (*0-87413-499-4*) U Delaware Pr.
Purintun, Ann-E., jt. ed. see Kraft, Robert A.
Puritt, Paul, jt. auth. see Moore, Sally F.
Purj. 199 Things to Do with a Politician. Jackson, Mike et al, eds. (Illus.). 168p. (Orig.). 1994. pap. 5.95 (*1-56245-088-3*) Great Quotations.
Purkait, B. R. Indian Renaissance & Education. (C). 1992. 18.00 (*0-8364-2770-X*, Pub. by Firma KLM) S Asia.
Purkait, Biswa R. Administration of Primary Education under Montford Reforms & Its Impact on West Bengal. LC 84-902647. 1985. 14.50 (*0-8364-1273-7*, Pub. by Mukhopadhyaya II) S Asia.
Purkart, Josef, ed. see Boncompagno da Signa.
Purkayastha, jt. ed. see Daniel.
Purkayastha, R. P. & Chandra, Aindrila. Manual of Indian Edible Mushrooms. (International Bioscience Monographs: No. 16). 267p. 1985. 37.00 (*1-55528-070-6*, Messers Today & Tomorrow) Scholarly Pubns.
Purkayastha, R. P. & Chendra, Anidrila. Manual of Indian Edible Mushrooms. Jain, R. K., ed. (International Bioscience Monographs: Vol. 16). (Illus.). xvi, 267p. (C). 1985. lib. bdg. 37.00 (*1-55528-001-3*, Messers Today & Tomorrow) Scholarly Pubns.
Purkey, Ruth A. The Haunted Carousel. (Illus.). 22p. (Orig.). 1982. pap. 2.50 (*0-88680-080-3*) I E Clark.
Purkey, William & Stanley, Paula. Invitational Teaching: A Guide for Teaching, Learning, & Living. 64p. 1991. 10.95 (*0-8106-3049-4*) NEA.
Purkey, William W. & Novak, John M. Education: By Invitation Only. LC 88-60074. (Fastback Ser.: No. 268). 50p. (Orig.). 1988. pap. 1.25 (*0-87367-268-2*) Phi Delta Kappa.
— Inviting School Success: A Self-Concept Approach to Teaching & Learning. 2nd ed. 159p. (C). 1984. pap. 21.95 (*0-534-02891-8*) Intl Thomson.
***Purkey, William W. & Schmidt, John J.** Invitational Counseling: A Self-Concept Approach to Professional Practice. LC 95-8766. 1996. pap. 24.95 (*0-534-33902-6*) Brooks-Cole.
— Invitational Learning for Counseling & Development. 136p. 1990. pap. 16.95 (*1-56109-002-6*) ERIC Clearinghouse.
— The Inviting Relationship: An Expanded Perspective for Professional Counseling. (Illus.). 192p. (C). 1987. pap. text ed. 25.00 (*0-13-505538-5*) P-H.
Purkey, William W. & Stanley, Paula H. The Inviting School Treasury: 1001 Ways to Invite Student Success. LC 93-34724. 1995. 35.00x (*0-590-49717-0*, 210p87 1994) Scholastic Inc.

P Q

Purkey, William W. & Strahan, David B. Positive Discipline: A Pocketful of Ideas. 50p. 1986. 9.00 (*1-56090-031-8*) Natl Middle Schl.

Purkhardt, S. Caroline. Transforming Social Representations: A Social Psychology of Common Sense & Science. LC 92-47076. 224p. 1993. 65.00 (*0-415-07960-8*, B0863, Routledge NY) Routledge.

***Purkis, Christine.** Peta's Pence. (YA). 1994. pap. 6.99 (*0-7043-4923-X*) Interlink Pub.

Purkiser, W. T. Beacon Bible Expositions Vol. 11: Hebrews, James, Peter. Greathouse, William M. & Taylor, Willard H., eds. 232p. 1974. 12.50 (*0-8341-0322-2*) Beacon Hill.

— Called unto Holiness, Vol. 2. 368p. 1983. 19.95 (*0-8341-0868-2*) Beacon Hill.

— Exploring Christian Holiness, Vol. 1: The Biblical Foundations, 3 Vols. (Exploring Christian Holiness Ser.). 280p. 1983. 14.95 (*0-8341-0843-7*) Beacon Hill.

— The Lordship of Jesus. 70p. (Orig.). 1986. pap. 3.50 (*0-8341-1135-7*) Beacon Hill.

— A Primer on Prayer. (Christian Living Ser.). 48p. (Orig.). 1987. pap. 2.50 (*0-8341-1191-8*) Beacon Hill.

***Purkiss, Diane, ed.** Renaissance Women: The Plays for Elizabeth Carry & The Poems of Aemilia Lanyer. (Women's Classics Ser.). 256p. 1994. 37.50 (*1-85196-029-5*, Pub. by Pickering & Chatto UK) Ashgate Pub Co.

Purkiss, Dianne, jt. ed. see Brant, Clare.

***Purkitt, Helen, ed.** Annual Editions: World Politics, 95-96. 16th rev. ed. (Illus.). 288p. (C). 1995. pap. text ed. 12. 95x (*1-56134-376-5*) Dushkin Pub.

Purks, James. Habitat for Humanity: Building Around the World. Kroitzsh, Gregory, ed. (Illus.). 96p. (Orig.). 1991. pap. 18.95 (*0-9627262-3-0*) Five Corners.

Purl, Benjamin F. Republic of Texas, Second Class Headrights: March 2, 1836-October 1, 1837. 261p. 1994. reprint ed. lib. bdg. 32.50 (*0-8328-3873-X*) Higginson Bk Co.

Purma. Balanced Yoga. 1992. pap. 13.95 (*1-85230-325-5*) Element MA.

Purna. The Truth Will Set You Free. 160p. 1990. pap. 13.95 (*1-85230-015-9*) Element MA.

Purnell. Rhyme Time Books: Humpty Dumpty. (J). 1989. 1.98 (*0-671-09369-X*) S&S Trade.

Purnell, Geoff. The Motorcycle Restores Workshop Manual. (Illus.). 160p. 1992. 24.95 (*1-85260-393-3*) Haynes Pubns.

Purnell, Herbert C., ed. Miao & Yao Linguistic Studies: Selected Articles in Chinese. LC 73-155571. (Cornell University, Southeast Asia Program, Data Paper Ser.: No. 88). 306p. reprint ed. pap. 87.30 (*0-8357-3677-6*, 2036401) Bks Demand.

Purnell, Herbert C., Jr., ed. see Lombard, Sylvia J.

***Purnell, Larry.** Conversational Medical Spanish. 240p. (C). 1995. pap. text ed. 27.95 (*0-7872-0740-3*) Kendall-Hunt.

Purnell, Larry D. Clinical Spanish for Medical Professionals. 224p. 1993. spiral bd. 16.95 (*0-8403-8346-0*) Kendall-Hunt.

Purnell, R. Science Workout Teacher's Guide, No. 1. (C). 1989. 60.00 (*0-7487-0198-2*, Pub. by S Thornes Pubs UK); 220.00 (*0-7487-0486-8*, Pub. by S Thornes Pubs UK); 300.00 (*0-7487-0197-4*, Pub. by S Thornes Pubs UK) St Mut.

— Science Workout Teacher's Guide, No. 2. (C). 1990. 60. 00 (*0-7487-0200-8*, Pub. by S Thornes Pubs UK); 220.00 (*0-7487-0487-6*, Pub. by S Thornes Pubs UK); 300.00 (*0-7487-0199-0*, Pub. by S Thornes Pubs UK) St Mut.

Purnell, Richard F., jt. auth. see Gotts, Edward E.

***Purnell, Robert.** The Little Lost Wagon. DHP, Inc. Staff, ed. (Illus.). 16p. (J). (ps-1). 1995. pap. write for info. (*1-885531-15-X*) Doghouse Pubng.

Purnell, Rosentene B. Bridges: Ways to Understand Written Discourse. 112p. 1988. per. 22.95 (*0-8403-4724-3*) Kendall-Hunt.

***Purnell, Susanna, et al.** A Formative Assessment of the General Electric Foundation's College Bound Program. LC 94-3462. 1994. write for info. (*0-8330-1563-X*, MR463GEF) Rand Corp.

Purohit, B. D. Handbook of Reservation for Scheduled Castes & Scheduled Tribes. (C). 1990. 125.00 (*0-89771-296-X*) St Mut.

Purohit, B. D. & Purohit, S. D. Handbook Reservation for Scheduled Castes & Scheduled Tribes. (C). 1990. 38.00 (*81-85287-05-8*, Pub. by Ashish II) S Asia.

Purohit, Mahesh, et al. Fiscal Policy for the National Capital Region. 171p. 1993. text ed. 25.00 (*0-7069-6382-2*, Pub. by Vikas II) S Asia.

Purohit, R. K. Thermal Engineering (S. I. Unites) (C). 1992. text ed. 137.50 (*81-7233-048-0*, Pub. by Scientific Pubs II) St Mut.

Purohit, R. K., jt. auth. see Sharma, B. L.

Purohit, S. D., jt. auth. see Purohit, B. D.

Purohit, S. S., ed. Hormonal Regulation of Plant Growth & Development. LC 85-11634. (Advances in Agricultural Biotechnology Ser.). 1985. lib. bdg. 162.50 (*90-247-3198-4*) Kluwer Ac.

— Hormonal Regulation of Plant Growth & Development. (Advances in Agricultural Biotechnology Ser.). 1986. lib. bdg. 117.00 (*90-247-3435-5*) Kluwer Ac.

Purohit, Shri, tr. The Geeta: The Gospel of the Lord Shri Krishna. 96p. (Orig.). 1965. pap. 7.95 (*0-571-06157-5*) Faber & Faber.

Purohit, V. B., ed. Recent Advances in Ecology & Environment. (Recent Researches in Ecology, Environment & Pollution Ser.: Vol. 1). 200p. 1988. 35. 00 (*1-55528-157-5*, Messers Today & Tomorrow) Scholarly Pubns.

Puroy, James. Out with the Stars. 192p. 1993. 19.95 (*0-87286-287-9*) City Lights.

— Out with the Stars. 192p. (Orig.). 1993. pap. 9.95 (*0-614-04942-3*) City Lights.

Purpel, David, jt. auth. see Giroux, Henry.

Purpel, David, jt. ed. see Gress, James.

Purpel, David E. The Moral & Spiritual Crisis in Education: A Curriculum for Justice & Compassion in Education. LC 88-16602. (Critical Studies in Education). 192p. (Orig.). 1988. text ed. 55.00 (*0-89789-153-8*, H153, Bergin & Garvey); pap. text ed. 17.95 (*0-89789-152-X*, G152, Bergin & Garvey) Greenwood.

***Purpel, David E & Shapiro, Svi.** Beyond Liberation & Excellence: Reconstructing the Public Discourse on Education. LC 94-39191. (Critical Studies in Education & Culture). 256p. 1995. text ed. 59.95 (*0-89789-416-2*, Bergin & Garvey); pap. text ed. 18.95 (*0-89789-417-0*) Greenwood.

Purpel, David E., jt. auth. see Shapiro, H. Svi.

Purple, Samuel S. Records of the Dutch Reformed Church in New Amsterdam & New York. 1972. 50.00 (*0-8490-0936-7*) Gordon Pr.

Purpura, Philip. Retail Security & Shrinkage Protection. 361p. 1993. 39.95 (*0-7506-9274-X*) Buttrwrth-Heinemann.

Purpura, Philip P. Modern Security & Loss Prevention Management. 1989. text ed. 32.95 (*0-409-90036-2*) Buttrwrth-Heinemann.

— Security & Loss Prevention. 2nd ed. 384p. 1990. text ed. 36.95 (*0-409-90203-9*) Buttrwrth-Heinemann.

— The Security Handbook. 288p. 1991. teacher ed 10.00 (*0-8273-3826-0*); pap. text ed. 33.95 (*0-8273-3825-2*) Delmar.

Purrington, Robert D., jt. auth. see Durham, Frank.

Purrington, Sandra, et al. Music! Words! Opera!, 4 vols., Level 1. LC 90-19274. (Illus.). 264p. (J). (gr. k-2). 1990. One vol., 264p. teacher ed 65.00 (*0-918812-65-8*, SE0694) MMB Music.

— Music! Words! Opera!, 3 vols., Set, Level 1. LC 90-19274. (Illus.). 264p. (J). (gr. k-2). 1990. Three vols., 24p. ea. student ed 3.50 (*0-918812-67-4*, SE0695-SE0697) MMB Music.

Purseglove, J. W. Tropical Crops: Monocotyledons. 618p. 1986. pap. text ed. 83.95 (*0-470-20568-7*) Halsted Pr.

Purseglove, Jeremy. Taming the Flood: Rivers & Wetlands in Britain. (Illus.). 320p. 1988. 35.00 (*0-19-215891-0*) OUP.

Pursell. Pocket Manual of Intensive Nutritional Care. 3rd ed. 150p. (C). 1990. pap. 15.95 (*1-55664-225-3*) Mosby Yr Bk.

***Pursell, Carroll.** The Machine in America: A Social History of Technology. (Illus.). 256p. 1994. text ed. 45. 00x (*0-8018-4817-2*); pap. text ed. 15.95x (*0-8018-4818-0*) Johns Hopkins.

— White Heat: People & Technology. 1994. pap. 18.00 (*0-520-08905-7*) U CA Pr.

Pursell, Carroll W., Jr., ed. Technology in America: A History of Individuals & Ideas. 2nd ed. (Illus.). 300p. 1990. pap. 16.00 (*0-262-66067-9*) MIT Pr.

Pursell, Cleo. Facing Death & Dying. 1982. pap. 1.95 (*0-89265-080-X*) Randall Hse.

— Triumph Over Suffering. 1982. pap. 1.95 (*0-89265-079-6*) Randall Hse.

Pursell, Donald E. & Deichert, Jerome A. The Economic Impact of the University of Nebraska. 1984. write for info. (*0-318-58380-1*) Bur Busn Res U Nebr.

Pursell, Donald E., jt. auth. see Bare, Charles L.

Pursell, John W. Why Do They Call It Topeka? How Places Got Their Names. LC 94-17790. 1994. 9.95 (*0-8065-1588-0*, Citadel Pr) Carol Pub Group.

***Purser, Ann.** Pastures New: The Modern Miss Read. 320p. 1995. 24.95 (*1-85797-059-4*, Pub. by Orion) Trafalgar.

Purser, B. H., jt. ed. see Schroeder, J. H.

Purser, Bruce, et al, eds. Dolomites: A Volume in Honour of Dolomieu. LC 93-31068. (International Association of Sedimentologists Special Publication Ser.: No. 21). 432p. 1994. pap. 100.00 (*0-632-03787-3*) Blackwell Sci.

Purser, Harry & Rowley, David. Clinical Information Technology: A Practical Guide to Personal Computing for Healthcare Clinicians & Managers. 220p. 1988. 53.00 (*0-85066-639-2*); pap. 27.00 (*0-85066-637-6*) Singular Publishing.

Purser, John. Scotland's Music: A History of the Traditional & Classical Music of Scotland from the Earliest Times to the Present Day. (Illus.). 304p. 1993. 55.00 (*1-85158-426-9*, Pub. by Mnstream UK) Trafalgar.

Purser, John W. The Literary Works of Jack B. Yeats. (Princess Grace Irish Library Ser.). 220p. (C). 1990. text ed. 75.00 (*0-389-20929-5*) B&N Imports.

Purser, Louis C., ed. see Apuleius.

Purser, Michael. Data Communications for Programmers. 256p. (C). 1986. pap. text ed. 15.96 (*0-201-12918-3*) Addison-Wesley.

— Introduction to Error-Correcting Codes. LC 94-32112. 1994. 54.00 (*0-89006-784-8*) Artech Hse.

— Secure Data Networking. LC 93-7161. 1993. text ed. 66. 00 (*0-89006-692-2*) Artech Hse.

Purser, Paul E., et al, eds. Manned Spacecraft: Engineering Design & Operation. LC 64-24708. (Illus.). 523p. reprint ed. pap. 149.10 (*0-317-10860-3*, 2011745) Bks Demand.

Pursey, Barbara. The Gifts of the Holy Spirit. 40p. 1984. 3.00 (*0-934421-02-1*) Presby Renewal Pubns.

— Prayer Beyond the Beginnings: Exploring Contemplative Prayer. 40p. 1984. 3.00 (*0-934421-05-6*) Presby Renewal Pubns.

Pursey, Barbara A. The Charismatic Renewal & You. 43p. (Orig.). 1987. pap. 3.00 (*0-934421-08-0*) Presby Renewal Pubns.

Pursey, H. J. Merchant Ship Construction. (Illus.). (C). 1987. 120.00 (*0-685-45085-6*, Pub. by Brwn Son Ferg) St Mut.

— Merchant Ship Construction. 7th ed. 217p. 1983. 45.00 (*0-85174-454-0*) Sheridan.

— Merchant Ship Stability. 6th ed. (Illus.). 207p. 1992. 40. 00 (*0-85174-274-2*) Sheridan.

— Merchant Ship Stability: (Metric Edition) (C). 1987. 100. 00 (*0-85174-442-7*, Pub. by Brwn Son Ferg) St Mut.

Pursglove, Glyn. Francis Warner & Tradition: An Introduction to the Plays. 232p. 1981. 26.00 (*0-86140-083-6*, Pub. by Colin Smythe Ltd UK) Dufour.

— Francis Warner's Poetry: A Critical Assessment. 348p. 1989. 35.00 (*0-86140-271-5*, Pub. by Colin Smythe Ltd UK) Dufour.

Pursglove, Paul D., intro. Zen in the Art of Close Encounters: Crazy Wisdom & UFOs. (Illus.). 333p. (Orig.). (C). 1995. pap. 14.50 (*0-9638691-0-8*) New Being Proj.

Pursh, Frederick. Flora Americae Septentrionalis. (Historia Naturalis Classica Ser.: 104). 1979. reprint ed. lib. bdg. 80.00 (*3-7682-1242-4*) Lubrecht & Cramer.

Pursiful, Darrell J. The Cultic Motif in the Spirituality of the Book of Hebrews. LC 93-21560. 208p. 1993. text ed. 89.95 (*0-7734-2376-1*, Mellen Biblical Pr) E Mellen.

Pursifull, Carmen M. Carmen by Moonlight. Taylor, Louise, ed. LC 82-90053. (Illus.). 1982. 5.50 (*0-9607856-0-4*) C M Pursifull.

— Elsewhere in a Parallel Universe. Walker, Ruth S., ed. (Hawk Production Ser.). 124p. (Orig.). 1992. pap. 10.00 (*0-932884-99-7*) Red Herring.

— The Twenty-Four Hour Wake. Singer, Karen K., ed. (Chapbook Ser.: No. 16). (Illus.). 57p. (Orig.). 1989. pap. 4.95 (*0-932884-16-4*) Red Herring.

Pursifull, Carmen M. & Walker, Ruth S., eds. Matrix Fifteen: Anthology of Red Herring Poets. 15th ed. 156p. 1990. pap. 7.95 (*0-932884-45-8*) Red Herring.

— Matrix Sixteen: Anthology of Red Herring Poets. 16th ed. 72p. 1991. pap. 8.00 (*0-932884-46-6*) Red Herring.

Pursifull, Carmen M., ed. see Mihalas, Dimitri.

Pursley, Duane, jt. auth. see Deems, Eugene F., Jr.

Pursley, Michael B. Introduction to Digital Communications. (Electrical Engineering Ser.). (Illus.). 575p. (C). 1995. text ed. write for info. (*0-201-18493-1*) Addison-Wesley.

Pursley, Paul. The Bodhisatyas - Keys to Awakening. 1995. 29.95 (*0-8062-5107-7*) Carlton.

Pursley, Robert D. Introduction to Criminal Justice. (Illus.). 1116p. (C). 1990. Incl. instr's. manual, tests & study guide. student ed, teacher ed write for info. (*0-02-396931-8*) Free Pr.

— Introduction to Criminal Justice. 6th ed. LC 93-16649. (Criminal Justice Ser.). 768p. (C). 1993. text ed. write for info. (*0-02-396941-5*) Macmillan.

Pursley, Robert D., jt. auth. see Albanese, Jay S.

***Purtee, Les.** Death Dressed in White. 310p. 1995. 21.50 (*0-9644420-0-0*) Flag Pub.

Purtell, April, et al. The Yellow Pages Guide to Educational Field Trips. Harris, Gregg, ed. 206p. 1993. pap. text ed. 20.00 (*0-923463-90-9*) Noble Pub Assocs.

***Purtell, April L.** The Gospel Syllabus. (Illus.). 15p. (YA). 1993. pap. 3.50 (*0-913717-71-1*, 1904) Hewitt Res Fnd.

Purtell, L. P., jt. ed. see Dutton, J. C.

Purtill, John, Jr., ed. see CAAS Inc. Staff.

Purtill, Richard L. A Logical Introduction to Philosophy. 256p. (C). 1988. pap. text ed. write for info. (*0-13-539917-3*) P-H.

— Logical Thinking. 174p. (C). 1992. reprint ed. pap. text ed. 19.50 (*0-8191-8493-4*) U Pr of Amer.

— Thinking about Ethics. 160p. 1976. pap. text ed. write for info. (*0-13-917716-7*) P-H.

— Thinking about Religion: A Philosophical Introduction to Religion. 1978. pap. text ed. write for info. (*0-13-917724-8*) P-H.

Purtilo, Ruth B. Ethical Dimensions in the Health Professions. 2nd ed. LC 92-49438. (Illus.). 288p. 1993. pap. text ed. 25.95 (*0-7216-3550-4*) Saunders.

— Health Professional & Patient Interaction. 4th ed. (Illus.). 352p. 1990. text ed. 29.50 (*0-7216-7396-1*) Saunders.

Purtle, Helen R. & Ey, John A., Jr., eds. Billings Microscope Collection of the Medical Museum, Armed Forces Institute of Pathology. 2nd ed. (Illus.). 266p. 1990. reprint ed. pap. 23.00 (*0-16-001840-4*, S/N 008-023-000) USGPO.

Purtle, Jane H. Food from the Hills of East Texas. LC 90-84194. (Illus.). 228p. (Orig.). 1990. pap. 10.00 (*0-9627944-0-6*) FoxLair Pubns.

Purton, M., jt. auth. see Bradshaw, A. M.

Purton, Peter, et al. Butterworths Planning Law Service. 1990. U.K. ring bd. 440.00 (*0-406-34050-1*, U.K.) Butterworth Legal Pubs.

Purtschert, R., ed. Advances in Vaccination Against Virus Diseases. (Monographs in Pediatrics: Vol. 11). (Illus.). 1979. pap. 27.25 (*3-8055-3046-3*) S Karger.

Purushotham, P., jt. auth. see Moulik, T. K.

Purushothaman, Sahasranaman & Zwarico, Amy, eds. NAPAW '92: Proceedings of the First North American Process Algebra Workshop, Stony Brook, NY, 28 August 1992. LC 92-44291. 1993. 69.00 (*0-387-19822-9*) Spr-Verlag.

Purver, Jonathan M. & Taylor, Lawrence. Handling Criminal Appeals. LC 80-81271. 1980. 120.00 (*0-685-59836-5*) Clark Boardman Callaghan.

Purver, Jonathan M., et al. Trial Lawyer's Book: Preparing & Winning Cases. 1990. 95.00 (*0-317-02942-8*) Lawyers Cooperative.

— Trial Lawyer's Book: Preparing & Winning Cases. suppl. ed. 1993. Suppl. 1993. 32.50 (*0-317-04629-2*) Lawyers Cooperative.

Purves, Alan C. The Scribal Society: An Essay on Literacy & Schooling in the Information Age. 128p. (Orig.). (C). 1990. pap. text ed. 22.95 (*0-8013-0378-8*, 78157) Longman.

Purves, Alan C., ed. The Idea of Difficulty in Literature. LC 90-43101. (SUNY Series, Literacy, Culture, & Learning: Theory & Practice). 182p. 1991. 59.50 (*0-7914-0673-3*); pap. 19.95 (*0-7914-0674-1*) State U NY Pr.

— Writing Across Languages & Cultures: Issues in Contrastive Rhetoric. LC 88-80974. (Written Communication Annual Ser.: No. 2). 309p. reprint ed. pap. 88.10 (*0-7837-6720-X*, 2046347) Bks Demand.

Purves, Alan C. & Monson, Dianne L. Experiencing Children's Literature. (C). 1984. pap. text ed. 19.00 (*0-673-15348-7*) HarpCollege.

Purves, Alan C., jt. ed. see Jennings, Edward M.

Purves, Alan C., jt. ed. see Westbury, Ian.

Purves, Alan C., et al. How Porcupines Make Love: Readers, Texts, Cultures in the Reponse-Based Literature Classroom, Vol. III. 2nd rev. ed. LC 94-6629. 215p. (C). 1995. pap. text ed. 24.95 (*0-8013-1260-4*) Longman.

— How Porcupines Make Love II: Teaching a Response-Centered Literature Curriculum. rev. ed. 256p. (C). 1990. pap. text ed. 23.00 (*0-8013-0382-6*, 78161) Longman.

Purves, Alan C., et al, eds. Becoming Readers in a Complex Society. LC 83-62344. (National Society for the Study of Education Yearbook Ser.: No. 83). xii, 312p. (C). 1984. lib. bdg. 20.00 (*0-226-60137-4*) U Ch Pr.

— Encyclopedia of English Studies & Language Arts: A Project of the National Council of Teachers of English. LC 93-33627. 1995. 150.00 (*0-590-49268-3*, pe65.e47 1994) Scholastic Inc.

Purves, Alec A. Collecting Medals & Decorations. 237p. (C). 1987. 85.00 (*0-317-90453-1*, Pub. by Picton UK) St Mut.

Purves, Andrew. The Search for Compassion: Spirituality & Ministry. 156p. (Orig.). 1989. pap. 10.99 (*0-664-25065-3*) Westminster John Knox.

Purves, Bill. Barefoot in the Boardroom. 192p. 1992. pap. 19.95 (*1-86373-038-9*, Pub. by Allen Unwin AT) Paul & Co Pubs.

— Barefoot in the Boardroom: Venture & Misadventure in the People's Republic of China. 190p. (Orig.). 1992. pap. 14.95 (*1-55021-079-3*, Pub. by NC Press CN) U of Toronto Pr.

Purves, Bryan. The Austin Seven Source Book. (Source Book Ser.). (Illus.). 592p. 1990. 150.00 (*0-85429-557-7*, Pub. by J H Haynes & Co UK) Motorbooks Intl.

— Information Graphics. 160p. (C). 1987. 60.00 (*0-85950-674-6*, Pub. by S Thornes Pubs UK) St Mut.

Purves, D. Trace-Element Contamination of the Environment: Fundamental Aspects of Pollution Control & Environmental Science, 7. rev. ed. 244p. 1985. 105.25 (*0-444-42503-9*) Elsevier.

Purves, Dale. Body & Brain: A Trophic Theory of Neural Connections. LC 88-764. (Illus.). 272p. 1988. 46.50 (*0-674-07715-6*) HUP.

— Body & Brain: A Trophic Theory of Neural Connections. (Illus.). 240p. 1990. pap. 18.95 (*0-674-07716-4*) HUP.

— Neural Activity & the Growth of the Brain. LC 93-34582. (Lezioni Lincee Ser.). (Illus.). 120p. (C). 1994. 37.95 (*0-521-45496-4*); pap. 15.95 (*0-521-45570-7*) Cambridge U Pr.

Purves, Dale & Lichtman, Jeff W. Principles of Neural Development. LC 84-10566. (Illus.). 433p. 1985. text ed. 48.95 (*0-87893-744-7*) Sinauer Assocs.

Purves, Dale, jt. ed. see Patterson, Paul H.

Purves, George T. The Testimony of Justin Martyr to Early Christianity. 1977. lib. bdg. 59.95 (*0-8490-2735-7*) Gordon Pr.

Purves, Jock. Fair Sunshine. 206p. 1990. reprint ed. pap. 8.95 (*0-85151-136-8*) Banner of Truth.

— The Unlisted Legion. 1978. pap. 6.95 (*0-85151-245-3*) Banner of Truth.

Purves, John. Italian Dictionary. (Routledge Pocket Dictionaries Ser.). 862p. (ITA.). 1980. pap. 12.95 (*0-7100-0602-0*, RKP) Routledge.

— Italian-English, English-Italian Pocket Dictionary. 833p. (ENG & ITA.). 1980. pap. 16.95 (*0-8288-4706-1*, M9364) Fr & Eur.

Purves, Libby, et al. The English & Their Horses. 1989. 24. 95 (*0-370-31175-2*) Random.

Purves, Lloyd. Lloyd Purves on Closing Sales. 1978. 4.95 (*0-13-539130-X*, Parker Publishing Co) P-H.

— Lloyd Purves on Closing Sales. 1986. 5.95 (*0-13-539148-2*) P-H.

Purves, M. J. The Physiology of Cerebral Circulation. LC 70-169577. (Monographs of the Physiological Society: No. 28). 436p. reprint ed. pap. 124.30 (*0-318-34841-1*, 2031716) Bks Demand.

Purves, P. E. & Pilleri, G., eds. Echolocation in Whales & Dolphins. 1983. text ed. 112.00 (*0-12-567960-2*) Acad Pr.

Purves, Pamela. Decorating Eggs: In the Style of Faberge. Dace, Rosalind, ed. (Illus.). 96p. (Orig.). (YA). 1989. pap. 16.95 (*0-85532-644-1*, Pub. by Search Pr UK) A Schwartz & Co.

Purves, R. D. Microelectrode Methods for Intracellular Recording & Ionophoresis. (Biological Techniques Ser.). 1981. text ed. 66.00 (*0-12-567950-5*) Acad Pr.

***Purves, William K., et al.** Life, the Science of Biology. 4th ed. LC 94-24802. (C). 1995. text ed. 65.00 (*0-7167-2629-7*) W H Freeman.

Purvey, A. Coins & Tokens of Scotland. 1976. lib. bdg. 8.00 (*0-686-45253-4*, Pub. by Seaby UK) S J Durst.

Purvey, Frank. Collecting Coins. 1985. 15.00 (*0-900652-75-6*) Numismatic Fine Arts.

Purvey, P. F. Coins of England & the United Kingdom. (Illus.). 1991. lib. bdg. 22.00 (*0-900652-69-1*, Pub. by Seaby UK) S J Durst.

Purvey, P. F., jt. auth. see Dickinson, M.

***Purviance, Edwin.** The Best of Mable. 100p. 1995. pap. text ed. 4.00 (*0-9620694-4-2*) E & M Purviance.

Purviance, Edwin & Purviance, Mable. Preachers Do the Craziest Things! 150p. (Orig.). 1993. pap. text ed. 3.95 (*0-9620694-3-4*) E & M Purviance.

Purviance, John, jt. auth. see Meehan, Michael D.

An Asterisk (*) at the beginning of an entry indicates that the title is appearing in BIP for the first time.

Purviance, Mable, jt. auth. see Purviance, Edwin.

Purvin, George. The Scholary Inquires of Jonathan Fane. abr. ed. 460p. 1995. pap. 9.95 (*1-56901-402-7*) NW Pub.

Purvin, Robert. Franchise Fraud: How to Protect Yourself Before & After You Invest. 1994. text ed. 27.95 (*0-471-59947-6*) Wiley.

Purvins, John J., jt. auth. see Lesperance, Gary L.

Purvis, Alston W. Dutch Graphic Design: 1918-1945. (Illus.). 228p. 1992. text ed. 39.95 (*0-442-00444-3*) Van Nos Reinhold.

Purvis, C. J. The Offensive Art: The Liberation of Poetic Imagination in Augustan Satirre. 232p. (C). 1989. 100.00 (*0-907839-34-7*, Pub. by Brynmill Pr Ltd UK) St Mut.

Purvis, Cynthia, ed. see England, Pamela & Van Zelst, Lambertus.

Purvis, Cynthia, ed. see Museum of Fine Arts Curatorial Staff.

Purvis, Cynthia, ed. see Roehrig, Catherine.

Purvis, Cynthia, ed. see Simpson, William K. & The, Egyptian Dept. of the MFA, Boston.

Purvis, Cynthia, ed. see Stebbins, Theodore E., Jr., et al.

Purvis, Cynthia M., ed. see Stebbins, Theodore E., Jr.

Purvis, Hoyt. Interdependence: An Introduction to International Affairs. (C). 1992. text ed. write for info. (*0-318-69125-6*) HB Coll Pubs.

Purvis, Hoyt, ed. Foreign Economic Decisionmaking: Case Studies from the Johnson Administration & Their Implications. (Policy Research Project Report Ser.: No. 54). 383p. 1983. 11.95 (*0-89940-656-4*) LBJ Sch Pub Aff.

— The Presidency & the Press. (Symposia Ser.). 120p. 1976. pap. 3.00 (*0-89940-405-7*) LBJ Sch Pub Aff.

Purvis, Hoyt, jt. ed. see Kelley, Donald R.

Purvis, Hoyt, jt. ed. see Radin, Beryl A.

Purvis, Hoyt H., ed. The Press: Free & Responsible? (Symposia Ser.). 114p. 1982. 6.00 (*0-89940-411-1*) LBJ Sch Pub Aff.

Purvis, James D. Jerusalem, the Holy City: A Bibliography. LC 87-4758. (American Theological Library Association Monograph: No. 20). 513p. 1988. 42.50 (*0-8108-1999-6*) Scarecrow.

— Jerusalem, the Holy City, Vol. II: A Bibliography. (American Theological Library Association Monograph: No. 20). 545p. 1991. 49.50 (*0-8108-2506-6*) Scarecrow.

Purvis, Jim, ed. see Abbey, James R.

Purvis, Jim, ed. see Angelo, Rocco M. & Vladimir, Andrew N.

Purvis, Jim, ed. see Kavanaugh, Raphael R. & Ninemeier, Jack D.

Purvis, Jim, ed. see Ninemeier, Jack D.

Purvis, Jim, ed. see Stipanuk, David M. & Roffmann, Harold.

Purvis, June. Hard Lessons: The Lives & Education of Working-Class Women in Nineteenth-Century England. 314p. 1989. text ed. 49.95 (*0-8166-1822-4*) U of Minn Pr.

— A History of Women's Education in England. (Gender & Education Ser.). 160p. (C). 1991. pap. 29.00 (*0-335-09775-8*, Open Univ Pr) Taylor & Francis.

Purvis, June, jt. ed. see Griffin, Gabriele.

Purvis, June, ed. see Jackson, Margaret.

Purvis, June, jt. ed. see Maynard, Mary.

Purvis, June, jt. ed. see Oldfield, Sybil.

Purvis, Kenneth. The Male Sexual Machine: An Owner's Manual. 224p. 1993. pap. 10.95 (*0-312-09331-4*) St Martin.

***Purvis, Leslie K.** The P. R. E. P. Guide: To the Real Estate Licensing Exams. (Orig.). 1995. pap. text ed. 24.95 (*0-9638207-4-5*) Exam Prep.

— Real Estate Exams: Texas Study Guide. 5th ed. 1993. pap. 24.95 (*0-9638207-0-2*) Exam Prep.

Purvis, O. W., et al, eds. The Lichen Flora of Great Britain & Ireland. (Illus.). 781p. (C). Date not set. text ed. write for info. (*0-318-70137-5*) Cambridge U Pr.

Purvis, Patricia, jt. auth. see Shetler, Jo.

Purvis, Peggy, jt. auth. see Leeburg, Verlene.

Purvis, Ronald L., et al. Life-Cycle Cost Analysis for Protection & Rehabilitation of Concrete Bridges Relative to Reinforcement Corrosion. 289p. (Orig.). (C). 1994. pap. text ed. 25.00 (*0-309-05755-8*, SHRP-S-377) SHRP.

Purvis, Sally. The Power of the Cross: Foundations for a Christian Feminist Ethic of Community. LC 92-41372. 160p. (Orig.). 1993. pap. 14.95 (*0-687-33206-0*) Abingdon.

Purvis, Scott C., jt. auth. see Burton, Philip W.

Purvis, T. T. Hagar, the Singing Maiden: With Other Stories & Rhymes. LC 77-174289. reprint ed. 45.00 (*0-404-00100-9*) AMS Pr.

Purvis, Thomas L. The Economics of Gender. 512p. 1995. 54.95 (*1-55786-388-1*) Blackwell Pubs.

— Proprietors, Patronage, & Paper Money: Legislative Politics in New Jersey, 1703-1776. LC 85-27895. 360p. 1986. lib. bdg. 45.00 (*0-8135-1161-5*) Rutgers U Pr.

— Revolutionary America, 1763-1800. LC 93-38382. (Almanacs of Everyday Life Ser.). 1995. 65.00 (*0-8160-2528-2*) Facts on File.

Puryear, Anne. Stephen Lives! His Life, Suicide & Afterlife. Merrill, Pat, ed. (Illus.). 400p. (Orig.). 1993. pap. 14.95 (*0-9634964-3-3*) N Paradigm.

Puryear, Douglas A. Helping People in Crisis: A Practical, Family-Oriented Approach to Effective Crisis Intervention. LC 79-88108. (Social & Behavioral Science Ser.). 237p. 1979. 30.95x (*0-87589-421-6*) Jossey-Bass.

Puryear, Edgar F., Jr. Nineteen Stars: A Study in Military Character & Leadership. LC 81-14365. 468p. 1992. reprint ed. pap. 14.95 (*0-89141-148-8*) Presidio Pr.

Puryear, Herbert B. The Edgar Cayce Primer. 272p. (Orig.). 1985. mass mkt. 5.99 (*0-553-25278-X*) Bantam.

— Why Jesus Taught Reincarnation: A Better News Gospel. Merrill, Pat, ed. 262p. (Orig.). 1993. pap. 14.95 (*0-9634964-9-2*) N Paradigm.

Puryear, Herbert B. & Thurston, Mark. Meditation & the Mind of Man. rev. ed. 130p. 1975. pap. 10.95 (*0-87604-105-5*, 274) ARE Pr.

Puryear, Jeffrey M. Thinking Politics: Intellectuals & Democracy in Chile, 1973-1988. LC 93-47402. (C). 1994. text ed. 42.50 (*0-8018-4839-3*); pap. text ed. 13.95 (*0-8018-4841-5*) Johns Hopkins.

Puryear, Jeffrey M. & Burnner, Jose J., eds. Education, Equity & Economic Competitiveness in the Americas, Vol. 1. LC 94-877. (INTERAMER Collection, Educational Ser.: No. 37). 1994. write for info. (*0-8270-3314-1*) OAS.

***Puryear, Kay & Corry, Tracy.** Today's Wedding - San Antonio. Crowell, Lynda, ed. 260p. (Orig.). Date not set. pap. 21.95 (*0-938934-34-1*) LCN.

— Today's Wedding - San Antonio. Crowell, Lynda, ed. 225p. (Orig.). 1993. pap. 18.95 (*0-938934-31-7*) LCN.

— Today's Wedding-Austin. Crowell, Lynda, ed. 250p. 1995. pap. 21.95 (*0-938934-30-9*) LCN.

— Today's Wedding Dallas-Ft. Worth-Metroplex. Crowell, Lynda, ed. 260p. (Orig.). Date not set. pap. 21.95 (*0-938934-33-3*) LCN.

— Today's Wedding Houston. Crowell, Lynda, ed. 260p. (Orig.). Date not set. pap. 21.95 (*0-938934-32-5*) LCN.

Puryear, Vernon. France & the Levant from the Bourbon Restoration to the Peace of Kutiah. LC 42-89. (University of California Publications in Social Welfare: Vol. 27). 265p. reprint ed. pap. 75.60 (*0-317-29073-8*, 2021446) Bks Demand.

Pusateri, C. Joseph, jt. ed. see Dethloff, Henry C.

Pusateri, James A., et al, eds. Small Business Bankruptcy Reorganization. LC 94-20896. (Bankruptcy Practice Library). 1994. pap. text ed. 128.00 (*0-471-10228-8*) Wiley.

Pusateri, Joseph C. A History of American Business. 2nd ed. LC 87-32955. (Illus.). 462p. (C). 1988. text ed. write for info. (*0-88295-844-5*); pap. text ed. write for info. (*0-88295-859-3*) Harlan Davidson.

Puscariu, Sextil. Etudes de Linguistique Roumaine. xix, 508p. 1973. reprint ed. write for info. (*3-487-05005-6*, Pub. by Georg Olms GW) Lubrecht & Cramer.

Pusch, Hans. Working Together on Rudolf Steiner's Mystery Dramas. LC 80-67024. (Steiner's Mystery Dramas Ser.). (Illus.). 144p. (Orig.). 1980. 15.95 (*0-910142-90-4*); pap. 9.95 (*0-910142-91-2*) Anthroposophic.

Pusch, Hans, tr. see Steiner, Rudolf.

Pusch, Margaret D., ed. Multicultural Education: A Cross-Cultural Training Approach. LC 79-92379. 276p. (Orig.). 1979. pap. text ed. 13.95 (*0-933662-06-8*) Intercult Pr.

***Pusch, R.** Rock Mechanics on a Geological Base. LC 95-3973. (Developments in Geotechnical Engineering Ser.: Vol. 77). 1995. write for info. (*0-444-89613-9*) Elsevier.

— Waste Disposal in Rocks. LC 93-48194. (Developments in Geotechnical Engineering Ser.: Vol. 76). 1994. 177.25 (*0-444-89449-7*) Elsevier.

Pusch, Ruth, tr. see Gabert, Erich.

Pusch, Ruth, tr. see Steiner, Rudolf.

Puschel, Karen L. U. S.-Israel Strategic Cooperation. (JCSS Study Ser.). 186p. (C). 1992. pap. text ed. 33.00 (*0-8133-1417-8*) Westview.

Puschel, Ulrich, jt. ed. see Sandig, Barbara.

Puschett, Jules B. Disorders of Fluid & Electrolyte Balance: Diagnosis & Treatment. (Illus.). 259p. (Orig.). 1985. pap. text ed. 32.00 (*0-443-08318-5*) Churchill.

Puschett, Jules B. & Greenberg, Arthur, eds. Diuretics IV: Chemistry, Pharmacology, & Clinical Applications, Proceedings of the Fourth International Conference on Diuretics, Boca Raton, Florida, 11-16 October 1992. LC 93-10691. (International Congress Ser.: No. 1023). 1993. 248.50 (*0-444-89630-9*, Excerpta Medica) Elsevier.

Puschman, Theodor. A History of Medical Education. 1972. 69.95 (*0-8490-0335-0*) Gordon Pr.

Puschmann-Nalenz, Barbara. Science Fiction & Postmodern Fiction: A Genre Study. LC 91-21112. (American University Studies: General Literature: Ser. XIX, Vol. 29). 268p. (C). 1992. text ed. 46.95 (*0-8204-1670-3*) P Lang Pubs.

Pusey, Charles D., ed. Immunology of Renal Disease. (Immunology & Medicine Ser.). (C). 1991. lib. bdg. 115. 00 (*0-7923-8964-6*) Kluwer Ac.

Pusey, E. B., jt. auth. see Nicoll, A.

Pusey, Edward B. Daniel the Prophet. 592p. lib. bdg. 20.99 (*0-8254-5219-8*) Kregel.

Pusey, Edward B., tr. see St. Augustine.

Pusey, James R. China & Charles Darwin. (East Asian Monographs: No. 100). 556p. 1983. 28.00 (*0-674-11735-2*) HUP.

— Wu Han: Attacking the Present Through the Past. (East Asian Monographs: No. 33). 94p. 1969. pap. 11.00 (*0-674-96275-3*) HUP.

Pusey, Merlo J. The Supreme Court Crisis. LC 74-171699. (FDR & the Era of the New Deal Ser.). 108p. 1972. reprint ed. lib. bdg. 19.50 (*0-306-70389-0*) Da Capo.

Pusey, Michael. Economic Rationalism in Canberra: A Nation-Building State Changes Its Mind. 304p. (C). 1992. 64.95 (*0-521-33422-5*) Cambridge U Pr.

— Jurgen Habermas. 1987. pap. 12.95 (*0-7458-0117-X*) Routledge Chapman & Hall.

Pusey, Nathan M. Age of the Scholar: Observations on Education in a Troubled Decade. LC 63-19146. 216p. 1963. text ed. 26.50 (*0-674-01000-0*) Belknap Pr.

— American Higher Education 1945-1970: A Personal Report. 240p. 1978. 25.00 (*0-674-02425-7*) HUP.

Pusey, William A. The History & Epidemiology of Syphilis. LC 75-23753. reprint ed. 32.50 (*0-404-13359-2*) AMS Pr.

— The History of Dermatology. LC 75-23754. reprint ed. 55.00 (*0-404-13360-6*) AMS Pr.

Push, Kenneth. Learn C & Save Your Job: C for COBOL Programmers. 1993. pap. text ed. 29.95 (*0-471-58807-5*, GD4310) Wiley.

Pushcart Prize Editors. The Pushcart Prize IX: Best of the Small Presses, 1984-1985. Henderson, Bill, ed. LC 76-58675. 588p. 1984. 24.95 (*0-916366-26-X*) Pushcart Pr.

Pushcart Prize Editors, jt. ed. see Henderson, Bill.

***Pushcart Prize Staff & Henderson, Bill, eds.** Pushcart Prize XIX: Best of the Small Presses, 1994-95 Edition. 580p. 1995. pap. 15.00 (*0-916366-98-7*) Pushcart Pr.

Pushkarev, Boris S. & Zupan, Jeffrey M. Public Transportation & Land Use Policy. LC 76-29299. (Illus.). 256p. reprint ed. 35.00 (*0-253-34682-7*) Ind U Pr.

Pushkarev, Sergei. Rol' Pravoslavnoi Tserkvi V Istorii Rosii: The Role of the Orthodox Church in Russian History. LC 85-80831. 125p. (RUS.). 1985. 9.50 (*0-911971-13-0*) Effect Pub.

Pushkarev, V. A. Watercolours & Drawings: Akvareli i Risunki v Gosudarstvennom Russkom Muzee. (Illus.). 1982. 125.00 (*0-317-57493-0*, Pub. by Collets UK) St Mut.

Pushkarev, V. V., et al. Treatment of Oil-Containing Wastewater. LC 83-70667. viii, 214p. 1983. 42.50 (*0-89864-004-0*) Allerton Pr.

Pushkariov, V. Treasures of the Russian Museum. 266p. 1975. 39.00 (*0-317-14324-7*, Pub. by Collets UK) Pro-Am Music.

Pushkarov, D. I., ed. Quasiparticle Theory of Defects in Solids. 200p. (C). 1991. text ed. 36.00 (*981-02-0180-X*) World Scientific Pub.

***Pushker, Gloria T.** A Belfer Bar Mitzvah. (Illus.). 32p. (J). (gr. 3-5). 1995. 14.95 (*1-56554-095-6*) Pelican.

— Toby Belfer Never Had a Christmas Tree. LC 91-14514. (Illus.). 32p. (J). 1991. 14.95 (*0-88289-855-8*) Pelican.

— Toby Belfer's Seder: A Passover Story Retold. LC 93-5585. (Illus.). (J). 1994. 14.95 (*0-88289-987-2*) Pelican.

Pushkin. The Bronze Horseman: Mednyi Vsadnik. Little, T. E., ed. (C). reprint ed. pap. text ed. 12.95 (*1-85399-245-3*, Pub. by Brstl Class Pr UK) Focus Info Gr.

— The Captain's Daughter: Kapitanskaya Dochka. Gottschalk, Fruma, ed. (C). reprint ed. pap. text ed. 17. 95 (*0-900186-12-7*, Pub. by Duckworth UK) Focus Info Gr.

— Eugene Onegin: Eugenii Onegin. (C). 1991. reprint ed. pap. text ed. 18.95 (*1-85399-396-4*, Pub. by Brstl Class Pr UK) Focus Info Gr.

— Tales of the Late Ivan Petrovich Belkin: Povesti Pokoinogo Ivana Petrovicha Belkina. Unbegaun, B. O., ed. (C). 1991. reprint ed. pap. text ed. 18.95 (*1-85399-250-X*, Pub. by Brstl Class Pr UK) Focus Info Gr.

***Pushkin, et al.** Liubvi Bezumnoe Tomlen'e: Rasskazy I Povesti Russkikh Pisateli XIX Veka. Efimov, Igor, ed. LC 94-47189. (Klassiki Russkoi Literatury (Russian Classics) Ser.). 290p. (Orig.). (RUS.). 1995. pap. 12.00 (*1-55779-081-7*) Hermitage.

Pushkin, A. S. Secret Journal, 1836-1837. 2nd ed. Armalinsky, Mikhail, tr. & intro. by. 91p. 1991. reprint ed. pap. 7.00 (*0-916201-07-4*) M I P Co.

Pushkin, Aleksandr. Alexander Pushkin: Complete Prose Fiction. Debreczeny, Paul, tr. LC 81-85450. 560p. 1983. 52.50 (*0-8047-1142-9*); pap. 17.95 (*0-8047-1800-8*) Stanford U Pr.

— Boris Godunov. Terras, V, ed. (Library of Russian Classics). 190p. pap. text ed. 15.95 (*0-900186-63-1*, Pub. by Duckworth UK) Focus Info Gr.

— Boris Godunov. Barbour, Philip L., tr. LC 75-31441. (Columbia Slavic Studies). 196p. 1976. reprint ed. text ed. 38.50 (*0-8371-8522-X*, PUBG, Greenwood Pr) Greenwood.

— The Bronze Horseman. Little, E., ed. (Library of Russian Classics). 84p. pap. text ed. 15.95 (*0-631-14385-8*, Pub. by Duckworth UK) Focus Info Gr.

— Captain's Daughter & Other Stories. 1957. pap. 8.00 (*0-394-70714-1*, Vin) Random.

— The Captain's Daughter & Other Stories. 1992. 15.00 (*0-679-41331-6*, Everymans Lib) Knopf.

— Collected Narrative & Lyrical Poetry. Arndt, Walter, tr. 475p. 1984. pap. 18.95 (*0-88233-826-9*) Ardis Pubs.

— Eugene Onegin. (Classics Ser.). 1979. pap. 8.95 (*0-14-044394-0*, Penguin Classics) Viking Penguin.

— Eugene Onegin: A Novel in Verse. Nabakov, Vladimir, tr. LC 80-8730. (Bollingen Ser.: No. LXXII). 362p. (C). 1990. pap. text ed. 14.95 (*0-691-01905-3*) Princeton U Pr.

— Eugene Onegin: A Novel in Verse, 4 vols., Set. Nabokov, Vladimir, tr. LC 80-8730. (Bollingen Ser.: Vol. LXXII). 1460p. (C). 1981. reprint ed. 250.00x (*0-691-09744-5*) Princeton U Pr.

— Golden Cockerel. Hulick, Elizabeth C., tr. (Illus.). 1962. 10.95 (*0-8392-1039-6*) Astor-Honor.

— Lyrics & Narrative Poems. 416p. (C). 1978. 50.00 (*0-317-92467-2*, Pub. by Collets UK) Pro-Am Music.

— Mozart & Salieri: The Little Tragedies. Wood, Antony, tr. 96p. 1982. boxed 23.00 (*0-946162-02-6*, Pub. by Angel Bks UK) Dufour.

— Mozart & Salieri: The Little Tragedies. Wood, Antony, tr. LC 87-13480. 96p. 1987. pap. 15.95 (*0-8023-1282-9*) Dufour.

— Prose Tales. Keane, T., tr. LC 78-150484. (Short Story Index Reprint Ser.). 1977. reprint ed. 24.95 (*0-8369-3825-9*) Ayer.

— Pushkin on Literature. rev. ed. Wolff, Tatiana, ed. & tr. by. LC 85-51799. 580p. 1986. 52.50 (*0-8047-1322-7*) Stanford U Pr.

— Queen of Spades & Other Stories. Edmonds, Rosemary, tr. (Classics Ser.). 1978. pap. 9.95 (*0-14-044119-0*, Penguin Classics) Viking Penguin.

— Ruslan I. Liudmila. 134p. 1985. 95.00 (*0-317-61367-7*, Pub. by Collets UK) Pro-Am Music.

— The Snow Storm. Redpath, Ann, ed. (Creative's Classic Short Stories Ser.). 40p. (J). (gr. 6 up). 1983. lib. bdg. 13. 95 (*0-87191-923-0*) Creative Ed.

— Tales of Belkin. Aitken, Gillon & Budgen, David, trs. 1983. 27.00 (*0-946162-04-2*) Dufour.

— The Tales of Ivan Belkin. 15.95 (*0-8488-0111-3*, Amereon Hse) Amereon Ltd.

— Tayniye Zapiski: Eighteen Thirty Six-Eighteen Thirty Seven Godov. 2nd ed. LC 86-90457. 104p. (RUS.). 1991. pap. 5.00 (*0-916201-02-3*) M I P Co.

Pushkin, Aleksandr, ed. Captain's Daughter. 248p. 1987. 30. 00 (*0-317-92449-4*) St Mut.

— Selected Works. 480p. (C). 1987. 55.00 (*0-317-92436-2*, Pub. by Collets UK) Pro-Am Music.

Pushkin, Aleksandr, et al. Armenia Observed. Baliozian, Ara, ed. LC 79-21946. 1979. 10.95 (*0-933706-10-3*); pap. 5.95 (*0-933706-11-1*) Ararat Pr.

Pushkin, Aleksandr S. Evgenij Onegin: A Novel in Verse. LC 52-12257. 358p. 1953. reprint ed. pap. 102.60 (*0-7837-1684-2*, 2057214) Bks Demand.

Pushkin, Alexander. The Captain's Daughter & Other Stories. 22.95 (*0-89190-254-7*, Am Repr) Amereon Ltd.

— Eugene Onegin. Arndt, Walter, tr. & intro. by. 224p. 1993. reprint ed. pap. 8.95 (*0-87501-106-3*) Ardis Pubs.

— Eugene Onegin: A Novel in Verse. Falen, James E., tr. (World's Classics Ser.). 272p. 1995. pap. 7.95 (*0-19-282491-0*) OUP.

— Pushkin Threefold: Narrative, Lyric, Polemic & Ribald Verse. The Originals with Linear & Metric Translations. 2nd ed. Arndt, Walter, tr. & intro. by. 455p. 1993. reprint ed. pap. 18.95 (*0-87501-107-1*) Ardis Pubs.

— The Queen of Spades & Other Stories. Keane, T., tr. 128p. 1994. reprint ed. pap. 1.00 (*0-486-28054-3*) Dover.

***Pushkin, Alexander & Dargel, Nancy.** Ruslan & Ludmilla: A Novel in Verse. 1994. 14.95 (*0-930267-39-7*) Bergh Pub.

Pushkin, Alexander S., et al. Pushkin Plus: Lyric Poems of Eight Russian Poets. Smith, Vasser W., ed. Smith, Vassar W., tr. & intro. by. LC 92-90674. 100p. (Orig.). (C). 1992. pap. text ed. 6.95 (*1-880964-02-3*) Zapizdat Pubns.

Pushkin, V. N. Problems of Heuristics. 208p. 1972. text ed. 52.50 (*0-7065-1279-0*, Pub. by Keter Pub IS) Coronet Bks.

Pushkin, V. N., jt. auth. see Dubrov, A. P.

Pushman, Muriel G. We All Wore Blue. Denny, Winifred, ed. (Illus.). 208p. (Orig.). 1989. 22.95 (*0-940495-13-9*) Pickering Pr.

— We All Wore Blue: Funny, Romantic & Moving - a Young Girl's Adventures in the Wartime WAAF. 175p. 1995. pap. 10.95 (*0-86051-940-6*, Robson-Parkwest) Parkwest Pubns.

***Pushong, Carlyle A.** Tarot of the Magi. 1994. pap. 10.95 (*0-87877-192-1*) Newcastle Pub.

Pushpadanta. Siva-Mahimna Stotram (the Hymn on the Greatness of Siva) Pavitrananda, Swami, tr. pap. 1.00 (*0-87481-148-1*) Vedanta Pr.

Pushpamma, P. Choosing Sorghum as Food in the Semi-Arid Tropics: Studies in Dryland Communities. 91p. 1993. pap. 15.00 (*0-88936-657-8*, IDRC6578, Pub. by IDRC CN) UNIPUB.

Pushpanjal. Siva Mahimna Stotram. pap. 1.00 (*0-87481-075-2*) Vedanta Pr.

Pusic, Eugen. Social Welfare & Social Development. LC 79-189707. (Institute of Social Studies Publications: No. 5). (Illus.). 251p. (Orig.). 1972. pap. text ed. 19.25 (*90-279-1969-0*) Mouton.

Pusic, Milenko, jt. auth. see Vukovic, Milan.

***Pusins, Dolores W. & Ross, Steven C.** Understanding & Using Lotus 1-2-3 for Windows 5.0. 450p. 1995. spiral bd. write for info. (*0-314-04651-8*) West Pub.

Puskar, A. Microplasticity & Failure of Metallic Materials. (Materials Science Monographs: No. 56). 304p. 1990. 115.50 (*0-444-98841-6*) Elsevier.

— Threshold States of Materials & Components. (Materials Science Monographs: No. 62). 296p. 1990. 120.00 (*0-444-98840-8*) Elsevier.

— The Use of High-Intensity Ultrasonics. (Materials Science Monographs: Vol. 13). 304p. 1983. 97.50 (*0-444-99690-7*) Elsevier.

Puskar, A. & Golovin, S. A. Fatigue in Materials: Cumulative Damage Processes. (Materials Science Monographs: Vol. 24). 320p. 1984. 113.00 (*0-444-99597-8*) Elsevier.

Puskas, Charles B. An Introduction to the New Testament. LC 89-48242. 320p. 1989. text ed. 19.95 (*0-913573-45-0*) Hendrickson MA.

Puskas, Charles B., Jr. The Letters of Paul: An Introduction. (Good News Studies: Vol. 25). 232p. (Orig.). 1993. 14.95 (*0-8146-5690-0*, M Glazier) Liturgical Pr.

***Puskas, Ildiko.** India Bibliografia - India Bibliography: Bibliotheca Orientalis Hungarica 35. (Bibliotheca Orientalis Hungarica Ser.). 602p. (C). 1991. 140.00 (*963-05-5591-3*, Pub. by Akad Kiado HU) St Mut.

Puskina, Druz'TA. Perepiska, Vospominaniia, Dnevniki, 2 Vols. 642p. 1984. 75.00 (*0-685-12144-5*, Pub. by Collets UK) St Mut.

Pusser. Angelettes & Cosmic Sex. LC 88-81436. 120p. (Orig.). 1988. pap. 9.95 (*0-941404-86-2*) New Falcon Pubns.

Pust, Ron, jt. auth. see Krogh, Christopher.

Pustan, Regina, tr. see Gonzalez, Luisa.

Pustay, Michael W., jt. auth. see Griffin, Ricky W.

Pustejovsky, James, ed. Semantics & the Lexicon. 416p. (C). 1993. pap. text ed. 39.00 (*0-7923-2386-6*) Kluwer Ac.

— Semantics & the Lexicon. LC 92-28758. (Studies in Linguistics & Philosophy: Vol. 49). 416p. (C). 1993. lib. bdg. 140.00 (*0-7923-1963-X*) Kluwer Ac.

P Q

Pustejovsky, James, et al, eds. Lexical Semantics & Knowledge Representation: First SIGLEX Workshop, Berkeley, CA, U. S. A., June 1991, Proceedings. LC 92-26469. (Lecture Notes in Computer Science, Lecture Notes in Artificial Intelligence Ser.: Vol. 627). xiii, 381p. 1992. pap. 57.00 (*0-387-55801-2*) Spr-Verlag.

***Puster, Rolf W., ed.** Veritas Filia Temporis? Philosophiehistorie Zwischen Wahrheit und Geschichte. 319p. (GER.). (C). 1995. lib. bdg. 133.85 (*3-11-014170-1*) De Gruyter.

Pusterla, Fred. My First Magnifier Book. (Illus.). 12p. (J). (ps-1). 1993. bds. 9.95 (*1-56293-140-7*) McClanahan Bk.

Pusti, Maureen S. Neighbors. 400p. (Orig.). 1991. pap. 4.50 (*0-8439-3077-2*) Dorchester Pub Co.

Pustovalova, N., jt. auth. see Kolesova, I.

Pustylnik, B. I., ed. Heavy Ion Physics: Scientific Report, Flerov Laboratory of Nuclear Reactions of Jinr, Dubna, Russia. (Illus.). 420p. 1993. pap. text ed. 70.00 (*0-911767-67-3*) Hadronic Pr Inc.

Pustylnik, B. I., jt. ed. see Kristiak, J.

Pusztai, Arpad. Plant Lectins. (Chemistry & Pharmacology of Natural Products Ser.). 224p. (C). 1992. 79.95 (*0-521-32824-1*) Cambridge U Pr.

***Pusztai, Arpad & Bardocz, Susan, eds.** Lectins: Biomedical Perspectives. 368p. 1994. 99.50x (*0-7484-0177-6*, Pub. by Tay Francis Ltd UK) Taylor & Francis.

Pusztai, Joseph, jt. auth. see Sava, Michael.

***Pusztai, Lajos, et al, eds.** Cell Proliferation in Cancer: Regulatory Mechanisms of Neoplastic Cell Growth. (Illus.). 360p. 1995. 90.00 (*0-19-854791-9*) OUP.

Puta, Mircea. Hamiltonian Mechanical Systems & Geometric Quantization. LC 93-13189. (Mathematics & Its Applications Ser.: Vol. 260). 288p. (C). 1993. lib. bdg. 110.00 (*0-7923-2306-8*) Kluwer Ac.

Putanec, Valentin. French - Serbocroatian Dictionary: Francusko-Hrvatski ili Srpski Rjecnik. 1152p. (FRE & SER.). 1988. write for info. (*0-8288-1047-8*, F97152) Fr & Eur.

Putatunda, Susil K., jt. ed. see Strauss, Bernard M.

Putcha, Mohan S. Linear Algebraic Monoids. (London Mathematical Society Lecture Note Ser.: No. 133). 200p. 1988. pap. 34.95 (*0-521-35809-4*) Cambridge U Pr.

Puter, S. A. Looters of the Public Domain. LC 70-38833. (Illus.). 495p. 1972. reprint ed. lib. bdg. 59.50 (*0-306-70449-8*) Da Capo.

Puterbaugh, Donald L., jt. auth. see Fling, Paul N.

Puterbaugh, Geoff. Twins & Homosexuality: A Casebook. LC 90-31756. 164p. 1990. 25.00 (*0-8240-6149-7*, 627) Garland.

***Puterbaugh, Parke & Bisbort, Alan.** California Beaches. 550p. (Orig.). 1996. pap. 16.95 (*0-935701-00-1*) Foghorn Pr.

Puterman, Martin L. Markov Decision Processes: Discrete Stochastic Dynamic Programming. (Series in Probability & Mathematical Statistics). 768p. 1994. text ed. 89.95 (*0-471-61977-9*, Wiley-Interscience) Wiley.

Puth, Robert C. American Economic History. 3rd ed. LC 92-72940. 732p. (C). 1993. text ed. 56.00 (*0-03-096905-0*) Dryden Pr.

— Supreme Life: The History of a Negro Life Insurance Company. LC 75-41780. (Companies & Men: Business Enterprises in America Ser.). 1976. 27.95 (*0-405-08095-6*) Ayer.

Puthenparampil, J. Philip, jt. ed. see Bickley, Verner C.

Puthenpura, Sarat C., jt. auth. see Fang, Shu-Cherng.

Puthenpurakal, Joseph. Baptist Missions in Nagaland. 1984. 22.50 (*0-8364-1138-2*, Pub. by Mukhopadhyaya II) S Asia.

Puthli, Ram S., et al, eds. Proceedings of the Second (1992) International Offshore & Polar Engineering Conference, Vol. IV. LC 91-78280. 628p. (Orig.). 1992. pap. 100.00 (*1-880653-04-4*) ISOPE.

Putinar, M., jt. auth. see Eschmeier, J.

Putinar, M., jt. auth. see Martin, M.

Putinski, Nancy A. & Kocik, Michael J. A Farewell to Failure: Creating Quality in Our Schools. 200p. 1993. spiral bd. 29.95 (*1-883296-00-5*) Par Excell.

Putman. Diagnostic Imaging of the Lung. (Lung Biology in Health & Disease Ser.: Vol. 46). 752p. 1990. 225.00 (*0-8247-8318-2*) Dekker.

Putman, A. O. & Davis, K. E., eds. Advances in Descriptive Psychology, Vol. 5. 320p. 1990. 70.00 (*0-685-68006-1*) Descriptive Psych Pr.

Putman, Andree, ed. International Design Yearbook 7. (Illus.). 240p. 1992. 65.00 (*1-55859-285-7*) Abbeville Pr.

Putman, Bill. Daddy, I'm Pregnant. Brown, Jane, ed. LC 88-1431. 114p. 1988. pap. 7.99 (*0-88070-204-4*, Multnomah Bks) Questar Pubs.

Putman, Bluford H. & Wilford, D. Sykes, eds. The Monetary Approach to International Adjustment. rev. ed. LC 85-28314. 396p. 1986. text ed. 65.00 (*0-275-92024-0*, C2024, Praeger Pubs) Greenwood.

Putman, Bob, et al. Is This Missions Thing for Real? For Students Who Have Their Doubts. (Illus.). 128p. 1990. teacher ed, ring bd. 49.95 (*0-935797-32-7*) Harvest IL.

Putman, Byron W. Digital & Microprogram Electronics: Theory Application Troubleshooting. (Illus.). 416p. (C). 1986. text ed. 52.00 (*0-13-214354-2*) P-H.

— Microcomputer Hardware, Operation, & Trouble-Shooting with IBM PC Applications. (Illus.). 224p. (C). 1987. text ed. 72.00 (*0-13-581943-1*) P-H.

— RS-232 Simplified: Connecting, Interfacing & Troubleshooting Peripheral Devices. (Illus.). 264p. (C). 1986. pap. 27.00 (*0-13-783499-3*) P-H.

Putman, Charles E. & Ravin, Carl E. Textbook of Diagnostic Imaging, 2 vols. 2nd ed. LC 94-4061. (Illus.). 2368p. 1994. text ed. 295.00 (*0-7216-3697-7*) Saunders.

Putman, Hilary. Philosophical Papers, Set. 1986. pap. 64.95 (*0-521-31020-2*) Cambridge U Pr.

— Philosophical Papers, Vol. 1: Mathematics, Matter & Method. 2nd ed. (Illus.). 368p. 1979. 74.95 (*0-521-22553-1*); pap. 29.95 (*0-521-29550-5*) Cambridge U Pr.

— Philosophical Papers, Vol. 2: Language & Reality. (Illus.). 457p. 1975. 47.50 (*0-317-66588-X*); pap. 18.95 (*0-317-66589-8*) Cambridge U Pr.

— Philosophical Papers, Vol. 3: Reason, Truth & History. (Illus.). 312p. 1985. pap. 22.95 (*0-521-31394-5*) Cambridge U Pr.

Putman, Jeff, ed. see Bateman, Paul, et al.

Putman, Marc R., jt. auth. see Engstrom, Robert E.

Putman, R. J. Community Ecology. LC 93-33026. 178p. 1993. write for info. (*0-412-56690-7*, Chap & Hall NY); pap. 29.95 (*0-412-54500-4*, Chap & Hall NY) Chapman & Hall.

Putman, R. J. & Wratten, S. D. Principles of Ecology. LC 83-18028. 384p. (C). 1984. pap. 19.00 (*0-520-05254-4*) U CA Pr.

Putman, Rory. The Natural History of Deer. LC 88-22856. (Comstock Book - The Natural History of Mammals Ser.). (Illus.). 224p. 1989. 28.50 (*0-8014-2283-3*) Cornell U Pr.

Putman, Rory J., ed. Mammals As Pests. 272p. 1989. 65.00 (*0-412-32590-X*, A3830) Chapman & Hall.

Putman, Stephen H. Urban Residential Location Models. (Studies in Applied Regional Science: Vol. 13). 1979. lib. bdg. 49.50 (*0-89838-011-1*) Kluwer Ac.

Putnam, A., jt. auth. see Abrishaman, M.

Putnam, A. R. & Tang, C. S., eds. The Science of Allelopathy. LC 86-7822. 317p. 1986. text ed. 87.95 (*0-471-83027-5*) Wiley.

Putnam, Alan & Putnam, Sandy. Wine Magic: The Wine Guide for Funloving People. (Illus.). 256p. (Orig.). 1994. pap. 14.95 (*1-56044-305-7*) Falcon Pr MT.

Putnam, Annie C., ed. see Wynne, Madeline Y.

Putnam, Anthony O. Advances in Descriptive Psychology, Vol. 5. Davis, Keith E., ed. 320p. 1990. 70.00 (*0-9625661-0-1*) Descriptive Psych Pr.

— Marketing Your Services: A Step-by-Step Guide for Small Businesses & Professionals. 246p. 1990. text ed. 37.95 (*0-471-50948-5*) Wiley.

Putnam, Bertha H. The Place in Legal History of Sir William Shareshull. LC 85-48163. (Cambridge Studies in English Legal History). 346p. 1986. reprint ed. 81.00 (*0-912004-33-9*) W W Gaunt.

Putnam, Bertha H., ed. Enforcement of the Statutes of Labourers During the First Decade After the Black Death, 1349-59. LC 70-127447. (Columbia University Social Science Studies: No. 85). reprint ed. 37.50 (*0-404-51085-X*) AMS Pr.

Putnam, Bluford H. & Wilford, D. Sykes, eds. The Monetary Approach to International Adjustment. LC 78-19753. 299p. 1979. 36.95 (*0-275-90409-1*, C0409, Praeger Pubs); pap. 15.95 (*0-275-91480-1*, B1480, Praeger Pubs) Greenwood.

Putnam, Calvin R. Commutation Properties of Hilbert Space Operators & Related Topics. (Ergebnisse der Mathematik und Ihrer Grenzgebiete Ser.: Vol. 36). 1967. 64.00 (*0-387-03778-0*) Spr-Verlag.

Putnam, Carleton. Race & Reality. LC 67-19407. 192p. 1980. pap. 5.00 (*0-914576-14-3*) Howard Allen.

— Race & Reason. LC 61-8447. 125p. 1977. pap. 5.00 (*0-914576-08-9*) Howard Allen.

Putnam-Carlson. Diccionario de Arquitectura: Ingles - Espanol Construccion y Obras Publicas. (SPA.). 1991. write for info. (*0-7859-3685-8*, 8428315604) Fr & Eur.

Putnam, Cindy, jt. auth. see McCune, Nancy.

Putnam, Cindy, ed. see Peirce, Pamela.

Putnam, Claudia, jt. auth. see Malville, J. McKim.

***Putnam, Craig T.** Discovered Light. 56p. 1995. pap. 7.00 (*0-8059-3694-7*) Dorrance.

Putnam, E. History of the Putnam Family in England & America (Including "Putnam Leaflets"), 2 vols. in 1. (Illus.). 720p. 1989. reprint ed. lib. bdg. 117.00 (*0-8328-0998-5*); reprint ed. pap. 99.00 (*0-8328-0999-3*) Higginson Bk Co.

Putnam, E. C. & Putnam, J. J. Jackson: Honorable Jonathan Jackson & Hannah Tracy Jackson, Their Ancestors & Descendants. (Illus.). 70p. 1991. reprint ed. pap. 14.00 (*0-8328-1749-X*) Higginson Bk Co.

Putnam, Eben. Lt. Joshua Hewes, a New England Pioneer, & Some of His Descendants. (Illus.). 673p. 1989. reprint ed. lib. bdg. 109.00 (*0-8328-0653-6*); reprint ed. pap. 101.00 (*0-8328-0654-4*) Higginson Bk Co.

Putnam, Eben, ed. see Osgood, I.

Putnam, Elizabeth, jt. auth. see Cooke, Margaret.

Putnam, Emily J. Candaules' Wife, & Other Old Stories. LC 72-169559. (Short Story Index Reprint Ser.). 1977. reprint ed. 19.95 (*0-8369-4022-9*) Ayer.

Putnam, F. W. The Manufacture of Bone Fish Hooks in the Little Miami Valley. (Ohio History, Prehistoric Indians, Archaeology Ser.). (Illus.). 8p. (C). 1994. reprint ed. pap. 1.30 (*1-56651-105-4*) A W McGraw.

— The Serpent Mound of Ohio: Site Excavation & Park Construction. (Ohio History, Archaeology, Prehistoric Indians Ser.). (Illus.). 8p. (C). 1994. reprint ed. lib. bdg. 2.80 (*1-56651-091-0*) A W McGraw.

Putnam, Frank B., jt. auth. see Cleland, Robert G.

Putnam, Frank W. Diagnosis & Treatment of Multiple Personality Disorder. LC 88-11217. (Guilford Foundations of Modern Psychiatry Ser.). 351p. 1989. lib. bdg. 38.95 (*0-89862-177-1*) Guilford Pr.

Putnam, Frank W., ed. The Plasma Proteins: Structure, Function, & Genetic Control, Vol. 3. 2nd ed. 1977. text ed. 169.00 (*0-12-568403-7*) Acad Pr.

— The Plasma Proteins: Structure, Function & Genetic Control, Vol. 4. 2nd ed. 1984. text ed. 153.00 (*0-12-568404-5*) Acad Pr.

— The Plasma Proteins: Structure, Function & Genetic Control, Vol. 5. 2nd ed. 1987. text ed. 129.00 (*0-12-568405-3*) Acad Pr.

Putnam, Frederic W. The Archaeological Reports of Frederic Ward Putnam. LC 78-178422. (Harvard University. Peabody Museum of Archaeology & Ethnology. Antiquities of the New World Ser.: No. 8). (Illus.). reprint ed. 62.50 (*0-404-57308-8*) AMS Pr.

— The Selected Archaeological Papers of Frederic Ward Putnam. LC 76-178419. (Harvard University. Peabody Museum of Archaeology & Ethnology. Antiquities of the New World Ser.: No. 5). (Illus.). reprint ed. 110.00 (*0-404-57305-3*) AMS Pr.

Putnam, George H. Books & Their Makers During the Middle Ages, 2 vols. 1972. 200.00 (*0-87968-777-0*) Gordon Pr.

— The Censorship of the Church of Rome, 2 vols. 1972. 200.00 (*0-87968-826-2*) Gordon Pr.

— Censorship of the Church of Rome & Its Influence upon the Production & Distribution of Literature, 2 vols. LC 67-12455. 1972. reprint ed. 60.95 (*0-405-08869-8*) Ayer.

— Censorship of the Church of Rome & Its Influence upon the Production & Distribution of Literature, 2 vols., 1. LC 67-12455. 1976. reprint ed. 30.95 (*0-405-08870-1*) Ayer.

— Censorship of the Church of Rome & Its Influence upon the Production & Distribution of Literature, 2 vols., 2. LC 67-12455. 1976. reprint ed. 30.95 (*0-405-08871-X*) Ayer.

Putnam, George I. Old Number Four. (Illus.). 1987. 7.95 (*0-685-19460-4*) Equity Pubng NH.

Putnam, George P., ed. see Earhart, Amelia.

Putnam, Greta, jt. auth. see Finch, Karen.

Putnam, H. G., ed. see Olivo, C. Thomas.

Putnam, Herbert, et al. Essays Offered to Herbert Putnam by His Colleagues & Friends on His Thirtieth Anniversary As Librarian of Congress, April 5, 1929. LC 67-23214. (Essay Index Reprint Ser.). 1977. pap. 30.95 (*0-8369-0430-3*) Ayer.

Putnam, Hilary. The Many Faces of Realism. 1988. 24.95 (*0-8126-9042-7*); pap. 9.95 (*0-8126-9043-5*) Open Court.

— Philosophical Papers, 2 vols. Incl. Vol. 2. Mind, Language & Reality. 1979. pap. 29.95 (*0-521-29551-3*); 1975. write for info. (*0-318-51290-4*) Cambridge U Pr.

— Philosophical Papers, Vol. 3: Reason, Truth & History. LC 81-6126. 224p. 1981. 54.95 (*0-521-23035-7*); pap. 18.95 (*0-521-29776-1*) Cambridge U Pr.

— Philosophy of Mathematics: Selected Readings. 2nd ed. Benacerraf, Hilary, ed. LC 85-25257. 580p. 1984. pap. 32.95 (*0-521-29648-X*) Cambridge U Pr.

— Pragmatism: An Open Question. 128p. 1995. 39.95 (*0-631-19342-1*); pap. 15.95 (*0-631-19343-X*) Blackwell Pubs.

— Realism with a Human Face. 424p. (C). 1992. pap. 15.95 (*0-674-74945-6*) HUP.

— Renewing Philosophy. LC 92-10854. 234p. (Orig.). 1992. 29.00 (*0-674-76093-X*) HUP.

— Renewing Philosophy. 248p. (Orig.). (C). 1995. pap. text ed. 14.95 (*0-674-76094-8*) HUP.

— Representation & Reality. 160p. 1988. 27.50 (*0-262-16108-7*) MIT Pr.

— Representation & Reality. (Illus.). 1991. pap. 11.95 (*0-262-66074-1*) MIT Pr.

— Words & Life. Conant, James, ed. LC 93-39799. 607p. (Orig.). 1994. 47.50 (*0-674-95606-0*) HUP.

— Words & Life. Conant, James, ed. 608p. (Orig.). (C). 1995. pap. text ed. 19.95 (*0-674-95607-9*) HUP.

Putnam, Howard D. & Busnar, Gene. The Winds of Turbulence: A CEO's Reflections on Surviving & Thriving on the Cutting Edge of Corporate Crisis. 227p. (C). 1993. reprint ed. pap. 10.00 (*0-9637398-0-8*) H D Putnam Enter.

Putnam, J. J., jt. auth. see Putnam, E. C.

Putnam, Jackson K. Modern California Politics. 3rd ed. Hundley, Norris, Jr. & Schutz, John A., eds. (Golden State Ser.). (Illus.). 144p. 1990. 9.00 (*0-929651-37-5*) MTL.

— Old-Age Politics in California: From Richardson to Reagan. LC 70-107649. (Illus.). x, 212p. 1970. 32.50 (*0-8047-0734-0*) Stanford U Pr.

***Putnam, James.** Amazing Facts about Ancient Egypt. 1994. 9.95 (*0-8109-1953-2*) Abrams.

— Egyptology: An Introduction to the History, Culture & Art. 1990. 9.99 (*0-517-02336-9*) Random Hse Value.

— Pyramid. LC 94-8804. (Eyewitness Bks.). (Illus.). 64p. (YA). (gr. 5 up). 1994. 16.00 (*0-679-86170-X*); lib. bdg. 17.99 (*0-679-96170-4*) Knopf Bks Yng Read.

— Pyramid. (DK Action Packs Ser.). (Illus.). (J). (gr. 3-7). 1994. 19.95 (*1-56458-684-7*) Dorling Kindersley.

Putnam, James J. Human Motives. LC 73-2413. (Mental Illness & Social Policy; the American Experience Ser.). 1973. reprint ed. 19.95 (*0-405-05223-5*) Ayer.

— James Jackson Putnam & Psychoanalysis: Letters Between Putnam & Sigmund Freud, Ernest Jones, William James, Sandor Ferenczi & Morton Prince, 1877-1917. Hale, Nathan G., Jr., ed. Heller, Judith B., tr. LC 70-150010. (Commonwealth Fund Publications). (Illus.). 400p. 1971. 37.00 (*0-674-47170-9*) HUP.

Putnam, Jeff. Bottoms Up. LC 92-75410. 320p. 1993. 20.00 (*0-9627509-4-8*) Baskerville.

— By the Wayside. LC 91-77771. 343p. 1992. 19.00 (*0-9627509-5-6*) Baskerville.

— Demigod. LC 93-70994. 320p. 20.00 (*1-880909-09-X*) Baskerville.

— Good Men. 253p. 1992. 18.00 (*0-9627509-7-2*) Baskerville.

— Hot Cars Poster Book. 32p. (J). (gr. 3 up). 1992. pap. 3.99 (*0-87406-634-4*) Willowisp Pr.

— On the Edge Poster Book. 32p. (J). 1994. pap. 3.99 (*0-87406-709-X*) Willowisp Pr.

— Sellout. Chase, Sam, ed. 310p. 1995. 21.00 (*1-880909-35-9*) Baskerville.

Putnam, Jeff, ed. see Black, Simon.

Putnam, Jeff, ed. see Eisner, William.

Putnam, Jeff, ed. see Wheelis, Allen.

***Putnam, Jim.** The Joshua Chronicles. 310p. (Orig.). 1995. pap. 13.95 (*0-9645993-0-9*) Ivy Hollow.

— Mummy. LC 92-1591. (Eyewitness Bks.). 64p. (J). (gr. 5 up). 1993. 15.00 (*0-679-83881-3*); lib. bdg. 15.99 (*0-679-93881-8*) Knopf Bks Yng Read.

Putnam, Joanne. A Time to Grow. LC 85-20190. (Illus.). 112p. (Orig.). 1985. pap. 4.99 (*0-912315-92-X*) Word Aflame.

Putnam, JoAnne W., ed. Cooperative Learning & Strategies for Inclusion: Celebrating Diversity in the Classroom. LC 93-428. (Children, Youth, & Change Ser.). 208p. 1993. pap. 20.00 (*1-55766-134-0*) P H Brookes.

Putnam, Joyce G. & Burke, J. Bruce. Organizing & Managing the Classroom Learning Community: An Integrated Approach for the Clinician. 1992. text ed. write for info. (*0-07-051041-5*) McGraw.

Putnam, Lawrence. Measures for Excellence: Reliable Software on Time, Within Budget. 400p. 1991. text ed. 50.67 (*0-13-567694-0*) P-H.

***Putnam, Lillian R.** How to Become a Better Reading Teacher: Strategies for Assessment & Intervention. LC 94-44805. 1995. write for info. (*0-02-397045-6*, Merrill Pub Co) Macmillan.

Putnam, Linda L. & Roloff, Michael E. Communication & Negotiation. (Annual Reviews of Communication Research Ser.: Vol. 20). 304p. (C). 1992. text ed. 52.00 (*0-8039-4011-4*); pap. text ed. 24.00 (*0-8039-4012-2*) Sage.

Putnam, Mary T. Record of an Obscure Man. LC 70-82213. (Anti-Slavery Crusade in America Ser.). 1970. reprint ed. 25.95 (*0-405-00652-7*) Ayer.

Putnam, Michael C. Artifices of Eternity: Horace's Fourth Book of Odes. LC 85-25542. (Cornell Studies in Classical Philology - The Townsend Lecture Ser.). 320p. (C). 1986. 31.50 (*0-8014-1852-6*) Cornell U Pr.

— Essays on Latin Lyric, Elegy, & Epic. LC 81-47944. (Collected Essays Ser.). 440p. 1982. 53.50 (*0-691-06497-0*); pap. 18.95x (*0-691-01388-8*) Princeton U Pr.

— The Poetry of the Aeneid. LC 88-47774. 256p. 1988. pap. 12.95 (*0-8014-9518-0*) Cornell U Pr.

— Tibullus: A Commentary. (American Philological Association Ser.: Vol. 3). 222p. 1979. pap. 14.95 (*0-8061-1560-2*) U of Okla Pr.

***Putnam, Michael C.J.** Virgil's Aeneid--Essays in Interpretation & Influence. LC 94-19891. 420p. 1995. lib. bdg. 45.00x (*0-8078-2191-8*); pap. text ed. 17.95x (*0-8078-4499-3*) U of NC Pr.

Putnam, Oliver. Tracts on Sundry Topics of Political Economy. LC 68-56567. (Reprints of Economic Classics Ser.). viii, 156p. 1970. reprint ed. 29.50 (*0-678-00600-8*) Kelley.

Putnam, Paul A., ed. Handbook of Animal Science. (Illus.). 401p. 1991. text ed. 75.00 (*0-12-568300-6*) Acad Pr.

Putnam, R. E. Spanish-English Dictionary of Architecture & Construction: With English Vocabulary. (Illus.). 535p. 1988. pap. 65.00 (*84-283-1560-4*) IBD Ltd.

Putnam, R. E., jt. auth. see Durbahn, W. E.

Putnam, R. G., jt. auth. see Blackbourn, A.

***Putnam, Rita J.** As Your Parents Age: Your 94-Minute Guide to Information, Help, Peace of Mind, Set, book & audio tape. 124p. (Orig.). 1994. digital audio, pap. 21.95 (*1-886909-00-8*) Dynam Comm.

Putnam, Robert. Bricklaying Skill & Practice. 3rd ed. LC 73-84363. (Illus.). 272p. reprint ed. pap. 77.60 (*0-8357-7401-5*, 2006412) Bks Demand.

— Builder's Comprehensive Dictionary. 2nd ed. (Illus.). 528p. 1989. reprint ed. pap. 24.95 (*0-934041-50-4*) Craftsman.

— Building Trades Blueprint Reading. LC 85-11864. (C). 1983. teacher ed write for info. (*0-8359-0508-X*, Reston) P-H.

— Building Trades Blueprint Reading. LC 85-11864. (C). 1986. pap. text ed. 63.00 (*0-8359-0507-1*, Reston) P-H.

— Construction Blueprint Reading. (C). 1985. teacher ed write for info. (*0-8359-0951-4*, Reston); pap. text ed. 71.00 (*0-8359-0950-6*, Reston) P-H.

— Welding Print Reading. (Illus.). 384p. 1986. pap. text ed. 39.60 (*0-8359-8609-8*) P-H.

Putnam, Robert, jt. auth. see Webster, Jay.

Putnam, Robert D. The Beliefs of Politicians: Ideology, Conflict, & Democracy in Britain & Italy. LC 72-75207. (Yale Studies in Political Science: No. 24). 322p. reprint ed. pap. 91.80 (*0-8357-7121-0*, 2022032) Bks Demand.

— Democracy & the Civic Community: Tradition & Change in an Italian Experiment. (Illus.). 288p. 1992. text ed. 35.00 (*0-691-07889-0*) Princeton U Pr.

— Making Democracy Work: Civic Traditions in Modern Italy. 258p. 1994. pap. 14.95 (*0-691-03738-8*) Princeton U Pr.

Putnam, Robert D. & Bayne, Nicholas. Hanging Together: Co-operation & Conflict in the Seven-Power Summits. 2nd ed. (One-Off Ser.). 304p. (C). 1988. text ed. 45.00 (*0-8039-8101-5*); pap. text ed. 17.95 (*0-8039-8102-3*) Sage.

— Hanging Together: Cooperation & Conflict in the Seven-Power Summits. rev. ed. LC 87-23593. 296p. 1988. pap. 16.95 (*0-674-37226-3*) HUP.

— Hanging Together: The Seven-Power Summits. (Illus.). 276p. 1985. 32.00 (*0-674-37225-5*) HUP.

Putnam, Robert E. Basic Blueprint Reading: Residential. LC 80-80673. (Illus.). 256p. reprint ed. pap. 73.00 (*0-8357-5974-1*, 2017842) Bks Demand.

— Modern Masonry. 395p. (C). 1988. teacher ed write for info. (*0-15-562066-5*, MASON IM); text ed. 33.25 (*0-15-562065-7*, MASON) SCP.

P Q

Putnam, Robert E. & Burnett, John. Concrete Block Construction. 3rd ed. LC 73-75302. (Illus.). 232p. reprint ed. pap. 66.20 (0-317-10862-X, 2011567) Bks Demand.
Putnam, Roger, jt. auth. see Hopkins, David.
Putnam, Roy C. In It to Win It. 1973. pap. 3.95 (0-87508-440-0) Chr Lit.
— Those He Came to Save. LC 77-13764. reprint ed. 35.50 (0-8357-9029-0, 2016414) Bks Demand.
Putnam, Russell, jt. auth. see McKay, Ray.
Putnam, Ruth. Alsace & Lorraine from Caesar to Kaiser 58 B.C.-1871 A.D. LC 75-160988. (Select Bibliographies Reprint Ser.). 1977. reprint ed. 33.95 (0-8369-5856-X) Ayer.
— Charles the Bold. LC 73-14465. (Heroes of the Nations Ser.). reprint ed. 30.00 (0-404-58283-4) AMS Pr.
— William the Silent. LC 73-14466. (Heroes of the Nations Ser.). reprint ed. 30.00 (0-404-58284-2) AMS Pr.
Putnam, Ruth, tr. see Blok, Petrus J.
Putnam, S. An Empirical Model of Regional Growth. (Monograph er.: No. 6). 1975. 22.00 (1-55869-037-9) Regional Sci Res Inst.
Putnam, Samuel. Francois Rabelais, Man of the Renaissance: A Spiritual Biography. 1977. 31.95 (0-8369-7167-1, 7999) Ayer.
— Paris Was Our Mistress: Memoirs of a Lost & Found Generation. LC 73-93886. (Arcturus Books Paperbacks). 272p. 1970. pap. 6.95 (0-8093-0417-1) S Ill U Pr.
Putnam, Samuel, tr. see Cervantes Saavedra, Miguel de.
Putnam, Samuel, tr. see DaCunha, Euclides.
Putnam, Samuel, tr. see Freyre, Gilberto.
Putnam, Samuel, tr. see Huysmans, J. K.
Putnam, Sandy, jt. auth. see Putnam, Alan.
Putnam, Stan P. How I Made Four Hundred Twenty-Three Thousand Dollars with a "Fool Idea" A Proven Money Building Plan of Success in Real Estate, I. (Illus.). (Orig.). (C). 1987. pap. 10.00 (0-944047-01-7) Res Improvement Inst.
— How I Made Four Hundred Twenty-Three Thousand Dollars with a "Fool Idea" A Proven Money Building Plan of Success in Real Estate, II. (Illus.). (Orig.). (C). 1987. pap. 10.00 (0-944047-02-5) Res Improvement Inst.
— How I Made Four Hundred Twenty-Three Thousand Dollars with a "Fool Idea" A Proven Money Building Plan of Success in Real Estate, Set. (Illus.). (Orig.). (C). 1987. pap. 20.00 (0-944047-00-9) Res Improvement Inst.
— How to Analyze Handwriting for Fun & Profit: A Manual Showing How to Analyze, Interpret & Provide Behavior Modification Through Handwriting. (Illus.). 120p. 1987. 20.00 (0-318-22857-2); pap. 12.00 (0-318-22858-0) Res Improvement Inst.
— How to Never Be Fat Again: A Proven Physical Fitness Plan for Health, Looks & Physique Using Exercise, Diet & Behavior Modification. (Illus.). 120p. 1987. 20.00 (0-318-22859-9); pap. 12.00 (0-318-22860-2) Res Improvement Inst.
— How to Test & Improve Your Sex Appeal: A Psychographological (Handwriting Analysis) Plan to Test & Improve Basic Sex Appeal. (Illus.). (Orig.). 1987. pap. text ed. 10.00 (0-944047-03-3) Res Improvement Inst.
— Momento, Souvenir, Keepsake, & Collector's Kit on the Life & Music of Elvis. (Illus.). 1988. reprint ed. pap. 10. 00 (0-944047-08-4) Res Improvement Inst.
— Money Making Secrets of the Self-Made Millionaires: A Proven Plan for Structuring & Implementing a Path Toward Riches As Has Been Done by Self-Made Millionaires. (Illus.). (Orig.). 1987. pap. 10.00 (0-944047-04-1) Res Improvement Inst.
— New Found Facts & Memorabilia about Elvis Presley: A Manual on the Life & Times of Elvis Presley Using Psychographology (Handwriting Analysis) with Related Memorabilia. (Illus.). 100p. 1987. 20.00 (0-318-22861-0); pap. 12.00 (0-318-22862-9) Res Improvement Inst.
Putnam, Thelma, et al. Christian Religion among the Stockbridge-Munsee Band of Mohican Indians. rev. ed. (Illus.). 78p. (Orig.). (C). 1980. pap. text ed. 3.50 (0-935790-01-2) Muh-He-Con-Neew.
Putnam, Tim, jt. auth. see Alfrey, Judith.
Putnam, Walter, III. Paul Valery Revisited. LC 94-12619. (Twayne's World Author Ser.: No. 850). 200p. 1994. text ed. 22.95x (0-8057-8291-5, Twayne) Macmillan.
Putnam, Walter C., III. L' Aventure Litteraire de Joseph Conrad et d'Andre Gide. (Stanford French & Italian Studies: Vol. 67). 276p. (FRE.). 1991. pap. 46.50 (0-915838-83-4) Anma Libri.
Putnam, William. The Worst Weather on Earth. (Illus.). 266p. 1993. 29.50 (0-930410-35-1) Amer Alpine Club.
Putnam, William L. The Explorers of Mars Hill: A Centennial History of Lowell Observatory. LC 93-49057. (Illus.). 320p. 1994. 30.00 (0-914659-69-3) Phoenix Pub.
— The Great Glacier & Its House: The Story of the First Center of Alpinism in North America, 1885-1925. LC 80-69728. (Illus.). 224p. 1982. 35.00 (0-930410-13-0) Amer Alpine Club.
— Joe Dodge "One New Hampshire Institution" LC 86-874. (Illus.). 184p. 1986. 16.00 (0-914659-17-0) Phoenix Pub.
— A Yankee Image: The Life & Times of Roger Lowell Putnam. LC 91-36425. (Illus.). 172p. 1991. 25.00 (0-914659-55-3) Phoenix Pub.
Putnam, William L., jt. auth. see Kauffman, Andrew J.
Putnam, William L., jt. auth. see Kruszyna, Robert.
Putnam, William L., et al. Placenames of the Canadian Alps. (Illus.). 384p. 1990. 25.95 (0-9691621-4-6) Footprint Pub.
Putney & Bolognesi. AIDS Vaccine Research & Clinical Trials. 504p. 1990. 125.00 (0-8247-8221-6) Dekker.
Putney, Albert H. U. S. Constitutional History & Law. 599p. 1985. reprint ed. lib. bdg. 45.00 (0-8377-1021-9) Rothman.
Putney, Diane T. Ultra & the U. S. Army Air Forces. 197p. 1987. 8.00 (0-912799-46-3); pap. 8.00 (0-912799-45-5) Off Air Force.
Putney, James W., Jr. Inositol Phosphates & Calcium Signalling (Advances in Second Messenger & Phosphoprotein Research), Vol. 26. 416p. 1992. 100.00 (0-88167-883-X) Raven.
Putney, James W., Jr., jt. ed. see Mitchell, Robert H.
Putney, Martha S. Black Sailors: Afro-American Merchant Seamen & Whalemen Prior to the Civil War. LC 86-22822. (Contributions in Afro-American & African Studies: No. 103). (Illus.). 184p. 1987. text ed. 47.95 (0-313-25639-X, PBS/, Greenwood Pr) Greenwood.
— When the Nation Was in Need: Blacks in the Women's Army Corps During World War II. LC 92-24084. (Illus.). 245p. 1992. 35.00 (0-8108-2531-7) Scarecrow.
***Putney, Mary J.** Angel Rogue. 384p. (Orig.). 1995. mass mkt., pap. 5.99 (0-451-40598-6, Topaz) NAL-Dutton.
— Carousel of Hearts. (Regency Romance Ser.). 224p. 1989. pap. 3.99 (0-451-16267-6, Sig) NAL-Dutton.
— The Controversial Countess. braille ed. 539p. 1993. text ed. 43.12 (1-56956-495-7, BR9136) W A T Braille.
— Dancing on the Wind. 384p. (Orig.). 1994. pap. 4.99 (0-451-40486-6, Topaz) NAL-Dutton.
— Dearly Beloved. 416p. (Orig.). 1990. pap. 4.99 (0-451-40185-9) NAL-Dutton.
— The Diabolical Baron. 224p. 1993. lib. bdg. 20.00 (0-7278-4528-4) Severn Hse.
— Petals in the Storm. 384p. (Orig.). 1993. pap. 4.99 (0-451-40445-9, Topaz) NAL-Dutton.
— The Rake & the Reformer. 1989. pap. 4.99 (0-451-16143-2, Sig) NAL-Dutton.
— Silk & Secrets. (Orig.). 1992. pap. 4.99 (0-451-40301-0, Onyx) NAL-Dutton.
— Silk & Shadows. 432p. 1991. pap. 4.99 (0-451-40277-4, Onyx) NAL-Dutton.
— Thunder & Roses. 384p. (Orig.). 1993. pap. 4.99 (0-451-40367-3, Topaz) NAL-Dutton.
— Uncommon Vows. 384p. (Orig.). 1991. pap. 4.99 (0-451-40244-8, Onyx) NAL-Dutton.
— Veils of Silk. 384p. (Orig.). 1992. pap. 4.99 (0-451-40348-7, Onyx) NAL-Dutton.
— The Would-Be Widow. (Orig.). 1991. 18.95 (0-7278-4291-9) Severn Hse.
Putney, Susan & Wrightson, Berni. Spider-Man: Hooky. 64p. 1986. 6.95 (0-87135-154-4) Marvel Entmnt.
Putnicki, Patti. Celibacy Is Better Than Really Bad Sex: And Other Classic Rules for Single Women. (Illus.). 176p. 1994. pap. 9.95 (0-944042-35-X) CorkScrew Pr.
— Man School. 1992. pap. 6.95 (0-9625536-0-3) Patti Industries.
Putnik, Edwin. Art of Flute Playing. LC 75-146521. (Illus.). 96p. 1970. pap. 14.95 (0-87487-077-1) Summy-Birchard.
Putnis, Andrew. An Introduction to Mineral Sciences. LC 92-8420. (Illus.). 450p. (C). 1992. pap. 39.95 (0-521-42947-1) Cambridge U Pr.
— An Introduction to Mineral Sciences. LC 92-8420. (Illus.). 450p. (C). 1993. 100.00 (0-521-41922-0) Cambridge U Pr.
Putnis, Andrew & McConnell, J. D. Principles of Mineral Behavior. (Geological Studies: Vol. 1). 258p. 1980. pap. 46.75 (0-444-00444-0) Elsevier.
Putnum, A. W. History of Middle Tennessee, Or, Life & Times of Gen. James Robertson. LC 73-146412. (First American Frontier Ser.). (Illus.). 1971. reprint ed. 49.95 (0-405-02876-8) Ayer.
Putschar, Walter G., jt. auth. see Ortner, Donald J.
Putschke, W., jt. ed. see Hartweg, Frederic.
Putseys, Y., jt. auth. see De Geest, W.
Putseys, Y., jt. ed. see De Geest, W.
Putt, Allen D. & Springer, J. Frederick. Policy Research: Concepts, Methods, & Applications. 384p. (C). 1988. Casebound. text ed. write for info. (0-13-684051-5) P-H.
Putt, Arlene M., jt. auth. see Van Ort, Suzanne.
Putt, S. Gorley, ed. see James, Henry.
Puttaswamaiah, K. Cost Benefit Analysis for Irrigation & Drought Proofing. (C). 1988. 27.50 (81-204-0369-X, Pub. by Oxford IBH II) S Asia.
— Irrigation Projects in India: Towards a New Policy. (C). 1994. text ed. 28.00 (81-7387-007-1, Pub. by Indus Pub II) S Asia.
Puttaswamiah, K. Poverty & Rural Development. (C). 1989. 48.50 (0-685-33267-5, Pub. by Oxford IBH II) S Asia.
***Putte, Katherine R.** Our Town: A Community Simulation of Contemporary Issues. LC 94-42940. 1995. write for info. (1-56976-011-X) Zephyr Pr AZ.
Puttenham, George. The Arte of English Poesie. Willcock, Gladys D. & Walker, Alice, eds. 471p. reprint ed. pap. 134.30 (0-8357-5768-4, 2024510) Bks Demand.
— The Arte of English Poesie. LC 79-26413. (English Experience Ser.: No. 342). 258p. 1971. reprint ed. 30.00 (90-221-0342-0) Walter J Johnson.
Puttenham, Richard. The Arte of English Poesie: Contriued into Three Bookes: The First of Poets & Poesie, the Second of Proportion, the Third of Ornament. LC 71-85107. (Kent English Reprints, the Renaissance Ser.). 340p. reprint ed. pap. 96.90 (0-7837-6150-3, 2045872) Bks Demand.
***Putter, Ad.** Sir Gawain & the Green Knight & the French Arthurian Romance. 288p. 1995. 49.95 (0-19-818253-8) OUP.
Putter, Irving. La Derniere Illusion de Leconte de Lisle: Lettres Inedites a Emilie LeForestier. LC 68-65490. 172p. 1983. reprint ed. lib. bdg. 33.00x (0-89370-794-5) Borgo Pr.
Putter, Irving, tr. see De Chateaubriand, Francois-Rene.
Putter, Johann S. Versuch Einer Academischen Gelehrtengeschichte Von der Georg-Augustus-Universitat Zu Gottingen, 4 vols., Set. reprint ed. write for info. (0-318-71942-8, Pub. by Georg Olms GW) Lubrecht & Cramer.
Putterford, Mark. AC-DC: Illustrated Biography. (Illus.). 96p. 1992. pap. 19.95 (0-7119-2823-1, OP46671) Omnibus NY.
— Aerosmith: Live! (Illus.). (Orig.). (YA). (gr. 9 up). 1994. pap. 9.95 (0-7119-4246-3, OP47707) Omnibus NY.
— Aerosmith: The Fall & Rise of Aerosmith. (Illus.). 80p. 1991. pap. 19.95 (0-7119-2303-5, OP46028) Omnibus NY.
Putterman, Allen M., ed. Cosmetic Oculoplastic Surgery. 2nd ed. LC 92-49768. (Illus.). 400p. 1993. text ed. 105. 00 (0-7216-4499-6) Saunders.
***Putterman, Barry.** On Television & Comedy: Essays on Style, Theme, Performer & Writer. 240p. 1995. pap. 28. 50 (0-7864-0067-6) McFarland & Co.
Putterman, Lewis. Peasants, Collectives, & Choice: Economic Theory & Tanzania's Villages. LC 86-2915. (Contemporary Studies in Economic & Financial Analysis: Vol. 57). 408p. 1986. 73.25 (0-89232-684-0) Jai Pr.
Putterman, Louis. Continuity & Change in China's Rural Development: Collective & Reform Eras in Perspective. (Illus.). 384p. 1993. 49.95 (0-19-507872-1) OUP.
— Division of Labor & Welfare: An Introduction to Economic Systems. (Library of Political Economy). (Illus.). 264p. 1990. 59.00 (0-19-877299-8); pap. text ed. 19.95 (0-19-877298-X) OUP.
Putterman, Louis, ed. The Economic Nature of the Firm: A Reader. (Illus.). 384p. 1986. pap. 27.95 (0-521-31140-3) Cambridge U Pr.
— The Economic Nature of the Firm: A Reader. (Illus.). 384p. 1986. 74.95 (0-521-32278-2) Cambridge U Pr.
Putterman, Louis & Rueschemeyer, Dietrich, eds. State & Market in Development: Synergy or Rivalry? LC 92-17038. (Emerging Global Issues Ser.). 277p. 1992. lib. bdg. 40.00 (1-55587-311-1) Lynne Rienner.
Putterman, Louis, jt. auth. see Bonin, John P.
Puttfarken, Thomas. Roger de Piles' Theory of Art. LC 85-40467. (Illus.). 148p. 1985. 30.00 (0-300-03356-7) Yale U Pr.
Putti, Joseph. Theology as Hermeneutics: Paul Ricoeur's Theory of Text Interpretation & Method in Theology. LC 93-39087. 1994. 64.95 (1-883255-23-6); pap. 44.95 (1-883255-22-8) Intl Scholars.
Puttick & Simpson. Bibliotheca Mejicana. LC 71-168027. reprint ed. 40.00 (0-404-02388-6) AMS Pr.
Puttick, Elizabeth & Clarke, Peter B., eds. Women As Teachers & Disciples in Traditional & New Religions. LC 93-30865. (Studies in Women & Religion: Vol. 32). 152p. 1993. text ed. 69.95 (0-7734-9346-8) E Mellen.
Puttick, K. Challenging Delegated Legislation. (Waterlow Practitioner's Library). 336p. 1988. 59.00 (0-08-033071-1, K125, K130, Pergamon Pr) Elsevier.
Puttick, Keith. Wages & the Law. (C). 1988. pap. 125.00 (0-317-92374-9, Scientific) St Mut.
— Wages & the Law. 190p. (C). 1989. pap. 75.00 (0-7219-1110-2, Pub. by IPM Hse UK) St Mut.
Puttick, Keith, jt. auth. see Painter, Richard W.
Puttini, Sergio. Carrozzeria Boneschi. (Illus.). 160p. 55.00 (88-7911-018-7, Pub. by Giorgio Nada Editore IT) Howell Pr VA.
Puttock, J. S., ed. Stably Stratified Flow & Dense Gas Dispersion. (Institute of Mathematics & Its Applications Conference Series, New Ser.: New Series 15). (Illus.). 448p. 1988. 89.00 (0-19-853615-1) OUP.
Putuwar, Sunanda. The Buddhist Sangha: Paradigm of the Ideal Human Society. 136p. (C). 1991. lib. bdg. 34.00 (0-8191-8279-6); pap. text ed. 19.50 (0-8191-7842-X) U Pr of Amer.
Putz-Anderson, Vern, ed. Cumulative Trauma Disorders: A Manual for Musculoskeletal Diseases of the Upper Limbs. 112p. 1988. 26.00 (0-85066-405-5) Taylor & Francis.
Putz, C. Delos, Jr., jt. auth. see Minninger, Joan.
Putz, F. E. & Mooney, Harold A., eds. Biology of Vines. (Illus.). 448p. (C). 1992. 125.00 (0-521-39250-0) Cambridge U Pr.
Putz, George, Jr. The Shawano Paper Mill Centennial 1894-1994. (Illus.). 112p. 1994. write for info. (0-942495-41-1); pap. write for info. (0-942495-42-X) Amherst Pr.
Putz, George. Wood & Canvas Kayak Building. 1990. pap. text ed. 17.95 (0-87742-258-3) Intl Marine.
— Wood & Canvas Kayak Building. 1990. pap. text ed. 17. 95 (0-07-155939-6) McGraw.
Putz, George & Island Journal Staff, eds. Killick Stones: A Collection of Maine Island Writing, Vol. 1. (Illus.). 117p. (Orig.). 1987. pap. text ed. 6.95 (0-942719-05-0) Island Inst.
Putz, Martin. Language Contact & Language Conflict. LC 93-46217. xv, 254p. 1994. lib. bdg. 59.00 (1-55619-479-X) Benjamins North Am.
Putz, Martin, ed. Thirty Years of Linguistic Evolution: Studies in Honor of Rene Dirven on the Occasion of His 60th Birthday. LC 92-22941. xi, 632p. 1992. 106.00x (1-55619-462-5); pap. 39.95x (1-55619-463-3) Benjamins North Am.
Putz, Robyn, ed. see Maurer, Tracy M. & Woolf, Joni W.
Putzar, Edward. Japanese Literature: A Historical Outline. LC 70-189229. 278p. reprint ed. pap. 79.30 (0-317-09821-7, 2022754) Bks Demand.
Putzar, Edward, tr. Watcher from the Shore. 400p. 1990. 19.95 (0-87011-938-9) Kodansha.
Putzel, J., et al. Agrarian Reform & Official Development Assistance in the Philippines: Four Papers. (Occasional Papers). (Illus.). 135p. 1990. 15.00 (0-317-05274-8, Pub. by CSEAS UK) Cellar.
Putzel, James. A Captive Land: The Politics of Agrarian Reform in the Philippines. LC 92-12667. 1992. pap. 18. 00 (0-85345-842-1) Monthly Rev.
***Putzel, Max.** Genius of Place: William Faulkner's Triumphant Beginnings. LC 84-10057. (Southern Literary Studies). 352p. 1985. pap. 100.40 (0-7837-8515-1, 2049324) Bks Demand.
Putzel, Steven. Reconstructing Yeats: "The Secret Rose" & "The Wind among the Reeds" LC 85-22986. 256p. 1986. 53.00 (0-389-20600-8, N8158) B&N Imports.
Putzell, Sara M., jt. auth. see McGuire, Peter J.
Putzer, Thomas C., ed. Population & Related Organizations: International Address List. LC 93-49526. (APLIC Special Publication Ser.: No. 6). (Orig.). 1994. pap. write for info. (0-933438-20-6) APLIC Intl.
Puu, Tonu. The Allocation of Road Capital in Two-Dimensional Space: A Continuous Approach. (Studies in Regional Science & Urban Economics: Vol. 5). 216p. 1979. 51.50 (0-444-85324-3, North Holland) Elsevier.
— Nonlinear Economic Dynamics. (Lecture Notes in Economics & Mathematical Systems Ser.: Vol. 336). (Illus.). viii, 119p. 1989. pap. 17.80 (0-387-51438-4) Spr-Verlag.
— Nonlinear Economic Dynamics. 2nd enl. rev. ed. (Illus.). x, 151p. 1991. 39.00 (0-387-53351-6) Spr-Verlag.
— Nonlinear Economic Dynamics. 3rd enl. rev. ed. LC 92-35868. 1993. 59.00 (0-387-56145-5) Spr-Verlag.
Puu, Tonu, jt. auth. see Beckmann, Martin J.
***Puxley, Frank L.** In African Game Tracks: Wanderings with a Rifle Through Eastern Africa. (Illus.). 320p. Date not set. 65.00 (1-882458-01-X) Trophy Rm Bks.
***Puxley, Lavallin.** Samoyeds. deluxe ed. 80p. 1995. 20.00 (0-614-04550-9) Donald R Hoflin.
***Puxley, Ray.** Cockney Rabbit: A Dick'n'Arry of Rhyming Slang. 230p. 1995. pap. 10.95 (0-86051-827-2, Robson-Parkwest) Parkwest Pubns.
Puxley, W. Lavallin. Collies & Sheepdogs. 1992. lib. bdg. 79. 95 (0-8490-5223-8) Gordon Pr.
— Magic Land of the Maya. 1977. lib. bdg. 59.95 (0-8490-2194-4) Gordon Pr.
Puxty, A. G. The Social & Organizational Context of Management Accounting. (Advanced Management Accounting & Finance Ser.). (Illus.). 163p. 1993. pap. text ed. 14.95 (0-12-568660-9) Acad Pr.
Puxty, Anthony, jt. auth. see Tinker, Tony.
Puy-Costa, M. Modern Langenscheidt French-Spanish, Spanish-French Dictionary: Diccionario Moderno Langenscheidt Frances-Espanol-Frances. 11th ed. 512p. (FRE & SPA.). 1981. 19.95 (0-8288-0740-X, S39863) Fr & Eur.
***Puy-Costa, M., ed.** Dictionnaire Pratique. 2nd ed. 1966. write for info. (0-7859-8602-2, 203220620X); write for info. (2-03-220620-X) Fr & Eur.
Puzak, P. P., jt. ed. see Holt, John M.
Puzinauskas, V. P. Properties of Asphalt Cements. 72p. 1980. 15.00 (0-318-13396-2, RR-80-2) Asphalt Inst.
***Puzio & Johnson.** Practical Heating, Ventilation, & Air Conditioning. 96p. 1995. teacher ed 14.00 (0-8273-5592-0) Delmar.
— Practical Heating, Ventilation, & Air Conditioning: Workbook. 160p. 1995. student ed 16.95 (0-8273-7058-X) Delmar.
***Puzio, Henry & Johnson, Jim.** Practical Heating, Ventilation, Air Conditioning, & Refrigeration. LC 94-30878. 1995. 46.95 (0-8273-5591-2) Delmar.
Puzman, J. & Kubin, B. Public Data Networks: From Separate PDNs to the ISDN. (Illus.). x, 241p. 1991. pap. 104.00 (0-387-19580-7) Spr-Verlag.
Puzo, Mario. The Dark Arena. 1977. pap. 1.95 (0-449-23295-6, Crest) Fawcett.
— Fools Die. 1979. pap. 6.99 (0-451-16019-3, Sig) NAL-Dutton.
— The Fourth K. large type ed. 685p. 1991. reprint ed. lib. bdg. 22.95 (1-56054-191-1) Thorndike Pr.
— The Godfather. 1983. pap. 5.99 (0-451-16771-6, Sig) NAL-Dutton.
— The Godfather. 1969. 24.95 (0-399-10342-2, Putnam) Putnam Pub Group.
— Selected from The Godfather. abr. ed. (Writers' Voices Ser.). 64p. (Orig.). 1991. pap. text ed. 3.50 (0-929631-22-6, Signal Hill) New Readers.
— The Sicilian. 416p. 1985. mass mkt. 6.99 (0-553-25282-8) Bantam.
Puzo, Michael J., jt. auth. see Muir, Douglas A.
***Puzon, Bridget, ed.** Women Religious in Contemporary American Society: The Brookland Commission Report. 248p. 1995. pap. text ed. 44.95 (1-883255-76-7) Intl Scholars.
— Women Religious in Contemporary American Society: The Brookland Commission Report. 248p. 1995. text ed. 64.95 (1-883255-77-5) Intl Scholars.
Puzzle House Staff, ed. Picture Puzzles. (FunFax Ser.). (Illus.). 48p. (J). (gr. 3-6). 1992. pap. 2.95 (1-56680-007-2) Mad Hatter Pub.
— Pocket Puzzler. (FunFax Ser.). (Illus.). 48p. (J). (gr. 3-6). 1992. pap. 2.95 (1-56680-006-4) Mad Hatter Pub.
Puzzo, Dante. Peering into the Darkness. LC 92-62457. 118p. (Orig.). 1993. pap. 12.00 (0-9634503-0-1) Randatamp Pr.
***Puzzo, Dante A.** Myth & the Cold War. 98p. (Orig.). 1995. pap. 12.00 (0-9634503-2-8) Randatamp Pr.
— The Partisans & the War in Italy. LC 92-10256. (Studies in Modern European History: Vol. 7). 101p. (C). 1993. text ed. 38.95 (0-8204-1951-6) P Lang Pubs.
Puzzo, Dante A. Spain & the Great Powers, Nineteen Thirty-Six to Nineteen Forty-One. LC 72-3101. (Select Bibliographies Reprint Ser.). 1980. reprint ed. 23.95 (0-8369-6868-9) Ayer.
PWN, Polish Scientific Publishers Staff, ed. see Szmydt, Zofia.
PWN, Polish Scientific Publishers Staff, ed. see Topolski, Jerzy.

P Q

An Asterisk (*) at the beginning of an entry indicates that the title is appearing in BIP for the first time.

Pyadyshen, Boris D., ed. Russia & the World: New Views on Foreign Policy. 352p. 1991. 21.95 (*1-55972-087-5*, Birch Ln Pr) Carol Pub Group.

Pyarelal. Mahatma Gandhi, 4 vols., Set. Incl. Vol. I. Early Phase, 1869-1896. 875p. 1983. 40.00 (*0-934676-41-0*); Vol. II. Discovery of Satyagraha, 1896-1902. 445p. 1983. 45.00 (*0-934676-42-9*); Vol. V. Last Phase, 1946-8 (Part One Only) (Illus.). 742p. 1983. 30.00 (*0-934676-43-7*); Vol. III. Birth of Satyagraha, 1902-1906. 648p. 1983. 50.00 (*0-934676-73-9*); (Illus.). 1983. write for info. (*0-318-57040-8*) Greenlf Bks.

Pyarelal, et al. Gandhian Thought & Contemporary Society. Mathur, J. S., ed. 285p. 1983. 18.00 (*0-934676-31-3*) Greenlf Bks.

Pyarelel. Gandhian Techniques in the Modern World. 70p. (Orig.). 1983. pap. 2.00 (*0-934676-45-3*) Greenlf Bks.

Pyatakhin, M. V. & Suchkov, A. F. Spatiotemporal Characteristics of Laser Emission. (Proceedings of the Lebedev Physics Institute Ser.: Vol. 199). (Illus.). 249p. (C). 1994. lib. bdg. 89.00 (*1-56072-163-4*) Nova Sci Pubs.

Pyatetskii-Shapiro, I. I. Automorphic Functions & the Geometry of Classical Domains. (Mathematics & Its Applications Ser.). 272p. 1969. text ed. 169.00 (*0-677-20310-1*) Gordon & Breach.

Pyatnitskii, I. V. Cobalt. (Analytical Chemistry of the Elements Ser.). 264p. 1970. text ed. 66.00 (*0-7065-0746-0*, Pub. by Keter Pub IS) Coronet Bks.

Pyatt, D. W., jt. ed. see Ellis, F. A.

Pyatt, F. Graham & Roe, Alan. Social Accounting for Development Planning with Special Reference to Sri Lanka. LC 76-30553. 222p. reprint ed. pap. 63.30 (*0-317-30419-4*, 2024943) Bks Demand.

Pyatt, Graham & Round, Jeffery I., eds. Social Accounting Matrices: A Basis for Planning. (Symposium Ser.). 293p. 1985. 18.95 (*0-8213-0550-6*, 10550) World Bank.

Pyatt, Richard I. Magic Meals: Two Hundred Healing and Preventive Recipes for Today's Thirteen Most Common Health Conditions. LC 92-21198. 1993. Case. write for info. (*0-13-554684-2*, Parker Publishing Co); pap. write for info. (*0-13-554676-1*, Parker Publishing Co) P-H.

— Medical Breakthroughs. 288p. 1986. 21.95 (*0-13-572470-8*) P-H.

— People's Medical Answer Book: Plain Answers to One Thousand One Hundred Common Questions from Thirty-Six Leading Specialists. 1984. 21.95 (*0-13-656596-4*); pap. 10.95 (*0-13-656588-3*) P-H.

Pyatt, Rosina. Unquestionable Lady. 1990. pap. 3.95 (*0-8217-3151-3*) Zebra.

Pyatt, Sherman. Apartheid, 1979-1988: A Selected Annotated Bibliography. LC 89-7710. 190p. 1989. 29.00 (*0-8240-7637-0*, 55587) Garland.

Pyatt, Sherman E., comp. Martin Luther King, Jr. An Annotated Bibliography. LC 86-7593. (Bibliographies & Indexes in Afro-American & African Studies: No. 12). 166p. 1986. text ed. 49.95 (*0-313-24635-1*, PML/, Greenwood Pr) Greenwood.

Pyburn, Philip, jt. auth. see Gremillion, Lee.

***Pybus, Cassandra, ed.** Columbus' Blindness & Other Essays. 1994. pap. 16.95 (*0-7022-2745-5*, Pub. by Univ Queensland Pr AT) Intl Spec Bk.

Pybus, Elizabeth. Human Goodness: Generosity & Courage. 154p. 1991. 40.00 (*0-8020-5939-2*) U of Toronto Pr.

Pybus, Paul, see Paul Notrik, pseud..

***Pycior, Helena M., et al, eds.** Creative Couples in the Sciences. LC 94-41059. (Lives of Women in Science Ser.). (Illus.). 250p. (C). 1995. text ed. 50.00 (*0-8135-2187-4*); pap. text ed. 18.95 (*0-8135-2188-2*) Rutgers U Pr.

Pycock, C. J., jt. auth. see Kruk, Z. L.

Pye. China: An Introduction. (6th ed. (C). 1990. pap. text ed. 29.50 (*0-673-46486-5*) HarpCollege.

Pye, A. Kenneth. The Use of Troops in Civil Disturbances in the United States. LC 82-70103. (Occasional Paper Ser.: No. 10). 42p. 1982. 5.00 (*0-685-14091-1*) Ctr Intl Stud Duke.

Pye, Brian, jt. auth. see Button, David.

***Pye, Chris.** Carving on Turning. (Illus.). 176p. 1995. pap. 14.95 (*0-946819-88-2*, Pub. by Guild Mstr Craftsman UK) Sterling.

— Woodcarving Tools, Materials & Equipment. (Illus.). 362p. 1995. pap. 24.95 (*0-946819-49-1*) Sterling.

Pye, Christopher. The Regal Phantasm: Shakespeare & the Politics of Spectacle. 176p. 1990. 29.95 (*0-415-01575-8*, A3996) Routledge.

Pye, David. The Crazy World of Sex. (Crazy World Ser.). (Illus.). 80p. 1992. pap. 4.99 (*1-85015-360-4*) Exley Giftbooks.

— The Nature & Aesthetics of Design. (Illus.). 160p. 1995. pap. 19.95 (*0-9643999-1-1*) Cambium Pr.

— The Nature & Art of Workmanship. rev. ed. (Illus.). 160p. 1995. pap. 19.95 (*0-9643999-0-3*) Cambium Pr.

Pye, David L., et al, eds. The Physics of Non-Crystalline Solids. 900p. 1992. 135.00 (*0-7484-0050-8*, Pub. by Tay Francis Ltd UK) Taylor & Francis.

Pye, Douglas, jt. ed. see Cameron, Ian.

Pye, Ethel, ed. see Adrine-Robinson, Kenyette.

Pye, Ethel, ed. see Ceasor, Ebraska D.

Pye, Ethel, ed. see Durant, Charlotte T.

Pye, Geralyn, jt. auth. see Pettavino, Paula J.

Pye, K., ed. The Dynamics & Environmental Context of Aeolian Sedimentary Systems. (Geological Society Special Publications: No. 72). (Illus.). viii, 336p. (C). 1993. 97.00 (*0-903317-88-5*, Pub. by Geol Soc Pub Hse UK) AAPG.

Pye, K. & Lancaster, N., eds. Aeiolian Sediments. LC 92-36454. (International Association of Sedimentologists Special Publication Ser.: No. 16). 1993. pap. 65.00 (*0-632-03544-7*) Blackwell Sci.

Pye, K. & Yates, R. British Politics: Ideas & Concepts. (C). 1990. 100.00 (*0-7487-0227-X*, Pub. by S Thornes Pubs UK) St Mut.

Pye, Kenneth. Aeolian Dust & Dust Deposits. (Orig.). 1987. text ed. 102.00 (*0-12-568690-0*); pap. text ed. 49.00 (*0-12-568691-9*) Acad Pr.

Pye, Kenneth, ed. Sediment Transport & Depositional Processes. LC 93-17446. 330p. 1994. pap. 54.95 (*0-632-03112-3*) Blackwell Sci.

Pye, Kenneth & Tsoar, Haim. Aeolian Sand & Sand Dunes. 416p. 1990. 115.00 (*0-04-551125-X*) Routledge Chapman & Hall.

Pye, Kenneth, jt. ed. see Goudie, Andrew S.

Pye, L. D., et al, eds. Borate Glasses: Structure, Properties, Applications. LC 78-9108. (Materials Science Research Ser.: Vol. 12). 648p. 1978. 125.00 (*0-306-40016-2*, Plenum Pr) Plenum.

Pye, Lucian W. Chinese Negotiating Style: Commercial Approaches & Cultural Principles. LC 91-32748. 136p. 1992. text ed. 47.95 (*0-89930-724-8*, PCN/, Quorum Bks) Greenwood.

— Guerrilla Communism in Malaya: Its Social & Political Meaning. LC 81-4591. xvi, 369p. 1981. reprint ed. text ed. 65.00 (*0-313-23017-X*, PYGC, Greenwood Pr) Greenwood.

— The Mandarin & the Cadre: China's Political Cultures. LC 88-27727. (Michigan Monographs in Chinese Studies: No. 59). 224p. 1988. pap. text ed. 12.50 (*0-89264-083-9*) Ctr Chinese Studies.

— The Non-Western Political Process. (Reprint Series in Social Sciences). (C). 1993. reprint ed. pap. text ed. 1.00 (*0-8290-3099-9*, PS-351) Irvington.

— The Spirit of Chinese Politics. 2nd ed. 264p. (C). 1992. pap. text ed. 17.50 (*0-674-83240-X*) HUP.

Pye, Lucian W., ed. Communications & Political Development. (Studies in Political Development: Vol. 1). 1963. 55.00 (*0-691-07504-2*); pap. 17.95 (*0-691-02152-X*) Princeton U Pr.

— Political Science & Area Studies: Rivals or Partners? LC 74-15711. 253p. reprint ed. pap. 72.20 (*0-8357-9234-X*, 2015832) Bks Demand.

Pye, Lucian W. & Pye, Mary W. Asian Power & Politics: The Cultural Dimensions of Authority. LC 85-2581. 432p. 1988. reprint ed. pap. 17.50 (*0-674-04979-9*) HUP.

Pye, Lucian W., jt. ed. see Jackson, Karl D.

Pye, Marian, jt. auth. see Campbell, John.

Pye, Marion, jt. auth. see Campbell, John.

Pye, Mary W., jt. auth. see Pye, Lucian W.

Pye, Michael. Maximum City: The Biography of New York. (Illus.). 320p. (Orig.). 1993. 29.95 (*1-85619-093-5*, Sinclair-Stevenson) Trafalgar.

Pye, Michael, ed. The Continuum Dictionary of Religion. LC 93-36623. 352p. 1994. 34.95 (*0-8264-0639-4*) Continuum.

Pye, Michael & Morgan, Robert, eds. The Cardinal Meaning: Essays in Comparative Hermeneutics, Buddhism & Christianity. (Religion & Reason Ser.: No. 6). 203p. 1973. text ed. 29.35 (*90-279-7228-1*) Mouton.

Pye, Michael, tr. see Tominaga, Nakamoto.

Pye, Michael, ed. see Troeltsch, Ernst.

Pye, Michael, tr. see Troeltsch, Ernst.

Pye, Richard J., jt. ed. see Champion, Robert H.

Pye-Smith, Charlie, et al. The Wealth of Communities: Stories of Success in Local Environmental Management. LC 94-75606. (Library of Management for Development). (Illus.). x, 213p. (Orig.). 1994. pap. 18.95 (*1-56549-038-X*) Kumarian Pr.

Pyenson, Bruce, jt. auth. see White, Jane.

***Pyenson, Bruce S., ed.** Calculated Risk: A Provider's Guide to Assessing & Controlling the Financial Risk of Managed Care. 78p. 1995. pap. text ed. 32.00 (*1-55648-131-4*, 131001) AHPI.

Pyenson, Lewis. Civilizing Mission: Exact Sciences & French Overseas Expansion, 1830-1940. LC 92-22577. (Illus.). 352p. 1993. text ed. 45.00 (*0-8018-4421-5*) Johns Hopkins.

— Neohumanism & the Persistence of Pure Mathematics in Wilhelmian Germany. LC 82-72156. (American Philosophical Society, Memoirs Ser.: No. 150). 148p. reprint ed. pap. 42.20 (*0-7837-4333-5*, 2044044) Bks Demand.

— The Young Einstein: The Advent of Relativity. (Illus.). 272p. 1985. 59.00 (*0-85274-779-9*) IOP Pub.

Pyenson, Lewis, ed. see Infeld, Leopold.

Pyenson, Lewis, jt. ed. see McCormmach, Russell.

Pyenson, Louis L. & Barke, Harvey E. Laboratory Manual for Entomology & Plant Pathology. 2nd ed. (Illus.). (C). 1981. pap. 20.95 (*0-87055-393-3*) AVI.

Pyeritz, Reed E. Molecular Biology in Critical Medicine. 1994. pap. text ed. 30.00 (*0-07-051102-0*) McGraw.

***Pyeritz, Reed E. & Gasner, Cheryll.** The Marfan Syndrome. 4th ed. (Illus.). 48p. 1994. pap. 3.00 (*0-918335-09-4*) Natl Marfan Foun.

Pyes, Craig. Picnics of Provence: French Country-Style Picnics to Enjoy at Home or Abroad. LC 92-13109. 1993. 14.00 (*0-671-78536-2*) S&S Trade.

— Picnics of Tuscany. LC 93-34448. 1994. 14.00 (*0-671-87015-7*) S&S Trade.

Pyhrr, Stephen A., et al. Real Estate Investment: Strategy, Analysis, Decisions. 2nd ed. 962p. 1989. Net. text ed. write for info. (*0-471-87953-3*) Wiley.

Pykare, Nina C. Lost Duchess of Greyden Castle. 1990. pap. 3.95 (*0-8217-3046-0*) Zebra.

— No Time for Kisses. 192p. 1992. 13.95 (*0-8034-8971-4*, Avalon Bks) Bouregy.

Pyke, David, ed. see Medawar, Peter.

Pyke, Frank. Industrial Development Through Small-Firm Cooperation Theory & Practice. vi, 69p. (Orig.). 1992. pap. 10.00 (*92-2-108256-3*) Intl Labour Office.

Pyke, Helen G. Doctor, Doctor. LC 92-37123. 1993. write for info. (*0-8280-0683-0*) Review & Herald.

Pyke, Kaye & Landy, Lynne. Kay Pyke's Elegant Embroidery. (Illus.). 128p. 1993. 29.95 (*0-04-442357-8*, Pub. by Allen & Unwin Aust Pty AT) IPG Chicago.

Pyke, Kaye, et al. Kaye Pyke's Classic Cushions. (Illus.). 128p. 1993. 34.95 (*1-86373-332-9*, Pub. by Allen & Unwin Aust Pty AT) IPG Chicago.

Pyke, Magnus. Weird & Wonderful Science Facts. LC 83-24288. (Illus.). 128p. (J). (gr. 5 up). 1985. pap. 4.95 (*0-8069-6254-2*) Sterling.

Pyke, Sandra W. & McKAgnew, Neil. The Science Game: An Introduction to Research in the Social Science. 6th ed. LC 93-40931. 384p. 1993. pap. text ed. write for info. (*0-13-098583-X*) P-H.

***Pyke, Steve, photos.** Philosophers. (Illus.). 168p. 1995. 50.00 (*0-9518371-8-4*) Dist Art Pubs.

— Philosophers. (Illus.). 168p. 1995. reprint ed. pap. 27.50 (*0-9518371-7-6*) Dist Art Pubs.

***Pyke, Vivian R.** Shells. 100p. (Orig.). Date not set. pap. 7.95 (*0-7610-0366-5*) NW Pub.

Pykest, Lyn. The Improper Feminine: The Women's Sensation Novel & the New Woman Writing. 224p. 1992. 49.95 (*0-415-04928-8*, A7560) Routledge.

Pykett, Lyn. Emily Bronte. 200p. (C). 1989. text ed. 53.00 (*0-389-20880-9*); pap. 19.00 (*0-389-20881-7*) B&N Imports.

— Engendering Fictions: The English Novel in the Early Twentieth Century. (Writing in History Ser.). 224p. 1995. 59.50 (*0-340-64577-6*, Pub. by E Arnld UK); pap. 16.95 (*0-340-56277-3*, Pub. by E Arnld UK) St Martin.

— Sensations Novels. 1990. 40.00 (*0-7463-0720-9*, Pub. by Northcote UK); pap. 21.00 (*0-7463-0752-7*, Pub. by Northcote UK) St Mut.

Pylant, Della. Borrowed Joy: Victory over Tragedy. LC 90-83324. (Illus.). 144p. (Orig.). 1991. 14.95 (*0-9628285-3-X*); pap. 9.95 (*0-9628285-5-6*); Reaching Out to Children. write for info. (*0-9628285-1-3*); Help? Let Me Count the Ways. write for info. (*0-9628285-2-1*); Borrowed Joy - Small Version. write for info. (*0-9628285-4-8*) ABBA Pub.

Pylant, James, ed. Genealogies of Texas Families: Biographical Notes of Pioneer Settlers. LC 88-51835. (Illus.). 400p. (C). 1989. 37.50 (*0-9622746-1-5*) Datatrace Systems.

— Genealogies of Texas Families: Biographical Notes of Pioneer Settlers, Vol. 2. LC 92-81935. (Illus.). 200p. (C). 1992. text ed. 27.50 (*0-9622746-2-3*) Datatrace Systems.

Pyldmaa, V. K., ed. Actinometry & Atmospheric Optics. 392p. 1971. text ed. 96.50 (*0-7065-1125-5*, Pub. by Keter Pub IS) Coronet Bks.

***Pyle.** Where Bigfoot Walks: Crossing the Dark Divide. 1995. (*0-395-44144-7*) HM.

Pyle & Larson. Elementary Accounting II. 1979. pap. 12.00 (*0-256-02131-7*) Irwin.

Pyle, A. M. Trouble Making Toys. LC 84-29162. 192p. 1985. 13.95 (*0-8027-5610-7*) Walker & Co.

Pyle, Arthur G. Eel River Massacre at Plymouth-1676. (Pilgrim Society Notes Ser.: No. 6). 1956. 2.00 (*0-940628-14-7*) Pilgrim Soc.

Pyle, Christopher H. & Pious, Richard M., eds. The President, Congress & the Constitution: Power & Legitimacy in American Politics. LC 83-48643. 448p. (C). 1984. pap. 18.95 (*0-02-925380-2*) Free Pr.

Pyle, D. L. Separations for Biotechnology 2. 1990. 124.25 (*1-85166-545-5*) Elsevier.

Pyle, D. L., ed. Separations for Biotechnology, No. 2: Papers Presented at the International Symposium, Second, Univ. of Reading, U. K., 10-13 Sept. 1990. 658p. 1990. 124.25 (*0-685-47416-X*) Elsevier.

— Separations for Biotechnology 3: Proceedings of the International Symposium, Reading, UK, 1994. 618p. 1994. 175.00 (*0-85186-724-3*, R6724) CRC Pr.

***Pyle, David R. & Moore, Alan.** Graphical User Interface Design & Evaluation Guide: A Practical Process. LC 94-42184. 1995. pap. text ed. 39.00 (*0-13-315193-X*) P-H.

Pyle, Ernest. Home Country. 28.95 (*0-89190-771-8*, Am Reprt) Amereon Ltd.

Pyle, Ernest W. New Techniques for Welding & Extending Sprinkler Pipes. 1976. 2.50 (*0-686-17608-1*, TR 76-2) Society Fire Protect.

Pyle, Ernie. Brave Men. 29.95 (*0-89190-770-X*, Am Repr) Amereon Ltd.

— Brave Men. 320p. 1983. reprint ed. lib. bdg. 26.95 (*0-89966-464-4*) Buccaneer Bks.

— Brave Men. LC 74-70. 474p. 1974. reprint ed. text ed. 35.00 (*0-8371-7368-X*, PYBM, Greenwood Pr) Greenwood.

— Here Is Your War. Kohn, Richard H., ed. LC 78-22393. (American Military Experience Ser.). (Illus.). 1980. reprint ed. lib. bdg. 27.95 (*0-405-11869-4*) Ayer.

— Here Is Your War. (Military Heritage Press Reprints Ser.). (Illus.). 304p. 1990. reprint ed. 19.95 (*0-88029-405-1*) Dorset Pr.

Pyle, Forest. The Ideology of Imagination: Subject & Society in the Discourse of Romanticism. LC 94-20154. 1995. 35.00 (*0-8047-1649-8*) Stanford U Pr.

Pyle, Gayle, ed. see Shaw, Thomas E. & Klemke, Anita.

***Pyle, Gayle M.** Nut Salad: Bompa & Me. Shaw, Thomas & Klemke, Anita, eds. LC 94-68040. (Illus.). 116p. (Orig.). 1994. pap. 12.95 (*0-9633371-1-4*) Carson St Pub.

Pyle, Gerald F. The Diffusion of Influenza: Patterns & Paradigms. LC 86-1780. (Illus.). 240p. (C). 1986. 60.50 (*0-8476-7429-0*, R7429) Rowman.

— Heart Disease, Cancer & Stroke in Chicago: A Geographical Analysis with Facilities, Plans for 1980. LC 77-167941. (Research Papers Ser.: No. 134). (Illus.). 292p. (Orig.). 1971. pap. 12.00 (*0-89065-041-1*) U Chicago Comm Geo.

Pyle, Gerald F., ed. see Shannon, Gary W., et al.

Pyle, Gerald F., et al. The Spatial Dynamics of Crime. (Research Papers Ser.: No. 159). (Illus.). 221p. 1974. 12.00 (*0-89065-066-7*) U Chicago Comm Geo.

— The Spatial Dynamics of Crime. LC 74-80718. (University of Chicago, Department of Geography, Research Paper Ser.: No. 159). (Illus.). 234p. reprint ed. pap. 66.70 (*0-8357-3722-5*, 2036444) Bks Demand.

Pyle, Hilary. Jack B. Yeats: A Biography. (C). 1989. lib. bdg. 52.50 (*0-389-20892-2*, N 8449) B&N Imports.

— Jack B. Yeats: His Watercolours, Drawings & Pastels. (Illus.). 256p. (C). 1993. text ed. 95.00 (*0-7165-2477-5*, Pub. by Irish Acad Pr IE) Intl Spec Bk.

Pyle, Homer, see HTP, pseud..

Pyle, Howard. The Adventures of Robin Hood & His Merry Men. Reynolds, Kay, ed. (Illus.). 160p. 1988. pap. 12.95 (*0-89865-602-8*, Starblaze) Donning Co.

— The Adventures of Robin Hood & His Merry Men. limited ed. Reynolds, Kay, ed. (Illus.). 160p. 1988. 40.00 (*0-89865-601-X*, Starblaze) Donning Co.

— Empty Bottles. 1975. 9.50 (*0-686-23319-0*) Rochester Folk Art.

— The Garden Behind the Moon. (Illus.). 192p. (J). (gr. 6-8). 1988. reprint ed. 14.95 (*0-930407-06-7*) Parabola Bks.

— The Garden Behind the Moon: The Real Story of the Moon Angel. (Illus.). 176p. (J). (gr. 6-8). 1991. reprint ed. pap. 10.95 (*0-930407-22-9*) Parabola Bks.

— Howard Pyle's Book of Pirates. 25.95 (*0-8488-0758-8*) Amereon Ltd.

— King Arthur. Hinkle, Don, ed. LC 87-15461. (Illus.). 48p. (J). (gr. 3-6). 1988. lib. bdg. 12.89 (*0-8167-1213-1*); pap. 3.95 (*0-8167-1214-X*) Troll Assocs.

— King Arthur & the Magic Sword. LC 89-27793. 21p. (J). (gr. 2-7). 1990. 13.95 (*0-8037-0824-6*) Dial Bks Young.

— Men of Iron. (Airmont Classics Ser.). (Illus.). (J). (gr. 6 up). 1965. pap. 3.50 (*0-8049-0093-0*, CL-93) Airmont.

— Men of Iron. 20.95 (*0-8488-1131-3*) Amereon Ltd.

— Men of Iron. Jordan, Suzette, ed. (Pennant Ser.). 220p. (J). 1993. pap. 5.95 (*0-89084-694-4*) Bob Jones Univ Pr.

— Men of Iron. LC 89-33926. (Illustrated Classics Ser.). (Illus.). 48p. (J). (gr. 3-6). 1990. lib. bdg. 12.89 (*0-8167-1871-7*); pap. text ed. 3.95 (*0-8167-1872-5*) Troll Assocs.

— The Merry Adventures of Robin Hood. 160p. 1989. 19.95 (*0-89865-617-6*); pap. 12.95 (*0-685-25333-3*) Donning Co.

— The Merry Adventures of Robin Hood. 1986. pap. 4.50 (*0-451-52284-2*, Sig Classics) NAL-Dutton.

— The Merry Adventures of Robin Hood. (Illus.). (J). (gr. 4-8). 19.25 (*0-8446-2765-8*) Peter Smith.

— The Merry Adventures of Robin Hood. (Illus.). 288p. (J). (gr. 6-9). 1977. text ed. 45.00 (*0-684-14838-2*, C Scribner Sons Young) S&S Childrens.

— The Merry Adventures of Robin Hood. Mattern, Joanne, ed. LC 92-12702. (Illustrated Classics Ser.). (Illus.). 48p. (J). (gr. 3-6). 1992. lib. bdg. 12.89 (*0-8167-2858-5*); pap. text ed. 3.95 (*0-8167-2859-3*) Troll Assocs.

— Merry Adventures of Robin Hood. 25.95 (*0-8488-0858-4*) Amereon Ltd.

— The Merry Adventures of Robin Hood. LC 68-55820. (Illus.). xxii, 296p. (J). (gr. 3-6). 1968. reprint ed. pap. 6.95 (*0-486-22043-5*) Dover.

— Otto of the Silver Hand. (Illus.). xv, 173p. (J). (gr. 5-9). 1967. pap. 5.95 (*0-486-21784-1*) Dover.

— Otto of the Silver Hand. (J). (gr. 5-9). 19.25 (*0-8446-6400-6*) Peter Smith.

— Pepper & Salt: Seasoning for Young Folk. 1990. pap. 5.95 (*0-486-26032-1*) Dover.

— Robin Hood. abr. ed. (Illustrated Classics Ser.). (Illus.). 128p. (Orig.). (J). 1991. pap. 2.95 (*1-56156-028-6*) Kidsbks.

— Sixth Merry Adventure of Robin Hood. 1986. pap. 2.95 (*0-317-38208-X*, Sig Classics) NAL-Dutton.

— The Story of King Arthur & His Knights. (Illus.). xviii, 313p. (J). (gr. 7 up). pap. 6.95 (*0-486-21445-1*) Dover.

— The Story of King Arthur & His Knights. (Illus.). 1986. pap. 5.95 (*0-451-52488-8*, Sig Classics) NAL-Dutton.

— Story of King Arthur & His Knights. 23.95 (*0-89190-662-2*, Am Repr) Amereon Ltd.

— Story of King Arthur & His Knights. (YA). (gr. 6-12). 19.25 (*0-8446-2766-6*) Peter Smith.

— The Story of King Arthur & His Knights. deluxe ed. (Illus.). (YA). (gr. 7 up). 1978. reprint ed. lib. bdg. 12.00 (*0-932106-01-3*, Pub. by Marathon Press) S J Durst.

— The Story of King Arthur & His Knights. LC 84-50167. (Illus.). 344p. (J). 1984. reprint ed. text ed. 19.95 (*0-684-14814-5*, C Scribner Sons Young) S&S Childrens.

— The Story of Sir Launcelot & His Companions. (Illus.). 368p. (YA). (gr. 5 up). 1985. text ed. 19.95 (*0-684-18313-7*, C Scribner Sons Young) S&S Childrens.

— The Story of Sir Launcelot & His Companions. 1991. pap. 8.95 (*0-486-26701-6*) Dover.

— The Story of the Champions of the Round Table. 23.95 (*0-89190-661-4*, Am Repr) Amereon Ltd.

— The Story of the Champions of the Round Table. (Illus.). xviii, 329p. (J). (ps-4). 1968. pap. 7.95 (*0-486-21883-X*) Dover.

— The Story of the Champions of the Round Table. (Illus.). (YA). (gr. 6-12). 19.25 (*0-8446-0229-9*) Peter Smith.

— The Story of the Champions of the Round Table. LC 84-13881. (Illus.). 352p. (YA). (gr. 7 up). 1984. text ed. 19.95 (*0-684-18171-1*, C Scribner Sons Young) S&S Childrens.

— The Story of the Grail & the Passing of Arthur. LC 85-40302. (Illus.). 280p. (YA). (gr. 7 up). 1985. text ed. 19.95 (*0-684-18483-4*, C Scribner Sons Young) S&S Childrens.

— The Story of the Grail & the Passing of Arthur. unabridged ed. LC 92-29058. (Illus.). 272p. (J). 1992. reprint ed. pap. text ed. 7.95 (*0-486-27361-X*) Dover.

— Tales of Pirates & Buccaneers. LC 93-44689. (Illus.). (J). 1994. write for info. (*0-517-10162-9*) Random Hse Value.

P Q

— Wonder Clock. (Illus.). (J). (gr. 5 up). 19.75 (*0-8446-2767-4*) Peter Smith.
— The Wonder Clock or, Four & Twenty Marvelous Tales, Being One for Each Hour of the Day. (Illus.). xiv, 319p. (J). (gr. 3-6). pap. 7.95 (*0-486-21446-X*) Dover.
Pyle, Howard, ed. The Buccaneers & Marooners of America. (Illus.). 420p. 1990. reprint ed. pap. 15.00 (*0-87380-173-3*) Rio Grande.
Pyle, Howard & Greene, Ellin. The Swan Maiden. LC 93-34605. (Illus.). 32p. (J). (ps-3). 1994. lib. bdg. 15.95 (*0-8234-1088-9*) Holiday.
Pyle, Howard, ed. see Mallory, Thomas.
Pyle, I. C. Developing Safety Critical Systems with Ada. 250p. 1991. pap. 39.00 (*0-13-204298-3*, 270406) P-H.
Pyle, Ian, et al. Real Time Systems: Investigating Industrial Practice. (Software-Based Systems Ser.). 329p. 1993. text ed. 64.95 (*0-471-93553-0*) Wiley.
Pyle, Jack. Boost Your Credibility As a Leader. 24p. 1993. student ed 7.00 (*1-882843-02-9*) Perf Pub MI.
Pyle, Jack & Reese, Taylor. Raising with the Moon: The Complete Guide to Gardening & Living. Jackson, Dot, ed. LC 93-70246. (Illus.). 147p. (Orig.). 1993. pap. 13.95 (*1-878086-18-9*) Down Home NC.
Pyle, Jack R., jt. auth. see Reese, Taylor.
Pyle, Jean L. The State & Women in the Economy: Lessons from Sex Discrimination in the Republic of Ireland. LC 89-26160. (Series on Women in Work). 202p. 1990. 59.50 (*0-7914-0379-3*); pap. 19.95 (*0-7914-0380-7*) State U NY Pr.
Pyle, Jeanne L. The Best in Tent Camping, Washington & Oregon: A Guide for Campers Who Hate RVs, Concrete Slabs & Rednecks with Portable Stereos. LC 93-46046. 175p. 1994. pap. 12.95 (*0-89732-155-3*) Menasha Ridge.
Pyle, Joseph G. The Life of James J. Hill, 2 vols., Set. 24.00 (*0-8446-1369-X*) Peter Smith.
Pyle, K. Richard, ed. Guiding the Development of Foreign Students. LC 85-644751. (New Directions for Student Services Ser.: No. SS 36). (Orig.). 1986. pap. 16.95x (*1-55542-993-9*) Jossey-Bass.
Pyle, Kenneth B. The Japanese Question: Power & Purpose in a New Era. 181p. (C). 1992. 19.95 (*0-8447-3798-4*) Am Enterprise.
— The Making of Modern Japan. 2nd ed. 240p. (C). 1995. pap. text ed. write for info. (*0-669-20020-4*) Heath.
— The Making of Modern Japan: An Introduction. (Civilization & Society Ser.). 224p. 1977. pap. text ed. 10.50 (*0-669-84657-0*) Heath.
— The New Generation in Meiji Japan: Problems of Cultural Identity, 1885-1895. LC 69-13183. viii, 240p. 1969. 27.50 (*0-8047-0697-2*) Stanford U Pr.
Pyle, Lisa. Creating Lotus Notes Applications. 1994. pap. 29.95 (*1-56529-556-0*) Que.
Pyle, Michael A. Advanced Practice for the TOEFL. (Cliffs Test Preparation Guides Ser.). 259p. (Orig.). 1992. pap. text ed. 19.95 (*0-8220-2007-6*) Cliffs.
Pyle, Michael A. & Munoz, Mary E. TOEFL Preparation Guide. rev. ed. (Cliffs Test Preparation Ser.). 482p. (C). 1991. audio, pap. text ed. 14.95 (*0-8220-2024-6*) Cliffs.
Pyle, Peter, jt. auth. see DeSante, David.
Pyle, Peter, et al. Identification Guide to North American Passerines. LC 87-90700. (Illus.). 283p. (Orig.). 1987. pap. 19.50 (*0-9618940-0-8*) Slate Creek Pr.
Pyle, Ransford C. Family Law. LC 93-25985. (Paralegal Ser.). 482p. 1994. text ed. 40.95 (*0-8273-5479-7*) Delmar.
— Family Law: Instructor's Guide. 83p. 1994. 12.00 (*0-8273-5480-0*) Delmar.
— Foundations of Law for Paralegals. 1992. text ed. 42.95 (*0-8273-4572-0*) Delmar.
— Foundations of Law for Paralegals: Instructor's Guide. 1991. 11.00 (*0-8273-4573-9*) Delmar.
Pyle, Richard. Schwarzkopf in His Own Words. 1991. pap. 4.50 (*0-451-17205-1*, Sig) NAL-Dutton.
Pyle, Robert. All That Remains: A West Virginia Archaeologist's Discoveries. Wiley, Betty L., ed. 84p. (C). 1991. pap. write for info. (*0-9623153-2-X*) Cannon Graphics.
Pyle, Robert M. Field Guide to Insects Coloring Book. (J). 1993. pap. 5.95 (*0-395-67088-8*, Pub. by Hill Content Pubng AT) Seven Hills Bk.
— Handbook for Butterfly Watchers. (Illus.). 288p. 1992. pap. 11.95 (*0-395-61629-8*) HM.
— The Thunder Tree: Lessons from a Secondhand Landscape. LC 92-44574. 224p. 1993. 19.95 (*0-395-46631-8*) HM.
Pyle, Robert M. Watching Washington Butterflies. LC 73-94500. (Trailside Ser). (Illus.). 1974. pap. 4.50 (*0-914516-03-5*) Seattle Audubon Soc.
***Pyle, Robert M.** Where Bigfoot Walks: Crossing the Dark Divide. 288p. 1995. 22.95 (*0-395-44114-5*) HM.
Pyle, Robert M., jt. auth. see Audubon Society Staff.
Pyle, Robert W., jt. auth. see Svenson, Henry K.
Pyle, S. I., et al. Onsets, Completions, & Spans of the Osseous State of Development in Representative Bone Growth Centers of the Extremities. (SRCD M: Vol. 26, No. 1). 1961. 12.00 (*0-527-01588-1*) Periodicals Srv.
Pyle, S. Idell, jt. auth. see Greulich, William W.
Pyle, Stephen J., jt. auth. see Pyle, Susan N.
Pyle, Susan N. & Pyle, Stephen J. Michigan's Town & Country Inns. 3rd ed. (Illus.). 248p. 1989. pap. 15.95 (*0-472-08087-3*) U of Mich Pr.
Pyle, Theresa P. The Teacher's Dependency Load. LC 79-177172. (Columbia University. Teachers College. Contributions to Education Ser.: No. 782). reprint ed. 37.50 (*0-404-55782-1*) AMS Pr.
Pyle, Vera. Current Medical Terminology. 5th ed. 506p. 1994. 36.00 (*0-934385-56-4*) Hlth Prof Inst.
Pyle, Walter L., jt. auth. see Gould, George M.
Pyle, Wilf E. Hunting Predators for Hides & Profit. 256p. 1985. pap. 11.95 (*0-88317-131-7*) Stoeger Pub Co.
Pyle, William E., jt. auth. see Larson, Kermit D.
Pyle, William T. & Seals, Mary A., eds. Experiencing Ministry Supervision. LC 94-6860. 1995. 14.99 (*0-8054-1163-1*) Broadman.
***Pyle, William W. & Zin, Michael.** Initiation a la Comptabilite Financiere Administrative la Monographie. (C). 1975. 7.45 (*0-256-01766-2*) Irwin.
Pyler, Ernst J. Baking Science & Technology, 2 vols. (Illus.). 1988. Vol. 1, 588p. write for info. (*1-882005-00-7*); Vol. 2, 757p. write for info. (*1-882005-01-5*) Sosland Pub.
— Baking Science & Technology, 2 vols., Set. (Illus.). 1988. 78.00 (*1-882005-02-3*) Sosland Pub.
Pyles, Marian S. Death & Dying in Children's & Young People's Literature: A Survey & Bibliography. LC 87-46386. 187p. 1988. lib. bdg. 28.50x (*0-89950-335-7*) McFarland & Co.
Pyles, Rebecca A., jt. auth. see Duellman, William E.
Pyles, Stephan & Harisson, John. The New Texas Cuisine. LC 92-31496. 1993. 35.00 (*0-385-42336-5*) Doubleday.
Pyles, Thomas. Selected Essays on English Usage. Algeo, John, ed. LC 78-18833. 237p. 1983. reprint ed. pap. 81.00 (*0-7837-4904-X*, 2044569) Bks Demand.
Pyles, Thomas & Algeo, John. English: An Introduction to Language. 367p. (C). 1970. pap. text ed. 18.75 (*0-15-522642-8*) HB Coll Pubs.
— The Origins & Development of the English Language. 3rd ed. 383p. (C). 1982. teacher ed write for info. (*0-318-52971-8*); text ed. 34.75 (*0-15-567608-3*) HB Coll Pubs.
— The Origins & Development of the English Language. 4th ed. (Illus.). 425p. (C). 1992. text ed. write for info. (*0-318-68953-7*) HB Coll Pubs.
— The Origins & Development of the English Language. 4th ed. 416p. (C). 1993. lib. bdg. write for info. (*0-15-500168-X*) HB Coll Pubs.
Pylyshyn, Zenon, ed. The Robot's Dilemma: The Frame Problem in Artificial Intelligence. LC 86-10801. (Theoretical Issues in Cognitive Science Ser.: Vol. 4). 168p. 1987. text ed. 39.50 (*0-89391-371-5*) Ablex Pub.
Pylyshyn, Zenon & Demopoulos, William, eds. Meaning & Cognitive Structure. LC 86-10801. (Theoretical Issues in Cognitive Science Ser.: Vol. 3). 288p. (C). 1986. text ed. 52.50 (*0-89391-372-3*) Ablex Pub.
Pylyshyn, Zenon, ed. see Dennett, D., et al.
Pylyshyn, Zenon W. Computation & Cognition: Toward A Foundation for Cognitive Science. 320p. (C). 1985. pap. 15.95x (*0-262-66058-X*, Bradford Bks) MIT Pr.
Pylyshyn, Zenon W., ed. Computational Processes in Human Vision: An Interdisciplinary Perspective. (CIAR Series in Artificial Intelligence & Robotics: Vol. 1). 512p. (C). 1988. text ed. 65.00 (*0-89391-460-6*) Ablex Pub.
Pylyshyn, Zenon W. & Bannon, Liam. Perspectives on the Computer Revolution. rev. ed. LC 89-30213. 560p. (C). 1989. text ed. 75.00 (*0-89391-369-3*); pap. 36.50 (*0-89391-591-2*) Ablex Pub.
Pylyshyn, Zenon W., ed. see Goodale, Melvyn A.
Pym, jt. auth. see Nelms.
Pym, Anthony. Translation & Text Transfer: An Essay on the Principles of Intercultural Communication. LC 92-15375. 1992. write for info. (*3-631-44995-X*) P Lang Pubs.
Pym, Barbara. Civil to Strangers: And Other Writings. 396p. 1989. pap. 8.95 (*0-452-26138-4*, Plume) NAL-Dutton.
— Crampton Hodnet. 224p. 1986. pap. 8.95 (*0-452-25816-2*, Plume) NAL-Dutton.
— A Few Green Leaves. 256p. 1989. pap. 8.95 (*0-525-48511-2*, Obelisk) NAL-Dutton.
— A Glass of Blessings. 1989. pap. 8.95 (*0-525-48512-0*, Dutton) NAL-Dutton.
— Jane & Prudence. 228p. 1990. pap. 8.95 (*0-525-48570-8*, Obelisk) NAL-Dutton.
— Less Than Angels. 264p. 1990. pap. 8.95 (*0-525-48571-6*, Dutton) NAL-Dutton.
— Quartet in Autumn. 228p. 1988. pap. 7.95 (*0-525-48379-9*, Obelisk) NAL-Dutton.
— Quartet in Autumn. large type ed. LC 93-19406. 1993. 20.95 (*0-7927-1634-5*, Curley Lrg Print); pap. 18.95 (*0-7927-1633-7*, Curley Lrg Print) Chivers N Amer.
— Some Tame Gazelle. LC 92-53576. 256p. 1992. pap. 10.95 (*0-452-26919-9*, Plume) NAL-Dutton.
Pym, Denis, jt. ed. see Hassard, John.
Pym, Dennis, jt. ed. see Hassard, John.
Pym, Dora & Silver, Nancy. Alive on Men's Lips. 150p. (C). 1982. pap. text ed. 50.00 (*0-685-44231-4*, Pub. by Old Vicarage UK) St Mut.
Pym, Francis, et al. Europe, America, & South Africa. Treverton, Gregory F., ed. 144p. 1989. 35.00 (*0-8147-8180-2*) NYU Pr.
Pym, John. Film on Four: A Survey, 1982-1991. (Illus.). 228p. (C). 1993. 42.00 (*0-85170-345-3*, Pub. by British Film Inst UK) Ind U Pr.
— Merchant Ivory's English Landscape: Rooms, Views, & Anglo-Saxon Attitudes. LC 94-32106. 1995. write for info. (*0-8109-4275-5*) Abrams.
Pyman, Avril. A History of Russian Symbolism. LC 93-30418. 491p. (C). 1994. 79.95 (*0-521-24198-7*) Cambridge U Pr.
Pyman, Avril, ed. Alexander Blok: Selected Poems. LC 67-31506. 388p. (C). 1972. 155.00 (*0-08-012185-3*, Pub. by Pergamon Repr UK) Franklin.
— Mikhail Bulgakov: Selected Works. 259p. 1972. pap. 98.00 (*0-08-015506-5*, Pub. by Pergamon Repr UK) Franklin.
— Yevgeniy Shvarts: Three Plays. 288p. 1972. pap. 106.00 (*0-08-016294-0*, Pub. by Pergamon Repr UK) Franklin.
Pyman, Kit. Embroidered Landscapes. 1989. pap. 7.95 (*0-85532-635-2*, Pub. by Search Pr UK) A Schwartz & Co.
Pyman, Kit, ed. Every Kind of Smocking. (Illus.). 126p. (YA). 1989. pap. 17.95 (*0-85532-632-8*, Pub. by Search Pr UK) A Schwartz & Co.
***Pyman, Stephen J.** Annotated Queensland Building Services Authority Act. 138p. 1993. pap. 39.00 (*0-455-21218-X*, Pub. by Law Bk Co) W W Gaunt.
Pynchon, et al. Deadly Sins. LC 94-9135. (Illus.). 1994. 17.00 (*0-688-13690-7*) Morrow.
Pynchon, John. The Pynchon Papers, Vol. 1. Bridenbaugh, Carl, ed. LC 81-70057. (Publications of the Colonial Society of Massachusetts: No. 60-61). 378p. reprint ed. pap. 102.10 (*0-7837-3741-6*, 2043423) Bks Demand.
— The Pynchon Papers, Vol. 2. Bridenbaugh, Carl, ed. LC 81-70057. (Publications of the Colonial Society of Massachusetts: No. 60-61). 539p. reprint ed. pap. 153.70 (*0-7837-3742-4*) Bks Demand.
Pynchon, Thomas. The Crying of Lot Forty-Nine. 1994. reprint ed. lib. bdg. 32.95 (*1-56849-320-7*) Buccaneer Bks.
— The Crying of Lot Forty-Nine. LC 85-45221. 192p. 1986. reprint ed. pap. 10.00 (*0-06-091307-X*, PL 1307, PL) HarpC.
— The Crying of Lot 49: A Novel. LC 85-45221. 183p. (C). 1991. reprint ed. lib. bdg. 23.00x (*0-8095-9030-1*) Borgo Pr.
— Gravity's Rainbow. 768p. 1987. pap. 15.00 (*0-14-010661-8*, Penguin Bks) Viking Penguin.
— Gravity's Rainbow. 768p. 1991. pap. 12.95 (*0-14-099699-0*) Viking Penguin.
— Gravity's Rainbow. (Twentieth Century Classics Ser.). 1995. pap. 15.95 (*0-14-018859-2*, Penguin Bks) Viking Penguin.
— Slow Learner: Early Stories. LC 84-934. 208p. 1985. reprint ed. pap. 11.95 (*0-316-72443-2*) Little.
— V. 1994. reprint ed. lib. bdg. 39.95 (*1-56849-321-5*) Buccaneer Bks.
— V. LC 85-45222. 496p. 1986. reprint ed. pap. 12.50 (*0-06-091308-8*, PL 1308, PL) HarpC.
— V: A Novel. 492p. (C). 1991. reprint ed. lib. bdg. 27.00x (*0-8095-9031-X*) Borgo Pr.
— Vineland. 400p. 1991. pap. 9.95 (*0-14-014511-7*) Viking Penguin.
Pynchon, William. The Diary of William Pynchon of Salem. Oliver, Fitch E., ed. LC 75-31131. reprint ed. 52.50 (*0-404-13608-7*) AMS Pr.
Pyne, Frederick W. The John Pyne Family in America Being the Comprehensive Genealogical Record of the Descendants of John Pyne (1766-1813) of Charleston, South Carolina. LC 92-71301. (Illus.). 224p. 1992. 20.00 (*0-9632539-0-5*) F W Pyne.
Pyne, Henry, tr. England & France in the Fifteenth Century. LC 78-63491. reprint ed. 27.50 (*0-404-17139-7*) AMS Pr.
Pyne, K. D. All the Way to China. (Illus.). 16p. (J). (ps). 1993. 4.95 (*1-882185-06-4*) Crnrstone Pub.
Pyne, R. Professional Discipline in Nursing, Midwifery & Health Visiting. 2nd ed. 224p. 1992. pap. 29.95 (*0-632-02975-7*) Blackwell Sci.
***Pyne, R. David G.** Groundwater Recharge Through Wells: A Guide to Aquifer Storage Recovery. LC 94-27575. 1994. write for info. (*1-56670-097-3*) Lewis Pubs.
Pyne, Stephen J. Burning Bush: A Fire History of Australia. (Illus.). 520p. 1992. pap. 15.95 (*0-8050-2101-9*, Owl) H Holt & Co.
— Fire on the Rim: A Firefighter's Season at the Grand Canyon. 336p. (C). 1995. pap. 14.95 (*0-295-97483-4*) U of Wash Pr.
— Grove Karl Gilbert: A Great Engine of Research. LC 80-13881. (History of Science Ser.: No. 2). 312p. 1980. text ed. 22.50 (*0-292-72719-4*) U of Tex Pr.
— The Ice: A Journey to Antarctica. LC 86-4362. (Illus.). 454p. reprint ed. pap. 129.40 (*0-7837-1624-9*, 2041917) Bks Demand.
— Introduction to Wildland Fire: Fire Management in the United States. LC 83-17100. 455p. 1984. text ed. 79.95 (*0-471-09658-X*, Wiley-Interscience) Wiley.
Pyne, Steven J. World Fire. 1995. 30.00 (*0-8050-3247-9*) H Holt & Co.
Pyne, W. H. Rustic Vignettes. LC 77-80117. (Orig.). 1977. pap. 6.95 (*0-486-23547-5*) Dover.
Pyne, Walter. The Chronicles of Auderlin. Van Treese, James B., ed. 354p. 1993. pap. 9.95 (*1-56901-003-X*) NW Pub.
Pyne, William H. Microcosm. LC 68-56512. (Illus.). 1972. reprint ed. 27.95 (*0-405-08872-8*, Pub. by Blom Pubns UK) Ayer.
Pyne, Zoe K. Giovanni Pierluigi da Palestrina: His Life & Times. 232p. 1990. reprint ed. lib. bdg. 69.00 (*0-7812-9078-3*) Rprt Serv.
— Giovanni Pierluigi Da Palestrina, His Life & Times. LC 79-107828. (Select Bibliographies Reprint Ser.). 1977. 23.95 (*0-8369-5159-X*) Ayer.
Pynenburg, W. & De Tollenaere, F., eds. The Second International Round Table Conference on Historical Lexicography: Proceedings. viii, 353p. 1980. pap. 75.00 (*90-70176-21-1*) Mouton.
Pynes, Joan E. & Lafferty, Joan M. Local Government Labor Relations: A Guide for Public Administrators. LC 92-34943. 256p. 1993. text ed. 55.00 (*0-89930-783-3*, PLG, Quorum Bks) Greenwood.
Pynn, Roger & Riste, T., eds. Time-Dependent Effects in Disordered Materials. LC 87-28562. (NATO ASI Series B, Physics: Vol. 167). (Illus.). 518p. 1988. 110.00 (*0-306-42782-6*, Plenum Pr) Plenum.
Pynn, Roger & Skjeltorp, Arne, eds. Scaling Phenomena in Disordered Systems. (NATO ASI Series B, Physics: Vol. 133). 592p. 1986. 120.00 (*0-306-42112-7*, Plenum Pr) Plenum.
Pynn, Ronald. American Politics: Changing Expectations. 4th ed. 480p. (C). 1993. pap. text ed. write for info. (*0-697-12893-8*) Brown & Benchmark.
Pynoos, Jon. Breaking the Rules: Bureaucracy & Reform in Public Housing. (Environment, Development, & Public Policy: Public Policy & Social Services Ser.). 236p. 1986. 45.00 (*0-306-42302-2*, Plenum Pr) Plenum.
Pynoos, Jon & Cohen, Evelyn. Home Safety Guide for Older People: Check It Out Fix It Up. LC 90-60369. (Illus.). 70p. 1990. pap. text ed. 13.95 (*0-914125-01-X*) Serif Pr.
Pynoos, Jon, ed. see Regnier, Victor.
Pynoos, Jon, et al, eds. Housing Urban America. 2nd ed. LC 80-12108. 670p. 1980. lib. bdg. 59.95 (*0-202-32010-3*); pap. text ed. 36.95 (*0-202-32011-1*) Aldine de Gruyter.
Pynoos, Robert S., ed. & pref. Posttraumatic Stress Disorder: A Clinical Review. LC 93-87409. x, 134p. (Orig.). (C). 1994. pap. 13.95 (*0-9629164-4-7*) Sidran Pr.
Pynoos, Robert S., jt. auth. see Eth, Spencer.
Pynsent, P., et al, eds. Outcome Measures in Trauma. LC 94-9397. 1994. 35.00 (*0-7506-1653-9*) Buttrwrth-Heinemann.
Pynsent, R., tr. see Chnoupek, B. & Brusak, K.
Pynsent, Robert & Kanikova, S. I., eds. Reader's Encyclopedia of Eastern European Literature. 608p. 1993. 50.00 (*0-06-270007-3*, Harper Ref) HarpC.
Pynsent, Robert B. Questions of Identity: Czech & Slovak Ideas of Nationality & Personality. (Central European University Press Bks.). 256p. 1994. 45.00 (*1-85866-005-X*) OUP.
Pynsent, Robert B., ed. T. G. Masaryk (1850-1937), Vol. 2: Thinker & Critic. 400p. 1989. text ed. 55.00 (*0-312-02680-3*) St Martin.
Pynsent, Robert B., jt. auth. see Peter, Laszlo.
***Pyong Gap Min, ed.** Asian Americans: Contemporary Perspectives. (Focus Editions Ser.: Vol. 174). 304p. 1994. 49.95 (*0-8039-4335-0*) Sage.
— Asian Americans: Contemporary Perspectives. (Sage Focus Editions Ser.: Vol. 174). 304p. 1994. pap. 24.95 (*0-8039-4336-9*) Sage.
Pyorala, K., et al, eds. Changing Trends in Coronary Heart Disease: Journal: Cardiology, Vol. 72, Nos. 1 & 2. (Illus.). 104p. 1985. pap. 56.00 (*3-8055-4015-9*) S Karger.
***Pyper, Diane M. & Angione, Ronald, eds.** Optical Astronomy from the Earth & Moon No. 55. 320p. 1994. 40.00 (*0-937707-74-0*) Astron Soc Pacific.
***Pyper, Robert & Robins, Lynton, eds.** Governing the U. K. in the 1990s. LC 94-43330. 293p. 1995. 49.95 (*0-312-12552-6*) St Martin.
Pyper, Terry. French Dictionary of Information Technology. 800p. (ENG & FRE.). 1987. 150.00 (*0-8288-0235-1*, F103160) Fr & Eur.
— French Dictionary of Information Technology. 592p. 1989. 92.50 (*0-415-00244-3*, 07549) Routledge.
Pyrah, Barbara. History of the Yorkshire Museum. (C). 1989. pap. 30.00 (*1-85072-042-8*, Pub. by W Sessions UK) St Mut.
Pyrah, G. B. Imperial Policy & South Africa, 1902-1910. LC 74-9170. (Illus.). 272p. 1975. reprint ed. text ed. 59.75 (*0-8371-7619-0*, PYIP, Greenwood Pr) Greenwood.
Pyramis, Alpha. A Dime for Every Minute of Your Time, That It Takes to Finish a Rhyme: And Other Funraising Poems. 10p. 1985. pap. 21.95 (*0-913597-75-9*) Prosperity & Profits.
— Herbal Teas & Their Rhyming Cures. rev. ed. 12p. (Orig.). (C). 1993. pap. text ed. 19.95 (*0-913597-86-4*) Prosperity & Profits.
— Jean or Denim Garments: Recycling Poem Booklet. 4p. (Orig.). 1985. pap. 4.00 (*0-317-00913-3*) Prosperity & Profits.
— Real Estate Poetry, Bk. 1. 20p. 1985. pap. text ed. 3.95 (*0-913597-82-1*) Prosperity & Profits.
— Recipe Ingredient Substitution Cookbook. 60p. 1992. pap. text ed. 19.95 (*0-913597-23-6*) Prosperity & Profits.
Pyrcioch, E. J., et al. Production of Pipeline Gas by Hydrogasification of Coal: 1954-1964, Vol. 1. (Research Bulletin Ser.: No. 39). iv, 225p. 1972. 20.00 (*0-317-56891-4*) Inst Gas Tech.
***Pyrczak, Fred.** Making Sense of Statistics: A Conceptual Overview. 128p. (C). 1995. pap. text ed. 18.95 (*0-614-04816-8*) Pyrczak Pub.
— Research Applications Workbook. 1983. pap. text ed. 13.75 (*0-912736-28-3*) EDITS Pubs.
— Statistics with a Sense of Humor: A Humorous Workbook & Guide to Study Skills. Sasser, Linda & Finkle, Deborah, eds. (Illus.). 132p. (C). 1989. student ed 17.95 (*0-9623744-0-7*) Pyrczak Pub.
— Statistics with a Sense of Humor: Concise Key & Step-by-Step Key. Morman, Robert, ed. 60p. (C). 1989. teacher ed 5.50x (*0-9623744-1-5*) Pyrczak Pub.
Pyrczak, Fred & Bruce, Randall R. Writing Empirical Research Reports: A Basic Guide for Students of the Social & Behavioral Sciences. 128p. (C). 1992. pap. text ed. 16.50x (*0-9623744-3-1*) Pyrczak Pub.
Pyre, J. F., jt. ed. see Campbell, Oscar J.
Pyre, James F. Formation of Tennyson's Style. LC 68-8979. 252p. (C). 1968. reprint ed. 50.00 (*0-87753-033-5*) Phaeton.
— The Formation of Tennyson's Style, a Study. (BCL1-PR English Literature Ser.). 252p. 1992. reprint ed. lib. bdg. 79.00 (*0-7812-7698-5*) Rprt Serv.
Pyrhonen, Heta. Murder from an Academic Angle: An Introduction to the Study of the Detective Narrative. x, 138p. 1994. 59.00 (*1-879751-81-X*) Camden Hse.
Pyrnelle, Louise C. Miss Li'l' Tweetty. LC 72-4705. (Black Heritage Library Collection). 1977. reprint ed. 28.95 (*0-8369-9122-2*) Ayer.
Pyrnelle, Louise-Clarke. Diddie, Dumps & Tot. (Illus.). 117p. (J). (gr. 4-8). 1963. 14.95 (*0-911116-17-6*) Pelican.
Pyroasopoulos, M., ed. see Zurukzoglu, W., et al.
Pyrom, Jay. Complete Introduction to Frogs & Toads. (Complete Introduction to...Ser.). (Illus.). 128p. (Orig.). 1987. pap. 5.95 (*0-86622-395-9*, CO-041S) TFH Pubns.

P
Q

Pyron, C. Lee. How to Manage Data with Entity Codes & Data Dictionaries: The Keys to Quality Information Resources & Quality Business Processes. LC 94-92106. (Illus.). 216p. 1994. pap. 45.00 (*0-9641642-1-3*) Pyron Ent.

Pyron, Cherry, jt. ed. see Silitch, Clarissa M.

Pyron, Darden A. Southern Daughter: The Life of Margaret Mitchell. (Illus.). 576p. 1991. 30.00 (*0-19-505276-5*) OUP.

Pyron, Darden A., ed. Recasting: "Gone with the Wind" in American Culture. LC 82-20310. 242p. 1983. pap. 19.95 (*0-8130-0747-X*) U Press Fla.

Pyron, Tim. Using Microsoft Project for Windows. (Illus.). 750p. (Orig.). 1993. pap. 29.95 (*1-56529-151-4*) Que.

— Using Microsoft Project 4 for Windows. 1994. pap. 29.95 (*1-56529-594-3*) Que.

Pyros, John. Mike Gold: Dean of Am. Proletarian Literature. 218p. (Orig.). 1980. pap. 3.00 (*0-9604000-0-1*) Dramatika.

Pyrz, R., ed. see IUTAM Symposium on Microstructure-Property Interactions in Composite Materials Staff.

Pyshkalo, A. M. Geometry in Grades One-Four: Problems in the Formation of Geometric Concepts in Primary School Children. Wilson, James W. & McKillip, William D., eds. Teller, Joan W., tr. (Soviet Studies in Mathematics Education: Vol. 7). 310p. (C). 1992. text ed. write for info. (*0-936745-56-8*) U Chi Dept Educ.

Pysz, Stephen. Team Earth: Advanced ABC Environmental Coloring Book, No. 1. (Illus.). 56p. (J). (gr. k-1). 1991. pap. text ed. 2.95 (*0-9630186-7-1*) Team Earth.

— Team Earth: Show You Care, No. 2. Patton, Sarah, ed. (Illus.). 32p. (J). (gr. 2-5). 1992. student ed, pap. text ed. 2.95 (*0-9630186-1-2*) Team Earth.

Pyszczynski, T. & Greenberg, J. Hanging on & Letting Go: Understanding the Onset, Progression & Remission of Depression. (Illus.). 225p. 1992. 87.00 (*0-387-97756-2*) Spr-Verlag.

Pyszka, Gloria L., jt. auth. see Merritt, Richard L.

Pytches, David. Spiritual Gifts in the Local Church. LC 87-15128. 288p. (Orig.). 1987. pap. 9.99 (*0-87123-984-1*) Bethany Hse.

Pytel & Kiusalaas. Engineering Mechanics: Dynamics. (C). 1994. text ed. 45.00 (*0-06-045276-5*) HarpCollege.

— Engineering Mechanics: Dynamics. (C). 1995. 13.00 (*0-06-502213-0*) HarpCollege.

— Engineering Mechanics: Statics. (C). 1994. text ed. 45.00 (*0-06-045292-7*) HarpCollege.

— Engineering Mechanics: Statics. (C). 1994. Solutions manual. teacher ed 13.00 (*0-06-501946-6*) HarpCollege.

— Engineering Mechanics: Statics & Dynamics. (C). 1994. text ed. 59.50 (*0-06-045275-7*) HarpCollege.

Pytel, Andrew & Kiusalaas, Jaan. Engineering Mechanics: Statics & Dynamics. LC 93-21041. (C). 1990. 82.00 (*0-06-045175-0*) HarpCollege.

Pytel, Andrew & Singer, Ferdinand L. Strength of Materials. 4th ed. 592p. (C). 1990. text ed. 84.50 (*0-06-045313-3*) HarpCollege.

Pythagoras. The Pythagorean Writings: Hellenistic Texts from the 1st Century B.C. to 3rd Century A.D. Navon, Robert, ed. Guthrie, Kenneth & Taylor, Thomas, trs. (Great Works of Philosophy Ser.: Vol. 3). 190p. (Orig.). 1986. text ed. 42.00 (*0-933601-01-8*) Selene Bks.

— The Pythagorean Writings: Hellenistic Texts from the 1st Century B.C. to 3rd Century A.D. Navon, Robert, ed. Guthrie, Kenneth & Taylor, Thomas, trs. (Great Works of Philosophy Ser.: Vol. 3). 190p. (Orig.). 1986. reprint ed. pap. text ed. 25.00 (*0-933601-02-6*) Selene Bks.

Python, Monty. The Brand New Monty Python Papperbok. 1992. pap. 14.95 (*0-7493-1170-3*, A0643, Pub. by Mandarin UK) Heinemann.

— The Life of Brian. 124p. (C). 1992. pap. 19.95 (*0-7493-0997-0*, A0665, Pub. by Mandarin UK) Heinemann.

— Monty Python & the Holy Grail. (Illus.). (C). 1992. pap. 19.95 (*0-7493-1142-8*, A0666, Pub. by Mandarin UK) Heinemann.

— Monty Python & the Holy Grail. 1977. pap. 9.95 (*0-458-92970-0*) NAL-Dutton.

— Monty Python & the Holy Grail. 1977. pap. 17.95 (*0-416-00341-9*) Routledge Chapman & Hall.

— Monty Python's Big Red Book. (Illus.). 63p. (Orig.). 1991. pap. 11.95 (*0-413-29520-6*, A0454) Heinemann.

Pytowska, Zofia. The Threshold. 176p. 1982. 18.95 (*0-87073-518-7*); pap. 11.95 (*0-87073-519-5*) Schenkman Bks Inc.

Pywell, Geoff. Staging Real Things: The Performance of Ordinary Events. LC 93-44701. 1994. write for info. (*0-8387-5274-8*) Bucknell U Pr.

Pywell, Sharon L. Writing That Works. LC 93-9288. (Business Skills Express Ser.). 96p. 1993. pap. 10.00 (*1-55623-856-8*) Irwin Prof Pubng.

— Writing That Works. (AMI How-to Ser.). 100p. 1995. 9.95 (*1-884926-44-4*) Amer Media.

Pyx, Martin. Autumn Scandals. (Victorian Era Ser.). 1989. pap. 4.95 (*0-929654-40-4*, 58) Blue Moon Bks.

— Birch Fever. (Orig.). 1994. pap. 5.95 (*1-56201-055-7*) Blue Moon Bks.

— Spring Fevers. 1992. pap. 5.95 (*1-56201-027-1*, 124) Blue Moon Bks.

— Summer Frolics. (Orig.). 1989. pap. 4.50 (*0-929654-14-5*, 52) Blue Moon Bks.

— The Tutor's Bride. 1988. pap. 4.95 (*0-929654-44-7*, 30) Blue Moon Bks.

***Pyxis Creative Services Staff.** Automated Medication Management: Criteria for Evaluating a System. 66p. 1995. pap. text ed. 25.00 (*1-886954-00-3*) Pyxis Pr.

Pyykko, P. Relativistic Theory of Atoms & Molecules. (Lecture Notes in Chemistry Ser.: Vol. 41). ix, 389p. 1986. pap. 51.00 (*0-387-17167-3*) Spr-Verlag.

— Relativistic Theory of Atoms & Molecules 2: A Bibliography 1986-1992. LC 93-31082. (Lecture Notes in Chemistry Ser.: Vol. 60). 1993. 89.00 (*0-387-57219-8*) Spr-Verlag.

Pyzalski, Leo. The Holy Will of God: Source of Peace & Happiness. LC 90-71554. 163p. 1991. reprint ed. pap. 6.00 (*0-89555-411-9*) TAN Bks Pubs.

Pyzdek. WEESKA Quality Control. (What Every Engineer Should Know Ser.: Vol. 26). 272p. 1988. 59.75 (*0-8247-7966-5*) Dekker.

Pyzdek, Thomas. CQE Exam Study Guide. 1991. 39.95 (*0-930011-01-5*) Quality Am.

— Pyzdeks Guide to SPC: Vol. II - Applications & Special Topics. (Illus.). 250p. (C). 1991. pap. 34.75 (*0-930011-04-X*) Quality Am.

— Pyzdek's Guide to SPC, Vol. I: Fundamentals. (Pyzdek's Guide to SPC Ser.). (Illus.). 88p. (Orig.). 1989. student ed 14.35 (*0-930011-06-6*); pap. 29.75 (*0-930011-03-1*) Quality Am.

— An SPC Primer: Programmed Introduction to Statistical Process Control Techniques. Orig. Title: Applied Industrial Statistics. (Orig.). 1985. pap. text ed. 14.95 (*0-930011-00-7*) Quality Am.

— What Every Manager Should Know about Quality. 232p. 1991. 65.00 (*0-8247-8401-4*) Dekker.

Pyzdek, Thomas & Berger, R. W. Quality Engineering Handbook. (Quality & Reliability Ser.: Vol. 29). 640p. 1991. 99.75 (*0-8247-8132-5*) Dekker.

Pyzoha. Understanding Stormwater Management Programs: Practical Guide. 1994. 59.95 (*0-87371-470-9*, TD665) Lewis Pubs.

Q

Qa, Laura. The Voice of the Image. LC 92-61605. 64p. (Orig.). 1992. pap. 10.95 (*0-9633497-0-8*) Red Dragon VA.

Qadeer, Mohammad A. Urbanization in the Third World: A Case Study of Lahore, Pakistan. LC 82-15117. 300p. 1983. text ed. 65.00 (*0-275-91061-X*, C1061, Praeger Pubs) Greenwood.

Qader, S. A. Natural Gas Substitutes from Coal & Oil: Coal Science & Technology, No. 8. 414p. 1985. 123.00 (*0-444-42501-2*) Elsevier.

Qaderi, M. Taleem-Ul-Islam, 4. (J). pap. 7.50 (*0-933511-72-8*) Kazi Pubns.

Qadir, A. Experimental Gravitation: Proceedings of the International Symposium on Experimental Gravitation, June 26-July 2, 1993, Nathigali, Pakistan. Karim, M., ed. (Illus.). 400p. 1994. 170.00 (*0-7503-0303-4*) IOP Pub.

Qadir, Asghar. Relativity: An Introduction to the Special Theory. 140p. 1989. text ed. 36.00 (*9971-5-0612-2*) World Scientific Pub.

Qadir, C. A. Philosophy & Science in the Islamic World. 228p. 1990. pap. 17.50 (*0-415-00294-X*, A4582) Routledge.

Qadir, Shahid, jt. ed. see Gills, Barry.

Qadri, A. A. Commentaries on Dissolution of Muslim Marriage Act. 137p. 1961. 40.00 (*0-317-54678-3*) St Mut.

Qadri, A. Jamil. Intra-Societal Tension & National Integration: Psychological Assessment. 212p. (C). 1988. 27.00 (*81-7022-042-4*, Pub. by Concept II) S Asia.

Qadri, Anwar A. Justice in Historical Islam. 144p. 1992. 15.95 (*1-56744-449-0*) Kazi Pubns.

Qadri, Maulana. Translation of the Meanings of Hadith from Muslim & Bukhari (Lu'Lu wa Maarjan), Vols. I & II. 562p. 1985. 69.00 (*1-56744-405-9*) Kazi Pubns.

Qafisheh. Yemini Arabic. 1990. 22.00x (*0-685-51718-7*) Intl Bk Ctr.

Qafisheh, Hamdi. Arabic Yemeni Reference Grammar. LC 91-77058. 308p. 1992. 59.00 (*0-931745-83-7*) Dunwoody Pr.

— Basic Course in Gulf Arabic. 482p. 1975. 25.00 (*0-86685-048-1*) Intl Bk Ctr.

Qafisheh, Hamdi A. A Basic Course in Gulf Arabic. 482p. 1975. pap. 22.95 (*0-8165-0483-0*) U of Ariz Pr.

— Gulf Arabic: Intermediate Level. LC 79-18305. 296p. 1979. pap. text ed. 17.95 (*0-8165-0692-2*) U of Ariz Pr.

Qaim, S. M., ed. Nuclear Data for Science & Technology: Proceedings of an International Conference Held at the Forschungszentrum Julich, FRG, 13-17 May 1991. (Research Reports in Physics). 1100p. 1992. pap. 198.00 (*0-387-55100-X*) Spr-Verlag.

Qaisar, Ahsan J. Building Construction in Mughal India: The Evidence from Painting. (Illus.). 100p. 1989. 22.50 (*0-19-562260-X*) OUP.

Qamar, J. God's Existence & Contemporary Science. pap. 2.00 (*1-56744-026-6*) Kazi Pubns.

Qamaruddin Khan. Status of Women in Islam. 1989. text ed. 10.95 (*81-207-1060-6*, Pub. by Sterling Pubs II) Apt Bks.

Qamber, Akhtar. Sabbatical in Japan. 1976. 8.00 (*0-89253-819-8*); 4.00 (*0-89253-820-1*) Ind-US Inc.

Qamus, Madd A. & Lane, Edward. An Arabic-English Lexicon, 8 vols., Set. (ARA & ENG.). 1980. 370.00 (*0-685-02567-5*) Intl Bk Ctr.

Qarabaghi, Mirza J. A History of Qarabagh: An Annotated Translation of Mirza Jamal Javanshir Qarabaghi's Tarikh-e Qarabagh. Bournoutian, George A., ed. & tr. by. 206p. (C). 1993. lib. bdg. 24.95 (*1-56859-011-3*) Mazda Pubs.

Qaradawi, Yousaf A. Lawful & the Prohibited in Islam. pap. 12.50 (*1-56744-118-1*) Kazi Pubns.

Qaradawi, Yusuf A. Islamic Awakening Between Rejection & Extremism. pap. 12.95 (*1-56744-090-8*) Kazi Pubns.

— Kayfa Nata'amalu ma'a al Sunnah al Nabawiyah Ma'alim wa Dawabit: Ma'alim wa Dawabit - Outlines & Rules. 3rd ed. 187p. (ARA.). 1991. pap. 7.50 (*0-912463-50-3*) IIIT VA.

Qara'i, Ali Q., tr. see Mughniyyah, Allamah M.

Qara'i, Ali Q., tr. see Mutahhari, Murtaza.

***Qasim, Abd A.** Rites of Assent: Two Novellas. Theroux, Peter, tr. (Border Lines). 160p. (Orig.). (C). 1995. lib. bdg. 39.95 (*1-56639-353-1*); pap. text ed. 12.95 (*1-56639-354-X*) Temple U Pr.

Qasim, Mir. My Life & Times. (C). 1992. 24.00 (*81-7023-355-0*, Pub. by Allied II) S Asia.

Qasim, Sayed R. & Chiang, W. Walter. Sanitary Landfill Leachate: Generation, Control & Treatment. LC 94-60645. 335p. 1994. pap. 49.00 (*1-56676-129-8*) Technomic.

Qasim, Syed R. Wastewater Treatment Plants: Planning, Design & Operation. 704p. (C). 1985. text ed. 58.75 (*0-03-062449-5*) SCP.

— Wastewater Treatment Plants: Planning, Design, & Operation. LC 93-61610. 746p. 1994. text ed. 58.00 (*1-56676-134-4*) Technomic.

Qaukhchishvili, S. The Georgian Chronicle: The Period of Georgi Lasha. Vivian, Katharine, tr. xlvii, 198p. 1991. pap. 40.00 (*90-256-0965-1*, Pub. by A M Hakkert NE) Benjamins North Am.

Qayoumi, Mohammad H. Electrical Distribution & Maintenance. 272p. 1989. 35.00 (*0-685-24176-9*); pap. 50.00 (*0-913359-49-1*) APPA VA.

Qayum, A. Numerical Models of Economic Development: Proceeding of the Western Resources Conference, 3rd, Colorado State University, 1961. 106p. 1979. text ed. 110.00 (*0-677-61600-7*) Gordon & Breach.

Qayyum, A. On Striving to Be a Muslim. pap. 14.50 (*0-935782-10-9*) Kazi Pubns.

Qayyum, Abdul, tr. see Al-Ghazali, Muhammad.

Qazi, M. A. ABC Islamic Reader. (J). pap. 3.50 (*0-935782-07-9*) Kazi Pubns.

— Arabic Alphabet Coloring Book. 20p. (J). (ps). 1984. pap. 3.50 (*1-56744-220-X*) Kazi Pubns.

— Arabic for Daily Use. 20p. (Orig.). (ARA.). 1986. pap. 2.00 (*1-56744-221-8*) Kazi Pubns.

— Bilal in Hadith. pap. 1.50 (*0-935782-50-8*) Kazi Pubns.

— Color & Learn Islamic Terms. pap. 3.50 (*0-935782-57-5*) Kazi Pubns.

— Concise Dictionary of Islamic Terms: English-Arabic. 1979. 8.50 (*0-86685-276-X*) Intl Bk Ctr.

— Miracles of Prophet Muhammad. pap. 6.50 (*1-56744-139-4*) Kazi Pubns.

— Short Suras for Prayer. 16p. (Orig.). 1985. pap. 3.95 (*1-56744-384-2*) Kazi Pubns.

— What's in a Muslim Name? pap. 3.95 (*0-933511-91-4*) Kazi Pubns.

Qazi, M. N., ed. Physics & Contemporary Needs: Proceedings of the International Nathiagali Summer College, Islamabad, August 1982, Vol. 7. 312p. (C). 1985. 75.00 (*9971-966-83-2*) World Scientific Pub.

Qesai, C. S., et al, eds. Constitutive Laws for Engineering Materials. 957p. 1991. 200.00 (*0-7918-0024-5*, 800245) ASME Pr.

Qian, Sima. Historical Records. Dawson, Raymond, tr. & intro. by. LC 93-34053. (World's Classics Ser.). (Illus.). 208p. (C). 1994. pap. 10.95 (*0-19-283115-1*) OUP.

— Records of the Grand Historian: Han Dynasty & Qin Dynasty, 3 vols. rev. ed. Watson, Burton, tr. LC 92-34085. (Records of Civilization, Sources & Studies: No. 65). (C). 1993. Vol. I, 540p. write for info. (*0-231-08164-2*); Vol. II, 520p. write for info. (*0-231-08166-9*) Col U Pr.

— Records of the Grand Historian: Han Dynasty & Qin Dynasty, 3 vols., Set. rev. ed. Watson, Burton, tr. LC 92-34085. (Records of Civilization, Sources & Studies: No. 65). (C). 1993. text ed. 200.00 (*0-231-08240-1*); text ed. 75.00 (*0-685-62192-8*) Col U Pr.

— Records of the Grand Historian: Han Dynasty & Qin Dynasty, 3 vols., Vol. III. rev. ed. Watson, Burton, tr. LC 92-34085. (Records of Civilization, Sources & Studies: No. 65). 210p. (C). 1993. text ed. 60.00 (*0-231-08168-5*) Col U Pr.

***Qian, Xiao.** Chestnuts & Other Stories. 184p. 1995. lib. bdg. 27.00 (*0-8095-4506-3*) Borgo Pr.

***Qian, Zhaoming.** Orientalism & Modernism: The Legacy of China in Pound & Williams, 1913-1923. LC 95-6130. 1995. write for info. (*0-8223-1657-9*); pap. write for info. (*0-8223-1669-2*) Duke.

Qiang, Ji, et al, eds. The Dapoushang Section: An Excellent Section for the Devonian-Carboniferous Boundary Stratotype in China. 400p. 1990. 42.00 (*7-03-001428-6*, Pub. by Science Pr CH) Intl Spec Bk.

Qibin, Li. Frontiers of Astronomy in 1990's. 300p. 1993. text ed. 106.00 (*981-02-1514-2*) World Scientific Pub.

Qibrisi, Shaykh N. Mercy Ocean: (Teachings of Abdullah Al Faizi Ad-Daghestani) 1991. pap. 9.95 (*1-56744-136-X*) Kazi Pubns.

Qimao, Chen, jt. ed. see Scalapino, Robert A.

Qimron, Elisha & Strugnell, John, eds. Qumran Cave Four Vol. 4: Miqsat Ma'ase Ha-Torah HQ 394-399. (Discoveries in the Judaean Desert Ser.). (Illus.). 200p. (ENG & HEB.). 1994. 60.00 (*0-19-826344-9*) OUP.

Qin, Duo. The Formation of Econometrics: A Historical Perspective. 224p. 1993. 39.95 (*0-19-828388-1*) OUP.

Qing, Dai. Wang Shiwei & "Wild Lilies" Rectification & Purges in the Chinese Communist Party, 1942-1944. Apter, David E. & Cheek, Timothy, eds. Liu, Nancy & Sullivan, Lawrence R., trs. LC 93-34022. 224p. (C). 1994. pap. 24.95 (*1-56324-256-7*, East Gate Bk) M E Sharpe.

Qing-Nan, Meng. Land-Based Marine Pollution: International Law Development. 276p. 1987. lib. bdg. 99.50 (*0-86010-909-7*) Kluwer Ac.

Qing-Zhu, Fu. Fu Qing-Zhu's Gynecology. Shou-Zhong, Yang & Da-Wei, Liu, trs. LC 92-71293. (Orig.). 1992. pap. 21.95 (*0-936185-35-X*) Blue Poppy.

***Qingde, Kang.** Large Sets of Triple Systems & Related Designs. Du Dingzhu et al, eds. (Descrete Mathematics & Theoretical Computer Science Ser.: Vol. 3). 202p. 1995. 39.95 (*1-880132-13-3*) Sci Pr NY.

Qinghua, Du, ed. Boundary Elements: Proceedings of the International Conference, Bejing, China, 14-17 October 1986. 750p. 1986. 302.00 (*0-08-034357-0*) Franklin.

Qingkal Zhang. AIDS & Chinese Medicine. 1993. pap. 19.95 (*0-941942-31-7*) Orient Heal Arts.

Qingkui, Li, jt. auth. see Yi, Xiong.

Qingming, J., jt. ed. see Milliman, J. D.

Qingshan, Tan. The Making of U. S. China Policy: From Normalization to the Post-Cold War Era. LC 92-41402. 190p. 1992. pap. text ed. 16.95 (*1-55587-314-6*) Lynne Rienner.

Qingxi, L. Historic Chinese Architecture. (Illus.). 146p. (C). 1985. text ed. 195.00 (*0-685-40306-8*, Pub. by Collets) St Mut.

Qingzhao, Hua. From Yalta to Panmunjom: Truman's Diplomacy & the Four Powers, 1945-1953. (Cornell East Asia Ser.: No. 64). 284p. (Orig.). (C). 1993. pap. 15.00 (*0-939657-64-3*) Cornell East Asia Pgm.

Qiong Yu, jt. auth. see Sherwani, Naveed A.

Qiu, Haiming, jt. auth. see Rao, Ming.

***Qiu Zhong, Grace Yi & Sullivan, Patricia Noble.** TOEFL Supercourse. 3rd ed. LC 95-2445. 1995. write for info. (*0-02-860338-9*) Macmillan.

Qiuping Cao. Early Childhood Education in Comparative Perspective: A Select Bibliography. (Special Studies in Comparative Education). 40p. (Orig.). 1990. pap. text ed. 10.00 (*0-937033-22-7*) SUNY GSE Pubns.

Qjha, J. M. Cultural Communication in India: Role & Impact of Phonograms. (C). 1992. 18.00 (*81-7022-367-9*, Pub. by Concept II) S Asia.

Qld.Ex-POW Repatriation Committee Staff. Nippon Very Sorry-Man Men Must Die. 123p. (C). 1990. 60.00 (*0-86439-112-9*, Pub. by Boolarong Pubns AT) St Mut.

Qoyawayma, Al & Berger, Bruce. Al Qoyawayma: Hopi Potter. King, Alma S., ed. (Illus.). 32p. (Orig.). 1984. pap. 5.00 (*0-941430-07-3*) Santa Fe E Gallery.

Qoyawayma, Polingaysi, pseud. & Carlson, Vada F. No Turning Back: A Hopi Indian Woman's Struggle to Live in Two Worlds. LC 64-7652. (Illus.). 187p. 1977. reprint ed. pap. 11.95 (*0-8263-0439-7*) U of NM Pr.

Qsba, G. N. Fungi of Jammu Kashmir. (C). 1991. 122.50 (*81-7136-027-0*, Pub. by Periodical Expert India) St Mut.

Qu Geping & Li Jinchang. Population & the Environment in China. LC 93-40821. 217p. 1994. lib. bdg. 45.00 (*1-55587-435-5*) Lynne Rienner.

Qu Yuan, et al. The Songs of the South: An Ancient Chinese Anthology of Poems. Hawkes, David, tr. (Classics Ser.). 352p. 1986. mass mkt. 11.95 (*0-14-044375-4*, Penguin Bks) Viking Penguin.

Quaal. Comprehensive Intra-Aortic Balloon Pumping. 432p. 1983. pap. 31.95 (*0-8016-4090-3*) Mosby Yr Bk.

Quaal, Susan J. Comprehensive Intraaortic Balloon Counterpulsation. 2nd ed. LC 92-48411. 576p. 1993. pap. 32.95 (*0-8016-6656-2*) Mosby Yr Bk.

Quaal, Susan J., ed. Cardiac Mechanical Assistance Beyond Balloon Pumping. LC 92-25096. 395p. 1992. pap. 39.95 (*0-8016-6442-X*) Mosby Yr Bk.

Quaal, Ward L. & Brown, James A. Broadcast Management: Radio & Television. 2nd ed. (Illus.). 464p. 1976. pap. text ed. 15.00 (*0-8038-0764-3*) Hastings.

***Quack, Sibylle, ed.** Between Sorrow & Strength: Women Refugees of the Nazi Period. (Publications of the German Historical Insitute, Washington, D.C. Ser.). 368p. (C). 1995. 69.95 (*0-521-47081-1*) Cambridge U Pr.

Quackenbos, George P., tr. see Mayura.

Quackenbuch, Hiroko C. The Runaway Riceball. Ogawa & Tazawa, eds. (Kodansha's Nihongo Folktales Ser.). (Illus.). 32p. (J). 1993. pap. 7.00 (*4-7700-1762-6*) Kodansha.

Quackenbush, Hiroko C. The Grateful Crane. Ogawa & Tazawa, eds. (Kodansha's Nihongo Folktales Ser.). (Illus.). 32p. (J). 1993. pap. 7.00 (*4-7700-1761-8*) Kodansha.

— Momotaro, the Peach Boy. Ogawa & Tazawa, eds. (Kodansha's Nihongo Folktales Ser.). (Illus.). 32p. (J). 1993. pap. 7.00 (*4-7700-1760-X*) Kodansha.

Quackenbush, Howard, ed. see Rojas, Gonzalo.

Quackenbush, Jan. Inside Out. (Orig.). 1994. pap. 9.95 (*0-7145-0292-8*) Riverrun NY.

— Inside Out & Other Plays. 72p. 1968. 12.95 (*0-910278-41-5*) Boulevard.

Quackenbush, L. Howard, tr. see Samperio, Guillermo.

Quackenbush, Marcia & Sargent, Pamela. Teaching AIDS. rev. ed. 164p. 1988. pap. text ed. 19.95 (*0-941816-41-9*) ETR Assocs.

***Quackenbush, Marcia & Schonfeld, David.** Teaching Kids about How AIDS Works. (J). (gr. k-3). 1995. 25.00 (*1-56071-377-1*) ETR Assocs.

— Teaching Kids about How AIDS Works. (J). (gr. 4-6). 1995. 25.00 (*1-56071-378-X*) ETR Assocs.

Quackenbush, Marcia & Villarreal, Sylia. Does AIDS Hurt? Educating Your Children about AIDS. 2nd ed. LC 92-25691. 1992. write for info. (*1-56071-084-5*) ETR Assocs.

Quackenbush, Marcia & Villarreal, Sylvia. Does AIDS Hurt? Educating Young Children about AIDS. Nelson, Mary, ed. 148p. (Orig.). 1988. pap. 14.95 (*0-941816-52-4*) ETR Assocs.

Quackenbush, Marcia, et al. Risk & Recovery: AIDs, HIV & Alcohol: a Handbook for Providers. LC 92-26635. 1992. 16.95 (*0-89087-690-8*) Celestial Arts.

Quackenbush, Marcia, et al, eds. The AIDS Challenge: Prevention Education for Young People. 526p. 1988. 34. 95 (*0-941816-54-0*); pap. 24.95 (*0-941816-53-2*) ETR Assocs.

Quackenbush, Marian. Air, Sunlight, & a Bit of Land. (Illus.). 1982. 9.95 (*0-87770-275-6*) Ye Galleon.

Quackenbush, Robert. Arthur Ashe & His Match with History. (J). (gr. 4-7). 1994. pap. 4.95 (*0-671-88182-5*, S&S Bks Young Read) S&S Childrens.

— Arthur Ashe & His Match with History. LC 93-14945. (J). (gr. 5 up). 1994. pap. 14.00 (*0-671-86597-8*, S&S Bks Young Read) S&S Childrens.

— Benjamin Franklin & His Friends. (Illus.). 32p. (J). (gr. 2-5). 1991. 14.95 (*0-945912-14-5*) Pippin Pr.

— Bicycle to Treachery. (Miss Mallard Mystery Ser.). 48p. (J). (gr. 1-5). 1991. pap. 2.95 (*0-671-73346-X*, S&S Bks Young Read) S&S Childrens.

— Clara Barton & Her Victory over Fear. LC 94-18168. (J). 1995. 14.00 (*0-671-86598-6*, S&S Bks Young Read) S&S Childrens.

— Clara Barton & Her Victory over Fear. (Illus.). (J). (gr. 2-6). 1995. pap. 4.95 (*0-689-80124-6*, Aladdin Paperbacks) S&S Childrens.

— Clear the Cow Pasture: I'm Comin' In. LC 89-6164. (J). 1990. pap. 11.95 (*0-671-68548-1*, S&S Bks Young Read); pap. 3.95 (*0-671-69218-6*, S&S Bks Young Read) S&S Childrens.

— Danger in Tibet: A Miss Mallard Mystery. (Illus.). 32p. (J). (gr. 1-4). 1989. 15.95 (*0-945912-03-X*) Pippin Pr.

— Detective Mole & Halloween Mystery. (J). 1989. pap. 3.95 (*0-671-67830-2*, Litl Simon S&S) S&S Childrens.

— Detective Mole & the Haunted Castle Mystery. LC 84-20141. (Illus.). 32p. (J). (gr. k-3). 1985. lib. bdg. 14.93 (*0-688-04641-X*) Lothrop.

— Dogsled to Dread. LC 86-25394. (Miss Mallard Mystery Ser.). (Illus.). 48p. (J). (gr. 2-6). 1988. pap. 12.95 (*0-671-66518-9*, S&S Bks Young Read) S&S Childrens.

— Don't You Dare Shoot That Bear. LC 84-4693. (J). 1990. pap. 3.95 (*0-671-69440-5*) S&S Trade.

— Evil Under the Sea: A Miss Mallard Mystery. (Illus.). 32p. (J). (gr. 1-4). 1992. 15.95 (*0-945912-16-1*) Pippin Pr.

— First Grade Jitters. LC 81-47757. (Illus.). 32p. (J). (gr. k-2). 1982. lib. bdg. 12.89 (*0-397-31981-9*, Lipp Jr Bks) HarpC Child Bks.

— Henry Babysits. LC 93-15472. (Parents Magazine Read Aloud Original Ser.). (J). 1993. lib. bdg. 13.27 (*0-8368-0968-8*) Gareth Stevens Inc.

— Henry Babysits. LC 83-2247. (Illus.). 48p. (J). (ps-3). 1983. 5.95 (*0-8193-1107-3*); lib. bdg. 5.95 (*0-8193-1108-1*) Parents.

— Henry Babysits. (Gold Banner Bks.). (Illus.). 48p. (J). (ps-2). 1990. pap. 2.95 (*0-448-04338-6*, G&D) Putnam Pub Group.

— Henry Goes West. LC 82-7971. (Illus.). 48p. (J). (ps-3). 1982. 5.95 (*0-8193-1089-1*); lib. bdg. 5.95 (*0-8193-1090-5*) Parents.

— Henry's Awful Mistake. LC 80-20327. (Illus.). 48p. (J). (ps-3). 1981. 5.95 (*0-8193-1039-5*); lib. bdg. 5.95 (*0-8193-1040-9*) Parents.

— Henry's Important Date. LC 93-7772. (Parents Magazine Read Aloud Original Ser.). (J). 1993. lib. bdg. 14.60 (*0-8368-0969-6*) Gareth Stevens Inc.

— Henry's Important Date. LC 81-5026. (Illus.). 48p. (J). (ps-3). 1982. 5.95 (*0-8193-1067-0*); lib. bdg. 5.95 (*0-8193-1068-9*) Parents.

— Here a Plant, There a Plant, Everywhere a Plant, Plant! A Story of Luther Burbank. rev. ed. (Illus.). 36p. (J). (gr. 1-5). 1995. 11.00 (*0-9637883-1-0*) L Burbank Home.

— I Did It with My Hatchet: A Story of George Washington. (Illus.). 32p. (J). (gr. 2-6). 1989. 14.95 (*0-945912-04-8*) Pippin Pr.

— James Madison & Dolly Madison & Their Times. (Illus.). 40p. (J). (gr. 2-5). 1992. 14.95 (*0-945912-18-8*) Pippin Pr.

— John Adams & Abigail Adams & Their Times. (Illus.). 40p. (J). (gr. 2-5). Date not set. 14.95 (*0-945912-24-2*) Pippin Pr.

— Lost in the Amazon: A Miss Mallard Mystery. (Illus.). 32p. (J). (gr. 1-4). 1990. lib. bdg. 15.95 (*0-945912-11-0*) Pippin Pr.

— Mark Twain. 1990. pap. 4.95 (*0-671-69439-1*) S&S Trade.

— Mark Twain? What Kind of Name is That? A Story of Samuel Langhorn Clemens. LC 83-19086. (Illus.). 40p. (J). (gr. 2-6). 1984. pap. 13.00 (*0-671-66294-5*, S&S Bks Young Read) S&S Childrens.

— Once upon a Time! A Story of the Brothers Grimm. LC 85-9410. (Illus.). 40p. (J). (gr. 2-6). 1986. pap. 11.95 (*0-671-66296-1*, Litl Simon S&S) S&S Childrens.

— Pass the Quill; I'll Write a Draft: A Story of Thomas Jefferson. (Illus.). 32p. (J). (gr. 2-6). 1989. lib. bdg. 14.95 (*0-945912-07-2*) Pippin Pr.

— Quit Pulling My Leg. (J). 1987. pap. 11.95 (*0-671-66516-2*) S&S Trade.

— Quit Pulling My Leg. 1990. pap. 3.95 (*0-671-69441-3*) S&S Trade.

— Sherlock Chick & the Case of the Night Noises. LC 89-70984. (Illus.). 48p. (J). (ps-3). 1990. 5.95 (*0-8193-1194-4*) Parents.

— Sherlock Chick & the Giant Egg Mystery. LC 88-4093. (Illus.). (J). (ps-3). 1989. 5.95 (*0-8193-1178-2*) Parents.

— Sherlock Chick & the Peekaboo Mystery. LC 87-3591. (Illus.). 48p. (J). (ps-3). 1987. 5.95 (*0-8193-1149-9*) Parents.

— Sherlock Chick's First Case. LC 86-9398. (Illus.). 48p. (J). (ps-3). 1986. 5.95 (*0-8193-1148-0*) Parents.

— Stage Door to Terror. (Miss Mallard Mystery Ser.). 48p. (J). (gr. 1-5). 1991. pap. 2.95 (*0-671-73347-8*, S&S Bks Young Read) S&S Childrens.

— Stairway to Doom. LC 82-21484. (Miss Mallard Mystery Ser.). (Illus.). 48p. (J). (gr. 2-6). 1986. pap. 5.95 (*0-671-67053-0*, S&S Bks Young Read) S&S Childrens.

— Stairway to Doom: A Miss Mallard Mystery. LC 82-21484. (Illus.). 48p. (J). (ps-5). 1983. lib. bdg. 9.95 (*0-13-804595-X*) P-H.

— Stop the Presses, Nellie's Got a Scoop! A Story of Nellie Bly. LC 91-4408. (J). (gr. 4-7). 1992. pap. 13.00 (*0-671-76090-4*, S&S Bks Young Read); pap. 3.95 (*0-671-76091-2*, S&S Bks Young Read) S&S Childrens.

— Surfboard to Peril. LC 85-24430. (J). (gr. 4-7). 1991. pap. 2.95 (*0-671-73344-3*, S&S Bks Young Read) S&S Childrens.

— Who Let Muddy Boots into the White House? A Story of Andrew Jackson. LC 86-4989. (Illus.). 40p. (J). (gr. 2-6). 1986. pap. 11.95 (*0-671-66970-2*, S&S Bks Young Read) S&S Childrens.

Quackenbush, Robert, illus. It's Raining Cats & Dogs: Cat & Dog Jokes. 40p. (J). (gr. 2-6). 1988. 13.95 (*0-945912-01-3*) Pippin Pr.

Quackenbush, Robert M. Henry Goes West. LC 94-11353. (Read Aloud Original Ser.). (J). 1994. write for info. (*0-8368-0996-3*) Parents.

— Henry's Awful Mistake. LC 92-32870. (Parents Magazine Press Read-Aloud Library). (Illus.). 42p. (J). (ps-3). 1992. lib. bdg. 14.60 (*0-8368-0882-7*) Gareth Stevens Inc.

Quackenbush, Ross & Gastineau, Jerrel. Homework? My Locker Ate It! An Effective Method for Parents to Help Their Student Study at Home & Improve in School. (Illus.). 143p. (Orig.). (J). (gr. 6-12). 1988. pap. 19.95 (*0-9621701-0-0*) CWP.

Quad City Symphony, Jr. Bd. Return Engagement. 1989. 13.95 (*0-685-24341-9*) JBQCS.

Quadagno, jt. auth. see Denney, Nancy W.

Quadagno, Jill. The Transformation of Old Age Security: Class & Politics in the American Welfare State. (Illus.). 272p. 1988. 29.95 (*0-226-69923-4*) U Ch Pr.

— Unfinished Democracy: Race, Rights, & the War on Poverty. (Illus.). 240p. 1994. 24.00 (*0-19-507919-1*) OUP.

Quadagno, Jill, jt. ed. see Peterson, Warren A.

Quade, E. S. & Carter, G. M. Analysis for Public Decisions. 3rd ed. 410p. 1989. 42.75 (*0-444-01471-3*) P-H.

Quade, Edward S. & Boucher, W. I., eds. Systems Analysis & Policy Planning: Applications in Defense. LC 68-22241. 480p. reprint ed. pap. 136.80 (*0-685-15495-5*, 2026274) Bks Demand.

Quade, Edward S., jt. ed. see Miser, Hugh J.

Quade, Edward S., jt. auth. see Miser, Hugh.

Quade, Kenneth. Biotechnology: The Future of Motherhood & Sex. 1993. 11.95 (*0-533-10652-4*) Vantage.

— You Won't Understand If You Have to Ask Why. Date not set. 16.95 (*0-533-11343-1*) Vantage.

Quade, Quentin L., ed. The Pope & Revolution: John Paul II Confronts Liberation Theology. LC 82-4971. 205p. (C). 1982. pap. 20.50 (*0-89633-054-0*) Ethics & Public Policy.

Quade, Vicki. Laughing Eyes. (Illus.). (Orig.). 1979. pap. 5.00 (*0-9602604-0-4*) V Quade.

Quade, Vicki, jt. auth. see MacCready, Jean.

Quadgano, Jill, jt. ed. see Myles, John.

Quadir, C. A. Philosophy & Science in the Islamic World: From Origins to the Present Day. 224p. 1988. lib. bdg. 69.50 (*0-7099-2108-X*, Pub. by Croom Helm UK) Routledge Chapman & Hall.

Quadling, Douglas, jt. ed. see Shuard, Hilary.

Quadrio-Curzio, A., jt. ed. see Antonelli, G.

Quadrio Curzio, A., et al, eds. Innovation, Resources & Economic Growth. (Illus.). viii, 300p. 1994. 98.00 (*0-387-57737-8*) Spr-Verlag.

Quadrucci, E., jt. ed. see Walker, R.

Quadrupani, R. P. Light & Peace. LC 79-67860. 193p. 1980. reprint ed. pap. 5.00 (*0-89555-133-0*) TAN Bks Pubs.

Quaghebeur, D., et al, eds. Organic Contaminants in Waste Water, Sludge & Sediment: Occurance, Fate & Disposal: Proc. of a Workshop held in Brussels, Belgium, 26- 27 Oct. 1988, under the Auspices of COST (European Cooperation in Scientific & Technology Research) - COST 641 & 681. 214p. 1990. 45.00 (*1-85166-445-9*) Elsevier.

Quagliano, James V. & Vallarino, Lidia M. Chemistry. 3rd ed. (C). 1969. 34.95 (*0-685-03782-7*) P-H.

— Chemistry Answers to Selected Problems. 3rd ed. (C). 1969. 11.95 (*0-685-03783-5*) P-H.

Quagliano, Tony. Fierce Meadows. 24p. 1981. pap. 2.50 (*0-932136-04-4*) Petronium HI.

Quagliariello, E. & Palmieri, F., eds. Structure & Function of Membrane Proteins. (Developments in Bioenergetics & Biomembranes Ser.: Vol. 6). 378p. 1984. 121.00 (*0-444-80540-0*, I-453-83) Elsevier.

Quagliariello, E., jt. ed. see Palmieri, F.

Quagliariello, E., et al, eds. Achievements & Perspectives of Mitochondrial Research, Vol. 1. 542p. 1986. 197.50 (*0-444-80745-4*) Elsevier.

— Achievements & Perspectives of Mitochondrial Research, Vol. II. 482p. 1986. Vol. 2, Biogenesis, 482 pgs. 176.00 (*0-444-80746-2*) Elsevier.

— From Enzyme Adaptation to Natural Philosophy: Heritage from Jacques Monod. 238p. 1987. 87.25 (*0-444-80887-6*) Elsevier.

Quaglieri, Philip L. America's Labor Leaders. LC 87-46240. 304p. 1989. pap. 24.95 (*0-669-17427-0*) Free Pr.

Quaglini, Juliana. The Night of the Shepherds: A Christmas Experience. Flanagan, Anne J., tr. LC 93-25027. (Illus.). 32p. (Orig.). (J). (gr. 4 up). 1993. pap. 3.95 (*0-8198-5128-0*) Pauline Bks.

Quaglino, D. & Hayhoe, F. G. Haematological Oncology. (Illus.). 485p. 1992. text ed. 195.00 (*0-443-04297-7*) Churchill.

Quaglino, Dennis, jt. auth. see Hayhoe, Frank G.

Quagmire, Joshua. Betty Boop's Big Break. Erickson, Byron, ed. (Illus.). 48p. (Orig.). 1990. pap. 5.95 (*0-915419-49-1*) First Pub IL.

Quah, Euston. Economics & Home Production: Theory & Measurement. 256p. 1993. 59.95 (*1-85628-457-3*, Pub. by Avebury Pub UK) Ashgate Pub Co.

Quah, Jon S. Singapore. (World Bibliographical Ser.). 1989. lib. bdg. 52.50 (*1-85109-071-1*) ABC-CLIO.

Quah, Jon S., jt. auth. see Quah, Stella R.

Quah, Stella R. Between Two Worlds: Modern Wives in a Traditional Setting. 66p. 1988. pap. 10.00 (*9971-988-85-2*, Pub. by Inst SE Asian Studies SI) Ashgate Pub Co.

Quah, Stella R. & Quah, Jon S. Friends in Blue: The Police & the Public in Singapore. (Illus.). 228p. 1987. pap. 24. 95 (*0-19-588854-5*) OUP.

Quaid, Maeve. Job Evaluation: The Myth of Equitable Assessment. LC 93-93041. 283p. 1993. 45.00 (*0-8020-2904-3*) U of Toronto Pr.

Quaife, Art. Automated Development of Fundamental Mathematical Theories. LC 92-34849. (Automated Reasoning Ser.: Vol. 2). 1992. lib. bdg. 123.00 (*0-7923-2021-2*) Kluwer Ac.

***Quaife, Darlene B.** Days & Nights on the Amazon. 1995. pap. 12.95 (*0-88801-183-0*) InBook.

Quaife, G. R. Godly Zeal & Furious Rage: The Witch in Early Modern Europe. 256p. 1987. text ed. 39.95 (*0-312-00475-3*) St Martin.

***Quaife, M. M., ed.** Early Days of Rock Island (Ill.) & Davenport (Ia.) The Narratives of J. W. Spencer (1872) & J. M. D. Burrows (1888) 315p. 1995. reprint ed. lib. bdg. 37.50 (*0-8328-4670-8*) Higginson Bk Co.

Quaife, M. M., ed. see Davis, Britton.

Quaife, M. M., ed. see Kelly, Luther S.

***Quaife, Milo M., ed.** From the Cannon's Mouth: The Civil War Letters of General Alpheus S. Williams. (Illus.). 448p. 1995. pap. 15.00 (*0-8032-9777-7*, Bison Books) U of Nebr Pr.

— Southwestern Expedition of Zebulon M. Pike. LC 70-124252. (Select Bibliographies Reprint Ser.). 1977. 18.95 (*0-8369-5440-8*) Ayer.

Quaife, Milo M., ed. see Brush, Daniel H.

Quaife, Milo M., ed. see Burlend, Rebecca & Burlend, Edward.

Quaife, Milo M., ed. see Carson, Kit.

Quaife, Milo M., ed. see Conard, Howard L.

Quaife, Milo M., ed. see Custer, George A.

Quaife, Milo M., ed. see Gillett, James B.

Quaife, Milo M., ed. see Leonard, Zenas.

Quaife, Milo M., ed. see Spencer, O. M.

Quaife, Milo M., ed. see Tillson, Christina H.

Quaife, Milo M., ed. see Tilson, Christiana H.

Quaife, Milo M., ed. see Williams, Alpheus S.

Quail, Beverly J. Colorado Real Estate Forms, 3 vols. suppl. ed. 1993. 80.00 (*0-685-74607-0*) Butterworth Legal Pubs.

— Colorado Real Estate Forms, 3 vols., Set. 1660p. 1993. 5.25 hd, ring bd. 299.00 (*0-87189-058-5*) Michie Butterworth.

Quail, Junius. The Fat Chance Diet Book. LC 82-62878. 64p. 1983. pap. 3.95 (*0-9610764-0-2*) Quail Prods.

Quailes, Sandra L. The Legal Assistant's Notebook, Vol. 1: So. California. 305p. 1992. ring bd. 85.00 (*0-9629697-5-3*) ASAP Pubns.

— The Legal Assistant's Notebook, Vol. 1: So. California. annuals 305p. 1992. 70.00 (*0-685-60076-9*) ASAP Pubns.

— The Legal Assistant's Notebook, Vol. 2: No. California. 505p. 1992. ring bd. 90.00 (*0-9629697-6-1*) ASAP Pubns.

— The Legal Assistant's Notebook, Vol. 2: No. California. annuals 505p. 1992. 70.00 (*0-685-60077-7*) ASAP Pubns.

— WordPerfect Simplified: Shortcuts & Macros. 1992. pap. 29.95 (*0-9629697-8-8*) ASAP Pubns.

***Quain, Bill.** Recobrando el Sueno Americano: Claves para Alcanzar la Libertad Financiera. Monterrosa, Ricardo, tr. (Illus.). 124p. (Orig.). (SPA.). 1995. pap. 9.95 (*0-9623646-6-5*) Wales Pub.

Quain, Edwin A. The Medieval Accessus Ad Auctores. LC 86-80646. 60p. reprint ed. pap. 25.00 (*0-7837-5616-X*, 2045525) Bks Demand.

— Paradosis: Studies in Memory of Edwin A. Quain. LC 76-20905. 240p. reprint ed. pap. 68.40 (*0-7837-5617-8*, 2045526) Bks Demand.

Quain, Kay D. So Your Daughter Is Engaged: or Why the Mother of the Bride Oughtn't Be in Pictures. LC 89-51256. (Illus.). 64p. (Orig.). 1989. pap. write for info. (*0-9623646-0-6*) Wales Pub.

— Surviving Cancer. LC 88-62065. 126p. 1988. pap. 7.95 (*1-55612-156-3*) Sheed & Ward MO.

Quain, Kevin. The Elvis Reader: Texts & Sources on the King of Rock 'n' Roll. (Illus.). 352p. (Orig.). 1991. pap. 13.95 (*0-312-06966-9*) St Martin.

Quain, William J. Reclaiming the American Dream: The Keys to Financial Freedom. 144p. 1994. pap. 9.95 (*0-9623646-1-4*) Wales Pub.

Quain, William J. & Jarboe, Glen R. The Marketing Plan Project Manual. Leyh, ed. 130p. (C). 1993. pap. text ed. 17.75 (*0-314-01341-5*) West Pub.

Quaine, Anthony I. Crime: Index of Modern Information. LC 88-47548. 150p. 1988. 39.50 (*0-88164-820-5*); pap. 34.50 (*0-88164-821-3*) ABBE Pubs Assn.

— Crime & Riot Control: Index of Modern Authors & Subjects with Guide for Rapid Research. LC 90-56263. 180p. 1991. 44.50 (*1-55914-320-7*); pap. 39.50 (*1-55914-321-5*) ABBE Pubs Assn.

— Crime Research Index for 1983: With Medical Subject Analysis & Bibliography. LC 83-70092. 150p. 1984. 37. 50 (*0-88164-036-0*); pap. 29.50 (*0-88164-037-9*) ABBE Pubs Assn.

Quaintance, Cheryl, ed. see Bryant, Kim & Meloan, Becky.

Quakenbush, Margaret, jt. auth. see Porat, Frieda.

Quaker U. S. - U. S. S. R. Committee Staff. Human Experience: Contemporary American & Soviet Fiction & Poetry. 1991. pap. 12.95 (*1-877741-05-1*) J Odell Editions.

Quaker U. S. Staff & U. S. S. R. Committee & the Soviet Writers Union, eds. The Human Experience: Contemporary American & Soviet Fiction & Poverty. 1989. 19.95 (*0-394-57061-8*) Knopf.

***Quaknin, Marc-Alain.** The Burnt Book: Reading the Talmud. Brown, Llewellyn, tr. LC 94-39674. (ENG & FRE.). 1995. write for info. (*0-691-03729-9*) Princeton U Pr.

Qual-Tech Staff, ed. see Wills, John H.

Qualben, James. Christ-Care Leaders Commentary. 150p. 1992. pap. 6.95 (*1-880292-06-8*) LangMarc.

Qualben, James D. Peace in the Parish: How to Use Conflict Redemption Principles & Process. LC 91-214809. 302p. (Orig.). 1992. pap. text ed. 15.95 (*1-880292-00-9*) LangMarc.

Qualben, Lois. Christ-Care: Bible Study for Personal & Group Use. 124p. (Orig.). 1991. pap. text ed. 5.95 (*1-880292-01-7*) LangMarc.

— Sand Castles & Fortresses: Christian Relationships. (Illus.). 140p. (Orig.). 1992. pap. text ed. 5.95 (*1-880292-02-5*) LangMarc.

— Values Symphony: How to Harmonize Faith & Choices in Everyday Living. rev. ed. Roberts, R. J., ed. (Illus.). 169p. 1993. pap. 8.95 (*1-880292-17-3*) LangMarc.

Quale, G. Robina. Families in Context: A World History of Population. LC 91-35713. (Contributions to the Study of World History Ser.: No. 35). 480p. 1992. text ed. 62.50 (*0-313-27830-X*, QSH/, Greenwood Pr) Greenwood.

— A History of Marriage Systems. LC 87-24957. (Contributions in Family Studies: No. 13). 400p. 1988. text ed. 59.95 (*0-313-26010-9*, QHM/, Greenwood Pr) Greenwood.

Quale, Mark E., ed. see Peterson, Charles & Blei, Norbert.

Qualey, Carlton C. Norwegian Settlement in the United States. LC 70-129409. (American Immigration Collection, Ser. 2). 1978. reprint ed. 23.95 (*0-405-00563-6*) Ayer.

Qualey, Carlton C., ed. Thorstein Veblen: The Carleton College Veblen Seminar Essays. LC 68-28400. 170p. 1968. text ed. 40.00 (*0-231-03111-4*) Col U Pr.

Qualey, Marsha. Come in from the Cold. LC 93-42064. (J). 1994. 15.95 (*0-395-68986-4*) HM.

— Everybody's Daughter. 208p. (YA). (gr. 6 up). 1993. pap. 4.95 (*0-395-65746-6*) HM.

— Hometown. LC 94-49321. 1995. 14.95 (*0-395-72666-2*) HM.

— Revolutions of the Heart. LC 92-24528. 192p. (YA). (gr. 6 up). 1993. 13.95 (*0-395-64168-3*) HM.

Quality Costs Committee Staff. Quality Costs: Ideas & Applications, Vol. I. 2nd ed. Grimm, Andrew F., ed. (Illus.). 592p. 1988. pap. 45.95 (*0-87389-046-9*, H0565) ASQC Qual Pr.

Quality Education Data Staff. Microcomputer & VCR Usage in Schools. (School Trend Ser.). 204p. 1988. pap. 49.95 (*0-88747-217-6*, 2176Q) Quality Ed Data.

— QED's Guide to U. S. School Districts 1987-88. (School Trend Ser.). 400p. 1988. pap. 79.95 (*0-88747-295-8*, 2958Q) Quality Ed Data.

— Video Purchasing Patterns in Schools. (School Trend Ser.). 204p. 1988. pap. 49.95 (*0-88747-225-7*, 2257Q) Quality Ed Data.

Quality Family Entertainment, Inc. Staff. Shining Time Station: Station House. (Pop-Up Sound-Up Bks.). 2p. (J). (ps-2). 1993. write for info. (*1-883366-10-0*) YES Ent.

Quality Park Products Staff. Envelopes & Mailing. LC 94-65590. (Illus.). 1994. pap. 5.95 (*0-9640688-0-X*) Quality Park.

Qualley, Charles. Safety in the Artroom. LC 85-73421. 128p. 1987. pap. 13.50 (*0-87192-174-X*) Davis Mass.

Qualley, Donna J., jt. ed. see Sullivan, Patricia A.

Qualley, John R. Speak Without Fear & Without Notes. LC 93-79270. 112p. (Orig.). 1993. pap. 19.95 (*1-878710-87-7*) Qualley & Whitfield.

Qualline, Steve. Practical C Programming. 2nd ed. (Nutshell Handbook Ser.). (Illus.). 396p. 1993. pap. 24.95 (*1-56592-035-X*) OReilly & Assocs.

— Windows Programming with Borland C Plus Plus. 1993. pap. 39.95 (*1-55851-313-2*) M&T Bks.

Qualline, Steven, jt. auth. see Peter Norton Computing Group Staff.

***Qualls-Corbett.** Sacred Prostitute. 1995. pap. 18.00 (*0-919123-31-7*) Atrium Pubs.

Qualls, Dorothy. How to Buy & Sell Real Estate: A Do It Yourself Survivors Guide. LC 91-50693. 200p. 1992. pap. 12.95 (*0-88247-895-8*, 895-8) R & E Pubs.

Qualls, John R., ed. see Petrie, Bruce I., Jr.

Qualls, P. D., jt. ed. see Bain, J. S.

Qualls, Robert L. Entrepreneurial Wit & Wisdom. rev. ed. (Illus.). 48p. (Orig.). 1986. pap. 4.85 (*0-9615143-4-5*) Univ Central AR Pr.

Qualman, Al. Blood on the Half Shell. LC 82-73152. (Illus.). 168p. 1982. pap. 6.95 (*0-8323-0411-5*) Binford Mort.

Qualman, Jack. The Glamour Photographer Sourcebook. 160p. 1992. pap. text ed. 19.95 (*0-9634137-0-8*) Jax Photo Bks.

Qualter, Terence H. Advertising & Democracy in the Mass Age. LC 91-11299. 200p. 1991. text ed. 49.95 (*0-312-06507-8*) St Martin.

— Graham Wallas & the Great Society. LC 79-1374. 260p. 1980. text ed. 29.95 (*0-312-34213-6*) St Martin.

***Quamina, Alvan.** The Silent Revolution. rev. ed. 1995. 13. 95 (*0-8062-5079-8*) Carlton.

Quamina, Odida T. Mineworkers of Guyana: The Making of a Working Class. LC 87-14719. (C). 1987. text ed. 35.00 (*0-86232-307-X*, Pub. by Zed Books UK) Humanities.

PQ

Quamme, G. A., ed. Magnesium Homeostasis. (Journal: Mineral & Electrolyte Metabolism: Vol. 19, Nos. 4-5, 1993). (Illus.). 132p. 1993. pap. 74.50 (*3-8055-5881-3*) S Karger.

Quammen, David. Blood Line: Stories of Fathers & Sons. LC 87-81374. (Short Fiction Ser.). 178p. (Orig.). 1988. pap. 8.00 (*1-55597-100-8*) Graywolf.

— The Flight of the Iguana: A Sidelong Look at Science & Nature. 1989. mass mkt. 9.50 (*0-385-26327-9*, Anchor NY) Doubleday.

Quan, Cao, jt. auth. see Allen, Virginia F.

Quan, Judy. Legal Assistant's Guide to Alternative Dispute Resolution. LC 93-49766. (Paralegal Practice Ser.). 1994. ring bd. 75.00 (*0-87632-990-3*) Clark Boardman Callaghan.

***Quan, Judy & Katz, Joanne.** Fundamentals of Alternative Dispute Resolution. 1995. per. write for info. (*0-929563-24-7*) Pearson Pubns.

Quan, Robert S. Lotus among the Magnolias: The Mississippi Chinese. LC 81-23991. (Illus.). 180p. reprint ed. pap. 51.30 (*0-7837-1071-2*, 2041594) Bks Demand.

Quan Yanchi. Mao Zedong: Man, Not God. Wang Wenjiong, tr. 213p. 1992. 15.95 (*0-8351-2789-3*) China Bks.

Quanbeck, Alton H. Strategic Forces: Issues for the Mid-Seventies. LC 73-1088. (Brookings Institution Staff Paper Ser.). 104p. reprint ed. pap. 29.70 (*0-317-26347-1*, 2025400) Bks Demand.

Quanbeck, Alton H. & Wood, Archie L. Modernizing the Strategic Bomber Force: Why & How. LC 75-38890. (Studies in Defense Policy). (Illus.). 128p. reprint ed. pap. 36.50 (*0-317-08247-7*, 2022561) Bks Demand.

Quance, Frank M. Part-Time Types of Elementary Schools in New York City: A Comparative Study of Pupil Achievement. LC 72-177173. (Columbia University. Teachers College. Contributions to Education Ser.: No. 249). reprint ed. 37.50 (*0-404-55249-8*) AMS Pr.

Quance, Leroy, jt. ed. see Johnson, Glenn L.

Quanchi, Max. Pacific People & Change. (Pacific in the Twentieth Century Ser.). (Illus.). 80p. (C). 1991. pap. 16.95 (*0-521-37627-0*) Cambridge U Pr.

Quanchi, Max, ed. Culture Contact in the Pacific. LC 92-17851. (Illus.). 200p. (C). 1993. pap. 25.00 (*0-521-42284-1*) Cambridge U Pr.

Quandahl, Ellen, jt. ed. see Donahue, Patricia.

Quandt, R. E., jt. ed. see Peston, M. H.

Quandt, Richard E. The Collected Essays of Richard E. Quandt, 2 vols., Set. (Economists of the Twentieth Century Ser.). 800p. 1992. 149.95 (*1-85278-605-1*, Pub. by E Elgar Pub UK) Ashgate Pub Co.

Quandt, Richard E. & Asch, Peter. Racetrack Betting: The Professors' Guide to Strategies. LC 86-7871. 206p. 1986. text ed. 55.00 (*0-86569-147-9*, Auburn Hse) Greenwood.

Quandt, Richard E. & Rosen, Harvey S. The Conflict Between Equilibrium & Disequilibrium Theories: The Case of the U. S. Labor Market. LC 88-10618. 125p. 1988. text ed. 20.00 (*0-88099-061-9*); pap. text ed. 10.00 (*0-88099-060-0*) W E Upjohn.

Quandt, Richard E. & Triska, Dusan, eds. Optimal Decisions in Markets & Planned Economies. 331p. (C). 1990. pap. text ed. 67.00 (*0-8133-0994-8*) Westview.

Quandt, Richard E., jt. auth. see Asch, Peter.

Quandt, Richard E., jt. auth. see Henderson, James M.

Quandt, William B. Camp David: Peacemaking & Politics. LC 85-48174. 426p. 1986. 36.95 (*0-8157-7290-4*); pap. 16.95 (*0-8157-7289-0*) Brookings.

— Decade of Decisions: American Policy Toward the Arab-Israeli Conflict, 1967-1976. LC 77-73499. 1977. pap. 14.00 (*0-520-03536-4*) U CA Pr.

— Peace Process: American Diplomacy & the Arab-Israeli Conflict since 1967. 612p. (C). 1993. 38.95 (*0-520-08388-1*); pap. 15.95 (*0-520-08390-3*) Brookings.

— Saudi Arabia in the 1980's: Foreign Policy, Security, & Oil. LC 82-18086. 190p. 1981. 26.95 (*0-8157-7286-6*) Brookings.

— Saudi Arabia's Oil Policy. LC 82-73524. 46p. 1982. pap. 7.95 (*0-8157-7287-4*) Brookings.

— The United States & Egypt: An Essay on Policy for the 1990s. 82p. (C). 1990. pap. 7.95 (*0-8157-7295-5*) Brookings.

Quandt, William B., ed. The Middle East: Ten Years after Camp David. 450p. 1988. 39.95 (*0-8157-7294-7*); pap. 18.95 (*0-8157-7293-9*) Brookings.

Quandt, William B., jt. auth. see Bohi, Douglas R.

Quandt, William B., et al. The Politics of Palestinian Nationalism. (Rand Corporation Research Study). 1973. pap. 12.00 (*0-520-02372-2*) U CA Pr.

Quang, Pham T. & Chartier-Kastler, C. Merise in Practice. Sumner, F. H., ed. (Computer Science Ser.). (Illus.). 206p. (Orig.). (C). 1991. pap. text ed. 38.00 (*0-333-55020-X*, Pub. by Macmill Educ UK) Scholium Intl.

Quanide, Russ. Whos Who among Werewolves. 96p. 1994. per., pap. 12.00 (*1-56504-140-2*, 3401) White Wolf.

Quann, C. James, et al, eds. Admissions, Academic Records, & Registrar Services. LC 79-88109. (Jossey-Bass Series in Higher Education). (Illus.). 509p. reprint ed. pap. 145.10 (*0-8357-4918-5*, 2037848) Bks Demand.

Quanrud, Percy, tr. see Howard, Rick C.

Quansah, Peter K., jt. auth. see Djawotho, Kisa.

Quansey, James S. & Maniotes, John. Structured Basic Fundamentals & Style for the IBM PC & Compatibles. 504p. 1988. pap. 30.00 (*0-87835-289-9*) Boyd & Fraser.

Quanstrom, Linda. And Some Are Walked Home: Stories of Grace. 68p. 1994. pap. 4.95 (*0-8341-1478-X*) Beacon Hill.

Quant, Wilhelm, ed. see Orpheus.

***Quantic, Diane D.** The Nature of the Place: A Study of Great Plains Fiction. 290p. 1995. text ed. 25.00 (*0-8032-3800-2*) U of Nebr Pr.

— William Allen White. LC 93-70137. (Western Writers Ser.: No. 109). (Illus.). 52p. 1993. pap. 3.95 (*0-88430-108-7*) Boise St U W Writ Ser.

Quantitative Methods of Investigations in the Clinics of Neuromuscular Diseases International Symposium Staff. Studies on Neuromuscular Diseases: Proceedings of the Quantitative Methods of Investigations in the Clinics of Neuromuscular Diseases International Symposium, Giessen, April 1974. Kunze, K. & Desmedt, J. E., eds. 250p. 1975. 152.00 (*3-8055-1749-1*) S Karger.

Quantrill, Malcolm. Alvar Aalto: A Critical Study. (Illus.). 307p. (C). 1989. reprint ed. pap. 30.00 (*0-941533-35-2*) New Amsterdam Bks.

Quantrill, Malcolm & Webb, Bruce, eds. Urban Forms, Suburban Dreams. LC 92-43269. (Studies in Architecture & Culture: No. 2). (Illus.). 232p. 1993. 50.00 (*0-89096-535-8*) Tex A&M Univ Pr.

Quantrill, Malcolm & Webb, Bruce J., eds. Constancy & Change in Architecture. LC 90-23669. (Studies in Architecture & Culture: No. 1). (Illus.). 184p. 1991. 50.00 (*0-89096-472-6*) Tex A&M Univ Pr.

Quantrille, Thomas E. & Liu, Y. A. Artificial Intelligence in Chemical Engineering. (Illus.). 609p. 1992. text ed. 59.95 (*0-12-569550-0*) Acad Pr.

Quantum, Inc. Staff. Development of Copper Organic Gasoline Additives for Improvement of Automotive Engine Combustion Efficiency. 51p. 1962. 7.65 (*0-317-34511-7*, 15) Intl Copper.

Quantz, J. Q.

Quantz, Johann J. On Playing the Flute. 1985. pap. 10.95 (*0-02-871930-1*) Macmillan.

— On Playing the Flute. 1985. 23.95 (*0-02-871940-9*) Macmillan.

— On Playing the Flute. 2nd ed. Reilly, Edward R., tr. LC 75-10986. (Illus.). 416p. 1985. reprint ed. pap. 20.00 (*0-02-870160-7*) Schirmer Bks.

— On Playing the Flute. 2nd ed. Reilly, Edward R., ed. 448p. 1985. text ed. 25.00 (*0-02-872920-X*) Schirmer Bks.

Quanyu, Huang, et al. A Guide to Successful Business Relations with the Chinese: Opening the Great Wall's Gate. LC 93-19379. 1994. lib. bdg. 49.95 (*1-56024-868-8*) Haworth Pr.

Quaraishi, M. Tariq, ed. Some Aspects of Prophet Muhammad's Life. LC 83-71409. 89p. (Orig.). 1985. reprint ed. pap. 4.50 (*0-89259-045-9*) Am Trust Pubns.

Quarantelli, E. L. Chemical Disasters: Preparations & Responses at the Local Level. text ed. write for info. (*0-8290-1289-3*) Irvington.

— Delivery of Emergency Medical Services in Disasters: Assumptions & Realities. LC 83-13028. 190p. (C). 1985. text ed. 29.50 (*0-8290-0531-5*) Irvington.

Quarantelli, E. L., jt. auth. see Helfrich, M. L.

Quarantiello, Laura E. AIR-Waves: The Aviation Monitor's Handbook. 90p. 1992. pap. 17.95 (*0-936653-38-8*) Tiare Pubns.

— Citizen's Guide to Scanning. 100p. 1992. pap. 19.95 (*0-936653-44-2*) Tiare Pubns.

— Cop-Talk: Monitoring Law Enforcement Communications. 80p. 1992. pap. 17.95 (*0-936653-42-6*) Tiare Pubns.

— On Guard! How You Can Win the War Against the Bad Guys. LC 93-48851. 128p. 1994. 17.95 (*0-936653-50-7*, Limelight Bks) Tiare Pubns.

Quaratiello, Elizabeth L., jt. auth. see Collier, George A.

***Quardt, Robert.** Mothers of Priests: True Stories of the "Other Marys" Behind the "Other Christs" Angelus Press Staff, ed. Fisher, Marc S., tr. 57p. (Orig.). (GER.). 1995. pap. 3.95 (*0-935952-56-X*) Angelus Pr.

Quaritch Wales, H. G. Siamese State Ceremonies: With Supplementary Notes (1971) (Illus.). 340p. (C). 1931. text ed. 70.00 (*0-7007-0269-5*, Pub. by Curzon Pr UK) Humanities.

***Quark.** Star Trek: Deep Space Nine: The Ferengi Rules of Acquisition. Ryan, Kevin, ed. 96p. 1995. pap. 6.00 (*0-671-52936-6*) PB.

***Quarles.** Discus As a Hobby: Everything You Need to Know to Get Started. 1995. pap. text ed. 7.95 (*0-86622-405-X*) TFH Pubns.

Quarles, Benjamin. Black Abolitionists. (Quality Paperbacks Ser.). 310p. 1991. reprint ed. pap. 13.95 (*0-306-80425-5*) Da Capo.

— Black Mosaic: Essays in Afro-American History. LC 87-13929. 248p. (Orig.). (C). 1988. pap. 15.95x (*0-87023-605-9*) U of Mass Pr.

— Frederick Douglass. 1990. 25.00 (*0-87498-033-X*) Assoc Pubs DC.

— Lincoln & the Negro. (Quality Paperbacks Ser.). (Illus.). 275p. 1991. reprint ed. pap. 13.95 (*0-306-80447-6*) Da Capo.

— The Negro in the American Revolution. (Institute of Early American History & Culture Ser.). xvi, 231p. 1961. 29.95 (*0-8078-0833-4*) U of NC Pr.

— The Negro in the American Revolution. 256p. 1973. reprint ed. pap. 9.95 (*0-393-00674-3*) Norton.

— The Negro in the Civil War. (Quality Paperbacks Ser.). (Illus.). 402p. 1989. pap. 12.95 (*0-306-80350-X*) Da Capo.

— The Negro in the Making of America. 3rd ed. 352p. 1987. pap. 6.95 (*0-02-036140-8*) Macmillan.

Quarles, Benjamin, ed. Blacks on John Brown. LC 72-188132. (Illus.). 180p. reprint ed. pap. 51.30 (*0-8357-7306-X*, 2020221) Bks Demand.

Quarles, Benjamin, ed. see Douglass, Frederick.

Quarles, Chester L. School Violence: A Survival Guide for School Staff. 48p. 1989. 7.95 (*0-8106-0243-1*) NEA.

— Staying Safe at School. (New Survival Skills for Teachers Ser.). 96p. 1993. pap. 9.95 (*0-8039-6086-7*) Corwin Pr.

Quarles, Chester L., ed. Terrorism: Avoidance & Survival. 224p. 1991. text ed. 39.95 (*0-7506-9176-X*) Buttrwrth-Heinemann.

Quarles, Francis. Argalus & Parthenia. Freeman, David, ed. LC 86-45041. (Renaissance English Text Society Ser.: Series 6, No. 11). (Illus.). 240p. 1987. 30.00 (*0-918016-90-8*) Folger Bks.

— Complete Works in Prose & Verse, 3 vols., Set. (BCL1-PR English Literature Ser.). 1992. reprint ed. lib. bdg. 225.00 (*0-7812-7395-1*) Rprt Serv.

— Emblemes. LC 91-22286. 1991. 80.00 (*0-8201-1458-8*) Schol Facsimiles.

— Emblemes & Hieroglyphikes of the Life of Man. 381p. (GER.). 1991. reprint ed. write for info. (*3-487-09264-6*, Pub. by Georg Olms GW) Lubrecht & Cramer.

— Francis Quarles' "Divine Fancies" A Critical Edition. rev. ed. Liston, William T., ed. LC 91-44132. (Renaissance Imagination Ser.). 304p. 1992. 70.00 (*0-8153-0453-6*) Garland.

Quarles, G. J., ed. Solid State Lasers III. 1992. 77.00 (*0-8194-0773-9*, 1627) SPIE.

Quarles, Garland R. Some Worthy Lives. LC 88-51619. (Illus.). 280p. (C). 1988. 23.00 (*0-923198-00-8*) Winchester-Frederick Cty Hist Soc.

Quarles, J. C., tr. see Sullivan, James L.

Quarles, Jaime C., tr. see Brown, Jamieson-Fausett.

Quarles, Jaime C., tr. see Latourette, Kenneth S.

Quarles, Johnny. Fool's Gold. 368p. (Orig.). 1993. mass mkt. 4.50 (*0-380-76813-5*) Avon.

— No Man's Land. 368p. (Orig.). 1993. mass mkt. 4.99 (*0-380-76814-3*) Avon.

— Spirit Trail. 320p. (Orig.). 1995. mass mkt. 4.99 (*0-380-77656-1*) Avon.

Quarles, Lemuel C., tr. see Brown, Jamieson-Fausett.

Quarles, Lemuel C., tr. see Latourette, Kenneth S.

***Quarles, Lucille W.** Consumer Attitudes & Wishes about Health Care: Index of New Information with Authors, Subjects & Bibliography. rev. ed. 149p. 1995. 49.50 (*0-7883-0701-0*); pap. 39.50 (*0-7883-0702-9*) ABBE Pubs Assn.

— Consumer's Attitudes to Health Care: Index of Modern of Information. rev. ed. LC 88-47542. 155p. 1994. 44.50 (*0-7883-0692-8*); pap. 39.50 (*0-7883-0693-6*) ABBE Pubs Assn.

— Health Status Indicators: Guidebook for Medicine, Reference & Research. LC 83-46105. 150p. 1985. 37.50 (*0-88164-144-8*); pap. 34.50 (*0-88164-145-6*) ABBE Pubs Assn.

— Jurisprudence & Rights to Treatment: Index of Modern Information. LC 88-47582. 150p. 1988. 44.50 (*0-88164-762-4*); pap. 39.50 (*0-88164-763-2*) ABBE Pubs Assn.

Quarles, Mary D. & Meyer, Tommye Q. Kirby Kin: From the Sixteenth Century to the Present. 496p. (C). 1993. 45.00 (*0-9625367-0-9*) T Q Meyer & M D Quarles.

Quarles, Mike. Down & Dirty: Hollywood's Exploitation Filmmakers & Their Movies. LC 92-56683. (Illus.). 208p. 1993. lib. bdg. 29.95 (*0-89950-877-4*) McFarland & Co.

Quarles, Sandra L. The Legal Secretary's Notebook. 260p. (Orig.). 1991. pap. 65.00 (*0-9629697-0-2*) ASAP Pubns.

— Making WordPerfect More Perfect: Macros, Tips & Tricks for WordPerfect 5.X. LC 91-75818. 150p. (Orig.). 1992. disk, pap. 49.95 (*0-9629697-3-7*) ASAP Pubns.

Quarmby, F. Banknotes & Banking in the Isle of Man. 1971. 18.00 (*0-685-51509-5*) S J Durst.

Quarmby, Jacqueline, jt. ed. see Clough, Eric.

Quarrell, John. NAPF Pensions Legislation Service, 2 vols. U.K. ring bd. 324.00 (*0-406-10199-X*) Butterworth Legal Pubs.

Quarrell, John J. Quarrell: Law of Pension Fund Investment. 1990. 130.00 (*0-406-67819-7*) Butterworth Legal Pubs.

Quarrell, W. H., ed. see Lichtenberg, G. C.

Quarrick, Gene. Our Sweetest Hours: Recreation & the Mental State of Absorption. LC 88-43571. 256p. 1989. lib. bdg. 28.50x (*0-89950-404-3*) McFarland & Co.

***Quarrie.** Offshore Race Crew's Manual. 1995. 39.95 (*1-85310-510-4*) Voyageur Pr.

Quarrie, Bruce. German Airborne Troops 1939-45. (Men-at-Arms Ser.: No. 139). (Illus.). 48p. pap. 11.95 (*0-85045-480-8*, 9071, Pub. by Osprey UK) Stackpole.

— Hitler: The Victory That Nearly Was. (Illus.). 224p. 1989. 19.95 (*0-7153-9215-8*, Pub. by D & C Pub UK) Sterling.

— Lightning Death: The Story of the Waffen SS. (Illus.). 176p. 1991. 27.95 (*1-85260-075-6*) Haynes Pubns.

— The Waffen SS Soldier 1940-45. (Warrior Ser.: No. 2). (Illus.). 64p. pap. 12.95 (*1-85532-288-9*, 9601, Pub. by Osprey UK) Stackpole.

Quarrie, Gordon M. Last Stories of the Old Duck Hunters. 151p. 1994. 19.50 (*1-57223-005-3*) Outlook Pubng.

— More Stories of the Old Duck Hunters. 198p. 1994. 19.50 (*1-57223-004-5*) Outlook Pubng.

— Stories of the Old Duck Hunters. 223p. 1994. 19.50 (*1-57223-003-7*) Outlook Pubng.

Quarrie, P. R., tr. see Alfonsi, Petrus.

Quarrie, Paul. Treasures of Eton College Library. (Illus.). 122p. 1990. 24.95 (*0-87598-089-9*) Pierpont Morgan.

Quarrie, Stuart. Quarrie on Racing. (Illus.). 128p. 1994. pap. 16.95 (*1-85310-300-4*) Voyageur Pr.

Quarrier, Ian, jt. ed. see Borton, Mark C.

Quarrier, Ian, jt. ed. see Borton, Mark.

Quarrier, Ian, jt. ed. see Caruso, Donna.

Quarry, W. Edmund. Dictionary of Musical Compositions & Composers. 192p. 1991. reprint ed. 69.00 (*0-7812-9304-9*) Rprt Serv.

Quart, Barbara K. Women Directors: The Emergence of a New Cinema. LC 88-1141. 288p. 1988. text ed. 52.95 (*0-275-92962-0*, C2962, Praeger Pubs) Greenwood.

— Women Directors: The Emergence of a New Cinema. LC 88-1141. 288p. 1989. pap. text ed. 19.95 (*0-275-93477-2*, B3477, Praeger Pubs) Greenwood.

Quart, Irving. Environmental Stress Screening: Facts & Myths. (Illus.). 121p. (C). 1989. student ed 100.00 (*0-918247-05-5*) Tustin Tech.

Quart, Leonard, jt. auth. see Auster, Albert.

Quartapelle, L. Numerical Solution of the Incompressible Navier-Stokes Equations. LC 93-28305. (International Series of Numerical Mathematics: Vol. 113). 1993. 100.00 (*3-7643-2935-1*); 100.00 (*0-8176-2935-1*) Birkhauser.

***Quartararo, Anne T.** Women Teachers & Popular Education in Nineteenth Century France: Social Values & Corporate Identity at the Normal School Institution. LC 94-45047. (Illus.). 232p. 1995. 38.50 (*0-87413-545-1*) U Delaware Pr.

Quarterly, Cornell. The Essentials of Tableside Cookery. 72p. 8.95 (*0-318-41635-2*, 220) Am Bartenders.

Quarterly Journal Staff. Sourcebook on Asbestos Diseases Case Law Quarterly. 1989. 85.00 (*0-8240-7348-7*) Butterworth Legal Pubs.

Quartermain, Peter. Disjunctive Poetics: From Gertrude Stein & Louis Zukofsky to Susan Howe. (Cambridge Studies in American Literature & Culture: No. 59). 418p. (C). 1992. 54.95 (*0-521-41268-4*) Cambridge U Pr.

Quartermain, Peter, ed. American Poets, 1880 to 1945 First Series. (Dictionary of Literary Biography Ser.: Vol. 45). 514p. 1985. 128.00 (*0-8103-1723-0*) Gale.

— American Poets 1880 to 1945 Second Series. (Dictionary of Literary Biography Ser.: Vol. 48). 350p. 1986. 128.00 (*0-8103-1726-5*) Gale.

— American Poets 1880 to 1945 Third Series, 2 vols., Set. (Dictionary of Literary Biography Ser.: Vol. 54). (Illus.). 743p. 1986. 238.00 (*0-8103-1732-X*) Gale.

Quartermain, Peter, jt. ed. see Emony, Elliot.

Quartermaine, Peter. Thomas Keneally. (Modern Fiction Ser.). 128p. 1991. pap. 10.95 (*0-340-51826-X*, A6318, Pub. by E Arnold UK) Routledge Chapman & Hall.

Quarterman, John S. E-Mail Companion: Communications Effectively Via the Internet. 1995. pap. 19.95 (*0-201-40658-6*) Addison-Wesley.

— The Matrix: Computer Networks & Conferencing Systems Worldwide. (Illus.). 720p. (Orig.). 1989. pap. text ed. 49.95 (*1-55558-033-5*, EY C176E-DP, Digital DEC) Buttrwrth-Heinemann.

— UniForum Technology Guide: Network Applications. 34p. pap. text ed. 10.00 (*0-936593-13-X*) UniForum.

— UniForum Technology Guide: Network Substrata. 30p. pap. text ed. 10.00 (*0-936593-14-8*) UniForum.

— UNIX, POSIX, & Open Systems: The Open Standards Puzzle. (Illus.). 384p. (C). 1993. text ed. 44.25 (*0-201-52772-3*) Addison-Wesley.

Quarterman, John S. & Mitchell, Smoot C. The InterNet Connection: System Connectivity & Configuration. (Illus.). 224p. (C). 1994. pap. text ed. 32.25 (*0-201-54237-4*) Addison-Wesley.

Quarterman, John S., jt. auth. see Carl-Mitchell, Smoot.

Quartermaster General of the Army Staff. U. S. Army Uniforms & Equipment, 1889: Specifications for Clothing, Camp & Garrison Equipage, & Clothing & Equipage Materials. LC 86-6972. (Illus.). x, 375p. 1986. reprint ed. 30.00 (*0-8032-4552-1*); reprint ed. pap. 14.95 (*0-8032-9552-9*) U of Nebr Pr.

Quarteroni, A. & Valli, A. Numerical Approximation of Partial Differential Equations. LC 94-21763. (Computational Mathematics Ser.: Vol. 23). 1994. 89.00 (*0-387-57111-6*) Spr-Verlag.

Quarteroni, A., jt. ed. see Canuto, C.

Quarteroni, Alfio, ed. see Sixth International Conference on Domain Decomposition.

Quartim, Joao. Dictatorship & Armed Struggle in Brazil. Fernbach, David, tr. LC 71-178711. 250p. reprint ed. pap. 71.30 (*0-8357-6093-6*, 2034348) Bks Demand.

***Quartly, Marian, et al, eds.** Freedom Bound Vol. 1: Documents on Women in Colonial Australia. 240p. 1995. pap. 22.95 (*1-86373-735-9*) Paul & Co Pubs.

Quarto Books Staff. How to Make Your Own Doll & Doll's Clothes. 1993. 12.98 (*1-55521-920-9*) Bk Sales Inc.

— How to Make Your Own Doll Furniture. 1993. 12.98 (*1-55521-923-3*) Bk Sales Inc.

— How to Make Your Own Doll House. 1993. 12.98 (*1-55521-921-7*) Bk Sales Inc.

Quarton, Bill, jt. auth. see Barnard, Phil.

Quarton, Lori. Children in Watercolor. (How to Draw & Paint Ser.). (Illus.). 32p. (Orig.). 1990. pap. 5.95 (*1-56010-053-2*, HT224) W Foster Pub.

Quarton, Marjorie. Corporal Jack. large type ed. 512p. 1988. 15.95 (*0-7089-1840-9*) Ulverscroft.

— The Cow Watched the Battle. 100p. (J). (gr. 3-7). 1990. pap. 6.95 (*1-85371-084-9*, Pub. by Poolbeg Pr IE) Dufour.

— No Harp Like My Own. large type ed. 1990. 21.95 (*0-7089-2177-9*) Ulverscroft.

— One Dog, His Man & His Trials. (Illus.). 176p. 1993. pap. 12.95 (*0-85236-253-6*, Pub. by Farming Pr UK) Diamond Farm Bk.

— Renegade. 288p. 1992. 24.95 (*0-233-98722-3*, Pub. by A Deutsch UK) Trafalgar.

***Quartuccio, Anthony.** How I Found Peace-Joy-Happiness in a World of Insanity: An Artist Reflects on His Catholic Faith. LC 94-92017. (Illus.). 128p. (Orig.). 1995. pap. 12.00 (*0-9606934-3-2*) A Quartuccio.

— Rambling Through Baja California with Pen & Brush: Painting & Sketching Baja's Landscape & Missions. LC 83-90130. (Illus.). 120p. 1984. 12.00 (*0-9606934-1-6*) A Quartuccio.

— Santa Clara Valley-California: An Artist's View Today & Yesterday Painting & Sketching the Valley I Love. LC 85-90472. (Illus.). 128p. (Orig.). 1986. pap. 12.00 (*0-9606934-2-4*) A Quartuccio.

— Tony's Guide to Better Painting. (Illus.). 48p. (Orig.). 1982. pap. text ed. 7.95 (*0-9606934-0-8*) A Quartuccio.

Quartz, Karen H., jt. ed. see Oakes, Jeannie.

An Asterisk (*) at the beginning of an entry indicates that the title is appearing in BIP for the first time.

Quas, Vince. The Lean Body Promise: An Owner's Manual. LC 89-4162. (Illus.). 288p. (Orig.). 1990. pap. 15.95 (0-925572-36-5) Synesis Pr.
Quasem, Mohammad A. The Ethics of Al-Ghazali. LC 78-15259. (Monographs in Islamic Religion & Theology). 1978. 35.00 (0-88206-021-X) Caravan Bks.
Quasem, Muhammad A. Al-Ghazali on Islamic Guidance. 1979. 12.00 (0-318-00409-7) Quasem.
— The Ethics of al-Ghazali: A Composite Ethics in Islam. 1975. 17.85 (0-686-18952-3); pap. 9.00 (0-686-18953-1) Quasem.
— The Jewels of the Qur'an: Al-Ghazali's Theory. 1977. 12.00 (0-686-23467-7) Quasem.
— The Jewels of the Qur'an: Al-Ghazali's Theory. 240p. 1982. pap. 14.95 (0-7103-0034-4, Pub. by Kegan Paul Intl UK) Routledge Chapman & Hall.
— The Recitation & Interpretation of the Qur'an. 1979. 12.00 (0-318-00410-0) Quasem.
— The Recitation & Interpretation of the Qur'an: Al-Gharzali's Theory. 124p. (Orig.). 1982. pap. 14.95 (0-7103-0035-2, Pub. by Kegan Paul Intl UK) Routledge Chapman & Hall.
— Salvation of the Soul & Islamic Devotion. 1981. 19.95 (0-318-00411-9) Quasem.
— Salvation of the Soul & Islamic Devotion. 200p. 1982. pap. 14.95 (0-7103-0033-6, Pub. by Kegan Paul Intl UK) Routledge Chapman & Hall.
Quash & Rodwell. Covalently Modified Antigens & Antibodies in Diagnosis & Theory. (Targeted Diagnosis & Therapy Ser.: Vol. 2). 248p. 1989. 140.00 (0-8247-8107-4) Dekker.
Quasha, George. Giving the Lily Back Her Hands. LC 79-64920. 64p. (Orig.). 1980. pap. 4.45 (0-930794-10-9) Station Hill Pr.
— In No Time. (Illus.). 144p. (Orig.). 1988. pap. 7.95 (0-88268-033-1) Station Hill Pr.
— Monarch Notes on Beowulf. (Orig.). (C). pap. 3.95 (0-671-00550-2, Arco Test) P-H Gen Ref & Trav.
— Monarch Notes on Joyce's Portrait of the Artist As a Young Man & Dubliners. (Orig.). (C). pap. 3.95 (0-671-00563-4, Arco Test) P-H Gen Ref & Trav.
Quasha, George, ed. see Beaulieu, John.
Quasha, George, ed. see Blanchot, Maurice.
Quasha, George, ed. see Byrd, Don.
Quasha, George, ed. see Chester, Laura.
Quasha, George, ed. see Henderson, Julie.
Quasha, George, ed. see Jahan, Dean.
Quasha, George, ed. see Kelly, Robert.
Quasha, George, ed. see Padmasambhava.
Quasha, George, ed. see Phipps, Frances.
Quasha, George, ed. see Sondheim, Alan.
Quasha, George, ed. see Trager, Milton & Guadagno, Cathy.
Quasha, Jill. Marjorie Content. (Illus.). 128p. 1995. 29.95 (0-393-03682-0) Norton.
Quasha, Jill, intro. The Quillan Collection of Nineteenth & Twentieth Century Photographs. LC 91-60309. (Illus.). 148p. 1991. boxed 100.00 (0-933920-39-3) Hudson Hills.
Quasney. Learning to Use Lotus 1-2-3 Release 2.3. (Shelly Cashman Ser.). (Illus.). 330p. (C). 1992. teacher ed, per. 19.00 (0-87835-860-9) Boyd & Fraser.
— Programming in Microsoft BASIC. (Shelly Cashman Ser.). 1992. teacher ed, per. 7.00 (0-87835-931-1) Boyd & Fraser.
— Programming in QuickBASIC. (Shelly Cashman Ser.). 1992. teacher ed 7.00 (0-87835-777-7) Boyd & Fraser.
Quasney & Maniotes. QuickBASIC Fundamentals & Style. 576p. 1991. 30.00 (0-87835-519-7) Boyd & Fraser.
— Structured Microsoft BASIC: Essentials for Business. 304p. 1990. 20.50 (0-87835-452-2) Boyd & Fraser.
Quasney & Vermaat. Learning to Use Lotus 1-2-3 Release 2.2. (Shelly Cashman Ser.). (Illus.). 330p. (C). 1992. teacher ed, per. 19.00 (0-87835-738-6) Boyd & Fraser.
Quasney, jt. auth. see Waggoner.
Quasney, James S. Essential Computer Concepts with Microcomputer Applications: WordPerfect 5.0 - 5.1, Lotus 1-2-3 Release 2.2, dBASE III PLUS. (Shelly Cashman Ser.). 928p. 1991. pap. 32.00 (0-87835-740-8, BF7408) Boyd & Fraser.
Quasney, James S. & Maniotes, John. Applesoft Basic Fundamentals & Style. (Orig.). (C). 1986. teacher ed write for info. (0-87835-171-X); pap. text ed. 28.00 (0-87835-170-1) Boyd & Fraser.
— Complete BASIC: For the Short Course. (Illus.). 196p. 1985. write for info. (0-87835-158-2); pap. text ed. 19.50 (0-87835-151-5) Boyd & Fraser.
— QBASIC: Fundamentals & Style. LC 94-25925. 1994. write for info. (0-87709-459-4) Boyd & Fraser.
— QuickBASIC Fundamentals & Style. (C). 1991. pap. 51.95 (0-87835-517-0, BF5170) S-W Pub.
Quasney, James S., et al. QuickBASIC Using Subprograms. LC 92-30589. 592p. 1993. write for info. (0-87709-010-6) Boyd & Fraser.
Quast, Kevin. Reading the Corinthian Correspondence: An Introduction. LC 94-15074. 288p. 1994. pap. 14.95 (0-8091-3481-0) Paulist Pr.
— Reading the Gospel of John: An Introduction. LC 91-32111. 176p. 1992. pap. 8.95 (0-8091-3297-4) Paulist Pr.
Quasten. Music & Worship in Pagan & Christian Antiquity. 1983. 11.95 (0-9602378-7-9) Pastoral Pr.
Quasten & Plumpe, eds. Epistles of St. Clement of Rome & St. Ignatius of Antioch. Kleist, James A., tr. (Ancient Christian Writers Ser.: No. 1). 1946. 14.95 (0-8091-0038-X) Paulist Pr.
Quasten, ed. see Jerome.
Quasten, ed. see Paulinus of Nola.
Quasten, J., et al, eds. Poems of St. Paulinus of Nola. Walsh, P. G., tr. (Ancient Christian Writers Ser.: No. 40). 1975. 29.95 (0-8091-0179-3) Paulist Pr.
Quasten, J., ed. see Augustine.
Quasten, J., ed. see St. Augustine.
Quasten, Johannes. Patrology, 4 vols., 1. LC 83-72018. 1514p. 1983. pap. 15.00 (0-87061-084-8) Chr Classics.
— Patrology, 4 vols., 3. LC 83-72018. 1514p. 1983. pap. 21.00 (0-87061-086-4) Chr Classics.
— Patrology, 4 vols., 4. LC 83-72018. 1514p. 1983. pap. 39.95 (0-87061-127-5) Chr Classics.
— Patrology, 4 vols., Set. LC 83-72018. 1514p. 1983. pap. 85.00 (0-87061-141-0) Chr Classics.
Quasten, Johannes, ed. Patrology, 4 vols., Set. LC 83-72018. 1514p. 1983. Vol. 2. pap. 85.00 (0-87061-085-6, 6912) Chr Classics.
***Quasthoff, Uta M., ed.** Aspects of Oral Communication. LC 94-45206. (Research in Text Theory Ser.: No. 21). vi, 493p. (C). 1995. lib. bdg. 192.35 (3-11-014465-4) De Gruyter.
***Quastler, I. E.** Missouri Pacific Northwest: A History of the Kansas City Northwestern Railroad. (Illus.). 136p. 1994. pap. 31.95 (0-942035-30-5) South Platte.
— The Railroads of Lawrence, Kansas: 1854-1900. (Illus.). pap. 10.00 (0-87291-094-6) Coronado Pr.
Quastler, I. E., jt. auth. see Davies, R. E.
Quataert, Donald. Home, Workshop & Factory in the Ottoman Middle East, 1800-1914. (Middle East Library). (Illus.). 224p. (C). 1993. 59.95 (0-521-42017-2) Cambridge U Pr.
Quataert, Donald, ed. Manufacturing in the Ottoman Empire & Turkey, 1500-1950. LC 93-36571. (SUNY Series in the Social & Economic History of the Middle East). 175p. 1994. 59.50x (0-7914-2015-9); pap. 19.95x (0-7914-2016-7) State U NY Pr.
***Quataert, Donald & Zurcher, Erik J., eds.** Workers & Working Class in the Ottoman Empire & the Turkish Republic, 1839-1950. 224p. 1995. text ed. 59.50 (1-85043-875-7) St Martin.
Quataert, Donald, jt. ed. see Antoun, Richard T.
Quataert, Jean H. Reluctant Feminists in German Social Democracy, 1885-1917. LC 79-84011. 327p. reprint ed. pap. 93.20 (0-8357-3850-7, 2036583) Bks Demand.
Quataert, Jean H., jt. ed. see Boxer, Marilyn J.
Quate, Calvin F., jt. ed. see Khuri-Yakub, Butrus T.
Quaterman, John S., et al. The Design & Implementation of the 43BSD UNIX Operating System. (Illus.). 448p. (C). 1989. text ed. 48.50 (0-201-06196-1) Addison-Wesley.
Quatmann, Gail R. & Ewen, Patricia B. Building Blocks: An Infant-Toddler Handbook. rev. ed. LC 92-93262. (Illus.). 85p. (C). 1992. pap. text ed. write for info. (0-9631122-8-7) G R Quatmann.
— Building Blocks: An Infant Toddler Handbook. rev. ed. LC 92-93262. (Illus.). 85p. 1993. pap. write for info. (0-9631122-9-5) G R Quatmann.
Quatremere, M. Prolegomenes D'ebn-Khaldoun, 3 vols., Set. (ARA.). 105.00 (0-86685-165-8) Intl Bk Ctr.
Quatrine, Dennis. Digital Electronics Laboratory Manual. 116p. (C). 1994. pap. text ed., spiral bd. 14.95 (0-8403-9221-4) Kendall-Hunt.
***Quattlebaum, Bryan.** Managed Care in Dentistry. LC 94-23729. 1994. write for info. (0-87814-433-1) PennWell Bks.
Quattlebaum, M. M. Quattlebaum Family History. 280p. 1994. reprint ed. lib. bdg. 58.50 (0-8328-4078-5); reprint ed. pap. 48.50 (0-8328-4079-3) Higginson Bk Co.
Quattlebaum, Mary. Jackson Jones & the Puddle of Thorns. LC 93-11433. (Illus.). (J). (gr. 4-7). 1994. 13.95 (0-385-31165-6) Delacorte.
— Jackson Jones & the Puddle of Thorns. (Illus.). (J). (gr. 1-5). 1995. mass mkt. 3.50 (0-440-41066-5) Dell.
Quattrin, Kevin. Living in a Psychic's World: A True-Life Experience. 224p. (Orig.). 1994. pap. 9.95 (1-878901-94-X) Hampton Roads Pub Co.
Quattrini, Joseph A. Successful Business Presentations. (Illus.). 264p. 1989. 19.95 (0-8306-0335-2, Liberty Hse) TAB Bks.
— Successful Business Presentations. 1990. pap. 15.95 (0-8306-3055-4) TAB Bks.
Quattrocchi, Paul B. A Life for Unity: Sister Maria Gabriella. Jeremiah, Mary, tr. 184p. 1990. pap. 9.95 (0-911782-77-X) New City.
Quattrochi, Joseph. Federal Tax Research. 208p. (C). 1982. pap. text ed. 29.00 (0-15-527108-3) Dryden Pr.
Quattrocki, Carolyn. Frosty's Snowy Day. (Favorite Christmas Tales Ser.). (Illus.). 24p. (J). (ps-4). 1992. lib. bdg. 10.95 (1-56674-022-3, HTS Bks) Forest Hse.
— The Little Drummer Boy. (Favorite Christmas Tales Ser.). (Illus.). 24p. (J). (ps-4). 1992. lib. bdg. 10.95 (1-56674-023-1, HTS Bks) Forest Hse.
— The Nutcracker. (Favorite Christmas Tales Ser.). (Illus.). 24p. (J). (ps-4). 1992. lib. bdg. 10.95 (1-56674-024-X, HTS Bks) Forest Hse.
— Rudolph's Adventure. (Favorite Christmas Tales Ser.). (Illus.). 24p. (J). (ps-4). 1992. lib. bdg. 10.95 (1-56674-025-8, HTS Bks) Forest Hse.
— Santa Claus Is Coming to Town. (Favorite Christmas Tales Ser.). (Illus.). 24p. (J). (ps-4). 1992. lib. bdg. 10.95 (1-56674-026-6, HTS Bks) Forest Hse.
— Twas the Night Before Christmas. (Favorite Christmas Tales Ser.). (Illus.). 24p. (J). (ps-4). 1992. lib. bdg. 10.95 (1-56674-027-4, HTS Bks) Forest Hse.
Quay, Ann, pseud. Lend Me Your Eyes. 223p. 1991. pap. 12.95 (0-9629229-1-9) A L Quay.
Quay, Anna L., see Ann Quay, pseud..
Quay, Effie A. And Now Infanticide. 2nd ed. 64p. 1980. pap. 1.25 (0-937930-01-6) Sun Life.
Quay, Herbert C. Managing Adult Inmates: Classification for Housing & Program Assignments. (Illus.). 79p. (Orig.). 1984. pap. 15.25 (0-942974-64-6, 103) Am Correctional.
Quay, Herbert C., ed. Handbook of Juvenile Delinquency. LC 86-34008. (Personality Processes Ser.). 480p. 1987. text ed. 69.95 (0-471-81707-4) Wiley.
Quay, Herbert C. & Werry, John S., eds. Psychopathological Disorders of Childhood. 3rd ed. LC 86-11105. 690p. 1986. Net. text ed. write for info. (0-471-88974-1) Wiley.
Quay, John G. Diagnostic Interviewing for Consultants & Auditors. 104p. (Orig.). 1986. pap. 18.75 (0-9616062-0-7) Quay Assocs.
***Quay, Joyce C.** Early Promise, Late Reward: A Biography of Helen Hoover Santmyer. (Illus.). 135p. (Orig.). 1995. pap. write for info. (1-879198-15-0) Knwldg Ideas & Trnds.
Quay, Paul M. The Christian Meaning of Human Sexuality. LC 88-81092. 121p. 1988. reprint ed. pap. 9.95 (0-89870-212-7) Ignatius Pr.
— The Mystery Hidden for Ages in God. LC 93-17286. (American University Studies: Vol. 161). 456p. (C). 1995. text ed. 63.95 (0-8204-2221-5) P Lang Pubs.
Quay, Ray, jt. auth. see McClendon, Bruce W.
Quay, Richard H., comp. Index to Anthologies on Postsecondary Education, 1960-1978. LC 79-8286. 342p. 1980. text ed. 49.95 (0-313-21272-4, QPE/, Greenwood Pr) Greenwood.
Quay, Sunny, ed. see Ryan, Christopher.
Quay, Thomas L., et al, eds. The Seaside Sparrow, Its Biology & Management. (Occasional Papers of the North Carolina Biological Survey). (Illus.). 174p. 1983. pap. 15.00 (0-917134-05-2) NC Natl Sci.
Quaye, Christopher O. Liberation Struggles in International Law. 358p. 1991. 59.95 (0-87722-712-8) Temple U Pr.
Quayle, A., ed. Advances in Mass Spectrometry: Proceedings of a Conference Held in Brussels, September, 1970, Vol. 5. 798p. reprint ed. pap. 180.00 (0-8357-5173-2, 2023995) Bks Demand.
Quayle, A., ed. see Institute of Petroleum Staff.
Quayle, A., jt. ed. see Institute of Petroleum Staff.
Quayle, Amil. Pebble Creek. 80p. 1993. pap. 12.00 (0-9635559-0-1) Slow Tempo.
Quayle, Anthony. A Time to Speak. large type ed. (Non-Fiction Ser.). 624p. 1992. 23.95 (0-7089-8652-8) Ulverscroft.
Quayle, D. B. & Newkirk, G. F. Farming Bivalve Molluscs: Methods for Study & Development. Sandifer, P. A., ed. (Advances in World Aquaculture Ser.). (Illus.). 290p. (C). 1989. text ed. 50.00 (0-685-29351-3) World Aquaculture.
***Quayle, Dan.** Standing Firm: A Vice Presidential Memoir. 480p. 1995. mass mkt. 6.99 (0-06-109390-4) Zondervan.
Quayle, Louise. Citizenship Made Simple. 1991. 12.00 (0-385-26586-7) Doubleday.
— Martin Luther King, Jr. Dreams for a Nation. (Illus.). 128p. 1989. pap. 3.95 (0-449-90377-X, Columbine) Fawcett.
— Weather: Understanding the Forces of Nature. (Illus.). 128p. 1990. 14.99 (0-517-67663-X) Random Hse Value.
Quayle, Margaret S. A Study of Some Aspects of Satisfaction in the Vocation of Stenography. LC 76-177174. (Columbia University. Teachers College. Contributions to Education Ser.: No. 659). reprint ed. 37.50 (0-404-55659-0) AMS Pr.
Quayle, Marilyn T. & Northcott, Nancy T. Embrace the Serpent. 1992. 20.00 (0-517-58822-6, Crown) Crown Pub Group.
Quayle, Thomas. Poetic Diction: A Study of Eighteenth Century Verse. (BCL1-PR English Literature Ser.). 212p. 1992. reprint ed. lib. bdg. 79.00 (0-685-54571-7) Rprt Serv.
Quayle, Thomas E., ed. Jose' el Diablo: The World's Most Traveled Dog. (Illus.). 95p. (Orig.). (YA). 1985. pap. 3.00 (0-9623144-0-4) Vilate Pub.
Quayle, Thomas E., jt. auth. see Baker, Beatrice V.
Quayle, William A. Recovered Yesterdays in Literature. LC 74-117829. (Essay Index Reprint Ser.). 1977. 21.95 (0-8369-1678-6) Ayer.
Quban, Fahim I. Education & Science in the Arab World. 1979. 36.95 (0-405-10622-X) Ayer.
***Qubayya, Mohammed.** Dictionary Grammatical Analysis Holy Qur'an. 830p. (ARA.). 1995. 65.00 (0-86685-645-5) Intl Bk Ctr.
Qubein, Nido. Get the Best from Yourself. 100p. 1986. mass mkt. 4.99 (0-425-08537-6) Berkley Pub.
— What Works & What Doesn't in Youth Ministry. Zapel, Arthur L. & Pijanowski, Kathy, eds. LC 86-62111. (Illus.). 208p. 1986. pap. 7.95 (0-916260-40-2, B-103) Meriwether Pub.
Qudamas, Ibn. Censure of Speculative Theology: An Edition & Translation of Ibn Qudamas Tahrim An-Nazar Fi Kutub Ahl Al-Kalam. Makdisi, ed. (Gibb Memorial New Ser.: Vol. 23 Introduction & Notes). 1992. 45.00 (0-906094-16-X, Pub. by Aris & Phillips UK) David Brown.
Que Corporation Staff. WordPerfect Quick Reference. 160p. 1988. pap. 9.95 (0-88022-370-7) Que.
Que Development Group Staff. Access for Windows SureSteps. (Illus.). 350p. (Orig.). 1993. pap. 24.95 (1-56529-534-X) Que.
— Access 2.0 VisiRef. 1994. pap. 12.99 (1-56529-863-2) Que.
— Ami Pro 3.0 Quickstart. 1994. pap. 21.95 (1-56529-683-4) Que.
— AutoCAD Release 12 Quick Reference. (Quick Reference Ser.). (Illus.). (Orig.). 1992. pap. 9.95 (1-56529-024-0) Que.
— Batch File & Macros Quick Reference. 160p. 1991. pap. 9.95 (0-88022-699-4) Que.
— Building Windows 95 Applications with Visual Basic. (Illus.). 448p. (Orig.). 1995. pap. 39.99 (0-7897-0209-6) Que.
— CorelDRAW! VisiRef. (Illus.). 168p. (Orig.). 1994. pap. 12.99 (1-56529-861-6) Que.
— Crash Course in CC: Mail for DOS. (Illus.). 288p. (Orig.). 1993. pap. 12.95 (1-56529-527-7) Que.
— Crash Course in CC: Mail for Windows. (Illus.). 288p. (Orig.). 1993. pap. 12.95 (1-56529-528-5) Que.
— Crash Course in DOS. (Illus.). 256p. (Orig.). 1993. pap. 12.95 (1-56529-529-3) Que.
— Crash Course in Microsoft Mail for Windows. (Illus.). 288p. (Orig.). 1993. pap. 12.95 (1-56529-526-9) Que.
— Crash Course in Turbo C Plus Plus. (Illus.). 250p. (Orig.). 1993. pap. 16.95 (1-56529-168-9) Que.
— Crystal Clear Access for Windows. (Illus.). 352p. (Orig.). 1993. pap. 24.95 (1-56529-509-9) Que.
— Crystal Clear DOS. (Illus.). 352p. (Orig.). 1993. pap. 24.95 (1-56529-358-4) Que.
— Crystal Clear Excel. (Illus.). 352p. (Orig.). 1993. pap. 24.95 (1-56529-536-6) Que.
— Crystal Clear Windows. (Illus.). 352p. (Orig.). 1993. pap. 24.95 (1-56529-357-6) Que.
— Crystal Clear WordPerfect. (Illus.). 352p. (Orig.). 1993. pap. 24.95 (1-56529-359-2) Que.
— Crystal Clear Wordperfect 6 for Windows. (Illus.). 352p. (Orig.). 1993. pap. 24.95 (1-56529-508-0) Que.
— DR DOS 6 Quick Reference. (Quick Reference Ser.). (Illus.). 160p. (Orig.). 1992. pap. 9.95 (0-88022-827-X) Que.
— Easy Ami Pro. 2nd ed. 1994. pap. 19.95 (1-56529-624-9) Que.
— Easy Macintosh. (Easy Ser.). (Illus.). 200p. (Orig.). 1992. pap. 19.95 (0-88022-819-9) Que.
— Easy Paradox for Windows. 1993. pap. 19.95 (1-56529-076-3) Que.
— Easy PCs. 2nd ed. (Illus.). 256p. (Orig.). 1993. pap. 16.95 (1-56529-276-6) Que.
— Easy World Wide Web with Netscape. (Illus.). 208p. (Orig.). 1995. pap. 19.99 (0-7897-0279-7) Que.
— Easy 1-2-3. 3rd ed. 1994. pap. 19.95 (1-56529-637-0) Que.
— Excel Version 5.0 for Windows Quick Reference. 2nd ed. (Illus.). 224p. 1993. pap. 9.99 (1-56529-458-0) Que.
— Excel 4.0 for Windows Sure Steps. (Sure Steps Ser.). (Illus.). 300p. (Orig.). 1993. disk 24.95 (1-56529-241-3) Que.
— FoxPro for Windows Programming by Example. 1994. pap. 27.95 (1-56529-644-3) Que.
— Fun Programming with Visual Basic. 1992. pap. 24.95 (1-56529-106-9) Que.
— Graphics on the Net. (Illus.). 600p. (Orig.). 1995. pap. text ed. 29.99 (0-7897-0137-5) Que.
— Hands on MS-DOS 5: Learn by Doing. (Illus.). 400p. (Orig.). 1992. pap. 29.95 (0-88022-683-8) Que.
— The HitchHiker's Guide to Internet. (Illus.). 512p. (Orig.). pap. 24.95 (1-56529-353-3) Que.
— I Hate Access. (Illus.). 352p. (Orig.). 1993. pap. 16.95 (1-56529-535-8) Que.
— I Hate PCs: A Friendly Guide for the Frustrated User. (I Hate! Ser.). (Illus.). 300p. (Orig.). 1993. pap. 16.95 (1-56529-254-5) Que.
— I Hate Windows: A Friendly Guide for Windows. 1993. pap. 16.95 (1-56529-214-6) Que.
— Information Superhighway: Beyond the Internet. 1994. pap. 19.99 (1-56529-825-X) Que.
— Information Superhighway Illustrated. (Illus.). 1994. pap. 24.99 (1-56529-892-6) Que.
— Insider's Guide to the IBM PowerPC. 1994. pap. 24.95 (1-56529-625-7) Que.
— The Internet CD Tutor. (Illus.). 400p. (Orig.). 1995. pap. 39.99 (0-7897-0285-1) Que.
— Killer Borland C Plus Plus. (Illus.). 1024p. (Orig.). 1994. pap. 49.99 (1-56529-685-0) Que.
— Killer Chicago Utilities. 1994. cd-rom, pap. 39.99 (0-7897-0001-8) Que.
— Killer Excel Utilities. (Illus.). 1000p. (Orig.). 1993. pap. 39.95 (1-56529-325-8) Que.
— Killer Paradox for Windows. 1994. Incl. diskette. disk 49.99 (1-56529-886-1) Que.
— Killer WordPerfect 6 Utilities. (Illus.). 1000p. (Orig.). 1993. pap. 39.95 (1-56529-362-2) Que.
— Lotus 1-2-3 Release 4.X for Windows Quick Reference. 1994. pap. 9.99 (1-56529-889-6) Que.
— Lotus 1-2-3 Sure Steps. (Sure Steps Ser.). (Illus.). 300p. (Orig.). 1993. pap. 24.95 (1-56529-260-X) Que.
— Macintosh VisiRef. (Illus.). (Orig.). 1994. pap. 12.99 (1-56529-831-4) Que.
— Movies, Music & Entertainment on the Net. (Illus.). 480p. (Orig.). 1995. pap. text ed. 24.99 (0-7897-0122-7) Que.
— Networking Illustrated. (Illus.). 1994. pap. 24.99 (1-56529-893-4) Que.
— Norton Utilities Six Quick Reference. (Quick Reference Ser.). (Illus.). 160p. (Orig.). 1992. pap. 9.95 (0-88022-858-X) Que.
— Now You See It: Making Random Dot Stereograms. (Illus.). (Orig.). 1994. pap. 24.99 (1-56529-994-9) Que.
— 1-2-3 for Windows Professional Techniques. (Illus.). (Orig.). 1994. pap. 39.99 (1-56529-990-6) Que.
— One-Two-Three Power Macros. (Illus.). (Orig.). 1992. pap. 39.95 (0-88022-804-0) Que.
— Oops! for WordPerfect: What To Do When Things Go Wrong. (Illus.). 300p. (Orig.). 1993. pap. 16.95 (1-56529-196-4) Que.
— Optimizing Visual Basic Applications. (Illus.). 448p. (Orig.). 1995. pap. 39.99 (0-7897-0206-1) Que.
— PageMaker 5.0 for Windows VisiRef. 1994. pap. 12.99 (1-56529-890-X) Que.
— Paradox for Windows Power Programming. 2nd ed. (Illus.). 550p. 1994. pap. 29.99 (0-614-06068-0) Que.
— Paradox Four Quick Reference. 2nd ed. (Quick Reference Ser.). (Illus.). 160p. 1992. pap. 9.95 (0-88022-891-1) Que.
— Programming with Remote Procedure Calls. (Illus.). 800p. (Orig.). 1995. pap. text ed. 49.99 (0-7897-0182-0) Que.

P Q

— Q & A 4 Quick Reference. (Quick Reference Ser.). (Illus.). 160p. (Orig.). 1992. pap. 9.95 (*0-88022-828-8*) Que.
— Q & A 4 QuickStart. 400p. 1991. pap. 19.95 (*0-88022-653-6*) Que.
— QBASIC for Rookies. (Illus.). 256p. (Orig.). 1993. pap. 16.95 (*1-56529-235-9*) Que.
— QuarkXpress 3.1 Quick Reference. (Quick Reference Ser.). 160p. (Orig.). 1991. pap. 9.95 (*0-88022-769-9*) Que.
— Que's CD-ROM Buyer's Guide, 1995. 1994. pap. 19.99 (*1-56529-883-7*) Que.
— Que's Computer Buyer's Guide, 1993. (Illus.). 450p. (Orig.). 1992. pap. 16.95 (*1-56529-021-6*) Que.
— Que's Computer Software Buyer's Guide, 1994. (Illus.). 400p. (Orig.). 1993. pap. 16.95 (*1-56529-282-0*) Que.
— Que's First Look at Chicago. 1994. pap. 14.99 (*0-7897-0074-3*) Que.
— Que's MS-DOS 5 User's Guide, Special Edition. 1000p. 1991. pap. 29.95 (*0-88022-671-4*) Que.
— Quick & Dirty Word for Windows. (Quick & Dirty Ser.). (Illus.). 416p. (Orig.). 1993. pap. 24.95 (*1-56529-300-2*) Que.
— Religion on the Net. (Illus.). 400p. (Orig.). 1995. pap. 24.99 (*0-7897-0282-7*) Que.
— Running a Perfect Internet Site. (Illus.). 900p. (Orig.). 1995. pap. 49.99 (*0-7897-0255-X*) Que.
— Running a Perfect Web Site. (Illus.). 480p. (Orig.). 1995. pap. text ed. 29.99 (*0-7897-0210-X*) Que.
— Special Edition Using CompuServe. (Illus.). 1000p. (Orig.). 1995. pap. 39.99 (*0-614-07263-8*) Que.
— Special Edition Using CorelDRAW! 2nd ed. (Illus.). 1200p. (Orig.). 1995. pap. 39.99 (*0-7897-0295-9*) Que.
— Special Edition Using dBase 5.X for Windows. (Illus.). 800p. (Orig.). 1995. pap. 34.99 (*0-7897-0345-9*) Que.
— Special Edition Using Sybase. (Illus.). 832p. (Orig.). 1995. pap. 49.99 (*0-7897-0087-5*) Que.
— Special Edition Using the Internet. 2nd ed. (Illus.). 1216p. 1995. pap. 39.99 (*0-7897-0077-8*) Que.
— Special Edition Using the Internet with Your Mac. (Illus.). 1100p. (Orig.). 1995. pap. text ed. 39.99 (*0-7897-0212-6*) Que.
— Turbo C Plus Plus for Rookies. (Illus.). 256p. (Orig.). 1993. pap. 16.95 (*1-56529-473-4*) Que.
— Turbo C Plus Plus Games & More! (Illus.). 480p. (Orig.). 1993. pap. 29.95 (*1-56529-472-6*) Que.
— UNIX Shell Commands Quick Reference. 1990. pap. 8.95 (*0-88022-572-6*) Que.
— Upgrading to Windows 3.1. 1992. pap. 14.95 (*0-88022-965-9*) Que.
— Using Act! (Illus.). 320p. (Orig.). 1995. pap. 19.99 (*0-7897-0254-1*) Que.
— Using Alpha Four. 2nd ed. (Using Ser.). (Illus.). 500p. (Orig.). 1992. pap. 29.99 (*1-56529-557-9*) Que.
— Using AmiPro 3, Special Edition. (Illus.). (Orig.). 1992. pap. 27.95 (*1-56529-067-4*) Que.
— Using AutoCAD for Windows. 1994. pap. 39.99 (*1-56529-887-X*) Que.
— Using AutoCAD, Release 12. (Using Ser.). (Illus.). (Orig.). 1992. pap. 34.95 (*0-88022-941-1*) Que.
— Using CA-Simply Money. 1993. pap. 19.95 (*1-56529-643-5*) Que.
— Using Cello. (Illus.). 300p. (Orig.). 1995. pap. 19.99 (*0-7897-0252-5*) Que.
— Using Chicago Multimedia Special Edition. 1994. cd-rom, pap. 39.99 (*0-7897-0058-1*) Que.
— Using Chicago Special Edition. 1994. pap. 29.99 (*1-56529-921-3*) Que.
— Using ClarisWorks. (Illus.). (Orig.). 1992. pap. 24.95 (*1-56529-003-8*) Que.
— Using ClarisWorks 2.1 for Macintosh. (Illus.). 500p. (Orig.). pap. 24.95 (*1-56529-550-1*) Que.
— Using Filemaker Pro 2.0 for Windows. (Illus.). (Orig.). 1992. pap. 27.95 (*1-56529-066-6*) Que.
— Using Internet Works. (Illus.). 416p. (Orig.). 1995. pap. 19.99 (*0-7897-0283-5*) Que.
— Using Microsoft Works 3 for DOS. 550p. (Orig.). 1993. pap. 24.95 (*1-56529-098-4*) Que.
— Using MS-DOS 6: Platinum Edition. 1993. pap. 29.95 (*1-56529-020-8*) Que.
— Using MS-DOS 6: Special Edition. 1993. pap. 29.95 (*1-56539-020-2*) Color Cnty.
— Using Netscape. (Illus.). 350p. (Orig.). 1995. pap. text ed. 19.99 (*0-7897-0211-8*) Que.
— Using Norton Desktop for DOS. (Illus.). (Orig.). 1992. pap. 24.95 (*0-88022-970-5*) Que.
— Using One Two Three Release 2.4. (Using Ser.). (Illus.). (Orig.). 1992. pap. 29.95 (*0-88022-988-8*) Que.
— Using One-Two-Three Release 4 for Windows. 1993. pap. 29.95 (*1-56529-005-4*) Que.
— Using Paradox for DOS, Special Edition. (Illus.). (Orig.). Date not set. pap. 29.99 (*1-56529-867-5*) Que.
— Using Paradox 4.5 for DOS, Special Edition. 2nd ed. 1024p. 1993. pap. 29.95 (*1-56529-554-4*) Que.
— Using Powerpoint for Windows. 2nd ed. 1994. pap. 29.95 (*1-56529-651-6*) Que.
— Using Soundblaster Special Edition. 1994. cd-rom, pap. 39.99 (*0-7897-0057-3*) Que.
— Using the Macintosh. (Illus.). 120p. (Orig.). 1994. pap. 34.99 (*1-56529-826-8*) Que.
— Using Turbo C Plus Plus. (Illus.). 800p. (Orig.). 1993. pap. 29.95 (*1-56529-471-8*) Que.
— Using UNIX. (Illus.). 384p. (Orig.). 1995. pap. 19.99 (*0-7897-0290-8*) Que.
— Using USENET NewsGroups. (Illus.). 350p. (Orig.). 1995. pap. text ed. 19.99 (*0-7897-0134-0*) Que.
— Using Visual BASIC for Applications. 1994. pap. 29.99 (*1-56529-725-3*) Que.
— Using Windows Sound System. 1994. pap. 24.99 (*1-56529-812-8*) Que.
— Using Winfax Pro 3.0. 1994. pap. 24.95 (*1-56529-617-6*) Que.
— Using Word for Macintosh. 1994. pap. 29.99 (*1-56529-647-8*) Que.
— Using Word, Version 6.0 for Windows. 1994. pap. 29.99 (*1-56529-834-9*) Que.
— Using WordPerfect DOS. (Illus.). 400p. (Orig.). 1995. pap. 19.99 (*0-7897-0327-0*) Que.
— Using WordPerfect Presentations 2.0 for Windows. 1994. pap. 27.95 (*1-56529-652-4*) Que.
— Using WordPerfect 5.1, Special Edition. 900p. 1991. 27.95 (*0-88022-554-8*) Que.
— Using WordPerfect 5.2 for Windows, Special Edition. (Illus.). 1280p. (Orig.). 1992. pap. 29.95 (*1-56529-166-2*) Que.
— Using WordPerfect 6 for Windows, Special Edition. (Using Ser.). (Illus.). 1200p. (Orig.). 1993. pap. 29.95 (*1-56529-138-7*) Que.
— Using Your Mac. (Illus.). 450p. (Orig.). 1995. pap. text ed. 19.99 (*0-7897-0094-8*) Que.
— Using 1-2-3 Release X for DOS, Special Edition. 1994. pap. 29.95 (*1-56529-629-X*) Que.
— Using 1-2-3 Release 3.4: Special Edition. 1100p. (Orig.). 1993. pap. 29.95 (*1-56529-004-6*) Que.
— Visual Basic by Example, New Edition. (Illus.). (Orig.). 1995. pap. 29.99 (*0-7897-0000-X*) Que.
— Visual BASIC Expert Solutions. 1994. cd-rom, pap. 49.99 (*0-7897-0073-5*) Que.
— Visual Basic Windows API Programming. (Illus.). 1120p. (Orig.). 1995. pap. text ed. 49.99 (*0-7897-0177-4*) Que.
— Windows after Hours. (Illus.). 160p. (Orig.). 1992. pap. 19.95 (*1-56529-112-3*) Que.
— Windows Hot Tips. (Hot Tips Ser.). (Illus.). 256p. (Orig.). 1993. pap. 12.99 (*1-56529-179-4*) Que.
— Windows 3.1: Undocumented Secrets. 1994. pap. 24.95 (*1-56529-657-5*) Que.
— Windows 3.1 Quick Reference. (Quick Reference Ser.). (Illus.). 160p. (Orig.). 1992. pap. 9.95 (*0-88022-740-0*) Que.
— Windows 3.11 QuickStart. (Illus.). 246p. (Orig.). 1994. pap. 19.99 (*0-614-06067-2*) Que.
— Windows 95 Preview User's Guide. (Illus.). 448p. (Orig.). 1995. pap. text ed. 24.99 (*0-7897-0191-X*) Que.
— Word for the Mac Hot Tips. (Hot Tips Ser.). (Illus.). 1224p. (Orig.). 1993. pap. 12.99 (*1-56529-161-1*) Que.
— Word for Windows 2.0 SureSteps. (Sure Steps Ser.). (Illus.). 300p. (Orig.). 1993. pap. 24.95 (*1-56529-239-1*) Que.
— WordPerfect for Windows Hot Tips. (Hot Tips Ser.). (Illus.). 224p. (Orig.). 1993. pap. 12.99 (*1-56529-175-1*) Que.
— WordPerfect 5.1 Quick Reference. 1990. pap. 9.95 (*0-88022-576-9*) Que.
— WordPerfect 5.1 QuickStart. 500p. 1990. 21.95 (*0-88022-558-0*) Que.
— WordPerfect 6 for Windows Quickstart. (Illus.). 608p. (Orig.). 1993. pap. 21.95 (*1-56529-463-7*) Que.
— WordPerfect 6 Quick Start. 2nd ed. 600p. (Orig.). 1993. pap. 21.95 (*1-56529-085-2*) Que.
***Que Development Group Staff & Drips, Mike.** Insider's Guide to Windows 95 Programming. (Illus.). 608p. (Orig.). 1995. pap. text ed. 34.99 (*1-56529-679-6*) Que.
***Que Development Group Staff & Flanders, Linda.** Using Quicken for Windows, New Edition. (Illus.). (Orig.). 1994. pap. 19.99 (*1-56529-933-7*) Que.
Que Development Group Staff & Grace, Rich. Word for Windows Quick Reference. 2nd ed. 192p. 1993. pap. 9.99 (*1-56529-468-8*) Que.
Que Development Group Staff & Johnson, Yvonne. DOS 6.0 Sure Steps. (Sure Steps Ser.). (Illus.). 300p. (Orig.). 1993. Incl. disk. disk 24.95 (*1-56529-262-6*) Que.
***Que Development Group Staff & Kenney, Cathy.** Using Lotus Organizer for Windows. (Illus.). (Orig.). 1995. pap. 24.99 (*1-56529-891-8*) Que.
Que Development Group Staff & Perry, Paul. Using Visual C Plus Plus, Special Edition. (Illus.). 1024p. (Orig.). 1994. Incl. diskette. pap. 44.99 (*1-56529-810-1*) Que.
***Que Development Group Staff & Shafran.** Using Lotus SmartSuite, Special Edition. (Illus.). (Orig.). 1994. pap. 29.99 (*1-56529-747-4*) Que.
***Que Development Group Staff & Thompson.** Upgrading Your PC to Multimedia. (Illus.). (Orig.). 1994. pap. 24.99 (*1-56529-937-X*) Que.
***Que Development Group Staff & Toupin, Ed.** Crash Course in C. 2nd ed. (Illus.). 1994. pap. 19.99 (*1-56529-940-X*) Que.
— Crash Course in Q Basic. 2nd ed. (Illus.). 1994. pap. 19.99 (*1-56529-939-6*) Que.
Que Development Group Staff, jt. auth. see Stover, Susan.
Que Development Group Staff, et al. Que's Computer Programmer's Dictionary. 400p. (Orig.). 1992. pap. 19.95 (*1-56529-125-5*) Que.
— The Ultimate QuarkXPress Book for Version 3.2 for the Mac. (Illus.). 900p. (Orig.). 1993. pap. 39.95 (*1-56529-195-6*) Que.
— Using Windows NT: Special Edition. (Illus.). 1000p. 1993. pap. 29.95 (*1-56529-101-8*) Que.
Que Development Staff. Access Power Programming. 2nd ed. 1994. Incl. diskette. pap. 49.90 (*1-56529-763-6*) Que.
— Crash Course in Borland C Plus Plus 4.0. 1994. pap. 19.99 (*1-56529-773-3*) Que.
— Crash Course in Visual BASIC. 1994. pap. 19.99 (*1-56529-765-2*) Que.
— Easy Freelance Graphics 2.0 for Windows. 1994. pap. 19.99 (*1-56529-768-7*) Que.
— Easy Lotus Notes 3.0 for Windows. 1994. pap. 19.99 (*1-56529-769-5*) Que.
— Easy Macintosh. 2nd ed. 1994. pap. 19.99 (*1-56529-738-5*) Que.
— Easy PowerPoint for Windows. 1994. pap. 19.99 (*1-56529-737-7*) Que.
— Easy Works 3.0 for Windows. 1994. pap. 19.99 (*1-56529-755-5*) Que.
— Lotus SmartSuite Bundle. 1994. pap. 69.95 (*1-56529-559-5*) Que.
— Lotus SmartSuite Notes Bundle. 1994. pap. 100.00 (*1-56529-951-5*) Que.
— Microsoft Office Bundle. 1994. pap. 69.95 (*1-56529-228-6*) Que.
— Microsoft Office Bundle. 2nd ed. 1994. pap. 75.00 (*1-56529-843-8*) Que.
— Microsoft Office Bundle New Edition. 1994. pap. 69.95 (*1-56529-585-4*) Que.
— Microsoft Office Bundle with Access. 1994. pap. 100.00 (*1-56529-803-9*) Que.
— Microsoft Office Bundle with Access. 2nd ed. 1994. pap. 105.00 (*1-56529-852-7*) Que.
— MS-DOS 6.2 Quickstart. 1994. pap. 21.95 (*1-56529-754-7*) Que.
— Using Autocad for DOS Special Edition. 1994. pap. 37.99 (*1-56529-621-4*) Que.
— Using dBASE for DOS. 1994. pap. 29.99 (*1-56529-728-8*) Que.
— Using Macromedia Director. 1994. Incl. CD-ROM. cd-rom 29.99 (*1-56529-781-4*) Que.
— Using MS-DOS 6.2 Bundle. 1993. pap. 29.95 (*1-56529-646-X*) Que.
— Using Paradox for Windows. 1994. pap. 29.99 (*1-56529-758-X*) Que.
— Using Windows 3.1. 3rd ed. 1994. pap. 29.99 (*1-56529-807-1*) Que.
— Using 1-2-3 for Windows. 1994. pap. 29.99 (*1-56529-743-1*) Que.
— Windows VisiRef. 1994. pap. 12.99 (*1-56529-805-5*) Que.
— Word for Windows 6.0 Quickstart. 2nd ed. 1994. pap. 21.95 (*1-56529-791-1*) Que.
— WordPerfect 6.0 for Windows Quickstart. 2nd ed. 1994. pap. 21.99 (*1-56529-785-7*) Que.
Que Hee, Shane S. & Sutherland, Ronald G. The Phenoxyalkanoic Herbicides: Chemistry, Analysis & Environmental Pollution, Vol. I. 321p. 1981. 145.00 (*0-8493-5851-5*, SB952, CRC Reprint) Franklin.
Que, Lawrence, Jr., ed. Metal Clusters in Proteins. LC 88-14504. (ACS Symposium Ser.: No. 372). (Illus.). ix, 413p. 1988. 84.95 (*0-8412-1487-5*) Am Chemical.
***Que Staff.** Easy Lotus Smartsuite Bundle. 1994. pap. 60.00 (*0-7897-0042-5*) Que.
— Easy Microsoft Office Bundle. 1994. pap. 60.00 (*0-7897-0041-7*) Que.
— Lotus SmartSuite Bundle. 2nd ed. 1994. pap. 90.00 (*0-7897-0044-1*) Que.
— Lotus SmartSuite Quickstart Bundle. 1994. pap. 75.00 (*1-56529-969-8*) Que.
— Microsoft Office Quickstart Bundle. 1994. pap. 75.00 (*1-56529-967-1*) Que.
— Microsoft Office Quickstart Bundle with Access. 1994. pap. 105.00 (*1-56529-968-X*) Que.
— Microsoft Office VisiRef Bundle. 1994. pap. 39.00 (*0-7897-0043-3*) Que.
— Turbo C Plus Plus for Windows by Example. 1995. pap. 29.99 (*1-56529-836-5*) Que.
— Using Compuserve Special Edition. 1995. cd-rom, pap. (*0-7897-0280-0*) Que.
— Using Internet E-Mail Special Edition. 1995. pap. (*0-7897-0237-1*) Que.
Que Staff, jt. auth. see Branchek, Bob.
Que Staff, jt. auth. see Eager, Bill.
Que Staff, jt. auth. see Haltberg, B.
Que Staff, jt. auth. see McComb, Gordon.
Que Staff, jt. auth. see Miller, Mike.
Que Staff, jt. auth. see Schwartau, Winn.
Que Staff, jt. auth. see Steinberg, Gene.
Queano, Nonilon V. Ang Katutubo at Delawa Pang Dula. 128p. 1984. pap. 7.50 (*971-10-0119-5*, Pub. by New Day Pub PH) Cellar.
Quebec Brewers Association Staff. English - French Lexicon of Brewing. 101p. (ENG & FRE.). 1986. pap. 29.95 (*0-8288-9396-9*) Fr & Eur.
Quebedeaux, Richard. Prime Sources of California & Nevada Local History: 151 Rare & Important City, County & State Directories, 1850-1906. LC 91-74139. (Illus.). 238p. 1992. 65.00 (*0-87062-213-7*) A H Clark.
Queck, Lynn. Meeting Jesus in Holy Communion: Leader's Guide. 96p. 1984. pap. 3.95 (*0-89243-224-1*) Liguori Pubns.
Queen, Betty A., jt. auth. see Queen, H. L.
***Queen, Carol.** Exhibitionism for the Shy: Show off, Dress up & Talk Hot. LC 95-68995. 248p. 1995. pap. 12.50 (*0-940208-16-4*) Down There Pr.
***Queen, Christopher S. & King, Sallie B., eds.** Engaged Buddhism: Buddhist Liberation Movements in Asia. 416p. (C). 1996. text ed. 74.50x (*0-7914-2843-5*); pap. text ed. 24.95x (*0-7914-2844-3*) State U NY Pr.
Queen, Daniel R. Wake up Call: (Final Call) (Illus.). 128p. Date not set. pap. write for info. (*1-881328-01-5*) Queens Palace.
— Wings of the Whirlwind: (A Tribute to Marcus M. Garvey) rev. ed. 86p. 1992. pap. 10.00 (*1-881328-00-7*) Queens Palace.
***Queen, E.** Face to Face. 1994. pap. 3.99 (*0-517-13217-6*) Random Hse Value.
— Origin of Evil. 1994. pap. 3.99 (*0-517-13218-4*) Random Hse Value.
***Queen, Edward L., II, et al.** Encyclopedia of American Religious History. LC 95-2487. 1995. write for info. (*0-8160-2406-5*) Facts on File.
Queen, Edward L., II. In the South the Baptists are the Center of Gravity: Southern Baptists & Social Change, 1930-1980. LC 91-28027. (Chicago Studies in the History of American Religion Ser.: Vol. 17). 210p. 1991. 50.00 (*0-926019-53-8*) Carlson Pub.
Queen, Ellery. And on the Eighth Day. (Ellery Queen Mystery Ser.). 192p. 1994. pap. 8.00 (*0-06-097603-9*, PL) HarpC.
— Cat of Many Tails. LC 88-82351. 247p. 1988. reprint ed. pap. 4.95 (*0-930330-94-3*, Lib Crime Classics) Intl Polygonics.
— Cop Out. Bd. with Last Woman in His Life. 1982. Set pap. 2.50 (*0-451-11562-7*, AE1562, Sig) NAL-Dutton.
— Drury Lane's Last Case. LC 87-82441. 232p. 1987. reprint ed. pap. 4.95 (*0-930330-70-6*) Intl Polygonics.
— The Dutch Shoe Mystery: An Ellery Queen Mystery. 324p. 1995. reprint ed. pap. 6.95 (*1-883402-12-3*) S&S Trade.
— The Ellery Queen Omnibus. LC 88-82352. 700p. 1988. reprint ed. pap. 9.95 (*1-55882-001-9*, Lib Crime Classics) Intl Polygonics.
— Ellery Queen's More Eyewitnesses. large type ed. 1991. pap. 16.95 (*0-7927-1026-6*, CS0267, Curley Lrg Print) Chivers N Amer.
— Ellery Queen's Poetic Justice. 21.95 (*0-8488-0615-8*) Amereon Ltd.
— Ellerys Queen's Masters of Mystery. 1993. 11.98 (*0-88365-822-4*) Galahad Bks.
— Eyes of Mystery, Anthology II. large type ed. 1990. pap. 16.95 (*0-7927-0436-3*, C0490, Curley Lrg Print) Chivers N Amer.
— The Four of Hearts: An Ellery Queen Mystery. LC 93-27181. 224p. 1994. reprint ed. pap. 8.00 (*0-06-097604-7*, PL) HarpC.
— French Powder Mystery. 1995. pap. 7.00 (*1-883402-90-5*) S&S Trade.
— In the Queens' Parlor & Other Leaves from the Editors' Notebook. LC 70-79516. 1969. reprint ed. 25.00 (*0-8196-0238-8*) Biblo.
— Masters of Suspense. 1992. 9.98 (*0-88365-787-2*) Galahad Bks.
— Queen's Quorum. LC 68-56450. 146p. 1969. 25.00 (*0-8196-0229-9*) Biblo.
— The Roman Hat Mystery. 340p. 1994. reprint ed. 35.00 (*1-883402-19-0*) S&S Trade.
— The Scarlet Letters. Bd. with Glass Village. 1984. Set pap. 3.50 (*0-451-12887-7*, E9675, Sig) NAL-Dutton.
— The Siamese Twin Mystery. LC 93-8120. 1993. 6.95 (*1-883402-11-5*) S&S Trade.
— Ten Days Wonder: An Ellery Queen Mystery. LC 93-27192. 224p. 1994. reprint ed. pap. 8.00 (*0-06-097606-3*, PL) HarpC.
— There Was an Old Woman. Bd. with Origin of Evil. 1984. Set pap. 3.50 (*0-451-12683-1*, AE2683, Sig) NAL-Dutton.
— The Tragedy of X. 288p. 1986. pap. 5.95 (*0-930330-43-9*) Intl Polygonics.
— The Tragedy of Z. (Library of Crime Classics). 200p. 1987. pap. 4.95 (*0-930330-58-7*) Intl Polygonics.
Queen, Ellery, ed. Ellery Queen's a Multitiude of Sins. 21.95 (*0-89190-794-7*, Am Repr) Amereon Ltd.
— Ellery Queen's Circumstantial Evidence. 21.95 (*0-89190-790-4*, Am Repr) Amereon Ltd.
— Ellery Queen's Faces of Mystery. large type ed. 1992. pap. 16.95 (*0-7927-1295-1*, Curley Lrg Print) Chivers N Amer.
— Ellery Queen's Magicians of Mystery. large type ed. 1992. pap. 19.95 (*0-7927-1193-9*, Curley Lrg Print) Chivers N Amer.
— Ellery Queen's Masks of Mystery. 21.95 (*0-89190-793-9*, Am Repr) Amereon Ltd.
— Ellery Queen's Other Faces of Mystery. large type ed. LC 93-35528. 1994. 18.95 (*0-7927-1832-1*, Curley Lrg Print); pap. 16.95 (*0-7927-1831-3*, Curley Lrg Print) Chivers N Amer.
— Ellery Queen's Secrets of Mystery. 21.95 (*0-89190-791-2*, Am Repr) Amereon Ltd.
— Ellery Queen's The Golden Thirteen. 24.95 (*0-89190-792-0*, Am Repr) Amereon Ltd.
— Ellery Queen's Veils of Mystery. 21.95 (*0-89190-795-5*, Am Repr) Amereon Ltd.
— Ellery Queen's Windows of Mystery. large type ed. LC 94-15601. 1994. 22.95 (*0-7927-2123-3*, Curley Lrg Print); pap. 21.95 (*0-7927-2122-5*, Curley Lrg Print) Chivers N Amer.
— Ellery Queen's Wings of Mystery. 21.95 (*0-89190-796-3*, Am Repr) Amereon Ltd.
Queen, George S. The United States & the Materials Advance in Russia, 1881-1906. Bruchey, Stuart & Bruchey, Eleanor, eds. LC 76-5030. (American Business Abroad Ser.). (Illus.). 1976. lib. bdg. 24.95 (*0-405-09297-0*) Ayer.
Queen, H. L. Chronic Mercury Toxicity: New Hope Against an Endemic Disease. (Doctor's Guide for Lifestyle Counseling Ser.: Vol. 1). (Illus.). 302p. (C). 1988. text ed. 45.00 (*0-9620479-1-0*) Queen Co Hlth Comns.
Queen, H. L. & Queen, Betty A. The IV-C Mercury Tox Program: A Guide for the Doctor. (Doctor's Guide for Lifestyle Counseling Ser.). 76p. (Orig.). 1991. pap. text ed. 11.95 (*0-9620479-0-2*) Queen Co Hlth Comns.
— The IV-C Mercury Tox Program: A Guide for the Patient. (Doctor's Guide for Lifestyle Counseling Ser.). 72p. (Orig.). 1991. pap. text ed. 8.95 (*0-9620479-2-9*) Queen Co Hlth Comns.
Queen, J. Allen. Complete Karate. LC 93-24831. (Illus.). 192p. (YA). (gr. 10-12). 1993. 19.95 (*0-8069-8678-6*) Sterling.
— Complete Karate. (Illus.). 192p. 1994. pap. 12.95 (*0-8069-8679-4*) Sterling.
— Karate Basics. LC 92-25112. (Illus.). 128p. 1992. 16.95 (*0-8069-8676-X*) Sterling.
— Karate Basics. (Illus.). 128p. (J). (gr. 3 up). 1993. pap. 7.95 (*0-8069-8677-8*) Sterling.
— Karate for Kids. LC 93-45837. (Illus.). 96p. (J). 1994. 13.95 (*0-8069-0614-6*) Sterling.

PQ

An Asterisk (*) at the beginning of an entry indicates that the title is appearing in BIP for the first time.

— Karate for Kids. (Illus.). 96p. (J). 1995. pap. 5.95 (0-8069-0615-4) Sterling.
— Total Karate. LC 89-49313. (Illus.). 128p. (J). (gr. 4 up). 1991. pap. 7.95 (0-8069-6715-3) Sterling.
Queen, Janel, jt. auth. see Woodward, John C.
Queen Liliuokalani. Hawaii's Story by Hawaii's Queen. LC 63-23301. (Illus.). 432p. 1964. pap. 10.95 (0-8048-1066-4) C E Tuttle.
Queen, Margaret M. So You're off to Summer Camp: A Trunk Load of Tips for a Fun-Filled Camp Adventure. LC 93-77129. (Illus.). 136p. (J). (gr. 2-12). 1993. 14.95 (1-882959-55-8); per. 6.95 (1-882959-50-7) Foxglove TN.
Queen, N. M., tr. see Prudnikov, A. P., et al.
Queen, N. M., tr. see Sibgatullin, N. R.
Queen, Pat & Lang, Carol E. Handbook of Pediatric Nutrition. 500p. 1992. 68.00 (0-8342-0290-5, 20290) Aspen Pub.
Queen, Sandy. Wellness Activities for Youth. 154p. 1992. spiral bd. 19.95 (0-938586-70-X) Whole Person.
— Wellness Activities for Youth, Vol. 1. 160p. 1994. 19.95 (1-57025-026-X) Whole Person.
— Wellness Activities for Youth, Vol. 2. 160p. 1994. 19.95 (0-938586-98-X) Whole Person.
Queen, Stuart A. The American City. LC 73-138175. (Illus.). 383p. 1972. reprint ed. text ed. 75.00 (0-8371-5632-7, QUAC, Greenwood Pr) Greenwood.
Queen, Stuart A., jt. auth. see Chapin, Francis S.
Queenan. Management of High-Risk Pregnancy. 2nd ed. 752p. 1985. boxed 76.95 (0-87489-382-8) Med Economics.
Queenan, Carrie N., jt. ed. see Queenan, John T.
Queenan, J. T. Management of High-Risk Pregnancy. 3rd ed. (Illus.). 832p. 1994. 79.95 (0-86542-187-0) Blackwell Sci.
Queenan, J. T. & Hobbins, J. C. Protocols for High-Risk Pregnancies. 2nd ed. 449p. 1987. pap. 49.95 (0-86542-177-3) Blackwell Sci.
Queenan, James F., Jr., et al, eds. Chapter Eleven Theory & Practice: A Guide to Reorganization Includes Supplement for October 1994. LC 93-49092. (Bankruptcy Law Ser.). 6000p. 1994. ring bd. 775.00 (0-934753-99-7) LRP Pubns.
Queenan, Joe. If You're Talking to Me Your Career Must Be in Trouble: Movies, Mayhem, & Malice. LC 93-3873. 288p. 1994. 22.95 (1-56282-788-X) Hyperion.
Queenan, John T., ed. Managing Ob-Gyn Emergencies. 2nd ed. 308p. 1983. boxed 52.95 (0-87489-344-5) Med Economics.
Queenan, John T. & Hobbins, John C., eds. Protocols for High-risk Pregnancies. 2nd ed. 472p. 1987. pap. 36.95 (0-87489-429-8) Med Economics.
Queenan, John T. & Queenan, Carrie N., eds. A New Life: Pregnancy, Birth & Your Child's First Year. 1986. 24.95 (0-316-72892-6) Little.
— A New Life: Pregnancy, Birth, & Your Child's First Year - A Comprehensive Guide. 2nd rev. ed. (Illus.). 240p. 1992. 29.95 (0-316-72878-0) Little.
Queenan, Joseph. If You're Talking to Me, Your Career Must Be in Trouble: Movies, Mayhem, & Malice. 288p. 1995. pap. 12.95 (0-7868-8067-8) Hyperion.
— The Unkindest Cut: How a Hatchet-Man Critic Made His Own 7,000 Dollar Movie & Put It All on His Credit Card. 272p. 1996. 22.95 (0-7868-6090-1) Hyperion.
Queenborough, Lady. Occult Theocracy, 2 vols. 1972. 500.00 (0-8490-0751-8) Gordon Pr.
***Queener, Elizabeth.** How to Climb Your Family Tree: Without Going Out on a Limb. Courtney, Richard & McCombs, Maryglenn, eds. LC 94-61376. 40p. (Orig.). 1994. pap. 8.95 (0-9635026-9-7) Eggman Pub.
***Queeney, Donna S.** Assessing Needs in Continuing Education: An Essential Tool for Quality Improvement. LC 94-37102. (Higher & Adult Education Ser.). 304p. 1995. 30.95 (0-7879-0059-1) Jossey-Bass.
Queen's Own Hussars Editors, ed. The Queen's Own Hussars: Tercentenary Edition. (Illus.). 96p. 1985. pap. 16.50 (0-08-033595-0, P110, T120, Pergamon Pr) Elsevier.
Queens Spark Rate Book Group Staff. Brighton on the Rocks Monetarism & the Local State. 192p. 1988. 39.00 (0-317-43589-2, Bertrand Russell Soc) St Mut.
Queen's University at Kingston Staff. Discontinuous Solidification of an Aluminum-Copper Alloy. 81p. 1965. 12.15 (0-317-34515-X, 66) Intl Copper.
Queen's University, Faculty of the Arts Staff. Philosophical Essays Presented to John Watson. LC 70-156704. (Essay Index Reprint Ser.). 1977. reprint ed. 23.95 (0-8369-2291-3) Ayer.
Queensboro, Lady, see Edith S. Miller, pseud..
Queeny, Edgar M. Prairie Wings. (Illus.). 256p. 1979. reprint ed. 50.00 (0-916838-21-8) Schiffer.
— Prairie Wings: The Classic Illustrated Study of American Wildfowl in Flight. (Nature Ser.). 256p. 1984. reprint ed. pap. 14.95 (0-486-24544-6) Dover.
Queffelec, Henri. Un Homme d'Ouessant. 224p. (FRE.). 1974. pap. 8.95 (0-7859-4026-X, 2070365417) Fr & Eur.
— Tempete sur Douarnenez. (FRE.). 1973. pap. 10.95 (0-7859-4006-5) Fr & Eur.
Queffelec, M. Substitution Dynamical Systems - Spectral Analysis. (Lecture Notes in Mathematics Ser.: Vol. 1294). 240p. 1987. pap. 40.80 (0-387-18692-1) Spr-Verlag.
Queffelec, Yann. Charme Noir. (Folio Ser.: No. 1665). (FRE.). pap. 9.95 (2-07-037665-6) Schoenhof.
— Le Charme Noir. (FRE.). 1985. pap. 11.95 (0-7859-4225-4) Fr & Eur.
— Noces Barbares. (Folio Ser.: No. 1856). 308p. (FRE.). 1985. pap. 9.95 (2-07-037856-X) Schoenhof.
Quehl, Gary H., ed. see Chickering, Arthur W., et al.
Quehl, Gary H., jt. ed. see Fisher, James L.
Quehl, Gary H., ed. see Pilon, Daniel H. & Bergquist, William H.
Queinnec, C. & Chailloux, J., eds. Lisp Standardization & Evolution: Proceedings of the 1st International Workshop, Paris, France, 1988. (Frontiers in Artificial Intelligence & Applications Ser.: Vol. 2). 86p. 1988. pap. 37.00 (90-5199-008-1, Pub. by IOS Pr NE) IOS Press.
Queirozde. Iglesia Local y las Misiones: The Local Church & Missions. (SPA.). 4.50 (84-7645-412-0, 223546, Pub. by Edit Clie SP) TSELF.
Queisser, H. J., ed. X-Ray Optics: Applications to Solids. (Topics in Applied Physics Ser.: Vol. 22). (Illus.). 1977. 51.00 (0-387-08462-2) Spr-Verlag.
***Queisser, H. J., et al, eds.** Proceedings of the Symposium on the Degradation of Electronic Devices Due to Device Operation As Well As Crystalline & Process-Induced Defects. LC 93-72866. (Proceedings Ser.: Vol. 94-01). 328p. 1994. 37.00 (1-56677-037-8) Electrochem Soc.
Queisser, Hans. The Conquest of the Microchip. LC 87-2440. (Illus.). 272p. 1988. 34.50 (0-674-16296-X) HUP.
Queisser, W. & Fiebig, H. H., eds. New Drugs in Oncology. (Beitraege zur Onkologie Ser.: Vol. 37). (Illus.). 302p. 1989. 63.25 (3-8055-5047-2) S Karger.
Quekett, John. Practical Treatise on the Use of the Microscope. (History of Microscopy Ser.). 512p. 1987. reprint ed. 72.00 (0-940095-05-X) Sci Heritage Ltd.
Quelch, H., tr. see Marx, Karl.
***Quelch, John A.** Cases in Product Management. 450p. (C). 1994. text ed. 48.95 (0-256-16347-2) Irwin.
— How to Market to Consumers: Ten Ways to Win. 224p. 1989. text ed. 53.95 (0-471-61853-5) Wiley.
— Sales Promotion Management. 360p. 1989. text ed. 63.00 (0-13-788118-5) P-H.
Quelch, John A. & Farris, Paul W. Cases in Advertising & Promotion Management. 3rd ed. 800p. (C). 1990. text ed. 61.95 (0-256-09689-9) Irwin.
— Cases in Advertising & Promotion Management. 4th ed. LC 93-5170. 768p. (C). 1993. text ed. 65.95 (0-256-12272-5) Irwin.
Quelch, John A., jt. auth. see Buzzell, Robert D.
Quelch, John A., jt. auth. see Farris, Paul W.
Quelch, John A., jt. auth. see Smith, N. Craig.
Quelch, John A., et al. Cases in European Marketing Management. LC 93-41069. (Series in Marketing). 544p. (C). 1994. pap. text ed. 48.95 (0-256-15722-7) Irwin.
— The Marketing Challenge of Europe 1992. (Illus.). 410p. (C). 1991. pap. text ed. 27.95 (0-201-56400-9) Addison-Wesley.
— The Marketing Challenge of 1992. (Illus.). 350p. (C). 1989. pap. text ed. 21.50 (0-201-51562-8) Addison-Wesley.
— Marketing Management: Text & Cases. LC 92-31499. (Series in Marketing). (Illus.). 960p. (C). 1993. text ed. 67.95 (0-256-10955-9) Irwin.
Quelet, Lucien. Flore Mycologique de la France & des Pays Limitrophes. 1962. reprint ed. 40.00 (90-6123-123-X) Lubrecht & Cramer.
Quell, E., jt. auth. see Finger, J. H.
Quell, Lawrence A. Awaken Your Twelve Personal Powers. Patterson-Oriel, Patricia, ed. (Illus.). (Orig.). 1989. pap. write for info. (0-318-65233-1) DC Enterprises.
Quelle, Henri. Tertullianus - Concordance Verbale du "De Exhortatione Castitatis" de Tertullien. (Alpha-Omega, Reihe A Ser.: Bd. CXXXI). iv, 226p. (GER.). 1993. write for info. (3-487-09501-7, Pub. by Georg Olms GW) Lubrecht & Cramer.
Queller, jt. auth. see Durst.
Queller, Donald E. The Venetian Patriciate: Reality vs. Myth. LC 84-28041. 398p. 1985. 34.95 (0-252-01144-9) U of Ill Pr.
Quellet, H., ed. Tertullianus - Concordance Verbale du "De Patientia" de Tertullien. (Alpha-Omega, Reihe A Ser.: Vol. XCVII). iv, 346p. (GER.). 1988. write for info. (3-487-07994-1, Pub. by Georg Olms GW) Lubrecht & Cramer.
Quellet, Henri. Bibliographia Indicum, Lexicorum et Concordantiarum Auctorum Latinorum. ix, 262p. 1980. write for info. (3-487-07014-6, Pub. by Georg Olms GW) Lubrecht & Cramer.
— Le Gitagovinda de Jayadeva: Texte, Concordance et Index. 570p. 1978. write for info. (3-487-06515-0, Pub. by Georg Olms GW) Lubrecht & Cramer.
— Tertullianus - Concordance Verbale de Cultu Feminarum de Tertullien. (Alpha-Omega, Reihe A Ser.: Vol. LX). iv, 382p. (GER.). 1986. write for info. (3-487-07769-8, Pub. by Georg Olms GW) Lubrecht & Cramer.
Quellet, Henri, ed. Tertullianus - Concordance Verbale du "De Corona" de Tertullien. (Alpha-Omega, Reihe A Ser.: Vol. XXIII). 434p. (GER.). 1975. write for info. (3-487-05763-8, Pub. by Georg Olms GW) Lubrecht & Cramer.
Quellette, Fernand. A Biography of Edgard Varese. (Illus.). xiv, 270p. 1981. reprint ed. lib. bdg. 27.50 (0-306-76103-3) Da Capo.
Quellette, Robert P., jt. auth. see Cheremisinoff, Paul N.
Quellette, Robert P., jt. ed. see Cheremisinoff, Paul N.
Quellhorst, E., et al, eds. Trace Elements in Renal Insufficiency. (Contributions to Nephrology Ser.: Vol. 38). (Illus.). x, 206p. 1984. 91.25 (3-8055-3676-3) S Karger.
Quemada, G. Dictionary of New Scientific & Technical Terms. 626p. (ENG, FRE, GER & SPA.). 1983. 175.00 (0-8288-0685-3, M2021) Fr & Eur.
Quen, Jacques M., ed. The Psychiatrist in the Courtroom: Selected Papers of Bernard L. Diamond, M.D. 376p. 1994. 47.50 (0-88163-160-4) Analytic Pr.
Quencer, Robert M. MRI of the Spine. (MRI Teaching File Ser.). 242p. 1991. 70.00 (0-88167-703-5) Raven.
Quendo, Rene. Creativity in Education: The Waldorf Approach. 1982. pap. 9.95 (0-930420-05-5) H S Dakin.
***Queneau.** The Last Days. Date not set. 19.95 (0-916583-62-7) Dalkey Arch.
Queneau, Joan, ed. see Miro, Joan.
Queneau, P. E., jt. ed. see Anderson, J. N.
Queneau, R. Le Chiendent. (FRE.). 1974. pap. 13.95 (0-8288-3767-8, M3944) Fr & Eur.
Queneau, Raymond. Bark Tree. 1991. pap. 11.95 (0-7145-0108-5) Riverrun NY.
— Batons, Chiffres et Lettres. (Idees Ser.). 384p. (FRE.). 1965. 9.95 (2-07-035070-3) Schoenhof.
— Battre la Campagne. 216p. (FRE.). 1968. pap. 10.95 (0-7859-1336-X, 2070272974) Fr & Eur.
— The Blue Flowers. Wright, Barbara, tr. LC 84-25544. (Revived Modern Classics Ser.). 224p. 1985. reprint ed. pap. 8.95 (0-8112-0945-8, NDP595) New Directions.
— Bords: Mathematiciens, Precurseurs, Encyclopedistes. 144p. (FRE.). 1978. pap. 24.95 (0-7859-1607-5, 270565402X) Fr & Eur.
— Cent Mille Milliards de Poemes. (Gallimard Ser.). 38p. (FRE.). 1965. 59.95 (2-07-010467-2) Schoenhof.
— Chene et Chien & Petite Cosmongonie Portative, le Chant du Styrene. (Poesie Ser.). 192p. (FRE.). 1969. pap. 9.95 (2-07-030231-8) Schoenhof.
— Chene et Chien, Petite Cosmogonie Portative. (FRE.). 1969. pap. 10.95 (0-8288-3866-6, F120250) Fr & Eur.
— Chiendent. (Folio Ser.: No. 588). 431p. (FRE.). 1933. pap. 10.95 (2-07-036588-3) Schoenhof.
— Contes et Propos. (FRE.). 1990. pap. 12.95 (0-7859-2920-7) Fr & Eur.
— Contes et Propos. (Folio Ser.: No. 2127). (FRE.). pap. 9.95 (2-07-038220-6) Schoenhof.
— Courir les Rues. 200p. 1967. 5.95 (0-686-54665-2) Fr & Eur.
— Courir les Rues. Battre la Campagne. Fendre les Flots. (Poesie Ser.). (FRE.). 1981. pap. 16.95 (2-07-032204-1) Schoenhof.
— Courir les Rues, Battre le Compagne, Fendre Flots. (FRE.). 1981. pap. 10.95 (0-8288-3867-4, F120280) Fr & Eur.
— Les Derniers Jours: Roman. 232p. (FRE.). 1977. pap. 24.95 (0-7859-1590-7, 207010916X) Fr & Eur.
— Le Dimanche de la Vie. (FRE.). 1973. pap. 10.95 (0-8288-3768-6, M3945) Fr & Eur.
— Dimanche de la Vie. (Folio Ser.: No. 442). (FRE.). pap. 8.95 (2-07-036442-9) Schoenhof.
— Exercices de Style. (FRE.). 1982. pap. 10.95 (0-8288-3770-8, M1261) Fr & Eur.
— Exercices de Style. (Folio Ser.: No. 1363). 200p. (FRE.). 1970. 6.95 (2-07-037363-0) Schoenhof.
— Exercises in Style. 2nd ed. Wright, Barbara, tr. LC 80-26102. (Illus.). 208p. 1981. 12.95 (0-8112-0803-6); pap. 9.95 (0-8112-0789-7, ND513) New Directions.
— Les Fleurs Bleues. (FRE.). 1978. pap. 10.95 (0-8288-3771-6, M11325) Fr & Eur.
— Les Fleurs Bleues. (Folio Ser.: No. 1000). 280p. (FRE.). 1965. 8.95 (2-07-037000-3) Schoenhof.
— The Flight of Icarus. Wright, Barbara, tr. LC 73-76900. Orig. Title: Le Vol D'Icare. 192p. 1973. pap. 6.95 (0-8112-0483-9, NDP358) New Directions.
— Histoire des Litteratures: Litteratures Anciennes, Orientales et Orales, Vol. 1. (Historique Ser.). 2024p. 82.50 (0-686-56447-2) Fr & Eur.
— Histoire des Litteratures: Litteratures Francaises, Vol. 3. (Historique Ser.). 2128p. 82.50 (0-686-56449-9) Fr & Eur.
— Histoire des Litteratures: Litteratures Occidentales, Vol. 2. (Historique Ser.). 2156p. 53.95 (0-686-56448-0) Fr & Eur.
— Une Histoire Modele. 124p. 1966. 4.95 (0-686-54674-1); pap. 16.95 (0-7859-1301-7, 2070253236) Fr & Eur.
— Histoires des Litteratures, Vol 1: Anciennes, Orientales, Orales. (FRE.). 1978. lib. bdg. 145.00 (0-7859-3836-2) Fr & Eur.
— Histoires des Litteratures, Vol 2: Etrangers d'Europe. 2150p. (FRE.). 1956. lib. bdg. 140.00 (0-7859-3774-9, 2070104079) Fr & Eur.
— Histoires des Litteratures, Vol. 3: Francaises, Connexes et Marginales. (FRE.). 1978. lib. bdg. 140.00 (0-7859-3837-0) Fr & Eur.
— L' Instant Fatal & les Ziaux. (Poesie Ser.). 224p. (FRE.). 1966. 9.95 (2-07-030229-6) Schoenhof.
— L' Instant Fatal, les Ziaux. (FRE.). 1966. pap. 10.95 (0-8288-3868-2, F120340) Fr & Eur.
— The Last Days. Wright, Barbara, tr. LC 90-3075. 237p. 1991. reprint ed. pap. 9.95 (0-916583-63-5) Dalkey Arch.
— Loin de Rueil. (FRE.). 1976. pap. 10.95 (0-8288-3772-4, F107610) Fr & Eur.
— Loin de Rueil. (Folio Ser.: No. 849). 211p. (FRE.). 1976. 8.95 (2-07-036849-1) Schoenhof.
— Morale Elementaire. 152p. (FRE.). 1975. pap. 17.95 (0-7859-1345-9, 2070293505) Fr & Eur.
— Odile. Sanders, Carol, tr. & intro. by. LC 88-25051. 120p. 1989. 19.95 (0-916583-34-1) Dalkey Arch.
— Odile. 196p. (FRE.). 1992. pap. 14.95 (0-686-54679-2, 2070725472) Fr & Eur.
— Odile. (Imaginaire Ser.). (FRE.). 1992. pap. 13.95 (2-07-072547-2) Schoenhof.
— Oeuvres Completes, Tome 1. deluxe ed. (Pleiade Ser.). (FRE.). 109.95 (2-07-011168-7) Schoenhof.
— Oeuvres Completes, Vol. 1. Debon, Claude, ed. (FRE.). 1989. lib. bdg. 165.00 (0-7859-3887-7) Fr & Eur.
— Les Oeuvres Completes de Sally Mara. 364p. (FRE.). 1979. pap. 17.95 (0-7859-1341-6, 2070287521) Fr & Eur.
— On Est Toujours Trop Bon avec des Femmes. (FRE.). 1981. pap. 10.95 (0-8288-3773-2) Fr & Eur.
— On Est Toujours Trop Bon avec le Femmes: Un Roman Irlandais De Sally Mara. (Folio Ser.: No. 1312). 200p. (FRE.). 1971. pap. 8.95 (2-07-037312-6) Schoenhof.
— Pierrot Mon Ami. Wright, Barbara, tr. LC 87-72849. 160p. 1989. pap. 9.95 (0-916583-40-6) Dalkey Arch.
— Pierrot Mon Ami. (Folio Ser.: No. 226). 224p. (FRE.). 1972. pap. 8.95 (2-07-036226-4) Schoenhof.
— Pierrot, Mon Ami. (FRE.). 1989. pap. 10.95 (0-8288-3774-0, F120390) Fr & Eur.
— Raymond Queneau's Chene et Chien: A Translation with Commentary. Velguth, Madeleine, tr. LC 93-32269. 104p. (C). 1995. text ed. 33.95 (0-8204-2311-4) P Lang Pubs.
— Un Rude Hiver. (Imaginaire Ser.). 174p. (FRE.). 1977. 11.95 (2-07-029648-2) Schoenhof.
— Saint-Glinglin. (Imaginaire Ser.). 272p. (FRE.). 1948. 12.95 (2-07-029151-0) Schoenhof.
— Saint Glinglin. Sallis, James, tr. LC 92-29479. 192p. 1993. 19.95 (1-56478-027-9) Dalkey Arch.
— The Skin of Dreams. Kaplan, H. J., tr. LC 77-11668. 1979. reprint ed. 30.00 (0-86527-305-7) Fertig.
— The Sunday of Life. Wright, Barbara, tr. LC 76-49628. 1977. 5.95 (0-8112-0645-9) New Directions.
— Le Vol d'Icare. 260p. (FRE.). 1968. pap. 17.95 (0-7859-1277-0, 2070104699) Fr & Eur.
— Vol d'Icare. (Gallimard Ser.). (FRE.). pap. 29.95 (2-07-027298-2) Schoenhof.
— Zazie dans le Metro. (FRE.). 1972. pap. 10.95 (0-8288-3725-2, F120461) Fr & Eur.
— Zazie dans le Metro. (Folio Ser.: No. 108). (FRE.). 1972. 6.95 (2-07-036103-9) Schoenhof.
Queneau, Raymond, et al. Miro's Lithographs: Nineteen Fifty-Three to Nineteen Seventy-Two, 4 Vols. (Illus.). 1000p. 1981. 2,950.00 (0-915346-83-4) A Wofsy Fine Arts.
***Quenk, Alex T. & Quenk, Naomi L.** Dream Thinking: The Logic, Magic, & Meaning of Your Dreams. LC 95-8816. 232p. (Orig.). 1995. pap. 15.95 (0-89106-076-6, 7114) Davies-Black.
Quenk, Naomi L. Beside Ourselves: Our Hidden Personality in Everyday Life. LC 93-4373. 292p. 1993. pap. 14.95 (0-89106-062-6) Consulting Psychol.
Quenk, Naomi L., jt. auth. see Quenk, Alex T.
Quennell, Peter. Baudelaire & the Symbolists. LC 72-142689. (Essay Index Reprint Ser.). 1977. reprint ed. 18.95 (0-8369-2423-1) Ayer.
— Byron. LC 73-21772. (Studies in Byron: No. 5). 1974. lib. bdg. 75.00 (0-8383-1784-7) M S G Haskell Hse.
— Byron in Italy. 1977. 18.95 (0-8369-7147-7, 7979) Ayer.
— Caroline of England: An Augustan Portrait. 1977. 21.95 (0-8369-7148-5, 7980) Ayer.
— Hogarth's Progress. 1977. text ed. 24.95 (0-8369-8145-6, 8285) Ayer.
Quennell, Peter & Johnson, Hamish. Who's Who in Shakespeare. (Who's Who Ser.). 240p. 1995. pap. 14.95 (0-19-521081-6) OUP.
— Who's Who in Shakespeare. LC 94-26058. (Who's Who Ser.). 256p. 1995. pap. write for info. (0-415-11883-2, B4951, Routledge NY) Routledge.
Quennell, Peter, ed. see Baudelaire, Charles.
Quennell, Peter, ed. see Connolly, Cyril.
Quenot, Michel. The Icon: A Window on the Absolute. (Illus.). (Orig.). 1991. pap. 16.95 (0-88141-098-5) St Vladimirs.
Quenouille, M. H. Rapid Statistical Calculations: A Collection of Distributions-Free & Easy Methods of Estimation & Testing. 2nd ed. 1972. 12.50 (0-85264-214-8) Lubrecht & Cramer.
***Quensel, Warren P.** Parent-Teen Manual for Learning to Drive. (Illus.). 96p. (Orig.). 1994. pap. 9.50 (0-9636134-0-5) Safety Ent.
Quenstedt, Friedrich A. Handbuch der Petrefaktenkunde: Handbook for the Study of Fossile, 1. Gould, Stephen J., ed. LC 79-8345. (History of Paleontology Ser.). (Illus.). (GER.). 1980. reprint ed. lib. bdg. 68.95 (0-405-12745-6) Ayer.
— Handbuch der Petrefaktenkunde: Handbook for the Study of Fossile, 2. Gould, Stephen J., ed. LC 79-8345. (History of Paleontology Ser.). (Illus.). (GER.). 1980. reprint ed. lib. bdg. 68.95 (0-405-12749-9) Ayer.
— Handbuch der Petrefaktenkunde: Handbook for the Study of Fossile, Set. Gould, Stephen J., ed. LC 79-8345. (History of Paleontology Ser.). (Illus.). (GER.). 1980. reprint ed. lib. bdg. 136.95 (0-405-12739-1) Ayer.
Quenstedt, J. A. The Nature & Character of Theology. Poellet, Luther, tr. 208p. 1986. 14.95 (0-570-03984-3, 12-3011) Concordia.
Quenstedt, W. A., jt. auth. see Lambrecht, K.
Quentin. The Man in the Net. (Black Dagger Crime Ser.). 16.50 (0-86220-753-3, C0854, Black Dagger) Chivers N Amer.
Quentin, Patrick. Black Widow. 218p. pap. 8.95 (1-55882-111-2) Intl Polygonics.
— Puzzle for Players. 250p. 1989. reprint ed. pap. 5.95 (1-55882-008-6, Lib Crime Classics) Intl Polygonics.
— Puzzle for Puppets. LC 89-85719. 206p. 1989. pap. 7.95 (1-55882-020-5, Lib Crime Classics) Intl Polygonics.
— Puzzle for Wantons. LC 90-80764. 229p. 1990. reprint ed. pap. 7.95 (1-55882-063-9) Intl Polygonics.
— Run to Death. LC 91-70602. 192p. 1991. reprint ed. pap. 5.95 (1-55882-095-7, Lib Crime Classics) Intl Polygonics.
Quenzer, A., ed. High Power Co2 Laser Systems & Applications, Vol. 1020. 1989. 45.00 (0-8194-0055-6) SPIE.
Quenzer, A., jt. ed. see Gaillard, Michel L.
Quenzer, Linda F., jt. auth. see Feldman, Robert S.
Quenzer, Ronald W., jt. ed. see Brillman, Judith C.
Quer, Pio F. Diccionario de Botanica. 1284p. (SPA.). 1989. 105.00 (0-7859-5923-8, 8433558048) Fr & Eur.
Quera, Vicenc, jt. auth. see Bakeman, Roger.
Queral, Maria V. Violeta. LC 91-71263. (Coleccion Espejo de Paciencia Ser.). (Illus.). 56p. (Orig.). (SPA.). 1992. pap. 9.95 (0-89729-602-8) Ediciones.

PQ

***Queralt, Magaly.** The Social Environment & Human Behavior: A Multicultural Perspective. LC 95-11989. 1995. write for info. (*0-02-397191-6*) Allyn.

Queralt, Rosa, ed. see Pijuan, Hernandez.

Querard. La France Litteraire ou Dictionnaire Bibliographique des Savants, Historiens et Gens de Lettres de la France, 12 tomes, Set. 350.00 (*0-685-35981-6*) Fr & Eur.

— La Litterature Francaise Contemporaine, 6 tomes, Set. 262.50 (*0-685-35980-8*) Fr & Eur.

— Les Supercheries litteraires devoiles, 3 tomes, Set. 150.00 (*0-685-35983-2*) Fr & Eur.

Querard, Joseph M. Les Supercheries Litteraires Devoilees, 3 vols. rev. suppl. ed. xiv, 66p. 1965. reprint ed. Supplement, xiv, 66p. write for info. (*0-318-71394-2*, Pub. by Georg Olms GW) Lubrecht & Cramer.

— Les Supercheries Litteraires Devoilees, 3 vols., Set. 2nd ed. 1965. reprint ed. write for info. (*0-318-71859-6*, Pub. by Georg Olms GW) Lubrecht & Cramer.

— Les Supercheries Litteraires Devoilees, 3 vols., Set. 2nd rev. ed. xii, 1947p. 1965. reprint ed. write for info. (*0-318-71393-4*, Pub. by Georg Olms GW) Lubrecht & Cramer.

***Querard, Joseph-Marie.** Litterature Francaise Contemporaine. 3150p. (FRE.). 1965. 1,095.00 (*0-7859-5223-3*) Fr & Eur.

Quercia, Valerie & O'Reilly, Tim. X Window System User's Guide, Vol. 3: Standard Edition. 4th ed. (X Window System Ser.). (Illus.). 866p. 1993. pap. 34.95 (*1-56592-014-7*) OReilly & Assocs.

— X Window System User's Guide, Vol. 3M: Motif Edition. 2nd ed. (X Window System Ser.). (Illus.). 956p. 1993. pap. 34.95 (*1-56592-015-5*) OReilly & Assocs.

***Quercia, Valerie & Savetz, Kevin.** Internet User Tools. 600p. 1995. 49.95 (*1-56592-131-3*) OReilly & Assocs.

Quercia, Valerie, jt. auth. see Mui, Linda.

Querciolo, Valter. Pulse Width Modulated (PWM) Power Supplies. LC 93-7123. (Studies in Electrical & Electronic Engineering). 1993. write for info. (*0-444-89790-9*) Elsevier.

Quere, Y., jt. auth. see Leteurtre, J.

Quereshi, Ishtiaq H. The Administration of the Moghul Empire. 1990. reprint ed. 11.50 (*81-85418-00-4*, Pub. by Low Price II) S Asia.

Quereshi, M. A. Waqfs in India: A Study of Administration & Statutory Control. 1990. 78.50 (*81-212-0282-5*, Pub. by Gian Publng Hse II) S Asia.

Querexeta Gallostequi, Jaime. Diccionario Onomastico y Heraldico Vasco, Vol. 5. 288p. (SPA.). 1974. 79.95 (*0-8288-5998-1*, S50375) Fr & Eur.

***Querido, A., et al.** The Discipline of Medicine - Emerging Concepts & Their Impact upon Medical Research & Medical Education: Proceedings of the Symposium, May 25 & 26, 1993. LC 94-27792. 1994. write for info. (*0-444-85772-9*, North Holland) Elsevier.

Querido, R. M., tr. see Steiner, Rudolf.

Querido, Rene. The Golden Age of Chartres: The Teachings of the Mystery School & the Eternal Feminine. 176p. 1990. 19.95 (*0-88010-188-1*, 1217) Anthroposophic.

— The Mystery of the Holy Grail - A Modern Path of Initiation. 1991. pap. 14.95 (*0-945803-12-5*) R Steiner Col Pubns.

— Questions & Answers on Reincarnation & Karma. 1977. pap. 5.50 (*0-916786-18-8*, Saint George Pubns) R Steiner Col Pubns.

— The Wonder of Childhood - Stepping into Life. 1991. pap. 5.95 (*0-945803-08-7*) R Steiner Col Pubns.

Querido, Rene & Moore, Hilmar. Behold, I Make All Things New. 1990. 10.95 (*0-945803-07-9*) R Steiner Col Pubns.

Querido, Rene M., tr. see Steiner, Rudolf.

Quern, Jacqueline. Tools for the Carpenter. 1994. pap. 8.95 (*1-55673-897-8*) CSS OH.

Querner, I., et al, eds. An Economic Analysis of Severe Industrial Hazard. (Microeconomic Studies). (Illus.). xiv, 271p. 1993. pap. 59.00 (*0-387-91449-8*) Spr-Verlag.

Quero De Tossini. Una Dicha Merecida: A Happiness Deserved. (SPA.). 5.50 (*84-7228-605-3*, 220924, Pub. by Edit Clie SP) TSELF.

Querol, Daniel. Genetic Resources: A Practical Guide to their Conservation. LC 92-35019. (C). 1993. text ed. 55.00 (*1-85649-203-6*, Pub. by Zed Books UK); pap. 22.50 (*1-85649-204-4*, Pub. by Zed Books UK) Humanities.

Querry, Ron. The Death of Bernadette Lefthand: A Novel. LC 92-53886. 1993. 23.95 (*1-878610-25-2*) Red Crane Bks.

— The Death of Bernadette Lefthand: A Novel. LC 94-37264. 1995. pap. 9.95 (*0-553-37536-9*) Bantam.

— Native American Struggle for Equality. LC 92-7474. (YA). 1992. 22.60 (*0-86593-179-8*); 16.95 (*0-685-59320-7*) Rourke Corp.

Querry, Ronald B. I See by My Get-up. LC 93-38190. (Illus.). 176p. 1994. reprint ed. pap. 12.95 (*0-8061-2638-8*) U of Okla Pr.

Quershi, M. A., ed. Waqfs in India: A Study of Administrative & Statutory Control. (C). 1990. 275.00 (*0-89771-141-6*) St Mut.

Quertermous, ed. see Woods, B. J.

Quertermous, Steve. Pocket Guide to Handguns: Identification & Values, 1900 to Present. 1993. pap. 9.95 (*0-89145-571-X*) Collector Bks.

— Pocket Guide to Rifles: Identification & Values, 1900 to Present. 1993. pap. 9.95 (*0-89145-572-8*) Collector Bks.

— Pocket Guide to Shotguns: Identification & Values, 1900 to Present. 1993. pap. 9.95 (*0-89145-573-6*) Collector Bks.

Quertermous, Steven. Modern Guns: Indetification & Values. 10th ed. 1994. pap. 12.95 (*0-89145-617-1*) Collector Bks.

Querubin, Perfecto. E-Z Reader. LC 93-15850. (Illus.). 208p. 1994. pap. 14.95 (*0-942963-34-2*) Distinctive Pub.

***Query, John.** Approach Reading Improvement. 100p. (C). 1995. pap. text ed., ring bd. 15.95 (*0-7872-0952-X*) Kendall-Hunt.

Query, John H. An Individualized Approach to Reading Improvement. 104p. 1993. spiral bd. 12.95 (*0-8403-8488-2*) Kendall-Hunt.

Query, Roy D. Corvette: An American Legend. LC 86-70357. (Bloomington Gold Corvettes Ser.: Vol. I). (Illus.). 184p. 1986. 49.95 (*0-915038-51-X*, 3-AQ-0046) Auto Quarterly.

— Corvette: The Legend Lives On. LC 86-70357. (Bloomington Gold Corvettes Ser.: Vol. II). (Illus.). 192p. 1987. 49.95 (*0-915038-52-8*, 3-AQ-0048) Auto Quarterly.

Quesada de Rodriguez, Pura. Componentes de un Sistema de Practica Docente Renovada. LC 78-3641. 119p. 1978. pap. 3.20 (*0-8477-2742-4*) U of PR Pr.

Quesada, Fernando. Argentine Anarchism & La Protesta. 1975. lib. bdg. 250.00 (*0-87968-657-X*) Gordon Pr.

— Sacco & Vanzetti. 1976. lib. bdg. 250.00 (*0-8490-0984-7*) Gordon Pr.

Quesada, Maria S. Estancias: Las Grandes Haciendas al Argentina. (Illus.). 200p. (SPA.). 1992. 65.00 (*1-55859-398-5*) Abbeville Pr.

— Estancias: The Great Ranches of Argentina. 1993. 65.00 (*1-55859-421-3*) Abbeville Pr.

Quesada, Roberto. The Ships. St. Martin, Hardie, tr. LC 92-7988. 214p. 1992. 17.95 (*0-941423-65-4*) FWEW.

Quesenbury, Pat. Promise Is a Promise. 160p. 1989. pap. 4.25 (*0-89114-165-0*) Baptist Pub Hse.

— What's a Girl to Do? Wright, Bobby J., ed. (Illus.). 133p. (Orig.). (YA). (gr. 7 up). 1981. pap. 3.50 (*0-89114-108-1*) Baptist Pub Hse.

Quesnay, Francois. Economical Table (Tableau Economique). 1973. 250.00 (*0-87968-052-0*) Gordon Pr.

— Quesnay's Tableau Economique. 3rd ed. Kuczynski, Marguerite & Meek, Ronald L., trs. LC 78-157694. 160p. (FRE.). 1971. lib. bdg. 27.50 (*0-678-07007-5*) Kelley.

Quesnel, L. B., jt. ed. see Skinner, Frederick A.

Quesnell, Jack. Beyond Your Wedding Day. 209p. (Orig.). 1986. pap. 7.95 (*0-317-40176-9*) Family Visions.

Quesnell, John G. Holy Terrors & Holy Parents. 228p. 1976. 3.49 (*0-8199-0561-5*, Frncscn Herld) Franciscan Pr.

Quesnell, John Q. The Message of Christ & the Counselor. (Synthesis Ser.). 1975. 1.95 (*0-8199-0534-8*, Frncscn Herld) Franciscan Pr.

Quesnell, Quentin. The Authority for Authority. (Pere Marquette Lectures). 54p. 10.00 (*0-87462-517-3*) Marquette.

Quesson, Noel. Spirit of the Psalms. 1990. 14.95 (*0-8091-3199-4*) Paulist Pr.

Quest, Barry, jt. auth. see Morris, A. I.

Quest, Caroline. Equal Opportunities: A Feminist Fallacy. 114p. (C). 1992. text ed. 65.00 (*0-255-36272-2*, Pub. by Inst Economic Affairs UK) St Mut.

Quest, Erica. Cold Coffin. large type ed. (General Ser.). 432p. 1993. 21.95 (*0-7089-2830-7*) Ulverscroft.

— Death Walk. large type ed. (Mystery-Romance Ser.). 384p. 1992. 21.95 (*0-7089-2698-3*) Ulverscroft.

Quest National Center Staff, ed. Positive Prevention: Successful Approaches to Preventing Youthful Drug & Alcohol Use. (Orig.). (SPA.). 1991. 1.50 (*0-685-50174-4*, 021-00180) Am Assn Sch Admin.

Quest National Center Staff, ed. see Resnick, Hank.

Quest, Q. How to Buy Your Own Hotel. (C). 1984. 110.00 (*0-7487-0355-1*, Pub. by S Thornes Pubs UK) St Mut.

Questel, Lynn K. Federal Laws Prohibiting Employment Discrimination - for State & Local Officials. 104p. 1989. pap. 11.95 (*0-89854-136-0*) U of GA Inst Govt.

Quester, George H. Brazil & Latin-American Nuclear Proliferation: An Optimistic View. (CISA Working Paper Ser.: No. 17). 36p. (Orig.). Date not set. pap. 10.00 (*0-86682-016-7*) Ctr Intl Relations.

— Defense over Offense in Central Europe. 30p. (Orig.). 1978. pap. text ed. 9.00 (*0-8191-5841-0*, Aspen Inst for Humanistic Studies) U Pr of Amer.

— Deterrence Before Hiroshima. 214p. 1986. 32.95 (*0-88738-087-5*) Transaction Pubs.

— The Falklands & the Malvinas: Strategy & Arms Control. (CISA Working Paper Ser.: No. 46). 51p. (Orig.). Date not set. pap. 10.00 (*0-86682-059-0*) Ctr Intl Relations.

— The Future of Nuclear Deterrence. LC 85-45343. 352p. 1986. text ed. 27.95 (*0-669-11565-7*); text ed. 19.95 (*0-669-12321-8*) Free Pr.

— The International Politics of Television. (Issues in World Politics Ser.). 304p. 1990. text ed. 49.95 (*0-669-20992-9*); pap. 24.95 (*0-669-24456-2*) Free Pr.

— Offense & Defense in the International System. 239p. 1987. 32.95 (*0-88738-156-1*) Transaction Pubs.

— Peaceful P. A. L. (CISA Working Paper Ser.: No. 9). 23p. (Orig.). Date not set. pap. 10.00 (*0-86682-008-6*) Ctr Intl Relations.

— The Politics of Nuclear Proliferation. LC 73-8119. 264p. reprint ed. pap. 75.30 (*0-317-20467-X*, 2023002) Bks Demand.

— Politics of Public Sector Labor Relations: Some Predictions. (IPE Monograph: No. 1). 32p. 1973. pap. 2.25 (*0-87546-237-5*) ILR Pr.

Quester, George H., ed. The Nuclear Challenge in Russia and the New States of Eurasia. (International Politics of Eurasia: Newly Independent States Enter the Twenty-First Century Ser.: Vol. 6). (Illus.). 320p. 1995. pap. 22.95 (*1-56324-363-6*) M E Sharpe.

— Nuclear Proliferation: Breaking the Chain. LC 80-53960. 258p. (C). 1981. 32.50 (*0-299-08600-3*); pap. text ed. 11.95 (*0-299-08604-6*) U of Wis Pr.

Quester, George H., et al, eds. The Nuclear Challenge in Russia and the New States of Eurasia. (International Politics of Eurasia: Vol. 6). (Illus.). 320p. 1995. 59.95 (*1-56324-362-8*) M E Sharpe.

Questron Staff. Princeton Review: SAT Math. 1986. pap. 4.95 (*0-394-88624-0*) Random.

Quetel, Claude. The History of Syphilis. Braddock, Judith & Pike, Brian, trs. (Illus.). 342p. 1992. reprint ed. pap. text ed. 14.95 (*0-8018-4392-8*) Johns Hopkins.

Quetelet, Adolphe J. Letters Addressed to H. R. H. the Grand Duke of Saxe Coburg & Gotha, on the Theory of Probabilities. Cohen, I. Bernard, ed. LC 80-2143. (Development of Science Ser.). (Illus.). 1981. lib. bdg. 33.95 (*0-405-13950-0*) Ayer.

Quetelet, Lambert A. Treatise on Man & the Development of His Faculties, 1842. LC 77-81364. (History of Psychology Ser.). (Illus.). 1969. 50.00 (*0-8201-1061-2*) Schol Facsimiles.

Quetglas, G. Martin, et al. Applications of Computers in Cardiology: State of the Art & New Perspectives. 1984. 82.00 (*0-444-86824-0*, I-029-84) Elsevier.

Queval, Jean. Lexique de la Musique. 130p. (FRE.). 1968. 19.95 (*0-7859-0774-2*, F-11890) Fr & Eur.

— Marcel Carne. (Film Ser.). 1979. lib. bdg. 59.95 (*0-8490-2970-8*) Gordon Pr.

***Quevauviller, P., et al, eds.** Quality Assurance for Environmental Analysis: Method Evaluation Within the Measurements & Testing Programme (BCR) LC 94-40004. 1995. write for info. (*0-444-89955-3*) Elsevier.

Quevauviller, P. H., et al. Certification of the Contents (Mass Fractions) of AL CA CL FE K MG MN NA P. 72p. 1992. pap. 9.00 (*92-826-3626-7*, CD-NA-14062-EN-C, Pub. by Europ Com) UNIPUB.

— Certification of the Contents (Mass Fractions) of AS CO MO & SE in White Clover. 54p. 1992. pap. 9.00 (*92-826-3994-0*, CD-NA-14234-EN-C, Pub. by Europ Com) UNIPUB.

Quevauvilliers, J. & Perlemuter, L. Dictionnaire Medical de l'Infirmiere. 4th rev. ed. 1344p. (FRE.). 1992. 130.00 (*0-7859-4749-3*, M1900) Fr & Eur.

Quevedo, Francisco. La Vida del Buscon. Lathrop, Thomas et al, eds. 310p. 1988. pap. 11.00 (*0-936388-41-2*) Juan de la Cuesta.

Quevedo, Francisco de. Antologia Poetica. Jauralde Pou, Pablo, ed. (Nueva Austral Ser.: Vol. 186). (SPA.). 1991. pap. text ed. 15.95 (*84-239-1986-2*) Elliots Bks.

Quevedo, Francisco De & Ife, Barry. Francisco de Quevedo: La Vida del Buscon Llamado Don Pablos. 1977. 121.00 (*0-08-021855-5*, Pub. by Pergamon Repr UK) Franklin.

Quevedo y Villegas, Francisco G. de. Choice Humorous Satirical Works. Duff, Charles, ed. L'Estrange, Roger & Stevens, John, trs. LC 76-48454. (Library of World Literature Ser.). 1991. reprint ed. 38.00 (*0-88355-602-2*) Hyperion Conn.

Quezada, Adolfo. A Desert Place. (Illus.). 96p. (Orig.). 1982. pap. 4.95 (*0-914544-40-3*) Living Flame Pr.

— Through the Darkness. LC 92-74491. 260p. Date not set. 7.95 (*0-87029-256-0*) Abbey.

— Walking with God: Reflections on Life's Meaning. LC 90-60305. 96p. (Orig.). 1990. pap. 3.50 (*0-89243-320-5*) Liguori Pubns.

— Wholeness: The Legacy of Jesus. 89p. (Orig.). 1983. pap. 4.95 (*0-914544-48-9*) Living Flame Pr.

Quezada, Alfredo, tr. see Leavell, Ronald Q.

Quezada, Aolfo. Loving Yourself for God's Sake. LC 91-75430. pap. 4.95 (*0-87029-244-7*) Abbey.

Quezada, Jose R., jt. auth. see Andrews, Keith L.

Quezada, Sergio A., jt. ed. see Bagley, Bruce M.

Quezada, Shelley & Nickse, Ruth S. Community Collaborations for Family Literacy Handbook. LC 93-21017. 181p. 1993. pap. 35.00 (*1-55570-164-7*) Neal-Schuman.

Quezada, Victor A., tr. see Coleman, Lucien E., Jr.

Quezon, Manuel L. Good Fight. LC 76-161779. reprint ed. 34.50 (*0-404-09036-2*) AMS Pr.

Quiatt, Duane & Itani, Junichiro, eds. Hominid Culture in Primate Perspecitve. (Illus.). 320p. 1994. 32.50 (*0-87081-313-7*) Univ Pr Colo.

Quiatt, Duane & Reynolds, Vernon. Primate Behaviour: Information, Social Knowledge, & the Evolution of Culture. LC 92-16239. (Studies in Biological Anthropology: Vol. 12). (Illus.). 275p. (C). 1993. 74.95 (*0-521-35255-X*) Cambridge U Pr.

— Primate Behaviour: Information, Social Knowledge, & the Evolution of Culture. (Studies in Biological Anthropology: No. 12). (Illus.). 322p. (C). 1995. pap. 24.95 (*0-521-49832-5*) Cambridge U Pr.

Quible, Zane K. Administrative Office Management: An Introduction. 3rd ed. (C). 1984. teacher ed write for info. (*0-8359-0054-1*, Reston) P-H.

— Administrative Office Management: An Introduction. 5th ed. 624p. (C). 1991. pap. text ed. write for info. (*0-13-005935-8*) P-H.

Quible, Zane K., et al. Records Management Manual for Michigan Municipalities. LC 81-620018. 71p. 1981. 6.50 (*0-941872-32-7*) MSU Dept Res Dev.

***Quibria, M. G., ed.** Critical Issues in Asian Development: Theories, Experiences & Policies. 261p. 1995. text ed. 49.00 (*0-19-586606-1*) OUP.

— Rural Poverty in Asia: Priority Issues & Policy Options. (Illus.). 352p. 1994. 62.00 (*0-19-586003-9*); pap. 24.00 (*0-19-586004-7*) OUP.

***Quicherat, Louis.** Dictionnaire Francais-Latin. 1967. write for info. (*0-7859-7600-0*, 2010041844) Fr & Eur.

— Thesaurus Poeticus Linguae Latinae Ou Dictionnaire Prosodique et Poetique de la Langue Latine. xx, 1251p. 1967. reprint ed. write for info. (*0-318-72070-1*, Pub. by Georg Olms GW) Lubrecht & Cramer.

— Thesaurus Poeticus Linguae Latine Ou Dictionnaire Prosodique et Poetique de la Langue Latine. xx, 1251p. 1967. reprint ed. write for info. (*0-318-71206-7*, Pub. by Georg Olms GW) Lubrecht & Cramer.

— Thesaurus Poeticus Linguae Latine Ou Dictionnaire Prosodique et Poetique De la Langue Latine. xx, 1251p. 1922. reprint ed. write for info. (*0-318-71395-0*, Pub. by Georg Olms GW) Lubrecht & Cramer.

***Quick.** Mistress. 1995. mass mkt. 5.99 (*0-553-56940-6*) Bantam.

— Northern Edge. 1994. pap. 10.00 (*0-06-258521-5*, PL) HarpC.

Quick & Buck, Susan J. Strategic Planning for Exploration Management. 161p. 1988. text ed. 56.00 (*0-13-851809-2*) P-H.

Quick, Allen N. & Buck, Neal A. Strategic Planning for Exploration Management. LC 83-12710. (Illus.). 161p. 1984. 32.00 (*0-934634-66-1*) Intl Human Res.

Quick, Amanda. Dangerous. 1993. mass mkt. 5.99 (*0-553-29317-6*) Bantam.

— Dangerous. large type ed. LC 93-13495. 1993. Alk. paper. 21.95 (*1-56054-726-X*) Thorndike Pr.

— Deception. 1994. mass mkt. 5.99 (*0-553-56506-0*) Bantam.

— Deception. large type ed. LC 93-28767. (Romance Ser.). 1993. 22.95 (*1-56054-770-7*) Thorndike Pr.

— Desire. 1994. mass mkt. 5.99 (*0-553-56153-7*, Fanfare) Bantam.

— Desire. 1994. 25.95 (*1-56895-067-5*) Wheeler Pub.

— Mistress. LC 94-1244. 1994. 19.95 (*0-553-09352-5*); pap. 24.95 (*0-553-09663-X*) Bantam.

— Mystique. LC 95-2248. 1995. 21.95 (*0-553-09698-2*) Bantam.

— Mystique. LC 95-5608. 1995. write for info. (*0-7862-0454-0*) Thorndike Pr.

— Ravished. 1992. pap. 5.99 (*0-553-29316-8*) Bantam.

— Ravished. large type ed. LC 92-27922. 538p. 1993. reprint ed. lib. bdg. 20.95 (*1-56054-429-5*) Thorndike Pr.

— Reckless. 1992. mass mkt. 5.99 (*0-553-29315-X*) Bantam.

— Reckless. large type ed. LC 92-42499. (Romance Ser.). 528p. 1993. reprint ed. lib. bdg. 20.95 (*1-56054-657-3*) Thorndike Pr.

— Reckless. large type ed. 528p. 1993. reprint ed. pap. 12.95 (*1-56054-882-7*) Thorndike Pr.

— Rendezvous. 1991. 5.99 (*0-553-29325-7*) Bantam.

— Rendezvous. large type ed. LC 92-18581. (General Ser.). 463p. 1992. text ed. 20.95 (*0-8161-5453-8*, Large Print Bks); pap. 16.95 (*0-8161-5454-6*, Large Print Bks) Hall.

— Scandal. 1991. pap. 5.99 (*0-553-28932-2*) Bantam.

— Scandal. large type ed. 564p. 1991. reprint ed. lib. bdg. 20.95 (*1-56054-176-8*) Thorndike Pr.

— Seduction. 1990. pap. 5.99 (*0-553-28354-5*) Bantam.

— Seduction. large type ed. LC 94-12082. Date not set. lib. bdg. 21.95 (*0-7862-0259-9*) Thorndike Pr.

— Surrender. 1990. mass mkt. 5.99 (*0-553-28594-7*) Bantam.

— Surrender. large type ed. LC 94-17375. 1994. 24.95 (*1-56895-103-5*) Wheeler Pub.

Quick, Anne, jt. ed. see Leyerle, John.

Quick, Barbara. Northern Edge. 1990. 18.95 (*1-55611-173-8*) D I Fine.

Quick, Beeaje. Realities of Life: Not All Pigeons Move Out of the Way. LC 94-76355. (Illus.). 156p. (Orig.). 1994. pap. 19.95 (*0-9641668-0-1*) GMK Prods.

Quick, Charles, ed. see Hopkins, Ezekiel.

Quick, Charles W., jt. ed. see King, Donald B.

Quick, Daniel L. & Noton, Thomas A. Cry from the Mountain. 159p. 1986. pap. 5.95 (*0-89066-064-6*) World Wide Pubs.

Quick, Daryl E. The Healing Journey for Adult Children of Alcoholics. LC 90-39684. 216p. (Orig.). 1990. pap. 9.99 (*0-8308-1328-4*, 1328) InterVarsity.

***Quick, Donna.** A Place Called Antelope: The Rajneesh Story. 152p. 1995. pap. text ed. 11.50 (*0-9643118-0-1*) August Press.

Quick, Douglas L. Holy Adorning. 1994. pap. 8.95 (*0-533-10954-X*) Vantage.

Quick, Emma, jt. auth. see Twining, William.

Quick, G. & Buchele, W. The Grain Harvesters. (Illus.). 280p. 1978. pap. 15.95 (*0-916150-13-5*, H1278) Am Soc Ag Eng.

Quick, Herbert. Vandemark's Folly. LC 87-10800. (Bur Oak Bk.). 452p. 1987. reprint ed. pap. 14.95 (*0-87745-182-6*) U of Iowa Pr.

Quick, Howard. The Living Cathedral: St. John the Divine a History & Guide. (Illus.). 160p. 1993. 25.00 (*0-8245-1227-8*); pap. 14.95 (*0-8245-1237-5*) Crossroad NY.

Quick, James. Fishing the Nymph. LC 60-7610. 144p. reprint ed. pap. 41.10 (*0-317-28591-2*, 2055174) Bks Demand.

Quick, James, ed. Career Stress in Changing Times. LC 90-35840. (Prevention in Human Services Ser.: Vol. 8, No. 1). 261p. 1990. text ed. 39.95 (*0-86656-956-1*) Haworth Pr.

Quick, James C., jt. auth. see Nelson, Debra L.

Quick, James C., et al. Stress & Challenge at the Top: The Paradox of the Successful Executive. 208p. 1990. text ed. 52.95 (*0-471-91983-7*) Wiley.

Quick, James C., et al, eds. Stress & Well-Being at Work: Assessments & Interventions for Occupational Mental Health. 382p. 1992. pap. text ed. 35.00 (*1-55798-175-2*) Am Psychol.

— Work Stress: Health Care Systems in the Workplace. LC 86-30636. 346p. 1987. text ed. 59.95 (*0-275-92329-0*, C2329, Praeger Pubs) Greenwood.

Quick, John. Dog & Pony Shows: How to Make Winning Presentations When the Stakes Are High. 1992. pap. text ed. 16.95 (*0-07-051077-6*) McGraw.

— Fool's Hill: Childhood Days & Dreams in an Oregon Coastal Town. LC 95-15839. 1995. write for info. (*0-87071-385-X*) Oreg St U Pr.

***Quick, Jonathan D., et al, eds.** Managing Drug Supply. 2nd ed. (Library of Management for Development). (Illus.). 720p. 1996. pap. write for info. (*1-56549-047-9*) Kumarian Pr.

Quick, Kevin R. Pilgrimage Through the Watchtower. 112p. (Orig.). 1989. pap. 6.99 (*0-8010-7551-3*) Baker Bk.
Quick, M., jt. auth. see Croser, J.
Quick, Michael. An American Painter Abroad: Frank Duveneck's European Years. (Illus.). 108p. (Orig.). (C). 1987. 25.00 (*0-931537-07-X*) Cincinnati Mus.
Quick, Michael, jt. auth. see Fort, Ilene S.
Quick, Michael, et al. The Paintings of George Bellows. (Illus.). 272p. 1992. 49.50 (*0-8109-3119-2*) Abrams.
Quick, Robert. Essays on Educational Reformers. reprint ed. lib. bdg. 14.00 (*0-7812-0786-X*) Rprt Serv.
Quick, Robert H. Essays on Educational Reformers. Harris, W. T., ed. LC 78-129348. 1971. reprint ed. 14.00 (*0-403-00485-3*) Scholarly.
Quick, Thomas. Successful Team Building. (AMA Worksmart Ser.). 120p. (Orig.). 1992. pap. 10.95 (*0-8144-7794-1*) AMACOM.
Quick, Thomas L. Getting Good Results from Problem Employees. 1990. pap. 29.95 (*1-55840-669-7*) Exec Ent Pubns.
— How People Work Best. 1988. pap. 39.95 (*0-88057-824-6*) Exec Ent Pubns.
— Increasing Your Sales Success. 1984. pap. 45.00 (*0-88057-064-4*) Exec Ent Pubns.
— Increasing Your Sales Success. 1994. pap. text ed. 45.00 (*0-471-11310-7*) Wiley.
— Inspiring People at Work. 1986. pap. 39.95 (*0-88057-402-X*) Exec Ent Pubns.
— Inspiring People at Work: How to Make Participative Management Work for You. 1994. pap. text ed. 39.95 (*0-471-11275-5*) Wiley.
— Making Your Sales Team Number 1. 192p. 1992. pap. 19.95 (*0-8144-7741-0*) AMACOM.
— Manager's Guide to Lawful Terminations. 2nd ed. 1990. pap. 29.95 (*1-55840-516-X*) Exec Ent Pubns.
— The Manager's Motivation Desk Book. LC 84-19587. 462p. 1985. text ed. 59.95 (*0-471-88377-8*, Ronald Pr) Wiley.
— Managing for Peak Performance. 1989. ring bd. 75.00 (*1-55840-020-6*) Exec Ent Pubns.
— Managing for Peak Performance. 1994. text ed. 59.95 (*0-471-11316-6*) Wiley.
— Managing People at Work Desk Guide. 1993. pap. 59.95 (*0-7816-0324-2*) Exec Ent Pubns.
— Managing People at Work Desk Guide. 2nd ed. 1994. text ed. 59.95 (*0-471-11278-X*) Wiley.
— Mastering the Power of Persuasion. 1990. pap. 29.95 (*0-685-59307-X*) Exec Ent Pubns.
— The Persuasive Manager: How to Sell Yourself & Your Ideas. LC 80-70254. 204p. reprint ed. pap. 58.20 (*0-317-55807-2*, 2029389) Bks Demand.
— Training Managers So They Can Really Manage: Confessions of a Frustrated Trainer. LC 90-28765. (Management Ser.). 214p. 1991. 27.95 (*1-55542-341-8*) Jossey-Bass.
— Unconventional Wisdom: Irreverent Solutions for Tough Problems at Work. LC 89-45594. (Management Ser.). 202p. 1989. 26.95x (*1-55542-177-6*) Jossey-Bass.
Quick, Thomas L., jt. auth. see Higginson, Margaret V.
Quick, Tommy E. Who's Who in the Church of God in Christ, Vol. 1. 500p. 1990. text ed. 69.95 (*1-878123-00-9*) Recognitive Soc.
Quick, W. T. Dreams of Gods & Men. 304p. 1989. pap. 3.95 (*0-318-39985-7*, Sig) NAL-Dutton.
Quick, William D., jt. auth. see Wright, Mildred S.
Quicke, Andrew & Quicke, Juliet. Hidden Agendas: The Politics of Religious Broadcasting in Britain 1987-1991. 276p. (C). 1993. pap. 14.99 (*0-9635509-0-X*) Dominion Kings.
Quicke, Donald L. Principles & Techniques of Contemporary Taxonomy. LC 93-17123. (Tertiary Level Biology Ser.). 1993. write for info. (*0-7514-0019-X*, Pub. by Blackie Acad & Prof UK); pap. write for info. (*0-7514-0020-3*, Pub. by Blackie Acad & Prof UK) Routledge Chapman & Hall.
Quicke, John. Helping Children Understand Disabilities: Disability in Modern Children's Fiction. LC 84-19844. 176p. 1985. text ed. 17.95 (*0-914797-09-3*) Brookline Bks.
Quicke, John C. The Cautious Expert. 192p. 1982. 91.00 (*0-335-10110-0*, Open Univ Pr) Taylor & Francis.
Quicke, John C., et al. Challenging Prejudice Through Education: The Story of a Mental Handicap Awareness Project. (Disability, Handicap & Life Chances Ser.). 195p. 1990. 65.00 (*1-85000-692-X*, Falmer Pr); pap. 30.00 (*1-85000-693-8*, Falmer Pr) Taylor & Francis.
Quicke, Juliet, jt. auth. see Quicke, Andrew.
Quickmire, Carolyn, jt. ed. see Moore, Alex.
Quie, Paul G., jt. ed. see Gallin, John I.
Quiel, John M., jt. auth. see Gill, James H.
Quiesser, Hans. The Conquest of the Microchip. 272p. 1990. pap. text ed. 9.95 (*0-674-16297-8*) HUP.
Quieti, R., ed. Piling & Deep Foundations: Proceedings of the 4th International Conference, Stresa, Italy, April 1991, 2 vols., Set. (Illus.). 1000p. (C). 1991. text ed. 225.00 (*90-6191-185-0*, Pub. by A A Balkema NE) Ashgate Pub Co.
Quigely, Joseph V. Vision: How Leaders Develop It, Share It, & Sustain It. LC 93-9582. 1993. text ed. 24.95 (*0-07-051084-9*) McGraw.
***Quigg, Chis, ed.** Annual Review of Nuclear & Particle Science, Vol. 45. 1995. lib. bdg. 62.00 (*0-8243-1545-6*) Annual Reviews.
Quigg, Chris. Gauge Theories of the Strong, Weak, & Electromagnetic Interactions. (Frontiers in Physics Ser.). 334p. (C). 1983. text ed. 51.75 (*0-8053-6020-4*, Adv Bk Prog) Addison-Wesley.
Quigg, Chris, ed. see American Institute of Physics.
Quigg, Chris, et al, eds. Annual Review of Nuclear & Particle Science, 1994, Vol. 44. (Illus.). 1994. text ed. 62.00 (*0-8243-1544-8*) Annual Reviews.
Quigg, H. Gerald, ed. Successful Capital Campaign: From Planning to Victory Celebration. 188p. 1986. 37.00 (*0-89964-248-9*) Coun Adv & Supp Ed.
Quigg, Philip W. Antarctica: The Continuing Experiment. LC 85-81558. (Headline Ser.: No. 273). (Illus.). 64p. (Orig.). 1985. pap. 5.95 (*0-87124-100-5*) Foreign Policy.
Quigg, Philip W., ed. Africa: A Foreign Affairs Reader. LC 75-40999. 346p. 1977. reprint ed. text ed. 59.75 (*0-8371-8713-3*, QUAF, Greenwood Pr) Greenwood.
Quiggin, Alison H. A Survey of Primitive Money: The Beginnings of Currency. LC 76-44779. reprint ed. 36.50 (*0-404-15964-8*) AMS Pr.
Quiggin, E. C. Prolegomena to the Study of the Later Irish Bards, 1200-1500. (Studies in Irish Literature, No. 16). 1970. reprint ed. pap. 19.95 (*0-8383-0064-2*) M S G Haskell Hse.
Quiggin, E. C., ed. Essays & Studies Presented to William Ridgeway on His Sixtieth Birthday, 6 August 1913. LC 67-22093. (Essay Index Reprint Ser.). 1977. 42.95 (*0-8369-0421-4*) Ayer.
Quiggin, John. Generalized Expected Utility Theory: The Rank Dependent Model. 224p. (C). 1992. lib. bdg. 73.00 (*0-7923-9302-3*) Kluwer Ac.
Quiggin, John, jt. auth. see Langmore, John.
Quiggle, James W. & Redman, Lipman. Procedure Before the IRS. 6th suppl. ed. LC 84-72251. (Illus.). 269p. 1987. 96.00 (*0-8318-0449-1*, B449/B533) Am Law Inst.
— Procedure Before the IRS - Pocket Supplement. 15p. 1987. pap. text ed. 11.00 (*0-8318-0533-1*, B533) Am Law Inst.
Quiggle, Kevin. COMAL Library of Functions & Procedures. (Amazing Adventures of Captain COMAL Ser.). (Illus.). 71p. (Orig.). (J). (gr. 6 up). 1984. pap. 14.95 (*0-928411-03-6*) COMAL Users.
Quigley. Handbook of Emergency Chemical Management. 1995. write for info. (*0-8493-8908-9*) CRC Pr.
***Quigley, A. A.** Green Is My Sky. 1983. 8.95 (*0-8159-5625-8*) Devin.
Quigley, Audrey. Chinese Landscape Painting for Beginners: A Practical Course. LC 93-14078. (Illus.). 64p. 1993. reprint ed. pap. 7.95 (*0-8069-0500-X*) Sterling.
Quigley, Austin E. The Modern Stage & Other Worlds. 352p. 1986. 42.50 (*0-416-39310-1*, 9273); pap. 13.95 (*0-416-39320-9*, 9274) Routledge Chapman & Hall.
Quigley, B. Allan, ed. Fulfilling the Promise of Adult & Continuing Education. LC 85-644750. (New Directions for Adult & Continuing Education Ser.: No. ACE 44). 1989. 16.95 (*1-55542-841-X*) Jossey-Bass.
Quigley, Betty. Never Be Afraid to Love Again. LC 90-91674. 192p. (Orig.). 1990. pap. 9.95 (*0-9626735-0-1*) Rabeth Pub Co.
— Our Master's Prayers: A Brief Story of Jesus' Life Based on His Prayers. (Illus.). 160p. (YA). 1991. 12.95 (*0-9626735-1-X*); pap. 7.50 (*0-9626735-3-6*) Rabeth Pub Co.
Quigley, Betty, ed. see James, I. M., pseud.
Quigley, Carroll. Anglo-American Establishment. 354p. reprint ed. pap. 12.95 (*0-945001-01-0*) GSG & Assocs.
— The Evolution of Civilizations. LC 79-4091. 1979. reprint ed. 20.00 (*0-913966-56-8*); reprint ed. pap. 7.00 (*0-913966-57-6*) Liberty Fund.
— Tragedy & Hope: A History of the World in Our Time. 1348p. 1995. text ed. 39.95 (*0-945001-10-X*) GSG & Assocs.
Quigley, Christine, comp. Death Dictionary: Over Fifty-Five Hundred Clinical, Legal, Literary & Vernacular Terms. LC 93-28817. 207p. 1994. lib. bdg. 29.95 (*0-89950-869-3*) McFarland & Co.
Quigley, Colin. Music from the Heart: Compositions of a Folk Fiddler. LC 93-39721. (Illus.). 288p. 1995. 35.00 (*0-8203-1637-7*) U of Ga Pr.
Quigley, Conor, ed. Completing the Internal Market Community: 1992 Legislation. 1990. pap. text ed. 75.00 (*1-85333-416-2*) Kluwer Ac.
Quigley, Conor, jt. auth. see Brealey, Mark.
Quigley, Conor, jt. ed. see Brealey, Mark.
Quigley, Declan. The Interpretation of Caste. LC 92-27757. (Oxford Studies in Social & Cultural Anthropology). (Illus.). 200p. 1993. 52.00 (*0-19-827882-9*, Clarendon Pr) OUP.
— The Interpretation of Caste. (Oxford Studies in Social & Cultural Anthropology). (Illus.). 200p. 1995. pap. 21.00 (*0-19-828027-0*) OUP.
Quigley, Declan, jt. ed. see Gellner, David N.
Quigley, Delia & Pitchford, Polly. Starting Over: Learning to Cook with Natural Foods. LC 87-33007. (Illus.). 144p. (Orig.). 1988. pap. 10.95 (*0-913990-55-8*) Book Pub Co.
Quigley, Delia, jt. auth. see Pitchford, Polly.
Quigley, Eamonn M. & Sorrell, Michael F. The Gastrointestinal Surgical Patient: Preoperative & Postoperative Care. (Illus.). 583p. 1994. 85.00 (*0-683-07001-0*) Williams & Wilkins.
Quigley, Elaine, jt. auth. see Buchter, Carol.
Quigley, Ellie. Perl by Example. 384p. 1994. pap. text ed. 21.75 (*0-13-122839-0*) P-H.
Quigley, Gary H. Homeless & Street People: Index of Modern Information. LC 88-47851. 150p. 1988. 39.50 (*0-88164-954-6*); pap. 34.50 (*0-88164-955-4*) ABBE Pubs Assn.
Quigley, Harold S. China's Politics in Perspective. LC 72-14000. (Illus.). 266p. 1973. reprint ed. text ed. 67.50 (*0-8371-6745-0*, QUCP, Greenwood Pr) Greenwood.
— Nineteen Thirty-Seven to Nineteen Forty-One. LC 73-3017. (Illus.). 369p. 1973. reprint ed. text ed. 65.00 (*0-8371-6835-X*, QUFE, Greenwood Pr) Greenwood.
Quigley, Harold S. & Turner, John E. The New Japan: Government & Politics. LC 74-10473. (Illus.). 456p. 1974. reprint ed. text ed. 75.00 (*0-8371-7689-1*, QUNJ, Greenwood Pr) Greenwood.
Quigley, Herbert K., Jr., pref. Proceedings of the Fourth Annual Conference & Exposition of the National Computer Graphics Association, Inc. (Illus.). 750p. (Orig.). 1983. pap. 20.00 (*0-941514-02-1*) Natl Comp Graphics.
Quigley, Hugh. The Cross & the Shamrock: An Irish-American Tale. LC 79-104546. reprint ed. lib. bdg. 19.50 (*0-8398-1650-2*) Irvington.
Quigley, Hugh & Clark, R. J. Republican Germany: A Political & Economic Study, 1919-1928. 1976. lib. bdg. 69.95 (*0-8490-2518-4*) Gordon Pr.
Quigley, James F., jt. auth. see McGonigle, Thomas D.
Quigley, Joan. What Does Joan Say? My Seven Years as White House Astrologer to Nancy & Ronald Reagan. 1990. 17.95 (*1-55972-032-8*, Birch Ln Pr) Carol Pub Group.
— What Does Joan Say? My Seven Years as White House Astrologer to Nancy & Ronald Reagan. 1991. mass mkt. 4.95 (*1-55817-473-7*, Pinnacle NY) Windsor NY.
Quigley, John. Palestine & Israel: A Challenge to Justice. LC 89-39218. 345p. (Orig.). (C). 1990. lib. bdg. 45.50 (*0-8223-1011-2*); pap. text ed. 20.95 (*0-8223-1023-6*) Duke.
— The Ruses for War: American Interventionism Since World War II. LC 92-19288. 310p. (C). 1992. 25.95 (*0-87975-767-1*) Prometheus Bks.
Quigley, John J., ed. see Jenks, Jeremiah W. & Clark, Walter E.
Quigley, John M. Housing Demand in the Short Run: An Analysis of Polytomous Choice. (Explorations in Economic Research Three Ser.: No. 1). 27p. 1976. reprint ed. 35.00 (*0-685-61397-6*) Natl Bur Econ Res.
Quigley, John M., ed. Perspectives on Local Public Finance & Public Policy, Vol. 1. 242p. 1983. 73.25 (*0-89232-257-8*) Jai Pr.
— Perspectives on Local Public Finance & Public Policy, Vol. 2. 1984. 73.25 (*0-89232-326-4*) Jai Pr.
— Perspectives on Local Public Finance & Public Policy, Vol. 3. 1987. 73.25 (*0-89232-648-4*) Jai Pr.
— Perspectives on Local Public Finance & Public Policy, Vol. 4. 1988. 73.25 (*0-89232-857-6*) Jai Pr.
Quigley, John M. & Rubinfeld, Daniel L., eds. American Domestic Priorities: An Economic Appraisal. LC 84-28013. (California Series in Real Estate Economics & Finance: No. 2). 398p. 1985. pap. 19.00 (*0-520-05522-5*) U CA Pr.
Quigley, John M. & Smolensky, Eugene, eds. Modern Public Finance. LC 93-23838. 362p. 1994. 39.95 (*0-674-58054-0*) HUP.
Quigley, John M. & Stinson, Debra. Levels of Property Tax Exemption: Part I, Sources of Basic Data & Part II, Tax Exemption in Central Cities & Suburbs, a Comparison Across States, No. 840. 1975. 6.00 (*0-686-20363-1*) CPL Biblios.
Quigley, John M., jt. auth. see Kain, John F.
***Quigley, Joseph V.** Vision: How Leaders Develop It, Share It, & Sustain It. 1994. pap. text ed. 14.95 (*0-07-051766-5*) McGraw.
***Quigley, Kathy.** Tika the Tiger. (Friends of the Forest Adventure Bks.). (Illus.). (J). (ps-8). 1995. 16.95 (*0-9641742-8-6*) Pequot Pubng.
Quigley, Kevin F., jt. ed. see Nau, Henry R.
Quigley, Martin. The Crooked Pitch: An Account of the Curveball in American Baseball History. (Illus.). 212p. 1984. 16.95 (*0-912697-08-3*) Algonquin Bks.
— Crooked Pitch: The Curveball in American Baseball History. (Illus.). 212p. 1988. reprint ed. pap. 9.95 (*0-912697-82-2*) Algonquin Bks.
***Quigley, Martin & Monush, Barry, eds.** First Century of Film. (Illus.). 432p. 1995. 49.50x (*0-900610-54-9*) Quigley Pub Co.
Quigley, Martin M., jt. ed. see Wolf, Don P.
Quigley, Martin S. Peace Without Hiroshima: Secret Action at the Vatican in Spring, 1945. 300p. 1991. 22.95 (*0-8191-8056-4*) Madison Bks UPA.
***Quigley, Mary A.** Trenton: A Capital Place. 1984. 22.95 (*0-89781-079-1*) Preferred Mktg.
Quigley, Pat. Creative Writing I: A Handbook for Teaching Classes Wherever Adults Gather. (Illus.). 98p. (Orig.). 1982. pap. 6.95 (*0-932910-40-8*) Potentials Development.
— Creative Writing II: A Handbook of Techniques for Effective Writing, Vol. II. 145p. (Orig.). 1983. pap. text ed. 7.95 (*0-932910-45-9*) Potentials Development.
***Quigley, Pat & Shroyer, Marilyn.** Making It Through the Night: How Couples Can Survive a Crisis Together. 300p. (Orig.). 1992. lib. bdg. 33.00x (*0-8095-5864-5*) Borgo Pr.
— Making It Through the Night: How Couples Can Survive a Crisis Together. 300p. (Orig.). 1992. pap. 12.95 (*0-943233-33-X*) Conari Press.
Quigley, Paxton. Armed & Female: Twelve Million American Women Own Guns, Should You? 1993. mass mkt. 4.99 (*0-312-95150-7*) St Martin.
Quigley, Raymond, ed. see James, I. M., pseud.
Quigley, Robert, jt. auth. see Sears, William.
Quigley, Robert D. Civil War Spoken Here: A Dictionary of Mispronounced People, Places & Things of the 1860s. 216p. 1993. pap. 12.00 (*0-9637745-0-6*) C W Hist.
Quigley, Stacy. Do I Have To? LC 85-24350. (Life & Living from a Child's Point of View Ser.). (Illus.). 32p. (J). (gr. k-6). 1980. lib. bdg. 19.97 (*0-8172-1352-X*) Raintree Steck-V.
Quigley, Stephen & Paul, Peter V. Language & Deafness. (Illus.). 296p. (C). 1991. reprint ed. pap. text ed. 29.50 (*1-879105-01-2*, A059) Singular Publishing.
Quigley, Stephen P., jt. auth. see King, C. M.
Quigley, Stephen P., jt. auth. see King, Cynthia M.
Quigley, Stephen P., ed. see McAnally, Patricia L., et al.
Quigley, Stephen P., jt. auth. see Paul, Peter V.
Quigley, Theresia M. The Child Hero in the Canadian Novel. 192p. (Orig.). Date not set. pap. 17.95 (*1-55021-069-6*, Pub. by NC Press CN) U of Toronto Pr.
Quigley, Thomas. Johannes Brahms: An Annotated Bibliography of the Literature Through 1982. LC 89-48412. (Illus.). 763p. 1990. 79.50 (*0-8108-2196-6*) Scarecrow.
Quigley, Thomas E., ed. American Catholics & Vietnam. LC 68-54102. 197p. reprint ed. pap. 56.20 (*0-8357-5357-3*, 2012814) Bks Demand.
Quigly, Isabel, tr. see Svevo, Livia V.
Quignard, Pascal. Albucius. (FRE.). 1992. pap. 10.95 (*0-7859-3169-4*, 2253059560) Fr & Eur.
— Albucius. Boone, Bruce, tr. (Illus.). 188p. (C). 1993. 35.00 (*0-932499-69-4*) Lapis Pr.
— All the World's Mornings: A Novel. Kirkup, James, tr. LC 93-2161. 112p. 1993. pap. 9.00 (*1-55597-203-9*) Graywolf.
— Carus. (FRE.). 1990. pap. 13.95 (*0-7859-2923-1*) Fr & Eur.
— Carus. (Folio Ser.: No. 2211). (FRE.). pap. 10.95 (*2-07-038301-6*) Schoenhof.
— Escaliers de Chambord. (Folio Ser.: No. 2301). (FRE.). 1971. pap. 9.95 (*2-07-038415-2*) Schoenhof.
— Les Escaliers de Chambord. (FRE.). 1991. pap. 12.95 (*0-7859-2927-4*) Fr & Eur.
— LeSalon du Wurtemburg. (FRE.). 1988. pap. 13.95 (*0-7859-2915-0*) Fr & Eur.
— Salon du Wurtemberg. (Folio Ser.: No. 1928). 432p. (FRE.). 1986. pap. 10.96 (*2-07-037928-0*) Schoenhof.
— Les Tablettes de Buis d'Apronenia Avtia. (FRE.). 1989. pap. 15.95 (*0-7859-2940-1*) Fr & Eur.
Quignon-Fleuret, Dominique. Mathieu. (CAL Art Ser.). (Illus.). 1977. 14.95 (*0-517-53086-4*, Crown) Crown Pub Group.
Quijano, Anibal. Nationalism & Capitalism in Peru: A Study in Neo-Imperialism. Lane, Helen R., tr. LC 78-163117. 128p. reprint ed. pap. 36.50 (*0-317-29067-3*, 2019255) Bks Demand.
Quijano, Mary L. Bloodmaster. 1989. pap. 3.95 (*1-55817-251-3*, Pinnacle NY) Windsor NY.
Quiko, Edo. The ABCs of State & Local Government in America. LC 81-51458. (Illus.). 70p. 1982. 9.95 (*0-88247-602-5*) R & E Pubs.
Quikrete Companies Staff. Build & Repair with Concrete: The Complete Do-It-Yourself Manual. LC 85-30139. (Illus.). 165p. 1986. 6.95 (*0-937558-16-8*) Scharff Ltd.
— Build & Repair with Concrete: The Complete Do-It-Yourself Manual. 2nd ed. LC 85-30139. (Illus.). 165p. 1986. 7.95 (*0-937558-18-4*) Scharff Ltd.
Quilan, Hamid, ed. see Sabiq, As-Sayyed.
Quilici, Alec, jt. auth. see Miller, Larry.
Quilici, Alexander E., jt. auth. see Miller, Lawrence H.
Quilici, Folco. Italy from the Air. 1987. 49.50 (*0-8109-1117-5*) Abrams.
***Quilis, Antonio & Hernandez Alonso, C.** Linguistica Aplicada a la Terapia Del Lenguaje. 552p. (SPA.). 1993. 125.00 (*84-249-1427-9*) Elliots Bks.
Quilis, Antonio & Niederehe, Hans J. The History of Linguistics in Spain. LC 86-17314. (Studies in the History of the Language Sciences: No. 34). viii, 360p. 1986. 84.00x (*90-272-4517-7*) Benjamins North Am.
Quill, Jeffrey. Birth of a Legend: The Spitfire. LC 86-60544. (Illus.). 160p. 1986. 32.50 (*0-87474-776-7*, QUBL) Smithsonian.
Quill, Lawrence L., ed. see AEC Technical Information Center Staff.
***Quill, Monica.** Nun Plussed. 1995. pap. 3.99 (*0-373-26187-X*, Wrldwide Lib) Harlequin Bks.
— Nun Plussed: A Sister Mary Teresa Mystery. 224p. 1993. 18.95 (*0-312-09890-1*) St Martin.
Quill, Timothy E. Death & Dignity: Making Choices & Taking Charge. 196p. 1993. 21.95 (*0-393-03448-8*) Norton.
— Death & Dignity: Making Choices & Taking Charge. 1994. pap. 10.95 (*0-393-31140-6*) Norton.
Quillen. Laboratory Manual T-A Therapeutic Modalities. 3rd ed. 192p. 1994. 19.95 (*0-8016-7921-4*) Mosby Yr Bk.
Quillen, D. G., et al. The Interface of Mathematics & Particle Physics. (Institute of Mathematics & Its Applications Conference Series, New Ser.: New Series 24). (Illus.). 240p. 1990. 55.00 (*0-19-853626-7*) OUP.
Quillen, Jim. Alcatraz from Inside. (Illus.). 164p. (Orig.). 1992. pap. 11.95 (*0-9625206-1-6*) Gldn Gate Natl Park Assoc.
Quillen, Maureen, jt. ed. see Anderson, Marc.
Quillen, Rita. Looking for Native Ground: Contemporary Appalachian Poetry. LC 89-83315. 1989. pap. 9.95 (*0-913239-58-5*) Appalach Consortium.
***Quillen, Rita S.** Counting the Sums. 64p. (Orig.). 1995. pap. 11.00 (*1-885912-04-8*) Sows Ear Pr.
Quillen, Roger K., jt. auth. see Hirsch, Jeffrey L.
Quiller-Couch, Arthur. Beauty & the Beast. (Illus.). 64p. 1991. 6.99 (*0-517-06630-0*, Pub. by Gramercy) Random Hse Value.
Quiller-Couch, Arthur, ed. The Oxford Book of Ballads, 2 vols in one. 800p. reprint ed. 55.00 (*0-403-08625-6*) Somerset Pub.
Quiller-Couch, Arthur & Du Maurier, Daphne. Castle D'Or. reprint ed. lib. bdg. 21.95 (*0-88411-148-2*, Aeonian Pr) Amereon Ltd.
Quiller-Couch, Arthur, ed. see Shakespeare, William.
Quiller-Couch, Arthur T. Adventures in Criticism. 1975. 59.95 (*0-87968-578-6*) Gordon Pr.
— Adventures in Criticism. (BCL1-PR English Literature Ser.). 408p. 1992. reprint ed. lib. bdg. 99.00 (*0-7812-7017-0*) Rprt Serv.
— Adventures in Criticism. LC 12-37963. 1969. reprint ed. 9.00 (*0-403-00064-5*) Scholarly.

— The Age of Chaucer. LC 75-155616. reprint ed. 29.00 (*0-404-05201-0*) AMS Pr.
— Cambridge Lectures. LC 72-4723. (Essay Index Reprint Ser.). 1977. reprint ed. 20.95 (*0-8369-2970-5*) Ayer.
— Charles Dickens & Other Victorians. (BCL1-PR English Literature Ser.). 240p. 1992. reprint ed. lib. bdg. 79.00 (*0-7812-7121-5*) Rprt Serv.
— Delectable Duchy: Stories, Studies & Sketches. LC 78-125235. (Short Story Index Reprint Ser.). 1977. 19.95 (*0-8369-3602-7*) Ayer.
— I Saw Three Ships, & Other Winter's Tales. LC 77-103527. (Short Story Index Reprint Ser.). 1977. reprint ed. 21.95 (*0-8369-4023-7*) Ayer.
— Laird's Luck: And Other Fireside Tales. LC 72-10767. (Short Story Index Reprint Ser.). 1977. reprint ed. 29.95 (*0-8369-4223-X*) Ayer.
— A Lecture on Lectures. LC 74-7042. (English Literature Ser.: No. 33). 1974. lib. bdg. 75.00 (*0-8383-1994-7*) M S G Haskell Hse.
— Noughts & Crosses. LC 77-103527. (Short Story Index Reprint Ser.). 1977. 19.95 (*0-8369-3269-2*) Ayer.
— Old Fires & Profitable Ghosts: A Book of Stories. LC 72-10813. (Short Story Index Reprint Ser.). 1977. reprint ed. 24.95 (*0-8369-4224-8*) Ayer.
— The Poet As a Citizen, & Other Papers. LC 75-41219. reprint ed. 27.50 (*0-404-14585-X*) AMS Pr.
— Studies in Literature. (BCL1-PR English Literature Ser.). 324p. 1992. reprint ed. lib. bdg. 89.00 (*0-7812-7018-9*) Rprt Serv.
— Studies in Literature - Second Series. (BCL1-PR English Literature Ser.). 301p. 1992. reprint ed. lib. bdg. 89.00 (*0-7812-7019-7*) Rprt Serv.
Quiller-Couch, Arthur T., ed. English Sonnets. LC 68-58821. (Granger Index Reprint Ser.). 1977. 15.95 (*0-8369-6038-6*) Ayer.
Quiller, Stephen. Acrylic Painting Techniques: How to Master the Medium of Our Age. LC 94-17459. (Illus.). 144p. 1994. 29.95 (*0-8230-0105-9*) Watsn-Guptill.
— Color Choices. (Illus.). 144p. 1989. 29.95 (*0-8230-0696-4*, Watsn-Guptill) Watsn-Guptill.
Quillet Staff. Dictionnaire Encylopedique Quillet, 10 vols., Set. (FRE.). 1977. 1,295.00 (*0-8288-5387-8*, M6139) Fr & Eur.
— Dictionnaire Quillet de la Langue Francais, 4 vols., Set. 2132p. (FRE.). 495.00 (*0-7859-0390-9*, M6153) Fr & Eur.
— Encyclopedie Illustree Du Monde Animal. (Illus.). 600p. (FRE.). 29.95 (*0-7859-0395-X*, M6218) Fr & Eur.
— Encyclopedie Illustree du Monde Animal. 175.00 (*0-8288-8147-2*, M6210) Fr & Eur.
— Encyclopedie Pratique de la Construction Du Batiment et Des Travaux Publics, 3 vols., Set. 3587p. (FRE.). 350.00 (*0-7859-0396-8*, M6232) Fr & Eur.
— Nouvelle Encyclopedie Autodidactique Quillet, 6 vols., Set. 668p. (FRE.). 1977. 695.00 (*0-8288-5504-8*, M6434) Fr & Eur.
Quilliam, Susan. Sexual Body Talk. (Illus.). 128p. 1992. pap. 15.95 (*0-88184-757-7*) Carroll & Graf.
— Women on Sex. LC 94-25589. 1994. 14.95 (*1-56980-025-1*) Barricade Bks.
Quillian, Thelma B. A Branch of Qullians from Ireland: Through Georgia to the Texas Lineage. (Illus.). 1984. write for info. (*0-318-58984-2*) Myriad.
Quilligan, Edward J., jt. ed. see Flamm, Bruce L.
Quilligan, Edward J., jt. auth. see Zuspan, Frederick P.
Quilligan, Edward J., jt. ed. see Zuspan, Frederick P.
Quilligan, Maureen. The Allegory of Female Authority: Christine de Pizan's Cite des Dames. LC 91-55069. 304p. 1992. 42.95 (*0-8014-2552-2*); pap. 15.95 (*0-8014-9788-4*) Cornell U Pr.
— The Language of Allegory: Defining the Genre. LC 78-74216. 312p. 1992. pap. 14.95 (*0-8014-8051-5*) Cornell U Pr.
— Milton's Spenser: The Politics of Reading. LC 83-45149. 256p. 1983. 33.50 (*0-8014-1590-X*) Cornell U Pr.
Quillin, Emerson. Listen, Honey: A Tribal History from Lewis & Clark to Custer. (Illus.). 112p. (Orig.). 1986. pap. 8.95 (*0-933002-03-3*) Cin Post.
Quillin, Martha A. Aerobic Dance: Fitness for Life. 128p. (C). 1992. pap. text ed. 24.95 (*0-8403-7626-X*) Kendall-Hunt.
Quillin, Noreen, jt. auth. see Quillin, Patrick.
Quillin, Patrick. Healing Nutrients. 1989. pap. 13.00 (*0-679-72187-8*, Vin) Random.
— Safe Eating. LC 90-42603. 252p. 1990. 19.95 (*0-87131-619-6*) M Evans.
Quillin, Patrick, ed. Adjuvant Nutrition in Cancer Treatment. (Illus.). 400p. (C). 1993. write for info. (*0-9638263-0-1*) Cancer Treatment.
Quillin, Patrick & Quillin, Noreen. Beating Cancer with Nutrition. 272p. (Orig.). 1995. pap. 14.95 (*0-9638372-0-6*) Nutrit Times.
Quillin, Patrick, jt. auth. see Smith, R. Philip.
***Quillin, Viv.** Pussyfooting: Self Defence Procedures for Cats. (Illus.). 96p. 1995. 10.00 (*1-56836-078-9*) Kodansha.
Quillinan, Carol, see Capper Sample, pseud..
Quillinan, Edward. Consolation; a Poem Addressed to Lady Brydges. Bd. with Monthermer; a Poem. LC 75-31249.; Sacrifice of Isabel. A Poem. LC 75-31249.; Elegiac Verses, Addressed to a Lady. LC 75-31249.; Woodcuts & Verses. LC 75-31249.; Carmina Brugensiana. Domestic Poems. LC 75-31249. LC 75-31249. (Romantic Context: Poetry 1789-1830 Ser.: Vol. 98). 1978. reprint ed. Set lib. bdg. 57.00 (*0-8240-2197-5*) Garland.
Quillinan, James V., et al. Transferring Property Without Probate, Pts. 1 & 2: Winter Action Guide, 1992, Pt. 2. Lester, Ellen, ed. 74p. 1992. write for info. (*0-318-69100-0*) Cont Ed Bar-CA.
Quilliot, Claude, ed. see Camus, Albert.
Quilliot, Roger, ed. see Camus, Albert.
Quillman. Nutrition & Diet Therapy. (Notes Ser.). 208p. 1989. 14.95 (*0-87434-205-8*) Springhouse Pub.
— SN: Nutrition & Diet Therapy. 2nd ed. 1993. 14.95 (*0-87434-612-6*) Springhouse Pub.
***Quillo, Ronald.** Catholic Answers to Questions about the New Age Movement. 64p. 1995. pap. 2.95 (*0-89243-764-2*) Liguori Pubns.
— Companions in Consciousness: The Bible & the New Age Movement. LC 93-33422. 192p. 1994. 18.95 (*0-89243-655-7*, Triumph Books) Liguori Pubns.
— Companions in Consciousness: The Bible & the New Age Movement. 192p. 1995. pap. 12.95 (*0-89243-824-X*) Liguori Pubns.
— Two Cultures of Belief: The Fallacy of Christian Certitude (a Systems Approach). 176p. 1995. pap. 14.95 (*0-89243-819-3*) Liguori Pubns.
Quillot, Claire & Quillot, Roger. L' Homme sur le Pavois. (FRE.). 1982. pap. 13.95 (*0-7859-4178-9*) Fr & Eur.
Quillot, Roger, jt. auth. see Quillot, Claire.
Quilt National Staff. Fiber Expressions: The Contemporary Quilt. LC 86-63763. (Illus.). 88p. 1987. pap. 12.95 (*0-88740-093-0*) Schiffer.
— The Quilt: New Directions for an American Tradition. LC 83-50843. (Illus.). 80p. 1983. pap. 10.95 (*0-916838-92-7*) Schiffer.
— Quilt National: Contemporary Designs in Fabric. LC 95-6494. (Illus.). 112p. 1995. 19.95 (*0-937274-85-2*) Lark Books.
Quilt San Diego Staff. Visions: Quilts, Layers of Excellence. Graves, Stevii T., ed. LC 94-1203. 1994. 19.95 (*0-914881-82-5*) C & T Pub.
— Visions - The Art of the Quilt. Nadel, Harold, ed. LC 92-53799. (Illus.). 96p. 1992. pap. 11.00 (*0-914881-54-X*) C & T Pub.
Quilter, Deborah, jt. auth. see Pascarelli, Emil.
Quilter, E. S. Searoom Handbook with Radar Anti-Collision Tables. LC 76-240. 177p. 1976. text ed., spiral bd. 15.00 (*0-87033-221-X*) Cornell Maritime.
Quilter, Jeffrey. Life & Death at Paloma: Society & Mortuary Practices in a Preceramic Peruvian Village. LC 88-31276. (Illus.). 203p. 1989. text ed. 29.95 (*0-87745-194-X*) U of Iowa Pr.
Quilter, Jeffrey, ed. see Higham, Charles & Thosarat, Rachanie.
Quilter, Jeffrey, ed. see Patterson, Thomas C.
Quilter, Jeffrey, ed. see Sheets, Payson D.
Quilter's Newsletter Magazine Editors & Leman, Bonnie. Star Spangled Sampler Quilts: The Art of the States. (Illus.). 64p. (Orig.). 1993. pap. 16.95 (*0-685-71057-2*) Leman Pubns.
Quilter's Newsletter Magazine Editors & Townswick, Jane. Classic Country Quilts: Step-by-Step Directions for 25 All-Time Favorites. LC 92-29542. 256p. 1993. 26.95 (*0-87596-573-3*, 11-752-0) Rodale Pr Inc.
Quilter's Newsletter Magazine Editors, jt. auth. see Leman, Bonnie.
***Quimby, D. M.** One of the Last. 1995. 19.95 (*0-533-11154-4*) Vantage.
Quimby, David S. PC Power: A Guide to DOS & Windows Systems for Computer-Literate Users. LC 92-21801. 272p. 1993. pap. 12.00 (*1-878956-30-2*) CBM Bks.
Quimby, Edith H. Radioactive Nuclides in Medicine & Biology. 3rd ed. LC 68-18868. 402p. reprint ed. pap. 114.60 (*0-317-26277-7*, 2055701) Bks Demand.
Quimby, Fred W., jt. auth. see Loeb, Walter.
Quimby, George I. Indian Culture & European Trade Goods: The Archaeology of the Historic Period in the Western Great Lakes Region. LC 78-4996. 217p. 1978. reprint ed. text ed. 35.00 (*0-313-20379-2*, QUIC, Greenwood Pr) Greenwood.
— Indian Life in the Upper Great Lakes 11,000 B. C. to A. D. 1800. LC 60-11799. (Illus.). 197p. pap. 56.20 (*0-8357-8919-5*, 2056768) Bks Demand.
Quimby, George I., jt. ed. see Casteel, Richard W.
Quimby, H. C. Genealogical History of the Quinby (Quimby) Family in England & America. (Illus.). 604p. 1993. reprint ed. lib. bdg. 104.00 (*0-8328-3051-8*); reprint ed. pap. 94.00 (*0-8328-3052-6*) Higginson Bk Co.
***Quimby, Ian M.** American Silver at Winterthur. LC 95-14228. (Illus.). 512p. (C). 1995. text ed. 75.00 (*0-912724-32-3*) Winterthur.
Quimby, Ian M., ed. Ceramics in America: Winterthur Conference Report 1972. LC 72-96715. (Winterthur Conference Report). 374p. 1980. reprint ed. pap. 16.95 (*0-8139-0476-5*) U Pr of Va.
— A Winterthur Bk., No. 7. (Winterthur Bk.). (Illus.). 1978. lib. bdg. 19.95 (*0-226-92133-6*) U Ch Pr.
— Winterthur Portfolio, No. 11. (Winterthur Bk.). (Illus.). 1978. lib. bdg. 19.95 (*0-226-92137-9*) U Ch Pr.
— Winterthur Portfolio, No. 12. (Winterthur Bk.). (Illus.). 1978. lib. bdg. 19.95 (*0-226-92138-7*) U Ch Pr.
— Winterthur Portfolio, No. 8: Thematic Issue on Religion in America. (Winterthur Bk.). (Illus.). 1978. lib. bdg. 19.95 (*0-226-92134-4*) U Ch Pr.
Quimby, Ian M. & Earl, Polly A., eds. Technological Innovation & the Decorative Arts Catalog: An Exhibition at the Hagley Museum Co-Sponsored by the Henry Francis Du Pont Winterthur Museum. (Illus.). 80p. 1984. reprint ed. pap. 16.95 (*0-8139-0569-9*) U Pr of Va.
Quimby, Ian M., jt. auth. see Doud, Richard K.
Quimby, Maureen. Eleutherian Mills. (Illus.). 92p. 1985. pap. 5.95 (*0-914650-04-1*) Hagley Museum.
Quimby, Phineas P. Immanuel. 109p. 1960. reprint ed. spiral bd. 6.60 (*0-7873-0687-8*) Mokelumne.
— Phineas Parkhurst Quimby: The Complete Writings, 3 vols., Vol. 1. LC 80-70090. 436p. 1988. 25.00 (*0-87516-600-8*) DeVorss.
— Phineas Parkhurst Quimby: The Complete Writings, 3 vols., Vol. 2. LC 80-70090. 417p. 1988. 25.00 (*0-87516-601-6*) DeVorss.
— Phineas Parkhurst Quimby: The Complete Writings, 3 vols., Vol. 3. LC 80-70090. 436p. 1988. 25.00 (*0-87516-602-4*) DeVorss.
Quimby, Thomas H. Recycling: the Alternative to Disposal: A Case Study of the Potential for Increased Recycling of Newspapers & Corrugated Containers in the Washington Metropolitan Area. LC 74-6836. 144p. reprint ed. pap. 41.10 (*0-317-41739-8*, 2020949) Bks Demand.
Quimio, T. H., jt. ed. see Chang, S. T.
***Quin-Hamlin, Janet.** Trade Winds. Creative Media Applications Staff, ed. 256p. (Orig.). 1993. pap. text ed. write for info. (*1-884066-00-3*) NBC Inc.
Quin-Harki. Tess & All. (Friends Ser.: No. 4). 1991. mass mkt. 3.50 (*0-06-106066-6*, Harp PBks) HarpC.
Quin-Harkin. Apartment. 1994. mass mkt. 3.50 (*0-06-106153-0*, Harp PBks) HarpC.
— The Boy Next Door. (Love Stories Ser.: No. 4). 1995. mass mkt. 3.50 (*0-553-56663-6*) Bantam.
— Four's a Crowd. (TGIF Ser.: No. 3). (J). 1995. pap. 3.50 (*0-671-51019-3*) PB.
Quin-Harkin, Janet. Amazing Grace. 1993. mass mkt. 4.50 (*0-06-108020-9*, Harp PBks) HarpC.
— Boy Trouble for Tess & Ali. (Friends Ser.: No. 3). (YA). 1991. mass mkt. 3.50 (*0-06-106065-8*, Harp PBks) HarpC.
— Fool's Gold. 1991. mass mkt. 4.50 (*0-06-104040-1*, Harp PBks) HarpC.
— Friends: Starring Tess & Ali, Vol. 1. 1991. mass mkt. 3.50 (*0-06-106063-1*, Harp PBks) HarpC.
— Ginger's New Crush. LC 94-21666. (Boysie Bks.: No. 5). (Illus.). 176p. (J). (gr. 3-6). 1994. pap. text ed. 2.95 (*0-8167-3418-6*, Rainbow NJ) Troll Assocs.
— Graduation Day. (Senior Year Ser.: No. 4). (YA). 1992. mass mkt. 3.50 (*0-06-106096-8*, Harp PBks) HarpC.
— Homecoming Dance. (Senior Year Ser.: No. 1). (YA). 1991. mass mkt. 3.50 (*0-06-106093-3*, Harp PBks) HarpC.
— Karen's Perfect Match. LC 94-14327. (Boyfriend Club Ser.: No. 3). 176p. (J). (gr. 4-7). 1994. pap. 2.95 (*0-8167-3416-X*, Little Rainbow) Troll Assocs.
— Magic Growing Powder. LC 80-18019. (Illus.). 48p. (J). (ps-3). 1981. 5.95 (*0-8193-1037-9*); lib. bdg. 5.95 (*0-8193-1038-7*) Parents.
— My Phantom Love. (Changes Romance Ser.: No. 1). (YA). (gr. 7 up). 1992. mass mkt. 3.50 (*0-06-106770-9*, Harp PBks) HarpC.
— New Year's Eve. (Senior Year Ser.: No. 2). (YA). 1991. mass mkt. 3.50 (*0-06-106094-1*, Harp PBks) HarpC.
— Night of the Prom. (Senior Year Ser.: No. 3). (YA). (gr. 7 up). 1992. mass mkt. 3.50 (*0-06-106095-X*, Harp PBks) HarpC.
— On My Own. (Changes Romance Ser.: No. 10). (YA). 1992. mass mkt. 3.50 (*0-06-106722-9*, Harp PBks) HarpC.
— Queen Justine. LC 94-12252. (Boyfriend Club Ser.: Vol. 4). 176p. (J). (gr. 3-6). 1994. pap. 2.95 (*0-8167-3417-8*) Troll Assocs.
— Roni's Dream Boy, No. 2. LC 93-50680. (Boyfriend Club Ser.: No. 2). (Illus.). 176p. (J). (gr. 3-6). 1994. pap. 2.95 (*0-8167-3415-1*) Troll Assocs.
— Roni's Two-Boy Trouble. LC 94-27321. (Boyfriend Club Ser.). 176p. (J). (gr. 3-6). 1994. pap. text ed. 2.95 (*0-8167-3419-4*, Rainbow NJ) Troll Assocs.
— Septimus Bean & His Amazing Machine. LC 79-163. (Illus.). 48p. (J). (ps-3). 1980. 5.95 (*0-8193-0999-0*) Parents.
— Sutcliffe Diamonds. (YA). 1994. pap. 3.50 (*0-06-106192-1*) HarpC Child Bks.
— Tess & Ali & the Teeny Bikini. (Friends Ser.: No. 02). (YA). 1991. mass mkt. 3.50 (*0-06-106064-X*, Harp PBks) HarpC.
Quin, Louis D. & Verkade, John G., eds. Phosphorus Chemistry: Proceedings of the International Conference, 1981. LC 81-14956. (ACS Symposium Ser.: No. 171). 1981. 65.95 (*0-8412-0663-5*) Am Chemical.
— Phosphorus 31 NMR Spectral Properties in Compound Characterization & Structural Analysis. LC 94-13378. (Methods in Stereochemical Analysis Ser.). 455p. 1994. 150.00 (*1-56081-637-6*) VCH Pubs.
Quin, Louis D., jt. ed. see Verkade, John G.
Quin, Mike. The Big Strike. LC 79-14101. 1991. reprint ed. pap. 7.50 (*0-7178-0504-2*) Intl Pubs Co.
Quina, James. Effective Secondary Teaching: Going Beyond the Bell Curve. 494p. (C). 1990. text ed. 44.00 (*0-06-045473-3*) HarpCollege.
Quina, Kathryn & Carlson, Nancy. Rape, Incest, & Sexual Harassment: A Guide for Helping Survivors. LC 89-16160. 275p. 1989. text ed. 55.00 (*0-275-92533-1*, C2533, Praeger Pubs) Greenwood.
Quina, Kathryn, jt. ed. see Bronstein, Phyllis.
Quinan, Jack. Frank Lloyd Wright's Larkin Building: Myth & Fact. (Illus.). 118p. 1990. reprint ed. pap. 17.95 (*0-262-67003-8*) MIT Pr.
***Quinanes, Matthew M.** Win the War on Drugs Without Firing a Shot. 112p. (YA). Date not set. pap. 12.95 (*1-56167-214-9*) Am Literary Pr.
Quinault, Roland E., jt. ed. see O'Brien, Patrick K.
Quinava, Ruby M. Menopause: Medical Research & Reference Guidebook. LC 84-45168. 150p. 1985. 37.50 (*0-88164-170-7*); pap. 34.50 (*0-88164-171-5*) ABBE Pubs Assn.
Quinby, E. J. Ida Was a Tramp. (Illus.). 277p. 1975. 12.00 (*0-911868-78-X*, C78) Carstens Pubns.
— Interurban Interlude: NJRT. (Illus.). 98p. 1968. 14.95 (*0-911868-04-6*, C76) Carstens Pubns.
Quinby, Henry C., ed. New England Family History. (Illus.). 866p. 1992. reprint ed. lib. bdg. 88.00 (*0-8328-2436-4*) Higginson Bk Co.
Quinby, Lee. Anti-Apocalypse: Exercises in Genealogical Criticism. LC 93-28600. 1994. text ed. 44.95 (*0-8166-2278-7*); pap. 17.95 (*0-8166-2279-5*) U of Minn Pr.
— Freedom, Foucault, & the Subject of America. 192p. 1991. text ed. 27.50 (*1-55553-108-3*) NE U Pr.
***Quinby, Lee, ed.** Genealogy & Literature. LC 95-739. 1995. text ed. 49.95 (*0-8166-2560-3*); pap. text ed. 19.95 (*0-8166-2561-1*) U of Minn Pr.
Quinby, Lee, jt. ed. see Diamond, Irene.
Quinby, Marge M. I Found My Family: An Orphan's Search. Pappas, Irene, ed. LC 93-87456. (Illus.). 160p. (Orig.). 1994. pap. write for info. (*0-9627478-3-1*) Oceanside Pr.
— Simple Steps to U. S. Citizenship: Bilingual Spanish & English. Sowers, Marjorie, ed. Contreras, Olga, tr. LC 93-87459. (Illus.). 112p. 1994. pap. text ed. 16.95 (*0-9627478-2-3*) Oceanside Pr.
— Simple Steps to U. S. Citizenship: Complete Information Needed to Obtain U. S. Citizenship. Gallery, Lee, ed. LC 90-62900. (Illus.). 102p. (Orig.). 1990. pap. text ed. 12.95 (*0-9627478-0-7*) Oceanside Pr.
— Simple Steps to U. S. Citizenship: Complete Information Needed to Obtain U. S. Citizenship. rev. ed. Gallery, Lee, ed. LC 92-83769. (Illus.). 100p. (Orig.). 1993. pap. 14.95 (*0-9627478-1-5*) Oceanside Pr.
Quincannon, Alan, ed. Lifestyles of Colonial America. (Learning & Coloring Bks.). (Illus.). 24p. (Orig.). (J). (gr. k-6). 1992. pap. 3.95 (*1-878452-10-X*) Tory Corner Editions.
— More Soldiers of Colonial America. (Learning & Coloring Bks.). (Illus.). 24p. (Orig.). (J). (gr. k-6). 1992. pap. 3.95 (*1-878452-12-6*) Tory Corner Editions.
— People of Colonial America. (Learning & Coloring Bks.). (Illus.). 20p. (Orig.). (J). (gr. k-6). 1992. pap. 3.95 (*1-878452-09-6*) Tory Corner Editions.
— Soldiers of Colonial America. (Learning & Coloring Bks.). (Illus.). 24p. (Orig.). (J). (gr. k-6). 1992. pap. 3.95 (*1-878452-11-8*) Tory Corner Editions.
Quince, R. Strategic Programme for Innovation & Technology Transfer (Sprint) (EUR Ser.: No. 14643). 182p. 1993. pap. 25.00 (*92-826-5627-6*, CD-NA-14643-EN-C, Pub. by Europ Com) UNIPUB.
Quincy, Joseph. The History of Harvard University, 2 vols., 1. Metzger, Walter P., ed. LC 76-55188. (Academic Profession Ser.). (Illus.). 1977. reprint ed. lib. bdg. 56.95 (*0-405-10016-7*) Ayer.
— The History of Harvard University, 2 vols., 2. Metzger, Walter P., ed. LC 76-55188. (Academic Profession Ser.). (Illus.). 1977. reprint ed. lib. bdg. 56.95 (*0-405-10017-5*) Ayer.
— The History of Harvard University, 2 vols., Set. Metzger, Walter P., ed. LC 76-55188. (Academic Profession Ser.). (Illus.). 1977. reprint ed. lib. bdg. 111.95 (*0-405-10015-9*) Ayer.
Quincy, Josiah. Memoir of the Life of Josiah Quincy. LC 78-146274. (Era of the American Revolution Ser.). 1971. reprint ed. lib. bdg. 55.00 (*0-306-70098-0*) Da Capo.
Quincy, Josiah, Jr. Memoir of the Life of Josiah Quincy, Jr. (American Biography Ser.). 498p. 1991. reprint ed. lib. bdg. 89.00 (*0-7812-8319-1*) Rprt Serv.
Quincy, Keith. How Things Work: Notes on Economic Policy. 194p. (Orig.). (C). 1991. pap. text ed. 19.50 (*0-8191-8190-0*) U Pr of Amer.
— Samuel. 255p. (Orig.). 1991. pap. 5.95 (*0-9628648-0-3*) Smidgen Bks.
Quincy, Kieth. Hmong: History of a People. (Illus.). 216p. 1988. pap. 12.95 (*0-910055-07-6*) East Wash Univ.
Quincy, Matthew. Diet Right! The Consumer's Guide to Diet & Weight Loss Programs. 128p. (Orig.). 1991. reprint ed. lib. bdg. 23.00x (*0-8095-5855-6*) Borgo Pr.
Quincy, William S. The Three-Masted Schooner James Miller: A History & Model Maker's Source Book. (Illus.). 48p. 1986. pap. 9.95 (*0-913372-37-4*) Mystic Seaport.
Quindlen, Anna. Living out Loud. 272p. 1994. pap. 12.00 (*0-449-90912-3*, Columbine) Fawcett.
— Living out Loud. 272p. 1989. mass mkt. 5.99 (*0-8041-0527-8*) Ivy Books.
— Object Lessons. 1992. mass mkt. 5.99 (*0-8041-0946-X*) Ivy Books.
— Object Lessons. large type ed. LC 91-26508. 471p. 1991. reprint ed. lib. bdg. 20.95 (*1-56054-251-9*) Thorndike Pr.
— One True Thing. 1994. 22.00 (*0-679-40712-X*) Random.
— One True Thing. large type ed. LC 94-24046. (Wheeler Large Print Book Series). 1995. 25.95 (*1-56895-168-X*) Wheeler Pub.
— Thinking Out Loud: On the Personal, the Political, the Public, & the Private. 304p. 1993. 22.00 (*0-679-40711-1*) Random.
— Thinking Out Loud: On the Personal, the Political, the Public & the Private. 320p. 1994. pap. 12.00 (*0-449-90905-0*, Columbine) Fawcett.
— Thinking Out Loud: On the Personal, the Political, the Public & the Private. braille ed. 432p. 1993. vinyl bd. 34.56 (*1-56956-432-9*, BR9228) W A T Braille.
— The Tree That Came to Stay. LC 91-31957. (Illus.). 32p. (J). (ps-4). 1992. 14.00 (*0-517-58145-0*) Crown Bks Yng Read.
Quindry, Kenneth E. & Schoening, Niles. State & Local Tax Performance Nineteen Seventy-Eight. rev. ed. 1980. pap. 3.00 (*0-686-29037-2*) S Regional Ed.
Quine, Hector. Guitar Technique. (Illus.). 112p. 1990. 26.95 (*0-19-322323-6*) OUP.
Quine, Judith B. The Bridesmaids. Rubenstein, Julie, ed. 576p. 1990. mass mkt. 5.95 (*0-671-70770-1*) PB.
Quine, Lyn, jt. auth. see Rutter, D. R.
***Quine, Maria S.** Population Politics in Twentieth Century Europe: Fascist Dictatorships & Liberal Democracies. LC 95-8636. (Historical Connections Ser.). Date not set. write for info. (*0-415-08069-X*) Routledge.

P Q

An Asterisk (*) at the beginning of an entry indicates that the title is appearing in BIP for the first time.

Quine, W. V. Pursuit of Truth. rev. ed. LC 92-5606. 114p. (C). 1992. pap. text ed. 12.95 (0-674-73951-5) HUP.
— Selected Logic Papers. enl. ed. LC 94-28372. 320p. 1995. text ed. 45.00 (0-674-79836-8, QUISEL); pap. text ed. 16.95 (0-674-79837-6, QUISEY) HUP.
Quine, W. V. & Ullian, J. S. The Web of Belief. 2nd ed. 1978. text ed. write for info. (0-07-553609-9) McGraw.
Quine, Willard V. Algebraic Logic & Predicate Functors. LC 71-157092. 1971. reprint ed. pap. text ed. 3.95 (0-672-61267-4) Irvington.
— Elementary Logic. rev. ed. LC 80-81978. 144p. (C). 1980. pap. 10.95 (0-674-24451-6) HUP.
— Elementary Logic. rev. ed. LC 80-81978. 144p. (C). 1990. 23.45 (0-674-24450-8) HUP.
— From a Logical Point of View: Nine Logico-Philosophical Essays. 2nd rev. ed. LC 61-15277. 200p. 1961. 26.50 (0-674-32350-5) HUP.
— From a Logical Point of View: Nine Logico-Philosophical Essays. 2nd rev. ed. LC 61-15277. 200p. 1980. pap. 12.95 (0-674-32351-3) HUP.
— From Stimulus to Science. LC 95-14062. 144p. (C). 1995. text ed. 22.95 (0-674-32635-0) HUP.
— The Logic of Sequences: A Generalization of Principia Mathematica. (Harvard Dissertations in Philosophy Ser.). 304p. 1990. reprint ed. 25.00 (0-8240-3210-1) Garland.
— Mathematical Logic. rev. ed. LC 51-7541. 358p. 1981. pap. 15.00 (0-674-55451-5) HUP.
— Methods of Logic. 4th ed. (Illus.). 344p. 1982. pap. 16.95 (0-674-57176-2) HUP.
— Ontological Relativity & Other Essays. LC 72-91121. (John Dewey Lectures Ser.: No. 1). 1977. pap. text ed. 16.00 (0-231-08357-2) Col U Pr.
— Philosophical Problems Today, Vol. 1. Flistad, Guttorm, ed. LC 93-38219. 224p. (C). 1994. lib. bdg. 115.00 (0-7923-2564-8) Kluwer Ac.
— Philosophy of Logic. 2nd ed. 128p. 1986. pap. 10.95 (0-674-66563-5) HUP.
— Pursuit of Truth. 128p. 1990. 23.50 (0-674-73950-7) HUP.
— Quiddities: An Intermittently Philosophical Dictionary. LC 87-11974. 288p. 1987. 32.00 (0-674-74351-2) HUP.
— Quiddities: An Intermittently Philosophical Dictionary. 288p. 1989. reprint ed. pap. text ed. 9.95 (0-674-74352-0) HUP.
— Set Theory & Its Logic. rev. ed. LC 68-14271. 378p. 1969. pap. 14.95 (0-674-80207-1) Belknap Pr.
— Theories & Things. 225p. 1986. pap. 12.95 (0-674-87926-0) Belknap Pr.
— The Ways of Paradox & Other Essays. enl. rev. ed. LC 75-19554. 364p. 1976. pap. 14.95 (0-674-94837-8) HUP.
— Word & Object. 1960. pap. 15.00 (0-262-67001-1) MIT Pr.
Quine, Willard V. & Carnap, Rudolf. Dear Carnap, Dear Van: The Quine-Carnap Correspondence & Related Work. 499p. 1990. 45.00 (0-520-06847-5) U CA Pr.
Quine, Willard V. & Ullian, J. S. The Web of Belief. 2nd ed. 1978. pap. text ed. 10.50 (0-394-32179-0) Random.
Quine, Willard van Orman. The Time of My Life: An Autobiography. (Illus.). 384p. 1985. 35.00 (0-262-17003-5, Bradford Bks) MIT Pr.
Quiner, Barry, ed. see Lange, Steve.
Quiner, Barry, ed. see Quiner, Krista.
***Quiner, Krista.** Kim Zmeskal: Determination to Win. Quiner, Barry & Bailey, Cara, eds. LC 94-79473. (Illus.). 200p. (Orig.). (J). (gr. 5-12). 1995. pap. 9.95 (0-9643460-0-1) Bradford Bk.
— Shannon Miller: America's Most Decorated Gymnast. Quiner, Barry & Bailey, Cara, eds. (Illus.). 248p. (Orig.). (J). (gr. 5-12). 1995. pap. 11.95 (0-9643460-1-X) Bradford Bk.
Quinet, Bart. Cooked: Dope Poems. 32p. 1992. pap. 5.00 (1-885710-09-7) Geekspeak Unique.
— Trammeled. 20p. 1992. pap. 5.00 (1-885710-07-0) Geekspeak Unique.
Quiney, Anthony. English Domestic Architecture: Kent Houses. (Illus.). 300p. 1993. 69.50 (1-85149-153-8) Antique Collect.
— John Loughborough Pearson. LC 79-9832. 1979. 80.00 (0-300-02253-0) Yale U Pr.
— The Traditional Buildings of England. LC 89-51819. (Illus.). 224p. 1990. 29.95 (0-500-34110-9) Thames Hudson.
— The Traditional Buildings of England. LC 89-51819. (Illus.). 224p. 1995. per., pap. 18.95 (0-500-27661-7) Thames Hudson.
Quinghua, Du, jt. ed. see Tanaka, Masataka.
Quinion, D. W. & Quinion, G. R. Control of Groundwater. 50p. 1987. 10.00 (0-7277-0362-5, Pub. by T Telford UK) Am Soc Civil Eng.
Quinion, G. R., jt. auth. see Quinion, D. W.
Quinion, Michael B. Cidermaking. 1989. pap. 25.00 (0-85263-614-8, Pub. by Shire UK) St Mut.
Quinitchette, Lucille. Where Do Bumblebees Live? (Illus.). 13p. (Orig.). (J). (gr. 4). 1994. pap. 5.95 (0-9640122-1-9) Pen & Pr Unltd.
Quinlan, jt. auth. see Harrow.
Quinlan, Beverly A., jt. auth. see Letts, Marceil F.
Quinlan, Daniel A. & Prasad, Marehalli G., eds. Noise-Con 91: Twenty Years of Progress & Future Trends: Proceedings of Noise-Con 91. (Noise-Con Ser.). xviii, 766p. 1991. pap. 75.00 (0-931784-22-0) Noise Control.
Quinlan, David. The Illustrated Guide to Film Directors. LC 83-10572. (Illus.). 336p. 1983. 44.00 (0-389-20408-0, N7293) B&N Imports.
— Quinlan's Illustrated Directory of Film Character Actors. (Illus.). 160p. 1993. 39.95 (0-7134-7041-0, Pub. by Batsford UK) Trafalgar.
— Quinlan's Illustrated Guide to Film Directors. (Illus.). 336p. 1992. pap. 39.95 (0-7134-6833-5, Pub. by Batsford UK) Trafalgar.
— Quinlan's Illustrated Registry of Film Stars. (Illus.). 496p. 1991. 39.95 (0-8050-1839-5) H Holt & Co.
***Quinlan, Edwin G.** Flight Instructors Lesson Plan Handbook: Airline Pilot Training for Private-Commercial Instrument Certificates-Rating, Based on the FAA Practical Test Standards. 240p. 1995. spiral bd., pap. 34.95 (0-9641188-0-7) Aviators Pub.
Quinlan, Hamid, ed. see Abdul Fattah Rashid Hamid.
Quinlan, Hamid, ed. see Abdulhamid Jodah Al Sahhar.
Quinlan, Hamid, ed. see Abu-Saud, Mahmoud.
Quinlan, Hamid, ed. see Choudhury, Masudul A.
Quinlan, Hamid, ed. see El Liwaru, Saidi J. & El Liwaru, Maisha Z.
Quinlan, Hamid, ed. see Kishta, Leila.
Quinlan, J. Ross. Applications of Expert Systems, Vol. 1. 224p. (C). 1987. text ed. 26.95 (0-201-17449-9) Addison-Wesley.
— Applications of Expert Systems, Vol. 2. 1989. text ed. 36.75 (0-201-41655-7) Addison-Wesley.
Quinlan, James E. History of Sullivan County. rev. ed. Gold, David M., ed. & intro. by. LC 93-83400. xi, 239p. (Orig.). 1993. reprint ed. pap. 19.95 (0-9636097-0-X) Marielle Pr.
Quinlan, John. God Is with You: Hospital Notes & Prayers. 55p. (Orig.). 1986. pap. 1.95 (0-86217-252-7, Pub. by Veritas Publns IE) Ignatius Pr.
***Quinlan, Joseph P.** Vietnam: Business Opportunities & Risks. LC 94-67837. 178p. (Orig.). 1994. pap. 19.95 (1-881896-10-2) Pacific View Pr.
Quinlan, Kieran. John Crowe Ransom's Secular Faith. LC 88-7850. (Southern Literary Studies). xxii, 152p. 1989. text ed. 24.95 (0-8071-1471-5) La State U Pr.
Quinlan, Kimberly & Kelly, Maura, eds. College Admissions Data Handbook, 1993-94 Edition, 4 vols. 3300p. (Orig.). 1993. Northeast reg. vol. pap. 48.00 (1-878172-23-9); Southeast reg. vol. pap. 48.00 (1-878172-24-7); Midwest reg. vol. pap. 48.00 (1-878172-25-5); West reg. vol. pap. 48.00 (1-878172-26-3) Wintergrn-Orchard Hse.
— College Admissions Data Handbook, 1993-94 Edition, 4 vols., Set. 3300p. (Orig.). 1993. boxed, pap. 160.00 (1-878172-21-2); ring bd. 175.00 (1-878172-22-0) Wintergrn-Orchard Hse.
— College Admissions Index of Majors & Sports, 1993-94 Edition. 440p. (Orig.). 1993. pap. 28.00 (1-878172-27-1) Wintergrn-Orchard Hse.
Quinlan, Marge. Rescue of Landmark: Frank Lloyd Wright's Darwin Martin House. 1990. pap. 9.95 (0-9620314-7-X) Meyer Enter.
Quinlan, Maurice J. Samuel Johnson: A Layman's Religion. (Illus.). 256p. 1963. 20.00 (0-299-03030-X) U of Wis Pr.
— William Cowper: A Critical Life. LC 79-106670. 251p. 1970. reprint ed. text ed. 55.00 (0-8371-3425-0, QUWC, Greenwood Pr) Greenwood.
***Quinlan, Michael.** Little Lost Angel. Zion, Claire, ed. 320p. (Orig.). 1995. mass mkt. 5.50 (0-671-88468-9) PB.
— A Place of Dreams: The Lough Gur People. 156p. 1993. pap. 13.95 (0-86278-291-0, Pub. by OBrien Pr IE) Dufour.
Quinlan, Nonie. Champions in 3-D. Bell, Rob, ed. (Champions Ser.). (Illus.). 160p. (Orig.). (C). 1990. pap. 16.00 (1-55806-109-6, 411) Iron Crown Ent Inc.
Quinlan, P. M. Espanol Rapido. 170p. 1976. 30.00 (0-249-38828-6) St Mut.
Quinlan, Patricia. Anna's Red Sled. (Illus.). 24p. (J). (ps-2). 1989. 12.95 (1-55037-073-1, Pub. by Annick CN); pap. 4.95 (1-55037-072-3, Pub. by Annick CN) Firefly Bks Ltd.
— Emma's Sea Journey. (Illus.). 24p. (J). (ps-3). 1991. lib. bdg. 15.95 (1-55037-179-7, Pub. by Annick CN); pap. 5.95 (1-55037-177-0, Pub. by Annick CN) Firefly Bks Ltd.
— My Dad Takes Care of Me. (Illus.). 24p. (J). (ps-3). 1987. lib. bdg. 14.95 (0-920303-79-X, Pub. by Annick CN); pap. 4.95 (0-920303-76-5, Pub. by Annick CN) Firefly Bks Ltd.
— Planting Seeds. (Illus.). 24p. (J). (ps-2). 1988. lib. bdg. 14.95 (1-55037-007-3, Pub. by Annick CN); pap. 4.95 (1-55037-006-5, Pub. by Annick CN) Firefly Bks Ltd.
— Tiger Flowers. LC 93-15214. (J). 1994. 13.99 (0-8037-1407-6); lib. bdg. 13.89 (0-8037-1408-4) Dial Bks Young.
Quinlan, Paul D. Clash over Romania: British & American Policies Toward Romania, 1938-1947. (American Romanian Academy Ser.: Vol. II). 1977. 6.00 (0-686-23263-1) Am Romanian.
— The Playboy King: Carol II of Romania. LC 94-46945. (Contributions to the Study of World History Ser.: No. 52). 288p. 1995. text ed. 55.00 (0-313-29519-0, Greenwood Pr) Greenwood.
Quinlan, Paul D., et al. The United States & Romania: American-Romanian Relations in the 20th Century, Vol. VI. 180p. (Orig.). 1988. text ed. 22.00 (0-912131-07-1); pap. text ed. 17.00 (0-318-37920-1) Am Romanian.
Quinlan, Philip T. Connectionism & Psychology: A Psychological Perspective on New Connectionist Research. 320p. 1991. lib. bdg. 49.95 (0-226-69960-9); pap. text ed. 24.95 (0-226-69961-7) U Ch Pr.
Quinlan, Ray. Canal Walks of England & Wales. (Illus.). 576p. 1994. boxed 50.00 (0-7509-0608-1) A Sutton Pub.
Quinlan, Richard M., jt. auth. see Tanford, J. Alexander.
Quinlan, Ross. C4.5: Programs for Machine Learning. LC 92-32653. (Representation & Reasoning Ser.). 302p. 1992. 49.95 (1-55860-238-0) Morgan Kaufmann.
Quinlan, Sterling. Something in Between. LC 94-16295. 1994. 18.50 (0-8076-1364-9) Braziller.
Quinlan, Susan C. The Female Voice in Contemporary Brazilian Narrative. LC 91-27454. (American University Studies: Latin American Literature: Ser. XXII, Vol. 7). 205p. (C). 1992. text ed. 40.95 (0-8204-1281-3) P Lang Pubs.
***Quinlan, Susan E.** Case of Mummified Pigs: And Other Mysteries in Nature. (Illus.). 128p. (J). (gr. 3-6). 1995. 15.95 (1-878093-82-7) Boyds Mills Pr.
Quinlan, Tom. Who Are Your Today? A Survivors Handbook for Substitute Teachers. (Illus.). vi, 82p. 1985. pap. 6.95 (0-9615691-0-7) Queue Prodns.
Quinlen, Anna. Living out Loud. 1988. 17.95 (0-394-56964-4) Random.
Quinley, Eva D., et al, eds. Immunohematology: Principles & Practice. LC 92-49056. 1993. 44.95 (0-397-54915-6) Lippincott.
Quinley, Harold E. & Glock, Charles Y. Anti-Semitism In America. LC 83-4956. 259p. 1983. reprint ed. pap. 21.95 (0-87855-940-X) Transaction Pubs.
***Quinley, Kevin.** Winning Strategies for Negotiating Claims. 256p. (Orig.). 1995. pap. 29.95 (1-56842-045-5) Marshall & Swift.
Quinley, Kevin M. Claims Management: How to Select, Manage, & Save Money on Adjusting Services. LC 92-18594. 252p. 1992. 46.50 (0-934753-67-9) LRP Pubns.
— Litigation Management. 250p. 1995. pap. 49.99 (1-886813-00-0) Intl Risk Mgt.
— The Quality Plan: Practical Advice to Keep Claims Clients Coming Back. 204p. 1992. 29.95 (0-9634957-0-4) IW Pubns.
— Time Management for Claims Professionals. rev. ed. 168p. 1995. 19.95 (0-9634957-1-2) IW Pubns.
Quinlin, Michael P. Guide to the Boston Irish. (Illus.). 96p. (Orig.). 1985. pap. 4.50 (0-934665-00-1) Quinlin C Pubs.
— Guide to the New England Irish. (Illus.). 184p. 1987. pap. 7.95 (0-934665-08-7) Quinlin C Pubs.
Quinlin, Michael P. & Minogue, Colette M. Guide to the New England Irish. 3rd ed. 188p. 1994. pap. text ed. write for info. (0-934665-11-7) Quinlin C Pubs.
Quinlivan, Gary M., jt. auth. see Boxx, T. William.
Quinlivan-Hall, David, jt. auth. see Renner, Peter.
***Quinn.** Adolescents & ADD: Gaining the Advantage. 128p. 1995. pap. 12.95 (0-945354-70-3) Brunner-Mazel.
— Horace: The Odes. 1983. pap. text ed. 20.00 (0-312-39026-2) St Martin.
— Ishmael. 1995. pap. (0-553-37540-7) Bantam.
— Network Programming with WinSock. 1995. 39.75 (0-201-63372-8) Addison-Wesley.
— Practical Guide to Veterinary Microbiology. 1993. 89.50 (0-8151-6975-2) Mosby Yr Bk.
— Quinn's UCC Forms & Practice, 2 vols. 1986. 155.00 (0-88712-369-4); Supplemented semi-annually. write for info. (0-318-61518-5) Warren Gorham & Lamont.
— Quinn's UCC Forms & Practice, 2 vols., 1. 1986. write for info. (0-88712-507-7) Warren Gorham & Lamont.
— Quinn's UCC Forms & Practice, 2 vols., 2. 1986. write for info. (0-88712-508-5) Warren Gorham & Lamont.
— Say Uncle. 1995. pap. (0-452-27166-5, Plume) NAL-Dutton.
— Seashells: The Natural Treasures Collector's Kit. 1995. pap. (0-590-48486-9) Scholastic Inc.
— The Sixty-Eight Hundred Microprocessor. 526p. (C). 1990. write for info. (0-675-20515-8, Merrill Pub Co) Macmillan.
Quinn, jt. auth. see Donahue.
Quinn, jt. auth. see Magilligan.
Quinn, jt. auth. see Wolcott.
Quinn, Adrienne. Dreams of History That Came True. 224p. (Orig.). 1987. pap. 8.95 (0-9607172-3-4) Dream Res.
— Dreams Secret Messages from Your Mind. rev. ed. (Illus.). 140p. (Orig.). 1981. reprint ed. pap. 6.95 (0-9607172-1-8) Dream Res.
— My Dream Interpretation Workbook. 70p. (Orig.). 1986. audio 15.95 (0-9607172-2-6) Dream Res.
***Quinn, Al.** Movies That Inspire: A Discussion Guide for Families & Groups. 112p. 1994. 9.95 (0-89944-318-4) Don Bosco Multimedia.
***Quinn, Alexandra & Redonnet, Marie.** Candy Story. LC 95-10304. (European Women Writers Ser.). 112p. 1995. text ed. 20.00 (0-8032-3915-7) U of Nebr Pr.
***Quinn, Alfred O.** Iron Rails to Alaskan Copper: The Epic Triumph of Erastus Corning Hawkins. (Illus.). 275p. (Orig.). 1995. pap. write for info. (0-9646669-0-1) DAloquin Pub.
Quinn, Alfred O., jt. auth. see Church, Earl.
Quinn, Alice, ed. see Clampitt, Amy.
Quinn, Alison M., jt. ed. see Quinn, David B.
***Quinn, Anthony.** One Man Tango. (Illus.). 400p. 1995. 25.00 (0-06-018354-3, HarpT) HarpC.
Quinn, Antoinette. Patrick Kavanagh: A Critical Study. (Irish Studies). 512p. 1991. text ed. 39.95 (0-8156-2549-9) Syracuse U Pr.
Quinn, Arthur. Broken Shore: The Marin Peninsula in California History. (Illus.). 192p. 1987. reprint ed. pap. 9.95 (0-939061-00-7) Redwood Press.
— Figures of Speech: Sixty Ways to Turn a Phrase. x, 103p. 1993. pap. 7.50 (1-880393-02-6) Hermagoras Pr.
— A New World: An Epic of Colonial America from the Founding of Jamestown to the Fall of Quebec. LC 93-46455. 600p. 1994. 35.00 (0-571-19837-6) Faber & Faber.
— The Rivals: William Gwin, David Broderick & the Birth of California. LC 94-20495. (Library of the American West). 1994. 25.00 (0-517-59573-7, Crown) Crown Pub Group.
Quinn, Arthur & Kikawada, Isaac. Before Abraham Was: The Unity of Genesis 1-11. LC 88-83623. 144p. (C). 1989. reprint ed. pap. 11.95 (0-89870-239-9) Ignatius Pr.
Quinn, Arthur, jt. auth. see Bradbury, Nancy M.
Quinn, Arthur, jt. auth. see Nathan, Leonard.
Quinn, Arthur H. A History of the American Drama: From the Beginning to the Civil War. 2nd ed. (Illus.). (C). 1982. reprint ed. 44.50 (0-89197-218-8) Irvington.
— A History of the American Drama: From the Civil War to the Present Day. rev. ed. (Illus.). (C). 1982. reprint ed. 44.50 (0-89197-219-6) Irvington.
— Literature of the American People. 1177p. 1989. reprint ed. text ed. 137.50 (0-8290-2464-6) Irvington.
— Pennsylvania Stories. 1993. reprint ed. lib. bdg. 89.00 (0-7812-5820-0) Rprt Serv.
Quinn, Bernard. The Small Rural Parish. LC 79-56508. (Orig.). 1980. pap. 3.50 (0-914422-11-1) Glenmary Res Ctr.
Quinn, Bernard, et al. Churches & Church Membership in the U. S. 1980: An Enumeration by Region, State & County Based on Data Reported by 111 Church Bodies. LC 82-81978. 1982. pap. 24.00 (0-914422-12-X) Glenmary Res Ctr.
Quinn, Bernetta. Dancing in Stillness. 90p. (Orig.). 1983. pap. 5.00 (0-932662-44-7) St Andrews NC.
— Ezra Pound: An Introduction to the Poetry. LC 72-6830. (Introductions to Modern American Poetry Ser.). 225p. 1973. text ed. 42.00 (0-231-03282-X) Col U Pr.
— Metamorphic Tradition in Modern Poetry: Essay on the Work of Ezra Pound & Other Poets. LC 66-19365. 263p. 1966. reprint ed. 45.00 (0-87752-089-5) Gordian.
Quinn, Betty N., jt. auth. see Lawall, Gilbert.
Quinn, Betty N., jt. ed. see Lawall, Gilbert.
Quinn, Beverly Carlson. Experts Speaking to Nonexperts: The Skill of Technical Interpreting. rev. ed. LC 91-60663. 1994. pap. 15.95 (0-9628765-1-8) Typhoon Pr.
Quinn, Bob. Smokey Hollow. (Illus.). 170p. 1991. 24.00 (0-86278-269-4, Pub. by OBrien Pr IE) Dufour.
— Smokey Hollow: A Fictional Memoir. (Illus.). 170p. 1993. pap. 13.95 (0-86278-318-6, Pub. by OBrien Pr IE) Dufour.
Quinn, Brennan, jt. auth. see Ballard, Jimmy.
Quinn, Brian & Mott, Helen, eds. World Travel Guide, 1993-94. 12th ed. (Illus.). 1400p. 1993. 139.00 (0-946393-23-0, Pub. by Columbus Pr Ltd UK) SF Comns.
— World Travel Guide 1994-95. 13th ed. (Illus.). 1300p. 1994. 159.00 (0-946393-35-4, Pub. by Columbus Pr Ltd UK) SF Comns.
— World Travel Guide 1995-96. 14th ed. (Illus.). 1350p. 1995. 159.00 (0-946393-47-8) SF Comns.
Quinn, Bridie & Cashman, Seamus, eds. Wolfhound Book of Irish Poems for Young People. (Illus.). 192p. (J). (ps-8). 1975. pap. 9.95 (0-86327-002-6, Pub. by Wolfhound Pr IE) Dufour.
Quinn, C. Edward. Signers of the Constitution. (Bicentennial of U. S. Constitution Ser.). (Illus.). 112p. 1986. 20.00 (0-941980-18-9) Bronx County.
— Signers of the Declaration of Independence. Hermalyn, Gary D. & Ultan, LLoyd, eds. (Bicentennial of U. S. Constitution Ser.). (Illus.). 132p. 1988. reprint ed. 20.00 (0-685-25265-5) Bronx County.
Quinn, Carroll A. & Smith, Michael D. The Professional Commitment: Issues & Ethics in Nursing. 208p. 1987. pap. text ed. 26.95 (0-7216-1098-6) Saunders.
Quinn, Charles J., Jr., jt. ed. see Bachnik, Jane M.
Quinn, Charles U., tr. see Bouyer, Louis.
Quinn, Charlotte A. Mandingo Kingdoms of the Senegambia: Traditionalism, Islam, and European Expansion. LC 77-154831. 235p. reprint ed. 67.00 (0-8357-9463-6, 2015307) Bks Demand.
Quinn, Cheri L., jt. auth. see Moore, Kenneth D.
Quinn, Christopher. The Adventures of Jason. Coy, Stanley C., ed. (Illus.). 36p. (Orig.). (J). (gr. 3-5). 1994. pap. 5.95 (1-881459-13-6) Eagle Pr SC.
Quinn, Colleen. Colorado Flame. 1989. pap. 3.75 (0-8217-2801-6) Zebra.
— Unveiled. 352p. (Orig.). 1993. mass mkt. 4.99 (1-55773-891-2) Diamond.
Quinn, Colleen, et al. Loving Hearts. 336p. (Orig.). 1992. mass mkt. 4.99 (1-55773-666-9) Diamond.
Quinn, D. Michael. Mormon Hierarchy Vol. 1: Origins of Power. LC 94-14854. 700p. 1994. text ed. 29.95 (1-56085-056-6) Signature Bks.
— Mormon Hierarchy, Vol. 2: Extensions of Power. 500p. 1994. 29.95 (1-56085-060-4) Signature Bks.
Quinn, D. Michael, ed. The New Mormon History: Revisionist Essays on the Past. (Essays on Mormonism Ser.). 310p. 1992. pap. 18.95 (1-56085-011-6) Signature Bks.
Quinn, Dan. The Spirit Within. 150p. 1993. pap. 11.95 (1-882421-00-0) Insite Pub.
Quinn, Dan & Davis, Larry. Multiplication Memorization Made Fun & Easy. 128p. (J). (gr. 1-3). 1993. teacher ed 9.95 (0-9629746-1-7) Texas Trends.
Quinn, Daniel. Ishmael. 1992. 20.00 (0-553-07875-5) Bantam.
— Ishmael. 1993. mass mkt. 5.99 (0-553-56166-9) Bantam.
— Providence: The Story of a Fifty-Year Vision Quest. LC 94-43423. 1995. 19.95 (0-553-10018-1) Bantam.
***Quinn, Daniel & Whalen, Tom.** A New Comer's Guide to the Afterlife: On the Other Side Known As the Little Book. LC 94-24558. 1995. write for info. (0-553-09670-2) Bantam.
Quinn, David, jt. auth. see Boyd, Frances.
Quinn, David B. Explorers & Colonies: America, 1500-1625. 464p. 1990. boxed 60.00 (1-85285-024-8) Hambledon Press.
— The Lost Colonists: Their Fortune & Probable Fate. (America's 400th Anniversary Ser.). (Illus.). xviii, 53p. 1993. reprint ed. pap. 5.00 (0-86526-204-7) NC Archives.
— Roanoke Voyages 1584-1590. 1990. pap. 14.95 (0-486-26513-7) Dover.
— Roanoke Voyages, 1584-1590: Documents to Illustrate the English Voyages to North American under. 1990. pap. 14.95 (0-486-26512-9) Dover.
— Set Fair for Roanoke: Voyages & Colonies, 1584-1606. LC 84-2345. (Illus.). xxiv, 468p. 1985. pap. 16.95 (0-8078-4123-4) U of NC Pr.

P Q

Quinn, David B., ed. New American World, 5 vols., Set. (Individual Publications). 1978. lib. bdg. 299.50 (*0-405-10759-5*) Ayer.

Quinn, David B. & Quinn, Alison M., eds. The First Colonists: Documents on the Planting of the First English Settlements in North America, 1584-1590. (Illus.). xlvi, 199p. 1985. reprint ed. pap. 10.00 (*0-86526-195-4*) NC Archives.

Quinn, David B., ed. see Cavendish, Thomas.

Quinn, Dawn & Malachowski, Cindy. Faithful Followers: Celebrating a Decade of Bon Jovi. Mendel, Kathleen L., ed. LC 94-60066. (Illus.). 64p. (Orig.). 1994. pap. 14.95 (*1-878142-33-X*) Telstar TX.

Quinn, Dennis P. An Examination of Kant's Treatment of Transcendental Freedom. LC 88-9600. 100p. (Orig.). (C). 1988. lib. bdg. 28.50 (*0-8191-6968-4*); pap. text ed. 17.00 (*0-8191-6969-2*) U Pr of Amer.

— Restructuring the Automobile Industry: A Study of Firms & States in Modern Capitalism. (Columbia Studies in Business, Government & Society). (Illus.). 416p. 1988. text ed. 51.00 (*0-231-06524-8*) Col U Pr.

Quinn, Dermot. Patronage & Piety: The Politics of English Roman Catholicism, 1850-1900. LC 91-75051. 320p. (C). 1993. 42.50 (*0-8047-1996-9*) Stanford U Pr.

***Quinn, Dick & Quinn, Kelly. Quinns' Best: From HELP YOURSELF TO HEALTH, Vol. I. (Illus.). 200p. (Orig.). 1995. pap. 12.95 (*0-9632839-4-4*) Quinn Pub Co.**

Dick Quinn & his daughter Kelly are herbalists & patient advocates who have published the monthly journal, HELP YOURSELF TO HEALTH, since February 1993. Now they have gathered the best articles & letters from 1993 & 1994 into a single volume. QUINNS' BEST is a wide-ranging collection of more than 50 articles about common afflictions from cancer to coronaries. Every affliction is dealt with herbally. Readers are told about the herbs, how to take them & where to get them. Dick Quinn is the author of LEFT FOR DEAD (1992), the story of his 1978 heart attack, failed bypass surgery & subsequent recovery by taking Cayenne & other heart herbs. Kelly Quinn, health writer & mother of three, is the editor of HELP YOURSELF TO HEALTH. Herbs helped her survive & recover from near-fatal hepatitis. She now uses natural medicines for every family need. QUINNS' BEST is an interesting, well-written book you'll refer to over & over. Illustrated & thoroughly indexed, it's engaging, easy to read, funny, touching. It'll help you HELP YOURSELF TO HEALTH. Also available as a 90-minute audio cassette & a 60-page health manual about herbal remedies. (ISBN 0-9632839-2-8, $14.95). Order from R. F. Quinn Publishing Co., Box 17100, Minneapolis, MN 55417; 612-824-5348; 612-824-5542. ***Publisher Provided Annotation.***

Quinn, Dick, et al. Left for Dead. (Illus.). 200p. (Orig.). 1992. pap. 12.95 (*0-9632839-0-1*) Quinn Pub Co.

Quinn, Dominic, jt. auth. see Pratt, Lindsay L.

Quinn, Drew B., jt. auth. see Barton, Peggy P.

***Quinn, Edward.** Cote d'Azur Album. (Illus.). 1994. 39.95 (*1-881616-27-4*, Pub. by Scalo Pubs) Dist Art Pubs.

— Picasso: Photos Nineteen Fifty-One to Nineteen Seventy-Two. (Pocket Art Ser.). (Illus.). 1980. pap. 6.95 (*0-8120-2109-6*) Barron.

— Responsibilities: A College Reader. 396p. (C). 1990. pap. text ed. 20.50 (*0-06-045319-2*) HarpCollege.

Quinn, Elizabeth. Murder Most Grizzly. Marrow, Linda, ed. 224p. (Orig.). 1993. mass mkt. 4.99 (*0-671-74990-0*) PB.

Quinn, Elizabeth, jt. auth. see Moore, Lola.

Quinn, Eric S. Say Uncle. 352p. 1994. 20.95 (*0-525-93780-3*) NAL-Dutton.

Quinn, Esther C. The Penitence of Adam: (A Study of the Andrius MS.) Dufau, Micheline, tr. LC 79-19056. (Romance Monographs: No. 36). 192p. 1980. 25.00 (*84-499-3367-6*) Romance.

Quinn, Evie, jt. auth. see Young, Mary.

Quinn, F., jt. ed. see Humphreys, J.

Quinn, F. X., jt. auth. see Hatakeyama, T.

***Quinn, Francis M.** Principles & Practice of Nurse Education. 3rd ed. (Illus.). 496p. 1994. pap. text ed. 47.50 (*1-56593-295-1*, 0619) Singular Publishing.

Quinn, Frank, jt. auth. see Freedman, Michael.

Quinn, Frederick. That We May Heal the Earth. 160p. 1994. pap. 9.95 (*0-8358-0702-9*) Upper Room Bks.

Quinn, Frederick, ed. The Federalist Paper's Reader. LC 92-36944. 223p. (Orig.). 1993. 18.95 (*0-929765-17-6*); pap. 14.95 (*0-929765-35-4*) Seven Locks Pr.

Quinn, George. The Novel in Javanese: Aspects of Its Social & Literary Character. (Verhandelingen Ser.: No. 148). (Illus.). 330p. (Orig.). 1992. pap. 29.00 (*90-6718-033-5*, Pub. by KLTV Pr NE) Cellar.

Quinn, Gerald M., jt. auth. see Hansen, Hardy.

Quinn, Gerald V. The Camcorder Handbook. 1991. 2.30 (*0-8306-5305-8*) TAB Bks.

— The Fax Handbook. (Illus.). 144p. 1989. 16.95 (*0-8306-4341-9*); pap. 8.95 (*0-8306-3341-3*) TAB Bks.

— The FAX Handbook. 1989. pap. 8.95 (*0-07-155722-9*) McGraw.

Quinn, Gerard. The Clip Art Book: A Compilation of More. 1992. 15.99 (*0-517-01773-3*) Random Hse Value.

***Quinn, Greg H.** The Garden in Our Yard. (Read with Me Paperbacks Ser.). (Illus.). 32p. (J). (ps-2). 1995. pap. 2.50 (*0-590-48536-9*, Cartwheel) Scholastic Inc.

— Gift of a Tree: Book & Starter Kit. (J). (ps-3). 1994. pap. 5.95 (*0-590-48092-8*) Scholastic Inc.

Quinn, Hartwell L. Arthur Campbell: Pioneer & Patriot of the "Old Southwest" LC 89-43628. (Illus.). 207p. 1990. lib. bdg. 27.50x (*0-89950-509-0*) McFarland & Co.

Quinn, Herbert F. The Union Nationale: Quebec Nationalism from Duplessis to Levesque. 2nd enl. ed. LC 80-472454. 356p. reprint ed. pap. 101.50 (*0-8357-8359-6*, 2033981) Bks Demand.

Quinn, J., jt. auth. see Nadler, Sam B., Jr.

Quinn, Jack. Digital Data Communication. (Illus.). 319p. (C). 1995. text ed. 57.00 (*0-02-397240-8*) Macmillan.

Quinn, Jacquelin G. Soil Stitches. 83p. (Orig.). (C). 1991. 10.00 (*0-9628202-1-0*); pap. 6.00 (*0-685-49362-8*) J Gannon Quinn.

Quinn, James. The ABCs of Thoroughbred Handicapping. Ladenheim, Randy, ed. LC 88-10025. (Illus.). 416p. 1988. 22.95 (*0-688-06550-3*) Morrow.

— The Best of Thoroughbred Handicapping: Advice on Handicapping from the Experts. rev. ed. LC 87-11128. 288p. 1987. 22.00 (*0-688-07012-4*) Morrow.

— Class of the Field: New Performance Ratings for the Thoroughbreds. LC 86-28464. (Illus.). 160p. 1987. 13.95 (*0-688-06551-1*) Morrow.

— Class of the Field: New Performance Ratings for Thoroughbreds. (Illus.). 144p. 1992. pap. 10.00 (*0-688-11277-3*, Quill) Morrow.

— Figure Handicapping Revisited: A Practical Guide to the Interpretation & Use of Speed & Pace Figures. LC 92-9899. (Tom Ainslie - Winner's Circle Ser.). 1992. 25.00 (*0-688-10582-3*) Morrow.

— The Handicapper's Condition Book: An Advanced Treatment of Thoroughbred Class. LC 86-5255. (Illus.). 320p. Date not set. pap. write for info. (*0-688-05932-5*, Quill) Morrow.

— The Handicapper's Condition Book: An Advanced Treatment of Thoroughbred Class. LC 86-5255. (Illus.). 320p. 1986. 22.95 (*0-688-05931-7*) Morrow.

— Handicapper's Stakes Festival: Class Evaluation, Simulcasting, Cross-Track Betting. 1995. 25.00 (*0-688-12790-8*) Morrow.

— High-Tech Handicapping in the Information Age. LC 85-15404. 320p. 1986. 22.00 (*0-688-05388-2*) Morrow.

— The New Expert Handicappers. LC 89-32522. (Illus.). 387p. 1989. 22.95 (*0-688-07511-8*) Morrow.

— Recreational Handicapping: A Comprehensive Introduction to the Art & Science. 1990. 22.95 (*0-688-08964-X*) Morrow.

Quinn, James, jt. auth. see Holman, John.

Quinn, James B. Intelligent Enterprise. 224p. 1992. text ed. 32.95 (*0-02-925615-1*) Free Pr.

Quinn, James B. & Mintzberg, Henry. The Strategy Process: Cases. 2nd ed. LC 92-27505. 672p. (C). 1993. pap. text ed. 49.00 (*0-13-854068-3*) P-H.

Quinn, James B., jt. auth. see Mintzberg, Henry.

Quinn, James B., ed. see National Academy of Engineering Staff.

Quinn, James D. The Art of Survival. LC 93-93947. 112p. 1994. pap. 7.00 (*1-56002-357-0*, Univ Edtns) Aegina Pr.

***Quinn, James P.** Grandpa Was No Saint: Poems. 112p. (Orig.). 1995. pap. 8.95 (*1-56474-136-2*) Fithian Pr.

Quinn, Jane. Minorcans in Florida. LC 75-6573. (Illus.). 282p. 1975. 25.00 (*0-917553-05-5*); pap. 8.95 (*0-917553-06-3*) St Augustine Hist.

Quinn, Jane, ed. see Carnegie Council on Adolescent Development Staff.

Quinn, Jane B. Making the Most of Your Money: A Comprehensive Guide to Financial Planning. 384p. 1991. 27.50 (*0-671-65952-9*) S&S Trade.

Quinn, Jerome D. Letter to Titus: A New Translation with Notes & Commentary. 1990. 28.00 (*0-385-05900-0*) Doubleday.

Quinn, Jerome D. & Wacker, William C. The First & Second Letters to Timothy: A New Translation with Notes & Commentary. LC 93-36601. 1995. 48.00 (*0-385-26643-X*, Anchor Bible) Doubleday.

Quinn, Jim & Cohen, Barry. Rock One Hundred. 3rd suppl. ed. (Illus.). 1982. Suppl., 1982. write for info. (*0-917190-10-6*) Chartmasters.

— Rock One Hundred, Set. 3rd ed. (Illus.). 1981. pap. text ed. 6.00 (*0-917190-09-2*) Chartmasters.

Quinn, Jim, jt. auth. see Heartney, Eleanor.

Quinn, Joan. Successful Case Management in Long-Term Care. LC 92-49033. (Illus.). 176p. 1993. 26.95 (*0-8261-7750-6*) Springer Pub.

***Quinn, Jocey, et al, eds.** Changing the Subject: Women in Higher Education. 240p. 1994. 75.00x (*0-7484-0281-0*); pap. 27.00x (*0-7484-0282-9*) Taylor & Francis.

Quinn, John. Astrological Techniques, Vol. 1: Fundamental Considerations & Natal Astrology. LC 87-90722. (Illus.). 159p. (Orig.). 1988. pap. 19.95 (*0-944189-01-6*) Quinn TX.

— Duck & Swan. 142p. (J). (gr. 5-9). 1994. pap. 6.95 (*1-85371-317-1*, Pub. by Poolbeg Pr IE) Dufour.

— The Gold Cross of Killadoo. 106p. (J). (gr. 5 up). 1993. pap. 8.95 (*1-85371-220-5*, Pub. by Poolbeg Pr IE) Dufour.

— Jungle Tales: Celtic Memories of an Epic Stand. (Illus.). 188p. 1995. 22.95 (*1-85158-673-3*, Pub. by Mnstream UK) Trafalgar.

— The Letters of John Quinn to William Butler Yeats. Himber, Alan, ed. LC 83-9207. (Studies in Modern Literature: No. 28). 316p. reprint ed. pap. 90.10 (*0-8357-1464-0*, 2070553) Bks Demand.

— The Summer of Lily & Esme. 190p. (Orig.). (J). (gr. 6 up). 1992. pap. 8.95 (*1-85371-208-6*, Pub. by Poolbeg Pr IE) Dufour.

Quinn, John, ed. Employee Ownership Bibliography. rev. ed. 61p. 1991. pap. 15.00 (*0-926902-17-2*) NCEO.

Quinn, John, rev. Employee Ownership: Alternatives to ESOPs. rev. ed. 86p. (Orig.). (C). 1992. pap. text ed. 25.00 (*0-926902-10-5*) NCEO.

— The Employee Ownership Casebook. rev. ed. (C). 1992. pap. 25.00 (*0-926902-01-6*) NCEO.

Quinn, John & Crawford, J. M. The Christian Foundation of Criminal Responsibility: Historical-Comparative Approach to the Roots of Theological & Civil Law. LC 90-5638. (Toronto Studies in Theology: Vol. 40). 640p. 1991. lib. bdg. 129.95 (*0-88946-979-2*) E Mellen.

***Quinn, John F., anno. & comp.** The Loyola Book of Verse. 267p. (C). Date not set. reprint ed. 7.25 (*0-8294-0600-X*, Campion Bks) Loyola Univ Pr.

Quinn, John J., jt. auth. see Goold, Michael.

Quinn, John J., jt. auth. see Gould, Michael.

Quinn, John M. Praise in St. Augustine: Readings & Reflections. 220p. 1987. pap. 8.95 (*0-8158-0430-X*) Chris Mass.

Quinn, John P. Gambling & Gambling Devices. LC 69-14942. (Criminology, Law Enforcement, & Social Problems Ser.: No. 48). (Illus.). 1969. reprint ed. 20.00 (*0-87585-048-0*) Patterson Smith.

— Law Firm Accounting. 340p. 1986. boxed 65.00 (*0-318-22527-1*, 00602) Law Journal.

Quinn, John R. Fishwatching: Your Complete Guide to the Underwater World. LC 93-51025. (Illus.). 272p. (Orig.). 1994. pap. 18.00 (*0-88150-284-7*) Countryman.

— The Kid's Fish Book: How to Catch Keep & Observe Your Own Native Fish. LC 93-31691. (J). 1994. pap. text ed. 10.95 (*0-471-58601-3*) Wiley.

— One Square Mile on the Atlantic Coast: An Artist's Journal of the New Jersey Shore. LC 92-38190. (America in Microcosm Ser.). (Illus.). 224p. 1993. pap. 17.95 (*0-8027-7395-8*) Walker & Co.

— Our Native Fishes: The Aquarium Hobbyist's Guide to Observing, Collecting, & Keeping Them. LC 90-15080. (Illus.). 256p. (Orig.). 1990. pap. 14.95 (*0-88150-181-6*) Countryman.

— Piranhas, Fact & Fiction. 1992. 19.95 (*0-86622-172-7*) TFH Pubns.

— The Summer Woodlands. (Illus.). 1980. 9.95 (*0-85699-140-6*) Chatham Pr.

— Wildlife Survivors: The Flora & Fauna of Tomorrow. 1993. text ed. 21.95 (*0-07-051087-3*); pap. text ed. 12.95 (*0-07-051088-1*) McGraw.

— Wildlife Survivors: The Flora & Fauna of Tomorrow. 1993. 21.95 (*0-8306-4346-X*); pap. 12.95 (*0-8306-4345-1*) TAB Bks.

— The Winter Woods. LC 76-18486. (Illus.). 1976. 9.95 (*0-85699-138-4*) Chatham Pr.

Quinn, Joseph F., et al. Passing the Torch: The Influence of Economic Incentives on Work & Retirement. LC 90-12352. 240p. 1990. text ed. 25.00 (*0-88099-091-0*); pap. text ed. 15.00 (*0-88099-092-9*) W E Upjohn.

Quinn, Julia. Birthright. (Silhouette Intimate Moments Ser.). 1993. mass mkt. 3.50 (*0-373-07540-5*, 5-07540-3) Silhouette.

— Splendid. 400p. (Orig.). 1995. mass mkt. 4.99 (*0-380-78074-7*) Avon.

***Quinn, Justin.** The O' o'a'a Bird. 64p. 1995. pap. 14.95 (*1-85754-125-1*) Paul & Co Pubs.

Quinn, Karen E., jt. auth. see Stebbins, Theodore E., Jr.

Quinn, Karen J. & Quinn, Kenneth P. A Manual of Old English Prose. LC 83-48285. 454p. 1990. 51.00 (*0-8240-9032-2*, 453) Garland.

Quinn, Kay. Animals: Sixty Things I Can Draw. (J). 1990. 4.99 (*0-517-03564-2*) Random Hse Value.

— Dinosaurs & Prehistoric Animals. (Sixty Things I Can Draw Ser.). (Illus.). 64p. (J). (gr. 2-10). 1990. 4.99 (*0-517-03566-9*) Random Hse Value.

— Monsters: Sixty Things I Can Draw. (J). 1990. 4.99 (*0-517-03565-0*) Random Hse Value.

Quinn, Kaye. Animals. (Science Crossword Puzzles Ser.). (Illus.). 48p. (Orig.). (J). (gr. 2-6). 1990. pap. 2.95 (*0-8431-2293-5*) Price Stern.

— Aquarium Creatures. (Facts 'n Fun Ser.). 80p. (Orig.). (J). 1991. pap. 2.95 (*0-8431-2719-8*) Price Stern.

— Bizarre Bugs. (Science Crossword Puzzles Ser.). 48p. (Orig.). (J). 1990. pap. 2.95 (*0-8431-2811-9*) Price Stern.

— Preschool Skills. (Rainbow Skill Builders Ser.: Level 1). 80p. (Orig.). (J). (ps). pap. 2.95 (*0-8431-2508-X*) Price Stern.

— Reading Readiness. (Rainbow Skill Builders Ser.: Level 2). 80p. (Orig.). 1985. pap. 2.95 (*0-8431-2501-2*) Price Stern.

— Zoo Animals. (Facts 'n' Fun Bks.). (Illus.). 80p. (Orig.). (J). (gr. k-4). 1991. pap. 2.95 (*0-8431-2720-1*) Price Stern.

Quinn, Kaye, tr. see Nigro, Susan L.

Quinn, Kelly, jt. auth. see Quinn, Dick.

Quinn, Kenneth. Catullus, Poems: A Commentary. LC 76-94751. (C). 1971. pap. text ed. 23.00 (*0-312-12495-3*) St Martin.

Quinn, Kenneth P., jt. auth. see Quinn, Karen J.

Quinn, Kerker & Shattuck, Charles, eds. Accent Anthology: Selections from Accent, a Quarterly of New Literature, 1940-1945. LC 70-156601. (Essay Index Reprint Ser.). 1977. reprint ed. 38.95 (*0-8369-2302-2*) Ayer.

Quinn, Khalegl. Everyday Self-Defense: Protect Yourself with Attitude, Intuition, & Strategy. (Illus.). 256p. 1994. pap. 14.00 (*0-7225-2991-0*) Thorsons SF.

Quinn, Lee D. Challenging Mazes. LC 75-2822. (Illus.). 64p. 1975. reprint ed. pap. 3.50 (*0-486-21177-0*) Dover.

— Perplexing Mazes. (Illus.). 64p. (Orig.). 1992. pap. 3.95 (*0-486-26945-0*) Dover.

— Puzzling Mazes. (Illus.). (J). (gr. k-3). 1994. pap. 1.00 (*0-486-27980-4*) Dover.

Quinn, Malcolm. The Swastika: Constructing the Symbol. LC 94-4683. (Material Cultures Ser.). (Illus.). 192p. 1994. 45.00 (*0-415-10095-X*, B4879) Routledge.

Quinn, Mary A., contrib. Shelley's 1819-1821 Huntington Notebook, Vol. VI, No. HM 2176. LC 83-49271. (Manuscripts of the Younger Romantics & the Bodleian Shelley Manuscripts). 484p. 1994. 180.00 (*0-8240-5870-4*, SSSHELL) Garland.

Quinn, Mary A., ed. The Mask of Anarchy Drafts: Shelley's 1819-1820 Huntington Notebook. (Manuscripts of the Younger Romantics, Shelley: Vol. IV). 580p. 1990. reprint ed. 150.00 (*0-8240-6975-7*, HM 2177) Garland.

Quinn, Mary E., jt. auth. see Fathman, Ann K.

Quinn, Mary J. & Tomita, Susan K. Elder Abuse & Neglect: Causes, Diagnosis & Intervention Strategies. 336p. 1986. 34.95 (*0-8261-5120-5*) Springer Pub.

Quinn, Mary L. & Schleh, Eugene P., eds. Consumable Goods II: Papers from the North East Popular Culture Association Meeting, 1987. 343p. 1988. pap. 9.95 (*0-943373-01-8*) Natl Poet Foun.

Quinn, Michael A., et al. Lead Paint Poisoning in Urban Children: An Annotated Bibliography, No. 1130. 1976. 6.50 (*0-686-20406-9*) CPL Biblios.

Quinn, Michael J. Parallel Computing: Theory & Practice. 2nd ed. 1993. text ed. write for info. (*0-07-051294-9*) McGraw.

Quinn, Michael J., jt. auth. see Hatcher, Philip J.

Quinn, Michael L. The Semiotic Stage: Prague School Theatre Theory. LC 92-37227. (Pittsburgh Studies in Theatre & Culture: Vol. 1). 176p. (C). 1995. text ed. 42.95 (*0-8204-1877-3*) P Lang Pubs.

Quinn, Michelle. Katherine Gibbs Handbook of Business English. 288p. 1987. pap. 4.95 (*0-02-047440-7*, Pub. by Gebrueder Borntraeger GW) Macmillan.

Quinn, Mickey & Quinn, Terri. How to Pray with Your Children. 1989. pap. 30.00 (*0-905092-91-0*, Pub. by Veritas IE) St Mut.

— How to Talk to Your Child about Sex. 1989. pap. 22.00 (*0-86217-057-5*, Pub. by Veritas IE) St Mut.

Quinn-Musgrove, Sandra & Doherty, Edward J. Auctions for Amateurs. LC 93-71299. 166p. (Orig.). 1993. pap. 9.95 (*0-9628295-2-8*) Blue Hse TX.

Quinn-Musgrove, Sandra, jt. auth. see Allen, Lee M.

Quinn-Musgrove, Sandra L. How to Pass Objective Examinations: And Other Considerations for Study. 96p. (C). 1991. per. 10.95 (*0-8403-6535-7*) Kendall-Hunt.

Quinn, Nancy D., jt. auth. see Quinn, Robert J.

Quinn, Naomi, jt. ed. see Holland, Dorothy.

Quinn, Niall. The Cafe Cong. 164p. (Orig.). 1991. pap. 14.95 (*0-86327-303-3*, Pub. by Wolfhound Pr IE) Dufour.

— Stolen Air. LC 89-50973. (Illus.). 116p. 1989. 19.95 (*0-86327-157-X*); pap. 8.95 (*0-86327-158-8*) Dufour.

Quinn, Niall & Jenner, Peter, eds. Disorders of Movement: Clinical, Pharmacological & Physiological Aspects. 567p. 1989. text ed. 157.00 (*0-12-569685-X*) Acad Pr.

Quinn, P. & Harwood, J., eds. Plant Lipid Biochemistry, Structure & Utilization. 1991. 95.00 (*1-85578-003-8*, Pub. by Portland Pr Ltd UK) Ashgate Pub Co.

Quinn, P. J. & Cherry, R. J., eds. Structural & Dynamic Properties of Lipids & Membranes. (Monograph Ser.: Vol. 3). 224p. 1992. 70.00 (*1-85578-014-3*, Pub. by Portland Pr Ltd UK) Ashgate Pub Co.

Quinn, Patricia A. Better Than the Sons of Kings. (Studies in History & Culture: Vol. 2). 265p. (C). 1989. text ed. 59.00 (*0-8204-0472-1*) P Lang Pubs.

Quinn, Patricia O., ed. ADD & the College Student: A Guide for High School & College Students with Attention Deficit Disorder. LC 93-36668. 128p. 1994. pap. 13.95 (*0-945354-58-4*) Magination Pr.

Quinn, Patricia O. & Stern, Judith M. Putting on the Brakes: Young People's Guide to Understanding Attention Deficit Hyperactivity Disorder (ADHD) LC 91-20390. (Illus.). (J). (gr. 4-7). 1991. pap. 8.95 (*0-945354-32-0*) Magination Pr.

— The "Putting on the Brakes" Activity Book for Young People with ADHD. (Illus.). 88p. (J). (gr. 3-8). 1993. pap. 14.95 (*0-945354-57-6*) Magination Pr.

***Quinn, Patrick.** Thick as Thieves. LC 94-28424. 1995. 20.00 (*0-517-70009-3*, Crown) Crown Pub Group.

Quinn, Patrick F., ed. see Poe, Edgar Allan.

Quinn, Patrick J. The Great War & the Missing Muse: The Early Writings of Robert Graves & Siefried Sassoon. LC 92-56915. 1994. write for info. (*0-945636-49-0*) Susquehanna U Pr.

Quinn, Paul D. Journal of the Second Son: An Uncharted Lifetime in the World That Was. 1991. 16.95 (*0-533-08701-5*) Vantage.

***Quinn, Paula M.** Shadow on My Soul: Overcoming Addiction to Suicide. 188p. (Orig.). 1995. pap. 14.95 (*1-879198-13-4*) Knwldg Ideas & Trnds.

Quinn, Peter. Banished Children of Eve. LC 93-11184. 608p. 1994. 22.95 (*0-670-85076-4*, Viking) Viking Penguin.

— Banished Children of Eve. 624p. 1995. 12.95 (*0-14-023003-3*, Penguin Bks) Viking Penguin.

Quinn, Peyton. A Bouncer's Guide to Barroom Brawling: Dealing with the Sucker Puncher, Streetfighter, & Ambusher. (Illus.). 64p. 1990. pap. 17.95 (*0-87364-586-3*) Paladin Pr.

Quinn, Phil. From Victim to Victory: Prescriptions from a Survivor of Child Abuse. LC 94-79240. 240p. (Orig.). 1994. pap. 12.95 (*0-687-13655-5*) Abingdon.

Quinn, Phil E. Cry Out! 1988. pap. 11.95 (*0-687-10014-3*) Abingdon.

— The Golden Rule of Parenting: Using Discipline Wisely. LC 88-34138. 1989. pap. 11.95 (*0-687-15515-0*) Abingdon.
— Renegade Saint: A Story of Hope by a Child Abuse Survivor. 1986. pap. 12.95 (*0-687-36131-1*) Abingdon.
Quinn, Philip L. Divine Commands & Moral Requirements. (Clarendon Library of Logic & Philosophy). 1978. text ed. 59.00 (*0-19-824413-4*) OUP.
Quinn, R. M. Fernando Gallego & the Retablo of Ciudad Rodrigo. LC 60-15915. (Illus.). 117p. (ENG & SPA.). 1961. 8.50 (*0-8165-0034-7*) U of Ariz Pr.
***Quinn, Ravadi L.** Joy of Thai Cooking. (Illus.). (Orig.). 1990. pap. 14.95 (*0-9628783-0-8*) Emerald Siam.
Quinn, Richard. Jesse Jackson & the Politics of Race. 269p. 1985. 17.95 (*0-915463-08-3*, Jameson Bks) Green Hill.
***Quinn, Robert.** Ghosts in the Shadows. 104p. 1995. pap. 7.95 (*1-56901-318-7*) NW Pub.
Quinn, Robert E. Beyond Rational Management: Mastering the Paradoxes & Competing Demands of High Performance. LC 87-46339. (Management Ser.). 221p. 1988. 28.95x (*1-55542-075-3*) Jossey-Bass.
— Beyond Rational Management: Mastering the Paradoxes & Competing Demands of High Performance. LC 87-46339. (Management Ser.). 221p. 1991. pap. 19.00 (*1-55542-377-9*) Jossey-Bass.
Quinn, Robert E. & Bowditch, James L. Organizational Competency Set. (C). 1993. Net. pap. text ed. write for info. (*0-471-53148-0*) Wiley.
Quinn, Robert E., et al. Becoming a Master Manager: A Competency Framework. Thompson, Michael P. & McGrath, Michael R., eds. 345p. 1990. Net. pap. text ed. write for info. (*0-471-51577-9*) Wiley.
Quinn, Robert J. & Quinn, Nancy D. Figure Skating Pins. LC 87-60429. (Illus.). 152p. (Orig.). (J). (gr. 7-12). 1987. pap. 15.00 (*0-9618349-1-9*) Quin Tel Prodns.
Quinn, Robert M. An Intermediate Vietnamese Reader. 214p. (ENG & VIE.). reprint ed. pap. 61.00 (*0-7837-1665-6*, 2041964) Bks Demand.
— Introductory Vietnamese. 534p. reprint ed. pap. 152.20 (*0-8357-2560-X*, 2040251) Bks Demand.
Quinn, Robert P. & Staines, Graham L. Nineteen Seventy-Seven Quality of Employment Survey: Descriptive Statistics, with Comparison Data from the 1969-70 & 1972-73 Surveys. LC 78-71659. (Illus.). 364p. (Orig.). 1979. pap. 16.00 (*0-87944-231-X*) Inst Soc Res.
Quinn, Robert P., et al. The Chosen Few: A Study of Discrimination in Executive Selection. LC 68-64118. 55p. reprint ed. pap. 25.00 (*0-685-23489-4*, 2029134) Bks Demand.
— The Decision to Discriminate: A Study of Executive Selection. LC 68-65536. 162p. 1968. pap. 7.00 (*0-87944-062-7*) Inst Soc Res.
— The Decision to Discriminate: A Study of Executive Selection. LC 68-65536. 170p. reprint ed. pap. 48.50 (*0-7837-5272-5*, 2045010) Bks Demand.
Quinn, Sally. Happy Endings. 1993. mass mkt. 5.99 (*0-345-37802-4*) Ballantine.
— Happy Endings. large type ed. LC 92-20788. 1992. 24.95 (*0-7927-1378-8*, Eagle Lrg Print); pap. 21.95 (*0-7927-1377-X*, Eagle Lrg Print) Chivers N Amer.
— Regrets Only. 672p. 1993. mass mkt. 4.95 (*0-345-34459-6*) Ballantine.
***Quinn, Sandra L. & Kanter, Sanford.** America's Royalty: All the Presidents' Children. expanded rev. ed. LC 95-7545. 304p. 1995. text ed. 59.95 (*0-313-29535-2*, Greenwood Pr) Greenwood.
Quinn, Sandra L. & Kantner, Sanford. The Lowdown on Higher Education: Straight Talk to Returning Students. 125p. (C). 1988. text ed. 19.50 (*0-8290-1436-5*); pap. 9.95 (*0-8290-1437-3*) Irvington.
Quinn, Shelley M. The Historical Development of Surrealism & the Relationships Between Hemispheric Specializations of the Brain. LC 91-28392. (Studies in Comparative Literature: Vol. 16). 224p. 1991. lib. bdg. 89.95 (*0-7734-9738-2*) E Mellen.
Quinn, Shirley & Irvings, Susan F. Active Reading in the Arts & Sciences. 2nd ed. 500p. 1990. pap. text ed. write for info. (*0-205-13062-3*, H3062-0) Allyn.
***Quinn, Susan.** Marie Curie: A Life. 1995. 30.00 (*0-671-67542-7*) S&S Trade.
— A Mind of Her Own: The Life of Karen Horney. (Radcliffe Biography Ser.). (Illus.). 512p. 1988. pap. 12.45 (*0-201-15573-7*) Addison-Wesley.
Quinn, T., et al. Evaluation of the BCR Programme, Measurement & Testing in Europe, 1988-1992. 76p. 1993. pap. 12.00 (*92-826-5807-4*, CG-NA-15041-EN-C, Pub. by Europ Com) UNIPUB.
Quinn, T. A. & Salzman, Ed. California Public Administration. 2nd ed. (Illus.). 120p. 1982. pap. 4.95 (*0-930302-51-6*) Cal Journal.
Quinn, T. Anthony. Carving up California: A History of Redistricting, 1951-1984. 334p. 1985. pap. text ed. 40.00 (*1-883638-03-8*) Rose Inst.
— Into the Political Thicket: California's 1951 Reapportionment. 57p. 1980. pap. text ed. 13.50 (*1-883638-06-2*) Rose Inst.
— The Political Geography of California. 132p. 1981. pap. text ed. 23.75 (*1-883638-18-6*) Rose Inst.
— Power Unbridled: The Nineteen Sixty-One Redistricting of California. 50p. 1980. pap. text ed. 12.50 (*1-883638-05-4*) Rose Inst.
Quinn, T. F. Physical Analysis for Tribology. (Illus.). 480p. (C). 1991. 135.00 (*0-521-32602-8*) Cambridge U Pr.
Quinn, T. J. Temperature. 2nd ed. (Monographs in Physical Measurement). (Illus.). 495p. 1991. text ed. 116.00 (*0-12-569681-7*) Acad Pr.
Quinn, T. J. & McNamara, T. F. Issues in Second Language Learning, General & Particular. 132p. (C). 1988. 51.00 (*0-7300-0550-X*, Pub. by Deakin Univ AT) St Mut.
Quinn, T. J., jt. ed. see Crovini, L.
Quinn, T. J., et al. The Healthy Lifestyle. (Illus.). 220p. 1987. pap. 14.95 (*0-685-18371-8*) Mouvement Pubns.
Quinn, Tara T. Dare to Love. 1994. mass mkt. 3.50 (*0-373-70600-6*, 1-70600-1) Harlequin Bks.
— Jacob's Girls. (Superromance Ser.). 1995. mass mkt. 3.75 (*0-373-70661-8*, 1-70661-3) Harlequin Bks.
— No Cure for Love. (Superromance Ser.). 1994. mass mkt. 3.50 (*0-373-70624-3*, 1-70624-1) Harlequin Bks.
— Yesterday's Secrets. (Superromance Ser.). 1993. mass mkt. 3.50 (*0-373-70567-0*, 1-70567-2) Harlequin Bks.
Quinn, Terence, ed. see International Congress of Applied Linguistics Staff.
Quinn, Terri, jt. auth. see Quinn, Mickey.
Quinn, Thomas C. Sexually Transmitted Diseases. (Advances in Host Defense Mechanisms Ser.: Vol. 8). 352p. 1992. 94.50 (*0-88167-882-1*) Raven.
Quinn, Thomas M. Quinn's Uniform Commercial Code Commentary & Law Digest. (Commercial Law Ser.). 2100p. 1991. Cumulative Suppls. avail. 145.00 (*0-7913-0889-8*, 78-50306) Warren Gorham & Lamont.
— Quinn's Uniform Commercial Code Commentary & Law Digest. suppl. ed. (Commercial Law Ser.). 2100p. 1991. 58.00 (*0-685-55632-8*); Supplemented semi-annually. 62.00 (*0-685-55633-6*) Warren Gorham & Lamont.
— The Uniform Commercial Code Law Letter. 165.00 (*0-685-69642-1*, UCLL) Warren Gorham & Lamont.
Quinn, Thomas R. Old-Fashioned Homemade Ice Cream: With 58 Original Recipes. (Illus.). 48p. (Orig.). 1983. pap. 2.50 (*0-486-24495-4*) Dover.
Quinn, Tom. Collecting Fishing Tackle: A Beginner's Guide. (Illus.). 80p. 1994. pap. 17.95 (*0-948253-68-1*, Pub. by Sportsmans Pr UK) Trafalgar.
— Tales of the Old Soldiers: Ten Veterans of the First World War Remember Life & Death in the Trenches. LC 93-2959. (Illus.). 192p. 1993. 30.00 (*0-7509-0090-3*) A Sutton Pub.
— The Working Retrievers: Being an Illustrated Discourse on Retrievers; Their Selection, Breeding, Care & Handling, & New Information on Training Dogs for Hunting & Field Training. (Illus.). 257p. 1983. 37.95 (*0-525-93287-9*, Dutton) NAL-Dutton.
Quinn, Tom, ed. Fish Tales: A Collection of Angling Stories. (Illus.). 189p. (YA). (gr. 8-12). 1992. 28.00 (*0-7509-0091-1*) A Sutton Pub.
Quinn, V. Beautiful Mexico. 1976. lib. bdg. 69.95 (*0-8490-1481-6*) Gordon Pr.
Quinn, Victoria, jt. auth. see CFNPP Staff.
Quinn, Vincent. Hart Crane. (Twayne's United States Authors Ser.). 1963. pap. 13.95 (*0-8084-0151-3*, T35) NCUP.
— Hilda Doolittle. (Twayne's United States Authors Ser.). 1967. pap. 13.95 (*0-8084-0002-9*, T126) NCUP.
— Hilda Doolittle (H. D.) LC 67-28856. (Twayne's United States Authors Ser.). 1967. lib. bdg. 17.95 (*0-8057-0356-X*) Irvington.
***Quinn, Virginia N.** Applying Psychology. 1994. write for info. (*0-615-00106-8*) McGraw.
— Applying Psychology. 3rd ed. 1994. text ed. write for info. (*0-615-00105-X*) McGraw.
Quinn, Warren. Morality & Action. LC 93-2769. (Studies in Philosophy). 272p. (C). 1994. 54.95 (*0-521-44164-1*); pap. 18.95 (*0-521-44696-1*) Cambridge U Pr.
Quinn, William. The Salt Works of Historic Cape Cod. LC 92-83913. (Illus.). 256p. 1993. 29.95 (*0-940160-56-0*) Parnassus Imprints.
Quinn, William, tr. see Abelly, Louis.
Quinn, William A. Chaucer's Rehersynges: The Performability of the Legend of Good Women. LC 93-31914. 1994. 55.95 (*0-8132-0791-6*) Cath U Pr.
Quinn, William G., ed. see Westmoreland, Kathy.
Quinn, William P. Cape Cod Maritime Disasters. LC 90-91663. 240p. 1990. 35.00 (*0-936972-13-0*) Lower Cape.
— Shipwrecks along the Atlantic Coast. 240p. 1988. 34.95 (*0-940160-40-4*) Parnassus Imprints.
— Shipwrecks Around Cape Cod. LC 73-92326. (Illus.). 240p. 1973. pap. 23.50 (*0-936972-01-7*) Lower Cape.
— Shipwrecks Around Maine. pap. 23.50 (*0-936972-11-4*) Lower Cape.
— Shipwrecks Around New England. LC 79-88076. (Illus.). 240p. 1984. pap. 23.50 (*0-936972-05-X*) Lower Cape.
Quinn, William P., jt. auth. see Morris, Paul C.
Quinn, William W. Buffalo Bill Remembers. LC 91-5063. 468p. 1991. boxed 18.95 (*0-923568-23-9*) Wilderness Adventure Bks.
Quinnell, A. Man on Fire. 1987. pap. 3.95 (*0-449-21418-4*) Fawcett.
Quinnell, A. J. Blood Ties. large type ed. (Adventure Suspense Ser.). 416p. 1985. 23.95 (*0-7089-8286-7*, Charnwood) Ulverscroft.
— The Mahdi. large type ed. (Adventure Suspense Ser.). 416p. 1982. 23.95 (*0-7089-8081-3*, Charnwood) Ulverscroft.
— Man on Fire. large type ed. (Adventure Suspense Ser.). 422p. 1982. 23.95 (*0-7089-8045-7*, Charnwood) Ulverscroft.
— The Perfect Kill. large type ed. (Charnwood Ser.). 448p. 1994. 25.95 (*0-7089-8744-3*, Charnwood) Ulverscroft.
— Snapshot. large type ed. (Adventure Suspense Ser.). 432p. 1984. 23.95 (*0-7089-8178-X*, Trail West Pubs) Ulverscroft.
***Quinnett, Paul.** Darwin's Bass: The Evolutionary Psychology of Fishing Man. (Orig.). Date not set. pap. write for info. (*1-879628-11-2*) Keokee ID.
— Pavlov's Trout: The Incompleat Psychology of Everyday Fishing. 224p. 1994. pap. 12.95 (*1-879628-05-8*) Keokee ID.
— Pavlov's Trout: The Incompleat Psychology of Everyday Fishing. 224p. 1994. 21.95 (*1-879628-07-4*) Keokee ID.
***Quinnett, Paul G.** On Becoming a Health & Human Services Manager: A Practical Guide for Clinicians & Counselors. 192p. 1989. 19.95x (*0-8264-0508-8*) Crossroad NY.
— Suicide: the Forever Decision: For Those Thinking about Suicide, & For Those Who Know, Love, & Counsel Them. 144p. 1987. pap. 9.95 (*0-8245-1352-5*) Crossroad NY.
— When Self-Help Fails: A Consumer's Guide to Counseling Services. 204p. 1991. pap. 11.95 (*0-8245-1846-2*) Crossroad NY.
Quinney, jt. auth. see Clinard.
Quinney, D. Introduction to the Numerical Solution of Differential Equations. rev. ed. (Applied & Engineering Mathematical Ser.). 1987. text ed. 105.00 (*0-471-91599-8*) Wiley.
Quinney, D. A., jt. auth. see Harding, R. D.
Quinney, H. Arthur, et al, eds. Toward Active Living: Proceedings of the International Conference on Physical Activity, Fitness & Health. LC 93-29972. (Illus.). 312p. 1994. pap. 39.00x (*0-87322-523-6*, BQUI0523) Human Kinetics.
***Quinney, Laura.** Literary Power & the Criteria of Truth. LC 94-42895. 192p. (C). 1995. lib. bdg. 34.95 (*0-8130-1345-3*) U Press Fla.
Quinney, Richard. Journey to a Far Place. (Illus.). 152p. 1991. 29.95 (*0-87722-725-X*) Temple U Pr.
— Providence: Reconstruction of Social & Moral Order. 120p. 1986. 14.95 (*0-932930-72-7*) Anderson Pub Co.
Quinney, Richard, ed. Capitalist Society: Readings for a Critical Sociology. LC 78-70955. (Dorsey Series in Sociology). 450p. reprint ed. pap. 128.30 (*0-317-09052-6*, 2055673) Bks Demand.
Quinney, Richard & Wildeman, John. The Problem of Crime: A Peace & Social Justice Perspective. 3rd ed. LC 90-39575. 152p. (C). 1991. pap. text ed. 18.95 (*0-87484-908-X*) Mayfield Pub.
Quinney, Richard, jt. ed. see Pepinsky, Harold E.
***Quinn's Staff.** Handbook Deschutes River Canyon. 1993. pap. 24.95 (*1-878175-35-1*) F Amato Pubns.
— Handbook Illinois River Canyon. 1983. pap. 24.95 (*1-878175-42-4*) F Amato Pubns.
— Handbook Middle Fork Salmon River. 1993. pap. 24.95 (*0-944664-03-2*) F Amato Pubns.
— Handbook Rogue River Canyon. 1978. pap. 24.95 (*1-878175-50-5*) F Amato Pubns.
— Handbook to the Klamath River Canyon. (Illus.). 1983. pap. 24.95 (*1-878175-49-1*) F Amato Pubns.
Quinodoz, Jean-Michel. The Taming of Solitude: Separation Anxiety in Psychoanalysis. LC 93-9866. (New Library of Psychoanalysis: Vol. 20). 1993. write for info. (*0-415-09153-5*); pap. write for info. (*0-415-09154-3*) Routledge.
Quinones, Armida. Espanol Vivo: Curso Programado Para Espanol Basico. 4th ed. 260p. (Orig.). (SPA.). (C). 1991. reprint ed. pap. text ed. 12.95 (*1-56328-010-8*) Edit Plaza Mayor.
Quinones-Baldrich, William J., ed. Pharmacologic Suppression of Intimal Hyperplasia. (Medical Intelligence Unit Ser.). 132p. 1993. 89.95 (*1-879702-53-3*, LN0253) R G Landes.
Quinones De Benavente, Luis. Joco Seria. (Textos y Estudios Clasicos De las Literaturas Hispanicas Ser.). 243p. 1985. reprint ed. write for info. (*3-487-06723-4*, Pub. by Georg Olms GW) Lubrecht & Cramer.
Quinones, Ferdinand, ed. see International Symposium on Tropical Hydrology Staff.
Quinones, Manny, jt. ed. see Cuellar, Carol.
Quinones, Nathan, ed. see Silverstein, Ruth, et al.
Quinones, Peter. Rapture of the Flat. LC 92-91113. 80p. 1993. pap. 8.00 (*1-56002-268-X*, Univ Edtns) Aegina Pr.
Quinones, Ricardo J. The Changes of Cain: Violence & the Lost Brother in Cain & Abel Literature. 304p. 1991. text ed. 29.95 (*0-691-06883-6*) Princeton U Pr.
— Dante Alighieri. (World Authors Ser.: No. 563). 216p. 1979. text ed. 22.95 (*0-8057-6405-4*, Twayne) Macmillan.
— Foundation Sacrifice in Dante's Commedia. (Penn State Studies). 176p. (C). 1994. 29.95 (*0-271-01309-5*) Pa St U Pr.
— Mapping Literary Modernism: Time & Development. LC 84-42899. 288p. 1985. text ed. 45.00 (*0-691-06636-1*) Princeton U Pr.
Quinones, Wanda M., tr. see Fassler, David & McQueen, Kelly.
Quinonesk, Eloise. Codex Telleriano-Remensis: Ritual, Divination, & History in a Pictorial Aztec Manuscript. LC 93-46481. (Illus.). 382p. (C). 1995. text ed. 75.00x (*0-292-76901-6*) U of Tex Pr.
Quinonez, Lora A. & Turner, Mary D. The Transformation of American Catholic Sisters. (Women in the Political Economy Ser.). (C). 1991. 34.95 (*0-87722-865-5*) Temple U Pr.
— The Transformation of American Catholic Sisters. 224p. 1993. pap. 16.95 (*1-56639-074-5*) Temple U Pr.
Quinsey, Mary B. Why Does That Man Have Such a Big Nose? LC 85-63760. (Illus.). 32p. (Orig.). (J). (ps-1). 1986. lib. bdg. 16.95 (*0-943990-25-4*); pap. 5.95 (*0-943990-24-6*) Parenting Pr.
Quint, Alonzo. Historical Memoranda Concerning Persons & Places in Old Dover, N.H., Vol. 1. Scales, John, ed. iv, 474p. 1983. reprint ed. 35.00 (*0-917890-29-9*) Heritage Bk.
***Quint, Alonzo H.** Civil War Infantry, the Record of the 2nd Massachusetts Infantry, 1861-1865. (Illus.). 528p. 1995. reprint ed. lib. bdg. 55.00 (*0-8328-4633-3*) Higginson Bk Co.
Quint, Artemis & Storr, Sherman. The Duoist from Del Remo. 183p. (Orig.). 1991. pap. 8.00 (*1-56002-123-3*) Aegina Pr.
Quint, B. G. Clear & Simple Guide to Bookkeeping. (Clear & Simple Study Guides Ser.). (Illus.). 128p. (Orig.). (C). 1981. pap. 8.00 (*0-671-42108-5*, Arco Test) P-H Gen Ref & Trav.
Quint, Barbara. Wall Street Talk: How to Understand Your Broker. (Illus.). 1983. 11.95 (*0-8027-0754-8*); pap. 5.95 (*0-8027-7232-3*) Walker & Co.
Quint, Bruce, jt. auth. see Lindsey, William H.
Quint, David. Epic & Empire: Politics & Generic Form from Virgil to Milton. LC 92-21709. (Literature in History Ser.). 432p. (C). 1993. text ed. 55.00 (*0-691-06942-5*); pap. text ed. 16.95 (*0-691-01520-1*) Princeton U Pr.
— Origin & Originality in Renaissance Literature: Versions of the Source. LC 82-24789. 275p. reprint ed. pap. 78.40 (*0-7837-4528-1*, 2080191) Bks Demand.
Quint, David, tr. The Stanze of Angelo Poliziano. LC 92-35532. 128p. (C). 1993. reprint ed. pap. 14.95 (*0-271-00937-3*) Pa St U Pr.
Quint, David, tr. see Ariosto, Ludovico.
Quint, David, jt. ed. see Parker, Patricia.
Quint, David, et al, eds. Creative Imitation: New Essays on Renaissance Literature in Honor of Thomas M. Greene. (Medieval & Renaissance Texts & Studies: Vol. 95). 456p. 1993. 40.00 (*0-86698-109-8*) MRTS.
Quint, Emanuel. A Restatement of Rabbinic Civil Law: Laws of Collection of Debts, Laws of Collection from Heirs, Laws of Mortgages, Laws of Agency, Laws of Guarantee, Laws of Presumption of Ownership of Personalty, Vol. 4. LC 89-18546. 384p. 1993. 40.00 (*0-87668-197-6*) Aronson.
— A Restatement of Rabbinic Civil Law: Laws of Judges & Laws of Evidence, Vol. 1. LC 89-18546. 336p. 1990. 40.00 (*0-87668-799-0*) Aronson.
— A Restatement of Rabbinic Civil Law: Laws of Loans, Vol. 2. LC 89-18546. 352p. 1991. 40.00 (*0-87668-678-1*) Aronson.
— A Restatement of Rabbinic Civil Law: Laws of Partnerships, Laws of Agents, Laws of Sales, Acquisition of Personalty, Vol. 6. LC 89-18546. 416p. 1995. 50.00 (*1-56821-319-0*) Aronson.
— A Restatement of Rabbinic Civil Law: Laws of Pleading, Vol. 3. LC 89-18546. 288p. 1993. 40.00 (*0-87668-396-0*) Aronson.
— A Restatement of Rabbinic Civil Law: Laws of Presumption of Ownership of Realty, Laws of Injuries to Neighbors, Laws of Joint Ownership of Realty, Laws of Partition of Realty, Vol. 5. LC 89-18546. 336p. 1994. 50.00 (*1-56821-167-8*) Aronson.
Quint, Emanuel & Hecht, Neil S. Jewish Jurisprudence: Its Sources & Modern Applications Ser, Vol. 1. 268p. (C). 1980. text ed. 72.00 (*3-7186-0054-4*); pap. text ed. 33.00 (*3-7186-0055-2*) Gordon & Breach.
Quint, Emanuel B. & Hecht, Neil S. Jewish Jurisprudence: Its Sources & Modern Applications, Vol. 2. 193p. 1986. text ed. 85.00 (*3-7186-0064-1*); pap. text ed. 27.00 (*3-7186-0293-8*) Gordon & Breach.
***Quint, Eric T., et al, eds.** Tomography, Impedence Imaging & Integral Geometry: Proceedings of the 1993 AMS-SIAM Seminar in Applied Mathematics on Tomography, Impedance Imaging & Integral Geometry, June 7-18, 1993, Mt. Holyoke College, Massachusetts. LC 94-28800. (Lectures in Applied Mathematics: Vol. 30). 1994. write for info. (*0-8218-0337-9*) Am Math.
Quint, Marie. Progress Shorthand Passages, 4 bks., Bk. 1. LC 80-42139. (Longman Secretarial Studies). reprint ed. pap. 20.00 (*0-317-27729-4*, 2025226) Bks Demand.
— Progress Shorthand Passages, 4 bks., Bk. 2. LC 80-42139. (Longman Secretarial Studies). reprint ed. pap. 20.00 (*0-317-27730-8*) Bks Demand.
— Progress Shorthand Passages, 4 bks., Bk. 3. LC 80-42139. (Longman Secretarial Studies). reprint ed. pap. 20.00 (*0-317-27731-6*) Bks Demand.
— Progress Shorthand Passages, 4 bks., Bk. 4. LC 80-42139. (Longman Secretarial Studies). reprint ed. pap. 20.00 (*0-317-27732-4*) Bks Demand.
Quint, Neal. American Spy Story. 1989. pap. 3.95 (*0-8217-2753-2*) Zebra.
***Quint, Sharon.** Schooling Homeless Children: A Qualitative Study of One Urban School. LC 94-28783. 176p. (C). 1994. text ed. 30.00 (*0-8077-3392-X*); pap. 14.95x (*0-8077-3391-1*) Tchrs Coll.
Quintahlen, Patrique, ed. see Daves, Prentiss V.
Quintal, Claire, ed. La Femme Franco-Americaine: Franco-American Woman. 216p. (ENG & FRE.). 1994. pap. 14.95 (*1-880261-02-2*) FI Assump Coll.
Quintal, Claire, intro. La Litterature Franco-Americaine Ecrivains et Ecritures: Franco-American Literature Writers & Their Writings. 193p. (Orig.). (ENG & FRE.). (C). 1992. pap. text ed. 10.95 (*1-880261-00-6*) FI Assump Coll.
— Religion Catholique et Appartenance Franco-Americaine: Franco-Americans & Religion: Impact & Influence. 202p. (Orig.). (ENG & FRE.). (C). 1993. pap. text ed. 11.95 (*1-880261-01-4*) FI Assump Coll.
Quintana. Cuisine of the Water Gods: Mexican Seafood & Vegetable Cookery. 1994. 25.00 (*0-671-74898-X*) S&S Trade.
***Quintana, Alvina E.** Home Girls: Chicana Literary Motifs. 208p. (Orig.). (C). 1995. lib. bdg. 39.95 (*1-56639-372-8*); pap. text ed. 16.95 (*1-56639-373-6*) Temple U Pr.
Quintana, Arturo O. Pablo Casals in Puerto Rico. (Puerto Rico Ser.). 1979. lib. bdg. 59.95 (*0-8490-2981-3*) Gordon Pr.
Quintana, Bertha B. & Floyd, Lois G. Que Gitano! Gypsies of Southern Spain. Spindler, George & Spindler, Louise, eds. (Case Studies in Cultural Anthropology). (Illus.). 137p. (C). 1983. reprint ed. pap. text ed. 6.95 (*0-8290-0582-X*) Irvington.
— Que Gitano! Gypsies of Southern Spain. (Illus.). 126p. (C). 1986. reprint ed. pap. text ed. 8.95 (*0-88133-217-8*) Waveland Pr.

PQ

Quintana, Francisco. Una Cita Con el Diablo. LC 90-83578. 159p. 1991. 16.00 (*0-89729-576-5*) Ediciones.
Quintana, Francisco, tr. see Lebelson, Harry & Rush, Bette.
Quintana, Hilda, et al. Personalidad y Literatura Puertorriquenas. 5th ed. (Illus.). 384p. (SPA.). (C). 1992. reprint ed. pap. text ed. 14.95 (*1-56328-034-5*) Edit Plaza Mayor.
Quintana, Kathy & Miller, Danny. G-d, Israel, the Future & You: From the Fall of Jordan to the Rapture of the Church. 200p. (Orig.). 1988. pap. 10.00 (*0-9621155-0-9*) Shalom Colorado.
Quintana, Leroy V. The History of Home. LC 93-10204. 96p. 1993. pap. 9.00 (*0-927534-36-3*) Biling Rev-Pr.
— Interrogations. (Vietnam Generation Ser.). 104p. (Orig.). (C). 1990. pap. 10.00 (*0-9628524-5-7*) Burning Cities Pr.
Quintana, Leroy V. & Suarez, Virgil, eds. Paper Dance: Fifty-Five Latino Poets. 256p. (Orig.). 1995. pap. 14.00 (*0-89255-201-8*) Persea Bks.
Quintana, Marlou J., jt. auth. see Sherman, Lois.
***Quintana, Patricia.** The Best of Quintana. LC 94-45985. (Illus.). 128p. 1995. 22.50 (*1-55670-409-7*) Stewart Tabori & Chang.
— Mexico's Feasts of Life. LC 89-61234. 254p. (Orig.). 1994. pap. 24.95 (*1-57178-000-9*) Coun Oak Bks.
— The Taste of Mexico. Wilkinson, Marilyn, ed. LC 86-5817. (Illus.). 304p. 1986. 50.00 (*0-941434-89-3*) Stewart Tabori & Chang.
— The Taste of Mexico. LC 86-5817. (Illus.). 304p. 1993. pap. 24.95 (*1-55670-326-0*) Stewart Tabori & Chang.
Quintana, Ricardo. Eighteenth Century Plays. (Modern Library College Editions). (C). 1966. pap. text ed. write for info. (*0-07-553659-5*) McGraw.
— Swift: An Introduction. LC 79-17607. 204p. 1980. reprint ed. text ed. 55.00 (*0-313-22052-2*, QUST, Greenwood Pr) Greenwood.
— Two Augustans: John Locke, Jonathan Swift. LC 77-91059. 156p. 1978. 26.50 (*0-299-07420-X*) U of Wis Pr.
Quintana, Ricardo, ed. Two Hundred Poems. LC 74-80377. (Granger Index Reprint Ser.). 1977. 23.95 (*0-8369-6058-0*) Ayer.
Quintana, Ricardo, ed. see Swift, Jonathan.
Quintana, Richardo. The Mind & Art of Jonathan Swift. 12.75 (*0-8446-1370-3*) Peter Smith.
Quintanar, Derek, ed. see Ackerman, David, et al.
Quintanar, Derek, ed. see MacLimore, Guy.
Quintanar, Derek, ed. see Pondsmith, Michael, et al.
Quintanilha, A. La Probleme de la Sexualite Chez les Champignons: Recherches sur le Genre Coprinus. (Illus.). 1968. reprint ed. pap. 24.00 (*3-7682-0556-8*) Lubrecht & Cramer.
Quintanilha, A., ed. Reactive Oxygen Species in Chemistry, Biology, & Medicine. LC 87-38498. (Illus.). 240p. 1988. 75.00 (*0-306-42808-3*, Plenum Pr) Plenum.
Quintanilha, F. E. Sixty Portuguese Poems: Fernando Pessoa. 141p. 1971. 14.00 (*0-904730-73-5*, Pub. by U of Wales UK) Bks Intl VA.
Quintanilla, Efren. Aventuras de Bartolillo. (SPA.). 7.95 (*84-241-5634-X*) E Torres & Sons.
Quintanilla Fisac, Miguel A. Diccionario de Filosofia. 300p. 1991. pap. 39.95 (*0-7859-6145-3*, 8471517094) Fr & Eur.
Quintanilla, Quadalupe C., tr. see Wade, Mary D.
Quintard, Michel & Todorovic, Marija, eds. Heat & Mass Transfer in Porous Media. LC 92-14156. 1992. write for info. (*0-444-89498-5*) Elsevier.
***Quintas, Alfonso L.** Human Love: Its Meaning & Scope. LC 94-40761. (Cultural Heritage & Contemporary Change Series I: Culture & Values: Vol. 15). 1995. 45.00 (*1-56518-073-9*); pap. 17.50 (*1-56518-074-7*) Coun Res Values.
— The Knowledge of Values: A Methodological Introduction. LC 89-5597. (Cultural Heritage & Contemporary Life Series I. Culture & Values: Vol. 2). 116p. (Orig.). 1989. 45.00 (*0-8191-7418-1*); pap. 14.00 (*0-8191-7419-X*) Coun Res Values.
Quintas, Louis V., jt. ed. see Gewirtz, Allan.
Quintas, Louis V., jt. ed. see Kenndy, J. W.
Quintas, Paul, ed. Social Dimensions of Systems Engineering: People, Processes, Policies, & Software Development. (Interactive Information Systems Ser.). 350p. 1993. pap. text ed. 50.00 (*0-13-020306-8*) P-H.
Quintela, Helen W. Out of Ashes. LC 91-10447. 160p. 1991. pap. 8.95 (*0-8361-3554-7*) Herald Pr.
Quintella, Rogerio H. The Strategic Management of Technology in the Chemical & Petrochemical Industries. LC 93-21542. 1994. 69.00 (*1-85567-146-8*, Pub. by Pinter Pubs UK) St Martin.
Quintero, A. G., jt. auth. see Garcia, Gervasio L.
Quintero, Alvarez. Genio Alegre - Amores Yamorios - Muela Del Rey Farfan - La Reja. 297p. (SPA.). 1964. 7.95 (*0-8288-7177-9*) Fr & Eur.
— Genio Alegre - las de Cain. 286p. (SPA.). 1963. 1.50 (*0-8288-7144-2*) Fr & Eur.
— Puebla de Las Mujeres - Genio Alegre. 142p. (SPA.). 1979. 5.95 (*0-8288-7101-9*) Fr & Eur.
Quintero, Ana H. Que Me Pasa con las Matematicas? LC 85-24617. (Illus.). 119p. 1986. pap. 11.50 (*0-8477-2749-1*) U of PR Pr.
— Representaciones en la Ensenanza de las Matematicas. LC 87-25573. 240p. 1988. pap. 16.00 (*0-8477-2750-5*) U of PR Pr.
Quintero, Angel G. Conflictos de Clase y Politica en PR. (Cuadernos CEREP Ser.). 168p. 1981. pap. 6.75 (*0-940238-09-8*) Ediciones Huracan.
Quintero, Diomedes & Aiello, Annette, eds. Insects of Panama & Mesoamerica: Selected Studies. 960p. 1992. 195.00 (*0-19-854018-3*) OUP.
Quintero, Elizabeth, jt. ed. see Weinstein-Shr, Gail.
Quintero, Jorge A. Acid Base Balance: A Manual for Clinicians. 2nd ed. LC 77-81798. 152p. 1981. 12.50 (*0-87527-148-0*) Green.
— Laws, Theories & Values. 2nd ed. LC 79-50190. (Illus.). 144p. 1980. 8.90 (*0-87527-147-2*) Green.
Quintero, Jose. If You Don't Dance They Beat You. 320p. 1988. pap. 10.95 (*0-312-02222-0*) St Martin.
Quintero, Maria C. Poetry as Play: "Gongorismo" & the "Comedia" LC 91-40886. (Purdue University Monographs in Romance Languages: No. 38). xviii, 260p. 1991. 80.00x (*1-55619-304-1*); pap. 27.95 (*1-55619-305-X*) Benjamins North Am.
Quintero-Rivera, Angel. Workers' Struggle in Puerto Rico: A Documentary History. Belfrage, Cedric, tr. LC 76-40343. 236p. 1977. 11.95 (*0-85345-392-6*) Monthly Rev.
Quintero-Rivera, Angel G. Patricios & Plebeyos: Burgueses, Hacendados, Artesanos & Obreros: Las Relaciones de Clase en el Puerto Rico de Cambio de Siglo. LC 87-82379. (Nave y el Puerto Ser.). 332p. (SPA.). 1988. pap. 9.95 (*0-940238-93-4*) Ediciones Huracan.
Quintero, Roberto, ed. see Cornish, Patty Jo.
Quintero, Ruben. Literate Culture: Pope's Rhetorical Art. LC 90-50939. 192p. 1992. 36.50 (*0-87413-433-1*) U Delaware Pr.
Quintero, Serafin Y. El Genio Alegre. Puebla de las Mujeres. Nebrera, Gregorio T., ed. (Nueva Austral Ser.: Vol. 78). (SPA.). 1991. pap. text ed. 14.95 (*84-239-1878-5*) Elliots Bks.
Quinteros, Alvarez. Malvaloca - Dona Clarines. 148p. (SPA.). 1966. 9.95 (*0-8288-7106-X*) Fr & Eur.
Quinteros, Juan. El Caso Lefevre: The Lefevre Case. (SPA.). 3.00 (*84-7228-334-8*, 220147, Pub. by Edit Clie SP) TSELF.
Quintet Books Staff. Floral Needlepoint. 1993. 12.98 (*1-55521-969-1*) Bk Sales Inc.
— Natural Health Cat Care Manual. 1993. 12.98 (*1-55521-970-5*) Bk Sales Inc.
— Who Built That? 1993. 12.98 (*1-55521-927-6*) Bk Sales Inc.
Quintiere, J., jt. ed. see Cho, P.
Quintiere, J. G., et al, eds. Fire Dynamics & Heat Transfer. (Heat Transfer Ser.: Vol. 25). 138p. 1983. pap. text ed. 34.00 (*0-317-02619-4*, H00269) ASME.
***Quintieri, Beniamino.** Patterns of Trade, Competition & Trade Policies. 176p. 1995. boxed, pap. 59.95 (*1-85972-066-8*, Pub. by Avebury Pub UK) Ashgate Pub Co.
Quintilian. Institutionis Oratoriae, 2 vols., Vol. 1, Bks. 1-6. Winterbottom, M., ed. (Oxford Classical Texts Ser.). 1970. 38.00 (*0-19-814654-X*) OUP.
— Institutionis Oratoriae, 2 vols., Vol. 2, Bks. 7-12. Winterbottom, M., ed. (Oxford Classical Texts Ser.). 1970. 39.95 (*0-19-814655-8*) OUP.
— Training of an Orator, 4 vols. No. 124-127. write for info. (*0-318-53200-X*) HUP.
— Training of an Orator, 4 vols., 1. (Loeb Classical Library: No. 124-127). 568p. 1920. 18.95 (*0-674-99138-9*) HUP.
— Training of an Orator, 4 vols., 2. (Loeb Classical Library: No. 124-127). 538p. 1921. 18.95 (*0-674-99139-7*) HUP.
— Training of an Orator, 4 vols., 3. (Loeb Classical Library: No. 124-127). 504p. 1921. 18.95 (*0-674-99140-0*) HUP.
— Training of an Orator, 4 vols., 4. (Loeb Classical Library: No. 124-127). 556p. 1922. 18.95 (*0-674-99141-9*) HUP.
Quintiliani, Patricia S. My Treasury of Chaplets. 3rd ed. (Illus.). 240p. 1992. pap. 7.95 (*0-911218-25-4*) Ravengate Pr.
Quintilianus. Institutionis Oratoriae Liber I. Colson, Francis H., ed. xcviii, 208p. 1973. reprint ed. write for info. (*3-487-04611-3*, Pub. by Georg Olms GW) Lubrecht & Cramer.
— Institutionis Oratoriae Liber X. Peterson, W., ed. lxxx, 227p. 1967. reprint ed. 50.70 (*0-685-66507-0*, 05101664, Pub. by Georg Olms GW) Lubrecht & Cramer.
Quintilianus, Marcus F. De Institutione Oratoria Libri Duodecim, 6 vols., Set. ccxxxvi, 4175p. 1968. reprint ed. write for info. (*0-318-71207-5*, Pub. by Georg Olms GW) Lubrecht & Cramer.
— De Institutione Oratoria Libri Duodecim, Vol. 6: Lexicon Quintilianeum. Bonell, E., ed. lxxxiv, 1044p. 1962. reprint ed. write for info. (*0-318-71208-3*, Pub. by Georg Olms GW) Lubrecht & Cramer.
Quintillan, Manuel A. Diccionario Economia General y Empresa, 4 vols., Set. 112p. (SPA.). 1991. pap. write for info. (*0-7859-5993-9*, 8436806522) Fr & Eur.
— Diccionario Economia General y Empresa, Vol. 1. 112p. (SPA.). 1991. pap. write for info. (*0-7859-5994-7*, 8436806530) Fr & Eur.
— Diccionario Economia General y Empresa, Vol. 2. 112p. (SPA.). 1991. pap. write for info. (*0-7859-5995-5*, 8436806549) Fr & Eur.
— Diccionario Economia General y Empresa, Vol. 3. 112p. (SPA.). 1991. pap. write for info. (*0-7859-5996-3*, M2818) Fr & Eur.
— Diccionario Economia General y Empressa, 4 vols., Set. 448p. (SPA.). 1991. pap. write for info. (*0-7859-5992-0*, 8436806514) Fr & Eur.
— Diccionario Tematico de Antropologia. 316p. (SPA.). 1985. 49.95 (*0-8288-1285-3*, S60822) Fr & Eur.
Quintilone, Paul M. Brian Has a Winning Day. (J). (gr. 3-5). 1988. pap. write for info. (*0-9616980-2-0*) Quintilone Ent.
— Michael Learns New Words. (Illus.). (J). (gr. 3-5). 1988. pap. 2.98 (*0-9616980-1-2*) Quintilone Ent.
Quintin, Jonathan, des. Geometric Coloring Book, Vol. II. (Illus.). 64p. (Orig.). 1993. pap. 5.00 (*1-56170-066-5*, 1422) Hay House.
— Geometric Coloring Book for Adults. (Illus.). 64p. (Orig.). 1991. pap. 5.00 (*1-56170-038-X*, 142) Hay House.
Quinting, Gerd. Hesitation Phenomena in Adult Aphasic & Normal Speech. LC 75-170008. (Janua Linguarum, Series Minor: No. 126). 73p. 1971. pap. text ed. 14.75 (*90-279-1842-2*) Mouton.
Quinto, Eric T., jt. ed. see Grinberg, Eric.
Quinto, Leon, jt. auth. see Burrill, Claude.
Quinton & Robert, Jean. Systolic Algorithms & Architectures. 350p. 1991. text ed. 46.00 (*0-13-880790-6*) P-H.
Quinton, Ann. The Ragusa Theme. large type ed. (Romance Suspense Ser.). 416p. 1988. 21.95 (*0-7089-1777-1*) Ulverscroft.
Quinton, Anne. A Little Grave. 480p. 1994. (*0-7278-4492-X*) Severn Hse.
— Little Grave. 1994. 20.00 (*0-7278-4578-0*) Severn Hse.
— The Sleeping & the Dead. 1994. lib. bdg. 20.00 (*0-7278-4668-X*) Severn Hse.
Quinton, Anthony. The Nature of Things. 1978. reprint ed. pap. 19.95 (*0-7100-8903-1*, RKP) Routledge.
— Thoughts & Thinkers. LC 81-13372. 350p. 1982. 54.50 (*0-8419-0772-2*); pap. 29.50 (*0-8419-0773-0*) Holmes & Meier.
— Utilitarian Ethics. 128p. 1988. 32.95 (*0-8126-9051-6*); pap. 13.95 (*0-8126-9052-4*) Open Court.
Quinton, Anthony, ed. Political Philosophy. (Oxford Readings in Philosophy Ser.). (Orig.). 1978. pap. 14.95 (*0-19-875002-1*) OUP.
Quinton, P. M., jt. ed. see Mastella, G.
Quinton, P. M., et al, eds. Fluid & Electrolyte Abnormalities in Exocrine Glands in Cystic Fibrosis. (Illus.). 1982. 18.75 (*0-911302-45-X*) San Francisco Pr.
Quintos, James L. Dog Diseases: Research Index with Bibliography. rev. ed. LC 87-47684. 150p. 1988. 39.50 (*0-88164-639-3*); pap. 34.50 (*0-88164-640-7*) ABBE Pubs Assn.
Quintrell, Brian. Charles the First, 1625-1640. LC 92-28086. (Seminar Studies in History). (C). 1993. pap. text ed. 11.95 (*0-582-00354-7*) Longman.
Quintus, Curtius. History of Alexander, 2 vols., 1. (Loeb Classical Library: No. 368-369). 15.50 (*0-674-99405-1*) HUP.
— History of Alexander, 2 vols., 2. (Loeb Classical Library: No. 368-369). 636p. 1946. 18.95 (*0-674-99407-8*) HUP.
Quintus Smyrnaeus. Fall of Troy. (Loeb Classical Library: No. 19). 640p. 1913. 18.95 (*0-674-99022-6*) HUP.
Quintus, Smyrnaeus. The War at Troy: What Homer Didn't Tell. Combellack, Frederick M., tr. & intro. by. LC 67-24612. 288p. reprint ed. pap. 82.10 (*0-7837-1988-4*, 2042262) Bks Demand.
Quinzii, Martine. Increasing Returns & Economic Efficiency. (Illus.). 176p. 1993. 38.00 (*0-19-506553-0*) OUP.
Quirey, B. May I Have the Pleasure. (Ballroom Dance Ser.). 1985. lib. bdg. 74.00 (*0-87700-686-5*) Revisionist Pr.
— May I Have the Pleasure? (Ballroom Dance Ser.). 1986. lib. bdg. 79.95 (*0-8490-3359-4*) Gordon Pr.
Quiri, Patricia R. The Algonquians. LC 91-29111. (First Bks.). (Illus.). 64p. (J). (gr. 3-5). 1992. lib. bdg. 13.93 (*0-531-20065-5*) Watts.
— The Algonquians. (First Bks.). 64p. (J). (gr. 5-8). 1992. pap. 5.95 (*0-531-15633-8*) Watts.
— Dating. LC 89-5709. (Venture Bks.). (Illus.). 95p. (YA). (gr. 7-12). 1989. lib. bdg. 14.28 (*0-531-10806-6*) Watts.
— Dolley Madison. LC 92-28300. (First Bks.). (J). 1993. 13.93 (*0-531-20097-3*) Watts.
— Metamorphosis. LC 91-3104. (First Bks.). (Illus.). 64p. (J). (gr. 5-8). 1991. lib. bdg. 13.93 (*0-531-20042-6*) Watts.
Quirin, H., et al, eds. Historischer Handatlas von Brandenburg und Berlin: 1962-79. Incl. Facsimile 1-6. Facsimile 1 - 6. 72.00 (*3-11-000493-3*); Facsimile 7-12. Facsimile 7 - 12. 78.00 (*3-11-000499-2*); Facsimile 13-18. Facsimile 13 - 18. 78.00 (*0-317-19773-8*); Facsimile 19-24. Facsimile 19 - 24. 78.00 (*3-11-000511-5*); Facsimile 27-30. Facsimile 27 - 30. 52.00 (*3-11-002697-X*); Facsimile 31-34. Facsimile 31 - 34. 52.00 (*3-11-003887-0*); Facsimile 35-36. Facsimile 35 - 36. 26.00 (*3-11-004323-8*); Facsimile 37-41. Facsimile 37 - 41. 93.50 (*3-11-004336-X*); Facsimile 42-46. Facsimile 42 - 46. 100.00 (*3-11-004866-3*); Facsimile 47-49. Facsimile 47 - 49. 60.00 (*3-11-005963-0*); Facsimile 50-52. Facsimile 50 - 52. 64.00 (*3-11-006924-5*); Facsimile 53-56. Facsimile 53 - 56. 90.75 (*3-11-007472-9*); Facsimile 57-60. Facsimile 57 - 60. 90.75 (*3-11-007490-7*); Facsimile 1-6. Facsimile 1 - 6. 72.00 (*3-11-000493-3*); Facsimile 7-12. Facsimile 7 - 12. 78.00 (*3-11-000499-2*); Facsimile 13-18. Facsimile 13 - 18. 78.00 (*0-317-19773-8*); Facsimile 19-24. Facsimile 19 - 24. 78.00 (*3-11-000511-5*); Facsimile 27-30. Facsimile 27 - 30. 52.00 (*3-11-002697-X*); Facsimile 31-34. Facsimile 31 - 34. 52.00 (*3-11-003887-0*); Facsimile 35-36. Facsimile 35 - 36. 26.00 (*3-11-004323-8*); Facsimile 37-41. Facsimile 37 - 41. 93.50 (*3-11-004336-X*); Facsimile 42-46. Facsimile 42 - 46. 100.00 (*3-11-004866-3*); Facsimile 47-49. Facsimile 47 - 49. 60.00 (*3-11-005963-0*); Facsimile 50-52. Facsimile 50 - 52. 64.00 (*3-11-006924-5*); Facsimile 53-56. Facsimile 53 - 56. 90.75 (*3-11-007472-9*); Facsimile 57-60. Facsimile 57 - 60. 90.75 (*3-11-007490-7*); write for info. (*0-318-59219-3*) De Gruyter.
Quirin, James. The Evolution of the Ethiopian Jews: A History of the Beta Israel (Falasha) to 1920. LC 91-47665. (Ethnohistory Ser.). (Illus.). 360p. (C). 1992. text ed. 38.95 (*0-8122-3116-3*) U of Pa Pr.
Quirin, Jim, jt. auth. see Cohen, Barry.
Quirin, William, et al. The Greenwich Country Club, 1892-1992. LC 93-16831. 1993. write for info. (*0-89865-862-4*) Donning Co.
Quirin, William L. Handicapping by Example. LC 86-12486. 256p. 1986. 23.00 (*0-688-05929-5*) Morrow.
— The Knollwood Spirit, 1894-1994. 1994. text ed. write for info. (*0-89865-920-5*) Donning Co.
— Morris County Golf Club, 1894-1994. LC 94-24079. 1995. write for info. (*0-89865-928-0*) Donning Co.
— North Jersey Country Club. LC 94-47356. 1995. write for info. (*0-89865-929-9*) Donning Co.
— Thoroughbred Handicapping. LC 84-60211. 320p. 1984. 23.00 (*0-688-03064-5*) Morrow.
— Thoroughbred Handicapping: State of the Art. (Illus.). 336p. 1992. pap. 12.50 (*0-688-11215-3*, Quill) Morrow.
— Winning at the Races: Computer Discoveries in Thoroughbred Handicapping. LC 79-1271. (Tom Ainslie - Winner's Circle Ser.). (Illus.). 1979. 22.95 (*0-688-03400-4*) Morrow.
***Quiring, Ethel F. & Savage, Hugh W.** Slavery Is Alive - & We Are Not Well: How to Recognize & Escape Inter-Personal Control. LC 95-60207. 186p. (Orig.). (C). 1995. pap. 12.95 (*0-932796-69-9*) Ed Media Corp.
***Quiring, Isaac.** Strangled Roots. 186p. (Orig.). 1982. pap. 8.95 (*0-920490-26-3*) Temeron Bks.
Quiring, James P. In Pictures Mount St. Helens: The Continuing Story. LC 91-60040. 48p. 1991. 6.95 (*0-88714-055-6*) KC Pubns.
Quiring, Virginia M., ed. The Milton S. Eisenhower Years at Kansas State University. 120p. 1986. 25.00 (*0-685-18353-X*) Friends Lib KSU.
— The Milton S. Eisenhower Years at Kansas State University. limited ed. 120p. 1986. 50.00 (*0-9616658-0-7*) Friends Lib KSU.
Quirino, Carlos. Amang: The Life & Times of Eulogio Rodriguez, Sr. (Illus.). 302p. (Orig.). 1984. pap. 13.75 (*971-10-0141-1*, Pub. by New Day Pub PH) Cellar.
— Chick Parsons: America's Master Spy in the Philippines. (Illus.). 168p. (Orig.). 1984. pap. 12.50 (*971-10-0198-5*, Pub. by New Day Pub PH) Cellar.
Quirion, Remi, jt. ed. see Samson, Willis K.
Quirk. The Employee Handbook. 443p. 1991. 96.00 (*0-88730-474-5*, S74) Aspen Pub.
***Quirk, Charles E., ed.** The Encyclopedia of Sports Law. LC 94-35594. (Reference Library of Social Science, Vol. 765: Vol. 4). 1995. write for info. (*0-8153-0220-7*) Garland.
Quirk, Dantia. Q's Who in Pay-Per-View. 80p. 1988. 24.95 (*0-910767-17-3*) QV Pub.
— Q's Who in Television Sports. 130p. 1987. 19.95 (*0-910767-20-3*) QV Pub.
Quirk, Dantia & Whitestone, Patricia. The Shrinking Library Dollar. 170p. 1982. 27.95 (*0-685-47122-5*) G K Hall.
— The Shrinking Library Dollar. LC 81-12319. (Communications Library). 170p. 1982. 27.95 (*0-685-02844-5*) G K Hall.
Quirk, James & Fort, Rodney D. Pay Dirt: The Business of Professional Team Sports. (Illus.). 400p. 1992. text ed. 39.50 (*0-691-04255-1*) Princeton U Pr.
Quirk, James, et al, eds. Coal Models & Their Use in Government Planning. LC 81-21153. 288p. 1982. text ed. 55.00 (*0-275-90880-1*, C0880, Praeger Pubs) Greenwood.
Quirk, James P., jt. ed. see Horwich, George.
Quirk, John. CIA Entrance Examination. (Arco Professional Test Preparation Ser.). 1988. pap. 14.95 (*0-317-66872-2*, Arco Test) P-H Gen Ref & Trav.
Quirk, John E. No Red Ribbons. 1965. 10.00 (*0-8159-6306-8*) Devin.
Quirk, Lawrence. The Films of Lauren Bacall. 1990. pap. 15.95 (*0-8065-1193-1*, Citadel Pr) Carol Pub Group.
Quirk, Lawrence, ed. see Dickens, Homer.
Quirk, Lawrence J. The Complete Films of Ingrid Bergman. 1989. pap. 14.95 (*0-8065-0972-4*, Citadel Pr) Carol Pub Group.
— The Complete Films of Joan Crawford. rev. ed. (Illus.). 224p. 1988. pap. 14.95 (*0-8065-1078-1*, Citadel Pr) Carol Pub Group.
— The Complete Films of William Holden. rev. ed. (Illus.). 288p. 1986. pap. 12.95 (*0-8065-0987-2*, Citadel Pr) Carol Pub Group.
— The Complete Films of William Powell. (Illus.). 288p. (Orig.). 1986. pap. 15.95 (*0-8065-0998-8*, Citadel Pr) Carol Pub Group.
— Fasten Your Seat Belts: The Passionate Life of Bette Davis. (Illus.). 560p. 1990. pap. 5.95 (*0-451-16950-6*, Sig) NAL-Dutton.
— Films of Fredric March. (Illus.). 1971. 9.95 (*0-8065-0259-2*, Citadel Pr); pap. 7.95 (*0-8065-0413-7*, Citadel Pr) Carol Pub Group.
— The Films of Gloria Swanson. LC 83-20859. 256p. 19.95 (*0-8065-0874-4*, Citadel Pr) Carol Pub Group.
— The Films of Gloria Swanson. (Illus.). 256p. 1988. reprint ed. pap. 14.95 (*0-8065-1077-3*, Citadel Pr) Carol Pub Group.
— Films of Ingrid Bergman. 1970. 9.95 (*0-8065-0212-6*, Citadel Pr) Carol Pub Group.
— The Films of Myrna Loy. 1980. 16.95 (*0-8065-0735-7*, Citadel Pr); pap. 9.95 (*0-8065-0880-9*, Citadel Pr) Carol Pub Group.
— The Films of Paul Newman. 256p. 1986. reprint ed. pap. 12.95 (*0-8065-0986-4*, Citadel Pr) Carol Pub Group.
— The Films of Robert Taylor. (Illus.). 256p. 1975. 14.00 (*0-8065-0495-1*, Citadel Pr); pap. 7.95 (*0-8065-0667-9*, Citadel Pr) Carol Pub Group.
— The Films of Ronald Colman. (Illus.). 1977. 14.95 (*0-8065-0562-1*, Citadel Pr); pap. 7.95 (*0-8065-0668-7*, Citadel Pr) Carol Pub Group.
— The Films of Warren Beatty. 1990. pap. 15.95 (*0-8065-1194-X*, Citadel Pr) Carol Pub Group.
— The Films of William Holden. 256p. 1973. 12.00 (*0-8065-0375-0*, Citadel Pr); pap. 12.95 (*0-8065-0517-6*, Citadel Pr) Carol Pub Group.
— The Great Romantic Films. (Illus.). 256p. 1974. 12.00 (*0-8065-0401-3*, Citadel Pr); pap. 9.95 (*0-8065-0539-7*, Citadel Pr) Carol Pub Group.
— The Great War Films: From Tte Birth of the Nation to Today. LC 94-20343. 1994. pap. 17.95 (*0-8065-1529-5*, Citadel Pr) Carol Pub Group.
— Lauren Bacall: Her Films & Career. (Illus.). 224p. 1986. 19.95 (*0-8065-0935-X*, Citadel Pr) Carol Pub Group.

PO

An Asterisk (*) at the beginning of an entry indicates that the title is appearing in BIP for the first time.

— Some Lovely Image. 1989. pap. 9.95 (0-8216-2007-X, Univ Books) Carol Pub Group.
— Totally Uninhibited: The Life & Wild Times of Cher. LC 92-25340. 1993. 7.00 (0-688-12303-1, Quill) Morrow.
***Quirk, Mark E.** How to Learn & Teach in Medical School: A Learner-Centered Approach. LC 94-21620. 224p. 1994. pap. 29.95 (0-398-06512-8) C C Thomas.
— How to Learn & Teach in Medical School: A Learner-Centered Approach. LC 94-21620. (Illus.). 224p. (C). 1994. text ed. 48.95x (0-398-05925-X) C C Thomas.
Quirk, Patrick. When Spirits Touch. Van Treese, James B., ed. 480p. 1993. pap. 8.95 (1-56901-154-0) NW Pub.
***Quirk, Patrick E.** The Message. Hansen, Jenet, ed. 310p. 1994. 22.95 (0-9644284-0-7) Woodlnd Pr UT.
Quirk, Paul J. Industry Influence in Federal Regulatory Agencies. LC 80-8571. 264p. 1981. pap. 14.95 (0-691-02823-0) Princeton U Pr.
— Industry Influence in Federal Regulatory Agencies. LC 80-8571. Date not set. reprint ed. pap. 77.60 (0-7837-9427-4, 2060168) Bks Demand.
Quirk, Paul J., jt. auth. see Derthick, Martha.
Quirk, Peter J., et al. Floating Exchange Rates in Developing Countries: Experience with Auction & Interbank Markets. (Occasional Paper Ser.: No. 53). vi, 43p. 1987. pap. 7.50 (0-939934-89-2) Intl Monetary.
— Policies for Developing Forward Foreign Exchange Markets. (Occasional Paper Ser.: No. 60). 51p. 1988. pap. 7.50 (1-55775-017-3) Intl Monetary.
***Quirk, Randolph.** Grammatical & Lexical Variance in English. LC 94-46562. 1995. write for info. (0-582-25359-4, Pub. by Longman UK); pap. text ed. write for info. (0-582-25358-6, Pub. by Longman UK) Longman.
Quirk, Randolph & Greenbaum, Sidney. A Concise Grammar of Contemporary English. 484p. (C). 1973. text ed. 37.25 (0-15-512930-9) HB Coll Pubs.
Quirk, Randolph & Stein, Gabriele. English in Use. 272p. (C). 1990. pap. text ed. 31.50 (0-582-06613-1, 78923) Longman.
Quirk, Randolph & Svartik, Jan. Investigating Linguistic Acceptability. (Janua Linguarum, Ser. Minor: No. 54). (Orig.). 1966. pap. text ed. 21.35 (90-279-0585-1) Mouton.
Quirk, Randolph & Wren, C. L. An Old English Grammar. LC 93-39877. 186p. (C). 1994. reprint ed. pap. text ed. 12.00 (0-87580-560-4) N Ill U Pr.
Quirk, Randolph, jt. auth. see Crystal, David.
Quirk, Randolph, jt. auth. see Greenbaum, Sidney.
Quirk, Randolph, et al. A Comprehensive Grammar of the English Language. 1779p. (C). 1985. 139.75 (0-582-51734-6, 73723) Longman.
Quirk, Robert E. Fidel Castro. LC 92-39300. 1993. 35.00 (0-393-03485-2) Norton.
— Fidel Castro. (Illus.). 928p. 1995. pap. 16.00 (0-393-31327-1, Norton Paperbks) Norton.
— The Mexican Revolution & the Catholic Church, 1910-1929. LC 85-30209. 276p. 1986. reprint ed. text ed. 65.00 (0-313-25121-5, QUMC, Greenwood Pr) Greenwood.
Quirk, Roderic P., ed. Transition Metal Catalyzed Polymerizations: Ziegler-Natta & Metathesis Polymerizations. (Illus.). 880p. (C). 1989. 94.95 (0-521-33289-3) Cambridge U Pr.
Quirk, Ronald J. Serafin Estebanez Calderon: Bajo la Corteza de su Obra. LC 91-42499. (American University Studies: Romance Languages & Literature: Ser. II, Vol. 187). 223p. (C). 1992. text ed. 38.95 (0-8204-1748-3) P Lang Pubs.
Quirk, Thomas C. Reptiles & Amphibians Coloring Book. (Illus.). (J). (gr. k-3). 1981. pap. 2.95 (0-486-24111-4) Dover.
Quirk, Thomas J. Study Guide to Accompany Assael's Marketing: Principles & Strategy. 2nd ed. 220p. (C). 1993. student ed, pap. text ed. 21.00 (0-03-096624-8) Dryden Pr.
Quirk, Tom. Bergson & American Culture: The Worlds of Willa Cather & Wallace Stevens. LC 89-32355. xvi, 302p. (C). 1990. 49.95 (0-8078-1880-1) U of NC Pr.
— Coming to Grips with Huckleberry Finn: Essays on a Book, a Boy, & a Man. LC 93-25042. 184p. (C). 1993. text ed. 24.95 (0-8262-0920-3) U of Mo Pr.
Quirk, Tom & Scharnhorst, Gary, eds. American Realism & the Canon. LC 94-11782. 1995. write for info. (0-87413-524-9) U Delaware Pr.
Quirk, Tom, jt. auth. see Barbour, James.
Quirk, Tom, ed. see Twain, Mark.
Quirk, William J. A Company Policy Manual. Haffeman, JoAnne S., ed. 77p. 1991. pap. 34.95 (0-916592-96-0) Panel Pubs.
— A Company Policy Manual: Special Report - Critical Company Policy Issues. Haffeman, JoAnne S., ed. 80p. 1991. pap. text ed. 34.95 (1-878375-81-4) Panel Pubs.
— Hiring Handbook: Special Report - Critical Hiring Issues. Haffeman, JoAnne S., ed. 80p. 1991. pap. text ed. 45.00 (1-878375-80-6) Panel Pubs.
Quirk, William J. & Bridwell, R. Randall. Abandoned: The Betrayal of the American Middle Class since World War II. 468p. 1992. 21.95 (0-8191-8459-4) Madison Bks UPA.
— Abandoned: The Betrayal of the American Middle Class since World War II. 468p. 1993. pap. 16.95 (1-56833-022-7) Madison Bks UPA.
— Judicial Dictatorship. LC 95-821. 1995. write for info. (1-56000-225-5) Transaction Pubs.
***Quirke, Bill.** Communicating Change. LC 94-29585. (Quality in Action Ser.). 1994. text ed. 34.95 (0-07-707941-8) McGraw.
Quirke, N., ed. see Haile, J. M.
Quirke, Philip, ed. The Molecular Biology of Digestive Diseases. 112p. 1994. pap. text ed. 24.00 (0-685-72219-8, BMJ Pubng Grp) Amer Coll Phys.
Quirke, Philip, jt. auth. see Dixon, Michael F.
***Quirke, Ruth M., comp.** Joyce Mabel (Carter) Allan: Her Antecedents, Descendants & Relatives Including the Carter, Shattock, Calvert, Wilson, Yapp, Parker, Jones & Nott Lines. 128p. (Orig.). 1994. pap. 25.00 (0-944113-03-6) Quirke Quirke Assocs.
Quirke, Stephen. Ancient Egyptian Religion. 1993. pap. 14.95 (0-486-27427-6) Dover.
— Who Were the Pharoahs: A History of Their Names. 1991. pap. 6.95 (0-486-26586-2) Dover.
Quirke, Stephen & Spencer, Jeffrey, eds. The British Museum Book of Ancient Egypt. LC 92-80823. (Illus.). 240p. 1992. pap. 19.95 (0-500-01550-3) Thames Hudson.
Quirke, Stephen, jt. auth. see Parkinson, Richard.
Quirke, Terence T., Jr., comp. Alexander Foster McIlraith (1858-1945) Genealogy: Including the Foster, Charland, Gavin & Love Lines; Ontario, North Dakota, Washington, Quebec, Manitoba & Alberta. LC 87-60962. (Illus.). 275p. (Orig.). 1987. pap. 20.00 (0-944113-00-1) Quirke Quirke Assocs.
— Goble Genealogy & Family History: Rolvenden & Adjacent Parishes, Kent, England. LC 94-65860. 91p. (Orig.). 1994. 25.00 (0-944113-02-8) Quirke Quirke Assocs.
— Grace Genealogy & Family History: East Sussex, England. LC 94-65861. 83p. (Orig.). 1994. 25.00 (0-944113-01-X) Quirke Quirke Assocs.
Quiroga, Horacio. The Decapitated Chicken & Other Stories. Peden, Margaret S., tr. LC 75-40167. (Texas Pan American Ser.). (Illus.). 213p. (C). 1976. pap. 10.95 (0-292-71541-2) U of Tex Pr.
— The Exiles & Other Stories. Danielson, J. David, tr. LC 86-30722. (Texas Pan American Ser.). 168p. 1987. 17.95 (0-292-72050-5); pap. 10.95 (0-292-72051-3) U of Tex Pr.
Quiroga, Roberto, tr. see Albornoz, Fernando, ed.
Quiroga, Robin M., ed. see Romero, John S.
***Quiroga, Virginia A.** Occupational Therapy: The First 30 Years 1900 to 1930. 290p. (C). 1995. pap. write for info. (1-56900-025-5) Am Occup Therapy.
— Poor Mothers & Babies: A Social History of Childbirth & Child Care Institutions in Nineteenth-Century New York City. (Studies in Historical Demography). 184p. 1990. reprint ed. 15.00 (0-8240-4356-1) Garland.
Quiros, Alfredo C., tr. see Hildebrand, Peter & Poeg, Federico.
Quiros, M., jt. auth. see Tenreiro, R. Dominguez.
Quiros, T. E. Por Sendas Biblicas. 162p. (SPA.). 1985. reprint ed. pap. 5.25 (0-311-08753-1) Casa Bautista.
Quirot, Consuelo, tr. see Warren, D. Michael.
Quiroz, Adrian Gonzalez. Llegando al Alcoholico. 1986. reprint ed. pap. 1.95 (0-311-46077-1) Casa Bautista.
Quiroz, Alfonso W. Domestic & Foreign Finance in Modern Peru, 1850-1950: Financing Visions of Development. LC 92-36947. (Latin American Ser.). 312p. (C). 1993. text ed. 49.95 (0-8229-1174-4) U of Pittsburgh Pr.
Quiroz, R. S., ed. Meteorological Investigations of the Upper Atmosphere: Proceedings of the AMS Symposium on Meteorological Investigations above 70 Kilometers, Miami, Florida, May 31-June 2, 1967. (Meteorological Monograph Ser.: Vol. 9, No. 31). (Illus.). 231p. 1968. 23.00 (0-933876-29-7) Am Meteorological.
Quirt, John. The Press & the World of Money: How the News Media Cover Business & Finance, Panic & Prosperity & the Pursuit of the American Dream. LC 93-22766. 364p. 1993. 24.95 (0-9635504-0-3) Anton-CA-Courier Pub.
Quisenberry, Anderson C. Kentucky in the War of Eighteen Twelve. (Illus.). 242p. 1989. reprint ed. 19.95 (0-685-60353-9, 4730) Clearfield Co.
Quisenberry, Anderson C., ed. Revolutionary Soldiers in Kentucky. 278p. 1994. reprint ed. pap. 29.50 (0-8328-4013-0) Higginson Bk Co.
***Quisenberry, Dan.** Double Play: A Poem. Hickok, Gloria V., ed. 6p. (Orig.). 1995. pap. 3.00 (1-884235-16-6) Helicon Nine Eds.
Quisenberry, J. B. Changed Forever. 1991. pap. 2.50 (1-55673-283-X, 9116) CSS OH.
— The Final Triumph. 1991. pap. 2.95 (1-55673-395-X, 9211) CSS OH.
— A Great Light. 1992. pap. 3.25 (1-55673-458-1, 9251) CSS OH.
— A Service of Shadows. 1991. pap. 3.25 (1-55673-390-9, 9208) CSS OH.
— Voices: Six Dialogues & Orders of Service for Lent. LC 92-34836. 1992. pap. 5.75 (1-55673-572-3, 9318) CSS OH.
Quisenberry, James D., ed. & intro. Changing Family Lifestyles: Their Effect on Children. LC 82-20628. (Illus.). 64p. (C). 1982. reprint ed. pap. 7.50 (0-87173-100-2) ACEI.
Quisenberry, James D., et al, eds. Readings from Childhood Education, Vol. II. LC 91-23454. (Illus.). 390p. 1991. 24.50 (0-87173-121-5) ACEI.
Quisenberry, Nancy L., jt. auth. see Isenberg, Joan.
Quisenberry, Stacey H. The Little Angel Who Lost Faith. Gress, Jonna, ed. LC 93-74773. (Illus.). 24p. (J). (ps-1). 1994. pap. 4.95 (0-944943-51-9, CODE 24178-6) Current Inc.
Quishenberry, Mary, jt. auth. see Linde, Lavaun.
***Quisling, Vidkun.** Russia & Ourselves. Warner, James K., ed. (Illus.). 183p. (Orig.). Date not set. pap. 15.00 (0-89562-156-8) Sons Lib.
Quispel, A., jt. ed. see Eijsackers, H.
Quisquater, J. J. & Vandewalle, J., eds. Advances in Cryptology - EUROCRYPT '89: Proceedings of the Workshop on the Theory & Application of Cryptographic Techniques Houthalen, Belgium, April 10-13, 1989. (Lecture Notes in Computer Science Ser.: Vol. 434). x, 710p. 1990. pap. 71.00 (0-387-53433-4) Spr-Verlag.
Quist, Allen. The Abortion Revolution. 1980. 4.95 (0-8100-0115-2, 12N1721) Northwest Pub.
Quist, D., et al. Readings in Principles & Curriculum of Secondary Education. 1971. pap. text ed. 4.75 (0-8422-0178-5) Irvington.
Quist, Norman, ed. AIDS: Legal, Legislative, & Policy Issues. (Special Studies on AIDS). 448p. 1989. pap. text ed. 58.00 (1-55572-020-X) Univ Pub Group.
Quistorp, Heinrich. Calvin's Doctrine of the Last Things. Knight, Harold, tr. LC 83-45629. reprint ed. 27.50 (0-404-19846-5) AMS Pr.
Quitko, Betsy, et al. Childbirth: A Consumer's Perspective. Leth, Kathy, ed. (Illus.). 144p. (Orig.). 1988. pap. 6.95 (0-936320-20-6) LIFETIME.
Quitregard, David. Arabic Key Words: The Basic Two Thousand-Word Vocabulary Transliterated & Arranged by Frequency in a Hundred Units. (Language & Literature Ser.: Vol. 16). 144p. (Orig.). 1993. pap. 14.95 (0-906672-27-9) Oleander Pr.
Quitt, Andrea, ed. see Varga, Margaret H.
Quitt, Martin H. Virginia House of Burgesses, 1660-1706: The Social, Educational & Economic Bases of Political Power. (Outstanding Studies in Early American History). 408p. 1989. reprint ed. 25.00 (0-8240-6194-2) Garland.
***Quittel, Frances.** Fire Power: Quick Tips When Your Career Gets the Shaft. LC 94-30404. 256p. (Orig.). 1995. pap. 11.95 (0-89815-662-9) Ten Speed Pr.
Quittner, J. Masters of Deception. 1994. 23.00 (0-06-017030-1, HarpT) HarpC.
Quittner, Marvin, jt. auth. see Schachner, Robert V.
Quittner, P. A Practical Approach to Data Base Systems. 300p. Date not set. pap. 39.00 (963-05-6636-2, Pub. by A K HU) Intl Spec Bk.
***Quivers, Robin.** Quivers: Unmasked. 1995. 22.00 (0-06-039153-7) HarpC.
Quivey, Charles. What If. 191p. 1994. 16.00 (0-9641135-0-3) C Quivey.
Qumsiyeh, Mazin B. The Bats of Egypt. (Special Publications: No. 23). (Illus.). 102p. 1985. 40.00 (0-89672-138-8); pap. 18.00 (0-89672-137-X) Tex Tech Univ Pr.
Qunbos, Abdullhalim M. Dictionary of Arabic Homonyms: Arabic - Arabic. 1987. 22.00 (0-86685-437-1) Intl Bk Ctr.
Quintilone, Paul M. Michael Learns to Trade. (Illus.). 27p. (J). 1988. write for info. (0-9616980-0-4) Quintilone Ent.
Quntanna, Beatrex. Tarot: A Universal Language. (Illus.). 96p. (Orig.). 1989. pap. 14.95 (0-9625292-0-6) Art Ala Carte Pub.
Quo, James C. Concise Chinese - English Dictionary Romanized. LC 60-14372. 226p. (CHI & ENG.). 1961. pap. 7.95 (0-8048-0116-9) C E Tuttle.
— Concise Chinese-English Dictionary. 225p. (CHI & ENG.). 1980. pap. 9.95 (0-8288-1607-7, M14144) Fr & Eur.
— Concise English-Chinese Dictionary Romanized. LC 55-11585. 324p. (CHI & ENG.). 1960. pap. 7.95 (0-8048-0117-7) C E Tuttle.
— English-Chinese Dictionary Romanized. 323p. (CHI & ENG.). 1964. pap. 6.95 (0-8288-6772-0, M-9591) Fr & Eur.
— English-Chinese Dictionary, Romanized. 323p. (CHI & ENG.). 37.50 (0-87557-008-9, 008-9) Saphrograph.
Quoirez, Jacques, jt. auth. see Sagan, Francoise.
Quoist, Michel. New Prayers. 160p. (Orig.). 1990. pap. 11.95 (0-8245-0983-8) Crossroad NY.
— Prayers. LC 63-17141. 190p. 1985. reprint ed. pap. 8.95 (0-934134-46-4) Sheed & Ward MO.
Quon, Michael. Non-Traditional Design. 176p. 1993. pap. 29.95 (0-86636-234-7) PBC Intl Inc.
***Quon, Mike & Graphic Design U. S. A. Editors.** Corporate Graphics Vol. 1. (Illus.). 240p. 1995. 42.50 (0-86636-232-0) PBC Intl Inc.
Quong, Rose. Chinese Written Characters: Their Wit & Wisdom. (Illus.). 80p. 1994. 14.95 (0-939218-01-1) Chapman Billies.
***Quontamatteo, Tom.** Emptiness That Plays So Rough. LC 93-74142. 56p. 1995. pap. 10.00 (0-9636156-0-2) Broken Shadow.
Quraeshi, Samina. Lahore: The City Within. (Illus.). 292p. 1989. 75.00 (0-7103-0335-1) Routledge Chapman & Hall.
Quraishi, Huda, ed. see El-Amin, Mildred.
Quraishi, M. A. Drought Strategy. (C). 1989. 21.50 (81-7018-562-9, Pub. by BR Pub II) S Asia.
Quraishi, M. Tariq, ed. Islam: A Way of Life & a Movement. LC 83-71408. 221p. (Orig.). 1986. reprint ed. pap. 9.50 (0-89259-055-6) Am Trust Pubns.
Quraishi, Mohammed S. Biochemical Insect Control: Its Impact on Economy, Environment, & Natural Selection. LC 76-29701. 288p. reprint ed. pap. 82.10 (0-8357-7216-0, 2056304) Bks Demand.
Qureshi, A. H., jt. ed. see Sood, Arun K.
Qureshi, A. I. Economic History of Pakistan. 367p. 1993. 19.95 (1-56744-466-0) Kazi Pubns.
— Fiscal System of Islam. 1981. 10.50 (1-56744-010-X) Kazi Pubns.
— Islam & the Theory of Interest. 15.50 (1-56744-073-8) Kazi Pubns.
Qureshi, Ahmed, tr. see Prophet of Islam.
Qureshi, Asif H., ed. The Public International Law of Taxation: Text, Cases & Materials. LC 93-33344. 640p. (C). 1994. lib. bdg. 180.00 (1-85333-950-4, Pub. by Graham & Trotman UK) Kluwer Ac.
Qureshi, B. Transcultural Medicine: Principles & Practice. (C). 1989. lib. bdg. 55.50 (0-85200-938-0) Kluwer Ac.
Qureshi, B. A. English-Urdu (Advanced Twentieth Century) 800p. 1970. 20.00 (81-85360-37-5) IBD Ltd.
Qureshi, Bashir. Transcultural Medicine: Dealing with Patients from Different Cultures. 2nd ed. LC 93-45887. 228p. (C). 1994. lib. bdg. 47.50 (0-7923-8836-4) Kluwer Ac.
Qureshi, Donna I. Rape: Social Facts from England & America. 293p. 1979. pap. text ed. 8.60 (0-87563-178-9) Stipes.
Qureshi, Hafiz M. The Qur'an & Slavery. 39p. (Orig.). 1984. pap. 2.00 (0-942978-07-2) Am Soc Ed & Rel.
Qureshi, Hazel & Walker, Alan. The Caring Relationship: Elderly People & Their Families. (Health, Society, & Policy Ser.). (C). 1990. 34.95 (0-87722-663-6) Temple U Pr.
Qureshi, Hazel, et al. Helpers in Case-Managed Community Care. (Illus.). 245p. 1989. text ed. 56.95 (0-566-05809-X, Pub. by Gower UK) Ashgate Pub Co.
Qureshi, I. Administration of the Sultanate of Delhi. 5th ed. 1971. 28.50 (0-317-89899-X) Coronet Bks.
Qureshi, M. A. Waqfs in India: A Study of Administrative & Legislative Control. (C). 1990. 280.00 (0-89771-239-0) St Mut.
Qureshi, M. A., jt. auth. see Gopa, D.
Qureshi, Mohsin. Inorganic Ion Exchangers in Chemical Analysis. (Illus.). 296p. 1991. 216.00 (0-8493-5526-5, QD562) CRC Pr.
Qureshi, Muhammad T., jt. auth. see Gajic, Zoran.
***Qureshi, Regula B.** Sufi Music of India & Pakistan: Sound, Context, & Meaning in Qawwali. 281p. 1995. pap. text ed. 24.95 (0-226-70092-5) U Ch Pr.
Qureshi, Salahudin. Regional Perspective on Dry Farming. (C). 1989. 34.00 (81-7033-072-6, Pub. by Rawat II) S Asia.
Qureshi, Z. H. Arabic Writing for Beginners: Part One. pap. 3.75 (0-935782-06-0) Kazi Pubns.
— Arabic Writing for Beginners: Part Three. pap. 3.75 (0-935782-18-4) Kazi Pubns.
— Arabic Writing for Beginners: Part Two. pap. 3.75 (0-935782-11-7) Kazi Pubns.
Qureshi, Zia, jt. auth. see Shah, Anwar.
Qutb, Muhammad. Islam: The Misunderstood Religion. pap. 10.50 (1-56744-084-3) Kazi Pubns.
— Islam: The Misunderstood Religion. 199p. 1977. pap. 5.95 (0-939830-05-1, Pub. by IIFSO KW) New Era Publns MI.
Qutb, S. Milestone. 1981. pap. 8.50 (0-934905-14-2) Kazi Pubns.
Qutb, Sayyid. Basic Principles of Islamic World View. Mizan Press, tr. LC 93-4677. 1993. write for info. (0-933782-25-X) Mizan Pr.
— In the Shade of the Quran. Salahi, M. A. & Shamis, A. A., trs. 366p. Date not set. pap. write for info. (1-882837-18-5) Wamy Intl.
— Islam & Universal Peace. LC 77-89635. 1977. pap. 4.50 (0-89259-007-6) Am Trust Pubns.
— Islamic Concept & Its Characteristics. Siddiqui, Mohammed M., tr. 217p. (Orig.). (C). 1991. pap. 12.00 (0-89259-119-6) Am Trust Pubns.
— Milestones. 303p. (Orig.). 1978. pap. 5.95 (0-939830-07-8, Pub. by IIFSO KW) New Era Publns MI.
— Milestones. rev. ed. (Orig.). 1991. pap. 9.00 (0-89259-076-9) Am Trust Pubns.
— Social Justice in Islam. 1993. pap. 12.50 (0-915597-87-X) Amana Bks.
— This Religion of Islam. 104p. (Orig.). 1977. pap. 2.95 (0-939830-08-6, Pub. by IIFSO KW) New Era Publns MI.
***Quynh Dao.** Canh Nhan Co Don. Lieu Quoc Nhi, tr. (Illus.). 278p. (Orig.). (YA). 1994. pap. 13.00 (1-886535-00-0) Dong Van.
— Em La Canhhoa Roi. Lieu Quoc Nhi, tr. 260p. (Orig.). (YA). 1994. pap. 13.00 (1-886535-03-5) Dong Van.
Quynn, Katelyn L., jt. auth. see Jordan, Ronald R.
Qvarnstrom, Olle. Hindu Philosophy in Buddhist Perspective. (Lund Studies in African & Asian Religions: No. 4). 170p. (Orig.). 1989. pap. 66.50x (91-86668-30-7, Pub. by Almqv & Wiksell SW) Coronet Bks.
Qvortrup, Lars. The Social Significance of Telematics: An Essay on the Information Society. Edmonds, Philip, tr. LC 85-7493. (P&B Ser.: Vol. V, No. 7). xviii, 228p. (Orig.). 1984. pap. 78.00x (0-915027-04-6) Benjamins North Am.
Qvortrup, Lars, et al, eds. Social Experiments with Information Technology & the Challenges of Innovation. (C). 1987. lib. bdg. 121.50 (90-277-2488-1) Kluwer Ac.

R

R & B Enterprises Engineering Staff & Goldblum, Robert D. EMP Testing Handbook: Per MIL-STD-461C & MIL-STD-462, Notice 5. (Illus.). 201p. (Orig.). 1986. pap. 150.00 (0-940499-00-2) R & B Enter.
R. B. I. Staff. Exchange Control Facilities for Investment by Non-Resident Indians. (C). 1988. 35.00 (0-685-36500-X) St Mut.
R. Bin Wong, jt. auth. see Will, Pierre-Etienne.
***R. Bloom, Walter & Heyer, Herbert.** Harmonic Analysis of Probability Measures on Hypergroups, Vol. 20. (Studies in Mathematics). 607p. (C). 1994. lib. bdg. 171.00 (3-11-012105-0) De Gruyter.
R C Publications Staff. Print's Best Illustration & Photography. 30581p. 1994. 34.95 (0-915734-82-6, 30581) RC Pubns.
— Print's Best Letterheads & Business Cards 3. 192p. 1994. 34.95 (0-915734-84-2, 30579) RC Pubns.
— Print's Best Logos & Symbols 3. 192p. 1994. 34.95 (0-915734-85-0, 30580) RC Pubns.

R

R, Catherine, adapt. Black Beauty. (Illus.). 128p. 1994. write for info. (*0-307-12420-7*, Wave WI) Western Pub.

R. H. Myers Tenants Staff, jt. auth. see Menorah Park Residents Staff.

R. K. Math. Call of the Gita. 192p. 1987. pap. 2.95 (*0-87481-537-1*, Pub. by Ramakrishna Math II) Vedanta Pr.

***R, LAL.** Pesticides & Nitrogen Cycle, Vol. 3. LC 87-7985. 1988. 106.00 (*0-8493-4353-4*, CRC Reprint) Franklin.

R, Mark & L, Mary. Stepping Stones to Recovery from Cocaine - Crack Addiction. LC 90-20336. 154p. (Orig.). 1990. pap. 7.95 (*0-934125-10-4*) Hazelden.

R. McCarter, William, jt. auth. see Gilbert, Rita.

***R. Owen Pubs. Staff.** Books for Ready to Read Classrooms. 72p. (Orig.). 1995. pap. text ed. 16.95 (*1-878450-87-5*) R Owen Pubs.

R. Po-chia Hsia. Social Discipline in the Reformation: Central Europe, 1550-1750. (Christianity & Society in the Modern World Ser.). (Illus.). 224p. 1992. pap. 15.95 (*0-415-01149-3*, A6634) Routledge.

R. Ram Mohan Rao & Simhadri, S. Development Dynamics in Command Areas of Major Irrigation Project. (C). 1989. 36.50 (*81-210-0236-2*, Pub. by Inter-India Pubns) S Asia.

R. S. Means Co., Inc., Adaptive Environments Center Staff. ADA Compliance Pricing Guide: Costs for the Seventy-Five Most Needes ADA Compliance Projects. Greene, Mary & Waier, Phillip, eds. (Illus.). 200p. 1994. 69.95 (*0-87629-351-8*) R S Means.

R. S. Means Company, Inc. Staff. Means Estimating Handbook. (Illus.). 900p. 1990. 99.95 (*0-87629-177-9*, 67276) R S Means.

Ra & L. L. Research Staff. The Law of One, Bk. III. LC 90-72156. 196p. (Orig.). 1991. pap. 12.95 (*0-924608-08-0*, Whitford Pr) Schiffer.

Ra & L-L Research Staff. The Law of One, Book Four: By Ra an Humble Messenger. 144p. (Orig.). (C). 1983. pap. 12.95 (*0-945007-04-3*) L-L Resrch.

— The Law of One, Book One: By Ra an Humble Messenger. (Illus.). 164p. (Orig.). (C). 1981. pap. 12.95 (*0-945007-01-9*) L-L Resrch.

— The Law of One, Book Three: By Ra an Humble Messenger. 137p. (Orig.). (C). 1982. pap. 12.95 (*0-945007-03-5*) L-L Resrch.

— The Law of One, Book Two: By Ra, an Humble Messenger. 95p. (Orig.). (C). 1982. pap. 9.95 (*0-945007-02-7*) L-L Resrch.

Ra, Carol, ed. Behind the King's Kitchen Door. LC 91-66056. (Illus.). 56p. (J). (gr. 5 up). 1992. 18.95 (*1-56397-024-4*, Wordsong) Boyds Mills Pr.

Ra, Carol F. Trot, Trot to Boston. LC 86-7354. (Illus.). 32p. (J). (ps). 1987. 12.95 (*0-688-06190-7*); lib. bdg. 12.88 (*0-688-06191-5*) Lothrop.

Ra, Jong Oh. Labor at the Polls: Union Voting in Presidential Elections, 1952-1976. LC 77-90729. (Illus.). 192p. 1978. 25.00 (*0-87023-026-3*) U of Mass Pr.

Ra, Ruth, illus. Many Lands, Many Stories: Asian Folk Tales for Children. LC 87-50167. 96p. (J). 1987. 12.95 (*0-8048-1527-5*) C E Tuttle.

Ra Un Nefer Amen. The Ausar Auset Nutrition Handbook. 54p. (Orig.). 1988. pap. 6.00 (*0-317-93991-2*) Khamit.

— Metu Neter, Vol. 1: The Great Oracle of Tehuti & the Egyptian System of Spiritual Cultivation. 439p. 1990. pap. 15.00 (*1-877662-03-8*) Khamit.

— A Nutritional, Herbal, & Homeopathic Guide to Healing. 52p. (Orig.). 1988. pap. 6.00 (*0-317-93992-0*) Khamit.

— The Ritual Systems of Ancient Black Civilizations, Vol. 1: Introduction to Meditation. 51p. (Orig.). 1988. pap. 14.95 (*0-317-93993-9*) Khamit.

Raab, Andrea, jt. auth. see Barkalow, Carol.

Raab, B. H., jt. ed. see Barta, B. J.

Raab, Charles, jt. auth. see MacPherson, Andrew.

Raab, Charles, jt. auth. see McPherson, Andrew.

***Raab, Diana.** Getting Pregnant & Staying Pregnant: Overcoming Infertility & Managing Your High-Risk Pregnancy. 320p. 1992. lib. bdg. 33.00 (*0-8095-6324-X*) Borgo Pr.

— Getting Pregnant & Staying Pregnant: Overcoming Infertility & Managing Your High-Risk Pregnancy. 2nd rev. ed. LC 91-3051. (Illus.). 336p. 1991. reprint ed. pap. 12.95 (*0-89793-080-0*) Hunter Hse.

Raab, Earl. The Anatomy of Nazism. rev. ed. (Illus.). 2.50 (*0-88464-013-2*) ADL.

Raab, Earl, ed. American Jews into the 21st Century: A Leadership Challenge. 134p. 1991. 49.95 (*1-55540-622-X*, 14 50 88) Scholars Pr GA.

Raab, Earl, jt. auth. see Lipset, Seymour M.

Raab, Jonathan. Using Consensus Building to Improve Utility Regulation. LC 94-15737. 400p. (Orig.). (C). 1994. pap. 28.00 (*0-918249-19-8*) Am Coun Energy.

Raab, Lawrence. The Collector of Cold Weather. LC 76-3301. (American Poetry Ser.: Vol.9). 1976. pap. 9.95 (*0-912946-45-8*) Ecco Pr.

— Other Children. LC 86-70208. (Poetry Ser.). 80p. (C). 1987. 16.95 (*0-88748-028-4*); pap. 9.95 (*0-88748-029-2*) Carnegie-Mellon.

— What We Don't Know about Each Other. LC 93-2664. 96p. (Orig.). 1993. pap. 12.00 (*0-14-058701-2*, Penguin Bks) Viking Penguin.

Raab, Patricia B., ed. see Moynihan, Patricia M.

Raab, R. E., jt. auth. see De Lange, O. L.

Raab, Reginald, tr. see Wachsmuth, Guenther.

Raab, Rex, et al. Eloquent Concrete: How Rudolf Steiner Employed Reinforced Concrete. (Illus.). 141p. 1979. pap. 24.00 (*0-85440-354-X*, Steinerbks) Anthroposophic.

Raab, Robert A. Coping with Death. rev. ed. Rosen, Ruth, ed. (Coping Ser.). (YA). (gr. 7-12). 1989. lib. bdg. 15.95 (*0-8239-0960-3*) Rosen Group.

— Coping with Divorce. rev. ed. (J). (gr. 7-12). 1984. lib. bdg. 15.95 (*0-8239-0428-8*) Rosen Group.

Raab, Selwyn, jt. auth. see Ragano, Frank.

Raab, Steven S. & Matusky, Gregory. Blueprint for Franchising a Business. LC 87-15932. 244p. 1987. text ed. 45.00 (*0-471-85617-7*) Wiley.

Raab, Susan S. Author's Guide to Children's Book Promotion. rev. ed. 58p. 1990. pap. 9.95 (*0-9621211-1-8*) Raab Assocs.

***Raab, Susan S. & Bierwirth, Johanna.** An Author's Guide to Children's Book Promotion. rev. ed. 85p. 1994. pap. 12.95 (*0-9621211-3-4*) Raab Assocs.

Raabe, Kenneth A., et al. Income Shifting after Tax Return. LC 88-61005. 1200p. 1989. pap. 38.00 (*0-13-454372-6*, Busn) P-H.

Raabe, Marie. Insect Neurohormones. Marshall, Nissim, tr. LC 82-7535. (Illus.). 366p. 1982. 75.00 (*0-306-40782-5*, Plenum Pr) Plenum.

— Recent Developments in Insect Neurohormones. (Illus.). 484p. 1989. 110.00 (*0-306-43175-0*, Plenum Pr) Plenum.

Raabe, Mechthild, comp. Leser und Lekture des 18. Jahrnunderts Die Ausleihbucher der Herzog August Bibliothek wolfenbuttel, 1715-1800, 4 vols. 400p. (GER.). 1987. Band 2: Sachkatalog der entliehenen Bucher. write for info. (*0-318-61906-7*); Band 3: Verzeichnis der Leser Nach Berufsgruppen. write for info. (*0-318-61907-5*); Bank 4: Spezialverzeichnisse. write for info. (*0-318-61908-3*) K G Saur.

— Leser und Lekture des 18. Jahrnunderts Die Ausleihbucher der Herzog August Bibliothek wolfenbuttel, 1715-1800, 4 vols., Band 1: Einleitung-Alphabetischer Katalog. 400p. (GER.). 1987. lib. bdg. 160.00 (*3-598-10651-3*) K G Saur.

Raabe, Otto, ed. Internal Radiation Dosimetry-1994: Health Physics Summer School. (Illus.). 680p. (C). 1994. text ed. 65.00 (*0-944838-47-2*) Med Physics Pub.

Raabe, Pamela. Imitating God: The Allegory of Faith in Piers Plowman B. LC 89-28364. 208p. 1990. 30.00 (*0-8203-1205-3*) U of Ga Pr.

Raabe, Paul. Era of German Expressionism. (German Expressionist Ser.). 1980. pap. 13.95 (*0-7145-0699-0*) Riverrun NY.

Raabe, Paul, ed. The Era of German Expressionism. Ritchie, J. M., tr. LC 72-97580. 424p. 1986. 22.95 (*0-87951-010-2*); pap. 12.95 (*0-87951-233-4*) Overlook Pr.

Raabe, Paul & August, Herzog, eds. Acta Eruditorum, 117 vols. fiche write for info. (*0-318-70648-2*, Pub. by Georg Olms GW); fiche write for info. (*0-318-70649-0*, Pub. by Georg Olms GW) Lubrecht & Cramer.

— Acta Eruditorum, 117 vols., Vols. 1-10. write for info. (*0-318-70647-4*, Pub. by Georg Olms GW) Lubrecht & Cramer.

Raabe, Susanne M. Der Wortschatz in den deutschen Schriften Thomas Murners: Band 1: Untersuchengen - Band 2: Worterbuch. (Studia Linguistica Germanica: Band 29). xviii, 358p. (C). 1990. lib. bdg. 275.40 (*3-11-012456-4*) De Gruyter.

Raabe, Tom. Biblioholism: The Literary Addiction. LC 91-7260. (Illus.). 193p. (Orig.). 1991. pap. 8.95 (*1-55591-080-7*) Fulcrum Pub.

— Sports for the Athletically Impaired. LC 92-54764. (Illus.). 240p. (Orig.). 1993. pap. 10.95 (*1-55591-133-1*) Fulcrum Pub.

— Sports in the Twentieth Century. Baron, Bob, ed. LC 95-8767. (Millennium 2000 Ser.). 144p. 1995. 12.95 (*1-55591-276-1*) Fulcrum Pub.

Raabe, Wilhelm. Novels. Sander, Volkmar, ed. LC 82-22097. (German Library: Vol. 45). 320p. 1983. 29.50 (*0-8264-0280-1*); 14.95 (*0-8264-0281-X*) Continuum.

Raabe, William A. & Johnson, Ranae. Winters Flower. 276p. 1992. pap. write for info. (*0-9631506-0-X*) Raintree.

Raabe, William A. & Parker, James E. Tax Concepts for Decision Making. (Illus.). 766p. (C). 1985. text ed. 62.50 (*0-314-85289-1*) West Pub.

Raabe, William A., et al. Multistate Corporate Tax Guide, Vols. I & II: 1992 Edition, 1. Kaiser, Laura B., ed. 950p. 1991. write for info. (*1-878375-57-1*) Panel Pubs.

— Multistate Corporate Tax Guide, Vols. I & II: 1992 Edition, 2. Kaiser, Laura B., ed. 950p. 1991. write for info. (*1-878375-58-X*) Panel Pubs.

— Multistate Corporate Tax Guide, Vols. I & II: 1992 Edition, Set. Kaiser, Laura B., ed. 950p. 1991. pap. text ed. 185.00 (*1-878375-59-8*) Panel Pubs.

— West's Federal Tax Research. 2nd ed. Craig & Fenton, eds. 648p. (C). 1991. text ed. 57.50 (*0-314-78734-8*) West Pub.

— West's Federal Tax Research. 3rd ed. LC 93-24109. 650p. (C). 1994. text ed. 60.25 (*0-314-02650-9*) West Pub.

***Raack, R. C.** Stalin's Drive to the West, 1938-1945: The Origins of the Cold War. LC 95-4990. 1995. 45.00 (*0-8047-2415-6*) Stanford U Pr.

Raack, Richard C. Fall of Stein. LC 65-19828. (Historical Monographs: No. 58). 228p. 1965. 20.00 (*0-674-29200-6*) HUP.

Raad, Virginia. The Piano Sonority of Claude Debussy. LC 93-50847. (Studies in the History & Interpretation of Music: Vol. 34). 92p. 1993. 49.95 (*0-7734-9138-4*) E Mellen.

Raadsheer, Fred. Motor Automotive Technology Teacher's Resource Kit. 2nd ed. 1993. 99.95 (*0-8273-3810-4*) Delmar.

Raaen, Aagot. Grass of the Earth: Immigrant Life in the Dakota Country. LC 93-44859. 238p. 1994. pap. 12.95 (*0-87351-295-2*) Minn Hist.

***Raaf, Hermann.** Chemie Des Alltags A-Z: Ein Lexikon der Praktischen Chemie. 28th ed. 310p. (GER.). 1992. 59.95 (*0-7859-8375-9*, 3451218534) Fr & Eur.

Raaf, John, jt. ed. see Andrews, Jullie S.

Raaf, John H. Management of Soft Tissue Sarcoma. 483p. 1992. 95.00 (*0-8151-7003-3*, Yr Bk Med Pubs) Mosby Yr Bk.

Raaflaub, Kurt A., ed. Social Struggles in Archaic Rome: New Perspective on the Conflict of the Orders. 424p. (C). 1986. 70.00 (*0-520-05528-4*) U CA Pr.

Raaflaub, Kurt A. & Tober, Mark, eds. Between Republic & Empire: Interpretations of Augustus & His Principate. 1990. 80.00 (*0-520-06676-6*); pap. 25.00 (*0-520-08447-0*) U CA Pr.

Raah-ne-ah. May the Light & Love Flow. 160p. (C). 1988. pap. write for info. (*0-7212-0767-7*, Pub. by Regency Press) St Mut.

Raaheim, Kjell, et al. Helping Students to Learn: Teaching, Counseling, Research. rev. ed. 192p. 1991. reprint ed. 90.00 (*0-335-09320-5*, Open Univ Pr); reprint ed. pap. 32.00 (*0-335-09319-1*, Open Univ Pr) Taylor & Francis.

Raam, Shanthi, ed. Immunology of Steroid Hormone Receptors, Vol. 1. 176p. 1988. 100.00 (*0-8493-4983-4*, QP572, CRC Reprint) Franklin.

Ra'anan, Uri, ed. Ethnic Resurgence in Modern Democratic States: A Multidisciplinary Approach to Human Resources & Conflict. (Policy Studies). 1980. 88.00 (*0-08-024647-8*, Pergamon Pr) Elsevier.

— The Soviet Empire & the Challenge of National & Democratic Movements. 272p. 1990. text ed. 45.00 (*0-669-24677-8*); pap. 24.95 (*0-669-24676-X*) Free Pr.

Ra'anan, Uri & Lukes, Igor. Inside the Apparat: Perspectives on the Soviet System from Former Functionaries. 352p. (C). 1990. text ed. 49.95 (*0-669-21985-1*); pap. 24.95 (*0-669-24226-8*) Free Pr.

Ra'anan, Uri & Lukes, Igor, eds. Gorbachev's U. S. S. R. LC 89-70321. 140p. 1990. text ed. 49.95 (*0-312-04492-5*) St Martin.

Ra'anan, Uri & Perry, Charles M. The U. S. S. R. Today & Tomorrow: Problems & Challenges. LC 86-45960. 160p. 1986. text ed. 29.95 (*0-669-14813-X*) Free Pr.

Ra'anan, Uri, et al, eds. Hydra of Carnage: International Linkages of Terrorism: The Witnesses Speak. 656p. 1985. text ed. 49.95 (*0-669-11135-X*) Free Pr.

— Russian Pluralism, Now Irreversible? LC 92-28597. 224p. 1993. text ed. 39.95 (*0-312-08648-2*) St Martin.

— State & Nation in Multi-Ethnic Societies. LC 91-31631. 208p. 1992. text ed. 39.95 (*0-7190-3711-5*, Pub. by Manchester Univ Pr UK) St Martin.

Raasch, Maynard S., jt. auth. see Springer, Victor G.

Raask, Erich. Mineral Impurities in Coal Combustion: Behavior, Problems, & Remedial Measures. LC 83-26400. (Illus.). 467p. 1985. 113.00 (*0-89116-362-X*) Hemisp Pub.

Raask, Erich, ed. Erosion Wear in Coal Utilization. (Illus.). 621p. 1988. 172.00 (*0-89116-617-3*) Hemisp Pub.

Raat, W. Dirk. Mexico & the United States: Ambivalent Vistas. LC 91-43591. (United States & the Americas Ser.). (Illus.). 288p. 1992. 45.00 (*0-8203-1456-0*); pap. 18.50 (*0-8203-1457-9*) U of Ga Pr.

— Revoltosos: Mexico's Rebels in the United States, 1903-1923. LC 80-6109. (Illus.). 368p. 1981. 24.50 (*0-89096-114-X*) Tex A&M Univ Pr.

Raat, W. Dirk, ed. Mexico: From Independence to Revolution, 1810-1910. LC 81-10503. (Illus.). xiv, 308p. (C). 1982. pap. 15.00x (*0-8032-8904-9*) U of Nebr Pr.

Raat, W. Dirk & Beezley, William H., eds. Twentieth-Century Mexico. LC 85-14109. (Illus.). xviii, 318p. 1986. pap. 12.95 (*0-8032-8914-6*) U of Nebr Pr.

Raatz, S. Graph-Based Proof Procedures for Horn Clauses. (Progress in Computer Science & Applied Logic Ser.: Vol. 10). viii, 147p. 1990. 36.50 (*0-8176-3530-0*) Birkhauser.

Raatz, Ursula K. Secrets of Precious Stones: Guide to the Activation of the 7 Human Energy Centers Using Gemstones, Crystals & Minerals. 125p. (Orig.). (C). 1988. pap. 9.95 (*0-941524-38-8*) Lotus Light.

***Rab & Wood.** Child Care & the ADA: A Handbook for Inclusive Programs. 208p. 1995. pap. 25.00 (*1-55766-185-5*) P H Brookes.

Rabade, Raquel M., ed. The Cuban Flavor: A Cookbook. 2nd ed. 230p. 1981. pap. 8.95 (*0-941010-00-7*) Downtown Bk.

Rabago, Gregorio & Cooley, Denton A., eds. Heart Valve Replacement & Future Trends in Cardiac Surgery. (Illus.). 432p. 1987. 65.00 (*0-87993-298-8*) Futura Pub.

Rabalais, J. Wayne. Principles of Ultraviolet Photoelectron Spectroscopy. LC 76-28413. (Wiley-Interscience Monographs in Chemical Physics). 472p. reprint ed. pap. 134.60 (*0-685-10693-4*, 2055710) Bks Demand.

Rabalais, J. Wayne, ed. Low Energy Ion Surface Interactions. LC 93-21244. (Current Topics in Ion Chemistry & Physics Ser.). 400p. 1994. text ed. 139.00 (*0-471-93891-2*) Wiley.

Rabalais, N. N., jt. ed. see Boesch, D. F.

Rabalais, Raphael J., Jr. International Regulation of Finance & Investment. LC 92-61611. (Continues Transnational Economic & Monetary Law). 1993. ring bd. 150.00 (*0-379-01267-7*) Oceana.

Rabald, Erich. Corrosion Guide. 2nd rev. ed. 900p. 1968. 233.50 (*0-444-40465-1*) Elsevier.

Raban, A. J. Working in the European Communities. 210p. 1991. pap. 18.00 (*92-826-2085-9*, CY-60-90-369-EN-C) UNIPUB.

Raban, Bridie, jt. auth. see Moon, Cliff.

Raban, Colin, jt. ed. see Lawless, Paul.

Raban, Colin, jt. ed. see Lee, Phil.

Raban, Jonathan. Arabia. (Illus.). 352p. 1991. pap. 11.00 (*0-671-74880-7*, Touchstone Bks) S&S Trade.

— For Love & Money: A Writing Life. 1993. 20.75 (*0-8446-6686-6*) Peter Smith.

— Foreign Land. large type ed. 512p. 1986. 23.95 (*0-7089-8347-2*, Charnwood) Ulverscroft.

— Hunting Mister Heartbreak. large type ed. 653p. 1991. reprint ed. lib. bdg. 24.95 (*1-56054-224-1*) Thorndike Pr.

— Old Glory: An American Voyage. 1993. 21.75 (*0-8446-6684-X*) Peter Smith.

— Soft City. 1992. pap. 13.00 (*0-00-272778-1*) Collins SF.

Raban, Jonathan, ed. The Oxford Book of the Sea. 522p. 1992. 24.95 (*0-19-214197-X*) OUP.

— The Oxford Book of the Sea. LC 92-41179. 1993. 13.95 (*0-19-283148-8*) OUP.

Rabas, Deb, ed. Eden. Nonis, Michael, tr. (Illus.). 48p. 1994. 14.95 (*0-87816-267-4*) Kitchen Sink.

Rabas, Deb, ed. see Siro.

Rabas, Debra, ed. see Gimenez, Juan & Dal Pra, Roberto.

Rabas, T. J. & Webb, R. L., eds. Turbulent Enhanced Heat Transfer. (HTD Ser.: Vol. 239). 72p. 1993. 30.00 (*0-7918-1152-2*, G00796) ASME.

Rabas, T. J., jt. ed. see Sohal, M. S.

Rabasa, Jose. Inventing America: Spanish Historiography & the Formation of Eurocentrism. LC 92-34510. (Project for Discourse & Theory Ser.: Vol. 11). 1994. pap. 16.95 (*0-8061-2539-X*) U of Okla Pr.

Rabassa, Clementine C. Demetrio Aguilera-Malta & Social Justice: The Tertiary Phase of Epic Tradition in Latin American Literature. LC 78-75193. 304p. 1970. 32.50 (*0-8386-2079-5*) Fairleigh Dickinson.

Rabassa, Gregory. Cloudy Day in Gray Minor. Barkan, Stanley M., ed. (Review Chapbook Ser.: No. 35: American Poetry 8). 48p. 1989. 15.00 (*0-89304-870-4*); 15.00 (*0-685-26627-3*); pap. 5.00 (*0-89304-871-2*); pap. 5.00 (*0-685-26628-1*) Cross-Cultrl NY.

Rabassa, Gregory, intro. The World of Translation. vii, 382p. 1987. 10.95 (*0-934638-06-3*) PEN Am Ctr.

Rabassa, Gregory, tr. see Aguilera-Malta, Demetrio.

Rabassa, Gregory, tr. see Amado, Jorge.

Rabassa, Gregory, tr. see Benet, Juan.

Rabassa, Gregory, tr. see Cortazar, Julio.

Rabassa, Gregory, tr. see De Moraes, Vinicius.

Rabassa, Gregory, tr. see Donoso, Jose.

Rabassa, Gregory, tr. see Franca, Oswald, Jr.

Rabassa, Gregory, tr. see Garcia Marquez, Gabriel.

Rabassa, Gregory, tr. see Garcia-Marquez, Gabriel.

Rabassa, Gregory, tr. see Garcia Marquez, Gabriel.

Rabassa, Gregory, tr. see Lezama Lima, Jose.

Rabassa, Gregory, tr. see Lins, Osman.

Rabassa, Gregory, tr. see Lispector, Clarice.

Rabassa, Gregory, tr. see Marquez, Gabriel G.

Rabassa, Gregory, tr. see Valenzuela, Luisa.

Rabassa, Jorge, ed. Quaternary of South America & Antarctic Peninsula, Vol. 1. 166p. (C). 1982. text ed. 70.00 (*90-6191-513-9*, Pub. by A A Balkema NE) Ashgate Pub Co.

— Quaternary of South America & Antarctic Peninsula, Vol. 2. 224p. 1984. text ed. 70.00 (*90-6191-542-2*, Pub. by A A Balkema NE) Ashgate Pub Co.

— Quaternary of South America & Antarctic Peninsula, Vol. 6. 318p. (C). 1990. text ed. 70.00 (*90-6191-995-9*, Pub. by A A Balkema NE) Ashgate Pub Co.

— Quaternary of South America & Antarctic Peninsula, Vol. 7. 384p. (C). 1990. text ed. 70.00 (*90-6191-784-0*, Pub. by A A Balkema NE) Ashgate Pub Co.

— Quaternary of South America & Antarctic Peninsula: With Selected Papers of the International Symposium on Sea-Level Changes Quaternary Shorelines, Sao Paulo, 7-14 July 1986, Vol. 4. 344p. 1987. text ed. 70.00 (*90-6191-732-8*, Pub. by A A Balkema NE) Ashgate Pub Co.

— Quaternary of South America & Antarctic Peninsula: With Selected Papers of the XIIth INQUA Congress, Ottawa, 1987 on the Quaternary of South America, Vol. 5. 250p. (C). 1987. text ed. 70.00 (*90-6191-733-6*, Pub. by A A Balkema NE) Ashgate Pub Co.

— Quaternary of South America & Antarctic Penninsula: With Selected Papers of the International Symposium on Late Quaternary Sea-Level Changes & Coastal Evolution, Mar del Plata, 30 Sept. - 3 October 1984, Vol. 3. 232p. (C). 1986. text ed. 70.00 (*90-6191-591-0*, Pub. by A A Balkema NE) Ashgate Pub Co.

Rabassa, Jorge & Salemme, Monica, eds. Quaternary of South America & Antarctic Peninsula, Vol. 8: With Selected Papers of the International Symposium on Quarterrary Climates of South America, International Geological Correlation Program UNESCO, Project 281, Medellin, Colombia, 3-6 May 1990. (Illus.). 224p. 1993. text ed. 70.00 (*90-5410-140-7*, Pub. by A A Balkema NE) Ashgate Pub Co.

Rabasse, Maurice. Du Regime Des Fiefs En Normandie Au Moyen Age. LC 80-2006. reprint ed. 29.50 (*0-404-18588-6*) AMS Pr.

Rabate, Jean-Michael. Language, Sexuality, & Ideology in Ezra Pound's Cantos. LC 84-23926. 339p. 1986. 59.50 (*0-88706-036-6*); pap. 19.95 (*0-88706-037-4*) State U NY Pr.

Rabate, Jean-Michel. James Joyce, Authorized Reader. LC 90-49032. 256p. 1991. text ed. 33.50x (*0-8018-4140-2*) Johns Hopkins.

— Joyce upon the Void: The Genesis of Doubt. LC 90-44947. 165p. 1991. text ed. 39.95 (*0-312-05361-4*) St Martin.

***Rabatin, June, ed.** Count the Ties to Manassas. 85p. 1984. pap. 6.00 (*1-886826-03-X*) Manassas Mus.

Rabaudy, Nicholas, jt. auth. see Robuchon, Joel.

Rabazza, Gregory, tr. see Marquez, Gabriel G.

Rabb, jt. auth. see Apple.

***Rabb, Antonia P. Quiverings in the Net. 100p. 1994. pap. text ed. 10.00 (*0-9644280-0-8*); audio 10.00 (*0-9644280-1-6*) A P Rabb. QUIVERINGS IN THE NET, a fourth book of poetry by Antonia Phillips Rabb brings out the composite poet. Mother of six, grandmother of nine, she gives us words to be fingered like worrystones, tossed & ruminated upon, thumbed musingly deep in the pocket of**

An Asterisk (*) at the beginning of an entry indicates that the title is appearing in BIP for the first time.

one's mind. She writes of Grandbirth, that "aurora borealis" of joy, of loneliness that grips a woman with many children in midgrowth & no one to nudge in the dark to talk to. She writes of loss that comes with the death of one's parents & the inevitable acceptance of one's own majority. Titillated by life, Rabb looses herself in the intoxication of New England in the fall. She stands in awe of "this heroic" grove of beeches & follows the Kankamagus riding the "shoulders of the stream". And she writes about a quiet love still savoring all "the subtle signs of spring". QUIVERINGS IN THE NET is a book to be read many times, to keep, to give when no word says the right thing, to share with a friend, a child, a lover. A tape with guitar accompaniment, also entitled QUIVERINGS IN THE NET, is a collection of twenty-four poems selected from the book. You may obtain a signed copy of the book or a tape by contacting: Antonia Phillips Rabb, 33 Chatham St., Brookline, MA 02146. (617) 277-3072. Or KenCo Printing & Publishing, 459 High St. Medford, MA 02155. (617) 391-9500. ***Publisher Provided Annotation.***

Rabb, Hamid, jt. auth. see Sanders, Helen.

***Rabb, Jane M., ed.** Literature & Photography: Interactions, 1840-1990: a Critical Anthology. (Illus.). 708p. 1995. 80.00x (*0-8263-1561-5*); pap. 39.95x (*0-8263-1663-8*) Free Spirit Pub.

— Literature & Photography Interactions, 1840-1990: A Critical Anthology. LC 95-4369. (Illus.). 1995. write for info. (*0-8263-1541-0*) U of NM Pr.

Rabb, Kate M. National Epics. LC 76-84355. (Granger Index Reprint Ser.). 1977. 21.95 (*0-8369-6059-9*) Ayer.

Rabb, Margaret Y. The Presentation Design Book: Tips, Techniques & Advice for Creating Effective, Attractive Slides, Overheads, Screen Shows, Multimedia & More. 2nd ed. LC 93-9554. (Illus.). 320p. (C). pap. 24.95 (*1-56604-014-0*) Ventana Pr.

Rabb, Robert L., jt. ed. see Huffaker, Carl B.

Rabb, T. & Rotberg, R. I. Marriage & Fertility. (Studies in Interdisciplinary History). 1981. 57.50 (*0-691-05319-7*); pap. 15.95x (*0-691-00781-0*) Princeton U Pr.

Rabb, Theodore & Rotberg, Robert. Industrialization & Urbanization. LC 80-8675. (Studies in Interdisciplinary History). 310p. 1981. pap. 15.95 (*0-691-00785-3*) Princeton U Pr.

Rabb, Theodore K. Enterprise & Empire: Merchant & Gentry Investment in the Expansion of England, 1575-1630. LC 67-29629. 429p. reprint ed. pap. 122.30 (*0-7837-4126-X*, 2057949) Bks Demand.

— Origins of the Modern West: Essays & Sources in Early Modern European History to Accompany a Series of Fims Entitled Renaissance. Marshall, Sherrin D., ed. LC 92-43374. 1992. Study guide. student ed, pap. text ed. write for info. (*0-07-041232-4*) McGraw.

— Origins of the Modern West: Essays & Sources in Early Modern European History to Accompany a Series of Fims Entitled Renaissance. Marshall, Sherrin D., ed. LC 92-43374. 1993. pap. text ed. write for info. (*0-07-041231-6*) McGraw.

— The Struggle for Stability in Early Modern Europe. (Illus.). 1976. pap. 14.95 (*0-19-501956-3*) OUP.

Rabb, Theodore K., ed. The Thirty Years' War. 2nd ed. LC 80-6215. (Illus.). 190p. 1981. reprint ed. lib. bdg. 47.50 (*0-8191-1746-3*); reprint ed. pap. text ed. 16.50 (*0-8191-1747-1*) U Pr of Amer.

Rabb, Theodore K. & Seigel, Jerrold E., eds. Action & Conviction in Early Modern Europe: Essays in Memory of E. H. Harbison. LC 68-27407. 487p. reprint ed. pap. 138.80 (*0-8357-3388-2*, 2039644) Bks Demand.

Rabb, Theodore K., jt. ed. see Rotberg, Robert I.

Rabbani, Majid, ed. Selected Papers on Image Coding & Compression. LC 92-5748. (Milestone Ser.: Vol. 48). 1992. 124.00 (*0-8194-0888-3*); pap. 109.00 (*0-8194-0889-1*) SPIE.

Rabbani, Majid & Jones, Paul W. Digital Image Compression Techniques. 221p. 1991. 42.00 (*0-8194-0648-1*, VOL. TT07) SPIE.

Rabbani, Ruhiyyih. Prescription for Living. 2nd rev. ed. 272p. 1978. pap. 8.25 (*0-85398-003-9*) G Ronald Pub.

— The Priceless Pearl. (Illus.). 1969. pap. 9.95 (*0-900125-03-9*, 331-048) Bahai.

Rabbat, Basile G., ed. see Portland Cement Association Staff.

Rabbath, Antoine. Documents Inedits pour Servir a l'Histoire du Christianisme en Orient, 2 vols. LC 72-174293. reprint ed. lib. bdg. 125.00 (*0-404-05202-9*) AMS Pr.

Rabbe Nachman. Likutey Moharan, Vol. 3. Mykoff, Moshe & Bergman, Ozer, eds. Kramer, Chaim, tr. & intro. by. 360p. 1990. 18.00 (*0-930213-78-5*) Breslov Res Inst.

Rabbetts, John. From Hardy to Faulkner: Wessex to Yoknapatawpha. LC 88-26358. 256p. 1989. text ed. 45.00 (*0-312-02510-6*) St Martin.

Rabbetts, R. B., jt. auth. see Bennett, A. G.

Rabbi Aryeh Kaplan. Unitl the Mashiach: The Life of Rabbi Nachman. Shapiro, Dovid, ed. 379p. 1986. text ed. 15.00 (*0-930213-08-4*) Breslov Res Inst.

Rabbi Dr. Joseph Breuer Foundation Staff, ed. The Book of Yechezkel. LC 93-25424. (ENG & HEB.). 1993. 22.95 (*0-87306-956-0*) Feldheim.

Rabbi Ezriel Tauber. I Shall Not Want: The Torah Outlook on Working for a Living. Astor, Yaakov, ed. (Hashkafa Dialogue Ser.). 112p. (Orig.). 1990. pap. 6.00 (*1-878999-00-1*) Shelheves.

Rabbi Mindy Avra Portnoy. Ima on the Bima: My Mommy Is a Rabbi. LC 86-3023. (Illus.). 32p. (J). (ps-4). 1986. 10.95 (*0-930494-55-5*); pap. 4.95 (*0-930494-54-7*) Kar Ben.

Rabbi Nachman. Le Tikoun Haklali. Dimermanas, Alon, tr. 125p. (FRE.). 1986. pap. text ed. 3.00 (*0-930213-24-6*) Breslov Res Inst.

Rabbi Nachman of Breslov. The Aleph-Bet Book. Mykoff, Moshe, tr. & intro. by. 268p. 1986. text ed. 16.00 (*0-930213-15-7*) Breslov Res Inst.

— TSOHAR. Greenbaum, Avraham, tr. 64p. (Orig.). 1986. pap. text ed. 3.00 (*0-930213-26-2*) Breslov Res Inst.

Rabbi Nachman of Breslov & Rabbi Nathan of Breslov. Rabbi Nachman De Breslov. Dimermanas, Alon, ed. (Illus.). 442p. 1986. pap. 15.00 (*0-930213-20-3*) Breslov Res Inst.

Rabbi Nathan of Breslov, jt. auth. see Rabbi Nachman of Breslov.

Rabbi Obadiah of Bartenura. Pathway to Jerusalem. 96p. 1992. write for info. (*1-56062-130-3*); pap. write for info. (*1-56062-131-1*) CIS Comm.

Rabbi Reuven P. Bulka. Jewish Divorce Ethics: The Right Way to Say Goodbye. LC 92-70080. 290p. (Orig.). 1992. pap. text ed. 12.95 (*0-918921-03-1*) Ivy League Pr.

Rabbi Yehoshja Y. Neuwirth. Shemirath Sabbath, Vol. 1. Grangewood, W., tr. 360p. 1984. 16.95 (*0-87306-298-1*); pap. 13.95 (*0-87306-375-9*) Feldheim.

Rabbie, Edwin, jt. ed. see Nellen, Henk J. M.

***Rabbin, Robert.** The Sacred Hub: Living in Our Real Self. (Orig.). 1995. pap. text ed. write for info. (*0-9630390-8-3*) New Leaders.

Rabbinge, R. Simulation & Systems Management in Crop Protection. 434p. (C). 1991. text ed. 350.00 (*81-7089-135-3*, Pub. by Intl Bk Distr II) St Mut.

Rabbinowitz, Joseph, ed. see Marmorstein, Arthur.

***Rabbit.** The Bremen Town Musicians. Date not set. pap. 19.95 (*0-689-80236-6*) Macmillan.

— Creation. Date not set. pap. 19.95 (*0-689-80238-2*) Macmillan.

— Daniel in the Lion's Den. (J). Date not set. pap. 19.95 (*0-689-80239-0*, Aladdin Paperbacks) S&S Childrens.

— Firebird. Date not set. pap. 19.95 (*0-689-80240-4*) Macmillan.

— Five Chinese Brothers. Date not set. pap. 19.95 (*0-689-80241-2*) Macmillan.

— Follow the Drinking Gourd. Date not set. pap. 19.95 (*0-689-80242-0*) Macmillan.

— Jonah & the Whale. Date not set. 19.95 (*0-689-80243-9*) Macmillan.

— Mose the Fireman. Date not set. pap. 19.95 (*0-689-80227-7*, Aladdin Paperbacks) S&S Childrens.

— Moses in Egypt. Date not set. pap. 19.95 (*0-689-80226-9*, Aladdin Paperbacks) S&S Childrens.

— Moses the Lawgiver. Date not set. pap. 19.95 (*0-689-80228-5*, Aladdin Paperbacks) S&S Childrens.

— Parables that Jesus Told. Date not set. pap. 19.95 (*0-689-80229-3*, Aladdin Paperbacks) S&S Childrens.

— Pinocchio. (J). Date not set. pap. 19.95 (*0-689-80230-7*, Aladdin Paperbacks) S&S Childrens.

— Princess Scargo & the Birthday Pumpkin. (J). Date not set. pap. 19.95 (*0-689-80231-5*, Aladdin Paperbacks) S&S Childrens.

— Ruth in Canaan. (J). Date not set. pap. 19.95 (*0-689-80232-3*, Aladdin Paperbacks) S&S Childrens.

— The Song of Sacajawea. Date not set. pap. 19.95 (*0-689-80233-1*) Macmillan.

— Squanto & the First Thanksgiving. Date not set. pap. 19.95 (*0-689-80234-X*) Macmillan.

— Tobias & the Angel. Date not set. pap. 19.95 (*0-689-80237-4*) Macmillan.

— Tom Thumb. Date not set. pap. 19.95 (*0-689-80219-6*, Aladdin Paperbacks) S&S Childrens.

Rabbit, Peter. Ornithology. (Illus.). 57p. (Orig.). 1983. pap. 6.00 (*0-9615914-0-4*) Minor Heron.

***Rabbitt, John T. & Bergh, Peter.** The ISO 9000 Book: The Global Competitor's Guide to Compliance & Certification. 2nd ed. 166p. 1994. 26.95 (*0-8144-0267-4*) AMACOM.

Rabbitt, John T. & Bergh, Peter A. The ISO 9000 Book: A Global Competitor's Guide to Compliance & Certification. LC 93-14904. 1993. 26.95 (*0-527-91721-4*) Qual Resc.

— The ISO 9000 Book: A Global Competitor's Guide to Compliance & Certification. LC 93-14904. (Illus.). 176p. 1993. pap. 50.20 (*0-7837-8359-0*, 2049149) Bks Demand.

— The ISO 9000 Book: A Global Competitor's Guide to Compliance & Certification. 2nd ed. LC 94-15521. (Illus.). 224p. 1994. text ed. 26.95 (*0-527-76258-X*) Qual Resc.

Rabbitt, P. & Backman, L., eds. Cognitive Gerontology: A Special Issue. 112p. 1990. pap. 19.95 (*0-86377-157-2*) L Erlbaum Assocs.

Rabbitt, P., jt. auth. see Vel'Yaminov, B.

Rabbitt, Thomas. The Abandoned Country. LC 87-71454. (Poetry Ser.). 1988. 16.95 (*0-88748-062-4*); pap. 9.95 (*0-88748-063-2*) Carnegie-Mellon.

Rabbitts, Muriel J. Thought of Childhood. (J). 1991. 10.95 (*0-533-09371-6*) Vantage.

Rabbow, Arnold. Wie Sah das Erste Sternenbanner Aus? What Did the First U. S. Flag Look Like? 1980. 1.50 (*0-934021-36-8*) Natl Flag Foun.

Rabby, Rami & Croft, Diane. Take Charge: A Strategic Guide for Blind Job Seekers. 336p. (Orig.). 1990. pap. text ed. 23.95 (*0-939173-16-6*); audio 19.95 (*0-939173-18-2*); disk 19.95 (*0-939173-19-0*) Natl Braille Pr.

— Take Charge: A Strategic Guide for Blind Job Seekers. braille ed. 336p. (Orig.). 1990. 19.95 (*0-939173-17-4*) Natl Braille Pr.

***Rabe.** Memoirs, Obstetrics. 1994. pap. (*0-412-56080-1*) Chapman & Hall.

Rabe, Alan. Be in Health. 288p. (C). 1993. pap. text ed. 19.95 (*0-8403-8387-8*) Kendall-Hunt.

Rabe, Barry G. Beyond NIMBY: Hazardous Waste Siting in Canada & the United States. LC 94-19039. 199p. (C). 1994. 34.95x (*0-8157-7308-0*); pap. 14.95x (*0-8157-7307-2*) Brookings.

Rabe, Berniece. The Balancing Girl. LC 80-22100. (Unicorn Paperbacks Ser.). (Illus.). 32p. (J). (ps-2). 1988. pap. 4.99 (*0-525-44364-9*, 0382-120, DCB) Dutton Child Bks.

— The First Christmas Candy Cane: A Legend. LC 94-6197. (J). 1994. 7.95 (*0-681-00441-X*) Longmeadow Pr.

— Magic Comes in Its Time. LC 92-19260. (Illus.). (J). 1993. pap. 13.00 (*0-671-79454-X*, S&S Bks Young Read) S&S Childrens.

— A Smooth Move. Tucker, Kathleen, ed. LC 87-2099. (Albert Whitman Concept Bks.). (Illus.). (J). (gr. 1-4). 1987. lib. bdg. 11.95 (*0-8075-7486-4*) A Whitman.

— Tall Enough to Own the World. LC 88-39139. 160p. (J). (gr. 5-7). 1989. lib. bdg. 14.77 (*0-531-10681-0*) Watts.

— Where's Chimpy? Tucker, Kathleen, ed. LC 87-37259. (Illus.). 32p. (J). (ps-2). 1988. lib. bdg. 13.95 (*0-8075-8928-4*); pap. 5.95 (*0-8075-8927-6*) A Whitman.

Rabe, Claire. Sicily Enough & More. 128p. (C). 1989. reprint ed. lib. bdg. 27.00x (*0-8095-4048-7*) Borgo Pr.

Rabe, David. The Crossing Guard. 320p. 1995. 22.95 (*0-7868-6119-3*) Hyperion.

— Goose & Tomtom. LC 86-29432. 136p. 1987. pap. 7.95 (*0-8021-5193-0*) Grove-Atltic.

— Hurlyburly: A Play. 1991. pap. 9.95 (*0-8021-3251-0*) Grove-Atltic.

— Hurlyburly & Those the River Keeps: Two Plays. 336p. 1994. pap. 14.00 (*0-8021-3351-7*, Grove) Grove-Atltic.

— In the Boom Boom Room. 112p. 1986. pap. 8.95 (*0-8021-5194-9*) Grove-Atltic.

— Those the River Keeps: And, Hurlyburly: Two Plays. LC 94-39497. 1995. write for info. (*0-8021-1568-3*, Grove) Grove-Atltic.

— The Vietnam Plays, Vol. 1. LC 92-37145. 1993. 12.95 (*0-8021-3313-4*) Grove-Atltic.

— Vietnam Plays: Streamers & the Orphan, Vol. 2. 1993. pap. 12.95 (*0-8021-3345-2*) Grove-Atltic.

Rabe, Hugo, ed. see Philoponus, Ioannes.

Rabe, Jean. Krynnspace. (Advanced Dungeons & Dragons, Spelljammer Ser.). (Illus.). 1993. pap. 10.95 (*1-56076-560-7*, SJR7) TSR Inc.

— Night of the Tiger. (Endless Quest Ser.). (Illus.). 192p. (Orig.). (YA). 1995. pap. text ed. 3.95 (*0-7869-0114-4*) TSR Inc.

— Red Magic: Forgotten Realms. LC 90-71502. (Harpers Ser.: No. 3). 320p. (Orig.). 1991. pap. 4.95 (*1-56076-118-0*) TSR Inc.

— Secret of the Djinn. (Endless Quest, Al-Qadim Ser.: No. 3). 192p. (Orig.). 1994. pap. 3.95 (*1-56076-864-9*) TSR Inc.

— Swamplight. (Advanced Dungeons & Dragons, Second Edition; Al-Qadim Ser.). (Illus.). 1993. pap. 6.95 (*1-56076-588-7*) TSR Inc.

Rabe, Peter. Dig My Grave Deep. LC 87-72697. 144p. 1988. reprint ed. pap. 4.95 (*0-88739-092-7*, Blk Lizard) Creat Arts Bk.

— Kill the Boss Good-Bye. LC 92-50689. (Vintage Crime - Black Lizard Ser.). 1993. pap. 9.00 (*0-679-74069-4*, Vin) Random.

— Kill the Boss Goodbye. LC 87-72698. 128p. 1988. reprint ed. pap. 4.95 (*0-88739-091-9*, Blk Lizard) Creat Arts Bk.

— The Out Is Death. LC 87-72696. 128p. 1988. reprint ed. pap. 4.95 (*0-88739-093-5*, Blk Lizard) Creat Arts Bk.

Rabe, Sheila. The Accidental Bride. 224p. 1994. mass mkt. 3.99 (*0-8217-4597-2*) Zebra.

— Bringing Out Betsy. 256p. 1994. mass mkt. 3.99 (*0-8217-4788-6*) Zebra.

— Ghostly Charade. 1991. pap. 3.95 (*0-8217-3545-4*) Zebra.

— An Innocent Imposter. 224p. 1995. mass mkt. 4.50 (*0-8217-4944-7*) Windsor NY.

— Miss Plympton's Peril. 208p. (Orig.). 1994. pap. text ed. 3.99 (*0-515-11453-7*) Jove Pubns.

— The Wedding Deception. 208p. (Orig.). 1993. pap. 3.99 (*1-55773-897-1*) Diamond.

***Rabe, Sheila & Schneider, Eric.** Interactive Parties & Games: Fun for All Ages. Lent, Penny, ed. LC 94-79465. (Illus.). 150p. (Orig.). 1995. per., pap. text ed. 9.95 (*1-885371-08-X*) Kldoscope Pr.

Rabe, Stephen G. Eisenhower & Latin America: The Foreign Policy of Anticommunism. LC 87-12493. x, 238p. (C). 1988. 37.50 (*0-8078-1761-9*); pap. 12.95 (*0-8078-4204-4*) U of NC Pr.

— The Road to OPEC: United States Relations with Venezuela, 1919-1976. (Texas Pan American Ser.). 272p. (C). 1982. text ed. 27.50 (*0-292-76020-5*) U of Tex Pr.

Rabe, Stephen G., jt. ed. see Paterson, Thomas G.

Rabe, Steven G., jt. ed. see Brown, Richard D.

Rabe, Susan A. Faith, Art, & Politics at Saint-Riquier: The Symbolic Vision of Angilbert. (Middle Age Ser.). (Illus.). 256p. (C). 1995. text ed. 36.95 (*0-8122-3208-9*) U of Pa Pr.

Rabe, Tish. My Name Is Ernie. (Golden Little Look-Look Book Ser.). (Illus.). (J). (ps-00). 1991. pap. write for info. (*0-307-11513-5*, Golden Pr) Western Pub.

— My Name Is Grover. (Golden Little Look-Look Book Ser.). (Illus.). 24p. (J). (ps-00). 1992. pap. write for info. (*0-307-11534-8*, 11534, Golden Pr) Western Pub.

Rabe, Valentin H. The Home Base of American China Missions, 1880-1920. (East Asian Monographs: No. 75). 300p. 1978. 26.00 (*0-674-40581-1*) HUP.

Rabeeya, David. A Guide to Understanding Judaism & Islam: More Similarities Than Differences. 95p. 1992. pap. 14.95 (*0-9631746-1-4*) Maimuna Pr.

Rabeeya, David & Rueveni, Roni. Sephardic Recipes: Delicacies from Baghdad. (Illus.). 52p. 1992. pap. 14.95 (*0-9631746-0-6*) Maimuna Pr.

Rabek. Progress in Photochemistry & Photophysics, Vol. V. 1992. 156.00 (*0-8493-4045-4*, QD714) CRC Pr.

Rabek, J. F. Experimental Methods in Photochemistry & Photophysics, 2 pts, Pt. 1. LC 81-14787. (Illus.). 612p. reprint ed. Part 1. pap. 159.20 (*0-318-39732-3*, 2033090) Bks Demand.

— Experimental Methods in Photochemistry & Photophysics, 2 pts, Pt. 2. LC 81-14787. (Illus.). 612p. reprint ed. Part 2. pap. 137.10 (*0-318-39733-1*) Bks Demand.

— Mechanisms of Photophysical Processes & Photochemical Reactions in Polymers: Theory & Applications. LC 86-15693. (Illus.). 776p. reprint ed. pap. 180.00 (*0-8357-4627-5*, 2037556) Bks Demand.

— Photostabilization of Polymers: Principles & Applications. 596p. 1990. 153.00 (*1-85166-408-4*) Elsevier.

Rabek, J. F., jt. ed. see Allen, N. S.

Rabek, J. F., jt. ed. see Fouassier, J. P.

Rabek, J. F., jt. auth. see Ranby, Bengt G.

Rabek, J. F., jt. ed. see Ranby, Bengt G.

Rabek, Jan F. Experimental Methods in Polymer Chemistry: Physical Principles & Applications. LC 79-40511. 887p. reprint ed. pap. 180.00 (*0-317-55697-5*, 2029264) Bks Demand.

— Photochemistry & Photophysics, Vol. IV. 1991. 190.00 (*0-8493-4044-6*, QD714) CRC Pr.

Rabek, Jan F. & Scott, Gary W., eds. Photochemistry & Photophysics, Vol. I. 208p. 1989. 156.00 (*0-8493-4041-1*, QD714) CRC Pr.

— Photochemistry & Photophysics, Vol. II. 192p. 1989. 156.00 (*0-8493-4042-X*, QD714) CRC Pr.

Rabek, Jan F., jt. ed. see Fouassier, Jean-Pierre.

Rabel, Carmen R. Lope de Vega: El Arte Nuevo de Hacer "Novellas" (Monografias Ser.: No. A 150). 128p. (C). 1992. text ed. 45.00 (*1-85566-016-4*, Pub. by Tamesis Bks Ltd UK) Boydell & Brewer.

***Rabel, Eve.** Songs of Madness. 1994. 12.95 (*0-533-10476-9*) Vantage.

Rabel, Lili. Khasi: A Language of Assam. LC 61-15485. (Louisiana State University Studies, Humanities Ser.: No. 10). (Illus.). 273p. reprint ed. pap. 77.90 (*0-317-10148-X*, 2051657) Bks Demand.

Rabel, Roberto G. Between East & West: Trieste, the United States & the Cold War, 1941-1954. LC 87-31775. xvii, 222p. (C). 1988. lib. bdg. 36.95 (*0-8223-0831-2*) Duke.

Rabelais. The Life of Gargantua & the Heroic Deeds of Pantagruel. 1972. 69.95 (*0-8490-0530-2*) Gordon Pr.

Rabelais, Francois. L' Abbaye de Theleme. 2nd ed. 40p. (FRE.). 1949. pap. 14.95 (*0-7859-5376-0*, F31160) Fr & Eur.

— Le Cinquieme et Dernier Livre des Faits et Dicts Heroiques Du bon Pantagruel. 219p. (FRE.). 1977. pap. 180.00 (*0-7859-5377-9*) Fr & Eur.

— The Complete Works of Francois Rabelais. Frame, Donald M., tr. 1114p. 1991. 75.00 (*0-520-06400-3*) U CA Pr.

— Francois Rabelais: Quart Livre: Des Faict et Dicts Heroiques du Bon Pantagruel. Heath, Michael, ed. 309p. 1990. pap. 9.00 (*1-870725-06-9*, R2, Pub. by Runnymede) MRTS.

— Gargantua. Screech, M. A., ed. (Illus.). 458p. 1970. 17.50 (*0-686-54693-8*) Fr & Eur.

— Gargantua. 190p. (FRE.). 1987. pap. 10.95 (*0-7859-1270-3*, 2040166998) Fr & Eur.

— Gargantua. (Folio Ser.: No. 773). (FRE.). pap. 10.95 (*2-07-036773-8*) Schoenhof.

— Gargantua & Pantagruel. Cohen, John M., tr. (Classics Ser.). 1955. pap. 9.95 (*0-14-044047-X*, Penguin Classics) Viking Penguin.

— Gargantua & Pantagruel. Raffel, Burton, tr. 640p. 1991. pap. 17.95 (*0-393-30806-5*) Norton.

— Gargantua & Pantagruel, 3 Vols, 1. LC 01-8984. (Tudor Translations, First Ser.: Nos. 24-26). reprint ed. 57.50 (*0-404-51921-0*) AMS Pr.

— Gargantua & Pantagruel, 3 Vols, 2. LC 01-8984. (Tudor Translations, First Ser.: Nos. 24-26). reprint ed. 57.50 (*0-404-51922-9*) AMS Pr.

— Gargantua & Pantagruel, 3 Vols, 3. LC 01-8984. (Tudor Translations, First Ser.: Nos. 24-26). reprint ed. 57.50 (*0-404-51923-7*) AMS Pr.

— Gargantua & Pantagruel, 3 Vols, Set. LC 01-8984. (Tudor Translations, First Ser.: Nos. 24-26). reprint ed. 172.50 (*0-404-51920-2*) AMS Pr.

— Gargantua & Pantagruel: Selections. Gray, Floyd F., ed. & tr. by. (Crofts Classics Ser.). 160p. 1966. pap. text ed. write for info. (*0-88295-068-1*) Harlan Davidson.

— Gargantula & Pantagreul. 1994. 23.00 (*0-679-43137-3*, Everymans Lib) Knopf.

— Oeuvres, 6 vols. (Illus.). 400.00 (*0-686-54699-7*) Fr & Eur.

— Oeuvres: Avec: Le Cinquieme Livre, Vol. 5. Plattard, Jean, ed. 400p. (FRE.). 1948. pap. 12.95 (*0-7859-1459-5*, 2251360859) Fr & Eur.

— Oeuvres: Avec: Le Quart-Livre, Vol. 4. Plattard, Jean, ed. 338p. (FRE.). 1959. pap. 17.95 (*0-7859-1458-7*, 2251360840) Fr & Eur.

— Oeuvres: Avec: Le Tiers-Livre, Vol. 3. Plattard, Jean, ed. 78p. (FRE.). 1961. pap. 17.95 (*0-7859-1457-9*, 2251360832) Fr & Eur.

R

— Oeuvres: Pantagruel, Vol. 2. Plattard, Jean, ed. 220p. (FRE.). 1959. pap. 17.95 (*0-7859-1456-0*, 2251360824) Fr & Eur.
— Oeuvres Completes. Boulanger, Jacques, ed. 1072p. (FRE.). 1978. lib. bdg. 100.00 (*0-7859-3780-3*, 2070104702) Fr & Eur.
— Oeuvres Completes. deluxe ed. Boulenger & Scheler, eds. (Pleiade Ser.). (FRE.). 1934. 63.95 (*2-07-010470-2*) Schoenhof.
— Pantagruel. 1964. pap. 4.50 (*0-685-11475-9*, 1240) Fr & Eur.
— Pantagruel. Saulnier, V. L., ed. 448p. (FRE.). 1973. pap. 13.95 (*0-7859-4556-3*) Fr & Eur.
— Pantagruel. (Folio Ser.: No. 387). (FRE.). pap. 10.95 (*2-07-036387-2*) Schoenhof.
— Pantagrueline Prognostication Pour l'An 1533: Avec les Almanachs pour les Ans 1533, 1535 et 1541. la Grande et Vraye Pronostication Nouvelle De 1544. (Illus.). 180p. (FRE.). 1975. pap. 24.95 (*0-7859-5378-7*) Fr & Eur.
— Le Quart Livre. 256p. (FRE.). 1990. pap. 10.95 (*0-7859-1425-0*, 2080702408) Fr & Eur.
— Le Tiers Livre. Michel, Pierre, ed. 1973. 4.95 (*0-686-54704-7*) Fr & Eur.
— Le Tiers Livre. Screech, A. M., ed. 474p. (FRE.). 1991. pap. 11.95 (*0-7859-4557-1*) Fr & Eur.
— Tiers Livre (Original) (Folio Ser.: No. 462). (FRE.). pap. 9.95 (*2-07-036462-3*) Schoenhof.
— La Vie Tres Honorifique du Grand Gargantua, Vol. 1. 233p. (FRE.). 1973. pap. 180.00 (*0-7859-5379-5*) Fr & Eur.
— La Vie Tres Horrificque du Grand Gargantua. 248p. 1968. 14.95 (*0-8288-7423-9*) Fr & Eur.

Rabell, Edda, ed. see Ronnholm, Ursula O.

Raben, Estelle M. Major Strategies in Twentieth-Century Drama: Apocalyptic Vision, Allegory & Open Form. (American University Studies: English Language & Literature: Ser. IV, Vol. 67). 164p. (C). 1989. text ed. 21.50 (*0-8204-0567-1*) P Lang Pubs.

Rabenau, A., ed. Problems of Nonstoichiometry. 1970. 31.00 (*0-444-10047-4*, North Holland) Elsevier.

Rabenau, A., jt. ed. see Rodymans, C.

***Rabenau, Merten.** Studien Zum Buch Tobit. (Beihefte zur Zeitschrift fuer die Alttestamentliche Wissenschaft Ser.). viii, 249p. (GER.). (C). 1994. lib. bdg. 106.15 (*3-11-014125-6*) De Gruyter.

Rabeneck, jt. auth. see Ehrhardt.

Rabeneck, Malvern, jt. auth. see Ehrhardt, Roy.

Rabeneck, Malvern, jt. auth. see Erhardt, Roy.

Rabeneck, Red, jt. auth. see Ehrhardt, Roy.

Rabenhorst, Thomas & McDermott, Paul D. Applied Cartography: Introduction to Remote Sensing. 128p. (C). 1989. pap. write for info. (*0-675-20633-2*, Merrill Pub Co) Macmillan.
— Applied Cartography: Source Materials for Map Making. 168p. (C). 1989. pap. write for info. (*0-675-20533-6*, Merrill Pub Co) Macmillan.

Rabenold, Diana. Love, Politics, & "Rescue" in Lesbian Relationships. (Lesbian-Feminist Essay Ser.). 24p. (Orig.). 1987. pap. 3.50 (*0-939821-29-X*) HerBooks.

Rabenort, William L. Spinoza As Educator. LC 70-177175. (Columbia University. Teachers College. Contributions to Education Ser.: No. 38). reprint ed. 37.50 (*0-404-55038-X*) AMS Pr.

Rabenstein, Albert L. Elementary Differential Equations with Linear Algebra. 3rd ed. 518p. (C). 1982. text ed. 48.00 (*0-15-520982-5*) HB Coll Pubs.
— Elementary Differential Equations with Linear Algebra. 4th ed. 650p. (C). 1992. text ed. 61.25 (*0-15-520984-1*) SCP.

Rabeony, Ernest. Fanorona: The Classic Game of Tactical Skill from Madagascar. Fox, Leonard, tr. 1990. 20.00 (*0-932329-02-0*) Intl Fanorona.

Raber, Ann, ed. A Life of Wholeness: Reflections on Abundant Living. rev. ed. 160p. 1993. pap. 7.95 (*0-8361-3646-2*) Herald Pr.

Raber, Chester, jt. auth. see Stoesz, Edgar.

Raber, Douglas & Raber, Nancy. Organic Chemistry. 1445p. (C). 1988. text ed. 79.50 (*0-314-28508-3*) West Pub.

Raber, Laura L., jt. auth. see Lindon, James A.

Raber, Martin D. A. I. D. S. - Occurrence & Transmission: Medical Subject Analysis with Reference Bibliography. LC 85-48178. 150p. 1986. 39.50 (*0-88164-490-0*); pap. 34.50 (*0-88164-491-9*) ABBE Pubs Assn.
— AIDS: Diagnosis with Medical Subject Analysis & Reference Bibliography. LC 85-48191. 156p. 1985. reprint ed. 39.50 (*0-88164-488-9*); reprint ed. pap. 34.50 (*0-88164-489-7*) ABBE Pubs Assn.

Raber, Merill F. & Dyck, George. Managing Stress for Mental Fitness: A Guide to Emotional Health. 2nd rev. ed. Gerould, Philip, ed. (Fifty-Minute Ser.). 80p. (Orig.). 1993. pap. 9.95 (*1-56052-200-3*) Crisp Pubns.

Raber, Nancy, jt. auth. see Raber, Douglas.

Raber, Robert R., ed. Fluid Filtration: Gas, Vol. 1. LC 86-22237. (Special Technical Publication Ser.: No. 975). (Illus.). 430p. 1986. text ed. 39.00 (*0-8031-0945-8*, 04-975001-39) ASTM.

Raber, Robert R., et al, eds. Fluid Filtration, 2 vols., Set. LC 86-22237. (Special Technical Publication Ser.: No. 975). (Illus.). 624p. 1986. text ed. 55.00 (*0-8031-0926-1*, 04-975000-39) ASTM.

Raber, Rom. Bo Jackson: Pro Sports Superstar. (Sports Achievers Ser.). (Illus.). 64p. (J). (gr. 4-9). 1991. lib. bdg. 13.50 (*0-8225-0487-1*, Lerner Publctns); pap. 4.95 (*0-8225-9585-0*, Lerner Publctns) Lerner Group.

Raber, Thomas R. Election Night. (American Politics Ser.). (Illus.). 88p. (J). (gr. 4 up). 1988. lib. bdg. 14.95 (*0-8225-1751-5*, Lerner Publctns) Lerner Group.
— Joe Montana: Comeback Quarterback. (J). (gr. 4-9). 1990. pap. 4.95 (*0-8225-9572-9*, Lerner Publctns) Lerner Group.
— Michael Jordan: Basketball Skywalker. LC 92-8277. (Achievers Ser.). (J). (gr. 4-9). 1992. 13.50 (*0-8225-0549-5*, Lerner Publctns) Lerner Group.
— Michael Jordan: Basketball Skywalker. (J). (gr. 4-9). 1993. pap. 4.95 (*0-8225-9625-3*, Lerner Publctns) Lerner Group.
— Presidential Campaign. (American Politics Ser.). (Illus.). 88p. (J). (gr. 4 up). 1988. lib. bdg. 14.95 (*0-8225-1750-7*, Lerner Publctns) Lerner Group.

Raber, Tom. Joe Montana: Comeback Quarterback. (Sports Achievers Ser.). (Illus.). 64p. (J). (gr. 4-9). 1989. lib. bdg. 13.50 (*0-8225-0486-3*, Lerner Publctns) Lerner Group.
— Wayne Gretzky: Hockey Great. (Sports Achievers Ser.). (Illus.). 64p. (J). (gr. 4-9). 1991. lib. bdg. 13.50 (*0-8225-0539-8*, Lerner Publctns) Lerner Group.
— Wayne Gretzky: Hockey Great. (YA). 1992. pap. 4.95 (*0-8225-9601-6*, Lerner Publctns) Lerner Group.

Rabes, H., et al, eds. Metastasis: Basic Research & Its Clinical Application. (Beitraege zur Onkologie, Contributions to Oncology Ser.: Vol. 44). x, 394p. 1992. 63.25 (*3-8055-5610-1*) S Karger.

Rabesa, Arthur. Kumite: The Complete Fighting Text. LC 84-16609. (Illus.). 133p. (Orig.). 1984. pap. text ed. 10.00 (*0-930559-00-2*) Peabody Pub.

Rabette, P. M., jt. ed. see Davenas, J.

Rabey, David I. Howard Barker: Politics & Desire: An Expository Study of His Drama & Poetry, 1969-1987. LC 88-15795. 256p. 1989. text ed. 45.00 (*0-312-02351-0*) St Martin.

Rabey, Ed, jt. auth. see Beyer, Beverly.

Rabey, Gordon. In Charge: Supervising for the First Time. (Institute of Management Ser.). 224p. (Orig.). 1994. pap. 45.00x (*0-273-60426-0*, Pub. by Pitman Pubng UK) St Mut.

Rabey, Gordon, jt. auth. see Healey, Barry.

Rabey, Lois M. The Snare: Understanding Emotional & Sexual Entanglements. LC 87-63506. 242p. 1994. pap. 12.00 (*0-89109-832-1*) NavPress.

Rabgay, Lobsang, tr. see Donden, Yeshi.

Rabia, H. Fundamentals of Casing Design. (C). 1987. lib. bdg. 96.00 (*0-86010-863-5*, Pub. by Graham & Trotman UK) Kluwer Ac.
— Oilwell Drilling Engineering: Principles & Practice. 334p. 1986. lib. bdg. 108.00 (*0-86010-661-6*); pap. text ed. 60.00 (*0-86010-714-0*) G & T Inc.

Rabianski, Joseph, jt. auth. see Vernor, James D.

Rabianski, Joseph S., jt. auth. see Epley, Donald R.

***Rabicoff, Richard.** Tough Customers: Stories by Richard Rabicoff. (Petite Ser.). 76p. 1994. pap. 4.00 (*1-884754-10-4*) Potpourri Pubns.

Rabideau, Clyde M. Robidous in North America: Three Hundred Fifty Years (1643-1993) 608p. 1993. 18.00 (*0-9636684-0-4*) C Rabideau.

Rabideau, Peter W., ed. The Conformational Analysis of Cyclohexenes, Cyclohexadienes, & Related Hydroaromatic Compounds. LC 88-33970. (Methods in Stereochemical Analysis Ser.). 323p. 1989. lib. bdg. 100.00 (*0-89573-702-7*) VCH Pubs.

Rabie, A. A Bibliography of Criminal Law: General Principles. 96p. 1987. pap. 16.00 (*0-7021-1852-4*, Pub. by Juta SA) W W Gaunt.

Rabie, M. A., jt. auth. see Fuggle, R. F.

Rabie, Mohamed. Conflict: Resolution & Ethnicity. LC 94-6381. 240p. 1994. text ed. 55.00 (*0-275-94598-7*, Praeger Pubs) Greenwood.
— The Politics of Foreign Aid: U. S. Foreign Assistance & Aid to Israel. LC 88-3096. 200p. 1988. text ed. 55.00 (*0-275-93000-9*, C3000, Praeger Pubs) Greenwood.
— U. S. - PLO Dialogue: Secret Diplomacy & Conflict Resolution. LC 94-5294. 224p. 1995. lib. bdg. 34.95 (*0-8130-1326-7*) U Press Fla.

***Rabie, P. J.** The Law of Estoppel in South Africa. 130p. 1992. pap. 49.00 (*0-409-05000-8*, SA); boxed 85.00 (*0-409-05001-6*, SA) Butterworth Legal Pubs.

Rabier, J., et al, eds. Dislocations 93. (Solid State Phenomena Ser.: Vols. 35-36). (Illus.). 631p. (C). 1994. 170.00 (*3-908450-02-0*, Pub. by Trans Tech SZ) LPS Dist Ctr.

Rabier, Jacque-Rene, et al. Euro-Barometer 27: The Common Agricultural Policy & Cancer, March-May 1987. LC 89-811139. (Euro-Barometers Ser.). 378p. 1989. write for info. (*0-89138-874-5*) ICPSR.

Rabier, Jacques-Rene. Euro-Barometer 4: Consumer Attitudes in Europe, October November 1975. LC 79-83752. 1979. write for info. (*0-89138-988-1*) ICPSR.

Rabier, Jacques-Rene & Inglehart, Ronald. Euro-Barometer 10: National Priorities & the Institutions of Europe, October-November 1978. LC 80-84080. 1980. write for info. (*0-89138-955-5*) ICPSR.
— Euro-Barometer 10-A: Scientific Priorities in the European Community, October-November 1978. LC 81-84734. 1981. write for info. (*0-89138-944-X*) ICPSR.
— Euro-Barometer 11: The Year of the Child in Europe, April 1979. LC 81-84735. 1981. write for info. (*0-89138-943-1*) ICPSR.
— Euro-Barometer 12: European Parliamentary Elections, October-November 1979. LC 81-84736. 1981. write for info. (*0-89138-942-3*) ICPSR.
— Euro-Barometer 3: European Men & Women, May 1975. LC 79-83750. 1979. write for info. (*0-89138-989-X*) ICPSR.
— Euro-Barometer 5: Revenues, Satisfaction, & Poverty, May 1976. LC 79-83756. 1979. write for info. (*0-89138-987-3*) ICPSR.
— Euro-Barometer 6: Twenty Years of the Common Market, October-November 1976. LC 79-83757. 1979. write for info. (*0-89138-986-5*) ICPSR.
— Euro-Barometer 7: Science & Technology in the European Community, April 1977. LC 80-84077. 1980. write for info. (*0-89138-952-0*) ICPSR.
— Euro-Barometer 8: Men, Women, & Work Roles in Europe, October-November 1977. LC 80-84078. 1980. write for info. (*0-89138-953-9*) ICPSR.
— Euro-Barometer 9: Employment & Unemployment in Europe, April 1978. LC 80-84079. 1980. write for info. (*0-89138-954-7*) ICPSR.

Rabier, Jacques-Rene, jt. auth. see Inglehart, Ronald.

Rabier, Jacques-Rene, et al. Candidates for the European Parliament, April-May 1979. LC 84-62936. 1985. write for info. (*0-89138-893-1*) ICPSR.
— Euro-Barometer No. 26: Energy Problems, November 1986. LC 89-83656. 240p. 1989. write for info. (*0-89138-876-1*) ICPSR.
— Euro-Barometer 13: Regional Development & Integration, April 1980. LC 82-81760. 1982. write for info. (*0-89138-937-7*, ICPSR 7957) ICPSR.
— Euro-Barometer 14: Trust in the European Community, October 1980. LC 82-81761. 1982. write for info. (*0-89138-936-9*, ICPSR 7958) ICPSR.
— Euro-Barometer 15: Membership in the European Community, April 1981. LC 82-81762. 1982. write for info. (*0-89138-935-0*, ICPSR 7959) ICPSR.
— Euro-Barometer 16: Noise & Other Social Problems, October 1981. LC 83-83374. 1984. write for info. (*0-89138-906-7*) ICPSR.
— Euro-Barometer 17: Energy & the Future, April 1982. LC 83-83375. 1984. write for info. (*0-89138-905-9*) ICPSR.
— Euro-Barometer 18: Ecological Issues, October 1982. LC 83-83376. 1984. write for info. (*0-89138-904-0*) ICPSR.
— Euro-Barometer 19: Gender Roles in the European Community, April 1983. LC 84-80216. 1984. write for info. (*0-89138-903-2*) ICPSR.
— Euro-Barometer 20: Aid to Developing Nations, October 1983. LC 84-62937. 1985. write for info. (*0-89138-894-X*) ICPSR.
— Euro-Barometer 21: Political Cleavages in the European Community, April 1984. LC 85-80716. 1985. write for info. (*0-89138-889-3*) ICPSR.
— Euro-Barometer 22: Energy Problems & the Atlantic Alliance, October 1984. LC 86-82557. (Euro-Barometers Ser.). 174p. 1986. write for info. (*0-89138-884-2*) ICPSR.
— Euro-Barometer 23: The European Currency Unit & Working Conditions, April 1985. LC 86-82556. (Euro-Barometers Ser.). 168p. 1986. write for info. (*0-89138-883-4*) ICPSR.
— Euro-Barometer 25: Holiday Travel & Environmental Problems, April 1986. LC 88-81973. (Euro-Barometers Ser.). 288p. 1988. write for info. (*0-89138-877-X*) ICPSR.
— Euro-Barometer 28: Relations with Third World Countries & Energy Problems, November 1987. LC 89-81140. (Euro-Barometers Ser.). 438p. 1989. write for info. (*0-89138-873-7*) ICPSR.

Rabier, P. J. Topics in One-Parameter Bifurcation Problems. (Tata Institute Lectures on Mathematics Ser.). vi, 290p. 1985. pap. 29.00 (*0-387-13907-9*) Spr-Verlag.

Rabier, P. J. & Oden, J. Tinsley. Bifurcation in Rotating Bodies. Ciarlet, P. G. & Lions, J. L., eds. (Recherches en Mathematiques Appliquees Ser.: Vol. 11). vii, 150p. 1990. pap. 35.00 (*0-387-51551-8*) Spr-Verlag.

Rabiger, Michael. Directing: Film Techniques & Aesthetics. (Illus.). 412p. 1989. pap. 36.95 (*0-240-80011-7*, Focal) Buttrwrth-Heinemann.

Rabiger, Michael, ed. Directing the Documentary. 2nd ed. 382p. 1992. pap. 39.95 (*0-240-80126-1*, Focal) Buttrwrth-Heinemann.

Rabii, S. Physics of Four-Six Compounds & Alloys. 264p. 1974. text ed. 205.00 (*0-677-05070-4*) Gordon & Breach.

Rabil, Albert. Erasmus & the New Testament: The Mind of a Christian Humanist. LC 71-184768. (Trinity University Monograph Series in Religion: Vol. 1). 206p. reprint ed. pap. 58.80 (*0-317-08044-X*, 2022565) Bks Demand.

Rabil, Albert, Jr. Erasmus & the New Testament: The Mind of a Christian Humanist. LC 93-4903. 208p. (C). 1993. reprint ed. pap. text ed. 21.50 (*0-8191-9217-1*) U Pr of Amer.

Rabil, Albert. Merleau-Ponty, Existentialist of the Social World. LC 66-15954. 349p. reprint ed. pap. 99.50 (*0-317-09247-2*, 2005781) Bks Demand.

Rabil, Albert, Jr., ed. & tr. Knowledge, Goodness, & Power: The Debate Over Nobility Among Quattrocento Italian Humanists. (Medieval & Renaissance Texts & Studies: Vol. 88). 432p. 1991. 36.00 (*0-86698-100-4*) MRTS.

Rabil, Albert, Jr., ed. Renaissance Humanism, Vols. 1-3: Foundations, Forms & Legacy, 3 vols., Set. LC 87-13928. (Illus.). 1988. pap. 89.95 (*0-8122-1400-5*) U of Pa Pr.
— Renaissance Humanism, Vols. 1-3: Foundations, Forms & Legacy, 3 vols., Vol. 1. LC 87-13928. (Illus.). 710p. 1988. pap. 26.95 (*0-8122-1372-6*) U of Pa Pr.
— Renaissance Humanism, Vols. 1-3: Foundations, Forms & Legacy, 3 vols., Vol. 2. LC 87-13928. (Illus.). 430p. 1988. pap. 26.95 (*0-8122-1373-4*) U of Pa Pr.
— Renaissance Humanism, Vols. 1-3: Foundations, Forms & Legacy, 3 vols., Vol. 3. LC 87-13928. (Illus.). 508p. 1988. pap. 36.95 (*0-8122-1374-2*) U of Pa Pr.

Rabil, Albert, Jr., jt. ed. see King, Margaret L.

Rabin. AIP Conference Proceedings, No. 137. LC 85-73915. 302p. 1986. lib. bdg. 53.75 (*0-88318-336-6*) Am Inst Physics.

Rabin, ed. Handbook of Public Budgeting. (Public Administration & Public Policy Ser.: Vol. 46). 760p. 1992. 195.00 (*0-8247-8592-4*) Dekker.

Rabin & Jackowski. Handbook of Information Resource Management. (Public Administration & Public Policy Ser.: Vol. 31). 592p. 1988. 170.00 (*0-8247-7739-5*) Dekker.

Rabin & Lynch. Handbook on Public Budgeting & Financial Management. (Public Administration & Public Policy Ser.: Vol. 12). 640p. 1983. 175.00 (*0-8247-1253-6*) Dekker.

Rabin & Steinhauer, eds. Handbook on Human Service Administration. (Public Adminstration & Public Policy Ser.: Vol. 34). 624p. 1988. 180.00 (*0-8247-7924-X*) Dekker.

Rabin, jt. auth. see Golembiewski.

Rabin, et al. Handbook of Public Administration. (Public Administration & Public Policy Ser.: Vol. 35). 1120p. 1989. 220.00 (*0-8247-7964-9*) Dekker.
— Handbook on Strategic Management. (Public Administration & Public Policy Ser.: Vol. 38). 496p. 1989. 199.00 (*0-8247-8089-2*) Dekker.
— Managing Administration. (Public Administration & Public Policy Ser.: Vol. 26). 280p. 1984. 79.75 (*0-8247-7096-X*) Dekker.

Rabin, et al, eds. Handbook of Public Personnel Administration. (Public Administration & Public Policy Ser.: Vol. 58). 744p. 1995. 195.00 (*0-8247-9231-9*) Dekker.

Rabin, Alan A. & Yeager, Leland B. Monetary Approaches to the Balance of Payments & Exchange Rates. LC 82-15587. (Essays in International Finance Ser.: No. 148). 1982. pap. text ed. 8.00 (*0-88165-055-2*) Princeton U Int Finan Econ.

Rabin, Albert. Assessment with Projective Techniques: A Concise Introduction. LC 80-26229. 352p. 1981. 35.95 (*0-8261-3550-1*) Springer Pub.

Rabin, Albert I. Projective Techniques for Adolescents & Children. (Illus.). 384p. 1986. 38.95 (*0-8261-4920-0*) Springer Pub.

Rabin, Arnold. The Outing. 53p. (Orig.). (YA). 1992. pap. 5.00 (*0-87602-303-0*) Anchorage.

Rabin, Chaim. Qumran Studies. LC 76-40116. (Scripta Judaica Ser.: No. 2). 135p. 1977. reprint ed. text ed. 35.00 (*0-8371-9060-6*, RAQS, Greenwood Pr) Greenwood.

Rabin, D. M., ed. Infrared Solar Physics: Proceedings of the 154th Symposium of the International Astronomical Union, Held in Tucson, Arizona, U. S. A., March 2-6, 1992. LC 93-33129. 628p. (C). 1993. lib. bdg. 176.00 (*0-7923-2522-2*); pap. text ed. 88.00 (*0-7923-2523-0*) Kluwer Ac.

Rabin, David. Long-Term Care for the Elderly: A Factbook. (Illus.). 269p. 1986. pap. 19.95 (*0-19-504106-2*) OUP.

Rabin, Edward H. & Kwall, Roberta R. Modern Real Property, Fundamentals Of. 3rd ed. (University Casebook Ser.). 1092p. 1992. text ed. 45.95 (*0-88277-962-1*) Foundation Pr.
— Teacher's Manual for Fundamentals of Modern Real Property Law. 3rd ed. (University Casebook Ser.). 1992. pap. text ed. write for info. (*1-56662-002-3*) Foundation Pr.

Rabin, H. M. & Rosenbaum, Max, eds. How to Begin a Psychotherapy Group: Six Approaches. 144p. 1976. text ed. 49.00 (*0-677-15800-9*) Gordon & Breach.

Rabin, Jack. Handbook of Public Personnel: Administration & Labor Relations. (Public Administration & Public Policy Ser.: Vol. 15). 704p. 1983. 170.00 (*0-8247-1318-4*) Dekker.

Rabin, Jack & Bowman, James. Politics & Administration: Woodrow Wilson & American Public Administration. (Public Administration & Public Policy Ser.: Vol. 22). 344p. 1984. 79.75 (*0-8247-7068-4*) Dekker.

Rabin, Jack & Dodd, Don. State & Local Government Administration. (Public Administration & Public Policy Ser.: Vol. 28). 464p. 1985. 55.00 (*0-8247-7355-1*) Dekker.

Rabin, Jack, jt. ed. see Vocino, Thomas.

Rabin, Jack, et al. Budget Management: A Reader in Local Government Financial Management. (Public Budgeting Laboratory Ser.). 258p. (Orig.). 1983. pap. 16.95 (*0-89854-090-9*) U of GA Inst Govt.
— Deborah Budgeting & Financial Management: An Annotated Bibliography. LC 91-11176. (Public Affairs & Administration Ser.: Vol. 25). 1991. 22.00 (*0-8240-7595-1*) Garland.
— Handbook on Public Personnel Administration & Labor Relations. fac. ed. LC 83-1468. (Public Administration & Public Policy Ser.: No. 15). 687p. 1983. pap. 180.00 (*0-7837-8334-5*, 2049121) Bks Demand.
— Personnel: Managing Human Resources in the Public Sector. 248p. (C). 1985. pap. text ed. 20.00 (*0-15-570188-6*) HB Coll Pubs.
— Public Budgeting Laboratory. 1983. teacher ed 9.95 (*0-89854-088-7*); student ed 11.95 (*0-89854-087-9*); disk 11.95 (*0-89854-089-5*) U of GA Inst Govt.

***Rabin, Jack, et al, eds.** Handbook of Public Sector Labor Relations. LC 94-13202. (Public Administration & Public Policy Ser.: Vol. 56). 448p. 1994. 165.00 (*0-8247-9235-1*) Dekker.

Rabin, M. Automata on Infinite Objects & Church's Problem. LC 72-6749. (CBMS Regional Conference Series in Mathematics: No. 13). 22p. 1982. reprint ed. 18.00 (*0-8218-1663-2*, CBMS-13) Am Math.

Rabin, Robert J., et al. Labor & Employment Law: Problems, Cases & Materials in the Law of Work. (American Casebook Ser.). 1014p. 1988. text ed. 44.50 (*0-314-39695-0*); teacher ed, pap. text ed. write for info. (*0-314-46970-2*) West Pub.
— Labor & Employment Law: Problems, Cases, & Materials in the Law of Work. 2nd ed. LC 95-3407. (American Casebook Ser.). 1995. text ed. 48.00 (*0-314-05458-8*) West Pub.
— Labor & Employment Law: Statutory Supplement. (American Casebook Ser.). 212p. 1993. reprint ed. pap. text ed. 12.50 (*0-314-44487-4*) West Pub.

Rabin, Robert L. Perspectives on Tort Law. 2nd ed. 352p. (C). 1983. 12.00 (*0-316-73003-3*) Little.

R

An Asterisk (*) at the beginning of an entry indicates that the title is appearing in BIP for the first time.

Rabin, Robert L. & Sugarman, Stephen D., eds. Smoking Policy: Law, Politics, & Culture. LC 92-33045. 1993. 38. 00 (*0-19-507231-6*) OUP.

Rabin, Robert L., jt. auth. see Franklin, Marc A.

Rabin, Staton. Casey over There. LC 92-30322. (Illus.). (J). 1994. 14.95 (*0-15-253186-6*) HarBrace.

— Monster Myths: The Truth about Water Monsters. LC 91-34420. (New England Aquarium Bks.). (Illus.). 40p. (J). (gr. 5-8). 1992. lib. bdg. 16.87 (*0-531-11074-5*) Watts.

Rabin, Susan & Lagowski, Barbara J. How to Attract Anyone, Anytime, Anyplace: The Smart Single's Guide to Flirting in the '90s. LC 93-10133. 144p. (Orig.). 1993. pap. 8.95 (*0-452-27086-3*, Plume) NAL-Dutton.

Rabin, Y. & Bruinsma, R., eds. Soft Order in Physical Systems. (NATO ASI, Series B, Physics: Vol. 323). (Illus.). 216p. (C). 1994. 75.00 (*0-306-44678-2*) Plenum.

***Rabinbach.** Marxism. 1995. 26.95 (*0-8057-8620-1*, Twayne); pap. 14.95 (*0-8057-8621-X*, Twayne) Macmillan.

Rabinbach, Anson & Zipes, Jack D., eds. Germans & Jews since the Holocaust: The Changing Situation in West Germany. LC 85-14036. 300p. 1986. 39.95 (*0-8419-0924-5*); pap. 18.95 (*0-8419-0925-3*) Holmes & Meier.

Rabinback, Anson. Human Motor: Energy, Fatigue, & the Origins of Modernity. 1992. pap. 17.00 (*0-520-07827-6*) U CA Pr.

***Rabindranath Tagore Festival Committee Staff.** Tagore, Rabindranath, a Collection of His Life & Work. (Illus.). 80p. 1986. pap. 28.00 (*0-905836-56-1*, Pub. by Museum Modern Art UK) St Mut.

Rabine, Leslie W. Reading the Romantic Heroine: Text, History, Ideology. LC 85-13955. (Women & Culture Ser.). 238p. 1985. reprint ed. pap. 67.90 (*0-7837-5653-4*, 2059078) Bks Demand.

Rabine, Leslie W., jt. ed. see Melzer, Sara E.

Rabine, Leslie W., jt. auth. see Moses, Claire G.

Rabineau, Phyllis. Feather Arts: Beauty, Wealth, & Spirit from Five Continents. 2nd ed. Williams, Patricia, ed. LC 78-74595. (Illus.). 88p. 1980. pap. 7.95 (*0-914868-08-X*) Field Mus.

Rabiner, Donald, jt. auth. see Brown, Claudia.

Rabiner, Donald, ed. see Brown, Claudia & Chou, Ju-Hsi.

Rabiner, Lawrence R. & Rader, Charles N., eds. Digital Signal Processing. LC 72-90358. (Illus.). 528p. 1972. pap. 39.95 (*0-87942-018-9*, PP00182) Inst Electrical.

Rabiner, Lawrence R. & Schafer, Ronald W. Digital Processing of Speech Signals. (Signal Processing Ser.). 1978. text ed. 81.00 (*0-13-213603-1*) P-H.

Rabiner, Lawrence R., jt. auth. see Crochiere, Ronald E.

Rabinnowitch, M. & Goldwurm, H. Mishnah-Zeraim: Sheviis. Danziger, Y., ed. (ArtScroll Mishnah Ser.). (Illus.). 254p. 1987. 22.95 (*0-89906-326-8*) Mesorah Pubns.

Rabinovic, M. I., jt. auth. see Abarbanel, H. D.

***Rabinovich, Abe.** Teddy Kollek, Builder of Jerusalem. LC 95-15871. (Young Biography Ser.). (J). 1995. write for info. (*0-8276-0559-5*) JPS Phila.

Rabinovich, Abraham. The Battle for Jerusalem. 470p. 1987. pap. 17.95 (*0-8276-0285-5*) JPS Phila.

— Jerusalem on Earth: People, Passions, & Politics in the Holy City. 256p. 1988. text ed. 24.95 (*0-02-925740-9*) Free Pr.

***Rabinovich, Boris I., et al.** Vortex Processes & Solid Body Dynamics: Spacecraft & Magnetic Levitation Systems Dynamics Problems. LC 94-30833. 1994. lib. bdg. 136. 50 (*0-7923-3092-7*) Kluwer Ac.

Rabinovich, Isaiah. Major Trends in Modern Hebrew Fiction. Roston, M., tr. LC 68-15035. 300p. reprint ed. pap. 85.50 (*0-317-10153-6*, 2020149) Bks Demand.

Rabinovich, Itamar. The Road Not Taken: Early Arab-Israeli Negotiations. 272p. 1991. 22.95 (*0-19-506066-0*) OUP.

— The War for Lebanon: 1970-1985. rev. ed. LC 83-45935. 243p. (C). 1984. 35.95 (*0-8014-1870-4*); pap. 13.95 (*0-8014-9313-7*) Cornell U Pr.

Rabinovich, Itamar & Shaked, Haim, eds. From June to October: The Middle East Between 1967 & 1973. LC 76-45942. 550p. (C). 1977. text ed. 39.95 (*0-87855-230-8*) Transaction Pubs.

— Middle East Contemporary Survey: Vol. X, 1986, Vol. 10. 694p. 1988. text ed. 102.00 (*0-8133-0764-3*) Westview.

Rabinovich, Itamar, jt. ed. see Esman, Milton J.

Rabinovich, Itamar, jt. ed. see Fry, Michael G.

Rabinovich, Itamar, jt. ed. see Shaked, Haim.

Rabinovich, Itamar, et al, eds. Middle East Contemporary Survey, Vol. XI, 1987, Vol. 11. 710p. 1989. text ed. 94. 50 (*0-8133-0925-5*) Westview.

Rabinovich, Izrail, jt. auth. see Harris, David A.

Rabinovich, Izrail' B. Influence of Isotopy on the Physicochemical Properties of Liquids. LC 69-17695. (Illus.). 316p. reprint ed. pap. 90.10 (*0-317-09392-4*, 2020681) Bks Demand.

Rabinovich, M. I. & Trubetskov, D. I. Oscillations & Waves. (C). 1989. lib. bdg. 253.50 (*0-7923-0445-4*) Kluwer Ac.

Rabinovich, M. I., jt. auth. see Gaponov-Grekhov, A. V.

Rabinovich, Moysey. Soviet Conventional Arms Transfers to the Third World: Main Missile & Artillery Directorate (1966-1990) (Foreign Technology Assessment Ser.). ix, 49p. (Orig.). 1994. pap. 45.00 (*1-881874-09-5*) Global Cnslts.

Rabinovich, Semyon. Measurement Errors: Theory & Practice. Alferieff, M. E., tr. LC 92-28122. 1992. 100.00 (*0-88318-866-X*) Am Inst Physics.

— Measurement Errors: Theory & Practice. Alferieff, M. E., tr. LC 92-28122. (Illus.). 271p. (C). 1994. pap. text ed. 39.95x (*1-56396-323-X*, AIP Pr) Am Inst Physics.

Rabinovich, V. A., et al, eds. Thermophysical Properties of Neon, Argon, Krypton & Xenon. (National Standard Reference Data Service of the U. S. S. R.: A Series of Property Tables: Vol. 10). 605p. 1987. 199.50 (*0-89116-675-0*) Hemisp Pub.

Rabinovich, V. A., jt. auth. see Vasserman, A. A.

Rabinovich, Viktor Abramovich. Thermophysical Properties of Gases & Liquids. (Physical Constants & Properties of Substances Ser.: No. 1). 215p. reprint ed. pap. 61.30 (*0-317-08438-0*, 2004605) Bks Demand.

Rabinovitch, B. S., et al, eds. Annual Review of Physical Chemistry, Vol. 27. LC 51-1658. (Illus.). 1976. text ed. 44.00 (*0-8243-1027-6*) Annual Reviews.

— Annual Review of Physical Chemistry, Vol. 29. LC 51-1658. (Illus.). 1978. text ed. 44.00 (*0-8243-1029-2*) Annual Reviews.

— Annual Review of Physical Chemistry, Vol. 30. LC 51-1658. (Illus.). 1979. text ed. 44.00 (*0-8243-1030-6*) Annual Reviews.

— Annual Review of Physical Chemistry, Vol. 31. LC 51-1658. (Illus.). 1980. text ed. 44.00 (*0-8243-1031-4*) Annual Reviews.

— Annual Review of Physical Chemistry, Vol. 32. LC 51-1658. (Illus.). 1981. text ed. 44.00 (*0-8243-1032-2*) Annual Reviews.

— Annual Review of Physical Chemistry, Vol. 33. LC 51-1658. (Illus.). 1982. text ed. 44.00 (*0-8243-1033-0*) Annual Reviews.

— Annual Review of Physical Chemistry, Vol. 34. LC 51-1658. (Illus.). 1983. text ed. 44.00 (*0-8243-1034-9*) Annual Reviews.

— Annual Review of Physical Chemistry, Vol. 35. LC 51-1658. (Illus.). 1984. text ed. 44.00 (*0-8243-1035-7*) Annual Reviews.

— Annual Review of Physical Chemistry, Vol. 36. LC 51-1658. (Illus.). (C). 1985. text ed. 44.00 (*0-8243-1036-5*) Annual Reviews.

Rabinovitch, Itamar. Syria under the Ba'th, 1963-1966: Army-Party Symbiosis. 276p. 1972. boxed 39.95 (*0-87855-163-8*) Transaction Pubs.

Rabinovitch, M. Mishnah-Nashim: Nedarim. Arem, T. Z., ed. (ArtScroll Mishnah Ser.). (Illus.). 238p. 1985. 22.95 (*0-89906-279-2*) Mesorah Pubns.

Rabinovitch, M. & Kalatsky, Y. Mishnah-Nashim: Nazir-Sotah. Danziger, Y., ed. (ArtScroll Mishnah Ser.). (Illus.). 400p. 1985. 22.95 (*0-89906-281-4*) Mesorah Pubns.

Rabinovitch, Nachum L. Probability & Statistical Inference in Ancient & Medieval Jewish Literature. LC 79-187394. 219p. reprint ed. pap. 62.50 (*0-317-08544-1*, 2014349) Bks Demand.

Rabinovitch, Sacha, tr. see Lefebvre, Henri.

Rabinovitz, Frances F., jt. auth. see Fried, Robert C.

Rabinovitz, Francine F. & Trueblood, Felicity M., eds. Latin American Urban Research, Vol. 1. LC 78-103483. 314p. reprint ed. pap. 89.50 (*0-317-29596-9*, 2021942) Bks Demand.

— National-Local Linkages: The Interrelationship of Urban & National Polities in Latin America. LC 72-98042. (Latin American Urban Research Ser.: Vol. 3). 312p. reprint ed. pap. 89.00 (*0-317-29600-0*, 2021941) Bks Demand.

***Rabinovitz, Judy.** Justice Detained: Conditions at the Verick Street Immigration Detention Center. (Public Policy Report Ser.). 63p. (Orig.). 1993. pap. 5.00 (*0-914031-21-X*) Amer Civil Lib.

Rabinovitz, Lauren. Points of Resistance: Women, Power, & Politics in the New York Avant-Garde Cinema, 1943-71. (Illus.). 264p. 1991. 34.95 (*0-252-01744-7*); pap. 14. 95 (*0-252-06139-X*) U of Ill Pr.

Rabinovitz, Lauren, jt. ed. see Jeffords, Susan.

Rabinovitz, Rubin. The Development of Samuel Beckett's Fiction. LC 83-4850. 248p. 1984. 24.95 (*0-252-01095-7*) U of Ill Pr.

— Innovation in Samuel Beckett's Fiction. 200p. (C). 1992. 34.95 (*0-252-01941-5*) U of Ill Pr.

— Iris Murdoch. LC 68-19756. (Columbia Essays on Modern Writers Ser.: No. 34). (Orig.). 1968. pap. text ed. 7.50 (*0-231-03000-2*) Col U Pr.

— Samna: Luxury Word Processing. (Illus.). 288p. 1986. 24. 95 (*0-8306-0634-3*); pap. 16.95 (*0-8306-2734-0*, NO. 2734) TAB Bks.

Rabinovitz, Rubin, jt. auth. see Barale, Michele A.

Rabinovitz, Rubin, jt. ed. see Barale, Michele A.

Rabinow, Jacob. Inventing for Fun & Profit. (Illus.). 1990. 18.75 (*0-911302-64-6*) San Francisco Pr.

Rabinow, Paul. French Modern: Norms & Forms of the Social Environment. 448p. 1989. 44.00x (*0-262-18134-7*) MIT Pr.

— French Modern: Norms & Forms of the Social Environment. x, 454p. 1995. pap. 16.95x (*0-226-70174-3*) U Ch Pr.

— Reflections on Fieldwork in Morocco. LC 77-71066. (Quantum Bks.: No. 11). 1977. pap. 13.00 (*0-520-03529-1*) U CA Pr.

Rabinow, Paul & Sullivan, William M., eds. Interpretive Social Science: A Reader. LC 77-85743. 1979. pap. 15. 00 (*0-520-03834-7*) U CA Pr.

— Interpretive Social Science: A Second Look. 1988. 50.00 (*0-520-05836-4*); pap. 15.00 (*0-520-05838-0*) U CA Pr.

Rabinow, Paul, jt. auth. see Dreyfus, Hubert L.

Rabinow, Paul, ed. see Foucault, Michel.

Rabinowich, Nosson D., tr. The Iggeres of Rav Sherira Gaon: The Epistle of Rau Sherira Gaon. 175p. (C). 1992. 15.95 (*0-940118-60-2*) Moznaim.

Rabinowics, Wlodzimierz. Universalizability. (Synthese Library: No. 141). 1979. lib. bdg. 51.50 (*90-277-1020-1*) Kluwer Ac.

Rabinowicz, Ernest. Friction & Wear of Materials. LC 65-12704. (Science & Technology of Materials Ser.). (Illus.). 244p. 1965. text ed. 84.95 (*0-471-70340-0*) Wiley.

— Friction & Wear of Materials. 2nd ed. LC 94-32860. 1995. text ed. 49.95 (*0-471-83084-4*) Wiley.

Rabinowicz, Harry. Hasidism & the State of Israel. (Littman Library of Jewish Civilization). (Illus.). 346p. 1982. 12. 50 (*0-19-710049-X*, Pub. by Littman Lib Jew UK) Bnai Brith Bk.

— A World Apart: The Story of the Chasidim in Britain. LC 95-5666. 1995. write for info. (*0-85303-261-0*, Pub. by Vallentine Mitchell UK) Intl Spec Bk.

Rabinowicz, Harry M. Hasidism: The Movement & Its Masters. LC 87-37427. 472p. 1988. 35.00 (*0-87668-998-5*) Aronson.

Rabinowicz, Oscar K. Winston Churchill on Jewish Problems. LC 74-43. 231p. (C). 1974. reprint ed. text ed. 59.75 (*0-8371-7357-4*, RAWC, Greenwood Pr) Greenwood.

Rabinowicz, Tzvi. A Guide to Life: Jewish Laws & Customs of Mourning. LC 89-35085. 256p. 1989. 30.00 (*0-87668-833-4*) Aronson.

— A Guide to Life: Jewish Laws & Customs of Mourning. LC 89-35085. 256p. 1994. pap. 20.00 (*1-56821-143-0*) Aronson.

— The Prince Who Turned into a Rooster: One Hundred Tales from Hasidic Tradition. LC 93-31396. 280p. 1994. pap. 24.95 (*0-87668-685-4*) Aronson.

Rabinowicz, Tzvi M., ed. Encyclopedia of Hasidism. LC 94-3140. 1995. write for info. (*1-56821-123-6*) Aronson.

Rabinowitch, Alexander. Prelude to Revolution: The Petrograd Bolsheviks & the July, 1917, Uprising. LC 68-10278. 315p. reprint ed. 89.80 (*0-8357-9236-6*, 2055224) Bks Demand.

— Prelude to Revolution: The Petrograd Bolsheviks & the July 1917 Uprising. LC 91-8422. (Illus.). 314p. 1991. reprint ed. 35.00 (*0-253-34768-8*); reprint ed. pap. 12.95 (*0-253-20661-8*, MB-661) Ind U Pr.

Rabinowitch, Alexander, et al, eds. Revolution & Politics in Russia: Essays in Memory of B. I. Nicolaevsky. LC 79-183608. (Russian & East European Studies: No. 41). (Illus.). 428p. reprint ed. pap. 122.60 (*0-685-20433-2*, 2056435) Bks Demand.

Rabinowitch, David. The Collinasca Cycle. (Illus.). 56p. 1993. pap. 35.00 (*0-935875-11-5*) P Blum Edit.

— David Rabinowitch: Work 1967-1976. (Illus.). 200p. 1992. 60.00 (*3-89322-462-9*, Pub. by Edition Cantz GW) Dist Art Pubs.

Rabinowitch, David, jt. ed. see Von Wise, Stephan.

Rabinowitch, E. & Belford, R. Spectroscopy & Photochemistry of Uranyl Compounds. LC 63-10059. (International Series of Monographs on Nuclear Energy: Vol. 1). 1964. 156.00 (*0-08-010180-1*, Pub. by Pergamon Repr UK) Franklin.

Rabinowitch, E., jt. ed. see Rabinowitch, V.

Rabinowitch, Eugene I. The Dawn of a New Age: Reflections on Science & Human Affairs. LC 63-20898. 340p. reprint ed. pap. 96.90 (*0-317-09265-0*, 2020150) Bks Demand.

Rabinowitch, Haim D. & Brewster, James L., eds. Onions & Allied Crops, 3 vols., Vol. I. 288p. 1989. 204.00 (*0-8493-6300-4*, SB341) CRC Pr.

— Onions & Allied Crops, 3 vols., Vol. II. 320p. 1989. 204. 00 (*0-8493-6301-2*, SB341) CRC Pr.

— Onions & Allied Crops, 3 vols., Vol. III. 272p. 1989. 204. 00 (*0-8493-6302-0*, SB341) CRC Pr.

Rabinowitch, V. & Rabinowitch, E., eds. Views on Science, Technology & Development. LC 74-32201. 300p. (C). 1975. 126.00 (*0-08-018241-0*, Pub. by Pergamon Repr UK) Franklin.

Rabinowitch, Z. E. & Lupandin, K. K. English-Russian Textile Dictionary. 640p. (ENG & RUS.). 1961. 49.95 (*0-685-57824-0*, M-9111) Fr & Eur.

Rabinowitz, A. H. Israel: The Christian Dilemma. 82p. 1992. pap. 7.95 (*965-229-017-3*, Pub. by Gefen Pub Hse IS) Gefen Bks.

***Rabinowitz, Abraham H.** TaRYaG. Date not set. write for info. (*1-56821-449-9*) Aronson.

Rabinowitz, Alan. Chasing the Dragon's Tail: The Struggle to Save Thailand's Wild Cats. LC 92-1739. 1992. 12.00 (*0-385-41518-4*, Anchor NY) Doubleday.

— Jaguar: One Man's Battle to Establish the World's First Jaguar Preserve. 1991. pap. 12.00 (*0-385-41519-2*, Anchor NY) Doubleday.

— Land Investment & the Predevelopment Process: A Guide for Finance & Real Estate Professionals. LC 87-32594. 248p. 1988. text ed. 59.95 (*0-89930-326-9*, RZP/, Quorum Bks) Greenwood.

— Municipal Bond Finance & Administration: A Practical Guide to the Analysis of Tax-Exempt Securities. LC 71-81325. (Illus.). 272p. reprint ed. pap. 77.60 (*0-317-09356-8*, 2051574) Bks Demand.

— The Real Estate Gamble: Lessons From Fifty Years of Boom & Bust. LC 80-65706. 320p. reprint ed. pap. 91.20 (*0-317-26698-5*, 2023508) Bks Demand.

— Social Change Philanthropy in America. LC 89-24362. 248p. 1990. text ed. 55.00 (*0-89930-536-9*, RSD/, Greenwood Pr) Greenwood.

Rabinowitz, Carla B. & Coughlin, Robert E. Analysis of Landscape Characteristics Relevant to Preference. (Discussion Paper Ser.: No. 38). 1970. pap. 10.00 (*1-55869-009-3*) Regional Sci Res Inst.

— Some Experiments in Quantitative Measurement of Landscape Quality. (Discussion Paper Ser.: No. 43). 1971. pap. 10.00 (*1-55869-116-2*) Regional Sci Res Inst.

Rabinowitz, Clara, jt. ed. see Wortis, Helen.

Rabinowitz, Dorothy. About the Holocaust: What We Know & How We Know It. LC 79-51801. (Illus.). 48p. 1979. pap. 1.50 (*0-87495-014-7*) Am Jewish Comm.

— The Other Jews: Portraits in Poverty. LC 77-183251. (Institute of Human Relations Press Paperback Ser). 64p. (Orig.). 1972. 1.25 (*0-87495-015-5*) Am Jewish Comm.

Rabinowitz, Fredric E. & Cochran, Sam V. Man Alive: A Primer of Men's Issues. LC 93-28043. 1994. pap. 17.95 (*0-534-21792-3*) Brooks-Cole.

Rabinowitz, Harvey Z. Buildings in Use Study: Part 1: Technical Factors; Part 2: Functional Factors; Appendix: Field Tests Manual, 2 pts. (Publications in Architecture & Urban Planning: No. R75-1). (Illus.). v, 258p. 1985. reprint ed. 12.00 (*0-938744-37-2*) U of Wis Ctr Arch-Urban.

Rabinowitz, Henry & Schaap, Chaim. Portable C. 288p. 1989. pap. 29.95 (*0-13-685967-4*) P-H.

Rabinowitz, Howard N. First New South, 1865-1920. Franklin, John H. & Eisenstadt, A. S., eds. (American History Ser.). 150p. 1992. pap. text ed. write for info. (*0-88295-883-6*) Harlan Davidson.

— Race, Ethnicity, & Urbanization: Selected Essays. 376p. 1993. text ed. 42.50 (*0-8262-0930-0*) U of Mo Pr.

— Race Relations in the Urban South, 1865-1890. LC 79-28674. (Blacks in the New World Ser.). 461p. 1980. pap. 14.95 (*0-252-00811-1*) U of Ill Pr.

Rabinowitz, Howard N., ed. Southern Black Leaders of the Reconstruction Era. LC 81-11372. (Blacks in the New World Ser.). (Illus.). 448p. 1982. pap. 14.95 (*0-252-00972-X*) U of Ill Pr.

Rabinowitz, Isaac. A Witness Forever: Ancient Israel's Perception of Literature & the Resultant Hebrew Bible. Owen, David I., ed. (Occasional Publications of the Department of Near Eastern Studies & the Program of Jewish Studies, Cornell U.). 165p. (C). 1994. 20.00 (*1-883053-02-1*) CDL Pr.

Rabinowitz, Isaac, ed. The Book of the Honeycomb's Flow: Sepher Nopheth Suphim by Judah Messer Leon. LC 81-15273. (Critical Edition & Translation Ser.). 604p. 1983. 85.00 (*0-8014-0870-9*) Cornell U Pr.

Rabinowitz, Jacob, pref. Gaius Valerius Catullus's Complete Poetic Works. LC 91-11173. (Dunquin Ser.: No. 20). 150p. (Orig.). 1991. pap. 13.50 (*0-88214-220-8*) Spring Pubns.

Rabinowitz, Jacob J. Jewish Law: Its Influence on the Development of Legal Institutions. 1956. 20.00 (*0-8197-0173-4*) Bloch.

Rabinowitz, Jan. The Tzedakah Workbook. (Illus.). 32p. (Orig.). (J). (gr. 4-5). 1986. pap. text ed. 3.95 (*0-933873-07-7*) Torah Aura.

Rabinowitz, Jonathan, ed. see Barnes, Susan.

Rabinowitz, Joseph L., jt. auth. see Chase, Grafton D.

Rabinowitz, Max. The Day They Scrambled My Brains at the Funny Factory. 1978. pap. 1.95 (*0-89083-344-3*) Zebra.

Rabinowitz, Mitchell, ed. Cognitive Science Foundations of Instruction. 248p. 1993. text ed. 49.95 (*0-8058-1279-2*) L Erlbaum Assocs.

Rabinowitz, Nancy S. Anxiety Veiled: Euripides & the Traffic in Women. LC 93-17257. 264p. 1993. 37.50 (*0-8014-2845-9*); pap. 14.95 (*0-8014-8091-4*) Cornell U Pr.

Rabinowitz, Nancy S. & Richlin, Amy, eds. Feminist Theory & the Classics. LC 92-40745. (Thinking Gender Ser.). 288p. 1993. 49.95 (*0-415-90645-8*, A7581, Routledge NY); pap. 15.95 (*0-415-90646-6*, A7585, Routledge NY) Routledge.

Rabinowitz, Oskar K. Arnold Toynbee on Judaism & Zionism: A Critique. 372p. 1975. 25.00 (*0-8464-0149-5*) Beekman Pubs.

Rabinowitz, P. Minimax Methods in Critical Point Theory with Applications to Differential Equations. LC 86-7847. (CBMS Regional Conference Series in Mathematics: No. 65). 110p. 1988. reprint ed. pap. text ed. 23.00 (*0-8218-0715-3*, CBMS-65) Am Math.

Rabinowitz, P. D., jt. ed. see Coffin, M. F.

Rabinowitz, Paul H. & Zehnder, Eduard, eds. Analysis, et Cetera: Research Papers Published in Honor of Jurgen Moser's 60th Birthday. 694p. 1990. text ed. 109.00 (*0-12-574249-5*) Acad Pr.

Rabinowitz, Paula. Labor & Desire: Women's Revolutionary Fiction in Depression America. LC 91-50259. (Gender & American Culture Ser.). xiv, 212p. (C). 1991. 32.50 (*0-8078-1994-8*); pap. 13.95 (*0-8078-4332-6*) U of NC Pr.

— They Must Be Represented: History & the Rhetoric of Gender in American Political Documentaries. (Haymarket Ser.). (Illus.). 288p. 1994. 64.95 (*1-85984-925-3*, B4643, Pub. by Verso UK); pap. 19.95 (*1-85984-025-6*, B4647, Pub. by Verso UK) Routledge Chapman & Hall.

Rabinowitz, Paula, jt. ed. see Nekola, Charlotte.

Rabinowitz, Peter J. Before Reading: Narrative Conventions & the Politics of Interpretation. LC 87-47602. 272p. (C). 1987. 35.95 (*0-8014-2010-5*); pap. 13.95 (*0-8014-9472-9*) Cornell U Pr.

Rabinowitz, Peter J., jt. ed. see Phelan, James.

Rabinowitz, Philip, ed. Numerical Methods for Nonlinear Algebraic Equations. LC 78-115963. (Illus.). 212p. 1970. text ed. 121.00 (*0-677-14230-7*); pap. text ed. 48.00 (*0-677-14235-8*) Gordon & Breach.

Rabinowitz, Philip, jt. auth. see Davis, Philip J.

Rabinowitz, Philip D. & Schouten, Hans. Ocean Margin Drilling Program Atlases, Vol. 11. (Regional Atlas Ser.). 1985. pap. 195.00 (*0-86720-260-0*) Jones & Bartlett.

Rabinowitz, Philip D., jt. auth. see Ewing, John I.

Rabinowitz, Philip D., jt. ed. see Hayes, Dennis E.

Rabinowitz, Richard. The Spiritual Self in Everyday Life: The Transformation of Personal Religious Experience in Nineteenth-Century New England. (New England Studies). 315p. 1989. text ed. 40.00 (*1-55553-022-2*) NE U Pr.

— What Is War? Fifty Questions & Answers for Kids. (J). (gr. 4-7). 1991. pap. 2.95 (*0-380-76704-X*, Camelot) Avon.

R

An Asterisk (*) at the beginning of an entry indicates that the title is appearing in BIP for the first time.

Rabinowitz, Stanley. The Assembly: A Century in the Life of the Adas Israel Hebrew Congregation of Washington, D. C. LC 93-34048. 1993. write for info. (*0-88125-443-6*) Ktav.

Rabinowitz, Stanley, ed. Index to Mathematical Problems 1980-1984. LC 91-66461. (Indexes to Mathematical Problems Ser.: Vol. 1). 532p. 1992. 49.95 (*0-9626401-1-5*, QA43) MathPro Pr.

Rabinowitz, Stanley, tr. & intro. The Noise of Change: Russian Literature & the Critics (1891-1917) 244p. (C). 1986. pap. 14.95 (*0-88233-526-X*) Ardis Pubs.

Rabinowitz, Stanley J. Sologub's Literary Children: Keys to a Symbolist's Prose. (Illus.). 176p. 1980. pap. 15.95 (*0-89357-069-9*) Slavica.

Rabinowitz, Stanley J., jt. auth. see Griffiths, Frederick T.

Rabinowitz, Y. Mishnah-Nashim: Yevamos. Danziger, Y., ed. (ArtScroll Mishnah Ser.). (Illus.). 364p. 1984. 22.95 (*0-89906-275-X*) Mesorah Pubns.

Rabinowitz, Yaron S., et al. Color Atlas of Corneal Topography: Interpreting Videokeratography. LC 93-208. (Illus.). 96p. 1993. 125.00 (*0-89640-235-5*) Igaku-Shoin.

Rabinowitz, Yosef. Ezra-The Book of Ezra. (ArtScroll Tanach Ser.). 208p. 1984. 17.95 (*0-89906-089-7*); pap. 15.95 (*0-89906-090-0*) Mesorah Pubns.

Rabins, P. V., jt. ed. see Billig, N.

Rabins, Peter & Mace, Nancy L. The Thirty-Six Hour Day. (C). 1989. 45.00 (*0-340-37012-2*, Pub. by Age Concern Eng UK) St Mut.

Rabins, Peter V., jt. frwd. see Honel, Rosalie W.

Rabins, Peter V., jt. auth. see Mace, Nancy L.

Rabinsky, Leatrice & Mann, Gertrude. Journey of Conscience: Young People Respond to the Holocaust. 112p. reprint ed. 1.50 (*0-686-95073-9*) ADL.

Rabinwicz, Tuvi. Chassidic Rebbes: From the Baal Shem Tov to Modern Times. (Illus.). 376p. 1989. 17.95 (*0-944070-10-8*) Targum Pr.

***Rabior, William.** From My Youth: Prayers As I Grow Old. LC 94-75242. 128p. (Orig.). 1994. pap. 7.95 (*0-89243-630-1*) Liguori Pubns.

Rabior, William & Bedard, Vicki W. Catholics Experiencing Divorce: Grieving, Healing, & Learning to Live Again. LC 91-60945. 80p. (Orig.). 1991. pap. text ed. 3.95 (*0-89243-347-7*) Liguori Pubns.

— Handbook for Single Parents. 80p. (Orig.). 1990. pap. 4.95 (*0-89243-313-2*) Liguori Pubns.

— Prayers for Catholics Experiencing Divorce: Prayers for Healing. (Illus.). 96p. 1993. pap. 3.95 (*0-89243-528-3*) Liguori Pubns.

Rabior, William & Leipert, Jack. Marriage Makers, Marriage Breakers: Counseling for a Stronger Relationship. LC 91-76662. 112p. (Orig.). 1992. pap. 5.95 (*0-89243-423-6*) Liguori Pubns.

Rabizadeh, Masoud. Housing for the Elderly. LC 82-1991. 1982. 5.00 (*0-87114-088-8*) U of Oreg Bks.

Rabjohn, N. Organic Syntheses: Collective Volumes, Vol. 4. 1036p. 1963. Vols. 30-39. text ed. 103.00 (*0-471-70470-9*, 2-203) Wiley.

Rabkin, Anna, jt. auth. see Rabkin, Marty.

Rabkin, Eric & Smith, Macklin. Teaching Writing That Works. LC 90-39360. 224p. (C). 1990. pap. text ed. 15.95 (*0-472-06443-6*) U of Mich Pr.

Rabkin, Eric, jt. auth. see Glaspell, Susan.

Rabkin, Eric S. Arthur C. Clarke. 2nd ed. Schlobin, Roger C., ed. LC 79-84709. (Starmont Reader's Guide Ser.: Vol. 1). 80p. 1980. lib. bdg. 20.00 (*0-916732-22-3*); pap. 10.00 (*0-916732-21-5*) Borgo Pr.

— Stories. (C). 1994. text ed. 34.50 (*0-06-045327-3*) HarpCollege.

Rabkin, Eric S., ed. Fantastic Worlds: Myths, Tales, & Stories. 1979. pap. 14.95 (*0-19-502541-5*) OUP.

— Science Fiction: An Historical Anthology. 1983. pap. 13.95 (*0-19-503272-1*) OUP.

Rabkin, Eric S. & Silverman, Eugene M. It's a Gas: A Study of Flatulence. (Illus.). 164p. (Orig.). 1991. pap. 9.95 (*1-879378-03-5*) Rabkin-Silverman.

— It's a Gas! A Study of Flatulence. (Illus.). 160p. (C). 1991. reprint ed. lib. bdg. 23.00x (*0-8095-6121-2*) Borgo Pr.

Rabkin, Eric S., jt. ed. see Slusser, George E.

Rabkin, Eric S., jt. ed. see Slusser, George.

Rabkin, Eric S., et al, eds. The End of the World. LC 82-19365. (Alternatives Ser.). 240p. 1983. 19.95 (*0-8093-1033-3*) S Ill U Pr.

— No Place Else: Exploration in Utopian & Dystopian Fiction. LC 83-4265. (Alternatives Ser.). 288p. 1983. 19.95 (*0-8093-1113-5*) S Ill U Pr.

Rabkin, G. & Lauro, Al Di. Dirty Movies: An Illustrated History of the Stag Film 1915-1970. LC 76-43040. (Illus.). 160p. 1976. 15.00 (*0-87754-046-2*) Chelsea Hse.

Rabkin, Gerald. Drama & Commitment. LC 72-6866. (Studies in Drama: No. 39). (C). 1972. reprint ed. lib. bdg. 75.00 (*0-8383-1659-X*) M S G Haskell Hse.

Rabkin, Jacob. Current Law Forms with Tax Analysis, Looseleaf Updates Avail. 1948. write for info. (*0-8205-1240-0*) Bender.

Rabkin, Jacob & Johnson, Mark H. Federal Income, Gift & Estate Taxation, 15 vols., Set. 1942. Looseleaf set & updating monthly service. ring bd. write for info. (*0-8205-1590-6*) Bender.

***Rabkin, Judith G., et al.** Good Doctors, Good Patients: Partners in HIV Treatment. 212p. 1995. pap. 15.00 (*0-9643884-0-5*) NCM Pubs.

Rabkin, Leo, jt. auth. see McDonald, Robert.

Rabkin, Marty & Rabkin, Anna. Public Libraries: Travel Treasures of the West. (Illus.). 352p. 1993. pap. 19.95 (*1-55591-915-4*, North Amer Pr) Fulcrum Pub.

Rabkin, Norman. Shakespeare & the Problem of Meaning. LC 80-18538. 1982. pap. text ed. 5.95 (*0-226-70178-6*) U Ch Pr.

Rabkin, Norman, jt. auth. see Fraser, Russell A.

Rabkin, Peggy A. Fathers to Daughters: The Legal Foundations of Female Emancipation. LC 79-6830. (Contributions in Legal Studies: No. 11). ix, 214p. 1980. text ed. 38.50 (*0-313-20670-8*, RFD/, Greenwood Pr) Greenwood.

Rabkin, Sarah. My First Science Dictionary. (Illus.). 64p. (J). (gr. k-3). 1992. 10.95 (*1-56288-215-5*) Checkerboard.

— My First Science Dictionary. 1994. pap. 6.95 (*1-56565-266-5*) Lowell Hse.

Rabkin, Sol. A Landmark Decision on Segregation in Housing: Jones vs. Mayer. 96p. 1.50 (*0-686-74894-8*) ADL.

Rabkin, Ssarah. My First Science Dictionary. (Illus.). 64p. (J). 1994. pap. 5.95 (*1-56565-177-4*) Lowell Hse Juvenile.

Rabkin, Yakov & Robinson, Ira, eds. The Interaction of Scientific & Jewish Cultures in Modern Times. LC 94-9910. 272p. 1994. 89.95 (*0-7734-9063-9*) E Mellen.

Rabkin, Yakov M. Science Between the Superpowers: A Twentieth Century Fund Paper. 119p. 1988. 18.95 (*0-87078-223-1*); pap. 8.95 (*0-87078-222-3*) TCFP-PPP.

Rabking, Rhoda P. Cuban Politics: The Revolutionary Experiment. LC 90-38808. (Politics in Latin America Ser.). 256p. 1990. text ed. 49.95 (*0-275-93739-9*, C3739, Praeger Pubs) Greenwood.

Rabl, Ari. Active Solar Collectors & Their Applications. LC 84-14861. (Illus.). 517p. 1985. text ed. 59.00 (*0-19-503546-1*) OUP.

Rabl, Ari, jt. auth. see Kreider, Jan.

Rabl, S. S. Boatbuilding in Your Own Backyard. 2nd ed. LC 57-11361. (Illus.). 239p. 1958. 29.95 (*0-87033-009-8*) Cornell Maritime.

— Ship & Aircraft Fairing & Development: For Draftsman & Loftsmen & Sheet Metal Workers. LC 41-51932. (Illus.). 109p. 1941. text ed. 19.95x (*0-87033-096-9*) Cornell Maritime.

Rabl, Veronika, ed. see Electric Power Research Institute Staff.

Rable, George C. Civil Wars: Women & the Crisis of Southern Nationalism. (Women in American History Ser.). 416p. 1991. pap. 13.95 (*0-252-06212-4*) U of Ill Pr.

— The Confederate Republic: A Revolution Against Politics. LC 93-36491. (Civil War America Ser.). (Illus.). xii, 428p. (C). 1994. 34.95 (*0-8078-2144-6*) U of NC Pr.

Rabo, Annika. Change on the Euphrates: Villagers, Townsmen & Employees in Northeast Syria. (Illus.). 222p. (Orig.). 1986. pap. text ed. 61.00x (*91-85284-26-2*) Coronet Bks.

Rabo, Jule A., ed. Zeolite Chemistry & Catalysis. LC 76-17864. (ACS Monograph: No. 171). 1976. 87.95 (*0-8412-0276-1*) Am Chemical.

Raboff, Adeline, tr. see Peter, Katherine.

Raboff, Ernest. Albrecht Durer. LC 87-17702. (Trophy Nonfiction Art for Children Ser.). (Illus.). 32p. (J). (gr. 1 up). 1988. reprint ed. pap. 5.95 (*0-06-446071-1*, Trophy) HarpC Child Bks.

Raboff, Fran, jt. auth. see Bassler, Lynn.

Raboff, Fran, jt. auth. see Chesman, Andrea.

Raboff, Fran, jt. auth. see Shepherd, Renee.

Rabold, Ted & Fair, Phillip. New Jersey: Yesterday & Today. 110p. (Orig.). (J). (gr. 4). 1982. 9.95 (*0-931992-41-9*); pap. text ed. 4.95 (*0-931992-43-5*) Penns Valley.

Rabold, Ted F., jt. auth. see Jones, Clarence J.

Rabolt, J. F., jt. ed. see Chase, D. B.

Rabon, Don. Interviewing & Interrogation. LC 92-81207. 212p. (C). 1992. pap. 14.95 (*0-89089-488-4*) Carolina Acad Pr.

— Investigative Discourse Analysis: Statements, Letters, & Transcripts. LC 94-70062. 188p. (Orig.). (C). 1994. pap. text ed. 14.95 (*0-89089-569-4*) Carolina Acad Pr.

Rabon, Israel. The Street. Wolf, Leonard, tr. LC 90-14113. 192p. 1990. 9.95 (*0-941423-45-X*) FWEW.

Rabone, David. Haynes Norton 500, 600, 650 & 750 Twins Owners Workshop Manual, No. 187: '57-'70. 1979. 16.95 (*0-85696-187-6*) Haynes Pubns.

Raboni, Giovanni. The Coldest Year of Grace: Selected Poems of Giovanni Raboni. Friebert, Stuart & Rossi, Vinio, trs. LC 84-7363. (Wesleyan Poetry in Translation Ser.). 104p. 1985. 12.95 (*0-8195-5114-7*, Wesleyan Univ Pr) U Pr of New Eng.

Raborg, Frederick A., Jr. Hakata. (Amelia Chapbooks Ser.). (Illus.). 24p. (Orig.). 1992. pap. 5.95 (*0-936545-13-5*) Amelia.

— Posing Nude. (Amelia Chapbooks Ser.). 64p. (Orig.). 1990. pap. 10.95 (*0-936545-14-3*) Amelia.

— The Transient Nativity: A Christmas Story. (Amelia Chapbooks Ser.). 8p. 1987. pap. 4.00 (*0-936545-07-0*) Amelia.

— Tule. (Amelia Chapbooks Ser.). (Illus.). 24p. (Orig.). 1986. pap. 6.95 (*0-936545-01-1*) Amelia.

Raboteau, Albert, jt. ed. see Johnson, Clifton.

***Raboteau, Albert J.** A Fire in the Bones: Reflections on African-American Religious History. LC 94-36887. 1995. write for info. (*0-8070-0932-6*) Beacon Pr.

— Slave Religion: The Invisible Institution in the Antebellum South. (Illus.). 1980. pap. 13.95 (*0-19-502705-1*) OUP.

— Speak My Name: Black Men on Masculinity & the American Dream. Belton, Don, ed. LC 94-36887. 304p. (C). 1996. 24.00 (*0-8070-0936-9*) Beacon Pr.

Rabovsky, Daniel, jt. auth. see Kerlin, Gregg.

Rabow, Gerald. Peace Through Agreement: Replacing War with Non-Violent Dispute-Resolution Methods. LC 89-71110. 200p. 1990. text ed. 49.95 (*0-275-93505-1*, C3505, Greenwood Pr) Greenwood.

Rabow, Jerome, jt. auth. see Empey, LaMar T.

Rabow, Jerome, et al. Advances in Psychoanalytic Sociology: A Text & Reader. LC 83-86. 379p. (C). 1987. text ed. 35.50 (*0-89874-608-6*) Krieger.

— Learning through Discussion. LC 93-40761. (C). 1994. text ed. 24.00 (*0-8039-5411-5*); pap. text ed. 9.95 (*0-8039-5412-3*) Sage.

***Raboy, David G., ed.** Essays in Supply Side Economics. 172p. 1982. pap. 0.95 (*0-614-04370-0*) IRET.

Raboy, Isaac. Jewish Cowboy. Shapiro, Nathaniel, tr. 300p. (Orig.). 1989. pap. 11.95 (*0-945917-00-7*) Tradition Bks.

Raboy, Marc. Missed Opportunities: The Story of Canada's Broadcasting Policy. 472p. (C). 1990. lib. bdg. 55.00 (*0-7735-0743-4*, Pub. by McGill CN); pap. 22.95 (*0-7735-0775-2*, Pub. by McGill CN) U of Toronto Pr.

Raboy, Marc & Dagenais, Bernard. Media, Crisis & Democracy: Mass Communication & the Disruption of Social Order. (Media, Culture & Society Ser.). 224p. (C). 1992. text ed. 55.00 (*0-8039-8639-4*); pap. text ed. 19.95 (*0-8039-8640-8*) Sage.

Rabson, Carolyn. Orchestral Excerpts: A Comprehensive Index. LC 92-46475. (Reference Books in Music: No. 25). xi, 221p. 1993. 35.00 (*0-914913-26-3*) Fallen Leaf.

— Songbook of the American Revolution. 1974. pap. 4.00 (*0-911014-18-7*) Neo Pr.

Rabson, Carolyn, ed. Songs of Oberlin. LC 83-8152. (Illus.). 120p. 1983. reprint ed. 8.50 (*0-9611434-0-1*); reprint ed. pap. 5.00 (*0-9611434-1-X*) Oberlin Con Lib.

Rabson, Carolyn, et al. George Whitfield Andrews: A Catalog of His Compositions. LC 86-8591. vii, 27p. 1986. pap. 8.50 (*0-9611434-2-8*) Oberlin Con Lib.

Rabson, Steve, tr. see Tatsuhiro, Oshiro & Mineo, Higashi.

Rabten, Geshe. Echoes of Voidness. Batchelor, Stephen, ed. & tr. by. (Intermediate Book: White Ser.). (Illus.). 148p. (C). 1986. pap. 8.95 (*0-86171-010-X*) Wisdom MA.

— The Essential Nectar: Meditations on the Buddhist Path. Willson, Martin, ed. & tr. by. (Wisdom Basic Book, Orange Ser.). 306p. 1992. pap. 14.00 (*0-86171-013-4*) Wisdom MA.

— Song of the Profound View. 96p. 1989. pap. 10.95 (*0-86171-086-X*) Wisdom MA.

Rabten, Geshe & Dhargyey, Geshe. Advice from a Spiritual Friend. rev. ed. Beresford, Brian, ed. & tr. by. (Wisdom Basic Book, Orange Ser.). (Illus.). 160p. 1994. pap. 8.95 (*0-86171-017-7*) Wisdom MA.

Rabuazzo, Agata M., jt. auth. see Belfiore, F.

Rabuck, Mark. Minas Ithil. Ney, Jessica, ed. (Middle Earth Ser.). (Illus.). 112p. (Orig.). (C). 1991. pap. text ed. 18.00 (*1-55806-143-6*, 8302) Iron Crown Ent Inc.

Rabuilas, Andreas D., jt. auth. see Stefanis, Costas N.

Rabun, H. P. & Cheely, W. W. Back-Trailing on the Old Frontiers. 1986. reprint ed. 6.95 (*0-913150-55-X*) Pioneer Pr.

Rabura, Horst, jt. auth. see Barrack, Charles.

Rabura, Horst M., jt. auth. see Barrack, Charles M.

Rabura, Horst M., et al. Mosaik: Deutsche Kultur und Literatur. 3rd ed. 1992. text ed. write for info. (*0-07-003963-1*) McGraw.

Raburn, Dan. Blood Bounty. 1985. pap. 2.50 (*0-8217-1580-1*) Zebra.

Raburn, Terry. Starting Blocks: Running the Race A-G Style. LC 88-80813. (Radiant Life Ser.). 128p. (Orig.). (YA). (gr. 7 up). 1988. teacher ed 4.50 (*0-88243-200-1*, 32-0200); pap. 2.95 (*0-88243-860-3*, 02-0860) Gospel Pub.

Rabushka, Alvin. A Compelling Case for a Constitutional Amendment to Balance the Budget & Limit Taxes. 29p. 1984. pap. 2.50 (*0-318-02038-6*) Natl Taxpayers Union Found.

— From Adam Smith to the Wealth of America. (Illus.). 364p. (C). 1985. 37.95 (*0-88738-029-8*); pap. 21.95 (*0-88738-645-8*) Transaction Pubs.

— Hong Kong: A Study in Economic Freedom. 1979. lib. bdg. 10.00 (*0-918584-02-7*, 70187-5) U Ch Pr.

— Scorecard on the Israeli Economy: A Review of 1989. xvi, 73p. (Orig.). 1990. pap. write for info. (*0-923791-01-9*) IASPS.

— A Simplified Tax System: The Option for Mexico. LC 92-46379. (Essays in Public Policy Ser.: No. 38). 1993. 5.00 (*0-8179-5432-5*) Hoover Inst Pr.

— Ten Myths about Higher Taxes. LC 93-30446. (Essays in Public Policy Ser.: No. 43). 1993. 5.00 (*0-8179-5482-1*) Hoover Inst Pr.

Rabushka, Alvin & Hanke, Steve H., eds. Toward Growth: A Blueprint for Economic Rebirth in Israel. 110p. 1988. pap. 19.00 (*0-923791-00-0*) IASPS.

Rabushka, Alvin & Jacobs, Bruce. Old Folks at Home. LC 79-7637. 1980. 14.95 (*0-02-925670-4*) Free Pr.

Rabushka, Alvin & Ryan, Pauline. The Tax Revolt. (Publication Ser.: No. 270). 288p. 1982. 6.78 (*0-8179-7701-5*) Hoover Inst Pr.

Rabushka, Alvin & Weissert, William G. Caseworkers or Police? How Tenants See Public Housing. LC 77-78049. (Publication Ser.: No. 186). (Illus.). 1977. 9.95 (*0-8179-6861-X*) Hoover Inst Pr.

Rabushka, Alvin, jt. ed. see Duignan, Peter.

Rabushka, Alvin, jt. auth. see Hall, Robert E.

Rabuzzi, Daniel D., et al. Diagnosis & Management of Deep Neck Infections. (Self-Instructional Package Ser.). (Illus.). 61p. (Orig.). (C). 1993. pap. text ed. 25.00 (*1-56772-006-4*) AAO-HNS.

Raby, Burgess J., jt. auth. see Raby, William L.

Raby, Elizabeth. Camphorwood. Page, Carolyn, ed. & illus. by. 36p. (Orig.). 1992. pap. 6.00 (*1-879205-28-9*) Nightshade Pr.

— The Hard Scent of Peonies. 24p. (Orig.). 1990. pap. 5.00 (*0-9625348-2-X*) P Goodrich.

Raby, Julian. Venice, Durer & the Oriental Mode. (Hans Huth Memorial Studies: No. 1). (Illus.). 104p. 1983. text ed. 45.00 (*0-85667-162-2*) Sothebys Pubns.

Raby, Julian & Johns, Jeremy. Bayt-al-Maqdis Pt. I: Abd al-Malik's Jerusalem. (Studies in Islamic Art: Vol. IX). (Illus.). 176p. 1993. 55.00 (*0-19-728017-X*) OUP.

— Bayt-al-Maqdis Pt. II: Abd al-Malik's Jerusalem. (Oxford Studies in Islamic Art: No. IX). (Illus.). 160p. 1995. 45.00 (*0-19-728018-8*) OUP.

Raby, Julian, jt. auth. see Atasoy, Nurhan.

Raby, Namika. Kachcheri Bureaucracy in Sri Lanka: The Culture & Politics of Accessibility. (Foreign & Comparative Studies Program, South Asian Ser.: No. 10). (Orig.). 1985. pap. text ed. 10.50 (*0-915984-88-1*) Syracuse U Foreign Comp.

***Raby, Peter.** Importance of Being Ernest: A Reader's Companion. (Masterwork Studies Ser.: No. 144). 144p. 1994. text ed. 22.95x (*0-8057-8587-6*, Twayne); pap. 12.95 (*0-8057-8588-4*, Twayne) Macmillan.

— Samuel Butler: A Biography. LC 90-71600. (Illus.). 358p. 1991. 37.95x (*0-87745-331-4*) U of Iowa Pr.

Raby, Peter, ed. see Gogol, Nikolai V.

Raby, Peter, ed. see Wilde, Oscar.

Raby, S. & Walker, T. The Building Blocks of Creation-from Microfermis to Megaparsecs: Proceedings of 93 Theology Advanced Study Institute. 628p. 1994. text ed. 121.00 (*981-02-1592-4*) World Scientific Pub.

Raby, W. L., et al. Guide to Successful Tax Practice, 2 vols., 1. (Tax Practice Ser.). 1993. write for info. (*1-56433-279-9*) Prctnrs Pub Co.

— Guide to Successful Tax Practice, 2 vols., 2. (Tax Practice Ser.). 1993. write for info. (*1-56433-280-2*) Prctnrs Pub Co.

— Guide to Successful Tax Practice, 2 vols., Set. (Tax Ser.). 1993. ring bd. 120.00 (*1-56433-278-0*) Prctnrs Pub Co.

Raby, William L. & Raby, Burgess J. Tax Practice Management: Client Servicing. ring bd. write for info. (*0-318-61973-3*) P-H.

Raby, William L. & Tidwell, Victor H. Introduction to Federal Taxation 1984. (Illus.). 528p. 1983. text ed. 29.95 (*0-685-06826-9*); student ed 12.95 (*0-685-42582-7*) P-H.

— Introduction to Federal Taxation 1986. (Illus.). 560p. (C). 1985. text ed. write for info. (*0-318-59728-4*) P-H.

— Introduction to Federal Taxation 1987. 528p. (C). 1986. text ed. 29.95 (*0-317-45977-5*) P-H.

***Raby, William L., et al.** Guide to Seccessful Tax Practice, 3 vols., Set. 1994. ring bd. 129.00 (*1-56433-499-6*) Prctnrs Pub Co.

— Guide to Successful Tax Practice, 2 vols. rev. ed. Russe, Robin et al, eds. (Tax Practice Ser.). 900p. 1991. Vol. 1, 450p. write for info. (*1-56433-006-0*); Vol. 2, 450p. write for info. (*1-56433-007-9*) Prctnrs Pub Co.

— Guide to Successful Tax Practice, 2 vols., Set. rev. ed. Russe, Robin et al, eds. (Tax Practice Ser.). 900p. 1991. ring bd. 120.00 (*1-56433-005-2*) Prctnrs Pub Co.

— Guide to Successful Tax Practice Vol. 1. 1994. ring bd. write for info. (*1-56433-500-3*) Prctnrs Pub Co.

— Guide to Successful Tax Practice Vol. 2. 1994. ring bd. write for info. (*1-56433-501-1*) Prctnrs Pub Co.

— Guide to Successful Tax Practice Vol. 3. 1994. ring bd. write for info. (*1-56433-502-X*) Prctnrs Pub Co.

Rac, G. & Potter, T. Informal Reading Diagnosis: A Practical Guide for the Classroom Teacher. 2nd ed. 1981. text ed. write for info. (*0-13-464628-2*) P-H.

***Racagni, G. & Brunello, N., eds.** Critical Issues in the Treatment of Schizophrenia. (International Academy for Biomedical & Drug Research Ser.: Vol. 10). (Illus.). x, 190p. 1995. 174.00 (*3-8055-6199-7*) S Karger.

Racagni, G., ed. see Brunello, N., et al.

Racagni, G., jt. ed. see Mendlewicz, J.

Racagni, G., et al, eds. Recent Advances in the Treatment of Neurodegenerative Disorders & Cognitive Dysfunction. (International Academy for Biomedical & Drug Research Ser.: Vol. 7). (Illus.). viii, 264p. 1994. 238.50 (*3-8055-5838-4*) S Karger.

— Treatment of Age-Related Cognitive Dysfunction: Pharmacological & Clinical Evaluation. (International Academy for Biomedical & Drug Research Ser.: Vol. 2). (Illus.). vi, 154p. 1992. 111.25 (*3-8055-5551-2*) S Karger.

Racagni, Giorgio & Donoso, Alfredo O., eds. GABA & Endocrine Function. (Advances in Biochemical Psychopharmacology Ser.: Vol. 42). (Illus.). 320p. 1986. text ed. 88.50 (*0-88167-250-5*) Raven.

Racagni, Giorgio & Smeraldi, Enrico, eds. Anxious Depression: Assessment & Treatment. 256p. 1987. text ed. 50.00 (*0-88167-337-4*) Raven.

Racagni, Giorgio, jt. ed. see Costa, E.

Racagni, Giorgio, jt. ed. see Kemali, Dargut.

Racaniello, V. R., et al. Harvey Lecture Series 1987, 1991-1992. 192p. 1993. text ed. 63.95 (*0-471-59790-2*, B500) Wiley.

Raccagni, Michelle. The Modern Arab Woman: A Bibliography. LC 78-15528. 272p. 1978. lib. bdg. 25.00 (*0-8108-1165-0*) Scarecrow.

Race. Teach Yourself Computer Based Systems. (Teach Yourself Ser.). pap. 7.95 (*0-685-03265-5*) McKay.

Race, Donna. Favorite Mother Goose Songs: A Musical Pop-up Book with Five Different Melodies. (Illus.). 12p. (J). (ps-1). 1993. 12.95 (*0-689-71684-2*, Aladdin Paperbacks) S&S Childrens.

— Jolly Old St. Nicholas: A Holiday Book with Lights & Music. LC 91-43087. (Illus.). 12p. (J). (ps-1). 1992. pap. 11.95 (*0-689-71622-2*, Aladdin Paperbacks) S&S Childrens.

Race, Henrietta V. Improvability: Its Intercorrelations & Its Relations to Initial Ability. LC 73-177176. (Columbia University. Teachers College. Contributions to Education Ser.: No. 124). reprint ed. 37.50 (*0-404-55124-6*) AMS Pr.

Race, Jeffrey. War Comes to Long An: Revolutionary Conflict in a Vietnamese Province. LC 79-145793. 1972. pap. 15.00 (*0-520-02361-7*) U CA Pr.

R

An Asterisk (*) at the beginning of an entry indicates that the title is appearing in BIP for the first time.

Race Management Committee Staff, ed. see United States Sailing Asociation Staff.

Race, Phil. Five Hundred Tips for Students. 128p. 1993. pap. 19.95 (*0-631-18851-7*) Blackwell Pubs.

— The Open Learning Handbook: Promoting Quality in Designing & Delivering Flexible Learning. 2nd ed. LC 93-34975. 220p. 1993. pap. text ed. 39.95 (*0-89397-392-0*) Nichols Pub.

— The Open Learning Handbook: Promoting Quality in Designing & Delivering Flexible Learning. 2nd ed. LC 93-34975. 202p. 1994. pap. 39.95 (*0-7494-1109-0*, Pub. by Kogan Page Educ UK) Taylor & Francis.

Race, Phil & Brown, Sally. Five Hundred Tips for Tutors. 200p. 1993. pap. 35.00 (*0-7494-0987-8*, Pub. by Kogan Page Educ UK) Taylor & Francis.

Race, Phil, jt. auth. see Brown, Sally.

Race, Phil, jt. auth. see Saunders, Danny.

***Race, Phil, et al.** 500 Tips for Teachers. 160p. 1995. pap. 29.95x (*0-7494-1417-0*, Pub. by Kogan Page Educ UK) Taylor & Francis.

Race, Philip. Open Learning Handbook. 250p. 1989. 37.95 (*0-89397-341-6*) Nichols Pub.

Race, Steve. The Two Worlds of Joseph Race. large type ed. 1990. 21.95 (*0-7089-2143-4*) Ulverscroft.

Race, William H. Classical Genres & English Poetry. 240p. 1988. lib. bdg. 59.95 (*0-415-00326-1*, A1774) Routledge.

— Plato's Lysis. (Greek Commentaries Ser.). 59p. (Orig.). (C). 1983. pap. text ed. 6.00 (*0-929524-29-2*) Bryn Mawr Commentaries.

Raceanu, Mircea, jt. auth. see Kirk, Roger.

***Racek, Jaroslav.** Cell-Based Biosensors. 110p. 1994. text ed. 45.00 (*1-56676-190-5*) Technomic.

Racevskis, Karlis. Postmodernism & the Search for Enlightenment. LC 93-7338. 192p. 1993. 28.50 (*0-8139-1471-X*) U Pr of Va.

***Racey, Paul A. & Swift, Susan M., eds.** Ecology, Evolution, & Behavior of Bats. (Symposia of the Zoological Society of London Ser.: No. 67). (Illus.). 460p. 1995. 118.00 (*0-19-854945-8*) OUP.

Rachal, Patricia. Federal Narcotics Enforcement: Reorganization & Reform. LC 82-1722. 170p. (C). 1982. text ed. 45.00 (*0-86569-089-8*, Auburn Hse) Greenwood.

Rachal, Sharon. Rustic Charms, Vol. 1. 100p. 1987. pap. 6.50 (*1-56770-175-2*) S Scheewe Pubns.

— Rustic Charms, Vol. 2. 100p. 1988. pap. 7.50 (*1-56770-199-X*) S Scheewe Pubns.

— Rustic Charms, Vol. 3. 100p. 1990. pap. 6.50 (*1-56770-217-1*) S Scheewe Pubns.

— Rustic Charms, Vol. 4. 100p. 1991. pap. 7.50 (*1-56770-238-4*) S Scheewe Pubns.

Rachal, William M., ed. see Caldwell, John E.

Rachal, William M., ed. see Madison, James.

Rachals, Richard H. On Your Own As a Computer Professional: How to Get Started & Succeed As an Independent. Kashanski, Susan H., ed. LC 94-90130. 180p. (Orig.). 1994. pap. 29.00 (*0-9641054-0-3*) Turner Hse Pubns.

Rachamanov. German-Russian Dictionary of Synonyms: Deutsch-Russiches Synonymwoerterbuch. 704p. (GER & RUS.). 1983. 75.00 (*0-8288-1235-7*, F52790) Fr & Eur.

Rachbauer, M. A. Wolfram von Eschenbach. LC 73-140041. (Catholic University Studies in German: No. 4). reprint ed. 37.50 (*0-404-50224-5*) AMS Pr.

Rachele, Sal. Life on the Cutting Edge. 352p. 1994. pap. 14.95 (*0-9640535-0-0*) Liv Awareness.

Rachels, James. Created from Animals: The Moral Implications of Darwinism. 256p. 1990. 22.95 (*0-19-217775-3*) OUP.

— The Elements of Moral Philosophy. 158p. (C). 1986. pap. text ed. write for info. (*0-07-553939-X*) McGraw.

— The Elements of Moral Philosophy. 2nd ed. (Heritage Series in Philosophy). 208p. (C). 1993. pap. text ed. write for info. (*0-07-051098-9*) McGraw.

— Moral Problems. 3rd ed. (C). 1990. 23.00 (*0-06-387100-9*) HarpCollege.

— The Right Thing to Do: Basic Readings in Moral Philosophy. 1989. pap. text ed. write for info. (*0-07-557002-5*) McGraw.

Racheotes, Nicholas S., jt. auth. see Jarnis, George M.

Rachet, Guy. Dictionnaire de la Civilisation. 256p. (FRE.). 1992. 59.95 (*0-8288-7354-2*) Fr & Eur.

— Dictionnaire de la Civilisation Grecque. 272p. (FRE.). 1992. 59.95 (*0-8288-7353-4*) Fr & Eur.

— Dictionnaire de l'Archaeologie. 1060p. (FRE.). 1982. pap. 49.95 (*0-7859-7814-3*, 2221503228) Fr & Eur.

— Petite Encyclopedie Larousse. 1496p. (FRE.). 1977. 49.95 (*0-7859-0764-5*, M-6473) Fr & Eur.

Rachev, S. T., jt. ed. see Anastassiou, G.

Rachev, S. T., jt. auth. see Kalashnikov, Vladimir V.

Rachev, Svetlozar. Probability Metrics. (Series in Probability & Mathematics). 494p. 1991. text ed. 124.00 (*0-471-92877-1*) Wiley.

Rachewiltz, Mary D. Ezra Pound, Father & Teacher: Discretions. LC 73-143717. (Illus.). 336p. 1975. pap. 4.75 (*0-8112-0589-4*, NDP405) New Directions.

Rachfalski, Jane, jt. auth. see Miller, Melinda J.

Rachie, K. O., jt. ed. see Singh, S. R.

Rachilde. The Juggler. Hawthorne, Melanie, tr. & intro. by. LC 90-8070. (Illus.). 232p. (Orig.). (C). 1990. text ed. 18.95 (*0-8135-1594-7*); pap. 12.95 (*0-8135-1625-0*) Rutgers U Pr.

Rachleff, Owen. Image. 304p. 1986. reprint ed. pap. 3.50 (*0-8439-2405-5*) Dorchester Pub Co.

Rachleff, Owen S. Enigma. 256p. pap. 3.50 (*0-8439-2736-4*) Dorchester Pub Co.

Rachleff, Peter. Black Labor in Richmond, 1865-1890. LC 88-29432. 264p. 1989. reprint ed. pap. 11.95 (*0-252-06026-1*) U of Ill Pr.

— Hard-Pressed in the Heartland: The Hormel Strike & the Future of the Labor Movement. 250p. (Orig.). 1992. 30.00 (*0-89608-451-5*); pap. 12.00 (*0-89608-450-7*) South End Pr.

— Marxism & Council Communism: Modern Revolutionary Thought. 312p. 1974. 250.00 (*0-87700-227-4*) Revisionist Pr.

Rachlin, Allan. News As Hegemonic Reality: American Political Culture & the Framing of New Accounts. LC 88-12009. 168p. 1988. text ed. 49.95 (*0-275-92534-X*, C2534, Praeger Pubs) Greenwood.

Rachlin, Ann. Bach. LC 92-9520. (Famous Children Ser.). (Illus.). (J). 1992. 5.95 (*0-8120-4991-8*) Barron.

— Brahms. (Famous Children Ser.). (Illus.). 24p. (J). (gr. k-3). 1993. pap. 5.95 (*0-8120-1542-8*) Barron.

— Chopin. (Famous Children Ser.). (Illus.). 24p. (J). (gr. k-3). 1993. pap. 5.95 (*0-8120-1543-6*) Barron.

— Handel. LC 92-11497. (J). 1992. 5.95 (*0-8120-4992-6*) Barron.

— Haydn. LC 92-9521. (Famous Children Ser.). (Illus.). (J). 1992. 5.95 (*0-8120-4988-8*) Barron.

— Mozart. LC 92-10302. (Famous Children Ser.). (Illus.). (J). 1992. 5.95 (*0-8120-4989-6*) Barron.

— Schumann. LC 92-26965. (Famous Children Ser.). (Illus.). 24p. (J). (gr. k-3). 1993. pap. 5.95 (*0-8120-1544-4*) Barron.

— Tchaikovsky. (Famous Children Ser.). (Illus.). 24p. (J). (gr. k-3). 1993. pap. 5.95 (*0-8120-1545-2*) Barron.

Rachlin, Anne. Beethoven. (Famous Children Ser.). (Illus.). 24p. (J). (gr. k-3). 1994. pap. 5.95 (*0-8120-1996-2*) Barron.

— Schubert. (Famous Children Ser.). (Illus.). 24p. (J). (gr. k-3). 1994. pap. 5.95 (*0-8120-1995-4*) Barron.

Rachlin, Edward S., ed. Diagnosis & Comprehensive Management of Myofascial Pain. LC 93-36499. 500p. 1993. 55.00 (*0-8016-6817-4*) Mosby Yr Bk.

Rachlin, Harvey. Extraordinary Artifacts. LC 92-53660. 1993. 18.00 (*0-394-58013-3*, Villard Bks) Random.

— The Making of a Cop. Pfefferblit, Elaine, ed. 320p. (Orig.). 1991. reprint ed. mass mkt. 4.99 (*0-671-74740-1*) PB.

— The Making of a Detective. LC 95-6148. 1995. 25.00 (*0-393-03797-5*) Norton.

Rachlin, Harvey, ed. The Songwriter's Workshop. 86p. 1991. audio 24.95 (*0-89879-452-8*) Writers Digest.

Rachlin, Howard. Behavior & Mind: The Roots of Modern Psychology. LC 92-47398. (Illus.). 176p. 1994. 35.00 (*0-19-507979-5*) OUP.

— Introduction to Modern Behaviorism. 3rd ed. (C). 1995. pap. text ed. 19.95 (*0-7167-2176-7*) W H Freeman.

— Judgment, Decision & Choice: A Cognitive Behavioral Synthesis. LC 88-16329. (Psychology Ser.). 312p. (C). 1995. text ed. 31.95 (*0-7167-1990-8*) W H Freeman.

Rachlin, Israel, jt. auth. see Rachlin, Rachel.

***Rachlin, Jill.** Kiplinger's Handbook of Personal Law. 1994. pap. 14.95 (*0-938721-35-6*) Kiplinger Bks.

— Kiplinger's Handbook of Personal Law. Date not set. pap. 15.00 (*0-8129-2654-4*, Times Bks) Random.

Rachlin, Nahid. Foreigner. 1979. reprint ed. pap. 8.95 (*0-393-00961-0*) Norton.

— Married to a Stranger. 232p. (Orig.). 1993. pap. 9.95 (*0-87286-276-3*) City Lights.

— Married to a Stranger. 232p. (Orig.). 1993. pap. 9.95 (*0-614-04943-1*) City Lights.

— Veils: Short Stories. 180p. (Orig.). 1992. pap. 8.95 (*0-87286-267-4*) City Lights.

Rachlin, Norman S. & Cerwinske, Laura. Eleven Steps to Building a Profitable Accounting Practice. LC 82-10106. (Illus.). 320p. 1983. text ed. 45.00 (*0-07-051103-9*) McGraw.

Rachlin, Rachel & Rachlin, Israel. Sixteen Years in Siberia: Memoirs of Rachel & Israel Rachlin. De Weille, Birgitte M., tr. LC 86-25096. (Illus.). 264p. 1988. 27.95 (*0-8173-0357-X*) U of Ala Pr.

Rachlin, Robert. Profit Strategies for Business. LC 79-88674. 127p. 1980. 14.95 (*0-938712-01-2*) Marr Pubns.

— Return on Investment: Strategies for Profit. LC 75-44668. 124p. 1976. 14.95 (*0-938712-00-4*) Marr Pubns.

— Successful Techniques for Higher Profits. LC 80-85150. 260p. 1981. 16.95 (*0-938712-02-0*) Marr Pubns.

— Total Business Budgeting: A Step-by-Step Guide with Forms. 1991. text ed. 70.00 (*0-471-53754-3*) Wiley.

Rachlin, Robert & Sweeny, H. W. Handbook of Budgeting. 3rd ed. 800p. 1993. text ed. 125.00 (*0-471-57771-5*) Wiley.

Rachlin, Robert, jt. ed. see Sweeny, H. W.

Rachlin, Sidney L., ed. see Metlina, L. S.

***Rachlin, Sidney L., et al.** First Steps to Math: A Guide to Beginning Mathematics Activities for Parents & Primary Teachers. (Illus.). 105p. 1993. teacher ed 14.95 (*1-895411-47-5*) Peguis Pubs Ltd.

Rachlis, Eugene, jt. ed. see Levine, Mark.

Rachman, Arnold W. Incest Trauma. Date not set. write for info. (*1-56821-062-0*) Aronson.

— Sandor Ferenczi: The Psychotherapist of Tenderness & Passion. LC 94-32540. Date not set. text ed. 60.00 (*1-56821-100-7*) Aronson.

Rachman, D. Standard & Poor's How to Invest: A Guide for Buying Stocks, Bonds & Mutual Funds. 1992. pap. text ed. write for info. (*0-07-051337-6*) McGraw.

Rachman, David. Marketing Today. 3rd ed. LC 93-72830. 634p. (C). 1993. pap. 36.25 (*0-03-097648-0*) Dryden Pr.

— Marketing Today. 3rd ed. LC 93-72830. 634p. (C). 1994. disk 21.00 (*0-03-098466-1*); disk 14.50 (*0-03-098172-7*); disk 21.00 (*0-03-098171-9*) Dryden Pr.

Rachman, David J. Business Today. 5th ed. 1986. 14.95 (*0-685-25735-5*) McGraw.

— Marketing Today. 2nd ed. (Illus.). 650p. (C). 1988. text ed. 36.00 (*0-03-013573-7*) Dryden Pr.

Rachman, David J., et al. Business Today. 7th ed. LC 92-17433. 1992. 43.95 (*0-685-59721-0*) McGraw.

Rachman, S., ed. Contributions to Medical Psychology, Vol. 2. LC 80-40416. (Illus.). 352p. 1980. 145.00 (*0-08-024684-2*, R726, Pub. by Pergamon Repr UK) Franklin.

Rachman, S. & Maser, Jack D., eds. Panic Psychological Perspectives. 392p. 1988. text ed. 79.95 (*0-8058-0091-3*) L Erlbaum Assocs.

Rachman, S. J. Fear & Courage. 2nd ed. (Psychology Ser.). 416p. (C). 1995. pap. text ed. write for info. (*0-7167-2061-2*) W H Freeman.

Rachman, Stanley J., ed. Advances in Behavior Research & Therapy, Vol. 2. (Illus.). 186p. 1980. 100.00 (*0-08-027110-3*, Pergamon Pr) Elsevier.

— Contributions to Medical Psychology, 3 Vols. 1984. 110.00 (*0-08-030855-4*, Pergamon Pr) Elsevier.

Rachman, Stanley J. & Wilson, T., eds. Advances in Behavior Research & Therapy, Vol. 3. (Illus.). 206p. 1982. 125.00 (*0-08-029671-8*, Pergamon Pr) Elsevier.

— Advances in Behavior Research & Therapy, Vol. 4. (Illus.). 282p. 1984. 125.00 (*0-08-031502-X*, Pergamon Pr) Elsevier.

— Advances in Behavior Research & Therapy, Vol. 5. (Illus.). 258p. 1985. 145.00 (*0-08-032327-8*, Pergamon Pr) Elsevier.

— Advances in Behavior Research & Therapy, Vol. 6. (Illus.). 270p. 1986. 132.00 (*0-08-034143-8*, Pub. by PPL UK) Elsevier.

Rachman, Stanley J., jt. auth. see De Silva, Padmal.

Rachman, Stanley J., jt. ed. see Eysenck, Hans J.

Rachman, Stephen, jt. ed. see Rosenheim, Shawn.

Rachmaninoff, Serge. Piano Concertos, No. 1, 2 & 3. 1990. pap. 17.95 (*0-486-26350-9*) Dover.

Rachmaninoff, Sergei. Rachmaninoff's Recollections Told to Oskar Von Riesemann. LC 74-111100. (Select Bibliographies Reprint Ser.). 1977. 31.95 (*0-8369-5232-4*) Ayer.

Rachmann, Hinrich, jt. auth. see Anken, Ralf H.

Rachmanov, I. V. German-Russian Dictionary of Synonyms. 704p. (GER & RUS.). 1983. 59.95 (*0-8288-1241-1*, M 15173) Fr & Eur.

Rachmilewitz, D. Inflammatory Bowel Disease. 1982. lib. bdg. 103.00 (*90-247-2612-3*) Kluwer Ac.

Rachmilewitz, D., ed. Inflammatory Bowel Diseases 1986. (Development in Gastroenterology Ser.). 1986. lib. bdg. 143.00 (*0-89838-796-5*) Kluwer Ac.

— Inflammatory Bowel Diseases, 1994: Proceedings of the 72nd Falk Symposium Held in Strasbourg, France, September 6-8, 1993. LC 93-44397. 320p. (C). 1994. lib. bdg. 94.00 (*0-7923-8845-3*) Kluwer Ac.

Rachmilewitz, D. & Zimmerman, J., eds. Inflammatory Bowel Diseases, 1990: Proceedings of the Third International Symposium on Inflammatory Bowel Diseases. (Developments in Gastroenterology Ser.). (C). 1990. lib. bdg. 115.50 (*0-7923-0657-0*) Kluwer Ac.

Rachner, Mary J. Anita, Enemy of the People: Let's Take the Communism Out of Womynism. 102p. (Orig.). 1991. pap. 9.95 (*0-9623133-3-5*) Oxner Inst.

— Kerry's Thirteenth Birthday: Everything Your Parents & Their Friends Know about Sex but Are Too Polite to Talk about. rev. ed. LC 93-84599. 80p. (YA). (gr. 8 up). 1993. pap. text ed. 9.95 (*0-9623133-4-3*) Oxner Inst.

— Satanic Reverses. LC 89-61567. (Illus.). 153p. (Orig.). 1989. pap. 9.95 (*0-9623133-0-0*) Oxner Inst.

Rachocki, Andrzej. Alluvial Fans: An Attempt at an Empirical Approach. LC 80-42061. (Illus.). 171p. reprint ed. pap. 48.80 (*0-8357-3081-6*, 2039338) Bks Demand.

Rachocki, Andrzej H. & Church, Michael, eds. Alluvial Fans: A Field Approach. 391p. 1990. text ed. 255.00 (*0-471-91694-3*) Wiley.

Rachor, Jo A. Of These You May Freely Eat. 90p. 1986. pap. 3.95 (*0-912145-12-9*) MMI Pr.

Rachor, JoAnn. Of These Ye May Freely Eat: A Vegetarian Cookbook. rev. ed. 96p. 1991. pap. 2.95 (*1-878726-02-1*) Fam Hlth Pubns.

Rachow, Louis A., ed. Theatre & Performing Arts Collections. LC 81-6567. (Special Collections Ser.: Vol. 1, No. 1). 166p. 1981. text ed. 49.95 (*0-917724-47-X*) Haworth Pr.

Rachowiecki, Rob. Costa Rica: A Travel Survival Kit. 2nd ed. (Illus.). 420p. (Orig.). 1994. pap. 14.95 (*0-86442-205-9*) Lonely Planet.

— Ecuador & the Galapagos Islands: A Travel Survival Kit. 3rd ed. (Illus.). 480p. 1992. pap. 16.95 (*0-86442-148-6*) Lonely Planet.

— Peru: A Travel Survival Kit. 2nd ed. (Illus.). 392p. 1991. pap. 14.95 (*0-86442-095-1*) Lonely Planet.

— The Southwest: U. S. A. Guide. (Illus.). 816p. 1995. pap. 19.95 (*0-86442-255-5*) Lonely Planet.

***Rachowiecki, Rob & Wagenhauser, Betsy.** Climbing & Hiking in Ecuador. 3rd ed. (Illus.). 240p. 1995. pap. text ed. 15.95 (*1-56440-612-1*, Pub. by Bradt Pubns UK) Globe Pequot.

Rachveli, N. N., ed. Black Americans: Issues & Concerns. (Illus.). 221p. 1994. lib. bdg. 59.00 (*1-56072-173-1*) Nova Sci Pubs.

Rachwald, Arthur R. In Search of Poland: The Superpowers' Response to Solidarity, 1980-1989. (P. Ser.: No. 396). (Orig.). (C). 1990. text ed. 19.95 (*0-8179-8961-7*); pap. text ed. 14.95 (*0-8179-8962-5*) Hoover Inst Pr.

Raciborski, M. Parasitische Algen und Pilze Javas, 3 pts. in 1. 1973. reprint ed. 30.00 (*3-7682-0855-9*) Lubrecht & Cramer.

Racic, Z. Archimedes & Arthur. 300p. 1989. boxed, text ed. 53.33 (*0-13-044074-4*) P-H.

***Raciggso, Lianne.** A Winter's Knight. (Orig.). (YA). 1995. lib. bdg. 15.00 (*0-88092-290-7*); pap. 5.00 (*0-88092-289-3*) Royal Fireworks.

Racine. Bajazet. Hollinghurst, Alan, tr. (Chatto Playscript Ser.). 64p. 1992. pap. 19.95 (*0-7011-3853-X*, Pub. by Chatto & Windus UK) Trafalgar.

Racine, Drew, ed. Managing Technical Services in the 90's. LC 91-24386. (Journal of Library Administration). (Illus.). 165p. 1991. lib. bdg. 29.95 (*1-56024-166-7*) Haworth Pr.

Racine, Jean. Andromache. Korn, Eric, tr. (Old Vic Theatre Collection Ser.: Vol. 1). 116p. 1988. pap. 7.95 (*1-55783-021-5*) Applause Theatre Bk Pubs.

— Andromache. Wilbur, Richard, tr. 1982. pap. 4.75 (*0-8222-0048-1*) Dramatists Play.

— Oeuvres Completes, Vol. 1. Picard, Jacques, ed. 1216p. (FRE.). 1951. lib. bdg. 100.00 (*0-7859-3781-1*, 2070104710) Fr & Eur.

— Phaedra: One-Act Adaptation. (Illus.). 35p. 1966. pap. 10.00 (*0-88680-152-4*); pap. 2.00 (*0-88680-151-6*) I E Clark.

— Theatre Complet, Tome 1. (Folio Ser.: No. 1412). (FRE.). pap. 15.95 (*2-07-037412-2*) Schoenhof.

— Theatre Complet, Tome 2. (Folio Ser.: No. 1495). (FRE.). pap. 15.95 (*2-07-037495-5*) Schoenhof.

Racine, Jean B. Andromache. Wilbur, Richard, tr. 1984. pap. 6.95 (*0-15-607510-5*, Harvest Bks) HarBrace.

— Andromache & Other Plays. Cairncross, John, tr. (Classics Ser.). 288p. 1976. pap. 8.95 (*0-14-044195-6*, Penguin Classics) Viking Penguin.

— Andromaque. (Illus.). 1965. pap. 4.95 (*0-685-10999-2*, F41504) Fr & Eur.

— Andromaque. Knight, R. C. & Barnwell, H. T., eds. 210p. 1977. 33.95 (*0-686-54708-X*, FC1729) Fr & Eur.

— Athalie. (Illus.). 128p. (FRE.). 1985. pap. 10.95 (*0-7859-1587-7*, 204016071X) Fr & Eur.

— Bajazet. 128p. (FRE.). 1984. pap. 10.95 (*0-7859-1263-0*, 2040160728) Fr & Eur.

— Berenice. 224p. (FRE.). 1991. pap. 10.95 (*0-7859-1259-2*, 2038714037) Fr & Eur.

— Britannicus. (Illus.). (FRE.). 1991. pap. 10.95 (*0-7859-1260-6*, 2038714045) Fr & Eur.

— Britannicus; Phaedra; Athaliah. Sisson, Charles H., tr. (World's Classics Ser.). 236p. 1987. pap. 6.95 (*0-19-281758-2*) OUP.

— Esther. (FRE.). 1985. pap. 10.95 (*0-7859-1588-5*, 204016099X) Fr & Eur.

— Iphigenie. (Illus.). 128p. (FRE.). 1985. pap. 10.95 (*0-7859-1264-9*, 2040160752) Fr & Eur.

— Jules Cesar. 40p. 1962. 12.50 (*0-686-54709-8*) Fr & Eur.

— Lettres d'Uzes. (Illus.). 118p. (FRE.). 1991. pap. 24.95 (*0-7859-1557-5*, 2869713746) Fr & Eur.

— Mithridate. (Illus.). 146p. (FRE.). 1992. pap. 10.95 (*0-7859-1255-X*, 2038701474) Fr & Eur.

— Oeuvres, 3 vols., Set. (Illus.). 450.00 (*0-686-54711-X*) Fr & Eur.

— Oeuvres, 8 vols., Set. cxliv, 616p. 1973. reprint ed. write for info. (*3-487-05000-5*, Pub. by Georg Olms GW) Lubrecht & Cramer.

— Oeuvres Completes, Vol. 2. deluxe ed. Ricard, Raymond, ed. 1168p. (FRE.). 1952. 105.00 (*0-7859-3782-X*, 2070104729) Fr & Eur.

— Phedre. (Illus.). 208p. (FRE.). 1990. pap. 10.95 (*0-685-73320-3*, 2038714088) Fr & Eur.

— Phedre. Rawlings, Margaret, tr. 1962. mass mkt. 6.95 (*0-525-47099-9*, 0674-210, Dutton) NAL-Dutton.

— Phedre. Rawlings, Margaret, tr. & frwd. by. 192p. (ENG & FRE.). 1992. pap. 8.95 (*0-14-044591-9*, Penguin Classics) Viking Penguin.

— Plaideurs. (Illus.). 128p. (FRE.). 1984. pap. 10.95 (*0-7859-1265-7*, 2040160779) Fr & Eur.

— Les Plaideurs. (FRE.). 1987. pap. 10.95 (*0-7859-3138-4*) Fr & Eur.

— Theatre Complet, 3 vols., Set. (Illus.). 200.00 (*0-686-54715-2*) Fr & Eur.

— Theatre Complet, Vol. 1. (FRE.). 1982. pap. 19.95 (*0-7859-2901-0*) Fr & Eur.

— Theatre Complet: Avec Bajazet, Mithridate, Iphigenie, Phedre, Esther, Athalie, Vol. 2. Stegmann, Andre, ed. 378p. 1983. pap. 19.95 (*0-7859-2905-3*) Fr & Eur.

— Theatre Complet: Avec: La Thebaide, Alexandre le Grand, Andromaque, Les Plaideurs, Britannicus, Berenice, Vol. 1. Stegmann, Andre, ed. 436p. 5.95 (*0-686-54713-6*) Fr & Eur.

— Three Plays: Phaedra, Andromache, Britannicus. Dillon, George, tr. LC 61-15938. 1961. pap. text ed. 11.95 (*0-226-15077-1*, P76) U Ch Pr.

Racine, Michel L. The Arithmetics of Quadratic Jordan Algebras. LC 73-17270. (Memoirs Ser.: No. 1/136). 125p. 1973. pap. 17.00 (*0-8218-1836-8*, MEMO 1/136) Am Math.

Racine, Philip N., ed. Piedmont Farmer: The Journals of David Golightly Harris, 1855-1870. LC 89-22755. 616p. 1990. text ed. 49.95 (*0-87049-637-9*) U of Tenn Pr.

— Unspoiled Heart: The Journal of Charles Mattocks of the 17th Maine. LC 93-21274. (Voices of the Civil War Ser.). (Illus.). 472p. (C). 1994. 36.00 (*0-87049-834-7*) U of Tenn Pr.

Racine, Philip N., jt. ed. see Harwell, Richard.

Racinet, A. Encyclopedia of Ornament. 1988. 24.99 (*0-517-66297-3*) Random Hse Value.

Racinet, Albert. The Historical Encyclopedia of Costumes. (Illus.). 320p. 1988. 45.00 (*0-8160-1976-2*) Facts on File.

Racinet, Auguste. Full-Color Picture Sourcebook of Historic Ornaments: All 120 Plates from "L'Ornement Polychrome," Series II. (Illus.). 112p. 1989. pap. 14.95 (*0-486-26096-8*) Dover.

— Racinet's Full-Color Pictorial History of Western Costume: With 92 Plates Showing Over 950 Authentic Costumes from the Middle Ages to 1800. (Fine Arts Ser.). (Illus.). iv, 92p. (Orig.). 1987. reprint ed. pap. 14.95 (*0-486-25464-X*) Dover.

— Racinet's Historic Ornament in Full Color. 112p. 1988. pap. 14.95 (*0-486-25787-8*) Dover.

R

Racino, Julie A., et al, eds. Housing, Support, & Community: Choices & Strategies for Adults with Disabilities. (Community Participation Ser.: Vol. 2). 416p. (Orig.). (C). 1992. pap. text ed. 32.00 (*1-55766-090-5*) P H Brookes.
***Racionero.** Leonardo Da Vinci. 1995. text ed. 22.95 (*0-8057-4300-6*) Macmillan.
Racioppi, Linda. Soviet Policy Towards South Asia since 1970. (Cambridge Russian, Soviet & Post-Soviet Studies: No. 91). (Illus.). 256p. (C). 1994. 59.95 (*0-521-41457-1*) Cambridge U Pr.
Rack, Henry D. Reasonable Enthusiast: John Wesley & the Rise of Methodism. LC 93-15360. 658p. (C). 1993. pap. text ed. 29.95 (*0-687-35625-3*) Abingdon.
Rack, Mary. Ten Minute Guide to Quicken for Windows. (Orig.). 1993. pap. 10.95 (*1-56761-361-6*) Alpha Bks IN.
Rack, Philip. Race, Culture, & Mental Disorder. 300p. 1982. 33.00 (*0-422-78160-6*, NO. 3801, Pub. by Tavistock UK) Routledge Chapman & Hall.
Rackam, Neil & Ruff, Richard. Managing Major Sales: Practical Strategies for Improving Sales Effectiveness. 224p. 1991. 27.50 (*0-88730-508-3*) Harper Busn.
Rackauskas, A., jt. auth. see Paulauskas, V.
Rackauskas, Jonas, ed. Aleksandras Stulginskis: Reminiscences. LC 80-80852. (Illus.). 295p. 1980. 12.00 (*0-936694-41-6*) Lith Inst Educ.
Rackauskas, Jonas, jt. auth. see Peckus, Kestutis.
Racke, Kenneth D. & Coats, Joel R., eds. Enhanced Biodegradation of Pesticides in the Environment. LC 90-34194. (ACS Symposium Ser.: No. 426). (Illus.). 296p. 1990. 69.95 (*0-8412-1784-X*) Am Chemical.
Racke, Kenneth D. & Leslie, Anne R., eds. Pesticides in Urban Environments: Fate & Significance. LC 92-42060. (Symposium Ser.: Vol. 522). (Illus.). 385p. 1993. 94.95 (*0-8412-2627-X*) Am Chemical.
Racke, Reinhard. Lectures on Nonlinear Evolution Equations: Initial Value Problems. (Aspects of Mathematics Ser.). viii, 259p. (C). 1992. 52.00 (*3-528-06421-8*, Pub. by Vieweg & Sohn GW) Ballen Bkslr.
Racker, Efraim. Science & the Cure of Diseases: Letters to Members of Congress. LC 79-84012. 121p. reprint ed. pap. 34.50 (*0-8357-7014-1*, 2033403) Bks Demand.
Racker, Heinrich. Transference & Countertransference. 216p. 1968. text ed. 32.50 (*0-8236-6640-9*) Intl Univs Pr.
Rackham, Arthur. Mother Goose, the Old Nursery Rhymes. (Illus.). (J). (ps-6). 1978. reprint ed. lib. bdg. 12.00 (*0-932106-02-1*, Pub. by Marathon Press) S J Durst.
— Rackham's Color Illustrations for Wagner's Ring. LC 78-73985. (Illus.). 1979. pap. 9.95 (*0-486-23779-6*) Dover.
— Sleeping Beauty. (Illus.). 110p. (J). (gr. k-4). 1920. pap. 3.95 (*0-486-22756-1*) Dover.
Rackham, Arthur, illus. Aesop's Fables. (Fairy Tales & Fables Ser.). (J). (gr. 2-9). 1992. 7.99 (*0-517-17198-8*) Random Hse Value.
— The Arthur Rackham Fairy Book. 271p. (J). (gr. 2-10). 1991. 3.99 (*0-517-24213-3*) Random Hse Value.
— The Fairy Tales of the Brothers Grimm. 176p. 1984. 35.00 (*0-89835-247-9*) Abaris Bks.
— Sixty Fairy Tales of the Brothers Grimm. (Fairy Tales & Fables Ser.). (J). (gr. 2-7). 8.98 (*0-517-28525-8*) Random Hse Value.
Rackham, Bernard. The Glaisher Collection of Pottery & Porcelain in the Fitzwilliam Museum, Cambridge, 2 vols., Set. (Illus.). reprint ed. 275.00 (*1-85149-033-7*) Antique Collect.
— The Glaisher Collection of Pottery & Porcelain in the Fitzwilliam Museum, Cambridge, Vol. I. (Illus.). 520p. reprint ed. write for info. (*0-318-61732-3*) Antique Collect.
— The Glaisher Collection of Pottery & Porcelain in the Fitzwilliam Museum, Cambridge, Vol. II. (Illus.). 282p. reprint ed. write for info. (*0-318-61733-1*) Antique Collect.
Rackham, Bernard & Read, Herbert. English Pottery. (Illus.). 1977. reprint ed. 39.00 (*0-85409-924-7*) Charles River Bks.
Rackham, James. Animal Bones. LC 93-45789. 1994. pap. 10.00 (*0-520-08833-6*) U CA Pr.
Rackham, Jeff & Bertagnolli, Olivia. From Sight to Insight: Stages in the Writing Process. 4th ed. 558p. (C). 1991. pap. text ed. 23.50 (*0-03-052208-0*) HB Coll Pubs.
— Windows: Exploring Human Values Through Reading & Writing. LC 92-11049. (C). 1992. 28.50 (*0-06-043808-8*) HarpCollege.
Rackham, Jeff & Slaughter, Beverly J. The Rinehart Reader, Vol. II. 708p. (C). 1990. pap. text ed. 20.00 (*0-03-021609-5*) HB Coll Pubs.
— The Rinehart Reader Vol. II. 2nd ed. LC 94-75161. (Illus.). 740p. (C). 1994. pap. text ed. 26.75 (*0-15-501621-0*) HB Coll Pubs.
Rackham, Jeff, jt. ed. see Bertagnolli, Olivia.
Rackham, Neil. Major Account Sales Strategy. 1989. text ed. 22.95 (*0-07-051114-4*) McGraw.
— S.P.I.N. Selling. 224p. 1988. text ed. 24.95 (*0-07-051113-6*) McGraw.
Rackham, Oliver & Moody, Jennifer. The Making of the Cretan Landscape. LC 93-49016. 1994. text ed. write for info. (*0-7190-3646-1*, Pub. by Manchester Univ Pr UK); text ed. write for info. (*0-7190-3647-X*, Pub. by Manchester Univ Pr UK) St Martin.
Rackham, P. Jane's C4I Systems, October, 93-94. 1993. 245.00 (*0-7106-1073-4*) Janes Info Group.
— Jane's C41 Systems 95-96. 1995. 265.00 (*0-7106-1261-3*) Janes Info Group.
Rackham, T. W., ed. see Rukl, Antonin.
Rackin, Donald. Alice's Adventures in Wonderland & Through the Looking Glass: Nonsense, Sense & Meaning. (Twayne's Masterworks Ser.: No. 81). 176p. 1991. pap. 12.95 (*0-8057-8553-1*, Twayne) Macmillan.
— Alice's Adventures in Wonderland & Through the Looking Glass: Nonsense, Sense & Meaning. (Twayne's Masterworks Ser.: No. 81). 176p. 1991. text ed. 21.95 (*0-8057-9430-1*, Twayne) Macmillan.
Rackin, Phyllis. Shakespeare's Tragedies. LC 75-34216. (Literature & Life Ser.). (Illus.). 192p. 1978. 19.95 (*0-8044-2706-2*, F Ungar Bks) Continuum.
— Stages of History: Shakespeare's English Chronicles. LC 90-55196. 264p. 1990. 36.95 (*0-8014-2430-5*); pap. 13.95 (*0-8014-9698-5*) Cornell U Pr.
Rackleff, Owen S. Escoffier: King of Chefs. (Illus.). 40p. (Orig.). 1983. pap. 4.95 (*0-88145-000-6*) Broadway Play.
Rackley, Charles E. Critical Care Cardiology. LC 80-18893. (Cardiovascular Clinics Ser.: Vol. 11, No. 3). (Illus.). 228p. 1981. text ed. 40.00 (*0-8036-7242-X*) Davis Co.
Rackley, Charles E., ed. Advances in Critical Care Cardiology. LC 70-6558. (Cardiovascular Clinics Ser.: Vol. 16, No. 3). (Illus.). 242p. 1986. text ed. 50.00 (*0-8036-7243-8*) Davis Co.
— Challenges in Cardiology I. (Bakken Research Center Ser.). (Illus.). 226p. 1991. pap. 39.00 (*0-87993-515-4*) Futura Pub.

***Rackley, Geneva M. Words from the Heart. 35p. 1994. pap. 10.95 (*0-9642363-0-3*) Joan White. WORDS FROM THE HEART is a collection of poems which focus on the themes of Love, Pain & Devotion to God. Dreams which are mystical in nature, which communicate my thoughts, transcend my words. In the poem titled THE DREAM, these themes are apparent. I show that sometimes you need to get away from your troubles by simply escaping as in the poem ESCAPE. I show themes of sadness & depression as I search to understand my innermost feelings in the poem SHADES OF BLUE. I seek to understand life's problems as I search my inner psyche for peace & for happiness through my inner self & through my faith in God. WORDS FROM THE HEART has been read by my publisher & she tells me it definitely touches lives. As for the public that have read WORDS FROM THE HEART, they tell me there is something inside that touches everyone's lives. WORDS FROM THE HEART was written for my children as something to leave them of my life, but, as the public begins to read some of the poetry, they begin to tell me that WORDS FROM THE HEART is a collection of poetry that touches everyone's life. So with the inspiration of friends & the public, this book has been published. To order this book please contact: Joan White Publishing, P.O. Box 7065, Panama City Beach, FL 32413. (904) 233-3947, or Baker & Taylor.** *Publisher Provided Annotation.*

— Words from the Heart. Date not set. pap. 10.95 (*0-9623630-3-0*) Rainbow Nursery.
Rackley, Lurma, ed. see Caldwell, Earl.
Rackley, R. Robert. Accounting & Finance for CPCU Eight. rev. ed. (CPCU Ser.). 1985. 155.00 (*0-88171-104-7*) Insurance Achiev.
— Answers to the Study Guide for CFP 1. rev. ed. (CFP Answers Ser.). 1985. 40.00 (*0-88171-129-2*) Insurance Achiev.
— Answers to the Study Guide for CFP 2. rev. ed. (CFP Answers Ser.). 1985. 40.00 (*0-88171-125-X*) Insurance Achiev.
— Answers to the Study Guide for CFP 3. 2nd rev. ed. (CFP Answers Ser.). 1985. 40.00 (*0-88171-124-1*) Insurance Achiev.
— Answers to the Study Guide for CFP 4. rev. ed. (CFP Answers Ser.). 1985. 40.00 (*0-88171-136-5*) Insurance Achiev.
— Answers to the Study Guide for CFP 5. rev. ed. (CFP Answers Ser.). 1985. 40.00 (*0-88171-135-7*) Insurance Achiev.
— Answers to the Study Guide for CFP 6. rev. ed. (CFP Answers Ser.). 1985. 40.00 (*0-88171-133-0*) Insurance Achiev.
— Casualty Insurance for INS 23. rev. ed. 1984. 100.00 (*0-88171-063-6*, INS-23) Insurance Achiev.
— Commercial Liability Risk Management & Insurance for CPCU Four. 2nd rev. ed. 1985. 155.00 (*0-88171-106-3*) Insurance Achiev.
— Economics (for CPCU 9) 2nd rev. ed. (CPCU Ser.). 1984. 155.00 (*0-88171-081-4*) Insurance Achiev.
— Economics (for 322) 2nd rev. ed. (CLU Ser.). 1984. 155.00 (*0-88171-083-0*) Insurance Achiev.
— Employee Benefits & Retirement Planning (for CFP 5) rev. ed. (CFP Ser.). 1985. 155.00 (*0-88171-132-2*) Insurance Achiev.
— Employee Benefits for Three Hundred & Twenty-Seven. (ChFC Ser.). 1985. 155.00 (*0-88171-111-X*) Insurance Achiev.
— Estate & Gift Tax Planning (for 330) 3rd rev. ed. (CLU Ser.). 1985. 155.00 (*0-88171-134-9*) Insurance Achiev.
— Estate Planning (for CFP 6) rev. ed. (CFP Ser.). 1985. 155.00 (*0-88171-127-6*) Insurance Achiev.
— Financial & Estate Planning Applications (for 332) 2nd rev. ed. (ChFC Ser.). 1985. 155.00 (*0-88171-121-7*) Insurance Achiev.
— Financial Paraplanner Program. (Financial Paraplanner Ser.). 1985. 175.00 (*0-88171-112-8*) Insurance Achiev.
— Financial Services: Environment & Professions (for 320) 3rd rev. ed. (CLU Ser.). 1985. 155.00 (*0-88171-130-6*) Insurance Achiev.
— Financial Statement Analysis: Individual Insurance Benefits for 323. 2nd rev. ed. (CLU Ser.). 1985. 155.00 (*0-88171-108-X*) Insurance Achiev.
— General Principles of Insurance (for INS 21) 2nd rev. ed. (INS Ser.). 1984. 100.00 (*0-88171-091-1*) Insurance Achiev.
— Group Benefits & Social Insurance for 325. 3rd rev. ed. (CLU Ser.). 1985. 155.00 (*0-88171-118-7*) Insurance Achiev.
— Income Taxation for Three Hundred & Twenty-One. 3rd rev. ed. 1985. 155.00 (*0-88171-115-2*) Insurance Achiev.
— Insurance Company Operations (for CPCU 5) (CPCU Ser.). 1984. 155.00 (*0-88171-080-6*) Insurance Achiev.
— Insurance Environment & Operations (for 324) 2nd rev. ed. (CLU Ser.). 1984. 135.00 (*0-88171-084-9*) Insurance Achiev.
— Insurance Environment & Operations (for 324) 3rd rev. ed. (CLU Ser.). 1985. 155.00 (*0-88171-109-8*) Insurance Achiev.
— Insurance Issues & Professional Ethics for CPCU Ten. rev. ed. (CPCU Ser.). 1985. 155.00 (*0-88171-114-4*) Insurance Achiev.
— Introduction to Financial Planning (for CFP 1) 3rd rev. ed. (CFP Ser.). 1986. 155.00 (*0-88171-128-4*) Insurance Achiev.
— Investment Company Products & Variable Contracts for NASD Six. 3rd rev. ed. (NASD Ser.). 1985. 75.00 (*0-88171-119-5*) Insurance Achiev.
— Investments (for CFP 3) 2nd rev. ed. (CFP Ser.). 1985. 155.00 (*0-88171-122-5*) Insurance Achiev.
— Investments for Three Hundred & Twenty-Eight. 2nd rev. ed. 1985. 155.00 (*0-88171-116-0*) Insurance Achiev.
— The Legal Environment of Insurance for CPCU Six. rev. ed. (CPCU Ser.). 1985. 155.00 (*0-88171-105-5*) Insurance Achiev.
— Management. (CPCU-7 Ser.). 1983. 155.00 (*0-88171-006-7*) Insurance Achiev.
— Pensions & Other Retirement Plans for 326. 3rd rev. ed. (CLU Ser.). 1985. 155.00 (*0-88171-110-1*) Insurance Achiev.
— Personal Risk Management & Insurance for CPCU Two. rev. ed. (CPCU Ser.). 1985. 155.00 (*0-88171-113-6*) Insurance Achiev.
— Planning for Business Owners & Professionals for 331. 2nd rev. ed. (CLU Ser.). 1985. 155.00 (*0-88171-117-9*) Insurance Achiev.
— Principles of Risk Management & Insurance (for CPCU 1) (CPCU Ser.). 1984. 155.00 (*0-88171-079-2*) Insurance Achiev.
— Property Insurance (for INS 22) 2nd rev. ed. (INS Ser.). 1984. 100.00 (*0-88171-092-X*) Insurance Achiev.
— Risk Control (for RM 55) rev. ed. 1984. 100.00 (*0-88171-067-9*, RM-55) Insurance Achiev.
— Risk Financing (for RM 56) rev. ed. (ARM Ser.). 1984. 100.00 (*0-88171-098-9*) Insurance Achiev.
— Risk Management (for CFP 2) 2nd rev. ed. (CFP Ser.). 1985. 155.00 (*0-88171-126-8*) Insurance Achiev.
— Structure of the Risk Management Process (for RM 54) 2nd rev. ed. (ARM Ser.). 1984. 100.00 (*0-88171-093-8*) Insurance Achiev.
— Tax Planning & Management (for CFP 4) 3rd rev. ed. (CFP Ser.). 1985. 155.00 (*0-88171-131-4*) Insurance Achiev.
— Wealth Accumulation Planning (for 329) 3rd rev. ed. (ChFC Ser.). 1985. 155.00 (*0-88171-123-3*) Insurance Achiev.
Rackley, Robert R. Commercial Property Risk Management & Insurance (For CPCU 3) (CPCU Ser.). 1984. 155.00 (*0-88171-099-7*) Insurance Achiev.
Rackman, Arthur. Rackman's Fairy Tales Coloring Book. (Illus.). (J). (gr. k-3). 1980. pap. 2.95 (*0-486-23844-X*) Dover.
Rackman, Emanuel. Modern Halakhah for Our Time. LC 93-35397. 1993. write for info. (*0-88125-295-6*) Ktav.
Rackstraw, Richard. Learning to Speak. 64p. 1977. pap. 3.95 (*0-915996-02-2*) North Am Rev.
Rackwitz, R., et al, eds. Reliability & Optimization of Structural Systems: Proceedings of the Fourth IFIP WG 7.5 Conference, Munich, Germany, September 11-13, 1991. LC 92-16815. (Lecture Notes in Engineering Ser.: Vol. 76). (Illus.). vii, 485p. 1992. pap. 115.00 (*0-387-55403-3*) Spr-Verlag.
Racle, Fred. Introduction to Evolution. (Biology Ser.). (Illus.). 1979. pap. text ed. write for info. (*0-13-482869-0*) P-H.
Racquet & Tennis Club, New York Staff. Dictionary Catalogue of the Library of Sports in the Racquet & Tennis Club with Special Collections on Tennis, Lawn Tennis, & Early American Sports, 2 vols, Set. 1971. lib. bdg. 220.00 (*0-8161-0916-8*, Hall Library) G K Hall.
Racster, Olga. Chats on Violoncellos. (Illus.). 227p. 1988. reprint ed. pap. 25.00 (*0-87556-363-5*) Saifer.
— The Master of the Russian Ballet: The Memoirs of Cav. Enrico Cecchetti. LC 78-18777. (Series in Dance). (Illus.). 1978. reprint ed. lib. bdg. 35.00 (*0-306-77589-1*) Da Capo.
Racusen, Lorraine C., jt. ed. see Solez, Kim.
Racy, A. Jihad, jt. ed. see Porter, James.
***Racz, A.** Courts & Tribunals: A Comparative Study. 246p. (C). 1980. 57.00x (*963-05-1799-X*, Pub. by Akad Kiado HU) St Mut.
— Problems of Constitutional Development. 240p. 1993. 87.00 (*963-05-6543-9*, Pub. by Akad Kiado HU) St Mut.
Racz, Attila. Courts & Tribunals: A Comparative Study. 246p. 1980. 49.00 (*0-569-08623-X*, Pub. by Collets UK) Pro-Am Music.
Racz, E. Pannonhalma. (Illus.). 95p. (C). 1989. 80.00 (*0-685-37535-8*, Pub. by Collets) St Mut.
Racz, G. J., tr. see Galdos, Benito P.
Racz, I., jt. auth. see Daroczy, J.
***Racz, Istvan.** Drug Formulation. 416p. (C). 1989. 150.00x (*963-05-4676-0*, Pub. by Akad Kiado HU) St Mut.
Racz, Istvan, jt. auth. see Gyula, Laszlo.
Racz, L. Z. & Bokay, B. Power System Stability. (Studies in Electrical & Electronic Engineering: Vol. 30). 290p. 1988. 115.50 (*0-444-98965-X*) Elsevier.
Racz, P., et al, eds. Accessory Cells in HIV & Other Retroviral Infections. (Illus.). viii, 212p. 1991. 158.50 (*3-8055-5323-4*) S Karger.
— Animal Models of HIV & Other Retroviral Infections. (Illus.). viii, 200p. 1993. 58.50 (*3-8055-5677-2*) S Karger.
— Cytotoxic T Cells in HIV & Other Retroviral Infections. (Illus.). 178p. 1992. 153.75 (*3-8055-5469-9*) S Karger.
Racz, Twyla & Tammany, Rosina, eds. Management & Organization of the Acquisitions Department. (Acquisitions Librarian Ser.). (Illus.). 111p. 1994. lib. bdg. 29.95 (*1-56024-583-2*) Haworth Pr.
Racz, Twyla M., jt. ed. see Eide, Margaret.
***Raczek, Linda T.** The Night the Grandfathers Danced. Murphy, Erin, ed. (Illus.). 32p. (J). (ps up). 1995. 14.95 (*0-87358-610-7*) Northland AZ.
Raczka, R., jt. auth. see Barut, Asim O.
Raczka, R., jt. ed. see Maurin, Krzysztof.
***Raczkowski, George.** Principles of Machine Dynamics. fac. ed. LC 78-72995. (Illus.). 111p. Date not set. pap. 31.70 (*0-7837-7413-3*, 2047208) Bks Demand.
***Raczymow, Henri.** Writing the Book of Esther. Katz, Dori, tr. (French Expressions Ser.). 220p. 1994. 24.00 (*0-8419-1335-8*) Holmes & Meier.
Raczynski, ed. Computer Simulation in Industrial Engineering: 1992 Symposium (Mexico City) 124p. 1992. pap. 40.00 (*0-685-67785-0*, MEX92) Soc Computer Sim.
***Raczynski, Dagmar.** Strategies to Combat Poverty in Latin America. 225p. (Orig.). 1995. pap. text ed. 18.50 (*0-940602-95-4*) IADB.
Rad, P. F. I A H S International Symposium on Housing Problems, 1976: Proceedings, 2 vols. 1977. pap. 641.00 (*0-08-022121-1*, Pub. by Pergamon Repr UK) Franklin.
Rad, U. Von, jt. ed. see Stackelberg, U. Von.
Rada, jt. auth. see Warren, Mary P.
Rada, Georgene. Rada's Guide to Health & Fitness Getaways in the Southwest. LC 91-60053. 192p. (Orig.). 1991. pap. 12.95 (*0-9628203-0-X*) Rada Pubns.
Rada, J. F. & Pipe, G. R., eds. Communication Regulation & International Business: Proceedings of a Workshop of the International Management Institute (IMI), Geneva, Switzerland, April 1983. 266p. 1984. 77.00 (*0-444-87531-X*, I-306-84, North Holland) Elsevier.
***Rada, Roy.** Interactive Media. LC 95-3759. (Illus.). 256p. 1995. 29.95 (*0-387-94485-0*) Spr-Verlag.
— Software Reuse. 224p. (Orig.). 1994. pap. text ed. 29.95 (*1-871516-53-6*, Pub. by Intellect Bks UK) Cromland.
***Rada, Staefan E.** The Adventures of Road Kill Kitty. LC 95-68016. (Illus.). 32p. (Orig.). 1995. pap. 6.95 (*1-886023-10-7*) Coyote Pr NM.
Rada, Staefan E., jt. auth. see Harrison, Babs S.
Radabaugh, Joseph. Heaven's Flame: A Guidebook to Solar Cookers. (Illus.). 100p. (Orig.). 1991. pap. 10.00 (*0-9629588-0-8*) Home Power.
Radaelli, Giorgio. Exchange Rate Determination & Control. LC 94-3981. 128p. 1994. 55.00 (*0-415-11103-X*, B4133) Routledge.
Radaj, Dieter. Design & Analysis of Fatigue Resistant Welded Structures. 1990. text ed. 115.00 (*0-470-21695-6*) Halsted Pr.
— Heat Effects of Welding: Temperature Field, Residual Stress & Distortion. (Illus.). 344p. 1992. 98.00 (*0-387-54820-3*) Spr-Verlag.
Radakov, D. V. Schooling in the Ecology of Fish. 174p. 1973. text ed. 48.00 (*0-7065-1351-7*, Pub. by Keter Pub IS) Coronet Bks.
Radakovich, Anka. The Wild Girls Club: Tales from below the Belt. 1994. 18.00 (*0-517-59631-8*) Crown Pub Group.
— The Wild Girls Club: Tales from below the Belt. 240p. 1995. pap. 10.00 (*0-449-90985-9*) Fawcett.
Radan, G. T., jt. ed. see Lengyel, A.
Radan, George T. The Sons of Zebulon: Jewish Maritime History. LC 78-54621. 85p. (Orig.). (C). 1978. pap. 9.95 (*0-935982-24-8*, GTR-01) Spertus Coll.
Radano, Ronald M. New Musical Figurations: Anthony Braxton's Cultural Critique. LC 93-1878. (Illus.). 304p. 1993. lib. bdg. 49.95 (*0-226-70195-6*); pap. 16.95 (*0-226-70196-4*) U Ch Pr.
Radanovic, L., ed. Sensitivity Methods in Control Theory. 1966. 191.00 (*0-08-011827-5*, Pub. by Pergamon Repr UK) Franklin.
Radashkevich, Aleksandr. Shpalera. LC 84-60082. (Russica Poetry Ser.: No. 5). 90p. (Orig.). (RUS.). 1986. pap. 8.95 (*0-89830-073-8*) Russica Pubs.
Radau, Hugo. Ninib, the Determiner of Fates from the Temple Library of Nippur. (Publications of the Babylonian Section, Ser. A: Vol. 5-2). (Illus.). x, 73p. 1910. pap. 10.00 (*0-686-11919-3*) U PA Mus Pubns.
Radaus, Jelka. The Folk Costumes of Croatia. 135p. 1975. 20.00 (*0-918660-45-9*) Ragusan Pr.

An Asterisk (*) at the beginning of an entry indicates that the title is appearing in BIP for the first time.

Radauskas, Henrikas. Chimeras in the Tower: Selected Poems of Henrikas Radauskas. LC 84-20984. (Wesleyan Poetry in Translation Ser.). 72p. reprint ed. pap. 25.00 (*0-7837-0219-1*, 2040527) Bks Demand.

Radbruch, A., ed. Flow Cytometry & Cell Sorting. (Illus.). 208p. 1992. 69.00 (*0-387-55594-3*) Spr-Verlag.

Radchenko, O. A. Geochemical Regularities in the Distribution of Oil-bearing Regions of the World. (Illus.). 328p. 1968. text ed. 83.00 (*0-7065-0480-1*, Pub. by Keter Pub IS) Coronet Bks.

Radcliff. Calculation of Drug Dosages, No. 4. (Illus.). 384p. 1990. pap. 19.95 (*0-8016-5271-5*) Mosby Yr Bk.

Radcliff, Amy, jt. auth. see Radcliff, Benjamin.

Radcliff, Anthony, et al. Pharmer's Almanac II. rev. ed. (Illus.). 1993. pap. 11.95 (*0-910223-19-X*) MAC Pub.

Radcliff, Benjamin & Radcliff, Amy. Understanding Zen. LC 92-42624. 192p. (Orig.). 1993. pap. 14.95 (*0-8048-1808-8*) C E Tuttle.

Radcliff, Jennifer L., ed. Heritage: A Pictorial History of Independence Township & the Village of Clarkston. (Illus.). 100p. 1989. 15.00 (*0-685-24269-2*) Clarkston CHS.

— In Remembrance. (Illus.). 150p. 1989. 25.00 (*0-685-29045-X*) White Lk Twnship.

Radcliff, Sarah. Teen Esteem. 194p. (YA). 1992. 14.95 (*0-944070-80-9*) Targum Pr.

Radcliff-Umstead, Douglas. Birth of Modern Comedy in Renaissance Italy. LC 69-16904. 295p. reprint ed. pap. 84.10 (*0-8357-9642-6*, 2016985) Bks Demand.

— Carnival Comedy & Sacred Play: The Renaissance Dramas of Giovan Maria Cecchi. LC 85-999. 200p. 1986. text ed. 22.50 (*0-8262-0462-7*) U of Mo Pr.

— The Exile into Eternity: A Study of the Narrative Writings of Giorgio Bassani. LC 86-45739. 176p. 1987. 29.50 (*0-8386-3296-3*) Fairleigh Dickinson.

— Wait for Me, Little Girl! 165p. 1989. 25.00 (*0-9624254-0-0*) DeSoto Pr Inc.

Radcliff-Umstead, Douglas, jt. auth. see Rossi, Patrizio.

Radcliff-Unstead, Douglas. The Mirror of Our Anguish: A Study of Luigi Pirandello's Narrative Works. 329p. 1978. 39.50 (*0-8386-1930-4*) Fairleigh Dickinson.

Radcliffe, Alexander. Works of Captain Alexander Radcliffe. LC 81-9003. 1981. reprint ed. 50.00 (*0-8201-1365-4*) Schol Facsimiles.

***Radcliffe, Ann.** The Castles of Athlin & Dunbayne. Milbank, Alison, ed. (World's Classics Ser.). 152p. 1995. pap. 7.95 (*0-19-282357-4*) OUP.

— Castles of Athlin & Dunbayne: A Highland Story. LC 78-131336. (Gothic Novels Ser.). 1974. reprint ed. 51.95 (*0-405-00808-2*) Ayer.

— The Female Advocate. 173p. reprint ed. lib. bdg. 32.37 (*3-487-06724-2*, Pub. by Georg Olms GW) Lubrecht & Cramer.

— Gaston de Blondeville. Keeping Festival in Ardenne. St. Alban's Abbey: With Some Poetical Pieces, 4 vols. in 2, Set. (Anglistica & Americana Ser.: No. 160). 1976. reprint ed. 174.20 (*3-487-05903-7*, Pub. by Georg Olms GW) Lubrecht & Cramer.

— Gaston De Blondeville, Or, the Court of Henry 3rd, Keeping Festival in Ardenne, 2 Vols, Set. LC 71-131337. (Gothic Novels Ser.). 1979. reprint ed. 53.95 (*0-405-00815-5*) Ayer.

— The Italian. Garber, Frederick, ed. (World's Classics Ser.). 1982. pap. 8.95 (*0-19-281572-5*) OUP.

— A Journey Made in the Summer of 1794 Through Holland & the Western Frontier of Germany. (Anglistica & Americana Ser.: No. 121). 507p. 1975. reprint ed. 115.70 (*3-487-05753-0*, Pub. by Georg Olms GW) Lubrecht & Cramer.

— The Poetical Works of Ann Radcliffe, 2 vols. LC 70-37714. reprint ed. 85.00 (*0-404-56805-X*) AMS Pr.

— The Romance of the Forest. Chard, Chloe, ed. & intro. by. (World's Classics Ser.). 427p. 1986. pap. 7.95 (*0-19-281712-4*) OUP.

— The Romance of the Forest: Interspersed with Some Pieces of Poetry, 3 vols., Set. LC 73-22770. 794p. 1979. reprint ed. 94.95 (*0-405-06020-3*) Ayer.

— A Sicilian Romance. Milbank, Alison, ed. LC 92-25480. (World's Classics Ser.). (C). 1993. 8.95 (*0-19-282212-8*) OUP.

— Sicilian Romance. LC 75-131338. (Gothic Novels Ser.). 1972. reprint ed. 46.95 (*0-405-00809-0*) Ayer.

Radcliffe, Anthony. Bronzes 1500-1650: The Robert H. Smith Collection. (Illus.). 160p. 1994. 50.00 (*0-302-00636-2*, Pub. by P Wilson Pubs) Sothebys Pubns.

Radcliffe, Anthony, et al. Renaissance & Later Sculpture: The Thyssen-Bornemisza Collection. (Illus.). 400p. 1992. 250.00 (*0-85667-401-X*) Sothebys Pubns.

Radcliffe, Anthony B., et al. The Pharmer's Almanac. (Illus.). (Orig.). 1985. pap. 8.95 (*0-910223-05-X*) MAC Pub.

Radcliffe-Brown, A. R. On the Concept of Function in Social Science. (Reprint Series in Sociology). (C). 1993. reprint ed. pap. text ed. 1.00 (*0-8290-3815-9*, S-227) Irvington.

Radcliffe-Brown, A. R. & Forde, Daryll, eds. African Systems of Kinship & Marriage. (Illus.). 400p. 1994. pap. text ed. 25.50 (*0-7103-0234-7*, 02347, Pub. by Kegan Paul Intl UK) Routledge Chapman & Hall.

Radcliffe-Brown, Alfred R. Structure & Function in Primitive Society. 1965. 19.95 (*0-02-925630-5*); pap. 16.95 (*0-02-925620-8*) Free Pr.

Radcliffe, C. J., et al, eds. Active Control of Noise & Vibration - 1992. (DSC Ser.: Vol. 38). 372p. 1992. 65.00 (*0-7918-2093-9*, G00737) ASME.

Radcliffe, C. W., jt. auth. see Suh, C. H.

Radcliffe, Carolyn M. African Affair. 1994. 15.95 (*0-533-10866-7*) Vantage.

Radcliffe College Editors. Catalog of the Arthur & Elizabeth Schlesinger Library on the History of Women in America: The Manuscript Inventories & the Catalogs of Manuscripts, Books, & Periodicals, 10 vols. 2nd ed. 7500p. 1983. lib. bdg. 2,290.00 (*0-8161-0425-5*, Hall Library) G K Hall.

Radcliffe College, the Arthur & Elizabeth Schlesinger Library on the History of Women in America Staff. Manuscripts Inventory & the Catalogs of Manuscripts, Books & Pictures, 3 vols. 1974. lib. bdg. 330.00 (*0-8161-1053-0*, Hall Library) G K Hall.

***Radcliffe, D.** Hillary Rodham Clinton. Date not set. pap. 4.98 (*0-517-13161-7*) Random Hse Value.

Radcliffe, David H. Edmund Spenser: A Reception History. 1995. 49.95 (*0-685-72215-5*) Camden Hse.

— Forms of Reflection: Genre & Culture in Meditational Writing. LC 92-31654. 248p. 1993. text ed. 38.50 (*0-8018-4500-9*) Johns Hopkins.

Radcliffe, Donnie. Hillary Rodham Clinton: A First Lady for Our Time. 272p. 1994. mass mkt. 5.50 (*0-446-60063-6*) Warner Bks.

— Simply Barbara Bush: A Portrait of America's Candid First Lady. 256p. 1990. mass mkt. 4.95 (*0-446-36024-4*) Warner Bks.

Radcliffe, Elizabeth S. & White, Carol J., eds. Faith in Theory & Practice: Essays on the Justification of Religious Belief. LC 93-33067. 245p. 1993. 34.95 (*0-8126-9246-2*); pap. 16.95 (*0-8126-9247-0*) Open Court.

Radcliffe, Elsa J. Gothic Novels of the Twentieth Century: An Annotated Bibliography. LC 78-24357. 291p. 1979. lib. bdg. 25.00 (*0-8108-1190-1*) Scarecrow.

Radcliffe, Evelyn. Profits Without Honor: A New Look at the Something for Nothing Syndrome. Parker, Diane, ed. LC 90-64425. 128p. 1991. pap. 7.95 (*0-88247-868-0*) R & E Pubs.

Radcliffe, George L. Governor Thomas H. Hicks of Maryland & the Civil War. LC 78-63884. (Johns Hopkins University. Studies in the Social Sciences. Thirtieth Ser. 1912: Nos. 11-12). reprint ed. 17.00 (*0-404-61139-7*) AMS Pr.

Radcliffe, Graham. Cosmic Messenger. 160p. (C). 1990. 90.00 (*0-86439-140-4*, Pub. by Boolarong Pubns AT) St Mut.

Radcliffe, James. The Reorganisation of British Central Government. 236p. 1991. text ed. 55.95 (*1-85521-176-9*, Pub. by Dartmth Pub UK) Ashgate Pub Co.

Radcliffe, James C. & Farentinos, Robert C. Plyometrics: Explosive Power Training. 2nd ed. LC 85-14409. 140p. (C). 1985. pap. text ed. 15.95x (*0-87322-024-2*, BRAD0024) Human Kinetics.

— Plyometrics: Explosive Power Training for Every Sport. 2nd ed. 140p. 1985. vhs 49.00 (*0-87322-143-5*, MPLY0027) Human Kinetics.

Radcliffe, Joel, ed. see Walker, John H.

Radcliffe, Mark F., jt. auth. see Brinson, J. Dianne.

Radcliffe, Mary A. The Female Advocate. LC 93-46509. (Revolution & Romanticism, 1789-1834 Ser.). 1994. reprint ed. 49.50 (*1-85477-172-8*, Pub. by Woodstock Bks UK) Cassell.

Radcliffe, Mary-Anne. Manfrone: Or the One-Handed Monk, 2 Vols, Set. LC 79-131339. (Gothic Novels Ser.). 1979. reprint ed. 53.95 (*0-405-00818-X*) Ayer.

Radcliffe, Robert C. Investment: Concepts, Analysis, Strategy. 826p. (C). 1994. Study guide. student ed 21.00 (*0-673-46697-3*) HarpCollege.

— Investment: Concepts, Analysis, Strategy. 4th ed. 826p. (C). 1994. text ed. 69.00 (*0-673-46657-4*) HarpCollege.

Radcliffe, Samuel J., jt. auth. see Sedjo, Roger A.

Radcliffe, Sarah A. & Westwood, Sallie, eds. Viva: Women & Popular Protest in Latin America. LC 92-20274. (International Studies of Women & Places). 288p. 1993. 55.00 (*0-415-07312-X*, A7379, Routledge NY); pap. 16.95 (*0-415-07313-8*, A7383, Routledge NY) Routledge.

Radcliffe, Sarah C. Aizer Knegdo: Jewish Woman's Guide to Happiness in Marriage. 254p. 1989. 16.95 (*0-944070-08-6*) Targum Pr.

— Akeres Habayis: Realizing Your Potential as a Jewish Homemaker. 228p. 1991. 15.95 (*0-944070-64-7*) Targum Pr.

— Smooth Sailing: Navigating Life's Challenges. (Illus.). 191p. 1994. 14.95 (*1-56871-039-9*) Targum Pr.

Radcliffe, Stanley, tr. see Fontane, Theodor.

Radcliffe, Theresa. Shadow the Deer. (Illus.). 32p. (J). (ps-1). 1993. 13.99 (*0-670-83852-7*) Viking Child Bks.

— Snow Leopard. (Illus.). 32p. (J). (ps-1). 1994. 13.99 (*0-670-85052-7*) Viking Child Bks.

Radcliffe, Walter. Milestones in Midwifery Bound with the Secret Instrument: The Birth of the Midwifery Forceps. (Illus.). 193p. 1989. reprint ed. 75.00 (*0-930405-20-X*) Norman SF.

Radcliffe, William. Origin of the New System of Manufacture Commonly Called "Power-Loom Weaving" LC 68-30541. (Reprints of Economic Classics Ser.). 216p. 1974. reprint ed. 35.00 (*0-678-00877-9*) Kelley.

Radco. Vintage Motorcyclists' Workshop. LC 86-82145. 1986. 31.95 (*0-85429-472-4*, Pub. by G T Foulis Ltd) Haynes Pubns.

Radcure '84 (1984: Atlanta GA) Staff. Radcure '84: Conference Proceedings, September 10-13, 1984, Atlanta, GA. LC 84-51496. (Illus.). 618p. reprint ed. pap. 180.00 (*0-8357-6500-8*, 2035871) Bks Demand.

Raddatz, Fritz. The Survivor. Manheim, Ralph, tr. 1989. 15.95 (*0-316-73213-3*) Little.

Radday, Yehuda & Levi, Yaakov. An Analytical Linguistic Key-Word-in-Context Concordance to the Book of Exodus. Baird, Arthur J. & Freedman, David, eds. (Computer Bible Ser.: Vol. 28). (Orig.). 1985. 45.00 (*0-935106-23-5*) Biblical Res Assocs.

Radday, Yehuda T. An Analytical Linguistic Concordance to the Book of Isaiah. (Computer Bible Ser.: Vol. II). 1975. 20.00 (*0-935106-15-4*) Biblical Res Assocs.

— An Analytical, Linguistic Key-Word-in-Context Concordance to the Book of Judges. (Computer Bible Ser.: Vol. XI). 1977. pap. 20.00 (*0-935106-10-3*) Biblical Res Assocs.

Radde & Macleod. Pediatric Pharmacology & Therapeutics. 2nd ed. 656p. 1992. 67.00 (*1-55664-368-3*) Mosby Yr Bk.

Radde, Bruce. The Merritt Parkway. LC 93-9466. (Illus.). 176p. 1993. 25.00 (*0-300-05379-7*) Yale U Pr.

Radde, Karl H. Woerterbuch der Technik, Vol. 2. 5th ed. 812p. (GER & SPA.). 1989. 175.00 (*0-8288-5565-X*, S40501) Fr & Eur.

— Woerterbuch der Technik: Spanish-German. 716p. 1977. 95.00 (*0-7859-8467-4*, 3773655304) Fr & Eur.

— Woerterbuch der Technik Spanisch - Deutsch. 6th ed. 960p. (GER & SPA.). 1992. 195.00 (*0-8288-2116-X*, S39877) Fr & Eur.

***Radde, Karl-Heinz.** Oekonomisches Woerterbuch: Spanish-German. 640p. (GER & SPA.). 1989. 105.00 (*0-7859-7034-7*) Fr & Eur.

Radde, Paul O. Supervising: A Guide for All Levels. Davis, Larry N., ed. LC 81-1827. (Illus.). 236p. 1981. 27.95 (*0-89384-053-X*) Pfeiffer & Co.

— Supervision Decision! Employee Guide to Choosing a Supervisory Position. Davis, Larry N., ed. LC 81-1116. (Illus.). 100p. 1981. pap. text ed. 29.95 (*0-89384-060-2*) Pfeiffer & Co.

— The Supervision Transition! An Employee Guide to Choosing & Moving into a Supervisory Position. Davis, Larry N., ed. (Illus.). (Orig.). 1990. pap. 17.95 (*0-9625872-0-6*); pap. text ed. 15.95 (*0-685-35333-8*) Thriving Pubns.

— Thrival! - a Guide to Soaring with Your Spirit: Six Essential Steps to Thriving. Date not set. 21.95 (*0-9625872-1-4*) Thriving Pubns.

Radden, Jennifer. Madness & Reason. (Studies in Applied Philosophy). 176p. 1985. text ed. 55.00 (*0-04-170034-1*); pap. text ed. 16.95 (*0-04-170035-X*) Routledge Chapman & Hall.

Radder, J. K., et al. Pathogenesis & Treatment of Diabetes Mellitus. 1986. lib. bdg. 92.00 (*0-89838-828-7*) Kluwer Ac.

Radding, Charles M. The Origins of Medieval Jurisprudence: Pavia & Bologna 850-1150. LC 87-14237. 272p. reprint ed. pap. 77.60 (*0-7837-4539-7*, 2080286) Bks Demand.

— A World Made by Men: Cognition & Society, 400-1200. LC 85-1111. xi, 286p. 1985. 37.50 (*0-8078-1664-7*) U of NC Pr.

— A World Made by Men: Cognition & Society, 400-1200. LC 85-1111. (Illus.). reprint ed. pap. 85.00 (*0-7837-9036-8*, 2049787) Bks Demand.

Radding, Charles M. & Clark, William W. Medieval Architecture, Medieval Learning: Builders & Masters in the Age of Romanesque & Gothic. (Illus.). 184p. 1994. pap. 18.00 (*0-300-06130-7*) Yale U Pr.

Radding, Charles M., ed. see Petrucci, Armando.

Raddock, David M., ed. Navigating New Markets Abroad: Charting a Course for International Business. 272p. (C). 1993. lib. bdg. 55.50 (*0-8476-7843-1*) Rowman.

Raddon, Alan J. How to Make Rope Soled Footwear. (C). 1982. pap. 35.00 (*0-9508937-0-6*, Pub. by Aberarth Pub UK) St Mut.

Raddon, Charlene. Taming Jenna. 416p. 1994. mass mkt. 4.50 (*0-8217-4604-9*) Zebra.

— Tender Touch. 432p. 1994. mass mkt. 4.50 (*0-8217-4777-0*) Zebra.

Raddon, Ethel, jt. auth. see Sluyter, E. H.

Raddon, Gary A. Developing New Financial Products: From Needs Analysis to Profitable Rollout. LC 89-28981. 281p. 1990. boxed 69.95 (*0-942061-05-5*, Financial Sourcebks) Sourcebks.

Raddon, Rosemary & Dix, Pamela. Planning Learning Resource Centres in Schools & Colleges, No. 2. 2nd ed. 1989. text ed. 63.95 (*0-566-05753-0*, Pub. by Gower UK) Ashgate Pub Co.

Rade, Lennart & Westergren, Bertil. Beta Mathematics Handbook: Concepts, Theorems, Methods, Algorithms, Formulas, Graphs, Tables. 2nd ed. 1992. 39.95 (*0-8493-7758-7*, QA) CRC Pr.

Radebaugh, Lee H. & Gray, Sidney J. International Accounting & Multinational Enterprises. 3rd ed. 592p. 1993. Net. text ed. write for info. (*0-471-50634-6*) Wiley.

Radebaugh, Lee H., jt. auth. see Arpan, Jeffery S.

Radebaugh, Lee H., jt. auth. see Daniels, John D.

Radebaugh, Lee H., jt. ed. see Fry, Earl H.

Radecke, Mark. In Christ: A New Creation. Sherer, Michael L., ed. (Orig.). 1986. pap. 6.55 (*0-89536-821-8*, 6830) CSS OH.

***Radecke, Mark W.** God in Flesh Made Manifest: Sermons for Advent, Christmas, & Epiphany: Cycle A, Gospel Lesson Texts. LC 95-13428. 1995. write for info. (*0-614-05428-1*) CSS OH.

— In Many & Various Ways. 1985. 6.00 (*0-89536-721-1*, 5806) CSS OH.

Radecki, Steven. Multimedia with QuickTime: A Practical Guide to Creating Applications. (Illus.). 266p. 1993. pap. 32.95 (*0-12-574750-0*, AP Prof) Acad Pr.

Radek, Karl. Portraits & Pamphlets. LC 67-22113. (Essay Index Reprint Ser.). 1977. 21.95 (*0-8369-0804-X*) Ayer.

Radel, H. Turkey. 2nd ed. (Visitor's Guides Ser.). (Illus.). 256p. 1990. pap. 14.95 (*1-55650-234-6*) Hunter NJ.

Radel, J. Lucien. Reconstructing the Western Alliance: Europe & the U. S. A. LC 89-92795. (Illus.). 100p. (Orig.). (C). 1990. pap. 6.75 (*0-9625359-0-7*) Lakesider Pub.

Radel, Jouffroy-Lucien. Demise & Regenesis of East Central Europe: Roots of the Political Forces & Their Evolvement. (Illus.). 240p. (Orig.). (C). 1991. pap. text ed. 9.95 (*0-9625359-3-1*) Lakesider Pub.

Radel, Stanley R. & Navidi, Marjorie. Chemistry. Ricci, ed. 1070p. (C). 1990. text ed. 67.00 (*0-314-25179-0*) West Pub.

— Chemistry. 2nd ed. Pullins, ed. LC 93-11454. 1215p. (C). 1994. text ed. 74.00 (*0-314-02654-1*) West Pub.

Radeleff, Rudolph D. Veterinary Toxicology. 2nd ed. LC 74-85846. 365p. reprint ed. pap. 104.10 (*0-317-29245-5*, 2055440) Bks Demand.

Radelet, Louis A. Police & the Community. 5th ed. (Illus.). 608p. (C). 1994. text ed. write for info. (*0-02-319681-5*) Macmillan.

Radelet, Michael L., ed. Facing the Death Penalty. 264p. 1990. pap. 18.95 (*0-87722-721-7*) Temple U Pr.

Radelet, Michael L., jt. auth. see Miller, Kent S.

Radelet, Michael L., et al. In Spite of Innocence: Erroneous Convictions in Capital Cases. 400p. 1992. text ed. 37.50 (*1-55553-142-3*) NE U Pr.

— In Spite of Innocence: Erroneous Convictions in Capital Cases. 416p. 1994. reprint ed. pap. text ed. 16.95 (*1-55553-197-0*) NE U Pr.

Radell, Karen M., ed. Affirmation in a Moral Wasteland: A Comparison of Ford Madox Ford & Graham Greene. (American University Studies: English Language & Literature: Ser. IV, Vol. 54). 233p. (C). 1987. text ed. 33.00 (*0-8204-0499-3*) P Lang Pubs.

Radell, Rick & Vines, Mike. Lancaster: A Living Legend. (Illus.). 128p. 1993. 15.95 (*1-85532-267-6*, Pub. by Osprey Pubng Ltd UK) Motorbooks Intl.

Radeloff, D. J., jt. auth. see Charlesworth, R.

***Rademacher.** Lay Ministry Study Guide. Date not set. 7.95 (*0-8245-1236-7*) Crossroad NY.

Rademacher, Hans. Collected Papers of Hans Rademacher, 2 vols., 2. Grosswald, Emil, ed. (Mathematicians of Our Time Ser.: Vols. 1 & 2). 1356p. 1974. 70.00x (*0-262-07055-3*) MIT Pr.

— Collected Papers of Hans Rademacher, 2 vols., Set. Grosswald, Emil, ed. (Mathematicians of Our Time Ser.: Vols. 1 & 2). 1356p. 1974. 135.00 (*0-685-03383-X*) MIT Pr.

— Collected Papers of Hans Rademacher, 2 vols., Vol. 1. Grosswald, Emil, ed. (Mathematicians of Our Time Ser.: Vols. 1 & 2). 1356p. 1974. 70.00 (*0-262-07054-5*) MIT Pr.

— Enjoyment of Mathematics. 1990. pap. 5.95 (*0-486-26242-1*) Dover.

— Lectures on Elementary Number Theory. LC 76-30495. 156p. 1977. reprint ed. lib. bdg. 18.50 (*0-88275-499-8*) Krieger.

Rademacher, Hans, jt. auth. see Grosswald, Emil.

Rademacher, Robert A., jt. auth. see Gibson, Harry L.

Rademacher, Susan C., jt. auth. see Klem, Joan R.

Rademacher, Thomas E., ed. Advances in Glycobiology, Vol. 1. 1991. 90.25 (*1-55938-350-X*) Jai Pr.

Rademacher, Uwe. Die Bildkunst Des Tacitus. (Spudasmata Ser.: Bd. 29). xi, 298p. (GER.). 1975. write for info. (*3-487-05754-9*, Pub. by Georg Olms GW) Lubrecht & Cramer.

Rademacher, William & Rogers, Marliss. The New Practical Guide for Parish Councils. LC 88-50662. 272p. (Orig.). 1988. pap. 7.95 (*0-89622-371-X*) Twenty-Third.

Rademacher, William J. Answers for Parish Councillors. LC 81-51429. 1981. pap. 6.95 (*0-89622-134-2*) Twenty-Third.

— Lay Ministry. 288p. (C). 1990. 75.00 (*0-85439-378-1*, Pub. by St Paul Pubns UK) St Mut.

— Lay Ministry: A Theological, Spiritual & Pastoral Handbook. 288p. (Orig.). 1991. pap. 14.95 (*0-8245-1086-0*) Crossroad NY.

Raden Adjeng Kartini. Letters of a Javanese Princess. Geertz, Hildred, ed. Symmers, Agnes L., tr. 246p. 1985. reprint ed. pap. text ed. 22.00 (*0-8191-4758-3*, The Asia Society) U Pr of Amer.

Radencich, Marguerite C. Administration & Supervision of the Reading - Writing Program. 1994. 39.95 (*0-205-15217-1*, Longwood Div) Allyn.

Radencich, Marguerite C., ed. Adult Literacy: A Compendium of Articles from the Journal of Reading. 304p. 1994. pap. 19.00 (*0-87207-122-7*) Intl Reading.

***Radencich, Marguerite C. & McKay, Lyn J.** Flexible Grouping for Literacy in the Elementary Grades. LC 94-23629. 1995. text ed. 39.95 (*0-205-17497-3*, Longwood Div); pap. text ed. 29.95 (*0-205-16226-6*, Longwood Div) Allyn.

Radencich, Marguerite C., jt. auth. see Schumm, Jeanne S.

Radencich, Marguerite C., et al. A Handbook for the K to Twelve Reading Resource Specialist. LC 93-2920. 240p. 1993. pap. 38.50 (*0-205-14081-5*, Longwood Div) Allyn.

Radencici, Marguerite C. & Kaiser Johnson, Sue. How to Help Your Child with Homework: Every Caring Parent's Guide to Encouraging Good Study Habits & Ending the Homework Wars. Espeland, Pamela, ed. LC 88-19019. 208p. (Orig.). 1988. pap. 12.95 (*0-915793-12-1*) Free Spirit Pub.

Rader. A Modern Book of Esthetics. 5th ed. 563p. (C). 1979. text ed. 40.00 (*0-03-019331-1*) HB Coll Pubs.

Rader, Barbara A. & Zettler, Howard G., eds. The Sleuth & the Scholar: Origins, Evolution, & Current Trends in Detective Fiction. LC 87-24958. (Contributions to the Study of Popular Culture Ser.: No. 19). 151p. 1988. text ed. 39.95 (*0-313-26036-2*, ZSS/) Greenwood.

Rader, Ben, intro. Making It in the Gilded Age. 212p. (Orig.). (C). 1994. pap. text ed. 11.95 (*1-881089-15-0*) Brandywine Press.

Rader, Benjamin G. American Sports: From the Age of Folk Games to the Age of Televised Sports. 2nd ed. 400p. 1989. pap. text ed. 48.00 (*0-13-029133-1*) P-H.

R

— American Sports: From the Age of Folk Games to the Age of Televised Sports. 3rd ed. LC 95-15765. 1995. pap. text ed. 29.47 (0-13-111213-9) P-H.
— Baseball: A History of America's Game. (Illinois History of Sports Ser.: Vol. 2). (Illus.). 272p. (C). 1993. 24.95 (0-252-01737-4); pap. 11.95 (0-252-06395-3) U of Ill Pr.
— In Its Own Image: How Television Has Transformed Sports. LC 84-47856. 256p. 1984. 27.95 (0-02-925700-X) Free Pr.
Rader, Billie T., ed. see Multi-Amp Institute Staff.
Rader, Brian F. The Political Outsiders: Blacks & Indians in a Rural Oklahoma County. LC 77-94282. 1978. spiral bd. 17.00 (0-88247-517-7) R & E Pubs.
Rader, Carl. Fundamentals of Electronics Mathematics. LC 84-17051. 200p. (C). 1985. teacher ed 12.00 (0-8273-2322-0); pap. text ed. 24.95 (0-8273-2321-2) Delmar.
Rader, Charles, jt. auth. see Zoubek, Leslie.
Rader, Charles N., jt. ed. see Rabiner, Lawrence R.

***Rader, David. From Tip to Tail: The Layman's Guide to Basic Alpine Ski Tuning. 2nd ed. (Illus.). 65p. 1995. pap. 7.95 (0-9645550-1-8) Cornerstne Pub. FINALLY, A SIMPLE SOURCE FOR THE SKI ENTHUSIAST TO UNDERSTAND & APPLY! Readers will appreciate the simple approach given to alpine ski tuning in FROM TIP TO TAIL. Author & long-time professional ski technician David Rader offers a full-length lesson on ski tuning in layman's terms. STEP-BY-STEP INSTRUCTIONS coupled with CLEAR & SIMPLE LINE ILLUSTRATIONS offer detailed explanations of technique & hand & tool positions for base scraping, edge filing & beveling, base waxing, base structuring, binding maintenance & more. From TIP TO TAIL stands on the premise that anyone who wants to learn the art of ski tuning must first acquire a basic knowledge with hands-on experience. This book bypasses the avalanche of technical information often associated with instructional guides & provides the layman with a clear & easy understanding of alpine ski tuning. To order FROM TIP TO TAIL: THE LAYMAN'S GUIDE TO BASIC ALPINE SKI TUNING, contact Menasha Ridge Press, 3169 Cahaba Heights Road, Birmingham, AL 35243. 1-800-247-9437.** *Publisher Provided Annotation.*

***Rader, David J.** From Tip to Tail: The Layman's Guide to Basic Alpine Ski Tuning. 40p. 1994. pap. text ed. 7.95 (0-9645550-0-X) Cornerstne Pub.
Rader, Dick A. Christian Ethics in an African Context: A Focus on Urban Zambia. LC 90-21429. (American University Studies: Theology & Religion: Ser. VII, Vol. 128). 200p. (C). 1991. text ed. 36.95 (0-8204-1453-0) P Lang Pubs.
Rader, Hannelore B., ed. Academic Library Instruction: Objectives, Programs, & Faculty Involvement. LC 75-678. (Library Orientation Ser.: No. 5). 1975. 25.00 (0-87650-063-7) Pierian.
— Faculty Involvement in Library Instruction. LC 76-21914. (Library Orientation Ser.: No. 6). 1976. 25.00 (0-87650-070-X) Pierian.
— Library Instruction in the Seventies: State of the Art. LC 77-75678. (Library Orientation Ser.: No. 7). 1977. 25.00 (0-87650-078-5) Pierian.
Rader, Hannelore B. & Ridgeway, Trish. Teaching Information Literacy on Campus: A How-to-Do-It Manual for Librarians. (How-to-Do-It Ser.). 150p. 1993. 39.95 (1-55570-109-4) Neal-Schuman.
Rader, James. Penetrating the U. S. Auto Market: German & Japanese Strategies, 1965-1976. LC 80-15530. (Research for Business Decisions Ser.: No. 22). 210p. reprint ed. pap. 59.90 (0-685-44074-5, 2070143) Bks Demand.
***Rader, Janet S. & Rosenhein, Neil B., eds.** Ultrasonic Surgical Techniques for the Pelvic Surgeon. LC 94-21216. 1994. 60.00 (0-387-94244-0) Spr-Verlag.
***Rader, Jennifer.** The Rainy Day Activity Book: How to Make Play Dough, Bubbles, Monster Spray & More. LC 94-27587. 1995. 12.00 (0-385-47544-6) Doubleday.
***Rader, Joanne & Tornquist, Elizabeth, eds.** Individualized Dementia Care: Creative, Compassionate Approaches. 200p. 1995. write for info. (0-8261-8730-7) Springer Pub.
Rader, Laura. Mother Hubbard's Cupboard: A Mother Goose Surprise Book. LC 92-45103. (Illus.). 48p. (J). (ps up). 1993. 12.95 (0-688-12562-X, Tambourine Bks) Morrow.
— My First Christmas Carols. LC 94-17170. (Illus.). 32p. 1994. lib. bdg. 11.89 (0-8167-3596-4) Troll Assocs.
— My First Christmas Carols. LC 94-17170. (Illus.). (J). (gr. k-2). 1994. pap. 2.25 (0-8167-3513-1) Troll Assocs.
Rader, Laura, illus. Goldilocks & the Three Bears. LC 94-4986. (J). 1995. write for info. (0-688-13258-8, Tambourine Bks) Morrow.
— Goody New Shoes. 32p. (J). (ps-3). 1991. pap. 3.50 (0-14-054391-0, Puffin) Puffin Bks.
— The Pudgy Where Is Your Nose? Book. (Pudgy Board Bks.). 16p. (J). 1989. bds. 2.95 (0-448-02258-3, G&D) Putnam Pub Group.
— The Three Billy Goats Gruff. LC 94-4987. (J). 1995. write for info. (0-688-13259-6, Tambourine Bks) Morrow.
Rader, Laura, jt. auth. see Hall, Kirsten.
Rader, Marth H. & Kurth, Linda A. Business Communication with Contemporary Issues & Microcomputer Applications. 2nd ed. LC 92-17795. 1994. text ed. 55.95 (0-538-70665-1) S-W Pub.
Rader, Melvin. False Witness. LC 78-93027. 232p. 1979. reprint ed. pap. 9.95 (0-295-95660-7) U of Wash Pr.
— The Right to Hope: Crisis & Community. LC 81-51284. 148p. 1981. 25.00 (0-295-95836-7) U of Wash Pr.
Rader, Melvin M. Presiding Ideas in Wordsworth's Poetry. LC 68-8341. 94p. (C). 1968. reprint ed. 40.00 (0-87752-090-9) Gordian.
Rader, Melvin M. & Gill, Jerry H. The Enduring Questions: Main Problems of Philosophy. 5th ed. (C). 1991. pap. text ed. 33.25 (0-03-032949-3) HB Coll Pubs.
Rader, Patrick Z. Western Wilderness Haiku: High Plains Ditties, Prairie Poems. 1993. 12.95 (0-936204-92-3) Jelm Mtn.
Rader, Randall R., jt. ed. see McGuigan, Patrick B.
Rader, Randy W. S-He. 20p. 1983. pap. 2.00 (0-913719-65-X) High-Coo Pr.
Rader, Richard. Entelek Computer-Based Physics Lab. 133p. pap. text ed. 14.95 (0-87567-035-0) Entelek.
Rader, Robert J. Advanced Software Design Techniques. (Illus.). 172p. 1979. text ed. 19.95 (0-89433-046-2) Petrocelli.
Rader, Ronald A. & Young, Sally A. Federal Bio-Technology Transfer Directory. 678p. 1994. pap. 150.00 (0-9639573-0-9) Biotech Info.
Rader, Trout. The Economics of Feudalism. Lieberman, Bernhardt, ed. LC 77-132148. (Monographs & Texts in the Behavioral Sciences). (Illus.). 146p. (C). 1971. text ed. 81.00 (0-677-03280-3) Gordon & Breach.
— Economics with No Special Technology: Memorial Volume. 320p. 1995. lib. bdg. 84.00 (0-904870-27-8, Pub. by Input-Output Pub UK) Kelley.
Rader, William. The Church & Racial Hostility: A History of Interpretation of Ephesians 2, 11-22. 282p. 1978. 55.00 (3-16-140112-3, Pub. by J C B Mohr GW) Coronet Bks.
Radermacher, R., et al, eds. Proceedings of the International Heat Pump Absorption Conference: New Orleans, Louisiana - January 19-21, 1994. LC 94-74375. (AES Ser.: Vol. 31). 544p. 1994. 75.00 (0-7918-0698-7, I00361) ASME.
Radermacher, reinhard, jt. auth. see Alefeld, Georg.
Radermacher, Reinhard, jt. auth. see Herold, Keith E.
Raderman, Marlene, tr. see Simon, Njami.
Radermecker, J., jt. auth. see Van Bogaer, L.
Raders, Sheri & Newsom, Peggy. Seattle Career Hunter's Guide. (Illus.). 1978. pap. 5.95 (0-918480-07-8) Victoria Hse.
Radeschi, Loretta. This Business of Glass: The Complete Guide for Artists, Craftspeople & Retailers. Porcelli, Joe, ed. (Illus.). 320p. 1993. pap. 19.95 (0-9629053-3-X) Glass Pr.
Radest, Howard B. Can We Teach Ethics? LC 88-27512. 162p. 1989. text ed. 35.95 (0-275-92857-8, C2857, Praeger Pubs) Greenwood.
— Community Service: Encounter with Strangers. LC 93-17116. 216p. 1993. text ed. 52.95 (0-275-94186-8, C4186, Praeger Pubs) Greenwood.
— The Devil & Secular Humanism: The Children of the Enlightenment. LC 90-38843. 184p. 1990. text ed. 47.95 (0-275-93442-X, C3442, Praeger Pubs) Greenwood.
***Radetski, Marian.** Polish Hard Coal & European Energy Market Integration. 137p. 1995. boxed, pap. 51.95 (1-85975-140-7, Pub. by Avebury Pub UK) Ashgate Pub Co.
Radetsky, Peter. Invisible Invaders: The Story of the Emerging Age of Viruses. 1991. 22.95 (0-316-73216-8) Little.
— Invisible Invaders: The Story of the Emerging Age of Viruses Updated, with a New Chapter, Vol. 1. 1995. pap. 14.95 (0-316-73217-6) Little.
Radetzki, Marian. Aid & Development: A Handbook for Small Donors. LC 72-92892. (Special Studies in International Economics & Development). 1973. 39.50 (0-275-28694-0) Irvington.
— State Mineral Enterprises: An Investigation into Their Impact on International Mineral Markets. LC 85-2346. 150p. 1985. pap. text ed. 15.00 (0-915707-16-0) Resources Future.
— Uranium: Economic & Political Instability in a Strategic Commodity Market. 1981. text ed. 39.95 (0-312-83424-1) St Martin.
Radevsky, Anthony. A Practical Guide to Drafting Pleading. 214p. 1991. 70.00 (1-85190-141-8, Pub. by Tolley Pubng UK) St Mut.
***Radford.** Bernie Drives a Truck. LC 91-58718. (J). 1995. pap. text ed. 4.99 (1-56402-488-1) Candlewick Pr.
Radford & Haigh. Turbo Pascal for the IBM PC. (C). 1986. pap. 48.95 (0-534-06426-4) PWS Pubs.
Radford, A. S. Teach Yourself Computer Programming - FORTRAN. (Teach Yourself Ser.). 1975. pap. 5.95 (0-685-03266-3) McKay.
Radford, Albert E., et al. Manual of the Vascular Flora of the Carolinas. LC 68-28264. (Illus.). lxii, 1183p. 1968. 34.95 (0-8078-1087-8) U of NC Pr.
— Natural Heritage: Classification, Inventory, & Information. LC 80-23087. xxi, 485p. 1981. 45.00 (0-8078-1463-6) U of NC Pr.
Radford, Andrew. Syntactic Theory & the Acquisition of English Syntax: The Nature of Early Child Grammars of English. 304p. 1991. pap. text ed. 21.95 (0-631-16358-1) Blackwell Pubs.
— Transformational Grammar: A First Course. (Cambridge Textbooks in Linguistics Ser.). 600p. 1988. pap. 29.95 (0-521-34750-5) Cambridge U Pr.
***Radford, Carole M.** Hearts Go Home for the Holidays: A Collection of Holiday Recipes. 184p. 1994. spiral bd. 17.95 (1-886300-00-3) Heirlooms by Radford.
***Radford, Carole M., ed.** Hospitality Southern Style: A Collection of Treasured Southern Recipes. 164p. 1994. spiral bd. 17.95 (1-886300-01-1) Heirlooms by Radford.
Radford, Colin. The Examined Life. 191p. 1989. text ed. 68.95 (0-566-07008-1, Pub. by Avebury Pub UK) Ashgate Pub Co.
***Radford, Darrel.** New Castle: A Pictorial History. (Indiana Pictorial History Ser.). (Illus.). 1994. write for info. (0-943963-28-1) G Bradley.
Radford, Derek. Building Machines & What They Do. LC 91-71860. 32p. (J). (ps-3). 1994. pap. 4.99 (1-56402-364-8) Candlewick Pr.
— Cargo Machines & What They Do. LC 91-71823. (Illus.). 32p. (J). (ps up). 1992. 8.95 (1-56402-005-3) Candlewick Pr.
— Cargo Machines & What They Do. LC 91-71823. 1995. pap. 4.99 (1-56402-434-2) Candlewick Pr.
— Harry at the Airport. LC 91-16116. (Illus.). 32p. (J). (gr. k-3). 1991. bds. 10.95 (0-689-71504-8, Aladdin Paperbacks) S&S Childrens.
— Harry at the Garage. LC 94-25699. (J). (gr. 1-8). Date not set. write for info. (1-56402-564-0) Candlewick Pr.
Radford, E. & Radford, M. A. Death at the Chateau Noir. large type ed. 1975. 12.00 (0-85456-375-X) Ulverscroft.
— Death Has Two Faces. large type ed. (Mystery Ser.). 1975. 16.95 (0-85456-350-4) Ulverscroft.
— Death of a "Gentleman" large type ed. (Mystery Ser.). 1976. 15.95 (0-85456-447-0) Ulverscroft.
— The Greedy Killers. large type ed. (Mystery Ser.). 1976. 16.95 (0-85456-399-7) Ulverscroft.
— Murder Magnified. large type ed. (Mystery Library). 368p. 1995. pap. 14.95 (0-7089-7655-7, Linford) Ulverscroft.
Radford, Edwin & Radford, Mona A. Encyclopedia of Superstitions. LC 70-88993. 269p. 1969. reprint ed. text ed. 55.00 (0-8371-2115-9, RASU, Greenwood Pr) Greenwood.
Radford, Elaine. A Complete Introduction to Cockatiels. (Illus.). 128p. 1987. pap. 5.95 (0-86622-284-7, CO012S) TFH Pubns.
— A Step-by-Step Book about Finches. (Illus.). 64p. 1989. pap. 3.95 (0-86622-466-1, SK-010) TFH Pubns.
— A Step-by-Step Book about Parrots. (Step-by-Step Ser.). (Illus.). 64p. (YA). (gr. 9-12). 1988. pap. 3.95 (0-86622-484-X, SK-031) TFH Pubns.
— A Step-by-Step Book about Training Cockatiels. (Illus.). 64p. 1989. pap. 3.95 (0-86622-970-1, SK-026) TFH Pubns.
Radford, Elaine R. & Becker, Gary D. Diagnosis & Management of Inhalant Allergy. (Self-Instructional Package Ser.). (Illus.). 93p. (Orig.). 1993. pap. text ed. 25.00 (1-56772-004-8) AAO-HNS.
— Introduction to the Diagnosis & Treatment of Food Sensitivities. (Self-Instructional Package Ser.). (Illus.). 65p. (Orig.). (C). 1993. pap. text ed. 25.00 (1-56772-005-6) AAO-HNS.
Radford, Elizabeth, ed. New Villagers: Urban Pressure on Rural Areas in Worchester. (Illus.). 76p. 1970. 25.00 (0-7146-1585-4, Pub. by F Cass Pubs UK) Intl Spec Bk.
Radford, G. H. Shylock & Others: Eight Studies. LC 72-13311. (Essay Index Reprint Ser.). 1977. reprint ed. 18.95 (0-8369-8172-3) Ayer.
Radford, Georgia F. & Radford, Warren H. Sculpture in the Sun: Hawaii's Art for Open Spaces. LC 77-92972. 117p. 1978. pap. 3.95 (0-8248-0526-7) UH Pr.
Radford, Irene. The Glass Dragon. 352p. (Orig.). 1994. mass mkt. 4.99 (0-88677-634-1) DAW Bks.
Radford, Jan. Delightful Beaded Earring Designs. Knight, Denise, ed. LC 93-70574. (Illus.). 72p. (Orig.). 1994. per., pap. 8.95 (0-943604-37-0) Eagles View.
Radford, Jean. Dorothy Richardson. LC 91-24136. (Key Women Writers Ser.). 176p. 1992. text ed. 29.95 (0-253-30108-4); pap. text ed. 10.95 (0-253-25456-6) Ind U Pr.
Radford, Jean, ed. The Progress of Romance: The Politics of Popular Fiction. 224p. 1987. 32.50 (0-7102-0717-4, 07174, RKP); pap. 12.95 (0-7102-0963-0, 09630, RKP) Routledge.
Radford, Jeff. The Chaco Coal Scandal. (Illus.). 257p. (Orig.). (C). 1986. pap. 8.00 (0-936455-01-2) Rhombus Pub.
Radford, Jill & Russell, Diana E. Femicide: The Politics of Woman Killing. 300p. 1992. text ed. 29.95 (0-8057-9026-8, Pub. by Royal Botanic Garden UK); pap. 16.95 (0-8057-9028-4, Pub. by Royal Botanic Garden UK) Macmillan.
Radford, Jim, jt. ed. see Eden, Colin.
Radford, Joan. The Complete Book of Family Aromatherapy. 192p. Date not set. pap. 11.95 (0-572-01622-0, Pub. by W Foulsham UK) Trans-Atl Phila.
Radford, John, ed. An Indian Journal. 224p. 1994. text ed. 39.50 (1-85043-776-9, Pub. by I B Tauris UK) St Martin.
— Talent, Teaching & Achievement. 160p. 1991. pap. 29.95 (1-85302-111-3, Pub. by J Kingsley Pubs UK) Taylor & Francis.
Radford, John & Rose, David. A Liberal Science: Psychology Education Past, Present & Future. 192p. 1990. 95.00 (0-335-09503-8, Open Univ Pr); pap. 36.00 (0-335-09502-X, Open Univ Pr) Taylor & Francis.
Radford, John & Rose, David, eds. The Teaching of Psychology: Method, Content, & Context. LC 79-40824. 380p. reprint ed. pap. 108.30 (0-8357-7046-X, 2033621) Bks Demand.
Radford, K. J. Individual & Small Group Decisions. xiv, 174p. 1989. pap. 61.00 (0-387-97156-4) Spr-Verlag.
— Modern Managerial Decision Making. 1981. teacher ed write for info. (0-318-55520-4, Reston) P-H.
— Strategic & Tactical Decisions. 2nd ed. (Illus.). 215p. 1988. pap. 64.00 (0-387-96819-9) Spr-Verlag.
Radford, Ken, comp. Fire Burn: Tales of Witchery. LC 93-7745. 1993. 7.99 (0-517-09366-9, Pub. by Wings Bks) Random Hse Value.
Radford, M. A., jt. auth. see Radford, E.
Radford, Michael. How to Create a Championship Vision. 176p. 1994. per. 25.00 (0-8403-9390-3) Kendall-Hunt.
Radford, Mona A., jt. auth. see Radford, Edwin.
Radford, Penny. Designer's Guide to Surfaces & Finishes. (Illus.). 160p. 1991. pap. 22.50 (0-8230-1311-1, Whitney Lib) Watsn-Guptill.
Radford, Richard R. Drug Agent U. S. A. 1991. pap. 3.95 (0-312-92326-0) St Martin.
Radford, Robert. Art for a Purpose: The Artists' International Association 1933-1953. 205p. 1991. 17.95 (0-9506783-7-6, Pub. by Winchester Schl Art Pr UK) Paul & Co Pubs.
Radford, Robert, jt. auth. see Morris, Lynda.
Radford, Russel, jt. auth. see Noori, Hamid.
Radford, T. S., ed. see Institute of Petroleum, London Staff.
Radford, Tom S. What Makes a Project Marginal. (C). 1989. 140.00 (0-89771-730-9, Pub. by Lorne & MacLean Marine) St Mut.
— What Makes a Project "Marginal?" 1989. 125.00 (90-6314-862-3, Pub. by Lorne & MacLean Marine) St Mut.
Radford, Vicki, et al, eds. Light for the Day. 368p. 1989. spiral bd. 6.50 (0-9624991-0-2) NWestern Prods.
Radford, Warren H., jt. auth. see Radford, Georgia F.
Radford, William A. Old House Measured & Scaled Drawings for Builders & Carpenters: An Early 20th Century Pictorial Sourcebook, with 183 Detailed Plates. 2nd ed. (Illus.). 200p. 1983. reprint ed. pap. 9.95 (0-486-24438-5) Dover.
Radforth, Ian. Bushworkers & Bosses: Logging in Northern Ontario, 1900-1980. 367p. 1987. 45.00 (0-8020-2639-7); pap. 20.95 (0-8020-6653-4) U of Toronto Pr.
Radforth, Ian, jt. ed. see Greer, Allan.
Radforth, N. W., ed. see Muskeg Research Conference Staff.
Radha, Sivananda. The Divine Light Invocation. 2nd ed. LC 90-31896. (Illus.). 104p. 1990. pap. 10.95 (0-931454-17-4) Timeless Bks.
— From the Mating Dance to the Cosmic Dance: Sex, Love, & Marriage from a Yogic Viewpoint. Foran, Rita & MacKenzie, Ian, eds. LC 92-13848. (Illus.). 208p. 1992. 22.95 (0-931454-31-X); pap. 14.95 (0-931454-32-8) Timeless Bks.
— Hatha Yoga: The Hidden Language: Symbols, Secrets, & Metaphor. LC 94-45215. (Illus.). 320p. 1995. pap. 18.95 (0-931454-74-3) Timeless Bks.
— Hatha Yoga - The Hidden Language: Symbols, Secrets & Metaphor. LC 87-9955. (Illus.). 320p. (Orig.). 1987. 19.95 (0-931454-12-3) Timeless Bks.
— In the Company of the Wise: Remembering My Teachers, Reflecting the Light. McKay, Julie, ed. LC 91-7431. (Illus.). 242p. 1991. 22.95 (0-931454-23-9) Timeless Bks.
— In the Company of the Wise: Remembering My Teachers, Reflecting the Light. LC 91-7431. (Illus.). 242p. 1993. pap. 14.95 (0-931454-24-7) Timeless Bks.
— Kundalini Yoga for the West: A Foundation for Character Building, Courage & Awareness. (Illus.). 373p. 1993. reprint ed. pap. 18.95 (0-931454-38-7) Timeless Bks.
— Kundalini Yoga for the West: A Foundation for Character Building, Courage & Awareness. (Illus.). 373p. (C). 1993. reprint ed. 29.95 (0-931454-37-9) Timeless Bks.
— Mantras: Words of Power. rev. ed. Lenman, Karin, ed. LC 93-46477. (Illus.). 208p. 1994. pap. 14.95 (0-931454-66-2) Timeless Bks.
— Radha: Diary of a Woman's Search. 2nd ed. Foran, Rita, ed. LC 90-32272. (Illus.). 242p. (Orig.). 1990. pap. 13.95 (0-931454-19-0) Timeless Bks.
— Realities of the Dreaming Mind. LC 94-16766. (Illus.). 384p. 1994. 29.95 (0-931454-68-9); pap. 18.95 (0-931454-69-7) Timeless Bks.
— Seeds of Light. LC 90-49580. (Illus.). 116p. 1991. pap. 9.95 (0-931454-22-0) Timeless Bks.
— Seeds of Light. LC 85-20943. (Illus.). 116p. 1985. reprint ed. pap. 8.95 (0-931454-11-5) Timeless Bks.
Radhakrishna, S., ed. Science Technology & Global Problems-Views from the Developing World. (Illus.). 1980. 108.00 (0-08-024489-0, Pub. by Pergamon Repr UK) Franklin.
Radhakrishna, S. & Jain, S. C., eds. Physics of Semiconductor Devices: Proceedings of the Third International Workshop on Physics of Semiconductor Devices, Madras, India, Nov 27 - Dec 2, 1985. 500p. 1985. 78.00 (9971-5-0082-5) World Scientific Pub.
Radhakrishna, S. & Tan, B. C., eds. Laser Spectroscopy & Nonlinear Optics of Solids: Proceedings of the International Workshop Organized by the Institute for Advanced Studies, University of Malaya, & the Malaysian Institute of Physics (Kuala Lumpur, Malaysia) 500p. 1991. 58.00 (0-387-52943-8) Spr-Verlag.
Radhakrishna, S., jt. ed. see Jain, S. C.
Radhakrishna, S., et al, eds. Solid State Materials. 400p. 1992. 69.00 (0-387-54229-9) Spr-Verlag.
Radhakrishnan, C. Zero. (Indian Novels Ser.: Vol. 1). 110p. 1974. 4.95 (0-88253-462-9) Ind-US Inc.

An Asterisk (*) at the beginning of an entry indicates that the title is appearing in BIP for the first time.

Radhakrishnan, N., ed. Gandhian Perspective of Nation Building for World Peace. 166p. (C). 1992. text ed. 25.00 (*81-220-0272-2*, Pub. by Konark Pubs Pvt Ltd II) Advent Bks Div.

Radhakrishnan, P. Computer Numerical Control (CNC) Machine. (C). 1989. 75.00 (*0-89771-389-3*, Current Dist) St Mut.

— Peasant Struggles, Land Reforms & Social Change: Malabar, 1836-1982. 290p. (C). 1989. text ed. 24.00 (*0-8039-9593-8*) Sage.

Radhakrishnan, S. Indian Philosophy, Vol. 1. 740p. 1993. 19.95 (*0-19-562348-7*) OUP.

— Indian Philosophy, Vol. 1. 740p. 1989. 49.95 (*0-04-181009-0*) Routledge Chapman & Hall.

— Indian Philosophy, Vol. 2. 808p. 1993. 19.95 (*0-19-562349-5*) OUP.

— Principal Upanisads. (C). 1994. pap. text ed. 16.00 (*81-7223-124-5*, Pub. by Indus Pub II) S Asia.

— Recovery of Faith. (C). 1995. reprint ed. 8.00x (*81-7223-145-8*, Pub. by Indus Pub II) S Asia.

— Religion & Society. (C). 1995. 9.50x (*81-7223-163-6*, Pub. by Indus Pub II) S Asia.

Radhakrishnan, S., ed. The Principal Upanisads. LC 91-47550. (Humanities Paperback Library). 956p. (C). 1992. pap. 29.95 (*0-391-03479-0*) Humanities.

Radhakrishnan, S., tr. The Principal Upanishads. 960p. 1989. 49.95 (*0-04-294046-X*) Routledge Chapman & Hall.

Radhakrishnan, S. & Raju, P. T., eds. The Concept of Man: A Study in Comparative Philosophy. 546p. (C). 1992. 21.95 (*1-881338-16-9*) Nataraj Bks.

— The Concept of Man: A Study in Comparative Philosophy. (C). 1995. reprint ed. 12.50x (*81-7223-146-6*, Pub. by Indus Pub II) S Asia.

Radhakrishnan, S. & Ranjana, Kumari. Higher Education & Scheduled Caste Youth in India. 125p. 1989. text ed. 15.95 (*81-7027-118-5*, Pub. by Radiant Pubs II) S Asia.

Radhakrishnan, S., jt. auth. see Kumari, Ranjana.

Radhakrishnan, Sarvepalli. The Creative Life. 146p. 1976. 9.00 (*0-86578-200-8*); pap. 2.40 (*0-89253-049-9*) Ind-US Inc.

— Eastern Religions & Western Thought. (Oxford India Paperbacks Ser.). 410p. 1990. pap. 9.95 (*0-19-562456-4*) OUP.

— The Hindu View of Life. 92p. 1988. pap. 7.00 (*0-04-294115-6*) Harper SF.

— An Idealist View of Life. LC 77-27145. (Hibbert Lectures: 1929). 352p. reprint ed. 47.50 (*0-404-60425-0*) AMS Pr.

— An Idealist View of Life. (Unwin Paperbacks Ser.). 288p. 1988. reprint ed. pap. 12.95 (*0-04-141009-2*) Routledge Chapman & Hall.

— Indian Religions. (Orient Paperbacks Ser.). 196p. 1981. 8.95 (*0-86578-117-6*); pap. 3.95 (*0-86578-084-6*) Ind-US Inc.

— Living with a Purpose. 136p. 1982. 9.00 (*0-86578-204-0*); pap. 4.25 (*0-86578-137-0*) Ind-US Inc.

— Our Heritage. (Orient Paperbacks Ser.). 156p. (Orig.). 1973. 9.00 (*0-86578-205-9*); pap. 4.25 (*0-88253-249-9*) Ind-US Inc.

— Recovery of Faith. (Orient Paperbacks Ser.). 187p. 1981. reprint ed. 9.00 (*0-86578-201-6*); reprint ed. pap. 4.25 (*0-88253-073-9*) Ind-US Inc.

— Towards a New World. 149p. 1983. 9.00 (*0-86578-202-4*); pap. 4.25 (*0-86578-138-9*) Ind-US Inc.

Radhakrishnan, Sarvepalli & Moore, Charles A., eds. Sourcebook in Indian Philosophy. 1957. pap. 18.95 (*0-691-01958-4*) Princeton U Pr.

Radhakrishnan, Sarvepalli, tr. see Badarayana.

Radhakrishnan, T., jt. auth. see Mukherjee, R. R.

Radharamanan, R., ed. Robotics & Factories of the Future '87. (Illus.). xvii, 878p. 1988. 126.00 (*0-387-50025-1*) Spr-Verlag.

Radhayrapetian, Juliet. Iranian Folk Narrative: A Survey of Scholarship. LC 89-274158. (Folklore Library: Vol. 1). 212p. 1990. 20.00 (*0-8240-7145-X*, 1285) Garland.

Radhoff, Sandra. The Kyrian Letters: Transformative Messages for Higher Vision. 249p. (Orig.). 1992. pap. 12.00 (*1-882545-00-1*) Herit Pubns.

Radhuber, Stanley. Flying Over Greenland. Gale, Vi, ed. LC 77-83287. (First Book Ser.). (Illus.). 1977. pap. 5.00 (*0-915986-06-X*) Prescott St Pr.

— Flying Over Greenland. limited ed. Gale, Vi, ed. LC 77-83287. (First Book Ser.). (Illus.). 1977. 20.00 (*0-915986-05-1*) Prescott St Pr.

Radian, Alex. Resource Mobilization in Poor Countries: Implementing Tax Policies. LC 79-66440. 226p. 1980. 32.95 (*0-87855-304-5*) Transaction Pubs.

Radian Corporation Staff. Chemical Additives for the Plastics Industry: Properties, Applications, Toxcologies. LC 86-31155. (Illus.). 884p. 1987. 64.00 (*0-8155-1114-0*) Noyes.

— Municipal Waste Combustion Study: Assessment of Health Risks Associated with Municipal Waste Combustion Emissions. 248p. 1989. 67.00 (*0-89116-071-X*) Hemisp Pub.

— Polymer Manufacturing: Technology & Health Effects. LC 86-17977. (Illus.). 718p. 1987. 59.00 (*0-8155-1090-X*) Noyes.

Radic, S., ed. Technological Engineering Dictionary German-Serbocroatian. 495p. (CRO, GER & SER.). 1981. 95.00 (*0-8288-4678-2*, M9687) Fr & Eur.

Radic, S., jt. auth. see Vekaric, Stjepan.

Radic, Therese. G. W. L. Marshall-Hall: Portrait of a Lost Crusader. (Music Monograph: Vol. 5). (Illus.). xii, 58p. (Orig.). 1983. pap. 12.25 (*0-909751-73-0*, Pub. by Univ of West Aust Pr AT) Intl Spec Bk.

— Melba, the Voice of Australia. ix, 214p. 1986. 14.95 (*0-918812-45-3*, SB 0005) MMB Music.

Radical Statistics Race Group (BAHT) Staff & Ohri, Sushel. Britain's Black Population. 2nd ed. (New Perspective Ser.). 160p. 1988. text ed. 54.95 (*0-566-05179-6*, Pub. by Gower UK) Ashgate Pub Co.

Radicati, Sara. Electronic Mail: An Introduction to the X. 400 Message Handling Standards. 1992. text ed. 40.00 (*0-07-051104-7*) McGraw.

— X-500 Directory Services: Technology & Deployment. LC 93-45358. 1994. text ed. 39.95 (*0-442-01816-9*) Van Nos Reinhold.

— X.500 Standards for Directory Services. 1993. 34.00 (*0-13-145913-9*) P-H.

Radice, Barbara. Ettore Sottsass. LC 92-26799. (Illus.). 264p. 1993. 50.00 (*0-8478-1681-8*) Rizzoli Intl.

— Jewelry by Architects. LC 86-43191. (Illus.). 120p. 1987. 35.00 (*0-8478-0798-3*) Rizzoli Intl.

— Memphis: Research, Experiences, Failures, & Successes of New Design. LC 94-60789. (Illus.). 208p. 1995. pap. 29.95 (*0-500-27377-4*) Thames Hudson.

Radice, Barbara, ed. Terrazo, Vol. 5. (Illus.). 160p. 1990. 25.00 (*0-8478-5557-0*) Rizzoli Intl.

— Terrazzo, 1. (Illus.). 102p. 1988. pap. 25.00 (*0-8478-5520-1*) Rizzoli Intl.

— Terrazzo, 2. (Illus.). 102p. 1988. pap. 25.00 (*0-8478-5524-4*) Rizzoli Intl.

— Terrazzo, 3. (Illus.). 102p. 1988. pap. 25.00 (*0-8478-5532-5*) Rizzoli Intl.

— Terrazzo, Vol. 4. (Illus.). 160p. 1990. pap. 25.00 (*0-8478-5551-1*) Rizzoli Intl.

— Terrazzo, Vol. 6. (Illus.). 160p. 1991. pap. 25.00 (*0-8478-5558-9*) Rizzoli Intl.

— Terrazzo, Vol. 7. (Illus.). 160p. 1992. pap. 25.00 (*0-8478-5573-2*) Rizzoli Intl.

— Terrazzo, Vol. 8. (Illus.). 160p. 1992. pap. 25.00 (*0-8478-5614-3*) Rizzoli Intl.

Radice, Betty. Who's Who in the Ancient World. (Reference Ser.). (Orig.). 1973. pap. 11.00 (*0-14-051055-9*, Penguin Bks) Viking Penguin.

Radice, Betty, tr. The Letters of Abelard & Heloise. (Classics Ser.). 312p. 1974. mass mkt. 8.95 (*0-14-044297-9*, Penguin Classics) Viking Penguin.

— The Letters of the Younger Pliny. (Classics Ser.). 320p. 1963. mass mkt. 9.95 (*0-14-044127-1*, Penguin Classics) Viking Penguin.

Radice, Betty, tr. see Erasmus, Desiderius.

Radice, Betty, tr. see Erasmus.

Radice, Betty, jt. auth. see Terence.

Radice, Betty, tr. see Terence.

Radice, E. A., jt. auth. see Kaser, Michael C.

Radice, Giles. Labour's Path to Power: The New Revisionism. 207p. 1989. text ed. 45.00 (*0-312-03224-2*) St Martin.

— Offshore: Britain & the European Idea, March 1992. 256p. 1992. text ed. 22.95 (*1-85043-529-4*, Pub. by I B Tauris UK) St Martin.

Radice, Giles & Radice, Lisanne. Socialists in the Recession: The Search for Solidarity. LC 86-14265. 200p. 1986. text ed. 35.00 (*0-312-73748-3*) St Martin.

Radice, Giles, jt. auth. see Lapping, Brian.

Radice, Judi. Menu Design 5. (Illus.). 240p. 1992. 60.00 (*0-86636-180-4*) PBC Intl Inc.

— Restaurant & Food Graphics. LC 93-49501. 1994. 45.00 (*0-86636-287-8*) PBC Intl Inc.

Radice, Lisanne. Prelude to Appeasement: East European Central Diplomacy in the Early 1930's. (East European Quarterly Ser.: No. 80). 218p. 1981. text ed. 43.50 (*0-914710-74-5*) East Eur Quarterly.

Radice, Lisanne, jt. auth. see Radice, Giles.

Radice, Roberto & Runia, David T. Philo of Alexandria: An Annotated Bibliography, 1937-1986. LC 88-26242. (Supplements to Vigiliae Christianae Ser.: Vol. 8). (Illus.). xli, 469p. 1992. reprint ed. 123.00 (*90-04-08986-1*) E J Brill.

Radice, William. Teach Yourself Bengali. (BEN & ENG.). 1993. pap. 18.95 (*0-7859-1052-2*, 0-340-552573); pap. 29.95 (*0-7859-1058-1*, 0-340-56489X) Fr & Eur.

Radice, William, ed. see Tagore, Rabindranath.

Radice, William, tr. see Tagore, Rabindranath.

Radich, Anthony. Economic Impact of the Arts: A Sourcebook. 252p. 1991. pap. 15.00 (*1-55516-216-9*, 2106) Natl Conf State Legis.

Radics, Katalin. Typology & Historical Linguistics: Affixed Person-Marking Paradigms. (Studia Uralo-altaica Ser.: Vol. 24). 305p. (Orig.). 1985. pap. 83.00 (*0-685-33593-3*, Pub. by Attila Josef Univ HU) Benjamins North Am.

Radigan, Raymond, jt. auth. see Turano, Margaret V.

Radiguet, Raymond. Le Bal du Comte d'Orgel. (Folio Ser.: No. 1176). 208p. 1924. 8.95 (*2-07-037476-9*) Schoenhof.

— Cheeks on Fire. Stone, Alan, tr. 112p. (ENG & FRE.). 1986. 13.95 (*0-7145-3513-3*) Riverrun NY.

— Count D'Orgel's Ball. Cancogni, Annapaola, tr. LC 88-83032. 174p. 1989. reprint ed. 20.00 (*0-941419-31-2*, Eridanos Library); reprint ed. pap. 11.00 (*0-941419-30-4*, Eridanos Library) Marsilio Pubs.

— Le Diable au Corps. (Coll. Diamant). 118p. (FRE.). 1991. pap. 6.95 (*0-7859-1492-7*, 2277229695) Fr & Eur.

— Le Diable au Corps. (Folio Ser.: No. 1391). 192p. (FRE.). 1955. pap. 8.95 (*2-07-037391-6*) Schoenhof.

— Oeuvres Completes. 1978. 75.00 (*0-686-54719-5*) Fr & Eur.

Radimersky, George W. German Science Reader: An Analytical Approach to Translation Problems. LC 50-8071. 253p. reprint ed. pap. 72.20 (*0-317-09358-4*, 2012533) Bks Demand.

Radin, jt. auth. see Wright.

Radin, Alexander. Miniature Bearing Technologies in the U. S. S. R. (The Institute VNIPP & NIIChasprom) Tamberg, Andreas, ed. 151p. (Orig.). 1986. pap. text ed. 75.00 (*1-55831-038-X*) Delphic Associates.

Radin, B. A. & Howley, W. D. The Politics of Federal Reorganization: Creating the U. S. Department of Education. LC 87-6972. (Illus.). 250p. 1988. 40.00 (*0-08-033978-6*, Pergamon Pr); pap. 18.95 (*0-08-033977-8*, Pergamon Pr) Elsevier.

***Radin, Barbara.** Decision Dramas: Real Language for Real Life. 96p. (Orig.). 1992. pap. 10.95 (*0-943327-12-1*) JAG Pubns.

Radin, Beryl A. Implementation, Change, & the Federal Bureaucracy: School Desegregation Policy in HEW, 1964-1968. LC 76-58320. (Policy Analysis & Education Ser.). 255p. reprint ed. pap. 72.70 (*0-8357-3007-7*, 2039275) Bks Demand.

Radin, Beryl A. & Purvis, Hoyt, eds. Women in Public Life. (Symposia Ser.). 56p. 1976. pap. 3.50 (*0-89940-404-9*) LBJ Sch Pub Aff.

Radin, Bill. Breakaway Careers. 224p. (Orig.). 1994. pap. 12.95 (*1-56414-121-7*) Career Pr Inc.

— Take This Job & Leave It: How to Get Out of a Job You Hate & into a Job You Love. 192p. 1993. pap. 12.95 (*1-56414-057-1*) Career Pr Inc.

Radin, Carol, ed. see Radin, William G.

Radin, Dave. Building a Successful Software Business. Loukides, Mike, ed. (Illus.). 394p. (Orig.). 1994. pap. 19.95 (*1-56592-064-3*) OReilly & Assocs.

Radin, Doris. There Are Talismans. LC 91-16268. (Eileen W. Barnes Award Ser.). (Illus.). 64p. (Orig.). 1991. pap. 7.00 (*0-938158-12-0*) Saturday Pr.

Radin, Dorothea, tr. see Slowacki, Juliusz.

Radin, Dorothea P., tr. see Kochanowski, Jan.

Radin, Eric L., et al. Practical Biomechanics for the Orthopaedic Surgeon. 2nd ed. (Illus.). 216p. 1992. text ed. 47.50 (*0-443-08702-4*) Churchill.

Radin-Fox, Barbara, jt. auth. see Fox, Larry.

Radin, Grace. Virginia Woolf's "The Years" The Evolution of a Novel. LC 80-22590. 212p. 1981. 29.00x (*0-87049-307-8*) U of Tenn Pr.

Radin, Jessica, ed. see Blond, Anne G. & Janusz, Leslye.

Radin, Joseph, jt. auth. see Reiss, Levi.

Radin, Judi, jt. auth. see Wei, Katherine.

Radin, Judi, jt. auth. see Wei, Kathie.

Radin, Margaret J. Reinterpreting Property. LC 93-4908. 1994. 29.95 (*0-226-70227-8*); pap. text ed. 13.95 (*0-226-70228-6*) U Ch Pr.

Radin, Max. Handbook of Anglo-American Legal History. LC 93-78454. 638p. 1993. reprint ed. 125.00 (*1-56169-039-2*) W W Gaunt.

— The Jews among the Greeks & Romans. 1915. 22.00 (*0-8196-2074-2*) Biblo.

— The Jews Among the Greeks & Romans. LC 73-2224. (Jewish People; History, Religion, Literature Ser.). 1973. reprint ed. 36.95 (*0-405-05286-3*) Ayer.

— The Lawful Pursuit of Gain. LC 75-39268. (Getting & Spending: the Consumer's Dilemma Ser.). 1976. reprint ed. 19.95 (*0-405-08041-7*) Ayer.

Radin, Max, jt. auth. see Schiffer, Walter.

Radin, Norma, jt. auth. see Feld, Sheila.

Radin, Paul. African Folktales. LC 74-106800. (Bollingen Ser., Vol. 32). 338p. (Orig.). reprint ed. 96.40 (*0-8357-9491-1*, 2013034) Bks Demand.

— Autobiography of a Winnebago Indian. 1920. pap. 3.50 (*0-486-20096-5*) Dover.

— The Italians of San Francisco. LC 74-17945. (Italian American Experience Ser.). (Illus.). 200p. 1975. reprint ed. 18.95 (*0-405-06415-2*) Ayer.

— The Method & Theory of Ethnology. LC 86-29921. 388p. 1987. pap. text ed. 18.95 (*0-89789-118-X*, Bergin & Garvey) Greenwood.

— Primitive Religion: Its Nature & Origin. 1937. pap. text ed. 8.95 (*0-486-20393-X*) Dover.

— The Road of Life & Death: A Ritual Drama of the American Indians. (Mythos: The Princeton - Bollingen Series in World Mythology). 368p. 1991. pap. text ed. 15.95 (*0-691-01916-9*) Princeton U Pr.

— The Trickster: A Study in American Indian Mythology. LC 74-88986. 223p. 1987. pap. 12.00 (*0-8052-0351-6*) Schocken.

— Trickster: A Study in American Indian Mythology. LC 74-88986. 211p. 1969. reprint ed. text ed. 38.50 (*0-8371-2112-4*, RATT, Greenwood Pr) Greenwood.

— The Winnebago Tribe. LC 64-63594. (Illus.). xvi, 573p. 1990. reprint ed. pap. 18.95 (*0-8032-5710-4*, Bison Books) U of Nebr Pr.

Radin, Paul, ed. African Folktales. LC 82-10475. 344p. (Orig.). 1987. reprint ed. pap. 14.95 (*0-8052-0732-5*) Schocken.

Radin, Paul & Espinoza, A. M. Folklore de Oaxaca. LC 78-63215. (Folktale Ser.). reprint ed. 28.00 (*0-404-16299-1*) AMS Pr.

Radin, Paul, tr. see Vendryes, Joseph.

***Radin, R.** Carver. 1994. pap. 2.99 (*0-517-13315-6*) Random.

Radin, Ruth. From the Wooded Hill: Reading Level 1-3 & Above. LC 92-42219. (Illus.). 1993. 3.00 (*0-88336-039-X*) New Readers.

— Morning Streets: Reading Level 1-3 & Above. LC 92-42220. (Illus.). 1993. 3.00 (*0-88336-040-3*) New Readers.

— Sky Bridges & Other Poems: Reading Level 1-3 & Above. LC 92-46291. 1993. 3.50 (*0-88336-038-1*); audio 11.50 (*0-88336-070-5*); audio 9.00 (*0-88336-620-7*) New Readers.

Radin, Ruth Y. All Joseph Wanted. LC 91-12643. (Illus.). 80p. (J). (gr. 3-7). 1991. text ed. 13.95 (*0-02-775641-6*, Mac Bks Young Read) S&S Childrens.

— High in the Mountains. LC 88-13395. (Illus.). 32p. (J). (gr. k-4). 1989. text ed. 13.95 (*0-02-775650-5*, Mac Bks Young Read) S&S Childrens.

— Tac's Island. 80p. (J). (gr. 2-9). 1989. reprint ed. pap. 2.95 (*0-8167-1320-0*) Troll Assocs.

— Tac's Turn. 80p. (J). (gr. 2-9). 1989. reprint ed. pap. 2.95 (*0-8167-1319-7*) Troll Assocs.

Radin, Shelden & Folk, Robert. Physics for Scientists & Engineers. 2nd ed. 1992. pap. 46.25 (*0-536-58178-9*) Ginn Pr.

Radin, Stephen & Greenberg, Harold. Computers in the Doctor's Office. LC 84-8378. 160p. 1984. text ed. 45.00 (*0-275-91245-0*, C1245, Praeger Pubs) Greenwood.

Radin, William G. Billing Power! The Recruiter's Guide to Peak Performance. Temple, Thea & Radin, Carol, eds. LC 90-81180. (Illus.). 216p. (Orig.). 1990. pap. 39.95 (*0-9626147-1-8*) Innovative Consulting.

— The Recruiter's Almanac of Scripts, Rebuttals, & Closes. Lorber, Ruth & Scott, Lou, eds. 138p. (Orig.). 1990. pap. 49.95 (*0-9626147-2-6*) Innovative Consulting.

— Shut up & Make More Money: The Recruiter's Guide to Talking Less & Billing More. Smith, Betty, ed. (Illus.). 224p. 1995. pap. 49.95 (*0-9626147-3-4*) Innovative Consulting.

Radine, Lawrence B. The Taming of the Troops: Social Control in the United States Army. LC 76-5262. (Contributions in Sociology Ser.: No. 22). 276p. (Orig.). 1977. text ed. 59.95 (*0-8371-8911-X*, RTT/, Greenwood Pr) Greenwood.

***Radinger, Willy & Schick, Walter.** Messerschmitt Me 262: Development-Testing-Production. (Illus.). 112p. 1993. 24.95 (*0-88740-516-9*) Schiffer.

Radinsky, Leonard B. The Evolution of Vertebrate Design. LC 87-5959. (Illus.). xii, 196p. 1987. pap. text ed. 14.95 (*0-226-70236-7*) U Ch Pr.

Radio Broadcasting Research Project Staff. Studies in the Control of Radio, Nos. 1-6. LC 79-161174. (History of Broadcasting: Radio to Television Ser.). 1977. reprint ed. 31.95 (*0-405-03581-0*) Ayer.

Radio Control Car Action Editors. Basics of Radio Control Cars. Pratt, Doug, ed. 52p. 1986. pap. 12.95 (*0-911295-03-8*) Air Age.

***Radio Control Car Action Editors Staff.** Radio Control Car How To's, Vol. 2. Howell, John, ed. (Illus.). 98p. (Orig.). 1994. pap. 14.95 (*0-911295-32-1*) Air Age.

Radio-Electronics Editors. Radio-Electronics: From "Drawing Board" to Finished Project. (Illus.). 160p. 1989. 15.95 (*0-8306-9133-2*, 3133); pap. 9.95 (*0-8306-3133-X*, 3133) TAB Bks.

— Radio-Electronics' Guide to Computer Circuits. (Illus.). 170p. 1988. 14.95 (*0-8306-0333-6*); pap. 9.95 (*0-8306-9333-5*, 3033P) TAB Bks.

Radio Free Europe-Radio Liberty Staff. Glasnost & Empire: National Aspirations in the U. S. S. R. LC 88-30186. (Illus.). 60p. (Orig.). (C). 1989. lib. bdg. 20.50 (*0-929849-01-9*); pap. text ed. 10.50 (*0-929849-00-0*) RFE-RL Inc.

Radio Free Europe Staff. Scaling the Wall: Talking to Eastern Europe: The Best of Radio Free Europe. Urban, George R., ed. LC 64-18955. 303p. reprint ed. pap. 86.40 (*0-7837-3801-3*, 2043621) Bks Demand.

Radio Magazine Editors. Audio Anthology, Vol. 5: When Audio Was Young. (Illus.). 144p. (Orig.). 1993. reprint ed. pap. 16.95 (*1-882580-01-X*) Audio Amateur.

***Radio Poet.** Doris Klein: Poems & Paintings. 1995. write for info. (*0-681-00784-2*) Longmeadow Pr.

Radio Station KQWC Staff & Hamilton County Historical Society Staff. Hamilton County, IA History. (Illus.). 729p. 1986. 62.50 (*0-88107-049-1*) Curtis Media.

Radioisotopes & Radiation Effects Committee E-10. Space Radiation Effects on Materials. LC 62-20905. (American Society for Testing & Materials: No. 330). 71p. reprint ed. pap. 25.00 (*0-317-09203-0*, 2000123) Bks Demand.

Radiological Society of North America-RadioGraphics Staff. RSNA, 1992: Selected Scientific Exhibits. 1994. vdisk 500.00 (*1-56815-024-5*, 10024) Image Premast.

Radiquet, Raymond. Bal du Comte d'Orgel. 208p. 1924. write for info. (*0-318-63432-5*) Fr & Eur.

— Bal du Comte d'Orgel. 256p. (FRE.). 1984. pap. 10.95 (*0-7859-1646-6*, 2080704060) Fr & Eur.

Radiquet, Raymond, jt. auth. see Cocteau, Jean.

Radish, Kris. Run, Bambi, Run. 408p. 1992. pap. 5.50 (*0-451-40351-7*, Onyx) NAL-Dutton.

— Run, Bambi, Run: The Beautiful Ex-Cop Convicted of Murder Who Escaped to Freedom & Won America's Heart. (Illus.). 1992. 18.95 (*1-55972-103-0*, Birch Ln Pr) Carol Pub Group.

Radisson, Pierre E. Voyages of Peter Esprit Radisson, Being an Account of His Travels & Experiences among the North American Indians, from 1652 to 1684; Transcribed from Original Messages in the Bodleian Library & British Museum. (American Biography Ser.). 385p. 1991. reprint ed. lib. bdg. 79.00 (*0-7812-8320-5*) Rprt Serv.

Raditsa, Leo. Prisoners of a Dream: The South African Mirage. 500p. (Orig.). 1989. pap. 25.00 (*0-317-93477-5*) Prince Grg St.

Raditsa, Leo, tr. see Kessel, Joseph.

Radjavi, H. & Rosenthal, P. Invariant Subspaces. LC 73-77570. (Ergebnisse der Mathematik und Ihrer Grenzgebiete Ser.: Vol. 77). (Illus.). 230p. 1973. 65.00 (*0-387-06217-3*) Spr-Verlag.

Radke, Barbara R. & Stein, Barbara L. Creating Newsletters, Brochures, & Pamphlets: A How-to-Do-It Manual for School & Public Librarians. (How-to-Do-It Ser.). 144p. 1992. 32.50 (*1-55570-107-8*) Neal-Schuman.

***Radke, Detlef.** The German Social Market Economy: An Option for the Transforming & Developing Countries? (GDI Bks.: Vol. 4). 1994. pap. 22.50 (*0-7146-4153-7*) Intl Spec Bk.

Radke, Dietmar & Oppl, Hubert, eds. Soziale Beschfltigungsformen: Zur Zukunft der Arbeit. (Soziokulturelle Herausforderungen-Sozialpolitische Aufgaben: Aspekte Moderner Sozialarbeit Ser.: Vol. 3). 240p. (GER.). 1991. pap. 28.00 (*3-597-10684-6*) K G Saur.

R

Radke, Ellie, jt. auth. see O'Malley, Anne E.
Radke, Judith, tr. see Chedid, Andree.
Radke, Linda F. The Domestic Screening Kit. 31p. 1985. pap. 25.00 (0-9619853-0-5) Five Star AZ.
— The Economical Guide to Self-Publishing: How to Produce & Market Your Book on a Budget. Hawkins, Mary E., ed. 1995. pap. 19.95 (1-877749-16-8) Five Star AZ.
— Household Careers: Nannies, Butlers, Maids & More: The Complete Guide for Finding Household Employment or "If the Dog Likes You, You're Hired!" Hawkins, Mary E., ed. 1993. pap. 14.95 (1-877749-05-2) Five Star AZ.
— Nannies, Maids, & More: The Complete Guide for Hiring Household Help. Hawkins, Mary E., ed. LC 89-80249. (Illus.). 113p. 1989. pap. 14.95 (0-9619853-2-1) Five Star AZ.
— Options - A Directory of Child & Senior Services. 1987. pap. 6.00 (0-9619853-1-3) Five Star AZ.
— Options, Vol. II: A Directory of Child & Senior Services (Arizona Edition) 1989. pap. 9.95 (0-9619853-4-8) Five Star AZ.
— That Hungarian's in My Kitchen, One Hundred Twenty-Five Hungarian - American Recipes. Hawkins, Mary E., ed. 1990. pap. 9.95 (1-877749-01-X) Five Star AZ.
— That Hungarian's in My Kitchen, One Hundred Twenty-Five Hungarian - American Recipes. Hawkins, Mary E., ed. 179p. 1994. spiral bd. 12.50 (1-877749-02-8) Five Star AZ.
— That Hungarian's in My Kitchen, One Hundred Twenty-Five Hungarian - American Recipes. Hawkins, Mary E., ed. 179p. 1994. 24.95 (1-877749-10-9) Five Star AZ.
Radke, Martha E. The Cat Who Conducted with His Tail. LC 81-90803. (Illus.). 28p. (Orig.). (J). (ps-3). 1982. pap. 1.95 (0-9607994-0-0) G E Radke.
Radke, William J., jt. auth. see Chiasson, Robert B.
Radkevich, V., jt. auth. see Krapivnvi, A.
Radkey, Oliver H. Russia Goes to the Polls: The Election to the All-Russian Constituent Assembly, 1917. LC 89-42884. (Cornell Studies in Soviet History & Society - Studies of the Harriman Institute). 192p. 1989. 29.95 (0-8014-2360-0) Cornell U Pr.
Radko, Karren. Dreams & Wishes. 224p. (Orig.). 1993. pap. 2.95 (1-56597-070-5, Kismet) Meteor Pub.
Radl, Emanuel. The History of Biological Theories. 1988. reprint ed. lib. bdg. 75.00 (0-7812-0068-7) Rprt Serv.
— The History of Biological Theories. LC 30-28974. 498p. 1930. reprint ed. 69.00 (0-403-01791-2) Scholarly.
Radlanski, Ralf J. Contributions to the Development of Human Deciduous Tooth Primordia. LC 92-48439. 1993. pap. text ed. 58.00 (0-86715-261-3) Quint Pub Co.
Radlauer, Ed. Bears, Bears & More Bears. (Ed Radlauer Bks.). (Illus.). 32p. (J). (ps-4). 1991. lib. bdg. 10.95 (1-878363-34-4) Forest Hse.
— Cats, Cats, & More Cats. (Ed Radlauer Bks.). (Illus.). 32p. (J). 1991. lib. bdg. 10.95 (1-878363-35-2) Forest Hse.
— Wheels, Wheels, & More Wheels. (Ed Radlauer Bks.). (Illus.). 32p. (J). 1991. lib. bdg. 10.95 (1-878363-36-0) Forest Hse.
Radlauer, Edward. Shark Mania. (J). 1986. pap. 3.95 (0-516-47410-3) Childrens.
Radlauer, K., ed. see Fleishhacker, B., et al.
Radlauer, Ruth S. Breakfast by Molly. (J). (gr. k-3). 1991. pap. 2.25 (0-671-74021-0, Litl Simon S&S) S&S Childrens.
— Honor the Flag: A Guide to Its Care & Display. (United States & Its Flag Ser.). (Illus.). 48p. (J). (gr. 2 up). 1992. lib. bdg. 12.95 (1-878363-61-1, JC346) Forest Hse.
— Molly. (Illus.). (J). (gr. k-3). 1991. pap. 2.50 (0-671-74018-0, Litl Simon S&S) S&S Childrens.
— Molly at the Library. (Illus.). (J). (gr. k-3). 1991. pap. 2.25 (0-671-74019-9, Litl Simon S&S) S&S Childrens.
— Molly Goes Hiking. (Illus.). (J). (gr. k-3). 1991. pap. 2.25 (0-671-74022-9, Litl Simon S&S) S&S Childrens.
— Molly Goes Hiking. LC 86-18761. (Illus.). 32p. (J). (ps-3). 1987. pap. 10.95 (0-671-66860-9) S&S Trade.
Radlauer, Steven. Step-by-Step Keyboarding for the Personal Computer. 368p. 1984. pap. 9.95 (0-8120-2628-4); For IBM-PC, IBM-PCjr. disk 34.95 (0-8120-7200-6); For Commodore 64. disk 34.95 (0-8120-7198-0); For Apple IIe, Apple II, Apple II Plus. disk 34.95 (0-8120-7199-9) Barron.
Radler, Albert J. & Jacob, Friedhelm. German Transfer Pricing: German Guidelines, Translation & Comments; Prix de Transfert en Allemagne; les Instructions Allemandes, Traduction et Commentaire. LC 84-10066. (Series on International Taxation: No. 4). 1984. 60.00 (90-6544-143-3) Kluwer Law Tax Pubs.
Radler, Albert J., jt. tr. see Ajult, Hugh J.
Radler, Albert J., jt. tr. see Ault, Hugh J.
Radler, K-H., jt. auth. see Krause, F.
Radlett, Marty, jt. ed. see Mirsky, Judith.
Radley, Alan. The Body & Social Psychology. (Social Psychology Ser.). xi, 213p. 1991. 65.00 (0-387-97584-5) Spr-Verlag.
— In Social Relationships: An Introduction to the Social Psychology of Membership & Intimacy. 192p. 1991. 90.00 (0-335-15197-3, Open Univ Pr); pap. 32.00 (0-335-15196-5, Open Univ Pr) Taylor & Francis.
— Making Sense of Illness: The Social Psychology of Health & Disease. 256p. 1995. text ed. 65.00 (0-8039-8908-3); pap. text ed. 21.95 (0-8039-8909-1) Sage.
— Prospects of Heart Surgery. (Contributions to Psychology & Medicine Ser.). (Illus.). 250p. 1988. 87.00 (0-387-96721-4) Spr-Verlag.
Radley, Alan, ed. Worlds of Illness: Biographical & Cultural Perspectives on Health & Disease. LC 92-49154. (Illus.). 272p. 1993. 59.95x (0-415-06769-3, A9945) Routledge.
— Worlds of Illness: Biographical & Cultural Perspectives on Health & Disease. 1996. pap. write for info. (0-415-13152-9) Routledge.

Radley, Edward, jt. auth. see Dan, Uri.
Radley, Gail. The Golden Days. LC 92-19526. 160p. (J). (gr. 5 up). 1992. pap. 3.99 (0-14-036002-6) Puffin Bks.
— The Golden Days. LC 90-46935. 144p. (J). (gr. 3-7). 1991. text ed. 13.95 (0-02-775652-1, Mac Bks Young Read) S&S Childrens.
— Odd Man Out. LC 94-10858. (J). 1995. text ed. 13.95 (0-02-775792-7, Mac Bks Young Read) S&S Childrens.
— Special Strengths. (Illus.). 64p. (J). (gr. 2-6). 1984. pap. 6.50 (0-87743-702-5, Bellwood Pr) Bahai.
— The Spinner's Gift: A Tale. LC 94-25622. (Illus.). 32p. (J). (gr. k-3). 1994. 14.95 (1-55858-325-4); lib. bdg. 14.88 (1-55858-326-2) North-South Bks NYC.
Radley, J. A., ed. Examination & Analysis of Starch & Starch Products. (Illus.). 268p. 1976. 88.25 (0-85334-692-5, Pub. by Elsevier Applied Sci UK) Elsevier.
— Industrial Uses of Starch & Its Derivatives. 268p. 1976. 88.25 (0-85334-691-7, Pub. by Elsevier Applied Sci UK) Elsevier.
— Starch Production Technology. (Illus.). 287p. 1976. 167.50 (0-85334-662-3, Pub. by Elsevier Applied Sci UK) Elsevier.
Radley, Kenneth. Rebel Watchdog: The Confederate States Army Provost Guard. LC 88-30338. (Illus.). 392p. 1989. 29.95 (0-8071-1468-5) La State U Pr.
Radley, Philippe, tr. see Berberova, Nina.
Radley, Sheila. Blood on the Happy Highway. large type ed. 1985. 16.95 (0-7089-1316-4) Ulverscroft.
— Cross My Heart & Hope to Die: An Inspector Quantrill Mystery. (Quantrill Ser.: No. 8). 288p. 1992. text ed. 19.00 (0-684-19410-4, Scribners) S&S Trade.
— Fate Worse Than Death. large type ed. (Mystery Ser.). 432p. 1986. 16.95 (0-7089-1630-9) Ulverscroft.
Radley, Virginia L. Elizabeth Barrett Browning. (English Authors Ser.: No. 136). 160p. 1972. text ed. 21.95 (0-8057-1064-7, Pub. by Royal Botanic Garden UK) Macmillan.
— Samuel Taylor Coleridge. (English Authors Ser.: No. 36). 176p. 1967. text ed. 21.95 (0-8057-1100-7, Pub. by Royal Botanic Garden UK) Macmillan.
Radloff, Carla. Sentence Repetition Testing for Studies of Community Bilingualism. LC 91-68075. (Publications in Linguistics: No. 104). xvi, 214p. (Orig.). 1992. pap. 15.00 (0-88312-667-2) Summer Instit Ling.
— Sentence Repetition Testing for Studies of Community Bilingualism, Set 4. LC 91-68075. (Publications in Linguistics: No. 104). xvi, 214p. (Orig.). 1992. fiche 16.00 (0-88312-561-7) Summer Instit Ling.
Radloff, Roland & Helmreich, Robert. Groups under Stress: Psychological Research in Sealab 2. LC 68-19962. (Century Psychology Ser.). (Illus.). (C). 1968. 27.50 (0-89197-191-2) Irvington.
***Radlow, James.** Computers & the Information Society. 2nd ed. LC 94-27457. 608p. 1995. pap. text ed. 43.95 (0-534-23358-9) Boyd & Fraser.
Radmacher, Earl & Hodges, Zane C. The NIV Reconsidered: A Fresh Look at a Popular Translation. 155p. (Orig.). 1991. pap. 8.95 (0-9607576-9-4) Redencion Viva.
***Radmacher, Earl D.** You & Your Thoughts. Tso, Thomas & Huang, Tony, trs. 135p. (CHI.). 1981. pap. 3.50 (1-56582-093-2) Christ Renew Min.
Radmacher, Sally A., jt. auth. see Sheridan, Charles L.
Radman Associates Staff. The Radman Guide to the Ionising Radiations Regulations, 1985. (Handbook Ser.: No. 1). (C). 1986. 54.00 (0-948237-00-7, Pub. by H&H Sci Cnslts UK) St Mut.
***Radman, Zdravko, ed.** From a Metaphorical Point of View: A Multidisciplinary Approach to the Cognitive Content of Metaphor. LC 95-11399. (Philosophie & Wissenschaft-Transdisziplinaere Studien Ser.: Vol. 7). xi, 460p. (C). 1995. pap. text ed. 44.60 (3-11-014554-5) De Gruyter.
Radmore, P. M., jt. auth. see Stephenson, G.
Radnai, Rudolf & Kingham, Edward. Jone's Instrument Technology, Vol. 5: Automatic Instruments & Measuring Systems. (Illus.). 168p. 1986. pap. text ed. 52.95 (0-408-01532-2) Buttrwrth-Heinemann.
***Radnedge, Keir.** The Ultimate Encyclopedia of Soccer: The Definitive Illustrated Guide to World Soccer. LC 94-34097. (Illus.). 1995. write for info. (1-55958-702-4) Prima Pub.
Radner, Barbara, ed. see Nero, Ann B.
Radner, Daisie & Radner, Michael. Animal Consciousness. 253p. 1989. lib. bdg. 46.95 (0-87975-459-1) Prometheus Bks.
— Science & Unreason. 110p. (C). 1982. pap. 14.95 (0-534-01153-5) Intl Thomson.
***Radner, Ephraim & Reno, R. R., eds.** Inhabiting Unity: Theological Perspectives on the Proposed Lutheran-Episcopal Concordat. 230p. (Orig.). 1995. pap. 14.99 (0-8028-0815-8) Eerdmans.
Radner, Ephraim & Sumner, George R., eds. Reclaiming Faith: Essays on Orthodoxy in the Episcopal Church & the Baltimore Declaration. 296p. (Orig.). 1993. pap. 24.99 (0-8028-0677-5) Eerdmans.
Radner, Gilda. It's Always Something. 288p. 1990. mass mkt. 5.95 (0-380-71072-2) Avon.
Radner, Hilary. Shopping Around: Feminine Culture & the Pursuit of Pleasure. 224p. 1994. pap. 15.95 (0-415-90540-0, A6797, Routledge NY) Routledge.
— Shopping Around: Feminine Culture & the Pursuit of Pleasure. 224p. 1994. 55.00 (0-415-90539-7, A6793) Routledge.
Radner, Hilary, et al, eds. Film Theory Goes to the Movies: Cultural Analysis of Contemporary Film. (AFI Film Readers Ser.). 1992. 49.95 (0-415-90575-3, A7155, Routledge NY); pap. 15.95 (0-415-90576-1, A7159, Routledge NY) Routledge.

Radner, Joan N., ed. Feminist Messages: Coding in Women's Folk Culture. LC 92-15701. (Illus.). 344p. (C). 1993. 39.95 (0-252-01957-1); pap. 18.95 (0-252-06267-1) U of Ill Pr.
Radner, Joan N., jt. ed. see Owens, Coilin D.
Radner, Michael, jt. auth. see Radner, Daisie.
Radner, Roy, jt. auth. see Marschak, Jacob.
Radner, Roy, jt. ed. see McGuire, C. B.
Radnitzky, G. & Bernholz, Peter, eds. Das Okonomische Weltbild: Beitrage zu einer Neuen Politischen Okonomie. (International Carl Menger Library). 350p. (GER.). (C). 1991. 59.00 (3-88405-072-9) Philosophia Pr.
Radnitzky, Gerard, ed. Centripetal Forces in the Sciences, Vol. 2. LC 86-30389. 358p. 1989. 29.95 (0-89226-048-3, ICUS) Paragon Hse.
Radnitzky, Gerard & Anderson, Gunnar, eds. The Structure & Development of Science. (Boston Studies in the Philosophy of Science: No. 136). 1979. lib. bdg. 84.00 (90-277-0994-7) Kluwer Ac.
Radnitzky, Gerard & Bartley, W. W., III, eds. Evolutionary Epistemology, Rationality & the Sociology of Knowledge. LC 87-23589. 489p. 1987. pap. 22.95 (0-8126-9039-7) Open Court.
Radnitzky, Gerard & Bernholz, Peter, eds. Economic Imperialism: The Economic Method Applied Outside the Field of Economics. LC 86-12337. 421p. 1986. pap. 12.95 (0-943852-18-8) Paragon Hse.
***Radnitzky, Gerard & Bouillon, Hardy.** Value & Social Order: Society & Order, Vol. 2. 216p. 1995. 63.95 (1-85628-900-1, Pub. by Avebury Pub UK) Ashgate Pub Co.
— Value & Social Order: Values & Society, Vol. 1. 268p. 1995. 63.95 (1-85628-899-4, Pub. by Avebury Pub UK) Ashgate Pub Co.
Radnor, Hilary. Across the Curriculum. LC 93-42673. (Education Matters Ser.). 176p. 1994. 60.00 (0-304-32832-4) Cassell.
Radnoti, Miklos. Under Gemini: The Selected Poems of Miklos Radnoti with a Prose Memoir. Kessler, Jascha et al, trs. LC 83-23751. (Illus.). 108p. 1985. text ed. 20.00x (0-8214-0763-5); pap. text ed. 11.95x (0-8214-0764-3) Ohio U Pr.
***Rado, Erin H., ed.** The New Age Resources Directory. 225p. (Orig.). 1994. pap. 15.95 (1-886329-00-1) Goddess Pr.
Rado, Ivan J., ed. see Chooluck, Leon.
Rado, Lisa, intro. Rereading Modernism: New Directions in Feminist Criticism. LC 94-14784. (Reference Library of Humanities, Vol. 1677, Wellesley Studies in Critical Theory, Literary History & Culture: Vol. 4). 408p. 1994. 60.00 (0-8153-1189-3) Garland.
Rado, P. Introduction to the Technology of Pottery. 2nd ed. (Institute of Ceramics Textbook Ser.). (Illus.). 300p. 1988. pap. text ed. 37.00 (0-08-034930-7, Pergamon Pr) Elsevier.
Rado, Rudolf, jt. ed. see Romanov, A.
Rado, Sandor. Codename Dora. Underwood, J. A., tr. (Classics of World War II: The Secret War Ser.). (Illus.). 298p. 1990. reprint ed. write for info. (0-8094-8566-4); reprint ed. lib. bdg. write for info. (0-8094-8567-2) Time-Life.
***Rado, Sandor, et al, eds.** Adaptational Psychodynamics. LC 70-82528. 306p. 1995. reprint ed. pap. 27.50 (1-56821-505-3) Aronson.
Rado, Tibor. Length & Area. (American Mathematical Society, Colloquium Publications: Vol. 30). 579p. reprint ed. pap. 165.10 (0-317-08616-2, 2004936) Bks Demand.
Radocy, Rudolf E. & Boyle, J. David. Psychological Foundations of Musical Behavior. 2nd ed. (Illus.). 386p. (C). 1988. text ed. 56.95x (0-398-05514-9) C C Thomas.
Radocy, Rudolf E., jt. auth. see Boyle, David J.
***Radocy, Rudolf E., et al.** Psychological Foundations of Musical Behavior. 2nd ed. 386p. 1988. pap. 34.95 (0-398-06334-6) C C Thomas.
***Radoev, Ivan.** My Children Are Wards. Wilson, Don D., tr. 56p. (Orig.). 1994. pap. 7.50 (1-880286-32-7) Singular Speech Pr.
Radoff, Morris L., ed. see Land, Aubrey C. & Crowl, Phillip.
Radojcic, Svetozar. Geschichte der Serbischen Kunst von den Anfaengen bis zum Ende des Mittelalters. (Illus.). (GER.). (C). 1969. 86.95 (3-11-000267-1) De Gruyter.
Radojkovic, M., jt. ed. see Maksimovic, C.
Radok, J. R. M., ed. Problems of Continuum Mechanics. (Miscellaneous Bks.: No. 1). xx, 601p. 1961. text ed. 59.50 (0-89871-040-5) Soc Indus-Appl Math.
Radok, Rainer. Capes & Captains: An Anthology of the Australian Coast. 308p. (C). 1990. text ed. 79.00 (0-949324-28-0, Pub. by Surrey Beatty & Sons AT) St Mut.
***Radoll, Arrayyel.** Her Life with Herself. 1995. 14.95 (0-8062-5330-4) Carlton.
***Radom, Sandra.** Messages from the Journey. (Illus.). 81p. 1995. text ed. 24.95 (0-9645441-0-5) Pr of Journey.
Radomski, Mary V., jt. auth. see Dougherty, Pamela M.
***Radomsky, Nellie A.** Lost Voices: Women, Chronic Pain, & Abuse. LC 94-29611. 172p. 1995. lib. bdg. 29.95 (1-56024-921-8) Harrington Pk.
— Lost Voices: Women, Chronic Pain, & Abuse. LC 94-29611. 1995. pap. 12.95 (1-56023-864-X) Haworth Pr.
Radon, J. C. Fracture & Fatigue-Elasto-Plasticity, Thin Sheet & Micro-Mechanisms: Proceedings of the Third European Colloquium on Fracture, London, 8-10 September 1980. LC 80-40915. (Illus.). 450p. 1980. 200.00 (0-08-026161-2, Pub. by Pergamon Repr UK) Franklin.
Radon, Lisa. Now Hear This. 20p. (Orig.). 1994. pap. 3.00 (0-916397-36-X) Manic D Pr.

Rados, David L. Marketing for Non-Profit Organizations. LC 80-25948. (Illus.). 572p. (C). 1981. text ed. 49.95 (0-86569-055-3, Auburn Hse) Greenwood.
— Marketing for Nonprofit Organizations. 2nd ed. LC 95-13609. 1996. text ed. write for info. (0-86569-254-8, Auburn Hse) Greenwood.
— Pushing the Numbers in Marketing: A Real-World Guide to Essential Financial Analysis. LC 91-47643. 200p. 1992. text ed. 49.95 (0-89930-736-1, RPH, Quorum Bks) Greenwood.
Radosevich, G. E., et al. Evolution & Administration of Colorado Water Law: 1876-1976. LC 76-17952. 1976. reprint ed. 30.00 (0-918334-12-8) WRP.
Radosevich, H. R., jt. ed. see Kassicieh, S. K.
Radosevich, Steven R. & Holt, Jodie S. Weed Ecology: Implications for Vegetation Management. LC 83-23249. 265p. 1984. text ed. 79.95 (0-471-87674-7, Wiley-Interscience) Wiley.
Radostits, O. M., et al. Herd Health: Food, Animal, Production, Medicine. 2nd ed. LC 92-43548. (Illus.). 640p. 1993. text ed. 99.95 (0-7216-3655-1) Saunders.
Radouco-Thomas, C. & Garcin, F., eds. Progress in Neuropsychopharmacology, Vol. 4, No. 6. (Illus.). 110p. 1981. pap. 31.00 (0-08-027157-X, Pergamon Pr) Elsevier.
Radoui, Nicolas. My Journey. 544p. 1991. 22.95 (0-8187-0134-X) Harlo Press.
Radovanovic, D., jt. auth. see Reljic, L.
Radovanovic, M., ed. Fluidized Bed Combustion. (Proceedings of the International Center for Heat & Mass Transfer Ser.). 350p. (C). 1986. 110.00 (0-89116-409-X) Hemisp Pub.
Radovanovic, Milorad, ed. Yugoslav General Linguistics. LC 88-7614. (Linguistic & Literary Studies in Eastern Europe: Vol. 26). viii, 381p. (C). 1989. 148.00x (90-272-1531-6) Benjamins North Am.
Radovich, Milan & Rosenblatt, Judith, eds. Serbs in the United States & Canada: A Comprehensive Bibliography. 2nd enl. rev. ed. (Bibliography Ser.: No. 1). ix, 193p. 1992. 20.00 (0-932833-12-8) Immig His Res.
Radovsky, Frank J., et al, eds. Biogeography of the Tropical Pacific: Proceedings of a Symposium. (Illus.). 228p. 1984. 25.00 (0-942924-08-8); pap. 15.00 (0-942924-09-6) Assn Syst Coll.
Radspieler, A., tr. see Bardon, Franz.
Radstone, ed. Sweet Dreams: Sexuality, Gender & Popular Fiction. (C). 1988. pap. 19.95 (0-85315-672-7, Pub. by Lawrence & Wishart UK) Humanities.
Radstone, Susannah, jt. ed. see Kuhn, Annette.
Radszuweit, S. & Spalier, M. Kanurs Lexikon der Sinnverwandten Woerter. 560p. (GER.). 1982. 49.95 (0-8288-1981-5, F59970) Fr & Eur.
Radt, Wolfgang, jt. auth. see Nohlen, Klaus.
Radtchenko, Konstantiu. Developments in Soviet Metal Rolling. Gallant, Jonathan, ed. Squires, Elizabeth, tr. (Illus.). 125p. (Orig.). 1989. pap. text ed. 75.00 (1-55831-094-0) Delphic Associates.
Radtka, R., jt. auth. see Gunther, K.
Radtke, Becky. SunSational Bulletin Boards for Holidays & Special Occasions. (Illus.). 226p. 1992. student ed 13.95 (0-86653-685-X, 1419) Good Apple.
Radtke, Becky, jt. auth. see Whitacre, Deborah.
Radtke, Becky J. Easy Hidden Picture Coloring Book. (Illus.). (J). (gr. k-3). 1993. pap. 1.00 (0-486-27675-9) Dover.
Radtke, Bernd, jt. ed. see Thomassen, Einor.
Radtke, Dawn, jt. auth. see Morrison, Ruth.
Radtke, Dawn D., jt. auth. see Morrison, Ruth.
Radtke, G. A Step-by-Step Book about Budgerigars. (Step by Step Book about Ser.). (Illus.). 63p. (Orig.). 1987. pap. 3.95 (0-86622-463-7, SK-002) TFH Pubns.
Radtke, Georg A. Encyclopedia of Budgerigars. Friese, U. Erich, tr. 320p. 1981. 21.95 (0-86622-734-2, H-1027) TFH Pubns.
Radtke, George A. Budgerigars. Orig. Title: Wellensittiche-Mein Hobby. (Illus.). 1979. 9.95 (0-87666-984-4, KW-011) TFH Pubns.
Radtke, Kurt W. China's Relations with Japan, Nineteen Forty-Five to Nineteen Eighty-Three: The Role of Liao Chengzhi. LC 90-36569. (Studies on East Asia). 304p. 1990. text ed. 69.95 (0-7190-2795-0, Pub. by Manchester Univ Pr UK) St Martin.
Radtke, Kurt W. & Saich, Tony, eds. China's Modernisation: Westernisation & Acculturation. 202p. (Orig.). 1993. pap. 57.50 (3-515-06406-0) Coronet Bks.
Radtke, Lorraine & Stam, Henderikus J., eds. Power & Gender: Social Relations in Theory & Practice. 320p. (C). 1994. text ed. 49.95 (0-8039-8675-0); pap. text ed. 18.95 (0-8039-8674-2) Sage.
Radtke, Terry. The History of the Pennsylvania American Legion. (Illus.). 256p. 1993. 19.95 (0-8117-0818-7) Stackpole.
Radu, Michael. Eastern Europe & the Third World: East vs. South. LC 80-27494. 376p. 1981. text ed. 65.00 (0-275-90708-2, C0708, Praeger Pubs) Greenwood.
— The New Insurgencies: Anti-Communist Guerrillas in the Third World. 300p. 1990. 39.95 (0-88738-307-6) Transaction Pubs.
Radu, Michael, ed. Violence & the Latin American Revolutionaries. 246p. 1988. 34.95 (0-88738-195-2) Transaction Pubs.
Radu, Michael & Klinghoffer, Arthur J. The Dynamics of Soviet Policy in Sub-Saharan Africa. LC 89-34604. x, 160p. 1991. 22.50 (0-8419-1226-2) Holmes & Meier.
Radu, Michael, jt. auth. see Allen, Chris.
Radu, Michael, jt. ed. see Bissell, Richard E.
Radu, R. & Tismaneanu, V. Latin American Revolutionaries: Groups, Goals, Methods. 400p. 1989. 60.00 (0-08-037429-8) Brasseys Inc.
Radulescu, C., jt. auth. see Dinescu, T. A.

An Asterisk (*) at the beginning of an entry indicates that the title is appearing in BIP for the first time.

Radulescu, Domnica. Andre Malraux: The "Farfelu" As Expression of the Feminine & the Erotic. LC 93-23079. (American University Studies, II, Romance Language & Literature: Vol. 209). 216p. (C). 1994. text ed. 55.95 (0-8204-2296-7) P Lang Pubs.

Radulescu, Stella V. Blood & White Apples. LC 93-29557. 64p. 1993. pap. 12.95 (0-7734-2769-4, Mellen Poetry Pr) E Mellen.

Radulovic, Sigrid, ed. see Stafford, Peter.

Radunski, Peter, et al. West German Political Parties: CDU, CSU, FDP, SPD, the Greens. Livingston, Robert G. & Kielmannsegg, Peter G., eds. LC 86-73191. (German Issues Ser.: No. 4). 102p. 1986. pap. 7.50 (0-941441-00-8) Am Inst Contemp Ger Studies.

Raduta, A., ed. Symmetries & Semiclassical Features of Nuclear Dynamics. (Lecture Notes in Physics Ser.: Vol. 279). 1987. 46.00 (0-387-17926-7) Spr-Verlag.

Raduta, A. A., et al. New Trends in Theoretical & Experimental Nuclear Physics: Predeal International Summer School. 600p. 1992. text ed. 106.00 (981-02-0906-1) World Scientific Pub.

Radvany, Ruth, et al. Intermediate Algebra Study Aid. (J). 1974. pap. 2.50 (0-87738-038-4) Youth Ed.

Radvanyi, Janos. Psychological Operations & Political Warfare in Long-Term Strategic Planning. LC 90-31183. 168p. 1990. text ed. 45.00 (0-275-93623-6, C3623, Praeger Pubs) Greenwood.

Radvanyi, Janos, ed. The Pacific in the Nineteen Nineties: Economic & Strategic Change. 166p. (C). 1990. lib. bdg. 47.50 (0-8191-7900-0); pap. text ed. 22.50 (0-8191-7901-9) U Pr of Amer.

Radwan, Samir, jt. auth. see Hansen, Bent.

Radwan, Samir, jt. ed. see Mafeje, Archie.

Radwan, Samir, et al. Tunisia: Rural Labour & Structural Transformation. 128p. 1991. 65.00 (0-415-04274-7, A4710) Routledge.

Radwanski, George & Luttrell, Julia. The Will of a Nation: Awakening the Canadian Spirit. 208p. 1992. 22.95 (0-7737-2637-3, Pub. by Stoddart Pubng CN) Genl Dist Srvs.

Radway, Janice, jt. ed. see Grossberg, Lawrence.

Radway, Janice, jt. ed. see Moi, Toril.

Radway, Janice A. Reading the Romance: Women, Patriarchy & Popular Literature. 2nd ed. LC 91-50284. x, 296p. (C). 1991. reprint ed. pap. 11.95 (0-8078-4349-0) U of NC Pr.

Radway, Jerrold E., ed. Corrosion & Deposits from Combustion Gases: Abstracts & Index. LC 66-52838. 575p. 1985. 136.00 (0-89116-301-8) Hemisp Pub.

Radwin, George E. & D'Attilio, Anthony. Murex Shells of the World: An Illustrated Guide to the Muricidae. LC 75-7485. (Illus.). 111p. reprint ed. pap. 30.00 (0-7837-2164-1, 2042470) Bks Demand.

Rady, Martin. Romania in Turmoil. 256p. 1992. pap. text ed. 22.50 (1-85043-500-6, Pub. by I B Tauris UK) St Martin.

***Rady, Martyn.** Collapse of Communism in Eastern Europe. LC 95-11728. (Causes & Consequences Ser.). 1995. write for info. (0-8172-4052-7) Raintree Steck-V.

Rady, Martyn, jt. ed. see Duncan, Peter J.

Rady, Martyn C. Medieval Buda. 1985. text ed. 51.00 (0-88033-074-0) East Eur Quarterly.

Rady, Virginia B., jt. auth. see Swanson, Faith H.

Radyke, George A. Lovebirds: A Complete Introduction. (Complete Introduction to...Ser.). (Illus.). 128p. (Orig.). 1987. pap. 5.95 (0-86622-382-7, CO-030S) TFH Pubns.

Radzialowski, Frederick M., ed. Hypertension Research: Methods & Models. LC 81-17462. (Modern Pharmacology-Toxicology Ser.: No. 19). (Illus.). 464p. reprint ed. pap. 132.30 (0-7837-0757-6, 2041071) Bks Demand.

Radziemski & Cremers. Lasers-Induced Plasmas & Applications. (Optical Engineering Ser.: Vol. 21). 464p. 1989. 140.00 (0-8247-8078-7) Dekker.

Radzig, A. A. & Smirnov, B. M. Reference Data on Atoms, Molecules & Ions. (Chemical Physics Ser.: Vol. 31). (Illus.). 430p. 1985. 99.00 (0-387-12415-2) Spr-Verlag.

Radzik, Adam & Emek, Sharon. Answers for Managers. LC 90-55207. 240p. (Orig.). 1990. pap. 16.95 (0-8144-7744-5) AMACOM.

Radzik-Marsh, Kelly & Strutchens, Marilyn, eds. Multicultural Education: Inclusion of All. (Illus.). 298p. (Orig.). Date not set. pap. write for info. (0-9624818-2-3) U GA Coll Ed.

Radzilowski, John. Out on the Winds: Poles & Danes in Lincoln County, Minnesota, 1880-1905. (Illus.). 128p. 1992. pap. 11.95 (0-9614119-4-5) Crossings Pr.

Radzilowski, Thaddeus C. Feudalism, Revolution, & the Meaning of Russian History: An Intellectual Biography of N.P. Pavlov-Silvanskii. 320p. (C). 1993. text ed. 45.00 (0-88033-258-1, 361) Col U Pr.

Radzinowicz, Mary Ann, ed. see Milton, John.

Radzinowicz, L., ed. see Odgers, F. J. & McClintock, F. H.

Radzinowicz, Leon & Hood, Roger G. Criminology & the Administration of Criminal Justice: A Bibliography. LC 76-24998. 400p. (Orig.). 1977. text ed. 49.95 (0-8371-9068-1, RCA/, Greenwood Pr) Greenwood.

— A History of English Law & Its Administration from Seventeen Fifty: The Emergence of Penal Policy, Vol. 5: Victorian & Edwardian England. 864p. 1991. pap. 48.00 (0-19-825663-9) OUP.

Radzinowicz, Leon, ed. see Levi, Michael.

Radzinowicz, Mary A. Milton's Epics & the Book of Psalms. 256p. (C). 1989. text ed. 39.50 (0-691-06759-7) Princeton U Pr.

— Toward Samson Agonistes: The Growth of Milton's Mind. LC 77-85559. (Illus.). 461p. 1978. reprint ed. pap. 131.40 (0-7837-8180-6, 2047885) Bks Demand.

Radzinski, Kandy, illus. The Twelve Cats of Christmas. 32p. (J). 1992. 9.95 (0-8118-0102-0) Chronicle Bks.

Radzinsky, Edvard. The Last Tsar: The Life & Death of Nicholas II. large type ed. Schwartz, Marian, tr. LC 93-6618. (General Ser.). (ENG & RUS.). 1993. Alk. paper. 25.95 (0-8161-5770-7) G K Hall.

— The Last Tsar: The Life & Death of Nicholas II. Schwartz, Marian, tr. LC 93-16757. 1993. reprint ed. pap. 14.95 (0-385-46962-4, Anchor NY) Doubleday.

Radziunas, Eileen. Lupus: My Search for a Diagnosis. LC 89-24683. 144p. 1989. pap. 6.95 (0-89793-065-7) Hunter Hse.

— Lupus: My Search for a Diagnosis. 128p. (C). 1989. reprint ed. lib. bdg. 23.00x (0-8095-6313-4) Borgo Pr.

Rae, A., ed. Agricultural Management Economics: Activity Analysis & Decision Making. 358p. 1994. pap. 41.50 (0-85198-768-0) CAB Intl.

Rae, A. I. Quantum Mechanics. 3rd ed. (Illus.). 262p. 1992. pap. 27.00 (0-7503-0217-8) IOP Pub.

Rae, Alastair. Quantum Physics: Illusion or Reality? (Canto Book Ser.). (Illus.). 133p. (C). 1994. pap. 8.95 (0-521-46716-0) Cambridge U Pr.

Rae, Alexander C., jt. auth. see Owens, P. J.

***Rae, Andrew, et al, eds.** Software Evaluation for Certification: Principles, Practice, & Legal Liability. LC 94-29412. (Software Assurance Ser.). 1994. write for info. (0-07-709042-X) McGraw.

Rae, Barbara. Destiny in Doubt. 1994. pap. 7.95 (1-56901-143-5) NW Pub.

Rae, Carlos. Short Stories of Carlos Rae. (Petites Major Ser.). 56p. 1993. pap. 4.00 (1-884754-04-X) Potpourri Pubns.

Rae, Catherine M. Afterward. large type ed. LC 92-11681. 273p. 1992. reprint ed. lib. bdg. 19.95 (1-56054-422-8) Thorndike Pr.

— Brownstone Facade. large type ed. 240p. 1990. reprint ed. lib. bdg. 16.95 (1-56054-027-3) Thorndike Pr.

— Flight from Fifth Avenue. LC 94-37517. 1995. 18.95 (0-312-11788-4) St Martin.

— Flight from Fifth Avenue. large type ed. LC 95-14547. 291p. 1995. reprint ed. 19.95 (0-7862-0493-1) Thorndike Pr.

— Sarah Cobb. large type ed. LC 90-29874. 267p. 1991. reprint ed. lib. bdg. 17.95 (1-56054-125-3) Thorndike Pr.

— The Ship's Clock. 192p. 1993. 17.95 (0-312-09386-1) St Martin.

— The Ship's Clock: A Family Chronicle. large type ed. LC 93-22972. 1993. pap. 19.95 (0-7862-0000-6) Thorndike Pr.

Rae, Charles B. The Music of Lutoslawski. (Illus.). 256p. 1995. 39.95 (0-571-16450-1) Faber & Faber.

Rae, Cheri. East Mojave Desert: A Visitor's Guide. (Illus.). 208p. 1992. pap. 10.95 (0-934161-06-2) Olympus Pr.

Rae, Cheri, ed. Death Valley: The 1938 WPA Guide Updated for Today's Traveler. rev. ed. Orig. Title: Death Valley. (Illus.). 160p. reprint ed. pap. 10.95 (0-934161-08-9) Olympus Pr.

Rae, Cheri & McKinney, John. Walk Santa Barbara: City Strolls & Country Rambles. (Illus.). 176p. (Orig.). 1990. pap. 10.95 (0-934161-06-2) Olympus Pr.

Rae, Cheri, ed. see McKinney, John C.

Rae, Cheri, ed. see McKinney, John.

Rae, Cheri, jt. auth. see McKinney, John.

Rae, Cheri, ed. see WPA of Northern California, Federal Writers' Project Staff.

***Rae, Colleen M.** Movies in the Mind: How to Build a Short Story. (Illus.). 160p. (Orig.). 1995. pap. text ed. 19.95 (1-880382-01-6) A Pr of Ones.

— Perchance to Dream. 121p. (Orig.). 1992. pap. 7.95 (1-880382-00-8) A Pr of Ones.

— Trophies in the Line of Duty: Essays, Columns & Occasional Letters. 128p. (Orig.). 1995. pap. 7.95 (1-880382-02-4) A Pr of Ones.

Rae, Douglas. Equalities. LC 81-4157. (Illus.). 224p. (C). 1981. 32.00 (0-674-25980-7) HUP.

— Equalities. 224p. 1983. pap. 13.50 (0-674-25981-5) HUP.

Rae, E. The Country of the Moors. 368p. 1985. 250.00 (1-85077-030-1, Darf Pubs Ltd) St Mut.

Rae, Eleanor. Women, the Earth, the Divine. LC 93-47614. (Ecology & Justice Ser.). 150p. (Orig.). 1994. pap. 14.95 (0-88344-952-8) Orbis Bks.

Rae, Eleanor, jt. auth. see Marie-Daly, Bernice.

Rae-Ellis, Vivienne. Black Robinson: Protector of Aborigines. (Illus.). 308p. 1988. 39.95 (0-522-84346-8) Intl Spec Bk.

Rae-Ellis, Vivienne, ed. True Ghost Stories of Our Own Time. 265p. (Orig.). 1991. pap. 10.95 (0-571-14273-7) Faber & Faber.

Rae, Gwenneth, jt. auth. see Cohen, Stewart.

Rae, John. Life of Adam Smith. LC 63-23522. (Reprints of Economic Classics Ser.). xv, 449p. 1965. reprint ed. 57.50 (0-678-00101-4) Kelley.

— Statement of Some New Principles on the Subject of Political Economy: Exposing the Fallacies of the System of Free Trade. LC 65-10366. xvi, 414p. 1964. 45.00 (0-678-00065-4) Kelley.

Rae, John & Volti, Rudi. The Engineer in History. LC 93-22895. (Worcester Polytechnic Institute Studies in Science, Technology, & Culture: Vol. 14). 268p. (C). 1994. text ed. 49.95 (0-8204-2062-X) P Lang Pubs.

Rae, John, jt. ed. see Moss, Scott.

Rae, John B. The American Automobile Industry. LC 84-6744. (Evolution of American Business: Industries, Institutions, & Entrepreneurs Ser.). 1985. lib. bdg. 22.95 (0-8057-9803-X, Twayne); pap. 14.95 (0-8057-9808-0, Twayne) Macmillan.

— Development of Railway Land Subsidy in the United States. Bouchey, Stuart, ed. LC 78-53564. (Development of Public Land Law in the U. S. Ser.). 1979. lib. bdg. 26.95 (0-405-11366-8) Ayer.

Rae, Judy. Bye, Bye Boogieman. rev. ed. LC 83-70412. (Illus.). 42p. (Orig.). (J). (ps-3). 1984. pap. 3.95 (0-939728-09-5) Steppingstone Ent.

Rae, Leila, ed. see Christiansen, L. A., et al.

Rae, Leslie. Assessing Trainer Effectiveness. 342p. 1991. 74.95 (0-566-07264-5, Pub. by Gower UK) Ashgate Pub Co.

— Evaluating Trainer Effectiveness. LC 92-37513. 300p. 1993. 35.00 (1-55623-881-9) Irwin Prof Pubng.

— Fifty Activities for Developing Management Skills, Vol. 1. 352p. 1988. ring bd. 139.95 (0-566-02768-2, Pub. by Gower UK) Ashgate Pub Co.

— Let's Have a Meeting: A Comprehensive Guide to Making Your Meetings Work. LC 93-43264. 1994. 19.95 (0-07-707628-1) McGraw.

— Meetings Management: A Manual of Effective Training Material. LC 92-46124. (McGraw-Hill Training Ser.). 1993. 75.00 (0-07-707782-2) McGraw.

— The Skills of Interviewing: A Guide for Managers & Trainers. 222p. 1989. pap. text ed. 15.95 (0-7045-0620-3, Pub. by Gower UK) Ashgate Pub Co.

— Skills of Training. 2nd ed. 220p. 1990. text ed. 49.95 (0-566-02902-2, Pub. by Gower UK) Ashgate Pub Co.

— Techniques of Training. 3rd rev. ed. LC 94-47426. 1995. pap. write for info. (0-566-07629-2, Pub. by Gower UK) Ashgate Pub Co.

— Techniques of Training: A Guide for Managers & Practitioners. 304p. 1993. pap. 19.95 (0-566-07432-X, Pub. by Gower UK) Ashgate Pub Co.

Rae, Maggie, jt. auth. see Goodman, Leo.

Rae, Maggie, et al. First Rights: New Edition. 1986. 40.00 (0-946088-15-2, Pub. by NCCL UK) St Mut.

Rae, Malcolm, jt. auth. see Tansley, David V.

Rae, Mary, tr. St. John of the Cross: Selected Poems. LC 90-19808. 94p. (C). 1991. text ed. 14.95 (0-89341-644-4, Longwood Academic) Hollowbrook.

Rae, Mary M. Over in the Meadow: A Counting-Out Rhyme. (Picture Puffins Ser.). (Illus.). 32p. (J). (ps-00). 1986. pap. 3.95 (0-685-14199-3, Penguin Bks) Viking Penguin.

Rae, Michelle, ed. see Hartonczyk, William & Hartonszyk, Christina G.

Rae, Murray, et al, eds. Science & Theology: Questions at the Interface. LC 94-12331. 272p. (Orig.). 1994. pap. 29.99 (0-8028-0816-6) Eerdmans.

Rae, Nicol C. The Decline & Fall of the Liberal Republicans: From 1952 to the Present. 288p. 1989. 39.95 (0-19-505605-1) OUP.

— Southern Democrats. LC 93-32876. 224p. 1994. 39.95 (0-19-508708-9); pap. 14.95 (0-19-508709-7) OUP.

Rae, Norm, ed. see Birchard, John.

Rae, Norman, ed. see Baldwin, Edward A.

Rae, Norman, ed. see Lang, Susan.

Rae, Norman, ed. see Williams, Greg.

Rae, Patricia. Charge Nurse. (Orig.). 1982. pap. 2.95 (0-8217-1044-3) Zebra.

— Emergency Nurse. (Orig.). 1982. pap. 2.95 (0-8217-1045-1) Zebra.

— Maternity Nurse. (Orig.). 1983. pap. 2.95 (0-8217-1221-7) Zebra.

— Storm Tide. 1983. pap. 3.75 (0-685-07867-1) Zebra.

— Student Nurse. 1983. pap. 2.95 (0-8217-1123-7) Zebra.

— To Suffer in Silence. 1981. pap. 2.75 (0-89083-748-1) Zebra.

— The Touch. 448p. (Orig.). 1985. pap. 3.75 (0-8439-2187-0) Dorchester Pub Co.

— Trauma Nurse. (Orig.). 1982. pap. 2.95 (0-8217-1036-2) Zebra.

— Ways of the Wind. 1984. pap. 3.75 (0-8217-1456-2) Zebra.

Rae, Robert W. Into Thy Hands. (Visitation Pamphlet Ser.). 1988. pap. 1.95 (0-8361-3483-4) Herald Pr.

Rae, Saul F., jt. auth. see Gallup, George H.

Rae, Scott B. The Ethics of Commercial Surrogate Motherhood: Brave New Families? LC 93-17667. 200p. 1993. text ed. 49.95 (0-275-94679-7, Praeger Pubs) Greenwood.

Rae, Simon. Dorset of One Hundred Years Ago. (One Hundred Years Ago Ser.). (Illus.). 1993. 36.00 (0-7509-0263-9) A Sutton Pub.

Rae, Simon, ed. The Faber Book of Drink, Drinkers, & Drinking. 400p. 1992. 24.95 (0-571-16229-0) Faber & Faber.

— The Faber Book of Drink, Drinkers & Drinking. 554p. 1993. pap. 14.95 (0-571-16821-3) Faber & Faber.

— The Faber Book of Murder. 516p. 1994. 24.95 (0-571-16752-7) Faber & Faber.

— Faber Book of Murder. 592p. 1995. reprint ed. pap. 15.95 (0-571-17494-9) Faber & Faber.

Rae, Simon & Rushton, Willie. Soft Targets. 1991. pap. 15.95 (1-85224-165-9) Dufour.

Rae, Wesley D. Thomas Lodge. LC 67-25185. (Twayne's English Authors Ser.). 1967. lib. bdg. 17.95 (0-89197-964-6); pap. text ed. 5.95 (0-8290-2007-1) Irvington.

Rae, William. Edinburgh New Official Guide: Scotland's Capital City. (Illus.). 176p. 1994. pap. 9.95 (1-85158-605-9, Pub. by Mnstream UK) Trafalgar.

Rae, William F. Westward by Rail: The New Route to the East. LC 72-9465. (Far Western Frontier Ser.). 412p. 1973. reprint ed. 25.95 (0-405-04993-5) Ayer.

Rae, William H. & Pope, Alan, Jr. Low-Speed Wind Tunnel Testing. 2nd ed. LC 84-3700. 534p. 1984. text ed. 99.95 (0-471-87402-7, Wiley-Interscience) Wiley.

Raebeck, Barry. Transforming Middle Schools: A Guide to Whole-School Change. LC 92-64255. 180p. 1992. pap. text ed. 35.00 (0-87762-958-7) Technomic.

Raebeck, Lois & Wheeler, Lawrence. New Approaches to Music in the Elementary School. 4th ed. 432p. 1980. pap. write for info. (0-697-03421-6) Brown & Benchmark.

Raeber, John A. Clear Water Repellent Treatments for Concrete Masonry. 62p. 1993. pap. 10.00 (0-940116-25-1) Masonry Inst Am.

Raeburn, Ben, ed. Treasury for the Free World. LC 72-5771. (Essay Index Reprint Ser.). 1977. reprint ed. 27.95 (0-8369-7293-7) Ayer.

Raeburn, Ben, ed. see Green, Aaron G. & DeNevi, Donald P.

Raeburn, Ben, jt. ed. see Kaufman, Edgar.

***Raeburn, D. & Giembycz, M. A.** Airways Smooth Muscle: Structure, Innervation & Neurotransmission. (Respiratory Pharmacology & Pharmacotherapy Ser.). 336p. 1994. 149.00 (0-8176-5010-5) Spr-Verlag.

Raeburn, D. & Giembycz, M. A., eds. Airways Smooth Muscle: Development, & Regulation of Contractility. LC 94-8800. (Respiratory Pharmacology & Pharmacotherapy Ser.). 1994. 169.00 (0-8176-5011-3, Pub. by Birkhauser Vlg SZ) Birkhauser.

— Airways Smooth Muscle: Peptide Receptors, Ion Channels & Signal Transduction. LC 94-48621. (Respiratory Pharmacology & Pharmacotherapy Ser.). 1995. write for info. (0-8176-5140-3) Birkhauser.

Raeburn, David & Giembycz, Mark A., eds. Airways Smooth Muscle: Biochemical Control of Contraction & Relaxation. LC 94-20775. (Respiratory Pharmacology & Pharmacotherapy Ser.). viii, 351p. 1994. text ed. 159.00 (0-8176-5043-1) Birkhauser.

Raeburn, H. A., jt. auth. see Raeburn, Janet K.

***Raeburn, J. R.** Agriculture: Foundations, Principles & Development. fac. ed. LC 84-3619. 345p. 1984. reprint ed. pap. 98.40 (0-7837-8270-5, 2049051) Bks Demand.

Raeburn, Janet K. & Raeburn, H. A. Anatomy, Physiology & Hygiene. 4th ed. 1975. pap. text ed. 7.95 (0-7195-3213-2) Transatl Arts.

Raeburn, John. Fame Became of Him: Hemingway as Public Writer. LC 83-48831. 248p. 1984. 25.00 (0-253-12690-8) Ind U Pr.

Raeburn, Michael & Kendall, Alan, eds. Heritage of Music: Classical Music & Its Origins, Vol. I. (Illus.). 322p. 1992. 60.00 (0-19-505370-2) OUP.

— Heritage of Music: Classical Music & Its Origins; The Romantic Era; The 19th Century Legacy; Music in the 20th Century, 4 vols., Set. LC 85-21429. (Illus.). 1294p. 1989. 225.00 (0-19-520493-X) OUP.

— Heritage of Music: Music in the Twentieth Century, Vol. IV. (Illus.). 322p. 1992. 60.00 (0-19-505373-7) OUP.

— Heritage of Music: The Nineteenth-Century Legacy, Vol. III. (Illus.). 322p. 1992. 60.00 (0-19-505372-9) OUP.

— Heritage of Music: The Romantic Era, Vol. II. (Illus.). 322p. 1992. 60.00 (0-19-505371-0) OUP.

Raeburn, Michael, jt. auth. see Whitfield, Sarah.

Raeburn, Nancy. Mykonos: A Memoir. 1992. pap. 9.95 (0-89823-131-0) New Rivers Pr.

***Raeburn, Paul.** The Last Harvest: The Genetic Gamble that Threatens to Destroy American Agriculture. 1995. 24.00 (0-684-80365-8) S&S Trade.

***Raeburn, Richard, et al.** Organising & Controlling Your Treasury. 240p. 1994. 120.00 (0-273-60028-1, Pub. by Pitman Pubng UK) St Mut.

***Raedels, Alan R.** Value-Focused Supply Management: Getting the Most out of the Supply Function. LC 94-24842. (NAPM Professional Development Ser.: 3). 192p. 1994. 45.00 (0-7863-0237-2) Irwin Prof Pubng.

Raeder, Erich. My Life. Drexel, Henry W., tr. LC 79-6121. (Navies & Men Ser.). (Illus.). 1980. reprint ed. lib. bdg. 44.95 (0-405-13075-9) Ayer.

Raeder, Hans. Platons' Philosophische Entwicklung. LC 75-13288. (History of Ideas in Ancient Greece Ser.). (GER.). 1976. reprint ed. 29.95 (0-405-07331-3) Ayer.

Raeder, Jurgen, et al. Controlled Nuclear Fusion: Fundamentals of Its Utilization for Energy Supply. LC 85-12384. (Wiley-Interscience Publication Ser.). 328p. reprint ed. pap. 93.50 (0-7837-4519-2, 2044298) Bks Demand.

Raedle, Fidel, ed. Lateinische Ordensdramen Des XV-XVIII: Jahrhunderts mit deutschen Uebersetzungen. (Ausgaben Deutscher Literatur des XV bis XVIII Jahrhunderts Ser.). (C). 1979. 484.65 (3-11-003383-6) De Gruyter.

Raedler, A. & Raedler, E. Modulation von Zelloberflaechenstrukturen. (Bibliotheca Anatomica Ser.: No. 25). (Illus.). vi, 82p. 1984. 38.50 (3-8055-3755-7) S Karger.

Raedler, E., jt. auth. see Raedler, A.

Raedt, Luc, jt. ed. see Bergadano, Francesco.

Raeff, Marc. Michael Speransky: Statesman of Imperial Russia, 1772 to 1839. LC 78-59037. 1990. reprint ed. 36.00 (0-88355-709-6) Hyperion Conn.

— Origins of the Russian Intelligensia: The Eighteenth-Century Nobility. LC 66-19152. 256p. (Orig.). 1966. pap. 9.95 (0-15-670150-2, Harvest Bks) HarBrace.

— Political Ideas & Institutions in Imperial Russia. 404p. 1994. text ed. 49.95 (0-8133-1878-5) Westview.

— Understanding Imperial Russia: State & Society in the Old Regime. Goldhammer, Arthur, tr. LC 83-26241. 240p. 1986. pap. text ed. 16.00 (0-231-05843-8) Col U Pr.

Raeff, Marc, ed. Peter the Great Changes Russia. 2nd ed. (Problems in European Civilization Ser.). 228p. 1972. pap. text ed. 8.50 (0-669-82701-0) Heath.

— Russian Intellectual History: An Anthology. 416p. (C). 1978. reprint ed. pap. 25.00 (0-391-00905-2) Humanities.

Raeithel, Gert. Awful America: A Dictionary of 200 Years of European Abuse. Aman, Reinhold, ed. Zohn, Harry, tr. LC 76-5698. (Maledicta Press Publications Ser.: Vol.7). Date not set. 15.00 (0-916500-07-1) Maledicta.

Raekel, Hans-Herbert S. Die Musikalische Erscheinungsform der Trouverepoesie. 391p. 1977. pap. 35.00 (3-258-01149-4) Theodore Front.

Rael. Beautiful Painted Arrow. 1992. pap. 12.95 (1-85230-310-7) Element MA.

R

An Asterisk (*) at the beginning of an entry indicates that the title is appearing in BIP for the first time.

Rael, Elsa O. Marushka's Egg. LC 92-303. (Illus.). 40p. (J). (gr. k-4). 1993. text ed. 14.95 (*0-02-775655-6*, Four Winds Pr) S&S Childrens.

Rael, Joseph. Being & Vibration. LC 92-72320. (Illus.). 185p. 1993. pap. 14.95 (*0-933031-72-6*) Coun Oak Bks.

— Native American Teachings. 1994. audio 14.95 (*0-933031-95-5*) Coun Oak Bks.

Rael, Joseph E. & Sutton, Lindsay. Tracks of Dancing Light: A Native American Approach to Understanding Your Name. LC 93-41375. (Earth Quest Ser.). 1994. pap. 12.95 (*1-85230-434-0*) Element MA.

Rael, Juan B. Cuentos Espanoles De Colorado y Nuevo Mejico: Spanish Tales from Colorado & New Mexico, 2 vols., 1. Dorson, Richard M., ed. LC 77-70617. (International Folklore Ser.). 1977. lib. bdg. 58.95 (*0-405-10120-1*) Ayer.

— Cuentos Espanoles De Colorado y Nuevo Mejico: Spanish Tales from Colorado & New Mexico, 2 vols., 2. Dorson, Richard M., ed. LC 77-70617. (International Folklore Ser.). 1977. lib. bdg. 58.95 (*0-405-10121-X*) Ayer.

— Cuentos Espanoles De Colorado y Nuevo Mejico: Spanish Tales from Colorado & New Mexico, 2 vols., Set. Dorson, Richard M., ed. LC 77-70617. (International Folklore Ser.). 1977. lib. bdg. 116.95 (*0-405-10119-8*) Ayer.

Rael, Juan B., jt. auth. see Tully, Marjorie F.

Rael, Leyla & Rudhyar, Dane. Astrological Aspects. 244p. 1980. pap. 14.00 (*0-943358-00-0*) Aurora Press.

Raelin, Joseph A. Building a Career: The Effect of Initial Job Experiences & Related Work Attitudes on Later Employment. LC 80-24848. 178p. 1980. pap. 4.00 (*0-911558-73-X*) W E Upjohn.

— The Clash of Cultures: Managers Managing Professionals. 274p. 1991. pap. 12.95 (*0-87584-305-0*) Harvard Busn.

— The Clash of Cultures: Managers Managing Professionals. 1992. pap. text ed. 12.95 (*0-07-103316-5*) McGraw.

— The Salaried Professional: How to Make the Most of Your Career. LC 83-24796. 304p. 1984. text ed. 65.00 (*0-275-91246-9*, C1246, Praeger Pubs) Greenwood.

Raelin, Joseph A., ed. The Clash of Cultures Industries. 1986. text ed. 29.95 (*0-07-103264-9*) McGraw.

Raelson, Jeffrey. Getting to Know German Wines. (Illus.). 80p. pap. 4.95 (*0-916224-45-7*) Banyan Bks.

Raemsch, Dorothy C. House of Light: Poems. 32p. (Orig.). 1990. pap. 5.00 (*0-9605398-1-6*) D C Raemsch.

— October Dawn: Poems. 32p. (Orig.). 1980. pap. 5.00 (*0-9605398-0-8*) D C Raemsch.

— Spinning with Gold: Poems for Young & Old. (Illus.). 32p. (J). 1991. pap. 7.50 (*0-9605398-2-4*) D C Raemsch.

— Three Poems by W. H. Davies: Song Set. (Illus.). 12p. (Orig.). 1994. pap. 4.00 (*0-9605398-3-2*) D C Raemsch.

Raeper, William, ed. The Gold Thread: Essays on George MacDonald. 220p. 1990. 39.00 (*0-7486-0166-X*, Pub. by Edinburgh U Pr UK) Col U Pr.

— The Gold Thread: Essays on George MacDonald. 224p. 1992. pap. 25.00 (*0-7486-0208-9*, Pub. by Edinburgh U Pr UK) Col U Pr.

Raes, S., jt. ed. see Lemmens, P.

Raeschild, Sheila. Lessons in Leaving. 1974. pap. 2.50 (*0-912786-30-2*) Know Inc.

Raescild, Sheila. Trolley Song. (Orig.). 1981. pap. 3.50 (*0-89083-889-5*) Zebra.

Raese, Jon & Goldberg, J. H., eds. Algal Limestones Within the Minturn Formation, Meeker to Dotsero Area, Western Colorado. (Colorado School of Mines Quarterly Ser.: Vol. 78, No. 2). (Illus.). 14p. 1983. pap. 10.00 (*0-686-45171-6*) Colo Sch Mines.

Raese, Jon, ed. see Weimer, R. J., et al.

Raese, Jon W., ed. Oil Shale Symposium Proceedings Index 1964-82. LC 82-19839. 110p. 1982. pap. text ed. 30.00 (*0-918062-52-7*) Colo Sch Mines.

Raese, Jon W., ed. see Agapito, J. F.

Raese, Jon W., ed. see Blackstone, Sandra L.

Raese, Jon W., ed. see Bugbee, Edward E.

Raese, Jon W., ed. see Clark, George B.

Raese, Jon W., ed. see Huber, G. C.

Raese, Jon W., ed. see Li Itunda Yenge.

Raese, Jon W., ed. see McCalpin, James P.

Raese, Jon W., ed. see Parker, Joni M. & Maurer, Ruth A.

Raese, Jon W., ed. see Sonnenberg, Stephen A., et al.

Raese, Jon W., ed. see Wayman, Cooper H. & Genasci, Gail A.

Raese, Jon W., ed. see Willard, Beatrice L.

Raese, Jon W., ed. see Yenge, Li I.

Raeside, Fiona, ed. see Walker, Eric.

Raeside, Ian. Gadyaraja: A Fourteenth Marathi Version of the KRSNA Legend. (C). 1989. 49.50 (*0-7286-0108-7*, Pub. by Sch Orient & African Stud UK) S Asia.

Raess, B. U. & Tunnicliff, G., eds. The Red Cell Membrane: A Model for Solute Transport. LC 89-15438. (Contemporary Biomedicine Ser.). (Illus.). 496p. 1989. 89.50 (*0-89603-158-6*) Humana.

Raess, Beat U., jt. auth. see Tunnicliff, Godfrey.

Raeth, Peter G. Expert Systems: A Software Methodology for Modern Applications. LC 89-46387. 472p. 1990. 9.95 (*0-8186-8904-8*, 1904) IEEE Comp Soc.

Raethel, Heinz-Sigurd. The New Duck Handbook. (Illus.). 1989. pap. 8.95 (*0-8120-4088-0*) Barron.

Raether, Carl N., jt. ed. see Glennon, John P.

Raether, H. Surface Plasmons. (Tracts in Modern Physics Ser.: Vol. 111). (Illus.). 150p. 1988. 64.00 (*0-387-17363-3*) Spr-Verlag.

Raether, Howard C. The Funeral Director's Practice Management Handbook. 496p. 1989. text ed. 49.95 (*0-13-345315-4*) P-H.

Raether, Manfred, jt. auth. see Lazarus, David.

Raevsky-Hughes, Olga, ed. see Remizov, Aleksei M.

***Rafael, Marty.** Spiritual Vampires: The Use & Misuse of Spiritual Power. LC 95-75339. 272p. (Orig.). 1995. pap. 14.95 (*1-57282-006-3*) Message NM.

Rafael, Ruth K. The Western Jewish History Center: Guide to Archival & Oral History Collections. LC 86-50102. (Illus.). 1987. pap. 24.95 (*0-943376-35-1*) Magnes Mus.

***Rafael, Vicente, ed.** Discrepant Histories: Translocal Essays on Filipino Cultures. (Asian American History & Culture Ser.). 240p. (Orig.). (C). 1995. lib. bdg. 39.95 (*1-56639-355-8*) Temple U Pr.

— Discrepant Histories: Translocal Essays on Filipino Cultures. (Asian American History & Culture Ser.). 240p. (Orig.). (C). 1995. pap. text ed. 12.95 (*1-56639-356-6*) Temple U Pr.

Rafael, Vicente L. Contracting Colonialism: Translation & Christian Conversion in Tagalog Society under Early Spanish Rule. LC 87-23937. 248p. 1988. 32.50 (*0-8014-2065-2*) Cornell U Pr.

— Contracting Colonialism: Translation & Christian Conversion in Tagalog Society under Early Spanish Rule. LC 92-32739. (Illus.). 256p. 1993. pap. text ed. 15.95 (*0-8223-1341-3*) Duke.

***Rafaela, Judith.** Poems along the Path. 48p. (Orig.). 1994. pap. 10.00 (*0-9644196-0-2*) Sherman Asher.

Rafaelsen, Lise, jt. ed. see Pines, Malcolm.

Rafai, P., jt. auth. see Kovacs, F.

Rafal, Richard B. Radiologic Oral Examination: Questions & Guide. LC 93-26566. 464p. 1994. pap. 59.50 (*0-89640-246-0*) Igaku-Shoin.

Rafalko, Robert J. Logic for an Overcast Tuesday. 604p. (C). 1990. text ed. 39.95 (*0-534-12552-2*) Intl Thomson.

Rafalovich, Danita & Pellman, Kathryn A. Backart: On the Flip Side. (Illus.). 80p. 1991. pap. text ed. 19.95 (*0-942786-10-6*) Leone Pubns.

Rafanelli, M., et al, eds. Statistical & Scientific Database Management. (Lecture Notes in Computer Science Ser.: Vol. 339). ix, 454p. 1989. pap. 51.00 (*0-387-50575-X*) Spr-Verlag.

Rafati, Vahid, ed. The Collected Works of Dr. Davudi. (Illus.). (PER.). 1987. 22.50 (*0-933770-58-8*) Kalimat.

Rafe, Martin. The Boy Who Loved Mammoths. (Storytelling-Folklore Ser.). (Illus.). 64p. (Orig.). Date not set. pap. 10.95 (*0-938756-42-7*) Yellow Moon.

Rafe, Stephen C. How to Be Prepared to Think on Your Feet. 1992. pap. 13.00 (*0-88730-528-8*) Harper Busn.

— Training Your Dog for Birdwork. LC 86-19874. (Training Bks.). (Illus.). 96p. 1987. 24.95 (*0-87714-129-0*); pap. 16.95 (*0-87714-130-4*) Denlingers.

— Your New Baby & Bowser. (Other Dog Bks.). (Illus.). 1990. 9.95 (*0-87714-138-X*) Denlingers.

Rafel, Lisa. It Began in Kathmandu. Odom, Robert, Jr., ed. 1990. write for info. (*0-9626168-1-8*) Prometh Pr CA.

Rafelski, J., jt. ed. see Gutbrod, H. H.

Rafelson, jt. ed. see Bezkorovainy.

Rafelson, M. E., ed. Cellular & Humoral Defense against Disease. (Journal: Clinical Physiology & Biochemistry: Vol. 1, No. 2-5, 1983). (Illus.). 228p. 1983. pap. 104.00 (*3-8055-3693-3*) S Karger.

Rafelson, M. E., ed. see Dubin, A.

Rafelson, Max, Jr. Metal Metabolism & Disease. (Journal: Clinical Physiology & Biochemistry: Vol. 4, No. 1, 1986). (Illus.). 112p. 1986. pap. 33.75 (*3-8055-4264-X*) S Karger.

Rafer, Suzanne, ed. see Argus, Marilyn & Glynn, Diane.

Rafer, Suzanne, ed. see Green, Mark.

Rafer, Suzanne, ed. see Klein, Robert.

Rafer, Suzanne, ed. see Urvater, Michele.

Rafert, John A., jt. auth. see Long, Bruce W.

Raferty, Kim G. & Raftery, Kevin. Kids Gardening: A Kid's Guide to Messing Around in the Dirt. (Illus.). 84p. (Orig.). (J). 1989. pap. 13.95 (*0-932592-25-2*) Klutz Pr.

Raferty, Margaret M. Mary of Nemmegen. (Medieval & Renaissance Texts Ser.: No. 5). 85p. 1991. 32.00 (*90-04-09252-8*) E J Brill.

Raff, Beverly & Friesner, Arlyne. Quick Reference to Maternity Nursing. 352p. (C). 1989. 55.00 (*0-8342-0051-1*) Aspen Pub.

Raff, Beverly, jt. ed. see Anderson, Gene C.

Raff, Beverly S., ed. see Ramer, Leah.

Raff, Beverly S., ed. see Weiner, Susan M.

Raff, Daniel M., jt. ed. see Lamoreaux, Naomi R.

Raff, Elizabeth C., jt. ed. see Raff, Rudolf A.

Raff, Ellison S., ed. Computers & Operations Research: Environmental Applications. 1977. pap. 42.00 (*0-08-021348-0*, Pergamon Pr) Elsevier.

***Raff, Joseph.** Fielding's Britain. Knoles, Kathy, ed. (Travel Guides Ser.). (Illus.). 464p. (Orig.). 1994. pap. 16.95 (*1-56952-028-3*) Fielding Wrldwide.

— Fielding's Britain 1993. (Illus.). 416p. 1992. pap. 15.00 (*0-688-11161-0*) Morrow.

— Fielding's Europe. Knoles, Kathy, ed. (Travel Guides Ser.). (Illus.). 1070p. (Orig.). 1994. pap. 16.95 (*1-56952-059-3*) Fielding Wrldwide.

— Fielding's Europe 1993. (Illus.). 960p. 1993. pap. 15.00 (*0-688-04691-6*) Morrow.

***Raff, Joseph & Raff, Judith.** Fielding's Budget Europe. Knoles, Kathy, ed. (Travel Guides Ser.). (Illus.). 784p. (Orig.). 1994. pap. 16.95 (*1-56952-058-5*) Fielding Wrldwide.

— Fielding's Budget Europe 1993. (Illus.). 656p. 1993. pap. 12.00 (*0-688-04694-0*) Morrow.

— Fielding's Selective Shopping Guide to Europe 1993. 384p. 1992. pap. 13.00 (*0-688-04697-5*) Morrow.

Raff, Judith, jt. auth. see Raff, Joseph.

Raff, Rudolf A. & Kaufman, Thomas C. Embryos, Genes, & Evolution: The Developmental-Genetic Basis of Evolutionary Change. LC 90-5351. (Illus.). 424p. 1991. pap. 24.95 (*0-253-20642-1*, MB-642) Ind U Pr.

Raff, Rudolf A. & Raff, Elizabeth C., eds. Development As an Evolutionary Process, 1985, Vol. 198. 344p. 1987. text ed. 99.95 (*0-471-62922-7*) Wiley.

Raff, S. J. Microwave System Engineering Principles. 1977. 61.00 (*0-08-021797-4*, Pub. by Pergamon Repr UK) Franklin.

Raffa, Frederick A. Personal Injury Valuation. 1992. write for info. (*0-8205-1678-3*) Bender.

Raffa, Frederick A., et al, comps. United States Employment & Training Programs: A Selected Annotated Bibliography. LC 82-25108. xvi, 152p. 1983. text ed. 42.95 (*0-313-23872-3*, RUE/, Greenwood Pr) Greenwood.

Raffa, Jean B. The Bridge to Wholeness: A Feminine Alternative to the Hero Myth. Broucek, Marcia, ed. LC 92-10643. (Illus.). 208p. (Orig.). 1992. pap. 14.95 (*0-931055-88-1*) LuraMedia.

— Dream Theatres of the Soul: Empowering the Feminine Through Jungian Dreamwork. Geiger, Lura J., ed. 224p. (Orig.). 1994. pap. 15.45 (*1-880913-10-0*) LuraMedia.

Raffa, John, et al. Haynes Toyota Pickups & 4-Runner, 1979-1992: Automotive Repair Manual. rev. ed. LC 91-76624. (Illus.). 336p. 1991. pap. 16.95 (*1-56392-041-7*) Haynes Pubns.

Raffa, John B. & Haynes, John H. Chevrolet Camaro: Automotive Repair Manual. rev. ed. LC 91-76626. (Illus.). 344p. 1991. pap. 16.95 (*1-56392-017-4*) Haynes Pubns.

— Ford Pick-Ups & Bronco: Automotive Repair Manual. rev. ed. LC 91-76096. (Illus.). 388p. 1991. pap. 16.95 (*1-56392-009-3*) Haynes Pubns.

Raffa, Kenneth F., jt. ed. see Wagner, Michael.

Raffaele, Herbert A. Una Guia a las Aves de Puerto Rico y las Islas Virgenes. rev. ed. (Illus.). 358p. (SPA.). 1991. pap. 24.95 (*0-89825-000-5*) Pub Resces PR.

— A Guide to the Birds of Puerto Rico & the Virgin Islands. (Illus.). 220p. (C). 1990. 47.50 (*0-691-08554-4*); pap. 22.95 (*0-691-02424-3*) Princeton U Pr.

Raffaele, Joseph A. The Management of Technology: Change in a Society of Organized Advocacies. rev. ed. LC 79-63752. 1979. pap. text ed. 27.00 (*0-8191-0739-5*) U Pr of Amer.

— System & Unsystem: How American Society Works. 388p. 1974. 18.95 (*0-470-70274-5*); pap. 11.95 (*0-470-70483-7*) Schenkman Bks Inc.

Raffalli, Bernard, jt. auth. see Dumas, Alexandre.

Raffalovich, Isaiah. Our Inheritance: A Collection of Sermons & Addresses for All the Sabbaths & Festivals. 272p. 32.50 (*0-87559-146-9*) Shalom.

Raffan, John, tr. see Burkert, Walter.

Raffan, Richard. Turned-Bowl Design. LC 87-72008. (Illus.). 176p. 1987. pap. 21.95 (*0-918804-82-5*) Taunton.

— Turning Projects. 160p. 1991. pap. text ed. 19.95 (*0-942391-38-1*) Taunton.

— Turning Wood with Richard Raffan. LC 84-52130. (Illus.). 176p. 1985. pap. 19.95 (*0-918804-24-8*) Taunton.

Raffat, Donne, ed. & tr. The Prison Papers of Bozorg Alavi: A Literary Odyssey. LC 85-8053. (Contemporary Issues in the Middle East Ser.). (Illus.). 256p. 1985. 39.95 (*0-8156-0195-6*) Syracuse U Pr.

Raffauf, Robert F. A Handbook of Alkaloids & Alkaloid-containing Plants. LC 73-113713. 1230p. reprint ed. pap. 180.00 (*0-317-28188-7*, 2020190) Bks Demand.

Raffauf, Robert F., jt. auth. see Schultes, Richard E.

Raffe, David. Education & the Youth Labour Market: Schooling & Scheming. 225p. 1988. 70.00 (*1-85000-420-X*, Falmer Pr); pap. 35.00 (*1-85000-421-8*, Falmer Pr) Taylor & Francis.

Raffe, David, ed. Fourteen to Eighteen: The Changing Pattern of Schooling in Scotland. 276p. 1984. pap. text ed. 17.50 (*0-08-030374-9*, Pergamon Pr) Elsevier.

Raffel, Burton. Art of Translating Poetry. LC 87-43124. 220p. 1988. lib. bdg. 27.50 (*0-271-00626-9*) Pa St U Pr.

— The Art of Translating Prose. LC 93-20439. 184p. (C). 1994. 29.95 (*0-271-01080-0*) Pa St U Pr.

— Artists All: Creativity, the University, & the World. 160p. 1991. 23.50 (*0-271-00760-5*) Pa St U Pr.

— The Forked Tongue: A Study of the Translation Process. LC 79-154530. (De Proprietatibus Litterarum, Ser. Major: No. 14). 181p. 1971. text ed. 29.25 (*3-10-800272-4*) Mouton.

— From the Vietnamese: Ten Centuries of Poetry. 1968. 6.95 (*0-8079-0052-4*); pap. 4.25 (*0-8079-0053-2*) October.

— How to Read a Poem. LC 83-21978. 224p. 1984. pap. 7.95 (*0-452-00682-1*, Mer); pap. 10.95 (*0-452-01033-0*, Plume) NAL-Dutton.

— How to Read a Poem: Metrics. 260p. (YA). (gr. 9-12). 1989. pap. 8.95 (*0-452-00917-0*, Mer) NAL-Dutton.

— Mia Poems. 1968. 6.95 (*0-8079-0082-6*); pap. 4.25 (*0-8079-0083-4*) October.

— T. S. Eliot. 2nd ed. (Literature & Life Ser.). 192p. 1991. reprint ed. 19.95 (*0-8264-0515-0*, F Ungar Bks) Continuum.

Raffel, Burton, ed. Anthology of Modern Indonesian Poetry. 2nd ed. LC 68-19044. 278p. 1967. reprint ed. 44.50 (*0-87395-024-0*) State U NY Pr.

Raffel, Burton, ed. & tr. Art of Poetry. LC 78-171176. 83p. (ENG & LAT.). 1974. 19.50 (*0-87395-240-5*) State U NY Pr.

Raffel, Burton, ed. & intro. The Signet Classic Book of American Short Stories. 1985. pap. 5.95 (*0-451-52279-6*, Sig Classics) NAL-Dutton.

Raffel, Burton, ed. The Signet Classic Book of Contemporary American Short Stories. 1986. pap. 6.95 (*0-451-52430-6*, Sig Classics) NAL-Dutton.

Raffel, Burton, intro. Sir Gawain & the Green Knight. (Orig.). 1970. pap. 2.50 (*0-451-62456-4*, ME2312, Ment) NAL-Dutton.

Raffel, Burton, tr. Beowulf. (Orig.). 1987. pap. 2.50 (*0-451-62627-3*, Ment) NAL-Dutton.

Raffel, Burton, tr. & intro. Poems from the Old English. 2nd ed. LC 60-14776. 141p. reprint ed. pap. 40.20 (*0-7837-1832-2*, 2042032) Bks Demand.

Raffel, Burton, tr. Sir Gawain & the Green Knight. (Orig.). 1970. pap. 2.95 (*0-451-62624-9*) NAL-Dutton.

Raffel, Burton, tr. see Anwar, Chairil.

Raffel, Burton, tr. see Cervantes Saavedra, Miguel de.

Raffel, Burton, tr. see De Balzac, Honore.

Raffel, Burton, tr. see Espriu, Salvador.

Raffel, Burton, tr. see Horace.

Raffel, Burton, tr. see Rabelais, Francois.

Raffel, Dawn. In the Year of Long Division: Stories. LC 93-43940. 1995. 18.00 (*0-679-41581-5*) Knopf.

Raffel, Jeffrey A. The Politics of School Desegregation: The Metropolitan Remedy in Delaware. LC 80-10840. 312p. 1980. 34.95 (*0-87722-176-6*) Temple U Pr.

Raffel, Jeffrey A., jt. auth. see Varady, David P.

Raffel, Lisa, jt. ed. see Olsen, Laurie.

Raffel, Marshal W. & Raffel, Norma K. The U. S. Health System: Origins & Function. 3rd ed. 1989. pap. text ed. 37.95 (*0-8273-4336-1*) Delmar.

Raffel, Marshall, ed. Comparative Health Systems: Descriptive Analyses of Fourteen National Health Systems. LC 83-43032. (Illus.). 480p. 1984. 45.00 (*0-271-00363-4*) Pa St U Pr.

Raffel, Marshall M. & Raffel, Norma K., eds. Perspectives on Health Policy: Australia, New Zealand, United States. LC 87-2168. (Wiley-Medical Publication Ser.). 296p. reprint ed. pap. 84.40 (*0-8357-3477-3*, 2039736) Bks Demand.

Raffel, Marshall W. & Raffel, Norma K. The U. S. Health System: Origins & Functions. 4th ed. LC 93-11931. 302p. 1994. pap. text ed. 37.95 (*0-8273-5408-8*) Delmar.

Raffel, Norma K., jt. auth. see Raffel, Marshal W.

Raffel, Norma K., jt. ed. see Raffel, Marshall M.

Raffel, Norma K., jt. auth. see Raffel, Marshall W.

Raffelt, Albert, ed. see Rahner, Karl.

Raffensperger, John. Swenson's Pediatric Surgery. 5th ed. (Illus.). 994p. 1990. boxed 150.00 (*0-8385-8757-7*, A8757-5) Appleton & Lange.

Raffensperger, John G., jt. auth. see Beal, John M.

Raffer, Kunibert. Unequal Exchange & the Evolution of the World System: Reconsidering the Impact of Trade on North-South Relations. LC 86-31306. 336p. 1987. text ed. 45.00 (*0-312-00440-0*) St Martin.

Raffer, Kunibert & Salih, M. A., eds. The Least Developed & the Oil-Rich Arab Countries: Dependence, Interdependence, or Patronage? LC 92-4718. 264p. 1992. text ed. 69.95 (*0-312-08097-2*) St Martin.

Raffer, Kunibert, jt. ed. see Murshed, S. Mansoob.

Rafferty, Carin. Even Cowboys Get the Blues. (Temptation Ser.). 1994. mass mkt. 2.99 (*0-373-25605-1*, 1-25605-6) Harlequin Bks.

— Touch of Magic. 384p. (Orig.). 1995. pap. 4.99 (*0-451-40515-3*, Topaz) NAL-Dutton.

— Touch of Night. 348p. (Orig.). 1994. pap. 4.99 (*0-451-40443-2*, Topaz) NAL-Dutton.

***Rafferty, Charles.** The Man on the Tower: Poems. LC 94-37208. (Poetry Award Ser.). 1995. write for info. (*1-55728-339-7*); pap. write for info. (*1-55728-340-0*) U of Ark Pr.

— The Wave That Will Beach Us Both. Warren, Shirley, ed. 28p. 1994. pap. 5.00 (*1-877801-26-7*) Still Waters.

Rafferty, Frank T. Catalog of Psychiatric Procedures. 136p. 1988. 21.00 (*0-88048-314-8*) Am Psychiatric.

Rafferty, Kathleen, ed. The Dell Crossword Dictionary. (Orig.). 1984. mass mkt. 9.95 (*0-440-56318-6*, Dell Trade Pbks) Dell.

***Rafferty, Kathleen & Moore, Rosalind, eds.** The Dell Crossword Dictionary. large type ed. LC 94-44579. 1995. write for info. (*0-7838-1227-2*); pap. write for info. (*0-7838-1228-0*) Hall.

— The Essential Crossword Dictionary. LC 94-46604. 1995. 8.99 (*0-517-12437-8*) Random Hse Value.

Rafferty, Keen A., Jr. Methods in Experimental Embryology of the Mouse. LC 70-101642. (Illus.). 94p. 1970. 20.00 (*0-8018-1129-5*) Johns Hopkins.

Rafferty, Michael, ed. Skid Marks: Common Jokes about Lawyers. 96p. 1988. pap. 3.95 (*0-89815-283-6*) Ten Speed Pr.

Rafferty, Milton D. A Geography of World Tourism. 560p. 1993. text ed. 60.00 (*0-13-963927-6*) P-H.

— Historical Atlas of Missouri. LC 81-675048. (Illus.). 256p. 1982. 34.95 (*0-8061-1663-3*); pap. 18.95 (*0-8061-1732-X*) U of Okla Pr.

— Ouachita Mountains: A Guide for Fishermen, Hunters, & Travelers. LC 90-50695. (C). 1993. pap. 18.95 (*0-8061-2360-5*) U of Okla Pr.

— The Ozarks: Land & Life. LC 79-4738. (Illus.). 294p. 1985. pap. 18.95 (*0-8061-1960-8*) U of Okla Pr.

— The Ozarks Outdoors: A Guide for Fishermen, Hunters, & Tourists. LC 85-40478. (Illus.). 408p. 1988. 29.95 (*0-8061-1554-8*); pap. 18.95 (*0-8061-2088-6*) U of Okla Pr.

Rafferty, Milton D. & Catau, John C. The Ouachita Mountains: A Guide for Fishermen, Hunters, & Travelers. LC 90-50695. (Illus.). 304p. 1991. 35.00 (*0-8061-1722-2*) U of Okla Pr.

Rafferty, Oliver P. Catholicism in Ulster, 1603-1983: An Historical Introduction. LC 94-11849. 1994. write for info. (*1-57003-025-1*) U of SC Pr.

Rafferty, Patrick J., ed. The Industrial Hygienist's Guide to Indoor Air Quality Investigations. 76p. (C). 1993. pap. 25.00 (*0-932627-49-8*, 144-EQ-93) Am Indus Hygiene.

Rafferty, Robert R. Texas: The Texas Monthly Guidebook. 3rd ed. 1993. 29.95 (*0-87719-240-5*) Gulf Pub.

— Texas Coast & the Rio Grande Valley. 2nd ed. (Texas Monthly Guidebooks Ser.). 420p. 1991. pap. 16.95 (*0-87719-184-0*) Gulf Pub.

Rafferty, Robert R., et al, eds. Texas: The Newest, the Biggest, the Most Complete Guide to All of Texas! 3rd rev. ed. LC 92-45102. (Texas Monthly Guidebooks Ser.). 1993. 18.95 (*0-87719-209-X*) Gulf Pub.

Rafferty, S. S. Cork of the Colonies: The First American Detective. LC 84-80232. 314p. 1984. pap. 4.95 (*0-930330-11-0*) Intl Polygonics.

— Die Laughing. 200p. pap. 4.95 (*0-930330-16-1*) Intl Polygonics.

R

An Asterisk (*) at the beginning of an entry indicates that the title is appearing in BIP for the first time.

*Rafferty, Terence D. Basics of Transesophageal Echocardiography. LC 95-2999. 1995. write for info. (0-443-08922-1) Churchill.

Rafferty, Terrence. The Things Happens: Ten Years of Writing about the Movies. LC 92-25769. 1993. 24.95 (0-8021-1485-7) Grove-Atltic.

Rafferty, Tod. Harley-Davidson: The Ultimate Machine. LC 93-73959. (Illus.). 192p. 1994. 29.98 (1-56138-406-2) Courage Bks.

Raffery, Jeanne. Stepping Stones to Hell: A Love Story. The, Merit Group Staff, ed. (Orig.). 1989. pap. text ed. 14.95 (0-685-30397-7) Merit Group.

Raffi. Baby Beluga. LC 89-49367. (Raffi Songs to Read Ser.). (Illus.). 32p. (J). (ps-2). 1990. 14.00 (0-517-57839-5) Crown Bks Yng Read.

— Baby Beluga. LC 89-49367. (Raffi Songs to Read Ser.). (Illus.). 32p. (J). (ps-2). 1992. pap. 4.99 (0-517-58362-3) Crown Bks Yng Read.

— Baby Beluga. 1993. pap. 4.99 (0-517-11128-4) Random Hse Value.

— Bowling Song. write for info. (0-517-59382-3) Random Hse Value.

— Down by the Bay. (Raffi Songs to Read Ser.). (Illus.). 32p. (J). (ps-2). 1988. lib. bdg. 14.00 (0-517-56644-3) Crown Bks Yng Read.

— Down by the Bay. LC 87-750291. (Raffi Songs to Read Ser.). (Illus.). 32p. (J). (ps-2). 1988. pap. 4.99 (0-517-56645-1) Crown Bks Yng Read.

— Everything Grows. LC 88-37162. (Raffi Songs to Read Ser.). (Illus.). 32p. (J). (ps-2). 1989. 14.00 (0-517-57387-3) Crown Bks Yng Read.

— Everything Grows. LC 88-37162. (Raffi Songs to Read Ser.). (Illus.). 32p. (J). (ps-2). 1993. pap. 3.99 (0-517-88098-9) Crown Bks Yng Read.

— Five Little Ducks. (J). 1988. 12.00 (0-517-56945-0) Crown Bks Yng Read.

— Five Little Ducks. LC 88-3752. (Raffi Songs to Read Ser.). (Illus.). 32p. (J). (ps-2). 1992. pap. 4.99 (0-517-58360-7) Crown Bks Yng Read.

— Like Me & You. LC 93-9840. (Raffi Songs to Read Ser.). (Illus.). (J). (ps-2). 1994. 13.00 (0-517-59587-7); lib. bdg. 13.99 (0-517-59588-5) Crown Bks Yng Read.

— One Light, One Sun. LC 87-22256. (Raffi Songs to Read Ser.). (Illus.). 32p. (J). (ps-2). 1990. pap. 4.99 (0-517-57644-9) Crown Bks Yng Read.

— Raffi's Christmas Treasury: 14 Illustrated Songs & Musical Arrangements. (Illus.). (J). (ps up). 1988. lib. bdg. 17.95 (0-517-56806-3) Crown Bks Yng Read.

— Raffi's Top 10 Songs to Read. LC 95-196. (J). 1995. write for info. (0-517-70907-4, Crown) Crown Pub Group.

— Shake My Sillies Out. LC 87-750478. (Raffi Songs to Read Ser.). (Illus.). 32p. (J). (ps-2). 1988. pap. 4.99 (0-517-56647-8) Crown Bks Yng Read.

— Songs - Read-Premium. 1995. 39.92 (0-517-88300-7) Random.

— The Spider on the Floor. LC 92-33442. (Raffi Songs to Read Ser.). (Illus.). 32p. (J). (ps-3). 1993. 13.00 (0-517-59381-5); lib. bdg. 13.99 (0-517-59464-1) Crown Bks Yng Read.

— Tingalayo. LC 88-3562. (Raffi Songs to Read Ser.). (Illus.). 32p. (J). (ps-2). 1993. pap. 3.99 (0-517-88099-7) Crown Bks Yng Read.

— Wheels on the Bus. LC 87-30126. (Raffi Songs to Read Ser.). (Illus.). 32p. (J). (ps-2). 1990. pap. 4.99 (0-517-57645-7) Crown Bks Yng Read.

Raffi, J. J. & Belliardo, J. J. Potential New Methods of Detection of Irradiated Food, No. EUR 13331. 238p. 1991. pap. 30.00 (92-826-2238-X, CD-NA-13331-EN-C, Pub. by Europ Com) UNIPUB.

Raffield, Barney T., III, jt. auth. see Bingham, Frank G., Jr.

Raffin, Michelle, jt. auth. see Jongeward, Dorothy.

Raffin, Patrizia. America. (Illus.). 128p. 1993. 12.98 (0-8317-9069-5) Smithmark.

Raffini, Christine. The Second Sequence in Maurice Sceve's Delie: A Study of Numerological Composition in the Renaissance. LC 88-61803. (Illus.). 167p. (ENG & FRE.). 1989. lib. bdg. 24.95 (0-917786-62-9) Summa Pubns.

Raffini, James P. Student Apathy. (What Research Says to the Teacher Ser.). 32p. 1988. 3.95 (0-8106-1080-9) NEA.

— Winners Without Losers: Structures & Strategies for Increasing Student Motivation to Learn. 1992. pap. 34.95 (0-205-16707-1) Allyn.

Raffinot, Jean-Paul, tr. see Seely, Contee & Romijn, Elizabeth.

*Raffle, David L. A Grain of Salt: Getting A's in College in Ten Easy Lessons. 140p. (Orig.). (C). 1994. pap. text ed. 7.95 (0-9643534-0-7) Thumbprnt Pr.

Raffle, P. A., et al, eds. Hunter's Diseases of Occupations. 8th ed. LC 93-46316. 1994. write for info. (0-340-57173-X, Pub. by E Arnold UK) Routledge Chapman & Hall.

Raffler-Engel, Walburga, et al, eds. Studies in Language Origins, Vol. 2. LC 88-7542. xxi, 329p. 1991. 112.00x (1-55619-077-8) Benjamins North Am.

Raffler-Engel, Walburga von. The Perception of Nonverbal Behavior in the Career Interview. (Pragmatics & Beyond Ser.: Vol. IV, No. 4). viii, 148p. 1983. pap. 41.00x (90-272-2517-6) Benjamins North Am.

Raffler-Engel, Walburga von, ed. Doctor-Patient Interaction. LC 89-17883. (Pragmatics & Beyond New Ser.: No. 4). xxxiv, 300p. 1989. 89.00x (1-55619-079-4); pap. 29.00 (1-55619-080-8) Benjamins North Am.

Raffles, Sophia. Memoir of the Life & Public Services of Sir Thomas Stamford Raffles. LC 77-87000. reprint ed. 89.00 (0-404-16774-8) AMS Pr.

Raffles, Thomas S. The History of Java, 2 vols., Set. LC 77-87509. (Illus.). reprint ed. 95.00 (0-404-16770-5) AMS Pr.

Raffman, Diana. Language, Music, & Mind. (Illus.). 180p. 1993. pap. 22.50 (0-262-18150-9, Bradford Bks) MIT Pr.

Raffo, Dave. Football. LC 93-23274. (How to Play the All-Star Way Ser.). (J). 1993. lib. bdg. 22.13 (0-8114-5780-X) Raintree Steck-V.

Raffo, Lynne, illus. Sacristan's Manual. 4th rev. ed. 55p. (C). 1988. pap. text ed. 4.00 (0-685-28962-1) Lit Comm Pubs.

Raffoul, Francois, tr. see Nancy, Jean-Luc & Lacoue-Labarthe, Philippe.

Raffoul, Francois, jt. ed. see Pettigrew, David.

Raffucci de Garcia, Carmen I. El Gobierno Civil y la Ley Foraker (Antecedentes Historicos) LC 79-16454. Orig. Title: Las Instituciones de Gobierno Civil en la Elaboracion de la Ley Foraker y Sus Antecedentes Historicos. xi, 145p. (SPA.). 1981. pap. 5.60 (0-8477-0864-0) U of PR Pr.

Raffucci de Lockwood, Alicia M. Cuatro Poetas De la "Generacion Del 36" Miguel Hernandez, Serrano Plajo, Rosales y Panero. (UPREX, Estudios Literarios Ser.: No. 28). (C). 1974. pap. 1.50 (0-8477-0028-3) U of PR Pr.

Raffy, Sabine. Sarraute Romanciere: Espaces intimes. (American University Studies: Romance Languages & Literature: Ser. II, Vol. 60). 269p. (C). 1988. text ed. 47.00 (0-8204-0479-9) P Lang Pubs.

Rafikov, S. R., et al. Determination of Molecular Weights & Polydispersity of High Polymers. 368p. 1964. text ed. 88.00 (0-7065-0539-5, Pub. by Keter Pub IS) Coronet Bks.

Rafinesque, C. S. Atlantic Journal & Friend of Knowledge. (Illus.). 1946. pap. 20.00 (0-685-42244-5) Lubrecht & Cramer.

— Flora Telluriana, 4 pts. in 1. 1946. pap. 20.00 (0-934454-33-7) Lubrecht & Cramer.

— New Flora & Botany of North America, 4 pts. in 1 vol. 1946. reprint ed. pap. 20.00 (0-934454-66-3) Lubrecht & Cramer.

Rafinesque, Constantine. Ichthyologia Ohiensis, or, Natural History of the Fishes Inhabiting the River Ohio & Its Tributary Streams. LC 72-125760. (American Environmental Studies). 1977. reprint ed. 20.95 (0-405-02686-2) Ayer.

Rafinesque, Constantine S. Medical Flora; Or, Manual of the Medical Botany of the United States of North America, 2 vols., Set. LC 75-23755. (Illus.). reprint ed. 60.00 (0-404-13191-3) AMS Pr.

*Rafiq, Fauzia, ed. Aurat Durbar. Date not set. pap. 14.95 (0-929005-70-8) InBook.

Rafiq, O., ed. Protocol Test Systems, VI: Proceedings of the IFIP TC6-WG6.1 International Workshop Held in Pau, France, 28-30 September 1993. 293p. 1993. pap. 134.50 (0-444-81697-6, North Holland) Elsevier.

Rafique, M. Sri Aurobindo's Ideal of Human Life. 127p. (C). 1987. 17.50 (81-7024-074-3, Pub. by Ashish II) S Asia.

Rafique, Muhammad, jt. auth. see Saleem, Mohammad.

Rafiquizzaman. Microprocessors & Microcomputer-Based System Design. 1990. 24.95 (0-8493-4275-9, QA76) CRC Pr.

Rafiquzzaman, Mohamed. Introduction to Microprocessors & Microcomputer-Based Applications. 2nd ed. 672p. 1995. 69.95 (0-8493-4475-1, 4475) CRC Pr.

Rafiquzzaman, Mohamed & Chandra, Rajan. Modern Computer Architecture. 410p. (C). 1988. text ed. 70.75 (0-314-60174-0) West Pub.

Rafiuddin, F. Ideology of the Future. 19.00 (1-56744-052-5) Kazi Pubns.

*Rafkin. Street Smarts: A Personal Safety Guide for Women. 1995. pap. 9.00 (0-06-251211-0) Harper SF.

*Rafkin, Louise. Gay & Lesbian Couples & Parenting. Duberman, Martin, ed. (Issues in Gay & Lesbian Life Ser.). (Illus.). 196p. (YA). (gr. 9 up). 1995. lib. bdg. 24.95 (0-7910-2609-4); pap. 12.95 (0-7910-2960-3) Chelsea Hse.

— Queer & Pleasant Danger: Writing Out My Life. 180p. (Orig.). (C). 1992. 24.95 (0-939416-60-3); pap. 9.95 (0-939416-61-1) Cleis Pr.

Rafkin, Louise, ed. Different Daughters: A Book by Mothers of Lesbians. LC 86-72846. 160p. (Orig.). (C). 1987. 21.95 (0-939416-12-3); pap. 9.95 (0-939416-13-1) Cleis Pr.

— Different Mothers: Sons & Daughters of Lesbians Talk about Their Lives. 160p. (Orig.). 1990. 24.95 (0-939416-40-9); pap. 9.95 (0-939416-41-7) Cleis Pr.

— Unholy Alliances: New Women's Fiction. 168p. (Orig.). (C). 1988. 21.95 (0-939416-14-X); pap. 9.95 (0-939416-15-8) Cleis Pr.

Raflik, M., et al, eds. CAD-I Database: An Approach to an Engineering Database, Version 4.0. (Research Reports ESPRIT, Project 322, CAD Interfaces: Vol. 5). x, 147p. 1990. pap. 29.00 (0-387-53383-4) Spr-Verlag.

*Rafols-Casamada. Rafols-Casamada: El Passeig Del Poeta. limited ed. (Ediciones Especiales y de Bibliofio Ser.). (Illus.). 88p. (CAT.). 1993. 600.00 (0-614-00138-2) Elliots Bks.

— Rafols-Casamada: El Passeig Del Poeta. limited ed. (Ediciones Especiales y de Bibiofio Ser.). (Illus.). 88p. (CAT.). 1993. 2,750.00 (0-614-00242-7) Elliots Bks.

— Rafols-Casamada: El Passeig Del Poeta. limited ed. (Ediciones Especiales y de Bibliofilo Ser.). (Illus.). 88p. (CAT.). 1993. 600.00 (0-614-00243-5) Elliots Bks.

*Rafols-Casamada, Albert. Estrats. limited ed. (Illus.). (CAT.). 1993. 150.00 (0-614-00142-0) Elliots Bks.

— Estrats. limited ed. (Ediciones Especiales y de Bibliofilo Ser.). (Illus.). (CAT.). 1993. 1,750.00 (84-343-0451-1) Elliots Bks.

Rafoth, Bennett A. & Rubin, Donald. The Social Construction of Written Communication. Farr, Marcia, ed. LC 88-22347. (Writing Research Ser.: Vol. 17). 336p. (C). 1988. text ed. 49.50 (0-89391-436-3); pap. text ed. 27.50 (0-89391-549-1) Ablex Pub.

Rafoth, Mary A., et al. Strategies for Learning & Remembering: Study Skills Across the Curriculum. LC 93-589. (Analysis & Action Ser.). 152p. 1993. 14.95 (0-8106-3048-6) NEA.

Rafoth, Richard. Bicycling Fuel: Nutrition for Bicycle Riders. 3rd exp. rev. ed. LC 93-83824. (Illus.). 128p. 1993. pap. 9.95 (0-933201-54-0) Bicycle Books.

Rafroidi, Patrick. Irish Literature in English: Romantic Period, 1789-1850, 2 vols. 1980. write for info. (0-318-64384-7) Dufour.

— Irish Literature in English: Romantic Period, 1789-1850, 2 vols., 1. 1980. 50.00 (0-86140-272-3) Dufour.

— Irish Literature in English: Romantic Period, 1789-1850, 2 vols., 2. 1980. 50.00 (0-86140-273-1) Dufour.

Raftelis, George A. Comprehensive Guide to Financing & Pricing at Water & Wastewater Treatment Plants. 2nd ed. 1992. 65.00 (0-87371-904-2, HD4456) Lewis Pubs.

— Ernst & Young Guide to Water & Wastewater Finance & Pricing. (Illus.). 212p. 1989. 64.95 (0-87371-181-5, HD44) Lewis Pubs.

Rafter, B. B., tr. see Breuil, Henri & Lantier, Raymond.

Rafter, Nicole H. Partial Justice: Women in State Prisons, 1800-1935. LC 84-7990. (Illus.). 295p. 1985. 37.50 (0-930350-63-4) NE U Pr.

— Partial Justice: Women, Prisons & Social Control. 2nd ed. 342p. (C). 1990. pap. 19.95 (0-88738-826-4) Transaction Pubs.

Rafter, Nicole H., ed. White Trash: The Eugenics Family Studies, 1877-1919. 428p. 1988. 45.00 (1-55553-030-3) NE U Pr.

*Rafter, Nicole H. & Heidensohn, Frances, eds. International Feminist Perspectives in Criminology: Engendering a Discipline. LC 95-10580. 1995. write for info. (0-335-19389-7, Open Univ Pr); pap. write for info. (0-335-19388-9, Open Univ Pr) Taylor & Francis.

Rafter, Rosalie & Alaia, Cheri. Practice RCT Writing Exam, Set. rev. ed. 1991. 10.50 (0-937820-61-X); 10.50 (0-937820-62-8); 10.50 (0-937820-63-6); 10.50 (0-937820-64-4) WestSea Pub.

— RCT Writing: A Workbook. rev. ed. 204p. (YA). (gr. 9-12). 1990. 8.95 (0-937820-60-1) WestSea Pub.

Raftery, Barry. Celtic Art. (Illus.). 172p. 1991. 50.00 (2-08-013509-0, Pub. by Flammarion) Abbeville Pr.

— Pagan Celtic Ireland: The Archaeology of the Irish Iron Age. LC 93-61274. (Illus.). 240p. 1994. 39.95 (0-500-05072-4) Thames Hudson.

Raftery, Francis. The Teacher in the Catholic School. 2nd ed. 61p. 1988. 6.60 (1-55833-014-3) Natl Cath Educ.

Raftery, James, jt. ed. see Stevens, Andrew.

Raftery, John. Risk Analysis in Project Management. LC 93-32191. 1993. write for info. (0-419-18420-1, E & FN Spon) Routledge Chapman & Hall.

Raftery, Joseph, ed. Celts. 83p. 1991. reprint ed. pap. 9.95 (0-85342-852-2, Pub. by Mercier Pr IE) Dufour.

Raftery, Judith R. Land of Fair Promise: Politics & Reform in Los Angeles Schools, 1885-1941. LC 91-26888. (Illus.). 312p. (C). 1992. 37.50 (0-8047-1930-6) Stanford U Pr.

Raftery, Kevin, jt. auth. see Raferty, Kim G.

Raftery, Susan R., jt. auth. see Halasz, Ida M.

Raftery, William J. Government Accounting & Financial Reporting Manual. 1993. ring bd. 152.00 (0-685-69613-8, GARM) Warren Gorham & Lamont.

Raftis, Alkis. The World of Greek Dance. Doumas, Alexandra, tr. (Illus.). 249p. 1987. 63.70 (3-487-09131-3, Pub. by Georg Olms GW) Lubrecht & Cramer.

Raftis, Alkis, comp. Dance in Poetry: An International Anthology of Poems on Dance. LC 91-38801. 186p. 1991. reprint ed. pap. 18.95 (0-87127-177-X, Dance Horizons) Princeton Bk Co.

Raftis, Chris. C.R. Billiards Pool Series, 7 vols. (C.R. Billiards Pool Ser.). 1992. 70.00 (1-880135-05-1) C R Billiards.

Raftis, Christos E. Cue Tips on Pocket Billiards: Including Billiard Mathematics. (Illus.). 186p. (Orig.). (C). 1990. pap. 5.95 (0-9625197-9-0) C R Billiards.

— Teach Your Self Pool. (Illus.). 326p. (Orig.). (C). 1991. pap. text ed. 14.95 (1-880135-00-0) C R Billiards.

— Tricks & Tips for Experienced Players. (Illus.). 32p. (Orig.). (C). 1992. pap. text ed. 5.95 (1-880135-02-7) C R Billiards.

*Raftopoulos, Evangelos. The Barcelona Convention & Protocols. 381p. 1993. 85.00 (1-898029-01-6, Pub. by Simmonds & Hill Pubng UK) W W Gaunt.

*Rag, Cheri. The Santa Barbara Bargain Book. 94p. (Orig.). 1993. pap. 7.95 (0-945092-33-4) EZ Nature.

Ragab, S. A. & Piomelli, U., eds. Engineering Applications & Large Eddy Simulations. 1993. LC 93-71644. (FED Ser.: Vol. 162). 155p. 1993. pap. 37.50 (0-7918-0970-6, H00802) ASME.

Ragache, Claude-Catherine. Creation of the World. LC 90-25263. (Myths & Legends Ser.: Gp. 2). (Illus.). 48p. (J). (gr. 4-8). 1991. lib. bdg. 9.95 (0-685-52829-4) Marshall Cavendish.

Ragache, Gilles. Dragons. LC 90-25902. (Myths & Legends Ser.: Gp. 2). (Illus.). 48p. (J). (gr. 4-8). 1991. lib. bdg. 9.95 (1-85435-265-2) Marshall Cavendish.

Ragaini, R. C., jt. ed. see Avogadro, A.

Ragan, Andrew & Cummings, Cherilyn, eds. The Southern California Anthology, Vol. V. 144p. (Orig.). 1987. pap. 5.95 (0-9615108-2-X) USC MPWP.

Ragan, Bryant T., Jr. & Williams, Elizabeth A., eds. Recreating Authority in Revolutionary France. LC 91-45492. 260p. (C). 1992. text ed. 40.00 (0-8135-1841-5); pap. text ed. 15.00 (0-8135-1842-3) Rutgers U Pr.

Ragan, David. Movie Stars of the Forties: A Complete Reference Guide for the Film Historian or Trivia Buff. 1991. write for info. (0-318-59598-2) S&S Trade.

— Who's Who in Hollywood, 2 vols., Set. 1992. 195.00 (0-8160-2011-6) Facts on File.

Ragan, David P. William Faulkner's "Absalom, Absalom!" A Critical Study. Litz, A. Walton, ed. LC 87-23300. (Studies in Modern Literature: No. 85). 244p. reprint ed. 66.70 (0-8357-1840-9, 2070755) Bks Demand.

Ragan, Donal M. Structural Geology: An Introduction to Geometrical Techniques. 3rd ed. LC 84-19658. 405p. 1985. Net. pap. text ed. write for info. (0-471-08043-8) Wiley.

Ragan, Genie. Beads, The Art of Stringing. (Illus.). 58p. (Orig.). 1986. pap. text ed. 3.95 (0-935182-44-6) Gem Guides Bk.

Ragan, James. Womb Weary. 1990. 14.95 (1-55972-053-0, Birch Ln Pr) Carol Pub Group.

Ragan, James, jt. ed. see Todd, Albert C.

Ragan, James F., Jr. & Thomas, Lloyd B., Jr. Computerized Test Bank A to Accompany Principles of Economics. 2nd ed. (C). 1993. teacher ed, 3.5 hd 14.50 (0-03-097072-5); teacher ed, disk 25.00 (0-03-097074-1) Dryden Pr.

— Instructor's Manual to Accompany "Principles of Economics," Second Edition. 2nd ed. 439p. (C). 1993. pap. text ed. 7.00 (0-03-097070-9) Dryden Pr.

— Principles of Economics. (Illus.). 955p. (C). 1990. Test Bank A. pap. text ed. 5.50 (0-15-571603-4) Dryden Pr.

— Principles of Economics. 2nd ed. LC 92-81302. 1584p. (C). 1993. trans. 63.00 (0-03-097071-7) Dryden Pr.

— Principles of Economics. 2nd ed. LC 92-81302. 1584p. (C). 1993. disk 14.50 (0-03-097908-0) Dryden Pr.

— Principles of Economics. 2nd ed. LC 92-81302. 1584p. (C). 1993. teacher ed 173.00 (0-03-098211-1); student ed, text ed. 58.75 (0-03-096632-9) Dryden Pr.

— Principles of Economics. 2nd ed. LC 92-81302. 1584p. (C). 1993. disk 15.00 (0-03-097073-3) Dryden Pr.

— Principles of Economics. 2nd ed. LC 92-81302. 1584p. (C). 1993. disk 14.50 (0-03-097075-X) Dryden Pr.

— Principles of Economics. 2nd ed. LC 92-81302. 1584p. (C). 1993. disk 14.50 (0-03-097909-9) Dryden Pr.

— Principles of Macroeconomics. 450p. (C). 1990. pap. text ed. 39.75 (0-15-571599-2) HB Coll Pubs.

— Principles of Macroeconomics. 2nd ed. 986p. (C). 1993. student ed, pap. text ed. 41.25 (0-03-096634-5) Dryden Pr.

— Principles of Microeconomics. 450p. (C). 1990. pap. text ed. 39.75 (0-15-571600-X) HB Coll Pubs.

— Principles of Microeconomics. 2nd ed. LC 92-81302. 1007p. (C). 1993. student ed, pap. text ed. 41.25 (0-03-096633-7) Dryden Pr.

— Testbook A to Accompany "Principles of Economics," 2nd ed. 497p. (C). 1993. teacher ed. pap. text ed. 19.00 (0-03-097081-4) Dryden Pr.

Ragan, John D. Emiliano Zapata. (World Leaders - Past & Present Ser.). (Illus.). 112p. (YA). (gr. 5 up). 1989. 17.95 (1-55546-823-3) Chelsea Hse.

— The Explorers of Alaska. (World Explorers Ser.). (Illus.). 112p. (YA). (gr. 5 up). 1992. lib. bdg. 18.95 (0-7910-1311-1) Chelsea Hse.

Ragan, Larry. True Tales of Birmingham. (Illus.). 64p. (Orig.). 1992. pap. 6.95 (0-943994-19-5) Birmingham Hist Soc.

Ragan, Laura L. Meandering Paws & Cat Calls. (Illus.). 32p. 1993. 7.95 (1-56167-121-5) Am Literary Pr.

Ragan, Lise B., ed. see Blosser, Betsy J.

Ragan, Lise B., ed. see Blosser, Betsy.

Ragan, Lise B., ed. see Garcia, Mary H. & Gonzalez-Mena, Janet.

*Ragan, Mark K. Submarines, Sacrifice, & Success in the Civil War: A History of the Confederate Submarine Hunley. LC 95-69553. (Illus.). 208p. 1995. 19.95 (1-886391-04-1); pap. 14.95 (1-886391-05-X) Narwhal Pr.

Ragan-Reid, Gale. Divine. LC 93-60229. (Illus.). 44p. (J). (gr. 1-4). 1994. 7.95 (1-55523-606-5) Winston-Derek.

Ragan, Robert. Step-by-Step Bookkeeping: The Complete Handbook for the Small Business. rev. ed. LC 74-7814. (Illus.). 128p. (YA). (gr. 10-12). 1992. pap. 8.95 (0-8069-8690-5) Sterling.

*Ragan, Robert C. Step-by-Step Bookkeeping. rev. ed. (Illus.). viii, 134p. 1994. lib. bdg. 23.00x (0-8095-7625-2) Borgo Pr.

Ragan, Robert C. & Igbal, Zafar M. Financial Recordkeeping for Small Stores. (Small Business Management Ser.: No. 32). 139p. 1985. pap. 4.00 (0-16-004550-9, S/N 045-000-00239-0) USGPO.

Ragan, Ruth M. Voiceprints of Lincoln: Memories of an Old Massachusetts Town & Its Unique Response to Industrial America. 292p. 1991. text ed. 29.95 (0-944856-03-9) Lincoln Hist Soc.

Ragan, Sam. Collected Poems of Sam Ragan: Poet Laureate of North Carolina. Warren, Marsha W., ed. LC 91-60872. 286p. 1990. 14.95 (0-932662-94-3); pap. 9.95 (0-932662-95-1) St Andrews NC.

— Walk into April. 1986. 10.00 (0-932662-62-5) St Andrews NC.

Ragan, Sam, ed. see Bell, Mae W.

Ragan, Samuel T. Weymouth. (Illus.). 152p. (Orig.). 1987. 14.00 (0-932662-71-4) St Andrews Pr.

Ragan, Sandra. Interior Color by Design: Commercial. 160p. 1995. pap. 29.99 (1-56496-119-2) Rockport Pubs.

Ragan, Sandra L., jt. auth. see Pagano, Michael P.

Ragan, Tillman & Smith, Patricia. Programming Instructional Software: Applesoft BASIC Edition. LC 88-24584. (Illus.). 463p. 1989. disk 29.95 (0-87778-213-X) Educ Tech Pubns.

Ragan, Tillman J., jt. auth. see Smith, Patricia L.

*Ragan, Vicki & Barbash, Shepard. The Edible Alphabet Book. LC 94-47008. (Illus.). 64p. 1995. 13.95 (0-8212-2208-2) Bulfinch Pr.

Ragan, W. Gordon. Georgia Cookbook. 2nd ed. LC 78-70630. (Illus.). 1980. 9.95 (0-916620-50-6) Portals Pr.

Ragan, William B., jt. auth. see Shepherd, Gene D.

Ragano, Frank & Raab, Selwyn. Mob Lawyer: Including the Inside Account of Who Killed Jimmy Hoffa & JFK. Grossman, Barbara & Pileggi, Nicholas, eds. (Illus.). 320p. 1994. text ed. 22.00 (*0-684-19568-2*, Scribners) S&S Trade.

Ragatz, L. J. Guide for the Study of British Caribbean History, 1763-1834, Including the Abolitions & Emancipation Movements. LC 71-75275. (Law, Politics & History Ser.). 1970. reprint ed. lib. bdg. 75.00 (*0-306-71308-X*) Da Capo.

Ragatz, Oswald G. Organ Technique: A Basic Course of Study. LC 78-3244. (Illus.). 272p. 1980. spiral bd., pap. 19.50 (*0-253-17146-6*) Ind U Pr.

Ragaway, Martin. Don't Think About Retiring Until... (Illus.). 48p. (Orig.). 1982. pap. 2.95 (*0-8431-0413-9*) Putnam Pub Group.

— Sex Before Golf. (Illus.). 48p. (Orig.). 1982. pap. 2.95 (*0-8431-0313-2*) Putnam Pub Group.

— Things You Don't What to Hear in a Hospital. 64p. 1977. pap. 2.95 (*0-8431-0528-3*) Putnam Pub Group.

— You Don't Have to Count Your Birthdays Until... (Laughter Library). (Illus.). 1979. pap. 2.95 (*0-8431-0534-8*) Putnam Pub Group.

Ragaway, Martin A. The World's Worst Golf Jokes. 48p. (J). 1972. pap. 2.95 (*0-8431-0200-4*) Putnam Pub Group.

Ragay. F-102 Delta Dagger in Europe. (Specials Ser.). (Illus.). 80p. 1991. pap. 9.95 (*0-89747-220-9*, 6050) Squad Sig Pubns.

Ragaz, J. & Ariel, I. M., eds. High-Risk Breast Cancer: Therapy. (Illus.). 536p. 1991. 199.00 (*0-387-51092-3*) Spr-Verlag.

Ragaz, J., et al, eds. Preoperative (Neoadjuvant) Chemotherapy. (Recent Results in Cancer Research Ser.: Vol. 103). (Illus.). 196p. 1986. pap. 66.00 (*0-387-16129-5*) Spr-Verlag.

***Ragaza, Angelo.** Notable Asian Americans: Business, Politics, Science. LC 94-37528. (Asian American Experience Ser.). (J). 1995. 18.95 (*0-7910-2189-0*) Chelsea Hse.

Ragazzini, G. Italian-English - English-Italian Dictionary with a Glossary of Terms on Finance, Economy & Business Organizations. 2nd ed. 2320p. 1968. 157.00 (*88-08-04862-4*) IBD Ltd.

— Italian-English - English-Italian Technical Dictionary. 1278p. 1983. 100.00 (*88-425-1370-9*) IBD Ltd.

Ragazzini, G. & Gagliardelli, G. Italian-English - English-Italian Commercial Dictionary. rev. ed. 1167p. 1992. 123.00 (*88-425-1079-3*, Mursia) IBD Ltd.

Ragazzini, Giuseppe. English - Italian, Italian - English Commercial Dictionary: Concise Edition. 1991. 75.00 (*0-8288-8476-5*) Fr & Eur.

— Italian & English Commercial Dictionary: Dizionario Commerciale. 672p. (ENG & ITA.). 1984. 39.95 (*0-8288-0108-8*, M7808) Fr & Eur.

— Italian-English, English-Italian Commercial Dictionary: Dizionario Commerciale Italiano-Inglese-Italiano. 813p. (ENG & ITA.). 1981. 150.00 (*0-8288-0109-6*, M8457) Fr & Eur.

— The New Ragazzini English - Italian, Italian - English Dictionary: Il Nuovo Ragazzini Dizionario Inglese-Italiano: Italiano-Inglese. 2nd ed. 2144p. (ENG & ITA.). 1989. lib. bdg. 150.00 (*0-8288-3331-1*, F9072) Fr & Eur.

— Il Nuovo Ragazzini - Biagi Concise Dizionario Inglese e Italiano: Italian English. 2nd ed. 1991. 85.00 (*0-685-49364-4*, F10010) Fr & Eur.

— Il Nuovo Ragazzini Dizionario Inglese-Italiano Italiano-Inglese. 2nd ed. 2144p. (ENG & ITA.). 1989. lib. bdg. 150.00 (*0-685-48307-X*, F9072) Fr & Eur.

— Nuovo Ragazzini Gigante. 2nd ed. 2128p. (ITA.). Date not set. 250.00 (*0-8288-9420-5*, F9073) Fr & Eur.

— Nuovo Ragazzini Rossi. 2nd ed. 2352p. (ENG & ITA.). Date not set. 195.00 (*0-8288-9424-8*) Fr & Eur.

Ragazzini, Giuseppe & Biagi, Adele. The New Ragazzini, Biagi Concise Italian-English, English-Italian Dictionary: Il Nuovo Ragazzini - Biagi Concise Dizionario Inglese-Italiano Italiano-Inglese. 2nd ed. 1200p. (ENG & ITA.). 1986. lib. bdg. 85.00 (*0-8288-3332-X*, F10010) Fr & Eur.

***Rage, J. D.** Dear Grim Reaper. 80p. 1993. per., pap. 5.00 (*1-886206-06-6*) Venom Pr.

— Man Trouble. 73p. 1989. per., pap. 5.00 (*1-886206-01-5*) Venom Pr.

— Rage. 58p. 1989. per., pap. 4.00 (*1-886206-02-3*) Venom Pr.

— Relentless. (Illus.). 51p. (Orig.). 1994. pap. 4.00 (*1-886206-13-9*) Venom Pr.

***Rage, J. D., et al.** Flashes of Dreams: A Poetry Anthology. 49p. 1988. per., pap. 4.00 (*1-886206-00-7*) Venom Pr.

Rage, Jean-Claude. Serpentes. (Encyclopedia of Paleoherpetology Ser.: Pt. 11). (Illus.). 80p. 1984. pap. text ed. 70.00 (*3-437-30448-8*) Lubrecht & Cramer.

Rageau, Jean-Pierre, jt. auth. see Chaliand, Gerard.

Ragelis, Edward P. Seafood Toxins. LC 84-18551. (Symposium Ser.: No. 262). 472p. 1984. lib. bdg. 87.95 (*0-8412-0863-8*) Am Chemical.

Ragen, Alex. A Lexicon of C. 182p. 1987. 23.90 (*1-85058-090-1*, Pub. by Sigma Pr UK) Bk Clearing Hse.

Ragen, Brian A. A Wreck on the Road to Damascus: Innocence, Guilt & Conversion in Flannery O'Connor. 230p. 1989. 12.95 (*0-8294-0605-0*) Loyola Univ Pr.

Ragen, Naomi. Jephte's Daughter. LC 88-40183. 416p. 1990. mass mkt. 5.99 (*0-446-35862-2*) Warner Bks.

— The Sacrifice of Tamar. 1994. 24.00 (*0-517-59561-3*, Crown) Crown Pub Group.

— Sotah. 1993. mass mkt. 5.99 (*0-06-100707-2*, Harp PBks) HarpC.

— Sotah: A Novel. 464p. 1992. 22.00 (*0-517-58977-X*, Crown) Crown Pub Group.

Rager, Mike. Automotive Rebuilders Hazardous Materials Program Employee Training Manual. (Illus.). (Orig.). (C). 1989. pap. write for info. (*0-318-65936-0*) Amer Hazmat.

— Automotive Repair Shop Hazardous Materials Program Employee Training Manual. (Illus.). (Orig.). (C). 1989. pap. write for info. (*0-318-65934-4*) Amer Hazmat.

— Body Shop Hazardous Materials Program Employee Training Manual. (Illus.). (Orig.). (C). 1989. pap. write for info. (*0-318-65935-2*) Amer Hazmat.

— Business-Industry Hazardous Materials Program Employee Training Manual. (Illus.). (Orig.). (C). 1989. pap. write for info. (*0-318-65930-1*) Amer Hazmat.

— Dryclean-Laundry Managers Manual: Hazardous Materials Program. (Illus.). (Orig.). (C). 1989. pap. write for info. (*0-318-65929-8*) Amer Hazmat.

— Hazardous Materials Program Employee Training Manual. (Illus.). (Orig.). (C). 1989. pap. write for info. (*0-318-65933-6*) Amer Hazmat.

— Photofinishing Hazardous Materials Employee Training Manual. (Illus.). (Orig.). (C). 1989. pap. write for info. (*0-318-65932-8*) Amer Hazmat.

— Vehicle Maintenance Repair Shop Hazardous Materials Program Employee Training Manual. (Illus.). (Orig.). (C). 1989. pap. write for info. (*0-318-65931-X*) Amer Hazmat.

Ragette, Friedrich. Architecture in Lebanon. (Illus.). 200p. 1975. 50.00 (*0-8156-6044-8*, Am U Beirut) Syracuse U Pr.

— Architecture in Lebanon: The Lebanese House During the 18th & 19th Centuries. LC 80-14121. 1980. reprint ed. 75.00 (*0-88206-041-4*) Caravan Bks.

— Baalbek. LC 80-19626. (Illus.). 128p. 1981. 18.00 (*0-8155-5059-6*, NP) Noyes.

Ragette, Friedrich, ed. Beirut of Tomorrow: Planning for Reconstruction. (Illus.). 142p. 1983. pap. text ed. 9.95 (*0-8156-6069-3*, Am U Beirut) Syracuse U Pr.

— Engineering & Architecture & the Future Environment of Man. 1968. pap. 14.95 (*0-8156-6013-8*, Am U Beirut) Syracuse U Pr.

Ragg, Laura, jt. ed. see Ragg, Lonsdale.

Ragg, Laura, tr. see Ragg, Lonsdale & Ragg, Laura, eds.

Ragg, Lonsdale. Dante & His Italy. LC 72-2129. (Studies in Dante: No. 9). (Illus.). 1972. lib. bdg. 75.00 (*0-8383-1462-7*) M S G Haskell Hse.

Ragg, Lonsdale & Ragg, Laura, eds. The Gospel of Barnabas. Ragg, Laura, tr. 273p. 1993. pap. text ed. write for info. (*1-881316-15-7*) A&B Bks.

***Ragg, Mark.** Body & Soul: Children, Teenagers & Cancer. 350p. (Orig.). 1995. pap. 16.95 (*0-85572-252-5*, Pub. by Hill Content Pubng AT) Seven Hills Bk.

Raggatt, Peter & Unwin, Lorna, eds. Change & Intervention: Vocational Education & Training. 224p. 1991. 65.00 (*1-85000-694-6*, Falmer Pr); pap. 27.00 (*1-85000-695-4*, Falmer Pr) Taylor & Francis.

Ragge. Immediate Eye Care. 208p. 1991. 92.00 (*0-8151-7008-4*, Yr Bk Med Pubs) Mosby Yr Bk.

Raggett, G., tr. see Brugsch, Emile & Maspero, Gaston.

Raggio, Grier & Stutman, Michael. How to Divorce in New York: Negotiating Your Divorce Settlement Without Tears Or Trial. enl. rev. ed. 224p. (Orig.). 1993. pap. 15.95 (*0-312-09273-3*) St Martin.

Raghariah, Jaiprakash. Basel Mission Industries in Malabar & South Canara, 1834-1914: A Study of Its Social & Economic Impact. 1990. 16.50 (*81-212-0324-4*, Pub. by Gian Publng Hse II) S Asia.

Raghava, Sulochana R. Sociology of Indian Literature. (C). 1987. lib. bdg. 26.00 (*81-7033-011-4*, Pub. by Rawat II) S Asia.

Raghavachari, V. T. Appellate Remedies under Excise & Customs. (C). 1990. 65.00 (*0-89771-222-6*) St Mut.

Raghavagosvami. Srila Raghava Gosvami's Sri Krsna-Bhakti-Ratna-Prakasa: The Jewel of Krsna-Bhakti, 2 vols. Kusakrathadasa, tr. (Krsna Library: Vols. 34-35). 432p. (Orig.). (C). 1988. pap. text ed. 24.00 (*0-944833-33-0*) Krsna Inst.

— Srila Raghava Gosvami's Sri Krsna-Bhakti-Ratna-Prakasa, Vol. 1: The Jewel of Krsna-Bhakti. Kusakrathadasa, tr. (Krsna Library: Vol. 34). 184p. (Orig.). (C). 1988. pap. text ed. 12.00 (*0-944833-31-4*) Krsna Inst.

— Srila Raghava Gosvami's Sri Krsna-Bhakti-Ratna-Prakasa, Vol. 2: The Jewel of Krsna-Bhakti. Kusakrathadasa, tr. (Krsna Library: Vol. 35). 248p. (Orig.). (C). 1988. pap. text ed. 12.00 (*0-944833-32-2*) Krsna Inst.

Raghavaiyangar, S. Srinivasa. Memorandum on the Progress of the Madras Presidency During the Last Forty Years of British Administration. (C). 1988. reprint ed. 54.00 (*81-206-0384-2*, Pub. by Asian Educ Servs II) S Asia.

Raghavan & Jones. Well Test Analysis. 300p. 1993. text ed. 80.00 (*0-13-953365-6*) P-H.

***Raghavan & Ozkan.** A Method for Computing Unsteady Flows in Porous Media. (Pitman Research Notes in Mathematics). 1995. pap. text ed. 49.95 (*0-470-23487-3*) Wiley.

Raghavan, D. An Introduction to Book Publishing. x, 333p. (C). 1988. text ed. 45.00 (*81-207-0739-7*, Pub. by Sterling Pubs II) Apt Bks.

Raghavan, G. N. Introducing India. 130p. 1983. 10.95 (*0-318-37002-6*) Asia Bk Corp.

— The Making of Modern India: Rammohun Roy to Gandhi & Nehru. (C). 1988. 24.00 (*81-212-0112-8*, Pub. by Gian Publng Hse II) S Asia.

Raghavan, J. V., ed. Higher Education in the Eighties (India) 1985. 25.00 (*0-8364-1346-6*, Pub. by Lancer II) S Asia.

Raghavan, Prabhakar, jt. auth. see Motwani, Rajeev.

Raghavan, R. K. Indian Police: Problems, Planning & Perspectives. (C). 1989. 31.00 (*81-85054-60-6*, Pub. by Manohar II) S Asia.

Raghavan, S., ed. see Husemoller, D.

Raghavan, S., ed. see Ivic, A.

Raghavan, S. V., ed. Local Area Networks: Proceedings of the IFIP TC6 International Conference (INDOLAN 1990), Madras, India, 30-31 Jan., 1990. 316p. 1990. 84.50 (*0-444-88761-X*, North Holland) Elsevier.

Raghavan, S. V., et al, eds. Computer Networks, Architecture & Applications: Proceedings, India, October 1992. LC 93-15617. (IFIP Transactions C: Communications Systems Ser.: Vol. C-13). x, 298p. 1993. pap. 100.00 (*0-444-89968-5*, North Holland) Elsevier.

Raghavan, T. E., ed. Stochastic Games & Related Topics: In Honor of Professor L. S. Shapley. (Theory & Decision Library: Vol. C). (C). 1991. lib. bdg. 102.50 (*0-7923-1016-0*) Kluwer Ac.

Raghavan, V. Embryogenesis in Angiosperms: A Developmental & Experimental Study. (Developmental & Cell Biology Ser.: No. 17). (Illus.). 304p. 1986. 64.95 (*0-521-26771-4*) Cambridge U Pr.

Raghavan, V., ed. & pref. Phase Diagrams of Ternary Iron Alloys, Pt. 1. (Monograph Series on Alloy Phase Diagrams). (Illus.). 219p. (C). 1990. reprint ed. text ed. 186.00 (*0-87170-230-4*) ASM.

Raghavan, V., ed. The Ramayana Tradition in Asia. 1982. 18.00 (*0-8364-0899-3*, Pub. by National Sahitya Akademi) S Asia.

Raghavan, V., ed. see Bhoja.

Raghavarao, D., jt. auth. see Desu, M. M.

Raghavarao, Damaraju. Constructions & Combinatorial Problems in Design of Experiments. 416p. 1988. reprint ed. pap. 10.95 (*0-486-65685-3*) Dover.

Raghavaro. Exploring Statistics. (Statistics: Vol. 92). 296p. 1988. 55.00 (*0-8247-7952-5*) Dekker.

***Raghaven, G. N.** The Press in India: A New History. (C). 1994. 28.50 (*81-212-0482-8*, Pub. by Gian Publng Hse II) S Asia.

Raghaven, V. Developmental Biology of Fern Gametophytes. (Illus.). 250p. (C). 1989. 89.95 (*0-521-33022-X*) Cambridge U Pr.

Raghavendra, A. S. Physiology of Trees. 528p. 1991. text ed. 125.00 (*0-471-50110-7*) Wiley.

Raghavendra, A. S., jt. ed. see Sethuraj, M. R.

Raghavendra, C. S., jt. auth. see Varma, Anujan.

Raghavulu, C. V., jt. ed. see Arora, Ramesh K.

***Ragheb, Mounir, et al.** Free Time Boredom: Manual & Testing Tool. 25p. (Orig.). (C). 1995. pap. 20.00 (*1-882883-19-5*) Idyll Arbor.

Ragheb, Sanaa, tr. see Ezeldin, Ahmed G.

Raghu, R. Palat. Tax Planning for the Salaried Employees. (C). 1990. 55.00 (*0-89771-259-5*) St Mut.

Raghunandan, Lakshmi. Contemporary Indian Poetry in English: With Special Emphasis on Nissim Ezekiel, Kamala Das, R. Parthasarathy & A. K. Ramanujan. 1990. text ed. 37.50 (*81-85047-68-5*, Pub. by Reliance Pub Hse II) Apt Bks.

Raghunathadasagosvami. Srila Raghunatha dasa Gosvami's Sri Stavavali, Collected Prayers, 4 Vols. Kuskrathadasa, tr. (Krsna Library: Vols. 93, 4, 94, 95). (Orig.). 1990. pap. text ed. 32.00 (*1-56130-002-0*) Krsna Inst.

— Srila Raghunatha dasa Gosvami's Sri Stavavali, Vol. 4: Collected Praayers. Kusakrathadasa, tr. (Krsna Library: Vol. 95). 136p. (Orig.). 1990. pap. text ed. 8.00 (*0-944833-98-5*) Krsna Inst.

— Srila Raghunatha dasa Gosvami's Sri Stavavali, VOl. 1: Collected Prayers. Kusakrathadasa, tr. (Krsna Library: Vol. 93). 112p. (Orig.). 1990. pap. text ed. 8.00 (*0-944833-96-9*) Krsna Inst.

— Srila Raghunatha dasa Gosvami's Sri Stavavali, Vol. 3: Collected Prayers. Kusakrathadasa, tr. (Krsna Library: Vol. 94). 128p. (Orig.). 1990. pap. text ed. 8.00 (*0-944833-97-7*) Krsna Inst.

— Srila Raghunatha dasa Gosvami's Sri Vraja-vilasa-stava: Prayers Glorifying the Lord's Pastimes in Vraja. Kusakrathadasa, tr. (Krsna Library: Vol. 4). 97p. (Orig.). (C). 1987. pap. text ed. 8.00 (*0-944833-03-9*) Krsna Inst.

— Srila Ragunatha dasa Gosvami's Sri Dana-Keli-Cintamani: The Cintamani Jewel of the Toll Pastime. Kusakrathadasa, tr. (Krsna Library: Vol. 111). 103p. (Orig.). 1990. pap. text ed. 8.00 (*1-56130-020-9*) Krsna Inst.

Raghunathan, M. S. Discrete Subgroups of Lie Groups. LC 71-189389. (Ergebnisse der Mathematik und Ihrer Grenzgebiete Ser.: Vol. 68). 240p. 1972. 42.00 (*0-387-05749-8*) Spr-Verlag.

Raghupathy, Raj, jt. ed. see Talwar, Gursaran P.

Raghuram, C., jt. auth. see Upadhyay, K. S.

Raghuram, R. Computer Simulation of Electronic Circuits. 246p. 1990. text ed. 57.95 (*0-470-21331-0*) Halsted Pr.

***Raghuramaiah, K. Lakshmi.** Hurricane: Autobiography of a Woman. (C). 1994. 28.00x (*81-7001-100-0*, Pub. by Chanakya II) S Asia.

— Night Birds: Indian Prostitutes from Devadasis to Call Girls. (C). 1991. text ed. 19.50 (*81-7001-084-5*, Pub. by Chanakya II) S Asia.

***Raghvan, G. S.** Warning of Kashmir. (C). 1993. reprint ed. 14.00x (*81-7041-824-0*, Pub. by Anmol II) S Asia.

Ragin, Bryant T., Jr., tr. see Calvi, Giulia.

Ragin, Charles. Constructing Social Research. 128p. 1994. pap. 15.95 (*0-8039-9021-9*) Pine Forge.

Ragin, Charles C. The Comparative Method: Moving Beyond Qualitative & Quantitative Strategies. LC 86-30800. 218p. 1987. pap. 13.00 (*0-520-06618-9*) U CA Pr.

— The Comparative Method: Moving Beyond Qualitative & Quantitative Strategies. LC 86-30800. 203p. reprint ed. pap. 57.90 (*0-7837-4698-9*, 2044485) Bks Demand.

Ragin, Charles C. & Becker, Howard S., eds. What Is a Case? Exploring the Foundations of Social Inquiry. (Illus.). 240p. (C). 1992. pap. 17.95 (*0-521-42188-8*) Cambridge U Pr.

— What Is a Case? Exploring the Foundations of Social Inquiry. (Illus.). 240p. (C). 1992. 59.95 (*0-521-42050-4*) Cambridge U Pr.

Ragini, Sri. Hindu Dances (Nrityanjali) 84p. 1982. 14.95 (*0-318-36310-0*) Asia Bk Corp.

Ragins, Marianne. Winning Scholarships for College: An Insider's Guide. 1994. pap. 10.95 (*0-8050-3072-7*) H Holt & Co.

Ragins, Sanford. Jewish Responses to Anti-Semitism in Germany, 1870-1914: A Study in the History of Ideas. LC 80-13202. (Alumni Series of the Hebrew Union College Press). 240p. reprint ed. pap. 68.40 (*0-8357-3455-2*, 2039716) Bks Demand.

Raginsky, Nina, et al, illus. Aperture, Issue 88. (Fine Photography Ser.). 80p. 1982. pap. 18.50 (*0-89381-099-1*) Aperture.

Ragionieri, Rodolfo, jt. ed. see Cerutti, Furio.

Ragir, John. La Svengali. 58p. 1992. pap. 5.95 (*1-56850-002-5*) Chicago Plays.

Raglan, FitzRoy. The Hero: A Study in Tradition, Myth, & Drama. LC 75-23424. 296p. 1975. reprint ed. text ed. 65.00 (*0-8371-8138-0*, RATH, Greenwood Pr) Greenwood.

Ragland. Spreading the Word: Mississippi Newspaper Abstracts of Genealogical Interest, 1825-1935. 255p. (Orig.). 1991. pap. 20.00 (*1-55613-451-7*) Heritage Bk.

Ragland, Ellie. Essays on the Pleasures of Death: From Freud to Lacan. 240p. 1994. pap. 16.95 (*0-415-90722-5*, A9909, Routledge NY) Routledge.

— Essays on the Pleasures of Death: From Freud to Lacan. 240p. 1994. 55.00 (*0-415-90721-7*, A9905, Routledge NY) Routledge.

***Ragland, Joyce C. & Hill, Marie S.** Women As Educational Leaders: Opening Windows, Pushing Ceilings. 144p. 1995. 38.00 (*0-8039-6136-7*); pap. 18.00 (*0-8039-6137-5*) Corwin Pr.

Ragland, Kay. Guinea Pigs. (Illus.). 128p. 1989. 9.95 (*0-86622-830-6*, KW-016) TFH Pubns.

— Kittens. 1988. 9.95 (*0-87666-857-0*, KW019) TFH Pubns.

Ragland, Margaret. Full of Joy. 1980. pap. 6.25 (*0-89137-415-9*) Quality Pubns.

— What's It Worth? Probing Our Values with Questions Jesus Asked. 1977. pap. 6.25 (*0-89137-409-4*) Quality Pubns.

Ragland, Mary L. & Williams, Jane J. Warren County, Mississippi, Probate Index. 242p. (Orig.). 1993. pap. text ed. 21.00 (*0-685-70624-9*) Heritage Bk.

Ragland, P. C., jt. ed. see Puffer, J. H.

Ragland, Paul C. Basic Analytical Petrology. (Illus.). 384p. (C). 1989. pap. text ed. 21.95 (*0-19-504535-1*) OUP.

Ragland, Sheila, ed. see Shirley, Anita G.

Ragland-Sullivan, Ellie. Jacques Lacan & the Philosophy of Psychoanalysis. LC 84-16125. 384p. 1987. pap. 13.95 (*0-252-01465-0*) U of Ill Pr.

Ragland-Sullivan, Ellie, ed. Lacan & the Subject of Language. 256p. 1991. 42.50 (*0-415-90307-6*, A4430, Routledge NY); pap. 14.95 (*0-415-90308-4*, A4434, Routledge NY) Routledge.

Ragland, Teresa, illus. Baby Days & Lullabye Nights. 48p. (J). 1993. 17.95 (*0-8249-8619-9*, Ideals Child); audio, boxed 24.95 (*0-8249-7629-0*, Ideals Child) Hambleton-Hill.

Ragland, Teresa B., illus. Cooking in the Kitchen with Santa. (Favorite Christmas Tales Ser.). 32p. (J). (ps up). 1992. lib. bdg. 11.95 (*1-56674-028-2*) Forest Hse.

— Cooking in the Kitchen with Santa. 32p. (J). 1992. pap. 4.95 (*0-8249-3096-7*, Ideals Child) Hambleton-Hill.

Ragland, Thomas E. The Faces of Fear: An Inside Look at Fear Itself. Libb, Melva, ed. (Illus.). 240p. (Orig.). 1988. pap. text ed. 6.95 (*0-936369-15-9*) Son-Rise Pubns.

Ragle, Nina S. Even Monkeys Fall Out of Trees: John Naka's Collection of Japanese Proverbs. LC 87-60655. 256p. 1987. 13.95 (*0-9618475-0-6*) Nippon Art Frms.

Raglin, Tim, illus. Pecos Bill. LC 88-11581. 36p. (J). (ps up). 1991. pap. 14.95 (*0-88708-081-2*, Rabbit); audio 19.95 (*0-88708-086-3*, Rabbit) S&S Childrens.

Ragman Rolls Staff. Instrumenta Publica Sive Processus Super Fidelitatibus et Homagiis Scotorum Domino Regi Angliae Factis A.D. MCCXCI MCCXCVI. Thomson, Thomas, ed. LC 76-174294. (Bannatyne Club, Edinburgh. Publications: No. 47). reprint ed. 27.50 (*0-404-52757-4*) AMS Pr.

Ragnarsson, Ingemar & Nilsson, Sven G. Shapes & Shells in Nuclear Structure. (Illus.). 432p. (C). 1994. write for info. (*0-521-37377-8*) Cambridge U Pr.

Rago, David, ed. see Montgomery, Susan J.

Rago, Linda. Dooryard Herbs. Knott, Susan, ed. LC 83-62799. (Illus.). 144p. (Orig.). 1984. pap. 12.95 (*0-938634-04-6*) Carabelle.

Rago, Linda O. A Dooryard Herb Cookbook. LC 88-60522. (Illus.). 128p. 1988. pap. 7.95 (*0-933126-92-1*) Pictorial Hist.

— Herbal Almanac. 1992. 12.95 (*0-912347-99-6*) Fulcrum Pub.

— Mugworts in May: A Folklore of Herbs. (Illus.). 121p. (Orig.). 1995. pap. 14.95 (*0-9646197-0-9*) Quarrier Pr.

Rago, Spephen A. UNIX System Five Network Programming. LC 92-45276. (Professional Computing Ser.). 784p. 1993. 45.95 (*0-201-56318-5*) Addison-Wesley.

Ragon, Michel. The Space of Death: A Study of Funerary Architecture, Decoration, & Urbanism. Sheridan, Alan, tr. LC 83-5958. (Illus.). 336p. reprint ed. pap. 95.80 (*0-8357-3129-4*, 2039391) Bks Demand.

***Ragone, David A.** Thermodynamics of Materials, 2 vols., Vol. 1. 1994. text ed. 75.95 (*0-471-30885-4*) Wiley.

***Ragone, David V.** Thermodynamics of Materials, 2 vols., Vol. 2. 1994. text ed. (*0-471-30886-2*) Wiley.

Ragone, Helena. Surrogate Motherhood: Conception in the Heart. LC 93-44717. 1994. text ed. 58.00 (*0-8133-1978-1*) Westview.

R

An Asterisk (*) at the beginning of an entry indicates that the title is appearing in BIP for the first time.

— Surrogate Motherhood: Conception in the Heart. (C). 1994. pap. text ed. 19.95 (0-8133-1979-X) Westview.
Ragones, Sergio & Evanier. Groo Bazaar, Vol. II. (Illus.). 96p. 1991. pap. 8.95 (0-87135-766-6) Marvel Entmnt.
Ragonese, Paul. Soul of a Cop. 1992. mass mkt. 4.99 (0-312-92816-5) St Martin.
***Ragonese, Roger & Dipierro, Joseph.** Principles of Biology. 544p. (C). 1995. pap. text ed., spiral bd. 42.95 (0-7872-0619-9) Kendall-Hunt.
Ragonese, Roger R. Principles of Biology: Biology 109-110. 5th ed. 496p. 1992. spiral bd. 38.95 (0-8403-7741-X) Kendall-Hunt.
Ragoni, Robert, ed. see Shotwell, James M.
***Ragoonath, Aldwin.** How Shall They Hear? The Art of Effective Biblical Preaching. (Orig.). 1995. pap. 7.95 (0-88270-689-6) Bridge Pub.
Ragosta, Marjorie, et al. Computer-Assisted Instruction & Compensatory Education: The ETS-Los Angeles Unified School District Study. 35.00 (0-317-67869-8) Educ Testing Serv.
Ragosta, Ray. The Act Proves Untenable. Kaplan, Peter, ed. 1976. 3.00 (0-915176-18-1) Pourboire.
— Sherds. deluxe ed. (Burning Deck Poetry Chapbooks Ser.). 32p. (Orig.). 1982. pap. 10.00 (0-930901-08-8) Burning Deck.
— Varieties of Religious Experience. (Burning Deck Poetry Ser.). 80p. (Orig.). 1993. pap. 8.00 (0-930901-83-5) Burning Deck.
— Varieties of Religious Experience. deluxe ed. (Burning Deck Poetry Ser.). 80p. (Orig.). 1993. pap. 15.00 (0-930901-84-3) Burning Deck.
Ragotzkie, Robert A., ed. Man & the Marine Environment. 200p. 1983. 119.00 (0-8493-5759-4, GC21, CRC Reprint) Franklin.
Ragozin, Zenaide A., tr. see Leroy-Beaulieu, Anatole.
Ragsdale, Bruce A. The House of Representatives. (Know Your Government Ser.). (Illus.). 96p. (J). (gr. 5 up). 1989. lib. bdg. 14.95 (1-55546-112-3) Chelsea Hse.
Ragsdale, Bruce A. & Treese, Joel D. Black Americans in Congress, Eighteen Seventy to Nineteen Eighty-Nine. LC 89-600409. (Illus.). 1990. per., pap. 12.00 (0-16-018476-2, S/N 052-071-008); boxed 16.00 (0-16-018477-0, S/N 052-071-00892-6) USGPO.
Ragsdale, Crystal S. The Women & Children of the Alamo. LC 93-41998. (Illus.). 114p. (J). 1994. 21.95 (1-880510-11-1); pap. 14.95 (1-880510-12-X) State House Pr.
Ragsdale, Crystal S., jt. auth. see Crawford, Ann F.
Ragsdale, Elizabeth. Poetic Notions. 16p. 1993. pap. text ed. 6.00 (0-9641217-0-0) Sea-Lark Print.
Ragsdale, Elizabeth S., jt. auth. see Moss, John R.
Ragsdale, Grady. Steve McQueen: The Final Chapter. LC 83-14681. 1983. 13.95 (0-88449-105-6, A524534) Vision Hse.
Ragsdale, Hugh. Tsar Paul & the Question of Madness: An Essay in History & Psychology. LC 88-24677. (Contributions to the Study of World History Ser.: No. 13). 284p. 1988. text ed. 59.95 (0-313-26608-5, RTS/, Greenwood Pr) Greenwood.
Ragsdale, Hugh & Ponomarev, Valerii N., eds. Imperial Russian Foreign Policy. (Woodrow Wilson Center Press Ser.). 400p. (C). 1993. 59.95 (0-521-44229-X) Cambridge U Pr.
Ragsdale, James G., jt. auth. see Karam, Thomas J.
Ragsdale, John. Camper's Guide to Outdoor Cooking: Tips, Techniques, & Delicious Eats. (Illus.). 130p. 1989. pap. 8.95 (0-87201-626-9) Gulf Pub.
Ragsdale, John G. Dutch Oven Cooking. 2nd ed. (Illus.). 80p. (Orig.). 1988. pap. 4.95 (0-88415-224-3) Gulf Pub.
— Dutch Ovens Chronicled. (Illus.). 104p. 1991. 14.95 (1-55728-220-X); pap. 7.95 (1-55728-221-8) U of Ark Pr.
— Growing Up in Union County, Arkansas. 1994. pap. 8.95 (0-87483-370-1) August Hse.
Ragsdale, John P. Protestant Mission Education in Zambia: Eighteen Eighty to Nineteen Fifty-Four. LC 85-40505. 192p. 1987. 36.50 (0-941664-09-0) Susquehanna U Pr.
Ragsdale, Kenneth B. Quicksilver: Terlingua & the Chisos Mining Company. LC 75-4081. (Illus.). 366p. 1995. pap. 13.95 (0-89096-188-3) Tex A&M Univ Pr.
— Wings over the Mexican Border: Pioneer Military Aviation in the Big Bend. (Illus.). 294p. 1984. 24.50 (0-292-79025-2) U of Tex Pr.
— The Year America Discovered Texas: Centennial '36. LC 86-30041. (Centennial Series of the Association of Former Students: No. 23). (Illus.). 352p. 1987. 18.95 (0-89096-299-5) Tex A&M Univ Pr.
Ragsdale, Lyn, jt. auth. see King, Gary.
Ragsdale, Nancy N. & Kuhr, Ronald J., eds. Pesticides: Minimizing the Risks. LC 87-1842. (ACS Symposium Ser.: No. 336). (Illus.). vii, 186p. 1987. 34.95 (0-8412-1022-5) Am Chemical.
Ragsdale, Nancy N. & Menzer, Robert E., eds. Carcinogenicity & Pesticides: Principles, Issues, & Relationships. LC 89-18052. (Symposium Ser.: No. 414). (Illus.). 237p. 1989. 54.95 (0-8412-1703-3) Am Chemical.
***Ragsdale, Nancy N., et al, eds.** Eighth International Congress of Pesticide Chemistry: Options 2000: Proceedings of a Conference Sponsored by the American Chemical Society & the International Union of Pure & Applied Chemistry, Washington, D. C., July 4-9, 1994. LC 94-42675. (Conference Proceedings Ser.). 1994. write for info. (0-8412-2995-3) Am Chemical.
Ragsdale, Ronald G. Permissible Computing in Education: Values, Assumptions, & Needs. LC 87-35964. 304p. 1988. text ed. 55.00 (0-275-92894-2, C2894, Praeger Pubs) Greenwood.
Ragsdale, Susann. Parallel Programming. 160p. (C). 1991. text ed. 30.00 (0-07-051186-1) McGraw.
Ragsdale, Tod A. Once a Hermit Kingdom: Ethnicity & Education & National Integration in Nepal. 252p. (C). 1989. 300.00 (0-89771-043-6, Pub. by Ratna Pustak Bhandar) St Mut.
— Once a Hermit Kingdom: Ethnicity, Education & National Integration in Nepal. (C). 1989. 34.00 (81-85054-75-4, Pub. by Manohar II) S Asia.
Ragsdale, Toda A. Once a Hermit Kingdom: Ethnicity & Education & National Integration in Nepal. 1989. 75.00 (0-7855-0232-7, Pub. by Ratna Pustak Bhandar) St Mut.
Ragsdale, Winifred, ed. A Sea of Upturned Faces: Proceedings of the Third Pacific Rim Conference on Children's Literature. LC 88-26534. 306p. 1989. 32.50 (0-8108-2108-7) Scarecrow.
Ragsdell, K. M., ed. see American Society of Mechanical Engineers Staff.
Ragucci. Voces de Hispanoamerica. 49.95 (0-686-56674-2, S-33067); 55.00 (0-8288-7948-6, S33067) Fr & Eur.
Raguet, Condy. Principles of Free Trade: Illustrated in a Series of Short & Familiar Essays. 2nd ed. LC 68-56569. (Reprints of Economic Classics Ser.). xix, 439p. 1969. reprint ed. 45.00 (0-678-00529-X) Kelley.
— Treatise on Currency & Banking. 2nd ed. LC 65-26375. (Library of Money & Banking History). xiv, 323p. 1967. reprint ed. 39.50 (0-678-00215-0) Kelley.
Raguin, Virginia C., ed. Conservation & Restoration of Stained Glass: An Owner's Guide. (Illus.). 40p. (Orig.). 1988. pap. 3.00 (0-317-93881-9) Census Stained.
***Raguin, Virginia C., et al, eds.** Artistic Integration in Gothic Buildings. (Illus.). 384p. 1995. 65.00 (0-8020-0457-1) U of Toronto Pr.
— Artistic Integration in Gothic Buildings. (Illus.). 384p. 1995. pap. 24.95 (0-8020-7477-4) U of Toronto Pr.
Ragulskis, K. M. & Yurkauskas, A. Y. Vibration of Bearings. (Applications of Vibration Ser.). (Illus.). 120p. 1989. 67.00 (0-89116-829-X) Hemisp Pub.
Ragulskis, K. M., ed. see Vulfson, I.
Ragulskis, K. M., et al. Vibromotors for Precision Microrobots. (Applications of Vibration Ser.). 400p. 1988. 105.00 (0-89116-549-5) Hemisp Pub.
Ragusa, John. Triggerman: The First Volume of John Ragusa's Mafia Secrets. 1994. pap. 5.99 (1-56171-335-X) Sure Sellers.
***Ragusa, Maria & Wolf, Juliette, eds.** The Alternative Pick, 1992. 390p. 1995. boxed 50.00 (0-9632606-3-4) Storm Music.
Ragusa, Olga. Comparative Perspectives on Manzoni. 38p. 1986. pap. 4.95 (0-913298-78-6) S F Vanni.
— Essential Italian Grammar. (Orig.). 1963. pap. 3.50 (0-486-20779-X) Dover.
— First Readings in Italian Literature - Letture Facili. (C). 1990. pap. 8.95 (0-913298-06-9) S F Vanni.
— Italian Verbs - Regular & Irregular. 1984. pap. 4.50 (0-913298-27-1) S F Vanni.
— Mallarme in Italy: Literary Influence & Critical Response. 1957. 10.95 (0-913298-34-4) S F Vanni.
— Narrative & Drama: Essays in Modern Italian Literature from Verga to Pasolini. (De Proprietatibus Litterarum, Ser. Practica: No. 110). 1976. pap. text ed. 40.00 (90-279-3474-6) Mouton.
— Pirandello: An Introduction to His Theatre. 198p. 1980. 18.00 (0-85224-373-1, Pub. by Edinburgh U Pr UK) Col U Pr.
— Say It in Italian. pap. 3.50 (0-486-20806-0) Dover.
— Teach Yourself Italian: Essential Grammar. (Teach Yourself Ser.). 1992. 14.95 (0-8288-8364-5) Fr & Eur.
— Verga's Milanese Tales. 1964. 10.95 (0-913298-33-6) S F Vanni.
Raguse, Dan. Prayer. (Active Bible Curriculum Ser.). 48p. (Orig.). 1990. pap. 9.99 (1-55945-104-1) Group Pub.
Raguso, Viola M. Olympian Plays: A Comprehensive Introduction to Greek Mythology Written in Television Script Form. LC 87-91373. (Illus.). 646p. (gr. 9-12). 1987. reprint ed. text ed. 11.95 (0-9619674-0-4) Olympian Plays.
Ragussis, Michael. Acts of Naming: The Family Plot in Fiction. 256p. 1987. 42.00 (0-19-504070-8) OUP.
— Figures of Conversion: The Jewish Question & English National Identity. LC 94-38191. (Post-Contemporary Interventions Ser.). (Illus.). 352p. 1995. lib. bdg. 49.95 (0-8223-1559-9); pap. text ed. 16.95 (0-8223-1570-X) Duke.
— The Subterfuge of Art: Language & the Romantic Tradition. LC 78-5845. 256p. reprint ed. pap. 73.00 (0-8357-6623-3, 2035269) Bks Demand.
Raguya-Robbins, Ann, ed. see Addison, Rita, et al.
Ragvald, Lars, jt. auth. see Lang, Graeme.
***Ragz.** Gotcha! (J). 1995. pap. 3.50 (0-671-88412-3) PB.
Ragz, M. M. Eyeballs for Breakfast. MacDonald, Patricia, ed. 128p. (Orig.). (J). (gr. 4-7). 1990. pap. 2.99 (0-671-68567-8, Minstrel Bks) PB.
— Eyeballs for Lunch. MacDonald, Patricia, ed. 114p. (Orig.). 1992. pap. 2.99 (0-671-75882-9, Minstrel Bks) PB.
— Eyeballs for Midnight Snack. MacDonald, Pat, ed. 144p. (Orig.). (J). 1994. pap. 3.50 (0-671-88411-5, Minstrel Bks) PB.
— French Fries up Your Nose. MacDonald, Pat, ed. 160p. (Orig.). (J). 1994. pap. 2.99 (0-671-88410-7, Minstrel Bks) PB.
— Sewer Soup. MacDonald, Patricia, ed. 128p. (Orig.). 1992. pap. 3.50 (0-671-75881-0) PB.
— Stiff Competition. MacDonald, Patricia, ed. 144p. (Orig.). 1991. pap. 2.99 (0-671-72522-X, Minstrel Bks) PB.
Raha, M. K. Polyandry in India. (C). 1987. 61.00 (81-212-0105-5, Pub. by Gian Publng Hse II) S Asia.
— Tribal Situation in West Bengal. (C). 1990. 47.50 (0-8364-2648-7, Pub. by Firma KLM) S Asia.
Raha, M. K. & Commar, P. C., eds. Tribal India: Problem Development Prospect, 2 vols., Set. 400p. 1989. write for info. (81-212-0273-6, Pub. by Gian Publng Hse II) S Asia.
Raha, Manis K. Matriliny to Patriliny: A Study of the Rabha Society. (C). 1989. 49.00 (81-212-0244-2, Pub. by Gian Publng Hse II) S Asia.
***Raha, Manis K. & Khan, Iar A., eds.** Polity, Political Process & Social Control in South Asia: The Tribal & Rural Perspectives. (C). 1993. 32.00 (81-212-0413-5, Pub. by Gian Publng Hse II) S Asia.
Raha, Manisk. The Himalaya Heritage. (C). 1987. 48.00 (81-212-0082-2, Pub. by Gian Publng Hse II) S Asia.
Raha, S., jt. auth. see Sinha, Bikas K.
Rahaee, Farhang, ed. The Iran-Iraq War: The Politics of Aggression. LC 92-33379. 256p. 1993. lib. bdg. 39.95 (0-8130-1176-0); pap. 19.95 (0-8130-1177-9) U Press Fla.
Raham, R. Gary. Dinosaurs in the Garden: A Naturalist's Guide to Backyard Biology & Evolution. (Illus.). 280p. 1988. 22.95 (0-937548-10-3) Plexus Pub.
— Sillysaurs: Dinosaurs That Could Have Been. (Illus.). 16p. (Orig.). (J). (gr. k-4). 1990. write for info. (0-9626301-0-1) Biostration.
Rahaman, A. Quranic Sciences. 19.95 (0-933511-32-9) Kazi Pubns.
***Rahaman, Vashanti.** A Little Salmon for Witness. LC 95-726. (Illus.). (J). 1996. write for info. (0-525-67521-3, Lodestar Bks) Dutton Child Bks.
Rahamimoff, Rami & Katz, Bernard, eds. Calcium Neuronal Function & Transmitter Release. 1986. lib. bdg. 122.50 (0-89838-791-4) Kluwer Ac.
Rahardjo, Budi. Buku Pegangan Sistem Unix Dan Internet. 266p. (IND.). 1994. pap. 19.95 (1-885130-11-2) Open Pathways.
Rahardjo, Haianto, jt. auth. see Fredlund, Delwyn G.
Rahat, Naveedi. Male Out Migration & Matri-Weighted Households: A Case Study of a Junjab Village in Pakistan. (C). 1990. text ed. 26.00 (81-7075-015-6, Pub. by Hindustan IA) S Asia.
Rahau, Giora, jt. auth. see Shoham, Shlomo G.
Rahbar, Daud & Schimmel, Anne M., eds. Urdu Letters of Mirza Asadu'llah Khan Ghalib. Schimmel, Anne M., tr. LC 87-6447. 628p. 1987. 59.50 (0-88706-412-4) State U NY Pr.
Rahdent, George K. & Roth, Larry M. Appeals to the Eleventh Circuit, 1984-1994, 3 vols., Set. 1000p. 1994. ring bd. 180.00 (0-409-26067-3) Michie Butterworth.
— Appeals to the Fifth Circuit, 1977-1994, 2 vols. 1000p. 1994. ring bd. 175.00 (0-409-26070-3) Michie Butterworth.
Rahdert, George K. & Roth, Larry M. Appeals to the Eleventh Circuit, 1984-1994, 3 vols. suppl. ed. 1000p. 1994. 42.50 (0-685-43647-0, D & S Pub) Butterworth Legal Pubs.
— Appeals to the Eleventh Circuit, 1984-1994. suppl. ed. 1994. ring bd. 47.00 (0-614-03174-5) Butterworth Legal Pubs.
— Appeals to the Fifth Circuit, 1977-1994, 2 vols. suppl. ed. 1000p. 1994. 50.00 (0-685-73809-4) Butterworth Legal Pubs.
Rahdert, Mark C. Covering Accident Costs: Insurance, Liability & Tort Reforms. LC 94-830. 288p. (C). 1994. text ed. 54.95 (1-56639-232-2); pap. text ed. 29.95 (1-56639-233-0) Temple U Pr.
Rahe, Harves. Index to Doctoral Dissertations. 107p. (C). 1975. pap. text ed. 10.00 (0-9603064-1-2) Delta Pi Epsilon.
— Index to Doctoral Dissertations in Business Education, Supplement, 1975-1980. 2nd ed. 71p. (C). 1981. pap. text ed. 8.00 (0-685-50912-5) Delta Pi Epsilon.
Rahe, Jurgen, jt. auth. see Kopal, Zdenek.
Rahe, Paul A. Republics Ancient & Modern Vol. I: The Ancient Regime in Classical Greece. LC 94-5728. 380p. 1994. pap. text ed. 22.95x (0-8078-4473-X) U of NC Pr.
— Republics Ancient & Modern, Vol. II: New Modes & Orders in Early Modern Political Thought. LC 94-5728. 490p. (C). 1994. pap. text ed. 24.95x (0-8078-4474-8) U of NC Pr.
— Republics Ancient & Modern, Vol. III: Inventions of Prudence: Constituting the American Regime. LC 94-5728. 380p. (C). 1994. pap. text ed. 19.95x (0-8078-4475-6) U of NC Pr.
***Raheb, Mitri.** I Am a Palestinian Christian. Gritsch, Ruth C., tr. LC 95-5483. 1995. write for info. (0-8006-2663-X, Fortress Pr) Augsburg Fortress.
Raheel. Protective Clothing Systems & Materials. (Occupational Safety & Health Ser.: Vol. 25). 272p. 1994. 125.00 (0-8247-9118-5) Dekker.
Raheem, Aminah. Soul Return: Integrating Body, Psyche & Spirit. rev. ed. LC 90-43487. (Illus.). 214p. 1991. pap. 12.95 (0-944031-10-2) Aslan Pub.
Raheja, Dev G. Assurance Technologies: Principles & Practices. (Engineering & Technology Management Ser.). 1991. text ed. 55.00 (0-07-051212-4) McGraw.
Raheja, Gloria G. The Poison in the Gift: Ritual, Prestation, & the Dominant Caste in North Indian Village. (Illus.). xiv, 286p. 1988. lib. bdg. 42.50 (0-226-70728-8); pap. text ed. 16.95 (0-226-70729-6) U Ch Pr.
Raheja, Gloria G. & Gold, Ann G. Listen to the Heron's Words: Reimagining Gender & Kinship in North India. LC 93-12586. 1994. 45.00 (0-520-08370-9); pap. 17.00 (0-520-08371-7) U CA Pr.
Rahim, Abdur. The Principles of Muhammadan Jurisprudence According to the Hanali, Maliki, Shafi'i & Hanbali Schools. LC 79-2879. 443p. 1981. reprint ed. 34.50 (0-8305-0047-2) Hyperion Conn.
Rahim, Enayetur. Scholar's Guide to Washington, D. C. for South Asian Studies: Afghanistan, Bangladesh, Bhutan, India, Maldives, Nepal, Pakistan, & Sri Lanka. LC 81-607847. (Scholar's Guide to Washington D.C. Ser.: No. 8). 430p. 1981. text ed. 29.95 (0-87474-778-3, Johns Hopkins); pap. 12.95 (0-87474-777-5, Johns Hopkins) W Wilson Ctr Pr.
Rahim, M. A. Jesus the Prophet of Islam. pap. 14.95 (1-56744-500-4) Kazi Pubns.
Rahim, M. Afzalur. Managing Conflict in Organizations. 2nd ed. LC 92-7479. 248p. 1992. text ed. 49.95 (0-275-93680-5, C3680, Praeger Pubs) Greenwood.
Rahim, M. Afzalur, ed. A Bibliography of Doctoral Dissertations & Masters' Theses on Conflict, 1975-86. 17p. (C). 1987. 5.00 (0-9623337-0-0) Intl ACM.
— Managing Conflict: An Interdisciplinary Approach. LC 88-14104. 348p. 1989. text ed. 59.95 (0-275-92683-4, C2683, Praeger Pubs) Greenwood.
— Theory & Research in Conflict Management. LC 90-31212. 256p. 1990. text ed. 55.00 (0-275-93173-0, C3173, Praeger Pubs) Greenwood.
Rahim, M. Afzalur & Blum, Albert A., eds. Global Perspectives on Organizational Conflict. LC 93-11874. 168p. 1994. text ed. 55.00 (0-275-93828-X, Praeger Pubs) Greenwood.
Rahim, M. Afzalur & Kaufman, Sanda, eds. A Bibliography of Doctoral Dissertations & Masters' Theses on Conflict, 1975-89. 2nd ed. 46p. (C). 1989. 10.00 (0-9623337-1-9) Intl ACM.
Rahim, Syed A. & Wedemeyer, Dan J., eds. Telecom Pacific. 200p. 1983. pap. text ed. 12.50 (0-8248-0918-1) Pac Telecom.
Rahimi, M., jt. ed. see Karwowski, Waldemar.
Rahimi, Mansour & Karwowski, Waldemar, eds. Human-Robot Interaction. 400p. 1992. 110.00 (0-85066-809-3, Pub. by Tay Francis Ltd UK) Taylor & Francis.
Rahimieh, Nasrin. Oriental Responses to the West: Comparative Essays in Select Writers from the Muslim World. x, 124p. 1990. pap. 37.25 (90-04-09177-7) E J Brill.
***Rahimov, Ibrahim.** Random Sums & Branching Stochastic Processes. LC 95-2595. (Lecture Notes in Statistics: Vol. 96). 1995. write for info. (0-387-94446-X) Spr-Verlag.
Rahimtoola, jt. ed. see Kulick.
Rahimtoola, S. H., jt. ed. see Gersh, B. J.
Rahimtoola, Shahbudin H. Coronary Bypass Surgery. LC 77-8284. (Cardiovascular Clinics Ser.: Vol. 8, No. 2). 287p. 1977. text ed. 35.00 (0-8036-7270-5) Davis Co.
Rahimtoola, Shahbudin H., ed. Controversies in Coronary Artery Disease. LC 82-7373. (Cardiovascular Clinics Ser.: Vol. 13, No. 1). (Illus.). 367p. 1983. 45.00 (0-8036-7272-1) Davis Co.
Rahimuddin, Muhammad, tr. see Salik, S. A.
Rahina, Rustam N. A Manual of English-Gujarati Dictionary. 1981. write for info. (0-8288-1769-3) Fr & Eur.
Rahinantti, K. Finnish-Portuguese-Finnish Dictionary. 359p. (FIN & POR.). 1975. pap. 69.95 (0-8288-5889-6, M9649) Fr & Eur.
Rahm, Debra L., jt. auth. see Burger, Leslie.
Rahm, Dianne, jt. ed. see Lambright, Henry.
Rahm, Dianne, jt. ed. see Lambright, W. Henry.
Rahm, Dick, jt. auth. see Tamburin, Henry J.
Rahman, A. Encyclopaedia of Seerah 1-8. 65.00 (0-935782-95-8); 65.00 (0-685-73782-9); 65.00 (0-685-73783-7); 65.00 (0-685-73784-5); 65.00 (0-685-73785-3); 65.00 (0-685-73786-1); 65.00 (0-685-73787-X); 65.00 (0-685-73788-8) Kazi Pubns.
— Essentials of Islam. pap. 5.50 (0-935782-97-4) Kazi Pubns.
— Maharaja Swawi Jai Singh II & Indian Renaissance. (C). 1987. 21.00 (81-7013-041-7, Pub. by Navrang) S Asia.
— Muhammad As a Military Leader. pap. 14.95 (1-56744-146-7) Kazi Pubns.
— Muhammad, the Educator of Mankind. pap. 18.00 (1-56744-150-5) Kazi Pubns.
— One & Two-Dimensional NMR Spectroscopy. 578p. 1989. 182.00 (0-444-87316-3) Elsevier.
— Prayer, Its Significance & Benefits. pap. 14.50 (1-56744-182-3) Kazi Pubns.
— Studies in Natural Products Chemistry: Stereoselective Synthesis, Pt. E. (Studies in Natural Products Chemistry: Vol. 8). 1991. 200.00 (0-444-88967-1) Elsevier.
— Studies in Natural Products Chemistry: Structure Elucidation, Vol. 5 No. 2. 1990. 256.50 (0-444-88336-3) Elsevier.
— Studies in Natural Products Chemistry, Volume Three: Stereoselective Synthesis (Part B) 540p. 1989. 174.50 (0-444-87298-1) Elsevier.
— Subject Index of Holy Quran. 19.95 (0-933511-68-X) Kazi Pubns.
— Utility of Prayers. pap. 4.50 (0-933511-84-1) Kazi Pubns.
Rahman, A., ed. Handbook of Natural Products Data Vol. 1: Diterpenoid & Steroidal Alkaloids. 970p. 1990. 353.75 (0-444-88173-5) Elsevier.
— Stereoselective Synthesis, Part A. (Studies in Natural Products Chemistry: No. 1A). 520p. 1988. 228.25 (0-444-42970-0) Elsevier.
— Studies in Natural Products Chemistry: Structure & Chemistry. (Studies & Natural Products Chemistry: Vol. 7). 528p. 1990. 179.50 (0-444-88829-2) Elsevier.
— Studies in Natural Products Chemistry, Vol. 4: Stereoselective Synthesis, Part C. 760p. 1989. 231.00 (0-444-88033-X) Elsevier.
— Studies in Natural Products Chemistry, Volume 2: Structure Elucidation (Part A) 470p. 1989. 151.50 (0-444-43038-5) Elsevier.
— Studies in Products Chemistry, Vol. 6: Stereoselective Synthesis (Part D) 606p. 1990. 189.75 (0-444-88566-8) Elsevier.

R

Rahman, A. U. Handbook of Natural Products Data Vol. 3: Isoquinoline Alkaloids. 784p. 1994. 441.25 (*0-444-81888-X*) Elsevier.

Rahman, A. U., ed. Studies in Natural Products Chemistry, Vol. 14: Stereoselective Synthesis, Pt. 1. 938p. 1994. 442.75 (*0-444-81780-8*) Elsevier.

Rahman, A. U., jt. auth. see Ahmad, Viqar U.

Rahman, Afzular. Islam Ideology & a Way of Life. 1991. pap. 18.95 (*0-907052-04-5*) Kazi Pubns.

— Role of Muslim Woman in Society. 1991. pap. 18.95 (*0-933511-43-4*) Kazi Pubns.

Rahman, Anisur. East & West Pakistan: A Problem in the Political Economy of Regional Planning. LC 74-38766. (Harvard University. Center for International Affairs. Occasional Papers in International Affairs: No. 20). reprint ed. 27.50 (*0-404-54620-X*) AMS Pr.

— Expressive Form in the Poetry of Kamala Das. 1981. 10.00 (*0-8364-0730-X*, Pub. by Abhinav II) S Asia.

— Form & Value in the Poetry of Nissim Ezekiel. 1981. 10.00 (*0-8364-0731-8*, Pub. by Abhinav II) S Asia.

— People's Self Development: Perspectives on Participatory Action Research. LC 93-37607. 256p. (C). 1993. text ed. 55.00 (*1-85649-079-3*, Pub. by Zed Books UK); pap. 19.95 (*1-85649-080-7*, Pub. by Zed Books UK) Humanities.

Rahman, Asheq R. & Brief, Richard. The Australian Accounting Standards Review Board: The Establishment of Its Participative Review Process. LC 91-41423. (New Works in Accounting History, 1992). 568p. 1992. 90.00 (*0-8153-0802-7*) Garland.

Rahman, Atiur. Peasants & Classes: A Study in Differentiation in Bangladesh. 272p. (C). 1987. text ed. 49.95 (*0-86232-345-2*, Pub. by Zed Books UK); pap. 17.50 (*0-86232-346-0*, Pub. by Zed Books UK) Humanities.

Rahman, Atta-ur, ed. Advances in Natural Product Chemistry. LC 92-23126. 1992. text ed. 140.00 (*3-7186-5319-2*) Gordon & Breach.

***Rahman, Atta-ur & Choudhary, Muhammad I.** Solving Problems with NMR Spectroscopy. LC 95-15392. 1995. pap. write for info. (*0-12-066320-1*) Acad Pr.

Rahman, Azia-ur. Teach Yourself Urdu in Two Months. 1990. 6.95 (*0-87052-913-7*) Hippocrene Bks.

Rahman, F., ed. see Avicenna.

Rahman, Fazlur. Islam. 2nd ed. LC 78-68547. 1979. pap. text ed. 11.95 (*0-226-70281-2*) U Ch Pr.

— Islam & Modernity: Transformation of an Intellectual Tradition. LC 82-2720. (Publications of the Center for Middle Eastern Studies: No. 15). 184p. 1984. pap. text ed. 10.95 (*0-226-70284-7*) U Ch Pr.

— Major Themes of the Qur'an. LC 79-54189. 1980. 25.00 (*0-88297-051-8*); pap. 16.00 (*0-88297-046-1*) Bibliotheca.

— The Philosophy of Mulla Sadra Shirazi. LC 75-31693. 277p. 1976. 49.50 (*0-87395-300-2*) State U NY Pr.

Rahman, G. Arthur. Sea of Mystery. (Illus.). 1981. 5.95 (*0-940244-14-4*) Flying Buffalo.

***Rahman, H.** A British Defence Problem in the Middle East 1946-7. 220p. 1995. 75.00 (*0-86372-186-9*, Pub. by Ithaca UK) Paul & Co Pubs.

Rahman, Habib U. Chronology of Islamic History. 256p. (C). 1989. text ed. 45.00 (*0-8161-9067-4*, Hall Reference) Macmillan.

***Rahman, Hossain Zillur & Hossain, Mahabub, eds.** Rethinking Rural Poverty: Bangladesh As a Case Study. LC 94-23400. 1994. 25.95 (*0-8039-9205-X*) Sage.

Rahman, Inam-Ur, jt. auth. see Shieh, Paulinus S.

Rahman, Leila B., ed. Singapore Property Tax Cases (1959-1986) xxii, 413p. 1987. 99.00 (*9971-70-057-3*) Butterworth Legal Pubs.

Rahman, M. Applied Differential Equations for Scientists & Engineers, 2 vols., Set. LC 91-76270. 1991. 210.00 (*1-56252-056-3*) Computational Mech MA.

— Applied Differential Equations for Scientists & Engineers, 2 vols., Vol. 2: Partial Differential Equations. LC 91-76270. 356p. 1991. 73.00 (*1-56252-058-X*) Computational Mech MA.

— Water Waves: Relating Modern Theory to Advanced Engineering Practice, 3. (Institute of Mathematics & Its Applications Monograph). (Illus.). 220p. 1995. 79.00 (*0-19-853478-7*) OUP.

***Rahman, M., ed.** Laminar & Turbulent Boundary Layers. (Advances in Fluid Mechanics Ser.). 300p. 1996. 118.00 (*1-85312-294-7*) Computational Mech MA.

— Ocean Waves Engineering: M. Rahman. LC 94-70414. (Advances in Fluid Mechanics Ser.: Vol. 2). 240p. 1994. 104.00 (*1-56252-209-4*) Computational Mech MA.

Rahman, M., jt. auth. see Gasper, G.

***Rahman, M. A., ed.** Potential Fluid Flow. (Advances in Fluid Mechanics Ser.). 300p. 1995. 118.00 (*1-56252-279-5*) Computational Mech MA.

Rahman, M. M., et al, eds. Amorphous & Crystalline Silicon Carbide II. (Proceedings in Physics Ser.: Vol. 43). (Illus.). x, 232p. 1989. 65.00 (*0-387-51656-5*, 3515) Spr-Verlag.

Rahman, M. Samsur. Administrative Elite in Bangladesh. (Illus.). vii, 361p. 1991. 27.00 (*81-85445-02-8*, Pub. by Manak Pubns Pvt Ltd) Nataraj Bks.

Rahman, Matiur. Applied Differential Equations for Scientists & Engineers, 2 vols., Vol. 1: Ordinary Differential Equations. LC 91-76270. 656p. 1991. 170.00 (*1-56252-057-1*) Computational Mech MA.

— Hydrodynamics of Waves & Tides with Some Applications. LC 88-70754. (Topics in Engineering Ser.). 322p. 1989. pap. 86.00 (*0-931215-19-6*) Computational Mech MA.

Rahman, Mohammed M., ed. The Freudian Paradigm: Psychoanalysis & Scientific Thought. LC 73-89486. 1977. 37.95 (*0-911012-89-3*); pap. 23.95 (*0-88229-461-X*) Nelson-Hall.

Rahman, Muhammad A., jt. ed. see Fals-Borda, Orlando.

Rahman, Munibur. Visitations. Fitzsimmons, Thomas, ed. 208p. (Orig.). 1988. 19.95 (*0-942668-16-2*); pap. 14.95 (*0-942668-17-0*) Katydid Bks.

***Rahman, Mushtaqur.** Divided Kashmir. 1995. lib. bdg. 40.00 (*1-55587-598-X*) Lynne Rienner.

Rahman, Mushtaqur, ed. Muslim World: Geography & Development. LC 87-14087. (Illus.). 202p. (Orig.). (C). 1987. lib. bdg. 38.00 (*0-8191-6558-1*); pap. text ed. 21.50 (*0-8191-6559-X*) U Pr of Amer.

Rahman, N. From Molecular Dynamics to Combustion Chemistry: Proceedings of the Conference. 368p. 1992. text ed. 105.00 (*981-02-1146-5*) World Scientific Pub.

Rahman, N. A. A Course in Theoretical Statistics. 542p. 1968. text ed. 26.95 (*0-85264-068-4*) Lubrecht & Cramer.

— Practical Exercises in Probability & Statistics: With Answers & Hints on Solutions. 1972. 26.95 (*0-85264-217-2*) Lubrecht & Cramer.

— Theoretical Exercises in Probability & Statistics. (Charles Griffin Book Ser.). 259p. 1987. pap. 35.00 (*0-19-520582-0*) OUP.

Rahman, N. K. & Guidotti, C., eds. Collisions & Half-Collisions with Lasers. 443p. 1984. text ed. 205.00 (*3-7186-0192-3*) Gordon & Breach.

— Photon-Assisted Collisions & Related Topics. 377p. 1982. text ed. 169.00 (*3-7186-0130-3*) Gordon & Breach.

Rahman, Philip J., ed. see Wandrei, Donald.

Rahman, S. A. Punishment of Apostasy in Islam. pap. 9.00 (*1-56744-199-8*) Kazi Pubns.

***Rahman, S. S. & Chilingarian, G. V.** Casing Design: Theory & Practice. LC 94-39740. (Developments in Petroleum Science Ser.: Vol. 42). 1994. write for info. (*0-444-81743-3*) Elsevier.

Rahman, Shamsur. Selected Poems. Chowdhury, Kabir, tr. (Writers Workshop Redbird Ser.). 61p. 1975. 9.00 (*0-89253-621-7*); 4.80 (*0-89253-622-5*) Ind-US Inc.

Rahman, Sultan H. Macroeconomic Performance, Stabilization & Adjustment: The Experience of Bangladesh in the 1980s. (C). 1992. 12.00 (*81-85182-74-4*, Pub. by Indus Pub II) S Asia.

Rahman, Syedur, jt. auth. see Baxter, Craig.

Rahman, Tariq. The Legacy & Other Short Stories. Narang, Harish, ed. (C). 1989. 29.00 (*0-8364-2472-7*) S Asia.

Rahmani, Bijan M., jt. auth. see Hogan, William W.

***Rahmani, L. Y.** A Catalogue of Jewish Ossuaries: In the Collections of the State of Israel. (Illus.). 466p. 1994. text ed. 60.00x (*0-614-03629-1*, Ctr Judaic Studies) Eisenbrauns.

Rahmani, Levy. Soviet Psychology: Philosophical, Theoretical & Experimental Issues. LC 72-182041. 560p. 1973. text ed. 50.00 (*0-8236-6110-5*) Intl Univs Pr.

Rahmani, M. & Strutt, J. E. Hydrodynamic Modelling of Corrosion of Carbon Steels & Cast Irons in Sulphuric Acid. 212p. reprint ed. pap. 60.50 (*0-8357-6992-5*, 2037565) Bks Demand.

Rahmani, Ray A. & Flores, Romeo M., eds. Sedimentology of Coal & Coal-Bearing Sequences. 396p. 1985. pap. 71.50 (*0-632-01286-2*) Blackwell Sci.

Rahmann, H., ed. Gangliosides & Modulation of Neuronal Functions. (NATO ASI Series H: Vol. 7). xvi, 647p. 1987. 153.00 (*0-387-17587-3*) Spr-Verlag.

Rahmann, H. & Rahmann, M. The Neurobiological Basis of Memory & Behavior. (Illus.). 272p. 1992. 87.00 (*0-387-97545-4*) Spr-Verlag.

Rahmann, Heinrich, ed. Fundamentals of Memory Formation: Neuronal Plasticity & Brain Function. (Progress in Zoology Ser.: Vol. 37). 431p. 1990. text ed. 195.00 (*0-89574-297-7*, Pub. by Gustav Fischer Verlag); 165.00 (*0-685-58518-2*, Pub. by Gustav Fischer Verlag) VCH Pubs.

Rahmann, M., jt. auth. see Rahmann, H.

Rahmas, D. Steve, ed. see Badrig, Robert H.

Rahmas, D. Steve, ed. see Barger, James.

Rahmas, D. Steve, ed. see Buchanan, John G.

Rahmas, D. Steve, ed. see Cevasco, G. A.

Rahmas, D. Steve, ed. see Duin, Nancy E.

Rahmas, D. Steve, ed. see Finke, Blythe F.

Rahmas, D. Steve, ed. see Fleissner, Else M.

Rahmas, D. Steve, ed. see Fredman, Lionel E.

Rahmas, D. Steve, ed. see Fredman, Lionel E. & Kurland, Gerald.

Rahmas, D. Steve, ed. see Hecht, Robert A.

Rahmas, D. Steve, ed. see Kurland, Gerald.

Rahmas, D. Steve, ed. see Laing, Martha.

Rahmas, D. Steve, ed. see Lichello, Robert.

Rahmas, D. Steve, ed. see Longo, Lucas.

Rahmas, D. Steve, ed. see Mallin, Jay.

Rahmas, D. Steve, ed. see Mushkat, Jerome.

Rahmas, D. Steve, ed. see Paley, Alan L.

Rahmas, D. Steve, ed. see Paley, Alan.

Rahmas, D. Steve, ed. see Roucek, Joseph S.

Rahmas, D. Steve, ed. see Roucek, Joseph.

Rahmas, D. Steve, ed. see Salsini, Barbara.

Rahmas, D. Steve, ed. see Schoen, Celin V.

Rahmas, D. Steve, ed. see Shatraw, Harriett.

Rahmas, D. Steve, ed. see Shivanandan, Mary.

Rahmas, D. Steve, ed. see Smith, Pattie S.

Rahmas, D. Steve, ed. see Victor, R. F.

Rahmas, D. Steve, ed. see Whitney, R. W.

Rahmas, D. Steve, ed. see Zierau, Lillee D.

Rahmas, Sigrid. Mother Sun & Her Planet Children. (Illus.). 32p. (Orig.). (J). (ps-3). 1991. 6.25 (*0-87157-099-8*); pap. 2.95 (*0-87157-599-X*) Story Hse Corp.

Rahmas, Sigurd C., ed. see Finke, Blythe F.

Rahmas, Sigurd C., ed. see Green, Bill.

Rahmas, Sigurd C., ed. see Hecht, Robert A.

Rahmas, Sigurd C., ed. see Jones, William M.

Rahmas, Sigurd C., ed. see Kurland, Gerald.

Rahmas, Sigurd C., ed. see Longo, Lucas.

Rahmas, Sigurd C., ed. see Musso, Louis, III.

Rahmas, Sigurd C., ed. see Paley, Alan.

Rahmas, Sigurd C., ed. see Reynolds, Moira D.

Rahmas, Sigurd C., ed. see Richie, Claude G.

Rahmas, Sigurd C., ed. see Westphal, Ethel.

Rahmas, Steve, ed. see Abbazia, Patrick.

Rahmat-Samii, Yahya, jt. auth. see Hoppe, Daniel J.

***Rahmatian, Sassan.** Management Information Systems: Learning Exercises & Applications. LC 94-32648. (William R. King Series in Information Management). 1994. pap. text ed. write for info. (*0-13-172702-8*) P-H.

***Rahmato.** Agrarian Reform in Ethiopia. Date not set. per. 7.95 (*0-932415-07-5*) Red Sea Pr.

Rahmatullah Khan. The Iran-United States Claims Tribunal: Controversies, Cases & Contribution. (C). 1990. lib. bdg. 126.50 (*0-7923-0633-3*) Kluwer Ac.

Rahmel, A., jt. ed. see Holmes, David R.

Rahmel, Dan, jt. auth. see Rahmel, Ronald.

***Rahmel, Ronald & Rahmel, Dan.** Interfacing to the PowerPC. (Illus.). 450p. (Orig.). 1995. pap. text ed. 45.00 (*0-672-30548-8*) Sams.

Rahming, D'Arcy. Advanced Combat Ju-Jutsu: Entrance to Secrets. LC 92-61754. (Illus.). (Orig.). 1993. pap. 24.95 (*0-9627898-3-6*) Mdrn Bu-Jutsu.

— The College Student's Complete Guide to Self-Protection. Baarman, Jennifer H., ed. (Illus.). 160p. (Orig.). 1992. pap. 14.95 (*0-9627898-2-8*) Mdrn Bu-Jutsu.

— A College Student's Guide to Self Protection. (Illus.). 100p. 1991. pap. 14.95 (*0-9627898-1-X*) Mdrn Bu-Jutsu.

— Combat Ju-Jutsu: The Lost Art. LC 90-92024. (Illus.). 1990. 24.95 (*0-9627898-0-1*) Mdrn Bu-Jutsu.

— Secrets of Advanced Combat Ju-jutsu. 2nd ed. Baarman, Jenifer H., ed. (Illus.). 228p. 1994. pap. 24.95 (*0-9627898-8-7*) Mdrn Bu-Jutsu.

— Secrets of Miyama Rya Combat: Combat Ju-jutsu-the Cost Art. 2nd ed. 160p. 1995. pap. 18.95 (*1-886219-00-1*) Mdrn Bu-Jutsu.

Rahming, D'Arcy, jt. auth. see Hinton, William.

Rahmings, Keith. Printouts. 36p. (Orig.). 1981. pap. 5.50 (*0-937013-06-4*) Potes Poets.

Rahmlow, Harold F. The Teaching-Learning Unit. Langdon, Danny G., ed. LC 77-25107. (Instructional Design Library). (Illus.). 88p. 1978. 23.95 (*0-87778-122-2*) Educ Tech Pubns.

Rahmlow, Harold F., et al. Plato. Langdon, Danny G., ed. LC 79-26395. (Instructional Design Library). 112p. 1980. 23.95 (*0-87778-150-8*) Educ Tech Pubns.

Rahmy, M., jt. auth. see Droz, R.

Rahn, jt. ed. see Bischel.

Rahn, Ann W., jt. auth. see Raper, Kenneth B.

Rahn, Armin. The Basics of Soldering. 400p. 1993. text ed. 85.00 (*0-471-58471-1*) Wiley.

Rahn, Arthur & Heartwell, Charles, Jr. Textbook of Complete Dentures. 5th ed. (Illus.). 600p. 1993. text ed. 65.95 (*0-8121-1523-6*) Williams & Wilkins.

***Rahn, B. J., ed.** Ngaio Marsh: The Woman & Her Work. LC 95-5785. (Illus.). 274p. 1995. 32.50 (*0-8108-3023-X*) Scarecrow.

Rahn, C. J. Hornberger: Genealogical Information Regarding the Families of Hornberger & Yingling, & Related Families of Eckert, Lenhart, Steffy, Gerwig & Rahn. 164p. 1992. reprint ed. lib. bdg. 38.00 (*0-8328-2670-7*); reprint ed. pap. 28.00 (*0-8328-2671-5*) Higginson Bk Co.

Rahn, Carl.

Rahn, Frank J., et al. A Guide to Nuclear Power Technology: A Resource for Decision Making. LC 91-22459. 1000p. (C). 1992. reprint ed. lib. bdg. 145.00 (*0-89464-652-4*) Krieger.

Rahn, Herman & Prakash, Omar, eds. Acid-Base Regulation & Body Temperature. (Developments in Critical Care, Medicine, & Anesthesiology Ser.). 1985. lib. bdg. 101.50 (*0-89838-708-6*) Kluwer Ac.

Rahn, Herman, jt. ed. see Fenn, Wallace O.

Rahn, Joan E. More Plants That Changed History. LC 84-21563. 136p. (J). (gr. 5 up). 1985. text ed. 13.95 (*0-689-31099-4*, Atheneum Bks Young) S&S Childrens.

Rahn, John. Basic Atonal Theory. 158p. 1987. pap. 18.00 (*0-02-873160-3*) Schirmer Bks.

Rahn, John, ed. Perspectives on Musical Aesthetics. (C). 1994. 35.00 (*0-393-03614-6*); pap. 18.95 (*0-393-96508-2*) Norton.

Rahn, K. A., ed. Arctic Air Chemistry: Proceedings of the Second Symposium, Graduate School of Oceanography, University of Rhode Island, 6-8 May, 1980. (Atmospheric Environment Ser.: Vol. 15, No. 8). iv, 172p. 1981. pap. 36.00 (*0-08-026288-0*, Pergamon Pr) Elsevier.

Rahn, K. H., jt. auth. see Bonner, Gerd.

Rahn, Perry H. Engineering Geology: An Environmental Approach. 608p. 1986. 60.25 (*0-444-00942-6*); text ed. 74.00 (*0-13-052770-X*) P-H.

***Rahn, Suzanne.** Rediscoveries in Children's Literature. LC 94-39594. (Children's Literature & Culture Ser.: Vol. 2). (Illus.). 224p. 1995. 30.00 (*0-8153-0930-9*, SS862) Garland.

***Rahnama-Moghadam, Mashaalah, et al.** Doing Business in Less Developed Countries: Financial Opportunities & Risks. LC 94-24986. 224p. 1995. text ed. 59.95 (*0-89930-854-6*, Quorum Bks) Greenwood.

Rahnema, Ali, ed. Pioneers of Islamic Revival. (Studies in Islamic Society). 272p. (C). 1994. text ed. 59.95 (*1-85649-253-2*, Pub. by Zed Books UK); pap. 25.00 (*1-85649-254-0*, Pub. by Zed Books UK) Humanities.

Rahnema, Ali & Nomani, Farhad. The Secular Miracle: Religion, Politics & Economic Policy in Iran. LC 90-46689. 432p. (C). 1990. text ed. 60.00 (*0-86232-938-8*, Pub. by Zed Books UK); pap. 25.00 (*0-86232-939-6*, Pub. by Zed Books UK) Humanities.

Rahnema, Ali & Nomani, Fouad. Islamic Economic Systems. 256p. (C). 1994. text ed. 60.00 (*1-85649-057-2*, Pub. by Zed Books UK); pap. 25.00 (*1-85649-058-0*, Pub. by Zed Books UK) Humanities.

***Rahnema, Saeed.** Iran after the Revolution: Crisis of an Islamic State. 1995. text ed. 59.50 (*1-85043-905-2*, Pub. by I B Tauris UK) St Martin.

***Rahner.** Spirit of the Church. Date not set. 3.95 (*0-8164-2189-7*) Crossroad NY.

Rahner, Hugo. Church & State in Early Christianity. Davis, Leo D., tr. LC 91-76752. 342p. 1992. pap. 16.95 (*0-89870-377-8*) Ignatius Pr.

— Greek Myths & Christian Mystery. LC 79-156736. (Illus.). 1971. reprint ed. 25.00 (*0-8196-0270-1*) Biblo.

— Ignatius the Theologian. 2nd ed. LC 90-60756. 246p. 1990. pap. text ed. 15.95 (*0-89870-290-9*) Ignatius Pr.

— The Spirituality of St. Ignatius Loyola: An Account of Its Historical Development. Smith, Francis J., tr. LC 53-5586. 1968. reprint ed. 4.95 (*0-8294-0066-4*) Loyola Univ Pr.

Rahner, Karl. Anointing of the Sick. 1979. pap. 4.95 (*0-87193-108-7*) Dimension Bks.

— Baptism. 1979. pap. 4.95 (*0-87193-120-6*) Dimension Bks.

— Confirmation. 1979. pap. 4.95 (*0-87193-123-0*) Dimension Bks.

— The Content of Faith: The Best of Karl Rahner's Theological Writings. Lehmann, Karl et al, eds. 600p. 1993. 42.50 (*0-8245-1221-9*) Crossroad NY.

— Encounters with Silence. 92p. 1984. reprint ed. pap. 6.95 (*0-87061-097-X*, 6938) Chr Classics.

— Eternal Yes. 1979. pap. 4.95 (*0-87193-119-2*) Dimension Bks.

— Eucharist. 1970. pap. 4.95 (*0-87193-106-0*) Dimension Bks.

— Faith in a Wintry Season: Conversations & Interviews with Karl Rahner in the Last Years of His Life. 216p. 1990. 22.95 (*0-8245-0909-9*) Crossroad NY.

— Foundations of Christian Faith: An Introduction to the Idea of Christianity. LC 82-4663. 492p. 1982. pap. 19.95 (*0-8245-0523-9*) Crossroad NY.

— The Great Church Year: The Best of Karl Rahner's Homilies, Sermons, & Meditations. Raffelt, Albert & Egan, Harvey D., eds. LC 93-3930. 384p. 1994. reprint ed. 29.95 (*0-8245-1228-6*); reprint ed. pap. 19.95 (*0-8245-1430-0*) Crossroad NY.

— Hearer of the Word. Richards, Michael, tr. LC 93-38427. 192p. 1994. pap. text ed. 18.95 (*0-8264-0648-3*) Continuum.

— Herder Theological Lexicon: Herder Theologisches Taschenlexikon. 9th ed. 460p. (GER.). 1983. 225.00 (*0-8288-2309-X*, M7463) Fr & Eur.

— Is Christian Life Possible Today? 1984. pap. 9.95 (*0-87193-210-5*) Dimension Bks.

— Karl Rahner in Dialogue. 352p. 1986. 22.50 (*0-8245-0749-5*) Crossroad NY.

— Kleines Theologisches Woerterbuch. (GER.). Date not set. 29.95 (*0-7859-8372-4*, 3451088339) Fr & Eur.

— The Love of Jesus & the Love of Neighbour. (C). 1988. 39.00 (*0-85439-224-6*, Pub. by St Paul Pubns UK) St Mut.

— Marriage. 1970. pap. 4.95 (*0-87193-118-4*) Dimension Bks.

— Meditations on Hope & Love. 1977. pap. 4.95 (*0-8164-2155-2*) Harper SF.

— On Prayer. LC 92-44000. 136p. 1993. 6.95 (*0-8146-2171-6*) Liturgical Pr.

— Petit Dictionnaire De Theologie Catholique. 512p. (FRE.). 1970. 85.00 (*0-7859-7622-1*, 2020032392) Fr & Eur.

— The Practice of Faith: A Handbook of Contemporary Spirituality. rev. ed. 336p. 1986. pap. 17.95 (*0-8245-0779-7*) Crossroad NY.

— Prayers for a Lifetime. Raffelt, Albert, ed. 170p. 1995. pap. 14.95 (*0-8245-0730-4*) Crossroad NY.

— Spirit in the World. 448p. 1994. pap. text ed. 24.95 (*0-8264-0647-5*) Continuum.

— Theological Investigations, Vol. 22: Humane Society & the Church of Tomorrow. 288p. 1987. 29.50 (*0-8245-0924-2*) Crossroad NY.

— Theological Investigations, Vol. 23: Final Writings. 240p. 1992. 29.50 (*0-8245-1165-4*) Crossroad NY.

— Theology Investment SCI CHR, Vol. 21. (Theological Investigations Ser.: Vol. 21). 352p. 1988. 29.50 (*0-8245-0888-2*) Crossroad NY.

Rahner, Karl & Vorgrimler, Herbert. Small Theological Dictionary: Kleines Theologisches Woerterbuch. 15th ed. 460p. (GER.). 1985. pap. 24.95 (*0-8288-2310-3*, M7508) Fr & Eur.

Rahner, Karl, jt. auth. see Fries, Heinrich.

Rahola, Ricardo C. One Unique Cooking Manual. 77p. 1993. pap. text ed. 9.95 (*0-9637618-0-3*) Rotisserie Pub.

Rahr, Alexander. A Biographical Directory of One Hundred Leading Soviet Officials. 211p. (C). 1991. text ed. 51.50 (*0-8133-8015-4*) Westview.

Rahr, Alexander G., jt. auth. see Azrael, Jeremy R.

Rahr, Richard R. & Niebuhr, Bruce R. Physician's Assistant Examination Review & Patient Management Problems. 2nd ed. 1992. pap. 25.00 (*0-8385-8026-2*, A8026-5) Appleton & Lange.

Raht, Carlysle G. Romance of Davis Mountains & Big Bend Country. 1993. reprint ed. lib. bdg. 75.00 (*0-7812-5896-0*) Rprt Serv.

***Rahtjen, Bruce D.** Biblical Truth & Today's World. 1995. pap. 12.95 (*0-9647079-1-8*) Trefoil Pr.

Rahtore, N. S. & Sukhadia, M. L., eds. Natural Resource Base Development. (C). 1991. 250.00 (*0-685-60030-0*, Pub. by Scientific Pubs II) St Mut.

Rahtz, Philip. English Heritage Book of Glastonbury. (Illus.). 152p. 1994. 55.00 (*0-7134-6866-1*, Pub. by Batsford UK); pap. 29.95 (*0-7134-6865-3*, Pub. by Batsford UK) Trafalgar.

Rahtz, Philip & Johnston. Invitation to Archaeology. 2nd ed. (Invitation Ser.). (Illus.). 192p. 1985. pap. 15.95x (*0-631-18067-2*) Blackwell Pubs.

Rahtz, Sebastian, jt. ed. see Reilly, Paul.

***Rahul, Ram.** Dalai Lama: The Institution. (C). 1995. 17.00 (*0-7069-8788-8*, Pub. by Vikas II) S Asia.

R

An Asterisk (*) at the beginning of an entry indicates that the title is appearing in BIP for the first time.

— Modern Tibet. (C). 1992. 12.00 (*0-8364-2800-5*, Pub. by Munshiram Manoharial II) S Asia.

— Mongolia: Between China & the U. S. S. R. 1989. 16.00 (*0-685-37831-4*, Pub. by Munshiram Manoharial II) S Asia.

Rahula, Walpola. What the Buddha Taught. rev. ed. (Illus.). 192p. 1987. pap. 9.95 (*0-8021-3031-3*) Grove-Atltic.

Rahuler, M. New Problems in Differential Geometry. (Series on Soviet & East European Mathematics: Vol. 8). 200p. (C). 1993. text ed. 44.00 (*981-02-0819-7*) World Scientific Pub.

Rahv, Philip. Image & Idea: Fourteen Essays on Literary Themes. LC 77-26061. 164p. 1978. reprint ed. text ed. 48.50 (*0-313-20082-3*, RAII, Greenwood Pr) Greenwood.

— Literature in America: An Anthology of Literary Criticism. 16.50 (*0-8446-2776-3*) Peter Smith.

*__Rahv, Philip, ed.__ The Great Short Novels of Henry James. 800p. 1996. pap. 17.95 (*0-7867-0265-6*) Carroll & Graf.

Rahv, Philip, ed. see James, Henry.

Rahwan, Ralf G. & Witiak, Donald T. Calcium Regulation by Calcium Antagonists. LC 82-16451. (ACS Symposium Ser.: No. 201). 210p. 1982. lib. bdg. 38.95 (*0-8412-0744-5*) Am Chemical.

Rai, Amar N., ed. Handbook of Symbiotic Cyanobacteria. 272p. 1989. 195.95 (*0-8493-3275-3*, QR99) CRC Pr.

Rai, B. C. History of Indian Education. 413p. 1981. 9.95 (*0-318-36823-4*) Asia Bk Corp.

*__Rai, Dhanwant K.__ Developments in Training in Social Services. 1994. pap. 21.00 (*0-902789-91-0*, Pub. by Natl Inst Soc Work) St Mut.

Rai, Hakumat, ed. Measurement of Photosynthetic Pigments in Freshwaters & Standardization of Methods: Proceedings of the Workshop Held at Plon, West Germany, 1978, Vol. 1. (Limnology Report: No. 14). (Illus.). 106p. (Orig.). 1980. pap. text ed. 47.50 (*3-510-47012-5*, Pub. by E Schweizerbartsche GW) Lubrecht & Cramer.

*__Rai, L. C. & Gaur, J. P., eds.__ Algae & Water Pollution. (Advances in Limnology Ser.: No. 42). (Illus.). 304p. 1994. pap. text ed. 110.00 (*3-510-47043-5*, Pub. by Schweitzerbart'sche GW) Lubrecht & Cramer.

Rai, Lajpat. History of the Arya Samaj: An Account of Its Origin, Doctrines & Activities with a Biographical Sketch of the Founder. (C). 1992. reprint ed. text ed. 20.00 (*81-215-0578-X*, Pub. by Munshiram Manoharial II) S Asia.

*__Rai, Lal D.__ Human Rights in the Hindu-Buddhist Tradition. xii, 192p. 1995. 20.00 (*81-85693-46-3*, Pub. by Nirala Pubns II) Nataraj Bks.

Rai, Lala L. The Arya Samaj: An Account of Its Origins, Doctrines & Activities. xxvi, 200p. 1991. text ed. 30.00 (*81-85047-77-4*, Pub. by Reliance Pub Hse II) Apt Bks.

— Swami Dayananda Saraswati: His Biography & Teachings. Bhatia, S. K., ed. iv, 104p. 1991. text ed. 22.50 (*81-85047-76-6*, Pub. by Reliance Pub Hse II) Apt Bks.

*__Rai, Milan.__ Chomsky's Politics. 160p. 1995. 59.95x (*1-85984-916-4*, Pub. by Verso UK); pap. 16.95 (*1-85984-011-6*, C0497, Pub. by Verso UK) Routledge Chapman & Hall.

Rai, Navin K. Living in a Lean-To: Philippine Negrito Foragers in Transition. LC 89-12557. (Anthropological Papers: No. 80). xi, 184p. (Orig.). 1990. pap. 12.00 (*0-915703-17-3*) U Mich Mus Anthro.

Rai, Priya M., comp. Sikhism & the Sikhs: An Annotated Bibliography. LC 88-38308. (Bibliographies & Indexes in Religious Studies: No. 13). 272p. 1989. text ed. 75.00 (*0-313-26130-X*, RSI/, Greenwood Pr) Greenwood.

Rai, R. K., ed. Environmental Management: Physio-Ecological Facets, 2 vols., I. (C). 1992. write for info. (*81-7033-152-8*, Pub. by Rawat II) S Asia.

— Environmental Management: Physio-Ecological Facets, 2 vols., II. (C). 1992. write for info. (*81-7033-153-6*, Pub. by Rawat II) S Asia.

— Environmental Management: Physio-Ecological Facets, 2 vols., Set. (C). 1992. 72.00 (*81-7033-154-4*, Pub. by Rawat II) S Asia.

Rai, R. Mohan. Sant Sai Baba. 1992. pap. 7.95 (*81-207-1509-8*, Pub. by Sterling Pubs II) Apt Bks.

— Satya Sai Avtar: Glimpses of Divinity. 132p. 1988. text ed. 25.00 (*81-207-0707-9*, Pub. by Sterling Pubs II) Apt Bks.

Rai, R. N. Theory of Drama: A Comparative Study of Aristotle & Bharata. (C). 1992. 29.50 (*81-7054-155-7*, Pub. by Classical Pub II) S Asia.

Rai, R. P., jt. auth. see Pant, Niranjan.

Rai, Raghu, photos. Delhi. (Illus.). 1994. 65.00 (*81-7223-092-3*) Harper SF.

Rai, S. S. Red Star & the Lotus: The Political Dynamics of Indo-Soviet Relations. 400p. 1990. text ed. 37.50 (*81-220-0177-7*, Pub. by Konark Pubs Pvt Ltd II) Advent Bks Div.

Rai, Shirin. Resistance & Reaction: University Politics in Post-Mao China. LC 91-28959. 224p. 1991. text ed. 65.00 (*0-312-07187-6*) St Martin.

Rai, Shirin, et al, eds. Women in the Face of Change. LC 91-44517. 208p. 1992. 67.50 (*0-415-07540-8*, A7458); pap. 15.95 (*0-415-07541-6*, A7462) Routledge.

Rai, Sudha. V. S. Naipaul: A Study in Expatriate Sensibility. (Indian Writers Ser.: Vol. 19). 136p. 1982. 12.00 (*0-86578-143-5*) Ind-US Inc.

Rai, Suresh & Agrawal, Dharma P. Advances in Distributed System Reliability. LC 89-45997. 347p. 1990. 9.95 (*0-8186-8907-2*, 1907) IEEE Comp Soc.

— Distributed Computing Network Reliability. LC 89-45995. 357p. 1990. 9.95 (*0-8186-8908-0*, 1908) IEEE Comp Soc.

Rai, V. T. S. Eliot's "The Waste Land" A Critical Study. 1974. lib. bdg. 69.95 (*0-8490-1173-6*) Gordon Pr.

Raia, Roman V. A Hostage. LC 91-75213. 91p. 1992. 7.95 (*1-55523-463-1*) Winston-Derek.

*__Raia, William A.__ Milwaukee Road in Color, Vol. 1. (Illus.). 1995. 49.95 (*1-878887-46-7*) Morning NJ.

Raibert, Marc. Legged Robots That Balance. (Artificial Intelligence Ser.). (Illus.). 275p. 1985. 35.00x (*0-262-18117-7*) MIT Pr.

*__Raible, Chris.__ Hymns for the Celebration of Strife. enl. rev. ed. 19p. 1990. pap. 3.50 (*0-9624431-1-5*) Dumont Pr.

— Muddy York Mud: Scansal & Scurrility in Upper Canada. (Illus.). 289p. Date not set. pap. 18.99 (*0-614-06783-9*) Dun.

Raible, Erwin. Fin de Siecle Prints, Posters & Prose: The Collection of Erwin Raible & Robert Hoskins. LC 90-62623. (Illus.). 44p. (Orig.). 1990. pap. 10.00 (*0-915577-21-6*) Taft Museum.

Raible, Karl-Friedrich, jt. ed. see Dopfer, Kurt.

Raiborn, Cecily A., et al. Management Accounting. Leyh, ed. LC 92-29592. 900p. (C). 1993. text ed. 69.25 (*0-314-01169-2*) West Pub.

Raichaudhuri, Srabani. Dimensions of Political Communication West Bengal: Nineteen Seventies. 1986. 17.50 (*0-317-47415-4*, Pub. by KP Bagchi IA) S Asia.

*__Raiche, Annabelle & Biermaier, Ann M., contribs.__ They Came to Teach. 300p. 1994. 19.95 (*0-87839-088-X*) North Star.

Raichelson, Richard, ed. see Doran, James M.

Raichert, Lane. D.C. Hopper, the First Starbunny. LC 91-23055. (Illus.). 32p. (J). (gr. 2-6). 1992. 15.95 (*1-880009-81-1*, DC-P1) Blue Zero Pub.

Raichle, Donald R. From a Normal Beginning: The Origins of Kean College of New Jersey. (Illus.). 432p. 1980. 30.00 (*0-8386-4500-3*) Fairleigh Dickinson.

— New Jersey's Union College. LC 83-45027. (Illus.). 272p. 1983. 25.00 (*0-8386-3198-3*) Fairleigh Dickinson.

Raichle, Marcus E., jt. auth. see Posner, Michael I.

Raichle, Marcus E., jt. ed. see Powers, William J.

Raichlen, Steven. Dining In - Boston. rev. ed. (Dining in Ser.). 194p. 1987. pap. 8.95 (*0-89716-124-6*) P B Pubng.

— High-Flavor, Low-Fat Cooking. (Illus.). 256p. 1994. reprint ed. 18.95 (*0-14-024123-X*, Penguin Bks) Viking Penguin.

— High-Flavor, Low-Fat Vegetarian Cooking. (Illus.). 304p. 1995. 24.95 (*0-670-85782-3*, Viking) Viking Penguin.

— Miami Spice: The New Florida Cuisine. LC 93-25446. (Illus.). 352p. (Orig.). 1993. 22.95 (*1-56305-519-8*, 3519); pap. 12.95 (*1-56305-346-2*, 3346) Workman Pub.

— Taste of the Mountains Cooking School Cookbook. 1986. pap. write for info. (*0-671-54429-2*) S&S Trade.

Raichler, Joseph. Baseball Encyclopedia. 29.95 (*0-02-578970-8*) Macmillan.

Raidchaudhuri, S. P., ed. Recent Advances in Medicinal, Aromatic & Spice Crops, Vol. 1: International Conference Held at New Delhi, India, Jan. 1989. (Illus.). 272p. 1991. text ed. 59.00 (*81-7019-372-9*, Pub. by Today Tomorrow II) Lubrecht & Cramer.

Raider, Melvyn, jt. auth. see Steele, William.

*__Raider, S. I., et al, eds.__ Proceedings of the Symposium on Low Temperature Electronics & High Temperature Superconductivity. LC 93-70073. (Proceedings Ser.: Vol. 93-22). 600p. 1993. 58.00 (*1-56677-071-8*) Electrochem Soc.

*__Raidt, Beley.__ Hairy Britches Goal Setting Techniques. LC 95-60592. (Illus.). 128p. (J). (gr. 3-8). 1996. pap. 7.95 (*1-55523-742-8*) Winston-Derek.

Raifeld, Y. E. Asymmetric Epoxidation: Mech Tech. & Synthetic App. 1995. write for info. (*0-8493-8929-1*) CRC Pr.

Raiff, Norma R. & Shore, Barbara K. Advanced Case Management: New Strategies for the Nineties. (Human Services Guides Ser.: Vol. 66). (Illus.). 180p. (C). 1993. text ed. 39.95 (*0-8039-5308-9*); pap. text ed. 17.95 (*0-8039-3872-1*) Sage.

Raiffa, Howard. Analysis for Decision Making: (Complete Program), 10 notebks. 821p. (C). 1987. reprint ed. Set. audio, ring bd. 795.00 (*1-55678-012-5*) Learn Inc.

— Analysis for Decision Making, Module 1: Decision Trees. 83p. (C). 1987. reprint ed. audio, ring bd. 70.00 (*1-55678-013-3*) Learn Inc.

— Analysis for Decision Making, Module 10: Case Analysis: Caroline Development & the Stephen Douglas. 104p. (C). 1987. reprint ed. audio, ring bd. 70.00 (*1-55678-022-2*) Learn Inc.

— Analysis for Decision Making, Module 2: New Information: Effect on Uncertainties. 73p. (C). 1987. reprint ed. audio, ring bd. 70.00 (*1-55678-014-1*) Learn Inc.

— Analysis for Decision Making, Module 3: Strategies & the Value of Information. 79p. (C). 1987. reprint ed. audio, ring bd. 70.00 (*1-55678-015-X*) Learn Inc.

— Analysis for Decision Making, Module 4: Case Analysis: The Rositex Company. 89p. (C). 1987. reprint ed. audio, ring bd. 70.00 (*1-55678-016-8*) Learn Inc.

— Analysis for Decision Making, Module 5: Utility Theory: Basic Concepts. 81p. (C). 1987. reprint ed. audio, ring bd. 70.00 (*1-55678-017-6*) Learn Inc.

— Analysis for Decision Making, Module 6: Utility Theory: The Assessment Problem. 80p. (C). 1987. reprint ed. audio, ring bd. 70.00 (*1-55678-018-4*) Learn Inc.

— Analysis for Decision Making, Module 7: Case Analysis: Edgartown Fisheries & J. B. Robinson. 55p. (C). 1987. reprint ed. audio, ring bd. 70.00 (*1-55678-019-2*) Learn Inc.

— Analysis for Decision Making, Module 8: Subjective Probability. 60p. (C). 1987. reprint ed. audio, ring bd. 70.00 (*1-55678-020-6*) Learn Inc.

— Analysis for Decision Making, Module 9: The Atr & Science of Probability Assessment. 117p. (C). 1987. reprint ed. audio, ring bd. 70.00 (*1-55678-021-4*) Learn Inc.

— The Art & Science of Negotiation. 384p. 1985. pap. text ed. 16.50 (*0-674-04813-X*) Belknap Pr.

— Decision Analysis: Introductory Lectures on Choices under Uncertainty. (Orig.). (C). 1968. pap. text ed. write for info. (*0-07-554866-6*) McGraw.

Raiffa, Howard, jt. auth. see Keeney, Ralph L.

Raiha, Kari-Jouko. The Design of Relational Databases. (C). 1992. pap. text ed. 37.75 (*0-201-56523-4*) Addison-Wesley.

Raiha, Niels C., ed. Protein Metabolism During Infancy. LC 94-1490. (Nestle Nutrition Workshop Ser.: Vol. 33). 272p. 1994. 60.00 (*0-7817-0215-1*) Raven.

Raihall, Richard. The Winner's Edge: The Inside Guide to Betting Pro Football. (Guides to Sports Betting Ser.). 180p. (Orig.). 1984. pap. 9.95 (*0-915643-07-3*); write for info. (*0-915643-09-X*) Santa Barb Pr.

Raijan, A. New Technology & Employment in Insurance Banking & Building Societies. (C). 1984. 275.00 (*0-685-32708-6*, Pub. by Witherby & Co UK) St Mut.

Raikes, Philip. Modernising Hunger: Famine, Food Surplus & Farm Policy in the EEC & Africa. LC 90-26661. vii, 280p. (C). 1991. text ed. 40.00 (*0-435-08030-X*, 08030); pap. text ed. 27.50 (*0-435-08058-X*, 08058) Heinemann.

Raiklin, Ernest. After Gorbachev? (Journal of Social, Political & Economic Studies Monograph Ser.: No. 20). 128p. (Orig.). 1989. pap. 15.00 (*0-930690-23-0*) Coun Soc Econ.

Raikov, Bozhidar. The Abagar of Philip Stanislavov: Rome 1651. 54p. 1979. 193.00 (*0-569-08620-5*, Pub. by Collets UK) Pro-Am Music.

Raikov, I. B. The Protozoan Nucleus: Morphology & Evolution. Bobrov, Nicholas & Verkhovsteva, M., trs. (Cell Biology Monographs: Vol. 9). (Illus.). 450p. 1982. 175.00 (*0-387-81678-X*) Spr-Verlag.

Rail, Axel. Mexico. Nobles, Pat, ed. & illus. by. 224p. (Orig.). 1986. write for info. (*0-938105-00-0*) Seabird Pub.

Rail, Chester D. Groundwater Contamination: Sources, Control, & Preventive Measures. LC 88-51817. 158p. 1989. 39.00 (*0-87762-594-8*) Technomic.

*__Rail, Robert.__ Defense Without Damage: A Photo-Illustrated Guide to Low Liability Arrest & Control Skills. (Illus.). 184p. (Orig.) (C). 1994. pap. 39.95 (*0-7881-1350-X*) Diane Pub.

Raile, A. L., pseud. A Defense of Uranian Love. LC 78-22240. (Gay Experience Ser.). reprint ed. 11.50 (*0-404-61531-7*) AMS Pr.

Raileanu, Lia, tr. see Seely, Contee & Romijn, Elizabeth.

Raileanu, Lia, tr. see Segal, Bertha E.

Railey, Douglas. Exacta Expose. (Orig.). 1992. 29.95 (*0-9614168-6-6*) Cynthia Pub Co.

Railey, Jim H. & Railey-Tschauner, Peggy. Instructor's Manual for Managing Physical Education, Fitness, & Sport Programs. 2nd ed. (C). 1993. teacher ed write for info. (*1-55934-174-2*) Mayfield Pub.

Railey, Jim H. & Railey-Tschauner, Peggy A. Managing Physical Education, Fitness, & Sport Programs. 2nd ed. 340p. (C). 1993. text ed. 42.95 (*1-55934-173-4*) Mayfield Pub.

Railey-Tschauner, Peggy, jt. auth. see Railey, Jim H.

Railey-Tschauner, Peggy A., jt. auth. see Railey, Jim H.

Railey, William E. History of Woodford County, Kentucky. (Illus.). 449p. 1990. reprint ed. 23.50 (*0-685-60379-2*, 4745) Clearfield Co.

Railfan Magazine Staff. Stephans' Railroad Directory: Railroad Magazine, 1929-1927, Vol. 3. 600p. pap. 43.00 (*0-685-35153-X*) Tioga Pubns.

Railing, Joy. Remembered Moments. 110p. 1993. 15.95 (*1-882188-03-9*) Magnolia Mktg.

Railings, Patricia, jt. auth. see Lissitzky, El.

Raillard, Hanni, tr. see Furtwangler, Elisabeth.

Raillard, Hans, tr. see Furtwangler, Elisabeth.

Raillery, Bonnie, ed. The Reader's Guide to Unavailable Literature & Other Omitted Media. LC 94-76412. (Illus.). 96p. (Orig.). 1994. per. 6.50 (*0-9641544-0-4*, RGB-1) Monitor Pubns.

Railo, Eilo. The Haunted Castle: A Study of the Elements of the English Romanticism. 1973. 300.00 (*0-87968-072-5*) Gordon Pr.

*__Railsback, Brian E.__ Parallel Expeditions: Charles Darwin & the Art of John Steinbeck. 1995. pap. 24.95 (*0-89301-177-0*) U of Idaho Pr.

Railton, Stephen. Authorship & Audience: Literary Performance in the American Renaissance. 247p. 1992. text ed. 37.50 (*0-691-06925-5*); pap. text ed. 13.95 (*0-691-01516-3*) Princeton U Pr.

Raiman, Jennifer, jt. ed. see Wilson-Barnett, Jennifer.

Raimbaut de Vaqueiras. The Poems of the Troubadour Raimbaut de Vaqueiras. Linskill, Joseph, ed. LC 80-2190. reprint ed. 45.00 (*0-404-19014-6*) AMS Pr.

Raimer, David A. The Joseph Principle. (Illus.). (Orig.). 1989. pap. write for info. (*0-9623058-0-4*) Trinity Pub Grp.

Raimes, Ann. Exploring Through Writing: A Process Approach to ESL Composition. 2nd ed. LC 90-71609. 318p. (C). 1992. pap. text ed. 0.44 (*0-312-04769-X*) St Martin.

— Focus on Composition. (Illus.). 1978. pap. 12.95 (*0-19-502238-6*) OUP.

— Grammar Troublespots: An Editing Guide for Students. 2nd ed. LC 90-61133. 115p. (C). 1992. pap. text ed. 7.50 (*0-312-06518-3*) St Martin.

— How English Works: A Grammar Handbook with Readings. LC 88-63058. 378p. (Orig.). (C). 1990. pap. text ed. 17.50 (*0-312-01276-4*); pap. text ed. 0.39 (*0-312-01277-2*) St Martin.

— Problems & Teaching Strategies in ESL Composition. (Language in Education Ser.: No. 14). 24p. (C). 1986. pap. text ed. 3.67 (*0-13-711987-9*) P-H.

— Techniques in Teaching Writing. (Techniques in Teaching English As a Second Language Ser.). (Illus.). 176p. (Orig.). (C). 1983. pap. text ed. 10.50 (*0-19-434131-3*) OUP.

Raimes, H. P. Fate Accompli. large type ed. 1990. 12.95 (*0-7451-9922-4*, C0639, Atlantic Lrg Print); pap. 15.95 (*0-7927-0371-5*, C0833, Atlantic Lrg Print) Chivers N Amer.

Raimes, James. Columbia Quiz Book. 1993. pap. 17.50 (*0-231-08079-4*) Col U Pr.

Raimi, Ralph A. The Philomathic Debating Club. xii, 153p. (Orig.). 1991. pap. 25.00 (*0-9609370-1-3*) Raimi.

— Vested Interests. xiv, 209p. 1982. 14.95 (*0-9609370-0-5*) Raimi.

Raimo, John W., ed. Biographical Directory of American Colonial & Revolutionary Governors, 1607-1789. LC 80-13279. 536p. 1980. text ed. 125.00 (*0-313-28133-5*, RAK/, Greenwood Pr) Greenwood.

— Biographical Directory of the Governors of the United States, 1978-1983. LC 84-20717. 400p. 1985. text ed. 75.00 (*0-313-28098-3*, RBM/, Greenwood Pr) Greenwood.

— A Guide to Manuscripts Relating to America in Great Britain & Ireland. LC 78-12672. 488p. 1979. text ed. 165.00 (*0-313-28135-1*, RMR/, Greenwood Pr) Greenwood.

Raimon, Peire. Le Poesie Di Peire Raimon De Tolosa. Cavaliere, Alfredo, ed. LC 80-2181. reprint ed. 29.50 (*0-404-19010-3*) AMS Pr.

Raimond, Jean & Watson, Richard, eds. A Handbook to English Romanticism. LC 91-41426. 328p. 1992. text ed. 59.95 (*0-312-07914-1*) St Martin.

Raimond, Paul. Management Projects: Design, Research, & Presentation. LC 93-14820. 1993. write for info. (*0-412-46810-7*) Chapman & Hall.

Raimondi, A. J., ed. Concepts in Pediatric Neurosurgery, No. 3. (Illus.). xxii, 226p. 1983. 158.50 (*3-8055-3580-5*) S Karger.

Raimondi, Anthony J. Pediatric Neurosurgery. (Illus.). 550p. 1987. 395.00 (*0-387-96408-8*) Spr-Verlag.

Raimondi, Anthony J., et al, eds. Posterior Fossa Tumors. LC 92-49986. (Principles of Pediatric Neurosurgery Ser.). 1993. 153.00 (*0-387-97915-8*) Spr-Verlag.

Raimondi, Anthony J., et al. The Dandy-Walker Syndrome. (Illus.). viii, 84p. 1983. 46.50 (*3-8055-1722-X*) S Karger.

Raimondi, Anthony J., et al, eds. Cerebrovascular Diseases in Children. (Principles of Pediatric Neurosurgery Ser.). (Illus.). xi, 256p. 1992. 138.00 (*0-387-97626-4*) Spr-Verlag.

— Head Injuries in the Newborn & Infant. (Principles of Pediatric Neurosurgery Ser.). (Illus.). 270p. 1986. 88.00 (*0-387-96208-5*) Spr-Verlag.

— Intracranial Cyst Lesions. LC 92-2314. (Principles of Pediatric Neurosurgery Ser.). (Illus.). 256p. 1993. 149.00 (*0-387-97869-0*) Spr-Verlag.

— The Pediatric Spine, Vol. 1. (Principles of Pediatric Neurosurgery Ser.). (Illus.). 220p. 1989. 148.00 (*0-387-96835-0*) Spr-Verlag.

— The Pediatric Spine, Vol. 2. (Principles of Pediatric Neurosurgery Ser.). (Illus.). 255p. 1989. 174.00 (*0-387-96861-X*) Spr-Verlag.

— The Pediatric Spine, Vol. 3. (Principles of Pediatric Neurosurgery Ser.). (Illus.). 205p. 1989. 148.00 (*0-387-96804-0*) Spr-Verlag.

Raimondi, Pietro. Il Ventaglio: Libretto by Domenico Gilardoni, after Carlo Goldoni Music by Pietro First Performance Naples, Teatro, Nuovo, 19 April 1831. LC 89-753856. (Italian Opera 1810-1840 Ser.: Vol. 40). 368p. 1990. 119.00 (*0-8240-6589-1*) Garland.

Raimondo, Henry J. Economics of State & Local Government. LC 91-7783. 288p. 1991. text ed. 59.95 (*0-275-93122-6*, C3122, Praeger Pubs); pap. text ed. 19.95 (*0-275-93937-5*, B3937, Praeger Pubs) Greenwood.

Raimondo, Joe, jt. auth. see Thoma, Rich.

Raimondo, Lois. The Little Lama of Tibet. LC 93-13627. (Illus.). 40p. (J). (ps-4). 1994. 15.95 (*0-590-46167-2*) Scholastic Inc.

*__Raimundo, Daniel E.__ Habla el Coronel Orlando Piedra. LC 94-70900. (Coleccion Cuba y sus Jueces). (Illus.). 230p. (Orig.). (SPA.). 1994. pap. 19.95 (*0-89729-479-3*) Ediciones.

Raimy, Victor. Misunderstandings of the Self. LC 74-28917. (Jossey-Bass Behavioral Science Ser.). 232p. reprint ed. pap. 66.20 (*0-8357-6884-8*, 2037936) Bks Demand.

Rain, D. A. The Water Book. (Illus.). 1993. 29.95 (*0-8283-1956-1*) Branden Pub Co.

Rain, Jennifer, pseud. Your Husband, My Lover. Frost, Anne, ed. 350p. (Orig.). 1989. pap. text ed. 12.95 (*0-9614624-6-9*) Frost Pub.

Rain, Mary S. Ancient Echoes: The Anasazi Book of Chants. (Illus.). 216p. (Orig.). 1993. pap. 10.95 (*1-878901-87-7*) Hampton Roads Pub Co.

— Daybreak. 1991. pap. 14.95 (*1-878901-14-1*) Hampton Roads Pub Co.

— Dreamwalker. 1993. 9.95 (*1-878901-63-X*) Hampton Roads Pub Co.

— Earthway. Zion, Claire, ed. 442p. 1992. pap. 14.00 (*0-671-70667-5*) PB.

— Mountains, Meadows & Moonbeams. 1992. pap. 10.95 (*1-878901-39-7*) Hampton Roads Pub Co.

— Phantoms Afoot. 1993. 10.95 (*1-878901-64-8*) Hampton Roads Pub Co.

— Phoenix Rising. (Orig.). 1993. 9.95 (*1-878901-62-1*) Hampton Roads Pub Co.

— The Seventh Mesa: A Novel. 304p. 1994. text ed. 19.95 (*1-57174-012-0*) Hampton Roads Pub Co.

— Soul Sounds. 1992. pap. 11.95 (*1-878901-33-8*) Hampton Roads Pub Co.

— Spirit Song. (Orig.). 1993. 10.95 (*1-878901-61-3*) Hampton Roads Pub Co.

— Whispered Wisdom. 1992. pap. 18.95 (*1-878901-49-4*) Hampton Roads Pub Co.

Rain, Patricia. The Artichoke Cookbook. LC 85-5771. (Illus.). 180p. (Orig.). 1985. pap. 11.95 (*0-89087-415-8*) Celestial Arts.

R

— The Vanilla Cookbook. LC 85-29149. (Illus.). 160p. (Orig.). 1986. pap. 11.95 (*0-89087-453-0*) Celestial Arts.

Rain, Patricia, ed. see Riedner, Ulrich.

Rain, Thomas. Browning for Beginners. LC 72-3194. (Studies in Browning: No. 4). 1972. reprint ed. lib. bdg. 75.00 (*0-8383-1518-6*) M S G Haskell Hse.

Raina, A., jt. auth. see Kac, Victor G.

Raina, Ashok, jt. auth. see Bobb, Dilip.

Raina, B. L. Health Science in Ancient India. (C). 1990. 44.00 (*81-7169-089-0*, Commonwealth) S Asia.

— Introduction to Malaria Problems in India: Prevedic Times to Early 1950's. (C). 1991. 23.00 (*81-7169-108-0*, Pub. by Commonwealth II) S Asia.

— Planning Family in India Prevedic Times to Early 1950's. 1990. 42.00 (*81-7169-060-2*, Commonwealth) S Asia.

— Population Challenge. (C). 1994. 21.50x (*81-7018-763-X*, Pub. by BR Pub II) S Asia.

— Quest for a Small Family. (C). 1991. 44.00 (*81-7169-125-0*, Pub. by Commonwealth II) S Asia.

— Social Situation in India. 1990. 55.00 (*81-7169-054-8*, Commonwealth) S Asia.

Raina, Badri. Dickens & the Dialectic of Growth. LC 85-40767. 208p. 1986. text ed. 27.50 (*0-299-10610-1*) U of Wis Pr.

Raina, Dina N. Unhappy Kashmir: The Hidden Story. 1990. text ed. 30.00 (*81-85047-69-3*, Pub. by Reliance Pub Hse II) Apt Bks.

— Unhappy Kashmir: The Hidden Story. (C). 1990. text ed. 29.00 (*0-685-39106-X*, Pub. by BR Pub II) S Asia.

Raina, J. L. Structural & Functional Changes in the Joint Family System: A Study Based on D.O.M. Workers. (C). 1989. 25.00 (*81-7022-237-0*, Pub. by Concept II) S Asia.

Raina, K. L. Dictionary of Electrical Engineering. 1989. 33.50 (*81-7041-162-9*, Pub. by Anmol II) S Asia.

Raina, M. K., ed. Creativity Research: International Perspective. 332p. 1980. 18.95 (*0-318-37231-2*) Asia Bk Corp.

Raina, N. N. Kashmir Politics & Imperialist Maneuvres, 1846-1980. 1988. 32.00 (*0-317-90514-7*, Patriot) S Asia.

Raina, Trilokinath, ed. An Anthology of Modern Kashmiri Verse 1930-1960. Raina, Trithokinath, tr. 280p. 1974. lib. bdg. 12.50 (*0-88253-469-6*) Ind-US Inc.

Raina, Trithokinath, tr. see Raina, Trilokinath, ed.

Rainbird Editors. Gardener's Palette. LC 86-6364. 160p. 1987. pap. 25.00 (*0-385-23357-4*) Doubleday.

Rainbird, Helen & Syben, Gerd, eds. Restructuring a Traditional Society: Construction Employment & Skills in Europe. 296p. 1991. 68.00 (*0-85496-585-8*) Berg Pubs.

Rainboldt, Jo, jt. auth. see Gingras, Louie.

Rainbolt, George W., jt. auth. see McInerney, Peter K.

Rainbolt, Jo. The Last Cowboy: Twilight Era of the Horseback Cowhand 1900-1940. (Illus.). 192p. (Orig.). 1992. pap. 12.95 (*1-56037-012-2*) Am Wrld Geog.

***Rainbolt, Jo & Brumback, Dorothy.** History of Missoula, Montana. (Illus.). 554p. 1991. 64.50 (*0-88107-178-1*) Curtis Media.

Rainbolt, Martha & Fleetwood, Janet, eds. On the Contrary: Essays by Men & Women. LC 82-19421. 340p. (C). 1984. pap. 14.95x (*0-87395-720-2*) State U NY Pr.

Rainbolt, Richard. The Plan to Heal the World. 98p. (Orig.). 1989. pap. 10.00 (*0-317-93650-6*) Peace Curriculum.

***Rainbolt, William.** Moses Rose. Danbury, Richard S., III, ed. 200p. (Orig.). 1995. pap. 8.95 (*0-89754-125-1*) Dan River Pr.

Rainbow, A. K. Why Recycle? Proceedings of the Recycling Council Annual Seminar, Birmingham, U. K., February 1994. (Illus.). (C). 1994. text ed. 95.00 (*90-5410-367-1*, Pub. by A A Balkema NE) Ashgate Pub Co.

Rainbow, A. K., ed. Reclamation, Treatment, & Utilization of Coal Mining Wastes: Proceedings of Second International Conference on the Reclamation, Treatment, & Utilization of Coal Mining Wastes, Nottingham, UK, Sept. 7-11, 1987. (Advances in Mining Science & Technology Ser.: Vol. 2). 668p. 1987. 151.50 (*0-444-42876-3*) Elsevier.

— Reclamation, Treatment & Utilization of Coal Mining Wastes: Proceedings of the Third International Symposium, Glasgow, 3-7 September 1990. (Illus.). 544p. (C). 1990. text ed. 130.00 (*90-6191-154-0*, Pub. by A A Balkema NE) Ashgate Pub Co.

Rainbow, Carol. Monitoring the Critically Ill Patient: Patient Problems & Nursing Care. 192p. 1990. pap. text ed. 39.95 (*0-433-00084-8*) Buttrwrth-Heinemann.

Rainbow, Edward L. & Froehlich, Hildegard C. Research in Music Education: An Introduction to Systematic Inquiry. (Illus.). 330p. (C). 1987. text ed. 47.00 (*0-02-870320-0*) Schirmer Bks.

Rainbow, Izo M., jt. auth. see Fleming, Hilary.

Rainbow, Jonathan H. The Will of God & the Cross: John Calvin & the Doctrine of Limited Redemption. LC 90-30695. (Princeton Theological Monograph Ser.: No. 22). 217p. (Orig.). 1990. pap. 24.00 (*1-55635-005-8*) Pickwick.

Rainbow, Philip S., jt. ed. see Fincham, A. A.

Rainbow, Philip S., jt. auth. see Phillips, David J.

***Rainbow Staff.** A Rainbow of Hope. 336p. 1994. 19.95 (*0-933657-26-9*) Rainbow Studies.

Rainbow, Stephen. Green Politics. (Critical Issues in New Zealand Society). 124p. 1994. pap. 23.00 (*0-19-558272-1*) OUP.

Raindance, A., ed. Radical Software, 4 vols., Set. 90p. 1990. text ed. 54.00 (*0-677-15385-6*) Gordon & Breach.

— Radical Software, Vol. 1, No. 6. 108p. 1971. text ed. 33.00 (*0-677-15375-9*) Gordon & Breach.

— Radical Software, Vol. 2. 72p. 1972. text ed. 26.00 (*0-677-41005-0*) Gordon & Breach.

— Radical Software, Vol. 2. 64p. 1973. text ed. 26.00 (*0-677-41015-8*); text ed. 26.00 (*0-677-41025-5*); text ed. 26.00 (*0-677-41035-2*); text ed. 26.00 (*0-677-41045-X*) Gordon & Breach.

— Radical Software, Vol. 2. 68p. 1974. text ed. 36.00 (*0-677-41055-7*) Gordon & Breach.

Rainders, Reinder & Paul, Kees, eds. Carvel Construction Technique. (Oxbow Monographs in Archaeology). (Illus.). 189p. 1991. pap. 42.00 (*0-946897-34-4*, Pub. by Oxbow Bks UK) David Brown.

***Raine.** Autobiographies, Vol. 1. 1995. pap. 24.95 (*1-871438-41-1*) Atrium Pubs.

Raine, A. E., ed. Advances in Renal Medicine. LC 92-49499. (Oxford Medical Publications). 1993. 105.00 (*0-19-262102-5*); pap. 52.50 (*0-19-262101-7*) OUP.

Raine, Adrian. The Psychopathology of Crime: Criminal Behavior As a Clinical Disorder. LC 93-911. (Illus.). 377p. 1993. text ed. 59.95 (*0-12-576160-0*) Acad Pr.

***Raine, Adrian, et al, eds.** Schizotypal Personality. (Illus.). 300p. (C). 1995. write for info. (*0-521-45422-0*) Cambridge U Pr.

Raine, Andy, jt. auth. see Skinner, John.

Raine, Cedric S., jt. intro. see Scheinberg, Labe.

Raine, Craig. History: The Home Movie. LC 94-16525. 1994. 22.00 (*0-385-47656-6*) Doubleday.

Raine, Craig, ed. see Kipling, Rudyard.

Raine, D. J. The Isotropic Universe. (Monographs on Astronomical Subjects: No. 7). (Illus.). 267p. 1981. 70.00 (*0-85274-370-X*) IOP Pub.

Raine, David F. Islands of Bermuda. (Caribbean Guides Ser.). (Illus.). 170p. (Orig.). 1990. pap. 12.95 (*0-333-51623-0*) Hunter NJ.

***Raine, David S.** Plays in Ten. Date not set. 3.00 (*0-87129-588-1*, P95) Dramatic Pub.

Raine, Derek J. & Heller, Michael. The Science of Space-Time. (Astronomy & Astrophysics Ser.: Vol. 9). (Illus.). 256p. 1981. text ed. 38.00 (*0-912918-12-8*, 0012) Pachart Pub Hse.

Raine, Harmony. The Baroness Orczy Collector Guide. (Orig.). (C). 1984. pap. 4.95 (*0-89966-502-0*) Buccaneer Bks.

— The Dorothy Dunnett Collector Guide. (Orig.). (C). 1984. pap. 4.95 (*0-89966-504-7*) Buccaneer Bks.

— The Dorothy Emily Stevenson Collector Guide. (Orig.). (C). 1984. pap. 4.95 (*0-89966-500-4*) Buccaneer Bks.

— The Georgette Heyer Compendium. 95p. (Orig.). 1984. pap. 5.95 (*0-89966-325-7*) Buccaneer Bks.

— The Harold Bell Wright Collector Guide. (Orig.). 1984. pap. 3.95 (*0-89966-498-9*) Buccaneer Bks.

— The Joseph Altsheler Collector Guide. (Orig.). (C). 1984. pap. 4.95 (*0-89966-503-9*) Buccaneer Bks.

— The Martha Finley Collector Guide. (Orig.). (C). 1984. pap. 4.95 (*0-89966-499-7*) Buccaneer Bks.

Raine, Harmony & Heyer, Georgette. The Georgette Heyer Compendium. (Orig.). 1979. 5.95 (*0-89967-000-8*) Harmony Raine.

Raine, James, ed. The Historians of the Church of York & Its Archbishops, 3 vols., Set. (Rolls Ser.: No. 71). 1969. reprint ed. 240.00 (*0-8115-1139-1*) Periodicals Srv.

— Historical Papers & Letters from the Northern Registers. (Rolls Ser.: No. 61). 1969. reprint ed. 80.00 (*0-8115-1129-4*) Periodicals Srv.

Raine, James W. Land of Saddlebags: A Study of the Mountain People of Appalachia. 1995. reprint ed. 35.00 (*1-55888-378-9*) Omnigraphics Inc.

Raine, Kathleen. Defending Ancient Springs. 198p. 1985. reprint ed. pap. 8.95 (*0-940262-13-4*) Lindisfarne Pr.

— Golgonooza: City of Imagination: Last Studies in William Blake. 182p. (Orig.). 1991. pap. 14.95 (*0-940262-42-8*) Lindisfarne Pr.

— India Seen Afar. 294p. 1991. 22.95 (*0-8076-1268-5*) Braziller.

— The Inner Journey of the Poet. LC 81-21675. 208p. 1982. 20.00 (*0-8076-1039-9*) Braziller.

— Oracle in the Heart. 1991. pap. 11.95 (*0-85105-347-5*, Pub. by Dolmen Pr IE) Dufour.

— The Presence: Poems Nineteen Eighty-Four to Nineteen Eighty-Nine. 80p. 1987. 14.95 (*0-940262-20-7*) Lindisfarne Pr.

— Selected Poems. 160p. 1988. pap. 12.95 (*0-940262-19-3*) Lindisfarne Pr.

— William Blake. (World of Art Ser.). (Illus.). 216p. 1985. pap. 14.95 (*0-500-20107-2*) Thames Hudson.

Raine, Kathleen, ed. see Blake, William.

***Raine, Linnea & Cilluffo, Frank.** Global Organized Crime: The New Empire of Evil. LC 94-41954. (CSIS Report Ser.). 185p. (C). (gr. 13). 1994. pap. text ed. 19.95 (*0-89206-312-2*) CSI Studies.

Raine, Norman R. Tugboat Annie. 15.95 (*0-89387-010-2*) Amereon Ltd.

Raine, P. A., jt. ed. see Morton, N. S.

Raine, W. MacLeod. Powder Smoke Feud. large type ed. (Western Ser.). 1978. 21.95 (*0-7089-0140-9*) Ulverscroft.

Raine, W. R. The Last Shot. 1976. reprint ed. lib. bdg. 18.95 (*0-88411-553-4*, Aeonian Pr) Amereon Ltd.

Raine, William M. Bonanza. 1976. reprint ed. lib. bdg. 23.95 (*0-88411-551-8*, Aeonian Pr) Amereon Ltd.

— Bucky Follows a Cold Trail. large type ed. LC 91-19656. 376p. 1991. reprint ed. lib. bdg. 15.95 (*1-56054-214-4*) Thorndike Pr.

— Colorado. 1976. reprint ed. lib. bdg. 22.95 (*0-88411-557-7*, Aeonian Pr) Amereon Ltd.

— Dry Gulch Trail. large type ed. 337p. 1992. reprint ed. lib. bdg. 17.95 (*1-56054-569-0*) Thorndike Pr.

— Famous Sheriffs & Western Outlaws. 19.95 (*0-89190-544-8*) Amereon Ltd.

— The Fighting Edge. large type ed. LC 90-11285. 376p. 1990. reprint ed. lib. bdg. 16.95 (*1-56054-077-X*) Thorndike Pr.

— Gunsight Pass. large type ed. 400p. 1991. reprint ed. lib. bdg. 16.95 (*1-56054-213-6*) Thorndike Pr.

— High Grass Valley. large type ed. LC 90-25147. 263p. 1991. reprint ed. lib. bdg. 15.95 (*1-56054-108-3*) Thorndike Pr.

— King of the Bush. 1976. reprint ed. lib. bdg. 25.95 (*0-88411-552-6*, Aeonian Pr) Amereon Ltd.

— Man-Size. large type ed. LC 93-21817. 363p. 1993. bds. 17.95 (*1-56054-582-8*) Thorndike Pr.

— On the Dodge. large type ed. LC 92-36433. (Western Ser.). 342p. 1993. reprint ed. lib. bdg. 17.95 (*1-56054-581-X*) Thorndike Pr.

— Run of the Brush. 1976. reprint ed. lib. bdg. 21.95 (*0-88411-554-2*, Aeonian Pr) Amereon Ltd.

— Square Shooter. 1976. reprint ed. lib. bdg. 21.95 (*0-88411-555-0*, Aeonian Pr) Amereon Ltd.

— Steve Yeager. 1976. reprint ed. lib. bdg. 21.95 (*0-88411-556-9*, Aeonian Pr) Amereon Ltd.

Rainer. Classic Music Expression. 1985. 35.00 (*0-02-872020-2*) Macmillan.

***Rainer, Arnulf, ed.** Hiroshima, Pictures Taken after the First Atomic Bomb Was Dropped on Hiroshima on August 6th, 1945. (Illus.). 1985. pap. 52.00 (*3-923791-01-1*, Pub. by Museum Modern Art UK) St Mut.

Rainer, George. Understanding Infrastructure: A Guide for Architects & Planners. 278p. 1990. text ed. 64.95 (*0-471-50546-3*) Wiley.

Rainer, H., jt. ed. see Jakesz, R.

Rainer, Howard. Proud Moments. (Illus.). 144p. 1994. reprint ed. pap. 24.95 (*0-89802-648-2*) Beautiful Am.

— A Song for Mother Earth. (Illus.). 192p. 1995. pap. 34.95 (*0-89802-661-X*) Beautiful Am.

Rainer, John D., et al, eds. Genetic Disease: The Unwanted Inheritance. LC 89-20100. (Loss, Grief & Care Ser.: Vol. 3, Nos. 3 & 4). (Illus.). 213p. 1989. text ed. 39.95 (*0-86656-953-7*) Haworth Pr.

Rainer, Kathleen. Yeats the Initiate: Essays on Certain Themes in the Work of W. B. Yeats. (Illus.). 449p. (C). 1990. text ed. 83.00 (*0-389-20951-1*) B&N Imports.

Rainer, Peter, ed. Love & Hisses: The National Society of Film Critics Sound Off on the Hottest Movie Controversies. LC 92-11175. 464p. 1992. pap. 16.95 (*1-56279-031-5*) Mercury Hse Inc.

Rainer, Pineas. Monarch Notes on Shakespeare's As You Like It. (Orig.). (C). pap. 3.95 (*0-671-00631-2*, Arco Test) P-H Gen Ref & Trav.

Rainer, Thom S. The Book of Church Growth: History, Theology, & Principles. LC 92-29944. 1993. 19.99 (*0-8054-1157-7*) Broadman.

— Eating the Elephant: Bite-Sized Steps to Achieve Long-Term Growth in Your Church. LC 94-499. 1994. 16.99 (*0-8054-6140-X*) Broadman.

— Giant Awakenings: Nine Surprising Trends You Can Use to Benefit Your Church. LC 94-23668. 1995. 17.99 (*0-8054-6173-6*) Broadman.

Rainer, Tristine. The New Diary: How to Use a Journal for Self-Guidance & Expanded Creativity. LC 76-62677. 324p. 1979. reprint ed. pap. 9.95 (*0-87477-150-1*) J P Tarcher.

Rainer, Yvonne. The Films of Yvonne Rainer. LC 88-46035. (Theories of Representation & Difference Ser.). (Illus.). 226p. 1989. 35.00 (*0-253-34906-0*); pap. 12.95 (*0-253-20542-5*) Ind U Pr.

Raineri, A., et al. The State & Future Directions of Acute Myocardial Infarction. 490p. 1988. text ed. 215.00 (*3-7186-4808-3*) Gordon & Breach.

Raineri, Vivian M. The Red Angel: The Life & Times of Elaine Black Yoneda, 1906-1988. LC 91-15038. (Illus.). xiv, 332p. 1991. 19.00 (*0-7178-0688-X*); pap. 9.95 (*0-7178-0686-3*) Intl Pubs Co.

Raines, Barbara, ed. see Ireland, Patricia, et al.

Raines, Cadwell W. Analytical Index to the Laws of Texas, 1823-1905 (Both Dates Inclusive) 559p. 1987. reprint ed. lib. bdg. 47.50 (*0-8377-2534-8*) Rothman.

Raines, Charles A. Monarch Notes on Rawlings' the Yearling. (Orig.). (C). pap. 3.95 (*0-671-00859-5*, Arco Test) P-H Gen Ref & Trav.

Raines, Claire. Visual Aids in Business. Crisp, Michael G., ed. LC 88-92738. (Fifty-Minute Ser.). (Illus.). 96p. (Orig.). 1989. pap. 9.95 (*0-931961-77-7*) Crisp Pubns.

Raines, Claire, jt. auth. see Bradford, Lawrence J.

Raines, Gar, ed. Forms for the Eighties: How to Design & Produce Them. LC 79-90511. 1980. 29.50 (*0-912920-54-8*) North Am Pub Co.

Raines, Howell. Fly Fishing Through the Midlife Crisis. LC 94-18465. 1994. 12.95 (*0-385-47519-5*, Anchor NY) Doubleday.

— Fly Fishing Through the Midlife Crisis. LC 93-15162. 1993. 22.00 (*0-688-10346-4*) Morrow.

— My Soul Is Rested: Movement Days in the Deep South Remembered. 472p. 1983. pap. 12.95 (*0-14-006753-1*, Penguin Bks) Viking Penguin.

Raines, Jeff. The Big Island. 224p. 1989. pap. 3.95 (*0-380-70552-4*) Avon.

— Unbalanced Acts. 272p. 1990. mass mkt. 4.50 (*0-380-76008-8*) Avon.

Raines, Lizz. Widowmaker: A Mystery Thriller. 1994. pap. 5.95 (*0-9625632-4-2*) NUVENTURES Pub.

Raines, Richard C. Handling Depositions, Pts. 1 & 2: Summer 1992, Action Guide. 108p. 1992. pap. text ed. 52.00 (*0-88124-545-3*, CP-11053) Cont Ed Bar-CA.

Raines, Robert A. New Life in the Church. rev. ed. LC 61-5267. (Harper's Ministers Paperback Library). 192p. 1980. pap. 4.50i (*0-06-066773-7*, RD 309) Harper SF.

Raines, Shirley. A Guide to Early Learning. LC 81-86352. 125p. 1982. pap. 16.95 (*0-88247-664-5*) R & E Pubs.

— Never, Ever, Serve Sugary Snacks on Rainy Days: The Official Little Instruction Book for Teachers of Young Children. LC 95-12515. 192p. (Orig.). 1995. pap. 6.95 (*0-87659-175-6*) Gryphon Hse.

***Raines, Shirley, ed.** Whole Language Across the Curriculum. (Language & Literacy Ser.). 240p. (J). (gr. 1-3). 1995. pap. text ed. 19.95 (*0-8077-3446-2*) Tchrs Coll.

Raines, Shirley & Isbell, Rebecca. Stories: Children's Literature in Early Education. 31p. 1994. teacher ed 14.00 (*0-8273-5510-6*) Delmar.

— Stories: Children's Literature in the Early Childhood Classroom & Curriculum. LC 93-28119. 416p. 1994. text ed. 39.95 (*0-8273-5509-2*) Delmar.

Raines, Shirley C. Four Hundred Fifty More Story Stretchers for the Primary Grades: Activities to Expand Children's Favorite Books. LC 94-9450. 256p. 1994. 14.95 (*0-87659-167-5*) Gryphon Hse.

— More Story Stretchers. 1991. pap. 14.95 (*0-87659-153-5*) Gryphon Hse.

— Story Stretchers for the Primary Grades. 1992. pap. 14.95 (*0-87659-157-8*) Gryphon Hse.

Raines, Shirley C. & Canady, Robert J. Story S-t-r-e-t-c-h-e-r-s: Activities to Expand Children's Favorite Books. Charner, Kathy, ed. 265p. 1989. pap. 14.95 (*0-87659-119-5*) Gryphon Hse.

— The Whole Language Kindergarten. (Early Childhood Education Ser.: No. 30). 304p. (C). 1990. pap. text ed. 18.95 (*0-8077-3049-1*) Tchrs Coll.

Rainey, Anson F., ed. Egypt, Israel, Sinai: Archaeological & Historical Relationships in the Biblical Period. (Books from the American University of Beirut Press). (Illus.). 174p. (C). 1988. pap. text ed. 7.95 (*0-8156-7054-0*) Syracuse U Pr.

Rainey, Anson F., tr. see Aharoni, Yohanan.

Rainey, Barbara, jt. auth. see Rainey, Dennis.

Rainey, Bill. Protocol & Etiquette of Golf: The Golfer's Guide to Proper Behavior on the Golf Course. (Orig.). 1993. pap. 9.95 (*1-55958-358-4*) Prima Pub.

Rainey, Buck. Heroes of the Range: Yesterday's Saturday Matinee Movie Cowboys. LC 85-20971. (Illus.). 366p. 1987. 47.50 (*0-8108-1804-3*) Scarecrow.

— The Life & Films of Buck Jones: The Silent Era. (Illus.). 263p. 1988. pap. 14.95 (*0-936505-07-9*) World Yesterday.

— The Life & Films of Buck Jones: The Sound Era. (Illus.). 388p. (Orig.). 1991. pap. 24.95 (*0-936505-08-7*) World Yesterday.

— The Reel Cowboy: Essays on the Myth in Movies & Literature. 400p. 1995. lib. bdg. 39.95 (*0-7864-0106-0*) McFarland & Co.

— The Shoot-Em-Ups Ride Again: A Supplement to Shoot-Em-Ups. LC 90-34151. (Illus.). 319p. 1990. 62.50 (*0-8108-2132-X*) Scarecrow.

— The Shoot-Em-Ups Ride Again: A Supplement to Shoot-Em-Ups. LC 90-34151. (Illus.). 309p. 1990. pap. 19.95 (*0-936505-12-5*) World Yesterday.

— Sweethearts of the Sage: Biographies & Filmographies of 258 Actresses Appearing in Western Movies. LC 91-52639. 652p. 1992. lib. bdg. 95.00 (*0-89950-565-1*) McFarland & Co.

— Those Fabulous Serial Heroines. (Illus.). 523p. 1990. pap. text ed. 29.95 (*0-936505-10-9*) World Yesterday.

— Those Fabulous Serial Heroines: Their Lives & Films. LC 88-11369. (Illus.). 537p. 1990. 62.50 (*0-8108-1911-2*) Scarecrow.

Rainey, Chuck. The Complete Electric Bass Player, Bk. 1: The Method. (Illus.). 200p. 1985. pap. 15.95 (*0-8256-2425-8*, AM37250) Music Sales.

— The Complete Electric Bass Player, Bk. 2: Playing Concepts & Dexterity. (Illus.). 80p. 1985. pap. 9.95 (*0-8256-2426-6*, AM37268) Music Sales.

— The Complete Electric Bass Player, Bk. 3: Electric Bass Improvisation. (Illus.). 64p. 1985. pap. 9.95 (*0-8256-2427-4*, AM37284) Music Sales.

— The Complete Electric Bass Player, Bk. 4: Slapping Techniques. (Illus.). 64p. 1985. pap. 9.95 (*0-8256-2428-2*, AM37276) Music Sales.

— The Complete Electric Bass Player, Bk. 5: Bass Chording. (Illus.). 48p. 1985. pap. 9.95 (*0-8256-2429-0*, AM39405) Music Sales.

***Rainey, Clarice H.** Mountain of Death. 260p. 1995. pap. 8.95 (*0-7610-0041-0*) NW Pub.

Rainey, Dennis. Staying Close. 1992. pap. write for info. (*0-8499-3343-9*) Word Inc.

Rainey, Dennis & Rainey, Barbara. The Questions Book for Marriage Intimacy. 80p. reprint ed. 9.95 (*0-9619022-0-5*) Family Ministry.

— Reconstruyendo la Auto-Estima de Tu Pareja - Building Your Mates' Self-Esteem. (Marriage Ser.). 316p. (SPA.). 1992. pap. 7.95 (*84-7645-570-4*) TSELF.

Rainey, Froelich. Reflections of a Digger: Fifty Years of World Archaeology. LC 92-12150. (Illus.). 324p. 1992. 22.50 (*0-924171-15-4*) U PA Mus Pubns.

Rainey, Froelich G. Excavations in the Ft. Liberte Region, Haiti. LC 76-44780. reprint ed. 21.00 (*0-404-15965-6*) AMS Pr.

Rainey, Hal G. Understanding & Managing Public Organizations. LC 90-28985. (Public Administration - Management Ser.). 359p. 1991. 36.95 (*1-55542-344-2*) Jossey-Bass.

Rainey, Homer P., et al. How Fare American Youth? LC 74-1700. (Children & Youth Ser.). 186p. 1974. reprint ed. 21.95 (*0-405-05977-9*) Ayer.

Rainey, John L. Camelot Island, 1858-1964. 1992. 17.95 (*0-533-10234-0*) Vantage.

Rainey, Lawrence S. Ezra Pound & the Monument of Culture: Text, History, & the Malatesta Cantos. LC 90-44410. (Illus.). 328p. 1991. 29.95 (*0-226-70316-9*) U Ch Pr.

Rainey, Margaret, tr. see Hergren, Per.

Rainey, Penelope. Medieval Latin Lyric, No. 2. (Latin Commentaries Ser.). 67p. (Orig.). (C). 1993. pap. text ed. 6.00 (*0-929524-78-0*) Bryn Mawr Commentaries.

R

An Asterisk (*) at the beginning of an entry indicates that the title is appearing in BIP for the first time.

— Medieval Latin Lyric, No. 3. (Latin Commentaries Ser.). 75p. (Orig.). (C). 1993. pap. text ed. 6.00 (0-929524-79-9) Bryn Mawr Commentaries.
— Medieval Latin Lyric, Vol. 1. (Latin Commentaries Ser.). 75p. (Orig.). (C). 1993. pap. text ed. 6.00 (0-929524-76-4) Bryn Mawr Commentaries.
— Plato: Laches. 1985. pap. text ed. 6.00 (0-929524-28-4) Bryn Mawr Commentaries.
Rainey, R. C. Migration & Meteorology: Flight Behaviour & the Atmospheric Environment of Migrant Pests. (Illus.). 344p. 1990. 150.00 (0-19-854541-X) OUP.
***Rainey, R. L.** Portraits from Paul's Pen. 1994. pap. text ed. 6.25 (0-937396-96-6) Walterick Pubs.
Rainey, Ralph E. Wallace A. Rainey & Jessie I. Ringer: Their Ancestors, Descendants & Allied Families. LC 85-90199. (Illus.). 402p. 1985. 35.00 (0-9615061-0-5) Rainey R.
Rainey, Reuben M. Freud As Student of Religion: Perspectives on the Background & Development of His Thought. LC 75-17536. (American Academy of Religion. Dissertation Ser.: No. 7). 184p. reprint ed. pap. 52.50 (0-317-08045-8, 2017548) Bks Demand.
Rainey, Rich. Haunted History. (Orig.). 1992. mass mkt. 4.99 (0-446-36179-8) Warner Bks.
Rainey, Richard. The Monster Factory. LC 92-26191. (Illus.). 128p. (J). (gr. 6 up). 1993. text ed. 13.95 (0-02-775663-7, Mac Bks Young Read) S&S Childrens.
Rainey, Ross. Capsule Comments on the Cults. 1988. pap. 2.50 (0-937396-72-9) Walterick Pubs.
Rainey, Russ. Shame. 72p. 1991. pap. 2.99 (0-945276-37-0) Rapha Pub.
Rainey, Shannon. Anger. (Institute of Biblical Counseling Discussion Guides Ser.). 72p. (Orig.). 1992. pap. 5.00 (0-89109-687-6) NavPress.
Rainey, Susan. Creating Picturesque America - 1870-1874: Monument to the Natural & Cultural Landscape. LC 94-33484. (Illus.). (C). 1994. 34.95 (0-8265-1257-7) Vanderbilt U Pr.
Rainey, Thomas E., Jr. The Flute Manual. (Illus.). 240p. pap. 12.95 (0-936369-28-0) Son-Rise Pubns.
Rainey, Virginia, jt. auth. see Carroll, John P.
Rainforth, Beverly, et al. Collaborative Teams for Students with Severe Disabilities: Integrating Therapy & Educational Services. 304p. (Orig.). (C). 1992. pap. text ed. 32.00 (1-55766-088-3) P H Brookes.
Rainger, P., et al. Satellite Broadcasting. LC 85-9366. 326p. 1985. text ed. 75.00 (0-471-90421-X) Wiley.
Rainger, Ronald. An Agenda for Antiquity: Henry Fairfield Osborn & Vertebrate Paleontology at the American Museum of Natural History 1890-1935. LC 90-25167. (History of American Science & Technology Ser.). 536p. (C). 1991. 39.50 (0-8173-0536-X) U of Ala Pr.
Rainger, Ronald, et al, eds. The American Development of Biology. 380p. (C). 1991. pap. text ed. 18.00 (0-8135-1702-8) Rutgers U Pr.
***Raingruber, Bob & Maser, Lou.** The King's Gambit As White. Long, Robert B., ed. (Illus.). 205p. 1995. pap. 22.95 (0-938650-47-5) Thinkers Pr.
Rainich, Gabrielle & Kuipers, A. H., eds. Russian-English Vocabulary with Grammatical Sketch. 66p. (ENG & RUS.). 1990. reprint ed. pap. 17.00 (0-8218-0037-X, REV) Am Math.
Rainis, Kenneth G. Environmental Science Projects for Young Scientists. (Projects for Young Scientists Ser.). (Illus.). 128p. (YA). (gr. 9-12). 1994. lib. bdg. 14.77 (0-531-11194-6) Watts.
— Exploring with a Magnifying Glass. LC 91-18329. (Venture Bks.). (Illus.). 144p. (YA). (gr. 9-12). 1991. lib. bdg. 14.77 (0-531-12508-4) Watts.
— Nature Projects for Young Scientists. (J). 1989. pap. 6.95 (0-531-15135-2) Watts.
Rainolde, Richard. A Booke Called the Foundacion of Rhetorike. LC 78-6210. (English Experience Ser.: No. 91). 1969. reprint ed. 30.00 (90-221-0091-X) Walter J Johnson.
Rains, jt. auth. see Palmer.
Rains, Alvin L. & Palmer, Michael J. Local Area Networking with Novell Software. 2nd ed. LC 93-8136. (C). 1994. text ed. 32.95 (0-87709-041-6, BF0416) S-W Pub.
Rains, Darell L. Major Home Appliances: A Common Sense Repair Manual. (Illus.). 160p. (Orig.). 1987. pap. 15.95 (0-8306-2747-2) TAB Bks.
Rains, John. Cruising Ports: Florida to California Via Panama. rev. ed. LC 82-10855. (Illus.). 208p. 1992. pap. 19.95 (0-930030-27-3) Western Marine Ent.
— Cruising Ports: Florida to California via Panama (Guidebook) (Illus.). 272p. 1995. 22.95 (0-9638470-0-7) Pt Loma Pubng.
— MexWX (Weather-Radio for Boaters in Mexico) 1995. 12.95 (0-9638470-1-5) Pt Loma Pubng.
***Rains, John & Miller, Patricia.** Boating Guide to Mexico: West Coast Edition (Guidebook) 304p. 1995. 39.95 (0-9644783-1-5) Pt Loma Pubng.
— Boating in Spanish (Lexicon for Adventurers) 1995. 22.95 (0-9638470-5-8) Pt Loma Pubng.
— Passagemaking Handbook: A Guide for Delivery Skippers & Boatowners. (Illus.). 288p. 1989. text ed. 27.50 (0-915160-99-4) Seven Seas.
Rains, Prue & Teram, Eli. Normal Bad Boys: Public Policies, Institutions, & the Politics of Client Recruitment. 192p. 1992. 44.95 (0-7735-0906-2, Pub. by McGill CN) U of Toronto Pr.
Rains, Rob. The Cardinals Fan's Little Book of Wisdom. 1994. pap. 5.95 (0-912083-77-8) Diamond Communications.
Rains, Theodore C., jt. ed. see Dean, John A.
Rainsberger, Richard, ed. see FERPA II Committee Members Staff.
Rainsbery, F. B. A History of Children's Television in English Canada, 1952-1986. LC 87-28773. (Illus.). 320p. 1988. 32.50 (0-8108-2079-X) Scarecrow.
Rainsbury, Paul A., jt. ed. see Brinsden, Peter R.
Rainsbury, Robert. Written English: An Introduction for Beginning Students of English As a Second Language. 1977. pap. text ed. 16.95 (0-13-970673-9) P-H.
Rainsford. Advances in Anti-Rheumatic Therapy. 1994. write for info. (0-8493-4937-0) CRC Pr.
— Cytokines as Targets for Novel Anti-Rheumatic Drugs. 1995. write for info. (0-8493-4935-4) CRC Pr.
Rainsford, K. D., ed. Anti-Inflammatory & Anti-Rheumatic Drugs: Anti-Rheumatic Drugs, Experimental Agents, & Clinical Aspects of Drug Use, Vol. III. 264p. 1985. 168.00 (0-8493-6232-6, RB405, CRC Reprint) Franklin.
— Anti-Inflammatory & Anti-Rheumatic Drugs Vol. 1: Inflammation Mechanisms & Actions of Traditional Drugs. 208p. 1985. 156.00 (0-8493-6230-X, RM405, CRC Reprint) Franklin.
— Anti-Inflammatory & Anti-Rheumatic Drugs Vol. 2: Newer Anti-Inflammatory Drugs. 296p. 1985. 191.00 (0-8493-6231-8, RM405, CRC Reprint) Franklin.
— Azapropazone: Twenty Years of Clinical Use. 256p. 1990. lib. bdg. 94.00 (0-7923-8911-5) Kluwer Ac.
Rainsford, K. D. & Brune, Kay, eds. Symposium on Aspirin & Related Drugs: Their Actions & Uses. Whitehouse, M. W., tr. (Agents & Actions Supplements Ser.: No. 1). 118p. 1980. pap. 31.00 (0-8176-0902-4) Birkhauser.
Rainsford, K. D. & Velo, G. P., eds. New Developments in Anti-Rheumatic Drugs. (Inflammation & Drug Therapy Ser.). 272p. (C). 1989. lib. bdg. 101.50 (0-7462-0080-3) Kluwer Ac.
— Side-Effects of Anti-Inflamatory Drugs 3. (Inflammation & Drug Therapy Ser.). (C). 1992. lib. bdg. 149.50 (0-7923-8966-2) Kluwer Ac.
Rainsford, K. D., jt. ed. see Ford-Hutchinson, A.
Rainsford, Kim, jt. ed. see Morley, John.
Rainsford, Kim D. & Velo, Giampaolo, eds. Side-Effects of Antiinflammatory-Analgesic Drugs. (Advances in Inflammation Research Ser.: Vol. 6). (Illus.). 320p. 1984. text ed. 86.00 (0-89004-971-8) Raven.
Rainsford, Marcus. Our Lord Prays for His Own: Thoughts on John 17. LC 85-8095. 476p. 1985. pap. 14.99 (0-8254-3617-6) Kregel.
Rainsford, Peter & Bangs, David H., Jr. Restaurant Planning Guide. 176p. 1992. pap. 19.95 (0-936894-35-0) Upstart Pub.
Rainsford, W. S. Story of a Varied Life. LC 70-126249. (Select Bibliographies Reprint Ser.). (Illus.). 1977. 25.95 (0-8369-5476-9) Ayer.
Rainsley, Glen E. Words of Worship: Resources for Sharing the Good News. LC 91-17439. 184p. (Orig.). 1991. pap. 12.95 (0-8298-0899-X) Pilgrim OH.
Raintree, Diane. The Household Book of Hints & Tips. 216p. 1986. pap. 8.95 (0-8246-0304-4) Jonathan David.
Raintree, Diane, ed. The Household Book of Hints & Tips. 272p. 1980. pap. 2.25 (0-345-28927-7) Ballantine.
Raintree, John B., ed. Land, Trees & Tenure: Proceedings of an International Workshop on Tenure Issues in Agroforestry, Nairobi, May 27-31, 1985. 435p. 1987. pap. 15.00 (0-934519-01-3) U of Wis Land.
Raintree, John B. & Taylor, David A., eds. Research on Farmer's Objectives for Tree Breeding: Report of a Workshop Following a Regional Study in Asia. 127p. (Orig.). 1992. pap. 15.00 (0-933595-69-7) Winrock Intl.
Raintree Publishers Inc. Volcanoes. LC 87-27785. (Science & Its Secrets Ser.). (Illus.). 64p. (Orig.). (J). (gr. 5-9). 1988. lib. bdg. 11.95 (0-8172-3081-5) Raintree Steck-V.
— Weather. LC 87-28715. (Science & Its Secrets Ser.). (Illus.). 64p. (Orig.). (J). (gr. 5-9). 1988. lib. bdg. 11.95 (0-8172-3079-3) Raintree Steck-V.
Raintree Publishers Inc. Staff. Dolphins. LC 87-28717. (Science & Its Secrets Ser.). (Illus.). 64p. (Orig.). (J). (gr. 5-9). 1988. lib. bdg. 11.95 (0-8172-3085-8) Raintree Steck-V.
— Energy. LC 87-28699. (Science & Its Secrets Ser.). (Illus.). 64p. (Orig.). (J). (gr. 5-9). 1988. lib. bdg. 11.95 (0-8172-3076-9) Raintree Steck-V.
— Prehistoric Animals. (Science & Its Secrets Ser.). (Illus.). 64p. (Orig.). (J). (gr. 5-9). 1988. lib. bdg. 11.95 (0-8172-3082-3) Raintree Steck-V.
Raintree Publishers Staff. Animals. LC 87-28712. (Science & Its Secrets Ser.). (Illus.). 64p. (Orig.). (J). (gr. 5-9). 1988. lib. bdg. 11.95 (0-8172-3083-1) Raintree Steck-V.
— Animals at the Water's Edge. LC 87-20687. (Animals & Their Homes Ser.). (Illus.). 48p. (J). (gr. k-6). 1987. lib. bdg. 10.95 (0-8172-3115-3) Raintree Steck-V.
— Animals in Cities & Parks. LC 87-20684. (Animals & Their Homes Ser.). (J). (gr. k-6). 1987. 10.95 (0-8172-3116-1) Raintree Steck-V.
— Animals in Houses & Gardens. LC 87-20775. (Animals & Their Homes Ser.). (Illus.). (J). (gr. k-6). 1987. lib. bdg. 10.95 (0-8172-3114-5) Raintree Steck-V.
— Animals in Rivers & Ponds. LC 87-20685. (Animals & Their Homes Ser.). (Illus.). 48p. (J). (gr. k-6). 1987. lib. bdg. 10.95 (0-8172-3113-7) Raintree Steck-V.
— Animals in the Forest. LC 87-20689. (Animals & Their Homes Ser.). (Illus.). 48p. (J). (gr. k-6). 1987. lib. bdg. 10.95 (0-8172-3111-0) Raintree Steck-V.
— Animals in the Mountains. LC 87-20688. (Animals & Their Homes Ser.). (Illus.). 48p. (J). (gr. k-6). 1987. lib. bdg. 10.95 (0-8172-3112-9) Raintree Steck-V.
— Archaeology. LC 87-28634. (Science & Its Secrets Ser.). (Illus.). 64p. (Orig.). (J). (gr. 5-9). 1988. lib. bdg. 11.95 (0-8172-3077-7) Raintree Steck-V.
— Astronomy. LC 87-28780. (Science & Its Secrets Ser.). (Illus.). 64p. (Orig.). (J). (gr. 5-9). 1988. lib. bdg. 11.95 (0-8172-3080-7) Raintree Steck-V.
— Birds. LC 87-28786. (Science & Its Secrets Ser.). (Illus.). 64p. (Orig.). (J). (gr. 5-9). 1988. lib. bdg. 11.95 (0-8172-3084-X) Raintree Steck-V.
Raintree Steck-Vaughn Staff. Atlas of the Environment. Coote, Roger, ed. LC 92-8196. (Illus.). 96p. (J). (gr. 6-7). 1992. lib. bdg. 26.99 (0-8114-7250-7) Raintree Steck-V.
Rainville, Earl D. Special Functions. LC 70-172380. (Illus.). xii, 365p. 1972. reprint ed. text ed. 27.50 (0-8284-0258-2) Chelsea Pub.
Rainville, Earl D. & Bedient, Phillip E. Elementary Differential Equations. 7th ed. 548p. (C). 1989. write for info. (0-02-397860-0) Macmillan.
— Short Course in Differential Equations. 6th ed. (C). 1981. write for info. (0-02-397760-4) Macmillan.
Rainville, Raymond E. Dreams Across the Lifespan. 234p. (C). 1988. pap. text ed. 16.95x (0-89641-177-X) American Pr.
Rainville, Rita. Alone at Last. (Silhouette Romance Ser.: No. 873). 1992. pap. 2.69 (0-373-08873-6, 5-08873-7) Silhouette.
— Bedazzled. (Desire Ser.). 1995. pap. 3.25 (0-373-05918-3, 1-05918-7) Silhouette.
— High Spirits. (Silhouette Desire Ser.). 1993. mass mkt. 2.99 (0-373-05792-X, 5-05792-2) Silhouette.
— Hot Property: (Centerfolds) (Desire Ser.). 1994. mass mkt. 2.99 (0-373-05874-8, 1-05874-2) Harlequin Bks.
— Paid in Full. large type ed. 1994. 17.95 (0-373-58847-X, Silhouette Lrg Print); pap. 16.95 (0-373-59069-5, Silhouette Lrg Print) Chivers N Amer.
— Tumbleweed & Gibraltar. (Silhouette Desire Ser.). 1993. mass mkt. 2.99 (0-373-05828-4, 5-05828-4) Silhouette.
Rainwater, Agnes B. Therapeutic Recreation for Chemically Dependent Adolescents & Adults: Programming & Activities. (Illus.). 208p. (Orig.). 1992. pap. text ed. 24.95 (0-88314-523-5) AAHPERD.
Rainwater, Brenda, jt. auth. see Swanson, Thomas G.
Rainwater, Catherine & Scheick, William J., eds. Contemporary American Women Writers: Narrative Strategies. LC 85-9116. 240p. 1985. pap. 12.00 (0-8131-0168-9) U Pr of Ky.
Rainwater, Dorothy, jt. auth. see Felger, Donna H.
Rainwater, Dorothy T. American Jewelry Manufacturers. LC 87-63485. (Illus.). 280p. 1988. pap. 45.00 (0-88740-120-1) Schiffer.
— Encyclopedia of American Silver Manufacturers. 3rd rev. ed. LC 85-61525. (Illus.). 258p. 1986. reprint ed. pap. 19.95 (0-88740-046-9) Schiffer.
Rainwater, Dorothy T. & Felger, Donna H. Spoons from Around the World. LC 92-60628. (Illus.). 288p. 1992. text ed. 59.95 (0-88740-425-1) Schiffer.
Rainwater, Dorothy T. & Rainwater, H. Ivan. American Silverplate. enl. rev. ed. LC 72-7998. (Illus.). 480p. 1988. 37.50 (0-88740-128-7) Schiffer.
Rainwater, H. Ivan, jt. auth. see Rainwater, Dorothy T.
***Rainwater, Harold.** Two Wheels & a Pair of Nuts. LC 95-60238. 304p. (Orig.). 1995. pap. 10.95 (0-9645385-0-4) Wiregrass Pubs.
Rainwater, Janette. You're in Charge: A Guide to Becoming Your Own Therapist. LC 82-9104. 221p. 1985. reprint ed. pap. 11.00 (0-87516-552-4) DeVorss.
Rainwater, Judy. Micro Magic. 200p. (Orig.). 1988. spiral bd. 11.95 (0-9622066-0-1) Ranrai Pub.
— Nutrition for the Nineties. 1992. spiral bd., pap. 13.50 (0-9622066-1-X) Ranrai Pub.
Rainwater, Lee. And the Poor Get Children: Sex, Contraception, & Family Planning in the Working Class. LC 84-12770. xiv, 202p. 1984. reprint ed. text ed. 55.00 (0-313-24452-9, RAPG, Greenwood Pr) Greenwood.
— Behind Ghetto Walls: Black Family Life in a Federal Slum. LC 77-113083. 458p. 1970. text ed. 49.95 (0-202-30113-3); pap. text ed. 29.95 (0-202-30114-1) Aldine de Gruyter.
Rainwater, Lee, ed. Black Experience: Soul. LC 72-87669. 266p. 1973. reprint ed. pap. text ed. 18.95 (0-87855-561-7) Transaction Pubs.
— Social Problems & Public Policy: Deviance & Liberty. 445p. (C). 1974. lib. bdg. 49.95 (0-202-30263-6) Aldine de Gruyter.
Rainwater, Lee, jt. ed. see Rein, Martin.
Rainwater, Lee, et al. Workingman's Wife: Her Personality, World & Life Style. Coser, Lewis A. & Powell, Walter W., eds. LC 79-7014. (Perennial Works in Sociology Ser.). 1980. reprint ed. lib. bdg. 21.95 (0-405-12113-X) Ayer.
Rainwater, Mara, jt. ed. see Kearney, Richard.
Rainwater, Marvenea. Slow of Heart. 1989. pap. 10.00 (0-941179-19-2) Latitudes Pr.
Rainwater, Percy L. Mississippi: Storm Center of Secession, 1856-1861. LC 72-84188. (American Scene, Comments & Commentators Ser.). 1969. reprint ed. lib. bdg. 29.50 (0-306-71614-3) Da Capo.
Rainwater, Robert, ed. Max Ernst: Beyond Surrealism. (Illus.). 192p. 1986. pap. 19.95 (0-87104-290-8) NY Pub Lib.
— On Paper. 1990. 19.95 (0-87104-425-0) NY Pub Lib.
Rainy, Charlotte, tr. see Boehme, Jacob.
Rainy, Charlotte A., jt. tr. see Behman, Jacob.
Raioahadur, R., jt. auth. see Dey, K. L.
Rairden, Anthony, jt. auth. see Konicki, Steve.
Rais, Elliot. Stealing the Borders. 1994. pap. 5.50 (1-56171-325-2, S P I Bks) Sure Sellers.
Rais, Kathleen. Albert Payson Terhune: A Bibliography of Primary Works. (Illus.). 1994. 50.00 (0-685-70378-9) Kathleen Rais.
Rais, Rasul B. The Indian Ocean & the Superpowers. LC 86-22306. 270p. (C). 1987. 57.00 (0-389-20695-4, N8253) B&N Imports.
— War Without Winners: Afghanistan's Uncertain Transition after the Cold War. (Illus.). 301p. 1994. 27.00 (0-19-577535-X) OUP.
Raisanen, Heikki. Beyond New Testament Theology. LC 89-48393. 224p. (Orig.). (C). 1990. pap. 14.95 (0-334-01907-9) TPI PA.
— The Messianic Secret in Mark's Gospel. Riches, John, ed. Tuckett, Christopher, tr. (Studies of the New Testament & Its World). 320p. 1990. 43.95 (0-567-09529-0, Pub. by T & T Clark UK) Bks Intl VA.
— The Messianic Secret in Mark's Gospel. Tuckett, Christopher, tr. 320p. 1994. pap. text ed. 24.95 (0-567-29253-3, Pub. by T & T Clark UK) Bks Intl VA.
Raisbeck, B. L., ed. Evidence. 260p. (C). 1990. pap. 60.00 (1-85352-790-4, Pub. by HLT Pubns UK) St Mut.
Raise Language Group Staff. The Raise Method Manual. 480p. 1995. pap. text ed. 46.00 (0-13-752700-4) P-H.
Raisenan, Heikki. Jesus Paul & Torah: Collected Essays. Orton, David E., tr. (JSNT Supplement Ser.: No. 43). 300p. (C). 1992. 30.00 (1-85075-237-0, Pub. by Sheffield Acad UK) CUP Services.
Raish, Martin. Key Guide to Electronic Resources: Fine Arts. Ensor, Pat, ed. 150p. 1995. pap. text ed. 35.00 (0-88736-957-X) Learned Info.
Raish, Martin H., jt. auth. see Sorenson, John L.
Raish, Peggy & Klaus, Billie J., eds. Every Nurses Guide to Physical Assessment: A Primary Care Focus. LC 86-34007. (Red Bks.). 500p. 1987. pap. text ed. 25.95 (0-8273-4213-6) Delmar.
Raisin, Max. Great Jews I Have Known. LC 71-117331. (Biography Index Reprint Ser.). 1977. 24.95 (0-8369-8023-9) Ayer.
***Raiskin, Judith.** Now on the Cane Fields: Women's Writing & Creole Subjectivity. 320p. 1995. text ed. 49.95 (0-8166-2300-7); pap. text ed. 19.95 (0-8166-2301-5) U of Minn Pr.
Raisman. Canopic Equipment in the Petrie Collection. 1984. pap. 44.00 (0-85668-268-3, Pub. by Aris & Phillips UK) David Brown.
***Raisman, Neal A., ed.** Directing General Education Outcomes. LC 85-644753. (New Directions for Community Colleges Ser.: No. 81). 107p. (Orig.). 1993. pap. 16.95 (1-55542-686-7) Jossey-Bass.
***Raison, Jennifer & Goldie, Michael.** Caraboo: The Servant Girl Princess: The Real Story of the Grand Hoax. LC 94-42794. 1995. pap. write for info. (1-56656-179-5) Interlink Pub.
Raison, Laura. Florence & Tuscany. 1994. pap. 16.95 (0-8442-9961-8, Passport Bks) NTC Pub Grp.
Raison, Timothy. Tories & the Welfare State: A History of Conservative Social Policy since the Second World War. LC 89-37094. 236p. 1990. text ed. 55.00 (0-312-04079-2) St Martin.
Raisor, Gary. Less Than Human. Hinchberger, Lauri, ed. (Illus.). 256p. (Orig.). (C). 1992. 29.95 (0-9633397-0-2) Overlook Connect.
— Less Than Human. deluxe limited ed. Hinchberger, Lauri, ed. (Illus.). 256p. (Orig.). (C). 1992. boxed 150.00 (0-9633397-1-0) Overlook Connect.
Raisor, Gary, ed. Obsessions. 1991. 20.95 (0-913165-55-7) Dark Harvest.
Raissiguier, Catherine. Becoming Women, Becoming Workers: Identity Formation in a French Vocational School. LC 93-40597. (Power, Social Identity & Education Ser.). 211p. (C). 1994. text ed. 49.50 (0-7914-2085-X); pap. 16.95 (0-7914-2086-8) State U NY Pr.
Raissman, Bob, jt. auth. see Montana, Joe.
Raistrick, Arthur. Dynasty of Iron Founders. (Illus.). 347p. (C). 1988. 105.00 (0-685-37102-6, Pub. by W Sessions UK) St Mut.
— Dynasty of Iron Founders: Standard Work on the Ironbridge Gorge, Shropshire. rev. ed. (C). 1989. pap. 32.00 (1-85072-058-4, Pub. by W Sessions UK) St Mut.
— Quakers in Science & Industry: Being an Account of Quaker Contributions to Science & Industry During the 17th & 18th Centuries. LC 68-18641. (Illus.). 361p. 1968. reprint ed. 39.50 (0-678-05622-6) Kelley.
Raistrick, Arthur & Roberts, Arthur. Life & Work of the Northern Lead Miner. (Illus.). 128p. 1991. 30.00 (0-86299-826-3) A Sutton Pub.
Raistrick, Donald. Index to Legal Citations & Abbreviations. 2nd ed. LC 94-141395. 497p. 1993. lib. bdg. 100.00 (1-85739-061-X) Bowker-Saur.
— Lawyers' Law Books. 3rd rev. ed. 600p. 1995. 125.00 (1-85739-087-3) Bowker-Saur.
Raisz, jt. auth. see Martin.
Raisz, Erwin J. Principles of Cartography. (Geography Ser.). (C). 1962. text ed. 33.00 (0-07-051151-9) McGraw.
Rait, Robert S. Life in the Medieval University. 1973. 69.95 (0-8490-0526-4) Gordon Pr.
***Raiten, Daniel J., ed.** Vitamin B-6 Metabolism in Pregnancy, Lacation & Infancy. LC 94-32693. 1995. write for info. (0-8493-4594-4) CRC Pr.
Raiter, Franklin R., jt. auth. see Carroll, Francis M.
Raith, Joachim, jt. auth. see Enninger, Werner.
Raithby. Transition Metal Cluster Carbonyls. 200p. 1993. 55.00 (0-13-927989-X) P-H.
Raithelhuber, J. Flora Mycologica Argentina, Hongos I. (Illus.). 371p. (SPA.). (C). 1987. pap. text ed. 42.00 (3-9801550-1-3) Lubrecht & Cramer.
— Flora Mycologica Argentina: Hongos II (Fungi II) (Illus.). 287p. (SPA.). 1988. pap. 35.00 (3-9801550-2-1) Lubrecht & Cramer.
Raiti, Salvatore & Tolman, Robert A., eds. Human Growth Hormone. LC 86-3288. 676p. 1986. 135.00 (0-306-42053-8, Plenum Pr) Plenum.
Raitiere, Martin N. Faire Bitts: Sir Philip Sydney & Continental Political Theory. LC 83-11705. (Duquesne Studies: Language & Literature Ser.: Vol. 4). 180p. 1984. text ed. 25.00x (0-8207-0162-9) Duquesne.
Raitport, Eli. Nineteen Eighties: The United States in Crisis. Duplantier, F. R., ed. (First Ser.). (Illus.). 216p. (Orig.). 1989. pap. text ed. 19.50 (0-685-48471-8) Raitport Co.

R

— 1980's the United States in Crisis: United States in Crisis. Duplantier, F. R., ed. (United States in Crises Ser.). 214p. (Orig.). (C). 1989. reprint ed. pap. 19.50x (*0-944182-01-1*) Raitport Co.

— The United States--Vulnerable. 2nd ed. Duplantier, F. R., ed. (United States in Crises Ser.). 221p. (Orig.). (C). 1989. reprint ed. pap. 19.50x (*0-944182-02-X*) Raitport Co.

— United States in Crisis, Vol. I. (Nineteen Eighty-Six to Nineteen Eighty-Seven Ser.). (Illus.). 192p. (Orig.). 1988. pap. 19.50 (*0-944182-00-3*) Raitport Co.

***Raitt.** Christian Spirituality, Vol. 2. Date not set. 43.50 (*0-8245-0765-7*) Crossroad NY.

Raitt, David I., jt. ed. see Ching-Chih, Chen.

***Raitt, George D., et al.** Masonic History of Unadilla, N.Y. Goerlich, Shirley B., ed. (Illus.). 59p. 1995. reprint ed. pap. 20.00 (*1-887530-00-2*) RSG Pub.

Raitt, Helen & Wayne, Mary C., eds. We Three Came West. LC 74-81909. (Illus.). 272p. 1974. 10.00 (*0-914488-03-1*) Rand-Tofua.

— We Three Came West. 2nd rev. ed. LC 74-81909. (Illus.). 272p. 1975. pap. 4.95 (*0-914488-08-2*) Rand-Tofua.

Raitt, Helen, jt. auth. see Gerstle, Donna.

Raitt, Jill. The Colloquy of Montbeliard: Religion & Politics in the Sixteenth Century. 304p. 1993. 49.95 (*0-19-507566-8*) OUP.

— The Eucharistic Theology of Theodore Beza: Development of the Reformed Doctrine. LC 74-188907. (American Academy of Religion. Studies in Religion: No. 4). 91p. reprint ed. pap. 26.00 (*0-7837-5490-6*, 2045255) Bks Demand.

Raitt, Jill, ed. Shapers of Religious Traditions in Germany, Switzerland, & Poland, Fifteen Sixty to Sixteen Hundred. LC 80-23287. 256p. (C). 1981. text ed. 37.50 (*0-300-02457-6*) Yale U Pr.

Raitt, Jill, et al, eds. Christian Spirituality, Vol. II: High Middle & Reformation. (World Spirituality Ser.: Vol. 17). (Illus.). 528p. 1989. pap. 19.95 (*0-8245-0967-6*) Crossroad NY.

Raitt, Lia N. Garrett & the English Muse. (Series A: Monagrafias, XCIV). 146p. (C). 1983. 35.00 (*0-7293-0145-1*, Pub. by Tamesis Bks Ltd UK) Boydell & Brewer.

Raitt, Robert L. Campus on the Hill, a History of Santa Paula High School: & Century of Community Yesterdays. (Illus.). 280p. (C). 1988. 21.50 (*0-9620212-8-8*) Santa Paula HS Alumni.

Raitt, Suzanne. Virginia Woolf's "To the Lighthouse" LC 90-46984. (Critical Studies of Key Texts). 143p. 1990. text ed. 39.95 (*0-312-05654-0*); pap. 12.95 (*0-312-05655-9*) St Martin.

— Vita & Virginia: The Work & Friendship of V. Sackville-West & Virginia Woolf. 210p. 1993. pap. 13.95 (*0-19-812277-2*) OUP.

Raitta, C., jt. ed. see Greve, Erik L.

Raitz, Karl, jt. auth. see Murray-Wooley, Carolyn.

***Raitz, Karl B., ed.** The Theater of Sport. (Illus.). 384p. 1995. text ed. 45.00x (*0-8018-4908-X*); pap. 19.95 (*0-8018-4909-8*) Johns Hopkins.

Raives, Barbara, jt. auth. see Luongo, Pino.

Raivio, Kari O., et al, eds. Respiratory Distress Syndrome. 1984. text ed. 113.00 (*0-12-576180-5*) Acad Pr.

***Raiz, Carmela.** Blue Star Over Red Square. LC 94-39654. 1994. write for info. (*0-87306-616-2*); pap. text ed. write for info. (*0-87306-617-0*) Feldheim.

Raizada, M. B. Flora of Mussoorie, Vol. 1. 645p. (C). 1978. 195.00 (*0-685-21857-0*, Pub. by Intl Bk Distr II); text ed. 250.00 (*0-89771-646-9*, Pub. by Intl Bk Distr II) St Mut.

— Grasses of Upper Gangetic Plaint, Pt. 3. (C). 1988. text ed. 40.00 (*0-685-44241-1*, Scientific) St Mut.

— Orchids of Mussorie. (C). 1988. 250.00 (*0-685-22329-9*, Scientific) St Mut.

— Supplement to Duthie's Flora of the Upper Gangetic Plain & of the Adjacent Siwalik & Sub Himalayan Tracks. 355p. (C). 1976. text ed. 75.00 (*0-89771-643-4*, Pub. by Intl Bk Distr II) St Mut.

Raizada, M. B., ed. Correction & Nomenclatural Changes to the Forest Flora of the Bombay Presidency & Sind, 2 vols., Set. (C). 1976. text ed. 65.00 (*0-89771-645-0*, Pub. by Intl Bk Distr II) St Mut.

— Supplement to Duthie's Flora of the Upper Gangetic Plain & of the Adjacent Siwalik & Sub-Himalayan Tracts. 355p. (C). 1976. 75.00 (*0-685-21741-8*, Pub. by Intl Bk Distr II) St Mut.

Raizada, M. K. & LeRoith, D., eds. Molecular Biology & Physiology of Insulin & Insulin-Like Growth Factors. (Advances in Experimental Medicine & Biology Ser.: Vol. 293). (Illus.). 498p. 1991. 135.00 (*0-306-43928-X*, Plenum Pr) Plenum.

Raizada, M. K., jt. ed. see LeRoith, D.

Raizada, M. K., et al, eds. Insulin, Insulin-Like Growth Factors, & Their Receptors in the Central Nervous System. LC 87-20337. (Illus.). 366p. 1987. 85.00 (*0-306-42666-8*, Plenum Pr) Plenum.

Raizada, Mohan K. & LeRoith, Derek, eds. Current Directions in Insulin-Like Growth Factor Research. LC 93-46649. (Advances in Experimental Medicine & Biology Ser.: Vol. 343). (Illus.). 417p. 1994. 110.00 (*0-306-44622-7*, Plenum Pr) Plenum.

— The Role of Insulin-Like Growth Factors in the Nervous System. LC 93-11672. (Annals Ser.: Vol. 692). 348p. 1993. write for info. (*0-89766-789-1*); pap. 95.00 (*0-89766-790-5*) NY Acad Sci.

Raizada, Mohan K., jt. ed. see Mukhopadhyay, Amal K.

Raizda, Mohan K., et al, eds. Cellular & Molecular Neurobiology of Renin-Angiotensin System. 1993. 189. 95 (*0-8493-4622-3*, QP572) CRC Pr.

Raizen, Senta A. & Jones, Lyle V., eds. Indicators of Precollege Education in Science & Mathematics: A Preliminary Review. LC 85-3028. 210p. reprint ed. pap. 59.90 (*0-7837-1263-4*, 2041402) Bks Demand.

Raizen, Senta A. & Michelsohn, Arie M., eds. The Future of Science in Elementary Schools: Educating Prospective Teachers. LC 93-41154. (Education-Higher Education Ser.). 206p. 1994. 27.95 (*1-55542-824-7*) Jossey-Bass.

Raizen, Senta A., ed. see National Research Council.

***Raizen, Senta A., et al.** Technology in the Classroom: Understanding the Designed World. (Educational Ser.). 1995. 32.95 (*0-7879-0178-4*) Jossey-Bass.

Raizer, Yu. P. Gas Discharge Physics. (Illus.). xi, 449p. 1991. 105.00 (*0-387-19462-2*) Spr-Verlag.

***Raizer, Yuri P., et al, eds.** Radio-Frequency Capacitive Discharges. 320p. 1995. 115.00 (*0-8493-8644-6*, 8644) CRC Pr.

Raizis, M. Byron & Papas, A. Greek Revolution & the American Muse: A Collection of Philhellenic Poetry 1821-1828. xx, 168p. (Orig.). 1986. reprint ed. pap. text ed. 32.50 (*0-317-57961-4*, Pub. by A M Hakkert SP) Coronet Bks.

Raiziss, Sona. Metaphysical Passion: Seven Modern American Poets & the Seventeenth Century Tradition. LC 73-194227. 327p. 1970. reprint ed. text ed. 59.75 (*0-8371-3343-2*, RAMP, Greenwood Pr) Greenwood.

Raiziss, Sonia. Bucks County Blues. (Illus.). 1977. per. 2.50 (*0-912284-90-0*) New Rivers Pr.

Raiziss, Sonia, tr. see De Palchi, Alfredo.

Raizman, Marjorie, jt. auth. see Cross, Thomas B.

***Raizman, Richard E. Stones Unfolding from the Garden of Time. 150p. (Orig.). 1994. pap. 8.95 (*0-9642627-0-3*) Mountn Meadw Pr.**

STONES UNFOLDING FROM THE GARDEN OF TIME is a richly textured new work of historical fiction. It is a collection of stories that relate through myth, folklore, & eastern European Jewish mysticism, the era when nineteenth-century Prussian Germany rose in parallel to the decaying grandeur of the Hapsburg empire. (Publisher's note) "In these stories, History itself is a major character. In its many complexities, History is symbolized by the graveyards that have gathered the generations within the confused boundaries of Europe. How the author creates patterns within that confusion - patterns that reach into the past to provide ironic explanations for the future, is the lyrical charm of these stories." "The garden of graves was outside of Time, as he knew it. The Jews kept within their gates, the splendor of the soul...The iron gates contain an unseen tower. It does not follow the physical laws as we know them, & that is its wonder. It spans a continuum between the depths of the earth & the heavens, to gleams of light that we call stars." - from "Das Ratsel des Lebens" (The Riddle of Life) - an excerpt from the collection. Mountain Meadow Press, 5736 W. Woodland Rd., Pittsburgh, PA 15232; 412-521-5804. Price $8.95. ***Publisher Provided Annotation.***

Raizner, Bernard I. Insult to Injury. 224p. 1989. pap. 3.95 (*0-380-70697-0*) Avon.

Raj. Pain Management: A Comprehensive Review. 1994. 39. 50 (*0-8016-7998-2*) Mosby Yr Bk.

— A Practical Treatment of Pain. (SPA.). 1994. 204.55 (*0-8016-7209-0*) Mosby Yr Bk.

Raj, A. Shiv. An Introduction to Physiology of Cereal Crops. (C). 1987. 17.50 (*81-204-0189-1*, Pub. by Oxford IBH II) S Asia.

Raj, B., jt. auth. see Dufour, J. M.

Raj, Baldev, ed. Advances in Econometrics & Modelling. (C). 1989. lib. bdg. 88.00 (*0-7923-0299-0*) Kluwer Ac.

— Henri Theil's Contributions to Economics & Econometrics, Set. (Advanced Studies in Theoretical & Applied Econometrics). (C). 1992. lib. bdg. 336.00 (*0-7923-1666-5*) Kluwer Ac.

— Henri Theil's Contributions to Economics & Econometrics, Vol. I: Econometric Theory & Methodology. (Advanced Studies in Theoretical & Applied Econometrics). 616p. (C). 1992. lib. bdg. 181.50 (*0-7923-1548-0*) Kluwer Ac.

— Henri Theil's Contributions to Economics & Econometrics, Vol. II: Consumer Demand Analysis & Information Theory. (Advanced Studies in Theoretical & Applied Econometrics). 487p. (C). 1992. lib. bdg. 131.50 (*0-7923-1664-9*) Kluwer Ac.

— Henri Theil's Contributions to Economics & Econometrics, Vol. III: Economic Policy & Forecasts, & Management Science. 350p. (C). 1992. lib. bdg. 112.50 (*0-7923-1665-7*) Kluwer Ac.

Raj, Baldev & Ullah, Aman. Econometrics: A Varying Coefficients Approach. 384p. 1981. text ed. 39.95 (*0-312-22632-2*) St Martin.

Raj, Baldev, et al, eds. Panel Data Analysis. (Studies in Empirical Economics). (Illus.). viii, 220p. 1992. 98.00 (*0-387-91416-1*) Spr-Verlag.

Raj, G., jt. auth. see Yadav, M.

Raj, Gagan. Dictionary of Literary Terms. 1990. 33.50 (*81-7041-284-6*, Pub. by Anmol II) S Asia.

Raj, Hans. Protection of Foreign Investment, Property & Nationalisation in India. (C). 1989. 250.00 (*0-685-27935-9*) St Mut.

Raj, K. N. Organizational Issues in Indian Agriculture. 236p. 1990. 26.00 (*0-19-562520-X*) OUP.

Raj, K. N., ed. see Narain, Dharm.

Raj, Maithreyi K. Women's Studies in India: Some Perspectives. 1986. 28.50 (*0-86132-135-9*, Pub. by Popular Prakashan II) S Asia.

Raj, Mulkh, jt. ed. see Gaudin, Jean-Pierre.

Raj, N. Desinga. Development Programmes in Agriculture & the Weaker Sections. 217p. 1987. 26.00 (*81-85076-16-2*, Pub. by Chugh Pubns II) S Asia.

Raj, P. Prithvi. Current Review of Pain. (Illus.). 272p. 1994. text ed. 109.95 (*1-878132-06-7*) Current Med.

— Practical Management of Pain. 2nd ed. 1152p. 1991. 165. 00 (*0-8151-7012-2*) Mosby Yr Bk.

Raj, P. Prithvi, ed. Clinical Practice of Regional Anesthesia. (Illus.). 543p. 1991. text ed. 124.00 (*0-443-08685-0*) Churchill.

Raj, Prakash A. Nepal. (Insider's Guides Ser.). (Illus.). 150p. (Orig.). 1991. pap. 9.95 (*0-87052-026-1*) Hippocrene Bks.

— Nepali-English English-Nepali Concise Dictionary. (Concise Language Dictionaries Ser.). 400p. (Orig.). 1991. pap. 8.95 (*0-87052-106-3*) Hippocrene Bks.

— Pokhara: A Valley in the Himalayas. (C). 1993. 23.00 (*0-7855-0203-3*, Pub. by Ratna Pustak Bhandar) St Mut.

Raj, Rishi, ed. see ASM Materials Science Seminar Staff.

Raj, Santosh. Understanding Sikhs & Their Religion: A Christian Perspective. 70p. (Orig.). 1991. pap. 3.95 (*0-919797-99-7*) Kindred Prods.

Raj, Sheela. Mediaevelism to Modernism: Socio Economic & Cultural History of Hyderabad, 1869-1911. (C). 1987. 36.00 (*0-86132-143-X*, Pub. by Popular Prakashan II) S Asia.

Raj, V. Manuel. Santal Theology of Liberation. 1990. 22.00 (*81-85024-81-2*, Pub. by Uppal Pub Hse II) S Asia.

Raj, Veni. A Diamond in the Darkness. (Illus.). 32p. 1984. pap. 4.50 (*0-85398-161-2*) G Ronald Pub.

***Raj, Victor A.** The Hindu Connection: Roots of the New Age. LC 94-43623. (Scholarship Today Ser.). 1995. write for info. (*0-570-04802-8*) Concordia.

Raja. Living Inspirations. 1994. 11.95 (*1-85230-557-6*) Element MA.

Raja, Gopal B., jt. auth. see Subramanyam, S. V.

Raja, K. Kunjunni, jt. auth. see Coward, Harold C.

Raja, Om P. The Words of Om Raja. LC 89-84563. 127p. (Orig.). 1990. pap. 7.95 (*0-9623163-0-X*) FL Pubs.

Raja, P. Folk Tales of Pondicherry. 112p. 1987. text ed. 15. 95 (*81-207-0683-8*, Pub. by Sterling Pubs II) Apt Bks.

— Many Worlds of Manoj Das. (Orig.). (C). 1993. 8.50x (*81-7018-761-3*, Pub. by BR Pub II) S Asia.

Raja, R. Tales of Mulla Nasruddin. (New World Literature Ser.: No. 18). (C). 1989. 18.00 (*81-7018-559-9*, Pub. by BR Pub II) S Asia.

Raja, R. & Yoh, John. The Batavia Meeting: Proceedings of the 1992 Meeting of the Division of Particles & Fields of the APS, 2 vols., Set. 750p. 1993. text ed. 178.00 (*981-02-1323-9*) World Scientific Pub.

Raja, Rao. Kanthapura. LC 77-3040. 244p. 1977. reprint ed. text ed. 47.50 (*0-8371-9573-X*, RAKA, Greenwood Pr) Greenwood.

Raja Rao, V. N. Perspectives in Phycology. (Illus.). 500p. 1991. 69.00 (*1-55528-192-3*, Pub. by Today & Tomorrows P & P II) Scholarly Pubns.

Rajab, Jehan. Palestinian Folk Costume. 200p. 1988. lib. bdg. 65.00 (*0-7103-0283-5*, Pub. by Kegan Paul Intl UK) Routledge Chapman & Hall.

Rajab, Jehan S. Invasion Kuwait: An English Woman's Tale. (Illus.). 224p. 1994. text ed. 39.50 (*1-85043-775-0*, Pub. by I B Tauris UK) St Martin.

Rajabov, Y. U., tr. see Entelis, S. G., et al.

Rajacic, Roy. The Best Poems of Roy Rajacic. Maljkovic-Petkovic, Djuro & Kostic, Katarina, eds. (Illus.). 80p. (Orig.). 1982. 7.95 (*0-943898-00-5*); pap. 6.95 (*0-943898-01-3*) Gospic Realty.

***Rajadhyaksha, Ashish & Willemen, Paul.** Encyclopedia of Indian Cinema. 544p. 1994. text ed. 49.95 (*0-85170-455-7*) Ind U Pr.

Rajaee, Farhang, ed. see Shari'ati, Ali, et al.

Rajaee, Farhang, tr. see Taleqani, Mahmood.

Rajagapalachari, Chakravarti, tr. see Vyasa.

Rajagopal. Entrepreneurship & Rural Markets. (C). 1992. text ed. 15.00 (*81-7033-167-6*, Pub. by Rawat II) S Asia.

***Rajagopal, et al.** Organizing Rural Business: Policy, Planning & Management. LC 94-32848. 180p. (C). 1995. 22.95 (*0-8039-9200-9*) Sage.

Rajagopal, Arvind, jt. ed. see Goldman, Robert.

Rajagopal, D., ed. see Krishnamurti, Jiddu.

Rajagopal, D., jt. auth. see Veeresh, G. K.

Rajagopal, G. & Ramakrishnan, S. Practical Biochemistry for Medical Students. (Illus.). 80p. (Orig.). 1983. pap. text ed. 8.95 (*0-86131-415-8*, Pub. by Orient Longman Ltd II) Apt Bks.

Rajagopal, K. P. Mechanics of Mixtures. 250p. 1995. text ed. 53.00 (*981-02-1585-1*) World Scientific Pub.

***Rajagopal, K. R., ed.** Recent Advances in Elasticity, Viscoelasticity & Inelasticity: Festschrift Volume in Honor of Professor Tse-Chien Woo on the Occasion of His 70th Birthday. LC 94-23839. (Series on Advances in Mathematics for Applied Sciences). 248p. 1995. text ed. 99.00 (*981-02-2103-7*) World Scientific Pub.

Rajagopal, K. R., jt. ed. see Massoudi, M.

Rajagopal, L. V. Critique of Vedanta. (C). 1993. text ed. 27. 00 (*81-215-0592-5*, Pub. by Munshiram Manoharial II) S Asia.

Rajagopal, R., ed. Environmental Mediation & Conflict Management: A Selection of Papers Presented at the 5th Annual Conference of the NAEP, Washington Dc, April 21-23 1980. 120p. 1981. pap. 12.00 (*0-08-026261-9*, Pergamon Pr) Elsevier.

Rajagopala, Rao T. A Historical Sketch of Telugu Literature, Vol. 6. 162p. 1986. reprint ed. 15.00 (*0-8364-1693-7*, Pub. by Manohar II) S Asia.

Rajagopalachari, C. Mahabharata. 1979. pap. 6.95 (*0-89744-929-0*) Auromere.

— Ramakrishna Upanishad. 1953. pap. 1.95 (*0-87481-430-8*, Pub. by Ramakrishna Math II) Vedanta Pr.

— Ramayana. 1979. pap. 6.95 (*0-89744-930-4*) Auromere.

Rajagopalachari, Chakravarti, ed. see Valmiki.

Rajagopalachari, Chakravarti, ed. see Vyasa.

Rajagopalachari, M. The Novels of Bernard Malamud. 222p. 1988. text ed. 27.50 (*81-85218-02-1*, Pub. by Prestige II) Advent Bks Div.

— The Novels of Manohar Malgonkar. 104p. 1990. text ed. 18.95 (*81-85218-16-1*, Pub. by Prestige II) Advent Bks Div.

Rajagopalachari, Parthasarathi. Down Memory Lane. 384p. 1993. 15.00 (*0-945242-23-9*) Shri Ram Chandra.

— The Fruit of the Tree. 250p. 1987. pap. text ed. 10.00 (*0-945242-01-8*) Shri Ram Chandra.

— Heart of the Lion. 196p. 1993. 10.00 (*0-945242-24-7*) Shri Ram Chandra.

— Heart to Heart. 358p. 1989. pap. 12.00 (*0-945242-06-9*) Shri Ram Chandra.

— Heart to Heart, Vol. II. 344p. 1991. 15.00 (*0-945242-07-7*) Shri Ram Chandra.

— Heart to Heart Vol. III. 292p. 1994. 15.00 (*0-945242-25-5*) Shri Ram Chandra.

— In His Footsteps. 344p. 1988. pap. 15.00 (*0-945242-03-4*) Shri Ram Chandra.

— In His Footsteps, Vol. II. 416p. 1993. 15.00 (*0-945242-17-4*) Shri Ram Chandra.

— My Master. 184p. 1989. reprint ed. 10.00 (*0-945242-12-3*) Shri Ram Chandra.

— A Preceptor's Guide, 1989, Vol. II. 312p. 1990. 10.00 (*0-945242-14-X*) Shri Ram Chandra.

— A Preceptor's Guide, 1990, Vol. III. 216p. 1990. 10.00 (*0-945242-15-8*) Shri Ram Chandra.

— Religion & Spirituality. 152p. 1992. 10.00 (*0-945242-18-2*) Shri Ram Chandra.

— Role of the Master in Human Evolution. 182p. 1994. 10. 00 (*0-945242-29-8*) Shri Ram Chandra.

— What Is Sahaj Marg. rev. ed. 248p. 1994. 12.00 (*0-945242-26-3*) Shri Ram Chandra.

Rajagopalan. Computer-Aided Analysis of Power Electronic Systems. (Electrical Engineering & Electronics Ser.: Vol. 40). 552p. 1987. 165.00 (*0-8247-7706-9*) Dekker.

Rajagopalan, K. Finite Element Buckling Analysis of Stiffened Cylindrical Shells. (Illus.). 175p. 1993. text ed. 75.00 (*90-5410-232-2*, Pub. by A A Balkema NE) Ashgate Pub Co.

— Storage Structures. (Illus.). 397p. (C). 1990. text ed. 95.00 (*90-6191-947-9*, Pub. by A A Balkema NE) Ashgate Pub Co.

— Storage Structures. (C). 1989. 23.50 (*81-204-0443-2*, Pub. by Oxford IBH II) S Asia.

Rajagopalan, R., jt. ed. see Chen, S. H.

Rajagopalan, S. Guide to Simple Sanitary Measures for the Control of Enteric Diseases. 1974. 12.80 (*92-4-154047-8*) World Health.

Rajah, jt. auth. see Choong.

Rajah, K. K., jt. ed. see Moran, D. P.

***Rajak, Harry & Davis, Richard.** Insolvency: A Business by Business Guide. 352p. 1994. pap. text ed. 99.00 (*0-406-02231-3*, UK) Butterworth Legal Pubs.

Rajak, R. L., et al. Plant Parasitic Nematodes - A Check List 1981-1985. (International Bioscience Monographs: Vol. XVIII). (Illus.). 135p. 1987. 17.00 (*1-55528-143-5*, Messers Today & Tomorrow) Scholarly Pubns.

Rajala, Reuben, jt. auth. see Proudman, Robert D.

Rajam, R. V. & Rangiah, P. N. Donovanosis. (Monograph Ser.: No. 24). 1954. 2.80 (*92-4-140024-2*) World Health.

Rajam, V. S. A Reference Grammar of Classical Tamil Poetry. LC 91-76989. (Memoirs Ser.: Vol. 199). 672p. (C). 1992. 45.00 (*0-87169-199-X*, M199-RAV) Am Philos.

Rajamanickam, C. & Packer, Lester, eds. Biomembranes: Structure, Biogenesis & Transport Proceedings of Biomembrane Symposium. (Current Trends in Life Sciences Ser.: Vol. XIII). (Illus.). 358p. 1987. 95.00 (*1-55528-142-7*, Messers Today & Tomorrow) Scholarly Pubns.

Rajamanickam, C., et al, eds. Biological Macro Molecules: Structure & Function: Proceedings of Indo-Soviet Binational Symposium, Madurai. 250p. 1985. 79.00 (*0-685-59946-9*, Messers Today & Tomorrow) Scholarly Pubns.

Rajan, A. & Fryatt, J., eds. Create or Abdicate: City's Human Resource Choice for the 1990's. (C). 1988. 250. 00 (*0-685-32837-6*, Pub. by Witherby & Co UK) St Mut.

Rajan, Amin. Job Subsidies: Do They Work? 80p. 1985. text ed. 49.95 (*0-566-05053-6*) Ashgate Pub Co.

Rajan, Amin & Fryatt, Julie, eds. Create or Abdicate: The City's Human Resource Choice for the 90's. 240p. 1988. 250.00 (*0-948691-66-2*, Pub. by Witherby & Co UK) St Mut.

Rajan, B. T. S. Eliot: A Study of His Writings by Several Hands. LC 65-15865. (Studies in T. S. Eliot: No. 11). 1969. reprint ed. lib. bdg. 75.00 (*0-8383-0545-8*) M S G Haskell Hse.

Rajan, Balachandra. The Form of the Unfinished: English Poetics from Spenser to Pound. LC 84-6637. 230p. 1985. text ed. 47.50 (*0-691-06637-X*) Princeton U Pr.

R

An Asterisk (*) at the beginning of an entry indicates that the title is appearing in BIP for the first time.

— The Overwhelming Question: A Study of the Poetry of T. S. Eliot. LC 75-32519. 161p. reprint ed. pap. 45.90 (*0-317-55724-6*, 2029346) Bks Demand.

— Too Long in the West. 1961. pap. 2.00 (*0-88253-175-1*) Ind-US Inc.

Rajan, Balachandra, ed. Paradise Lost: A Tercenenary Tribute. LC 77-429833. 154p. reprint ed. pap. 43.90 (*0-317-27001-X*, 2023659) Bks Demand.

Rajan, Chandra, tr. see Sarma, Visnu.

***Rajan, Gayatri.** The Story of Santoshi Devi. (Illus.). 40p. (Orig.). (J). (gr. k-6). Date not set. pap. write for info. (*0-9644226-0-3*) Buddhi Pubns.

***Rajan, Gita & Mohanram, Radhika, eds.** Postcolonial Discourse & Changing Cultural Contexts Theory & Criticism. LC 95-16019. (Contributions to the Study of World Literature: Vol. 64). 1995. text ed. write for info. (*0-313-29693-6*, Greenwood Pr) Greenwood.

Rajan, Janaki, jt. ed. see Arslan, Mehdi.

Rajan, K., et al, eds. Dislocations & Interfaces in Semiconductors. LC 88-61505. (Illus.). 210p. 1988. 10. 00 (*0-87339-046-6*, 325) Minerals Metals.

Rajan, K. N. Advanced Medical Radiation Dosimetry. 522p. 1992. pap. 20.00 (*0-87692-706-1*) Med Physics Pub.

Rajan, K. T., jt. ed. see Richards, R. J.

Rajan, K. U. Mechanics of City & Village in Ancient India. (C). 1986. 42.50 (*81-85055-96-3*, Pub. by Sundeep II) S Asia.

Rajan, K. V. Art of South India: Tamilnadu & Kerala. (C). 1988. 32.50 (*0-8364-2465-4*, Pub. by Sundeep II) S Asia.

— Indian Temple Styles: The Personality of Hindu Architecture. 1972. reprint ed. 38.50 (*0-8364-2604-5*, Pub. by Munshiram Manoharial II) S Asia.

— Secularism in Indian Art. (C). 1988. 48.50 (*81-7017-245-4*, Pub. by Abhinav II) S Asia.

Rajan, Krishna, ed. see Metallurgical Society Staff.

Rajan, M. A. Land Reforms in Karnataka. 178p. 1986. 17.50 (*0-8364-1938-3*, Pub. by Hindustan IA) S Asia.

Rajan, M. S. The Future of Nonalignment & the Nonaligned Movement: Some Reflective Essays. 136p. 1990. text ed. 18.95 (*81-220-0189-0*, Pub. by Konark Pubs Pvt Ltd II) Advent Bks Div.

— India & the Commonwealth: Some Studies. 192p. 1990. text ed. 27.50 (*81-220-0187-4*, Pub. by Konark Pubs Pvt Ltd II) Advent Bks Div.

Rajan, M. S., jt. auth. see Appadorai, A.

Rajan, M. S., et al, eds. The Nonaligned & the United Nations. 388p. 1987. 22.50 (*81-7003-073-0*, Pub. by S Asia Pubs II) S Asia.

Rajan, Mohan S. Atoms of Hope. 155p. 1980. 15.95 (*0-940500-39-6*, Pub. by Allied Pubs II) Asia Bk Corp.

Rajan, P. K. The Growth of the Novel in India. (C). 1989. 22.00 (*81-7017-259-4*, Pub. by Abhinav II) S Asia.

— Studies in Mulk Raj Anand. viii, 122p. 1986. 11.00 (*81-7017-207-1*, Pub. by Abhinav II) S Asia.

Rajan, R. Sundara. The Primacy of the Political. 224p. 1992. 12.95 (*0-19-562729-6*) OUP.

Rajan, R. Sundara, ed. see Krishna, Daya.

Rajan, Rajeswari S. Real & Imagined Women: Gender, Culture, & Postcolonialism. LC 93-6923. (Illus.). 176p. 1994. 59.95 (*0-415-08503-9*, B2277); pap. 16.95 (*0-415-08504-7*, B2281) Routledge.

Rajan, Rajeswari S., ed. The Lie of the Land: English Literary Studies in India. 320p. 1992. 11.95 (*0-19-562829-2*) OUP.

— The Lie of the Land: English Literary Studies in India. 326p. 1994. reprint ed. pap. 7.95 (*0-19-563361-X*) OUP.

***Rajan, S. Irudaya.** Catholics in Bombay: A Historical Demographic Study of the Roman Catholic Population in the Archdiocese of Bombay. (C). 1993. 44.00x (*81-85408-08-4*, Pub. by Firma KLM) S Asia.

Rajan, Tilottama. Dark Interpreter: The Discourse of Romanticism. 288p. 1980. pap. 13.95 (*0-8014-9369-2*) Cornell U Pr.

— Myth in a Metal Mirror. (Writers Workshop Redbird Ser.). 1975. 8.00 (*0-88253-580-3*); pap. text ed. 4.80 (*0-88253-579-X*) Ind-US Inc.

— The Supplement of Reading: Figures of Understanding in Romantic Theory & Practice. LC 90-55122. 368p. 1990. 46.95 (*0-8014-2045-8*); pap. 15.95 (*0-8014-9749-3*) Cornell U Pr.

Rajan, Tilottama & Clark, David L., eds. Intersections: Nineteenth-Century Philosophy & Contemporary Theory. LC 94-15204. (SUNY Series, The Margins of Literature). 386p. (C). 1995. 64.50 (*0-7914-2257-7*); pap. 21.95 (*0-7914-2258-5*) State U NY Pr.

Rajan, V. N. Victimology in India. 136p. 1981. 16.95 (*0-940500-86-8*, Pub. by Allied Pubs II) Asia Bk Corp.

Rajan, Vithal. Rebuilding Communities. (Illus.). 288p. (Orig.). 1993. pap. 14.95 (*1-870098-50-1*, Pub. by Green Bks UK) Seven Hills Bk.

Rajanayagam, M. J. The Law of Negotiable Instruments in Australia. 2nd ed. Conrick, Brian, ed. 280p. (C). 1989. Australia. 76.00 (*0-409-49527-1*); Australia. pap. 56.00 (*0-409-49528-X*) Butterworth Legal Pubs.

Rajanen. Of Finnish Ways. 1992. pap. 10.00 (*0-06-092382-2*) HarpC.

Rajani, Shasbi & Gregory, Keith. Tolley's Corporate Insolvency Handbook. 2nd ed. 500p. 1993. 200.00 (*0-85459-748-4*, Pub. by Tolley Pubng UK) St Mut.

Rajaonarimanana, Narivelo. Dictionnaire Francais-Malgache. 192p. (FRE.). 1993. pap. 39.95 (*0-7859-5666-2*, 2901795544) Fr & Eur.

Rajapakse, Y., jt. ed. see Achenbach, J. D.

Rajapakse, Y. D., ed. Mechanics of Thick Composites. LC 93-71576. (AMD Ser.: Vol. 162). 267p. 1993. pap. 55.00 (*0-7918-1141-7*, G00785) ASME.

Rajapurohit, A. R., ed. Land Reforms in India. 1985. 20.00 (*0-8364-1295-8*, Pub. by Ashish II) S Asia.

Rajaram, Anand. Reforming Prices: The Experience of China, Hungary, & Poland. (Discussion Paper Ser.: No. 144). 46p. 1992. 6.95 (*0-8213-1991-4*, 11991) World Bank.

Rajaraman, Dharma. Computer: A Child's Play. 120p. (J). 1989. reprint ed. pap. text ed. 12.95 (*0-9615336-9-2*) Silicon Pr.

Rajaraman, R. Solitons & Instantons: An Introduction to Solitons & Instantons in Quantum Field Theory. 412p. 1982. 105.25 (*0-444-86229-3*, North Holland) Elsevier.

— Solitons & Instantons: An Introduction to Solitons & Instantons in Quantum Field Theory. (North-Holland Personal Library). 410p. 1987. pap. 35.00 (*0-444-87047-4*, North Holland) Elsevier.

Rajaraman, V., ed. CAD CAM CAE for Industrial Progress: Proceedings of the IFIP TC 5 International Fonference, Bangalore, India, 29-30 June 1985. 298p. 1986. 72.00 (*0-444-70000-5*) Elsevier.

Rajaratnam, N. Turbulent Jets. (Developments in Water Science Ser.: Vol. 5). 304p. 1976. 107.75 (*0-444-41372-3*) Elsevier.

Rajaratnam, T. W. A Judiciary in Crisis? The Trial of Zulfikar Ali Bhutto. (C). 1988. 65.00 (*0-685-36504-2*) St Mut.

Rajaretnam, M., ed. The Aquino Alternative. 158p. 1986. pap. text ed. 17.25 (*9971-988-46-1*, Pub. by Inst SE Asian Studies SI) Ashgate Pub Co.

Rajasekaran, B. A Framework for Incorporating Indigenous Knowledge Systems into Agricultural Research, Extension, & NGOs for Sustainable Agricultural Development. (Studies in Technology & Social Change: No. 22). 52p. (Orig.). (C). 1994. pap. 7.00 (*0-945271-32-8*) ISU-TSCP.

Rajasekhar, D. Land Transfers & Family Partitioning. (C). 1988. 11.50 (*81-204-0305-3*, Pub. by Oxford IBH II) S Asia.

Rajasekhara, S. Masterpieces of Vijayanarara Art. (Illus.). 100p. 1983. text ed. 40.00 (*0-86590-115-5*) Apt Bks.

Rajasekharaiah, T. R. The Roots of Whitman's Grass. LC 76-85762. 522p. 1975. 50.00 (*0-8386-7493-3*) Fairleigh Dickinson.

Rajashekarappa, K. G. Engineering Mechanics: Applied Mechanics. Bhavikatti, S. S., ed. LC 92-36073. 537p. 1994. text ed. 39.95 (*0-470-22054-6*) Halsted Pr.

Rajasingham, Lalita, jt. auth. see Tiffin, John.

Rajat, Sanyal. Voluntary Associations & the Urban Public Life in Bengal. 1983. 16.50 (*0-8364-0980-9*, Pub. by Rddhi IA) S Asia.

Rajbahak, R. P. Nepal-India Open Border: A Bond of Shaved Aspirations. (C). 1992. 48.00 (*0-7855-0199-1*, Pub. by Ratna Pustak Bhandar) St Mut.

Rajbman, N. S., ed. Identification & System Parameter Estimation: Proceedings of the IFAC Symposium, 4th, Tbilisi, U. S. S. R., September 1976, 3 vols., Set. 2178p. 1978. 274.00 (*0-444-85096-1*, North Holland) Elsevier.

Rajbman, N. S. & Chadeev, V. M. Identification of Industrial Processes: The Application of Computers in Research & Production Control. 436p. 1980. 97.50 (*0-444-85181-X*, North Holland) Elsevier.

Rajchman, John. Identity in Question. 1994. pap. 15.95 (*0-415-90618-0*, Pub. by Tavistock UK) Routledge Chapman & Hall.

— Philosophical Events: Essays of the Eighties. 192p. 1990. text ed. 33.50 (*0-231-07210-4*) Col U Pr.

— Truth & Eros: Foucault, Lacan & the Question of Ethics. 192p. 1991. 42.50 (*0-415-90379-3*, A2331, Routledge NY); pap. 13.95 (*0-415-90380-7*, A2335, Routledge NY) Routledge.

***Rajchman, John, ed. & intro.** The Identity in Question. LC 94-24832. 1995. 49.50 (*0-415-90617-2*) Routledge.

Rajchman, John & West, Cornel, eds. Post-Analytic Philosophy. LC 85-377. 304p. 1985. text ed. 52.50 (*0-231-06066-1*); pap. text ed. 18.00 (*0-231-06067-X*) Col U Pr.

Rajcsanyi, Elisabeth, jt. auth. see Rajcsanyi, Peter M.

Rajcsanyi, Peter M. & Rajcsanyi, Elisabeth. High-Speed Liquid Chromatography. LC 75-29922. (Chromatographic Science Ser.: No. 6). 211p. reprint ed. pap. 60.20 (*0-7837-3894-3*, 2043742) Bks Demand.

Rajecki, D. W. Attitudes. 2nd rev. ed. LC 89-38465. (Illus.). 522p. (C). 1990. pap. text ed. 27.95 (*0-87893-787-0*) Sinauer Assocs.

— Comparing Behavior: Studying Man Studying Animals. 304p. (C). 1983. 69.95 (*0-89859-259-3*) L Erlbaum Assocs.

Rajeev, S., jt. auth. see Krishnamoorthy, C. S.

Rajeeva, R., ed. An Introduction to the Tribal Development in India. 150p. 1989. 65.00 (*81-7089-109-4*, Pub. by Intl Bk Distr II) St Mut.

Rajendra, Cecil. Dove on Fire: Poems on Peace, Justice & Ecology. (Risk Book Ser.: No. 33). (Illus.). 92p. (Orig.). 1987. pap. 5.75 (*2-8254-0899-9*) Wrld Coun Churches.

Rajendra, Vijeya. Australia. LC 91-15864. (Cultures of the World Ser.: Group 3). (Illus.). 128p. (J). (gr. 5-9). 1991. lib. bdg. 21.95 (*1-85435-400-0*) Marshall Cavendish.

Rajendra, Vijeya & Kaplan, Gisela. Iran. LC 92-10207. (Cultures of the World Ser.). (J). 1992. 21.95 (*1-85435-534-1*) Marshall Cavendish.

Rajeshwar, M. The Novels of Wole Soyinka. 96p. 1990. text ed. 17.95 (*81-85218-21-8*, Pub. by Prestige II) Advent Bks Div.

Rajeshwari, D. R. Sakti Iconography. (C). 1988. 65.00 (*81-7076-015-1*, Pub. by Intellectual II) S Asia.

***Rajewski, Brian, ed.** Countries of the World Yearbook, 1995. suppl. ed. 450p. 1995. 85.00 (*0-8103-6843-9*) Gale.

Rajfer. Common Problems in Infertility & Impotence. 416p. 1989. 69.00 (*0-8151-6991-4*, Yr Bk Med Pubs) Mosby Yr Bk.

Rajfer, Jacob. Urologic Endocrinology. (Illus.). 448p. 1986. text ed. 98.95 (*0-7216-7426-7*) Saunders.

Rajgopal, P. R. Communal Violence in India. 141p. 1987. 34.95 (*0-318-37208-8*) Asia Bk Corp.

— Communal Violence in India. (C). 1987. 24.00 (*81-85024-14-6*, Pub. by Uppal Pub Hse II) S Asia.

— Social Change & Violence: The Indian Experience. 227p. (C). 1987. 35.00 (*81-85024-27-8*, Pub. by Uppal Pub Hse II) S Asia.

Rajhans, G. S., jt. auth. see Blackwell, David S.

Rajiv, Sudhi. Forms of Black Consciousness. 189p. 1992. text ed. 25.00 (*0-89891-062-5*) Advent Bks Div.

Rajiva, Stanley E. The Permanent Element. 8.00 (*0-89253-720-5*); 4.80 (*0-89253-721-3*) Ind-US Inc.

Rajka, G. Essential Aspects of Atopic Dermatitis. (Illus.). xvi, 261p. 1989. 133.00 (*0-387-51165-2*) Spr-Verlag.

Rajki, Sandor. Proceedings of a Workshop on Agricultural Potentiality Directed by Nutritional Needs June 5th-9th, 1978 Martonvaoar. 238p. 1979. 93.00 (*0-569-08563-2*, Pub. by Collets UK) Pro-Am Music.

Rajkumar, Ragunathan, ed. Synchronization in Real-Time Systems: A Priority Inheritance Approach. 208p. (C). 1991. lib. bdg. 65.50 (*0-7923-9211-6*) Kluwer Ac.

Rajkumar, S. & Toback, C. Principles & Practice of Ambulatory Pediatrics. 824p. 1988. 150.00 (*0-306-42500-9*, Plenum Med Bk) Plenum.

Rajkumar, Tajpertab. Cross-Cultural Reader. 2nd ed. 240p. 1993. per. 25.95 (*0-8403-8969-8*) Kendall-Hunt.

***Rajnavolgyi.** Synthetic Peptides in the Search for T & B Cell Epitopes. (Molecular Biology Intelligence Unit Ser.). 200p. 1994. 89.95 (*1-57059-160-1*) R G Landes.

Rajneesh Academy Staff, ed. see Rajneesh, Osho.

Rajneesh Foundation International, ed. see Rajneesh, Osho.

Rajneesh Foundation International Staff, ed. see Rajneesh, Osho.

Rajneesh, Osho. After Middle Age: A Limitless Sky. Amoore, Mary, ed. (Introduction to the Teachings of Osho Ser.). 96p. 1992. 6.95 (*0-918963-02-8*) Osho Chidvilas.

— Ah This! Rajneesh Foundation International Staff, ed. LC 82-24026. (Zen Ser.). 268p. (Orig.). 1982. pap. 8.95 (*0-88050-502-8*) Osho Chidvilas.

— And Now, & Here, Vol. 1. Mahasattva, Swami Satya, ed. LC 84-42798. (Early Discourses & Writings Ser.). 320p. (Orig.). 1984. pap. 4.95 (*0-88050-709-8*) Osho Chidvilas.

— And Now, & Here, Vol. II. Vedant, Swami S., ed. LC 84-42798. (Early Writings & Discourses Ser.). 384p. (Orig.). 1985. pap. 4.95 (*0-88050-712-8*) Osho Chidvilas.

— Bodhidharma, the Greatest Zen Master. Gitika, Ma D. & Sarito, Ma D., eds. (Zen Ser.). (Illus.). 780p. 1988. 21.95 (*3-89338-025-6*, Pub. by Rebel Hse GW) Osho Chidvilas.

— The Book of the Books, Vol. 1. Rajneesh Foundation International, ed. LC 82-50462. (Buddha Ser.). 360p. (Orig.). 1982. pap. 9.95 (*0-88050-513-3*) Osho Chidvilas.

— Book of the Books, Vol. 2. Asha, Ma P., ed. LC 82-50462. (Buddha Ser.). 352p. (Orig.). 1983. pap. 4.95 (*0-88050-514-1*) Osho Chidvilas.

— The Book of the Books, Vol. 3. Ma P. Karima, ed. LC 82-50462. (Buddha Ser.). 352p. (Orig.). 1984. pap. 4.95 (*0-88050-515-X*) Osho Chidvilas.

— The Book of the Books, Vol. 4. Krishna, Swami P., ed. LC 82-50462. (Buddha Ser.). 384p. (Orig.). 1985. pap. 4.95 (*0-88050-516-8*) Osho Chidvilas.

— The Book of the Secrets, Vol. IV. 2nd ed. Rajneesh Foundation International Staff, ed. LC 75-36733. (Tantra Ser.). 408p. 1982. pap. 7.95 (*0-88050-528-1*) Osho Chidvilas.

— The Book of Wisdom, Vol. 2. Swami Krishna Prabhu, ed. LC 82-23142. (Atisha Ser.). 416p. (Orig.). 1984. pap. 5.95 (*0-88050-531-1*) Osho Chidvilas.

— The Buddha: The Emptiness of the Heart. Sarito, Deva & Ashik, Deva, eds. (Zen Ser.). 288p. 1989. 12.95 (*3-89338-055-8*, Pub. by Rebel Hse GW) Osho Chidvilas.

— Come, Come, Yet Again Come. Sagar, Ma D., ed. (Questions & Answers Ser.). 301p. 1991. 21.95 (*3-89338-108-2*, Pub. by Rebel Hse GW) Osho Chidvilas.

— A Cup of Tea. 2nd ed. Somendra, Swami Anand, ed. LC 83-43215. (Early Discourses & Writings Ser.). 272p. 1983. pap. 4.95 (*0-88050-538-9*) Osho Chidvilas.

— Don't Let Yourself Be Upset by the Sutra: Rather Upset the Sutra Yourself. Prabhu, Swami Krishna, ed. LC 85-43054. (Initiation Talks Ser.). 560p. (Orig.). 1985. pap. 5.95 (*0-88050-584-2*) Osho Chidvilas.

— Don't Look Before You Leap. Rajneesh Foundation International Staff, ed. LC 83-3282. (Initiation Talks Ser.). 480p. (Orig.). 1983. pap. 4.95 (*0-88050-554-0*) Osho Chidvilas.

— From Darkness to Light. Devaraj, Sambuddha S. & Maneesha, Sambodhi M., eds. (Talks in America Ser.). 408p. 1988. 24.95 (*3-89338-020-5*, Pub. by Rebel Hse GW) Osho Chidvilas.

— From Sex to Superconsciousness. 2nd ed. Prem, Krishna & Burt, Anand, eds. 180p. (Orig.). 1989. 12.95 (*3-89338-062-0*, Pub. by Rebel Hse GW) Osho Chidvilas.

— Glimpses of a Golden Childhood. Sambuddha, Swami Devaraj & Mahasattva, Swami Devageet, eds. LC 85-43069. (Autobiography Ser.). 788p. (Orig.). 1985. pap. 9.95 (*0-88050-715-2*) Osho Chidvilas.

— The Goose Is Out. Rajneesh Foundation International Staff, ed. LC 82-60497. (Questions & Answers Ser.). 324p. (Orig.). 1982. pap. 10.95 (*0-88050-571-0*) Osho Chidvilas.

— The Great Pilgrimage: From Here to Here. Prabhu, Krishna & Taranga, Ma P., eds. (Question & Answer Ser.). 356p. 1988. 21.95 (*3-89338-016-7*, Pub. by Rebel Hse GW) Osho Chidvilas.

— Great Secret: Talks on the Songs of Kabir. Prem, Krishna, ed. (Kabir Ser.). 384p. 1992. 17.95 (*3-89338-087-6*, Pub. by Rebel Hse GW) Osho Chidvilas.

— The Great Zen Master Ta Hui. Prabhu, Krishna et al, eds. (Zen Ser.). 544p. 1988. 24.95 (*3-89338-027-2*, Pub. by Rebel Hse GW) Osho Chidvilas.

— Guest. Sudha, Ma Yoga, ed. LC 82-203740. (Kabir Ser.). (Illus.). 604p. (Orig.). 1981. pap. 14.95 (*0-88050-574-5*) Osho Chidvilas.

— Guida Spirituale. Rajneesh Foundation International Staff, ed. LC 83-4435. (Western Mystics Ser.). 400p. (Orig.). 1983. pap. 4.95 (*0-88050-575-3*) Osho Chidvilas.

— Hari Om Tat Sat: The Divine Sound That Is the Truth. Suvarna, Shivam, ed. (Mantra Ser.). (Illus.). 328p. 1989. 21.95 (*3-89338-046-9*, Pub. by Rebel Hse GW) Osho Chidvilas.

— I Teach Religiousness, Not Religion. Amoore, Mary, ed. (Introduction to the Teachings of Osho Ser.). 126p. 1992. 6.95 (*0-918963-01-X*) Osho Chidvilas.

— In Search of the Miraculous, Vol. 1. Sambuddha, Swami Anand, ed. LC 84-42869. (Early Discourses & Writings Ser.). 368p. (Orig.). 1984. pap. 4.95 (*0-88050-710-1*) Osho Chidvilas.

— The Invitation. Sagar, Ma D. & Robin, Anand, eds. (Mystery School Ser.). 384p. 1988. 21.95 (*3-89338-035-3*, Pub. by Rebel Hse GW) Osho Chidvilas.

— Jesus Crucified Again, This Time in Ronald Regan's America. Sarito, Ma D., ed. (Compilation Ser.). 320p. 1988. 18.95 (*3-89338-039-6*, Pub. by Rebel Hse GW) Osho Chidvilas.

— Just Around the Corner. Mahasattva, Swami Krishna, ed. LC 84-42870. (Initiation Talks Ser.). 224p. (Orig.). 1984. pap. 3.95 (*0-88050-588-5*) Osho Chidvilas.

— Krishna: The Man & His Philosophy. Sambuddha, Swami Anand, ed. LC 85-43055. (Early Writings & Discourses Ser.). 880p. 1985. pap. 5.95 (*0-88050-713-6*) Osho Chidvilas.

— The Language of Existence. Suvarna, Shivan, ed. (Zen Ser.). (Illus.). 288p. 1989. 12.95 (*3-89338-054-X*, Pub. by Rebel Hse GW) Osho Chidvilas.

— The Last Testament, Vol. I. Svadesh, Swami et al, eds. LC 85-63289. (Interview Ser.). (Illus.). 832p. (Orig.). (C). 1986. pap. 9.95 (*0-88050-250-9*) Osho Chidvilas.

— Light on the Path. (Talks in the Himalayas Ser.). 416p. 1988. 24.95 (*3-89338-030-2*, Pub. by Rebel Hse GW) Osho Chidvilas.

— Live Zen: A New Therapy Is Born, Therapy Through Gibberish. Sagar, Ma D., ed. (Zen Ser.). (Illus.). 320p. 1988. 12.95 (*3-89338-032-9*, Pub. by Rebel Hse GW) Osho Chidvilas.

— The Long & the Short & the All. Prabhu, Swami Krishna, ed. LC 84-42806. (Early Writings & Discourses Ser.). 320p. 1984. pap. 4.95 (*0-88050-708-X*) Osho Chidvilas.

— The Messiah: Commentaries on Kahlil Gibran's the Prophet, Vol. 1. Sarito, Dhyan, ed. (Mystery School Ser.). 520p. (Orig.). 1987. 27.95 (*3-89338-002-7*, Pub. by Rebel Hse GW); pap. 14.95 (*3-89338-009-4*, Pub. by Rebel Hse GW) Osho Chidvilas.

— The Messiah: Commentaries on Kahlil Gibran's the Prophet, Vol. 2. Melissa, Ma P. & Taranga, Ma P., eds. (Mystery School Ser.). 519p. (Orig.). 1987. 27.95 (*3-89338-003-5*, Pub. by Rebel Hse GW); pap. 14.95 (*3-89338-010-8*, Pub. by Rebel Hse GW) Osho Chidvilas.

— The Miracle. (Zen Ser.). 288p. 1989. 12.95 (*3-89338-053-1*, Pub. by Rebel Hse GW) Osho Chidvilas.

— More Gold Nuggets. (Compilation Ser.). (Illus.). 192p. 1989. 12.95 (*3-89338-076-0*, Pub. by Rebel Hse GW) Osho Chidvilas.

— The New Dawn. (Mystery School Ser.). 432p. 1989. 21. 95 (*3-89338-023-X*, Pub. by Rebel Hse GW) Osho Chidvilas.

— The New Man: The Only Hope for the Future. 112p. (Orig.). 1987. pap. 6.95 (*3-89338-005-1*, Pub. by Rebel Hse GW) Osho Chidvilas.

— No Mind the Flowers of Eternity. Sarito, Deva & Robin, Anand, eds. (Zen Ser.). (Illus.). 276p. 1992. 28.95 (*3-89338-060-4*, Pub. by Rebel Hse GW) Osho Chidvilas.

— Om Mani Padme Hum: The Sound of Silence: The Diamond in the Lotus. Sarito, Deva, ed. & intro. by. (Mantra Ser.). 242p. 1990. 21.95 (*3-89338-050-7*, Pub. by Rebel Hse GW) Osho Chidvilas.

— Om Shantih Shantih Shantih: The Soundless Sound Peace, Peace, Peace. Sagar, Dhyan & Nirvesha, Deva, eds. (Mantra Ser.). (Illus.). 290p. 1990. 19.95 (*3-89338-048-5*, Pub. by Rebel Hse GW) Osho Chidvilas.

— On Basic Human Rights. Ma Deva Sarito, ed. (Introduction to the Teachings of Osho Ser.). 70p. (Orig.). 1987. pap. 5.95 (*3-907757-03-3*) Osho Chidvilas.

— The Original Man. (Zen Ser.). 288p. 1989. 12.95 (*3-89338-056-6*, Pub. by Rebel Hse GW) Osho Chidvilas.

— Osho Neo Tarot. (Illus.). 85p. 1986. pap. 19.95 (*3-89338-129-5*, Pub. by Rebel Hse GW) Osho Chidvilas.

— The Path of the Mystic. Shanti, Ma A. & Kaveesha, Ma P., eds. (Talks in Uruguay Ser.). 480p. 1988. 24.95 (*3-89338-040-X*, Pub. by Rebel Hse GW) Osho Chidvilas.

— Philosophia Perennis, Vol. 1. Anurag, Ma Yoga, ed. (Western Mystics Ser.). (Illus.). 392p. (Orig.). 1981. pap. 14.95 (*0-88050-115-4*) Osho Chidvilas.

— Philosophia Perennis, Vol. 2. Anurag, Ma Yoga, ed. (Western Mystics Ser.). (Illus.). 436p. (Orig.). 1981. pap. 14.95 (*0-88050-616-4*) Osho Chidvilas.

— Priests & Politicians: The Mafia of the Soul. 112p. (Orig.). 1988. pap. text ed. 6.95 (*3-89338-000-0*, Pub. by Rebel Hse GW) Osho Chidvilas.

R

An Asterisk (*) at the beginning of an entry indicates that the title is appearing in BIP for the first time.

— The Rainbow Bridge. Prabhu, Krishna, ed. LC 85-42535. (Initiation Talks Ser.). 368p. (Orig.). (C). 1985. pap. 4.95 (*0-88050-618-0*) Osho Chidvilas.

— The Rajneesh Bible, Vol. II. Rajneesh Academy Staff, ed. LC 85-42539. (Talks in America Ser.). 839p. (Orig.). 1985. pap. 9.95 (*0-88050-201-0*) Osho Chidvilas.

— The Rajneesh Bible, Vol. III. Rajneesh Academy Staff, ed. LC 85-42539. (Talks in America Ser.). 1072p. (Orig.). 1985. pap. 9.95 (*0-88050-202-9*) Osho Chidvilas.

— The Rebellious Spirit. Pankaja, Ma P. et al, eds. LC 87-42814. (Mystery School Ser.). 325p. (Orig.). 1987. pap. 14.95 (*3-907757-16-5*) Osho Chidvilas.

— Sat Chit Anand: Truth-Consciousness-Bliss. (Mantra Ser.). 416p. 1989. 21.95 (*3-89338-042-6*, Pub. by Rebel Hse GW) Osho Chidvilas.

— Satyam Shivam Sundram: Truth-Godliness-Beauty. Prabhu, Krishna & Shabda, Ma V., eds. (Mantra Ser.). (Illus.). 368p. 1989. 21.95 (*3-89338-031-0*, Pub. by Rebel Hse GW) Osho Chidvilas.

— Sermons in Stones. Sarito, Ma D., ed. LC 87-42569. (Mystery School Ser.). 900p. (Orig.). 1987. pap. 9.95 (*3-907757-04-1*) Osho Chidvilas.

— The Shadow of the Bamboo. Maneesha, Ma Prem, ed. LC 84-42807. (Initiation Talks Ser.). 240p. (Orig.). 1984. pap. 3.95 (*0-88050-630-X*) Osho Chidvilas.

— Snap Your Fingers, Slap Your Face & Wake Up! Sarito, Ma Deva, ed. LC 84-43011. (Initiation Talks Ser.). 256p. (Orig.). 1984. pap. 3.95 (*0-88050-632-6*) Osho Chidvilas.

— Socrates Poisoned Again after 25 Centuries. Lisa, M. P. & Sarar, M. D., eds. (Talks in Greece Ser.). 433p. 1988. 24.95 (*3-89338-018-3*, Pub. by Rebel Hse GW) Osho Chidvilas.

— Tao: The Golden Gate, Vol. 1. Asha, Ma Prem, ed. LC 84-42615. (Tao Ser.). 336p. (Orig.). 1984. pap. 4.95 (*0-88050-646-6*) Osho Chidvilas.

— Tao: The Golden Gate, Vol. 2. Prabhu, Swami Krishna, ed. LC 84-42615. (Tao Ser.). 304p. (Orig.). 1985. pap. 4.95 (*0-88050-647-4*) Osho Chidvilas.

— Tao: The Three Treasures, Vol. I. 2nd ed. Veena, Ma Prem, ed. LC 83-10910. (Tao Ser.). 336p. (Orig.). 1983. reprint ed. pap. 4.95 (*0-88050-650-4*) Osho Chidvilas.

— That Art Thou. Sagar, Ma D., ed. (Early Talks Ser.). (Illus.). (Orig.). 1987. pap. 17.95 (*3-89338-011-6*, Pub. by Rebel Hse GW) Osho Chidvilas.

— Theologia Mystica. Asha, Ma Prem, ed. LC 83-11086. (Western Mystics Ser.). 400p. (Orig.). 1983. pap. 4.95 (*0-88050-655-5*) Osho Chidvilas.

— This, This, a Thousand Times This: The Very Essence of Zen. Govind, Mahasattva S., ed. (Zen Ser.). (Illus.). 288p. 1988. 12.95 (*3-89338-013-2*, Pub. by Rebel Hse GW) Osho Chidvilas.

— The Transmission of the Lamp. Ashik, Deva, ed. (Talks in Uruguay Ser.). 464p. 1989. 24.95 (*3-89338-049-3*, Pub. by Rebel Hse GW) Osho Chidvilas.

— Turning in. Sudha, Yoga & Shabda, Veet, eds. (Zen Ser.). (Illus.). 288p. 1989. 12.95 (*3-89338-059-0*, Pub. by Rebel Hse GW) Osho Chidvilas.

— Walking in Zen, Sitting in Zen. Rajneesh Foundation International Staff, ed. LC 82-24025. (Responses to Questions Ser.). 444p. (Orig.). 1982. pap. 10.95 (*0-88050-668-7*) Osho Chidvilas.

— The Wild Geese & the Water. Prabhu, Swami Krishna, ed. LC 85-43053. (Responses to Questions Ser.). 416p. (Orig.). 1985. pap. 4.95 (*0-88050-673-3*) Osho Chidvilas.

— Words from a Man of No Words. Avirbhava, Ma S., ed. (Compilation Ser.). (Illus.). 132p. 1989. 9.95 (*3-89338-024-8*, Pub. by Rebel Hse GW) Osho Chidvilas.

— Yoga Science of the Soul, Vol. 2. 1984. pap. 4.95 (*0-88050-678-4*) Osho Chidvilas.

— Yoga Science of the Soul, Vol. 3. 1984. pap. 4.95 (*0-88050-679-2*) Osho Chidvilas.

— You Ain't Seen Nothing Yet. Maneesha, Ma Prem, ed. LC 84-42614. (Initiation Talks Ser.). 304p. (Orig.). 1984. pap. 4.95 (*0-88050-687-3*) Osho Chidvilas.

— Zen: The Diamond Thunderbolt. (Zen Ser.). (Illus.). 288p. 1988. 12.95 (*3-89338-043-4*, Pub. by Rebel Hse GW) Osho Chidvilas.

— Zen: The Quantum Leap from Mind to No-Mind. Robin, Anand, ed. (Zen Ser.). (Illus.). 288p. 1988. 12.95 (*3-89338-045-0*, Pub. by Rebel Hse GW) Osho Chidvilas.

— Zen: The Solitary Bird, Cuckoo of the Forest. Sarito, Ma D., ed. (Zen Ser.). (Illus.). 288p. 1988. 12.95 (*3-89338-044-2*, Pub. by Rebel Hse GW) Osho Chidvilas.

Rajneesh, Osho B. Revolution, Rebellion & Religiousness. LC 89-82415. 200p. (Orig.). 1990. pap. 12.95 (*0-941404-63-3*) New Falcon Pubns.

Rajoppi, Joanne. Women in Office: Getting There & Staying There. LC 93-18135. 200p. 1993. text ed. 45.00 (*0-89789-343-3*, H343, Bergin & Garvey) Greenwood.

Rajotte, Pierre. Belgian Ale. (Classic Beer Style Ser.). (Illus.). 176p. 1992. pap. 11.95 (*0-937381-31-4*) Brewers Pubns.

***Rajput, Pam & Swarup, Hem L., eds.** Women & Globalisation: Reflections, Options & Strategies. xxxiv, 393p. (C). 1994. 49.00 (*81-7024-669-5*, Pub. by Ashish Pub Hse II) Nataraj Bks.

***Rajs, Jake.** The Hudson River: From Tear of the Clouds to Manhattan. Adams, Arthur G., ed. (Illus.). 272p. 1995. 60.00 (*1-885254-10-5*) Monacelli Pr.

— The Hudson River: From Tear of the Clouds to Manhattan, 4 vols., Set. Adams, Arthur G., ed. (Illus.). 272p. 1995. 240.00 (*1-885254-17-2*) Monacelli Pr.

Rajs, Jake, illus. America. LC 90-8169. 256p. 1990. 50.00 (*0-8478-1244-8*) Rizzoli Intl.

Rajs, Jake, photos. Manhattan: An Island in Focus. LC 85-43056. (Illus.). 256p. 1985. 60.00 (*0-8478-0670-7*) Rizzoli Intl.

Rajshekar, V. T. & Kly, Y. N. Dalit: The Black Untouchables of India. LC 87-71663. 100p. (Orig.). 1987. pap. 7.95 (*0-932863-05-1*) Clarity Pr.

Rajskub, MaryLynn. The Big Picture. 10p. 1993. pap. 1.00 (*1-884047-51-3*) Mass Extinct.

Rajsuman, R., jt. auth. see Malaiya, Y. K.

***Rajsuman, Rochit.** IDDQ Testing for CMOS VLSI. LC 94-21066. 1994. 65.00 (*0-89006-726-0*) Artech Hse.

Rajsuman, Rochit, ed. Digital Hardware Testing: Transistor-Level Fault Modeling & Testing. (Telecommunications Engineering Ser.). 270p. 1992. text ed. 78.00 (*0-89006-580-2*) Artech Hse.

***Rajtar, Steve.** Hiking Trails, Eastern United States: Address, Phone Number & Distances for 5,000 Trails, with Indexing of over 200 Guidebooks. 368p. 1995. pap. 39.95 (*0-7864-0142-7*) McFarland & Co.

Raju, B. R. Developmental Migration: A Processual Analysis of Inter State Rural-Rural Migration. (C). 1989. 22.50 (*81-7022-205-2*, Pub. by Concept II) S Asia.

***Raju, C. K.** Time: Towards a Consistent-Theory, 65. LC 94-32856. (Fundamental Theories of Physics Ser.). 272p. (C). 1994. lib. bdg. 114.00 (*0-7923-3103-6*) Kluwer Ac.

Raju, K. V., jt. auth. see Maloney, Clarence.

Raju, M. K. Managerial Perspectives. 185p. 1992. 25.00 (*0-86311-261-7*, Pub. by Orient Longman Ltd II) Apt Bks.

— W. H. Auden - The Commissar & the Yogi: A Study of His Plays & Longer Poems. 200p. 1991. text ed. 30.00 (*81-85218-25-0*, Pub. by Prestige II) Advent Bks Div.

Raju, N. Krishna. Design of Bridges. (C). 1988. 16.50 (*81-204-0344-4*, Pub. by Oxford IBH II) S Asia.

— Structural Design & Drawing: Reinforced Concrete & Steel. 1993. 37.50 (*0-86311-189-0*, Pub. by Universities Pr II) Apt Bks.

Raju, P. K., ed. Vibro-Acoustic Characterization of Materials & Structures. (NCA Ser.: Vol. 14). 242p. 1992. 57.50 (*0-7918-1125-5*, G00769) ASME.

Raju, P. K. & Gibson, R. F., eds. Dynamic Characterization of Advanced Materials. LC 93-73264. 215p. Date not set. pap. 60.00 (*0-7918-1028-3*) ASME.

Raju, P. T. Introduction to Comparative Philosophy. xii, 364p. (C). 1992. 14.95 (*1-881338-17-7*) Nataraj Bks.

— Introduction to Comparative Philosophy. LC 62-7870. (Arcturus Books Paperbacks). 376p. 1970. pap. 9.95 (*0-8093-0419-8*) S Ill U Pr.

— The Philosophical Traditions of India. 256p. (C). 1992. 14.95 (*1-881338-18-5*) Nataraj Bks.

— Spirit, Being & Self. (Studies in Indian & Western Philosophy). 285p. 1982. 29.95 (*0-940500-98-1*, Pub. by S Asian Pubs II) Asia Bk Corp.

— Spirit, Being & Self: Studies in Indian & Western Philosophy. 284p. 1986. 20.00 (*0-8364-1853-0*, Pub. by S Asia Pubs II) S Asia.

— Spirit, Being, & Self: Studies in Indian & Western Philosophy. 285p. 1982. 29.95 (*0-318-37031-X*) Asia Bk Corp.

— Structural Depths of Indian Thought. (SUNY Series in Philosophy). 599p. 1985. 59.50 (*0-88706-139-7*); pap. 19.95 (*0-88706-140-0*) State U NY Pr.

Raju, P. T., jt. ed. see Radhakrishnan, S.

Raju, R., jt. auth. see Jhala, J.

Raju, R. K. A Mystic Link with India: Life Story of Two Pilgrims Painters of Hungary. (C). 1991. 22.00 (*81-7023-317-8*, Pub. by Allied II) S Asia.

Raju, Saraswati & Bagchi, Deipica, eds. Women & Work in South Asia: Regional Patterns & Perspectives. LC 93-10554. 1994. 49.95 (*0-415-04249-6*) Routledge.

Raju, Seshadri. Surgical & Medical Management of Venous Disease. 1995. 110.00 (*0-683-07111-4*) Williams & Wilkins.

Raju, Suryanarayana S. Analysis of Productivity Levels & Economic Efficiency in Agriculture. 1987. 41.00 (*81-85076-12-X*, Pub. by Chugh Pubns II) S Asia.

Raju Umapathi Datla, tr. see Jnanananda, Swami.

Raju, V. B. Commentaries on Evidence Act. 4th ed. (C). 1991. 110.00 (*0-685-39711-4*) St Mut.

— Commentaries on the Constitution of India. 992p. 1973. 120.00 (*0-317-54672-4*) St Mut.

— Indian Penal Code. (C). 1990. 100.00 (*0-685-39348-8*) St Mut.

— Indian Penal Code, Eighteen-Sixty: Nineteen Eighty-Two Bound in One Book W-S 1986, 2 vols., Set. 4th ed. (C). 1986. 200.00 (*0-685-36420-8*) St Mut.

— Indian Penal Code, 1860, Set. 4th ed. 1982. 660.00 (*0-317-54665-1*) St Mut.

— Indian Penal Code, 1860, 1982 Edition, 2 vols. in 1. 4th ed. (C). 1990. 200.00 (*0-685-39589-8*) St Mut.

***Raju, V. Rajendra.** Role of Women in India's Freedom Struggle. (C). 1994. text ed. 20.00 (*81-7141-238-6*, Pub. by Discovery Pub Hse II) S Asia.

Rajwade, A. R. Squares. (London Mathematical Society Lecture Note Ser.: No. 171). 300p. (C). 1993. pap. 42.95 (*0-521-42668-5*) Cambridge U Pr.

Rajwar, G. S. Advances in Himalayan Ecology. (Recent Researches in Ecology, Environment & Pollution Ser.: Vol. 6). (Illus.). 360p. 1991. 59.00 (*1-55528-241-5*, Messers Today & Tomorrow) Scholarly Pubns.

Rajwar, G. S., ed. Garhwal Himalaya: Ecology & Environment. (Illus.). xii, 263p. 1993. 32.00 (*81-7024-559-1*, Pub. by Ashish Pub Hse II) Nataraj Bks.

Rajyalakshmi, P. Tribal Food Habits. (C). 1991. 18.50 (*81-212-0337-6*, Pub. by Gian Publng Hse II) S Asia.

Rak, Charles, jt. auth. see Weiner, Jack.

Rak, Mary K. Cowman's Wife. 1993. 29.95 (*0-87611-126-6*); pap. 19.95 (*0-87611-127-4*) Tex St Hist Assn.

Rakas, Frank G. Italian for the Business Traveler. 2nd ed. LC 93-30810. (Foreign Language Business Dictionaries Ser.). 600p. (ENG & ITA.). 1994. pap. 9.95 (*0-8120-1771-4*) Barron.

Rakauski, Casimir. Computer Aided Design Explained. (Series 860). 1981. student ed, pap. 5.00 (*0-8064-0345-4*, 860); audio 179.00 (*0-8064-0346-2*) Bergwall.

***Rake, Alan.** One Hundred Great Africans. LC 94-25934. (Illus.). 441p. 1994. text ed. 59.50 (*0-8108-2929-0*) Scarecrow.

— Who's Who in Africa: Leaders for the Nineteen Nineties. LC 92-8166. 456p. 1992. 59.50 (*0-8108-2557-0*) Scarecrow.

Rakel. Yearbook of Family Practice, 1990. 536p. 1990. 54.95 (*0-8151-7227-3*, Yr Bk Med Pubs) Mosby Yr Bk.

Rakel, R. E., jt. ed. see Schuckit, M. A.

***Rakel, Robert E.** Conn's Current Therapy, 1995. 1312p. 1994. text ed. 55.00 (*0-7216-4052-4*) Saunders.

— Essentials of Family Practice. (Illus.). 486p. 1992. pap. text ed. 54.95 (*0-7216-4227-6*) Saunders.

— Patient Care Procedures For Your Practice. Driscoll, Charles E., ed. 264p. (Orig.). 1988. pap. 32.95 (*0-87489-444-1*) Med Economics.

— Textbook of Family Practice. 4th ed. (Illus.). 1952p. 1990. text ed. 142.50 (*0-7216-3115-0*) Saunders.

— Textbook of Family Practice. 5th ed. (Illus.). 1760p. 1995. text ed. 115.00 (*0-7216-4053-2*) Saunders.

***Rakel, Robert E., ed.** Saunders Manual of Medical Practice. LC 95-6354. 1995. write for info. (*0-7216-5192-5*) Saunders.

— Year Book of Family Practice, 1989. (Illus.). 552p. 1989. 54.95 (*0-8151-7226-5*, Yr Bk Med Pubs) Mosby Yr Bk.

Rakel, Robert E., jt. auth. see Driscoll, Charles E.

Raker, Dan. One Minute CAD Manager. 98p. 1992. pap. 14.95 (*0-934605-25-4*, OnWord Pr) High Mtn.

***Raker, J. W. & Shukla, R. S.** Hindi-English - English-Hindi Dictionary. 673p. 1995. 18.50 (*81-86264-21-3*) IBD Ltd.

Rakes, Charles D. Alarms: Fifty-Five Electronic Projects & Circuits. (Illus.). 160p. 1988. 19.95 (*0-8306-2096-6*, 2996) TAB Bks.

Rakesh, Hooja. Administrative Interventions in Rural Development. 1987. 10.95 (*0-8364-2237-6*, Pub. by Rawat II) S Asia.

Rakesh, Mohan. Lingering Shadows. Ratan, Jai, tr. 214p. 1970. pap. 2.50 (*0-88253-075-5*) Ind-US Inc.

Rakesh, R., ed. Law of Sexual Offences. (C). 1988. 180.00 (*0-685-44801-0*) St Mut.

Rakesh, Ram D. Cultural Heritage of Nepal Terai. xiv, 221p. 1994. 20.00 (*81-85693-26-9*, Pub. by Nirala Pubns II) Nataraj Bks.

Rakesh, Virendra P. Sir William Wedderburn & Indian Freedom Movement. 1989. 26.00 (*0-8364-2538-3*, Commonwealth) S Asia.

Rakestraw, Donald A. For Honor or Destiny: The Anglo-American Crisis over the Oregon Territory. LC 93-46250. (American University Studies: Vol. 160). 256p. (C). 1995. text ed. 58.95 (*0-8204-2454-4*) P Lang Pubs.

Rakestraw, Lawrence. A History of Forest Conservation in the Pacific Northwest, 1891-1913. Bruchey, Stuart, ed. LC 78-56660. (Management in Public Lands in the U. S. Ser.). 1979. lib. bdg. 18.95 (*0-405-11351-X*) Ayer.

Rakestraw, N. W. & Kieffer, W. F., eds. Cumulative Index to Journal of Chemical Education, 4 vols. Vol. 2, 1961. 16.50 (*0-910362-11-4*, 1949-1958) Chem Educ.

Rakestraw, Robert V., jt. ed. see Clark, David K.

Rakhe, S. M. Education in Ancient India. (Sri Garib Dass Oriental Ser.: No. 135). (C). 1992. text ed. 16.00 (*81-7030-312-5*) S Asia.

Rakhmatulin, K. A. & Dem'yanov, y. A. Strength under High Transient Loads. 352p. 1966. text ed. 86.00 (*0-7065-0529-8*, Pub. by Keter Pub IS) Coronet Bks.

Rakic, Bogdan, tr. see Andric, Ivo.

Rakic, P. & Singer, W., eds. Neurobiology of the Neocortex LS42: Report of the Dahlem Workshop on Neurobiology of Neocortex, Berlin 1987, May 17-22. LC 87-33983. (Dahlem Workshop Reports). 461p. 1988. text ed. 239.95 (*0-471-91776-1*, Wiley-Interscience) Wiley.

Rakich, J. & Darr, K., eds. Hospital Organization & Management: Text & Readings. 3rd ed. LC 77-24710. (Health Systems Management Ser.: Vol. 16). 684p. 1983. text ed. 29.95 (*0-88331-151-8*) Luce.

Rakich, Johnathon S., et al. Managing Health Services Organizations. 2nd ed. (Illus.). 550p. 1985. 42.50 (*0-7216-2045-0*) Saunders.

Rakich, Jonathon S., et al. Instructor's Manual for Managing Health Services Organizations. 3rd ed. 176p. 1992. pap. text ed. 22.00 (*1-878812-13-0*) Hlth Prof Pr.

— Managing Health Services Organizations. 3rd ed. 768p. 1992. 53.00 (*1-878812-09-2*) Hlth Prof Pr.

***Rakich, Jonathon S., et al, eds.** Cases in Health Services Management. 3rd ed. 368p. 1994. pap. text ed. 30.00 (*1-878812-19-X*) Hlth Prof Pr.

Rakipov, N. G. & Geyer, B., comps. Elsevier's Dictionary of Agriculture & Food Production: Russian-English. LC 93-48591. (ENG & RUS.). 1994. 228.50 (*0-444-89929-4*) Elsevier.

Rakkar, J. S. Muslim Politics in the Punjab. 1986. 36.00 (*0-8364-1904-9*, Pub. by Deep) S Asia.

Raknes, Ola, jt. auth. see Grondahl, Illit.

Rako, Susan & Mazer, Harvey, eds. Semrad: The Heart of a Therapist. LC 84-45091. 208p. 1983. 30.00 (*0-87668-684-6*) Aronson.

Rakoczy, Sharon, jt. auth. see Natarajan, K. V.

Rakoczy, Susan, ed. Common Journey, Different Paths: Spiritual Direction in Cross-Cultural Perspective. LC 91-40977. 1992. pap. 18.95 (*0-88344-789-4*) Orbis Bks.

***Rakodi, Carole.** Harare: Inheriting a Settler-Colonial City: Change Or Continuity. LC 95-3850. (Belhaven World Cities Ser.). 1995. text ed. 49.95 (*0-471-94951-5*) Wiley.

Rakodi, Carole, jt. auth. see Devas, Nick.

***Rakoff, Dena O.** Choosing a Career in the Law. rev. ed. 88p. 1991. pap. 13.00 (*0-943747-15-5*) Harvard OCS.

Rakoff, Jed S. & Goldstein, Howard W., eds. RICO: Civil & Criminal, Law & Strategy. 650p. 1989. ring bd. 110.00 (*0-317-05402-3*, 00609) NY Law Pub.

Rakoff, Jed S., et al, eds. Organizational Sentencing Guidelines: Compliance & Mitigation. 1993. ring bd. 85.00 (*0-317-05401-5*, 00619) NY Law Pub.

Rakoff, V., jt. ed. see Persad, E.

Rakofsky, Marc. Fractional Arthrography of the Shoulder. Stielle, Z., tr. LC 87-14951. (Illus.). 259p. 1987. lib. bdg. 115.00 (*0-89574-247-0*) G F Verlag.

Rakos, Jennie, ed. see Dunnahoo, Terry.

Rakos, John. Software Project Management for Small to Medium Sized Projects. 1990. text ed. 61.00 (*0-13-826173-3*) P-H.

Rakos, Richard F. Assertive Behaviour. (International Series on Communication Skills). 288p. 1990. 67.00 (*0-415-00041-6*, A4831); pap. 19.95 (*0-415-00042-4*, A4835) Routledge.

Rakos, Sandor. Catullan Games. Korosy, Maria, tr. LC 89-60942. 80p. (Orig.). 1989. pap. 9.00 (*0-910395-53-5*) Marlboro Pr.

Rakosi, Carl. Amulet. 88p. 1967. pap. 1.50 (*0-87685-248-7*) Black Sparrow.

— Collected Poems. LC 84-62266. (Poets Ser.). 550p. (Orig.). 1986. 35.00 (*0-915032-35-X*); pap. 15.95 (*0-915032-36-8*) Natl Poet Foun.

— Collected Prose of Carl Rakosi. LC 83-62144. 150p. 1984. pap. 12.95 (*0-915032-21-X*) Natl Poet Foun.

— Droles De Journal. LC 80-28307. 20p. (Orig.). 1981. 30.00 (*0-915124-43-2*); pap. 5.00 (*0-915124-44-0*) Coffee Hse.

— Ere-Voice. LC 75-159737. 92p. 1971. 4.50 (*0-87685-251-7*); pap. 2.45 (*0-87685-250-9*) Black Sparrow.

Rakosi, Carl & Crozier, Andrew, eds. Poems 1923-1941. (Sun & Moon Classics Ser.: No. 64). 205p. (Orig.). 1995. pap. 12.95 (*1-55713-185-6*) Sun & Moon CA.

Rakosi, Thomas & Jonas, Irmtrud. Orthodontic Diagnosis. LC 92-49147. (Color Atlas of Dental Medicine Ser.). 1993. 159.00 (*0-86577-450-1*) Thieme Med Pubs.

Rakosnik, J., jt. auth. see Tichy, M.

Rakove, Jack N. The Beginnings of National Politics: An Interpretive History of the Continental Congress. LC 82-15186. 512p. (Orig.). (C). 1982. reprint ed. pap. text ed. 15.95 (*0-8018-2864-3*) Johns Hopkins.

— James Madison & the Creation of the American Republic. (C). 1989. pap. text ed. 16.00 (*0-673-39994-X*) HarpCollege.

— James Madison & the Creation of the American Republic. (Library of American Biography). 200p. 1995. pap. 15.95 (*1-886746-20-6*) Talman Pub.

Rakove, Jack N., ed. Interpreting the Constitution: The Debate over Original Intent. 1990. text ed. 45.00 (*1-55553-079-6*); pap. text ed. 16.95 (*1-55553-081-8*) NE U Pr.

Rakove, Milton L. Don't Make No Waves--Don't Back No Losers: An Insider's Analysis of the Daley Machine. LC 75-1939. 318p. reprint ed. pap. 90.70 (*0-7837-3724-6*, 2057902) Bks Demand.

Rakovic, Miroslav, tr. see Kneppo, I., ed.

Rakowski, Marc. Towards an East European Marxism. LC 77-18171. 1978. text ed. 24.95 (*0-312-81048-2*) St Martin.

Rakovszky, Zsuzsa. New Life. Szirtes, George, tr. 64p. 1994. pap. 11.95 (*0-19-283089-9*) OUP.

Rakow, Lana, ed. see Bowen, Sheryl P. & Wyatt, Nancy.

Rakow, Lana F. Gender on the Line: Women, the Telephone, & Community Life. (Illinois Studies in Communications). 184p. 1992. 24.95 (*0-252-01807-9*) U of Ill Pr.

Rakow, Lana F., ed. Women Making Meaning: New Feminist Directions in Communication. 1992. 49.95 (*0-415-90629-6*, A7421, Routledge NY); pap. 15.95 (*0-415-90630-X*, A7425, Routledge NY) Routledge.

Rakow, Lana F. & Kramarae, Cheris, eds. The Revolution in Words: Righting Women, 1868-1871. (Women's Source Library). 304p. 1990. 35.00 (*0-415-90298-3*, A1693, Routledge NY) Routledge.

Rakow, Phyllis L. Contact Lenses. LC 87-42948. (Ophthalmic Technical Skills Ser.: Vol. I). 156p. 1988. pap. 40.00 (*1-55642-024-2*) SLACK Inc.

Rakow, Steven J. Teaching Science As Inquiry. LC 86-61751. (Fastback Ser.: No. 246). 50p. (Orig.). 1986. pap. 1.25 (*0-87367-246-1*) Phi Delta Kappa.

Rakow, Sue F. & Carpenter, Carol B. Signs of Sharing: An Elementary Sign Language & Deaf Awareness Curriculum. LC 92-46219. (Illus.). 380p. (Orig.). 1993. spiral bd. 47.95x (*0-398-05851-2*) C C Thomas.

Rakow, Sue F., jt. auth. see Carpenter, Carol B.

Rakowicz-Szulczynska, Ewa M., ed. Nuclear Localization of Growth Factors & of Monoclonal Antibodies. LC 93-12471. 224p. 1993. 149.95 (*0-8493-4713-0*, QP552) CRC Pr.

Rakowitz, Elly & Rubin, Gloria S. Living with Your New Baby. 3rd ed. 400p. 1987. pap. 4.95 (*0-425-10875-9*) Berkley Pub.

Rakowska-Harmstone, Teresa. Russia & Nationalism in Central Asia: The Case of Tadzhikistan. Published in Cooperation with the Institute for Sino-Soviet Studies, the George Washington University. LC 69-13722. 342p. reprint ed. pap. 97.50 (*0-317-41760-6*, 2025866) Bks Demand.

Rakowska-Harmstone, Teresa, ed. Communism in Eastern Europe. 2nd ed. LC 83-49501. (Illus.). 400p. 1984. 35.00 (*0-253-31391-0*); pap. 12.95 (*0-253-20328-7*, MB-328) Ind U Pr.

Rakowski, Cathy A., ed. Contrapunto: The Informal Sector Debate in Latin America. LC 93-26767. (SUNY Series in Power & Political Economy). 336p. 1994. 64.50 (*0-7914-1905-3*); pap. 21.95 (*0-7914-1906-1*) State U NY Pr.

An Asterisk (*) at the beginning of an entry indicates that the title is appearing in BIP for the first time.

Rakowski, Cathy A., jt. auth. see Saulniers, Suzanne S.

Rakowski, Eric. Equal Justice. 400p. 1993. reprint ed. pap. 21.00 (*0-19-824079-1*) OUP.

Rakowski, James P., ed. Transportation Economics: A Guide to Information Sources. LC 73-17584. (Economics Information Guide Ser.: Vol. 5). 232p. 1976. 68.00 (*0-8103-1307-3*) Gale.

Rakowski, John. Cooking on the Road. LC 78-65977. (Illus.). 176p. 1980. pap. 5.95 (*0-89037-200-4*) Anderson World.

Rakowski, M. & Kalecki, Michal. Efficiency of Investment in a Socialist Economy. LC 65-15379. 1966. 224.00 (*0-08-011174-2*, Pub. by Pergamon Repr UK) Franklin.

Rakowski, Z. Geomechanics 93 - Water Jet Cutting: Proceedings of the International Conference, Hradec-Ostrava, Czechia, September 1993. (Illus.). 480p. (C). 1994. text ed. 95.00 (*90-5410-354-X*, Pub. by A A Balkema NE) Ashgate Pub Co.

Rakowski, Zikmund, ed. Geomechanics, 1991: Proceedings of the International Conference on Geomechanics 1991, Hradec, Ostrava, Czecho-Slovakia, 24-26 September 1991. (Illus.). 384p. (C). 1992. text ed. 75.00 (*90-5410-039-7*, Pub. by A A Balkema NE) Ashgate Pub Co.

Rakshit, Mihir. Trade, Mercantile Capital & Economic Development. 1993. pap. 10.00 (*0-86311-368-0*, Pub. by Orient Longman Ltd II) Apt Bks.

Rakshit, Mihir, ed. Studies in the Macroeconomics of Developing Countries. (Illus.). 200p. 1989. 16.95 (*0-19-562340-1*) OUP.

Rakshit, P. C. Elementary Physical Chemistry. 1985. 79.00 (*0-317-38763-4*, Current Dist) St Mut.

— Thermodynamics. 1985. 79.00 (*0-317-38807-X*, Current Dist) St Mut.

Rakshit, R., jt. auth. see Chattopadhyay, C.

Rakshit, S. C. Molecular Symmetry Groups & Chemistry. 1985. 79.00 (*0-317-38786-3*, Current Dist) St Mut.

Raktoe, B. L. & Hubert, J. J. Basic Applied Statistics. LC 79-727. (Statistics, Textbooks & Monographs: No. 27). (Illus.). 440p. reprint ed. pap. 125.40 (*0-7837-5982-7*, 2045788) Bks Demand.

Rakusan, Jeromira, jt. auth. see Cowan, William.

Rakusan, K., et al, eds. Oxygen Transport to Tissue, No. XI. (Advances in Experimental Medicine & Biology Ser.: Vol. 247). (Illus.). 812p. 1989. 165.00 (*0-306-43156-4*, Plenum Pr) Plenum.

Rakusen, Michael L., et al. Distribution of Matrimonial Assets on Divorce. 3rd ed. 1989. boxed 122.00 (*0-406-51021-0*, UK) Butterworth Legal Pubs.

Rakusin, Stephen. Florida Construction Lien Law, 5 vols., Set. 2000p. 1994. ring bd. 350.00 (*0-409-26052-5*) Michie Butterworth.

— Florida Creditors' Rights Manual, 5 vols., Set. 2000p. 1994. ring bd. 350.00 (*0-409-26093-2*) Michie Butterworth.

Rakusin, Stephen B. Florida Construction Lien Law, 5 vols. suppl. ed. 1994. Suppl. 01/1991. ring bd. 45.00 (*0-685-43657-8*) Butterworth Legal Pubs.

— Florida Creditors' Rights Manual. suppl. ed. 1994. ring bd. 51.00 (*0-685-43215-7*) Butterworth Legal Pubs.

Raland, Craig, jt. auth. see Hines, Andrew.

Ralbovsky, Ed & Treichler, Fran. Automotive Computer Systems & Circuits. (Illus.). 176p. (C). 1988. pap. text ed. 22.00 (*0-13-054230-X*) P-H.

Ralebipi, Matabole D., ed. Inventory of Marriage & Family Literature, Vol. 13. 1400p. 1988. 45.00 (*0-916174-23-9*) Natl Coun Family.

Ralebipi, Matabole D., intro. Inventory of Marriage & Family Literature, Vol. 14. 879p. (C). 1989. 45.00 (*0-916174-24-7*) Natl Coun Family.

— Inventory of Marriage & Family Literature, Vol. 15. 976p. (C). 1990. 70.00 (*0-916174-28-X*) Natl Coun Family.

Ralebipi, Matabole D., jt. ed. see Touliatos, John.

Raleigh, A. S. Hermetic Fundamentals Revealed. 127p. 1993. pap. 14.95 (*1-56459-370-3*) Kessinger Pub.

— Hermetic Fundamentals Revealed. 57p. 1974. reprint ed. spiral bd. 5.50 (*0-7873-1178-2*) Mokelumne.

— Hermetic Science of Motion & Number. 68p. 1993. reprint ed. spiral bd. 6.60 (*0-7873-0688-6*) Mokelumne.

— Metaphysical Healing, 2 vols., Set. 1991. lib. bdg. 199.95 (*0-8490-5133-9*) Gordon Pr.

— Metaphysical Healing, 2 vols. in 1, Vols. 1 & 2. 87p. 1974. reprint ed. spiral bd. 16.50 (*0-7873-1204-5*) Mokelumne.

— Occult Geometry; & Hermetic Science of Motion & Number. 208p. 1991. reprint ed. pap. 9.95 (*0-87516-639-3*) DeVorss.

— Science of Alchemy. 172p. 1992. reprint ed. pap. 16.95 (*1-56459-007-0*) Kessinger Pub.

— Scientifica Hermetica: An Introduciton to the Science of Alchemy. 109p. 1974. reprint ed. spiral bd. 5.50 (*0-7873-1049-2*) Mokelumne.

— Scientifica Hermetica: An Introduction to the Science of Alchemy. 115p. 1995. reprint ed. pap. 15.95 (*1-56459-492-0*) Kessinger Pub.

— The Shepherd of Men: An Official Commentary on the Sermon of Hermes Trismegistos. 145p. 1995. reprint ed. pap. 16.95 (*1-56459-493-9*) Kessinger Pub.

— Speculative Art of Alchemy. 191p. 1992. reprint ed. pap. 16.95 (*1-56459-006-2*) Kessinger Pub.

Raleigh, C. B., jt. ed. see Behr, H. J.

Raleigh, Donald J. Revolution on the Volga: 1917 in Saratov. LC 85-12792. (Cornell Studies in Soviet History & Science). (Illus.). 376p. 1986. 39.95 (*0-8014-1790-2*) Cornell U Pr.

Raleigh, Donald J., ed. A Russian Civil War Diary: Alexis V. Babine in Saratov, 1917-1922. LC 88-3967. (Illus.). xxiv, 264p. 1988. lib. bdg. 31.95 (*0-8223-0835-5*) Duke.

— Soviet Historians & Perestroika: The First Phase. LC 89-10724. 300p. 1990. text ed. 42.50 (*0-87332-554-0*) M E Sharpe.

Raleigh, Donald J., ed. see Burdzhalov, E. N.

***Raleigh, Duane.** Ice: Tools & Technique. (Illus.). 128p. 1995. pap. text ed. 11.95 (*1-887216-00-6*) Elk Mtn Pr.

Raleigh, Duane, jt. auth. see Benge, Michael.

Raleigh, Eugene, jt. auth. see Pasternak, Grigory I.

Raleigh, John H., ed. see Frederic, Harold.

Raleigh, John H., ed. see Scott, Walter.

***Raleigh, Lori E. & Roginsky, Rachel J., eds.** Hotel Investments: Issues & Perspectives. 1994. write for info. (*0-86612-088-2*) Educ Inst Am Hotel.

Raleigh, Michael. The Maxwell Street Blues. LC 94-16795. 1994. 20.95 (*0-312-11394-3*) St Martin.

Raleigh, Sir Walter. Selections from His Historie of the World, His Letters, Etc. (BCL1-PR English Literature Ser.). 212p. 1992. reprint ed. lib. bdg. 79.00 (*0-7812-7218-1*) Rprt Serv.

Raleigh, Walter. A Declaration of the Demeanor & Cariage of Sir W. Raleigh As Well in His Voyage, As in His Returne. LC 71-25674. (English Experience Ser.: No. 288). 68p. 1970. reprint ed. 9.50 (*90-221-0288-2*) Walter J Johnson.

— The Discoverie of the Large, Rich & Bewtiful Empire of Guiana, Performed in the Yeare 1595, by Sir W. Ralegh. LC 68-27482. (English Experience Ser.: No. 3). 112p. 1968. reprint ed. 11.50 (*90-221-0003-0*) Walter J Johnson.

— England & the War: Being Sundry Addresses Delivered During the War. LC 67-30228. (Essay Index Reprint Ser.). 1977. 17.95 (*0-8369-0805-8*) Ayer.

— English Novel: Being a Short Sketch of Its History from Earliest Times... 1988. reprint ed. lib. bdg. 59.00 (*0-7812-0200-0*) Rprt Serv.

— English Novel: Being a Short Sketch of Its History from the Earliest Times to the Appearance of Waverly. LC 72-131810. 1970. reprint ed. 29.00 (*0-403-00697-X*) Scholarly.

— Milton. LC 67-13336. 1972. reprint ed. 19.95 (*0-405-08873-6*) Ayer.

— The Ocean to Cynthia: Poems. (Illus.). 1984p. 20.00 (*0-317-40774-0*) Abattoir.

— On Writing & Writers: Being Extracts from His Notebooks. Gordon, G., ed. LC 68-22939. (Essay Index Reprint Ser.). 1977. 19.95 (*0-8369-0806-6*) Ayer.

— The Prerogative of Parliaments in England: Proved in a Dialogue. LC 74-80207. (English Experience Ser.: No. 686). 68p. 1974. reprint ed. 7.00 (*90-221-0686-1*) Walter J Johnson.

— A Report of the Truth of the Fight about the Iles of Acores. LC 72-26280. (English Experience Ser.: No. 183). 32p. 1969. reprint ed. 30.00 (*90-221-0183-5*) Walter J Johnson.

— Shakespeare. LC 74-182702. (English Men of Letters Ser.). reprint ed. 32.50 (*0-404-05206-1*) AMS Pr.

— Sir Walter Raleigh's Speech from the Scaffold: A Translation of the 1619 Dutch Edition, & Comparison with English Texts. Parker, John & Johnson, Carol A., eds. Johnson, Carol A., tr. & intro. by. (Illus.). 80p. (C). 1995. text ed. 15.00 (*0-9601798-5-2*) Assocs James Bell.

— Some Authors. LC 68-55855. (Essay Index Reprint Ser.). 1977. 23.95 (*0-8369-0807-4*) Ayer.

Raleigh, Walter A. Milton. (BCL1-PR English Literature Ser.). 286p. 1992. reprint ed. lib. bdg. 79.00 (*0-7812-7389-7*) Rprt Serv.

— Shakespeare. (BCL1-PR English Literature Ser.). 233p. 1992. reprint ed. lib. bdg. 79.00 (*0-7812-7283-1*) Rprt Serv.

— Six Essays on Johnson. (BCL1-PR English Literature Ser.). 184p. 1992. reprint ed. lib. bdg. 69.00 (*0-7812-7368-4*) Rprt Serv.

— Wordsworth. (BCL1-PR English Literature Ser.). 232p. 1992. reprint ed. lib. bdg. 79.00 (*0-7812-7682-9*) Rprt Serv.

— Wordsworth. LC 76-131811. 1970. reprint ed. 29.00 (*0-403-00698-8*) Scholarly.

Raleight, Duane, jt. auth. see Long, John.

***Ralescu, Anca L., ed.** Applied Research in Fuzzy Technology: Results of the Laboratory for International Fuzzy Engineering (LIFE) LC 94-34459. (International Series in Intelligent Technologies). 480p. (C). 1994. lib. bdg. 120.00 (*0-7923-9496-8*) Kluwer Ac.

— Fuzzy Logic in Artificial Intelligence: Proceedings of the IJCAI '93 Workshop, Chambery, France, August 28, 1993. LC 94-33308. (Lecture Notes in Computer Science, Vol. 810; Lecture Notes in Artificial Intelligence: 847). 1994. 28.00 (*3-540-58409-9*) Spr-Verlag.

Ralescu, Anca L., ed. see International Joint Conference on Artificial Intelligence.

Ralevic, Simo. The Tongue - Our Measure. 62p. 1987. pap. 4.50 (*0-85151-507-X*) Banner of Truth.

Ralevic, V. & Burnstock, G. Neural-Endothelial Interactions in the Control of Local Vascular Tone. (Medical Intelligence Unit Ser.). 124p. 1993. 89.95 (*1-879702-59-2*, LN0259) R G Landes.

Raley, Harold. Responsible Vision: The Philosophy of Julian Marfas. 1980. 20.00 (*0-89217-004-2*); pap. 8.95 (*0-89217-005-0*) American Hispanist.

Raley, Harold C., tr. see Marias, Julian.

Raley, Nancy & Carter, Laura, eds. New Guide to Effective Media Relations. 101p. 1988. 32.00 (*0-89964-255-1*) Coun Adv & Supp Ed.

Raley, Patricia E. Making Love: How to Be Your Own Sex Therapist. 288p. 1980. pap. 12.95 (*0-380-48819-1*) Avon.

Raley, Tom. Country! Cowboys, Rodeo, Women Like Never Before. (Illus.). 170p. (Orig.). 1993. pap. 9.95 (*0-935752-03-X*) Latigo Pr.

***Ralf, Sube & Eisenreich, Guenther.** Dictionary of Physics: English-German. 1008p. (ENG & GER.). 1987. 225.00 (*0-7859-7072-X*) Fr & Eur.

— Dictionary of Physics: English-German-French-Russian. 2nd ed. 2896p. (ENG, FRE & GER.). 1984. 750.00 (*0-7859-7069-X*) Fr & Eur.

Ralfe, James. The Naval Biography of Great Britain: Consisting of Historical Memoirs of Those Officers of the British Navy Who Distinguished Themselves During the Reign of His Majesty George III, 4 vols., Set. LC 72-20833. (American Revolutionary Ser.). (Illus.). reprint ed. lib. bdg. 310.00 (*0-8398-1773-8*) Irvington.

— The Naval Biography of Great Britain: Consisting of Historical Memoirs of Those Officers of the British Navy Who Distinguished Themselves During the Reign of His Majesty George III, 4 vols., Vol. 1. LC 72-20833. (American Revolutionary Ser.). (Illus.). 456p. reprint ed. lib. bdg. 75.00 (*0-8290-1850-6*) Irvington.

— The Naval Biography of Great Britain: Consisting of Historical Memoirs of Those Officers of the British Navy Who Distinguished Themselves During the Reign of His Majesty George III, 4 vols., Vol. 2. LC 72-20833. (American Revolutionary Ser.). (Illus.). 534p. reprint ed. lib. bdg. 80.00 (*0-8290-1851-4*) Irvington.

— The Naval Biography of Great Britain: Consisting of Historical Memoirs of Those Officers of the British Navy Who Distinguished Themselves During the Reign of His Majesty George III, 4 vols., Vol. 3. LC 72-20833. (American Revolutionary Ser.). (Illus.). 406p. reprint ed. lib. bdg. 75.00 (*0-685-02674-4*) Irvington.

— The Naval Biography of Great Britain: Consisting of Historical Memoirs of Those Officers of the British Navy Who Distinguished Themselves During the Reign of His Majesty George III, 4 vols., Vol. 4. LC 72-20833. (American Revolutionary Ser.). (Illus.). 551p. reprint ed. lib. bdg. 80.00 (*0-8290-1853-0*) Irvington.

Ralfel, B. Evenly Distributed Rubble. write for info. (*0-943216-05-2*) MoonsQuilt Pr.

Ralfs, J. British Desmidieae. (Illus.). 1962. 52.00 (*3-7682-0144-9*) Lubrecht & Cramer.

***Ralhan, O. P.** Indian National Movement-Punjabi Martyrs of Freedom, Set. (C). 1995. 225.00x (*81-7041-923-9*, Pub. by Anmol II) S Asia.

Rall, David P., ed. see Institute of Medicine, Committee on the Survey of the Health Effects of Mustard Gas & Lewisite Staff.

Rall, David P., ed. see Institute of Medicine Staff.

Rall, I. B. Automatic Differentiation: Techniques & Applications. (Lecture Notes in Computer Science Ser.: Vol. 120). 165p. 1981. pap. 23.00 (*0-387-10861-0*) Spr-Verlag.

Rall, J. E. & Kopin, Irwin J. The Thyroid & Biogenic Amines. (Methods in Investigative & Diagnostic Endocrinology Ser.: Vol. 1). 1972. 187.25 (*0-444-10371-6*, North Holland) Elsevier.

Rall, Louis B. Computational Solution of Nonlinear Operator Equations. LC 78-2378. 236p. (Orig.). 1979. reprint ed. 17.50 (*0-88275-667-2*) Krieger.

Rall, Ted. Waking up in America. 128p. (Orig.). 1992. pap. 6.95 (*0-312-08518-4*) St Martin.

Rall, Theodore W. Goodman & Gilman's Essentials of Pharmacology. (Illus.). 800p. 1994. pap. text ed. 37.00 (*0-07-105430-8*) McGraw.

Rall, W. Anatomy & Function. 1990. 75.00 (*0-8176-3502-5*) Birkhauser.

Ralley, Thomas G., jt. auth. see Dudewicz, Edward J.

Ralli, Augustus. Guide to Carlyle, 3 vols. LC 74-92979. (Reference Ser.: No. 44). 1970. reprint ed. lib. bdg. 89.95 (*0-8383-0999-2*) M S G Haskell Hse.

Ralli, Augustus J. Critiques. LC 67-22114. (Essay Index Reprint Ser.). 1977. 20.95 (*0-8369-0808-2*) Ayer.

— Later Critiques. LC 68-26469. (Essay Index Reprint Ser.). 1977. reprint ed. 18.95 (*0-8369-0809-0*) Ayer.

Ralli, Mary P., jt. auth. see Ordman, Kathryn A.

Rallides, Charles. The Tense Aspect System of the Spanish Verb As Used in Cultivated Bogata Spanish. LC 73-147933. (Janua Linguarum, Ser. Practica: No. 119). 66p. 1971. pap. text ed. 12.90 (*0-686-22488-4*) Mouton.

Rallin, Beryl, contrib. Federal Policies for Equal Educational Opportunity: Conflict & Confusion. (Policy Research Project Report Ser.: No. 23). 147p. 1977. 3.50 (*0-89940-616-5*) LBJ Sch Pub Aff.

Ralling, Christopher. The Kon-Tiki Man: Thor Heyerdahl. large type ed. 292p. 1991. 12.47 (*1-85089-297-0*, Pub. by ISIS UK) Transaction Pubs.

Rallings, Colin & Thrasher, Michael. Britain Votes Five. (Parliamentary Research Services Ser.). 226p. 1993. text ed. 55.95 (*0-900178-36-1*, Pub. by Dartmth Pub UK) Ashgate Pub Co.

Rallis, S. L-Functions & the Oscillator Representation. (Lecture Notes in Mathematics Ser.: Vol. 1245). xv, 239p. 1987. pap. 34.00 (*0-387-17694-2*) Spr-Verlag.

Rallis, Sharon F., jt. auth. see Goldring, Ellen B.

Rallis, Sharon F., jt. ed. see Reichardt, Charles S.

***Rallis, Sharon F., et al.** Dynamic Teachers: Leaders of Change. (Illus.). 176p. 1995. 39.95 (*0-8039-6235-5*); pap. 18.95 (*0-8039-6236-3*) Corwin Pr.

Rallis, Stephen & Schiffmann, Gerard. Weil Representation I: Intertwining Distributions & Discrete Spectrum. LC 80-12191. (Memoirs of the American Mathematical Society Ser.: No. 25/231). 203p. 1980. pap. 17.00 (*0-8218-2231-4*, MEMO 25/231) Am Math.

Rallis, Tom. City Transport in Developed & Developing Countries. LC 86-29789. 210p. 1988. text ed. 45.00 (*0-312-00450-8*) St Martin.

Rallison, Marvin L. Growth Disorders in Infants, Children & Adolescents. LC 85-6487. 476p. 1986. 43.00 (*0-471-08567-7*) Churchill.

Rallo, John A., jt. auth. see Ma, Marina.

Rallo, Joseph C. Defending Europe in the 1990's: The New Divide of High Technology. LC 86-22245. 1986. text ed. 35.00 (*0-312-19112-X*) St Martin.

Ralls, Kenneth M., et al. Introduction to Materials Science & Engineering. LC 76-10813. 665p. (C). 1976. Net. text ed. write for info. (*0-471-70665-5*) Wiley.

Ralls, Philip W., jt. ed. see Jeffrey, R. Brooke.

RaLonde, R. & Paust, B. Developing a Mariculture Business in Alaska: Information & Resources. (Aquaculture Note Ser.: No. 15). 40p. (Orig.). 1993. pap. 4.00 (*1-56612-020-9*) AK Sea Grant CP.

Ralov, Kirsten, ed. The Bournonville School, Pt. 4: Labanotation. LC 78-9554. (Dance Program Ser.: Vol. 12). 137p. reprint ed. Pt. 4 - Labanotation. pap. 39.10 (*0-8357-7370-1*, 2027074) Bks Demand.

***Ralovich, B.** Listeriosis Research: Present Situation & Perspective. 222p. (C). 1984. 75.00x (*963-05-3657-9*, Pub. by Akad Kiado HU) St Mut.

Ralph, Brian, jt. auth. see Kurzydlowski, Krzysztof J.

Ralph, James. Case of Authors by Profession or Trade, 1758, Champion 1739. LC 66-10008. 1966. 50.00 (*0-8201-1037-X*) Schol Facsimiles.

— Case of Our Present Theatrical Disputes Fairly Stated. LC 70-174295. reprint ed. lib. bdg. 39.50 (*0-404-05208-8*) AMS Pr.

— Northern Protest: Martin Luther King, Jr., Chicago, & the Civil Rights Movement. LC 92-45231. 352p. 1993. text ed. 27.95 (*0-674-62687-7*) HUP.

Ralph, Jerry. Somewhat Normal? 1992. 14.95 (*0-533-10035-6*) Vantage.

***Ralph, Judy & Gompf, Ray.** The Peanut Butter Cookbook for Kids. LC 94-37852. (Illus.). 96p. (YA). (gr. 3 up). 1995. lib. bdg. 14.89 (*0-7868-2110-8*); pap. 10.95 (*0-7868-1028-9*) Hyprn Child.

Ralph, Julian. Alone in China & Other Stories. LC 70-101819. (Short Story Index Reprint Ser.). 1977. 30.95 (*0-8369-3207-2*) Ayer.

— Our Great West. LC 75-126250. (Select Bibliographies Reprint Ser.). 1977. 30.95 (*0-8369-5477-7*) Ayer.

— Prince of Georgia, & Other Tales. LC 74-142274. (Short Story Index Reprint Ser.). 1977. 19.95 (*0-8369-3758-9*) Ayer.

Ralph, Margaret. Historias Que Jesus Conto. (Serie Jirafa). Orig. Title: Stories Jesus Told. 28p. (J). (gr. 4 up). 1979. 2.75 (*0-311-38537-0*, Edit Mundo) Casa Bautista.

— Jesus: Historias de su Vida. LaValle, Teresa, tr. (Serie Jirafa). Orig. Title: The Life of Jesus. (Illus.). 28p. (J). (gr. 4). 1979. 2.75 (*0-311-38536-2*, Edit Mundo) Casa Bautista.

— Personas Escogidas de Dios. (Serie Jirafa). Orig. Title: God's Special People. 28p. 1979. 2.75 (*0-311-38535-4*, Edit Mundo) Casa Bautista.

Ralph, Margaret N. And God Said What? An Introduction to Biblical Literary Forms for Bible Lovers. 1986. pap. 10.95 (*0-8091-2780-6*) Paulist Pr.

— Discovering Old Testament Origins: The Books of Genesis, Exodus, & Samuel. LC 92-8494. (Discovering the Living Word Ser.). 1992. pap. 12.95 (*0-8091-3322-9*) Paulist Pr.

— Discovering Prophecy & Wisdom: The Books of Isaiah, Job, Proverbs & Psalms. LC 93-10245. (Discovering the Living Word Ser.: Vol. IV). 336p. 1993. pap. 12.95 (*0-8091-3402-0*) Paulist Pr.

— Discovering the First Century Church: The Acts of the Apostles, Letters of Paul & the Book of Revelation. (Discovering the Living Word Ser.). 1991. pap. 12.95 (*0-8091-3254-0*) Paulist Pr.

— Discovering the Gospels: Four Accounts of the Good News. (Discovering the Living Word Ser.). 1990. 11.95 (*0-8091-3200-1*) Paulist Pr.

— Plain Word about Biblical Images: Growing in Our Faith Through the Scriptures. 1989. pap. 10.95 (*0-8091-3045-9*) Paulist Pr.

Ralph, Phyllis C. Victorian Transformations: Fairy Tales, Adolescence, & the Novel of Female Development. (American University Studies: English Language & Literature: Ser. IV, Vol. 96). 176p. (C). 1989. text ed. 31.95 (*0-8204-1039-X*) P Lang Pubs.

Ralph, R., jt. auth. see Brown, B.

Ralph, Richard. The Life & Works of John Weaver. LC 82-83649. (Illus.). 1075p. 1985. 125.00 (*0-87127-139-7*, Dance Horizons) Princeton Bk Co.

***Ralph, Sharon.** The Alphabet Book: An ABC Book of AA, Rhymes, Patterns, & Activities. Britt, Leslie, ed. (Illus.). 96p. (Orig.). (J). (gr. k-2). 1995. pap. text ed. 9.95 (*0-86530-307-X*, 1P307-0) Incentive Pubns.

Ralphs, J. D., et al, eds. Principles & Practice of Multi-Frequency Telegraphy. 216p. 1985. boxed 107.00 (*0-86341-022-7*, TE011) Inst Elect Eng.

Ralphs, John D. Exploring the Fourth Dimension: Secrets of the Paranormal. LC 92-920. (Illus.). 272p. 1992. pap. 9.95 (*0-87542-655-7*) Llewellyn Pubns.

Ralphs, Lady & Norman, Geoffrey. The Magistrate as Chairman. 2nd ed. 224p. 1992. U.K. pap. 22.00 (*0-406-00118-9*) Butterworth Legal Pubs.

Ralsey, Alicia. Poetic Justice. 320p. 1994. mass mkt. 3.99 (*0-8217-4599-9*) Zebra.

Ralston, jt. auth. see Naylor.

Ralston, A. & Young, Gail S., eds. The Future of College Mathematics: Proceedings. (Illus.). 278p. 1983. 49.00 (*0-387-90813-7*) Spr-Verlag.

Ralston, A., jt. auth. see Maurer, Stephen B.

Ralston, Anthony, ed. Discrete Mathematics in the First Two Years. 112p. 1989. 5.00 (*0-88385-064-8*, NTE-15) Math Assn.

***Ralston, Anthony & Reilly, Edwin D., eds.** Encyclopedia of Computer Science. 3rd ed. 1992. 129.95 (*0-7803-0432-2*) Inst Electrical.

R

Ralston, Anthony & Reilly, Edwin D., Jr., eds. Encyclopedia of Computer Science & Engineering. 3rd rev. ed. (Illus.). 2000p. 1993. text ed. 125.00 (*0-442-27679-6*) Van Nos Reinhold.

Ralston, Anthony & Wilf, Herbert S., eds. Mathematical Methods for Digital Computers, Vol. 1. 305p. reprint ed. pap. 87.00 (*0-317-26226-2*, 2055669) Bks Demand.

Ralston, Anthony & Wilf, Herberts, eds. Mathematical Methods for Digital Computers, Vol. 3. LC 60-6509. 464p. reprint ed. pap. 132.30 (*0-685-20942-3*, 2056554) Bks Demand.

Ralston, Birgitta. Sisters: Photographic Portraits - An Exhibition. LC 88-51842. 32p. (Orig.). 1989. pap. 7.00 (*0-9621886-0-3*) Univ WI Art Gal.

Ralston, Charles W., jt. ed. see Convery, Frank J.

Ralston, David B. Importing the European Army: The Introduction of European Military Techniques & Institutions into the Extra-European World, 1600-1914. 216p. 1990. 29.95 (*0-226-70318-5*) U Ch Pr.

Ralston, Dennis, et al. Dennis Ralston's Tennis Workbook. (Illus.). 225p. 1991. 12.95 (*0-13-198607-4*) P-H.

Ralston, Diane D. & Ralston, Henry J., III. The Nerve Cell. Head, J. J., ed. LC 84-45836. (Carolina Biology Readers Ser.: No. 157). (Illus.). 16p. (Orig.). (YA). (gr. 10 up). 1988. pap. text ed. 2.75 (*0-89278-357-5*, 45-9757) Carolina Biological.

Ralston, Elizabeth W., jt. ed. see Montgomery, Susan.

Ralston, Esther. Some Day We'll Laugh: An Autobiography. LC 85-2482. (Filmmakers Ser.: No. 11). (Illus.). 244p. 1985. 20.00 (*0-8108-1814-0*) Scarecrow.

***Ralston, Faith.** Hidden Dynamics: How Emotions Affect Business Performance & How You Can Harness Their Power for Positive Results. LC 95-3940. 192p. 1995. 19.95 (*0-8144-0272-0*) AMACOM.

Ralston, G. B., jt. ed. see Hilderson, H. J.

Ralston, Gregory B., jt. auth. see Kuchel, Philip W.

Ralston, Helen. The Christian Ashrams: A New Religious Movement in Contemporary India. LC 87-21019. (Studies in Religion & Society: Vol. 20). 150p. 1987. lib. bdg. 69.95 (*0-88946-854-0*) E Mellen.

Ralston, Henry J., III, jt. auth. see Ralston, Diane D.

Ralston, Ian, jt. ed. see Hunter, John.

Ralston, James. The Choice of Emptiness. 2nd ed. LC 87-63357. 170p. 1988. pap. 5.99 (*0-945073-00-3*) Nightsun MD.

— The Night After. 2nd ed. 100p. 1986. pap. text ed. 6.00 (*0-945073-01-1*) Nightsun MD.

— The Poet's Car: Poems. LC 91-62670. 60p. (Orig.). 1992. pap. 7.00 (*0-945073-15-1*) Nightsun MD.

Ralston, Kathleen. A Man for Antarctica: The Early Life of Phillip Law. 1993. 29.95 (*1-875657-13-4*, Pub. by Hyland Hse AT) Intl Spec Bk.

Ralston, Kenneth M. & Schwed, Mechtild. Alltaksverb im Blickpunkt. 1995. pap. text ed. write for info. (*0-07-051325-2*) McGraw.

Ralston, Margaret C. Fashion Outlines: Dress Cutting by the Block Pattern System. Kliot, Jules & Kliot, Kaethe, eds. (Illus.). 80p. (C). 1990. reprint ed. pap. 9.50 (*0-916896-32-3*) Lacis Pubns.

Ralston, Marion. An Exchange of Gifts. (Pippin Teacher's Library). 88p. (C). 1993. pap. text ed. 12.50 (*0-88751-040-X*, 00737) Heinemann.

Ralston, Nancy C. & Jordan, Marynor. The Brown County Cookbook. LC 83-47917. (Illus.). 96p. (Orig.). 1992. pap. 6.95 (*0-253-21250-2*) Ind U Pr.

— The New Zucchini Cookbook: And Other Squash. LC 89-46018. (Illus.). 176p. 1990. pap. 10.95 (*0-88266-589-8*, Garden Way Pub) Storey Comm Inc.

Ralston, Peter. Ancient Wisdom, New Spirit: Investigations into Being Alive. LC 94-25348. 238p. 1994. pap. 12.95 (*1-883319-21-8*) Frog CA.

— Ancient Wisdom, New Spirit: Investigations into Being Alive. 300p. (C). 1994. pap. 12.95 (*0-685-72179-5*) North Atlantic.

— Cheng Hsin: Principles of Effortless Power. rev. ed. 236p. 1988. pap. 12.95 (*1-55643-048-5*) North Atlantic.

— Cheng Hsin Tui Shou: The Principles of Effortless Power. (Illus.). 380p. 1990. 30.00 (*1-55643-115-5*); pap. 18.95 (*1-55643-094-9*) North Atlantic.

— Reflections of Being. 80p. 1991. pap. 9.95 (*1-55643-119-8*) North Atlantic.

Ralston, Richard E., ed. Communism: Its Rise & Fall in the 20th Century. 256p. 1991. 37.50 (*0-87510-218-2*) Christian Sci.

Ralston, Richard S. Bankruptcy Stays: A Practitioner's Guide to Stays & Release from Stays. 1989. write for info. (*0-318-66005-9*) Bk Pub Co WA.

Ralston, Richard W., jt. ed. see Weinstock, Harold.

Ralston, Rick. Cast Iron Floor Trains: An Encyclopedia with Rarity & Price Guide. Engebretson, George, ed. LC 93-92799. (Illus.). 336p. 1994. 89.95 (*0-9638315-0-X*) Ralston Pubng.

Ralston, Sonia. Plowshares: A Contemporary Fable of Peace & War. LC 86-2443. 80p. 1986. pap. 4.95 (*0-8091-2788-1*) Paulist Pr.

Ralston, Trudy, jt. auth. see Foster, Eric.

Ralston, W. R. Songs of the Russian People: As Illustrative of Slavonic Mythology & Russian Social Life. LC 77-132444. (Studies in Music: No. 42). 1970. reprint ed. lib. bdg. 75.00 (*0-8383-1224-1*) M S G Haskell Hse.

— Tibetan Tales Derived from Indian Sources. 368p. 1989. reprint ed. pap. 30.00 (*957-9482-21-7*) Oriental Bk Store.

Ralston, W. R., jt. tr. see Von Schiefner, F. Anton.

Ralston, William S. Russian Folk-Tales. Dorson, Richard M., ed. LC 77-70619. (International Folklore Ser.). 1977. reprint ed. lib. bdg. 33.95 (*0-405-10122-8*) Ayer.

Raluy, Poudevida A. Porrua Dictionary of the Spanish Language: Diccionario Porrua de la Lengua Espanola. 26th ed. 849p. (SPA.). 1985. 10.95 (*0-8288-2057-0*, S12281) Fr & Eur.

Raluy Poudevila, Antonio. Diccionario Porrua de la Lengua Espanola. Monterde, Francisco, ed. (SPA.). pap. 10.95 (*0-686-56694-7*, S-12281) Fr & Eur.

— Diccionario Porrua de la Lengua Espanola Para Escuelas Primarias. Monterde, Francisco, ed. 461p. (SPA.). pap. 8.95 (*0-7859-0712-2*, S-12282) Fr & Eur.

Ralya, Jerry, jt. auth. see Parker, Charles S.

Ram, jt. auth. see Tyle.

Ram, Akrishan, jt. auth. see Shah, Amit.

***Ram, Ashwin & Leake, David B., eds.** Goal-Driven Learning. (Illus.). 500p. 1994. 55.00 (*0-262-18165-7*, Bradford Bks) MIT Pr.

Ram, Ashwin, jt. ed. see DesJardins, Marie.

***Ram, Aswin & Eiselt, Kurt, eds.** Proceedings of the Sixteenth Annual Conference of the Cognitive Science Society: Atlanta, Georgia, 1994. 1016p. 1994. pap. 135.00 (*0-8058-1803-0*) L Erlbaum Assocs.

Ram, Atma. Perspectives on Arthur Miller. (C). 1988. 14.50 (*81-7017-240-3*, Pub. by Abhinav II) S Asia.

Ram Atvar Agnihotri. Social & Political Study of Modern Hindi Cinema. 1990. 48.50 (*81-7169-049-1*, Commonwealth) S Asia.

Ram Avtar Vir. Learn to Play on Sitar. (Illus.). 56p. 1980. 12.95 (*0-940500-41-8*) Asia Bk Corp.

Ram, Bhanu P., et al, eds. Immunology: Clinical, Fundamental & Therapeutic Aspects. LC 89-24846. (Immunology, Biochemistry & Biotechnology: Vol. 1). 364p. 1990. text ed. 85.00 (*0-89573-763-9*) VCH Pubs.

Ram, D. Sundar. Role of Opposition Parties in Indian Politics: The Andhra Pradesh Experience. (C). 1992. 29.50 (*81-7100-412-1*, Pub. by Deep) S Asia.

Ram, F., jt. auth. see Pathak, K. B.

Ram, G. M. The Bible of Hinduism. 532p. (C). 1985. 27.50 (*0-317-90509-0*, Pub. by Allied II) S Asia.

Ram, Haggay. Myth & Mobilization in Revolutionary Iran: The Use of the Friday Congregational Sermon. 278p. (C). 1994. lib. bdg. 55.00 (*1-879383-21-7*) Am Univ Pr.

Ram, James. The Science of Legal Judgment: A Treatise Designed to Show the Materials Whereof, & the Process by Which, Courts Construct Their Judgments; & Adapted to Practical & General Use in the Discussion & Determination of Questions of Law. 456p. 1988. reprint ed. lib. bdg. 42.50 (*0-8377-2539-9*) Rothman.

Ram, James & Townshend, John N. A Treatise on Facts As Subjects of Inquiry by a Jury. 3rd ed. 486p. 1982. reprint ed. lib. bdg. 35.00 (*0-8377-1033-2*) Rothman.

Ram, K. Sri. Basic Nuclear Engineering. 1990. 32.00 (*81-224-0130-9*, Pub. by Wiley Eastern II) S Asia.

Ram, Kalpana. Mukkuvar Women: Gender, Hegemony & Capitalist Transformation in a South Indian Fishing Village. (Women in Asia Ser.). 304p. (C). 1991. text ed. 57.95 (*1-85649-031-9*, Pub. by Zed Books UK) Humanities.

Ram, M. D., ed. Surgery Review: A Self-Assessment Study Manual. LC 87-14466. 225p. 1987. pap. 32.50 (*0-941022-09-9*) Appleton Davies.

Ram, Mahabal. High Yielding Varieties of Crops. 2nd ed. (C). 1986. 18.00 (*81-204-0095-X*, Pub. by Oxford IBH II) S Asia.

Ram, Manatha, jt. auth. see Murthy, T.

Ram-Mar, pseud. Romances Del Alma. LC 93-74228. (Coleccion Espejo de Paciencia Ser.). 112p. (Orig.). (SPA.). 1993. pap. 9.95 (*0-89729-714-8*) Ediciones.

Ram, Monder. Managing to Survive: Working Lives in Small Firms. (Warwick Studies in Industrial Relations). 256p. (C). 1994. 54.95 (*0-631-19109-7*) Blackwell Pubs.

***Ram, N. Sri.** Way of Wisdom. 1995. 22.95 (*81-7059-133-3*, Quest) Theos Pub Hse.

***Ram, Nandu.** Beyond Ambedkar: Essays on Dalits in India. (C). 1995. 44.00 (*81-241-0239-2*, Pub. by Har-Anand Pubns II) S Asia.

Ram Nath, Uma. Smoking: Third World Alert. (Illus.). 1986. 29.95 (*0-19-261402-9*) OUP.

Ram, Neil M., et al, eds. Significance & Treatment of VOCs in Water Supplies. (Illus.). 500p. 1989. 88.95 (*0-87371-123-8*, TD449) Lewis Pubs.

***Ram, Nin.** Iris's School Essays. 1995. 16.95 (*0-8062-5353-3*) Carlton.

Ram, Paras. Rep.-Additional Advance & Impex Pass Book Licences. (C). 1989. 125.00 (*0-685-27936-7*) St Mut.

Ram, Raghunath. Soviet Policy Towards Pakistan. 224p. 1989. 35.00 (*0-317-52156-X*, Pub. by S Chand II) St Mut.

***Ram, Raja.** Agricultural Development: Command Area Approach. (C). 1993. 32.00x (*81-7017-299-3*, Pub. by Abhinav II) S Asia.

Ram, Sodhi. Indian Immigrants in Great Britain. 1989. 80.00 (*81-210-0242-7*, Pub. by Inter-India Pubns) S Asia.

RAM Staff. William Lesch: Expansions. Kawaii, K., ed. (Illus.). 102p. (ENG & JPN.). 1992. 49.95 (*4-8457-0667-9*, Pub. by Treville Co Ltd JA) Res Art Media.

Ram, Uri. The Changing Agenda of Israeli Sociology: Theory, Ideology, & Identity. (SUNY Series in Israeli Studies). 264p. (C). 1995. text ed. 59.50x (*0-7914-2301-8*); pap. text ed. 19.95x (*0-7914-2302-6*) State U NY Pr.

Ram, Venkata S., jt. ed. see Kaplan, Norman M.

Rama. Love & Family Life. LC 92-37512. 130p. (Orig.). pap. 9.95 (*0-89389-133-9*) Himalayan Pubs.

Rama, tr. Japji: Meditation in Sikhism. LC 87-26865. 90p. 1987. pap. 5.95 (*0-89389-107-X*) Himalayan Pubs.

Rama, Jager. Hemorrhoids: A Book for Silent Sufferers. 164p. 1990. pap. 8.95 (*0-9625295-0-8*) Colon & Rectal Care.

***Rama, K.** Buddhist Art of Nagarjunakonda. (C). 1995. 88.00x (*81-85067-90-2*, Pub. by Sundeep II) S Asia.

Rama, Mani. The Physically Handicapped in India: Policy & Programme. 223p. (C). 1988. 26.50 (*81-7024-164-2*, Pub. by Ashish II) S Asia.

Rama, P. R., et al, eds. Progress in Fracture Research, 1985. (International Series of Monographs on the Strength & Fracture of Materials & Structures). (Illus.). 114p. 1987. 59.00 (*0-08-035903-5*, Pub. by Pergamon Repr UK) Franklin.

Rama Prasada, tr. see Patanjali.

Rama Rao Pappu & Puligandia, R. Indian Philosophy: Past & Future. (C). 1982. 28.00 (*0-8364-0670-2*); text ed. 18.50 (*0-8364-0789-X*) S Asia.

Rama Rao Pappu, S. S., ed. The Dimensions of Karma. (C). 1987. 38.50 (*81-7001-025-X*, Pub. by Chanakya II) S Asia.

Rama, Ruth. Investing in Food. 290p. (Orig.). 1992. pap. 55.00 (*92-64-13747-5*) OECD.

Rama, Swami. Enlightenment Without God (Mandukya Upanishad) LC 82-83391. 124p. (Orig.). (C). 1982. pap. 7.95 (*0-89389-084-7*) Himalayan Pubs.

— Exercise Without Movement. LC 84-20500. (Illus.). 88p. (Orig.). 1984. pap. 5.95 (*0-89389-089-8*) Himalayan Pubs.

— Freedom from the Bondage of Karma. 2nd ed. 92p. 1977. pap. 5.95 (*0-89389-031-6*) Himalayan Pubs.

— Love Whispers. LC 86-19475. 85p. 1986. 9.95 (*0-89389-099-5*) Himalayan Pubs.

— Path of Fire & Light, Vol. Two: A Practical Companion to Volume One. LC 86-7586. 226p. (Orig.). 1988. pap. 10.95 (*0-89389-112-6*) Himalayan Pubs.

— Perennial Psychology of the Bhagavad Gita. LC 84-25137. 480p. (C). 1982. pap. 14.95 (*0-89389-090-1*) Himalayan Pubs.

— Wisdom of the Ancient Sages: Mundaka Upanishad. LC 90-48615. 181p. (Orig.). 1990. pap. 10.95 (*0-89389-120-7*) Himalayan Pubs.

Rama, Swami, ret. The Valmiki Ramayana, 2 Vols., 1. LC 93-26312. 1993. write for info. (*0-89389-136-3*) Himalayan Pubs.

— The Valmiki Ramayana, 2 Vols., 2. LC 93-26312. 1993. write for info. (*0-89389-138-X*) Himalayan Pubs.

— The Valmiki Ramayana, 2 Vols., Vol. 1. LC 93-26312. 1993. Vol.1. pap. write for info. (*0-89389-137-1*) Himalayan Pubs.

— The Valmiki Ramayana, 2 Vols., Vol. 2. LC 93-26312. 1993. Vol.2. pap. write for info. (*0-89389-139-8*) Himalayan Pubs.

Ramabai, Pandita. The High Caste Hindu Woman. LC 74-33954. (Pioneers of the Woman's Movement: an International Perspective Ser.). (Illus.). 142p. 1976. reprint ed. 16.00 (*0-88355-273-6*) Hyperion Conn.

Ramacciotti, Mary D. Syntax of Il Fiore & of Dante's Inferno As Evidence in the Question of the Authorship of Il Fiore. LC 72-115356. (Catholic University of America. Studies in Romance Languages & Literatures: No. 12). reprint ed. 23.00 (*0-685-05985-5*) AMS Pr.

***Ramacciotti, Mary D., Sr.** Syntax of Il Fiore & of Dante's Inferno As Evidence in the Question of the Authorship of Il Fiore. LC 72-115356. (Catholic University of America: No. 12). Date not set. reprint ed. 37.50 (*0-404-50312-8*) AMS Pr.

Ramachandra Dikshitar, V. R. War in Ancient India. (C). 1987. reprint ed. 26.00 (*81-208-0382-5*, Pub. by Motilal Banarsidass II) S Asia.

***Ramachandra, Vande M.** Satyartha Prakash in English with Comments: Spot Light on Truth. xii, 328p. 1988. text ed. 25.00x (*0-614-00504-3*, Pub. by Sarvadeshik Arya II) Nataraj Bks.

Ramachandran. Sri Sankara Vijayam. 1977. pap. 1.50 (*0-89744-123-0*) Auromere.

Ramachandran & Mahadevan, eds. Gandhi: His Relevance for Our Times. 408p. 1983. 20.00 (*0-934676-32-1*) Greenlf Bks.

Ramachandran, B. & Lau, Ka-Sing. Functional Equations in Probability Theory. (Probability & Mathematical Statistics Ser.). (Illus.). 249p. 1991. text ed. 77.00 (*0-12-437730-0*) Acad Pr.

Ramachandran, C. N. Self-Conscious Structure: A Study of the British Theatre from Buchingham Through Fielding & Sheridan. 210p. 1987. 17.50 (*81-202-0183-3*, Pub. by Ajanta II) S Asia.

Ramachandran, H., ed. Environmental Issues in Agricultural Development. 1990. 26.00 (*81-7022-294-X*, Pub. by Concept II) S Asia.

Ramachandran, H., ed. see De Campos Guimaraes, J. P.

Ramachandran, J. Thin Shells: Theory & Problems. 1993. text ed. 27.50 (*0-86311-272-2*, Pub. by Universities Pr II) Apt Bks.

Ramachandran, K., jt. auth. see Baker, Selwyn J.

Ramachandran, K. S. Archaeology of South India: Tamilnadu. 1980. 40.00 (*0-8364-0669-9*, Pub. by Sundeep II) S Asia.

— Gulf War & Environmental Problems. (C). 1991. text ed. 32.00 (*81-7024-399-8*, Pub. by Ashish II) S Asia.

— Inflation: The Critical Issues. viii, 204p. (C). 1992. 27.95 (*0-7069-5693-1*, Pub. by Vikas II) S Asia.

Ramachandran, K. S., ed. Development Perspectives. 1991. text ed. 25.00 (*0-7069-5332-0*, Pub. by Vikas II) S Asia.

Ramachandran, L. Constipation & Indigestion: Prevention & Cure. 284p. 1985. 14.95 (*0-318-36360-7*) Asia Bk Corp.

— Food Planning: Some Vital Aspects. 392p. 1982. 22.95 (*0-940500-68-X*, Pub. by Allied Pubs II) Asia Bk Corp.

— Handbook of Management for Primary Health Care Centre Personnel. 1993. 15.95 (*0-7069-6820-4*, Pub. by Vikas II) S Asia.

Ramachandran, P. & Oommen, M. A., eds. Some Issues in Development Administration. 223p. (C). 1987. 18.00 (*0-317-89537-0*, Pub. by Oxford IBH II) S Asia.

Ramachandran, P. A. Boundary Element Methods in Transport Phenomena. LC 93-72570. 424p. 1993. 160.00 (*1-56252-184-5*) Computational Mech MA.

— Boundary Element Methods in Transport Phenomena. 400p. 1993. 160.00 (*1-85861-026-5*, Pub. by Elsevier Applied Sci UK) Elsevier.

Ramachandran, P. A. & Chaudhari, R. V. Three-Phase Catalytic Reactors. LC 81-23521. (Topics in Chemical Engineering Ser.: Vol. 2). (Illus.). 440p. 1983. text ed. 218.00 (*0-677-05650-8*) Gordon & Breach.

Ramachandran, R. Urbanization & Urban Systems in India. (Illus.). 380p. 1990. 24.95 (*0-19-562140-9*) OUP.

Ramachandran, R., ed. Recent Advances in Theoretical Physics: Proceedings of the Silver Jubille Workshop, ITT, Kanpur, 5-16 December, 1984. 464p. 1985. 78.00 (*9971-5-0014-0*) World Scientific Pub.

Ramachandran, Suguna, ed. Krishna Chaitanya: A Profile & Selected Papers. xii, 284p. 1991. 30.00 (*81-220-0230-7*) Advent Bks Div.

Ramachandran, T. M. & Rukmini, S., eds. Seventy Years of Indian Cinema, Nineteen Thirteen to Nineteen Eighty-Three. (Illus.). 1985. 49.50 (*0-86132-090-5*) IBD Ltd.

Ramachandran, V., jt. auth. see Lindsay, J. F.

Ramachandran, V. G. Administrative Law. 1100p. 1984. 600.00 (*0-317-54662-7*) St Mut.

— Administrative Law. 2nd ed. (C). 1984. 200.00 (*0-685-36419-4*) St Mut.

— Contempt of Court. (C). 1992. 170.00 (*81-7012-483-2*, Pub. by Eastern Book II) St Mut.

— Fundamental Rights & Constitutional Remedies, Set. 2nd ed. 2452p. 1982. 300.00 (*0-317-54649-X*) St Mut.

— Fundamental Rights & Constitutional Remedies, 2 vols., Set. 2nd ed. (C). 1982. 150.00 (*0-685-39696-7*) St Mut.

— Law of Agency. (C). 1985. 175.00 (*0-685-39762-9*) St Mut.

— Law of Contract, 3 vols., Set. 2nd suppl. ed. (C). 1989. 500.00 (*0-685-36418-6*) St Mut.

— Law of Contract in Three Vols. (C). 1989. 500.00 (*0-89771-776-7*, Pub. by Eastern Book II); pap. 300.00 (*0-685-60269-9*, Pub. by Eastern Book II) St Mut.

— Law of Land Acquisition & Compensation. 7th ed. 1985. 65.00 (*0-317-56736-5*) St Mut.

— Law of Land Acquisition & Compensation, 2 vols., Set. 7th ed. (C). 1990. 425.00 (*0-685-36437-2*) St Mut.

— Law of Land Acquisition & Compensation, with Supplement, 2 vols. 7th ed. (C). 1990. text ed. 425.00 (*0-89771-504-7*) St Mut.

— Law of Limitation in Three Volumes. (C). 1989. 500.00 (*0-89771-788-0*, Pub. by Eastern Book II); pap. 300.00 (*0-685-60268-0*, Pub. by Eastern Book II) St Mut.

— The Law of Parliamentary Privileges in India. 912p. 1972. 135.00 (*0-317-54637-6*) St Mut.

— Law of Writs. 5th rev. ed. (C). 1993. 225.00 (*81-7012-504-9*, Pub. by Eastern Book II) St Mut.

Ramachandran, V. G. & Gopalan. Contempt of Court. 5th ed. 1146p. 1983. 420.00 (*0-317-54659-7*) St Mut.

— Contempt of Court. 6th ed. (C). 1991. 110.00 (*0-685-39766-1*) St Mut.

Ramachandran, V. K. Wage Labour & Unfreedom in Agriculture: An Indian Case Study. (WIDER Studies in Development Economics). 352p. 1991. 79.00 (*0-19-828647-3*) OUP.

Ramachandran, V. S., ed. Encyclopedia of Human Behavior, 4 vols., 1. LC 93-34371. (Illus.). 2765p. 1994. text ed. 149.00 (*0-12-226921-7*) Acad Pr.

— Encyclopedia of Human Behavior, 4 vols., Set. LC 93-34371. (Illus.). 2765p. 1994. text ed. 595.00 (*0-12-226920-9*) Acad Pr.

Ramachandron, C. M. Problems of Higher Education in India. 1987. 27.50 (*0-8364-2218-X*, Pub. by Mittal II) S Asia.

Ramacharaka, Y. The Philosophies & Religions of India. 212p. 1963. 11.95 (*0-318-37149-9*) Asia Bk Corp.

Ramacharaka, Yogi. Advanced Course in Yogi Philosophy. 12.00 (*0-911662-02-2*) Yoga.

— The Bhagavad Gita. 184p. 1978. 6.00 (*0-318-37175-8*) Asia Bk Corp.

— Bhagavad Gita. 9.00 (*0-911662-10-3*) Yoga.

— Fourteen Lessons in Yoga Philosophy. 12.00 (*0-911662-01-4*) Yoga.

— Gnani Yoga. 12.00 (*0-911662-04-9*) Yoga.

— Hatha Yoga. 12.00 (*0-911662-06-5*) Yoga.

— Hindu-Yogi Breathing Exercises. 1976. 9.00 (*0-911662-62-6*) Yoga.

— Hindu-Yogi Practical Water Cure. pap. text ed. 6.00 (*0-911662-12-X*) Yoga.

— Life Beyond Death. 12.00 (*0-911662-09-X*) Yoga.

— Mystic Christianity. 12.00 (*0-911662-08-1*) Yoga.

— Philosophies & Religions of India. 12.00 (*0-911662-05-7*) Yoga.

— Psychic Healing. 12.00 (*0-911662-07-3*) Yoga.

— Raja Yoga. 12.00 (*0-911662-03-0*) Yoga.

— Science of Breath. 9.00 (*0-911662-00-6*) Yoga.

— Science of Breath. 88p. 1969. reprint ed. spiral bd. 3.30 (*0-7873-0691-6*) Mokelumne.

— The Science of Psychic Healing. 190p. 1972. reprint ed. spiral bd. 6.60 (*0-7873-0689-4*) Mokelumne.

— Spirit of the Upanishads. 9.00 (*0-911662-11-1*) Yoga.

— Yogi Philosophy & Oriental Occultism: Correspondence Class Course, Lessons 1 Through VII. (Yogi Bks.). 139p. 1972. reprint ed. spiral bd. 4.95 (*0-7873-0690-8*) Mokelumne.

Ramacher, Shirley I., jt. ed. see Standiford, Richard B.

***Ramacitti.** Do It Yourself Publicity. 1994. 5.99 (*0-517-13619-8*) Random Hse Value.

Ramacitti, David. Do-It-Yourself Marketing. 192p. 1994. 18.95 (*0-8144-7800-X*) AMACOM.

Ramacitti, David F. Do-It-Yourself Advertising. 250p. (Orig.). 1992. pap. 18.95 (*0-8144-7743-7*) AMACOM.

— Do-It-Yourself Publicity. LC 89-81026. 200p. 1991. pap. 17.95 (*0-8144-7773-9*) AMACOM.

Ramackers, Guus J. Integrated Object Modelling: An Executable Specification Framework for Business Analysis & Information System Design. 250p. 1994. pap. 26.50 (*90-5170-244-2*, Pub. by Thesis Pubs NE) IBD Ltd.

Ramadas, S. R., et al. Methods of Synthesis of Thia Analogues of Gonasteroids; Review of Some Recent Syntheses, Reactions & Bioactivities of Pyridyl Sulfides. Senning, A., ed. (Sulfer Report Ser.: Vol. 7, No. 4). 70p. 1987. pap. text ed. 54.00 (3-7186-0442-6) Gordon & Breach.

***Ramade, Francois.** Dictionnaire Encyclopedique de l'Ecologie et des Sciences De. 1993. write for info. (0-7859-8052-0, 2-84074-037-0) Fr & Eur.

— Ecology of Natural Resources. Duffin, W. J., tr. LC 84-3678. 245p. reprint ed. pap. 69.90 (0-7837-0115-2, 2040392) Bks Demand.

— Ecotoxicology. Hodgson, L. J., tr. LC 84-26999. 272p. reprint ed. pap. 77.60 (0-7837-3214-7, 2043232) Bks Demand.

Ramadhan, S. Islam & Nationalism. pap. 2.00 (1-56744-067-3) Kazi Pubns.

Ramadhyani, Rachel, ed. Indians & a Changing Frontier: The Art of George Winter. LC 92-43041. (Illus.). xiv, 270p. 1993. 49.95 (0-87195-097-9) Ind Hist Soc.

Ramadori, G., jt. ed. see Gressner, A. M.

Ramadori, R. Biological Phosphate Removal From Wastewaters: Proceedings of the IAWPRC Specialized Conference Held in Rome, Italy, 28-30 September 1987. (Advances in Water Pollution Control Ser.). 440p. 1987. 90.00 (0-317-66313-5, Pergamon Pr) Elsevier.

Ramadurai, jt. auth. see Biswas.

Ramadurai, S., jt. ed. see O'Sullivan, D.

Ramage, Andrew. Lydian Houses & Architectural Terracottas. LC 78-15507. (Archaeological Exploration of Sardis, Monograph Ser.: No. 5). 104p. 1978. reprint ed. pap. 29.70 (0-7837-2317-2, 2057405) Bks Demand.

Ramage, Andrew, jt. auth. see Ramage, Nancy H.

Ramage, Burr J. Local Government & Free Schools in South Carolina. LC 78-63741. (Johns Hopkins University. Studies in Social Sciences. First Ser. 1882-1883: 12). reprint ed. 11.50 (0-404-61011-0) AMS Pr.

Ramage, C. T. Beautiful Thoughts from French & Italian Authors. 1972. 70.00 (0-87968-713-4) Gordon Pr.

— Beautiful Thoughts from German & Spanish Authors. 1972. 70.00 (0-87968-714-2) Gordon Pr.

Ramage, Craufurd T. Ramage in South Italy. Clay, Edith, ed. (Illus.). 232p. 1986. reprint ed. 20.00 (0-89733-217-2); reprint ed. pap. 10.00 (0-89733-216-4) Academy Chi Pubs.

Ramage, Crawford T. Beautiful Thoughts from Greek Authors. 1973. 69.95 (0-87968-715-0) Gordon Pr.

Ramage, E. S., et al. Roman Satirists & Their Satire: The Fine Art of Criticism in Ancient Rome. LC 74-81538. 212p. 1974. 12.50 (0-8155-5028-6, NP) Noyes.

Ramage, Edwin S. Nature & Purpose of Augustus' "Res Gestae" (Historia Einzelschriften Ser.: No. 54). 160p. (Orig.). 1987. pap. 38.00 (3-515-04892-8) Coronet Bks.

Ramage, Edwin S., ed. Atlantis, Fact or Fiction? LC 77-23624. 224p. reprint ed. pap. 63.90 (0-8357-5836-2, 2056248) Bks Demand.

Ramage, Edwin T., jt. ed. see Bright, David F.

Ramage, James A. John Wesley Hunt: Pioneer Merchant, Manufacturer, & Financier. LC 74-7881. (Kentucky Bicentennial Bookshelf Ser.). 115p. reprint ed. pap. 32.80 (0-7837-2422-5, 2042568) Bks Demand.

— Rebel Raider: The Life of General John Hunt Morgan. 320p. 1995. pap. 18.95 (0-8131-0839-X) U Pr of Ky.

Ramage, Janet. Energy: A Guidebook. (Illus.). 345p. 1983. pap. 17.50 (0-19-289157-X) OUP.

Ramage, Jesse. War Toys. LC 81-84846. 1982. 8.95 (0-87212-160-7) Libra.

Ramage, John D. & Bean, John C. Writing Arguments. 2nd ed. (Illus.). 816p. (C). 1991. pap. write for info. (0-02-398120-2) Macmillan.

— Writing Arguments: A Rhetoric with Readings. 3rd abr. ed. 512p. (C). 1995. pap. write for info. (0-02-398141-5) Macmillan.

— Writing Arguments: A Rhetoric with Readings. 3rd ed. 800p. (C). 1995. pap. write for info. (0-02-398145-8) Macmillan.

Ramage, Michael S. Pennsylvania Elder Law Handbook. (Orig.). 1994. pap. 9.95 (0-9640206-7-X) Elder Law Pr.

Ramage, Nancy H. & Ramage, Andrew. Roman Art: Romulus to Constantine. (Illus.). 304p. 1991. 49.50 (0-8109-3755-7) Abrams.

— Roman Art: Romulus to Constantine. 1990. pap. text ed. 46.67 (0-13-782947-7, 620102) P-H.

Ramage, R. The Companies Acts - Table A, 1856-1986. 2nd ed. 1985. 70.00 (0-406-35124-4, U.K.) Butterworth Legal Pubs.

Ramage, R. W., ed. Kelly's Draftsman. 16th ed. 900p. 1993. U. K. 180.00 (0-406-00190-1); write for info. (0-406-00191-X) Butterworth Legal Pubs.

Ramage, Timothy G., ed. see Stoner, Michael W. & Reichow, Alan W.

Ramahlo, Jose A. One Hundred Eleven Clipper Functions, Set. LC 91-37357. (General-Advanced Ser.). (Illus.). 320p. (Orig.). 1992. disk, pap. 29.95 (1-55622-246-7) Wordware Pub.

Ramaiah, G. Sundara. A Philosophical Study of the Mysticism of Sankara. 1983. 12.00 (0-686-88924-X, Pub. by KP Bagchi IA) S Asia.

Ramaiah, L. S. Communicative Language Teaching: A Bibliographical Survey of Resourses. 1986. 17.50 (0-8364-1556-6, Pub. by Indian Doc Serv II) S Asia.

— Documentation & Bibliographic Control of the Humanities in India. (C). 1992. 32.00 (81-85689-06-7, Pub. by Aditya Prakashan II) S Asia.

Ramaiah, L. S., jt. auth. see Pathak, Vijay.

Ramaiya, A. Guide to Companies Act. (C). 1988. 340.00 (0-685-25703-7) St Mut.

— Guide to Companies Act. 11th ed. (C). 1988. 440.00 (0-685-36538-7) St Mut.

— Guide to the Companies Act. (C). 1990. 220.00 (0-89771-220-X) St Mut.

Ramaiya, R. Company Law Digest, 1956-1990. (C). 1990. 400.00 (0-89771-221-8) St Mut.

Ramakant & Upretty. Indo-Nepal Relations. (C). 1991. text ed. 60.00 (0-7855-0143-6, Pub. by Ratna Pustak Bhandar) St Mut.

Ramakant, M. A. & Phil, D. China & South Asia. 1988. 17.50 (81-7003-092-7) South Asia Pubns.

Ramakant, R. Indo-Nepalese Relations. 1968. text ed. 35.00 (0-685-14080-6) Coronet Bks.

Ramakrihna, P., ed. Proceedings of the International Conference Advances in Composite Materials. (C). 1991. 74.00 (81-204-0572-2, Pub. by Oxford IBH II) S Asia.

Ramakrishn-Ananda, jt. auth. see Dobbie-Bateman, A. F.

Ramakrishna. God & Divine Incarnations. 1947. pap. 2.50 (0-87481-445-6, Pub. by Ramakrishna Math II) Vedanta Pr.

***Ramakrishna, Kilaparti.** Global Warming & International Law: A Review of Strategies. 450p. 1995. text ed. 49.95 (1-55963-413-8) Island Pr.

— Global Warming & International Law: A Review of Strategies. 450p. (C). 1995. pap. text ed. 29.95 (1-55963-414-6) Island Pr.

Ramakrishna, Sri. Sayings of Sri Ramakrishna. pap. 4.95 (0-87481-431-6, Pub. by Ramakrishna Math II) Vedanta Pr.

— Tales & Parables of Sri Ramakrishna. 1943. pap. 4.95 (0-87481-493-6) Vedanta Pr.

— Teachings of Sri Ramakrishna. (C). 1934. pap. 4.95 (0-87481-133-3, Pub. by Advaita Ashrama II) Vedanta Pr.

— Words of the Master. Brahmananda, Swami, ed. 1932. pap. 1.50 (0-87481-135-X, Pub. by Advaita Ashrama II) Vedanta Pr.

Ramakrishna, Swami. Tales from Ramakrishna. (Illus.). 54p. (Orig.). (J). (gr. 1-5). 1975. pap. 1.95 (0-87481-152-X, Pub. by Advaita Ashrama II) Vedanta Pr.

Ramakrishnam, K. Introducing India. 88p. 1982. 10.95 (0-940500-95-7, Pub. by Pubns Div II) Asia Bk Corp.

Ramakrishnan, Alladi, ed. see Institute of Mathematical Sciences (India).

Ramakrishnan, P., ed. Metal, Ceramic & Composite Powders. (C). 1990. 24.00 (81-204-0533-1, Pub. by Oxford IBH II) S Asia.

— Powder Metallurgy Alloys: Proceedings of the Symposium on Powder Metallurgy Alloys Held at I. I. T. Bombay on 11th October, 1980. 124p. (C). 1982. text ed. 70.00 (90-6191-406-X, Pub. by A A Balkema NE) Ashgate Pub Co.

— Powder Metallurgy & Related High Temperature Materials. 500p. 1988. text ed. 184.00 (0-87849-577-0, Pub. by Trans Tech GW) LPS Dist Ctr.

— Powder Metallurgy Opportunity for Engineering Industries. (C). 1987. 18.00 (81-204-0173-5, Pub. by Oxford IBH II) S Asia.

Ramakrishnan, P. S. Shifting Agriculture & Sustainable Development. (Man & the Biosphere Ser.: Vol. 10). (Illus.). 550p. (C). 1992. 85.00 (1-85070-383-3) Prthnon Pub.

Ramakrishnan, Prema. King Kamel. (Illus.). 24p. (Orig.). (J). (gr. k-3). 1980. pap. 2.50 (0-89744-210-5, Pub. by Childrens Bk Trust II) Auromere.

***Ramakrishnan, Raghu, ed.** Applications of Logic Databases. (International Series in Engineering & Computer Science, Natural Language Processing & Machine Translation). 304p. (C). 1994. lib. bdg. 95.00 (0-7923-9533-6) Kluwer Ac.

Ramakrishnan, S. Cytotoxic Conjugates. LC 93-4767. (Medical Intelligence Unit Ser.). 1993. 89.95 (1-879702-60-6) R G Landes.

Ramakrishnan, S., jt. auth. see Rajagopal, G.

Ramakrishnananda, Swami. For Thinkers on Education. 226p. 1949. 3.95 (0-87481-450-2) Vedanta Pr.

— Krishna: Pastoral & Kingmaker. 1909. pap. 1.95 (0-87481-447-2) Vedanta Pr.

Ramakrishna's Disciples Staff. Message of Our Master. 1936. pap. 1.95 (0-87481-102-3) Vedanta Pr.

— Spiritual Talks. 1936. pap. 3.95 (0-87481-103-1, Pub. by Advaita Ashrama II) Vedanta Pr.

Ramakrisnan, S., et al. Landlords & Land Reform: Socio-Economic Impact on Landlords in Taiwan. 115p. reprint ed. pap. 32.80 (0-7837-3872-2, 2043708) Bks Demand.

Ramakrisnananda, Swami. Life of Sri Ranauja. 1979. pap. 4.95 (0-87481-446-4) Vedanta Pr.

Ramakrshna, Kilaparti & Woodwell, George M., eds. World Forests for the Future: Their Use & Conservation. LC 92-34492. 208p. (C). 1993. text ed. 20.00 (0-300-05749-0) Yale U Pr.

Ramakumar, R. Engineering Reliability: Fundamentals & Applications. 496p. 1992. text ed. 78.00 (0-13-276759-7) P-H.

— Technical Demography. (C). 1987. pap. 9.50 (0-85226-743-6, Pub. by Wiley Eastern II) S Asia.

Ramal, jt. auth. see Kolar.

Ramal, Walter, pseud. Songs of Childhood. (Granger Poetry Library). 184p. 1985. reprint ed. 19.75 (0-89609-257-7) Roth Pub Inc.

Ramaley, Judith, et al. Molecular & Biochemical Aspects of Progesterone Function. 173p. 1972. text ed. 29.75 (0-8290-2380-1) Irvington.

Ramaley, William C. Applied Calculus. 736p. (C). 1994. text ed. write for info. (0-697-21635-7) Wm C Brown Pubs.

— Functional Calculus: Brief Calculus for Management, Life, & Social Sciences. 592p. (C). 1994. text ed. write for info. (0-697-21625-X) Wm C Brown Pubs.

Ramaley, William C. & Foard, Pat. Student's Solutions Manual to Accompany Functional Calculus & Applied Calculus. 128p. (C). 1995. spiral bd. write for info. (0-697-21629-2) Wm C Brown Pubs.

Ramalho, R. S. Introduction to Wastewater Treatment Processes. 2nd ed. 1983. text ed. 89.00 (0-12-576560-6) Acad Pr.

Ramalingam, T., jt. auth. see Goel, Prem K.

Ramalingam, Vimala, et al. Medicinal Plants, Vol. 1. Singh, N. & Mital, H. C., eds. 161p. 1974. text ed. 22.50 (0-8422-7240-2) Irvington.

Ramalingham, R., jt. ed. see Kops, L.

Ramamani, V. S. Tribal Economy: Problems & Prospects. 1988. 34.00 (0-317-90510-4, Pub. by Chugh Pubns II) S Asia.

Ramamoorthy, S. & Baddaloo, E. Evaluation of Environmental Data for Regulatory & Impact Assessment. (Studies in Environmental Science: No. 41). 466p. 1991. 171.50 (0-444-88530-7) Elsevier.

***Ramamoorthy, S. & Baddaloo, E. G.** Handbook of Chemical Toxicity Profiles of Biological Species Vol. 1: Aquatic Species. LC 94-41896. 464p. 1995. 95.00 (1-56670-013-2, L1013) Lewis Pubs.

Ramamoorthy, S., jt. auth. see Moore, J. W.

Ramamoorthy, T. P., et al, eds. Biological Diversity of Mexico: Origins & Distributions. (Illus.). 856p. 1993. 79.95 (0-19-506674-X) OUP.

Ramamoorty, M., ed. Automation & Instrumentation for Power Plants: Proceedings of the IFAC Symposium, December 15-17, 1986, Bangalore, India. (IFPS Proceedings Ser.: No. 8700). 360p. 1989. 140.00 (0-08-034197-7, Pergamon Pr) Elsevier.

Ramamritham, Krithi, jt. auth. see Stankovic, John A.

Ramamurthy, Vaidhyanathan, ed. Photochemistry in Organized & Constrained Media. 526p. 1991. lib. bdg. 135.00 (0-89573-775-2) VCH Pubs.

Ramamurti, Ravi & Vernon, Raymond. Privatization & Control of State-Owned Enterprises. (EDI Development Study). 344p. 1991. 21.95 (0-8213-1863-2, 11863) World Bank.

Ramamurty, A. The Central Philosophy of the Rig-Veda. (C). 1991. 32.00 (81-202-0306-2, Pub. by Ajanta II) S Asia.

Ramamurty, P. The Problems of Indian Polity. 487p. 1986. 28.00 (81-212-0042-3, Pub. by Gian Publng Hse II) S Asia.

Ramamyya, N. Venkata. Studies in the History of the Third Dynasty of Vijayanagara. 568p. 1986. 30.00 (81-212-0066-0, Pub. by Gian Publng Hse II) S Asia.

***Raman.** Oh Cards. 1995. 34.95 (1-896018-02-5) Atrium Pubs.

— Probate & Administration in Singapore & Malaysia - Law & Practice. 1991. 122.00 (0-409-99602-5) Butterworth Legal Pubs.

— Saga. 1995. 17.50 (1-896018-24-6) Atrium Pubs.

Raman, A. & Labine, P., eds. Reviews on Corrosion Inhibitors Science & Technology. LC 92-61226. 716p. 1993. pap. 120.00 (1-877914-42-8) NACE Intl.

Raman, A., jt. auth. see Ananthakrishnan, T. N.

Raman, B. V. Ashtakavarga System of Prediction. (C). 1993. text ed. 6.50 (81-85674-25-6, Pub. by UBS Pubs Dist II) S Asia.

— Female Horoscopy: Strijataka. rev. ed. (C). 1992. pap. 5.00 (81-85674-40-X, Pub. by UBS Pubs Dist II) S Asia.

— Hindu Astrology & the West. (BVR Astrology Ser.). (C). 1992. pap. 6.00 (81-85273-97-9, Pub. by UBS Pubs Dist II) S Asia.

— Hindu Predictive Astrology. (C). 1992. 6.00 (81-85273-93-6, Pub. by Ranjan Pubs II) S Asia.

— How to Judge a Horoscope, 2 vols. 1991. reprint ed. pap. write for info. (0-318-68535-3) S Asia.

— How to Judge a Horoscope, 2 vols., 1. 1991. reprint ed. pap. 12.50 (0-685-72493-X) S Asia.

— How to Judge a Horoscope, 2 vols., 2. 1991. reprint ed. pap. 12.50 (81-208-0845-2) S Asia.

— Manual of Hindu Astrology: Correct Casting of Horoscopes. (BVR Astrology Ser.). (C). 1992. pap. 4.50 (81-85674-29-9, Pub. by UBS Pubs Dist II) S Asia.

— Muhurtha (Electional Astrology) (C). 1993. 6.50x (81-85674-68-X, Pub. by UBS Pubs Dist II) S Asia.

— My Experiences in Astrology. (BVR Astrology Ser.). (C). 1992. 6.00 (81-85273-73-1, Pub. by UBS Pubs Dist II) S Asia.

— Notable Horoscopes. (C). 1991. reprint ed. 14.00 (81-208-0900-9, Pub. by Motilal Banarsidass II) S Asia.

— Planetary Influences on Human Affairs. (C). 1992. 4.50 (81-85273-90-1, Pub. by Ranjan Pubs II) S Asia.

— Prasna Marga, Pt. 2. (ENG & SAN.). (C). 1992. text ed. 17.50 (81-208-1034-1, Pub. by Motilal Banarsidass II); pap. text ed. 11.50 (81-208-1035-X, Pub. by Motilal Banarsidass II) S Asia.

— Prasna Marga, Part 1: English Translation with Original Text in Devanagri & Notes. (C). 1991. reprint ed. 12.50 (81-208-0918-1, Pub. by Motilal Banarsidass II); reprint ed. 12.52 (81-208-0914-9, Pub. by Motilal Banarsidass II) S Asia.

— Raman's One Hundred Ten Year Ephemeris of Planetary Positions (1891-2000 AD) (BVR Astrology Ser.). (C). 1992. pap. 6.00 (81-85273-92-8, Pub. by UBS Pubs Dist II) S Asia.

— Three Hundred Important Combinations: Indian Astrology. (C). 1991. reprint ed. 12.50 (81-208-0843-6, Pub. by Motilal Banarsidass II) S Asia.

— Varshaphal or the Hindu Progressed Horoscope. (BVR Astrology Ser.). (C). 1992. pap. 5.00 (81-85674-24-8, Pub. by UBS Pubs Dist II) S Asia.

***Raman, Bangalore V.** Hindu Predictive Astrology. (C). 1993. 6.50x (81-85273-54-5, Pub. by UBS Pubs Dist II) S Asia.

— Sri Neelakanta's Prasna Tantra: Horary Astrology. Astrological Magazine Staff, ed. (Orig.). (C). 1993. pap. text ed. 6.50x (81-85674-66-3, Pub. by UBS Pubs Dist II) S Asia.

Raman, C. V. Scientific Papers of C. V. Raman, Vol. 1: Scattering of Light. Ramaseshan, S., ed. (Illus.). 608p. 1989. 49.95 (81-85324-01-8) OUP.

— Scientific Papers of C. V. Raman, Vol. 2: Acoustics. Ramaseshan, S., ed. (Illus.). 668p. 1989. 49.95 (81-85324-02-6) OUP.

— Scientific Papers of C. V. Raman, Vol. 3: Optics. Ramaseshan, S., ed. (Illus.). 576p. 1989. 49.95 (81-85324-03-4) OUP.

— Scientific Papers of C. V. Raman, Vol. 4: Optics of Minerals & Diamond. Ramaseshan, S., ed. (Illus.). 766p. 1989. 49.95 (81-85324-04-2) OUP.

— Scientific Papers of C. V. Raman, Vol. 5: Physics of Crystals. Ramaseshan, S., ed. (Illus.). 874p. 1989. 49.95 (81-85324-05-0) OUP.

— Scientific Papers of C. V. Raman, Vol. 6: Floral Colors & Visual Perception. Ramaseshan, S., ed. (Illus.). 636p. 1989. 49.95 (81-85324-06-9) OUP.

Raman, Chandrasekhara V. New Physics. LC 73-128292. (Essay Index Reprint Ser.). 1977. 19.95 (0-8369-2020-1) Ayer.

***Raman, Ely.** Persona. 1995. 24.95 (1-896018-32-7) Atrium Pubs.

Raman, G. Venkat, jt. auth. see Lee, H. A.

Raman, K. Venkatesha. Project Management Techniques for R & D in Agriculture. 1993. 30.00 (81-207-1471-7, Pub. by Sterling Pubs II) Apt Bks.

Raman, N., jt. auth. see Natarajan, K.

Raman, N. S. Shri Varadrajswamy Temple-Kanchi. (Illus.). 206p. 1975. 29.95 (0-318-36252-X) Asia Bk Corp.

Raman, Narayan. Real Time Scheduling Problems in a General Flexible Manufacturing System. LC 93-49427. (Studies on Industrial Productivity). 136p. 1994. 38.00 (0-8153-1672-0) Garland.

Raman, Papri Sri, jt. auth. see Sen, Abhijit.

Raman, R. Chemical Process Computations. 592p. 1985. 144.00 (0-85334-341-1, Pub. by Elsevier Applied Sci UK) Elsevier.

Raman, Rajeswari. Hatha Yoga for All. (C). 1991. reprint ed. 5.00 (81-208-0937-8, Pub. by Motilal Banarsidass II) S Asia.

Raman, S. Capture Gamma-Ray Spectroscopy & Related Topics 1984: International Symposium, Knoxville, Tennessee. LC 84-73303. (AIP Conference Proceedings Ser.: No. 125). 984p. 1985. lib. bdg. 65.50 (0-88318-324-2) Am Inst Physics.

Raman, Sunder. Constitutional Amendments in India, 1950-1989. (C). 1990. 85.00 (0-89771-198-X) St Mut.

Raman, V. Glimpses of Indian Heritage. 1989. 31.00 (0-86132-181-2, Pub. by Popular Prakashan II) S Asia.

Ramana, D. V. Economics of Sericulture & Silk Industry in India. (C). 1987. 21.00 (81-7100-034-7, Pub. by Deep) S Asia.

Ramana, M. V. Inter-State River Water Disputes in India. 1993. 15.95 (0-86311-343-5, Pub. by Orient Longman Ltd II) Apt Bks.

Ramanadham, V. V. The Economics of Public Enterprise. 432p. (C). 1991. text ed. 89.95 (0-415-04332-8, A4891) Routledge.

— Privatisation in the UK. 256p. (C). 1988. lib. bdg. 69.50 (0-415-00150-1) Routledge.

— Public Enterprises & Income Distribution. 160p. 1989. 57.50 (0-415-00916-2) Routledge.

— Studies in Public Enterprise. 275p. 1986. 42.00 (0-7146-3267-8, Pub. by F Cass Pubs UK) Intl Spec Bk.

— The Yugoslav Enterprise. (ICPE Monograph: No. 2). 61p. 1981. pap. 10.00 (92-9038-901-X, Pub. by Intl Ctr Pub Ent XV) Kumarian Pr.

Ramanadham, V. V., ed. Constraints & Impacts of Privatization. LC 93-9827. 1993. write for info. (0-415-09826-2) Routledge.

— Joint Ventures & Public Enterprises in Developing Countries. 231p. 1980. pap. 20.00 (92-9038-040-3, Pub. by Intl Ctr Pub Ent XV) Kumarian Pr.

— Privatisation: A Global Perspective. 480p. 1992. 89.95 (0-415-07566-1, A7521) Routledge.

— Privatisation in Developing Countries. 400p. 1989. 67.50 (0-415-03815-4, A3675) Routledge.

— Privatization & After: Monitoring & Regulation. LC 94-3978. 256p. 1994. 89.95x (0-415-11112-9, B4300) Routledge.

— Privatization & Equity. LC 94-28093. 272p. 1995. 75.00x (0-415-11898-0, C0108) Routledge.

— Public Enterprise: Studies in Organisational Structure. 275p. 1986. 35.00 (0-7146-3248-1, Pub. by F Cass Pubs UK) Intl Spec Bk.

Ramanamma, A. Women in Indian Industry. 232p. 1987. 27.50 (0-8364-2085-3, Pub. by Mittal II) S Asia.

Ramanamurty, Y. V., jt. ed. see Rawer, Karl.

Ramanan, K. Venkata. Nagarjuna's Philosophy. 409p. (C). 1987. reprint ed. 18.00 (81-208-0159-8, Pub. by Motilal Banarsidass II) S Asia.

Ramanan, S., ed. Proceedings of the Hyderabad Conference on Algebraic Groups. 546p. 1991. 60.00 (81-231-0090-6, HCAG/1C) Am Math.

Ramanan, S., ed. see Van der Kallen, W. L.

Ramanarayanan, R., ed. Particle Design Via Crystallization. LC 91-29216. (AIChE Symposium Ser.: Vol. 87, No. 284). 203p. 1991. pap. text ed. 60.00 (0-8169-0553-3) Am Inst Chem Eng.

***Ramanarayanan, T. A., et al, eds.** Proceedings of the International Symposium on Ionic & Mixed Conducting Ceramics, 2nd. LC 94-70844. (Proceedings Ser.: Vol. 94-12). 652p. 1994. 68.00 (1-56677-044-0) Electrochem Soc.

Ramanathan, Indira. China & the Ethnic Chinese in Malaysia & Indonesia 1949-1992. (C). 1994. 18.50 (81-7027-196-7, Pub. by Radiant Pubs II) S Asia.

Ramanathan, Ramu. Introduction to Econometrics with Applications. 2nd ed. 650p. (C). 1992. text ed. 57.25 (0-15-546489-2) Dryden Pr.

R

An Asterisk (*) at the beginning of an entry indicates that the title is appearing in BIP for the first time.

— Introductory Econometrics with Applications. 614p. (C). 1988. text ed. 53.25 (*0-15-546485-X*); 1.25 (*0-15-546486-8*) HB Coll Pubs.
— Statistical Methods in Econometrics. (Illus.). 405p. 1993. text ed. 55.00 (*0-12-576830-3*) Acad Pr.
Ramanathan, Sivam. Obstetric Anesthesia. LC 87-17293. 432p. reprint ed. pap. 123.20 (*0-7837-2742-9*, 2043122) Bks Demand.
Ramanayya, N. Venkata. Vijayanagara Origin of the City & the Empire. (C). 1990. 19.00 (*81-206-0545-4*, Pub. by Asian Educ Servs II) S Asia.
Ramanayyan, Venkata. An Essay on the Origin of the South Indian Temples. (Illus.). 92p. 1986. reprint ed. 15.00 (*0-8364-1725-9*, Pub. by Manohar II) S Asia.
Ramanda, S. Communications with Reality. 1993. pap. 12.95 (*0-533-10354-1*) Vantage.
Ramani, P. S. Stop Worrying about Backache. 102p. 1983. 8.95 (*0-318-36400-X*) Asia Bk Corp.
***Ramani, R. V., ed.** Longwall-Shortwall Mining, State of the Art. fac. ed. LC 81-67436. (Illus.). 306p. 1981. reprint ed. pap. 87.30 (*0-7837-7849-X*, 2047608) Bks Demand.
Ramani, R. V. & Ghose, A. K. Longwall Thick Seam Mining. 1988. 26.00 (*81-204-0267-7*, Pub. by Oxford IBH II) S Asia.
Ramani, R. V., jt. ed. see Frantz, R. L.
Ramani, R. V., ed. see International Symposium on the Application of Computers & Operations Research in the Mineral Industries Staff.
***Ramani, R. V., et al.** Computers in Mineral Industry. (Illus.). 366p. (C). 1994. text ed. 55.00 (*90-5410-242-X*) Ashgate Pub Co.
Ramani, Raja V., ed. Longwall-Shortwall Mining: State-of-the-Art. LC 81-67436. (Illus.). 296p. 1981. 5.00 (*0-89520-288-3*) SMM&E Inc.
Ramani, Raja V. & Ghose, Ajoy K., eds. Longwall Thick Seam Mining: Proceedings of the Indo-U. S. Seminar on Longwall Mining Systems for Thick Seam Mining - Assessment of Progress & Needs, Indian School of Mines, Dhanbad, 11-13 January 1986. 270p. (C). 1988. text ed. 105.00 (*90-6191-901-0*, Pub. by A A Balkema NE) Ashgate Pub Co.
Ramani, S., ed. Data Communication & Computer Networks. 310p. 1981. 46.75 (*0-685-01549-1*, North Holland) Elsevier.
Ramani, S., et al, eds. Knowledge Based Computer Systems: International Conference KBCS '89, Bombay, India, December 11-13, 1989 Proceedings. (Lecture Notes in Artificial Intelligence Ser.: Vol. 444). x, 546p. 1990. pap. 51.50 (*0-387-52850-4*) Spr-Verlag.
— Proceedings of the International Conference on Computer Communication, 10th, New Delhi, 4-9 November 1990. 800p. 1991. 115.00 (*0-387-53449-0*) Spr-Verlag.
Ramaniah, J. Temples of South India: A Study of Hindu, Jain & Buddhist Monuments of the Deccan. (C). 1989. 52.00 (*81-7022-223-0*, Pub. by Concept II) S Asia.
Ramankutty, Ramesh, jt. auth. see Brandon, Carter.
Ramanuja Research Society Staff. Vishishtadvaita: Philosophy & Religion. 273p. 1975. 10.75 (*0-88253-683-4*) Ind-US Inc.
Ramanujachari, C., tr. see Tyagaraja.
Ramanujam, G. Indian Labour Movement: An History. 348p. 1990. text ed. 50.00 (*81-207-1096-7*, Pub. by Sterling Pubs II) Apt Bks.
***Ramanujan, A. K.** The Collected Poems of A. K. Ramanujan. 300p. 1995. 29.95 (*0-19-563561-2*) OUP.
— Poems of Love & War: From the Eight Anthologies & the Ten Songs of Classical Tamil. LC 84-12182. 320p. 1985. pap. text ed. 17.50 (*0-231-05107-7*) Col U Pr.
— Second Sight. 72p. 1986. pap. 5.95 (*0-19-561874-2*) OUP.
Ramanujan, A. K., ed. Folktales from India. (Fairy Tale & Folklore Library). (Illus.). 384p. 1994. reprint ed. pap. 16.00 (*0-679-74832-6*) Pantheon.
Ramanujan, A. K., tr. The Interior Landscape: Love Poems from a Classical Tamil Anthology. (India Paperbacks Ser.). 130p. 1994. pap. 7.95 (*0-19-563501-9*) OUP.
— Speaking of Siva. (Classics Ser.). 200p. 1973. pap. 9.95 (*0-14-044270-7*, Pub. by Penguin Classics) Viking Penguin.
Ramanujan, A. K. & Krishnamurthi, M. G., eds. Some Kannada Poems. 1975. pap. 8.00 (*0-88253-636-2*) Ind-US Inc.
Ramanujan, A. K., tr. see Adiga, M. G.
Ramanujan, A. K., jt. ed. see Dharwadker, Vinay.
Ramanujan, A. K., et al, eds. When God Is a Customer: Telugu Courtesan Songs by Ksetrayya & Others. LC 93-28264. (C). 1994. 25.00 (*0-520-08068-8*); pap. 12.00 (*0-520-08069-6*) U CA Pr.
Ramanujan, G. The Honey Bee: Towards a New Concept in Industrial Relations. 124p. 1984. text ed. 13.95 (*0-86590-181-3*, Pub. by Sterling Pubs II) Apt Bks.
Ramanujan, M. S., jt. auth. see Dubinsky, Ed.
Ramanujan, S. R. The Lost Notebook. xxvi, 419p. 1988. 64.00 (*0-387-18726-X*) Spr-Verlag.
Ramas, D. Steve, ed. see Finke, Blythe F.
Ramasami, T. Education & Personality Development. (Illus.). x, 159p. 1993. 18.00 (*81-7024-515-X*, Pub. by Ashish Pub Hse II) Nataraj Bks.
Ramasamy, A. History of Pondicherry. 1987. text ed. 35.00 (*81-207-0645-5*, Pub. by Sterling Pubs II) Apt Bks.
Ramasamy, C., jt. ed. see Hazell, Peter B.
Ramasamy, P. Plantation Labour, Unions, Capital, & the State in Peninsular Malaysia. (South-East Asian Social Science Monographs). (Illus.). 320p. 1994. 42.00 (*967-65-3031-X*) OUP.
Ramasarma, T., jt. auth. see Singhal, G. S.
Ramasay, John. Dog Tales. LC 87-80984. (Illus.). 107p. (Orig.). 1987. pap. 5.95 (*0-935680-35-7*) Kentucke Imprints.
Ramaseder, Josef, tr. see Ricard, Rene.
Ramaseshan, S., ed. see Raman, C. V.
Ramashray, Roy. Democracy in Two Nations - U. S. A. & India. 403p. 1982. 29.95 (*0-318-37232-0*) Asia Bk Corp.
— Gandhi: Soundings in Political Philosophy. 1984. 16.00 (*0-8364-1104-8*, Pub. by Chanakya II) S Asia.
Ramasubramanian, R., jt. auth. see Nickalls, R. W.
Ramasut, Arlene, ed. Whole-School Approaches: Meeting the Special Educational Needs of All Children - A Guide to Teachers. 280p. 1989. 75.00 (*1-85000-569-9*, Falmer Pr); pap. 35.00 (*1-85000-570-2*, Falmer Pr) Taylor & Francis.
Ramaswami, Murali & Moeller, Susan E. Investing in Financially Distressed Firms: A Guide to Pre-& Post-Bankruptcy Opportunities. LC 89-10749. 183p. 1990. text ed. 55.00 (*0-89930-404-4*, RRO/, Greenwood Pr) Greenwood.
Ramaswami, N. S. Indian Monuments. 1986. 16.00 (*0-8364-1843-3*, Pub. by Abhinav II) S Asia.
— Political History of Carnatic under the Nawabs. 1985. 40.00 (*0-8364-1262-1*, Pub. by Abhinav II) S Asia.
***Ramaswamy, A. E.** The Rayon Spinners: The Strategic Management of Industrial Relations. 196p. 1995. 22.00 (*0-19-563537-X*) OUP.
Ramaswamy, E. A. The Worker & His Union: A Study in South India. 1977. 9.00 (*0-88386-991-8*) S Asia.
Ramaswamy, G. S. Design & Construction of Concrete Shell Roofs. rev. ed. LC 81-19299. 758p. 1984. lib. bdg. 74.50 (*0-89874-001-0*) Krieger.
— Modern Prestressed Concrete Design. (Illus.). 1976. text ed. 29.95 (*0-8464-0639-X*); pap. 29.95 (*0-686-77190-7*) Beekman Pubs.
Ramaswamy, G. S. & Rao, V. V. S I Units: A Source Book. 1973. text ed. 15.00 (*0-07-096575-7*) McGraw.
Ramaswamy, N. S. Indian Monuments. 187p. 1979. 31.95 (*0-318-37001-8*) Asia Bk Corp.
Ramaswamy, P. New Delhi & Sri Lanka. 300p. 1987. 27.00 (*0-8364-2057-8*, Pub. by Allied II) S Asia.
Ramaswamy, Sundar, jt. auth. see Ramaswamy, Sunita.
Ramaswamy, Sunita & Ramaswamy, Sundar. Vedic Heritage Teaching Program, Vol. III. Schleicher, Irene, ed. 280p. (Orig.). (C). 1994. pap. text ed. write for info. (*1-882325-05-2*) Arsha Vidya.
— Vedic Heritage Teaching Program Teaching Manual, Vol. I. Schleicher, Irene, ed. (Illus.). 294p. (Orig.). 1992. pap. text ed. write for info. (*1-882325-00-1*) Arsha Vidya.
— Vedic Heritage Teaching Program Teaching Manual, Vol. II. Schleicher, Irene, ed. 236p. (Orig.). (C). 1993. pap. text ed. write for info. (*1-882325-03-6*) Arsha Vidya.
***Ramaswamy, T. N.** Essentials of Indian Statecraft: Kautilya's Arthasastra for Contemporary Readers. (C). 1994. text ed. 15.00 (*81-215-0655-7*, Pub. by Munshiram Manoharial II) S Asia.
Ramat, Anna G., et al, eds. Papers from the Seventh International Conference on Historical Linguistics. LC 87-8100. (Current Issues in Linguistic Theory Ser.: Vol. 48). xvi, 672p. (C). 1987. 139.00x (*90-272-3542-2*) Benjamins North Am.
Ramat, Paolo. Linguistic Typology. (Empirical Approaches to Language Typology Ser.: No. 1). (Illus.). xii, 244p. (C). 1987. lib. bdg. 65.35 (*0-89925-085-8*) Mouton.
Ramat, Paolo, jt. ed. see Harris, Martin.
Ramat, Paolo, et al, eds. The History of Linguistics in Italy. LC 86-17407. (Studies in the History of Linguistics: SiHol 33). x, 364p. 1986. 84.00x (*90-272-4515-0*) Benjamins North Am.
— Linguistic Reconstruction & Indo-European Syntax: Proceedings of the Colloquium of the "Indogermanische Gesellschaft", University of Pavia, 6-7 September 1979. (Current Issues in Linguistic Theory Ser.: No 19). viii, 263p. 1980. 59.00x (*90-272-3512-0*) Benjamins North Am.
Ramathal, Jotsna, ed. see Ramathal, Solomon N.
Ramathal, Solomon N. The Story Makers of Those Tormenting Days, Vol. I. Ramathal, Jotsna, ed. LC 89-84858. (Illus.). 440p. (C). 1989. 30.00 (*0-9623406-0-X*) Karnataka Pub.
Ramaurti, Ravi. State-Owned Enterprises in High Technology Industries: Studies in India & Brazil. LC 85-30751. 319p. 1987. text ed. 65.00 (*0-275-92156-5*, C2156, Praeger Pubs) Greenwood.
Ramayana of Kampan. The Forest Book of the Ramayana of Kampan. Hart, George L. & Heifetz, Hank, trs. 336p. (C). 1988. 42.50 (*0-520-06088-1*) U CA Pr.
Ramayya, A. V. & Greiner, Walter. Nuclear Physics of Our Times. 584p. 1993. text ed. 114.00 (*981-02-1358-1*) World Scientific Pub.
***Ramayya, N. Narashimha.** Linguistic Entropy in Othello of Shakespeare. 95p. (C). 1994. 30.00x (*81-85880-22-0*, Pub. by Print Hse II) St Mut.
Ramazani, Jahan. Poetry of Mourning: The Modern Elegy from Hardy to Heaney. LC 93-31581. 1994. pap. text ed. 16.95 (*0-226-70340-1*) U Ch Pr.
— Poetry of Mourning: The Modern Elegy from Hardy to Heaney. LC 93-31581. 1994. lib. bdg. 42.00 (*0-226-70339-8*) U Ch Pr.
— Yeats & the Poetry of Death: Elegy, Self-Elegy & the Sublime. 240p. (C). 1990. text ed. 27.00 (*0-300-04804-1*) Yale U Pr.
Ramazani, P. K. The Persian Gulf & the Strait of Hormuz. (International Straits of the World Ser.: No. 3). 200p. 1979. 35.00 (*0-685-04604-4*) Kluwer Ac.
Ramazani, R. K. Beyond the Arab-Israeli Settlement: New Directions for U. S. Policy in the Middle East. LC 77-87564. (Foreign Policy Reports). 69p. 1977. 11.95 (*0-89549-006-4*) Inst Foreign Policy Anal.
Ramazani, R. K., et al. The Gulf Cooperation Council: Record & Analysis. LC 87-37170. (Illus.). 256p. 1988. 45.00 (*0-8139-1148-6*) U Pr of Va.
Ramazani, R. K. Revolutionary Iran: Challenge & Response in the Middle East. LC 86-45440. 304p. 1987. text ed. 49.50 (*0-8018-3377-9*) Johns Hopkins.
— Revolutionary Iran: Challenge & Response in the Middle East. LC 86-45440. 352p. 1988. reprint ed. pap. text ed. 14.95 (*0-8018-3610-7*) Johns Hopkins.
Ramazani, R. K., ed. Iran's Revolution: The Search for Consensus. LC 89-7516. (Illus.). 160p. 1990. 27.50 (*0-253-34796-3*); pap. 8.95 (*0-253-20548-4*, MB-548) Ind U Pr.
Ramazani, Rouhollah K. Foreign Policy of Iran, Fifteen Hundred to Nineteen Forty-One: A Developing Nation in World Affairs. LC 66-12469. 330p. 1966. 35.00 (*0-8139-0200-2*) U Pr of Va.
— Iran's Foreign Policy, 1941-1973: A Study of Foreign Policy in Modernizing Nations. LC 74-16467. 507p. 1975. 40.00 (*0-8139-0594-X*) U Pr of Va.
— Middle East & the European Common Market. LC 64-13718. 175p. reprint ed. 49.90 (*0-8357-9810-0*, 2013658) Bks Demand.
— The Persian Gulf: Iran's Role. LC 72-77262. (Illus.). 175p. reprint ed. pap. 49.90 (*0-317-08537-9*, 2002291) Bks Demand.
Ramazani, Vaheed K. The Free Indirect Mode: Flaubert & the Poetics of Irony. LC 88-5572. 250p. (C). 1989. text ed. 30.00 (*0-8139-1179-6*) U Pr of Va.
Ramazanoglu, Caroline. Feminism & the Contradictions of Oppression. 196p. 1989. 49.95 (*0-415-02835-3*); pap. 13.95 (*0-415-02836-1*) Routledge.
Ramazanoglu, Caroline, ed. Up Against Foucault: Explorations of Some Tensions Between Foucault & Feminism. LC 93-9861. 1993. write for info. (*0-415-05010-3*); pap. write for info. (*0-415-05011-1*) Routledge.
Ramazanoglu, Gulseren. Turkish Cookery. 4th ed. (Illus.). 120p. (ENG & TUR.). 1993. reprint ed. pap. 9.95 (*975-7489-00-X*, Pub. by Ramazanoglu Yayinlari TU) Bosphorus Bks.
— Turkish Cooking. 2nd ed. Edmonds, Anna G., ed. (Illus.). 96p. (ENG & TUR.). 1992. reprint ed. pap. text ed. 14.95 (*975-7489-05-0*, Pub. by Ramazanoglu Yayinlari TU) Bosphorus Bks.
— Turkish Embroidery. 2nd ed. (Illus.). 104p. 1987. reprint ed. pap. 13.95 (*0-442-26799-1*, Pub. by Ramazanoglu Yayinlari TU) Bosphorus Bks.
Ramazanoglu, Huseyin, ed. Turkey in the World Capitalist System: A Study of Industrialisation, Power & Class. 300p. 1985. text ed. 47.95 (*0-566-05049-8*) Ashgate Pub Co.
Rambach, Peggy. When the Animals Leave. LC 86-70220. 48p. 1986. pap. 4.00 (*0-935331-00-X*) Ampersand RI.
Rambachan, Anantanand. Accomplishing the Accomplished: The Vedas As a Source of Valid Knowledge in Sankara. LC 91-10279. (Society for Asian & Comparative Philosophy Monographs: No. 10). 182p. (C). 1991. pap. text ed. 15.00 (*0-8248-1358-8*) UH Pr.
— Bharata: Love & Justice in the Ramayana. 76p. (Orig.). 1993. pap. 5.00 (*0-9634164-3-X*) Vijnana Pubns.
— Gitamrtam: The Essential Teachings of Bhagavadgita. (C). 1993. pap. 9.50 (*81-208-1167-4*, Pub. by Motilal Banarsidass II) S Asia.
— Hanuman: The Devotee of God. 85p. 1991. pap. 5.00 (*0-9634164-2-1*) Vijnana Pubns.
— Hanuman: The Messenger of God. 94p. 1990. pap. 5.00 (*0-9634164-1-3*) Vijnana Pubns.
— The Hindu Vision. (C). 1992. text ed. 7.00 (*81-208-1059-7*, Pub. by Motilal Banarsidass II) S Asia.
— The Limits of Scripture: Vivekananda's Reinterpretation of the Authority of the Vedas. 186p. 1993. text ed. 31.00 (*0-8248-1542-4*) UH Pr.
— Love & Truth in the Ramayana of Tulsidas. 72p. 1989. pap. 5.00 (*0-9634164-0-5*) Vijnana Pubns.
— Rama Gita: The Dialogues of Rama. 100p. 1994. pap. 5.00 (*0-9634164-4-8*) Vijnana Pubns.
Rambali, Paul. In the Cities & Jungles of Brazil. LC 93-30666. 1994. 23.00 (*0-8050-3079-4*) H Holt & Co.
— In the Cities & Jungles of Brazil. 1995. pap. 12.95 (*0-8050-3078-6*) H Holt & Co.
Rambaud, Alfred N. History of Russia from the Earliest Time to 1882, 3 Vols, Set. enl. ed. Dole, Nathan H., ed. Lang, Leonora B., tr. LC 73-124766. (Illus.). reprint ed. 205.00 (*0-404-05230-4*) AMS Pr.
Rambaut, Paul. Space Medicine. Head, J. J., ed. LC 84-45837. (Carolina Biology Readers Ser.: No. 166). (Illus.). 16p. (Orig.). (YA). (gr. 10 up). 1985. pap. text ed. 2.75 (*0-89278-366-4*, 45-9766) Carolina Biological.
Rambeau, P. Hope. Roman in the Inviolate Realm. (Illus.). 98p. (Orig.). 1994. pap. 14.95 (*0-9638501-9-9*) S David Pubs.
Rambeaud, J. J. & Vincent, F., eds. Local Prostatic Carcinoma. (Contributions to Oncology Ser.: Vol. 47). (Illus.). viii, 146p. 1995. 112.00 (*3-8055-5973-9*) S Karger.
***Rambeck, Richard.** Andre Agassi. (Sports Superstars Ser.). (Illus.). 24p. (J). (gr. 2-6). 1995. lib. bdg. 21.36 (*1-56766-202-1*) Childs World.
— Atlanta Falcons. (NFL Today Ser.). (Illus.). 48p. (J). (gr. 4 up). 1991. lib. bdg. 14.95 (*0-88682-359-5*) Creative Ed.
— Atlanta Hawks. rev. ed. (NBA Today Ser.). (Illus.). 32p. (J). (gr. 4 up). 1993. lib. bdg. 14.95 (*0-88682-560-1*) Creative Ed.
— Babe Ruth. (Sports Superstars Ser.). (ENG & SPA.). (J). (gr. 2-6). 1992. lib. bdg. 21.36 (*0-89565-962-X*) Childs World.
— Babe Ruth. (Sports Superstars Ser.). (ENG & SPA.). (J). (gr. 2-6). 1992. lib. bdg. 21.36 (*1-56766-054-1*) Childs World.
— Baltimore Orioles. (Baseball: The Great American Game Ser.). 48p. (J). (gr. 4-10). 1992. lib. bdg. 14.95 (*0-88682-451-6*) Creative Ed.
— Barry Bonds. (Sports Superstars Ser.). (Illus.). 24p. (J). (gr. 2-6). 1995. lib. bdg. 21.36 (*1-56766-201-3*) Childs World.
— Bonnie Blair. (Sports Superstars Ser.). (Illus.). (J). (gr. 2-6). 1995. lib. bdg. 14.95 (*0-614-04748-X*) Childs World.
— Boston Red Sox. (Baseball: The Great American Game Ser.). 48p. (J). (gr. 4-10). 1992. lib. bdg. 14.95 (*0-88682-450-8*) Creative Ed.
— Cal Ripken. (Sports Biographies Ser.). (ENG & SPA.). (J). (gr. 2-6). 1992. lib. bdg. 21.36 (*0-89565-867-4*) Childs World.
— Cal Ripken. (ENG & SPA.). (J). (gr. 2-6). 1992. lib. bdg. 21.36 (*1-56766-052-5*) Childs World.
— California Angels. (Baseball: The Great American Game Ser.). 48p. (J). (gr. 4-10). 1992. lib. bdg. 14.95 (*0-88682-449-4*) Creative Ed.
— Charlotte Hornets. (NBA Today Ser.). (YA). (gr. 5 up). 1993. lib. bdg. 14.95 (*0-88682-559-8*) Creative Ed.
— Chicago White Sox. (Baseball: The Great American Game Ser.). 48p. (J). (gr. 4-10). 1992. lib. bdg. 14.95 (*0-88682-448-6*) Creative Ed.
— Cincinnati Bengals. (NFL Today Ser.). (J). (gr. 4 up). 1991. lib. bdg. 14.95 (*0-88682-362-5*) Creative Ed.
— Cleveland Browns. (NFL Today Ser.). 48p. (J). (gr. 4 up). 1991. lib. bdg. 14.95 (*0-88682-363-3*) Creative Ed.
— Cleveland Cavaliers. rev. ed. (NBA Today Ser.). (Illus.). 32p. (J). (gr. 4 up). 1993. lib. bdg. 14.95 (*0-88682-527-X*) Creative Ed.
— Cleveland Indians. (Baseball: The Great American Game Ser.). 48p. (J). (gr. 4-10). 1992. lib. bdg. 14.95 (*0-88682-439-7*) Creative Ed.
— Detroit Lions. (NFL Today Ser.). 48p. (J). (gr. 4 up). 1991. lib. bdg. 14.95 (*0-88682-366-8*) Creative Ed.
— Detroit Pistons. rev. ed. (NBA Today Ser.). (Illus.). 32p. (J). (gr. 4 up). 1993. lib. bdg. 14.95 (*0-88682-521-0*) Creative Ed.
— Detroit Tigers. (Baseball: The Great American Game Ser.). 48p. (J). (gr. 4-10). 1991. lib. bdg. 14.95 (*0-88682-447-8*) Creative Ed.
— Hakeem Alajuwon. (Sports Superstars Ser.). (Illus.). 32p. (J). (gr. 2-6). 1995. lib. bdg. 21.36 (*1-56766-200-5*) Childs World.
— Indiana Pacers. (NBA Today Ser.). (Illus.). 32p. (J). (gr. 4 up). 1993. lib. bdg. 14.95 (*0-88682-522-9*) Creative Ed.
— The Indianapolis Colts. (NFL Today Ser.). (J). (gr. 4 up). 1991. lib. bdg. 14.95 (*0-88682-369-2*) Creative Ed.
— Jerry Rice. (Sports Superstars Ser.). (Illus.). 24p. (J). (gr. 2-6). 1995. lib. bdg. 21.36 (*1-56766-204-8*) Childs World.
— Jim Abbott. LC 92-43044. (Sports Superstars Ser.). 32p. (ENG & SPA.). (J). 1993. 21.36 (*1-56766-072-X*) Childs World.
— Jim Abbott. LC 92-43044. (Sports Superstars Ser.). 32p. (ENG & SPA.). (J). 1993. pap. 21.36 (*1-56766-111-4*) Childs World.
— Kansas City Chiefs. (NFL Today Ser.). (J). (gr. 4 up). 1991. lib. bdg. 14.95 (*0-88682-370-6*) Creative Ed.
— Kansas City Royals. (Baseball: The Great American Game Ser.). 48p. (J). (gr. 4-10). 1992. lib. bdg. 14.95 (*0-88682-440-0*) Creative Ed.
— Kristi Yamaguchi. LC 92-43058. 32p. (ENG & SPA.). (J). (gr. 2-6). 1993. 21.36 (*1-56766-071-1*) Childs World.
— Kristi Yamaguchi. LC 92-43058. 32p. (ENG & SPA.). (J). (gr. 2-6). 1993. lib. bdg. 21.36 (*1-56766-109-2*) Childs World.
— Los Angeles Clippers. rev. ed. (NBA Today Ser.). (Illus.). 32p. (J). (gr. 4 up). 1993. lib. bdg. 14.95 (*0-88682-526-1*) Creative Ed.
— Los Angeles Rams. (NFL Today Ser.). (J). (gr. 4 up). 1991. lib. bdg. 14.95 (*0-88682-372-2*) Creative Ed.
— Lou Gehrig. LC 92-40673. (Sports Superstar Ser.). (ENG & SPA.). (J). (gr. 2-6). 1993. lib. bdg. 21.36 (*1-56766-110-6*) Childs World.
— Lou Gehrig. LC 92-40673. (Sports Superstar Ser.). (ENG & SPA.). (J). (gr. 2-6). 1993. lib. bdg. 21.36 (*1-56766-073-8*) Childs World.
— Miami Heat. (NBA Today Ser.). (J). (gr. 5 up). 1993. lib. bdg. 14.95 (*0-88682-561-X*) Creative Ed.
— Milwaukee Brewers. (Baseball: The Great American Game Ser.). 48p. (J). (gr. 4-10). 1992. lib. bdg. 14.95 (*0-88682-441-9*) Creative Ed.
— Minnesota Timberwolves. (NBA Today Ser.). (J). (gr. 5 up). 1993. lib. bdg. 14.95 (*0-88682-524-5*) Creative Ed.
— Minnesota Twins. (Baseball: The Great American Game Ser.). 48p. (J). (gr. 4-10). 1992. lib. bdg. 14.95 (*0-88682-446-X*) Creative Ed.
— New England Patriots. (NFL Today Ser.). 48p. (J). (gr. 4 up). 1991. lib. bdg. 14.95 (*0-88682-375-7*) Creative Ed.
— New York Yankees. (Baseball: The Great American Game Ser.). 48p. (J). (gr. 4-10). 1992. lib. bdg. 14.95 (*0-88682-445-1*) Creative Ed.
— Oakland A's. (Baseball: The Great American Game Ser.). 48p. (J). (gr. 4-10). 1992. lib. bdg. 14.95 (*0-88682-444-3*) Creative Ed.
— Oksana Baiul. (Sports Superstars Ser.). (Illus.). (J). (gr. 2-6). 1995. lib. bdg. 21.36 (*1-56766-205-6*) Childs World.
— Orlando Magic. (NBA Today Ser.). (J). (gr. 5 up). 1993. lib. bdg. 14.95 (*0-88682-558-X*) Creative Ed.
— Philadelphia Eagles. (NFL Today Ser.). 48p. (J). (gr. 4 up). 1991. lib. bdg. 14.95 (*0-88682-379-X*) Creative Ed.
— Phoenix Cardinals. (NFL Today Ser.). 48p. (J). (gr. 4 up). 1991. lib. bdg. 14.95 (*0-88682-381-1*) Creative Ed.
— Phoenix Suns. rev. ed. (NBA Today Ser.). (Illus.). 32p. (J). (gr. 4 up). 1992. lib. bdg. 14.95 (*0-88682-520-2*) Creative Ed.
— Portland Trailblazers. (NBA Today Ser.). (Illus.). 38p. (J). (gr. 4 up). 1993. lib. bdg. 14.95 (*0-88682-518-0*) Creative Ed.
— San Antonio Spurs. (NBA Today Ser.). (J). (gr. 5 up). 1993. lib. bdg. 14.95 (*0-88682-519-9*) Creative Ed.
— San Diego Chargers. (NFL Today Ser.). (J). (gr. 4 up). 1991. lib. bdg. 14.95 (*0-88682-382-X*) Creative Ed.
— Seattle Seahawks. (NFL Today Ser.). (J). (gr. 4 up). 1991. lib. bdg. 14.95 (*0-88682-384-6*) Creative Ed.

R

An Asterisk (*) at the beginning of an entry indicates that the title is appearing in BIP for the first time.

— Shaquille O'Neal. (Sports Superstars Ser.). (Illus.). 24p. (J). (gr. 2-6). 1995. lib. bdg. 21.36 (*1-56766-199-8*) Childs World.

— Tampa Bay Buccaneers. (NFL Today Ser.). (Illus.). 48p. (J). (gr. 4-12). 1991. lib. bdg. 14.95 (*0-88682-385-4*) Creative Ed.

— Texas Rangers. (Baseball: The Great American Game Ser.). 48p. (J). (gr. 4-10). 1992. lib. bdg. 14.95 (*0-88682-443-5*) Creative Ed.

— Toronto Blue Jays. (Baseball: The Great American Game Ser.). 48p. (J). (gr. 4-10). 1992. lib. bdg. 14.95 (*0-88682-442-7*) Creative Ed.

— Utah Jazz. (NBA Today Ser.). 32p. (J). (gr. 4). 1993. lib. bdg. 14.95 (*0-88682-525-3*) Creative Ed.

— Washington Redskins. (NFL Today Ser.). (J). (gr. 4 up). 1991. lib. bdg. 14.95 (*0-88682-386-2*) Creative Ed.

— Wayne Gretsky. (Sports Superstars Ser.). (Illus.). 24p. (J). (gr. 2-6). 1995. lib. bdg. 21.36 (*1-56766-203-X*) Childs World.

Ramberg, Bennett. Nuclear Energy in War: The Implications of Israel's Reactor Strike. (CISA Working Paper Ser.: No. 34). 34p. (Orig.). Date not set. pap. 10.00 (*0-86682-045-0*) Ctr Intl Relations.

— Nuclear Power Plants As Weapons for the Enemy: An Unrecognized Military Peril. 250p. 1985. pap. 12.00 (*0-520-04969-1*) U CA Pr.

Ramberg, Bennett, ed. Arms Control Without Negotiation: From the Cold War to the New World Order. LC 93-9339. 285p. 1993. lib. bdg. 44.00 (*1-55587-376-6*) Lynne Rienner.

Ramberg, Bennett, jt. ed. see Thomas, Raju G.

Ramberg, Bjorn T. Donald Davidson's Philosophy of Language: An Introduction. 240p. 1989. pap. text ed. 24.95 (*0-631-16786-2*) Blackwell Pubs.

Ramberg, Hans. Gravity, Deformation & the Earth's Crust: In Theory, Experiments & Geological Application. 2nd ed. LC 80-41317. 1981. text ed. 148.00 (*0-12-576860-5*) Acad Pr.

Ramberg, Ivar B. & Neumann, Else-Ragnhild, eds. Tectonics & Geophysics of Continental Rifts. (NATO Advanced Study Institute Ser.: No. 37). 1978. lib. bdg. 89.00 (*90-277-0867-3*) Kluwer Ac.

Ramberg, Ivar B., jt. ed. see Neumann, Else-Ragnhild.

Ramberg, Jan. Incoterms in the Era of Electronic Data Interchange. (Forum Internationale Ser.: No. 13). 1989. 24.00 (*90-6544-430-0*) Kluwer Law Tax Pubs.

Rambert, Judy. All New Beautiful Braids. (Illus.). 64p. 1993. spiral bd. 5.98 (*1-56173-231-1*, 3612102) Pubns Intl Ltd.

— Beautiful Braids. 1990. pap. 5.98 (*0-88176-925-8*) Pubns Intl Ltd.

Ramble, Charles, jt. ed. see Rustomji, N. K.

Ramble, Charles, tr. see Rustomji, N. K. & Ramble, Charles, eds.

Rambler. Guide to Florida. LC 64-66300. (Floridiana Facsimile & Reprint Ser.). (Illus.). 1964. reprint ed. 18.95 (*0-8130-0193-5*) U Press Fla.

Rambler, Mitchell B., et al, eds. Global Ecology: Towards a Science of the Biosphere. 204p. 1989. text ed. 49.00 (*0-12-576890-7*) Acad Pr.

Rambler's Association Staff. The Rambler's Yearbook & Accommodation Guide, 1993. 240p. Date not set. pap. 8.95 (*0-900613-74-2*) Atrium Pubs.

— The Rambler's Yearbook & Accommodation Guide 1995. 1995. pap. 9.95 (*0-900613-78-5*) Atrium Pubs.

Rambo, A. Terry. Primitive Polluters: Semang Impact on the Malaysian Tropical Rain Forest. (Anthropological Papers: No. 76). (Illus.). 104p. (Orig.). 1986. pap. 8.00 (*0-915703-04-1*) U Mich Mus Anthro.

Rambo, A. Terry & Gillogly, Kathleen, eds. Profiles in Cultural Evolution: Papers from a Conference in Honor of Elman R. Service. LC 90-25676. (Anthropological Papers: No. 85). xviii, 450p. (Orig.). 1991. pap. 20.00 (*0-915703-23-8*) U Mich Mus Anthro.

Rambo, A. Terry, jt. ed. see Le, Trong Cuc.

Rambo, A. Terry, et al, eds. Ethnic Diversity & the Control of Natural Resources in Southeast Asia. LC 87-62020. (Michigan Papers on South & Southeast Asia: No. 32). (Illus.). 320p. 1987. 31.95 (*0-89148-043-9*); pap. 17.95 (*0-89148-044-7*) Ctr S&SE Asian.

Rambo, Anne H., et al. Practicing Therapy: Exercises for Growing Therapists. 180p. (C). 1993. pap. 14.95 (*0-393-70161-1*) Norton.

— Practicing Therapy: Exercises for Growing Therapists. 180p. (C). 1993. 22.95 (*0-393-70159-X*) Norton.

Rambo, Beverly J. Adaptation Nursing: Assessment & Intervention. (Illus.). 432p. 1984. pap. text ed. 44.00 (*0-7216-1048-X*) Saunders.

— Ward Clerk Skills. LC 77-1819. (Nursing & Allied Health Ser.). 1977. text ed. 25.95 (*0-07-051176-4*) McGraw.

Rambo, Beverly J. & Watson, Diane. Your Career in Health Care. 1976. text ed. 30.95 (*0-07-051166-7*) McGraw.

Rambo, Buck. Legacy of Buck & Dottie Rambo. 1993. 15.99 (*1-56233-041-1*, Star Song Contemp) Star Song TN.

Rambo, Dorothy, ed. see Ceasor, Ebraska D.

Rambo, Elizabeth L. Colonial Ireland in Medieval English Literature. LC 93-46784. 1994. write for info. (*0-945636-61-X*) Susquehanna U Pr.

Rambo, Lewis R. Understanding Religious Conversion. LC 92-39404. 224p. (C). 1993. text ed. 27.00 (*0-300-05283-9*) Yale U Pr.

Rambo, Mary E., jt. auth. see Rambo, Simmeon B.

Rambo, Sarah. Private Pilot-Airplane. LC 82-21299. (Illus.). 194p. 1983. pap. 15.95 (*0-8138-1382-4*) Iowa St U Pr.

Rambo, Simmeon B. & Rambo, Mary E. The Rambo Heritage. (Illus.). 188p. 1983. 25.00 (*0-89308-385-2*, BFH 17) Southern Hist Pr.

***Rambo, William M.** The Student's Textbook of Surgery. LC 95-12316. (Medical Bks.). 1995. text ed. write for info. (*0-393-71032-7*) Norton.

Rambold, G. A Monograph of the Saxicolous Lecideoid Lichens of Australia (excl. Tasmania) (Bibliotheca Lichenologica Ser.: Vol. 34). (Illus.). 346p. 1989. pap. text ed. 91.00 (*3-443-58013-0*, Pub. by Gebruder Borntraeger GW) Lubrecht & Cramer.

Rambold, G. & Triebel, Dagmar. The Inter-Lecanoralean Associations. (Bibliotheca Lichenologica Ser.: Vol. 48). (Illus.). 204p. 1993. pap. text ed. 65.00 (*3-443-58027-0*, Pub. by Cramer-Borntraeger GW) Lubrecht & Cramer.

Ramboli, jt. auth. see Glahder.

Rambon, Sheppard. School Dropouts: Everybody's Problem. Lewis, Anne & Usdan, Michael D., eds. 58p. (Orig.). 1986. pap. 7.50 (*0-937846-91-0*) Inst Educ Lead.

Rambova, N., jt. ed. see Piankoff, A.

Ramboz, I. W., ed. Spanish Verbs & Essentials of Grammar. (C). 1988. 55.00 (*0-8442-7214-0*, Pub. by S Thornes Pubs UK) St Mut.

Ramboz, Ina W. Christmas Songs in Spanish. 32p. (SPA.). (J). (gr. 6-9). 1985. pap. 7.95 (*0-8442-7097-0*, Passport Bks) NTC Pub Grp.

Rambusch, Erik H., jt. auth. see Wilson, Robert F.

Rambusch, V., ed. Lighting for Houses of Worship. (Recommended Practices Ser.). 56p. 1992. pap. text ed. 50.00 (*0-87995-086-2*, RP-25-91) Illum Eng.

***Rambusch, Viggo B.** Lighting the Liturgy. (Meeting House Essays Ser.). 62p. (Orig.). 1994. pap. 6.00 (*1-56854-061-2*, LITLIT) Liturgy Tr Pubns.

Rambuss, Richard. Spenser's Secret Career. LC 92-8539. (Studies in Renaissance Literature & Culture: Vol. 3). (Illus.). 200p. (C). 1993. 49.95 (*0-521-41663-9*) Cambridge U Pr.

Ramchandani, R., jt. auth. see Ali, Shanti S.

Ramchandani, R. R., ed. India Africa Economic Relations, in the Context of Economic Co-Operation among Developing Countries, Vol. 2. (Illus.). xii, 380p. 1990. 33.00 (*81-85163-12-X*, Pub. by Kalinga Pubns) Nataraj Bks.

— India Africa Relations, Vol. 1: Issues & Policy Options. vi, 405p. 1990. 37.00 (*81-85163-11-1*, Pub. by Kalinga Pubns) Nataraj Bks.

Ramchandani, R. R., jt. ed. see Ali, Shanti S.

Ramcharan, B. G. The Concept & Present Status of the International Protection of Human Rights. (C). 1989. lib. bdg. 207.50 (*90-247-3759-1*) Kluwer Ac.

— Humanitarian Good Offices in International Law. 1983. lib. bdg. 39.50 (*0-686-39789-4*) Kluwer Ac.

— The International Law & Practice of Early-Warning & Preventive Diplomacy: The Emerging Global Watch. (C). 1991. lib. bdg. 87.00 (*0-7923-1338-0*) Kluwer Ac.

— The International Law Commission. 1977. pap. text ed. 70.00 (*90-247-1984-4*) Kluwer Ac.

— Keeping Faith with the United Nations. (C). 1987. lib. bdg. 92.00 (*90-247-3516-5*) Kluwer Ac.

Ramcharan, R. G., ed. Human Rights: Thirty Years After the Universal Declaration. 1979. lib. bdg. 94.00 (*90-247-2145-8*) Kluwer Ac.

Ramcharan, Shail K. Balancing on the Edge of Nowhere & Forever. 32p. 1991. 6.95 (*0-8059-3192-9*) Dorrance.

— Fire & Lace. 40p. 1994. 8.00 (*0-8059-3595-9*) Dorrance.

Ramdahl, jt. auth. see Bjorseth.

Ramdas, Swami. In the Vision of God, Vol. 1: The Continuing Saga of an Extraordinary Pilgrimage. 200p. 1994. 19.95 (*1-884997-02-3*); pap. 9.95 (*1-884997-03-1*) Blue Dove Pr.

— In the Vision of God, Vol. 2: The Continuing Saga of an Extraordinary Pilgrimage. 200p. 1994. 19.95 (*1-884997-04-X*); pap. 9.95 (*1-884997-05-8*) Blue Dove Pr.

Ramdass, jt. ed. see Gopalakrishnan, K. C.

Ramdin, Ron. West Indies. LC 91-7490. (World in View Ser.). (Illus.). 96p. (YA). (gr. 6-12). 1991. lib. bdg. 24.26 (*0-8114-2442-1*) Raintree Steck-V.

Rame, Franca & Fo, Dario. A Woman Alone & Other Plays. Hood, Stuart, ed. Hanna, Gillian et al, trs. (Methuen Modern Plays Ser.). 206p. (Orig.). 1991. pap. 13.95 (*0-413-64030-2*, AO562, Pub. by Methuen UK) Heinemann.

Rameau, Jean-Philipe. Treatise on Harmony. Gossett, Philip, tr. 11.95 (*0-486-22461-9*) Dover.

Rameau, Jean-Philippe. Castor et Pollux. De Lajarte, Theodore, ed. (Chefs-d'oeuvre classiques de l'opera francaise Ser.: Vol. 30). (Illus.). 318p. (FRE.). 1970. reprint ed. pap. 35.00 (*0-8450-1130-8*) Broude.

— Dardanus. Poisot, Charles, ed. (Chefs-d'oeuvre classiques de l'opera francaise Ser.: Vol. 31). (Illus.). 372p. (FRE.). 1970. reprint ed. pap. 37.50 (*0-8450-1131-6*) Broude.

— Les Festes d'Hebe. De Lajarte, Theodore, ed. (Chefs-d'oeuvre classiques de l'opera francaise Ser.: Vol. 32). (Illus.). 300p. (FRE.). 1970. reprint ed. pap. 35.00 (*0-8450-1132-4*) Broude.

— Hippolyte et Aricie. Poisot, Charles, ed. (Chefs-d'oeuvre classiques de l'opera francaise Ser.: Vol. 33). (Illus.). 340p. (FRE.). 1970. reprint ed. pap. 35.00 (*0-8450-1133-2*) Broude.

— Les Indes Galantes. Poisot, Charles, ed. (Chefs-d'oeuvre classiques de l'opera francaise Ser.: Vol. 34). (Illus.). 334p. (FRE.). 1970. reprint ed. pap. 35.00 (*0-8450-1134-0*) Broude.

— Platee, ou Junon Jalouse. Poisot, Charles, ed. (Chefs-d'oeuvre classiques de l'opera francaise Ser.: Vol. 35). (Illus.). 316p. (FRE.). 1970. reprint ed. pap. 35.00 (*0-8450-1135-9*) Broude.

— Zoroastre. Poisot, Charles & Pougin, Arthur, eds. (Chefs-d'oeuvre classiques de l'opera francaise Ser.: Vol. 36). (Illus.). 338p. (FRE.). 1970. reprint ed. pap. 35.00 (*0-8450-1136-7*) Broude.

Ramee, jt. ed. see White.

Ramee, Stephen R., jt. auth. see White, Christopher J.

Rameh, Clea, jt. auth. see Abreu, Maria I.

Rameh, Clea, ed. see Georgetown University Round Table on Languages & Linguistics Staff.

Ramel, Charlotte, illus. The Bake-a-Cake Book: Beat the Batter, Measure the Flour, Bake a Cake with the Cakebakers. LC 93-40877. (J). (ps-3). 1994. 16.95 (*0-8118-0693-6*) Chronicle Bks.

Ramel, Claes & Norden, Bengt, eds. Interaction Mechanisms of Low-Level Electromagnetic Fields in Living Systems. (Illus.). 312p. 1992. 85.00 (*0-19-857759-1*) OUP.

Ramelb, Carol, ed. Biography East & West. (Literary Studies: East & West: No. 3). 256p. (Orig.). 1990. pap. text ed. 18.00 (*0-8248-1284-0*) UH Pr.

Ramella, Franco, jt. ed. see Baily, Samuel L.

***Ramelli, Agostino.** The Various & Ingenious Machines of Agostino Ramelli: A Classic Sixteenth-Century Illustrated Treatise on Technology. (Illus.). 608p. 1994. pap. text ed. 24.95 (*0-486-28180-9*) Dover.

— The Various & Ingenious Machines of Agostino Ramelli: A Classic Sixteenth-Century Illustrated Treatise on Technology. (Illus.). 608p. 1987. reprint ed. 34.95 (*0-486-25497-6*) Dover.

Ramenofsky, Elizabeth. From Charcoal to Banking: The Solomons of Arizona. (Illus.). 1984. 19.95 (*0-87026-060-X*) Westernlore.

***Ramer, Andrew.** Angel Answers: A Joyful Guide to Creating Heaven on Earth. Bestler, Emily, ed. 192p. (Orig.). 1995. pap. 10.00 (*0-671-52589-1*) PB.

Ramer, Andrew, jt. auth. see Cunningham, Donna.

Ramer, Jeanette C., jt. auth. see Miller, Geoffrey.

Ramer, Leah. Culturally Sensitive Caregiving & Childbearing Families. Raff, Beverly S. & Fiore, Ellen, eds. LC 92-13293. (Nursing Issues for the Twenty-First Century Ser.: No. 4, Module 1). 1992. pap. write for info. (*0-86525-054-5*) March of Dimes.

Ramer, Samuel C., tr. see Kochina, Elena I.

Ramesh, A., ed. Contributions to Indian Geography, Vol. 5: Resource Geography. 1985. 38.50 (*0-8364-1303-2*, Pub. by Heritage IA) S Asia.

Ramesh, A., jt. auth. see Misra, R. P.

Ramesh, G. Aesthetics & Education. (C). 1988. 17.50 (*81-7003-094-3*, Pub. by S Asia Pubs II) S Asia.

Ramesh, J. Mobilizing Technology for World Development. LC 79-53493. 234p. 1979. text ed. 69.50 (*0-275-90410-5*, C0410, Praeger Pubs) Greenwood.

***Ramesh, Jain, et al.** Machine Vision. LC 95-3771. 1995. text ed. write for info. (*0-07-032018-7*) McGraw.

Ramesh, Jairam & Weiss, Charles, Jr., eds. Mobilizing Technology for World Development. LC 79-5349. 240p. 1979. pap. 6.95 (*0-03-055451-9*) Overseas Dev Council.

Ramesh, K. Human Relations in an Indian University: An Organizational Perspective. (C). 1991. 21.00 (*81-202-0304-6*, Pub. by Ajanta II) S Asia.

Ramesh, K. T., ed. Experimental Techniques in the Dynamics of Deformable Solids. LC 93-71579. (AMD Ser.: Vol. 165). 1993. pap. 35.00 (*0-7918-1144-1*, G00788) ASME.

Ramesh, K. V., ed. Indian History & Epigraphy. 1990. 125.00 (*0-8364-2597-9*, Pub. by Agam II) S Asia.

Ramesh, R., et al, eds. Epitaxial Oxide Thin Films & Heterostructures: Materials Research Society Symposium Proceedings, Vol. 341. 1994. text ed. 48.00 (*1-55899-241-3*) Materials Res.

Ramesh, Richard. Population of Heaven: A Biblical Response to the Inclusivist Position on Who Will Be Saved. 1994. pap. 9.99 (*0-8024-3946-2*) Moody.

***Ramesh, Srinivasan & Gupta, Arun.** Venture Capital & the Indian Financial Sector. 250p. 1995. 24.00 (*0-19-563633-3*) OUP.

Rameshray, Roy. Perspectives on Indian Politics. 489p. 1987. 48.50 (*0-8364-2014-4*, Pub. by Usha II) S Asia.

Ramet, Pedro. Cross & Commissar: The Politics of Religion in Eastern Europe & the U. S. S. R. LC 86-46165. (Illus.). 256p. (C). 1987. 24.95 (*0-253-31575-1*) Ind U Pr.

— Eastern Christianity & Politics in the Twentieth Century. LC 87-27029. (Christianity under Stress Ser.). vii, 471p. (C). 1988. lib. bdg. 52.95 (*0-8223-0827-4*) Duke.

— Nationalism & Federalism in Yugoslavia, 1963-1983. LC 83-49055. 319p. reprint ed. pap. 91.00 (*0-8357-6685-3*, 2056864) Bks Demand.

Ramet, Pedro, ed. Catholicism & Politics in Communist Societies. LC 89-39178. 463p. (Orig.). (C). 1990. lib. bdg. 52.95 (*0-8223-1010-4*); pap. text ed. 23.95 (*0-8223-1047-3*) Duke.

— Religion & Nationalism in Soviet & East European Politics. enl. rev. ed. LC 88-21132. 560p. (C). 1988. lib. bdg. 72.50 (*0-8223-0854-1*); pap. text ed. 26.95 (*0-8223-0891-6*) Duke.

Ramet, Sabrina P. Balkan Babel: Politics, Culture, & Religion in Yugoslavia. 230p. (C). 1992. text ed. 49.95 (*0-8133-8184-3*) Westview.

— Nationalism & Federalism in Yugoslavia, 1962-1991. 2nd ed. LC 91-23623. (Illus.). 352p. 1992. text ed. 39.95 (*0-253-34794-7*); pap. text ed. 17.95 (*0-253-20703-7*, MB-703) Ind U Pr.

— Rocking the State: Rock Music & Politics in Eastern Europe & the Soviet Union. 1994. text ed. 63.00 (*0-8133-1762-2*) Westview.

— Rocking the State: Rock Music & Politics in Eastern Europe & the Soviet Union. (C). 1994. pap. text ed. 19.95 (*0-8133-1763-0*) Westview.

— Social Currents in Eastern Europe: The Sources & Consequences of the Great Transformation. 2nd ed. 624p. 1995. lib. bdg. 65.00 (*0-8223-1551-3*); pap. text ed. 23.95 (*0-8223-1548-3*) Duke.

— Social Currents in Eastern Europe: The Sources & Meaning of the Great Transformation. LC 90-24049. 447p. 1991. lib. bdg. 52.95 (*0-8223-1129-1*); pap. text ed. 24.95 (*0-8223-1148-8*) Duke.

Ramet, Sabrina P., ed. Adaptation & Transformation in Communist & Post-Communist Systems. 326p. (C). 1992. pap. text ed. 52.50 (*0-8133-1423-2*) Westview.

— Beyond Yugoslavia: Politics, Economics, & Culture in a Shattered Community. (Eastern Europe After Communism Ser.). 484p. (C). 1995. text ed. 49.95 (*0-8133-7953-9*) Westview.

— Protestantism & Politics in Eastern Europe & Russia: The Communist & Post-Communist Eras. LC 92-9418. (Christianity under Stress Ser.: Vol. 3). 408p. 1992. 39.95 (*0-8223-1241-7*) Duke.

— Religious Policy in the Soviet Union. 350p. (C). 1993. 69.95 (*0-521-41643-4*) Cambridge U Pr.

***Ramet, Sabrina P. & Treadgold, Donald W., eds.** Render unto Caesar: The Religious Sphere in World Politics. 500p. (C). 1995. pap. 29.95 (*1-879383-44-6*) Am Univ Pr.

— Render unto Caesar: The Religious Sphere in World Politics. 500p. (C). 1995. 69.50 (*1-879383-43-8*) Am Univ Pr.

Ramette, Peggy L. & Sternberg, Dick. America's Favorite Fish Recipes. LC 92-6416. (Hunting & Fishing Library). 160p. 1992. 19.95 (*0-86573-039-3*) Cy De Cosse.

Ramette, Richard W. Chemical Equilibrium & Analysis. (Chemistry Ser.). (Illus.). 672p. (C). 1981. text ed. write for info. (*0-201-06107-4*) Addison-Wesley.

***Ramey, Ardella & Sniffen, Carl E.** A Company Policy & Personnel Workbook. 3rd ed. (Successful Business Library). 338p. 1995. pap. 29.95 (*1-55571-365-3*); ring bd. 49.95 (*1-55571-364-5*) Oasis Pr OR.

***Ramey, Ardella & Sniffen, Carl R.** A Company Policy & Personnel Workbook. 2nd ed. (Successful Business Library). 338p. 1991. ring bd. 49.95 (*1-55571-183-9*) Oasis Pr OR.

— A Company Policy & Personnel Workbook. 2nd rev. ed. (Successful Business Library). 338p. 1991. pap. 29.95 (*1-55571-184-7*) Oasis Pr OR.

— A Company Policy & Personnel Workbook. 2nd rev. ed. (Successful Business Library). 338p. 1992. disk, ring bd. 125.95 (*1-55571-315-7*) Oasis Pr OR.

— Developing Company Policies: Ready-to-Use Models for Small Business. (Successful Business Library). 170p. (Orig.). 1991. pap. 19.95 (*1-55571-125-1*) Oasis Pr OR.

Ramey, Bern C. The Great Wine Grapes & the Wines They Make. (Illus.). 49.95 (*0-8436-2257-1*) Great Wine Grapes.

Ramey, David. Empowering Leaders. LC 91-35001. 256p. (Orig.). (C). 1991. pap. 14.95 (*1-55612-372-8*) Sheed & Ward MO.

— Horsefeathers: Facts vs. Myths about Your Horses Health. (Illus.). 192p. 1995. 25.00 (*0-87605-986-8*) Howell Bk.

Ramey, Emmett & Wong, Alex. The Loan Package. (Successful Business Library). 286p. 1990. reprint ed. ring bd. 39.95 (*0-916378-13-6*) Oasis Pr OR.

Ramey, Henry J., et al. Gas Well Test Analysis Under Water-Drive Conditions. 312p. 1973. 12.00 (*0-318-12634-6*, L00311) Am Gas Assn.

Ramey, J. J. West of Paradise Run. 192p. 1989. pap. 2.95 (*0-345-35700-0*) Ballantine.

Ramey, James W., jt. auth. see Calderone, Mary S.

Ramey, Jerry & Stewart, Ed. How to Go to Work on Your Faith. 131p. 1992. pap. 7.95 (*0-8341-1430-5*) Beacon Hill.

***Ramey, Jim.** Jr. (Illus.). 80p. 1995. pap. 8.00 (*0-8059-3745-5*) Dorrance.

Ramey, Mary. Adult Children, Adult Choices: Outgrowing Codependency. LC 92-12728. 168p. (Orig.). 1992. pap. 10.95 (*1-55612-406-6*, LL1406) Sheed & Ward MO.

Ramey, Mary A. Library Skills Reference Book. 4th ed. (Illus.). 40p. 1992. pap. text ed. 7.95x (*0-89892-103-1*) Contemp Pub Co of Raleigh.

Ramey, Mary A., jt. ed. see Reichel, Mary.

Ramey, Mary L., jt. auth. see Thomas, M. Angele.

Ramey, Ralph. Fifty Hikes in Ohio: Walks, Hikes & Backpacking Trips Throughout the Buckeye State. LC 90-40939. 256p. 1990. pap. 13.00 (*0-88150-165-4*, Backcountry) Countryman.

— Walks & Rambles in Southwestern Ohio: From the Stillwater to the Ohio River. (Walks & Rambles Ser.). (Illus.). 192p. (Orig.). 1994. pap. 12.00 (*0-88150-250-2*, Backcountry) Countryman.

***Ramey, Robert, Jr.** The Pastor's Start-up Manual: Beginning a New Pastorate. (Leadership Insight Ser.). 144p. (Orig.). 1995. pap. 11.95 (*0-687-01486-7*) Abingdon.

Ramey, Robert H., Jr. & Johnson, Ben C. Living the Christian Life: A Guide to Reformed Spirituality. 208p. (Orig.). 1992. pap. 12.99 (*0-664-25286-9*) Westminster John Knox.

Ramfjord, Sigurd, jt. auth. see Ash, Major M.

Ramfjord, Sigurd P. & Ash, M., Jr. Periodontology & Periodontics: Modern Theory & Practice. rev. ed. 1989. 59.50 (*0-912791-40-3*) Ishiyaku Euro.

Ramgulam, P. Mauritius. (World Bibliographical Ser.). 1992. lib. bdg. 70.00 (*1-85109-153-X*) ABC-CLIO.

Ramholz, James, ed. see Baek, Sung.

Rami, Sonia. Antiquity Street. 224p. 1992. 20.00 (*0-374-10534-0*) FS&G.

Ramie, Florence. Toyland. 400p. (Orig.). 1989. reprint ed. pap. 3.95 (*0-8439-2883-2*) Dorchester Pub Co.

Ramierez, Gonzalo, Jr. & Ramierez, Jan L. Multiethnic Children's Literature. LC 93-39662. 158p. 1994. pap. text ed. 24.95 (*0-8273-5433-9*) Delmar.

Ramierez, Jan L., jt. auth. see Ramierez, Gonzalo, Jr.

***Ramierz, Anthony.** The Best of Latin American Short Stories - A Bilingual Edition: Los Mejores Cuentos Hispanoamericanos. Hamel, Bernard H., ed. 114p. (Orig.). 1994. spiral bd., pap. 10.95 (*1-886835-02-0*) Bilingual Bk Pr.

Ramig, R. F., ed. Current Topics in Microbiology & Immunology: Rotaviruses. 330p. 1994. 129.00 (*0-387-56761-5*) Spr-Verlag.

R

Ramin, Terese. Accompanying Alice. large type ed. (Silhouette Special Edition Ser.). 1993. 17.95 (0-373-58837-2, Silhouette Lrg Print); pap. 16.95 (0-373-58929-8, Silhouette Lrg Print) Chivers N Amer.
— A Certain Slant of Light. (Intimate Moments Ser.). 1995. mass mkt. 3.75 (0-373-07634-7, 1-07634-8) Silhouette.
— Five Kids, One Christmas. 1995. pap. 3.75 (0-373-07680-0, 1-07680-1) Silhouette.
— Winter Beach. (Silhouette Intimate Moments Ser.). 1993. mass mkt. 3.39 (0-373-07477-8, 5-07477-8) Silhouette.
Ramio, Christian, jt. auth. see Mention, Philippe.
Ramiorez, J. Yankee Duchess. Date not set. mass mkt. 4.50 (0-06-108075-6, Harp PBks) HarpC.
Ramirez. Psychotherapy & Counseling. (Practitioner Guidebook Ser.). 1991. pap. 25.95 (0-205-14461-6, H4461, Longwood Div) Allyn.
Ramirez, Alfonso R., ed. Four Generations of Velas. (Illus.). 96p. 1986. 15.00 (0-935071-01-6) New Santander.
Ramirez, Anthony, Jr. Romualdo Pacheco: Governor of California. (Illus.). 1974. 5.00 (0-911302-26-3, PS3-6) San Francisco Pr.
Ramirez, Arnulfo G. Bilingualism Through Schooling: Cross-Cultural Education for Minority & Majority Students. LC 83-24246. 275p. 1985. 64.50 (0-87395-891-8); pap. 21.95 (0-87395-892-6) State U NY Pr.
— Creating Contexts for Second Language Acquisition: Theory & Methods. LC 94-6628. 395p. (C). 1995. pap. text ed. 32.95 (0-8013-0480-6, 78313) Longman.
Ramirez, Bernardo & Lastiri, Santiago, eds. Casos en Administracion de Servicios de Salud: Un Enfoque para la Solucion de Problemas. (Illus.). 180p. (Orig.). (SPA.). (C). 1989. pap. text ed. 14.55 (0-910591-23-7) AUPHA Pr.
Ramirez, Bernardo & Parra-Elliott, Ligia, eds. Educacion en Administracion de Salud en America Latina y El Caribe. LC 87-72570. 140p. (Orig.). 1987. pap. text ed. 8.00 (0-910591-06-7) AUPHA Pr.
Ramirez, Blandina C., jt. auth. see Cardenas, Jose A.
Ramirez, Bruce & Ortiz, Alba A., eds. Schools & the Culturally Diverse Exceptional Student: Promising Practices & Future Directions. 176p. 1988. 21.70 (0-86586-182-X, P326) Coun Exc Child.
Ramirez, Bruno. When Workers Fight: The Politics of Industrial Relations in the Progressive Era, 1898-1916. LC 77-83895. (Contributions in Labor History Ser.: No. 2). 241p. 1978. text ed. 55.00 (0-8371-9826-7, RAW/, Greenwood Pr) Greenwood.
Ramirez, C. Manual & Atlas of Penicillia. 874p. 1982. 247.25 (0-444-80369-6) Elsevier.
Ramirez-Christensen, Esperanza. Heart's Flower: The Life & Poetry of Shinkei. LC 93-17305. 1994. 50.00 (0-8047-2253-6) Stanford U Pr.
Ramirez de Arellano, Annette B. & Seipp, Conrad. Colonialism, Catholicism, & Contraception: A History of Birth Control in Puerto Rico. LC 82-13646. xiv, 219p. 1983. 29.95 (0-8078-1544-6) U of NC Pr.
— Colonialism, Catholicism, & Contraception: A History of Birth Control in Puerto Rico. LC 82-13646. reprint ed. pap. 65.90 (0-7837-9029-5, 2049780) Bks Demand.
Ramirez de Arellano, E., ed. Algebraic Geometry & Complex Analysis. (Lecture Notes in Mathematics Ser.: Vol. 1414). vi, 180p. 1990. pap. 30.60 (0-387-52175-5, 3875) Spr-Verlag.
Ramirez De Arellano, Rafael. Folklore Portoriqueno. LC 78-63213. (Folktale Ser.). reprint ed. 25.50 (0-404-16154-5) AMS Pr.
Ramirez de Carias, Maria. La Cocina Dominicana: Edicion Para Coleccionistas. (Illus.). 200p. (SPA.). 1993. write for info. (0-318-69984-2) Pilon FL.
Ramirez, Donald E., jt. auth. see Dunkl, Charles F.
Ramirez, Doreen, jt. auth. see Manuel, Ted.
Ramirez, Doreen, ed. see Manuel, Ted.
Ramirez, E. V. & Weiss, M. Microprocessing Fundamentals: Hardware & Software. 1980. text ed. 36.95 (0-07-051172-1) McGraw.
Ramirez, Edelmina, ed. see Gorostiza, Jose.
Ramirez, Elizabeth C. Footlights Across the Border: A History of Spanish-Language Professional Theatre on the Texas Stage. (American University Studies: Theatre Arts: Ser. XXVI, Vol. 1). 206p. (C). 1989. text ed. 43.95 (0-8204-1035-7) P Lang Pubs.
Ramirez, Enrique. Encounter of Two Worlds: The Mexican Experience. 480p. (C). 1992. pap. text ed. 29.95 (0-8403-7559-X) Kendall-Hunt.
Ramirez, Francisco O., ed. Rethinking the Nineteenth Century: Contradictions & Movements. LC 87-17791. (Contributions in Economics & Economic History Ser.: No. 76). 256p. 1988. text ed. 55.00 (0-313-25997-6, RRK/, Greenwood Pr) Greenwood.
Ramirez, Frank. Adventure of the Discerning Thespian. LC 82-91140. (Illus.). 64p. 1983. 28.00 (0-88014-064-X) Mosaic Pr OH.
— The Third Letter. Chirich, Nancy, ed. LC 90-1851. 166p. 1991. pap. 8.95 (0-912761-33-4) Cliffhanger Pr.
Ramirez, Gloria, tr. see Mann, Peggy.
Ramirez, Jeanette. Lady of Lochabar. 1993. mass mkt. 4.50 (0-06-108073-X, Harp PBks) HarpC.
Ramirez, Jose, III. Things about the Guitar. Teresita, tr. (Illus.). 229p. 1994. pap. 32.50 (0-933224-88-5, Pub. by Soneto Ediciones SP) Bold Strummer Ltd.
Ramirez, Jose, tr. see Scholtes, Peter R.
Ramirez, Lynette, ed. see Miller, P. B.
Ramirez, Lynette, ed. see Wallach, Paul.
Ramirez, Mari C., ed. El Taller Torres-Garcia: The School of the South & Its Legacy. LC 91-20731. (Illus.). 411p. 1992. 55.00 (0-292-78121-0); pap. 29.95 (0-292-78122-9) U of Tex Pr.
***Ramirez, Mari C., et al, contribs.** Encounters - Displacements: Luis Camnitzer, Alfredo Jarr, Cildo Meireles. (Illus.). 77p. 1992. pap. 24.00 (0-935213-23-6) A M Huntington Art.
Ramirez, Mario A. Refugee Policy Challenges: The Case of Nicaraguans in Costa Rica. 58p. (Orig.). 1990. pap. 7.50 (0-924046-12-0) Ctr EPRA.
Ramirez Mattei, Aida E. Carmelina Vizcarrondo: Vida, Obra y Antologia. (UPREX, Estudios Literarios Ser.: No. 8). 261p. (C). 1972. pap. 1.50 (0-8477-0008-9) U of PR Pr.
Ramirez-Mattei, Aida E. La Narrativa de Carlos Fuentes: Afan por la Armonia en la Multiplicidad Antagonica del Mundo. LC 83-1322. xv, 437p. (Orig.). (SPA.). (C). 1983. pap. 8.50 (0-8477-3507-9) U of PR Pr.
***Ramirez, Micahel R. & Sawaya, Linda.** The Little Ant - La Hormiga Chiquita. LC 95-10282. (Illus.). 32p. (ENG & SPA.). (J). 1995. 12.95 (0-8478-1922-1) Rizzoli Intl.
Ramirez, Miguel D. Development Banking in Mexico: The Case of the Nacional Financiera, S. A. LC 85-16700. 252p. 1985. text ed. 59.95 (0-275-92032-1, C2032, Praeger Pubs) Greenwood.
— Mexico's Economic Crisis: Its Origins & Consequences. LC 88-30738. 164p. 1989. text ed. 49.95 (0-275-92867-5, C2867, Praeger Pubs) Greenwood.
Ramirez, Noel, jt. auth. see Lindenberg, Marc.
Ramirez, Noemi, jt. auth. see Eoff, Sherman H.
Ramirez, Nora. The Southwestern Livestock Show & Rodeo. (Southwestern Studies: No. 32). 1972. pap. 10.00 (0-87404-140-6) Tex Western.
***Ramirez, O. M. & Daniel, R. K.** Endoscopic Aesthetic Surgery: A Video Manual, PAL Version. 80p. 1995. pap. 225.00 (3-540-92626-7) Spr-Verlag.
Ramirez, O. T., jt. ed. see Galindo, E.
***Ramirez, Oscar M. & Daniel, Rollin K.** Manual of Endoscopic Aesthetic Surgery. LC 94-30008. 1994. 225.00 (0-387-92623-2) Spr-Verlag.
***Ramirez, Oscar M. & Daniel, Rollin K., eds.** Endoscopic Techniques in Plastic & Aesthetic Surgery. LC 95-16149. 1995. write for info. (0-387-94466-4) Spr-Verlag.
Ramirez, Rafael, jt. auth. see Normann, Richard.
Ramirez, Rafael E. El Arrabal y la Politica. Lopez-Chiclana, Margarita, tr. LC 76-40124. (Centro de Investigaciones Sociales Ser.). Orig. Title: Politics & the Urban Poor. (Illus.). (Orig.). (SPA.). 1977. 4.80 (0-8477-2484-0) U of PR Pr.
Ramirez, Rafael L. Dime Capitan: Raflexiones Sobre la Masculinidad. LC 93-74310. 133p. (Orig.). 1993. pap. 7.95 (0-929157-18-4) Ediciones Huracan.
Ramirez, Rafael L. & Deliz, Wenceslao S., eds. Crisis y Critica de las Ciencias Sociales en Puerto Rico. 310p. 1980. pap. 5.95 (0-8477-2465-4) U of PR Pr.
Ramirez, Rafael L., jt. auth. see Rivera-Medina, Eduardo.
***Ramirez, Ricardo.** Fiesta, Worship & Family. 56p. 1981. write for info. (0-614-04868-0) Mex Am Cult.
Ramirez, Robert W. The FFT: Fundamentals & Concepts. (Illus.). 192p. (C). 1984. text ed. 73.00 (0-13-314386-4) P-H.
Ramirez, Ron & Prosise, Michael. Philco Radio, 1928-1942. (Illus.). 160p. 1993. pap. 29.95 (0-88740-547-9) Schiffer.
Ramirez, Sabet, tr. see Serbin, Andres.
***Ramirez, Santiago & Cohen, Robert S., eds.** Mexican Studies in the History & Philosophy of Science. LC 95-13783. (Boston Studies in the Philosophy of Science: Vol. 172). 1995. write for info. (0-7923-3462-0) Kluwer Ac.
***Ramirez, Sergio.** Hatful of Tigers: Reflections on Art, Culture & Politics. Flakoll, D. J., tr. 148p. 1995. 15.00 (0-915306-98-0) Curbstone.
— Stories from Nicaragua. Caistor, Nick, tr. (Readers International Ser.). (Illus.). 130p. (Orig.). (C). 1987. pap. 7.95 (0-930523-29-6) Readers Intl.
— To Bury Our Fathers: A Novel of Nicaragua. Caistor, Nick, tr. LC 84-61849. (Illus.). 250p. (Orig.). (C). 1985. pap. 11.95 (0-930523-03-2) Readers Intl.
Ramirez, Sharon & Scheie, David. Cops & Neighbors: An Evaluation of the Whittier Community-Based Policing Project. 70p. (Orig.). (C). 1994. pap. text ed. 40.00 (0-7881-0753-4) Diane Pub.
Ramirez, Stephen. Health Promotion for All: Strategies for Reaching Diverse Populations at the Workplace. 128p. (Orig.). 1994. pap. 25.00 (0-9628334-3-6) WELCOA.
Ramirez, Susan E., ed. see MacLeod, Murdo J., et al.
Ramirez Villareal, Humberto. Diccionario Ilustrado de Electronica. 192p. (SPA.). 24.95 (0-7859-0708-4, S-25248) Fr & Eur.
Ramirez, W. F. Application of Optimal Control Theory to Enhanced Oil Recovery. (Developments in Petrolem Science Ser.: No. 21). 244p. 1987. 79.50 (0-444-42835-6) Elsevier.
Ramirez, W. Fred. Computational Methods for Process Simulation. (Illus.). 501p. 1989. text ed. 59.95 (0-409-90184-9) Buttrwrth-Heinemann.
— Process Control & Identification. (Illus.). 424p. 1993. text ed. 64.95 (0-12-577240-8) Acad Pr.
Ramis, Guillermo, jt. auth. see Cerda, Victor.
Ramis, J. P., jt. ed. see Gerard, R.
Ramis, Jean-Pierre. Theoremes d'indices Gevrey pour les equations differentielles ordinaires. LC 83-27157. (Memoirs Ser.: No. 48/296). 95p. 1984. pap. 17.00 (0-8218-2296-9, MEMO 48/296) Am Math.
***Ramis, Magali G.** Happy Days, Uncle Sergio. Esteves, Carmen C., tr. (Secret Weapons Ser.: Vol. 8). 170p. (Orig.). 1995. pap. 12.00 (1-877727-52-0) White Pine.
Ramji, Dipak, jt. ed. see Gacesa, Peter.
Ramke, Bin. The Difference Between Night & Day. LC 77-16790. (Younger Poets Ser.: No. 73). 1978. 17.00 (0-300-02225-5) Yale U Pr.
— The Erotic Light of Gardens. LC 88-28070. (Wesleyan Poetry Ser.). 71p. 1989. 22.50 (0-8195-2171-X, Wesleyan Univ Pr); pap. 10.95 (0-8195-1174-9, Wesleyan Univ Pr) U Pr of New Eng.
— The Language Student. Poems. LC 86-7439. 58p. 1986. text ed. 13.95 (0-8071-1344-1) La State U Pr.
— Massacre of the Innocents. LC 94-37407. (Iowa Poetry Prize). 95p. (Orig.). 1995. pap. 10.95 (0-87745-492-2) U of Iowa Pr.
— White Monkeys. LC 80-24582. (Contemporary Poetry Ser.). 104p. 1981. pap. 7.95 (0-8203-0551-0) U of Ga Pr.
Ramkinshina, D., ed. Neal R. Amundson: A Special Issue in His Honor - A Special Issue of the Journal Chemical Engineering Communications. 486p. 1987. pap. text ed. 469.00 (2-88124-256-1) Gordon & Breach.
Ramkumar, K., jt. auth. see Satyam, M.
Ramkumar, Usha, jt. auth. see Tara, S. Nayana.
Ramlin, Carol, jt. auth. see Marriot, Alice.
Ramlu, M. A. Mine Disasters & Mine Rescue. (Illus.). 408p. (C). 1991. text ed. 95.00 (90-6191-964-9, Pub. by A A Balkema NE) Ashgate Pub Co.
— Mine Disasters & Mine Rescue. (C). 1991. 60.00 (81-204-0526-9, Pub. by Oxford IBH II) S Asia.
Ramm. Multidimensional Inverse Scattering Problems. (Pitman Monographs & Surveys in Pure & Applied Mathematics: No. 1774). 379p. 1992. text ed. 250.00 (0-470-21851-7) Halsted Pr.
Ramm, A. Theory & Applications of Some New Classes of Integral Equations. 344p. 1980. pap. 31.50 (0-685-04732-6) Spr-Verlag.
Ramm, A. G. Iterative Methods of Calculating Static Fields & Wave Scattering by Small Bodies. (Illus.). 124p. 1982. 59.00 (0-387-90682-7) Spr-Verlag.
— Scattering by Obstacles. 1986. lib. bdg. 163.00 (90-277-2103-3) Kluwer Ac.
Ramm, Agatha. Europe in the Twentieth Century, Vol. 1. 7th ed. (Grant & Temperley's Europe in the 19th & 20th Centuries Ser.). 432p. (C). 1984. pap. text ed. 25.50 (0-582-49028-6, 73445) Longman.
— William Ewart Gladstone. Morgan, K. O., ed. (Political Portraits Ser.). xi, 131p. 1989. 25.95 (0-7083-1044-3, Pub. by U of Wales UK); pap. 9.95 (0-7083-1045-1, Pub. by U of Wales UK) Bks Intl VA.
Ramm, Bernard. Diccionario de Teologia Contemporanea. Valle, Roger V., tr. 143p. 1984. reprint ed. pap. 4.50 (0-311-09064-8) Casa Bautista.
— Protestant Biblical Interpretation. 1970. 17.99 (0-8010-7600-5) Baker Bk.
— Protestant Biblical Interpretation. Chan, Silas, tr. (CHI.). (C). 1984. pap. write for info. (0-941598-10-1) Living Spring Pubns.
— Salida - Los Caminos de Dios: His Way Out. (SPA.). 5.50 (84-7228-223-6, 220784, Pub. by Edit Clie SP) TSELF.
Ramm, Bernard L. After Fundamentalism: The Future of Evangelical Theology. LC 82-47792. 226p. 1984. pap. 9.95 (0-06-066789-3) Harper SF.
— God's Way Out. rev. ed. Stewart, Ed, ed. LC 87-12872. 214p. 1987. pap. 6.99 (0-8307-1215-1, S416154) Regal.
Ramm, Charles A. Meditations on the Mystery of Christmas. Lilly, Catherine M., ed. LC 59-15709. (Illus.). 1959. 10.00 (0-87015-092-8) Pacific Bks.
Ramm, H. Roman York from AD 71: A Pictorial Guide with Map & Suggested Roman Walk. (C). 1990. 35.00 (1-85072-001-0, Pub. by W Sessions UK) St Mut.
Ramm, Hartmut. The Marxism of Regis Debray: Between Lenin & Guevara. LC 77-17915. xii, 240p. 1978. 25.00 (0-7006-0170-8) U Pr of KS.
Ramm, Heinrich J. Fluid Dynamics for the Study of Transonic Flow. (Oxford Engineering Science Ser.: No. 23). (Illus.). 216p. 1990. 45.00 (0-19-506097-0) OUP.
Ramm, Herman. Roman York from A.D. 71. (C). 1989. 45.00 (1-85072-084-3, Pub. by W Sessions UK) St Mut.
Rammel, Hal. Aero into the Aether: Surrealist Comics & Poems. (Illus.). 28p. 1980. pap. 12.00 (0-941194-14-0) Black Swan Pr.
— Nowhere in America: The Big Rock Candy Mountain & Other Comic Utopias. (Folklore & Society Ser.). (Illus.). 184p. 1990. 25.95 (0-252-01717-X) U of Ill Pr.
Rammerstorfer, F., ed. Nonlinear Analysis of Shells by Finite Elements. (CISM International Centre for Mechanical Sciences Ser.: Vol. 328). (Illus.). v, 283p. 1992. pap. 72.00 (0-387-82416-2) Spr-Verlag.
Rammerstorfer, F. G., jt. auth. see Hult, J.
Rammig, F. J. Electronic Design Automation Frameworks. 1991. 100.00 (0-444-88917-5) Elsevier.
Rammig, F. J., ed. Tool Integration & Design Environments: Proceeding of the IFIP WG10.2 Workshop on Tool Integration & Design Environments, Paderborn, FRG, 26-27 Nov., 1987. 334p. 1988. 77.00 (0-444-70446-9, North Holland) Elsevier.
Rammig, F. J., jt. ed. see Darringer, J. A.
Ramming, H. G. & Kowalik, Z. Numerical Modelling of Marine Hydrodynamics: Applications to Dynamic Physical Processes. (Oceanography Ser.: Vol. 26). 368p. 1980. 100.00 (0-444-41849-0) Elsevier.
Ramminger, Johann, ed. see Avitus, Alcimus E.
Rammohun Roy, R. The English Works of Raja Ramohun Roy. Ghose, Jogendra C., ed. LC 75-41220. reprint ed. 72.50 (0-404-14738-0) AMS Pr.
Rammuny, Raji. Advanced Business Arabic. 1994. 22.95x (0-86685-416-9) Intl Bk Ctr.
— Advanced Standard Arabic: Through Authentic Tests & Audiovisual Materials, Pt. 2. 116p. 1994. pap. text ed. 19.95 (0-472-08262-0) U of Mich Pr.
— Advanced Standard Arabic: Through Authentic Texts & Audiovisual Materials, Pt. 1. 326p. 1994. pap. text ed. 24.95 (0-472-08261-2) U of Mich Pr.
— Programmed Arabic-Islamic Reader, Bk. I. 1991. student ed 5.95x (0-317-66014-4); audio 59.95x (0-86685-545-9) Intl Bk Ctr.
— Programmed Arabic Islamic Reader I. 1988. 16.95x (0-86685-412-6) Intl Bk Ctr.
Rammuny, Raji, jt. auth. see McCarus, Ernest N.
Rammuny, Raji, jt. auth. see McCarus, Ernest.
Rammuny, Raji M. Advanced Arabic Composition & Conversation. 1980. 16.95 (0-86685-410-X); student ed 16.95 (0-86685-411-8) Intl Bk Ctr.
— Investigating Arabic. 298p. (C). 1994. pap. text ed. 24.95 (1-57074-108-5) Greyden Pr.
— Programmed Arabic-Islamic Reader, Bk. 2. (ARA & ENG.). 1988. 19.95 (0-86685-431-2); teacher ed 5.95 (0-86685-635-8); audio 99.95 (0-86685-546-7) Intl Bk Ctr.
— Standard Achievement Tests. 102p. 1994. pap. text ed. 10.95 (1-57074-141-7) Greyden Pr.
— Supplementary Enrichment Vocabulary. 100p. (C). 1994. pap. text ed. 8.00 (1-57074-145-X) Greyden Pr.
Ramnath, S. Rings in a Tree Trunk. (Writers Workshop Redbird Ser.). 46p. 1976. 8.00 (0-86578-271-7); 4.00 (0-86578-272-5) Ind-US Inc.
Ramnujan, A. K., tr. see Murthy, U. R.
Ramo, Simon. America's Technology Slip. LC 80-21525. 304p. reprint ed. pap. 86.70 (0-8357-5410-3, 2021503) Bks Demand.
— What's Wrong with Our Technological Society - & How to Fix It. LC 83-696. 320p. 1983. text ed. 24.95 (0-07-051169-1) McGraw.
Ramo, Simon, et al. Fields & Waves in Communication Electronics. 3rd ed. LC 93-34415. 844p. 1994. text ed. 77.95 (0-471-58551-3) Wiley.
Ramo, Simon, et al, eds. Peacetime Uses of Outer Space. LC 76-52430. (Illus.). 279p. 1977. reprint ed. text ed. 38.50 (0-8371-9368-0, RAPU, Greenwood Pr) Greenwood.
***Ramon.** Psychiatric Hospital Closure: Myths & Realities. 224p. 1992. pap. 47.75 (1-56593-048-7) Singular Publishing.
Ramon-Medrano, M., jt. ed. see Julve, J.
Ramon, Shulamit, ed. Psychiatry in Transition. (C). 1990. pap. text ed. 18.95 (0-7453-0470-2) Westview.
Ramon, Shulamit & Giannichedda, Maria G., eds. Psychiatry in Transition: The British & Italian Experiences. 288p. (C). 1990. text ed. 74.50 (0-7453-0177-0, Pub. by Pluto Pr UK) Westview.
Ramon y Cajal, Santiago. Cajal's Histology of the Nervous System, 2 vols. Swanson, Larry W., ed. Swanson, Neely, tr. LC 93-35437. (History of Neuroscience Ser.: No. 6). (Illus.). 1664p. 1995. 195.00 (0-19-507401-7) OUP.
— New Ideas on the Structure of the Nervous System in Man & Vertebrates. Swanson, Larry W. & Swanson, Neely, trs. 200p. 1990. pap. 32.50 (0-262-18141-X) MIT Pr.
— Recollections of My Life. LC 88-11713. (Genes Cells & Organisms Ser.). 656p. 1988. 25.00 (0-8240-1385-9) Garland.
— Reglas y Consejos Sobre Investigacion Cientifica. (Nueva Austral Ser.: Vol. 232). (SPA.). 1991. pap. text ed. 24.95x (84-239-7232-1) Elliots Bks.
Ramona Pioneer Historical Society Staff. Let's Eat. 1975. pap. 2.50 (0-916552-03-9) Acoma Bks.
Ramond, P. & Stora, R., eds. Architecture of Fundamental Interactions at Short Distances, Pt. I. 418p. 1987. Part I, 418pp. 115.50 (0-444-87053-9, North Holland) Elsevier.
— Architecture of Fundamental Interactions at Short Distances, Pt. II. 642p. 1987. Part II, 642pp. 164.00 (0-444-87054-7, North Holland) Elsevier.
— Architecture of Fundamental Interactions at Short Distances, Set. 1060p. 1987. 243.75 (0-444-87026-1, North Holland) Elsevier.
Ramond, Pierre. Field Theory: A Modern Primer. 2nd ed. (Frontiers in Physics Ser.). (Illus.). 352p. 1988. text ed. 43.25 (0-201-15772-1, Adv Bk Prog) Addison-Wesley.
— Field Theory: A Modern Primer. 2nd rev. ed. 352p. (C). 1990. 45.95 (0-201-54611-6, 130A01, Adv Bk Prog) Addison-Wesley.
Ramondetta, P. J. Facies & Stratigraphy of the San Andres Formation, Northern & Northwestern Shelves of the Midland Basin, Texas & New Mexico. (Report of Investigations Ser.: RI 128). (Illus.). 56p. 1982. 2.50 (0-318-03277-5) Bur Econ Geology.
Ramondino, Salvatore, ed. New World Spanish-English, English-Spanish Dictionary. 1232p. (ENG & SPA.). 1969. pap. 5.50 (0-451-15994-2, AE1312, Sig) NAL-Dutton.
Ramos. Diccionario de la Naturaleza. 976p. (SPA.). 1987. lib. bdg. 49.95 (0-7859-5016-8, 8423969495) Fr & Eur.
Ramos, jt. auth. see Kaiser.
Ramos, Aaron G., ed. Las Ideas Anexionistas en Puerto Rico Bajo la Dominacion Norteamericana. LC 87-82378. (Clasicos Huracan Ser.). 183p. (SPA.). 1987. pap. 7.50 (0-940238-92-6) Ediciones Huracan.
Ramos, Abiud R. Vocabulario Tecnico de Contabilidad Moderna. 159p. 1992. pap. 8.95 (0-8477-2645-2) U of PR Pr.
Ramos, Adam & Ramos, Joseph. California Brandy: The Wine Drinker's Spirit. (Illus.). 160p. 1990. 14.95 (0-929935-08-X) Countrywomans Pr.
— Mixed Wine Drinks: Seven Hundred Recipes for Punches, Hot Drinks, Coolers & Cocktails. 2nd ed. LC 74-25080. (Illus.). 160p. 1990. pap. 9.95 (0-02-003504-7) Countrywomans Pr.
Ramos, Alberto G. The New Science of Organizations: A Reconceptualization of the Wealth of Nations. 224p. 1984. pap. 17.95 (0-8020-6561-9) U of Toronto Pr.
— The New Science of Organizations: A Reconceptualization of the Wealth of Nations. LC 81-178962. 224p. reprint ed. pap. 63.90 (0-685-15277-4, 2026469) Bks Demand.
***Ramos, Andreas.** Your Personal Computer. (Illus.). 352p. (Orig.). 1995. pap. 15.00 (0-87573-062-0) Jain Pub Co.
Ramos, Angel, ed. Diccionario de la Naturaleza: Hombre, Ecologio, Paisaje. (Illus.). 1032p. (SPA.). 1989. 239.50 (84-239-6949-5) Elliots Bks.

R

An Asterisk (*) at the beginning of an entry indicates that the title is appearing in BIP for the first time.

Ramos-Arizpe, Miguel. Report That Dr. Miguel Ramos de Arizpe, Priest of Borbon, & Deputy in the Present General & Special Cortes of Spain for the Province of Coahuila, One of the Four Eastern Interior Provinces of the Kingdom of Mexico, Presents to the August Congress. Benson, Nettie L., tr. & intro. by. LC 69-19011. xiii, 61p. 1970. reprint ed. text ed. 49.75 (*0-8371-1036-X*, TLRR) Greenwood.

Ramos, Arnoldo. El Salvador. (C). 1990. pap. 19.95 (*0-393-30645-3*) Norton.

Ramos, Artur. The Negro in Brazil. Pattee, Richard, tr. LC 80-25342. (Perspectives in Latin American History Ser.: No. 3). xx, 203p. 1981. reprint ed. lib. bdg. 35.00 (*0-87991-604-4*) Porcupine Pr.

Ramos, Elias T. Dualistic Unionism & Industrial Relations. 250p. (Orig.). (C). 1990. pap. 13.75 (*971-10-0415-1*, Pub. by New Day Pub PH) Cellar.

Ramos, Emilio & Schroeder, Al. Concepts of Data Communication. LC 93-30171. (Illus.). 249p. (Orig.). (C). 1993. pap. write for info. (*0-02-407774-7*) Macmillan.

Ramos, Emilio, jt. auth. see Schroeder, Al.

Ramos, Emilio, et al. Data Communications & Networking Fundamentals Using Novell Netware. (Illus.). 473p. (Orig.). (C). 1992. teacher ed write for info. (*0-318-69336-4*); pap. write for info. (*0-02-407791-7*) Macmillan.

— Data Communications & Networking Fundamentals Using Novell NetWare 3.11. LC 93-8780. 475p. (C). 1994. pap. write for info. (*0-02-407766-6*) Macmillan.

— Networking Using Novell NetWare: Release 3.11. LC 93-30153. (Illus.). 268p. (Orig.). (C). 1993. pap. write for info. (*0-02-408025-X*) Macmillan.

— Programming in Visual Basic: A Beginner's Approach. (Illus.). 350p. (C). 1995. pap. text ed. write for info. (*0-201-80884-6*) Addison-Wesley.

Ramos-Escobar, Jose L. Sintigo. LC 85-80225. (Coleccion Sur). 121p. (SPA.). 1985. pap. 7.25 (*0-940238-81-0*) Ediciones Huracan.

***Ramos, Fely.** Pearl from the Orient. 1995. 25.95 (*0-8062-5059-3*) Carlton.

Ramos, Francisco J. Hacer: Pensar. 1994. 22.95 (*0-8477-0184-0*) U of PR Pr.

Ramos-Garcia, Luis, ed. see Colaizzi, Giuliana.

Ramos-Garcia, Luis, jt. ed. see Oliphant, Dave.

Ramos-Garcia, Luis, ed. see Talens, Jenaro.

Ramos-Garcia, Luis, ed. see Talens, Jenaro & Nerlich, Michael.

Ramos-Garcia, Luis A., ed. A South American Trilogy: Osman Lins, Felisberto Hernandez & Luis Fernando Vidal. (ENG, POR & SPA.). 1982. 5.95 (*0-934840-04-0*) Studia Hispanica.

— Southwest Graduate Symposium of Spanish & Portuguese, Literature & Language at the University of Texas. 1980. 5.00 (*0-934840-03-2*) Studia Hispanica.

— Tales from Austin. 1980. 5.95 (*0-934840-02-4*) Studia Hispanica.

Ramos-Garcia, Luis A. & Lugones, Nestor, eds. Studia Hispanica I in Honor of Rodolfo Cardona. 1982. 12.95 (*0-934840-01-6*) Studia Hispanica.

Ramos-Garcia, Luis A. & O'Hara, Edgar, eds. The Newest Peruvian Poetry in Translation. 1979. 4.95 (*0-934840-00-8*) Studia Hispanica.

Ramos-Garcia, Luis A., jt. ed. see Klee, Carol A.

Ramos-Gomez, F., ed. Statistical Physics. 160p. (C). 1991. text ed. 59.00 (*981-02-0584-8*) World Scientific Pub.

Ramos, Graciliano. Barren Lives. Dimmick, Ralph E., tr. LC 65-16468. (Texas Pan American Ser.). (Illus.). 165p. 1965. 12.95 (*0-292-73172-8*); pap. 9.95 (*0-292-70133-0*) U of Tex Pr.

Ramos, I., jt. ed. see Diaz, J.

Ramos, I., jt. ed. see Tjoa, A. M.

Ramos, J. I. Internal Combustion Engine Modeling. (Illus.). 460p. 1989. 73.00 (*0-89116-157-0*) Hemisp Pub.

Ramos, J. M. Combat Raceguns: The World's Best Custom Pistols. (Illus.). 168p. 1993. pap. 25.00 (*0-87364-750-5*) Paladin Pr.

— The CZ-75 Family: The Ultimate Combat Handgun. (Illus.). 1990. 16.00 (*0-87364-566-9*) Paladin Pr.

— Forty-Five Caliber ACP Super Guns: Modified .45 Autos for Competition, Hunting, & Personal Defense. (Illus.). 144p. 1991. pap. 24.00 (*0-87364-636-3*) Paladin Pr.

— World's Deadliest Rimfire Battleguns. (Illus.). 184p. 1989. pap. 16.00 (*0-87364-504-9*) Paladin Pr.

Ramos, J. R. California Land Use Procedure. 1050p. 1991. ring bd. 175.00 (*0-685-70496-3*) Shepards-McGraw.

Ramos-Jimenez, Pilar, jt. auth. see Gastardo-Conaco, M. Cecilia.

Ramos, Joseph. Neoconservatives Economics in the Southern Cone of Latin America, 1973-1983. LC 86-165. (Studies in Development). 240p. 1986. text ed. 32.50x (*0-8018-3040-0*) Johns Hopkins.

Ramos, Joseph, jt. auth. see Ramos, Adam.

Ramos, Juan A. En Casa de Guillermo Tell. (Biblioteca de Autores de Puerto Rico Ser.). 104p. (Orig.). (SPA.). 1991. pap. text ed. 5.95 (*1-56328-004-3*) Edit Plaza Mayor.

— El Manual del Buen Modal y Otras Ocurrencias "Light" 1993. 7.95 (*0-8477-0185-9*) U of PR Pr.

Ramos, Juanita, comp. Companera: Latina Lesbians: An Anthology. (Illus.). 294p. (Orig.). pap. 8.95 (*0-9619450-0-1*) LLHP.

— Companeras: Latina Lesbians: An Anthology. LC 94-4288. 1994. write for info. (*0-415-90925-2*, Routledge NY); pap. write for info. (*0-415-90926-0*, Routledge NY) Routledge.

Ramos, Julio, ed. Amor y Anarquia: Los Escritos de Luisa Capetillo. LC 91-78121. (Clasicos Huracan Ser.). 222p. (SPA.). 1992. pap. 7.95 (*0-929157-15-X*) Ediciones Huracan.

Ramos, Lindsey. Four Chinese Children's Stories. (Illus.). (J). 1991. 14.95 (*0-9628563-0-4*) Lttle Peop Pr.

Ramos, Luis A. & Armas, Jose, eds. Angela de Hoyos: A Critical Look. (Illus.). 53p. 1979. pap. 3.50 (*0-918358-08-6*) Pajarito Pubns.

Ramos, M. Los Acontecimientos del Fin (Finding Events) (SPA.). Date not set. 1.79 (*1-56063-120-1*, 498143) Editorial Unilit.

— Los Acontecimientos del Principio (Beginning Events: How It All Began) (SPA.). 1.79 (*1-56063-318-2*, 498157) Editorial Unilit.

— Relaciones Humanas: Sanas y Positivas (Safe & Positive Human Relations) (SPA.). Date not set. 1.79 (*1-56063-125-2*, 498137) Editorial Unilit.

Ramos, Manuel. The Ballad of Gato Guerrero. 192p. 1994. 18.95 (*0-312-10935-0*, Pub. by Thomas Dunne Bks) St Martin.

— Death of a Martyr: The Ballad of Rocky Ruiz. 208p. 1993. 17.95 (*0-312-09271-7*, Pub. by Thomas Dunne Bks) St Martin.

Ramos, Manuel, jt. auth. see Glass, Elliot.

Ramos, Marcos A. La Pastoral del Divorcio en la Historia de la Iglesia. 198p. (SPA.). 1988. pap. 5.50 (*0-89922-244-7*) Edit Caribe.

— Protestantism & Revolution in Cuba. 168p. 1989. pap. 16.95 (*0-935501-17-7*, CP321) U Miami N-S Ctr.

Ramos, Marcos A., ed. Panorama del Protestantismo en Cuba. 668p. (Orig.). (SPA.). 1986. pap. 14.50 (*0-89922-241-2*) Edit Caribe.

Ramos, Margaret M., ed. see Englekirk, John E.

Ramos, Mary A. Greek Orthodox Faith in Poetry. 200p. (Orig.). 1994. pap. 9.95 (*1-880971-02-X*) Light&Life Pub Co MN.

***Ramos, Mary G., ed.** Texas Almanac 1996-97: State Industrial Guide. (Illus.). (C). 1995. 17.95 (*0-914511-22-X*); pap. 12.95 (*0-914511-21-1*) Dallas Morning.

Ramos, Miguel. Ase Omo Osayin...Ewe Aye. 113p. (Orig.). (SPA.). (C). 1982. pap. 11.99 (*0-685-26085-2*) M W Ramos.

— Seminario De Dilogun Owo Merindilogun. 60p. (Orig.). (SPA.). 1989. pap. write for info. (*0-318-65225-0*) M W Ramos.

Ramos, Miguel W. Seminario De Religion Yoruba: Santeria. 54p. (Orig.). (SPA.). (C). 1988. pap. 12.99 (*0-685-26086-0*) M W Ramos.

Ramos Mimoso, Adriana. Vida & Poesia en Jose Antonio Davila. (UPREX, Estudios Literarios Ser.: No. 71). 409p. 1986. pap. 6.00 (*0-8477-0071-2*) U of PR Pr.

Ramos, Myra, tr. see Freire, Paulo.

Ramos, Myra B., tr. see Freire, Paulo.

Ramos Oliveira, Antonio. Politics, Economics & Men of Modern Spain, 1808-1946. Hall, Teener, tr. LC 72-4285. (World Affairs Ser.: National & International Viewpoints). 720p. 1972. reprint ed. 41.95 (*0-405-04578-6*) Ayer.

Ramos-Poqui, Guillem. The Technique of Icon Painting. (Illus.). 80p. 1991. pap. 17.95 (*0-8192-1624-0*) Morehouse Pub.

Ramos-Ramos, Abiud. Stocks & Bonds. LC 80-20002. (Illus.). 30p. (C). 1980. pap. 2.80 (*0-8477-2637-1*) U of PR Pr.

Ramos, Roberto. Bibliografia de la Revolucion Mexicana, 3 vols. 1976. lib. bdg. 300.00 (*0-8490-1494-8*) Gordon Pr.

Ramos, Teresita & Bautista, Maria. Handbook of Tagalog Verbs: Inflections, Modes, & Aspects. LC 86-6983. 306p. 1986. pap. text ed. 11.00 (*0-8248-1018-X*) UH Pr.

Ramos, Teresita & Goulet, Rosalina M. Intermediate Tagalog: Developing Cultural Awareness Through Language. LC 81-16037. (PALI Language Texts, Philippines Ser.). 542p. (C). 1981. pap. text ed. 17.00 (*0-8248-0776-6*) UH Pr.

Ramos, Teresita V. Conversational Tagalog: A Functional-Situational Approach. LC 84-8612. 358p. 1985. pap. text ed. 15.00 (*0-8248-0944-0*) UH Pr.

— Tagalog Dictionary. LC 71-152471. (PALI Language Texts, Philippines Ser.). 374p. (Orig.). (TAG.). (C). 1971. pap. text ed. 10.00 (*0-87022-676-2*) UH Pr.

— Tagalog Structures. LC 75-152472. (PALI Language Texts, Philippines Ser.). 186p. (Orig.). (C). 1971. pap. text ed. 8.50 (*0-87022-677-0*) UH Pr.

Ramos, Teresita V. & Cena, Resty M. Modern Tagalog: Grammatical Explanations & Exercises for Non-Native Speakers. LC 90-15577. 184p. (C). 1990. pap. text ed. 10.50 (*0-8248-1332-4*) UH Pr.

Ramos, Teresita V. & Clausen, Josie. Filipino Word Book. (Illus.). 112p. (ENG, ILO & TAG.). (J). (gr. k-6). 1993. pap. 11.95 (*1-880188-44-9*) Bess Pr.

— Filipino Word Book. (Illus.). 112p. (ILO & TAG.). (J). (gr. k-6). 1993. 15.95 (*1-880188-54-6*) Bess Pr.

Ramos, Teresita V. & De Guzman, Videa P. Tagalog for Beginners. LC 77-148651. (Pacific & Asian Linguistics Institute. PALI Language Texts: Philippines Ser.). 875p. reprint ed. pap. 180.00 (*0-317-55727-0*, 2029584) Bks Demand.

Ramounachou Moon, Germaine L. Barstow Depots & Harvey Houses. LC 80-80936. (Illus.). 42p. (Orig.). (C). 1980. pap. text ed. 3.50 (*0-918614-02-3*) Mojave Riv Val.

Ramp, Philip, tr. see Kazantzakis, Nikos.

Ramp, Wilma. Fantastic Oatmeal Recipes. 160p. 1988. pap. 5.50 (*0-941016-45-5*) Penfield.

***Rampa, T. Lobsang.** Candlelight. 1994. lib. bdg. 23.95x (*1-56849-438-6*) Buccaneer Bks.

— Cave of the Ancients. 1978. mass mkt. 4.95 (*0-345-27614-0*) Ballantine.

— Chapters of Life. 1994. lib. bdg. 23.95x (*1-56849-436-X*) Buccaneer Bks.

— Doctor from Lhasa. 1991. 10.95 (*0-938294-95-4*) Glob Comm-Inner Lght.

— Feeding the Flame. 190p. 1990. 9.95 (*0-938294-89-X*) Glob Comm-Inner Lght.

— Hermit. 1990. pap. 9.95 (*0-938294-96-2*) Glob Comm-Inner Lght.

— My Visit to Venus. 1992. 5.95 (*0-938294-61-X*) Glob Comm-Inner Lght.

— The Rampa Story. rev. ed. 224p. 10.95 (*0-938294-09-1*) Glob Comm-Inner Lght.

— The Third Eye. 1986. mass mkt. 4.95 (*0-345-34038-8*) Ballantine.

— Thirteenth Candle. 1994. lib. bdg. 23.95x (*1-56849-437-8*) Buccaneer Bks.

— Wisdom of the Ancients. 192p. 1991. reprint ed. lib. bdg. 23.95 (*0-89966-776-7*) Buccaneer Bks.

— You Forever. 288p. (Orig.). 1990. pap. 9.95 (*0-87728-717-1*) Weiser.

— You-Forever. 224p. 1991. reprint ed. lib. bdg. 19.95 (*0-89966-775-9*) Buccaneer Bks.

Rampage, John, intro. International Coal Engineering Conference, 1990. (Illus.). 326p. (Orig.). 1990. pap. 81.75 (*0-85825-499-9*, Pub. by Inst Engrs Aust-EA Bks AT) Accents Pubns.

Rampal, Jean-Pierre & Wise, Deborah. Music My Love: An Autobiography. 1989. 18.95 (*0-318-42516-5*) Random.

Rampal, P., jt. ed. see Scarpignato, C.

Rampal, S. N. Indian Women & Sex. 192p. 1978. 14.95 (*0-318-37064-6*) Asia Bk Corp.

Rampal, V. V. & Mehta, P. C. Lasers & Holography. 450p. 1993. text ed. 99.00 (*981-02-1214-3*) World Scientific Pub.

Rampaul, Hoobasar. Pipe Welding Procedures. LC 73-7849. (Illus.). 238p. 1973. 26.95 (*0-8311-1100-3*) Indus Pr.

***Rampersad, Arnold.** Langston Hughes: The Man, His Art, & His Continuing Influence. Trotman, C. James, ed. LC 95-15708. (Critical Studies in Black Life & Culture: Vol. 29). (Illus.). 175p. 1995. 27.00 (*0-8153-1763-8*, H1872) Garland.

— The Life of Langston Hughes: Vol. 1: 1902-1941: I, Too, Sing America. (Illus.). 448p. 1988. pap. 13.95 (*0-19-505426-1*) OUP.

— The Life of Langston Hughes, Vol. I, 1902-1941: I, Too, Sing America. (Illus.). 448p. 1986. 39.95 (*0-19-504011-2*); pap. 9.95 (*0-685-13534-9*) OUP.

— The Life of Langston Hughes, Vol. II, 1941-1967: I Dream a World. (Illus.). 528p. 1988. reprint ed. 39.95 (*0-19-504519-X*) OUP.

— The Life of Langston Hughes, Vol. II, 1941-1967: I Dream a World. (Illus.). 528p. 1989. reprint ed. pap. 15.95 (*0-19-506169-1*) OUP.

***Rampersad, Arnold, ed.** Richard Wright: A Collection of Critical Essays. LC 94-19515. 216p. 1994. write for info. (*0-13-036120-8*) P-H.

Rampersad, Arnold & Roessel, David, eds. The Collected Poems of Langston Hughes. LC 94-14509. 1994. 30.00 (*0-679-42631-0*) Knopf.

Rampersad, Arnold, jt. auth. see Ashe, Arthur.

Rampersad, Arnold, jt. ed. see McDowell, Deborah E.

Rampersad, Arnold, ed. see Wright, Richard.

***Rampersad, Hubert K.** Integrated & Simultaneous Design for Robotic Assembly. LC 94-28301. 1994. text ed. 34.95 (*0-471-95018-1*) Wiley.

Ramphal, Shridath. Our Country, the Planet: Forging a Partnership for Survival. LC 91-43320. 293p. (Orig.). 1992. 32.00 (*1-55963-165-1*); pap. 15.00 (*1-55963-164-3*) Island Pr.

Ramphal, Shridath, frwd. Banking on Apartheid: The Financial Links Report. 96p. 1990. pap. text ed. 15.00 (*0-435-08044-X*, 08044) Heinemann.

Ramphele, Mamphela. A Bed Called Home: Life in the Migrant Labor Hostels of Cape Town. LC 93-19117. (Illus.). 176p. (Orig.). (C). 1993. pap. text ed. 21.95 (*0-8214-1063-6*) Ohio U Pr.

Rampini, Charles J. Letters from Jamaica the Lands of Streams & Woods. 1977. text ed. 17.95 (*0-8369-9246-6*, 9100) Ayer.

Rampino, Michael R., et al, eds. Climate: History, Periodicity, & Predictability. (Illus.). 608p. 1987. text ed. 95.00 (*0-442-27866-7*) Chapman & Hall.

Rampling, Anne. Exit to Eden. 1986. mass mkt. 5.99 (*0-440-12392-5*) Dell.

Rampling, Anne, ed. see Rice, Anne.

Rampo, Edogawa. Japanese Tales of Mystery & Imagination. Harris, James B., tr. LC 56-6804. (Illus.). 232p. (YA). (gr. 9 up). 1956. pap. 12.95 (*0-8048-0319-6*) C E Tuttle.

Rampp, Lary C., jt. auth. see Anderson, Craig.

***Rampton, Ben.** Crossing: Language & Ethnicity among Adolescents. LC 94-29266. (Real Language Ser.). 400p. (C). 1995. text ed. 57.95 (*0-582-21790-3*, 77024, Pub. by Longman UK); pap. text ed. 27.95 (*0-582-21791-1*, 77023, Pub. by Longman UK) Longman.

Rampton, David. Vladimir Nabokov. LC 93-16140. (Modern Novelists Ser.). 160p. 1993. text ed. 29.95 (*0-312-09629-1*) St Martin.

Rampton, Glenn M., jt. ed. see Wiskoff, Martin F.

Rampton, Richard & Sharp, Victoria. Duncan & Neill: Defamation. 3rd ed. Neill, Brian, ed. 1992. 169.00 (*0-406-17831-3*, U.K.) Butterworth Legal Pubs.

Rampton, Sheldon, jt. auth. see Chilsen, Liz.

Rampton, Sheldon, jt. auth. see Stauber, John.

Rampton, Thomas G. River Guide to Desolation & Gray Canyons on the Green River, Utah. LC 92-97528. (Illus.). 72p. (Orig.). 1992. pap. 9.95 (*0-9634799-0-3*) Blacktail Ent.

Rampulla, Ciro, et al, eds. Cardiopulmonary Rehabilitation. LC 93-13742. (Current Topics in Rehabilitation Ser.). 1993. 45.00 (*0-387-19836-9*) Spr-Verlag.

Ramquist, Grace. Four Dramas for Christmas. 1978. 4.25 (*0-685-68594-2*, MC-251) Lillenas.

— Four Services for Easter. 1974. 4.25 (*0-685-68661-2*, ME-20) Lillenas.

Ramquist, Grace, comp. Christmas Program Builder, No. 22. 1969. 4.25 (*0-685-68582-9*, MC-122) Lillenas.

— Christmas Program Builder, No. 23. 1970. 4.25 (*0-8341-9138-5*, MC-123) Lillenas.

— Christmas Program Builder, No. 24. 1971. 4.25 (*0-685-68580-2*, MC-124) Lillenas.

— Christmas Program Builder, No. 25. 1972. 4.25 (*0-8341-9139-3*, MC-125) Lillenas.

— Christmas Program Builder, No. 26. 1973. 4.25 (*0-685-68578-0*, MC-126) Lillenas.

— Christmas Program Builder, No. 27. 1974. 4.25 (*0-8341-9140-7*, MC-127) Lillenas.

— Christmas Program Builder, No. 28. 1975. 4.25 (*0-8341-9141-5*, MC-128) Lillenas.

— Christmas Program Builder, No. 29. 1976. 4.25 (*0-685-68575-6*, MC-129) Lillenas.

— Christmas Program Builder, No. 30. 1977. 4.25 (*0-8341-9142-3*, MC-130) Lillenas.

— Christmas Program Builder, No. 31. 1978. 4.25 (*0-685-68573-X*, MC-131) Lillenas.

— Christmas Program Builder, No. 32. 1979. 4.25 (*0-685-68572-1*, MC-132) Lillenas.

— Christmas Programs for All Ages. 1978. 4.25 (*0-8341-9148-2*, MC-252) Lillenas.

— Easter Program Builder, No. 9. 1962. 4.25 (*0-685-68674-4*, ME-109) Lillenas.

— Easter Program Builder, No. 10. 1964. 4.25 (*0-685-68673-6*, ME-110) Lillenas.

— Easter Program Builder, No. 11. 1965. 4.25 (*0-8341-9200-4*, ME-111) Lillenas.

— Easter Program Builder, No. 12. 1968. 4.25 (*0-685-68671-X*, ME-112) Lillenas.

— Easter Program Builder, No. 13. 1970. 4.25 (*0-685-68670-1*, ME-113) Lillenas.

— Easter Program Builder, No. 14. 1976. 4.25 (*0-8341-9201-2*, ME-114) Lillenas.

— Easter Program Builder, No. 15. 1978. 4.25 (*0-685-68668-X*, ME-115) Lillenas.

— Four Services for Christmas. 1975. 4.25 (*0-685-68609-4*, MC-248) Lillenas.

— Mother's Day & Father's Day Program Builder, No. 2. 1954. 4.25 (*0-685-68769-4*, MP-302) Lillenas.

— Mother's Day & Father's Day Program Builder, No. 3. 1960. 4.25 (*0-685-68768-6*, MP-303) Lillenas.

— Mother's Day & Father's Day Program Builder, No. 4. 1965. 4.25 (*0-685-68767-8*, MP-304) Lillenas.

— Mother's Day & Father's Day Program Builder, No. 5. 1971. 4.25 (*0-685-68766-X*, MP-305) Lillenas.

Ramraj, Victor J., ed. Concert of Voices: An Anthology of World Writing in English. 400p. 1994. pap. write for info. (*1-55111-025-3*) Broadview Pr.

Ramras-Rauch, Gila. Aharon Appelfeld: The Holocaust & Beyond. LC 93-5016. 1994. 35.00 (*0-253-34831-5*) Ind U Pr.

— The Arab in Israeli Literature. LC 88-46017. (Jewish Literature & Culture Ser.). 256p. 1989. 35.00 (*0-253-34832-3*) Ind U Pr.

Ramras-Rauch, Gila & Michman-Melkman, Joseph, eds. Facing the Holocaust. 292p. 1986. 24.95 (*0-8276-0253-7*) JPS Phila.

Ramsaier, Yves, jt. auth. see Bronkhorst, Jahannes.

Ramsar Convention Bureau Staff. A Directory of Wetlands of International Importance. 796p. 1990. 50.00 (*2-8317-0014-0*, Pub. by IUCN SZ) Island Pr.

Ramsaran, Ramesh F. The Challenge of Structural Adjustment in the Commonwealth Caribbean. LC 91-37505. 224p. 1992. text ed. 57.95 (*0-275-94209-0*, C4209, Praeger Pubs) Greenwood.

— U. S. Direct Investment in the Latin American-Caribbean Region: Trends & Issues. LC 84-18364. 224p. 1985. text ed. 39.95 (*0-312-83317-2*) St Martin.

Ramsaran, Susan M., ed. Studies in the Pronunciation of English: A Commemorative Volume in Honour of A. C. Gimson. 350p. 1989. 82.50 (*0-415-00313-X*) Routledge.

Ramsay. New Ideas Efforting School Improvement. 250p. 1990. 75.00 (*1-85000-696-2*, Falmer Pr); pap. 35.00 (*1-85000-697-0*, Falmer Pr) Taylor & Francis.

— Ramsay: Hawaii Landmark Collection. LC 88-83768. (Illus.). 64p. (Orig.). 1989. pap. 25.00 (*0-317-93360-4*) In Black Inc.

Ramsay, A. T. Oceanic Micropalaeontology, Vol. 1. 1977. text ed. 288.00 (*0-12-577301-3*) Acad Pr.

Ramsay, Agnes D. Everyday Life in Turkey. LC 77-87636. reprint ed. 24.00 (*0-404-16461-7*) AMS Pr.

Ramsay, Alan & Ramsay, Leslie. The MAX: A Personal Financial Management System. 72p. 1983. vinyl bd. 15.00 (*0-932925-00-6*) Cactus Max.

Ramsay, Allan. Ever Green, 2 Vols, 1. LC 74-144532. reprint ed. write for info. (*0-404-08685-3*) AMS Pr.

— Ever Green, 2 Vols, 2. LC 74-144532. reprint ed. write for info. (*0-404-08686-1*) AMS Pr.

— Ever Green, 2 Vols, Set. LC 74-144532. reprint ed. 47.50 (*0-404-08684-5*) AMS Pr.

— Poems of Allan Ramsay, 2 Vols, 1. LC 71-144498. reprint ed. write for info. (*0-404-08585-7*) AMS Pr.

— Poems of Allan Ramsay, 2 Vols, 2. LC 71-144498. reprint ed. write for info. (*0-404-08586-5*) AMS Pr.

— Poems of Allan Ramsay, 2 Vols, Set. LC 71-144498. reprint ed. 110.00 (*0-404-08584-9*) AMS Pr.

— Tea-Table Miscellany: Or, a Collection of Choice Songs, Scots & English. 12th ed. LC 73-144572. reprint ed. 41.50 (*0-404-08687-X*) AMS Pr.

Ramsay, Allan, ed. The Logical Structure of English. 224p. (C). 1990. text ed. 190.00 (*0-273-03287-9*, Pub. by Pitman Pubng UK) St Mut.

Ramsay, Allan & Tenant, William. The Gentle Shepherd: A Pastoral Comedy. LC 78-72783. reprint ed. 19.50 (*0-404-17679-8*) AMS Pr.

R

An Asterisk (*) at the beginning of an entry indicates that the title is appearing in BIP for the first time.

Ramsay, Allan M. Formal Methods in Artificial Intelligence. (Cambridge Tracts in Theoretical Computer Science Ser.: No. 6). 288p. (C). 1988. 69.95 (*0-521-35236-3*) Cambridge U Pr.
— Formal Methods in Artificial Intelligence. (Cambridge Tracts in Theoretical Computer Science Ser.: No. 6). 336p. (C). 1991. pap. 32.95 (*0-521-42421-6*) Cambridge U Pr.
Ramsay, Anna. The Legend of Dr. Markland. large type ed. 257p. 1992. 21.95 (*0-7505-0391-2*, Pub. by Magna Print Bks) Ulverscroft.
Ramsay, Anna A. Sir Robert Peel. LC 72-95076. (Select Bibliographies Reprint Ser.). 1977. 24.95 (*0-8369-5076-3*) Ayer.
— Sir Robert Peel. LC 72-95076. (Select Bibliographies Reprint Ser.). 1982. reprint ed. lib. bdg. 21.50 (*0-8290-0839-X*) Irvington.
Ramsay, Ansil & Mungkandi, Wiwat, eds. Thailand - U. S. Relations: Changing Political, Strategic, & Economic Factors. LC 88-8027. (Research Papers & Policy Studies: No. 23). 330p. (Orig.). 1988. pap. 10.00 (*1-55729-001-6*) IEAS.
Ramsay, Arlan & Richtmyer, Robert D. Introduction to Hyperbolic Geometry. LC 94-25789. (Universitext Ser.). 1994. 39.00 (*0-387-94339-0*) Spr-Verlag.
Ramsay, Caroline C. International Directory of Resources for Artisans, 1992. 2nd ed. Mooney, Sheila, ed. 181p. 1991. 49.95 (*0-9625480-0-6*) Crafts Ctr.
Ramsay, Caroline C. & Mooney, Sheila A. International Directory of Resources for Artisans. 1990. 100.00 (*0-318-50018-3*) Crafts Ctr.
Ramsay, Clay. The Ideology of the Great Fear: The Soissonnais in 1789. LC 91-17676. (Studies in Historical & Political Science: 109th Series, No. 2 (1991)). (Illus.). 352p. 1991. text ed. 49.95x (*0-8018-4197-6*) Johns Hopkins.
***Ramsay, Craig, ed.** U. S. Health Policy Groups: Institutional Profiles. LC 94-27942. 488p. 1995. text ed. 79.50 (*0-313-28618-3*) Greenwood.
Ramsay, Cynthia R. Hawaii's Hidden Treasures. LC 93-6307. 1993. 12.95 (*0-87044-909-5*) Natl Geog.
Ramsay, D. A., ed. see Mulliken, Robert S.
Ramsay, D. C. Engineering Instrumentation & Control. 264p. (C). 1984. pap. 33.00x (*0-85950-225-2*, Pub. by S Thornes Pubs UK) St Mut.
Ramsay, D. C., jt. auth. see Kiddle, P. F.
Ramsay, David. The History of the American Revolution, 2 vols. LC 89-14583. (Illus.). (C). 1990. reprint ed. text ed. 25.00 (*0-86597-078-5*); reprint ed. pap. 15.00 (*0-86597-081-5*) Liberty Fund.
Ramsay, Diana. Four Steps to Death. large type ed. LC 90-40508. 290p. 1990. reprint ed. lib. bdg. 7.95 (*1-56054-037-0*) Thorndike Pr.
— Killing Words. 192p. 1994. 18.95 (*0-312-11015-4*) St Martin.
Ramsay, Diane P. Voyage to Discovery: An Activity Guide to the Age of Exploration. (Illus.). 275p. (Orig.). 1992. pap. text ed. 25.00 (*1-56308-063-X*) Teacher Ideas Pr.
Ramsay, E. Mary. Christian Science & Its Discoverer. LC 35-18957. 137p. 1963. 14.95 (*0-87510-162-3*); pap. 9.95 (*0-87510-108-9*) Christian Sci.
Ramsay, Freda, anno. The Day Book of Daniel Campbell of Shawfield 1767: With Relevant Papers Concerning the Estate of Islay. 1991. 39.90 (*0-08-040933-4*, Pub. by Aberdeen U Pr) Macmillan.
Ramsay, G. D. Wiltshire Woollen Industry in the Sixteenth & Seventeenth Centuries. 2nd rev. ed. 165p. 1965. reprint ed. 35.00 (*0-7146-1355-X*, Pub. by F Cass Pubs UK) Intl Spec Bk.
Ramsay, Harvie, jt. ed. see Beirne, Martin.
Ramsay, Iain, ed. Consumer Law. (International Library of Essays in Law & Legal Theory). 500p. 1992. text ed. 150.00 (*0-8147-7423-7*) NYU Pr.
***Ramsay, J. G.** England, This England: In the Steps of J. B. Priestley. (Illus.). 344p. 1995. 39.95 (*1-85619-329-2*, Sinclair-Stevenson) Trafalgar.
***Ramsay, Jack C., Jr.** Jean Laffite: Prince of Pirates. LC 95-5782. 1995. write for info. (*1-57168-029-2*, Eakin Pr) Sunbelt Media.

—Photographer...Under Fire: The Story of George S. Cook 1819-1902. limited ed. (Illus.). 192p. 1994. 29.95 (*0-9642511-0-8*) J Ramsay Jr. George Cook set up his camera on Fort Sumter's walls in the face of deadly fire. Despite heavy artillery directed at him, he captured combat on a glass plate. This feat was described by the CHARLESTON DAILY COURIER, September 12, 1863 as "One of the most remarkable acts ever recorded in the history of war." Based on unpublished manuscripts including a journal from his son, PHOTOGRAPHER...UNDER FIRE details the daring of the South's premier photographer & records the human drama of a family caught in the disruption of war, the trauma of a raid by Sherman's foragers on their home & the continuing turmoil of the Reconstruction years. Cook balanced love of adventure with a unique ability to picture both the drama of war & the beauty of the human face. His story is as interesting as are his photographs that survived the burning of Columbia. Exhaustive research, endnotes, bibliography, index, & an extensive sampling of Cook's photographs never before published. $29.95, check or money order, Historical Resources Press, 2420-6 Eastman Ave., Green Bay, WI 54302. ***Publisher Provided Annotation.***

— Sunshine on the Prairie: The Story of Cynthia Ann Parker. Eakin, Edwin M., ed. (Illus.). 224p. 1990. 16.95 (*0-89015-686-7*) Sunbelt Media.
Ramsay, James H. The Angevin Empire: or The Three Reigns of Henry II, Richard I, & John, 1154-1216. LC 76-29840. (Illus.). reprint ed. 72.50 (*0-404-15426-3*) AMS Pr.
— The Foundations of England: Or, Twelve Centuries of British History, 2 vols., 1. LC 80-2215. reprint ed. write for info. (*0-404-18781-1*) AMS Pr.
— The Foundations of England: Or, Twelve Centuries of British History, 2 vols., 2. LC 80-2215. reprint ed. write for info. (*0-404-18782-X*) AMS Pr.
— The Foundations of England: Or, Twelve Centuries of British History, 2 vols., Set. LC 80-2215. reprint ed. 125.00 (*0-404-18780-3*) AMS Pr.
Ramsay, James W. Basic Skills for Academic Reading. (Illus.). 288p. (C). 1986. pap. text ed. 17.50 (*0-13-066036-1*) P-H.
Ramsay, Jay. Raw Spiritual: Selected Poems, Nineteen Eighty to Nineteen Eighty-Five. (C). 1986. pap. 38.00 (*0-947612-20-3*, Pub. by Rivelin Grapheme Pr) St Mut.
Ramsay, Jay, ed. The White Poem. (Illus.). 48p. (C). 1988. 60.00 (*0-947612-29-7*, Pub. by Rivelin Grapheme Pr); pap. 39.00 (*0-947612-30-0*, Pub. by Rivelin Grapheme Pr) St Mut.
Ramsay, Jay, jt. auth. see Palmer, Martin.
Ramsay, Jo, jt. auth. see Jordan, Louise.
Ramsay, John. American Potters & Pottery. LC 76-22944. (Illus.). 1976. reprint ed. 34.95 (*0-89344-006-X*) Ars Ceramica.
— Scotland & Scotsmen in the Eighteenth Century: From the Memoirs of John Ramsay Esq. of Ochtertyre, 2 vols. Allardyce, Alexander, ed. LC 78-67537. reprint ed. 97.50 (*0-404-17520-1*) AMS Pr.
Ramsay, John G. & Huber, Martin. The Techniques of Modern Structural Geology, Vol. 1. 1984. text ed. 109.00 (*0-12-576901-6*); teacher ed. text ed. 10.00 (*0-12-576911-3*); pap. text ed. 49.00 (*0-12-576921-0*) Acad Pr.
— Techniques of Modern Structural Geology: Folds & Fractures, Vol. 2. 400p. 1987. pap. text ed. 49.00 (*0-12-576922-9*) Acad Pr.
Ramsay, John R., jt. ed. see Jackson, Michael B.
Ramsay, L. Cobdon. Feudatory States of Orissa. 1983. reprint ed. 22.00 (*0-8364-0960-4*, Pub. by Mukhopadhyaya II) S Asia.
Ramsay, Leslie, jt. auth. see Ramsay, Alan.
Ramsay, Linda M. Interior Design Furnishings Directory of Discounted 800- Number & Hard-to-Find Companies: Insider's Home Decorating Directory of Lower-Priced & Little Known Companies That Offer You Substantial Savings & Higher Values. Matthews, Mary Jo, ed. 169p. 1995. pap. 19.99 (*0-9629918-2-1*) Touch Design.
— Secrets of Success for Today's Interior Designers & Decorators: Easily Sell the Job, Plan It Correctly & Keep the Customer Coming Back for Repeat Sales. 3rd rev. ed. Bachelis, Faren, ed. LC 91-91011. (Illus.). 336p. 1992. reprint ed. pap. text ed. 39.99 (*0-9629918-3-X*, Baker & Taylor) Touch Design.
— Start Your Own Interior Design Business & Keep It Growing! Your Guide to Business Success. Bachelis, Faren, ed. LC 93-93833. 384p. (Orig.). (C). 1994. pap. text ed. 39.99 (*0-9629918-0-5*, Baker & Taylor) Touch Design.
— Successful Window Dressing & Interior Design: Your Guide to Achieving Excellent Results. Matthews, Mary Jo, ed. (Illus.). 336p. 1995. pap. 24.99 (*0-9629918-1-3*) Touch Design.
Ramsay, Maggy. Magic Motif Crochet. LC 87-5381. (Illus.). 160p. 1987. 16.95 (*0-87131-519-X*) M Evans.
Ramsay, Margaret H. The Grand Union (1970-1976) An Improvisational Performance Group. LC 91-17013. (Artists & Issues in the Theatre Ser.). 195p. (C). 1992. text ed. 41.95 (*0-8204-1547-2*) P Lang Pubs.
***Ramsay, Marina, tr.** Notes on Russian America Pt. 2-5: Kad'iak, Unalashka, Atkha, Pribylov Islands. (Alaska History Ser.: No. 43). 1994. 35.00x (*1-895901-02-2*) Limestone Pr.
Ramsay, Marina, tr. see Alekseev, Aleksandr I.
Ramsay, Marina, tr. see Shelikhov, Grigorii I.
Ramsay, Marion L. Pyramids of Power: The Story of Roosevelt, Insull & the Utility Wars. (FDR & the Era of the New Deal Ser.). (Illus.). 342p. 1975. reprint ed. lib. bdg. 37.50 (*0-306-70707-1*) Da Capo.
Ramsay, Marjorie. Golden Prince. LC 77-79266. (Illus.). 1977. 4.95 (*0-917182-04-9*) Triumph Pub.
Ramsay, Marjorie B. Nyra. (Illus.). (J). (gr. 4-7). 1979. 4.95 (*0-917182-10-3*) Triumph Pub.
Ramsay, Mary. Christian Science & Its Discoverer. (GER.). pap. 9.95 (*0-87510-280-8*); pap. 9.95 (*0-87510-281-6*) Christian Sci.
Ramsay, Maureen. Human Needs & the Market. 229p. 1992. 63.95 (*1-85628-258-9*, Pub. by Avebury Pub UK) Ashgate Pub Co.
***Ramsay, Meredith.** Community, Culture, & Economic Development: The Social Roots of Local Action. (Democracy in American Politics Ser.). 160p. (C). 1995. text ed. 49.50x (*0-7914-2749-8*); pap. 16.95x (*0-7914-2750-1*) State U NY Pr.
Ramsay, Nigel, jt. ed. see Blair, John.
Ramsay, Nigel, et al, eds. St. Dunstan: His Life, Times & Cult. (Illus.). 376p. (C). 1992. text ed. 130.00 (*0-85115-301-1*) Boydell & Brewer.
Ramsay, O. Bertrand, jt. auth. see Nicholson, Elva Mae.
Ramsay, Ogden B., ed. Van't Hoff - Le Bel Centennial: A Symposium Sponsored by the Division of the History of Chemistry at the 168th Meeting of the American Chemical Society, Atlantic City, NJ, September 11-12, 1974. LC 75-9656. (ACS Symposium Ser.: No. 12). (Illus.). 208p. reprint ed. pap. 59.30 (*0-8357-4123-0*, 2052334) Bks Demand.
Ramsay, Pamela. Early Childhood Planner: Year-Round Activities & Planning Tips. (J). 1992. pap. 18.70 (*0-201-81784-5*) Addison-Wesley.
Ramsay, Patricia C., et al. Multicultural Education: A Source Book. LC 88-31061. (Source Books on Education). 192p. 1989. 27.00 (*0-8240-8558-2*) Garland.
Ramsay, Paul. Lochs & Glens of Scotland. 1994. 27.50 (*1-55859-867-7*) Abbeville Pr.
Ramsay, R. L. The Place Names of Boone County, Missouri. (Publications of the American Dialect Society: No. 18). (Illus.). 52p. 1952. pap. 5.35 (*0-8173-0618-8*) U of Ala Pr.
Ramsay, Raylene L. Robbe-Grillet & Modernity: Science, Sexuality, & Subversion. LC 92-12415. (University of Florida Humanities Monographs: No. 66). (Illus.). 336p. 1992. lib. bdg. 39.95 (*0-8130-1145-0*) U Press Fla.
Ramsay, Robert L. Our Storehouse of Missouri Place Names. LC 73-79512. 160p. 1973. pap. 10.95 (*0-8262-0586-0*) U of Mo Pr.
Ramsay, T. S., ed. Oceanic Micropalaeontology, Vol. 2. 1978. text ed. 257.00 (*0-12-577302-1*) Acad Pr.
Ramsay, Verna, ed. see Academy of Motion Picture Arts & Sciences Staff.
Ramsay, W. E., ed. Studies in the History & Art of the Eastern Provinces of the Roman Empire. No. 20. xvi, 391p. Date not set. write for info. (*0-318-71210-5*, Pub. by Georg Olms GW) Lubrecht & Cramer.
***Ramsay, W. M.** The Letters to the Seven Churches. rev. ed. Wilson, Mark W., ed. LC 94-33869. (Illus.). 336p. 1994. pap. 19.95 (*1-56563-059-9*) Hendrickson MA.
— Pauline & Other Studies in Early Christian History. 1977. lib. bdg. 59.95 (*0-8490-2416-1*) Gordon Pr.
Ramsay, W. M. & Bell, Gertrude L. The Thousand & One Churches. (Illus.). xvi, 580p. reprint ed. lib. bdg. 100.00 (*0-89241-121-X*) Caratzas.
Ramsay, William. Asianic Elements in Greek Civilization. 303p. 1976. 30.00 (*0-89005-173-9*) Ares.
— Unpaid Costs of Electrical Energy: Health & Environmental Impacts from Coal & Nuclear Power. LC 78-15668. 180p. 1978. pap. 14.95 (*0-8018-2230-0*) Resources Future.
Ramsay, William H. The Education of Christ. LC 80-84438. (Shepherd Illustrated Classics Ser.). (Illus.). 156p. pap. 5.95 (*0-8254-5318-6*) Kregel.
Ramsay, William M. Asianic Elements in Greek Civilisation, Gifford Lecture in the University of Edinburgh, 1915-1916. LC 77-97894. reprint ed. 35.00 (*0-404-05209-6*) AMS Pr.
— The Cities & Bishoprics of Phrygia. LC 75-7336. (Roman History Ser.). (Illus.). 1975. reprint ed. 63.95 (*0-405-07055-1*) Ayer.
— Four Modern Prophets: Walter Rauschenbusch, Martin Luther King, Jr., Gustavo Gutierrez, Rosemary Radford Ruether. LC 86-45351. 108p. (Orig.). 1986. pap. 8.99 (*0-8042-0811-5*, John Knox) Westminster John Knox.
— The Layman's Guide to the New Testament. LC 79-87742. 273p. (Orig.). 1980. pap. 12.99 (*0-8042-0322-9*, John Knox) Westminster John Knox.
— The Social Basis of Roman Power in Asia Minor. Anderson, J. G., ed. 317p. reprint ed. lib. bdg. 52.50 (*0-685-13381-8*, Pub. by A M Hakkert SP) Coronet Bks.
— The Westminster Guide to the Books of the Bible. 608p. 1994. 30.00 (*0-664-22061-4*) Westminster John Knox.
Ramsaye, Terry. Motion Picture Almanac of 1930. 1976. lib. bdg. 700.00 (*0-8490-2288-6*) Gordon Pr.
— Motion Picture Almanac of 1933. 1976. lib. bdg 79.95 (*0-8490-2289-4*) Gordon Pr.
— Motion Picture Almanac of 1935-1936. 1976. lib. bdg 99.50 (*0-8490-2290-8*) Gordon Pr.
— Motion Picture Almanac of 1937-1938. 1976. lib. bdg. 120.00 (*0-8490-2291-6*) Gordon Pr.
Ramsberger, Jack. The Battle History of the Four Hundred Seventy-Third U. S. Infantry in World War Two. 22p. 1981. reprint ed. 4.95 (*0-932572-08-1*) Phillips Pubns.
Ramsberger, Peter F., jt. auth. see Laurence, Janice H.
Ramsbotham, Oliver, jt. auth. see McCall, Malcolm.
Ramsbottom, A. E. Depth Charts of the Cumbrian Lakes. 1976. 30.00 (*0-900386-25-8*) St Mut.
Ramsdale, David & Ramsdale, Ellen. Sexual Energy Ecstasy: A Practical Guide to Lovemaking Secrets of the East & West. LC 93-10329. (Illus.). 1993. pap. 16.95 (*0-553-37231-9*) Bantam.
Ramsdale, David A. & Dorfman, Ellen J. Sexual Energy Ecstasy: A Guide to the Ultimate Intimate Sexual Experience. LC 84-60801. (Illus.). 288p. (Orig.). 1985. pap. 9.95 (*0-917879-00-7*) Peak Skill.
Ramsdale, David A. & Ramsdale, Ellen J. Sexual Energy Ecstasy: A Practical Guide to Lovemaking Secrets of the East & West. 2nd rev. ed. (Illus.). 384p. 1991. 24.95 (*0-917879-04-X*) Peak Skill.
Ramsdale, Ellen, jt. auth. see Ramsdale, David.
Ramsdale, Ellen J., jt. auth. see Ramsdale, David A.
Ramsdale, Jeanne. Long-Haired Cats. (Illus.). 80p. 1984. pap. text ed. 5.95 (*0-86622-231-6*, PB-116) TFH Pubns.
— Persian Cats & Other Longhairs. (Illus.). 1964. 19.95 (*0-86622-718-0*, H-918) TFH Pubns.
Ramsdale, P. A., jt. auth. see Slade, M. G.
Ramsdale, S. A., et al. Status of Research & Modelling of Water-Pool Scrubbing Final Report: Shared-Cost. (EUR Ser.: No. 14566). 172p. 1993. pap. 25.00 (*92-826-5107-X*, CD-NA-14566-EN-C, Pub. by Europ Com) UNIPUB.
Ramsdell. What Do I Read Next? 2nd ed. 1991. 82.00 (*0-8103-5405-5*) Gale.
— What Do I Read Next? 3rd ed. 1992. 82.00 (*0-8103-5406-3*) Gale.
Ramsdell, Charles. Reconstruction in Texas. 1993. reprint ed. lib. bdg. 75.00 (*0-7812-5897-9*) Rprt Serv.
Ramsdell, Charles, tr. see Sierra, Justo.
Ramsdell, Charles W. Reconstruction in Texas. (Texas History Paperbacks Ser.: No. 6). 324p. 1970. reprint ed. pap. 8.95 (*0-292-70031-8*) U of Tex Pr.
Ramsdell, Daniel B. The Japanese Diet: Stability & Change in the Japanese House of Representatives, 1890-1990. 256p. (C). 1992. lib. bdg. 44.50 (*0-8191-8494-2*) U Pr of Amer.
Ramsdell, Donald C., jt. ed. see Caruso, Frank L.
Ramsdell, Marcia, jt. auth. see Lord, Linda A.
Ramsdell, Melissa. A New Leaf: A Handbook for Preserving Michigan's Environment. 144p. 1991. pap. text ed. 4.95 (*0-933112-16-5*) Mich United Conserv.
Ramsdell, Melissa, ed. My First Year as a Doctor: Real World Stories from America's M. D.s. LC 94-4990. (First Year Career Ser.). 1994. 19.95 (*0-8027-1290-8*); pap. 9.95 (*0-8027-7418-0*) Walker & Co.
Ramsdell, William. Ramsdell Family: William Ramsdell Genealogy. 60p. 1994. reprint ed. pap. 12.00 (*0-8328-4184-6*) Higginson Bk Co.
Ramsden, Caroline. Racing Without Tears: Horses. (Illus.). 5.00 (*0-87556-247-7*) Saifer.
Ramsden, D., jt. auth. see Watt, D.
Ramsden, E. C., tr. see Undset, Sigrid.
Ramsden, E. H., tr. Letters of Michelangelo, Vols. 1 & 2. (Illus.). 1963. Set; Vol. 1, lxv, 317p.; Vol. 2, lxv, 338p. 99.50 (*0-8047-0183-0*) Stanford U Pr.
Ramsden, E. H. & Eates, Margot, eds. Eidos: A Journal of Painting, Sculpture & Design, Set, Nos. 1-3. LC 68-9237. (Contemporary Art Ser.). (Illus.). 1968. reprint ed. Set. 24.95 (*0-405-00718-3*) Ayer.
Ramsden, E. N. A-Level Chemistry. 784p. (C). 1988. pap. 95.00 (*0-85950-154-X*, Pub. by S Thornes Pubs UK) St Mut.
— Calculations for A-Level Chemistry. 288p. (C). 1988. 100.00 (*0-85950-755-6*, Pub. by S Thornes Pubs UK) St Mut.
— Calculations for GCSE Chemistry. (C). 1987. text ed. 40.00 (*0-85950-667-3*, Pub. by S Thornes Pubs UK) St Mut.
— Extending Science, No. 5: Metals & Alloys. (C). 1985. 30.00 (*0-85950-193-0*, Pub. by S Thornes Pubs UK) St Mut.
— Food. 96p. (C). 1988. 39.00 (*0-85950-820-X*, Pub. by S Thornes Pubs UK) St Mut.
— A Level Chemistry. 2nd ed. (C). 1990. text ed. 150.00 (*0-7487-0154-0*, Pub. by S Thornes Pubs UK) St Mut.
— A New First Chemistry Course. (C). 1987. text ed. 50.00 (*0-685-39384-4*, Pub. by S Thornes Pubs UK) St Mut.
— A New First Chemistry Course. 192p. (C). 1994. pap. 21.00x (*0-85950-758-0*, Pub. by S Thornes Pubs UK) St Mut.
— Revision Notes in Chemistry. (C). 1981. text ed. 40.00 (*0-85950-498-0*, Pub. by S Thornes Pubs UK) St Mut.
Ramsden, E. N. & Lee, R. E. Air. 64p. (C). 1987. 39.00 (*0-85950-388-7*, Pub. by S Thornes Pubs UK) St Mut.
— Extending Science, No. 1: Air. (C). 1990. 40.00 (*0-7487-0449-3*, Pub. by S Thornes Pubs UK) St Mut.
— Extending Science, No. 2: Water. (C). 1984. 30.00 (*0-85950-389-5*, Pub. by S Thornes Pubs UK) St Mut.
Ramsden, Eileen. Key Science: Chemistry. (Illus.). 384p. (Orig.). 1994. teacher ed 33.00 (*0-7487-1721-8*, Pub. by Stanley Thornes UK); pap. 33.00 (*0-7487-1675-0*, Pub. by Stanley Thornes UK) Trans-Atl Phila.
Ramsden, Francis, ed. see O'Dell, Jennifer.
Ramsden, H., ed. see Garcia Lorca, Federico.
Ramsden, Jean, ed. see MacNeill, Carol.
***Ramsden, John.** The Age of Churchill & Eden: A History of the Conservative Party, 1940-1957. LC 95-9778. 368p. (C). 1996. text ed. 69.95 (*0-582-50463-5*) Longman.
Ramsden, John, jt. auth. see Cook, Christopher.
Ramsden, John, jt. ed. see Cook, Christopher.
Ramsden, John, jt. auth. see Williams, Glyn.
Ramsden, Pamela & Zacharias, Joan. Action Profiling. 386p. 1993. 88.95 (*0-566-02727-5*, Pub. by Gower UK) Ashgate Pub Co.
Ramsden, Paul. Learning to Teach in Higher Education. LC 91-20971. 256p. (Orig.). 1991. 69.50 (*0-415-06414-7*, A6586); pap. 19.95 (*0-415-06415-5*, A6590) Routledge.
Ramsden, Paul, ed. Improving Learning: New Perspectives. 290p. 1988. 39.95 (*0-89397-309-2*) Nichols Pub.
Ramsden, Paul, jt. auth. see Percy, Keith.
Ramsell, John. Questions & Answers. 128p. (Orig.). Date not set. pap. 10.95 (*0-8464-4277-9*) Beekman Pubs.
Ramsett, David. American Capitalism: A Macro View. 208p. (C). 1992. pap. text ed. 32.95 (*0-8403-8150-6*) Kendall-Hunt.
Ramsey. Accident Prevention & Investigation. 1995. text ed. 69.95 (*0-442-01839-8*) Van Nos Reinhold.
— Ethics at the Edges of Life: Medical & Legal Intersections. LC 77-76308. 1980. pap. 18.00 (*0-300-02141-0*) Yale U Pr.
— Five Hundred & One Ways to Boost Your Child's Self-Esteem. 1995. pap. 6.95 (*0-8092-3391-6*, Tribune) Contemp Bks.
***Ramsey & Sleeper.** Architectural Graphics Standards: 1995 Supplement. 9th ed. 1995. pap. text ed. 75.00 (*0-471-11472-3*) Wiley.
Ramsey, jt. auth. see Frederic, Harold.
Ramsey, A. H. The Nameless War. 1978. pap. 5.00 (*0-911038-38-8*) Noontide.

An Asterisk (*) at the beginning of an entry indicates that the title is appearing in BIP for the first time.

Ramsey, A. S. Newtonian Attraction: Cambridge Science Classics. LC 81-18130. 184p. (C). 1982. pap. 24.95 (*0-521-09193-4*) Cambridge U Pr.

Ramsey, Arthur S. An Introduction to the Theory of Newtonian Attraction. LC 41-15935. 194p. reprint ed. pap. 55.30 (*0-317-08670-7*, 2051354) Bks Demand.

Ramsey, Bennett. Submitting to Freedom: The Religious Vision of William James. (Religion in America Ser.). 208p. 1993. 27.50 (*0-19-507426-2*) OUP.

Ramsey, Bets. Old & New Quilt Patterns in the Southern Tradition. LC 87-25182. 132p. 1987. 19.95 (*0-934395-92-6*); pap. 9.95 (*0-934395-63-2*) Rutledge Hill Pr.

Ramsey, Bets & Trechsel, Gail. Southern Quilts: A New View. LC 91-425. (Illus.). 96p. (Orig.). 1991. pap. 12.50 (*0-939009-52-8*) EPM Pubns.

Ramsey, Bets & Waldvogel, Merikay. The Quilts of Tennessee: Images of Domestic Life Prior to 1930. LC 86-14263. (Illus.). 1986. 22.95 (*0-934395-30-6*) Rutledge Hill Pr.

Ramsey, Boniface. Beginning to Read the Fathers. 288p. (Orig.). 1985. pap. 15.95 (*0-8091-2691-5*) Paulist Pr.

Ramsey, Boniface, tr. & anno. The Sermons of St. Maximus of Turin. (Ancient Christian Writers Ser.: No. 50). 1989. 22.95 (*0-8091-0423-7*) Paulist Pr.

Ramsey, Boniface, tr. see Cassian, John.

Ramsey, Boniface, tr. see Kasper, Walter.

Ramsey, Boniface, tr. see Ratzinger, Joseph C.

Ramsey, Brian, ed. The Fiber Optic LAN Handbook. 3rd ed. (Illus.). 467p. (C). 1991. pap. text ed. 17.95 (*0-9626933-3-2*) Codenoll Tech.

Ramsey, Brian & Zack, Tim, eds. The Fiber Optic LAN Handbook. 4th ed. (Illus.). 449p. 1991. pap. 17.95 (*0-9626933-4-0*) Codenoll Tech.

Ramsey, Buck. And As I Rode Out on the Morning. 64p. (Orig.). 1993. pap. 9.95 (*0-89672-310-0*); audio, pap. 18.95 (*0-89672-313-5*); audio 9.95 (*0-89672-312-7*) Tex Tech Univ Pr.

***Ramsey, Caroline C.** International Directory of Resources for Artisans. 3rd ed. 1994. lib. bdg. 100.00 (*0-9625480-1-4*) Crafts Ctr.

Ramsey, Charles G. & Sleeper, Harold R. Architectural Graphic Standards. deluxe ed. 233p. 1990. text ed. 125.00 (*0-471-51940-5*) Wiley.

— Architectural Graphic Standards. 8th suppl. ed. LC 87-31746. 320p. 1993. pap. 81.50 (*0-471-59456-3*) Wiley.

— Architectural Graphic Standards Facsimile. 233p. 1990. text ed. 195.00 (*0-471-51556-6*) Wiley.

— Residential & Light Construction from Architectural Graphic Standards. 8th ed. 467p. 1991. text ed. 115.00 (*0-471-54371-3*) Wiley.

— Site Details from Architectural Graphic Standards. 8th ed. (Ramsey-Sleeper Architectural Graphic Standards Ser.: No. 1955). 336p. 1992. text ed. 115.00 (*0-471-57060-5*) Wiley.

Ramsey, Charles G., et al. Traditional Details for Building Restoration, Renovation & Rehabilitation: From the 1932-1951 Editions of Architectural Graphic Standards. Hoke, John & Kliment, Stephen, eds. 285p. 1991. text ed. 115.00 (*0-471-52956-7*) Wiley.

Ramsey, Charles G., et al, eds. Construction Details from Architectural Graphic Standards. 8th ed. (Ramsey-Sleeper Architectural Graphic Standards Ser.: No. 1955). 408p. 1991. text ed. 115.00 (*0-471-54899-5*) Wiley.

Ramsey, Christian N., Jr., ed. Family Systems in Medicine. LC 88-24477. (Guilford Family Therapy Ser.). (Illus.). 615p. 1989. lib. bdg. 75.00 (*0-89862-103-8*) Guilford Pr.

Ramsey, Dan. Automotive Repair Service: Start & Run a Money-Making Business. LC 93-38576. 1994. pap. text ed. 17.95 (*0-07-051363-5*) TAB Bks.

— Budget Flying: A Private Pilot's Guide. 2nd ed. (Illus.). 192p. 1989. 24.95 (*0-8306-9448-X*) TAB Bks.

— Builder's Guide to Foundations & Framing. LC 94-48314. 1995. text ed. 44.00 (*0-07-051814-9*) McGraw.

— Building a Log Home From Scratch or Kit. 2nd ed. (Illus.). 302p. (Orig.). 1987. pap. 16.95 (*0-8306-2858-4*) TAB Bks.

— Building a Log Home from Scratch or Kit. 2nd ed. 1987. pap. 16.95 (*0-07-155212-X*) McGraw.

— The Complete Foundation & Floor Framing Book. (Illus.). 220p. 1987. pap. 15.95 (*0-8306-2878-9*) TAB Bks.

— Doors, Windows & Skylights. 2nd ed. (Illus.). 240p. 1990. 14.95 (*0-8306-8248-1*, 3248); pap. 14.95 (*0-8306-3248-4*) TAB Bks.

— Electrical Contractor: Start & Run a Money-Making Business. 1993. pap. text ed. 17.95 (*0-07-051289-2*) McGraw.

— Electrical Contractor: Start & Run a Money-Making Business. LC 93-23867. 1993. pap. text ed. 17.95 (*0-8306-4467-9*) TAB Bks.

— Fences, Decks & Other Backyard Projects. 1992. pap. 14.95 (*0-07-051276-0*) McGraw.

— Fences, Decks & Other Backyard Projects. 2nd ed. (Illus.). 304p. 1988. 22.95 (*0-8306-0478-2*); pap. 15.95 (*0-8306-2778-2*) TAB Bks.

— Fences, Decks, & Other Backyard Projects. 3rd ed. 288p. 1992. 24.95 (*0-8306-3494-0*, 4071); pap. 14.95 (*0-8306-3493-2*, 4071) TAB Bks.

— Hardwood Floors. 2nd ed. 1990. pap. 14.95 (*0-07-155314-2*) McGraw.

— Hardwood Floors. 2nd ed. (Illus.). 160p. 1991. 22.95 (*0-8306-7529-9*, 3529); pap. 14.95 (*0-8306-3529-7*) TAB Bks.

— Home Improvements. 1991. 23.95 (*0-8306-5315-5*) TAB Bks.

— Home Improvements: Fifty-Two Weekend Projects. 1989. pap. 14.95 (*0-685-26866-7*) TAB Bks.

— How to Build Great Decks: 50 Great Designs with Complete Plans & Instructions. (Illus.). 128p. 1996. pap. 14.95 (*0-8117-2447-6*) Stackpole.

— Painting Contractor: Start & Run a Money-Making Business. 1993. pap. text ed. 17.95 (*0-07-051299-X*) McGraw.

— Painting Contractor: Start & Run a Money-Making Business. LC 93-23869. 1993. pap. 17.60 (*0-8306-4466-0*) TAB Bks.

— Tile Floors. 2nd ed. (Illus.). 164p. 1991. 22.95 (*0-8306-7535-3*, 3535); pap. 13.95 (*0-8306-3535-1*) TAB Bks.

— UPS Guide to Owning & Managing a Desktop Publishing Business. 250p. 1994. pap. 15.95 (*0-936894-68-7*, 610060-01, Upstart) Dearborn Finan.

— UPS Guide to Owning & Managing a Resume Service. 250p. 1994. pap. 15.95 (*0-936894-69-5*, 6100-6201, Upstart) Dearborn Finan.

— Weather Forecasting: A Young Meteorologist's Guide. (Illus.). 144p. (YA). 1990. 19.95 (*0-8306-8338-0*, 3338); pap. 10.95 (*0-8306-3338-3*) TAB Bks.

— Weather Forecasting: Young Meteorologist's Guide. 1990. pap. 10.95 (*0-07-155685-0*) McGraw.

— Woodworker's Guide to Pricing Your Work. LC 94-33313. 160p. 1995. pap. 18.99 (*1-55870-372-1*) Betterway Bks.

Ramsey, Dave. Financial Peace. 188p. 1992. pap. text ed. write for info. (*0-9635712-0-6*) Lampo Pr.

Ramsey, Dennis A., jt. auth. see Nowicki, Edward J.

Ramsey, Donald O. Your Tax Return: How to Organize & Prepare It. 140p. 1991. student ed 15.95 (*0-9630667-0-6*) KISS Enter.

Ramsey, Donna, jt. auth. see Meier, Regula S.

Ramsey, Doug. Jazz Matters. LC 88-26165. 336p. 1989. 22.95 (*1-55728-060-6*); pap. 12.95 (*1-55728-061-4*) U of Ark Pr.

Ramsey, Doug, ed. see Lowe, Deborah, et al.

Ramsey, Doug, ed. see Wartenberg, Daniel.

Ramsey, Douglas L., jt. auth. see Skroch, Larry E.

***Ramsey, Edwin P. & Rivele, Stephen J.** Lieutenant Ramsey's War. (Illus.). 336p. 1990. reprint ed. pap. 17.95 (*1-57488-052-7*) Brasseys Inc.

Ramsey, Elizabeth M. The Placenta: Human & Animal. LC 81-23372. 204p. 1982. text ed. 65.00 (*0-275-91378-3*, C1378, Praeger Pubs) Greenwood.

Ramsey, Frances M., ed. English Episcopal Acta, Vol. X: Bath & Wells, 1061-1205. (British Academy Ser.). (Illus.). 344p. 1995. 82.00 (*0-19-726131-0*) OUP.

Ramsey, Frank P. On Truth: Original Manuscript Materials from the Ramsey Collection at the University of Pittsburgh (1927-1929) (Episteme Ser.). (C). 1991. lib. bdg. 71.50 (*0-7923-0857-3*) Kluwer Ac.

Ramsey, Frederic, Jr. A Guide to Longplay Jazz Records. LC 77-9065. (Roots of Jazz Ser.). (Illus.). 1977. reprint ed. lib. bdg. 32.50 (*0-306-70891-4*) Da Capo.

Ramsey, Frederic & Smith, Charles E., eds. Jazzmen. LC 78-181233. 360p. 1939. reprint ed. 39.00 (*0-403-01654-1*) Scholarly.

Ramsey, Frederick & Edward, Smith C., eds. Jazzmen. LC 84-26121. (Illus.). 376p. 1985. pap. 9.95 (*0-87910-039-7*) Limelight Edns.

Ramsey, G. Let's Get Talking. (C). 1983. 35.00 (*0-7175-1140-5*, Pub. by S Thornes Pubs UK) St Mut.

Ramsey, Gaynor & Rutman, Michael. Scenes & Themes. 64p. (C). 1985. 40.00 (*0-7175-1306-8*, Pub. by S Thornes Pubs UK) St Mut.

Ramsey, Gerald G. Morning, Noon & Night Cookbook & Menu Planning Guide. rev. ed. LC 80-27662. 262p. 1981. reprint ed. 12.50 (*0-87074-178-0*) SMU Press.

Ramsey, Guy. Postmarked Washington: Pierce County. LC 81-620032. (Illus.). 123p. 1982. 8.50 (*0-917048-54-7*) Wash St Hist Soc.

Ramsey, Guy R. Postmarked Iowa. LC 75-26264. (Illus.). 553p. 1976. 34.00 (*0-916170-02-0*) J-B Pub.

Ramsey Head Pr. Staff. Eating & Drinking in Edinburgh. 1987. 50.00 (*0-902859-90-0*) St Mut.

Ramsey, I. T., ed. see Locke, John.

Ramsey, Iain. Debtors & Creditors - A Socio-Legal Perspective. 1986. U.K. text ed. 56.00 (*0-86205-101-0*) Butterworth Legal Pubs.

Ramsey, Ian T., ed. Prospect for Metaphysics: Essays of Metaphysical Exploration. LC 72-97318. 240p. 1970. reprint ed. text ed. 55.00 (*0-8371-2557-X*, RAME, Greenwood Pr) Greenwood.

***Ramsey, Ida T.** Ida's in the Kitchen. (Illus.). 174p. (Orig.). 1994. pap. text ed. 9.95 (*0-9646860-0-7*) Viola Hilltop Pub.

Ramsey, J. G. Annals of Tennessee to the End of the Eighteenth Century. LC 77-146413. (First American Frontier Ser.). (Illus.). 1971. reprint ed. 55.95 (*0-405-02877-6*) Ayer.

Ramsey, J. G., jt. auth. see Thomas, Jane H.

Ramsey, J. T. Sallust's Bellum Catilinae. LC 81-21281. (American Philological Association Textbook Ser.). 272p. (C). 1984. pap. 15.00 (*0-89130-560-2*, 40 03 09) Scholars Pr GA.

Ramsey, Jackson E. Research & Development: Project Selection Criteria. rev. ed. Farmer, Richard, ed. LC 86-16085. (Research for Business Decisions Ser.: No. 80). 222p. reprint ed. 63.00 (*0-8357-1708-9*, 2070412) Bks Demand.

Ramsey, James. Objections to the Abolition of the Slave Trade with Answers. LC 73-83873. (Black Heritage Library Collection). 1977. 14.95 (*0-8369-8644-X*) Ayer.

— Winter Watch. (Illus.). 154p. (Orig.). (YA). (gr. 10). 1989. pap. 9.95 (*0-88240-329-X*) Alaska Northwest.

Ramsey, James B. Economic Forecasting - Models or Markets? LC 80-21911. (Cato Papers: No. 15). 112p. 1980. pap. 1.00x (*0-932790-28-3*) Cato Inst.

— The Economics of Exploration for Energy Resources. Altman, Edward I. & Walter, Ingo, eds. LC 80-82477. (Contemporary Studies in Economic & Financial Analysis: Vol. 26). 400p. 1981. 73.25 (*0-89232-159-8*) Jai Pr.

— The Oil Middle: Control vs. Competition. 144p. 1985. reprint ed. pap. text ed. 8.50 (*0-8191-4483-5*) U Pr of Amer.

— Revelation: An Exposition of the First Eleven Chapters. (Geneva Commentaries Ser.). 1977. 26.95 (*0-85151-256-9*) Banner of Truth.

Ramsey, James B., ed. see Walter, Ingo I.

Ramsey, James G. Autobiography & Letters. Hesseltine, William B., ed. LC 54-63080. 385p. reprint ed. pap. 109.80 (*0-8357-5906-7*, 2022216) Bks Demand.

***Ramsey, James L.** Who Am I Now That I Am Alone? 3rd ed. (Orig.). 1994. pap. 49.95 (*0-614-04768-4*); pap. 10.95 (*0-614-04769-2*) ABT Inc.

Ramsey, James L., jt. auth. see Bommarito, Patricia S.

Ramsey, James P., jt. auth. see MacBrayne, Lewis.

Ramsey, James R. Architectural, Building, & Mechanical System Acoustics: A Guide to Technical Literature, Volume I Applications. LC 86-63348. viii, 95p. 1986. 28.00 (*0-940737-00-0*) RT Books.

— Architectural, Building, & Mechanical System Acoustics: A Guide to Technical Literature, Volume II Technology. LC 86-63349. viii, 83p. 1986. 25.00 (*0-940737-01-9*) RT Books.

— Sound & Vibration Engineered Environments - Manufacturers & Fabricators of Architectural, Building & Mechanical System Products. vi, 246p. 1988. 28.00 (*0-940737-03-5*) RT Books.

— Wondrous Things: Ancient American Art from the Patterson Collection. (Illus.). 60p. (Orig.). 1993. pap. 19.95 (*0-940561-18-2*) White Rose Pr.

Ramsey, Janet E. Feature & Magazine Article Writing. 384p. 1994. pap. write for info. (*0-697-13832-1*) Brown & Benchmark.

***Ramsey, Jarold.** Hand-Shadows. (QRL Poetry Book Ser.: Vols. XXVIII-XXIX). 20.00 (*0-614-06428-7*); pap. 10.00 (*0-614-06429-5*) Quarterly Rev.

— Reading the Fire: Essays in the Traditional Indian Literatures of the Far West. LC 82-21775. xxii, 250p. 1983. 25.00 (*0-8032-3864-9*) U of Nebr Pr.

Ramsey, Jarold, ed. Coyote Was Going There: Indian Literature of the Oregon Country. LC 76-49158. (Illus.). 336p. 1977. pap. 16.95 (*0-295-95731-X*) U of Wash Pr.

— The Stories We Tell: An Anthology of Oregon Folk Literature. (Oregon Literature Ser.: Vol. 5). (Illus.). 352p. (Orig.). 1994. text ed. 35.95 (*0-87071-379-5*); pap. 21.95 (*0-87071-380-9*) Oreg St U Pr.

***Ramsey, Jeff.** Global Studies: Africa. 6th ed. 288p. 1995. pap. text ed. 13.95 (*1-56134-377-3*) Dushkin Pub.

Ramsey, John. Clarity. LC 83-91303. (Illus.). 160p. (Orig.). 1985. pap. 10.00 (*0-9613286-1-4*) Brainchild Bks.

— Clarity, 3 cass., Set. LC 83-91303. (Illus.). 160p. (Orig.). 1985. audio 20.00 (*0-317-14112-0*) Brainchild Bks.

— Sailing Savannah 1996. LC 93-45965. (Illus.). 128p. 1995. pap. 15.95 (*0-913720-96-8*) Beil.

Ramsey, John, et al. A Science-Technology-Society Case Study: Municipal Solid Waste. 152p. (C). 1989. pap. text ed. 14.60 (*0-87563-339-0*) Stipes.

Ramsey, John T., jt. auth. see Barnes, E. J.

Ramsey, Johnny, ed. Story of the Bible. 1983. pap. 5.50 (*0-89137-543-0*) Quality Pubns.

Ramsey, Jonathan, jt. ed. see Hall, Spencer.

Ramsey-Klee, Diane M., ed. Aids to Biological Communication: Prosthesis & Synthesis. 392p. 1970. 173.00 (*0-677-13410-X*) Gordon & Breach.

— Information & Control Processes in Living Systems: Molecular Coding Problems. 262p. 1967. 123.00 (*0-677-65060-4*) Gordon & Breach.

Ramsey, Lee C. Chivalric Romances: Popular Literature in Medieval England. LC 83-47659. 256p. 1983. 27.50 (*0-253-31360-0*) Ind U Pr.

Ramsey, Leroy. Remembering the Messman at Pearl Harbor: The Story of Doris Miller. (Illus.). 285p. (Orig.). 1992. pap. 14.95 (*0-930355-19-9*) ELRAMCO Enter.

Ramsey, Leroy, ed. see Dillon, Avis Y.

Ramsey, Leroy, ed. see Fanuele, Fran.

Ramsey, Linda L. Plant Biology: Investigations & Explorations. 208p. (C). 1993. spiral bd. 18.95 (*0-8403-8684-2*) Kendall-Hunt.

Ramsey, Lon W. Golf: The Mind Game. rev. ed. LC 87-2550. (Illus.). 40p. 1988. pap. 4.95 (*0-87576-137-2*) Pilot Bks.

***Ramsey, Marcy D.** Rosie's Posies. (Illus.). 36p. (J). (ps-3). 1995. pap. 14.95 (*0-87033-472-7*, Tidewtr Pubs) Cornell Maritime.

Ramsey, Marjorie, jt. ed. see Dittmann, Laura L.

Ramsey, Marjorie E., ed. It's Music! LC 84-435. (Illus.). 56p. (J). (ps-9). 1984. 7.50 (*0-87173-104-5*) ACEI.

***Ramsey, Martha.** Blood Stories. (CSU Poetry Ser.: No. XLIX). 75p. (Orig.). 1996. pap. 10.00 (*1-880834-44-8*) Cleveland St Univ Poetry Ctr.

Ramsey, Matthew. Professional & Popular Medicine in France, 1770-1830: The Social World of Medical Practice. (Cambridge History of Medicine Ser.). (Illus.). 368p. 1988. 69.95 (*0-521-30517-9*) Cambridge U Pr.

Ramsey, Michael. Be Still & Know: A Study in the Life of Prayer. LC 83-4765. 120p. (Orig.). 1993. reprint ed. pap. 9.95 (*1-56101-083-9*) Cowley Pubns.

— The Christian Priest Today. rev. ed. 112p. 1994. pap. 9.95 (*1-56101-106-1*) Cowley Pubns.

— The Gospel & the Catholic Church. LC 89-48207. (Classics Ser.). 234p. 1990. 19.95 (*1-56101-006-5*); pap. 11.95 (*0-936384-91-3*) Cowley Pubns.

— Modern Spirituality Series. 96p. 1990. pap. 4.95 (*0-87243-178-9*) Templegate.

Ramsey, Michael & Coleman, Dale. The Anglican Spirit. LC 91-6599. 175p. (Orig.). 1991. pap. 11.95 (*1-56101-027-8*) Cowley Pubns.

Ramsey, Michael & Griffiss, James, prefs. Holy Spirit: A Biblical Study. LC 92-25733. (Cowley Classic Ser.). 140p. 1992. pap. 9.95 (*1-56101-069-3*) Cowley Pubns.

Ramsey, Myriam & Dixon, Paul. Uma Concordancia do Romance Grande Sertao: Veredas de Joao Guimaraes Rosa. LC 88-36934. (Studies in the Romance Languages & Literatures: No. 235). 1989. fiche 27.50 (*0-8078-9239-4*) U of NC Pr.

Ramsey, Norman, jt. auth. see Kleppner, Daniel.

Ramsey, Norman F. Molecular Beams. (International Series of Monographs on Physics). (Illus.). 466p. 1990. reprint ed. pap. 42.50 (*0-19-852021-2*) OUP.

Ramsey, Paige. In the Middle of Muddle. (Illus.). 95p. (Orig.). 1991. pap. 5.95 (*1-879366-05-3*) Hearthstone OK.

Ramsey, Patricia. A Killin. 18p. (Orig.). 1990. pap. 2.50 (*0-87129-011-1*, K22) Dramatic Pub.

— Making Friends in School: Promoting Peer Relationships in Early Childhood. (Early Childhood Education Ser.: Vol. 32). 1991. text ed. 40.95 (*0-8077-3128-5*); pap. text ed. 18.95 (*0-8077-3127-7*) Tchrs Coll.

Ramsey, Patricia G. Teaching & Learning in a Diverse World: Multicultural Education for Young Children. (Early Childhood Education Ser.). (C). 1986. text ed. 29.95 (*0-8077-2830-6*); pap. text ed. 17.95 (*0-8077-2828-4*) Tchrs Coll.

Ramsey, Paul. The Art of John Dryden. LC 70-80088. (South Atlantic Modern Language Association Award Study). 224p. reprint ed. pap. 63.90 (*0-8357-5762-5*, 2030055) Bks Demand.

— Basic Christian Ethics. (Library of Theological Ethics). 416p. 1993. pap. 14.99 (*0-664-25324-5*) Westminster John Knox.

— Deeds & Rules in Christian Ethics. LC 83-10257. 256p. (C). 1983. reprint ed. pap. text ed. 23.00 (*0-8191-3355-8*) U Pr of Amer.

— The Essential Paul Ramsey: A Collection. Werpehowski, William & Crocco, Stephen, eds. LC 93-35449. 320p. (C). 1994. 30.00 (*0-300-05815-2*) Yale U Pr.

— Fabricated Man: The Ethics of Genetic Control. LC 78-123395. (Yale Fastback Ser.: No. 6). 182p. reprint ed. pap. 51.90 (*0-7837-2783-6*, 2043175) Bks Demand.

— The Fickle Glass: A Study of Shakespeare's Sonnets. LC 77-15910. (Studies in the Renaissance: No. 4). 1979. 34.50 (*0-404-16032-8*) AMS Pr.

— The Just War: Force & Political Responsibility. 524p. (C). 1991. pap. text ed. 19.95 (*0-8226-3014-1*) Littlefield.

Ramsey, Paul, 1913. Limits of Nuclear War: Thinking About the Do-Able & the Un-Do-Able. LC 63-17701. (Ethics & Foreign Policy Ser.). 1963. pap. 0.50 (*0-87641-106-5*) Carnegie Ethics & Intl Affairs.

Ramsey, Paul. Nine Modern Moralists: Paul Tillich, Karl Marx, H. Richard Niebuhr, Fyodor Dostoevski, Reinhold Niebuhr, Jacques Maritain, Jean-Paul Sartre, Emil Brunner, Edmond Cahn. 284p. (C). 1983. reprint ed. pap. text ed. 24.00 (*0-8191-3414-7*) U Pr of Amer.

— The Patient as Person: Explorations in Medical Ethics. LC 77-118737. (Lyman Beecher Lectures at Yale University). 305p. reprint ed. pap. 87.00 (*0-8357-8260-3*, 2033863) Bks Demand.

— Speak up for Just War or Pacifism: A Critique of the United Methodist Bishop's Pastoral Letter "In Defense of Creation" LC 87-21295. 256p. 1988. lib. bdg. 30.00 (*0-271-00619-6*); pap. 12.95 (*0-271-00639-0*) Pa St U Pr.

— Study of Religion in Colleges & Universities. Wilson, John F., ed. LC 70-90957. 336p. 1970. 55.00x (*0-691-07161-6*) Princeton U Pr.

— War & the Christian Conscience: How Shall Modern War Be Conducted Justly? LC 61-10666. xxiv, 331p. 1961. reprint ed. pap. 14.95 (*0-8223-0361-2*) Duke.

— War & the Christian Conscience: How Shall Modern War be Conducted Justly? LC 61-10666. 353p. reprint ed. pap. 100.70 (*0-317-26099-5*, 2023766) Bks Demand.

— Window for New York. 1968. pap. 10.00 (*0-912136-01-4*) Twowindows Pr.

Ramsey, Paul, ed. Contemporary Religious Poetry. 224p. 1987. pap. 9.95 (*0-8091-2883-7*) Paulist Pr.

***Ramsey, Paul & Wilson, John F., eds.** The Study of Religion in Colleges & Universities. LC 70-90957. Date not set. reprint ed. pap. 104.10 (*0-7837-9429-0*, 2060170) Bks Demand.

Ramsey, Paul, ed. see Edwards, Jonathan.

Ramsey, Paul, jt. ed. see McCormick, Richard A.

Ramsey, Paul G. & Larson, Eric B. Medical Therapeutics. 2nd ed. LC 92-17196. (Illus.). 651p. 1992. pap. text ed. 18.95 (*0-7216-3496-6*) Saunders.

***Ramsey, R. D.** Mother's Wisdom: A Book of Thoughts & Encouragements. 288p. 1995. 12.00 (*0-8092-3433-5*) Contemp Bks.

Ramsey, Richard. Am I Good Enough: Learning to Live by God's Grace. (Illus.). 98p. (Orig.). 1992. student ed, pap. 4.99 (*0-87552-395-1*) Presby & Reformed.

***Ramsey, Rick.** All About Administering NIS. 2nd ed. 480p. 1994. pap. text ed. 42.00 (*0-13-309576-2*) P-H.

Ramsey, Robert. Five Hundred One Ways to Boost Your Child's Self-Esteem. LC 93-38723. 1994. pap. 5.95 (*1-56943-037-3*, Tribune) Contemp Bks.

***Ramsey, Robert D.** Administrator's Complete School Discipline Guide: Creating an Environment Where All Kids Can Learn. LC 94-31881. 1994. pap. (*0-13-079401-5*) P-H.

— Educator's Discipline Handbook. LC 81-38402. 284p. 1981. text ed. 24.95 (*0-13-240788-4*, Parker Publishing Co) P-H.

— Management Techniques for Solving School Personnel Problems. 192p. 1984. text ed. 32.95 (*0-13-549841-4*, Busn) P-H.

Ramsey, Robert W. Carolina Cradle: Settlement of the Northwest Carolina Frontier, 1747-1762. LC 64-22530. xvii, 251p. 1987. reprint ed. pap. 14.95 (*0-8078-4189-7*) U of NC Pr.

Ramsey, Roy V. The Manly-Rickert Text of the Canterbury Tales. LC 93-50809. 716p. 1994. 139.95 (*0-7734-9128-7*) E Mellen.

R

An Asterisk (*) at the beginning of an entry indicates that the title is appearing in BIP for the first time.

Ramsey, Russell W. God's Joyful Runner: The Story of Eric Liddell. LC 87-71167. 225p. (Orig.). 1987. pap. 7.95 (0-88270-624-1) Bridge Pub.
— Lady - A Peacemaker. 1988. 17.95 (0-8283-1910-3) Branden Pub Co.
— On Law & Country: The Biography & Speeches of Russell Archibald Ramsey. (Illus.). 200p. 1993. pap. 12.95 (0-8283-1970-7) Branden Pub Co.
Ramsey, Russell W. & Khromov, Yuri G. Ten Soviet Sports Stars. (Illus.). 1990. pap. 11.95 (0-8283-1930-8) Branden Pub Co.
Ramsey, Russell W., ed. see Holley, Joseph W.
Ramsey, Ruth G. Diagnostic Radiology of the Brain: CT, DSA, NMR. 2nd ed. (Advanced Exercises in Diagnostic Radiology Ser.: Vol. 9). (Illus.). 320p. 1984. pap. text ed. 55.95 (0-7216-1177-X) Saunders.
— Neuroradiology. 3rd ed. LC 93-26474. (Illus.). 1056p. 1994. text ed. 159.00 (0-7216-3657-8) Saunders.
Ramsey, S., jt. auth. see MacBeth, A.
Ramsey, S. Robert. The Languages of China. (Illus.). 353p. 1990. pap. 18.95 (0-691-01468-X) Princeton U Pr.
Ramsey, Samuel. English Language & English Grammar: An Historical Study. LC 68-24968. (Studies in Language: No. 41). 1969. reprint ed. lib. bdg. 75.00 (0-8383-0231-9) M S G Haskell Hse.
Ramsey, Stanley C. & Harvey, J. D. Small Georgian Houses & Their Details. (Illus.). 100p. 1977. pap. 54.95 (0-85139-248-2, Butterwrth Archit) Buttrwrth-Heinemann.
Ramsey, Sylvia. Favorite Recipe Index. 102p. (Orig.). pap. 6.95 (0-318-18420-6) S Ramsey.
Ramsey, Thomas L. Elementary Instrumental Teachers' Handbook. Pellerin, R. G., ed. & illus. by. 104p. (Orig.). 1986. pap. text ed. 10.00 (0-9615350-0-8) Intro Musicaids.
Ramsey, Verna, ed. see Academy of Motion Picture Arts & Sciences Staff.
Ramsey-Wilkes. Success Strategies for Women in Business. 224p. 1993. pap. text ed. 19.95 (0-8403-8166-2) Kendall-Hunt.
Ramsey, Willard A. Zion's Glad Morning. (Illus.). 320p. (Orig.). 1990. 15.95 (0-9625220-0-7); pap. 9.95 (0-9625220-1-5) Millennium Three Pubs.
Ramsey, William, et al, eds. Philosophy & Connectionist Theory. 336p. (C). 1991. text ed. 69.95 (0-8058-0592-3); pap. 34.50 (0-8058-0883-3) L Erlbaum Assocs.
Ramsey-Woodward, Maureen, ed. see Woodward, Dan.
Ramseyer, Alice R., jt. auth. see Ramseyer, Robert.
Ramseyer, J. Mark & Rosenbluth, Frances M. Japan's Political Marketplace. LC 92-33647. (Illus.). 272p. 1993. 42.50 (0-674-47280-2) HUP.
— The Politics of Oligarchy: Institutional Choice in Imperial Japan. (Political Economy of Institutions & Decisions Ser.). (Illus.). 256p. (C). 1995. write for info. (0-521-47397-7) Cambridge U Pr.
Ramseyer, J. Mark, jt. auth. see Klein, William A.
Ramseyer, Robert & Ramseyer, Alice R. Mennonites in China. rev. ed. Funk, Herta & Kelsey, Betty, eds. (Illus.). 114p. 1989. reprint ed. pap. 6.00 (1-877736-02-3) MB Missions.
Ramseyer, Robert L. Mission & the Peace Witness. LC 79-16738. (Mennonite Missionary Study Ser.: No. 7). 152p. 1979. pap. 7.95 (0-8361-1896-0) Herald Pr.
Ramseyer, William L. Jellyfish Mask. 64p. 1992. pap. 9.95 (1-882620-01-1) Buy Yourself.
Ramsfield, Jill J., jt. auth. see Ray, Mary B.
Ramshaw, Elaine. The Godparent Book. LC 93-29858. 96p. 1993. 15.95 (1-56854-037-X); pap. 8.95 (1-56854-015-9) Liturgy Tr Pubns.
— Ritual & Pastoral Care. LC 85-45487. (Theology & Pastoral Care Ser.). 128p. 1987. pap. 11.00 (0-8006-1738-X, 1-1738, Fortress Pr) Augsburg Fortress.
Ramshaw, Gail. God beyond Gender: Feminist Christian God Language. LC 94-17695. 1995. 12.00 (0-8006-2774-1, Fortress Pr) Augsburg Fortress.
— A Metaphorical God. rev. ed. (Illus.). 90p. 1995. pap. 6.95 (1-56854-071-X, METGOD) Liturgy Tr Pubns.
— Sunday Morning. (Illus.). 46p. 1993. 15.95 (1-56854-005-1, SUN/AM) Liturgy Tr Pubns.
— Sunday Morning. (Illus.). 48p. (J). 1994. pap. 8.95 (1-56854-081-7, PSUNAM) Liturgy Tr Pubns.
— Words Around the Fire: Reflections on the Scriptures of the Easter Vigil. (Illus.). 77p. (Orig.). 1990. pap. 6.95 (0-929650-14-X) Liturgy Tr Pubns.
— Words Around the Font. LC 94-24022. (Illus.). 110p. (Orig.). 1995. pap. 8.95 (1-56854-063-9, WFONT) Liturgy Tr Pubns.
— Words Around the Table. (Illus.). 122p. (Orig.). 1990. pap. 8.95 (0-929650-28-X) Liturgy Tr Pubns.
— Words That Sing. 167p. (Orig.). 1992. pap. 9.95 (0-929650-42-5) Liturgy Tr Pubns.
Ramshaw, Gail, ed. Homilies for the Christian People, Cycles A, B, C. 572p. 1992. pap. 25.00 (0-8146-6092-4, Pueblo Bks) Liturgical Pr.
— Intercessions for the Christian People, Cycles A, B, C. 216p. 1992. pap. 17.50 (0-8146-6091-6, Pueblo Bks) Liturgical Pr.
— Richer Fare for the Christian People, Cycles A, B, C. 245p. pap. 18.50 (0-8146-6102-5, Pueblo Bks) Liturgical Pr.
Ramshaw, Gail, jt. auth. see Lathrop, Gordon.
Ramshaw, Gail, jt. ed. see Lathrop, Gordon.
Ramshaw, Paul, et al, eds. Intervention on Trial: The New York War Crimes Tribunal on Central America & the Caribbean. LC 86-30342. 218p. 1987. text ed. 55.00 (0-275-92188-3, C2189, Praeger Pubs); pap. 14.95 (0-275-92189-1, B2189, Praeger Pubs) Greenwood.
***Ramshaw, Raymond.** Power Electronics Semiconductor Switches. 2nd ed. LC 94-133716. 458p. 1994. pap. 29.50 (0-412-28870-2) Chapman & Hall.
Ramshaw, Raymond S. & Van Heeswijk, R. G. Energy Conversion: Electric Motors & Generators. 633p. (C). 1990. text ed. 62.75 (0-03-003399-3); Solutions manual. teacher ed. write for info. (0-03-003402-7) SCP.
Ramshaw-Schmitt, Gail. Worship: Searching for Language. 213p. (Orig.). 1988. pap. 11.95 (0-912405-49-X) Pastoral Pr.
Ramsland, Clement, jt. ed. see Bowditch, John.
***Ramsland, Katherine.** The Anne Rice Trivia Book. (Orig.). 1994. mass mkt. 5.99 (0-345-39251-5) Ballantine.
— Prism of the Night: A Biography of Anne Rice. LC 92-5355. (Illus.). 432p. 1992. pap. 12.00 (0-452-26862-1, Plume) NAL-Dutton.
— Prism of the Night: A Biography of Anne Rice. 432p. 1994. pap. 12.95 (0-452-27331-5, Plume) NAL-Dutton.
— Vampire Companion. (Illus.). 640p. 1995. 17.95 (0-345-39739-8) Ballantine.
— The Vampire Companion: The Official Guide to Anne Rice's The Vampire Chronicles. LC 93-2378. 512p. 1994. 29.95 (0-345-37922-5, Ballantine Trade) Ballantine.
— The Witches' Companion: The Official Guide to Anne Rice's Lives of the Mayfair Witches. LC 94-9747. 528p. 1994. 29.95 (0-345-38947-6) Ballantine.
Ramsland, Katherine M. The Art of Learning: A Self-Help Manual for Students. 236p. (C). 1992. 39.50 (0-7914-0921-X); pap. 12.95 (0-7914-0922-8) State U NY Pr.
— Engaging the Immediate: Kierkegaard's Indirect Communication & Psychotherapy. LC 87-46432. 136p. 1989. 29.50 (0-8387-5152-0) Bucknell U Pr.
Ramslove. The Magical Circle. rev. ed. (Illus.). 96p. 1985. spiral bd., pap. 24.95 (0-9614605-0-4) Trout Gulch Pr.
Ramson, W. S., ed. The Australian Concise Oxford Dictionary. 2nd ed. 1424p. 1993. 35.00 (0-19-553442-5) OUP.
— The Australian National Dictionary: A Dictionary of Australianisms on Historical Principles. 830p. 1989. 85.00 (0-19-554736-5) OUP.
Ramsower, Reagan M. Telecommuting: The Organizational & Behavioral Effects of Working at Home. Farmer, Richard, ed. LC 84-28095. (Research for Business Decisions Ser.: No. 75). 208p. reprint ed. pap. 59.00 (0-8357-1628-7, 2070413) Bks Demand.
Ramstack, Janet & Rosenbaum, Ernest H. Nutrition for the Chemotherapy Patient. 380p. 1990. pap. 18.95 (0-915950-99-5) Bull Pub.
Ramstad, C. J. Legend: Arctic Cat's First Quarter Century. (Illus.). 194p. (Orig.). 1987. pap. text ed. 17.95 (0-9603786-0-X) PPM Bks.
Ramstad, C. J. & Satran, Bob. Of Ice & Engines: Twenty-Five Years of Eagle River World's Championship Snowmobile Derby Racing. (Illus.). 146p. (Orig.). 1988. pap. text ed. 15.00 (0-9603786-2-6) PPM Bks.
Ramstad, P. E., jt. ed. see Watson, S. A.
***Ramstad, T. A., et al.** Subband Compression of Images: Principles & Examples. 394p. 1995. 157.25 (0-444-89431-4) Elsevier.
Ramstedt, Gustav J. Seven Journeys Eastward Eighteen Ninety-Eight to Nineteen Twelve. Krueger, John R., tr. (Mongolia Society Occasional Papers: No. 9). Orig. Title: Seitseman Retkea Itaan. 1978. pap. 15.00 (0-910980-19-5) Mongolia.
***Ramstetter, Mary.** Over the Mountains of the Moon: An American Novel. LC 94-93954. 458p. (Orig.). 1995. per., pap. 14.00 (0-9643283-0-5) C Lazy Three.
Ramsurrun, Pahlad. Folk Tales of Mauritius. 120p. 1988. text ed. 15.95 (81-207-0733-8, Pub. by Sterling Pubs II) Apt Bks.
Ramteke, Timothy. Networks. LC 93-41893. 482p. 1993. text ed. 66.00 (0-13-958059-X) P-H.
Ramtha. I Am Ramtha. 1987. 24.95 (0-941831-11-6) Beyond Words Pub.
— Ramtha. Weinberg, Steven L., ed. LC 85-61768. 224p. 1986. 19.95 (0-932201-11-3) Sovereignty.
— Ramtha. Weinberg, Steven L., ed. 224p. 1994. pap. 12.50 (0-932201-03-2) Sovereignty.
— Ramtha: An Introduction. Weinberg, Steve L., ed. LC 87-60651. 208p. (Orig.). 1988. pap. 9.95 (0-932201-76-8) Sovereignty.
Ramtha & Mahr, Douglas J. The Ominous Dragoon. LC 84-62175. (Illus.). 48p. 1985. 7.95 (0-931317-12-6) Masterwrks Inc.
— The Ominous Dragoon. deluxe ed. LC 84-62175. (Illus.). 48p. 1985. 24.95 (0-931317-13-4) Masterwrks Inc.
Ramtin, Ramin. Capitalism & Automation: Revolution in Technology & Capitalist Breakdown. 211p. (C). 1991. text ed. 73.50 (0-7453-0370-6, Pub. by Pluto Pr UK) Westview.
Ramu, G. N. Family Structure & Fertility: Emerging Patterns in an Indian City. 188p. (C). 1988. text ed. 20.00 (0-8039-9547-4) Sage.
— Women, Work & Marriage in Urban India: A Study of Dual- & Single-Earner Couples. 200p. (C). 1990. text ed. 24.00 (0-8039-9626-8) Sage.
Ramulu, R. & Komanduri, R., eds. Machining of Advanced Composites. LC 93-73268. 227p. Date not set. pap. 60.00 (0-7918-1033-X) ASME.
Ramundo, Bernard A. The Bargaining Manager: Enhancing Organizational Results Through Effective Negotiation. LC 93-32881. 176p. 1994. text ed. 49.95 (0-89930-805-8, Quorum Bks) Greenwood.
— Effective Negotiation: A Guide to Dialogue Management & Control. LC 91-40961. 216p. 1992. text ed. 52.95 (0-89930-727-2, REM, Quorum Bks) Greenwood.
— Peaceful Coexistence: International Law in the Building of Communism. LC 67-12421. 262p. 1967. 38.00x (0-8018-0542-2) Johns Hopkins.
***Ramundo, Michael.** The Complete Customer Service Model Letter & Memo Book. LC 94-29915. (C). 1994. text ed. 32.95 (0-13-335803-8) P-H.
Ramundo, Peggy, jt. auth. see Kelly, Kate.
Ramunny, Murkot. World of Nagas. 1993. reprint ed. 30.00 (81-7211-035-9, National Bk Ctr) S Asia.
Ramus, Charles, ed. see Daumier, Honore.
Ramus, Daniel. New England Who, What, When & Where Book. 1994. 9.98 (0-88365-855-0) Galahad Bks.
***Ramus, David.** Thief of Light: A Novel. 1995. 23.00 (0-06-017664-4, HarpT) HarpC.
Ramus, Erica, jt. auth. see Frank, Norman.
Ramus, J. W. Contract Practice for Quantity Surveyors. 2nd ed. 224p. 1989. pap. 39.95 (0-434-91677-3) Buttrwrth-Heinemann.
Ramus, Petrus, pseud. Grammatica. 119p. 1991. reprint ed. write for info. (0-318-71466-3, Pub. by Georg Olms GW) Lubrecht & Cramer.
Ramus, Petrus. Scholae in Liberales Artes. Ong, W. J., ed. xvi, 1166p. 1970. reprint ed. write for info. (0-318-71275-X, Pub. by Georg Olms GW) Lubrecht & Cramer.
— Scholae in Liberales Artes. xvi, 1166p. (GER.). 1970. reprint ed. write for info. (0-318-70504-4, Pub. by Georg Olms GW); reprint ed. write for info. (0-318-71467-1, Pub. by Georg Olms GW) Lubrecht & Cramer.
— Scholarum Mathematicarum Libri Unus et Triginta. 314p. reprint ed. write for info. (0-318-71468-X, Pub. by Georg Olms GW) Lubrecht & Cramer.
Ramus, Petrus & Talaeus, Audomarus. Collectaneae Praefationes, Epistolae, Orationes. xxviii, 625p. 1969. reprint ed. write for info. (0-318-71465-5, Pub. by Georg Olms GW) Lubrecht & Cramer.
Ramusack, Barbara N. The Princes of India in the Twilight of Empire: Dissolution of a Patron-Client System, 1914-1939. LC 78-18161. (Illus.). 344p. 1978. 49.50 (0-8142-0272-1) Ohio St U Pr.
Ramuz, C. F. Cezanne: Form. (Rhythem & Color Two Ser.). 1970. 9.95 (0-8288-9515-5) Fr & Eur.
Ramwell, Dave & Madge, Tim. A Ship Too Far: The Truth about the Loss of the Derbyshire. 256p. 1992. 34.95 (0-340-56997-2, Pub. by H & S UK) Trafalgar.
Ramwell, P., et al, eds. Sex Steroids & the Cardiovascular System. LC 92-49749. (Schering Foundation Workshop Ser.: Vol. 5). (Illus.). xii, 201p. 1993. 59.00 (3-540-55728-8); 52.00 (0-387-55728-8) Spr-Verlag.
Ramwell, Peter W., jt. ed. see O'Flaherty, Joseph T.
Ramzaev, P. V., ed. Medical Consequences of the Chernobyl Nuclear Accident. 237p. 1994. lib. bdg. 89.00 (1-56072-111-1) Nova Sci Pubs.
Ramzy, Ashraf. How to Advertise Your Hotel to Success: The Marketing Guide to Hotel Advertising. LC 91-65993. 174p. (Orig.). (C). 1991. pap. 39.95 (0-9630095-0-8) Townhouse FL.
Ramzy, Ibrahim. Clinical Cytopathology & Aspiration Biopsy. (Illus.). 427p. 1989. boxed 95.00 (0-8385-1279-8, A1279-7) Appleton & Lange.
***Ran, Bin & Boyce, David E.** Dynamic Urban Transportation Network Models: Theory & Implications for Intelligent Vehicle-Highway Systems. LC 94-22844. 1994. write for info. (0-387-58360-2) Spr-Verlag.
Ran-Moseley, Faye. The Tragicomic Passion: Clowns, Fools & Madmen in Drama, Film & Literature. LC 92-27556. (American University Studies: Comparative Literature: Ser. III, Vol. 40). 208p. (C). 1993. text ed. 43.95 (0-8204-1551-0) P Lang Pubs.
Ran, Nachman. Journeys to the Promised Land. 1989. 19.99 (0-517-68916-2) Random Hse Value.
Rana, I. M. Economic System under Umer the Great. 14.50 (0-935782-86-9) Kazi Pubns.
Rana, Indi. The Roller Birds of Rampur. 1994. mass mkt. 3.99 (0-449-70434-3, Juniper) Fawcett.
— The Roller Birds of Rampur. 304p. (YA). (gr. 7 up). 1993. 15.95 (0-8050-2670-3, Bks Young Read) H Holt & Co.
Rana, Kiran S., tr. see Schuurman, C. J.
Rana, M. S. Writings on Indian Constitution, 1861-1985. 548p. (C). 1987. 57.50 (0-8364-2093-4, Pub. by Usha II) S Asia.
***Rana, Margo.** Barbie Exclusives, Identification & Values. 160p. 1995. pap. 18.95 (0-89145-632-5, 3957) Collector Bks.
Rana, Padma J. Life of Maharaja Sir Jung Bahadur of Nepal. 1980. 75.00 (0-7855-0317-X, Pub. by Ratna Pustak Bhandar) St Mut.
Rana, Pradumna B. Exchange Rate Risk under Generalized Floating: Eight Asian Countries. 20p. (Orig.). 1980. pap. text ed. 10.00 (9971-902-19-2, Pub. by Inst SE Asian Studies SI) Ashgate Pub Co.
Rana, Pradumna B. & Alburo, Florian A., eds. Economic Stablization Policies in ASEAN Countries. 169p. 1987. text ed. 11.35 (9971-988-48-8, Pub. by Inst SE Asian Studies SI) Ashgate Pub Co.
Rana, Pradumna B. & Hamid, Naved, eds. From Centrally Planned to Market Economies: The Asian Approach. LC 93-47050. (C). 1994. write for info. (0-19-586620-7); pap. write for info. (0-19-586621-5) OUP.
— From Centrally Planned to Market Economies: The Asian Approach, Vol. I: An Overview. 160p. 1995. 45.00 (0-19-586602-9) OUP.
— From Centrally Planned to Market Economies: The Asian Approach, Vol. II: People's Republic of China & Mongolia. 280p. 1995. 49.95 (0-19-586603-7) OUP.
— From Centrally Planned to Market Economies: The Asian Approach, Vol. III: Lao PDR, Myanamar, & Viet Nam. 400p. 1995. 65.00 (0-19-586604-5) OUP.
Rana, Pudma J. Life of Maharaja Sir Jung Bahadur of Nepal. 1980. 75.00 (0-7855-0259-9, Pub. by Ratna Pustak Bhandar) St Mut.
— Life of Maharaja Sir Jung Bahadur of Nepal. 314p. (C). 1980. 100.00 (0-89771-112-2, Pub. by Ratna Pustak Bhandar); 100.00 (0-89771-064-9, Pub. by Ratna Pustak Bhandar) St Mut.
Rana, V. V., et al, eds. Advanced Metallization for ULSI Applications. (Materials Research Society Conference Proceedings Ser.: Vol. VLSI-7). 577p. 1992. text ed. 62.00 (1-55899-152-2) Materials Res.
Ranabhumi, R. The Bending Reed. (C). 1993. 21.00 (0-7855-0173-8, Pub. by Ratna Pustak Bhandar) St Mut.
Ranada, Julie G. The Economic Impact of Rising Oil Prices: A Survey of Theory & Methodology. (Working Paper Ser.: No. 82-15). 76p. reprint ed. pap. 25.00 (0-317-41999-4, 2025973) Bks Demand.
Ranade, Ashok D. Indology & Ethnomusicology: Conturs of the Indo-British Relationship. 93p. 1992. 8.95 (1-881338-01-0) Nataraj Bks.
— On Music & Musicians of Hindoostan. 1984. 40.00 (0-8364-1156-0, Pub. by Promilla) S Asia.
Ranade, Jay. C++ Primer for C Programmers. 1992. disk, pap. text ed. 39.95 (0-07-051216-7) McGraw.
— C++ Primer for C Programmers. 2nd ed. 1994. pap. text ed. 34.95 (0-07-051487-9) McGraw.
— DB2: Concepts, Programming & Design. 1991. text ed. 48.00 (0-07-051265-5) McGraw.
— Elements of C Programming Style. 1992. pap. text ed. 29.95 (0-07-051278-7) McGraw.
— J. Ranade UNIX Primer. 1993. text ed. 45.00 (0-07-051141-1); pap. text ed. 29.95 (0-07-051249-3) McGraw.
— VSAM: Concept, Programming, & Design. 2nd ed. 1992. text ed. 45.00 (0-07-051244-2) McGraw.
— VSAM: Performance, Design, & Fine Tuning. 1987. text ed. 43.00 (0-07-583963-6) McGraw.
— VSAM Concepts, Programming And Design. 1986. text ed. 40.00 (0-07-051198-5) McGraw.
Ranade, Jay & Bobak, Angelo R. DOS to OS-2: Conversion, Migration, Application Design, Set. 640p. 1991. text ed. 50.00 (0-07-051264-7) McGraw.
Ranade, Jay & Sackett, George. Advanced SNA Networking: A Guide to Using VTAM-NCP. (Ranade Ser.). (Illus.). 256p. 1991. text ed. 48.00 (0-07-051143-8) McGraw.
— Introduction to SNA Networking: A Guide for Using VTAM-NCP. (Ranade Ser.). (Illus.). 304p. 1989. text ed. 48.00 (0-07-051144-6) McGraw.
— Introduction to SNA Networking: A Professional Guide to VTAM - NCP. 2nd ed. 1995. text ed. 50.00 (0-07-051506-9) McGraw.
Ranade, Prabha S. Population Dynamics in India. 1990. 32.50 (81-7024-307-6, Pub. by Ashish II) S Asia.
Ranade, R. D. Jnaneshwar: The Guru's Guru. 211p. (C). 1994. pap. 9.95 (0-7914-2090-6) State U NY Pr.
— Mysticism in India: The Poet-Saints of Maharashtra. LC 82-10458. (Illus.). 494p. 1983. reprint ed. 44.50 (0-87395-669-9); reprint ed. pap. 14.95 (0-87395-670-2) State U NY Pr.
— Mysticism in Maharashtra (Indian Mysticism) (C). 1988. 31.00 (81-208-0575-5, Pub. by Motilal Banarsidass II) S Asia.
— Tukaram. 231p. (C). 1994. pap. 9.95 (0-7914-2092-2) State U NY Pr.
Ranade, Subhash. Natural Healing Through Ayurveda. 238p. 1993. pap. 14.95 (1-878423-13-4) Morson Pub.
Ranadive, Gail. Writing Re-Creatively: A Spiritual Quest for Women. LC 92-81603. 1992. pap. text ed. 7.95 (0-9632859-0-4) Columbine Pr.
— Writing Re-Creatively: A Spiritual Quest for Women. 104p. 1994. 10.00 (1-55896-276-X) Unitarian Univ.
Ranaghan, Dorothy. A Day in Thy Courts. LC 84-70866. 144p. (Orig.). 1984. pap. 4.95 (0-943780-05-5, 8055) Charismatic Ren Servs.
Ranaghan, Dorothy, jt. auth. see Ranaghan, Kevin.
Ranaghan, Dorothy G. A Closer Look at the Enneagram. LC 89-83732. 42p. (Orig.). 1989. pap. 3.95 (0-937779-10-5) Greenlawn Pr.
Ranaghan, Kevin. In the Power of the Spirit: Effective Catholic Evangelization. LC 91-61640. 96p. (Orig.). 1991. pap. 6.95 (1-878718-05-3) Resurrection.
Ranaghan, Kevin & Ranaghan, Dorothy. Catholic Pentecostals Today. rev. ed. LC 83-70963. 196p. 1983. pap. 4.95 (0-943780-03-9, 8039) Charismatic Ren Servs.
Ranai, K. & Srinivasan, B., eds. Visual Editing on Unix. 200p. (C). 1989. text ed. 55.00 (9971-5-0770-6) World Scientific Pub.
Ranai, K., jt. ed. see Srinivasan, B.
Ranaivo, Flavien. The Poetic Works of Flavien Ranaivo: L'Ombre et le Vent, Mes Chansons de Tourjours, Le Retour au Bercail. (B. E. Ser.: No. 29). 1962. Three works in one unit. 18.00 (0-8115-2980-0) Periodicals Srv.
Ranald, Joseph. Pens & Personalities. 16.95 (0-685-01130-5) NCUP.
Ranald, Margaret L. The Eugene O'Neill Companion. LC 83-22671. xi, 827p. 1984. text ed. 95.00 (0-313-22551-6, REO/, Greenwood Pr) Greenwood.
— John Webster. (English Authors Ser.: No. 465). 197p. 1989. text ed. 25.95 (0-8057-6976-5, TEAS 465, Pub. by Royal Botanic Garden UK) Macmillan.
— Monarch Notes on Shakespeare's Selected Comedies. (Orig.). (C). pap. 4.25 (0-671-00629-0, Arco Test) P-H Gen Ref & Trav.
— Monarch Notes on Shakespeare's Taming of the Shrew. (Orig.). (C). pap. 3.95 (0-671-00654-1, Arco Test) P-H Gen Ref & Trav.
— Monarch Notes on Shakespeare's Winter's Tale. (Orig.). (C). pap. 3.95 (0-671-00656-8, Arco Test) P-H Gen Ref & Trav.
— Shakespeare & His Social Context: Essays in Osmotic Knowledge & Literary Interpretation. LC 83-45279. (Studies in the Renaissance: No. 10). 1987. 42.50 (0-404-62280-1) AMS Pr.

R

An Asterisk (*) at the beginning of an entry indicates that the title is appearing in BIP for the first time.

Ranald, Margaret L., et al. A Style Manual for College Students: A Guide to Written Assignments & Papers. rev. ed. 1982. reprint ed. pap. 1.00 (*0-930146-07-7*) Queens Coll Pr.

Ranald, Ralph A. Monarch Notes on James' Washington Square. (Orig.). (C). pap. 3.95 (*0-671-00846-3*, Arco Test) P-H Gen Ref & Trav.

— Monarch Notes on Shakespeare's the Tempest. (Orig.). (C). pap. 3.95 (*0-671-00644-4*, Arco Test) P-H Gen Ref & Trav.

***Ranaldo, Lee.** Bookstore & Others. (Illus.). 90p. (Orig.). 1995. pap. 7.00 (*1-885175-06-X*) Hozomeen Pr.

Ranalli, Giorgio. Rheology of the Earth: Deformation & Flow Processes in Geophysics & Geodynamics. LC 86-17311. 388p. 1987. text ed. 100.00 (*0-04-551110-1*); pap. text ed. 39.95 (*0-04-551111-X*) Routledge Chapman & Hall.

Ranamurthy. Decision Making in Pain Management. 305p. 1992. 52.00 (*1-55664-370-5*) Mosby Yr Bk.

Ranande, Rekha. Sir Bartle Frere & His Times. (C). 1990. text ed. 18.50 (*81-7099-222-2*, Pub. by Mittal II) S Asia.

***Ranard, Donald A. & Pfleger, Margot, eds.** From the Classroom to the Community: A Fifteen Year Experiment in Refugee Education. LC 95-7785. (Language in Education Ser.: Vol. 86). (Illus.). 144p. (Orig.). 1995. pap. text ed. 14.95 (*0-937354-55-4*) Delta Systems.

Ranawake, Silvia, jt. auth. see James, Dorothy.

Ranawat, C. S., ed. Total-Condylar Knee Arthroplasty. (Illus.). 250p. 1985. 109.00 (*0-387-96043-0*) Spr-Verlag.

Ranby, Bengt G. & Rabek, J. F. Photodegradation, Photo-Oxidation, & Photostabilization of Polymers: Principles & Applications. LC 74-2498. 585p. reprint ed. pap. 166.80 (*0-317-09017-8*, 2016183) Bks Demand.

Ranby, Bengt G. & Rabek, J. F., eds. Singlet Oxygen: Reactions with Organic Compounds & Polymers. LC 77-2793. 341p. reprint ed. pap. 97.20 (*0-685-20685-8*, 2030475) Bks Demand.

Rancan, Janet. How to Draw Cats. LC 81-52121. (Illus.). 32p. (J). (gr. 2-6). 1982. lib. bdg. 10.65 (*0-89375-679-2*); pap. text ed. 1.95 (*0-89375-680-6*) Troll Assocs.

Rancati, Gino. Ferrari, the Man. rev. ed. Wallace, Angelo, tr. 12.00 (*0-9606804-5-4*) Wallace Pub.

Rance, Adrian. Fast Boats & Flying Boats: A Biography of Hubert Scott-Paine. (C). 1989. 39.00 (*1-85455-026-8*, Pub. by Ensign Pubns & Print UK) St Mut.

Rance, H. F. Raw Materials & Processing of Paper Making. (Handbook of Paper Science: Vol. 1). 298p. 1980. 120.50 (*0-444-41778-8*) Elsevier.

— Structure & Physical Properties of Paper. (Handbook of Paper Science: Vol. 2). 288p. 1982. 120.50 (*0-444-41974-8*) Elsevier.

Rance, Joseph & Kato, Arei. Bullet Train. large type ed. 410p. 1980. 12.00 (*0-7089-0697-4*) Ulverscroft.

Rance, Nicholas. Wilkie Collins & Other Sensation Novelists: Walking the Moral Hospital. LC 90-48390. 1991. 36.50 (*0-8386-3444-3*) Fairleigh Dickinson.

Rance, Sheila. Heron's Reach. large type ed. (Linford Romance Library). 240p. 1992. pap. 14.95 (*0-7089-7201-2*, Trailtree Bookshop) Ulverscroft.

Rances, Atilano. Diccionario Ilustrado de la Lengua Espanola. 480p. (SPA.). 1983. pap. 14.95 (*0-7859-5108-3*) Fr & Eur.

Ranchan, Rahul. Night Sea Journey. vii, 46p. 1989. text ed. 12.50 (*81-220-0157-2*, Pub. by Konark Pubs Pvt Ltd II) Advent Bks Div.

Ranchan, Som. New Sights on the Gita. (C). 1987. 11.00 (*81-202-0184-1*, Pub. by Ajanta II) S Asia.

Ranchan, Som. P. An Adventure in Vedanta: J. D. Salingers The Glass Family. 1989. 14.50 (*81-202-0245-7*, Pub. by Ajanta II) S Asia.

Ranchan, Som P. America with Love: An Epic Tantric Poem. 120p. 1989. text ed. 18.95 (*81-220-0048-7*, Pub. by Konark Pubs Pvt Ltd II) Advent Bks Div.

— An Anatomy of Indian Psyche. (C). 1987. 15.00 (*81-202-0172-8*, Pub. by Ajanta II) S Asia.

— Anteros - Poems: Opus Alchymicum on Friendship. 90p. 1992. text ed. 15.95 (*81-220-0266-8*, Pub. by Konark Pubs Pvt Ltd II) Advent Bks Div.

— Aurobindran Yoga: A Revisioning. 1993. 12.95 (*81-220-0308-7*, Pub. by Konark Pubs Pvt Ltd II) Advent Bks Div.

— Jawaharlal Nehru: Puer Aeternus. 109p. 1992. text ed. 15.95 (*81-220-0256-0*, Pub. by Konark Pubs Pvt Ltd II) Advent Bks Div.

— Nigamas: For the Age. 93p. 1989. text ed. 15.95 (*81-220-0156-4*, Pub. by Konark Pubs Pvt Ltd II) Advent Bks Div.

— Revisioning Gita. 200p. 1991. text ed. 27.50 (*81-220-0216-1*, Pub. by Konark Pubs Pvt Ltd II) Advent Bks Div.

Ranchan, Som P. & Gupta, K. D. Sri Aurobindo As a Political Thinker: An Interdisciplinary Study. 113p. 1989. text ed. 15.95 (*81-220-0111-4*, Pub. by Konark Pubs Pvt Ltd II) Advent Bks Div.

Rancier, Esther. Matchcovers: A Guide to Collecting. LC 76-23699. (Illus.). 1976. pap. 10.50 (*0-87282-102-1*) Am Life Foun.

Ranciere, Jacques. The Ignorant Schoolmaster: Five Lessons in Intellectual Emancipation. Ross, Kristin, tr. 176p. 1991. 37.50 (*0-8047-1874-1*); pap. 12.95 (*0-8047-1969-1*) Stanford U Pr.

— The Names of History: On the Poetics of Knowledge. Melehy, Hassan, tr. LC 94-7212. (ENG & FRE.). 1994. text ed. 39.95 (*0-8166-2401-1*); pap. 16.95 (*0-8166-2403-8*) U of Minn Pr.

— The Nights of Labor: The Workers' Dream in Nineteenth-Century France. Drury, John, tr. 448p. (C). 1989. 44.95 (*0-87722-625-3*) Temple U Pr.

— Nights of Labor: The Worker's Dream in Nineteenth Century France. Drury, John, tr. 448p. 1991. pap. 19.95 (*0-87722-833-7*) Temple U Pr.

— On the Shores of Politics. Heron, Liz, tr. (Phronesis Ser.). 256p. 1994. 59.95 (*0-86091-467-4*, B3628, Pub. by Verso UK); pap. 17.95 (*0-86091-637-5*, B3632, Pub. by Verso UK) Routledge Chapman & Hall.

Ranck, George W. Boonesborough: Its Founding, Pioneer Struggles, Indian Experiences, Transylvania Days, & Revolutionary Annals. LC 70-146414. (First American Frontier Ser.). (Illus.). 1971. reprint ed. 30.95 (*0-405-02878-4*) Ayer.

Ranck, Glenn N. Pictures from Northwest History. (Shorey Historical Ser.). 38p. reprint ed. pap. 3.95 (*0-8466-0115-X*, S115) Shorey.

Ranck, James B. Albert Gallatin Brown: Radical Southern Nationalist. LC 73-16349. (Perspectives in American History Ser.: No. 20). (Illus.). 320p. 1974. reprint ed. lib. bdg. 39.50 (*0-87991-347-9*) Porcupine Pr.

Ranck, Joanne, jt. auth. see Pellman, Rachel T.

Ranck, Katherine H., jt. auth. see Cavan, Ruth S.

Ranck, Katherine Q. Portrait of Dona Elena. LC 82-83842. 1982. pap. 3.00 (*0-89229-012-9*) TQS Pubns.

Ranck, Shirley A. Cakes for the Queen of Heaven. 176p. (Orig.). 1995. pap. 13.95 (*1-878980-10-6*) Delphi IL.

Rancour-Laferriere, Daniel. Signs of the Flesh: An Essay on the Evolution of Hominid Sexuality. LC 91-6785. (Illus.). 488p. 1992. pap. text ed. 17.95 (*0-253-20673-1*) Ind U Pr.

— Signs of the Flesh: An Essay on the Evolution of Homonid Sexuality. (Approaches to Semiotics Ser.: No. 71). x, 473p. 1986. 120.00 (*0-89925-121-8*) Mouton.

— The Slave Soul of Russia: Moral Masochism & the Cult of Suffering. 336p. 1995. 35.00 (*0-8147-7458-X*) NYU Pr.

Rancour-Laferriere, Daniel, ed. Russian Literature & Psychoanalysis. LC 89-280. (Linguistic & Literary Studies in Eastern Europe: Vol. 31). x, 485p. 1989. 130.00x (*90-272-1536-7*); pap. 32.95 (*90-272-1540-5*) Benjamins North Am.

— Self-Analysis in Literary Study: Exploring Hidden Agendas. (Literature & Psychoanalysis Ser.). 240p. 1994. 45.00 (*0-8147-7439-3*) NYU Pr.

Rancourt, Karen L. Yeah but, Children Need... 144p. 1978. 18.95 (*0-87073-959-X*) Schenkman Bks Inc.

Rancourt, Muriel M. Creation Speaks. (Illus.). 40p. (Orig.). 1988. pap. 4.95 (*0-936015-17-9*) Pocahontas Pr.

Rancourt, Sylvie. Melody, Bk. One: The Orgies of Abitibi. Schreiner, Dave, ed. Boivin, Jacques, tr. & illus. by. (Melody; the True Stories of a Nude Dancer Ser.). 128p. 1991. 29.95 (*0-87816-140-6*); pap. 14.95 (*0-87816-141-4*) Kitchen Sink.

Rancurello, Anto, tr. see Brentano, Franz.

***Rand.** Conozco: Las Banderas. 1995. pap. (*0-528-83739-7*) Rand McNally.

Rand, jt. auth. see Bowman.

Rand, Andrew. Explore Seattle: A Guide Book. 192p. 1992. pap. 8.95 (*0-9631315-0-8*) Silver Pen.

Rand, Ann & Rand, Paul. Little One. (Illus.). 32p. (J). 1991. reprint ed. 16.95 (*0-8109-3558-9*) Abrams.

— Sparkle & Spin. (Illus.). 32p. (J). 1991. reprint ed. 16.95 (*0-8109-3822-7*) Abrams.

Rand, Austin L., jt. auth. see Archbold, Richard.

Rand, Ayn. Anthem. LC 52-5216. 1953. 10.95 (*0-87004-124-X*) Caxton.

— Anthem. 1961. pap. 4.99 (*0-451-16683-3*, Sig) NAL-Dutton.

— Anthem. aniversary ed. LC 95-9854. 1995. 22.95 (*0-525-94015-4*, Dutton) NAL-Dutton.

— Anthem: 50th Anniversary Edition. 128p. 1995. mass mkt. 5.99 (*0-451-18532-3*, Sig) NAL-Dutton.

— Atlas Shrugged. 1992. pap. 6.99 (*0-451-17192-6*, Sig) NAL-Dutton.

— Atlas Shrugged. 1957. 34.50 (*0-394-41576-0*) Random.

— Atlas Shrugged. 35th anniversary ed. 1088p. 1992. 35.00 (*0-525-93418-9*, Dutton) NAL-Dutton.

—The Ayn Rand Column: A Collection of Her Weekly Newspaper Articles, Written for the Los Angeles Times. LC 89-63827. 138p. (Orig.). 1992. pap. 14.95 (*1-56114-099-6*, AR15B) Second Renaissance.

Can a newspaper column written nearly three decades ago be relevant today? When the columnist is Ayn Rand - you bet it can! From one of the foremost thinkers of the twentieth century - creator of ATLAS SHRUGGED, champion of the individual, & fountainhead of Objectivism - comes a newly collected series of articles illustrating what a proper analysis of world events can & should be. As Peter Schwartz notes in the Introduction: "Her perspective on the news is not that of the daily reporter, but that of the grand historian, whose time frame is the centuries & whose function is to explain the world by reference to universal truths." What is the appeal of Ayn Rand? Ayn Rand was dedicated to the power of ideas & perceived that philosophy affected every man, whether he knew it or not. Through her novels, The Ayn Rand Institute, & student study groups, her ideas continue to influence millions around the world.

THE AYN RAND COLUMN will appeal to anyone who cares about his life. From a review by Robert Paglia: "This book is must-reading for anyone who respects his mind." Order from: Second Renaissance Books, 143 West Street, P.O. Box 1988, New Milford, CT 06776. Tel. 800-729-6149, FAX: 203-355-7161. ***Publisher Provided Annotation.***

— The Ayn Rand Letter: 1971-1976, Vols. 1-4. 5th ed. LC 90-616721. 400p. 1990. reprint ed. lib. bdg. 29.95 (*1-56114-147-X*) Second Renaissance.

— Capitalism: The Unknown Ideal. 1986. pap. 5.99 (*0-451-14795-2*, Sig) NAL-Dutton.

— The Early Ayn Rand. 448p. 1986. pap. 5.99 (*0-451-14607-7*, Sig) NAL-Dutton.

— For the New Intellectual. 1963. pap. 3.95 (*0-451-14103-2*, AE3181, Sig); pap. 5.50 (*0-451-16308-7*) NAL-Dutton.

— For the New Intellectual. 1961. 14.95 (*0-394-42526-X*) Random.

— Fountainhead. 744p. 1985. text ed. 40.00 (*0-02-600910-2*) Macmillan.

— Fountainhead. 1952. pap. 5.99 (*0-451-15823-7*, Sig) NAL-Dutton.

— The Fountainhead. 752p. 1994. pap. 14.95 (*0-452-27333-1*, Plume) NAL-Dutton.

— The Fountainhead. 50th anniversary ed. 696p. 1952. pap. 6.99 (*0-451-17512-3*, Sig) NAL-Dutton.

— Introduction to Objectivist Epistemology. 2nd exp. ed. Peikoff, Leonard & Binswanger, Harry, eds. 1990. pap. 12.95 (*0-452-01030-6*, Mer) NAL-Dutton.

— Letters of Ayn Rand. Berliner, Michael S., ed. 504p. 1995. 34.95 (*0-525-93946-6*, Dutton) NAL-Dutton.

— The New Left. 1993. pap. 10.00 (*0-452-01125-6*, Mer) NAL-Dutton.

— New Left: The Anti-Industrial Revolution. (Orig.). 1971. pap. 4.50 (*0-451-14982-3*, Sig) NAL-Dutton.

— Night of January Sixteenth. 15.95 (*0-89190-772-6*, Am Repr) Amereon Ltd.

— Night of January Sixteenth. 1971. pap. 8.00 (*0-452-26486-3*, Plume) NAL-Dutton.

— The Night of January Sixteenth: A Play Book. Play Bk. 3.95 (*0-679-39051-0*); 7.00 (*0-679-39100-2*) McKay.

— Night of January 16th. 1971. mass mkt. 6.95 (*0-452-25995-9*, Plume) NAL-Dutton.

— Philosophy: Who Needs It? LC 82-4320. 288p. 1984. write for info. (*0-672-52725-1*); pap. write for info. (*0-672-52795-2*) Macmillan.

— Philosophy: Who Needs It? 1984. pap. 5.99 (*0-451-13893-7*, Sig) NAL-Dutton.

— Romantic Manifesto. 1971. pap. 4.99 (*0-451-14916-5*, AE2374, Sig) NAL-Dutton.

— Virtue of Selfishness. 1964. pap. 4.50 (*0-451-15699-4*, Sig) NAL-Dutton.

— The Virtue of Selfishness. 1964. pap. 4.99 (*0-451-16393-1*) NAL-Dutton.

— We the Living. 1960. pap. 6.99 (*0-451-15860-1*, Sig) NAL-Dutton.

— We the Living: 60th Anniversary Edition. aniversary ed. 464p. 1995. 25.95 (*0-525-94054-5*, Dutton) NAL-Dutton.

Rand, Ayn & Peikoff, Leonard. The Voice of Reason: Essays in Objectivist Thought. (Ayn Rand Library Ser.: Vol. V). 372p. 1990. pap. 13.95 (*0-452-01046-2*, Mer) NAL-Dutton.

Rand, Benjamin. Berkeley's American Sojourn. LC 75-3329. reprint ed. 8.50 (*0-404-59323-2*) AMS Pr.

Rand, Benjamin, ed. see Shaftesbury, Anthony A.

Rand, Christopher C., tr. see Ts'ao.

Rand, Clayton. Sons of the South. LC 61-8069. (Illus.). 212p. 1961. 13.95 (*0-911116-76-1*) Pelican.

Rand, D. A. & Bond, A. M. Electrochemistry: The Interfacing Science. (Studies in Physical & Theoretical Chemistry: Vol. 34). 482p. 1984. 172.00 (*0-444-42304-4*) Elsevier.

Rand, D. A., jt. ed. see McNicol, B. D.

Rand, D. A., et al, eds. Progress in Electrochemistry. (Studies in Physical & Theoretical Chemistry). 470p. 1981. reprint ed. 141.00 (*0-444-41955-1*) Elsevier.

Rand, E. K. & Jones, L. W. Earliest Book of Tours. (Mediaeval Academy of America Publications: Vol. 20). 1934. 130.00 (*0-527-01692-6*) Periodicals Srv.

Rand, E. K., et al. Serviani in Aeneidem Commentarii: Editio Harvardiana, Vol. 3 - Aeneid III-V. (American Philological Association Special Publications Ser.). 1974. 39.50 (*0-89130-718-4*, 40 05 01) Scholars Pr GA.

Rand, E. W. The Journal of Earl Wadsworth Rand: From There to Here - From Then until Now. 1991. 13.95 (*0-533-09590-5*) Vantage.

Rand, Earl. The Syntax of Mandarin Interrogatives. LC 78-626766. (University of California Publications in Social Welfare: Vol. 55). (Illus.). 123p. reprint ed. pap. 35.10 (*0-317-10083-1*, 2011788) Bks Demand.

Rand, Edward A. The Tent in the Notch. LC 72-2040. (Black Heritage Library Collection). 1977. reprint ed. 24.95 (*0-8369-9054-4*) Ayer.

Rand, Edward K. Cicero in the Courtroom of Saint Thomas Aquinas. (Aquinas Lectures). 1945. 10.00 (*0-87462-109-7*) Marquette.

— Ovid. LC 63-10269. (Our Debt to Greece & Rome Ser.). reprint ed. 28.50 (*0-8154-0187-6*) Cooper Sq.

Rand, Elizabeth, ed. see Johl, Karen.

Rand, Elizabeth, ed. see Seales, John B.

Rand, Elizabeth, ed. see Wheeler, Grace.

Rand, Elizabeth H., ed. see Boyko, Walter N.

Rand, Elizabeth H., ed. see Schwartz, Henry.

***Rand, Erica.** Barbie's Queer Accessories. Barale, Michele A. et al, eds. LC 94-38509. (Series Q). (Illus.). 256p. 1995. lib. bdg. 45.95 (*0-8223-1604-8*); pap. 15.95 (*0-8223-1620-X*) Duke.

Rand, Erika. Lying Eyes. (Intrigue Ser.). 1994. mass mkt. 2.99 (*0-373-22259-9*, 1-22259-5) Harlequin Bks.

Rand, Frank P. The Story of David Grayson. 160p. 1963. 9.95 (*0-686-31118-3*) Jones Lib.

Rand, G. K., ed. Operational Research Nineteen Eighty-Seven: Proceedings of the 11th IFORS International Conference, Buenos Aires, Argentina, 10-14 Aug., 1987. 972p. 1988. 179.50 (*0-444-70280-6*, North Holland) Elsevier.

Rand, G. K. & Eglese, R. W., eds. Further Developments in Operational Research. 1985. text ed. 59.00 (*0-08-033361-3*, Pub. by PPL UK) Franklin.

Rand, G. K., jt. ed. see Eglese, R. W.

Rand, Gary M., ed. Fundamentals of Aquatic Toxic: Effects, Environmental Fate & Risk Assessment. 2nd ed. 1150p. 1995. 160.00x (*1-56032-090-7*); pap. 79.95x (*1-56032-091-5*) Taylor & Francis.

Rand, Gary M. & Petrocelli, Sam R., eds. Fundamentals of Aquatic Toxicology: Methods & Applications. LC 84-4529. (Illus.). 666p. (C). 1985. 83.00 (*0-89116-302-6*); pap. 59.50 (*0-89116-382-4*) Hemisp Pub.

Rand, Gertrude.

Rand, Glenn M. & Litschel, David R. Black & White Photography. Jucha, ed. LC 93-14290. 300p. (C). 1994. pap. text ed. 28.25 (*0-314-02460-3*) West Pub.

Rand, Gloria. The Cabin Key. LC 93-10398. (Illus.). (J). 1994. 14.95 (*0-15-213884-6*) HarBrace.

— Prince William. LC 91-25180. (Illus.). 32p. (J). (gr. 1-3). 1992. 14.95 (*0-8050-1841-7*, Bks Young Read) H Holt & Co.

— Prince William. LC 91-25180. (J). (ps-3). 1994. pap. 5.95 (*0-8050-3384-X*) H Holt & Co.

— Salty Dog. LC 88-13453. (Illus.). 32p. (J). (ps-2). 1991. pap. 4.95 (*0-8050-1847-6*, Bks Young Read) H Holt & Co.

— Salty Sails North. LC 89-39063. (Illus.). 32p. (J). (ps-3). 1992. pap. 4.95 (*0-8050-2188-4*, Owlet BYR) H Holt & Co.

— Salty Takes Off. LC 90-46371. (Salty Ser.). (Illus.). 32p. (J). (ps-2). 1991. 14.95 (*0-8050-1159-5*, Bks Young Read) H Holt & Co.

— Willie Takes a Hike. LC 95-13698. (Illus.). (J). 1996. write for info. (*0-15-200272-3*) HarBrace.

Rand, Graham, jt. auth. see Chambers, Andrew.

Rand, Harry. Arshile Gorky: The Implications of Symbols. LC 90-47360. (Illus.). 270p. 1991. 60.00 (*0-520-06371-6*); pap. 25.00 (*0-520-06345-7*) U CA Pr.

— The Beginning of Things: Translations from Genesis. (Illus.). 1983. pap. 8.95 (*0-931848-53-9*) Dryad Pr.

— Color: Suite in Four Parts. deluxe limited ed. (Illus.). 56p. 1993. ring bd. 3,000.00 (*0-9638014-0-6*) Dov Press.

— Louis Ribak, the Late Paintings. 36p. 1984. pap. 10.00 (*0-914983-00-8*) Roswell Mus.

— Manet's Contemplation at the Gare Saint-Lazare. LC 86-25077. (Illus.). 168p. 1987. 37.50 (*0-520-05967-0*) U CA Pr.

— Manet's Contemplation at the Gare Saint-Lazare. (Illus.). 168p. 1991. reprint ed. pap. 18.00 (*0-520-07658-3*) U CA Pr.

— Paul Manship. LC 88-15594. (Illus.). 216p. (C). 1989. 55.00 (*0-87474-834-8*) Smithsonian.

— Stokely Webster: Paintings Nineteen Twenty-Three to Nineteen Eighty-Four. Libby, Gary R., ed. LC 85-60099. (Illus.). 104p. (Orig.). 1985. pap. 5.00 (*0-933053-00-2*) Museum Art Sciences.

Rand, Howard B. Behold, He Cometh. 1955. 5.00 (*0-685-08798-0*) Destiny.

— Digest of the Divine Law. 1943. 8.00 (*0-685-08802-2*) Destiny.

— Hour Cometh. 1966. 5.00 (*0-685-08805-7*) Destiny.

— Marvels of Prophecy. 1959. 5.00 (*0-685-08810-3*) Destiny.

— Primogenesis. 1953. 15.00 (*0-685-08813-8*) Destiny.

— Study in Daniel. 1948. 12.00 (*0-685-08814-6*) Destiny.

— Study in Hosea. 1955. 5.00 (*0-685-08815-4*) Destiny.

— Study in Jeremiah. 1947. 12.00 (*0-685-08816-2*) Destiny.

— Study in Revelation. 1941. 12.00 (*0-685-08817-0*) Destiny.

Rand, Jacki T. Wilma Mankiller. LC 92-12813. (American Indian Stories Ser.). (Illus.). 32p. (J). (gr. 4-5). 1992. lib. bdg. 19.97 (*0-8114-6576-4*); pap. 4.95 (*0-8114-4097-4*) Raintree Steck-V.

Rand, James A., ed. Total Knee Arthroplasty. LC 92-12132. 480p. 1993. 136.50 (*0-88167-930-5*) Raven.

Rand, James R. Fire Department Management: Scope & Method Study Guide. Davis, Stewart, ed. 188p. 1972. reprint ed. pap. 10.95 (*0-945250-03-7*) Davis Pub Co.

Rand, Jim, ed. Jordanhill College of Education. (C). 1989. 45.00 (*1-85098-145-0*, Pub. by Jordanhill College UK) St Mut.

Rand, Joyce. A Hippo with Feathers. LC 92-9952. (Light Line Ser.). (Illus.). 1992. pap. 4.95 (*0-89084-627-8*) Bob Jones Univ Pr.

Rand, Ken. Elementary Algebra: Solving the Mystery. 576p. 1989. per. 50.95 (*0-8403-5623-4*) Kendall-Hunt.

Rand, Laurance B. High Stakes: The Life & Times of Leigh S. J. Hunt. (American University Studies: History: Ser. IX, Vol. 76). 352p. (C). 1989. text ed. 51.00 (*0-8204-0992-8*) P Lang Pubs.

Rand, Lydia, tr. see Bomani, Asake & Rooks, Belvie, eds.

Rand, M. J. & Raper, C. Pharmacology. (International Congress Ser.: Vol. 750). 1987. 217.50 (*0-444-80949-X*) Elsevier.

Rand, Marguerite C. Ramon Perez de Ayala. (Twayne's World Authors Ser.). 175p. (C). 1971. lib. bdg. 17.95 (*0-8290-1734-8*) Irvington.

An Asterisk (*) at the beginning of an entry indicates that the title is appearing in BIP for the first time.

***Rand, Maria.** A. K. A. Ruby Brooklyn. (Illus.). 390p. (Orig.). 1994. pap. 13.95 (*0-9642457-3-6*) Goddesses We Aint.

Rand, Mary E. & Burger, Irene T. The Dog Owner's Guide to Washington. LC 92-97113. 224p. (Orig.). 1992. pap. 14.95 (*0-9628685-1-5*) Edington-Rand.

Rand McNally & Company Staff. Rand McNally Children's Atlas of the United States. (Illus.). 112p. (J). (gr. 3-6). 1991. reprint ed. lib. bdg. 18.95 (*1-878363-37-9*) Forest Hse.

— Rand McNally Children's Atlas of the World. rev. ed. LC 92-24028. (Illus.). (J). (gr. 4-7). 1992. pap. 7.95 (*0-528-83541-6*) Rand McNally.

***Rand McNally Staff.** Atlas for Today's World. Date not set. pap. 7.95 (*0-528-83777-X*) Rand McNally.

— Atlas of American History. 1991. pap. 6.95 (*0-528-83456-8*) Rand McNally.

— Atlas of the World: Masterpiece Edition. LC 94-22280. 1994. write for info. (*0-528-83715-X*) Rand McNally.

— Atlas of World History. 1995. 45.00 (*0-528-83780-X*); pap. 24.95 (*0-528-83779-6*) Rand McNally.

— Best Travel Activity Book Ever! (Backseat Bks.). (Illus.). 320p. (J). (gr. 1-6). 1994. pap. 3.95 (*0-528-81410-9*) Rand McNally.

— Business Traveler's Road Atlas, 1996. 216p. 1995. ring bd. 9.95 (*0-528-81480-X*) Rand McNally.

— Children's Atlas of Earth Through Time. Fagan, Elizabeth, ed. (Illus.). 80p. (J). 1990. 14.95 (*0-528-83415-0*) Rand McNally.

— Children's Atlas of the Environment. (J). (gr. 4-7). 1991. 14.95 (*0-528-83438-X*) Rand McNally.

— Children's Atlas of the Universe. (Illus.). (J). (gr. 3-7). 1990. 14.95 (*0-528-83408-8*) Rand McNally.

— Compact Road Atlas, 1996: United States, Canada, Mexico. 1995. pap. 6.95 (*0-528-81489-3*) Rand McNally.

— Deluxe Motor Carriers' Road Atlas, 1996: United States, Canada, Mexico. 1995. pap. 79.95 (*0-528-81479-6*) Rand McNally.

— Deluxe Road Atlas & Travel Guide, 1996. 216p. 1995. ring bd. 7.95 (*0-528-81485-0*) Rand McNally.

— Dist-O-Map. 1995. 7.95 (*0-528-88369-0*) Rand McNally.

— Easy-to-Read Travel Atlas 1996. 1995. pap. 14.95 (*0-528-81482-6*) Rand McNally.

— Family World Atlas. LC 93-48823. (J). 1995. 11.95 (*0-528-83782-6*) Rand McNally.

— First Atlas. LC 93-37528. (Illus.). (J). 1994. write for info. (*0-528-83679-X*) Rand McNally.

— Giant Atlas of the U. S. A. (J). (gr. 4-7). 1992. pap. 27.95 (*0-528-83495-9*) Rand McNally.

— Goode's World Atlas. 19th ed. 1995. 24.95 (*0-528-83130-5*) Rand McNally.

— Historical Atlas & Guide. LC 93-11581. 1993. 14.95 (*0-528-83624-2*) Rand McNally.

— Historical Atlas & Guide. LC 93-11581. 1993. pap. 9.95 (*0-528-83623-4*) Rand McNally.

— International Geographic Atlas. rev. ed. 1993. 19.95 (*0-528-83629-3*) Rand McNally.

— Luminous Star Finder. 1989. 5.95 (*0-528-83374-X*) Rand McNally.

— New International Atlas. deluxe ed. (Illus.). 1994. 200.00 (*0-528-83694-3*) Rand McNally.

Rand-McNally Staff. New York Quik-Finder. 1991. pap. 4.95 (*0-88433-005-2*) Geographia.

***Rand McNally Staff.** Pocket Road Atlas, 1996. (Illus.). 1996. pap. 2.95 (*0-528-81490-7*) Rand McNally.

— Pocket World Atlas. 1992. pap. 2.50 (*0-528-83517-3*) Rand McNally.

— Quick Reference World Atlas. 1993. pap. 4.95 (*0-528-83622-6*) Rand McNally.

— Rand McNally Animal Sticker Atlas. (Illus.). (J). (ps-3). 1993. pap. 4.95 (*0-528-83586-6*) Rand McNally.

— Rand McNally Dinosaur Sticker Atlas. (Illus.). (J). (ps-3). 1993. pap. 4.95 (*0-528-83585-8*) Rand McNally.

— Rand McNally New Universal World Atlas. LC 94-3532. 1994. 49.95 (*0-528-83717-6*) Rand McNally.

— Rand McNally Road Atlas: U. S., Canada & Mexico. 1991. 8.95 (*0-685-83176-0*) Wehman.

— Rand McNally Streetfinder: Los Angeles. 1994. pap. 17.95 (*0-528-91323-9*) Rand McNally.

— Rand McNally Streetfinder: Nashville. 1994. pap. 14.95 (*0-528-91321-2*) Rand McNally.

— Rand McNally Zip Code Finder, 1996. 1995. pap. 7.95 (*0-528-81601-2*) Rand McNally.

— Traveler's World Atlas & Guide. LC 93-11580. 1993. 14.95 (*0-528-83626-9*); pap. 9.95 (*0-528-83625-0*) Rand McNally.

— The World Afganistan to Zimbabwe. 1995. 49.95 (*0-528-83773-7*) Rand McNally.

— World Facts & Maps, 1996. 1995. pap. 10.95 (*0-528-83776-1*) Rand McNally.

Rand McNally Staff & Reddy, Francis. Children's Atlas of Native Americans Rand McNally: Native Cultures of North & South America. Adelman, Elizabeth, ed. (United States & Its Flag Ser.). (Illus.). 78p. (J). (gr. 3-12). Date not set. 14.95 (*0-685-66563-1*); lib. bdg. 18.95 (*1-878363-99-9*) Forest Hse.

***Rand McNally Staff & Zapenski, David, eds.** Commercial Atlas & Marketing Guide, 1996. (Illus.). 568p. Date not set. 395.00 (*0-528-81602-0*) Rand McNally.

Rand, Miriam, jt. auth. see Porter, Ona L.

Rand, Muriel K., jt. ed. see Burks, Susan P.

Rand, Nicholas, tr. see Abraham, Nicolas & Torok, Maria.

Rand, Nicholas T., tr. see Abraham, Nicolas & Torok, Maria.

Rand, Pamela. French for Kids. (Illus.). 35p. (Orig.). (J). (ps-6). 1988. digital audio, pap. 19.95 (*1-878245-02-3*) OptimaLearning.

— Spanish for Kids. (Illus.). 31p. (Orig.). (J). (ps-6). 1990. digital audio, pap. 19.95 (*1-878245-01-5*) OptimaLearning.

Rand, Paul. Design, Form, & Chaos. (Illus.). 224p. (C). 1993. 45.00 (*0-300-05553-6*) Yale U Pr.

Rand, Paul, jt. auth. see Rand, Ann.

Rand, R. H. & Armbruster, D. Perturbation Methods, Bifurcation Theory & Computer Algebra. (Applied Mathematical Sciences Ser.: Vol. 65). (Illus.). 255p. 1987. pap. 39.00 (*0-387-96589-0*) Spr-Verlag.

Rand, Richard. Topics in Nonlinear Dynamics with Computer Algebra. LC 94-2869. (Computers in Education Ser.: Vol. 1). 1994. text ed. 48.00 (*2-88449-113-9*); pap. text ed. 22.00 (*2-88449-114-7*) Gordon & Breach.

Rand, Richard, ed. Logomachia: The Conflict of the Faculties Today. LC 92-6977. 420p. 1992. 30.00 (*0-8032-3884-3*); pap. 13.95 (*0-8032-8940-5*) U of Nebr Pr.

Rand, Richard, tr. see Derrida, Jacques.

Rand, Richard S., Jr. Instructor's Manual to Accompany Knechel's Monopoly Game Practice Set. 72p. (C). 1992. teacher ed, pap. text ed. 5.00 (*0-15-500305-4*) Dryden Pr.

Rand-Riley, Candy. Fifty Ways to Please Your Lover: A Woman's Guide to a Mutually Pleasurable Love Relationship. 173p. (Orig.). 1990. pap. 14.95 (*0-9625452-0-1*) Persimmon CA.

Rand, Ritch, jt. auth. see Reynolds, Bill.

Rand, Robert. Comrade Lawyer: Inside Soviet Justice in an Era of Reform. (Illus.). 166p. 1991. text ed. 52.00 (*0-8133-7991-1*) Westview.

— Comrade Lawyer: Inside Soviet Justice in an Era of Reform. (Illus.). 166p. (C). 1991. pap. text ed. 17.95 (*0-8133-1192-6*) Westview.

— Strange Sins. 1995. 22.00 (*0-671-78689-X*) S&S Trade.

Rand, Ron. For Fathers Who Aren't in Heaven. Klope, Joan Bay, ed. LC 86-27979. 224p. (Orig.). 1987. text ed. 7.99 (*0-8307-1187-2*, 5418983) Regal.

Rand, Roy E. Recirculating Electron Acclerators. (Nuclear Physics Ser.: Vol. 3). 275p. 1984. text ed. 168.00 (*3-7186-0183-4*) Gordon & Breach.

Rand, Royden N., et al, eds. Quality Assurance in Health Care: A Critical Appraisal of Clinical Chemistry. LC 80-66260. 460p. 1980. 15.00 (*0-915274-11-6*) Am Assn Clinical Chem.

Rand, Sharon R. The French Imparfait & Passe Simple in Discourse. LC 93-60371. xii, 136p. 1993. pap. 15.00 (*0-88312-822-5*); fiche 12.00 (*0-88312-579-X*) Summer Instit Ling.

***Rand, Silas T.** English-Micmac Dictionary. 1994. 50.00x (*1-895959-16-0*) IBD Ltd.

Rand, T., jt. auth. see Bunting, Eve.

Rand, Theodore H. Treasury of Canadian Verse. LC 76-75717. (Granger Index Reprint Ser.). 1977. 23.95 (*0-8369-6039-4*) Ayer.

Rand, W. & Lee, Z. Teach Yourself Czech. (Teach Yourself Ser.). 1992. 19.95 (*0-8288-8310-6*) Fr & Eur.

Rand, W. W. Diccionario de la Santa Biblia. (Illus.). 768p. (SPA.). 1969. reprint ed. pap. 16.25 (*0-89922-003-7*) Edit Caribe.

***Rand, William L.** The Reiki Class: First & Second Degree Audio Cassette Tapes. 1994. audio, pap. 29.95 (*1-886785-01-5*) Vision Pub.

— Reiki the Healing Touch: First & Second Degree Manual. 44p. 1992. 12.95 (*0-9631567-0-5*) Vision Pub.

— Spiritual Protection & Healing. 1995. audio, pap. 16.95 (*1-886785-00-7*) Vision Pub.

Randal, Jude. A Miracle for Bryan. (Silhouette Romance Ser.). 1994. pap. 2.75 (*0-373-08986-4*, 5-08986-7) Silhouette.

Randall. Marketing to the Retail Trade. 1990. pap. text ed. 34.95 (*0-434-91719-2*) Buttrwrth-Heinemann.

Randall, jt. auth. see Huang.

Randall, jt. auth. see Shull.

Randall, jt. auth. see Stillwell.

Randall, Adrian. Before the Luddites: Custom, Community & Machinery in the English Woollen Industry, 1776-1809. (Illus.). 336p. (C). 1991. 69.95 (*0-521-39042-7*) Cambridge U Pr.

Randall, Alan. Resource Economics: An Economic Approach to Natural Resource & Environmental Policy. 2nd ed. LC 84-15174. 434p. 1987. Net. text ed. write for info. (*0-471-87468-X*) Wiley.

Randall, Albert B. The Mystery of Hope in the Philosophy of Gabriel Marcel (1888-1973) Hope & "Homo Viator" LC 92-26572. (Problems in Contemporary Philosophy Ser.: Vol. 33). 420p. 1992. text ed. 109.95 (*0-7734-9160-0*) E Mellen.

Randall, Alexander & Bennett, Steven J. Alex Randall's Used Computer Handbook. 1990. pap. 14.95 (*1-55615-267-1*) Microsoft.

Randall, Alice E. The Sources of Spenser's Classical Mythology. 1972. 35.00 (*0-8490-1092-6*) Gordon Pr.

— Sources of Spenser's Classical Mythology. LC 72-115364. reprint ed. 21.50 (*0-404-05223-1*) AMS Pr.

***Randall, Allan D. & Johnson, A. Ivan, eds.** The Northeast Glacial Aquifers: Papers Presented at AWRA Symposium on Monitoring, Modeling, & Mediating Water Quality, May 17-20, 1987, Syracuse, New York. (AWRA Monograph Ser.: Vol. 11). reprint ed. pap. 45.60 (*0-7837-9277-8*, 2060015) Bks Demand.

Randall, Ann. The Search for God: Finding the Key to Happiness, Purpose, & Peace. 147p. 1993. pap. 9.95 (*0-9639041-9-1*) Amery Pr.

Randall, Anthony G. The Time Museum Catalogue of Chronometers. Chandler, Bruce, ed. (Illus.). x, 366p. 1992. 139.00 (*0-912947-03-9*) Time Museum.

Randall, Bernice. When Is a Pig a Hog. 1993. pap. 10.00 (*0-671-87471-3*) P-H Gen Ref & Trav.

Randall, Bernice, tr. see Ada, Alma F.

Randall, Brian. The B Book. LC 93-40927. 96p. 1994. 22.95 (*0-446-51801-8*) Warner Bks.

Randall, C. & Clepper, Henry. Famous & Historic Trees. 4.50 (*0-686-26725-7*, 21) Am Forests.

Randall, C., jt. auth. see Youngman, W.

Randall, C. J. A Color Atlas of Diseases & Disorders of the Domestic Fowl & Turkey. 2nd ed. LC 90-85707. (Illus.). 176p. (C). 1991. text ed. 79.95 (*0-8138-0376-4*) Iowa St U Pr.

Randall, Caitlin. Roses. 224p. (Orig.). 1991. pap. 2.75 (*1-878702-36-X*, Kismet) Meteor Pub.

Randall, Carter. Up on the Market with Carter Randall: Wisdom, Insights & Advice from a Lifetime on Wall Street. 250p. 1992. 22.95 (*1-55738-263-8*) Probus Pub Co.

Randall, Charles A., Jr., ed. Extra-Terrestrial Matter. LC 69-15447. (Illus.). 331p. 1969. 22.00 (*0-87580-009-2*) N Ill U Pr.

Randall, Charles E. & Clepper, Henry. Famous & Historic Trees. rev. ed. LC 76-39710. (Illus.). 90p. 1977. pap. 4.50 (*0-685-46351-6*) Am Forests.

Randall, Charles E., jt. auth. see Youngman, Wilbur H.

***Randall, Charles H. & Bushnell, Joan L.** Hisses, Boos & Cheers. Date not set. 12.95 (*0-87129-421-4*, H49) Dramatic Pub.

— Trapped by a Treacherous Twin. 1982. 5.00 (*0-87129-498-2*, T56) Dramatic Pub.

Randall, Charles T. The Encyclopedia of Window Fashions: A Visual Guide to the World of Window Treatments. rev. ed. LC 91-90537. (Illus.). 146p. 1992. pap. 19.95 (*0-9624736-3-4*) Randall Intl.

— The Encyclopedia of Window Fashions: A Visual Guide to the World of Window Treatments. 3rd rev. ed. LC 91-90537. (Illus.). 146p. 1992. spiral bd. 39.95 (*0-9624736-2-6*) Randall Intl.

Randall, Clifford W., jt. auth. see Benefield, Larry D.

Randall, Clifford W., et al, eds. Design & Retrofit of Wastewater Treatment Plants for Biological Nutrient Removal. LC 92-53521. (Water Quality Management Library: Vol. 5). 375p. 1992. text ed. 75.00 (*0-87762-922-6*) Technomic.

Randall, Clyde L., jt. auth. see Nichols, David H.

Randall, D., jt. auth. see Betz, A.

Randall, D. D., et al, eds. Current Topics in Plant Biochemistry & Physiology, Vol. 6. (Illus.). 190p. (Orig.). 1987. 12.00 (*0-936463-05-8*) U MO Plant Bio.

— Current Topics in Plant Biochemistry & Physiology, Vol. 7. (Illus.). 258p. (Orig.). 1988. 12.00 (*0-685-35120-3*) U MO Plant Bio.

— Current Topics in Plant Biochemistry & Physiology, Vol. 8. (Illus.). 316p. (Orig.). 1989. 15.00 (*0-936463-07-4*) U MO Plant Bio.

— Current Topics in Plant Biochemistry & Physiology, Vol. 9. (Illus.). (Orig.). 1990. 17.50 (*0-936463-08-2*) U MO Plant Bio.

— Current Topics in Plant Biochemistry & Physiology: Symposium Proceedings, Vol. 5. (Illus.). 216p. (Orig.). 1986. 12.00 (*0-936463-04-X*) U MO Plant Bio.

Randall, D. J. Type A Personality: Index of Authors & Subjects with Guide for Rapid Research. rev. ed. 1994. 44.50 (*0-7883-0182-9*); pap. 39.50 (*0-7883-0183-7*) ABBE Pubs Assn.

Randall, D. J., jt. ed. see Hoar, W. S.

Randall, D. J., et al. The Evolution of Air Breathing in Vertebrates. LC 80-462. (Illus.). 176p. 1981. 44.95 (*0-521-22259-1*) Cambridge U Pr.

Randall, D. V. Once upon the Eighth Day. 325p. 1993. write for info. (*0-9636838-0-2*) D V Randall.

Randall, Dale B. Gentle Flame: The Life & Verse of Dudley, Fourth Lord North. LC 82-21143. xviii, 255p. (C). 1983. text ed. 45.50 (*0-8223-0491-0*) Duke.

— The Golden Tapestry: A Critical Survey of Non-Chivalric Spanish Fiction in English Translation, 1543-1657. LC 63-13313. 272p. reprint ed. pap. 77.60 (*0-317-20426-2*, 2023438) Bks Demand.

— Joseph Conrad & Warrington Dawson: The Record of a Friendship. LC 68-56068. 258p. reprint ed. pap. 73.60 (*0-317-20424-6*, 2023439) Bks Demand.

— Winter Fruit: English Drama, 1642-1660. LC 95-7634. (Illus.). 456p. 1995. text ed. 39.95 (*0-8131-1925-1*) U Pr of Ky.

Randall, Dale B., ed. see Southeastern Renaissance Conference Staff.

Randall, Daniel R. A Puritan Colony in Maryland. LC 78-63763. (Johns Hopkins University. Studies in the Social Sciences. Thirtieth Ser. 1912: 6). reprint ed. 11.50 (*0-404-61031-5*) AMS Pr.

***Randall, David & Shoraka-Blair, Suzanne, eds.** An Evaluation of the Cost of Incinerating Wastes Containing PVC. 85p. 1994. 35.00 (*0-7918-1214-6*) ASME.

Randall, Deborah. Sin-Eater. 1989. pap. 11.95 (*1-85224-041-5*, Pub. by Bloodaxe Bks UK) Dufour.

— White Eyes, Dark Ages. (Illus.). 64p. 1994. pap. 12.95 (*1-85224-222-1*, Pub. by Bloodaxe Bks UK) Dufour.

Randall, Denise J. Management of Personnel in Health Sciences: Index of New Information with Authors & Subjects. 180p. 1993. 49.50 (*1-55914-858-6*); pap. 39.50 (*1-55914-859-4*) ABBE Pubs Assn.

— Psychological Adaptations in Life & Work: Subject Analysis Index with Reference Bibliography. LC 85-47866. 150p. 1987. 44.50 (*0-88164-406-4*); pap. 39.50 (*0-88164-407-2*) ABBE Pubs Assn.

— Psychophysiology: Guidebook for Medicine, Reference & Research. LC 83-46104. 150p. 1985. 37.50 (*0-88164-142-1*); pap. 34.50 (*0-88164-143-X*) ABBE Pubs Assn.

Randall, Doanda, comp. Buddhist & Hindu Art in the Collection of John H. Mann. (Illus.). 285p. (Orig.). 1981. 65.00 (*0-940492-01-6*) Asian Conserv Lab.

Randall, Dudley. Cities Burning. LC 68-18623. (YA). (gr. 12 up). 1966. pap. 3.00 (*0-685-00860-6*) Broadside Pr.

— A Litany of Friends: New & Selected Poems. 2nd ed. LC 83-82770. 103p. (YA). (gr. 9-12). 1983. per. 6.00 (*0-916418-50-2*) Lotus.

Randall, Dudley, ed. The Black Poets. (Illus.). 384p. 1985. mass mkt. 5.95 (*0-553-27563-1*, Bantam Classics) Bantam.

— Homage to Hoyt Fuller. LC 84-72587. 356p. (YA). (gr. 12 up). 1984. 20.00 (*0-910296-22-7*); pap. 15.00 (*0-910296-24-3*) Broadside Pr.

Randall, Dudley & Burroughs, Margaret G., eds. For Malcolm: Poems on the Life & Death of Malcolm X. 2nd ed. LC 74-78642. (YA). (gr. 12 up). 1969. pap. 7.00 (*0-685-00863-0*) Broadside Pr.

Randall, E. O. The Separatist Society of Zoar: An Experiment in Communism - from Its Commencement to Its Conclusion. (Ohio History, Communism Ser.). (Illus.). 128p. 1990. reprint ed. lib. bdg. 31.80 (*1-56651-020-1*); reprint ed. pap. 14.80 (*1-56651-019-8*) A W McGraw.

— Serpent Mound - Adams County, Ohio: Mystery of the Mound & History of the Serpent. (Ohio History, Prehistoric Indians, Serpent Worship Ser.). (Illus.). 56p. (C). 1993. reprint ed. lib. bdg. 25.65 (*1-56651-088-0*); reprint ed. pap. 7.55 (*1-56651-087-2*) A W McGraw.

Randall, E. T. Cosmic Kidnappers. LC 84-8579. (Alien Adventures Ser.). (Illus.). 128p. (J). (gr. 3-7). 1985. lib. bdg. 9.49 (*0-8167-0328-0*); pap. text ed. 2.95 (*0-8167-0329-9*) Troll Assocs.

— Target: Earth. LC 84-2740. (Alien Adventures Ser.). (Illus.). 128p. (J). (gr. 3-7). 1985. lib. bdg. 9.49 (*0-8167-0326-4*); pap. text ed. 2.95 (*0-8167-0327-2*) Troll Assocs.

— Thieves from Space. LC 84-8538. (Alien Adventures Ser.). (Illus.). 128p. (J). (gr. 3-7). 1985. lib. bdg. 9.49 (*0-8167-0330-2*); pap. text ed. 2.95 (*0-8167-0331-0*) Troll Assocs.

— Town in Terror. LC 84-5617. (Alien Adventures Ser.). (Illus.). 128p. (J). (gr. 3-7). 1985. lib. bdg. 9.49 (*0-8167-0332-9*); pap. 2.95 (*0-8167-0333-7*) Troll Assocs.

Randall, E. Vance. Private Schools & Public Power: A Case for Pluralism. 240p. (C). 1994. text ed. 34.00 (*0-8077-3344-X*) Tchrs Coll.

Randall, Edith & Campbell, Florence. Sacred Symbols of the Ancients. (Illus.). 200p. 1982. reprint ed. spiral bd. 21.95 (*0-87516-487-0*) DeVorss.

Randall, Edith M., jt. auth. see Stillwell, Susan B.

Randall, Elinor, tr. see Marti, Jose.

Randall, Elinor, tr. see Tibol, Raquel.

Randall, Elinor, tr. see Zamora, Daisy.

Randall, Emilius O. History of Ohio, 5 vols., Set. 1993. reprint ed. lib. bdg. 375.00 (*0-7812-5397-7*) Rprt Serv.

— History of the Zoar Society. 3rd ed. LC 75-134427. 1972. reprint ed. 31.50 (*0-404-08467-2*) AMS Pr.

— History of the Zoar Society. 1993. reprint ed. lib. bdg. 89.00 (*0-7812-5396-9*) Rprt Serv.

Randall, Everett D., ed. Issues in Insurance, 2 vols. 4th ed. LC 87-71983. 1034p. 1987. reprint ed. text ed. 26.00 (*0-89463-050-4*) Am Inst FCPCU.

Randall, F. A. Randall & Allied Families: William Randall, 1609-1693 of Scituate & His Descendants with Ancestral Families. (Illus.). 596p. 1993. reprint ed. lib. bdg. 99.00 (*0-8328-3732-6*); reprint ed. pap. 89.00 (*0-8328-3733-4*) Higginson Bk Co.

Randall, F. H. Psychology: The Cultivation & Development of Mind & Will by Positive & Negative Processes, the Primacy of Will Power. 1991. lib. bdg. 75.00 (*0-8490-4065-5*) Gordon Pr.

Randall, Frances. Denali Diary: Letters from McKinley. (Illus.). 160p. (Orig.). 1987. pap. 9.95 (*0-938567-01-2*) Cloudcap.

Randall, Francis B. N. G. Chernyshevskii. LC 67-19353. (Twayne's World Authors Ser.). 1967. lib. bdg. 17.95 (*0-8057-2212-2*) Irvington.

Randall, Frank A. History of the Development of Building Construction in Chicago. LC 72-5070. (Technology & Society Ser.). (Illus.). 400p. 1978. reprint ed. 33.95 (*0-405-04720-7*) Ayer.

Randall, Frank H. Psychology: The Cultivation & Development of Mind & Will by Positive & Negative Processes, the Primacy of Will Power. 193p. 1973. reprint ed. spiral bd. 7.70 (*0-7873-0692-4*) Mokelumne.

— Your Mesmeric Forces & How to Develop Them. 151p. 1971. reprint ed. spiral bd. 5.50 (*0-7873-0693-2*) Mokelumne.

Randall, Geoffrey. Effective Marketing. LC 94-2995. (Self Development for Managers Ser.). 128p. 1994. pap. 14.95 (*0-415-10236-7*, B4119) Routledge.

— The Principles of Marketing. LC 92-45846. (Series in the Principles of Management). 1993. write for info. (*0-415-07266-2*, Routledge NY) Routledge.

— Trade Marketing Strategies: The Partnership Between Manufacturers, Brands & Retailers. 2nd ed. (Professional Development Ser.). 250p. 1994. pap. 32.95 (*0-7506-2012-9*) Buttrwrth-Heinemann.

Randall, Glenn. Cold Comfort: Keeping Warm in the Outdoors. (Illus.). 144p. (Orig.). 1987. pap. 10.95 (*0-941130-46-0*) Lyons & Burford.

— Modern Backpacker's Handbook. (Illus.). 288p. 1993. pap. 14.95 (*1-55821-248-5*) Lyons & Burford.

— Mount McKinley Climber's Handbook. (Illus.). 128p. (Orig.). 1993. pap. 18.00 (*0-934641-55-2*) Chockstone Pr.

— The Outward Bound Map & Compass Book. (Illus.). 160p. (Orig.). 1989. pap. 8.95 (*1-55821-022-9*) Lyons & Burford.

Randall, Glenn R. & Lutz, Ellen L. Serving Survivors of Torture. 218p. 1991. 18.00 (*0-87168-433-0*, 91-42S) AAAS.

Randall, H. Advanced Level Accounting. 464p. (C). 1990. 50.00 (*1-870941-36-5*) St Mut.

An Asterisk (*) at the beginning of an entry indicates that the title is appearing in BIP for the first time.

Randall, Hal. Publicity Photography. (Illus.). 108p. (Orig.). 1989. pap. 25.00 (*0-934420-08-4*) Studio Pr Twain Harte.

Randall, Harriet H., ed. The Backstretch. 120p. 1989. 14.00 (*0-318-16780-8*) United Thoroughbred Trnrs.

Randall, Henry S. Life of Thomas Jefferson, 3 Vols, Set. LC 72-117890. (Select Bibliographies Reprint Ser.). 1977. 108.95 (*0-8369-5343-6*) Ayer.

— The Life of Thomas Jefferson, 3 vols, Set. LC 79-172011. (American Scene Ser.). (Illus.). 1972. reprint ed. lib. bdg. 175.00 (*0-306-70250-9*) Da Capo.

Randall, J. Personal Defense Weapons. LC 92-72813. 102p. (Orig.). 1992. pap. 10.00 (*1-55950-087-5*, 19188) Loompanics.

Randall, J. E. Microcomputers & Physiological Simulation. 1980. pap. write for info. (*0-201-06128-7*) Addison-Wesley.

Randall, J. G. & Current, Richard N. Lincoln the President: Last Full Measure. 440p. 1991. 39.95 (*0-252-01785-4*) U of Ill Pr.

Randall, J. Herman. The Power of Suggestion. 71p. 1975. reprint ed. spiral bd. 4.40 (*0-7873-1066-2*) Mokelumne.

Randall, J. K. Something Medieval. LC 80-80808. (Illus.). 48p. 1988. 14.50 (*0-939044-24-2*) Lingua Pr.

Randall, J. K., jt. auth. see Boretz, Benjamin.

Randall, James. California Personal Injury Forms, 1987-1990, 2 vols. annuals suppl. ed. 130.00 (*0-8321-0004-8*) Bancroft Whitney Co.

Randall, James C., ed. NMR & Macromolecules: Sequence, Dynamic, & Domain Structure. LC 84-366. (ACS Symposium Ser.: No. 247). 181p. 1984. lib. bdg. 43.95 (*0-8412-0829-8*) Am Chemical.

Randall, James E. Microcomputers & Physiological Simulation. 2nd ed. 304p. 1987. text ed. 50.00 (*0-88167-292-0*) Raven.

Randall, James G. Lincoln & the South. LC 80-22084. (Walter Lynwood Fleming Lectures in Southern History). (Illus.). viii, 161p. 1980. reprint ed. text ed. 49.75 (*0-313-22843-4*, RALS, Greenwood Pr) Greenwood.

Randall, James G. & Donald, David H. The Civil War & Reconstruction. 2nd rev. ed. 866p. (C). 1969. pap. text ed. 21.00 (*0-669-06428-9*) Heath.

Randall, Joan, jt. auth. see Randall, Stan.

Randall, Joel. Essence. 219p. 1994. pap. write for info. (*1-882400-10-0*) Featherweed.

Randall, John. The Book of Revelation: What Does It Really Say? 87p. (Orig.). 1976. pap. 5.95 (*0-914544-16-0*) Living Flame Pr.

— Feature Films on a Low Budget. (Illus.). 152p. 1991. pap. 24.95 (*0-240-80097-4*, Focal) Buttrwrth-Heinemann.

— Plato: Dramatist of the Life of Reason. LC 71-106565. 288p. reprint ed. pap. 82.10 (*0-317-30468-2*, 2024826) Bks Demand.

— Tojo Virus. 512p. 1991. mass mkt. 4.95 (*0-8217-3436-9*) Zebra.

— Wisdom Instructs Her Children: The Power of the Spirit & the Word. 146p. (Orig.). 1981. pap. 5.95 (*0-914544-36-5*) Living Flame Pr.

Randall, John, jt. auth. see Petrie, Ted.

Randall, John, et al. Mary: Pathway to Fruitfulness. (Orig.). 1978. pap. 6.95 (*0-914544-28-4*) Living Flame Pr.

Randall, John C. How to Save Time ... & Worry Less. LC 79-92477. (Illus.). 65p. (Orig.). 1980. pap. 24.95 (*0-935864-01-6*, 804) Hotline Multi-Ent.

Randall, John D. Jihad Ultimatum. 1989. mass mkt. 4.50 (*1-55817-260-2*, Pinnacle NY) Windsor NY.

Randall, John D., jt. auth. see Petrie, Ted.

Randall, John E. The Diver's Guide to Fishes of the Maldives. 192p. (C). 1990. 125.00 (*0-907151-53-1*, Pub. by IMMEL Pubng UK) St Mut.

— Guide to Hawaiian Reef Fishes. LC 85-24551. (Illus.). 84p. 1985. 21.95 (*0-915180-07-3*); pap. 18.95 (*0-915180-29-4*) Harrowood Bks.

— Red Sea Reef Fishes. 192p. (C). 1990. pap. 135.00 (*0-907151-04-3*, Pub. by IMMEL Pubng UK) St Mut.

— Sharks of Arabia. 148p. (C). 1990. 125.00 (*0-907151-09-4*, Pub. by IMMEL Pubng UK) St Mut.

— The Underwater Guide to Hawaiian Reef Fishes. LC 79-27625. (Illus.). 1980. spiral bd. 16.95 (*0-915180-02-2*) Harrowood Bks.

Randall, John E., et al. Fishes of the Great Barrier Reef & Coral Sea. LC 90-38987. (Illus.). 564p. (C). 1991. text ed. 60.00 (*0-8248-1346-4*) UH Pr.

Randall, John H. Aristotle. LC 60-6030. (C). 1962. text ed. 50.00 (*0-231-02359-6*); pap. text ed. 17.00 (*0-231-08529-X*) Col U Pr.

Randall, John H., Jr. Career of Philosophy, Vol. 2. 1965. text ed. 67.50 (*0-685-62748-9*) Col U Pr.

Randall, John H. The Career of Philosophy, Vol. 2: From the German Enlightenment to the Age of Darwin. LC 62-10454. 687p. reprint ed. pap. 180.00 (*0-8357-6048-0*, 2034191) Bks Demand.

— How Philosophy Uses Its Past. LC 63-20464. (Matchette Lectures: No. 14). 120p. reprint ed. pap. 34.20 (*0-317-09222-7*, 2007203) Bks Demand.

— How Philosophy Uses Its Past. LC 83-12754. xiv, 106p. 1983. reprint ed. text ed. 45.00 (*0-313-24127-9*, RAHO, Greenwood Pr) Greenwood.

Randall, John H., 3rd. The Landscape & the Looking Glass: Willa Cather's Search for Value. LC 72-6207. (Illus.). 425p. 1973. reprint ed. text ed. 35.00 (*0-8371-6466-4*, RALG, Greenwood Pr) Greenwood.

Randall, John H., Jr. The Making of the Modern Mind: A Survey of the Intellectual Background of the Present Age. LC 76-20740. 720p. 1976. reprint ed. text ed. 78.50 (*0-231-04142-X*); reprint ed. pap. text ed. 29.50 (*0-231-04143-8*) Col U Pr.

Randall, John H. Nature & Historical Experience: Essays in Naturalism & the Theory of History. LC 57-11694. (C). 1962. pap. text ed. 20.00 (*0-231-08537-0*) Col U Pr.

Randall, John H., Jr. Philosophy After Darwin: Chapters for the Career of Philosophy & Other Essays, Vol. 3. Singer, Beth J., ed. LC 62-10454. 1977. text ed. 50.00 (*0-231-04114-4*) Col U Pr.

— Problem of Group Responsibility to Society. LC 72-89760. (American Labor, from Conspiracy to Collective Bargaining Ser., No. 1). 296p. 1974. reprint ed. 19.95 (*0-405-02145-3*) Ayer.

— The Role of Knowledge in Western Religion. 160p. 1986. reprint ed. pap. text ed. 19.50 (*0-8191-5167-X*) U Pr of Amer.

Randall, John H., Jr., ed. see Woodbridge, Frederick J.

Randall, John L. Childhood & Sexuality: A Radical Christian Approach. 304p. 1992. 16.95 (*0-8059-3284-4*) Dorrance.

Randall, Joyce. Beading & Bonding in Ribbon Embroidery. (Illus.). 56p. 1994. 14.95 (*0-86417-563-9*, Pub. by Kangaroo Pr AT) Seven Hills Bk.

— Floral Designs for Ribbon Embroidery. (Illus.). 48p. 1993. 12.95 (*0-86417-431-4*, Pub. by Kangaroo Pr AT) Seven Hills Bk.

Randall, Judson, ed. see Stanford, Phil.

Randall, Jules T. Good-Bye, Darling Ting: A Musical Tragedy. 1990. 10.95 (*0-533-08810-0*) Vantage.

Randall, Julia. Moving in Memory. Poems. LC 86-27623. 51p. 1987. pap. 6.95 (*0-8071-1388-3*) La State U Pr.

— The Path to Fairview: New & Selected Poems. LC 92-19003. 224p. 1992. text ed. 24.95 (*0-8071-1782-X*); pap. 14.95 (*0-8071-1783-8*) La State U Pr.

Randall, Kenneth C. Federal Courts & the International Human Rights Paradigm. LC 90-2877. 303p. (C). 1990. text ed. 48.00 (*0-8223-1038-4*) Duke.

Randall, Laura. The Political Economy of Brazilian Oil. LC 92-15781. 328p. 1993. text ed. 59.95 (*0-275-94091-8*, C4091, Praeger Pubs) Greenwood.

— The Political Economy of Mexican Oil. LC 89-16099. 238p. 1989. text ed. 55.00 (*0-275-93372-5*, C3372, Praeger Pubs) Greenwood.

— The Politics Economoy of Venezuelan Oil. LC 87-15848. 260p. 1987. text ed. 59.95 (*0-275-92823-3*, C2823, Praeger Pubs) Greenwood.

***Randall, Laura, ed.** Changing Structure of Mexico: Political, Social & Economic Prospects. (Columbia University Seminars Ser.). 350p. 1995. 69.95 (*1-56324-641-4*); pap. 24.95 (*1-56324-642-2*) M E Sharpe.

Randall, LaVeta, jt. ed. see Evans, Robert L.

Randall, Laveta

Randall, Lee. The Garth Brooks Scrapbook. (Illus.). 240p. 1992. pap. 18.95 (*0-8065-1300-4*, Citadel Pr) Carol Pub Group.

— The Madonna Scrapbook. (Illus.). 224p. 1992. pap. 15.95 (*0-8065-1297-0*, Citadel Pr) Carol Pub Group.

— Michael Bolton: Time, Love, & Tenderness. LC 93-23942. 1993. pap. 12.00 (*0-671-87304-0*, Fireside) S&S Trade.

Randall, Lilian M. Medieval & Renaissance Manuscripts in the Walters Art Gallery, Vol. II: France, 1420-1540, 2 vols. (Illus.). 832p. 1993. text ed. 135.95 (*0-8018-2870-8*) Johns Hopkins.

— Medieval & Renaissance Manuscripts in the Walters Art Gallery, Vol. 1: France, 875-1420. LC 88-45410. (Illus.). 432p. 1989. text ed. 85.00 (*0-8018-2869-4*) Johns Hopkins.

Randall, Lillian M. The Diary of George A. Lucas: An American Art Agent in Paris, 1857-1909, 2 vols., Set. LC 77-85561. (Illus.). 1292p. 1978. 131.00 (*0-691-03933-X*) Princeton U Pr.

— Illuminated Manuscript: Masterpieces in Miniature. 44p. 1984. pap. 10.00 (*0-911886-29-X*) Walters Art.

Randall, Lindsay. Desire's Storm. 512p. 1986. pap. 3.95 (*0-8217-1920-3*) Zebra.

— Miss Marcie's Mischief. 224p. 1995. mass mkt. 3.99 (*0-8217-4814-9*) Zebra.

— Miss Meredith's Marriage. 288p. 1995. pap. 3.99 (*0-8217-5051-8*) Zebra.

— Silversword. 368p. (Orig.). 1990. pap. 3.95 (*0-8439-2948-0*) Dorchester Pub Co.

Randall, Louise A. Bible Heroes: Stories for Children Ages One to Six. LC 87-82112. 56p. (J). (ps). 1988. pap. 4.98 (*0-88290-316-0*) Horizon Utah.

— Scripture Stories for Tiny Tots: Read-Aloud Stories from the Bible for Children 1 to 6. LC 83-83429. 38p. (Orig.). (J). (gr. k-3). 1983. pap. 4.98 (*0-88290-209-1*) Horizon Utah.

Randall, Lyman K. Notes from Midlife & other Poems. LC 86-800088. 70p. 1986. pap. 5.95 (*0-317-52124-1*) Freeman Farms.

***Randall, Lyn & Senior, M.** Managing & Improving Service Quality & Delivery. (C). 1994. 150.00x (*0-946655-64-2*, Pub. by S Thornes Pubs UK) St Mut.

Randall, Lyn, jt. auth. see Bond, John.

Randall, Lynda E. The Student Teacher's Handbook for Physical Education. LC 92-19454. 160p. 1992. spiral bd. 13.00x (*0-87322-365-9*, BRAN0365) Human Kinetics.

— Systematic Supervision for Physical Education. LC 92-2930. (Illus.). 264p. 1992. text ed. 42.00x (*0-87322-363-2*, BRAN0363) Human Kinetics.

Randall, Lynn M. Litigation Organization & Management for Paralegals. LC 92-36836. 352p. 1993. text ed. 95.00 (*0-471-58798-2*) Wiley.

Randall-Maciver, D. Libyan Notes. 176p. 1987. 250.00 (*1-85077-169-3*, Darf Pubs Ltd) St Mut.

Randall, Margaret. Albuquerque: Coming Back to the U. S. A. 350p. (Orig.). 1986. pap. 12.95 (*0-919573-53-3*) Left Bank.

— Christians in the Nicaraguan Revolution. (Illus.). 240p. (Orig.). 1984. pap. 4.00 (*0-919573-15-0*) Left Bank.

— Christians in the Nicaraguan Revolution. 240p. (Orig.). (C). 1983. reprint ed. pap. 7.95 (*0-939306-48-4*) Left Bank.

— Coming Home: Peace without Complacency. (Illus.). 52p. (Orig.). 1990. pap. 5.95 (*0-931122-57-0*) West End.

— The Coming Home Poems. 32p. 5.00 (*0-942986-04-0*) LongRiver Bks.

— Dancing with the Doe: New & Selected Poems, 1986-91. 74p. (Orig.). 1992. pap. 9.95 (*0-931122-70-8*) West End.

— Gathering Rage: The Failure of Twentieth Century Revolutions to Develop a Feminist Agenda. LC 92-29712. 224p. (C). 1992. text ed. 28.00 (*0-85345-860-X*); pap. text ed. 12.00 (*0-85345-861-8*) Monthly Rev.

— Memory Says Yes. LC 87-73442. 80p. 1988. pap. 7.95 (*0-915306-77-8*) Curbstone.

— The Old Cedar Bar. (Fine Art Ser.). (Illus.). 100p. 1992. 150.00 (*0-89556-092-5*) Gateways Bks & Tapes.

— Our Voices Our Lives: Stories of Women from Central America & the Caribbean. 200p. 1995. text ed. 29.95 (*1-56751-047-7*); pap. text ed. 12.95 (*1-56751-046-9*) Common Courage.

— Part of the Solution: Portrait of a Revolutionary. LC 72-93974. 1973. pap. 2.95 (*0-8112-0471-5*, NDP350) New Directions.

— Risking a Somersault in the Air: Conversations with Nicaraguan Writers. Alexander, Floyce, ed. Mills, Christina, tr. LC 86-10052. (Illus.). 215p. 1984. pap. 8.00 (*0-942638-12-3*, 27L) New Amer Pr.

— Risking a Somersault in the Air: Conversations with Nicaraguan Writers. Alexander, Floyce, ed. Mills, Christina, tr. LC 86-10052. (Illus.). 220p. reprint ed. pap. 9.95 (*0-915306-92-1*) Curbstone.

— Sandino's Daughters: Testimonies of Nicaraguan Women in Struggle. LC 95-8563. 224p. (C). 1995. pap. text ed. 18.95 (*0-8135-2214-5*) Rutgers U Pr.

— Sandino's Daughters Revisited: Feminism in Nicaragua. LC 93-10819. (Illus.). 311p. (C). 1994. text ed. 47.00 (*0-8135-2024-X*); pap. 16.95 (*0-8135-2025-8*) Rutgers U Pr.

— This Is about Incest. LC 87-412. (Illus.). 72p. (Orig.). 1987. lib. bdg. 18.95 (*0-932379-30-3*); pap. 8.95 (*0-932379-29-X*) Firebrand Bks.

— Twenty-Five Stages of My Spine. 1967. 3.00 (*0-685-01011-2*) Elizabeth Pr.

— Walking to the Edge: Essays of Resistance. 220p. (Orig.). 1991. 25.00 (*0-89608-398-5*); pap. 12.00 (*0-89608-397-7*) South End Pr.

— We. 1978. pap. 1.50 (*0-918266-10-6*) Smyrna.

— Women in Cuba-Twenty Years Later. LC 80-54055. (Illus.). 182p. (C). 1981. 19.95 (*0-918266-15-7*); pap. 8.95 (*0-918266-14-9*) Smyrna.

Randall, Margaret, tr. see Borge, Tomas.

Randall, Margaret, tr. see Castillo, Otto R.

Randall, Margaret, jt. auth. see Hubbard, Ruth.

Randall, Margaret, tr. see Zamora, Daisy.

Randall, Marta. John F. Kennedy. (World Leaders - Past & Present Ser.). 112p. 1988. 17.95 (*0-87754-586-3*); pap. 9.95 (*0-7910-0580-1*) Chelsea Hse.

— The Sword of Winter. LC 83-4830. 271p. 1983. 25.00 (*0-89366-160-0*) Ultramarine Pub.

Randall, Marta, ed. New Dimensions, No. 13. (Orig.). pap. 3.50 (*0-671-44227-9*) PB.

Randall-McIver, David. Mediaeval Rhodesia. 106p. 1971. reprint ed. 40.00 (*0-7146-1885-3*, Pub. by F Cass Pubs UK) Intl Spec Bk.

Randall, Mercedes M. Improper Bostonian: Emily Greene Balch. LC 64-25058. (Illus.). 475p. 1964. 29.50 (*0-8290-0178-6*) Irvington.

Randall, Mike. The Funny Side of the Street. 182p. 1989. 34.95 (*0-7475-0086-X*, Pub. by Bloomsbury Pub Ltd UK) Trafalgar.

***Randall, Monica.** Phantoms of the Hudson Valley: The Glorious Estates of a Lost Era. (Illus.). 224p. 1995. 45.00 (*0-87951-617-8*) Overlook Pr.

***Randall, Neil.** Plug-n-Play Internet: The Instant Internet Signup Kit for Windows. (Illus.). 500p. (Orig.). 1995. pap. text ed. 35.00 (*0-672-30669-7*) Sams.

— Teach Yourself the Internet: Around the World in 21 Days. 2nd ed. (Illus.). 700p. (Orig.). 1995. pap. 25.00 (*0-672-30735-9*) Sams.

— X-Com Strategies & Secrets. 1995. 12.99 (*0-7821-1671-X*) Sybex.

***Randall, Neil & Savetz, Kevin.** The Internet Surfer CD-ROM. (Illus.). 500p. (Orig.). 1995. pap. 39.99 (*0-672-30716-2*) Sams.

Randall, Oran E. History of Chesterfield, New Hampshire, from 1776 to 1881, with Family Histories. 525p. 1988. reprint ed. lib. bdg. 53.00 (*0-8328-0047-3*) Higginson Bk Co.

Randall, P. J., et al, eds. Genetic Aspects of Plant Mineral Nutrition: The Fourth International Symposium on Genetic Aspects of Plant Mineral Nutrition, Canberra, Australia, 30 September - 4 October 1991, Vol. 50. LC 92-43811. 400p. (C). 1993. lib. bdg. 195.50 (*0-7923-2118-9*) Kluwer Ac.

Randall, P. K. Genealogy of a Branch of the Randall Family, 1666 to 1879. 389p. 1989. reprint ed. lib. bdg. 51.00 (*0-8328-1000-2*); reprint ed. pap. 43.00 (*0-8328-1001-0*) Higginson Bk Co.

Randall, Paul. Baby Photos of the Country Stars. (Illus.). 200p. (Orig.). 1987. pap. 12.95 (*0-911679-01-4*) Union & Confed Inc.

Randall, Paul, jt. auth. see Williams, Douglas.

Randall, Peter, tr. see Boesak, Allan.

Randall, Peter, jt. auth. see Tree, Christina.

Randall, Peter E. Hampton: A Century of Town & Beach, 1888-1988. (History of Hampton, New Hampshire, 1638-1988 Ser.: Vol. III). (Illus.). 904p. 1989. 40.00 (*0-914339-23-0*) P E Randall Pub.

— Mount Washington: A Guide & Short History. 3rd ed. (Illus.). 224p. 1992. pap. 9.95 (*0-88150-220-0*) Countryman.

— Out on the Shoals: Co-Founder of Brook Farm. (Illus.). 64p. (Orig.). 1994. pap. 15.00 (*0-914339-51-6*) P E Randall Pub.

— Out on the Shoals: Twenty Years of Photography on the Isles of Shoals. (Illus.). 64p. 1995. pap. 16.50 (*0-914339-52-4*) P E Randall Pub.

— There Are No Victors Here: A Local Perspective on the Treaty of Portsmouth. LC 85-16986. (Portsmouth Marine Society Ser.: No. 8). (Illus.). 96p. 1985. 19.95 (*0-915819-07-4*) Portsmouth Marine Soc.

Randall, Peter G. & Bennett, Steven J. Total 1-2-3 Release 3.0. (Illus.). 700p. 1989. 24.95 (*0-13-925728-4*) Brady Compu Bks.

Randall, Peter G. & Scherrer, J. Portable Selling. (Illus.). (Orig.). 1992. pap. 34.95 (*1-56686-019-9*) Brady Compu Bks.

Randall, Peter G., jt. auth. see Bennett, Steven J.

Randall, Phyllis R., ed. Caryl Churchill: Critical Essays. LC 88-24473. (Casebooks on Modern Dramatists Ser.: Vol. 3). 214p. 27.00 (*0-8240-5841-0*, H736) Garland.

Randall, R. C., ed. Cancer Treatments & Marijuana Therapy: Marijuana's Use in the Reduction of Nausea & Vomiting & for Appetite Stimulation in Cancer Patients. Testimony from Historic Federal Hearings. LC 90-81972. 384p. (Orig.). 1990. pap. 39.95 (*0-936485-05-1*, Galen Pr DC) Lkng Glass Pubns.

— Marijuana, Medicine & the Law, Vol. II: Legal Briefs, Oral Arguments & Decision of the Judge. LC 88-80330. 502p. (Orig.). 1989. 55.00 (*0-936485-04-3*, Galen Pr) Lkng Glass Pubns.

— Marijuana, Medicine & the Law, Vol. 1: Direct Testimony. LC 88-80330. 502p. (Orig.). 1988. pap. 65.00 (*0-936485-02-7*, Galen Pr DC) Lkng Glass Pubns.

— Muscle Spasm, Pain & Marijuana Therapy: Testimony from Federal & State Court Proceedings on Marijuana's Medical Use. (Marijuana, Medicine & the Law Ser.). 200p. 1991. pap. text ed. write for info. (*0-936485-06-X*, Galen Pr DC) Lkng Glass Pubns.

***Randall, Richard C.** Randall's Practical Guide to ISO 9000: Implementation, Registration, & Beyond. (Engineering Process Improvement Ser.). 400p. 1995. pap. 31.95 (*0-201-63379-5*) Addison-Wesley.

Randall, Richard E., jt. auth. see Khan, Hashim.

Randall, Richard H., Jr. American Furniture in the Museum of Fine Arts, Boston. LC 65-24149. 278p. 1965. reprint ed. pap. 29.95 (*0-87846-003-9*) Mus Fine Arts Boston.

— The Golden Age of Ivory: Gothic Carvings in North American Collections. LC 93-19466. (Illus.). 160p. 1993. 75.00 (*1-55595-076-0*) Hudson Hills.

Randall, Richard H., Jr., et al. Objects of Adornment: Five Thousand Years of Jewelry from the Walters Art Gallery, Baltimore. (Illus.). 190p. 1984. pap. 17.50 (*0-917481-76-3*) Am Fed Arts.

Randall, Richard S. Censorship of the Movies: The Social & Political Control of a Mass Medium. LC 68-14035. 296p. 1968. 27.50 (*0-299-04731-8*); pap. 14.50 (*0-299-04734-2*) U of Wis Pr.

— Freedom & Taboo: Pornography & the Politics of a Self Divided. 400p. 1989. 32.50 (*0-520-06379-1*) U CA Pr.

— Freedom & Taboo: Pornography & the Politics of a Self Divided. 1992. pap. 15.00 (*0-520-08034-3*) U CA Pr.

Randall, Rick, jt. auth. see Hagee, John C.

Randall, Rick, ed. see Hagee, John C.

Randall, Robert. What People Expect from Church: Why Meeting the Needs of People Is More Important Than Church Meetings. LC 92-33162. (Ministry for the Third Millennium Ser.). 128p. (Orig.). 1993. pap. 11.95 (*0-687-13387-4*) Abingdon.

Randall, Robert, jt. ed. see Fahey, Liam.

Randall, Robert C., comp. Marijuana & AIDS: Pot, Politics & PWAS in America. LC 91-77140. 190p. (Orig.). 1992. pap. 12.95 (*0-936485-07-8*, Galen Pr DC) Lkng Glass Pubns.

Randall, Robert L. The Eternal Triangle: Pastor, Spouse, & Congregation. LC 91-42375. 176p. (Orig.). 1992. pap. 12.00 (*0-8006-2588-9*, 1-2588, Fortress Pr) Augsburg Fortress.

— Pastor & Parish: The Psychological Care of Ecclesiastical Conflicts. LC 86-27176. 172p. 1987. 38.95 (*0-89885-348-6*) Human Sci Pr.

— The Time of Your Life: Self-Time Management for Pastors. LC 93-45856. 144p. (Orig.). 1994. pap. 12.95 (*0-687-37137-6*) Abingdon.

Randall, Ron. Trekker Collection. (Illus.). 112p. 1988. pap. 5.95 (*1-56971-013-9*) Dark Horse Comics.

Randall, Ron, jt. auth. see Verheiden, Mark.

Randall, Rona. Arrogant Duke. large type ed. (Romance Ser.). 416p. 1993. 21.95 (*0-7089-2918-4*) Ulverscroft.

— Curtain Call. large type ed. (Romance Ser.). 720p. 1993. 21.95 (*0-7089-2960-5*) Ulverscroft.

— Glenrannoch. large type ed. (Romance Ser.). 464p. 1993. 21.95 (*0-7089-2992-3*) Ulverscroft.

— Knight's Keep. large type ed. (Romance Suspense Ser.). 432p. 1993. 21.95 (*0-7089-2973-7*) Ulverscroft.

— The Ladies of Hanover Square. large type ed. (Charnwood Large Print Ser.). 1994. 26.95 (*0-7089-8795-8*) Ulverscroft.

— The Potter's Niece. large type ed. 1990. 18.95 (*0-7089-2130-2*) Ulverscroft.

***Randall, Ronne.** Birthday Fun: Great Things to Make & Do. (Illus.). 32p. (J). (gr. 2-6). 1995. pap. 4.95 (*1-85697-548-7*, Kingfisher LKC) LKC.

— Gingerbread Man. (First Fairy Tales Ser.: No. S852-9). (J). 1988. boxed 3.95 (*0-7214-5102-0*) Ladybird Bks.

— Little Red Hen. (Favorite Tales Ser.). (Illus.). 28p. (J). 1994. 2.99 (*0-7214-5394-5*) Ladybird Bks.

— My Christmas Book. (Golden Naptime Tales Ser.). (Illus.). 18p. (J). 1994. write for info. (*0-307-12427-4*, Golden Bks) Western Pub.

— My Hanukkah Book. (Golden Naptime Tales Ser.). (Illus.). 18p. (J). 1994. write for info. (0-307-12428-2, Golden Bks) Western Pub.
— Thanksgiving Fun: Great Things to Make & Do. LC 93-48615. (Illus.). 32p. (J). (gr. 3-7). 1994. pap. 4.95 (1-85697-500-2, Kingfisher LKC) LKC.
Randall, Ronne P. Baby Forest Animals. (Happytime Storybks.). (Illus.). 24p. (J). (ps-00). 1987. pap. 1.25 (0-7214-9546-X, S871-2) Ladybird Bks.
— Marcus & Lionel. (Teddy Bear Tales Ser.: No. S897-5). (J). 1989. boxed 3.95 (0-7214-5228-0) Ladybird Bks.
— One to Ten. (Happytime Ser.). (Illus.). 24p. (J). (ps). 1987. pap. 1.25 (0-7214-9554-0, S871-10) Ladybird Bks.
— Opposites. (Happytime Ser.). (Illus.). 24p. (J). (ps). 1987. pap. 1.25 (0-7214-9556-7, S871) Ladybird Bks.
Randall, Ruth & Geiger, Keith. School Choice: Issues & Answers. 228p. (Orig.). 1991. pap. 21.95 (1-879639-02-5) Natl Educ Serv.
Randall, Stan & Randall, Joan. Steep Holm Through the Centuries. 256p. 1993. pap. 19.99 (0-7509-0323-6) A Sutton Pub.
Randall, Stephen J. Colombia & the United States: Hegemony & Interdependence. LC 91-17739. (United States & the Americas Ser.). (Illus.). 344p. 1992. 40.00 (0-8203-1401-3); pap. 17.50 (0-8203-1402-1) U of Ga Pr.
— The Diplomacy of Modernization: Colombian-American Relations 1920-1940. LC 77-4480. 251p. reprint ed. pap. 71.60 (0-685-43698-5, 2026440) Bks Demand.
— United States Foreign Oil Policy, 1919-1948: For Profits & Security. 336p. 1985. 49.95 (0-7735-0449-4, Pub. by McGill CN) U of Toronto Pr.
Randall, Stephen J., jt. auth. see Thompson, John H.
Randall, Steve, ed. see Tulku, Tarthang.
Randall, Tom, jt. auth. see Culbertson, Judi.
Randall, Vicky. Women & Politics. LC 82-10657. 237p. 1984. pap. 11.95 (0-312-88728-0) St Martin.
— Women & Politics: An International Perspective. xii, 362p. 1988. pap. text ed. 15.95 (0-226-70392-4) U Ch Pr.
— Women & Politics: An International Perspective. 2nd ed. xii, 362p. 1988. lib. bdg. 32.50 (0-226-70391-6) U Ch Pr.
Randall, Vicky, ed. Political Parties in the Third World. (One-Off Ser.). 256p. (C). 1988. text ed. 45.00 (0-8039-8143-0); pap. text ed. 16.95 (0-8039-8144-9) Sage.
Randall, Vicky & Theobald, Robin. Political Change & Underdevelopment: A Critical Introduction to Third World Politics. LC 85-10176. ix, 215p. 1985. 41.95 (0-8223-0564-X); pap. text ed. 15.95 (0-8223-0662-X) Duke.
Randall, Vicky, jt. auth. see Lovenduski, Joni.
Randall, Walter C., ed. Nervous Control of Cardiovascular Function. (Illus.). 1984. text ed. 45.00 (0-19-503390-6) OUP.
Randall, Warren R. Manual of Oregon Trees & Shrubs. 1981. reprint ed. pap. text ed. 5.75 (0-88246-019-6) Oreg St U Bkstrs.
Randall, Willard S. Benedict Arnold: Patriot & Traitor. LC 90-5656. (Illus.). 667p. 1990. 27.95 (1-55710-034-9) Morrow.
— Benedict Arnold: Patriot & Traitor. (Illus.). 672p. 1991. pap. 15.00 (0-688-10968-3, Quill) Morrow.
— George Washington. 1996. 35.00 (0-8050-2779-3) H Holt & Co.
— Thomas Jefferson: A Life. 736p. 1993. 35.00 (0-8050-1577-9, J Macrae Bks) H Holt & Co.
***Randall, William L.** The Stories We Are: An Essay on Self-Creation. 288p. 1995. 45.00 (0-8020-0564-0); pap. 17.95 (0-8020-6986-X) U of Toronto Pr.
Randau, Karen. Anxiety Attacks. 66p. 1991. pap. 2.99 (0-945276-25-7) Rapha Pub.
— Conquering Fear. 164p. 1991. pap. 9.99 (0-945276-22-2) Rapha Pub.
Randazzo, Angela. Bats in the Bellfry. 1975. 4.95 (0-87129-360-9, B12) Dramatic Pub.
***Randazzo, Sal.** Mythmakers: How Advertisers Apply the Power of Old Myths to Create Modern Day Legends. 275p. 1995. 22.95 (1-55738-895-4) Probus Pub Co.
Rande, Jay. Best of BYTE: Two Decades on the Leading Edge. 1993. pap. text ed. 24.95 (0-07-051344-9) McGraw.
***Rande, Wallace L.** Introduction to Foodservice Management. Date not set. text ed. write for info. (0-471-57746-4) Wiley.
Randel, Don M. Harvard Concise Dictionary of Music. LC 78-5948. (Illus.). 584p. 1978. text ed. 22.50 (0-674-37471-1); pap. text ed. 14.00 (0-674-37470-3) Belknap Pr.
— Harvard Dictionary of Music: Diccionario Harvard de Musica. 559p. (SPA.). 1984. 49.95 (0-8288-2184-4, F138171) Fr & Eur.
— An Index to the Chant of the Mozarabic Rite. LC 72-5384. (Princeton Studies in Music: No. 6). 692p. reprint ed. pap. 180.00 (0-317-09926-4, 2011400) Bks Demand.
Randel, Don M., ed. The New Harvard Dictionary of Music. LC 86-4780. (Illus.). 1024p. 1990. text ed. 37.50 (0-674-61525-5) Belknap Pr.
Randel, Mary G. The Historical Prose of Fernando de Herrera. (Serie A: Monagrafias, XX). 206p. (Orig.). (C). 1970. pap. 45.00 (0-900411-16-3, Pub. by Tamesis Bks Ltd UK) Boydell & Brewer.
Randel, William. Edward Eggleston. (Twayne's United States Authors Ser.). 1963. pap. 13.95 (0-8084-0116-5, T45) NCUP.
Randel, William, ed. see Eggleston, Edward.
Randell, Brian, ed. The Origins of Digital Computers. 3rd ed. (Texts & Monographs in Computer Science). (Illus.). 598p. 1982. 69.00 (0-387-11319-3) Spr-Verlag.
Randell, Gerry, jt. auth. see Wilpert, Bernhard.
Randell, Gerry, et al. Staff Appraisal: A First Step to Effective Leadership. rev. ed. 128p. (C). 1984. 48.00 (0-85292-333-3, Pub. by IPM Hse UK) St Mut.
Randell, J., jt. ed. see Hardy, L.
***Randell, Joan.** Crystal Clear. 176p. 1995. 34.95 (0-7872-1001-3) Kendall-Hunt.
Randell, Neil, jt. auth. see Zelazny, Roger.
Randell, R. Singularities. LC 89-6662. (CONM Ser.: Vol. 90). 359p. 1989. pap. text ed. 50.00 (0-8218-5096-2, CONM-90) Am Math.
Randell, Stephen, et al, eds. North America Without Borders? Integrating Canada, the United States & Mexico. 350p. (Orig.). 1992. pap. text ed. 24.95 (1-895176-18-2, Pub. by Univ Calgary CN) Paul & Co Pubs.
RanDelle, B. J. & Marshbum, Sandra. Lessons in Love. LC 24-476. (Illus.). 64p. (J). (gr. k-4). 1982. text ed. 5.95 (0-910445-00-1) Randelle Pubns.
Randelman, Mary U. & Schwartz, Joan. Memories of a Cuban Kitchen. (Illus.). 352p. 1992. text ed. 25.00 (0-02-600911-0) Macmillan.
Randeraad, N. Authority in Search of Liberty: The Prefects in Liberal Italy. (Scrinium (Monographs on History, Archaeology & Art History. Published under the Auspices of the Netherlands Institute & the Foundation of Friends of the Dutch Institute in Rome) Ser.: Vol. VII). 224p. 1993. 53.00 (90-5170-218-3) IBD Ltd.
Randeria, Jer D. The Parsi Mind: A Zoroastrian Asset to Culture. 175p. (C). 1993. 33.50 (81-215-0560-7, Pub. by M Manoharial II) Coronet Bks.
Randers, Jorgen, ed. Elements of the System Dynamics Method. LC 79-20019. 344p. (C). 1979. reprint ed. pap. text ed. 50.00 (0-915299-39-9) Prod Press.
Randers-Pehrson, Justine D. Barbarians & Romans: The Birth Struggle of Europe A. D. 400-700. LC 82-20025. 400p. 1993. pap. 14.95 (0-8061-2511-X) U of Okla Pr.
Randers-Pherson, Justine D. Barbarians & Romans: The Birth Struggle of Europe, A.D. 400-700. LC 82-20025. (Illus.). 416p. 1983. 37.95 (0-8061-1818-0) U of Okla Pr.
Randerson, K., et al. Influence of Segregation on Hydrogen Cracking in Structural Steels, EUR 13958. 92p. 1992. pap. 12.00 (92-826-3619-4, CD-NA-13958-EN-C, Pub. by Europ Com) UNIPUB.
Randesi, Stephen J. & Czubek, Donald H. IBM's System Application Architecture. (Illus.). 352p. 1991. pap. 49.95 (0-442-00468-0) Van Nos Reinhold.
— SNA: IBM's System Network Architecture. (Illus.). 384p. 1992. pap. 44.95 (0-442-00504-0) Van Nos Reinhold.
Randey, Pajendra. Social Inequality: Features, Forms & Functions. 317p. 1982. 34.95 (0-317-13625-9, Pub. by Anuj Pubns India) Asia Bk Corp.
Randhawa, Bikkar S. & Coffman, William E., eds. Visual Learning, Thinking, & Communication. (Cognition & Perception Ser.). 1978. text ed. 47.00 (0-12-579450-9) Acad Pr.
Randhawa, Bikkar S., jt. ed. see Leong, Che K.
Randhawa, D. S., jt. auth. see Randhawa, M. S.
Randhawa, G. S. Ornamental Horticulture in India. (Illus.). 144p. 1973. 8.00 (1-55528-089-7, Pub. by Today & Tomorrows P & P II) Scholarly Pubns.
Randhawa, G. S. & Mukhopadhyay, A. Floriculture in India. 1986. 38.00 (81-7023-057-8, Pub. by Allied II) S Asia.
Randhawa, G. S. & Srivastava, K. C. Citriculture in India. (C). 1986. 62.00 (0-8364-2420-4, Pub. by Hindustan IA) S Asia.
Randhawa, M. S. Basohli Painting. 116p. 1981. 49.95 (0-940500-92-2, Pub. by Pubns Div II) Asia Bk Corp.
— Kangra Paintings of the Bihari Sat Sai. (Illus.). 87p. 1982. 49.95 (0-318-36339-9) Asia Bk Corp.
— Kangra Paintings of the Gita Govinda. (Illus.). 132p. 1982. 85.00 (0-318-36340-2) Asia Bk Corp.
— Kangra Valley Painting. (Illus.). 68p. 1982. 34.95 (0-318-36341-0) Asia Bk Corp.
— Paintings of the Babur Nama. 139p. 1983. 80.00 (0-318-36345-3) Asia Bk Corp.
Randhawa, M. S. & Randhawa, D. S. Guler Paintings. (Illus.). 60p. 1982. 32.95 (0-318-36336-4) Asia Bk Corp.
— Kishangarh Painting. (Illus.). 46p. 1980. 32.95 (0-318-36342-9) Asia Bk Corp.
Randhawa, Maninder S. The Rural & Urban Aged. (C). 1991. 28.00 (81-85135-55-X, Pub. by Natl Bk Org II) S Asia.
Randhawa, Ravinder. A Wicked Old Woman. 1990. pap. 8.95 (0-7043-4078-X, Pub. by Womens Pr UK) Interlink Pub.
Randhawa, Simran P. Eurofashion... Unleashing the Designer in You. LC 92-70333. (Illus.). 180p. (Orig.). 1992. pap. 24.95 (0-9631974-9-5) Immis Pub.
Randi, James. Conjuring. (Illus.). 336p. 1993. pap. 19.95 (0-312-09771-9) St Martin.
— The Encyclopedia of Lies, Frauds & Hoaxes of the Occult & Supernatural: James Randi's Decidedly Skeptical Definitions of Alternate Realities. (Illus.). 336p. 1995. 24.95 (0-312-13066-X) St Martin.
— The Faith Healers. LC 87-17241. 318p. 1989. 20.95 (0-87975-369-2); pap. 19.95 (0-87975-535-0) Prometheus Bks.
— Flim-Flam! The Truth about Unicorns, Parapsychology, & Other Delusions. LC 82-60953. (Illus.). 342p. 1982. reprint ed. pap. 17.95 (0-87975-198-3) Prometheus Bks.
— Magic World of Amazing Randi. 168p. 1989. pap. 10.95 (1-55850-982-8) Adams Pubng.
— The Mask of Nostradamus: The Prophecies of the World's Most Famous Seer. LC 92-41554. (Illus.). 256p. (C). 1993. reprint ed. pap. 16.95 (0-87975-830-9) Prometheus Bks.
— The Truth about Uri Geller. rev. ed. LC 82-60951. (Illus.). 234p. 1982. pap. 19.95 (0-87975-199-1) Prometheus Bks.
Randic, M. & Trinajstic, N. On the Relative Stabilities of Conjugated Heterocycles Containing Divalent Sulfur (SR) 48p. 1986. pap. text ed. 33.00 (3-7186-0372-1) Gordon & Breach.
Randic, M., jt. ed. see Klein, D. J.
***Randich, Keith.** Carving the Little Guys: An Introductory Text by Keith Randich. LC 91-91341. (Illus.). 60p. (Orig.). 1991. pap. 9.00 (0-9642327-0-7) K Randich Pubng.
— Carving the Little Sailors: An Introductory Text by Keith Randich. LC 93-92743. (Illus.). 80p. (Orig.). 1993. pap. 10.00 (0-9642327-1-5) K Randich Pubng.
— Old Time Whittling: An Introductory Text by Keith Randich. LC 94-92208. (Illus.). 60p. (Orig.). 1994. pap. 9.00 (0-9642327-2-3) K Randich Pubng.
***Randisi.** Deadly Allies II. 1995. mass mkt. 4.99 (0-553-56317-3) Bantam.
Randisi, Jennifer L. On Her Way Rejoicing: The Fiction of Muriel Spark. LC 90-32628. (Contexts & Literature Ser.: Vol. 3). 129p. 1991. text ed. 29.95 (0-8132-0730-4) Cath U Pr.
— A Tissue of Lies: Eudora Welty & the Southern Romance. LC 82-45042. 198p. (Orig.). (C). 1982. lib. bdg. 55.00 (0-8191-2451-6); pap. text ed. 24.00 (0-8191-2452-4) U Pr of Amer.
***Randisi, Robert J.** Alone with the Dead. LC 95-1758. 1995. 21.95 (0-312-13022-8, Pub. by Thomas Dunne Bks) St Martin.
— Full Contact. 1986. pap. 2.95 (0-380-69984-2) Avon.
— Hard Look: A Miles Jacoby Mystery. 1993. 21.00 (0-8027-1251-7) Walker & Co.
— Separate Cases. 192p. 1990. 18.95 (0-8027-5723-5) Walker & Co.
— Stand-Up: A Miles Jacoby Mystery. LC 94-18377. 1994. 20.95 (0-8027-3196-1) Walker & Co.
Randisi, Robert J., ed. An Eye for Justice. 224p. 1989. 16. 95 (0-89296-979-2); pap. 9.95 (0-685-67688-9) Mysterious Pr.
— The Eyes Have It: The First Private Eye Writers of America Anthology. 336p. 1987. pap. 8.95 (0-89296-906-7) Mysterious Pr.
— The Eyes Still Have It: The Shamus Award-Winning Stories. LC 95-15521. 256p. 1995. 21.95 (0-525-93988-1, Dutton) NAL-Dutton.
— Justice for Hire: The Fourth Private Eye Writers of American Anthology. 256p. 1990. 18.95 (0-89296-371-9) Mysterious Pr.
— Justice for Hire: The Fourth Private Eye Writers of American Anthology. deluxe limited ed. 256p. 1990. 75. 00 (0-89296-425-1) Mysterious Pr.
— Mean Streets: The Second Private Eye Writers of American Anthology. 240p. 1987. 16.95 (0-89296-169-4); pap. 8.95 (0-89296-924-5) Mysterious Pr.
Randisi, Robert J. & Dunlap, Susan, eds. Deadly Allies II: Private Eye Writers of America-Sisters in Crime Collaborative Anthology. LC 93-31344. 1994. 18.95 (0-385-42468-X) Doubleday.
Randjbar-Daemi, S., et al, eds. Recent Developments in Conformal Field Theories: Trieste Conference. 320p. (C). 1990. pap. 37.00 (981-02-0280-6) World Scientific Pub.
Randjbar-Daemi, S. & Lu, Yu. Quantum Field Theory & Condensed Matter Physics: Proceedings of the 4th Trieste Conference on Quantum Field. 148p. 1994. text ed. 53.00 (981-02-1622-X) World Scientific Pub.
Randklev, James. Georgia Images of Wildness. 1992. pap. 19.95 (1-56579-008-1) Westcliffe Pubs Inc.
— Wild & Scenic Florida: A Photographic Portfolio. (Illus.). 128p. 1995. 39.95 (1-56313-702-X) BrownTrout Pubs Inc.
Randle, Damian. Natural Resources. LC 93-25195. (Young Geographer Ser.). (Illus.). 32p. (J). (gr. 4-6). 1993. 14.95 (1-56847-056-8) Thomson Lrning.
Randle, Deatrice. Lessons for Today's Kids. rev. ed. 1994. 7.95 (0-8062-4969-2) Carlton.
Randle, John & Watanabe, Mariko. Coping with Japan. 184p. 1987. pap. 13.95 (0-631-15443-4) Blackwell Pubs.
Randle, Kevin. The Citadel. 192p. (Orig.). 1994. pap. 4.50 (0-441-00056-8) Ace Bks.
— Galactic MI. 208p. (Orig.). 1993. pap. 4.50 (0-441-27238-X) Ace Bks.
— The Rat Trap. (Galactic MI Ser.: No. 2). 1993. pap. 4.50 (0-441-27243-6) Ace Bks.
***Randle, Kevin D.** A History of UFO Crashes. 296p. (Orig.). 1995. mass mkt. 5.50 (0-380-77666-9) Avon.
— The October Scenario. LC 88-1669. (Illus.). 192p. (Orig.). pap. 9.95 (0-934523-35-5) Middle Coast Pub.
— To Touch the Light. 320p. 1994. mass mkt. 4.99 (0-7860-0047-3) Windsor NY.
— Truth about the UFO Crash at Roswell. 1994. 19.95 (0-87131-761-3) M Evans.
— The UFO Casebook. 256p. (Orig.). 1989. mass mkt. 5.50 (0-446-35715-4) Warner Bks.
Randle, Kevin D. & Schmitt, Don R. UFO Crash at Roswell. 352p. (Orig.). 1991. mass mkt. 5.50 (0-380-76196-3) Avon.
***Randle, Kevin D. & Schmitt, Donald R.** The Truth about the UFO Crash at Roswell. 336p. (Orig.). 1994. mass mkt. 5.99 (0-380-77803-3) Avon.
Randle, Kevin J. Spanish Gold. LC 90-42202. (Novel of the West Ser.). 192p. 1990. 15.95 (0-87131-615-3) M Evans.
Randle, Kristen D. On the Side of the Angels. 12.95 (0-88494-690-8) Bookcraft Inc.
— The Only Alien on the Planet. LC 93-34594. (YA). 1995. 14.95 (0-590-46309-8) Scholastic Inc.
— Why Did Grandma Have to Die? (J). pap. 5.95 (0-88494-621-5) Bookcraft Inc.
Randle, Michael & Rogers, Paul. Alternatives in European Security. (Illus.). 184p. 1990. text ed. 48.95 (1-85521-050-9, Pub. by Dartmth Pub UK) Ashgate Pub Co.
Randle, Michael C., ed. Birmingham's Best. (Illus.). 125p. (Orig.). 1989. pap. 4.95 (1-878225-01-4) First Pub Inc.
Randle, Mike & McWhorter, Mitzi, eds. Birmingham's Commercial Real Estate - Review & Forecast. (Illus.). 1989. pap. 2.95 (0-685-29149-9) First Pub Inc.
Randle, Mike & White, Colleen, eds. Birmingham's Health Care - Review & Forecast. (Illus.). 1989. pap. 2.95 (0-685-29150-2) First Pub Inc.
Randle, P. J. & Denton, R. M. Hormones & Cell Metabolism. 2nd ed. Head, J. J., ed. LC 78-69515. (Carolina Biology Readers Ser.: No. 79). (Illus.). 16p. (C). (gr. 10 up). 1982. pap. 2.75 (0-89278-279-X, 45-9679) Carolina Biological.
Randle, P. J., et al, eds. Carbohydrate Metabolism & Its Disorders, Vol. 3. LC 68-17670. 1981. text ed. 220.00 (0-12-579703-6) Acad Pr.
Randle, Robert. Making Peace with Germany, 1918: The Pre-Armistice Negotiations. (Pew Case Studies in International Affairs). 50p. (C). 1993. pap. text ed. 2.50 (1-56927-435-5) Geo U Inst Dplmcy.
Randle, Robert F. Issues in the History of International Relations: The Role of Issues in the Evolution of the State System. LC 87-14614. 336p. 1987. text ed. 69.50 (0-275-92700-8, C2700, Praeger Pubs) Greenwood.
Randle, V. & Wills, H. H. The Measurement of Grain Boundary Geometry. (Electron Microscopy in Materials Science Ser.). (Illus.). 184p. 1993. 120.00 (0-7503-0235-6) IOP Pub.
Randle, Valerie. Microtexture Determination & Its Application. 192p. 1992. 80.00 (0-901716-35-9, Pub. by Inst Materials UK) Ashgate Pub Co.
***Randles, Bill.** Making War in the Heavenlies: A Different Look at Spiritual Warfare. (Illus.). 193p. (Orig.). Date not set. pap. 10.00 (0-9646626-0-4) B Randles.
— Weighed & Found Wanting: Putting the Toronto Blessing in Context. (Illus.). 249p. (Orig.). Date not set. pap. 10. 00 (0-9646626-1-2) B Randles.
Randles, Harry. Stories for Tight Places. LC 89-91744. 156p. (Orig.). 1990. pap. 7.95 (0-9623219-0-7) H Randles.
Randles, Jenny. Alien Abductions. 1990. pap. 10.95 (0-938294-65-2) Glob Comm-Inner Lght.
— Alien Contacts & Abductions: The Real Story from the Other Side. LC 94-20750. (Illus.). 196p. 1994. pap. 9.95 (0-8069-0751-7) Sterling.
— From Out of the Blue. 256p. (Orig.). 1993. mass mkt. 4.99 (0-425-13803-8) Berkley Pub.
— From Out of the Blue: The Incredible UFO Cover-up at Bentwaters NATO Air Base. 200p. 1992. 10.95 (0-938294-08-3) Glob Comm-Inner Lght.
— Sixth Sense: Psychic Powers & Your Five Senses. 240p. (C). 1987. 75.00 (0-7090-2802-4) St Mut.
— Star Children: The True Story of Alien Offspring among Us. LC 95-30212. 224p. 1995. pap. 10.95 (0-8069-3856-0) Sterling.
— Strange & Unexplained Mysteries of the 20th Century. LC 93-45608. Orig. Title: The Unexplained. (Illus.). 144p. 1994. pap. 14.95 (0-8069-0768-1) Sterling.
— Time Travel: Fact, Fiction & Possibility. (Illus.). 208p. 1994. 24.95 (0-7137-2402-1, Pub. by Blandford Pr UK) Sterling.
— Time Travel: Fact, Fiction & Possibility. (Illus.). 224p. 1995. pap. 9.95 (0-7137-2404-8, Pub. by Blandford Pr UK) Sterling.
— UFO Retrievals: The Recovery of Alien Spacecraft. (Illus.). 200p. 1995. pap. 9.95 (0-7137-2493-5, Pub. by Blandford Pr UK) Sterling.
— UFOs & How to See Them. (Illus.). 144p. 1993. pap. 14. 95 (0-8069-0297-3) Sterling.
Randles, Jenny & Hough, Peter. The Afterlife. 240p. 1994. reprint ed. pap. 10.00 (0-425-14212-4, Berkley Trade) Berkley Pub.
— Spontaneous Human Combustion. 272p. (Orig.). 1994. pap. text ed. 4.99 (0-425-14184-5) Berkley Pub.
Randles, Jenny & Hough, Peter A. World's Best "True" UFO Stories. LC 94-19807. (Illus.). 96p. 1994. 13.95 (0-8069-1258-8) Sterling.
— World's Best "True" UFO Stories. (Illus.). 96p. (Orig.). 1995. pap. 3.95 (0-8069-1259-6) Sterling.
Randles, Ronald H. & Wolfe, Douglas A. Introduction to the Theory of Nonparametric Statistics. 464p. (C). 1991. reprint ed. lib. bdg. 59.95 (0-89464-543-9) Krieger.
***Randlesome, Collin.** The Business Culture in Germany. 288p. 1994. pap. 24.95 (0-7506-1833-7) Buttrwrth-Heinemann.
Randlesome, Collin, ed. Business Cultures in Europe. 2nd ed. 320p. 1993. pap. 34.95 (0-7506-0872-2) Buttrwrth-Heinemann.
Randlev, Karen. Light Runner. (New Alaskan Poets Ser.). 128p. 1987. 5.95 (0-914221-08-6) Fireweed Pr AK.
***Rando, Caterina.** Words of Women: Quotations for Success. (Orig.). 1995. spiral bd., pap. 6.95 (0-9644906-0-9) PowerDynamics.
Rando, Emily N., jt. auth. see Napoli, Donna J.
Rando, Emily N., jt. ed. see Napoli, Donna J.
Rando, Guy L., jt. auth. see Jones, Rees L.
Rando, Guy L., jt. auth. see Muirhead, Desmond.
Rando, Therese A. Grief, Dying, & Death: Clinical Interventions for Caregivers. LC 84-60903. 490p. (Orig.). (C). 1984. pap. text ed. 19.95 (0-87822-232-4, 2324) Res Press.
— Grieving: How to Go on Living When Someone You Loves Dies. 348p. 1988. text ed. 24.95 (0-669-17021-6) Free Pr.
— How to Go on Living When Someone You Love Dies. 352p. 1991. pap. 11.95 (0-553-35269-5) Bantam.

R

An Asterisk (*) at the beginning of an entry indicates that the title is appearing in BIP for the first time.

— Treatment of Complicated Mourning. LC 90-64044. 768p. (Orig.). (C). 1992. text ed. 39.95 (*0-87822-329-0*, 4428) Res Press.

Rando, Therese A., ed. Loss & Anticipatory Grief. LC 85-45082. 256p. 1986. text ed. 35.00 (*0-669-11144-9*) Free Pr.

— Parental Loss of a Child. LC 86-61549. 570p. (Orig.). 1986. pap. text ed. 19.95 (*0-87822-281-2*, 2812) Res Press.

Randolf, Barbara. Country Kitchens: Decorating, Cooking & Entertaining. (American Country Living Ser.). 1992. 14.99 (*0-517-06115-5*) Random Hse Value.

Randoll, Wilma V. Back Pain & Spinal Problems: Index of New Information with Authors, Subjects & References. 150p. 1994. 49.50 (*1-55914-518-8*); pap. 39.50 (*1-55914-519-6*) ABBE Pubs Assn.

Randolph. American Nursing Review for Psych. & Mental Health Nursing Certification. 1993. 26.95 (*0-87434-513-8*) Springhouse Pub.

Randolph, jt. auth. see Clough.

Randolph, Alan & Posner, Barry Z. Getting the Job Done! Managing Project Teams & Task Forces for Success. 192p. 1991. text ed. write for info. (*0-13-616285-1*) P-H.

Randolph, Alan, jt. auth. see Posner, Barry Z.

Randolph, Alan D. & Larsen, Maurice A., eds. Theory of Particulate Processes: Analysis & Techniques of Continuous Crystallization. 2nd ed. 369p. 1988. text ed. 92.00 (*0-12-579652-8*) Acad Pr.

Randolph, Barbara. Christmas: Recipes, Crafts & More. (American Country Living Ser.). 1991. 14.99 (*0-517-02014-9*) Random Hse Value.

Randolph, Barbara, jt. auth. see Vaillant, Janet.

Randolph, Blythe. Amelia Earhart. LC 90-49175. (American Cavalcade Ser.). (Illus.). 160p. (J). (gr. 6-10). 1991. lib. bdg. 9.95 (*1-55905-078-0*) Marshall Cavendish.

Randolph, Bob. I Am Writing of Hand Grenades, Butterflies & Kisses. (Illus.). 214p. (Orig.). 1991. pap. 10.00 (*1-881969-25-8*) Randolph Hse.

Randolph, Boris. Bible Verses in Verse. LC 80-67992. 144p. 1980. pap. 3.95 (*0-87516-424-2*) DeVorss.

Randolph, Brenda, jt. auth. see Vaillant, Janet.

Randolph, Carman F. The Law of Eminent Domain in the United States. cxxv, 462p. 1991. reprint ed. lib. bdg. 55.00 (*0-8377-2545-3*) Rothman.

***Randolph, David.** This Is Music: A Guide to the Pleasures of Listening. rev. ed. 236p. 1995. pap. 12.50 (*0-88739-110-9*) Creat Arts Bk.

Randolph, David J. Power That Heals: Love Healing & the Trinity. LC 93-31888. 160p. (Orig.). 1994. pap. 10.95 (*0-687-33207-9*) Abingdon.

Randolph, Dennis A. Civil Engineering for the Community. LC 93-12282. 96p. 1993. 20.00 (*0-87262-845-0*) Am Soc Civil Eng.

Randolph, Edmund. Beef, Leather & Grass. LC 80-18818. (Illus.). 286p. 1981. 28.95 (*0-8061-1517-3*) U of Okla Pr.

Randolph, Elizabeth. The Basic Book of Fish Keeping. 240p. (Orig.). 1990. pap. 3.95 (*0-449-21776-0*) Fawcett.

— How to Be Your Cat's Best Friend. 288p. 1989. mass mkt. 4.95 (*0-449-21824-4*, Crest) Fawcett.

— How to Help Your Puppy Grow Up To Be a Wonderful Dog. 288p. 1988. reprint ed. mass mkt. 4.95 (*0-449-21503-2*, Crest) Fawcett.

— Rabbits & Other Furry Pets. (Orig.). 1992. mass mkt. 4.99 (*0-449-22033-8*, Crest) Fawcett.

Randolph, Elizabeth, jt. auth. see Dibra, Bashkim.

Randolph, Elizabeth, jt. auth. see Kay, William J.

Randolph, Ellen. Threads of Love. large type ed. (Romance Ser.). 288p. 1993. 21.95 (*0-7089-2993-1*) Ulverscroft.

Randolph, Forrest A. The Confederate, No. 2: Ride Beyond Glory. pap. 2.50 (*0-8217-1357-4*) Zebra.

Randolph, Francis L. Studies for a Byron Bibliography. LC 79-13752. 144p. 1979. 25.00 (*0-915010-26-7*) Sutter House.

Randolph, Howard S. & Rankin, Russell B., eds. Paramus, Bergen County, New Jersey, Reformed Dutch Church Baptisms, 1740-1850: Together with Records from the Gravestones in the Church Yard & a List of Church Members. Versteeg, Dingman, tr. 224p. 1992. reprint ed. lib. bdg. 41.00 (*1-56012-124-6*) Kinship Rhinebeck.

Randolph, I. & Clokey, J. The Grasshopper: A Tragic Tale. 20p. 1965. 3.95 (*0-87487-708-3*) Summy-Birchard.

Randolph, J., tr. see Trismegistus, Hermes.

Randolph, J. Thornton. Cabin & Parlor: Or, Slaves & Masters. LC 77-149876. (Black Heritage Library Collection). 1977. 28.95 (*0-8369-8756-X*) Ayer.

Randolph, Jacob. Memoirs of the Life & Character of Philip Syng Physick. 1993. reprint ed. lib. bdg. 89.00 (*0-7812-5821-9*) Rprt Serv.

Randolph, James C., jt. ed. see Randolph, Polley A.

Randolph, Jan T. Onion Snow. 1988. pap. 7.00 (*0-941179-11-7*) Latitudes Pr.

Randolph, Jean, ed. see Prince, Robert H.

Randolph, Jerry, jt. auth. see Taylor, James B.

Randolph, Joan. True Stories by Three Men of the Sea. Sappey, Maureen, ed. 192p. (Orig.). 1990. pap. 10.95 (*0-9627510-0-6*) Island Harbor Pr.

Randolph, Judson G., ed. The Injured Child: Surgical Management. LC 79-21432. (Illus.). 434p. reprint ed. pap. 123.70 (*0-8357-7599-2*, 2056921) Bks Demand.

Randolph, Julian F. Anthology of the Romancero Nuevo (1580-1600) (American University Studies: Romance Languages & Literature: Ser. II, Vol. 88). 150p. (C). 1988. text ed. 30.00 (*0-8204-0704-6*) P Lang Pubs.

***Randolph, K. B.** Lover's Handbook. 144p. (Orig.). 1995. pap. 7.99 (*0-614-00664-3*) Hawkins Kelly Pub.

***Randolph, L.** Child Abuse & Neglect: ECE 112 Course. 286p. (C). 1994. write for info. (*0-933195-66-4*) Allied Hlth Pubns.

Randolph, L. F. Basics of Radio Control Airplanes. Uravitch, Richard, ed. (Illus.). 80p. 1990. pap. 12.95 (*0-911295-10-0*) Air Age.

Randolph, L. V. Fitz Randolph Traditions: A Story of a Thousand Years. (Illus.). 134p. 1993. reprint ed. lib. bdg. 34.00 (*0-8328-3312-6*); reprint ed. pap. 24.00 (*0-8328-3313-4*) Higginson Bk Co.

Randolph, Lamar P. Forecasting: Index of Modern Information. LC 88-47564. 150p. 1990. 39.50 (*1-55914-160-3*); pap. 34.50 (*1-55914-161-1*) ABBE Pubs Assn.

Randolph, Larry. Crosspatch. 1973. pap. 2.50 (*0-87129-080-4*, C36) Dramatic Pub.

Randolph, Leonard. Scar Tissue. (Hollow Spring Poetry Ser.). (Illus.). 64p. (C). 1984. pap. text ed. 5.00 (*0-318-00815-7*) Hollow Spring Pr.

Randolph, Lillian. The Fundamental Laws of Governmental Organization. 1971. pap. 15.95 (*0-8084-0141-6*) NCUP.

Randolph Macon Woman's College Staff. Masterpieces of American Painting from Randolph-Macon Woman's College. 1990. pap. 19.95 (*0-486-26384-3*) Dover.

***Randolph, Mary.** The Deeds Book. 3rd ed. LC 94-34110. (Illus.). 1994. pap. 16.95 (*0-87337-279-4*) Nolo Pr.

— Dog Law. 2nd rev. ed. LC 88-63101. 272p. (Orig.). 1993. pap. 12.95 (*0-87337-216-6*) Nolo Pr.

— Living Trust Maker 2.0. 1994. disk 79.95 (*0-87337-275-1*); mac hd 79.95 (*0-87337-293-X*) Nolo Pr.

— The Virginia House-Wife. Hess, Karen, ed. LC 83-19869. 417p. 1984. 24.95 (*0-87249-423-3*) U of SC Pr.

— The Virginia Housewife: or Methodical Cook: A Facsimile of an Authentic Early American Cookbook. LC 93-32924. 192p. 1993. reprint ed. pap. text ed. 4.95 (*0-486-27772-0*) Dover.

Randolph, Mary, ed. see Nissley, Julia.

Randolph, Mary, ed. see Steingold, Fred S.

Randolph, Norman. Gangs, My Town & the Nation. Date not set. write for info. (*1-55691-119-X*) Learning Pubns.

Randolph, P. B. Dealings with the Dead: The Human Soul, Its Migrations & Its Transmigrations. 156p. 1959. spiral bd. 8.80 (*0-7873-0694-0*) Mokelumne.

— Soul: Soul World. 1932. 9.95 (*0-686-05882-8*) Philos Pub.

Randolph, Pascal B. Sexual Magic. North, Robert, tr. (Illus.). 180p. 1989. 14.95 (*0-318-42501-7*) Magickal Childe.

Randolph, Paschal B. After Death: The Disembodiment of Man. reprint ed. spiral bd. 7.70 (*0-7873-0701-7*) Mokelumne.

— After Death: The Immortality of Man. 272p. 1970. write for info. (*0-932785-00-X*) Philos Pub.

— Beyond the Veil: Posthumous Work of Paschal Beverly Randolph. reprint ed. spiral bd. 8.80 (*0-7873-0696-7*) Mokelumne.

— Eulis: History of Love. 2nd ed. reprint ed. 7.00 (*0-685-71655-4*) Mokelumne.

— Hermes Mercurius Trismegistus: His Divine Pymander. reprint ed. spiral bd. 6.60 (*0-7873-0700-9*) Mokelumne.

— The Immortality of Love. Clymer, Emerson M. et al, eds. 290p. 1978. 9.95 (*0-932785-17-4*) Philos Pub.

— Pre-Adamite Man: Demonstrating the Existence of the Human Race. 6th ed. 408p. 1970. reprint ed. spiral bd. 10.45 (*0-7873-0695-9*) Mokelumne.

— Ravalette: The Rosicrucian's Story. 283p. 1939. 7.95 (*0-932785-40-9*) Philos Pub.

— Ravalette the Rosicrucian's Story. reprint ed. spiral bd. 7.70 (*0-7873-0698-3*) Mokelumne.

— Seership: Soul Sight. reprint ed. spiral bd. 7.70 (*0-7873-0697-5*) Mokelumne.

— Soul! The Soul World! Clymer, R. Swinburne, ed. 246p. 1932. 9.95 (*0-932785-45-X*) Philos Pub.

— The Soul World: The Home of the Dead. reprint ed. spiral bd. 9.35 (*0-7873-0699-1*) Mokelumne.

Randolph, Paschal B., tr. Ancient Kaldi Oracle: Rosicrucian Predictive Symph. reprint ed. spiral bd. 1.65 (*0-7873-0702-5*) Mokelumne.

Randolph, Paul B. One-Third of What Is Known about Natural Philosophy. 103p. (C). 1989. pap. text ed. 4.50 (*0-317-93248-9*) Randolph Dallas.

Randolph, Polley A. & Randolph, James C., eds. Readings in Ecology. (Illus.). (C). 1973. text ed. 39.50 (*0-8422-5085-9*) Irvington.

Randolph, Priscilla S. Lifehunter: Selected Stories, Poems & Essays. 326p. 1994. text ed. 19.95 (*0-9642113-0-0*) Beecher Pr.

Randolph, R., jt. auth. see Hammett, H.

Randolph, R. I., jt. auth. see Carter, R. R.

Randolph, R. Sean. The United States & Thailand: Alliance Dynamics, 1950-1985. LC 86-82389. (Research Papers & Policy Studies: No. 12). (Illus.). x, 246p. (Orig.). 1987. pap. 7.50 (*0-912966-92-0*) IEAS.

Randolph, Randy. R-C Airplane Building Techniques. 146p. 1991. 14.95 (*0-911295-13-5*) Air Age.

Randolph, Renee, jt. auth. see Christino, Karen.

Randolph, Ruth E., jt. auth. see Roses, Lorraine E.

***Randolph, S.** Woodrow Wilson. Date not set. 3.98 (*0-517-13423-3*) Random Hse Value.

Randolph, Sallie. Gerald R. Ford: President. LC 86-16333. 128p. (J). (gr. 5 up). 1987. 12.95 (*0-8027-6666-8*); lib. bdg. 13.85 (*0-8027-6667-6*) Walker & Co.

— Richard M. Nixon, President. (Presidential Biography Ser.). 128p. (J). (gr. 5 up). 1989. 13.95 (*0-8027-6848-2*); lib. bdg. 14.85 (*0-8027-6849-0*) Walker & Co.

— Woodrow Wilson. (Presidential Biography Ser.). 128p. (J). (gr. 6-9). 1992. 14.95 (*0-8027-8143-8*); lib. bdg. 15.85 (*0-8027-8144-6*) Walker & Co.

Randolph, Sallie & Bolick, Nancy. Shaker Inventions. (Illus.). (J). (gr. 4-7). 1990. 12.95 (*0-8027-6933-0*); lib. bdg. 13.85 (*0-8027-6934-9*) Walker & Co.

Randolph, Sallie G., jt. auth. see Bolick, Nancy O.

Randolph, Sarah N. The Domestic Life of Thomas Jefferson. LC 78-14312. (Illus.). 452p. 1979. pap. 16.95 (*0-8139-0718-7*) U Pr of Va.

Randolph, Shirley L., et al. Kids Learn from the Inside Out: How to Enhance the Human Matrix. Terra, Jean, ed. LC 93-80615. (Illus.). 256p. 1994. pap. 18.95 (*0-9625040-4-1*) Legendary Pub.

***Randolph, Spring & Snyder, Mary.** The Seafood List: FDA's Guide to Acceptable Market Names for Seafood Sold in Interstate Commerce 1993. 69p. (Orig.). (C). 1994. pap. text ed. 40.00x (*0-7881-1324-0*) Diane Pub.

Randolph, Susan, jt. auth. see Harik, Iliya.

Randolph, Theron G. Human Ecology & Susceptibility to the Chemical Environment. (Illus.). 160p. 1981. 31.95x (*0-398-01548-1*) C C Thomas.

— Human Ecology & Susceptibility to the Chemical Environment. (Illus.). 160p. 1981. pap. 16.95 (*0-398-06335-4*) C C Thomas.

Randolph, Theron G. & Moss, Ralph W. An Alternative Approach to Allergies: The New Field of Clinical Ecology Unravels the Environmental Causes of Mental & Physical Ills. rev. ed. LC 88-45902. 352p. 1990. reprint ed. pap. 13.00 (*0-06-091693-1*, PL) HarpC.

Randolph, Thomas. Poetical & Dramatic Works of Thomas Randolph, 2 Vols. Hazlitt, William C., ed. LC 68-57192. 1972. reprint ed. 48.95 (*0-405-08874-4*) Ayer.

Randolph, Vance. Blow the Candle Out: "Unprintable" Ozark Folksongs & Folklore, Vol. II: Folk Rhymes & Other Lore. LC 91-17685. 392p. 1992. 45.00 (*1-55728-237-4*) U of Ark Pr.

— Ozark Folksongs. Cohen, Norm, ed. LC 81-4403. (Music in American Life Ser.). 624p. 1982. pap. 16.95 (*0-252-00952-5*) U of Ill Pr.

— Ozark Magic & Folklore. Orig. Title: Ozark Superstition. 1947. pap. 7.95 (*0-486-21181-9*) Dover.

— Pissing in the Snow & Other Ozark Folktales. LC 76-18181. 192p. 1976. pap. 6.95 (*0-252-01364-6*) U of Ill Pr.

— Roll Me in Your Arms, Vol. 1: "Unprintable" Ozark Folksongs & Folklore. Legman, G., ed. LC 91-17685. 582p. 1992. 50.00 (*1-55728-231-5*) U of Ark Pr.

— We Always Lie to Strangers. LC 74-12852. (Illus.). 309p. 1974. reprint ed. text ed. 35.00 (*0-8371-7765-0*, RAAL, Greenwood Pr) Greenwood.

Randolph, Vance & McCann, Gordon. Ozark Folklore: An Annotated Bibliography, Vol. II. LC 86-16071. 376p. 1987. text ed. 40.00 (*0-8262-0486-4*, 83-36232) U of Mo Pr.

Randolph, Vance & Wilson, George P. Down in the Holler: A Gallery of Ozark Folk Speech. 330p. 1979. pap. 15.95 (*0-8061-1535-1*) U of Okla Pr.

Randolph, W. Alan, jt. auth. see Miles, Robert H.

***Random.** American Watercolors. 1995. 16.99 (*0-517-12081-X*) Random Hse Value.

— Jungle Jaunts. 1995. pap. 3.99 (*0-679-87671-5*) Random.

— Little Gingerbread House. LC 93-86032. 1995. (*0-679-84916-5*) Random.

— Safari Adventures. 1995. pap. 3.99 (*0-679-87670-7*) Random.

— Search for Zini. 1995. pap. 3.50 (*0-679-87592-1*) Random.

— Three Little Pigs. 1995. (*0-679-84914-9*) Random.

Random, Candice F. Jimmy Crack Corn. LC 93-16657. (Illus.). (J). (gr. 2-5). 1993. 18.95 (*0-87614-786-4*, Carolrhoda) Lerner Group.

Random House College Dictionary Staff. The Random House College Dictionary. rev. ed. 1975. 16.45 (*0-394-43500-1*); Thumb-indexed ed. 17.45 (*0-394-43600-8*); 16.95 (*0-394-51192-1*) Random.

— The Random House College Dictionary. rev. ed. 1982. 14.95 (*0-394-52762-3*) Random.

Random House Editorial Staff. Random House Unabridged Dictionary: Print & Electronic Versions. rev. ed. (Illus.). 2550p. 1994. CD-ROM version. cd-rom 79.00 (*0-679-74979-9*, Random Ref) Random.

— Random House Unabridged Dictionary: Print & Electronic Versions. 2nd rev. ed. (Illus.). 2550p. 1994. 100.00 (*0-679-42917-4*, Random Ref) Random.

— Random House Webster's College Dictionary. rev. ed. 1995. 22.95 (*0-676-50205-9*, Random Ref) Random.

— Random House Webster's College Dictionary with Macintosh Electronic Version. 1994. 40.00 (*0-679-43064-4*, Random Ref) Random.

— Random House Webster's School & Office Dictionary. rev. ed. 1995. pap. 9.95 (*0-679-76158-6*, Random Ref) Random.

— Random House Webster's School & Office Thesaurus. 1995. pap. 9.95 (*0-679-76157-8*, Random Ref) Random.

Random House Editors. Random House Webster's College Dictionary. 1993. 30.00 (*0-679-42915-8*, Random Ref) Random.

***Random House Home Video Staff.** Brown Bears & Truth. 1988. pap. 6.99 (*0-394-81957-8*) Random.

***Random House, Inc. Staff.** Illustrated Dog's Life. (Illus.). Date not set. pap. 12.99 (*0-517-12163-8*) Random.

— Love Sories. Date not set. 9.99 (*0-517-12426-2*) Random.

— Marilyn Monroe. Date not set. pap. 8.99 (*0-517-12148-4*) Random.

— Natural History of North America. (Illus.). Date not set. pap. 19.99 (*0-517-12164-6*) Random.

— Raising a Vegetarian Child. Date not set. pap. text ed. 14.99 (*0-517-12152-2*) Random.

— The Random House Dictionary: Concise Edition. 1980. 2.38 (*0-394-51200-6*) Random.

— Shopping Basket. 1995. pap. 2.99 (*0-517-12161-1*) Random.

— Songs & Carols. Date not set. pap. 7.99 (*0-517-12439-4*) Random.

— Stories of Inspiration. Date not set. pap. 9.99 (*0-517-12427-0*) Random.

— Tool Box. 1995. pap. 2.99 (*0-517-12162-X*) Random.

— Toy Box. 1995. pap. 2.99 (*0-517-12160-3*) Random Hse Value.

***Random House Reference Staff.** Random House English Language Desk Reference. 1995. 18.00 (*0-679-43898-X*) Random.

Random House Staff. At Random, Vol. 4. 1992. pap. write for info. (*0-394-25151-2*) Random.

— At Random, Vol. 6. 1993. write for info. (*0-394-25757-X*) Random.

— At Random, Vol. 9. 1994. write for info. (*0-394-26747-8*) Random.

— At Random, Vol. 11. 1995. pap. write for info. (*0-394-27238-2*) Random.

— Build Your Own Farm. (J). 1994. 5.99 (*0-517-10248-X*) Random Hse Value.

— Build Your Own Town. (J). 1994. 5.99 (*0-517-10249-8*) Random Hse Value.

— Come Back Bunny. (Hide & Seek Board Bks.). (J). 1994. bds. 2.99 (*0-517-10270-6*) Random Hse Value.

— Elvis Presley. Date not set. pap. 8.99 (*0-517-12149-2*) Random.

— Grant Wood. (American Art Ser.). (Illus.). 1994. 15.99 (*0-517-10298-6*) Random Hse Value.

— Hide & Seek Kitten. (Hide & Seek Board Bks.). (J). 1994. bds. 2.99 (*0-517-10259-5*) Random Hse Value.

— How to Get Better Test Scores on Elementary School Standardized Tests. (Elementary School Study Guides Ser.). (Illus.). 152p. (Orig.). (J). (gr. 5-6). 1991. pap. 9.00 (*0-679-82109-0*) Random Bks Yng Read.

— How to Get Better Test Scores on Elementary School Standarized Tests. (Elementary School Study Guides Ser.). (Illus.). 152p. (Orig.). (J). (gr. 3-4). 1991. pap. 9.00 (*0-679-82108-2*) Random Bks Yng Read.

— My Runaway Pony. (Hide & Seek Board Bks.). (J). 1994. bds. 2.99 (*0-517-10271-4*) Random Hse Value.

— New International Bartender's Guide. 1993. 8.00 (*0-394-57615-2*) Random.

— Nursery Rhymes from Mother Goose. (J). 1994. pap. 8.99 (*0-517-11857-2*) Random Hse Value.

— Nursery Songs & Games. (J). 1994. pap. 8.99 (*0-517-10191-2*) Random Hse Value.

— Plain-Edged. 1991. 17.50 (*0-679-40110-5*) Random.

— Random House Biographical Dictionary. 1992. pap. 6.00 (*0-679-41580-7*, Random Ref) Random.

— Random House Dictionary of Health & Medicine: The Random House Pocket Dictionaries & Guides. 1992. pap. 7.00 (*0-679-41590-4*, Random Ref) Random.

— Random House Encyclopedia. rev. ed. 1990. 129.95 (*0-394-58450-3*) Random.

— Random House Geographical Dictionary. 1992. pap. 7.00 (*0-679-41570-X*, Random Ref) Random.

— The Random House Timetables of History. rev. ed. 1993. 6.00 (*0-679-42395-8*, Random Ref) Random.

— Random House Unabridged Dictionary Book. 2nd ed. 1994. cd-rom 100.00 (*0-679-75748-1*) Random.

— Random House Webster's College Dictionary. deluxe ed. 1991. 24.50 (*0-679-40130-X*) Random.

— Random House Webster's College Dictionary & Random House College Thesaurus Desk Set. 1992. 37.00 (*0-679-41700-1*, Random Ref) Random.

— Random House Webster's Concise Dictionary. 1993. 7.00 (*0-679-41690-0*, Random Ref) Random.

— Random House Webster's Dictionary & the Random House Thesaurus, the Random House Basic. 1993. pap. 259.40 (*0-345-38353-2*) Ballantine.

— Random House Webster's School & Office Dictionary. 1993. pap. 8.00 (*0-679-74420-7*, Random Ref) Random.

— Sing along Piano Fun. (J). 1994. 7.99 (*0-517-10246-3*) Random Hse Value.

— Where's My Puppy? (Hide & Seek Board Bks.). (J). 1994. bds. 2.99 (*0-517-10258-7*) Random Hse Value.

Random House Staff, ed. Random House Timetables of History. 1991. pap. 6.00 (*0-679-40293-4*) Random.

***Random House Value Publishing Staff.** Great Baseball Stories. 1994. 7.99 (*0-517-12068-2*) Random Hse Value.

— Webster's Atlas of the World. 1994. 12.99 (*0-517-12071-2*) Random Hse Value.

Randon, Anita, jt. auth. see Perri 6.

Randour, Mary L. Women's Psyche, Women's Spirit: The Reality of Relationships. LC 86-17180. 240p. 1988. text ed. 37.00 (*0-231-06250-8*); pap. text ed. 15.50 (*0-231-06251-6*) Col U Pr.

Randour, Mary L., et al, eds. Exploring Sacred Landscapes: Religious & Spiritual Experiences in Psychotherapy. 216p. (C). 1993. text ed. 40.00 (*0-231-07000-4*) Col U Pr.

Randriamasimanana, Charles. The Causatives of Malagasy. (Oceanic Linguistics Special Publications: No. 21). 704p. 1986. pap. text ed. 30.00 (*0-8248-1079-1*) UH Pr.

Rands, Jeffrey. Seattle Style Guide: Cultural Imperatives of the Hot Seattle Scene. 125p. (Orig.). 1993. pap. 9.95 (*0-9636753-0-3*) J Rands.

Rands, William B., see Matthew Browne, pseud..

Rands, William J. & Shifman, Julie C. Couse's Ohio Form Book, Vol. 1. 6th rev. ed. Booth, Robert A., ed. 1078p. 1990. text ed. 85.00 (*0-87084-170-X*) Anderson Pub Co.

Randsborg, Klaus. The First Millennium A.D. in Europe & the Mediterranean: An Archaeological Essay. (Illus.). 248p. (C). 1991. 69.95 (*0-521-38401-X*); pap. 19.95 (*0-521-38787-6*) Cambridge U Pr.

***Randy, Donald C. & Gillette, M. L.** Determining the Dissociation Constant of a Weak Acid Using pH Measurements. Neidig, H. A., ed. (Modular Laboratory Program in Chemistry Ser.). 16p. (C). 1989. pap. text ed. 1.25x (*0-87540-376-X*) Chem Educ Res.

Randy, Rieffeld. Joey Lawrence. (YA). 1993. mass mkt. 3.99 (*0-671-88719-X*) PB.

Rane, Bill. Talfulano. LC 75-27249. 104p. (Orig.). 1976. pap. 7.00 (*0-912292-39-3*) The Smith.

Ranelagh, E. L. The Past We Share: The Near Eastern Ancestry of Western Folk Literature. (Illus.). 288p. 1981. 21.95 (*0-7043-2234-X*, Pub. by Quartet UK) Charles River Bks.

R

An Asterisk (*) at the beginning of an entry indicates that the title is appearing in BIP for the first time.

Ranelagh, John. The Agency: The Rise & Decline of the CIA. 1987. pap. 17.00 (*0-671-63994-3*, Touchstone Bks) S&S Trade.
***Ranelagh, John O.** A Short History of Ireland. 320p. (C). 1995. pap. 17.95 (*0-521-46944-9*) Cambridge U Pr.
— A Short History of Ireland. 320p. (C). 1995. 64.95 (*0-521-47548-1*) Cambridge U Pr.
RaNelle, Wallace & Taylor, Curtis. The Burning Within: The Story of My Life & Death. LC 94-260. 218p. 1994. 16.95 (*1-882723-05-8*) Gold Leaf Pr.
***Ranes, Barbara.** From Baba to Tovarishch: The Bolshevik Revolution & Soviet Women's Struggle for Liberation. (Illus.). 128p. 1994. per., pap. 15.00 (*0-86714-027-5*) Marxist-Leninist.
***Ranew, Nathael.** Solitude Improved by Divine Meditation. 1995. reprint ed. 17.00 (*0-614-06633-6*) Soli Deo Gloria.
***Ranew, Nathanael.** Solitude Improved by Divine Meditation. 350p. 1995. reprint ed. 24.95 (*1-57358-012-0*) Soli Deo Gloria.
Raney, jt. auth. see Brashear.
Raney, Charles. If You Are Born Again: You Can Not Think Evil. 28p. 1983. pap. 2.00 (*0-9610842-0-0*) La-Ran Pub Co.
Raney, Ken. It's Probably Good That Dinosaurs Are Extinct. LC 92-33739. (J). 1993. 14.00 (*0-671-86576-5*, Green Tiger S&S) S&S Childrens.
— Stick Horse. (Illus.). 32p. (J). (ps-1). 1991. 9.95 (*0-9625261-4-2*, Green Tiger S&S) S&S Childrens.
Raney, Laura, jt. auth. see Subbarao, K.
Raney, Mark. Believing in the Wind. 235p. 1981. 10.00 (*0-933272-02-2*) Hurricane Co.
— Breathe All Seasons. (Illus.). 241p. 1977. 10.00 (*0-933272-00-6*) Hurricane Co.
— This Soil of Sand. (Illus.). 26p. 1978. 20.00 (*0-933272-01-4*) Hurricane Co.
Ranfagni, A. Trajectories & Rays: The Path - Summation in Quantum Mechanics & Optics. Mugnai, D. et al, eds. 240p. (C). 1990. text ed. 70.00 (*9971-5-0781-1*) World Scientific Pub.
Ranft, B., ed. Ironclad to Trident: 100 Years of Defence Commentary, Brassey's 1886-1986. 272p. 1986. 65.00 (*0-08-031191-1*, Pergamon Pr) Elsevier.
Ranft, B. McL. The Beatty Papers: Selections from the Private & Official Correspondence of Admiral of the Fleet Earl Beatty, Vol. I: 1902-1918. 500p. 1989. text ed. 69.95 (*0-85967-807-5*, Pub. by Scolar Pr UK) Ashgate Pub Co.
Ranft, Bryan & Till, Geoffrey. The Sea in Soviet Strategy. 2nd ed. LC 88-61128. (Illus.). 275p. 1988. 31.95 (*0-87021-992-8*) Naval Inst Pr.
Ranft, Bryan, jt. ed. see Hill, J. R.
Ranft, Bryan M. The Beatty Papers, Vol. II: 1916-1927. (Navy Records Ser.). 1993. 79.95 (*0-85967-964-0*, Pub. by Scolar Pr UK) Ashgate Pub Co.
Ranft, Katherine, ed. see Camp, Robert.
Rang. Kausalitat und Motivation. (Phaenomenologica Ser.: No. 53). 1973. lib. bdg. 70.00 (*90-247-1353-6*) Kluwer Ac.
Rang, H. P. & Dale, M. M. Pharmacology. 2nd ed. (Illus.). 955p. (Orig.). 1991. pap. text ed. 55.00 (*0-443-04110-5*) Churchill.
***Rang, H. P., et al.** Pharmacology. LC 94-47182. 1995. text ed. write for info. (*0-443-07560-3*) Churchill.
Rang, Jack C. How to Read the Bible Aloud: Oral Interpretation of Scripture. 224p. 1994. pap. 10.95 (*0-8091-3493-4*) Paulist Pr.
Rang, Mary L. Manual of Newborn Care Plans. (Spiral Manual Ser. - Nursing). 1981. 14.00 (*0-316-73380-6*) Little.
Rang, Mercer, ed. Children's Fractures. 2nd ed. (Illus.). 300p. 1983. text ed. 79.50 (*0-397-50476-4*, 65-06182, Lippincott Medical) Lippincott.
Rang, Mercer, jt. auth. see Wenger, Dennis R.
Rangachari, K., jt. auth. see Thurston, Edgar.
***Rangacharya, Adya.** Quest for Wisdom: Thoughts on the Bhagawadgita. (C). 1993. 22.00x (*81-7154-709-5*, Pub. by Popular Prakashan II) S Asia.
Rangacharya, K., jt. ed. see Mahadeva, A.
Rangacharya, M. Hindu Philosophy of Conduct. (Lectures on the Bhagavadgita: Vol. Two). 410p. 1990. 42.50 (*81-215-0469-4*, Pub. by M Manoharial II) Coronet Bks.
— Hindu Philosophy of Conduct. (Lectures on the Bhagavadgita: Vol. One). 637p. 1989. reprint ed. 48.50 (*0-317-99950-8*, Pub. by M Manoharial II) Coronet Bks.
— Hindu Philosophy of Conduct, Vol. 3. (C). 1991. 35.00 (*0-685-50021-7*, Pub. by Munshiram Manoharial II) S Asia.
— The Hindu Philosophy of Conduct-Lectures on the Bhagavadgita, Vol. 1. (C). 1989. 58.50 (*0-685-30709-3*, Pub. by Munshiram Manoharial II) S Asia.
Rangacharya, M. & Aiyangar, M. B., trs. The Vedantasutras with the Sribhasya of Ramanujacarya, Vol. 1. (C). 1988. 36.00 (*81-215-0091-5*, Pub. by Munshiram Manoharial II) S Asia.
Rangan, Haripriya, jt. ed. see Friedmann, John.
***Rangan, Kasturi, et al, eds.** Business Marketing Strategy: Cases, Concepts, & Applications. LC 94-22561. (Marketing Ser.). 864p. (C). 1994. text ed. 70.95 (*0-256-16911-X*) Irwin.
Rangan, U. Srinivasan, jt. auth. see Yoshino, Michael Y.
***Rangan, V. K., et al, eds.** Business Marketing Strategy: Concepts & Applications. LC 94-22562. (Marketing Ser.). 192p. (C). 1995. 38.95 (*0-256-16910-1*) Irwin.
Rangan, Venkat P., ed. Network & Operating System Support for Digital Audio & Video: Third International Workshop, La Jolla, California, U. S. A., November 1992, Proceedings. LC 93-11825. (Lecture Notes in Computer Science Ser.: Vol. 712). 1993. 60.00 (*0-387-57183-3*) Spr-Verlag.
***Ranganathan, B. G.** Origins? 37p. 1988. pap. 1.95 (*0-85151-535-5*) Banner of Truth.
Ranganathan, N. VLSI Algorithms & Architecture: Advanced Concepts. 320p. 1993. text ed. 40.00 (*0-8186-4402-8*, 4402) IEEE Comp Soc.
— VLSI Algorithms & Architectures: Fundamentals. LC 93-2125. 305p. 1993. Case. text ed. 40.00 (*0-8186-4392-7*, 4392) IEEE Comp Soc.
***Ranganathan, S., et al, eds.** Interfaces - Structure & Properties. 400p. 1993. text ed. 106.00 (*0-87849-613-0*) LPS Dist Ctr.
Ranganathan, S. R. Cataloguing Practice. 2nd ed. 517p. reprint ed. text ed. 50.00 (*81-85273-14-6*, Pub. by Sarada Ranganathan Endowment for Library Science II) Advent Bks Div.
— Classification & Communication. 291p. 1990. pap. 13.95 (*81-85273-27-8*, Pub. by Sarada Ranganathan Endowment for Library Science II) Advent Bks Div.
— Classified Catalogue Code: With Additional Rules for Dictionary Catalogue Code. 5th ed. 844p. (C). 1988. reprint ed. text ed. 50.00 (*81-85273-06-5*, Pub. by Sarada Ranganathan Endowment for Library Science II) Advent Bks Div.
— Colon Classification. rev. ed. 400p. (C). 1988. reprint ed. pap. text ed. 50.00 (*81-85273-11-1*, Pub. by Sarada Ranganathan Endowment for Library Science II) Advent Bks Div.
— Elements of Library Classification. 108p. 1990. reprint ed. text ed. 20.00 (*81-85273-30-8*, Pub. by Sarada Ranganathan Endowment for Library Science II) Advent Bks Div.
— The Five Laws of Library Science. 2nd ed. 449p. (C). 1988. reprint ed. pap. 18.95 (*81-85273-07-3*, Pub. by Sarada Ranganathan Endowment for Library Science II) Advent Bks Div.
— Library Administration. 678p. 1990. reprint ed. pap. 25.00 (*81-85273-22-7*, Pub. by Sarada Ranganathan Endowment for Library Science II) Advent Bks Div.
— Library Book Selection. 436p. 1990. reprint ed. text ed. 50.00 (*81-85273-26-X*, Pub. by Sarada Ranganathan Endowment for Library Science II) Advent Bks Div.
— Library Catalogue: Fundamentals & Procedures. (Library Science Ser.). 1980. lib. bdg. 75.00 (*0-8490-3168-0*) Gordon Pr.
— Library Manual: For Library Authorities, Librarians & Library Workers. rev. ed. 414p. (C). 1990. reprint ed. pap. 18.95 (*81-85273-03-0*, Pub. by Sarada Ranganathan Endowment for Library Science II) Advent Bks Div.
— Philosophy of Library Classification. 133p. 1990. pap. 5.95 (*81-85273-33-2*, Pub. by Sarada Ranganathan Endowment for Library Science II) Advent Bks Div.
— Prolegomena to Library Classification, Vol. I. 640p. 1990. reprint ed. pap. 30.00 (*81-85273-16-2*, Pub. by Sarada Ranganathan Endowment for Library Science II) Advent Bks Div.
— Reference Service. 432p. 1990. reprint ed. pap. 18.95 (*81-85273-20-0*, Pub. by Sarada Ranganathan Endowment for Library Science II) Advent Bks Div.
Ranganathan, V., ed. see AFREPREN Staff.
Ranganathananda, Swami. Human Being in Depth: A Scientific Approach to Religion. Nelson, Elva L., ed. LC 90-43594. 159p. (C). 1991. 49.50 (*0-7914-0679-2*); pap. 16.95 (*0-7914-0680-6*) State U NY Pr.
— Ramakrishna Math & Mission: Its Ideals & Activities. (Illus.). 1954. pap. 1.00 (*0-87481-448-0*) Vedanta Pr.
— Science & Religion. 1979. pap. 3.50 (*0-87481-190-2*, Pub. by Advaita Ashrama II) Vedanta Pr.
Rangarajan, Haripriya. Spread of Vaisnavism in Gujarat up to 1600 AD: A Study with Special Reference to the Iconic Forms of Visnu. (C). 1991. 72.00 (*81-7039-192-X*, Pub. by Somaiya) S Asia.
Rangarajan, L. N. Commodity Conflict: The Political Economy of International Commodity Negotiations. LC 77-22674. 362p. 1978. 42.50 (*0-8014-1154-8*) Cornell U Pr.
Rangarao, B. V. & Chaubey, N. P., eds. Social Perspective of Development of Science & Technology in India. 1983. 22.00 (*0-8364-0931-0*, Pub. by Heritage IA) S Asia.
Rangarao, S. Good Food from India. 284p. 1985. 9.95 (*0-318-36291-0*) Asia Bk Corp.
Rangaswami, Vanaja. Story of Integration: A New Interpretation of Princely States in India. 1982. 34.00 (*0-8364-0876-4*, Pub. by Manohar II) S Asia.
Rangaswamy, N. S., jt. auth. see Shivanna, K. R.
Rangayyan, R. M. Telecommunication for Health Care, Vol. 1355: Telemetry, Teleradiology, & Telemedicine (Jul 1990, Calgary, Canada) 1990. 53.00 (*0-8194-0416-0*) SPIE.
Rangdrol, Tsele N. Lamp of Mahamudra. LC 88-34344. 128p. (Orig.). 1989. pap. 9.95 (*0-87773-487-9*) Shambhala Pubns.
Range, Dale G., jt. auth. see Kohut, Sylvester, Jr.
Range, Maggie, jt. auth. see Kindervatter, Suzanne.
Range, R. M. Holomorphic Functions & Integral Representations in Several Complex Variables. (Graduate Texts in Mathematics Ser.: Vol. 108). (Illus.). 375p. 1986. 49.90 (*0-387-96259-X*) Spr-Verlag.
Range, Willard. Jawaharlal Nehru's World View: A Theory of International Relations. LC 61-15570. 149p. reprint ed. pap. 42.50 (*0-318-34866-7*, 2031038) Bks Demand.
— The Rise & Progress of Negro Colleges in Georgia, 1865-1949. LC 51-14571. (University of Georgia Phelps-Stokes Fellowship Studies: No. 15). 264p. reprint ed. pap. 75.30 (*0-318-34878-0*, 2031088) Bks Demand.
Rangel, Carlos. The Latin Americans: Their Love-Hate Relationship with the United States. rev. ed. 322p. 1987. pap. 21.95 (*0-88738-692-X*) Transaction Pubs.
— Third World Ideology & Western Reality: Manufacturing Political Myth. 180p. 1986. pap. 19.95 (*0-88738-601-6*) Transaction Pubs.
Rangel-Guerrero, Daniel. Gil Vicente: Comedia Sobre a Divisa da Cidade de Coimbra. LC 79-24434. (Romance Monographs: No. 38). 84p. 1980. 15.00 (*84-499-3496-6*) Romance.
***Rangel-Ribeiro, Lea.** Time, Measurement, & Money. Evento, Susan, ed. (Macmillan Early Skills Program - Conversion Ser.). 64p. (J). (ps-2). Date not set. pap. text ed. 9.95 (*1-56784-509-6*) Newbridge Comms.
***Rangel-Ribeiro, Lea & Rangel-Ribeiro, Victor.** Wonderful World. Evento, Susan, ed. (Macmillan Early Skills Program - Conversion Ser.). 64p. (J). (ps-2). Date not set. pap. text ed. 9.95 (*1-56784-514-2*) Newbridge Comms.
Rangel-Ribeiro, Victor & Markel, Robert. Chamber Music: A Guide to Works & Their Instrumentation. 352p. 1992. lib. bdg. 45.00 (*0-8160-2296-8*) Facts on File.
Rangel-Ribeiro, Victor, jt. auth. see Rangel-Ribeiro, Lea.
Rangeley, Robert, jt. auth. see Kirmani, Syed.
Rangeley, Robert, et al. International River Basin Organizations in Sub-Saharan Africa. LC 94-12868. 1994. write for info. (*0-8213-2871-9*) World Bank.
Rangell, Leo. The Human Core: The Intrapsychic Base of Behavior, Vol. 1. 478p. 1990. 60.00 (*0-8236-2365-3*) Intl Univs Pr.
— The Human Core: The Intrapsychic Base of Behavior, Vol. 2. 500p. 1990. 60.00 (*0-8236-2366-1*) Intl Univs Pr.
Ranger, Charles. Gray's Inn Journal, 1752-1754. 312p. 1977. 60.00 (*0-379-20369-3*) Oceana.
Ranger, G., ed. Eurojet: European Jetliner Directory. 125p. (C). 1993. text ed. 195.00 (*0-9516105-0-3*, Pub. by Euravia Bks) St Mut.
***Ranger, Laurel A.** Low Mid-Volume Competitive Analysis. Kasper, Juneann, ed. (Copier Productivity Ser.). 45p. (Orig.). 1994. pap. 45.00 (*0-9629936-2-X*) Minnella Ent.
Ranger, P. Performance: Practical Examinations in Speech & Drama. 200p. 1990. pap. 22.95 (*0-419-14460-9*, A3884, E & FN Spon) Routledge Chapman & Hall.
Ranger, Terence. Chingaira Makoni's Head: Myth, History & the Colonial Experience. (Hans Wolff Memorial Lecture Ser.). 27p. 1988. 5.00 (*0-941934-52-7*) Indiana Africa.
***Ranger, Terence & Slack, Paul, eds.** Epidemics & Ideas: Essays on the Historical Perception of Pestilence. (Past & Present Publications). 356p. (C). 1995. pap. write for info. (*0-521-55831-X*) Cambridge U Pr.
Ranger, Terence & Slack, Paul A., eds. Epidemics & Ideas: Essays on the Historical Perception of Pestilence. (Past & Present Publications). 300p. (C). 1992. 59.95 (*0-521-40276-X*) Cambridge U Pr.
Ranger, Terence, jt. ed. see Bhebe, Ngwabi.
Ranger, Terence, jt. ed. see Hobsbawm, Eric J.
Ranger, Terence O. Peasant Consciousness & Guerilla War in Zimbabwe: A Comparative Study. LC 85-40286. (Perspectives on Southern Africa Ser.: No. 37). 399p. reprint ed. pap. 113.80 (*0-7837-4693-8*, 2044440) Bks Demand.
Ranger, Terence O. & Kimambo, I. N., eds. The Historical Study of African Religion. LC 76-186104. 317p. reprint ed. pap. 90.40 (*0-685-23565-3*, 2029060) Bks Demand.
Rangiah, P. N., jt. auth. see Rajam, R. V.
Rangnath, Molly, ed. see Fallon, Joan M.
***Rangnow, Warren.** Hut Two. 224p. 1994. text ed. 15.95 (*1-57087-076-4*) Prof Pr NC.
Rango, A., jt. ed. see Johnson, Arnold I.
Rangra, Ranavir. Interviews with Indian Writers. (New World Literature Ser.: No. 48). (C). 1992. 24.00 (*81-7018-699-4*, Pub. by BR Pub II) S Asia.
Rangwala, S. S., jt. ed. see Jouaneh, M.
Ranhofer, Charles. Epicurean. 1971. 34.95 (*0-486-22680-8*) Dover.
Rani, Bilimoria. Female Criminality. 1985. 65.00 (*0-317-56734-9*) St Mut.
— Female Criminality. (C). 1989. 50.00 (*0-89771-764-3*, Pub. by Eastern Book II) St Mut.
— Female Criminality a Socio-Legal Study, 1987: With Supplement. (C). 1990. 60.00 (*0-685-39705-X*) St Mut.
Rani, Bilmoria. Female Criminality. (C). 1987. 35.00 (*0-685-39350-X*) St Mut.
Rani Gopal, K. Economics of Health & Nutrition: Some Aspects of Growth & Welfare. (C). 1987. 22.50 (*81-85076-18-9*, Pub. by Chugh Pubns II) S Asia.
Rani, Seema & Malviya, Achla. Communication & Rural Women. (Illus.). x, 148p. 1991. 13.00 (*81-85445-15-X*, Pub. by Manak Pubns Pvt Ltd) Nataraj Bks.
Ranicki, A. Algebraic L-Theory & Topological Manifolds. (Tracts in Mathematics Ser.: No. 102). 350p. (C). 1993. 69.95 (*0-521-42024-5*) Cambridge U Pr.
Ranicki, A. A. Lower K & L-Theory. (London Mathematical Society Lecture Note Ser.: No. 178). 192p. (C). 1992. pap. 32.95 (*0-521-43801-2*) Cambridge U Pr.
Ranicki, A. A., et al, eds. Algebraic & Geometric Topology. (Lecture Notes in Mathematics Ser.: Vol. 1126). v, 423p. 1985. pap. 49.60 (*0-387-15235-0*) Spr-Verlag.
Ranicki, Andrew. Exact Sequences in the Algebraic Theory of Surgery. LC 80-18277. (Mathematical Notes Ser.: No. 26). 516p. 1981. pap. 35.00 (*0-691-08276-6*) Princeton U Pr.
Ranier, Chris. Keepers of the Spirit: Stories of Nature & Humankind. Berry, Paul, ed. (Illus.). 1992. 50.00 (*0-941831-76-0*) Beyond Words Pub.
Ranieri, Helene. Let's "Unhook" the French Verbs (and 77 Quick Grammar, Syntax & Pronunciation "Tips") 2nd rev. ed. LC 77-85156. (Illus.). 1974. 10.50 (*0-686-24866-X*) H Ranieri.
Ranieri, Joe. Diary of the Lord's Place. 128p. (Orig.). 1992. pap. 7.95 (*0-9631517-5-4*) Jeremiah Pr.
***Ranieri, John J.** Eric Voegelin & the Good Society. 320p. 1995. 39.95 (*0-8262-1012-0*) U of Mo Pr.
Ranieri, Ralph E. The Road Ultimately Traveled: Death & the Spiritual Journey. 64p. (Orig.). 1993. pap. text ed. 3.95 (*0-89243-519-4*) Liguori Pubns.
Ranieri, Ralph F. Meditations from Downtown: A Counselor's Reflections on Life. LC 90-61149. 64p. (Orig.). 1990. pap. 1.95 (*0-89243-326-4*) Liguori Pubns.
Ranina, H. P., ed. Business & Corporate Taxation: A Handbook, with Supplement Containing 7 New Chapters on Tax Planning for Partnership Firms. (C). 1990. 175.00 (*0-89771-265-X*) St Mut.
Ranis, Gustav. The United States & the Developing Economies. rev. ed. (Problems of Modern Economy Ser.). (C). 1973. text ed. 8.95 (*0-393-05461-6*); pap. text ed. 5.95 (*0-393-09999-7*) Norton.
Ranis, Gustav, ed. Government & Economic Development. LC 79-140537. (Economic Growth Center, Yale University Publication Ser.). (Illus.). 581p. reprint ed. pap. 165.60 (*0-8357-8148-8*, 2033864) Bks Demand.
Ranis, Gustav & Mahmood, Syed. The Political Economy of Development Policy Change. abr. ed. (Illus.). 200p. (C). 1991. text ed. 39.95 (*1-55786-250-8*) Blackwell Pubs.
Ranis, Gustav, ed. see Barros, Ricardo, et al.
Ranis, Gustav, jt. auth. see Fei, John C.
Ranis, Gustav, et al. Linkages in Developing Economies: A Philippine Study. LC 89-48871. 83p. 1990. pap. 9.95 (*1-55815-049-8*) ICS Pr.
***Ranis, Gustavo, ed.** En Route to Modern Growth: Latin American in the 1990s - Essays in Honor of Carlos Diaz-Alejandro. (Inter-American Development Bank Ser.). 154p. (Orig.). 1994. 21.00x (*0-940602-85-7*) IADB.
Ranis, Peter. Argentine Workers: Peronism & Contemporary Class Consciousness. LC 91-35602. (Latin American Ser.). 336p. 1992. 49.95 (*0-8229-3703-4*) U of Pittsburgh Pr.
***Ranis, Peter, ed.** Class, Democracy & Labor in Contemporary Argentina. rev. ed. LC 94-26252. Orig. Title: Argentine Workers. 352p. 1994. pap. 21.95 (*1-56000-775-3*) Transaction Pubs.
***Ranish, J. M. & Struck, C. W., eds.** Proceedings of the International Symposium on High Temperature Lamp Chemistry, 3rd. LC 93-72869. (Proceedings Ser.: Vol. 93-16). 280p. 1993. 37.00 (*1-56677-040-8*) Electrochem Soc.
***Ranjan, Kumud.** Women & Modern Occupation in India. (C). 1993. 42.00 (*81-85613-78-8*, Pub. by Chugh Pubns II) S Asia.
Ranjana, Bodhisattva M., ed. see Osho.
Ranjana, Kumari, jt. auth. see Radhakrishnan, S.
Ranjeva, R. & Boudet, A. M., eds. Signal Perception & Transduction in Higher Plants. (NATO ASI Series H: Cell Biology: Vol. 47). (Illus.). ix, 344p. 1990. 115.00 (*0-387-51772-3*) Spr-Verlag.
Ranjhan, S. K. Animal Nutrition & Feeding Practices. 4th ed. Date not set. 40.00 (*0-7069-7101-9*, Pub. by Vikas II) S Asia.
— Animal Nutrition in Tropics. 446p. 1980. 19.95 (*0-7069-1005-2*) Asia Bk Corp.
Rank. Head & Hands. 1987. 37.50 (*0-906923-12-3*) Mosby Yr Bk.
Rank, Hugh. Pep Talk: How to Analyze Political Language. LC 83-15318. (Illus.). 215p. (Orig.). 1984. pap. 11.95 (*0-943468-01-9*) Counter-Prop Pr.
— Persuasion Analysis: A Companion to Composition. LC 88-25696. 160p. (Orig.). 1988. pap. text ed. 10.00 (*0-943468-02-7*) Counter-Prop Pr.
— The Pitch. 2nd rev. ed. (Illus.). 160p. 1991. pap. text ed. 14.95 (*0-943468-03-5*, HF5821.R26) Counter-Prop Pr.
Rank, Hugh, ed. see Wedekind, Frank.
Rank, Mark R. Living on the Edge: The Realities of Welfare in America. LC 93-22818. 266p. 1994. 29.95 (*0-231-08424-2*); pap. write for info. (*0-231-08425-0*) Col U Pr.
***Rank, Mark R. & Kain, Edward L., eds.** Diversity & Change in Families: Patterns, Prospects & Policies. LC 94-28524. 480p. 1994. pap. text ed. write for info. (*0-13-219668-9*) P-H.
Rank, Maureen. Dealing with the Dad of Your Past. 160p. (Orig.). 1990. pap. 7.99 (*0-87123-622-2*) Bethany Hse.
— Free to Grieve: Coping with the Trauma of Miscarriage. LC 85-11273. 176p. 1985. pap. 8.99 (*0-87123-806-3*) Bethany Hse.
Rank, Maureen, jt. auth. see Chapman, Annie.
Rank, Otto. Art & Artist. 1989. pap. 15.95 (*0-393-30574-0*) Norton.
— Beyond Psychology. pap. text ed. 6.95 (*0-486-20485-5*) Dover.
— The Double: A Psychoanalytic Study. 120p. 1971. reprint ed. pap. 21.95 (*0-946439-58-3*, Pub. by Karnac Bks UK) Brunner-Mazel.
— The Incest Theme in Literature & Legend. Richter, Gregory C., tr. LC 91-19651. 672p. 1991. text ed. 65.00 (*0-8018-4176-3*) Johns Hopkins.
— The Trauma of Birth. LC 93-21385. (Illus.). 256p. reprint ed. pap. 7.95 (*0-486-27974-X*) Dover.
Rank, Otto, jt. auth. see Ferenczi, Sandor.
Rank, Otto, et al. In Quest of the Hero. 210p. (C). 1990. pap. text ed. 10.95 (*0-691-02062-0*) Princeton U Pr.
Rank, Richard. Criminal Justice Systems of the Latin-American Nations: A Bibliography of the Primary & Secondary Literature. (New York University Criminal Law Education & Research Center Monograph: Vol. 11). xxxiii, 576p. 1974. text ed. 45.00 (*0-8377-1026-X*) Rothman.
Ranka, S. & Sahni, S. Hypercube Algorithms: With Applications to Image Processing & Pattern Recognition. (Bilkent University Lecture Ser.). 256p. 1990. 43.00 (*0-387-97322-2*) Spr-Verlag.
Rankama, K. Isotope Geology. 229.00 (*0-08-009007-9*, Pub. by Pergamon Repr UK) Franklin.
Ranke-Heine, Uta. Putting Away Childish Things. 1995. pap. 13.00 (*0-06-066861-X*, PL) HarpC.

R

Ranke-Heinemann, Uta. Eunuchs for the Kingdom of Heaven: Women, Sexuality, & the Catholic Church. 368p. 1991. reprint ed. pap. 11.95 (*0-14-016500-2*, Penguin Bks) Viking Penguin.
— Putting Away Childish Things. LC 93-33896. 304p. 1994. 24.00 (*0-06-066860-1*) Harper SF.

Ranke, Hermann. Die Aegyptischen Personennamen. Incl. List of Names. 90.00 (*0-685-71722-4*); Form, Meaning, History of Names. 128.00 (*0-685-71723-2*); List of Components. 75.00 (*0-685-71721-6*); write for info. (*0-318-53734-6*) J J Augustin.
— Early Babylonian Personal Names from the Published Tablets of the So-Called Hammurabi Dynasty 2000 B. C. (Publications of the Babylonian Section, Ser. A: Vol. 3). xiii, 255p. 1905. pap. 16.00 (*0-686-11916-9*) U PA Mus Pubns.

Ranke, Kurt. Die Welt der einfachen Formen: Studien zur Motiv- Wort- und Quellenkunde. (C). 1978. 176.95 (*3-11-007420-6*) De Gruyter.

Ranke, Kurt, ed. Enzyklopaedie des Maerchens: Handwoerterbuch zur historischen und vergleichenden Erzaehlforschung, 12 vols. 144p. (C). 340.00 (*3-11-008201-2*) De Gruyter.
— Enzyklopaedie des Maerchens: Handwoerterbuch zur historischen und vergleichenden Erzaehlforschung, 12 vols., Vol. 1. 703p. (C). 1977. 340.00 (*3-11-006781-1*) De Gruyter.
— Enzyklopaedie des Maerchens: Handwoerterbuch zur historischen und vergleichenden Erzaehlforschung, 12 vols., Vol. 3. 723p. (C). 1981. 340.00 (*3-11-008091-5*) De Gruyter.
— Enzyklopaedie des Maerchens: Handwoerterbuch zur historischen und vergleichenden Erzaehlforschung, 12 vols., Vol. 4. 720p. (C). 1984. 340.00 (*3-11-009566-1*) De Gruyter.

Ranke, Leopold. Civil Wars & Monarchy in France: In the Sixteenth & Seventeenth Centuries; A History of France Principally During That Period, 2 vols. Garvey, M. A., tr. LC 78-38365. (Select Bibliographies Reprint Ser.). 1977. reprint ed. 57.95 (*0-8369-6782-8*) Ayer.

Ranken, M. D. & Kill, R. C., eds. Food Industries Manual. 23th ed. LC 93-3707. 1993. write for info. (*0-7514-0015-7*, Pub. by Blackie Acad & Prof UK) Routledge Chapman & Hall.

Ranki, G., jt. auth. see Berend, T. I.

Ranki, George. Hungarian History-World History: Indiana University Studies on Hungary. 316p. 1984. 90.00 (*0-569-08837-2*, Pub. by Collets UK) Pro-Am Music.

***Ranki, Gy.** Hungarian History-World History. (Indiana University Turkish Studies: No. 1). 316p. (C). 1984. 56. 00x (*963-05-3997-7*, Pub. by Akad Kiado HU) St Mut.

Ranki, Gyorgy. Economy & Foreign Policy. (East European Monographs: No. 141). 224p. 1983. text ed. 42.00 (*0-88033-032-5*) East Eur Quarterly.

Ranki, Gyorgy, jt. auth. see Berend, Ivan T.

Ranki, Gyorgy, jt. tr. see Berend, Ivan T.

Rankilor, Peter R. Membranes in Ground Engineering. LC 80-40504. (Illus.). 387p. reprint ed. pap. 110.30 (*0-8357-3827-2*, 2036551) Bks Demand.

***Rankin.** Tarantulas & Scorpions. 1995. pap. text ed. (*0-7938-0259-8*) TFH Pubns.

Rankin, ed. The Presidency in Transition. 1949. pap. 7.50 (*0-317-27710-3*) Kallman.

Rankin & Ingersoll. Organization & Administration of Athletic Team. 416p. 1994. 34.95 (*0-8016-7698-3*) Mosby Yr Bk.

Rankin, jt. auth. see Lightbourne.

Rankin, Anne M., ed. Explaining the Service Contract Act. (National Contract Management Association Workshop Ser.). 76p. (Orig.). 1992. pap. 10.95 (*0-940343-35-5*) Natl Contract Mgmt.
— Practical Small Purchasing. 2nd ed. (National Contract Management Association Workshop Ser.). 71p. 1993. pap. 10.95 (*0-940343-41-X*) Natl Contract Mgmt.

Rankin, Anne M., ed. see Belev, George C.

Rankin, Anne M., ed. see Bolos, Joseph T., et al.

Rankin, Anne M., ed. see National Contract Management Association Staff.

Rankin, Anne M., ed. see Rumbaugh, Margaret G.

Rankin, Anne M., ed. see Smith, John A.

Rankin, Anne M., ed. see Wells, Rita L.

Rankin, Anne M., ed. see Wexler, Bonnie F.

Rankin, Arthur C. The Poetry of Stevie Smith: "Little Girl Lost" LC 84-16896. (Illus.). 120p. 1985. 43.00 (*0-389-20508-7*, BNB-08066) B&N Imports.

***Rankin-Box, Denise F., ed.** The Nurses' Handbook of Complementary Therapies. LC 94-41151. 1995. write for info. (*0-443-05180-1*) Churchill.

Rankin, Carroll W. Dandelion Cottage. 4th ed. 1982. reprint ed. 8.95 (*0-938746-00-6*) Marquette Cnty.

***Rankin, Chris.** Christmas Wreaths: Twenty-Seven Festive Easy-to-Make Wreaths, Garlands & Swags. LC 94-30697. 1995. write for info. (*0-8069-1279-0*) Sterling.
— Country Decorating with Fabric: More Than Eighty Projects to Add Country Style, Charm & Color to Every Room in Your Home. (Illus.). 160p. 1992. 24.95 (*0-8069-8380-9*) Sterling.
— Country Decorating with Fabric: More Than 80 Projects to Add Country Style, Charm & Color to Every Room in Your Home. (Illus.). 160p. 1993. pap. 14.95 (*0-8069-8381-7*) Sterling.
— Decorating Table Linens: Sixty Tablecloths, Place Mats, & Napkins to Applique, Paint, Cross-Stitch, Embroider & Sew. (Illus.). 144p. 1993. pap. 14.95 (*0-8069-8599-2*) Sterling.
— The Filet Crochet Book. LC 89-21904. 160p. 1992. pap. 14.95 (*0-8069-5823-5*) Sterling.
— Gift Knits: More Than Seventy Wearable & Decorative Projects. LC 92-37393. (Illus.). 144p. 1993. 24.95 (*0-8069-8842-8*) Sterling.
— Gift Knits: More Than Seventy Wearable & Decorative Projects. (Illus.). 144p. 1994. pap. 14.95 (*0-8069-8843-6*) Sterling.
— Glorious Cross Stitch: More Than Fifty Stunning Projects for Every Room in Your Home. (Illus.). 128p. 1994. pap. 14.95 (*0-8069-0292-2*, Lark Books) Sterling.
— Gorgeous Cross-Stitch: More Than 60 Enchanting Projects to Decorate Every Room. LC 94-24193. (Illus.). 144p. 1995. 24.95 (*0-8069-0974-9*) Sterling.
— Great Pillows! Sixty Original Projects: Simple Sewing, Fabric Painting, Crochet, Quilting, Applique, Embroidery, Cross-Stitch. LC 95-4556. (Illus.). 128p. 1995. 24.95 (*0-8069-3162-0*, Lark Bks) Sterling.
— Sew Many Gifts, Sew Little Time: More Than 50 Special Projects to Be Cherished & Enjoyed. LC 93-44538. (Illus.). 128p. 1994. 24.95 (*0-8069-0606-5*) Sterling.
— Splendid Samplers: 35 Unusual Projects. LC 95-11548. 1995. write for info. (*0-8069-3164-7*) Sterling.

Rankin, Chris, jt. auth. see Theiss, Nola.

***Rankin, David.** Tertullian & the Church. 270p. (C). 1995. write for info. (*0-521-48067-1*) Cambridge U Pr.

Rankin, David, jt. auth. see Christensen, Alice.

Rankin, David L., jt. auth. see Wilcox, Earl J.

Rankin, David O. So Great a Cloud of Witnesses. LC 78-2584. (Illus.). (Orig.). 1978. pap. 6.95 (*0-89407-014-2*) Strawberry Hill.

Rankin, Deborah, jt. auth. see Consumer Reports Books Editors.

Rankin, Diana. Metropolitan Dayton: Flying High. (Illus.). 280p. 1992. 34.95 (*0-89781-450-9*) Preferred Mktg.

Rankin, Dianne M. Financial Planning: A Home Study Course. (Home Study Ser.). 43p. 1987. student ed 30.00 (*0-939926-40-7*); audio (*0-939926-39-3*) Fruition Pubns.

Rankin, Don. Answers to Fifty of the Most Often Asked Questions about Watercolor Glazing Techniques. (Illus.). 144p. 1991. 29.95 (*0-8230-4489-0*, Watsn-Guptill) Watsn-Guptill.
— Painting from Sketches, Photographs & the Imagination. (Illus.). 144p. 1990. pap. 18.95 (*0-8230-3637-5*, Watsn-Guptill) Watsn-Guptill.

Rankin, Dorothy. Pestos! Cooking With Herb Pastes. LC 85-17121. (Specialty Cookbook Ser.). (Illus.). 144p. (Orig.). 1985. pap. 8.95 (*0-89594-180-5*) Crossing Pr.

Rankin, Elizabeth. Seeing Yourself As a Teacher: Conversations with Five New Teachers in a University Writing Program. 137p. 1994. write for info. (*0-8141-4298-2*) NCTE.

Rankin, Ernest H. The Indians of Gitchi Gumee. (Illus.). 24p. (Orig.). 1975. pap. 2.00 (*0-938746-08-1*) Marquette Cnty.

Rankin, Ernest H., jt. ed. see Carter, James L.

Rankin, H. C., jt. auth. see Barbour, Charlotte.

Rankin, H. D. Antisthenes Sokratikos. vi, 210p. 1986. 44. 00 (*90-256-0896-5*, Pub. by A M Hakkert NE) Benjamins North Am.
— Archilochus of Paros. LC 77-6157. (Noyes Classical Studies). 136p. 1978. 15.00 (*0-8155-5053-7*, NP) Noyes.
— Celts & the Classical World. 336p. 1987. 48.95 (*0-918400-06-6*) Areopagitica.

Rankin, Hattie L. I Saw It Happen to China. 1960. 10.00 (*0-87511-684-1*) Claitors.

Rankin, Howard, jt. auth. see Miller, Peter M.

Rankin, Hugh F. The North Carolina Continentials. LC 79-135311. 440p. reprint ed. pap. 125.40 (*0-8357-3866-3*, 2036598) Bks Demand.
— Pirates of Colonial North Carolina. (Illus.). viii, 72p. 1994. reprint ed. pap. 5.00 (*0-86526-100-8*) NC Archives.

Rankin, Hugh F., jt. auth. see Scheer, George F.

Rankin, Ian. The Black Book: An Inspector Rebus Novel. LC 94-8929. 288p. 1994. reprint ed. text ed. 21.00 (*1-883402-77-8*) S&S Trade.
— Hide & Seek. large type ed. (General Ser.). 464p. 1993. 21.95 (*0-7089-2734-3*) Ulverscroft.
— Hide & Seek: A John Rebus Mystery. 288p. 1994. reprint ed. 21.00 (*1-883402-74-3*) S&S Trade.
— Strip Jack: An Inspector Rebus Novel. 272p. 1994. 20.95 (*0-312-10553-3*, Pub. by Thomas Dunne Bks) St Martin.

Rankin, Jack, jt. auth. see Ronck, Ronn.

Rankin, Jeanne, jt. auth. see Rankin, Paul.

Rankin, Jimmie R. As Perceived by the Patient: Introduction to the Literature of Patient Response. LC 93-26011. (Literature of Patient Response Ser.: Vol. I). 70p. 1993. per., pap. 12.95 (*1-883938-02-3*) Dry Bones Pr.
— Disability, Stigma, & Recovery: The Patient As Anthropologist. (Literature of a Patient Response Ser.). 75p. 1994. pap. 14.95 (*1-883938-13-9*) Dry Bones Pr.
— Disparate Voices. 30p. 1993. pap. 4.95 (*1-883938-08-2*) Dry Bones Pr.
— Listening with the "Third Ear" Reading What Patients Write - a Basic Course. (Literature of Patient Response Ser.). 100p. 1994. pap. 29.95 (*1-883938-16-3*) Dry Bones Pr.
— Listening with the "Third Ear" Reading What Patients Write - a Basic Course. (Literature of Patient Response Ser.). 100p. 1995. pap., vhs 29.95 (*1-883338-21-2*) Dry Bones Pr.
— Not Wonder but Fear: The Patient As Investigative Reporter. (Literature of Patient Response Ser.: Vol. III). 80p. 1993. pap. 12.95 (*1-883938-04-X*) Dry Bones Pr.
— The Nursing Diagnosis, "Swallowing Impaired" The Bedside Assessment of Swallowing in Neurologically-Involved Cases. 150p. 1993. pap. 19.95 (*1-883938-06-6*); 5.25 hd 4.95 (*1-883938-07-4*) Dry Bones Pr.
— Recovery Room! A Nurse's Guide to Care of the Patient, Post Anesthesia. 150p. 1994. pap. 24.95 (*1-883938-15-5*) Dry Bones Pr.
— Talking Head: The Novelist & Gullain-Barre. (Literature of a Patient Response Ser.). 770p. 1994. pap. 14.95 (*1-883938-14-7*) Dry Bones Pr.
— Who's in Charge Here? The Patient As Primary Caregiver. (Literature of Patient Response Ser.: Vol. II). 70p. 1993. pap. 12.95 (*1-883938-05-8*) Dry Bones Pr.

***Rankin, Jimmie R., ed.** Bill Graham Presents & the Family Dog: Dry Bones Research Database, Numbered Posters, Tickets & Memorabilia. 100p. (Orig.). 1996. pap. 25.00 (*1-883938-20-1*) Dry Bones Pr.

***Rankin, Jimmie R. & Aquino, Marifi.** Staff Developments: The Director of Staff Development in Long Term Case, a 24 Hour Course. (Illus.). 150p. (Orig.). 1995. ring bd. 49.95 (*1-883938-19-8*) Dry Bones Pr.

Rankin, Jimmie R., ed. see Gandhi, Mohandas K.

Rankin, John. Letters on American Slavery, Addressed to Mister Thomas Rankin, Merchant at Middlebrook, Augusta County, Virginia. LC 73-82214. (Anti-Slavery Crusade in America Ser.). 1970. reprint ed. 13.95 (*0-405-00653-5*) Ayer.

Rankin, John C. & Jensen, Frank B., eds. Fish Ecophysiology. LC 92-37628. (Fish & Fisheries Ser.: Vol. 9). 1993. write for info. (*0-412-45920-5*) Chapman & Hall.

Rankin, John R. Computer Graphics Software Construction. (Illus.). 448p. (C). 1988. text ed. 49.20 (*0-13-162793-7*) P-H.

***Rankin, Joyce.** Children's Running: An After-School Program for Elementary School Children. Ohlrich, Warren H., ed. LC 94-61609. (Illus.). 88p. 1995. pap. 15. 00 (*1-882426-02-9*) W H O Pr.

Rankin, Karl L. China Assignment. LC 64-20488. (Illus.). 363p. 1964. 20.00 (*0-295-73742-5*) U of Wash Pr.

Rankin, Kenneth. The Recovery of the Soul: An Aristotelian Essay on Self-Fulfillment. 1991. 49.95 (*0-7735-0796-5*, Pub. by McGill CN) U of Toronto Pr.

Rankin, Kim. Christian Crafts from Eggs. (Christian Craft Ser.). (Illus.). 64p. 1992. 8.95 (*0-86653-642-6*, SS1899, Shining Star Pubns) Good Apple.
— Heroes of the Old Testament. (Bible Story Puzzle Ser.). 1992. 7.95 (*0-86653-710-4*, SS2846, Shining Star Pubns) Good Apple.
— New Testament Story Mazes. (Bible Story Puzzle Ser.). (Illus.). 48p. (J). (gr. k-6). 1994. 6.95 (*1-56417-000-4*, SS3822, Shining Star Pubns) Good Apple.

Rankin, Laura. The Handmade Alphabet. (J). 1991. 14.99 (*0-8037-0974-9*); lib. bdg. 14.89 (*0-8037-0975-7*) Dial Bks Young.

Rankin, Lee, jt. auth. see Martin, Ray.

Rankin, Lee, jt. auth. see Rankin, Peg.

Rankin, Lee, jt. auth. see Strom, Mark.

Rankin, Lois, jt. ed. see Abrahams, Roger D.

Rankin, Lois, ed. see Brettell, Rick, et al.

Rankin, Louise. Daughter of the Mountains. LC 92-26793. (Newbery Library). (Illus.). 192p. (J). (gr. 5 up). 1993. pap. 4.99 (*0-14-036335-1*) Puffin Bks.

Rankin, Marie. Children's Interests in Library Books of Fiction. LC 70-177178. (Columbia University. Teachers College. Contributions to Education Ser.: No. 906). reprint ed. 37.50 (*0-404-55906-9*) AMS Pr.

Rankin, Marjorie. Trends in Educational Occupations. LC 74-177179. (Columbia University. Teachers College. Contributions to Education Ser.: No. 412). reprint ed. 37.50 (*0-404-55412-1*) AMS Pr.

Rankin, Martha, jt. auth. see Whitlock, Sarah.

Rankin, Mary B. Early Chinese Revolutionaries: Radical Intellectuals in Shanghai & Chekiang, 1902-1911. LC 76-115479. 354p. 1971. pap. 13.95 (*0-674-22004-8*) HUP.
— Elite Activism & Political Transformation in China: Zhejiang Province, 1865-1911. LC 86-5875. 448p. 1986. 47.50 (*0-8047-1321-9*) Stanford U Pr.

Rankin, Mary B., jt. ed. see Esherick, Joseph W.

***Rankin, Myra.** Danger in Paradise. 144p. 1994. pap. 6.95 (*1-57087-102-7*) Prof Pr NC.

Rankin, Neil, jt. ed. see Dixon, Huw.

Rankin, Oliver S. Jewish Religious Polemic in Narrative, Poetry, Letters & Debate. rev. ed. 1969. 25.00 (*0-87068-007-2*) Ktav.

***Rankin, Paul & Rankin, Jeanne.** Gourmet Ireland. Gooch, Annette, ed. (Cole Group Ser.). (Illus.). (Orig.). 1995. pap. 29.95 (*1-56426-073-9*) Cole Group.

Rankin, Paula. Augers. LC 80-70565. (Poetry Ser.). 1981. pap. 9.95 (*0-915604-46-9*) Carnegie-Mellon.
— By the Wreckmaster's Cottage. LC 77-80343. (Poetry Ser.). 1977. pap. 9.95 (*0-915604-13-2*) Carnegie-Mellon.
— Divorce: A Romance. 56p. (Orig.). 1991. pap. 9.95 (*0-88748-111-6*) Carnegie-Mellon.
— To the House Ghost. LC 84-72993. (Poetry Ser.). 56p. 1985. 16.95 (*0-88748-013-6*); pap. 9.95 (*0-88748-014-4*) Carnegie-Mellon.

Rankin, Peg. How to Care for the World & Still Take Care of Yourself. LC 94-2431. 1994. 9.99 (*0-8054-5370-9*) Broadman.
— Yet Will I Trust Him: Accepting the Sovereignty of God in Times of Need. rev. ed. Beckwith, Mary, ed. LC 79-91705. 180p. 1988. reprint ed. pap. 7.99 (*0-8307-1279-8*, 5419458) Regal.

Rankin, Peg & Rankin, Lee. Your Marriage: Making It Work: Ten Consumer-Tested Principles for a Lasting Marriage. 140p. (Orig.). 1986. pap. 6.99 (*0-7459-1007-6*) Lion USA.

Rankin, R. Introduction to Math Analysis. LC 61-10656. 1963. 253.00 (*0-08-010182-8*, Pub. by Pergamon Repr UK) Franklin.

Rankin, Richard. Ambivalent Churchmen & Evangelical Churchwomen: The Religion of the Episcopal Elite in North Carolina, 1800-1860. 218p. (C). 1993. text ed. 39. 95 (*0-87249-887-5*) U of SC Pr.

Rankin, Robert S. When Civil Law Fails. LC 39-16186. reprint ed. 29.50 (*0-404-05224-X*) AMS Pr.

Rankin, Robert S. & Dallmayr, Winfried R. Freedom & Emergency Powers in the Cold War. LC 63-21213. (C). 1964. reprint ed. pap. text ed. 14.95 (*0-89197-531-4*) Irvington.

Rankin, Russell B., jt. ed. see Randolph, Howard S.

Rankin, S., jt. auth. see Gedroyc, W.

Rankin, Sally H. & Stallings, Karen D. Patient Education: Issues, Principles, & Practices. 2nd ed. (Illus.). 404p. 1990. text ed. 26.00 (*0-397-54789-7*) Lippincott.
— Patient Education: Issues, Principles, Practices. 3rd ed. LC 95-10728. 1995. write for info. (*0-397-55194-0*) Lippincott.

Rankin-Smith, Pamela. Perfectly Candid: Photographs of Famous People. 1994. 45.00 (*0-88268-150-8*) Station Hill Pr.

Rankin, Susan & Hiley, David, eds. Music in the Medieval English Liturgy: Plainsong & Mediaeval Music Society Centennial Essays. (Illus.). 528p. 1993. 82.00 (*0-19-316125-7*) OUP.

Rankin, T. E., et al. Fred Newton Scott Anniversary Papers, Contributed by Former Students & Colleagues of Professor Scott & Presented to Him in Celebration of His Thirty-Eighth Year of Distinguished Service in the University of Michigan, 1888-1926. LC 68-29205. (Essay Index Reprint Ser.). 1977. reprint ed. 21.95 (*0-8369-0459-1*) Ayer.

***Rankin, Thomas M.** Stonewall Jackson's Romney Campaign, January 1 - February 20, 1862. (Virginia Civil War Battles & Leaders Ser.). (Illus.). 192p. 1994. 25.00 (*1-56190-070-2*) H E Howard.
— Thirty-Seventh Virginia Infantry. (Virginia Regimental Histories Ser.). (Illus.). 150p. 1987. 19.95 (*0-930919-44-0*) H E Howard.
— Twenty Third Virginia Infantry. (Virginia Regimental Histories Ser.). (Illus.). 141p. 1985. 19.95 (*0-930919-14-9*) H E Howard.

Rankin, Tom. New Forms of Work Organization: The Challenge for North American Unions. 168p. 1990. 40. 00 (*0-8020-2698-2*) U of Toronto Pr.
— New Forms of Work Organization: The Challenge for North American Unions. 168p. 1992. pap. 17.95 (*0-8020-7398-0*) U of Toronto Pr.
— Sacred Space: Photographs from the Mississippi Delta. LC 93-6973. (Illus.). 96p. 1993. text ed. 35.00 (*0-87805-640-8*); pap. 19.95 (*0-87805-641-6*) U Pr of Miss.

Rankin, Tom, ed. see Sayre, Maggie L.

Rankin, W. Parkman. The Practice of Newpaper Management. LC 85-28099. 176p. 1986. text ed. 55.00 (*0-275-92051-8*, C2051, Praeger Pubs) Greenwood.

Rankin, William . Come Hibernate with Me. (Illus.). 214p. (Orig.). (YA). (gr. 9 up). 1989. 30.00 (*0-9623948-0-7*) M Camphouse.

Rankin, William J., ed. see Office of Commissioner Federal Judicial Affairs Staff.

Rankin, William P. & Waggaman, Eugene S., Jr. Business Management of General Consumer Magazines. 2nd ed. LC 84-1908. 208p. 1984. text ed. 55.00 (*0-275-91745-2*, C1745, Praeger Pubs) Greenwood.

Rankin, William W. Confidentiality & Clergy: Churches, Ethics & the Law. LC 90-37966. 176p. (Orig.). 1990. pap. 8.95 (*0-8192-1530-9*) Morehouse Pub.
— Cracking the Monolith: The Struggle for the Soul of America - A Peace & Justice Manifesto. 160p. (Orig.). 1994. pap. 10.95 (*0-8245-1439-4*) Crossroad NY.

Rankine, Claudia. Nothing in Nature Is Private. Archer, Nuala, ed. (CSU Poetry Ser.: Vol. XLIV). 88p. (Orig.). Date not set. pap. 10.00 (*1-880834-09-X*) Cleveland St Univ Poetry Ctr.
— Nothing in Nature Is Private. Archer, Nuala, ed. (CSU Poetry Ser.: Vol. XLIV). 88p. (Orig.). 1995. 15.00 (*1-880834-10-3*) Cleveland St Univ Poetry Ctr.

Rankine, David, jt. auth. see Block, Janice.

Rankine, Graeme & Stice, Earl K. Readings & Applications in Financial Accounting. 2nd ed. LC 92-36014. 1992. pap. text ed. write for info. (*0-13-156803-5*) P-H.

Rankins, William.

Rankins, William H., jt. auth. see Wilson, David A.

Rankoff, P. Bulgarian-German Pocket Dictionary: Taschenwoerterbuch Bulgarisch-Deutsch. 11th ed. 367p. (BUL & GER.). 1987. 14.95 (*0-8288-0999-2*, F34910) Fr & Eur.
— German-Bulgarian Pocket Dictionary: Taschenwoerterbuch Deutsch-Bulgarisch. 12th ed. 315p. (BUL & GER.). 1987. 14.95 (*0-8288-1000-1*, F34920) Fr & Eur.

***Rankonen, Carl, ed.** World Music in the Music Library. 77p. 1994. 24.00 (*0-914954-49-0*) Music Library Assn.

Rankov, Boris. The Praetorian Guard. (Elite Ser.). (Illus.). 64p. 1994. pap. 12.95 (*1-85532-361-3*, 9465, Pub. by Osprey UK) Stackpole.

Rankov, N. B., jt. auth. see Austin, N. J.

Rankova, M. English-Bulgarian Dictionary, 2 vols., Set. 1086p. (C). 1987. 295.00 (*0-89771-905-0*, Pub. by Collets) St Mut.

Ranky, Paul G. Computer Integrated Manufacturing: An Introduction. (Illus.). 528p. (C). 1985. text ed. 87.00 (*0-13-165655-4*) P-H.
— The Design & Operation of Flexible Manufacturing Systems. xiv, 348p. 1984. 74.00 (*0-444-86819-4*, North Holland) Elsevier.

Ranlet, Philip. Enemies of the Bay Colony. LC 93-39513. (American University Studies: Ser. IX, Vol. 157). 344p. (C). 1995. text ed. 59.95 (*0-8204-2439-0*) P Lang Pubs.
— The New York Loyalists. LC 85-29601. (Illus.). 320p. (C). 1986. text ed. 36.00x (*0-87049-503-8*) U of Tenn Pr.

Ranlett, William. The Architect, 2 vols. LC 69-16664. (Architecture & Decorative Art Ser.). (Illus.). 1976. reprint ed. lib. bdg. 110.00 (*0-306-70799-3*) Da Capo.

R

An Asterisk (*) at the beginning of an entry indicates that the title is appearing in BIP for the first time.

***Ranly, Don.** Principles American Journalism. (C). 1995. per., pap. text ed. 48.95 (*0-7872-0748-9*) Kendall-Hunt.
— Publication Editing. 240p. (C). 1991. teacher ed 10.95 (*0-8138-1134-1*); pap. text ed. 19.95 (*0-8138-1133-3*) Iowa St U Pr.
Rann, Agatha, ed. Beloved & Darling Child. 256p. 1991. 40. 00 (*0-86299-880-8*) A Sutton Pub.
***Rann, D.** Z: A Beginner's Guide. 1994. pap. 29.95 (*0-412-55660-X*, Blackie & Son-Chapman NY) Routledge Chapman & Hall.
Rann, Sheila. Anything for Love. 288p. 1995. 21.95 (*0-446-51830-1*) Warner Bks.
Rann, W. S., ed. History of Chittendon County, Vermont. (Illus.). 867p. 1993. reprint ed. lib. bdg. 87.50 (*0-8328-3171-9*) Higginson Bk Co.
Rann, W. S., jt. auth. see Smith, H. P.
***Rannells, Jackson.** PNG: A Fact Book on Modern Papua New Guinea. 2nd ed. (Illus.). 224p. 1995. pap. 35.00 (*0-19-553679-7*) OUP.
Ranney, Austin. The American Elections of 1980. LC 81-7907. (AEI Studies: No. 327). 408p. reprint ed. pap. 116.30 (*0-8357-4433-7*, 2037267) Bks Demand.
— The American Elections of 1984. LC 85-24573. (Illus.). 382p. reprint ed. pap. 108.90 (*0-8357-4434-5*, 2037268) Bks Demand.
— The Doctrine of Responsible Party Government, Its Origins & Present State. LC 82-15517. (Illus.). ix, 176p. 1982. reprint ed. text ed. 35.00 (*0-313-22873-6*, RADR, Greenwood Pr) Greenwood.
— Governing: An Introduction to Political Science. 6th ed. LC 92-10547. 544p. (C). 1992. text ed. write for info. (*0-13-361049-7*) P-H.
— Pathways to Parliament: Candidate Selection in Britain. 314p. 1965. 25.00 (*0-299-03560-3*) U of Wis Pr.
Ranney, Austin, ed. The American Elections of Nineteen Eighty-Four. LC 85-24573. (At the Polls Ser.). (Illus.). xii, 368p. 1985. 41.95 (*0-8223-0230-6*); pap. 18.95 (*0-8223-0697-2*) Duke.
— Britain at the Polls, 1983: A Study of the General Election. LC 84-24646. (At the Polls Ser.). xiv, 227p. 1985. 37.00 (*0-8223-0619-0*); pap. 16.95 (*0-8223-0620-4*) Duke.
— Britain at the Polls, 1983: A Study of the General Election. LC 84-24646. (Illus.). 239p. reprint ed. pap. 68.20 (*0-8357-4438-8*, 2037272) Bks Demand.
— Essays on the Behavioral Study of Politics. LC 62-7120. 265p. reprint ed. pap. 75.60 (*0-317-07754-6*, 2019047) Bks Demand.
— The Referendum Device: A Conference. LC 80-25657. (AEI Symposia Ser.: No. 80G). 208p. reprint ed. pap. 59.30 (*0-7837-1085-2*, 2041617) Bks Demand.
Ranney, Austin & Penniman, Howard R. Democracy in the Islands: The Micronesian Plebiscites of 1983. LC 85-3895. (AEI Studies: No. 420). (Illus.). 160p. reprint ed. pap. 45.60 (*0-8357-4461-2*, 2037305) Bks Demand.
Ranney, Austin & Sartori, Giovanni, eds. Eurocommunism: The Italian Case. LC 78-17068. (AEI Symposia Ser.: 78G). (Illus.). 208p. reprint ed. pap. 59.30 (*0-8357-4475-2*, 2037323) Bks Demand.
Ranney, Austin, jt. ed. see Butler, David E.
Ranney, Austin, jt. ed. see Butler, David.
Ranney, Austin, et al. Linking the Governors & the Governed. Taylor, Richard W., ed. (Illus.). 238p. 1981. pap. text ed. 9.95 (*0-933522-09-6*) Kent Popular.
Ranney, Brooks. The Odyssey of Thomas Ranny. (Illus.). 420p. 1994. write for info. (*0-9618939-3-1*); pap. write for info. (*0-9618939-4-X*) B Ranney.
— The Origin & Education of a Doctor. (Illus.). 396p. 1990. 25.00 (*0-9618939-1-5*); pap. 17.00 (*0-9618939-2-3*) B Ranney.
— To Cross the River Barriers. (Illus.). 450p. 1987. 15.00 (*0-9618939-0-7*) B Ranney.
Ranney, Edward & Mondejar, Publio L., intros. Martin Chambi: Photographs, 1920-1950. LC 92-62314. (Illus.). 115p. (Orig.). 1993. pap. 39.95 (*1-56098-244-6*) Smithsonian.
Ranney, Garner, ed. see Kenner, Duncan F.
Ranney, James T. Pennsylvania Criminal Law & Practice, 3 vols., Set. 1990. write for info. (*0-8205-1697-X*, 697) Bender.
***Ranney, Karen.** Tapestry. 384p. 1995. mass mkt. 4.99 (*0-8217-4902-1*) Windsor NY.
Ranney, M. W. Specialized Curing Methods for Coatings & Plastics-Recent Advances. LC 77-71928. (Chemical Technology Review Ser.: No. 88). (Illus.). 1977. 39.00 (*0-8155-0660-0*) Noyes.
Ranney, M. William, ed. Functional Fluids for Industry, Transportation & Aerospace. LC 80-10550. (Chemical Technology Review Ser.: No. 155). (Illus.). 364p. 1980. 45.00 (*0-8155-0789-5*) Noyes.
Ranney-Marinelli, Alesia, jt. auth. see Saggese, Nicholas P.
Ranney, Victoria P., et al, eds. Papers of Fredrick Law Olmsted, Vol. V: The California Frontier, 1863-1865. LC 89-15315. (Illus.). 848p. 1990. text ed. 55.00 (*0-8018-3885-1*) Johns Hopkins.
Ranney, Wayne. Canyon Country. (Plateau Ser.). 32p. 1993. pap. 6.95 (*0-89734-113-9*) Mus Northern Ariz.
— Sedona Through Time: Geology of the Red Rocks. (Illus.). 97p. 1993. pap. 12.95 (*0-9611678-9-0*) Red Lake Bks.
— The Verde Valley: A Geological History. (Plateau Ser.: Vol. 60, No. 3). 32p. 1989. pap. 4.95 (*0-89734-096-5*) Mus Northern Ariz.
Ranniaia, Tom I., tr. see Bulgakov, Mikhail.
Rannie, David W. Scenery in Shakespeare's Plays & Other Studies. LC 70-153346. reprint ed. 45.00 (*0-404-05225-8*) AMS Pr.
— Wordsworth & His Circle. LC 72-3432. (Studies in Wordsworth: No. 29). (Illus.). 1972. reprint ed. lib. bdg. 69.95 (*0-8383-1537-2*) M S G Haskell Hse.
Rannigan, Remley L. Minnesota Multiphasic Personality Inventory (MMPI) Index of Modern Authors & Subjects with Guide for Rapid Research. 200p. 1991. 44.50 (*1-55914-280-4*); pap. 39.50 (*1-55914-281-2*) ABBE Pubs Assn.
— MMPI (Minnesota Multiphasic Personality Inventory) in Testing, Medicine & Psychology: Guidebook for Reference & Research. LC 84-45215. 150p. 1985. 37.50 (*0-88164-186-3*); pap. 34.50 (*0-88164-187-1*) ABBE Pubs Assn.
Rannit, Aleksis. Cantus Firmus. Lyman, Henry, tr. 1978. 50. 00 (*0-685-90033-9*) Elizabeth Pr.
— Donum Estonicum. 1976. 16.00 (*0-685-79486-5*); pap. 8.00 (*0-685-79487-3*) Elizabeth Pr.
Ranny, M. Thin-Layer Chromatography with Flame Ionization Detection. (C). 1987. lib. bdg. 92.00 (*90-277-1973-X*) Kluwer Ac.
***Rano, Balbino.** Augustinian Origins, Charism, & Spirituality. LC 94-32757. (Augustinian Ser.: Vol. 3). 1994. write for info. (*0-941491-75-7*); pap. text ed. write for info. (*0-941491-76-5*) Augustinian Pr.
Ranocchia, Diane D., ed. Rochester Applications Conference, 1983: Proceedings. 300p. 1983. pap. 25.00 (*0-914593-00-5*) Inst Appl Forth.
— Rochester Forth Applications Conference, 1984: Proceedings. 1984. pap. 25.00 (*0-914593-05-6*) Inst Appl Forth.
Ranolph, J. Petroleum in Mexico. 1976. lib. bdg. 34.95 (*0-8490-2427-7*) Gordon Pr.
Rans, Geoffrey. Cooper's Leather-Stocking Novels: A Secular Reading. LC 91-10607. xiii, 282p. (C). 1991. 37.50 (*0-8078-1975-1*) U of NC Pr.
Rans, Laurel, jt. auth. see Sturgeon, Susan.
Ransel, David L. Mothers of Misery: Child Abandonment in Russia. (Illus.). 285p. (Orig.). 1990. text ed. 49.50 (*0-691-05522-X*); pap. text ed. 14.95 (*0-691-00848-5*) Princeton U Pr.
— The Politics of Catherinian Russia: The Panin Party. LC 74-29736. 337p. reprint ed. pap. 96.10 (*0-8357-8276-X*, 2033865) Bks Demand.
Ransel, David L., ed. The Family in Imperial Russia: New Lines of Historical Research. LC 78-17579. 352p. reprint ed. pap. 100.40 (*0-7837-5742-5*, 2045403) Bks Demand.
Ransel, David L., ed. see Semyonova Tian-Shanskaia.
Ransford, Edward H. Race & Class in American Society. rev. ed. pap. 18.95 (*0-87047-069-8*) Schenkman Bks Inc.
— Race & Class in American Society. 2nd rev. ed. 29.95 (*0-87047-068-X*) Schenkman Bks Inc.
Ransford, H. Edward. Race & Class in American Society: Black, Chicano, Anglo. LC 74-84674. 200p. 1977. pap. text ed. 11.95 (*0-87073-041-X*) Schenkman Bks Inc.
Ransford, Lynn, et al. ABC Crafts & Cooking. (Illus.). 64p. (J). (ps-2). 1987. student ed 7.95 (*1-55734-090-0*) Tchr Create Mat.
Ransford, Lynn. Creepy Crawlies for Curious Kids. (Illus.). 48p. (J). (gr. k-3). 1987. student ed 6.95 (*1-55734-217-2*) Tchr Create Mat.
— Happy Healthy Bodies. (Illus.). 48p. (J). (gr. 1-4). 1987. student ed 6.95 (*1-55734-223-7*) Tchr Create Mat.
Ransford, Rosalind, ed. The Early Charters of the Augustinian Canons of Waltham Abbey, Essex, 1062-1230. (Studies in Medieval Religion: Vol. 2). 608p. (C). 1989. 99.00 (*0-85115-516-2*) Boydell & Brewer.
Ransford, Sandy. Global Warming: A Pop-up Book of Our Endangered Planet. (J). (ps-3). 1992. pap. 15.00 (*0-671-77080-2*, S&S Bks Young Read) S&S Childrens.
— Master Magician: An Action Book. (Illus.). 64p. (J). 1994. 19.95 (*1-56138-460-7*) Running Pr.
Ransford, Tessa. A Dancing Innocence. (C). 1989. 39.00 (*0-86334-063-6*, Pub. by Saltire Soc) St Mut.
***Ransford, Thomas.** Potential Theory in the Complex Plane. (London Mathematical Society Student Texts Ser.: No. 28). 244p. (C). 1995. 49.95 (*0-521-46120-0*); pap. 19.95 (*0-521-46654-7*) Cambridge U Pr.
Ranshofen-Wertheimer, E. F. The International Secretariat: A Great Experiment in International Administration. (Studies in the Administration of International Law & Organization). 1969. reprint ed. 45.00 (*0-527-00881-8*) Periodicals Srv.
Ransick, Gary, jt. auth. see Forsthoefel, John.
Ransil, M. Michele, ed. see Gruber, Mark.
Ransmayr, Christoph. The Last World. Rosenman, Jane, ed. 256p. 1992. reprint ed. pap. 10.00 (*0-671-74962-5*, WSP) PB.
Ransohoff, Rita. Venus after Forty: Sexual Myths, Men's Fantasies & Truths about Middle Aged Women. LC 87-12233. 289p. 1990. 11.95 (*0-88282-064-8*) New Horizon NJ.
Ransohoff, Rita M. Venus after Forty: Sexual Myths, Men's Fantasies, & Truths about Middle-Aged Women. LC 87-12233. 289p. 1987. 20.95 (*0-88282-034-6*) New Horizon NJ.
Ransom. Sabrina. (Orig.). (J). 1993. pap. 2.75 (*0-685-66034-6*) Scholastic Inc.
Ransom, Angela, et al. Improving Higher Education in Developing Countries. LC 92-28785. (EDI Seminar Report Ser.). 90p. 1993. 7.95 (*0-8213-2216-8*, 12216) World Bank.
Ransom, Arthur. Oscar Wilde: A Critical Study. LC 79-151283. (English Literature Ser.: No. 33). 1971. reprint ed. lib. bdg. 75.00 (*0-8383-1230-6*) M S G Haskell Hse.
***Ransom, Bill.** Burn. LC 95-9747. 320p. (Orig.). 1995. text ed. 19.95 (*0-441-00246-3*) Ace Bks.
— Learning the Ropes: A Creative Autobiography. LC 95-4342. 1995. write for info. (*0-87421-190-5*) Utah St U Pr.
— Viravax. LC 92-21148. 320p. 1993. 17.95 (*0-441-86476-7*) Ace Bks.
— Viravax. 320p. 1994. pap. text ed. 4.99 (*0-441-00083-5*) Ace Bks.
Ransom, Bill, jt. auth. see Herbert, Frank.
Ransom, Bruce R., jt. auth. see Kettenmann, Helmut.
Ransom, Candice. The Big Green Pocketbook. LC 92-29393. (Laura Geringer Bk.). (Illus.). 32p. (J). (ps-2). 1993. lib. bdg. 14.89 (*0-06-020849-X*) HarpC Child Bks.
— The Big Green Pocketbook. LC 92-29393. (Illus.). 32p. (J). (ps-3). 1995. pap. 4.95 (*0-06-443395-1*, Trophy) HarpC Child Bks.
— The Man on Stilts. LC 92-39358. (Illus.). (J). 1994. write for info. (*0-399-22537-4*, Philomel Bks) Putnam Pub Group.
— Third Grade Detectives. LC 93-41364. (Tales from Third Grade Ser.). (Illus.). 128p. (J). (gr. 2-4). 1994. lib. bdg. 9.89 (*0-8167-2992-1*); pap. 2.95 (*0-8167-2993-X*) Troll Assocs.
Ransom, Candice F. Between Two Worlds. (J). (gr. 4-7). 1994. pap. 3.25 (*0-590-45755-1*) Scholastic Inc.
— Listening to Crickets: A Story about Rachel Carson. (Creative Minds Biographies Ser.). (Illus.). (J). (gr. 3-6). 1993. 15.95 (*0-87614-727-9*, Carolrhoda) Lerner Group.
— Listening to Crickets: A Story about Rachel Carson. (J). (gr. 3-6). 1993. pap. 5.95 (*0-87614-615-9*, Carolrhoda) Lerner Group.
— More Than a Name. LC 94-28592. 1995. write for info. (*0-02-775795-1*, Mac Bks Young Read) S&S Childrens.
— One Christmas Dawn. LC 93-39751. (Illus.). 32p. (J). (gr. k-3). 1995. lib. bdg. 14.95 (*0-8167-3384-8*) BrdgeWater.
— Shooting Star Summer. (Illus.). 32p. (J). (ps-3). 1992. lib. bdg. 14.95 (*1-56397-005-8*) Boyds Mills Pr.
— Sixth Grade High. 176p. (J). (gr. 3-7). 1991. reprint ed. pap. 3.50 (*0-590-43891-3*, Apple Paperbacks) Scholastic Inc.
— So Young to Die: The Story of Hannah Senesh. (J). (gr. 4-7). 1993. pap. 2.95 (*0-685-65620-9*) Scholastic Inc.
— The Spitball Class. MacDonald, Pat, ed. 160p. (Orig.). (J). 1994. pap. 2.99 (*0-671-72910-1*, Minstrel Bks) PB.
— Third Grade Stars: Tales from Third Grade. LC 93-7868. (Illus.). 128p. (J). (gr. 2-4). 1993. lib. bdg. 9.89 (*0-8167-2994-8*); pap. 2.95 (*0-8167-2995-6*) Troll Assocs.
— Thirteen. 192p. (Orig.). (J). (gr. 6-8). 1990. pap. 2.95 (*0-590-43742-9*) Scholastic Inc.
— We're Growing Together. LC 92-7424. (Illus.). 32p. (J). (ps-2). 1993. text ed. 14.95 (*0-02-775666-1*, Bradbury S&S) S&S Childrens.
— When the Whippoorwill Calls. LC 94-41567. (Illus.). (J). 1995. write for info. (*0-688-12729-0*); pap. write for info. (*0-688-12730-4*, Tambourine Bks) Morrow.
— Who Needs Third Grade? LC 92-30754. (Tales from Third Grade Ser.). 128p. (J). (gr. 2-4). 1992. lib. bdg. 9.89 (*0-8167-2988-3*); pap. text ed. 2.95 (*0-8167-2989-1*) Troll Assocs.
— Why Are Boys So Weird? LC 93-6222. (Tales from the Third Grade Ser.). (Illus.). 128p. (J). (gr. 2-6). 1994. lib. bdg. 9.89 (*0-8167-2990-5*); pap. text ed. 2.95 (*0-8167-2991-3*) Troll Assocs.
Ransom, Dana. Alexandra's Ecstasy. 1989. pap. 3.75 (*0-8217-2773-7*) Zebra.
— Dakota Dawn. 1991. mass mkt. 4.50 (*0-8217-3597-7*) Zebra.
— Dakota Desire. 1992. mass mkt. 4.50 (*0-8217-3768-6*) Zebra.
— Dakota Destiny. 448p. 1993. mass mkt. 4.50 (*0-8217-4060-1*) Zebra.
— Dakota Promises. 480p. 1993. mass mkt. 4.50 (*0-8217-4255-8*) Zebra.
— Liar's Promise. 1990. mass mkt. 4.25 (*0-8217-2881-4*) Zebra.
— Lifetime Investment. (Lucky in Love Ser.: No. 27). 288p. 1993. pap. 3.50 (*0-8217-4113-6*) Zebra.
— Love's Own Reward. (Lucky in Love Ser.). 320p. 1992. mass mkt. 3.99 (*0-8217-3836-4*) Zebra.
— Rebel Vixen. (Heartfire Romance Ser.). 1987. pap. 3.75 (*0-8217-2222-0*) Zebra.
— Temptation's Trail. 448p. 1994. mass mkt. 4.50 (*0-8217-4458-5*) Zebra.
— Texas Destiny. 448p. 1994. mass mkt. 4.50 (*0-8217-4652-9*) Zebra.
— Totally Yours. 320p. 1993. mass mkt. 3.99 (*0-8217-4053-9*) Zebra.
— Wild Savage Love. 1990. mass mkt. 4.25 (*0-8217-3055-X*) Zebra.
— Wild Texas Bride. 384p. 1995. pap. 4.99 (*0-8217-4833-5*) Zebra.
— Wild Wyoming Love. 384p. 1991. mass mkt. 4.25 (*0-8217-3427-X*) Zebra.
Ransom, Daniel. Daddy's Little Girl. 1985. pap. 3.50 (*0-8217-1606-9*) Zebra.
— The Fugitive Stars. 288p. (Orig.). 1995. mass mkt. 4.99 (*0-88677-625-2*) DAW Bks.
— Toys in the Attic. 336p. 1986. pap. 3.95 (*0-8217-1862-2*) Zebra.
Ransom, Daniel J. Poets at Play: Irony & Parody in the Harley Lyrics. LC 85-544. 160p. (C). 1985. 29.95 (*0-937664-67-7*) Pilgrim Bks OK.
Ransom, David F. George Keller: Architect. (Illus.). 218p. 1978. pap. 12.00 (*0-917482-14-X*) Stowe-Day.
Ransom, Donald. Nothin' but the 'Boo. (Illus.). 20p. (Orig.). 1981. pap. text ed. 2.50 (*0-686-32817-5*) Skydog OR.
Ransom, Evelyn. Complementation: Its Meaning & Forms. LC 86-3554. (Typological Studies in Language: Vol. 10). xii, 226p. 1986. 59.00x (*0-915027-87-9*); pap. 29.95x (*0-915027-88-7*) Benjamins North Am.
Ransom, Harry, ed. People's Architects. LC 64-15812. 156p. reprint ed. pap. 44.50 (*0-8357-9652-3*, 2016991) Bks Demand.
Ransom, Harry H. The Conscience of the University & Other Essays. Ransom, Hazel H., ed. 120p. 1982. text ed. 14.95 (*0-292-71078-X*) U of Tex Pr.
— The Conscience of the University & Other Essays. limited ed. Ransom, Hazel H., ed. 120p. 1982. Limited ed. 125. 00 (*0-292-71080-1*) U of Tex Pr.
— The Intelligence Establishment. enl. rev. ed. LC 70-115480. 327p. 1970. reprint ed. pap. 93.20 (*0-7837-2318-0*, 2057406) Bks Demand.
— The Other Texas Frontier. Ransom, Hazel H., ed. (Illus.). 75p. 1984. 19.95 (*0-292-71101-8*) U of Tex Pr.
Ransom, Hazel H., ed. see Ransom, Harry H.
Ransom, J. C., ed. Annual Index, 1990. 524p. 1990. pap. text ed. 29.95 (*0-914899-08-2*) Current Lit Pubns.
Ransom, Jackie. A Dog Owner's Guide to Standard, Miniature & Toy Poodles. (Illus.). 119p. 10.95 (*3-923880-63-4*, 16024) Tetra Pr.
— A Dog Owner's Guide to Yorkshire Terriers. (Illus.). 119p. 10.95 (*3-923880-99-5*, 16043) Tetra Pr.
Ransom, Jane Reavill. Without Asking. (Roerich Poetry Prize Winner Ser.). 49p. 1989. pap. 9.95 (*0-934257-29-9*) Story Line.
Ransom, Janet H. & Ortaldo, John, eds. Leukolysins & Cancer. LC 87-17221. (Illus.). 360p. 1988. 79.50 (*0-89603-125-X*) Humana.
Ransom, John. John Ransom's Andersonville Diary. Orig. Title: John Ransom's Diary. 304p. 1988. pap. 4.95 (*0-425-10554-7*) Berkley Pub.
— John Ransom's Andersonville Diary. Orig. Title: John Ransom's Diary. 304p. 1994. pap. 10.00 (*0-425-14146-2*, Berkley Trade) Berkley Pub.
Ransom, John C. Beating the Bushes: Selected Essays, 1941-1970. LC 79-159738. (New Directions Bks.). 186p. reprint ed. pap. 53.10 (*0-8357-7086-9*, 2026174) Bks Demand.
— College Primer of Writing. 1943. 15.00 (*0-686-17405-4*) R S Barnes.
— The New Criticism. LC 78-31133. 339p. 1979. reprint ed. text ed. 65.00 (*0-8371-9079-7*, RANC, Greenwood Pr) Greenwood.
— Selected Essays of John Crowe Ransom. fac. ed. Young, Thomas D. & Hindle, John, eds. LC 83-12041. (Southern Literary Studies). 368p. 1984. reprint ed. pap. 104.90 (*0-7837-7816-3*, 2047572) Bks Demand.
— Selected Poems. 3rd ed. 1991. 21.50 (*0-679-40257-8*) Knopf.
— The World's Body. fac. ed. LC 68-7658. (Louisiana Paperbacks Ser.: No. L-28). 408p. 1968. reprint ed. pap. 116.30 (*0-7837-7931-3*, 2047687) Bks Demand.
Ransom, John L. Andersonville Diary. LC 73-21807. (American History & Americana Ser.: No. 47). 1974. lib. bdg. 75.00 (*0-8383-1783-9*) M S G Haskell Hse.
Ransom, Jon C. Nephrology & Transplantation, 1986. 1986. pap. text ed. 24.95 (*0-914899-04-X*) Current Lit Pubns.
— Nephrology & Transplantation, 1987. 340p. 1987. pap. text ed. 24.95 (*0-914899-05-8*) Current Lit Pubns.
— Nephrology & Transplantation, 1988. 436p. 1988. pap. text ed. 29.95 (*0-914899-06-6*) Current Lit Pubns.
— Nephrology, Nineteen Eighty-Five. 337p. 1985. pap. text ed. 24.95 (*0-914899-03-1*) Current Lit Pubns.
— Nephrology, Nineteen Eighty-Four. 338p. (Orig.). 1984. pap. text ed. 24.95 (*0-914899-01-5*) Current Lit Pubns.
Ransom, Jon C., ed. Annual Index, 1989. 472p. 1989. pap. text ed. 29.95 (*0-914899-07-4*) Current Lit Pubns.
Ransom, Judith. Blessings & Bible Stories: For the Family Table. Rolfes, Ellen, ed. 96p. 1992. spiral bd. 5.95 (*1-879958-20-1*) Tradery Hse.
Ransom, Judy. The Courage to Care. 192p. 1994. pap. 9.95 (*0-8358-0701-0*) Upper Room Bks.
Ransom, Judy G. & Henderson, James G. To Be the Hands of God. LC 91-67170. 144p. (Orig.). 1992. pap. 9.95 (*0-8358-0657-X*) Upper Room Bks.
Ransom, M. A. & Engle, Eloise K. Sea of the Bear. LC 79-6122. (Navies & Men Ser.). (Illus.). 1980. reprint ed. lib. bdg. 24.95 (*0-405-13076-7*) Ayer.
Ransom, Marion, ed. see Ives, James L.
Ransom, McAllister. Fuzzy Mules, Pink Slippers, Vol. I: Came a Clown. LC 88-80849. 883800p. (Orig.). 1992. pap. 5.95 (*0-945969-00-7*) Kohinoor Bks.
***Ransom, Patti & Towne, Kathleen.** I'm Afraid to Go Home: A Program to Help Students Cope with Violent Families or Violent Neighborhoods. (Illus.). 52p. 1994. 10.95 (*1-884063-27-6*) Mar Co Prods.
***Ransom, Paul.** Job Security & Social Stability: The Impact of Mass Unemployment on Expectations of Work. 188p. 1995. 55.95 (*1-85628-966-4*, Pub. by Avebury Pub UK) Ashgate Pub Co.
Ransom, R. Handbook of Drosophila Development. 290p. 1982. 177.00 (*0-444-80366-1*); pap. 71.00 (*0-444-80418-8*) Elsevier.
***Ransom, Reverdy.** Pilgrimage of Harriet Ransom's Son. (American Autobiography Ser.). 336p. 1995. reprint ed. lib. bdg. 89.00 (*0-7812-8622-0*) Rprt Serv.
Ransom, Richard, jt. auth. see Beattie, Gregory.
Ransom, Robert & Matela, Ray. Computers in Biology: An Introduction. 160p. 1985. pap. 40.00 (*0-335-15018-7*, Open Univ Pr) Taylor & Francis.
***Ransom, Robert C.** Practical Formation Evaluation. LC 95-11161. 1995. write for info. (*0-471-10755-7*) Wiley.
Ransom, Robert J. Computers & Embryos: Models in Developmental Biology. LC 81-197475. 224p. reprint ed. pap. 63.90 (*0-318-34727-X*, 2031941) Bks Demand.
Ransom, Roger L. Conflict & Compromise: The Political Economy of Slavery, Emancipation, & the American Civil War. (Illus.). (C). 1989. 59.95 (*0-521-32343-6*); pap. 17.95 (*0-521-31167-5*) Cambridge U Pr.
Ransom, Roger L., ed. Research in Economic History, Vol. 12. 239p. 1989. 73.25 (*1-55938-007-1*) Jai Pr.
Ransom, Ron. Angel Carving. LC 88-64157. (Illus.). 80p. 1989. pap. text ed. 9.95 (*0-88740-147-3*) Schiffer.
— Carving Santas with Special Interests. LC 91-65655. (Illus.). 64p. 1991. pap. 12.95 (*0-88740-328-X*) Schiffer.
— Ron Ransom Carves Athletic Santa Mini-Cheers: Step-by-Step Instructions Plus Patterns for 5 Original Santas. LC 95-7003. (Book for Woodcarvers Ser.). (Illus.). 64p. (Orig.). 1995. pap. 12.95 (*0-88740-825-7*) Schiffer.

R

An Asterisk (*) at the beginning of an entry indicates that the title is appearing in BIP for the first time.

— Santa Carving. (Illus.). 48p. 1987. pap. 8.95 (*0-88740-107-4*) Schiffer.
— Santa Mini-Cheers: Carving Miniature Santas. LC 95-7246. (Illus.). 64p. (Orig.). 1995. pap. 12.95 (*0-88740-824-9*) Schiffer.
Ransom, Timothy W. The Beach Troop of the Gombe. LC 77-92573. (Illus.). 319p. 1979. 46.50 (*0-8387-1704-7*) Bucknell U Pr.
Ransom, Victoria & Bernstein, Henrietta. The Crone Oracles: Initiate's Guide to the Ancient Mysteries. 176p. (Orig.). 1994. pap. 12.95 (*0-87728-800-3*) Weiser.
Ransom, W. H. Building Failures. 2nd ed. 200p. 1981. text ed. 45.00 (*0-419-14260-6*, E & FN Spon); pap. text ed. 19.95 (*0-419-14270-3*, E & FN Spon) Routledge Chapman & Hall.
Ransom, Will. Private Presses & Their Books. LC 75-41221. reprint ed. 32.50 (*0-404-14732-1*) AMS Pr.
— Selective Check Lists of Press Books. 420p. 1992. 75.00 (*1-882860-03-9*) J Cummins Bksell.
Ransom, William L. Majority Rule & the Judiciary. LC 78-166099. (American Constitutional & Legal History Ser). 1971. reprint ed. lib. bdg. 22.50 (*0-306-70205-3*) Da Capo.
***Ransom, Wyllys C.** Ransom Historical Outline of the Ransom Family of America, & Genealogical Records of the Colchester, Ct., Branch. (Illus.). 408p. 1995. lib. bdg. 72.00 (*0-8328-4454-3*) Higginson Bk Co.
— Ransom Historical Outline of the Ransom Family of America, & Genealogical Records of the Colchester, Ct., Branch. (Illus.). 408p. 1995. reprint ed. pap. 62.00 (*0-8328-4455-1*) Higginson Bk Co.
Ransome, A. Edgar Allan Poe: A Critical Study. LC 72-3534. (Studies in Poe: No. 23). 1972. reprint ed. lib. bdg. 75.00 (*0-8383-1548-8*) M S G Haskell Hse.
Ransome, Arthur. Coot Club. LC 88-46106. (Illus.). 352p. (J). (gr. 4-6). 1989. pap. 11.95 (*0-87923-787-2*) Godine.
— Favroite Russian Fairy Tales. LC 94-45619. (Children's Thrift Classics Ser.). (Illus.). 96p. (J). 1995. pap. text ed. 1.00 (*0-486-28632-0*) Dover.
— The Fool of the World & the Flying Ship. LC 68-54105. (Illus.). 48p. (J). (ps-3). 1968. 16.00 (*0-374-32442-5*) FS&G.
— The Fool of the World & the Flying Ship: A Russian Tale. (Sunburst Ser.). (Illus.). (J). (ps up). 1987. pap. 6.95 (*0-374-42438-1*) FS&G.
— Old Peter's Russian Tales. (Puffin Novels Ser.). (Illus.). 256p. (J). (gr. 5-9). 1975. pap. 3.50 (*0-14-030696-X*) Viking Child Bks.
— Peter Duck. LC 86-46247. (Illus.). 414p. 1987. pap. 11.95 (*0-87923-660-4*) Godine.
— Pigeon Post. 372p. (YA). 1992. pap. 11.95 (*0-87923-864-X*) Godine.
— Secret Water. 376p. (J). 1995. pap. 12.95 (*1-56792-064-0*) Godine.
— Swallowdale. LC 84-48802. (Illus.). 448p. 1985. pap. 11.95 (*0-87923-572-1*) Godine.
— Swallows & Amazons. LC 84-48803. 352p. 1985. pap. 11.95 (*0-87923-573-X*) Godine.
— Tontimundo y el Barco Volador. Negroni, Maria, tr. (Mirasol Ser.). (Illus.). 48p. (SPA.). (J). (ps-3). 1991. 15.95 (*0-374-32443-3*) FS&G.
— Tontimundo y el Barco Volador: Un Cuento Ruso. braille ed. 30p. (J). 1993. vinyl bd. 2.40 (*1-56956-443-4*, BR8877) W A T Braille.
— We Didn't Mean to Go to Sea. 344p. 1994. pap. 12.95 (*0-87923-991-3*) Godine.
Ransome, F. L. Mines of the Goldfield, Bullfrog & Other Southern Nevada Districts. (Illus.). 144p. pap. 14.95 (*0-913814-60-1*) Nevada Pubns.
Ransome, Hilda M. The Sacred Bee in Ancient Times & Folklore. 1976. lib. bdg. 250.00 (*0-8490-2552-4*) Gordon Pr.
Ransome, Ian G., jt. ed. see De Wit, Maarten J.
Ransome, Julia. The Book of Sandwiches. (Book of...Ser.). (Illus.). 120p. (Orig.). 1989. pap. 12.00 (*0-89586-789-3*, HP Books) Berkley Pub.
***Ranson, Charles E.** Statesman of Harper's Ferry. LC 95-68286. 180p. 1995. 14.95 (*0-9636320-3-5*) Nuggets Wisdom.
Ranson, Charles W. A Missionary Pilgrimage. LC 88-7021. (Illus.). 212p. reprint ed. pap. 60.50 (*0-8357-4367-5*, 2037196) Bks Demand.
Ranson, Daniel. The Forsaken. 1988. pap. 3.50 (*0-318-35176-5*) St Martin.
Ranson, Nicholas, jt. ed. see Merrix, Robert P.
Ranson, P. Healthy Housing: A Practical Guide. 1991. pap. 32.95 (*0-442-31430-2*) Chapman & Hall.
Ranson, R. Healthy Housing: A Design Guide. (Illus.). 288p. 1991. pap. write for info. (*0-419-15400-0*, E & FN Spon) Routledge Chapman & Hall.
Ranson, Rebecca, ed. Theater in the South. (Southern Exposure Ser.). (Illus.). 120p. (Orig.). 1986. pap. 4.00 (*0-943810-21-3*) Inst Southern Studies.
Ranson, Robert. Advertising Is A Waste of Money. 1994. pap. 12.95 (*0-87425-971-1*) Human Res Dev Pr.
— East Coast Florida Memoirs 1837 to 1886. Martin, Val, ed. (Florida Classics Ser.). (Illus.). 48p. reprint ed. pap. 4.95 (*0-912451-09-2*) Florida Classics.
Ranson, Ron. Big Brush Watercolour. (Illus.). 128p. 1993. 24.95 (*0-7153-9301-4*, Pub. by D & C Pub UK) Sterling.
— Distilling the Scene. (Illus.). 128p. 1995. 24.95 (*0-7153-0067-9*, Pub. by D & C Pub UK) Sterling.
— Edward Seago. 1994. 55.00 (*0-7153-9001-5*, Pub. by D & C Pub UK) Sterling.
— Edward Seago: The Vintage Years. (Illus.). 96p. 1992. 55.00 (*0-7153-9927-6*, Pub. by D & C Pub UK) Sterling.
— Learn Watercolor the Edgar Whitney Way. (Illus.). 144p. 1994. 27.95 (*0-89134-494-2*) North Light Bks.
— The Maritime Paintings of Montague Dawson. (Illus.). 96p. 1994. 55.00 (*0-7153-0045-8*, Pub. by D & C Pub UK) Sterling.
— Perfecting Your Watercolors. (Ron Ranson's Painting School Ser.). (Illus.). 120p. 1995. 22.95 (*1-85470-211-4*, Pub. by Anaya Pubs UK) Trafalgar.
— Ron Ranson's Painting School: Watercolors. (Illus.). 128p. (Orig.). 1993. pap. 19.95 (*0-89134-545-0*, 30550) North Light Bks.
— Watercolour Fast & Loose. 1994. 24.95 (*0-7153-0120-9*, Pub. by D & C Pub UK) Sterling.
— Watercolour Impressionists. 1994. 34.95 (*0-7153-9338-3*, Pub. by D & C Pub UK) Sterling.
— Watercolour Painting: The Ron Ranson Technique. rev. ed. (Illus.). 192p. 1992. pap. 16.95 (*0-289-80070-6*, Pub. by Blandford Pr UK) Sterling.
Ranson, Stewart. Towards the Learning Society. (Education Ser.). 224p. 1994. 70.00 (*0-304-32770-0*); pap. 24.95 (*0-304-32769-7*) Cassell.
***Ranson, Stewart & Stewart, John.** Management for the Public Domain: Enabling the Learning Society. LC 94-25479. 1994. write for info. (*0-312-12284-5*) St Martin.
Ranson, Stewart, jt. ed. see Nixon, Jon.
Ranson, Will. Private Presses & Their Books. 493p. 1992. 75.00 (*1-882860-05-5*) J Cummins Bksell.
Ransone, Coleman B., Jr. The American Governorship. LC 81-6653. (Contributions in Political Science Ser.: No. 69). (Illus.). 216p. 1982. text ed. 55.00 (*0-313-22977-5*, RAG/, Greenwood Pr) Greenwood.
— Office of Governor in the United States. LC 78-130564. (Select Bibliographies Reprint Ser.). 1977. 26.95 (*0-8369-5537-4*) Ayer.
Rant, Lilian V., jt. auth. see Pounds, V. H.
***Ranta, Aarne.** Type-Theoretical Grammar. (Indices 1 Ser.). (Illus.). 260p. 1995. 72.00 (*0-19-853857-X*) OUP.
Ranta, D. E., ed. Applied Mining Geology: Ore Reserve Estimation. LC 86-61399. 212p. (Orig.). reprint ed. pap. 60.50 (*0-8357-3483-8*, 2039742) Bks Demand.
Ranta, J., ed. Analysis, Design & Evaluation of Man-Machine Systems, 1988: Selected Papers from the Third IFAC-IFIP-IEA-IFORS Conference, Oulu, Finland, 14-16 June, 1988. (IFAC Proceedings Ser.). 442p. 1989. 235.00 (*0-08-036226-5*, Pergamon Pr) Elsevier.
Ranta, Rachel & Ward, Elizabeth. Lawndale Live! A Retrospective 1979-1990. LC 93-80111. (Illus.). 72p. 1993. 15.00 (*1-883754-00-3*) Lawndale Art.
Rantala, Judy A. Laos: A Personal Portrait from the Mid-1970s. LC 93-38746. 254p. 1994. pap. 21.95 (*0-89950-939-8*) McFarland & Co.
Rantala, P. K. & Luonsi, A. A., eds. Anaerobic Treatment of Forest Industry Wastewaters: Proceedings of the First IAWPRC Symposium on Forest Industry Wastewaters, Tampere, Finland, 11-15 June 1984. (Illus.). 326p. 1985. pap. 59.00 (*0-08-032729-X*, Pub. by PPL UK) Elsevier.
Rantala, P. K., jt. auth. see Luonsi, A. A.
Rants-Rodriguez, Deanna, jt. auth. see Stringer, Gayle M.
Rantz, J. M., ed. Proceedings of the International Symposium of Nitrogen in Grapes & Wine. 323p. (C). 1991. lib. bdg. 50.00 (*0-9630711-0-6*) Am Soc Enology.
— Proceedings of the International Symposium on Table Grape Production. (Illus.). (C). 1994. pap. text ed. 40.00 (*0-9630711-1-4*) Am Soc Enology.
Rantz, Marilyn & Miller, Tari V. Quality Documentation for Long-Term Care: A Nursing Diagnosis Approach. 250p. 1993. ring bd. 115.00 (*0-8342-0384-7*, S75) Aspen Pub.
Ranucci, Ernest R. & Rollins, Wilma E. Brain Drain, 2 bks. 70p. (J). (gr. 6-12). 7.50 (*0-685-74212-1*); Bk. A, 1975. write for info. (*1-878669-10-9*, 4301); Bk. B, 1978. write for info. (*0-318-66932-3*, 4420) Crea Tea Assocs.
— Brain Drain, 2 bks., Bks. A & B. 70p. (J). (gr. 6-12). teacher ed write for info. (*1-878669-09-5*, 4301) Crea Tea Assocs.
Ranucci, Michael, jt. auth. see Cunningham, Janet.
***Ranuga, Thomas K.** The New South Africa & the Socialist Vision: Positions & Perspectives Toward a Post-Apartheid Society. 152p. (C). 1995. text ed. 39.95 (*0-391-03926-1*) Humanities.
Ranulf, Svend. The Jealousy of the Gods & Criminal Law at Athens: A Contribution to the Sociology of Moral Indignation, 2 vols. in 1. LC 73-14176. 486p. 1974. reprint ed. 27.95 (*0-405-05519-6*) Ayer.
Ranum, Orest. Artisans of Glory: Writers & Historical Thought in Seventeenth-Century France. LC 79-19248. (Illus.). xiii, 355p. 1980. 37.50 (*0-8078-1413-X*) U of NC Pr.
— The Fronde: A French Revolution, 1648-1652. LC 93-6816. 1993. 35.00 (*0-393-03550-6*) Norton.
Ranum, Orest, jt. auth. see Forster, Robert.
Ranum, Orest, jt. ed. see Forster, Robert.
Ranum, Orest A., ed. National Consciousness, History, & Political Culture in Early-Modern Europe. LC 74-6837. (Johns Hopkins Symposia in Comparative History Ser.: No. 5). (Illus.). 192p. reprint ed. pap. 54.80 (*0-8357-4328-4*, 2037128) Bks Demand.
Ranum, Orest A., jt. ed. see Forster, Robert.
Ranum, Patricia, tr. see Aries, Philippe.
Ranum, Patricia, tr. see Forster, Robert & Ranum, Orest.
Ranum, Patricia, tr. see Forster, Robert & Ranum, Orest A., eds.
Ranum, Patricia, tr. see Le Goff, Jacques.
Ranum, Patricia M., tr. see Braudel, Fernand.
Ranum, Patricia M., tr. see Forster, Robert & Ranum, Orest, eds.
Ranweiler, Robert, jt. auth. see Behrenfeld, William H.
Ranwez, Alain D. Jean-Paul Sartre's "Les Temps Modernes" LC 80-50077. 163p. 1980. 15.00 (*0-87875-191-2*) Whitston Pub.
Ranz, Charlotte A., jt. auth. see McLamb, Jess R.
***Ranzoni, Patricia.** Claiming. Hunting, Constance, ed. 65p. (Orig.). 1995. pap. 8.95 (*0-913006-59-9*) Puckerbrush.
Rao. Conditional Measures & Applications. (Pure & Applied Mathematics Ser.: Vol. 177). 424p. 1993. 150.00 (*0-8247-8884-2*) Dekker.
— Flowering Plants of Travencore. 502p. (C). 1976. reprint ed. 275.00 (*0-685-21738-8*, Pub. by Intl Bk Distr II) St Mut.
— The Role of the Cell Surface in Development, 2 vols., Set. 1987. 229.95 (*0-8493-4687-8*, QH601) CRC Pr.
— The Role of the Cell Surface in Development, 2 vols., Vol. II. 144p. 1987. 130.00 (*0-8493-4689-4*, QH601) CRC Pr.
Rao & Rizvi. Engineering Properties of Food. (Food Science & Technology Ser.: Vol. 19). 408p. 1986. 140.00 (*0-8247-7526-0*) Dekker.
Rao & Rizvi, eds. Engineering Properties of Food. 2nd expanded rev. ed. (Food Science & Technology Ser.: Vol. 63). 552p. 1995. 150.00 (*0-8247-8943-1*) Dekker.
Rao, jt. auth. see Schwartzberg.
Rao, A. Amruth. Personnel Management & Municipal Administration in India. 1985. 32.50 (*0-8364-1389-X*, Pub. by Ashish II) S Asia.
Rao, A. Amruth, jt. ed. see Rao, V. Bhaskara.
Rao, A. G. & Rao, T. V., eds. Fatigue & Fracture in Steel & Concrete Structures: Proceedings of the International Symposium, 19-21 December 1991, Madras, India, 2 vols. (Illus.). 1618p. (C). 1992. text ed. 210.00 (*90-5410-205-5*, Pub. by A A Balkema NE) Ashgate Pub Co.
Rao, A. K., jt. auth. see Naidu, D. S.
Rao, A. M., tr. see Vol, N. E. & Kagan, I. K.
Rao, A. N., et al. Journal of Plant Anatomy & Morphology. 1988. 150.00 (*0-317-62332-X*, Scientific) St Mut.
Rao, A. Narasimha, jt. auth. see Melkote, Rama S.
Rao, A. R. A Taxonomy for Texture Description & Identification. Jain, R. C., ed. (Perception Engineering Ser.). (Illus.). 208p. 1990. 44.00 (*0-387-97302-8*) Spr-Verlag.
Rao, A. R. & Shukla, Priti. Pollen Flora of the Gangetic Plain. (Indian Pollen Spore Flora Ser.: Vol. I). 140p. 1977. 15.00 (*0-88065-179-2*, Messers Today & Tomorrow) Scholarly Pubns.
Rao, A. Ramakrishna, ed. Comparative Perspectives on Indian Literature. 160p. (C). 1992. 25.00 (*81-85218-64-1*, Pub. by Prestige II) Advent Bks Div.
Rao, A. S. Modern Commercial Drafting. (C). 1989. 200.00 (*0-685-54204-1*) St Mut.
Rao, A. S., ed. Commentaries on Delhi Apartment Ownership Act, 1986: With Supplement. (C). 1989. 90.00 (*0-685-47808-4*) St Mut.
***Rao, Adapa R. & Sivaramkrishna, M., eds.** When East Meets West: Indian Thought in Anglo-Indian & Indo-English Fiction. (C). 1995. 20.00x (*81-207-1513-6*, Pub. by Sterling Plns Pvt II) S Asia.
Rao, Anthony. Cut & Make Animal Masks. (J). 1989. pap. 4.95 (*0-486-25199-3*) Dover.
— Dinosaur Coloring Book. (Illus.). (J). (gr. k-3). 1980. pap. 2.50 (*0-486-24022-3*) Dover.
Rao, Anthony, illus. The Cow in the Kitchen. LC 90-85905. 24p. (J). (ps-2). 1991. reprint ed. 8.95 (*1-878093-45-2*) Boyds Mills Pr.
— Nursery Rhymes. LC 90-85900. 32p. (J). (ps-1). 1991. reprint ed. 8.95 (*1-878093-24-X*) Boyds Mills Pr.
Rao, Aparna, jt. ed. see Casimir, Michael J.
Rao, Aruna, ed. Women's Studies International: Nairobi & Beyond. LC 90-48653. 376p. 1991. 35.00 (*1-55861-031-6*); pap. 15.95 (*1-55861-032-4*) Feminist Pr.
Rao, Aruna, et al, eds. Gender Analysis in Development Planning: A Case Book. LC 91-31013. (Library of Management for Development). (Illus.). 103p. (Orig.). 1991. teacher ed 10.95 (*0-931816-62-9*); pap. 15.95 (*0-931816-61-0*) Kumarian Pr.
Rao, Ashok. Capacity Management Training Aid. LC 82-72090. 39p. 1982. 35.00 (*0-935406-18-2*) Am Prod & Inventory.
Rao, B. Bhaskar. Metamorphic Petrology. 190p. (C). 1986. text ed. 70.00 (*90-6191-483-3*, Pub. by A A Balkema NE) Ashgate Pub Co.
— Metaporphic Petrology. (C). 1987. 18.50 (*81-204-0127-1*, Pub. by Oxford IBH II) S Asia.
Rao, B. Bhaskara, ed. Cointegration: Expository Essays for the Applied Economist. LC 94-5981. 1994. text ed. 75.00 (*0-312-12177-6*) St Martin.
Rao, B. Bhaskara, jt. auth. see Srivastava, V. K.
Rao, B. K., ed. Profitable Condition Monitoring. 330p. 1992. lib. bdg. 184.50 (*0-7923-2098-0*) Kluwer Ac.
Rao, B. L. Asymptotic Theory of Statistical Inference. LC 86-15735. (Probability & Mathematical Statistics Ser.). 464p. 1987. text ed. 127.00 (*0-471-84335-0*) Wiley.
***Rao, B. Narahari.** A Semiotic Reconstruction of Ryle's Critique of Cartesianism. LC 94-31008. (Quellen Und Studien Zur Philosophie: Bd. 38). xiv, 165p. (C). 1994. lib. bdg. 96.35 (*3-11-014156-6*) De Gruyter.
Rao, B. V. History of Europe, Fourteen-Fifty to Eighteen-Fifteen. 320p. (C). 1989. text ed. 30.00 (*81-207-0874-1*, Pub. by Sterling Pubs II) Apt Bks.
— World History. 466p. (C). 1984. text ed. 30.00 (*0-86590-808-7*, Pub. by Sterling Pubs II); pap. 15.95 (*0-86590-315-8*, Pub. by Sterling Pubs II) Apt Bks.
Rao, Balakrishna. Landscape Problem Management. LC 92-71121. 153p. 1992. pap. 39.95 (*0-929870-03-4*) Advanstar Commns.
Rao, Bhaskara K. Theories of Charges: A Study of Finitely Additive Measures. (Pure & Applied Mathematics Ser.). 1983. text ed. 134.00 (*0-12-095780-9*) Acad Pr.
Rao, Bindu R. C Plus Plus & the OOP Paradigm. 1992. text ed. 40.00 (*0-07-051140-3*) McGraw.
— Object-Oriented Databases: Technology, Applications, & Products. 1994. pap. text ed. 40.00 (*0-07-051279-5*) McGraw.
Rao, C. & Lahiri, D. Contributions to Statistics. LC 63-21723. 218.00 (*0-08-011026-6*, Pub. by Pergamon Repr UK) Franklin.
Rao, C. H. Agricultural Growth, Rural Poverty & Environmental Degradation in India. (Illus.). 288p. 1994. 23.00 (*0-19-563343-1*) OUP.
Rao, C. Hayavadana. Indian Caste System: A Study. (C). 1988. reprint ed. 11.50 (*81-206-0270-6*, Pub. by Asian Educ Servs II) S Asia.
Rao, C. M. Manohar Malgonkar & Portrait of the Hero in His Novels. 1993. text ed. 25.00 (*81-85047-11-1*, Pub. by Reliance Pub Hse II) Apt Bks.
Rao, C. M., tr. see Glazovskaya, M. A.
Rao, C. N. Advances in Solid State Chemistry: Proc of the Insa Golden Jubilee Symp. 428p. 1987. 85.00 (*9971-5-0137-6*) World Scientific Pub.
— Chemical & Structural Aspects of High Temperature Superconductors. 248p. (C). 1988. pap. 39.00 (*9971-5-0608-4*) World Scientific Pub.
— Chemical Approaches to the Synthesis of Inorganic Materials. LC 94-21800. 1995. text ed. 27.95 (*0-470-23431-8*) Wiley.
Rao, C. N., ed. Bismuth & Thallium Cuprate Superconductors: A Special Issue of the Journal Phase Transitions. 96p. 1989. pap. text ed. 165.00 (*0-677-25930-1*) Gordon & Breach.
— Chemistry of High-Temperature Superconductors. 400p. (C). 1991. text ed. 104.00 (*981-02-0805-7*) World Scientific Pub.
— Solid State Chemistry. LC 73-82705. (Illus.). 923p. reprint ed. pap. 180.00 (*0-7837-0918-8*, 2041223) Bks Demand.
***Rao, C. N. & Raveau, B.** Transition Metal Oxides. LC 95-10717. 1995. write for info. (*1-56081-647-3*) VCH Pubs.
Rao, C. N., jt. ed. see Agterberg, Frederik P.
Rao, C. N., jt. ed. see Edwards, P. P.
Rao, C. N., jt. auth. see Graziani, M.
Rao, C. N. R. & Mashelkar, R. A. Solid State Chemistry. Joshi, S. K., ed. LC 94-34672. (Twentieth Century Chemistry Ser.). 600p. 1995. text ed. 86.00 (*981-02-1808-7*) World Scientific Pub.
Rao, C. Nagaraja. Dr. S. Radhakrishnan: His Life & Work. 1986. 12.50 (*0-8364-2566-9*, Pub. by Mittal II) S Asia.
Rao, C. R. Essays on Econometrics & Planning. 1965. 146.00 (*0-08-011025-8*, Pub. by Pergamon Repr UK) Franklin.
Rao, C. R., ed. Computational Statistics. LC 93-7155. (Handbook of Statistics Ser.: Vol. 9). 1045p. 1993. 190.00 (*0-444-88096-8*, North Holland) Elsevier.
— Indian Response to African Literature. 1993. text ed. 15.95 (*81-85218-71-4*, Pub. by Prestige II) Advent Bks Div.
— Multivariate Analysis: Future Directions. LC 93-16230. (Series in Statistics & Probability: Vol. 5). 478p. 1993. 154.25 (*0-444-89687-2*, North Holland) Elsevier.
Rao, C. R. & Chakraborty, R., eds. Handbook of Statistical Methods in Biological & Medical Sciences. (Handbook of Statistics Ser.: No. 8). 500p. 1991. 120.00 (*0-444-88095-X*, North Holland) Elsevier.
Rao, C. R. & Kleffe, J. Estimation of Variance Components & Applications. (North Holland Series in Statistics & Probability: Vol. 3). 1988. 82.00 (*0-444-70023-4*) Elsevier.
Rao, C. R. & Rao, M. M., eds. Multivariate Statistics & Probability: Essays in Memory of Paruchuri R. Krishnaiah. 500p. 1989. text ed. 92.00 (*0-12-580205-6*) Acad Pr.
Rao, C. R., jt. ed. see Cuadras, C. M.
Rao, C. R., jt. ed. see Krishaiah, P. R.
Rao, C. R., jt. ed. see Krishnaiah, P. R.
Rao, C. R., jt. ed. see Patil, G. P.
Rao, C. Radhakrishna. Linear Statistical Inference & Its Applications. 2nd ed. LC 72-13093. (Probability & Mathematical Statistics Ser.). 625p. 1973. text ed. 134.95 (*0-471-70823-2*) Wiley.
Rao, C. Radhakrishna & Shanbhag, D. N. Choquet-Deny Type Functional Equations with Applications to Stochastic Models. LC 94-10080. (Series in Probability & Mathematical Statistics). 1994. text ed. 72.95 (*0-471-95104-8*) Wiley.
Rao, C. S. Environmental Pollution Control Engineering. 431p. 1992. text ed. 57.95 (*0-470-21763-4*) Halsted Pr.
— Environmental Pollution Control Engineering. (C). 1992. pap. 18.50 (*81-224-0301-8*, Pub. by Wiley Eastern II) S Asia.
Rao, D. Gopal. Population Education: A Guide to Curriculum & Teacher Education. xii, 136p. 1974. 6.75 (*0-88386-470-3*) S Asia.
Rao, D. N., et al, eds. Perspectives in Environmental Botany, Vol. 2. (Illus.). xiv, 325p. 1988. 69.00 (*1-55528-098-6*, Pub. by Today & Tomorrows P & P II) Scholarly Pubns.
Rao, D. Panduranga, ed. Dimensions of Rural Transportation. (C). 1989. 78.50 (*81-210-0235-4*, Pub. by Inter-India Pubns) S Asia.
***Rao, D. Ratnagiri.** Cultural Advancement of Orissa under the Gangas of Kalinga. (C). 1995. 34.00x (*81-85094-80-2*, Pub. by Punthi Pus II) S Asia.
Rao, D. V. & Vinay, Mudda. Regional Development. 1990. 20.00 (*81-7001-075-6*, Pub. by Chanakya II) S Asia.
Rao, Dandamudi V., et al, eds. Physics of Nuclear Medicine: Recent Advances: Proceedings of the AAPM 1983 Summer School Held at Farleigh Dickinson University, Madison, New Jersey, July 24-29, 1983. (American Association of Physicists in Medicine Symposium Ser.: No. 10). 570p. 1984. 60.00 (*0-88318-440-0*) Am Inst Physics.
Rao, Dandina H., jt. ed. see Gupta, Madan M.
Rao, Dileep. Development Finance Source Guide. 154p. 1993. pap. write for info. (*1-884147-01-1*) InterFinance.
— Fast Track Business Plans. 250p. 1993. pap. write for info. (*1-884147-02-X*) InterFinance.
— Find Financing Frustration-Free. 1993. pap. write for info. (*1-884147-03-8*) InterFinance.

R

— Smarter Business Finance. 298p. 1993. pap. write for info. (*1-884147-00-3*) InterFinance.

Rao, Doreen, intro. Choral Music for Children. annot. ed. 176p. (Orig.). (C). 1990. pap. 13.50 (*0-940796-80-5*, 1502) Music Ed Natl.

Rao, E. Nageswara, ed. John Keats: An Anthology of Recent Criticism. 1993. 30.00 (*81-85753-02-4*, Pub. by Pencraft International II) Advent Bks Div.

Rao, Eleonora. Strategies for Identity: The Fiction of Margaret Atwood. LC 93-14218. (Writing about Women Ser.: Vol. 9). 204p. (Orig.). 1994. pap. text ed. 31.95 (*0-8204-2216-9*) P Lang Pubs.

Rao, G. Gopal, jt. auth. see Skelton, Mary L.

Rao, G. Lakshmana. Brain Drain & Foreign Students. LC 78-10903. (Illus.). 1979. text ed. 32.50 (*0-312-09437-X*) St Martin.

Rao, G. N., intro. Communications Conference, 1990: Electronic Communications in the 1990's - A New Era. (Illus.). 246p. (Orig.). 1990. pap. 67.25 (*0-85825-507-3*) Accents Pubns.

Rao, G. P. Piecewise Constant Orthogonal Functions & Their Application to Systems & Control. (Lecture Notes in Control & Information Sciences Ser.: Vol. 55). 254p. 1983. pap. 32.00 (*0-387-12556-6*) Spr-Verlag.

Rao, G. P., jt. auth. see Saha, D. C.

Rao, G. P., jt. ed. see Sinha, Naresh K.

Rao, G. P., jt. auth. see Unbehauen, H.

Rao, G. Parthasardhy. Alankaratnakara of Sobhakaramitra: A Study. (C). 1992. text ed. 50.00 (*81-7099-406-3*, Pub. by Mittal II) S Asia.

Rao, G. Stayanarayan. The Telegu Chodas of Kanduru: History, Art & Architecture. 1987. 34.00 (*0-8364-2205-8*, New Era Bks) S Asia.

Rao, Gopal K. Multilevel Interconnection Technology. LC 93-20583. 224p. 1993. text ed. 55.00 (*0-07-051224-8*) McGraw.

Rao, H. P. The Psychology of Music. (Illus.). 80p. 1986. reprint ed. 15.00 (*0-8364-1765-8*, Pub. by Abhinav II) S Asia.

Rao, H. S., jt. ed. see Ghose, Ajoy K.

Rao, Hanumantha. Unstable Agriculture & Droughts. 155p. 1988. text ed. 25.00 (*0-7069-4041-5*, Pub. by Vikas II) S Asia.

Rao, Hemlata. Rural Energy Crisis: A Diagnostic Analysis. 1990. 32.50 (*81-7024-275-4*, Pub. by Ashish II) S Asia.

— Scheduled Castes & Tribes: Socio-Economic Upliftment Programmes. Babu, M. Devendra, ed. (Illus.). vi, 150p. (C). 1994. 16.00x (*81-7024-566-4*, Pub. by Ashish Pub Hse II) Nataraj Bks.

Rao, Hy. Teach Yourself. . . Windows NT. 1995. pap. 21.95 (*1-55828-269-6*) MIS Press.

Rao, J. S. Advanced Theory of Vibrations: Nonlinear Vibration, One-Dimensional Machine Members & Structures. LC 92-14502. 1992. text ed. 54.95 (*0-470-21861-4*) Halsted Pr.

— Turbomachine Blade Vibration. 445p. 1991. text ed. 64.95 (*0-470-21764-2*) Halsted Pr.

Rao, J. S., ed. see Indian Society of Theoretical & Applied Mechanics, 20th Congress, India, 1975.

Rao, Joe & Abel, Ken. Your Complete Guide to the Solar Eclipse of Jan. 4, 1992. (Illus.). 64p. (Orig.). 1991. pap. text ed. 4.95 (*0-944214-00-2*) ABELexpress.

***Rao, Josyula R.** Extensions of the UNITY Methodology: Compositionality, Fairness & Probability in Parallelism. LC 95-10413. (Lecture Notes in Computer Science: Vol. 908). 1995. write for info. (*0-387-59173-7*) Spr-Verlag.

Rao, K. B. Husband, Lover, Holy Man: An Intercultural Comedy. LC 92-9171. 184p. (Orig.). 1992. pap. 14.95 (*0-933662-98-X*) Intercult Pr.

Rao, K. Bhasker & Chowdhury, N. N. Clinical Gynecology. 360p. 1984. pap. text ed. 25.00 (*0-86131-471-9*, Pub. by Orient Longman Ltd II) Apt Bks.

Rao, K. Damodar. Novels of Ayi Kwei Armah. 1993. 15.95 (*81-85218-75-7*, Pub. by Prestige II) Advent Bks Div.

Rao, K. K., ed. Food Consumption & Planning. 1976. 208.00 (*0-08-016459-5*, Pub. by Pergamon Repr UK) Franklin.

Rao, K. K., jt. auth. see Hall, D. D.

Rao, K. L. Mahatma Gandhi & Comparative Religion. rev. ed. 1990. 15.00 (*81-208-0755-3*, Pub. by Motilal Banarsidass II) S Asia.

Rao, K. L., ed. Marketing Perspectives of Public Enterprises in Developing Countries. (ICPE Bks.). 220p. 1986. 20.00 (*92-9038-090-X*, Pub. by Intl Ctr Pub Ent XV) Kumarian Pr.

— State, Public Enterprise & the Marketplace. 1988. pap. 20.00 (*92-9038-091-8*, Pub. by Intl Ctr Pub Ent XV) Kumarian Pr.

***Rao, K. N.** Learn Vedic Astrology Without Tears. (C). 1995. 9.00x (*0-8364-2906-0*, Pub. by Ranjan Pubs II) S Asia.

— The Rotation & Lorentz Groups & Their Representations for Physicists. (C). 1988. 35.00 (*81-224-0056-6*, Pub. by Wiley Eastern II) S Asia.

Rao, K. N., ed. Textbook of Tuberculosis. 607p. 1981. 24.95 (*0-318-36372-0*) Asia Bk Corp.

Rao, K. N., jt. auth. see Bloomer, O. T.

Rao, K. Narahari & Weber, Alfons, eds. Spectroscopy of the Earth's Atmosphere & Interstellar Medium. (Illus.). 526p. 1992. text ed. 150.00 (*0-12-580645-0*) Acad Pr.

Rao, K. Narahari, jt. auth. see Guelachvili, Guy.

Rao, K. P. Deccan Megaliths. 175p. (C). 1988. 48.00 (*81-85067-07-4*, Pub. by Sundeep II) S Asia.

***Rao, K. R., ed.** Codes & Standards for Quality Engineering: Proceedings of the Pressure Vessels & Piping Conference, Minneapolis, MN, 11994. LC 94-71664. (PVP Ser.: vol. 285). 279p. 1994. pap. 60.00 (*0-7918-1358-4*) ASME.

***Rao, K. R. & Todd, J. A., eds.** Changing Priorities of Codes & Standards: Failure, Fatigue & Creep; Proceedings of the Pressure Vessels & Piping Conference, Minneapolis, MN, 1994. LC 94-71665. (PVP Ser.: Vol. 286). 175p. 1994. pap. 50.00 (*0-7918-1359-2*) ASME.

Rao, K. R., jt. auth. see Bapna, S. L.

Rao, K. R., jt. ed. see Deepak, Adarsh.

Rao, K. R., jt. auth. see Sailaja, P.

Rao, K. Raghavendra. Society, Culture & Population Policy in India. 1989. 19.50 (*81-202-0241-4*, Pub. by Ajanta II) S Asia.

Rao, K. Raghavendra, tr. see Bhyrappa, S. L.

Rao, K. Raghavendra, tr. see Bhyrappan, S. L.

Rao, K. Ramakrishna, ed. Charles Honorton & the Impoverished State of Skepticism: Essays on a Parapsychological Pioneer. (Illus.). 237p. 1994. lib. bdg. 39.95 (*0-7864-0003-X*) McFarland & Co.

— Cultivating Consciousness: Enhancing Human Potential, Wellness, & Healing. LC 92-43428. 248p. 1993. text ed. 55.00 (*0-275-94515-4*, C4515, Praeger Pubs) Greenwood.

Rao, K. Ramamohan. Perspectives of Archeology, Art & Culture in Early Andhra Desa. (C). 1992. text ed. 42.00 (*81-85689-01-6*, Pub. by Aditya Prakashan II) S Asia.

Rao, K. Ramamohan, ed. Discrete Transforms & Their Applications. LC 89-48054. 350p. 1990. reprint ed. 54.50 (*0-89464-442-4*) Krieger.

Rao, K. Ramamohan & Yip, P. Discrete Cosine Transform: Algorithms, Advantages, Applications. 490p. 1990. text ed. 59.95 (*0-12-580203-X*) Acad Pr.

Rao, K. Ramamohan, jt. auth. see Elliott, Douglas F.

Rao, K. S. & Rasjeswari, V. Quantum Theory of Angular Momentum: Selected Topics. xxiii, 315p. 1993. 69.00 (*0-387-56308-3*) Spr-Verlag.

Rao, K. S., jt. auth. see Van Dijck, Pitou.

Rao, K. Srinivasa. Public Sector Banks in India & the Productivity Question. (C). 1989. 34.00 (*81-7024-252-5*, Pub. by Ashish II) S Asia.

Rao, K. Sudha & Chowdhary, N. K. Catch Them Young: Vocationalisation for Higher Employability. viii, 120p. (C). 1992. 22.50 (*81-207-1398-2*, Pub. by Sterling Pubs II) Apt Bks.

Rao, K. U. A Dictionary of Bharatnatyam. (Illus.). 92p. 1980. 16.95 (*0-318-36307-0*) Asia Bk Corp.

Rao, K. Uma. Kuchipudi Bharatam or Kuchipudi Dance: A South Indian Classical Tradition. (C). 1992. 28.50 (*81-7030-291-9*) S Asia.

Rao, K. V. Research Methodology in Commerce & Management. 1992. 30.00 (*81-207-1422-9*, Pub. by Sterling Pubs II) Apt Bks.

Rao, K. V., jt. auth. see Halli, Shivalingappa S.

Rao, K. Vaninadha, jt. auth. see Wicks, Jerry W.

Rao, K. Venkateswara. Leprosy in Rural India. (Illus.). xii, 500p. 1992. 34.00 (*81-85445-43-5*, Pub. by Manak Pubns Pvt Ltd) Nataraj Bks.

Rao, Krishna. A Dictionary of Bharata Natya. (Illus.). 100p. 1980. text ed. 15.95 (*0-86131-155-8*, Pub. by Orient Longman Ltd II) Apt Bks.

Rao, Krishna P., ed. Weather Satellites: Systems, Data, & Environmental Applications. (Illus.). 518p. 1990. 95.00 (*0-933876-87-4*) Am Meteorological.

Rao, Krisna, et al. MRI & CT of the Spine. (Illus.). 608p. 1994. 135.00 (*0-683-07133-5*) Williams & Wilkins.

***Rao, Linda R.** Eagles Flying High. LC 94-28705. (Eagle Wings Ser.). 288p. (Orig.). 1995. pap. 8.99 (*0-8007-5548-0*) Revell.

— Ordeal at Iron Mountain. LC 95-14311. (Eagle Wings Ser.). 1995. pap. write for info. (*0-8007-5568-5*) Revell.

Rao, M. Integrated System for Intelligent Control. (Lecture Notes in Control & Information Sciences Ser.: Vol. 167). (Illus.). 144p. 1992. pap. 36.00 (*0-387-54913-7*) Spr-Verlag.

Rao, M., ed. Social Movements in India: Peasant & Backward Classes Movements, Vol. 1. 1980. 17.50 (*0-8364-0199-9*) S Asia.

Rao, M. & Stetkaer, H. An Invitation to Complex Analysis. 252p. (C). 1991. text ed. 37.00 (*981-02-0375-6*); pap. text ed. 21.00 (*981-02-0376-4*) World Scientific Pub.

Rao, M. B. Integrated Rural Development & Areas Planning in India. (C). 1991. text ed. 24.00 (*81-7041-499-7*, Pub. by Anmol II) S Asia.

Rao, M. Gangadhar, et al. Organizational Behaviour: Text & Cases. 584p. 1990. text ed. 40.00 (*81-220-0040-1*, Pub. by Konark Pubs Pvt Ltd II) Advent Bks Div.

Rao, M. Govinda, et al. Sales Taxation in Madhya Pradesh. 1990. text ed. 22.50 (*0-7069-5327-4*, Pub. by Vikas II) S Asia.

Rao, M. Kodanda. Cultural & Structural Dimensions of Family: A Study of Jalari Fisherman. 1990. 20.00 (*81-7022-270-2*, Pub. by Concept II) S Asia.

Rao, M. M. Probability Theory with Applications. (Probability & Mathematical Statistics Ser.). (C). 1984. text ed. 105.00 (*0-12-580480-6*) Acad Pr.

Rao, M. M., ed. Real & Stochastic Analysis. 362p. (C). 1986. lib. bdg. 44.95 (*0-471-82969-2*) Wiley.

Rao, M. M. & Ren, Z. D. Theory of Orlicz Spaces. (Pure & Applied Mathematics Ser.: Vol. 146). 472p. 1991. 180.00 (*0-8247-8478-2*) Dekker.

Rao, M. M., jt. ed. see Rao, C. R.

Rao, M. R. Flowering Plants of Travancore. 502p. (C). 1976. text ed. 275.00 (*0-89771-647-7*, Pub. by Intl Bk Distr II) St Mut.

Rao, M. S. Social Movements & Social Transformation. (C). 1987. reprint ed. 27.50 (*0-8364-2133-7*, Pub. by Manohar II) S Asia.

— Studies in Migration: Internal & International Migration in India. 410p. 1986. 34.00 (*81-85054-08-8*, Pub. by Manohar II) S Asia.

Rao, M. S., ed. Social Movements in India: Tribal, Sectarian & Women's Movements, Vol. 2. 1981. 17.50 (*0-8364-0787-3*, Pub. by Manohar II) S Asia.

Rao, M. S., jt. ed. see Frankel, Francine R.

Rao, M. S., jt. ed. see Khare, R. S.

Rao, M. S., et al, eds. A Reader in Urban Sociology. 425p. (C). 1991. 40.00 (*0-86311-151-3*, Pub. by Orient Longman Ltd II) Apt Bks.

Rao, M. S. A., jt. ed. see Frankel, Francine R.

Rao, Malathi. Khajuraho & Other Poems. 1976. 8.00 (*0-89253-821-X*); 4.80 (*0-89253-822-8*) Ind-US Inc.

Rao, Mangesh, jt. auth. see Watsa.

Rao, Maya, ed. see Lockridge, Frances & Lockridge, Richard.

Rao, Ming & Qiu, Haiming. Process Control Engineering: A Textbook for Chemical, Mechanical & Electrical Engineers. 1993. text ed. 60.00 (*2-88124-628-1*) Gordon & Breach.

***Rao, Ming, et al.** Modeling & Advanced Control for Process Industries: Applications to Paper Making Processes. LC 94-26235. (Advances in Industrial Control Ser.). 1994. 56.00 (*0-387-19881-4*) Spr-Verlag.

Rao, Mohini. Teach Yourself Hindi. (Language Bks.). 207p. (C). 1989. pap. 7.95 (*0-87052-831-9*) Hippocrene Bks.

Rao, Mukunda. The Mahatma: A Novel. 1993. pap. 7.95 (*0-86311-369-9*, Pub. by Disha Bks II) Apt Bks.

Rao, Myers & Rao, Raja. Images of India in English Fiction: Studies on Kipling. (C). 1991. 28.00 (*81-7018-609-9*, Pub. by BR Pub II) S Asia.

Rao, N. B. Family Planning in India. 132p. 1976. 7.95 (*0-318-36837-4*) Asia Bk Corp.

Rao, N. N. Elements of Engineering Electromagnetics. 4th ed. 1993. text ed. 74.00 (*0-13-948746-8*) P-H.

Rao, N. P. Terrorism, Violence & Human Destruction: Causes, Effects, & Control Measures. (C). 1992. 15.00 (*81-7041-568-3*, Pub. by Anmol II) S Asia.

Rao, N. R., tr. see Vyasa.

Rao, N. S. Biofertilizers in Agriculture & Forestry. (C). 1993. reprint ed. 32.00 (*81-204-0791-1*, Pub. by Oxford IBH II) S Asia.

— Soil Microorganisms & Plant Growth. 350p. 1995. text ed. 29.95 (*1-886106-18-5*) Science Pubs.

Rao, N. Subba. Fisheries Development & Management in India, 1785-1986: A Bibliography. 1989. 44.00 (*81-85119-60-0*, Pub. by Northern Bk Ctr II) S Asia.

Rao, N. Venkat, tr. see Amurskii, G. I., et al.

Rao, Nannapaneni N. Elements of Engineering Electromagnetics. 2nd ed. (Illus.). 544p. 1986. text ed. 60.00 (*0-13-264193-3*) P-H.

— Elements of Engineering Electromagnetics. 3rd ed. 656p. 1990. text ed. 74.00 (*0-13-251604-7*) P-H.

Rao, Narasinga. Handbook of Kanarese Proverbs. 1988. reprint ed. 5.50 (*81-206-0317-6*, Pub. by Asian Educ Servs II) S Asia.

Rao, Natti S. Computer Aided Design of Plasticating Screws: Programs in Fortran & Basic. 134p. (C). 1986. text ed. 47.50 (*1-56990-082-5*) Hanser-Gardner.

— Design Formulas for Plastics Engineers. 135p. (C). 1991. text ed. 27.95 (*1-56990-084-1*) Hanser-Gardner.

— Designing Machines & Dies for Polymer Processing with Computer Programs. 208p. (C). 1981. text ed. 47.50 (*1-56990-083-3*) Hanser-Gardner.

— Designing Machines & Dies for Polymer Processing with Computer Programs: Fortran & Basic. (Illus.). 208p. 1981. 44.00 (*0-686-48155-0*, 1907) T-C Pubns CA.

***Rao, Nirmala.** The Making & Unmaking of Local Self-Government. 180p. 1995. text ed. 59.95 (*1-85521-635-3*, Pub. by Dartmth Pub UK) Ashgate Pub Co.

Rao, P. B., ed. Textbook of Diseases of Nose, Throat & Ear. 340p. (C). 1990. 90.00 (*0-685-57271-4*, Pub. by Interprint II) St Mut.

***Rao, P. Chandrasekhara.** The Indian Constitution & International Law. 248p. (C). 1995. lib. bdg. 86.50 (*0-7923-2739-X*, Pub. by M Nijhoff) Kluwer Ac.

Rao, P. D., ed. Focus on Alaska's Coals '86 - Proceedings of the Conference. (MIRL Report Ser.: No. 72). 396p. 1987. 20.00 (*0-911043-00-4*) UAKF Min Ind Res Lab.

Rao, P. D., jt. auth. see Lin, H. K.

Rao, P. D., jt. auth. see Walsh, Daniel E.

Rao, P. Dharma, et al. Characterization & Washability Studies of Raw Coal from the Little Tonzona Field, Alaska. (MIRL Report Ser.: No. 88). 120p. (Orig.). 1991. pap. 7.00 (*0-911043-11-X*) UAKF Min Ind Res Lab.

Rao, P. K. Professional Crime in India. 256p. 1983. text ed. 27.50 (*0-685-14724-X*) Coronet Bks.

Rao, P. M., tr. see Akramkhodzhaev, A. M., et al.

Rao, P. M., tr. see McHedlidze, G. A.

Rao, P. N. Fundamentals of Indian Philosophy. 205p. 1981. 16.95 (*0-318-37020-4*) Asia Bk Corp.

Rao, P. R. Ancient & Medieval History of Andhra Pradesh. 1993. 15.95 (*81-207-1495-4*, Pub. by Sterling Pubs II) Apt Bks.

— History of Modern Andhra Pradesh. 4th enl. rev. ed. 250p. 1989. text ed. 27.50 (*81-207-0878-4*, Pub. by Sterling Pubs II) Apt Bks.

— Indian Heritage & Culture. 104p. 1989. text ed. 12.95 (*81-207-0929-2*, Pub. by Sterling Pubs II) Apt Bks.

***Rao, P. Raghunadha.** History of Modern Andhra Pradesh. (C). 1993. pap. 7.50 (*81-207-1547-0*, Pub. by Sterling Plns Pvt II) S Asia.

Rao, P. Subba. Human Resource Management: Environmental Influence. (C). 1989. 44.00 (*81-85076-59-6*, Pub. by Chugh Pubns II) S Asia.

Rao, P. Syamasundar. Tricuspid Atresia. 2nd ed. (Illus.). 480p. 1992. 98.00 (*0-87993-518-9*) Futura Pub.

Rao, P. Syamasundar, ed. Transcatheter Therapy in Pediatric Cardiology. 528p. 1993. text ed. 132.00 (*0-471-58827-X*) Wiley.

Rao, P. V., jt. auth. see Sood, P.

***Rao, P. V. Narasimah.** India & the Asian-Pacific: Forging a New Relationship. (Singapore Lecture Ser.). 46p. 1994. pap. text ed. 11.95 (*981-3016-96-5*, Pub. by Inst SE Asian Studies SI) Ashgate Pub Co.

Rao, Peggy L. & Mahoney, Jean. Japanese Accents in Western Interiors. LC 87-82851. (Illus.). 168p. 1990. 24.95 (*0-87040-762-7*) Japan Pubns USA.

— Nature on View: Homes & Gardens Inspired by Japan. (Illus.). 192p. 1993. 29.95 (*0-8348-0299-6*) Weatherhill.

Rao, Peggy L., jt. auth. see Mahoney, Jean.

Rao, Prakasa. Urbanization in India: Spatial Dimensions. 1983. 24.00 (*0-8364-1033-5*) S Asia.

Rao, Prakasa, jt. ed. see Basawa, Ishwar V.

Rao, R., jt. ed. see Pappu, S. S.

Rao, R. G. Bhrigu Nandi Nadi. (C). 1991. reprint ed. text ed. 24.00 (*0-8364-2878-1*, Pub. by Ranjan Pubs II) S Asia.

— Your Destiny in Thumb. (Illus.). 1991. write for info. (*0-318-68201-X*, Pub. by Ranjan Pubs II) S Asia.

Rao, R. P., ed. Luminescence: Phenomena, Materials & Devices. (Solid State Physics, Luminescence Ser.). 448p. (C). 1991. text ed. 145.00 (*1-56072-013-1*) Nova Sci Pubs.

Rao, R. R. & Razi, B. A. A Synoptic Flora of Mysore District. (International Bioscience Monographs: No. 7). 694p. 1981. 65.00 (*0-88065-180-6*, Messers Today & Tomorrow) Scholarly Pubns.

Rao, R. R., jt. auth. see Baishya, A. J.

Rao, R. R., jt. auth. see Baishya, A. K.

Rao, R. R., jt. auth. see Haridasan, K.

Rao, R. R., jt. auth. see Jain, S. K.

Rao, R. Rama. India's Energy Scene: Options for the Future. (Illus.). 120p. 1988. text ed. 20.00 (*81-7027-122-3*, Pub. by Radiant Pubs II) S Asia.

Rao, R. S. Flora of Goa, Div, Daman, Dadra & Nagarhaveli, 1. (C). 1987. text ed. 40.00 (*0-685-22098-2*, Scientific) St Mut.

— Flora of Goa, Div, Daman, Dadra & Nagarhaveli, 2. (C). 1987. text ed. 50.00 (*0-685-22099-0*, Scientific) St Mut.

Rao, R. V. Rural Industrialisation in India. 1987. reprint ed. 10.50 (*0-8364-2258-9*, Pub. by Concept II) S Asia.

Rao, Raghavendra. Poems. 8.00 (*0-89253-722-1*); 4.00 (*0-89253-723-X*) Ind-US Inc.

Rao, Raj B. & Hope, A. D., eds. Conditioning Monitoring & Diagnostic Engineering Management 91: Proceedings from the 3rd International Congress, Southampton, 2-4 July 1991. (Illus.). 560p. 1991. 174.00 (*0-7503-0154-6*) IOP Pub.

Rao, Raja. The Chessmaster & His Moves. (C). 1988. 45.00 (*0-8364-2365-8*, Pub. by Vision) S Asia.

— Comrade Kirillov. (Orient Paperbacks Ser.). 132p. 1976. pap. 2.75 (*0-86578-080-3*) Ind-US Inc.

— Kanthapura. LC 63-18637. 1967. pap. 10.95 (*0-8112-0168-6*, NDP224) New Directions.

— The Serpent & the Rope. LC 85-13628. 408p. 1986. 22.50 (*0-87951-220-2*) Overlook Pr.

— The Serpent & the Rope. 408p. 1988. Tusk. pap. 9.95 (*0-87951-243-1*) Overlook Pr.

— The Serpent & the Rope. 408p. 1968. reprint ed. pap. 6.00 (*0-88253-766-0*) Ind-US Inc.

Rao, Raja, jt. auth. see Rao, Myers.

Rao, Rama K. AIDS (Disease) in Asia, Africa & the U. S. A Bibliography. (Social Science Resource Guides Ser.: No. 7). 27p. (C). 1991. 8.95 (*0-9628998-7-9*) Ramdil.

— An Annotated & Classified Bibliography on Parenting: Current Literature 1980-1990. (Social Science Resource Guides Ser.: No. 1). 31p. (C). 1991. pap. text ed. 9.95 (*0-9628998-0-1*) Ramdil.

— Asian Minorities in American Schools, Colleges & Universities: A Classified Bibliography. (Social Science Resource Guides Ser.: No. 5). 19p. (C). 1991. 6.95 (*0-9628998-4-4*) Ramdil.

— Breast Cancer: Current Literature for Nonmedical People: A Bibliography. (Social Science Resource Guides Ser.: No. 8). 30p. (C). 1992. pap. text ed. 9.95 (*0-9628998-6-0*) Ramdil.

— Current Literature on Job Hunting: An Annotated & Classified Bibliography. (Social Science Resource Guides Ser.: No. 2). 35p. (C). 1991. pap. text ed. 8.95 (*0-9628998-1-X*) Ramdil.

— Current Literature on Starting & Staying Successful in Business: An Annotated & Classified Bibliography. (Social Science Resource Guides Ser.: No. 3). 30p. (C). 1991. pap. text ed. 8.95 (*0-9628998-2-8*) Ramdil.

— Elderly: Abuse & Issues: Bibliography (1985-Present) (Social Science Resource Guides Ser.: No. 9). 24p. (C). 1993. 7.50 (*1-883215-04-8*) Ramdil.

— Family Violence-Alcohol & Drug Abuse: Correlation: Current Literature '85-'94. (RAMDIL Bibliographies Ser.: No. 8). 11p. (C). 1994. 8.00 (*1-883215-08-0*) Ramdil.

— Home Schooling: A Bibliography Current Literature, '85 - Present. (Bibliographies Ser.: No. 2). 20p. 1992. 6.50 (*0-9628998-9-5*) Ramdil.

— Homelessness & Drug Abuse: A Correlation: A Bibliography. (Social Science Resource Guides Ser.: No. 6). 19p. (C). 1991. 6.95 (*0-9628998-5-2*) Ramdil.

— Illiteracy - a Global Problem: A Classified Bibliography. (Social Science Resource Guides Ser.: No. 4). 27p. (C). 1991. pap. text ed. 7.95 (*0-9628998-3-6*) Ramdil.

— Incontinence, Urinary: Bibliography, 1985-1992. (Bibliographies Ser.: No. 5). 12p. 1993. 3.50 (*1-883215-05-6*) Ramdil.

— Literacy in the United States: A Bibliography. (Bibliographies Ser.: No. 1). 20p. (C). 1992. 6.50 (*0-9628998-8-7*) Ramdil.

— Rape & Alcoholism: A Bibliography. (RAMDIL Bibliographies Ser.: No. 7). 6p. Date not set. 3.50 (*1-883215-07-2*) Ramdil.

— Social, Economic & Biological Aspects of Global Warming: Bibliography. (Bibliographies Ser.: No. 3). 15p. (C). 1992. 6.00 (*1-883215-02-1*) Ramdil.

Rao, Ramakrishna. India's Borders: Ecology & Security Perspectives. (C). 1991. 24.00 (*81-85515-02-6*, Pub. by Promilla II) Nataraj Bks.

R

Rao, Ramesh K. Financial Management: Concepts & Applications. 2nd ed. (Illus.). 880p. (C). 1992. text ed. write for info. (*0-02-398241-1*); student ed, pap. write for info. (*0-02-398248-9*) Macmillan.
— Financial Management: Concepts & Applications. 3rd ed. LC 94-22216. 1994. write for info. (*0-534-21930-6*) S-W Pub.
— Fundamentals of Financial Management. 1200p. (C). 1989. text ed. write for info. (*0-02-398151-2*); student ed write for info. (*0-02-398157-1*) Macmillan.
Rao, Ranga R., jt. auth. see Bhattacharya, R. N.
Rao, Ratna N. Social Organization in an Indian Slum. 1990. 37.50 (*81-7099-186-2*, Pub. by Mittal II) S Asia.
Rao, Rolla S. Flora of Goa, Diu, Daman, Dadra & Nagarhaveli, Vol. 1. (Flora of India Ser.: No. 2). 198p. 1985. text ed. 35.00 (*0-945345-52-6*, Pub. by Mahendra Pal Singh II) Lubrecht & Cramer.
— Flora of Goa, Diu, Daman, Dadra & Nagarhaveli, Vol. 2. (Flora of India Ser.: No. 2). 546p. 1986. text ed. 35.00 (*0-945345-53-4*, Pub. by Mahendra Pal Singh II) Lubrecht & Cramer.
Rao, S. Interoperability in Broadband Networks. LC 94-75948. 458p. 1994. 109.00 (*90-5199-160-6*) IOS Press.
Rao, S., ed. Interworking in Broadband Networks. LC 93-78257. 500p. 1993. 115.00 (*90-5199-135-5*, Pub. by IOS Pr NE) IOS Press.
Rao, S. Balachandra & Shantha, C. K. Numerical Analysis with Programs in BASIC, FORTRAN & PASCAL. 1993. pap. 20.00 (*0-86311-370-2*, Pub. by Universities Pr II) Apt Bks.
Rao, S. K. Encyclopaedia of Indian Medicine, Vol. 1: Historical Perspectives. (C). 1985. 31.00 (*0-8364-2322-4*, Pub. by Popular Prakashan II) S Asia.
— Encyclopaedia of Indian Medicine, Vol. 2: Basic Concepts. (C). 1987. 47.50 (*0-8364-2323-2*, Pub. by Popular Prakashan II) S Asia.
— Encyclopaedia of Indian Medicine, Vol. 3: Clinical Examination & Diagnostic Methods. (C). 1987. 42.50 (*0-8364-2324-0*, Pub. by Popular Prakashan II) S Asia.
Rao, S. K., jt. ed. see Reddy, J. M.
Rao, S. Kishan. Contributions to Post-Keynesian Economics: A Resume & Critique. 77p. 1987. text ed. 15.95 (*81-207-0703-6*, Pub. by Sterling Pubs II) Apt Bks.
Rao, S. Kishen, jt. ed. see Reddy, J. Mahendra.
Rao, S. Krishna. Planning for Stability, Equity & Employment. 1992. 25.00 (*81-207-1401-6*, Pub. by Sterling Pubs II) Apt Bks.
Rao, S. P. & Sinha, V. M., eds. Professionalism in Public Administration. 1990. text ed. 27.50 (*0-685-31755-2*, Pub. by Associated Pub Hse II) Advent Bks Div.
Rao, S. R. Dawn & Devolution of the Indus Civilization. (C). 1991. 120.00 (*81-85179-74-3*, Pub. by Aditya Prakashan II) S Asia.
— Electrical Gadgets & Their Repairs. 290p. 1990. 48.00 (*81-209-0683-7*, Pub. by Pitambar Pub II) St Mut.
Rao, S. R., ed. Coal Preparation & Use--A World Review: International Coal Preparation Congress, New Delhi, India, 9th, 1982. 259p. (C). 1982. text ed. 160.00 (*90-6191-256-3*, Pub. by A A Balkema NE) Ashgate Pub Co.
Rao, S. R., jt. ed. see Dobby, G. S.
Rao, S. Ramachandra. Xanthates & Related Compounds. LC 77-141626. 512p. reprint ed. pap. 146.00 (*0-685-16367-9*, 2027130) Bks Demand.
Rao, S. V., ed. Women's Studies in India: A Directory of Research Institutions. (Illus.). viii, 123p. 1993. 13.00 (*81-7024-569-9*, Pub. by Ashish Pub Hse II) Nataraj Bks.
***Rao, S. V., et al.** Women at Work in India Vol. 2: An Annotated Bibliography. 324p. 1994. 25.00 (*0-8039-9173-8*) Sage.
Rao, S. Vasudeva. Status of Women & Children in Slums: A Study of Hyderabad City. (C). 1992. 15.00 (*81-7013-094-8*, Pub. by Navarang II) S Asia.
Rao, S. Venogopal, ed. Perspectives in Criminology. 250p. 1988. text ed. 40.00 (*0-7069-4000-8*, Pub. by Vikas II) S Asia.
Rao, S. Venugopal. Criminal Justice: Problems & Perspectives in India. xiv, 310p. 1991. 35.00 (*81-220-0233-1*) Advent Bks Div.
Rao, Salem S., ed. Acid Stress & Aquatic Microbial Interactions. 192p. 1989. 156.00 (*0-8493-5168-5*, QR105) CRC Pr.
Rao, Shanta R. Children of God. 165p. 1992. pap. 10.00 (*0-86311-190-4*, Pub. by Orient Longman Ltd II) Apt Bks.
— The Mahabharata. (Illus.). 150p. 1992. pap. 6.95 (*0-86311-282-X*, Pub. by Orient Longman Ltd II) Apt Bks.
— Seethu: A Novel. 160p. 1980. pap. text ed. 3.95 (*0-86131-178-7*, Pub. by Orient Longman Ltd II) Apt Bks.
Rao, Singiresu S. The Finite Element Method in Engineering. 2nd ed. (Illus.). 650p. 1989. text ed. 87.00 (*0-08-033420-2*, Pub. by PPL UK); pap. text ed. 33.00 (*0-08-033419-9*, Pub. by PPL UK) Elsevier.
— Mechanical Vibrations. 2nd ed. (Illus.). 624p. (C). 1990. text ed. 72.25 (*0-201-50156-2*) Addison-Wesley.
— Mechanical Vibrations. 3rd ed. LC 93-3311. (C). 1995. text ed. 70.95 (*0-201-52686-7*) Addison-Wesley.
— Reliability Based Design. 1992. text ed. 60.00 (*0-07-051192-6*) McGraw.
Rao, Singiresu S., ed. The Finite Element Method in Engineering. LC 80-40817. 400p. 1981. text ed. 96.00 (*0-08-025467-5*, Pergamon Pr); pap. text ed. 30.95 (*0-08-025466-7*, Pergamon Pr) Elsevier.
Rao, Singiresu S., jt. auth. see San Diego State University Staff.
Rao, Stephen M., ed. Neurobehavioral Aspects of Multiple Sclerosis. (Illus.). 288p. 1990. 39.95 (*0-19-505400-8*) OUP.
Rao, Subba. Jurisprudence & Legal Theory. (C). 1991. 40.00 (*0-89771-798-8*, Pub. by Eastern Book II) St Mut.
— Shastra evam Vidhi ke Sidhant (Jurisprudence & Legal Theory in Hindi) 377p. 1981. 52.50 (*0-317-54630-9*) St Mut.
Rao, Sudha V. Education & Rural Development. 320p. (C). 1986. text ed. 25.00 (*0-8039-9491-5*) Sage.
Rao, T. A., jt. auth. see Banerjee, L. K.
Rao, T. Ananda. Compendium of Foliar Sclerids in Angiosperms: Morphology & Taxonomy. (C). 1991. 62.00 (*81-224-0067-1*, Pub. by Wiley Eastern II) S Asia.
Rao, T. K., et al, eds. Genotoxicology of N-Nitroso Compounds. LC 83-23716. (Topics in Chemical Mutagenesis Ser.: Vol. 1). 288p. 1984. 75.00 (*0-306-41445-7*, Plenum Pr) Plenum.
***Rao, T. Nageswara.** Inviolable Air: Canadian Poetic-Modernism in Perspective. (C). 1994. 20.00x (*81-7018-779-6*, Pub. by BR Pub II) S Asia.
Rao, T. V. Economic Efficiency of the Organizational Decisions of the Firm. (Illus.). 240p. 1989. pap. 64.00 (*0-387-51570-4*, 3423) Spr-Verlag.
— Readings in Human Resource Development. (C). 1991. text ed. 29.50 (*81-204-0585-4*, Pub. by Oxford IBH II) S Asia.
Rao, T. V. & Bhatt, Anil. Adult Education for Social Change. 1980. 15.00 (*0-685-04704-0*, Pub. by Manohar II) S Asia.
Rao, T. V. & Pereira, D. F. Recent Experiences in Human Resources Development. (C). 1986. 18.50 (*81-204-0120-4*, Pub. by Oxford IBH II) S Asia.
Rao, T. V., jt. ed. see Rao, A. G.
Rao, U. R., ed. see Gandhi, M. K.
Rao, U. S. Panorama of Indian Dances. (Raga Nrtya Ser.: No. 6). (C). 1993. 68.50 (*81-7030-330-3*) S Asia.
Rao, Usha. Women in a Developing Society, India. 1984. 14.00 (*0-8364-1057-2*, Pub. by Ashish II) S Asia.
Rao, V. Bhaskara. Public Administration in India. (C). 1989. 31.00 (*81-202-0233-3*, Pub. by Ajanta II) S Asia.
Rao, V. Bhaskara & Rao, A. Amruth, eds. Nehru & Administration. (C). 1989. 34.00 (*81-202-0231-7*, Pub. by Ajanta II) S Asia.
Rao, V. K. Organisational & Financial Management of Religious Institutions. (C). 1992. 34.00 (*0-8364-2807-2*, Pub. by Deep) S Asia.
Rao, V. Krishna, jt. auth. see Jatkar, S. D.
Rao, V. M. & Aziz, Abdul. Poverty Alleviation in India: Programmes & Action. (C). 1989. 30.00 (*81-7024-255-X*, Pub. by Ashish II) S Asia.
Rao, V. R. Selected Doctrines from Indian Philosophy. (C). 1987. 21.50 (*81-7099-000-9*, Pub. by Mittal II) S Asia.
Rao, V. S. & Narayana, P. S. Management Concepts & Thoughts. 2nd rev. ed. 556p. 1990. text ed. 45.00 (*81-220-0154-8*, Pub. by Konark Pubs Pvt Ltd II) Advent Bks Div.
Rao, V. V. Graham Greene's Comic Vision. 1990. text ed. 27.95 (*81-85047-59-6*, Pub. by Reliance Pub Hse II) Apt Bks.
Rao, V. V., jt. auth. see Ramaswamy, G. S.
Rao, Valluru. C Plus Plus Neural Networks & Fuzzy Logic. 1993. pap. 29.95 (*1-55828-298-X*) MIS Press.
Rao, Vasant, et al. Switch-Level Timing Simulation of MOS VLSI Circuits. (C). 1988. lib. bdg. 73.50 (*0-89838-302-1*) Kluwer Ac.
Rao, Velcheru N. & Roghair, Gene H., trs. Siva's Warriors: The Basava Purana of Palkuriki Somanatha. 325p. 1990. text ed. 55.00 (*0-691-05591-2*) Princeton U Pr.
Rao, Velcheru N., et al. Symbols of Substance: Court & State in Nayaka Period Tamilnadu. (Illus.). 388p. 1993. 39.95 (*0-19-563021-1*) OUP.
Rao, Vijay M., et al. MRI & CT Atlas of Correlative Imaging in Otolaryngology. 383p. 1992. boxed 125.00 (*0-8385-6526-3*, A6526-6) Appleton & Lange.
Rao, Vimala. Banaras, Nineteen Seventy-Four Poems. 1976. 8.00 (*0-89253-827-9*); 4.80 (*0-89253-828-7*) Ind-US Inc.
***Rao, Vithala R.** New Science of Marketing: State-of-the-Art Tools for Anticipating & Tracking the Market. 1995. 42.50 (*1-55738-539-4*) Probus Pub Co.
Rao, Vithala R., jt. auth. see McLaughlin, Edward W.
Rao, Y. A. The Paper Industry in India. (C). 1989. 34.00 (*81-204-0441-6*, Pub. by Oxford IBH II) S Asia.
Rao, Y. Kris, jt. ed. see Kudryk, Val.
Rao, Y. V. Communication & Development: A Study of Two Indian Villages. LC 66-21940. 152p. reprint ed. pap. 43.40 (*0-317-42280-4*, 2055898) Bks Demand.
Raouf, A. & Ahmad, S. I., eds. Flexible Manufacturing: Recent Developments in FMS, Robotics CAD-CAM, CIM. (Manufacturing Research & Technology Ser.: Vol. 1). 256p. 1985. 97.50 (*0-444-42504-7*) Elsevier.
***Raouf, A. & Ben-Daya, M.** Flexible Manufacturing Systems: Recent Developments. LC 94-48220. (Manufacturing Research & Technology Ser.: Vol. 23). 1995. write for info. (*0-444-89798-4*) Elsevier.
Raouf, A., jt. auth. see Dhillon, B. S.
Raoul, Bill. Stock Scenery Construction Handbook. 250p. 1991. pap. 12.95 (*0-911747-23-0*) Broadway Pr.
Raoul, Gordon, ed. Puerto Rico: A Guide to the Island of Boriguen. 1976. lib. bdg. 75.00 (*0-8490-1375-5*) Gordon Pr.
Raoul, Valerie. Distinctly Narcissistic: Diary Fiction in Quebec. (Theory - Culture Ser.). 336p. 1993. 55.00 (*0-8020-2882-9*) U of Toronto Pr.
Raoult, Didier. Antimicrobial Agents & Intracellular Pathogens. LC 93-2668. 1993. 189.95 (*0-8493-4924-9*, RM409) CRC Pr.
Raoult, J. C., et al, eds. CAAP '92. (Lecture Notes in Computer Science Ser.: Vol. 581). 361p. 1992. pap. 52.00 (*0-387-55251-0*) Spr-Verlag.
Rap, Le. Bonjour, Mr. McGrue. (Nursery Rhymes Ser.). 15p. (J). (gr. k-2). 1991. pap. text ed. 23.00 (*1-56843-040-X*); pap. text ed. 4.50 (*1-56843-087-6*) BGR Pub.
— Little Betty Blue. (Nursery Rhymes Ser.). 15p. (J). (gr. k-2). 1991. pap. text ed. 23.00 (*1-56843-042-6*); pap. text ed. 4.50 (*1-56843-089-2*) BGR Pub.
— A Lost Little Pig. (Nursery Rhymes Ser.). 15p. (J). (gr. k-2). 1991. pap. text ed. 23.00 (*1-56843-038-8*); pap. text ed. 4.50 (*1-56843-085-X*) BGR Pub.
— The Secret of the Sheep. (Nursery Rhymes Ser.). 15p. (J). (gr. k-2). 1991. pap. text ed. 23.00 (*1-56843-037-X*); pap. text ed. 4.50 (*1-56843-084-1*) BGR Pub.
— Sherman Be Nimble. (Nursery Rhymes Ser.). 15p. (J). (gr. k-2). 1991. pap. text ed. 23.00 (*1-56843-044-2*); pap. text ed. 4.50 (*1-56843-091-4*) BGR Pub.
— Who's in the Shoe? (Nursery Rhymes Ser.). 15p. (J). (gr. k-2). 1991. pap. text ed. 23.00 (*1-56843-041-8*); pap. text ed. 4.50 (*1-56843-088-4*) BGR Pub.
Rapaccini, L. Parlo Italiano. (Monnier Ser.). 27.95 (*88-00-85275-0*) Schoenhof.
Rapacki, Lyle J. Satanism: The Not So New Problem. (Illus.). 65p. (Orig.). 1988. pap. 10.00 (*0-9621597-0-0*) Crossroads Ministries.
Rapaczynski, Andrzej. Nature & Politics: Liberalism in the Philosophies of Hobbes, Locke, & Rousseau. LC 87-5451. 312p. (C). 1987. pap. 14.95 (*0-8014-9606-3*) Cornell U Pr.
Rapaczynski, Andrzej, jt. auth. see Frydman, Roman.
Rapahel, Sally J. & Abadie, M. J. Finding Love. 1988. pap. 3.95 (*0-515-09796-9*) Jove Pubns.
Rapakko, A. Base Company Taxation. 272p. 1990. 83.00 (*90-6544-431-9*) Kluwer Law Tax Pubs.
Rapalje, Stewart. A Treatise on Contempt Including Civil & Criminal Contempts of Judicial Tribunals, Justices of the Peace, Legislative Bodies, Municipal Boards, Committees, Notaries, Commissioners, Referees & Other Officers Exercising Judicial & Quasi-judicial Functions: With Practice & Forms. xliv, 273p. 1981. reprint ed. lib. bdg. 32.50 (*0-8377-1030-8*) Rothman.
Rapanos, George A. In Search of the Hidden Treasure: The Pearl of Great Worth. LC 92-75844. (Spiritual Autobiography & Poetry & Wisdom Tales Ser.). 203p. 1994. pap. 8.95 (*0-9634591-0-4*) Lifetime Bks.
— The Tao of Tribute Money: The Truth Lies Beyond the Paradox. LC 92-75845. (Philosophy-Metaphysics-Religion-Mysticism Ser.). 233p. 1994. pap. 9.95 (*0-9634591-1-2*) Lifetime Bks.
Rapant, Larry. Children at the Beach: Poems. 64p. (Orig.). Date not set. pap. text ed. 9.95 (*1-55605-225-1*) Wyndhall Pr.
— Collecting the Empties: Poems. LC 92-20423. 64p. 1992. pap. 12.95 (*0-7734-9519-3*) E Mellen.
— Flesh Colors. Schultz, Patrica, ed. LC 89-12171. (Lewiston Poetry Ser.: Vol. 9). 64p. 1989. pap. 12.95 (*0-88946-898-2*) E Mellen.
Rapaport, et al. Early Child Care in Israel. (International Monographs on Early Child Care). 212p. 1976. text ed. 86.00 (*0-677-05270-7*) Gordon & Breach.
Rapaport, Alan M. & Sheftell, Fred D., eds. Headache: A Clinician's Guide to Diagnosis, Pathophysiology & Treatment Strategies. LC 93-17688. 288p. 1993. 50.00 (*1-56262-009-6*) PMA Pub Corp.
Rapaport, Anatol, ed. Game Theory As Theory of Conflict Resolution. LC 73-91434. (Theory & Decision Library: No. 2). 289p. 1974. lib. bdg. 89.00 (*90-277-0424-4*) Kluwer Ac.
Rapaport, David. The History of the Concept of Association of Ideas. LC 73-89438. 120p. 1974. text ed. 27.50 (*0-8236-2330-0*) Intl Univs Pr.
— Structure of Psychoanalytic Theory: A Systematizing Attempt. (Psychological Issues Monograph: No. 6, Vol. 2, No. 2). 158p. (Orig.). 1967. text ed. 26.00 (*0-8236-6180-6*) Intl Univs Pr.
Rapaport, David, tr. see Hartmann, Heinz.
Rapaport, David, jt. auth. see Shakow, David.
Rapaport, David, et al. Diagnostic Psychological Testing. LC 68-16993. 562p. 1968. text ed. 65.00 (*0-8236-1260-0*) Intl Univs Pr.
Rapaport, Diane S. How to Make & Sell Your Own Record. 3rd rev. ed. Fluegelman, Andrew, ed. LC 87-82953. (Illus.). 183p. 1988. reprint ed. pap. 14.95 (*0-685-12102-X*) Jerome Headlands.
— How to Make & Sell Your Own Recording: A Complete Guide for Independent Labels. 4th ed. LC 92-26110. (Jerome Headlands Press Bk.). Orig. Title: How to Make & Sell Your Own Record. 200p. 1992. pap. 29.95 (*0-13-402314-5*) P-H.
Rapaport, E., tr. Hungarian Problem Book 1: Based on the Eotvos Competition. LC 63-16149. (New Mathematical Library: No. 11). 111p. 1963. pap. 10.00 (*0-88385-611-5*, 63-16149) Math Assn.
Rapaport, Elizabeth, ed. see Mill, John Stuart.
Rapaport, Elliot. Cardiology Update, 1983: Reviews for Physicians. 360p. 1983. 47.50 (*0-318-32521-7*) Elsevier.
Rapaport, Elliot, ed. Cardiology & Co-Existing Disease. (Illus.). 352p. 1994. 85.00 (*0-443-08887-X*) Churchill.
— Cardiology Update: Reviews for Physicians. 1,990th ed. 400p. 1990. 85.00 (*0-444-01517-5*) Elsevier.
— Early Interventions in Acute Myocardial Infarction. (Developments in Cardiovascular Medicine Ser.). (C). 1989. lib. bdg. 121.00 (*0-7923-0175-7*) Kluwer Ac.
Rapaport, Felix T., jt. ed. see Waltzer, Wayne C.
Rapaport, Herman. Between the Sign & the Gaze. (Illus.). 312p. 1993. 41.50 (*0-8014-2898-X*); pap. 16.95 (*0-8014-8133-3*) Cornell U Pr.
— Heidegger & Derrida: Reflections on Time & Language. LC 88-4748. x, 293p. 1991. pap. 12.95 (*0-8032-8927-8*) U of Nebr Pr.
— Milton & the Postmodern. LC 82-21935. (Illus.). xiv, 270p. 1983. 25.00 (*0-8032-3862-2*) U of Nebr Pr.
Rapaport, J., et al, eds. Neutron-Nucleus Collisions. A Probe of Nuclear Structure: Burr Oak State Park, Ohio, 1984. LC 84-73216. (AIP Conference Proceedings Ser.: No. 124). 548p. 1985. lib. bdg. 52.00 (*0-88318-323-4*) Am Inst Physics.
Rapaport, Jacques, et al. Small States & Territories: Status & Problems. LC 72-140128. (UNITAR Studies). 1971. 65.95 (*0-405-02237-9*) Ayer.
Rapaport, Lowell, jt. auth. see Berkel, Bob.
Rapaport, Matthew. Computer Mediated Communications: Bulletin Boards, Computer Conferencing, Electronic Mail & Information Retrieval. 373p. 1991. pap. text ed. 39.95 (*0-471-51642-2*) Wiley.
Rapaport, Samuel I. Introduction to Hematology. 2nd ed. LC 65-10036. (Illus.). 624p. 1987. text ed. 29.95 (*0-397-50838-7*, Lippincott Medical) Lippincott.
Rapaport, Stanley, ed. see Fenichel, Otto.
Rapaport, Valery. Arkhangel Skoye: Country Estate of the 18th & 19th Centuries. 148p. 1984. 104.00 (*0-317-61209-3*, Pub. by Collets UK) Pro-Am Music.
Rapapport, Felix T., jt. auth. see Sheil, A. G.
Raparaz, M. C. & Oosterveld-Egas. Legal Dictionary Dutch - Spanish: With Spanish - Dutch Index. 371p. (DUT & SPA.). 1992. 295.00 (*0-8288-9435-3*) Fr & Eur.
Rapatz, F. & Roll, F. Diccionario Enciclopedico Tecnico: Materiales Siderurgicos. 260p. (SPA.). 1968. 49.95 (*0-8288-6624-4*, S-33724) Fr & Eur.
Rapcewicz, K., jt. ed. see Paszkiewicz, T.
Rape & Abuse Crisis Center Staff. Annie. rev. ed. (Illus.). 21p. (J). (ps up). 1985. pap. text ed. 2.50 (*0-914633-03-1*) Rape Abuse Crisis.
— Gente Bandera Roja y Gente Bandera Verde: Red Flag Green Flag People. Peterson, Francisca E., tr. (Illus.). 36p. (SPA.). (J). (gr. k-5). 1987. student ed 4.00 (*0-914633-13-9*) Rape Abuse Crisis.
— Red Flag Green Flag People. (Illus.). 28p. (J). (gr. k up). 1985. student ed, pap. 4.00 (*0-914633-10-4*) Rape Abuse Crisis.
Rapee, Erno. Encyclopedia of Music for Pictures. LC 77-124034. (Literature of Cinema Ser.). 1978. reprint ed. 27.95 (*0-405-01634-4*) Ayer.
— Motion Picture Moods for Pianists & Organists, a Rapid Reference Collection of Selected Pieces. LC 70-124035. (Literature of Cinema, Ser. 1). 1979. reprint ed. 48.95 (*0-405-01635-2*) Ayer.
Rapee, Ronald M. & Barlow, David H., eds. Chronic Anxiety: Generalized Anxiety Disorder & Mixed Anxiety-Depression. LC 91-24737. 214p. 1991. lib. bdg. 26.95 (*0-89862-771-0*) Guilford Pr.
Rapee, Ronald M., jt. auth. see Barlow, David H.
Rapela, C. W., jt. auth. see Harmon, R. S.
Rapela, C. W., jt. ed. see Kay, S. M.
Raper, Arthur F. Preface to Peasantry: A Tale of Two Black Belt Counties. LC 72-137183. (Poverty U. S. A. Historical Record Ser.). 1971. reprint ed. 33.95 (*0-405-03121-1*) Ayer.
— Tenants of the Almighty. LC 76-137184. (Poverty U. S. A. Historical Record Ser.). 1971. reprint ed. 30.95 (*0-405-03122-X*) Ayer.
— Tragedy of Lynching. LC 72-90191. (Mass Violence in America Ser.). 1969. reprint ed. 19.95 (*0-405-01334-5*) Ayer.
— Tragedy of Lynching. LC 69-14943. (Criminology, Law Enforcement, & Social Problems Ser.: No. 25). 1969. reprint ed. 16.00 (*0-87585-025-1*) Patterson Smith.
— The Tragedy of Lynching. LC 69-16568. (Illus.). 499p. 1969. reprint ed. text ed. 35.00 (*0-8371-1145-5*, RAL&, Greenwood Pr) Greenwood.
Raper, Bill & Raper, June. Sail to Freedom: A Handbook for Extended Cruising. 96p. (C). 1939. text ed. 59.00 (*0-906754-91-7*, Pub. by Fernhurst Bks UK) St Mut.
Raper, C., jt. auth. see Rand, M. J.
Raper, Horace W. William W. Holden: North Carolina's Political Enigma. LC 84-2353. (James Sprunt Studies in History & Political Science: Vol. 59). xvi, 376p. 1985. 35.00 (*0-8078-5060-8*) U of NC Pr.
Raper, Jonathan, ed. Three-Dimensional Applications in G. I. S. 260p. 1989. 75.00 (*0-85066-776-3*) Taylor & Francis.
***Raper, Julius R.** From the Sunken Garden: The Fiction of Ellen Glasgow, 1916-1945. fac. ed. LC 79-16703. (Southern Literary Studies). 228p. 1980. reprint ed. pap. 65.00 (*0-7837-7817-1*, 2047573) Bks Demand.
— Narcissus from Rubble: Competing Models of Character in Contemporary British & American Fiction. LC 91-32604. 200p. (C). 1992. text ed. 30.00 (*0-8071-1712-9*) La State U Pr.
Raper, Julius R., ed. Ellen Glasgow's Reasonable Doubts: A Collection of Her Writings. LC 87-32491. (Southern Literary Studies). xix, 262p. 1988. text ed. 35.00 (*0-8071-1412-X*) La State U Pr.
Raper, Julius R., et al, eds. Lawrence Durrell: Comprehending the Whole. 224p. 1995. 39.95 (*0-8262-0982-3*) U of Mo Pr.
Raper, June. The Beaufort Scale Cook Book: Boat Cuisine for All Weathers. (Illus.). 96p. 1989. pap. 12.95 (*0-906754-43-7*) TAB Bks.
Raper, June, jt. auth. see Raper, Bill.
Raper, Kenneth B. & Rahn, Ann W. The Dictyostelids. LC 83-43089. (Illus.). 448p. 1984. 95.00 (*0-691-08345-2*) Princeton U Pr.
Raper, Richard, comp. Consolidated Index to the Oxford History of England. (Oxford History of England Ser.: Vol. 16). 632p. 1991. 56.00 (*0-19-821786-2*) OUP.
Rapf, Joanna E. & Green, Gary L. Buster Keaton: A Bio-Bibliography. LC 94-21062. (Popular Culture Bio-Bibliographies Ser.). 272p. 1995. text ed. 55.00 (*0-313-25148-7*, Greenwood Pr) Greenwood.
Rapgay, Lobsang. The Tibetan Book of Healing. 1995. pap. 14.95 (*1-878423-21-5*) Passage Pr.

Raph, Alan. The Double Valve Bass Trombone A Method. (Illus.). 64p. 1949. pap. 10.95 (*0-8258-0190-7*, 0-4808) Fischer Inc NY.
Raph, Alan, jt. auth. see Watrous, Bill.
Raph, Theodore, ed. The American Song Treasury: One Hundred Favorites. 416p. 1986. reprint ed. pap. 12.95 (*0-486-25222-1*) Dover.
***Raphael.** Ancient Egypt: Drawing History. (Illus.). 1995. pap. (*0-590-48082-0*) Scholastic Inc.
— Ancient Greece: Drawing History. (Illus.). 1995. pap. (*0-590-22729-7*) Scholastic Inc.
— Ancient Rome: Drawing History. (Illus.). 1995. pap. (*0-590-25090-6*) Scholastic Inc.
— Book of the Stars. reprint ed. spiral bd. 9.35 (*0-7873-0706-8*) Mokelumne.
— Drawings of Raphael. Longstreet, Stephen, ed. (Master Draughtsman Ser.). (Illus.). (Orig.). 1962. 10.95 (*0-87505-028-X*); pap. 4.95 (*0-87505-181-2*) Borden.
— GRE, Psychology. 1994. pap. 15.00 (*0-671-87462-4*, Arco Test) P-H Gen Ref & Trav.
— The Guide to Astrology, Vol. 1. reprint ed. spiral bd. 8.25 (*0-7873-0705-X*) Mokelumne.
— The Key to Astrology. reprint ed. spiral bd. 4.40 (*0-7873-0704-1*) Mokelumne.
— Pathway of Fire: Initiation to the Kabbalah. (Illus.). 96p. (Orig.). 1993. pap. 10.00 (*0-87728-771-6*) Weiser.
— The Pathway of Non-Duality (Advaitavada) An Approach to Some Key-Points of Gaudapada's Asparsavada & Samkara's Advaita Vedanta by Means of a Series of Questions Answered by an Asparsin. xi, 88p. 1992. 10.95 (*1-881338-19-3*) Nataraj Bks.
— Pocahontas: Princess of the River Tribes. 1995. pap. (*0-590-44372-0*) Scholastic Inc.
— Proudhon Marx Picasso. (C). 1979. pap. 18.50 (*0-85315-549-6*, Pub. by Lawrence & Wishart UK) Humanities.
— Raphael: Tables of Houses. 9.95 (*0-685-38474-8*) Wehman.
— Raphael's Astro Ephemeris (Any Year) pap. 9.95 (*0-685-22085-0*) Wehman.
— Raphael's Guide to Astrology - Containing a Complete System of Genethliacal Astrology. 132p. 1991. pap. 15.00 (*0-89540-189-4*, SB-189, Sun Bks) Sun Pub.
— Raphael's Horary Astrology; By Which Every Question Relating to the Future May Be Answered. 4th ed. reprint ed. spiral bd. 4.40 (*0-7873-0703-3*) Mokelumne.
— Raphael's Key to Astrology. 118p. 1991. pap. 12.00 (*0-89540-142-8*, SB-142, Sun Bks) Sun Pub.
— Raphael's Medical Astrology. 88p. 1991. reprint ed. pap. 10.00 (*0-89540-180-0*, SB-180, Sun Bks) Sun Pub.
— Raphael's Mundane Astrology. 80p. 1994. pap. 7.00 (*0-89540-231-9*, SB-231, Sun Bks) Sun Pub.
— Self & Non-Self: The Drigdrisyaviveka Attributed to Sankara. 140p. 1990. 35.00 (*0-7103-0377-7*, A4515, Pub. by Kegan Paul Intl UK) Routledge Chapman & Hall.
— Tat Tvam Asi - That Thou Art: The Path of Fire According to Asparsa-Yoga. xiii, 122p. 1992. 12.95 (*1-881338-20-7*) Nataraj Bks.
Raphael, A. Cheirosophy (the Hand) A Scientific Treatise on Palmistry. reprint ed. spiral bd. 7.70 (*0-7873-0707-6*) Mokelumne.
***Raphael, Adam.** Ultimate Risk: The Inside Story of the Lloyd's Catastrophe. LC 95-11797. 1995. 21.00 (*1-56858-056-8*) FWEW.
Raphael, Alan. Criminal Procedure. 508p. (C). 1993. 46.00 (*1-879581-09-4*) Lupus Pubns.
— Criminal Procedure. rev. ed. 542p. (C). 1995. ring bd. 46.50 (*1-879581-20-5*) Lupus Pubns.
Raphael, Alan J., jt. auth. see Reichenberg, Norman.
Raphael, Albert. Earthology, Humanity Characterized. reprint ed. spiral bd. 6.60 (*0-7873-0708-4*) Mokelumne.
Raphael, Alice. Things That Are: Poems. 1969. 4.95 (*0-8079-0155-5*); pap. 1.95 (*0-8079-0156-3*) October.
Raphael, Antoine A. Concern, No. 3: Harmony & Contrast. 216p. (Orig.). 1992. text ed. 11.99 (*0-9631764-0-4*); pap. text ed. 9.99 (*0-9631764-1-2*) A A Raphael.
— Le Drame Haitien. rev. ed. 200p. (FRE.). (C). 1992. 24.95 (*0-9631764-2-0*); pap. 19.95 (*0-9631764-3-9*) A A Raphael.
— Fateful Encounters. 2nd ed. 142p. (YA). 1991. 9.05 (*0-9631764-7-1*); text ed. 11.95 (*0-9631764-8-X*); pap. text ed. 8.00 (*0-9631764-9-8*) A A Raphael.
Raphael, B., jt. ed. see Wilson, J. P.
Raphael, Beverly. The Anatomy of Bereavement. LC 94-66571. 454p. 1994. pap. 35.00 (*1-56821-270-4*) Aronson.
Raphael, Bishop. Anglican-Orthodox Intercommunion. pap. 0.25 (*0-89981-004-7*) Eastern Orthodox.
Raphael, Carolyn B. The Writing Reader. 432p. (C). 1986. pap. write for info. (*0-02-398280-2*) Macmillan.
Raphael, Chaim. A Feast of History: The Drama of Passover Through the Ages: With a New Translation of the Haggadah for Use at the Seder. LC 93-4770. 250p. 1993. reprint ed. 35.00 (*0-910250-26-X*) Bnai Brith Intl.
— Memoirs of a Special Case. rev. ed. LC 62-9548. 208p. 1985. reprint ed. 12.95 (*0-940646-16-1*); reprint ed. pap. 7.95 (*0-940646-17-X*) Rossel Bks.
— Minyan: Ten Jewish Lives in Twenty Centuries of History. enl. ed. Simon, Joseph, ed. LC 92-14078. (Illus.). 128p. 1992. 27.50 (*0-934710-28-7*) J Simon.
— The Sephardi Story: A Celebration of Jewish History. 1991. text ed. 27.00 (*0-85303-247-5*, Pub. by Vallentine Mitchell UK); pap. text ed. 15.00 (*0-85303-251-3*, Pub. by Vallentine Mitchell UK) Intl Spec Bk.
Raphael, Chaim, intro. The Jewish Manual: Or, Practical Information in Jewish & Modern Cookery with a Collection of Valuable Recipes & Hints Relating to the Toilette (Edited by a Lady) LC 83-2405. 288p. 1983. reprint ed. 22.00 (*0-911389-01-6*); reprint ed. pap. 12.95 (*0-911389-00-8*) NightinGale Res.
Raphael, Chester M., ed. see Reich, Wilhelm.

Raphael, D. D. Moral Philosophy. 2nd ed. 160p. (Orig.). 1994. pap. 11.95 (*0-19-289246-0*) OUP.
— Problems of Political Philosophy. 2nd enl. rev. ed. LC 90-4249. 240p. (C). 1990. pap. 17.50 (*0-391-03685-8*) Humanities.
Raphael, D. D., intro. British Moralists, 1650-1800, 2 vols. 1991. reprint ed. Vol. I, Hobbes-Gay. write for info. (*0-318-68108-0*); reprint ed. Vol. II, Hume-Bentham. write for info. (*0-318-68109-9*); reprint ed. Vol. I, Hobbes-Gay. write for info. (*0-318-68110-2*); reprint ed. Vol. II, Hume-Bentham. write for info. (*0-318-68111-0*) Hackett Pub.
— British Moralists, 1650-1800, 2 vols., Set. LC 90-85423. 1991. reprint ed. lib. bdg. 67.50 (*0-87220-121-X*); reprint ed. pap. text ed. 25.00 (*0-87220-120-1*) Hackett Pub.
Raphael, Dan. Polymerge. 24p. (Orig.). 1979. pap. text ed. 4.00 (*0-686-35895-3*) Skydog OR.
— Zone du Jour. 28p. (Orig.). 1981. pap. 5.50 (*0-937013-00-5*) Potes Poets.
Raphael, Dana, ed. Being Female: Reproduction, Power, & Change. (World Anthropology Ser.). xvi, 294p. 1975. 26.75 (*90-279-7599-X*) Mouton.
Raphael, Dana & Davis, Flora. Only Mothers Know: Patterns of Infant Feeding in Traditional Cultures. LC 84-15742. (Contributions in Women's Studies: No. 54). (Illus.). xvii, 159p. 1985. text ed. 45.00 (*0-313-24541-X*, RBR/, Greenwood Pr) Greenwood.
Raphael, David. The Alhambra Decree. LC 88-71589. 360p. (C). 1988. 18.00 (*0-9620772-0-8*) Carmi Hse Pr.
— Cavalier of Malaga. 190p. 1989. 15.00 (*0-9620772-1-6*) Carmi Hse Pr.
— El Decreto de la Alhambra: Novela Historica Sobre la Expulsion de los Judios de Espana en 1492. Santacruz, Daniel, tr. 357p. (SPA.). 1992. 25.00 (*0-9620772-4-0*); pap. 15.00 (*0-9620772-5-9*) Carmi Hse Pr.
Raphael, David D. Paradox of Tragedy. LC 77-128293. (Essay Index Reprint Ser.). 1977. 18.95 (*0-8369-2021-X*) Ayer.
Raphael, David T., intro. The Expulsion Fourteen Ninety-Two Chronicles: An Anthology of Medieval Chronicles Relating to the Expulsion of the Jews from Spain & Portugal. LC 91-76641. 222p. 1992. 35.00 (*0-9620772-3-2*) Carmi Hse Pr.
Raphael, Edwin. The Complete Book of Dreams. 344p. (Orig.). 1995. pap. 11.95 (*0-572-01714-6*, Pub. by Foulsham UK) Atrium Pubs.
***Raphael, Elaine & Bolognese, Don.** Daniel Boone, Frontier Hero. LC 95-8465. (Drawing America Ser.). (J). 1996. write for info. (*0-590-47900-8*) Scholastic Inc.
— Pocahontas, Princess of the River Tribes. LC 92-41990. (J). 1993. 12.95 (*0-590-44371-2*) Scholastic Inc.
— Sacajawea: The Journey West. LC 93-49002. (Drawing America Ser.). (J). 1994. 12.95 (*0-590-47898-2*) Scholastic Inc.
— The Story of the First Thanksgiving. (J). 1992. 3.95 (*0-590-44374-7*, Cartwheel) Scholastic Inc.
Raphael, Elaine, jt. auth. see Bolognese, Don.
Raphael, Frederic. France: The Four Seasons. 1994. 29.95 (*1-55859-869-3*) Abbeville Pr.
Raphael, Frederic, tr. see Aeschylus.
Raphael, Frederick. Darling: An Original Screenplay, Directed by Richard Lester. Garrett, George P. et al, eds. LC 71-135273. (Film Scripts Ser.). 1989. pap. text ed. 19.95 (*0-89197-719-8*) Irvington.
Raphael, Harold J. & Olsson, David L. Management of the Packaging Function. LC 76-55109. (American Management Associations. Management Briefing Ser.). 38p. reprint ed. pap. 25.00 (*0-317-11091-8*, 2051305) Bks Demand.
Raphael, Harold J., jt. auth. see Olsson, David L.
Raphael, Jesse, jt. auth. see Fox, Ivan.
Raphael, Jesse S. The Uniform Commercial Code Simplified. LC 67-15469. 416p. reprint ed. pap. 118.60 (*0-317-09564-1*, 2012370) Bks Demand.
Raphael, Lawrence J., jt. ed. see Bell-Berti, Fredericka.
Raphael, Lawrence J., et al, eds. Language & Cognition: Essays in Honor of Arthur J. Bronstein. LC 83-22987. (Cognition & Language Ser.). 306p. 1984. 70.00 (*0-306-41433-3*, Plenum Pr) Plenum.
Raphael, Lev. Dancing on Tisha B'av. (Stonewall Inn Editions Ser.). 240p. 1991. pap. 8.95 (*0-312-06326-1*) St Martin.
— Winter Eyes. 256p. 1993. 8.95 (*0-312-10576-2*, Stonewall Inn) St Martin.
Raphael, Lev, jt. auth. see Kaufman, Gershen.
Raphael, Marc L. Abba Hillel Silver: A Profile in American Judaism. LC 89-7581. 282p. 1989. 49.50 (*0-8419-1059-6*) Holmes & Meier.
— A History of the United Jewish Appeal, 1939-1982. LC 82-3327. (Brown Judaic Studies). (C). 1982. pap. 14.50 (*0-89130-575-0*, 140034) Scholars Pr GA.
— Jews & Judaism in a Midwestern Community: Columbus, Ohio, 1840-1975. (Illus.). 296p. 1979. 10.00 (*0-318-00876-9*) Ohio Hist Soc.
— Understanding American Jewish Philanthropy. 25.00 (*0-87068-689-5*) Ktav.
Raphael, Marc L., ed. Approaches to Modern Judaism, Vol. II. (Brown Judaic Studies: No. 56). 128p. (C). 1985. 20.95 (*0-89130-793-1*, 14 00 56); pap. 17.95 (*0-89130-794-X*) Scholars Pr GA.
— Approaches to Modern Judaism. (Brown Judaic Studies). 1983. pap. 16.00 (*0-89130-647-1*, 14 00 49) Scholars Pr GA.
Raphael, Max. The Demands of Art: With an Appendix, Toward an Empirical Theory of Art. LC 65-10431. (Bollingen Ser.: No. 78). (Illus.). 293p. reprint ed. pap. 83.60 (*0-317-10221-4*, 2051182) Bks Demand.

Raphael, Morris. The Battle in the Bayou Country. (Illus.). 199p. (J). (gr. 5-12). 1976. 12.95 (*0-9608866-0-5*) M Raphael.
— A Gunboat Named Diana: And Other Exciting Stories of Civil War Battles Which Raged in South Louisiana. (Illus.). 216p. 1994. 19.95 (*0-9608866-9-9*) M Raphael.
— Halo for a Devil. 120p. 1989. 14.95 (*0-9608866-6-4*) M Raphael.
— How Do You Know When You're in Acadiana. (Illus.). 32p. (Orig.). (J). (gr. 5 up). 1984. pap. 3.95 (*0-9608866-3-X*) M Raphael.
— The Loup-Garou of Cote Gelee. (Illus.). 48p. (J). (gr. 3-9). 1990. 12.95 (*0-9608866-7-2*) M Raphael.
— Maria: Goddess of the Teche. (Illus.). 48p. (J). (gr. 4-9). 1991. 13.95 (*0-9608866-8-0*) M Raphael.
— Murder on the Teche Queen. LC 86-82822. 128p. 1987. 12.95 (*0-9608866-5-6*) M Raphael.
— Mystic Bayou. LC 85-81338. 88p. 1985. 9.95 (*0-9608866-4-8*) M Raphael.
— Weeks Hall: The Master of the Shadows. LC 81-90439. (Illus.). 207p. (J). (gr. 5-12). 1981. 14.95 (*0-9608866-1-3*) M Raphael.
— The Weeks Hall Tapes. LC 83-91286. 90p. (Orig.). 1983. pap. 7.95 (*0-9608866-2-1*) M Raphael.
Raphael, Neil & Raphael, Ray. Comic Cops. 182p. (Orig.). (J). (gr. 4-8). 1992. pap. 6.95 (*1-881102-13-0*) Real Bks.
Raphael, Ray. Cash Crop: An American Dream. LC 85-8376. (Illus.). 179p. (Orig.). (C). 1985. pap. 8.00 (*0-934203-03-2*) Ridge Times Pr.
— An Everyday History of Somewhere: Being the True Story of Indians, Deer, Homesteaders, Potatoes, Loggers, Trees, Fishermen, Salmon, & Other Living Things in the Backwoods of Northern California. LC 92-8470. (Illus.). 192p. 1992. reprint ed. pap. 15.95 (*1-881102-25-4*) Real Bks.
— Little White Father: Redick McKee on the California Frontier. LC 93-8515. 1993. pap. write for info. (*1-883254-00-0*) Humboldt Cnty.
— The Men from the Boys: Rites of Passage in Male America. LC 88-17369. xvii, 228p. 1988. reprint ed. 25.00 (*0-8032-3888-6*); reprint ed. pap. 8.95 (*0-8032-8937-5*) U of Nebr Pr.
— Tree Talk: The People & Politics of Timber. LC 81-2835. (Illus.). 287p. (Orig.). 1981. pap. 14.95 (*0-933280-10-6*) Island Pr.
Raphael, Ray, jt. auth. see Raphael, Neil.
Raphael, Sally J. & Proctor, Pam. Sally: Unconventional Success. (Illus.). 264p. 1991. mass mkt. 4.99 (*0-312-92522-0*) St Martin.
Raphael, Sandra. The Oak Spring Garden Library, Vol. 2: An Oak Spring Pomon. 300p. (C). 1991. text ed. 60.00 (*0-300-04936-6*) Yale U Pr.
— An Oak Spring Sylva. (Oak Spring Garden Library: Vol. 1). 160p. 1989. text ed. 45.00 (*0-300-04652-9*) Yale U Pr.
Raphael, Sandra, jt. auth. see Blunt, Wilfrid.
Raphael, Simcha P. Jewish Views of the Afterlife. LC 94-10597. 512p. 1995. 40.00 (*0-87668-768-1*) Aronson.
Raphael, Stanley S. Lynch's Medical Laboratory Technology. 4th ed. (Illus.). 864p. 1983. text ed. 80.50 (*0-7216-7465-8*) Saunders.
Raphael, Sylvia, ed. see De Balzac, Honore.
Raphael, Sylvia, tr. see De Balzac, Honore.
Raphael, Sylvia, tr. see Sand, George.
Raphael, Winifred. Patients & Their Hospitals. King Edward's Hospital Fund Staff, ed. 46p. 1977. pap. 19.95 (*0-8464-1297-7*) Beekman Pubs.

Raphaell, Katrina. Crystal Healing: The Therapeutic Application of Crystals & Stones. 220p. 1987. pap. 14.95 (*0-943358-30-2*) Aurora Press.
— The Crystalline Transmission - A Synthesis of Light, Vol. III. 300p. 1989. 16.95 (*0-943358-33-7*) Aurora Press.
Raphaelson, Joel, jt. auth. see Roman, Kenneth.
Raphaelson, Josh. I Worship the Very Dirt She Treats Me Like: The Story of a Warm, Caring Guy. 1992. pap. 4.99 (*1-56171-103-9*, S P I Bks) Sure Sellers.
— I Worship the Very Dirt She Treats Me Like: The Story of a Warm, Caring Guy in a Society. 1991. pap. 7.95 (*1-56171-040-7*) Sure Sellers.
Raphaelson, Samson. Three Screen Comedies by Samson Raphaelson: Trouble in Paradise, The Shop Around the Corner, Heaven Can Wait. LC 81-50948. 512p. 1983. 22.50 (*0-299-08780-8*) U of Wis Pr.
Raphaely, Russell C., jt. ed. see Swedlow, David B.
Raphals, Lisa. Knowing Words: Wisdom & Cunning in the Classical Traditions of China & Greece. LC 91-55554. (Myth & Poetics Ser.). 304p. 1992. 39.95 (*0-8014-2619-7*) Cornell U Pr.
Raphel, Mary. Money, Emotions & the Recovery Process. 96p. 1993. pap. 10.95 (*0-9639287-0-8*) M Raphel.
Raphel, Murray. Mind Your Own Business: Rules, Guidelines, Examples, Stories & Exhortations. 1992. 19.95 (*0-9624808-4-3*) Raphel Mktg.
Raphel, Murray & Erdman, Ken. The Do-It-Yourself Direct Mail Handbook. LC 86-63913. 1986. 19.95 (*0-939951-01-0*) Marketers Bookshelf.
Raphel, Murray, jt. auth. see Raphel, Neil.
***Raphel, Neil & Raphel, Murray.** Up the Loyalty Ladder: Turning Some-Time Customers into Full-Time Advocates for Your Business. 288p. 1995. 23.00 (*0-88730-725-6*) Harper Busn.
Raphelson, Samson. Skylark. 1942. pap. 13.00 (*0-8222-1319-2*) Dramatists Play.
***Rapi, Nina.** Making Out: The Complete Book of Lesbian Sexuality. 1995. pap. 24.00 (*0-04-440932-X*) Routledge Chapman & Hall.
Rapid Excavation & Tunneling Conference Staff. Rapid Excavation & Tunneling Conference, Proceeding: Chicago, Illinois, June 12-16, 1983, 2 vols. LC 83-70933. (Illus.). 74p. reprint ed. Index, 74p. pap. 25.00 (*0-7837-1101-8*, 2041631) Bks Demand.
— Rapid Excavation & Tunneling Conference, Proceeding: Chicago, Illinois, June 12-16, 1983, 2 vols., Vol. 1. LC 83-70933. (Illus.). 673p. reprint ed. pap. 180.00 (*0-7837-1099-2*, 2041631) Bks Demand.
— Rapid Excavation & Tunneling Conference, Proceeding: Chicago, Illinois, June 12-16, 1983, 2 vols., Vol. 2. LC 83-70933. (Illus.). 611p. reprint ed. pap. 174.20 (*0-7837-1100-X*, 2041631) Bks Demand.
— Rapid Excavation & Tunneling Conference Proceedings, 1979, 2 vols. Hustrulid, William A. & Maevis, Alfred C., eds. LC 79-52280. (Illus.). 1819p. 1979. 60.00 (*0-89520-266-2*) SMM&E Inc.
Rapier, R. C. Atlantis Two, Three, Four, Five & One -- Includes Atlantis Times Two, Back Flash & Sky Mite in One Volume. (Illus.). 1978. 30.00 (*0-9600589-2-3*) R C Rapier.
— Heir to the Castle, or The Guilt of Cinderac. 1971. 20.00 (*0-614-06250-0*) R C Rapier.
— Night of the Moon Children. 1970. 30.00 (*0-614-06251-9*) R C Rapier.
— Return of Viking II: Sequellae to: Atlantis 2, 3, 4, 5 & 1. 48p. 1994. 10.00 (*0-614-06249-7*) R C Rapier.
— Tales Out of Tilt, Or Tales Out of Time, Vol. II. 1983. 20.00 (*0-9600584-5-1*) R C Rapier.
Rapier, Regina. Music in Mourning: A Novel of the Gulf Coast. (Illus.). 196p. 1991. reprint ed. 20.00 (*0-685-48990-6*) R C Rapier.
— Saga of Felix Senac: Being the Legend & Biography of a Confederate Agent in Europe. (Illus.). 216p. 1972. 30.00 (*0-9600584-1-9*) R C Rapier.
— Tales Out of Time, Vol. 1: The Mad Compactor & Other Science Fiction Short Stories. 1980. 20.00 (*0-685-04205-7*) R C Rapier.
***Rapin, I. & Segalowitz, S. J., eds.** Handbook of Neuropsychology: Child Neuropsychology (Part 1), Vol. 6. 1994. pap. 103.00 (*0-444-82060-4*) Elsevier.
— Handbook of Neuropsychology: Child Neuropsychology (Part 2), Vol. 7. 1994. pap. 103.00 (*0-444-82059-0*) Elsevier.
Rapin, Isabelle. Children with Brain Dysfunction: Neurology, Cognition, Language, & Behavior. (International Review of Child Neurology Ser.). 300p. 1982. text ed. 83.00 (*0-89004-844-4*) Raven.
Rapin, J. R., jt. ed. see Le Poncin-Lafitte, M.
Rapin, M., jt. ed. see Tinker, J.
***Rapin, Maurice.** Dictionnaire Encyclopedique Medical. 1986. write for info. (*0-7859-8636-7*, 225710482x) Fr & Eur.
Rapin, Rene. Comparaison Des Poemes d'Homere et De Virgile. xvi, 167p. 1973. reprint ed. write for info. (*3-487-04807-8*, Pub. by Georg Olms GW) Lubrecht & Cramer.
— Reflexions Sur la Philosophie Ancienne et Moderne, et Sur l'Usage Qu'on En Doit Faire Pour la Religion. xx, 263p. reprint ed. write for info. (*0-318-71396-9*, Pub. by Georg Olms GW) Lubrecht & Cramer.
— Reflexions Sur la Poetique d'Aristote, et Sur les Ouvrages Des Poetes Anciens et Modernes. xx, 257p. 1973. reprint ed. write for info. (*3-487-04818-3*, Pub. by Georg Olms GW) Lubrecht & Cramer.
Rapinchuk, Andrei, jt. auth. see Platonov, Vladimir.
Rapini, Ronald P. & Jordon, Robert E., eds. Atlas of Dermatopathology. (Illus.). 456p. 1987. 115.00 (*0-8151-7087-4*, ATD-1, Yr Bk Med Pubs) Mosby Yr Bk.
Rapisarda, Mario. Precision Metal Technology. 800p. (C). 1991. text ed. 47.00 (*0-15-571075-3*) SCP.

R

An Asterisk (*) at the beginning of an entry indicates that the title is appearing in BIP for the first time.

Rapisardi, Carmel J. Then Now & Forever. 271p. 1992. pap. write for info. (*0-9632702-0-6*) Lightning.
Rapkin, Alec. Under Stone. (C). 1989. 30.00 (*0-685-63395-0*, Pub. by Dragonheart Pr UK) St Mut.
Rapkin, Andrea & Tonnessen, Diana. A Woman Doctor's Guide to PMS: Essential Facts & Up-to-the-Minute Information on Premenstrual Syndrome. LC 93-10992. (Illus.). 160p. 1994. pap. 9.95 (*1-56282-810-X*) Hyperion.
Rapkin, David P., ed. World Leadershp & Hegemony. (International Political Economy Yearbook Ser.: Vol. 5). 286p. 1990. lib. bdg. 42.00 (*1-55587-189-5*) Lynne Rienner.
***Rapkin, David P. & Avery, William P., eds.** National Competitiveness in a Global Economy. LC 94-43543. (International Political Economy Yearbook Ser.: Vol. 8). 235p. 1995. lib. bdg. 49.95 (*1-55587-542-4*) Lynne Rienner.
Rapkin, David P., jt. ed. see Avery, William P.
Rapkin, Julie, jt. auth. see Shapiro, Robert.
Rapley, Elizabeth. The Devotes: Women & Church in Seventeenth-Century France. (Studies in the History of Religion). (Illus.). 320p. (C). 1990. pap. 19.95 (*0-7735-1101-6*, Pub. by McGill CN) U of Toronto Pr.
Rapley, Janice, jt. auth. see Nash, Grace C.
Rapley, John. Ivoirien Capitalism: African Entrepreneurs in Cote d'Ivoire. LC 93-9245. 198p. 1993. Alk. paper. lib. bdg. 38.00 (*1-55587-397-9*) Lynne Rienner.
Rapley, Linda, jt. auth. see Pipe, David.
Rapley, Ralph & Walker, Matthew R., eds. Molecular Diagnostics: Research Towards Application. LC 92-43669. 1993. 100.00 (*0-632-03528-5*) Blackwell Sci.
Rapley, Ralph, jt. ed. see Walker, Matthew R.
***Rapley, Robin J.** Colt Percussion Accoutrements 1834-1873: Including Cartridge Conversions & Their Valves. 432p. 1994. pap. 39.95 (*1-882824-08-3*) Graphic Pubs.
Rapolla, Antonio & Keller, George V., eds. Geophysics of Geothermal Areas: State of the Art & Future Development: Proceedings of the Third Course Held at the School of Geophysics, International Centre for Scientific Culture, Erice, Italy, May 1980. (Illus.). 306p. 1984. text ed. 25.00 (*0-918062-57-8*) Colo Sch Mines.
Rapone, Anita. The Guardian Life Insurance Company 1860-1920: A History of a German-American Enterprise. 228p. 1987. 50.00x (*0-8147-7401-6*) NYU Pr.
Rapopart, Robert N., et al. Community As Doctor. Grob, Gerald N., ed. LC 78-22587. (Historical Issues in Mental Health Ser.). (Illus.). 1980. reprint ed. lib. bdg. 25.95 (*0-405-11938-0*) Ayer.
Rapoport, A. General System Theory: Essential Concepts & Applications. LC 85-8749. (Cybernetics & Systems Ser., Abacus Bks.). 270p. (C). 1986. text ed. 107.00 (*0-85626-172-6*) Gordon & Breach.
— History & Precedent in Environmental Design. (Illus.). 580p. 1990. 65.00 (*0-306-43429-6*, Plenum Med Bk); pap. 32.50 (*0-306-43445-8*, Plenum Med Bk) Plenum.
Rapoport, A., et al. Coalition Formation by Sophisticated Players. (Lecture Notes in Economics & Mathematical Systems Ser.: Vol. 169). 1979. pap. 27.00 (*0-387-09249-8*) Spr-Verlag.
Rapoport, Alan M. & Sheftell, Fred D. Headache Relief. 288p. 1991. pap. 10.00 (*0-671-74803-3*, Fireside) S&S Trade.
— Headache Relief for Women: How You Can Manage & Prevent Pain. LC 95-6757. 1996. 24.95 (*0-316-73393-8*); pap. 12.95 (*0-316-73391-1*) Little.
Rapoport-Albert, Adda, ed. Essays in Jewish Historiography. 1991. 69.95 (*1-55540-561-4*) Scholars Pr GA.
Rapoport, Amnon. Experimental Studies of Interactive Decisions. (C). 1990. lib. bdg. 154.00 (*0-7923-0685-6*) Kluwer Ac.
Rapoport, Amnon, jt. auth. see Kahan, James P.
Rapoport, Amnon, et al. Response Models for Detection of Change. (Theory & Decision Library: No. 18). 1979. lib. bdg. 64.00 (*90-277-0934-3*) Kluwer Ac.
Rapoport, Amos. Cross-Cultural Studies & Urban Form. (Urban Studies Monograph Ser.: No. 10). 64p. 7.50 (*0-913749-20-6*) U MD Urban Stud.
— House Form & Culture. LC 69-14550. (Geography Ser.). 1969. pap. text ed. write for info. (*0-13-395673-3*) P-H.
— Human Aspects of Urban Form: Towards a Man-Environment Approach to Urban Form & Design. 1977. 187.00 (*0-08-017974-6*, Pub. by Pergamon Repr UK) Franklin.
— Meaning of the Built Environment: A Nonverbal Communication Approach. LC 90-10742. 253p. 1990. reprint ed. pap. 15.95 (*0-8165-1176-4*) U of Ariz Pr.
Rapoport, Amos, ed. The Mutual Interaction of People & Their Built Environment: A Cross-Cultural Perspective. (World Anthropology Ser.). (Illus.). xvi, 506p. 1976. 58.50 (*3-10-800169-8*) Mouton.
Rapoport, Anatol. Decision Theory & Decision Behaviour. (C). 1989. lib. bdg. 201.00 (*0-7923-0297-4*) Kluwer Ac.
— Fights, Games, & Debates. (Illus.). 416p. 1974. reprint ed. pap. 18.95 (*0-472-08741-X*) U of Mich Pr.
— The Origins of Violence: Approaches to the Study of Conflict. rev. ed. LC 94-12483. 589p. (C). 1994. pap. 24.95 (*1-56000-783-4*) Transaction Pubs.
— Peace: An Idea Whose Time Has Come. 190p. (C). 1992. text ed. 34.50 (*0-472-10315-6*) U of Mich Pr.
— Science & the Goals of Man: A Study in Semantic Orientation. LC 70-138126. 262p. 1971. reprint ed. text ed. 35.00 (*0-8371-4142-7*, RASG, Greenwood Pr) Greenwood.
Rapoport, Anatol & Chammah, Albert M. Prisoner's Dilemma. LC 65-11462. (Illus.). 1965. 34.50 (*0-472-75602-8*) U of Mich Pr.
— Prisoner's Dilemma. (Illus.). 1970. pap. 12.95 (*0-472-06165-8*, 165, Ann Arbor Bks) U of Mich Pr.
Rapoport, Bernard & Adams, Mark. How to Live with an Uneasy Conscience. (Shortcuts to Ignorance Ser.). 20p. 1983. pap. 1.95 (*0-915433-08-7*) Packrat WA.
Rapoport, Bonnie. Dining in Baltimore, Vol. II. (Dining in Cookbooks Ser.). 189p. 1988. pap. 8.95 (*0-89716-172-6*) P B Pubng.
Rapoport, David C., ed. Inside Terrorist Organizations. 260p. 1988. text ed. 47.50 (*0-231-06720-8*); pap. text ed. 15.50 (*0-231-06721-6*) Col U Pr.
Rapoport, David C. & Alexander, Jonah, eds. The Morality of Terrorism: Religious & Secular Justifications. (Morningside Bk.). 377p. 1989. text ed. 66.00 (*0-231-06752-6*); pap. text ed. 18.50 (*0-231-06753-4*) Col U Pr.
Rapoport, David C. & Alexander, Yonah, eds. The Morality of Terrorism: Religious Origins & Ethical Implications. (Policy Studies on International Politics). 280p. 1982. 47.00 (*0-08-026347-X*, Pergamon Pr) Elsevier.
— The Rationalization of Terrorism. LC 81-70296. 210p. 1982. text ed. 39.95 (*0-313-27098-8*, U7098, Greenwood Pr) Greenwood.
Rapoport, Eduardo H. Areography: Geographical Strategies of Species. (Publications of Fundacion Bariloche: Vol. 1). (Illus.). 250p. 1982. 120.00 (*0-08-028914-2*, G135, H110, Pub. by Pergamon Repr UK) Franklin.
Rapoport, Henry, jt. auth. see Cason, James.
Rapoport, John, et al. Understanding Health Care Economics. LC 81-14987. 554p. (C). 1982. text ed. 70.00 (*0-89443-380-6*) Aspen Pub.
Rapoport, John D. & Zevnik, Brian L. The Employee Strikes Back! LC 93-40437. 324p. 1994. pap. 11.00 (*0-02-036160-2*, Collier S&S) S&S Trade.
Rapoport, Judith L. The Boy Who Couldn't Stop Washing: The Experience & Treatment of Obesessive-Compulsive Disorder. 272p. 1990. pap. 9.95 (*0-452-26365-4*, Plume) NAL-Dutton.
— Boy Who Couldn't Stop Washing: The Experience & Treatment of Obsessive-Compulsive Disorder. 304p. 1991. pap. 5.99 (*0-451-17202-7*, Sig) NAL-Dutton.
Rapoport, Judith L., ed. Obsessive-Compulsive Disorder in Children & Adolescents. LC 88-6282. 355p. 1989. text ed. 45.00 (*0-88048-282-6*) Am Psychiatric.
Rapoport, Judith L. & Ismond, Deborah R. DSM-III-R Training Guide for Diagnosis of Childhood Disorders. rev. ed. LC 89-10005. 175p. 1989. 28.50 (*0-87630-509-5*); pap. 19.95 (*0-87630-563-X*) Brunner-Mazel.
— DSM-IV Training Guide for Diagnosis of Childhood Disorders. 1995. write for info. (*0-87630-766-7*) Brunner-Mazel.
Rapoport, Louis. Redemption Song: The Story of Operation Moses. LC 85-30489. (Illus.). 320p. 1986. 18.95 (*0-15-176120-5*) HarBrace.
— Shake Heaven & Earth: Peter Bergson & the Rescue of the Jews of Europe. 1988. 21.95 (*0-940461-06-4*) Seth Pr.
— Stalin's War Against the Jews: The Doctor's Plot & the Soviet Solution. (Illus.). 1990. text ed. 27.95 (*0-02-925821-9*) Free Pr.
Rapoport, M., et al, eds. Beilinson's Conjectures on Special Values of L-Functions. (Perspectives in Mathematics Ser.: Vol. 4). 373p. 1988. text ed. 79.00 (*0-12-581120-9*) Acad Pr.
Rapoport, Maxine & Graybill, Nina. Hearty Salads. LC 89-11623. 168p. (Orig.). 1989. pap. 10.95 (*0-918535-08-5*) Farragut Pub.
Rapoport, Maxine, jt. auth. see Graybill, Nina.
Rapoport, Mitchell, jt. ed. see Chaffetz, David.
Rapoport, Mitchell, jt. ed. see Levin, Arthur.
Rapoport, Nathan. Sculptures & Monuments. LC 80-52914. (Illus.). 96p. 1981. 30.00 (*0-88400-072-9*) Shengold.
Rapoport, Nessa. Woman's Book of Grieving. 1994. 15.00 (*0-688-10947-0*) Morrow.
Rapoport, Nessa, jt. ed. see Solotaroff, Ted.
Rapoport, Paul. Sorabji: A Critical Celebration. 250p. 1992. 69.95 (*0-85967-923-3*, Pub. by Scolar Pr UK) Ashgate Pub Co.
Rapoport, Robert N. New Interventions for Children & Youth: Action-Research Approaches. (Illus.). 336p. 1987. 59.95 (*0-521-34122-1*) Cambridge U Pr.
Rapoport, Robert N., ed. Children, Youth, & Families: The Action Research Relationship. (Illus.). 320p. 1985. 49.95 (*0-521-30143-2*) Cambridge U Pr.
Rapoport, Roger. Great Cities of Eastern Europe. 256p. 1991. pap. 16.95 (*1-56261-012-0*) John Muir.
— Into the Sunlight: Life After the Iron Curtain. 128p. 1991. reprint ed. lib. bdg. 23.00x (*0-8095-4957-3*) Borgo Pr.
— Two to Twenty-Two Days in California: The Itinerary Planner. (Two to Twenty-Two Days Ser.). (Illus.). 192p. (Orig.). 1993. pap. 10.95 (*1-56261-113-5*) John Muir.
— Two to Twenty-Two Days in California: The Itinerary Planner 1993. rev. ed. (Two to Twenty-Two Days Ser.). (Illus.). 192p. 1992. pap. 9.95 (*1-56261-051-1*) John Muir.
— Two to Twenty-Two Days in California, 1995 Edition. (Two to Twenty-Two Days Itinerary Planner Ser.). (Illus.). 192p. 1995. pap. 11.95 (*1-56261-203-4*) John Muir.
— Two to Twenty-Two Days in the Rockies: The Itinerary Planner 1993. rev. ed. (Two to Twenty-Two Days Ser.). (Illus.). 192p. Date not set. pap. 10.95 (*1-56261-081-3*) John Muir.
— Two to Twenty-Two Days in the Rockies: The Itinerary Planner, 1994. (Two to Twenty-Two Days Ser.). 192p. (Orig.). 1993. pap. 10.95 (*1-56261-138-0*) John Muir.
— Two to Twenty-Two Days in the Rockies, 1995 Edition. (Two to Twenty-Two Days Itinerary Planner Ser.). (Illus.). 192p. 1995. pap. 11.95 (*1-56261-208-5*) John Muir.
— Ultimate Maui. LC 91-65700. (Ultimate Guidebook Ser.). (Illus.). 192p. (Orig.). 1994. pap. 11.95 (*0-915233-46-0*) Ulysses Pr.
Rapoport, Roger & Castanera, Marguerita, eds. I Should Have Stayed Home: The Worst Trips of Great Writers. LC 94-70039. 256p. (Orig.). 1994. pap. 13.95 (*1-57143-014-8*, Book Passage Pr) RDR Bks.
***Rapoport, Roger & Lenhart, Maria.** Hidden Oregon: The Adventurer's Guide. LC 95-60713. (Hidden Travel Ser.). (Illus.). 252p. (Orig.). 1995. pap. 12.95 (*1-56975-037-8*) Ulysses Pr.
Rapoport, Roger & Willes, Burl. Twenty-Two Days Around the World: The Itinerary Planner 1993. 1,993th ed. (Two to Twenty-Two Days Ser.). (Illus.). 256p. (Orig.). 1992. pap. 12.95 (*1-56261-050-3*) John Muir.
— Twenty-Two Days (or More) Around the World: The Itinerary Planner. (Two to Twenty-Two Days Ser.). (Illus.). 264p. (Orig.). 1993. pap. 13.95 (*1-56261-119-4*) John Muir.
— Two to Twenty Two Days in Asia: The Itinerary Planner. (Two to Twenty-Two Days Ser.). (Illus.). 176p. 1993. pap. 10.95 (*1-56261-111-9*) John Muir.
— Two to Twenty-Two Days in Asia: The Itinerary Planner 1993. rev. ed. (Two to Twenty-Two Days Ser.). (Illus.). 176p. 1993. pap. 9.95 (*1-56261-055-4*) John Muir.
Rapoport, Roger, jt. auth. see Logsdon, Wendy.
Rapoport, Roger, et al. Ultimate Washington. Pearlman, Joanna, ed. LC 93-60066. (Ultimate Guidebook Ser.). (Illus.). 328p. (Orig.). 1993. pap. 11.95 (*0-915233-85-1*) Ulysses Pr.
Rapoport, Ron, ed. A Kind of Grace: A Treasury of Sportswriting by Women. LC 94-60001. 385p. (Orig.). 1994. pap. 14.95 (*1-57143-013-X*, Zenobia Pr) RDR Bks.
Rapoport, Ronald B., et al, eds. The Life of the Parties: Activists in Presidential Politics. LC 85-22510. 256p. 1986. 28.00 (*0-8131-1559-0*) U Pr of Ky.
Rapoport, S. & Schewe, T. Processing & Turnover of Proteins & Organelles in Cell. LC 78-41025. (Proceedings FEBS Meeting, Dresden 1978 Ser.: Vol. 53: S6). 1979. 86.00 (*0-08-023177-2*, Pub. by Pergamon Repr UK) Franklin.
Rapoport, S., jt. auth. see Federation European Staff.
Rapoport, S., jt. ed. see Jacobasch, G.
Rapoport, Samuel M. The Reticulocyte. 256p. 1986. 216.00 (*0-8493-6538-4*, QP96) CRC Pr.
Rapoport, Stanley I. Blood-Brain Barrier in Physiology & Medicine. LC 75-26280. 328p. 1976. 80.00 (*0-89004-079-6*) Raven.
Rapoport, Vitaly. Introduction of Management Information Systems in the U. S. S. R. The Ministry of the Electrical Equipment Industry - A Case Study. Tamberg, Andreas, ed. Tamberg, Nora, tr. (Delphic Monograph Ser.). (Illus.). 95p. (Orig.). 1989. pap. text ed. 75.00 (*1-55831-088-6*) Delphic Associates.
Rapoport, Vitaly & Alexeev, Yuri. High Treason: Essays on the History of the Red Army, 1918-1938. Treml, Vladimir G. & Adams, Bruce, eds. LC 85-16322. (Illus.). xvii, 436p. 1985. 45.50 (*0-8223-0647-6*) Duke.
Rapoport, Yaakov M. The Light from Dvinsk: Rav Meir Simcha, the Ohr Somayach. 144p. 12.95 (*0-944070-56-6*) Targum Pr.
Rapoport, Yaakov M., tr. see Chayoun, Yehudah.
Rapoport, Yaakov M., tr. see Grossman, Reaven.
Rapoport, Yakov. The Doctors' Plot of Nineteen Fifty-Three. LC 90-4812. (Illus.). 281p. 1991. text ed. 32.00 (*0-674-21477-3*, RAPDOC) HUP.
Raposa, Michael L. Peirce's Philosophy of Religion. LC 88-46016. 192p. 1989. 25.00 (*0-253-34833-1*) Ind U Pr.
Raposa, Peter J. Reassurance: Should I Worry about My Heart Skipping Beats? Van Treese, James B., ed. 206p. 1992. pap. 9.95 (*1-880416-65-4*) NW Pub.
Raposo, Joe. Bein' Green. (Sing-a-Song Storybooks Ser.). (Illus.). 24p. (J). 1993. 9.95 (*0-7935-1680-3*, 00183008) H Leonard.
— C Is for Cookie. (Xylotone Fun! Ser.). (Illus.). 16p. (J). 1993. spiral bd. 9.95 (*0-7935-2155-6*, 00824048) H Leonard.
— C Is for Cookie & Other Kids' Favorites. (Sing 'n' Color Fun! Ser.). (Illus.). (J). 1993. spiral bd. 6.95 (*0-7935-1954-3*, 00823016) H Leonard.
— Sing. (Sing-a-Song Storybooks Ser.). (Illus.). 24p. (J). 1993. 9.95 (*0-7935-1860-1*, 00183012) H Leonard.
— Sing & Other Kids' Favorites. (Sing 'n' Color Fun! Ser.). (Illus.). (J). 1993. spiral bd. 6.95 (*0-7935-1955-1*, 00823020) H Leonard.
Rapoza, J. A., ed. The Psychic Bible: The Apocryphal Scriptures of Genesis Porridge & Psychic TV. 192p. 1994. pap. 14.99 (*0-9641136-0-0*) Etherworld Pub.
***Rapp & Collins.** Beyond MaxiMarketing: The New Power of Caring & Daring. 1995. pap. text ed. 14.95 (*0-07-015338-8*) McGraw.
Rapp, Adam. Missing the Piano. 160p. (YA). (gr. 7 up). 1994. 14.99 (*0-670-95340-7*) Viking Child Bks.
— Missing the Piano: A Novel. LC 93-44110. (J). 1994. 14.99 (*0-670-85340-2*, Viking) Viking Penguin.
Rapp, Adrian M., jt. auth. see Dodgen, Lynda I.
Rapp, Augustus. The Life & Times of Augustus Rapp, the Small Town Showman: Written by Himself. Boggs, Marcia, ed. (Illus.). 201p. 1991. 28.95 (*0-916638-44-8*); pap. 18.95 (*0-916638-45-6*) Meyerbooks.
***Rapp, Barbara, ed.** Biotechnology Sources: North & South America. 144p. 1994. pap. 32.50 (*0-938734-87-3*) Learned Info.
***Rapp, Bernard.** Larousse Dictionnaire des Films: 10,000 Films du Monde Entier. (FRE.). 1993. 125.00 (*0-7859-7672-8*, 2035123151) Fr & Eur.
Rapp, Burt. Armed Defense: Gunfight Survival for the Householder & Businessman. LC 89-84029. 205p. 1989. pap. text ed. 14.95 (*1-55950-014-X*) Loompanics.
— The B & E Book. LC 89-63211. 160p. 1989. pap. text ed. 14.95 (*1-55950-021-2*) Loompanics.
— Check Fraud Investigation. LC 91-60413. (Illus.). 176p. (Orig.). 1991. pap. 16.95 (*1-55950-065-4*, 40072) Loompanics.
— Credit Card Fraud. LC 90-63591. 136p. (Orig.). 1991. pap. 13.95 (*1-55950-055-7*, 49024) Loompanics.
— Deep Cover: Police Intelligence Operations. 136p. 1989. pap. 14.00 (*0-87364-507-3*) Paladin Pr.
— Homicide Investigation. LC 89-63201. 184p. 1989. pap. text ed. 14.95 (*1-55950-020-4*) Loompanics.
— Interrogation. LC 87-81101. 160p. (Orig.). 1987. pap. 14.95 (*0-915179-59-8*) Loompanics.
— The Police Sniper: A Complete Handbook. LC 88-45201. (Illus.). 200p. (Orig.). 1988. pap. text ed. 14.95 (*0-915179-77-6*, 55073) Loompanics.
— Professional Killers: An Inside Look. LC 90-63507. 168p. (Orig.). 1990. pap. 14.95 (*1-55950-054-9*, 34057) Loompanics.
— Sex Crimes Investigation. LC 87-83444. 200p. (Orig.). 1988. pap. 14.95 (*0-915179-72-5*, 55071) Loompanics.
— Shadowing & Surveillance: A Complete Guide Book. LC 85-82012. 152p. (Orig.). 1985. pap. 14.95 (*0-915179-33-4*) Loompanics.
— Shoplifting & Employee Theft Investigation. LC 88-46126. 178p. 1989. pap. text ed. 13.95 (*0-915179-87-3*) Loompanics.
— S.W.A.T. Team Operations. LC 90-60904. (Illus.). 160p. (Orig.). 1990. pap. 16.95 (*1-55950-035-2*, 58065) Loompanics.
— The Two Eleven Book: Armed Robbery Investigation. 184p. 1989. pap. text ed. 14.95 (*1-55950-019-0*) Loompanics.
— Undercover Work: A Complete Handbook. LC 85-82011. 152p. (Orig.). 1985. pap. 12.95 (*0-915179-32-6*) Loompanics.
— Vehicle Theft Investigation: A Complete Handbook. LC 88-83740. 128p. (Orig.). 1989. pap. text ed. 12.95 (*1-55950-010-7*) Loompanics.
Rapp, Carl. William Carlos Williams & Romantic Idealism. LC 83-40561. 175p. 1984. text ed. 25.00 (*0-87451-290-5*) U Pr of New Eng.
Rapp, Catherine. Burgher & Peasant. LC 75-140039. (Catholic University Studies in German: No. 7). reprint ed. 37.50 (*0-404-50227-X*) AMS Pr.
Rapp, Charles A. & Poertner, John. Social Administration: A Client-Centered Approach. 308p. (C). 1992. teacher ed write for info. (*0-8013-0450-4*, 78262); pap. text ed. 45.95 (*0-8013-0435-0*, 78244) Longman.
Rapp, David, jt. auth. see Congressional Quarterly, Inc.
Rapp, Dean. Samuel Whitbread 1764-1815: A Social & Political Study. McNeill, William H. & Stansky, Peter, eds. (Modern European History Ser.). 512p. 1987. lib. bdg. 15.00 (*0-8240-7829-2*) Garland.
Rapp, Donald E., Jr. Guide to Commercial Real Estate Loan Documentation. 336p. 1990. 69.95 (*0-13-370842-X*) P-H.
Rapp, Doris. Is This Your Child: Discovering & Treating Unrecognized Food Allergies. 1991. 23.00 (*0-688-08623-3*) Morrow.
— Recognize & Manage Your Allergies. (Self-Care Health Library). 32p. (Orig.). 1987. pap. 2.50 (*0-87983-396-3*) Keats.
Rapp, Doris G. Healing the Injured Church. Nehring, Donna, ed. 120p. (Orig.). 1993. pap. 9.95 (*0-9637200-0-7*) Daniels Hse.
Rapp, Doris J. Allergies & Your Family. 352p. 1990. reprint ed. pap. 12.95 (*0-9616318-2-1*) Practical Allergy.
— Is This Your Child? Discovering & Treating Unrecognized Allergies. LC 92-8944. 1992. pap. 12.00 (*0-688-11907-7*, Quill) Morrow.
— Is This Your School? For Students, for Teachers. (Illus.). 750p. 1994. 23.00 (*1-880509-04-0*); Video cass. vhs 15.00 (*1-880509-05-9*) Practical Allergy.
— El Nino Insoportable. Zaragoza, Lydia J., tr. Orig. Title: The Impossible Child. (Illus.). 170p. (SPA.). 1988. pap. 12.95 (*1-880509-01-6*); vhs 16.95 (*1-880509-02-4*) Practical Allergy.
— Why an Environmentally Clean Classroom for Children? (Illus.). 248p. (Orig.). 1991. pap. 30.00 (*0-9616318-9-9*) Practical Allergy.
Rapp, Doris J. & Bamberg, Dorothy L. The Impossible Child - in School, at Home. (Illus.). 136p. 1986. lib. bdg. 8.95 (*0-9616318-0-5*) Practical Allergy.
— The Impossible Child in School, at Home: A Guide for Caring Teachers & Parents. 2nd rev. ed. LC 87-63550. (Illus.). 160p. 1988. pap. 10.95 (*0-9616318-1-3*) Practical Allergy.
Rapp, F. Gesetz & Determination in der Sowjetphilosophie: Zur Gesetzeskonzeption des Dialectischen Materialismus unter Besonderer Beruecksichtigung der Diskussion ueber Dynamische & Statistische Gesetzmaessigkeit in der Zeitgenoessischen Sowjetphilosophie. (Sovietica Ser.: No. 26). 174p. (GER.). 1968. lib. bdg. 42.50 (*90-277-0065-6*) Kluwer Ac.
Rapp, F., ed. Frontiers in Virology: In Honour of Joseph L. Melnick on the Occasion of His 60th Birthday. (Progress in Medical Virology Ser.: Vol. 21). (Illus.). 250p. 1975. 79.25 (*3-8055-2202-9*) S Karger.
Rapp, Fred, ed. On Cogenic Herpesviruses, Vol. 1. 208p. 1980. 98.95 (*0-8493-5619-9*, QR400, CRC Reprint) Franklin.
— On Cogenic Herpesviruses, Vol. 2. 152p. 1980. 87.95 (*0-8493-5620-2*, CRC Reprint) Franklin.
Rapp, Friedrich. Analytical Philosophy of Technology. xiv, 199p. 1981. lib. bdg. 62.00 (*90-277-1221-2*) Kluwer Ac.
Rapp, Friedrich & Wiehl, Reiner, eds. Whitehead's Metaphysics of Creativity. LC 89-4479. 223p. 1990. 59.50 (*0-7914-0202-9*); pap. 19.95 (*0-7914-0203-7*) State U NY Pr.

Rapp, G., Jr. & Mulholland, S. C., eds. Phytolith Systematics: Emerging Issues. (Advances in Archaeological & Museum Science Ser.: Vol. 1). (Illus.). 360p. (C). 1992. 49.50 (0-306-44208-6, Plenum Pr) Plenum.

Rapp, George, Jr. & Gifford, John A., eds. Archaeological Geology. LC 84-40201. 455p. 1985. reprint ed. pap. 129.70 (0-7837-3326-7, 2057732) Bks Demand.

Rapp, George & Gifford, John A., eds. Troy: The Archaeological Geology. LC 50-9752. (Illus.). 232p. 1982. 95.00x (0-691-03559-8) Princeton U Pr.

Rapp, George R., Jr., jt. ed. see McDonald, William A.

Rapp-Hunt, Tawney. The Boo Boo Zoo. (First Book Ser.). 36p. (J). 1993. text ed. 11.95 (0-9638882-0-X) Tawney Pubng.

Rapp, James. Successful Sales Meetings: How to Plan, Conduct & Make Sales Meetings Pay Off. 250p. 1990. pap. 32.95 (0-85013-171-5) Dartnell Corp.

Rapp, James A. Education Law, 4 vols. 1984. Updates avail. ring bd. write for info. (0-8205-1397-0) Bender.

— Illinois Corporations System. 1984. write for info. (0-8205-1447-0) Bender.

Rapp, James A., jt. auth. see Hunter, Robert S.

Rapp, Jay. Dog Training Is Kid Stuff. LC 77-87768. (Training Bks.). 1978. pap. 4.95 (0-87714-056-1) Denlingers.

— Dog Training Is Kid Stuff Coloring Book. 1978. pap. 2.95 (0-87714-068-5) Denlingers.

— How to Train Dogs for Police Work. LC 77-87767. (Training Bks.). 1979. 22.95 (0-87714-071-5); pap. 16.95 (0-87714-057-X) Denlingers.

— Rappid Obedience & Watchdog Training. LC 77-87766. (Training Bks.). 1978. 7.95 (0-87714-070-7); pap. 4.95 (0-87714-055-3) Denlingers.

Rapp, Jim. Successful Sales Meetings. 250p. 1990. ring bd. 91.50 (0-85013-190-1) Dartnell Corp.

Rapp, Joel. Let's Get Growing: Twenty-Five Quick & Easy Gardening Projects for Kids. (J). 1992. pap. 7.00 (0-517-58880-3, Crown) Crown Pub Group.

Rapp, Joel, jt. auth. see Rapp, Lynn.

Rapp, Lynn & Rapp, Joel. Mother Earth's Hassle-Free Indoor Plant Book. (Illus.). 144p. 1990. pap. 8.95 (0-449-90428-8, Columbine) Fawcett.

Rapp, Marrin, jt. auth. see Weaver, Herbert.

Rapp, Marvin A. Canal Water & Whiskey: Tall Tales of the Erie Canal Country. rev. ed. (Illus.). 398p. (C). 1992. pap. 19.95 (1-878097-07-5) Canisius Coll Pr.

***Rapp, Paul.** The Silver Sabre. 340p. 1995. pap. 9.95 (1-56901-876-6) NW Pub.

Rapp, R. & Samso, F., eds. Determination of the Geoid. (International Association of Geodesy Symposia Ser.: Vol. 106). (Illus.). 496p. 1991. pap. 76.00 (0-387-97470-9) Spr-Verlag.

Rapp, R. H., jt. ed. see Grafarend, E. W.

Rapp, Rayna, jt. ed. see Ginsburg, Faye D.

Rapp, Rayna, jt. ed. see Schneider, Jane.

Rapp, Richard T. Industry & Economic Decline in Seventeenth Century Venice. (Historical Monographs: No. 69). (Illus.). 224p. 1976. 20.00 (0-674-44545-7) HUP.

Rapp, Rosemary & Twohig, Maureen A. American Paintings from Nature: Flower, Fruit, & Leaf. (Illus.). 36p. (Orig.). 1988. 14.95 (0-9620585-0-5) Cahoon Mus Amer Art.

Rapp, Sandy. God's Country: A Case Against Theocracy. LC 91-7771. (Illus.). 160p. 1991. lib. bdg. 32.95 (1-56024-103-9); pap. 12.95 (0-918393-94-9) Haworth Pr.

Rapp, Stan. Beyond MaxiMarketing: The New Power of Caring & Daring. 1993. text ed. 21.95 (0-07-051343-0) McGraw.

Rapp, Stan & Collins, L. Maximarketing: The New Direction in Advertising, Promotion, & Marketing Strategy. 256p. 1987. text ed. 26.95 (0-07-051191-8) McGraw.

Rapp, Stan & Collins, Tom. The Great Marketing Turnaround. 368p. 1990. 22.95 (0-13-365560-1) P-H.

— The Great Marketing Turnaround: The Age of the Individual - & How to Profit from It. 352p. 1992. reprint ed. pap. 12.95 (0-452-26749-8, Plume) NAL-Dutton.

— Maximarketing: The New Direction in Advertising, Promotion & Marketing Strategy. 1989. pap. 12.00 (0-452-26238-0, Plume) NAL-Dutton.

Rapp, William F. An Annotated Catalog of Louisiana Railroads. (Railway History Monograph). (Illus.). 34p. 1990. pap. 8.00 (0-916170-37-3) J-B Pub.

— Atlas of Hand Cancels, 1875-1975. (Illus.). 95p. (Orig.). 1991. pap. 5.50 (0-916170-39-X) J-B Pub.

— Brickmaking in Nebraska. (Illus.). 88p. 1993. pap. 9.00 (0-916170-28-4) J-B Pub.

— A Catalog of Burlington & Missouri River RR & C. B. & Q. RR Employee Timetables in the Archives of the Nebraska State Historical Society. (Railway History Monograph). (Illus.). (Orig.). 1985. pap. 6.00 (0-916170-26-8) J-B Pub.

— The Chicago & Northwestern: The Nebraska Division Operation. (Railway History Monograph). (Illus.). 62p. (Orig.). 1991. pap. 12.00 (0-916170-41-1) J-B Pub.

— The Galveston, Houstan & Henderson Railroad. (Railway History Monograph). (Illus.). 49p. (Orig.). 1987. pap. 10.50 (0-916170-36-5) J-B Pub.

— Railway History Via Post Cards: How We Got There. 52p. (Orig.). 1992. pap. 14.00 (0-916170-40-3) J-B Pub.

— The Spiders of Galveston Island (Texas) (Novitates Arthropodae Ser.). 10p. 1984. pap. 3.00 (0-916170-23-3) J-B Pub.

Rapp, William F. & Beranek, Susan K. An Industrial Archaeology of Nebraska. LC 76-8317. (Illus.). 155p. 1984. 15.00 (0-916170-00-4) J-B Pub.

Rapp, William F., jt. auth. see Koval, Andrew C.

Rapp, William G. Construction of Structural Steel Building Frames. 2nd ed. LC 87-16605. 416p. (C). 1988. reprint ed. lib. bdg. 62.50 (0-89464-241-3) Krieger.

Rappaport, Alain, jt. ed. see Schorr, Herbert.

Rappaport, Alain, ed. see Smith, Reid.

Rappaport, Alfred. Creating Shareholder Value. 272p. 1986. text ed. 35.00 (0-02-925720-4) Free Pr.

Rappaport, Alfred, ed. Information for Decision Making: Readings in Cost & Managerial Accounting. 3rd ed. (Illus.). 416p. (C). 1982. pap. text ed. write for info. (0-13-464354-2) P-H.

Rappaport, Ann. Development & Transfer of Pollution Prevention Technology. LC 93-292. 224p. 1993. text ed. 55.00 (0-89930-816-3, Q816, Quorum Bks) Greenwood.

Rappaport, Ann & Flaherty, Margaret F. Corporate Responses to Environmental Challenges: Initiatives by Multinational Management. LC 91-44706. 216p. 1992. text ed. 49.95 (0-89930-715-9, RMJ/, Quorum Bks) Greenwood.

Rappaport, Anna M. & Schieber, Sylvester J., eds. Demography & Retirement in the 21st Century. LC 92-46552. 344p. 1993. text ed. 57.95 (0-275-94248-1, C4248, Praeger Pubs) Greenwood.

Rappaport, Armin. The British Press & Wilsonian Neutrality. 1951. 11.25 (0-8446-1378-9) Peter Smith.

— The Navy League of the United States. LC 62-8227. 284p. reprint ed. pap. 81.00 (0-7837-3684-3, 2043558) Bks Demand.

Rappaport, Armin, ed. Monroe Doctrine. LC 64-25181. 1964. pap. 9.50 (0-03-048705-6) Krieger.

Rappaport, Armin, ed. see Bailey, Thomas A.

Rappaport, Arthur. Mozart's Ear. 1995. write for info. (0-89189-301-6) Am Soc Clinical.

Rappaport, Bruce M. The Open Adoption Book: A Guide to Adoption Without Tears. 256p. 1992. text ed. 20.00 (0-02-601105-0) Macmillan.

Rappaport, Claudia. How to Make & Market Costume Jewelry for Fun or Profit. 24p. 1992. 4.95 (0-9634225-0-2) C Rappaport.

Rappaport, Donald, jt. auth. see Butler, Robert E.

Rappaport, Doreen. The Alger Hiss Trial. LC 92-46155. (Be the Judge - Be the Jury Ser.). (Illus.). 192p. (J). (gr. 5 up). 1993. 15.00 (0-06-025119-0); lib. bdg. 14.89 (0-06-025120-4); pap. 4.95 (0-06-446115-7, Trophy) HarpC Child Bks.

— American Women: Their Lives in Their Words. LC 89-77621. (Trophy Nonfiction Bk.). (Illus.). 336p. (YA). (gr. 7 up). 1992. pap. 7.95 (0-06-446127-0, Trophy) HarpC Child Bks.

— The Boston Coffee Party. LC 87-45301. (Harper I Can Read Bk.). (Illus.). 64p. (J). (gr. k-3). 1988. lib. bdg. 14.89 (0-06-024825-4) HarpC Child Bks.

— The Boston Coffee Party. LC 87-45301. (Trophy I Can Read Bk.). (Illus.). 64p. (J). (gr. k-3). 1990. pap. 3.50 (0-06-444141-5, Trophy) HarpC Child Bks.

— But She's Still My Grandma! LC 81-20236. (Illus.). 32p. (J). (gr. 1-5). 1982. 16.95 (0-89885-072-X) Human Sci Pr.

— Escape from Slavery: Five Journeys to Freedom. LC 90-38170. (Illus.). 128p. (J). (gr. 4-7). 1991. 13.95 (0-06-021631-X); lib. bdg. 13.89 (0-06-021632-8) HarpC Child Bks.

— Journey of Meng. (J). (ps-3). 1991. 13.95 (0-8037-0895-5); lib. bdg. 13.89 (0-8037-0896-3) Dial Bks Young.

— Living Dangerously: American Women Who Risked Their Lives for Adventure. LC 90-28915. (Illus.). 128p. (J). (gr. 4-7). 1991. 14.95 (0-06-025108-5); lib. bdg. 14.89 (0-06-025109-3) HarpC Child Bks.

— The Lizzie Borden Trial. LC 91-23232. (Be the Judge - Be the Jury Ser.). (Illus.). 176p. (J). (gr. 5 up). 1992. lib. bdg. 13.89 (0-06-025114-X) HarpC Child Bks.

— The Sacco-Vanzetti Trial. LC 91-47509. (Be the Judge - Be the Jury Ser.). (Illus.). 176p. (J). (gr. 5 up). 1992. lib. bdg. 13.89 (0-06-025116-6) HarpC Child Bks.

— The Sacco-Vanzetti Trial. LC 91-47509. (Be the Judge - Be the Jury Ser.). (Illus.). 176p. (J). (gr. 5 up). 1994. pap. 4.95 (0-06-446113-0, Trophy) HarpC Child Bks.

— A Scary Day. (J). (ps-1). 1988. 8.49 (0-87386-056-X); pap. 1.95 (0-87386-052-7); audio 16.99 (0-685-25200-0); audio 9.95 (0-685-25201-9) Jan Prods.

— Tinker vs. Des Moines: Student Rights on Trial. LC 92-25019. (Be the Judge - Be the Jury Ser.). (Illus.). 160p. (J). (gr. 5 up). 1993. lib. bdg. 14.89 (0-06-025118-2) HarpC Child Bks.

— Tinker vs. Des Moines: Student Rights on Trial. LC 92-25019. (Be the Judge - Be the Jury Ser.). (Illus.). 160p. (J). (gr. 5 up). 1994. pap. 4.95 (0-06-446114-9, Trophy) HarpC Child Bks.

Rappaport, Doreen, ed. American Women: Their Lives in Their Words. LC 89-77621. (Illus.). 336p. (YA). (gr. 7 up). 1990. 18.00 (0-690-04819-X, Crowell Jr Bks); lib. bdg. 17.89 (0-690-04817-3, Crowell Jr Bks) HarpC Child Bks.

Rappaport, E., tr. Hungarian Problem Book 2: Based on the Eotvos Competition. LC 63-16149. (New Mathematical Library: No. 12). 120p. 1963. pap. 11.00 (0-88385-612-3) Math Assn.

Rappaport, Elana, ed. see Carlebach, Shlomo.

Rappaport, Ernest A. Anti-Judaism: A Psychohistory. LC 75-36297. 312p. 1976. 12.50 (0-9603382-0-9) Perspective Chicago.

Rappaport, Fred. Farewell to Vienna. (Illus.). 344p. (Orig.). 1985. 16.50 (0-915911-02-7) Publishers Assocs.

Rappaport, Gilbert C. Grammatical Function & Syntactic Structure: The Adverbial Participle of Russian. (UCLA Slavic Studies: Vol. 9). 218p. 1984. pap. 18.95 (0-89357-133-4) Slavica.

Rappaport, Harold M., tr. see Basrani, Enrique.

Rappaport, Harvey M., et al. The Guidebook for Patient Counseling. LC 93-79389. 90p. 1993. pap. text ed. 24.50 (1-56676-089-5) Technomic.

Rappaport, Helen, tr. see Chekhov, Anton.

Rappaport, Joanne. Cumbe Reborn: An Andean Ethnography of History. LC 93-4909. (Illus.). 256p. 1993. pap. text ed. 15.95 (0-226-70526-9) U Ch Pr.

— Cumbe Reborn: An Andean Ethnography of History. LC 93-4909. (Illus.). 256p. 1993. lib. bdg. 41.95 (0-226-70525-0) U Ch Pr.

— The Politics of Memory: Native Historical Interpretation in the Colombian Andes. (Cambridge Latin American Studies: No. 70). (Illus.). 200p. (C). 1990. 64.95 (0-521-37345-X) Cambridge U Pr.

Rappaport, Jon, ed. see Cantwell, Alan, Jr.

Rappaport, Julian. Community Psychology: Values, Research, & Action. LC 76-55422. 482p. (C). 1977. text ed. 42.75 (0-03-006441-4) HB Coll Pubs.

Rappaport, Julian & Hess, Robert, eds. Studies in Empowerment: Steps Toward Understanding & Action. LC 84-4461. (Prevention in Human Services Ser.: Vol. 3, Nos. 2-3). 230p. 1984. text ed. 49.95 (0-86656-283-4) Haworth Pr.

Rappaport, Julian, jt. ed. see Seidman, Edward.

Rappaport, Roy A. Ecology, Meaning, & Religion. 259p. 1988. 25.00 (0-938190-28-8); pap. 12.95 (0-938190-27-X) North Atlantic.

— Pigs for the Ancestors: Ritual in the Ecology of a New Guinea People. 2nd ed. LC 83-51294. (Illus.). 496p. 1984. text ed. 40.00 (0-300-03204-8); pap. 18.00 (0-300-03205-6) Yale U Pr.

Rappaport, S. Perspectives in Judaism: South Africa. 378p. 1986. 17.95 (0-8197-0523-3) Bloch.

Rappaport, S. A., jt. ed. see Van den Heuvel, E. P.

Rappaport, Sheldon R. Public Education for Children with Brain Dysfunction. LC 69-17693. (Illus.). 257p. reprint ed. pap. 73.30 (0-8357-3983-X, 2036681) Bks Demand.

Rappaport, Stephen, jt. ed. see Leighland, James.

Rappaport, Stephen P. Affluent Investor: Investment Strategies for All Markets. 1990. 24.95 (0-13-018375-X) P-H.

— The Affluent Investor: Investment Strategies for All Markets. 1990. 24.95 (0-317-03937-7) NY Inst Finance.

Rappaport, Stephen P., jt. auth. see Lamb, Robert.

Rappaport, Stephen S. Age Discrimination: A Legal & Practical Guide for Employers. 1989. 95.00 (1-55871-136-8, BSP 129) BNA.

Rappaport, Suki, jt. auth. see Jay, Ira.

Rappaport, Susan. Traveler's Guide to Museum Exhibitions, 1989: U. S. Edition. Preciado, Kathleen, ed. (Illus.). 160p. (Orig.). 1988. pap. 8.95 (0-923041-00-1) Mus Guide Pubns Inc.

***Rappaport, Susan S.** Nineteen Ninety-Five Traveler's Guide to Art Museum Exhibitions. 1994. pap. 12.95 (0-8109-2586-9) Abrams.

Rappaport, Theodore S. Mobile Cellular Communications. (Illus.). write for info. (0-7803-0344-X, HL0455-6) Inst Electrical.

***Rappaport, Theodore S., ed.** Cellular Radio & Personal Communications: Selected Readings. LC 94-40139. 522p. 1995. pap. 39.95 (0-7803-2283-5) IEEE Comp Soc.

Rappaport, Theodore S., jt. ed. see Feuerstein, Martin J.

Rappaport, Theodore S., et al, eds. Wireless Personal Communications: Trends & Challenges. LC 93-50913. (International Series in Engineering & Computer Science, VLSI, Computer Architecture, & Digital Screen Processing: Vol. 262). 280p. (C). 1994. lib. bdg. 95.00 (0-7923-9430-5) Kluwer Ac.

Rappard, Hans V., et al, eds. Annals of Theoretical Psychology, Vol. 8. LC 84-644088. 306p. 1993. 79.50 (0-306-44564-6, Plenum Pr) Plenum.

— Annals of Theoretical Psychology, Vol. 9. LC 84-644088. (Illus.). 280p. 1993. 79.50 (0-306-44624-3, Plenum Pr) Plenum.

Rappard, William E. Collective Security in Swiss Experience, 1291-1948. LC 84-10758. xvi, 150p. 1984. reprint ed. text ed. 49.75 (0-313-24381-6, RACS, Greenwood Pr) Greenwood.

— International Relations As Viewed from Geneva. LC 72-4290. (World Affairs Ser.: National & International Viewpoints). 238p. 1972. reprint ed. 23.95 (0-405-04582-4) Ayer.

Rapparini, R. Health Service Market in Europe Hospital Equipment. 1984. 75.00 (0-444-80561-3, I-185-84) Elsevier.

Rappay, George. Proteinases & Their Inhibitors in Cells & Tissues. (Progress in Histochemistry & Cytochemistry Ser.: Vol. 18, No. 4). 60p. 1989. pap. text ed. 50.00 (0-89574-281-0, Pub. by Gustav Fischer Verlag); 40.00 (0-685-56004-X, Pub. by Gustav Fischer Verlag) VCH Pubs.

Rappaz, J., jt. auth. see Crouzeix, M.

Rappaz, M., et al, eds. Modeling of Casting, Welding & Advanced Solidification Processes Five. (Illus.). 925p. 1991. 165.00 (0-87339-172-1, 409) Minerals Metals.

Rappe, C., et al, eds. Chlorinated Dioxins & Dibenzofurans in Perspective. (Illus.). 589p. 1986. 86.95 (0-87371-056-8, TD196, CRC Reprint) Franklin.

— Environmental Carcinogens: Methods of Analysis & Exposure Measurement, Vol. 11: Oolychlorinated Dioxins & Dibenzofurans. (IARC Scientific Publications: No. 108). (Illus.). 400p. 1992. 120.00 (92-832-2108-7) OUP.

Rappel, Yoel, ed. Yearning for the Holy Land: Hasidic Tales of Israel. Himmelstein, Shmuel, tr. (Illus.). 176p. 1987. reprint ed. 11.95 (0-317-56162-6, Watts); reprint ed. pap. 9.95 (0-915361-86-8, Watts) Modan-Adama Bks.

Rappel, Yoel & Ben-Dov, Meir. Mosaics in the Holy Land: Christian, Moslem & Jewish. Himmelstein, Shmuel, tr. (Illus.). 148p. 1987. 15.95 (0-915361-54-X) Modan-Adama Bks.

— Mosaics in the Holy Land: Christian, Moslem, & Jewish. (Illus.). 148p. (J). (ps up). 1987. 15.95 (0-318-32655-8, Watts) Modan-Adama Bks.

Rappelfeld, Joel. The Complete Blader. (Illus.). 144p. (Orig.). 1992. pap. 8.95 (0-312-06936-7) St Martin.

Rappen, Ulrich, jt. auth. see MacLean, George.

***Rapping, Elayne.** The Culture of Recovery: Making Sense of the Self-Help Movement in Women's Lives. LC 95-14095. 256p. (C). 1996. 24.00 (0-8070-2716-2) Beacon Pr.

— The Looking Glass World of Non Fiction Television. LC 86-27944. 201p. (Orig.). 1987. 25.00 (0-89608-282-2); pap. 9.00 (0-89608-281-4) South End Pr.

— Media-tions: Forays into the Culture & Gender Wars. 250p. (Orig.). (C). 1994. pap. 15.00 (0-89608-478-7) South End Pr.

— Media-tions: Forays into the Culture & Gender Wars. 250p. (Orig.). (C). 1994. lib. bdg. 35.00 (0-89608-479-5) South End Pr.

— The Movie of the Week: Private Stories - Public Events. (American Culture Ser.: Vol. 5). 208p. (C). 1992. text ed. 39.95 (0-8166-2017-2); pap. text ed. 14.95 (0-8166-2018-0) U of Minn Pr.

Rapping, Leonard A. International Reorganization & American Economic Policy. 208p. 1989. pap. 18.50 (0-8147-7416-4) NYU Pr.

***Rappleye, Charles & Becker, Ed.** All American Mafioso: The Johnny Rosselli Story. rev. ed. LC 94-46832. 1995. pap. 14.95 (1-56980-027-8) Barricade Bks.

Rappleyea, Alan, ed. Federal Fisheries Management Update, No. 2: A Guidebook to the Magnuson Fishery Conservation & Management Act. rev. ed. (Illus.). (C). 1989. pap. text ed. 4.50 (0-945216-02-5) U OR Ocean & Law Ctr.

***Rappold, Edward A.** Reflections of Old Cedarburg. 3rd ed. (Illus.). 156p. 1994. pap. 14.95 (0-9625597-2-5) Cedarburg Cultural Ctr.

***Rappole, John B.** The Ecology of Migrant Birds: A Neotropical Perspective. LC 95-10214. 1995. write for info. (1-56098-514-3); pap. write for info. (1-56098-513-5) Smithsonian.

Rappole, John H. & Blacklock, Gene W. Birds of Texas: A Field Guide. LC 93-8448. (W. L. Moody, Jr. Natural History Ser.: Vol. 14). (Illus.). 372p. 1994. 39.95 (0-89096-544-7); pap. 14.95 (0-89096-545-5) Tex A&M Univ Pr.

— Birds of the Texas Coastal Bend: Abundance & Distribution. LC 84-40567. (W. L. Moody, Jr. Natural History Ser.: No. 7). (Illus.). 184p. 1985. 19.50 (0-89096-221-9) Tex A&M Univ Pr.

Rappole, John H., jt. auth. see DeGraaf, Richard M.

Rappole, John H., et al. Aves Migratorias Nearticas En los Neotropicos. 348p. 1993. 19.00 (0-9638408-0-0) C & RC Nat Zool.

Rappolt, Hedwig, tr. see Buchner, Georg.

Rappolt, Hedwig, tr. see Mussmann, Linda.

Rappolt, Hedwig, tr. see Wolf, Christa.

Rappolt, Miriam. Queen Emma: A Woman of Vision. (Illus.). (Orig.). (YA). 1991. pap. 12.95 (0-916630-68-4) Pr Pacifica.

Rappolt, Miriam E. One Paddle, Two Paddle: Hawaiian Teen Age Mystery & Suspense Stories. Pultz, Jane W., ed. LC 82-24048. (Illus.). 190p. (YA). (gr. 7-12). 1993. pap. 10.95 (0-916630-69-2) Pr Pacifica.

Rappopport, A. S., tr. see Peretz, Isaac L.

Rappoport, Albert, jt. auth. see Burgess, Ernest M.

Rappoport, Angelo S. Dictionary of Socialism. 1976. lib. bdg. 44.00 (0-8490-1723-8) Gordon Pr.

— The Love Affairs of the Vatican. 1972. 35.00 (0-8490-0561-2) Gordon Pr.

— Myth & Legend of Ancient Israel, 3 Vols, Set. rev. ed. 1966. 49.50 (0-87068-099-4) Ktav.

Rappoport, David S. Cave Life. 1991. pap. 4.75 (0-8222-0192-5) Dramatists Play.

Rappoport, Doreen. The Night the Minute Hand Stopped. LC 88-81466. (Illus.). 32p. (Orig.). (J). (ps-2). 1988. pap. 8.95 (0-937124-16-8) Kimbo Educ.

Rappoport, James, et al, eds. Office Planning & Design Desk Reference. 352p. 1991. text ed. 79.95 (0-471-50820-9) Wiley.

Rappoport, Jon. AIDS Inc: Scandal of the Century. LC 88-80560. (Illus.). 275p. 1988. pap. 13.95 (0-941523-03-9) Human Energy Pr.

Rappoport, Ken. Bobby Bonilla. LC 92-34583. (Illus.). 144p. (J). (gr. 5 up). 1993. 14.95 (0-8027-8255-8); lib. bdg. 15.85 (0-8027-8256-6) Walker & Co.

— Nolan Ryan: The Ryan Express. LC 92-3244. (Taking Part Ser.). (Illus.). 64p. (J). (gr. 3 up). 1992. text ed. 13.95 (0-87518-524-X, Dillon Silver Burdett) Silver Burdett Pr.

— Shaquille O'Neal. LC 93-38561. 128p. (YA). 1994. 15.95 (0-8027-8294-9); lib. bdg. 16.85 (0-8027-8295-7) Walker & Co.

— The Syracuse Football Story. LC 75-6096. (College Sports Book Ser.). 1975. 10.95 (0-87397-061-6) Strode.

— Tar Heel, North Carolina Football. LC 76-19968. (College Sports Book Ser.). (Illus.). 1980. 10.95 (0-87397-029-2) Strode.

— Top Ten Basketball Legends. LC 94-32060. (Sports Top Ten Ser.). (Illus.). 48p. (J). (gr. 4-10). 1995. lib. bdg. 15.95 (0-89490-610-0) Enslow Pubs.

— Wake up the Echoes: Notre Dame Football. rev. ed. (College Sports Book Ser.). (Illus.). 464p. 1988. 19.95 (0-318-42033-3) Strode.

Rappoport, L. & Summers, D. Human Judgement & Social Interaction. LC 72-84872. 416p. 1973. 13.00 (0-8290-2305-4) Irvington.

Rappoport, Leon H., jt. auth. see Kren, George M.

Rappoport, Lisa B., ed. see Jones, Courtney R.

Rappoport, Paul S. Value for Value Psychotherapy: The Economic & Therapeutic Barter. LC 82-16573. 208p. 1983. text ed. 49.95 (0-275-91724-X, C1724, Praeger Pubs) Greenwood.

***Rappoport, Pavela.** Building the Churches of Kievan Russia. 300p. 1995. 59.50 (0-86078-327-8, Pub. by Variorum UK) Ashgate Pub Co.

Rappoport, Wendy Van Biert. Premenstrual Syndrome: A Self Help Guide. (Illus.). 96p. (Orig.). 1984. pap. 4.95 (0-936320-19-2) Compact Books.

Rappoport, Zui, jt. ed. see Patai, Saul E.

***Rappoport, Zvi.** The Chemistry of Cyclopropyl Groups Part 2. LC 87-10440. (The Chemistry of Functional Groups Ser.). 944p. reprint ed. pap. 180.00 (0-7837-8274-8, 2049054) Bks Demand.

— The Chemistry of the Cyclopropyl Group Part 1. LC 87-10440. (The Chemistry of Functional Groups Ser.). 822p. 1987. reprint ed. pap. 180.00 (0-7837-8273-X, 2049054) Bks Demand.

Rappoport, Zvi, ed. The Chemistry of Enamines. (Chemistry of Functional Groups Ser.). 800p. 1994. text ed. 875.00 (0-471-93339-2) Wiley.

— Chemistry of Enols. (Chemistry of Functional Groups Ser.). 823p. 1990. text ed. 620.00 (0-471-91720-6) Wiley.

— The Chemistry of the Cyano Group. LC 70-116165. (Chemistry of Functional Groups Ser.: Vol. 8). (Illus.). 1059p. reprint ed. pap. 180.00 (0-685-23865-2, 2056648) Bks Demand.

— The Chemistry of the Quinonoid Compounds, Vol. 2. LC 86-32494. (Chemistry of Functional Groups Ser.). 1740p. 1988. Set. text ed. 1,950.00 (0-471-91916-0) Wiley.

— Handbook of Tables for Organic Compound Identification. 3rd ed. 1966. 76.95 (0-8493-0303-6, QD1966) CRC Pr.

Rappoport, Zvi, ed. see Ogliaruso, Michael A. & Wolfe, James F.

Rappoport, Zvi, jt. auth. see Patai, Saul E.

Rappoport, Zvi, jt. ed. see Patai, Saul E.

Rappoport, Zvi, jt. ed. see Patai, Saul.

Rappoport, Zvi, ed. see Schank, K., et al.

***Rapport, David J., et al, eds.** Evaluating & Monitoring the Health of Large-Scale Ecosystems: Proceedings of the NATO Advanced Research Workshop, Held at Montebello, Quebec, Canada, October 10-15, 1993. LC 94-43600. (NATO ASI Ser.: Series I, Global Environmental Change: Vol. 28). 1995. write for info. (3-540-58805-1) Spr-Verlag.

Rapport, Leonard & Northwood, Arthur, Jr. Rendezvous with Destiny. (Illus.). 1977. 20.00 (0-686-26296-4) One Hund First Air.

***Rapport, Maurice M. & Gorio, Alfredo, eds.** Gangliosides in Neurological & Neuromuscular Function, Development, & Repair. fac. ed. LC 81-48322. (Illus.). 296p. Date not set. pap. 84.40 (0-7837-7200-9, 2047099) Bks Demand.

Rapport, Nigel. Diverse World Views in an English Village. 224p. 1993. 55.00 (0-7486-0417-0, Pub. by Edinburgh U Pr UK) Col U Pr.

— The Prose & the Passion: Anthropology, Literature, & the Writing of E. M. Forster. LC 93-28178. 1994. text ed. 79.95 (0-7190-3616-X, Pub. by Manchester Univ Pr UK) St Martin.

Rapport, Nigel, jt. ed. see Cohen, Anthony P.

Rapport, Steve, jt. auth. see Waller, Johnny.

Rapport, Virginia, ed. see Association for Childhood Education International.

Rappuoli, R., et al, eds. Bacterial Protein Toxins: Fourth European Workshop, Urbino, July 3-6, 1989. (International Medical Microbiology Ser.: Supplement 19). 551p. 1990. 95.00 (0-685-48100-X); lib. bdg. 110.00 (0-89574-315-9) G F Verlag.

***Rappuoli, Rino.** Signal Transduction & Bacterial Virulence. LC 95-6581. (Medical Intelligence Unit Ser.). 157p. 1995. 69.00 (1-57059-231-4) R G Landes.

Raps, Beth G., tr. see Dibango, Manu & Rouard, Danielle.

Raps, Beth G., tr. see Gibbal, Jean-Marie.

Rapsch, Jurgen & Najock, Dietmar, eds. Sallust - Concordantia in Corpus Sallustianum, 2 vols., Set. (Alpha-Omega, Reihe A Ser.: Bd. IX). xii, 1472p. (GER.). 1990. write for info. (3-487-09384-7, Pub. by Georg Olms GW) Lubrecht & Cramer.

***Rapske, Brian.** The Book of Acts & Paul in Roman Custody. Winter, Bruce W., ed. LC 94-34745. (Book of Acts in Its First Century Setting: Vol. 3). 600p. 1994. text ed. 37.50 (0-8028-2435-8) Eerdmans.

Rapsomanikis, jt. auth. see Harrison.

Rapson, jt. auth. see Hatfield.

***Rapson, E. J.** Ancient India from Earliest Times to the First Century Ad. 208p. Date not set. 25.00 (0-89005-493-2) Ares.

Rapson, Richard L. American Yearnings: Love, Money, & Endless Possibility. LC 88-17216. 282p. (Orig.). (C). 1988. pap. text ed. 25.00 (0-8191-7089-5) U Pr of Amer.

Rapson, Richard L., ed. Major Interpretations of the American Past. LC 72-149210. (Literature of History Ser.). (Orig.). (C). 1971. 29.50 (0-89197-284-6); pap. text ed. 9.95 (0-89197-285-4) Irvington.

Rapson, Richard L., jt. auth. see Hatfield, Elaine.

Rapson, Rip, jt. auth. see Proescholdt, Kevin.

Rapsus, Ginger. The United States Clad Coinage. (Illus.). 184p. (Orig.). 1992. pap. text ed. 12.95 (0-943161-42-8) Bowers & Merena.

Raptaosh, Diane. Just West of Now. (Essential Poets Ser.). 64p. 1993. pap. 8.00 (0-920717-71-3) Guernica Editions.

Raptis, Michael. Revolution & Counter Revolution in Chile. LC 74-82175. 160p. (C). 1975. text ed. 35.00 (0-312-67970-X) St Martin.

Raptis, Michel. Socialism, Democracy & Self Management: Political Essays. LC 79-56924. 172p. 1980. text ed. 29.95 (0-312-73653-3) St Martin.

Raqaz, jt. auth. see Ackerman, A. Bernard.

***Raquepali, James.** Lia Dan Stone of Destiny. 350p. (Orig.). 1995. pap. 9.95 (1-56901-785-9) NW Pub.

Raquin, Michele, jt. auth. see Bookmaker.

Raraty, ed. Hoffman: Prinzessin Brambill. (Bristol German Texts Ser.). (GER.). pap. 12.95 (0-631-01880-8, Pub. by Brstl Class Pr UK) Focus Info Gr.

Raraty, Maurice, tr. see Von Drygalski, Erich.

Rardin, Ronald L., jt. ed. see Parker, R. Gary.

Rardon, jt. auth. see Zipes.

Rardon, James R., jt. auth. see Kroes, Michael J.

Rare Books & Manuscripts Section, Bibliographic Standards Committee Staff. Examples to Accompany Descriptive Cataloging of Rare Books. 148p. 1993. 29.95 (0-8389-7672-7) Assn Coll & Res Libs.

Rarick, Holly M. Progressive Vision: The Planning of Downtown Cleveland 1903-1930. LC 86-12950. 96p. 1986. pap. 16.95 (0-910386-86-2) Cleveland Mus Art.

Raridon, Susan. Basics for Writing Your Law Firm Brochure. 36p. 1987. pap. 19.95 (0-89707-347-9, 511-0223) Amer Bar Assn.

Rarique, M. Indian & Muslim Philosophy: A Comparative Study. 1988. 13.00 (81-7024-171-5, Pub. by Ashish II) S Asia.

Rarirkar, H., jt. ed. see Poitevin, G.

Raritan Arsenal Staff. Modern Ordnance Materiel 1943. (Illus.). 216p. 1992. reprint ed. pap. 30.00 (0-910667-30-6) Northstar Bks.

***Rarwood, Hebert, Jr.** Baltimore's Light Rail. 1995. pap. 15.95 (0-915276-55-0) Quadrant Pr.

Ras & Zemankova, M. Intelligent Systems: State of the Art & Future Directions. 400p. 1990. boxed write for info. (0-13-465931-7) P-H.

Ras, Barbara, intro. Costa Rica: A Traveler's Literary Companion. (Traveler's Literary Companions Ser.). 256p. (Orig.). 1994. pap. 12.95 (1-883513-00-6) Whereabouts.

Ras, J. J. & Robson, S. O., eds. Variation, Transformation & Meaning: Studies on Indonesian Literatures in Honour of A. Teeuw. (KLTV Verhandelingen Ser.: No. 144). 236p. (Orig.). 1992. pap. 23.00 (90-6718-027-0, Pub. by KLTV Pr NE) Cellar.

Ras, Jim. Write TSRs Now with Borland's Turbo Assembler, Turbo C, Turbo Pascal. LC 93-14077. (Popular Applications Ser.). 200p. (Orig.). 1993. pap. 15.95 (1-55622-335-8) Wordware Pub.

Ras, V. Shalapati & Melnick, Joseph L., eds. Human Viruses in Sediments, Sludges, & Soils. 272p. 1987. 119.00 (0-8493-6572-4, RA644) CRC Pr.

***Ras, Z. W. & Zemankova, M., eds.** Methodologies for Intelligent Systems: Proceedings of the 8th International Symposium, ISMIS '94, Charlotte, North Carolina, USA, October 16-19, 1994. (Lecture Notes in Computer Science: Lecture Notes in Artificial Intelligence: Vol. 869). x, 610p. 1994. 82.00 (3-540-58495-1) Spr-Verlag.

Ras, Z. W., jt. ed. see Komorowski, J.

Ras, Z. W., et al, eds. Methodologies for Intelligent Systems: 6th International Symposium, ISMIS '91 Charlotte, NC, U. S. A., October 16-19, 1991 Proceedings. (Lecture Notes in Artifical Intelligence, Subseries of Lecture Notes in Computer Science: Vol. 542). x, 644p. 1991. pap. 61.00 (0-387-54563-8) Spr-Verlag.

Ras, Zbigniew W., ed. see International Symposium on Methodologies for Intelligent Systems.

Rasa, Anne E., et al, eds. The Sociobiology of Sexual & Reproductive Strategies. 300p. 1989. 69.95 (0-412-33780-0, A3098) Chapman & Hall.

Rasbach, Hubert H. The Dinkywinkies & Snickity Snackety Snort. LC 79-89378. (Illus.). (J). (ps-4). 1982. 6.95 (0-934822-05-0) Plus One Pub.

***Rasband, Judith.** Fabulous Fit. 1994. 27.00 (0-614-04518-5) Conselle Inst.

— Fabulous Fit. (Illus.). 200p. (C). 1992. pap. text ed. 19.50 (0-685-59695-8) Fairchild.

— Wardrobe Strategies for Women. LC 94-8251. 1995. write for info. (0-8273-6159-9) Delmar.

***Rasband, Judith A.** Wardrobe Strategies for Women. 1995. 29.95 (0-614-04519-3) Conselle Inst.

Rasband, S. Neil. The Chaotic Dynamics of Nonlinear Systems. 230p. 1990. text ed. 64.95 (0-471-63418-2) Wiley.

— Dynamics. 286p. 1990. reprint ed. 43.95 (0-89464-445-9) Krieger.

Rasberry, Leslie. Copyfitting with a Small Calculator. LC 77-83812. 83p. 1977. 11.50 (0-910158-26-6) Art Dir.

Rasberry, Robert W. & Lindsay, Laura L. Effective Managerial Communication. 2nd ed. LC 93-2578. 688p. 1994. text ed. 49.95 (0-534-21468-1) S-W Pub.

Rasberry, Robert W., jt. auth. see Flacks, Niki.

***Rasberry, Salli & Elwyn, Padi S.** Living Your Life Out Loud: How to Unlock Your Creativity & Unleash Your Joy. Miller, Tom, ed. 1995. pap. 12.00 (0-671-89805-1) PB.

Rasberry, Salli, jt. auth. see Phillips, Michael.

Rasberry, Salli, jt. auth. see Whitmyer, Claude.

***Rasburry, Kaitlin.** The Cat Sat. (Illus.). 32p. (J). (gr. k-3). 1995. pap. 8.95 (1-884825-15-X) Raspberry Pubns.

— The Cat Sat: A Study in Short & Long Vowels. (Illus.). 32p. (J). (gr. k-3). 1994. lib. bdg. 14.95 (1-884825-02-8) Raspberry Pubns.

— Hillary's Book of ABC's. (Illus.). 32p. (J). (ps-1). 1994. lib. bdg. 14.95 (1-884825-00-1) Raspberry Pubns.

— Hillary's Book of ABC's. 2nd ed. (Illus.). 32p. (J). (ps-1). 1994. pap. 8.95 (1-884825-09-5) Raspberry Pubns.

— A Monster in My Mouth: My Retainer. (Illus.). 24p. (J). (gr. 1-3). 1994. lib. bdg. 14.95 (1-884825-01-X) Raspberry Pubns.

— A Monster in My Mouth: My Retainer. 2nd ed. (Illus.). 24p. (J). (gr. 1-3). 1995. pap. 8.95 (1-884825-10-9) Raspberry Pubns.

***Rascal.** Orson. LC 94-75732. (J). (ps-3). 1994. 15.00 (0-688-13462-9) Lothrop.

— Socrates. (J). (ps-3). 1995. pap. 6.95 (0-8118-1047-X) Chronicle Bks.

Rascal & Bogaerts, Gert. Socrates. LC 92-24120. (J). 1993. 13.95 (0-8118-0314-7) Chronicle Bks.

Rasch, Arthur R. Manual for SIS Micro-Computer Software System. Ussery, Robert, ed. (Illus.). 101p. (C). 1987. 45.00 (0-317-91111-2, SIS030-M) Summa Info Systs.

Rasch, D., et al, eds. Elsevier's Dictionary of Biometry: In English, French, Spanish, Dutch, German, Italian, & Russian. LC 94-1645. (ENG & MUL.). 1994. 225.75 (0-444-81495-7) Elsevier.

Rasch, Deborah K. & Webster, Dawn E. Clinical Manual of Pediatric Anesthesia. (Clinical Manual Ser.). (Illus.). 624p. 1994. pap. text ed. 37.50 (0-07-051119-5) Hlth Prof Div.

Rasch, Dieter & Herrendorfer, Gunter. Experimental Design: Sample Size Determination & Block Designs. LC 85-18285. 1986. lib. bdg. 80.50 (90-277-1684-6) Kluwer Ac.

Rasch, Dieter & Tiku, Moti L., eds. Robustness of Statistical Methods & Nonparametric Statistics. 1986. lib. bdg. 109.00 (90-277-2076-2) Kluwer Ac.

Rasch, G. Probabilistic Models for Some Intelligence & Attainment Tests. LC 80-16546. 208p. 1980. lib. bdg. 21.00 (0-226-70553-6) U Ch Pr.

Rasch, Georg. Probabilistic Models for Some Intelligence & Attainment Tests. LC 80-16546. (Illus.). 222p. (C). 1993. reprint ed. pap. text ed. 20.00 (0-941938-05-0) Mesa Pr.

Rasch, John D. Rehabilitation of Workers' Compensation & Other Insurance Claimants: Case Management, Forensic, & Business Aspects. (Illus.). 222p. 1985. 41.95 (0-398-05087-2) C C Thomas.

Rasch, Joseph. Handling Federal Estate & Gift Taxes, 3 vols., Set. 4th ed. LC 84-81703. 1984. 330.00 (0-685-59864-0) Clark Boardman Callaghan.

— New York Landlord & Tenant: Rent Control & Rent Stabilization. 2nd ed. LC 87-80713. 1987. 90.00 (0-317-01506-0) Lawyers Cooperative.

— New York Landlord & Tenant: Rent Control & Rent Stabilization. 2nd suppl. ed. LC 87-80713. 1993. Suppl. 1993. 52.50 (0-317-03311-5) Lawyers Cooperative.

— New York Landlord & Tenant, Summary Proceedings, 3 Vols. 3rd ed. LC 71-154362. 1988. 270.00 (0-317-03188-0) Lawyers Cooperative.

— New York Landlord & Tenant, Summary Proceedings, 3 Vols. 3rd suppl. ed. LC 71-154362. 1993. Suppl. 1993. 60.00 (0-317-03189-9) Lawyers Cooperative.

— New York Law & Practice of Real Property, 3 vols. 2nd ed. LC 62-4443. 270.00 (0-317-00514-6) Lawyers Cooperative.

— New York Law & Practice of Real Property, 3 vols. 2nd suppl. ed. LC 62-4443. 1993. Suppl. 1993. 50.00 (0-317-05565-8) Lawyers Cooperative.

***Rasch, Philip J.** Trailing Billy the Kid. DeArment, Robert K., ed. LC 95-12960. (Outlaw-Lawman Research Ser.: Vol. 1). 1995. write for info. (0-935269-19-3) Natl Assn Outlaw.

— Weight Training. 5th ed. 128p. 1990. pap. write for info. (0-697-10417-6) Brown & Benchmark.

Rasch, Philip J., ed. Kinesiology & Applied Anatomy. 7th ed. LC 88-26649. (Illus.). 286p. 1989. text ed. 41.00 (0-8121-1132-X) Williams & Wilkins.

Rasch, Rudolf. Johannes de Garlandia en de Voor-Franconische Notatie. (Wissenschaftliche Abhandlungen-Musicological Studies: Vol. 20). 250p. (DUT.). 1969. lib. bdg. 54.00 (0-912024-90-9) Inst Mediaeval Mus.

Rasch, Tony. Lupine Walker. (Illus.). 88p. (Orig.). 1992. pap. 11.95 (1-56044-144-5) Falcon Pr MT.

***Rasche, Jeffrey A.** Devotional Companion to the International Lessons 1995-96. 112p. (Orig.). 1995. pap. 8.95 (0-687-00420-9) Abingdon.

Rasche, Robert H. & Johannes, James M. Controlling the Growth of Monetary Aggregates. (C). 1987. lib. bdg. 65.50 (0-89838-226-2) Kluwer Ac.

***Rasche, Ruth W.** The Deaconess Heritage: One Hundred Years of Caring, Healing & Teaching. 350p. 1994. pap. 9.95 (0-9642849-0-1) Deaconess Fnd.

Raschen, Dan. Send Port & Pyjamas! 245p. (C). 1988. 35.00 (0-7212-0763-4, Pub. by Regency Press) St Mut.

— Wrong Again Dan! Karachi to Krakatoa. 256p. 1984. 40.00 (0-7212-0638-7, Pub. by Regency Press) St Mut.

***Raschka, Chris.** Can't Sleep. LC 94-48805. (Illus.). 32p. (J). (ps-1). 1995. 14.95 (0-531-09479-0); lib. bdg. 14.99 (0-531-08779-4) Orchard Bks Watts.

— Charlie Parker Played Be Bop. LC 91-38420. (Illus.). 32p. (J). (ps-1). 1992. 14.95 (0-531-05999-5); lib. bdg. 14.99 (0-531-08599-6) Orchard Bks Watts.

— Elizabeth Imagined an Iceberg. LC 93-4875. (Illus.). 32p. (J). (ps-2). 1994. 14.95 (0-531-06817-X); lib. bdg. 14.99 (0-531-08667-4) Orchard Bks Watts.

— R & R: A Story about Two Alphabets. (Illus.). (J). 1989. 7.95 (0-87178-731-8) Brethren.

— Yo! Yes? LC 92-25644. (Illus.). 32p. (J). (ps-1). 1993. 14.95 (0-531-05469-1); lib. bdg. 14.99 (0-531-08619-4) Orchard Bks Watts.

Raschke, Carl. Theological Thinking. LC 87-26604. (Studies in Religion). 169p. 1988. 20.95 (1-55540-187-2, 01-00-53); pap. 13.95 (1-55540-188-0) Scholars Pr GA.

Raschke, Carl, ed. see Fehr, Wayne L.

Raschke, Carl A. The Alchemy of the Word: Language & the End of Theology. LC 79-15490. (American Academy of Religion. Studies in Religion: No. 20). 106p. reprint ed. pap. 30.30 (0-7837-5476-0, 2045241) Bks Demand.

— The Bursting of New Wineskins: Reflection on Religion & Culture at the End of Affluence. LC 78-16604. (Pittsburgh Theological Monographs: No. 24). 1978. 10.75 (0-915138-34-4) Pickwick.

— Fire & Roses: Postmodernity & the Thought of the Body. LC 95-4242. (SUNY Series, Postmodern Culture). 192p. (C). 1995. text ed. 49.50x (0-7914-2729-3); pap. text ed. 16.95x (0-7914-2730-7) State U NY Pr.

— The Interruption of Eternity: Modern Gnosticism & the Origins of the New Religious Consciousness. LC 79-16460. 280p. 1980. 29.95 (0-88229-374-5) Nelson-Hall.

— Painted Black. 1992. mass mkt. 5.50 (0-06-104080-0, Harp PBks) HarpC.

Raschke, Carl A., ed. New Dimensions in Philosophical Theology. (American Academy of Religion, Thematic Studies). 1982. 30.95 (0-89130-682-X, 01-24-91) Scholars Pr GA.

Raschke, E., et al, eds. Solar Radiation Atlas of Africa: Global & Diffuse Radiation Fluxes at Ground Level Derived from Imaging Data of the Geostationary Satellite METEOSAT 2. (Illus.). 172p. (C). 1991. text ed. 160.00 (90-5410-109-1, Pub. by A A Balkema NE) Ashgate Pub Co.

Raschke, Ehrhard, et al, eds. Remote Sensing of Atmosphere & Oceans. (Advances in Space Research Ser.: No. 9). 474p. 1989. pap. 70.00 (0-08-040149-X, 2208; 2307; 2309, Pergamon Pr) Elsevier.

Raschke, U. Fachwoerterbuch Sozialrecht und Arbeitsschutz. 195p. (ENG, FRE & GER.). 1987. pap. 75.00 (0-8288-7951-6) Fr & Eur.

Raschke, Wendy J., ed. The Archaeology of the Olympics: The Olympics & Other Festivals in Antiquity. LC 87-40150. (Wisconsin Studies in Classics). 312p. reprint ed. pap. 89.00 (0-7837-1984-1, 2042258) Bks Demand.

Rasco, Jose I. Hispanidad y Cubanidad. LC 87-82479. (Coleccion Cuba y Sus Jueces Ser.). 42p. (Orig.). (SPA.). 1987. pap. 6.00 (0-89729-461-0) Ediciones.

— Jacques Maritain y la Democracia Cristiana. LC 80-68468. 63p. (Orig.). (SPA.). 1980. pap. 4.95 (0-89729-274-X) Ediciones.

Rascoe, B. Theodore Dreiser. LC 72-3569. (American Literature Ser.: No. 49). (C). 1972. reprint ed. lib. bdg. 49.95 (0-8383-1545-3) M S G Haskell Hse.

Rascoe, Bailey, Jr. & Hyne, Norman J., eds. Petroleum Geology of the Mid-Continent. (Illus.). 162p. (C). 1988. 75.00 (0-945087-00-4) Tulsa Geol Soc.

Rascoe, Burton. Prometheans: Ancient & Moderns. LC 70-156707. (Essay Index Reprint Ser.). 1977. reprint ed. 20.95 (0-8369-2855-5) Ayer.

— Titans & Prometheans, 2 vols., Set. 1972. 100.00 (0-8490-1216-3) Gordon Pr.

— Titans of Literature from Homer to the Present. LC 76-121502. (Essay Index Reprint Ser.). 1977. 23.95 (0-8369-1775-8) Ayer.

***Rascon, Armando.** Xicano Progeny: Investigative Agents, Executive Council, & Other Representatives from the Sovereign State of Aztlan. Lipsett, Suzanne, ed. (Illus.). (Orig.). (SPA.). 1995. pap. 10.00 (1-880508-03-6) Mexican Museum.

Rascon, Bonnie & Levy, Judith. Feasting on an Allergy Diet. (Illus.). 224p. (Orig.). 1985. lib. bdg. 8.95 (0-9615136-4-0) Cuissential.

***Rascovsky, Arnaldo.** Filicide: The Murder, Humiliation, Mutilation, & Abandonment of Children by Parents. Rogers, Susan H., tr. LC 94-46705. 1995. pap. 25.00 (1-56821-456-1) Aronson.

Rase, Howard F. Chemical Reactor Design for Process Plants: Principles & Techniques, Vol. 1. LC 77-1285. (Illus.). 784p. 1977. reprint ed. pap. 180.00 (0-685-23826-1, 2056607) Bks Demand.

— Chemical Reactor Design for Process Plants, Vol. 2: Case Studies & Design Data. LC 77-1285. 258p. 1977. reprint ed. pap. 73.60 (0-7837-1462-9, 2056607) Bks Demand.

— Fix-Bed Reactor Design & Diagnostics: Gas-Phase Reactions. 376p. 1990. text ed. 62.95 (0-409-90003-6) Buttrwrth-Heinemann.

— The Philosophy & Logic of Chemical Engineering. LC 61-18166. (Illus.). 176p. reprint ed. pap. 50.20 (0-685-23791-5, 2032882) Bks Demand.

— Piping Design for Process Plants. LC 89-24404. (Illus.). 312p. 1990. reprint ed. 73.00 (0-89464-424-6) Krieger.

Rase, Howard F. & Barrow, M. H. Project Engineering of Process Plants. LC 57-5929. 708p. reprint ed. pap. 180.00 (0-317-27812-6, 2055947) Bks Demand.

Rase, Howard F. & Cunningham, William A. Chemical Engineering at the University of Texas 1910-1990. (Illus.). 282p. (C). 1990. 40.00 (0-9627614-0-0) UTX Austin DCE.

Raser, Harold E. Phoebe Palmer: Her Life & Thought. LC 86-31251. (Studies in Women & Religion: Vol. 22). 392p. 1987. lib. bdg. 99.95 (0-88946-527-4) E Mellen.

***Raser, Jamie B.** Raising Children You Can Live With: A Guide for Frustrated Parents. (Illus.). 152p. (Orig.). 1995. per., pap. 10.95 (1-886298-08-4) Bayou Pubng.

Raser, Lois. Carol Builds a House. Pierce, Glen, ed. LC 92-70674. 96p. (Orig.). 1992. pap. 6.95 (0-916035-48-4) Evangel Indiana.

Rasetti, M. Modern Methods in Equilibrium Statistical Mechanics. (Series on Advances in Statistical Mechanics: Vol. 2). 270p. 1986. text ed. 47.00 (9971-966-27-1); pap. text ed. 28.00 (9971-966-29-8) World Scientific Pub.

Rasetti, M., ed. The Hubbard Model: Recent Results. (Advances in Statistical Mechanics Ser.: Vol. 7). 240p. (C). 1991. text ed. 83.00 (981-02-0623-2); pap. 28.00 (981-02-0624-0) World Scientific Pub.

Rasetti, M. & Montorsi, A., eds. Integrable Systems in Statistical Mechanics. (Series on Advances in Statistical Mechanics: Vol. 1). 250p. 1985. text ed. 47.00 (9971-978-11-3); pap. text ed. 30.00 (9971-978-14-8) World Scientific Pub.

R

An Asterisk (*) at the beginning of an entry indicates that the title is appearing in BIP for the first time.

Rasetti, M. G., ed. New Problems, Methods & Techniques in Quantum Field Theory & Statistical Mechanics. 232p. (C). 1990. text ed. 61.00 (*981-02-0225-3*); pap. text ed. 33.00 (*981-02-0226-1*) World Scientific Pub.

Rasevic, Marc, jt. ed. see Druart, Therese-Anne.

Rasevskii, P. K., et al. Transactions of the Moscow Mathematical Society, Vol. 30 (1974) LC 65-7413. 260p. 1976. 70.00 (*0-8218-1630-6*, MOSCOW-30) Am Math.

Rasey, Marie I., ed. The Nature of Being Human. LC 58-12082. (Franklin Lectures of 1956-1957 Ser.). 129p. reprint ed. pap. 36.80 (*0-7837-3672-X*, 2043546) Bks Demand.

Rasey Simpson, Ruth M. Hand-Hewn in Old Vermont. 240p. 1993. pap. 12.95 (*1-881548-05-8*) Crane Hill AL.

— Out of the Saltbox. 220p. 1993. pap. 12.95 (*1-881548-06-6*) Crane Hill AL.

Rash, Ansley F. The Message of the Minor Prophets. 2nd ed. 48p. 1989. reprint ed. pap. 3.00 (*0-934666-30-X*) Artisan Sales.

Rash, Bryson B. Footnote Washington: Tracking the Engaging, Humorous & Surprising Bypaths of Capital History. LC 83-1572. (Illus.). 128p. 1983. pap. 8.95 (*0-914440-62-4*) EPM Pubns.

Rash, Felicity J. French & Italian Lexical Influences in German-Speaking Switzerland (1550-1650) (Studia Linguistica Germanica: No. 25). xii, 411p. (C). 1989. lib. bdg. 138.50x (*0-89925-526-4*) De Gruyter.

— French & Italian Lexical Influences in German-Speaking Switzerland (1550-1650) (Studia Linguistica Germanica: No. 25). 9xii, 411p. (C). 1989. lib. bdg. 138.50x (*3-11-011862-9*) De Gruyter.

Rash, Francis C., jt. auth. see Block, Robert W.

Rash, James N. Meter & Language in the Lyrics of the Suppliants of Aeschtlus. rev. ed. Connor, W. R., ed. LC 80-2665. (Monographs in Classical Studies). 1981. lib. bdg. 34.95 (*0-405-14049-5*) Ayer.

Rash, Nancy. The Painting & Politics of George Caleb Bingham. (Illus.). 304p. (C). 1991. text ed. 37.50 (*0-300-04731-2*) Yale U Pr.

Rash, Ron. The Night the New Jesus Fell to Earth & Other Stories from Cliffside, North Carolina. LC 94-18350. 1994. pap. 14.95 (*0-930769-11-2*) Bench Pr SC.

Rash, Wayne & Kenner, Hugh. Writing Well in the Real World: The Official Guide to Grammatik. 1992. 40.00 (*0-679-74112-7*) Random.

Rashad, Adib. Aspects of Eurocentric Thought. 220p. (C). 1991. pap. text ed. 15.95 (*1-56411-012-5*) Untd Bros & Sis.

***Rashad, Adib, pseud.** Islam, Black Nationalism & Slavery: A Detailed History. 1995. pap. 13.00 (*0-9627854-8-2*) Writers Inc.

***Rashad, Adib, ed.** Elijah Muhammad & the Ideological Foundation of the Nation of Islam. (Illus.). 290p. (Orig.). 1994. pap. 11.00 (*1-56411-065-6*) Untd Bros & Sis.

Rashad, Ahmad. Selected from Rashad: Mikes, Vikes & Something on the Backside. abr. ed. (Writers' Voices Ser.). 64p. (Orig.). 1991. pap. text ed. 3.50 (*0-929631-30-7*, Signal Hill) New Readers.

Rashad, Johari. Steppin' over the Glass: Life Journeys in Poetry & Prose. 80p. (Orig.). 1991. pap. 9.95 (*1-879260-05-0*) Evanston Pub.

Rashad, M. N. Anesthesia Review: Basic Science. 320p. 1991. pap. 24.95 (*1-56262-011-8*) PMA Pub Corp.

Rashad, Phylicia, jt. ed. see Scott, Arunika.

Rashap, Arthur & Braly, Beverly, eds. Seventh North American Ginseng Conference: Proceedings. 200p. 1986. pap. text ed. 10.00 (*0-9613800-1-2*) Ginseng Res Inst.

Rashap, Arthur W., et al, eds. The Ginseng Research Institute's Indexed Bibliography. LC 84-81467. 120p. 1984. pap. 65.00 (*0-9613800-0-4*) Ginseng Res Inst.

Rashba, E. I. & Sturge, M. D. Excitons. (Modern Problems in Solid State Physics Ser.: Vol. 2). 866p. 1982. 241.00 (*0-444-86202-1*, I-121-82, North Holland) Elsevier.

Rashba, E. I. & Sturge, M. D., eds. Excitons: Selected Chapters from the Book "Excitons" (Modern Problems in Condensed Matter Sciences Ser.: Vol. 2). 600p. 1987. pap. 36.00 (*0-444-87052-0*, North Holland) Elsevier.

Rashba, E. I., jt. ed. see Landwehr, G.

Rashbaum, Beth, jt. auth. see Silverstein, Olga.

Rashbrook, F., jt. auth. see Civardi, Anne.

Rashdall, Hastings. Ideas & Ideals. Major, H. D. & Cross, F. L., eds. LC 68-16970. (Essay Index Reprint Ser.). 1977. reprint ed. 19.95 (*0-8369-0810-4*) Ayer.

— Philosophy & Religion: Six Lectures Delivered at Cambridge. LC 79-98791. 1970. text ed. 38.50 (*0-8371-3025-5*, RAPR, Greenwood Pr) Greenwood.

Rashed, Roshdi. The Development of Arabic Mathematics: Between Arithmetic & Algebra. Armstrong, Angela, tr. LC 93-39784. (Boston Studies in the Philosophy of Science: Vol. 156). 1994. lib. bdg. 115.00 (*0-7923-2565-6*) Kluwer Ac.

— Optique et Mathematiques: Recherches Sur l'Historie de la Pensee Scientifique en Arabe. (Collected Studies: Vol. CS378). 352p. 1992. 105.00 (*0-86078-330-8*, Pub. by Variorum UK) Ashgate Pub Co.

Rasheed, Asalia. The Order of the Universe: Who is the Messiah? 52p. (Orig.). (C). 1991. pap. text ed. 10.00 (*0-317-04219-X*) Darby Pub.

***Rasheed, Sadig.** Development Management in Africa: Toward Dynamism, Empowerment, & Entrepreneurship. 283p. (C). 1994. pap. text ed. 49.95 (*0-8133-2147-6*) Westview.

Rasheed, Sadig, et al, eds. Public Enterprise Performance in Africa: Lessons from Country Case Studies. 304p. (Orig.). 1994. pap. 30.00 (*92-9038-053-5*) Kumarian Pr.

Rasheev, Velcho. English-French-German-Russian-Bulgarian Textile Dictionary. 1038p. (BUL, ENG, FRE, GER & RUS.). 1977. 125.00 (*0-317-59475-3*, Pub. by Collets UK) Pro-Am Music.

Rasher, Arthur A. Study Guide to Accompany Raymond McLeod Management Information Systems. 5th ed. (Illus.). 192p. (C). 1993. pap. write for info. (*0-02-398450-3*) Macmillan.

Rashevsky, Nicolas, ed. see Richardson, Lewis F.

Rashford, Nicholas & Coghlan, David. The Dynamics of Organizational Levels: A Change Framework for Managers & Consultants. (Organization Development Ser.). (Illus.). 120p. (C). 1994. pap. text ed. 26.95 (*0-201-54323-0*) Addison-Wesley.

Rashid, A. Cell Physiology & Genetics of Higher Plant, 2 vols. 1988. Vol. I, Cell Multiplication Cell Differentiation, Cell Totipotency, 208 pgs. 106.00 (*0-8493-6062-5*, QK725, CRC Reprint); Vol. II, Protoplast--Isolation & Cell Regeneration, 224 pgs. 117. 00 (*0-8493-6063-3*, QK725, CRC Reprint) Franklin.

Rashid, Ahmed. The Resurgence of Central Asia: Islam or Nationalism? (Politics in Contemporary Asia Ser.). 160p. (C). 1994. text ed. 59.95 (*1-85649-131-5*, Pub. by Zed Books UK); pap. 25.00 (*1-85649-132-3*, Pub. by Zed Books UK) Humanities.

Rashid al Madfai, Madiha. Jordan, the United States & the Middle East Peace Process, 1974-1991. (Middle East Library: No. 28). 296p. (C). 1993. 64.95 (*0-521-41523-3*) Cambridge U Pr.

***Rashid, Bob, photos & intro.** Wisconsin's Rustic Roads: A Road Less Travelled. LC 95-14187. (Illus.). 1995. 29.95 (*1-883755-02-6*) Lost Riv Pr.

***Rashid, Hani & Couture, Lise A.** Asymptote: Architecture at the Interval. LC 94-45009. (Illus.). 160p. (Orig.). 1995. pap. 27.50 (*0-8478-1861-6*) Rizzoli Intl.

Rashid, M. A. Geochemistry of Marine Humic Compounds. LC 85-14692. (Illus.). xii, 300p. 1985. 139.00 (*0-387-96135-6*) Spr-Verlag.

Rashid, Mark. Considering the Horse: Tales of Problems Solved & Lessons Learned. LC 93-2522. (Illus.). 224p. (Orig.). 1993. pap. 15.95 (*1-55566-118-1*) Johnson Bks.

Rashid, Muhammad H. SPICE for Circuits & Electronics Using PSpice. 2nd ed. LC 94-17481. 1994. pap. text ed. 26.00 (*0-13-124652-6*) P-H Gen Ref & Trav.

— SPICE for Electronics Using PSPICE. 304p. 1989. pap. text ed. 27.00 (*0-13-834672-0*) P-H.

Rashid, Muhammad H., jt. auth. see Lindsay, James F.

Rashid, Muhammed. SPICE for Power Electronics. 464p. 1993. pap. text ed. 30.00 (*0-13-030420-4*) P-H.

Rashid, Muhammed H. Power Electronics: Circuits, Devices, & Applications. 2nd ed. 650p. 1993. text ed. 66.00 (*0-13-678996-X*) P-H.

***Rashid, Naji A.** The Resurrection of Afrikan People in Amerika. 52p. (Orig.). 1994. pap. 6.95 (*1-56411-095-8*) Untd Bros & Sis.

Rashid, Nasser I. & Shaheen, Esber I. King Fahd & Saudi Arabia's Great Evolution. (Current Events, Historical-Societal Progress Ser.). (Illus.). 342p. 1987. 22.95 (*0-940485-00-1*) Intl Inst Tech.

— Saudi Arabia: All You Need to Know. LC 95-5829. 1995. 39.95 (*0-940485-02-8*) Intl Inst Tech.

— Saudi Arabia & the Gulf War. LC 92-9853. (Illus.). 564p. 1992. 22.95 (*0-940485-01-X*) Intl Inst Tech.

Rashid, Richard F., ed. CMU Computer Science: A Twenty-Fifth Anniversary Commemorative. (ACM Press Anthology Ser.). (Illus.). 448p. (C). 1991. text ed. 44.25 (*0-201-52899-1*) Addison-Wesley.

Rashid, Salim. Economies with Many Agents: An Approach Using Nonstandard Analysis. LC 86-45442. 192p. 1987. text ed. 30.00 (*0-8018-3379-5*) Johns Hopkins.

Rashidd, Amir & Williams, L. V. Breath of Blood & Milk: Dry Long So Poems. LC 88-70764. 64p. (Orig.). 1989. pap. 10.95 (*0-943767-05-9*) Audacious Pr.

Rashidi, Runoko, ed. see Van Sertima, Ivan.

Rashiduzzaman, Mohammed. Politics & Government in the New World. 380p. 1993. per. 44.95 (*0-8403-8734-2*) Kendall-Hunt.

***Rashish, Peter S., ed.** Partnership for Growth: Reshaping Trade & Investment Patterns: New Approaches to Assisting Central & Eastern Europe. LC 94-71785. 136p. (Orig.). 1994. pap. 15.00 (*0-9628287-7-7*) European Inst.

— Regionalism or Globalism? A Report of the September 1994 Seminar: Transatlantic Trade & Investment: Factors for Stability. 76p. (Orig.). 1995. pap. 15.00 (*0-9628287-0-X*) European Inst.

***Rashke.** Escape from Sobibor. LC 94-47590. 1995. pap. text ed. 16.95 (*0-252-06479-8*) U of Ill Pr.

Rashke, Richard. Escape from Sobibor. (Illus.). 1987. pap. 3.95 (*0-380-75394-4*) Avon.

— Runaway Father: One Family's Seventeen-Year Search. 271p. 1988. 17.95 (*0-15-179040-X*) HarBrace.

Rashkevich, J. English - Latvian Dictionary. (ENG & LAV.). 1985. 59.95 (*0-8288-2485-1*) Fr & Eur.

Rashkin, Esther. Family Secrets & the Psychoanalysis of Narrative. 224p. 1992. text ed. 25.00 (*0-691-06951-4*) Princeton U Pr.

***Rashkind, Alan B. & Rowe, Gerard P.** Virginia Insurance Case Finder. 800p. 1994. 95.00 (*1-55834-146-3*) Michie Butterworth.

Rashkis, Harold A. & Tashjian, Levon D. Understanding Your Parents. LC 78-60444. (Illus.). 154p. (J). (gr. 9-12). 1978. 6.95 (*0-397-53067-6*) Lippincott.

Rashkovich, L. N. KDP-Family Single Crystals. (Optics & Optoelectronics Ser.). (Illus.). 212p. 1991. 103.00 (*0-7503-0105-8*) IOP Pub.

Rashkovsky, Avigail, ed. see Dovlatov, Sergei.

Rashkow, Ilona N. The Phallacy of Genesis: A Feminist & Psychoanalytic Approach. (Literary Currents in Biblical Interpretation Ser.). 144p. (Orig.). 1993. pap. 14.99 (*0-664-25250-8*) Westminster John Knox.

Rashotte, Michael E., jt. auth. see Amsel, Abram.

Rashwan, A., jt. auth. see Shawaki, I.

Rashwan, A., jt. ed. see Shawaki, I.

Rasi, Humberto. Life of Jesus. 1985. 3.99 (*0-8163-0573-0*) Pacific Pr Pub Assn.

— Life of Jesus, 1. 1985. 3.99 (*0-8163-0574-9*) Pacific Pr Pub Assn.

— Life of Jesus, 2. 1985. 3.99 (*0-8163-0608-7*) Pacific Pr Pub Assn.

— Life of Jesus, 3. 1985. 3.99 (*0-8163-0609-5*) Pacific Pr Pub Assn.

— Life of Jesus, Set. 1985. 9.99 (*0-685-10862-7*) Pacific Pr Pub Assn.

***Rasi, Richard A. & Rodriguez-Nogues, Lourdes, eds.** Out in the Workplace: Gay & Lesbian Professionals Tell Their Stories. 220p. (Orig.). 1995. pap. 12.95 (*1-55583-251-2*) Alyson Pubns.

***Rasiah, Rajah.** Foreign Capital & Industrialization in Malaysia. LC 94-31773. (Studies in the Economies of East & Southeast Asia Ser.). 1995. write for info. (*0-312-12440-6*) St Martin.

— Foreign Capital & Industrialization in Malaysia. (Studies in the Economies of East & Southeast Asia). 272p. 1995. 69.95 (*0-312-12405-8*) St Martin.

Rasic, J., jt. auth. see Kurmann, J.

Rasic, Mirko R. Postal History & Postage Stamps of Serbia, 1841-1921. (Illus.). 276p. 1979. 18.00 (*0-912574-25-9*) Collectors.

Rasico, Philip D. The Minorcans of Florida: Their History, Language, & Culture. LC 90-30600. (Illus.). 200p. (C). 1990. 50.00 (*1-877633-05-4*); pap. write for info. (*1-877633-07-0*) Luthers.

***Rasie, Lawrence.** Directory of Business Information. 1995. text ed. 85.00 (*0-471-59816-X*) Wiley.

***Rasikananda.** Srila Rasikananda's Sri Syamananda-Sataka: A Hundred Verses Glorifying Sri Syamahanda. Kusakrathadasa, tr. (Krsna Library Volume). 77p. (Orig.). 1995. pap. text ed. 6.00 (*1-56130-159-0*) Krsna Inst.

***Rasinski, Tim & Padak, Nancy, eds.** The Yearbook of the College Reading Association. annuals (Reading & Literacy Education Ser.). 200p. (C). 1994. lib. bdg. 15.00 (*1-883604-00-1*) Coll Read Assn.

Rasinski, Timothy, jt. auth. see Vacca, Richard T.

Rasinski, Timothy V. Parents & Teachers: Helping Children Learn to Read & Write. (Illus.). 200p. (Orig.). (C). 1994. pap. text ed. write for info. (*0-15-501315-7*) HB Coll Pubs.

Rasinski, Timothy V. & Gillespie, Cindy. Sensitive Issues: An Annotated Guide to Children's Literature K-6. 288p. 1992. pap. 29.95 (*0-89774-777-1*) Oryx Pr.

Rasis, E. P. Technical Reference Handbook. 2nd ed. (Illus.). 220p. 1991. 19.96 (*0-8269-3451-X*) Am Technical.

Rasjeswari, V., jt. auth. see Rao, K. S.

Raskas, Bernard S. Heart of Wisdom, Bk. III. 1986. 10.50 (*0-317-55245-7*) United Synagogue.

— Heart of Wisdom-One. 1962. 8.50 (*0-8381-2102-0*) United Syn Bk.

— Heart of Wisdom-Two. 1979. 9.50 (*0-8381-2104-7*) United Syn Bk.

Raskas, Bernard S., ed. Living Thoughts. LC 76-22418. 1976. 12.50 (*0-87677-145-2*) Hartmore.

Raskevics, J., et al. English-Latvian-Russian Dictionary. 718p. (ENG, LAV & RUS.). 1977. 50.00 (*0-686-82324-9*, Pub. by Collets UK) St Mut.

— English-Latvian-Russian Phraseological Dictionary. 718p. (ENG, LAT & RUS.). 1977. 35.00 (*0-317-59474-5*, Pub. by Collets UK) Pro-Am Music.

Raskiewicz. Woodturners Art. 1985. 24.95 (*0-684-18329-3*, Scribners) S&S Trade.

***Raskin.** First Principles. Date not set. 24.00 (*0-02-874107-2*) Free Pr.

— For the Hell of It: The Life & Times of Abbie Hoffman. 1992. write for info. (*0-15-165208-2*) HarBrace.

— Your Child's Education: Total Planning on Your Computer. 1995. pap. text ed. 24.95 (*1-56276-314-8*) Ziff-Davis.

Raskin, Abram. Petrodvorets: Palaces, Gardens, Fountains, Sculpture. 346p. 1979. 155.00 (*0-317-57407-8*, Pub. by Collets UK) St Mut.

Raskin, Allen, jt. ed. see Gershon, Samuel.

Raskin, Barbara. Current Affairs. 336p. 1991. mass mkt. 5.95 (*0-8041-0537-5*) Ivy Books.

— Current Affairs. 288p. 1990. 19.95 (*0-394-57994-1*) Random.

— Hot Flashes. 1991. mass mkt. 5.99 (*0-312-92801-7*) St Martin.

— A List. 1990. 18.95 (*0-685-33569-0*) Random.

— Loose Ends. 1988. mass mkt. 4.95 (*0-312-91348-6*) St Martin.

Raskin, David, ed. Psychological Methods in Criminal Investigation & Evidence. 416p. 1989. 44.95 (*0-8261-6450-1*) Springer Pub.

Raskin, Ellen. Figgs & Phantoms. LC 73-17309. (Illus.). 160p. (J). (gr. 4 up). 1974. pap. 15.95 (*0-525-29680-8*, 01063-320, DCB) Dutton Child Bks.

— Figgs & Phantoms. (Illus.). 160p. (J). (gr. 5-9). 1989. pap. 5.99 (*0-14-032944-7*, Puffin) Puffin Bks.

— The Mysterious Disappearance of Leon (I Mean Noel) (Illus.). 160p. (J). (gr. 5-9). 1989. pap. 4.99 (*0-14-032945-5*, Puffin) Puffin Bks.

— Nothing Ever Happens on My Block. LC 89-31342. (Illus.). 32p. (J). (gr. k-4). 1989. reprint ed. pap. 4.95 (*0-689-71335-5*, Aladdin Paperbacks) S&S Childrens.

— Spectacles. 2nd ed. LC 88-10363. (Illus.). 48p. (J). (gr. k-4). 1988. pap. 4.95 (*0-689-71271-5*, Aladdin Paperbacks) S&S Childrens.

— Twenty-Two, Twenty-Three. LC 76-5475. (Illus.). 32p. (J). (gr. k-3). 1976. lib. bdg. 12.95 (*0-689-30529-X*, Atheneum Bks Young) S&S Childrens.

— The Westing Game. (Illus.). 192p. (YA). (gr. 7 up). 1984. pap. 3.50 (*0-380-67991-4*, Flare) Avon.

— The Westing Game. (J). (gr. 5-9). 1978. 15.99 (*0-525-42320-6*, DCB) Dutton Child Bks.

— The Westing Game. 192p. (J). (gr. 5 up). 1992. pap. 3.99 (*0-14-034991-X*) Puffin Bks.

Raskin, Eugene. Architecturally Speaking. (Illus.). 1970. reprint ed. pap. 7.95 (*0-8197-0003-7*) Bloch.

— Citronella. 1980. 10.95 (*0-686-98251-7*); pap. 4.95 (*0-8197-0483-0*) Bloch.

Raskin, Herbert, jt. auth. see Krystal, Henry.

Raskin, Herbert A., jt. auth. see Krystal, Henry.

Raskin, Jonah. James D. Houston. LC 91-55033. (Western Writers Ser.: No. 99). (Illus.). 48p. 1991. 3.95 (*0-88430-098-6*) Boise St U W Writ Ser.

Raskin, Linda, jt. auth. see Lawrence, Jan.

***Raskin, Marcus, comp.** Visions & Revisions: Reflections on Culture & Democracy at the End of the Century. LC 94-25203. (Voices & Visions Ser.). 1994. pap. 16.95 (*1-56656-172-8*, Olive Branch Pr) Interlink Pub.

Raskin, Marcus, ed. Next Steps for a New Administration. 48p. 1976. pap. 17.95 (*0-87855-657-5*) Transaction Pubs.

Raskin, Marcus & Hartman, Chester, eds. Winning America: Ideas & Leadership for the 1990s. LC 88-42556. 414p. (Orig.). 1988. 40.00 (*0-89608-344-6*); pap. 16.00 (*0-89608-343-8*) South End Pr.

Raskin, Marcus G. Abolishing the War System. 1992. lib. bdg. 30.00 (*0-9623718-9-0*); pap. 14.00 (*0-9623718-8-2*) Aletheia Pr.

— Essays of a Citizen: From National Security State to Democracy. LC 90-9074. 336p. 1991. 41.95 (*0-87332-764-0*) M E Sharpe.

— The Politics of National Security. LC 78-55935. (Issues in Contemporary Civilization Ser.). 320p. 1979. 34.95 (*0-87855-239-1*) Transaction Pubs.

Raskin, Marcus G., et al, eds. New Ways of Knowing: The Sciences, Society & Reconstructive Knowledge. 352p. 1987. pap. 26.50 (*0-8476-7463-0*) Rowman.

Raskin, Markus. Visions & Revisions: Reflections on Culture & Democracy at the End of the Century. 320p. XOlive Branch Pr. 39.95 (*1-56656-171-X*, Olive Branch Pr); pap. 16.95 (*0-685-73062-X*) Interlink Pub.

Raskin, Michael M. Comparative Abdominal & Pelvic Anatomy by Computed Tomography & Ultrasound. 304p. 1979. 86.95 (*0-8493-5369-6*, RC944, CRC Reprint) Franklin.

Raskin, Milton. Isometrics for Drummers. (Illus.). 20p. 1972. pap. text ed. 4.95 (*0-89915-016-0*) Playback Mus Pub.

— Isometrics for Guitarists. (Howard Roberts Guitar Manuals Ser.). (Illus.). 24p. 1971. pap. text ed. 5.95 (*0-89915-001-2*) Playback Mus Pub.

— Isometrics for Pianists. pap. 4.95 (*0-685-75234-8*) Cherry Lane.

— Isometrics for Pianists. (Illus.). 28p. 1972. pap. text ed. 4.95 (*0-89915-009-8*) Playback Mus Pub.

Raskin, Miriam S. Empirical Studies in Field Instruction. LC 88-24670. (Clinical Supervisor Ser.: Vol. 6, Nos. 3 & 4). (Illus.). 399p. 1989. text ed. 49.95 (*0-86656-869-7*) Haworth Pr.

Raskin, Miriam S., jt. ed. see Daley, Dennis C.

Raskin, Neil H. Headache. 2nd ed. LC 88-2848. (Illus.). 406p. reprint ed. pap. 115.80 (*0-7837-2561-2*, 2042720) Bks Demand.

***Raskin, Nord.** Colonoscopy: Principles & Techniques. 1995. write for info. (*0-89640-277-0*) Igaku-Shoin.

Raskin, Patricia. Success, Your Dream & You: A Personal Success Guide to Marketing. LC 90-52808. 224p. 1991. 19.95 (*0-915677-51-2*) Roundtable Pub.

Raskin, Philip, jt. ed. see Rifkin, Harold.

Raskin, Robin & Ellison, Carol. Parents, Kids & Computers: An Activity Guide for Family Fun & Learning. LC 92-23044. 1992. pap. 20.00 (*0-679-73910-6*) Random.

Raskin, Robin, jt. auth. see Christian, Kaare.

Raskin, Saul. Hagadah for Passover: Drawings by Saul Raskin. 92p. 1994. 39.95 (*0-8197-0605-1*) Bloch.

— Our Father, Our King: Drawings by Saul Raskin. 96p. 1966. 39.95 (*0-8197-0603-5*) Bloch.

— Pirke Aboth: Sayings of the Fathers: Drawings by Saul Raskin. 136p. 1994. 39.95 (*0-8197-0608-6*) Bloch.

Raskin, Selma. Once over Lightly. 1989. write for info. (*0-938509-04-7*) Pretty Penny Pr.

— So Simple So Good! 1989. write for info. (*0-938509-05-5*) Pretty Penny Pr.

— Vittles & Verse: A Unique Cookbook of Delicious Verse & Poetic Food. 128p. 1989. pap. 9.95 (*0-938509-02-0*) Pretty Penny Pr.

Raskin, Selma, jt. auth. see Cate, Jean M.

Raskin, Valerie D., jt. auth. see Kleima, Karen R.

Raskin, Victor & Weiser, Irwin. Language & Writing: Applications of Linguistics to Rhetoric & Composition. LC 86-17753. 304p. 1987. text ed. 49.50 (*0-89391-405-3*) Ablex Pub.

Raskin, Victor, jt. auth. see Bjarkman, Peter C.

Rasko, I. & Downes, C. S. Genes & Medicine: Molecular Biology & Human Genetic Disorders. (Illus.). 200p. 1993. text ed. 45.00 (*0-412-37340-8*) Chapman & Hall.

***Raskob, Tony.** The Sex Backpack. (Illus.). (YA). (gr. 7-12). 1994. pap. 9.95 (*0-9642469-0-2*) Lrning to Lrn.

— Truth & Consequences. (Orig.). 1989. write for info. (*0-318-65039-8*) YNot Read.

Raskodt, Mark C., jt. auth. see Zuckerman, Tod I.

Raskoff, Mark C., jt. auth. see Zuckerman, Tod I.

Raskop, Heinrich, jt. auth. see Pieper, Josef.

Raskova, H., ed. Pharmacology & Toxicology of Naturally Occurring Toxins, 2 vols, 1. LC 77-130797. 1971. 164. 00 (*0-08-016319-X*, Pub. by Pergamon Repr UK) Franklin.

— Pharmacology & Toxicology of Naturally Occurring Toxins, 2 vols, 2. LC 77-130797. 1971. 136.00 (*0-08-016798-5*, Pub. by Pergamon Repr UK) Franklin.

— Pharmacology & Toxicology of Naturally Occurring Toxins, 2 vols, Set. LC 77-130797. 1971. 300.00 (*0-08-016797-7*, Pub. by Pergamon Repr UK) Franklin.

An Asterisk (*) at the beginning of an entry indicates that the title is appearing in BIP for the first time.

Raskova, H. & Rocha E Silva, M. Mechanisms of Drug Toxicity: Proceedings of the 3rd International Pharmacological Meeting, Sao Paulo, July 1966, Vol. 4. LC 67-19416. 1968. 50.00 (0-08-012370-8, Pub. by Pergamon Repr UK) Franklin.

Raskova, H., jt. auth. see Krayer, O.

***Rasler, Karen A. & Thompson, William R.** The Great Powers & Global Struggle, 1490-1990. LC 94-31406. 280p. 1995. lib. bdg. 35.00x (0-8131-1889-1) U Pr of Ky.

— War & State Making: The Shaping of the Global Powers. (Studies in International Conflict: Vol. 2). 272p. 1989. text ed. 55.00 (0-04-445097-4) Routledge Chapman & Hall.

Rasley, Alicia. A Midsummer's Delight. 320p. 1993. mass mkt. 3.99 (0-8217-4230-2) Zebra.

— A Royal Escapade. 320p. 1992. mass mkt. 3.99 (0-8217-3968-9) Zebra.

Rasmer, Raymond, ed. see Oscard, Anne.

***Rasmueen.** Diversity: ASTD Trainer's Sourcebook. 1995. pap. text ed. 39.95 (0-07-053438-1) McGraw.

Rasmus, Carolyn J. In the Strength of the Lord I Can Do All Things. LC 89-78380. 120p. 1990. 9.95 (0-87579-308-8) Deseret Bk.

Rasmusen, Eric. Games & Information: An Introduction to Game Theory. (Illus.). 400p. 1989. text ed. 34.95 (0-631-15709-3) Blackwell Pubs.

— Games & Information: An Introduction to Game Theory. 2nd ed. LC 93-40356. (Illus.). 375p. 1994. 37.95 (1-55786-502-7) Blackwell Pubs.

Rasmuson, Mark R., et al. Communication for Child Survival. 144p. 1988. pap. 8.00 (0-685-59932-9) Acad Educ Dev.

Rasmussen. Jesus & Power. Date not set. 25.00 (0-06-066746-X, HarpT); pap. 20.00 (0-06-066846-6, PL) HarpC.

— The Last Chapter. 288p. 1993. pap. 2.99 (0-88368-021-1) Whitaker Hse.

Rasmussen, jt. auth. see Chadam, John M.

Rasmussen, A. E. Financial Management in Cooperative Enterprise. 1975. pap. 9.50 (0-88817-000-9) NCBA.

Rasmussen, Anne M., tr. see Willumsen, Dorrit.

***Rasmussen, Anne Marie B.** History of the Quaker Movement in Africa. (Illus.). 224p. 1995. text ed. 54.50 (1-85043-904-4) St Martin.

Rasmussen, B. & Caratti, G. Wind Energy, No. 2: Proceedings of the Second Contractor's Meeting, Brussels, November 23-24, 1987. 434p. 1988. text ed. 135.00 (3-7186-4843-1) Gordon & Breach.

Rasmussen, Barbara. Absentee Landowning & Exploitation in West Virginia, 1760-1920. LC 94-5096. 224p. 1994. lib. bdg. 29.95x (0-8131-1880-8) U Pr of Ky.

Rasmussen, Bill. Sports Junkies Rejoice! The Birth of ESPN. 256p. 1983. 14.95 (0-318-00106-3) QV Pub.

Rasmussen, Carl, tr. see Nygren, Anders.

Rasmussen, Carl G. The Zondervan NIV Atlas of the Bible. 1989. 39.99 (0-310-25160-5) Zondervan.

Rasmussen, D. Tab & Schopf, eds. The Origin & Evolution of Humans & Humanness. LC 93-6741. 160p. 1993. pap. text ed. 31.25 (0-86720-857-0) Jones & Bartlett.

Rasmussen, David, ed. Universalism vs. Communitarianism: Contemporary Debates in Ethics. 250p. 1990. 32.50 (0-262-18140-1); pap. 17.95 (0-262-68063-7) MIT Pr.

Rasmussen, David, jt. ed. see Bernauer, James W.

Rasmussen, David, jt. ed. see Kemp, T. Peter.

Rasmussen, David, jt. auth. see Rasmussen, Steven.

Rasmussen, David M. Reading Habermas. 256p. 1990. 54.95 (0-631-15273-3); pap. 21.95 (0-631-15274-1) Blackwell Pubs.

Rasmussen, David W. Agriculture in the U. S. A Documentary History, 4 vols., 1. (Documentary Reference Collections). 1977. text ed. 95.00 (0-313-20148-X, RAAG1) Greenwood.

— Agriculture in the U. S. A Documentary History, 4 vols., Set. LC 74-9643. (Documentary Reference Collections). 1977. text ed. 295.00 (0-313-20147-1, RAAG) Greenwood.

— Agriculture in the U. S. A Documentary History, 4 vols., Vol. 2. (Documentary Reference Collections). 1977. text ed. 95.00 (0-313-20149-8, RAAG2) Greenwood.

— Agriculture in the U. S. A Documentary History, 4 vols., Vol. 3. (Documentary Reference Collections). 1977. text ed. 95.00 (0-313-20150-1, RAAG3) Greenwood.

— Agriculture in the U. S. A Documentary History, 4 vols., Vol. 4. (Documentary Reference Collections). 1977. text ed. 95.00 (0-313-20151-X, RAAG4) Greenwood.

Rasmussen, David W. & Benson, Bruce L. The Economic Anatomy of a Drug War: Criminal Justice in the Commons. 260p. (C). 1994. lib. bdg. 54.00 (0-8476-7909-8); pap. text ed. 22.95 (0-8476-7910-1) Rowman.

Rasmussen, Dennis. The Lord's Question. LC 85-50505. 112p. 1985. 6.95 (0-933413-00-9) Keter Found.

— Poetry & Truth. LC 74-75364. (De Proprietatibus Litterarum, Ser. Minor: No. 20). 123p. 1974. pap. text ed. 20.80 (90-279-3462-2) Mouton.

***Rasmussen, Donald P.** Doing Something for Someone Else: A History of the Wisconsin Lions. Goc, Michael J., ed. 288p. Date not set. 25.00 (0-938627-27-9) New Past Pr.

Rasmussen, Douglas & Den Uyl, Douglas. Liberty & Nature: An Aristotelian Defense of Order. LC 90-20965. (C). 1991. 49.95 (0-8126-9119-9); pap. 24.95 (0-8126-9120-2) Open Court.

Rasmussen, Douglas & Sterba, James. Catholic Bishops & the Economy: A Dialog. 150p. 1987. 19.95 (0-912051-15-9); pap. 18.95 (0-912051-16-7) Transaction Pubs.

Rasmussen, Douglas B., jt. intro. see Den Uyl, Douglas J.

Rasmussen, Ellis T. A Latter-Day Saint Commentary on the Old Testament. LC 93-47675. (Illus.). 718p. 1994. 25.95 (0-87579-712-1) Deseret Bk.

***Rasmussen, Else B.** Seven Months Till April. 200p. (Orig.). Date not set. pap. 7.95 (0-7610-0105-0) NW Pub.

Rasmussen, Eric. A Textual Companion to Doctor Faustus. LC 93-18696. (Revels Plays Companion Library). 1994. text ed. 69.95 (0-7190-1562-6, Pub. by Manchester Univ Pr UK) St Martin.

Rasmussen, Eric, ed. see Marlowe, Christopher.

Rasmussen, Erik. Complementarity & Political Science: An Essay on Fundamentals of Political Science Theory & Research Strategy. 137p. (Orig.). 1987. pap. 37.50x (87-7492-628-4, Pub. by Odense Universitets Forlag DK) Coronet Bks.

Rasmussen, Gerald R. Adams Middle School Principal Monroe City Schools Simulation Entire Simulation Package. (Illus.). (Orig.). (C). 1986. audio, pap. text ed. 185.00 (0-922971-49-8, AMS 116) Univ Council Educ Admin.

— Adams Middle School Principalship Adams Middle School Background Materials Monroe City Simulation Faculty Handbook. (Orig.). (C). 1986. pap. text ed. 5.50 (0-922971-38-2, AMS 103) Univ Council Educ Admin.

— Adams Suburban District Simulation: Entire Simulation Package. (Illus.). (Orig.). (C). 1986. audio, pap. text ed. 230.00 (1-55996-140-6) Univ Council Educ Admin.

— Longfellow Elementary School Monroe City Schools Simulation: Primary-Elementary Rules, Regulations & Procedures for Monroe City. 48p. (C). 1983. pap. text ed. 5.60 (0-922971-28-5, MCE 204) Univ Council Educ Admin.

— Longfellow Elementary School Monroe City Schools Simulation Data Bank Materials. (Illus.). 50p. (C). 1983. pap. text ed. 5.90 (0-922971-29-3, MCE-205) Univ Council Educ Admin.

— Longfellow Elementary School Monroe City Schools Simulation License Fee. (Illus.). (C). 1983. pap. text ed. 100.00 (0-922971-36-6, MCE-217) Univ Council Educ Admin.

Rasmussen, Greta. Brain Stations: A Center Approach to Thinking Skills. (Illus.). 112p. (Orig.). 1989. teacher ed 11.95 (0-936110-07-4) Tin Man Pr.

— The Great Unbored Blackboard Book. LC 85-51757. 56p. (Orig.). (J). (gr. 2-6). 1985. pap. 6.95 (0-936110-05-8) Tin Man Pr.

— The Great Unbored Bulletin Board, Book II. LC 80-52305. (Illus.). (J). (gr. 2-6). 1984. pap. 6.95 (0-936110-04-X) Tin Man Pr.

— The Great Unbored Bulletin Board Book. LC 80-52305. (Illus.). 56p. (Orig.). (J). (gr. 2-6). 1984. pap. 6.95 (0-936110-01-5) Tin Man Pr.

— Is It Friday Already? Learning Centers That Work. LC 79-92710. (Illus.). 230p. (Orig.). (J). (gr. 2-6). 1980. pap. 16.95 (0-936110-00-7) Tin Man Pr.

— Nifty Fifty: Five Hundred Thinking Challenges about 50 Familiar Things. LC 87-51619. (Illus.). 112p. 1988. pap. text ed. 11.95 (0-936110-06-6) Tin Man Pr.

— OPQ: Offbeat Adventures with the Alphabet. rev. ed. LC 81-82798. (Illus.). 63p. (Orig.). (J). (gr. 2-6). 1994. pap. 8.95 (0-936110-03-1) Tin Man Pr.

— Play by the Rules: Creative Practice in Direction-Following. LC 89-51969. (Illus.). 112p. 1990. pap. text ed. 11.95 (0-936110-09-0) Tin Man Pr.

— Waiting for Lunch. LC 81-82797. (Illus.). 63p. (Orig.). (J). (gr. 2-6). 1981. pap. 7.95 (0-936110-02-3) Tin Man Pr.

***Rasmussen, Greta & Rasmussen, Ted.** Ideas to Go: Fifty Ready-to-Use Thinking Challenges. LC 92-80381. (Illus.). 112p. 1992. pap. 11.95 (0-936110-14-7) Tin Man Pr.

— Smart Snips: Hands-on Adventures in Thinking, Reading & Direction-Following. 112p. 1993. pap. 11.95 (0-936110-15-5) Tin Man Pr.

— T Is for Think: Thinking Fun with the Alphabet. LC 94-61645. (Illus.). 64p. 1995. pap. 8.95 (0-936110-17-1) Tin Man Pr.

— WakerUppers: A Spirited Collection of Thinking Activities. LC 93-95045. (Illus.). 112p. 1994. pap. 11.95 (0-936110-16-3) Tin Man Pr.

Rasmussen, H. On Law & Policy in the European Court of Justice. 1986. lib. bdg. 228.50 (90-247-3217-4) Kluwer Ac.

***Rasmussen, Hanne N.** Terrestrial Orchids: From Seed to Mycotrophic Plant. (Illus.). 332p. (C). 1995. write for info. (0-521-45165-5) Cambridge U Pr.

Rasmussen, Henning, jt. auth. see Chadam, John M.

Rasmussen, Henning, jt. ed. see Chadam, John M.

***Rasmussen, Henry.** D-Day Plus Fifty Years. 1994. 39.95 (1-879301-06-7) Top Ten Pub.

— International McCormick Tractors: Reliable Red-Farmall, Deering & Case International. (Illus.). 96p. 1989. pap. text ed. 14.95 (0-87938-372-0) Motorbooks Intl.

Rasmussen, Henry, photos & text. Corvette: Cream of the Crop. (Top Ten Ser.). (Illus.). 132p. 1992. 29.95 (1-879301-01-6) Top Ten Pub.

— D-Day Plus Fifty Years: The Normandy Beaches Revisited. (Illus.). 192p. 1994. 39.95 (1-879301-05-9) Top Ten Pub.

— Ferrari: Salute to the Spyder. (Top Ten Ser.). (Illus.). 132p. 1992. 29.95 (1-879301-00-8) Top Ten Pub.

— Porsche: Six Cylinder Supercars. (Illus.). 132p. 1992. 29.95 (1-879301-02-4) Top Ten Pub.

— Porsche 356 & 550: A Pictorial History. (Illus.). 160p. 1992. 29.95 (1-879301-03-2) Top Ten Pub.

Rasmussen, Henry R. Automobiles of Distinction: The Imperial Palace Collection, Las Vegas, Nevada. (Illus.). 192p. 1990. 300.00 (0-87938-461-1) Motorbooks Intl.

Rasmussen, Howard. Cell Communication in Health & Disease: Readings from Scientific American. (Scientific American Reader Ser.). (Illus.). 144p. (C). 1995. text ed. write for info. (0-7167-2224-0) W H Freeman.

Rasmussen, J. Lewis & Oakley, Robert B. Conflict Resolution in the Middle East: Simulating a Diplomatic Negotiation Between Israel & Syria. LC 92-30410. (Orig.). 1992. pap. 6.95 (1-878379-19-4) US Inst Peace.

Rasmussen, Jane. Musical Taste As a Religious Question in Nineteenth Century America: The Development of Episcopal Church Hymnody. LC 86-12774. (Studies in American Religion: Vol. 20). 632p. 1986. lib. bdg. 129.95 (0-88946-664-5) E Mellen.

Rasmussen, Janet E. New Land, New Lives: Scandinavian Immigrants to the Pacific Northwest. LC 93-22999. (Illus.). 344p. 1993. 24.95 (0-295-97288-2) U of Wash Pr.

Rasmussen, Jaye, ed. Merger Yearbook. 11th ed. 550p. 1989. 189.00 (0-939008-13-0) Cambridge Corp.

Rasmussen, Jens & Rouse, William B., eds. Human Detection & Diagnosis of System Failures. LC 81-8699. (NATO Conference Series III, Human Factors: Vol. 15). 726p. 1981. 125.00 (0-306-40744-2, Plenum Pr) Plenum.

Rasmussen, Jens & Zunde, Pranas, eds. Empirical Foundations of Information & Software Science, Vol. 3. LC 87-12275. (Illus.). 280p. 1987. 65.00 (0-306-42585-8, Plenum Pr) Plenum.

Rasmussen, Jens, et al. Cognitive Systems Engineering. LC 93-46162. (A Wiley-Interscience Publication Ser.). 378p. 1994. text ed. 59.95 (0-471-01198-3) Wiley.

Rasmussen, Jens, et al, eds. Distributed Decision Making: Cognitive Models for Cooperative Work. (New Technologies & Work Ser.). 397p. 1991. text ed. 142.95 (0-471-92828-3) Wiley.

— New Technology & Human Error. fac. ed. LC 86-5607. (New Technologies & Work Ser.). 370p. 1987. reprint ed. pap. 105.50 (0-7837-8271-3, 2049052) Bks Demand.

Rasmussen, John H., tr. see Grane, Leif, ed.

Rasmussen, Jorgen S. The British Political Process: Concentrated Power vs. Accountability. 256p. (C). 1993. pap. 16.95 (0-534-20064-8) Intl Thomson.

Rasmussen, Jorgen S. & Moses, Joel C. Major European Governments. 9th ed. LC 94-17290. 710p. 1995. text ed. 47.95 (0-534-22212-9) Intl Thomson.

***Rasmussen, K. B.** The School Foundation Workbook. Date not set. 72.00 (1-56925-015-4, TSFW) Capitol Publns.

Rasmussen, Knud J. Across Arctic America, Narrative of the Fifth Thule Expedition. LC 68-55213. 388p. 1970. reprint ed. text ed. 35.00 (0-8371-1489-6, RAAA, Greenwood Pr) Greenwood.

— The Alaska Eskimos As Described in the Posthumous Notes of Knud Rasmussen. LC 76-21645. (Thule Expedition, 5th, 1921-1924 Ser.: Vol. 10, No. 3). 1976. reprint ed. 60.00 (0-404-58327-X) AMS Pr.

— Alaskan Eskimo Words. LC 76-21784. (Thule Expedition, 5th, 1921-1924 Ser.: Vol. 3 No. 4). reprint ed. 30.00 (0-404-58314-8) AMS Pr.

— Greenland by the Polar Sea. LC 74-5867. (Illus.). reprint ed. 67.50 (0-404-11674-4) AMS Pr.

— Intellectual Culture of the Copper Eskimos. LC 76-21675. (Thule Expedition, 5th, 1921-1924 Ser.: No. 9). (Illus.). reprint ed. 74.50 (0-404-58324-5) AMS Pr.

— Intellectual Culture of the Hudson Bay Eskimos, 3 vols., Set. (Fifth Thule Expedition Ser.: Vol. 7). reprint ed. 160.00 (0-404-58320-2) AMS Pr.

— Intellectual Culture of the Iglulik Eskimos. LC 76-22535. (Fifth Thule Expedition Ser.: Vol. 7, No. 1). reprint ed. 105.00 (0-404-58321-0) AMS Pr.

— Knud Rasmussen's Posthumous Notes on East Greenland Legends & Myths. Osterman, H., ed. LC 74-19913. reprint ed. 27.00 (0-404-12296-5) AMS Pr.

— Knud Rasmussen's Posthumous Notes on the Life & Doings of the East Greenlanders in Olden Times. Osterman, H., ed. LC 74-19915. (Illus.). reprint ed. 37.50 (0-404-12297-3) AMS Pr.

— The Mackenzie Eskimos. LC 76-21643. (Thule Expedition, 5th, 1921-1924 Ser.: Vol. 10, No. 2). reprint ed. 42.50 (0-404-58326-1) AMS Pr.

— The Netsilik Eskimos. LC 76-21685. (Thule Expedition, 5th, 1921-1924 Ser.: No. 8, Pts. 1-2). reprint ed. 105.00 (0-404-58323-7) AMS Pr.

— Observations on the Intellectual Culture of the Caribou Eskimos. Bd. with Iglulik & Caribou Eskimo Texts. LC 76-22536. LC 76-22536. (Fifth Thule Expedition Ser.: Vol. 7, No. 2 & No. 3). reprint ed. write for info. (0-404-58322-9) AMS Pr.

— The People of the Polar North: A Record... Herring, G., ed. LC 74-5868. (Illus.). reprint ed. 56.50 (0-404-11675-2) AMS Pr.

Rasmussen, Larry. Reinhold Niebuhr: Theologian of Public Life. LC 91-14239. (Making of Modern Theology Ser.). 312p. 1991. pap. 14.00 (0-8006-3407-1, 1-3407) Augsburg Fortress.

Rasmussen, Larry & Bethge, Renate. Dietrich Bonhoeffer - His Significance for North Americans. LC 89-36037. 192p. (Orig.). 1989. pap. 15.00 (0-8006-2400-9, 1-2400) Augsburg Fortress.

Rasmussen, Larry L. Moral Fragments & Moral Community: A Proposal for Church in Society. LC 93-18155. 144p. 1993. pap. 11.00 (0-8006-2757-1, Fortress Pr) Augsburg Fortress.

Rasmussen, Larry L., jt. auth. see Birch, Bruce C.

Rasmussen, Lissi. Christian & Muslim Relations in Africa: The Cases of Northern Nigeria & Tanzania Compared. 200p. 1993. text ed. 59.50 (1-85043-641-X, Pub. by I B Tauris UK) St Martin.

Rasmussen, Louis J. California Wagon Train List. 400p. 1994. 20.95 (0-911792-79-1) SF Hist Records.

— San Francisco Ship Passenger Lists, Vol. 2. 1966. 20.95 (0-685-71025-4) SF Hist Records.

Rasmussen, M. L., jt. auth. see Reddy, J. N.

Rasmussen, Margaret, ed. see Bain, Winifred E.

Rasmussen, Margaret, ed. see Smith, Agnes.

Rasmussen, Marion R. The Language of Stroke. 72p. 1990. pap. 4.95 (0-9622455-2-6) Courage Ctr.

Rasmussen, Maurice. Hypersonic Flow. LC 93-39714. 1994. text ed. 74.95 (0-471-51102-1) Wiley.

Rasmussen, Michael R. & Rasmussen, Ronda L. The Kids' Encyclopedia of Things to Make & Do. LC 88-39449. (Illus.). 244p. 1989. reprint ed. pap. 17.95 (0-934140-51-0) Redleaf Pr.

Rasmussen, Norman C., jt. auth. see Oldenberg, Otto.

Rasmussen, P., jt. auth. see Macedo, E. A.

Rasmussen, Paul. Massage Parlor Prostitution. 163p. text ed. write for info. (0-8290-1029-7) Irvington.

Rasmussen, Peter, jt. auth. see King, Julie.

Rasmussen, Peter, ed. see Suppes, Patrick.

***Rasmussen, R. Kent.** Mark Twain A to Z: The Essential Reference to His Life & Writings. LC 94-39156. 1995. 45.00 (0-8160-2845-1) Facts on File.

Rasmussen, R. Kent & Rubert, Steven C. Historical Dictionary of Zimbabwe. 2nd ed. LC 90-45366. (African Historical Dictionaries Ser.: No. 46). (Illus.). 542p. 1990. 55.00 (0-8108-2337-3) Scarecrow.

Rasmussen, R. Kent, jt. auth. see Lipschultz, Mark R.

Rasmussen, R. Kent, ed. see Schuyler, George S.

Rasmussen, Richard. The Branemark System of Oral Reconstruction: A Clinical Atlas. Hacke, Gregory, ed. (Illus.). 305p. 1992. text ed. 75.00 (1-56386-003-1) Ishiyaku Euro.

— Extraterrestrial Life. LC 91-15564. (Overview Ser.). (Illus.). 112p. (J). (gr. 5-8). 1991. lib. bdg. 16.95 (1-56006-126-X) Lucent Bks.

Rasmussen, Richard M. The UFO Challenge. LC 90-32962. (Overview Ser.). (Illus.). 96p. (J). (gr. 5-8). 1990. lib. bdg. 16.95 (1-56006-122-7) Lucent Bks.

Rasmussen, Richard M., ed. Recorded Concert Band Music, 1950-1987: A Selected, Annotated Listing. LC 88-42522. 456p. 1988. lib. bdg. 49.95x (0-89950-318-7) McFarland & Co.

Rasmussen, Robert. Mountain Biking the Coast Range, Guide 11: Orange County & Cleveland National Forest. 1992. 9.95 (0-938665-17-0) Fine Edge Prods.

Rasmussen, Robert R., tr. see Nentvig, Juan.

Rasmussen, Roderick C. Paw Paw Lake, Michigan: A One Hundred Year Resort History (1890's-1990's) 144p. (Orig.). 1994. 27.30 (0-9640093-0-7); pap. 15.85 (0-9640093-1-5) SW Mich Pubns.

Rasmussen, Ronda L., jt. auth. see Rasmussen, Michael R.

Rasmussen, Roy H., ed. Golfers Travel Guide: Great Lakes Edition, Vol. 1, No. 1. 208p. (Orig.). 1987. pap. 12.95 (0-940703-00-9) RSG Pub MI.

— Illinois Golfers Travel Guide. 34p. (Orig.). 1992. pap. 6.95 (0-940703-04-1) RSG Pub MI.

— Indiana Golfers Travel Guide. 33p. (Orig.). 1992. pap. 6.95 (0-940703-03-3) RSG Pub MI.

— Michigan Golfers Travel Guide. 36p. (Orig.). 1992. pap. 6.95 (0-940703-01-7) RSG Pub MI.

— Minnesota - Wisconsin Golfers Travel Guide. 40p. (Orig.). 1992. pap. 6.95 (0-940703-05-X) RSG Pub MI.

— Ohio Golfers Travel Guide. 35p. (Orig.). 1992. pap. 6.95 (0-940703-02-5) RSG Pub MI.

Rasmussen, Shelley. An Introduction to Statistics with Data Analysis. 672p. (C). 1992. text ed. 54.95 (0-534-13578-1) Intl Thomson.

Rasmussen, Steen E. Experiencing Architecture. 2nd ed. (Illus.). 1962. pap. 10.95x (0-262-68002-5) MIT Pr.

— London, the Unique City. rev. ed. 1982. pap. 19.95 (0-262-68027-0) MIT Pr.

— Towns & Buildings. 1969. pap. 16.95 (0-262-68011-4) MIT Pr.

Rasmussen, Steven. Key to Fractions Reproducible Test. rev. ed. 32p. 1991. pap. 9.95 (0-913684-96-1) Key Curr Pr.

— Key to Fractions Reproducible Tests. 32p. 1985. pap. 9.95 (0-317-31629-X) HM.

— Key to Fractions Series. Incl. Bk. 1. Fraction Concepts. 37p. 1980. 2.00 (0-913684-91-0); Bk. 2. Multiplying & Dividing. 37p. 1980. 2.00 (0-913684-92-9); Bk. 3. Adding & Subtracting. 37p. 1980. 2.00 (0-913684-93-7); Bk. 4. Mixed Numbers. 37p. 1980. 2.00 (0-913684-94-5); Key to Fractions Answer Book. 37p. 1980. pap. 2.30 (0-913684-97-X); (gr. 4-12). 1980. write for info. (0-318-53984-5) Key Curr Pr.

Rasmussen, Steven & Rasmussen, David. Key to Percents Reproducible Tests. 23p. 1988. 9.95 (0-913684-95-3) Key Curr Pr.

— Key to Percents Series. Incl. Bk. 1: Percent Concepts. 45p. 1988. pap. text ed. 2.00 (0-913684-57-0); Bk. 2: Percents & Fractions. 45p. 1988. pap. text ed. 2.00 (0-913684-58-9); Bk. 3: Percents & Decimals. 45p. 1988. pap. text ed. 2.00 (0-913684-59-7); Bk. 3: Percents & Decimals. 45p. 1988. 2.30 (0-913684-61-9); (J). (gr. 4-12). 1988. write for info. (0-318-63295-0) Key Curr Pr.

Rasmussen, Steven & Rosekrans, Spreck. Key to Decimals Reproducible Tests. 32p. 1985. pap. 9.95 (0-913684-26-0) Key Curr Pr.

Rasmussen, Steven & Rosekraus, Spreck. Key to Decimals Series. Incl. Bk. 1. Decimal Concepts. 45p. 1985. pap. 2.00 (0-913684-21-X); Bk. 2. Adding, Subtracting, Multiplying. 45p. 1985. pap. 2.00 (0-913684-22-8); Bk. 3. Dividing. 45p. 1985. pap. 2.00 (0-913684-23-6); Bk. 4. Using Decimals. 45p. 1985. pap. 2.00 (0-913684-24-4); Answers & Notes. 45p. 1985. pap. 2.30 (0-913684-25-2); (gr. 4-12). 1985. write for info. (0-318-59210-X) Key Curr Pr.

***Rasmussen, Susan J.** Spirit Possession & Personhood among the Kel Ewey Tuareg. (Cambridge Studies in Social & Cultural Anthropology: No. 94). 192p. (C). 1995. 49.95 (0-521-47007-2) Cambridge U Pr.

Rasmussen, Tarald. Inimici Ecclesiae, Das Ekklesiologische Feinbild in Luther's "Dictata Super Psalterium" (1513-1515) im Horizont der Theologischen Tradition. LC 89-37288. (Studies in Medieval & Reformation Thought: Vol. 44). x, 242p. (GER.). 1989. 68.75 (90-04-08837-7) E J Brill.

R

An Asterisk (*) at the beginning of an entry indicates that the title is appearing in BIP for the first time.

Rasmussen, Ted, jt. auth. see Rasmussen, Greta.

***Rasmussen, Theodore & Marino, Raul, Jr., eds.** Functional Neurosurgery. fac. ed. LC 77-85871. (Illus.). 288p. Date not set. pap. 82.10 (0-7837-7178-9, 2047121) Bks Demand.

Rasmussen, Theodore, jt. auth. see Andermann, Frederick.

Rasmussen, Thomas H., jt. auth. see Peterson, Steven A.

Rasmussen, Tom. Bucchero Pottery from Southern Etruria. LC 78-13464. (Cambridge Classical Studies). (Illus.). 1979. 59.95 (0-521-22316-4) Cambridge U Pr.

Rasmussen, Tom & Spivey, Nigel J., eds. Looking at Greek Vases. (Illus.). 296p. (C). 1991. 64.95 (0-521-37524-X); pap. 19.95 (0-521-37679-3) Cambridge U Pr.

Rasmussen, Tom, ed. see Nicholls, Richard.

***Rasmussen, Waldo.** Latin American Artists of the Twentieth Century: Fourteen Essays by Critics & Scholars. 1993. 65.00 (0-87070-431-1) Mus of Modern Art.

Rasmussen, Wayne D. Taking the University to the People: Seventy-Five Years of Cooperative Extension. LC 88-37672. (Illus.). 310p. 1989. 26.95 (0-8138-0419-1) Iowa St U Pr.

***Rasmusson, Arne.** The Church As Polis: From Political Theology to Theological Politics. LC 94-45054. (C). 1995. text ed. 34.95x (0-268-00810-8) U of Notre Dame Pr.

***Rasmusson, Arne, et al.** The Church as Polis: From Political Theology to Theological Politics as Exemplified by Jurgen Moltmann & Stanley Hauerwas. LC 94-45054. 1995. write for info. (0-268-00809-4) U of Notre Dame Pr.

Rasmusson, D. C. Barley. 522p. 1985. 40.00 (0-89118-085-0) Am Soc Agron.

Rasmusson, R. L. The Cardiac Resting, Pacemaker & Action Potentials. (Medical Intelligence Unit Ser.). write for info. (1-57059-142-3) R G Landes.

Rasnake, Roger N. Domination & Cultural Resistance: Authority & Power among Andean People. LC 87-35834. xi, 323p. (C). 1988. lib. bdg. 41.95 (0-8223-0809-6) Duke.

Raso, Jack. Alternative Healthcare: A Comprehensive Guide. 267p. (C). 1994. 26.95 (0-87975-891-0) Prometheus Bks.

Raso, Jack & Barrett, Stephen. Mystical Diets: Paranormal, Spiritual, & Occult Nutrition & Practices. (Consumer Health Ser.). 291p. 1992. 23.95 (0-87975-761-2) Prometheus Bks.

Rasof, Henry, ed. see Bleifeld, Maurice.

Rasolondraibe, Peri, jt. auth. see Lazareth, William H.

Rasool, A. F. On the Wings of Poetry. 1995. 6.95 (0-533-09004-0) Vantage.

Rasool, Joan, et al. Critical Thinking: Reading & Writing in a Diverse World. 311p. (C). 1993. pap. 29.95 (0-534-12818-1) Intl Thomson.

Rasool, S. I., jt. ed. see Jastrow, R.

Rasooli, Jay M. & Allen, Cady H. Dr. Sa'eed of Iran: Kurdish Physician to Princes & Peasants, Nobles & Nomads. LC 57-13245. (Illus.). 192p. 1983. reprint ed. pap. 6.95 (0-87808-743-5) William Carey Lib.

Rasor. Consumer Finance Law. 1985. write for info. (0-8205-0121-2, 212); teacher ed write for info. (0-8205-0122-0) Bender.

Rasor, Eugene L. The Battle of Jutland: A Bibliography. LC 91-24368. (Bibliographies of Battles & Leaders Ser.: No. 7). 192p. 1991. text ed. 49.95 (0-313-28124-6, RJU, Greenwood Pr) Greenwood.

— British Naval History since Eighteen Fifteen: A Guide to Literature. LC 90-3310. (Military History Bibliographies Ser.: Vol. 13). 864p. 1990. 90.00 (0-8240-7735-0, 1069) Garland.

— The Falklands-Malvinas Campaign: A Bibliography. LC 91-24365. (Bibliographies of Battles & Leaders Ser.: No. 6). 216p. 1991. text ed. 55.00 (0-313-28151-3, RFK, Greenwood Pr) Greenwood.

— The Spanish Armada of Fifteen Eighty-Eight: Historiography & Annotated Bibliography. LC 92-31759. (Bibliographies of Battles & Leaders Ser.: No. 10). 295p. 1992. text ed. 65.00 (0-313-28303-6, RXS, Greenwood Pr) Greenwood.

Rasor, Eugene L., ed. General Douglas MacArthur, 1880-1964: Historiography & Annotated Bibliography. LC 93-43711. (Bibliographies of Battles & Leaders Ser.: Vol. 12). 224p. 1994. text ed. 59.50 (0-313-28873-9, Greenwood Pr) Greenwood.

Rasor, Paul B. Kansas Law of Sales under the Uniform Commercial Code. LC 81-84870. 1981. 80.00 (0-942357-06-X) KS Bar CLE.

— Kansas Law of Sales under the Uniform Commercial Code. suppl. ed. LC 81-84870. 1989. Supplement, 1989. 85.00 (0-942357-31-0) KS Bar CLE.

Rasor, Richard, jt. auth. see Bartz, Wayne.

Rasovsky, Yuri, jt. auth. see Adorjan, Carol.

***Rasp, Barbara.** The Lines of Light: With Prayers for the Heart. (Illus.). 128p. (Orig.). 1995. pap. 9.95 (0-9643006-6-4) Equalite Pr.

Rasp, Richard A. Redwood: The Story Behind the Scenery. LC 88-80122. (Illus.). 48p. 1988. pap. 6.95 (0-88714-022-X) KC Pubns.

Raspa, Anthony. The Emotive Image: Jesuit Poetics in the English Renaissance. LC 83-502. 174p. (C). 1983. 19.50 (0-912646-65-9) Tex Christian.

Raspa, Anthony, ed. see Donne, John.

Raspa, Richard, jt. auth. see Mathias, Elizabeth.

Raspail, Jean. Blue Island. Leggatt, Jeremy, tr. LC 90-49381. 192p. 1991. 17.95 (0-916515-99-0) Mercury Hse Inc.

— The Camp of the Saints. 313p. 1975. 15.00 (0-936247-06-1) Amer Immigration.

— The Camp of the Saints. Shapiro, Norman, tr. 311p. 1994. pap. 12.95 (1-881780-07-4) Social Contract.

— The Camp of the Saints: The End of the White Race. 1984. lib. bdg. 250.00 (0-87700-584-2) Revisionist Pr.

Raspall de Cauhe, Joana, et al. Diccionari Usual de Sinonims Catalans: Mots i Frases. 572p. (CAT.). 1975. 29.95 (0-8288-5801-2, S50048) Fr & Eur.

Raspall Juanola, Joana. Diccionari d'Homonims i Paronims. 256p. 1988. 19.95 (0-7859-6233-6, 8475334334) Fr & Eur.

Raspanti, Celeste. I Never Saw Another Butterfly. 1971. 4.95 (0-87129-276-9, I22) Dramatic Pub.

— I Never Saw Another Butterfly - One Act. 1982. 2.75 (0-87129-319-6, I33) Dramatic Pub.

— No Fading Star. 1979. 2.50 (0-87129-250-5, N24) Dramatic Pub.

***Raspberry Publications Staff.** Young Authors Guide to Publishers: Getting Manuscripts Published. 60p. (J). (gr. 1-12). 1994. pap. 8.95 (1-884825-03-6) Raspberry Pubns.

Raspberry, William. Looking Backward at Us. LC 91-21565. 1991. 20.00 (0-87805-535-5) U Pr of Miss.

Raspe, G., ed. Life Science Monograph, No. 2. Long, J. et al, trs. 221p. 1972. 101.00 (0-08-017596-1, Pub. by Pergamon Repr UK) Franklin.

Raspe, G. & Brosig, W. International Symposium Treatment Carcinoma of the Prostate, Berlin 11-69. LC 76-172395. (Life Science Monographs: Vol. 1). 1971. 96.00 (0-08-017572-4, Pub. by Pergamon Repr UK) Franklin.

Raspe, Rudolph E. Baron Munchausen. 3rd ed. (Dedalus European Fiction Classics Ser.). (Illus.). 287p. Date not set. pap. 11.95 (1-873982-35-6) Hippocrene Bks.

Rasper, Vladimir F. & Preston, Ken R., eds. The Extensigraph Handbook. LC 91-73488. (Illus.). 50p. 1991. 59.00x (0-913250-72-4) Am Assn Cereal Chem.

Rasper, Vladimir F., jt. ed. see Faridi, Hamed.

Raspler, D., ed. see Grant, A. & Dixon, C.

Raspler, D., ed. see Grant, Alan.

Raspler, Dan & Hill, Michael C., eds. Lobo's Greatest Hits. (Illus.). 176p. 1992. pap. 12.95 (1-56389-013-5) DC Comics.

Rasponi, Lanfranco. Last Prima Donnas. LC 84-26129. (Illus.). 656p. 1985. pap. 22.00 (0-87910-040-0) Limelight Edns.

Rasporich, A. W., jt. ed. see Corbet, E. A.

Rasputin, pseud. Bridge over Troubled Waters. Kelsey, Avonelle, ed. 207p. (Orig.). (GER.). 1994. pap. 9.95 (0-9640610-0-7) Cheval Intl.

Rasputin, Maria. My Father. 1970. 5.00 (0-8216-0120-2, Univ Bks) Carol Pub Group.

Rasputin, Valentin. Farewell to Matyora. Bouis, Antonina W., tr. 227p. 1991. reprint ed. pap. 12.95 (0-8101-0997-2) Northwestern U Pr.

— Live & Remember. Bouis, Antonina W., tr. 225p. 1992. reprint ed. pap. 14.95 (0-8101-1053-9) Northwestern U Pr.

— Siberia on Fire: Stories & Essays by Valentin Rasputin. Mikkelson, Gerald & Winchell, Margaret, trs. 252p. 1989. 30.00 (0-87580-152-8); pap. 12.50 (0-87580-547-7) N Ill U Pr.

***Rasputnis & Tartakosky.** PowerBuilder 4 Expert Solutions. (Illus.). 1000p. (Orig.). 1995. pap. 60.00 (0-7897-0346-7) Que.

***Rasquinha, J.** Managerial Issues in the Reformed NHS. Malek, M. et al, eds. 1993. text ed. 85.95 (0-471-94033-X) Wiley.

Rass, Rebecca. The Fairy Tales of My Mind. LC 78-53828. (Illus.). 145p. (Orig.). 1978. 8.00 (0-931642-03-5); pap. 5.00 (0-931642-02-7) Lintel.

— Monarch Notes: Simone De Beauvoir's the Second Sex. 128p. 1988. pap. 4.50 (0-671-67126-X, Arco Test) P-H Gen Ref & Trav.

— The Mountain. (Illus.). 145p. 1982. 10.00 (0-931642-10-8); pap. 6.95 (0-931642-13-2) Lintel.

Rass, Rebecca & Brafman, Morris. From Moscow to Jerusalem. LC 75-18142. 1976. 12.95 (0-88400-010-9) Shengold.

Rassam, A. Yasmine. Women in the Domicile: The Treatment of Women's Work in International Law. LC 93-655022. (MacArthur Scholar Ser.: No. 24). 67p. (Orig.). 1994. pap. 4.50 (1-881157-26-1) In Ctr Global.

Rassam, Amal, jt. auth. see Bates, Daniel.

***Rassam, Clive.** Design & Corporate Success. (Design Council - Strategies for Product Development Ser.: No. 3). 176p. 1995. 59.95 (0-566-07534-2, Pub. by Gower UK) Ashgate Pub Co.

Rassam, Clive, jt. auth. see Barham, Kevin.

Rassam, G. N. Multilingual Thesaurus of Geosciences. 516p. (ENG, FRE, GER, ITA, RUS & SPA.). 1988. 195.00 (0-8288-7952-4) Fr & Eur.

Rassel, Gary R., jt. auth. see O'Sullivan, Elizabethann.

Rassi, Judith A. & McElroy, Margaret D., eds. The Education of Audiologists & Speech-Language Pathologists. LC 92-16758. 496p. 1992. text ed. 49.50 (0-912752-30-0) York Pr.

Rassia, J. M. Lecture Notes on Mixed Type Partial Differential Equations. 152p. (C). 1990. text ed. 43.00 (981-02-0275-X); pap. text ed. 23.00 (981-02-0406-X) World Scientific Pub.

Rassias. Differential Geometry, Calculus of Variations & Their Applications: Calculus of Variations & Their Applications. (Lecture Notes in Pure & Applied Mathematics Ser.: Vol. 100). 544p. 1985. 140.00 (0-8247-7267-9) Dekker.

— Le Francais: Depart-Arrivee. 3rd ed. 1992. text ed. 49.95 (0-8384-3726-5) Heinle & Heinle.

— Le Francais: Depart-Arrivee. 3rd ed. 1992. student ed, pap. 28.95 (0-8384-3729-X) Heinle & Heinle.

Rassias, G., jt. ed. see Stratopoulos, G.

Rassias, G. M. Differential Topology-Geometry & Related Fields. 376p. (C). 1985. 130.00 (0-685-36899-8, Pub. by Collets) St Mut.

— The Mathematical Heritage of C. F. Gauss. 550p. (C). 1991. text ed. 118.00 (981-02-0201-6) World Scientific Pub.

Rassias, G. M., ed. Morse Theory & Its Applications. 400p. (C). 1994. text ed. 58.00 (9971-5-0977-6) World Scientific Pub.

Rassias, J. M. Counter-Examples in Differential Equations & Related Topics. 192p. 1991. text ed. 48.00 (981-02-0460-4); pap. text ed. 25.00 (981-02-0461-2) World Scientific Pub.

Rassias, J. M., ed. Geometry, Analysis & Mechanics. 500p. (C). 1995. text ed. 95.00 (981-02-0757-3) World Scientific Pub.

Rassias, John. Mixed Type Equations. 312p. (C). 1986. 160.00 (0-685-36886-6, Pub. by Collets) St Mut.

Rassias, John M., ed. Functional Analysis, Approximation Theory & Numerical Analysis. 500p. (C). 1994. text ed. 114.00 (981-02-0737-9) World Scientific Pub.

Rassias, T. M. Constantin Caratheodory: An International Tribute, 2 Vols. 1468p. 1991. text ed. 301.00 (981-02-0544-9) World Scientific Pub.

— Topics in Mathematical Analysis. 992p. (C). 1989. pap. 55.00 (9971-5-0801-X) World Scientific Pub.

Rassias, T. M., ed. Constantin Caratheodory: An International Tribute, 2 vols. 1468p. (C). 1991. text ed. 230.00 (0-685-58547-6) World Scientific Pub.

— Constantin Caratheodory: An International Tribute, 2 vols., Set. 1468p. (C). 1991. text ed. 238.00 (0-685-58546-8) World Scientific Pub.

— Nonlinear Analysis. 572p. 1988. text ed. 99.00 (9971-5-0140-6) World Scientific Pub.

— The Problem of Plateau: A Tribute to Jesse Douglas & Tibor Rado. 400p. (C). 1992. text ed. 130.00 (981-02-0556-2) World Scientific Pub.

Rassias, T. M., jt. auth. see Prastaro, A.

Rassias, T. M., jt. ed. see Srivastava, H. M.

Rassias, T. M., et al. Topics in Polynomials of One & Several Variables & Their Applications. 500p. (C). 1993. text ed. 127.00 (981-02-0614-3) World Scientific Pub.

***Rassias, Themistocles M. & Simsa, Jaromir.** Finite Sums Decompositions in Mathematical Analysis. LC 94-42852. (Pure & Applied Mathematics Ser.). 1995. text ed. 49.95 (0-471-94827-6) Wiley.

Rassias, Themistocles M. & Tabor, Jozef, eds. Stability of Mappings of Hyers-Ulam Type. 160p. 1994. text ed. 90.00 (0-911767-82-7); pap. text ed. 60.00 (0-911767-64-9) Hadronic Pr Inc.

Rassinier, Paul. The Holocaust Story & the Lies of Ulysses. 450p. 1989. pap. 12.00 (0-939484-26-9) Inst Hist Rev.

— The Real Eichmann Trial. 170p. 1980. pap. 7.50 (0-911038-48-5) Inst Hist Rev.

Rasskazov, L. N., jt. auth. see Goldin, A. L.

Rassmusen, Bonnie. Volcanology. rev. ed. (Learning Packets - Anthropology Ser.). (Illus.). 92p. (J). (gr. k-8). 1983. pap. text ed. 19.95 (0-913705-07-1) Zephyr Pr AZ.

Rassmussen, Richard M. Mysteries of Space: Opposing Viewpoints. LC 93-13592. 1994. lib. bdg. 16.95 (1-56510-097-2) Greenhaven.

Rassner, Gernot. Atlas of Dermatology. 3rd ed. (Illus.). 512p. 1993. text ed. 85.00 (0-8121-1601-1) Williams & Wilkins.

Rassoull, Abass. The Jacobite Scheme. 76p. (Orig.). 1992. pap. text ed. 6.95 (1-56411-016-8) Untd Bros & Sis.

Rassudova, O. Aspectual Usage in Modern Russian. 200p. (C). 1984. 55.00 (0-685-33701-4, Pub. by Collets); 33.00 (0-685-39370-4, Pub. by Collets) St Mut.

Rassudova, O. P. & Stepanova, L. V. Temp Two: Intensive Course of Russian. 140p. (C). 1986. teacher ed 40.00 (0-317-92422-2, Pub. by Collets UK) Pro-Am Music.

Rassuli, Kathleen, jt. ed. see Hollander, Stanley.

Rassweiler, Anne D. The Generation of Power: The History of Dneprostroi. (Illus.). 262p. 1988. 42.00 (0-19-505166-1) OUP.

Rast, N. Applied Geophysics U. S. S. R. LC 60-53385. 1962. 176.00 (0-08-009662-X, Pub. by Pergamon Repr UK) Franklin.

Rast, N. & Delaney, F. M., eds. Profiles of Orogenic Belts. (Geodynamics Ser.: Vol. 10). 310p. 1983. 36.00 (0-87590-510-2) Am Geophysical.

Rast, N., jt. ed. see Horton, J. W., Jr.

Rast, N., ed. see Nalivkin, Dmitrii V.

Rast, W., jt. auth. see Ryding, S.

Rast, W., et al, eds. Assessment & Control of Non-Point Source Pollution of Aquatic Systems: A Practical Approach. (Man & the Biosphere Ser.: Vol. 14). 300p. 1995. 75.00 (1-85070-384-1) Prthnon Pub.

Rast, Walter E. Through the Ages in Palestinian Archaeology: An Introductory Handbook. LC 92-33156. 1992. pap. 15.95 (1-56338-055-2) TPI PA.

Rast, Walter E., ed. Preliminary Reports of ASOR-Sponsored Excavations 1980-84. LC 86-11482. (BASOR Supplements Ser.: No. 24). 164p. 1986. pap. text ed. 20.00 (0-89757-324-2, Eisenbrauns) Am Sch Orient Res.

— Preliminary Reports of ASOR-Sponsored Excavations 1981-83. LC 85-12851. (Bulletin of the American Schools of Oriental Research, Supplement Ser.: No. 23). 135p. 1985. pap. 17.50 (0-89757-323-4, Eisenbrauns) Am Sch Orient Res.

Rast, Walter E., jt. auth. see Schaub, R. Thomas.

Rastall, P. R. Empirical Phonology & Cartesian Tables. LC 93-28814. 108p. 1993. text ed. 59.95 (0-7734-9327-1, Mellen Univ Pr) E Mellen.

— A Functional View of English Grammar. LC 95-11024. 164p. 1996. text ed. 79.95 (0-7734-8922-3) E Mellen.

Rastall, Peter. Postprincipia: Gravitation for Physicists & Astronomers. 300p. (C). 1991. text ed. 48.00 (981-02-0778-6) World Scientific Pub.

***Rastall, Richard.** The Heaven Singing: Music in Early English Religious Drama. 352p. (C). 1996. text ed. 63.00 (0-85991-428-3) Boydell & Brewer.

Rastell, John. Nature of the Four Elements. LC 71-133725. (Tudor Facsimile Texts. Old English Plays Ser.: No. 7). reprint ed. 49.50 (0-404-53307-8) AMS Pr.

— Les Termes de la Ley: or Certain Difficult & Obscure Words & Terms of the Common & Statute Laws of England. iv, 392p. 1993. reprint ed. lib. bdg. 85.00 (0-8377-2575-5) Rothman.

— Three Rastell Plays. Axton, Richard, ed. (Tudor Interludes Ser.: No. 1). 175p. 1979. 59.00 (0-85991-047-4) Boydell & Brewer.

Rastellini, M. M., ed. Search & Rescue Survival Training. (Air Force Regulation Ser.: No. 64-4, V. 1). (Illus.). 579p. 1985. pap. 19.00 (0-16-002206-1, S/N 008-070-00560-3) USGPO.

— Survival Training: Search & Rescue. (Illus.). 579p. (Orig.). (C). 1994. pap. text ed. 75.00 (0-7881-0314-8) Diane Pub.

Rastetter, J. W., jt. auth. see Begemann, H.

Rastier, Francois. Ideologie et Theorie des Signes. (Approaches to Semiotics Ser.). (Illus.). 168p. 1972. text ed. 36.95 (90-279-2114-8) Mouton.

Rastogi, B., jt. auth. see Gupta, H.

Rastogi, Navjivan. Introduction to the Tantraloka: A Study in Structure. 589p. 1987. 36.00 (81-208-0180-6, Pub. by Motilal Banarsidass II) S Asia.

Rastogi, Navjivan, ed. see Gupta, Abhina.

Rastogi, P. N. Ethnic Tensions in Indian Society. 1986. 38.00 (0-8364-1931-6, Pub. by Mittal II) S Asia.

— Policy Analysis & Problem-Solving for Social Systems: Toward Understanding, Monitoring, & Managing Complex Real World Problems. (Illus.). 150p. (C). 1992. 27.50 (0-8039-9425-7) Sage.

— Productivity, Innovation, Management & Development: A Study in the Productivity Cultures of Nations & System Renewal. 273p. (C). 1988. text ed. 28.00 (0-8039-9563-6) Sage.

Rastogi, Pramod K. Holographic Interferometry: Principles & Methods. LC 93-39992. (Series in Optical Sciences: Vol. 68). (Illus.). 410p. 1994. 65.00 (0-387-57354-2) Spr-Verlag.

Rastogi, T. C. Islamic Mysticism Sufism. 126p. 1982. 23.95 (0-318-37184-7) Asia Bk Corp.

— Muslim World (Islam Breaks Fresh Ground) 1986. 29.00 (81-7024-039-5, Pub. by Ashish II) S Asia.

— Western Influence in Iqbal. (C). 1987. 34.00 (81-7024-080-8, Pub. by Ashish II) S Asia.

Rastogi, V. B. Modern Biology, Vol. 1. 408p. 1992. 75.00 (81-209-0442-7, Pub. by Pitambar Pub II) St Mut.

Rastogi, V. G. Modern Biology, Vol. 2. 792p. 1992. 120.00 (81-209-0496-6, Pub. by Pitambar Pub II) St Mut.

Raston, Emily, ed. see Dunnan, Nancy.

Rastorfer, Darl, jt. ed. see Holod, Renata.

Rastovski, A. Storage of Potatoes, Post-Harvest Behaviour, Store Design, Storage Practical Handling. 1989. 300.00 (81-7089-111-6, Pub. by Intl Bk Distr II) St Mut.

Rastyannikov, V. G. Food for Developing Countries in Asia & North Africa. Watts, George S., tr. LC 75-26311. (World Food Supply Ser.). (Illus.). 1976. reprint ed. 15.95 (0-405-07789-0) Ayer.

Rasula, Jed. Tabula Rasula. LC 85-30378. (Illus.). 96p. 1986. pap. 5.50 (0-930794-62-1) Station Hill Pr.

Rasuso, John N. Atlantic Wrecks, Bk. 1. Barrett, Linda, ed. (Fisherman Library). (Illus.). 176p. (Orig.). 1992. pap. text ed. 17.95 (0-923155-15-5) Fisherman Lib.

Rasvan, V, jt. auth. see Halanay, A.

Raswan, Carl & Seydel, R. H. Der Araber und Sein Pferd. (Documenta Hippologica Ser.). (Illus.). 166p. 1990. reprint ed. write for info. (3-487-08234-9, Pub. by Georg Olms GW) Lubrecht & Cramer.

Raswan, Carl R. Escape from Baghdad. (Illus.). 278p. 1978. reprint ed. 50.70 (3-487-08158-X, Pub. by Georg Olms GW) Lubrecht & Cramer.

— Im Land der Schwarzen Zelte. (Illus.). 167p. 1990. reprint ed. write for info. (3-487-08136-9, Pub. by Georg Olms GW) Lubrecht & Cramer.

— Sohne der Wuste. (Documenta Hippologica Ser.). (Illus.). 132p. 1977. write for info. (3-487-08134-2, Pub. by Georg Olms GW) Lubrecht & Cramer.

— Trinker der Lufte. (Illus.). 154p. 1990. write for info. (3-487-08140-7, Pub. by Georg Olms GW) Lubrecht & Cramer.

Rat, ed. see De Montaigne, Michel E.

Rat, Maurice. Larousse Dictionnaire des Locutions Francaises. 464p. (FRE.). 1970. 49.95 (0-7859-4628-4) Fr & Eur.

Rat, Maurice, ed. see Musset, Alfred.

Ratajack, Joan A. Words of Love. (Words to Live By Ser.). 1992. 4.99 (0-517-07364-1) Random Hse Value.

Ratajack, Joan E. Words of Happiness & Laughter. (Words to Live By Ser.). 1992. 4.99 (0-517-07366-8) Random Hse Value.

Ratajczak, H., et al, eds. Molecular Interactions, 3 vols., 1. LC 79-40825. (Illus.). 437p. reprint ed. pap. 124.60 (0-685-20690-4, 2030480) Bks Demand.

— Molecular Interactions, 3 vols., 2. LC 79-40825. (Illus.). 651p. reprint ed. pap. 180.00 (0-685-20691-2, 2030480) Bks Demand.

— Molecular Interactions, 3 vols., 3. LC 79-40825. (Illus.). 583p. reprint ed. pap. 166.20 (0-685-20692-0, 2030480) Bks Demand.

Ratajewicz, Zbigniew, jt. auth. see Tomasik, Piotr.

Ratan, Jai. The Angry Goddess. 8.00 (0-89253-634-9) Ind-US Inc.

***Ratan, Jai, ed.** Contemporary Urdu Short Stories: An Anthology. (C). 1992. 9.00x (81-207-1304-4, Pub. by Sterling Plns Pvt II) S Asia.

***Ratan, Jai, tr.** Anthology of Hindi Short Stories. (C). 1993. 18.00x (81-7201-527-5, Pub. by Sahitya Akademi II) S Asia.

R

— Contemporary Hindi Short Stories. (Writers Workshop Saffronbird Ser.). 180p. 1975. 12.00 (*0-88253-518-8*) Ind-US Inc.
— Krishan Chander: Selected Short Stories. (C). 1990. 12.50 (*0-8364-2618-5*, Pub. by Sahitya Akademi II) S Asia.
— Modern Hindi Short Stories. (C). 1991. 24.00 (*81-7023-187-6*, Pub. by Allied II) S Asia.
— Modern Urdu Short Stories. vi, 200p. 1987. 13.50 (*0-8364-2049-7*, Pub. by Allied II) S Asia.
Ratan, Jai, tr. see Askh, Upendranath.
Ratan, Jai, tr. see Chander, Krishan.
Ratan, Jai, tr. see Rakesh, Mohan.
Ratan, Jai, tr. see Sahni, Bhisham.
Ratan, Jai, tr. see Varma, Shrikant.
Ratan, Jai, tr. see Yadav, Rajendra.
Ratanlal, Mishra. Epigraphical Studies of Rajasthan Inscriptions. 1990. 44.50 (*81-7018-596-3*, Pub. by BR Pub II) S Asia.
Ratanov, V. F., jt. auth. see Zakladnoi, G. A.
Ratanova, V. F., jt. auth. see Zakladnoi, G. A.
Ratay, Robert T., ed. Temporary Structures in Construction Operations. 156p. 1987. 17.00 (*0-87262-592-3*) Am Soc Civil Eng.
Ratch, Jerry. Hot Weather: Poems Selected & New. Peters, Robert B., ed. LC 81-21473. (Poets Now Ser.: No. 3). 202p. 1982. 13.50 (*0-8108-1511-7*) Scarecrow.
— Lenin's Paintings. (Orig.). 1987. pap. 10.00 (*0-89807-148-8*) Illuminati.
— Lenin's Paintings. deluxe limited ed. (Orig.). 1987. 20.00 (*0-89807-149-6*) Illuminati.
— Light. 64p. 1988. 8.00 (*0-929022-06-8*) O Bks.
Ratcheson, Robert A., jt. auth. see Wirth, Fremont P.
Ratchford, B. U. American State Debts. LC 71-182704. reprint ed. 30.00 (*0-404-05226-6*) AMS Pr.
Ratchford, Paula G. Instruction in Singlesness. 124p. Date not set. student ed 13.00 (*0-9641801-1-1*); pap. text ed. 8.00 (*0-9641801-0-3*) P G Ratchford.
Ratchford, Walt. How to Be a Successful Bachelor: A Humorous Guide to Your New Life. 198p. 1995. pap. 12.95 (*0-9640027-0-1*) Virgin Pubng.
Ratchnevsky, Paul. Genghis Khan: His Life & Legacy. Haining, Thomas N., tr. 272p. (C). 1991. 34.95 (*0-631-16785-4*) Blackwell Pubs.
— Genghis Khan: His Life & Legacy. 272p. 1993. pap. 17.95 (*0-631-18949-1*) Blackwell Pubs.
Ratcliffe, Stephen. Distance. LC 86-71933. 112p. (Orig.). 1986. pap. 6.00 (*0-939691-00-0*) Avenue B.
Ratcliff. Oedipus Trilogy (Sophocles) (Book Notes Ser.). (C). 1984. pap. 2.50 (*0-8120-3430-9*) Barron.
Ratcliff, Bryan. Introducing Specification Using Z: A Practical Case Study Approach. LC 93-33831. (International Series in Software Engineering). 1994. 17. 95 (*0-07-707965-5*) McGraw.
Ratcliff, Carter. Alex Katz: Cutouts. (Illus.). 34p. 1979. pap. 5.00 (*0-944680-31-3*) R Miller Gal.
— Andy Warhol. LC 83-3835. (Modern Masters Ser.). (Illus.). 128p. 1986. 29.95 (*0-89659-385-1*); pap. 19.95 (*1-55859-257-1*) Abbeville Pr.
— The Fate of a Gesture: Jackson Pollock & Postwar American Art. LC 95-12081. (Illus.). 400p. 1995. 30.00 (*0-374-22331-9*) FS&G.
— Fever Coast. 7.00 (*0-686-09757-2*); pap. 3.50 (*0-686-09758-0*) Kulchur Foun.
— Give Me Tomorrow. (Illus.). 48p. 1983. text ed. 24.00 (*0-931428-03-3*) Vehicle Edns.
— John Singer Sargent. LC 82-6779. (Illus.). 256p. 1986. 39. 98 (*0-89660-014-9*, Artabras) Abbeville Pr.
— Jorge Castillo: Dibujo, Pintura, Escultura. (Grandes Monografias). (Illus.). 412p. (SPA.). 1993. 350.00 (*84-343-0476-7*) Elliots Bks.
— Komar & Melamid. (Illus.). 208p. 1989. 19.98 (*0-89659-891-8*); 3,500.00 (*0-89659-954-X*) Abbeville Pr.
— Lynda Benglis & Keith Sonnier: A Ten Year Retrospective, 1977-1987. Hammill, Audrey, ed. LC 87-19544. (Illus.). 56p. (Orig.). 1987. pap. text ed. 14.00 (*0-944564-00-3*) Alex Mus.
— Mia Westerlund Roosen. Blank, Shoshana, ed. (Illus.). 22p. (Orig.). 1989. pap. text ed. 10.00 (*0-317-93161-X*) Shoshana Wayne Gall.
— Pressures of the Hand: Expressionist Impulses in Recent American Art. (Illus.). 36p. 1984. pap. 12.50 (*0-942746-05-8*) SUNYP R Gibson.
— Venet. (Illus.). 200p. 1993. 60.00 (*1-55859-699-2*, Cross Riv Pr) Abbeville Pr.
Ratcliff, Carter & Rosenblum, Robert. Gilbert & George: The Singing Sculpture. Wolmer, Bruce, ed. LC 92-82072. (Illus.). 64p. 1993. 35.00 (*0-9635649-0-0*) A McCall NY.
Ratcliff, Carter, jt. auth. see McFadden, Sarah.
Ratcliff, Carter, jt. auth. see Reuter, Laurel.
Ratcliff, Carter, jt. auth. see Schweizer, Paul D.
Ratcliff, Carter, et al. Aperture, Issue 91. (Fine Photography Ser.). (Illus.). 80p. 1983. pap. 18.50 (*0-89381-127-0*) Aperture.
Ratcliff, Clarence E. North Carolina Taxpayers, Sixteen Seventy-Nine to Seventeen-Ninety. 230p. 1990. 20.00 (*0-8063-1204-1*, 4762) Genealog Pub.
— North Carolina Taxpayers, 1701-1786. LC 84-80487. 228p. 1993. 20.00 (*0-8063-1079-0*) Genealog Pub.
Ratcliff, Donald. Christian Views of Sociology. 1994. pap. text ed. 19.90 (*1-56226-168-1*) CT Pub.
Ratcliff, Donald, ed. Handbook of Children's Religious Education. LC 91-43038. 285p. (Orig.). 1992. pap. 17.95 (*0-89135-085-3*) Religious Educ.
— Handbook of Preschool Religious Education. LC 88-30868. 306p. (Orig.). 1989. pap. 17.95 (*0-89135-068-3*) Religious Educ.
Ratcliff, Donald & Davies, James A., eds. Handbook of Youth Ministry. 318p. (Orig.). 1990. pap. 17.95 (*0-89135-079-9*) Religious Educ.
Ratcliff, Donald & Fitch, Stanley. Insights into Child Development. 495p. (C). 1991. pap. text ed. 39.95 (*1-56226-070-7*) CT Pub.
Ratcliff, Donald & Neff, Blake. A Complete Guide to Religious Education Volunteers. 280p. (Orig.). 1993. pap. 16.95 (*0-89135-089-6*) Religious Educ.
Ratcliff, Donald, jt. ed. see Neff, Blake J.
Ratcliff, E. C., ed. Exposito Antiquae Liturgiae Gallicanae. (Publications of the Henry Bradshaw Society Ser. No. XCIV (94)). 1970. 30.00 (*0-907077-15-3*) Boydell & Brewer.
Ratcliff, Graham, jt. ed. see Farah, Martha.
Ratcliff, J. & Papworth, N. Single Camera Stereo Sound. (Illus.). 144p. 1992. pap. 37.95 (*0-240-51307-X*, Focal) Buttrwrth-Heinemann.
Ratcliff, James, ed. ASHE Reader on Community Colleges. 1992. 26.50 (*0-536-58226-2*) Ginn Pr.
Ratcliff, James L. & Jones, Elizabeth A., eds. Assessment & Curriculum Reform. LC 85-644752. (New Directions for Higher Education Ser.: No. HE 80). 100p. 1992. 16.95 (*1-55542-735-9*) Jossey-Bass.
Ratcliff, John. Timecode: A User's Guide. (Illus.). 272p. 1993. pap. 30.00 (*0-240-51334-7*, Focal) Buttrwrth-Heinemann.
Ratcliff, John D. Lives & Dollars. LC 70-111859. (Essay Index Reprint Ser.). 1977. 21.95 (*0-8369-2022-8*) Ayer.
— Modern Miracle Men. LC 79-37770. (Essay Index Reprint Ser.). 1977. reprint ed. 26.95 (*0-8369-2619-6*) Ayer.
Ratcliff, Kathryn S., ed. Healing Technology: Feminist Perspectives. 1989. 42.50 (*0-472-09395-9*); pap. 16.95 (*0-472-06395-2*) U of Mich Pr.
***Ratcliff, Mel.** Keys of Succession: A Guide for Spouses, Children, &-or Successor Trustees. 320p. 1995. boxed 44.95 (*0-9646347-1-6*) Possiblts Pr.
Ratcliff, Phyllis E. Satyagraha. 52p. (Orig.). 1992. pap. 5.95 (*0-910303-39-8*) Writers Pub Serv.
Ratcliff, R. E. English-French Dictionary of Naval Terminology. 168p. (ENG & FRE.). 1983. pap. 75.00 (*0-8288-1580-1*, F25470) Fr & Eur.
Ratcliff, Richard. Research in Social Movements, Conflicts & Change, Vol. 6. 73.25 (*0-89232-311-6*) Jai Pr.
Ratcliff, Richard E., jt. auth. see Zeitlin, Maurice.
Ratcliff, Ronald E. & Peck, Michael A. Dictionary of Naval Terminology-Dictionnaire de Terminologie Navale: English-French; Anglais-Francais. (Illus.). 160p. (Orig.). 1983. pap. text ed. 30.00 (*2-85206-200-3*) Sheridan.
Ratcliff, Ruth. Scottish Folk Tales. 1977. 40.00 (*0-685-87557-1*) St Mut.
***Ratcliffe.** ADA Yearbook 1995. LC 95-75768. 1995. 82.00 (*90-5199-218-1*) IOS Press.
Ratcliffe, A. The Truth about Hitler & the Roman Catholic Church. 1982. lib. bdg. 59.95 (*0-87700-362-9*) Revisionist Pr.
Ratcliffe, A., ed. see Zakhvatkin, A. A.
Ratcliffe, Amy, ed. see Jankowski, Dennis A. & Butler, L. Rick.
Ratcliffe, Ann. Chemistry: The Experience. LC 92-27306. 324p. 1993. Net. pap. text ed. write for info. (*0-471-57707-3*) Wiley.
Ratcliffe, Betram, jt. auth. see Ysaye, Antoine.
***Ratcliffe, Bill.** The Art of Senior Golf. LC 94-61584. (Illus.). 124p. (Orig.). 1995. 10.95 (*1-884570-20-8*) Research Triangle.
Ratcliffe, Carter. Michael Lucero: Recent Sculpture. (Illus.). 32p. (Orig.). 1989. write for info. (*0-318-64754-0*) ACA Galleries.
Ratcliffe, Derek. The Peregrine Falcon. LC 80-65963. (Illus.). 1980. 25.00 (*0-931130-05-0*) Harrell Bks.
Ratcliffe, Derek A. Bird Life of Mountain & Upland. (Bird Life Ser.). (Illus.). 280p. (C). 1991. 44.95 (*0-521-33123-4*) Cambridge U Pr.
— The Peregrine Falcon. 2nd ed. (Illus.). 488p. 1993. text ed. 39.95 (*0-85661-060-7*, Pub. by Poyser UK) Acad Pr.
Ratcliffe, Dolores. Women Entrepreneurs, Networking & Sweet Patato Pie: Business Survival Guide. (YA). (gr. 10-12). 1987. pap. 14.95 (*0-933016-03-4*) Corita Comm.
Ratcliffe, Elisabeth. A Country Parish Neen Savage in 1981. 112p. (C). 1989. 39.00 (*0-86157-140-1*, Pub. by S A Baldwin UK) St Mut.
Ratcliffe, F. N., jt. auth. see Fenner, Frank J.
Ratcliffe, Florence M. Myself When Young. (C). 1989. text ed. 39.00 (*1-872795-42-0*, Pub. by Pentland Pr UK) St Mut.
***Ratcliffe, Georgetta.** How to Buy Your First Computer. 2nd rev. ed. 200p. 1995. pap. 10.00 (*1-881818-05-5*) TBL.
Ratcliffe, Georzetta. How to Buy Your First Computer, 1994. 150p. (Orig.). 1993. pap. 10.00 (*1-881818-03-9*) TBL.
Ratcliffe, James M. Good Samaritan & the Law. 11.50 (*0-8446-2783-6*) Peter Smith.
Ratcliffe, John, jt. auth. see Crooke, Philip.
Ratcliffe, John A. The Magneto-Ionic Theory & Its Applications to the Ionosphere: A Monograph. LC 59-896. 216p. reprint ed. pap. 61.60 (*0-317-11075-6*, 2050747) Bks Demand.
Ratcliffe, John G. Foundations of Hyperbolic Manifolds. LC 94-8958. (Graduate Texts in Mathematics Ser.). 768p. 1994. 69.95 (*0-387-94249-1*) Spr-Verlag.
— Foundations of Hyperbolic Manifolds. (Graduate Texts in Mathematics Ser.). 768p. 1994. pap. text ed. 49.95 (*0-615-00203-X*) Spr-Verlag.
***Ratcliffe, Krista.** Anglo-American Feminist Challenges to the Rhetorical Traditions: Virginia Woolf, Mary Daly, & Adrienne Rich. LC 94-40053. 248p. (C). 1995. 29.95x (*0-8093-1934-9*) S Ill U Pr.
Ratcliffe, Marjorie. Jimena: A Woman in Spanish Literature. 250p. Date not set. 63.50 (*0-916379-94-9*) Scripta.
Ratcliffe, Mitch. Newton's Law: The Brave New World of Apple's Personal Digital Assistant. 1993. pap. 24.00 (*0-679-74647-1*) Random.
Ratcliffe, Mitch, jt. auth. see Gore, Andrew.
Ratcliffe, N. A. & Rowley, A. F., eds. Invertebrate Blood Cells: Anthropods to Urchordates Invertebrates & Vertebrates Compared, Vol. 2. LC 80-41248. 1981. text ed. 212.00 (*0-12-582102-6*) Acad Pr.
— Invertebrate Blood Cells: General Aspects, Animals Without True Circulatory Systems to Cephalopods, Vol. 1. LC 80-41248. 1981. text ed. 212.00 (*0-12-582101-8*) Acad Pr.
Ratcliffe, N. A., jt. ed. see Chantler, E.
Ratcliffe, N. A., jt. ed. see Rowley, A. F.
Ratcliffe, Peter, ed. Race, Ethnicity & Nation: International Perspectives on Social Conflict. LC 94-12567. 1994. 75. 00 (*1-85728-099-7*, Pub. by UCL Pr UK) Taylor & Francis.
Ratcliffe, R. An Introduction to Town & Country Planning. (C). 1989. text ed. 110.00 (*0-09-144021-1*, Pub. by S Thornes Pubs UK) St Mut.
Ratcliffe, Robert H., ed. Great Cases of the Supreme Court. (Illus.). (gr. 7-8). 1975. teacher ed 5.56 (*0-685-02291-9*) HM.
— Vital Issues of the Constitution. (Trailmarks of Liberty Ser.). (Illus.). 150p. (gr. 11-12). 1975. pap. 25.40 (*0-395-20125-X*) HM.
Ratcliffe, Ronald. Steinway. (Illus.). 196p. 1989. 40.00 (*0-87701-592-9*) Chronicle Bks.
Ratcliffe, Sam D. Painting Texas History to Nineteen Hundred. LC 92-9752. (American Studies Ser.). (Illus.). 190p. 1992. 29.95 (*0-292-78113-X*) U of Tex Pr.
Ratcliffe, Stephen. New York Notes. 32p. (Orig.). 1983. pap. text ed. 3.50 (*0-939180-22-7*) Tombouctou.
— Spaces in the Light Said to Be Where One Comes From. 88p. (Orig.). 1993. pap. 9.50 (*0-937013-42-0*) Potes Poets.
— Where Late the Sweet Birds Sang. LC 88-62610. 88p. 1989. 8.00 (*0-929022-03-3*) O Bks.
Ratcliffe, Susan, ed. The Little Oxford Book of Quotations. 468p. 1995. 11.95 (*0-19-866207-6*) OUP.
Ratcliffe, Thomas A., jt. auth. see Munter, Paul.
***Rateaver, Bargyla & Rateaver, Gylver.** Organic Method Primer: The Basics: Special Edition. (Conservation Gardening & Farming Ser.). (Illus.). 100p. 1994. pap. 25. 00 (*0-915966-04-2*) Rateavers.
— Organic Method Primer Update: Special Edition. (Conservation Gardening & Farming Ser.). (Illus.). 700p. 1993. 125.00 (*0-915966-01-8*) Rateavers.
Rateaver, Bargyla, ed. see Cotten, Emmi.
Rateaver, Bargyla, ed. see Hills, Lawrence D.
Rateaver, Bargyla, ed. see Turner, F. Newman.
Rateaver, Gylver, ed. see Corley, Hugh.
Rateaver, Gylver, ed. see Cotten, Emmi.
Rateaver, Gylver, ed. see Hainsworth, P. H.
Rateaver, Gylver, ed. see Hills, Lawrence D.
Rateaver, Gylver, ed. see Leatherbarrow, Margaret.
Rateaver, Gylver, jt. auth. see Rateaver, Bargyla.
Rateaver, Gylver, ed. see Stephenson, W. A.
Rateaver, Gylver, ed. see Sykes, Friend.
Rateaver, Gylver, ed. see Turner, F. Newman.
Rateitschak, K., et al. Color Atlas of Periodontology. 2nd rev. ed. Hassell, Thomas, tr. (Dental Medicine Ser.). (Illus.). 400p. 1989. text ed. 159.00 (*0-86577-318-1*) Thieme Med Pubs.
Rateitschak, Klaus H., ed. see Spiekermann, Hubertus.
Ratel, J. Dictionary of Childhood Health: Diccionario de la Salud Infantil. 480p. (SPA.). 1983. pap. 19.95 (*0-8288-1875-4*, S60549) Fr & Eur.
Rateliff, John D., jt. ed. see Weber, Valerie.
Rater, Alan F., ed. Anthology of Magazine Verse & Yearbook of American Poetry for 1984. 1984. 35.00 (*0-917734-10-6*) Monitor Bk.
Ratera, Rosario K. A Gift. (Illus.). (J). (gr. 1-3). 1972. 3.00 (*0-686-09524-3*, Pub. by New Day Pub PH) Cellar.
Ratermann, Dale. Basketball Crosswords. 2nd ed. LC 94-19943. (Illus.). 192p. 1994. pap. 12.95 (*1-57028-004-5*, Spalding Sports) Masters Pr IN.
— Football Crosswords. 2nd ed. (Illus.). 192p. 1994. pap. 12. 95 (*1-57028-002-9*) Masters Pr IN.
— Hockey Crosswords. LC 94-41466. (Illus.). 192p. 1994. pap. 12.95 (*1-57028-006-1*, Spalding Sports) Masters Pr IN.
***Ratermann, Dale & Mullen, Mike.** How to Get a Job in Sports. (Illus.). 128p. (Orig.). 1995. pap. 12.95 (*1-57028-043-6*) Masters Pr IN.
Ratermann, Dale & Ociepka, Bob. Basketball Playbook: Plays from the Pros. LC 95-7520. (Illus.). 160p. 1995. pap. 12.95 (*1-57028-008-8*, Spalding Sports) Masters Pr IN.
Ratey, John, jt. auth. see Hallowell, Edward M.
***Ratey, John J.** Neuropsychiatry of Personality Disorders. (Neuropsychiatry Ser.). (Illus.). 304p. 1994. (*0-86542-293-1*) Blackwell Sci.
Ratey, John J., ed. Mental Retardation: Developing Pharmacotherapies. LC 90-14485. (Progress in Psychiatry Ser.: No. 32). 160p. 1991. 29.50 (*0-88048-452-7*, CG1A8452) Am Psychiatric.
Rath, B. B. & Misra, M. S., eds. Role of Interfaces on Material Dumping: Proceedings of an International Symposium Held in Conjunction with ASM's Materials Week & TMS-AIME Fall Meeting, 13-17 October 1985, Toronto, Ontario, Canada. LC 86-71998. (Illus.). 131p. reprint ed. pap. 37.40 (*0-318-39723-4*, 2033081) Bks Demand.
Rath, Bhakta B., ed. see AIME, Metallurgical Society Staff.
Rath, Daniel D., jt. ed. see Mayers, Marvin K.
Rath, Eric. Container Systems. LC 72-13139. (Materials Handling & Packaging Ser.). 595p. 1973. reprint ed. pap. 169.60 (*0-7837-3464-6*, 2057792) Bks Demand.
Rath, Erna. Splendid Soft Toy Book. 1991. pap. 14.95 (*0-85532-540-2*, Pub. by Search Pr UK) A Schwartz & Co.
— The Splendid Soft Toy Book. rev. ed. Bedoyere, Charlotte de la, ed. (Illus.). 128p. 1984. 18.95 (*0-85532-537-2*, Pub. by Search Pr UK) A Schwartz & Co.
Rath, Gustave & Shawchuck, Norman. Benchmarks of Quality in the Church. 144p. (Orig.). 1994. pap. 14.95 (*0-687-34912-5*) Abingdon.
Rath, H. J., ed. Microgravity Fluid Mechanics: IUTAM Symposium, Bremen, 1991. (International Union of Theoretical & Applied Mechanics Symposia Ser.). xxii, 611p. 1992. 139.00 (*0-387-55122-0*) Spr-Verlag.
Rath, H. M., et al. Reproduction in Camels. (Animal Production & Health Papers: No. 82). 60p. 1990. pap. 12.00 (*92-5-102969-5*, F9695) UNIPUB.
***Rath, Matthias.** Why Animals Don't Get Heart Attacks. (Illus.). (Orig.). (YA). 1994. pap. 7.95 (*0-9638768-1-3*) Health Now.
Rath, Patricia, et al. Introduction to Fashion Merchandising. LC 92-39192. 1993. 36.95 (*0-8273-4871-1*) Delmar.
Rath, Patricia M., et al. Fashion Forecaster for Introduction to Fashion Merchandising. 277p. 1994. student ed 15.95 (*0-8273-5065-1*) Delmar.
— Introduction to Fashion Merchandising. 156p. 1994. teacher ed 14.00 (*0-8273-5064-3*) Delmar.
Rath, R., et al, eds. Diversity & Unity in Cross-Cultural Psychology. vi, 374p. 1982. 32.75 (*90-265-0431-4*, Pub. by Swets Pub Serv NE) Taylor & Francis.
Rath, R. K. Fresh Water Aquaculture. (C). 1992. text ed. 200.00 (*81-7233-055-3*, Pub. by Scientific Pubs II) St Mut.
Rath, Rabindranath, jt. auth. see Das, Hari H.
Rath, Ralph. After Death: Judgment or Recycling? (Get the Facts Ser.: Series I). 30p. (Orig.). 1993. pap. 2.95 (*0-9640167-3-7*) Peter Pubns.
— Christian Community: A Reporter's Inside Look. (Get the Facts Ser.: Series II). 32p. (Orig.). 1994. pap. 2.95 (*0-9640167-6-1*) Peter Pubns.
— The Devil: An Old Fashioned Belief? (Get the Facts Ser.: Series I). 30p. (Orig.). 1992. pap. 2.95 (*0-9640167-0-2*) Peter Pubns.
— Get the Facts Series I, Set. (Orig.). 1993. pap. 11.80 (*0-9640167-8-8*) Peter Pubns.
— Get the Facts Series II, Set. (Orig.). 1995. pap. 11.80 (*0-9640167-9-6*) Peter Pubns.
— God: Almighty or All Me? (Get the Facts Ser.: Series II). 32p. (Orig.). 1995. pap. 2.95 (*0-9640167-7-X*) Peter Pubns.
— God Is at Work in You: A Practical Guide to Growth in the Spirit. LC 89-83731. 89p. (Orig.). 1989. pap. 5.95 (*0-937779-11-3*) Greenlawn Pr.
— Homosexuality: What Are the Issues? (Get the Facts Ser.: Series II). 32p. (Orig.). 1993. pap. 2.95 (*0-9640167-4-5*) Peter Pubns.
— Inner Guides: OK for Catholics? (Get the Facts Ser.: Series I). 30p. (Orig.). 1992. pap. 2.95 (*0-9640167-1-0*) Peter Pubns.
— Jesus: Guru or God? (Get the Facts Ser.: Series II). 32p. (Orig.). 1994. pap. 2.95 (*0-9640167-5-3*) Peter Pubns.
— Mantras: Helpful or Harmful? (Get the Facts Ser.: Series I). 30p. (Orig.). 1993. pap. 2.95 (*0-9640167-2-9*) Peter Pubns.
— The New Age: A Christian Critique. LC 90-80211. viii, 343p. (Orig.). 1990. pap. 8.95 (*0-937779-15-6*) Greenlawn Pr.
Rath, Reuben J. The Provisional Austrian Regime in Lombardy- Venetia, 1814-1815. LC 69-18808. 426p. reprint ed. pap. 121.50 (*0-8357-7756-1*, 2036114) Bks Demand.
— The Viennese Revolution of 1848. LC 56-11770. 440p. reprint ed. pap. 125.40 (*0-8357-7757-X*, 2036115) Bks Demand.
Rath, Sara. About Cows. (Illus.). 256p. 1987. 14.95 (*0-942802-75-6*) NorthWord.
***Rath, Sharada, et al, eds.** Role of Elites & Citizens in Rural Development of India. 198p. (C). 1993. 60.00x (*81-85880-18-2*, Pub. by Print Hse II) St Mut.
***Rath, Sura P. & Shaw, Mary N., eds.** Flannery O'Connor: New Perspectives. LC 94-48867. 1995. write for info. (*0-8203-1749-7*) U of Ga Pr.
Rathaur, Majula. Unmarried Working Women. 165p. 1988. text ed. 18.95 (*81-7027-134-7*, Pub. by Radiant Pubs II) S Asia.
***Rathbone.** Surviving Workplace Violence: Before, During & After. 1999. write for info. (*0-7506-9671-0*, Focal) Buttrwrth-Heinemann.
Rathbone, Andrew, jt. auth. see Moseley, Marshall L.
Rathbone, Andy. More Windows for Dummies. (More...for Dummies Ser.). (Illus.). 416p. 1994. pap. 19.95 (*1-56884-048-9*) IDG Bks.
— Multimedia & CD-ROMS. 2nd ed. 1995. boxed 29.99 (*1-56884-909-5*) IDG Bks.
— Multimedia & CD-ROMs for Dummies. 1994. pap. 19.95 (*1-56884-089-6*) IDG Bks.
— Multimedia & CD-ROMS for Dummies. 2nd ed. 1995. pap. 19.99 (*1-56884-907-9*) IDG Bks.
— Multimedia & CD-ROMs for Dummies Interactive Multimedia Value Pack. 1994. pap. 29.95 (*1-56884-225-2*) IDG Bks.
— OS-2 for Dummies. 1993. pap. 19.95 (*1-878058-76-2*) IDG Bks.
— OS-2 Warp for Dummies. 2nd ed. 1995. pap. 19.99 (*1-56884-205-8*) IDG Bks.
— PCs for Dummies. 3rd ed. 1995. pap. 16.99 (*1-56884-904-4*) IDG Bks.
— Upgrading & Fixing PCs for Dummies. (Illus.). 356p. 1993. pap. 19.95 (*1-56884-002-0*) IDG Bks.
— Upgrading & Fixing PCs for Dummies. 2nd ed. 1995. pap. 19.99 (*1-56884-903-6*) IDG Bks.

R

— VCRs & Camcorders for Dummies. 1994. pap. 14.99 (*1-56884-229-5*) IDG Bks.

— Windows for Dummies. (Illus.). 352p. 1993. pap. 16.95 (*1-878058-61-4*) IDG Bks.

— Windows 3.1 for Dummies. 2nd ed. 1994. pap. 16.95 (*1-56884-182-5*) IDG Bks.

— Windows 3.1 for Dummies 101. 1995. pap. 24.99 (*1-56884-627-4*) IDG Bks.

— Windows 3.11 for Dummies. 3rd ed. 1995. pap. 16.95 (*1-56884-370-4*) IDG Bks.

— Windows 95 for Dummies. 1995. pap. 19.99 (*1-56884-240-6*) IDG Bks.

Rathbone, Andy & Gookin, Dan. PCs for Dummies. 2nd ed. (For Dummies Ser.). (Illus.). 360p. 1994. pap. 16.95 (*1-56884-078-0*) IDG Bks.

Rathbone, Andy, jt. auth. see Goodin, Dan.

Rathbone, Andy, jt. auth. see Gookin, Dan.

Rathbone, B. J. & Heatley, R. V. Helicobacter Pylori & Gastroduodenal Disease. 2nd ed. (Illus.). 312p. 1992. 140.00 (*0-632-03346-0*) Blackwell Sci.

Rathbone, Basil. In & Out of Character. 15.95 (*0-8488-1113-5*) Amereon Ltd.

— In & Out of Character. 379p. 1983. reprint ed. lib. bdg. 16.95 (*0-686-47484-8*) Buccaneer Bks.

— In & Out of Character. LC 88-21531. (Illus.). 288p. 1989. reprint ed. pap. 14.95 (*0-87910-119-9*) Limelight Edns.

***Rathbone, Belinda.** Walker Evans: Message from the Interior. Evans, Walker, ed. LC 95-3711. (Illus.). 338p. 1995. 25.00 (*0-395-59072-8*) HM.

Rathbone, Belinda, et al, eds. Two Lives - Georgia O'Keeffe & Alfred Stieglitz: A Conversation in Paintings & Photographs. LC 92-36411. (Illus.). 144p. 1992. pap. 28.00 (*0-943044-17-0*) Phillips Coll.

Rathbone, Charles, et al. Multiage Portraits: Teaching & Learning in Mixed-Age Classroom. 202p. (Orig.). 1993. pap. 24.95 (*0-9627389-7-2*, Crystal Spgs) Soc Dev Educ.

Rathbone, Charles H. It's the Climate. LC 71-134974. (Short Story Index Reprint Ser.). (Illus.). 1977. 18.95 (*0-8369-3705-8*) Ayer.

Rathbone, Charles H., jt. auth. see Hyman, Ronald T.

Rathbone, Dominic. Economic Rationalism & Rural Society in Third-Century AD Egypt: The Heroninos Archive & the Appianus Estate. (Classical Studies). (Illus.). 496p. (C). 1991. 84.95 (*0-521-40149-6*) Cambridge U Pr.

Rathbone, Eliza, et al. Nicolas de Stael in America. LC 90-35478. (Illus.). 192p. 1992. pap. 30.00 (*0-943044-15-4*) U of Wash Pr.

Rathbone, Eliza E. Bill Jensen. LC 87-27312. (Illus.). 45p. 1987. pap. 15.00 (*0-943044-10-3*) Phillips Coll.

Rathbone, Irene. We That Were Young. LC 88-31029. 528p. 1989. 35.00 (*1-55861-001-4*); pap. 10.95 (*1-55861-002-2*) Feminist Pr.

Rathbone, Jean P. Ecuador, the Galapagos, & Colombia: Cadogan Guides. LC 91-21692. (Illus.). 352p. 1991. pap. 17.95 (*0-87106-248-8*) Globe Pequot.

Rathbone, Julian. Sand Blind. 1994. pap. 12.99 (*1-85242-281-5*) Serpents Tail.

— Wellington's War: His Peninsular Dispatches. (Illus.). 352p. 1995. pap. 14.95 (*0-7181-3841-4*, Penguin Bks) Viking Penguin.

Rathbone, Lee, ed. see Blum, Miriam D.

Rathbone-McCuan, Eloise & Fabian, Dorothy R., eds. Self-Neglecting Elders: A Clinical Dilemma. LC 91-36343. 216p. 1992. text ed. 47.95 (*0-86569-047-2*, T047, Auburn Hse) Greenwood.

Rathbone-McCuan, Eloise & Havens, Betty, eds. North American Elders: United States & Canadian Perspectives. LC 87-15048. (Contributions to the Study of Aging Ser.: No. 8). 320p. 1988. text ed. 59.95 (*0-313-25484-2*, REL/, Greenwood Pr) Greenwood.

Rathbone, R., ed. Ghana - Pt. 2: 1952-1957: British Documents on the End of Empire, Series B, Vol. 1. 443p. 1992. 120.00 (*0-11-290526-9*, HMO5264, Pub. by HMSO UK) UNIPUB.

Rathbone, R. Andrew, jt. auth. see Moseley, Marshall L.

Rathbone, Richard. Murder & Politics in Colonial Ghana. (Illus.). 256p. (C). 1993. text ed. 35.00 (*0-300-05504-8*) Yale U Pr.

Rathbone, Robert R. Communicating Technical Information. LC 66-25632. (Engineering Ser.). (Illus.). (Orig.). 1966. pap. write for info. (*0-201-06305-0*) Addison-Wesley.

Rathbone, Tina. Modems for Dummies. (Illus.). 512p. 1993. pap. 16.95 (*1-56884-001-2*) IDG Bks.

— Modems for Dummies. 2nd ed. 1994. pap. 19.99 (*1-56884-223-6*) IDG Bks.

— More Modems & On-Line Services For. 1995. pap. 19.99 (*1-56884-365-8*) IDG Bks.

Rathbun. Eyelid Surgery. 1990. 200.00 (*0-316-73437-3*) Little.

Rathbun, Carole. The Village in the Turkish Novel & Short Story 1920-1955. (Near & Middle East Monographs: No. 2). 192p. 1972. text ed. 56.95 (*90-279-2327-2*) Mouton.

Rathbun, Carolyn R. Sara Bear's Surprise. (Land of Pleasant Dreams Ser.). (Illus.). (Orig.). (J). (ps). 1993. 12.95 (*0-9634808-0-4*); pap. 4.50 (*0-9634808-1-2*) Endless Love.

Rathbun, Galen, jt. auth. see Nicoll, Martin E.

Rathbun, Gilbert. Monarch Notes on Williams' Glass Menagerie. (Orig.). (C). pap. 3.95 (*0-671-00700-9*, Arco Test) P-H Gen Ref & Trav.

— Monarch Notes on Williams' Street-Car Named Desire. (Orig.). (C). pap. 3.95 (*0-671-00701-7*, Arco Test) P-H Gen Ref & Trav.

Rathbun, John W. & Grecu, Monica M., eds. American Literary Critics & Scholars, 1850-1880, Vol. 64. (Dictionary of Literary Biography Ser.: Vol. 64). 450p. 1987. 128.00 (*0-8103-1742-7*) Gale.

Rathbun, Jonathan. Narrative of Jonathan Rathbun of the Capture of Fort Griswold with Accurate Accounts of the Capture of Groton Fort, the Massacre That Followed, & the Sacking & Burning of New London, September 6, 1781 by the British Forces Under the Command of the Traitor Benedict Arnold. LC 76-140878. (Eyewitness Accounts of the American Revolution Ser., No. 1). 1971. reprint ed. 21.95 (*0-405-01217-9*) Ayer.

Rathbun, Katharine C., jt. auth. see Richards, Edward P., III.

Rathbun, Linda & Ringrose, Linda. Foothills to Mount Evans: West of Denver Trailguide. (Illus.). 80p. (Orig.). 1980. pap. 6.95 (*0-9606108-0-4*) Wordsmiths.

Rathbun, Mary & Peron, Dennis. Brownie Mary's Marijuana Cookbook: Recipes for Social Change. 65p. (Orig.). 1993. pap. 9.95 (*0-685-71003-3*) Trail of Smoke.

Rathbun, Mary C., jt. auth. see Hayes, Bartlett H., Jr.

Rathbun, Mary J., jt. auth. see Edmondson, C. H.

Rathbun, Paula, jt. auth. see Wright, Christopher.

Rathbun, Pete. Just Say No: The Role of Material Bans in Integrated Waste Management. 100p. 1990. 10.00 (*0-685-56589-0*) CPA Washington.

Rathbun, Robert D., ed. Shopping Centers & Malls. (Illus.). 192p. 1986. 44.95 (*0-685-13287-0*) Retail Report.

— Shopping Centers & Malls, No. 4. (Illus.). 224p. 1992. 49.95 (*0-934590-45-1*) Retail Report.

— Shopping Centers & Malls, Vol. II. (Illus.). 192p. 1988. 44.95 (*0-934590-25-7*) Retail Report.

Rathbun, Robert D., intro. Shopping Centers & Malls, Vol. III. (Illus.). 224p. 1990. 49.95 (*0-934590-34-6*) Retail Report.

***Rathbun, Ron.** The Way Is Within: A Spiritual Journey. LC 94-68656. (Illus.). 271p. (Orig.). 1995. pap. 14.95 (*0-9643519-4-3*) Quiescence CA.

Rathbun, Ted A. & Buikstra, Jane E., eds. Human Identification: Case Studies in Forensic Anthropology. (Illus.). 456p. (C). 1984. 82.95 (*0-398-04875-4*) C C Thomas.

— Human Identification: Case Studies in Forensic Anthropology. (Illus.). 456p. 1984. pap. 42.95 (*0-398-06337-0*) C C Thomas.

Rathbun, W. B., jt. ed. see Hockwin, O.

Rathbun, William. Beyond the Tanabata Bridge: Traditional Japanese Textiles. LC 93-60436. (Illus.). 208p. 1993. 45.00 (*0-500-01586-4*) Thames Hudson.

Rathburn. History of Thurston County, Washington from 1845-1895. (Shorey Historical Ser.). 130p. reprint ed. pap. 8.95 (*0-8466-0237-7*, S237) Shorey.

Rathburn, Thomas A., ed. Modeling on Micros & Workstations, 1991. 10th ed. 104p. 1991. pap. 48.00 (*0-911801-84-7*, MSM91) Soc Computer Sim.

Rathe, Gustave. The Wreck of the Barque Stefano off the North West Cape of Australia in 1875. (Illus.). 160p. (YA). 1992. 17.00 (*0-374-38585-8*) FS&G.

Rathe, John C. & Elliott, Paul. Radiologic Tumor Localizer. 71p. (C). 1982. 6.00 (*0-87527-249-5*) Green.

Rathe, John F. Bibliography of the Typophile Chap Books 1935-1992. Lerner, Abe, ed. (Typophile Chap Bks.: No. 60). 94p. 1992. 27.50 (*0-945074-02-6*) Dawsons.

Rathe, Kurt. Die Ausdrucksfunktion Extrem Verkurzter Figren. (Warburg Institute Studies: Vol. 8). 1972. reprint ed. 30.00 (*0-8115-1386-6*) Periodicals Srv.

Rathegeber, David. Selling Your Home in Northern Virginia, 1994 Edition. 152p. 1994. pap. 9.95 (*0-9635337-2-X*) Rathco Realty Res.

Rather, Dan. Camera Never Blinks Twice: The Further Adventures of a Television Journalist. 1994. 23.00 (*0-688-09748-0*) Morrow.

***Rather, Dan & Herskowitz, Mickey.** The Camera Never Blinks Twice: The Further Adventures of a Television Journalist. large type ed. LC 94-48913. 1995. write for info. (*0-7862-0414-1*) Thorndike Pr.

Rather, L., ed. see Virchow, Rudolph.

Rather, L. J. The Genesis of Cancer: A Study in the History of Ideas. LC 78-2785. 280p. reprint ed. pap. 79.80 (*0-8357-6624-1*, 2035270) Bks Demand.

— Reading Wagner: A Study in the History of Ideas. LC 89-37814. 368p. 1990. text ed. 40.00 (*0-8071-1557-6*) La State U Pr.

Rather, L. J., et al. Johannes Mueller & the Nineteenth-Century Origins of Tumor Cell Theory. LC 86-6616. 1987. 15.00 (*0-88135-080-X*) Watson Pub Intl.

Rather, Lelland J. A Commentary on the Medical Writings of Rudolf Virchow: Based on Schwalbe's Virchow-Bibliographie, 1843-1901. (Bibliography Ser.: No. 3). (Illus.). 236p. 1990. 125.00 (*0-930405-19-6*) Norman SF.

Rather, Lelland J., tr. see Virchow, Rudolf.

Rather, Lois. Bonanza Theater. limited ed. (Illus.). 1977. 25.00 (*0-686-20514-6*) Rather Pr.

— Dunsmuir House. limited ed. (Illus.). 1982. 25.00 (*0-686-37970-5*) Rather Pr.

— Henry George: Printer to Author. limited ed. (Illus.). 1978. 25.00 (*0-686-22963-0*) Rather Pr.

— J. Ross Browne: Adventurer. limited ed. (Illus.). 1978. 25.00 (*0-686-05279-X*) Rather Pr.

— Lotta's Fountain. limited ed. (Illus.). 1979. 25.00 (*0-686-15713-3*) Rather Pr.

— The Man with the Hoe. limited ed. (Illus.). 1977. 25.00 (*0-686-20513-8*) Rather Pr.

— Miss Kate: Kate Douglas Wiggin in San Francisco. limited ed. (Illus.). 1980. 25.00 (*0-686-26424-X*) Rather Pr.

— R. W. Emerson, Tourist. limited ed. (Illus.). 1979. 25.00 (*0-686-26147-X*) Rather Pr.

— Rather a Small Press. limited ed. (Illus.). 1976. 12.50 (*0-686-20625-8*) Rather Pr.

— West Is West: Rudyard Kipling in San Francisco. limited ed. (Illus.). 1976. 25.00 (*0-686-20624-X*) Rather Pr.

Rather, Marsha L., jt. ed. see Dickelmann, Nancy L.

Rather, Susan. Archaism, Modernism, & the Art of Paul Manship. LC 92-14217. (American Studies Ser.). (Illus.). 284p. (C). 1993. text ed. 42.50 (*0-292-76035-3*) U of Tex Pr.

Rathert, Donna. Advent Is for Waiting. (Illus.). 24p. (J). (ps). 1987. pap. 2.99 (*0-570-04140-6*, 56-1569) Concordia.

Rathert, Donna & Prahlow, Lois. Time for Church. 24p. (J). (gr. 2-5). 1985. pap. 2.99 (*0-570-04129-5*, 56-1540) Concordia.

Rathert, Donna R. Job. (Arch Bks.). (Illus.). 24p. (J). (ps-2). 1989. pap. 1.99 (*0-570-09017-2*, 59-1440) Concordia.

— Lent Is for Remembering. LC 56-1613. 24p. (Orig.). (J). (ps-1). 1987. pap. 2.99 (*0-570-04147-3*, 56-1613) Concordia.

Rathert, P., et al. Urinary Cytology: Manual & Atlas. 2nd rev. ed. Telger, Terry C., tr. LC 92-49568. 1992. 129.00 (*0-387-53312-5*) Spr-Verlag.

Rathert-Phillips, Annette, see Alexandria Uriel, pseud..

Rathet, Mike & Smith, Don R. The Pro Football Hall of Fame Presents Their Deeds & Dogged Faith. LC 84-11188. (Illus.). 1984. 24.95 (*0-917439-02-3*) Balsam Pr.

Rathgaber, Eileen, ed. see St. Anthony of Padua Mother's Guild Staff.

Rathgeb, Marlene M. Sexual Astrology. 304p. (Orig.). 1993. pap. 10.00 (*0-380-76888-7*) Avon.

— Success Signs. (Illus.). 224p. 1981. pap. 5.95 (*0-312-77486-9*) St Martin.

***Rathgeb, Steven & Lipsky, Michael.** Nonprofits for Hire: The Welfare State in the Age of Contracting. (Illus.). 312p. 1995. pap. 16.95 (*0-674-62639-7*, SMINOX) HUP.

Rathgeber. Drug Consultant & Interaction Guide. 1992. 15.95 (*1-878060-04-X*) Mosby Yr Bk.

Rathgeber, David. Buying a Home in Northern Virginia, 1994 Edition. 184p. 1994. pap. 9.95 (*0-9635337-1-1*) Rathco Realty Res.

— Buying a Home in the Washington, D. C. Metropolitan Area. 164p. 1995. pap. 9.95 (*0-9635337-3-8*) Rathco Realty Res.

— Selling Your Home in the Washington, D.C. Metropolitan Area. 134p. 1995. pap. 9.95 (*0-9635337-4-6*) Rathco Realty Res.

Rathgeber, David G. Selling Your Home in Northern Virginia Today. 144p. 1992. pap. 9.95 (*0-9635337-0-3*) Rathco Realty Res.

Rathgeber, Eva-Maria, jt. auth. see Altbach, Philip G.

Rathi, Manohar L., ed. Current Perinatology. (Illus.). 290p. 1988. 93.00 (*0-387-96758-3*) Spr-Verlag.

— Current Perinatology Two. (Illus.). xii, 230p. 1990. 93.00 (*0-387-97214-5*) Spr-Verlag.

Rathi, Manohar L. & Kumar, S. Perinatal Medicine, 2 Vols., 1. 1982. text ed. 35.00 (*0-07-051204-3*) McGraw.

— Perinatal Medicine, 2 Vols., 2. 1982. text ed. 39.50 (*0-07-051208-6*) McGraw.

Rathi, Manohar L., jt. ed. see Kumar, S.

Rathi, Rajendra P. Image Processing Using a Two-Dimensional Digital Convolution Filter. 141p. 1984. 13.50 (*0-317-01486-2*) Am-Nepal Ed.

***Rathie, William & Murphy, Cullen.** Rubbish! The Archaeology of Garbage. braille ed. 581p. 1994. text ed. 46.48 (*1-56956-475-2*, BR9320) W A T Braille.

Rathjan, Don, jt. auth. see Doherty, Paul.

Rathje, Linda. AppleWorks for Educators: A Beginning & Intermediate Workbook 2.0. rev. ed. Orig. Title: AppleWorks for Educators: A Beginners Workbook. 365p. 1988. disk, pap. text ed. 22.95 (*0-924667-48-6*) Intl Society Tech Educ.

— AppleWorks for Educators: A Beginning & Intermediate Workbook 3.0. 3rd ed. 456p. 1990. disk, pap. text ed. 26.95 (*0-924667-75-3*) Intl Society Tech Educ.

Rathje, William & Murphy, Cullen. Rubbish! The Archaeology of Garbage. LC 91-50452. (Illus.). 256p. 1993. pap. 12.00 (*0-06-092228-1*, PL) HarpC.

Rathje, William L. & Schiffer, Michael B. Archaeology. 434p. (C). 1982. text ed. 42.75 (*0-15-502950-9*) HB Coll Pubs.

Rathjen, Frederick W., ed. Panhandle-Plains Historical Review: Annual Journal. 104p. (Orig.). 1994. pap. 10.00 (*0-685-57471-7*) Panhandle.

Rathjen, Joseph E. Locksmithing: From Apprentice to Master. 1994. pap. text ed. write for info. (*0-07-051645-6*) McGraw.

Rathjens, C., jt. ed. see Muller, P.

***Rathke, David E & Edwards, Clayton J., eds.** A Review of Trends in Lake Erie Water Quality with Emphasis on the 1978-1979 Intensive Survey: Report to the Surveillance Work Group. fac. ed. LC 86-103207. (Illus.). 139p. 1985. pap. 39.70 (*0-7837-8627-1*, 2075241) Bks Demand.

Rathke, Ewald, jt. ed. see Hering, Karl H.

Rathkey, Paul. Time Innovations & the Development of Manpower: Attitudes & Options. (Illus.). 149p. 1990. text ed. 68.95 (*0-566-07121-5*, Pub. by Avebury Pub UK) Ashgate Pub Co.

Rathkopf, Charles A., et al. Rathkopf's Law of Zoning & Planning, 5 vols. 4th ed. LC 56-2013. (Real Property-Zoning Ser.). 1975. ring bd. 550.00 (*0-87632-020-5*) Clark Boardman Callaghan.

Rathlef, Ernst L. Geschichte Jetztlebender Gelehrter, Als eine Fortsetzung des Jetztlebenden Gelehrten Europa, 3 vols., Set. 1972. reprint ed. write for info. (*3-487-04384-X*, Pub. by Georg Olms GW) Lubrecht & Cramer.

***Rathlev, Mary & Riley, Martha.** Youth & HIV: It's Up to You & Me: A Reference Guide for Service Providers. (YA). 1994. pap. 7.95 (*0-9634295-0-7*) Childs Hosp.

Rathlev, Mary, jt. auth. see Parrott, Robert H.

***Rathman.** Ruby, Mono Ve, Mono Hace: Ruby the Copycat. 1995. pap. (*0-590-50211-5*) Scholastic Inc.

Rathman, Helena R. Yin Deficiency & Yin-Yang: Index of New Information & Research Guide. 150p. 1994. 44.50 (*0-7883-0106-3*); pap. 39.50 (*0-7883-0107-1*) ABBE Pubs Assn.

Rathman, Lothar, jt. ed. see Barthel, Gunter.

Rathman, Peggy. Ruby the Copycat. (J). (ps-3). 1993. pap. 4.95 (*0-590-47423-5*) Scholastic Inc.

Rathman, Peggy, tr. see Rathmann, Peggy.

Rathman, R. Annabel, ed. see Dean, Bob.

Rathman, R. Annabel, ed. see Flynn, Lucine H.

Rathman, R. Annabel, ed. see Grossman, Alvin.

Rathman, R. Annabel, ed. see Pferd, William, III.

Rathman, R. Annabel, ed. see Riddle, Maxwell.

Rathman, R. Annabel, ed. see Sanford, John A.

Rathman, R. Annabel, ed. see Travis, John W.

Rathman, R. Annabel, ed. see Walkowicz, Chris.

Rathman, R. Annabel, ed. see Widdrington, Gay.

Rathmann, Peggy. Goodnight, Gorilla. Rathman, Peggy, tr. LC 92-29020. (Illus.). 40p. (J). (ps-1). 1994. 12.95 (*0-399-22445-9*, Putnam) Putnam Pub Group.

— Officer Buckle & Gloria. LC 93-43887. (J). 1995. write for info. (*0-399-22616-8*, Putnam) Putnam Pub Group.

— Ruby the Copycat. 32p. (J). 1991. 13.95 (*0-590-43747-X*, Scholastic Hardcover) Scholastic Inc.

Rathmayer, H. G. & Saari, K. H., eds. Improvement of Ground: Proceedings of the Eighth European Conference on Soil Mechanics & Foundation Engineering, Helsinki 23-26 May 1983, 3 vols. 1398p. 1983. text ed. 480.00 (*90-6191-240-7*, Pub. by A A Balkema NE) Ashgate Pub Co.

Rathmill, K., ed. Flexible Manufacturing Systems 2: Proceedings of the International Conference, 2nd, London, U. K., Oct. 1983. 700p. 1984. 115.50 (*0-444-86815-1*, I-509-83, North Holland) Elsevier.

— Robotic Assembly. (International Trends in Manufacturing Technology Ser.). 350p. 1985. 78.00 (*0-387-15483-3*) Spr-Verlag.

Rathmill, K. & Macconaill, P. A., eds. Computer Integrated Manufacturing. (Illus.). 280p. 1988. 123.00 (*0-387-18758-8*) Spr-Verlag.

Rathmill, K., et al, eds. Robot Technology & Applications. (Illus.). 203p. 1985. 69.00 (*0-387-13960-5*) Spr-Verlag.

***Rathmussen, Roland.** Not Wrath, But Tribulation! LC 95-68987. 1995. pap. text ed. 10.00 (*0-932050-46-8*) New Puritan.

Rathnaiah, K. Social Change among Malsa: An Ex-Untouchable Caste in South India. (C). 1991. 24.50 (*81-7141-137-1*) S Asia.

Rathnam, P. V. Rathnam's Cost & Management Accounting: Problems & Solutions. 3rd rev. ed. 780p. 1989. text ed. 45.00 (*0-685-21871-6*, Pub. by Sterling Pubs II) Apt Bks.

Rathnow, Ron. Chattooga River Section Four Flip Map. LC 86-28475. (Great American Rivers Flip Map Ser.). (Illus.). 36p. 1986. pap. text ed. 5.95 (*0-89732-047-6*) Menasha Ridge.

— West Branch of the Penobscot & the Kennebec Gorge Flip Map. LC 87-34978. (Great American Rivers Flip Map Ser.). (Illus.). 57p. 1989. pap. 5.95 (*0-89732-081-6*) Menasha Ridge.

— Youghiogheny River Flip Map. LC 86-12654. (Great American Rivers Flip Map Ser.). (Illus.). 36p. 1987. pap. text ed. 5.95 (*0-89732-056-5*) Menasha Ridge.

Rathore. Handbook of Chromatography: Liquid Chromatography Polylyclicclcl. 1993. 179.95 (*0-8493-3005-X*, QD341) CRC Pr.

Rathore, H. C. Management of Distance Education in India. (Illus.). x, 225p. 1993. 26.00 (*81-7024-532-X*, Pub. by Ashish Pub Hse II) Nataraj Bks.

***Rathore, H. S.** Reliability of Metals in Electronics. 1995. pap. 42.00 (*1-56677-097-1*, PV 95-3) Electrochem Soc.

Rathore, H. S., et al, eds. Reliability of Semiconductor Devices - Interconnections & Dielectric Breakdown, Vol. 92-4. LC 92-70488. (Proceedings Ser.). 350p. 1992. 42.00 (*1-56677-003-3*) Electrochem Soc.

Rathore, L. S. & Haqqi, S. A. Principles of Political Theory & Organization. (C). 1988. 60.00 (*0-685-39584-7*) St Mut.

Rathore, L. S. & Haqqi, S. H. Political Theory & Organisation. (C). 1988. 50.00 (*0-685-25675-8*) St Mut.

Rathore, N. S. Natural Resources Base Development. (C). 1992. text ed. 138.00 (*81-7233-032-4*, Pub. by Scientific Pubs II) St Mut.

Rathore, R. & Haqqi, H. Political Theory & Organisation for Law Students. (C). 1991. text ed. 60.00 (*0-89771-505-5*) St Mut.

***Raths, James.** NCATE Accreditation: A Framework for Preparing Section II of the Institutional Report. 1993. 21.00 (*0-89333-106-6*) AACTE.

Raths, James, jt. ed. see Katz, Lilian G.

Raths, Louis, et al. Teaching for Thinking: Theory, Strategies, & Activities for the Classroom. 2nd ed. 240p. (C). 1986. pap. 18.95 (*0-8077-2814-4*) Tchrs Coll.

Rathus, Spencer A. Essentials of Psychology. 3rd ed. (Illus.). 525p. (C). 1991. pap. text ed. 36.00 (*0-03-052248-X*) HB Coll Pubs.

— Essentials of Psychology. 4th ed. LC 93-79351. 619p. 1994. pap. 36.00 (*0-15-500739-4*) HarBrace.

— Psychology. 4th ed. 768p. (C). 1990. text ed. 49.25 (*0-03-034597-9*) HB Coll Pubs.

— Psychology & the Challenges of Life: Adjustment & Growth. 4th ed. (Illus.). (C). 1989. text ed. 40.00 (*0-03-025464-7*) HB Coll Pubs.

Rathus, Spencer A. & Favaro, Peter. Understanding Child Development. (Illus.). 688p. (C). 1988. text ed. 46.75 (*0-03-001837-4*) HB Coll Pubs.

Rathus, Spencer A. & Fichner-Rathus, Lois. Making the Most of College. 2nd ed. LC 93-12890. 414p. 1993. pap. text ed. 27.40 (*0-13-045956-9*) P-H.

Rathus, Spencer A. & Nevid, Jeffrey. BT--Behavior Therapy. 1978. pap. 2.95 (*0-451-09949-4*, E9949, Sig) NAL-Dutton.

Rathus, Spencer A. & Nevid, Jeffrey S. Adjustment & Growth: The Challenges of Life. 5th ed. Howard, Eve, ed. (Illus.). 600p. (C). 1992. text ed. 42.75 (0-03-074418-0) HB Coll Pubs.

Rathus, Spencer A., et al. Abnormal Psychology. 2nd ed. LC 93-13056. 1993. text ed. write for info. (0-13-044918-0) P-H Gen Ref & Trav.

— Human Sexuality in a World of Diversity. 1993. write for info. (0-318-69680-0) Allyn.

***Rathvon, Henry, et al.** Boston Globe Sunday Crosswords Vol. 2. 1995. pap. 8.00 (0-8129-2539-4, Times Bks) Random.

***Rathwell, Tom, et al, eds.** Tipping the Balance Towards Primary Health Care: A Pan-European Analysis. 200p. 1995. 55.95 (1-85628-941-9, Pub. by Avebury Pub UK) Ashgate Pub Co.

Ratigan, V. & Swidler, A., eds. A New Phoebe: Perspectives on Roman Catholic Women & the Permanent Diaconate. LC 90-60898. 120p. (Orig.). (C). 1990. pap. 7.95 (1-55612-357-4) Sheed & Ward MO.

Ratigan, William. Great Lakes Shipwrecks. 1994. 10.98 (0-88365-853-4) Galahad Bks.

— Great Lakes Shipwrecks & Survivals. 1960. pap. 14.99 (0-8028-7010-4) Eerdmans.

Rational Data Systems, Inc. Staff. NetWare for AOS - VS, 5 bks., Set. 1992. disk, pap. 375.00 (1-881378-14-4) Rational Data.

— NetWare for AOS - VS Concepts. 1992. disk, pap. 75.00 (1-881378-07-1) Rational Data.

— NetWare for AOS - VS Installation. 1992. disk, pap. 75. 00 (1-881378-10-1) Rational Data.

— NetWare for AOS - VS System Administration. 1992. disk, pap. 75.00 (1-881378-09-8) Rational Data.

— NetWare for AOS - VS System Messages. 1992. disk, pap. 75.00 (1-881378-11-X) Rational Data.

— NetWare for AOS - VS Utilities. 1992. disk, pap. 75.00 (1-881378-08-X) Rational Data.

— PC - Mail User's Guide. 99p. 1992. disk 3.50 (1-881378-06-3) Rational Data.

— PC - Remote User's Guide. 192p. 1992. disk 4.00 (1-881378-01-2) Rational Data.

— PC - VS System Managers Guide. 84p. 1992. disk 10.00 (1-881378-03-9) Rational Data.

— PC - VS System Managers Guide: PC - VS 5. 1992. disk 10.00 (1-881378-15-2) Rational Data.

— PC - VS User's Guide. 194p. 1992. disk 4.00 (0-685-55375-2) Rational Data.

— PopTerm - NVT for MS-DOS User's Guide. 40p. 1992. disk 5.50 (1-881378-04-7) Rational Data.

— PopTerm - NVT for Windows User's Guide. 30p. 1992. disk 5.50 (1-881378-05-5) Rational Data.

— PopTerm User's Guide. 84p. 1992. disk 4.00 (1-881378-00-4) Rational Data.

— Report on PC Integration, 1991. 118p. 1992. 5.00 (1-881378-12-8) Rational Data.

— Report on PC Integration, 1992. 136p. 1992. 24.95 (1-881378-13-6) Rational Data.

Rational Development Committee. Sri Lanka: The Ethnic Conflict: Myths, Realities & Perspectives. 1985. 35.00 (0-8364-1292-3, Pub. by Navrang) S Asia.

Ratisbonne, Theodore. St. Bernard of Clairvaux: Oracle of the 12th Century (1091-1153) Abbot, Confessor & Doctor of the Church. LC 91-67795. Orig. Title: The Life & Times of St. Bernard. 437p. 1991. reprint ed. pap. 16.50 (0-89555-453-4) TAN Bks Pubs.

Ratiu, T., ed. The Geometry of Hamiltonian Systems: Proceedings of a Workshop held June 5-16, 1989. (Lecture Notes in Mathematics Ser.: Vol. 22). (Illus.). x, 527p. 1991. 55.00 (0-387-97608-6) Spr-Verlag.

Ratiu, Tudor S., jt. auth. see Marsden, Jerrold E.

Ratkevich, Ronald P., jt. auth. see Casanova, Richard L.

Ratkowsky. Handbook of Nonlinear Regression Models. (Statistics: Vol. 107). 264p. 1990. 89.75 (0-8247-8189-9) Dekker.

— Nonlinear Regression Modeling: A Unified Practical Approach. (Statistics: Vol. 48). 288p. 1983. 95.00 (0-8247-1907-7) Dekker.

Ratkowsky, David A., et al. Cross-over Experiments: Design, Analysis & Application. (Statistics: Vol. 135). 480p. 1993. 125.00 (0-8247-8892-3) Dekker.

Ratledge, C., jt. ed. see Kyle, D. J.

Ratledge, Colin, ed. Biochemistry of Microbial Degradation. LC 93-10260. 584p. (C). 1994. lib. bdg. 265.00 (0-7923-2273-8) Kluwer Ac.

— Physiology of Biodegradative Microorganisms. 142p. 1991. lib. bdg. 115.00 (0-7923-1132-9) Kluwer Ac.

Ratledge, Colin & Stanford, John L., eds. The Biology of the Mycobacteria, Vol. 1. 1982. text ed. 189.00 (0-12-582301-0) Acad Pr.

— Biology of the Mycobacteria Vol. 2: Immunological & Environmental Aspects. 1983. text ed. 189.00 (0-12-582302-9) Acad Pr.

Ratledge, Colin & Wilkinson, S. G., eds. Microbial Lipids, Vol. 1. 450p. 1988. text ed. 300.00 (0-12-582304-5) Acad Pr.

— Microbial Lipids, Vol. 2. 726p. 1989. 190.00 (0-685-29291-6) Acad Pr.

Ratledge, Colin, et al, eds. The Biology of the Mycobacteria Vol. 3: Clinical Aspects of Mycobacterial Disease. 621p. 1989. text ed. 187.00 (0-12-582303-7) Acad Pr.

— Biotechnology for the Oils & Fats Industry. 298p. 1984. 40.00 (0-935315-08-X) AOCS Pr.

Ratledge, Edward C. & Jacoby, Joan E. Handbook on Artificial Intelligence & Expert Systems in Law Enforcement. LC 89-7467. (Illus.). 216p. 1989. text ed. 55.00 (0-313-26461-9, RHX/, Greenwood Pr) Greenwood.

Ratledge, M. W., ed. Don't Become the Victim: A Guide to Effective Anti-Crime Measures. 1986. lib. bdg. 79.95 (0-8490-3681-X) Gordon Pr.

Ratledge, Marcus W. Hot Cars! An Inside Look at the Auto Theft Industry. (Illus.). 136p. 1982. pap. 15.00 (0-87364-220-1) Paladin Pr.

Ratliff. The Prince (Machiavelli) (Book Notes Ser.). (C). 1985. pap. 2.95 (0-8120-3536-4) Barron.

Ratliff, A. H., et al. Selected References in Elective Orthopaedics. xviii, 204p. 1991. pap. 39.00 (0-387-19682-X) Spr-Verlag.

— Selected References in Orthopaedic Trauma. xvii, 124p. 1989. pap. 31.00 (0-387-19556-4) Spr-Verlag.

Ratliff, Donald E. Map, Compass, & Campfire: A Handbook for the Outdoorsman. LC 64-8453. (Illus.). 64p. 1993. reprint ed. pap. 7.95 (0-8323-0129-9) Binford Mort.

Ratliff, Floyd. Mach Bands: Quantitative Studies on Neural Networks in the Retina. LC 65-10436. 1965. 38.00 (0-8162-7045-7) Holden-Day.

— Paul Signac & Color in Neo-Impressionism. (Illus.). 317p. 1992. 49.95 (0-87470-050-7) Rockefeller.

Ratliff, Floyd, ed. Studies on Excitation & Inhibition in the Retina. LC 73-89539. (Illus.). 688p. 1974. 17.50 (0-685-42323-9) Rockefeller.

Ratliff, Gerald L. Coping with Stage Fright. (Illus.). 119p. (gr. 7-12). 1985. 15.95 (0-8239-0638-8) Rosen Group.

— Playing Scenes: A Sourcebook for Performers. Zapel, Theodore O., ed. LC 93-11356. (Illus.). 450p. (Orig.). 1993. pap. 14.95 (0-916260-89-5, B109) Meriwether Pub.

Ratliff, Gerald L., ed. Playscript Interpretation & Production. (Theatre Student Ser.). 114p. 1985. lib. bdg. 14.95 (0-8239-0608-6) Rosen Group.

Ratliff, Gerald L. & Troth, Susan. Onstage, Producing Musical Theatre. (Theatre Student Ser.). (Illus.). 109p. (YA). (gr. 7-12). 1988. lib. bdg. 14.95 (0-8239-0697-3) Rosen Group.

***Ratliff, Hurbert S.** R.S.V.P. Gulliver. 240p. Date not set. pap. 8.95 (0-7610-0266-9) NW Pub.

Ratliff, J. Bill. When You Are Facing Change: Resources for Living. 132p. (Orig.). 1989. pap. 9.99 (0-664-25048-3) Westminster John Knox.

Ratliff, Joe S. Church Planting in the African-American Community. (Orig.). 1993. pap. 6.95 (0-8054-6071-3) Broadman.

Ratliff, Martha. Meaningful Tone: A Study of Tonal Morphology in Compounds, Form Classes, & Expressive Phrases in White Hmong. (Special Report Ser.: No. 27). 275p. 1992. 22.00 (1-877979-77-5) North Ill U Ctr SE Asian.

Ratliff, R., et al. Internal Auditing: Principles & Techniques. 950p. 1988. teacher ed write for info. (0-318-63169-5); text ed. 79.50 (0-89413-167-2) Inst Inter Aud.

***Ratliff, Randy.** Data Communications: With Network Management. Freeman, Whitney, ed. (Illus.). 450p. (C). 1994. write for info. (1-884268-04-8); teacher ed 29.00 (1-884268-05-6); pap. text ed. 54.00 (1-884268-03-X) Marcraft Intl.

Ratliff, Susan. How to Be a Weekend Entrepreneur: Making Money at Craft Fairs, Trade Shows & Swap Meets. (Illus.). 112p. (Orig.). 1991. pap. 9.95 (0-9624798-2-9) Mktg Methods Pr.

Ratliff, Susan, jt. auth. see Lambeis, Barbara.

Ratliff, T., jt. ed. see Catalona, William J.

Ratliff, Thomas A., Jr. The Laboratory Assurance System: A Manual of Quality Procedures & Forms. 2nd ed. LC 92-43678. 1993. text ed. 69.95 (0-442-01470-8) Van Nos Reinhold.

— Laboratory Quality Assurance Systems. 1990. text ed. 49. 95 (0-442-23459-7) Van Nos Reinhold.

Ratliff, Timothy L. & Catalona, William J., eds. Genitourinary Cancer. (Cancer Treatment & Research Ser.). 1987. lib. bdg. 146.00 (0-89838-830-9) Kluwer Ac.

Ratliff, Wayne. Emerald Bay: A Guide to Multi-User Applications. 1989. pap. 24.95 (0-13-274416-3) P-H.

Ratliff, Wayne & Byers, Robert A. Emerald Bay: The Guide to Multi-user Applications. 400p. 1989. pap. 18.95 (0-318-41956-4) P-H.

Ratliff, William, ed. & intro. A Half Century of Peronism, 1943-1993: An International Bibliography. (Bibliographical Ser.: No. 76). 370p. 1993. pap. text ed. 19.95 (0-8179-2762-X) Hoover Inst Pr.

Ratliff, William & Fontaine, Roger. Argentina's Capitalist Revolution Revisited: Confronting the Social Costs of Statist Mistakes. LC 93-28402. (Essays in Public Policy Ser.: No. 41). 55p. 1993. pap. 5.00 (0-8179-5462-7) Hoover Inst Pr.

Ratliff, William, jt. auth. see Miranda, Roger.

Ratliff, William E. Castroism & Communism in Latin America, 1959-1976: The Varieties of Marxist-Leninist Experience. LC 76-28554. (AEI-Hoover Policy Studies: No. 19). 260p. reprint ed. pap. 74.10 (0-8357-4444-2, 2037279) Bks Demand.

— Following the Leader in the Horn: The Soviet-Cuban Presence in East Africa. 1986. 3.00 (0-317-90496-5) Cuban Amer Natl Fndtn.

Ratliff, William E., et al. The Selling of Fidel Castro: The Media & the Cuban Revolution. 193p. 1986. 32.95 (0-88738-104-9); pap. 19.95 (0-88738-649-0) Transaction Pubs.

Ratliff, William F., et al. Cara a Cara: A Basic Reader for Communication. 2nd ed. 240p. (SPA.). (C). 1982. pap. text ed. 21.00 (0-03-057597-4) HB Coll Pubs.

Ratliff, William G. Faithful to the Fatherland: Julius Curtius & Weimar Foreign Policy. (American University Studies: History: Ser. IX, Vol. 62). 216p. (C). 1989. text ed. 43. 95 (0-8204-0948-0) P Lang Pubs.

***Ratliffe, Kate.** Recipes from My Gascon Village. 144p. 1995. 15.95 (0-89815-753-6) Ten Speed Pr.

Ratliffe, Laraine M., jt. auth. see Ratliffe, Thomas.

Ratliffe, Sharon & Stech, Ernest. Effective Group Communication. 320p. 1985. pap. 15.95 (0-8442-5146-1, NTC Busn Bks) NTC Pub Grp.

Ratliffe, Sharon A. & Hudson, David D. Communication for Everyday Living. 256p. (C). 1988. pap. text ed. write for info. (0-13-154386-5) P-H.

— Skill Building for Interpersonal Competence. 320p. (C). 1988. pap. text ed. 18.00 (0-03-012602-9) HB Coll Pubs.

Ratliffe, Thomas & Ratliffe, Laraine M. Teaching Children Fitness: Becoming a Master Teacher. LC 93-42449. (Illus.). 128p. 1994. pap. text ed. 14.00x (0-87322-478-7, BRAT0478) Human Kinetics.

Ratna, Jai, ed. & tr. Contemporary Urdu Short Stories. 224p. 1991. text ed. 30.00 (81-207-1317-6, Pub. by Sterling Pubs II) Apt Bks.

Ratna Pustak Bhandar Staff, ed. Ratna Trekker's Pocket-Pal: Nepali Word & Phrase Guide. (C). 1986. 22.00 (0-89771-081-9, Pub. by Ratna Pustak Bhandar) St Mut.

Ratna Pustak Bhandar Staff, tr. Cooking in Nepal: A Selection of International & Nepali Recipes. 204p. (C). 1982. 75.00 (0-89771-094-0, Pub. by Ratna Pustak Bhandar); pap. 55.00 (0-685-51090-5, Pub. by Ratna Pustak Bhandar) St Mut.

Ratnam, et al, eds. Endometriosis. (Advances in Fertility & Sterility Ser.: Vol. 5). 236p. 1987. 55.00 (1-85070-155-5) Prthnon Pub.

Ratnam, K. J., jt. auth. see Milne, R. S.

Ratnam, Perala. Afghanistan's Uncertain Future. 100p. 1981. 18.95 (0-940500-18-3, Pub. by Tulsi Pub Hse) Asia Bk Corp.

— Laos & the Super Powers. 167p. 1980. 15.95 (0-940500-19-1, Pub. by Tulsi Pub Hse) Asia Bk Corp.

Ratnam, S. S., jt. ed. see Landy, Uta.

Ratnam, S. S., ed. see Microsurgery Workshop Staff.

Ratnam, S. S., et al. Contributions to Obstetrics & Gynaecology, No. 1. (Illus.). 258p. (Orig.). 1991. pap. text ed. write for info. (0-443-04669-7) Churchill.

— Contributions to Obstetrics & Gynaecology, No. 2. (Illus.). 232p. (Orig.). 1991. pap. text ed. 84.00 (0-443-04670-0) Churchill.

Ratnam, S. S., et al, eds. Contraception. (Advances in Feritlity & Sterility Ser.: Vol. 6). 196p. 1987. 55.00 (1-85070-156-3) Prthnon Pub.

— In Vitro Fertilisation & Other Alternative Methods of Conception. (Advances in Fertility & Sterility Ser.: Vol. 2). 244p. 1987. 55.00 (1-85070-152-0) Prthnon Pub.

— Infertility - Males & Female. (Advances in Fertility & Sterility Ser.: Vol. 4). 240p. 1987. 55.00 (1-85070-154-7) Prthnon Pub.

— Obstetrics & Gynecology for Postgraduates, Vol. 1. 1993. text ed. 50.00 (0-86311-308-7, Pub. by Orient Longman Ltd II) Apt Bks.

— Ovulation - & Early Pregnancy. (Advances in Fertility & Sterility Ser.: Vol. 1). 230p. 1987. 55.00 (1-85070-151-2) Prthnon Pub.

— Releasing Hormones: Genetics & Immunology in Human Reproduction. (Advances in Fertility & Sterility Ser.: Vol. 3). 204p. 1987. 55.00 (1-85070-153-9) Prthnon Pub.

Ratnapala, Nandasena. Buddhist Sociology. (Bibliotheca Indo-Buddhica Ser.: No. 117). 1993. 21.00 (81-7030-363-X) S Asia.

— Crime & Punishment in the Buddhist Tradition. (C). 1993. 22.00x (81-7099-463-2, Pub. by Mittal II) S Asia.

— The Police of Sri Lanka: Police-Public Relations. (Illus.). 100p. (C). 1988. reprint ed. pap. text ed. 6.00 (0-942511-13-1) OICJ.

Ratnapala, Suri, jt. ed. see Stephenson, M. A.

Ratnatunga, P. D. & Davidson, S. S. Pali Text Society Journal Index 1882-1927. (C). 1973. pap. 6.00 (0-86013-058-4, Pub. by Pali Text) Wisdom MA.

Ratner. Institutional Investors. 1978. text ed. 33.00 (0-88277-446-8) Foundation Pr.

— Something to Say: Student Essays for Freshman English. 1991. 12.00 (0-536-57932-6) Ginn Pr.

Ratner, Buddy D., ed. Surface Characterization of Biomaterials. (Progress in Biomedical Engineering Ser.: No. 6). 346p. 1988. 118.00 (0-444-43016-4) Elsevier.

Ratner, C. Vygotsky's Sociohistorical Psychology: A Paradigm for Today. LC 90-25506. (Psycholinguistics Ser.). (Illus.). 370p. 1991. 49.50 (0-306-43656-6, Plenum Pr) Plenum.

Ratner, David L. Securities Regulation in a Nutshell. 4th ed. LC 92-18886. (Nutshell Ser.). 326p. (C). 1992. pap. text ed. 17.00 (0-314-00930-2) West Pub.

— Securities Regulation, Selected Statutes, Rules & Forms: 1995 Edition. Hazen, Thomas L., ed. 1246p. 1994. pap. text ed. 26.00 (0-314-04766-2) West Pub.

Ratner, David L. & Hazen, Thomas L. Securities Regulation: Materials for a Basic Course On. 4th ed. (American Casebook Ser.). 1062p. (C). 1990. text ed. 50. 00 (0-314-79326-7) West Pub.

— Securities Regulations, Cases & Materials. 4th ed. (American Casebook Ser.). 41p. (C). 1991. pap. text ed. write for info. (0-314-92863-4) West Pub.

Ratner, David L. & Mazen, Thomas L. Securities Regulation: Cases & Materials Containing Problems & New Cases & Materials, 1994 Supplement. 4th ed. (American Casebook Ser.). 62p. 1993. pap. text ed. 8.00 (0-314-03030-1) West Pub.

Ratner, Elaine, jt. auth. see Dodge, Jim.

Ratner, Elaine, ed. see Jones, James L.

Ratner, Elaine, ed. see Roman, Sanaya & Packer, Duane.

Ratner, Elaine, ed. see Roman, Sanaya.

Ratner, Ellen. Savory Soups. LC 88-70045. (Allergy Kitchen Ser.: Vol. 1). (Illus.). 128p. 1988. pap. 7.95 (0-9616708-7-8) Allergy Pubns.

Ratner, Ellis, jt. ed. see Coler, Mark.

Ratner-Gantshar, Barbara. Philadelphia: The City & the Bell. Miller, Wynne, ed. LC 76-43573. (Grasshopper Ser.). (Illus.). (J). (gr. 4-8). 1976. 3.98 (0-686-16319-2); teacher ed 3.48 (0-686-16320-6) Artistic Endeavors.

Ratner, Jerrold, jt. ed. see Siddens, Robert.

***Ratner, Jonathan.** Prescription Drugs: Spending Controls in Four European Countries. (Illus.). 100p. (Orig.). (C). 1994. pap. text ed. 45.00x (0-7881-1172-8) Diane Pub.

Ratner, Joseph, ed. see Dewey, John.

Ratner, Jules J. Stress: Index for Medicine & Research with Bibliography. LC 88-47629. 150p. 1988. 44.50 (0-88164-662-8); pap. 39.50 (0-88164-663-6) ABBE Pubs Assn.

Ratner, Leonard G. Classic Music: Expression, Form & Style. 496p. 1985. pap. 22.00 (0-02-872690-1) Schirmer Bks.

— Romantic Music: Sound & Syntax. 368p. 1992. text ed. 45.00 (0-02-872065-2) Schirmer Bks.

Ratner, Lorman A. James Kirke Paulding. LC 92-8846. (Contributions in American History Ser.: No. 146). 168p. 1992. text ed. 45.00 (0-313-28550-0, RJP, Greenwood Pr) Greenwood.

Ratner, Lorman A., jt. ed. see Buenker, John D.

Ratner, Marilyn & Chamlin, Susan. Straight Talk: Sexuality Education for Parents & Kids. 48p. (gr. 4-7). 1987. mass mkt. 5.00 (0-14-009413-X, Penguin Bks) Viking Penguin.

Ratner, Mark A., jt. auth. see Schatz, George C.

Ratner, Megan, jt. auth. see Billing, Billie.

Ratner, Michael, jt. auth. see Stephens, Beth.

Ratner, Mitchell S., ed. Crack Pipe As Pimp: An Ethnographic Investigation of Sex-for-Crack Exchanges. LC 92-29042. 1992. text ed. 35.00 (0-02-925725-5) Free Pr.

Ratner, Nan B., jt. ed. see Gleason, Jean B.

Ratner, Rochelle. Bobby's Girl. LC 86-20794. 116p. (Orig.). 1986. pap. 9.95 (0-918273-22-6) Coffee Hse.

— Combing the Waves. LC 79-2276. (Illus.). 1979. pap. 6.00 (0-914610-16-3) Hanging Loose.

— Hide & Seek. (Offset Offshoot Ser.: No. 2). 50p. 1979. pap. 4.00 (0-317-06438-X) Ommation Pr.

— The Lion's Share. LC 91-24085. 174p. (Orig.). 1991. pap. 10.95 (0-918273-87-0) Coffee Hse.

— Practicing to Be a Woman: New & Selected Poems. Peters, Robert B., ed. LC 81-21472. (Poets Now Ser.: No. 2). 152p. 1982. 13.50 (0-8108-1510-9) Scarecrow.

— Quarry. (Orig.). 1978. pap. 1.75 (0-912284-98-6) New Rivers Pr.

— Someday Songs. LC 92-4608. 64p. 1992. 9.50 (0-933532-89-X) BkMk.

— Trying to Understand What It Means to Be a Feminist: Essays on Women Writers. (Chapbook Ser.). 100p. (Orig.). (C). 1983. pap. 5.00 (0-936556-10-2) Contact Two.

Ratner, Rochelle, ed. see Drachler, Rose.

Ratner, Ronnie S., ed. Equal Employment Policy for Women: Strategies for Implementation in the United States, Canada & Western Europe. LC 79-19509. 544p. 1980. 37.95 (0-87722-156-1) Temple U Pr.

Ratner, S., ed. Mechanisms of Lymphocyte Extravasation. (Journal: Invasion & Metastasis: Vol. 12, No. 2, 1992). (Illus.). 92p. 1992. pap. 48.00 (3-8055-5657-8) S Karger.

Ratner, Sidney, ed. The New American State Papers: Public Finance, 1789-1860 Subject Set, 32 vols., Set. LC 72-95580. 1973. lib. bdg. 1,850.00 (0-8420-1610-4) Scholarly Res Inc.

Ratner, Sidney, ed. see Bentley, Arthur F.

Ratner, Sidney R., et al. The Evolution of the American Economy: Growth, Welfare & Decision Making. 2nd ed. LC 92-11088. (Illus.). 704p. (C). 1993. text ed. write for info. (0-02-398680-8) Macmillan.

***Ratner, Steven R.** The New UN Peacekeeping: Building Peace in Lands of Conflict after the Cold War. LC 94-35326. 1995. text ed. 45.00 (0-312-12415-5) St Martin.

Ratner, V. A. & Kolchanov, N. A., eds. Modelling & Computer Methods in Molecular Biology & Genetics. 475p. (C). 1993. lib. bdg. 98.00 (1-56072-077-8) Nova Sci Pubs.

Ratner, Vivienne L. & Harris, Laura R. Understanding Language Disorders: The Impact on Learning. LC 93-23636. 1994. text ed. 47.00 (0-930599-90-X) Thinking Pubns.

***Ratnett, Michael.** Monster of Class Seven. (Illus.). 32p. (Orig.). (J). (gr. 1-4). 1995. pap. 4.99 (1-56790-513-7) Cool Hand Comms.

— Monsters of Class 7. LC 95-10614. (Illus.). 32p. (J). (gr. 1-4). 1995. 14.95 (1-56790-512-9, Cool Kids Pr) Cool Hand Comms.

Ratney, Ronald S., ed. Hazard Assessment & Control Technology in Semiconductor Manufacturing, Vol. II. (Illus.). (C). 1993. pap. text ed. 65.00 (1-882417-02-X) Am Conf Govt Indus Hygienist.

Ratnoff & Forbes. Disorders of Hemostasis. 2nd ed. 624p. 1990. text ed. 145.00 (0-7216-3432-X) Saunders.

***Ratnoff, Oscar D. & Forbes, Charles D., eds.** Disorders of Hemotasis. 3rd ed. LC 95-2349. 1996. write for info. (0-7216-5273-5) Saunders.

Rato, Khyongla. My Life & Lives. 2nd rev. ed. 238p. 1991. reprint ed. pap. 17.95 (0-9630293-0-4) Rato Pubns.

Ratsch, Christian. Sacred & Magical Plants. 1992. lib. bdg. 55.00 (0-87436-716-6) ABC-CLIO.

Ratschow, Carl H., ed. Paul Tillich Main Works, Vol. 5. (Writings on Religion). xvii, 325p. 1987. lib. bdg. 75.40 (0-89925-381-4) De Gruyter.

— Paul Tillich Main Works, Vol. 5. (Writings on Religion). xvii, 325p. 1987. lib. bdg. 75.40 (3-11-011541-7) De Gruyter.

Ratschow, Carl H., ed. see Tillich, Paul.

***Ratschow, Carl H., et al, eds.** Paul Tillich's Main Works in Six Volumes - Hauptwerke in 6 Banden Vol. 1: Philosophical Writings. xiv, 424p. (GER.). (C). 1989. lib. bdg. 103.10x (3-11-011533-6) De Gruyter.

— Paul Tillich's Main Works in Six Volumes - Hauptwerke in 6 Banden, Vol. 1: Philosophical Writings. xiv, 424p. (ENG & GER.). (C). 1989. lib. bdg. 103.10x (0-89925-563-9) De Gruyter.

Ratsoy, Eugene W., jt. auth. see Richards, Donald M.

Rattan, Ram. Gandhi's Thought & Action. ix, 348p. 1991. 30.00 (*81-85163-21-9*, Pub. by Kalinga Pubns) Nataraj Bks.

Rattan, S. S. Resupinate Aphyllophorales of the Northwestern Himalayas. (Bibliotheca Mycologica Ser.: No. 60). (Illus.). 1977. lib. bdg. 78.00 (*3-7682-1172-X*) Lubrecht & Cramer.

Rattan, S. S. & Khurana, I. P. S. The Clavaria of the Sikkim Himalayas. (Bibliotheca Mycologica Ser.: No. 66). (Illus.). 1978. pap. text ed. 18.00 (*3-7682-1212-2*) Lubrecht & Cramer.

Rattansi, ed. Rethinking Radical Education: Essays in Honour of Brian Simon. (C). 1992. pap. 19.95 (*0-85315-717-0*, Pub. by Lawrence & Wishart UK) Humanities.

Rattansi, Ali, ed. Ideology, Method & Marx. 256p. 1989. pap. 19.95 (*0-415-02862-0*, A3494) Routledge.

***Rattansi, Ali & Westwood, Sallie, eds.** Racism Modernity & Identity on the Western Front. 350p. 1995. 54.95 (*0-7456-0941-4*) Blackwell Pubs.

— Racism Modernity & Identity on the Western Front. 350p. 1995. pap. 21.95 (*0-7456-0942-2*) Blackwell Pubs.

Rattansi, Ali, jt. ed. see Boyne, Roy.

Rattansi, Ali, jt. auth. see Donald, James.

Rattansi, Piyo, jt. ed. see Clericuzio, Antonio.

Rattay, F. Electrical Nerve Stimulation: Theory, Experiments & Applications. (Illus.). iv, 264p. 1991. pap. 65.00 (*0-387-82247-X*) Spr-Verlag.

Rattay-Prade, Regina. Die Vegetation auf Strassenbegleitstreifen in verschiedenen Naturraeumen Suedbadens. Ihre Bewertung fuer den Naruschutz und ihre Bedeutung fuer ein Biotopverbundsystem. (Dissertationes Botanicae Ser.: Vol. 114). (Illus.). 230p. (GER.). 1988. pap. text ed. 84.50 (*3-443-64026-5*) Lubrecht & Cramer.

Rattazzi, Priscilla, illus. Children. LC 91-50744. 128p. 1992. 30.00 (*0-8478-1498-X*) Rizzoli Intl.

Ratte, John, ed. see Peabody, Robert E.

Rattee, Michael. Calling Yourself Home. 67p. (Orig.). 1986. pap. 6.00 (*0-914946-59-5*) Cleveland St Univ Poetry Ctr.

Rattenborg, C. C. Clinical Use of Mechanical Ventilation. 2nd ed. (Illus.). 1989. pap. 24.95 (*0-8151-7071-8*, Yr Bk Med Pubs) Mosby Yr Bk.

Rattenborg, Christen C., ed. Clinical Use of Mechanical Ventilation. LC 80-25269. (Illus.). 383p. reprint ed. pap. 109.20 (*0-8357-7629-8*, 2056952) Bks Demand.

Rattenbury, J. Ernest. The Eucharistic Hymns of John & Charles Wesley. rev. ed. Crouch, Timothy J., ed. 256p. 1990. 24.95 (*1-878009-05-2*, OSL Pubns) Order St Luke Pubns.

Rattenbury, Judith. Introduction to the IBM 360 Computer & OS-JCL (Job Control Language) rev. ed. LC 73-620248. 113p. reprint ed. pap. 32.30 (*0-7837-5258-X*, 2044995) Bks Demand.

— Introduction to the IBM 360 Computer & OS-JCL (Job Control Language) rev. ed. LC 73-620248. 103p. 1974. 8.00 (*0-87944-011-2*) Inst Soc Res.

Rattenbury, Judith & Pelletier, Paula. Data Processing in the Social Sciences with OSIRIS. LC 74-620138. (Illus.). 253p. reprint ed. pap. 72.20 (*0-7837-5273-3*, 2045011) Bks Demand.

— Data Processing in the Social Sciences with OSIRIS III. LC 74-620138. 245p. 1974. 15.00 (*0-87944-163-1*); pap. 10.00 (*0-87944-162-3*) Inst Soc Res.

Rattenbury, Judith, et al. Computer Processing of Social Science Data Using OSIRIS IV. 196p. (Orig.). (C). 1984. pap. text ed. 20.00 (*0-87944-295-6*) Inst Soc Res.

— Computer Processing of Social Science Data Using OSIRIS IV. LC 84-2727. 194p. (Orig.). reprint ed. pap. 55.30 (*0-7837-5276-8*, 2045014) Bks Demand.

Rattenbury, Ken. Duke Ellington, Jazz Composer. 384p. (C). 1991. text ed. 47.50 (*0-300-04428-3*) Yale U Pr.

— Duke Ellington, Jazz Composer. (Illus.). 384p. (C). 1993. reprint ed. pap. text ed. 19.00 (*0-300-05507-2*) Yale U Pr.

Rattenbury, Richard C. Packing Iron: Gunleather of the Frontier West. Begley, Janet, ed. LC 93-17019. (Illus.). 216p. 1993. 45.00 (*0-939549-08-5*) Zon Intl Pub.

Ratteray, Joan D. & Shujaa, Mwalimu. Dare to Choose: Parental Choice at Independent Neighborhood Schools. (Illus.). 216p. 1987. pap. text ed. 25.00 (*0-941001-03-2*); pap. text ed. 4.50 (*0-941001-04-0*) Inst Indep Educ.

Ratteray, Oswald M., ed. see Nichols, Edwin J., et al.

Ratterman, Ernest, jt. auth. see Krar, Steve F.

Ratterman, P. H. The Emerging Catholic University: With a Commentary on the Joint Statement on the Rights & Freedoms of Students. LC 68-8746. 191p. reprint ed. pap. 54.50 (*0-7837-0464-X*, 2040787) Bks Demand.

Ratterree, John. Diving & Snorkeling Guide to the Red Sea. 96p. 1994. 11.95 (*1-55992-081-5*, PISCES) Gulf Pub.

Ratterree, John, jt. auth. see Rosenberg, Steve.

Rattey, B. K. A Short History of the Hebrews: From the Patriarchs to Herod the Great. 3rd ed. (Illus.). 1976. pap. 14.95 (*0-19-832121-X*) OUP.

Ratti, jt. auth. see Westbrook.

Ratti, Carlo G. & Morassi, Antonio, trs. Alessandro Magnasco. (Illus.). 64p. 1967. pap. 3.00 (*0-912303-03-4*) Michigan Mus.

Ratti, J. S., jt. auth. see Goodman, A. W.

Ratti, John. Samson's Riddle. 1985. pap. 6.00 (*0-914610-41-4*) Hanging Loose.

Ratti, John T., et al, comps. Waterfowl Ecology & Management: Selected Readings. LC 82-70782. (Illus.). xvi, 1328p. (Orig.). (C). 1982. pap. 29.00 (*0-933564-09-0*) Wildlife Soc.

Ratti, Marianne. Workbook for Elements of English Grammar. 172p. 1991. 18.95 (*0-931541-40-9*) Mancorp Pub.

Ratti, O., jt. auth. see Westbrook, A. M.

Ratti, Oscar & Westbrook, Adele. Secrets of the Samurai: The Martial Arts of Feudal Japan. LC 72-91551. (Illus.). 483p. 1991. pap. 19.95 (*0-8048-1684-0*) C E Tuttle.

Ratti, Oscar, tr. see Arano, Luisa C., ed.

Ratti, Rakesh, ed. A Lotus of Another Color: An Unfolding of the South Asian Gay & Lesbian Experience. LC 92-36791. (Illus.). 302p. (Orig.). 1993. pap. 9.95 (*1-55583-171-0*) Alyson Pubns.

Rattigan, Alf. Industry Assistance: The Inside Story. 328p. 1986. 34.95 (*0-522-84313-1*) Intl Spec Bk.

Rattigan, Jama K. Dumpling Soup. 32p. (J). (gr. 4-8). 1993. 15.95 (*0-316-73445-4*) Little.

— Truman's Aunt Farm. LC 93-4860. (Illus.). (J). 1994. 13.95 (*0-395-65661-3*) HM.

Rattigan, Neil. Images of Australia: One Hundred Films of the New Australian Cinema. LC 90-52662. (Illus.). 320p. 1991. 24.95 (*0-87074-312-0*); pap. 15.95 (*0-87074-313-9*) SMU Press.

Rattigan, Terence. Man & Boy. 101p. 1964. 10.95 (*0-910278-42-3*) Boulevard.

— O Mistress Mine. 116p. 1949. 10.95 (*0-910278-43-1*) Boulevard.

— The Sleeping Prince. 126p. 1954. 12.95 (*0-910278-44-X*) Boulevard.

— The Winslow Boy. 1950. pap. 4.75 (*0-8222-1264-1*) Dramatists Play.

Rattigan, W. H., tr. see Von Savigny, Friedrich K.

Rattiner, Dan. The Eat All You Want & Still Lose Weight Cookbook. LC 80-82070. (Illus.). 64p. 1980. pap. 3.95 (*0-932966-11-X*) Permanent Pr.

— Who's Here. 1994. pap. 15.00 (*0-916366-91-X*) Pushcart Pr.

Rattiner, Dan, jt. auth. see Atkinson, Susan.

Rattingan, W. H. De Jure Personarum: or, a Treatise on the Roman Law of Persons. LC 93-79723. 362p. 1994. reprint ed. 85.00 (*1-56169-081-3*) W W Gaunt.

Rattinger, Hans, jt. ed. see Dewitt, David.

Rattinger, Hans, jt. ed. see Flynn, Gregory.

Rattle, Cora N. Creative Crochet Originals, Vol. 2. 1993. 14.95 (*0-533-10360-6*) Vantage.

Rattlehead, David. The Life & Adventures of an Arkansaw Doctor. McNeil, W. K., ed. LC 89-4692. 200p. 1989. 20.00 (*1-55728-086-X*); pap. 12.00 (*1-55728-079-7*) U of Ark Pr.

Rattner, Donald M. The Classical Architecture Orders. (Illus.). 144p. 1992. pap. 19.95 (*0-8306-4284-6*, 4313, Design Pr) TAB Bks.

Rattner, Joseph. Alfred Adler. Zohn, Harry, tr. LC 82-40251. (Literature & Life Ser.). 226p. (C). 1983. 19.95 (*0-8044-5988-6*, F Ungar Bks) Continuum.

Rattner, R. S., tr. see Makrinenko, Leonid I.

Ratto, Andrea, jt. auth. see Eells, James.

Ratto, Linda L. Coping with a Physically Challenged Brother Or Sister. Rosen, Ruth, ed. (Coping Ser.). (YA). (gr. 7-12). 1992. 15.95 (*0-8239-1492-5*) Rosen Group.

— Coping with Being Physically Challenged. Rosen, Ruth, ed. (Coping Ser.). (YA). (gr. 7-12). 1991. lib. bdg. 15.95 (*0-8239-1344-9*) Rosen Group.

Ratto, R. Aes Grave Italique. (Illus.). 33p. 1974. 15.00 (*0-915018-06-3*) Attic Bks.

— Collection Claudius Cote: Monnaies de Tarente. (Illus.). 42p. 17.90 (*0-915018-09-8*) Attic Bks.

Rattray, C. & Van Rijsbergen, C. J., eds. Specification & Verification of Concurrent Systems. (Workshops in Computing Ser.). 624p. 1990. pap. 59.00 (*0-387-19581-5*) Spr-Verlag.

Rattray, Charles & Clark, Robert G., eds. The Unified Computation Laboratory: Modelling, Specifications, & Tools. (Institute of Mathematics & Its Applications Conference Series, New Ser.: New Series 34). (Illus.). 480p. 1992. 98.00 (*0-19-853684-4*) OUP.

Rattray, Charles, jt. auth. see Rus, Teodor.

Rattray, David. Opening the Eyelid. deluxe ed. LC 90-84027. 96p. (Orig.). 1991. pap. 9.95 (*0-9627430-1-1*); pap. 500.00 (*0-9627430-2-X*) diwan.

— Opening the Eyelid. limited ed. LC 90-84027. 96p. (Orig.). 1991. 35.00 (*0-9627430-0-3*) diwan.

Rattray, David, tr. see Gilbert-Lecomte, Roger.

Rattray, Evelyn. The Teotihuacan Burials & Offerings: A Commentary & Inventory. Spores, Ronald et al, eds. (Publications in Anthropology: No. 42). 254p. (Orig.). 1992. pap. 23.00 (*0-935462-33-3*) Vanderbilt Pubns.

Rattray, Everett. Jeremiah Dimon: A Novel of Old East Hampton. LC 85-60911. 1990. pap. 9.95 (*0-916366-51-0*) Pushcart Pr.

— The South Fork. 1989. pap. 12.95 (*0-916366-41-3*) Pushcart Pr.

Rattray, James B., ed. Biotechnology of Plant Fats & Oils. 184p. (C). 1991. 70.00 (*0-935315-33-0*) AOCS Pr.

Rattray, Jamie, et al. Kids & Alcohol. 200p. 1983. pap. 5.95 (*0-932194-13-3*, 22H93) Health Comm.

— Kids & Drugs. 208p. 1983. pap. text ed. 5.95 (*0-932194-19-2*, 22H98) Health Comm.

— Kids & Smoking. 199p. 1983. pap. text ed. 5.95 (*0-932194-14-1*, 22H49) Health Comm.

Rattray, Robert F. Bernard Shaw: A Chronicle. LC 74-30342. (George Bernard Shaw Ser.: No. 92). 1974. lib. bdg. 52.95 (*0-8383-1892-4*) M S G Haskell Hse.

— Samuel Butler. LC 73-21671. (English Biography Ser.: No. 31). 1974. lib. bdg. 43.95 (*0-8383-1782-0*) M S G Haskell Hse.

Rattray, Robert S. Akan-Ashanti Folk-Tales. LC 78-63214. (Folktale Ser.). (Illus.). 320p. 1983. reprint ed. 34.50 (*0-404-16155-3*) AMS Pr.

— Ashanti. LC 73-92759. (Illus.). 348p. 1971. reprint ed. text ed. 35.00 (*0-8371-2201-5*, RAA&, Negro U Pr) Greenwood.

— Religion & Art in Ashanti. LC 76-44781. reprint ed. 34.50 (*0-404-15878-1*) AMS Pr.

***Rattue, James.** The Living Stream: Holy Wells in Historical Context. 144p. 1995. text ed. 45.00 (*0-85115-601-0*) Boydell & Brewer.

Ratushinkaya, Irina. No, I'm Not Afraid. McDuff, David, tr. 142p. 1992. 26.00 (*1-85224-057-1*, Pub. by Bloodaxe Bks UK); pap. 16.95 (*0-906427-95-9*, Pub. by Bloodaxe Bks UK) Dufour.

Ratushinskaya, Irina. Beyond the Limit. Brent, Frances P. & Avins, Carol, trs. 121p. (ENG & RUS.). 1987. pap. 10.95 (*0-8101-0749-X*) Northwestern U Pr.

— Dance with a Shadow. McDuff, David, tr. 77p. 1993. 25.00 (*1-85224-232-9*, Pub. by Bloodaxe Bks UK); pap. 13.95 (*1-85224-233-7*, Pub. by Bloodaxe Bks UK) Dufour.

— Grey Is the Color of Hope. Kojevnikov, Alyona, tr. (Vintage International Ser.). 1989. pap. 8.95 (*0-685-30682-8*, Vin) Random.

— Grey Is the Color of Life. Kojevnikov, Alyona, tr. 1989. pap. 8.95 (*0-685-26532-3*, Vin) Random.

— Pencil Letter. 1989. pap. 9.95 (*0-679-72600-4*, Vin) Random.

— Stikhi, Poems, Poemes. Devergnas, Meery et al, trs. LC 84-12974. 134p. (ENG, FRE & RUS.). 1984. pap. text ed. 8.50 (*0-938920-54-5*) Hermitage.

— A Tale of Three Heads. Ignashev, Diane N., tr. & intro. by. LC 86-25623. 128p. (ENG & RUS.). 1986. pap. 7.50 (*0-938920-83-9*) Hermitage.

Raty, Loren, jt. auth. see Spielman, Patricia.

Raty, Loren, jt. auth. see Spielman, Patrick.

Ratych, Joanna M., tr. see Pinthus, Kurt, ed.

Ratz de Tagyos, Paul. A Coney Tale. (Illus.). 32p. (J). (gr. k-3). 1992. 14.95 (*0-395-58834-0*, Clarion Bks) HM.

— Showdown at Lonesome Pellet. LC 93-25733. (J). 1994. 14.95 (*0-395-67645-2*, Clarion Bks) HM.

Ratz, John L. Lasers in Cutaneous Medicine & Surgery. (Illus.). 128p. 1986. 49.95 (*0-8151-7074-2*, GKZ-1, Yr Bk Med Pubs) Mosby Yr Bk.

Ratz, O., jt. auth. see Eisenbarth, M. A.

Ratzan, Scott C., ed. AIDS: Effective Health Communicaton for the 90's. LC 92-17933. 1992. 39.50 (*1-56032-273-X*) Hemisp Pub.

Ratzan, Scott C., jt. auth. see Payne, J. Gregory.

Ratzel, F. History of Mankind, 3 vols. 1702p. 1989. 1,200.00 (*81-7158-084-X*, Pub. by Scientific Pubs II) St Mut.

Ratzel, Friedrich. History of Mankind, 3 vols. 1972. 750.00 (*0-8490-0333-4*) Gordon Pr.

Ratzenhofer, Gustav. Die Sociologische Erkenntnis: Sociological Knowledge: The Positive Philosophy of Social Life. LC 74-25775. (European Sociology Ser.). 372p. 1975. reprint ed. 31.95 (*0-405-06529-9*) Ayer.

Ratzenhofer, M., ed. see Hoefler, H. & Walter, G. F.

Ratzin-Jackson, Catherine G., ed. Nutrition for the Recreational Athlete. LC 94-19402. (Nutrition in Exercise & Sport). 1994. write for info. (*0-8493-7914-8*) CRC Pr.

Ratzinger, Cardinal J. Seek That Which Is Above. Harrison, Graham, tr. LC 86-81553. 133p. 1986. 9.95 (*0-89870-101-5*) Ignatius Pr.

Ratzinger, Joseph. The Church, Ecumenism, & Politics. 256p. (C). 1988. 19.95 (*0-8245-0859-9*) Crossroad NY.

— Church, Ecumenism & Politics. 278p. (C). 1990. 75.00 (*0-85439-267-X*, Pub. by St Paul Pubns UK) St Mut.

— To Look on Christ. 120p. (C). 1990. 35.00 (*0-85439-330-7*, Pub. by St Paul Pubns UK) St Mut.

Ratzinger, Joseph C. Behold the Pierced One. LC 86-80103. 128p. 1986. pap. 9.95 (*0-89870-087-6*) Ignatius Pr.

— Church, Ecumenism & Politics. (C). 1988. 50.00 (*0-685-22284-5*, Pub. by St Paul Pubns UK) St Mut.

— Co-Workers of Truth. McCarthy, Mary F. & Krauth, Lothar, trs. LC 92-71960. 415p. 1992. pap. 17.95 (*0-89870-409-X*) Ignatius Pr.

— Dogma & Preaching. O'Connell, Matthew J., tr. 1983. 5.95 (*0-8199-0819-3*, Frncscn Herld) Franciscan Pr.

— Eschatology: Death & Eternal Life. Nichols, Aidan, ed. Waldstein, Michael, tr. LC 87-35107. (Dogmatic Theology Ser.: Vol. 9). 307p. 1988. 29.95 (*0-8132-0632-4*); pap. 14.95 (*0-8132-0633-2*) Cath U Pr.

— The Feast of Faith. Harrison, Graham, tr. LC 85-82175. Orig. Title: Das Fest des Glaubens. 153p. (Orig.). 1986. pap. 9.95 (*0-89870-056-6*) Ignatius Pr.

— The God of Jesus Christ. Cunningham, Robert, tr. 1978. 6.95 (*0-8199-0697-2*, Frncscn Herld) Franciscan Pr.

— In the Beginning... A Catholic Understanding of the Story of Creation & the Fall. Ramsey, Boniface, tr. LC 89-62499. 108p. (Orig.). 1990. pap. 5.95 (*0-87973-438-8*, 438) Our Sunday Visitor.

— Introduction to Christianity. Foster, J. R., tr. LC 90-82991. 280p. 1990. pap. text ed. 15.95 (*0-89870-316-6*) Ignatius Pr.

— Journey Toward Easter. 160p. 1987. 12.95 (*0-8245-0803-3*) Crossroad NY.

— Journey Towards Easter. (C). 1988. 39.00 (*0-85439-258-0*, Pub. by St Paul Pubns UK) St Mut.

— The Meaning of Christian Brotherhood. 2nd ed. Glen-Doeple, W. A., tr. LC 92-65064. 115p. 1993. pap. 9.95 (*0-89870-446-4*) Ignatius Pr.

— The Nature & Mission Theology. 134p. Date not set. pap. 14.95 (*0-89870-538-X*) Ignatius Pr.

— Principles of Catholic Theology: Building Stones for Fundamental Theology. McCarthy, Mary F., tr. LC 86-83133. 398p. (Orig.). 1986. 31.95 (*0-89870-133-3*) Ignatius Pr.

— Theology of History According to St. Bonaventure. Hayes, Zachary, tr. 268p. 1989. 12.50 (*0-8199-0415-5*, Frncscn Herld) Franciscan Pr.

— To Look on Christ: Exercises in Faith, Hope, & Love. 128p. 1991. 13.95 (*0-8245-1064-X*) Crossroad NY.

— Turning Point for Europe. LC 93-78528. 177p. Date not set. pap. 12.95 (*0-89870-461-8*) Ignatius Pr.

Ratzinger, Joseph C. & Messori, Vittorio. The Ratzinger Report. Attanasio, Salvator & Harrison, Graham, trs. LC 85-81218. 197p. (Orig.). (GER & ITA.). 1985. pap. 10.95 (*0-89870-080-9*) Ignatius Pr.

Ratzinger, Joseph C. & Schonborn, Christoph. Introduction to the Catechism of the Catholic Church. LC 94-75081. 95p. Date not set. pap. 9.95 (*0-89870-485-5*) Ignatius Pr.

Ratzinger, Joseph C., et al. The Church & Women: A Compendium. Krauth, Lothar et al, trs. LC 88-81309. 277p. (Orig.). 1988. pap. 14.95 (*0-89870-164-3*) Ignatius Pr.

— Principles of Christian Morality. Harrison, Graham, tr. LC 85-82176. Orig. Title: Prinzipien Chrislicher Moral. 104p. (Orig.). 1986. pap. 7.95 (*0-89870-086-8*) Ignatius Pr.

Ratzlaff, Don, jt. auth. see Johnson, Rose.

Ratzlaff, J. T., ed. Tesla: Complete Patents. (Nikola Tesla Ser.). 1986. lib. bdg. 125.00 (*0-8490-3838-3*) Gordon Pr.

Ratzlaff, John T. Tesla Said. LC 83-72252. (Illus.). 292p. (Orig.). 1984. pap. text ed. 28.00 (*0-914119-00-1*) Tesla Bk Co.

Ratzlaff, John T., comp. Dr. Nikola Tesla - Complete Patents, 2 vols. 2nd ed. LC 79-67722. (Illus.). 500p. lib. bdg. 43.50 (*0-9603536-8-2*); 35.00 (*0-914119-27-3*) Tesla Bk Co.

— Dr. Nikola Tesla - Complete Patents, 2 vols., Vol. I. 2nd ed. LC 79-67722. (Illus.). 500p. write for info. (*0-914119-10-9*) Tesla Bk Co.

— Dr. Nikola Tesla - Complete Patents, 2 vols., Vol. II. 2nd ed. LC 79-67722. (Illus.). 500p. write for info. (*0-914119-11-7*) Tesla Bk Co.

Ratzlaff, John T. & Anderson, Leland I. Dr. Nikola Tesla Bibliography. LC 78-66027. 248p. 1979. pap. 18.00 (*0-918660-08-4*) Ragusan Pr.

— Dr. Nikola Tesla Bibliography. 248p. Date not set. reprint ed. pap. 23.50 (*0-9636012-6-1*) Twty Frst Cent.

Ratzlaff, John T. & Jost, Fred A. Dr. Nikola Tesla, 3 pts. LC 79-67377. (Illus.). (Orig.). 1979. pap. 20.00 (*0-9603536-0-7*) Tesla Bk Co.

Ratzlaff, Keith. New Winter Night. Zarucchi, Roy, ed. (Chapbook Ser.). (Illus.). 24p. (Orig.). 1994. pap. 6.00 (*1-879205-47-5*) Nightshade Pr.

Ratzlaff, Kenneth L. Introduction to Computer-Assisted Experimentation. LC 86-19011. 464p. 1987. text ed. 91.95 (*0-471-86525-7*) Wiley.

Ratzlaff, Leslie A. Education Regulations Library: A Guide to the Making of Federal Education Laws & Rules. LC 87-110637. 22p. 1986. pap. 9.95 (*0-937925-14-4*) Capitol VA.

Ratzlaff, Leslie A., ed. The Education Evaluator's Workbook: How to Assess Education Programs, Vol. I. 100p. (Orig.). 1987. 32.00 (*0-937925-16-0*, EE) Capitol VA.

— The Education Evaluator's Workbook: How to Assess Education Programs, Vol. II. 145p. (Orig.). 1986. 30.00 (*0-937925-17-9*, EEW) Capitol VA.

— The Education Evaluator's Workbook: How to Assess Education Programs, Vol. III. 120p. (Orig.). 1987. 29.00 (*0-937925-18-7*, EEN) Capitol VA.

Ratzlaff, Patricia, jt. auth. see National Association of Home Builders Staff.

Ratzlaff, Robert K. John Rutledge, Jr. South Carolina Federalist, 1766-1819. 1981. 29.95 (*0-405-14104-1*) Ayer.

Ratzlatf, John T., ed. Dr. Nikola Tesla - Selected Patent Wrappers from the National Archives, 4 vols. LC 80-83299. (Illus.). 940p. 1981. pap. 60.00 (*0-9603536-2-3*) Tesla Bk Co.

Ratzleff, Edith. The Power of the Lamb. 48p. 1988. Pgs. 48, 07/1988. student ed 2.50 (*0-919797-72-5*) Kindred Prods.

Ratzloff, John. North Cabin Gallery. 1992. 12.95 (*0-934860-87-4*) Adventure Pubns.

Ratzlow, Helen. Edelmira Hernandez & the Kissing Dog. LC 92-25018. 24p. (J). 1992. 8.95 (*0-944957-38-2*) Rivercross Pub.

Rau. Respiratory Care Pharmacology. 376p. 1988. pap. 35.95 (*0-8151-7077-7*, Yr Bk Med Pubs) Mosby Yr Bk.

— Understanding Chest Radiographers. 1985. 23.95 (*0-8016-4026-1*) Mosby Yr Bk.

Rau, A. R., jt. auth. see Fano, U.

Rau, Albert G. & David, Hans T. Catalogue of Music by American Moravians, 1742-1842. LC 76-134283. reprint ed. 29.50 (*0-404-07206-2*) AMS Pr.

Rau, Bill. From Feast to Famine: Official Cures & Grass Roots Remedies to Africa's Food Crisis. LC 90-38990. 192p. (C). 1991. text ed. 49.95 (*0-86232-926-4*, Pub. by Zed Books UK); pap. 15.00 (*0-86232-927-2*, Pub. by Zed Books UK) Humanities.

Rau, Bob. The Collectors: Anecdotes & Answers about Antiques & Collectibles. Powell, Karla, ed. LC 88-82193. (Illus.). 104p. 1988. 19.95 (*0-932575-98-6*) Gr Arts Ctr Pub.

Rau, Bob, jt. auth. see Fisher, Joseph A.

***Rau, Dana M.** Robin at Hickory Street. (Smithsonian's Backyard Ser.). (Illus.). 32p. (J). (ps-3). 1995. 15.95 (*1-56899-168-1*); 4.95 (*1-56899-169-X*); 29.95 (*1-56899-170-3*); 12.95 (*1-56899-171-1*); audio 19.95 (*1-56899-172-X*) Soundprints.

Rau, Diantha C. Dear Angels. (Illus.). 61p. (Orig.). 1985. pap. 5.95 (*0-935557-00-8*) D C Rau.

Rau, Jon, ed. Applied Finance for Natural Resources: United Nations Interregional Seminar, Bangkok, 1991. (Illus.). 373p. (Orig.). (C). 1993. pap. text ed. write for info. (*0-9633833-1-0*) UN Dept Econ & Soc Dev.

Rau, Joseph L. Respiratory Care Pharmacology. 4th ed. 350p. 1994. pap. 32.95 (*0-8016-7184-1*) Mosby Yr Bk.

Rau, Joseph L. & Rau, Mary Y. Fundamental Respiratory Therapy Equipment: Principles of Use & Operation. LC 77-73776. (Illus.). 214p. reprint ed. pap. 61.00 (*0-317-58148-1*, 2029739) Bks Demand.

R

Rau, Joseph L., Jr. Respiratory Therapy Pharmacology. 3rd ed. (Illus.). 316p. 1988. 29.95 (*0-685-34790-7*, Yr Bk Med Pubs) Mosby Yr Bk.

Rau, Lucy, jt. auth. see Postman, Leo J.

Rau, M. Chalapathi. Indian Drama: Traditional Societies in Transition. 1983. 13.50 (*0-8364-1014-9*, Pub. by Allied II) S Asia.

Rau, Margaret. The Gray Kangaroo at Home. LC 77-14942. (Illus.). (J). (gr. 5-8). 1978. lib. bdg. 6.99 (*0-394-93451-2*) Knopf Bks Yng Read.

— The Snow Monkey at Home. LC 78-31550. (Illus.). (J). (gr. 4-7). 1979. lib. bdg. 6.99 (*0-394-93976-X*) Knopf Bks Yng Read.

— World's Scariest "True" Ghost Stories. LC 94-16579. (Illus.). 96p. 1994. pap. 3.95 (*0-8069-0796-7*) Sterling.

— Young Women in China. LC 88-31045. (Illus.). 160p. (J). (gr. 6 up). 1989. lib. bdg. 18.95 (*0-89490-170-2*) Enslow Pubs.

Rau, Marie T. Coping with Communication Challenges in Alzheimer's Disease. LC 92-41712. (Coping with Aging Ser.). (Illus.). 222p. (Orig.). (C). 1993. pap. text ed. 18. 95 (*1-879105-76-4*) Singular Publishing.

Rau, Mary Y., jt. auth. see Rau, Joseph L.

Rau, Nicholas J., jt. ed. see Pearce, David W.

Rau, Pip. Ikats: Woven Silks from Central Asia. (Pip Rau Collection Ser.). 96p. 1988. pap. 29.95 (*0-631-16171-6*) Blackwell Pubs.

Rau, Pradaeep A., jt. auth. see Ryans, John K., Jr.

Rau, R., ed. Low-Dose Methotrexate-Therapy in Rheumatic Diseases. (Rheumatology Ser.: Vol. 9). (Illus.). xii, 268p. 1986. 143.25 (*3-8055-4236-4*) S Karger.

Rau, Ron. Sage Lake Road. 126p. 1983. 15.00 (*0-932558-17-8*) Willow Creek Pr.

Rau, Rudolph, jt. auth. see Rauff, Rebecca.

Rau, Sara S., ed. Woman to Woman: Entrepreneurial Advice for All Week Long from Ash to Zunkel. (Illus.). 55p. (Orig.). 1992. pap. 8.95 (*0-9633089-0-4*) Phillippe-Fenton.

***Rau, Zbigniew.** Contractarianism vs. Holism: Reinterpreting Locke's Two Treatises of Government. LC 95-6234. 1995. write for info. (*0-8191-9929-X*); pap. write for info. (*0-8191-9930-3*) U Pr of Amer.

Rau, Zbigniew, ed. The Reemergence of Civil Society in Eastern Europe & the Soviet Union. 183p. (C). 1991. text ed. 46.00 (*0-8133-8404-4*) Westview.

Raub, John J. Who Told You That You Were Naked? Freedom from Judgement, Guilt & Fear of Punishment. 160p. (C). 1990. 49.00 (*0-85439-423-0*, Pub. by St Paul Pubns UK) St Mut.

— Who Told You That You Were Naked? Freedom from Judgment, Guilt, & Fear of Punishment. 128p. (Orig.). 1992. pap. 10.95 (*0-8245-1203-0*) Crossroad NY.

Raub, Joyce. Cain & Abel. (Arch Bks.). (Illus.). 24p. (J). (gr. k-4). 1986. pap. 1.99 (*0-570-06199-7*, 59-1422) Concordia.

Raub, Patricia. Yesterday's Stories: Popular Women's Novels of the Twenties & Thirties. LC 94-4794. (Contributions in American Studies). 160p. 1994. text ed. 49.95 (*0-313-29259-0*, Greenwood Pr) Greenwood.

Raub, T. L., jt. ed. see Audus, K. L.

***Raube, K.** Health & Social Support of the Elderly. 124p. (Orig.). (C). 1994. pap. text ed. 40.00x (*0-7881-1056-X*) Diane Pub.

Raubicheck, Walter & Srebnick, Walter, eds. Hitchcock's Rereleased Films: From Rope to Vertigo. LC 90-49240. (Contemporary Film & Television Ser.). (Illus.). 303p. (C). 1991. text ed. 39.95 (*0-8143-2325-1*); pap. text ed. 18.95 (*0-8143-2326-X*) Wayne St U Pr.

Raubitschek, A. E. The School of Hellas: Essays on Greek History, Archaeology, & Literature. Obbink, Dirk & Waerdt, P. A., eds. (Illus.). 416p. 1991. 55.00 (*0-19-505691-4*) OUP.

Raucat, Thomas. L' Honorable Partie de Campagne. (FRE.). 1984. pap. 11.95 (*0-7859-4213-0*) Fr & Eur.

***Raucci, Richard.** Mosaic for Windows: A Hands-on Configuration & Set-up Guide to Popular Web Browsers. LC 95-11636. (Illus.). 192p. 1995. 19.95 (*0-387-97996-4*) Spr-Verlag.

Rauch, jt. auth. see Thompson.

Rauch, A. H., ed. see American Society for Metals Staff.

Rauch, Anne, jt. auth. see Fegan, Lydia.

Rauch, Basil. Roosevelt: From Munich to Pearl Harbor. LC 74-34446. (FDR & the Era of the New Deal Ser.). 527p. 1975. reprint ed. lib. bdg. 45.00 (*0-306-70739-X*) Da Capo.

Rauch, Erich. Diagnostics According to F. X. Mayr: Criteria of Good, Marginal & Ill Health. Fogg, David M., tr. (Illus.). 129p. (Orig.). 1993. pap. text ed. 25.00 (*2-8043-4004-X*, Pub. by Edits Haug Intl) Medicina Bio.

— Health Through Inner Body Cleansing: The Famous MAYR Intestinal Therapy From Europe. 3rd ed. Peters, Mollie C., tr. (Illus.). 89p. 1990. pap. 9.95 (*3-7760-1179-3*, Pub. by K F Haug Pubs) Medicina Bio.

— Naturopathic Treatment of Colds & Infectious Diseases. Fogg, David M., tr. (Illus.). 83p. (Orig.). 1993. pap. 9.95 (*2-8043-4003-1*, Pub. by K F Haug Pubs) Medicina Bio.

Rauch, Friedrich. Psychology; or, a View of the Human Soul, Including Anthropology. LC 74-22335. (History of Psychology Ser.). 1975. 60.00 (*0-8201-1142-2*) Schol Facsimiles.

Rauch, Friedrich, ed. Iconsource. (Illus.). 1990. write for info. (*0-318-71805-7*, Pub. by Georg Olms GW) Lubrecht & Cramer.

Rauch, H. E., jt. auth. see IFAC Symposium Staff.

Rauch, H. E., ed. see IFAC Symposium Staff.

Rauch-Hindin, Wendy B. A Guide to Commercial Artificial Intelligence: Fundamentals & Real-World Applications. (Illus.). 592p. 1987. 29.95 (*0-13-368770-8*) P-H.

Rauch, Irmengard. The Old Saxon Language: Grammar, Epic Narrative, Linguistic Formation. LC 92-20320. (Berkeley Models of Grammar Ser.: Vol. 1). xliii, 416p. (C). 1993. text ed. 60.95 (*0-8204-1893-5*) P Lang Pubs.

Rauch, Irmengard & Carr, Gerald F., eds. Language Change. LC 82-48626. 286p. 1983. reprint ed. pap. 81.60 (*0-7837-6106-6*, 2059152) Bks Demand.

— Linguistic Method: Essays in Honor of Herbert Penzl. (Janua Linguarum, Series Major: No. 79). 1979. text ed. 142.35 (*90-279-7767-4*) Mouton.

— The Semiotic Bridge: Trends from California. (Approaches to Semiotics Ser.: No. 86). x, 428p. (C). 1989. lib. bdg. 142.35 (*0-89925-626-0*) Mouton.

— The Signifying Animal: The Grammar of Language & Experience. LC 79-3624. (Advances in Semiotics Ser.). (Illus.). 304p. reprint ed. pap. 86.70 (*0-8357-6696-9*, 2056876) Bks Demand.

***Rauch, Irmengard & Moore, Cornelia N., eds.** Across the Oceans: Studies from East to West in Honor of Richard K. Seymour. LC 95-14377. 208p. (C). 1995. pap. text ed. 25.00x (*0-8248-1693-5*) UH Pr.

Rauch, Irmengard & Scott, Charles T., eds. Approaches in Linguistic Methodology. 168p. 1967. 21.50 (*0-299-04240-5*) U of Wis Pr.

Rauch, Irmengard, et al, eds. On Germanic Linguistics: Issues & Methods. LC 92-21566. (Trends in Linguistics, Studies & Monographs: No. 68). viii, 416p. (C). 1992. lib. bdg. 152.35 (*3-11-013000-9*) Mouton.

Rauch, J. Partial Differential Equations. Ewing, J. H. et al, eds. (Graduate Texts in Mathematics Ser.: Vol. 128). (Illus.). 256p. 1991. 39.95 (*0-387-97472-5*) Spr-Verlag.

Rauch, James, ed. Kline Guide to the Ink Industry. LC 81-84941. (Illus.). 140p. 1982. pap. 85.00 (*0-917148-18-5*) Kline.

Rauch, James, jt. ed. see Deitsch, Marian.

Rauch, James A., ed. Rauch Guide to the U. S. Ink Industry. (Illus.). 142p. 1987. 189.00 (*0-932157-02-5*) Rauch Assocs.

— Rauch Guide to the U. S. Packaging Industry. (Illus.). 280p. 1989. 225.00 (*0-932157-03-3*) Rauch Assocs.

— Rauch Guide to the U. S. Paint Industry. (Illus.). 250p. 1989. 173.00 (*0-932157-00-9*) Rauch Assocs.

— Rauch Guide to the U. S. Plastics Industry. (Illus.). 375p. 1989. 173.00 (*0-932157-04-1*) Rauch Assocs.

Rauch, Jonathan. Demosclerosis: The Silent Killer of American Government. 1994. 22.00 (*0-8129-2257-3*, Times Bks) Random.

— Kindly Inquisitors: The New Attacks on Free Thought. LC 92-35805. 176p. (C). 1993. 17.95 (*0-226-70575-7*) U Ch Pr.

— Kindly Inquisitors: The New Attacks on Free Thought. xx, 180p. 1995. pap. 9.95 (*0-226-70576-5*) U Ch Pr.

— The Outnation: A Search for the Soul of Japan. LC 91-37946. 182p. 1992. 18.95 (*0-87584-320-4*) Harvard Busn.

— The Outnation: A Search for the Soul of Japan. LC 93-18499. 1993. pap. 10.95 (*0-316-73447-0*) Little.

— The Outnation: A Search for the Soul of Japan. 1992. text ed. 18.95 (*0-07-103370-X*) McGraw.

Rauch, Julia B., ed. Assessment: A Sourcebook for Social Work Practice. LC 93-27098. 416p. 1993. pap. 27.95 (*0-87304-267-0*) Families Intl.

Rauch, Karen, jt. auth. see Fessler, Jeff.

Rauch, Leo. Monarch Notes on Plato's the Republic & Selected Dialogues. (C). pap. 3.95 (*0-671-00505-7*, Arco Test) P-H Gen Ref & Trav.

Rauch, Leo, tr. see Hegel, Georg W.

Rauch, Nicolas. Bibliography of the Major French Artist Books, 1867-1957: Les Peintres et Livre, 1867-1957. rev. ed. (Illus.). 228p. (FRE.). 1991. 100.00 (*1-55660-127-1*) A Wofsy Fine Arts.

Rauch, Paul H. How to Be Your Own Contractor: Remodeling, Additions, Alterations, & Building a New Home. 3rd ed. LC 88-6986. 1994. pap. 9.95 (*0-931790-74-3*) Brick Hse Pub.

Rauch, Robert S. Smile: Be True to Your Teeth & They'll Never be False to You. rev. ed. (Illus.). 105p. 1991. pap. text ed. 4.95 (*0-9624076-0-7*) R S Rauch.

Rauch, Seymour. Legalized Stealing: The American Way of Life. (American University Studies: Economics: Ser. XVI, Vol. 2). 334p. (C). 1989. text ed. 43.00 (*0-8204-0625-2*) P Lang Pubs.

Rauch, Sidney J. Barnaby Brown: Home from Erehwon. (Barnaby Brown Bks.: Bk. 5). (Illus.). 80p. (Orig.). (J). (gr. 2-4). 1990. pap. 4.95 (*1-55743-162-0*) Berrent Pubns.

— The Further Adventures of Barnaby Brown. (Barnaby Brown Bks.: Bk. 4). (Illus.). 63p. (Orig.). (J). (gr. 2-4). 1990. pap. 4.95 (*1-55743-159-0*) Berrent Pubns.

— The Return of B. B. (Barnaby Brown Bks.: Bk. 2). (Illus.). 48p. (Orig.). (J). (gr. 2-4). 1989. pap. 4.95 (*1-55743-153-1*) Berrent Pubns.

— A Visit to B. B.'s Planet. (Barnaby Brown Bks.: Bk. 3). (Illus.). 64p. (Orig.). (J). (gr. 2-4). 1989. pap. 4.95 (*1-55743-156-6*) Berrent Pubns.

— The Visitor from Outer Space. (Barnaby Brown Bks.: Bk. 1). (Illus.). 48p. (Orig.). (J). (gr. 2-4). 1989. pap. 4.95 (*1-55743-150-7*) Berrent Pubns.

Rauch, Sidney J. & Sanacore, Joseph, eds. Handbook for the Volunteer Tutor. 2nd ed. LC 84-15723. 147p. (Orig.). reprint ed. pap. 41.90 (*0-7837-4735-7*, 2044543) Bks Demand.

Rauch, W. Hardy & Henderson, James D. Guidelines for the Development of a Security Program. (Illus.). 278p. (Orig.). 1988. pap. 31.75 (*0-942974-91-3*) Am Correctional.

Rauchbauer, Otto, ed. Ancestral Voices: The Big House in Anglo-Irish Literature. (Illus.). 327p. 1992. 50.70 (*3-487-09531-9*, Pub. by Georg Olms GW) Lubrecht & Cramer.

Raucher, Alan R. Paul G. Hoffman: Architect of Foreign Aid. LC 85-13406. 224p. 1985. 25.00 (*0-8131-1555-8*) U Pr of Ky.

Raucher, Herman. Summer of Forty-Two. 1991. reprint ed. lib. bdg. 21.95 (*1-56849-079-8*) Buccaneer Bks.

— Summer of '42. 21.95 (*0-8488-0310-8*) Amereon Ltd.

Rauchut, E. A., jt. comp. see Elton, W. R.

Rauchway, Alan. Relating: Reflections of a Psychologist. (Illus.). 108p. 1985. pap. 9.95 (*0-89529-290-4*) Avery Pub.

Rauchweger, Boaz & Rauchweger, Greta. How to Turn Your Time Into Gold. 216p. (Orig.). 1984. pap. 9.95 (*0-917873-00-9*) Tiberias Inst.

Rauchweger, Greta, jt. auth. see Rauchweger, Boaz.

Rauckman, E. J. & Padilla, George, eds. The Isolated Hepatocyte: Use in Toxicology & Xenobiotic Biotransformations. (Cell Biology Ser.). 292p. 1987. text ed. 126.00 (*0-12-582870-5*) Acad Pr.

Raudabaugh, James E., jt. auth. see Heilman, Karl J.

Raudenbush, Stephen W. & Willms, J. Douglas, eds. Schools, Classrooms, & Pupils: International Studies of Schooling from a Multilevel Perspective. (Illus.). 260p. 1991. text ed. 42.00 (*0-12-582910-8*) Acad Pr.

Raudenbush, Stephen W., jt. auth. see Bryk, Anthony S.

Raudkivi, A. J. Hydrology. 1979. 200.00 (*0-08-024261-8*, Pub. by Pergamon Repr UK) Franklin.

— Loose Boundary Hydraulics. 3rd ed. (Civil Engineering Ser.). (Illus.). 400p. 1990. text ed. 86.00 (*0-08-034074-1*, Pergamon Pr); pap. text ed. 42.00 (*0-08-034073-3*, Pergamon Pr) Elsevier.

Raudkivi, A. J., jt. auth. see Breusers, H. N.

Raudkivi, Arved J. Sedimentation: Exclusion & Removal of Sediment from Diverted Water. (Hydraulic Structures Design Manual Ser.: No. 6). (Illus.). 176p. 1993. text ed. 85.00 (*90-5410-132-6*, Pub. by A A Balkema NE) Ashgate Pub Co.

Raudsepp, Jaanus. Gogol v KGB. LC 91-76741. 141p. (Orig.). (RUS.). 1992. pap. 12.00 (*0-911971-72-6*) Effect Pub.

***Raue, F., ed.** Hypercalcemia of Malignancy. (Recent Results in Cancer Research Ser.: Vol. 137). 170p. 1994. text ed. 89.00 (*0-387-57631-2*) Spr-Verlag.

Raue, F., et al, eds. Medullary Thyroid Carcinoma. LC 92-2297. (Recent Results in Cancer Research Ser.: Vol. 125). (Illus.). 232p. 1992. 98.00 (*0-387-55372-X*) Spr-Verlag.

Rauf, A. Hadith for Children. pap. 6.50 (*0-933511-14-0*) Kazi Pubns.

— Quran for Children. pap. 7.50 (*0-935782-08-7*) Kazi Pubns.

— Story of Islamic Culture. 1981. 3.00 (*0-933511-65-5*) Kazi Pubns.

Rauf, Abdul. Bilal Ibn Rabah. LC 76-49691. 1977. pap. 3.95 (*0-89259-008-4*) Am Trust Pubns.

Rauf, M. A. Arabic for English Speaking Students. 1991. 22. 95 (*0-935782-21-4*) Kazi Pubns.

Rauf, Muhammad A. Arabic for English Speaking Students. rev. ed. 434p. (C). 1993. reprint ed. pap. text ed. 20.00 (*1-881963-00-4*) Al-Saadawi Pubns.

Rauf, S. A. Advice to a Friend. pap. 3.95 (*0-935782-25-7*) Kazi Pubns.

Rauf, S. A., tr. see Amin Ahsan Islahi.

Raufer, Roger K. & Feldman, Stephen L. Acid Rain & Emissions Trading: Implementing a Market Approach to Pollution Control. 176p. (C). 1988. 45.50 (*0-8476-7555-6*) Rowman.

***Rauff, James V.** Math Matters. LC 94-42054. 1995. pap. text ed. write for info. (*0-471-30452-2*) Wiley.

Rauff, Rebecca & Rau, Rudolph. Everyday Situations for Communicating English: Full-Color Cultural Scenes & Activities for Developing Language Skills: Advanced Beginning Through Intermediate. (Illus.). 128p. 1993. teacher ed 11.95 (*0-8442-0677-6*, Natl Textbk); pap. 18. 60 (*0-8442-0676-8*, Natl Textbk) NTC Pub Grp.

Raugh, Harold E., Jr. Wavell in the Middle East, 1939-1941: A Study in Generalship. (Illus.). 348p. 1992. 54.00 (*0-08-040983-0*, Pub. by Brasseys UK) Brasseys Inc.

Rauh, H. & Steinhausen, H. C., eds. Psychobiology & Early Development. 298p. 1987. 105.25 (*0-444-70256-3*, North Holland) Elsevier.

Rauh, Nicholas K. The Sacred Bonds of Commerce: Religion, Economy, & Trade Society at Hellenistic Roman Delos. xxiv, 376p. 1994. lib. bdg. 74.00 (*90-5063-156-8*, Pub. by Gieben NE) Benjamins North Am.

Rauhut, J. Brent & Darter, Michael I. Early Analyses of LTPP General Pavement Studies Data. 32p. (Orig.). (C). 1993. pap. text ed. 10.00 (*0-309-05774-4*, SHRP-P-392) SHRP.

Rauk, Arvi. Orbital Interaction Theory of Organic Chemistry. LC 93-27021. 1994. text ed. 59.95 (*0-471-59389-3*) Wiley.

Raul, K. B. Naked to the Night. rev. ed. 176p. 1986. reprint ed. pap. 7.95 (*0-917342-20-8*) Gay Sunshine.

Raulerson, John D., jt. auth. see Wong, Martin R.

Raulet, Sylvie. Van Cleef & Arpels. LC 86-42721. (Illus.). 330p. 1987. 110.00 (*0-8478-0754-1*) Rizzoli Intl.

Raulin, F., jt. ed. see Levasseur-Regourd, A. C.

Raulin, Michael L., jt. auth. see Graziano, Anthony M.

Raulston, J. C., jt. auth. see Tripp, Kim E.

Raulston, J. Leonard & Livingood, James W. Sequatchie: A Story of the Southern Cumberlands. LC 73-17360. (Illus.). 313p. reprint ed. pap. 89.30 (*0-7837-5391-8*, 2045155) Bks Demand.

Raulston, Ruth N., ed. see Sinks, Charles.

Rauluskiewicz, J., et al. Physics of Narrow Gap Semiconductors. 1978. 102.75 (*0-444-99801-2*) Elsevier.

Rauluszkiewicz, J., et al, eds. Physics of Magnetic Materials: Proceedings of the 2nd International Conference. 592p. 1985. 100.00 (*9971-978-34-2*) World Scientific Pub.

***Raum, O. F.** Chaga Childhood: A Description. (Classics in African Anthropology Ser.). (C). 1996. text ed. 64.50 (*3-89473-690-9*); pap. text ed. 25.50 (*3-89473-874-X*) Westview.

Raum, Otto F. Chaga Childhood: A Description of Indigenous Education in an East African Tribe. LC 76-44782. reprint ed. 30.00 (*0-404-15966-4*) AMS Pr.

— Chaga Childhood: A Description of Indigenous Education in an East African Tribe. LC 41-12399. 435p. reprint ed. pap. 124.00 (*0-8357-6966-6*, 2039026) Bks Demand.

— The Social Functions of Avoidances & Taboos among the Zulu. (Illus.). (C). 1973. 211.55 (*3-11-003460-3*) De Gruyter.

Raum, Otto F., tr. see Kecskesi, Maria.

Rauman, Richard. For the Reputation of Truth: Politics, Religion, & Conflict Among the Pennsylvanian Quakers, 1750-1800. LC 79-143626. 280p. reprint ed. pap. 79.80 (*0-317-39712-5*, 2025828) Bks Demand.

Raun, Alo. Essays in Finno-Ugric & Finnic Linguistics. (Uralic & Altaic Ser.: Vol. 107). 1971. pap. text ed. 12. 00 (*0-87750-152-1*) Res Inst Inner Asian Studies.

Raun, Alo, jt. ed. see Sebouk, Thomas.

Raun, Melanie. Quantum Leap: Knights of the Morningstar. 224p. (Orig.). 1994. pap. text ed. 4.99 (*0-441-00092-4*) Ace Bks.

Raun, Toivo U. Estonia & the Estonians. 2nd ed. 350p. 1991. pap. 18.95 (*0-8179-9132-8*); pap. text ed. 38.95 (*0-8179-9131-X*) Hoover Inst Pr.

Raundelen, Magne, jt. auth. see Dodge, Cole P.

Rauner, Judy A. Helping People Volunteer. LC 80-82556. (Illus.). 96p. (Orig.). 1980. pap. 9.95 (*0-9604594-0-5*) Marlbrgh Pubns.

Rauner, Judy A., jt. auth. see Trost, Arty.

Rauner, Julie N. Caribbean Basin Financing Opportunities: A Guide to Financing Trade & Investment in Central America & the Caribbean. 118p. 1990. per., pap. 5.50 (*0-16-022051-3*, S/N 003-009-005) USGPO.

Raunikar, Robert & Huang, Chung-Liang, eds. Food Demand Analysis: Problems, Issues, & Empirical Evidence. LC 86-30534. 302p. (C). 1987. text ed. 28.95 (*0-8138-1841-9*) Iowa St U Pr.

Raunkiaer, Christen. The Life Forms of Plants & Statistical Plants Geography. Egerton, Frank N., 3rd, ed. Gilbert-Carter, H. et al, trs. LC 77-74249. (History of Ecology Ser.). (Illus.). 1978. reprint ed. lib. bdg. 56.95 (*0-405-10418-9*) Ayer.

Raup, David M. Extinction: Bad Genes or Bad Luck? 224p. 1992. pap. 9.95 (*0-393-30927-4*) Norton.

— The Nemesis Affair: A Story of the Death of Dinosaurs & the Ways of Science. (Illus.). 224p. 1987. pap. 8.95 (*0-393-30409-4*) Norton.

Raup, David M. & Stanley, Steven M. Principles of Paleontology. 2nd ed. LC 77-17443. (Illus.). 481p. (C). 1995. text ed. write for info. (*0-7167-0022-0*) W H Freeman.

Raup, H., jt. auth. see Johnson, F.

Raup, H. F., ed. see Hamy, Ernest T.

Raup, Omar B., et al. Geology Along Going-to-the-Sun Road Glacier National Park Montana. Porte, Sannat, ed. (Illus.). 64p. (Orig.). 1983. pap. 4.95 (*0-685-07263-0*) Glacier Nat Hist Assn.

Raup, Omer B., et al. Geology Along Going-to-the-Sun Road Glacier National Park, Montana. LC 82-84746. (Illus.). 62p. 1983. pap. 8.95 (*0-934318-11-5*) Falcon Pr MT.

Raup, Ruth M. Intergovernmental Relations in Social Welfare. LC 70-168966. 234p. 1972. reprint ed. pap. 65.00 (*0-8371-6239-4*, RASW, Greenwood Pr) Greenwood.

Raupach, Manfred, jt. auth. see Dechert, Hans W.

Raupach, Manfred, jt. ed. see Dechert, Hans W.

Raupach, Manfred, jt. ed. see Dechert, Hans.

Raupp, Michael J., jt. ed. see Tallamy, Douglas W.

Raurell, Lydia. Aria. 12p. (Orig.). 1975. pap. 1.00 (*0-934776-01-6*) Bard Pr.

Raus, J., jt. ed. see Lowenthal, A.

Raus, J., jt. ed. see Vandenbark, A.

Raus, Jef, jt. auth. see Zhang, Jingwu.

Rausa, Rosario. The Blue Angels: An Illustrated History. (Illus.). 104p. 1979. 14.50 (*0-685-03409-7*) Moran Pub Corp.

— Gold Wings, Blue Sea: A Naval Aviator's Story. LC 80-26954. (Illus.). 200p. 1981. 21.95 (*0-87021-219-2*) Naval Inst Pr.

Rausa, Rosario, jt. auth. see Mogensen, Allan H.

Rausand, Marvin, jt. auth. see Hyland, Arnljot.

Rausch, D. O., et al, eds. Lead-Zinc Update. LC 77-83619. (Illus.). 414p. 1977. text ed. 5.00 (*0-89520-250-6*) SMM&E Inc.

Rausch, David. Fundamentalist-Evangelicals & Anti-Semitism. LC 93-3923. 256p. (Orig.). 1993. pap. 15.95 (*1-56338-049-8*) TPI PA.

Rausch, David A. Arno C. Gaebelein, Eighteen Sixty-One to Nineteen Forty-Five: Irenic Fundamentalist & Scholar. LC 83-9364. (Studies in American Religion: Vol. 10). (Illus.). 318p. 1984. lib. bdg. 99.95 (*0-88946-652-1*) E Mellen.

— Communities in Conflict: Evangelicals & Jews. LC 91-24449. 216p. (Orig.). (C). 1991. pap. 14.95 (*1-56338-029-3*) TPI PA.

— A Legacy of Hatred: Why Christians Must Not Forget the Holocaust. 2nd ed. LC 90-45918. 256p. 1991. pap. text ed. 13.99 (*0-8010-7758-3*) Baker Bk.

— Messianic Judaism: Its History, Theology, Polity. LC 82-20382. (Texts & Studies in Religion: Vol. 14). 304p. 1983. lib. bdg. 99.95 (*0-88946-802-8*) E Mellen.

— The Middle East Maze: A Guide to Israel & Her Neighbors. 1991. pap. 9.99 (*0-8024-5191-8*) Moody.

R

— Zionism Within Early American Fundamentalism, 1878-1918: A Convergence of Two Traditions. LC 79-66371. (Texts & Studies in Religion: Vol. 4). viii, 386p. 1980. lib. bdg. 99.95 (*0-88946-875-3*) E Mellen.

Rausch, David A. & Schlepp, Blair. Native American Voices. LC 93-45564. 192p. (Orig.). 1994. pap. 10.99 (*0-8010-7773-7*) Baker Bk.

Rausch, David A. & Voss, Carl H. World Religions: Our Quest for Meaning. LC 93-21711. (Orig.). 1993. pap. 15.00 (*1-56338-069-2*) TPI PA.

Rausch, David A., jt. auth. see Craig, Russell L.

Rausch, Don. Nuts, Bolts & Carnations. 58p. 1977. pap. 4.00 (*0-88680-143-5*) I E Clark.

***Rausch, Donald O., et al, eds.** Lead Zinc Update. LC 77-83619. (Illus.). reprint ed. pap. 120.30 (*0-7837-9179-8*, 2049878) Bks Demand.

Rausch, Erwin. Balancing Needs of People & Organizations: The Linking Elements Concept. 321p. 1978. 26.50 (*0-87179-274-5*) Didactic Syst.

— Financial Analysis. (Simulation Game Ser.). 1972. pap. 26.25 (*0-89401-026-3*) Didactic Syst.

— Win-Win Performance Management-Appraisal: A Problem Solving Approach. LC 85-12201. 311p. 1985. text ed. 64.95 (*0-471-86777-2*) Wiley.

Rausch, Erwin & Rausch, George. Leading Groups to Better Decisions. (Simulation Game Ser.). 1971. pap. 26.25 (*0-89401-046-8*); pap. 21.50 (*0-685-78113-5*); pap. 24.90 (*0-89401-047-6*); pap. 21.50 (*0-685-78114-3*); pap. 35.00 (*0-89401-048-4*); pap. write for info. (*0-685-78115-1*) Didactic Syst.

Rausch, Erwin & Wohlking, Wallace. Handling Conflict in Hospital Management: Conflict Among Peers (Game I) (Simulation Game Ser.). 1973. pap. 26.25 (*0-89401-036-0*); pap. write for info. (*0-685-78117-8*) Didactic Syst.

— Handling Conflict in Hospital Management: Superior - Subordinate Conflict (Game III) (Simulation Game Ser.). 1974. pap. 26.25 (*0-89401-043-3*); pap. write for info. (*0-685-78123-2*) Didactic Syst.

— Handling Conflict in Management: Conflict Among Peers-Game 1. (Simulation Game Ser.). 1969. pap. 26.25 (*0-89401-035-2*); pap. 35.00 (*0-685-78109-7*) Didactic Syst.

— Handling Conflict in Management: Superior - Subordinate Conflict Game 111. (Simulation Game Ser.). 1969. pap. 26.25 (*0-89401-098-0*); pap. 35.00 (*0-89401-041-7*); pap. 35.00 (*0-89401-042-5*) Didactic Syst.

— Handling Conflict in Management: Superior-Subordinate-Group Conflict Game II. 35.00 (*0-89401-039-5*); pap. write for info. (*0-685-85552-X*) Didactic Syst.

Rausch, Erwin, jt. auth. see Lieberman, Harvey.

Rausch, G. Jay, jt. auth. see Mundell, E. H., Jr.

Rausch, George, jt. auth. see Rausch, Erwin.

Rausch, Gerald, jt. auth. see Tonnis, John.

Rausch, Jane M. The Llanos Frontier in Colombian History, 1830-1930. LC 92-480. (Illus.). 416p. 1993. 57.50x (*0-8263-1396-5*) U of NM Pr.

Rausch, Jane M., jt. ed. see Weber, David J.

Rausch, Joseph P. LP-CD Master: Record Album Reference & Price Guide 1940-1987. LC 87-92216. 378p. (Orig.). 1988. pap. 39.95 (*0-9620095-0-4*) Standard Music.

Rausch, R. The Phosphating of Metals. 418p. 1991. 295.00 (*0-904477-11-8*, Pub. by FMJ Intl UK) St Mut.

Rausch, Ralph, jt. auth. see Morner, Kathleen.

Rausch, Ronald D., jt. ed. see Culp, Robert D.

Rausch, Thomas. Authority & Leadership in the Church: Past Directions & Future Possibilities. LC 88-24621. 158p. (Orig.). 1988. 15.95 (*0-8146-5745-1*) Liturgical Pr.

Rausch, Thomas P. Priesthood Today: An Appraisal. LC 92-747. 160p. 1992. pap. 9.95 (*0-8091-3326-1*) Paulist Pr.

— Radical Christian Communities. (Illus.). 216p. 1990. pap. 14.95 (*0-8146-5008-2*) Liturgical Pr.

— Roots of the Catholic Tradition. (Theology & Life Ser.: Vol. 16). 247p. 1986. pap. 14.95 (*0-8146-5538-6*) Liturgical Pr.

Rausch, Thomas P., ed. The College Students' Introduction to Theology. 216p. (Orig.). 1993. pap. text ed. 14.95 (*0-8146-5841-5*, M Glazier) Liturgical Pr.

Rausch, Werner. The Phosphating of Metals. 2nd ed. (Illus.). 418p. 1990. 131.00 (*0-685-53393-X*, 6389U) ASM.

***Rauschenbach, Boris V.** Hermann Oberth: The Father of Space Flight. Zavrel, B. John, ed. Kvinnesland, Lynne, tr. (Illus.). 256p. (Orig.). 1994. pap. 15.00 (*0-914301-14-4*) West-Art.

— Hermann Oberth: The Father of Space Flight. deluxe ed. Zavrel, B. John, ed. Kvinnesland, Lynne, tr. (Illus.). 256p. (Orig.). 1994. pap. 80.00 (*0-914301-15-2*) West-Art.

Rauschenberg, Christopher. Photographs, Nineteen Seventy-Three to Nineteen Eighty. LC 82-81916. (Illus.). 139p. (Orig.). 1982. pap. 10.00 (*0-943446-00-7*) Pair O Dice.

Rauschenberg, Christopher, ed. Drugstore Photographs: A Collection of Anonymous Snapshots. (Illus.). 64p. (Orig.). 1976. pap. 2.95 (*0-943446-01-5*) Pair O Dice.

Rauschenberger, Maria. Shakespeare's Imagery: Versuch einer Definition. (Bochum Studies in English: No. 11). x, 731p. (Orig.). (GER.). 1981. pap. 50.00 (*90-6032-203-7*) Benjamins North Am.

Rauschenbusch, Walter. Christianity & the Social Crisis. (Library of Theological Ethics). 448p. 1992. reprint ed. pap. 14.99 (*0-664-25321-0*) Westminster John Knox.

— Dare We Be Christians? 2nd rev. ed. LC 93-11041. (William Bradford Collection). (Illus.). 64p. 1993. 8.95 (*0-8298-0960-0*) Pilgrim OH.

Rauscher, Donald. Paul Simon for Flute & Piano. 1979. pap. 9.95 (*0-8256-2703-6*) Music Sales.

— Paul Simon for Trumpet & Piano. 1979. pap. 9.95 (*0-8256-2704-4*) Music Sales.

Rauscher, Elizabeth & Grotz, Toby, eds. International Tesla Symposium Proceedings, 1984. (Illus.). 160p. (C). 1992. pap. 35.00 (*0-9620394-0-3*) Intl Tesla Society Inc.

Rauscher, Elizabeth A. Electromagnetic Phenomena in Complex Geometrics & Nonlinear Phenomena, Non-Hertzian Waves & Magnetic Monopoles. LC 83-50845. 141p. (Orig.). 1983. pap. text ed. 15.50 (*0-9603536-9-0*) Tesla Bk Co.

Rauscher, Freya. Cruising Guide to Belize & Mexico's Caribbean Coast, Including Guatemala's Rio Dulce. Wilensky, Julius M., ed. LC 90-71942. (Illus.). 288p. 1991. pap. 34.95 (*0-918752-11-6*) Wescott Cove.

Rauscher, G., jt. ed. see Laude, L. D.

Rauscher, Gerhard, tr. see Edmunds, Adeline, ed.

Rauscher, H. Michael, jt. auth. see Schmoldt, Daniel L.

Rauscher, Tomlinson G. & Ott, Linda M. Software Development & Management for Microprocessor-Based Systems. (Illus.). 256p. 1987. text ed. 32.95 (*0-317-56706-3*) P-H.

Rauschkolb, Roy S. & Hornsby, Arthur G. Nitrogen Management in Irrigated Agriculture. (Illus.). 252p. 1994. 49.95 (*0-19-507835-7*) OUP.

Rauschning. Laser Anatomy: Lumbar Spine & Sacrum. 1991. 595.00 (*91-88142-00-0*) Mosby Yr Bk.

Rauschning, Hermann. Hitler Speaks: A Series of Political Conversations with Adolf Hitler on His Real Aims. LC 92-38341. (ENG.). 1995. reprint ed. write for info. (*0-86527-416-9*) Fertig.

— Men of Chaos. LC 71-167405. (Essay Index Reprint Ser.). 1977. reprint ed. 23.95 (*0-8369-2471-1*) Ayer.

— The Revolution of Nihilism: Warning to the West. Dickes, E. W., tr. LC 72-180666. reprint ed. 28.50 (*0-404-56402-X*) AMS Pr.

— The Revolution of Nihilism: Warning to the West. LC 72-4291. (World Affairs Ser.: National & International Viewpoints). 318p. 1972. reprint ed. 23.95 (*0-405-04583-2*) Ayer.

***Rausenberger, Mark.** A Somalia Journal. 96p. (Orig.). Date not set. pap. 12.95 (*1-878044-26-5*) Mayhaven Pub.

Raush, Charlotte L., jt. auth. see Raush, Harold L.

Raush, Harold L. Communication, Conflict & Marriage. LC 73-18506. (Jossey-Bass Behavioral Science Ser.). 264p. reprint ed. pap. 75.30 (*0-317-08634-0*, 2013751) Bks Demand.

Raush, Harold L. & Raush, Charlotte L. Halfway House Movement: A Search for Sanity. LC 68-18037. (Century Psychology Ser.). (C). 1968. 27.50 (*0-89197-197-1*) Irvington.

Raush, Harold L., jt. ed. see Levinger, George.

Raushenbush, Stephen. March of Fascism. 1939. 69.50 (*0-686-83616-2*) Elliots Bks.

Raushenbush, Winifred. Robert E. Park: Biography of a Sociologist. LC 77-88063. 220p. reprint ed. pap. 62.70 (*0-317-55491-3*, 2052212) Bks Demand.

Rausiri, Supa. The Beautiful Chick. Rodriguez, Gloria F., ed. Pinta, Thanom, tr. (Illus.). (J). (gr. k-2). 1979. pap. 3.00 (*0-686-26620-X*, Pub. by New Day Pub PH) Cellar.

Rauss, Erhard & Natzmer, Oldwig. The Anvil of War: German Generalship on the Eastern Front. Tsouras, Peter G., ed. 320p. 1994. 34.95 (*1-85367-181-9*, 5403) Stackpole.

***Rauss, Erhard, et al.** Fighting in Hell: The German Ordeal on the Eastern Front. Tsouras, Peter G., ed. (Illus.). 288p. 1995. 34.95 (*1-85367-218-1*, Pub. by Greenhill Bks UK) Stackpole.

Rausser. New Directions in Econometric Modelling & Forecasting in U. S. Agriculture. 830p. 1983. 135.00 (*0-444-00736-9*) P-H.

Rausser, Gordon & Hochman, Eleanor. Dynamic Agricultural Systems: Economic Prediction & Control. (Dynamic Economics Ser.: Vol. 3). 364p. 1980. 56.75 (*0-444-00274-X*, North Holland) Elsevier.

***Rausser, Gordon C., et al.** GATT Negotiations & the Political Economy of Policy Reform. LC 94-33513. 1994. write for info. (*0-387-58470-6*) Spr-Verlag.

Rautarharju, P., jt. auth. see MacFarlane, P. W.

Rautbord, Sugar. Sweet Revenge. 1992. 19.50 (*0-679-41387-1*, Villard Bks) Random.

Rautenbach, F. Labour Litigation: Practical Guide to Procedure & Tactics. 1993. write for info. (*0-7021-2992-5*, Pub. by Juta SA) W W Gaunt.

Rautenbach, Frans, ed. Noter-up to the Industrial Law Journal. 34p. 1992. pap. write for info. (*0-7021-2813-9*, Pub. by Juta SA) W W Gaunt.

Rautenbach, R. & Albrecht, R. Membrane Separation Processes. LC 87-23211. 459p. 1989. text ed. 350.00 (*0-471-91110-0*) Wiley.

***Rautenberg, Arne.** Dislimitations. (Illus.). 34p. (Orig.). 1995. pap. 5.00 (*1-57141-009-0*) Runaway Spoon.

Rautenberg, W., ed. Omega-Bibliography of Mathematical Logic, Vol. 1. (Perspectives in Mathematical Logic Ser.). xxxix, 483p. 1987. 197.00 (*0-387-17321-8*) Spr-Verlag.

— Omega-Bibliography of Mathematical Logic, Vol. II. (Perspectives in Mathematical Logic Ser.). xxxvii, 468p. 1987. 197.00 (*0-387-15521-X*) Spr-Verlag.

Rauter, Peter, photos. English Cottage Interiors. LC 89-42806. (Illus.). 160p. 1989. 27.50 (*0-8478-1113-1*) Rizzoli Intl.

Rautian, S. G., ed. Nonlinear Optics. 537p. (C). 1992. lib. bdg. 135.00 (*1-56072-074-3*) Nova Sci Pubs.

Rautian, S. G. & Shalagin, A. M., eds. Kinetic Problems of Nonlinear Spectroscopy. 430p. 1991. 151.50 (*0-444-88357-6*, North Holland) Elsevier.

Rautkallio, Hannu. Finland & the Holocaust: The Finnish Experience. 1987. 20.95 (*0-89604-120-4*); pap. 13.95 (*0-89604-121-2*) Holocaust Pubns.

Rautmenn, R., ed. Approximation Methods for Navier-Stokes Problems: Proceedings. (Lecture Notes in Mathematics Ser.: Vol. 771). 581p. 1980. pap. 49.00 (*0-387-09734-1*) Spr-Verlag.

Rauton, Jane, jt. auth. see Miles, Curtis.

Rauwendaal, Chris. Polymer Extrusion. 568p. (C). 1990. text ed. 57.95 (*1-56990-085-X*) Hanser-Gardner.

— Polymer Extrusion. 3rd rev. ed. 1994. write for info. (*1-56990-140-6*) Hanser-Gardner.

— SPC-Statistical Process Control in Extrusion. 224p. (C). 1992. text ed. 54.50 (*1-56990-086-8*) Hanser-Gardner.

Rauwendaal, Chris, ed. Mixing in Polymer Processing. (Plastics Engineering Ser.: Vol. 23). 496p. 1991. 199.00 (*0-8247-8521-5*) Dekker.

Rauzon, Mark. Horns, Antlers, Fangs, & Tusks. LC 90-49726. (J). (ps-3). 1993. 13.00 (*0-688-10230-1*); lib. bdg. 12.93 (*0-688-10231-X*) Lothrop.

— Skin, Scales, Feathers, & Fur. LC 90-409858. (J). (ps-3). 1993. 13.00 (*0-688-10232-8*); lib. bdg. 12.93 (*0-688-10233-6*) Lothrop.

Rauzon, Mark J. Catch a Comet by the Tail. (Illus.). 48p. (J). (gr. 5-10). 1985. pap. 6.95 (*0-935181-00-8*) Marine Endeavors.

— Eyes & Ears, Vol. 1. (J). (ps-3). 1994. 13.00 (*0-688-10237-9*) Morrow.

— Feet, Flippers, Hooves, & Hands. LC 93-86330. (J). (ps-3). 1994. 13.00 (*0-688-10234-4*); 12.93 (*0-688-10235-2*) Lothrop.

— The Last Condor. (Illus.). 24p. (Orig.). (J). (gr. 5 up). 1986. pap. 3.95 (*0-935181-02-4*) Marine Endeavors.

Rauzon, Mark J. & Bix, Cynthia O. Water, Water Everywhere. LC 92-34521. (Illus.). 32p. (J). (gr. 1-4). 1994. 14.95 (*0-87156-598-6*) Sierra.

— Water, Water Everywhere. (Illus.). 32p. (J). (gr. 1-4). 1995. pap. 5.95 (*0-87156-383-5*) Sierra.

Ravage, Jack. Singletree. (Illus.). 300p. (Orig.). 1990. pap. 12.95 (*0-936204-67-2*) Jelm Mtn.

Ravage, John. Time Out: Time Management Strategies for the Real Estate Professional. 224p. 1991. 19.95 (*0-7931-0210-3*, 2703-11) Dearborn Finan.

Ravage, M. E. The Rothschilds: Five Men of Frankfurt. 1973. reprint ed. lib. bdg. 300.00 (*0-8490-0975-8*) Gordon Pr.

Ravaglioli, A. & Krajewski, A. Bioceramics: Materials, Properties, Applications. 416p. 1991. 125.00 (*0-412-34960-4*, A6082) Chapman & Hall.

***Ravagnan, G. & Chiesa, C., eds.** Yersinia. (Contributions to Microbiology & Immunology Ser.: Vol. 13). (Illus.). x, 330p. 1995. 246.00 (*3-8055-6138-5*) S Karger.

Ravai, Nazanine, jt. auth. see Forestier, Nadege.

***Ravaioli, Carla.** Economists & the Environment: A Diverse Dialogue. Bates, Richard, tr. 192p. (C). 1995. text ed. 55.00 (*1-85649-277-X*, Pub. by Zed Books UK) Humanities.

— Economists & the Environment: A Diverse Dialogue. Bates, Richard, tr. 192p. (C). 1995. pap. 17.50 (*1-85649-278-8*) Interlink Pub.

Ravaioli, Umberto, jt. auth. see Cancellieri, Giovanni.

Ravaisson, Felix. Essai Sur la Metaphysique d'Aristote, 2 vols., Set. xiii, 1183p. 1963. reprint ed. write for info. (*0-318-71397-7*, Pub. by Georg Olms GW) Lubrecht & Cramer.

Raval, Hasmukh. Bhagavad Gita: A Philosophical System. (Illus.). 112p. 1990. 15.00 (*0-87527-484-6*) Green.

Raval, M. H., jt. auth. see Possehl, Gregory L.

Raval, P. J. Going to the U. S. A. A Newcomer's Practical Reference Book for Travel, Study, Work & Business in America. LC 90-82585. x, 142p. (Orig.). 1990. pap. 9.95 (*0-9628660-0-8*) Crown Apar Ent.

Ravald, Bertild. The Art of Swedish Massage. (Illus.). 120p. 1984. pap. 14.95 (*0-930267-18-4*) Bergh Pub.

— Get Fit for Golf. (Illus.). 96p. 1985. pap. 8.95 (*0-930267-04-4*) Bergh Pub.

Ravallion, Martin. Does Undernutrition Respond to Incomes & Prices? Dominance Tests for Indonesia. (Living Standards Measurement Study Working Paper Ser.: No. 82). 44p. 1991. 6.95 (*0-8213-1883-7*, 11883) World Bank.

— Markets & Famines. (Illus.). 216p. 1990. reprint ed. pap. 22.00 (*0-19-828727-5*) OUP.

— Poverty Comparisons. LC 93-14943. 1994. pap. text ed. 22.00 (*3-7186-5402-4*) Gordon & Breach.

— Poverty Comparisons: A Guide to Concepts & Methods. (LSMS Working Paper Ser.: No. 88). 134p. 1992. 8.95 (*0-8213-2036-X*, 12036) World Bank.

— Reaching the Poor Through Rural Public Employment: A Survey of Theory & Evidence. (Discussion Paper Ser.: No. 94). 68p. 1990. 7.95 (*0-8213-1622-2*, 11622) World Bank.

Ravallion, Martin & Datt, Gaurav. Growth & Redistribution Components of Changes in Poverty Measures: A Decomposition with Applications to Brazil & India in the 1980s. (Living Standards Measurement Study Working Paper Ser.: No. 83). 40p. 1991. 6.95 (*0-8213-1940-X*, 11940) World Bank.

Ravallion, Martin, jt. auth. see Datt, Gaurav.

Ravan, Pam. Sock Hunting & Other Pursuits of the Working Mother. (Heart Issues Ser.). 160p. 1991. pap. 9.95 (*0-932305-89-X*, 535010) Aglow Communs.

Ravanesi, Bill, et al. Breath Taken: The Landscape & Biography of Asbestos. (Illus.). 50p. 1991. pap. 20.00 (*1-879842-91-2*) Ctr Vis Arts.

Ravani, B., ed. CAD Based Programming for Sensory Robots. (NATO Asi Series F: Vol. 50). 580p. 1988. 118.00 (*0-387-50415-X*) Spr-Verlag.

Ravani, Bahram, jt. ed. see Lenarcic, Jadran.

Ravasio, P., et al. Local Computer Networks. 504p. 1982. 84.75 (*0-444-86386-9*, North Holland) Elsevier.

Raveau, B., jt. auth. see Rao, C. N.

Raveau, Bernard, et al. Crystal Chemistry of High Tc Superconducting Copper Oxides. Gonser, U. et al, eds. (Materials Science Ser.: Vol. 15). (Illus.). 352p. 1991. 106.00 (*0-387-51545-3*) Spr-Verlag.

Raveed, Sion. Joint Ventures Between U. S. Multinational Firms & Host Governments in Selected Developing Countries. Bruchey, Stuart, ed. LC 80-590. (Multinational Corporations Ser.). (Illus.). 1981. lib. bdg. 31.95 (*0-405-13381-2*) Ayer.

Raveed, Sion, jt. auth. see Renforth, William.

Raveh, Yael-Anna, jt. auth. see Weinshall, Theodore D.

Raveill, Ken. North Carolina Plantation & Historic Homes Cookbook. 32p. (Orig.). (C). 1992. pap. 4.50 (*0-935031-68-5*) Aerial Photo.

Raveill, Ken, ed. & photos. Georgia, Plantation & Historic Homes Cookbook. (Illus.). (Orig.). 1990. pap. 3.95 (*0-936672-80-3*) Aerial Photo.

Ravel, Maurice. Piano Masterpieces of Maurice Ravel. 128p. 1986. pap. 7.95 (*0-486-25137-3*) Dover.

Ravel, O. E. Numismatique Grecque Falsifications Moyens Pour les Reconnaitre. 105p. (FRE.). 1980. reprint ed. 20.00 (*0-916710-71-8*) Obol Intl.

— Les "Poulains" de Corinthe. (Illus.). 1979. text ed. 80.00 (*0-916710-47-5*) Obol Intl.

Ravel, O. E. & Vlastos, M. P. Descriptive Catalogue of the Collection of Tarantine Coins. (Illus.). 1977. 70.00 (*0-916710-30-0*) Obol Intl.

Ravel, Richard. Clinical Laboratory Medicine. 5th ed. 752p. 1988. 36.95 (*0-8151-7098-X*, Yr Bk Med Pubs) Mosby Yr Bk.

— Clinical Laboratory Medicine: Clinical Application of Laboratory Data. 6th ed. LC 94-30386. 1994. write for info. (*0-8151-7148-X*) Mosby Yr Bk.

Ravel, Sally & Wolfe, Lee A. Retirement Living: A Guide to the Best Residences in Northern California. (Illus.). 256p. (Orig.). 1991. reprint ed. lib. bdg. 33.00x (*0-8095-5861-0*) Borgo Pr.

— Southern California Retirement Living: A Guide to the Best Residences. (Illus.). 300p. (Orig.). 1992. reprint ed. lib. bdg. 37.00x (*0-8095-5862-9*) Borgo Pr.

Ravelli, Louise, jt. ed. see Davies, Martin.

Ravelli, Robert J., ed. Car-Free in New York City: The Regional Public Transit Guide, 1994-1995. LC 92-34898. (Car-Free Ser.). 220p. (Orig.). 1994. pap. 7.95 (*0-940159-17-1*) Camino Bks.

— Car-Free in Philadelphia: The Regional Public Transit Guide, 1993-1994. LC 92-22255. (Car-Free Ser.). (Illus.). 176p. (Orig.). 1993. pap. 6.95 (*0-940159-16-3*) Camino Bks.

Raven. Tragic Illusion: Educational Testing. 1991. pap. 10.00 (*0-89824-523-0*) Trillium Pr.

— Understanding Biology. 3rd ed. 1994. 45.95 (*0-8016-7843-9*) Mosby Yr Bk.

Raven & Johnson. Biology. 4th ed. 1994. write for info. (*0-8016-6908-1*) Mosby Yr Bk.

— Biology: Special Edition. 2nd ed. 1264p. 1991. 51.95 (*0-8016-6371-7*) Mosby Yr Bk.

— Understanding Biology. 2nd ed. (Illus.). 1264p. (C). 1989. text ed. 49.95 (*0-8016-4041-5*); International ed. text ed. 47.95 (*0-8016-3531-4*); student ed 14.95 (*0-8016-5288-X*) Mosby Yr Bk.

— Understanding Biology. 2nd ed. (Illus.). 1120p. (C). 1991. 52.95 (*0-8016-2524-6*) Mosby Yr Bk.

Raven & Vodopich. Biology No. 3: Raven Text Plus Vodopich Lab Manual. 1992. 67.95 (*0-8016-7267-8*) Mosby Yr Bk.

Raven, Alan. Essex-Class Carriers. LC 88-15590. (Warship Design History Ser.). (Illus.). 125p. 1988. 36.95 (*0-87021-021-1*) Naval Inst Pr.

— The Fletcher-Class Destroyers. LC 86-12559. (Warship Design History Ser.). (Illus.). 158p. 1986. 32.95 (*0-87021-193-5*) Naval Inst Pr.

***Raven, Ann.** Clinical Trials: An Introduction. 1996. pap. 15.95 (*1-85775-035-7*) Scovill Paterson.

Raven, Arlene. Crossing Over: Feminism & Art of Social Concern. Kuspit, Donald, ed. & pref. by. LC 87-25545. (Contemporary American Art Critics Ser.: No. 10). (Illus.). 242p. reprint ed. pap. 64.80 (*0-8357-2017-9*) Bks Demand.

Raven, Arlene, ed. Art in the Public Interest. (Illus.). 380p. 1993. reprint ed. pap. 14.95 (*0-306-80539-1*) Da Capo.

Raven, Arlene, intro. Art in the Public Interest. LC 89-16719. (Studies in the Fine Arts: Criticism: No. 32). 380p. 1990. pap. 108.10 (*0-8357-1970-7*, 2070756) Bks Demand.

— Giftwraps by Artists: Raoul Dufy. (Joost Elffers Bks.). (Illus.). 136p. 1986. pap. 14.95 (*0-8109-2953-8*) Abrams.

— Giftwraps by Artists: Vienna Style (Wiener Werkstatte) (Joost Elffers Bks.). (Illus.). 136p. 1985. pap. 14.95 (*0-8109-2951-1*) Abrams.

— Giftwraps by Artists: William Morris. (Joost Elffers Bks.). (Illus.). 136p. 1985. pap. 14.95 (*0-8109-2950-3*) Abrams.

Raven, Arlene, et al, eds. Feminist Art Criticism: An Anthology. LC 91-50514. 256p. 1991. reprint ed. pap. text ed. 16.00 (*0-06-430216-4*, Icon Edns) HarpC.

Raven, Bertram H., ed. Policy Studies Review Annual, Vol. 4. 768p. 1980. text ed. 69.95 (*0-8039-1119-X*) Transaction Pubs.

Raven, C. Oogenesis: Storage of Developmental Information. LC 61-17281. (International Series of Monographs on Pure & Applied Mathematics: Vol. 10). 1961. 122.00 (*0-08-009539-9*, Pub. by Pergamon Repr UK) Franklin.

Raven, C. & Harris, James R. Morphogenesis: Analysis of Molluscan Development. LC 57-14446. (International Series of Monographs on Pure & Applied Mathematics: Vol. 2). 1958. 134.00 (*0-08-011704-X*, Pub. by Pergamon Repr UK) Franklin.

Raven, C. P. Outline of Developmental Physiology. 3rd ed. 1966. 95.00 (*0-08-011343-5*, Pub. by Pergamon Repr UK) Franklin.

Raven, Charles. Apollinarianism: An Essay on the Christology of the Early Church. LC 77-84706. reprint ed. 38.00 (*0-404-16113-8*) AMS Pr.

— Science, Religion & the Future. Howatch, Susan, ed. LC 94-31712. (Yes: Library of Anglican Spirituality Ser.). 144p. 1995. pap. 9.95 (*0-8192-1633-X*) Morehouse Pub.

Raven, Charles E. Christian Socialism 1848-1854. LC 68-56058. xii, 396p. 1968. reprint ed. 45.00 (*0-678-05148-8*) Kelley.

R

An Asterisk (*) at the beginning of an entry indicates that the title is appearing in BIP for the first time.

— Christian Socialism, 1848-1854. 396p. 1968. reprint ed. 35.00 (0-7146-2129-3, Pub. by F Cass Pubs UK) Intl Spec Bk.
— John Ray, Naturalist: His Life & Works. 2nd ed. (Cambridge Science Classics Ser.). (Illus.). 532p. 1986. pap. 39.95 (0-521-31083-0) Cambridge U Pr.
— Natural Religion & Christian Theology: First & Second Series, 2 vols., Set. LC 77-27176. (Gifford Lectures: 1951-52). reprint ed. 37.50 (0-404-60540-0) AMS Pr.
Raven, Diederick, et al, eds. Cognitive Relativism & Social Science. 150p. (C). 1992. 39.95 (0-88738-425-0) Transaction Pubs.
Raven, E. Toussaint. Cattle Footcare & Claw Trimming. (Illus.). 128p. (Orig.). 1985. pap. 27.95 (0-85236-149-1, Pub. by Farming Pr UK) Diamond Farm Bk.
***Raven, Ellen M.** Gupta Gold Coins with a Garuda-Banner, 2 vols., Set. (Gonda Indological Studies: No. 1). (Illus.). 1994. pap. text ed. 142.00 (90-6980-065-9, Pub. by Egbert Forsten NE) Benjamins North Am.
Raven, Ellen M., et al, eds. Panels of the Seventh World Sanskrit Conference, Vol. 10: Indian Art & Archaeology. LC 91-28801. (Illus.). 135p. 1991. 68.75 (90-04-09553-5) E J Brill.
Raven, Francis H. Automatic Control Engineering. 5th ed. LC 94-10701. (McGraw-Hill Series in Mechanical Engineering). 1994. text ed. write for info. (0-07-051341-4) McGraw.
Raven, Frithjof A., tr. see Von Humboldt, Wilhelm.
Raven, Frithjof A., et al, eds. Germanic Studies in Honor of Edward Henry Sehrt: Presented by His Colleagues, Students, & Friends. LC 68-12422. (Miami Linguistics Ser.: No. 1). (Illus.). 1968. 10.95 (0-87024-078-1) U of Miami Pr.
Raven, Greg. Volkswagen Water-Cooled, Front-Drive Preformance Handbook. (Illus.). 256p. 1987. pap. 18.95 (0-87938-268-6) Motorbooks Intl.
Raven-Hansen, jt. auth. see Shreve.
Raven-Hansen, Peter. First Use of Nuclear Weapons: Under the Constitution, Who Decides? LC 86-33655. (Contributions in Legal Studies: No. 38). 259p. 1987. text ed. 59.95 (0-313-25520-2, RVF/, Greenwood Pr) Greenwood.
Raven-Hansen, Peter, jt. auth. see Shreve, Gene R.
Raven-Hasen, Peter, jt. auth. see Banks, William.
Raven, J. E. Pythagoreans & Eleatics. 196p. 1981. 20.00 (0-89005-367-7) Ares.
Raven, James. British Fiction, 1750-1770: A Chronological Check-List of Prose Fiction Printed in Britain & Ireland. LC 87-6041. 360p. 1987. 50.00 (0-87413-324-6) U Delaware Pr.
— Judging New Wealth: Popular Publishing & Responses to Commerce in England 1750-1800. 360p. 1992. 60.00 (0-19-820237-7) OUP.
Raven, John. A Botanist's Garden, 1992. 224p. (C). 1989. 90.00 (1-85183-034-0, Silent Bks) St Mut.
Raven, John A. Energetics & Transport in Aquatic Plants. LC 84-12525. (MBL Lectures in Biology Ser.: Vol. 4). 598p. (C). 1984. 110.00 (0-8451-2203-7) Krieger.
Raven, John E. Plato's Thought in the Making: A Study of the Development of His Metaphysics. LC 65-25585. 268p. reprint ed. pap. 76.40 (0-317-08827-0, 2050781) Bks Demand.
Raven, John E., pseud. Plato's Thought in the Making: A Study of the Development of His Metaphysics. LC 85-10074. xii, 256p. 1985. reprint ed. text ed. 59.75 (0-313-24958-X, RAPT, Greenwood Pr) Greenwood.
Raven, Lee. Hands on Spinning. LC 86-83427. (Illus.). 120p. 1987. pap. 8.95 (0-934026-27-0) Interweave.
***Raven, Margot.** Angels in the Dust. LC 95-3627. (Illus.). 32p. (J). (gr. k-3). 1996. lib. bdg. 13.95 (0-8167-3806-8) BrdgeWater.
Raven, Mark. Barrow. LC 86-82477. (Illus.). 191p. 1987. 16. 95 (0-9617588-0-5) Huttman Co.
Raven, P. H., jt. auth. see Zardini, E. M.
Raven, Peter & Johnson, George. Biology. 2nd ed. 1260p. (C). 1993. student ed write for info. (0-697-23506-8) Wm C Brown Pubs.
— Biology. 3rd ed. 1260p. (C). 1993. write for info. (0-697-23498-3); text ed. write for info. (0-697-23494-0) Wm C Brown Pubs.
— Understanding Biology. 2nd ed. 850p. 1991. student ed write for info. (0-318-71646-1) Wm C Brown Pubs.
— Understanding Biology. 2nd ed. 850p. (C). 1993. student ed write for info. (0-697-23505-X); text ed. write for info. (0-697-23503-3) Wm C Brown Pubs.
— Understanding Biology. 2nd ed. 416p. (C). 1995. student ed, spiral bd. write for info. (0-697-22217-9) Wm C Brown Pubs.
— Understanding Biology. 3rd ed. 64p. 1995. student ed, spiral bd. write for info. (0-697-25031-8) Wm C Brown Pubs.
— Understanding Biology. 3rd ed. 384p. (C). 1995. student ed, pap. text ed. write for info. (0-697-22216-0) Wm C Brown Pubs.
Raven, Peter & Johnson, George B. Understanding Biology. 3rd ed. 968p. (C). 1995. text ed. write for info. (0-697-22213-6) Wm C Brown Pubs.
Raven, Peter H. Native Shrubs of Southern California. (California Natural History Guides Ser.: No. 15). (Illus.). 1966. pap. 8.00 (0-520-01050-7) U CA Pr.
Raven, Peter H. & Axelrod, Daniel J. Origin & Relationships of the California Flora. (Publications in Botany: Vol. 72). 1978. pap. 22.00 (0-520-09573-1) U CA Pr.
Raven, Peter H. & Johnson. Biology, No. 3. 1344p. 1991. 56.95 (0-8016-6372-5) Mosby Yr Bk.
Raven, Peter H, jt. ed. see Gilbert, Lawrence E.
Raven, Peter H., jt. auth. see Osterbrock, Donald E.
Raven, Peter H., et al. Biology of Plants. 5th ed. 791p. 1992. text ed. 62.95x (0-87901-532-2); Laboratory Topics in Botany by Every & Eichhorn. pap. 25.95x (0-87901-521-7) Worth.
Raven, R. W. An Atlas of Oncology. (Encyclopedia of Visual Medicine Ser.). (Illus.). 200p. 1993. 85.00 (1-85070-363-9) Prthnon Pub.
— Rehabilitation & Continuing Care in Cancer. 172p. 1986. 39.00 (1-85070-105-9) Prthnon Pub.
— The Theory & Practice of Oncology: Historical Evolution & Present Principles. (History of Medicine Ser.). (Illus.). 366p. 1990. 95.00 (1-85070-179-2) Prthnon Pub.
Raven, Ronald W., ed. A Practical Guide to Rehabilitation Oncology. (Illus.). 200p. (C). 1992. 48.00 (1-85070-294-2) Prthnon Pub.
Raven, Ronald W., et al. Cancer Care: An International Survey. LC 86-9247. 340p. reprint ed. pap. 96.90 (0-7837-4506-0, 2044283) Bks Demand.
Raven, Susan. Rome in Africa. rev. ed. LC 92-13208. (Illus.). 1993. 65.00 (0-415-08261-7, A9615, Routledge NY); pap. 17.95 (0-415-08150-5, A9619, Routledge NY) Routledge.
Raven, Trevor. The Class Joke. LC 92-62013. (Illus.). 64p. 1993. pap. 8.00 (1-56002-231-0, Univ Edtns) Aegina Pr.
Ravenal, Earl C. Large-Scale Foreign Policy Change: The Nixon Doctrine as History & Portent. LC 89-84417. (Policy Papers in International Affairs Ser.: No. 35). viii, 89p. 1989. pap. 8.50 (0-87725-535-0) U of Cal IAS.
— NATO: The Tides of Discontent. LC 85-80223. (Policy Papers in International Affairs Ser.: No. 23). vii, 95p. 1985. pap. 7.50 (0-87725-523-7) U of Cal IAS.
Ravenal, Earl C., ed. Peace with China? U. S. Decisions for Asia. LC 71-162433. 1971. pap. 2.95 (0-87140-257-2) Liveright.
Ravenal, John B., jt. auth. see Miller-Keller, Andrea.
Ravender, Goyal. Monolithic Microwave Integrated Circuits: Technology & Design. (Microwave Library). (Illus.). 842p. 1989. text ed. 85.00 (0-89006-309-5) Artech Hse.
Ravenel, D. C., jt. ed. see Miller, H. R.
Ravenel, Daniel. List of French & Swiss: Settled in Charleston, on the Santee, & at the Orange Quarter in Carolina. (Illus.). 77p. 1990. reprint ed. pap. 8.50 (0-685-60515-9, 4770) Clearfield Co.
Ravenel, Douglas C. Complex Cobordism & Stable Homotopy of Spheres. (Pure & Applied Mathematics Ser.). 1986. text ed. 70.00 (0-12-583430-6) Acad Pr.
— Nilpotence & Periodicity in Stable Homotopy Theory. LC 92-26785. (Annals of Mathematics Studies: No. 128). 209p. (C). 1993. text ed. 69.50 (0-691-08792-X); pap. text ed. 24.95 (0-691-02572-X) Princeton U Pr.
Ravenel, Marion R. Rivers Delivers. (Illus.). 1995. 19.95 (0-941711-24-2) Wyrick & Co.
Ravenel, Mazyck P., ed. Half Century of Public Health: Jubilee Historical Volume of the American Public Health Association in Commemoration of the Fiftieth Anniversary Celebration of Its Foundation, New York City, November 14-18, 1921. LC 74-112569. (Rise of Urban America Ser.). (Illus.). 1976. reprint ed. 35.95 (0-405-02472-X) Ayer.
Ravenel, Rose P. Charleston Recollections & Receipts: Rose P. Ravenel's Cookbook. Harrigan, Elizabeth R., ed. (Illus.). 91p. 1989. reprint ed. 14.95 (0-87249-647-3) U of SC Pr.
***Ravenel, Shannon.** New Stories from the South: The Year's Best 1994. 368p. 1994. pap. 10.95 (1-56512-088-4) Algonquin Bks.
***Ravenel, Shannon, ed.** New Stories from the South: Best of the Year, 1995. (New Stories from the South Ser.). 300p. 1995. write for info. (1-56512-123-6) Algonquin Bks.
— New Stories from the South: The Year's Best, 1986. LC 86-7971. 241p. 1986. 14.95 (0-912697-40-7); pap. 9.95 (0-912697-49-0) Algonquin Bks.
— New Stories from the South: The Year's Best, 1987. 264p. 1987. 16.95 (0-912697-66-0); pap. 10.95 (0-912697-73-3) Algonquin Bks.
— New Stories from the South: The Year's Best, 1988. LC 88-6175. 264p. 1988. 19.95 (0-912697-90-3); pap. 8.95 (0-912697-93-8) Algonquin Bks.
— New Stories from the South: The Year's Best, 1989. 252p. 1989. pap. 9.95 (0-945575-27-0) Algonquin Bks.
— New Stories from the South: The Year's Best, 1990. 240p. 1990. pap. 9.95 (0-945575-52-1) Algonquin Bks.
— New Stories from the South: The Year's Best, 1993. 1993. pap. 10.95 (1-56512-053-1) Algonquin Bks.
Ravenel, Shannon, intro. The Best American Short Stories 1980-89. 384p. 1990. pap. 10.95 (0-395-52223-4) HM.
— New Stories from the South: The Year's Best 1992. 240p. 1992. pap. 9.95 (1-56512-011-6) Algonquin Bks.
— New Stories from the South, Nineteen Ninety-One: The Year's Best. 264p. 1991. pap. 9.95 (0-945575-82-3) Algonquin Bks.
Ravenel, Shannon, ed. see Brown, Larry.
Ravenel, Shannon, jt. ed. see Carver, Raymond.
Ravenel, Shannon, jt. ed. see Ford, Richard.
Ravenel, Shannon, ed. see Goodman, Richard.
Ravenel, Shannon, ed. see McCorkle, Jill.
Ravenel, Shannon, ed. see Nordan, Lewis.
Ravenette, A. T. Dimensions of Reading Difficulties. 1968. 53.00 (0-08-012956-0, Pub. by Pergamon Repr UK) Franklin.
Ravenhill, John. Collective Clientelism: The Lome Conventions & North-South Relations. LC 84-17674. 460p. 1985. text ed. 51.00 (0-231-05804-7) Col U Pr.
Ravenhill, John, ed. Africa in Economic Crisis. LC 85-26972. 320p. 1986. text ed. 52.50 (0-231-06382-2); pap. text ed. 18.50 (0-231-06383-0) Col U Pr.
— No Longer an American Lake? Alliance Problems in the South Pacific. LC 89-7612. (Research Ser.: No. 73). (Illus.). 240p. 1989. pap. 14.95 (0-87725-173-8) U of Cal IAS.
— The Political Economy of East Asia, 3 vols. Incl. Vol. 1. Japan, 2 bks. set. LC 95-7194. 1995. 309.95 (1-85898-252-9, Pub. by E Elgar Pub UK); Vol. 2. China, Korea & Taiwan, 2 bks. set. LC 95-7192. 1995. 309.95 (1-85898-253-7, Pub. by E Elgar Pub UK); Vol. 3. Singapore, Indonesia, Malaysia, the Philippines & Thailand, 2 bks. set. LC 95-7193. 1995. 309.95 (1-85898-254-5, Pub. by E Elgar Pub UK); 899.95 (1-85898-031-3, Pub. by E Elgar Pub UK) Ashgate Pub Co.
Ravenhill, John, jt. ed. see Callaghy, Thomas M.
Ravenhill, John, jt. ed. see Mack, Andrew.
Ravenhill, John, jt. auth. see Moss, Joanna.
Ravenhill, Leonard. America Is Too Young to Die. LC 79-19229. 128p. 1979. pap. 6.99 (0-87123-013-5, 210013) Bethany Hse.
— Meat for Men. 144p. 1979. pap. 6.99 (0-87123-362-2) Bethany Hse.
— Porque No Llega el Avivamiento. 144p. 1980. 3.95 (0-88113-250-0) Edit Betania.
— Reconquista de Tu Cuidad. (SPA.). Date not set. pap. 6.99 (0-88113-023-0) Edit Betania.
— Requisitos Para un Avivamiento. Araujo, Juan S., tr. 112p. (SPA.). (C). 1988. pap. 3.95 (0-88113-014-1) Edit Betania.
— Revival Gods Way. LC 83-15589. 160p. (Orig.). 1983. pap. 7.99 (0-87123-620-6) Bethany Hse.
— Revival Praying. 176p. 1962. pap. 7.99 (0-87123-482-3) Bethany Hse.
— Sodom Had No Bible. 208p. 1979. reprint ed. pap. 7.99 (0-87123-496-3) Bethany Hse.
— Tried & Transfigured. LC 81-71752. 144p. 1982. pap. 6.99 (0-87123-544-7) Bethany Hse.
— Why Revival Tarries. 176p. 1979. pap. 7.99 (0-87123-607-9) Bethany Hse.
Ravenhill, Philip L. The Art of the Personal Object. LC 91-33970. (Exploring African Art Ser.). (Illus.). 32p. 1992. pap. 9.95 (0-295-97171-1) U of Wash Pr.
— The Self & the Other: Personhood & Images among the Baule, Cote d'Ivoire. (Monograph Ser.: No. 28). (Illus.). 48p. 1994. pap. 15.00 (0-614-06236-5) UCLA Fowler Mus.
Ravenscraft, David J. & Scherer, F. M. Mergers, Sell-Offs, & Economic Efficiency. LC 87-14018. 290p. 1987. 34.95 (0-8157-7348-X); pap. 14.95 (0-8157-7347-1) Brookings.
Ravenscraft, Sue A., jt. auth. see Marini, John J.
Ravenscroft, Anna. Reader's Digest Calligraphy School. 1994. 21.00 (0-89577-524-7) RD Assn.
Ravenscroft, Donald, jt. auth. see Ravenscroft, Margaret.
Ravenscroft, Donald R. Taxation & Foreign Currency: Supplement One, 1973-1981. LC 81-19391. 233p. 1982. pap. 30.00 (0-915506-25-4) Harvard Law Intl Tax.
— Taxation & Foreign Currency: The Income Tax Consequences of Foreign Exchange Transactions & Exchange Rate Fluctuations. LC 72-81277. (Illus.). 888p. 1973. 50.00 (0-915506-15-7) Harvard Law Intl Tax.
Ravenscroft, John H., jt. ed. see Kostura, John R.
***Ravenscroft, Margaret & Ravenscroft, Donald.** Handbook for Voters & Liberal Democratic Candidates. LC 95-6391. viii, 106p. 1995. pap. 8.00 (0-86663-210-7) Ide Hse.
***Ravenscroft, Peter J. & Cavanaugh, John.** A Guide to Symptom Relief in Advanced Cancer. 160p. 1995. text ed. 19.95 (0-07-470134-7) Hlth Prof Div.
Ravenscroft, Raphael. The Complete Saxophone Player, Bk. 1. (Illus.). 48p. 1987. pap. 8.95 (0-7119-0887-7, AM62712) Music Sales.
— The Complete Saxophone Player, Bk. 2. (Illus.). 48p. 1987. pap. 8.95 (0-7119-0888-5, AM62720) Music Sales.
— The Complete Saxophone Player, Bk. 3. (Illus.). 48p. 1987. pap. 8.95 (0-7119-0889-3, AM62738) Music Sales.
— The Complete Saxophone Player, Bk. 4. (Illus.). 48p. 1987. pap. 8.95 (0-7119-0890-7, AM62746) Music Sales.
Ravenscroft, Thomas. A Briefe Discourse of the True (but Neglected) Use of Charact'ring the Degrees... (Monuments of Music & Music Literature in Facsimile: Series II, Vol. 22). 1976. reprint ed. lib. bdg. 45.00 (0-8450-2222-9) Broude.
Ravenscroft, Trevor. The Spear of Destiny. LC 82-60165. 400p. 1982. pap. 12.95 (0-87728-547-0) Weiser.
Ravenscroft, Trevor & Wallace-Murphy, T. The Mark of the Beast. 256p. 1992. pap. 12.95 (0-8065-1322-5, Citadel Pr) Carol Pub Group.
Ravenscroft, W. The Comacines. 120p. 1992. reprint ed. pap. 12.95 (1-56459-054-2) Kessinger Pub.
Ravenshear, Kit. Simplified V-Springs: A Guncraftsmanship Manual. 1991. 2.00 (0-685-51019-0) Pioneer Pr.
Ravenstein, Charles A. Organization & Lineage of the United States Air Force. LC 84-27361. (USAF Warrior Studies). (Illus.). 103p. (Orig.). 1986. pap. 7.50 (0-16-002212-6, S/N 008-070-00570-1) USGPO.
— The Organization & Lineage of the United States Air Force. Kohn, Richard H. & Harahan, Joseph P., eds. 77p. 1986. 7.50 (0-912799-17-X) Off Air Force.
Ravenstein, Charles A., ed. The Lineage & Honors History of Air Force-Controlled (AFCON) Combat Wings: 1947-1977. 317p. 1984. write for info. (0-912799-12-9) Off Air Force.
Ravenstein, E. G. The Laws of Migration: Papers 1 & 2. LC 75-38142. (Demography Ser.). (Illus.). 1976. reprint ed. 17.95 (0-405-07995-8) Ayer.
Ravenstein, E. G., ed. The Strange Adventures of Andrew Battell of Leigh in Angola & the Adjoining Regions. Bd. with Concise History of Kongo & Angola. (Hakluyt Society Works Ser.: No. 2, Vol. 6). (Illus.). 1974. reprint ed. 40.00 (0-8115-0329-1) Periodicals Srv.
Ravenstone, Piercy. Few Doubts As to the Correctness of Some Opinions Generally Entertained on the Subjects of Population & Political Economy. LC 64-22243. (Reprints of Economic Classics Ser.). 1966. reprint ed. 49.50 (0-678-00124-3) Kelley.
— Thoughts on the Funding System & Its Effects. LC 66-28961. (Reprints of Economic Classics Ser.). 80p. 1966. reprint ed. 19.50 (0-678-00192-8) Kelley.
Ravenswood, Fritzen. The Spawning. 352p. 1989. pap. 3.95 (0-8217-2554-8) Zebra.
— Witching. 1989. pap. 3.95 (0-8217-2657-9) Zebra.
Ravenswood Publ. Ltd. Staff. Hospitals in the EEC. (C). 1987. 99.00 (0-685-28613-4) St Mut.
— Law on Accidents to Health Service Staff & Volunteers. (C). 1987. 125.00 (0-901812-23-4); pap. 89.00 (0-901812-24-2) St Mut.
— Legal Liability for Claims Arising from Hospital Treatment. (C). 1987. pap. 89.00 (0-685-28608-8); write for info. (0-901812-14-5) St Mut.
— Occupies's Liability Act Nineteen Fifty-Seven & Liability of Hospitals. (C). 1957. 125.00 (0-901812-20-X); pap. 110.00 (0-901812-19-6) St Mut.
Ravenswood Publications Ltd. Staff. French Hospitals & European Health Care. (C). 1987. 79.00 (0-901812-15-3) St Mut.
***Ravensworth, Olivia M.** The Mistress of Castle Rohmenstadt. (Orig.). 1996. mass mkt., pap. 5.95 (1-56333-372-4) Masquerade.
Raventon, Edward. Island in the Plains: A Black Hills Natural History. LC 94-17996. (Illus.). 280p. (Orig.). 1994. pap. 16.95 (1-55566-132-7) Johnson Bks.
***Raventos, Gold.** Random House New Spanish-English, English-Spanish Dictionary. (ENG & SPA.). 1995. 18.00 (0-679-43897-1) Random.
Raventos, M. H. Teach Yourself Spanish Dictionary. (Teach Yourself Ser.). (SPA.). 1974. pap. 9.95 (0-679-10230-2) McKay.
***RavenWolf, Silver.** Beneath a Mountain Moon. LC 95-11763. 408p. 1995. pap. 13.00 (1-56718-722-6) Llewellyn Pubns.
— HexCraft: Dutch Country Pow-Wow Magick. LC 95-2100. (Llewellyn's Practical Magick Series). 1995. pap. 15.95 (1-56718-723-4) Llewellyn Pubns.
— To Ride a Silver Broomstick: New Generation Witchcraft. LC 92-38151. (Illus.). 320p. 1993. pap. 14.95 (0-87542-791-X) Llewellyn Pubns.
***Raver.** Magic & Loss. 1994. 18.95 (1-57174-017-1) Hampton Roads Pub Co.
***Raver, Ann.** Deep in the Green: An Exploration of Country Pleasures. 1995. 24.00 (0-679-43483-6) Knopf.
***Raver-Lampman, Greg.** Magic & Loss. 176p. (Orig.). 1994. pap. 9.95 (1-57174-015-5) Hampton Roads Pub Co.

***Raver, Mary F. Women's Health Diary: The Essential Health Record for Every Woman Aged 35 to 55. 52p. (Orig.). 1995. pap. 4.95 (1-886245-00-2) Adelante CA.**
This book is designed to provide each of the over two million women a year experiencing PMS, perimenopausal, or menopausal symptoms with the means necessary to take control of their health. This book is for every woman who has experienced the frustration of forgetting to ask questions while in the doctor's office or has only been able to provide vague, nonspecific answers to the doctor's questions about her symptoms. In five minutes a day, a woman can record her symptoms & make quick notes about other events or activities in her life. Within a few weeks, a woman has created a database of health information which not only details her symptoms & the effect that different activities have on them, but provides the necessary information her doctor needs to effectively detect, diagnose & treat problems affecting her health. The diary's contents include: an example of weekly record keeping, pages for recording basic health information (e.g. blood pressure, cholesterol level, & immunizations), a medical appointment information section with space for writing questions for the doctor, a glossary of symptoms & a bibliography of books available on the subjects of PMS, Perimenopause & Menopause. To order contact: Adelante Publishing, P.O. Box 501584, San Diego, CA 92150-1584, Phone: (619) 748-6192, FAX: (619) 748-3033. ***Publisher Provided Annotation.***

Raver, Sharon A. Strategies for Teaching At-Risk & Handicapped Infants & Toddlers. 460p. (C). 1991. text ed. write for info. (0-675-21202-2, Merrill Pub Co) Macmillan.
Ravera, O., ed. Ecological Assessment of Environmental Degradation, Pollution & Recovery: Lectures of a Course Held at the Joint Research Centre, Ispra, Italy, 12-16 Oct., 1987. 370p. 1989. 151.50 (0-444-87361-9) Elsevier.

R

Ravera, O., jt. auth. see Mislin.
Raverat, Gwen. Period Piece. (Ann Arbor Paperbacks Ser.). (Illus.). 290p. (C). 1991. reprint ed. pap. text ed. 14.95 (*0-472-06475-4*) U of Mich Pr.
Raverty, H. C., tr. see Al-din, Minhaj.
Raverty, H. G. A Dictionary of the Puk'hto, Pus'hto, or Language of the Afghans; with Remarks on the Originality of the Language & Its Affinity to the Semitic & Other Oriental Tongues. 1987. reprint ed. 52.00 (*81-206-0286-2*, Pub. by Asian Educ Servs II) S Asia.
— Dictionary of the Pushto Language: Pushto - English Dictionary. 1140p. 1987. 79.95 (*0-8288-8477-3*) Fr & Eur.
— A Grammar of the Puk'hto, Pus'hto, or Language of the Afghans. (C). 1987. reprint ed. 36.00 (*0-8364-2400-X*, Pub. by Asian Educ Servs II) S Asia.
— Grammar of the Puk'tho-Pus'hto. 204p. 1987. 18.00 (*0-88431-029-9*) IBD Ltd.
— The Pushto Manual. 257p. 1986. 28.00 (*0-88431-180-5*) IBD Ltd.
— Selection of Poetry of the Afghans. (C). 1988. 135.00 (*1-85077-197-9*, Darf Pubs Ltd) St Mut.
Ravesloot, John C. Mortuary Practices & Social Differentiation at Casas Grandes, Chihuahua, Mexico. LC 88-15385. (Anthropological Papers). 113p. 1988. pap. 25.00 (*0-8165-1048-2*) U of Ariz Pr.
Ravesloot, John C., jt. ed. see Woosley, Anne I.
Ravetllat, Pere J. Block Housing. (Illus.). 192p. 1992. 59.95 (*84-252-1567-6*) Rizzoli Intl.
Ravetto, C. & Boccato, P. Fine-Needle Aspiration Cytodiagnosis: A Color Atlas. 210p. 1984. text ed. 64.00 (*1-57235-031-8*) Piccin NY.
Ravetto, Carlo & Boccato, Paolo. Fine-Needle Aspiration Cytodiagnosis: A Color Atlas. (Illus.). 212p. 1984. 145.00 (*0-407-01054-8*) Buttrwrth-Heinemann.
Ravetz, J. R. The Merger of Knowledge with Power: Essays in Critical Science. 352p. 1990. text ed. 80.00 (*0-7201-2021-7*, Mansell Pub) Cassell.
Ravetz, J. R., jt. auth. see Fincham, John.
Ravetz, Jerome R., jt. auth. see Funtowicz, Silvio O.
Ravi, Jennifer. Notable North Carolina Women. LC 92-70165. (Illus.). 160p. (Orig.). 1992. pap. 9.95 (*1-878177-03-6*) Bandit Bks.
Ravi, K. V., ed. see Electrochemical Society Staff.
Ravi, K. V., jt. ed. see Khattak, C. P.
***Ravi, K. V., et al.** Diamond Materials: Fourth International Symposium. 1995. 72.00 (*1-56677-098-X*, PV 95-4) Electrochem Soc.
Ravi, P. Agarwal. Inequalities & Applications. 604p. 1994. text ed. 104.00 (*981-02-1830-3*) World Scientific Pub.
Ravi, V. A. & Srivatsan, T. S., eds. Processing & Fabrication of Advanced Materials for High Temperature Applications. (Illus.). 418p. 1992. 106.00 (*0-87339-182-9*, 426) Minerals Metals.
— Processing & Fabrication of Advanced Materials for High Temperature Applications II. (Illus.). 700p. 1993. 128.00 (*0-87339-215-9*, 464) Minerals Metals.
***Ravi, V. A., et al, eds.** Processing & Frabrication of Advanced Materials III: Proceedings. 884p. 1994. 218.00 (*0-87339-231-0*) Minerals Metals.
Raviart, P. A., jt. auth. see Girault, V.
Ravich, M. G. & Kamenev, E. N. Crystalline Basement of the Antarctic Platform. 592p. 1974. text ed. 138.00 (*0-7065-1401-7*, Pub. by Keter Pub IS) Coronet Bks.
Ravich, M. G., et al. Geological Structure of Mac. Robertson Land (East Antarctica) Ghosh, S. P., tr. 266p. (ENG.). (C). 1985. text ed. 85.00 (*90-6191-439-6*, Pub. by A A Balkema NE) Ashgate Pub Co.
Ravich, Uri I., et al. Semiconducting Lead Chalcogenides. Stillbans, L. S. & Tybulewicz, Albin, eds. LC 77-107542. (Monographs in Semiconductor Physics: Vol. 5). 393p. reprint ed. pap. 112.10 (*0-685-15851-9*, 2026308) Bks Demand.
Ravichandran, N. Stochastic Methods in Reliability Theory. 1991. text ed. 58.95 (*0-470-21681-6*) Halsted Pr.
Ravicz, R. Marisol, jt. auth. see Struyk, Raymond J.
Ravicz, Robert. The Japanese Artist's Book: Wood Block Impressions 17th - 20th Centuries. Zangar, Catherine, ed. (Illus.). 20p. (Orig.). (C). 1988. pap. 7.95 (*1-880269-04-X*) D H Sheehan.
Ravid, Benjamin, ed. see Rawidowicz, Simon.
Ravid, Dorit D. Language Change in Child & Adult Hebrew: A Psycholinguistic Perspective. (Oxford Studies in Sociolinguistics). 256p. 1995. 45.00 (*0-19-508893-X*); pap. 22.00 (*0-19-509036-5*) OUP.
Ravid, Joyce. Here & There: Photographs. 1993. 30.00 (*0-679-40399-X*) Knopf.
Ravid, Ruth. Practical Statistics for Educators. LC 94-4720. 366p. (Orig.). Date not set. lib. bdg. 48.50 (*0-8191-9498-0*); pap. text ed. 29.50 (*0-8191-9499-9*) U Pr of Amer.
Ravier, Andre. A Do-It-at-Home Retreat: The Spiritual Exercises of St. Ignatius of Loyola. Buckley, Cornelius, tr. LC 90-85500. 233p. (Orig.). 1991. pap. 12.95 (*0-89870-363-8*) Ignatius Pr.
— Francis de Sales: Sage & Saint. LC 87-83532. 270p. (Orig.). 1988. pap. 12.95 (*0-89870-193-7*) Ignatius Pr.
— St. Jeanne de Chantal: Noble Lady, Holy Woman. LC 89-84205. (Illus.). 231p. (Orig.). 1989. pap. text ed. 12.95 (*0-89870-267-4*) Ignatius Pr.
Ravier, Roger, ed. see Saint Francois de Sales.
Raviez, Marilyn E. Early Colonial Religious Drama in Mexico: From Tzompantli to Golgotha. LC 77-76157. 273p. reprint ed. pap. 77.90 (*0-685-17846-3*, 2029506) Bks Demand.
Ravignant, Patrick, jt. auth. see Aubier, Catherine.
Ravikovitch, Dahlia. A Dress of Fire. Bloch, Chana, tr. LC 77-95139. 52p. 1978. pap. 7.95 (*0-8180-1546-2*) Sheep Meadow.
— The Window: New & Selected Poems. Bloch, Chana & Bloch, Ariel, trs. LC 88-34896. 117p. (Orig.). 1989. 15.95 (*0-935296-81-6*); pap. 10.95 (*0-935296-82-4*) Sheep Meadow.
Ravikumar, C. P. Parallel Methods for VLSI Layout Design. Zobrist, George W., ed. (Computer Engineering & Computer Science Ser.). 216p. (C). 1995. 47.50 (*0-89391-828-8*) Ablex Pub.
Ravikumar, T. S. Novel Regional Therapies for Liver Tumors. (Medical Intelligence Unit Ser.). write for info. (*1-879702-99-1*) R G Landes.
Ravikumar, V. M. Play the Benko Gambit. (Chess Library). (Illus.). 120p. 1991. write for info. (*0-08-029767-6*, Pub. by CHES UK); pap. 19.95 (*0-08-029766-8*, Pub. by CHES UK) Macmillan.
Ravikumar, Vaidyanathan. Play the Benko Gambit. 1991. 15.00 (*1-85744-014-5*, Maxwell Macmillan) Macmillan.
Ravilious, James & Ravilious, Robin. The Heart of the Country. 1980. pap. 17.95 (*0-85967-627-7*, Pub. by Scolar Pr UK) Ashgate Pub Co.
Ravilious, Robin. Two in a Pocket. (J). (ps-3). 1991. 14.95 (*0-316-73449-7*) Little.
Ravilious, Robin, jt. auth. see Ravilious, James.
Ravin, Abe, et al. Auscultation of the Heart. 3rd ed. LC 76-53227. 297p. reprint ed. pap. 84.70 (*0-8357-5886-9*, 2026506) Bks Demand.
Ravin, Carl E., ed. Imaging & Invasive Radiology in the Intensive Care Unit. LC 92-49509. (Illus.). 181p. 1993. text ed. 64.00 (*0-443-08868-3*) Churchill.
Ravin, Carl E., jt. auth. see Putman, Charles E.
Ravin, Carl E., et al, eds. Review of Radiology. 2nd ed. LC 93-3351. (Illus.). 400p. 1993. pap. text ed. 49.95 (*0-7216-5028-7*) Saunders.
Ravin, Thomas, jt. auth. see Dorman, Thomas A.
Ravin, Yael. Lexical Semantics Without Thematic Roles. 256p. 1990. 55.00 (*0-19-824831-8*) OUP.
Ravindra, H, jt. ed. see Cropley, A. J.
Ravindra, R. Yoga of Christ: In the Gospel According to St. John. 1993. pap. 14.95 (*1-85230-139-2*, Pub. by Element Bks UK) Element MA.
***Ravindra, Ravi.** Krishnamurti: Two Birds on One Tree. 90p. (Orig.). 1995. pap. 8.00 (*0-8356-0718-6*, Quest) Theos Pub Hse.
— Whispers from the Other Shore. LC 84-40164. 170p. (Orig.). 1984. pap. 6.50 (*0-8356-0589-2*, Quest) Theos Pub Hse.
Ravindra, Ravi, ed. Science & Spirit. LC 90-6962. (ICUS Ser.). 433p. (C). 1990. text ed. 29.95 (*0-89226-085-8*, ICUS); pap. text ed. 14.95 (*0-89226-082-3*, ICUS) Paragon Hse.
Ravindran, A., et al. Operations Research: Principles & Practice. 2nd ed. LC 86-5561. 637p. 1987. Net. text ed. write for info. (*0-471-08608-8*) Wiley.
Ravindran, C., ed. see Conference on Process Control & Reliability Analysis Staff.
Ravindran, D. J., ed. A Handbook on Training Paralegals: Report of a Seminar on Training of Paralegals, TagaTay City, Philippines, 5-9 December, 1988. 49p. reprint ed. pap. 25.00 (*0-7837-0093-8*, 2040370) Bks Demand.
Ravindran, T. K. On the Other Shore Poems. 104p. 1991. text ed. 10.00 (*81-220-0214-5*, Pub. by Konark Pubs Pvt Ltd II) Advent Bks Div.
Ravindranath, P. K. Sharad Pawar: The Making of a Modern Maratha. (C). 1992. 14.00 (*81-85674-46-9*, Pub. by UBS Pubs Dist II) S Asia.
Ravindranathan, T. R. Bakunin & the Italians. 342p. (C). 1988. text ed. 55.00 (*0-7735-0646-2*, Pub. by McGill CN) U of Toronto Pr.
Raving Beauties Staff. In the Pink: The Raving Beauties. rev. ed. (Illus.). 128p. 1993. pap. 9.95 (*0-7043-3920-X*) InBook.
Raviola, jt. auth. see Fawcett.
Raviola, Elio. Bloom & Fawcett: A Textbook of Histology. 12th rev. ed. Fawcett, Don W., ed. (Illus.). 250p. 1993. text ed. 89.00 (*0-412-04691-1*) Chapman & Hall.
Raviola, Roberto, see Magnus, pseud..
Ravise, J. S. Tableaux Culturels de la France. (C). 1984. 75.00 (*0-85950-206-6*, Pub. by S Thornes Pubs UK) St Mut.
Ravishankar, K., jt. auth. see Burton, Dudley J.
Ravitch, jt. auth. see Steichen.
Ravitch, D. American Reader. 1992. 35.00 (*0-06-270065-0*, HarpT) HarpC.
***Ravitch, Diane.** Debating the Future of American Education. 200p. (C). Date not set. 12.95x (*0-8157-7353-6*) Brookings.
— National Standards in American Education: A Citizen's Guide. 220p. (C). 1995. 22.95x (*0-8157-7352-8*) Brookings.
— The Schools We Deserve: Reflections on the Educational Crisis of Our Time. LC 84-45303. 352p. 1987. pap. text ed. 16.00 (*0-465-07234-8*) Basic.
— Troubled Crusade: American Education 1945-1980. 384p. 1985. pap. text ed. 18.00 (*0-465-08757-4*) Basic.
Ravitch, Diane, ed. The American Reader: Words That Moved a Nation. LC 89-46553. 400p. 1991. reprint ed. pap. 14.00 (*0-06-272016-3*, Harper Ref) HarpC.
Ravitch, Diane & Thernstrom, Abigail M., eds. The Democracy Reader: Classic & Modern Speeches, Essays, Poems, Declarations, & Documents on Freedom & Human Rights Worldwide. LC 91-55393. (Illus.). 352p. 1993. pap. 13.00 (*0-06-272035-X*, Harper Ref) HarpC.
***Ravitch, Diane & Vinovskis, Maris A., eds.** Learning from the Past: What History Teaches Us about School Reform. LC 94-27015. 440p. 1994. text ed. 48.50x (*0-8018-4920-9*); pap. text ed. 16.95x (*0-8018-4921-7*) Johns Hopkins.
Ravitch, Diane, ed. see Conference on Needs & Opportunities for the Study of Educational History in New York City Staff.
Ravitch, Diane, jt. ed. see Goodenow, Ronald K.
Ravitch, Mark M. A Century of Surgery 1880-1980, 2 vols., Set. (Illus.). 1600p. 1981. text ed. 225.00 (*0-397-50479-9*, Lippincott Medical) Lippincott.
Ravitch, Mark M., ed. The Papers of Alfred Blalock, 2 Vols. (Illus.). 1966. 195.00 (*0-8018-0544-9*) Johns Hopkins.
Ravitch, Mark M. & Steichen, Felician M. Atlas of General Thoracic Surgery. (Illus.). 400p. 1988. text ed. 195.00 (*0-7216-7474-7*) Saunders.
Ravitch, Mark M., et al. The Current Practice of Surgical Stapling. LC 90-5932. (Illus.). 324p. 1991. text ed. 95.00 (*0-8121-1328-4*) Williams & Wilkins.
***Ravitch, Melech.** Night Prayers & Other Poems. Mayne, Seymour & Augenfeld, Rivka, trs. 24p. 1995. lib. bdg. 20.00 (*0-8095-4829-1*) Borgo Pr.
Ravitch, Norman. The Catholic Church & the French Nation: 1685-1985. 240p. 1990. 59.95 (*0-415-00170-6*, A4739) Routledge.
— Sword & Mitre: Government & Episcopate in France & England in the Age of Aristocracy. 1966. text ed. 35.40 (*0-686-22467-1*) Mouton.
Ravitz, Abe C. Alfred Henry Lewis. LC 78-52560. (Western Writers Ser.: No. 32). 46p. 1978. pap. 3.95 (*0-88430-056-0*) Boise St U W Writ Ser.
— David Graham Phillips. (Twayne's United States Authors Ser.). 1966. lib. bdg. 17.95 (*0-8290-0006-2*); pap. text ed. 4.95 (*0-685-42217-8*) Irvington.
— David Graham Phillips. (Twayne's United States Authors Ser.). 1966. pap. 13.95x (*0-8084-0098-3*, T96) NCUP.
— Leane Zugsmith: Thunder on the Left. LC 92-16381. 130p. 1992. pap. 6.95 (*0-7178-0702-9*) Intl Pubs Co.
— Rex Beach. (Western Writers Ser.: No. 113). (Illus.). 52p. 1994. pap. 3.95 (*0-88430-112-5*) Boise St U W Writ Ser.
Ravitz, Leonard J., Jr. Electrodynamic Man: Electromagnetic Field Measurements in Biology, Medicine, Hypnosis & Psychiatry. Russell, Edward W., ed. LC 92-46056. (Orig.). 1995. 29.99 (*0-935834-96-6*); pap. 19.95 (*0-935834-95-8*) Rainbow Books.
Raviv, Dan & Melman, Yossi. Every Spy a Prince: The Complete History of Israel's Intelligence Community. 512p. 1991. reprint ed. pap. 12.95 (*0-395-58120-6*) HM.
— Friends in Deed: Inside the U. S.-Israel Alliance. LC 93-42416. 560p. 1994. 27.95 (*0-7868-6006-5*) Hyperion.
Raviv, Dan, jt. auth. see Melman, Yossi.
Raviv, J., ed. Computer Communication Technologies for the Nineties: Proceedings of the Ninth International ICCC Conference on Computer Communication, Tel Aviv, Israel, 30 October to 3 November, 1988. 606p. 1989. 123.00 (*0-444-70539-2*, North Holland) Elsevier.
— Uses of Computers in Aiding the Disabled: Proceedings of the IFIP-IMIA Working Conference, Haifa, Israel, November 3-5, 1981. 446p. 1982. 72.00 (*0-444-86436-9*, North Holland) Elsevier.
Raviv, J., et al, eds. Computer Aided Tomography & Ultrasonics in Medicine. 320p. 1979. 56.50 (*0-444-85299-9*, North Holland) Elsevier.
Ravizza, Ken, jt. auth. see Hanson, Tom.
Ravizza, Luigi, et al, eds. Psychiatry & Advanced Technologies. LC 92-48413. 324p. 1993. 63.00 (*0-7817-0003-5*) Raven.
Ravizza, Mark, jt. auth. see Fischer, John M.
Ravizza, Mark, jt. ed. see Fischer, John M.
Ravnitzky, Yehoshua H., jt. ed. see Bialik, Hayim N.
Ravoira, LaWanda & Cherry, Andrew L., Jr. Social Bonds & Teen Pregnancy. LC 92-9821. 200p. 1992. text ed. 45.00 (*0-275-94179-5*, C4179, Praeger Pubs) Greenwood.
Ravoofs, A. A. Meet Mr. Jinnah. pap. 9.50 (*1-56744-135-1*) Kazi Pubns.
Ravosa, Mathew J. & Gomez, Anne M., eds. Ontogenic Perspectives on Primate Evolutionary Biology. (Illus.). 300p. 1993. pap. text ed. 43.00 (*0-12-583470-5*) Acad Pr.
Ravve, A. Organic Chemistry of Macromolecules: An Introductory Textbook. LC 67-17006. (Illus.). 512p. reprint ed. pap. 146.00 (*0-7837-0902-1*, 2041207) Bks Demand.
***Ravve, Abe.** Principles of Polymer Chemistry. 490p. 1995. 59.50 (*0-306-44873-4*, Plenum Pr) Plenum.
Raw, Anthony, jt. auth. see O'Toole, Christopher.
Raw, Barbara C. Anglo-Saxon Crucifixion Iconography & the Art of the Monastic Revival. (Cambridge Studies in Anglo-Saxon England: No. 1). (Illus.). 288p. (C). 1990. 79.95 (*0-521-36370-5*) Cambridge U Pr.
Raw, M., jt. auth. see Grunsell, C.
Raw, M. E. & Parkinson, T. J., eds. The Veterinary Annual Thirty-Two. (Illus.). 320p. (C). 1992. text ed. 178.95 (*0-8464-4163-2*) Beekman Pubs.
Raw, M. E., jt. ed. see Grunsell, C. S.
Raw, Mary E. & Parkinson, T. J., eds. The Veterinary Annual, No. 34. (Illus.). 256p. 1994. write for info. (*0-86542-809-3*) Blackwell Sci.
Raw, Mary-Elizabeth. The Veterinary Annual, 1991. 31th ed. Grunsell, C. S. et al, eds. (Illus.). 232p. 1991. 95.00 (*0-632-03264-2*) Blackwell Sci.
Raw, Mary-Elizabeth & Parkinson, T. J. The Veterinary Annual, No. 32. 32th ed. (Illus.). 320p. 1992. 135.00 (*0-632-03406-8*) Blackwell Sci.
Rawal, Munni. Dadabhai Naoroji: A Prophet of Indian Nationalism. 1989. 21.00 (*0-685-46917-4*, Pub. by Anmol II) S Asia.
Rawal, Narinder & Coombs, Dennis W., eds. Spinal Narcotics. (Current Management of Pain Ser.). (C). 1989. lib. bdg. 87.50 (*0-7923-0374-1*) Kluwer Ac.
Rawat, Ajay S. History of Forestry in India. (C). 1991. 44.00 (*81-85182-57-4*, Pub. by Indus Pub II) S Asia.
Rawat, Ajay S., ed. Indian Forestry: A Perspective. (C). 1993. 44.00 (*81-85182-78-7*, Pub. by Indus Pub II) S Asia.
Rawat, B. & Zhou Siyong, eds. Recent Advances in Microwave Technology (IAP) Proceedings of the 2nd International Symposium on Recent Advances in Microwave Technology, Beijing, China, 4-8 September 1989. (International Academic Publishers Ser.). 800p. 1990. 230.00 (*0-08-040184-8*, Pub. by IAP UK) Elsevier.
***Rawcliffe, Carole, tr. & intro.** Sources for the History of Medicine in Medieval England. LC 94-45554. (Documents of Practice Ser.). 1995. write for info. (*1-879288-54-0*) Medieval Inst.
Rawcliffe, D. H. Occult & Supernatural Phenomena. Orig. Title: Psychology of the Occult. (Illus.). 551p. 1987. reprint ed. pap. 10.95 (*0-486-25551-4*) Dover.
Rawcliffe, Michael. Timeline: The Welfare State. (Weighing up the Evidence Ser.). (Illus.). 72p. (J). (gr. 7 up). 1990. 19.95 (*0-7134-9806-4*, Pub. by Batsford UK) Trafalgar.
— Victorian Town Life. (How It Was Ser.). (Illus.). 48p. (YA). (gr. 7-10). Date not set. 19.95 (*0-7134-6355-4*, Pub. by Batsford UK) Trafalgar.
— Where You Live. (Changing Britain Ser.). (Illus.). 48p. (J). (gr. 6-9). 1994. 19.95 (*0-7134-6714-2*, Pub. by Batsford UK) Trafalgar.
Rawding, F. W. Gandhi. LC 79-11008. (Cambridge Introduction to World History Topic Bks.). (Illus.). 48p. (YA). (gr. 7 up). 1980. pap. 8.25 (*0-521-20715-0*) Cambridge U Pr.
— The Rebellion in India, 1857. (Cambridge Introduction to World History Topic Bks.). (Illus.). 48p. (YA). (gr. 7 up). 1977. pap. 8.25 (*0-521-20683-9*) Cambridge U Pr.
***Rawdon, Douglas S. & Cousin, Larry D.** Final Abomination. Ingram, tr. 330p. 1996. pap. 9.95 (*0-7610-0449-1*) NW Pub.
***Rawer, et al.** Off Median Phenomena & International Reference Ionosphere. (Advances in Space Research Ser.: Vol. 15, No. 2). 1994. pap. 100.00 (*0-08-042537-2*, Pergamon Pr) Elsevier.
***Rawer, K., et al, eds.** The High Latitudes in the International Reference Ionosphere. (Advances in Space Research (RJ) Ser.: Vol. 16). 186p. 1995. pap. 94.00 (*0-08-042621-2*, Pergamon Pr) Elsevier.
Rawer, Karl. Wave Propagation in the Ionosphere. LC 92-24066. (Developments in Electromagnetic Theory & Application Ser.: No. 5). 424p. (C). 1993. lib. bdg. 175.00 (*0-7923-0775-5*) Kluwer Ac.
Rawer, Karl, ed. Geophysics Three. (Encyclopedia of Physics Ser., Gruppe 10-Geophysik: Band 49, Teil 7). (Illus.). 720p. 1985. 350.00 (*0-387-11425-4*) Spr-Verlag.
Rawer, Karl & Bradley, P. A., eds. Ionospheric Informatics & Empirical Modelling. (Advances in Space Research Ser.: No. 10). (Illus.). 144p. 1990. pap. 105.00 (*0-08-040165-1*, Pergamon Pr) Elsevier.
Rawer, Karl & Cospar. Methods of Measurements & Results of Lower Ionosphere Structure: Proceedings of Symposium Constance 5-73. LC 73-94253. 1974. 197.00 (*0-08-021995-0*, Pub. by Pergamon Repr UK) Franklin.
Rawer, Karl & Piggott, W. R., eds. Development of IRI-90: Proceedings of a Workshop Held in Abingdon, UK, 7-9 August 1989. (Advances in Space Research Ser.: Vol. 10). 1991. pap. 105.00 (*0-08-040785-4*, Pergamon Pr) Elsevier.
— Enlarged Space & Ground Data Base for Ionospheric Modelling: Proceedings of the Topical Meeting of the COSPAR Interdisciplinary Scientific Commission, 28th Plenary Meeting Held in the Hague, the Netherlands, 25 June-6 July 1990. (Advances in Space Research Ser.). (Illus.). 206p. 1991. pap. 160.00 (*0-08-041166-5*, ASR 11, NO. 10, Pergamon Pr) Elsevier.
Rawer, Karl & Ramanamurty, Y. V., eds. International Reference Ionosphere - Status 1985-86: Proceedings of the URSI-COSPAR Workshop on the International Reference Ionosphere Held in Louvain-la-Neuve, Belgium, 25 October - 1st November. 138p. 1986. pap. 52.00 (*0-08-034026-1*, Pergamon Pr) Elsevier.
Rawer, Karl, et al. Ionospheric Informatics: Proceedings of an International (URSI & COSPAR Sponsored) Workshop Held in Novgorod, USSR, 25-29 May 1987. LC 83-645550. (Advances in Space Research Ser.: No. 8). (Illus.). 254p. 1988. pap. 60.00 (*0-08-036868-9*, Pergamon Pr) Elsevier.
Rawer, Karl, et al, eds. Models of the Atmosphere & Ionosphere: Proceedings of Workshops VIII & X of the COSPAR 25th Plenary Meeting held in Graz, Austria, 25 June-7 July 1984. (Illus.). 242p. 1985. pap. 54.00 (*0-08-033196-3*, Pub. by PPL UK) Elsevier.
Rawick, George P. From Sundown to Sunup: The Making of the Black Community, Vol. 11. LC 71-105986. (Contributions in Afro-American & African Studies: No. 11). 208p. 1973. pap. text ed. 14.95 (*0-8371-6747-7*, RSM, Greenwood Pr) Greenwood.

R

An Asterisk (*) at the beginning of an entry indicates that the title is appearing in BIP for the first time.

Rawick, George P., ed. The American Slave: A Composite Autobiography, 19 vols., Set. Incl. Vol. 1. LC 71-38591. 208p. 1971. text ed. 75.00 (*0-8371-6299-8*, RSM&, Greenwood Pr); Vol. 2. LC 71-38591. 1972. text ed. 75.00 (*0-8371-6300-5*, RSN&, Greenwood Pr); Vol. 3. LC 71-38591. 1972. text ed. 75.00 (*0-8371-6301-3*, RSO&, Greenwood Pr); Vol. 4. LC 71-38591. 1972. text ed. 75.00 (*0-8371-6302-1*, RSP&, Greenwood Pr); Vol. 5. LC 71-38591. 1972. text ed. 75.00 (*0-8371-6303-X*, RSQ&, Greenwood Pr); Vol. 6. LC 71-38591. 1972. text ed. 75.00 (*0-8371-6304-8*, RSR&, Greenwood Pr); Vol. 7. LC 71-38591. 1971. text ed. 75.00 (*0-8371-6305-6*, RSS&, Greenwood Pr); Vol. 8. LC 71-38591. 1972. text ed. 75.00 (*0-8371-6306-4*, RST&, Greenwood Pr); Vol. 2. LC 71-38591. 1972. text ed. 75.00 (*0-8371-6307-2*, RSU&, Greenwood Pr); Vol. 3. LC 71-38591. 1972. text ed. 75.00 (*0-8371-6308-0*, RSV&, Greenwood Pr); Vol. 4. LC 71-38591. 1972. text ed. 75.00 (*0-8371-6309-9*, RSW&, Greenwood Pr); Vol. 5. LC 71-38591. 1972. text ed. 75.00 (*0-8371-6310-2*, RSX&, Greenwood Pr); Vol. 6. LC 71-38591. 1972. text ed. 75.00 (*0-8371-6311-0*, RSY&, Greenwood Pr); Vol. 7. LC 71-38591. 1972. text ed. 75.00 (*0-8371-6312-9*, RSZ&, Greenwood Pr); Vol. 8. LC 71-38591. 1972. text ed. 75.00 (*0-8371-6313-7*, RSA&, Greenwood Pr); Vol. 9. LC 71-38591. 1972. text ed. 75.00 (*0-8371-6314-5*, RSB&, Greenwood Pr); Vol. 10. LC 71-38591. 1972. text ed. 75.00 (*0-8371-6315-3*, RSC&, Greenwood Pr); Vol. 11. LC 71-38591. 1972. text ed. 75.00 (*0-8371-6316-1*, RSD&, Greenwood Pr); Vol. 12. LC 71-38591. 1972. text ed. 75.00 (*0-8371-6317-X*, RSE&, Greenwood Pr); LC 71-38591. (Contributions in Afro-American & African Studies: No. 11). 1972. Set text ed. 495.00 (*0-8371-3314-9*, RSL & RSF, Greenwood Pr) Greenwood.

— The American Slave: A Composite Autobiography, Vols. 1-7, Vols. 1-7. Incl. Vol. 1. LC 71-38591. 208p. 1971. text ed. 75.00 (*0-8371-6299-8*, RSM&, Greenwood Pr); Vol. 2. LC 71-38591. 1972. text ed. 75.00 (*0-8371-6300-5*, RSN&, Greenwood Pr); Vol. 3. LC 71-38591. 1972. text ed. 75.00 (*0-8371-6301-3*, RSO&, Greenwood Pr); Vol. 4. LC 71-38591. 1972. text ed. 75.00 (*0-8371-6302-1*, RSP&, Greenwood Pr); Vol. 5. LC 71-38591. 1972. text ed. 75.00 (*0-8371-6303-X*, RSQ&, Greenwood Pr); Vol. 6. LC 71-38591. 1972. text ed. 75.00 (*0-8371-6304-8*, RSR&, Greenwood Pr); Vol. 7. LC 71-38591. 1971. text ed. 75.00 (*0-8371-6305-6*, RSS&, Greenwood Pr); Vol. 8. LC 71-38591. 1972. text ed. 75.00 (*0-8371-6306-4*, RST&, Greenwood Pr); Vol. 2. LC 71-38591. 1972. text ed. 75.00 (*0-8371-6307-2*, RSU&, Greenwood Pr); Vol. 3. LC 71-38591. 1972. text ed. 75.00 (*0-8371-6308-0*, RSV&, Greenwood Pr); Vol. 4. LC 71-38591. 1972. text ed. 75.00 (*0-8371-6309-9*, RSW&, Greenwood Pr); Vol. 5. LC 71-38591. 1972. text ed. 75.00 (*0-8371-6310-2*, RSX&, Greenwood Pr); Vol. 6. LC 71-38591. 1972. text ed. 75.00 (*0-8371-6311-0*, RSY&, Greenwood Pr); Vol. 7. LC 71-38591. 1972. text ed. 75.00 (*0-8371-6312-9*, RSZ&, Greenwood Pr); Vol. 8. LC 71-38591. 1972. text ed. 75.00 (*0-8371-6313-7*, RSA&, Greenwood Pr); Vol. 9. LC 71-38591. 1972. text ed. 75.00 (*0-8371-6314-5*, RSB&, Greenwood Pr); Vol. 10. LC 71-38591. 1972. text ed. 75.00 (*0-8371-6315-3*, RSC&, Greenwood Pr); Vol. 11. LC 71-38591. 1972. text ed. 75.00 (*0-8371-6316-1*, RSD&, Greenwood Pr); Vol. 12. LC 71-38591. 1972. text ed. 75.00 (*0-8371-6317-X*, RSE&, Greenwood Pr); LC 71-38591. (Contributions in Afro-American & African Studies: No. 11). 1972. Set lib. bdg. 250.00 (*0-685-42146-5*, Greenwood Pr) Greenwood.

— The American Slave: A Composite Autobiography, Vols. 8-19, Vols. 8-19. Incl. Vol. 1. LC 71-38591. 208p. 1971. text ed. 75.00 (*0-8371-6299-8*, RSM&, Greenwood Pr); Vol. 2. LC 71-38591. 1972. text ed. 75.00 (*0-8371-6300-5*, RSN&, Greenwood Pr); Vol. 3. LC 71-38591. 1972. text ed. 75.00 (*0-8371-6301-3*, RSO&, Greenwood Pr); Vol. 4. LC 71-38591. 1972. text ed. 75.00 (*0-8371-6302-1*, RSP&, Greenwood Pr); Vol. 5. LC 71-38591. 1972. text ed. 75.00 (*0-8371-6303-X*, RSQ&, Greenwood Pr); Vol. 6. LC 71-38591. 1972. text ed. 75.00 (*0-8371-6304-8*, RSR&, Greenwood Pr); Vol. 7. LC 71-38591. 1971. text ed. 75.00 (*0-8371-6305-6*, RSS&, Greenwood Pr); Vol. 8. LC 71-38591. 1972. text ed. 75.00 (*0-8371-6306-4*, RST&, Greenwood Pr); Vol. 2. LC 71-38591. 1972. text ed. 75.00 (*0-8371-6307-2*, RSU&, Greenwood Pr); Vol. 3. LC 71-38591. 1972. text ed. 75.00 (*0-8371-6308-0*, RSV&, Greenwood Pr); Vol. 4. LC 71-38591. 1972. text ed. 75.00 (*0-8371-6309-9*, RSW&, Greenwood Pr); Vol. 5. LC 71-38591. 1972. text ed. 75.00 (*0-8371-6310-2*, RSX&, Greenwood Pr); Vol. 6. LC 71-38591. 1972. text ed. 75.00 (*0-8371-6311-0*, RSY&, Greenwood Pr); Vol. 7. 1972. text ed. 75.00 (*0-8371-6312-9*, RSZ&, Greenwood Pr); Vol. 8. LC 71-38591. 1972. text ed. 75.00 (*0-8371-6313-7*, RSA&, Greenwood Pr); Vol. 9. LC 71-38591. 1972. text ed. 75.00 (*0-8371-6314-5*, RSB&, Greenwood Pr); Vol. 10. LC 71-38591. 1972. text ed. 75.00 (*0-8371-6315-3*, RSC&, Greenwood Pr); Vol. 11. LC 71-38591. 1972. text ed. 75.00 (*0-8371-6316-1*, RSD&, Greenwood Pr); Vol. 12. LC 71-38591. 1972. text ed. 75.00 (*0-8371-6317-X*, RSE&, Greenwood Pr); LC 71-38591. (Contributions in Afro-American & African Studies: No. 11). 1972. Set lib. bdg. 445.00 (*0-685-42147-3*, Greenwood Pr) Greenwood.

— The American Slave: A Composite Autobiography, Supplement Series 1, 12 vols., Set. Incl. Vol. 1. Alabama Supplement. LC 77-88899. 1978. text ed. 69.50 (*0-8371-9761-9*, RAA/01, Greenwood Pr); Vol. 2. Arkansas Collected Supplement. LC 77-88899. 1978. text ed. 69.50 (*0-8371-9762-7*, RAA/02, Greenwood Pr); Vol. 3. Georgia, Supplement 1. LC 77-88899. 1978. text ed. 69.50 (*0-8371-9763-5*, RAA/03, Greenwood Pr); Vol. 4. Georgia, Supplement 2. LC 77-88899. 1978. text ed. 69.50 (*0-8371-9764-3*, RAA/04, Greenwood Pr); Vol. 5. Ind-Ohio Supplement. LC 77-88899. 1978. text ed. 69.50 (*0-8371-9765-1*, RAA/05, Greenwood Pr); Vol. 6. Mississippi, Supplement 1. LC 77-88899. 1978. text ed. 69.50 (*0-8371-9766-X*, RAA/06, Greenwood Pr); Vol. 7. Mississippi, Supplement 2. LC 77-88899. 1978. text ed. 69.50 (*0-8371-9767-8*, RAA/07, Greenwood Pr); Vol. 8. Mississippi, Supplement 3. LC 77-88899. 1978. text ed. 69.50 (*0-8371-9768-6*, RAA/08, Greenwood Pr); Vol. 9. Mississippi, Supplement 4. LC 77-88899. 1978. text ed. 69.50 (*0-8371-9769-4*, RAA/09, Greenwood Pr); Vol. 10. Mississippi, Supplement 5. LC 77-88899. 1978. text ed. 69.50 (*0-8371-9770-8*, RAA/10, Greenwood Pr); Vol. 11. North Carolina-South Carolina Supplement. LC 77-88899. 1978. text ed. 69.50 (*0-8371-9771-6*, RAA/11, Greenwood Pr); Vol. 12. Oklahoma Supplement. LC 77-88899. 1978. text ed. 69.50 (*0-8371-9772-4*, RAA/12, Greenwood Pr); LC 77-88899. (Contributions in Afro-American & African Studies: No. 35). 1978. Set text ed. 795.00 (*0-8371-9756-2*, RAA/, Greenwood Pr) Greenwood.

— The American Slave: A Composite Autobiography, Supplement Series 2, 10 vols., Set. Incl. Vol. 1. LC 79-12456. 1979. text ed. 69.50 (*0-313-21979-6*, RAB/01, Greenwood Pr); Vol. 2. LC 79-12456. 1979. text ed. 69.50 (*0-313-21980-X*, RAB/02, Greenwood Pr); Vol. 3. LC 79-12456. 1979. text ed. 69.50 (*0-313-21981-8*, RAB/03, Greenwood Pr); Vol. 4. LC 79-12456. 1979. text ed. 69.50 (*0-313-21982-6*, RAB/04, Greenwood Pr); Vol. 5. LC 79-12456. 1979. text ed. 69.50 (*0-313-21983-4*, RAB/05, Greenwood Pr); Vol. 6. LC 79-12456. 1979. text ed. 69.50 (*0-313-21984-2*, RAB/06, Greenwood Pr); Vol. 7. LC 79-12456. 1979. text ed. 69.50 (*0-313-21985-0*, RAB/07, Greenwood Pr); Vol. 8. LC 79-12456. 1979. text ed. 69.50 (*0-313-21986-9*, RAB/08, Greenwood Pr); Vol. 9. LC 79-12456. 1979. text ed. 69.50 (*0-313-21987-7*, RAB/09, Greenwood Pr); Vol. 10. LC 79-12456. 1979. text ed. 69.50 (*0-313-21988-5*, RAB/10, Greenwood Pr); LC 79-12456. (Contributions in Afro-American & African Studies: No. 49). 1980. Set text ed. 675.00 (*0-313-21423-9*, RAB/, Greenwood Pr) Greenwood.

Rawicz, Leonard, jt. auth. see Nash, Ralph C., Jr.

Rawicz, Slavomir. The Long Walk. 224p. 1988. pap. 12.95 (*0-941130-86-X*) Lyons & Burford.

Rawidowicz, Simon. Israel: The Ever-Dying People & Other Essays. Ravid, Benjamin, ed. & tr. by. LC 84-46115. 248p. 1987. 37.50 (*0-8386-3253-X*) Fairleigh Dickinson.

Rawidowicz, Simon, ed. The Chicago Pinkas. 319p. (ENG & HEB.). (C). 1952. 7.95 (*0-935982-05-1*, SR-01) Spertus Coll.

***Rawksi, Thomas G., ed.** Economics & the Historian. LC 94-24931. 1996. 45.00 (*0-520-07268-5*) U CA Pr.

Rawle, Graham. Wonder Book of Fun. 1994. pap. 11.95 (*0-15-600094-6*) HarBrace.

Rawle, Tim. Cambridge Architecture. (Illus.). 224p. 1993. pap. 29.95 (*0-233-98818-1*, Pub. by A Deutsch UK) Trafalgar.

Rawle, William. View of the Constitution of the United States of America. LC 70-109548. (American Constitutional & Legal History Ser). 1970. reprint ed. lib. bdg. 39.50 (*0-306-71902-9*) Da Capo.

Rawlence, G. Jane Austen. LC 74-39869. (Jane Austen Ser.: No. 69). 1972. reprint ed. lib. bdg. 49.95 (*0-8383-1405-8*) M S G Haskell Hse.

Rawles, Beverly A. Human Resource Management in Small Libraries. LC 81-20834. 136p. 1982. 27.50 (*0-208-01966-9*, Lib Prof Pubns); pap. 21.00 (*0-208-01950-2*, Lib Prof Pubns) Shoe String.

Rawles, J. Atrial Fibrillation. (Illus.). xii, 243p. 1991. 105.00 (*0-387-19699-4*) Spr-Verlag.

Rawles, Jess, ed. The House That Jack Built. (Illus.). 32p. (J). 1994. pap. 3.95 (*1-879384-24-8*) Cypress Hse.

Rawles, John. Political Liberalism. 401p. (C). 1993. 29.95 (*0-231-05248-0*) Col U Pr.

Rawles, William A. Centralizing Tendencies in the Administration of Indiana. (Columbia University. Studies in the Social Sciences: No. 44). 1968. reprint ed. 24.50 (*0-404-51044-2*) AMS Pr.

***Rawley, Donald.** Duende: Poems. LC 94-22714. 1994. pap. 13.95 (*0-941749-32-0*) Black Tie Pr.

— Malibu Stories. LC 91-2465. 68p. (Orig.). 1991. pap. 12.50 (*0-941749-23-1*) Black Tie Pr.

— Mecca. LC 91-10123. 108p. (Orig.). 1991. pap. 12.95 (*0-941749-24-X*) Black Tie Pr.

— Steaming. LC 93-19965. 1993. pap. 12.50 (*0-941749-30-4*) Black Tie Pr.

Rawley, James A. Secession: The Disruption of the American Republic, 1844-1861. LC 89-2505. (Anvil Ser.). 276p. (Orig.). 1990. pap. 13.50 (*0-89464-249-9*) Krieger.

— Turning Points of the Civil War. LC 89-4873. xvi, 230p. 1989. pap. 9.95 (*0-8032-8935-9*, Bison Books) U of Nebr Pr.

Rawley, James A., ed. Lincoln & Civil War Politics. LC 77-8812. (American Problem Studies). 136p. 1977. reprint ed. pap. text ed. 9.50 (*0-88275-576-5*) Krieger.

Rawley, Michael. Book. (Illus.). 128p. 1982. 9.95 (*0-938580-00-0*) Please Pr.

Rawling, Bill. Surviving Trench Warfare: Technology & the Canadian Corps, 1914-1918. 320p. 1992. 50.00 (*0-8020-5017-4*); pap. 19.95 (*0-8020-6002-1*) U of Toronto Pr.

Rawlings, C., jt. ed. see Craig, I.

Rawlings, C., jt. ed. see Solomon, E.

Rawlings, C. J., jt. ed. see Bishop, M. J.

Rawlings, Charles A. Electrocardiography: Biophysical Measurements. 129p. (C). 1991. 28.00 (*0-9627449-1-3*) SpaceLabs.

Rawlings, Clarence A. Heartworm Disease in Dogs & Cats. (Illus.). 329p. 1986. text ed. 45.50 (*0-7216-1221-0*) Saunders.

Rawlings, Edna I. & Carter, Dianne K. Psychotherapy for Women: Treatment Toward Equality. (Illus.). 500p. 1977. 55.95 (*0-398-03584-9*) C C Thomas.

— Psychotherapy for Women: Treatment Toward Equality. (Illus.). 500p. 1977. pap. 33.95 (*0-398-06338-9*) C C Thomas.

Rawlings, Edwin. Born to Fly: The Story of General Edwin Rawlings. LC 87-82697. (Illus.). 309p. (C). 1987. 16.95 (*0-9619320-0-7*) Great Way Pub.

Rawlings, Eleanor, ed. Godey Costume Plates in Color for Decoupage & Framing. (Illus.). 1980. pap. 4.95 (*0-486-23879-2*) Dover.

Rawlings, Eleanor H., ed. Audubon's Birds in Color for Decoupage. LC 77-70050. (Pictorial Archive Ser.). (Illus.). 1977. pap. 4.95 (*0-486-23492-4*) Dover.

— The Cornucopia of Design & Illustration for Decoupage & Other Arts & Crafts. (Illus.). 160p. (Orig.). 1984. pap. 8.95 (*0-486-24486-5*) Dover.

— Decoupage: The Big Picture Sourcebook. LC 75-11080. (Pictorial Archive Ser.). (Illus.). 176p. 1975. pap. 8.50 (*0-486-23182-8*) Dover.

— Old English Country Illustrations: For Decoupage & Other Crafts. LC 77-70051. (Pictorial Archive Ser.). (Illus.). 1977. pap. 4.95 (*0-486-23491-6*) Dover.

— One Thousand & One Scrolls, Ornaments & Borders: Ready-to-Use Illustrations for Decoupage & Other Crafts. (Illus.). 1979. pap. 5.95 (*0-486-23795-8*) Dover.

Rawlings, Ellen. A Convenient Marriage. 208p. (Orig.). 1993. pap. 3.99 (*1-55773-918-8*) Diamond.

Rawlings, Hunter R. The Structure of Thucydides' History. LC 80-8572. 293p. reprint ed. pap. 83.60 (*0-8357-7898-3*, 2036317) Bks Demand.

***Rawlings, James B., ed.** Chemical Engineering Faculties, 1994-1995. 198p. 1995. pap. 70.00 (*0-8169-0654-8*, D-29) Am Inst Chem Eng.

Rawlings, John O. Applied Regression Analysis: A Research Tool. LC 88-20638. 553p. (C). 1988. text ed. 62.95 (*0-534-09246-2*) Intl Thomson.

Rawlings, Joseph. SCM for Network Development Environments. 1993. text ed. 40.00 (*0-07-051101-2*) McGraw.

***Rawlings, Linda, ed.** Dear General: The Private Letters of Annie E. Kennedy & John Bidwell, 1866-1868. LC 93-74235. (Illus.). 212p. 1994. text ed. 19.95 (*0-941925-12-9*) Cal Parks Rec.

Rawlings, Louisa. Scarlet Woman. (Historical Ser.). 1993. mass mkt. 3.99 (*0-373-28794-1*, 1-28794-5) Harlequin Bks.

Rawlings, Margaret, tr. see Racine, Jean B.

Rawlings, Marjorie. South Moon Under. 23.95 (*0-89190-773-4*, Am Repr) Amereon Ltd.

Rawlings, Marjorie K. Cross Creek. 21.95 (*0-8488-0700-6*) Amereon Ltd.

— Cross Creek. (Illus.). 384p. 1987. pap. 5.95 (*0-02-023820-7*, Collier S&S) S&S Trade.

— Cross Creek Cookery. LC 42-25465. 256p. 1971. reprint ed. pap. 11.00 (*0-684-71876-6*, Scribners) S&S Trade.

— Golden Apples. 23.95 (*0-8488-0701-4*) Amereon Ltd.

— The Marjorie Rawlings Reader. 504p. 1989. reprint ed. lib. bdg. 19.95 (*0-935259-05-8*) San Marco Bk.

— The Secret River. 3rd ed. (Illus.). 57p. (J). (gr. 3-6). 1987. reprint ed. lib. bdg. 12.95 (*0-935259-02-3*) San Marco Bk.

— Short Stories by Marjorie Kinnan Rawlings. Tarr, Rodger L., ed. LC 93-30649. (Illus.). 392p. (C). 1994. lib. bdg. 44.95 (*0-8130-1252-X*); pap. 24.95 (*0-8130-1253-8*) U Press Fla.

— Sojourner. 22.95 (*0-8488-0616-6*) Amereon Ltd.

— The Sojourner. LC 90-27830. 336p. 1991. reprint ed. 24.95 (*0-87797-228-1*) Cherokee.

— When the Whippoorwill. 21.95 (*0-89190-686-X*, Am Repr) Amereon Ltd.

— The Yearling. LC 85-40301. (Scribner's Illustrated Classics Ser.). (Illus.). 416p. (J). 1985. text ed. 25.00 (*0-684-18461-3*, C Scribner Sons Young) S&S Childrens.

— The Yearling. 2nd ed. LC 86-20743. (Illus.). 448p. (YA). (gr. 5 up). 1988. reprint ed. pap. 5.95 (*0-02-044931-3*, Collier Bks Young) S&S Childrens.

— The Yearling. 250p. (YA). 1991. reprint ed. lib. bdg. 19.95 (*0-89966-841-0*) Buccaneer Bks.

Rawlings, Maurice. Beyond Death's Door. 1991. mass mkt. 4.99 (*0-553-22970-2*) Bantam.

Rawlings, Paul. Fade to Black. (Crime Court Mystery Ser.). 240p. (Orig.). 1986. pap. 2.95 (*0-8439-5003-X*) Dorchester Pub Co.

Rawlings, Peter, ed. Critical Essays on Henry James. (Critical Thoughts Ser.: Vol. 5). 460p. 1993. 55.95 (*0-85967-953-5*, Pub. by Scolar Pr UK) Ashgate Pub Co.

Rawlings, Peter, ed. see James, Henry.

Rawlings, Philip. Drunks, Whores & Idle Apprentices: Criminal Biographies of the Eighteenth Century. LC 91-46370. 272p. 1992. 79.95 (*0-415-05056-1*, A7964) Routledge.

Rawlings, Richard, jt. auth. see Harlow, Carol.

Rawlings, Shirley. Whippets: An Owners Companion. (Illus.). 1992. 39.95 (*1-85223-279-X*, Pub. by Crowood Pr UK) Trafalgar.

Rawlings, Stuart, tr. see Cayer, Marc.

Rawlings, Stuart, jt. auth. see Wolf, Juri.

Rawlingson, F. Chinese Ethical Ideals: A Study of the Ethical Values in China's Literary, Social & Religious Life. 1972. lib. bdg. 79.95 (*0-87968-551-4*) Krishna Pr.

Rawlins. Comp Package of Rawlins Mental Health-Psychiatric. 3rd ed. 1993. write for info. (*0-8016-7359-3*) Mosby Yr Bk.

— Text - Clinical Manual Package. 2nd ed. 1992. 67.95 (*0-8016-7360-7*) Mosby Yr Bk.

— What? (C). 1995. text ed. write for info. (*0-7167-8279-0*) W H Freeman.

Rawlins, Bert J. The Parish Churches & Nonconformist Chapels of Wales: Their Records & Where to Find Them, Vol. 1: Includes: Cardigan, Carmarthen & Pembroke Counties. (Illus.). 648p. 1987. pap. text ed. 28.95 (*0-685-24267-6*) Celtic Heritage Pub.

Rawlins, Bruce, jt. auth. see Rawlins, David.

Rawlins, C. L. Sky's Witness. 1994. pap. 12.95 (*0-8050-3208-8*) H Holt & Co.

— Sky's Witness: A Year in Wyoming's Wind River Range. LC 92-8698. 336p. 1993. 23.95 (*0-8050-1597-3*, J Macrae Bks) H Holt & Co.

Rawlins, C. L., jt. auth. see Dorman, L. S.

Rawlins, Carol. The Grand Canyon. (Wonders of the World Ser.). (Illus.). 64p. (J). (gr. 5-8). 1994. lib. bdg. 24.26 (*0-8114-6364-8*) Raintree Steck-V.

Rawlins, Claudia. Business Communications. LC 92-54688. (Outline Ser.). 256p. 1993. pap. 12.00 (*0-06-467155-0*, Harper Ref) HarpC.

— Introduction to Management. (College Outline Ser.). 464p. (Orig.). (C). 1992. pap. 12.00 (*0-06-467127-5*, Harper Ref) HarpC.

Rawlins, David & Rawlins, Bruce. Protect Yourself Against Crime: Important Hints for Prevention of Crime Against Children, Family, Belongings, Yourself. 2nd ed. (Illus.). 208p. 1989. reprint ed. pap. 9.95 (*0-936417-19-6*) Axelrod Pub.

***Rawlins, Debbi.** Marriage Incorporated: (In Name Only) (American Romance Ser.). 1995. mass mkt. 3.50 (*0-373-16580-3*, 1-16580-3) Harlequin Bks.

***Rawlins, Duane.** More Than a Father: Breaking Down the Barriers to Intimacy with God. 132p. (Orig.). 1993. pap. 7.99 (*1-883002-00-1*) Emerald WA.

Rawlins, George & Rich, Jillian. Look, Listen & Trust: A Framework for Learning Through Drama. LC 91-51056. 192p. (Orig.). 1992. pap. 17.00 (*0-88734-618-9*) Players Pr.

Rawlins, Gregory J. Compared to What? An Introduction to the Analysis of Algorithms. LC 91-30850. 536p. (C). 1995. text ed. 50.95 (*0-7167-8243-X*, Computer Sci Pr) W H Freeman.

— Foundations of Genetic Algorithms. 1991. 45.95 (*1-55860-170-8*) Morgan Kaufmann.

Rawlins, Jack. Demon Prince: The Dissonant Worlds of Jack Vance. LC 81-21600. (Milford Series: Popular Writers of Today: Popular Writers of Today: Vol. 40). 104p. 1986. lib. bdg. 25.00x (*0-89370-163-7*); pap. 15.00 (*0-89370-263-3*) Borgo Pr.

Rawlins, Jack P. The Writer's Way, 2 Vols. 2nd ed. (C). 1991. pap. 27.16 (*0-395-43226-X*) HM.

Rawlins, John C., jt. auth. see Fulton, Stanley R.

Rawlins, LeeAnn. Loving Your Husband for Life. LC 88-64189. 112p. (C). 1989. pap. 5.99 (*0-88419-232-6*, Creation Hse) Strang Comms Co.

Rawlins, M. D., jt. ed. see Wilkinson, G. R.

Rawlins, Nancy V. Silent Rain: A Search for the Child Within. 232p. 1993. 14.95 (*1-879908-04-2*) Milton Pub.

Rawlins, Richard G. & Kessler, Matt J., eds. The Cayo Santiago Macaques: History, Behavior, & Biology. LC 86-19616. (Primatology Ser.). 306p. (Orig.). (C). 1986. 74.50 (*0-88706-135-4*); pap. 24.95 (*0-88706-136-2*) State U NY Pr.

Rawlins, Ruth P. Clinical Manual of Psychiatric Nursing. 2nd ed. LC 92-12910. 401p. 1992. spiral bd. 27.95 (*0-8016-6333-4*) Mosby Yr Bk.

Rawlins, Ruth P., et al, eds. Mental Health - Psychiatric Nursing: A Holistic Life-Cycle Approach. 3rd ed. LC 92-49347. 960p. 1992. 49.95 (*0-8016-6331-8*) Mosby Yr Bk.

Rawlins, W. H., jt. auth. see Kerruish, C. M.

Rawlins, William K. Friendship Matters: Communication, Dialectics, & the Life Course. (Communication & Social Order Ser.). 320p. 1992. lib. bdg. 46.95 (*0-202-30403-5*); pap. text ed. 21.95 (*0-202-30404-3*) Aldine de Gruyter.

Rawlins, Winifred. If Flowers of Kindness Bloom: Poems. LC 91-62505. 52p. 1991. pap. 4.50 (*0-938875-27-2*) Pittenbruach Pr.

— The Inner Islands. (C). 1953. pap. 3.00 (*0-87574-073-1*) Pendle Hill.

— Occasions for Joy: Poems. LC 95-67768. 49p. 1995. pap. 4.50 (*0-938875-34-5*) Pittenbruach Pr.

Rawlinson, David, ed. The Oxford Book of Friendship. 384p. 1992. pap. 13.95 (*0-19-282967-X*) OUP.

Rawlinson, David, jt. ed. see Enright, D. J.

Rawlinson, G., tr. see Herodotus.

Rawlinson, Geore. Phoenicia. LC 70-39206. (Select Bibliographies Reprint Ser.). 1977. reprint ed. 30.95 (*0-8369-6808-5*) Ayer.

Rawlinson, George. The Religions of the Ancient World. reprint ed. spiral bd. 7.70 (*0-7873-0709-2*) Mokelumne.

— Reyes de Israel & Juda: Kings of Israel & Judah. (SPA.). 6.95 (*84-7645-072-9*, 223131, Pub. by Edit Clie SP) TSELF.

— Vida y los Tiempos de Moises: Life & Times of Moses. (SPA.). 6.95 (*84-7645-080-X*, 223142, Pub. by Edit Clie SP) TSELF.

Rawlinson, George, tr. see Herodotus.

Rawlinson, Graham, jt. auth. see Brown, Sally.

R

An Asterisk (*) at the beginning of an entry indicates that the title is appearing in BIP for the first time.

Rawlinson, H. Site Surveying & Levelling: Level 2. LC 81-8122. (Longman Technician Series, Construction & Civil Engineering). (Illus.). 173p. reprint ed. pap. 49.40 (*0-685-20303-4*, 2030342) Bks Demand.

Rawlinson, H. G. Intercourse Between India & the Western World: From the Earliest Times to the Fall of Rome. (C). 1992. 20.00 (*81-85565-06-6*, Pub. by Uppal Pub Hse II) S Asia.

Rawlinson, Hugh G. Bactria: The History of a Forgotten Empire. LC 77-93189. reprint ed. 32.50 (*0-404-05227-4*) AMS Pr.

— Makers of India. LC 77-134126. (Essay Index Reprints - Living Names Ser.). 1977. reprint ed. 15.95 (*0-8369-2251-4*) Ayer.

Rawlinson, Hugh G., ed. see Hall, Basil.

Rawlinson, J. Cruisers. (Sea Power Library). (Illus.). 48p. (J). (gr. 3-8). 1989. lib. bdg. 18.60 (*0-86625-085-9*) Rourke Corp.

— Hunter-Killer Submarines. (Sea Power Library). (Illus.). 48p. (J). (gr. 3-8). 1989. 13.95 (*0-685-58644-8*); lib. bdg. 18.60 (*0-86625-086-7*) Rourke Corp.

— Nuclear Carriers. (Sea Power Library). (Illus.). 48p. (J). (gr. 3-8). 1989. 13.95 (*0-685-58646-4*); lib. bdg. 18.60 (*0-86625-084-0*) Rourke Corp.

— Space to Seabed. (Great Adventure Ser.). (Illus.). 32p. (J). (gr. 4 up). 1988. 12.95 (*0-685-58292-2*); lib. bdg. 17.27 (*0-86592-872-X*) Rourke Corp.

— Titanic. (Great Adventure Ser.). (Illus.). 32p. (J). (gr. 4 up). 1988. lib. bdg. 17.27 (*0-86592-873-8*); lib. bdg. 12. 95 (*0-685-58290-6*) Rourke Corp.

Rawlinson, Jean, ed. see Nijinska, Bronislava.

Rawlinson, Jean, tr. see Nijinska, Bronislava.

Rawlinson, John L. China's Struggle for Naval Development, 1839-1895. LC 66-10127. (Harvard East Asian Ser.: No. 25). 329p. reprint ed. pap. 93.80 (*0-7837-3962-1*, 2043791) Bks Demand.

— Rawlinson, The Recorder & China's Revolution: A Topical Biography of Frank Joseph Rawlinson, 1871-1937, 2 vols., Vol. 1. (Illus.). 520p. 1991. 39.50 (*0-940121-12-3*) Cross Cultural Pubns.

— Rawlinson, The Recorder & China's Revolution: A Topical Biography of Frank Joseph Rawlinson, 1871-1937, 2 vols., Vol. 2. (Illus.). 520p. 1991. 39.50 (*0-940121-13-1*) Cross Cultural Pubns.

Rawlinson, Jon, jt. auth. see Walmer, Max.

Rawlinson, Jorge. Esdras y Nehemias: Ezra & Nehemiah. (SPA.). 6.50 (*84-7645-079-6*, 223141, Pub. by Edit Clie SP) TSELF.

Rawlinson, Michael, jt. auth. see Wells, Peter.

***Rawlinson, Peter.** Hatred & Contempt. large type ed. 528p. 1995. 23.95 (*0-7089-3247-9*) Ulverscroft.

Rawlinson, W. & Cornwell-Kelly, M. P. Essentials of EEC Law. (Waterlow Practitioner's Library). 400p. (Orig.). 1990. pap. 39.95 (*0-08-033103-3*, Waterlow) Macmillan.

— European Community Law. (Waterlow Practitioner's Library). 256p. 1990. 35.95 (*0-685-32856-2*, Pergamon Pr) Elsevier.

***Rawlinson, William & Cornwell-Kelly, Malachy P.** European Community Law Vol. 1. 2nd ed. 1994. pap. text ed. 80.00 (*0-421-50320-3*, Pub. by Sweet & Maxwll) W W Gaunt.

Rawls, Bea O. Drugs & Anger. LC 94-1906. (Drug Abuse Prevention Library). (YA). (gr. 5 up). 1994. 15.95 (*0-8239-1706-1*) Rosen Group.

Rawls, Bea O. & Johnson, Gwen. Drugs & Where to Turn. Rosen, Ruth, ed. (Drug Abuse Prevention Library). (YA). (gr. 7-12). 1993. 15.95 (*0-8239-1466-6*) Rosen Group.

Rawls, Greg, ed. Computers in Health & Safety. 255p. 1990. 40.00 (*0-932627-39-0*) Am Indus Hygiene.

Rawls, J. James. California Interpretive History. 6th ed. 1993. pap. text ed. write for info. (*0-07-004269-1*) McGraw.

Rawls, James J. Indians of California: The Changing Image. LC 83-21710. (Illus.). 312p. 1986. reprint ed. pap. 14.95 (*0-8061-2020-7*) U of Okla Pr.

— Never Turn Back: Father Serra's Mission. LC 92-12814. (Stories of America Ser.). (Illus.). 52p. (J). (gr. 2-5). 1992. lib. bdg. 21.36 (*0-8114-7221-3*) Raintree Steck-V.

— New Directions in California History: A Book of Readings. 320p. 1988. pap. text ed. write for info. (*0-07-051253-1*) McGraw.

Rawls, James J., ed. see Egger-Bovet, Howard & Smith-Baranzini, Marlene.

Rawls, James L., ed. see Egger-Bovet, Howard & Smith-Baranzini, Marlene.

***Rawls, Jim.** California Dreaming: More Stories from Dr. History. 1994. pap. 13.95 (*0-07-052029-1*) McGraw.

— Dame Shirley & the Gold Rush. LC 92-18083. (Stories of America Ser.). (Illus.). (J). (gr. 2-5). 1992. lib. bdg. 21.36 (*0-8114-7222-1*) Raintree Steck-V.

— Dr. History's Whiz Bang: Favorite Stories of California's Past. LC 91-27640. (Illus.). 118p. (Orig.). 1991. pap. 9.95 (*0-935382-77-1*) Tioga Pub Co.

Rawls, John. Justice As Fairness. (Reprints in Philosophy Ser.). (C). 1991. reprint ed. pap. text ed. 2.50 (*0-8290-2600-2*, F-174) Irvington.

— Theory of Justice. LC 73-168432. (Illus.). 607p. 1971. 38. 00 (*0-674-88010-2*); pap. text ed. 17.95 (*0-674-88014-5*) Belknap Pr.

— Two Concepts of Rules. (Reprints in Philosophy Ser.). (C). 1991. reprint ed. pap. text ed. 1.00 (*0-8290-2601-0*) Irvington.

***Rawls, Rod.** AutoLISP Programming: Principles & Techniques. LC 95-8369. 500p. 1995. text ed. 33.00 (*1-56637-196-1*) Goodheart.

Rawls, Walter C., Jr., jt. auth. see Davis, Albert R.

Rawls, Walton. Disney Dons Dogtags: The Best of Disney Military Insignia from World War II. 96p. 1992. 21.95 (*1-55859-401-9*) Abbeville Pr.

— Tiny Folios: Currier & Ives' America. (Illus.). 320p. 1991. 10.95 (*1-55859-229-6*) Abbeville Pr.

Rawls, Wilson. Summer of the Monkeys. (J). (gr. 4-7). 1992. mass mkt. 4.50 (*0-553-29818-6*) Bantam.

— Summer of the Monkeys. LC 75-32295. (J). 1989. pap. 14.95 (*0-385-11450-8*) Doubleday.

— Where the Red Fern Grows. (J). 1984. mass mkt. 4.50 (*0-553-27429-5*) Bantam.

— Where the Red Fern Grows. (YA). (gr. 7 up). 1992. 16.95 (*0-553-08900-5*, Starfire) Bantam.

***Rawlyk, G. A.** The Canada Fire: Radical Evangelicalism in British North America, 1775-1812. 272p. 1994. 49.95 (*0-7735-1221-7*, Pub. by McGill CN); pap. 18.95 (*0-7735-1277-2*, Pub. by McGill CN) U of Toronto Pr.

Rawlyk, G. A., ed. Canadian Baptists & Christian Higher Education. 142p. (C). 1988. text ed. 39.95 (*0-7735-0677-2*, Pub. by McGill CN); pap. text ed. 17.95 (*0-7735-0684-5*, Pub. by McGill CN) U of Toronto Pr.

Rawlyk, George & Noll, Mark A., eds. Amazing Grace: Evangelicalism in Australia, Britain, Canada, & the United States. LC 92-331996. 416p. (Orig.). 1994. pap. 19.99 (*0-8010-7772-9*) Baker Bk.

— Amazing Grace: Evangelicalism in Australia, Britain, Canada, & the United States. (McGill-Queen's Studies in the History of Religion). 416p. (Orig.). (C). 1994. 44.95 (*0-7735-1207-1*, Pub. by McGill CN); pap. text ed. 22.95 (*0-7735-1214-4*, Pub. by McGill CN) U of Toronto Pr.

Rawlyk, George A. Champions of the Truth: Fundamentalism, Modernism, & the Maritime Baptists. 136p. (C). 1990. 37.95 (*0-7735-0760-4*, Pub. by McGill CN); pap. 17.95 (*0-7735-0783-3*, Pub. by McGill CN) U of Toronto Pr.

— Ravished by the Spirit: Religious Revivals, Baptists, & Henry Alline. 190p. 1984. 39.95 (*0-7735-0439-7*, Pub. by McGill CN); pap. 16.95 (*0-7735-0440-0*, Pub. by McGill CN) U of Toronto Pr.

— Wrapped up in God: A Study of Several Canadian Revivals & Revivalists. 184p. 1988. pap. 15.95 (*0-7735-1131-8*, Pub. by McGill CN) U of Toronto Pr.

Rawlyk, George A., ed. The Canadian Protestant Experience, 1760-1990. 254p. 1990. pap. 19.95 (*0-7735-1132-6*, Pub. by McGill CN) U of Toronto Pr.

— Henry Alline: Selected Writings. (Sources of American Spirituality Ser.: Vol. 8). 384p. 1987. 19.95 (*0-8091-0396-6*) Paulist Pr.

Rawn, J. David, jt. auth. see Kask, Uno.

Rawn, Melanie. Dragon Prince. (Dragon Prince Ser.: No. 1). 576p. 1988. reprint ed. mass mkt. 6.99 (*0-88677-450-0*) DAW Bks.

— The Dragon Token. (Dragon Star Ser.: Bk. 2). 656p. 1993. mass mkt. 5.99 (*0-88677-542-6*) DAW Bks.

— Exiles, Vol. 1. 480p. 1994. 20.95 (*0-88677-619-8*) DAW Bks.

— Skybowl. (Dragon Star Ser.: Bk. 3). 776p. 1994. mass mkt. 5.99 (*0-88677-595-7*) DAW Bks.

— The Star Scroll. (Dragon Prince Ser.: Bk. 2). 592p. 1989. reprint ed. mass mkt. 6.99 (*0-88677-349-0*) DAW Bks.

— Stronghold. (Dragon Star Ser.: Bk. 1). 486p. 1990. 21.95 (*0-88677-440-3*) DAW Bks.

— Stronghold. (Dragon Star Ser.: Bk. 1). 592p. 1991. mass mkt. 5.99 (*0-88677-482-9*) DAW Bks.

— Sunrunner's Fire. (Dragon Prince Ser.: Bk. 3). 480p. 1990. mass mkt. 5.99 (*0-88677-403-9*) DAW Bks.

Rawnsley, Allan, ed. Manual of Industrial Marketing Research: Prepared under the Auspices of the Industrial Marketing Research Association. LC 77-7272. (Illus.). 206p. reprint ed. pap. 58.80 (*0-8357-3082-4*, 2039339) Bks Demand.

Rawnsley, Ellis. Roses. (Illus.). 48p. 1984. 20.00 (*0-88014-070-4*) Mosaic Pr OH.

Rawnsley, H. Memories of Tennysons. LC 72-675. (Studies in Tennyson: No. 27). 1972. reprint ed. lib. bdg. 64.95 (*0-8383-1417-1*) M S G Haskell Hse.

Rawnsley, Howard M., jt. auth. see Mitruka, Brij M.

Rawnsley, J., jt. auth. see Robinson, P.

Rawnsley, J. H., jt. auth. see Burstall, F. E.

***Rawnsley, Judith H.** Total Risk: Nick Leeson and the Fall of the Barings Bank. 288p. 1995. 24.00 (*0-88730-781-7*) Harper Busn.

Rawnsley, L. Scott & McWhirter, Jay D. Selective Bibliography of Outer Space Law: A Bibliography of Materials in the English Language. (Collection of Bibliographic & Research Resources). 280p. 1987. pap. 50.00 (*0-379-20910-1*) Oceana.

Raworth, Jenny. Dried Flowers for All Seasons: A Complete Guide to Selecting, Drying & Arranging Flowers Throughout the Year. LC 93-5026. (Illus.). 128p. 1993. 23.00 (*0-89577-522-0*, Random) RD Assn.

Raworth, Philip. The Legislative Process In the European Community. LC 93-7393. 1993. write for info. (*90-6544-690-7*) Kluwer Law Tax Pubs.

***Raworth, Philip, ed.** European Union Law Guide. 1994. ring bd. 165.00 (*0-379-10175-0*) Oceana.

— WTO: Final Text of the GATT, Uruguay Round Agreements, Article-by-Article Analysis & Summary with a Fully Searchable Diskette. (The Practitioner's Deskbook Ser.). 1995. disk, pap. text ed. 69.95 (*0-379-21354-0*) Oceana.

Raworth, Tom. Emptily. 1994. 4.00 (*0-935724-64-8*) Figures.

— Eternal Sections. (Sun & Moon Classics Ser.: No. 23). 72p. (Orig.). 1992. pap. 9.95 (*1-55713-129-5*) Sun & Moon CA.

— Tottering State: Selected & New Poems 1963-1983. 240p. 1984. pap. 11.50 (*0-935724-19-2*) Figures.

— The Vein. 16p. 1991. 4.00 (*0-935724-50-8*) Figures.

— Visible Shivers. LC 87-90687. 88p. 1987. 8.00 (*0-917585-15-1*) O Bks.

Rawsi, Thomas G. Economic Growth in Prewar China. 1989. 60.00 (*0-520-06372-4*) U CA Pr.

Rawski, Conrad H., tr. see Petrarca, Francesco.

Rawski, Evelyn S. Agricultural Change & the Peasant Economy of South China. LC 77-173407. (Harvard East Asian Ser.: No. 66). 300p. reprint ed. pap. 85.50 (*0-7837-1525-0*, 2041802) Bks Demand.

Rawski, Evelyn S., jt. auth. see Naquin, Susan.

Rawski, Evelyn S., jt. ed. see Watson, James L.

Rawski, Thomas G. China's Transition to Industrialism: Producer Goods & Economic Development in the Twentieth Century. (Studies on China). (Illus.). 226p. 1980. 32.50x (*0-472-08755-X*) U of Mich Pr.

***Rawski, Thomas G., ed.** Economics & the Historian. LC 94-24931. 1996. pap. 17.00 (*0-520-07269-3*) U CA Pr.

Rawski, Thomas G. & Li, Lillian M., eds. Chinese History in Economic Perspective. (Studies on China: Vol. 13). (C). 1992. 45.00 (*0-520-07068-2*) U CA Pr.

Rawson. Disguise & Make-Up. (Spy Guides Ser.). (J). (gr. 2-5). 1979. pap. 4.50 (*0-86020-166-X*, Usborne) EDC.

— How Machines Work. (Children's World Ser.). (J). (gr. 2-5). 1976. lib. bdg. 14.96 (*0-88110-115-X*); pap. 7.95 (*0-86020-197-X*) EDC.

Rawson, jt. auth. see Hindley.

Rawson, Beryl, ed. The Family in Ancient Rome: New Perspectives. LC 85-18976. 280p. (C). 1986. 39.95 (*0-8014-1873-9*); pap. 14.95 (*0-8014-9460-5*) Cornell U Pr.

— Marriage, Divorce & Children in Ancient Rome. (Illus.). 282p. 1991. 69.00 (*0-19-814918-2*) OUP.

Rawson, C. & Spector, J. Riding & Pony Care. (Horses Ser.). 32p. (J). (gr. 2 up). 1987. lib. bdg. 15.96 (*0-88110-297-0*); pap. 9.95 (*0-7460-0111-8*) EDC.

Rawson, Claude. Gulliver & the Gentle Reader: Studies in Swift & Our Time. LC 91-16181. 208p. (C). 1991. pap. 18.50 (*0-391-03710-2*) Humanities.

— Henry Fielding & the Augustan Ideal under Stress. LC 91-16182. 288p. (C). 1991. pap. 19.95 (*0-391-03711-0*) Humanities.

— Order from Confusion Sprung: Studies in Eighteenth Century Literature from Swift to Cowper. 272p. 1985. text ed. 19.95 (*0-04-800019-1*) Routledge Chapman & Hall.

— Order from Confusion Sprung: Studies in Eighteenth-Century Literature from Swift to Cowper. LC 92-5336. 448p. (C). 1992. reprint ed. pap. 25.00 (*0-391-03745-5*) Humanities.

— Satire & Sentiment, 1660-1830. LC 92-30428. 290p. (C). 1994. 64.95 (*0-521-38395-1*) Cambridge U Pr.

Rawson, Claude, ed. The Character of Swift's Satire: A Revised Focus. LC 81-72062. 344p. 1983. 45.00 (*0-87413-209-6*) U Delaware Pr.

— Jonathan Swift: A Collections of Critical Essays. LC 94-4782. (New Century Views Ser.). 307p. 1994. write for info. (*0-13-091299-9*) P-H.

Rawson, Claude & Lock, F. P., eds. Collected Poems of Thomas Parnell. LC 85-41023. (Illus.). 720p. 1989. 89.50 (*0-87413-154-5*) U Delaware Pr.

Rawson, Claude, ed. see Beaver, Harold.

Rawson, Claude, ed. see Byrd, Max.

Rawson, Claude, ed. see Dickens, Charles.

Rawson, Claude, ed. see Makin, Peter.

Rawson, Claude, ed. see Riley, E. C.

Rawson, Clayton. Death from a Top Hat. (Black Dagger Crime Ser.). 288p. 16.50 (*0-86220-731-2*, Black Dagger) Chivers N Amer.

— Death from a Top Hat. 288p. 1986. pap. 4.95 (*0-930330-44-7*) Intl Polygonics.

— The Footprints on the Ceiling. 256p. 1987. pap. 4.95 (*0-930330-45-5*) Intl Polygonics.

— The Headless Lady. (Library of Crime Classics). 300p. 1987. pap. 4.95 (*0-930330-60-9*) Intl Polygonics.

— No Coffin for the Corpse. LC 87-82444. 256p. 1987. reprint ed. pap. 4.95 (*0-930330-74-9*) Intl Polygonics.

Rawson, Don C. Russian Rightists & the Revolution of Nineteen Hundred Five. LC 94-8850. (Russian, Soviet & Post-Soviet Studies: No. 95). (Illus.). 300p. (C). 1995. 64.95 (*0-521-46487-0*) Cambridge U Pr.

Rawson, Elizabeth. Roman Culture & Society: Collected Papers. 384p. 1991. 135.00 (*0-19-814752-X*, 12235) OUP.

— The Spartan Tradition in European Thought. (Illus.). 408p. 1991. pap. 32.00 (*0-19-814733-3*) OUP.

Rawson, Eric G., ed. Selected Papers on Fiber Optic Local Area Networks. LC 93-42627. (Milestone Ser.: Vol. 91). 1994. write for info. (*0-8194-1503-0*); pap. write for info. (*0-8194-1502-2*) SPIE.

Rawson, H. Glasses & Their Applications. 174p. 1991. 70.00 (*0-901462-89-6*, Pub. by Inst Materials UK) Ashgate Pub Co.

— Properties & Applications of Glass. (Glass Science & Technology Ser.: Vol. 3). 318p. 1980. 95.00 (*0-444-41922-5*) Elsevier.

Rawson, Hugh. Devious Derivations. LC 92-34135. 1993. 22.50 (*0-517-58066-7*, Crown) Crown Pub Group.

— Devious Derivations. 1994. pap. 12.00 (*0-517-88128-4*, Crown) Crown Pub Group.

— A Dictionary of Euphemisims. Date not set. 14.00 (*0-517-88297-3*) Random.

— Wicked Words. 1989. 24.95 (*0-517-57334-2*, Crown) Crown Pub Group.

— Wicked Words: A Treasury of Curses, Insults, Put-Downs, & Other Formerly Unprintable Terms from Anglo-Saxon Times to the Present. 448p. 1992. pap. 14. 00 (*0-517-59089-1*, Crown) Crown Pub Group.

Rawson, Hugh, ed. A Dictionary of Quotations from Shakespeare. 528p. 1994. pap. 5.99 (*0-451-18186-7*, Sig) NAL-Dutton.

— The New International Dictionary of Quotations. 2nd ed. 496p. 1994. pap. 5.99 (*0-451-17597-2*, Sig) NAL-Dutton.

Rawson, Hugh & Miner, Margaret, eds. The New International Dictionary of Quotations. 544p. 1988. pap. 4.50 (*0-451-15153-4*, Sig) NAL-Dutton.

Rawson, J. On Reflection. (C). 1990. 39.00 (*0-7223-2568-1*, Pub. by A H S Ltd UK) St Mut.

Rawson, J., ed. see Silone, Ignazio.

Rawson, Jessica. Chinese Jade Thru the Ages. (Illus.). 152p. 1975. pap. 25.00 (*0-87556-754-1*) Saifer.

— Chinese Ornament: The Lotus & the Dragon. LC 84-43047. (Illus.). 248p. 1985. 44.50 (*0-8419-1022-7*); pap. write for info. (*0-8419-1023-5*) Holmes & Meier.

Rawson, Jessica, ed. The British Museum Book of Chinese Art. LC 92-61337. (Illus.). 396p. 1993. pap. 24.95 (*0-500-27700-1*) Thames Hudson.

Rawson, Judith A., ed. see Machiavelli, Niccolo.

Rawson, K. J. & Tupper, E. C. Basic Ship Theory. 4th ed. LC 94-9031. 1994. pap. text ed. 59.95 (*0-470-23388-5*) Halsted Pr.

— Basic Ship Theory, 1. 3rd ed. LC 82-20395. (Illus.). 400p. 1986. pap. text ed. 59.95 (*0-582-30528-4*) Wiley.

— Basic Ship Theory, Vol. 2. LC 82-20395. (Illus.). 346p. 1986. pap. text ed. 49.95 (*0-582-30527-6*) Wiley.

— Basic Ship Theory Vol. 2: Ship Dynamics & Design, Vol. 2. 4th ed. 1995. pap. text ed. 57.95 (*0-470-23429-6*) Halsted Pr.

Rawson, Marion, tr. see Lussu, Emilio.

Rawson, P. F., tr. see Cope, J. C., et al, eds.

Rawson, P. F., ed. see International Symposium on the Boreal Lower Cretaceous Staff.

Rawson, Pam, jt. auth. see Lilburn, Pat.

Rawson, Philip. The Art of Southeast Asia: Cambodia, Vietnam, Thailand, Laos, Burma, Java & Bali. LC 89-52204. (World of Art Ser.). (Illus.). 252p. 1990. pap. 14. 95 (*0-500-20060-2*) Thames Hudson.

— Art of Tantra. (World of Art Ser.). (Illus.). 216p. 1985. pap. 14.95 (*0-500-20166-8*) Thames Hudson.

— Ceramics. LC 83-12480. (Illus.). 203p. 1983. reprint ed. pap. 17.95 (*0-8122-1156-1*) U of Pa Pr.

— Design. (Illus.). 320p. (C). 1988. pap. text ed. 38.95 (*0-13-199886-2*) P-H.

— Drawing. 2nd ed. LC 87-10929. (Illus.). 336p. 1987. reprint ed. pap. text ed. 20.95 (*0-8122-1251-7*) U of Pa Pr.

— Sacred Tibet. LC 90-70359. (Art & Imagination Ser.). (Illus.). 96p. 1991. pap. 14.95 (*0-500-81032-X*) Thames Hudson.

— Tantra: The Indian Cult of Ecstasy. (Art & Imagination Ser.). (Illus.). 1984. pap. 15.95 (*0-500-81001-X*) Thames Hudson.

Rawson, Philip & Legeza, Laszlo. Tao: The Chinese Philosophy of Time & Change. (Art & Imagination Ser.). (Illus.). 1984. pap. 14.95 (*0-500-81002-8*) Thames Hudson.

Rawson, Rodney E. Value Travel Passport Nineteen Eighty-Eight. rev. ed. 486p. 1988. pap. 16.95 (*0-941761-01-0*) Aeon Pub.

Rawson, Rosemary & Trent, Zoa, eds. Creative Source Book. 216p. (Orig.). 1986. pap. 7.95 (*0-936633-01-8*) Gnsis Pubns Tucson.

Rawson, Ruth. Acting. LC 68-21664. (Theatre Student Ser.). (Illus.). (YA). (gr. 7 up). 1970. lib. bdg. 14.95 (*0-8239-0151-3*) Rosen Group.

Rawson-Wade, Henry W. Towards Adminstrative Justice. LC 63-9896. (Michigan Legal Publications). vii, 138p. 1985. reprint ed. lib. bdg. 34.00 (*0-89941-390-0*, 303600) W S Hein.

Rawsthorne, A., tr. see Davalo, Eric & Naim, Patrick.

Rawstron, D. & Cullen, D. Child Care Law: A Summary of the Law in England & Wales. (C). 1989. 60.00 (*0-903534-64-9*, Pub. by Brit Ag for Adopt & Fost UK) St Mut.

Rawstron, D. D., ed. Rights of Children. (C). 1989. 39.00 (*0-903534-35-5*, Pub. by Brit Ag for Adopt & Fost UK) St Mut.

Ray. Focus on Phytochemical Pesticides, Vol. II. 1992. 99. 50 (*0-8493-4102-7*, CRC Reprint) Franklin.

— Food Biopreservatives of Microbial Origin. 1992. 184.00 (*0-8493-4943-5*, QR115) CRC Pr.

— Lasting Love Relationships. 1995. 16.95 (*1-879323-23-0*) Sound Horizons AV.

— Sweet Deceiver. 1995. mass mkt. 4.99 (*0-06-108379-8*, Harp PBks) HarpC.

— Undeniable. 1995. mass mkt. 4.99 (*0-7860-0125-9*, Pinnacle NY) Windsor NY.

Ray & Lainiotis, eds. Distributed Parameter Systems: Identification, Estimation & Control. (Control & Systems Theory Ser.: Vol. 6). 616p. 1978. 195.00 (*0-8247-6601-6*) Dekker.

Ray & Lewis. Exploring Professional Cooking. (gr. 9-12). 1986. student ed 9.16 (*0-02-667960-4*); teacher ed 13.32 (*0-02-667980-9*) Bennett IL.

— Exploring Professional Cooking. rev. ed. (gr. 9-12). 1986. text ed. 24.80 (*0-02-667950-7*) Bennett IL.

Ray, jt. auth. see Sen, S. P.

Ray, A. & Velusamy, R., eds. Supernovae & Stellar Evolution: Proceedings of the School & Workshop, Goa, Indian, 10-17 March 1989. 340p. (C). 1991. text ed. 104. 00 (*981-02-0657-7*) World Scientific Pub.

Ray, A. B. Students & Politics in India. 232p. 1977. 15.95 (*0-318-36618-5*) Asia Bk Corp.

Ray, A. K. Widows Are Not for Burning. 1985. 24.95 (*0-318-37316-5*) Asia Bk Corp.

Ray, A. S. An Outline of Indian Culture. 112p. 1978. 8.95 (*0-318-36962-1*) Asia Bk Corp.

Ray, Acharya P., jt. ed. see Ray, Priyadaranjian.

Ray, Al. Passion Pit Murders. Asher, Ross, ed. LC 92-61672. 224p. 1992. 19.95 (*0-931662-02-8*) Photo-Go Pr.

— Virgins of the Sun. 908p. 1992. 24.95 (*0-931662-08-7*) Photo-Go Pr.

Ray, Amalendu. Calcutta: An Annotated Bibliography. 1990. 17.50 (*0-8364-2626-6*, Pub. by Asiatic Bk Agency JA) S Asia.

Ray, Ami. Apocalypso. 10.00 (*0-89253-637-3*); 5.00 (*0-89253-638-1*) Ind-US Inc.

An Asterisk (*) at the beginning of an entry indicates that the title is appearing in BIP for the first time.

Ray, Amitava. Political Utopianism: Some Philosophical Problems. 1979. 11.00 (0-8364-0499-8) S Asia.

Ray, Anandarup. Cost-Benefit Analysis: Issues & Methodologies. LC 83-49367. 176p. 1984. pap. text ed. 11.95 (0-8018-3069-9) Johns Hopkins.

— Cost Benefit Analysis: Issues & Methodologies. 208p. 1984. 11.95 (0-614-02764-0, 43069) World Bank.

— Cost-Benefit Analysis: Issues & Methodologies. LC 83-49367. 166p. reprint ed. pap. 47.40 (0-685-15553-6, 2026707) Bks Demand.

Ray, Andy. A Candle in the Rain. 179p. (Orig.). 1990. pap. 9.95 (0-9621856-0-4) Panther Pr.

Ray, Angeln. Angels Ascending & Descending. 176p. 1984. 12.95 (0-915763-00-1) Starseed Pubns.

Ray, Angie. Ghostly Enchantment. 1994. mass mkt. 4.50 (0-06-108209-0, Harp PBks) HarpC.

Ray, Anil. Students & Politics: A Case Study of Benares Hindu University, India. 1978. 14.00 (0-88386-789-3) S Asia.

Ray, Ann, ed. see Hills, Christopher.

Ray, Ann, jt. auth. see Ray, Robert J.

Ray, Annada S. Yes, I Saw Gandhi. 215p. 1994. 15.00 (0-934676-78-X) Greenlf Bks.

***Ray, Anthony.** Liverpool Printed Tiles. (Illus.). 72p. 1994. 69.95 (0-9512140-7-1, Pub. by J Horne UK) Antique Collect.

Ray, Arthur J. The Canadian Fur Trade in the Industrial Age. 284p. 1990. 40.00 (0-8020-2699-0); pap. 19.95 (0-8020-6743-3) U of Toronto Pr.

— Indians in the Fur Trade: Their Role As Trappers, Hunters, & Middle Man in the Lands Southwest of Hudson Bay, 1660-1860. LC 73-89848. (Illus.). 1974. pap. 16.95 (0-8020-6226-1) U of Toronto Pr.

Ray, Arthur J. & Freeman, Donald B. Give Us Good Measure: An Economic Analysis of Relations Between the Indians & the Hudson's Bay Company Before 1763. LC 79-304038. (Illus.). 316p. reprint ed. pap. 90.10 (0-8357-8146-1, 2033987) Bks Demand.

Ray, Asok, jt. auth. see Nayak, Nitin.

Ray, B. Two-Six Compounds. LC 72-93126. (C). 1969. 118.00 (0-08-006624-0, Pub. by Pergamon Repr UK) Franklin.

Ray, B. C., ed. Tribals of Orissa: The Changing Socio-Economic Profile. 170p. 1989. 16.00 (81-212-0270-1, Pub. by Gian Publng Hse II) S Asia.

Ray, Barbara. The Best of Barbara Ray. 160p. 1989. write for info. (0-318-65419-9) Rayve Prodns.

Ray, Barbara, jt. auth. see Ray, Norm.

Ray, Benjamin C. African Religions: Symbol, Ritual & Community. 1975. pap. text ed. write for info. (0-13-018622-8) P-H.

— Myth, Ritual, & Kingship in Buganda. (Illus.). 264p. 1991. 47.50 (0-19-506436-4) OUP.

***Ray, Bharati.** From the Seams of History: Essays on Indian Women. (Gender-Women's Studies). 328p. 1995. 29.95 (0-19-563226-5) OUP.

— Hyderabad & British Paramountcy. (Illus.). 250p. 1989. 19.95 (0-19-562231-6) OUP.

Ray, Bibek, ed. Injured Index & Pathogenic Bacteria: Occurrence & Detection in Foods, Water, & Feeds. 224p. 1989. 180.00 (0-8493-4928-1, QR115) CRC Pr.

Ray, Bidyut L. Studies in Jagannatha-Cult. (C). 1993. text ed. 19.50 (81-7054-176-X, Pub. by Classical Pub II) S Asia.

***Ray, Bill T.** Environmental Engineering. LC 94-26681. (Engineering Ser.). 608p. (C). 1995. text ed. 64.95 (0-534-20652-2) PWS Pubs.

Ray, Binavendranath. Consciousness in Neo-Realism. LC 75-3330. reprint ed. 11.50 (0-404-59324-0) AMS Pr.

Ray, Binita, jt. auth. see Das, R. R.

Ray, Blaine. Look, I Can Talk! Student Notebook in English. (Illus.). 100p. 1991. teacher ed, pap. text ed. 12.95 (1-56018-456-6); trans. 21.00 (1-56018-458-2) Sky Oaks Prodns.

— Look, I Can Talk! Student Notebook in Spanish. Asher, James J., ed. (Illus.). 96p. (Orig.). (SPA.). 1992. student ed, pap. text ed. 12.95 (1-56018-459-0) Sky Oaks Prodns.

— Look, I Can Talk! Teacher's Guidebook. 2nd ed. Asher, James J., ed. 52p. 1995. pap. text ed. 9.95 (1-56018-488-4) Sky Oaks Prodns.

— Look, I Can Talk! (Schau, Ich Kann Reden!: Deutsches Schuler Arbeitsbuch) Student Notebook in German. Asher, James J., ed. (Illus.). 96p. (Orig.). (GER.). 1991. pap. text ed. 12.95 (1-56018-461-2) Sky Oaks Prodns.

***Ray, Blaine & Buchan, Greg.** Look, I Can Talk! Student Notebook in French. Asher, James J., ed. (Illus.). 100p. (Orig.). (FRE.). 1995. student ed, pap. text ed. 12.95 (1-56018-497-3) Sky Oaks Prodns.

Ray, Blaine, et al. Look, I Can Talk More! In English - Student Textbook. Asher, James J., ed. (Illus.). 120p. (Orig.). 1993. pap. text ed. 12.95 (1-56018-489-2) Sky Oaks Prodns.

— Look, I Can Talk More! - Mirame, Puedo Hablar Mas! In Spanish - Student Textbook. (Illus.). 120p. (Orig.). 1993. pap. text ed. 12.95x (1-56018-490-6) Sky Oaks Prodns.

— Look, I Can Talk More! - Regardez-Moi, Je Peux Parler Plus! In French - Student Textbook. (Illus.). 120p. (Orig.). 1993. pap. text ed. 12.95 (1-56018-491-4) Sky Oaks Prodns.

Ray, Blair. Introduction to Professional Communication. 384p. (C). 1989. pap. text ed. write for info. (0-13-493149-1) P-H.

Ray, Bruce. Withhold Not Correction. 1978. pap. 5.99 (0-87552-400-1) Presby & Reformed.

Ray, Bruce A. No Rehuses el Corregir: Withold Not Correction. (SPA.). 4.25 (84-7228-934-6, 223008, Pub. by Edit Clie SP) TSELF.

Ray, C. The Evolution of Relativity. (Illus.). 224p. 1987. 80.00 (0-85274-423-4) IOP Pub.

Ray, C., ed. AIDS, Stories of Living Longer. 32p. (Orig.). 1991. pap. 3.25 (0-9616792-9-8) Taterhill.

Ray, C. & Baum, M. Psychological Aspects of Early Breast Cancer. (Contributions to Psychology & Medicine Ser.). (Illus.). 160p. 1985. 51.00 (0-387-96122-4) Spr-Verlag.

Ray, C. A. La Vida Responsable: Orientacion Biblica Sobre Nuestro Estilo De Vivir. Lopez, Albert C., tr. Orig. Title: Living the Responsible Life. 160p. 1982. reprint ed. 2.75 (0-311-46079-8) Casa Bautista.

Ray, Cecil A. Living the Responsible Life. Hogg, G. A., ed. 160p. 1983. pap. text ed. 12.50 (0-311-72371-3) Casa Bautista.

Ray, Charles. Conversations Chinoises Prises sur le Vif, 2 vols. (Asian Folklore & Social Life Monographs: Nos. 47-48). 746p. (FRE.). 1973. 24.00 (0-89986-045-1) Oriental Bk Store.

— Marvellous Ministry, A. 1985. pap. 4.95 (1-56186-217-7) Pilgrim Pubns.

— Mrs. C. H. Spurgeon. 1979. pap. 4.95 (1-56186-305-X) Pilgrim Pubns.

Ray, Charles, jt. auth. see Adkins, Myrna A.

Ray, Charles L. How to Start & Operate an Electrical Contracting Business. 176p. 1988. text ed. 40.00 (0-07-051243-4) McGraw.

Ray-Chaudhuri, D., et al, eds. Coding Theory & Design Theory: Part I - Coding Theory. (IMA Volumes in Mathematics & Its Applications Ser.: Vol. 20). xiv, 239p. 1990. 36.00 (0-387-97228-5) Spr-Verlag.

— Coding Theory & Design Theory: Part II - Design Theory. (IMA Volumes in Mathematics & Its Applications Ser.: Vol. 21). xiii, 378p. 1990. 43.00 (0-387-97231-5) Spr-Verlag.

Ray-Chaudhuri, D. K., ed. Relations Between Combinatorics & Other Parts of Mathematics. LC 78-25979. (Proceedings of Symposia in Pure Mathematics Ser., Humboldt State University, Arcata, CA, July 29-August 16, 1974: Vol. 34). 378p. 1986. reprint ed. pap. 44.00 (0-8218-1434-6, PSPUM-34) Am Math.

Ray, Christiana I. The Bond Market: Trading & Risk Management. 553p. 1992. text ed. 75.00 (1-55623-289-6) Irwin Prof Pubng.

Ray, Christopher. Time, Space & Philosophy. (Philosophical Issues in Science Ser.). (Illus.). 288p. 1991. 55.00 (0-415-03221-0, A5750); pap. 15.95 (0-415-03222-9, A5754) Routledge.

Ray, Clayton E., ed. Geology & Paleontology of the Lee Creek Mine, North Carolina, Pt. I. LC 82-600265. (Smithsonian Contributions to Paleobiology Ser.: No. 53). 535p. reprint ed. pap. 152.50 (0-317-29733-3, 2022203) Bks Demand.

***Ray, Cyril.** Cyril Ray's Compleat Imbiber, No. 16. 192p. 1992. 24.95 (1-85732-944-9, Pub. by Reed Illust Books UK) Antique Collect.

— Robert Mondavi of the Napa Valley. 192p. 1986. pap. 12.95 (0-446-38322-8) Warner Bks.

Ray, D. B. The Baptist Succession. 1984. reprint ed. 22.00 (0-317-11348-8) Church History.

— Text-Book on Campbellism. 1991. reprint ed. 19.50 (0-685-40811-6) Church History.

Ray, Daniel. Alexandrine Scripts: A Stretch of Sand & Other Stories. 168p. 1989. 19.95 (0-86327-177-4, Pub. by Wolfhound Pr IE) Dufour.

Ray, Daniel K. Water Works: A Survey of Great Lakes - St. Lawrence River Waterfront Development. Botts, Paul, ed. (Illus.). 72p. (Orig.). (C). 1991. 16.95 (0-921578-06-7) Harbor Hse MI.

***Ray, Darrell W. & Bronstein, Howard.** Teaming Up: Making the Transition to a Self-Directed, Team-Based Organization. LC 94-33604. 1995. text ed. 24.95 (0-07-051646-4) McGraw.

Ray, Darryal W., ed. see Jones, Joey.

***Ray, Dave.** Inside Brother's Check-Up. 151p. 1994. student ed 19.95 (1-57326-018-5) Core Ministries.

— The Liberating Devotional: Daily Planner-Compact Pak. 200p. 1993. student ed 24.95 (1-57326-003-7) Core Ministries.

— The Liberating Devotional: Intro-Pak. 70p. 1994. student ed 6.95 (1-57326-004-5) Core Ministries.

— The Liberating Devotional: Soft Cover Pak. 110p. 1993. student ed 19.95 (1-57326-001-0) Core Ministries.

— The Liberating Devotional: Standard Version. 200p. 1993. student ed 29.95 (1-57326-000-2) Core Ministries.

— The Liberating Devotional: The Executive Version. 200p. 1993. student ed 79.95 (1-57326-002-9) Core Ministries.

— Man's Check-Up. 56p. 1994. student ed 9.95 (1-57326-015-0) Core Ministries.

— Pastor's Check-Up. 36p. 1994. student ed 9.95 (1-57326-016-9) Core Ministries.

***Ray, Dave & Schmees, Paul.** Job Search Check-Up. 68p. 1994. student ed 10.95 (1-57326-017-7) Core Ministries.

Ray, David. The Farm in Calabria & Other Poems. Sklar, Morty, ed. LC 80-123410. (Outstanding Author Ser.: No. 3). (Illus.). 32p. (Orig.). 1980. per., pap. 2.00 (0-930370-08-2) Spirit That Moves.

— Kangaroo Paws: Poems Written in Australia. 145p. (Orig.). 1995. boxed 25.00 (0-943549-35-3) TJU Pr.

— Kangaroo Paws: Poems Written in Australia. LC 94-47568. (Orig.). 1995. pap. write for info. (0-943549-34-5) TJU Pr.

— The Maharani's New Wall & Other Poems. LC 88-10650. (Wesleyan Poetry Ser.). 80p. 1989. 22.50 (0-8195-2164-7, Wesleyan Univ Pr); pap. 10.95 (0-8195-1165-X, Wesleyan Univ Pr) U Pr of New Eng.

— On Wednesday I Cleaned out My Wallet. 32p. (Orig.). (C). 1985. 10.95 (0-942908-08-2); pap. 5.95 (0-942908-07-4) Pancake Pr.

— Pumpkin Light. LC 92-25118. (Illus.). 32p. (J). (ps-3). 1993. 14.95 (0-399-22028-3, Philomel Bks) Putnam Pub Group.

— Sam's Book. LC 86-9195. (Wesleyan Poetry Ser.). 95p. 1987. pap. 10.95 (0-8195-6180-0, Wesleyan Univ Pr) U Pr of New Eng.

Ray, David, ed. New Letters: A Book of Translations. (New Letters Ser.). (Illus.). 184p. (Orig.). 1985. pap. 4.00 (0-938652-09-5) New Letters MO.

— New Letters: Reader One. (New Letters Ser.). 288p. (Orig.). 1983. pap. 7.50 (0-938652-07-9) New Letters MO.

— New Letters, Fall 1984, Vol. 51, No. 1. (Illus.). 1984. pap. 4.00 (0-317-17179-8) New Letters MO.

— New Letters, Fall 1985, Vol. 52, No. 1. (Illus.). 136p. 1985. pap. 4.00 (0-317-44322-4) New Letters MO.

— New Letters Reader Two. (New Letters Ser.). 288p. (Orig.). 1984. pap. 7.50 (0-938652-08-7) New Letters MO.

Ray, David, tr. & intro. Not Far from the River: Poems from the Gatha-Saptasati. LC 90-81354. 96p. (Orig.). 1990. pap. 10.00 (1-55659-034-2) Copper Canyon.

Ray, David & Ray, Judy, eds. New Asian Writing: A New Letters Anthology. (Writers Workshop Greybird Ser.). 101p. 1979. 16.00 (0-86578-270-9) Ind-US Inc.

Ray, David & Singh, Amritjit, eds. India. (New Letters Ser.). 272p. (Orig.). 1982. pap. 5.00 (0-938652-05-2) New Letters MO.

Ray, David, ed. see Mayo, E. L.

Ray, David R. The Big Small Church Book. LC 92-30774. 256p. (Orig.). 1992. pap. 14.95 (0-8298-0936-8) Pilgrim OH.

Ray, Deborah W. & Stewart, Gloria P. Loyal to the Land: The History of a Greenwich Connecticut Family. LC 90-46740. (Illus.). 192p. 1990. 45.00 (0-914659-50-2) Phoenix Pub.

Ray, Deborah Wing & Stewart, Gloria P. Norwalk, Being an Historical Account of That Connecticut Town. LC 78-24441. (Illus.). 1979. 13.95 (0-914016-56-3) Phoenix Pub.

Ray, Debra & Walley, Patti. James & the Giant Peach: A Study Guide. (Novel-Ties Ser.). 1988. student ed, teacher ed 15.95 (0-88122-077-9) Lrn Links.

Ray, Debraj, jt. auth. see Mookherjee, Dilip.

Ray, Delia. Behind the Blue & Gray: The Soldier's Life in the Civil War. (Young Readers' History of the Civil War Ser.). (Illus.). 112p. (J). (gr. 5-9). 1991. 16.99 (0-525-67333-4, Lodestar Bks) Dutton Child Bks.

Ray, Delmas D. Accounting & Business Fluctuations. LC 60-6718. 196p. reprint ed. pap. 55.90 (0-7837-4925-2, 2044591) Bks Demand.

***Ray, Deng D.** The Politics of Two Sudans: The South & the North, 1821-1969. 183p. 1994. pap. 42.50 (91-7106-344-7, Pub. by Almqv & Wiksell SW) Coronet Bks.

***Ray, Diane T.** Fashion Doll Dream Castle. 146p. 1994. pap. 14.95 (0-9638031-3-1) Needlecrft Shop.

Ray, Dixy L., ed. Marine Boring & Fouling Organisms. LC 59-14772. (Illus.). 548p. 1959. 20.00 (0-295-73840-5) U of Wash Pr.

Ray, Dixy L. & Guzzo, Lou. Environmental Overkill: Whatever Happened to Common Sense? LC 92-39903. 260p. 1993. 19.95 (0-89526-512-5) Regnery Pub.

— Environmental Overkill: Whatever Happened to Common Sense? 272p. 1994. reprint ed. pap. 12.00 (0-06-097598-9, PL) HarpC.

— Trashing the Planet: How Science Can Help Us Deal with Acid Rain, Depletion of the Ozone, & Nuclear Waste (Among Other Things) 1992. pap. 12.00 (0-06-097490-7, PL) HarpC.

Ray, Dixy L. & Guzzo, Louis R. Trashing the Planet: How Science Can Help Us Deal with Acid Rain, Depletion of the Ozone, & Nuclear Waste (Among Other Things) LC 90-8344. 210p. 1990. 19.95 (0-89526-544-3) Regnery Pub.

Ray, Don. A Public Records Primer & Investigator's Handbook: California 1991 Edition. rev. ed. 196p. (Orig.). 1991. pap. 14.95 (0-9629552-0-5) ENG Pr.

— A Public Records Primer & Investigator's Handbook 1992-1993: California Edition. rev. ed. Aref, Dalia, ed. 220p. 1992. pap. 16.95 (0-9629552-1-3) ENG Pr.

Ray, Donald I. Dictionary of the African Left: Parties, Movements & Groups. 2nd ed. 290p. 1989. text ed. 59.95 (1-85521-014-2, Pub. by Dartmth Pub UK) Ashgate Pub Co.

Ray, Donnalee, ed. see Nijinsky, Tamara.

Ray, Dorothy J. The Eskimos of Bering Strait, 1650-1898. LC 91-28577. (Illus.). 360p. 1991. reprint ed. pap. 16.95 (0-295-97122-3) U of Wash Pr.

— Ethnohistory in the Arctic: The Bering Strait Eskimo. Pierce, Richard A., ed. (Alaska History Ser.: No. 23). (Illus.). 280p. 1983. 29.95 (0-919642-98-5) Limestone Pr.

— Setting It Free: An Exhibition of Modern Alaskan Eskimo Ivory Carving. Larsen, Dinah, ed. (Illus.). 110p. (Orig.). 1982. pap. 10.00 (0-931163-08-0) U Alaska Museum.

Ray, Douglas & Poonwassie, Deo H., eds. Education & Cultural Differences: New Perspectives. LC 91-45117. (Reference Books in International Education: Vol. 15). 586p. 1992. 78.00 (0-8240-6047-4, SS#594) Garland.

Ray, E. B. & Donohew, L., eds. Communication & Health: Systems & Applications. 224p. 1990. pap. 22.50 (0-8058-0697-0) L Erlbaum Assocs.

— Communication & Health: Systems & Applications. 224p. 1990. 49.95 (0-8058-0154-5) L Erlbaum Assocs.

Ray, Edward J. U. S. Protectionism & the World Debt Crisis. LC 89-3774. 259p. 1989. text ed. 59.95 (0-89930-367-6, RUP/, Quorum Bks) Greenwood.

Ray, Eileen B., ed. Case Studies in Health Communication. (Communication Textbooks, Applied Communication Subseries). 328p. (C). 1992. text ed. 79.95 (0-8058-1108-7); pap. 24.95 (0-8058-1109-5) L Erlbaum Assocs.

Ray, Eleanor & Marinacci, Barbara. Vineyards in the Sky: The Life of Legendary Vintner Martin Ray. LC 92-74051. (Illus.). 448p. 1993. 28.95 (0-9623048-4-0); pap. 18.95 (0-9623048-5-9) Heritage West.

Ray, Eric. Sofer: The Story of a Torah Scroll. LC 85-52420. (Illus.). 32p. (Orig.). (J). (ps-4). 1986. pap. 4.95 (0-933873-04-2) Torah Aura.

Ray, Eric & Grishaver, Joel L. Sofer: The Story of a Torah Scroll. (Illus.). 32p. (Orig.). 1988. text ed. 12.95 (0-933873-24-7) Torah Aura.

Ray, Francis. Fallen Angel. 1992. pap. 4.75 (1-878634-08-9) Odyssey Bks.

— Forever Yours. 1994. mass mkt. 4.99 (0-7860-0025-2, Pinnacle NY) Windsor NY.

— Undeniable. 256p. 1995. pap. 4.99 (0-8217-0125-8) Zebra.

Ray, Fred O. The New Poverty Row: Independent Filmmakers As Distributors. LC 91-52743. 240p. 1991. lib. bdg. 32.50x (0-89950-628-3) McFarland & Co.

Ray, Frederic. Old Fort Niagara: An Illustrated History. rev. ed. (Illus.). 16p. (J). 1988. reprint ed. pap. 1.25 (0-941967-06-9) Old Fort Niagara Assn.

Ray, Frederic E. Our Special Artist: Alfred R. Waud's Civil War. (Illus.). 192p. 1994. 22.95 (0-8117-1194-3) Stackpole.

Ray, G. Carleton & Robins, C. Richard. A Field Guide to Atlantic Coast Fishes. (Peterson Field Guide Ser.). (Illus.). 482p. 1986. 24.95 (0-395-31852-1); pap. 16.95 (0-395-39198-9) HM.

Ray, G. F., jt. ed. see Nabseth, Lars.

Ray Garfield Staff. Life & Love. 184p. (Orig.). 1983. pap. 5.95 (0-9609856-0-3) Garfield Pubns.

***Ray, George.** Poems of Life & Nature. Date not set. pap. 4.95 (1-57087-048-9) Prof Pr NC.

Ray, George, ed. Energy Management: Can We Learn from Others? (Joint Energy Programme Ser.). 80p. 1985. text ed. 43.95 (0-566-05015-3) Ashgate Pub Co.

Ray, Gordon N. The Art of the French Illustrated Book, 1700-1914. (Illus.). 608p. 1986. reprint ed. pap. 24.95 (0-486-25086-5) Dover.

— Buried Life. LC 74-6372. (Thackeray Ser.: No. 91). 1974. lib. bdg. 59.95 (0-8383-1984-X) M S G Haskell Hse.

— H. G. Wells & Rebecca West. LC 74-77990. (Illus.). 241p. reprint ed. pap. 68.70 (0-8357-8161-5, 2033918) Bks Demand.

— The Illustrator & the Book in England from 1790 to 1914. (Illus.). 384p. 1992. reprint ed. pap. 24.95 (0-486-26955-8) Dover.

— William Makepeace Thackeray: Contributions to the Morning Chronicle. LC 55-6945. 232p. 1966. reprint ed. pap. 11.95 (0-252-72736-3) U of Ill Pr.

Ray, Gordon N., ed. see James, Henry & Wells, H. G.

Ray, Gordon N., ed. see Thackeray, William Makepeace.

Ray, Gordon N., ed. see Wells, H. G.

Ray H. Bennett Lumber Co., Inc. Staff. Bennett's Small House Catalog, 1920. LC 93-40012. (Illus.). 80p. 1993. reprint ed. pap. text ed. 8.95 (0-486-27809-3) Dover.

Ray, H. P. Trade & Diplomacy in India-China Relations: A Study of Bengal During the 15th Century. 1993. text ed. 25.00 (81-7027-202-5, Pub. by Radiant Pubs II) S Asia.

Ray, H. S. Kinetics of Metallurgical Reactions. 312p. (C). 1993. 29.95 (1-881570-05-3) Intl Sci Pub.

Ray, Harmon & Ogunnaike, Babatund A. Introduction to Process Dynamics & Control. 1993. text ed. 64.00 (0-13-030784-X) P-H.

Ray, Harold L., jt. auth. see Palmatier, Robert A.

Ray, Harold L., jt. auth. see Palmatier, Robert S.

Ray, Hem C. Dynastic History of Northern India (Early Medieval Period), 2 vols., Set. (Illus.). reprint ed. text ed. 92.50 (0-685-13419-9) Coronet Bks.

Ray, Hem S., jt. auth. see Ghosh, Ahindra.

Ray, Hemen. China & Eastern Europe. 150p. 1988. text ed. 25.00 (81-7027-115-0, Pub. by Radiant Pubs II) S Asia.

— The Enduring Friendship: Soviet-Indian Relations in Mrs. Gandhi's Days. (C). 1989. 21.50 (81-7017-249-7, Pub. by Abhinav II) S Asia.

— Sino-Soviet Conflict over India. (C). 1988. 16.00 (81-7017-206-3, Pub. by Abhinav II) S Asia.

***Ray, Himanshu P.** The Winds of Change: Buddhism & the Early Maritime Links of South Asia. (Illus.). 240p. 1995. 24.00 (0-19-563551-5) OUP.

Ray, Hugh & Branch, Ben. Bankruptcy Investing: How to Profit from Distressed Companies. 286p. 1992. 29.95 (0-7931-0206-5, 560840) Dearborn Finan.

Ray, Irene R. & Gupta, Mallika C. Story of Vivekananda. (Illus.). (J). (gr. 4-7). 1971. pap. 1.95 (0-87481-125-2, Pub. by Advaita Ashrama II) Vedanta Pr.

Ray, Isaac. Contributions to Mental Pathology (1873). LC 73-9908. (History of Psychology Ser.). 576p. 1973. reprint ed. lib. bdg. 85.00 (0-8201-1120-1) Schol Facsimiles.

— A Treatise on the Medical Jurisprudence of Insanity. 5th ed. LC 75-16732. (Classics in Psychiatry Ser.). 1977. reprint ed. 54.95 (0-405-07453-0) Ayer.

— A Treatise on the Medical Jurisprudence of Insanity. (Historical Foundations of Forensic Psychiatry & Psychology Ser.). xvi, 480p. 1983. reprint ed. lib. bdg. 45.00 (0-306-76181-5) Da Capo.

Ray, Isaac & Earle, Pliny. American Psychiatrists Abroad: An Original Anthology. LC 75-16679. (Classics in Psychiatry Ser.). 1976. 30.95 (0-405-07411-5) Ayer.

Ray, J. & Davis, L. Computers in Educational Administration. 1991. pap. text ed. write for info. (0-07-051257-4) McGraw.

Ray, J. & Hagerty, J., eds. The Course of British History, Bk. 3: 1714 to the Present Day. (C). 1987. 40.00 (0-09-172701-4, Pub. by S Thornes Pubs UK) St Mut.

Ray, J. & Hagerty, James. History for You: The Twentieth Century World. (C). 1986. pap. 21.00 (0-09-160911-9, Pub. by S Thornes UK) Dufour.

R

An Asterisk (*) at the beginning of an entry indicates that the title is appearing in BIP for the first time.

Ray, J. P. & Engelhardt, F. R., eds. Produced Water: Technological - Environmental Issues & Solutions. (Environmental Science Research Ser.: Vol. 46). (Illus.). 610p. (C). 1993. 129.50 (0-306-44358-9, Plenum Pr) Plenum.

Ray, James. Entrepreneur's Handbook: A Complete Guide to Venture Selection & Business Planning. 384p. 1994. pap. 50.00 (0-7863-0326-3) Irwin Prof Pubng.

***Ray, James C.** The Most Valuable Corporate Forms You'll Ever Need. 225p. (Orig.). 1995. pap. 24.95 (1-57248-007-6) Sphinx Pub FL.

Ray, James E. Who Killed Martin Luther King? The True Story by the Alleged Assassin. 285p. 1993. pap. 12.95 (1-882605-02-0) Natl Pr Bks.

Ray, James L. The Future of American-Israeli Relations: A Parting of the Ways. LC 85-706. 167p. reprint ed. pap. 47.60 (0-7837-5813-8, 2045480) Bks Demand.

Ray, James L., jt. ed. see Smith, Dale L.

***Ray, James Lee.** Democracy & International Conflict: An Evaluation of the Democratic Peace Proposition. LC 95-4339. (Studies in International Relations). 1995. write for info. (1-57003-041-3) U of SC Pr.

***Ray, Jane.** Day Book. (J). (ps-3). 1994. 12.99 (0-525-45259-1) NAL-Dutton.

— Noah's Ark. LC 90-32786. (Illus.). 32p. (J). (ps up). 1990. 14.95 (0-525-44653-2, DCB) Dutton Child Bks.

Ray, Jane, illus. La Historia de Navidad. LC 91-578. 32p. (SPA.). (J). (ps up). 1991. 16.00 (0-525-44830-6, DCB) Dutton Child Bks.

— Magical Tales from Many Lands. LC 93-12164. 128p. (J). 1993. 19.99 (0-525-45017-3, DCB) Dutton Child Bks.

— The Story of Christmas: Words from the Gospels of Matthew & Luke. LC 91-11357. 32p. (J). (ps up). 1991. 15.95 (0-525-44768-7, DCB) Dutton Child Bks.

Ray, Jane, illus. & photos. The Story of the Creation: Words from Genesis. LC 92-20862. 32p. (J). (gr. 1 up). 1993. 16.00 (0-525-44946-9, DCB) Dutton Child Bks.

Ray, Jane, photos. The Story of the Creation: Words from Genesis. LC 92-20862. (Illus.). 32p. (J). (gr. 1 up). 1993. Spanish ed. 16.00 (0-525-45055-6, DCB) Dutton Child Bks.

***Ray, Jerry L.** Narrative Irony in Luke-Acts: The Paradoxical Interaction of Prophetic Fulfillment & Jewish Rejection. LC 95-12483. 200p. 1996. 79.95 (0-7734-2359-1, Mellen Biblical Pr) E Mellen.

Ray, Joan K. & Ray, Robert D. Integrating Aerospace Science into the Curriculum: K-12. (Illus.). 150p. 1992. pap. text ed. 21.50 (0-87287-924-0) Teacher Ideas Pr.

Ray, Jocelyn, intro. N. A. Tink Tinkham: Watchmaker, Music Maker. 126p. 1981. lib. bdg. 29.00 (1-56475-210-0); fiche write for info. (1-56475-211-9) U NV Oral Hist.

Ray, Joel, jt. auth. see Marino, Andrew.

Ray, John. Battle of Britain New Perspectives: Behind the Scenes of the Great Air War. (Illus.). 208p. 1994. 24.95 (1-85409-229-4) Sterling.

— The Correspondence of John Ray. Lankester, Edwin R., ed. LC 74-26287. (History, Philosophy & Sociology of Science Ser.). 1975. reprint ed. 42.95 (0-405-06613-9) Ayer.

— Miscellaneous Discourses Concerning the Dissolution & Changes of the World. (Anglistica & Americana Ser.: No. 10). 259p. 1968. reprint ed. 50.70 (0-685-66508-9, 05102001, Pub. by Georg Olms GW) Lubrecht & Cramer.

— Synopsis Methodica Animalium Quadrupedum et Serpentini Generis. Sterling, Keir B., ed. LC 77-81111. (Biologists & Their World Ser.). (LAT.). 1978. reprint ed. lib. bdg. 31.95 (0-405-10694-7) Ayer.

— Synopsis Methodica Avium & Piscium. Derham, William & Sterling, Keir B., eds. LC 77-81111. (Biologists & Their World Ser.). (Illus.). (LAT.). 1978. reprint ed. lib. bdg. 39.95 (0-405-10695-5) Ayer.

— Three Physico-Theological Discourses: Primitive Chaos, & Creation of the World, the General Deluge, Its Causes & Effects. Albritton, Claude C., Jr., ed. LC 77-6538. (History of Geology Ser.). 1978. reprint ed. lib. bdg. 37.95 (0-405-10457-X) Ayer.

— The Wisdom of God Manifested in the Works of Creation. (Anglistica & Americana Ser.: No. 122). 250p. 1974. reprint ed. 50.70 (3-487-05403-5, Pub. by Georg Olms GW) Lubrecht & Cramer.

— The Wisdom of God Manifested in the Works of the Creation: Heavenly Bodies, Elements, Meteors, Fossils, Vegetables, Animals. Egerton, Frank N., 3rd, ed. LC 77-74250. (History of Ecology Ser.). 1978. reprint ed. lib. bdg. 44.95 (0-405-10419-7) Ayer.

Ray, John & Hagerty, James. Course of British History: Tudors & Stuarts. (Illus.). 96p. 1987. pap. 13.95 (0-09-170781-1, Pub. by S Thornes UK) Dufour.

***Ray, John E.** Managing Official Export Credits: The Quest for a Global Regime. LC 95-6146. 1995. write for info. (0-88132-207-5) Inst Intl Eco.

Ray, John R. & Warden, Kathleen. Technology, Computers F&TE Special Needs Learner. LC 94-6812. 224p. 1994. pap. text ed. 25.95 (0-8273-6476-8) Delmar.

Ray, Jordan B., jt. auth. see Gleim, Irvin N.

Ray, Judith A. A Single Lady's Guide to Bar Games. 65p. (Orig.). 1989. pap. 4.00 (0-9622689-0-9) J A Ray.

Ray, Judy. Pebble Rings. 64p. 1980. pap. 3.00 (0-912678-42-9, Greenfld Rev Pr) Greenfld Rev Lit.

— Pigeons in the Chandeliers. (Illus.). 75p. (Orig.). 1993. pap. 10.00 (0-944048-04-8) Timberline Missouri.

— Token: A Poem. Hickok, Gloria V., ed. 8p. (Orig.). 1995. pap. 3.00 (0-614-04935-0) Helicon Nine Eds.

Ray, Judy, jt. ed. see Ray, David.

Ray, Juliana & Bokoli, Madeleine. Crochet Designs from Hungary. Kinmond, Jean, ed. 71p. 1973. reprint ed. pap. 3.50 (0-486-20391-3) Dover.

Ray, Karen. Come Home to Darkness. 1991. mass mkt. 4.50 (0-8217-3542-X) Zebra.

— To Cross a Line. LC 93-11813. 160p. (YA). (gr. 7 up). 1994. 15.95 (0-531-06831-5); lib. bdg. 15.99 (0-531-08681-X) Orchard Bks Watts.

— To Cross a Line. 160p. (YA). (gr. 7 up). 1995. pap. 3.99 (0-14-037587-2) Puffin Bks.

Ray, Karen, jt. auth. see Winer, Michael.

***Ray, Kathleen, ed.** Experience Teaches: A Teacher's Journey Through the School Year, 1995-96. 48p. 1995. pap. 15.00 (0-912099-15-1) Kappa Delta Pi.

Ray, Keith & McClary, Cheryl. Wellness & the Liberal Arts. 112p. (C). 1994. per. 19.95 (0-8403-9212-5) Kendall-Hunt.

Ray, Keith, jt. auth. see McClary, Cheryl.

Ray, Keka D. Political Upsurges in Post-War India, 1945-6. (C). 1992. 15.00 (0-685-63242-3, Pub. by Intellectual II) S Asia.

***Ray, Krishna D.** India: A Journey Through the Ages. 1995. 19.95 (0-533-11149-8) Vantage.

Ray, L. P. Twice Sold, Twice Ransomed. LC 76-173613. (Black Heritage Library Collection). 1977. reprint ed. 28.95 (0-8369-8905-8) Ayer.

Ray, Larry. Critical Sociology: The Formation of a Critical Theory of Society. (Schools of Thought in Sociology Ser.). 400p. 1990. text ed. 121.95 (1-85278-166-1, Pub. by E Elgar Pub UK) Ashgate Pub Co.

— Formal Sociology: The Work of George Simmel. (Schools of Thought in Sociology Ser.). 354p. 1991. text ed. 119.95 (1-85278-298-6, Pub. by E Elgar Pub UK) Ashgate Pub Co.

Ray, Larry & Reed, Michael. Organizing Modernity: New Weberian Perspectives on Work, Organizations, & Society. LC 94-7259. 240p. 1994. 65.00 (0-415-08916-6, B4462, Routledge NY); pap. 17.95 (0-415-08917-4, B4466, Routledge NY) Routledge.

Ray, Larry J. Rethinking Critical Theory: Emancipation in the Age of Global Social Movements. (Illus.). 256p. 1993. 59.95 (0-8039-8363-8); pap. 21.95 (0-8039-8364-6) Sage.

Ray, Leslie. Oil Spill Prevention & Response: How to Comply with OPA & OSPRA. LC 93-40393. 250p. 1994. 72.95 (0-87814-389-0, S4525) PennWell Bks.

Ray, Lila. Entrance. (Redbird Ser.). 1976. 6.75 (0-89253-512-1); 4.00 (0-89253-124-X) Ind-US Inc.

Ray, Lila, tr. see Ray, Satyajit.

Ray, Lillian. Modern Ballroom Dancing. (Ballroom Dance Ser.). 1986. lib. bdg. 79.95 (0-8490-3330-6) Gordon Pr.

— Modern Ballroom Dancing. (Ballroom Dance Ser.). 1985. lib. bdg. 79.95 (0-87700-657-1) Revisionist Pr.

Ray, Lisa. Southern Women Artists: From the Collection of the Columbia Museum of Art. 38p. (Orig.). 1990. pap. 3.00 (0-9627858-0-6) Columbia Mus Art.

Ray, Lou. The Burros of Mavrick Gulch. (Illus.). 44p. (Orig.). (J). (gr. k-5). 1983. pap. 7.95 (0-9612346-0-1, 83-090410) Ray-Foster.

Ray, M. Catherine. I'm Here to Help: A Hospice Worker's Guide to Communicating with Dying People & Their Loved Ones. (Illus.). 72p. 1992. reprint ed. pap. 7.00 (0-9636311-0-1) McRay.

Ray, M. L. Pumpkins. Root, Barry, ed. (J). 1992. 13.95 (0-15-252252-2, Gulliver Bks) HarBrace.

Ray, M. S. & Johnston, D. W. Chemical Engineering Design Project: A Case Study Approach. xxvi, 358p. 1989. 90.00 (2-88124-712-1); text ed. 124.00 (2-88124-713-X) Gordon & Breach.

Ray, M. Tipton, jt. auth. see Schleien, Stuart J.

Ray, Malibika, ed. Environmental Protection & Afforetions: National Seminar Visva-Bharati, Sanitiniketan. 250p. 1990. 45.00 (0-685-59954-X, Messers Today & Tomorrow) Scholarly Pubns.

***Ray, Man.** Man Ray, 1890-1976. LC 95-5561. 1995. write for info. (0-8109-4277-1) Abrams.

— Man Ray in Fashion. (Illus.). 96p. (Orig.). 1991. pap. 24.95 (0-933642-14-8, U of Wash Pr) Intl Ctr Photo.

— Photographs by Man Ray: Nineteen Twenty to Nineteen Thirty-Four. LC 79-50461. (Illus.). 1980. reprint ed. pap. 10.95 (0-486-23842-3) Dover.

Ray, Margaret & Shalleck, Allan J. Curious George Goes to an Ice Cream Shop. (Illus.). 32p. (J). (ps-2). 1989. pap. 3.95 (0-395-51937-3) HM.

Ray, Marilyn A., jt. ed. see Watson, Jean.

Ray, Marilyn C. Applied Immunodermatology. LC 91-20900. (Topics in Clinical Dermatology Ser.). (Illus.). 232p. 1992. 80.00 (0-89640-191-X) Igaku-Shoin.

Ray, Martin. Joseph Conrad. LC 93-24481. (Modern Fiction Ser.). 1993. 11.99 (0-7131-6559-6, Pub. by E Arnold UK) Routledge Chapman & Hall.

Ray, Martin, ed. Joseph Conrad: Interviews & Recollections. LC 89-52160. 254p. 1990. text ed. 34.95 (0-87745-290-3) U of Iowa Pr.

Ray, Martin, ed. see Conrad, Joseph.

Ray, Marty. Writers Block. Ingram, tr. 250p. 1995. pap. 8.95 (1-56901-319-5) NW Pub.

Ray, Martyn S. Chemical Engineering Bibliography, 1967-1988. LC 89-77185. 887p. 1990. 98.00 (0-8155-1241-4) Noyes.

— Chemical Process & Plant Design Bibliography, 1959-1989. LC 90-22371. 196p. 1991. 54.00 (0-8155-1272-4) Noyes.

— Engineering Experimentation: Ideas, Techniques & Presentation. 1988. text ed. write for info. (0-07-084184-5) McGraw.

Ray, Mary. Cooking for A Crowd: Menus, Recipes, & How-to's For Church Kitchens. LC 94-33297. 128p. (Orig.). 1995. pap. 9.95 (0-687-00253-2) Abingdon.

Ray, Mary, et al, eds. Gloucester, Massachusetts, Town & City Records Guide: Including Other Related Material. 151p. 1992. lib. bdg. 29.50 (0-8328-2581-6); pap. 19.50 (0-8328-2582-4) Higginson Bk Co.

Ray, Mary B. & Cox, Barbara J. Beyond the Basics: A Text for Advanced Legal Writing. 427p. 1993. reprint ed. pap. text ed. 22.00 (0-314-85410-X) West Pub.

— Beyond the Basics: A Text for Advanced Legal Writing. 375p. (C). 1993. reprint ed. teacher ed, pap. text ed. write for info. (0-314-92269-5) West Pub.

Ray, Mary B. & Ramsfield, Jill J. Legal Writing: Getting It Right & Getting It Written. 2nd ed. LC 93-22762. 361p. 1993. pap. text ed. 19.50 (0-314-02255-4) West Pub.

Ray, Mary-Ellen J. Flash: A Pause for the Menopause. LC 84-4836. (Illus.). 56p. (Orig.). 1984. pap. 4.50 (0-917047-00-1) Rising Pub.

Ray, Mary F. & Dondi, Beda. Professional Cooking & Baking. (Illus.). 450p. (C). 1981. teacher ed 9.28 (0-02-665440-7); text ed. 19.96 (0-02-665430-X); student ed 7.20 (0-02-665450-4) Bennett IL.

***Ray, Mary H. & Nicholls, Robert P., eds.** A Guide to Significant & Historic Gardens of America. LC 82-74400. (Illus.). 327p. (Orig.). 1984. pap. 9.95 (0-9612486-0-2) Garden GA.

— The Traveler's Guide to American Gardens. rev. ed. (Illus.). xv, 375p. 1988. 12.95 (0-8078-1787-2) U of NC Pr.

Ray, Mary L. Alvah & Arvilla. LC 93-31874. (Illus.). (J). 1994. 14.95 (0-15-202655-X) HarBrace.

— Angel Baskets: A Little Story about the Shakers. LC 87-50789. (Illus.). 32p. (Orig.). (J). 1987. pap. write for info. (0-9609384-3-5) M Wetherbee.

— Mud. LC 94-28711. (Illus.). (J). 1996. write for info. (0-15-256263-X) HarBrace.

— My Carousel Horse. LC 93-45876. (J). 1900. write for info. (0-15-200023-2) HarBrace.

— Pianna. LC 91-14609. (J). (ps-3). 1994. 14.95 (0-15-261357-9, HB Juv Bks) HarBrace.

— A Rumbly Tumbly Glittery Gritty Place. LC 92-20084. (Illus.). (J). 1993. 13.95 (0-15-292861-8, HB Juv Bks) HarBrace.

— Shaker Boy. LC 93-1333. (Illus.). (J). 1994. 15.95 (0-15-276921-8) HarBrace.

Ray, Mary L., ed. see Wetherbee, Martha & Taylor, Nathan.

Ray, Mary W., jt. auth. see Brown, William L.

Ray, MaryEllen B. City of Watts: Nineteen Seven to Nineteen Twenty-Six. LC 85-8336. (Illus.). 96p. (Orig.). 1985. pap. 6.95 (0-917047-01-X) Rising Pub.

Ray, Maurice, ed. Recruitment Advertising: A Means of Communication. 240p. (C). 1980. 85.00 (0-85292-259-0, Pub. by IPM Hse UK) St Mut.

Ray, Michael & Rinzler, Alan, eds. The New Paradigm in Business: Emerging Strategies for Leadership & Organizational Change. LC 92-26205. 320p. 1994. pap. 13.95 (0-87477-726-7, J P T-Putnam) Putnam Pub Group.

Ray, Michael, jt. auth. see Catford, Lorna.

Ray, Michael, jt. auth. see Littman, Barbara.

***Ray, Michael J.** Boeing 757-767 Simulator Checkride: The Line Pilot's Survival Guide. 250p. 1995. pap. write for info. (1-885591-88-8) Morris Pubng.

— The Line Pilots Similator Checkride Survival Guide. 250p. 1995. 49.95 (0-936283-02-5) U Temecula Pr.

— Rivers of Time: A Graphic Chronology of Man. 280p. (C). write for info. (0-936283-01-7) U Temecula Pr.

— Then & Now: Cartoons about Airline Pilots. 96p. (Orig.). 1986. pap. 6.95 (0-936283-00-9) U Temecula Pr.

Ray, Michael L., ed. Measurement Readings for Marketing Research. LC 84-9385. 382p. (Orig.). reprint ed. pap. 108.90 (0-7837-2492-6, 2042657) Bks Demand.

Ray, Michael L. & Meyers, Rochelle. Creativity in Business. 1989. pap. 12.00 (0-385-24851-2) Doubleday.

Ray, Michael L. & Ward, Scott, eds. Communicating with Consumers: The Information Processing Approach. LC 75-32370. (Sage Contemporary Social Science Issues Ser.: No. 21). 142p. reprint ed. pap. 40.50 (0-317-09979-5, 2021943) Bks Demand.

Ray, Michael L., jt. auth. see Peter, J. Paul.

Ray, Mrs. Sam. Post Cards from Old Kansas City. LC 80-84468. (Illus.). 48p. 1980. pap. 9.50 (0-685-02273-0) Hist Kansas City.

***Ray, Muriel.** Creative Art Ideas for Teachers. 1995. 9.95 (0-8062-5307-X) Carlton.

Ray, N. Idea & Image in Indian Art. (Illus.). 1973. text ed. 26.00 (0-685-13741-4) Coronet Bks.

Ray, N., et al. Normal Structures & Bordism Theory, with Applications to MSP. LC 77-10134. (Memoirs Ser.: No. 12/193). 66p. 1977. 21.00 (0-8218-2193-8, MEMO 12/193) Am Math.

Ray, N. H. Inorganic Polymers. 1978. text ed. 99.00 (0-12-583550-7) Acad Pr.

Ray, N. R., ed. Dictionary of National Biography, Supplement Vol. 1. (C). 1986. 54.00 (0-8364-2364-X) S Asia.

— Himalaya Frontier in Historical Perspectives. 399p. 1986. 22.50 (0-8364-2000-4, Pub. by Usha II) S Asia.

Ray, N. R. & Chakrabarti, P. N., eds. Studies in Cultural Development of India. (C). 1991. 44.00 (81-85094-43-8, Pub. by Punthi Pus II) S Asia.

Ray, Nicholas. Cambridge Architecture: A Concise Guide. (Illus.). 125p. (C). 1994. pap. 18.95 (0-521-45855-2) Cambridge U Pr.

— Cambridge Architecture: A Concise Guide. (Illus.). 125p. (C). 1994. 54.95 (0-521-45222-8) Cambridge U Pr.

— I Was Interrupted: Nicholas Ray on Making Movies. LC 92-35003. 1993. 25.00 (0-520-08233-8) U CA Pr.

— I Was Interrupted: Nicholas Ray on Making Movies. Ray, Susan, ed. & intro. by. (Illus.). 243p. 1995. pap. 14.00 (0-520-20169-8) U CA Pr.

***Ray, Nicholas D.** Arab Islamic Banking & the Renewal of Islamic Law. LC 95-9842. (Arab & Islamic Law Ser.). 1995. write for info. (1-85966-104-1, Pub. by Graham & Trotman UK) Kluwer Ac.

Ray, Nigel & Walker, Grant, eds. Proceedings of the Adams Memorial Symposium on Algebraic Topology: Vol. 1. (London Mathematical Society Lecture Note Ser.: No. 175). (Illus.). 300p. (C). 1992. 42.95 (0-521-42074-1) Cambridge U Pr.

— Proceedings of the Adams Memorial Symposium on Algebraic Topology: Vol. 2. (London Mathematical Society Lecture Note Ser.: No. 176). (Illus.). 300p. (C). 1992. 42.95 (0-521-42153-5) Cambridge U Pr.

Ray, Nihar-Ranjan. Brahmanical Gods in Burma: A Chapter of Indian Art & Iconography. LC 77-87020. reprint ed. 16.50 (0-404-16852-3) AMS Pr.

— An Introduction to the Study of Theravada Buddhism in Burma: A Study of Indo-Burmese Historical & Cultural Relations from the Earliest Times to the British Conquest. LC 77-87021. reprint ed. 25.00 (0-404-16853-1) AMS Pr.

— Sanskrit Buddhism in Burma. LC 78-70112. reprint ed. 22.00 (0-404-17367-5) AMS Pr.

Ray, Niharranjan. The Sikh Gurus & the Sikh Society. 1975. 14.50 (0-8364-2615-0, Pub. by Munshiram Manoharlal II) S Asia.

Ray, Nisith R. Calcutta: The Profile of a City. 1986. 11.50 (0-317-56328-9, Pub. by KP Bagchi IA) S Asia.

— Dimensions of National Integration: The Experiences & Lessons of Indian History. (C). 1993. 40.00 (81-85094-62-4, Pub. by Punthi Pus II) S Asia.

— Growth of Public Opinion in India: 19th & Early 20th Centuries. (C). 1989. 34.00 (81-85109-94-X, Pub. by Naya Prokash IA) S Asia.

— The Urban Experience: Essays in Honour of Professor Nisith R. Ray. 1987. 17.50 (0-8364-2276-7, Pub. by Rddhi IA) S Asia.

Ray, Nisith R., ed. Atmacarit: Autobiography of Sivnath Sastri. 1988. 16.00 (81-85292-03-5, Pub. by Rddhi IA) S Asia.

Ray, Norm. Easy Financials for Your Home-Based Business: The Friendly Guide to Successful Management Systems for Busy Home Entrepreneurs. LC 92-50682. (Illus.). 184p. (Orig.). 1993. pap. 19.95 (1-877810-92-4) Rayve Prodns.

Ray, Norm & Ray, Barbara. Lifetimes, the Life Experiences Journal. LC 89-92021. 288p. 1989. 49.95 (1-877810-34-7) Rayve Prodns.

Ray, Oakley & Ksir, Charles. Drugs, Society, & Human Behavior. 6th ed. LC 92-27621. 462p. 1992. pap. 29.95 (0-8016-6563-9) Mosby Yr Bk.

Ray, Olden M., Sr. Black Valentine. 100p. 1988. 6.95 (0-9616488-4-8) Alef Bet Comns.

Ray, P. K. Advances in Immunity & Cancer Therapy, Vol. 2. (Illus.). 305p. 1986. 91.00 (0-387-96258-1) Spr-Verlag.

— Agricultural Insurance: Principles & Organization & Application to Developing Countries. LC 66-178100. 1967. 141.00 (0-08-011513-6, Pub. by Pergamon Repr UK) Franklin.

— Agricultural Insurance: Theory & Practice & Application to Developing Countries. 2nd ed. (Illus.). 360p. 1981. 190.00 (0-08-025787-9, Pub. by Pergamon Repr UK) Franklin.

— A Practical Guide to Multi-Risk Crop Insurance for Developing. (C). 1991. text ed. 21.50 (81-204-0604-4, Pub. by Oxford IBH II) S Asia.

Ray, P. Orman. Repeal of the Missouri Compromise. 1965. reprint ed. 12.50 (0-910324-07-7) Canner.

Ray, Paul C. The Surrealist Movement in England. LC 70-145626. 331p. 1971. 20.00 (0-685-10518-0) Lib Soc Sci.

Ray, Pearl J. Beyond Today. 288p. (Orig.). (C). 1986. pap. 6.95 (0-9616405-0-2) Harvest Age.

Ray, Peter, jt. auth. see Coleman, Brian.

Ray, Peter, et al. Botany. 784p. (C). 1983. text ed. 54.00 (0-03-089942-7) SCP.

Ray, Peter S., ed. Mesoscale Meteorology & Forecasting. (Illus.). 793p. (C). 1987. reprint ed. text ed. 66.25 (0-933876-66-1) Am Meteorological.

Ray, Prasanta K., ed. Immunobiology & Transplantation, Cancer & Pregnancy. 500p. 1983. 200.00 (0-08-025994-4, Pergamon Pr) Elsevier.

Ray, Priyadaranjian & Ray, Acharya P., eds. History of Chemistry in Ancient & Medieval India, Incorporating the History of Hindu Chemistry. LC 79-8619. reprint ed. 42.50 (0-404-18483-9) AMS Pr.

Ray, Punya S., et al. Bengali Language Handbook. LC 66-29717. (Language Handbook Ser.). 155p. reprint ed. pap. 44.20 (0-8357-3357-2, 2039594) Bks Demand.

Ray, R., et al. Role & Status of Women in India. 167p. 1978. 11.95 (0-318-37071-9) Asia Bk Corp.

Ray, Rabindra. The Naxalites & Their Ideology. 262p. 1993. reprint ed. pap. 7.95 (0-19-563125-0) OUP.

Ray, Rajat. Urban Roots of Indian Nationalism. 246p. 1979. 18.95 (0-318-36867-6) Asia Bk Corp.

Ray, Rajat K., ed. Entrepreneurship & Industry in India, 1800-1947. (Oxford in India Readings: Themes in Indian History Ser.). 276p. 1992. 16.95 (0-19-562806-3) OUP.

***Ray, Ralph & Redman, John.** Practical Inheritance Tax Planning. 3rd ed. 1994. pap. 45.00 (0-406-02417-0) Butterworth Legal Pubs.

Ray, Ralph P. & Redman, John E. Practical Inheritance Tax Planning. 2nd ed. 342p. 1991. pap. 79.00 (0-406-00451-X, U.K.) Butterworth Legal Pubs.

Ray, Randolph, ed. One Hundred Great Religious Poems. LC 78-80378. (Granger Index Reprint Ser.). 1977. 18.95 (0-8369-6060-2) Ayer.

Ray, Ratnalakha. Change in Bengal Agrarian Society, Seventeen Sixty to Eighteen Fifty. 1980. 20.00 (0-8364-0646-X, Pub. by Manohar II) S Asia.

Ray, Rayburn W. & Ray, Rose A. Wedding Anniversary Idea Book. 96p. (Orig.). 1985. pap. 7.95 (0-939298-43-0, 430) J M Prods.

Ray, Rayburn W. & Ray, Rose Ann. The Groom's Wedding Guidebook. 96p. (Orig.). 1983. pap. 7.95 (0-939298-22-8, 228) J M Prods.

R

An Asterisk (*) at the beginning of an entry indicates that the title is appearing in BIP for the first time.

— When Your Daughter Marries. 96p. (Orig.). 1982. pap. 7.95 (*0-939298-14-7*, 147) J M Prods.

Ray, Raymond L. Anybody Seen Soldier? LC 88-83634. 116p. (Orig.). 1989. pap. text ed. 7.00 (*0-916383-84-9*) Aegina Pr.

Ray, Rebecca L. Bridging Both Worlds: The Communication Consultant in Corporate America. LC 93-28996. 194p. (Orig.). (C). 1993. lib. bdg. 49.50 (*0-8191-9278-3*); pap. text ed. 27.50 (*0-8191-9279-1*) U Pr of Amer.

Ray, Reginald A. Buddhist Saints in India: A Study in Buddhist Values & Orientations. 528p. 1994. 49.95 (*0-19-507202-2*) OUP.

***Ray, Richard.** Case Studies in Athletic Training Administration. LC 94-28362. (Illus.). 104p. (Orig.). 1995. pap. text ed. 14.00x (*0-87322-675-5*, nRAY0675) Human Kinetics.

— Management Strategies in Athletic Training. LC 93-5167. (Illus.). 280p. 1994. 32.00 (*0-87322-582-1*, BRAY0582) Human Kinetics.

Ray, Richard & MacCaskey, Michael. Roses. LC 80-82532. (Gardening Ser.). (Illus.). (Orig.). 1984. pap. 14.95 (*0-89586-079-1*) Price Stern.

Ray, Richard P., jt. ed. see Elton, David J.

***Ray, Robert B.** The Avant-Garde Finds Andy Hardy. LC 95-13646. (Illus.). 272p. (C). 1996. text ed. 39.95 (*0-674-05537-3*); pap. text ed. 18.95 (*0-674-05538-1*) HUP.

— A Certain Tendency of the American Cinema: 1930-1980. LC 84-42901. (Illus.). 405p. 1985. pap. 19.95 (*0-691-10174-4*) Princeton U Pr.

Ray, Robert D., jt. auth. see Ray, Joan K.

***Ray, Robert H.** A George Herbert Companion. LC 94-30947. (Garland Reference Library of the Humanities Ser.: Vol. 921). 240p. Date not set. 35.00 (*0-8240-4849-0*, H921) Garland.

Ray, Robert H., ed. Approaches to Teaching Shakespeare's King Lear. LC 86-12734. (Approaches to Teaching World Literature Ser.: No. 12). x, 166p. 1986. 37.50 (*0-87352-497-7*, AP12C); pap. 18.00x (*0-87352-498-5*, AP12P) Modern Lang.

Ray, Robert J. The Weekend Novelist. LC 93-15108. 1994. 10.95 (*0-440-50594-1*) Dell.

Ray, Robert J. & Ray, Ann. The Art of Reading: A Handbook on Writing. 174p. (Orig.). 1968. pap. 8.50 (*0-471-00453-7*) Wiley.

Ray, Roberta K. The Power of Listening. 126p. (C). 1993. spiral bd. 18.95 (*0-8403-9127-7*) Kendall-Hunt.

Ray, Roger B. Indians of Maine & the Atlantic Provinces: A Bibliographic Guide. Morris, Gerald E., ed. (Maine History Bibliographical Guide Ser.). 1977. pap. 4.00 (*0-915592-29-0*) Maine Hist.

Ray, Ronald D., jt. auth. see U. S. Government Accounting Office Staff.

Ray, Rose A., jt. auth. see Ray, Rayburn W.

Ray, Rose Ann, jt. auth. see Ray, Rayburn W.

Ray, Rose M. Superwomen Do It Less...A Guide to Having It All: Children, a Career, & a Loving Relationship. Baird, Nelle, ed. LC 91-65759. (Illus.). (Orig.). 1992. pap. 9.95 (*0-9629361-0-3*) Yankee Pub.

Ray, Ruth E. The Practice of Theory: Teacher Research in Composition. 191p. (Orig.). 1993. pap. 14.95 (*0-8141-3660-5*) NCTE.

Ray, S., jt. ed. see Kiceniuk, J. W.

Ray, S. Alan. Modern Soul: Michel Foucault & the Theological Discourse of Gordon Kaufman & David Tracey. LC 87-21094. (Harvard Dissertations in Religion Ser.). 208p. (Orig.). 1988. pap. 16.00 (*0-8006-7073-6*, 1-7073, Fortress Pr) Augsburg Fortress.

Ray, S. Dutta. Psychological Disorders of Young Children. 259p. 1980. 19.95 (*0-318-36940-0*) Asia Bk Corp.

Ray, S. N. Communication & Rural Development in India: The Changing Perceptions & the Search for a New Public Policy. (C). 1992. pap. text ed. 5.00 (*81-7304-030-3*, Pub. by Manohar II) S Asia.

Ray, S. S. Reinforced Concrete: Analysis & Design. LC 94-13306. (Illus.). 576p. 1994. 66.00 (*0-632-03724-5*, Pub. by Blckwell Sci Pubns UK) Blackwell Sci.

Ray, Samuel N. Job Hunting after Fifty: Strategies for Success. 203p. 1991. pap. text ed. 14.95 (*0-471-53344-0*) Wiley.

— Resumes for the Over-50 Job Hunter. 216p. 1993. text ed. 42.50 (*0-471-57422-8*); pap. text ed. 14.95 (*0-471-57423-6*) Wiley.

***Ray, Sandra K.** Making Waves in Zion. LC 95-11597. 1995. write for info. (*1-881320-27-8*) Black Belt Pr.

Ray, Sandy. The Lamb. Sytsma, Cheryle, ed. (Illus.). 15p. (Orig.). (J). 1991. pap. write for info. (*1-879068-10-9*) Ray-Ma Natsal.

— The Little Seed. Sytsma, Cheryle, ed. LC 90-63623. (Illus.). 30p. (Orig.). (J). (gr. k-5). 1991. pap. write for info. (*1-879068-01-X*) Ray-Ma Natsal.

— Sir Joshua, Himself. Sytsma, Cheryle, ed. LC 90-63622. (Illus.). 30p. (Orig.). (J). (gr. k-5). 1991. pap. write for info. (*1-879068-02-8*) Ray-Ma Natsal.

— Songs of My Heart. Sytsma, Cheryle, ed. (Illus.). 160p. (Orig.). 1991. pap. 7.98 (*1-879068-07-9*) Ray-Ma Natsal.

— Songs of Sorrow Songs of Praise. Sytsma, Cheryle, ed. LC 90-91937. (Illus.). 160p. (Orig.). 1990. pap. 7.98 (*1-879068-00-1*) Ray-Ma Natsal.

— Words from My Father. Sytsma, Cheryle, ed. (Illus.). 192p. (Orig.). 1991. pap. 8.95 (*1-879068-03-6*) Ray-Ma Natsal.

Ray, Satyajit. Brave Professor Shonku. 108p. 1986. 7.95 (*0-318-36944-3*) Asia Bk Corp.

— Our Films, Their Films. 219p. 1983. 19.95 (*0-86125-637-9*) Asia Bk Corp.

— Our Films, Their Films. 224p. 1994. 22.95 (*0-7868-6122-3*) Hyperion.

— Phatik Chand. Ray, Lila, tr. 108p. (J). (gr. 6-8). 1984. pap. 8.00 (*0-86578-230-X*) Ind-US Inc.

Ray, Satyajit, jt. auth. see Ray, Sukumar.

Ray, Satyajit, tr. see Ray, Sukumar & Ray, Satyajit.

Ray, Shreela. Night Conversations with None Other. (American Dust Ser.: No. 6). 85p. 1977. 6.95 (*0-913218-32-4*); pap. 2.95 (*0-913218-31-6*) Dustbooks.

Ray, Sibnarayan. Autumnal Equinox. (Redbird Ser.). 1975. 10.00 (*0-89253-601-2*); pap. text ed. 4.80 (*0-88253-711-3*) Ind-US Inc.

Ray, Sibnarayan, ed. For a Revolution from Below. (C). 1989. 17.50 (*81-85195-15-3*, Pub. by Minerva II) S Asia.

— Selected Works of M. N. Roy, 1917-1922, Vol I. (Illus.). 596p. 1988. 39.95 (*0-19-562038-0*) OUP.

— Vak: An Anthology of Australian, European & Indian Verse. 14.00 (*0-89253-623-3*); pap. 8.00 (*0-86578-108-7*) Ind-US Inc.

Ray, Sibnarayan, ed. see Roy, M. N.

***Ray, Sidney E., ed.** Photographic Data. (Focal Press Pocketbooks Ser.). 256p. 1994. pap. 19.95 (*0-240-51385-1*, Focal) Buttrwrth-Heinemann.

Ray, Sidney F. Applied Photographic Optics: Lenses & Optical Systems for Photography, Film, Video, & Electronic Imaging. 2nd ed. LC 93-44367. 576p. 1994. 65.00 (*0-240-51350-9*, Focal) Buttrwrth-Heinemann.

— Photographic Chemistry & Processing. (Focal Press Pocketbooks Ser.). 256p. 1994. 19.95 (*0-240-51386-X*, Focal) Buttrwrth-Heinemann.

— Photographic Imaging & Electronic Photography. (Focal Press Pocketbooks Ser.). 256p. 1994. 19.95 (*0-240-51393-2*, Focal) Buttrwrth-Heinemann.

— The Photographic Lens: Media Manual. 2nd ed. (Illus.). 355p. 1992. pap. 16.95 (*0-240-51329-0*, Focal) Buttrwrth-Heinemann.

— Photographic Lenses & Optics. (Focal Press Pocketbooks Ser.). 256p. 1994. 19.95 (*0-240-51387-8*, Focal) Buttrwrth-Heinemann.

— Photographic Printing & Enlarging. (Focal Press Pocketbooks Ser.). 256p. 1994. 19.95 (*0-240-51388-6*, Focal) Buttrwrth-Heinemann.

***Ray, Sidney F., ed.** Photographic Technology & Imaging Science. (Focal Press Pocketbooks Ser.). 256p. 1994. pap. 19.95 (*0-240-51389-4*, Focal) Buttrwrth-Heinemann.

Ray, Sidney H. A Comparative Study of the Melanesian Island Languages. LC 75-35151. reprint ed. 87.50 (*0-404-14166-8*) AMS Pr.

Ray, Sidney H. & Haddon, Alfred C. A Study of the Languages of Torres Straits. LC 75-35153. reprint ed. 27.00 (*0-404-14168-4*) AMS Pr.

Ray, Sidney H. & Riley, E. B. A Grammar of the Kiwai Language, Fly Delta, Papua, with a Kiwai Vocabulary. LC 75-35152. reprint ed. 15.00 (*0-404-14167-6*) AMS Pr.

Ray, Siva P. Turning of the Wheel. Ghosh, A., ed. (Illus.). 132p. (Orig.). 1987. pap. 6.95 (*0-9611614-2-6*) A Ghosh.

Ray, Slim. The Canoe Handbook: Techniques for Mastering the Sport of Canoeing. LC 91-16032. (Illus.). 224p. 1992. pap. 15.95 (*0-8117-3032-8*) Stackpole.

Ray, Slim, jt. auth. see Bechdel, Les.

Ray, Sondra. Celebration of Breath. LC 83-1770. 192p. 1983. pap. 8.95 (*0-89087-355-0*) Celestial Arts.

— Drinking the Divine. LC 84-45361. 192p. (Orig.). 1984. pap. 9.95 (*0-89087-460-3*) Celestial Arts.

— How to Be Chic, Fabulous, & Live Forever. LC 89-85828. 1989. 18.95 (*0-89087-564-2*) Celestial Arts.

— I Deserve Love. LC 75-28774. 128p. 1987. 7.95 (*0-89087-909-5*) Celestial Arts.

— Ideal Birth. LC 84-71025. 272p. (Orig.). 1985. pap. 8.95 (*0-89087-364-X*) Celestial Arts.

— Inner Communion. LC 90-82187. 96p. (Orig.). 1990. pap. 8.95 (*0-89087-621-5*) Celestial Arts.

— Interludes with the Gods. 128p. (Orig.). 1991. pap. 8.95 (*0-89087-635-5*) Celestial Arts.

— Loving Relationships. LC 79-55633. 1980. pap. 8.95 (*0-89087-244-9*) Celestial Arts.

— Loving Relationships, No. II. 192p. 1992. pap. text ed. 9.95 (*0-89087-661-4*) Celestial Arts.

— The Only Diet There Is. LC 80-70795. 156p. 1981. pap. 7.95 (*0-89087-321-6*) Celestial Arts.

— Pure Joy. LC 86-26911. 216p. 1988. pap. 9.95 (*0-89087-491-3*) Celestial Arts.

Ray, Sondra & Mandel, Bob. Birth & Relationships: How Your Birth Affects Your Relationships. LC 86-28404. 172p. 1987. pap. 8.95 (*0-89087-486-7*) Celestial Arts.

Ray, Sondra, jt. auth. see Orr, Leonard.

Ray, Stephen & Murdoch, Kathleen. The Ant Nest. LC 92-34254. (Voyages Ser.). (Illus.). (J). 1993. 4.25 (*0-383-03614-3*) SRA Schl Grp.

— Have You Ever Found a Beetle? LC 92-27265. (Voyages Ser.). (Illus.). (J). 1993. 3.75 (*0-383-03627-5*) SRA Schl Grp.

— In the Forest. LC 92-27266. (Voyages Ser.). (Illus.). (J). 1993. 3.75 (*0-383-03635-6*) SRA Schl Grp.

— Just Right for the Night. LC 92-21398. (Illus.). (J). (gr. 4 up). 1993. 4.25 (*0-383-03580-5*) SRA Schl Grp.

— Snake. LC 92-21453. (Illus.). (J). 1993. 4.25 (*0-383-03653-4*) SRA Schl Grp.

— Some Snakes. LC 93-113. (J). 1994. pap. write for info. (*0-383-03715-8*) SRA Schl Grp.

— Tall Stories about Snakes. LC 93-6630. (J). 1994. pap. write for info. (*0-383-03716-6*) SRA Schl Grp.

Ray, Subhash C., jt. auth. see Lott, William F.

Ray, Sukumar. Folk-Music of Eastern India. (C). 1988. 24.00 (*81-85109-81-8*, Pub. by Naya Prokash IA) S Asia.

— Music of Eastern India. 1986. 20.00 (*0-8364-1581-7*, KL Mukhopadhyay) S Asia.

Ray, Sukumar & Ray, Satyajit. Nonsense Rhymes. Ray, Satyajit, tr. (Writers Workshop Saffronbird Ser.). 1975. 8.00 (*0-88253-588-9*); pap. text ed. 4.00 (*0-88253-587-0*) Ind-US Inc.

Ray, Sunandra, jt. auth. see Berer, Marge.

Ray, Susan, jt. auth. see Isaak, Gudrum.

Ray, Susan, ed. see Ray, Nicholas.

Ray, Suzanne S., et al, comps. Preliminary Guide to Pre-Nineteen Hundred & Four County Records in the Virginia State Library & Archives. xxv, 331p. 1994. reprint ed. pap. 12.00 (*0-88490-179-3*) VA State Lib.

Ray, Syamal K. Indian Bureaucracy at the Crossroads. 407p. 1979. 25.95 (*0-940500-58-2*, Pub. by Sterling II) Asia Bk Corp.

***Ray, T P.** Predoctoral Astrophysics School (5th: 1992: Berlin, Germany) Star Formation & Techniques in Infrared & mm-Wave Astronomy: Lectures Held at the Predoctoral Astrophysics School V, Organized by the European Astrophysics Doctoral Network (EADN) in Berlin, Germany, 21 September-20October 1992. Beckwith, S., ed. LC 94-25872. 1994. 65.00 (*0-387-58196-0*) Spr-Verlag.

Ray, Thomas P., jt. ed. see Sandqvist, Aage.

***Ray, Ujjal.** From Diffidence to Reliance: Journey of a Colonial Intellectual 1839-94. (C). 1993. 14.00x (*81-85195-51-X*, Pub. by Minerva II) S Asia.

Ray, Uma. Indian Music for English Speaking Singers. (Illus.). 125p. 1995. text ed. 35.00 (*0-89341-736-X*); pap. text ed. 18.50 (*0-89341-737-8*) Hollowbrook.

Ray, Verne F. Cultural Relations in the Plateau of Northwestern America. LC 76-43807. reprint ed. 35.00 (*0-404-15664-9*) AMS Pr.

— The Sanpoil & Nespelem: Salishan Peoples of Northeastern Washington. LC 76-43809. (Univ. of Washington Publications in Anthropology: Vol. 5). reprint ed. 45.00 (*0-404-15663-0*) AMS Pr.

Ray, Verne F., ed. Cultural Stability & Cultural Change: American Ethnological Society Proceedings, 1957. LC 84-45544. 1988. reprint ed. pap. 35.00 (*0-404-62651-3*) AMS Pr.

— Intermediate Societies, Social Mobility, & Communication: American Ethnological Society Proceedings, 1959. LC 84-45546. 1988. reprint ed. pap. 35.00 (*0-404-62653-X*) AMS Pr.

— Systems of Political Control & Bureaucracy in Human Societies: American Ethnological Society Proceedings, 1958. LC 84-45545. 1988. reprint ed. pap. 35.00 (*0-404-62652-1*) AMS Pr.

Ray, Verne F., ed. see Teicher, Morton I.

Ray, Veronica. Choosing Happiness: The Art of Living Unconditionally. LC 90-55300. 176p. (Orig.). 1991. pap. 10.00 (*0-06-255356-9*, Hazelden SF) Harper SF.

— Design for Growth: Twelve Steps for Adult Children. 1993. mass mkt. 4.99 (*0-345-38517-9*) Ballantine.

— Green Spirituality. 128p. 1992. 9.00 (*0-89486-808-X*, 5184A) Hazelden.

— Other Peoples Successes: Moving Beyond Envy & Jealousy. 1993. pap. 1.95 (*0-89486-800-4*, 5245A) Hazelden.

— Personal Evolution: The Art of Living with Purpose. 160p. 1992. pap. 10.00 (*0-89486-811-X*, 5187A) Hazelden.

Ray, W. H., jt. ed. see Arkun, Y.

Ray, W. Harmon, jt. auth. see Ogunnaike, Babatunde A.

Ray, Walter R. Poems of the Heart. LC 84-73412. 64p. 1985. 6.50 (*0-8233-0407-8*) Golden Quill.

Ray, Wendel A. & Keeney, Bradford. Resource Focused Therapy. (Systemic Thinking & Practice Ser.). 112p. 1993. pap. 22.95 (*1-85575-049-X*, Pub. by Karnac Bks UK) Brunner-Mazel.

Ray, Wendel A., jt. auth. see Silberman, Bernice S.

Ray, Wendel A., jt. ed. see Weakland, John H.

Ray, William. Literary Meaning: From Phenomenology to Deconstruction. 300p. 1984. pap. 21.95 (*0-631-13458-1*) Blackwell Pubs.

— Story & History: Narrative Authority & Social Identity in the Eighteenth-Century French & English Novel. 400p. 1990. pap. 21.95 (*0-631-17512-1*) Blackwell Pubs.

Ray, William B. FCC: The Ups & Downs of Radio-TV Regulation. 214p. 1990. 26.95 (*0-8138-0227-X*) Iowa St U Pr.

Ray, William J. Methods Toward a Science of Behavior & Experience. 4th ed. (C). 1993. text ed. 52.95 (*0-534-17838-3*) Brooks-Cole.

Ray, William W. Graduate Student Research in Planning, Urban Design & Urban Affairs: 1974-76, No. 1176. 1976. 9.50 (*0-686-20418-2*) CPL Biblios.

Ray, Willis H. & Szekely, Julian. Process Optimization: With Applications in Metallurgy & Chemical Engineering. LC 73-936. (Wiley-Interscience Publication Ser.). (Illus.). 382p. reprint ed. pap. 108.90 (*0-7837-3465-4*, 2057793) Bks Demand.

Ray, Winifred, tr. see Heiden, Konrad.

***Ray, Worth S.** Austin Colony Pioneers: Including History of Bastrop, Fayette, Grimes, Montgomery & Washington Counties, Texas. (Illus.). 378p. 1995. reprint ed. 30.00 (*0-8063-1473-7*) Genealog Pub.

— Lost Tribes of North Carolina: Colonial Granville County (North Carolina) & Its People, Pt. 2. (Illus.). 120p. 1993. reprint ed. pap. 13.50 (*0-685-65685-3*, 4780) Clearfield Co.

— Lost Tribes of North Carolina: Index & Digest to Hathaway's "North Carolina Historical & Genealogical Register", Pt. 1. 192p. 1993. reprint ed. pap. 19.50 (*0-685-65683-7*, 4795) Clearfield Co.

— Lost Tribes of North Carolina: Old Albemarle & Its Absentee Landlords, Pt. 4. (Illus.). 156p. 1993. reprint ed. pap. 15.00 (*0-685-65687-X*, 4790) Clearfield Co.

— Lost Tribes of North Carolina: The Mecklenburg Signers & Their Neighbors, Pt. 3. (Illus.). 246p. 1993. reprint ed. pap. 22.50 (*0-685-65686-1*, 4785) Clearfield Co.

— Tennessee Cousins: A History of Tennessee People. LC 68-24685. (Illus.). 819p. 1994. reprint ed. 40.00 (*0-8063-0289-5*, 4800) Genealog Pub.

***Raya, Joseph.** Abundance of Love: The Incarnation & Byzantine Tradition. (Illus.). 143p. (Orig.). 1989. pap. 6.95 (*1-56125-015-5*) Educ Services.

— Acathist Hymn to the Name of Jesus. deluxe ed. Vinck, Jose de, ed. 40p. 1989. reprint ed. 5.75 (*0-911726-46-2*, CODE NJB) Alleluia Pr.

— Byzantine Church & Culture. De Vinck, Jose M., ed. LC 91-77254. 72p. (Orig.). 1992. 9.75 (*0-911726-54-3*, CODE CCC); pap. 6.75 (*0-911726-55-1*, CODE CCB) Alleluia Pr.

— Crowning: The Rite of Marriage. LC 91-78219. (Illus.). 64p. (Orig.). 1992. 9.75 (*0-911726-56-X*, CODE CMC); pap. 6.75 (*0-911726-57-8*, CODE CMB) Alleluia Pr.

Raya, Joseph & De Vinck, Jose. Byzantine Altar Gospel. 350p. 1979. 87.50 (*0-911726-35-7*, CODE AGU); 127.50x (*0-911726-34-9*, CODE AGC); 187.50x (*0-911726-51-9*, CODE AGL) Alleluia Pr.

— Byzantine Daily Worship. 2nd ed. 1036p. 1992. Black imitation morocco. 48.75 (*0-911726-07-1*, CODE BDW) Alleluia Pr.

— Byzantine Epistles Lectionary: Apostolos. 550p. 1981. Unsewn folded sheets. 67.50 (*0-911726-38-1*, CODE AEU); Red cloth. 87.50 (*0-911726-37-3*, CODE AEC); Silk Moire end-sheets. 105.00 (*0-911726-50-0*, CODE AEL) Alleluia Pr.

***Raya, Joseph M.** The Face of God: Essays in Byzantine Spirituality. 220p. (Orig.). 1984. pap. text ed. 10.00 (*1-887158-00-6*) Educ Services.

— Passage to Heaven: An Appreciation of the Divine Liturgy. 2nd rev. ed. (Illus.). 40p. 1991. pap. 6.95 (*1-56125-017-1*) Educ Services.

Rayan, Krishna. Sahitya, a Theory. 88p. 1991. text ed. 15.95 (*81-207-1175-0*, Pub. by Sterling Pubs II) Apt Bks.

Rayappa, P. Hanumantha. Backwardness & Welfare of Scheduled Castes & Scheduled Tribes in India. 1986. 18.00 (*81-7024-059-X*, Pub. by Ashish II) S Asia.

Rayaprol, Srinivas. Bones & Distances. 2nd ed. (Redbird Ser.). 1976. 8.00 (*0-89253-117-7*); 4.00 (*0-89253-135-5*) Ind-US Inc.

— Married Love & Other Poems. (Writers Workshop Redbird Ser.). 1976. 8.00 (*0-89253-724-8*); pap. text ed. 4.00 (*0-89253-725-6*) Ind-US Inc.

Rayar, Louise, et al, trs. The Dutch Penal Code. rev. ed. LC 93-46355. 1994. write for info. (*0-8377-0050-7*) Rothman.

Rayback, Joseph G. History of American Labor. LC 59-5344. 1966. pap. 18.95 (*0-02-925850-2*) Free Pr.

Rayback, Robert J. Millard Fillmore: Biography of a President. LC 91-78015. (Signature Ser.). (Illus.). 470p. 1992. reprint ed. 32.50 (*0-945707-04-5*) Amer Political.

Raybaud, C. R., et al, eds. Pediatric Oncology. (International Congress Ser.: Vol. 570). 408p. 1982. 117.50 (*0-444-90247-3*, Excerpta Medica) Elsevier.

Raybould, David. Comparative Law of Monopolies. (C). 1988. lib. bdg. 541.00 (*1-85333-074-4*, Pub. by Graham & Trotman UK); pap. text ed. 450.50 (*1-85333-073-6*, Pub. by Graham & Trotman UK) Kluwer Ac.

— Comparative Law of Monopolies: 1989 Basic Work & 1989 Supplement Services. (C). 1989. ring bd. 324.00 (*0-86010-941-0*, Pub. by Graham & Trotman UK) Kluwer Ac.

— Comparative Law of Monopolies: 1991 Basic Work & 1991 Supplement Service. 400p. 1991. 400.00 (*1-85333-515-0*, Pub. by Graham & Trotman UK) Kluwer Ac.

— Comparative Law of Monopolies Vols. 1-2: 1995 Basic Work, 2 vols., Set. 1000p. 1995. ring bd. 346.00 (*1-85333-826-5*, Pub. by Graham & Trotman UK) Kluwer Ac.

— Comparative Law of Monopolies, Vols. 1 & 2: 1992 Basic Work & 1992 Supplement Service. 600p. 1992. ring bd. 332.00 (*1-85333-669-6*, Pub. by Graham & Trotman UK) Kluwer Ac.

Raybould, David, ed. Comparative Law of Monopolies: Basic Work & Supplement Service, 1990. 1990. ring bd. 350.00 (*1-85333-326-3*, Pub. by Graham & Trotman UK) Kluwer Ac.

Raybould, David M. & Firth, Alison. Law of Monopolies: Competition Law & Practice in the U. S. A., E. E. C., Germany & the U. K. 592p. (C). 1991. lib. bdg. 140.00 (*1-85333-624-6*, Pub. by Graham & Trotman UK) Kluwer Ac.

Raybould, Edward, jt. auth. see Solity, Jonathan.

Raybould, Helen, jt. ed. see Mayer, Emeran A.

Raybould, S. Universities, Adult Education & Social Criticism. (Tolley Medal Ser.). 1970. 1.50 (*0-686-52207-9*, WPT 3) Syracuse U Cont Ed.

Raybrook, Roy B., et al. Russian Warrior. (Osprey Ser.). (Illus.). 128p. 1993. 15.95 (*1-85532-293-5*) Motorbooks Intl.

Rayburn. Quick Reference 3. 1991. 6.95 (*0-8016-6815-8*) Mosby Yr Bk.

Rayburn, et al. Laboratory Exercises in Biology. 2nd ed. 224p. (C). 1994. spiral bd. 22.95 (*0-8403-9300-8*) Kendall-Hunt.

***Rayburn, Alan.** Naming Canada: Stories About Place Names from Canadian Geographic. (Illus.). 300p. 1994. 55.00 (*0-8020-0569-1*); pap. 16.95 (*0-8020-6990-8*) U of Toronto Pr.

Rayburn, Cherie. Elizabeth's Castle Adventure: A Just Suppose(TM) Story. Gress, Jonna, ed. (Illus.). 4p. (J). (gr. 1-7). 1992. 18.80 (*0-944943-07-1*, CODE 18899-9) Current Inc.

— Fee Fiddle Foo What Should We Do? Gress, Jonna, ed. LC 92-76154. (Illus.). 14p. (J). (ps-3). 1993. pap. 16.20 (*0-944943-23-3*, CODE 22494-7) Current Inc.

— The Voyage of the Mayflower: A Teacher's Guide. Krall, Sharon, ed. (Illus.). 16p. 1994. pap. text ed. 10.95 (*0-944943-52-7*, CODE 23831-7) Current Inc.

— Where's Kitty. Gress, Jonna, ed. (Illus.). 12p. (J). (ps-5). 1994. pap. 8.25 (*0-944943-45-4*, 23304-5) Current Inc.

Rayburn, Cherie, ed. see Polhamus, Jean B.

Rayburn, Cherie, ed. see Swaby, Barbara.

Rayburn, Francis M., jt. auth. see Lindsey, Bonnie J.

R

An Asterisk (*) at the beginning of an entry indicates that the title is appearing in BIP for the first time.

Rayburn, John. Gregorian Chant: A History of Controversy Concerning Its Rhythm. LC 80-27616. xiv, 90p. 1981. reprint ed. text ed. 35.00 (*0-313-22811-6*, RAGR, Greenwood Pr) Greenwood.

Rayburn, John C., et al, eds. Century of Conflict, 1821-1913: Incidents in the Lives of William Neale & William A. Neale, Early Settlers in South Texas. LC 76-1556. (Chicano Heritage Ser.). (Illus.). 1977. reprint ed. 16.95 (*0-405-09520-1*) Ayer.

*__Rayburn, L. Gayle.__ Cost Accounting, International: Using a Cost Management Approach. 5th ed. 1024p. (C). 1992. text ed. 36.50 (*0-256-10809-9*) Irwin.

Rayburn, Letricia G. Principles of Cost Accounting: Using a Cost Management Approach. 5th ed. LC 92-18559. 1024p. (C). 1992. text ed. 69.95 (*0-256-08649-4*) Irwin.

Rayburn, Richard. Elections. (Illus.). 96p. (Orig.). (J). (gr. 4-8). 1992. student ed 10.95 (*1-55734-069-2*) Tchr Create Mat.

Rayburn, Richard, jt. auth. see Hale, Janet.

Rayburn, S. R. The Foundations of Laboratory Safety. (Contemporary Bioscience Ser.). (Illus.). xiii, 418p. 1989. 65.00 (*0-387-97125-4*) Spr-Verlag.

Rayburn, William, ed. Obstetrics. (House Officer Ser.). (Illus.). 272p. 1988. pap. text ed. 20.00 (*0-683-07159-9*) Williams & Wilkins.

Rayburn, William, jt. auth. see Appraisal Institute Staff.

Rayburn, William B. & Tosh, Dennis S. Uniform Standards of Profesisonal Appraisal Practice: Applying the Standards. 2nd ed. 1993. pap. 19.95 (*0-7931-0848-9*, 1556-1802) Dearborn Trade.

Rayburn, William B., jt. auth. see Tosh, Dennis S., Jr.

Rayburn, William B., jt. auth. see Tosh, Dennis S.

Rayburn, William F. & Zuspan. Drug Therapy in Obstetrics & Gynecology. 3rd ed. 661p. 1991. 55.00 (*0-8016-4052-0*) Mosby Yr Bk.

Raychahduri, S. P. & Verma, J. P., eds. Review of Tropical Plant Pathology: Diseases of Fruits, Vol. 2. iv, 406p. 1986. 99.00 (*1-55528-081-1*, Pub. by Today & Tomorrows P & P II) Scholarly Pubns.

Raychard, Al. Al Raychard's Fly Fishing in Maine: The Complete Guide to the Best Fly Fishing in Maine. rev. ed. LC 80-12126. (Illus.). 184p. 1990. pap. 9.95 (*0-945980-20-5*) Nrth Country Pr.

— Al Raychard's Guide to Remote Trout Ponds in Maine. LC 88-22524. (Illus.). 211p. (Orig.). 1984. pap. 9.95 (*0-945980-06-X*) Nrth Country Pr.

— Fly Fishing the Salt: A Guide to Saltwater Fly Fishing from Maine to the Chesapeake Bay. LC 89-3084. (Illus.). 169p. (Orig.). 1989. pap. 8.95 (*0-945980-08-6*) Nrth Country Pr.

— Flying-In for Trout: A Guide to Fishing the Remote Waters of Maine, Quebec, & Labrador. LC 87-7844. (Illus.). 168p. (Orig.). 1987. pap. 7.95 (*0-89621-108-8*) Nrth Country Pr.

— Salar, Vol. 1: An Angling Guide to Landlocked Salmon. LC 94-20776. 1994. pap. 14.95 (*0-945980-45-0*) Nrth Country Pr.

— Trout & Salmon Fishing in Northern New England: A Guide to Selected Waters in Maine, New Hampshire, Vermont & Massachusetts. LC 82-5930. (Illus.). 206p. (Orig.). 1982. pap. 9.95 (*0-945980-42-6*) Nrth Country Pr.

Raychaudhuri, A. K., et al. General Relativity, Relativistic Astrophysics & Cosmology. Harwit, Martin D. et al, eds. (Astronomy & Astrophysics Library). (Illus.). 320p. 1992. 59.00 (*0-387-97813-5*) Spr-Verlag.

Raychaudhuri, Hemchandra. Political History of Ancient India. LC 78-174301. reprint ed. 49.50 (*0-404-05228-2*) AMS Pr.

Raychaudhuri, S. P. Recent Advances in Medicinal Aromatic & Spice Crops, 2 vols., Set. (Illus.). 1000p. 1991. 150.00 (*1-55528-260-1*, Pub. by Today & Tomorrows P & P II) Scholarly Pubns.

Raychaudhuri, S. P., ed. Recent Advances in Medicinal, Aromatic & Spice Crops: International Conference Held on 28-31, January 1989, at New Delhi, India, Vol. 1. (Illus.). 280p. 1992. 59.00 (*1-55528-229-6*, Pub. by Today & Tomorrows P & P II) Scholarly Pubns.

— Recent Advances in Medicinal, Aromatic & Spice Crops: International Conference Held on 28-31, January 1989, at New Delhi, India, Vol. 2. 568p. 1992. 59.00 (*1-55528-266-0*, Pub. by Today & Tomorrows P & P II) Scholarly Pubns.

Raychaudhuri, S. P. & Varma, Anupam, eds. Plant Diseases Caused by Fastidious Prokaryotes: Third Regional Workshop on Plant Mycoplasma. viii, 139p. 1989. 59.00 (*1-55528-179-6*, Messers Today & Tomorrow) Scholarly Pubns.

Raychaudhuri, S. P. & Verma, J. P. Review of Tropical Plant Pathology: Diseases of Cereals, Maize & Millet, Vol. 1. (Illus.). 564p. 1984. 79.00 (*1-55528-080-3*, Pub. by Today & Tomorrows P & P II) Scholarly Pubns.

— Review of Tropical Plant Pathology, Vol. 5: Diseases of Fibre & Oilseed Crops. (Illus.). vi, 316p. 1989. 95.00 (*1-55528-173-7*, Messers Today & Tomorrow) Scholarly Pubns.

Raychaudhuri, S. P. & Verma, J. P., eds. Hall of Fame. (Review of Tropical Plant Pathology Ser.: Vol. 7). 275p. 1992. 95.00 (*1-55528-232-6*, Pub. by Today & Tomorrows P & P II) Scholarly Pubns.

— Review of Tropical Plant Pathology: Diseases of Plantation Crops & Forest Trees, Vol. IV. (Illus.). 350p. 1988. 99.00 (*1-55528-092-7*, Pub. by Today & Tomorrows P & P II) Scholarly Pubns.

— Review of Tropical Plant Pathology: Diseases of Vegetables, Vol. 3. (Illus.). 586p. 1987. 95.00 (*1-55528-144-3*, Pub. by Today & Tomorrows P & P II) Scholarly Pubns.

Raychaudhuri, S. P., jt. ed. see Maramorosch, Karl.

Raychaudhuri, S. P., jt. ed. see Singh, B. P.

Raychaudhuri, Tapan. Bengal under Akbar & Jahangir: An Introductory Study in Social History. 275p. 1969. text ed. 25.00 (*0-685-43637-3*) Coronet Bks.

— Europe Reconsidered: Perceptions of the West in Nineteenth-Century Bengal. 388p. 1989. 28.00 (*0-19-562066-6*) OUP.

— Europe Reconsidered: Perceptions of the West in Nineteenth Century Bengal. 388p. 1990. reprint ed. pap. 9.95 (*0-19-562441-6*) OUP.

Raychaudhuri, Tapan & Habib, Irfan, eds. The Cambridge Economic History of India: Volume 1, c. 1200 - c. 1750. LC 80-40454. (Illus.). 600p. 1982. 125.00 (*0-521-22692-9*) Cambridge U Pr.

Raycher, Jeanne. Birth Plan Guide. (Illus.). (Orig.). (C). 1988. pap. 9.95 (*0-944252-00-1*) CC Services.

Raycraft, Carol. Collector's Guide to Country Stoneware. 1990. pap. 14.95 (*0-89145-420-9*) Collector Bks.

Raycraft, Carol, jt. auth. see Raycraft, Don.

Raycraft, Don. The American Country Store: A Wallace-Homestead Price Guide. 1994. pap. 14.95 (*0-87069-723-4*) Chilton.

— Collecting Baseball Player Autographs. 1991. pap. 9.95 (*0-89145-445-4*) Collector Bks.

— Value Guide to Baseball Collectibles. 1992. pap. 16.95 (*0-89145-506-X*) Collector Bks.

*__Raycraft, Don & Raycraft, Carol.__ American Stoneware: A Wallace-Homestead Price Guide. 1995. pap. 16.95 (*0-87069-714-5*) Chilton.

— Country & Folk Antiques. (Illus.). 176p. (Orig.). 1995. pap. 29.95 (*0-88740-828-1*) Schiffer.

— Country Stoneware & Pottery. (Illus.). 160p. 1989. pap. 9.95 (*0-89145-289-3*) Collector Bks.

— Wallace-Homestead Price Guide to American Country Antiques. 13th ed. (Illus.). 272p. 1993. pap. 15.95 (*0-87069-586-X*, Wallace-Hmestead) Chilton.

Raycraft, Mary B., tr. see Perdrizet, Marie-Pierre.

Raycroft, Carol, jt. auth. see Raycroft, Don.

*__Raycroft, Don & Raycroft, Carol.__ W. H. Price Guide to American Country Antiques, Bk. 14. 14th ed. 264p. 1995. pap. 15.95 (*0-87069-720-X*) Chilton.

Raydo, Linda, jt. auth. see Eddy, Mary L.

Raye, Don. Pipe Dreams. King, Una & Moon, Delia, eds. LC 81-2507. 110p. 1980. pap. 12.00 (*0-686-75463-8*) Family Pub CA.

Raye, Helen, jt. auth. see Saunders, Richard.

Raye, Marina. Do You Have an Owner's Manual for Your Brain? 320p. (Orig.). 1991. pap. 12.95 (*1-878010-00-X*) Allen.

— Sexuality: the Sacred Journey: An Awakening to Ecstasy. (Illus.). 224p. (Orig.). 1994. pap. 12.95 (*1-878010-01-8*) Allen.

Rayed, Amal. The Nehru Legacy: An Appraisal. 1991. 28.00 (*81-204-0556-0*, Pub. by Oxford IBH II) S Asia.

Rayer, John, et al. Robson Rhodes: Personal Financial Planning Manual 1991-92. 7th ed. 312p. 1991. pap. 59.00 (*0-406-00203-7*) Butterworth Legal Pubs.

Rayes, Joseph. Living Religious Vows: A Personal Pilgrimage. 84p. (Orig.). 1987. pap. 5.95 (*0-86716-063-2*) St Anthony Mess Pr.

Rayess, George. Art of Lebanese Cooking. 1992. 17.95x (*0-86685-038-4*) Intl Bk Ctr.

Rayevskii, N. & Barrett, D. Measurement of Mechanical Parameters in Machines. LC 63-21449. 1965. 99.00 (*0-08-010184-4*, Pub. by Pergamon Repr UK) Franklin.

Rayevsky, Paulina. Tak Eto Bylo - It Was Like This: One Family Story, Russia - U. S. A., 1950-1990. LC 92-72486. (Illus.). 370p. (Orig.). (RUS.). 1992. 16.00 (*0-911971-73-4*) Effect Pub.

Rayevsky, Robert, illus. Androcles & the Lion: And Other Aesop's Fables. LC 90-19173. 40p. (J). (ps up). 1991. 13.95 (*0-688-09682-4*); lib. bdg. 13.88 (*0-688-09683-2*) Morrow Jr Bks.

— Three Sacks of Truth: A Story from France. 32p. (J). (ps-3). 1993. lib. bdg. 15.95 (*0-8234-0921-X*) Holiday.

— A Word to the Wise: And Other Proverbs. LC 93-26836. 40p. (J). (ps up). 1994. 15.00 (*0-688-12065-2*); lib. bdg. 14.93 (*0-688-12066-0*) Morrow Jr Bks.

Rayez, Andre. Dictionnaire de Spiritualite: Dictionary of Spirituality, 12 vols., Set. (FRE.). 1970. 4,995.00 (*0-8288-6518-3*, M-6125) Fr & Eur.

Rayfiel, Thomas. Split Levels. 1994. 20.00 (*0-671-86522-6*) S&S Trade.

Rayfield, Donald. The Cherry Orchard: Catastrophe & Comedy. LC 93-29455. (Twayne's Masterwork Studies: No. 131). 168p. 1994. text ed. 22.95 (*0-8057-8364-4*, Twayne); pap. 12.95 (*0-8057-4451-7*, Twayne) Macmillan.

— The Literature of Georgia: A History. 376p. 1995. text ed. 55.00 (*0-19-815191-8*) OUP.

Rayfield, Elliot J. & Solimini, Cheryl. Diabetes: Beating the Odds: The Doctor's Guide to Reducing Your Risk. LC 92-14725. (Illus.). 198p. 1992. pap. 8.61 (*0-201-57784-4*) Addison-Wesley.

Rayfield, J. R. Languages of a Bilingual Community. LC 73-106457. (Janua Linguarum, Ser. Practica: No. 77). 1970. pap. text ed. 40.80 (*90-279-0730-7*) Mouton.

Rayfield, Joan R., tr. see Maquet, Jacques P.

Rayfield, Julie K. The Office Interior Design Guide: An Introduction for Facilities Managers & Designers. 250p. 1993. text ed. 54.95 (*0-471-57286-1*) Wiley.

Rayfield, Robert, et al. Public Relations Writing: Strategies & Skills. 456p. (C). 1991. pap. write for info. (*0-697-03174-8*) Brown & Benchmark.

Rayfield, Susan. Marine Painting: Techniques of Modern Masters. (Illus.). 144p. 1991. 29.95 (*0-8230-3006-7*, Watsn-Guptill) Watsn-Guptill.

— Painting Birds. (Illus.). 144p. 1991. pap. 18.95 (*0-8230-3561-1*, Watsn-Guptill) Watsn-Guptill.

— Wildlife Painting: Techniques of Modern Masters. (Illus.). 144p. 1990. pap. 18.95 (*0-8230-5748-8*, Watsn-Guptill) Watsn-Guptill.

*__Rayfield, Sylvia & Manning, Loretta.__ Nursing Made Insanely Easy. (Illus.). 248p. 1995. pap. 24.95 (*0-9643622-0-1*) ICAN LA.

Rayfield, Sylvia, et al. NCLEX-RN 101: How to Pass! LC 93-83437. 500p. 1993. pap. 23.95 (*0-9628210-2-0*) Nursing Ed Consultants.

Rayford, Julian L. Cottonmouth. (Library of Alabama Classics). 424p. 1991. pap. 19.95 (*0-8173-0529-7*) U of Ala Pr.

Rayfus, Rosemary, ed. ICSID Reports: (Reports of Cases Decided under the Convention on the Settlement of Investment Disputes Between States & Nationals of Other States, 1965), Vol. 1. 750p. (C). 1993. text ed. 570.00 (*1-85701-009-4*, Pub. by Grotius Pubns UK) St Mut.

— ICSID Reports: (Reports of Cases Decided under the Convention on the Settlement of Investment Disputes Between States & Nationals of Other States, 1965), Vol. 2. 350p. (C). 1993. text ed. 456.00 (*1-85701-010-8*, Pub. by Grotius Pubns UK) St Mut.

*__Rayfuse, Rosemary, ed.__ ICSID Reports Vol. 3. (Grotius ICSID Reports). 420p. (C). 1995. 200.00 (*0-521-47512-0*) Cambridge U Pr.

Raygor, Alton L., ed. see Lewick-Wallace, Mary.

Raygor, Robin D. & Bateson, Robert N. BASIC Programming for the IBM PC. (Illus.). 318p. (Orig.). (C). 1986. text ed. 36.50 (*0-314-93407-3*); teacher ed, pap. text ed. write for info. (*0-314-97148-3*) West Pub.

Raygor, Robin D., jt. auth. see Bateson, Robert N.

Rayha, Bonnie J., ed. see Degroodt, Mary P.

Rayher, Ed. Alice's Flip Book. (Illus.). 38p. (J). 1982. per., pap. 1.75 (*0-934714-19-3*) Swamp Pr.

— Flight of the Mantas. (Illus.). 12p. 1986. pap. 5.00 (*0-934714-11-8*) Swamp Pr.

— Off with Their Heads. (Illus.). 38p. 1982. pap. 1.75 (*0-685-40710-1*) Swamp Pr.

Raykher, Esfir. Natural Gas Transport in the U. S. S. R. Young, Maureen, ed. 103p. (Orig.). 1983. pap. text ed. 75.00 (*1-55831-039-8*) Delphic Associates.

Raykov, Mariana. Beginner's Bulgarian. (Eurolingua Beginner's Languages Ser.). 200p. 1994. pap. 7.95 (*0-7818-0300-4*) Hippocrene Bks.

Rayl, Eric. Lotus Notes Developer's Guide. (Illus.). 800p. (Orig.). 1994. Incl. diskette. pap. 44.95 (*0-672-30500-3*) Sams.

Rayle, James F. Stay Out of the Wheat Field. Montague, Diana M., ed. 269p. (Orig.). 1993. pap. 10.95 (*1-883868-00-9*) Am Vision Pub.

Rayleigh, Robert J. Life of John William Strutt, Third Baron Rayleigh, O.M., F.R.S. LC 68-16063. 467p. reprint ed. pap. 133.10 (*0-317-41615-4*, 2023722) Bks Demand.

Rayleigh, Strutt. Theory of Sound, 2 vols., 1. pap. 10.95 (*0-486-60292-3*) Dover.

— Theory of Sound, 2 vols., 2. pap. 10.95 (*0-486-60293-1*) Dover.

Raylor, R., ed. see Schibsbye, K. & Kossmann, H.

Raylor, Timothy. Cavaliers, Clubs, & Literary Culture: Sir John Mennes, James Smith, & the Order of the Fancy. LC 93-37277. (C). 1994. write for info. (*0-87413-523-0*) U Delaware Pr.

Raylor, Timothy, jt. ed. see Leslie, Michael.

*__Rayman, Jack R., ed.__ The Changing Role of Career Services. LC 85-644751. (New Directions for Student Services Ser.: No. 62). 114p. (Orig.). 1993. pap. 16.95 (*1-55542-699-9*) Jossey-Bass.

Rayman, Paula. The Kibbutz Community & Nation Building. LC 81-47152. 323p. reprint ed. pap. 92.10 (*0-7837-1414-9*, 2041768) Bks Demand.

Rayman, Paula & Brett, Belle. Pathways for Women in the Sciences, Pt. 1: The Wellesley Report. 177p. 1993. 20.00 (*0-9641921-0-1*) WC Ctr Res Women.

Rayman, Paula, jt. ed. see Bruyn, Severyn T.

Rayman, Paula M. The Kibbutz Community & Nation Building. LC 81-47152. (Illus.). 320p. 1981. 47.50 (*0-691-09391-1*); pap. 17.95 (*0-691-10124-8*) Princeton U Pr.

Rayman, Rebecca. The Body in Brief: Essentials for Health Care. 2nd ed. (Illus.). 400p. 1993. 26.95 (*0-944132-76-6*) Skidmore Roth Pub.

— Nurse's Trivia Calendar, 1995. 370p. 1994. 9.95 (*1-56930-013-5*) Skidmore Roth Pub.

Raymer, Dan, jt. auth. see Watman, Kenneth.

Raymer, Daniel P. Aircraft Design: A Conceptual Approach. 2nd ed. (Educ Ser.). 739p. 1992. 66.95 (*0-930403-51-7*) AIAA.

— RDS-Student: Software for Aircraft Design, Sizing, & Performance, Version 3.0. (Educ Ser.). 71p. 1992. student ed, disk 69.95 (*1-56347-047-0*) AIAA.

Raymer, Steve. St. Petersburg. LC 94-8374. 1994. 39.95 (*1-878685-48-1*) Turner Pub GA.

Raymist, Malkah. The Stiff Necked City. 400p. 1992. pap. 15.95 (*965-229-038-6*, Pub. by Gefen Pub Hse IS) Gefen Bks.

*__Raymo, C.__ The Dork of Cork. Date not set. pap. 3.98 (*0-517-13158-7*) Random Hse Value.

Raymo, Chet. The Dork of Cork. (Fresh Voices Ser.). 368p. 1994. pap. 9.99 (*0-446-67000-6*) Warner Bks.

— In the Falcon's Claws: A Novel of the Year 1000. 1990. 17.95 (*0-685-31428-6*) Viking Penguin.

— The Soul of the Night: An Astronomical Pilgrimage. write for info. (*0-318-59586-9*) S&S Trade.

Raymo, Chet & Raymo, Maureen E. Written in Stone: A Geological History of the Northeastern United States. (Illus.). 192p. 1991. pap. 14.95 (*0-87106-320-4*) Globe Pequot.

Raymo, Maureen E., jt. auth. see Raymo, Chet.

Raymon, Loren A. Petrology: The Study of Igneous, Sedimentary & Metamorphic Rocks. 240p. (C). 1995. student ed, spiral bd. write for info. (*0-697-05976-6*) Wm C Brown Pubs.

Raymond. Writing: An Unnatural Act. (C). 1990. pap. text ed. 29.00 (*0-06-045341-9*) HarpCollege.

Raymond, Agnes. Jean Giraudoux: The Theatre of Victory & Defeat. LC 65-26238. 216p. 1966. pap. 15.95x (*0-87023-013-1*) U of Mass Pr.

Raymond, Al. Swinging Big Bands: Into the Nineties. 245p. 1992. pap. 20.00 (*0-9634600-0-5*) Harmony Pr PA.

*__Raymond, Alan G.__ The HMO Health Care Companion: A Consumer's Guide to Managed Care Networks. LC 94-29554. 1994. pap. 10.00 (*0-06-095080-3*, HarpT) HarpC.

Raymond, Alex. Flash Gordon: "The Tides of Battle" Schreiner, Dave, ed. LC 90-549. (Illus.). 112p. 1992. 34.95 (*0-87816-161-9*); pap. 21.95 (*0-87816-162-7*) Kitchen Sink.

— Flash Gordon: "Three Against Ming" Schreiner, Dave, ed. LC 90-5049. (Illus.). 112p. 1991. 34.95 (*0-87816-120-1*); pap. 19.95 (*0-87816-139-2*) Kitchen Sink.

— Flash Gordon: The Fall of Ming. Schreiner, Dave, ed. LC 90-549. (Flash Gordon Ser.: Vol. 4). (Illus.). 112p. 1992. 34.95 (*0-87816-167-8*); pap. 21.95 (*0-87816-168-6*) Kitchen Sink.

— Flash Gordon: 1941-1943 Between Worlds at War, Vol. 5. Poplaski, Peter, ed. 112p. 1993. 34.95 (*0-87816-176-7*); pap. 21.95 (*0-87816-177-5*) Kitchen Sink.

— Triumph in Tropica. Schreiner, Dave & Poplaski, Pete, eds. LC 90-549. (Flash Gordon Ser.: Vol. 6). (Illus.). 96p. 1993. 34.95 (*0-87816-198-8*); pap. 21.95 (*0-87816-199-6*) Kitchen Sink.

Raymond, Alex, jt. auth. see Hammett, Dashiell.

*__Raymond, Andrew.__ Secrets of the Sphinx: Mysteries of the Ages Revealed. (Illus.). 160p. (Orig.). 1995. pap. 12.95 (*0-9646954-6-4*) UNI Prods.

Raymond, C. Elizabeth. George Wingfield: Owner & Operator of Nevada. LC 92-17980. (Wilbur S. Shepperson Series in History & Humanities: No. 34). (Illus.). 368p. (C). 1992. 31.95 (*0-87417-197-0*) U of Nev Pr.

Raymond, Carole. Love in a Lunchbox. (Illus.). 96p. (Orig.). 1994. pap. 12.95 (*0-89802-616-4*) Beautiful Am.

Raymond, Clarinda H. License Renewal for the Blind. 24p. (Orig.). 1994. pap. 8.00 (*0-939121-03-4*) Cooper Hse.

Raymond, Clarinda H., ed. see Fein, Richard.

Raymond, Clarinda H., ed. see Langille, Carol.

Raymond, Daniel. Elements of Political Economy: In Two Parts with Additions from the 3rd Edition of 1836, 2 vols., Set. 2nd ed. LC 63-22260. (Reprints of Economic Classics Ser.). 1964. reprint ed. 75.00 (*0-678-00067-0*) Kelley.

Raymond, Derek. Crust on Its Uppers. 1993. pap. 11.99 (*1-85242-268-8*) Serpents Tail.

— A State of Denmark. (Mask Noir Ser.). 272p. (Orig.). 1995. pap. 12.99 (*1-85242-315-3*) Serpents Tail.

Raymond, Diana. House of the Dolphin. large type ed. 352p. 1987. 16.95 (*0-7089-1646-5*) Ulverscroft.

Raymond, Diane. Existentialism & the Philosophical Tradition. 432p. (C). 1990. pap. text ed. write for info. (*0-13-295775-2*) P-H.

Raymond, Diane, ed. Sexual Politics & Popular Culture. LC 90-82104. 249p. (C). 1990. text ed. 37.95 (*0-87972-501-X*); pap. text ed. 18.95 (*0-87972-502-8*) Bowling Green Univ.

Raymond, Diane, jt. auth. see Blumenfeld, Warren J.

Raymond, Dick. Down-to-Earth Gardening Know-How for the '90s: Vegetables & Herbs. rev. ed. Watson, Ben, ed. LC 90-50416. (Illus.). 192p. 1991. pap. 12.95 (*0-88266-649-5*, Garden Way Pub) Storey Comm Inc.

— Down-to-Earth Natural Lawn Care. Watson, Ben, ed. LC 92-53950. (Illus.). 176p. 1993. 27.95 (*0-88266-812-9*, Garden Way Pub); pap. 16.95 (*0-88266-810-2*, Garden Way Pub) Storey Comm Inc.

— Garden Way's Joy of Gardening. LC 82-12075. (Illus.). 384p. 1983. pap. 19.95 (*0-88266-319-4*, Garden Way Pub) Storey Comm Inc.

Raymond, Dora N. British Policy & Opinion During the Franco-Prussian War. LC 21-20208. (Columbia University. Studies in the Social Sciences: No. 227). reprint ed. 27.50 (*0-404-51227-5*) AMS Pr.

— Captain Lee Hall of Texas. LC 73-5131. (Illus.). 384p. 1982. 29.95 (*0-8061-0086-9*) U of Okla Pr.

— Oliver's Secretary. LC 71-174302. reprint ed. 26.50 (*0-404-05229-0*) AMS Pr.

Raymond, Dorothy. How to Catch & Cook Shellfish. LC 73-9493. (Illus.). (Orig.). 1973. pap. 1.95 (*0-8200-0805-2*) Great Outdoors.

— Stalking the Stone Crab. Pope, Patricia, ed. LC 75-6886. (Illus.). 32p. 1975. pap. 1.00 (*0-8200-0119-8*) Great Outdoors.

Raymond, E. The Gem Stones in the Breastplate. (Illus.). 48p. (Orig.). 1987. pap. 3.00 (*0-934666-18-0*) Artisan Sales.

Raymond, E. Neill. Victorian Viceroy. 346p. 1984. 39.00 (*0-7212-0599-2*, Pub. by Regency Press) St Mut.

Raymond, E. T. Man of Promise: Lord Rosebery. LC 72-1276. (Select Bibliographies Reprint Ser.). 1977. reprint ed. 18.95 (*0-8369-6834-4*) Ayer.

Raymond, E. T. & Chenoweth, C. C. Aircraft Flight Control Actuation System Design. 325p. 1993. 85.00 (*1-56091-376-2*, R-123) Soc Auto Engineers.

Raymond, Eleanor. Early Domestic Architecture of Pennsylvania. LC 77-92980. (Illus.). 158p. 1979. reprint ed. 25.00 (*0-916838-11-0*) Schiffer.

Raymond, Eric S., ed. The New Hacker's Dictionary. 2nd ed. (Illus.). 530p. 1993. 14.95 (*0-262-68079-3*) MIT Pr.

Raymond, Ernest. Two Gentlemen of Rome: Keats & Shelley. 1972. 69.95 (*0-8490-1238-4*) Gordon Pr.

*__Raymond, Florian.__ Living Can Be Hazardous to Your Health. 1996. 10.95 (*0-943873-43-6*) Elder Bks.

Raymond, Florian. Surviving Alzheimer's: A Guide for Families. 1994. 10.95 (*0-943873-00-2*) Elder Bks.

R

An Asterisk (*) at the beginning of an entry indicates that the title is appearing in BIP for the first time.

Raymond, Frank E. Rivers to Remember: A Guide to Northern California's Great Outdoors by a Famous Storyteller. (Illus.). 76p. (Orig.). 1988. pap. 7.95 (*0-9621614-0-3*) Siskiyou Trail Pr.
— Rowayton on the Half Shell: The History of a Connecticut Coastal Village. LC 90-7392. (Illus.). 240p. 1990. 20.00 (*0-914659-48-0*) Phoenix Pub.
Raymond, George L. Fundamentals in Education, Art & Civics: Essays & Addresses. LC 67-23263. (Essay Index Reprint Ser.). 1977. 23.95 (*0-8369-0811-2*) Ayer.
— Memoirs of Robert William Elliston, 2 Vols. in 1. LC 77-81218. 1972. 48.95 (*0-405-08875-2*, Pub. by Blom Pubns UK) Ayer.
— The Orator's Manual: A Practical & Philosophical Treatise on Vocal Culture, Emphasis & Gesture. rev. ed. LC 72-434. (Granger Index Reprint Ser.). 1977. reprint ed. 23.95 (*0-8369-6368-7*) Ayer.
***Raymond, Gino.** Andre Malraux: Politics & the Temptation of Myth. 210p. 1995. 59.95 (*1-85972-132-X*, Pub. by Avebury Pub UK) Ashgate Pub Co.
Raymond, Gino G., ed. France During the Socialist Years. 296p. 1994. 59.95 (*1-85521-518-7*, Pub. by Dartmth Pub UK) Ashgate Pub Co.
Raymond, Gregory A. Conflict Resolution & the Structure of the State System: An Analysis of Arbitrative Settlements. LC 79-53702. (Illus.). 122p. 1980. text ed. 41.00 (*0-916672-12-3*) Rowman.
— Salvador Allende & the Peaceful Road to Socialism. (Pew Case Studies in International Affairs). 50p. (C). 1992. pap. text ed. 2.50 (*1-56927-451-7*) Geo U Inst Dplmcy.
Raymond, Gregory A., jt. auth. see Kegley, Charles W., Jr.
Raymond, Gregory A., jt. auth. see Kegley, Charles W.
Raymond, Gregory A., jt. ed. see Taylor, Phillip.
Raymond, H. R. Delaware Wing-T: An Order of Football. 1986. 21.95 (*0-13-198326-1*) P-H.
Raymond, Henry N. Learn in Your Car - Japanese Level Two. 1993. 15.95 (*1-56015-143-9*) Penton Overseas.
— Learn in Your Car, French, 3 vols., Set. Date not set. 39.95 (*1-56015-138-2*) Penton Overseas.
— Learn in Your Car, German, 3 vols., Set. Date not set. 39.95 (*1-56015-139-0*) Penton Overseas.
— Learn in Your Car, Italian, 3 vols., Set. Date not set. 39.95 (*1-56015-140-4*) Penton Overseas.
— Learn in Your Car Japanese, Level 3. 1993. 15.95 (*1-56015-145-5*) Penton Overseas.
— Learn in Your Car, Japanese, 3 vols., Set. 1993. 39.95 (*1-56015-146-3*) Penton Overseas.
— Learn in Your Car Japanese, Level 1. (JPN.). Date not set. 15.95 (*1-56015-137-4*) Penton Overseas.
— Learn in Your Car Russian, 3 vols. (RUS.). Date not set. 39.95 (*1-56015-148-X*) Penton Overseas.
— Learn in Your Car Russian, Level 1. 1993. 15.95 (*1-56015-142-0*) Penton Overseas.
— Learn in Your Car Russian, Level 2. 1994. 15.95 (*1-56015-144-7*) Penton Overseas.
— Learn in Your Car Russian, Level 3. (RUS.). Date not set. 15.95 (*1-56015-147-1*) Penton Overseas.
— Learn in Your Car, Spanish, 3 vols., Set. Date not set. 39.95 (*1-56015-141-2*) Penton Overseas.
Raymond, Irving W. Teaching of the Early Church on the Use of Wine & Strong Drink. LC 79-120207. (Columbia University. Studies in the Social Sciences: No. 286). reprint ed. 20.00 (*0-404-51286-0*) AMS Pr.
Raymond, Irving W., tr. Medieval Trade in the Mediterranean World: Illustrative Documents. 458p. 1990. text ed. 58.00 (*0-231-01865-7*); pap. text ed. 12.50 (*0-231-09626-7*) Col U Pr.
Raymond, J., jt. ed. see Laurie, G.
Raymond, Jack. Robert O. Anderson: Oil Man-Environmentalist & His Leading Role in the International Environmentalist Movement. 64p. (Orig.). (C). 1988. pap. text ed. 10.50 (*0-8191-7043-7*, Aspen Inst for Humanistic Studies) U Pr of Amer.
— Show Music on Record: The First One Hundred Years. rev. ed. LC 91-23483. 440p. 1992. 45.00 (*1-56098-151-2*) Smithsonian.
Raymond, Jacque, jt. auth. see Banerji, Dilip.
Raymond, James C., ed. see McMillan, James B.
Raymond, Janice G. A Passion for Friends: Toward a Philosophy of Female Affection. LC 85-47942. 320p. (C). 1987. pap. 15.00x (*0-8070-6739-3*, BP 754) Beacon Pr.
— The Transsexual Empire: The Making of the She-Male. LC 93-46771. (Athene Ser.: No. 39). 256p. (C). 1994. pap. text ed. 17.95 (*0-8077-6272-5*) Tchrs Coll.
— Women as Wombs: Reproductive Technologies & the Battle Over Women's Freedom. LC 92-56139. 288p. 1993. reprint ed. 22.00 (*0-06-250898-9*) Harper SF.
— Women as Wombs: Reproductive Technologies & the Battle Over Women's Freedom. LC 92-56139. 288p. 1994. reprint ed. pap. 12.00 (*0-06-250899-7*) Harper SF.
Raymond, Janice G., jt. auth. see Leidholdt, Dorchen.
Raymond, Janice G., jt. ed. see Leidholdt, Dorchen.
Raymond, Janice G., et al. RU 486: Myths, Misconceptions & Morals. 160p. 1991. pap. 10.95 (*0-9630083-0-7*) Inst Women Tech.
Raymond, Jehan. Decorative Floral Designs for Needleworkers & Craftspeople. (Pictorial Archive Ser.). iv, 59p. 1986. reprint ed. pap. 4.50 (*0-486-25134-9*) Dover.
Raymond, Joad, ed. Making the News: An Anthology of the Newsbooks of Revolutionary England, 1941-1660. LC 93-1629. 1993. text ed. 45.00 (*0-312-10093-0*) St Martin.
Raymond, Jocelyn M. The Nursery World of Dr. Blatz. 280p. 1991. 35.00 (*0-8020-2793-8*) U of Toronto Pr.
Raymond, Kathleen Z., jt. auth. see Newman, Jim.
Raymond, Larry. Reinventing Communication: A Guide to Using Visual Language for Planning, Problem Solving, & Reengineering. LC 94-18254. 1994. pap. 30.00 (*0-87389-288-7*) ASQC Qual Pr.
***Raymond, Larry, illus.** Drugs: The Social Impact Series, 3 vols., Set. 88p. (J). (gr. 5-8). 1994. lib. bdg. 44.94 (*0-8050-3450-1*) TFC Bks NY.
Raymond, Laurie & Rosbrow-Reich, Susan. Psychoanalytic Reflections. Date not set. 40.00 (*0-87668-513-0*) Aronson.
Raymond, Lilo, photos. Linens & Lace. (Illus.). 1990. 22.50 (*0-517-57680-5*, C P Pubs) Crown Pub Group.
Raymond, Linda. Rocking the Babies. LC 94-8795. 288p. 1994. 21.95 (*0-670-85263-5*, Viking) Viking Penguin.
— Rocking the Babies. 272p. 1995. pap. 10.95 (*0-14-023254-0*, Penguin Bks) Viking Penguin.
Raymond, Loren A. Petrology: The Study of Igneous, Sedimentary & Metamorphic Rocks. 672p. (C). 1994. text ed. write for info. (*0-697-00190-3*) Wm C Brown Pubs.
Raymond, Loren A., ed. Melanges: Their Nature, Origin, & Significance. (Special Paper Ser.: No. 198). (Illus.). 175p. 1985. pap. 6.50 (*0-8137-2198-9*) Geol Soc.
Raymond, Lou, ed. Hydrogen Embrittlement: Prevention & Control, STP 962. LC 88-3490. (Special Technical Publication (STP) Ser.). (Illus.). 441p. 1988. text ed. 54.00 (*0-685-21955-0*, 04-962000-26) ASTM.
Raymond, M. Burnt out Incense: The Saga of Citeaux America Epoch. 445p. 1988. reprint ed. write for info. (*0-8198-1117-3*); reprint ed. pap. write for info. (*0-8198-1118-1*) Pauline Bks.
— The Family That Overtook Christ. LC 86-19670. 1986. 6.95 (*0-8198-2626-X*); pap. 5.50 (*0-8198-2625-1*) Pauline Bks.
— These Women Walked with God: The Saga of Citeaux Third Epoch. 255p. 1988. reprint ed. write for info. (*0-8198-7341-1*); reprint ed. pap. write for info. (*0-8198-7342-X*) Pauline Bks.
— Three Religious Rebels: Founding Fathers of the Cistercians. LC 88-6992. 407p. 1992. reprint ed. pap. 9.95 (*0-8198-7340-3*) Pauline Bks.
— Your Hour. 216p. 1995. reprint ed. text ed. 19.95 (*0-912141-23-9*) Roman Cath Bks.
Raymond, M. D. Gray Genealogy: Being a Genealogical Record & History of the Descendants of John Gray of Beverly, Massachusetts, & Including Sketches of Other Gray Families. 316p. 1994. reprint ed. lib. bdg. 57.50 (*0-8328-4093-9*); reprint ed. pap. 47.50 (*0-8328-4094-7*) Higginson Bk Co.
Raymond, M. Susan. Health & Policymaking in the Arab Middle East. 70p. (Orig.). 1978. pap. text ed. 4.00 (*0-932568-00-9*) GU Ctr CAS.
Raymond, Marsha P., ed. see Swain, Adrian.
Raymond-Martimbeau, Pauline. Phlebologia Houston Ninety-One: Proceedings of the Intensive Practical Course in Phlebologia. 438p. 1991. write for info. (*1-880693-00-3*) P Ray-Mart.
Raymond, Mary. Change of Heart. large type ed. (Romance Ser.). 304p. 1985. 21.95 (*0-7089-1330-X*) Ulverscroft.
— Girl in a Mask. large type ed. (Linford Romance Library). 336p. 1985. pap. 11.95 (*0-7089-6126-6*, Trailtree Bookshop) Ulverscroft.
— Grandma Tyson's Legacy. large type ed. (Romance Ser.). 336p. 1984. 21.95 (*0-7089-1230-3*) Ulverscroft.
— Her Part of the House. large type ed. (General Ser.). 336p. 1993. 21.95 (*0-7089-2866-8*) Ulverscroft.
— Hide My Heart. large type ed. (Linford Romance Library). 304p. 1985. pap. 11.95 (*0-7089-6101-0*, Trailtree Bookshop) Ulverscroft.
— I Have Three Sons. large type ed. (Linford Romance Library). 320p. 1985. pap. 11.95 (*0-7089-6107-X*, Trailtree Bookshop) Ulverscroft.
— Island of the Heart. large type ed. (Romance Ser.). 336p. 1985. 21.95 (*0-7089-1393-8*) Ulverscroft.
— The Long Journey Home. large type ed. (Linford Romance Library). 320p. 1985. pap. 11.95 (*0-7089-6071-5*, Linford) Ulverscroft.
— Love Be Wary. large type ed. (Linford Romance Library). 320p. 1986. pap. 11.95 (*0-7089-6179-7*, Linford) Ulverscroft.
— The Pimpernel Project. large type ed. (Linford Romance Library). 288p. 1989. pap. 11.95 (*0-7089-6654-3*, Linford) Ulverscroft.
— Shadow of a Star. large type ed. (Romance Ser.). 304p. 1987. 16.95 (*0-7089-1591-4*) Ulverscroft.
— The Silver Girl. large type ed. (Linford Romance Library). 304p. 1985. pap. 11.95 (*0-7089-6117-7*, Trailtree Bookshop) Ulverscroft.
— Surety for a Stranger. large type ed. (Linford Romance Library). 304p. 1986. pap. 11.95 (*0-7089-6166-5*, Linford) Ulverscroft.
— Take-Over. large type ed. 304p. 1986. 21.95 (*0-7089-1546-9*) Ulverscroft.
— That Summer. large type ed. (Romance Ser.). 288p. 1986. 21.95 (*0-7089-1507-8*) Ulverscroft.
— Villa of Flowers. large type ed. (Linford Romance Library). 288p. 1985. pap. 11.95 (*0-7089-6056-1*, Trailtree Bookshop) Ulverscroft.
Raymond, Meredith B. & Sullivan, Mary R., eds. Elizabeth Barrett Browning: Selected Poetry & Prose. 150p. (C). 1993. pap. 15.95 (*0-939464-52-7*) Labyrinth Pr.
Raymond, Mike. The Human Side of Diabetes: Beyond Doctors, Diets & Drugs. LC 91-50644. 326p. (Orig.). 1991. pap. 13.95 (*1-879360-09-8*) Noble Pr.
Raymond, Mike, jt. auth. see Dickson, Wayne.
Raymond, Miner. Advertising That Sells: A Primer for Product Managers. (Illus.). 160p. (Orig.). 1989. pap. 24.95 (*0-685-28874-9*) Blk Rose Pub.
— Advertising That Sells: A Primer for Product Managers. Raymond, Elizabeth, ed. (Illus.). 160p. (Orig.). 1990. write for info. (*0-9624575-0-7*) Blk Rose Pub.
Raymond, P. A., et al, eds. Systems Approaches to Developmental Neurobiology. (NATO ASI Series A, Life Sciences: Vol. 192). (Illus.). 204p. 1990. 69.50 (*0-306-43594-2*, Plenum Pr) Plenum.
Raymond, Patrick. Daniel & Esther. LC 89-49588. 176p. (YA). (gr. 7 up). 1990. text ed. 13.95 (*0-689-50504-3*, McElderry) S&S Childrens.
Raymond, Percy E. The Appendages, Anatomy, & Relationships of Trilobites. (Connecticut Academy of Arts & Sciences Ser., Trans.: Vol. 7). 1920. pap. 200.00 (*0-685-22866-5*) Elliots Bks.
Raymond, Peter. Rowing for the Hell of It: A Manual for Recreational Rowers. (Illus.). 154p. 1982. 11.95 (*0-89182-048-5*) Charles River Bks.
Raymond, Richard D. Myth of the Appalachian Brain Drain. LC 72-187762. 78p. 1972. pap. 13.00 (*0-937058-06-8*) West Va U Pr.
Raymond, Robert. From Bees to Buzz Bombs: Robert Raymond's Boyhood-to-Blitz Memoirs. (Orig.). 1992. pap. 24.95 (*0-7022-2449-9*, Pub. by Univ Queensland Pr AT) Intl Spec Bk.
— Out of the Fiery Furnace: The Impact of Metals on the History of Mankind. LC 86-2367. (Illus.). 1986. pap. 10.00 (*0-271-00441-X*) Pa St U Pr.
Raymond, Robert, jt. ed. see Fair, Donald E.
***Raymond, Robert G.** Scouting, Cavorting, & Other World War II Memories. (Illus.). (Orig.). Date not set. pap. write for info. (*0-9645021-0-0*) R G Raymond.
Raymond, Robert L. At a Dollar a Year: Ripples on the Edge of the Maelstrom. LC 76-157794. (Short Story Index Reprint Ser.). 1977. reprint ed. 19.95 (*0-8369-3906-9*) Ayer.
Raymond, Ronald R., Jr., et al. Grow Your Roots Anywhere, Anytime. 1980. 12.95 (*0-89256-152-1*, Rawson Assocs) Macmillan.
Raymond, Rossiter W. Peter Cooper. LC 72-1252. (Select Bibliographies Reprint Ser.). 1977. reprint ed. 15.95 (*0-8369-6835-2*) Ayer.
Raymond, S. Genealogy of the Raymond Family of New England 1630 to 1886, with a Historical Sketch of Some of the Raymonds of Early Times. (Illus.). 304p. 1989. reprint ed. lib. bdg. 54.00 (*0-8328-1006-1*); reprint ed. pap. 46.00 (*0-8328-1007-X*) Higginson Bk Co.
Raymond, Steve. Bowling Madness: Hey Pops, You Hustled Me. LC 88-83761. 278p. (Orig.). 1989. pap. 8.95 (*0-927707-16-0*) FL Bay Pubs.
— Kamloops: An Angler's Study of the Kamloops Trout. (Illus.). 148p. 1994. 39.95 (*1-878175-74-2*); pap. 24.95 (*1-878175-73-4*) F Amato Pubns.
— Steelhead Country. (Illus.). 196p. 1991. 19.95 (*1-55821-126-8*) Lyons & Burford.
— Steelhead Country: Angling in Northwest Waters. 228p. 1994. reprint ed. pap. 9.95 (*1-57061-014-2*) Sasquatch Bks.
— The Year of the Angler. rev. ed. (Illus.). 256p. 1995. pap. 12.95 (*1-57061-023-1*) Sasquatch Bks.
— Year of the Angler & Year of the Trout, 2 vols., Set. 1995. pap. 25.00 (*1-57061-032-0*) Sasquatch Bks.
— The Year of the Trout. rev. ed. (Illus.). 288p. 1995. pap. 11.95 (*1-57061-022-3*) Sasquatch Bks.
***Raymond, Steve & Karman, Mal.** The Poison River: An Unbelievable True Story of Betrayal & Redemption. (Illus.). 354p. (Orig.). (C). 1994. 19.95 (*0-9642533-9-9*); pap. 12.95 (*0-9642533-8-0*) New Amstrdm Pr.
Raymond, Susan G. Aleph Through Tav - Chalkboard Games. Solomon, Richard D. & Solomon, Elaine C., eds. (Illus.). 100p. (C). 1989. pap. text ed. 25.00 (*0-9617198-9-3*) NIRT Inc.
Raymond, Susan G., et al. Jewish Handbook for Group Discussion. 65p. 1988. pap. text ed. 15.00 (*0-9617198-8-5*) NIRT Inc.
Raymond, Susan U., jt. ed. see Greenberg, Henry M.
Raymond, Valerie. Surviving Proposition Thirteen: Fiscal Crisis in California Counties. LC 88-2766. 84p. (Orig.). (C). 1988. pap. 9.95 (*0-87772-315-X*) UCB IGS.
Raymond, W. F. & Larvor, P., eds. Alternative Uses for Agricultural Surpluses: Proceedings of a Seminar, Brussels, Belgium, June 25-27, 1985. 134p. 1987. 41.50 (*1-85166-084-4*, Pub. by Elsevier Applied Sci UK) Elsevier.
Raymond, W. F., et al. Forage, Conservation & Feeding. 4th ed. (Illus.). 192p. 1986. 27.95 (*0-85236-139-4*, Pub. by Farming Pr UK) Diamond Farm Bk.
Raymond, Walter J. The Attitudes of Voters & Planning Commissioners Toward Regional Planning, No. 1088. 1976. 5.50 (*0-686-20403-4*) CPL Biblios.
— Dictionary of Politics: Selected American & Foreign Political & Legal Terms. 7th ed. LC 92-14215. (Illus.). 762p. 1992. 60.00 (*1-55618-008-X*) Brunswick Pub.
— Substate Regional Planning in Virginia: A Bibliographical Essay, No. 1086. 1976. 5.00 (*0-686-20402-6*) CPL Biblios.
Raymond, Walter J., jt. ed. see Belyakov, Vladimir V.
Raymond, Walter M. Rebels of the New South. LC 72-2027. (Black Heritage Library Collection). (Illus.). 1977. reprint ed. 19.95 (*0-8369-9055-2*) Ayer.
Raymond, William O. The Infinite Moment, & Other Essays in Robert Browning. 2nd ed. LC 65-1834. (Canadian University Paperbooks Ser.: No. 32). 272p. reprint ed. pap. 77.60 (*0-8357-4167-2*, 2036941) Bks Demand.
Raymondo, James C. Population Estimation & Projection: Methods for Marketing, Demographic, & Planning Personnel. LC 91-45709. 224p. 1992. text ed. 55.00 (*0-89930-663-2*, RPF, Quorum Bks) Greenwood.
Raymont, Andre, ed. see Rousseau, Jean-Jacques.
Raymont, J. E. Plankton & Productivity in the Oceans: Zooplankton, Vol. 2. 2nd ed. (Illus.). 700p. 1983. 342.00 (*0-08-024404-1*, Pub. by Pergamon Repr UK) Franklin.
Raymont, Michael E., ed. Sulfur: New Sources & Uses. LC 82-1645. (ACS Symposium Ser.: No. 183). 1982. 37.95 (*0-8412-0713-5*) Am Chemical.
Raymund, Bernard. Hidden Waters. LC 76-144720. (Yale Series of Younger Poets: No. 13). reprint ed. 18.00 (*0-404-53813-4*) AMS Pr.
Rayn, Jay. Butch. 194p. (Orig.). 1992. pap. text ed. 10.95 (*0-9633031-0-4*) RMG Ent.
— Butch. LC 93-29580. 160p. (Orig.). 1993. reprint ed. pap. 7.95 (*1-55583-316-0*) Alyson Pubns.
— Butch II. 190p. (Orig.). 1994. pap. 8.95 (*1-55583-317-9*, Lace MA) Alyson Pubns.
Rayna, Gerhard. Reduce: Software for Algebraic Computation. LC 87-20535. 335p. 1987. pap. 49.00 (*0-387-96598-X*) Spr-Verlag.
Raynack, Elton. Not So Free to Choose: The Political Economy of Milton Friedman & Ronald Reagan. LC 86-21276. 224p. 1986. text ed. 55.00 (*0-275-92363-0*, C2363, Praeger Pubs) Greenwood.
Raynal, Guillaume T. The Revolution of America. Billias, George, ed. LC 72-10134. (American Revolutionary Ser.). 1979. reprint ed. lib. bdg. 39.50 (*0-8398-1774-6*) Irvington.
Raynal, Jose, ed. Hydrology & Water Resources Education Training & Management. 485p. 1992. text ed. 45.00 (*0-918334-73-X*) WRP.
Raynal, Maurice. Modern French Painters. LC 76-91374. (Contemporary Art Ser.). 1970. reprint ed. 23.95 (*0-405-00735-3*) Ayer.
Raynal, Michel. Algorithms for Mutual Exclusion. (Scientific Computation Ser.). 160p. 1985. 30.00x (*0-262-18119-3*) MIT Pr.
— Distributed Algorithms & Protocols. LC 87-25409. (Computing Ser.). 163p. 1988. pap. text ed. 64.95 (*0-471-91754-0*) Wiley.
— Networks & Distributed Computation: Concepts, Tools & Algorithms. (Computer Systems Ser.). 200p. 1988. 32.50 (*0-262-18130-4*) MIT Pr.
Raynal, Michel & Helary, Jean-Michel. Synchronization & Control of Distributed Systems & Programs. (Parallel Computing Ser.). 124p. 1990. text ed. 84.95 (*0-471-92453-9*) Wiley.
Raynal, Michel, jt. ed. see Bermond, J. C.
Raynaud, C., ed. Nuclear Medicine & Biology Advances: Proceedings of the Third World Congress on Nuclear Medicine & Biology, August 29 - September 2, 1982, Paris, France, 7 Vols., Set. 3685p. 1983. 1,556.00 (*0-08-026405-0*, Pub. by Pergamon Repr UK) Franklin.
Raynaud, Ernest. La Melee Symboliste, 3 vols. in 1. LC 77-11474. reprint ed. 37.50 (*0-404-16336-X*) AMS Pr.
Raynaud, Fernand. Heureux! (FRE.). 1976. pap. 11.95 (*0-7859-4066-9*) Fr & Eur.
Raynaud, Gaston. Recueil De Motets Francais Des Twelfth et Thirteenth Siecles. (Bibliotheque Francaise Du Moyen Age Ser.: No. 1-2). liv, 811p. 1972. reprint ed. write for info. (*3-487-04274-6*, Pub. by Georg Olms GW) Lubrecht & Cramer.
Raynaud, M. & Shioda, T., eds. Algebraic Geometry. (Lecture Notes in Mathematics Ser.: Vol. 1016). 528p. 1983. pap. 49.60 (*0-387-12685-6*) Spr-Verlag.
Rayne, Martha L. What Can a Woman Do; Or, Her Position in the Business & Literary World. LC 74-3970. (Women in America Ser.). (Illus.). 584p. 1974. reprint ed. 44.95 (*0-405-06118-8*) Ayer.
Rayner, A. & Boddy, L. Fungal Decomposition of Wood: Its Biology & Ecology. LC 87-30966. 587p. 1988. text ed. 275.00 (*0-471-10310-1*) Wiley.
Rayner, A. J. & Colman, David, eds. Current Issues in Agricultural Economics. LC 92-30623. (Current Issues in Economics Ser.). 320p. 1993. text ed. 45.00 (*0-312-09091-9*) St Martin.
Rayner, A. J., jt. ed. see Milner, Chris.
Rayner, Alice. Comic Persuasion: Moral Structure in British Comedy from Shakespeare to Stoppard. LC 86-28281. (Illus.). 181p. reprint ed. pap. 51.60 (*0-7837-4699-7*, 2044446) Bks Demand.
— To Act, to Do, to Perform: Drama & the Phenomenology of Action. LC 94-3828. (Theater--Theory-Text-Performance Ser.). 168p. 1994. text ed. 32.50 (*0-472-10537-X*) U of Mich Pr.
Rayner, Anthony C. & Little, Ian M. Higgledy Piggledy Growth Again: An Investigation of the Predictability of Company Earnings & Dividends in the U. K. 1951-1961. LC 66-73566. (Illus.). 111p. 1966. 25.00 (*0-678-06261-7*) Kelley.
Rayner, B. H., jt. auth. see Kibble, B. P.
Rayner-Canham, Geoffrey, et al. Foundations of Chemistry. LC 82-18486. (Illus.). 525p. (C). 1983. teacher ed write for info. (*0-201-10414-8*); teacher ed write for info. (*0-201-10416-4*); text ed. write for info. (*0-201-10284-6*) Addison-Wesley.
Rayner-Canham, Geoffrey W., jt. auth. see Rayner-Canham, Marelene F.
Rayner-Canham, Marelene F. & Rayner-Canham, Geoffrey W. Harriet Brooks: Pioneer Nuclear Scientist. LC 91-90627. (Illus.). 192p. 1992. 37.95 (*0-7735-0881-3*) U of Toronto Pr.
— Harriet Brooks: Pioneer Nuclear Scientist. LC 91-90627. (Illus.). 168p. 1994. pap. 15.95 (*0-7735-1254-3*, Pub. by McGill CN) U of Toronto Pr.
Rayner, Claire. Bedford Row. large type ed. (Orig.). 1991. 21.95 (*0-7089-2557-X*) Ulverscroft.
— Charing Cross. 320p. 1982. pap. 3.25 (*0-8439-1023-2*) Dorchester Pub Co.
— Charing Cross. large type ed. (General Fisheries Council of the Mediterranean (GFCM): Studies & Reviews). 672p. 1992. 21.95 (*0-7089-2631-2*) Ulverscroft.
— Chelsea Reach. large type ed. (General Fiction Ser.). 576p. 1992. 21.95 (*0-7089-2700-9*) Ulverscroft.
— Dangerous Things. large type ed. (Charnwood Large Print Ser.). 1994. 25.95 (*0-7089-8801-6*) Ulverscroft.
— The Don't Spoil Your Body Book. King, Tony, tr. (Illus.). 48p. (J). (gr. 3 up). 1989. pap. 4.95 (*0-8120-6098-9*) Barron.
— Flanders: The Poppy Chronicles II. large type ed. 466p. 1989. 23.95 (*0-7089-8518-1*, Charnwood) Ulverscroft.

R

— The House on the Fen. large type ed. (Linford Mystery Library). 272p. 1989. pap. 11.95 (0-7089-6731-0, Linford) Ulverscroft.

— Jubilee: The Poppy Chronicles I. large type ed. 624p. 1988. 23.95 (0-7089-8479-7, Charnwood) Ulverscroft.

— Life & Love & Everything. (Children's Questions Ser.). (Illus.). 96p. (J). (gr. 2-5). 1995. 9.95 (1-85626-112-3, Pub. by C Kyle) Trafalgar.

— Long Acre. large type ed. 592p. 1992. 21.95 (0-7089-2593-6) Ulverscroft.

— Piccadilly. large type ed. (General Fiction Ser.). 560p. 1992. 21.95 (0-7089-2776-9) Ulverscroft.

— Postscripts. large type ed. 1992. 20.95 (0-7927-1355-9, Eagle Lrg Print) Chivers N Amer.

— Postscripts. large type ed. 1993. pap. 17.95 (0-7927-1354-0, Paragon Lrg Print) Chivers N Amer.

— Seven Dials. large type ed. (General Ser.). 592p. 1993. 21.95 (0-7089-2812-9) Ulverscroft.

— Shaftesbury Avenue. large type ed. (General Fiction Ser.). 544p. 1992. 21.95 (0-7089-2735-1) Ulverscroft.

— Sixties: (Poppy Chronicles VI) large type ed. (Charnwood Ser.). 432p. 1994. 25.95 (0-7089-8751-6, Charnwood) Ulverscroft.

— The Strand. large type ed. (General Fiction Ser.). 576p. 1992. 21.95 (0-7089-2669-X) Ulverscroft.

— Trafalgar Square. Orig. Title: The Strand. 320p. 1982. reprint ed. pap. 3.25 (0-8439-1152-2) Dorchester Pub Co.

*Rayner, Derek. Road Rollers. 1989. pap. 25.00 (0-7478-0153-3, Pub. by Shire UK) St Mut.

Rayner, Desmond. The Dawlish Season. large type ed. (General Ser.). 656p. 1993. 21.95 (0-7089-2792-0) Ulverscroft.

— The Husband. 512p. 1993. lib. bdg. 22.00 (0-7278-4400-8) Severn Hse.

Rayner, Emma. Handicapped among the Free. 1977. text ed. 19.95 (0-8369-9252-0, 9105) Ayer.

Rayner, Eric. The Independent Mind in British Psychoanalysis. LC 91-6403. 360p. 1991. 45.00x (0-87668-560-2) Aronson.

— Unconscious Logic: An Introduction to Matte Blanco's Bi-Logic & Its Uses. LC 94-45146. (New Library of Psychoanalysis). 176p. 1995. 59.95x (0-415-12725-4, C0565); pap. 18.95 (0-415-12726-2, C0566) Routledge.

Rayner, J. C. & Best, D. J. Smooth Tests of Goodness of Fit. (Oxford Statistical Science Ser.). (Illus.). 176p. 1989. 39.95 (0-19-505610-8) OUP.

Rayner, J. M. & Wootton, R. J., eds. Biomechanics in Evolution. (Society for Experimental Biology Seminar Ser.: Vol. 36). 288p. 1992. 74.95 (0-521-34421-2) Cambridge U Pr.

Rayner, John D., jt. auth. see Goldberg, David J.

Rayner, John N., jt. ed. see Golledge, Reginald G.

Rayner, Keith, ed. Eye Movements in Reading: Perceptual & Language Processes. LC 82-11565. (Perspectives in Neurolinguistics, Neuropsychology & Psycholinguistics Ser.). 1983. text ed. 118.00 (0-12-583680-5) Acad Pr.

*Rayner, Keith & Pollatsek, Alexander. The Psychology of Reading. 536p. 1994. pap. 39.95 (0-8058-1872-3) L Erlbaum Assocs.

Rayner, Keith & Whitaker, H. A., eds. Eye Movements & Visual Cognition: Scene Perception & Reading. (Neuropsychology Ser.). (Illus.). 480p. 1992. 87.00 (0-387-97711-2) Spr-Verlag.

Rayner, Kenneth. Listing Securities in the United States & the United Kingdom: A Comparative Guide to the Regulatory & Accounting Requirements. 288p. 1991. lib. bdg. 120.50 (1-85333-565-7, Pub. by Graham & Trotman UK) Kluwer Ac.

Rayner, Lee J. Legends of the Kings of Ireland. 109p. 1988. pap. 9.95 (0-85342-857-3, Pub. by Mercier Pr IE) Dufour.

Rayner, Lois. The Adopted Child Comes of Age. 1980. 40. 00 (0-317-05782-0, Pub. by Natl Inst Soc Work) St Mut.

Rayner, Lynn, jt. auth. see Butler, Kurt.

Rayner, Mary. Garth Pig & the IceCream Lady. LC 77-1647. (Illus.). 32p. (J). (gr. k-3). 1978. text ed. 14.95 (0-689-30598-2, Atheneum Bks Young) S&S Childrens.

— Garth Pig Steals the Show. LC 92-24508. (Illus.). (J). (ps-3). 1993. 13.99 (0-525-45023-8, DCB) Dutton Child Bks.

— Mr. & Mrs. Pig's Evening Out. LC 76-4476. (Illus.). 32p. (J). (gr. k-3). 1976. lib. bdg. 14.95 (0-689-30530-3, Atheneum Bks Young) S&S Childrens.

— Mrs. Pig Gets Cross & Other Stories. LC 86-13433. (Unicorn Paperback Ser.). (Illus.). 64p. (J). (ps-3). 1991. pap. 5.95 (0-525-44705-9, Puffin) Puffin Bks.

— Mrs. Pig's Bulk Buy. LC 80-19875. (Illus.). 32p. (J). (gr. k-3). 1981. text ed. 14.95 (0-689-30831-0, Atheneum Bks Young) S&S Childrens.

— Oh, Paul! (Banana Bks.). (Illus.). 42p. (J). (gr. 2-4). 1989. 3.95 (0-8120-6145-4) Barron.

— One by One: Garth Pig's Rain Song. (Illus.). 24p. (J). (ps-1). 1994. 5.99 (0-525-45240-0) Dutton Child Bks.

— Ten Pink Piglets: Garth Pig's Wall Song. (Illus.). 24p. (J). (ps-1). 1994. 5.99 (0-685-70795-4, DCB) Dutton Child Bks.

Rayner, Michael, jt. ed. see Wiegand, Patrick.

Rayner, Mike, jt. auth. see Longfield, Jeanette.

Rayner, Nicholas. Jewels of the Duchess of Windsor. LC 87-14218. (Illus.). 208p. 1987. 50.00 (0-86565-089-6) Vendome.

Rayner, P. Alan. English Silver Coinage since Sixteen Forty-Nine. (Illus.). 252p. 1992. 45.00 (1-85264-053-7, Pub. by Seaby UK) Trafalgar.

Rayner, R. Pilze Erkennen-Leicht Gemancht. (Illus.). (GER.). 1979. pap. text ed. 7.95 (3-440-04748-2) Lubrecht & Cramer.

Rayner, R., tr. see Moser, Meinhard.

*Rayner, Shoo. Cat in a Flap. (Illus.). 22p. (J). 1995. pap. 4.99 (0-14-054860-2) Puffin Bks.

— The Lydia Books: Lydia & Her Garden; Lydia & the Letters; Lydia & the Present; Lydia & Her Cat; Lydia at the Shops; Lydia & the Ducks, 6 bks., Set. (Oxford Reading Tree Ser.). (Illus.). 96p. (J). (gr. k-k). 1994. pap. 9.95 (0-19-916171-2) OUP.

— My First Picture Joke Book. (Illus.). 32p. (J). (ps-1). 1993. pap. 3.99 (0-14-050925-9) Puffin Bks.

— The Victor Books: Victor the Hero; Victor & the Kite; Victor the Champion; Victor & the Computer Cat; Victor & the Sail-Kart; Victor & the Martian. (Oxford Reading Tree Ser.). (Illus.). 96p. (J). (gr. k-k). 1994. pap. 9.95 (0-19-916225-5) OUP.

Rayner, Stephen, ed. Butterworths Privatisation in Central & Eastern Europe. 1992. U.K. pap. 150.00 (0-406-00840-X) Butterworth Legal Pubs.

— Butterworths Trade & Finance in Central & Eastern Europe. 255p. 1993. pap. 160.00 (0-406-02088-4, U.K.) Butterworth Legal Pubs.

Rayner, Steve, jt. auth. see Flanagan, James G.

Rayner, Steve, jt. auth. see Gross, Jonathan L.

Rayner, Steven R. Recreating the Workplace: The Pathway to High Performance Work Systems. LC 92-85209. 281p. 1993. 27.50 (0-939246-32-5) Oliver Wight.

— Team Traps: Survival Stories & Lessons from Team Disasters, Mishaps & Other Near-Death Experiences. 256p. 1995. 25.00 (0-939246-79-1) Oliver Wight.

Rayner, Susan. The Theory of Contracts in Islamic Law: A Comparative Analysis with Particular Reference to Modern Legislation in Kuwait, Bahrain & the U. A. E. 454p. (C). 1991. lib. bdg. 115.00 (1-85333-617-3, Pub. by Graham & Trotman UK) Kluwer Ac.

Rayner, Victoria. Clinical Cosmetology: A Medical Approach to Esthetics Procedures. (Illus.). 440p. (C). 1993. text ed. 39.95 (1-56253-056-9) Milady Pub.

*Rayner, Victoria L. The Survival Guide for Today's Career Woman. 208p. (Orig.). 1994. pap. 19.95 (0-924272-06-6) Info Net Pub.

Raynes, Bert. Birds of Grand Teton: And the Surrounding Area. Broadus, Debbie, ed. (Illus.). 90p. (Orig.). reprint ed. pap. 7.95 (0-931895-00-6) Grand Teton NHA.

Raynes, Harold E. Social Security in Britain: A History-A Greenwood Archival Edition. 2nd ed. LC 76-40057. 264p. 1977. reprint ed. text ed. 79.50 (0-8371-9055-X, RASSB, Greenwood Pr) Greenwood.

Raynes, Livia, ed. see Stiles, Tom.

Raynes, Marybeth, ed. see Schow, Ron.

Raynes, Norma, et al. Homes for Mental Handicapped People. 240p. 1988. text ed. 65.00 (0-422-60770-3, Pub. by Tavistock UK) Routledge Chapman & Hall.

Raynes, Norma V., jt. ed. see Hogg, James.

Raynes, Norma V., et al. Organisational Structure & the Care of the Mentally Retarded. LC 79-83740. (Praeger Special Studies). 240p. 1979. text ed. 59.95 (0-275-90411-3, C0411, Praeger Pubs) Greenwood.

Raynes, Polly. Watercolor. (Workstations Ser.). (Illus.). 48p. (J). (gr. 9 up). 1993. 21.95 (0-8431-3663-4) Price Stern.

Rayney, Peter, jt. auth. see Hart, Gerry.

Raynolds, Eleanor, jt. auth. see Raynolds, John F., III.

Raynolds, John F., III & Raynolds, Eleanor. Beyond Success: How Volunteer Service Can Help You Begin Making a Life Instead of Just a Living. 1989. 19.95 (0-942361-04-0); pap. 9.95 (0-942361-14-8) MasterMedia Ltd.

*Raynor, Bill & Bay, Roger R., eds. Proceedings of the Workshop on Research Methodologies & Applications for Pacific Island Agroforestry. (Illus.). 86p. (Orig.). (C). 1994. pap. text ed. 45.00x (0-7881-1073-X) Diane Pub.

Raynor, G. Physical Metallurgy of Magnesium & Its Alloys. LC 58-9829. (International Series of Monographs on Metals Physics & Physical Metallurgy: Vol. 5). 1959. 225.00 (0-08-013603-6, Pub. by Pergamon Repr UK) Franklin.

Raynor, G., jt. auth. see Pearson, W.

Raynor, G. V. An Introduction to the Electron Theory of Metals. 96p. 1988. text ed. 21.00 (0-901462-37-3, Pub. by Inst Materials UK) Ashgate Pub Co.

Raynor, J. & Entin, E. Motivation, Career Striving & Aging. 1981. pap. text ed. 24.95 (0-07-051274-4) McGraw.

Raynor, Joyce, et al. The Coins of Ancient Meiron. LC 87-19135. (Meiron Excavation Project Ser.: Vol. 4). vii, 140p. 1988. text ed. 27.50 (0-89757-208-4); pap. text ed. 19.50 (0-89757-209-2) Am Sch Orient Res.

Raynor, Lois. The Adopted Child Comes of Age. LC 79-41348. (London. National Institute for Social Work Training. National Institute Social Services Library: No. 36). 176p. reprint ed. pap. 50.20 (0-8357-5117-1, 2023180) Bks Demand.

Raynor, Louise A., jt. auth. see Kerr, Carolyn H.

Raynor, Peter. Probation As an Alternative to Custody: A Case Study. 214p. 1988. text ed. 59.50 (0-566-05588-0, Pub. by Avebury Pub UK) Ashgate Pub Co.

Raynor, Sherry & Drouillard, Richard. Get a Wiggle On. Alonso, Lou, ed. (Illus.). 80p. 1978. pap. 5.00 (0-88314-077-2) AAHPERD.

— Move It!!! Alonso, Lou, ed. (Illus.). 96p. 1978. pap. 5.00 (0-88314-132-9) AAHPERD.

Raynor, Tom, jt. ed. see Cannastra, Lyn.

Raynor, Victoria. Clinical Cosmetology: A Medical Approach to Esthetics Procedures. 1993. 34.95 (1-56293-056-7) Phoenix Soc.

Raynould, Andre C., jt. auth. see OECD Staff.

Raynovich, William, jt. auth. see Gonsoulin, Sheryl M.

Rayns, Tony, jt. ed. see Field, Simon.

Rayo. Vonu: The Search for Personal Freedom. Fisher, Jon, ed. (Illus.). 1983. pap. 7.95 (0-915179-96-2) Loompanics.

Rayor, Diane, tr. Sappho's Lyre: Archaic Lyric & Women Poets of Ancient Greece. LC 90-48642. (Illus.). 234p. 1991. 35.00 (0-520-07335-5); pap. 12.00 (0-520-07336-3) U CA Pr.

Rayor, Diane, jt. tr. see Lombardo, Stanley.

*Rayor, Diane J. & Batstone, William W., eds. Latin Lyric & Elegiac Poetry: An Anthology of New Translations. LC 94-37902. (Reference Library of the Humanities). 384p. 1995. 56.00 (0-8153-0087-5, H1425); pap. 18.95 (0-8153-1540-6, H1425) Garland.

Rayoumi, Magdy A., ed. Parallel Algorithms & Architectures for DSP Applications. 304p. (C). 1991. lib. bdg. 78.50 (0-7923-9209-4) Kluwer Ac.

Rayser, V. Fred. The Seven Secrets for Getting What You Want. LC 75-12106. 160p. 1976. pap. 8.95 (0-915922-00-2) Winged Lion.

Rayside, David M. A Small Town in Modern Times: Alexandria, Ontario. 360p. (C). 1991. text ed. 44.95 (0-7735-0826-0, Pub. by McGill CN) U of Toronto Pr.

Raysman, Richard & Brown, Peter. Computer Law: Drafting & Negotiating Forms & Agreements. 1984. 145.00 (0-318-12028-3) NY Law Pub.

*Raysman, Richard, et al. Multimedia Law: Forms & Analysis. (Commercial Law Intellectual Property Ser.). 1994. write for info. (0-615-00120-3) Law Journal.

Raysman, Victor. Say It in Polish. (Orig.). 1954. pap. 2.95 (0-486-20808-7) Dover.

Rayson, Ann. Modern Hawaiian History. LC 83-73465. (Illus.). 288p. 1984. student ed 7.95 (0-935848-29-0) Bess Pr.

— Modern Hawaiian History. rev. ed. LC 83-73465. (Illus.). 304p. 1994. pap. 19.95 (1-880188-89-9) Bess Pr.

Rayson, Ann, jt. auth. see Wong, Helen.

Rayson, Ethel. Polish Music & Chopin, Its Laureate. 64p. 1991. reprint ed. lib. bdg. 59.00 (0-7812-9344-8) Rprt Serv.

Rayson, Jane, jt. auth. see Mallender, Paul.

Raysor, Thomas M., ed. see Wordsworth, William & Coleridge, Samuel Taylor.

Raysuni, Ahmad A. Nazariyat al Maqasid 'inda al Imam al Shatibi: The Theory of the Law's Objectives According to al Shatibi. 2nd ed. LC 92-8243. (Silsilat al Rasa'il al Jami'iyah Ser.: No. 1). 383p. (ARA.). 1993. 18.00 (1-56564-036-5); pap. 12.00 (1-56564-037-3) IIIT VA.

Rayudu, C. S. Agricultural Credit & Rural Development in Drought Regions: A Study of Cooperative Banks of A. P. (C). 1992. text ed. 21.00 (81-7022-385-7, Pub. by Concept II) S Asia.

Rayudu, C. S., jt. auth. see Balan, K. R.

Rayudu, Garimella V., ed. Radiotracers for Medical Applications, Vol. I. 1983. 155.00 (0-8493-6015-3, R895) CRC Pr.

— Radiotracers for Medical Applications, Vol. II. 304p. 1983. 155.00 (0-8493-6016-1, R895, CRC Reprint) Franklin.

Raywalt, James K. Barnhart: The Descendants of John & Mariah (Hiveley) Barnhart: a Genealogy of the Ancestors & Descendants of John Barnhart & Mariah Hively of Eastern Ohio to the Present. (Illus.). 109p. 1992. reprint ed. lib. bdg. 29.50 (0-8328-2408-9); reprint ed. pap. 19.50 (0-8328-2409-7) Higginson Bk Co.

— Lane ... & a Cast of Thousands: A History of the Lane Family of Canada & the U. S. from Their Arrival in 1819 to the Present. (Illus.). 751p. 1992. reprint ed. lib. bdg. 99.50 (0-8328-2406-2); reprint ed. pap. 89.50 (0-8328-2407-0) Higginson Bk Co.

— Morgan: A History of the Descendants of Henry Oscar Morgan & Ellen Jane Mandigo. (Illus.). 203p. 1992. reprint ed. lib. bdg. 39.00 (0-8328-2410-0); reprint ed. pap. 29.00 (0-8328-2411-9) Higginson Bk Co.

— Shove: An English Ancestry: an Account of the Ancestry of Edward Melvin Shove & His Siblings. (Illus.). 149p. 1992. reprint ed. lib. bdg. 31.00 (0-8328-2412-7); reprint ed. pap. 21.00 (0-8328-2413-5) Higginson Bk Co.

Rayward, W. B. International Organization & Dissemination of Knowledge: Selected Essay of Paul Otlet. 256p. 1990. 115.50 (0-444-88678-8) Elsevier.

Rayward, W. Boyd, ed. see Chicago University, Graduate Library School Staff.

Rayward, W. Boyd, ed. see Metcalf, John W.

Rayyan, Omar, illus. Rimonah of the Flashing Sword: A North African Tale. LC 93-40091. 32p. (J). (ps-3). 1995. lib. bdg. 15.95 (0-8234-1093-5) Holiday.

Raz. Project Planning & Computer Models. 1995. pap. 32.95 (0-442-01843-6) Van Nos Reinhold.

Raz, Hilda. What Is Good. 64p. (Orig.). 1988. pap. 5.95 (0-939395-09-6) Thorntree Pr.

Raz, Joseph. The Authority of Law: Essays on Law & Morality. 1983. pap. 26.00 (0-19-825493-8) OUP.

— The Concept of a Legal System: An Introduction to the Theory of a Legal System. 2nd ed. 1980. pap. 29.95 (0-19-825363-X) OUP.

— The Morality of Freedom. 448p. 1988. pap. 24.95 (0-19-824807-5) OUP.

— Practical Reason & Norms. 218p. (C). 1990. text ed. 45. 00 (0-691-07851-3); pap. text ed. 13.95 (0-691-02320-4) Princeton U Pr.

— Practical Reason & Norms. LC 89-78127. reprint ed. pap. 62.70 (0-7837-9282-4, 2060021) Bks Demand.

Raz, Joseph, ed. Authority. (Readings in Social & Political Theory Ser.). 330p. 1990. 50.00 (0-8147-7414-8); pap. 20.00 (0-8147-7415-6) NYU Pr.

Raz, Joseph, jt. ed. see Hacker, P. M.

Raz, Joseph, ed. see Hart, H. L.

Raz, Mirla G. Help Me Talk Right: A Guide to Stuttering & Disfluent Speech in the Two to Five Year Old Child. (Orig.). pap. write for info. (0-9635426-2-1) Gersten Weitz.

— Help Me Talk Right: How to Correct a Child's Lisp in 15 Easy Lessons. LC 92-63349. (Illus.). 112p. (Orig.). 1993. pap. 24.95 (0-9635426-0-5) Gersten Weitz.

— Help Me Talk Right: Teach a Child to Say the "R" Sound in 15 Easy Lessons. (Illus.). (Orig.). Date not set. pap. 24.95 (0-9635426-1-3) Gersten Weitz.

Raz, S. Tigre Grammar & Texts. LC 81-71735. (Afroasiatic Dialects Ser.: Vol. 4). 163p. (C). 1983. pap. 24.50 (0-89003-097-9) Undena Pubns.

Raz, Shlomo. Female Urology. (Illus.). 464p. 1983. text ed. 142.00 (0-7216-7483-6) Saunders.

Raz, Simcha. The Sayings of Menahem Mendel of Kotsk. Levin, Edward, tr. LC 94-28313. 232p. 1995. 25.00 (1-56821-297-6) Aronson.

— A Tzaddik in Our Time. Wengrow, Charles, tr. (Illus.). 1976. 17.95 (0-87306-130-6) Feldheim.

Raz, Tzvi & Thomas, Marlin U., eds. Design of Inspection Systems - Selected Readings. (Inspection Ser.). (Illus.). 354p. 1990. 19.95 (0-87389-082-5) ASQC Qual Pr.

Raz, Z. W. & Saitta, L., eds. Methodologies for Intelligent Systems, Vol. 3: Proceedings of the 3rd International Symposium, October 12-15, 1988, Turin, Italy. 512p. 1988. 103.00 (0-444-01461-6, North Holland) Elsevier.

*Raza, Asmi. Pakistan's Quest for Food Security. (C). 1993. cd-rom 18.50x (81-7024-550-8, Pub. by Ashish II) S Asia.

Raza, Mehdi, jt. auth. see Shafi, Mohammad.

Raza, Mehdi, jt. ed. see Shafi, Mohammad.

Raza, Monis. Atlas of Tribal India: With Computed Tables of District-Level Data & Its Geographic Interpretation. 1990. 100.00 (0-685-34762-1, Pub. by Concept II) S Asia.

Raza, Moonis. Higher Education in India: A Comprehensive Bibliography. (C). 1991. 62.50 (81-7022-346-6, Pub. by Concept II) S Asia.

Raza, Moonis, ed. Renewable Resources for Regional Development. (C). 1988. 52.00 (81-7022-229-X, Pub. by Concept II) S Asia.

Raza, Moonis, jt. ed. see Misra, R. P.

Razaboni, Rosa M., ed. see Salmon, Michel.

*Razavi, Amir H. ArcView Developer's Guide. (Illus.). 300p. 1995. pap. 49.95 (1-56690-059-X, 4202, OnWord Pr) High Mtn.

Razavi, B. Trends in Lower Power Electronics. (Current Topics in Electronics & System). 200p. 1994. text ed. 48.00 (981-02-1863-X) World Scientific Pub.

*Razavi, Behzad. Principles of Data Conversion System Design. LC 94-26694. 1995. 54.95 (0-7803-1093-4) Inst Electrical.

Razavi, Hossein & Fesharaki, Fereidun. Fundamentals of Petroleum Trading. LC 91-8072. 232p. 1991. text ed. 65. 00 (0-275-93920-0, C3920, Praeger Pubs) Greenwood.

Razdan, M. N., jt. auth. see Bhojwani, S. S.

Razdolskaya, Vera. Rubens. (Masters of World Painting Ser.). (C). 1983. text ed. 60.00 (0-569-08768-6, Pub. by Collets) St Mut.

Razeghi, M. Physical Concepts of Materials for Novel Optoelectronic Device Applications I, Vol. 1361: Materials Growth & Characterization (Nov 1990, Aachen, FRG) 1991. 132.00 (0-8194-0422-5) SPIE.

— Physical Concepts of Materials for Novel Optoelectronic Device Applications II, Vol. 1362: Device Physics & Applications (Nov 1990, Aachen, FRG) 1991. 132.00 (0-8194-0423-3) SPIE.

Razeghi, M., ed. Optoelectronic Materials & Device Concepts. 1991. 67.00 (0-8194-0530-2); pap. 52.00 (0-8194-0533-7) SPIE.

Razeghi, Manijeh, jt. ed. see Wong, Ka-Kha.

Razek, Joseph & Hosch, Gordon. Introduction to Government & NFP Accounting. 2nd ed. 512p. (C). 1990. Casebound. text ed. write for info. (0-13-484718-0) P-H.

*Razek, Joseph R. & Hosch, Gordon A. Introduction to Governmental & Not-for-Profit Accounting. 3rd ed. LC 95-10465. 1995. text ed. write for info. (0-13-064296-7) P-H.

Razgon, Lev. True Stories, Memoirs of Lev Razgon. Crowfoot, J., tr. 1995. 24.95 (0-87501-108-X) Ardis Pubs.

Razheghi, Manijeh. The MOCVD Challenge, Vol. 1: A Survey of GaInAsP-InP for Photonic & Electronic Applications. 340p. 1989. 139.00 (0-85274-161-8) IOP Pub.

Razi, B. A., jt. auth. see Rao, R. R.

Razi, F. D. The Modern Persian-Urdu-English Dictionary. 250p. (ENG, PER & URD.). 1981. 29.95 (0-8288-1454-6, M14111) Fr & Eur.

Razi, Sayyid, ed. see Talib, Ali B. Abi.

Razia Akter Banu, U. A., ed. Islam in Contemporary Bangladesh. LC 91-19061. (International Studies in Sociology & Social Anthropology: No. 58). xviii, 194p. 1992. pap. 43.00 (90-04-09497-0) E J Brill.

Razik, Sail I. A History of the Imams & Seyyids of Oman. 592p. 1986. 350.00 (1-85077-129-4, Darf Pubs Ltd) St Mut.

Razik, Taher A., ed. & comp. Bibliography of Programmed Instruction & Computer-Assisted Instruction. LC 76-125875. (Educational Technology Bibliography Ser.: Vol.1). 288p. 1971. 34.95 (0-87778-013-7) Educ Tech Pubns.

*Razik, Taher A. & Swanson, Austin D. Fundamental Concepts of Educational Leadership & Management. (Illus.). 640p. 1994. write for info. (0-02-398732-4, Merrill Pub Co) Macmillan.

Razin, A., et al, eds. DNA Methylation. (Molecular Biology Ser.). (Illus.). xiii, 392p. 1984. 119.00 (0-387-96038-4) Spr-Verlag.

Razin, Andrew M., jt. auth. see Gurman, Alan S.

Razin, Andrew M., et al. Helping Cardiac Patients: Biobehavioral & Psychotherapeutic Approaches. LC 84-47995. (Joint Publication in the Jossey-Bass Social & Behavioral Science Series & the Jossey-Bass Health Ser.). 230p. reprint ed. pap. 65.60 (0-7837-2533-7, 2042692) Bks Demand.

Razin, Assaf & Sadka, Efraim. The Economy of Modern Israel: Malaise & Promise. LC 93-3054. (Illus.). 168p. (C). 1993. Alk. paper. 34.95 (0-226-70589-7) U Ch Pr.

An Asterisk (*) at the beginning of an entry indicates that the title is appearing in BIP for the first time.

— Population Economics. LC 94-27773. 250p. 1995. 30.00x (*0-262-18160-6*) MIT Pr.

Razin, Assaf & Sadka, Efraim, eds. Economic Policy in Theory & Practice. 350p. 1987. text ed. 39.95 (*0-312-23453-8*) St Martin.

Razin, Assaf & Slemrod, Joel, eds. Taxation in the Global Economy. LC 90-30262. (National Bureau of Economic Research Project Report Ser.). (Illus.). ix, 443p. 1991. pap. text ed. 19.95 (*0-226-70592-7*) U Ch Pr.

— Taxation in the Global Economy. LC 90-30262. (National Bureau of Economic Research Project Report Ser.). (Illus.). 453p. reprint ed. pap. 129.20 (*0-7837-4095-6*, 2057916) Bks Demand.

Razin, Assaf, jt. auth. see Frenkel, Jacob A.

Razin, Assaf, jt. ed. see Helpman, Elhanan.

Razin, Assaf, jt. ed. see Leiderman, Leonardo.

Razin, S. & Barile, M. F., eds. The Mycoplasmas: Mycoplasma Pathogenicity, Vol. 4. 1985. text ed. 143. 00 (*0-12-078404-1*) Acad Pr.

***Razin, Shmuel & Tully, Joseph G., eds.** Molecular & Diagnostic Procedures in Mycoplasmology Vol. 1: Molecular Characterization. (Illus.). 600p. 1995. boxed write for info. (*0-12-583805-0*) Acad Pr.

Razin, Shmuel, jt. ed. see Tully, Joseph G.

Razis, Vic. The American Connection: The Influence of U. S. Business on South Africa. LC 85-25026. 300p. 1986. text ed. 45.00 (*0-312-02203-4*) St Martin.

Razkova, S. & Remesh, T. Early Soviet Photographs. (C). 1990. pap. 75.00 (*0-685-34320-0*, Pub. by Collets) St Mut.

Razmyslov, Iurii P. Identities of Algebras & Their Representations. LC 94-20766. (Translations of Mathematical Monographs: Vol. 138). 1994. 120.00 (*0-8218-4608-6*) Am Math.

Razquin, M. C., jt. auth. see Baert, A. E.

Razso, Imre. English-Hungarian Technical Dictionary-Angol-Magyar Muszaki Szotar. (ENG & HUN.). 49.50 (*0-87557-041-0*, 041-0) Saphrograph.

Razumikhin, B. S. Classical Principles & Optimization Problems. (C). 1987. lib. bdg. 198.50 (*90-277-2605-1*) Kluwer Ac.

— Physical Models & Equilibrium Methods in Programming & Economics. (Mathematics & Its Applications, Soviet Ser.). 372p. 1984. lib. bdg. 132.00 (*90-277-1644-7*) Kluwer Ac.

Razumovskii, S. D. & Zaikov, G. E. Ozone & Its Reactions with Organic Compounds. (Studies in Organic Chemistry: Vol. 15). 1984. 154.00 (*0-444-42369-9*, I-034-84) Elsevier.

Razumovsky, Maria. Marina Tsvetayeva. Gibson, Aleksey, tr. 363p. 1995. reprint ed. 65.00 (*1-85224-045-8*, Pub. by Bloodaxe Bks UK) Dufour.

Razvalyaev, A. V. Continental Rift Formation & Its Prehistory. Chakraverty, R., ed. (Russian Translation Ser.: No. 87). (Illus.). 208p. (C). 1991. text ed. 70.00 (*90-6191-991-6*, Pub. by A A Balkema NE) Ashgate Pub Co.

***Razvan.** Lemon Whip. (Illus.). (J). (ps-1). 1995. 14.95 (*0-02-775668-8*, Mac Bks Young Read) S&S Childrens.

— Two Little Shoes. Stupple, Deborah, tr. LC 92-40814. (Illus.). 32p. (J). (ps-1). 1993. lib. bdg. 14.95 (*0-02-775667-X*, Bradbury S&S) S&S Childrens.

Razvan, E., ed. River Intakes & Diversion Dams. (Developments in Civil Engineering Ser.: No. 25). 510p. 1989. 146.25 (*0-444-87315-5*) Elsevier.

Razvayaev, Av. Continental Rift Formation & Its Prehistory. (C). 1991. 38.00 (*81-204-0601-X*, Pub. by Oxford IBH II) S Asia.

Razwy, Sayed A. Salman el-Farsi. 1985. pap. 3.95 (*0-933543-02-6*) Aza Khana.

— Salman El-Farsi. rev. ed. LC 83-50152. 1990. pap. text ed. 5.95 (*0-940368-29-3*, 67) Tahrike Tarsile Quran.

Razwy, Sayed A., ed. Khadija-Tul-Kubra: (The Wife of Prophet Muhammed) LC 89-50010. 120p. 1989. pap. 5.95 (*0-940368-93-5*, 15) Tahrike Tarsile Quran.

Razzaq, Roshi. Low Fat Indian Cookbook. 1993. 12.98 (*1-55521-898-9*) Bk Sales Inc.

Razzell, Mary. The Secret Code of DNA. (Illus.). 36p. (J). (ps-8). 1986. 7.95 (*0-920806-83-X*, Pub. by Penumbra Pr CN) U of Toronto Pr.

Razzell, Peter. Victorian Working Class: Selections from the "Morning Chronicle" Wainwright, R. W., ed. (Illus.). 380p. 1973. 37.50 (*0-7146-2957-X*, Pub. by F Cass Pubs UK) Intl Spec Bk.

Razzi, Jim. The Ghost in the Mirror: And Other Ghost Stories. (Illus.). 64p. (J). 1990. pap. 2.95 (*0-448-40058-8*, G&D) Putnam Pub Group.

— The Haunted Playground & Other Stories. LC 89-20281. (Horror Show Ser.). 96p. (YA). (gr. 7 up). 1990. lib. bdg. 9.89 (*0-8167-1688-9*); pap. text ed. 2.95 (*0-8167-1689-7*) Troll Assocs.

— Mighty Max. (J). Date not set. 5.99 (*0-679-87407-0*) Random.

— Nightmare Island: And Other Real-Life Mysteries. LC 92-32638. (Trophy Bk.). (Illus.). 96p. (J). (gr. 3-7). 1993. pap. 3.95 (*0-06-440426-9*, Trophy) HarpC Child Bks.

— Polly Pocket. (J). Date not set. 5.99 (*0-679-87406-2*) Random.

— The Restless Dead: More Strange Real-Life Mysteries. LC 93-34745. (Trophy Bk.). (Illus.). 96p. (J). (gr. 3-7). 1994. pap. 3.95 (*0-06-440427-7*, Trophy) HarpC Child Bks.

— Terror in the Mirror. LC 89-5230. (Horror Show Ser.). 96p. (YA). (gr. 7 up). 1990. lib. bdg. 9.89 (*0-8167-1684-6*); pap. text ed. 2.95 (*0-8167-1685-4*) Troll Assocs.

— The Very Best Christmas Present. LC 87-83045. (Golden Look-Look Bks.). (Illus.). 24p. (Orig.). (J). (ps-3). 1988. pap. write for info. (*0-307-11711-1*) Western Pub.

Razzi, Jim, adapt. Disney's Mickey's Christmas Carol. LC 91-58970. (Animated Film Picture Bks.). (Illus.). (J). 1992. 12.95 (*1-56282-238-1*); lib. bdg. 12.89 (*1-56282-236-5*); pap. 3.50 (*1-56282-239-X*) Disney Pr.

— Walt Disney's Snow White & the Seven Dwarfs. LC 92-53431. (Junior Novel Ser.). (Illus.). 64p. (J). (gr. 2-6). 1993. pap. 3.50 (*1-56282-364-7*) Disney Pr.

— Walt Disney's the Jungle Book. LC 91-58975. (Junior Novel Ser.). (Illus.). 64p. (J). 1992. pap. 3.50 (*1-56282-243-8*) Disney Pr.

RCA Service Company Staff. Electrical Circuits in Gas Appliances. 61p. 1964. pap. 1.50 (*0-318-12605-2*, X55564) Am Gas Assn.

RCA Staff. RCA Electro-Optics Handbook. (Illus.). 1974. 4.95 (*0-913970-11-5*, EOH-11) RCA Solid State.

***Rcaf.** Royal Canadian Air Force Exercise Plans for Physical Fitness. 1990. mass mkt. 5.50 (*0-671-72755-9*) PB.

RCC Pilotage Foundation Staff. The Atlantic Crossing Guide. 2nd ed. Allen, Philip, ed. (Illus.). 280p. 1988. 29. 95 (*0-87742-979-0*) Intl Marine.

— Atlantic Islands: Azores, Madeira, Canaries & Cape Verde Islands. 2nd ed. (Illus.). 232p. 1994. 74.95 (*0-85288-267-X*, Pub. by Imray Laurie Norie & Wilson UK) Bluewater Bks.

— Faeroes Iceland Greenland Cruising Guide. (Illus.). 100p. 1995. ring bd. 37.95 (*0-85288-268-8*, Pub. by Imray Laurie Norie & Wilson UK) Bluewater Bks.

RCC Pilotage Foundation Staff, et al. North Biscay Pilot: Brest to the Gironde Estuary. 4th ed. (Illus.). 326p. (C). 1990. 160.00 (*0-229-11808-9*, Pub. by Imray Laurie Norie & Wilson UK) St Mut.

RCC Pilotage Foundation Staff & Coles, K. Adlard. North Biscay Pilot: Ouessant to La Gironde. 6th ed. (Illus.). 224p. 1994. 79.95 (*0-85288-245-9*, Pub. by Imray Laurie Norie & Wilson UK) Bluewater Bks.

RCG-Hagler, Bailly, Inc. Staff, ed. see U. S. Department of Energy, Office of Industrial Programs Staff.

Rchowdari, B. V., et al. Solid State Ionic Materials: Proceedings of the 4th Asian Conference on Solid State Ionics. 472p. 1994. text ed. 109.00 (*981-02-1861-3*) World Scientific Pub.

RCL Team, jt. auth. see Katzenbach, Jon.

RDD Inc. Staff. Process Architecture, No. 113: Design for Gathering People. (Illus.). 155p. 1994. pap. 46.95 (*4-89331-113-1*, Pub. by Process Archit JA) Bks Nippan.

***RDD Pilotage Foundation Staff.** North Biscay Pilot. 4th ed. (Illus.). 284p. 1990. 79.50 (*0-229-11809-7*) Sheridan.

Re, Edward D. & Krauss, Stanton D. Remedies, Cases & Materials. 3rd ed. (University Casebook Ser.). 1296p. (C). 1991. text ed. 43.95 (*0-88277-945-1*) Foundation Pr.

— Remedies, Teacher's Manual to Accompany Cases & Materials On. 3rd ed. (University Casebook Ser.). 126p. 1992. pap. text ed. write for info. (*0-88277-988-5*) Foundation Pr.

Re, Edward D. & Re, Joseph R. Brief Writing & Oral Argument. 7th ed. LC 87-22068. 384p. 1993. lib. bdg. 37.50 (*0-379-20425-8*) Oceana.

— Brief Writing & Oral Argument. 7th ed. LC 87-22068. 384p. 1993. pap. text ed. 24.95 (*0-379-21203-X*) Oceana.

Re, Edward D., jt. auth. see Chafee, Zechariah, Jr.

Re, Frank M. Re Views. 80p. 1975. pap. 2.95 (*0-686-14654-9*) F M Re.

Re, Joseph. Earn & Learn: Cooperative Education Opportunities Offered by the Federal Government, 1989-1990. 16th ed. 36p. 1994. 4.00 (*0-945981-87-2*) Octameron Assocs.

Re, Joseph, ed. Financial Aid Fin-Ancer: Expert Answers to College Financing Questions. 6th ed. 36p. 1994. 4.00 (*0-945981-92-9*) Octameron Assocs.

Re, Joseph R., jt. auth. see Re, Edward D.

Re, Judith & Schneider, Meg F. Social Savvy. (Illus.). 208p. 1992. pap. 11.00 (*0-671-74198-5*, Fireside) S&S Trade.

Re, Lucia. Calvino & the Age of Neorealism: Fables of Estrangement. LC 89-49547. 432p. 1990. 37.50 (*0-8047-1650-1*) Stanford U Pr.

Re, Paul. The Dance of the Pencil: Serene Art by Paul Re. LC 92-91089. 128p. 1993. write for info. (*0-9634902-0-6*) P B Re.

Re, Richard N. Bioburst: The Impact of Modern Biology on the Affairs of Man. LC 86-7422. (Illus.). xvi, 254p. 1986. text ed. 29.95 (*0-8071-1289-5*) La State U Pr.

Rea, Alayna, jt. auth. see Rea, John D.

Rea, Alexander. South Indian Buddhist Antiquities: Including the Stups of Bhattiprolu, Gudivada, & Ghanta Sala & Other Ancient Sites in the Krishna District Madras Presidency; with Notes on Dome Construction; Andhra Numismatics & Marble Sculpture. (C). 1989. reprint ed. 18.00 (*81-206-0512-8*, Pub. by Asian Educ Servs II) S Asia.

Rea, Amadeo, ed. see Unitt, Philip.

Rea, Amadeo M. Once a River: Bird Life & Habitat Changes on the Middle Gila. LC 82-23815. (Illus.). 285p. 1983. 35.00 (*0-8165-0799-6*) U of Ariz Pr.

Rea, C. British Basidomysetaceae: A Handbook to the Larger British Fungi. 1968. pap. 60.00 (*3-7682-0561-4*) Lubrecht & Cramer.

Rea, Cross & Auchincloss Staff. Transportation of Hazardous Materials: A Compliance & Practice Guide for Safe Transportation of Hazardous Materials. 2nd ed. 300p. 1992. pap. text ed. 79.00 (*0-86587-286-4*) Gov Insts.

Rea, David, jt. ed. see Duncan, Robert.

Rea, Dean, ed. see Barna, George.

Rea, Dean, ed. see London, H. B., Jr. & Wiseman, Neil B.

Rea, Dean, ed. see Towns, Elmer L.

Rea, Denis & Jacques, Rodney. Beginner's Guide to Car Maintenance, Fault-finding & Repair. 1987. pap. 26.95 (*0-434-90898-3*) Buttrwrth-Heinemann.

Rea, G. & Miller, C., eds. Spinal Trauma - Current Evaluation & Management. (Illus.). 200p. 1993. 90.00 (*1-879284-19-7*) Am Assn Neuro.

***Rea, G. Thomas, ed.** 6th International Symposium on Vulcanospeleology. (Illus.). 286p. 1991. pap. 11.00 (*1-879961-02-4*) Natl Speleological.

Rea, Gavin A., jt. auth. see Jones, Keith E.

Rea, John. Across the Channel. LC 85-62783. (Illus.). 80p. 1986. pap. write for info. (*0-918702-07-0*) Eilean Ban Pub.

— Around Ireland. LC 82-84237. 1982. pap. 7.00 (*0-918702-05-4*) Eilean Ban Pub.

— Around Scotland. LC 78-54125. 1978. pap. 4.00 (*0-918702-03-8*) Eilean Ban Pub.

— Celts, Will Travel. LC 81-71404. (Illus.). 136p. 1981. 11. 00 (*0-918702-04-6*) Eilean Ban Pub.

— Celts, Will Travel, 3 vols., Set. LC 81-71404. (Illus.). 144p. 1986. 13.00 (*0-918702-09-7*) Eilean Ban Pub.

— Celts, Will Travel, Vol. 3. LC 81-71404. (Illus.). 144p. 1986. Vol.3. 13.00 (*0-918702-08-9*) Eilean Ban Pub.

— The Holy Spirit in the Bible. LC 89-80826. 394p. (Orig.). 1989. pap. 19.99 (*0-88419-261-X*, Creation Hse) Strang Comms Co.

— A Look at Scotland & the Macdonalds. LC 75-24937. 1976. 8.95 (*0-918702-01-1*) Eilean Ban Pub.

— Trains & Scotland. LC 77-4806. 1977. pap. 3.00 (*0-918702-02-X*) Eilean Ban Pub.

Rea, John D. Patterns of the Whole, Vol. 1: Healing & Quartz Crystals (A Journey with our Souls) (Illus.). 376p. (Orig.). 1986. pap. 12.95 (*0-938183-01-X*) Two Trees Pub.

Rea, John D. & Rea, Alayna. The Twelve Days of Christmas: The Twelve Stages of a Soul (The Creation of a Universe) 40p. (Orig.). 1987. pap. 4.95 (*0-938183-04-4*) Two Trees Pub.

Rea, Kathryn, jt. auth. see Lientz, Benent P.

Rea, Kenneth J. The Prosperous Years: The Economic History of Ontario 1939-1975. (Ontario Historical Studies). 304p. 1985. pap. 14.95 (*0-8020-6592-9*) U of Toronto Pr.

— The Prosperous Years: The Economic History of Ontario, 1939-1975. LC 86-182022. (Ontario Historical Studies Ser.). 301p. reprint ed. pap. 85.80 (*0-8357-3771-3*, 2036500) Bks Demand.

Rea, Leonard O. The Financial History of Baltimore, 1900-1926. LC 78-64132. (Johns Hopkins University. Studies in the Social Sciences. Thirtieth Ser. 1912: 3). 128p. 1983. reprint ed. 24.50 (*0-404-61245-8*) AMS Pr.

Rea, Louis M. & Parker, Richard A. Designing & Conducting Survey Research: A Comprehensive Guide. LC 91-30033. (Public Administration Ser.). 280p. 1992. 32.95 (*1-55542-404-X*) Jossey-Bass.

Rea, Mark S., ed. Selected Papers on Architectural Lighting. LC 92-19412. (Milestone Ser.: Vol. 58). 1992. write for info. (*0-8194-0991-X*); pap. write for info. (*0-8194-0992-8*) SPIE.

Rea, Michael. American Story: The Rea Award for the Short Story. 1993. 25.00 (*0-88001-341-9*) Ecco Pr.

Rea, Nicky & TSR, Inc. Staff. Age of Heroes Sourcebook. (Illus.). 1994. 18.00 (*1-56076-814-2*) TSR Inc.

***Rea, Peter W. & Irving, David K.** Producing & Directing the Short Film & Video. (Illus.). 352p. 1995. pap. 34.95 (*0-240-80188-1*, Focal) Buttrwrth-Heinemann.

Rea, R. Sam. Attorney's Master Guide to Successful Solo Law Practice. LC 83-18652. 288p. 1983. text ed. 49.50 (*0-87624-024-4*, Inst Busn Plan) P-H.

Rea, Richard C., ed. see American Institute of Certified Public Accountants Staff.

Rea, Richard G. & Gray, John W. Parliamentary Procedure: A Programmed Introduction. 2nd ed. 124p. 1993. per. 13.95 (*0-8403-8882-9*) Kendall-Hunt.

Rea, Rober R., jt. ed. see Coker, William S.

Rea, Robert R. Major Robert Farmar of Mobile. 200p. 1991. 31.95 (*0-8173-0505-X*) U of Ala Pr.

Rea, Robert R., jt. ed. see Newton, Wesley P.

Rea, Robert R., jt. ed. see Servies, James A.

Rea, Robert R., jt. auth. see Ware, John D.

Rea, S. A., jt. auth. see Pesando, James E.

***Rea, Sara W.** The Koreshan Story. Bigelow, Jo, ed. (Illus.). 72p. (Orig.). 1994. pap. 10.00 (*0-9632676-0-4*) Koreshan Unity.

***Rea Staff.** Careers for the Nineties & Beyond. 1994. pap. 17.95 (*0-87891-959-7*) Res & Educ.

Rea, Tom, ed. Caving Basics. LC 82-61922. 128p. 1987. pap. 11.00 (*0-9615093-1-7*) Natl Speleological.

Rea, Val, jt. auth. see Martin, Mike.

Rea, Walter T. The White Lie. LC 81-83353. (Illus.). 409p. (Orig.). 1982. 16.95 (*0-9607424-0-9*); pap. 13.95 (*0-9607424-1-7*) M & R Pubns.

Rea, William J. Chemical Sensitivity, 4 vols., I. 1992. 75.00 (*0-87371-541-1*, RB152) Lewis Pubs.

— Chemical Sensitivity, 4 vols., II. 1992. 75.00 (*0-87371-963-8*) Lewis Pubs.

— Chemical Sensitivity, 4 vols., III. 848p. 1995. 89.95 (*0-87371-964-6*, L964) Lewis Pubs.

— Chemical Sensitivity, 4 vols., IV. 1992. write for info. (*0-87371-965-4*) Lewis Pubs.

Reach & Schwartz. Softball Everyone. 2nd ed. 172p. 1992. pap. text ed. 12.95 (*0-88725-162-5*) Hunter Textbks.

Reach, Russell, ed. Big Road Interstate Exit Guide, 1992: United States Eastern Edition. (Illus.). 300p. (Orig.). 1992. pap. 9.95 (*1-880477-00-9*) Inter Am Pub.

Reachem, Richard G., jt. auth. see Cairncross, Sandy.

Read. The Christmas Mouse. 150p. 1986. reprint ed. lib. bdg. 16.95 (*0-89966-537-3*) Buccaneer Bks.

— Clinical Skills in Medicine. 6th ed. 1989. 24.95 (*0-7236-1163-7*, Pub. by John Wright UK) Buttrwrth-Heinemann.

— Gossip from Thrush Green. large type ed. LC 92-25219. 1992. 18.95 (*0-7927-1376-1*, Eagle Lrg Print) Chivers N Amer.

— Market Square. (Illus.). 224p. 1988. reprint ed. pap. 9.00 (*0-89733-318-7*) Academy Chi Pubs.

— The Multimedia Handbook. 1993. pap. 29.95 (*0-442-01756-1*) Van Nos Reinhold.

— News from Thrush Green. large type ed. LC 92-40907. (General Ser.). 1993. 20.95 (*0-8161-5503-8*, Large Print Bks) Hall.

— News from Thrush Green. 291p. 1983. reprint ed. lib. bdg. 16.95 (*0-89966-465-2*) Buccaneer Bks.

— Preventing Breast Cancer: The Politics of an Epidemic. 1995. pap. 13.00 (*0-04-440909-5*) Harper SF.

— Return to Thrush Green. large type ed. 1992. 18.95 (*0-7927-1267-6*, Eagle Lrg Print) Chivers N Amer.

— Thrush Green. large type ed. 1992. pap. 14.95 (*0-7927-0867-9*, Paragon Lrg Print) Chivers N Amer.

Read, A. E., et al, eds. Modern Medicine. 600p. (C). 1975. pap. text ed. 45.00 (*0-8464-0637-3*) Beekman Pubs.

***Read, Alan.** Theatre & Everyday Life. 304p. 1995. pap. 17. 95 (*0-415-06941-6*, A7978) Routledge.

— Theatre & Everyday Life: A Theoretical Introduction. LC 92-11913. (Illus.). 244p. 1993. 49.95 (*0-415-06940-8*, A7974) Routledge.

Read, Alan E. & Jones, John V., eds. Essential Medicine. LC 93-2560. 544p. 1993. pap. 24.95 (*0-443-04595-X*) Churchill.

Read, Alan E., et al. Basic Gastroenterology. 3rd ed. (Illus.). 558p. (C). 1981. pap. text ed. 44.95 (*0-7236-0551-3*, Pub. by John Wright UK) Buttrwrth-Heinemann.

Read, Alexander. A Treatise of the First Part of Chirurgerie. LC 76-57411. (English Experience Ser.: No. 826). 1977. reprint ed. lib. bdg. 24.00 (*90-221-0826-0*) Walter J Johnson.

Read, Alice. Read: The Reads & Their Relatives, Being an Account of Col. Clemens & Madam Read of Bushy Forest, Lunenburg County, Virginia, Their Eight Children, Their Descendants, & Allied Families. (Illus.). 688p. 1993. reprint ed. lib. bdg. 109.50 (*0-8328-3388-6*); reprint ed. pap. 99.50 (*0-8328-3389-4*) Higginson Bk Co.

Read, Allen W. Classic American Graffiti: Lexical Evidence from Folk Epigraphy in Western North America; a Glossarial Study of the Low Element in the English Vocabulary. LC 76-5697. (Maledicta Press Publications Ser.: Vol. 6). 96p. (C). 1977. reprint ed. pap. 7.50 (*0-916500-06-3*) Maledicta.

Read, Andrew P., jt. auth. see Davies, Kay E.

Read, Ann K., jt. auth. see Garrison, Linda.

Read, Anothy & Fisher, David. Kristallnacht: The Unleashing of the Holocaust. (Illus.). 294p. 1990. pap. 10.95 (*0-87226-237-5*) P Bedrick Bks.

Read, Anthony. Berlin Rising: Biography of a City. 1994. 35. 00 (*0-393-03606-5*) Norton.

— Deadly Embrace. 1989. pap. 12.95 (*0-393-30651-8*) Norton.

Read, Anthony & Fisher, David. The Fall of Berlin. 524p. 1993. 29.95 (*0-393-03472-0*) Da Capo.

— The Fall of Berlin. (Illus.). 535p. 1995. reprint ed. pap. 16.95 (*0-306-80619-3*) Da Capo.

Read, Anthony, jt. auth. see Fisher, David.

Read, Bendict, ed. Pre-Raphaelite Sculpture: Nature & Imagination in British Sculpture 1848-1914. (British Sculptors & Sculpture Ser.). (Illus.). 176p. (C). 1991. 70. 00 (*0-85331-609-0*, Pub. by Lund Humphries UK) Antique Collect.

Read, Benedict. Victorian Sculpture. LC 83-70483. (Paul Mellon Centre for Studies in British Art). (Illus.). 416p. 1984. reprint ed. pap. 32.00 (*0-300-03177-7*) Yale U Pr.

Read, Benedict, ed. Herbert Read: A British Vision of World Art. (Illus.). 160p. (C). 1993. pap. 39.95 (*0-85331-643-0*, Pub. by Lund Humphries UK) Antique Collect.

Read, Benjamin. History of Swanzey, New Hampshire, from 1734 to 1890. (Illus.). 585p. 1988. reprint ed. lib. bdg. 59.50 (*0-8328-0057-0*, NH0025) Higginson Bk Co.

— Pressures on the Edges: Jackson Hole & Planning in the 1990s. LC 95-2891. (Center Bks.: Vol. 2). 1995. write for info. (*1-886402-01-9*) Jackson Hole Mus.

Read, Benjamin M. Illustrated History of New Mexico. Cortes, Carlos E., ed. LC 76-1562. (Chicano Heritage Ser.). (Illus.). 1977. reprint ed. 58.95 (*0-405-09521-X*) Ayer.

Read, Bernard E. Chinese Materia Medica: Animal Drugs. 1982. reprint ed. 25.00 (*0-89986-308-6*) Oriental Bk Store.

— Chinese Materia Medica: Dragon & Snake Drugs. 1979. lib. bdg. 300.00 (*0-8490-3063-3*) Krishna Pr.

— Chinese Materia Medica: Insect Drugs, Dragons & Snake Drugs, Fish Drugs. (Chinese Material Medica Ser.: No. 2). 1982. reprint ed. 30.00 (*0-89986-321-3*) Oriental Bk Store.

— Chinese Materia Medica: Turtle & Shellfish Drugs, Avian Drugs, a Compendium of Minerals & Stones. (Chinese Material Medica Ser.: No. 3). 1982. reprint ed. 30.00 (*0-89986-330-2*) Oriental Bk Store.

— Chinese Medicinal Plants from the Pen T'sao Kang Mu. 1977. 30.00 (*0-89986-317-5*) Oriental Bk Store.

— Famine Foods List in the Chiu Huang Pen Ts'ao. 1977. 25.00 (*0-89986-318-3*) Oriental Bk Store.

***Read, Bobbie.** How to Enjoy a Healthy Family: Even in Stressful Times. LC 94-39362. (How To Family Ser.). 1995. pap. 7.99 (*0-570-04691-2*) Concordia.

— Single Adult Journey. 1992. pap. 15.95 (*0-87162-616-0*, D7001) Warner Pr.

— Single Parent Journey. 1992. pap. 15.95 (*0-87162-614-4*, D7000) Warner Pr.

Read, Bryan E. & Dean, G. D. The Determination of Dynamic Properties of Polymers & Composites. LC 79-302865. 217p. reprint ed. pap. 61.90 (*0-317-10725-9*, 2022564) Bks Demand.

Read, Campbell, jt. auth. see Patel, Jagdish K.

Read, Charles. Children's Creative Spelling. (International Library of Psychology). (Illus.). 192p. (C). 1986. 39.95 (*0-7100-9802-2*, 98022, RKP) Routledge.

R

Read, Charles, jt. auth. see Kent, Ray D.

Read, Charles H. & Dalton, Ormonde M. Antiquities from the City of Benin & from Other Parts of West Africa in the British Museum. LC 71-143360. (Illus.). 1973. reprint ed. 90.00 (0-87817-079-0) Hacker.

Read, Christopher. Culture & Power in Revolutionary Russia. 264p. 1990. text ed. 59.95 (0-312-03681-7) St Martin.

Read, Clark P. Parasitism & Symbiology: An Introductory Text. LC 75-110390. 326p. reprint ed. 93.00 (0-8357-9947-6, 2055139) Bks Demand.

Read, Colin. The Rising in Western Upper Canada, 1837-8: The Duncombe Revolt & After. LC 82-168779. 339p. reprint ed. pap. 96.70 (0-8357-6366-8, 2035720) Bks Demand.

Read, Conyers. The Government of England under Elizabeth. LC 79-65980. (Folger Guides to the Age of Shakespeare Ser.). 1979. pap. 4.95 (0-918016-07-X) Folger Bks.

— Mr. Secretary Walsingham & the Policy of Queen Elizabeth, 3 vols., Set. LC 75-41223. reprint ed. 145.00 (0-404-13490-4) AMS Pr.

— Tudors: Personalities & Practical Politics in Sixteenth Century England. LC 68-24854. (Essay Index Reprint Ser.). 1977. 20.95 (0-8369-0812-0) Ayer.

Read, Conyers, ed. see Lambarde, William.

Read, D., ed. Chemval Project Report on Stages Three & Four Testing of Coupled Chemical Transport, No. EUR 13675. 234p. 1991. pap. 25.00 (92-826-2889-2, CD-NA-13675-EN-C) UNIPUB.

Read, D. J., et al. Mycorrhizas in Ecosystems. 419p. 1992. 104.50 (0-85198-786-9) CAB Intl.

Read, D. T. & Reed, R. P., eds. Fracture Mechanics: Eighteenth Symposium. LC 87-30666. (Special Technical Publication Ser.: No. 945). (Illus.). 1135p. 1988. 120.00 (0-8031-0949-0, 04-945000-30) ASTM.

***Read, David B.** The Lives of the Judges of Upper Canada & Ontario: From 1971 to the Present Time, Vol. 1. 486p. 1995. 98.00 (1-56169-110-0) W W Gaunt.

Read, David H. The Christian Faith. large type ed. 1985. pap. 9.95 (0-8027-2515-5) Walker & Co.

Read, Donal R. Harvard Graphics Made Easy. (Illus.). 256p. 1989. pap. 17.95 (0-8306-3401-0, Windcrest) TAB Bks.

Read, Donald. The Age of Urban Democracy: England 1868-1914. 2nd rev. ed. LC 93-20486. (History of England Ser.). 536p. (C). 1994. pap. text ed. 27.50 (0-582-08921-2, 76256) Longman.

— The Power of News: The History of Reuters, 1849-1989. (Illus.). 480p. 1992. 30.00 (0-19-821776-5) OUP.

— Press & People, 1790-1850: Opinion in Three English Cities. (Modern Revivals in Economic & Social History Ser.). 225p. (C). 1993. text ed. 54.95 (0-7512-0245-2, Pub. by Gregg Revivals UK) Ashgate Pub Co.

Read, Donald A. The Concept of Health. 3rd ed. (C). 1978. write for info. (0-318-57216-8, H56872) Allyn.

Read, Donald A. & Greene, Walter H. Creative Teaching in Health. 3rd ed. (Illus.). 436p. (C). 1989. reprint ed. pap. text ed. 23.95x (0-88133-394-8) Waveland Pr.

Read, Donald R. Mastering Harvard Graphics for Windows. 1993. pap. 22.95 (0-07-051288-4) McGraw.

— Mastering Harvard Graphics for Windows. (Illus.). 352p. 1993. pap. 22.95 (0-8306-4049-5, 4186, Windcrest) TAB Bks.

— Mastering Harvard Graphics 3.0. (Illus.). 376p. 1992. pap. 18.95 (0-8306-3602-1, 3602, Windcrest) TAB Bks.

— ObjectVision Programming for Windows. 1993. 34.95 (0-07-051292-2); pap. text ed. 24.95 (0-07-051293-0) McGraw.

— ObjectVision Programming for Windows. (Illus.). 352p. 1993. text ed. 34.95 (0-8306-4194-7, 4258, Windcrest); pap. 24.95 (0-8306-4193-9, 4258, Windcrest) TAB Bks.

Read, Edward M. & Daley, Dennis C. Getting High & Doing Time: What's the Connection? A Recovery Guide for Alcoholics & Drug Addicts in Trouble with the Law. (Illus.). 80p. (Orig.). 1990. pap. 10.00 (0-929310-31-4, 416) Am Correctional.

Read, Edward M., jt. auth. see Daley, Dennis C.

Read, Elfreida. Plays for Special Days: Ten One-Act Christmas & Easter Plays for Young People. 72p. 1993. 20.00 (1-55896-312-X) Unitarian Univ.

Read, Elizabeth. Let's Cook It Metric. LC 75-5395. (Illus.). 1975. pap. 5.00 (0-9600996-1-1) E Read.

— Twenty-First Century Guide to Building Your Vocabulary. 1995. pap. 5.99 (0-440-21721-0) Dell.

***Read, F. W.** Egyptian Religion & Ethics. (African Heritage Classical Research Studies Ser.). Date not set. 25.00 (0-938818-34-1) ECA Assoc.

Read, Forrest. Seventy Six: One World & the Cantos of Ezra Pound. LC 80-15892. 488p. reprint ed. pap. 139.10 (0-8357-4406-X, 2037226) Bks Demand.

Read, Francoise, tr. see Kende, Pierre & Strmiska, Zdenek, eds.

Read, Frank H. Electromagnetic Radiation. LC 79-41484. (Manchester Physics Ser.). (Illus.). 315p. reprint ed. pap. 89.80 (0-7837-6392-1, 2046105) Bks Demand.

Read, G. Westhill Project - Christianity: Teacher's Manual. (C). 1986. text ed. 95.00 (0-86158-895-9, Pub. by S Thornes Pubs UK) St Mut.

— Westhill Project - Christians: Pupils Book 2. (C). 1987. text ed. 40.00 (1-871402-34-4, Pub. by S Thornes Pubs UK) St Mut.

— Westhill Project - Christians: Pupils Book 3. (C). 1987. text ed. 35.00 (0-86158-696-4, Pub. by S Thornes Pubs UK) St Mut.

— Westhill Project - Christians: Pupils Book 4. (C). 1987. text ed. 50.00 (0-86158-697-2, Pub. by S Thornes Pubs UK) St Mut.

— Westhill Project - How Do I Teach R. E? (C). 1986. text ed. 70.00 (0-86158-894-0, Pub. by S Thornes Pubs UK) St Mut.

— Westhill Project - Islam: Photopack. (C). 1988. text ed. 190.00 (1-85234-072-X, Pub. by S Thornes Pubs UK) St Mut.

— Westhill Project - Islam: Teacher's Manual. (C). 1988. text ed. 95.00 (1-85234-071-1, Pub. by S Thornes Pubs UK) St Mut.

— Westhill Project - Jews: Pupils Book 3. (C). 1990. text ed. 35.00 (1-871402-20-4, Pub. by S Thornes Pubs UK) St Mut.

— Westhill Project - Jews: Pupils Book 4. (C). 1990. text ed. 50.00 (1-871402-21-2, Pub. by S Thornes Pubs UK) St Mut.

— Westhill Project - Judaism: Photopack. (C). 1990. text ed. 190.00 (1-871402-22-0, Pub. by S Thornes Pubs UK) St Mut.

— Westhill Project - Life Themes in the Early Years - Pack 1. (C). 1990. text ed. 350.00 (1-871402-24-7, Pub. by S Thornes Pubs UK) St Mut.

— Westhill Project - Life Themes in the Early Years - Pack 2. (C). 1990. text ed. 350.00 (1-871402-25-5, Pub. by S Thornes Pubs UK) St Mut.

— Westhill Project - Life Themes in the Early Years - Pack 3. (C). 1990. text ed. 350.00 (1-871402-26-3, Pub. by S Thornes Pubs UK) St Mut.

— Westhill Project - Muslims: Pupils Book 1. (C). 1988. text ed. 42.00 (1-85234-073-8, Pub. by S Thornes Pubs UK) St Mut.

— Westhill Project - Muslims: Pupils Book 2. (C). 1988. text ed. 42.00 (1-85234-074-6, Pub. by S Thornes Pubs UK) St Mut.

— Westhill Project - Muslims: Pupils Book 3. (C). 1988. text ed. 42.00 (1-85234-075-4, Pub. by S Thornes Pubs UK) St Mut.

— Westhill Project Judaism: Teacher's Manual. (C). 1990. text ed. 95.00 (1-871402-23-9, Pub. by S Thornes Pubs UK) St Mut.

Read, Gardner. Compendium of Modern Instrumental Techniques. LC 92-17854. 280p. 1993. text ed. 59.95 (0-313-28512-8, RCZ, Greenwood Pr) Greenwood.

— Modern Rhythmic Notation. LC 77-9860. 211p. reprint ed. pap. 60.20 (0-7837-1506-4, 2057296) Bks Demand.

— Music Notation. LC 68-54213. (Illus.). (C). 1979. reprint ed. pap. 19.95 (0-8008-5453-5, Crescendo) Taplinger.

— Source Book of Proposed Music Notation Reforms. LC 86-14315. (Music Reference Collection Ser.: No. 11). 489p. 1987. text ed. 69.50 (0-313-25446-X, RHN/, Greenwood Pr) Greenwood.

— Style & Orchestration. LC 77-15884. (Illus.). reprint ed. pap. 91.20 (0-7837-9011-2, AU00463) Bks Demand.

— Thesaurus of Orchestral Devices. LC 69-14045. 631p. 1969. reprint ed. text ed. 45.00 (0-8371-1884-0, REOD, Greenwood Pr) Greenwood.

— Twentieth-Century Microtonal Notation. LC 90-2782. (Contributions to the Study of Music & Dance Ser.: No. 18). 216p. 1990. text ed. 49.95 (0-313-27398-7, RCD/, Greenwood Pr) Greenwood.

***Read, Garth, et al.** How Do I Teach Religious Education? 2nd ed. 80p. (C). 1992. pap. 39.00x (0-7478-1470-8, Pub. by S Thornes Pubs UK) St Mut.

Read, Grace. Doctor's Diagnosis. large type ed. 1990. 17.95 (0-7451-9915-1, C0631, Atlantic Lrg Print); pap. 15.95 (0-7927-0363-4, C0825, Atlantic Lrg Print) Chivers N Amer.

— The Market Square. large type ed. 1991. 17.95 (0-7927-0559-9, E0002, Eagle Lrg Print) Chivers N Amer.

Read, H. H. & Gribble, Colin D. Rutley's Elements of Minerology. rev. ed. 512p. 1988. pap. text ed. 27.95 (0-04-549011-2) Routledge Chapman & Hall.

— Rutley's Elements of Minerology. 27th rev. ed. 512p. 1988. text ed. 75.00 (0-04-549010-4) Routledge Chapman & Hall.

Read, H. H. & Watson, Janet. Introduction & Geology, 2 vols. Incl. Vol. 2. , 2 pts. 1975. (0-318-52891-6); Pt. 1. Early Stages of Earth History. 221p. 24.95 (0-470-71165-5); Pt. 2. Later Stages of Earth History. 371p. 34.95 (0-470-71166-3); write for info. (0-318-52890-8) Halsted Pr.

Read, Hadley & Andersen, Mary K. Just Be My Friend. (Illus.). 90p. 1989. pap. 6.50 (0-9617924-0-X) M K Andersen.

Read, Harriet. From My Pen. (Illus.). xii, 98p. 1986. write for info. (0-913529-01-X) Homestead MI.

— Just Rememberin' LC 83-10672. (Illus.). xiv, 106p. 1983. 10.95 (0-913529-00-1) Homestead MI.

Read, Helen J., jt. auth. see Hopkin, Stephen P.

Read, Herbert. Coleridge As Critic. LC 65-15891. 40p. (C). 1964. text ed. 75.00 (0-8383-0613-6) M S G Haskell Hse.

Read, Herbert & Stangos, Nikos. The Thames & Hudson Dictionary of Art & Artists. rev. ed. LC 93-61272. (World of Art Ser.). (Illus.). 352p. 1994. pap. 14.95 (0-500-20274-5) Thames Hudson.

Read, Herbert, jt. auth. see Rackham, Bernard.

Read, Herbert E. Ambush. LC 74-7020. (English Literature Ser.: No. 33). 1974. lib. bdg. 75.00 (0-8383-1996-3) M S G Haskell Hse.

— Annals of Innocence & Experience. LC 74-7019. (English Literature Ser.: No. 33). 1974. lib. bdg. 75.00 (0-8383-1993-9) M S G Haskell Hse.

— Aristotle's Mother. (Dramascripts Ser.: Vol. 1). 1961. pap. 4.95 (0-900891-03-3) Oleander Pr.

— Collected Essays in Literary Criticism. LC 78-14137. 1985. reprint ed. 32.00 (0-88355-811-4) Hyperion Conn.

— Concise History of Modern Painting. LC 84-51313. (World of Art Ser.). (Illus.). 396p. 1985. pap. 14.95 (0-500-20141-2) Thames Hudson.

— Green Child. LC 48-9595. 1966. 12.95 (0-8112-0365-4); pap. 8.95 (0-8112-0172-4, NDP208) New Directions.

— In Defence of Shelley & Other Essays. LC 68-26470. (Essay Index Reprint Ser.). 1977. reprint ed. 18.95 (0-8369-0813-9) Ayer.

— An Introduction to Herbert Read's Work by Several Hands. 1972. 59.95 (0-8490-0417-9) Gordon Pr.

— The Limits of Permissiveness in Art. 50p. 1968. pap. 1.00 (0-8477-2105-1) U of PR Pr.

— Lord Byron at the Opera. (Dramascripts Ser.: Vol. 3). 1963. 4.95 (0-900891-02-5) Oleander Pr.

— The Meaning of Art. 2nd ed. (Illus.). 280p. 1984. pap. 11. 95 (0-571-09658-1) Faber & Faber.

— Meet Kropotkin, the Master. 1973. 59.95 (0-8490-0602-3) Gordon Pr.

— Modern Sculpture. (World of Art Ser.). (Illus.). 310p. 1985. pap. 14.95 (0-500-20014-9) Thames Hudson.

— Nature of Literature. LC 74-105034. (Essay Index Reprint Ser.). 1977. 26.95 (0-8369-1478-3) Ayer.

— Philosophy of Modern Art. LC 70-128294. (Essay Index Reprint Ser.). 1977. 24.95 (0-8369-2023-6) Ayer.

— The Philosophy of Modern Art. 278p. 1964. pap. 9.95 (0-571-06506-6) Faber & Faber.

— Poems: Nineteen Eleven to Nineteen Thirty-One. LC 78-64052. (Des Imagistes: Literature of the Imagist Movement Ser.). reprint ed. 18.00 (0-404-17092-7) AMS Pr.

— Poetry & Anarchism. 1972. 59.95 (0-8490-0857-3) Gordon Pr.

— Poetry & Anarchism. LC 72-290. (Essay Index Reprint Ser.). 1977. reprint ed. 13.95 (0-8369-2819-9) Ayer.

— Reason & Romanticism. LC 72-6856. (English Literature Ser.: No. 33). 1974. lib. bdg. 75.00 (0-8383-1640-9) M S G Haskell Hse.

— Sense of Glory: Essays in Criticism. LC 67-26773. (Essay Index Reprint Ser.). 1977. 19.95 (0-8369-0814-7) Ayer.

— Tenth Muse. LC 73-99646. (Essay Index Reprint Ser.). 1977. 29.95 (0-8369-1427-9) Ayer.

— To Hell with Culture: And Other Essays on Art & Society. LC 72-3370. (Essay Index Reprint Ser.). 1977. reprint ed. 18.95 (0-8369-2918-7) Ayer.

— The True Voice of Feeling: Studies in English Romantic Poetry. LC 75-30010. reprint ed. 29.50 (0-404-14016-5) AMS Pr.

— Wordsworth. LC 83-1723. 194p. (C). 1983. reprint ed. text ed. 49.75 (0-313-23321-7, REWO, Greenwood Pr) Greenwood.

Read, Herbert E. & Stangos, Nikos, eds. The Thames & Hudson Dictionary of Art & Artists. rev. ed. LC 87-50342. (World of Art Ser.). (Illus.). 1988. 19.95 (0-500-52340-1) Thames Hudson.

Read, Herbert E., ed. see Orage, Alfred R.

Read, Herbert E., et al. Five European Sculptors. LC 75-86444. (Museum of Modern Art Publications in Reprint). 1969. reprint ed. 26.95 (0-405-01541-0) Ayer.

Read, Hollis. Negro Problem Solved: Or, Africa As She Was, As She Is, & As She Shall Be, Her Curse & Her Cure. LC 77-83874. (Black Heritage Library Collection). 1977. 20.95 (0-8369-8645-8) Ayer.

Read, Horace E. Recognition & Enforcement of Foreign Judgments in the Common Law Units of the British Commonwealth. LC 38-18887. (Harvard Studies in the Conflict of Laws: Vol. 2). xiv, 371p. 1978. reprint ed. lib. bdg. 47.50 (0-89941-127-4, 302790) W S Hein.

Read, Horace E., et al. Materials on Legislation. 4th ed. LC 81-17479. (University Casebook Ser.). 953p. (C). 1981. text ed. 35.00 (0-88277-045-4) Foundation Pr.

***Read, Ian G.** The Bush: A Guide to the Vegetated Landscapes of Australia. (Illus.). 1995. pap. 22.95 (0-86840-254-0, Pub. by New South Wales Univ Pr AT) Intl Spec Bk.

Read, J. Gate Arrays: Design Techniques & Applications. 368p. 1985. text ed. 48.00 (0-07-051286-8) McGraw.

Read, J. W. In Clear English: An Intermediate Course in Comprehension & Composition. 344p. 1982. 29.00 (0-7223-1061-7, Pub. by A H S Ltd UK) St Mut.

Read, James, jt. auth. see Bullock, Nicholas.

Read, James M. Atrocity Propaganda, 1914-1919. LC 72-4676. (International Propaganda & Communications Ser.). 333p. 1977. reprint ed. 20.95 (0-405-04760-6) Ayer.

Read, Jan. Chilean Wine. LC 87-60746. (Illus.). 176p. 1988. 39.95 (0-85667-343-9, Pub. by P Wilson Pubs) Sothebys Pubns.

— Sherry & the Sherry Bodegas. LC 88-60434. (Illus.). 208p. 1988. 45.00 (0-85667-349-8, Pub. by P Wilson Pubs) Sothebys Pubns.

— The Simon & Schuster Pocket Guide to the Wines of Spain. LC 92-19089. 1993. pap. 13.00 (0-671-79708-5, Fireside) S&S Trade.

— Wines of Portugal. 2nd ed. (Books on Wine Ser.). (Illus.). 220p. (Orig.). 1988. pap. 11.95 (0-571-15003-9) Faber & Faber.

— Wines of Spain. 2nd ed. (Books on Wine Ser.). 272p. (Orig.). 1986. pap. 13.95 (0-571-14621-X) Faber & Faber.

— Wines of the Rioja. LC 84-50546. (Illus.). 184p. 1984. 29. 95 (0-85667-186-X, Pub. by P Wilson Pubs) Sothebys Pubns.

***Read, Jan & Manjon, Maite.** Catalonia, Traditions, Places, Wind & Food. (Illus.). 324p. 1992. pap. 19.95 (1-871569-42-7, Herbert Pr UK) New Amsterdam Bks.

***Read, Jane.** Counselling for Fertility Problems. (Counselling in Practice Ser.). 240p. 1995. text ed. 44.00 (0-8039-8949-0); pap. text ed. 19.95 (0-8039-8950-4) Sage.

Read, Jenny. Jenny Read: In Pursuit of Art & Life. Johnson, Dallas & Doyle, Kathleen, eds. LC 82-73449. (Illus.). 176p. (Orig.). 1982. 18.95 (0-914064-17-7); pap. 13.95 (0-914064-18-5) Celo Pr.

Read, Jesse, jt. auth. see Burkitt, Lemuel.

Read, Joan R. The Norfolk Terrier. (Illus.). 344p. 1989. 29. 95 (0-9623261-0-0) J R Read.

— The Norfolk Terrier. 2nd rev. ed. LaMar, Nat R., ed. 1994. write for info. (0-9623261-1-9) J R Read.

Read, John. The Alchemist in Life, Literature, & Art. (Illus.). 120p. 1992. pap. text ed. 17.95 (1-56459-210-3) Kessinger Pub.

— The Alchemist in Life, Literature & Art. LC 79-8620. reprint ed. 29.50 (0-404-18486-3) AMS Pr.

— From Alchemy to Chemistry. LC 95-6387. 1995. pap. write for info. (0-486-28690-8) Dover.

— Humour & Humanism in Chemistry. LC 79-8621. reprint ed. 42.50 (0-404-18487-1) AMS Pr.

— Prelude to Chemistry: An Outline of Alchemy, Its Literature & Relationships. LC 79-8622. (Illus.). reprint ed. 48.00 (0-404-18488-X) AMS Pr.

— Prelude to Chemistry: An Outline of Alchemy, its Literature & Relationships. 328p. 1992. reprint ed. pap. 24.95 (1-56459-015-1) Kessinger Pub.

— Through Alchemy to Chemistry. 206p. 1992. reprint ed. pap. 19.95 (1-56459-013-5) Kessinger Pub.

— Through Alchemy to Chemistry: A Procession of Ideas & Personalities. LC 79-8623. (Illus.). reprint ed. 29.00 (0-404-18489-8) AMS Pr.

Read, Karen, jt. auth. see Marrs, Texe.

Read, Katherine, et al. Early Childhood Programs: Human Relationships & Learning. 8th ed. 432p. (C). 1987. text ed. 38.75 (0-03-007172-0) HB Coll Pubs.

— Early Childhood Programs: Human Relationships & Learning. 9th ed. 448p. (C). 1993. write for info. (0-03-074166-1) HB Coll Pubs.

Read, Ken, ed. Improving Secondary School Management in an Era of Change Special Issue of School Organization, 6.1. 120p. 1986. 14.00 (0-8002-4177-0) Taylor & Francis.

Read, Kenneth E. The High Valley. 265p. 1980. reprint ed. pap. text ed. 17.00 (0-231-05035-6) Col U Pr.

— Return to the High Valley: Coming Full Circle. LC 85-16385. (Studies in Melanesian Anthropology: No. 4). (Illus.). 225p. 1986. 32.00 (0-520-05664-7); pap. 13.00 (0-520-06468-2) U CA Pr.

Read, Lenet H. How We Got the Bible. LC 85-72842. 132p. 1985. 8.95 (0-87747-799-X) Deseret Bk.

Read, Leonard E. Castles in the Air. 191p. 1975. 12.95 (0-910614-52-0) Foun Econ Ed.

— Deeper Than You Think. 208p. 1967. 12.95 (0-910614-38-5) Foun Econ Ed.

— Freedom Freeway. 128p. 1979. pap. 8.95 (0-910614-62-8) Foun Econ Ed.

— How Do We Know? 128p. 1981. 12.95 (0-910614-68-7) Foun Econ Ed.

— Let Freedom Reign. 167p. 1969. 12.95 (0-910614-40-7) Foun Econ Ed.

— Then Truth Will Out. 177p. 1971. 8.95 (0-910614-27-X) Foun Econ Ed.

— To Free or Freeze. 224p. 1972. pap. 12.95 (0-910614-44-X) Foun Econ Ed.

— Vision. 160p. 1978. 12.95 (0-910614-59-8) Foun Econ Ed.

— Who's Listening? 208p. 1973. 12.95 (0-910614-48-2) Foun Econ Ed.

***Read, M. & Jones, R.** Teacher, This Book's for You. 150p. (Orig.). 1995. pap. 7.95 (1-56626-147-3) Country Rds.

Read, M. D. & Wellby, Diana. A Practical Guide for the Obstetric Team. LC 84-15257. 197p. reprint ed. pap. 56. 20 (0-7837-1879-9, 2042080) Bks Demand.

Read, M. M., tr. see De Tourtoulon, Pierre.

***Read Magazine Staff, comp.** Dear Author: Students Write about the Books That Changed Their Lives. 150p. (Orig.). (YA). (gr. 6-12). 1995. pap. 9.95 (1-57324-003-6) Conari Press.

Read, Malcolm K. Language, Text, Subject: A Critique of Hispanism. LC 92-15636. 216p. 1992. 29.00 (1-55753-027-0) Purdue U Pr.

Read, Malcom K. Jorge Luis Borges & His Predecessors: Notes Towards a Materialist Historiography of Linguistic Idealism. LC 92-80589. (Studies in the Romance Languages & Literatures: No. 242). 210p. (C). 1992. pap. 25.00 (0-8078-9246-7) U of NC Pr.

— Visions in Exile: The Body in Spanish Literature & Linguistics. LC 89-17736. xii, 211p. 1990. 65.00x (1-55619-071-9); pap. 27.95 (1-55619-072-7) Benjamins North Am.

Read, Margaret. Children of Their Fathers: Growing up Among the Ngoni of Malawi. Spindler, George & Spindler, Louise, eds. 112p. 1982. reprint ed. pap. text ed. 6.95 (0-8290-0320-7) Irvington.

— Children of Their Fathers: Growing up among the Ngoni of Malawi. (Illus.). 97p. (C). 1987. reprint ed. pap. text ed. 7.95 (0-88133-288-7) Waveland Pr.

— The Ngoni of Nyasaland. LC 57-994. 218p. reprint ed. pap. 62.20 (0-8357-3223-1, 2057117) Bks Demand.

Read, Margery. Steel, Smoke & Steam: A Guide to America's Most Scenic Railroads. LC 91-77860. (Illus.). 120p. (Orig.). 1992. pap. 12.95 (0-9630646-3-0) Country Rds.

Read, Margery, jt. auth. see Will, Richard.

Read, Maureen H. Earthen Vessel: James Hay, Ordinary Man. 188p. 1993. pap. 7.95 (1-883294-01-0) Olde Sprgfld.

— The Least One. (Illus.). 192p. (Orig.). 1989. pap. 7.95 (0-8361-3491-5) Herald Pr.

Read, Melvyn, jt. auth. see Marsh, David C.

Read, Michael, ed. Ancestral Dialogues: The Photographs of Albert Chong. (Untitled Ser.: No. 57). (Illus.). 64p. 1994. pap. 18.95 (0-933286-63-5) Frnds Photography.

***Read, Michael & Jenkins, Steven, eds.** Points of Entry: Tracing Cultures. (Illus.). 94p. 1995. 18.95 (0-933286-69-4) Frnds Photography.

Read, Michael, ed. see Willis, Deborah.

Read, Michael D. & Mellor, Stuart. Obstetrics in Outline. LC 85-9367. (Illus.). 264p. reprint ed. pap. 75.30 (0-8357-3828-0, 2036552) Bks Demand.

R

An Asterisk (*) at the beginning of an entry indicates that the title is appearing in BIP for the first time.

***Read, Mike & Allsop, Jake.** The Barn Owl. (Illus.). 128p. 1995. 24.95 (*0-7137-2349-1*, Pub. by Blandford Pr UK) Sterling.

Read-Miller, Cynthia. Main Street U. S. A., in Early Photographs: 113 Detroit Publishing Co. Views. 128p. 1988. pap. 10.95 (*0-486-25841-6*) Dover.

Read, Miss. Celebrations at Thrush Green. LC 93-38894. 1994. 18.95 (*0-7927-1921-2*, Eagle Lrg Print); pap. write for info. (*0-7927-1920-4*, Eagle Lrg Print) Chivers N Amer.

— Changes at Fairacre. large type ed. 1994. pap. 18.95 (*0-7927-1592-6*, Paragon Lrg Print) Chivers N Amer.

— Christmas Mouse. (J). 15.95 (*0-8488-1452-5*) Amereon Ltd.

— Farewell to Fairacre. large type ed. (Illus.). 1994. 20.95 (*0-7862-0332-3*) Thorndike Pr.

— Fresh from the Country. (J). 16.95 (*0-8488-1453-3*) Amereon Ltd.

— Howards of Caxley. (J). 15.95 (*0-8488-1454-1*) Amereon Ltd.

— News from Thrush Green. (J). 15.95 (*0-8488-1455-X*) Amereon Ltd.

— Winter in Thrush Green. (J). 18.95 (*0-8488-1456-8*) Amereon Ltd.

Read, N. W. Irritable Bowel Syndrome: New Ideas & Insights into Pathophysiology. (Illus.). 256p. 1991. 90.00 (*0-632-02555-7*) Blackwell Sci.

Read, Nicholas W., ed. Irritable Bowel Syndrome. 288p. 1985. text ed. 67.50 (*0-8089-1669-6*, 793529, Grune) Saunders.

Read, Opie. Confessions of a Negro Preacher. LC 73-18597. reprint ed. 21.50 (*0-404-11408-3*) AMS Pr.

— My Young Master. Novel. LC 86-27443. (Library of Southern Civilization). 352p. 1987. text ed. 30.00 (*0-8071-1380-8*); pap. text ed. 11.95 (*0-8071-1395-6*) La State U Pr.

Read, Opie & Pixley, Frank. The Carpetbagger: A Novel. LC 72-2070. (Black Heritage Library Collection). 1977. reprint ed. 27.95 (*0-8369-9056-0*) Ayer.

Read, P. A. Commercial Law. 276p. (C). 1990. pap. 40.00 (*1-85352-782-3*, Pub. by HLT Pubns UK) St Mut.

Read, P. A., ed. Commercial Law, Vol. 1: Sale of Goods, Consumer Credit & Agency. 390p. (C). 1991. 76.00 (*1-85352-382-8*, Pub. by HLT Pubns UK) St Mut.

— Contract Law. 222p. (C). 1990. pap. text ed. 60.00 (*1-85352-755-6*, Pub. by HLT Pubns UK) St Mut.

— General Principles of English Law. 400p. (C). 1991. pap. 400.00 (*1-85352-928-1*, Pub. by HLT Pubns UK) St Mut.

— Sale of Goods & Credit. 365p. (C). 1991. 110.00 (*1-85352-907-9*, Pub. by HLT Pubns UK) St Mut.

Read, P. A., jt. ed. see Lichtenstein, E. A.

Read, Patricia & Kincaid, Lucy. Milanese Lace: An Introduction. (Illus.). 144p. 1989. 39.95 (*0-7134-5707-4*, Pub. by Batsford UK) Trafalgar.

— Milanese Lace: New Designs & Braids. (Illus.). 168p. 1994. 39.95 (*0-7134-7192-1*, Pub. by Batsford UK) Trafalgar.

Read, Paul, jt. auth. see Preece, John E.

Read, Peter. Responding to Global Warming: The Technology, Economics & Politics of Sustainable Energy. LC 93-18986. 256p. (C). 1994. text ed. 59.95 (*1-85649-161-7*, Pub. by Zed Books UK); pap. 25.00 (*1-85649-162-5*, Pub. by Zed Books UK) Humanities.

Read, Peter, ed. Down There with Me on the Cowra: An Oral History of Erambie Aboriginal Reserve Cowra, New South Wales. (Illus.). 144p. 1985. text ed. 22.00 (*0-08-029856-7*, Pergamon Pr) Elsevier.

Read, Peter B., jt. ed. see Izard, Carroll E.

Read, Peter G. Dictionary of Gemmology. 2nd ed. (Illus.). 256p. 1988. text ed. 59.95 (*0-408-02925-0*) Buttrwrth-Heinemann.

— Dictionary of Gemmology. 2nd ed. (Illus.). 272p. 1994. pap. 29.95 (*0-7506-1675-X*) Buttrwrth-Heinemann.

— Gemmology. (Illus.). 392p. 1991. text ed. 67.95 (*0-7506-1066-2*) Buttrwrth-Heinemann.

— Gemmology. (Illus.). 372p. 1995. pap. 32.95 (*0-7506-2290-3*, Focal) Buttrwrth-Heinemann.

Read, Peter G., jt. auth. see Sinkankas, John.

Read, Phyllis J. & Witlieb, Bernard. The Book of Women's Firsts: Break-Through Achievements of Over 1000 American Women. LC 92-16872. 1992. 24.00 (*0-679-40975-0*, Random Ref); pap. 16.00 (*0-679-74280-8*, Random Ref) Random.

Read, Phyllis J., et al. Strategies for Learning. 2nd ed. 144p. 1991. spiral bd. 16.95 (*0-8403-6528-4*) Kendall-Hunt.

Read, Piers P. Ablaze: The Story of Chernobyl. LC 92-56840. 416p. 1993. 25.00 (*0-679-40819-3*) Random.

— Alive: The Story of the Andes Survivors. 1979. mass mkt. 5.99 (*0-380-00321-X*) Avon.

— On the Third Day. 1991. 19.50 (*0-679-40089-3*) Random.

— The Patriot. LC 95-11598. 1996. 24.00 (*0-679-44544-7*) Random.

— A Season in the West. large type ed. (General Fiction Ser.). 496p. 1992. 21.95 (*0-7089-2632-0*) Ulverscroft.

Read, R. Secrets of Art & Nature. 350p. 1992. reprint ed. pap. 27.50 (*1-56459-004-6*) Kessinger Pub.

Read, Ralph H., ed. Younger Churchmen Look at the Church. LC 74-156708. (Essay Index Reprint Ser.). 1977. reprint ed. 23.95 (*0-8369-2330-8*) Ayer.

Read, Ralph R., tr. see Bienek, Horst.

Read, Randy, jt. auth. see Rusk, Tom.

Read, Richard, jt. auth. see Morse-Cluley, Elizabeth.

Read, Roger E., jt. auth. see Graham, Ron.

Read, Roland H., jt. auth. see Waesche, James F.

Read, Ronald C. Tangrams: Three Hundred & Thirty Puzzles. 1978. pap. 3.95 (*0-486-21483-4*) Dover.

Read, Samuel. Political Economy: An Inquiry into the Natural Grounds of Right to Vendible Property. LC 68-56570. (Reprints of Economic Classics Ser.). 1976. reprint ed. 49.50 (*0-678-00959-7*) Kelley.

Read, Stephen. Thinking about Logic: An Introduction to the Philosophy of Logic. 192p. 1995. pap. 14.95 (*0-19-289238-X*) OUP.

Read, Stephen, ed. see Nineth European Symposium on Medieval Logic & Semantics Staff.

Read, Susan & Empringham, David. Chiltern Images. (Images Ser.). (Illus.). 192p. 1992. 33.00 (*0-7509-0007-5*) A Sutton Pub.

Read, Susan, ed. see Taunt, Henry.

Read, T. R. & Cressie, N. Goodness-of-Fit Statistics for Discrete Multivariate Data. (Series in Statistics). (Illus.). 260p. 1988. 49.00 (*0-387-96682-X*) Spr-Verlag.

Read, Thomas B. Sheridan's Ride. LC 92-16225. (Illus.). 32p. (J). 1993. 14.00 (*0-688-10873-3*); lib. bdg. 13.93 (*0-688-10874-1*) Greenwillow.

Read, Thomas T., jt. auth. see Bain, Foster H.

Read, W. A. Florida Place Names of Indian Origin & Seminole Personal Names. 1977. lib. bdg. 59.95 (*0-8490-1845-5*) Gordon Pr.

Read, W. L., jt. auth. see Chappell, C.

Read, W. L., jt. auth. see Chappell, R. T.

Read, W. S. The Making of Modern New Guinea-with Special Reference to Culture Contact in the Mandated Territory. LC 43-7044. (American Philosophical Society, Memoirs Ser.: Vol. 18). 353p. reprint ed. pap. 100.70 (*0-317-11254-6*, 2000364) Bks Demand.

Read, William A. Florida Place-Names of Indian Origin & Seminole Personal Names. LC 32-28107. (Louisiana State University Studies: No. 11). 97p. reprint ed. pap. 27.70 (*0-317-28664-1*, 2055313) Bks Demand.

— Indian Place Names in Alabama. rev. ed. LC 84-2593. (Library of Alabama Classics). 1984. reprint ed. pap. 11.50 (*0-8173-0231-X*) U of Ala Pr.

***Read, William H.** America's Mass Media Merchants. LC 76-17231. 222p. 1976. pap. 63.30 (*0-7837-7457-5*, 2049179) Bks Demand.

***Read, William W.** Eddie Buss' Rocks. LC 93-93780. 280p. (Orig.). 1995. pap. 8.00 (*1-56002-315-5*, Univ Edtns) Aegina Pr.

Reade, Arthur. Tea & Tea Drinking. (Illus.). 174p. 1985. reprint ed. 12.95 (*0-936253-00-2*) Attic Pr Discoveries.

Reade, Bob. Coaching Successful Football. LC 93-1272. (Illus.). 192p. 1994. pap. 18.95 (*0-87322-518-X*, PREA0518) Human Kinetics.

Reade, C. Cornewall: The House of Cornewall Family in England. (Illus.). 316p. 1993. reprint ed. lib. bdg. 57.50 (*0-8328-3659-1*); reprint ed. pap. 47.50 (*0-8328-3660-5*) Higginson Bk Co.

— Read. (Illus.). 148p. 1991. reprint ed. pap. 23.50 (*0-8328-2162-4*) Higginson Bk Co.

— Smith Family: Being a Popular Account of Most Branches of the Names - However Spelt. (Illus.). 324p. 1990. reprint ed. lib. bdg. 56.00 (*0-8328-1536-5*); reprint ed. pap. 48.00 (*0-8328-1537-3*) Higginson Bk Co.

Reade, Charles. Peg Woffington & Christie Johnstone. (BCL1-PR English Literature Ser.). 329p. 1992. reprint ed. lib. bdg. 89.00 (*0-7812-7621-7*) Rprt Serv.

— Works of Charles Reade, 17 Vols, Set. LC 73-118070. reprint ed. 1,232.50 (*0-404-05260-6*) AMS Pr.

Reade, Chris. Elements of Functional Programming. (International Computer Science Ser.). (Illus.). 464p. (C). 1989. text ed. 37.75 (*0-201-12915-9*) Addison-Wesley.

Reade, Eric. Britain & Sweden: Current Issues in Local Government. xii, 170p. (Orig.). 1989. pap. 53.25x (*91-540-9318-X*, Pub. by Almqv & Wiksell SW) Coronet Bks.

— History & Heartburn: The Saga of Australian Film, 1896-1978. 353p. 1980. 60.00 (*0-8386-3082-0*) Fairleigh Dickinson.

— Practical Work in Planning Education. (C). 1981. 35.00 (*0-685-30290-3*, Pub. by Oxford Polytechnic UK) St Mut.

Reade, Eric, ed. British Town & Country Planning. 288p. 1987. 90.00 (*0-335-15509-X*, Open Univ Pr); pap. 34.00 (*0-335-15508-1*, Open Univ Pr) Taylor & Francis.

Reade, Eugene, ed. see Smith, Carl B.

Reade, Eugene W., ed. see Smith, Carl B.

Reade, Eugene W., jt. auth. see Smith, Carl B.

Reade, Isabel, tr. see Anderson Imbert, Enrique.

Reade, J. E., jt. ed. see Curtis, J. E.

Reade, John B. An Introduction to Mathematical Analysis. 140p. 1986. 35.00 (*0-19-853258-X*) OUP.

Reade, Julian. Assyrian Sculpture. (British Museum Paperbacks Ser.). (Illus.). 72p. 1983. pap. 12.50 (*0-674-05016-9*) HUP.

— Mesopotamia. (British Museum Paperbacks Ser.). 72p. (C). 1991. pap. 12.50 (*0-674-56958-X*) HUP.

Reade, Kathleen M. The Plaintiff's Personal Injury Handbook. LC 94-163. (Paralegal Practice Ser.). 1994. ring bd. 75.00 (*0-87632-993-8*) Clark Boardman Callaghan.

Reade, Marjorie. Historic Buildings, Ann Arbor, Michigan. rev. ed. (Illus.). 96p. 1986. reprint ed. pap. 3.00 (*1-882574-01-X*) Ann Arbor Hist.

Reade, Marjorie & Wineberg, Susan. Historic Buildings, Ann Arbor, Michigan. 2nd ed. 250p. 1992. pap. 14.95 (*1-882574-00-1*) Ann Arbor Hist.

Reade, W. W. The Veil of Isis, Mysteries of the Druids. 1991. lib. bdg. 79.95 (*0-8490-4960-1*) Gordon Pr.

Reade, W. Winwood. The Veil of Isis: Mysteries of the Druids. reprint ed. spiral bd. 9.90 (*0-7873-0710-6*) Mokelumne.

— Veil of Isis or Mysteries of the Druids. 1992. pap. 9.95 (*0-87877-176-X*) Newcastle Pub.

Reade, Winwood. The Martyrdom of Man. 1981. lib. bdg. 69.95 (*0-686-71630-2*) Revisionist Pr.

Readel, Fred W. All Heavens Ranges. (Orig.). 1986. pap. 4.95 (*0-9616822-3-X*) F W Readel.

Readence, John E., et al. Content Area Reading: An Integrated Approach. 3rd ed. 384p. 1992. per. 32.95 (*0-8403-6735-X*) Kendall-Hunt.

Reader, jt. auth. see Richardson.

Reader, Alice, jt. auth. see Morrison, Kathy.

Reader, Dennis. I Want One! (J). (ps-3). 1992. pap. 4.95 (*0-8249-8581-8*, Ideals Child) Hambleton-Hill.

Reader, Dennis J. Coming Back Alive. 256p. 1983. pap. 2.25 (*0-380-61416-2*, 61416-2, Flare) Avon.

Reader, Dennis J., jt. ed. see Hallwas, John E.

Reader, Diane & Franz, Marion. Pass the Pepper Please! Healthy Meal Planning for People on Sodium Restricted Diets. LC 87-20209. 66p. 1988. pap. 3.95 (*0-937721-17-4*) Chronimed.

Reader, Ian. Religion in Contemporary Japan. 320p. 1991. pap. text ed. 16.00 (*0-8248-1354-5*) UH Pr.

Reader, Ian, et al. Japanese Religions: Past & Present. LC 93-2725. (Illus.). 136p. 1991. text ed. 36.00 (*0-8248-1545-9*); pap. text ed. 16.00 (*0-8248-1546-7*) UH Pr.

Reader, J. The Divine Mystery. 79p. pap. 4.95 (*0-88172-117-4*) Believers Bkshelf.

Reader, Jimmy. Breaking Through Your Highest Potential. 1988. pap. 8.95 (*1-56292-490-7*) Honor Bks OK.

Reader, John. Man on Earth. (Corrie Herring Hooks Ser.: No. 10). (Illus.). 320p. 1988. 29.95 (*0-292-75101-X*) U of Tex Pr.

— Missing Links: The Hunt for Earliest Man. 304p. 1989. pap. 11.95 (*0-14-013973-7*, Penguin Bks) Viking Penguin.

***Reader, Keith.** Regis Debray: The Writing of Commitment. LC 95-14373. (Modern European Thinkers Ser.). 1995. write for info. (*0-7453-0821-X*, Pub. by Pluto Pr UK); pap. write for info. (*0-7453-0822-8*, Pub. by Pluto Pr UK) Westview.

— Teach Yourself the Cinema. 1979. pap. 4.95 (*0-679-12056-4*) McKay.

Reader, Keith A. Intellectuals & the Left in France since 1968. 208p. 1987. text ed. 29.95 (*0-312-41894-9*) St Martin.

Reader, Keith A. & Wadia, Khursheed. The May Nineteen Sixty-Eight Events in France: Reproductions & Interpretations. LC 92-27879. 240p. 1993. text ed. 65.00 (*0-312-09014-5*) St Martin.

Reader, Larry, jt. auth. see Barber, George.

Reader, Ralph, ed. see Conference on Canberra, 1973.

Reader, W. J. At Duty's Call: A Study in Obsolete Patriotism. LC 87-32142. (Studies in Imperialism). 160p. 1988. text ed. 59.95 (*0-7190-2395-5*, Pub. by Manchester Univ Pr UK) St Martin.

— At Duty's Call: A Study in Obsolete Patriotism. LC 87-32142. (Studies in Imperialism). 160p. 1991. text ed. 19.95 (*0-7190-2409-9*, Pub. by Manchester Univ Pr UK) St Martin.

— Bowater: A History. LC 81-7681. (Illus.). 312p. 1981. 89.95 (*0-521-24165-0*) Cambridge U Pr.

Reader, Willie. Back Packing. 1975. 1.50 (*0-936814-02-0*) New Collage.

***Reader's Digest Association Staff.** Exploring the Secrets of Nature: The Amazing World of Animals & Plants. 1995. 32.00 (*0-276-42107-8*, Pub. by RD Assn UK) RD Assn.

***Reader's Digest Association Staff, ed.** Fruits & Vegetables. LC 95-12022. (Successful Gardening Ser.). (Illus.). 1995. write for info. (*0-89577-824-6*) RD Assn.

***Reader's Digest Editor.** Book of Facts: People, Places, Science & Technology, Animals & Plants, Arts & Entertainment, the Earth, the Universe. 1995. 30.00 (*0-89577-692-8*) RD Assn.

— Complete Guide to Sewing: Step-by-Step Techniques for Making Clothes & Home Furnishings. rev. ed. 1995. 30.00 (*0-88850-247-8*) RD Assn.

Reader's Digest Editors. A to Z of Annuals, Biennials & Bulbs. LC 93-37667. (Successful Gardening Ser.). (Illus.). 176p. 1994. 18.98 (*0-89577-584-0*) RD Assn.

— A-Z of Deciduous Trees & Shrubs. LC 94-13100. (Successful Gardening Ser.). (Illus.). 176p. 1994. 18.98 (*0-89577-615-4*) RD Assn.

— A-Z of Evergreen Trees & Shrubs. LC 94-47610. (Successful Gardening Ser.). (Illus.). 176p. 1995. 18.98 (*0-89577-698-7*) RD Assn.

— A-Z of Perennials. LC 93-26149. (Successful Gardening Ser.). (Illus.). 176p. 1993. 18.98 (*0-89577-554-9*) RD Assn.

— ABCs of Nature. LC 83-60796. (Illus.). 336p. 1984. 27.95 (*0-89577-169-1*, Random) RD Assn.

— ABCs of the Bible. LC 90-45962. (Illus.). 336p. 1991. 32.00 (*0-89577-375-9*, Random) RD Assn.

— ABC's of the Human Body. LC 85-14470. (Illus.). 336p. 1987. 28.00 (*0-89577-220-5*, Random) RD Assn.

— ABCs of the Human Mind. LC 89-36711. (Illus.). 336p. 1990. 28.00 (*0-89577-345-7*, Random) RD Assn.

— After Jesus: The Triumph of Christianity. LC 91-8873. (Illus.). 352p. 1992. 30.00 (*0-89577-392-9*, Random) RD Assn.

— America: Land of Beauty & Splendor. LC 91-27098. (Illus.). 432p. 1992. 35.00 (*0-89577-404-6*, Random) RD Assn.

— American Folklore & Legend. LC 77-80638. (Illus.). 448p. 1978. 27.00 (*0-89577-045-8*, Random) RD Assn.

— America's Fascinating Indian Heritage. LC 78-55614. (Illus.). 416p. 1990. reprint ed. 30.00 (*0-89577-372-4*, Random) RD Assn.

— America's Historic Places. LC 87-4757. (Illus.). 352p. 1988. 28.00 (*0-89577-265-5*, Random) RD Assn.

— Antarctica: The Extraordinary History of Man's Conquest of the Frozen Continent. 2nd ed. (Illus.). 320p. 1990. 32.95 (*0-86438-167-0*, Random) RD Assn.

— Atlas of the Bible: An Illustrated Guide to the Holy Land. LC 80-53426. (Illus.). 256p. 1982. 30.00 (*0-89577-097-0*) RD Assn.

— The Australian Wildlife Year: A Month-by-Month Guide to Nature. (Illus.). 336p. 1989. 34.95 (*0-86438-071-2*, Random) RD Assn.

— Back Roads & Hidden Corners. LC 93-8254. (Illus.). 144p. 1993. 16.98 (*0-89577-545-X*) RD Assn.

— Back to Basics: How to Learn & Enjoy Traditional American Skills. LC 80-50373. (Illus.). 456p. 1981. 26.00 (*0-89577-086-5*, Random) RD Assn.

— Bizarre Phenomena. LC 92-31739. (Quest for the Unknown Ser.). (Illus.). 144p. 1992. 16.98 (*0-89577-464-X*) RD Assn.

— Book of Christmas. LC 73-84158. (Illus.). 304p. 1973. 24.99 (*0-89577-013-X*) RD Assn.

— Book of North American Birds. LC 89-70261. (Illus.). 576p. 1990. 32.95 (*0-89577-351-1*, Random) RD Assn.

— The Busy Cook's Cookbook. LC 92-43506. (Books for Cooks Ser.). (Illus.). 144p. 1993. 19.95 (*0-89577-489-5*, Readers Digest Kids) RD Assn.

— Caring for Your Plants. (Successful Gardening Ser.). (Illus.). 176p. 1994. 18.98 (*0-89577-603-0*) RD Assn.

— Charting the Future. LC 92-8818. (Quest for the Unknown Ser.). (Illus.). 144p. 1992. 16.98 (*0-89577-441-0*) RD Assn.

— Color Round the Year. LC 93-45391. (Successful Gardening Ser.). (Illus.). 176p. 1994. 18.98 (*0-89577-602-2*) RD Assn.

— Complete Guide to Needlework. LC 78-71704. (Illus.). 504p. 1981. 28.00 (*0-89577-059-8*, Random) RD Assn.

— Complete Guide to Sewing. LC 75-32406. (Illus.). 528p. 1976. 28.00 (*0-89577-026-1*) RD Assn.

— The Complete Manual of Fitness & Well-Being. LC 87-9735. (Illus.). 352p. 1988. 28.00 (*0-89577-270-1*, Random) RD Assn.

— Consumer Adviser: An Action Guide to Your Rights. rev. ed. LC 88-32437. 416p. 1989. 24.95 (*0-89577-326-0*, Random) RD Assn.

— Cook Now, Serve Later. LC 88-36564. (Illus.). 320p. 1990. 24.95 (*0-89577-314-7*, Random) RD Assn.

— Country Ways. LC 87-23308. (Illus.). 304p. 1988. 25.95 (*0-89577-290-6*, Random) RD Assn.

— Crafts & Hobbies. LC 79-63118. (Illus.). 456p. 1981. 24.95 (*0-89577-063-6*) RD Assn.

— Did You Know? New Insights into a World that is Full of Astonishing Facts & Astonishing Stories. (Illus.). 384p. 1993. 32.95 (*0-276-42014-4*, Random) RD Assn.

— Discovering America's Past: Customs, Legends, History & Lore of Our Great Nation. LC 93-3508. (Illus.). 400p. 1993. 32.95 (*0-89577-520-4*, Random) RD Assn.

— Discovering the Wonders of Our World: A Guide to Nature's Scenic Marvels. (Illus.). 456p. 1994. 30.00 (*0-276-42108-6*, Pub. by RD Assn UK) RD Assn.

— Earth's Mysterious Places. LC 92-34961. (Quest for the Unknown Ser.). (Illus.). 144p. 1992. 16.98 (*0-89577-470-4*) RD Assn.

— Eat Better, Live Better: A Commonsense Guide to Nutrition & Good Health. LC 82-60100. (Illus.). 416p. 1982. 30.00 (*0-89577-141-1*, Random) RD Assn.

— Emergency: Reader's Digest Action Guide. LC 88-18537. (Illus.). 354p. 1988. 24.95 (*0-89577-319-8*, Random) RD Assn.

— Encyclopedia of Animals: Mammals, Birds, Reptiles, Amphibians. 688p. 1994. 50.00 (*1-875137-49-1*) RD Assn.

— Everyday Life Through the Ages. (Illus.). 384p. 1992. 35.00 (*0-276-42035-7*, Random) RD Assn.

— Facts & Fallacies. LC 87-20627. (Illus.). 448p. 1988. 30.00 (*0-89577-273-6*, Random) RD Assn.

— The Family Favorites Cookbook. LC 93-16408. (Books for Cooks Ser.). (Illus.). 144p. 1993. 19.95 (*0-89577-490-9*) RD Assn.

— Family Guide to Natural Medicine: How to Stay Healthy the Natural Way. LC 92-6163. (Illus.). 416p. 1993. 32.95 (*0-89577-433-X*, Random) RD Assn.

— Family Guide to the Bible: A Concordance & Reference Companion to the King James Version. LC 84-13261. (Illus.). 832p. 1984. 27.00 (*0-89577-192-6*, Random) RD Assn.

— The Family Handyman Easy Repair: Over 100 Simple Solutions to the Most Common Household Problems. LC 94-14896. (Illus.). 192p. 1994. 19.95 (*0-89577-624-3*) RD Assn.

— The Family Handyman Helpful Hints: Quick & Easy Solutions, Timesaving Tips, Tricks of the Trade. LC 94-1807. (Illus.). 384p. 1995. 30.00 (*0-89577-617-0*) RD Assn.

— Family Handyman Outdoor Projects: Over 20 Easy Ways to Make the Most of Your Outdoor Living Space. (Illus.). 192p. 1994. 19.95 (*0-89577-623-5*) RD Assn.

— The Family Handyman Weekend Improvements: Over 30 Do-It-Yourself Projects for the Home. LC 94-46623. (Illus.). 192p. 1995. 19.95 (*0-89577-685-5*) RD Assn.

— The Family Handyman Woodworking; Room by Room: Furniture, Cabinetry, Built-Ins, & Other Projects for the Home. LC 94-45302. (Illus.). 192p. 1995. 19.95 (*0-89577-686-3*) RD Assn.

— Family Word Finder. LC 75-18006. 896p. 1975. 23.97 (*0-89577-023-7*) RD Assn.

— Fix-It-Yourself Manual. LC 77-73634. (Illus.). 480p. 1981. 26.00 (*0-89577-040-7*, Random) RD Assn.

— Garden for All Seasons. (Illus.). 432p. 1991. 30.00 (*0-89577-380-5*, Random) RD Assn.

— Ghosts & Hauntings. LC 92-39630. (Quest for the Unknown Ser.). (Illus.). 144p. 1993. 16.98 (*0-89577-493-3*) RD Assn.

— The Good Health Fact Book. LC 91-44169. (Illus.). 480p. 1992. 27.00 (*0-89577-416-X*, Random) RD Assn.

— Great Disasters. LC 88-26504. (Illus.). 320p. 1989. 30.00 (*0-89577-321-X*, Random) RD Assn.

— Great Recipes for Good Health. LC 88-6733. (Illus.). 304p. 1989. 24.95 (*0-89577-306-6*, Random) RD Assn.

— Growing Your Favorite Plants. LC 93-20907. (Successful Gardening Ser.). (Illus.). 176p. 1993. 18.98 (*0-89577-577-8*) RD Assn.

R

An Asterisk (*) at the beginning of an entry indicates that the title is appearing in BIP for the first time.

— Historic Places. LC 93-21872. (Explore America Ser.). (Illus.). 144p. 1993. 16.98 (*0-89577-506-9*) RD Assn.

— Home Improvements Manual. LC 81-84488. (Illus.). 384p. 1991. 30.00 (*0-89577-132-2*, Random) RD Assn.

— Home Improvements Manual. LC 81-84488. (Illus.). 384p. 1992. 28.00 (*0-89577-410-0*) RD Assn.

— Household Hints & Handy Tips. LC 87-16356. (Illus.). 480p. 1988. 26.95 (*0-89577-276-0*, Random) RD Assn.

***Readers Digest Editors.** Household Hints & Handy Tips. LC 87-16356. 480p. 1994. pap. 14.95 (*0-89577-663-4*) RD Assn.

Reader's Digest Editors. How in the World? LC 90-30663. (Illus.). 448p. 1990. 32.00 (*0-89577-353-8*, Random) RD Assn.

— The How-to Book of Healthy Cooking. LC 95-5940. 1995. write for info. (*0-89577-789-4*) RD Assn.

— How to Do Just about Anything. LC 85-14446. (Illus.). 448p. 1986. 30.00 (*0-89577-218-3*, Random) RD Assn.

— Illustrated Reverse Dictionary. LC 90-39606. (Illus.). 608p. 1991. 25.00 (*0-89577-352-X*, Random) RD Assn.

— The Indoor Garden. LC 94-35382. (Successful Gardening Ser.). (Illus.). 176p. 1995. 18.98 (*0-89577-684-7*) RD Assn.

— Jesus & His Times. LC 86-24857. (Illus.). 336p. 1987. 32.95 (*0-89577-257-4*, Random) RD Assn.

— Know Your Rights & How to Make Them Work for You. LC 95-9561. 1995. write for info. (*0-89577-831-9*) RD Assn.

— Legal Problem Solver: A Quick-&-Easy Action Guide to the Law. LC 93-27340. 640p. 1994. 32.95 (*0-89577-550-6*) RD Assn.

— Life Beyond Death. LC 91-25399. (Quest for the Unknown Ser.). (Illus.). 144p. 1992. 16.98 (*0-89577-399-6*) RD Assn.

— Live Longer Cookbook. LC 92-17030. (Illus.). 352p. 1992. 30.00 (*0-89577-395-3*, Random) RD Assn.

— Live Longer, Live Better: Adding Years to Your Life & Life to Your Years. LC 93-31829. (Illus.). 368p. 1995. 35.00 (*0-89577-578-6*) RD Assn.

— Magic & Medicine of Plants. LC 85-30101. (Illus.). 464p. 1986. 27.95 (*0-89577-221-3*, Random) RD Assn.

— Man & Beast. LC 92-47142. (Quest for the Unknown Ser.). (Illus.). 144p. 1993. 16.98 (*0-89577-496-8*) RD Assn.

— Mind Power. LC 92-4413. (Quest for the Unknown Ser.). (Illus.). 144p. 1992. 16.98 (*0-89577-421-6*) RD Assn.

— Mysteries of the Ancient Americas. LC 84-15038. (Illus.). 320p. 1986. 30.00 (*0-89577-183-7*, Random) RD Assn.

— Mysteries of the Ancients. LC 93-8399. (Quest for the Unknown Ser.). (Illus.). 144p. 1993. 16.98 (*0-89577-529-8*) RD Assn.

— Mysteries of the Bible. LC 87-32402. (Illus.). 384p. 1989. 30.00 (*0-89577-293-0*, Random) RD Assn.

— Mysteries of the Unexplained. LC 82-60791. (Illus.). 320p. 1983. 30.00 (*0-89577-146-2*) RD Assn.

— National Parks. LC 92-35785. (Explore America Ser.). (Illus.). 144p. 1993. 16.98 (*0-89577-477-1*) RD Assn.

— Natural Wonders of the World. LC 80-50353. (Illus.). 464p. 1980. 27.00 (*0-89577-087-3*, Random) RD Assn.

— Nature in America. LC 90-46146. (Illus.). 456p. 1991. 32.95 (*0-89577-376-7*, Random) RD Assn.

— New Age Healing. LC 92-16462. (Quest for the Unknown Ser.). (Illus.). 144p. 1992. 16.98 (*0-89577-463-1*) RD Assn.

— New Complete Do-It-Yourself Manual. LC 90-46830. (Illus.). 528p. 1991. 30.00 (*0-89577-378-3*, Random) RD Assn.

— North American Wildlife. LC 81-50919. (Illus.). 576p. 1982. 28.95 (*0-89577-102-0*) RD Assn.

— Off the Beaten Path: A Guide to More Than 1,000 Scenic & Interesting Places Still Uncrowded & Inviting. LC 86-11372. (Illus.). 384p. 1987. 28.00 (*0-89577-253-1*, Random) RD Assn.

— On the Road, U. S. A. LC 88-31763. (Illus.). 240p. 1989. 24.95 (*0-89577-323-6*, Random) RD Assn.

— One-Dish Meals the Easy Way. LC 91-10972. (Illus.). 352p. 1991. 28.00 (*0-89577-389-9*, Random) RD Assn.

— One Hundred One Do-It-Yourself Projects. LC 82-61581. (Illus.). 384p. 1993. 28.00 (*0-89577-163-2*) RD Assn.

— Our Glorious Century. LC 94-14328. (Illus.). 512p. 1994. 40.00 (*0-89577-616-2*) RD Assn.

— Our National Parks: America's Spectacular Wilderness Heritage. LC 89-33561. (Illus.). 352p. 1989. 30.00 (*0-89577-336-8*, Random) RD Assn.

— The Practical Gardener. LC 93-19529. (Successful Gardening Ser.). (Illus.). 176p. 1993. 18.98 (*0-89577-539-5*) RD Assn.

— Practical Guide to Home Landscaping. LC 72-157525. (Illus.). 479p. 1984. 26.00 (*0-89577-005-9*) RD Assn.

— Practical Problem Solver. LC 89-27729. (Illus.). 448p. 1991. 28.00 (*0-89577-346-5*, Random) RD Assn.

— Quest for the Past. LC 83-60795. (Illus.). 320p. 1984. 25.95 (*0-89577-170-5*, Random) RD Assn.

— Quick & Delicious: How to Fix Great Meals in Minutes. LC 92-34604. (Illus.). 400p. 1994. 28.00 (*0-89577-491-7*) RD Assn.

— Reader's Digest - Bartholomew Illustrated Atlas of the World. 2nd rev. ed. (Illus.). 176p. 1994. 24.00 (*0-89577-613-8*) RD Assn.

— Reader's Digest Atlas of the World. LC 87-675016. (Illus.). 240p. 1987. 34.96 (*0-89577-264-7*) RD Assn.

— Reader's Digest Book of Facts. LC 86-29744. (Illus.). 416p. 1987. 29.00 (*0-89577-256-6*, Random) RD Assn.

— Reader's Digest Book of Skills & Tools. LC 92-28686. (Illus.). 360p. 1993. 30.00 (*0-89577-469-0*, Random) RD Assn.

— The Reader's Digest Children's Atlas of World History. LC 93-4320. (Illus.). 128p. (J). (gr. 4-7). 1993. 20.00 (*0-89577-526-3*) RD Assn.

— Reader's Digest Guide to Creative Gardening. LC 87-128856. (Illus.). 384p. 1987. 32.00 (*0-276-35223-8*) RD Assn.

— The Reader's Digest Illustrated Book of Cats. (Illus.). 256p. 1993. 25.00 (*0-88850-198-6*) RD Assn.

— The Reader's Digest Illustrated Book of Dogs. 2nd rev. ed. (Illus.). 384p. 1989. 24.95 (*0-89577-340-6*, Random) RD Assn.

— Reader's Digest Illustrated Book of Dogs. 2nd rev. ed. (Illus.). 1993. 27.00 (*0-88850-205-2*) RD Assn.

— Reader's Digest Illustrated Encyclopedic Dictionary, 2 vols., Set. LC 87-9650. (Illus.). 1920p. 1987. 59.96 (*0-89577-269-8*) RD Assn.

— Reader's Digest Illustrated Guide to Ireland. (Illus.). 1992. 35.00 (*0-276-42033-0*, Random) RD Assn.

— Reader's Digest Illustrated Guide to the Game Parks & Nature Reserves of Southern Africa. (Illus.). 1993. 30.00 (*0-947008-66-7*, Random) RD Assn.

— The Reader's Digest Illustrated History of South Africa. 2nd ed. (Illus.). 512p. 1995. 30.00 (*0-947008-90-X*) RD Assn.

— The Reader's Digest Legal Question & Answer Book. LC 87-25963. 704p. 1988. 32.00 (*0-89577-291-4*, Random) RD Assn.

— Reader's Digest Visitors' Guide to the Great Barrier Reef. (Illus.). 168p. 1989. pap. 19.95 (*0-86438-073-9*, Random) RD Assn.

— Remembering the Fifties: One Hundred Top Hits to Play & Sing. (Illus.). 276p. 1992. spiral bd. 30.00 (*0-89577-429-1*, Random) RD Assn.

— Secrets of the Natural World. LC 93-435. (Quest for the Unknown Ser.). (Illus.). 144p. 1993. 16.98 (*0-89577-498-4*) RD Assn.

— Sharks: Silent Hunters of the Deep. LC 87-670009. (Illus.). 208p. 1986. 19.95 (*0-86438-014-3*, Random) RD Assn.

— Southern Africa Spectacular World of Wildlife. (Illus.). 272p. 1994. 35.00 (*1-874912-05-X*) RD Assn.

— The Story of Jesus. LC 92-42206. (Illus.). 384p. 1993. 33.00 (*0-89577-472-0*, Random) RD Assn.

— Story of the Great American West. LC 76-23542. (Illus.). 384p. 1977. 30.00 (*0-89577-039-3*, Random) RD Assn.

— Strange Stories, Amazing Facts. LC 76-2966. (Illus.). 608p. 1976. 25.95 (*0-89577-028-8*) RD Assn.

— Strange Stories, Amazing Facts of America's Past. LC 88-11515. (Illus.). 416p. 1989. 32.95 (*0-89577-307-4*, Random) RD Assn.

— Success with House Plants. LC 78-59802. (Illus.). 480p. 1979. 26.00 (*0-89577-052-0*) RD Assn.

— Success with Words. LC 82-62542. 704p. 1983. 24.95 (*0-89577-168-3*, Random) RD Assn.

— Touring Guide to Britain. 1993. 30.00 (*0-276-42031-4*, Random) RD Assn.

— Travel Guide U. S. A. LC 93-5857. (Illus.). 432p. 1994. 32.95 (*0-89577-564-6*, Random) RD Assn.

— Treasures of Britain. (Illus.). 680p. 1991. 45.00 (*0-276-42022-5*, Random) RD Assn.

— Treasures of China: An Armchair Journey to 352 Legendary Landmarks. (Illus.). 336p. 1989. 29.95 (*0-89577-325-2*, Random) RD Assn.

— Treasury of Great Show Tunes. (Illus.). 288p. 1993. 32.00 (*0-89577-495-X*, Random) RD Assn.

— UFO: The Continuing Enigma. LC 91-22275. (Quest for the Unknown Ser.). (Illus.). 144p. 1991. 16.98 (*0-89577-397-X*) RD Assn.

— Unsolved Mysteries of the Past. LC 90-28809. (Quest for the Unknown Ser.). (Illus.). 144p. 1991. 16.98 (*0-89577-359-7*) RD Assn.

— Who's Who in the Bible: An Illustrated Biographical Dictionary. LC 94-17591. (Illus.). 480p. 1994. 32.00 (*0-89577-618-9*) RD Assn.

— Wild Australia. (Illus.). 488p. 1988. 39.95 (*0-86438-069-0*, Random) RD Assn.

— The Wildlife Year: Life Cycles of Nature Around the World. (Illus.). 360p. 1993. 35.00 (*0-276-42012-8*, Random) RD Assn.

— The World at Arms: The Reader's Digest Illustrated History of World War II. (Illus.). 512p. 1989. 29.95 (*0-89577-333-3*, Random) RD Assn.

— Write Better, Speak Better. LC 75-183859. 730p. 1972. 21.99 (*0-89577-006-7*) RD Assn.

Reader's Digest Editors, des. Daily Life in Colonial America. LC 93-2719. (Journeys into the Past Ser.). (Illus.). 144p. 1993. 18.98 (*0-89577-497-6*) RD Assn.

Reader's Digest Editors, ed. All-Occasion Cookbook: Books for Cooks. LC 94-64. 1994. 19.95 (*0-89577-592-1*) RD Assn.

— Down Home Cooking the New, Healthier Way. LC 94-13511. (Illus.). 384p. 1995. 28.00 (*0-89577-646-4*) RD Assn.

— The Easy Way to Play One Hundred Unforgettable Hits. (Illus.). 224p. 1991. Lie-flat spiral bdg. spiral bd. 30.00 (*0-89577-385-6*, Random) RD Assn.

— Family Songbook. LC 70-84403. (Illus.). 252p. 1981. spiral bd. 29.95 (*0-89577-002-4*, Random) RD Assn.

— Family Songbook of Faith & Joy: 129 All-Time Inspirational Favorites. LC 74-26223. (Illus.). 288p. 1981. spiral bd. 29.95 (*0-89577-021-0*) RD Assn.

— Festival of Popular Songs. LC 77-24818. (Illus.). 288p. 1981. spiral bd. 29.95 (*0-89577-035-0*, Random) RD Assn.

— The Garden Problem Solver. LC 94-30615. (Successful Gardening Ser.). (Illus.). 176p. 1994. 18.98 (*0-89577-675-8*) RD Assn.

— Great Music's Greatest Hits: Ninety-Seven Unforgettable Classics for Piano & Organ. LC 79-53751. (Illus.). 252p. 1980. spiral bd. 29.95 (*0-89577-066-0*, Random) RD Assn.

— Parade of Popular Hits. (Illus.). 252p. 1989. spiral bd. 29.95 (*0-89577-327-9*, Random) RD Assn.

— The Pioneers: Novels of the American Frontier. LC 85-23236. (Illus.). 640p. 1988. 19.95 (*0-89577-229-9*) RD Assn.

— Plant Partners. LC 94-13509. (Successful Gardening Ser.). (Illus.). 176p. 1994. 18.98 (*0-89577-614-6*) RD Assn.

— Popular Classics. (Illus.). 252p. 1988. spiral bd. 29.95 (*0-89577-274-4*, Random) RD Assn.

— Popular Songs That Will Live Forever. LC 81-84487. (Illus.). 252p. 1982. spiral bd. 29.95 (*0-89577-104-7*, Random) RD Assn.

— The Reader's Digest Children's Songbook. (Illus.). 252p. (J). (ps up). 1985. spiral bd. 29.95 (*0-89577-214-0*, Random) RD Assn.

— The Reader's Digest Country & Western Songbook. (Illus.). 252p. 1983. spiral bd. 29.95 (*0-89577-147-0*, Random) RD Assn.

— The Reader's Digest Merry Christmas Songbook. LC 81-51285. (Illus.). 252p. 1981. spiral bd. 29.95 (*0-89577-105-5*, Random) RD Assn.

— Remembering Yesterday's Hits. (Illus.). 252p. 1986. spiral bd. 29.95 (*0-89577-249-3*, Random) RD Assn.

— Treasury of Best Loved Songs: 114 All-Time Family Favorites. LC 71-183858. (Illus.). 288p. 1981. spiral bd. 29.95 (*0-89577-007-5*, Random) RD Assn.

— Unforgettable Musical Memories. (Illus.). 252p. 1984. spiral bd. 29.95 (*0-89577-178-0*, Random) RD Assn.

— The World's Best Fairy Tales, 2 vols., Set. LC 79-89496. (Illus.). 832p. 1981. 24.99 (*0-89577-078-4*) RD Assn.

— The World's Last Mysteries. LC 77-87127. (Illus.). 320p. 1978. 23.97 (*0-89577-044-X*) RD Assn.

***Reader's Digest Editors, et al, eds.** See the U. S. A. the Easy Way: 136 Loop Tours to 1200 Great Places. LC 94-36959. (Illus.). 352p. 1995. 32.95 (*0-89577-682-0*) RD Assn.

Reader's Digest Editors, sel. Family Favorites from Reader's Digest, 4 bks. Incl. I Am Joe's Body. 1982. pap. 2.95 (*0-425-07689-X*); Word Power. 256p. 1982. pap. 2.95 (*0-425-07492-7*); Secrets of the Past. 1982. pap. 2.75 (*0-425-05765-8*); 1982. Boxed Set. Set pap. 10.00 (*0-425-05211-7*) Berkley Pub.

***Reader's Digest Editors Staff.** Creative Garden Design: Successful Gardening. LC 94-39325. (Successful Gardening Ser.). (Illus.). 176p. 1995. 18.98 (*0-89577-693-6*, J Morris NY) RD Assn.

Reader's Digest Seleccione Staff. Family Medical Dictionary: Diccionario Medico Familiar. 756p. (SPA.). 1981. 95.00 (*0-8288-1878-9*, S34982) Fr & Eur.

Reader's Digest Staff. Reader's Digest Illustrated Guide. 1989. 30.00 (*0-394-21707-1*) Random.

Reader's Digest Staff, sel. Le Dictionnaire Plus. 703p. (FRE.). 1992. 110.00 (*0-7859-1004-2*, 2709803704) Fr & Eur.

Readers House Staff, ed. Changes: An Anthology by New Writers. (New Writers' Voices Ser.). 64p. (Orig.). 1993. pap. text ed. 3.50 (*1-56853-006-4*, Signal Hill) New Readers.

— Never Say Good-bye: An Anthology by New Writers in Prison. (New Writers' Voices Ser.). 64p. (Orig.). 1993. pap. text ed. 3.50 (*1-56853-005-6*, Signal Hill) New Readers.

— Speaking to One Another: An Anthology by New Writers. (New Writers' Voices Ser.). 64p. 1993. pap. text ed. 3.50 (*1-56853-007-2*, Signal Hill) New Readers.

Readers House Staff, ed. see Attenborough, David.

Readers House Staff, ed. see Belgrade, Belen & Friedman, Isatu.

Readers House Staff, ed. see Heyerdahl, Thor.

Readers House Staff, ed. see Holder, Andre.

Readers House Staff, ed. see Sagan, Carl.

Readers of Harrowsmith Magazine Editors. Harrowsmith Cookbook, Vol. I: Classic & Creative Cuisine from Harrowsmith Kitchens. (Illus.). 320p. (Orig.). 1982. reprint ed. 17.95 (*0-920656-19-6*, Pub. by Camden Hse CN) Firefly Bks Ltd.

Readett, A. G., jt. auth. see Herbst, R.

Readett, Alan G., jt. auth. see Herbst, Robert.

Readett, Alan G., jt. ed. see Herbst, Robert.

Readey, H. & Readey, W. Mathematical Concepts in Nursing: A Workbook. 1980. pap. text ed. 17.56 (*0-201-06166-X*, Health Sci) Addison-Wesley.

Readey, W., jt. auth. see Readey, H.

Readhead, Paul A., ed. Vacuum Science & Technology: Pioneers of the 20th Century. LC 93-28714. (History of Vacuum Science & Technology Ser.: Vol. 2). (Illus.). 300p. 1993. pap. text ed. 35.00 (*1-56396-248-9*, AIP Pr) Am Inst Physics.

Readicker-Henderson, Ed. Adventure Guide to the Alaska Highway. (Adventure Guides Ser.). (Illus.). 224p. (Orig.). 1991. pap. 15.95 (*1-55650-457-8*) Hunter NJ.

— The Traveler's Guide to Japanese Pilgrimages. (Illus.). 240p. (Orig.). 1994. pap. 14.95 (*0-8348-0291-0*) Weatherhill.

Readicker-Henderson, Ed, jt. auth. see Readicker-Henderson, Lynn.

Readicker-Henderson, Lynn & Readicker-Henderson, Ed. The Adventure Guide to Coastal Alaska & the Inside Passage. (Adventure Guides Ser.). (Illus.). 224p. (Orig.). 1994. pap. 14.95 (*1-55650-630-9*) Hunter NJ.

***Reading, Alison J., et al.** Humid Tropical Environments. LC 94-27803. (Natural Environment Ser.). 384p. 1994. 74.95 (*0-631-17287-4*); pap. 29.95 (*0-631-19174-7*) Blackwell Pubs.

Reading, Anthony, ed. Psychological Aspects of Infertility. 1994. text ed. 34.95 (*0-471-52792-0*) Wiley.

Reading Catalog of the Library of the American Museum of Natural History Staff. Research Catalog of the Library of the American Museum of Natural History: Classed Catalog. 1978. lib. bdg. 1,155.00 (*0-8161-0238-4*, Hall Library) G K Hall.

Reading, Chris M. & Meillon, Ross S. Your Family Tree Connection. Orig. Title: Relatively Speaking. (Illus.). 288p. (Orig.). 1988. reprint ed. pap. 9.95 (*0-87983-483-8*) Keats.

Reading, Clive. Strategic Business Planning: An Action Program for Forward-Looking Businesses. 400p. 1993. text ed. 47.95 (*0-89397-391-2*) Nichols Pub.

Reading, Gerald R. The South Sea Bubble. LC 73-109972. (Illus.). 176p. 1978. reprint ed. text ed. 49.75 (*0-8371-4480-9*, RESO, Greenwood Pr) Greenwood.

Reading, H. Sedimentary Environments & Facies. 3rd ed. 1994. write for info. (*0-632-03627-3*) Blackwell Sci.

Reading, H. G. Sedimentary Environments & Facies. 2nd ed. (Illus.). 680p. 1986. pap. text ed. 59.95 (*0-632-01223-4*) Blackwell Sci.

Reading, J. P. Summer of Sassy Jo. (YA). 1993. pap. 4.95 (*0-395-66956-1*) HM.

Reading, Joseph H. A Voyage along the Western Coast or Newest Africa; a Descripton of Newest Africa; or the Africa of Today & the Immediate Future. LC 72-5528. (Black Heritage Library Collection). 1977. reprint ed. 25.95 (*0-8369-9147-8*) Ayer.

Reading Laboratory Staff. Double Your Reading Speed. 1986. pap. write for info. (*0-449-44250-0*, Prem) Fawcett.

Reading, M. K. Bowne: William Bowne of Yorkshire, England & His Descendants. (Illus.). 47p. 1994. reprint ed. pap. 10.00 (*0-8328-4199-4*) Higginson Bk Co.

— Bowne - William Bowne of Yorkshire, England & His Descendants. (Illus.). 47p. 1994. reprint ed. lib. bdg. 20.00 (*0-8328-4515-9*); reprint ed. pap. 10.00 (*0-8328-4516-7*) Higginson Bk Co.

Reading, Peter. Evagatory. 48p. 1992. pap. 13.95 (*0-7011-3924-2*, Pub. by Chatto & Windus UK) Trafalgar.

— Last Poems. 45p. 1995. pap. 15.95 (*0-7011-6100-0*, Pub. by Chatto & Windus UK) Trafalgar.

— Three-in-One: Diplopic, Ukelele Music. 176p. 1992. pap. 17.95 (*0-7011-3689-8*, Pub. by Chatto & Windus UK) Trafalgar.

— Ukulele Music - Perduta Gente. (TriQuarterly Bks.). 112p. (Orig.). 1994. 26.95 (*0-8101-5030-1*); pap. 11.95 (*0-8101-5005-0*) Northwestern U Pr.

Reading Research Dept. Staff. Atlantis. (Library: Vol. 22). 480p. 1987. 24.95 (*0-87604-204-3*, 1122) ARE Pr.

— Egypt, Pt. I. (Library: Vol. 23). 340p. 1989. 24.95 (*0-87604-220-5*, 1123) ARE Pr.

— Egypt, Pt. II. (Library: Vol. 24). 362p. 1989. 24.95 (*0-87604-228-0*, 1124) ARE Pr.

Reading, Susan. Desert Plants. (Plant Life Ser.). 64p. (YA). 1990. 15.95 (*0-8160-2421-9*) Facts on File.

Readings, Bill. Introducing Lyotard: Art & Politics. (Critics of the Twentieth Century Ser.). 224p. 1991. 54.95 (*0-415-02196-0*, A4850); pap. 15.95 (*0-415-05536-9*, A4854) Routledge.

Readings, Bill, tr. see Lyotard, Jean-Francois.

Readings, Bill, jt. ed. see Melville, Stephen.

Readings Research Dept. Staff. Astrology, Pt. 1, Vol. 18. (Library). 611p. 1985. lib. bdg. 24.95 (*0-87604-159-4*, 1118) ARE Pr.

— Astrology, Pt. 2, Vol. 19. (Library). 330p. 1985. lib. bdg. 22.95 (*0-87604-176-4*, 1119) ARE Pr.

— Mind, Vol. 20. (Library). 346p. 1986. lib. bdg. 22.95 (*0-87604-180-2*, 1120) ARE Pr.

Readings, William & Schaber, Bennet, eds. Postmodernism Across the Ages. 320p. 1993. text ed. 39.95 (*0-8156-2577-4*); pap. text ed. 16.95 (*0-8156-2581-2*) Syracuse U Pr.

Readio, Skip. How to Do Electrical Systems. (Illus.). 125p. 1993. pap. 19.95 (*1-884089-02-X*) CarTech.

Readman, Alison, jt. auth. see McCallum, R. B.

***Readman, Jo.** Muck & Magic: Start Your Own Natural Garden with Colorful, Simple Projects. (J). (gr. 4-7). 1994. pap. 12.95 (*0-85532-757-X*, Pub. by Search Pr UK) A Schwartz & Co.

Readman, Mark C. Flexible Joint Robots. 158p. 1994. 49.95 (*0-8493-2601-X*, 2601) CRC Pr.

Readshaw, G. R. & Wood, R. Looking Up: Looking Back at Old Brisbane Watercolours. 80p. (C). 1990. 90.00 (*0-86439-032-7*, Pub. by Boolarong Pubns AT) St Mut.

Readshaw, Grahame. Keep It Simple System for Water Colour Painting. (C). 1990. 90.00 (*0-86439-144-7*, Pub. by Boolarong Pubns AT) St Mut.

Readus, James H. The Big Hit. (Orig.). 1975. pap. 2.25 (*0-87067-218-5*, BH218) Holloway.

— Black Renegades. (Orig.). 1976. pap. 2.50 (*0-87067-294-0*, BH294) Holloway.

— Death Merchants. 382p. 1991. pap. 3.95 (*0-87067-323-8*, BH323) Holloway.

Readwell. English - Assamese Dictionary. 1992. reprint ed. 19.95 (*0-8288-8478-1*) Fr & Eur.

Ready, Anna. Mississippi. LC 92-31056. (Hello U. S. A. Ser.). (J). (gr. 3-6). 1993. lib. bdg. 17.50 (*0-8225-2743-X*, Lerner Publctns) Lerner Group.

Ready, Anna D. A Cat's Life: Dulcy's Story. large type ed. LC 92-43512. 1993. pap. 16.95 (*0-7927-1522-5*, Curley Lrg Print) Chivers N Amer.

Ready, Dee, teller. A Cat's Life: Dulcy's Story. (Illus.). 96p. 1992. 12.00 (*0-517-58872-2*, Crown) Crown Pub Group.

Ready, Dolores. Meeting Jesus. (Discovering Program Ser.). (Illus.). 66p. (Orig.). 1989. teacher ed 6.00 (*0-88489-191-7*); text ed. 2.80 (*0-88489-190-9*) St Marys.

— Praying. (Discovering Program Ser.). (Illus.). 67p. (Orig.). 1989. teacher ed 6.00 (*0-88489-195-X*); text ed. 2.80 (*0-88489-194-1*) St Marys.

— Understanding Myself. (Discovering Program Ser.). (Illus.). 61p. (Orig.). 1989. 2.80 (*0-88489-196-8*); teacher ed 6.00 (*0-88489-197-6*) St Marys.

Ready, J. Lee. Forgotten Allies: The Military Contribution of the Colonies, Exiled Governments, & Lesser Powers to the Allied Victory in World War II, Set. LC 84-42608. 1985. lib. bdg. 62.50x (0-89950-117-6) McFarland & Co.

— Forgotten Allies: The Military Contribution of the Colonies, Exiled Governments, & Lesser Powers to the Allied Victory in World War II, Vol. 1: The European Theater. LC 84-42608. 488p. 1985. lib. bdg. 32.00 (0-89950-129-X) McFarland & Co.

— Forgotten Allies: The Military Contribution of the Colonies, Exiled Governments, & Lesser Powers to the Allied Victory in World War II, Vol. 2: The Asian Theater. LC 84-42608. 229p. 1985. lib. bdg. 23.00 (0-89950-130-3) McFarland & Co.

— The Forgotten Axis: Germany's Partners & Foreign Volunteers in World War II. LC 87-42519. 575p. 1987. lib. bdg. 55.00x (0-89950-275-X) McFarland & Co.

Ready, John F. Effects of High-Power Laser Radiation. 1971. text ed. 136.00 (0-12-583950-2) Acad Pr.

Ready, John F., ed. Lasers in Modern Industry. LC 79-66705. (Illus.). 276p. reprint ed. pap. 78.70 (0-8357-6489-3, 2035860) Bks Demand.

Ready, Kathryn J., jt. ed. see Bognanno, Mario F.

Ready, Keith F., jt. auth. see Burke, Louise L.

Ready, Kevin E. Credit Sense: How to Borrow Money & Manage Debt. 250p. 1989. pap. 12.60 (0-8306-3025-2, 30025, Liberty Hse) TAB Bks.

Ready, Mark, tr. see Johnson, Thomas M.

Ready, Mark, tr. see Johnson, Thomas M., et al.

Ready, Mark, tr. see Johnson, Thomas M.

Ready, Milton. Asheville: Land of the Sky. LC 86-23368. (Illus.). 136p. 1986. 22.95 (0-89781-168-2) Preferred Mktg.

Ready, Milton, jt. ed. see Coleman, Kenneth.

Ready, Milton L. The Castle Builders: Georgia's Economy Under the Trustees, 1732-1754. LC 77-14750. (Dissertations in American Economic History Ser.). 1978. 37.95 (0-405-11053-7) Ayer.

Ready, N. P. Ship Registration. 1991. 100.00 (1-85044-326-2) Lloyds London Pr.

Ready, Robert. Hazlitt at Table. LC 79-22811. 126p. 1981. 24.50 (0-8386-2414-6) Fairleigh Dickinson.

Ready-Smith, John. Living in Spain. 5th ed. (Illus.). 223p. 1990. 33.50 (0-7090-4100-4) Trans-Atl Phila.

Ready, Timothy. Latino Immigrant Youth: Passages from Adolescence to Adulthood. LC 91-19038. (Studies in Education & Culture: Vol. 5). 282p. 1991. 38.00 (0-8153-0057-3, SS728) Garland.

Ready, William B. Files on Parade: A Memoir. LC 81-23310. (Illus.). 274p. 1982. 25.00 (0-8108-1516-8) Scarecrow.

Reagan. Ronald Regan Talks to America. 1985. 12.95 (0-8159-6719-5) Devin.

Reagan & Smith. Metal Spinning Projects. (Illus.). 80p. 1991. reprint ed. 20.00 (1-877767-56-5); reprint ed. pap. 10.00 (1-877767-55-7) Univ Publng Hse.

Reagan, jt. auth. see Fu.

Reagan, Alice E. H. I. Kimball, Entrepreneur. LC 82-73598. (Illus.). 184p. 1983. 9.95 (0-87797-064-5) Cherokee.

Reagan, Charles E., jt. ed. see Richter, William L.

Reagan, Christopher J. & Seneca, Lucius A. Seneca, Lucius Annaeus: A Concordance to the Epigrams Attributed to Seneca the Younger. (Alpha-Omega, Reihe A Ser.: No. XXVII). vi, 118p. 1972. 25.87 (3-487-04493-5, Pub. by Georg Olms GW) Lubrecht & Cramer.

***Reagan, Danial.** Where's Bill? Missing in Action. 24p. 1994. pap. 10.95 (1-886504-00-8) Funny Bone FL.

Reagan, Daniel, ed. see Melville, Herman.

Reagan, David. Jesus Is Coming Again! 1993. pap. 5.99 (0-89081-989-0) Harvest Hse.

— The Master Plan. 1993. pap. 7.99 (1-56507-074-7) Harvest Hse.

***Reagan, David R.** Trusting God: Learning to Walk by Faith. 2nd rev. ed. LC 94-79447. 264p. (Orig.). 1994. pap. 8.95 (0-945593-03-1) Lamb Lion Minstrs.

Reagan, David R., jt. auth. see Hedger, Leslie K.

***Reagan, Dian C.** Home for the Howl-idays. (J). (gr. 4-7). 1994. pap. 2.95 (0-590-48772-8) Scholastic Inc.

Reagan, J. E., ed. see Petroleum Mechanical Engineering Workshop & Conference Staff.

Reagan, James & Smith, Earl. Metal Spinning: Metal Spinning for Craftsman, Instructors & Students. 80p. reprint ed. pap. 8.95 (0-917914-83-X) Lindsay Pubns.

Reagan, Jim. Castle King-Four. LC 89-38938. 336p. (Orig.). 1990. pap. 10.95 (0-931832-37-3) Fithian Pr.

— The Scene: And Other Stories. 176p. 1994. pap. 9.95 (1-56474-103-6) Fithian Pr.

Reagan, John H. Memoirs, with Special Reference to Secession & the Civil War. McCaleb, Walter F., ed. LC 79-174304. reprint ed. 29.50 (0-404-04620-7) AMS Pr.

Reagan, Julie C. Scarf Tying Made Easy: It's the Easy Way to Look Good! (Illus.). 210p. (Orig.). (C). 1988. pap. 14.95 (0-317-93908-4) J Claire Inc.

Reagan, Maureen & Herrmann, Dorothy. First Father, First Daughter: A Memoir. (Illus.). 288p. 1989. 19.95 (0-316-73631-7) Little.

Reagan, Michael & Hyams, Joe. On the Outside Looking In. 1988. 17.95 (0-8217-2392-8); mass mkt. 4.95 (0-8217-2839-3) Zebra.

***Reagan, Michael & Phillips, Bob.** The All-American Quote Book. LC 94-48344. (Orig.). 1995. pap. 8.99 (1-56507-346-0) Harvest Hse.

Reagan, Michael D. Curing the Crisis: Options for America's Health Care. LC 92-15706. 196p. (C). 1992. pap. text ed. 17.95 (0-8133-8180-0) Westview.

— The Managed Economy. LC 81-13262. ix, 288p. 1982. reprint ed. text ed. 59.75 (0-313-23154-0, REME, Greenwood Pr) Greenwood.

— Regulation: The Politics of Policy. (C). 1987. pap. text ed. 17.75 (0-673-39471-9) HarpCollege.

Reagan, Nancy. My Turn. large type ed. LC 90-41187. 650p. 1990. reprint ed. lib. bdg. 22.95 (1-56054-056-7) Thorndike Pr.

— To Love a Child. 1982. 14.95 (0-02-601180-8) Macmillan.

Reagan, Nancy & Novak, William. My Turn: The Memoirs of Nancy Reagan. (Illus.). 1989. 21.95 (0-394-56368-9) Random.

Reagan, Patrick D. & Wortman, Roy T. For the General Welfare: Essays in Honor of Robert H. Bremner. (American University Studies: History: Ser. IX, Vol. 48). 402p. (C). 1989. text ed. 48.00 (0-8204-0796-8) P Lang Pubs.

Reagan, Patrick D., jt. ed. see Brown, Jerold E.

Reagan, Priscilla, ed. see James, Robert.

Reagan, Robin, ed. see Knapp, Robert H.

Reagan, Ron. Siamese Cats. 1988. 9.95 (0-87666-860-0, KW062) TFH Pubns.

Reagan, Ronald. The Public Speeches of Ronald Reagan. Kiewe, Amos & Houch, Davis W., eds. LC 92-35918. 372p. 1993. text ed. 59.95 (0-313-28491-1, HAI/) Greenwood.

— Reagan on Cuba: Selected Statements by the President. 1986. 4.00 (0-317-90497-3) Cuban Amer Natl Fndtn.

— Ronald Reagan Talks to America. 2nd rev. ed. LC 68-26085. 226p. 1982. 12.95 (0-8159-5222-8) Devin.

Reagan, Sally, et al, eds. Writing With: New Directions in Collaborative Teaching, Learning, & Research. (Feminist Theory in Education Ser.). 311p. 1994. text ed. 65.50x (0-7914-1841-3); pap. text ed. 21.95x (0-7914-1842-1) State U NY Pr.

Reagan, Sally B., et al. Writing from A to Z: The Easy-to-Use Reference Handbook. LC 93-39639. 513p. (C). 1994. spiral bd. 21.95 (1-55934-025-8) Mayfield Pub.

***Reagan, Van.** That's It...It's Radical. LC 94-66569. (Illus.). 88p. (Orig.). 1994. pap. 7.00 (0-9641860-5-5) Reagan Pr.

Reagan, Wesley C., ed. see Durham, Ron, et al.

Reagan, Wesley C., ed. see Rondurham, et al.

Reagar, Daniel, ed. see Melville, Herman.

Reage, jt. auth. see Crepax.

***Reage, Pauline.** Return to the Chateau. 1995. pap. 10.00 (0-345-39465-8) Ballantine.

— Story of O. 1981. mass mkt. 4.95 (0-345-30111-0) Ballantine.

— Story of O. (Orig.). 1994. pap. 9.95 (1-56201-082-4, North Star Line) Blue Moon Bks.

Reagen, Michael V. & Chertow, Doris S., eds. The Challenge of Modern Church-Public Relations. LC 72-5637. (Occasional Papers: No. 33). 68p. (Orig.). 1972. pap. 3.00 (0-87060-056-7, OCP 33) Syracuse U Cont Ed.

Reagh, Kevin P., jt. auth. see Lockhart, Shawna D.

***Reagin, Nancy R.** Lucrative Differences: Gender, Class & the Work of the Women's Movement in Hanover, 1880-1933. LC 94-39348. 1995. write for info. (0-8078-2210-8); pap. write for info. (0-8078-4525-6) U of NC Pr.

Reagle, Merl. Merl Reagle's Sunday Crosswords, Vol. 1. Rosen, David, ed. (Illus.). 56p. (Orig.). 1995. pap. 7.95 (0-9630828-0-9) PuzzleWorks.

— Merl Reagle's Sunday Crosswords, Vol. 2. 56p. (Orig.). 1995. pap. 7.95 (0-9630828-1-7) PuzzleWorks.

— Merl Reagle's Sunday Crosswords, Vol. 3. 56p. (Orig.). 1995. pap. 7.95 (0-9630828-2-5) PuzzleWorks.

Reagon, Bernice J., ed. Black American Culture & Scholarship: Contemporary Issues. (Illus.). 184p. (Orig.). (C). 1985. pap. text ed. 3.00 (0-929847-00-8) Natl Mus Am.

— We'll Understand It Better By & By: Pioneering African American Gospel Composers. LC 91-37954. (Illus.). 432p. 1993. 49.95 (1-56098-166-0); pap. 19.95 (1-56098-167-9) Smithsonian.

Reagon, Bernice J. & Sweet Honey in the Rock. We Who Believe in Freedom: Sweet Honey in the Rock - Still on the Journey. LC 93-20308. 1993. pap. 16.95 (0-385-46862-8, Anchor NY) Doubleday.

Reak, Jack. Kanuga - Story of a Gathering Place. Gooch, Albert S., Jr. et al, eds. LC 93-80360. (Illus.). 192p. 1993. 16.95 (0-9639021-0-5) Kanuga Confer.

Real Academia Espanola Staff, ed. Diccionario Manual e Ilustrado de la Lengua Espanola. 4th ed. (Illus.). 1666p. (SPA.). 1989. 275.00x (84-239-5978-3) Elliots Bks.

Real Academia de Ciencias. Scientific & Technical Vocabulary: Vocabulario Cientifico y Tecnico. 503p. (SPA.). 1983. 175.00 (0-8288-2145-3, S60131) Fr & Eur.

Real Academia de Ciencias Morales y Politicas Staff. Acerca de "Centesimus Annus" (Nueva Austral Ser.: Vol. 245). (SPA.). 1991. pap. text ed. 24.95x (84-239-7245-3) Elliots Bks.

Real Academia de la Lengua Espanol Staff. Diccionario de la Lengua Espanol, 2 vols., Set. 19th ed. 1456p. (SPA.). 1986. 295.00 (0-8288-4402-X, S12257) Fr & Eur.

— Diccionario Manuel e Ilustrado de la Lengua Espanol, 5 vols., Set. 4th ed. 1666p. (SPA.). 1989. 195.00 (0-8288-2736-2, S38002) Fr & Eur.

— Esbozo de una Neuva Gramatica de la Lengua Espanola. 13th ed. 1991. pap. 59.95 (0-7859-5215-2) Fr & Eur.

Real Academia Espano. Diccionario Manual. 4th ed. 1668p. 1989. 195.00 (0-7859-5752-9) Fr & Eur.

Real Academia Espano Staff. Diccionario Manual e Ilustrado de la Lengua Espanola, 1. 1983. 45.00 (0-7859-5754-5) Fr & Eur.

— Diccionario Manual e Ilustrado de la Lengua Espanola, 2. 1983. 45.00 (0-7859-5755-3) Fr & Eur.

— Diccionario Manual e Ilustrado de la Lengua Espanola, 3. 1983. 45.00 (0-7859-5756-1) Fr & Eur.

— Diccionario Manual e Ilustrado de la Lengua Espanola, 5. 1983. 45.00 (0-7859-5758-8) Fr & Eur.

— Diccionario Manual e Ilustrado de la Lengua Espanola, 6. 1983. 45.00 (0-7859-5759-6) Fr & Eur.

Real Academia Espanola Staff. Diccionario de la Lengua Espanola, 2 Vols. 20th ed. (SPA.). 1984. 220.00 (84-239-4774-2) Colton Bk.

— Diccionario de la Real Academia Expanola. 2nd ed. 980p. 1991. 275.00 (0-7859-6048-1, 8460076059) Fr & Eur.

— Diccionario Historico de la Lengua Espanola: Fascicles 1-10, Bound Together. (SPA.). 1991. 650.00 (84-600-3782-7) Elliots Bks.

— Diccionario Historico de la Lengua Espanola (Faciculos) 156p. 1984. pap. 29.95 (0-7859-6046-5, 8460037835) Fr & Eur.

— Esbozo de una Nueva Gramatica de la Lengua Espanola. 592p. (SPA.). 1991. pap. 57.50x (84-239-4759-9) Elliots Bks.

Real Academia Espanola Staff, ed. Diccionario de la Lengua Espanola. 21th ed. 1548p. (SPA.). 1992. 289.50x (84-239-4399-2) Elliots Bks.

— Diccionario de la Lengua Espanola, 2 vols., Set. 21th ed. 2192p. (SPA.). 1994. pap. text ed. 89.50x (84-239-9200-4) Elliots Bks.

— Esbozo de una Nueva Gramatica de la Lengua Espanola. 592p. (SPA.). 1991. 89.50x (84-239-4762-9) Elliots Bks.

— Fuero Juzgo. 131p. (SPA.). 1968. pap. 250.00 (0-614-00126-9) Elliots Bks.

Real Academia Espanola Staff, ed. see Alarcos Llorach, Emilio.

Real Academia Galega Staff. Diccionario da Lingua Galega. 840p. 1990. 69.95 (0-7859-6047-3, 8460075095) Fr & Eur.

Real, Antony. The Story of the Stick: Folklore & Anthropology. 1977. lib. bdg. 250.00 (0-8490-2691-1) Gordon Pr.

Real Estate Record Association Staff. History of Real Estate, Building & Architecture in New York City. LC 67-23061. (Illus.). 1967. reprint ed. 46.95 (0-405-00054-5) Ayer.

Real Estate Research Corporation Staff. Air Rights & Highways. LC 78-97085. (Urban Land Institute, Technical Bulletin Ser.: No. 64). (Illus.). 84p. reprint ed. pap. 25.00 (0-8357-8014-7, 2033953) Bks Demand.

Real Estate Section Council Staff. Commercial Real Estate Transactions Practice Manual & Forms Diskette. 590p. 1989. ring bd. 90.00 (0-88726-010-1); disk 25.00 (0-88726-011-X) AZ St Bar.

Real Estate Timesharing & the Property Tax Staff. Real Estate Timesharing & the Property Tax. Bloch, Stuart M., ed. (Lincoln Institute Monograph Ser.: No. 85-4). 115p. reprint ed. pap. 32.80 (0-7837-2159-5, 2042462) Bks Demand.

Real Estate Valuation Colloquium Staff. Real Estate Valuation Colloquium, 1984: A Redefinition of Real Estate Appraisal Precepts & Processes. Kinnard, William N., Jr., ed. LC 86-1388. (Lincoln Institute of Land Policy Book Ser.). 415p. reprint ed. pap. 118.30 (0-7837-3268-6, 2043287) Bks Demand.

Real Goods Staff & Schaeffer, John. Alternative Energy Sourcebook 1990: The Complete Guide to Renewable Energy Technologies & Sustainable Living. 8th ed. (Real Goods Independent Living Bks.). (Illus.). 672p. (Orig.). 1994. pap. 23.00 (0-930031-68-7) Real Goods Pub.

Real, H. G., jt. auth. see Fox, R. M.

Real, Herrmann J. Jonathan Swift, the Battle of the Books. (Quellen und Forschungen zur Sprach und Kulturgeschichte der Germanischen Voelker Ser.: Vol. 71). (C). 1978. 107.10 (3-11-006985-7) De Gruyter.

Real, Katarina, comment. A Cultural Mosaic, the Folk Arts of Brazil. (Illus.). 56p. 1978. 10.00 (0-317-68012-9) Mingei Intl Mus.

Real, Lavergne, jt. ed. see Momar-Coumba, Diop.

Real, Leslie & Brown, James H., eds. Foundations of Ecology: Classic Papers with Commentaries. 1000p. 1991. pap. text ed. 29.50 (0-226-70594-3) U Ch Pr.

Real, Leslie A., ed. Behavioral Mechanisms in Evolutionary Biology. LC 94-14131. 1994. lib. bdg. 80.00 (0-226-70595-1); pap. text ed. 29.95 (0-226-70597-8) U Ch Pr.

— Ecological Genetics. LC 93-4762. (Illus.). 272p. 1994. text ed. 49.50 (0-691-03241-6); pap. text ed. 24.95 (0-691-00066-2) Princeton U Pr.

Real, Michael. Super Media: A Cultural Studies Approach. (Communication & Human Values Ser.). (Illus.). 282p. (C). 1989. text ed. 49.95 (0-8039-3313-4); pap. text ed. 24.00 (0-8039-3314-2) Sage.

Real Property Law Institute & Institute of Continuing Legal Education, Georgia. Program Materials for Real Property Law Institute: May 8-10, 1986, St. Simons, May 22-23, 1986, Atlanta. LC 86-623182. 1986. 23.00 (0-685-18536-2) ICLE Georgia.

Real Ramos, Cesar, ed. see Melendez Valdes, Juan.

Real, Rory. A Baseball Dream. (Sports Mites Ser.). (Illus.). 32p. (J). (ps-3). 1990. pap. 3.95 (0-8120-4395-2) Barron.

— The Fishing Derby. (Sports Mites Ser.). (Illus.). 32p. (J). (ps-3). 1990. pap. 3.95 (0-8120-4394-4) Barron.

Real, Willy, ed. see Herzfeld, Hans.

Reale, A., jt. ed. see Lichtlen, P. R.

Reale, D. L., ed. see Thomas-Trautman.

Reale, Giovanni. The Concept of First Philosophy & the Unity of the Metaphysics of Aristotle. Catan, John R., ed. & tr. by. LC 79-13867. 513p. 1980. 59.50 (0-87395-385-1); pap. 29.95 (0-87395-443-2) State U NY Pr.

— A History of Ancient Philosophy II: Plato & Aristotle. Catan, John R., ed. & tr. by. LC 84-16310. (SUNY Series in Philosophy). 437p. 1990. 74.50 (0-7914-0516-8); pap. 24.95 (0-7914-0517-6) State U NY Pr.

— A History of Ancient Philosophy III: Systems of the Hellenistic Age. Catan, John R., ed. & tr. by. LC 79-13867. (SUNY Series in Philosophy). 499p. (C). 1985. 64.50 (0-88706-027-7); pap. 21.95 (0-88706-008-0) State U NY Pr.

— A History of Ancient Philosophy IV: The Schools of the Imperial Age. Catan, John R., ed. & tr. by. LC 84-16310. (SUNY Series in Philosophy). 548p. 1990. 64.50 (0-7914-0128-6); pap. 21.95 (0-7914-0129-4) State U NY Pr.

— History of Ancient Philosophy, Vol. 1: From the Origins to Socrates. Catan, John R., ed. & tr. by. LC 84-14559. (SUNY Series in Philosophy). 425p. (C). 1987. 64.50 (0-88706-292-X); pap. 21.95 (0-88706-290-3) State U NY Pr.

Reale, Paul J. South Shore Stories, Vol. 3. 62p. Date not set. write for info. (0-9637415-3-5) Peejay Pub.

— South Shore Stories, Vol. 1. rev. ed. (Illus.). 60p. 1992. write for info. (0-9637415-1-9) Peejay Pub.

— South Shore Stories, Vol. 2. 62p. 1994. write for info. (0-9637415-2-7) Peejay Pub.

Reale, Robert, jt. auth. see Reale, Willie.

Reale, Willie. Many Happy Returns & Fast Women: Two One Act Plays, Acting Edition. 1983. pap. 2.75 (0-8222-0729-X) Dramatists Play.

***Reale, Willie, ed.** The Bedtime Zone. 1995. 20.00 (0-8222-1443-1) Dramatists Play.

— The Butler Did It! 1995. pap. 30.00 (0-8222-1442-3) Dramatists Play.

— The 52nd Street Project Kid Theater Kit: Plays, Projects & Programs for Young People. 1995. 195.00 (0-8222-1440-7) Dramatists Play.

— Plays for Pairs. 1995. 15.00 (0-8222-1444-X) Dramatists Play.

— The Spring Thing. 1995. 15.00 (0-8222-1445-8) Dramatists Play.

***Reale, Willie & Reale, Robert.** The Dinosaur Musical. 1995. 25.00 (0-8222-1446-6) Dramatists Play.

— Quark Victory. 1995. 25.00 (0-8222-1447-4) Dramatists Play.

***Reale, Willie, et al, eds.** 52 Pick-Up: A Practical Guide to Doing Theatre with Children. 1995. 35.00 (0-8222-1441-5) Dramatists Play.

***Realmuto, George.** Psychological Problems of Priests & Seminarians. 1995. pap. 10.95 (0-533-11233-8) Vantage.

Reals, Willis H. A Study of the Summer High School. LC 79-177180. (Columbia University. Teachers College. Contributions to Education Ser.: No. 337). reprint ed. 37.50 (0-404-55337-0) AMS Pr.

Ream, Lanny. Idaho Minerals. (Illus.). 329p. 1993. 34.95 (0-928693-03-1); pap. 14.95 (0-928693-02-3) L R Ream.

Ream, Lanny R. A Family's Guide to Discovering North Idaho, Vol. I. (Illus.). 51p. (Orig.). 1992. pap. 6.95 (0-928693-04-X) L R Ream.

— The Gem, Mineral & Fossil Collector's Guide to Montana, Vol. 1. (Illus.). 40p. (Orig.). 1992. pap. 4.95 (0-928693-06-6) L R Ream.

— Gems & Minerals of Washington. rev. ed. (Illus.). 216p. 1984. pap. 7.95 (0-918499-00-3) Jackson Mtn.

Ream, Lenny R. Northwest Volcanoes: A Roadside Geologic Guide. (Illus.). 123p. (Orig.). 1983. pap. 6.95 (0-918499-05-4) Jackson Mtn.

Ream, S. L., ed. Focus on Laser Materials Processing. (Illus.). 280p. 1988. 153.00 (0-387-19005-8) Spr-Verlag.

Reaman, G. Elmore. The Trail of the Huguenots: In Europe, the United States, South Africa, & Canada. (Illus.). 318p. 1993. reprint ed. 25.00 (0-8063-0290-9, 4810) Genealog Pub.

Reamer, Frederic G. AIDs & Ethics. 1993. pap. 15.00 (0-231-07359-3) Col U Pr.

— Ethical Dilemmas in Social Service. 2nd ed. 288p. 1989. text ed. 26.00 (0-231-06968-5) Col U Pr.

— Ethical Dilemmas in Social Service: A Guide for Social Workers. 2nd ed. 266p. 1993. pap. 22.00 (0-231-06969-3) Col U Pr.

— The Philosophical Foundations of Social Work. 288p. 1993. text ed. 46.00 (0-231-07126-4) Col U Pr.

— Social Work Malpractice & Liability: Strategies for Prevention. LC 94-7628. 1994. pap. 22.50 (0-231-08263-0) Col U Pr.

— Social Work Values & Ethics. LC 94-38229. 1995. write for info. (0-231-09990-8) Col U Pr.

Reamer, Frederic G., ed. AIDS & Ethics. 384p. 1991. text ed. 29.50 (0-231-07358-5) Col U Pr.

— The Foundations of Social Work Knowledge. LC 94-7273. (Illus.). 496p. 1994. 37.50 (0-231-08034-4) Col U Pr.

Reamer, Frederic G., jt. auth. see Shireman, Charles H.

***Reamer, Frederick G.** Social Work Values & Ethics. LC 94-38229. 1995. pap. write for info. (0-231-09991-6) Col U Pr.

Reamer, Judy. Feelings Women Rarely Share. Arthur, Donna, ed. 208p. (Orig.). 1987. pap. text ed. 2.99 (0-88368-186-2) Whitaker Hse.

Reames, Cheryl. Parenting. (Lifesearch Ser.). 64p. (Orig.). 1994. pap. 4.95 (0-687-77868-9) Abingdon.

Reames, Nancy. Scrap Basket Crafts: Over Fifty Quick & Easy Projects to Make from Fabric Scraps. (Illus.). 288p. 1994. 27.95 (0-87596-620-9) Rodale Pr Inc.

Reames, Sherry L. The Legenda Aurea: A Reexamination of Its Paradoxical History. LC 84-40502. (Illus.). 336p. 1985. 40.00 (0-299-10150-9) U of Wis Pr.

Reams, Bernard, ed. see Keasbey, E. Quinton.

Reams, Bernard D. American International Law Cases, Second Series, 27 vols., Set. LC 86-33167. 1986. 1,540.00 (0-685-73851-5) Oceana.

Reams, Bernard D., Jr. Insider Trading & Securities Fraud Enforcement: A Legislative History of the Insider Trading & Securities Fraud Enforcement Act of 1988, Pub. Law No. 100-704, 6 vol. LC 89-85648. (Federal Legislative Histories of Economics, Monetary Policy & Stock Market Ser.: Pt. 4). 7000p. 1989. 450.00 (0-89941-716-7, 306100) W S Hein.

Reams, Bernard D. Insider Trading & the Law: A Legislative History of the Insider Trading Sanctions Act of 1984, Pub. Law No. 98-376: Federal Legislative Histories of Laws & Legislation on Economics, Monetary Policy & Stock Market Regulation, Pt. 2. LC 89-7532. viii, 590p. 1989. lib. bdg. 82.00 (*0-89941-688-8*, 305860) W S Hein.

Reams, Bernard D., Jr. Medical Waste Tracking Act of Nineteen Eighty-Eight, 5 vols. LC 93-78606. 4068p. 1993. 375.00 (*0-89941-848-1*, 307940) W S Hein.

— Reader in Law Librarianship. LC 87-82949. xv, 375p. 1987. reprint ed. lib. bdg. 45.00 (*0-89941-589-X*, 305430) W S Hein.

— The Stock Market Crash of October 1987: Federal Documents & Materials on the Stock Market & Stock Index Futures Markets, 2 vols. LC 88-81970. 2100p. 1988. lib. bdg. 180.00 (*0-89941-656-X*, 305650) W S Hein.

— Technology Transfer Law: The Export Administration Acts of the United States, 1969-1985 Federal Laws, Legislative Histories, &..., 15 vols. in 33 bks., Set. 1986. reprint ed. 1,750.00 (*0-89941-437-0*, 303790) W S Hein.

— United States & International Aviation Law Reports, 1991, 4 vols. LC 93-78620. 1960p. 1993. 295.00 (*0-89941-846-5*, 307820) W S Hein.

— University-Industry Research Partnerships: The Major Legal Issues in Research & Development Agreements. LC 85-9589. (Illus.). 365p. 1986. text ed. 69.50 (*0-89930-121-5*, RUI/, Quorum Bks) Greenwood.

Reams, Bernard D., Jr., comp. Federal Price & Wage Control Programs, 1917-1979: Legislative Histories, Laws & Administrative Documents, 77 vols, 50 bks., Set. LC 79-93088. 1980. lib. bdg. 2,495.00 (*0-89941-052-9*, 301260) W S Hein.

— Individuals with Disabilities Education Act: A Legislative History of Public Law 101-476 As Amended by Public Law 102-119, 5 vols. LC 93-29859. (Federal Legislative Histories of the Law of Disabled Persons Ser.). 4394p. 1994. 450.00 (*0-89941-849-X*, 307930) W S Hein.

Reams, Bernard D., Jr., ed. American International Law Cases: Sources & Documents, 1979-1989, 7 vols. LC 91-50825. (Second Series, 1979-1989). 1991. Set. lib. bdg. 420.00 (*0-379-21059-2*) Oceana.

— American International Law Cases, 3rd Series, 24 vols. 3rd ed. 1993. lib. bdg. 1,560.00 (*0-379-21250-1*) Oceana.

— Congress & the Courts: A Legislative History, 1985-1992, the 99th Through the 102d Congresses, Set. LC 94-4821. 1994. 1,850.00 (*0-89941-868-6*, 308110) W S Hein.

— Education of the Handicapped: Laws, Legislative Histories & Administrative Documents, 55 vols., Set. LC 82-81360. (Federal Legislative Histories of the Law of Disabled Persons Ser.). 1982. lib. bdg. 2,640.00 (*0-89941-157-6*, 302020) W S Hein.

— Federal Laws of the Mentally Handicapped: Laws, Legislative Histories, & Administrative Documents,, 42 vols., Set. LC 81-83898. (Legislative Histories of the Law of Disabled persons Ser.: Pt. 1). 1981. 1,950.00 (*0-89941-106-1*, 302010) W S Hein.

Reams, Bernard D., ed. Federal Legislative Histories: An Annotated Bibliography & Index to Officially Published Sources. LC 93-38809. (Bibliographies & Indexes in Law & Political Science Ser.: No. 21). 624p. 1994. text ed. 105.00 (*0-313-23092-7*, Greenwood Pr) Greenwood.

Reams, Bernard D., Jr., ed. General & Plastic Surgery Devices Panel Breast Implants Transcript of the FDA Panel Meeting on November 12, 13 & 14, 1991. LC 92-49827. 1294p. 1993. reprint ed. 125.00 (*0-89941-806-6*, 307590) W S Hein.

— General & Plastic Surgery Devices Panel Transcript of the FDA Meeting on Silicone Gel-Filled Breast Implants on February 18, 19 & 20, 1992. LC 92-49830. 1390p. 1993. reprint ed. 125.00 (*0-89941-805-8*, 307600) W S Hein.

— Health Care Quality Improvement Act of 1986: A Legislative History of Pub. Law No. 99-660. LC 89-83918. (Federal Health Law Ser.). 730p. 1990. lib. bdg. 65.00 (*0-89941-693-4*, 306000) W S Hein.

— Historical Reprints in Jurisprudence & Classical Legal Literature, 20 bks., Set. 1984. reprint ed. lib. bdg. write for info. (*0-89941-248-3*, 303270) W S Hein.

— Internal Revenue Acts of the United States: 1909-1950 Legislative Histories & Administrative Documents, 144 vols. in 146 bks., Set. LC 78-71405. 176000p. 1978. reprint ed. student ed, lib. bdg. 7,500.00 (*0-930342-69-0*, 301270) W S Hein.

— Internal Revenue Acts of the United States: 1950-1951 Legislative Histories, Laws & Administrative Documents, 7 vols. in 9, Set. LC 82-81278. 1986. fiche 298.00 (*0-89941-703-5*, 301971) W S Hein.

— Internal Revenue Code of 1954, 2 vols., Set. LC 92-39056. 2512p. 1993. 195.00 (*0-89941-830-9*, 307580) W S Hein.

— The Law of Hospital & Health Care Administration: Cases & Materials. LC 93-14239. 201p. (Orig.). (C). 1993. pap. 36.00 (*0-910701-94-6*, 0929) Health Admin Pr.

— Medicare & Medicaid Patient & Program Protection Act of 1987: A Legislative History of Pub. Law No. 98-507, 3 vols., Set. LC 89-83920. (Federal Health Law Ser.). 1932p. 1990. lib. bdg. 175.00 (*0-89941-695-0*, 305960) W S Hein.

— Monopoly Problems in Regulated Industries: Hearings Before the House Committee on the Judiciary, 84th Congress, Serial No. 22, 8 vols., Set. LC 91-72318. (Illus.). 6656p. 1991. lib. bdg. 695.00 (*0-89941-765-5*, 307190) W S Hein.

— Monopoly Problems in Regulated Industries: Hearings Before the House Committee on the Judiciary, 84th Congress, Serial No. 22, 8 vols., Set. LC 91-72268. (Illus.). 8378p. 1991. reprint ed. lib. bdg. 645.00 (*0-89941-766-3*, 307180) W S Hein.

— Monopoly Problems in Regulated Industries: Hearings Before the 87th Congress, Serial No. 10, 2 vols., Set. LC 91-72670. (Illus.). 2004p. 1991. reprint ed. lib. bdg. 195.00 (*0-89941-764-7*, 307150) W S Hein.

— National Organ Transplant Act of 1984: A Legislative History of Pub. Law No. 98-507, 3 vols., Set. LC 89-83919. (Federal Health Law Ser.). 2466p. 1990. lib. bdg. 210.00 (*0-89941-691-8*, 305920) W S Hein.

— Peer Review Improvement Act of 1982: A Legislative History of Pub. Law No. 97-248. LC 89-83917. (Federal Health Law Ser.). 564p. 1990. lib. bdg. 55.00 (*0-89941-692-6*, 305930) W S Hein.

— Professional Standards Review Act: A Legislative History of Title Eleven of the Social Securities Amendments of 1972 Pub. Law No. 92-603, 2 vols., Set. LC 89-84259. (Federal Health Law Ser.). 1636p. 1990. lib. bdg. 145.00 (*0-89941-694-2*, 305950) W S Hein.

— Tax Reform, 1969: A Legislative History of the Tax Reform Act of 1969, 25 vols., Set. LC 91-71948. 27000p. 1991. lib. bdg. 2,250.00 (*0-89941-762-0*, 306130) W S Hein.

— Trade Agreements Program of the United States: Annual Reports to the President. LC 89-83415. 3074p. 1989. lib. bdg. 395.00 (*0-89941-711-6*, 306080) W S Hein.

Reams, Bernard D. & Couture, Faye L., eds. Revenue Reconciliation Act of 1990: Title XI Omnibus Budget Reconciliation Act of 1990, Public Law 101-508. LC 94-15648. 8748p. 1994. 760.00 (*0-89941-873-2*, 308180) W S Hein.

Reams, Bernard D., Jr. & Ferguson, J. Ray. Federal Consumer Protection: Laws, Rules & Regulations, 5 bdrs. LC 78-11285. 1978. ring bd. 695.00 (*0-379-10025-8*) Oceana.

Reams, Bernard D., Jr. & Gary, Carol J., eds. Government Securities Law: A Legislative History of the Government Securities Act of 1986, Pub Law No. 99-571, 10 vols. LC 89-84148. (Federal Legislative Histories of Laws & Legislation on Trade Law & Economic Policy Ser.). 9800p. 1989. lib. bdg. 595.00 (*0-89941-696-9*, 305970) W S Hein.

Reams, Bernard D., Jr. & Gray, Carol J. Human Experimentation: A Bibliography of Materials on Federal Policy & Related Issues. (Collection of Bibliographic & Research Resources). 126p. 1987. pap. text ed. 35.00 (*0-379-20913-6*) Oceana.

Reams, Bernard D., Jr. & House, Emelyn B., eds. Tax Reform, 1976: A Legislative History of the Tax Reform Act of 1976 (Public Law 94-455), 17 vols., Set. 1992. 1,525.00 (*0-89941-773-6*, 307020) W S Hein.

Reams, Bernard D., Jr. & McDermott, Margaret H. Deficit Control & the Gramm-Rudman-Hollings Act: History of the Balanced Budget & Emergency Deficit Control Act of 1985 (P.L. 99-177), 5 vols., Set. LC 86-80964. 1986. lib. bdg. 250.00 (*0-89941-484-2*, 304110) W S Hein.

— Tax Reform 1986: A Legislative History of the Tax Reform Act of 1986, 64 vols. 1987. lib. bdg. 3,985.00 (*0-89941-621-7*, 305450) W S Hein.

Reams, Bernard D., Jr. & McDermott, Margaret H., eds. Federal Deficit Control: The Legislative History of the Balanced Budget & Emergency Deficit Control Reaffirmation Act of 1987, 32 vols. in 33 bks., Set. 30000p. 1989. lib. bdg. 1,920.00 (*0-89941-672-1*, 305790) W S Hein.

Reams, Bernard D., Jr. & Nelson, Mary A. Trade Reform Legislation, 1988: A Legislative History of the Omnibus Trade & Competitiveness Act of 1988, 10 vols., Set. LC 91-75494. 1991. 985.00 (*0-89941-777-9*, 306760) W S Hein.

Reams, Bernard D., Jr. & Nelson, Mary A., eds. United States-Canada Free Trade Act: A Legislative History of the US-Canada Free Trade Agreement Implementation Act of 1988, Pub. L. 100-449, 13 vols. LC 89-81792. (Federal Legislative Histories of Laws & Legislation on Trade Law & Economic Policy Ser.). 12084p. 1990. lib. bdg. 910.00 (*0-89941-728-0*, 306450) W S Hein.

Reams, Bernard D., Jr. & Nelson, Mary Ann. Export Trading Company Act of 1982: Including the Foreign Trade Antitrust Improvement Act, 9 vols., Set. LC 88-83622. (Federal Legislative Histories of Laws & Legislation on Trade Law & Economic Policy Ser.: Pt. 1). 8900p. 1988. lib. bdg. 675.00 (*0-89941-666-7*, 305760) W S Hein.

Reams, Bernard D., Jr. & Wypyski, Eugene M. Bankruptcy Reform Amendments: A Legislative History of the Bankruptcy Amendments & Federal Judgeship Act of 1984, Public Law 98-353, 10 vols. LC 91-40244. 1992. 895.00 (*0-89941-783-3*, 307300) W S Hein.

Reams, Bernard D., Jr. & Yoak, Stuart D. The Constitution of the U. S. A Guide & Bibliography to Current Scholarly Research. 545p. 1987. 65.00 (*0-379-20858-X*) Oceana.

Reams, Bernard D., Jr., ed. see Ames, James B.

Reams, Bernard D., Jr., ed. see Ault, Warren O.

Reams, Bernard D., Jr., ed. see Choate, George F.

Reams, Bernard D., Jr., ed. see Coke, Edwardo.

Reams, Bernard D., Jr., ed. see Goffin, R. J.

Reams, Bernard D., Jr., ed. see Gray, John C.

Reams, Bernard D., Jr., ed. see Hoffman, David.

Reams, Bernard D., Jr., ed. see Holdsworth, William S.

Reams, Bernard D., Jr., ed. see Jameson, J. Franklin.

Reams, Bernard D., Jr., jt. auth. see Kutten, L. J.

Reams, Bernard D., Jr., jt. auth. see Livermore, Samuel.

Reams, Bernard D., Jr., ed. see Maine, Henry J.

Reams, Bernard D., Jr., ed. see McClelland, Ralph A.

Reams, Bernard D., ed. see Pike, Luke O.

Reams, Bernard D., Jr., ed. see Pomeroy, John N. & Mann, John C.

Reams, Bernard D., Jr., ed. see Reed, Alfred Z.

Reams, Bernard D., Jr., ed. see Reeve, Tapping.

Reams, Bernard D., Jr., ed. see Russell, Elmer B.

Reams, Bernard D., Jr., ed. see Street, Thomas A.

Reams, Bernard D., Jr., ed. see Sullivan, James.

Reams, Bernard D., Jr., jt. ed. see Swindler, William F.

Reams, Bernard D., Jr., ed. see Taylor, John N.

Reams, Bernard D., Jr., ed. see Thomas, J. H.

Reams, Bernard D., Jr., ed. see Wood, Horace G.

Reams, Bernard D., Jr., jt. ed. see Wypyski, Eugene M.

Reams, Bernard D., et al. Disability Law in the United States: A Legislative History of the Americans with Disabilities Act of 1990, Public Law 101-336, 6 vols. LC 92-28987. (Federal Disabilities Laws Ser.). 3470p. 1992. 550.00 (*0-89941-797-3*, 307400) W S Hein.

Reams, Bernard D., Jr., et al, eds. Internal Revenue Acts, 1909-1950 Guide & Analytical Index. LC 79-2486. xii, 400p. 1979. lib. bdg. 200.00 (*0-930342-94-1*, 301280) W S Hein.

Reams, Bernard J., Jr., jt. ed. see Helmholz, R. H.

Reamy. Travelability. 1978. 13.95 (*0-02-601170-0*) Macmillan.

Reamy, Martha, ed. see Brown, George S.

Reamy, Tom. Blind Voices. LC 78-3817. 254p. 1978. 25.00 (*0-399-12240-0*) Ultramarine Pub.

— San Diego Lightfoot Sue & Other Stories. LC 79-54396. (Illus.). 1979. 16.95 (*0-935128-00-X*) Ursus Imprints.

Reamy, William, ed. see Brown, George S.

Reaney. Colours in the Dark. (NFS Canada Ser.). 1993. pap. 11.95 (*0-88922-001-8*, Pub. by Talonbooks CN) InBook.

Reaney, P. H. The Origin of English Surnames. 1980. pap. 12.95 (*0-7100-0353-6*, RKP) Routledge.

***Reaney, P. H. & Wilson, R. M.** A Dictionary of English Surnames. 3rd ed. 584p. 1995. pap. 15.95 (*0-19-863146-4*) OUP.

— A Dictionary of English Surnames. 3rd ed. 640p. 1991. 75.00 (*0-685-49859-X*, A5791) Routledge.

Reanney, D. C., jt. ed. see Chambon, Pierre.

***Reanney, Darryl.** Living Forever: A New Future for Human Consciousness. LC 95-13186. 1995. write for info. (*0-688-14420-9*) Morrow.

— Music of the Mind: An Adventure into Consciousness. 200p. 1994. 14.95 (*0-85572-240-1*, Pub. by Hill Content Pubng AT) Seven Hills Bk.

Reanult, Michael, ed. see Rolliet, D. G.

Reap, Charles A., Jr. Complete Handbook for Dental Auxiliaries. (Illus.). 150p. (C). 1981. pap. text ed. 34.00 (*0-931386-44-6*) Quint Pub Co.

Reapsome, James. Exodus: Learning to Trust God. LC 89-15299. (LifeGuide Bible Studies). 110p. (Orig.). 1989. pap. 4.99 (*0-8308-1023-4*, 1023) InterVarsity.

— Growing Through Life's Challenges. (Fisherman Bible Studyguide Ser.). 1995. pap. 4.99 (*0-87788-381-5*) Shaw Pubs.

— Hebrews: Race to Glory. (LifeGuide Bible Studies). 64p. (Orig.). 1991. pap. 4.99 (*0-8308-1017-X*, 1017) InterVarsity.

— Romans: The Christian Story. (Fisherman Bible Studyguide Ser.). 96p. 1989. 4.99 (*0-87788-734-9*) Shaw Pubs.

***Reapsome, James & Reapsome, Martha.** Discipleship: The Growing Christian's Lifestyle. Ting, Yi-Hsin, tr. 57p. (CHI.). 1990. pap. 3.50 (*1-56582-009-6*) Christ Renew Min.

— Effective Prayer. (Discipleship Ser.). 48p. 1992. pap. 4.99 (*0-310-54731-8*) Zondervan.

— Marriage: God's Design for Intimacy. (LifeGuide Bible Studies). 64p. (Orig.). 1986. pap. 4.99 (*0-8308-1056-0*, 1056) InterVarsity.

— Spiritual Warfare. (Discipleship Ser.). 48p. 1992. pap. 4.99 (*0-310-54771-7*) Zondervan.

Reapsome, James W., jt. auth. see Barrett, David B.

Reapsome, Jim & Reapsome, Martha. Senior Saints: Growing Older in God's Family. (Fisherman Bible Studyguide Ser.). 80p. (Orig.). 1993. 4.99 (*0-87788-746-2*) Shaw Pubs.

Reapsome, Martha. Colossians & Philemon: Finding Fulfillment in Christ. LC 89-15298. (LifeGuide Bible Studies). 63p. (Orig.). 1989. pap. 4.99 (*0-8308-1014-5*, 1014) InterVarsity.

— The Journey of a Lifetime: Discovering the Joy of Walking with God. LC 92-44923. 1994. 8.99 (*0-87788-416-1*) Shaw Pubs.

Reapsome, Martha, jt. auth. see Jim.

Reapsome, Martha, jt. auth. see Reapsome, James.

Reapsome, Martha, jt. auth. see Reapsome, Jim.

Rearden, Jim. Alaska's Salmon Fisheries. (Alaska Geographic Ser.: Vol. 10, No. 3). (Illus.). 128p. 1983. pap. 15.95 (*0-88240-174-2*) Alaska Geog Soc.

— Castner's Cutthroats: Saga of the Alaska Scouts. (Illus.). 380p. 1990. 28.95 (*0-935632-93-X*) Wolfe Pub Co.

— Tales of Alaska's Big Bears. 238p. (Orig.). 1989. pap. 12.95 (*0-935632-83-2*) Wolfe Pub Co.

— Wind on the Water. 280p. 1990. pap. 19.95 (*0-937708-19-4*) Great Northwest.

Rearden, Jim, jt. auth. see Conkle, Bud.

***Rearden, Myles.** You Are Mine: A View of the Spiritual Life. 142p. (Orig.). 1994. pap. 14.95 (*1-85607-105-7*, Pub. by Columba Pr IE) Twenty-Third.

Rearden, Steven L., jt. auth. see Thompson, Kenneth W.

Rearden, Steven L., jt. ed. see Thompson, Kenneth W.

Rearden, Steven L., jt. auth. see Williamson, Samuel R., Jr.

Reardon. Big Time Tommy Sloane. 1988. pap. 3.95 (*0-317-67578-8*) St Martin.

Reardon, A. A Study of Humor in Greek Tragedy. 1972. 59.95 (*0-8490-1153-1*) Gordon Pr.

Reardon, Agnes. Personality & Morality: A Developmental Approach. (Illus.). 122p. (Orig.). 1983. pap. 8.95 (*0-931474-26-4*) TBW Bks.

Reardon-Anderson, James. Pollution, Politics, & Foreign Investment in Taiwan: The Lukang Rebellion. LC 92-29888. (Taiwan in the Modern World Ser.). 134p. 1992. 36.95 (*0-87332-702-0*) M E Sharpe.

— The Study of Change: Chemistry in China, 1840-1949. (Illus.). 464p. (C). 1991. 69.95 (*0-521-39150-4*) Cambridge U Pr.

— Unites States-China Nuclear Cooperative Agreement of 1985. (Pew Case Studies in International Affairs). 50p. (C). 1993. pap. text ed. 2.50 (*1-56927-110-0*) Geo U Inst Dplmcy.

— Yenan & the Great Powers. LC 79-23343. 1980. text ed. 39.50 (*0-231-04784-3*) Col U Pr.

Reardon, Anne M. & Chambers, Kate. Called to Live Justly Social Justice in Luke-Acts. (Illus.). 36p. 1984. 2.95 (*0-934134-20-0*) Sheed & Ward MO.

— Follow Me: Becoming a Disciple According to Matthew's Gospel. (Illus.). 32p. 1985. 2.95 (*0-934134-81-2*) Sheed & Ward MO.

Reardon, B. P. The Form of Greek Romance. 223p. 1991. text ed. 35.00 (*0-691-06838-0*) Princeton U Pr.

Reardon, B. P., ed. Collected Ancient Greek Novels. 1989. 42.50 (*0-520-06417-8*); pap. 24.95 (*0-685-54179-7*) U CA Pr.

— Collected Ancient Greek Novels. 1989. 80.00 (*0-520-04303-0*); pap. 25.00 (*0-520-04306-5*) U CA Pr.

Reardon, B. P., tr. see Lucian.

Reardon, Bernard G. Kant As Philosophical Theologian. 192p. 1987. 50.00 (*0-389-20759-4*, N8318) B&N Imports.

Reardon, Bernard M. Religion in the Age of Romanticism: Studies in Early Nineteenth Century Thought. 320p. 1985. 74.95 (*0-521-30088-6*); pap. 29.95 (*0-521-31745-2*) Cambridge U Pr.

— Religious Thought in the Reformation. 2nd ed. 1995. pap. text ed. 20.95 (*0-582-25959-2*) Wiley.

— Religious Thought in the Reformation. 2nd ed. LC 94-36908. (C). 1995. text ed. 50.95 (*0-582-25960-6*) Longman.

— Religious Thought in the Victorian Age: A Survey from Coleridge to Gore. 2nd ed. LC 95-15347. (C). 1995. text ed. 52.95 (*0-582-26514-2*, Pub. by Longman UK); pap. text ed. 22.95 (*0-582-26516-9*, Pub. by Longman UK) Longman.

— Religious Thoughts in the Reformation. (C). 1981. pap. text ed. 25.50 (*0-582-49031-6*, 73448) Longman.

Reardon, Bernard M., ed. Liberal Protestantism. 244p. 1968. 32.50 (*0-8047-0647-6*) Stanford U Pr.

— Roman Catholic Modernism. 254p. 1970. 32.50 (*0-8047-0750-2*) Stanford U Pr.

Reardon, Betty. Comprehensive Peace Education: Educating for Global Responsibility. 136p. 1988. text ed. 25.95 (*0-8077-2886-1*); pap. text ed. 13.95 (*0-8077-2885-3*) Tchrs Coll.

— Discrimination, Vol. 2: No. 2. 111p. 1977. 5.00 (*0-910365-03-2*) Decade Media.

— Educating for Human Dignity: Learning about Rights & Responsibilities. (Pennsylvania Studies in Human Rights Ser.). 340p. 1995. text ed. 48.95 (*0-8122-3306-9*) U of Pa Pr.

— Educating for Human Dignity: Learning about Rights & Responsibilities. (Pennsylvania Studies in Human Rights Ser.). 340p. 1995. pap. text ed. 24.95 (*0-8122-1524-9*) U of Pa Pr.

— Sexism & the War System. LC 85-12619. 128p. (Orig.). (C). 1985. pap. text ed. 13.95 (*0-8077-2769-5*) Tchrs Coll.

Reardon, Betty, ed. Educating for Global Responsibility: Teacher-Designed Curricula for Peace Education, K-12. 216p. (C). 1987. pap. text ed. 15.95 (*0-8077-2879-9*) Tchrs Coll.

Reardon, Betty A. Women & Peace: Feminist Visions of Global Security. LC 92-9682. (SUNY Series, Global Conflict & Peace Education). 209p. 1993. 49.50 (*0-7914-1399-3*); pap. 16.95 (*0-7914-1400-0*) State U NY Pr.

***Reardon, Betty A., ed.** Educating for Global Responsibility: Teacher-Designed Curricula for Peace Education, K-12. LC 87-18017. reprint ed. pap. 61.60 (*0-7837-9601-3*, 2060358) Bks Demand.

Reardon, Betty A. & Nordland, Eva, eds. Learning Peace: The Promise of Ecological & Cooperative Education. (SUNY Series, Global Conflict & Peace Education). 234p. (C). 1994. 57.50x (*0-7914-1755-7*); pap. 18.95x (*0-7914-1756-5*) State U NY Pr.

Reardon, Carol. Soldiers & Scholars: The U. S. Army & the Uses of Military History, 1865-1920. LC 90-50111. (Modern War Studies). viii, 272p. 1990. 35.00 (*0-7006-0466-9*) U Pr of KS.

Reardon, Colleen. Agostino Agazzari & Music at Siena Cathedral, 1597-1641. (Oxford Monographs on Music). (Illus.). 224p. 1994. 45.00 (*0-19-816272-3*) OUP.

Reardon, D. F. In or Out of the Military: How to Make Your Own Best Decision. LC 92-61683. (Illus.). 144p. 1993. per. 14.95 (*1-882287-44-4*, Shelf-Life Bks) Pepper Pr.

***Reardon, David.** Aborted Women: Silent No More. LC 87-17074. 373p. (C). 1987. 17.95 (*0-8294-0578-X*, Campion Bks) Loyola Univ Pr.

— Aborted Women: Silent No More. LC 87-17074. (C). 1987. pap. 10.95 (*0-8294-0579-8*, Campion Bks) Loyola Univ Pr.

Reardon, Dennis C. S Corporations: Estate, Business, & Compensation Planning. LC 91-68030. 312p. (Orig.). 1992. pap. 29.95 (*0-87218-489-7*) Natl Underwriter.

Reardon, James. Big Time Tommy Sloane. LC 86-31957. 320p. 1987. 18.95 (*0-88191-043-0*) Freundlich.

Reardon, Joan. M. F. K. Fisher, Julia Child, & Alice Waters: Celebrating the Pleasures of the Table. LC 94-8650. 1994. 25.00 (*0-517-57748-8*, Harmony) Crown Pub Group.

R

An Asterisk (*) at the beginning of an entry indicates that the title is appearing in BIP for the first time.

— Poetry by American Women, 1975-1989: A Bibliography. LC 90-21020. 242p. 1990. 29.50 (*0-8108-2366-7*) Scarecrow.

Reardon, Joan & Thorsen, Kristine A. Poetry by American Women, 1900-1975: A Bibliography. LC 78-11944. 631p. 1979. 37.50 (*0-8108-1173-1*) Scarecrow.

Reardon, John J. America & the Multinational Corporation: The History of a Troubled Partnership. LC 92-12211. 194p. 1992. text ed. 49.95 (*0-275-93918-9*, C3918, Praeger Pubs) Greenwood.

— Peyton Randolph, 1721-1775: One Who Presided. LC 81-70431. (Illus.). 112p. 1982. lib. bdg. 12.95 (*0-89089-201-6*) Carolina Acad Pr.

Reardon, Judy A. & Smock, Raymond W. The Western Civilization Slide Collection. (Illus.). 253p. (Orig.). (YA). (gr. 7 up). 1988. reprint ed. pap. 25.00 (*0-685-24654-X*); reprint ed. sl. 895.00 (*0-923805-02-8*) Instruc Resc MD.

— The Western Civilization Slide Collection Master Guide. rev. ed. 253p. (Orig.). (YA). (gr. 7 up). 1988. 25.00 (*0-923805-01-X*) Instruc Resc MD.

Reardon, Judy A., jt. ed. see Smock, Raymond W.

Reardon, Kathleen K. Persuasion in Practice. 2nd ed. (Illus.). 232p. 1991. 38.95 (*0-8039-3316-9*); pap. 17.95 (*0-8039-3317-7*) Sage.

— They Don't Get It, Do They: Closing the Communication Gap Between Women & Men in the, Vol. 1. 1995. 21.95 (*0-316-73641-4*) Little.

Reardon, L. F., jt. auth. see Kleinberg, Howard.

Reardon, Marge. How to Flatten Your Tush. 1979. 2.00 (*0-87980-369-X*) Wilshire.

Reardon, Patricia, jt. auth. see Lippman, Helen.

Reardon, Paul C. The Plymouth Patents. (Pilgrim Society Notes Ser.: No. 27). 1988. 2.00 (*0-940628-35-X*) Pilgrim Soc.

***Reardon, Ray.** Universal Reflections. 90p. 1993. pap. 120.00 (*0-949823-33-3*, Pub. by Deakin Univ AT) St Mut.

Reardon, Robert. This Is the Way It Was. 1991. pap. 3.95 (*0-87162-995-X*, D4002) Warner Pr.

Reardon, Robert C., jt. ed. see Sampson, James P., Jr.

Reardon, Roy, ed. see Fallada, Hans.

***Reardon, Ruth.** Listening to a Teenager. (Illus.). 64p. 1995. 7.95 (*0-8378-8830-1*) Gibson.

— Listening to the Littlest. (Illus.). 48p. 1984. 7.95 (*0-8378-1749-8*) Gibson.

Reardon, Ruth & Rodegast, Roland. Listen to My Feelings. (Illus.). (J). 1992. 8.95 (*0-8378-2499-0*) Gibson.

Reardon, Timothy A., jt. auth. see Baumgold, Sharon.

Reardon, William R. & Pawley, Thomas D. Black Teacher & the Dramatic Arts: A Dialogue, Bibliography & Anthology. LC 73-90789. 487p. 1970. text ed. 65.00 (*0-8371-1850-6*, RET&, Negro U Pr) Greenwood.

***Rearick, Charles.** Pleasures of the Belle Epoque: Entertainment & Festivity in Turn-of-the-Century France. LC 85-40468. 263p. 1985. pap. 75.00 (*0-7837-8653-0*, 2082366) Bks Demand.

— Pleasures of the Belle Epoque: Entertainment & Festivity in Turn-of-the-Century France. LC 85-40468. 240p. (C). 1988. reprint ed. 22.00 (*0-300-04381-3*) Yale U Pr.

Rearick, Elizabeth C. Dances of the Hungarians. LC 72-177181. (Columbia University. Teachers College. Contributions to Education Ser.: No. 770). reprint ed. 37.50 (*0-404-55770-8*) AMS Pr.

Rearick, W. R., et al. Jacopo Bassano, 1510-1592. Marini, Paola, ed. & intro. by. (Illus.). 594p. 1993. 115.00 (*0-912804-28-9*) Kimbell Art.

Reasenberg, R. D. & Vessot, R. F., eds. Relativistic Gravitation: Proceedings of Symposium 15 of the COSPAR Twenty-Seventh Plenary Meeting Held in Espoo, Finland, 18-29 July 1988. (Advances in Space Research Ser.: No. 9). (Illus.). 158p. 1989. pap. 100.00 (*0-08-040151-1*, 1702; 1709; 2308, Pergamon Pr) Elsevier.

Reaser, Jamie, jt. auth. see Greenberg, Russell.

Reash, Janice M. Early Vows. 2nd ed. reprint ed. pap. 6.00 (*0-9616908-0-1*) Piedmont Pr OH.

Reaske, Christopher R. & Knott, John R., Jr., eds. Mirrors: An Introduction to Literature. 3rd ed. 801p. (C). 1990. pap. text ed. 40.00 (*0-06-043742-1*) HarpCollege.

Reaske, Herbert. Monarch Notes on Tolstoy's Anna Karenina. (Orig.). (C). pap. 3.95 (*0-671-00571-5*, Arco Test) P-H Gen Ref & Trav.

Reason, James. Human Error. 400p. (C). 1990. 64.95 (*0-521-30669-8*); pap. 24.95 (*0-521-31419-4*) Cambridge U Pr.

Reason, James, jt. auth. see Fisher, Shirley.

Reason, Joseph H. Inquiry into the Structural Style & Originality of Chrestien's Yvain. LC 79-174304. (Catholic University of America. Studies in Romance Languages & Literatures: No. 57). reprint ed. 37.50 (*0-404-50357-8*) AMS Pr.

Reason, Peter, ed. Human Inquiry in Action: Developments in New Paradigm Research. 272p. (C). 1989. text ed. 45.00 (*0-8039-8089-2*); pap. text ed. 17.95 (*0-8039-8090-6*) Sage.

— Participation in Human Inquiry. 240p. 1995. 69.95 (*0-8039-8831-1*) Sage.

— Participation in Human Inquiry. 240p. 1995. pap. 21.95 (*0-8039-8832-X*) Sage.

Reason, Peter & Rowan, John, eds. Human Inquiry: A Sourcebook of New Paradigm Research. LC 80-41585. 530p. 1981. pap. text ed. 52.95 (*0-471-27936-6*, Wiley-Interscience) Wiley.

Reason, Rea & Boote, Rene. Helping Children with Reading & Spelling: A Special Needs Manual. 2nd ed. LC 94-1685. (Illus.). 144p. 1994. pap. 17.95 (*0-415-10733-4*, B4571) Routledge.

Reason, Rea, jt. ed. see Pumfrey, Peter D.

Reason, Sharon, ed. see Zakutinsky, Ruth.

Reasoner. The Diablo Grant. 240p. (Orig.). 1995. mass mkt. 4.99 (*0-671-87142-0*) PB.

— Medicine Creek. (Wind River Ser.: No. 4). 1995. mass mkt. 3.99 (*0-06-100774-9*, Harp PBks) HarpC.

Reasoner, Charles. Alphabite! A Funny Feast from A to Z. LC 89-65563. 36p. (J). (ps). 1989. 9.95 (*0-8431-2361-3*) Price Stern.

— First-Aid Kit, 4 bks., Set. LC 93-87682. (Little Box Bks.). (Illus.). 8p. (J). (ps up). 1995. bds. 8.95 (*0-8431-3756-8*) Price Stern.

— Lunch Box. (Little Box Bks.). (Illus.). 8p. (J). (ps up). 1995. bds. 8.95 (*0-614-03672-0*) Price Stern.

— Lunch Box, 4 bks., Set. LC 93-87683. (Little Box Books Ser.). (Illus.). 1995. 8.95 (*0-8431-3755-X*) Price Stern.

— The Magic Amber. LC 93-43180. (Legends of the World Ser.). (Illus.). 32p. (J). (gr. 2-5). 1994. lib. bdg. 11.89 (*0-8167-3407-0*); pap. text ed. 3.95 (*0-8167-3408-9*) Troll Assocs.

— Number Munch! (Illus.). 36p. (J). (ps). 1993. bds. 9.95 (*0-8431-3674-X*) Price Stern.

— Who's Hatching? LC 93-87680. (Sliding Surprise Bks.). (Illus.). 12p. (J). (ps). 1994. bds. 9.95 (*0-8431-3717-7*) Price Stern.

— Who's in the Sea? LC 94-68514. (Sliding Surprise Bks.). (Illus.). 1995. 9.95 (*0-8431-3912-9*) Price Stern.

— Who's Peeking? (Sliding Surprise Bks.). (Illus.). 12p. (J). (ps). 1993. 9.95 (*0-8431-3478-X*) Price Stern.

— Who's There? (Sliding Surprise Bks.). (Illus.). 12p. (J). (ps). 1993. 9.95 (*0-8431-3479-8*) Price Stern.

— Whose House Is This? (Sliding Surprise Bks.). (Illus.). 12p. (J). 1995. bds. 9.95 (*0-8431-3911-0*) Price Stern.

— Whose Mommy Is This? LC 93-87681. (Sliding Surprise Bks.). (Illus.). 12p. (J). (ps). 1994. bds. 9.95 (*0-8431-3718-5*) Price Stern.

***Reasoner, Charles, ed. & illus.** Night Owl & the Rooster: A Haitian Legend. LC 95-9983. 32p. (J). (gr. 1-4). 1995. teacher ed 3.95 (*0-8167-3750-9*); lib. bdg. 11.89 (*0-8167-3749-5*) Troll Assocs.

***Reasoner, Charles, illus.** Fun Toys & Fun Foods, 12 bks., Set. LC 94-68502. (Bunch of Board Bks.). 6p. (J). (ps up). 1995. bds. 4.95 (*0-8431-3097-0*) Price Stern.

— My First Musical Piggy Bank Book. (Electronic Board Bks.). 6p. (J). (ps-2). 1992. bds. 9.95 (*1-56293-139-3*) McClanahan Bk.

— The Princess Who Lost Her Hair: An Akamba Legend. LC 92-13273. 32p. (J). (gr. 2-5). 1992. lib. bdg. 11.89 (*0-8167-2815-1*); pap. 3.95 (*0-8167-2816-X*) Troll Assocs.

Reasoner, Charles, jt. auth. see Warren, Vic.

Reasoner, Chuck. The Big Busy Building. (Illus.). 10p. (J). (ps up). 1994. bds. 12.95 (*0-8431-3659-6*) Price Stern.

***Reasoner, J. L.** The Healer's Road, Bk. 1. 352p. (Orig.). 1995. pap. 5.99 (*0-515-11762-5*) Jove Pubns.

— Rivers of Gold: A Novel of the California Gold Rush. 352p. (Orig.). 1995. pap. text ed. 5.50 (*0-515-11524-X*) Jove Pubns.

Reasoner, James. Stark's Justice. 1994. mass mkt. 3.99 (*0-671-87140-4*) PB.

— Stark's Justice. large type ed. LC 94-35471. 1994. write for info. (*1-56895-153-1*) Wheeler Pub.

— Thunder Wagon. (Wind River Ser.: No. 2). 1994. mass mkt. 3.50 (*0-06-100772-2*) HarpC.

— Wind River. 1994. mass mkt. 3.50 (*0-06-100771-4*, Harp PBks) HarpC.

— Wolf Shadow. (Wind River Ser.: No. 3). 1994. pap. 3.50 (*0-06-100773-0*, Harp PBks) HarpC.

Reasoner, James, jt. auth. see Lovisi, Gary.

Reasoner, Robert W. Building Self-Esteem in the Elementary Schools. 2nd rev. ed. 1992. 105.00 (*0-89106-056-1*) Consulting Psychol.

Reasoner, Robert W. & Dusa, Gail S. Building Self-Esteem in the Secondary Schools. 1991. 90.00 (*0-89106-054-5*) Consulting Psychol.

Reasoner, Victor P. The Hole in the Holiness Movement. 149p. (Orig.). 1991. pap. 4.95 (*0-9629383-3-5*) Fundmntl Wesleyan.

Reasonner, James M. The Hawthorne Legacy. Grad, Doug, ed. (Orig.). 1994. mass mkt. 4.99 (*0-671-87141-2*) PB.

Reasonover, Ila. Lottie Daughter of the Depression. Caroland, Mary, ed. LC 90-71004. 154p. (J). (gr. 4-8). 1991. 7.95 (*1-55523-365-1*) Winston-Derek.

Reat, N. Ross. Buddhism: A History. LC 93-1792. (Religions of the World). 336p. (C). 1993. text ed. 60.00 (*0-87573-001-9*, Asian Human Pr); pap. text ed. 25.00 (*0-87573-002-7*, Asian Human Pr) Jain Pub Co.

— Origins of Indian Psychology. LC 90-48484. 400p. (C). 1990. text ed. 60.00 (*0-89581-923-6*, Asian Human Pr); pap. 25.00 (*0-89581-924-4*, Asian Human Pr) Jain Pub Co.

Reat, N. Ross & Perry, Edmund F. A World Theology: The Central Spiritual Reality of Humankind. 340p. (C). 1991. 59.95 (*0-521-33159-5*) Cambridge U Pr.

Reater, John. Rise of Life: The First Three & a Half Billion Years. 1990. 14.99 (*0-517-05173-7*) Random Hse Value.

***Reau, Louis.** Dictionnaire Polyglotte des Termes d'Art et d'Archeologie. 1977. write for info. (*0-7859-8668-5*, 3535015502) Fr & Eur.

— Dictionnaire Polyglotte des Termes d'Art et d'Archeologie. 961p. (FRE.). 1977. reprint ed. 595.00 (*0-8288-9540-6*, M6612) Fr & Eur.

— Iconographie de l'Chretien: Paris, 1955-1959, 3. vols. 1969. 630.00 (*0-8115-0046-2*) Periodicals Srv.

Reaugh, Frank. Frank Reaugh: Painter to the Longhorns. LC 85-40051. (Joe & Betty Moore Texas Art Ser.: No. 7). (Illus.). 148p. 1985. 29.95 (*0-89096-236-7*) Tex A&M Univ Pr.

Reaume, Chuck, jt. auth. see Knight, E. Leslie.

Reaveley, Mabel. Weathervane Secrets. LC 83-25854. (Illus.). (Orig.). 1984. pap. 6.95 (*0-87233-075-3*) Bauhan.

Reaven. Clinician's Guide to Non-Insulin-Dependent Diabetes Mellitus Pathogenesis & Treatment. 152p. 1989. 65.00 (*0-8247-8083-3*) Dekker.

Reaver, Chap. Bill. (J). 1994. 14.95 (*0-385-31175-3*) Delacorte.

— A Little Bit Dead. LC 92-7185. 192p. (J). (gr. 6 up). 1992. 15.00 (*0-385-30801-9*) Delacorte.

— Little Bit Dead. (YA). 1994. mass mkt. 3.99 (*0-440-21910-8*) Dell.

— A Little Bit Dead. large type ed. LC 93-42210. (J). 1994. pap. 15.95 (*0-7862-0139-8*) Thorndike Pr.

Reaver, J. Russell, ed. Florida Folktales. 192p. 1987. pap. text ed. 19.95 (*0-8130-0870-0*) U Press Fla.

Reaver, Joseph R. Emerson as Mythmaker. LC 54-8431. 116p. reprint ed. pap. 33.10 (*0-7837-4997-X*, 2044664) Bks Demand.

Reaves, Celia C. Quantitative Research for the Behavioral Sciences. 416p. (C). 1991. Net. text ed. write for info. (*0-471-61683-4*) Wiley.

Reaves, Diane C. The Egyptian Cat. 200p. (Orig.). 1993. pap. text ed. 4.99 (*0-9630046-3-8*) Lydian Comm.

Reaves, George A., jt. auth. see Frank, Joseph A.

Reaves, Graham. A Stranger to Manhood. 120p. (Orig.). 1993. pap. text ed. 8.95 (*0-9630046-2-X*) Lydian Comm.

— The Unemployment Primer. 65p. (Orig.). 1992. pap. text ed. 4.95 (*0-9630046-1-1*) Lydian Comm.

Reaves, J. Graham. A Stranger to Myself: An Adult Guide to Higher Self-Esteem & Creative Living. 120p. 1991. pap. text ed. 8.95 (*0-9630046-0-3*) Lydian Comm.

Reaves, James N. Black Cops. Wartman, William, ed. (Illus.). 216p. 1991. 21.95 (*0-9627161-4-6*) QLP Phila PA.

Reaves, Marilyn & Schulte, Eliza. Brush Lettering: An Instructional Manual of Western Brush Lettering. 128p. 1993. pap. 19.95 (*1-55821-269-8*) Lyons & Burford.

Reaves, Marilyn, jt. auth. see Schulte, Eliza.

Reaves, Michael. Night Hunter. 256p. 1995. 21.95 (*0-312-85318-1*) Tor Bks.

Reaves, Sam. Bury it Deep. LC 93-3242. 272p. 1993. 21.95 (*0-399-13870-6*, Putnam) Putnam Pub Group.

— Bury It Deep. 272p. 1994. mass mkt. 4.99 (*0-380-72266-6*) Avon.

— Fear Will Do It. 352p. 1994. mass mkt. 4.99 (*0-380-72034-5*) Avon.

— Get What's Coming. LC 94-33195. 1995. write for info. (*0-399-14018-2*, Putnam) Putnam Pub Group.

— A Long Cold Fall. 304p. 1992. mass mkt. 4.50 (*0-380-71641-0*) Avon.

Reaves, Shiela. Wisconsin: Pathways to Prosperity. (Illus.). 336p. (YA). (gr. 7 up). 1988. 32.95 (*0-89781-236-0*) Preferred Mktg.

Reaves, Verne. Heading South: A Guide to Budget Travel in Latin America. LC 81-52888. 142p. 1982. pap. 6.95 (*0-9607036-0-8*) Sec Thoughts OR.

Reaves, Verne, ed. see Baehr, Russell.

Reavey, George, ed. New Russian Poets. 1966. 15.00 (*0-8079-0095-8*); pap. 7.95 (*0-8079-0096-6*) October.

Reavey, George, ed. & tr. The New Russian Poets. 320p. 1981. pap. 9.95 (*0-7145-2715-7*) M Boyars Pubs.

Reavey, George, tr. see Berdiaev, Nikolai A.

Reavey, George, tr. see Mayakovsky, Vladimir.

Reavey, George, tr. see Turgenev, Ivan S.

Reavey, George, tr. see Yevtushenko, Yevgeny.

***Reavey, Patrick G.** Legal Malpractice: A Research guide for Lawyers & Law Students. LC 95-15352. 1995. write for info. (*0-89941-933-X*) W S Hein.

Reavill, Gil. Compass American Guide: Hollywood: Los Angeles & Beyond. 2nd ed. (Compass American Guides Ser.). 1994. pap. 16.95 (*1-878867-71-7*, Compass Amrcn) Fodors Travel.

— Compass American Guide: Los Angeles. Jensen, Jamie, ed. (Discover America Ser.). (Illus.). 320p. (Orig.). 1992. 22.95 (*1-878867-25-3*, Compass Amrcn) Fodors Travel.

— Los Angeles. Jensen, Jamie, ed. (Discover America Ser.). (Illus.). 320p. (Orig.). 1992. pap. 14.95 (*1-878867-17-2*) Fodors Travel.

Reavis, Charles. Cooking with Fresh Sausage. 1989. pap. 2.95 (*0-88266-530-8*, Garden Way Pub) Storey Comm Inc.

— Dash of Elegance. 1994. 22.00 (*0-02-601210-3*) Macmillan.

— Hardwood Grilling Tips & Recipes. 1990. pap. 2.95 (*0-88266-627-4*) Storey Comm Inc.

— Home Sausage Making: Healthy Low-Salt, Low-Fat Recipes. rev. ed. Oxley, Constance, tr. LC 87-45094. 176p. (Orig.). 1987. pap. 13.95 (*0-88266-477-8*, Garden Way Pub) Storey Comm Inc.

Reavis, Charles, ed. Ecology of Successful Schools: One Approach to Restructuring. LC 91-65918. (Yearbook of the Texas Association for Supervision & Curriculum Development, 1991 Ser.). viii, 128p. (Orig.). 1991. pap. 6.00 (*0-934955-21-2*) Watercress Pr.

Reavis, Charles & Griffith, Harry. Restructuring Schools: Theory & Practice. LC 91-66130. 215p. 1992. text ed. 45.00 (*0-87762-849-1*) Technomic.

Reavis, Charles A. Extraordinary Educators: Lessons in Leadership. LC 88-60071. (Fastback Ser.: No. 271). 50p. (Orig.). 1988. pap. 1.25 (*0-87367-271-2*) Phi Delta Kappa.

Reavis, Cheryl. One of Our Own: (That Special Woman!) (Special Edition Ser.). 1994. mass mkt. 3.50 (*0-373-09901-0*, 1-09901-9) Harlequin Bks.

— Promise Me a Rainbow. braille ed. 567p. 1993. Braille. vinyl bd. 45.36 (*1-56956-385-3*, BR8729) W A T Braille.

***Reavis, Dick J.** Compass American Guide: Texas. LC 94-27287. (Illus.). 1995. 17.95 (*1-878867-64-4*) Fodors Travel.

— Conversations with Moctezuma: Ancient Shadows over Modern Life in Mexico. LC 89-34923. (Illus.). 356p. 1990. 19.95 (*0-688-07999-7*) Morrow.

— Conversations with Moctezuma: The Soul of Modern Mexico. (Illus.). 304p. 1991. pap. 12.00 (*0-688-10738-9*, Quill) Morrow.

Reavis, Dick J., tr. see Perez, Ramon T.

Reavis, Donna. Assessing Students with Multiple Disabilities: Practical Guidelines for Practitioners. (Illus.). 110p. (C). 1990. text ed. 29.95x (*0-398-05683-8*) C C Thomas.

— Assessing Students with Multiple Disabilities: Practical Guidlines for Practitioners. (Illus.). 110p. 1990. pap. 15.95 (*0-398-06339-7*) C C Thomas.

Reavis, George H. The Animal School. (Illus.). 28p. (Orig.). 1988. pap. 3.95 (*0-935493-15-8*, RRB 424) Programs Educ.

— Factors Controlling Attendance in Rural Schools. LC 76-177182. (Columbia University. Teachers College. Contributions to Education Ser.: No. 108). reprint ed. 37.50 (*0-404-55108-4*) AMS Pr.

Reavis, Larry. The Master Homeowner. (Illus.). 256p. (Orig.). 1991. pap. 12.98 (*0-9617523-1-9*) Hathaway Pub.

Reavis, Ralph. Martin Luther: Martin Luther King Jr. & the Black Experience. 1982. pap. 5.95 (*0-933184-42-5*) Flame Intl.

Reay, B., ed. see McGregor, J. F.

Reay, C., jt. auth. see Kumar, Bakul.

Reay, D. A., ed. Energy Economics & Management in Industry: Proceedings of the European Congress Held Algarve, Portugal, 2-5 April 1984. 80p. 1985. pap. 22.00 (*0-08-032548-3*, Pergamon Pr) Elsevier.

— Innovation For Energy Efficiency. (Illus.). 400p. 1987. 97.00 (*0-317-66351-8*, Pergamon Pr) Elsevier.

Reay, D. A. & MacMichael, D. B. Heat Pumps. 2nd ed. 350p. 1988. text ed. 125.00 (*0-08-033463-6*, Pergamon Pr); pap. text ed. 51.00 (*0-08-033462-8*, Pergamon Pr) Elsevier.

Reay, D. A. & Wright, A. Innovation for Energy Efficiency: Proceedings of the European Conference, Newcastle Tyne U. K. 10-87. LC 87-19016. 1988. 172.00 (*0-08-034798-3*, Pub. by Pergamon Repr UK) Franklin.

Reay, D. A., jt. auth. see Dunn, P. D.

Reay, D. A., jt. auth. see International Heat Pipe Conference Staff.

Reay, D. W., jt. ed. see Jenkins, J. D.

Reay, David. Evaluating Training. (Competent Trainer's Toolkit Ser.). 96p. (Orig.). 1994. pap. 24.95 (*0-89397-426-9*) Nichols Pub.

— Identifying Training Needs. (Competent Trainer's Toolkit Ser.). 96p. (Orig.). 1994. pap. 24.95 (*0-89397-427-7*) Nichols Pub.

— Implementing Training. (Competent Trainer's Toolkit Ser.). 96p. (Orig.). 1994. pap. 24.95 (*0-89397-428-5*) Nichols Pub.

— Planning a Training Strategy. (Competent Trainer's Toolkit Ser.). 96p. (Orig.). 1994. pap. 24.95 (*0-89397-429-3*) Nichols Pub.

— Selecting Training Methods. (Competent Trainer's Toolkit Ser.). 96p. (Orig.). 1994. pap. 24.95 (*0-89397-425-0*) Nichols Pub.

— Understanding How People Learn. (Competent Trainer's Toolkit Ser.). 96p. (Orig.). 1994. pap. 24.95 (*0-89397-430-7*) Nichols Pub.

— Understanding the Training Function. (Competent Trainer's Toolkit Ser.). 96p. (Orig.). 1994. pap. 24.95 (*0-89397-431-5*) Nichols Pub.

Reay, David A. History of Man-Powered Flight. 1977. 146.00 (*0-08-021738-9*, Pub. by Pergamon Repr UK) Franklin.

Reay, J. A Guide to Catering Organization. (C). 1983. 60.00 (*0-85950-122-1*, Pub. by S Thornes Pubs UK) St Mut.

***Reay, Joanne.** Bumpa Rumpus & the Rainy Day. LC 94-28258. (Illus.). (J). 1995. 14.95 (*0-395-71038-3*) HM.

Reay, John R. Generalizations of a Theorem of Caratheodory. LC 52-42839. (Memoirs Ser.: No. 1/54). 50p. 1965. pap. 16.00 (*0-8218-1254-8*, MEMO 1/54) Am Math.

Reay, Julia. A Guide to Catering Organisation. 176p. (C). 1983. pap. 52.00 (*0-685-33830-4*, Pub. by S Thornes Pubs UK) St Mut.

Reay, Lee. Incredible Passage Through the Hole-in-the-Rock. 128p. 1980. 6.95 (*0-317-59293-9*, 8426) Pubs Bk Sales.

Reba, jt. auth. see Diksic.

Reba, Richard, et al. Diagnostic Imaging Medicine. 1983. lib. bdg. 186.50 (*90-247-2798-7*) Kluwer Ac.

Rebac, Zoran. Thai Boxing Dynamite: The Explosive Art of Muay Thai. (Illus.). 120p. 1987. reprint ed. pap. 14.00 (*0-87364-426-3*) Paladin Pr.

Rebach, H. M. & Bruhn, J. G., eds. Handbook of Clinical Sociology. LC 90-7998. (Illus.). 380p. 1991. 60.00 (*0-306-43559-4*, Plenum Pr); pap. 32.50 (*0-306-43579-9*, Plenum Pr) Plenum.

Rebach, Howard M., et al. Substance Abuse among Ethnic Minorities in America: A Critical, Annotated Bibliography. LC 91-45032. (Library of Sociology: Vol. 20). 480p. 1992. 72.00 (*0-8153-0066-2*, SS#737) Garland.

Reban, Milan J., jt. ed. see Klein, George.

Reband, P. L. Related Mathematics for Carpenters. 2nd ed. (Illus.). 218p. 1973. pap. 11.96 (*0-8269-2332-1*) Am Technical.

Rebane, George. Financial Model for Interactive Systems: Focus on Electronic Retailing. (Monitor Report Ser.). 52p. (Orig.). (C). 1987. student ed 50.00 (*0-938907-05-0*); pap. 185.00 (*0-938907-04-2*); Floppy disk. disk 150.00 (*0-938907-06-9*) Future Syst.

Rebarchek, Ray. Why I Came to Alaska. 1994. pap. 7.95 (*0-533-10726-1*) Vantage.

Rebaric, Joyce A. Nocturne. 143p. 1993. pap. 17.00 (*0-9635084-0-7*) Nightshadow Prods.

Rebarto, Manuel. Spanish Cooking. 1993. 12.98 (*1-55521-928-4*) Bk Sales Inc.

Rebay, Luciano. Alberto Moravia. LC 77-126544. (Columbia Essays on Modern Writers Ser.: No. 52). (Orig.). 1971. pap. text ed. 7.50 (*0-231-02762-1*) Col U Pr.

R

— Introduction to Italian Poetry. 1991. pap. 3.95 (*0-486-26715-6*) Dover.
*Rebber, Elizabeth. Seymour: A Pictorial History. (Indiana Pictorial History Ser.). 1990. write for info. (*0-614-04652-1*) G Bradley.
Rebbert, Richard L. Instructor's Manual to Accompany Experiments in Chemistry. 3rd ed. 104p. (C). 1989. pap. text ed. 28.50 (*0-15-506464-9*) HB Coll Pubs.
Rebbi, C., ed. Lattice Gauge Theories & Monte Carlo Simulations. 658p. 1983. text ed. 89.00 (*9971-950-70-7*); pap. text ed. 46.00 (*9971-950-71-5*) World Scientific Pub.
Rebbi, C. & Soliani, G., eds. Solitons & Particles. 836p. 1984. text ed. 121.00 (*9971-966-42-5*); pap. text ed. 52.00 (*9971-966-43-3*) World Scientific Pub.
Rebec, George, jt. auth. see Groves, Philip.
Rebeiz, Constantin A., jt. ed. see Duke, Stephen O.
Rebeiz, Gabriel M., jt. auth. see Eleftheriades, George V.
Rebel, Hermann. Peasant Classes: The Bureaucratization of Property & Family Relations under Early Absolutism, 1511-1636. LC 82-47610. 400p. 1983. 55.00x (*0-691-05366-9*) Princeton U Pr.
— Peasant Classes: The Bureaucratization of Property & Family Relations under Early Habsburg Absolutism, 1511-1636. LC 82-47610. (Illus.). Date not set. reprint ed. pap. 106.40 (*0-7837-9431-2*, 2060173) Bks Demand.
Rebel Montgomery Temple Staff. Shadow of the Eagles. (Illus.). 157p. (Orig.). (J). 1982. pap. 3.75 (*0-89279-045-8*, TXU 90-499) S&S Trade.
Rebel, Thomas P. Sea Turtles & the Turtle Industry of the West Indies, Florida, & the Gulf of Mexico. LC 73-159293. 224p. 1974. 14.95 (*0-87024-217-2*) U of Miami Pr.
Rebell, Gerbert & Taplin, David, eds. Dermatophytes: Their Recognition & Identification. 2nd rev. ed. LC 70-130448. (Illus.). 1974. pap. 19.95 (*0-87024-185-0*) U of Miami Pr.
Rebell, Michael A. & Block, Arthur R. Educational Policy-Making & the Courts: An Empirical Study of Judicial Activism. LC 81-16225. (Illus.). 336p. 1982. 30.00 (*0-226-70598-6*) U Ch Pr.
— Equality & Education: Federal Civil Rights Enforcement in the New York City School System. LC 85-42700. 312p. 1985. 52.50 (*0-691-07692-8*) Princeton U Pr.
— Equality & Education: Federal Civil Rights Enforcement in the New York City School System. LC 85-42700. reprint ed. pap. 100.70 (*0-7837-9301-4*, 2060040) Bks Demand.
Rebellion, Boxer. The Invisible Man & The Butler. Abell, Joan, ed. & illus. by. (YA). (gr. 8 up). 1992. lib. bdg. 25.00 (*1-56611-013-0*); pap. 15.00 (*1-56611-149-8*) Jonas.
Rebello, Stephen. Alfred Hitchcock & the Making of Psycho. LC 89-30988. 1990. 24.95 (*0-942637-14-3*, Dembner NY) Barricade Bks.
— Alfred Hitchcock & the Making of Psycho. LC 90-55514. (Illus.). 224p. 1991. reprint ed. pap. 12.00 (*0-06-097366-8*, PL) HarpC.
Rebello, Stephen & Allen, Richard. Reel Art: Great Posters from the Golden Age of the Silver Screen. (Illus.). 342p. Date not set. 29.98 (*0-89660-033-5*, Artabras) Abbeville Pr.
— Reel Art: Great Posters from the Golden Age of the Silver Screen. (Illus.). 342p. 1988. 49.98 (*0-89659-869-1*, Artabras) Abbeville Pr.
— Tiny Folios: Reel Art. 288p. 1992. 10.95 (*1-55859-403-5*) Abbeville Pr.
Rebello, Stephen, jt. auth. see Margulies, Edward.
*Rebello, Steven. Art of Pocahontas. (Illus.). 200p. 1995. 50.00 (*0-7868-6158-4*) Hyperion.
Rebennack, Mac, see Dr. John, pseud..
Rebens. William Richard Lethaby. 1986. 47.95 (*0-85139-350-0*, Butterwrth Archit) Buttrwrth-Heinemann.
*Reber. Eerie Canal: An Historical Adventure. 1990. 5.00 (*0-614-04729-3*) Royal Fireworks.
Reber, Arthur S. Implicit Learning & Tacit Knowledge: An Essay on the Cognitive Unconscious. LC 92-30709. (Oxford Psychology Ser.: No. 19). (Illus.). 200p. 1993. 35.00 (*0-19-505942-5*) OUP.
— The Penguin Dictionary of Psychology. (Reference Ser.). 864p. 1986. pap. 12.95 (*0-14-051079-6*, Penguin Bks) Viking Penguin.
Reber, Howard A., ed. Atlas of Pancreatic Surgery. (Illus.). 265p. 1988. 79.95 (*0-8151-7160-9*, ATR-1, Yr Bk Med Pubs) Mosby Yr Bk.
Reber, Jan & Shaw, Paul. Executive Protection Manual. 1976. 29.95 (*0-916070-02-6*, MTI Film & Video); pap. 19.95 (*0-686-70710-9*, MTI Film & Video) Coronet.
Reber, Robert E. Linking Faith & Daily Life (Leader's Guide) An Educational Program for Lay People. LC 91-72969. 55p. (Orig.). 1991. student ed, pap. 19.95 (*1-56699-045-9*, AL126L) Alban Inst.
— Linking Faith & Daily Life (Participant's Packet) An Educational Program for Lay People, Set. LC 91-72969. 223p. (Orig.). 1991. student ed, pap. 35.00 (*1-56699-047-5*, AL126P) Alban Inst.
Reber, Vera B. British Mercantile Houses in Buenos Aires, 1810-1880. LC 78-15743. (Studies in Business History: No. 29). (Illus.). 217p. 1979. 29.00 (*0-674-08245-1*) HUP.
Reberdy, Janet, jt. auth. see Benziger, Marieli.
Reberg, Evelyne. A Devil in the Grog Garage. (I Love to Read Collection). (Illus.). (J). (gr. 3-8). 1992. lib. bdg. 12.79 (*0-89565-893-3*) Childs World.
— The Old Woman & the Ghost. (I Love to Read Collection). (Illus.). 48p. (J). 1991. lib. bdg. 12.79 (*0-89565-814-3*) Childs World.
Reberioux, Madeleine, jt. auth. see Mayeur, Jean-Marie.
Rebers, Paul, jt. ed. see Cothern, C. Richard.
Rebert, Jo & O'Hara, Jean. Copper Enameling. 1956. 2.95 (*0-934706-00-X*) Prof Pubns Ohio.
Rebert, Sandi Z. Seventy Times Seven. 180p. (Orig.). 1982. pap. 3.95 (*0-89084-156-X*) Bob Jones Univ Pr.
*Rebeschi, Lisa & Brown, Mary. The Pediatric Nurse's Survival Guide. (Nurse's Survival Guide Ser.). 400p. (Orig.). (C). Date not set. pap. text ed. 24.95 (*1-56930-018-6*) Skidmore Roth Pub.
Rebholz, R. A., ed. see Wyatt, Thomas.
Rebhorn, Marlette. Screening America: Using Hollywood Films to Teach History. (American University Studies: History: Ser. IX, Vol. 42). 211p. 1988. 34.50 (*0-8204-0726-7*) P Lang Pubs.
*Rebhorn, Wayne A. The Emperor of Men's Minds: Literature & the Renaissance Discourse of Rhetoric. LC 94-34553. (Rhetoric & Society Ser.). (Illus.). 304p. 1995. 35.00x (*0-8014-2562-X*) Cornell U Pr.
— Foxes & Lions: Machiavelli's Confidence Men. LC 87-47824. 288p. 1988. 31.50 (*0-8014-2095-4*) Cornell U Pr.
Rebhun, Joseph. The Embers of Michael: An Historical Epic. 411p. 1993. Perfect bdg. per. 15.00 (*0-9614162-2-X*) OR Pub.
— God & Man in Two Worlds. 1985. lib. bdg. 16.95 (*0-9614162-1-1*) OR Pub.
— Witness to History: Man & God in Two Worlds. Kravetz, Nathan, ed. LC 95-5340. (Studies in Judaica & the Holocaust: No. 16). 1995. pap. text ed. write for info. (*0-8095-1403-6*) Borgo Pr.
*Rebhun, Joseph & Kravetz, Nathan, eds. Witness to History: Man & God in Two Worlds. rev. ed. LC 95-5340. (Studies in Judaica & the Holocaust: No. 16). 1995. write for info. (*0-8095-0403-0*) Borgo Pr.
Rebhun, Linda-Anne, jt. auth. see Parker, Robert N.
*Rebhun, William C. Diseases of Dairy Cattle. LC 94-44191. 1995. write for info. (*0-683-07193-9*) Williams & Wilkins.
ReBibo, Kathy, ed. see Kannan, Narisimhan P.
Rebisz, Jacqueline, ed. see Metz, Mary S. & Helstrom, Jo.

Reblitz, Arthur A. Piano Servicing, Tuning, & Rebuilding: For the Professional, the Student, the Hobbyist. 2nd ed. LC 92-13175. (Illus.). 340p. 1993. 39.95 (*1-879511-02-9*); pap. 29.95 (*1-879511-03-7*) Vestal.
The first edition of this now world-famous book came into being in 1976 for one simple reason -- to put into clear & understandable pictures & language how anyone handy with tools can repair, regulate, maintain, & even do a complete rebuild of a piano. The late John Steinway (then president of Steinway Piano Company) was so impressed that he told us so in writing, & we've been proud to print his letter in each book -- the First Edition of which sold over 45,000 copies. This new edition features a more comprehensive section on soundboard repair, detailed photos showing installation of hammers, & a completely new chapter on evaluating the quality, age & condition of an old piano. The chapter on tuning procedures has been expanded & revised to incorporate the popular & easy-to-learn temperaments taught by George Defebaugh & Randy Potter. Clearer typesetting, a more reader-friendly layout, 650 invaluable illustrative photos & diagrams, & meticulous table of contents, index & bibliography make this edition even more accessible to readers at all levels of expertise. Professionals & hobbyists alike will appreciate this reference guide on how to bring a piano from a badly-neglected state to top form. Elaine Stuart, The Vestal Press, Inc., 320 North Jensen Road, P.O. Box 97, Vestal, NY 13851-0097. Phone: (607) 797-4872. ***Publisher Provided Annotation.***

— Player Piano Servicing & Rebuilding. LC 85-3140. (Illus.). 224p. 1985. 29.95 (*0-911572-41-4*); pap. 24.95 (*0-911572-40-6*) Vestal.
Rebmann, Gerhard. Dictionary of Garment Terminology. 450p. (ENG, FRE & GER.). 1984. 295.00 (*0-8288-0747-7*, M6966) Fr & Eur.
Rebne, Douglas. Determinants of Individual Productivity: A Study of Academic Researchers. (Monograph & Research Ser.: No. 53). 155p. 1990. pap. 12.50 (*0-89215-162-5*) U Cal LA Indus Rel.
Reboiras, J. J. Basic Concepts of Medical Terminology: Conceptos Basicos de Terminologia Medica. 157p. (SPA.). 1982. 27.95 (*0-8288-1876-2*, S12385) Fr & Eur.
Rebok, George W. Lifespan Cognitive Development. 592p. (C). 1987. text ed. 40.00 (*0-03-064182-9*) HB Coll Pubs.
*Rebolledo, Francisco. Rasero: A Novel. Lane, Helen R., tr. 568p. (C). 1995. 29.95 (*0-8071-2004-9*) La State U Pr.
Rebolledo, R., jt. ed. see Del Pino, G.
*Rebolledo, Tey D. Women Singing in the Snow: A Cultural Analysis of Chicana Literature. 250p. 1995. lib. bdg. 35.00x (*0-8165-1520-4*); pap. 16.95 (*0-8165-1546-8*) U of Ariz Pr.
Rebolledo, Tey D. & Rivero, Eliana S., eds. Infinite Divisions: An Anthology of Chicana Literature. LC 92-45101. 387p. (Orig.). 1993. pap. 19.95 (*0-8165-1384-8*) U of Ariz Pr.
Rebollo Torio, Miguel A. Vocabulario Politico Republicano y Franquista: Republican & Franco-ite Political Vocabulary, 1931-1971. 184p. (SPA.). 1978. 24.95 (*0-8288-5277-4*, S50122) Fr & Eur.
Rebore, Ronald W. Personnel Administration in Education: A Management Approach. 2nd ed. (Illus.). 368p. (C). 1987. text ed. write for info. (*0-13-657719-9*) P-H.
— Personnel Administration in Education: A Management Approach. 4th ed. LC 94-11077. 1994. text ed. write for info. (*0-205-15772-6*) Allyn.
— Personnel Administration in Education: A Management Approach for Educational Organizations. (Illus.). 336p. (C). 1982. write for info. (*0-13-657742-3*) P-H.
Rebore, Ronald W., jt. auth. see Rebore, William T.
Rebore, Ronald W., jt. auth. see Travers, Paul D.
Rebore, William T. & Rebore, Ronald W. Introduction to Financial & Business Administration in Public Education. 400p. (C). 1993. text ed. write for info. (*0-205-13509-9*, H35090) Allyn.
Reboucas, Marcelo J., ed. see MacCallum, Malcolm A., et al.
Reboul, Antoine. Thou Shall Not Kill. Craig, Stephanie, tr. LC 77-77312. Orig. Title: Tu Ne Tueras Point. (J). (gr. 5-8). 1969. 22.95 (*0-87599-161-0*) S G Phillips.
Reboul, P., jt. auth. see Wordingham, J. A.
Reboul, Pierre, ed. see De Chateaubriand, Rene.
Reboullet, et al. Methode Orange, Bk 1. (Methode Orange Ser.). (Illus.). (FRE.). (gr. 7-12). 1979. pap. text ed. 5.25 (*0-88345-406-8*) Prentice ESL.
— Methode Orange-Workbook 1. (Methode Orange Ser.). (Illus.). (FRE.). (gr. 7-12). 1979. teacher ed 6.75 (*0-88345-411-4*); pap. text ed. 3.50 (*0-88345-408-4*); audio 85.00 (*0-686-60844-5*) Prentice ESL.
Rebourgeon, P., ed. Tennis Dictionary: Dictionnaire de Tennis. 160p. (FRE.). 1981. 89.95 (*0-8288-4442-9*, M9769) Fr & Eur.
Rebovich, Donald J. Dangerous Ground: The World of Hazardous Waste Crime. 168p. (C). 1992. text ed. 34.95 (*1-56000-014-7*) Transaction Pubs.
Rebreanu, Liviu. Ion. 1965. 30.00 (*0-7206-4650-2*) Dufour.
— Uprising. 1964. 30.00 (*0-7206-9382-9*) Dufour.
Rebreau, Liviu. Ion. Aderman, Ralph M., ed. LC 67-25190. 1967. 13.50 (*0-8057-5695-7*) Irvington.
Rebrisz, J., ed. see Protase, E. Woodford & Kernan, Doris.
Rebrovich, Victor E. Star Menu: A Professional Menu & System Management Program for the IBM PC-XT-AT-PS2. rev. ed. Nugent, Kathy, ed. (Illus.). 80p. (C). 1990. disk 79.95 (*0-9626641-0-3*) AstroSoft Data.
Rebsamen, Frederick. Beowulf: A Verse Translation. LC 91-55103. 1992. mass mkt. 4.50 (*0-06-430212-1*, PL) HarpC.
Rebucci, G. G., et al, eds. Symposium on Lucunar Infarcts: Clinical Aspects & Diagnostic Examinations: Ravenna, April 1989. (Journal: European Neurology: Vol. 29, Suppl. 2, 1989). 50p. (C). 1989. pap. 22.50 (*3-8055-5124-X*) S Karger.
Rebuck, Debra, jt. auth. see Woodall, Jack.
Rebuck, Linda & Fettke, Tom. Gettin' Ready for the Miracle. (J). 1985. 4.95 (*0-685-71358-X*, MC-57); audio 10.98 (*0-685-71359-8*, TA-9071C) Lillenas.
— To See a Miracle. 1983. 5.25 (*0-685-68647-7*, MB-522); audio 10.98 (*0-685-68648-5*, TA-9049C); audio 60.00 (*0-685-68649-3*, MU-9049C); 86.00 (*0-685-68650-7*, OR-9049) Lillenas.
— To Tell the Truth. (J). 1985. 5.25 (*0-685-68203-X*, MB-546); audio 10.98 (*0-685-68204-8*, TA-9065C) Lillenas.
Rebuck, Linda, jt. auth. see Fettke, Tom.
Rebuck, Linda, et al. Not a Creature Was Stirring. (J). (gr. 2 up). 1990. 4.95 (*0-685-68517-9*, MC-72); audio 10.98 (*0-685-68518-7*, TA-9119C) Lillenas.
Reby, Jacob & Douglas, James A. Banking & Lending Institution Forms with Commentary. 4th ed. 1992. 245.00 (*0-685-69634-0*, MBF) Warren Gorham & Lamont.
Recalde, L. Sallaberry. Seasons of Our Years. (Illus.). 84p. (Orig.). 1989. pap. 3.00 (*0-929688-15-5*) Bear Hse Pub.
Recamier, Jeanne F. Memoirs & Correspondence of Madame Recamier. LC 73-37715. (Illus.). reprint ed. 55.00 (*0-404-56808-4*) AMS Pr.
Recanati, Francois. Direct Reference: A Philosophical Essay on Meaning. LC 92-29857. 350p. 1993. 49.95 (*0-631-18154-7*) Blackwell Pubs.
— Meaning & Force: The Pragmatics of Performative Utterances. (Cambridge Studies in Philosophy). 272p. 1988. 64.95 (*0-521-30353-2*) Cambridge U Pr.
Recardo, Ronald J. & Peluso, Luigi A. The People Dimension: Managing the Transition to World-Class Manufacturing. LC 92-11950. 224p. 1992. text ed. 29.95 (*0-527-91666-8*, 916668) Qual Resc.
Reccenda, Ann B., ed. see Roede, Ann.
Recchia, Cheri, ed. see Bel'kovitch, V. M. & Sh'ekotov, M. N.
Recent & Fossil Marine Diatoms Staff. Proceedings of the Recent & Fossil Marine Diatoms, 3rd Symposium, 1975. Simonsen, R., ed. 1975. 150.00 (*3-7682-5453-4*) Lubrecht & Cramer.
Recent & Fossil Marine Diatoms Symposium Staff. Proceedings of the Recent & Fossil Marine Diatoms Symposium, 1st, 1972. Simonsen, R., ed. 1972. 90.00 (*3-7682-5439-9*) Lubrecht & Cramer.
— Proceedings of the Recent & Fossil Marine Diatoms, 2nd, 1974. Simonsen, R., ed. 1974. 150.00 (*3-7682-5445-3*) Lubrecht & Cramer.
Recent Advances in Optimization Techniques Symposium Staff. Recent Advances in Optimization Techniques: Proceedings of the Symposium, Carnegie Institute of Technology, 1965. Lavi, Abrahim et al, eds. LC 66-4421. 670p. reprint ed. pap. 180.00 (*0-317-08576-X*, 2006349) Bks Demand.
*Receveur, Betty L. Kentucky Home. 1995. mass mkt. 5.99 (*0-345-37118-1*) Ballantine.
— Oh, Kentucky! 1992. mass mkt. 5.99 (*0-345-31717-3*) Ballantine.
Rech, R. H. & Gudelsky, G. A., eds. Five-HT Antagonists As Psychoactive Drugs. LC 88-61898. (Illus.). 308p. 1988. write for info. (*0-916182-06-1*) NPP Bks.
Rechcigi, M. Nutrient Elements & Toxicants. (Comparative Animal Nutrition Ser.: Vol. 2). (Illus.). 1977. 78.50 (*3-8055-2351-3*) S Karger.
Rechcigl, Jack E., ed. Influence of Soil Amendments on Biotic Systems. LC 94-17628. (Agriculture & Environment Ser.). 1994. write for info. (*0-87371-860-7*) Lewis Pubs.
— Soil Amendments & Environmental Quality. 448p. 1995. 95.00 (*0-87371-859-3*, L859) Lewis Pubs.
Rechcigl, M. Diets, Culture, Media & Food Supplements: Culture Media for Cells, Organs & Embryos. LC 77-6287. (Handbook Series in Nutrition & Food: Vol. 4, Sec. G). 1978. 99.95 (*0-8493-2739-3*) CRC Pr.
— Diets, Culture, Media & Food Supplements: Diets for Mammals. LC 77-6287. (Handbook Series in Nutrition & Food: Vol. 1, Sec. G). 1977. 107.95 (*0-8493-2736-9*) CRC Pr.
— Diets, Culture, Media & Food Supplements: Food Habits, Diets, Invertibrate, Vertebrates, Zoo Diets. LC 77-6287. (Handbook Series in Nutrition & Food: Vol. 2, Sec. G). 1978. 99.95 (*0-8493-2737-7*) CRC Pr.
— Diets, Culture, Media, Food Supplement Section G, 3 vols., Set. LC 77-6287. 1977. 833.00 (*0-8493-2735-0*) CRC Pr.
— Handbook Series in Nutrition & Food, 4 vols., Set. LC 77-6287. 1977. 1,122.00 (*0-8493-2700-8*) CRC Pr.
— World Food Problem: Selective Bibliography of Reviews. LC 74-30748. 1975. 53.00 (*0-8493-5098-0*) CRC Pr.
Rechcigl, M., Jr., ed. Carbohydrates, Lipids & Accessory Growth Factors. (Comparative Animal Nutrition Ser.: Vol. 1). (Illus.). 1976. 78.50 (*3-8055-2268-1*) S Karger.
Rechcigl, M., ed. Food, Nutrition & Health. (World Review of Nutrition & Dietetics Ser.: Vol. 16). (Illus.). 350p. 1973. 144.00 (*3-8055-1398-4*) S Karger.
Rechcigl, M., Jr., ed. Handbook of Nutritive Value of Processed Food: Food for Human Use, Vol. I. 696p. 1982. 172.00 (*0-8493-3951-0*, TX551, CRC Reprint) Franklin.
— Nitrogen, Electrolytes Water & Metabolism. (Comparative Animal Nutrition Ser.: Vol. 3). (Illus.). 1979. 104.00 (*3-8055-2829-9*) S Karger.
— Physiology of Growth & Nutrition. (Comparative Animal Nutrition Ser.: Vol. 4). (Illus.). xii, 344p. 1981. pap. 199.25 (*3-8055-1199-X*) S Karger.
Rechcigl, Miloslav, Jr. Handbook of Agricultural Productivity, Vol. I: Plant Productivity. 464p. 1982. 168.95 (*0-8493-3961-8*, S494, CRC Reprint) Franklin.
Rechcigl, Miloslav, Jr., ed. CRC Handbook of Nutritive Value of Processed Food: Animal Foodstuffs, Vol. II. 520p. 1982. 155.00 (*0-8493-3953-7*, TX551, CRC Reprint) Franklin.
— Czechoslovak Contribution to World Culture. 1964. text ed. 115.40 (*90-279-1032-4*) Mouton.
— Czechoslovakia Past & Present, Set. Incl. Vol. 1. Political, International, Social & Economic Aspects. 1968. (*0-318-54400-8*); Vol. 2. Essays on the Arts & Sciences. 1968. (*0-318-54401-6*); 1968. Set text ed. 347.00 (*0-686-22479-5*) Mouton.
— Handbook of Foodborne Diseases of Biological Origin. 535p. 1983. 152.95 (*0-8493-3964-2*, RA1258, CRC Reprint) Franklin.
— Handbook of Naturally Occurring Food Toxicants. 360p. 1983. 152.95 (*0-8493-3965-0*, TX531, CRC Reprint) Franklin.
— Handbook of Nutrition & Food. (Comparative & Qualitative Requirements Ser.). (Illus.). 576p. 1977. 99.00 (*0-8493-2721-0*, QH519, CRC Reprint) Franklin.
Rechcigl, Miloslav, ed. Handbook of Nutritional Requirements in a Functional Context, Vol. I. 560p. 1981. Vol. 1: Development & Conditions of Physiological Stress, 560p. 151.00 (*0-8493-3956-1*, QP82, CRC Reprint) Franklin.
— Handbook of Nutritional Requirements in a Functional Context, Vol. II. 616p. 1981. Vol. 2: Hematopoiesis, Metabolic Function & Resistence to Physical Stress, 616p. 198.00 (*0-8493-3958-8*, QP82, CRC Reprint) Franklin.
Rechcigl, Miloslav, Jr., ed. Handbook of Nutritional Supplements, 2 Vols., Vol. I: Human Use. 576p. 1984. 201.95 (*0-8493-3969-3*, TX553, CRC Reprint) Franklin.
— Handbook of Nutritional Supplements, 2 Vols., Vol. II: Agricultural Use. 424p. 1984. 180.95 (*0-8493-3970-7*, CRC Reprint) Franklin.
Rechcigl, Miroslav, ed. Nutrition & Food Deficiencies Animals. 1978. 110.00 (*0-8493-2797-0*, RC620, CRC Reprint) Franklin.
— Nutrition & Food Deficiencies Animals, Vol. III. 388p. 1978. 70.50 (*0-8493-2798-9*, CRC Reprint) Franklin.
Rechelbacher, Horst. Rejuvenation. (Illus.). 224p. 1987. pap. 12.95 (*0-89281-248-6*) Inner Tradit.
Rechenauer, Georg. Thuykdides und die Hippokratische Medizin. (Spudasmata Ser.: Bd. XLVII). xii, 396p. (GER.). 1991. write for info. (*3-487-09226-3*, Pub. by Georg Olms GW) Lubrecht & Cramer.
Rechenbach, Charles W. & Gesuga, Angelica W. Swahili-English Dictionary. LC 67-31438. 653p. reprint ed. pap. 180.00 (*0-318-39759-5*, 2033133) Bks Demand.
Rechenberg, H., jt. auth. see Mehra, Jagdish.

An Asterisk (*) at the beginning of an entry indicates that the title is appearing in BIP for the first time.

Rechenberg, Helmut, jt. auth. see Mehra, Jagdish.

Rechin & Wilder, Dan. Here's Sand in Nose. (Crock Ser.: No. 11). 1986. pap. 2.25 (*0-449-12960-8*) Fawcett.

Rechin, Bill. Who Pulled My Plug. 1984. pap. 1.95 (*0-449-12643-9*) Fawcett.

Rechin, Bill, et al. You'll Pay for This...All of You! 1979. pap. 1.95 (*0-449-14121-7*, GM) Fawcett.

Rechinger, K. H. Flora of Lowland Iraq. 1964. 95.00 (*3-7682-0217-8*) Lubrecht & Cramer.

Rechlin, Charles F. Securities Credit Regulation. LC 93-44704. (Securities Law Ser.). 1994. ring bd. 145.00 (*0-87632-984-9*) Clark Boardman Callaghan.

Rechlin, Fred, jt. auth. see Rechlin, Harriet.

Rechlin, Harriet & Rechlin, Fred. Pioneer Jews: A New Life in the Far West. (Illus.). 256p. 1986. pap. 18.95 (*0-395-42639-1*) HM.

Rechnitz, G. & Belcher, R. Controlled-Potential Analysis. LC 63-19612. (International Series of Monographs on Analytical Chemistry: Vol. 13). 1963. 42.00 (*0-08-013135-2*, Pub. by Pergamon Repr UK) Franklin.

Rechs, Robert J. Balloon Construction: Design Critera, Vol. 1. (Illus.). 176p. (Orig.). 1987. pap. 35.00 (*0-937568-15-5*, TL 638 R43 V1) Rechs Pubns.

— Balloon Construction: Materials & Suppliers, Vol. 2. (Illus.). 176p. (Orig.). 1987. pap. text ed. 35.00 (*0-937568-16-3*, TL 638 R43 V2) Rechs Pubns.

— Balloon Construction: Plans & Construction, Vol. 3. (Illus.). 176p. (Orig.). 1987. pap. text ed. 35.00 (*0-937568-17-1*, TL 638 R43 V3) Rechs Pubns.

— Who's Who of Ballooning: 1783-1983. 362p. (Orig.). 1982. 35.00 (*0-937568-26-0*, TL 615 R43); pap. text ed. 20.00 (*0-937568-27-9*) Rechs Pubns.

Rechsteiner, M., ed. Ubiquitin. LC 88-9809. (Illus.). 364p. 1988. 75.00 (*0-306-42850-4*, Plenum Pr) Plenum.

Recht, Christine. Herbs. (Mini Fact Finders Ser.). 64p. 1991. spiral bd. 4.95 (*0-8120-4453-3*) Barron.

Recht, Christine & Wetterwald, Max. Bamboos. (Illus.). 160p. 1992. 32.95 (*0-88192-268-4*) Timber.

***Recht, Marilyn.** She Must Have Been a Giant. 41p. (Orig.). 1994. pap. write for info. (*1-877649-22-8*) Tesseract SD.

Rechtin, Eberhardt. Systems Architecting: Creating & Building Complex Systems. 352p. 1990. text ed. 75.00 (*0-13-880345-5*) P-H.

***Rechtschaffen, Joseph S. & Carola, Robert.** Dr. Rechtschaffen's Diet for Lifetime Weight Control & Better Health. 224p. 1995. pap. 10.00 (*1-56836-077-0*) Kodansha.

— Minding Your Body: 100 Ways to Live & Be Well. 256p. 1995. 18.00 (*1-56836-076-2*) Kodansha.

Rechtschaffen, Scott D., et al. Employee Handbook: How to Write One for Your Company. (Orig.). (C). 1994. pap. text ed. 59.00 (*1-878630-53-9*) CA Chamber Commerce.

Rechung, Ven R., ed. & tr. Tibetan Medicine: Illustrated in Original Text. 346p. 1973. reprint ed. pap. 16.00 (*0-520-03048-6*) U CA Pr.

Rechy, John. Bodies & Souls. 386p. (Orig.). 1983. pap. 8.95 (*0-88184-004-1*); pap. 4.50 (*0-88184-102-1*) Carroll & Graf.

— City of Night. 400p. 1988. pap. 10.95 (*0-8021-3083-6*) Grove-Atltic.

— The Fourth Angel. 158p. 1983. pap. 6.95 (*0-8021-5197-3*) Grove-Atltic.

— The Miraculous Day of Amalia Gomez. 256p. 1993. pap. 9.95 (*1-55970-203-6*) Arcade Pub Inc.

— Numbers. 272p. 1990. pap. 11.95 (*0-8021-5198-1*) Grove-Atltic.

— The Sexual Outlaw: A Documentary. 304p. 1990. pap. 9.95 (*0-8021-3163-8*) Grove-Atltic.

Reciniello, Richard. A Cynic's Dictionary of Modern American Terms. 1992. 10.00 (*0-533-10253-7*) Vantage.

Recinos, Adrian, et al, trs. Popol Vuh: The Sacred Book of the Ancient Quiche Maya: Spanish Version of the Original Maya. LC 50-6643. (Civilization of the American Indian Ser.: No. 29). 288p. 1991. reprint ed. 26.95 (*0-8061-0205-5*); reprint ed. pap. 12.95 (*0-8061-2266-8*) U of Okla Pr.

Recinos, Adrian & Goetz, Delia, trs. The Annals of the Cakchiquels. Bd. with Title of the Lords of Totonicapan. (Civilization of the American Indian Ser.: Vol. 37). 217p. 1974. Set pap. 9.95 (*0-8061-1152-6*) U of Okla Pr.

Recinos, Hal J. Jesus Weeps: Global Encounter on Our Doorstep. 112p. (Orig.). 1992. pap. 10.95 (*0-687-03185-0*) Abingdon.

Recio, L. M., ed. see Menendez Pidal, Ramon.

Recio, T., jt. ed. see Dubois, D. W.

Reciputi, Natalie S. Dante's Ratchet. 74p. (Orig.). 1993. pap. 7.00 (*0-944920-06-3*) Bellowing Ark Pr.

Reck, Andrew J. Introduction to William James: An Essay & Selected Texts. LC 67-25137. (Midland Book Ser.: No. MB105). 220p. reprint ed. pap. 62.70 (*0-317-09895-0*, 2055212) Bks Demand.

Reck, Andrew J., ed. see Mead, George H.

Reck, Brian, ed. see Bunn, T. Davis.

Reck, Carleen. The Small Catholic Elementary School: Advantages & Opportunities. 119p. (Orig.). 1988. pap. 10.60 (*1-55833-008-9*) Natl Cath Educ.

Reck, Carleen, ed. AIDS: A Catholic Educational Approach to HIV - Teacher's Manual. rev. ed. (Illus.). 176p. 1992. pap. 16.60 (*1-55833-111-5*); 5.00 (*1-55833-112-3*) Natl Cath Educ.

Reck, Carleen & Coreil, Judith, eds. Verifying the Vision: A Self-Evaluation for the Catholic Elementary School. 2nd ed. 150p. 1988. reprint ed. pap. 14.00 (*1-55833-003-8*) Natl Cath Educ.

Reck, Carleen, jt. ed. see Hall, Suzanne E.

Reck, Carleen, jt. auth. see Heft, James.

Reck, Gregory C. In the Shadow of Tlaloc: Life in a Mexican Village. (Illus.). 224p. (C). 1986. reprint ed. pap. text ed. 9.95 (*0-88133-244-5*) Waveland Pr.

Reck, Hanne G. Aleman Para Estudiantes de Habla Espanola: Deutsch fur Studenten der Spanischer Sprache, Vol. II. 7.00 (*0-8477-3340-8*) U of PR Pr.

— Deutsch Fur Studenten Spicher Sprache-Aleman Para Estudiantes De Habla Espanola, Vol. 1. LC 78-18825. 193p. 1979. pap. text ed. 6.00 (*0-8477-3321-1*) U of PR Pr.

Reck, JoAnn M., jt. auth. see Siskin, H. Jay.

Reck, Jurgen. Diccionario Rioduero Matematica. 2nd ed. 224p. (SPA.). 1982. write for info. (*0-7859-5069-9*) Fr & Eur.

— Herder-Lexikon Mathematik. 238p. (GER.). 1974. 39.95 (*0-8288-6050-5*, M7445) Fr & Eur.

Reck, Michael, tr. see Homer.

Reck, Rima D. Drieu La Rochelle & the Picture Gallery Novel: French Modernism in the Interwar Years. LC 89-48255. (Illus.). 272p. 1990. text ed. 34.95 (*0-8071-1584-3*) La State U Pr.

Reck, Ross R. Win-Win Negotiator. 1989. pap. 8.00 (*0-671-67698-9*) PB.

Reck, Ross R. & Long, Brian. Negotiating Techniques: How to Work Toward a Constructive Agreement. Guder, Robert, ed. 1985. 14.95 (*0-910187-05-3*) Economics Pr.

Reck, Ross R. & Long, Brian G. The Win-Win Negotiator: How to Negotiate Favorable Agreements That Last. LC 87-61727. (Illus.). 1987. 15.00 (*0-9616722-1-8*, RR-1) Spartan MI.

Reck, Ruth A. & Hummel, John R., eds. Interpretation of Climate & Photochemical Models, Ozone & Temperature Measurements: AIP Conference Proceedings, No. 82, La Jolla Institute, March 9-11, 1981. LC 82-71345. 320p. 1982. 33.00 (*0-88318-181-9*) Am Inst Physics.

***Reck, Sue, ed.** Search of the Soul. (Discovery Ser.). 1995. teacher ed 9.95 (*0-7814-5201-5*, 29538) Cook.

— Search of the Soul Journal. (Discovery Ser.). (YA). 1995. 9.95 (*0-7814-5202-3*, 29538) Cook.

Reck, Sue, ed. see Baldry, Cherith.

Reck, Sue, ed. see Boyce, Kim & Abraham, Ken.

Reck, Sue, ed. see Erickson, Mary.

Reck, Sue, ed. see Fraser, Wynnette.

Reck, Sue, ed. see Kennedy, Pamela.

Reck, Sue, ed. see Levene, Nancy S.

Reck, Sue, ed. see Lord, Wendy.

Reck, Sue, ed. see McHenry, Janet H.

Reck, Sue, ed. see Sattgast, L. J.

Reck, Vera T. Boris Pil'niak: A Soviet Writer in Conflict with the State. LC 76-356287. 255p. reprint ed. pap. 72.70 (*0-8357-7355-8*, 2023857) Bks Demand.

Reck, Vera T., tr. see Pilnyak, Boris.

Reck, W. Emerson. A. Lincoln: His Last Twenty Four Hours. LC 85-43587. 240p. 1987. lib. bdg. 23.95x (*0-89950-216-4*) McFarland & Co.

— A. Lincoln: His Last Twenty-Four Hours. (Illus.). 256p. (C). 1994. reprint ed. pap. 14.95 (*1-57003-008-1*) U of SC Pr.

Reck, William A. Thoughts: On Apparitions, Chastisements, the Church. LC 93-83447. 92p. (Orig.). 1993. pap. 2.00 (*1-877678-23-6*) Riehle Found.

Recke, Walther-Albert M. Bucherkunde Zur Geschichte und Literatur des Konigreichs Polen. xi, 242p. reprint ed. write for info. (*0-318-71861-8*, Pub. by Georg Olms GW) Lubrecht & Cramer.

Recker, Jo A., jt. auth. see Siskin, H. Jay.

Recker, Jo Ann. The "Appelle-moi 'Pierrot'": Wit & Irony in "Lettres" of Madame de Sevigne. LC 86-20777. (Purdue University Monographs in Romance Languages: No. 21). ix, 128p. (Orig.). 1986. pap. 33.00x (*0-915027-70-4*) Benjamins North Am.

Recker, Robert R., ed. Bone Histomorphometry: Techniques & Interpretation. 312p. 1983. 168.00 (*0-8493-5373-4*, QM569, CRC Reprint) Franklin.

Recker, Wilfred W., jt. auth. see Paaswell, Robert E.

Reckert, Stephen. Beyond Chrysanthemums: Perspectives on Poetry East & West. LC 92-26818. 1993. 52.00 (*0-19-815165-9*, Clarendon Pr) OUP.

Reckford, Kenneth J. Aristophanes' Old-&-New Comedy, Vol. 1: Six Essays in Perspective. LC 86-16188. xiv, 567p. (C). 1987. 45.00 (*0-8078-1720-1*) U of NC Pr.

Reckford, Kenneth J., tr. see Euripides.

Reckford, Thomas J., jt. auth. see Palmer, Ronald D.

Reckhow, Kenneth H. & Chapra, Steven. Engineering Approaches for Lake Management, 2 vols., Set. LC 79-56115. 200p. 1983. text ed. 125.00 (*0-250-40516-4*) Buttrwrth-Heinemann.

— Engineering Approaches for Lake Management, 2 vols., Vol. 1: Data Analysis & Empirical Modeling. LC 79-56115. 200p. 1983. text ed. 66.95 (*0-250-40344-7*) Buttrwrth-Heinemann.

Reckinger, Nancy. Parents' Record of Educational Progress: How to Insure Your Child's Success in School. 78p. (Orig.). 1982. pap. 10.00 (*0-943346-00-2*) Ctr Ed Alternatives.

Reckitt, B. N. Diary of Anti-Aircraft Defence, 1938-1944. (C). 1990. 35.00 (*0-7223-2459-6*, Pub. by A H S Ltd UK) St Mut.

Reckitt, B. N., ed. Diary of Military Government in Germany, 1945. 78p. (C). 1989. 35.00 (*0-7223-2301-8*, Pub. by A H S Ltd UK) St Mut.

Reckitt, Basil N. William Reckitt: An Eighteenth Century Quaker Traveller in America, France & West Indies from 1756. (C). 1989. pap. 21.00 (*1-85072-057-6*, Pub. by W Sessions UK) St Mut.

Reckless, Walter C. Vice in Chicago. LC 69-16243. (Criminology, Law Enforcement, & Social Problems Ser.: No. 84). 1969. reprint ed. 18.00 (*0-87585-084-7*) Patterson Smith.

Reckling. Orthopedic Anatomy & Surgical Approaches. 544p. 1990. 99.95 (*0-8151-7120-X*, Yr Bk Med Pubs) Mosby Yr Bk.

Recknagel. Message. 1988. 12.95 (*1-55774-024-0*) Modan-Adama Bks.

Recknagel, A. B. Forest Management. 269p. (C). 1981. text ed. 900.00 (*0-685-52007-2*, Pub. by Intl Bk Distr II) St Mut.

— Forest Management. 269p. 1985. 225.00 (*81-7089-034-9*, Pub. by Intl Bk Distr II) St Mut.

Recknagel, Carl. Just off the Ground: Memoirs of an Aviator. (Illus.). 176p. (Orig.). 1993. pap. 19.95 (*1-56474-067-6*) Fithian Pr.

Recknagel, E. & Soares, J. C., eds. Nuclear Physics Applications on Materials Science. (C). 1988. lib. bdg. 179.50 (*90-247-3703-6*) Kluwer Ac.

Recknagel, E., jt. ed. see Echt, O.

Reckner, James R. Teddy Roosevelt's Great White Fleet. (Illus.). 384p. 1988. 28.95 (*0-87021-697-X*) Naval Inst Pr.

Reckner, Jerald H. & Norton, Jeni F. The Power Within: Living with Your Full Potential. LC 87-71541. (Illus.). (Orig.). (C). 1987. pap. 8.95 (*0-943889-00-6*) Assoc Beta Cos.

Recktenwald, Charles. Helping Children Succeed: How to Help Children Succeed in School & in Life. LC 88-80401. 138p. (Orig.). 1989. pap. 6.95 (*0-929089-00-6*) East Fork Pub Co.

Recktenwald, Horst C. Dictionary of Economics: Woerterbuch der Wirtschaft. 10th ed. 706p. (GER.). 1987. 59.95 (*0-8288-1279-9*, M6941) Fr & Eur.

Reclus, E. The Earth & Its Inhabitants, 21 Vols. 1975. lib. bdg. 2,500.00 (*0-8490-0077-7*) Gordon Pr.

— Evolution & Revolution. 1972. 200.00 (*0-8490-0142-0*) Gordon Pr.

Reclus, Elisee. Plant Physiognomies. 1973. 69.95 (*0-8490-0840-9*) Gordon Pr.

Recognition Systems Staff. Providing Recognition: A Handbook of Ideas. 1974. ring bd. 24.90 (*0-89401-103-0*) Didactic Syst.

***Recommended Country Inns Series Staff.** Recommended Romantic Inns of America. 2nd ed. LC 92-39760. (Recommended Country Inns Ser.). (Illus.). 320p. 1995. pap. 14.95 (*1-56440-515-X*) Globe Pequot.

***Record.** High Octane. 1995. (*0-7858-0327-0*) Bk Sales Inc.

— Hot Rods & Dragsters: Ultimate Speed Machines. 1995. (*0-7858-0342-4*) Bk Sales Inc.

Record, Jeffrey. Force Reductions in Europe: Starting Over. LC 80-83753. (Special Report Ser.). 92p. 1980. 11.95 (*0-89549-027-7*) Inst Foreign Policy Anal.

— Hollow Victory: A Contrary View of the Gulf War. LC 92-26885. 192p. 1993. 23.00 (*0-02-881046-5*) Brasseys Inc.

— NATO'S Theater Nuclear Force Modernization Program: The Real Issues. LC 81-84988. (Special Report Ser.). 102p. 1981. 11.95 (*0-89549-038-2*) Inst Foreign Policy Anal.

— The Rapid Deployment Force & U. S. Military Intervention in the Persian Gulf. 2nd ed. LC 83-81086. (Special Report Ser.). 83p. 1983. 11.95 (*0-89549-053-6*) Inst Foreign Policy Anal.

— Sizing up the Soviet Army. LC 75-26941. (Studies in Defense Policy). 61p. reprint ed. pap. 25.00 (*0-685-23652-8*, 2027971) Bks Demand.

— Strategic Bombers: How Many Are Enough? LC 86-6. (National Security Papers: No. 3). 26p. 1986. 7.50 (*0-89549-069-2*) Inst Foreign Policy Anal.

— U. S. Nuclear Weapons in Europe: Issues & Alternatives. LC 74-23433. (Studies in Defense Policy). 70p. 1974. pap. 7.95 (*0-8157-7365-X*) Brookings.

— U. S. Strategic Airlift: Requirements & Capabilities. LC 85-23927. (National Security Papers: No. 2). 43p. 1986. 7.50 (*0-89549-068-4*) Inst Foreign Policy Anal.

Record, Jeffrey, ed. The Future of the U. S. Military Commitment to Europe. 172p. (Orig.). (C). 1989. pap. text ed. 10.95 (*0-685-37970-1*) Hudson Instit IN.

Record, Jeffrey & Hanks, Robert J. U. S. Strategy at the Crossroads: Two Views. LC 82-82774. (Foreign Policy Reports). 69p. 1982. 11.95 (*0-89549-044-7*) Inst Foreign Policy Anal.

Record, Jeffrey, jt. auth. see Binkin, Martin.

Record, Jeffrey, jt. auth. see Lawrence, Richard D.

Record, Jeffrey, et al. The INF Treaty: Pro & Con. 70p. (Orig.). (C). 1988. pap. 5.00 (*1-55813-032-2*) Hudson Instit IN.

Record, Robert. The Castle of Knowledge. LC 74-28882. (English Experience Ser.: No. 760). 1975. reprint ed. 44.00 (*90-221-0760-4*) Walter J Johnson.

— The Grounde of Artes, Teachying the Worke & Practise of Arithmetike. LC 77-26032. (English Experience Ser.: No. 174). (Illus.). 1969. reprint ed. 35.00 (*90-221-0174-6*) Walter J Johnson.

— The Path-Way to Knowledge, Containing the First Principles of Geometrie. LC 74-80206. (English Experience Ser.: No. 687). 1974. reprint ed. 25.00 (*90-221-0687-X*) Walter J Johnson.

Record, Samuel J. & Hess, Robert W. Timbers of the New World. LC 73-140611. (Use & Abuse of America's Natural Resources Ser.). (Illus.). 718p. 1975. reprint ed. 63.95 (*0-405-02806-7*) Ayer.

Record, Sandra H., ed. see Atkinson, Chuck.

***Records, Laban S.** Cherokee Outlet Cowboy: Recollections of Laban S. Records. Wheeler, Ellen J., ed. LC 94-37534. (Illus.). 370p. 1995. 24.95 (*0-8061-2694-9*) U of Okla Pr.

Records, Pam. Once upon a Rhyme: A Wizard's Wacky Story Time. (Shuffle-a-Book Ser.). (Illus.). 21p. (J). (ps). 1993. pap. 10.95 (*0-9639839-0-3*) MP Records.

Recouly, Raymond. Third Republic. Buckley, E. F., tr. LC 28-23849. (National History of France Ser.: No. 10). reprint ed. 45.00 (*0-404-50800-6*) AMS Pr.

Recourse Systems, Inc. Staff, jt. auth. see INFORM, Inc. Staff.

Recovery Alliance, Inc. Staff. The Impossible Diet Cookbook. LC 92-61954. 196p. 1992. pap. 12.95 (*0-9629391-0-2*) Recovery Alliance.

Recreation & Sport Dept. Staff. Heysen Trail Guide Book, Pt. 1. 128p. (C). 1989. pap. text ed. 30.00 (*0-89771-020-7*, Pub. by Bob Mossel AT) St Mut.

— Heysen Trail Guide Book, Pt. 11: Parachilna to Hawker. (C). 1989. pap. text ed. 30.00 (*0-89771-033-9*, Pub. by Bob Mossel AT) St Mut.

Recruiting New Teachers, Inc. Staff. The RNT Careers in Teaching Handbook. (Illus.). 104p. 1993. write for info. (*1-884139-02-7*) Recruit New Tchrs.

— State Policies to Improve the Teacher Workforce: Shaping the Profession That Shapes America's Future. (Illus.). 48p. 1993. write for info. (*1-884139-00-0*) Recruit New Tchrs.

— Teaching's Next Generation. (Illus.). 160p. 1993. write for info. (*1-884139-01-9*) Recruit New Tchrs.

Recski, A. Matroid Theory & Its Applications in Electric Network Theory & Statics. (Algorithms & Combinatorics Ser.: Vol. 6). 350p. 1989. 89.50 (*0-387-15285-7*) Spr-Verlag.

Recski, A., jt. ed. see Lovasz, L.

Rectanus, Cheryl. Math by All Means: Geometry, Grade 3. 1994. pap. 19.95 (*0-941355-10-1*) M Burns Educ Assocs.

Rectanus, Mark W. & Hiller, Renate. Prisma: Dokumente, Literatur, Kommunikation. 314p. (GER.). (C). 1992. pap. text ed. write for info. (*0-669-20492-7*) Heath.

Rector. Complications of Chronic Liver Disease. 383p. 1991. 69.00 (*0-8151-7236-2*, Yr Bk Med Pubs) Mosby Yr Bk.

Rector, Andy. Five Minutes 'til Bedtime: Twelve Quick-As-a-Wink Bible Stories. LC 93-7339. (Illus.). 32p. (Orig.). (J). 1993. pap. 5.99 (*0-7847-0110-5*, 24-03670) Standard Pub.

— Old Testament Bedtime Bible Stories for Toddlers. 1993. 4.99 (*0-685-70269-3*) Standard Pub.

— Quick-As-a-Wink New Testament Bedtime Stories. (Illus.). 12p. (J). (ps). 1993. bds. 4.99 (*0-7847-0112-1*, 24-03102) Standard Pub.

— Quick-As-a-Wink Old Testament Bedtime Bible Stories. (Illus.). 12p. (J). (ps). 1993. bds. 4.99 (*0-7847-0111-3*, 24-03101) Standard Pub.

— The Secret Room. Stortz, Diane, ed. (Really Reading! Bks.). (Illus.). 48p. (Orig.). (J). (ps-3). 1994. pap. 4.49 (*0-7847-0179-2*, 24-03939) Standard Pub.

Rector, Andy, ed. see Beegle, Shirley.

Rector, Andy, ed. see Boender, Caroline.

Rector, Andy, jt. ed. see Lierman, Deonna.

Rector, Andy, ed. see Tiner, John H.

Rector, Brent E. Developing Windows 3.1 Applications with Microsoft C - C Plus Plus. 2nd ed. (Illus.). 1992. pap. 39.95 (*0-672-30166-0*) Sams.

Rector, C. H. The Story of Beautiful Puerto Rico: By Pen & Camera. 200p. 1974. lib. bdg. 250.00 (*0-8490-1128-0*) Gordon Pr.

Rector, Floyd C., Jr., jt. auth. see Brenner, Barry M.

Rector, Harry E. Guidelines for Monitoring Indoor Air Quality. (Illus.). 270p. (C). 1986. 58.00 (*0-89116-385-9*) Hemisp Pub.

Rector, Hartman, Jr. Already to Harvest. 91p. 1985. pap. 5.95 (*0-934126-73-9*) CFI Dist.

— To a Chosen Generation. 6.95 (*0-88494-564-2*) Bookcraft Inc.

Rector, Janice. How to Recognize & Overcome Depression: A Woman's Personal Experience. LC 93-85051. 112p. (Orig.). 1994. pap. 10.95 (*0-9637222-0-4*) Sunrise Internat.

Rector, Johnny. Deluxe Encyclopedia of Guitar Chord Progressions. 1993. 8.95 (*0-87166-030-X*, 93416); audio 9.98 (*1-56222-588-X*, 93416) Mel Bay.

— Deluxe Encyclopedia of Jazz Guitar Runs, Fills, Licks, & Lines. 1993. 8.95 (*0-87166-955-2*, 93976) Mel Bay.

Rector, Lee T. Americana. Tibbetts, Kathleen & Tibbetts, Laurene, eds. LC 81-90246. 168p. 1981. write for info. (*0-9606170-0-0*) Rector Pub.

— Melodies of the Wind & Other Poems. 89p. 1984. write for info. (*0-318-58392-5*) Rector Pub.

— Yesteryears. 117p. 1982. write for info. (*0-318-58391-7*) Rector Pub.

Rector, Liam. American Prodigals. 1994. 19.95 (*0-685-72739-4*); pap. 11.95 (*0-685-72740-8*) Story Line.

— The Sorrow of Architecture. LC 83-20685. 75p. 1984. 14.00 (*0-937872-16-4*); pap. 6.00 (*0-937872-17-2*) Dragon Gate.

Rector, Liam, ed. The Day I Was Older: Writings on the Poetry of Donald Hall. 288p. (Orig.). 1989. 24.95 (*0-934257-20-5*); pap. 15.95 (*0-934257-19-1*) Story Line.

Rector, Margaret, ed. Cowboy Life on the Texas Plains: The Photographs of Ray Rector. LC 82-5902. (Illus.). 124p. 1992. pap. 19.95 (*0-89096-529-3*) Tex A&M Univ Pr.

Rector, Margaret H. The Lady & the Commissioner of Airports. LC 93-28279. 1993. 4.00 (*0-88734-325-2*) Players Pr.

— The Lady & the Mortician. LC 93-28300. 1993. 4.00 (*0-88734-326-0*) Players Pr.

— The Wishfork Wedding. LC 95-10803. 1995. pap. write for info. (*0-88734-327-9*) Players Pr.

***Rector-Page, Linda.** Body Cleansing & Detoxification. rev. ed. (Healthy Healing Library Ser.). 32p. 1993. 2.95 (*1-884334-31-8*) Hlthy Healing.

— Colds & Flu & You. (Healthy Healing Library Ser.). 32p. 1993. pap. 2.95 (*1-884334-03-2*) Hlthy Healing.

— Cooking for Healthy Healing: Diets & Recipes for Alternative Healing. 3rd ed. 708p. 1993. reprint ed. pap. 27.95 (*1-884334-51-2*) Hlthy Healing.

— Do You Want to Have a Baby: Conception & Natural Prenatal Care. (Healthy Healing Library Ser.). 32p. 1993. pap. 2.95 (*1-884334-02-4*) Hlthy Healing.

— The Energy Crunch & You. (Helathy Healing Library Ser.). 28p. 1993. 2.95 (*1-884334-07-5*) Hlthy Healing.

R

— Fighting Infections with Herbs: Sexually Transmitted Infections. (Healthy Healing Library Ser.). 32p. 1993. pap. 2.95 (*1-884344-04-6*) Hlthy Healing.

— Renewing Female Balance. (Healthy Healing Library Ser.). 32p. 1993. (*1-884334-25-3*) Hlthy Healing.

— Renewing Male Health & Energy with Herbs. (Healthy Healing Library Ser.). 32p. 1993. pap. 2.95 (*0-685-70777-6*) Hlthy Healing.

***Rector-Page, Linda & Van, Douglas.** Party Lights: Healthy Party Foods & Environmentally Conscious Decorations. (Illus.). (Orig.). 1994. pap. 19.95 (*1-884334-53-9*) Hlthy Healing.

***Rector-Page, Linda G.** Healthy Healing. 9th ed. 1994. write for info. (*0-912331-21-6*) Golden-Lee.

Rector, William F., III, ed. Leadership in Space for Benefits on Earth. LC 57-43769. (Advances in the Astronautical Sciences Ser.: Vol. 47). (Illus.). 310p. 1982. lib. bdg. 45.00 (*0-87703-168-1*, Pub. by Am Astro Soc); pap. text ed. 35.00 (*0-87703-169-X*, Pub. by Am Astro Soc) Univelt Inc.

Rector, William F., III & Penzo, Paul A., eds. Space Shuttle: Dawn of an Era. (Advances in the Astronautical Sciences Ser.: Vol. 41). 1980. pap. 35.00 (*0-87703-112-6*, Pub. by Am Astro Soc); pap. 40.00 (*0-87703-114-2*, Pub. by Am Astro Soc) Univelt Inc.

— Space Shuttle: Dawn of an Era. suppl. ed. (Advances in the Astronautical Sciences Ser.: Vol. 41). 1980. fiche 10.00 (*0-87703-136-3*, Pub. by Am Astro Soc) Univelt Inc.

— Space Shuttle: Dawn of an Era, Pt. 1. (Advances in the Astronautical Sciences Ser.: Vol. 41). 452p. 1980. Part 1, 452pp. lib. bdg. 45.00 (*0-87703-111-8*, Pub. by Am Astro Soc) Univelt Inc.

— Space Shuttle: Dawn of an Era, Pt. 2. (Advances in the Astronautical Sciences Ser.: Vol. 41). 528p. 1980. Part 2, 528pp. lib. bdg. 55.00 (*0-87703-113-4*, Pub. by Am Astro Soc) Univelt Inc.

Recuerda, J. Martin. Salvajes En Puente San Gil. 290p. (SPA.). 1978. 9.50 (*0-8288-7046-2*) Fr & Eur.

Recuerda, Jose M. The Theatre of Jose Martin Recuerda, Spanish Dramatist: Dramas of Franco & Post-Franco Spain. Torres, Sixto E., ed. LC 93-30131. (Hispanic Literature Ser.: Vol. 22). 408p. 1993. 109.95 (*0-7734-9356-5*) E Mellen.

Recuero, Pascal. Dicionario Basico Ladino - Espanol: Basic Ladino - Spanish Dictionary. 153p. (LAD & SPA.). 1977. pap. 29.95 (*0-8288-9419-1*, S36126) Fr & Eur.

Recycling Consortium Staff. Coconut Uses: Uses for the Coconut. rev. ed. 1992. pap. text ed. 14.95 (*0-317-04791-4*, Recycling Consort) Prosperity & Profits.

— Corn Uses: Uses for Corn. rev. ed. 1992. pap. text ed. 14.95 (*0-317-04792-2*, Recycling Consort) Prosperity & Profits.

— Dandelion Uses: Uses for the Dandelion. rev. ed. 1992. pap. text ed. 14.95 (*0-317-04793-0*, Recycling Consort) Prosperity & Profits.

— Egg Uses: Uses for Eggs. rev. ed. 1992. pap. text ed. 14.95 (*0-317-04794-9*, Recycling Consort) Prosperity & Profits.

— Homes for the Moving: Recyclable Home Possibilities. rev. ed. 1992. pap. 17.95 (*0-317-04781-7*) Prosperity & Profits.

— Lemon Uses: Uses for the Lemon. rev. ed. 1992. pap. text ed. 14.95 (*0-317-04795-7*, Recycling Consort) Prosperity & Profits.

— Orange Uses: Uses for the Orange. rev. ed. 1992. pap. text ed. 14.95 (*0-317-04796-5*, Recycling Consort) Prosperity & Profits.

— Potato Uses: Uses for the Potato. rev. ed. 1992. pap. text ed. 14.95 (*0-317-04797-3*, Recycling Consort) Prosperity & Profits.

— Recycling Commodity Exchange Encyclopedia. 1985. ring bd. 39.95 (*0-317-00916-8*) Prosperity & Profits.

— Roses Uses: Uses for the Rose. rev. ed. 1992. pap. text ed. 14.95 (*0-317-04798-1*, Recycling Consort) Prosperity & Profits.

— Solicit, Remake & Resell: The Jeans & Denim Recycling Fundraising Project Workbook. 1991. ring bd. 17.95 (*0-318-03755-6*, Recycling Consort) Prosperity & Profits.

— Solicit, Remake & Resell: The Panty Hose Recycling Fundraising Project Workbook. 1991. ring bd. 17.95 (*0-318-03754-8*, Recycling Consort) Prosperity & Profits.

— Watermelon Uses: Uses for the Watermelon. rev. ed. 1992. pap. text ed. 14.95 (*0-317-04799-X*, Recycling Consort) Prosperity & Profits.

Red. Pilgrim Hymnal. LC 58-1015. 1958. 10.95 (*0-8298-0107-3*) Pilgrim OH.

Red, Carmine. The Magic Binoculars: An Odyssey to Infinity. LC 94-82025. (Illus.). 60p. (J). (gr. 3-6). 1994. 12.95 (*0-9640506-7-6*) Rock-It Pr.

Red, David D. Rational Design. 148p. 1990. pap. 10.95 (*0-533-08511-X*) Vantage.

Red Hawk. The Sioux Dog Dance. (CSU Poetry Ser.: No. XXXV). 60p. (Orig.). 1991. pap. 8.00 (*0-914946-90-0*) Cleveland St Univ Poetry Ctr.

Red Hawk, Richard. ABCs the American Indian Way. (Illus.). 55p. (Orig.). (J). (ps-8). 1988. pap. 6.95 (*0-940113-15-5*) Sierra Oaks Pub.

— Grandfather's Story of Navajo Monsters. (Illus.). (Orig.). (J). (ps-7). 1988. pap. 6.95 (*0-940113-11-2*) Sierra Oaks Pub.

— A Trip to a Pow Wow. (Illus.). 45p. (Orig.). (J). (gr. k-3). 1988. pap. 6.95 (*0-940113-14-7*) Sierra Oaks Pub.

Red, Henrietta. Rival Sisters. Bd. with Garth of Tregillis.; Intruder at Windgates. (Romances Ser.). 576p. 1983. Set mass mkt. 3.95 (*0-373-20078-1*) Harlequin Bks.

Red, James. The American Original Home Recipe Collection Series, 4 vols., Set. Lynn, Mary, ed. (Illus.). (Orig.). 1991. pap. 15.95 (*1-879490-04-8*) Timberline NM.

Red, William S. Texas Colonists & Religion, 1821-1836. 1993. reprint ed. lib. bdg. 75.00 (*0-7812-5947-9*) Rprt Serv.

Reda, jt. auth. see Kamel Al Wajiz.

Reda, jt. auth. see Kamel De Poche.

Reda, Jacques, illus. Sempe on Holiday. 88p. 1990. pap. 19.95 (*3-7913-1099-2*, Pub. by Prestel) TeNeues.

Reda, Janet E. The Village Pantry's: Treasury of Homemade Liqueurs. rev. ed. (Illus.). 115p. (Orig.). 1986. pap. 6.95 (*0-9618109-0-4*) Village Pantry.

Reda, Mario, et al, eds. Systems & Processes: Collected Works in Sociology. (C). 1968. pap. 19.95 (*0-8084-0292-7*) NCUP.

Reda, Youssef M. Dictionnaire Francais - Arabe Detaille: Al-Kamel al-Wasit. 1990. 45.00 (*0-86685-463-0*) Intl Bk Ctr.

Redbeard, Ragnar. Might Is Right. 1972. 250.00 (*0-87700-187-1*) Revisionist Pr.

— Might Is-Right. LC 84-81634. 154p. 1984. reprint ed. pap. 7.95 (*0-915179-12-1*) Loompanics.

Redbook Florist Services Educational Advisory Committee Staff. Encyclofiora (TM) Series, 12 vols., Set. (Illus.). Date not set. text ed. 347.52 (*1-56963-000-3*) Redbk Florist.

Redbook Florist Services Educational Advisory Committee. Advanced Floral Design. LC 92-80132. (Encyclofiora Ser.). (Illus.). 326p. (Orig.). 1992. pap. text ed. 34.95 (*1-56963-024-0*) Redbk Florist.

— Basic Floral Design. LC 91-61275. (Encyclofiora Ser.). (Illus.). 286p. (Orig.). 1991. pap. text ed. 34.95 (*1-56963-014-3*) Redbk Florist.

— Designing with Balloons & Flowers. LC 91-66385. (Encyclofiora Ser.). (Illus.). 176p. (Orig.). 1991. pap. text ed. 34.95 (*1-56963-020-8*) Redbk Florist.

— Floral Design for the Holidays. LC 91-73528. (Encyclofiora Ser.). (Illus.). 566p. (Orig.). 1991. pap. text ed. 39.95 (*1-56963-019-4*) Redbk Florist.

— Green & Blooming Plants. LC 92-60180. (Encyclofiora Ser.). (Illus.). 296p. (Orig.). 1992. pap. text ed. 34.95 (*1-56963-015-1*) Redbk Florist.

— Marketing & Promoting Floral Products. LC 92-85370. (Encyclofiora Ser.). (Illus.). 468p. (Orig.). 1993. pap. text ed. 39.95 (*1-56963-018-6*) Redbk Florist.

— Purchasing & Handling Fresh Flowers & Foliage. LC 91-66386. (Encyclofiora Ser.). (Illus.). 332p. (Orig.). 1992. pap. text ed. 34.95 (*1-56963-013-5*) Redbk Florist.

— Retail Flower Shop Operation. LC 91-73529. (Encyclofiora Ser.). (Illus.). 478p. (Orig.). 1991. pap. text ed. 39.95 (*1-56963-016-X*) Redbk Florist.

— Selling & Designing Party Flowers. LC 92-64275. (Encyclofiora Ser.). (Illus.). 404p. (Orig.). 1992. pap. text ed. 34.95 (*1-56963-021-6*) Redbk Florist.

— Selling & Designing Sympathy Flowers. LC 92-60503. (Encyclofiora Ser.). (Illus.). 222p. (Orig.). 1992. pap. text ed. 34.95 (*1-56963-023-2*) Redbk Florist.

— Selling & Designing Wedding Flowers. LC 91-60000. (Encyclofiora Ser.). (Illus.). 304p. (Orig.). 1991. pap. text ed. 34.95 (*1-56963-022-4*) Redbk Florist.

— Visual Merchandising for the Retail Florist. LC 91-67527. (Encyclofiora Ser.). (Illus.). 246p. (Orig.). 1992. pap. text ed. 34.95 (*1-56963-017-8*) Redbk Florist.

Redburn, F. Steven, et al, eds. Revitalizing the U. S. Economy. LC 85-30166. 242p. 1986. text ed. 55.00 (*0-275-92101-8*, C2101, Praeger Pubs) Greenwood.

Redburn, F. Stevens & Buss, Terry. Public Policies for Communities in Economic Crisis. 1981. pap. 12.00 (*0-918592-54-2*) Pol Studies.

Redburn, F. Stevens & Buss, Terry F. Responding to America's Homeless: Public Policy Alternatives. LC 86-21186. 170p. 1986. text ed. 45.00 (*0-275-92231-6*, C2231, Praeger Pubs) Greenwood.

Redburn, F. Stevens, jt. auth. see Buss, Terry F.

Redburn, H. Ashley, jt. auth. see Langworth, Richard M.

Redburn, Ray, et al. Confessions of Empowering Organizations: Who's Doing It & How. LC 91-77165. (Illus.). 224p. (Orig.). 1992. pap. 19.95 (*0-9631461-0-6*) Assn Qual & Part.

Redcliffe Press, Ltd. Staff, ed. Dorset Essays. 168p. 1983. 39.00 (*0-905459-53-9*, Pub. by Redcliffe Pr Ltd) St Mut.

Redclift, M. R. Agrarian Reform & Peasant Organization on the Ecuadorian Coast. (Institute of Latin American Studies Monographs: No. 8). (Illus.). 186p. (C). 1978. text ed. 44.50 (*0-485-17708-0*, Pub. by Athlone Pr UK) Humanities.

Redclift, Michael. Development & the Environment Crisis: Red or Green Alternatives. (Development & Underdevelopment Ser.). 176p. 1984. pap. 14.95 (*0-416-32140-2*, NO. 4020) Routledge Chapman & Hall.

— Sustainable Development: Exploring the Contradictions. 200p. 1987. lib. bdg. 47.50 (*0-416-90240-5*); pap. 14.95 (*0-415-05085-5*) Routledge Chapman & Hall.

Redclift, Michael & Benton, Ted, eds. Social Theory & the Global Environment. LC 93-44072. (Global Environmental Change Ser.). 288p. 1994. 59.95x (*0-415-11169-2*, B3819, Routledge NY); pap. 17.95 (*0-415-11170-6*, B3823, Routledge NY) Routledge.

Redclift, Michael & Sage, Colin, eds. Strategies for Sustainable Development: Local Agendas for the Southern Hemisphere. LC 93-32721. 1994. text ed. 69.95 (*0-471-94278-2*) Wiley.

Redclift, Michael, jt. auth. see Goodman, David S.

Redclift, Michael R. Development Policymaking in Mexico: The Sistema Alimentario Mexicano (SAM) (Research Report Ser.: No. 24). 26p. (Orig.). (C). 1981. pap. 5.00 (*0-935391-23-1*, RR-24) UCSD Ctr US-Mex.

Redclift, Nanneke & Sinclair, M. Thea, eds. Working Women: International Perspectives on Labour & Gender Ideology. 256p. 1991. 52.50 (*0-415-01842-0*, A5099); pap. 16.95 (*0-415-01843-9*, A5103) Routledge.

Redd. Revelations: Expository Essays by & about Blacks. 1991. 20.00 (*0-536-57971-7*) Ginn Pr.

Redd, Ann, jt. auth. see Redd, Robert.

Redd, James B., et al. Quality Control Manual for Citrus Processing Plants: Processing & Operating Procedures, Blending Techniques, Formulating, Citrus Mathematics & Costs, Vol. 2. 290p. (C). 1992. text ed. 57.00 (*0-9631397-0-3*) AgScience.

Redd, Jim. The Illinois & Michigan Canal: A Contemporary Perspective in Essays & Photographs. LC 91-2220. (Illus.). 144p. (C). 1992. 29.95 (*0-8093-1660-9*) S Ill U Pr.

Redd, Kathleen M. & Harkins, Arthur M., eds. Education: A Time for Decisions: Selections from the Second Conference of the World Future Society's Education Section. 1980. 6.95 (*0-930242-12-2*) World Future.

Redd, Lorraine. Only in Mississippi: A Guide for the Adventurous Traveler. LC 93-32607. (Illus.). 96p. 1993. 5.95 (*0-937552-54-2*) Quail Ridge.

Redd, Mary A. The World of Holly Prickle: For Women Who Have Worked for Men. LC 93-92632. 290p. (Orig.). 1993. pap. 10.00 (*0-9636548-0-2*) Shenandoah Bks.

Redd, Preston. From Horseback to Cadillac, I'm Still a Cowboy: True Tales of the Old West. Tegeler, Dorothy, ed. (Illus.). 355p. 1989. 27.50 (*0-9621360-2-6*) Tavas Cash Pr.

Redd, Rahn. The Final Challenge. LC 88-92273. 177p. (Orig.). 1988. pap. 10.95 (*0-922969-01-9*) Pebble Beach Pub.

Redd, Robert & Redd, Ann. Whimsey, Wit & Wisdom: For the Wonderful Years after Fifty. 128p. 1990. pap. text ed. 8.95 (*1-877756-03-2*) Thornapple Pub.

Redd, Robert O. Achievers Never Quit - How to Create a Life Plan for the Years after Fifty: A Book for People Who Can't Quit. LC 89-50123. (Illus.). 150p. (Orig.). 1989. pap. 6.95 (*1-877756-00-8*) Thornapple Pub.

Redd, True. La Rose: An Intimacy of Roses. (Illus.). 100p. 1990. 35.00 (*0-941283-08-9*); pap. 19.95 (*0-941283-07-0*) Western Eye Pr.

Redd, William H., et al. Behavior Modification: Behavioral Approaches to Human Problems. 1978. text ed. write for info. (*0-394-32134-0*) Random.

Redda, Kinfe K., et al, eds. Cocaine, Marijuana, Designer Drugs: Chemistry, Pharmacology, & Behavior. 256p. 1989. 144.00 (*0-8493-6853-7*, RM316) CRC Pr.

Reddall, Henr. Fact, Fancy & Fable. 1995. reprint ed. 40.00 (*1-55888-973-6*) Omnigraphics Inc.

Reddan, Minnie & Clapham, Alfred W. The Church of St. Helen, Bishopsgate, Pt. 1. LC 74-6179. (London County Council. Survey of London Ser.: No. 9). reprint ed. 84.50 (*0-404-51659-9*) AMS Pr.

Reddaway, William. Frederick the Great & the Rise of Prussia. LC 68-25262. (Studies in German Literature: No. 13). 1969. reprint ed. lib. bdg. 75.00 (*0-8383-0232-7*) M S G Haskell Hse.

Reddaway, William F. Frederick the Great & the Rise of Prussia. 1904. reprint ed. 13.00 (*0-403-00037-8*) Scholarly.

— Problems of the Baltic. LC 75-41224. reprint ed. 27.50 (*0-404-14588-4*) AMS Pr.

Reddel, Carl W., ed. Military History Symposium Series of the United States Air Force Academy. (Orig.). 1993. write for info. (*1-879176-14-9*) Imprint Pubns.

Reddell, Rayford C. The Rose Bible. LC 92-40231. 1994. 50.00 (*0-517-58821-8*, Harmony) Crown Pub Group.

Redden, Charlotte A. A Comparative Study of Colombian & Costa Rican Emigrants to the United States. Cortes, Carlos E., ed. LC 79-6218. (Hispanics in the United States Ser.). (Illus.). 1981. lib. bdg. 23.95 (*0-405-13166-6*) Ayer.

Redden, Charlotte A., jt. auth. see Switzer, Kenneth A.

***Redden, J. C.** The Best & the Rest of Redden's Rules of Thumb: Almost 200 Money-Saving, Money-Making Tips for the Cemetery/Mortuary Industry. 82p. 1993. 20.00 (*1-879111-24-1*); text ed. 20.00 (*0-614-04564-9*) Lincoln-Bradley.

Redden, Joseph. Emotional Overload. LC 91-75214. 459p. 1992. pap. 9.95 (*1-55523-466-6*) Winston-Derek.

Redden, Kenneth R. Modern Legal Systems Cyclopedia, 10 vols. in 21 bks. LC 83-82953. 1984. 195.00 (*0-685-07910-4*); 250.00 (*0-685-73597-4*) W S Hein.

— Modern Legal Systems Cyclopedia, 10 vols. in 21 bks., Set. LC 83-82953. 1984. ring bd. 1,995.00 (*0-89941-300-5*, 302990) W S Hein.

— Punitive Damages: With 1991 Cumulative Supplement, 2 vols. suppl. ed. 1991. 40.00 (*0-87473-789-3*) Michie Butterworth.

Redden, Kenneth R. & Beyer, Gerry W. Modern Dictionary for the Legal Profession, 1994. suppl. ed. LC 92-35678. xiii, 802p. 1993. pap. 65.00 (*0-89941-829-5*, 307770) W S Hein.

— Modern Dictionary for the Legal Profession, 1994. suppl. ed. LC 92-35678. 78p. 1994. 55.00 (*0-614-04746-3*, 307770) W S Hein.

— Modern Dictionary for the Legal Profession, 1994. suppl. ed. 1995. pap. 25.00 (*0-614-07155-0*) W S Hein.

Redden, Mary, jt. ed. see Stuart-Smith, Stephen.

Reddi, A. H., jt. ed. see Piez, K. A.

Reddi, A. Harri, jt. auth. see Habal, Mutaz B.

Reddick, Allen. The Making of Johnson's Dictionary, 1746-1773. (Studies in Publishing & Printing History). (Illus.). 296p. (C). 1990. 69.95 (*0-521-36160-5*) Cambridge U Pr.

Reddick, DeWitt C. The Mass Media & the School Newspaper. 2nd ed. 448p. (C). 1985. text ed. 22.95 (*0-534-03256-7*) Intl Thomson.

***Reddick, Don.** Dawson City Seven. 1994. pap. 14.95 (*0-86492-158-6*, Pub. by Goose Ln Edits CN) InBook.

Reddick, Eddie J., et al, eds. An Atlas of Laparoscopic Surgery. LC 92-14363. 128p. 1993. 103.00 (*0-88167-932-1*, 2408); sl. 236.50 (*0-88167-979-8*) Raven.

***Reddick, J. Rex, ed.** F. W. Assmann & Sohne Sales Catalog. (Illus.). 108p. 1993. pap. 17.95 (*0-9624883-3-X*) Reddick Enterp.

Reddick, J. Rex, jt. auth. see Evans, C. Scott.

Reddick, J. Rex, ed. see Hicks, Kelly.

Reddick, J. Rex, ed. see Wilson, Kit.

Reddick, John. The Danzig Trilogy of Gunter Grass: A Study of the Tin Drum, Cat & Mouse, & Dog Years. LC 74-11027. 290p. 1975. pap. 5.95 (*0-15-623829-2*, Harvest Bks) HarBrace.

— Georg Buchner: The Shattered Whole. 350p. 1995. 65.00 (*0-19-815812-2*) OUP.

Reddick, John, tr. see Buchner, Georg.

Reddick, Marshall E., jt. auth. see Cohen, William A.

***Reddick, Randy & King, Elliot.** The Online Journalist: Using the Internet & Other Electronic Resources. (Illus.). 240p. (C). 1995. pap. text ed. 16.00 (*0-15-502018-8*) HB Coll Pubs.

Reddicliffe, Sheila. The Cornish Mistress. 148p. (C). 1992. pap. 29.95 (*1-871330-04-1*, Pub. by Lightbody Pubns UK) St Mut.

Reddie, James. Inquiries Elementary & Historical in the Science of Law. viii, 216p. 1982. reprint ed. lib. bdg. 24.00 (*0-8377-1034-0*) Rothman.

Reddiford, Gordon, jt. ed. see Beveridge, Michael.

Reddig, Jill S., jt. ed. see Eisel, Deborah D.

Reddig, William M. Tom's Town: Kansas City & the Pendergast Legend. LC 85-20888. 400p. 1986. pap. 19.95 (*0-8262-0498-8*) U of Mo Pr.

Reddin, A. R. Esther What Time Is It. 64p. (Orig.). 1987. pap. 2.50 (*0-89114-161-8*) Baptist Pub Hse.

Reddin, Chitra P. Forms of Evil in the Gothic Novel. Varma, Devendra P., ed. LC 79-8472. (Gothic Studies & Dissertations). 1980. lib. bdg. 35.95 (*0-405-12669-7*) Ayer.

Reddin, Joan. Secret Promise. 320p. 1992. mass mkt. 3.99 (*0-8217-4014-8*) Zebra.

Reddin, Keith. Big Time & After School Special. 61p. (Orig.). 1987. pap. 4.95 (*0-88145-063-4*) Broadway Play.

— Black Snow. 1993. 4.75 (*0-8222-1371-0*) Dramatists Play.

— Desperadoes, Throwing Smoke, Keyhole Lover. 1986. pap. 4.75 (*0-8222-0301-4*) Dramatists Play.

— Innocents' Crusade. 1993. 4.75 (*0-8222-1332-X*) Dramatists Play.

— Life & Limb. 1985. pap. 4.75 (*0-8222-0658-7*) Dramatists Play.

— Life During Wartime. 1991. pap. 4.75 (*0-8222-0659-5*) Dramatists Play.

Reddin, Mike & Pilch, Michael. Can We Afford Our Future. (C). 1989. 35.00 (*0-86242-038-5*, Pub. by Age Concern Eng UK) St Mut.

Reddin, William J. Using Tests to Improve Training: The Complete Guide to Selecting, Developing, & Using Training Instruments. LC 94-5600. 1994. write for info. (*0-13-108556-5*) P-H.

Redding, J. McLaren. (Kimberley's Grand Prix Guide: No. 14). (Illus.). 24p. 1986. pap. 6.98 (*0-946132-28-3*) Motorbooks Intl.

Redding, J. Saunders. Stranger & Alone. (Northeastern Library of Black Literature). 320p. 1989. reprint ed. text ed. 37.50 (*1-55553-055-9*); reprint ed. pap. text ed. 12.95 (*1-55553-053-2*) NE U Pr.

— To Make a Poet Black. LC 86-47630. 184p. 1987. 29.95 (*0-8014-1982-4*); pap. 9.95 (*0-8014-9438-9*) Cornell U Pr.

— Troubled in Mind: J. Saunders Redding's Early Years in Wilmington. (Illus.). 90p. (Orig.). 1991. pap. write for info. (*0-924117-03-6*) Delaware HP.

Redding, J. Saunders & Joyce, Joyce A. The New Cavalcade I: African American Writing. Davis, Arthur P. et al, eds. 1991. 42.95 (*0-88258-130-9*); pap. 32.95 (*0-88258-133-3*) Howard U Pr.

Redding, Jay S. To Make a Poet Black. 8.00 (*0-405-18495-6*) Ayer.

— To Make a Poet Black. (BCL1-PS American Literature Ser.). 142p. 1993. reprint ed. lib. bdg. 69.00 (*0-7812-6567-3*) Rprt Serv.

Redding, John C. & Catalanello, Ralph F. Strategic Readiness: The Making of A Learning Organization. LC 93-48673. (Business-Management Ser.). 200p. 1994. 26.95 (*1-55542-633-6*) Jossey-Bass.

Redding, M. W. Scarlet Book of Freemasonry: Containing, a Thrilling & Authentic Account of the Imprisonment, Torture, & Martyrdom of Freemasons & Knights Templars, for the Past Six Hundred Years; Also an Authentic Account of the Education, Remarkable Career & Tragic Death of the Renowned Philospher Pythagoras, Recent Remarkable Discovery of Masonic Emblems on an Ancient Obelisk in Egypt. 517p. 1992. pap. 36.00 (*1-56459-283-9*) Kessinger Pub.

Redding, Phil. Tuning In: A Layman's Guide to Youth Ministry. 153p. 1990. pap. 5.95 (*1-882449-21-5*) Messenger Pub.

Redding, Richard W. & Knecht, Charles E. An Atlas of Electro-Encephalography in the Dog & Cat. LC 83-13693. (Illus.). 400p. 1984. text ed. 75.00 (*0-275-91448-8*, C1448, Praeger Pubs) Greenwood.

Redding, Robert. One Man's Homestead. Clark, Marvin, ed. (Illus.). 120p. (Orig.). (YA). 1990. pap. 10.95 (*0-937708-23-2*) Great Northwest.

Redding, Rodney J., jt. auth. see Miller, Paul B.

Redding, S. Gordon. The Spirit of Chinese Capitalism. (Studies in Organization: No. 22). xiv, 267p. (C). 1993. pap. text ed. 24.95 (*3-11-013794-1*) De Gruyter.

Redding, S. Gordon, jt. ed. see Clegg, Stewart R.

Redding, Spencer W. & Montgomery, Michael T., eds. Dentistry in Systemic Disease: Diagnostic & Therapeutic Approach to Patient Management. LC 89-64175. (Illus.). 348p. 1990. pap. text ed. 21.95 (*0-945892-00-4*) JBK Pub.

An Asterisk (*) at the beginning of an entry indicates that the title is appearing in BIP for the first time.

Redding-Stewart, Deborah. The Soft Voice of the Rain. LC 91-67097. 55p. 1992. pap. 5.95 (*1-55523-475-5*) Winston-Derek.

Redding, Trilba N., ed. see Wilson, Charles A.

Redding, Trilba N., jt. ed. see Wilson, Charles A.

Redding, W. Charles. How to Conduct a Readership Survey: A Guide for Organizational Editors & Communications Managers. LC 81-86059. (Communications Library). 152p. 1982. pap. 30.00 (*0-931368-08-1*) Ragan Comm.

Reddington, Marge. Health, Happiness & Human Needs: An Introduction to Symbolization. LC 94-60127. 254p. 1994. pap. 19.95 (*0-9640594-0-1*) TDC Pubng.

Reddish, D. J., jt. auth. see Whittaker, Barry N.

Reddish, Mitchell G., ed. Apocalyptic Literature: A Reader. LC 89-18342. 320p. 1990. pap. 24.95 (*0-687-01566-9*) Abingdon.

Reddish, V. C. Stellar Formation. 225p. 1978. 91.00 (*0-08-018062-0*, Pub. by Pergamon Repr UK) Franklin.

Reddit, Paul L. Haggai, Zechariah, Malachi. (New Century Bible Commentary Ser.). 224p. (Orig.). (C). 1994. pap. text ed. 14.99 (*0-8028-0748-8*) Eerdmans.

Redditt, Jo Ann T., ed. see Steidel, Kitty.

Redditt-Lyon, Elizabeth. Mabel: The Story of One Midwife. (Illus.). 159p. 1982. pap. 6.50 (*0-941894-01-0*) Red Lyon Pubns.

Reddix, Valerie. Dragon Kite of the Autumn Moon. LC 91-1506. (J). (ps-3). 1992. 14.00 (*0-688-11030-4*); lib. bdg. 14.93 (*0-688-11031-2*) Lothrop.

— Millie & the Mud Hole. LC 90-21147. (Illus.). 32p. (J). (ps-3). 1992. 14.00 (*0-688-10212-3*); lib. bdg. 13.93 (*0-688-10213-1*) Lothrop.

Reddock, Rhoda. Women, Labour & Politics in Trinidad & Tobago: A History. 304p. (C). 1994. text ed. 60.00 (*1-85649-153-6*, Pub. by Zed Books UK); pap. 25.00 (*1-85649-154-4*) Humanities.

Reddon, Kenneth R., jt. auth. see Schlueter, Linda L.

Reddy. Offshore Structures, 2 vols., Set. 694p. 1991. 175.00 (*0-89464-386-X*) Krieger.

— Offshore Structures, Vol. I. LC 89-2712. 408p. 1991. 120.00 (*0-89464-206-5*) Krieger.

— Offshore Structures, Vol. II. 286p. 1991. 95.00 (*0-89464-385-1*) Krieger.

Reddy, ed. Phytates in Cereals & Legumes. 1989. 144.00 (*0-8493-6108-7*, QP801) CRC Pr.

Reddy, A. K. Technology, Development & the Environment: A Re-Appraisal. (Illus.). 60p. 1979. pap. 26.00 (*0-08-025693-7*, Pub. by Pergamon Repr UK) Franklin.

Reddy, A. Rathna. The Political Philosophy of Swami Vevekawada. 210p. (C). 1984. text ed. 22.50 (*0-86590-281-X*, Pub. by Sterling Pubs II) Apt Bks.

Reddy, A. V. The Political Philosophy of the Bhagvad Gita. 176p. 1993. text ed. 27.50 (*81-207-1338-9*, Pub. by Sterling Pubs II) Apt Bks.

Reddy, A. Vinayak. Modernisation of Indian Agriculture: With Special Reference to Andhra Pradesh. (C). 1991. text ed. 21.00 (*0-685-50089-6*, Pub. by Mittal II) S Asia.

Reddy, Allan C. Total Quality Marketing: The Key to Regaining Market Shares. LC 94-15885. 200p. 1994. text ed. 49.95 (*0-89930-893-7*, Quorum Bks) Greenwood.

Reddy, Allan C. & Campbell, David P. Marketing's Role in Economic Development. LC 93-27715. 160p. 1993. text ed. 49.95 (*0-89930-766-3*, Quorum Bks) Greenwood.

Reddy, Amulya K. & Bhalla, Ajit S., eds. The Technological Transformation of Rural India. LC 93-29554. 192p. 1994. text ed. 45.00 (*0-312-09595-3*) St Martin.

Reddy, Anne W. & Riffe, Andrew L., IV, eds. Richmond County, Virginia Marriage Books, 1797-1853. 158p. 1994. reprint ed. pap. 16.00 (*0-8328-4016-5*) Higginson Bk Co.

Reddy, Bandaru S. & Cohen, Leonard A., eds. Diet, Nutrition & Cancer: A Critical Evaluation. 184p. 1986. Vol. I, 184p. 144.00 (*0-8493-6332-2*, RC268); Vol. II, 208p. 106.00 (*0-8493-6333-0*) Franklin.

Reddy, Bayapa. Studies in Indian Writing in English. 128p. 1990. text ed. 20.00 (*81-85218-26-9*, Pub. by Prestige II) Advent Bks Div.

Reddy, C. A., ed. see International Symposium on Microbial Ecology (3rd: 1983: Michigan State University) Staff.

Reddy, C. Channa, ed. see Madyastha, K. M.

Reddy, C. Channa, et al, eds. Biological Oxidation Systems, Vol. 2. (Illus.). 532p. 1990. text ed. 105.00 (*0-12-584552-9*) Acad Pr.

Reddy, C. M. Gene Structure & Function in Higher Plants. (C). 1987. 32.50 (*81-204-0097-6*, Pub. by Oxford IBH II) S Asia.

Reddy, C. Narayana. Viswambhara. 66p. 1987. text ed. 15.95 (*81-207-0578-5*, Pub. by Sterling Pubs II) Apt Bks.

Reddy, D. P., ed. Seismic Design Technology for Breeder Reactor Structures: Special Topics in Earthquake Ground Motion, Vol. 1. LC 83-50358. 277p. 1983. pap. 36.50 (*0-87079-542-2*, DOE/SF/01011-T25, VOL. 1, DE84004808); fiche 9.00 (*0-87079-543-0*, DOE/SF/01011-T25, VOL. 1, DE84004808) DOE.

— Seismic Design Technology for Breeder Reactor Structures: Special Topics in Piping & Equipment, Vol. 4. 215p. 1983. pap. 36.50 (*0-87079-548-1*, DOE/SF/01011-T25, VOL. 4, DE84004811); fiche 9.00 (*0-87079-549-X*, DOE/SF/01011-T25, VOL. 4, DE84004811) DOE.

— Seismic Design Technology for Breeder Reactor Structures: Special Topics in Reactor Structures, Vol. 3. 167p. 1983. pap. 27.00 (*0-87079-546-5*, DOE/SF/01011-T25, VOL. 3, DE84004810); fiche 9.00 (*0-87079-547-3*, DOE/SF/01011-T25, VOL. 3, DE84004810) DOE.

— Seismic Design Technology for Breeder Reactor Structures: Special Topics in Soil Structure Interaction Analyses, Vol. 2. LC 83-50358. 134p. 1983. pap. 27.00 (*0-87079-544-9*, DOE/SF/01011-T25, VOL. 2, DE84004309); fiche 9.00 (*0-87079-545-7*, DOE/SF/01011-T25, VOL. 2, DE84004309) DOE.

Reddy, D. Subramanyam. Agrarian Relations & Peasant in Modern Andhra. 1990. 16.00 (*81-7035-073-5*, Pub. by Daya Pub Hse II) S Asia.

Reddy, E. P., et al, eds. The Oncogene Handbook. 560p. 1988. 210.25 (*0-444-80937-6*) Elsevier.

Reddy, E. S. Oliver Tambo & the Struggle Against Apartheid. 172p. 1988. text ed. 27.50 (*81-207-0779-6*, Pub. by Sterling Pubs II) Apt Bks.

Reddy, E. S., ed. Liberation of Southern Africa: Speeches of Olaf Palme. 1990. text ed. 18.95 (*0-7069-5317-7*, Pub. by Vikas II) Advent Bks Div.

— Nelson Mandela: Symbol of Resistance & Hope for a Free South Africa. 121p. 1991. text ed. 25.00 (*81-207-1291-9*, Pub. by Sterling Pubs II) Apt Bks.

— Oliver Tambo: Apartheid & the International Community. 1991. text ed. 25.00 (*0-685-56302-2*, Pub. by Sterling Pubs II) Apt Bks.

— Socialism, Peace & Solidarity: Speeches of Olaf Palme. 1990. text ed. 25.00 (*0-7069-5316-9*, Pub. by Vikas II) S Asia.

Reddy, E. S., ed. see Dadoo, Yusuf M.

Reddy, Francis. Discovery Atlas of Dinosaurs & Prehistoric Creatures. LC 93-43086. Orig. Title: Rand McNally Children's Atlas of Earth Through Time. (Illus.). (J). 1994. 4.95 (*0-528-83677-3*) Rand McNally.

Reddy, Francis & Walz-Chojnacki, Greg. Celestial Delights: The Best Astronomical Events Through 2001. (Illus.). 192p. 1992. pap. 16.95 (*0-89087-675-4*) Celestial Arts.

Reddy, Francis, jt. auth. see Rand McNally Staff.

Reddy, G. Lokanadha. Education for Unorganised Sector. (C). 1992. 39.00 (*81-7024-490-0*, Pub. by Ashish II) S Asia.

Reddy, G. Ram. Patterns of Panchayati Raj in India. 1977. 9.50 (*0-8364-0046-1*) S Asia.

Reddy, G. Ram, ed. Government & Public Enterprise: Essays in Honour of Professor V. V. Ramanadham. 224p. 1985. 37.50 (*0-7146-3258-9*, Pub. by F Cass Pubs UK) Intl Spec Bk.

— Open Universities: The Ivory Towers Thrown Open. 270p. 1988. text ed. 37.50 (*0-318-35446-2*, Pub. by Sterling Pubs II) Apt Bks.

***Reddy, Indra K., ed.** Ocular Therapeutics & Drug Delivery: A Multi-Disciplinary Approach. LC 94-60709. 525p. 1995. text ed. 89.00 (*1-56676-213-8*) Technomic.

Reddy, J., jt. auth. see Scarpelli, D.

Reddy, J. M. & Rao, S. K., eds. Indian Economy in the Medium Term: Problems & Prospects. 1990. text ed. 27.50 (*81-207-1190-4*, Pub. by Sterling Pubs II) Apt Bks.

Reddy, J. M., ed. see Upadhyay, K. S. & Raghuram, C.

Reddy, J. M., et al, eds. Seventh Five-Year Plan: Performance & Perspectives. xvi, 254p. 1989. text ed. 30.00 (*81-207-1021-5*, Pub. by Sterling Pubs II) Apt Bks.

Reddy, J. Mahender. Demand & Supply of Pulses & Oilseeds: A Case Study of Andhra Pradesh. 188p. 1991. text ed. 27.50 (*81-207-1314-1*, Pub. by Sterling Pubs II) Apt Bks.

Reddy, J. Mahendra & Rao, S. Kishen, eds. Agricultural Development & Rural-Urban Disparities. 288p. (C). 1991. text ed. 27.95 (*81-207-1315-X*, Pub. by Sterling Pubs II) Apt Bks.

Reddy, J. N. Applied Functional Analysis & Variational Methods in Engineering. 560p. (C). 1991. reprint ed. lib. bdg. 59.50 (*0-89464-585-4*) Krieger.

— Energy & Variational Methods in Applied Mechanics. LC 84-3605. 545p. 1984. text ed. 99.95 (*0-471-89673-X*, Wiley-Interscience) Wiley.

— An Introduction to the Finite Element Method. 2nd ed. LC 92-29532. (McGraw-Hill Series in Mechanical Engineering). 1993. text ed. write for info. (*0-07-051355-4*) McGraw.

***Reddy, J. N., ed.** Mechanics of Composite Materials: Selected Works of Nicholas J. Pagano. LC 94-30334. (Solid Mechanics & Its Applications Ser.). 1994. lib. bdg. 198.00 (*0-7923-3041-2*) Kluwer Ac.

Reddy, J. N. & Gartling, D. K. The Finite Element Method in Heat Transfer & Fluid Dynamics. LC 94-8277. 1994. write for info. (*0-8493-9410-4*) CRC Pr.

Reddy, J. N. & Murty, A. V., eds. Composite Structures: Testing, Analysis & Design. (Illus.). 350p. 1993. 149.00 (*0-387-55879-9*) Spr-Verlag.

Reddy, J. N. & Rasmussen, M. L. Advanced Engineering Analysis. 504p. (C). 1990. reprint ed. 59.50 (*0-89464-498-X*) Krieger.

Reddy, J. N. & Reifsnyder, K. L., eds. Local Mechanics Concepts for Composite Material Systems: IUTAM Symposium, Blacksburg, VA, 1991. LC 92-17944. (International Union of Theoretical & Applied Mechanics Symposia Ser.). xi, 412p. 1992. 139.00 (*0-387-55547-1*) Spr-Verlag.

Reddy, J. N., jt. auth. see Ochoa, O. O.

Reddy, K. C. Sickness in Small Scale Industries. (C). 1988. 32.00 (*81-7024-212-6*, Pub. by Ashish II) S Asia.

Reddy, K. J., ed. Practical Exercises for Bar Students. 300p. (C). 1991. 80.00 (*1-85352-893-5*, Pub. by HLT Pubns UK) St Mut.

Reddy, K. Madhusudan, ed. see Melkote, Rama S. & Rao, A. Narasimha.

Reddy, K. N., jt. auth. see Kline, Daniel L.

Reddy, K. R. & Smith, W. H., eds. Aquatic Plants for Water Treatment & Resource Recovery. LC 87-61397. (Illus.). 1088p. 1987. 140.00 (*0-941463-00-1*) Magnolia FL.

Reddy, K. Venkata. Major Indian Novelists. 1991. text ed. 22.50 (*81-85218-29-3*, Pub. by Prestige II) Advent Bks Div.

***Reddy, M. Atchi.** Lands & Tenants in South India: A Study of Nellore District, 1850-1990. 224p. 1995. 19.95 (*0-19-563660-0*) OUP.

Reddy, M. S. & Daniel, D. F., eds. Latest Advances in Power Generating Facilities Design, Operation & Maintenance & Environmental Improvements. (PWR Ser.: Vol. 22). 176p. 1993. 37.50 (*0-7918-0997-8*, H00829) ASME.

Reddy, Marlita A., ed. American Salaries & Wages Survey, 1993: Statistical Data Derived from More Than 300 Government, Business & News Sources. 1000p. 1993. 105.00 (*0-8103-8591-0*, 101401) Gale.

— Statistical Record of Native North Americans: Current & Historical Data. 750p. 1993. 89.50 (*0-8103-8963-0*, 101755) Gale.

***Reddy, Marlita A. & Lazich, Robert S., eds.** World Market Share Reporter 1: A Compilation of Reported World Market Share Data & Rankings on Companies Products & Services. 620p. 1994. 295.00 (*0-8103-9641-6*) Gale.

Reddy, Marlita A., jt. ed. see Darnay, Arsen J.

Reddy, Maureen, et al, eds. Mother Journeys: Feminists Write about Mothering. LC 94-18338. 300p. 1994. 29.95 (*1-883523-04-4*) Spinsters Ink.

Reddy, Maureen T. Crossing the Color Line: Race, Parenting & Culture. LC 94-535. 215p. (C). 1994. 22.95 (*0-8135-2105-X*) Rutgers U Pr.

Reddy, Maureen T., jt. ed. see Daly, Brenda O.

Reddy, Maureen T., et al, eds. Mother Journeys: Feminists Write about Mothering. LC 94-18338. (Illus.). 352p. (C). 1994. pap. 15.95 (*1-883523-03-6*) Spinsters Ink.

Reddy, Michael T. Securities Operations: A Guide to Operations & Information Systems in the Securities Industry. 1990. 75.00 (*0-13-799123-1*) NY Inst Finance.

— Securities Operations: A Guide to Operations & Information Systems in the Securities Industry. 1995. 75.00 (*0-13-161044-9*) P-H.

Reddy, N. K. Social History of Andhra Pradesh. 1991. 44.00 (*0-685-48716-4*, Pub. by Agam Kala Prakashan) S Asia.

Reddy, N. Krishna. Intaglio Simultaneous Color Printmaking: Significance of Materials & Processes. LC 88-1516. (Illus.). 142p. 1988. 74.50 (*0-88706-739-5*); pap. 24.95 (*0-88706-740-9*) State U NY Pr.

Reddy, N. R., et al. Legume-Based Fermented Foods. 272p. 1986. 228.00 (*0-8493-6286-5*, TX558, CRC Reprint) Franklin.

Reddy, N. Y. Values & Attitudes of Indian Youth. 244p. 1980. 24.95 (*0-940500-10-8*, Pub. by Light & Life Pubs II) Asia Bk Corp.

Reddy, P. Chenna. Guilds in Medieval Andhra Desa. (C). 1991. text ed. 49.50 (*81-85067-70-8*, Pub. by Sundeep Prakashan II) S Asia.

Reddy, P. Chinnappa. Physics of Sports: Basketball. (C). 1992. text ed. 20.00 (*81-7024-511-7*, Pub. by Ashish II) S Asia.

Reddy, P. S., et al, eds. Pericardial Disease. LC 81-23539. (Illus.). 391p. reprint ed. pap. 111.50 (*0-7837-7097-9*, 2046926) Bks Demand.

Reddy, R. G. & Weizenbach, R., eds. The Paul E. Queneau International Symposium-Extractive Metallurgy of Copper, Nickel & Cobalt: Fundamental Aspects, Vol. 1. (Illus.). 1735p. 1993. 220.00 (*0-87339-218-3*, 455) Minerals Metals.

Reddy, R. G., et al, eds. Residues & Effluents: Processing & Environmental Considerations. (Illus.). 750p. 1992. 182.00 (*0-87339-144-6*, 427) Minerals Metals.

Reddy, Rama & Ziegler, Carol. FORTRAN 77 with FORTRAN 90 Applications for Scientists & Engineers. 2nd ed. Conty, ed. LC 93-33046. 650p. (C). 1994. pap. text ed. 52.00 (*0-314-02861-7*) West Pub.

Reddy, Rama N. & Ziegler, Carol. PL-1: Structured Programming & Problem Solving. (Illus.). 739p. (C). 1986. text ed. 59.75 (*0-314-93915-6*) West Pub.

Reddy, Ramana G., ed. see Metallurgical Society of AIME Staff.

Reddy, Ramana G., ed. see Minerals, Metals & Materials Society Staff.

Reddy, Sigrid, ed. see Hodges, Maud.

Reddy, Srinivas K., jt. ed. see Pellegrini, Luca.

Reddy, Srivanas K., jt. ed. see Pellegrini, Luca.

Reddy, Suma N. Institutionalised Children. (C). 1989. 44.00 (*81-85076-57-X*, Pub. by Chugh Pubns II) S Asia.

Reddy, T. Agami. The Design & Sizing of Active Solar Thermal Systems. (Illus.). 416p. 1987. 95.00 (*0-19-859016-4*) OUP.

Reddy, T. Ramakrishna. India's Policy in the United Nations. LC 67-26816. 164p. 1975. 24.50 (*0-8386-6755-4*) Fairleigh Dickinson.

Reddy, Terrence R., jt. auth. see Long, Huey B.

Reddy, Tom. Murder Will Out: A Book of Irish Murder Cases. 256p. 1990. pap. 13.95 (*0-7171-1787-1*, Pub. by Gill & MacMill IE) Irish Bks Media.

Reddy, V. Madhusudan. Integral Yoga Psychology. 148p. (Orig.). 1990. pap. 7.95 (*0-941524-92-2*) Lotus Light.

Reddy, V. Ramakrishan. Economic History of Hyderabad State: Warangal Suba (1911-1950) 834p. 1987. 40.00 (*81-212-0099-7*, Pub. by Gian Publng Hse II) S Asia.

Reddy, V. Rami. Elements of Prehistory. (C). 1987. 20.00 (*81-7099-013-0*, Pub. by Mittal II) S Asia.

— Neolithic & Post-Neolithic Cultures. (C). 1991. text ed. 15.00 (*81-7099-311-3*, Pub. by Mittal II) S Asia.

***Reddy, Vikram M., ed.** Soil Organisms & Litter Decomposition in the Tropics. LC 95-14219. 1995. write for info. (*0-8133-8940-2*) Westview.

Reddy, Vishu, ed. Powder Coating Applications. (Illus.). 250p. 1990. 44.00 (*0-87263-378-0*) SME.

Reddy, Vishu, jt. ed. see Dawson, Sam.

Reddy, W. Brendan. Intervention Skills: Process Consultation for Small Groups & Teams. LC 94-65468. 256p. 1994. 39.95 (*0-88390-434-9*) Pfeiffer & Co.

Reddy, W. Brendan & Henderson, Clenard C., Jr., eds. Training Theory & Practice. LC 87-62132. 300p. (Orig.). 1987. pap. text ed. 19.00 (*0-9610392-4-8*) NTL Inst.

Reddy, W. Brendan & Jamison, Kaleel, eds. Team Building: Blueprints for Productivity & Satisfaction. 225p. (Orig.). 1988. pap. text ed. 19.00 (*0-9610392-5-6*) NTL Inst.

Reddy, William M. Money & Liberty in Modern Europe: A Critique of Historical Understanding. (Illus.). 320p. 1987. pap. 16.95 (*0-521-31509-3*) Cambridge U Pr.

— The Rise of Market Culture: The Textile Trade & French Society, 1750-1900. (Illus.). 352p. 1984. 69.95 (*0-521-25653-4*) Cambridge U Pr.

— The Rise of Market Culture: The Textile Trade & French Society, 1750-1900. (Illus.). 352p. 1987. pap. 19.95 (*0-521-34779-3*) Cambridge U Pr.

Reddy, Y. R. & Sinha, Dharni P., eds. Business Scenarios for the Nineties: Strategic Perspectives. 168p. (C). 1992. 25.00 (*0-7069-5876-4*, Pub. by Vikas II) S Asia.

***Reddy, Y. Ramachandra.** Grass-Root Democracy: Anantapur Area Under Madras Presidency. (C). 1993. 18.00x (*0-8364-2898-6*, Pub. by New Era) S Asia.

Reddy, Y. Venugopal. Public Enterprise Reform & Privatization. 1992. 30.00 (*81-7040-471-1*, Pub. by Himalaya II) Apt Bks.

— World Bank: Borrowers Perspective. 143p. 1986. text ed. 20.00 (*81-207-0032-5*, Pub. by Sterling Pubs II) Apt Bks.

Redeen, Kira S. I Never Say Goodbye. 2nd ed. 364p. 1988. pap. 8.00 (*0-9615501-0-4*) K Singh Pub.

— Istina I Mirazh. 256p. (Orig.). (RUS.). 1992. pap. 14.00 (*0-934923-03-5*) Hermitage.

Redefinition, Inc. Staff. Efficient Housecleaning. LC 93-4822. (Do It! Ser.). 112p. 1994. ring bd. 9.95 (*0-8118-0625-1*) Chronicle Bks.

Redefinition Inc Staff. Essential Car Care. LC 93-2191. (Do It! Ser.). 112p. 1994. ring bd. 9.95 (*0-8118-0600-6*) Chronicle Bks.

Redefinition Inc. Staff. Everyday Home Repairs. LC 93-2190. (Do It! Ser.). 112p. 1994. ring bd. 9.95 (*0-8118-0594-8*) Chronicle Bks.

— Fix Your Plumbing. LC 93-2189. (Do It! Ser.). 112p. 1994. ring bd. 9.95 (*0-8118-0599-9*) Chronicle Bks.

— Grow Great Annuals. LC 93-2188. (Do It! Ser.). 112p. 1994. ring bd. 9.95 (*0-8118-0574-3*) Chronicle Bks.

— Household Emergencies. LC 93-2181. (Do It! Ser.). 112p. 1994. ring bd. 9.95 (*0-8118-0580-8*) Chronicle Bks.

Redefinition Inc Staff. Quick Bike Repairs. LC 93-2180. (Do It! Ser.). 112p. 1994. ring bd. 9.95 (*0-8118-0559-X*) Chronicle Bks.

Redefinition Inc Staff. Start a Garden. LC 93-2179. (Do It! Ser.). 112p. 1994. ring bd. 9.95 (*0-8118-0561-1*) Chronicle Bks.

***Redei, K.** Zyrian Folklore Texts. (Bibliotheca Uralica: No. 3). 652p. (C). 1978. 171.00x (*963-05-1506-7*, Pub. by Akad Kiado HU) St Mut.

Redei, Karoly. Zyrian Folklore Texts. 652p. 1978. 163.00 (*0-569-08501-2*, Pub. by Collets UK) Pro-Am Music.

Redei, L. Algebra, Vol. 1. 1967. 337.00 (*0-08-010954-3*, Pub. by Pergamon Repr UK) Franklin.

Redeker, Hans. Bruno Bruni. Ayers, Helge, tr. (Bibliophilen Taschenbucher Ser.). (Illus.). 247p. (Orig.). 1981. pap. 15.00 (*3-921785-16-2*) J Szoke Graphics.

Redeker, James R. Discipline, Policies & Procedure. LC 83-6053. 290p. reprint ed. pap. 82.70 (*0-7837-4609-1*, 2044328) Bks Demand.

— Employee Discipline: Policies & Practices. LC 88-38546. 426p. 1989. pap. text ed. 36.00 (*0-87179-595-7*, 0595) BNA.

***Redeker, Patty.** The History & Development of the Saleen Mustang. LC 94-71001. (Illus.). 206p. (Orig.). 1994. pap. 12.95 (*0-9624908-8-1*) CA Mustang Sales.

Redekop, Calvin. Mennonite Society. LC 88-32013. 456p. (C). 1989. text ed. 48.50 (*0-8018-3729-4*); pap. text ed. 15.95 (*0-8018-3871-1*) Johns Hopkins.

— Strangers Become Neighbors. LC 80-13887. (Studies in Anabaptist & Mennonite History: No. 22). (Illus.). 312p. 1980. 24.95 (*0-8361-1228-8*) Herald Pr.

Redekop, Calvin, jt. ed. see Burkholder, John R.

***Redekop, Calvin, et al.** Mennonite Entrepreneurs. LC 94-46177. 320p. 1995. text ed. 34.95x (*0-8018-5003-7*) Johns Hopkins.

Redekop, Calvin W. The Old Colony Mennonites: Dilemmas of Ethnic Minority Life. LC 69-13192. 322p. reprint ed. pap. 91.80 (*0-317-08392-9*, 2021737) Bks Demand.

Redekop, John H. The Christian & Civil Disobedience. (Faith & Life Ser.). 42p. 1991. pap. text ed. 2.50 (*0-921788-12-6*) Kindred Prods.

— A People Apart: Ethnicity & the Mennonite Brethren. 198p. 1987. pap. 2.95 (*0-919797-68-7*) Kindred Prods.

— Two Sides, the Best of Personal Opinion, 1964-1984. 306p. (Orig.). 1984. 15.95 (*0-685-73759-4*); pap. 2.00 (*0-919797-13-X*) Kindred Prods.

Redekop, Magdalene. Mothers & Other Clowns: The Stories of Alice Munro. LC 91-33773. 256p. 1992. 69.95 (*0-415-01097-7*, A5997); pap. 15.95 (*0-415-01098-5*, 9717) Routledge.

Redekop, Vernon W. A Life for a Life? The Death Penalty on Trial. (Peace & Justice Ser.: Vol. 9). 104p. (Orig.). 1990. pap. 5.95 (*0-8361-3516-4*) Herald Pr.

Redel, D. Color Blood Flow Imaging of the Heart. (Illus.). 140p. 1988. 199.00 (*0-387-16521-5*) Spr-Verlag.

***Redel, Victoria.** Already the World: Poems. LC 95-4151. (Wick Poetry First Bks.: No. 1). 128p. 1995. text ed. 17.00x (*0-87338-530-6*); pap. 9.50 (*0-87338-531-4*) Kent St U Pr.

— Where the Road Bottoms Out: Stories. 1995. 20.00 (*0-679-42071-1*) Knopf.

Redelinghuis, A., et al. Quantitative Methods for Managerial Decision Making. 2nd ed. 479p. 1989. pap. text ed. 49.95 (*0-409-10961-4*) Buttrwrth-Heinemann.

R

Redemann, Hans. Innovations in Aircraft Construction: Thirty-Seven Influential Designs. Force, Edward, tr. LC 91-62736. (Illus.). 248p. 1991. 29.95 (0-88740-338-7) Schiffer.

Redemptorist Pastoral Publication Staff. Handbook for Today's Catholic: Fully Indexed to the Catechism of the Catholic Church. rev. ed. LC 94-75247. 112p. 1994. pap. 2.95 (0-89243-671-9) Liguori Pubns.

— How You Live with Jesus: Catechism for Today's Young Catholic. LC 81-80097. 96p. (J). (gr. 4-6). 1981. pap. 4.95 (0-89243-137-7) Liguori Pubns.

— The Illustrated Catechism. LC 80-84312. 112p. (Orig.). 1980. pap. 7.95 (0-89243-135-0) Liguori Pubns.

— Jesus Loves You: A Catholic Catechism for the Primary Grades. LC 82-8. 96p. (J). (gr. 1-3). 1982. pap. 5.95 (0-89243-157-1) Liguori Pubns.

— Peace Be with You. rev. ed. (Illus.). 16p. 1987. pap. 1.95 (0-89243-417-1) Liguori Pubns.

***Redemptorist Pastoral Publications Staff.** Your Child's First Communion. (Illus.). 16p. 1990. pap. 2.95 (0-89243-328-0) Liguori Pubns.

Redemptorists of London Province Staff. Your Faith: A Popular Presentation of Catholic Belief. rev. ed. LC 93-79048. 88p. (Orig.). 1993. pap. 7.95 (0-89243-617-4) Liguori Pubns.

Redemptorists Pastoral Publication Staff. El Bautismo De Su Bebe: Your Baby's Baptism. (Redemptorist Pastoral Publicaitons). 16p. 1994. pap. 2.95 (0-89243-627-1) Liguori Pubns.

Redemptorists Staff & Liquori, Alfonso M. The Mission-Book of the Congregation of the Most Holy Redeemer. 1978. 42.95 (0-405-10843-5, 11848) Ayer.

Redenbach, Sandi. Self-Esteem; The Necessary Ingredient for Success: A Student-Centered Approach to Restructuring Education. Cole, Carol S., ed. LC 91-90017. (Illus.). 135p. (Orig.). 1991. pap. 14.00 (0-9632112-0-X) Esteem Sem.

Redenbacher, Fritz. Platen-Bibliographie. viii, 186p. 1972. reprint ed. write for info. (3-487-04095-6, Pub. by Georg Olms GW) Lubrecht & Cramer.

Redenbacher, Orville, et al. Higher Than the Top. LC 92-33944. 96p. (Orig.). 1993. pap. 7.00 (0-687-17002-8) Dimen for Liv.

Redenbarger, Wayne J. Articulator Features & Portuguese Vowel Height. (Studies in Romance Languages: No. 37). (Illus.). 197p. (C). 1981. pap. 9.00 (0-674-04815-6) HUP.

Redenbaugh. Synseeds: Applications of Synthetic Seeds to Crop Improvement. 1992. 219.00 (0-8493-4906-0) CRC Pr.

Redenius, Charles M., et al. American Republic: Politics, Institutions & Policies. LC 86-24695. (Illus.). 353p. (Orig.). (C). 1987. pap. text ed. 40.50 (0-314-28509-1); teacher ed. pap. text ed. write for info. (0-314-35236-8) West Pub.

Redenius, Ken. McMaster's Horses. 1980. pap. 1.75 (0-8439-0832-7) Dorchester Pub Co.

***Reder.** Seventy-Five Business Practices for Socially Responsible Companies. 1995. pap. text ed. 10.95 (0-87477-783-6) J P Tarcher.

Reder, Alan. In Pursuit of Principle & Profit: Business Success Through Social Responsibility. 304p. 1994. 22.95 (0-87477-781-X, J P T-Putnam) Putnam Pub Group.

— In Pursuit of Principle & Profit: Business Success Through Social Responsibility. LC 95-2370. 1995. pap. 13.95 (0-87477-812-3, Putnam) Putnam Pub Group.

— 75 Best Business Practices for Socially Responsible Companies. LC 95-13772. 1995. write for info. (0-87477-817-4) J P Tarcher.

Reder, Alan, jt. auth. see Brill, Jack A.

***Reder, Barry.** The Dusty Road. (Illus.). 32p. (Orig.). (J). (gr. k-3). 1994. pap. 12.95 (0-9641863-1-4) Understand Busn.

***Reder, C.** Grandpa's Mountain. 1994. pap. 3.99 (0-517-13322-9) Random.

Reder, Melvin W. Studies in the Theory of Welfare Economics. LC 68-54288. (Columbia University. Studies in the Social Sciences: No. 534). reprint ed. 20.00 (0-404-51534-7) AMS Pr.

Reder, Melvin W., jt. auth. see Hogarth, Robin M.

***Reder, Peter & Lucey, Clare, eds.** Assessment of Parenting: Psychiatric & Psychological Contributions. LC 95-7618. 1995. write for info. (0-415-11453-5); pap. write for info. (0-415-11454-3) Routledge.

Reder, Peter, et al. Beyond Blame: Child Abuse Tragedies Revisited. (Illus.). 240p. 1993. 65.00 (0-415-06678-6, A7788); pap. 19.95 (0-415-06679-4, A7792) Routledge.

REDEX Staff. Solar SNG: The Estimated Availability of Resources for Large-Scale Production of SNG by Anaerobic Digestion of Specially Grown Plant Material. 450p. 1979. pap. 15.00 (0-318-12701-6, M80779) Am Gas Assn.

Redey, George & Spatz, Eugene. A Comprehensive Diagnostic Test to Evaluate Motor & Cognitive Ability for the Ambulatory Severely Mentally Retarded. LC 76-23718. 100p. 1976. 5.00 (0-935484-00-0) Universe Pub Co.

Redfearn, D. H. Redfearn: History of the Redfearn Family. rev. ed. (Illus.). 377p. 1992. reprint ed. lib. bdg. 66.00 (0-8328-2710-X); reprint ed. pap. 56.00 (0-8328-2711-8) Higginson Bk Co.

Redfearn, David. Tolstoy: Principles for a New World Order. 192p. 1992. text ed. 18.95 (0-85683-134-4, Pub. by Shepheard-Walwyn Pubs UK) Paul & Co Pubs.

— Tolstoy: Principles for a New World Order. 196p. 1992. pap. 18.95 (0-685-70315-0, Pub. by Shephrd-Walwyn UK) Schalkenbach.

Redfearn, J. W. Parting, Clinging, Individuation. 1985. 20.00 (0-317-62214-5) St Mut.

Redfearn, Joe. The Exploding Self: The Creative & Destructive Nucleus of the Personality. 312p. (Orig.). 1992. pap. 16.95 (0-933029-60-8) Chiron Pubns.

Redfern, Angela, jt. auth. see Edward, Viv.

Redfern, Angela, jt. auth. see Edwards, Viv.

Redfern, Darren. The Maple Handbook. 400p. 1993. write for info. (3-540-94054-5) Spr-Verlag.

— The Maple Handbook. LC 93-27726. 400p. 1994. pap. 29.00 (0-387-94054-5) Spr-Verlag.

— The Maple Handbook. 2nd ed. LC 94-25796. 1995. 29.00 (0-387-94331-5) Spr-Verlag.

— Matlab Handbook. 1994. pap. 29.95 (0-387-94200-9) Spr-Verlag.

Redfern, E., jt. auth. see Allenby, R. B.

Redfern, E. J. Introduction to Pascal for Computational Mathematics. (Computer Science Ser.). (Illus.). 300p. (C). 1988. text ed. 90.00 (0-333-44430-2, Pub. by Macmill Press UK); pap. text ed. 35.00 (0-333-44431-0, Pub. by Macmill Press UK) Scholium Intl.

Redfern, H. B. Questions in Aesthetic Education. Snelders, Philip & Wringe, Colin, eds. 120p. 1986. pap. text ed. 14.95 (0-04-370163-9) Routledge Chapman & Hall.

Redfern, James. A Lexical Study of Raeto-Romance & Contiguous Italian Dialect Areas. LC 70-159469. (Janua Linguarum, Ser. Practica: No. 120). (Illus.). 105p. (Orig.). 1971. pap. text ed. 76.95 (90-279-1908-9) Mouton.

Redfern, James G. Into Poeta's Eyes. LC 90-55241. 106p. (Orig.). 1991. pap. 7.95 (1-56002-050-4) Aegina Pr.

Redfern, John C. The New Wave & Human Rights of Constitutional Law Against the Dark Age in America: God's Truth Against the Secular Machine. LC 87-60754. 131p. (Orig.). (C). 1988. pap. 19.95 (0-9618238-0-1) Small Busn Consult.

Redfern, Jon, jt. ed. see David, Jack.

Redfern, P. H., et al, eds. Circadian Rhythms in the Central Nervous System. LC 85-17970. (Satellite Symposia of the 9th IUPHAR Congress). (Illus.). 270p. 1985. lib. bdg. 115.00 (0-89573-507-5) VCH Pubs.

Redfern, Paul. The Love Diseases. (Illus.). 150p. 1981. reprint ed. pap. 4.95 (0-8065-0772-1, Citadel Pr) Carol Pub Group.

Redfern, Ray & Harmon, Barbara S. The Paintings of F. Grayson Sayre, 1879-1939. (Illus.). 76p. 1986. pap. 35.00 (0-939370-06-9) DeRu's Fine Art.

Redfern, Sally J., ed. Nursing Elderly People. 2nd ed. (Illus.). 600p. (Orig.). 1991. pap. text ed. 54.00 (0-443-04138-5) Churchill.

Redfern, Walter. Cliches & Coinages. (Crystal: The Language Ser.). (Illus.). 336p. 1989. 32.95 (0-631-15691-7) Blackwell Pubs.

— Feet First: Jules Valles. 240p. 1993. 60.00 (0-85261-315-6, Pub. by Univ of Glasgow UK) St Mut.

Redfern, Walter D. Private World of Jean Giono. LC 67-20396. 217p. reprint ed. 61.90 (0-8357-9115-7, 2017924) Bks Demand.

Redfield, A. C., et al. Interaction of Sea & Atmosphere: A Group of Contributions. (Meteorological Monograph Ser.: Vol. 2, No. 10). (Illus.). 75p. (Orig.). 1957. pap. 17.00 (0-933876-05-X) Am Meteorological.

Redfield, Alden, ed. see Hulan, Richard & Lawrence, Stephen S.

Redfield, Bessie G., ed. Gods: A Dictionary of the Deities of All Lands Including Supernatural Beings, Mythical Heroes & Kings & Sacred Books of Religions. 1977. lib. bdg. 300.00 (0-8490-1893-5) Gordon Pr.

Redfield, Bryan. A Bartender's Guide on How to Pick-Up Women: With a Special Section for Women Only. (Illus.). 345p. (Orig.). 1990. pap. 19.95 (0-9626455-0-8) New Atlan CA.

Redfield, Dana. Ezekiel's Chariot. 1991. pap. 9.95 (1-878901-10-9) Hampton Roads Pub Co.

Redfield, Isaac F. A Practical Treatise upon the Law of Railways. 2nd ed. LC 70-37982. (American Law Ser.: The Formative Years). 850p. 1972. reprint ed. 53.95 (0-405-04025-3) Ayer.

Redfield, James. The Celestine Prophecy. 256p. 1994. 17.95 (0-446-51862-X) Warner Bks.

— The Celestine Prophecy. large type ed. LC 94-19119. 1994. 26.95 (1-56895-113-2) Wheeler Pub.

— The Tenth Insight. 1996. 19.95 (0-446-51908-1) Warner Bks.

Redfield, James & Adrienne, Carol. The Celestine Prophecy: An Experiential Guide. 304p. 1995. pap. 8.99 (0-446-67122-3) Warner Bks.

Redfield, James, tr. see Borgeaud, Philippe.

Redfield, James F. The Celestine Prophecy: An Adventure. 256p. (Orig.). 1993. pap. 13.95 (0-944353-00-2) Satori.

Redfield, James M. Nature & Culture in the "Iliad" The Tragedy of Hector. LC 93-32349. 336p. 1993. lib. bdg. 49.95 (0-8223-1409-6); pap. text ed. 19.95 (0-8223-1422-3) Duke.

Redfield, Kent D. Cash Cleut: Political Money in Illinois Legislative Elections. 290p. 1994. pap. write for info. (0-938943-05-7) Sangamon Pub Affairs.

Redfield, Kent D., jt. auth. see Van Der Slik, Jack R.

Redfield, Margaret P., ed. see Redfield, Robert.

Redfield, Nayan L., tr. see D'Olivet, Fabre.

Redfield, Robert. The Folk Culture of Yucatan. 1976. lib. bdg. 59.95 (0-8490-1848-X) Gordon Pr.

— The Folk Culture of Yucatan. LC 41-15380. (University of Chicago Publications in Anthropology. Social Anthropology). 440p. reprint ed. pap. 125.40 (0-685-15652-4, 2026740) Bks Demand.

— The Folk Society. (Reprint Series in Sociology). (C). 1993. reprint ed. pap. text ed. 1.00 (0-8290-2622-3, S-229) Irvington.

— The Little Community & Peasant Society & Culture. 288p. 1989. pap. text ed. 18.95 (0-226-70670-2, Midway Reprint) U Ch Pr.

— Papers of Robert Redfield, 2 vols., 2. Redfield, Margaret P., ed. LC 62-10995. (Illus.). 301p. reprint ed. pap. 85.80 (0-8357-6250-5, 2056818) Bks Demand.

— Papers of Robert Redfield, 2 vols., Vol. 1: Human Nature & the Study of Society. Redfield, Margaret P., ed. LC 62-10995. (Illus.). 523p. reprint ed. Vol. 1, Human Nature & the Study of Society, 523p. pap. 149.10 (0-8357-6249-1, 2056818) Bks Demand.

— The Primitive World & Its Transformations. 198p. 1957. pap. 9.95 (0-8014-9028-6) Cornell U Pr.

— Tepoztlan, a Mexican Village: A Study of Folk Life. LC 30-15556. (Midway Reprint Ser.). 271p. reprint ed. pap. 77.30 (0-685-15784-9, 2026783) Bks Demand.

Redfield, Robert & Franz, Wanda K. AIDS & Young People. 32p. (YA). (gr. 9-12). 1987. pap. 4.00 (0-89526-774-8) Regnery Pub.

Redfield, Robert & Rojas, Alfonso V. Chan Kom: A Mayan Village. abr. ed. (Illus.). 236p. (C). 1989. reprint ed. pap. text ed. 9.95 (0-88133-488-X) Waveland Pr.

Redfield, Robert & Villa Rojas, Alfonso. Chan Kom, a Maya Village. LC 62-2616. 246p. reprint ed. pap. 70.20 (0-317-20695-8, 2024062) Bks Demand.

Redfield, Susan S. & Kupetsky, Lisa. Developing Subjective Test Items. (Illus.). 40p. (Orig.). 1987. pap. 16.50 (0-87683-917-0, A917-0) GP Pub.

Redfield, W. C. Genealogical History of the Redfield Family in the United States, Being a Revision & Extension of the Genealogical Tables Compiled in 1839. (Illus.). 345p. 1989. reprint ed. lib. bdg. 65.00 (0-8328-1010-X); reprint ed. pap. 55.00 (0-8328-1011-8) Higginson Bk Co.

Redfield, William. Letters from an Actor. LC 83-26627. 256p. 1984. pap. 7.95 (0-87910-007-9) Limelight Edns.

Redfinn, Michael. Being. 368p. (Orig.). 1988. pap. 3.95 (0-8439-2643-0) Dorchester Pub Co.

Redford, A. H., jt. auth. see Mills, B.

Redford, Arthur. The Economic History of England, 1760-1860: A Greenwood Archival Edition. LC 73-15244. 244p. 1974. reprint ed. text ed. 65.00 (0-8371-7166-0, REEH, Greenwood Pr) Greenwood.

— Labour Migration in England, 1800-1850. 2nd ed. Chaloner, W. H., ed. LC 68-6093. (Illus.). xx, 209p. 1968. lib. bdg. 35.00 (0-678-06766-X) Kelley.

— Manchester Merchants & Foreign Trade, Vol. 1, 1794-1858. Incl. Vol. 1. 1794-1858. LC 73-1675. xii, 251p. 1973. (0-318-53954-3); LC 73-1675. xii, 251p. 1973. reprint ed. 35.00 (0-678-00750-0) Kelley.

Redford, Bruce. The Converse of the Pen: Acts of Intimacy in the Eighteenth Century Familiar Letter. LC 86-11237. (Illus.). 252p. 1987. lib. bdg. 28.00 (0-226-70678-8); pap. text ed. 11.95 (0-226-70679-6) U Ch Pr.

Redford, Bruce, ed. The Letters of Samuel Johnson, Vol. IV: 1782-1784. (Illus.). 1994. write for info. (0-691-06977-8) Princeton U Pr.

— The Letters of Samuel Johnson, Vol. V: Appendices & Comprehensive Index. (Illus.). 1994. 29.95 (0-691-06978-6) Princeton U Pr.

— The Letters of Samuel Johnson: Volume I: 1731-1772, Volume II: 1773-1776, Volume III: 1777-1781, 3 vols. (Illus.). 1992. text ed. write for info. (0-318-68401-2) Princeton U Pr.

— The Letters of Samuel Johnson: Volume I: 1731-1772, Volume II: 1773-1776, Volume III: 1777-1781, 3 vols., Vol. I. (Illus.). 431p. 1992. text ed. 35.00 (0-691-06881-X) Princeton U Pr.

— The Letters of Samuel Johnson: Volume I: 1731-1772, Volume II: 1773-1776, Volume III: 1777-1781, 3 vols., Vol. II. (Illus.). 389p. 1992. text ed. 35.00 (0-691-06928-X) Princeton U Pr.

— The Letters of Samuel Johnson: Volume I: 1731-1772, Volume II: 1773-1776, Volume III: 1777-1781, 3 vols., Vol. III. (Illus.). 399p. 1992. text ed. 35.00 (0-691-06929-8) Princeton U Pr.

Redford, Bruce, ed. see Sheridan, R. B.

Redford, D. B., jt. ed. see Wevers, J. W.

Redford, D. B., jt. ed. see Wevers, John W.

Redford, Donald. Egypt, Canaan, & Israel in Ancient Times. (Illus.). 480p. 1992. text ed. 55.00 (0-691-03606-3) Princeton U Pr.

Redford, Donald B. Akhenaten: The Heretic King. LC 83-22960. (Illus.). 281p. 1987. pap. 19.95 (0-691-00217-7) Princeton U Pr.

— Egypt, Canaan, & Israel in Ancient Times. (Illus.). 505p. 1993. pap. text ed. 16.95 (0-691-00086-7) Princeton U Pr.

Redford, Emmette S. The Never-Ending Search for the Public Interest. (Reprint Series in Social Sciences). (C). 1993. reprint ed. pap. text ed. 2.30 (0-8290-3667-9, PS-236) Irvington.

Redford, Emmette S., contrib. Water Resource Development & Management in the Edwards Aquifer Region. (Policy Research Project Report Ser.: No. 1). 63p. 1972. 3.00 (0-89940-600-9) LBJ Sch Pub Aff.

Redford, Emmette S. & McCulley, Richard T. White House Operations: The Johnson Presidency. LC 85-26437. (Administrative History of the Johnson Presidency Ser.). 261p. 1986. text ed. 30.00 (0-292-79033-3) U of Tex Pr.

Redford, Emmette S., ed. see Hammond, Paul Y.

Redford, Emmette S., ed. see Herring, George C.

Redford, Emmette S., ed. see Welborn, David M.

Redford, John. Play of Wit & Science. (Tudor Facsimile Texts. Old English Plays Ser.: No. 18). reprint ed. 49.50 (0-404-53318-3) AMS Pr.

Redford, John, jt. ed. see Pasco, Rowanne.

Redford, Kent H. & Eisenberg, John F. Mammals of the Neotropics, Vol. 2: The Southern Cone: Chile, Argentina, Uruguay, & Paraguay. (Illus.). 272p. 1992. lib. bdg. 95.00 (0-226-70681-8); pap. text ed. 39.50 (0-226-70682-6) U Ch Pr.

Redford, Kent H. & Padoch, Christine, eds. Conservation of Neotropical Forests: Working from Traditional Resource Use. (Biological Resource Management in the Tropics Ser.). (Illus.). 432p. 1992. text ed. 45.00 (0-231-07602-9) Col U Pr.

Redford, Kent H., jt. ed. see Robinson, John G.

Redford, M. H., et al, eds. The Condom: Increasing Utilization in the U. S. (Illus.). 1974. 10.00 (0-911302-25-5); pap. 7.50 (0-317-58587-8) San Francisco Pr.

Redford, Robert, pref. The Legacy of Wildness: The Photographs of Robert Glenn Ketchum. 120p. 1993. 65.00 (0-89381-498-9) Aperture.

Redgate, S., ed. see International Symposium on Brain-Pituitary-Adrenal Interrelationships Staff.

Redgment, J. The Law Student's Companion: A Guide to the Study & Practice of Law. 2nd ed. 232p. 1988. pap. write for info. (0-7021-2211-4, Pub. by Juta SA) W W Gaunt.

Redgrave, G. R., jt. ed. see Pollard, Alfred W.

Redgrave, Lynn. This Is Living: How I Found Health & Happiness. 400p. 1992. pap. 5.99 (0-451-17307-4, Sig) NAL-Dutton.

Redgrave, Michael. Actor's Ways & Means. 1979. pap. 9.95 (0-87830-516-5, Theatre Arts Bks) Routledge Chapman & Hall.

— The Actor's Ways & Means. 2nd ed. (Illus.). 160p. 1995. pap. 13.95 (0-87830-059-7, B7285, Theatre Arts Bks) Routledge Chapman & Hall.

Redgrave, Richard & Redgrave, Samuel. A Century of British Painters. Todd, Ruthven, ed. (Landmarks in Art History Ser.). (Illus.). 622p. 1981. pap. 19.95 (0-8014-9217-3) Cornell U Pr.

Redgrave, Samuel, jt. auth. see Redgrave, Richard.

Redgrave, Vanessa. Vanessa Redgrave: An Autobiography. LC 94-14307. (Illus.). 419p. 1994. 25.00 (0-679-40216-0) Random.

Redgrove, H. Stanley. Alchemy Ancient & Modern. 141p. 1992. pap. 17.95 (1-56459-143-3) Kessinger Pub.

— The Belief in Talismans. reprint ed. pap. 6.95 (1-55818-200-4, Sure Fire) Holmes Pub.

— Bygone Beliefs: An Excursion into the Occult & Alchemical Nature of Man. (Excursion into the Occult & Alchemical Nature of Man Ser.). 287p. 1981. pap. 20.00 (0-89540-078-2, SB-078) Sun Pub.

— Magic & Mysticism: Studies in Bygone Beliefs. 1970. 7.95 (0-8216-0111-3, Univ Bks) Carol Pub Group.

— Roger Bacon: Christian Mystic & Alchemist. 1994. pap. 6.95 (1-55818-303-5, Pub. by Alchemical Pr) Holmes Pub.

Redgrove, Peter. The Cyclopean Mistress: Selected Short Fiction 1960-1990. 156p. 1994. pap. 16.95 (1-85224-207-8, Pub. by Bloodaxe Bks UK) Dufour.

— The Mudlark Poems & Grand Buveur. (Illus.). 64p. (C). 1986. pap. 38.00 (0-947612-21-1, Pub. by Rivelin Grapheme Pr) St Mut.

Redgrove, Stanley. Magic & Mysticism. pap. 2.95 (0-8065-0301-7, Citadel Pr) Carol Pub Group.

Redhawk, Randy. The Pow Wow Book: A Must for Every Pow Wow. 2nd rev. ed. LC 94-92187. (Illus.). 22p. (J). (gr. 3 up). 1994. pap. 5.00 (0-9641861-0-1) Redhawk Pubng.

Redhawk, Richard. Grandfather Origin Story: The Navajo Indian Begining. (Orig.). (J). (gr. 3-6). 1988. pap. 6.95 (0-940113-07-4) Sierra Oaks Pub.

— Grandmother's Christmas Story: A True Tale of the Quechan Indians. (Illus.). (J). (ps-5). 1987. pap. 6.95 (0-940113-08-2) Sierra Oaks Pub.

Redhead. The Big Block of Chocolate. (J). 1989. pap. 19.95 (0-590-50157-7) Scholastic Inc.

Redhead, Brian. Manchester: A Celebration. (Illus.). 170p. 1994. 45.00 (0-233-98816-5, Pub. by A Deutsch UK) Trafalgar.

Redhead, Brian, ed. Political Thought from Plato to NATO. 288p. (C). 1988. pap. 17.95 (0-534-10801-6) Intl Thomson.

Redhead, Brian, jt. auth. see Gumley, Frances.

Redhead, D. N. & Chalmers, N. Imaging. LC 94-11040. (Colour Guide Ser.). Date not set. write for info. (0-443-05020-1) Churchill.

Redhead, Janet S. Something Special for Miss Margery. LC 93-6632. (Voyages Ser.). (Illus.). (J). 1994. write for info. (0-383-03673-9) SRA Schl Grp.

Redhead, Keith & Hughes, Steward. Financial Risk Management. 200p. 1988. text ed. 59.95 (0-566-02652-X) Ashgate Pub Co.

Redhead, Mark, jt. auth. see Drewett, Richard.

***Redhead, Michael.** From Physics to Metaphysics. (Illus.). 150p. (C). 1995. write for info. (0-521-47405-1) Cambridge U Pr.

— Incompleteness, Nonlocality, & Realism: A Prolegomenon to the Philosophy of Quantum Mechanics. 200p. 1987. reprint ed. 49.95 (0-19-824937-3) OUP.

— Incompleteness, Nonlocality, & Realism: A Prolegomenon to the Philosophy of Quantum Mechanics. 200p. 1989. reprint ed. pap. 21.00 (0-19-824238-7) OUP.

Redhead, P. A., et al. The Physical Basis of Ultrahigh Vacuum. LC 92-46643. (AVS Classics of Vacuum Science & Technology Ser.). 1993. write for info. (1-56396-122-9) Am Inst Physics.

Redhead, Steve. The End-of-the-Century Party: Youth & Pop Towards 2000. 1990. text ed. 17.95 (0-7190-2827-2, Pub. by Manchester Univ Pr UK) St Martin.

— Unpopular Culture: The Birth of Law & Popular Culture. 1995. text ed. 19.95 (0-7190-3652-6) St Martin.

Redhead, Steve, ed. The Passion & the Fashion: Football Fandom in the New Europe. LC 93-3864. (Popular Cultural Studies). 238p. 1993. 54.95 (1-85628-462-X, Pub. by Avebury Pub UK) Ashgate Pub Co.

R

An Asterisk (*) at the beginning of an entry indicates that the title is appearing in BIP for the first time.

— Rave Off: Politics & Deviance in Contemporary Youth Culture. (Popular Culture in the City Ser.). 202p. 1993. 54.95 (*1-85628-463-8*, Pub. by Avebury Pub UK); pap. 21.95 (*1-85628-465-4*, Pub. by Avebury Pub UK) Ashgate Pub Co.

Redheffer. Differential Equations - Suggestions for Use. 1991. pap. 10.00 (*0-86720-201-7*) Jones & Bartlett.

— Introduction to Differential Equations. (Math Ser.). 480p. (C). 1992. boxed 50.00 (*0-86720-289-0*) Jones & Bartlett.

Redheffer, jt. auth. see Redheffer, Gordon.

Redheffer, Gordon & Redheffer. Linear Algebra Issue 2. (Math Ser.). 400p. (C). 1995. 50.00 (*0-86720-288-2*) Jones & Bartlett.

Redheffer, R. M., jt. auth. see Sokolnikoff, Ivan S.

Redheffer, Raymond. Differential Equations. 800p. 1991. boxed 53.75 (*0-86720-200-9*) Jones & Bartlett.

Redheffer, Raymond, jt. auth. see Levinson, Norman.

Redhouse, J. W., tr. see Shah, Nasir A.

Redhouse, James. A Turkish & English Lexicon. 1987. 95.00x (*0-86685-127-5*) Intl Bk Ctr.

Redhouse, James, ed. Legends of the Sufis. 1977. pap. 9.50 (*0-7229-5051-9*) Theos Pub Hse.

Redhouse, James W. Redhouse English Turkish Dictionary. 17th ed. 1152p. (ENG & TUR.). 1990. lib. bdg. 95.00 (*0-7859-0640-1*, M2050) Fr & Eur.

— Turkish-English Dictionary, 3 pts., Set. (ENG & TUR.). 1977. reprint ed. 297.95 (*0-518-19005-6*) Ayer.

Redi, H., jt. ed. see Schlag, G.

Redican, Kerry, et al. Organization of School Health Programs. 2nd ed. 496p. (C). 1993. boxed write for info. (*0-697-13129-7*) Brown & Benchmark.

Redican, Kerry J., et al. Dimensions of Consumer Health. LC 94-526. 1994. text ed. write for info. (*0-13-217415-4*) P-H.

Redick, S. S. & Lazzell, K. M. The Handicapped: Our Mission. 1978. 2.50 (*0-911365-07-9*, A261-08444) Home Econ Educ.

Redig, Patrick T., et al, eds. Raptor Biomedicine. 288p. (C). 1993. text ed. 39.95 (*0-8166-2219-1*) U of Minn Pr.

— Raptor Biomedicine. LC 92-40604. 265p. (C). 1993. text ed. 39.95x (*0-8166-2220-5*) U of Minn Pr.

Rediger, G. Lloyd. Ministry & Sexuality: Cases, Counseling, & Care. LC 90-33422. 176p. (Orig.). 1990. pap. 14.00 (*0-8006-2418-1*, 1-2418) Augsburg Fortress.

***Rediger, Pat.** Great African Americans in Business. (Great African Americans Ser.). (Illus.). 80p. (J). (gr. 4-11). 1995. lib. bdg. 18.70 (*0-86505-803-2*); pap. 7.95 (*0-86505-817-2*) Crabtree Pub Co.

— Great African Americans in Civil Rights. (Great African Americans Ser.). (Illus.). 80p. (J). (gr. 4-11). 1995. lib. bdg. 18.70 (*0-86505-798-2*); pap. 7.95 (*0-86505-812-1*) Crabtree Pub Co.

— Great African Americans in Entertainment. (Great African Americans Ser.). (Illus.). 80p. (J). (gr. 4-11). 1995. lib. bdg. 18.70 (*0-86505-799-0*); pap. 7.95 (*0-86505-813-X*) Crabtree Pub Co.

— Great African Americans in Literature. (Great African Americans Ser.). (Illus.). 80p. (J). (gr. 4-11). 1995. lib. bdg. 18.70 (*0-86505-802-4*); pap. 7.95 (*0-86505-816-4*) Crabtree Pub Co.

— Great African Americans in Music. (Great African Americans Ser.). (Illus.). 80p. (J). (gr. 4-11). 1995. lib. bdg. 18.70 (*0-86505-800-8*); pap. 7.95 (*0-86505-814-8*) Crabtree Pub Co.

— Great African Americans in Sports. (Great African Americans Ser.). (Illus.). 80p. (J). (gr. 4-11). 1995. lib. bdg. 18.70 (*0-86505-801-6*); pap. 7.95 (*0-86505-815-6*) Crabtree Pub Co.

Rediker, Marcus. Between the Devil & the Deep Blue Sea: Merchant Seamen, Pirates & the Anglo-American Maritime World, 1700-1750. LC 87-6304. (Illus.). 340p. 1987. 44.95 (*0-521-30342-7*) Cambridge U Pr.

— Between the Devil & the Deep Blue Sea: Merchant Seamen, Pirates, & the Anglo-American Maritime World, 1700-1750. (Canto Book Ser.). (Illus.). 352p. (C). 1993. pap. 11.95 (*0-521-45720-3*) Cambridge U Pr.

Redin, Mats A. Word-Order in English Verse from Pope to Sassoon. 1977. lib. bdg. 59.95 (*0-8490-2842-6*) Gordon Pr.

Redinbaugh, Larry D. & Neu, Clyde W. Small Business Management: A Planning Approach. (Illus.). 475p. 1980. text ed. 53.75 (*0-314-52971-3*); teacher ed, pap. text ed. write for info. (*0-314-52998-5*) West Pub.

Reding, Andrew, ed. see Borge, Tomas.

Reding, Andrew A. & Whalen, Christopher. Fragil Estabilidad: Reforma y Represion Bajo el Regimen de Carlos Salinas. (North America Project Special Report Ser.). 37p. (SPA.). 1992. 5.00 (*0-911646-51-5*) World Policy.

— Fragile Stability: Reform & Repression in Mexico under Carlos Salinas. (North America Project Special Report Ser.). 33p. 1992. 5.00 (*0-911646-50-7*) World Policy.

Reding, Andrew A., ed. see Levinson, Jerome I.

Reding, Andrew A., tr. see Santos de la Garza, Luis.

***Reding, Jaclyn.** Chasing Dreams. (Historical Romance Ser.). 384p. 1995. pap. 5.50 (*0-451-40559-5*, Topaz) NAL-Dutton.

— Deception's Bride. 336p. (Orig.). 1993. mass mkt. 4.99 (*1-55773-966-8*) Diamond.

— Tempting Fate. 384p. 1995. 4.99 (*0-451-40558-7*, Topaz) NAL-Dutton.

Reding, Malcolm E. Flood Insurance: The Insecurity Blanket. 1994. pap. 6.95 (*0-9638709-1-2*) Shade Tree Pr.

Reding, Malcolm E., ed. see Butcher, Clyde.

Reding, Malcolm E., ed. see Teger, Allan T.

***Reding, Todd L., ed.** Rockhurst Review - 1992 Vol. V: A Fine Arts Journal. 50p. 1992. pap. 5.00 (*1-886761-04-3*) Rockhurst Col.

Redinger, Teresa, ed. Money Fund Vision. Date not set. write for info. (*0-913755-24-9*) Donoghue Organ Inc.

Redington, Catherine. Perfect Picnics. (Illus.). 128p. 1991. pap. 10.95 (*0-926684-01-9*) Eclectic Oregon.

Redington, Charles B. Redington Field Guides to Biological Interactions: Plants in Wetlands. 432p. (C). 1993. ring bd. 28.95 (*0-8403-8983-3*) Kendall-Hunt.

Redington, James F., jt. auth. see Klimenko, Nicholas A.

Redisch, Edward F., jt. ed. see Risley, John S.

Redish, Edward W. & Risley, John S. The Conference on Computers in Physics Instruction Proceedings. (Illus.). 608p. (C). 1990. 49.95 (*0-201-16306-3*, Adv Bk Prog) Addison-Wesley.

Redish, Janice C., jt. auth. see Dumas, Joseph F.

Redish, Martin H. The Constitution As Political Structure. LC 93-42364. 224p. 1995. 39.95 (*0-19-507060-7*) OUP.

— Federal Courts: Cases, Comments & Questions. 2nd ed. (American Casebook Ser.). 1122p. 1988. text ed. 45.00 (*0-314-43919-6*) West Pub.

— The Federal Courts in the Political Order: Judicial Jurisdiction & American Political Theory. LC 90-85345. 200p. 1991. 24.95 (*0-89089-411-6*) Carolina Acad Pr.

— Federal Jurisdiction. 2nd ed. (Black Letter Ser.). 234p. 1990. pap. text ed. 19.00 (*0-314-79273-2*) West Pub.

— Federal Jurisdiction: Tensions in the Allocation of Judicial Power. 2nd ed. 423p. 1990. 35.00 (*0-87473-516-5*) Michie Butterworth.

Redish, Martin H. & Nichol, Gene R. Federal Courts - Cases, Comments & Questions. (American Casebook Ser.). 83p. (C). 1993. reprint ed. pap. text ed. 9.50 (*0-314-01098-X*) West Pub.

Redishl, Martin H. & Nichol, Gene R. Federal Courts: Cases, Comments & Questions. 3rd ed. (American Casebook Ser.). 995p. 1994. text ed. 48.00 (*0-314-03990-2*) West Pub.

Redjou, Pat C. No-Gluten Solution: Children's Cookbook. (Illus.). (J). (gr. 4 up). 1991. pap. 22.00 (*0-9626052-2-0*) Rae Pub.

— The "No-Gluten" Solution: Cooking Guide for People Who Are Sick & Tired of Being Sick & Tired. (Illus.). (Orig.). 1990. pap. 23.95 (*0-9626052-0-4*) Rae Pub.

Redkey, Edwin S., ed. A Grand Army of Black Men: Letters from African-American Soldiers in the Union Army, 1861-1865. LC 92-14632. (Cambridge Studies in American Literature & Culture: No. 63). 320p. (C). 1992. pap. 17.95 (*0-521-43998-1*) Cambridge U Pr.

— Respect Black: The Writings & Speeches of Henry McNeal Turner. LC 79-138695. 1971. 11.95 (*0-405-01984-X*) Ayer.

Redknap, Mark, jt. ed. see Gaimster, David.

Red'ko, Kliment, comp. Art of the Early Soviet Period. 16p. (C). 1987. 40.00 (*0-569-09033-4*, Pub. by Collets UK) Pro-Am Music.

Redl, et al. Electronics: Dictionary of Technical Information, 2 vols. 1270p. (C). 1983. 205.00 (*0-569-08782-1*, Pub. by Collets) St Mut.

Redl, E. & Oldal, E. Dictionary of Electronics, Telecommunications & Vacuum Technology, 2 vols., Set. 1269p. (ENG, FRE, GER, HUN & RUS.). 1983. 75.00 (*0-8288-0315-3*, M6649) Fr & Eur.

— Electronics, Telecommunications, Vacuum Technology Vols. 50-53, 2 vols. 1270p. 1983. 60.00x (*963-05-2674-3*, Pub. by Akad Kiado HU) St Mut.

Redl, Fritz. Pre-Adolescents: What Makes Them Tick? 17p. 1974. pap. 1.25 (*0-686-12276-3*) Jewish Bd Family.

— When We Deal with Children: Selected Writings. 1972. pap. 16.95 (*0-02-925880-4*) Free Pr.

Redl, Fritz & Wineman, David. Children Who Hate: The Disorganization & Breakdown of Behavior Controls. LC 51-13784. 1965. pap. 14.95 (*0-02-925960-6*) Free Pr.

— Controls from Within: Techniques for the Treatment of the Aggressive Child. LC 52-8161. 1965. text ed. 22.95 (*0-02-926030-2*); pap. 16.95 (*0-02-926040-X*) Free Pr.

Redl, H., jt. ed. see Schlag, G.

Redl, Maureen, jt. auth. see Hayes, Jody.

***Redl, Siegmund H., et al.** An Introduction to GSM. LC 94-23893. 1995. write for info. (*0-89006-785-6*) Artech Hse.

Redl, William A., ed. Noise & Vibration Measurement: Proceedings of a Symposium Sponsored by the Environmental Engineering Division. 145p. 1985. 19.00 (*0-87262-445-5*) Am Soc Civil Eng.

Redlake, Kevin. The Sorrows below Apollyon, Vol. 1. Stohlmberg, Jacob, ed. (Illus.). 74p. 1995. pap. 9.00 (*0-9639186-0-5*) Stohlmberg Pubng.

Redleaf, Rhoda. Busy Fingers, Growing Minds: Finger Plays, Verses & Activities for Whole Language Learning. LC 93-39636. (Illus.). 164p. (Orig.). (J). (ps). 1993. pap. 18.95 (*0-934140-79-0*) Redleaf Pr.

— Open the Door, Let's Explore: Neighborhood Field Trips for Young Children. LC 83-70035. (Illus.). 200p. (Orig.). 1983. pap. 15.95 (*0-934140-20-0*) Redleaf Pr.

— Teachables II. LC 87-50215. (Illus.). 224p. (Orig.). 1987. pap. 14.95 (*0-934140-41-3*) Redleaf Pr.

Redlich, Frederick C., jt. auth. see Hollinghead, August B.

Redlich, Fredrick C., jt. ed. see Brody, Eugene B.

Redlich, Josef. Austrian War Government. (Economic & Social History of the World War Ser.). 1929. 100.00 (*0-685-69855-6*) Elliots Bks.

Redlich, Josef & Hirst, Francis W. History of Local Government in England, Bk. 1. 2nd ed. LC 71-110121. xvii, 284p. 1970. lib. bdg. 39.50 (*0-678-07005-9*) Kelley.

Redlich, Joseph. Osterreichische Regierung Und Verwaltung Im Weltkriege. (Wirtschafts-Und Sozialgeschichte des Weltkrieges (Osterreichische Und Ungarische Serie)). (GER.). 1925. 100.00 (*0-317-27532-1*) Elliots Bks.

— Procedure of the House of Commons, 3 Vols, Set. Steinthal, A. Ernest, tr. LC 77-77895. reprint ed. 165.00 (*0-404-05280-0*) AMS Pr.

Redlich, Norman. Professional Responsibility: A Problem Approach. 2nd ed. 1983. 22.00 (*0-316-73657-0*) Little.

— Standards of Professional Conduct for Lawyers & Judges. (C). 1984. pap. 16.00 (*0-316-73658-9*) Little.

Redlich, Otto. Thermodynamics: Fundamentals, Applications. 278p. 1976. 95.00 (*0-444-41487-8*) Elsevier.

Redlich, Rosemarie, jt. auth. see Scherman, David E.

Redlich, Shimon. Propaganda & Nationalism in Wartime Russia: The Jewish Anti-Fascist Committee in the U. S. S. R., 1941-1948. (East European Monographs: No. 108). 236p. 1982. text ed. 42.00 (*0-88033-001-5*) East Eur Quarterly.

Redlin, Michael H. & Stipanuk, David M. Managing Hospitality Engineering Systems. Eaton, Timothy J., ed. LC 87-15712. (Illus.). 275p. (C). 1987. text ed. 57.95 (*0-86612-037-8*) Educ Inst Am Hotel.

Redman, Alvin, ed. see Wilde, Oscar.

Redman, Arthur, ed. see Kuypers, Marcus E., et al.

Redman, B. R., tr. see Gobineau, Joseph A.

Redman, Barbara K. The Process of Patient Education. 7th ed. LC 92-12909. 368p. 1992. pap. 29.95 (*0-8016-6670-8*) Mosby Yr Bk.

Redman, Barbara K., ed. see American Association of Colleges of Nursing Staff.

Redman, Barbara K., et al, eds. Educating RNs for the Baccalaureate: Programs & Issues. LC 90-9533. (Teaching of Nursing Ser.: Vol. 12). 248p. 1990. 39.95 (*0-8261-7210-5*) Springer Pub.

Redman, Ben. Edwin Arlington Robinson. LC 74-1444. (Studies in Poetry: No. 38). 1974. lib. bdg. 49.95 (*0-8383-2045-7*) M S G Haskell Hse.

Redman, Ben R. Edwin Arlington Robinson. 1972. 59.95 (*0-8490-0098-X*) Gordon Pr.

Redman, Ben R., ed. see Voltaire, Francois-Marie de.

Redman, C. W., et al. The Human Placenta. (Illus.). 608p. 1993. 185.00 (*0-632-02721-5*) Blackwell Sci.

Redman, Charles L. People of the Tonto Rim: Archaeological Discovery in Prehistoric Arizona. LC 92-25213. (Illus.). 224p. 1993. 39.95 (*1-56098-193-8*); pap. 14.95 (*1-56098-192-X*) Smithsonian.

Redman, Charles L., ed. Medieval Archeology. (Medieval & Renaissance Texts & Studies: Vol. 60). 320p. 1989. 24.00 (*0-86698-044-X*) MRTS.

Redman, Charles L., jt. ed. see Minnis, Paul E.

Redman, Chris & Walker, Isabel. Pre-Eclampsia: The Hidden Threat to Pregnancy. (Facts Ser.). (Illus.). 208p. 1992. 29.95 (*0-19-262012-6*) OUP.

Redman, Deborah A. A Reader's Guide to Rational Expectations: A Survey & Comprehensive Annotated Bibliography. 176p. 1992. text ed. 63.95 (*1-85278-567-5*, Pub. by E Elgar Pub UK) Ashgate Pub Co.

Redman, Deborah A., comp. Economic Methodology: A Bibliography with References to Works in the Philosophy of Science, 1860-1988. LC 89-17195. (Bibliographies & Indexes in World History Ser.: No. 9). 301p. 1989. text ed. 79.50 (*0-313-26859-2*, REG/, Greenwood Pr) Greenwood.

Redman, Eric. The Dance of Legislation. 1974. pap. 11.00 (*0-671-21746-1*, Touchstone Bks) S&S Trade.

Redman, George L. Building Self-Esteem in Children: A Skill & Strategy Workbook for Parents. rev. ed. Gorham, Kerstin, ed. (Illus.). 95p. 1992. 19.95 (*1-879276-02-X*) Parent Tching Pubns.

— Building Self-Esteem in Students: A Skill & Strategy Workbook for Teachers. Gorham, Kerstin, ed. (Illus.). 91p. 1992. 19.95 (*1-879276-01-1*) Parent Tching Pubns.

Redman, Harry, Jr. Major French Milton Critics of the Nineteenth Century. LC 93-39661. (Duquesne Studies: Language & Literature Ser.: Vol. 14). 400p. (C). 1994. text ed. 48.00x (*0-8207-0249-8*) Duquesne.

— The Roland Legend in Nineteenth-Century French Literature. LC 90-26581. 264p. 1991. text ed. 32.00 (*0-8131-1732-1*) U Pr of Ky.

Redman, Helen C., jt. auth. see Fisch, Allan E.

Redman, Helen C., jt. auth. see Weinreb, Jeffrey C.

Redman, Helen C., et al. Emergency Radiology. (Illus.). 554p. 1992. text ed. 105.00 (*0-7216-7491-7*) Saunders.

Redman, John. Understanding State Economies Through Industry Studies. LC 94-5574. 1994. write for info. (*0-934842-70-1*) CSPA.

Redman, John & Thomason, Michael E. John Redman's Essentials of the Golf Swing. (Illus.). 144p. 1994. pap. 12.95 (*0-452-27302-1*, Plume) NAL-Dutton.

Redman, John, jt. ed. see Lacher, Mortimer J.

Redman, John, jt. auth. see Ray, Ralph.

Redman, John E., jt. auth. see Ray, Ralph P.

Redman, Lenn. How to Draw Caricatures. (Illus.). 176p. (Orig.). 1984. pap. 18.95 (*0-8092-5685-1*) Contemp Bks.

Redman, Lipman, jt. auth. see Quiggle, James W.

Redman, Martin. Illustrated AJS Matchless Buyers Guide. (MBI Illustrated Buyer's Guide Ser.). (Illus.). 160p. 1992. pap. 16.95 (*0-946627-84-3*) Motorbooks Intl.

Redman, Michael, jt. auth. see Walker, D. J.

Redman, Michael E., et al. Traveling America: An Activity Book for the Whole Family. 56p. (Orig.). 1993. pap. write for info. (*0-9637442-0-8*) Mstr Designs.

Redman, Robert E., jt. auth. see Ripley, Earle A.

Redman, Stuart & Ellis, Robert. A Way with Words, Level 1: Vocabulary Development Activities for Learners of English. McCarthy, Mike, ed. (Illus.). 112p. (C). 1990. teacher ed, pap. 12.95 (*0-521-35918-X*) Cambridge U Pr.

— A Way with Words, Level 1: Vocabulary Development Activities for Learners of English. McCarthy, Mike, ed. (Illus.). 106p. (C). 1990. student ed, pap. 9.95 (*0-521-35917-1*); pap. 15.95 (*0-521-35026-3*) Cambridge U Pr.

Redman, T. F. Lecture Notes on Midwifery. 4th ed. (Illus.). 331p. 1985. pap. 30.00 (*0-7236-0812-1*, Pub. by John Wright UK) Buttrwrth-Heinemann.

Redman, Tim. Ezra Pound & Italian Fascism. (Cambridge Studies in American Literature & Culture: No. 47). 350p. (C). 1991. 47.95 (*0-521-37305-0*) Cambridge U Pr.

Redman, Warren. Portfolios for Development: A Guide for Trainers & Managers. 192p. (Orig.). 1994. pap. text ed. 27.95 (*0-89397-394-7*) Nichols Pub.

— Portfolios for Development Guide for Trainers & Managers. 224p. (C). 1994. pap. 45.00x (*0-7494-1158-9*, Pub. by IPM Hse UK) St Mut.

Redmann, J. M. Death by the Riverside. LC 90-42741. 256p. (Orig.). 1990. pap. 9.95 (*0-934678-27-8*) New Victoria Pubs.

— Deaths of Jocasta. LC 92-14648. 288p. (Orig.). 1992. pap. 9.95 (*0-934678-39-1*) New Victoria Pubs.

— The Intersection of Law & Desire: A Mystery. 352p. 1995. 22.00 (*0-393-03793-2*) Norton.

Redmann, R. E., jt. auth. see Ripley, E. A.

Redmayne, Ann. A Time to Forget. large type ed. (Linford Romance Library). 1989. pap. 11.95 (*0-7089-6791-4*, Trailtree Bookshop) Ulverscroft.

— To Speak of Love. large type ed. (Linford Romance Library). 1991. pap. 13.95 (*0-7089-6988-7*, Trailtree Bookshop) Ulverscroft.

Redmayne, Barbara. Ambitious Angel. large type ed. (Romance Ser.). 336p. 1988. 15.95 (*0-7089-1855-7*) Ulverscroft.

— Lovely Day. large type ed. (Romance Ser.). 320p. 1988. 15.95 (*0-7089-1747-X*) Ulverscroft.

Redmayne, Robert A. British Coal-Mining Industry During the War: R. A. S. Redmayne. (Economic & Social History of the World War Ser.). 1923. 125.00 (*0-686-37864-4*) Elliots Bks.

Redmill. SPC Digital Telephone Exchanges. 1990. 109.00 (*0-86341-147-9*, TE021) Inst Elect Eng.

Redmill, F. J., ed. Dependability of Critical Computer Systems: Guidelines Produced by the European Workshop on Industrial Computer Systems, No. 1. 296p. 1989. 75.75 (*1-85166-203-0*) Elsevier.

— Dependability of Critical Computer Systems 2: Guidelines Produced by the European Workshop on Industrial Computer Systems Technical Committee, No. 7. 288p. 1990. 81.00 (*1-85166-381-9*) Elsevier.

Redmill, F. J. & Valdar, A. R. SPC Digital Telephone Exchanges. rev. ed. (Telecommunications Ser.: No. 21). 537p. 1994. pap. 45.00 (*0-86341-298-X*, Pub. by Peregrinus UK); boxed 109.00 (*0-86341-301-3*, Pub. by Peregrinus UK) Inst Elect Eng.

***Redmill, Felix & Anderson, Tom, eds.** Achievement & Assurance of Safety: Proceedings of the Third Safety-Critical Systems Symposium, Brighton, UK, 7-9 February, 1995. LC 94-46761. 1995. pap. 69.00 (*3-540-19922-5*) Spr-Verlag.

— Directions in Safety-Critical Systems: Proceedings of the First Safety-Critical Systems Symposium, the Watershed Media Centre, Bristol, 9-11 February 1993. LC 92-43311. 1992. 69.00 (*0-387-19817-2*) Spr-Verlag.

— Safety-Critical Systems: Current Issues, Techniques, & Standards. LC 92-47352. 1993. write for info. (*0-412-54820-8*) Chapman & Hall.

— Technology & Assessment of Safety-Critical Systems: Proceedings of the Second Safety-Critical Systems Symposium, Birmingham, UK, 8-10 February 1994. LC 93-50853. 1994. pap. text ed. 75.00 (*0-387-19859-8*) Spr-Verlag.

Redmon, Curtis. Anointed Praise: The Ministry of Music in the Church Today. (Practical Church Ser.). 54p. 1992. pap. text ed. 4.95 (*1-881685-00-4*) LUA Stand Minist.

— Just Servants: The Ministry of the Deacon & the Usher. (Practical Church Ser.). (Orig.). 1993. pap. text ed. 5.95 (*1-881685-02-0*) LUA Stand Minist.

— What about the Children: The Ministry of the Sunday School. (Practical Church Ser.). (Orig.). 1993. pap. text ed. 5.95 (*1-881685-01-2*) LUA Stand Minist.

Redmon, Gerald W., jt. auth. see Redmon, Tina L.

Redmon, Hugo. Campamentos y Retiros Cristianos - Christian Camps & Retreats. 128p. (Orig.). (SPA.). 1992. pap. 3.85 (*0-311-11051-7*) Casa Bautista.

Redmon, Ronald. Panzergrenadiers in Action. (Combat Troops in Action Ser.). (Illus.). 1995. pap. 8.95 (*0-89747-096-6*, 3005) Squad Sig Pubns.

Redmon, Tina L. & Redmon, Gerald W. The Inventor's Handbook on Patent Applications. 1993. pap. 18.95 (*0-533-10405-X*) Vantage.

Redmon, William K. & Dickinson, Alyce M. Promoting Excellence Through Performance Management. LC 90-4369. (Journal of Organizational Behavior Management: Vol. 11, No. 1). 289p. 1990. Acid-free paper. text ed. 39.95 (*1-56024-015-6*) Haworth Pr.

Redmond. Most Beautiful Horse. 1994. mass mkt. 3.50 (*0-06-106204-9*, Harp PBks) HarpC.

Redmond, Anthony D., jt. auth. see Robertson, Colin E.

Redmond, Anthony D., jt. auth. see Robertson, Colin.

Redmond, Barbara, jt. auth. see Thomas, Eberle.

Redmond, C. F., jt. ed. see Lodge, H. C.

Redmond, Christopher. In Bed with Sherlock Holmes: Sexual Elements in Arthur Conan Doyle's Stories of the Great Detective. 1993. 30.00 (*0-88924-142-2*, Pub. by Simon & Pierre Pub CN) Empire Pub Srvs.

— A Sherlock Holmes Handbook. 250p. 1994. 30.00 (*0-88924-246-1*, Pub. by Simon & Pierre Pub CN) Empire Pub Srvs.

— Welcome to America, Mr. Sherlock Holmes: Victorian America Meets Arthur Conan Doyle. 236p. (Orig.). 1993. pap. 20.00 (*0-88924-184-8*, Pub. by Simon & Pierre Pub CN) Empire Pub Srvs.

Redmond, Don, jt. auth. see Gregory, John.

Redmond, Donald A. Sherlock Holmes: A Study in Sources. 375p. 1982. 39.95 (*0-7735-0391-9*, Pub. by McGill CN) U of Toronto Pr.

— Sherlock Holmes among the Pirates: Copywright & Conan Doyle in America 1890-1930. LC 89-27280. (Contributions to the Study of World Literature Ser.: No. 36). 304p. 1990. text ed. 59.95 (*0-313-27230-1*, RSH/, Greenwood Pr) Greenwood.

R

An Asterisk (*) at the beginning of an entry indicates that the title is appearing in BIP for the first time.

Redmond, Elsa M. A Fuego y Sangre: Early Zapotec Imperialism in the Cuicatlan Canada, Oaxaca. (Memoirs Ser.: No. 16). (Illus.). 214p. 1983. pap. 15.00 (*0-932206-97-2*) U Mich Mus Anthro.
— Tribal & Chiefly Warfare in South America. LC 94-18061. (Memoirs, Studies in Latin American Ethnohistory & Archaeology: No. 28, Vol. 5). 1994. 25.00 (*0-915703-35-1*) U Mich Mus Anthro.
Redmond, Eugene B. The Eye in the Ceiling: Selected Poems. 156p. (Orig.). 1992. 22.00 (*0-86316-308-4*); pap. 12.00 (*0-86316-307-6*) Writers & Readers.
Redmond, G. P., ed. Lipids & Women's Health. (Illus.). 272p. 1990. 54.00 (*0-387-97318-4*) Spr-Verlag.
***Redmond, Geoffrey P.** Androgenic Disorders. 356p. 1995. 89.00 (*0-7817-0274-7*) Raven.
— The Good News about Women's Hormones: Complete Information & Proven Solutions for the Most Common Hormonal Problems. 528p. 1995. pap. 12.99 (*0-446-39454-8*) Warner Bks.
Redmond, Geoffrey P., jt. ed. see Soyka, Lester F.
Redmond, Gerald. The Sporting Scots of Nineteenth-Century Canada. LC 80-67124. (Illus.). 352p. 1982. 40.00 (*0-8386-3069-3*) Fairleigh Dickinson.
Redmond, Gerald, ed. Sport & Politics. LC 85-18114. 240p. 1986. text ed. 36.00x (*0-87322-007-2*, BRED0007) Human Kinetics.
Redmond, Gerry. Wayne Gretzky: A Biography. (Illus.). 112p. (Orig.). 1993. pap. 9.95 (*1-55022-190-6*, Pub. by ECW Pr CN) InBook.
Redmond, Gertrude T. & Ouellette, Frances. Concept & Case Studies Nursing: A Life Cycle Approach. 1983. pap. write for info. (*0-201-06207-0*, Health Sci) Addison-Wesley.
Redmond, Howard A. Christian Hedonism. LC 89-12344. (American University Studies: Theology & Religion: Ser. VII, Vol. 67). 156p. 1990. text ed. 34.95 (*0-8204-1117-5*) P Lang Pubs.
Redmond, Ian. Elephant. LC 92-20855. (Eyewitness Bks.: Vol. 44). 64p. (J). (gr. 5 up). 1993. 16.00 (*0-679-83880-5*); lib. bdg. 16.99 (*0-679-93880-X*) Knopf Bks Yng Read.
— Elephant Book. 1991. 16.95 (*0-87951-432-9*) Overlook Pr.
— The Elephant in the Bush. LC 89-11297. (Animal Habitats Ser.). (Illus.). 32p. (J). (gr. 4-6). 1989. lib. bdg. 17.27 (*0-8368-0116-4*) Gareth Stevens Inc.
Redmond, James, ed. Drama & Nemesis. LC 79-9054. (Themes in Drama Ser.: No. 2). (Illus.). 1980. write for info. (*0-521-22179-X*) Cambridge U Pr.
— Drama & Symbolism. LC 81-10250. (Themes in Drama Ser.: No. 4). (Illus.). 280p. 1982. write for info. (*0-521-22181-1*) Cambridge U Pr.
— Drama, Dance & Music. (Themes in Drama Ser.: No. 3). (Illus.). 260p. 1981. write for info. (*0-521-22180-3*) Cambridge U Pr.
— Drama in Society. LC 77-54723. (Themes in Drama Ser.: No. 1). (Illus.). 1979. write for info. (*0-521-22076-9*) Cambridge U Pr.
Redmond, James, ed. see Morris, William.
Redmond, John. Great Golf Courses of Ireland. 1993. 19.99 (*0-517-08755-3*) Random Hse Value.
— The Next Mediterranean Enlargement of the European Community: Turkey, Cyprus & Malta? 166p. 1993. 57.95 (*1-85521-281-1*, Pub. by Dartmth Pub UK) Ashgate Pub Co.
Redmond, John, ed. The External Relations of the European Community: The International Response to 1992. LC 92-4253. 200p. 1992. text ed. 65.00 (*0-312-08051-4*) St Martin.
***Redmond, LaGroon, ed.** Campbell County, Georgia Superior Court Deeds & Mortgages Grantee-Grantor Index 1829-1931. LC 94-60683. 1078p. 1994. text ed. 53.25 (*1-883793-04-1*) W H Wolfe.
Redmond, Liam. Death Is So Kind. 1959. 9.95 (*0-8159-5301-1*) Devin.
Redmond, Lindy. The Young Story Maker. 1991. 29.95 (*0-88047-282-0*, D9105-K) DOK Pubs.
Redmond, Lula M. Surviving When Someone You Love Was Murdered: A Professional's Guide to Group Grief Therapy for Families & Friends of Murder Victims. 170p. (Orig.). (C). 1989. pap. 24.95 (*0-9624592-0-8*) Psychological Consult.
Redmond, Marie, jt. ed. see Barrett, Edward.
Redmond, Marilyn. Henry Hamilton, Graduate Ghost. LC 81-22693. (Illus.). 159p. (J). (gr. 6 up). 1982. 11.95 (*0-88289-303-3*) Pelican.
— Henry Hamilton in Outer Space. LC 90-25176. (J). (gr. 4-7). 1991. 11.95 (*0-88289-820-5*) Pelican.
Redmond, Michael. Sixty Second Sells: Ninety-Nine Hot Radio Spots for Retail Businesses. LC 92-56684. 109p. 1993. lib. bdg. 19.95 (*0-89950-792-1*) McFarland & Co.
Redmond, P. W. & Shears, Peter. General Principles of English Law. 7th ed. 496p. 1993. pap. 49.50 (*0-7121-0858-0*, Pub. by Pitman Pub Ltd UK) Trans-Atl Phila.
Redmond, Patricia, jt. ed. see Baker, Houston A., Jr.
Redmond, Paul. Companies & Securities Law: Commentary & Materials. lxi, 912p. 1988. 120.00 (*0-455-20765-8*, Pub. by Law Bk Co); pap. 79.00 (*0-455-20766-6*, Pub. by Law Bk Co) W W Gaunt.
Redmond, R., ed. General Principles of English Law. 392p. (C). 1990. 130.00 (*0-685-39832-3*, Inst Pur & Supply) St Mut.
Redmond, R. & Lawson, L. An Introduction to Business Law. 320p. (C). 1990. 125.00 (*0-685-47809-2*, Inst Pur & Supply) St Mut.
Redmond, Shirley-Raye. Grampa & the Ghost. 96p. (Orig.). (J). (gr. 3 up). 1994. pap. 3.50 (*0-380-77382-1*, Camelot Young) Avon.

***Redmond, Stephen. The Fountain of Youth: Slowing the Aging Process. (Illus.). 308p. (Orig.). 1995. pap. 14.95 (*0-9643754-0-0*) Ridgeback Pr.**
This new book shows readers how to use the most up-to-date information on preventive nutrition, exercise, supplements of vitamins & minerals, self-guided imagery, & personal preventive health strategies to slow the aging process. It is packed with practical information in a format that is easy to read. A model of The Life Tree Matrix is utilized as a map for reaching the Fountain of Youth. It also explains a unique method of using self-guided imagery as a tool to effect change in oneself in a pleasant & effective way. By harnessing the power of self-guided imagery, it is possible to tap into the inner mind & use it to channel changes to improve personal nutrition, use of vitamin & mineral supplements, exercising, relaxation, interests such as hobbies, & relationships with family & friends. Available from Ridgeback Press, Inc., 305 Vineyard Town Center, #295, Morgan Hill, CA 95037; 408-683-2008. ***Publisher Provided Annotation.***

Redmond, Tim. Not in Our Backyard: People & Events That Shaped America's Environmental Movement, 1969-1990. 1993. 27.50 (*0-688-10644-7*) Morrow.
Redmond, Tim, jt. auth. see Mason, John.
Redmond, Tony. All-in-One: A Technical Odyssey. (Office Automation Ser.). (Illus.). 551p. (Orig.). 1991. pap. 44.95 (*1-55558-086-6*, EY-H952E-DP, Digital DEC) Buttrwrth-Heinemann.
— All-in-One: Managing & Programming in V3.0. LC 92-27295. (All-in-One Ser.). (Illus.). 552p. (Orig.). 1992. pap. text ed. 52.95 (*1-55558-101-3*, EYM522EDP, Digital DEC) Buttrwrth-Heinemann.
— Working with Teamlinks. (Networking & Data Communications Ser.). (Illus.). 446p. 1993. pap. 44.95 (*1-55558-116-1*, EY-P942E-DP, Digital DEC) Buttrwrth-Heinemann.
Redmont, Bernard S. Risks Worth Taking: The Odyssey of a Foreign Correspondent. 264p. (C). 1992. lib. bdg. 47.50 (*0-8191-8797-6*); pap. text ed. 24.00 (*0-8191-8852-2*) U Pr of Amer.
Redmont, Jane. Generous Lives: American Catholic Women Today. 1992. 23.00 (*0-688-06707-7*) Morrow.
— Generous Lives: American Catholic Women Today. LC 93-15400. 384p. 1993. reprint ed. pap. text ed. 14.95 (*0-89243-576-3*, Triumph Books) Liguori Pubns.
Redmont, P. W. Mercantile Law. 296p. (C). 1989. 80.00 (*0-685-36150-0*, Inst Pur & Supply) St Mut.
Redmore, G. B. Under the Southern Cross: South America, Australia, Africa. (Life & Livelihood Geographies Ser.: Bk. 2). (Illus.). pap. 8.95 (*0-685-20646-7*) Transatl Arts.
Redmount, R. S., et al. Grievance-Response Mechanisms in the Ghetto. LC 74-151046. (Symposia on Law & Society Ser.). 1971. reprint ed. lib. bdg. 19.50 (*0-306-70117-0*) Da Capo.
Redner, Harry. The Ends of Science: An Essay in Scientific Authority. 344p. 1987. pap. text ed. 85.00 (*0-8133-0452-0*) Westview.
— A New Science of Representation: Towards an Integrated Theory of Representation in Science, Politics, & Art. LC 94-14892. (C). 1994. text ed. 59.50 (*0-8133-2211-1*) Westview.
Redner, Harry, ed. An Heretical Heir of the Enlightenment: Politics, Policy, & Science in the Work of Charles E. Linblom. LC 93-19808. 378p. (C). 1993. text ed. 68.50 (*0-8133-1669-3*) Westview.
Rednour, Shar, ed. Virgin Territory. (Orig.). 1995. pap. 12.95 (*1-56333-238-8*) Masquerade.
Redon, Odilon. To Myself. 1986. 16.95 (*0-8076-1145-X*) Braziller.
Redondi, P., ed. Science: The Renaissance of a History: (Proceedings of the International Conference, Paris, June 1986) (History & Technology Ser.). iv, 582p. 1987. pap. text ed. 146.00 (*3-7186-0441-8*) Gordon & Breach.
Redondi, Pietro. Galileo Heretic. Rosenthal, Raymond, tr. (Illus.). 366p. 1990. pap. 16.95 (*0-691-02426-X*) Princeton U Pr.
Redondi, Pietro & Fox, R., eds. French Institutions from the Revolution to the Restoration. (Special Issue of the Journal History & Technology Ser.: Vol. 5, Nos. 2-4). 232p. (C). 1988. pap. text ed. 235.00 (*3-7186-4845-8*) Gordon & Breach.
Redondi, Pietro, jt. ed. see Bhattacharya, Sabyasachi.
Redondo, Mary. California Directory of Attorneys, 1993, 2 vols. 1992. pap. 27.50 (*1-55943-131-8*) Butterworth Legal Pubs.
Redondo, Mary, ed. Parker's California Directory of Attorneys, 1994. 2390p. 1993. 40.00 (*0-250-47263-5*) Butterworth Legal Pubs.
— Parker's Directory of California Attorneys, 1994, 2 vols. 1430p. 1993. disk 28.50 (*0-250-47214-7*) Butterworth Legal Pubs.
— Texas Directory of Attorneys. 5th ed. 1993. pap. 28.00 (*1-55943-203-9*) Butterworth Legal Pubs.
***Redonnet, Marie.** Candy Store. (European Women Writers Ser.). 112p. 1995. pap. 10.00 (*0-8032-8958-8*) U of Nebr Pr.
— Forever Valley. Stump, Jordan, tr. LC 94-1315. (European Women Writers Ser.). 120p. 1994. pap. 10.00 (*0-8032-8951-0*, Bison Books) U of Nebr Pr.
— Hotel Splendid. Stump, Jordan, tr. LC 94-1314. (European Women Writers Ser.). 1994. pap. 10.00 (*0-8032-8953-7*, Bison Books) U of Nebr Pr.
— Rose Mellie Rose. Stump, Jordan, tr. LC 94-1313. (European Women Writers Ser.). 1994. pap. 10.00 (*0-8032-8952-9*, Bison Books) U of Nebr Pr.
Redonnet, Marie, jt. auth. see Quinn, Alexandra.
Redor, Dominique. Wage Inequalities in East & West. (Illus.). 240p. (C). 1993. 59.95 (*0-521-39531-3*) Cambridge U Pr.
Redoseyev, P. Marxist Philosophy & Our Time. (Social Science Today Problems of the Contemporary World Ser.: No.109). 256p. 1983. pap. 21.25 (*0-317-53803-9*, Pub. by Collets) St Mut.
Redoute, Pierre. Lilies & Related Flowers. LC 81-11021. (Illus.). 240p. 1982. 65.00 (*0-87951-135-4*) Overlook Pr.
Redoute, Pierre J. The Most Beautiful Flowers. (Illus.). 304p. 1991. pap. 37.50 (*0-914427-08-3*, Tabard Pr) W S Konecky Assocs.
Redpath, Alan. The Bible Speaks to Our Times: The Christian's Victory in Christ. (Alan Redpath Library). 124p. 1993. reprint ed. pap. 9.99 (*0-8007-5492-1*) Revell.
— Blessings Out of Buffetings: Studies in Second Corinthians. (Alan Redpath Library). 240p. 1993. reprint ed. pap. 11.99 (*0-8007-5488-3*) Revell.
— Faith for the Times: Studies in the Book of Isaiah. (Alan Redpath Library). 368p. 1994. reprint ed. pap. 12.99 (*0-8007-5518-9*) Revell.
— Law & Liberty: The Ten Commandments for Today. LC 77-14980. (Alan Redpath Library). 128p. 1994. reprint ed. pap. 9.99 (*0-8007-5515-4*) Revell.
— The Making of a Man of God: Studies in the Life of David. LC 62-10731. (Alan Redpath Library). 256p. 1994. reprint ed. pap. 11.99 (*0-8007-5516-2*) Revell.
— The Royal Route to Heaven: Studies in First Corinthians. (Alan Redpath Library). 248p. 1993. reprint ed. pap. 11.99 (*0-8007-5491-3*) Revell.
— Victorious Christian Faith: Lessons in the Higher Christian Life. LC 84-4719. (Alan Redpath Library). 192p. 1994. reprint ed. pap. 11.99 (*0-8007-5514-6*) Revell.
— Victorious Christian Living: Studies in the Book of Joshua. (Alan Redpath Library). 254p. 1993. reprint ed. pap. 11.99 (*0-8007-5490-5*) Revell.
— Victorious Christian Service: Studies in the Book of Nehemiah. LC 58-11020. (Alan Redpath Library). 192p. 1994. reprint ed. pap. 11.99 (*0-8007-5517-0*) Revell.
— Victorious Praying: Studies in the Lord's Prayer. (Alan Redpath Library). 151p. 1993. reprint ed. pap. 9.99 (*0-8007-5489-1*) Revell.
Redpath, Ann. What Happens If You Become Homeless. (Real Facts for Growing up Ser.). (Illus.). 48p. (J). (gr. 3-6). Date not set. lib. bdg. 12.95 (*1-56065-132-6*) Capstone Pr.
— What Happens If You Go to Jail? (Real Facts for Growing up Ser.). (Illus.). 48p. (J). (gr. 3-6). Date not set. lib. bdg. 12.95 (*1-56065-135-0*) Capstone Pr.
— What Happens If You Have a Baby? (Real Facts for Growing up Ser.). (Illus.). 48p. (J). (gr. 3-6). Date not set. lib. bdg. 12.95 (*1-56065-138-5*) Capstone Pr.
— What Happens If You Join a Street Gang? (Real Facts for Growing up Ser.). (Illus.). 48p. (J). (gr. 3-6). Date not set. lib. bdg. 12.95 (*1-56065-139-3*) Capstone Pr.
— What Happens If You Quit School? (Real Facts for Growing up Ser.). (Illus.). 48p. (J). (gr. 3-6). Date not set. lib. bdg. 12.95 (*1-56065-136-9*) Capstone Pr.
— What Happens If You Run Away from Home? (Real Facts for Growing up Ser.). (Illus.). 48p. (J). (gr. 3-6). Date not set. lib. bdg. 12.95 (*1-56065-133-4*) Capstone Pr.
— What Happens If You Shoplift? (Real Facts for Growing up Ser.). (Illus.). 48p. (J). (gr. 3-6). Date not set. lib. bdg. 12.95 (*1-56065-137-7*) Capstone Pr.
— What Happens If You Use Drugs? (Real Facts for Growing up Ser.). (Illus.). 48p. (J). (gr. 3-6). Date not set. lib. bdg. 12.95 (*1-56065-134-2*) Capstone Pr.
Redpath, Ann, ed. see Asimov, Isaac.
Redpath, Ann, ed. see Broun, Heywood.
Redpath, Ann, ed. see Chekhov, Anton.
Redpath, Ann, ed. see De Maupassant, Guy.
Redpath, Ann, ed. see Einstein, Albert.
Redpath, Ann, ed. see Gallaz, Chrsitophe.
Redpath, Ann, ed. see Gandhi, Mahatma.
Redpath, Ann, ed. see Murtha, Philly.
Redpath, Ann, ed. see Poe, Edgar Allan.
Redpath, Ann, ed. see Pushkin, Aleksandr.
Redpath, Ann, ed. see Russell, Bertrand.
Redpath, Ann, ed. see Stevenson, Robert Louis.
Redpath, H. A., jt. auth. see Hatch, E.
Redpath, Henry A., jt. auth. see Hatch, Edwin.
Redpath, James. Echoes of Harper's Ferry. LC 77-82215. (Anti-Slavery Crusade in America Ser.). 1970. reprint ed. 23.95 (*0-405-00654-3*) Ayer.
— Public Life of Captain John Brown. LC 79-126251. (Select Bibliographies Reprint Ser.). 1977. 34.95 (*0-8369-5478-5*) Ayer.
Redpath, Peter, ed. From Twilight to Dawn: The Cultural Vision of Jacques Maritain. LC 90-50611. 320p. (C). 1991. pap. text ed. 15.00 (*0-268-00979-1*) U of Notre Dame Pr.
Redpath, Peter A. Help Me! My Child Is Missing! LC 84-71207. 106p. (Orig.). 1985. pap. 9.95 (*0-936049-00-6*) Child Savers.
— A Simplified Introduction to the Wisdom of St. Thomas. LC 80-5230. 180p. 1980. pap. text ed. 21.00 (*0-8191-1059-0*) U Pr of Amer.
Redpath, Philip. William Golding: A Structural Reading of His Fiction. LC 86-10710. 224p. 1986. 58.50 (*0-389-20647-4*, N8204) B&N Imports.
Redshaw, L. C., ed. see Ilyushin, A. A. & Lenskii, V. S.
Redshaw, Mavis, jt. ed. see Orville-Thomas, W. J.
Redshaw, S. C., jt. auth. see Rushton, K. R.
Redshaw, Tom. Site Agent's Handbook: Construction under the ICE Conditions. 183p. 1990. text ed. 58.50 (*0-7277-1540-2*, Pub. by T Telford UK) Am Soc Civil Eng.
Redsicker, D. R., ed. The Practical Methodology of Forensic Photography. (Illus.). 292p. 1991. 44.95 (*0-444-01597-3*, TR822) CRC Pr.
Redslob, Edwin. Schicksal und Dichtung: Goethe Aufsaetze Ed. by Wieland Schmidt. 145p. (GER.). 1985. 63.10 (*3-11-010472-5*) De Gruyter.
Redstone, Lilian J., ed. Parish of All Hallows, Pt. 1. LC 74-138273. (London County Council. Survey of London Ser.: No. 12). reprint ed. 84.50 (*0-404-51662-9*) AMS Pr.
Redstone, Louis G. New Dimensions in Shopping Centers & Stores. LC 82-6546. 344p. 1983. reprint ed. 37.50 (*0-89874-508-X*) Krieger.
— The New Downtowns: Rebuilding Business Districts. LC 82-17111. 352p. (C). 1983. reprint ed. lib. bdg. 37.50 (*0-89874-560-8*) Krieger.
Redway, A. R., jt. auth. see Brennan, Neil.
Redway, I. R. Life Is Not a Bed of Roses. 32p. 1993. pap. 5.95 (*0-8059-3391-3*) Dorrance.
Redway, Jacques W. Making of the Empire State. 263p. 1993. reprint ed. lib. bdg. 79.00 (*0-7812-5196-6*) Rprt Serv.
Redway, Kathryn. How to Be a Rapid Reader. LC 90-62788. 128p. 1991. pap. 6.95 (*0-8442-5174-7*, VGM Career Bks) NTC Pub Grp.
Redwine, Carole C. Basic Research Skills: A Review Handbook. 58p. (Orig.). (C). 1994. pap. text ed. 6.00 (*0-87563-498-2*) Stipes.
***Redwine, Cooper.** Upgrading to FORTRAN 90. LC 95-12917. (Illus.). 416p. 1995. pap. 39.95 (*0-387-97995-6*) Spr-Verlag.
Redwine, Mary F. Substitute Teacher's Handbook: Activities & Projects for Kindergarten Through Grade Six. 1970. pap. 6.99 (*0-8224-6600-7*) Fearon Teach Aids.
Redwine, Robert P., jt. auth. see Enge, Harald A.
***Redwine, Samuel T. & Withey, James V., eds.** Methods of Technology Transfer (3-95) (S-W Process Improvement Ser.). 150p. 1995. 20.00 (*0-8186-6830-X*, BP06830) IEEE Comp Soc.
— Responsibilities & Functions of Change Agents (3-95) (S-W Process Improvement Ser.). 150p. 1995. 20.00 (*0-8186-6820-2*, BP06820) IEEE Comp Soc.
— Software Process Improvement for Technology Transfer (3-95) (S-W Process Improvement Ser.). 150p. 1995. 20.00 (*0-8186-6825-3*, BP06825) IEEE Comp Soc.
— Software Process Improvement Series, 3 bks., Set. 1995. 55.00 (*0-614-03793-X*, BP06835) IEEE Comp Soc.
***Redwood, Charles.** D. C. Edgar Cayce's Holistic Health Program. Barilla, Jean, ed. (Good Health Guide Ser.). 1995. 3.95 (*0-87983-661-X*) Keats.
Redwood, Christopher. Delius Companion. 1991. pap. 11.95 (*0-7145-3826-4*) Riverrun NY.
Redwood, Christopher, ed. A Delius Companion: A 70th Birthday Tribute to Eric Fenby. LC 76-57756. (Music Reprint Ser.). (Illus.). 1977. reprint ed. lib. bdg. 35.00 (*0-306-70880-9*) Da Capo.
Redwood Cultural Work & Community Music & Friends Staff. Note by Note: A Guide to Concert Production. Shoemaker, Joanie, ed. 288p. (Orig.). (C). 1989. pap. 15.95 (*0-9608774-3-6*) Redwood Records.
Redwood, Daniel. A Time to Heal: How to Reap the Benefits of Holistic Health. 251p. (Orig.). 1993. pap. 12.95 (*0-87604-310-4*, 383) ARE Pr.
Redwood, H., jt. ed. see Taylor, B.
Redwood, John. Popular Capitalism. 208p. (C). 1988. lib. bdg. 52.50 (*0-415-00114-5*) Routledge.
Redwood, John, 3rd. World Bank Approaches to the Environment in Brazil. LC 93-14544. (Operations Evaluation Study Ser.). 90p. 1993. 7.95 (*0-8213-2511-6*, 12511) World Bank.
Redwood, Ray. QTC: I Have a Message for You. Noe, Tom, ed. LC 88-90627. (Illus.). 376p. (Orig.). 1989. 15.00 (*0-945845-00-6*); pap. 9.95 (*0-945845-01-4*) Sequoia Pr TX.
Redwood, Rosaline. On Copra Ships & Coral Isles. large type ed. 352p. 1992. 21.95 (*0-7089-2614-2*) Ulverscroft.
— Stranger from Shanghai. large type ed. (Linford Mystery Library). 384p. 1992. pap. 14.95 (*0-7089-7218-7*, Trailtree Bookshop) Ulverscroft.
Redworth, Glyn. In Defence of the Church Catholic: The Life of Stephen Gardiner. 288p. 1990. text ed. 49.95 (*0-631-16392-1*) Blackwell Pubs.
Ree. Lemon Twist: No Salt Added Cookbook. LC 87-92238. 204p. 1989. 19.45 (*0-929622-02-2*); pap. text ed. 14.95 (*0-929622-00-6*) Nutrit Unltd Pubns.
Ree, Harry. Educator Extrordinary: The Life & Achievement of Henry Morris 1889-1961, 163p. 1985. pap. 17.95 (*0-7206-0700-0*, Pub. by P Owen Ltd UK) Dufour.
Ree, Harry, ed. The Henry Morris Collection. 112p. 1985. 54.95 (*0-521-26612-2*) Cambridge U Pr.
Ree, Jonathan. Concise Encyclopedia of Western Philosophy & Philosophers. 3rd ed. Urmson, J. O., ed. 256p. (C). 1990. text ed. 44.95 (*0-685-46018-5*); pap. text ed. 16.95 (*0-685-46019-3*) Routledge Chapman & Hall.
— Philosophical Tales. 192p. 1987. pap. text ed. 12.95 (*0-416-42620-4*) Routledge Chapman & Hall.
Ree, Jonathan, ed. see Sartre, Jean-Paul.
Ree, Jonathan, jt. ed. see Urmson, J. O.

R

An Asterisk (*) at the beginning of an entry indicates that the title is appearing in BIP for the first time.

*Reece. Pollyanna Comes Home. 1995. pap. text ed. 2.97 (*1-55748-657-3*) Barbour & Co.
— Pollyanna Plays the Game. 1995. pap. text ed. 2.97 (*1-55748-658-1*) Barbour & Co.
Reece, Albert & Coustan, Donald R., eds. Diabetes Mellitus in Pregnancy: Principles & Practice. (Illus.). 652p. 1988. text ed. 98.00 (*0-443-08470-X*) Churchill.
Reece, Albert E., et al. Handbook of Medicine of the Fetus & Mother. (Illus.). 512p. 1994. 39.95 (*0-397-51347-X*) Lippincott.
Reece, B. & Manning, G. Wilson RV: An In-Basket Simulation. (C). 1976. text ed. 13.40 (*0-07-051485-2*) McGraw.
Reece, Barry L. & Brandt, Rhonda. Effective Human Relations in Organizations, 3 Vols. 3rd ed. LC 86-80602. 575p. (C). 1986. text ed. 52.36 (*0-395-35711-X*); Experiencing human relations. student ed, pap. 17.96 (*0-395-42574-3*) HM.
— Effective Human Relations in Organizations, 4 Vols. 4th ed. (C). 1989. student ed 17.16 (*0-395-52991-3*) HM.
— Human Relations: Principles & Practices. (C). 1990. pap. 23.16 (*0-395-52994-8*) HM.
— Human Relations: Principles & Practices. (C). 1990. pap. 3.96 (*0-395-52995-6*) HM.
— Human Relations: Principles & Practices, 2 Vols. (C). 1993. pap. 21.56 (*0-395-52996-4*) HM.
Reece, Barry L., jt. auth. see Manning, Gerald L.
Reece, Byron H. Ballad of the Bones & Other Poems. LC 85-21338. 96p. 1985. reprint ed. 14.95 (*0-87797-100-5*) Cherokee.
— Better a Dinner of Herbs: A Novel by Byron Herbert Reece. LC 92-22952. (Brown Thrasher Bks.). 240p. 1992. reprint ed. pap. 14.95 (*0-8203-1489-7*) U of Ga Pr.
— Bow down in Jerico. LC 85-21335. 160p. 1985. reprint ed. 15.95 (*0-87797-102-1*) Cherokee.
— The Hawk & the Sun: A Novel. LC 85-2238. (Brown Thrasher Bks.). 200p. 1994. reprint ed. pap. 14.95 (*0-8203-1656-3*) U of Ga Pr.
— Season of Flesh. LC 85-21333. 96p. 1985. reprint ed. 14. 95 (*0-87797-104-8*) Cherokee.
— Song of Joy & Other Poems. LC 85-22355. 128p. 1985. reprint ed. 15.95 (*0-87797-105-6*) Cherokee.
Reece, Colleen. The Calling of Elizabeth Courtland & Honor Bound, 2 bks. in 1. (Romance Reader Ser.: No. 1). 7.95 (*1-55748-089-3*) Barbour & Co.
— A Girl Called Cricket & The Hills of Hope, 2 bks. in 1. (Romance Reader Ser.: No. 8). 7.95 (*1-55748-228-4*) Barbour & Co.
— Legacy of Silver & Angel of the North, 2 bks. in 1. (Romance Reader Ser.: No. 6). 7.95 (*1-55748-163-6*) Barbour & Co.
— Mark of Our Moccasins. (Indian Culture Ser.). 1982. 5.95 (*0-686-81747-8*) Coun India Ed.
— To Love & Cherish & Storm Clouds over Chantel, 2 bks. in 1. (Romance Reader Ser.: No. 4). 7.95 (*1-55748-132-6*) Barbour & Co.
Reece, Colleen L. Interrupted Flight & Delayed Dream. (Present Tense Collections: No. 1). 1992. 7.95 (*1-55748-257-8*) Barbour & Co.
— Mi Primer Libro de el Dia de las Brujas: My First Halloween Book. Kratky, Lada, tr. LC 85-31396. (Spanish Edition--My First Holiday Bks.). (Illus.). 32p. (SPA.). (J). (ps-3). 1986. lib. bdg. 11.55 (*0-516-32902-2*); pap. 3.95 (*0-516-52902-1*) Childrens.
— My First Christmas Book. LC 84-9431. (My First Holiday Bks.). (Illus.). 32p. (J). (ps-2). 1984. pap. 3.95 (*0-516-42901-9*) Childrens.
— My First Halloween Book. LC 84-9431. (My First Holiday Bks.). (Illus.). 32p. (J). (ps-2). 1984. pap. 3.95 (*0-516-42902-7*) Childrens.
— Saying Thank You. LC 82-21992. (Moods & Emotions Ser.). (Illus.). 32p. (J). (ps-2). 1983. lib. bdg. 21.36 (*0-89565-249-8*) Childs World.
— Writing Smarter, Not Harder: The Workbook Way. Lent, Penny, ed. (Illus.). 112p. (Orig.). 1995. pap. 17.99 (*1-885371-13-6*) Kldoscope Pr.
Reece, Connie, ed. see Hagee, John C.
Reece, Debra. Make-Up Magic: A Complete Guide to a Beautiful New You. Settel, Trudy, ed. (Illus.). 64p. (Orig.). 1987. pap. 3.95 (*0-932523-01-3*) Briarcliff Pr.
Reece, E. Albert. Medicine of Fetus & Mother. 1992. Text Review Package. 155.00 (*0-397-51339-9*) Lippincott.
***Reece, E. Albert & Coustan, Donald R., eds.** Diabetes Mellitus in Pregnancy. 2nd ed. LC 95-12415. 1995. write for info. (*0-443-08979-5*) Churchill.
Reece, E. Albert, et al. Medicine of the Fetus & Mother. (Illus.). 1488p. 1992. text ed. 145.00 (*0-397-51013-6*) Lippincott.
— Review for Medicine of the Fetus & Mother. LC 92-25643. 1992. 19.95 (*0-397-51331-3*) Lippincott.
— Ultrasound in Obstetrics & Gynecology. (Illus.). 272p. (C). 1994. text ed. 65.00 (*0-8385-9247-3*, A9247-6) Appleton & Lange.
Reece, Gerow, tr. see Kawai, Hayao.
Reece, Ira T. Homicide - Index of Modern Authors & Subjects with Guide for Rapid Research. LC 90-56268. 200p. 1991. 44.50 (*1-55914-304-5*); pap. 39.50 (*1-55914-305-3*) ABBE Pubs Assn.
— Prisoners: Health & Medical Subject Analysis with Reference Bibliography. LC 85-48088. 150p. 1987. 44.50 (*0-88164-448-X*); pap. 39.50 (*0-88164-449-8*) ABBE Pubs Assn.
Reece, J. McGee, jt. auth. see Caplow, Theodore.
Reece, James S., jt. auth. see Anthony, Robert N.
Reece, June E. Jimmy & the Sun Drop. (Illus.). 24p. (Orig.). (J). (ps-3). 1992. pap. 3.50 (*0-9631934-0-6*) Sun Drop.
Reece, Katherine E., jt. auth. see Frascona, Oliver E.
Reece, Louise. Thank You Lord. (Illus.). 164p. (Orig.). 1983. pap. 3.95 (*0-9614264-0-3*) Lovejoy Pr.
Reece, Nancy S., ed. see Mitchell, Richard L.
***Reece-Podgorski, Ashley.** Ultimate Performance System. LC 94-90309. 270p. 1993. 49.95 (*0-9644303-0-4*) Ultimate Perf.
— Ultimate Performance System, II. LC 94-90308. 344p. (C). 1994. 89.95 (*0-9644303-1-2*) Ultimate Perf.
Reece, Ray. The Sun Betrayed: A Report on the Corporate Seizure of U. S. Solar Energy Development. LC 79-66992. 234p. 1979. 35.00 (*0-89608-072-2*); pap. 7.50 (*0-89608-071-4*) South End Pr.
Reece, Richard. Coinage in Roman Britain. (Illus.). 144p. 1987. 39.95 (*0-900652-86-1*, Pub. by Seaby UK) Trafalgar.
— Identifying Roman Coins. (Illus.). 48p. 1986. 17.95 (*0-900652-79-9*, Pub. by Seaby UK) Trafalgar.
Reece, Richard & Casey, John, eds. Coins & the Archaeologist. rev. ed. (Illus.). 306p. 1988. reprint ed. 39.95 (*1-85264-011-1*, Pub. by Seaby UK) Trafalgar.
Reece, Robert D. & Siegel, Harvey A. Studying People: A Primer in the Ethnics of Social Research. LC 86-18059. 272p. (Orig.). 1986. 29.95 (*0-86554-220-1*, H198); pap. 18.75 (*0-86554-221-X*, P28) Mercer Univ Pr.
Reece, Robert H. Night Bombing with the Bedouins. (Great War Ser.: No. 12). (Illus.). 120p. 1991. reprint ed. 27.95 (*0-89839-161-X*) Battery Pr.
Reece, Robert M. Child Abuse: Medical Diagnosis & Management. (Illus.). 450p. 1993. text ed. 69.50 (*0-8121-1498-1*) Williams & Wilkins.
Reece, Sachiko, tr. see Kawai, Hayao.
Reece, Steve. The Stranger's Welcome: Oral Theory & the Aesthetics of the Homeric Hospitality Scene. (Monographs in Classical Antiquity). 240p. (C). 1992. text ed. 39.50 (*0-472-10386-5*) U of Mich Pr.
Reece, Thom. Magic Methods of Recruiting: How to Recruit Dealers, Distributors, Agents, Commission Salespeople, Direct Sales Teams & Multi Level Sales Organizations. (Illus.). 1987. pap. 39.95 (*0-944865-00-3*) Pel-I-Can Pr.
Reece, Trevor. Radio Control Model Racing Yachts. (Illus.). 160p. 1989. pap. 19.95 (*0-85242-972-X*, Pub. by Argus Pubs UK) Motorbooks Intl.
Reece, Trudy, jt. auth. see Pritikin, Enid.
Reece, William O. Physiology of Domestic Animals. LC 90-5543. (Illus.). 372p. 1991. pap. text ed. 39.50 (*0-8121-1307-1*) Williams & Wilkins.
Reece, William O., jt. ed. see Swenson, Melvin J.
Reecher, David, ed. see Sackheim, Maxwell.
Reeck, Darrell. Ethics for the Professions: A Christian Perspective. LC 81-52282. 176p. (Orig.). 1982. pap. 15. 99 (*0-8066-1914-7*, 10-2088, Augsburg) Augsburg Fortress.
***Reed.** Between Thought. 4.99 (*0-517-13654-6*) Random Hse Value.
— The Deception. write for info. (*0-517-70156-1*) Random Hse Value.
— Graceland Book Club. Date not set. 45.00 (*0-00-255448-8*, HarpT) HarpC.
— Keeping the Faith: The Can-Do Spirit of Modern America. Date not set. 25.00 (*0-02-874106-4*) Free Pr.
— Nineteen Eighty-Four (Orwell) (Book Notes Ser.). (C). 1984. pap. 2.95 (*0-8120-3449-X*) Barron.
— Nurse Education. 1993. 51.50 (*1-56593-212-9*, 0540) Singular Publishing.
— Presenting Harry Mazer. 1996. text ed. 21.95 (*0-8057-4512-2*) Macmillan.
Reed, jt. auth. see Pauls.
Reed, et al. Diseases of the Fetus & Newborn. 1989. 175.00 (*0-8016-5800-4*) Mosby Yr Bk.
Reed, A. Unmanned Aircraft. 110p. 1979. 35.95 (*0-08-027026-3*, Pergamon Pr) Elsevier.
Reed, Adele. Old Mammoth. Smith, Genny, ed. LC 82-60130. (Illus.). 200p. 1982. 17.50 (*0-931378-05-2*) Genny Smith Bks.
Reed, Adolph, Jr., ed. Race, Politics & Culture: Critical Essays on the Radicalism of the 1960s. LC 85-27162. (Contributions in Afro-American & African Studies: No. 95). 304p. 1986. text ed. 59.95 (*0-313-24480-4*, RRA/, Greenwood Pr) Greenwood.
Reed, Adolph L., Jr. The Jesse Jackson Phenomenon: The Crisis of Purpose in Afro-American Politics. LC 85-26499. 138p. (Orig.). 1986. text ed. 22.50 (*0-300-03543-8*) Yale U Pr.
***Reed, Alan B.** Collector's Encyclopedia of Pickard China. 216p. 1995. 24.95 (*0-89145-646-5*, 3964) Collector Bks.
Reed, Alan J. How You Save Money on Your Home Improvements. 2nd ed. LC 88-80114. (Illus.). 96p. 1988. pap. 9.95 (*0-945173-00-8*) IMAGETECTS.
Reed, Alan P. & Kaplan, Joel A. Clinical Cases in Anesthesia. (Illus.). 344p. 1989. pap. text ed. 39.95 (*0-443-08595-1*) Churchill.
Reed, Albert, tr. see Biorklund, Elis.
Reed, Alden. Weapons of Righteousness. 80p. (Orig.). 1993. pap. 5.99 (*1-56043-751-0*) Destiny Image.
Reed, Alette E., et al. Drafting Wills & Trusts in Massachusetts. LC 89-64081. 500p. 1990. ring bd. 95.00 (*0-944490-17-4*) Mass CLE.
Reed, Alfred Z. Present-Day Law Schools in the United States & Canada. LC 75-22836. (America in Two Centuries Ser.). 1976. reprint ed. 51.95 (*0-405-07707-6*) Ayer.
— Present-Day Law Schools in the United States & Canada. LC 87-80146. (Historical Writings in Law & Jurisprudence Ser.: No. 12). xv, 508p. 1987. reprint ed. lib. bdg. 45.00 (*0-89941-546-6*, 305100) W S Hein.
— Territorial Basis of Government under the State Constitutions. LC 68-56685. (Columbia University. Studies in the Social Sciences: No. 106). reprint ed. 39. 50 (*0-404-51106-6*) AMS Pr.
— Training for the Public Profession of the Law. LC 75-22837. (America in Two Centuries Ser.). 1976. reprint ed. 42.95 (*0-405-07708-4*) Ayer.
— Training for the Public Profession of the Law. Helmholz, R. H. & Reams, Bernard D., Jr., eds. LC 86-62932. (Historical Writings in Law & Jurisprudence Ser.: No. 2). xviii, 498p. 1986. reprint ed. lib. bdg. 45.00 (*0-89941-516-4*, 304520) W S Hein.
***Reed, Allan P., ed.** Clinical Cases in Anesthesia. 2nd ed. LC 94-23730. 1995. write for info. (*0-443-08899-3*) Churchill.
Reed, Allen C. Grand Circle Adventure. rev. ed. LC 94-75108. (Illus.). 48p. 1994. pap. 6.95 (*0-88714-082-3*) KC Pubns.
Reed, Alma. Jose Clemente Orozco. LC 76-6319. (Illus.). 272p. 1985. reprint ed. lib. bdg. 50.00 (*0-87817-204-1*) Hacker.
Reed, Alonzo & Kellogg, Brainerd. Higher Lessons in English. LC 87-4980. (American Linguistics, 1700-1900 Ser.). 1987. 50.00 (*0-8201-1422-7*) Schol Facsimiles.
Reed, Anderson. Shouting at the Wolf: A Guide to Identifying & Warding off Evil in Everyday Life. 1990. pap. 11.95 (*0-8065-1170-2*, Citadel Pr) Carol Pub Group.
***Reed, Andrew & Herron, Jeffrey.** Dan Screams. (Illus.). 64p. (Orig.). 1994. pap. 10.95 (*0-9633307-3-X*) Poets Farm Pr.
Reed, Ann, jt. auth. see Low, John.
Reed, Arden, ed. Romanticism & Language. LC 84-45146. 320p. 1984. pap. 16.95 (*0-8014-9891-0*) Cornell U Pr.
Reed, Arthea. Comics to Classics: A Parent's Guide to Books for Teens & Preteens. 130p. 1988. pap. 6.95 (*0-87207-798-5*) Intl Reading.
Reed, Arthea J. Reaching Adolescents. LC 84-12905. 490p. (C). 1985. text ed. 32.75 (*0-03-069342-X*) HB Coll Pubs.
— Reaching Adolescents: The Young Adult Book & the School. (Illus.). 502p. (Orig.). (C). 1993. pap. write for info. (*0-02-398861-4*, Merrill Pub Co) Macmillan.
***Reed, Arthea J. & Bergemann, Verna E.** A Guide to Participation & Observation in the Classroom. (Illus.). 208p. (Orig.). (C). 1995. pap. text ed. 11.95 (*1-56134-320-X*) Dushkin Pub.
— In the Classroom: An Introduction to Education. (Illus.). 686p. 1995. 38.95 (*0-614-06947-5*) Dushkin Pub.
Reed, Arthea J. S. Comics to Classics: A Guide to Books for Teens & Preteens. LC 94-5094. 256p. 1994. 9.95 (*0-14-023712-7*, Penguin Bks) Viking Penguin.
Reed, B. E., jt. ed. see Brown, R. P.
Reed, B. J. & Swain, John. Public Finance Administration. 320p. (C). 1989. text ed. write for info. (*0-13-737511-5*) P-H.
Reed, Barbara. Nutritional Guidelines for Correcting Behavior. rev. ed. 1984. pap. 10.00 (*0-939956-07-1*) Natural Pr.
Reed, Barbara, et al. Food, Teens & Behavior. 307p. 1983. pap. 7.00 (*0-939956-04-7*) Natural Pr.
Reed, Barbara F. Beyond the Great Darkness. 1987. pap. 4.95 (*9971-972-55-7*) OMF Bks.
Reed, Barry. Choice. 1992. mass mkt. 5.99 (*0-312-92883-1*) St Martin.
— The Indictment. LC 94-8346. 1994. 22.00 (*0-517-59433-1*, Crown) Crown Pub Group.
— Verdict. 1992. mass mkt. 4.99 (*0-312-92954-4*) St Martin.
Reed, Bella & Roth, Kevin. The Good Friends Song Book. 86p. 1985. pap. 9.95 (*0-931759-02-1*) Centerstream Pub.
Reed, Beth G. & Garvin, Charles D., eds. Groupwork with Women - Groupwork with Men: An Overview of Gender Issues in Social Groupwork Practice. LC 83-12745. (Social Work with Groups Ser.: Vol. 6, Nos. 3-4). 195p. 1983. text ed. 39.95 (*0-86656-258-3*); pap. text ed. 17.95 (*0-86656-274-5*) Haworth Pr.
Reed, Bika. The Field of Transformations: A Quest for the Immortal Essence of Human Awareness. 224p. (Orig.). 1987. pap. 12.95 (*0-89281-154-4*) Inner Tradit.
— Rebel in the Soul. (Illus.). 144p. 1979. pap. 10.95 (*0-89281-172-2*) Inner Tradit.
Reed, Billy, ed. The Final Four: Reliving America's Basketball Classic. (Illus.). 240p. 1987. 29.95 (*1-879688-06-9*) Host Comns Inc.
Reed, Bobbie. Dear Lord, I Can't Do It All. 96p. (Orig.). 1991. pap. 6.99 (*0-570-04199-6*) Concordia.
— How to Prepare Your Kids for Dating. LC 95-7305. (How to Family Ser.). 1995. write for info. (*0-570-04826-5*) Concordia.
— I Didn't Plan to Be a Single Parent! 1981. pap. 7.99 (*0-570-03837-5*, 12YY2927) Concordia.
— Life after Divorce. 196p. (Orig.). 1993. pap. 9.99 (*0-570-04614-9*) Concordia.
— Longing for a Child: Coping with Infertility. LC 93-38562. 1994. 10.99 (*0-8066-2672-0*, 9-2672) Augsburg Fortress.
— Making the Most of Single Life. 1980. pap. 7.99 (*0-570-03809-X*, 12-2918) Concordia.
— Merging Families: A Step by Step Guide for Blended Families. 152p. 1992. pap. 7.99 (*0-570-04566-5*) Concordia.
— Pleasing You Is Destroying Me: How to Stop Being Controlled by Your People-Pleasing Addiction. LC 92-8367. 204p. 1992. pap. 10.99 (*0-8499-3347-1*) Word Inc.
— Single on Sunday: A Manual for Successful Single Adult Ministries. 1979. pap. 7.99 (*0-570-03781-6*, 12-2735) Concordia.
Reed, Bobbie, jt. auth. see Marlowe, Monroe.
Reed, Brenda L. Easy-to-Make Decorative Paper Snowflakes. 64p. (Orig.). 1987. pap. 2.95 (*0-486-25408-9*) Dover.
Reed, Brian E. & Sack, William A., eds. Hazardous & Industrial Wastes: Proceedings of the Mid-Atlantic Industrial Waste Conference, 24th. 776p. 1992. pap. 85. 00 (*0-87762-974-9*) Technomic.
***Reed, Bruce.** The Task of the Church & the Role of Its Members. Date not set. pap. 5.95 (*1-56699-097-1*, OD69) Alban Inst.
Reed, Bruce W. Record That Rental: A Video Directory. 160p. 1991. write for info. (*0-9629797-0-8*) Reedcorp Intl.
Reed, C. E. English Archaisms in Pennsylvania German. Bd. with Word List from the Appalachians & the Piedmont Area of North Carolina. (Publications of the American Dialect Society: No. 19). 19p. 1953. Set pap. 2.50 (*0-8173-0619-6*) U of Ala Pr.
Reed, Carlynn. And We Have Danced: The History of the Sacred Dance Guild, 1958-1978. Adams, Doug, ed. 1978. 5.95 (*0-941500-00-4*) Sharing Co.
Reed, Carol L. Wardrobes at Work: A Woman's Professional Dress Guide. (Illus.). 64p. (Orig.). 1983. pap. 6.25 (*0-910347-02-6*) Chatham Comm Inc.
Reed, Carroll E.
Reed, Carson & Hawk, Doug. The Colorado Community College & Occupational Education System: A Silver Anniversary History. Van Lew, Carol & Fetter, Rosemary, eds. (Illus.). 163p. (C). 1994. pap. 15.00 (*0-9635787-0-7*) CO Comm Coll.
Reed, Cartwright, jt. auth. see Mark, Dave.
Reed, Catherine. Environment. LC 92-12423. (Science Fair Ser.). (YA). 1992. 15.94 (*0-86625-431-5*); 11.95 (*0-685-59385-1*) Rourke Pubns.
Reed, Cecil & Donovan, Priscilla. Fly in the Buttermilk: The Life Story of Cecil Reed. LC 93-18624. (Singular Lives: The Iowa Series in North American Autobiography). (Illus.). 208p. 1993. text ed. 29.95 (*0-87745-415-9*); pap. 12.95 (*0-87745-416-7*) U of Iowa Pr.
Reed, Charles A., ed. Origins of Agriculture. (World Anthropology Ser.). (Illus.). xvi, 1014p. 1977. 113.85 (*90-279-7919-7*) Mouton.
Reed, Charles B. The First, Great, Canadian: The Story of Pierre Le Moyne, Sieur d'Iberville. 1977. 27.95 (*0-8369-6987-1*, 7864) Ayer.
Reed, Charles E., jt. ed. see Dempsey, Jerome A.
Reed, Charles F., et al, eds. Psychopathology: A Source Book. LC 58-10405. (Illus.). 815p. 1958. 77.50 (*0-674-72200-0*) HUP.
Reed, Chip. Resource Track: Applying Biblical Principles to Personal Finances. (Illus.). 74p. (Orig.). 1989. student ed, pap. 10.00 (*0-9621353-1-3*) C Reed Assocs.
Reed, Chris. Computer Law. 2nd ed. 340p. 1993. pap. 40.00 (*1-85431-227-8*, Pub. by Blackstone Pr UK) W W Gaunt.
— KC-135 Stratotanker in Action. (Aircraft in Action Ser.). (Illus.). 50p. 1991. pap. 8.95 (*0-89747-268-3*, 1118) Squad Sig Pubns.
Reed, Christine, jt. auth. see Reed, J. D.
Reed, Christine M., jt. auth. see Bruce, Willa M.
Reed, Cleota. Henry Chapman Mercer & the Moravian Pottery & Tile Works. (Illus.). 280p. 1987. 64.95 (*0-8122-8076-8*) U of Pa Pr.
Reed, Cleota, ed. Henry Keck Stained Glass Studio, 1913-1974. LC 85-2593. (New York State Bks.). (Illus.). 200p. 1985. pap. 24.95 (*0-8156-0194-8*) Syracuse U Pr.
Reed, Clyde G. Price Data & European Economic History: England 1300-1600. Bruchey, Stuart, ed. LC 80-2826. (Dissertations in European Economic History Ser.: No. II). (Illus.). 1981. lib. bdg. 17.95 (*0-405-14010-X*) Ayer.
Reed, Colin, jt. auth. see Trent, Dennis R.
Reed, Colin, jt. ed. see Trent, Dennis.
Reed, Cory A. The Novelist As Playwright: Cervantes & the Entremes Nuevo. LC 92-25216. (Studies on Cervantes & His Times: Vol. 4). 224p. (C). 1993. text ed. 43.95 (*0-8204-1989-3*) P Lang Pubs.
Reed, Crafton C., III. Thiu Soo-Pr Pum-Kn: The Super Pumpkin. (Illus.). (J). (gr. 2-5). 1980. pap. text ed. 3.50 (*0-87881-091-9*) Mojave Bks.
Reed, Craig. The Cost of War, Vol. 1. Strunk, Janet, ed. 240p. (Orig.). (C). 1989. pap. text ed. write for info. (*0-318-65794-5*) Hurricane Ridge.
***Reed, Cynthia M.** Phlebotomist Test Preparation. LC 94-45960. (Test Prep Ser.). 1995. pap. 18.00 (*0-8359-4945-1*, Arco Test) P-H Gen Ref & Trav.
Reed, D. The Controversy of Zion. 1982. lib. bdg. 250.00 (*0-87700-419-6*) Revisionist Pr.
Reed, D. W. Eastern Dialect Words in California. Bd. with Supplementary List of South Carolina Words & Phrases. (Publications of the American Dialect Society: No. 21). 49p. 1954. Set pap. 3.85 (*0-8173-0621-8*) U of Ala Pr.
Reed, Dale, jt. comp. see Palm, Charles G.
Reed, Dan. The American Eagle: The Ascent of Bob Crandall & American Airlines. LC 92-44216. (Thomas Dunne Book Ser.). (Illus.). 302p. 1993. 23.95 (*0-312-08696-2*) St Martin.
Reed, Dana. Deathbringer. 400p. (Orig.). 1987. 3.95 (*0-8439-2562-0*) Dorchester Pub Co.
— Demon Within. 368p. (Orig.). 1993. reprint ed. pap. 4.50 (*0-8439-3382-8*) Dorchester Pub Co.
— The Gatekeeper. 400p. 1991. pap. 3.95 (*0-8439-2500-0*) Dorchester Pub Co.
— Hell Board. 368p. (Orig.). 1990. pap. 3.95 (*0-8439-2959-6*) Dorchester Pub Co.
— Margo. 368p. pap. 3.95 (*0-8439-2771-2*) Dorchester Pub Co.
— The Summoning. 368p. (Orig.). 1988. pap. 3.95 (*0-8439-2656-2*) Dorchester Pub Co.
Reed, Daniel A. & Fujimoto, Richard M. Multicomputer Networks: Message-Based Parallel Processing. (Scientific Computation Ser.). 400p. 1987. 52.50 (*0-262-18129-0*) MIT Pr.
Reed, David. Education for Building a People's Movement. LC 81-51388. 300p. (Orig.). 1981. 20.00 (*0-89608-122-2*); pap. 7.50 (*0-89608-121-4*) South End Pr.
— Figures of Thought: Mathematics & Mathematical Texts. LC 94-356. 224p. 1995. 49.95x (*0-415-08146-7*, B4555) Routledge.

R

— Milwaukee's New Architecture: A Downtown Trail. (Publications in Architecture & Urban Planning: No. R86-2). (Illus.). 6p. 1986. 1.00 (*0-938744-48-8*) U of Wis Ctr Arch-Urban.

— Reponse Biblique Aux Temoins D. 160p. (FRE.). 1991. 4.95 (*0-8297-1108-2*) Life Pubs Intl.

— Respuestas Biblicas - Testigos D. 144p. (SPA.). 1990. 3.95 (*0-8297-0390-X*) Life Pubs Intl.

Reed, David, ed. Structural Adjustment & the Environment. pap. text ed. write for info. (*1-85383-153-0*, Pub. by Kogan Page Educ UK) Taylor & Francis.

— Structural Adjustment & the Environment. LC 92-23516. 209p. (C). 1992. pap. text ed. 42.50 (*0-8133-8702-7*) Westview.

Reed, David & Basualdo, Carlos. Two Bedrooms in San Francisco. Echavarren, Roberto, tr. (Illus.). 12p. (Orig.). (ENG & SPA.). 1992. pap. 5.00 (*0-930495-17-9*) San Fran Art Inst.

Reed, David, jt. ed. see Ryhn, Douglas.

Reed, David A. Behind the Watchtower Curtain. 160p. (Orig.). 1989. pap. write for info. (*0-925703-08-7*) Crown MA.

— How to Rescue Your Loved One from the Watchtower. 168p. (Orig.). 1989. pap. 8.99 (*0-8010-7752-4*) Baker Bk.

— Jehovah's Witness Literature: A Critical Guide to Publications from the Watchtower. 192p. 1993. pap. 8.99 (*0-8010-7768-0*) Baker Bk.

— Jehovah's Witnesses Answered Verse by Verse. 1987. pap. 6.99 (*0-8010-7739-7*) Baker Bk.

— No Blood! 144p. (Orig.). 1995. pap. 7.95 (*0-9637448-2-8*) Comments Friends.

Reed, David A. & Cornell, John, eds. Index of Watchtower Errors. 160p. (Orig.). 1990. pap. 7.99 (*0-8010-7756-7*) Baker Bk.

Reed, David A. & Farkas, John R. How to Rescue Your Loved One from Mormonism. LC 94-3942. 208p. (Orig.). 1994. pap. 8.99 (*0-8010-7771-0*) Baker Bk.

— Mormons Answered Verse by Verse. 160p. (Orig.). 1992. pap. 6.99 (*0-8010-7761-3*) Baker Bk.

Reed, David A., jt. auth. see Farkas, John R.

Reed, David P. Residential Fiber Optic Networks: An Engineering & Economic Analysis. (Telecommunications Library). 376p. 1992. text ed. 69.00 (*0-89006-600-0*) Artech Hse.

Reed, Dena. Guides to Living. 1991. 16.95 (*0-533-09504-2*) Vantage.

Reed, Dennis & Wilson, Michael. Pictorialism in California: Photographs 1900-1940. (Illus.). 160p. 1994. pap. 30.00x (*0-89236-313-4*) J P Getty Trust.

Reed, Dennis, jt. auth. see Wilson, Michael G.

Reed, Dick A. The Complete Investor's Guide to Silver Dollar Investing. 1982. 18.95 (*0-911349-00-6*) English Fact.

Reed, Doel. Doel Reed Makes an Aquatint. (Illus.). 1965. pap. 9.95 (*0-89013-012-4*) Museum NM Pr.

Reed, Dolores M. Fight City Hall & Win. 86p. (Orig.). 1985. pap. text ed. write for info. (*0-935543-00-7*) Inst Political Res.

— Kingmaker-Kingbreaker: A Political Campaign Primer. Polgar, Antoine, ed. (Inaugural Ser.). (Illus.). 128p. (Orig.). 1986. pap. text ed. 12.85 (*0-935543-01-5*) Inst Political Res.

— No More Setasides: Women, Minorities, Business, & Politics. Polgar, Antoine, ed. (Inaugural Ser.). 19p. pap. text ed. 5.90 (*0-318-20009-0*) Inst Political Res.

Reed, Don C. The Dolphins & Me. (J). 1990. pap. 2.95 (*0-590-43294-X*) Scholastic Inc.

— Kraken. 224p. (J). (gr. 3-6). 1995. 15.95 (*1-56397-216-6*) Boyds Mills Pr.

***Reed, Donn. The Home School Source Book. 2nd rev. ed. (Illus.). 293p. 1994. pap. 15.00 (*0-919761-26-7*) Brook Farm Bks.**
"...bursting with ideas, opinions, books, games, materials, & resources for enriching the home schooling environment...Even parents who send their children to public school need to supplement their children's learning experience, & this book is a great collection of the basic tools." (REAL GOOD NEWS). "...the only major home education resource guide we have seen that does not emphasize fundamentalist religious books & materials...It places emphasis on comparative religions, cultural literacy, ecology, conservation, & global awareness. We recommend it." (BACKWOODS HOME MAGAZINE). "This book lives up to its title. It tries to be a WHOLE EARTH CATALOG for homeschoolers, & does a darn good job. (293) pages packed full of resources, reviews, & rant." (MILLENNIUM WHOLE EARTH CATALOG). "...a wealth of information for beginning & experienced homeschoolers". (Pat Farenga, publisher of GROWING WITHOUT SCHOOLING). "...a veritable smorgasbord of articles, resources, essays, letters, insights, honest (& sometimes scathing) reviews, notes & commentaries on home education." (HOME EDUCATION MAGAZINE). Available from Brook Farm Books, Box 246BP, Bridgewater, ME 04735. Standard trade discounts. STOP 40% plus $2 postage. ***Publisher Provided Annotation.***

***Reed, Donna.** Daddy's Little Girl: For Dad's & Little Girls of All Ages. (Illus.). 34p. (Orig.). 1994. pap. 8.00 (*0-9641434-1-0*) Westbury Pubng.

— Loving Me-Loving You: Loving Me Frees Me for Loving You. 151p. 1993. pap. 10.00 (*0-9641434-0-2*) Westbury Pubng.

Reed, Donna K. The Novel & the Nazi Past. LC 83-49004. (American University Studies: Germanic Languages & Literature: Ser. I, Vol. 28). 216p. (C). 1985. text ed. 26.50 (*0-8204-0064-5*) P Lang Pubs.

Reed, Doris, see Dorian Robb, pseud..

Reed, Douglas. Battle for Rhodesia. 1967. 9.95 (*0-8159-5102-7*) Devin.

— Behind the Scene, Pt. 2. 1976. Part 2 of Far & Wide. pap. 6.95 (*0-911038-41-8*) Noontide.

— Behind the Scenes. 1982. lib. bdg. 75.00 (*0-87700-433-1*) Revisionist Pr.

— The Controversy of Zion. 588p. 1987. 12.95 (*0-939482-03-7*) Noontide.

— Disgrace Abounding. 1982. lib. bdg. 75.00 (*0-87700-432-3*) Revisionist Pr.

— Far & Wide. 398p. pap. 5.00 (*0-913022-22-5*) Angriff Pr.

— The Grand Design. 1977. pap. 5.00 (*0-911038-49-3*) Noontide.

— Insanity Fair. 1982. lib. bdg. 75.00 (*0-87700-440-4*) Revisionist Pr.

— Somewhere South of Suez. 9.95 (*0-8159-6816-7*) Devin.

Reed, Duffer. Golf Lovers' Edition - From Wishes to Wealth in Four Easy Steps: Plus the Idea Factory. (Illus.). 52p. (Orig.). 1992. pap. 4.98 (*1-881878-04-X*) Gift Bks Am.

Reed, E. H. The Silver Arrow & Other Indian Romances of the Dune Country. 1977. lib. bdg. 59.95 (*0-8490-2605-9*) Gordon Pr.

Reed, Earl H. The Dune Country. (Illus.). 1979. reprint ed. 10.50 (*0-915056-09-7*) Hardscrabble Bks.

Reed, Ed. Requiem for a Kingfish. LC 86-71787. 250p. 1986. 24.95 (*0-9617384-0-5*) Award Pubns.

Reed, Edward. Masque: Photographs of Halloween. LC 80-54591. (Illus.). 60p. 1981. pap. 8.95 (*0-89822-012-2*) Visual Studies.

Reed, Edward, ed. see Center for the Study of Democratic Institutions Staff.

Reed, Edward A., jt. auth. see Eary, Donald F.

Reed, Edward B. English Lyrical Poetry. LC 67-30805. 1970. reprint ed. lib. bdg. 99.00 (*0-8383-0703-5*) M S G Haskell Hse.

— English Lyrical Poetry from Its Origins to the Present Time. (BCL1-PR English Literature Ser.). 616p. 1992. reprint ed. lib. bdg. 109.00 (*0-7812-7081-2*) Rprt Serv.

Reed, Edward P. Agrarian Reform & Rural Reconstruction: A Seminar Report. 66p. pap. text ed. 6.50 (*0-942717-00-7*) Intl Inst Rural.

Reed, Edward S. Revolution in Perception: The Ecological Psychology of James J. Gibson. (C). 1989. 40.00 (*0-300-04289-2*) Yale U Pr.

***Reed, Edward S., et al, eds.** Values & Knowledge. (Jean Piaget Symposia Ser.). 270p. 1996. text ed. 45.00 (*0-8058-1521-X*) L Erlbaum Assocs.

Reed, Edwin. Francis Bacon Our Shake-speare. 250p. 1992. pap. 24.95 (*1-56459-136-0*) Kessinger Pub.

Reed, Eleanor C. Battle Invisible, & Other Stories. LC 71-125236. (Short Story Index Reprint Ser.). 1977. 19.95 (*0-8369-3603-5*) Ayer.

Reed, Ellen C. The Goddess & the Tree, Bk. I: The Witches Qabala. 2nd rev. ed. LC 84-48088. (Modern Witchcraft Ser.). (Illus.). 192p. (Orig.). 1989. pap. 7.95 (*0-87542-666-2*) Llewellyn Pubns.

— Invocation of the Gods: Ancient Egyptian Magic for Today. LC 91-32383. (Illus.). 312p. (Orig.). 1992. 12.95 (*0-87542-667-0*) Llewellyn Pubns.

— The Witches Tarot, Bk. II: The Witches Qabala. LC 88-45181. (Modern Witchcraft Ser.). (Illus.). 320p. (Orig.). 1989. pap. 9.95 (*0-87542-668-9*) Llewellyn Pubns.

***Reed, Elroy.** Rage of a People. 240p. 1995. 23.95 (*0-9645448-0-6*); pap. 8.95 (*0-9645448-1-4*) Soaring Eagle.

Reed, Emily. Emily's Guides to the San Juan Islands - Washington. (Emily's Guides Ser.). 1993. 9.95 (*1-882625-00-5*) Gus Pubns.

— Emily's Guides to the San Juan Islands-Washington, 3 bks., Set. 4th ed. 48p. 1995. 10.95 (*1-882625-04-8*) Gus Pubns.

Reed, Emily F. The Penry Penalty: Capital Punishment & Offenders with Mental Retardation. LC 92-44124. 1993. 48.50 (*0-8191-9019-5*); pap. 28.50 (*0-8191-9020-9*) U Pr of Amer.

Reed, Emily F., jt. auth. see Barnett, Larry D.

Reed, Erik K. Excavations in Mancos Canyon, Colorado. (Utah Anthropological Papers: No. 35). reprint ed. 40.00 (*0-404-60635-0*) AMS Pr.

Reed, Esther. Life of Esther De Berdt, Afterwards Esther Reed, of Pennsylvania. LC 72-140877. (Eyewitness Accounts of the American Revolution Ser., No. 1). 1971. reprint ed. 23.95 (*0-405-01208-X*) Ayer.

Reed, Eugene S., ed. see Callahan, Richard J.

Reed, Evelyn. Is Biology Woman's Destiny? 2nd ed. 31p. 1989. reprint ed. 3.00 (*0-87348-258-1*) Pathfinder NY.

— Problems of Women's Liberation: A Marxist Approach. LC 78-143808. 131p. (Orig.). 1993. reprint ed. lib. bdg. 30.00 (*0-87348-166-6*); reprint ed. pap. 12.95 (*0-87348-167-4*) Pathfinder NY.

— Sexism & Science. LC 77-92144. (Illus.). 1993. reprint ed. lib. bdg. 45.00 (*0-87348-540-8*); reprint ed. pap. 15.95 (*0-87348-541-6*) Pathfinder NY.

— Woman's Evolution: From Matriarchal Clan to Patriarchal Family. LC 74-26236. 491p. 1993. reprint ed. lib. bdg. 65.00 (*0-87348-421-5*); reprint ed. pap. 22.95 (*0-87348-422-3*) Pathfinder NY.

Reed, Evelyn D. Coyote Tales from the Indian Pueblos. LC 86-14544. (Illus.). 96p. (J). (gr. 4 up). 1988. pap. 8.95 (*0-86534-094-3*) Sunstone Pr.

Reed, F. Morton. Odd & Curious. (Illus.). 1979. lib. bdg. 12.50 (*0-685-04428-9*); pap. 7.00 (*0-915262-37-1*) S J Durst.

Reed, Fran. A Dream with Storms: Reading Level 3. (Sundown Fiction Collection). 64p. 1993. 3.75 (*0-88336-207-4*); audio 13.50 (*0-88336-226-0*); audio 10.50 (*0-88336-264-3*) New Readers.

Reed, Frances. Experiencing Guidance: Inner Help in Life's Struggles. 240p. (Orig.). 1993. pap. 14.95 (*0-9627954-1-0*) Life Time.

Reed, Frances K. Hilo Legends. (Illus.). 52p. (Orig.). 1987. pap. 4.95 (*0-912180-45-5*) Petroglyph.

Reed, Frances M., ed. see Wilde, Oscar.

Reed, Francis. The ABC of Stage Lighting. (Illus.). 144p. (C). 1992. pap. text ed. 16.95 (*0-89676-119-3*) Drama Bk.

Reed, Frank C., jt. auth. see Firestone, David B.

***Reed, Fred A.** Persian Postcards. 1994. pap. 15.95 (*0-88922-351-3*) InBook.

Reed, G., jt. auth. see Rehm, H. J.

Reed, G., jt. ed. see Rehm, H. J.

Reed, G. H. Refrigeration: A Practical Manual for Apprentices. 3rd ed. (Illus.). 153p. 1974. reprint ed. 32.50 (*0-85334-605-4*, Pub. by Elsevier Applied Sci UK) Elsevier.

Reed, G. M., jt. auth. see Roscoe, A. W.

Reed, G. M., jt. ed. see Van Mill, Jan.

Reed, G. M., et al, eds. Topology & Category Theory in Computer Science. 408p. (C). 1991. 75.00 (*0-19-853760-3*) OUP.

Reed-Gach, Michael. The Bum Back Book. LC 83-71044. 144p. 1983. pap. 8.95 (*0-89087-417-4*) Celestial Arts.

***Reed, Gail, ed.** Island in the Storm: Cuban Communist Party's 4th Congress. (Illus.). 200p. 1993. pap. 13.95 (*1-875284-48-6*, Pub. by Ocean Pr AT) Talman.

Reed, Gail, ed. see Frank, Marc.

Reed, Gail S. Transference Neurosis & Psychoanalytic Experience: Perspectives on Contemporary Clinical Practice. LC 94-1406. 240p. 1994. 30.00 (*0-300-05957-4*) Yale U Pr.

Reed, Gary. RDF Accelerated Training Program. Marciniszyn, Alex & Cartier, Randi, eds. (Robotech RPG Adventures Ser.). (Illus.). 56p. (Orig.). (YA). (gr. 8 up). 1988. pap. 7.95 (*0-916211-32-0*, 555) Palladium Bks.

***Reed, Gary & Davis, Guy.** Baker Street: Children of the Night. (Graphic Novel Ser.). (Illus.). 176p. 1993. write for info. (*0-941613-43-7*) Stabur Pr.

— Baker Street: Honour among Punks. (Graphic Novel Ser.). (Illus.). 176p. 1993. write for info. (*0-941613-42-9*) Stabur Pr.

Reed, Geoffrey, jt. auth. see Sodersten, Bo.

Reed, George. Dark Sky Legacy: Astronomy's Impact on the History of Culture. 199p. 1989. 28.95 (*0-87975-541-5*) Prometheus Bks.

— Murdered by Isaac Newton. 216p. 1984. 14.95 (*0-89697-146-5*) Intl Univ Pr.

Reed, Gerald. Enzymes in Food Processing. 2nd ed. 1975. text ed. 165.00 (*0-12-584852-8*) Acad Pr.

— Prescott & Dunn's Industrial Microbiology. 4th ed. (Illus.). 1982. text ed. 119.99 (*0-87055-374-7*) AVI.

Reed, Gerlad, jt. ed. see Nagodawithana, Tilak.

Reed, Germaine M. Crusading for Chemistry: The Professional Career of Charles Holmes Herty. LC 94-25816. (Illus.). 496p. 1995. 45.00 (*0-8203-1671-7*) U of Ga Pr.

Reed, Gervais, jt. auth. see Moseley, Spencer.

Reed, Glenn, ed. see Simms, William G.

Reed, Gordon K. Living Life By God's Law. 124p. (Orig.). 1984. pap. 6.00 (*0-317-03221-6*) Word Ministries Inc.

Reed, Graham. The Psychology of Anomalous Experience. rev. ed. 207p. 1988. pap. 21.95 (*0-87975-435-4*) Prometheus Bks.

Reed, Graham F. Obsessional-Compulsive Disorders: A Cognitive-Structural Approach. 1985. text ed. 69.00 (*0-12-584830-7*) Acad Pr.

***Reed, Gregory A.** An Historical Geographical Analysis of the Modoc Indian War. 124p. 1994. 13.50 (*0-614-05683-7*) Assn NC Records.

Reed, Gregory J. Economic Empowerment Through the Church: A Blueprint for Progressive Community Development. LC 94-1895. 1994. pap. 14.99 (*0-310-48951-2*) Zondervan.

— Negotiation's Behind Closed Doors. 135p. Date not set. text ed. 22.00 (*1-882806-07-7*); pap. text ed. 19.00 (*1-882806-08-5*) New Natl Pub.

— Progressive Cleric. 170p. 1992. text ed. 35.00 (*1-882806-09-3*); pap. text ed. 35.00 (*1-882806-10-7*) New Natl Pub.

— This Business of Boxing & Its Secrets. 300p. 1981. text ed. 20.00 (*1-882806-03-4*); pap. text ed. 20.00 (*1-882806-04-2*) New Natl Pub.

— This Business of Celebrity Estates. 1992. text ed. 25.00 (*1-882806-06-9*); pap. text ed. 19.50 (*1-882806-05-0*) New Natl Pub.

— This Business of Entertainment & Its Secrets. 295p. 1985. text ed. 25.50 (*1-882806-01-8*); pap. text ed. 19.50 (*1-882806-02-6*) New Natl Pub.

Reed, Gregory J., jt. auth. see Parks, Rosa.

Reed, Gretchen M. & Sheppard, Vincent F. Basic Structures of the Head & Neck: A Programmed Instruction in Clinical Anatomy for Dental Professionals. LC 75-298. (Illus.). 716p. 1976. pap. text ed. 47.50 (*0-7216-7516-6*) Saunders.

Reed, Harry. Platform for Change: The Foundations of the Northern Black Community, 1775-1865. LC 93-37526. 1993. 29.95 (*0-87013-341-1*) Mich St U Pr.

Reed, Harry A., jt. ed. see Henderson, John P.

Reed, Helen H. The Reader in the Picaresque Novel. (Serie A: Monagrafias, CXIV). 120p. (C). 1984. 27.00 (*0-7293-0204-0*, Pub. by Tamesis Bks Ltd UK) Boydell & Brewer.

Reed, Helen M. A Diet Pill, a Pretty Rock & a Live Snake for the Teacher. 100p. 1991. 8.95 (*0-9630217-0-2*) H M Reed.

Reed, Helen R. All about You: A Religious Physiology & Hygiene for Parents to Read to Their Children. (J). 1992. 7.95 (*0-533-10079-8*) Vantage.

Reed, Henry. Collected Poems. Stallworthy, Jon, ed. 192p. 1988. pap. 14.95 (*0-19-282072-9*) OUP.

— Collected Poems. Stallworthy, Jon, ed. 192p. 1991. 42.50 (*0-19-212298-3*) OUP.

— Edgar Cayce on Channeling Your Higher Self. Cayce, Charles T., ed. 288p. 1989. mass mkt. 5.50 (*0-446-34980-1*) Warner Bks.

— Getting Help from Your Dreams. (Illus.). 144p. (Orig.). 1985. pap. 9.95 (*0-917483-04-9*) InnerVision.

— Lectures on English History & Tragic Poetry. LC 72-174305. reprint ed. 36.50 (*0-404-05234-7*) AMS Pr.

Reed, Henry, tr. see De Balzac, Honore.

Reed, Henry, ed. see Wordsworth, Christopher.

Reed, Henry H. The New York Public Library: Its Architecture & Decoration. (Illus.). 1986. pap. 16.95 (*0-393-30336-5*) Norton.

Reed, Henry H., Jr., jt. ed. see Coles, William A.

Reed, Henry H., jt. auth. see Farber, Joseph.

Reed, Henry H., jt. auth. see Gillon, Edmund V.

Reed, Henry M. The A. B. Frost Book. (Illus.). 176p. 1993. 49.95 (*0-941711-13-7*) Wyrick & Co.

Reed-Hill, R. E., et al, eds. Deformation Twining: Proceedings, Gainesville, Florida, March 21-22, 1963. LC 64-8380. (Metallurgical Society Conference Ser.: Vol. 25). 476p. reprint ed. pap. 135.70 (*0-317-10405-5*, 2001513) Bks Demand.

Reed-Hill, Robert E. & Abbaschian, Reza. Physical Metallurgy Principles. 3rd ed. (C). 1992. text ed. 80.95 (*0-534-92173-6*) PWS Pubs.

Reed, Horace B. & Loughran, Elizabeth L., eds. Beyond Schools: Education for Economic, Social & Personal Development. LC 84-70668. (Illus.). 253p. (C). 1984. pap. text ed. 15.00 (*0-934210-10-1*) Devlp Commy.

— Beyond Schools: Education for Economic, Social & Personal Development. (Illus.). 266p. 1985. reprint ed. pap. text ed. 27.00 (*0-8191-5174-2*) U Pr of Amer.

Reed, Ione. Pioneering in Oregon's Coast Range: Surviving the Depression Years. (Illus.). 140p. (Orig.). 1983. pap. 7.95 (*0-934784-31-0*) Calapooia Pubns.

Reed, Ishmael. Airing Dirty Laundry. LC 93-13874. 1993. 19.23 (*0-201-62462-1*) Addison-Wesley.

— Airing Dirty Laundry. 304p. 1995. pap. 11.54 (*0-201-40832-5*) Addison-Wesley.

— Flight to Canada. 180p. 1989. pap. 11.00 (*0-689-70733-9*, Pub. by Ctrl Bur voor Schimmel NE) Macmillan.

— Japanese by Spring. Fehr, Don, ed. 192p. 1993. text ed. 20.00 (*0-689-12072-9*, Pub. by Ctrl Bur voor Schimmel NE) Macmillan.

— The Last Days of Louisiana Red. 192p. 1989. pap. 8.95 (*0-689-70731-2*, Atheneum S&S) S&S Trade.

— Mumbo Jumbo. 256p. 1989. pap. 11.00 (*0-689-70730-4*, Atheneum S&S) S&S Trade.

— New & Collected Poems. 256p. 1989. pap. 9.95 (*0-689-12004-4*, Atheneum S&S) S&S Trade.

— A Secretary to the Spirits. (Poets Ser.). (Illus.). 42p. 1977. 11.95 (*0-88357-057-2*); pap. 4.95 (*0-88357-058-0*) NOK Pubs.

— Shrovetide in Old New Orleans. 300p. 1989. pap. 10.95 (*0-689-70729-0*, Atheneum S&S) S&S Trade.

— The Terrible Threes. 224p. 1989. text ed. 16.95 (*0-689-11893-7*, Atheneum S&S) S&S Trade.

— The Terrible Twos. 192p. 1988. pap. 9.95 (*0-689-70727-4*, Pub. by Ctrl Bur voor Schimmel NE) Macmillan.

— Writin' Is Fightin' Thirty-Seven Years of Boxing on Paper. 192p. 1991. pap. 9.95 (*0-689-70734-7*, Pub. by Ctrl Bur voor Schimmel NE) Macmillan.

Reed, Ishmael, et al, eds. The Before Columbus Foundation Fiction Anthology: Selections from the American Book Awards 1980-1990. 400p. 1991. 22.95 (*0-393-03055-5*); pap. 14.95 (*0-393-30832-4*) Norton.

— The Before Columbus Foundation Poetry Anthology: Selections from the American Book Awards 1980-1990. 320p. 1991. 22.95 (*0-393-03056-3*); pap. 14.95 (*0-393-30833-2*) Norton.

Reed, J. Moby Dick (Melville) (Book Notes Ser.). (C). 1984. pap. 2.50 (*0-8120-3428-7*) Barron.

***Reed, J. & Proctor, S.** Practitioner Research in Health Care: The Inside Story. (Illus.). 224p. 1994. pap. text ed. 42.50 (*1-56593-189-0*, 0504) Singular Publishing.

Reed, J., jt. ed. see Black, M.

Reed, J., tr. see Nasrallah, Ibrahim.

Reed, J. C. Bcl-2 Gene & the Molecular Basis of B Cell Malignancy. (Medical Intelligence Unit Ser.). write for info. (*1-57059-096-6*) R G Landes.

— Martin Luther King, Jr. A Big Biography. 16p. (J). (gr. 2-4). 1994. pap. text ed. 14.95 (*1-56784-350-6*) Newbridge Comms.

Reed, J. D. & Reed, Christine. Exposure. LC 86-29772. 242p. 1987. 14.95 (*0-939149-00-1*) Soho Press.

Reed, J. E., jt. auth. see Herriott, W.

Reed, J. J., jt. auth. see Chamberlain, Nugent F.

Reed, J. L. The Reed Genealogy, Descendants of William Reade of Weymouth, Mass., from 1635-1902. (Illus.). 786p. 1989. reprint ed. lib. bdg. 117.00 (*0-8328-1014-2*); reprint ed. pap. 109.00 (*0-8328-1015-0*) Higginson Bk Co.

An Asterisk (*) at the beginning of an entry indicates that the title is appearing in BIP for the first time.

R

Reed, J. Ronald. The Craftmanship Revival in Interior Design: How Today's Artisans Preserve Yesterday's Skills. (Illus.). 144p. 1991. 14.99 (*0-517-05474-4*) Random Hse Value.

Reed, J. W. History of the Reed Family in Europe & America. (Illus.). 596p. 1989. reprint ed. lib. bdg. 97.00 (*0-8328-1012-6*); reprint ed. pap. 89.00 (*0-8328-1013-4*) Higginson Bk Co.

Reed, Jake. The Promise of the Seed. LC 91-72729. 800p. 1991. text ed. 19.95 (*1-56467-165-8*); pap. text ed. 12.95 (*1-56467-166-6*) Elan Pubns.

Reed, James. The Birth Control Movement & American Society: From Private Vice to Public Virtue, with a New Preface on the Relationship Between Historical Scholarship & Feminist Issues. LC 83-60459. 482p. reprint ed. pap. 137.40 (*0-7837-1420-3*, 2041775) Bks Demand.

— The Missionary Mind & American East Asia Policy, 1911-1915. (East Asian Monographs: No. 104). 300p. 1983. 28.00 (*0-674-57657-8*) HUP.

— State Legislation Relating to Native Americans, 1991. (State Legislative Reports: Vol. 16, No. 9). 19p. 1991. pap. text ed. 5.00 (*1-55516-308-4*, 7302-1609) Natl Conf State Legis.

Reed, James, jt. auth. see Corrado, Joseph.

Reed, James, jt. auth. see Furneaux, David.

Reed, James B. & Calhoon, John A. The California Framework for Science Education. (State Legislative Reports: Vol. 17, No. 2). 7p. 1992. pap. text ed. 5.00 (*1-55516-310-6*, 7302-1702) Natl Conf State Legis.

Reed, James B. & Mahoney, Katherine A. Federal Training Assistance for the Transportation of Spent Fuel. (State Legislative Reports: Vol. 17, No. 10). 5p. 1992. pap. text ed. 5.00 (*1-55516-282-7*, 7302-1710) Natl Conf State Legis.

***Reed, James B. & Zelio, Judy A.** State-Tribal Relations: Into the 21st Century. 100p. 1995. 25.00 (*1-55516-929-5*, 9354) Natl Conf State Legis.

Reed, James C. Chest Radiology: Plain Film Patterns & Differential Diagnosis. 3rd ed. 464p. 1990. 79.00 (*0-8151-7220-6*, Yr Bk Med Pubs) Mosby Yr Bk.

Reed, James E. History of Erie County, Pennsylvania, 2 vols. (Illus.). 1288p. 1994. reprint ed. lib. bdg. 130.00 (*0-8328-4007-6*) Higginson Bk Co.

Reed, James E. & Provost, Ronnie. A History of Christian Education. 1993. text ed. 24.99 (*0-8054-6586-3*) Broadman.

Reed, James H., jt. auth. see Williams, Walter E.

Reed, James N., et al. The Black Man's Guide to Food Health: Essential Advice for the Special Concerns of African-American Men. Shucker, Charlene & Shulman, Neil B., eds. LC 94-13443. 288p. (Orig.). 1994. pap. 12.00 (*0-399-52138-0*, Perigree Bks) Berkley Pub.

Reed, James S. Introduction to the Principles of Ceramic Processing. LC 87-25310. 486p. 1988. text ed. 74.95 (*0-471-84554-X*) Wiley.

— Principles of Ceramics Engineering. 2nd ed. LC 94-20838. 1995. text ed. 69.95 (*0-471-59721-X*) Wiley.

***Reed, Jan & Procter, Sue, eds.** Practitioner Research in Health Care. 208p. 1995. pap. 40.00 (*0-412-49810-3*) Chapman & Hall.

Reed, Jane L., ed. Toward Independence: A Century of Indonesia Photographed. LC 91-71572. (Illus.). 120p. (Orig.). 1992. pap. 24.95 (*0-933286-58-9*, U of Wash Pr) Friends Photography.

***Reed, Jane Levy & Grundberg, Andy.** David Ireland: Skellig. 60p. 1995. pap. 40.00 (*0-933286-65-1*) Frnds Photography.

Reed, Janet. Psychology of Dress. 46.60 (*0-8273-6519-5*); teacher ed 8.00 (*0-8273-6520-9*) Delmar.

Reed, Jeanne. Business English. 4th ed. 1985. text ed. 24.15 (*0-07-051503-4*) McGraw.

Reed, Jeanne & Finch, R. Business Writing, a Gregg Text-Kit in Adult Education. 1970. text ed. 24.75 (*0-07-051480-1*) McGraw.

Reed, Jeanne, et al. Business English: A Gregg Text-Kit in Continuing - Adult Education. 4th ed. 1986. write for info. (*0-07-051507-7*) McGraw.

Reed, Jeffrey G. & Baxter, Pam M. Library Use: A Handbook for Psychology. 2nd ed. 192p. (Orig.). (C). 1992. pap. text ed. 19.95 (*1-55798-144-2*) Am Psychol.

***Reed, Jeremy.** Diamond Nebula: A Novel. 200p. 1995. 28.00 (*0-7206-0891-0*, Pub. by P Owen Ltd UK) Dufour.

— Dicing for Pearls. 38p. (Orig.). 1990. 25.00 (*1-870612-85-X*, Pub. by Enitha Pr UK); pap. 10.95 (*1-870612-80-9*, Pub. by Enitha Pr UK) Dufour.

— Inhabiting Shadows. 120p. 1990. 30.00 (*0-7206-0787-6*, Pub. by P Owen Ltd UK) Dufour.

— Isidore: A Novel about the Comte de Lautreamont. (Illus.). 150p. 1991. 29.00 (*0-7206-0831-7*, Pub. by P Owen Ltd UK) Dufour.

— Lipstick, Sex & Poetry: An Autobiography. 119p. 1991. 32.00 (*0-7206-0817-1*, Pub. by P Owen Ltd UK) Dufour.

— Madness - The Price of Poetry. LC 90-80803. 208p. 1990. 36.00 (*0-7206-0744-2*, Pub. by Peter Owen Ltd UK) Dufour.

— Red-Haired Android. 280p. (Orig.). 1993. pap. 12.95 (*0-87286-283-6*) City Lights.

— When the Whip Comes Down: A Novel about De Sade. 136p. 1993. 29.00 (*0-7206-0857-0*, Pub. by P Owen Ltd UK); pap. 17.95 (*0-7206-0858-9*, Pub. by P Owen Ltd UK) Dufour.

Reed, Jeremy, tr. see Cocteau, Jean.

Reed, Jeremy, tr. see Friedrich von Hardenberg, Georg P.

Reed, Jeremy, jt. auth. see Montale, Eugenio.

Reed, Jim, jt. ed. see Jemison, Marie S.

Reed, Jim H. The Three Sons of Han. 390p. (Orig.). 1994. pap. 13.50 (*1-885411-00-6*) Columbia Lit.

Reed, Jimi, jt. auth. see McGilvrey, Carole.

Reed, Jo, jt. ed. see Kimmett, Joseph.

Reed, Joel L. Trump - The Man - The Myth - The Scandal. (Illus.). 192p. (Orig.). 1990. pap. 4.95 (*1-878320-17-3*) Masquerade.

***Reed, John.** The Collected Works of John Reed. LC 94-32160. 1995. write for info. (*0-679-60114-7*, Modern Lib) Random.

— The Collected Works of John Reed. 1995. 20.00 (*0-679-60144-9*, Modern Lib) Random.

— Daughter of the Revolution, & Other Stories. LC 75-134975. (Short Story Index Reprint Ser.). 1977. 16.95 (*0-8369-3707-4*) Ayer.

— The Education of John Reed. Stuart, John, ed. 224p. 1972. reprint ed. pap. 2.75 (*0-7178-0354-6*) Intl Pubs Co.

— Insurgent Mexico. LC 69-14047. 325p. 1969. reprint ed. text ed. 59.50 (*0-8371-0633-8*, REIM, Greenwood Pr) Greenwood.

— Insurgent Mexico. LC 69-17616. 292p. 1994. reprint ed. pap. 7.95 (*0-7178-0099-7*) Intl Pubs Co.

— The Schubert Song Companion. 528p. 1994. pap. 34.95 (*0-571-17013-7*) Faber & Faber.

Reed, John, et al. Successful Remodeling. LC 94-65697. (Illus.). 112p. (Orig.). 1994. pap. 9.95 (*0-89721-269-X*, UPC 05988) Ortho Info.

Reed, John. Ten Days That Shook the World. (Classics Ser.). 301p. 1992. mass mkt. 4.95 (*0-553-21268-0*, Bantam Classics) Bantam.

— Ten Days That Shook the World. 1982. lib. bdg. 75.00 (*0-8490-3225-3*) Gordon Pr.

— Ten Days That Shook the World. LC 67-27252. (Illus.). 445p. (C). 1989. pap. 6.95 (*0-7178-0200-0*) Intl Pubs Co.

— Ten Days That Shook the World. 1990. pap. 7.95 (*0-14-018293-4*, 612, Penguin Classics) Viking Penguin.

— Ten Days That Shook the World. 1992. reprint ed. lib. bdg. 21.95 (*0-89968-271-5*, Lghtyr Pr) Buccaneer Bks.

Reed, John, jt. auth. see Grant, Reg.

Reed, John, tr. see Oyono, Ferdinand.

Reed, John, tr. see Senghor, Leopold S.

Reed, John, ed. see Vance, Rupert.

Reed, John C. Conduct of Lawsuits Out of & in Court: Practically Teaching, & Copiously Illustrating, the Preparation & Forensic Management of Litigated Cases of All Kinds. LC 94-17732. xxvii, 434p. 1994. reprint ed. lib. bdg. 52.50 (*0-8377-2576-3*) Rothman.

Reed, John C., jt. auth. see Love, J. D.

Reed, John C., Jr., et al, eds. Precambrian: Conterminous U. S. LC 92-30479. (DNAG, Geology of North America Ser.: Vol. C2). 1993. 98.00 (*0-8137-5218-3*) Geol Soc.

Reed, John E. History of Erie County, Pennsylvania, 2 vols., Set. (Illus.). 1288p. 1993. reprint ed. lib. bdg. 125.00 (*0-8328-3222-7*) Higginson Bk Co.

Reed, John F. Campaign to Valley Forge. 1980. reprint ed. 12.95 (*0-913150-42-8*) Pioneer Pr.

— Root & Shoot Growth of Shortleaf & Loblolly Pines in Relation to Certain Environmental Conditions. LC 40-13430. (Duke University, School of Forestry Bulletin Ser.: No. 4). 54p. reprint ed. pap. 25.00 (*0-7837-6052-3*, 2045865) Bks Demand.

— Valley Forge, Crucible of Victory. LC 70-76769. (Revolutionary War Bicentennial Ser.). (Illus.). 1969. lib. bdg. 11.95 (*0-912480-04-1*) Freneau.

Reed, John H. The Application of Operations Research to Court Delay. LC 72-89647. (Special Studies in U. S. Economic, Social & Political Issues). 1973. 39.50 (*0-275-06690-8*) Irvington.

— Directory of Back Issue Treasure Magazine Buyers, Sellers, & Traders. 41p. (Orig.). 1987. pap. 6.95 (*0-940519-02-X*) Res Discover Pubns.

— Directory of Treasure Hunting, Prospecting & Related Organizations. LC 86-63262. 191p. 1987. pap. 12.95 (*0-940519-00-3*) Res Discover Pubns.

— Treasure Hunting Bibliography & Index to Periodical Articles. 425p. (Orig.). 1989. pap. 29.95 (*0-940519-04-6*) Res Discover Pubns.

Reed, John P. When You Feel Insecure: Resources for Living. Lester, Andrew D., ed. 132p. (Orig.). 1989. pap. 9.99 (*0-664-25049-1*) Westminster John Knox.

Reed, John R. Decadent Style. LC 84-16545. (Illus.). xiv, 284p. (C). 1985. text ed. 35.00 (*0-8214-0793-7*) Ohio U Pr.

— Dickens & Thackeray: Punishment & Forgiveness. 550p. (C). 1995. text ed. 59.95x (*0-8214-1117-9*) Ohio U Pr.

— The Natural History of H. G. Wells. LC 81-11261. x, 294p. 1982. lib. bdg. 30.00 (*0-8214-0628-0*) Ohio U Pr.

— Old School Ties: The Public School in British Literature. LC 64-23341. 344p. reprint ed. pap. 98.10 (*0-8357-3980-5*, 2036678) Bks Demand.

— Stations of the Cross. (Illus.). 32p. (Orig.). 1992. pap. text ed. 5.00 (*1-56439-012-8*) Ridgeway.

— Thirteen Mountain. 224p. 1995. 19.95 (*0-312-11341-2*) St Martin.

— Victorian Conventions. LC 73-92908. xiii, 561p. 1985. 40.00 (*0-8214-0147-5*); pap. text ed. 24.95 (*0-8214-0828-3*) Ohio U Pr.

— Victorian Will. LC 88-33695. 500p. 1989. lib. bdg. 39.95 (*0-8214-0928-X*) Ohio U Pr.

— The Winter of the Robot. 100p. 1996. pap. 7.95 (*0-7610-0474-2*) NW Pub.

Reed, John S. The Enduring South: Subcultural Persistence in Mass Society. LC 86-40031. xxi, 150p. 1986. pap. 10.95 (*0-8078-4162-5*) U of NC Pr.

— Kicking Back: Further Dispatches from the South. 192p. 1995. 22.50 (*0-8262-1004-X*) U of Mo Pr.

— My Tears Spoiled My Aim. 1994. pap. 8.95 (*0-15-600006-7*) HarBrace.

— My Tears Spoiled My Aim, & Other Reflections on Southern Culture. LC 92-37623. (Illus.). 168p. (C). 1993. 17.95 (*0-8262-0886-X*) U of Mo Pr.

— One South: An Ethnic Approach to Regional Culture. LC 81-19387. xxii, 218p. (C). 1982. pap. text ed. 11.95 (*0-8071-1038-8*) La State U Pr.

— Southern Folk, Plain & Fancy: Native White Social Types. LC 86-1479. (Mercer University Lamar Memorial Lecture Ser.: No. 29). (Illus.). 136p. 1986. 20.00 (*0-8203-0862-5*) U of Ga Pr.

— Southern Folk, Plain & Fancy: Native White Social Types. LC 86-1479. (Brown Thrasher Bks.). (Illus.). 136p. 1988. pap. 9.95 (*0-8203-1023-9*) U of Ga Pr.

— Surveying the South: Studies in Regional Sociology. LC 93-8561. 168p. (Orig.). (C). 1993. text ed. 29.95 (*0-8262-0914-9*); pap. text ed. 14.95 (*0-8262-0915-7*) U of Mo Pr.

— Whistling Dixie: Dispatches from the South. 1992. pap. 9.95 (*0-15-696174-1*, Harvest Bks) HarBrace.

— Whistling Dixie: Dispatches from the South. 264p. 1990. 24.95 (*0-8262-0758-8*) U of Mo Pr.

***Reed, John S. & Watson, Harry L., eds.** Southern Humor. (Special Issue of Southern Cultures Ser.: Vol. 1, No. 4). 110p. 1995. pap. 8.00 (*0-8223-6427-1*) Duke.

Reed, John S., jt. auth. see Black, Merle.

***Reed, John T.** Aggressive Tax Avoidance for Real Estate Investors: How to Make Sure You Aren't Paying One. 14th enl. ed. 267p. 1995. pap. 23.95 (*0-939224-34-8*) John T Reed.

— Coaching Youth Football Defense. LC 92-93048. 220p. (Orig.). 1993. pap. 19.95 (*0-939224-27-5*) John T Reed.

— How to Buy Real Estate for at Least 20% below Market Value. 262p. pap. 19.95 (*0-939224-24-0*) John T Reed.

— How to Increase the Value of Real Estate. 208p. 1986. pap. 39.95 (*0-939224-10-0*) John T Reed.

— How to Manage Residential Property: For Maximum Cash Flow & Resale Value. 4th ed. 308p. 1995. pap. 23.95 (*0-939224-33-X*) John T Reed.

— How to Use Leverage to Maximize Your Real Estate Investment Return. 300p. 1991. pap. 19.95 (*0-939224-12-7*) John T Reed.

— Office Building Acquisition Handbook: Checklists for Making Sure You Don't Overlook Anything Important When You Buy an Office Building. LC 85-90317. 170p. 1985. ring bd. 39.95 (*0-939224-17-8*) John T Reed.

— Real Estate Investment Strategy: Selected Articles from the National Newsletter. 290p. 1991. pap. 39.95 (*0-939224-23-2*) John T Reed.

— Residential Property Acquisition Handbook: Checklists for Making Sure You Don't Overlook Anything Important When You Buy a House, Condo, Apartment Building. 250p. 1991. pap. 39.95 (*0-939224-22-4*) John T Reed.

Reed, Jonas. A History of Rutland, Worcester County, Massachusetts, from Its Earliest Settlement, with a Biography of Its First Settlers. 168p. 1992. reprint ed. lib. bdg. 24.50 (*0-8328-2522-0*) Higginson Bk Co.

Reed, Jonathan, jt. ed. see Brown, Ashley.

Reed, Joseph, ed. see Reed, Kit.

Reed, Joseph R., jt. auth. see Field, Homer H.

Reed, Joseph W. American Scenarios: The Uses of Film Genre. LC 88-27930. (Illus.). 376p. 1989. 30.00 (*0-8195-5215-1*, Wesleyan Univ Pr) U Pr of New Eng.

Reed, Joseph W., Jr. English Biography in the Early Nineteenth Century: 1801-1838. 1966. 59.50 (*0-685-45652-8*) Elliots Bks.

Reed, Joseph W. Three American Originals: John Ford, William Faulkner, & Charles Ives. LC 83-23349. (Illus.). 255p. 1984. text ed. 30.00 (*0-8195-5101-5*, Wesleyan Univ Pr); pap. 13.95x (*0-8195-6186-X*, Wesleyan Univ Pr) U Pr of New Eng.

Reed, Joseph W., Jr., ed. see Walpole, Horace.

Reed, Joy. An Inconvenient Engagement. 320p. 1994. mass mkt. 3.99 (*0-8217-4442-9*) Zebra.

Reed, Joyce G. Take a Whistler's Walk. (Illus.). 77p. (J). (gr. 4-9). 1988. 12.95 (*0-943487-08-0*); pap. 4.95 (*0-943487-07-2*) Sevgo Pr.

Reed, Judith, illus. Lauren Groveman's Kitchen: Nurturing Food for Family & Friends. LC 94-13263. write for info. (*0-8118-0609-X*) Chronicle Bks.

Reed, Karen S. Betty Neuman: The Neuman Systems Model. (Notes on Nursing Theories Ser.: Vol. 11). (Illus.). 64p. (C). 1993. text ed. 18.95 (*0-8039-4861-1*); pap. text ed. 8.95 (*0-8039-4862-X*) Sage.

Reed, Kathleen. Holiday to East Africa. 1992. 13.95 (*0-533-09609-X*) Vantage.

Reed, Kathlyn L. Quick Reference to Occupational Therapy. LC 91-18038. 300p. 1991. 45.00 (*0-8342-0237-9*) Aspen Pub.

Reed, Kathlyn L. & Nelson, Sharon R. Concepts of Occupational Therapy. 3rd ed. (Illus.). 410p. 1992. 36.00 (*0-683-07207-2*) Williams & Wilkins.

Reed, Kathryn L., jt. ed. see Copel, Joshua A.

Reed, Kathryn L., et al. Fetal Echocardiography: An Atlas. 146p. 1988. text ed. 99.95 (*0-471-61733-4*) Wiley.

Reed, Keith. Hell's Angel. Richardson, Betty, ed. (Orig.). 1990. pap. 7.95 (*0-9625526-0-7*) Dokatoke Pub.

***Reed, Keith A. & Mignin, Robert J., eds.** Chicagoland Employment Law Manual. 456p. 1994. pap. 75.00 (*0-614-06735-9*) Amer CC Pubs.

— Employment Discrimination: How to Comply. 160p. 1993. pap. 65.00 (*0-923606-04-1*) Amer CC Pubs.

— Federal Employment Laws & Regulations: How to Comply. 356p. 1993. pap. 65.00 (*0-685-67823-7*) Amer CC Pubs.

Reed, Keith A., et al, eds. New York State Employment Laws & Regulations: How to Comply. 140p. 1993. pap. 65.00 (*0-923606-01-7*) Amer CC Pubs.

Reed, Ken. Lectures in Psychiatry: The Functional Psychoses, Vol. 1. (Illus.). 304p. 1985. 37.50 (*0-87527-339-4*) Green.

Reed, Ken C. & Graves, Jennifer A., eds. Mammalian Sex Chromosomes & Sex-Determining Genes. LC 92-1483. 1993. text ed. 98.00 (*3-7186-5276-5*) Gordon & Breach.

***Reed, Kenneth A.** In the Nurture & Admonition of the Lord: Parenting Basics. 136p. (Orig.). 1995. pap. write for info. (*1-885591-92-6*) Morris Pubng.

Reed, Kenneth T. Truman Capote. (United States Authors Ser.: No. 388). 152p. (C). 1981. text ed. 21.95 (*0-8057-7321-5*, Pub. by Royal Botanic Garden UK) Macmillan.

Reed, Kenny, tr. see Bogary, Hamza.

Reed, Kevin. A Season for Dreams. LC 89-90670. (Illus.). 152p. (J). (gr. 5-7). 1989. pap. 5.95 (*0-9614546-3-6*) Chowder Pr.

Reed, Kevin, jt. auth. see Warner, David C.

Reed, Kevin J. The Saratoga Yearling. Herold, Meri G., ed. (Illus.). 110p. (Orig.). (J). (gr. 5-9). 1985. pap. 3.95 (*0-9614546-0-1*) Chowder Pr.

Reed-King, Susan. Food & Farming. LC 93-3719. (Young Geographer Ser.). (Illus.). 32p. (J). (gr. 4-6). 1993. 14.95 (*1-56847-054-1*) Thomson Lrning.

Reed, Kit. Catholic Girls. LC 87-81418. 240p. 1987. 17.95 (*1-55611-063-4*) D I Fine.

— Fat. LC 73-22670. 1974. 7.95 (*0-672-51979-8*, Bobbs) Macmillan.

— Little Sisters of the Apocalypse: Black Ice Books. 1994. pap. 7.00 (*0-932511-95-3*) Fiction Coll.

— Mastering Fiction Writing. 142p. 1991. 18.95 (*0-89879-479-X*) Writers Digest.

— Story First: The Writer As Insider. Reed, Joseph, ed. 150p. 1982. 19.95 (*0-13-850487-3*) P-H.

— Thief of Lives. 192p. 1992. 19.95 (*0-8262-0850-9*) U of Mo Pr.

Reed, L. Wenzel's Menu Maker. 3rd ed. 1992. text ed. write for info. (*0-442-01283-7*) Van Nos Reinhold.

Reed, L. C. & Longnecker, O. M., Jr. The Geology of Hemphill County, Texas. (Bulletin Ser.: BULL 3231). (Illus.). 98p. 1932. 0.50 (*0-686-31764-5*) Bur Econ Geology.

Reed, Langford. Complete Limerick Book: The Origin, History & Achievements of the Limerick. (Illus.). 1995. reprint ed. 35.00 (*1-55888-943-4*) Omnigraphics Inc.

— Writer's Rhyming Dictionary. LC 61-16086. 1985. pap. 8.95 (*0-87116-143-5*) Writer.

Reed, Lawrence W. A Lesson from the Past: The Silver Panic of 1893. vii, 86p. (Orig.). 1993. pap. 9.95 (*0-910614-90-3*) Foun Econ Ed.

Reed, Lawrence W. & Haywood, Dale M. When We Are Free. 3rd ed. 403p. 17.50 (*0-87359-054-6*) Northwood Univ.

Reed, Lena F., jt. auth. see Brey, Catherine F.

Reed, Lena F., ed. see Tolhurst, William D.

Reed, Leslie, jt. auth. see Peyton, Joy K.

Reed, Leslie A. Please Dear God Open the Door. LC 88-50761. 60p. 1988. 5.95 (*1-55523-152-7*) Winston-Derek.

Reed, Lester. Old Time Cattlemen: And Other Pioneers of the Anza-Borrego Area. 3rd ed. 146p. 1986. reprint ed. pap. 7.95 (*0-910805-02-4*) Anza-Borrego.

Reed, Lewis. Specs: The Comprehensive Foodservice Purchasing & Specification Manual. 2nd ed. LC 92-12414. 1993. text ed. 99.95 (*0-442-00705-1*) Van Nos Reinhold.

Reed, Linda. Simple Decency & Common Sense: The Southern Conference Movement, 1938-1963. LC 91-7803. (Blacks in the Diaspora Ser.). (Illus.). 288p. 1991. text ed. 29.95 (*0-253-34895-1*) Ind U Pr.

— Simple Decency & Common Sense: The Southern Conference Movement, 1938-1963. LC 91-7803. (Blacks in the Diaspora Ser.). (Illus.). 288p. 1994. pap. 10.95 (*0-253-20912-9*) Ind U Pr.

Reed, Linda A. Education in the People's Republic of China & U. S. - China Educational Exchanges. 200p. (Orig.). 1989. pap. text ed. 18.00 (*0-912207-42-6*) NAFSA Washington.

Reed, Linda A., jt. auth. see Turner-Gottschang, Karen.

Reed, Lorena. Blue Water Women. (Illus.). 320p. 1993. write for info. (*0-933858-12-4*) Kennebec River.

Reed, Lori S. & Reed, Paul F., eds. Cultural Diversity & Adaptation: The Archaic, Anasazi, & Navajo Occupation of the San Juan Basin. (Cultural Resources Ser.: No. 9). (Illus.). 182p. (Orig.). 1992. 8.00 (*1-878178-10-5*) Bureau of Land Mgmt NM.

Reed, Louis. Burning Springs. LC 85-51953. 280p. 1987. pap. 9.95 (*0-916383-05-9*, Univ Edtns) Aegina Pr.

— The Wicks & the Wacks. LC 85-70443. (J). (ps-2). 1985. pap. 5.00 (*0-916383-00-8*, Univ Edtns) Aegina Pr.

Reed, Lyman E. Preparing Missionaries for Intercultural Communication. LC 84-23060. (Illus.). 204p. (Orig.). 1985. pap. text ed. 7.95 (*0-87808-438-X*) William Carey Lib.

***Reed, Lynn R.** Pedro, His Perro & the Alphabet Sombrero. large type ed. LC 94-28215. (Illus.). 32p. (J). (ps-3). 1995. 14.95 (*0-7868-0071-2*); lib. bdg. 14.89 (*0-7868-2058-6*) Hyprn Child.

Reed, Mabel, jt. auth. see Arnold, Mary E.

Reed, Marcelina. Seven Clans of the Cherokee Society. (Illus.). 32p. (Orig.). 1993. pap. 3.50 (*0-935741-17-8*) Cherokee Pubns.

Reed, Marietta, jt. auth. see Timberlake, Lewis.

Reed, Mark, jt. ed. see Spaulding, Malcolm L.

Reed, Mark A. & Kirk, Wiley P., eds. Nanostructure Physics & Fabrication. 544p. 1989. text ed. 92.00 (*0-12-585000-X*) Acad Pr.

Reed, Mark A., jt. ed. see Kirk, Wiley P.

Reed, Mark L. Wordsworth: The Chronology of the Early Years, 1770-1799. LC 66-21344. 383p. 1967. reprint ed. pap. 109.20 (*0-7837-4182-0*, 2059031) Bks Demand.

— Wordsworth: The Chronology of the Middle Years, 1800-1815. LC 74-77179. 768p. 1975. 46.50 (*0-674-95777-6*) HUP.

Reed, Mark L., ed. see Nichols, Gary.

Reed, Mark L., ed. see Wordsworth, William.

Reed, Martin H. Skeletal Radiology. (Illus.). 696p. 1992. 150.00 (*0-683-07212-9*) Williams & Wilkins.

Reed, Mary. Fruits & Nuts in Symbolism & Celebration. LC 92-23681. (Illus.). 248p. (Orig.). (C). 1992. pap. 21.95 (*0-89390-238-1*) Resource Pubns.

R

Reed, Mary & Simon-Smolinski, Carole. Researching Local History. (Local History Technical Leaflets Ser.). (Illus.). 22p. (Orig.). 1985. pap. 1.50 (0-931406-08-0) Idaho State Soc.

Reed, Mary E. Carol Ryrie Brink. LC 91-55034. (Western Writers Ser.: No. 100). (Illus.). 51p. 1991. 3.95 (0-88430-099-4) Boise St U W Writ Ser.

Reed, Mary E., jt. auth. see Petersen, Keith C.

Reed, Mary H. IEG Legal Guide to Sponsorship. 498p. 1989. 79.00 (0-944807-01-1) IEG.

Reed, Mary M. An Investigation of Practices in First Grade Admission & Promotion. LC 70-177183. (Columbia University. Teachers College. Contributions to Education Ser.: No. 290). reprint ed. 22.50 (0-685-27470-5) AMS Pr.

***Reed, Maxine, comp.** And Baby Makes Three: Wise & Witty Observations on the Joys of Parenthood. 144p. 1995. 7.95 (0-8092-3496-3) Contemp Bks.

Reed, Maxine K. & Reed, Robert M. Career Opportunities in Television, Cable & Video. 3rd ed. (Career Opportunities Ser.). 272p. 1990. 27.95 (0-8160-2318-2) Facts on File.

— Career Opportunities in Television, Cable & Video. 3rd ed. (Career Opportunities Ser.). 272p. 1991. reprint ed. pap. 14.95 (0-8160-2341-7) Facts on File.

Reed, Maxine K., jt. auth. see Reed, Robert M.

Reed, Melania, ed. see Moses Monk of the Holy Mountain.

Reed, Merl E. Seedtime for the Modern Civil Rights Movement: The President's Committee on Fair Employment Practice, 1941-1946. LC 90-39656. 344p. 1991. text ed. 39.95 (0-8071-1617-3); pap. text ed. 16.95 (0-8071-1688-2) La State U Pr.

Reed, Merl E., jt. ed. see Fink, Gary M.

Reed, Merl E., jt. ed. see Fink, Gary M.

Reed, Merl E., et al, eds. Southern Workers & Their Unions, Eighteen Eighty to Nineteen Seventy-Five: Selected Papers, the Second Southern Labor History Conference, 1q78. LC 80-24724. (Contributions in Economics & Economic History Ser.: No. 39). (Illus.). 256p. 1981. text ed. 59.95 (0-313-22701-2, RSW/) Greenwood.

Reed, Meryl, et al. Guide to Troubled Businesses & Bankruptcy, 2 vols. 1993. ring bd. 120.00 (1-56433-415-5) Prctnrs Pub Co.

— Guide to Troubled Businesses & Bankruptcy, 2 vols., Vol. 1. 1993. write for info. (1-56433-416-3) Prctnrs Pub Co.

— Guide to Troubled Businesses & Bankruptcy, 2 vols., Vol. 2. 1993. write for info. (1-56433-417-1) Prctnrs Pub Co.

Reed, Meryl L., jt. auth. see Carmichael, Douglas R.

***Reed, Meryl L., et al.** Guide to Installing Microcomputer Systems, 2 vols., Vol. 2. 1994. ring bd. 29.00 (1-56433-563-1) Prctnrs Pub Co.

— Guide to Troubled Businesses & Bankruptcies, 2 vols., Set. 1994. ring bd. 125.00 (1-56433-529-1) Prctnrs Pub Co.

— Guide to Troubled Businesses & Bankruptcies, Vol. 1. 1994. ring bd. write for info. (1-56433-530-5) Prctnrs Pub Co.

— Guide to Troubled Businesses & Bankruptcies, Vol. 2. 1994. ring bd. write for info. (1-56433-531-3) Prctnrs Pub Co.

Reed, Michael. Educating Hearing Impaired Childrren. 208p. 1984. pap. 32.00 (0-335-10422-3, Open Univ Pr) Taylor & Francis.

— The Landscape of Britain: From the Beginnings to 1914. (Illus.). 368p. (C). 1990. text ed. 83.00 (0-389-20933-3) B&N Imports.

— Redirections in Organizational Analysis. 180p. 1985. pap. 18.95 (0-422-78940-2, 9589, Pub. by Tavistock UK) Routledge Chapman & Hall.

Reed, Michael, ed. The Ipswich Probate Inventories, 1583-1631. (Suffolk Records Society Ser.: No. XXII). 160p. 1970. 28.00 (0-85115-148-5) Boydell & Brewer.

Reed, Michael & Hughes, Michael. Rethinking Organization: New Directions in Organization Theory & Analysis. 320p. (C). 1992. text ed. 62.00 (0-8039-8287-9); pap. text ed. 22.00 (0-8039-8288-7) Sage.

Reed, Michael & Simon, Barry. Methods of Modern Mathematical Physics, 4 vols. Incl. Vol. 2. Fourier Analysis Self-Adjointness. 1975. text ed. 59.95 (0-12-585002-6); Vol. 3. Scattering Theory. 1979. text ed. 72.00 (0-12-585003-4); Vol. 4. 1978. text ed. 60.00 (0-12-585004-2); write for info. (0-318-50309-3) Acad Pr.

Reed, Michael & Simon, Barry, eds. Methods of Modern Mathematical Physics: Functional Analysis, Vol. 1. 2nd enl. rev. ed. 1980. text ed. 59.95 (0-12-585050-6) Acad Pr.

Reed, Michael, jt. auth. see Ray, Larry.

Reed, Mick & Wells, Roger, eds. Class, Conflict & Protest in the English Countryside, 1700-1800. 236p. 1990. text ed. 35.00 (0-7146-3343-7, Pub. by F Cass Pubs UK) Intl Spec Bk.

Reed, Millard & Forman, Jan R. It's Your Serve: A Practical Leadership for Pastors & Sunday School Superintendents. (Illus.). 176p. 1989. pap. 14.95 (0-8341-1293-0) Beacon Hill.

Reed, Mort. Coinology. 1985. 4.50 (0-89637-005-4) American Numismatic.

Reed, Mortimer. Complete Guide to Residential Remodeling. (Illus.). 320p. 1983. 19.95 (0-13-160663-8) P-H.

Reed, Morton. Proof of Innocence. 416p. (Orig.). 1994. mass mkt. 5.99 (0-515-11353-0) Jove Pubns.

— Shattered Lullabies. 1989. mass mkt. 4.50 (1-55817-228-9, Pinnacle NY) Windsor NY.

Reed, Myril B., jt. auth. see Maxwell, Lee M.

Reed, Myrtle. Flower of the Dusk. 1976. lib. bdg. 15.75 (0-89968-109-3, Lghtyr Pr) Buccaneer Bks.

— Lavender & Old Lace. 1976. lib. bdg. 13.50 (0-89968-110-7, Lghtyr Pr) Buccaneer Bks.

— A Spinner in the Sun. 1976. lib. bdg. 17.25 (0-89968-111-5, Lghtyr Pr) Buccaneer Bks.

Reed, Nancy A. Cockatiels! Pets - Breeding - Showing. Erhart, Rainer R., ed. (Illus.). 256p. 1990. lib. bdg. 19.95 (0-86622-640-0, TS-140) TFH Pubns.

***Reed, Nat.** Danny the Champion of the World. Friedland, J. & Kessler, R., eds. (Novel-Ties Ser.). (J). (gr. 4-6). 1993. student ed, pap. text ed. 15.95 (0-88122-897-4) Lrn Links.

— Homer Price. Friedland, J. & Kessler, R., eds. (Novel-Ties Ser.). (J). (gr. 4-6). 1994. student ed, pap. text ed. 15.95 (1-56982-069-4) Lrn Links.

Reed, Nathanial. The Life of Texas Jack; Eight Years a Criminal - 41 Years Trusting in God. (American Biography Ser.). 66p. 1991. reprint ed. lib. bdg. 59.00 (0-7812-8321-3) Rprt Serv.

Reed, Nelson. The Caste War of Yucatan. (Illus.). xii, 308p. 1964. reprint ed. 42.50 (0-8047-0164-4); reprint ed. pap. 13.95 (0-8047-0165-2) Stanford U Pr.

Reed, Nelson A. Family Papers. (Illus.). 1990. 29.95 (0-935284-78-8) Patrice Pr.

Reed, Nicholas. Camille Pissaro at Crystal Palace. 1993. pap. 29.95 (0-9515258-2-4, Pub. by Lilburne Pr UK) St Mut.

— Pissarro in Essex. 1990. pap. 29.95 (0-9515258-4-0, Pub. by Lilburne Pr UK) St Mut.

— Pissarro in West London. 1990. pap. 29.95 (0-685-70498-X, Pub. by Lilburne Pr UK) St Mut.

— Richmond & Kew Green: A Souvenir Guide. 1992. pap. 29.95 (0-9515258-6-7, Pub. by Lilburne Pr UK) St Mut.

— Sisley & the Thames. 1992. pap. 29.95 (0-9515258-5-9, Pub. by Lilburne Pr UK) St Mut.

Reed, Norman. A Place Fit Only for Refuse: Stories of Dump-Picking on Martha's Vineyard Island. 2nd ed. 1986. write for info. (0-318-61140-6) Quill Pubns GA.

Reed, Norman S. A Place Fit Only for Refuse. (Illus.). 63p. 1985. pap. 12.95 (0-317-53582-X); pap. 7.95 (0-317-53583-8) Quill Pubns GA.

— A Place Where the Eelgrass Flows. Vineyard Gazette Editors, ed. (Illus.). 81p. pap. 7.95 (0-685-18165-0) Quill Pubns GA.

Reed, O. Lee. The Legal & Regulatory Environment of Business. 9th ed. 1993. pap. text ed. write for info. (0-07-013319-0) McGraw.

Reed, O. Lee, jt. auth. see Corley, Robert N.

Reed, Orrel P., Jr. German Expressionist Art: The Rifkind Collection. (Illus.). 392p. 1977. pap. 75.00 (0-915346-28-1) A Wofsy Fine Arts.

Reed, Oscar F. Beacon Bible Expositions Vol. 7: Corinthians. Greathouse, William M. & Taylor, Willard H., eds. 298p. 1976. 12.50 (0-8341-0318-4) Beacon Hill.

Reed, P. & Brown, R. H. Marine Reinsurance. (C). 1981. 210.00 (0-685-32723-X, Pub. by Witherby & Co UK) St Mut.

Reed, P. B., jt. auth. see Thomas, P. I.

Reed, P. I. & Hill, M. J., eds. Gastric Carcinogenesis: Proceedings of the 6th Annual Symposium of the European Organisation for Cooperation in Cancer Prevention Studies (ECP), London, UK, 7-8 March 1988. (International Congress Ser.: No. 795). 270p. 1988. 92.50 (0-444-81019-6, Excerpta Medica) Elsevier.

Reed, P. I., et al, eds. New Trends in Gastric Cancer. (Developments in Oncology Ser.). (C). 1990. lib. bdg. 81.00 (0-7923-8917-4) Kluwer Ac.

Reed, Parker M. History of Bath, Maine. (Illus.). 526p. 1993. reprint ed. lib. bdg. 54.00 (0-8328-3112-3) Higginson Bk Co.

Reed, Pat. Kismet. LC 90-60631. 96p. 1991. 8.00 (1-882022-03-3) O Bks.

Reed, Patti. Reed's Guide to Farms & Barns in Eastern Pennsylvania, New Jersey, & Delaware. (Illus.). 112p. 1993. per. 10.95 (0-9637181-0-X) Horse Tales.

***Reed, Paul.** Cats Are from Jupiter Dogs Are from Pluto. 1994. pap. 8.00 (0-671-52002-4) PB.

— Longing. LC 88-14994. 160p. 1988. 14.95 (0-89087-540-5) Celestial Arts.

— Longing. LC 88-14994. 192p. 1990. pap. 7.95 (0-89087-597-9) Celestial Arts.

— Les Mains Sales, Satre: Critical Monographs in English. 64p. 1993. pap. 32.00 (0-85261-247-8, Pub. by Univ of Glasgow UK) St Mut.

— The Q Journal: A Treatment Diary. LC 90-2571. 172p. (Orig.). 1991. pap. 8.95 (0-89087-628-2) Celestial Arts.

— The Savage Garden: A Journal. 176p. 1994. 20.00 (0-9641006-0-6) Hse of Lillian.

— Serenity: Support & Guidance for People with HIV, Their Families, Friends, & Caregivers. 2nd ed. LC 90-38097. 128p. 1990. pap. 6.95 (0-89087-604-5) Celestial Arts.

Reed, Paul, ed. Fire-Emergency Services Sourcebook, 1990-91. 2nd ed. Orig. Title: Fire Service Directory of Training & Information Sources. 650p. 1990. text ed. 79. 95 (0-940613-01-8) Special Pubn Serv.

Reed, Paul F., jt. ed. see Reed, Lori S.

Reed, Paula & Tate, Grover T. The Tenderfoot Bandits: Sam Bass & Joel Collins, Their Lives & Hard Times. (Great West & Indian Ser.: Vol. 51). (Illus.). 1987. 26.95 (0-87026-066-9) Westernlore.

Reed, Peter, ed. Glasgow: The Forming of a City. (Illus.). 335p. 1992. text ed. 110.00 (0-7486-0246-1, Pub. by Edinburgh U Pr UK) Col U Pr.

***Reed, Peter & Leeds, Marc, eds.** The Vonnegut Chronicles: Interviews & Essays. LC 95-4670. (Contributions to the Study of World Literature Ser.: Vol. 65). 1996. text ed. write for info. (0-313-29719-3, Greenwood Pr) Greenwood.

Reed, Peter & Rothenberg, David, eds. Wisdom in the Open Air: The Norwegian Roots of Deep Ecology. (Illus.). 288p. (C). 1992. text ed. 44.95 (0-8166-2150-0); pap. text ed. 18.95 (0-8166-2182-9) U of Minn Pr.

Reed, Peter, jt. auth. see Brown, Robert.

Reed, Philip, ed. & anno. The Diaries of Peter Pears, 1939-1979. (Aldeburgh Studies in Music: No. 2). 160p. (C). 1995. text ed. 45.00 (0-85115-364-X) Boydell & Brewer.

***Reed, Philip, ed.** On Mahler & Britten: Essays in Honour of Donald Mitchell on His 70th Birthday. (Aldeburgh Studies in Music). 374p. (C). 1995. text ed. 63.00 (0-85115-382-8) Boydell & Brewer.

Reed, Philip, jt. ed. see Cooke, Mervyn.

Reed, Philip, jt. ed. see Mitchell, Donald.

Reed, Phillip. Ten Minute Guide to CompuServe. 176p. 1994. 10.99 (1-56761-427-2) Alpha Bks IN.

Reed, Porter B. National List of Plant Species That Occur in Wetlands: National Summary. 250p. 1988. pap. 12.00 (0-16-003585-6, S/N 024-010-00682-0) USGPO.

Reed, Prentiss B., Sr., jt. auth. see Thomas, Paul I.

Reed, Presley. The Medical Disability Advisor: Workplace Guidelines for Disability Duration. LC 91-14155. 1994. 275.00 (0-934753-52-0) LRP Pubns.

Reed, R. Banker or Retailer? (C). 1989. 39.00 (0-85297-245-8, Pub. by Inst Bankers UK) St Mut.

Reed, R., ed. see Carmichael, Viola S.

Reed, R., ed. see Cavasina, Richard G.

Reed, R., ed. see Grantham, Charles E.

Reed, R., ed. see Hofeller, Kathleen H.

Reed, R., ed. see Kinard, E. Milling.

Reed, R., ed. see Mahan, Sue.

Reed, R., ed. see Michel, M. & Dauphin, M.

Reed, R., ed. see Morgan, Steven M.

Reed, R. C. Train Wrecks. 1988. 10.99 (0-517-32897-6) Random Hse Value.

Reed, R. I. Recent Topics in Mass Spectrometry. 368p. (C). 1971. text ed. 295.00 (0-677-14800-3) Gordon & Breach.

Reed, R. P. & Fickett, F. R., eds. Advances in Cryogenic Engineering, Vol. 36. (Illus.). 1426p. 1990. 185.00 (0-306-43598-5, Plenum Pr) Plenum.

Reed, R. P., jt. ed. see Clark, A. F.

Reed, R. P., jt. ed. see Fickett, F. R.

Reed, R. P., jt. ed. see Read, D. T.

Reed, Ralph D. Geology of California. 1992. reprint ed. lib. bdg. 75.00 (0-7812-5076-5) Rprt Serv.

***Reed, Ralph E.** Politically Incorrect: What Religious Conservatives Really Think. LC 94-28095. 1994. 19.99 (0-8499-1172-9) Word Inc.

Reed, Rebecca T. Six Months in a Convent: The Narrative of Rebecca Theresa Reed & Supplement. LC 76-46097. (Anti-Movements in America Ser.). 1977. reprint ed. lib. bdg. 39.95 (0-405-09970-3) Ayer.

Reed, Rex. Rex Reed's Guide to Movies on TV & Video. 640p. (Orig.). 1992. mass mkt. 6.99 (0-446-36206-9) Warner Bks.

Reed, Richard, jt. auth. see Luffman, George A.

Reed, Richard C. Managing a Law Practice: The Human Side. LC 88-70279. 95p. 1988. pap. 34.95 (0-89707-351-7, 511-0248) Amer Bar Assn.

Reed, Richard J. North American Combustion Handbook: Combustion, Fuels, Stoichiometry, Heat Transfer, Fluid Flow, Vol. 1. 3rd ed. LC 86-11635. 1986. 30.00 (0-9601596-2-2) North Am Mfg Co.

Reed, Richard J., ed. see Gill, James H. & Quiel, John M.

Reed, Richard J., jt. auth. see Harkin, James C.

Reed, Richard K. Prophets of Agroforestry: Guarani Communities & Commercial Gathering. LC 94-10634. (Illus.). 264p. (C). 1995. text ed. 37.50x (0-292-77067-7) U of Tex Pr.

Reed, Richard P. & Clark, Alan F., eds. Materials at Low Temperature. LC 82-73607. (Illus.). 608p. reprint ed. pap. 173.30 (0-7837-1873-X, 2042074) Bks Demand.

Reed, Robert. Beyond the Veil of Stars. 352p. 1994. 21.95 (0-312-85730-6) Tor Bks.

— Beyond the Veil of Stars. 320p. 1995. mass mkt. 4.99 (0-8125-2406-3) Tor Bks.

— Black Milk. 336p. 1989. 18.95 (1-55611-115-0) D I Fine.

— Collector's Guide to Trading Cards: Identification & Values. 128p. 1993. pap. 17.95 (0-89145-542-6, 3438) Collector Bks.

— Essential Buyer's Guide to Paper Collectibles. LC 94-27448. 176p. 1995. 17.95 (0-87069-718-8, Wallace-Hmestead) Chilton.

— An Exaltation of Larks. 1995. 21.95 (0-312-85888-4) Tor Bks.

— The Hormone Jungle. LC 87-46033. 304p. 1988. 17.95 (1-55611-066-9) D I Fine.

— The Leeshore. LC 86-82106. 256p. 1987. 16.95 (0-917657-98-5) D I Fine.

— Old Washington, D. C., in Early Photographs. LC 79-52841. (Illus.). (Orig.). 1980. pap. 10.95 (0-486-23869-5) Dover.

Reed, Robert, jt. ed. see Reed, Tina.

Reed, Robert D. A. I. D. S. A Bibliography. 1986. pap. 11. 00 (0-88247-757-9) R & E Pubs.

— A. I. D. S. How & Where to Find Facts & Do Research. 1986. pap. 5.00 (0-88247-758-7) R & E Pubs.

— Furnace Operations. 3rd ed. LC 80-26274. 240p. reprint ed. pap. 68.40 (0-8357-2574-X, 2040265) Bks Demand.

— How & Where to Find Information & Get Help for Alzheimer's Disease. LC 87-90418. 32p. (Orig.). 1987. pap. 4.95 (0-88247-769-2) R & E Pubs.

— How & Where to Research & Find Information on Aging in America. LC 82-60572. 50p. (Orig.). 1984. pap. 6.50 (0-88247-698-X) R & E Pubs.

— How & Where to Research Your Ethnic-American Cultural Heritage, 12 bks. Incl. Japanese Americans. 1979. 4.50 (0-318-55381-3); Native Americans. 1979. 4.50 (0-318-55382-1); Black Americans. 1979. 4.50 (0-318-55384-8); Mexican Americans. 1979. 4.50 (0-318-55385-6); Polish Americans. 1979. 4.50 (0-318-55386-4); Italian Americans. 1979. 4.50 (0-318-55387-2); German Americans. 1979. 4.50 (0-318-55388-0); Jewish Americans. 1979. 4.50 (0-318-55389-9); Scandinavian Americans. 1979. 4.50 (0-318-55390-2); Russian Americans. 1979. 4.50 (0-318-55391-0); 1979. write for info. (0-318-55379-1) R & E Pubs.

Reed, Robert D. & Kaus, Danek. A. I. D. S. Your Child & the School. 1986. pap. 5.00 (0-88247-756-0) R & E Pubs.

— Cults: How & Where to Find Facts & Get Help. Parker, Diane, ed. LC 94-68699. (Abuse Ser.). 50p. (Orig.). 1994. 4.50 (1-56875-083-8, 083-8) R & E Pubs.

— Finding Your Afro-American Roots: A Guide to Researching Your Ethnic-American Cultural Heritage. Parker, Diane, ed. LC 92-50960. 1993. pap. 4.50 (1-56875-012-9) R & E Pubs.

— Finding Your Austrian-American Roots: A Guide to Researching Your Ethnic-American Cultural Heritage. Parker, Diane, ed. LC 92-50982. 1993. pap. 4.50 (1-56875-034-X) R & E Pubs.

— Finding Your Chinese-American Roots: A Guide to Researching Your Ethnic-American Cultural Heritage. Parker, Diane, ed. LC 92-50961. 1993. pap. 4.50 (1-56875-013-7) R & E Pubs.

— Finding Your Croatian-American Roots: A Guide to Researching Your Ethnic-American Cultural Heritage. Parker, Diane, ed. LC 92-50986. 1993. pap. 4.50 (1-56875-038-2) R & E Pubs.

— Finding Your Cuban-American Roots: A Guide to Researching Your Ethnic-American Cultural Heritage. Parker, Diane, ed. LC 92-50980. 1993. pap. 4.50 (1-56875-032-3) R & E Pubs.

— Finding Your Dutch-American Roots: A Guide to Researching Your Ethnic-American Cultural Heritage. Parker, Diane, ed. LC 92-50962. 1993. pap. 4.50 (1-56875-014-5) R & E Pubs.

— Finding Your English-American Roots: A Guide to Researching Your Ethnic-American Cultural Heritage. Parker, Diane, ed. LC 92-50963. 1993. pap. 4.50 (1-56875-015-3) R & E Pubs.

— Finding Your Estonian-American Roots: A Guide to Researching Your Ethnic-American Cultural Heritage. Parker, Diane, ed. LC 92-50985. 1993. pap. 4.50 (1-56875-037-4) R & E Pubs.

— Finding Your Filipino-American Roots: A Guide to Researching Your Ethnic-American Cultural Heritage. Parker, Diane, ed. LC 92-50971. 1993. pap. 4.50 (1-56875-023-4) R & E Pubs.

— Finding Your French-American Roots: A Guide to Researching Your Ethnic-American Cultural Heritage. Parker, Diane, ed. LC 92-50964. 1993. pap. 4.50 (1-56875-016-1) R & E Pubs.

— Finding Your German-American Roots: A Guide to Researching Your Ethnic-American Cultural Heritage. Parker, Diane, ed. LC 92-50965. 1993. pap. 4.50 (1-56875-017-X) R & E Pubs.

— Finding Your Hungarian-American Roots: A Guide to Researching Your Ethnic-American Cultural Heritage. Parker, Diane, ed. LC 92-50981. 1993. pap. 4.50 (1-56875-033-1) R & E Pubs.

— Finding Your Irish-American Roots: A Guide to Researching Your Ethnic-American Cultural Heritage. Parker, Diane, ed. LC 92-50966. 1993. pap. 4.50 (1-56875-018-8) R & E Pubs.

— Finding Your Italian-American Roots: A Guide to Researching Your Ethnic-American Cultural Heritage. Parker, Diane, ed. LC 92-50967. 1993. pap. 4.50 (1-56875-019-6) R & E Pubs.

— Finding Your Japanese-American Roots: A Guide to Researching Your Ethnic-American Cultural Heritage. Parker, Diane, ed. LC 92-50968. 1993. pap. 4.50 (1-56875-020-X) R & E Pubs.

— Finding Your Jewish-American Roots: A Guide to Researching Your Ethnic-American Cultural Heritage. Parker, Diane, ed. LC 92-50969. 1993. pap. 4.50 (1-56875-021-8) R & E Pubs.

— Finding Your Latvian-American Roots: A Guide to Researching Your Ethnic-American Cultural Heritage. Parker, Diane, ed. LC 92-50988. 1993. pap. 4.50 (1-56875-035-8) R & E Pubs.

— Finding Your Lithuanian-American Roots: A Guide to Researching Your Ethnic-American Cultural Heritage. Parker, Diane, ed. LC 92-50984. 1993. pap. 4.50 (1-56875-036-6) R & E Pubs.

— Finding Your Mexican-American Roots: A Guide to Researching Your Ethnic-American Cultural Heritage. Parker, Diane, ed. LC 92-50970. 1993. pap. 4.50 (1-56875-022-6) R & E Pubs.

— Finding Your Native-American Roots: A Guide to Researching Your Ethnic-American Cultural Heritage. Parker, Diane, ed. LC 92-50979. 1993. pap. 4.50 (1-56875-031-5) R & E Pubs.

— Finding Your Polish-American Roots: A Guide to Researching Your Ethnic-American Cultural Heritage. Parker, Diane, ed. LC 92-50972. 1993. pap. 4.50 (1-56875-024-2) R & E Pubs.

— Finding Your Portuguese-American Roots: A Guide to Researching Your Ethnic-American Cultural Heritage. Parker, Diane, ed. LC 92-50978. 1993. pap. 4.50 (1-56875-030-7) R & E Pubs.

— Finding Your Puerto-Rican-American Roots: A Guide to Researching Your Ethnic-American Cultural Heritage. Parker, Diane, ed. LC 92-50976. 1993. pap. 4.50 (1-56875-028-5) R & E Pubs.

An Asterisk (*) at the beginning of an entry indicates that the title is appearing in BIP for the first time.

— Finding Your Russian-American Roots: A Guide to Researching Your Ethnic-American Cultural Heritage. Parker, Diane, ed. LC 92-50973. 1993. pap. 4.50 (*1-56875-025-0*) R & E Pubs.

— Finding Your Scandinavian-American Roots: A Guide to Researching Your Ethnic-American Cultural Heritage. Parker, Diane, ed. LC 92-50974. 1993. pap. 4.50 (*1-56875-026-9*) R & E Pubs.

— Finding Your Spanish-American Roots: A Guide to Researching Your Ethnic-American Cultural Heritage. Parker, Diane, ed. LC 92-50977. 1993. pap. 4.50 (*1-56875-029-3*) R & E Pubs.

— Finding Your Vietnamese-American Roots: A Guide to Researching Your Ethnic-American Cultural Heritage. Parker, Diane, ed. LC 92-50975. 1993. pap. 4.50 (*1-56875-027-7*) R & E Pubs.

— Multiple Personality Disorder: How & Where to Find Facts & Get Help. Parker, Diane, ed. LC 93-85144. (Abuse Ser.). 50p. 1994. 4.50 (*1-56875-084-6*, 084-6) R & E Pubs.

Reed, Robert D. & Kaus, Danek S. Abortion: How & Where to Find Facts & Get Help. Parker, Diane, ed. LC 92-53758. (Abuse Ser.). 48p. 1993. pap. 4.50 (*0-88247-948-2*) R & E Pubs.

— Child Custody: How & Where to Find Facts & Get Help. Parker, Diane, ed. LC 92-53757. (Abuse Ser.). 48p. 1993. pap. 4.50 (*0-88247-947-4*) R & E Pubs.

— Child Sexual Abuse: How & Where to Find Facts & Get Help. Parker, Diane, ed. LC 92-53764. (Abuse Ser.). 48p. 1993. pap. 4.50 (*0-88247-941-5*) R & E Pubs.

— Domestic Violence - Battered Women: How & Where to Find Facts & Get Help. Parker, Diane, ed. LC 92-53763. (Abuse Ser.). 48p. 1993. pap. 4.50 (*0-88247-942-3*) R & E Pubs.

— Homelessness: How & Where to Find Facts & Get Help. Parker, Diane, ed. LC 92-53766. (Abuse Ser.). 48p. 1993. pap. 4.50 (*0-88247-939-3*) R & E Pubs.

— Hunger: How & Where to Find Facts & Get Help. Parker, Diane, ed. LC 92-53765. 48p. 1993. pap. 4.50 (*0-88247-940-7*) R & E Pubs.

— Missing Children: How & Where to Find Facts & Get Help. Parker, Diane, ed. LC 92-53769. (Abuse Ser.). 48p. 1993. pap. 4.50 (*0-88247-936-9*) R & E Pubs.

— Pornography: How & Where to Find Facts & Get Help. Parker, Diane, ed. LC 92-53767. (Abuse Ser.). 48p. 1993. pap. 4.50 (*0-88247-938-5*) R & E Pubs.

— Poverty: How & Where to Find Facts & Get Help. Parker, Diane, ed. LC 92-53755. (Abuse Ser.). 48p. 1993. pap. 4.50 (*0-88247-946-6*) R & E Pubs.

— Rape - Sexual Assault: How & Where to Find Facts & Get Help. Parker, Diane, ed. LC 92-53762. (Abuse Ser.). 48p. 1993. pap. 4.50 (*0-88247-943-1*) R & E Pubs.

— Ritual Child Abuse: How & Where to Find Facts & Get Help. Parker, Diane, ed. LC 92-53759. (Abuse Ser.). 48p. 1992. pap. 4.50 (*0-88247-949-0*) R & E Pubs.

— Runaway Children: How & Where to Find Facts & Get Help. Parker, Diane, ed. LC 92-53768. (Abuse Ser.). 48p. 1993. pap. 4.50 (*0-88247-937-7*) R & E Pubs.

— Sexual Harassment: How & Where to Find Facts & Get Help. Parker, Diane, ed. LC 92-53761. (Abuse Ser.). 48p. 1993. pap. 4.50 (*0-88247-944-X*) R & E Pubs.

— Single Parenting: How & Where to Find Facts & Get Help. Parker, Diane, ed. LC 92-53756. (Abuse Ser.). 48p. 1993. pap. 4.50 (*0-88247-945-8*) R & E Pubs.

— Suicide: How & Where to Find Facts & Get Help. Parker, Diane, ed. LC 92-53760. (Abuse Ser.). 48p. 1993. pap. 4.50 (*0-88247-950-4*) R & E Pubs.

***Reed, Robert D. & Roy, R. R.** Statistical Physics for Students of Science & Engineering. (Illus.). xi, 320p. 1995. pap. text ed. 10.95 (*0-486-68568-3*) Dover.

Reed, Robert G., III & Fesharaki, Fereidun, eds. The Oil Market in the 1990s: Challenges for the New Era. (Special Studies in International Economics & Development). 214p. (C). 1989. pap. text ed. 53.00 (*0-8133-0819-4*) Westview.

Reed, Robert M. Facts on File Dictionary of Television, Cable & Video. 256p. 1994. 24.95 (*0-8160-2947-4*) Facts on File.

Reed, Robert M. & Reed, Maxine K. The Encyclopedia of Television, Cable & Video. 704p. 1992. text ed. 64.95 (*0-442-00627-6*) Chapman & Hall.

Reed, Robert M., jt. auth. see Reed, Maxine K.

Reed, Robert R. Colonial Manila: The Context of Hispanic Urbanism & Process of Morphogenesis. LC 77-80476. (University of California Publications in Social Welfare: No. 22). 143p. reprint ed. pap. 40.80 (*0-685-23993-4*, 2031576) Bks Demand.

— Crime & God's Judgment in Shakespeare. LC 83-19701. 231p. reprint ed. pap. 65.90 (*0-685-44499-6*, 2031524) Bks Demand.

Reed, Robert W., jt. auth. see Brunelle, Richard L.

***Reed, Roberta G. & Kotz, John C.** Analyzing Food Products for Vitamin C. Neidig, H. A., ed. (Modular Laboratory Program in Chemistry Ser.). 12p. (C). 1994. pap. text ed. 1.25x (*0-87540-442-1*) Chem Educ Res.

Reed, Rod. The Cisco Kid. (U. S. Classics Ser.). (Illus.). 80p. (Orig.). 1983. pap. 5.95 (*0-912277-00-9*) K Pierce Inc.

Reed, Rodney J., jt. auth. see Guthrie, James W.

Reed, Roland. The Miser. (J). (gr. 4-12). 1973. 5.00 (*0-87602-158-5*) Anchorage.

Reed, Ronald, ed. I Wish That I Could Live Outdoors: Mohican Outdoor School Student Poetry Contest Winners & Others. (Illus.). 100p. (Orig.). (J). (gr. 4-7). 1992. pap. 18.95 (*0-685-53268-2*) Mohican Schl.

Reed, Ronald F. Rebecca: A Novel for Children. 37p. (Orig.). (J). (ps-4). 1990. pap. 8.00 (*0-924303-00-X*) TX Wesleyan Coll.

— Talking with Children. LC 83-9990. 123p. (Orig.). 1983. 11.95 (*0-912869-00-3*); pap. 6.95 (*0-912869-01-1*) Arden Pr.

Reed, Ronald F., jt. ed. see Sharp, Ann M.

Reed, Ronny L. Subtle Destruction. 1994. 11.95 (*0-8062-4992-7*) Carlton.

Reed, Rosalind & Lang, Thomas A. Health Behaviors. LC 85-26551. (Illus.). 602p. (C). 1986. teacher ed, pap. text ed. write for info. (*0-314-96653-6*) West Pub.

— Health Behaviors. 2nd ed. LC 85-26551. (Illus.). 602p. (C). 1986. pap. text ed. 46.00 (*0-314-93409-X*) West Pub.

Reed, Rose, adapt. The Velveteen Rabbit. (Big Golden Book Ser.). (Illus.). 24p. (J). (ps up). 1990. write for info. (*0-307-12105-4*, Golden Bks) Western Pub.

Reed, Rowena. Combined Operations in the Civil War. LC 92-37967. (Illus.). xxxvi, 468p. (C). 1993. pap. 17.95 (*0-8032-8943-X*, Bison Books) U of Nebr Pr.

Reed, Rowena, jt. auth. see Mullins, Michael.

Reed, Rowland I., ed. see NATO Advanced Study Institute Staff.

Reed, Roy. Looking for Hogeye. LC 85-28906. 142p. 1986. 13.95 (*0-938626-60-X*) U of Ark Pr.

Reed, Roy A., jt. auth. see Browning, Robert L.

Reed, Ruddell. Plant Layout: Factors, Principles & Techniques. LC 61-14497. (Erwin Series in Management). 473p. reprint ed. pap. 134.90 (*0-317-10732-1*, 2050147) Bks Demand.

***Reed, Ruth.** Blake the Snake. (Illus.). (J). (gr. 2). 1994. pap. text ed. 12.95 (*1-881116-48-4*) Black Forrest Pr.

— The Illegitimate Family in New York City: Its Treatment by Social & Health Agencies. LC 78-169397. (Family in America Ser.). 408p. 1972. reprint ed. 19.95 (*0-405-03874-7*) Ayer.

— Negro Illegitimacy in New York City. LC 68-57577. (Columbia University. Studies in the Social Sciences: No. 277). reprint ed. 20.00 (*0-404-51277-1*) AMS Pr.

Reed, Ruth A. Beyond the Egg Crate. 96p. 1993. pap. 5.95 (*1-880365-79-0*) Prof Pr NC.

Reed, Ruth R. Til Death Did Us Part. 1991. 16.95 (*0-533-09538-7*) Vantage.

***Reed, S.** Toxic Executive. 1994. pap. 5.99 (*0-517-13212-5*) Random Hse Value.

Reed, S. G. A History of the Texas Railroads & of Transportation Conditions under Spain & Mexico & the Republic & the State. Bruchey, Stuart, ed. LC 80-1339. (Railroads Ser.). (Illus.). 1981. reprint ed. lib. bdg. 77.95 (*0-405-13811-3*) Ayer.

Reed, S. J. Electron Microprobe Analysis. 2nd ed. LC 92-16263. (Illus.). 320p. (C). 1993. 79.95 (*0-521-41956-5*) Cambridge U Pr.

Reed, Sabrina, ed. see Layton, Irving & Creeley, Robert.

Reed, Sally G. Library Volunteers - Worth the Effort! A Program Manager's Guide. LC 94-4568. 128p. 1994. pap. 21.95 (*0-7864-0004-8*) McFarland & Co.

— Saving Your Library: A Guide to Getting, Using & Keeping the Power You Need. LC 91-51207. 144p. 1992. pap. 21.95x (*0-89950-719-0*) McFarland & Co.

— Small Libraries: A Handbook for Successful Management. LC 90-50813. 156p. 1991. lib. bdg. 21.95x (*0-89950-596-1*) McFarland & Co.

Reed, Sampson. Observations on the Growth of the Mind Including GENIUS. 5th ed. LC 72-4971. (Romantic Tradition in American Literature Ser.). 110p. 1972. reprint ed. 20.95 (*0-405-04641-3*) Ayer.

— Observations on the Growth of the Mind with Remarks on Other Subjects. LC 78-100126. 1970. reprint ed. 50.00 (*0-8201-1070-1*) Schol Facsimiles.

— Sampson Reed: Primary Source Material for Emerson Studies. (Swedenborg Studies: No. 1). 53, xiip. 1992. pap. text ed. 6.95 (*0-87785-180-8*) Swedenborg.

Reed, Scott. Miracle of Psycho Command Power: The New Way to Riches, Love & Happiness. 1972. 17.95 (*0-13-585679-5*, Reward); pap. 3.95 (*0-13-585596-9*, Reward) P-H.

Reed-Scott, J., jt. auth. see Oldham-Merrill, J.

Reed, Sharon. Sharon Shares from Where Eagles Soar. 95p. (Orig.). 1993. pap. text ed. 12.95 (*0-9629735-1-3*) Sharon Reed.

***Reed, Sharon, ed.** Pastoral Care. 144p. 1993. 14.95 (*0-89944-268-4*) Don Bosco Multimedia.

— Spirituality. 190p. 1991. 14.95 (*0-89944-210-2*) Don Bosco Multimedia.

***Reed, Sharon & Roberto, John.** Pastoral Care: Resource Manual. 64p. 1994. 7.95 (*0-89944-300-1*) Don Bosco Multimedia.

Reed, Sherwood C., et al. Natural Systems for Waste Management & Treatment. 2nd ed. 1995. text ed. 55.00 (*0-07-060982-9*) McGraw.

Reed, Smith, Shaw & McClay Staff. OSHA Compliance Handbook. 400p. (Orig.). 1992. pap. text ed. 79.00 (*0-86587-290-2*) Gov Insts.

Reed, Stanley F. Art of M & A: A Merger Acquisition Buyout Guide. 2nd ed. 1000p. 1994. text ed. 125.00 (*1-55623-722-7*) Irwin Prof Pubng.

— The Art of M & A: Merger Acquisition Buyout Guide. 960p. 1988. text ed. 100.00 (*1-55623-113-X*) Irwin Prof Pubng.

— The Toxic Executive. 320p. 1994. reprint ed. pap. 12.00 (*0-88730-693-4*) Harper Busn.

***Reed, Stephen A., et al, eds.** The Dead Sea Scrolls Catalogue: Documents, Photographs, & Museum Inventory Numbers. LC 94-29939. (SBL Resources for Biblical Study: No. 32). (Illus.). 606p. 1994. 89.95 (*0-7885-0017-1*, 060332); pap. 64.95 (*0-7885-0018-X*, 060332) Scholars Pr GA.

Reed, Stephen K. Cognition: Theory & Applications. 3rd ed. LC 91-14250. 400p. (C). 1992. text ed. 47.95 (*0-534-14760-7*) Brooks-Cole.

— Cognition: Theory & Applications. 4th ed. LC 95-15683. 1996. text ed. 47.95 (*0-534-21954-3*) Brooks-Cole.

Reed, Stephen W. The Making of Modern New Guinea. LC 75-30077. (Institute of Pacific Relations Ser.). (Illus.). 352p. 1982. reprint ed. 47.50 (*0-404-59554-5*) AMS Pr.

Reed, Steven R. Japan Election Data: The House of Representatives, 1947-1990. LC 92-2509. xx, 602p. 1992. 67.50 (*0-939512-57-2*); pap. 34.95 (*0-939512-58-0*) U MI Japan.

— Japanese Prefectures & Policymaking. LC 85-22528. (Series in Policy & Institutional Studies). 206p. 1986. 49.95 (*0-8229-3527-9*) U of Pittsburgh Pr.

— Making Common Sense of Japan. LC 93-12871. (Policy & Institutional Studies). 208p. (C). 1993. text ed. 49.95 (*0-8229-3757-3*); pap. text ed. 15.95 (*0-8229-5510-5*) U of Pittsburgh Pr.

Reed, Sue & Yates, Juanita. Journey of a Soul: In an MS Body. (Illus.). 92p. (Orig.). 1990. pap. 7.95 (*0-9627655-1-1*) J Yates.

Reed, Sue W. & Shapiro, Barbara S. Degas' Complete Graphic Work. (Painter As Printmaker Ser.). (Illus.). 344p. 1984. 125.00 (*1-55660-196-4*); pap. 75.00 (*0-915346-89-3*) A Wofsy Fine Arts.

— Edgar Degas: The Painter As Printmaker. Jupe, D. Margaret, ed. LC 84-61859. (Illus.). 272p. 1984. 30.00 (*0-87846-244-9*); pap. 24.95 (*0-87846-243-0*) Mus Fine Arts Boston.

Reed, Sue W. & Wallace, Richard. Italian Etchers of the Renaissance & Baroque. (Illus.). 352p. 1989. text ed. 65.00 (*0-87846-306-2*); pap. text ed. 34.50 (*0-87846-305-4*) Mus Fine Arts Boston.

Reed, T. Occupational Stress Guide to Control. 1991. text ed. write for info. (*0-442-00189-4*) Van Nos Reinhold.

Reed, T. G., jt. auth. see Smith, D. B.

Reed, T. J. The Classical Centre: Goethe & Weimar Seventeen Seventy-Five to Eighteen Thirty-Two. LC 79-54252. (Literary History of Germany Ser.: Vol. 5). 1980. text ed. 44.00 (*0-06-495825-6*, N6651) B&N Imports.

— Death in Venice: Making & Unmaking a Master. LC 94-4252. (Twayne's Masterwork Studies Ser.: No. 140). 125p. 1994. text ed. 23.95x (*0-8057-8069-6*, Twayne); pap. 12.95 (*0-8057-8114-5*, Twayne) Macmillan.

— Schiller. (Past Masters Ser.). 128p. 1991. pap. 7.95 (*0-19-287670-8*) OUP.

Reed, T. J., tr. see Heine, Heinrich.

Reed, T. V. Fifteen Jugglers, Five Believers: Literary Politics & the Poetics of American Social Movements. (New Historicism: Studies in Cultural Poetics: No. 22). (C). 1992. 32.00 (*0-520-07521-8*); pap. 16.00 (*0-520-07522-6*) U CA Pr.

***Reed, Teresa.** Keisha Leads the Way. Bodnar, Judit & Gould, Betsy, eds. (Magic Attic Club Ser.). (Illus.). 64p. (Orig.). (J). (gr. 2-6). 1995. 12.95 (*1-57513-016-5*); pap. 5.95 (*1-57513-017-3*) Magic Attic Club.

— Three Cheers for Keisha. Bodnar, Judit & Gould, Betsy, eds. (Magic Attic Club Ser.). (Illus.). 64p. (Orig.). (J). (gr. 2-6). 1995. 12.95 (*1-57513-008-4*); pap. 5.95 (*1-57513-009-2*) Magic Attic Club.

Reed, Terry & Cummings, John. Compromised: Clinton, Bush, & the CIA. 1993. 23.95 (*1-56171-249-3*) Sure Sellers.

— Compromised: Clinton, Bush & the CIA How the Presidency Was Co-Opted by the CIA. (Illus.). 704p. 1995. pap. 17.95 (*1-883955-02-5*) Penmarin Bks.

Reed, Thomas B., ed. see Swedish Academy of Engineering Staff.

Reed, Thomas J. & Ross, Eunice L. Will Contests. LC 92-72560. 1992. ring bd. 135.00 (*0-685-59866-7*) Clark Boardman Callaghan.

Reed, Thomas L. Lost Days: Children from Dysfunctional Families. Ingram, tr. 120p. 1994. pap. 7.95 (*1-56901-274-1*) NW Pub.

Reed, Thomas L., Jr. Middle English Debate Poetry & the Aesthetics of Irresolution. 480p. 1990. text ed. 43.00 (*0-8262-0733-2*) U of Mo Pr.

Reed, Thomas M., jt. auth. see Gubbins, Keith E.

Reed, Thomas S. A Profile of Brigadier General Alfred N. A. Duffie. 53p. 1982. 17.00 (*0-89126-109-5*) MA-AH Pub.

Reed, Thomas S., ed. Second MNMA Conference Proceedings, 1991: With Test Drive the New Notation Systems. LC 93-86922. 180p. (C). 1994. pap. 27.00 (*0-9638849-0-5*) Music Notation.

***Reed, Thomas W. & Cameron, Bradley J.** Above the Law: Covering Congress under Federal Employment Laws. 113p. 1994. 25.00 (*0-916559-53-X*, 2051-MO-4035) EPF.

Reed, Tina. Words of Love, No. II: The Romance Continues. 96p. 1994. pap. 6.95 (*0-399-51877-0*, Perigree Bks) Berkley Pub.

Reed, Tina, ed. Words of Love: A Celebration of Passion & Romance. 128p. (Orig.). 1993. pap. 6.95 (*0-399-51789-8*, Perigree Bks) Berkley Pub.

***Reed, Tina & Reed, Robert, eds.** Speaking of Marriage: Irreverent Reflections on Matrimony. LC 94-39474. 1995. pap. 10.00 (*0-399-51941-6*, Perigee Bks) Berkley Pub.

Reed, Tom. The Black Music History of Los Angeles - Its Roots: A Classical Pictorial History of Black Music in L. A. from 1920-1970. Graham, Julian, ed. (Illus.). 480p. (C). 1992. 60.00x (*0-9632908-6-X*) Black Accent.

Reed, Toni. Demon-Lovers & Their Victims in British Fiction. LC 88-18126. 184p. 1988. 20.00 (*0-8131-1663-5*) U Pr of Ky.

***Reed, Tony.** On the Wild Side. 200p. (Orig.). 1995. pap. write for info. (*1-885591-67-5*) Morris Pubng.

***Reed, V. Delbert.** Bear Bryant: What Made Him a Winner. (Illus.). 210p. 1995. 29.95 (*1-885219-01-6*) Vision AL.

Reed, Verner Z. Southern Ute Indians of Early Colorado. Jones, William R., ed. (Illus.). 1980. reprint ed. pap. 3.95 (*0-89646-067-3*) Vistabooks.

***Reed, Vernon.** Presiding & Leading: How to Be a President. 113p. 1994. 23.95 (*0-9641116-0-8*) Woodflower Pr.

Reed, Veronica M., jt. auth. see Turner, Margery A.

Reed, Vicki. Children with Language Disorders: An Introduction. LC 85-26409. 368p. 1986. write for info. (*0-02-399140-2*) Macmillan.

— An Introduction to Children with Language Disorders. 2nd ed. LC 93-2404. 526p. (C). 1994. text ed. write for info. (*0-02-399150-X*, Merrill Pub Co) Macmillan.

Reed, Vicki A. & Miles, Marcia. Adolescent Language Disorders: A Video Inservice for Educators, 8 bks., Set. 251p. (C). 1989. 450.00 (*0-930599-54-3*) Thinking Pubns.

Reed, Vilia. Photographic Retouching (E-97) LC 87-81377. (Illus.). 116p. 1987. pap. 24.95 (*0-87985-474-X*) Saunders Photo.

Reed, Virginia. Shady Gardens. Patrick, John, ed. (Lothian Australian Garden Ser.). (Illus.). 64p. (Orig.). 1995. pap. 9.95 (*0-85091-323-3*, Pub. by Lothian Pub AT) Seven Hills Bk.

Reed, W. F. The Descendants of Thomas Durfee, Vol. 2. (Illus.). 668p. 1989. reprint ed. lib. bdg. 107.00 (*0-8328-0504-1*); reprint ed. pap. 97.00 (*0-8328-0505-X*) Higginson Bk Co.

Reed, W. H. Reed. (Illus.). 529p. 1991. reprint ed. lib. bdg. 91.50 (*0-8328-2051-2*); reprint ed. pap. 81.50 (*0-8328-2052-0*) Higginson Bk Co.

Reed, W. L. & Bristow, M. J., eds. National Anthems of the World. 8th rev. ed. 528p. 90.00 (*0-304-34218-1*, Pub. by Cassell UK) Sterling.

Reed, W. L., jt. auth. see Winnett, Frederick V.

Reed, W. Michael & Burton, John K., eds. Educational Computing & Problem Solving. LC 87-2795. (Computers in the Schools Ser.: Vol. 4, Nos. 3-4). (Illus.). 217p. 1988. text ed. 49.95 (*0-86656-781-X*) Haworth Pr.

Reed, Walt. Illustrator in America, 1880-1980. 1984. 48.50 (*0-8230-5849-2*) Madison Square.

— The Magic Pen of Joseph Clement Coll. 2nd ed. (Illus.). 176p. Date not set. reprint ed. write for info. (*0-614-07421-5*) Illustration Hse.

Reed, Walter L. Dialogues of the Word: The Bible As Literature According to Bakhtin. LC 92-36420. 248p. (C). 1993. 39.95 (*0-19-507997-3*) OUP.

— Meditations on the Hero: A Study of the Romantic Hero in Nineteenth-Century Fiction. LC 74-77068. 217p. reprint ed. 61.90 (*0-8357-9384-2*, 2016760) Bks Demand.

Reed, Warren, jt. ed. see Little, Reg.

Reed, William. Ki: A Practical Guide for Westerners. LC 85-81367. 224p. (Orig.). 1986. pap. 18.00 (*0-87040-640-X*) Japan Pubns USA.

— Ki: A Road That Anyone Can Walk. (Illus.). 272p. (Orig.). 1992. pap. 24.00 (*0-87040-799-6*) Japan Pubns USA.

— The Phantom of the Poles. reprint ed. spiral bd. 13.75 (*0-7873-0711-4*) Mokelumne.

— The Phantom of the Poles: Mysteries of the Polar Regions & the Interior of the Earth. 1991. lib. bdg. 79.95 (*0-8490-4966-0*) Gordon Pr.

— Shodo: The Art of Coordinating Mind, Body, & Brush. LC 88-81760. (Illus.). 212p. (Orig.). 1990. pap. 22.00 (*0-87040-784-8*) Japan Pubns USA.

Reed, William B., et al. Condensed Analysis of the Ninth Air Force in the European Theater of Operations. Kohn, Richard H. & Harahan, Joseph P., eds. (USAF Warrior Studies). (Illus.). 148p. (C). 1984. reprint ed. write for info. (*0-912799-13-7*) Off Air Force.

Reed, William C. The Role of Traditional Rulers in Elective Politics in Nigeria. (Graduate Student Term Paper Ser.: No. 5). 1982. pap. text ed. 2.00 (*0-941934-41-1*) Indiana Africa.

Reed, William F. The Descendants of Thomas Durfee of Portsmouth, R. I., Vol. 1. (Illus.). 593p. 1989. reprint ed. lib. bdg. 99.00 (*0-8328-0502-5*); reprint ed. pap. 89.00 (*0-8328-0503-3*) Higginson Bk Co.

Reed, William H. Elgar. 1988. reprint ed. lib. bdg. 59.00 (*0-7812-0411-9*) Rprt Serv.

— Elgar. LC 71-181234. 227p. 1949. reprint ed. 29.00 (*0-403-01656-8*) Scholarly.

Reed, William S. Doctor's Thoughts on Healing. pap. 0.95 (*0-910924-33-3*) Macalester.

Reed, Willow. Succession: From Field to Forest. LC 90-3216. (Living World Ser.). (Illus.). 64p. (J). (gr. 6 up). 1991. lib. bdg. 15.95 (*0-89490-271-7*) Enslow Pubs.

Reed, Wornie L., ed. Complete Series of Assessment of the Status of African-Americans. 700p. (Orig.). 1990. pap. 39.95 (*1-878358-05-5*) U MA W M Trotter Inst.

— Critiques of the NRC Study, A Common Destiny: Blacks & American Society. (Assessment of the Status of African-Americans Ser.). 56p. (Orig.). (C). 1990. pap. 3.95 (*1-878358-06-5*) U MA W M Trotter Inst.

— Health & Medical Care of African-Americans. LC 92-30000. 184p. (Orig.). 1993. text ed. 49.95 (*0-86569-217-3*, T217, Auburn Hse); pap. text ed. 16.95 (*0-86569-218-1*, R218, Auburn Hse) Greenwood.

— Health & Medical Care of African-Americans, Vol. V. (Assessment of the Status of African-Americans Ser.). 150p. (Orig.). (C). 1990. pap. 8.95 (*1-878358-01-4*) U MA W M Trotter Inst.

— Social, Political, & Economic Issues in Black America, Vol. IV. (Assessment of the Status of African-Americans Ser.). 150p. (Orig.). (C). 1990. pap. 8.95 (*1-878358-03-0*) U MA W M Trotter Inst.

— Summary of the Assessment of the Status of African-Americans, Vol. I. 100p. (Orig.). (C). 1990. pap. 5.95 (*1-878358-04-9*) U MA W M Trotter Inst.

Reed, Wornie L. & Hill, Robert B., eds. Research on the African-American Family: A Holistic Perspective. LC 92-26624. 200p. 1993. text ed. 55.00 (*0-86569-019-7*, T019, Auburn Hse); pap. text ed. 15.95 (*0-86569-021-9*, R021, Auburn Hse) Greenwood.

Reed, Wornie L. & Simon, Mary E., eds. Cleveland's Children & Youth: A Status Report, 1993. 175p. 1993. pap. write for info. (*0-9638675-0-4*) CSU Urban Chld.

R

Reed, Wornie L., et al, eds. African-Americans: Essential Perspectives. LC 92-31298. 184p. 1993. text ed. 49.95 (*0-86569-221-1*, T221, Auburn Hse); pap. text ed. 16.95 (*0-86569-222-X*, R222, Auburn Hse) Greenwood.

Reed-Wright, E. Reed-Read Lineage: Captain John Reed of Providence, Rhode Island, & Norwalk, Connecticut, & His Descendants Through His Sons, John & Thomas, 1660-1909. (Illus.). 796p. 1989. reprint ed. lib. bdg. 117.00 (*0-8328-1016-9*); reprint ed. pap. 109.00 (*0-8328-1017-7*) Higginson Bk Co.

Reeday, T. G. The Law Relating to Banking. 5th ed. 1985. 58.00 (*0-406-64768-2*); pap. 46.00 (*0-406-64769-0*, U.K.) Butterworth Legal Pubs.

Reeday, T. G. & Smart, P. E. Legal Decisions Affecting Bankers, 1879-1990, 12 vols., Set. 1991. 1,100.00 (*0-86205-245-9*, U.K.) Butterworth Legal Pubs.

Reede, Silver. Atlanta's Business & Employment Guide. (Illus.). 240p. (C). 1991. per. 29.95 (*0-944449-08-5*) Silver Reede Servs.

— Florida's Business & Employer's Directory for Orlando & the Space Coast: Orlando, Jacksonville, Titusville. (Illus.). 144p. (C). 1989. per., pap. 32.95 (*0-944449-07-7*) Silver Reede Servs.

— Florida's Gold Coast Business & Employer's Directory: Palm Beach, Ft. Lauderdale, Miami Metro Areas. rev. ed. (Illus.). 240p. (C). 1989. per., pap. 34.95 (*0-944449-05-0*) Silver Reede Servs.

— Florida's Gulf Coast Business & Employer's Directory: Tampa, Clearwater, St. Pete Metro Areas. rev. ed. (Illus.). 144p. (C). 1988. per., pap. 29.95 (*0-944449-06-9*) Silver Reede Servs.

Reeder, Carolyn. Grandpa's Mountain. LC 90-27126. 176p. (J). 1993. reprint ed. pap. 3.99 (*0-380-71914-2*, Camelot) Avon.

— Moonshiner's Son. 208p. (J). 1995. pap. 3.99 (*0-380-72251-8*, Camelot) Avon.

— Moonshiner's Son. LC 92-39570. 208p. (J). (gr. 3-7). 1993. text ed. 14.95 (*0-02-775805-2*, Mac Bks Young Read) S&S Childrens.

— Shades of Gray. 160p. (J). 1991. pap. 3.99 (*0-380-71232-6*, Camelot) Avon.

— Shades of Gray. LC 89-31976. 160p. (J). (gr. 3-7). 1989. text ed. 13.95 (*0-02-775810-9*, Mac Bks Young Read) S&S Childrens.

— Shades of Gray. braille ed. 230p. 1991. Braille. vinyl bd. 18.40 (*1-56956-314-4*, BR8548) W A T Braille.

Reeder, Carolyn & Reeder, Jack. Shenandoah Heritage: The Story of the People Before the Park. LC 78-61240. 88p. 1988. 6.00 (*0-915746-10-7*) Potomac Appalach.

— Shenandoah Secrets. 184p. 1991. pap. 12.95 (*0-915746-41-7*) Potomac Appalach.

— Shenandoah Vestiges: What the Mountain People Left Behind. LC 80-81761. 72p. 1993. pap. 5.00 (*0-915746-14-X*) Potomac Appalach.

Reeder, Clarence A., Jr. The History of Utah's Railroads, Eighteen Sixty-Nine to Eighteen Eighty-Three. Bruchey, Stuart, ed. LC 80-1288. (Railroads Ser.). (Illus.). 1981. lib. bdg. 49.95 (*0-405-13759-1*) Ayer.

Reeder, Colin. West Meadow Books. Hayes, Barbara, ed. (Illus.). (C). 1989. 65.00 (*1-85183-009-X*, Silent Bks) St Mut.

Reeder, Dan. The Simple Screamer: A Guide to the Art of Papier & Cloth Mache. (Illus.). 96p. 1984. pap. 16.95 (*0-87905-163-9*, Peregrine Smith) Gibbs Smith Pub.

Reeder, David, ed. see Dyos, H. J.

Reeder, DeeAnn M., jt. ed. see Wilson, Don E.

***Reeder, Dottie.** From Blueberries to Wild Roses: A Northwoods Wild Foods Cookbook. (Illus.). 128p. (Orig.). 1995. pap. 9.95 (*1-879432-15-3*) Explorers Guide Pub.

Reeder, Edwin H. A Method of Directing Children's Study of Geography. LC 73-177184. (Columbia University. Teachers College. Contributions to Education Ser.: No. 193). reprint ed. 37.50 (*0-404-55193-9*) AMS Pr.

Reeder, Ellen D. Hellenistic Art in the Walters Art Gallery. Moss, Troy, ed. (Illus.). 260p. 1988. pap. 40.00 (*0-911886-35-4*) Walters Art.

Reeder, Ellen D., ed. Hellenistic Art in the Walters Art Gallery. 260p. 1989. text ed. 85.00 (*0-691-04069-9*) Princeton U Pr.

Reeder, Glenn, jt. ed. see Pryor, John.

Reeder, Harry P. The Work of Felix Kaufmann. (Current Continental Research Ser.: No. 220). 238p. (C). 1991. lib. bdg. 60.00 (*0-8191-7728-8*) U Pr of Amer.

Reeder, J. C., jt. auth. see Mowbray, E. J.

Reeder, Jack, jt. auth. see Reeder, Carolyn.

Reeder, Jefferson, ed. see Bouchard, Ronald A.

Reeder, Jefferson, ed. see National Association of College & University Business Officers Staff.

Reeder, John D. & Andelman, Samuel M. MRI Atlas of the Joints: Normal Anatomy & Pathology. (Illus.). 226p. 1992. 85.00 (*0-683-07214-5*) Williams & Wilkins.

Reeder, John P., Jr. Killing & Saving: Abortion, Hunger, & War. LC 93-2510. 1995. 35.00 (*0-271-01028-2*); pap. 16.95 (*0-271-01029-0*) Pa St U Pr.

Reeder, John P., Jr., jt. ed. see Outka, Gene.

***Reeder, Josh.** Indexing Genealogy Publications. Earnest, Corinne, ed. & pref. by. (Illus.). 48p. (Orig.). 1994. pap. 13.90 (*1-879311-08-9*) R D Earnest.

Reeder, Kenneth, ed. see Pellegrini, Anthony D.

Reeder, Maurice M. Reeder & Felson's Gamuts in Bone, Joint, & Spine Radiology: Comprehensive Lists of Roentgen Differential Diagnosis. xx, 501p. 1993. pap. 35.00 (*0-387-94016-2*) Spr-Verlag.

— Reeder & Felson's Gamuts in Cardiovascular Radiology: Comprehensive Lists of Radiographic & Angiographic Differential Diagnosis. LC 93-46633. 1994. 25.00 (*0-387-94219-X*) Spr-Verlag.

Reeder, Maurice M. & Bradley, William G., Jr. Reeder & Felson's Gamuts in Neuroradiology: Comprehensive Lists of roentgen & MRI Differential Diagnosis. LC 93-10195. 1993. Alk. paper. 30.00 (*0-387-94034-0*) Spr-Verlag.

— Reeder & Felson's Gamuts in Radiology: Comprehensive Lists of Roentgen Differential Diagnosis. 3rd ed. LC 92-49707. 640p. 1992. 79.00 (*0-387-97891-7*); write for info. (*3-540-97891-7*) Spr-Verlag.

Reeder, Pat. Using PC Tools 6. Hanson, Kevin C., ed. (LogicNotes Ser.). (Illus.). (Orig.). 1990. pap. text ed. write for info. (*0-929978-30-7*) M-USA Busn Systs.

Reeder, R. J., ed. Carbonates: Mineralogy & Chemistry. (Reviews in Mineralogy Ser.: Vol. 11). 394p. 1983. 17.00 (*0-939950-15-4*) Mineralogical Soc.

Reeder, R. L., et al. Investigations in the Lower Perche-Hinkson Drainage. (Illus.). xvii, 258p. 1983. 10.00 (*0-917111-00-1*) Mus Anthro MO.

Reeder, Rachael, ed. Liturgy: The Holy Cross. (Liturgy, the Quarterly Journal of the Liturgical Conference: Vol. 1, No. 1). (Illus.). 76p. 1980. pap. 7.95 (*0-918208-00-9*) Liturgical Conf.

Reeder, Rachel. Liturgy: Holy Places. (Quarterly Journal of The Liturgical Conference: Vol. 3, No. 4). (Illus.). 96p. (Orig.). 1983. pap. text ed. 7.95 (*0-918208-32-7*) Liturgical Conf.

Reeder, Rachel, ed. The Art of Celebration. (Liturgy Ser.). 96p. (Orig.). 1990. pap. 10.95 (*0-918208-50-5*) Liturgical Conf.

— Glad Shouts. (Liturgy Ser.). 104p. (Orig.). 1990. pap. 10.95 (*0-918208-52-1*) Liturgical Conf.

— A Life to Share. (Liturgy Ser.). 92p. (Orig.). 1990. 10.95 (*0-918208-53-X*) Liturgical Conf.

— Liturgy: Celebrating Marriage, Vol. 4, No. 2. (Illus.). 80p. 1984. pap. text ed. 8.95 (*0-918208-34-3*) Liturgical Conf.

— Liturgy: Central Symbols. (Quarterly Journal of The Liturgical Conference: Vol. 7, No. 1). (Illus.). 96p. (Orig.). 1988. pap. text ed. 9.95 (*0-918208-45-9*) Liturgical Conf.

— Liturgy: Covenant with the World. (Quarterly Journal of The Liturgical Conference: Vol. 6, No. 4). 112p. 1987. pap. 8.95 (*0-918208-44-0*) Liturgical Conf.

— Liturgy: Diakonia. (Journals of The Liturgical Conference: Vol. 2, No. 4). (Illus.). 84p. (Orig.). 1982. pap. 7.95 (*0-918208-28-9*) Liturgical Conf.

— Liturgy: Ethics & Justice. (Quarterly Journal of The Liturgical Conference: Vol. 7, No. 4). (Illus.). 111p. (Orig.). 1989. pap. text ed. 10.95 (*0-918208-48-3*) Liturgical Conf.

— Liturgy: Feasts & Fasting. (Quarterly Journal of The Liturgical Conference: Vol. 2, No. 1). (Illus.). 80p. (Orig.). 1981. pap. text ed. 7.95 (*0-918208-25-4*) Liturgical Conf.

— Liturgy: In Spirit & Truth. (Quarterly Journal of The Liturgical Conference: Vol. 5, No. 3). (Illus.). 96p. (Orig.). pap. text ed. 8.95 (*0-918208-39-4*) Liturgical Conf.

— Liturgy: Language & Metaphor, Vol. 4, No.4. (Quarterly Journal of The Liturgical Conference). (Illus.). 95p. (Orig.). 1985. pap. 8.95 (*0-918208-35-1*) Liturgical Conf.

— Liturgy: Ministries to the Sick. (Quarterly Journal of The Liturgical Conference: Vol. 2, No. 2 of Liturgy). (Illus.). 80p. 1982. 7.95 (*0-918208-26-2*) Liturgical Conf.

— Liturgy: One Church, Many Churches. (Quarterly Journal of The Liturgical Conference: Vol. 3, No. 2). (Illus.). 96p. (Orig.). 1983. pap. text ed. 7.95 (*0-918208-30-0*) Liturgical Conf.

— Liturgy: Putting on Christ, Vol. 4, No. 1. (Illus.). 80p. 1983. pap. text ed. 8.95 (*0-918208-33-5*) Liturgical Conf.

— Liturgy: Scripture & the Assembly. (Quarterly Journal of The Liturgical Conference: Vol. 2, No. 3 of Liturgy). (Illus.). 80p. 1982. 7.95 (*0-918208-27-0*) Liturgical Conf.

— Liturgy: Teaching Prayer. (Quarterly Journal of The Liturgical Conference: Vol. 5, No. 1). (Illus.). 96p. (Orig.). pap. text ed. 8.95 (*0-918208-37-8*) Liturgical Conf.

— Liturgy: The Calendar. (Liturgy, the Quarterly Journal of the Liturgical Conference: Vol. 1, No. 2). (Illus.). 92p. 1980. pap. 7.65 (*0-918208-01-7*) Liturgical Conf.

— Liturgy: The Healing Word. (Quarterly Journal of The Liturgical Conference: Vol. 7, No. 2). (Illus.). 104p. (Orig.). 1988. pap. text ed. 10.95 (*0-318-41831-2*) Liturgical Conf.

— Liturgy: The Power That Unites, Vol. 6, No. 2. (Illus.). 96p. (Orig.). 1986. pap. 8.95 (*0-918208-42-4*) Liturgical Conf.

— Liturgy: The Song of All Creation. (Quarterly Journal of The Liturgical Conference: Vol. 6 No. 3). (Illus.). 88p. (Orig.). 1987. pap. 8.95 (*0-918208-43-2*) Liturgical Conf.

— Liturgy: With All the Saints. (Quarterly Journal of The Liturgical Conference: Vol. 5, No. 2). (Illus.). 112p. (Orig.). pap. text ed. 8.95 (*0-918208-38-6*) Liturgical Conf.

— Liturgy: With Lyre & Harp. (Quarterly Journal of The Liturgical Conference: Vol. 3, No. 3). (Illus.). 88p. (Orig.). 1983. pap. text ed. 7.95 (*0-918208-31-9*) Liturgical Conf.

— Rhythms of Prayer. (Liturgy Ser.). 104p. (Orig.). 1990. pap. 10.95 (*0-918208-51-3*) Liturgical Conf.

Reeder, Ray. Bach English-Title Index. LC 92-37177. (Reference Books in Music: No. 20). viii, 184p. 1993. 33.00 (*0-914913-23-9*) Fallen Leaf.

Reeder, Robert H., jt. auth. see Fisher, Edward C.

Reeder, Robert R., et al. Industrial Marketing: Analysis, Planning, & Control. 2nd ed. 704p. (C). 1991. text ed. 39.00 (*0-13-457110-X*, 150106) P-H.

Reeder, Roberta. Anna Akhmatova: Poet & Prophet. 640p. 1994. 35.00 (*0-312-11241-6*) St Martin.

Reeder, Roberta, ed. & tr. Russian Folk Lyrics. LC 92-7155. (Illus.). 288p. 1992. 35.00 (*0-253-34623-1*); pap. 15.95 (*0-253-20749-5*, MB-749) Ind U Pr.

Reeder, Roberta, tr. see Lezhnev, A.

Reeder, Rudolph R. How Two Hundred Children Live & Learn. LC 74-1701. (Children & Youth Ser.). 252p. 1974. reprint ed. 25.95 (*0-405-05978-7*) Ayer.

Reeder, S. Gail. Creative Applique. (Illus.). 32p. 1984. pap. 7.95 (*0-910585-02-4*) Willcraft.

— Creative Cutwork. (Illus.). 16p. (Orig.). 1988. pap. 7.95 (*0-910585-05-9*) Willcraft.

Reeder, S. Gail, ed. Succesful Machine Applique. LC 78-72878. (Illus.). 48p. 1978. pap. 6.00 (*0-932946-01-1*) Burdett CA.

Reeder, Sharon J., jt. auth. see Martin, Leonide L.

Reeder, Sharon J., et al. Maternity Nursing: Family, Newborn & Women's Health Care. 17th ed. (Illus.). 1376p. 1992. text ed. 56.95 (*0-397-54813-3*) Lippincott.

Reeder, T. Jefferson, ed. Financial Accounting & Reporting Manual for Higher Education. 1990. 545.00 (*0-915164-57-4*) NACUBO.

Reeder, T. Jefferson, ed. see Hughes, K. Scott, et al.

Reeder, Tony. The Black Lotus. 175p. (C). 1990. 39.00 (*0-947333-17-7*, Pub. by Pascoe Pub AT) St Mut.

Reeder, W. Donald. Letters of John & Jude. (Teach Yourself the Bible Ser.). (C). 1965. pap. 3.99 (*0-8024-4674-4*) Moody.

Reeder, William G., ed. see Bruni, Mary A.

Reeders, J. W., et al. Ischaemic Colitis. (Illus.). 200p. 1984. lib. bdg. 122.50 (*0-89838-645-4*) Kluwer Ac.

Reeders, Jacques W. & Rosenbusch, Gerd. Clinical Radiology & Endoscopy of the Colon. Winter, Peter, ed. Bergman, Clifford et al, trs. LC 93-30486. (Illus.). 1993. 199.00 (*0-86577-508-7*) Thieme Med Pubs.

Reedijk, Jan. Bioinorganic Catalysis. 496p. 1993. 195.00 (*0-8247-9004-9*) Dekker.

Reedman, J. H. Techniques in Mineral Exploration. (Illus.). 526p. 1979. 142.25 (*0-85334-817-0*, Pub. by Elsevier Applied Sci UK); pap. 88.25 (*0-85334-851-0*, Pub. by Elsevier Applied Sci UK) Elsevier.

Reeds & Mitchell Staff. Standard Catalogue of British Coins. 30th ed. 1994. 24.95 (*0-7134-7671-0*, Pub. by Seaby UK) Trafalgar.

Reeds, Brian & Mitchell, Stephen. Standard Catalog of British Coins. 28th ed. (Illus.). 370p. 1993. 29.95 (*0-317-05150-4*, Pub. by Seaby UK) Trafalgar.

Reeds, Brian, jt. ed. see Mitchell, Stephen.

Reeds, Karen M. Botany in Medieval & Renaissance Universities. rev. ed. Gingerich, Owen, ed. LC 91-30721. (Harvard Dissertations in the History of Science Ser.). (Illus.). 392p. 1992. reprint ed. 86.00 (*0-8240-7449-1*) Garland.

Reeds, Roger C. Biblical Graphics. 1977. 6.95 (*0-89265-058-3*); pap. 5.95 (*0-89265-042-7*) Randall Hse.

— Pupil Profiles. (Sunday School Workers Training Course Ser.: No. 3). (C). 1973. pap. 6.95 (*0-89265-010-9*) Randall Hse.

Reedstrom, E. Lisle. Apache Wars: An Illustrated Battle History. LC 90-38971. (Illus.). 272p. (YA). (gr. 10-12). 1992. pap. 19.95 (*0-8069-7255-6*) Sterling.

— Custer's Seventh Cavalry: From Fort Riley to the Little Big Horn. LC 92-26524. (Illus.). 176p. (YA). (gr. 10-12). 1992. pap. 14.95 (*0-8069-8762-6*) Sterling.

— Note Cards of Color-Bearers. 7.95 (*0-685-71943-X*, J M C & Co) Amereon Ltd.

— Scrapbook of the American West. LC 90-43034. (Illus.). 1991. pap. 17.95 (*0-87004-303-X*) Caxton.

— Story of Baseball Coloring Book. (Illus.). (J). (gr. k-3). 1991. pap. 2.95 (*0-486-26748-2*) Dover.

Reedstrom, Ernest L. Bugles, Banners, & War Bonnets. LC 77-165608. 384p. reprint ed. pap. 109.50 (*0-8357-7461-9*, 2023062) Bks Demand.

Reedy & Miller. Allergic Skin Diseases in Dogs & Cats. 256p. 1989. pap. text ed. 32.95 (*0-7216-2432-4*) Saunders.

Reedy, Barry L. The New Health Practitioners in America: A Comparative Study. 1978. text ed. 27.95 (*0-8464-0671-3*) Beekman Pubs.

Reedy, Chandra L., jt. auth. see Reedy, Terry J.

Reedy, Daniel & Bustamante, Cecilia. Magda Portal's Truth & Hope: A XX Century Feminist of Latin America. (Seagreen Ser.). (Illus.). 200p. (C). 1989. pap. 12.95 (*0-685-30777-8*) Extramares Edit.

***Reedy, Dennis, ed.** School & Community History of Dickenson County, Virginia. (Illus.). 520p. 1994. 21.95 (*1-57072-010-X*) Overmountain Pr.

Reedy, E. K., jt. auth. see Eaves, J. L.

Reedy, G. V. Erotic Sculptures of Ancient India. (C). 1991. 42.00 (*81-210-0261-3*, Pub. by Inter-India Pubns) S Asia.

Reedy, George E. Twilight of the Presidency: From Johnson to Reagan. rev. ed. 208p. 1971. pap. 4.50 (*0-451-62510-2*, Sig) NAL-Dutton.

Reedy, Gerard. Robert South (1634-1716) An Introduction to His Life & Sermons. (Studies in Eighteenth-Century English Literature & Thought: No. 12). (Illus.). 200p. (C). 1992. 54.95 (*0-521-40164-X*) Cambridge U Pr.

Reedy, Jeremiah, tr. The Platonic Doctrines of Albinus. LC 91-25598. 81p. (Orig.). 1991. 20.00 (*0-933999-14-3*); pap. 12.00 (*0-933999-15-1*) Phanes Pr.

Reedy, Joel. Marketing to Consumers with Disabilities: How to Identify & Meet the Growing Market Needs of 43 Million Americans. 240p. 1993. 32.50 (*1-55738-478-9*) Probus Pub Co.

Reedy, Terry J. & Reedy, Chandra L. Statistical Analysis in Art Conservation Research: Research in Conservation, No. 1. LC 88-2994. (Technical Report Ser.). 108p. 1988. pap. 20.00 (*0-89236-097-6*) J P Getty Trust.

Reedy, Thomas. The Hand of Zerubbabel. 140p. (Orig.). 1993. pap. 7.99 (*1-56043-789-8*) Destiny Image.

Reedy, William J., ed. Becoming a Catholic Christian. 198p. pap. 10.80 (*0-8215-9326-9*) Sadlier.

Reef, Catherine. Albert Einstein. LC 91-7560. (Taking Part Ser.). (Illus.). 64p. (J). (gr. 3 up). 1991. text ed. 13.95 (*0-87518-462-6*, Dillon Silver Burdett) Silver Burdett Pr.

— Arlington National Cemetery. LC 91-17183. (Places in American History Ser.). (Illus.). 72p. (J). (gr. 4-6). 1991. text ed. 14.95 (*0-87518-471-5*, Dillon Silver Burdett) Silver Burdett Pr.

— Baltimore. LC 89-25695. (Downtown America Ser.). (Illus.). 60p. (J). (gr. 3 up). 1990. text ed. 13.95 (*0-87518-427-8*, Dillon Silver Burdett) Silver Burdett Pr.

— Baltimore. (Illus.). 60p. (J). (gr. 3 up). 1990. write for info. (*0-685-31388-3*, Mac Bks Young Read) S&S Childrens.

— Benjamin Davis, Jr. (African-American Soldiers Ser.). (Illus.). 80p. (J). (gr. 4-7). 1992. lib. bdg. 14.98 (*0-8050-2137-X*) TFC Bks NY.

— Black Fighting Men: A Proud History. (African-American Soldiers Ser.). (Illus.). 80p. (J). (gr. 4-7). 1994. bds. 14.98 (*0-8050-3106-5*) TFC Bks NY.

— The Buffalo Soldiers. (African-American Soldiers Ser.). (Illus.). 80p. (J). (gr. 4-7). 1993. lib. bdg. 14.98 (*0-8050-2372-0*) TFC Bks NY.

— Civil War Soldiers. (African-American Soldiers Ser.). (Illus.). 80p. (J). (gr. 4-7). 1993. lib. bdg. 14.98 (*0-8050-2371-2*) TFC Bks NY.

— Colin Powell. (African-American Soldiers Ser.). (Illus.). 80p. (J). (gr. 4-7). 1992. lib. bdg. 14.98 (*0-8050-2136-1*) TFC Bks NY.

— Eat the Right Stuff: Food Facts. LC 93-1370. 64p. (J). (gr. 4-7). 1993. lib. bdg. 15.98 (*0-8050-2442-5*) TFC Bks NY.

— Ellis Island. LC 91-18755. (Places in American History Ser.). (Illus.). 72p. (J). (gr. 4-6). 1991. text ed. 14.95 (*0-87518-473-1*, Dillon Silver Burdett) Silver Burdett Pr.

— Gettysburg. LC 91-43653. (Places in American History Ser.). (Illus.). 72p. (J). (gr. 4 up). 1992. text ed. 14.95 (*0-87518-503-7*, Dillon Silver Burdett) Silver Burdett Pr.

— Good Health Guidelines Series, 3 vols., Set. (Illus.). 64p. (J). (gr. 4-7). 1994. lib. bdg. 47.94 (*0-8050-3453-6*) TFC Bks NY.

— Henry David Thoreau: A Neighbor to Nature. (Earth Keepers Ser.). (Illus.). 72p. (J). (gr. 4-7). 1992. lib. bdg. 14.98 (*0-941477-39-8*) TFC Bks NY.

— Jacques Cousteau: Champion of the Sea. (Earth Keepers Ser.). (Illus.). 72p. (J). (gr. 4-7). 1992. lib. bdg. 14.98 (*0-8050-2114-0*) TFC Bks NY.

— John Steinbeck. LC 95-11500. (J). 1996. write for info. (*0-395-71278-5*, Clarion Bks) HM.

— The Lincoln Memorial. LC 93-13708. (Places in American History Ser.). (Illus.). 72p. (J). (gr. 4 up). 1994. text ed. 14.95 (*0-87518-624-6*, Dillon Silver Burdett) Silver Burdett Pr.

— Monticello. LC 91-15850. (Places in American History Ser.). (Illus.). 72p. (J). (gr. 4-6). 1991. text ed. 14.95 (*0-87518-472-3*, Dillon Silver Burdett) Silver Burdett Pr.

— Mount Vernon. LC 91-33494. (Places in American History Ser.). (Illus.). 72p. (J). (gr. 4 up). 1992. text ed. 14.95 (*0-87518-474-X*, Dillon Silver Burdett) Silver Burdett Pr.

— Rachel Carson: The Wonder of Nature. (Earth Keepers Ser.). (Illus.). 68p. (J). (gr. 4-7). 1992. lib. bdg. 14.98 (*0-941477-38-X*) TFC Bks NY.

— Ralph David Abernathy. LC 94-28623. (People in Focus Ser.). (Illus.). (J). (gr. 5). 1995. 13.95 (*0-87518-653-X*, Dillon Silver Burdett) Silver Burdett Pr.

— Stay Fit: Build a Strong Body. LC 93-19349. (Good Health Guidelines Ser.). 64p. (J). (gr. 4-7). 1993. 15.98 (*0-8050-2441-7*) TFC Bks NY.

— The Supreme Court. LC 93-21506. (Places in American History Ser.). (Illus.). 72p. (J). (gr. 4-7). 1994. lib. bdg. 14.95 (*0-87518-626-2*, Dillon Silver Burdett) Silver Burdett Pr.

— Think Positive: Cope with Stress. LC 93-3973. (Good Health Guidelines Ser.). (J). (gr. 4-7). 1993. 15.98 (*0-8050-2443-3*) TFC Bks NY.

— Walt Whitman. LC 94-7405. (J). 1995. 16.95 (*0-395-68705-5*, Clarion Bks) HM.

— Washington, D. C. LC 89-12025. (Downtown America Ser.). (Illus.). 60p. (J). (gr. 3 up). 1990. text ed. 13.95 (*0-87518-411-1*, Dillon Silver Burdett) Silver Burdett Pr.

***Reef, Catherine M.** Ralph David Abernathy. LC 94-28623. (People in Focus Ser.). (Illus.). (YA). (gr. 5 up). 1995. pap. 7.95 (*0-382-24965-8*, Dillon Silver Burdett) Silver Burdett Pr.

Reef, Pat. Bernard Langlais, Sculptor. LC 84-81337. (Illus.). 48p. (J). (gr. 3-7). 1985. pap. 9.95 (*0-933858-06-X*) Kennebec River.

Reef, Pat D. Dahlov Ipcar, Artist. (Maine Artists for Young Readers Ser.: No. 2). (Illus.). 48p. (J). (gr. 3-7). 1987. pap. 12.95 (*0-933858-20-5*) Kennebec River.

— William Thon, Painter. (Maine Artists for Young Readers Ser.: No. 3). (Illus.). 56p. (J). (gr. 4-7). 1991. pap. 12.95 (*0-933858-28-0*) Kennebec River.

Reefman, William E. How to Sell Your Own Invention. (Illus.). 1977. pap. 10.00 (*0-912256-11-7*) Halls of Ivy.

Reegan, S. L., jt. ed. see Frisch, Kurt C.

Reegen, S. L., jt. ed. see Frisch, K. C.

Reegen, S. L., jt. auth. see Frisch, Kurt C.

Reegen, Sidney L., jt. ed. see Frisch, Kurt C.

Reeh, Merrill J., et al. Ophthalmic Anatomy. (Illus.). 290p. 1981. 25.00 (*0-317-94082-1*) Am Acad Ophthal.

Reejal, P. R. Monetary & Credit Policies of the Nepal Rastra Bank & Their Impact on the Nepalese Economy. 1986. 75.00 (*0-7855-0248-3*, Pub. by Ratna Pustak Bhandar) St Mut.

Reejal, P. R., ed. Monetary & Credit Policies of the Nepal Rastra Bank & Their Impact on the Nepalese Economy. 100p. (C). 1987. 220.00 (*0-89771-051-7*, Pub. by Ratna Pustak Bhandar) St Mut.

Reejhsingani, Aroona. Vegetarian Wonders from Gujarat. 140p. 1978. 5.95 (*0-318-36306-2*) Asia Bk Corp.

R

An Asterisk (*) at the beginning of an entry indicates that the title is appearing in BIP for the first time.

Reejhsinghani, Aroona. The Art of South Indian Cooking. 141p. 1982. 6.95 (*0-318-36302-X*) Asia Bk Corp.
— Cookery Around India. 184p. 1984. pap. 4.50 (*0-86578-232-6*) Ind-US Inc.
— Cooking the Punjabi Way. 137p. 1990. 6.95 (*0-318-36283-X*) Asia Bk Corp.
— Delicious Bengali Dishes. 162p. 1980. 5.95 (*0-318-36285-6*) Asia Bk Corp.
— Delights from Goa. 135p. 1987. 5.95 (*0-318-36286-4*) Asia Bk Corp.
— Delights from Maharashtra. 162p. 1980. 5.95 (*0-318-36287-2*) Asia Bk Corp.
Reeker, Hans-Dieter. Die Landschaft in der Aeneis. Bd. XXVII. xii, 192p. 1971. write for info. (*0-318-71211-3*, Pub. by Georg Olms GW) Lubrecht & Cramer.
Reekie, Duncan W. & Weber, Michael H. Profits, Politics & Drugs. LC 78-24496. 185p. 1979. 49.50 (*0-8419-0461-8*) Holmes & Meier.
Reekie, H. Martin, jt. auth. see Murray, Alan F.
Reekie, Jennie. The London Ritz Book of Christmas: The Art & Pleasures of a Traditional Christmas. LC 90-61081. (Illus.). 64p. 1990. reprint ed. 10.95 (*0-688-10097-X*) Morrow.
Reekie, Robert. Llamados a Escribir (Called to Write) (SPA.). 1992. 3.99 (*1-56063-108-2*, 498421) Editorial Unilit.
Reekie, Robert, ed. Servant of Words: A Tribute to James L. Johnson, Mentor to Writer & Other Communicators. 1992. pap. 8.99 (*0-8024-7926-X*) Moody.
Reekie, Shirley H. Sailing Made Simple. LC 86-10393. (Illus.). 168p. (Orig.). 1986. pap. 16.95 (*0-88011-278-6*, PREE0278) Human Kinetics.
***Reekie, W. Duncan.** Government in Healthcare: Lessons from the U. K. (Illus.). 120p. (Orig.). 1995. pap. 6.95 (*1-883969-02-6*) CSU Smith Ctr.
— Industrial Economics: A Critical Introduction to Corporate Enterprise in Europe & America. 208p. 1989. text ed. 59.95 (*1-85278-074-6*, Pub. by E Elgar Pub UK) Ashgate Pub Co.
Reekie, W. Duncan & Allen, D. E. The Economics of Modern Business. 2nd ed. 248p. (C). 1991. pap. text ed. 32.95 (*0-631-17215-7*) Blackwell Pubs.
Reekie, W. Duncan & Crook, Jonathan N. Managerial Economics. 4th ed. LC 94-894. 1995. pap. text ed. 52.00 (*0-13-100520-0*) P-H.
Reekle, Gail. Temptations: Sex & Selling in the Department Store. (Illus.). 240p. 1993. pap. text ed. 19.95 (*1-86373-342-6*, Pub. by Allen Unwin AT) Paul & Co Pubs.
Reeks, Lindsay S. Ancestors of Reeks & Rogers, Christchurch, Dorset. LC 88-83492. (Illus.). 235p. 1989. 25.00 (*0-9616950-1-3*) L S Reeks.
— Ontario Loyalist Ancestors. LC 92-73836. (Illus.). 235p. 1992. 30.00 (*0-9616950-2-1*) L S Reeks.
— Scottish Coalmining Ancestors. LC 86-81614. (Illus.). 292p. 1986. 25.00 (*0-9616950-0-5*) L S Reeks.
***Reel, et al.** The Blood of Innocents. 432p. 1995. pap. 4.99 (*0-7860-0177-1*) Windsor NY.
Reel, Bill, jt. auth. see Newsday Staff.
Reel, Guy. Unequal Justice: Wayne Dumond, Bill Clinton & the Politics of Rape in Arkansas. 263p. 1993. 22.95 (*0-87975-841-4*) Prometheus Bks.
Reel, Jerome V., Jr. Index to Biographies of Englishmen, 1000-1485: Found in Dissertations & Theses. LC 74-19807. 689p. 1975. text ed. 79.50 (*0-8371-7846-0*, RIB/, Greenwood Pr) Greenwood.
Reel, Joseph P. Use Both Brains. LC 80-82602. (Illus.). 104p. (Orig.). 1980. pap. 14.95 (*0-938024-00-0*) Human Dev Pr.
Reel, Nancy. Macintosh Notebook: Chart. write for info. (*0-318-59656-3*) S&S Trade.
Reel, Richard. Two Gun Reel. LC 91-67925. 194p. 1993. pap. 12.95 (*1-56002-185-3*, Univ Edtns) Aegina Pr.
Reeling, Patricia & Varlejs, Jana, eds. Education for the Library - Information Profession: Strategies for the Mid-1990s. LC 92-51096. 96p. 1993. pap. 13.95 (*0-89950-892-8*) McFarland & Co.
***Reels, Hilda.** Go & Tell. 1995. 9.95 (*0-8062-5161-1*) Carlton.
Reeman, Douglas. Path of the Storm. large type ed. 1980. 12.00 (*0-7089-0486-6*) Ulverscroft.
— A Prayer for the Ship. large type ed. 1975. 15.95 (*0-85456-329-6*) Ulverscroft.
— Send a Gunboat. 256p. 1986. reprint ed. lib. bdg. 19.95 (*0-89966-557-8*) Buccaneer Bks.
— To Risks Unknown. large type ed. 576p. 1981. 15.95 (*0-7089-0893-4*) Ulverscroft.
Reemes, Dana M. Directed by Jack Arnold. LC 87-46382. (Illus.). 255p. 1988. lib. bdg. 32.50x (*0-89950-331-4*) McFarland & Co.
Re'emi, P., jt. auth. see Martin-Achard, R.
Re'emi, Paul S., jt. auth. see Coggins, Richard J.
Reemsnyder, H. S. & Throop, J. F., eds. Residual Stress Effects in Fatigue-- STP 776. 241p. 1982. 26.50 (*0-8031-0711-0*, 04-776000-30) ASTM.
Reen, D. R., jt. ed. see Gosling, J. P.
Reenan, Andrew M. The Chocolate Lover's Handbook: How to Eat & Enjoy Chocolate Without Guilt & Without Gaining Weight. rev. ed. Clark, Teresa J., ed. LC 93-71146. (Illus.). 260p. 1993. pap. text ed. 14.95 (*0-9636482-0-9*) Action Pubns.
Reenstjerna, Frederick R. Library Survival Skills: Beginning Research Techniques Using the James E. Morrow Library. 68p. 1990. spiral bd. 12.95 (*0-8403-6130-0*) Kendall-Hunt.
Reents-Budet, Dorie. Painting the Maya Universe: Royal Ceramics of the Classic Period. LC 93-29587. (Illus.). 404p. 1994. 75.00 (*0-8223-1434-7*); pap. 39.95 (*0-8223-1438-X*) Duke.
Reep, Diana. The Rescue & Romances: Popular Novels Before World War 1. LC 82-61169. 144p. 1982. 13.95 (*0-87972-211-8*); pap. 7.95 (*0-87972-212-6*) Bowling Green Univ.
Reep, Diana C. Margaret Deland. (United States Authors Ser.: No. 479). 152p. 1985. lib. bdg. 22.95 (*0-8057-7420-3*, Twayne) Macmillan.
— Technical Writing: Principles, Strategies, & Readings. 2nd ed. LC 93-29668. 619p. 1993. pap. text ed. 36.00 (*0-205-15513-8*) Allyn.
Reep, Edward. A Combat Artist in World War II. LC 86-22380. (Illus.). 224p. 1987. 25.00 (*0-8131-1602-3*) U Pr of Ky.
Reep, James W. & Reep, Reynold F. Reep Family Bibliography. LC 81-85071. (Illus.). 196p. 1985. 14.00 (*0-9614602-0-2*) James Reep.
Reep, Marianna L. & Plass, Richard M. New York State Regents Biology Laboratory Manual. (Illus.). 138p. (YA). (gr. 8-11). 1989. 5.95 (*0-685-29317-3*) Amer Scholastic.
Reep, R., ed. Relationship Between Prefrontal & Limbic Cortex: A Comparative Anatomical Review. (Journal: Brain, Behavior & Evolution: Vol. 25, Nos. 1-2). (Illus.). 80p. 1985. pap. 44.00 (*3-8055-4033-7*) S Karger.
Reep, Reynold F., jt. auth. see Reep, James W.
Reepen, Ronald. Lefty Meets Hefty. (Illus.). 40p. (J). (gr. 2-7). 1987. 6.95 (*0-930905-02-4*) Platypus Bks.
Rees. Credit Union Teller Handbook. 128p. (C). 1994. per., pap. text ed. 3.79 (*0-8403-5858-X*) Kendall-Hunt.
— Manual of Soccer Coaching. 1988. pap. text ed. 14.95 (*0-937347-19-1*) C & D Intl.
— Rhinoplasty Problems & Controversies: A Discussion with the Experts. 448p. 1986. 99.00 (*0-8016-4111-X*) Mosby Yr Bk.
***Rees & CUNA Staff.** Human Resource Management. 160p. 1994. per., pap. text ed. 10.42 (*0-7872-0181-2*) Kendall-Hunt.
Rees & Leiner, eds. Gradient-Index Optics & Miniature Optics: Critical Reviews. 1988. 48.00 (*0-89252-970-9*, 935) SPIE.
Rees, A. L. & Borzello, Frances, eds. The New Art History. LC 87-2997. 176p. (C). 1988. reprint ed. pap. 17.50 (*0-391-03552-5*) Humanities.
Rees, A. R. Ornamental Bulbs, Corms & Tubers. (Crop Production Science in Horticulture Ser.: No. 1). 220p. 1992. pap. 30.00 (*0-85198-656-0*) CAB Intl.
Rees, A. R., ed. see Society for the Environmental Therapy, Inaugural Conference, 1981: Oxford, Oxfordshire.
Rees, Alan M. Managing Consumer Health Information Services. 336p. 1991. pap. 39.50 (*0-89774-622-8*) Oryx Pr.
Rees, Alan M., ed. CHIS: Consumer Health Information Service, 1985 Index. 58p. 1985. pap. 25.00 (*0-8357-0700-8*) Univ Microfilms.
— Consumer Health Information Service, 1985-1987 Index. 120p. 1987. pap. 25.00 (*0-8357-0721-0*) Univ Microfilms.
— Consumer Health Information Service, 1987-1989 Index. 143p. 1989. pap. 25.00 (*0-8357-0808-X*) Univ Microfilms.
— Consumer Health Information Source Book. 4th ed. LC 94-26854. 240p. 1994. pap. 44.50 (*0-89774-796-8*) Oryx Pr.
— Consumer Health USA. LC 94-37594. 504p. 1994. boxed 59.40 (*0-89774-889-1*) Oryx Pr.
Rees, Albert. The Economics of Trade Unions. LC 88-4848. x, 204p. 1989. pap. text ed. 13.95 (*0-226-70710-5*) U Ch Pr.
— The Economics of Trade Unions. 2nd rev. ed. LC 77-1668. 1977. 12.50 (*0-226-70701-6*) U Ch Pr.
— New Measures of Wage-Earner Compensation in Manufacturing, 1914-57. (Occasional Papers: No. 75). 38p. 1960. reprint ed. 20.00 (*0-87014-389-1*); reprint ed. mic. film 20.00 (*0-685-61326-7*) Natl Bur Econ Res.
— Personal Health Reporter. 1992. 105.00 (*0-8103-8392-6*, 101230) Gale.
— Real Wages in Manufacturing: 1890-1914. LC 75-19735. (National Bureau of Economic Research Ser.). (Illus.). 1975. reprint ed. 20.95 (*0-405-07612-6*) Ayer.
— Real Wages in Manufacturing, 1890-1914. (General Ser.: No. 70). 179p. 1961. reprint ed. 46.60 (*0-87014-069-8*) Natl Bur Econ Res.
— Striking a Balance: Making National Economic Policy. LC 83-17881. (Illus.). x, 118p. 1984. 12.50 (*0-226-70707-5*) U Ch Pr.
— Striking a Balance: Making National Economic Policy. LC 83-17881. (Illus.). x, 118p. 1986. pap. text ed. 6.95 (*0-226-70708-3*) U Ch Pr.
Rees, Albert & Smith, Sharon P. Faculty Retirement in the Arts & Sciences. (Illus.). 103p. 1991. text ed. 25.00 (*0-691-04287-X*) Princeton U Pr.
Rees, Albert, jt. ed. see Ashenfelter, Orley.
Rees, Albert, jt. auth. see Hamermesh, Daniel S.
Rees, Allan H., et al. Pediatric Cardiology Handbook. (Illus.). 194p. 1987. 23.75 (*0-87527-348-3*) Green.
Rees, Alwyn & Rees, Brinley. Celtic Heritage: Ancient Tradition in Ireland & Wales. LC 78-63038. (Illus.). 1989. reprint ed. pap. 10.95 (*0-500-27039-2*) Thames Hudson.
Rees, Ann M. Consumer Handbook. (Illus.). 160p. 1992. pap. 20.95 (*0-632-00692-7*) Blackwell Sci.
Rees, Anthony R., et al, eds. Protein Engineering: A Practical Approach. LC 92-49381. (Practical Approach Ser.). (Illus.). 424p. (C). 1993. 79.00 (*0-19-963139-5*, IRL Pr); pap. 44.00 (*0-19-963138-7*, IRL Pr) OUP.
Rees, B. R. Pelagius: A Reluctant Heretic. 160p. (C). 1991. reprint ed. text ed. 70.00 (*0-85115-503-0*); reprint ed. pap. text ed. 25.00 (*0-85115-294-5*) Boydell & Brewer.
***Rees, Bill.** Financial Analysis. LC 95-13407. 1995. write for info. (*0-13-288283-3*) P-H.
Rees, Bill & Sheikh, Saleem. Pervasive Subjects. 250p. 1993. 34.00 (*1-85431-298-7*, Pub. by Blackstone Pr UK) W W Gaunt.
***Rees, Bob & Sherwood, Marika.** The Black Experience: In the U. S. A. & the Carribean. LC 94-38918. (Biographical History Ser.). (Illus.). 64p. (YA). (gr. 5 up). 1995. 16.95 (*0-87226-117-4*) P Bedrick Bks.
Rees, Brinley, jt. auth. see Rees, Alwyn.
Rees, C., et al, eds. Theory & Applications of Fourier Analysis. (Pure & Applied Mathematics Ser.: Vol. 59). 432p. 1981. 140.00 (*0-8247-6903-1*) Dekker.
Rees, C. Roger & Miracle, Andrew W., eds. Sport & Social Theory. LC 85-19758. 352p. 1986. pap. 22.00x (*0-87322-350-0*, BREE0350) Human Kinetics.
Rees, C. Roger, jt. auth. see Miracle, Andrew W., Jr.
Rees, C. W., jt. ed. see Capon, B.
Rees, C. W., jt. ed. see Katritzky, Alan R.
Rees, C. W., ed. see Simon, J. & Andre, J. J.
***Rees, Carol.** Hints for Upstairs, Downstairs. 134p. 1991. pap. text ed. 7.95 (*0-941162-02-8*) D Gibson.
— Household Hints for Upstairs, Downstairs, & All Around the House. LC 87-28864. 1988. pap. 7.95 (*0-8050-0765-2*, Owl) H Holt & Co.
— Household Hints for Upstairs, Downstairs & All Around the House. 1993. 5.98 (*0-88365-815-1*) Galahad Bks.
Rees, Charles S., et al. Plane Trigonometry with Tables. 7th ed. (Illus.). 1977. text ed. 23.95 (*0-685-03896-3*) P-H.
Rees, Charles W., ed. see Crossley, Roger J.
Rees, Chris. British Specialist Cars: Low Volume Production Cars & Kit Cars since World War II. (Illus.). 208p. 1993. 39.95 (*1-872004-22-9*, Pub. by Windrow & Green UK) Motorbooks Intl.
— The Complete Mini. (Illus.). 160p. 1995. 32.95 (*0-947981-88-8*, Pub. by Motor Racing UK) Motorbooks Intl.
***Rees, Christine.** Utopian Imagination & Eighteenth-Century Fiction. LC 95-13096. (Studies in Eighteenth & Nineteenth-Century Literature). (C). 1995. text ed. 49.95 (*0-582-06735-9*); pap. text ed. 19.95 (*0-582-06736-7*) Longman.
Rees, Claudia. The Bird with the Word Talks about Self-Control. (Illus.). (Orig.). (J). (gr. 1-3). 1987. pap. 0.98 (*0-89274-451-0*) Harrison Hse.
Rees, Compton, jt. auth. see Butler, Francelia.
Rees, D. Lectures on the Asymptotic Theory of Ideals. (London Mathematical Society Lecture Note Ser.: No. 113). 200p. 1988. pap. 34.95 (*0-521-31127-6*) Cambridge U Pr.
Rees, D., jt. ed. see Warwick, K.
Rees, D., et al, eds. Cospar International Reference Atmosphere: 1986: Middle Atmosphere Models, Pt. II. (Advances in Space Research Ser.: No. 10). (Illus.). 528p. 1991. pap. 105.00 (*0-08-040789-7*, Pergamon Pr) Elsevier.
Rees, D. A., ed. see Farguharson, Arthur.
Rees, D. A., ed. see Joachim, H. Henry.
Rees, D. Ben. The Life & Work of Owen Thomas, 1812-1891: A Welsh Preacher. LC 91-4083. (Welsh Studies: Vol. 3). 336p. 1991. lib. bdg. 99.95 (*0-7734-9710-2*) E Mellen.
***Rees, D. G.** Essential Statistics. 3rd ed. LC 89-31953. 265p. 1995. pap. 22.50 (*0-412-61280-1*) Chapman & Hall.
Rees, D. H. E., jt. ed. see Axford, J. S.
Rees, D. T., jt. auth. see Feeley, T.
Rees, Dafydd & Crampton, Luke. Rock Movers & Shakers: An A to Z of People Who Made Rock Happen. 608p. 1991. lib. bdg. 35.00 (*0-87436-661-5*) ABC-CLIO.
Rees, Dafyyd & Crampton, Luke. Rock Movers & Shakers: An A-Z of the People Who Made Rock Happen. enl. rev. ed. (Illus.). 608p. 1991. pap. 19.95 (*0-8230-7609-1*, Billboard Bks) Watsn-Guptill.
Rees, Daniel, jt. auth. see English Benedictine Congregation Members Staff.
Rees, Darren. Bird Impressions: A Personal View of Birds. (Illus.). 128p. 1994. 42.95 (*1-85310-286-5*) Voyageur Pr.
Rees, David. The Marble in the Water: Essays on Contemporary Writers of Fiction for Children & Young Adults. LC 80-16623. 224p. 1980. pap. 9.95 (*0-87675-281-4*) Horn Bk.
— Packing It In. 160p. (Orig.). 1992. pap. 13.95 (*1-873741-07-3*, Pub. by Millvres Bks UK) InBook.
— Painted Desert, Green Shade: Essays on Contemporary Writers for Children & Young Adults. LC 83-12996. 211p. 1984. pap. 13.95 (*0-87675-286-5*) Horn Bk.
— Sir Rhys Ap Thomas. 92p. 1992. pap. 21.00 (*0-86383-744-1*, Pub. by Gomer Pr UK) St Mut.
— The Soviet Seizure of the Kuriles. LC 84-18373. 204p. 1985. text ed. 55.00 (*0-275-90154-8*, C0154, Praeger Pubs) Greenwood.
— What Do Draculas Do? Essays on Contemporary Writers of Fiction for Children & Young Adults. LC 90-8669. 260p. 1990. 27.50 (*0-8108-2320-9*) Scarecrow.
— Words & Music. 220p. 1994. pap. 14.95 (*1-873741-11-1*, Pub. by Millvres Bks UK) InBook.
Rees, David, jt. auth. see Garrison, Terry.
Rees, David G. Essential Statistics. 256p. 1989. pap. 19.95 (*0-412-32030-4*, A3819) Chapman & Hall.
Rees, David W. Satellite Communications: the First Quarter Century of Service. 329p. 1990. text ed. 85.00 (*0-471-62243-5*) Wiley.
Rees, David W. & Smith, Simon D. Living with Tinnitus. (Living with Ser.). 176p. 1992. text ed. 24.95 (*0-7190-3366-7*, Pub. by Manchester Univ Pr UK) St Martin.
***Rees, E. A.** Stalinism & Soviet Rail Transport, 1928-41. LC 94-30652. (Studies in Soviet History & Society Ser.). 307p. 1995. 65.00 (*0-312-12381-7*) St Martin.
— State Control in Soviet Russia: The Rise & Fall of the Workers' & Peasants' Inspectorate, 1920-1934. LC 87-4777. 320p. 1987. text ed. 45.00 (*0-312-00767-1*) St Martin.
Rees, E. A., ed. The Soviet Communist Party in Disarray: The Twenty-Eighth Congress of the Communist Party of the Soviet Union. LC 92-14224. 1992. text ed. 59.95 (*0-312-08543-5*) St Martin.
Rees, E. G. Notes in Geometry. (Universitext Ser.). (Illus.). 109p. 1993. pap. 35.00 (*0-387-12053-X*) Spr-Verlag.
Rees, Eleanor. Hijacked Honeymoon. (Presents Ser.). 1994. mass mkt. 2.99 (*0-373-11645-4*, 1-11645-8) Harlequin Bks.
— Hijacked Honeymoon. large type ed. 1992. reprint ed. lib. bdg. 18.95 (*0-263-12900-4*) Thorndike Pr.
Rees, Elizabeth, jt. auth. see Jennings, Sue.
Rees, Ennis. Brer Rabbit & His Tricks. LC 93-32674. (Illus.). 48p. (J). (ps-4). 1994. pap. 5.95 (*1-56282-577-1*) Hyprn Ppbks.
— Brer Rabbit & His Tricks. (J). (ps-3). 1990. pap. 5.95 (*0-929077-10-5*) WaterMark Inc.
— Brer Rabbit & His Tricks. LC 93-32674. (Illus.). 56p. (J). (gr. k-5). 1992. reprint ed. 12.95 (*1-56282-215-2*) Hyprn Child.
— Fast Freddie Frog: And Other Tongue-Twister Rhymes. (J). (ps-3). 1993. 14.95 (*1-56397-038-4*) Boyds Mills Pr.
— More Brer Rabbit & His Tricks. (J). 1990. pap. 5.95 (*0-929077-11-3*) WaterMark Inc.
— More of Brer Rabbit's Tricks. LC 93-32676. (Illus.). 48p. (J). (ps-4). 1994. pap. 5.95 (*1-56282-578-X*) Hyprn Ppbks.
— More of Brer Rabbit's Tricks. LC 93-32676. (Illus.). 56p. (J). (gr. k-5). 1992. reprint ed. 13.95 (*1-56282-217-9*) Hyprn Child.
— The Odyssey of Homer. (C). 1991. pap. write for info. (*0-02-399141-0*) Macmillan.
Rees, Ennis, tr. Iliad of Homer. 544p. 1991. pap. 8.95 (*0-19-506826-2*) OUP.
Rees, Ennis, tr. see Homer.
Rees, Fran. How to Lead Work Teams: Facilitation Skills. LC 91-6561. 161p. 1991. pap. 24.95 (*0-88390-056-4*) Pfeiffer & Co.
Rees, Fran, intro. Twenty-Five Activities for Teams. LC 92-85291. 108p. (Orig.). 1993. pap. text ed. 34.95 (*0-88390-362-8*) Pfeiffer & Co.
Rees, Frederick. The Problem of Wales & Other Essays. 146p. 1963. 12.50 (*0-7083-0069-3*, Pub. by U of Wales UK) Bks Intl VA.
— Studies in Welsh History. 2nd ed. 184p. 1965. 12.50 (*0-7083-0079-0*, Pub. by U of Wales UK) Bks Intl VA.
Rees, G. Wyn, ed. International Politics in Europe: The New Agenda. LC 92-44820. 224p. 1993. 59.95 (*0-415-08282-X*, B2421, Routledge NY); pap. 17.95 (*0-415-08283-8*, B2425, Routledge NY) Routledge.
Rees, Gareth, jt. ed. see Day, Graham.
Rees, Gareth, et al. Cancer Practice. LC 92-49494. 328p. 1993. 60.00 (*0-7506-1404-8*) Buttrwrth-Heinemann.
Rees, Gareth J. Clinical Oncology. 368p. 1989. pap. 47.50 (*0-7194-0133-X*) OUP.
Rees, Garnet, ed. see Apollinaire, Guillaume.
Rees, Gary W. & Hoeber, Mary. A Catalogue of Sanborn Atlases at California State University, Northridge. LC 73-5773. (Occasional Papers: No. 1). (Illus.). 143p. (Orig.). 1973. pap. 4.00 (*0-939112-01-9*) Western Assn Map.
Rees, Geoffrey. Sex with Strangers. LC 93-1242. 1993. 20.00 (*0-374-26165-2*) FS&G.
Rees, Goronwy, tr. see Janouch, Gustav.
Rees, Graham L. Britain's Commodity Markets. 25.00 (*0-89979-002-X*) British Am Bks.
Rees, Gwendolen. Libraries for Children. (Library Science Ser.). 1980. lib. bdg. 55.00 (*0-8490-3131-1*) Gordon Pr.
Rees, H., jt. frwd. see Elliott, D.
Rees, H. Louis. The Czechs During World War One: The Path to Independence. 200p. 1992. text ed. 28.00 (*0-88033-236-0*) Col U Pr.
Rees, Hedley, jt. auth. see Hughes-Hallett, Andrew.
Rees, Helen G. Guytons Galore: From French Huguenots to Oregon Pioneers. LC 85-73595. (Illus.). 294p. 1986. 19.95 (*0-8323-0448-4*) Binford Mort.
— Shaniko: From Wool Capital to Ghost Town. 2nd ed. LC 81-70285. (Illus.). 176p. 1990. reprint ed. pap. 10.00 (*0-8323-0399-2*) Binford Mort.
— Shaniko People. LC 82-73596. (Illus.). 256p. 1982. 10.95 (*0-8323-0414-X*); pap. 7.95 (*0-8323-0415-8*) Binford Mort.
***Rees, Herbert.** Mold Engineering. LC 95-2590. 1995. write for info. (*1-56990-131-7*) Hanser-Gardner.
— Understanding Injection Molding Technology. 128p. 1994. pap. write for info. (*1-56990-130-9*) Hanser-Gardner.
Rees, Ioan B., intro. The Mountains of Wales: An Anthology in Verse & Prose. xvii, 299p. 1992. 50.00 (*0-7083-1162-8*, Pub. by U of Wales UK) Bks Intl VA.
Rees, Jacqui, jt. auth. see Lloyd, Clem.
Rees, James. Life of Edwin Forrest with Reminiscences & Personal Recollections. 524p. 1993. reprint ed. lib. bdg. 99.00 (*0-7812-5285-7*) Rprt Serv.
— Shakespeare & the Bible. LC 70-174307. reprint ed. 34.50 (*0-404-05235-5*) AMS Pr.
Rees, Jane & Rees, Mark, eds. British Planemakers from Seventeen Hundred. 3rd ed. (Illus.). 530p. 1993. 39.50 (*1-879335-43-3*) Astragal Pr.
***Rees, Jenny.** Looking for Mr. Nobody: The Secret Life of Goronwy Rees. (Illus.). 320p. 1995. 40.00 (*0-297-81430-3*, Pub. by Weidenfeld) Trafalgar.
Rees, Jim. Farewell to Famine. (Illus.). 165p. 1994. 33.95 (*0-9522029-0-5*, Pub. by Arklow Ent IE); pap. 19.95 (*0-9522029-5-6*, Pub. by Arklow Ent IE) Irish Bks Media.
***Rees, Jim, intro.** 2nd USENIX Symposium on Mobile & Location-Independent Computing Proceedings: Ann Arbor, MI. 132p. (Orig.). 1995. pap. text ed. 24.00 (*1-880446-69-3*) USENIX Assn.

Rees, Joan. Shakespeare & the Story: Aspects of Creation. 239p. (C). 1978. pap. 18.95 (0-485-12041-0, Pub. by Athlone Pr UK) Humanities.
— Sir Philip Sidney & Arcadia. LC 89-46411. 1991. 32.50 (0-8386-3406-0) Fairleigh Dickinson.
Rees, John. Idaho, Chronology, Nomenclature & Bibliography. (Shorey Historical Ser.). 127p. reprint ed. pap. 8.95 (0-8466-0104-4, S104) Shorey.
Rees, John, ed. Technology, Regions, & Policy. 336p. (C). 1986. 54.50 (0-8476-7409-6, R7409) Rowman.
Rees, John & Price, John. ABC of Asthma. 2nd ed. (Illus.). 34p. 1985. pap. 16.00 (0-7279-0226-1, Pub. by Brit Med Assn UK) Amer Coll Phys.
Rees, John, jt. auth. see Weinstein, Bernard L.
Rees, John, et al. Aids to Clinical Pharmacology & Therapeutics. 3rd ed. LC 92-49325. (Illus.). 350p. 1993. pap. text ed. write for info. (0-443-04698-0) Churchill.
Rees, John, et al, eds. Industrial Locations & Regional Systems: Spatial Organization and the Economic Sector. LC 80-28399. (Illus.). 272p. (C). 1981. text ed. 39.95 (0-89789-008-6, Greenwood Pr) Greenwood.
Rees, John F., ed. Contaminated Land Treatment Technologies. LC 92-28321. 1992. write for info. (1-85166-943-4, Pub. by Elsevier Applied Sci UK) Elsevier.
***Rees-Jones, Deryn.** The Memory Tray. 1995. 14.95 (0-614-07442-8, Pub. by Seren Bks UK) Dufour.
Rees, Joseph. Reforming the Workplace: A Study of Self-Regulation in Occupational Safety. LC 88-20822. (Law in Social Context Ser.). 320p. (C). 1988. text ed. 42.95x (0-8122-8132-2) U of Pa Pr.
Rees, Joseph V. Hostages of Each Other: The Transformation of Nuclear Safety since Three Mile Island. LC 93-35819. 1994. 24.95 (0-226-70687-7) U Ch Pr.
Rees, Judith. Natural Resources: Allocation, Economics & Policy. 2nd ed. 480p. 1990. 77.00 (0-415-05104-5, A4670); pap. 25.00 (0-415-05103-7, A4674) Routledge.
Rees, Kay, ed. see Khammash, Ammar.
Rees, L. H., jt. ed. see Van Wimersma Greidanus, T. B.
Rees, L. V., ed. see International Conference on Zeolites Staff.
Rees, Lesley H., jt. ed. see Bouloux, Pierre M.
Rees, Lloyd. Don't Stand So Close. 258p. 1994. pap. 16.95 (1-85411-097-7, Pub. by Poetry Wales Pr UK) Dufour.
Rees, Lucy. The Fundamentals of Riding. (Illus.). 160p. 1991. 24.95 (0-312-06750-X, Pub. by Thomas Dunne Bks) St Martin.
— The Horse's Mind. write for info. (0-318-59622-9) S&S Trade.
Rees, M. & Stoneham, R. Supernovae: A Survey of Current Research. 1982. lib. bdg. 149.50 (90-277-1442-8) Kluwer Ac.
Rees, M. H. Physics & Chemistry of the Upper Atmosphere. (Illus.). 350p. 1989. pap. 32.95 (0-521-36848-0) Cambridge U Pr.
— Physics & Chemistry of the Upper Atmosphere. (Illus.). 350p. 1989. 89.95 (0-521-32305-3) Cambridge U Pr.
Rees, Margaret A. Alfred de Musset. LC 73-120495. (Twayne's World Authors Ser.). 1971. lib. bdg. 17.95 (0-8057-2646-2) Irvington.
Rees, Maria, tr. see Toniolo, Gianni.
Rees, Mark, intro. The Preston Catalogue. (Illus.). 224p. 1991. reprint ed. pap. 19.95 (0-9618088-9-6) Astragal Pr.
Rees, Mark, jt. ed. see Rees, Jane.
***Rees, Martin.** Perspectives in Astrophysical Cosmology. (Lezioni Lincee Lectures). (Illus.). 96p. (C). 1995. 39.95 (0-521-47530-9); pap. 19.95 (0-521-47561-9) Cambridge U Pr.
Rees, Martin, et al. Black Holes, Gravitational Waves & Cosmology: Introduction to Current Research. 436p. 1974. text ed. 190.00 (0-677-04580-8) Gordon & Breach.
Rees, Mary, illus. & adapt. Ten in a Bed. (J). (ps-1). 1988. 13.95 (0-316-73708-9, Joy St Bks) Little.
Rees, Matthew. From the Deck to the Sea: Blacks & the Republican Party. LC 91-34055. 300p. 1992. text ed. 35.00 (0-89341-684-3, Longwood Academic) Hollowbrook.
Rees, Mel. Principles to Live By. (Illus.). 96p. (Orig.). 1993. pap. 4.95 (0-945383-47-9) Teach Servs.
Rees, Michael J., jt. auth. see Barron, David W.
Rees, Mike & Robson, David. Compiling Pascal S. (Illus.). 256p. (C). 1988. pap. text ed. 29.25 (0-201-18487-7) Addison-Wesley.
Rees-Mogg, Lord W., jt. auth. see Davidon, James D.
Rees-Mogg, William, jt. auth. see Davidson, James D.
***Rees, Nigel.** Brewer's Quotations: A Phrase & Fable Dictionary. 448p. 1995. 24.95 (0-304-34397-8, Pub. by Cassell UK) Sterling.
— Cassell Dictionary of Catchphrases. 240p. 1995. 21.95 (0-304-34563-6, Pub. by Cassell UK) Sterling.
— Cassell Dictionary of Word & Phrase Origins. 224p. 1994. pap. 8.95 (0-304-34422-2, Pub. by Cassell UK) Sterling.
— Epitaphs: A Dictionary of Grave Epigrams & Memorial Eloquence. 272p. 1994. pap. 10.95 (0-7867-0080-7) Carroll & Graf.
— The Politically Correct Phrasebook: What "They Say" You Can & Cannot Say in the 1990's. 152p. 1994. 17.95 (0-7475-1426-7, Pub. by Bloomsbury Pub Ltd UK) Trafalgar.
— Talent. 384p. 1989. pap. 9.95 (0-7472-3252-0, Pub. by Headline UK) Trafalgar.
Rees, Nona. St. David of Dewisland. (Illus.). (C). 1993. pap. 21.00x (0-86383-856-1, Pub. by Gomer Pr UK) St Mut.
***Rees, Owen.** Polyphony in Portugal c. 1530-c. 1620: Sources from the Monastery of Santa Cruz, Coimbra. LC 95-16153. (Outstanding Dissertations in Music from British Universities Ser.). (Illus.). 482p. 1995. 103.00 (0-8153-2029-9) Garland.
Rees, Pat. Positive Parenting: A Survival Guide. 1992. 31.00 (1-85549-018-8, Pub. by Attic Pr IE) St Mut.
Rees, Paul K., et al. Algebra & Trigonometry. 3rd ed. (Illus.). 576p. (C). 1975. text ed. write for info. (0-07-051723-1) McGraw.
— College Algebra. 10th ed. 576p. (C). 1990. text ed. write for info. (0-07-051741-X); Student solutions manual. student ed, pap. text ed. 13.96 (0-07-051744-4) McGraw.
— College Algebra with Trigonometry. 736p. (C). 1991. text ed. write for info. (0-07-051737-1) McGraw.
Rees, Paul S. The Warrior Saint. 1987. pap. 7.99 (0-88019-213-5) Schmul Pub Co.
Rees, Philip. Biographical Dictionary of the Extreme Right since 1890. 428p. 1991. 75.00 (0-13-089301-3) S&S Trade.
— Margaret Atwood: A Critical Inquiry. LC 84-433. (Women Writers Ser.). 352p. (C). 1984. 57.00 (0-389-20742-X, 08034) B&N Imports.
Rees, Philip H. Residential Patterns in American Cities: 1960. LC 78-12169. (Research Papers Ser.: No. 189). (Illus.). 1979. pap. 12.00 (0-89065-096-9) U Chicago Comm Geo.
Rees, Philip H., jt. ed. see Woods, Robert I.
Rees, R. A., jt. auth. see Styles, S. J.
Rees, R. C., ed. The Biology & Clinical Applications of Interleukin-2. (Illus.). 200p. 1991. 55.00 (0-19-963137-9, IRL Pr) OUP.
Rees, Ray, jt. auth. see McKenna, C. J.
Rees, Richard. Simone Weil: A Sketch for a Protrait. LC 77-24990. (Arcturus Books Paperbacks). 215p. 1978. reprint ed. pap. 6.95 (0-8093-0852-5) S Ill U Pr.
Rees, Richard, tr. see Monnerot, Jules.
Rees, Robert A., jt. ed. see Harbert, Earl N.
***Rees, Roberta.** Beneath the Faceless Mountain. 248p. 1995. pap. 12.95 (0-88995-106-3, Pub. by Red Deer CN) BookWorld Dist.
Rees, Roger, tr. see Turgenev, Ivan S. & Konovalov, S.
***Rees-Rohrbacher, Darhon.** Hands-Free Travel: How to Travel the World with Only Carry-on Luggage. 60p. (Orig.). 1996. pap. 7.50 (1-882712-48-X) Dragonflower.
— The Pocket Guide to Harp Composing. 2nd rev. ed. (Illus.). 80p. 1995. pap. text ed. 9.00 (1-882712-14-5) Dragonflower.
— A Spanish Diction Manual for Singers. 100p. (C). Date not set. pap. text ed. 10.00 (1-882712-01-3) Dragonflower.
***Rees-Rohrbacher, Darhon & Dutton, Thomas.** Classic Festival Preludes. 67p. (Orig.). 1995. pap. 15.00 (1-882712-42-0) Dragonflower.
Rees, Rolf S., ed. Graphs, Matrices, & Designs. LC 92-24370. (Lecture Notes in Pure & Applied Mathematics Ser.: Vol. 139). 344p. 1992. 140.00 (0-8247-8790-0) Dekker.
Rees, Ronald. Interior Landscapes: Gardens & the Domestic Environment. LC 92-536. (Illus.). 224p. 1993. 35.00 (0-8018-4467-3) Johns Hopkins.
Rees, Roweena & Ward, Mike. Computer Integrated Manufacturing. (Andersen Consulting Management Guides Ser.: No. 1). (Illus.). 176p. 1991. pap. write for info. (0-434-91754-0) Buttrwrth-Heinemann.
Rees, Saskiavan, et al. Women Giving Birth. (Illus.). 160p. (Orig.). 1992. pap. 18.95 (0-89087-668-1) Celestial Arts.
Rees, Shan & Graham, Roderick. Assertion Training: How to Be Who You Really Are. (Strategies for Mental Health Ser.). 176p. 1991. 59.95 (0-415-05816-3, A5405); pap. 16.95 (0-415-01073-X, A5409) Routledge.
Rees, Stuart. Social Work Face to Face: Clients & Social Workers' Perceptions of the Content & Outcome of Their Meetings. 1979. text ed. 36.50 (0-231-04764-9) Col U Pr.
Rees, Stuart, ed. Achieving Power. 216p. 1991. pap. 17.95 (0-04-442335-7, Pub. by Allen & Unwin Aust Pty AT) Paul & Co Pubs.
Rees, Teresa. Women & the Labour Market. LC 92-10512. 224p. 1993. 67.50 (0-415-03801-4); pap. write for info. (0-415-03802-2) Routledge.
Rees, Thomas D. & LaTrenta, Gregory S. Aesthetic Plastic Surgery, 2 vols., Set. 2nd ed. (Illus.). 1384p. 1994. text ed. 395.00 (0-7216-3712-4) Saunders.
Rees, Thomas R. The Technique of T. S. Eliot. LC 72-94500. (De Proprietatibus Litterarum, Ser. Practica: No. 39). (Illus.). 397p. (Orig.). 1974. pap. text ed. 53.10 (90-279-3190-9) Mouton.
Rees, Una, ed. The Cartulary of Haughmond Abbey. x, 294p. 1985. 39.95 (0-7083-0907-0, Pub. by U of Wales UK) Bks Intl VA.
Rees, W. D. Advances in Peptic Ulcer Pathogenesis. 250p. 1988. lib. bdg. 103.00 (0-7462-0062-5) Kluwer Ac.
Rees, W. G. Physical Principles of Remote Sensing. (Topics in Remote Sensing Ser.: No. 2). (Illus.). 250p. (C). 1990. 69.95 (0-521-35213-4); pap. 29.95 (0-521-35994-5) Cambridge U Pr.
— Physics by Example: Two Hundred Problems & Solutions. LC 93-34300. (Illus.). 325p. (C). 1994. 69.95 (0-521-44514-0); pap. 24.95 (0-521-44975-8) Cambridge U Pr.
***Rees, W. Michael, et al, eds.** Multimedia & Megachange: New Roles for Educational Computing. (Computers in the Schools Ser.). (Illus.). 438p. 1995. lib. bdg. 49.95 (1-56024-693-6) Haworth Pr.
Rees, William. A History of the Order of St. John of Jerusalem in Wales & on the Welsh Border: Including an Account of the Templars. LC 76-29839. (Illus.). reprint ed. 37.50 (0-404-15427-1) AMS Pr.
— Survey of the Duchy of Lancaster Lordships in Wales, 1609-1613. (History & Law Ser.: No. 12). xxxix, 303p. 1953. 28.50 (0-7083-0117-7, Pub. by U of Wales UK) Bks Intl VA.
Rees, William, ed. Calendar of Ancient Petitions Relating to Wales. (History & Law Ser.: No. 28). xxxviii, 559p. 1975. 28.50 (0-7083-0566-0, Pub. by U of Wales UK) Bks Intl VA.
Rees, William, intro. The Book of French Poetry, 1820-1950. 856p. 1991. pap. 16.95 (0-14-042357-5, Penguin Classics) Viking Penguin.
Rees, William & Wackernagel, Mathis. Our Ecological Footprint: Reducing Human Impact on the Earth. (Illus.). 144p. 1995. pap. 12.95 (0-86571-312-X) New Soc Pubs.
— Our Ecological Footprint: Reducing Human Impact on the Earth. (Illus.). 144p. 1995. lib. bdg. 34.95 (0-86571-311-1) New Soc Pubs.
Rees, William E. Sustainable Development & the Biosphere: Concepts & Principles. (Teilhard Studies). 1990. 3.50 (0-89012-061-7) Anima Pubns.
Rees, Yvonne. The Art of Balcony Gardening. (Illus.). 144p. 1991. 24.95 (0-7063-6999-8, Pub. by Ward Lock UK) Sterling.
— Caning & Rushwork. (Practical Home Restoration Ser.). (Illus.). 96p. 14.95 (0-7063-7048-1, Pub. by Ward Lock UK) Sterling.
— Cats. (Nature Library). (Illus.). 64p. (J). 1991. 4.99 (0-517-05153-2) Random Hse Value.
— Complete Book of Cats. 1993. 14.99 (0-517-06593-2) Random Hse Value.
— Curtains & Blinds. (Quick & Easy Ser.). (Illus.). 96p. 1995. 14.95 (0-7063-7346-4, Pub. by Ward Lock UK) Sterling.
— Dogs. (Nature Library). (Illus.). 64p. (J). 1991. 4.99 (0-517-05152-4) Random Hse Value.
— Gilding & Antique Finishes. (Practical Home Restoration Ser.). (Illus.). 96p. 14.95 (0-7063-7047-3, Pub. by Ward Lock UK) Sterling.
— Practical Conservatory Gardening. (Illus.). 64p. 1993. pap. 8.95 (1-85223-736-8, Pub. by Crowood Pr UK) Trafalgar.
— Practical Garden Design. (Illus.). 64p. Date not set. pap. 8.95 (1-85223-624-8, Pub. by Crowood Pr UK) Trafalgar.
— Practical Garden Features. (Illus.). 64p. 1995. pap. 8.95 (1-85223-856-9, Pub. by Crowood Pr UK) Trafalgar.
— Practical Patio Gardening. (Illus.). 64p. 1993. pap. 8.95 (1-85223-735-X, Pub. by Crowood Pr UK) Trafalgar.
— Practical Water Gardening. (Illus.). 64p. 1994. pap. 8.95 (1-85223-623-X, Pub. by Crowood Pr UK) Trafalgar.
— Practical Wildflower Gardening. (Illus.). 64p. 1994. pap. 8.95 (1-85223-778-3, Pub. by Crowood Pr UK) Trafalgar.
— Wildflower Gardening: Step by Step to Growing Success. (Crowood Gardening Guides Ser.). (Illus.). 128p. 1991. pap. 16.95 (1-85223-524-1, Pub. by Crowood Pr UK) Trafalgar.
— Window Style. 1990. text ed. 19.95 (0-442-30295-9) Van Nos Reinhold.
Rees, Yvonne & Herbert, Tony. Floor Style: A Sourcebook of Ideas for Transforming the World Beneath Your Feet. (Illus.). 160p. 1989. text ed. 16.98 (0-442-23923-8) Chapman & Hall.
Rees, Yvonne & Palliser, David. Container Gardening: All Year Round. (Crowood Gardening Guides Ser.). (Illus.). 128p. 1991. pap. 16.95 (1-85223-303-6, Pub. by Crowood Pr UK) Trafalgar.
— Patio Gardening: Step by Step to Growing Success. (Crowood Gardening Guides Ser.). (Illus.). 128p. 1992. pap. 16.95 (1-85223-507-1, Pub. by Crowood Pr UK) Trafalgar.
***Reese.** Dictionary of Philosophy & Religion. 2nd ed. (C). Date not set. text ed. write for info. (0-391-03864-8); pap. write for info. (0-391-03865-6) Humanities.
— Infectious Disease. 3rd ed. 1991. 73.95 (0-316-73717-8) Little.
Reese & Gasparis. Mental Health & Psychiatric Nursing. (Nursetest: A Review Ser.). 1991. 19.95 (0-87434-306-2) Springhouse Pub.
***Reese & Hoffman.** Play It Again, Sam. Date not set. 7.95 (0-910791-21-X, 0690) Devyn Pr.
Reese, et al. Revised 1993 Supplement to Conflict of Laws. 9th ed. 1993. pap. text ed. 4.95 (1-56662-132-1) Foundation Pr.
Reese, Alexander. Industrial Energy Conservation: Where Do We Go from Here? LC 77-93745. 54p. reprint ed. pap. 25.00 (0-7837-0331-7, 2040650) Bks Demand.
Reese, Andrew J., jt. auth. see Debo, Thomas N.
Reese, Becky D., jt. auth. see Hendricks, Patricia D.
Reese, Becky D., jt. auth. see Mayer, Susan M.
Reese, Bernie, et al. Tahquitz Exchange. (Orig.). (YA). (gr. 12). 1993. pap. write for info. (0-9628802-3-X) DeChamp CA.
Reese, Bob. ABCs. LC 92-12188. (School Days Ser.). (Illus.). 24p. (J). (ps-2). 1992. lib. bdg. 9.75 (0-516-05577-1) Childrens.
— Abert & Kaibab. (Grand Canyon Ser.). (Illus.). (J). (gr. k-6). 1987. 7.95 (0-89868-226-6); pap. 2.95 (0-89868-227-4); pap. 20.00 (0-685-50872-2) ARO Pub.
— Ape Escape. (Going Ape Ser.). (Illus.). (J). 1983. 7.95 (0-89868-147-2); pap. 2.95 (0-89868-146-4) ARO Pub.
— The Ape Team. (Going Ape Ser.). (Illus.). (J). 1983. 7.95 (0-89868-145-6); pap. 2.95 (0-89868-144-8) ARO Pub.
— Apricot Ape. (Going Ape Ser.). (Illus.). (J). 1983. 7.95 (0-89868-141-3); pap. 2.95 (0-89868-140-5) ARO Pub.
— Arbor Day. Jordan, Alton, ed. (Holiday Set). (Illus.). (J). (gr. k-3). 1984. 6.95 (0-89868-031-X, Read Res); pap. 3.50 (0-89868-064-6, Read Res) ARO Pub.
— Art. LC 92-12187. (School Days Ser.). (Illus.). 24p. (J). (ps-2). 1992. lib. bdg. 9.75 (0-516-05578-X) Childrens.
— Bubba Bear. (Yellowstone Ser.). (Illus.). (J). (gr. k-6). 1986. 7.95 (0-89868-173-1); pap. 2.95 (0-89868-174-X); pap. 20.00 (0-685-50871-4) ARO Pub.
— Buffa Buffalo. (Yellowstone Ser.). (Illus.). (J). (gr. k-6). 1986. 7.95 (0-89868-175-8); pap. 2.95 (0-89868-176-6) ARO Pub.
— Bugle Elk & Little Toot. (Yellowstone Ser.). (Illus.). (J). (gr. k-6). 1986. 7.95 (0-89868-177-4); pap. 2.95 (0-89868-178-2) ARO Pub.
— Camper Critters. (Yellowstone Ser.). (Illus.). (J). (gr. k-6). 1986. 7.95 (0-89868-169-3); pap. 2.95 (0-89868-170-7) ARO Pub.
— Can Do. (Ten Word Book Ser.). (Illus.). (J). (gr. k-3). 1994. lib. bdg. 9.25 (0-89868-247-9, Read Res) ARO Pub.
— Can Do. (Ten Word Book Ser.). (Illus.). (J). (gr. k-3). 1994. pap. 3.50 (0-89868-248-7, Read Res) ARO Pub.
— Cocos Berry Party. (Grand Canyon Ser.). (Illus.). (J). (gr. k-6). 1987. 7.95 (0-89868-193-6); pap. 2.95 (0-89868-194-4) ARO Pub.
— Coral Reef. LC 82-23610. (Critterland Ocean Adventures Ser.). (Illus.). 24p. (J). (ps-2). 1983. pap. 2.95 (0-516-42312-6) Childrens.
— Crab Apple. Wasserman, Dan, ed. (Ten Word Book Ser.). (Illus.). (J). (gr. k-1). 1979. 7.95 (0-89868-072-7); pap. 2.95 (0-89868-083-2) ARO Pub.
— The Critter Race. LC 81-3874. (Critterland Desert Adventures Ser.). (Illus.). 24p. (J). (ps-2). 1981. pap. 2.95 (0-516-42302-9) Childrens.
— Easter. Jordan, Alton, ed. (Holiday Set). (Illus.). (J). (gr. k-3). 1984. 6.95 (0-89868-032-8, Read Res); pap. 3.50 (0-89868-065-4, Read Res) ARO Pub.
— Field Trip. LC 92-12186. (School Days Ser.). (Illus.). 24p. (J). (ps-2). 1992. lib. bdg. 9.75 (0-516-05579-8) Childrens.
— For Keeps. (Ten Word Book Ser.). (Illus.). (J). (gr. k-3). 1994. lib. bdg. 9.25 (0-89868-251-7, Read Res) ARO Pub.
— For Keeps. (Ten Word Book Ser.). (Illus.). (J). (gr. k-3). 1994. pap. 3.50 (0-89868-252-5, Read Res) ARO Pub.
— Forty Word Yellowstone Series, 6 bks., Set. (Illus.). (J). (gr. k-6). 1986. 47.70 (0-89868-239-8) ARO Pub.
— Glasses. LC 92-12185. (School Days Ser.). (Illus.). 24p. (J). (ps-2). 1992. lib. bdg. 9.75 (0-516-05580-1) Childrens.
— Going Bananas. (Going Ape Ser.). (Illus.). (J). 1983. 7.95 (0-89868-143-X); pap. 2.95 (0-89868-142-1) ARO Pub.
— El Gusano Curioso. Schaffer-Melendez, Gloria, tr. (Libro de Diaz Palabras Ser.). (Illus.). (SPA.). (J). (gr. k-3). 1994. lib. bdg. 9.25 (0-89868-257-6, Read Res); pap. 3.50 (0-89868-258-4, Read Res) ARO Pub.
— Honest Ape. (Going Ape Ser.). (Illus.). (J). 1983. 7.95 (0-89868-149-9); pap. 2.95 (0-89868-148-0) ARO Pub.
— Huzzard Buzzard. LC 81-6118. (Critterland Desert Adventures Ser.). (Illus.). 24p. (J). (ps-2). 1981. pap. 2.95 (0-516-42303-7) Childrens.
— The Jungle Train. (Going Ape Ser.). (Illus.). (J). 1983. 7.95 (0-89868-151-0); pap. 2.95 (0-89868-150-2) ARO Pub.
— Jungle Train. (Big Zero Word Book Ser.). (Illus.). (J). (gr. k-3). 1983. pap. 20.00 (0-685-50868-4) ARO Pub.
— Little Dinosaur. Wasserman, Dan, ed. (Ten Word Book Ser.). (Illus.). (J). (gr. k-1). 1979. 7.95 (0-89868-070-0); pap. 2.95 (0-89868-081-6) ARO Pub.
— Mickey Moose. (Yellowstone Ser.). (Illus.). (J). (gr. k-6). 1986. 7.95 (0-89868-171-5); pap. 2.95 (0-89868-172-3) ARO Pub.
— Ocean Fish School. LC 82-23572. (Critterland Ocean Adventures Ser.). (Illus.). 24p. (J). (ps-2). 1983. pap. 2.95 (0-516-42314-2) Childrens.
— Old Faithful. (Yellowstone Ser.). (Illus.). (J). (gr. k-6). 1986. 7.95 (0-89868-167-7); pap. 2.95 (0-89868-168-5) ARO Pub.
— Pamba & the Bink. (Illus.). (J). (gr. k-6). 1984. 11.95 (0-89868-152-9) ARO Pub.
— Para Siempre. Schaffer-Melendez, Gloria, tr. (Libro de Diaz Palabras Ser.). (Illus.). (SPA.). (J). (gr. k-3). 1994. lib. bdg. 9.25 (0-89868-259-2, Read Res); pap. 3.50 (0-89868-260-6, Read Res) ARO Pub.
— Podemos. Schaffer-Melendez, Gloria, tr. (Libro de Diaz Palabras Ser.). (Illus.). (SPA.). (J). (gr. k-3). 1994. lib. bdg. 9.25 (0-89868-255-X, Read Res); pap. 3.50 (0-89868-256-8, Read Res) ARO Pub.
— Rapid Robert Roadrunner. LC 81-6090. (Critterland Desert Adventures Ser.). (Illus.). 24p. (J). (ps-2). 1981. pap. 2.95 (0-516-42305-3) Childrens.
— Raven's Roost. (Grand Canyon Ser.). (Illus.). (J). (gr. k-6). 1987. 7.95 (0-89868-195-2); pap. 2.95 (0-89868-196-0) ARO Pub.
— Recess. LC 92-12184. (School Days Ser.). (Illus.). 24p. (J). (ps-2). 1992. lib. bdg. 9.75 (0-516-05581-X) Childrens.
— Sack Lunch. LC 92-12183. (School Days Ser.). (Illus.). 24p. (J). (ps-2). 1992. lib. bdg. 9.75 (0-516-05582-8) Childrens.
— Scary Larry the Very Very Hairy Tarantula. LC 81-3871. (Critterland Desert Adventures Ser.). (Illus.). 24p. (J). (ps-2). 1981. pap. 2.95 (0-516-42306-1) Childrens.
— Sixty Word Grand Canyon Series, 6 bks., Set. (Illus.). (J). (gr. k-6). 1987. 47.70 (0-89868-241-X) ARO Pub.
— Slitherfoot Snake. (Grand Canyon Ser.). (Illus.). (J). (gr. k-6). 1987. 7.95 (0-89868-191-X); pap. 2.95 (0-89868-192-8) ARO Pub.
— St. Patrick's Day. Jordan, Alton, ed. (Holiday Set). (Illus.). (J). (gr. k-3). 1984. 6.95 (0-89868-030-1, Read Res); pap. 3.50 (0-89868-063-8, Read Res) ARO Pub.
— Sunshine. Wasserman, Dan, ed. (Ten Word Book Ser.). (Illus.). (J). (gr. k-1). 1979. 7.95 (0-89868-073-5); pap. 2.95 (0-89868-084-0) ARO Pub.
— Surefoot Mule. (Grand Canyon Ser.). (Illus.). (J). (gr. k-6). 1987. 7.95 (0-89868-197-9); pap. 2.95 (0-89868-198-7) ARO Pub.

An Asterisk (*) at the beginning of an entry indicates that the title is appearing in BIP for the first time.

— Who's a Silly Egg? Jordan, Alton, ed. (Buppet Bks.). (Illus.). (J). (gr. 1-4). 1980. 9.25 (*0-89868-092-1*, Read Res); pap. 3.50 (*0-89868-103-0*, Read Res) ARO Pub.

— Wild Turkey Run. (Grand Canyon Ser.). (Illus.). (J). (gr. k-6). 1987. 7.95 (*0-89868-199-5*); pap. 2.95 (*0-89868-225-8*) ARO Pub.

— Wonder Worm. (Ten Word Book Ser.). (Illus.). (J). (gr. k-3). 1994. lib. bdg. 9.25 (*0-89868-249-5*, Read Res); pap. 3.50 (*0-89868-250-9*, Read Res) ARO Pub.

— Zero Word Going Ape Series, 6 bks., Set. (Illus.). (J). 1983. 47.70 (*0-89868-139-1*); pap. 29.50 (*0-89868-138-3*) ARO Pub.

***Reese, Bob & Preece-Sandoval, Pam.** Libros de Diez Palabras Series, 4 bks., Set. Schaffer-Melendez, Gloria, tr. (Illus.). (J). (gr. k-3). 1994. lib. bdg. 37.00 (*0-89868-278-9*, Read Res); pap. 14.00 (*0-89868-279-7*, Read Res) ARO Pub.

— Ten Word Book Series, 4 bks., Set. (Illus.). (J). (gr. k-3). 1994. lib. bdg. 37.00 (*0-89868-273-8*, Read Res); pap. 14.00 (*0-89868-274-6*, Read Res) ARO Pub.

Reese, Bob & Reese, Nancy. Smiley Snake. Jordan, Alton, ed. (I Can Read Ser.). (Illus.). (J). (gr. k-3). 1984. 6.95 (*0-89868-010-7*, Read Res); pap. 3.50 (*0-89868-043-3*, Read Res) ARO Pub.

Reese, Bob, jt. auth. see Preece-Sandoval, Pam.

Reese, Bob, jt. auth. see Reese, Nancy.

Reese, Bob, et al. Big Big Book Series, 7 bks. (Illus.). (J). (gr. k-6). 1987. pap. 140.00 (*0-89868-244-4*) ARO Pub.

— I Can Read Underwater Series, 10 bks. Jordan, Alton, ed. (Illus.). (J). (gr. k-2). 1984. Set. 69.50 (*0-89868-000-X*, Read Res); Set. pap. 35.00 (*0-89868-033-6*, Read Res) ARO Pub.

— Ten Word Book Series, 10 bks., Set. (Illus.). (J). (gr. k-1). 1979. 35.00 (*0-89868-077-8*, Read Res) ARO Pub.

Reese, Charles D. Palm Beach Roots & Recipes. (Illus.). 120p. (Orig.). 1991. reprint ed. pap. 12.95 (*0-9629266-0-4*) Palm Bch Roots.

Reese, Craig E. Deregulation & Environmental Quality: The Use of Tax Policy to Control Pollution in North America & Western Europe. LC 82-11266. (Illus.). 495p. 1983. text ed. 65.00 (*0-89930-018-9*, RDE/, Quorum Bks) Greenwood.

Reese, David E. & Gross, Lynne S. Radio Production Worktext: Studio & Equipment. (Illus.). 146p. 1989. pap. 24.95 (*0-240-80045-1*, Focal) Buttrwrth-Heinemann.

Reese, David E., jt. auth. see Gross, Lynne S.

Reese, David M. Humbugs of New York. LC 77-37314. (Black Heritage Library Collection). 1977. reprint ed. 26.95 (*0-8369-8951-1*) Ayer.

***Reese, Dawnell & Vondrak, Elizabeth, eds.** Rockhurst Review - 1995 Vol. VIII: A Fine Arts Journal. 80p. 1995. pap. 6.00 (*1-886761-07-8*) Rockhurst Col.

Reese, E. Advances in Enzymic Hydrolysis of Cellulose & Related Materials: Proceedings of the Symposium of the American Chemical Society Army Research, March, 1962. LC 62-22051. 1963. 126.00 (*0-08-009947-5*, Pub. by Pergamon Repr UK) Franklin.

Reese, Ed. Beyond Selling. LC 87-63208. 1988. 19.95 (*0-916990-19-2*) META Pubns.

Reese, Edward, comp. The Reese Chronological Bible. 1620p. 1980. reprint ed. 37.99 (*0-87123-115-8*) Bethany Hse.

Reese, Ellen P., jt. auth. see Sulzer-Azaroff, Beth.

***Reese-Fejoku, Julia.** Simplified Theology: Radiance of Joy Glorifies the Lord. 66p. 1995. pap. 10.00 (*0-8059-3609-2*) Dorrance.

Reese, Francesca G., jt. ed. see Gardner, John W.

Reese, Gareth. New Testament History - Acts. 8th ed. (Bible Study Textbook Ser.). (Illus.). 1056p. 1976. 24.99 (*0-89900-055-X*) College Pr Pub.

Reese, Gary F. Origins of Place Names in Pierce County. LC 89-63005. (Illus.). 144p. (Orig.). 1988. pap. 22.95 (*0-9603666-7-9*) R & M Pr WA.

Reese, George, ed. Proceedings in the Court of Vice-Admiralty of Virginia: 1698-1775. xiii, 121p. 1983. 12.50 (*0-88490-113-0*) VA State Lib.

Reese, George, jt. ed. see Van Horne, John C.

Reese, George H., ed. Journals & Papers of the Virginia State Convention of 1861, 3 vols., Set. LC 65-7459. 1966. text ed. 49.95 (*0-88490-058-4*) VA State Lib.

— Proceedings of the Virginia State Convention of 1861, 4 vols., Set. LC 65-7459. 1965. text ed. 75.00 (*0-88490-057-6*) VA State Lib.

Reese, George H. & Hickin, Patricia, eds. Journal of the Senate of Virginia, November Session, 1793. (Journals of the Senate of Virginia 1792-1803). vii, 110p. 1972. 10.00 (*0-88490-051-7*) VA State Lib.

— Journal of the Senate of Virginia, Session of 1802-03. (Journals of the Senate of Virginia 1792-1803). vi, 131p. 1973. 10.00 (*0-88490-056-8*) VA State Lib.

Reese, Gerd, tr. see Kirzner, Israel M.

Reese, Gustave. Fourscore Classics of Music Literature. LC 78-87616. (Music Reprint Ser.). 1970. reprint ed. lib. bdg. 23.50 (*0-306-71620-8*) Da Capo.

— Music in the Middle Ages. (Illus.). (C). 1940. text ed. 45.00 (*0-393-09750-1*) Norton.

— Music in the Renaissance. rev. ed. (Illus.). (C). 1959. text ed. 39.95 (*0-393-09530-4*) Norton.

Reese, Gustave & Snow, Robert J., eds. Essays in Musicology: In Honor of Dragan Plamenac on His 70th Birthday. LC 77-4220. (Music Reprint Ser.). (Illus.). 1977. reprint ed. lib. bdg. 45.00 (*0-306-77408-9*) Da Capo.

Reese, Gustave, tr. see Einstein, Alfred, ed.

Reese, H. W. & Lipsitt, Lewis P., eds. Advances in Child Development & Behavior, Vol. 15. (Serial Publication Ser.). 1980. text ed. 116.00 (*0-12-009715-X*) Acad Pr.

Reese, Harry. The Sandragraph: Between Printing & Painting. (Illus.). 20p. (C). 1987. 3,000.00 (*0-923980-04-0*) Arundel Pr.

***Reese, Harvey.** Bouncing Back: How to Turn Business Crises into Success. 224p. 1994. 18.95 (*1-57101-014-9*) MasterMedia Ltd.

— How to License Your Million Dollar Idea: Everything You Need to Know to Make Money from Your New Product Idea. 240p. 1993. pap. text ed. 14.95 (*0-471-58050-3*) Wiley.

— How to License Your Million Dollar Idea: Everything You Need to Know to Make Money from Your New Product Idea. 240p. 1993. text ed. 49.95 (*0-471-58051-1*) Wiley.

Reese, Hayne W., ed. Advances in Child Development & Behavior, Vol. 20. (Serial Publication Ser.). 351p. 1987. text ed. 84.00 (*0-12-009720-6*) Acad Pr.

— Advances in Child Development & Behavior, Vol. 21. (Serial Publication Ser.). 300p. 1989. text ed. 80.00 (*0-12-009721-4*) Acad Pr.

— Advances in Child Development & Behavior, Vol. 22. (Serial Publication Ser.). 350p. 1989. text ed. 84.00 (*0-12-009722-2*) Acad Pr.

— Advances in Child Development & Behavior, Vol. 23. (Illus.). 298p. 1991. text ed. 72.00 (*0-12-009723-0*) Acad Pr.

— Advances in Child Development & Behavior, Vol. 24. (Illus.). 317p. 1993. text ed. 79.00 (*0-12-009724-9*) Acad Pr.

— Advances in Child Development & Behavior, Vol. 25. (Illus.). 385p. 1994. text ed. 74.95 (*0-12-009725-7*) Acad Pr.

Reese, Hayne W. & Lipsitt, Lewis P., eds. Advances in Child Development & Behavior, Vol. 16. (Serial Publication Ser.). 1982. text ed. 116.00 (*0-12-009716-8*) Acad Pr.

Reese, Hayne W. & Parrott, Linda J., eds. Behavior Science: Philosophical, Methodological, & Empirical Advances. 272p. 1986. text ed. 69.95 (*0-89859-766-8*) L Erlbaum Assocs.

Reese, Hayne W., jt. ed. see McCluskey, Kathleen A.

Reese, Hayne W., jt. ed. see Puckett, James M.

Reese, Herbert H. Kellogg Arabians: Their Background & Influence. 1958. 19.95 (*0-87505-114-6*) Borden.

Reese, James. The Book of Wisdom, Song of Songs. LC 82-83726. (Old Testament Message Ser.: Vol. 20). 1983. pap. 8.95 (*0-8146-5254-9*) Liturgical Pr.

Reese, James M. First & Second Thessalonians. LC 79-53889. (New Testament Message Ser.: Vol. 16). 113p. 1980. pap. 6.95 (*0-8146-5139-9*) Liturgical Pr.

— The Student's Guide to the Gospels. (Good News Studies: Vol. 24). 150p. (Orig.). 1992. pap. text ed. 11.95 (*0-8146-5689-7*) Liturgical Pr.

Reese, James T. & Goldstein, Harvey A., eds. Psychological Services for Law Enforcement. (Illus.). 563p. 1986. pap. 28.00 (*0-16-024242-8*, S/N 027-001-00055-6) USGPO.

Reese, Jeffrey G. Poems & Other Writings. (Illus.). (Orig.). 1994. pap. 20.00 (*0-9641717-0-8*) Am Vision Gallery.

***Reese, Joe.** Katie Dee & Katie Haw: Letters from a Texas Farm Girl. (Illus.). 184p. (Orig.). (YA). (gr. 8-12). 1995. pap. 8.95 (*0-925854-13-1*) Defiant Pr.

Reese, John. The Wild One. 1981. pap. 1.75 (*0-449-13953-0*, GM) Fawcett.

***Reese, John H.** Administrative Law: Principles & Practice. LC 94-49388. (American Casebook Ser.). 844p. (C). 1995. text ed. 47.00 (*0-314-04986-X*) West Pub.

— Administrative Law, Principles & Practice, Teacher's Manual to Accompany. (American Casebook Ser.). 65p. (C). 1995. pap. text ed. write for info. (*0-314-06261-0*) West Pub.

Reese, John W. Flaming Feuds of Colorado County, Texas. (Illus.). 1962. 35.00 (*0-685-05000-9*) A Jones.

Reese, Joyce A. & Valega, Thomas M., eds. Restorative Dental Materials: An Overview. 331p. 1986. pap. text ed. 56.00 (*1-85097-003-3*, 1385) Quint Pub Co.

Reese, Karen J., ed. see Johnson, Norman F.

Reese, Karen J., ed. see Meyer, Bernard S.

Reese, Karen J., ed. see North American Prairie Conference Staff.

Reese, Kenneth M., ed. A Century of Chemistry: The Role of Chemists & the American Chemical Society. LC 76-6126. 468p. 1976. 17.95 (*0-8412-0307-5*) Am Chemical.

***Reese, Laura.** Topping from Below. 368p. 1995. 22.95 (*0-312-12000-1*) St Martin.

Reese, Leslie A. Upside down Tapestry Mosaic History. LC 87-71058. 53p. (YA). (gr. 12 up). 1987. pap. 5.00 (*0-940713-00-4*) Broadside Pr.

Reese, Lizette W. Selected Poems. (BCL1-PS American Literature Ser.). 187p. 1992. reprint ed. lib. bdg. 69.00 (*0-7812-6839-7*) Rprt Serv.

***Reese, Lyn.** I Will Not Bow My Head: Documenting Women's Political Resistance in World History. Wilkinson, Jean & Dougherty, Mary A., eds. (Illus.). 112p. (Orig.). (YA). (gr. 9-12). 1995. student ed, pap. text ed. 16.95 (*0-9625880-3-2*) Women World CRP.

— Spindle Stories: World History Units for the Middle Grades, Bk. 1. Dougherty, Mary A. & Wilkinson, Jean B., eds. (Illus.). 90p. (J). (gr. 5-9). 1990. pap. text ed. 15.00 (*0-9625880-0-8*) Women World CRP.

— Spindle Stories: World History Units for the Middle Grades, Bk. 2. Dougherty, Mary & Wilkinson, Jean, eds. 1991. write for info. (*0-318-67277-4*) Women World CRP.

— Spindle Stories Bk. 3: Three Units on Women's World History. Wilkinson, Jean & Doughtery, Mary A., eds. (Spindle Stories Ser.). (Illus.). 125p. (Orig.). (YA). (gr. 6 up). 1994. pap. text ed. 15.00 (*0-9625880-2-4*) Women World CRP.

— Spindle Stories, Bk. Two: Three Units on Women's World History. Dougherty, Mary A. & Wilkinson, Jean B., eds. (Illus.). 118p. (J). (gr. 6-10). 1991. pap. text ed. 15.00 (*0-9625880-1-6*) Women World CRP.

Reese, Lyn & Wilkinson, Jean. Women in the World: Annotated History Resources for the Secondary Student. LC 87-16436. (Illus.). 228p. 1987. 27.50 (*0-8108-2050-1*) Scarecrow.

***Reese, Lyn, et al, eds.** I'm on My Way Running: Women Speak on Coming of Age. rev. ed. 304p. 1995. pap. 11.00 (*0-380-78050-X*) Avon.

Reese, M. R. Better Beer & How to Brew It. LC 81-7003. (Illus.). 128p. 1981. pap. 9.95 (*0-88266-257-0*, Garden Way Pub) Storey Comm Inc.

***Reese, Margaret.** The Matriarch. 300p. 1996. pap. 9.95 (*0-7610-0473-4*) NW Pub.

***Reese, Margaret C.** Abstract of Augusta County, Virginia Death Registers, 1853-1896. viii, 236p. 1983. pap. 12.50x (*0-935931-55-4*) Borgo Pr.

— Abstract of Augusta County, Virginia Death Registers, 1853-1896. viii, 236p. (C). 1983. reprint ed. lib. bdg. 31.00x (*0-8095-8210-4*) Borgo Pr.

Reese, Maryann. How to Walk What You Talk: Your Personal NLP Development Manual. 160p. 1989. student ed 39.95 (*0-9615502-3-6*) Southern Inst Pr.

Reese, Maryann & Yancar, Carol L. Practitioner Manual for Introductory Patterns of Neuro Linguistic Programming. 245p. 1986. 30.00 (*0-9615502-1-X*) Southern Inst Pr.

Reese, Michael, II. Autographs of the Confederacy. LC 81-68377. 225p. 1981. 54.95 (*0-940746-00-X*); 89.95 (*0-686-42866-8*) Cohasco.

Reese, Michael. Collector's Guide to Luger Values. 1972. pap. 2.00 (*0-911116-79-6*) Pelican.

Reese, Michael, II. Luger Tips. rev. ed. 1992. reprint ed. 10.95 (*0-913150-36-3*) Pioneer Pr.

— Nineteen Hundred Luger-U. S. Test Trials. 2nd rev. ed. Pioneer Press Staff, ed. LC 71-117532. (Illus.). 1976. pap. 4.95 (*0-913150-35-5*) Pioneer Pr.

— A Travel Letter, 1871. 1988. write for info. (*0-318-65536-5*) Cloister Pr.

Reese, Nancy. I Can Eat an Elephant. Jordan, Alton, ed. (I Can Eat an Elephant Ser.). (Illus.). (J). (gr. k-3). 1984. 6.95 (*0-89868-012-3*, Read Res); pap. 3.50 (*0-89868-045-X*, Read Res) ARO Pub.

— New Year's. Jordan, Alton, ed. (Holiday Set). (Illus.). (J). (gr. k-3). 1984. 6.95 (*0-89868-026-3*, Read Res); pap. 3.50 (*0-89868-059-X*, Read Res) ARO Pub.

— Silly Egg. Jordan, Alton, ed. (I Can Read Ser.). (Illus.). (J). (gr. k-3). 1984. 6.95 (*0-89868-004-2*, Read Res); pap. 3.50 (*0-89868-037-9*, Read Res) ARO Pub.

— Valentine's Day. Jordan, Alton, ed. (Holiday Set). (Illus.). (J). (gr. k-3). 1984. 6.95 (*0-89868-029-8*, Read Res); pap. 3.50 (*0-89868-062-X*, Read Res) ARO Pub.

Reese, Nancy & Reese, Bob. The Bee. Jordan, Alton, ed. (I Can Read Ser.). (Illus.). (J). (gr. k-3). 1984. 6.95 (*0-89868-005-0*, Read Res); pap. 3.50 (*0-89868-038-7*, Read Res) ARO Pub.

Reese, Nancy, jt. auth. see Reese, Bob.

Reese, Nancy, jt. auth. see Stadler, Bernice.

Reese, Nancy, et al. Elephant Set, 10 bks. Jordan, Alton, ed. (Illus.). (J). (gr. k-3). 1984. Set. 69.50 (*0-89868-011-5*, Read Res); Set. pap. 35.00 (*0-89868-044-1*, Read Res) ARO Pub.

***Reese, Nicholas.** Art in Focus: Washington. (Illus.). 128p. 1995. 12.95 (*0-8212-2233-3*) Bulfinch Pr.

Reese, Paul & Henderson, Joe. Ten Million Steps: The Incredible Journey of Paul Reese. (Illus.). 240p. 1993. pap. 12.95 (*1-56796-014-6*) WRS Group.

Reese, R. Thessalonians. 1989. pap. 21.00 (*0-86217-022-2*, Pub. by Veritas IE) St Mut.

Reese, R. Page. Don't Move. LC 94-75765. 325p. 1994. lib. bdg. 19.95 (*0-9609672-1-4*) Jeanies Classics.

Reese, Randy L. & Minirth, Frank. Growing into Wholeness: Putting Body, Mind & Spirit Back Together. 170p. 1993. 15.99 (*0-8024-3286-7*) Moody.

Reese, Reuben A. The True Doctrine of Ultra Vires in the Law of Corporations, Being a Concise Presentation of the Doctrine in Its Application to the Powers & Liabilities of Private & Municipal Corporations. lxxi, 338p. 1981. reprint ed. lib. bdg. 30.00 (*0-8377-1031-6*) Rothman.

Reese, Richard E. & Betts, Robert F. Handbook of Antibiotics. 2nd ed. LC 92-48900. (Little, Brown Handbook Ser.). 672p. 1993. 31.95 (*0-316-73719-4*) Little.

Reese, Richard G., III, jt. auth. see Reese, Suzanne L.

Reese, Rick. Greater Yellowstone: The National Park & Adjoining Wildlands. rev. ed. (Montana Geographic Ser.: No. 6). (Illus.). 104p. 1991. pap. 14.95 (*1-56037-004-1*) Am Wrld Geog.

— Montana Mountain Ranges. rev. ed. (Montana Geographic Ser.: No. 1). (Illus.). 104p. 1985. pap. 14.95 (*0-938314-17-3*) Am Wrld Geog.

Reese, Robert. Flying with One Wing. 176p. (Orig.). 1992. pap. 8.95 (*0-9633351-2-X*) Blue Pacific.

— Healing Fits: The Cure of an Epileptic. LC 87-27668. 175p. (Orig.). 1988. pap. 7.95 (*0-944592-00-7*) Big Sky Pr.

Reese, Robert T. & Kawahara, Wendell A. Handbook on Structural Testing. LC 93-9439. 1993. 95.00 (*0-88173-155-2*) Fairmont Pr.

Reese, Ron. Crazy Cat. Jordan, Alton, ed. (I Can Read Ser.). (Illus.). (J). (gr. k-3). 1984. 6.95 (*0-89868-002-6*, Read Res); pap. 3.50 (*0-89868-035-2*, Read Res) ARO Pub.

— Crazy Cat's Bad Day. Jordan, Alton, ed. (Buppet Bks.). (Illus.). (J). (gr. 1-4). 1980. 9.25 (*0-89868-090-5*, Read Res); pap. 3.50 (*0-89868-101-4*, Read Res) ARO Pub.

— Halloween. Jordan, Alton, ed. (Holiday Set). (Illus.). (J). (gr. k-3). 1984. 6.95 (*0-89868-023-9*, Read Res); pap. 3.50 (*0-89868-056-5*, Read Res) ARO Pub.

— Sammy Skunk. (I Can Read Ser.). (Illus.). (J). (gr. k-3). 1984. 6.95 (*0-89868-009-3*, Read Res) ARO Pub.

— Sammy Skunk. Jordan, Alton, ed. (I Can Read Ser.). (Illus.). (J). (gr. k-3). 1984. pap. 3.50 (*0-89868-042-5*, Read Res) ARO Pub.

— Toy Bear. Jordan, Alton, ed. (I Can Eat an Elephant Ser.). (Illus.). (J). (gr. k-3). 1984. 6.95 (*0-89868-016-6*, Read Res); pap. 3.50 (*0-89868-049-2*, Read Res) ARO Pub.

Reese, Ron, et al. Holiday Series, 10 bks. Jordan, Alton, ed. (Illus.). (J). (gr. k-3). 1984. Set. 69.50 (*0-89868-022-0*, Read Res); Set. pap. 35.00 (*0-89868-055-7*, Read Res) ARO Pub.

Reese, Stephen, jt. auth. see Shoemaker, Pamela.

Reese, Stephen D., jt. auth. see Shemaker, Pamela J.

Reese, Suzanne L. & Reese, Richard G., III. Pilots Guide to Southwestern Airports. (Illus.). 550p. 1982. Flight guide/airport directory. 34.95 (*0-9622494-0-8*) RGR Pubns.

Reese, T. Winning at Casino Gambling. 1979. pap. 4.99 (*0-451-16777-5*, ROC) NAL-Dutton.

***Reese, Taylor & Pyle, Jack R.** You & the Man in the Moon: The Almanac User's Complete Instruction Book. (Illus.). 150p. (Orig.). 1995. pap. 13.95 (*1-878086-44-8*) Down Home NC.

Reese, Taylor, jt. auth. see Pyle, Jack.

Reese, Terence. Begin Bridge with Reese. 1979. pap. 4.50 (*0-451-16292-7*, Sig) NAL-Dutton.

— Bridge for Ambitious Players. 144p. 1988. pap. 15.95 (*0-575-04176-5*, Pub. by V Gollancz UK) Trafalgar.

— Bridge for Bright Beginners. 144p. 1973. reprint ed. pap. 3.95 (*0-486-22942-4*) Dover.

— Brilliancies & Blunders in the European Bridge Championship. 1992. text ed. 11.95 (*1-85744-500-7*, Maxwell Macmillan) Macmillan.

— C. C. Wei's Precision System. 98p. (Orig.). 1970. pap. 2.50 (*0-87643-033-7*) M Lisa Precision.

— Do You Really Want to Win at Bridge? 159p. 1989. pap. 15.95 (*0-575-04404-7*, Pub. by V Gollancz UK) Trafalgar.

— Master Play in Contract Bridge. (Illus.). 144p. 1974. reprint ed. 3.95 (*0-486-20336-0*) Dover.

— Master Plays in a Single Suit. 8p. 1988. pap. 3.95 (*0-575-04132-3*, Pub. by V Gollancz UK) Trafalgar.

— Winning at Casino Gambling. 1979. pap. 3.95 (*0-451-15937-3*, AE3110, Sig) NAL-Dutton.

Reese, Terence & Bird, David. All You Need to Know about Bidding. (Illus.). 128p. 1993. 24.95 (*0-575-05378-X*, Pub. by V Gollancz UK) Trafalgar.

— All You Need to Know about Play. 128p. 1994. 24.95 (*0-575-05670-3*, Pub. by V Gollancz UK) Trafalgar.

— All You Need to Know about Play. LC 94-45165. (Master Bridge Ser.). 120p. 1995. pap. 9.95 (*0-395-72861-4*) HM.

— The Art of Good Bidding. 192p. (Orig.). 1993. pap. 10.95 (*0-571-16716-0*) Faber & Faber.

— Bridge - Tricks of the Trade. 144p. 1992. pap. 13.95 (*0-575-05024-1*, Pub. by V Gollancz UK) Trafalgar.

— Cardinal Sins. (Master Bridge Ser.). 128p. 1991. 24.95 (*0-575-04997-9*, Pub. by V Gollancz UK) Trafalgar.

— Doubled & Venerable: Further Miracles of Card Play. (Illus.). 183p. 1993. pap. 15.95 (*0-575-05425-5*, Pub. by V Gollancz UK) Trafalgar.

— Famous Hands from Famous Matches. LC 91-4060. (Maxwell Macmillan Bridge Ser.). 164p. 1991. pap. 15.95 (*1-85744-501-5*, Pub. by CHES UK) Macmillan.

— The Hidden Side of Bridge. 160p. 1987. pap. 7.95 (*0-571-14910-3*) Faber & Faber.

— Make a Start at Bridge. 224p. (Orig.). 1994. pap. 10.95 (*0-571-17112-5*) Faber & Faber.

— Miracles of Card Play. (Master Bridge Ser.). (Illus.). 128p. 1982. 18.95 (*0-575-03079-8*, Pub. by V Gollancz UK) Trafalgar.

— Miracles of Card Play. 160p. 1989. pap. 13.95 (*0-575-04505-1*, Pub. by V Gollancz UK) Trafalgar.

— That Elusive Extra Trick. 128p. 1995. pap. 13.95 (*0-575-05816-1*, Pub. by V Gollancz UK) Trafalgar.

— Unholy Tricks: More Miraculous Card Play. 128p. 1995. pap. 13.95 (*0-575-05944-3*, Pub. by V Gollancz UK) Trafalgar.

Reese, Terence & Dormer, Albert. The Complete Book of Bridge. 2nd ed. LC 84-28767. 475p. 1985. pap. 13.95 (*0-571-13528-5*) Faber & Faber.

Reese, Terence & Flint, Jeremy. Bridge with the Professional Touch. (Master Bridge Ser.). 128p. 1991. pap. 13.95 (*0-575-04998-7*, Pub. by V Gollancz UK) Trafalgar.

Reese, Terence & Pottage, Julian. The Extra Edge in Play. 112p. 1994. pap. 13.95 (*0-575-05737-8*, Pub. by V Gollancz UK) Trafalgar.

Reese, Terence & Trezel, Roger. The Art of Defence in Bridge. 80p. 1988. pap. 9.95 (*0-575-02598-0*, Pub. by V Gollancz UK) Trafalgar.

— Blocking & Unblocking Plays in Bridge. (Master Bridge Ser.). (Illus.). 128p. 1991. pap. 9.95 (*0-575-02749-5*, Pub. by V Gollancz UK) Trafalgar.

— Blocking, Unblocking, & Safety Plays in Bridge. LC 92-35310. 128p. 1993. pap. 8.95 (*0-395-65669-9*) HM.

— The Mistakes You Make at Bridge. (Master Bridge Ser.). 160p. 1992. pap. 9.95 (*0-395-62891-1*) HM.

— Safety Plays in Bridge. (Master Bridge Ser.). (Illus.). 64p. 1976. pap. 9.95 (*0-575-02748-7*, Pub. by V Gollancz UK) Trafalgar.

— Snares & Swindles in Bridge. 1977. pap. 8.95 (*0-575-02633-2*, Pub. by V Gollancz UK) Trafalgar.

— Those Extra Chances in Bridge. (Master Class Ser.). (Illus.). 128p. 1987. pap. 7.95 (*0-575-02634-0*, Pub. by V Gollancz UK) Trafalgar.

Reese, Terence & Watkins, A. T. How to Win at Poker. 1976. pap. 7.00 (*0-87980-070-4*) Wilshire.

Reese, Terence, tr. see Le Dentu, Jose.

Reese, Terence, jt. auth. see McNeil, Keith.

Reese, Terence, jt. auth. see Senior, Brian.

Reese, Thomas J. A Flock of Shepherds: The National Conference of Catholic Bishops. LC 92-13530. 416p. (Orig.). 1992. pap. 19.95 (*1-55612-557-7*, LL1557) Sheed & Ward MO.

— The Politics of Taxation. LC 79-8413. (Illus.). xxv, 237p. 1980. text ed. 49.95 (*0-89930-003-0*, RPT/, Quorum Bks) Greenwood.

Reese, Thomas J., ed. Episcopal Conferences: Historical, Canonical, & Theological Studies. LC 89-16784. 312p. 1989. 19.95 (*0-87840-493-7*) Georgetown U Pr.

Reese, Timothy J. Sykes' Regular Infantry Division, 1861-1864: A History of Regular United States Infantry Operations in the Civil War's Eastern Theater. LC 90-42746. 488p. 1990. lib. bdg. 49.95x (*0-89950-447-7*) McFarland & Co.

Reese, William B., jt. auth. see Hoss, E. E.

Reese, William D. & Landry, Garrie. Acadiana Flora: Native & Naturalized Woody Plants of South-Central Louisiana. (Illus.). 126p. 1992. 15.00 (*0-940984-77-6*) U of SW LA Ctr LA Studies.

Reese, William D., jt. auth. see Allen, Noris S.

Reese, William Dean. Mosses of the Gulf South: From the Rio Grande to the Apalachicola. LC 83-889. (Illus.). xvi, 252p. 1984. text ed. 35.00 (*0-8071-1110-4*) La State U Pr.

***Reese, William J.** The Origins of the American High School. LC 94-24975. 1995. write for info. (*0-300-06384-9*) Yale U Pr.

— Power & Promise of School Reform: Grass Roots Movements During the Progressive Era. (Critical Social Thought Ser.). 320p. (C). 1986. text ed. 39.95 (*0-7100-9952-5*, RKP); pap. text ed. 14.95 (*0-7102-0767-0*, RKP) Routledge.

Reese, William J., jt. ed. see McClellan, B. Edward.

Reese, William L. Dictionary of Philosophy & Religion: Eastern & Western Thought. LC 78-12561. 644p. (C). 1980. pap. 25.00 (*0-391-00941-9*) Humanities.

Reese, William S. The First Hundred Years of Printing in British North America: Printers & Collectors. 37p. 1990. reprint ed. pap. 5.00 (*0-944026-19-2*) Am Antiquarian.

— The Printers' First Fruits: An Exhibition of American Imprints, 1640-1742, from the Collections of the American Antiquarian Society. (Illus.). 52p. 1989. pap. 15.00 (*0-944026-15-X*) Am Antiquarian.

Reese, William S., jt. auth. see Field, Thomas W.

Reese, Willis L., et al. Conflict of Laws: Cases & Materials. 9th ed. (University Casebook Ser.). 1021p. 1990. text ed. 42.50 (*0-88277-789-0*) Foundation Pr.

— Conflict of Laws: Cases & Materials. 9th ed. (University Casebook Ser.). 186p. 1990. teacher ed, pap. text ed. write for info. (*0-88277-851-X*) Foundation Pr.

Reeser, Jacki, ed. see Madewell, Terry.

Reeser, M. P. Introduction to Public Utility Accounting. 407p. write for info. (*0-318-59899-X*) Am Gas Assn.

Reeser, Michael. Huan Ching & the Golden Fish. (Publish-a-Book Contest Ser.). (Illus.). 32p. (J). (gr. 2-4). 1988. lib. bdg. 19.97 (*0-8172-2751-2*); pap. 4.95 (*0-8114-5213-1*) Raintree Steck-V.

Reeser, Renee, ed. see Wrath.

Reesing, John. Milton's Poetic Art: A Mask, Lycidas, & Paradise Lost. LC 68-17632. 222p. reprint ed. 63.30 (*0-8357-9166-1*, 2017011) Bks Demand.

Reesink, Carole J., ed. Teacher-Made Aids for Elementary School Mathematics, Vol. 2: Readings from the Arithmetic Teacher. LC 73-21581. (Illus.). 185p. 1985. pap. 12.00 (*0-87353-225-2*) NCTM.

Reesink, Ger P. Structures & Their Functions in Usan: A Papuan Language of Papua New Guinea. LC 86-17518. (Studies in Language Companion: Vol. 13). xviii, 369p. 1987. 97.00x (*90-272-3015-3*) Benjamins North Am.

Reesink, H., ed. Hepatitis C Virus. (Current Studies in Hematology & Blood Transfusion: No. 61). (Illus.). viii, 212p. 1994. 193.75 (*3-8055-5866-X*) S Karger.

***Reesink, H. W., et al, eds.** International Society of Blood Transfusion, 23rd Congress, Amsterdam 1994: State of the Art Lectures, No. 67. (Journal: Vox Sanguinis Ser.: Supplement 3, 1994). (Illus.). iv, 274p. 1994. pap. 76.00 (*3-8055-6018-4*) S Karger.

***Reesman, Ann E.** The Americans with Disabilities Act: Disability As a Threshold Issue. 22p. 1990. pap. 10.00x (*0-614-06162-8*, 2023-PP-4040) EPF.

— The Americans with Disabilities Act: Medical Examinations & Inquiries. 18p. 1990. pap. 10.00x (*0-614-06164-4*, 2023B-PP-4040) EPF.

— The Americans with Disabilities Act: Qualified Individual with a Disability. 31p. 1990. pap. 10.00x (*0-614-06163-6*, 2023A-PP-4040) EPF.

— Should Federal Law Provide Monetary Damages for Harassment? 30p. 1991. pap. 10.00 (*0-614-06157-1*, 2028-PP-4040) EPF.

***Reesman, Ann E., ed.** Americans with Disabilities Act Desk Reference. 1160p. 1992. 90.00 (*0-916559-36-X*, 2002-MO-4035) EPF.

Reesman, Ann E., jt. auth. see Potter, Eddward E.

Reesman, Ann E., jt. auth. see Potter, Edward E.

Reesman, Ann E., jt. auth. see Yager, Daniel V.

Reesman, Jeanne C. American Designs: The Late Novels of James & Faulkner. LC 90-19272. 248p. (C). 1991. text ed. 29.95x (*0-8122-8253-1*) U of Pa Pr.

Reesman, Jeanne C., jt. auth. see Labor, Earl.

Reesor, Margaret E. The Nature of Man in Early Stoic Philosophy. LC 89-37509. 179p. 1989. text ed. 49.95 (*0-312-03579-9*) St Martin.

Reetz, Dorothea. Clara Zetkin As a Socialist Speaker. LC 86-27178. 76p. 1987. pap. 3.95 (*0-7178-0649-9*) Intl Pubs Co.

Reetz, Elaine. Come Back in Time, Vol. 2. (Illus.). 240p. 1982. pap. 9.95 (*0-939398-03-6*) Fox River.

Reetz, Elaine, et al. Come Back in Time: Communities, Vol. I. (Illus.). 184p. 1981. pap. 8.95 (*0-939398-00-1*) Fox River.

Reetz, Henry C. Electroplating. (Illus.). 99p. reprint ed. pap. 6.95 (*1-55918-008-0*) Lindsay Pubns.

Reetz, M. T. Organotitanium Reagents in Organic Synthesis. (Reactivity & Structure Ser.: Vol. 24). (Illus.). 240p. 1986. 109.00 (*0-387-15784-0*) Spr-Verlag.

Reeve, et al. Managerial Accounting. 3rd ed. (C). 1994. text ed. 51.95 (*0-538-82185-X*, AQ65CA) S-W Pub.

Reeve, Agnesa, comp. & intro. My Dear Mollie: Love Letters of a Texas Sheep Rancher. LC 90-41891. (Illus.). 192p. (J). (gr. 5 up). 1990. 17.95 (*0-937460-62-1*) Hendrick-Long.

Reeve, Agnesa & Reeve, Jack. Cooking with a Handful of Ingredients: Delicious Meals in the Palm of Your Hand. LC 91-77268. 272p. (Orig.). 1992. pap. 15.95 (*0-9631401-6-7*) Cimarron NM.

Reeve, Andrew, ed. Modern Theories of Exploitation. (Modern Politics Ser.: Vol. 14). 214p. (C). 1987. text ed. 45.00 (*0-8039-8072-8*); pap. text ed. 17.95 (*0-8039-8073-6*) Sage.

Reeve, Andrew & Ware, Alan. Electoral Systems: A Theoretical & Comparative Introduction. (Theory & Practice in British Politics Ser.). (Illus.). 272p. 1991. 67.50 (*0-415-01204-X*, A6670) Routledge.

Reeve, Andrew, jt. auth. see Goodin, Robert E.

Reeve, Andrew, jt. auth. see Lively, Jack.

Reeve, Andru J. Turn Me on, Dead Man: The Complete Story of the Paul McCartney Death Hoax. (Rock & Roll Remembrances Ser.: No. 12). (Illus.). 224p. 1994. lib. bdg. 40.00 (*1-56075-035-9*) Popular Culture.

Reeve, Anne & Screech, M. A., eds. Erasmus' Annotations on the New Testament: Acts, Romans, First & Second Corinthians - Facsimile of the Final Latin Text with All Earlier Variants. LC 89-15792. (Studies in the History of Christian Thought: Vol. XLII). xxxiv, 297p. 1989. 80.00 (*90-04-09124-6*) E J Brill.

— Erasmus' Annotations on the New Testament: Galatians to the Apocalypse, Facsimile of the Final Latin Text with All Earlier Variants. LC 93-29006. (Studies in the History of Christian Thought: No. 52). vii, 293p. 1993. 85.75 (*90-04-09906-9*) E J Brill.

Reeve, Arthur B. Poisoned Pen. LC 70-150561. (Short Story Index Reprint Ser.). (Illus.). 1977. reprint ed. 23.95 (*0-8369-3858-5*) Ayer.

— The Silent Bullet: The Adventures of Craig Kennedy, Scientific Detective. LC 75-32795. (Literature of Mystery & Detection Ser.). (Illus.). 1976. reprint ed. 34.95 (*0-405-07896-X*) Ayer.

Reeve, C. D. Philosopher-Kings: The Argument of Plato's "Republic" (Illus.). 400p. 1992. reprint ed. text ed. 55.00 (*0-691-07326-0*); reprint ed. pap. text ed. 17.95 (*0-691-02094-9*) Princeton U Pr.

— Practices of Reason: Aristotle's Nicomachean Ethics. 240p. 1992. 49.95 (*0-19-823984-X*) OUP.

— Practices of Reason: Aristotle's Nicomachean Ethics. 240p. 1995. pap. 21.00 (*0-19-823565-8*) OUP.

— Socrates in the Apology: An Essay on Plato's Apology of Socrates. LC 89-33069. (Illus.). 224p. 1989. 34.95 (*0-87220-089-2*); pap. 12.95 (*0-87220-088-4*) Hackett Pub.

Reeve, Catherine & Sward, Marilyn. The New Photography: A Guide to New Images, Processes, & Display Techniques for Photographers. (Quality Paperbacks Ser.). (Illus.). xiv, 242p. 1987. reprint ed. pap. 16.95 (*0-306-80295-3*) Da Capo.

Reeve, Charles & Watts, Jacqueline, eds. Groundwater, Drought, Pollution & Management: Proceedings of the International Conference, Brighton, 1994. (Illus.). 263p. (C). 1994. 95.00 (*90-5410-351-5*, Pub. by A A Balkema NE) Ashgate Pub Co.

Reeve, Cintra, jt. auth. see Gray, Rebecca.

Reeve, D. A. C. I. I. Pension Scheme Design & Administration, No. 170-060. (C). 1984. 240.00 (*0-685-33746-4*, Pub. by Witherby & Co UK) St Mut.

Reeve, F. A. The Cambridge That Never Was. (Cambridge Town, Gown & County Ser.: Vol. 8). (Illus.). 1976. pap. 4.95 (*0-902675-72-9*) Oleander Pr.

Reeve, F. D. Concrete Music. 88p. 1992. 18.00 (*1-881119-56-4*); pap. 11.00 (*1-881119-72-6*) Pyncheon Hse.

— Concrete Music & Other Poems. limited ed. 96p. 1993. 75.00 (*1-881119-84-X*) Pyncheon Hse.

— A Few Rounds of Old Maid & Other Stories. LC 94-79252. 144p. (Orig.). 1995. pap. text ed. 12.95 (*1-885214-00-6*) Azul Edits.

— The White Monk: An Essay on Dostoevsky & Melville. LC 89-35562. 192p. 1990. 22.50 (*0-8265-1234-8*) Vanderbilt U Pr.

Reeve, F. D., ed. & tr. Nineteenth-Century Russian Plays. (Library Ser.: No. N683). 464p. 1973. reprint ed. pap. 13.95 (*0-393-00683-2*) Norton.

Reeve, F. D. & Meek, Jay, eds. After the Storm: Poems on the Persian Gulf War. LC 92-11673. 1992. pap. 10.95 (*0-944624-16-2*) Maisonneuve Pr.

Reeve, Frank A. Cambridge College Walks. (Cambridge Town, Gown & County Ser.: Vol. 25). (Illus.). 1978. pap. 4.95 (*0-900891-42-4*) Oleander Pr.

— Cambridge College Walks French Edition. (Cambridge Town, Gown & County Ser.: Vol. 25). (Illus.). 1978. pap. 4.95 (*0-685-55599-2*) Oleander Pr.

— Cambridge College Walks German. (Cambridge Town, Gown & County Ser.: Vol. 25). (Illus.). 1978. pap. 4.95 (*0-685-55600-X*) Oleander Pr.

— The Cambridge Nobody Knows. (Cambridge Town, Gown & County Ser.: Vol. 14). (Illus.). 1977. pap. 4.95 (*0-900891-10-6*) Oleander Pr.

— Promenades a Cambridge. (Cambridge Town, Gown & County Ser.: Vol. 26). (Illus.). (FRE.). 1978. pap. 4.95 (*0-900891-43-2*) Oleander Pr.

— Spaziergange durch Cambridge. (Cambridge Town, Gown & County Ser.: Vol. 27). (Illus.). (GER.). 1978. pap. 4.95 (*0-900891-44-0*) Oleander Pr.

— Varsity Rags & Hoaxes. (Cambridge Town, Gown & County Ser.: Vol. 17). (Illus.). 1977. pap. 4.95 (*0-900891-16-5*) Oleander Pr.

Reeve, Frank D. Navajo Foreign Affairs: Seventeen Ninety-Five to Eighteen Forty-Six. 1983. pap. 4.00 (*0-912586-51-6*) Navajo Coll Pr.

Reeve, Franklin D., ed. Contemporary Russian Drama. LC 68-20138. 1968. 35.00 (*0-672-53521-1*); pap. text ed. 14.95 (*0-8290-2101-9*) Irvington.

Reeve, Helen, tr. see Zernova, Ruth.

Reeve, Helen H. Brown County, Indiana, Abstracts of Probate Records, 1836-1945. 607p. 1992. text ed. 75.00 (*0-9616808-5-7*) Brown Cnty Hist Soc.

— Brown County, Indiana Circuit Court Records, Civil & Criminal, 1836-1945. 905p. 1993. text ed. 100.00 (*0-9616808-6-5*) Brown Cnty Hist Soc.

— Brown County, Indiana Federal Census Index, 1840 through 1910. 500p. 1988. 35.00 (*0-9616808-4-9*) Brown Cnty Hist Soc.

— Brown County, Indiana Obituaries 1914-1984, 2 vols., I. 1708p. 1986. write for info. (*0-9616808-1-4*) Brown Cnty Hist Soc.

— Brown County, Indiana Obituaries 1914-1984, 2 vols., II. 1708p. 1986. write for info. (*0-9616808-2-2*) Brown Cnty Hist Soc.

— Brown County, Indiana Obituaries 1914-1984, 2 vols., Set. 1708p. 1986. 100.00 (*0-9616808-0-6*) Brown Cnty Hist Soc.

Reeve, Henry, tr. see De Tocqueville, Alexis.

Reeve, Jack, jt. auth. see Reeve, Agnesa.

Reeve, James H. Wolves in Sheeps' Clothing: How to Recognize False Prophets & Protect Your Family from Their Influence. (Orig.). 1994. pap. write for info. (*1-884781-00-4*) Quest For Excell.

Reeve, James K. The Art of Showing Art. rev. ed. LC 86-61319. (Illus.). 144p. (Orig.). 1992. pap. 14.95 (*0-933031-67-X*) Coun Oak Bks.

Reeve, John & Chattington, Jenny. The Anglo-Saxons Activity Book. (British Museum Activity Bks.). (Illus.). 16p. (J). 1994. pap. 5.95 (*0-500-27762-1*) Thames Hudson.

Reeve, John, et al. The Anglo-Saxons. (Illus.). (J). (gr. 2-6). pap. 4.95 (*0-7141-0537-6*, Pub. by Brit Mus UK) Parkwest Pubns.

Reeve, Johnmarshall. Understanding Motivation & Emotion. 544p. (C). 1992. text ed. 42.75 (*0-03-030512-8*) HB Coll Pubs.

Reeve, Joseph R., Jr., ed. Cholecystokinin. LC 94-4554. (Annals Ser.: Vol. 713). 1994. write for info. (*0-89766-857-X*); pap. 130.00 (*0-89766-858-8*) NY Acad Sci.

Reeve, Kay A. Santa Fe & Taos, Eighteen Ninety-Eight to Nineteen Forty-Two: An American Cultural Center. (Southwestern Studies: No. 67). (Illus.). 72p. 1982. pap. 10.00 (*0-87404-126-0*) Tex Western.

Reeve, M. R., jt. ed. see Grice, G. D.

Reeve, Mike & Zenith, Steven E., eds. Parallel Processing & Artificial Intelligence. LC 89-16532. (Wiley Communicating Process Architecture Ser.). (Illus.). 307p. reprint ed. pap. 87.50 (*0-7837-6393-X*, 2046106) Bks Demand.

Reeve, N. H. The Novels of Rex Warner: An Introduction. 190p. 1990. text ed. 45.00 (*0-312-03703-1*) St Martin.

Reeve, Pamela. Faith Is. . . 49p. 1970. pap. 5.99 (*0-930014-05-7*, Multnomah Bks) Questar Pubs.

— Faith Is-- LC 94-11231. 1994. 5.99 (*0-88070-691-0*, Multnomah Bks) Questar Pubs.

— Faith Is. rev. ed. 75p. 1994. pap. 12.99 (*0-88070-622-8*, Multnomah Bks) Questar Pubs.

— Parables by the Sea. LC 77-6209. (Illus.). 46p. 1976. pap. 6.99 (*0-930014-11-1*) Questar Pubs.

— Parables of the Forest. Libby, Larry, ed. LC 88-36472. (Illus.). 49p. (Orig.). 1989. pap. 6.99 (*0-88070-306-7*, Multnomah Bks) Questar Pubs.

Reeve, Paul, jt. auth. see Brown, Dave.

Reeve, R., ed. Chlamydial Infections. (Illus.). 145p. 1987. pap. 51.00 (*0-387-16552-5*) Spr-Verlag.

Reeve, Rachel, jt. ed. see Wintle, Michael.

Reeve, Richard M. An Annotated Bibliography on Carlos Fuentes: 1949-69. 56p. 1970. 2.00 (*0-318-12189-1*) AATSP.

Reeve, Roger N. Environmental Analysis. Barnes, John D., ed. LC 93-46292. 1994. pap. text ed. 34.95 (*0-471-93833-5*) Wiley.

Reeve, Stuart A., et al. An Archaeological & Historical Survey of Myrtle Point, St. Mary's County, Maryland. (Occasional Papers: No. 3). (Illus.). 209p. 1991. 18.00 (*1-878399-09-8*) Div Hist Cult Progs.

Reeve, T. G., jt. ed. see Proctor, R. W.

Reeve, Tapping. The Law of Baron & Femme: Of Parent & Child: Of Guardian & Ward: Of Master & Servant: & of the Powers of Court of Chancery. Helmholz, R H. & Reams, Bernard D., Jr., eds. LC 80-84865. (Historical Writings in Law & Jurisprudence Ser.: No. 11, bk. 14). x, 502p. 1981. reprint ed. lib. bdg. 52.50 (*0-89941-066-9*, 301320) W S Hein.

— A Treatise on the Law of Descents, in the Several United States of America. Helmholz, R. H. & Reams, Bernard D., Jr., eds. LC 80-84864. (Historical Writings in Law & Jurisprudence Ser.: No. 12, Bk. 15). iv, 515p. 1981. reprint ed. lib. bdg. 52.00 (*0-89941-067-7*, 301330) W S Hein.

***Reeve, Tim.** Action Robots: A Pop-Up Book Showing How They Work. LC 95-2543. (Illus.). (J). 1995. 16.95 (*0-8037-1843-8*) Dial Bks Young.

— Machines: A Book of Moving Pop-Ups. LC 92-5752. (Illus.). 22p. (J). (gr. 1 up). 1993. 15.95 (*0-399-21974-9*, Philomel Bks) Putnam Pub Group.

Reeve, W. Kannada-English. 2nd ed. 1040p. 1980. 38.00 (*0-88431-107-4*) IBD Ltd.

— Kannada-English Dictionary. rev. ed. 1040p. (ENG & KAN.). 1980. 75.00 (*0-8288-1144-X*, M 14009) Fr & Eur.

Reeve, W. D. Public Administration in Siam. LC 74-179236. reprint ed. 24.50 (*0-404-54863-6*) AMS Pr.

— The Republic of Korea: A Political & Economic Study. LC 79-9857. 197p. 1979. reprint ed. text ed. 49.75 (*0-313-21265-1*, RERK, Greenwood Pr) Greenwood.

Reeve, Whitham D. Subscriber Loop Signaling & Transmission Handbook: Analog. LC 91-19685. (Telecommunications Handbook Ser.). (Illus.). 304p. (C). 1992. text ed. 59.95 (*0-87942-274-2*, PC0268-3) Inst Electrical.

— Subscriber Loop Signaling & Transmission Handbook: Digital. (Telecommunications Handbook Series). 654p. 1994. 69.95 (*0-7803-0440-3*) Inst Electrical.

Reeve, William. Hammer, Compass & Traverse-Wheel. 175p. (C). 1989. text ed. 59.00 (*1-872795-33-1*, Pub. by Pentland Pr UK) St Mut.

Reeve, William C. George Buchner. LC 77-4599. (Literature & Life Ser.). (Illus.). 192p. (C). 1979. 19.95 (*0-8044-2711-9*, F Ungar Bks) Continuum.

— In Pursuit of Power: Heinrich von Kleist's Machiavellian Protagonists. 236p. 1987. 35.00 (*0-8020-5702-0*) U of Toronto Pr.

— Kleist on Stage, 1804-1987. (Illus.). 256p. 1993. 44.96 (*0-7735-0941-0*, Pub. by McGill CN) U of Toronto Pr.

— Kleist's Aristocratic Heritage & Das Kathchen von Heilbronn. 1991. 49.95 (*0-7735-0869-4*, Pub. by McGill CN) U of Toronto Pr.

Reeven, Reb. The Jewish Riddle Collection: A Yiddle's Riddle. (Illus.). 164p. 1990. pap. 7.95 (*0-933503-38-5*) Sure Sellers.

Reeves, jt. auth. see Weir.

***Reeves, Adrienne E.** Change of Heart. 288p. 1995. pap. 4.99 (*0-8217-0103-7*) Zebra.

— Change of Heart. 1995. pap. 4.99 (*0-7860-0103-8*, Pinnacle NY) Windsor NY.

— Willie & the Number Three Door & Other Adventures. (Illus.). 120p. (Orig.). (J). (gr. 1-3). 1991. pap. 8.95 (*0-87743-703-3*) Bahai.

Reeves, Alexander G. Disorders of the Nervous System: A Primer. LC 80-24086. (Internal Medicine Ser.). 252p. reprint ed. pap. 71.90 (*0-318-34997-3*, 2030851) Bks Demand.

Reeves, Alexander G., ed. Epilepsy & the Corpus Callosum. LC 85-3465. 520p. 1985. 125.00 (*0-306-41848-7*, Plenum Pr) Plenum.

Reeves, Andree E. Congressional Committee Chairmen: Three Who Made an Evolution. LC 92-34812. (Illus.). 280p. 1993. text ed. 39.00 (*0-8131-1816-6*) U Pr of Ky.

Reeves, Anne-Rose, jt. auth. see Barr, Randolph W.

Reeves, Arthur. The Golden Age of Crime. (Criminology Ser.). 1992. lib. bdg. 76.95 (*0-8490-5297-1*) Gordon Pr.

***Reeves, Barbara.** April Morning. Friedland, J. & Kessler, R., eds. (Novel-Ties Ser.). (YA). 1992. student ed, pap. text ed. 15.95 (*0-88122-714-5*) Lrn Links.

— Bunnicula: A Study Guide. Friedland, Joyce & Kessler, Rikki, eds. (Novel-Ties Ser.). (J). (gr. 2-5). 1991. pap. text ed. 15.95 (*0-88122-572-X*) Lrn Links.

— Cheaper by the Dozen. Friedland, J. & Kessler, R., eds. (Novel-Ties Ser.). (YA). (gr. 7-10). 1994. student ed, pap. text ed. 15.95 (*1-56982-073-2*) Lrn Links.

— The Civil War: A Study Guide. (Historical Ties Ser.). (J). (gr. 5-8). 1991. pap. text ed. 20.95 (*0-88122-688-2*) Lrn Links.

— The Dangerous Marquis. 240p. (Orig.). 1994. mass mkt. 3.99 (*0-380-77672-3*) Avon.

— Farewell to Manzanar: A Study Guide. Friedland, Joyce & Kessler, Rikki, eds. (Novel-Ties Ser.). (J). (gr. 7-10). 1991. pap. text ed. 14.95 (*0-88122-583-5*) Lrn Links.

— Georgina's Campaign. 180p. 1991. 19.95 (*0-8027-1185-5*) Walker & Co.

— Georgina's Campaign. (Regency Novel Ser.). 192p. 1993. reprint ed. mass mkt. 3.99 (*0-380-71968-1*) Avon.

— Hamlet. Friedland, J. & Kessler, R., eds. (Novel-Ties Ser.). (YA). (gr. 10-12). 1995. student ed, pap. text ed. 15.95 (*1-56982-322-7*) Lrn Links.

— Lacy's Dilemma. 224p. (Orig.). 1995. mass mkt. 3.99 (*0-380-77673-1*) Avon.

— Lantern in Her Hand. Friedland, J. & Kessler, R., eds. (Novel-Ties Ser.). (YA). 1992. student ed, pap. text ed. 15.95 (*0-88122-716-1*) Lrn Links.

— The Lilies of the Field: A Study Guide. Friedland, Joyce & Kessler, Rikki, eds. (Novel-Ties Ser.). (YA). (gr. 8-12). 1991. pap. text ed. 15.95 (*0-88122-585-1*) Lrn Links.

— The Much Maligned Lord. 192p. (Orig.). 1993. mass mkt. 3.99 (*0-380-77332-5*) Avon.

— Murder on the Orient Express. Friedland, J. & Kessler, R., eds. (Novel-Ties Ser.). (YA). 1992. student ed, pap. text ed. 15.95 (*0-88122-717-X*) Lrn Links.

— Number the Stars: A Study Guide. Friedland, Joyce & Kessler, Rikki, eds. (Novel-Ties Ser.). (J). (gr. 5-8). 1991. pap. text ed. 15.95 (*0-88122-579-7*) Lrn Links.

— Scandalous Courtship. 190p. 1993. 19.95 (*0-8027-1258-4*) Walker & Co.

— A Scandalous Courtship. 208p. 1994. mass mkt. 3.99 (*0-380-72151-1*) Avon.

— The Slave Dancer. Friedland, J. & Kessler, R., eds. (Novel-Ties Ser.). (J). (gr. 5-7). 1993. pap. text ed. 15.95 (*0-88122-905-9*) Lrn Links.

— Thunder at Gettysburg. Friedland, J. & Kessler, R., eds. (Novel-Ties Ser.). (J). (gr. 1-3). 1993. student ed, pap. text ed. 15.95 (*0-88122-881-8*) Lrn Links.

— The War Between the Classes: A Study Guide. Friedland, Joyce & Kessler, Rikki, eds. (Novel-Ties Ser.). (J). (gr. 7-10). 1991. pap. text ed. 15.95 (*0-88122-586-X*) Lrn Links.

— When the Legends Die. Friedland, J. & Kessler, R., eds. (Novel-Ties Ser.). (YA). (gr. 7-10). 1993. student ed, pap. text ed. 15.95 (*0-88122-898-2*) Lrn Links.

Reeves, Barbara, ed. see Friedland, Joyce & Kessler, Rikki.

***Reeves, Barbara M.** The French Riviera Cote d'Azur: Self-Guided Tours. (Illus.). 182p. (Orig.). Date not set. pap. write for info. (*0-9643520-0-1*) B Reeves.

Reeves, Betsy, ed. see Athology Reprints Staff.

***Reeves, Bill.** North Carolina Freedman's Savings & Trust Company Records. 598p. 1995. 30.00 (*0-614-04971-7*) N C Genealogical.

Reeves, C. C., Jr. Caliche-Origin Classification, Morphology & Uses. LC 76-2234. 1976. text ed. 39.95 (*0-686-16733-3*) Estacado Bks.

Reeves, C. N. After Tut 'Ankhamun: Research & Excavation in the Royal Necropolis at Thebes. LC 90-43443. 211p. 1992. 95.00 (*0-7103-0406-4*, Pub. by Kegan Paul Intl UK) Routledge Chapman & Hall.

Reeves, Carole. Egyptian Medicine. (Shire Egyptology Ser.). (Illus.). 72p. 1992. pap. 12.00 (*0-7478-0127-4*, Pub. by Shire Pubns UK) Lubrecht & Cramer.

Reeves, Carole, jt. auth. see Thornton, John L.

Reeves, Carolyn K., ed. The Choctaw Before Removal. LC 84-13090. 1985. 30.00 (*0-87805-244-5*) U Pr of Miss.

Reeves, Charles A. Problem-Solving Techniques Helpful in Math & Science. LC 87-12219. (Illus.). 35p. 1987. pap. 6.00 (*0-87353-246-5*) NCTM.

Reeves, Charles E. An Analysis of Janitor Service in Elementary Schools. LC 77-177185. (Columbia University. Teachers College. Contributions to Education Ser.: No. 167). reprint ed. 37.50 (*0-404-55167-X*) AMS Pr.

Reeves, Charles H., tr. see Lenhart, John N.

Reeves, Clement. The Psychology of Rollo May: Reflections & Commentary by Rollo May. LC 76-50708. (Jossey-Bass Behavioral Science Ser.). 352p. reprint ed. pap. 100. 40 (*0-8357-6885-6*, 2037937) Bks Demand.

Reeves, Colin. An Introduction to Logical Design of Digital Circuits. LC 77-182029. (Cambridge Computer Science Texts Ser.: No. 1). 198p. reprint ed. pap. 56.50 (*0-317-20798-9*, 2024532) Bks Demand.

— Modern Heuristic Techniques for Combinatorial Problems. 320p. 1993. text ed. 79.95 (*0-470-22079-1*) Halsted Pr.

Reeves, D. Avanzando: Estrategias Modernas De: Always Advancing: Church Growth. (SPA.). 5.25 (*84-7645-293-4*, 223361, Pub. by Edit Clie SP) TSELF.

Reeves, D. S., jt. ed. see Neu, H. C.

Reeves, Dale, ed. see Olshine, David.

Reeves, David, jt. ed. see Lewis, Dierde.

Reeves, David S. & Ullmann, Uwe, eds. High Performance Liquid Chromatography in Medical Microbiology, Vol. 2. 272p. (Orig.). 1986. pap. text ed. 65.00 (*0-89574-215-2*, Pub. by Gustav Fischer Verlag) VCH Pubs.

Reeves, Dennis & Wedding, Danny. The Clinical Assessment of Memory: A Practical Guide. LC 93-36920. 240p. 1993. 38.95 (*0-8261-7920-7*) Springer Pub.

Reeves, Diana. Introduction to Drawing the Nude. 1993. 14. 98 (*1-55521-901-2*) Bk Sales Inc.

Reeves, Diane L. Child Care: A Reference Handbook. (Contemporary World Issues Ser.). 200p. 1992. lib. bdg. 39.50 (*0-87436-645-3*) ABC-CLIO.

***Reeves, Don.** Supervisors' Handbook for Employee Assistance. 40p. 1995. pap. 20.00 (*1-884937-21-7*) Manisses Communs.

Reeves, Don, ed. see Reeves, Jeanne.

Reeves, Donald. Making Sense of Religion. 157p. 1992. pap. 7.95 (*0-563-20759-0*, BBC-Parkwest) Parkwest Pubns.

Reeves, Dorothea D. Resources for the Study of Economic History: A Preliminary Guide to Pre-Twentieth Century Printed Material in Collection. (Kress Library of Business & Economics Publication: No. 16). viiii, 62p. 1961. pap. 9.95 (*0-678-09917-0*, Kress Lib Business) Kelley.

Reeves, E. La Historia De Jesus (The Story of Jesus) (SPA.). Date not set. 5.99 (*1-56063-350-6*, 494011) Editorial Unilit.

Reeves, E. A. Cable Management Systems. (Illus.). 336p. 1992. 76.95 (*0-632-02808-4*) Blackwell Sci.

Reeves, E. A., ed. Newnes Electrical Pocket Book. 21th ed. (Illus.). 528p. 1992. pap. 32.95 (*0-7506-0513-8*) Buttrwrth-Heinemann.

Reeves, E. A., ed. see Bush, K. G.

Reeves, Earl. Aviation's Place in Tomorrow's Business. (Airlines History Project Ser.). reprint ed. 35.00 (*0-404-19331-5*) AMS Pr.

Reeves, Earl, jt. ed. see Filipovitch, Anthony.

***Reeves, Edward B.** The Hidden Government: Ritual, Clientelism, & Legitimation in Northern Egypt. LC 90-52748. 240p. 1990. pap. 68.40 (*0-7837-8557-7*) Bks Demand.

Reeves, Eira. Story of Jesus. (J). (ps). 1992. pap. 6.99 (*0-7814-0975-6*, Chariot Bks) Chariot Family.

Reeves, Eira, illus. Doing Things. LC 91-76214. (Let's Read Bks.). 12p. (J). (ps). 1992. bds. 3.99 (*0-8066-2590-2*, 9-2590, Augsburg) Augsburg Fortress.

— Going Places. LC 91-76215. (Let's Read Bks.). 12p. (J). (ps). 1992. 3.99 (*0-8066-2589-9*, 9-2589) Augsburg Fortress.

— Helping. LC 91-76216. (Let's Read Bks.). 12p. (J). (ps). 1992. bds. 3.99 (*0-8066-2588-0*, 9-2588, Augsburg) Augsburg Fortress.

— Playing. LC 91-76217. (Let's Read Bks.). 12p. (J). (ps). 1992. bds. 3.99 (*0-8066-2587-2*, 9-2587, Augsburg) Augsburg Fortress.

Reeves, Elton. How to Get along with (Almost) Everybody. 200p. 1975. reprint ed. pap. 3.95 (*0-8065-0479-X*, Citadel Pr) Carol Pub Group.

Reeves, Elton T. So You Want to Be an Executive. LC 73-138569. 254p. reprint ed. pap. 72.40 (*0-317-09942-6*, 2050398) Bks Demand.

Reeves, Emma B. Minutes of the District Court of Nacogdoches County (Texas) (Minute Bk. A). 152p. (Orig.). 1981. pap. 12.50 (*0-911013-06-7*) E B Reeves.

— Tennessee Smithology. (Illus.). 153p. 1975. pap. 12.50 (*0-317-05109-1*) E B Reeves.

— Three Centuries of Ballingers in America. LC 75-27993. (Illus.). 614p. 1977. lib. bdg. 20.00 (*0-911013-02-4*) E B Reeves.

***Reeves, F. Dale, ed.** Totally His: Ten Sessions on Servanthood for Teens. (Illus.). 1995. 29.99 (*0-7847-0333-7*, 26-03253) Standard Pub.

— Totally His: Ten Sessions on Servanthood for Teens. (Illus.). 112p. 1995. pap. 2.59 (*0-7847-0334-5*, 26-03254) Standard Pub.

***Reeves, Faye C.** The Birthday Wish Mystery. LC 94-18348. (Illus.). 64p. (J). (gr. 2-5). 1994. lib. bdg. 9.79 (*0-8167-3530-1*, Little Rainbow); pap. text ed. 2.95 (*0-8167-3531-X*, Little Rainbow) Troll Assocs.

— Howie Merton & the Magic Dust. LC 90-38341. (Stepping Stone Bks.). (Illus.). 64p. (Orig.). (J). (gr. 2-4). 1991. pap. 2.50 (*0-679-81527-9*) Random Bks Yng Read.

Reeves, Floyd W., et al, eds. Instructional Problems in the University. LC 71-168086. reprint ed. 34.50 (*0-404-05236-3*) AMS Pr.

Reeves, Francis. Business Ethics. 85p. (C). 1993. 13.78 (*1-56870-032-6*) RonJon Pub.

— Problems of Philosophy. 85p. (C). 1993. student ed 11.23 (*1-56870-033-4*) RonJon Pub.

Reeves, Frank. British Racial Discourse: A Study of British Political Discourse about Race & Race-Related Matters. LC 83-7273. (Comparative Ethnic & Race Relations Ser.). (Illus.). 300p. 1984. 69.95 (*0-521-25554-6*) Cambridge U Pr.

Reeves, Frank W. Race & Borough Politics. 318p. 1989. text ed. 58.95 (*0-566-05573-2*, Pub. by Avebury Pub UK) Ashgate Pub Co.

Reeves, Fred. A Baseball Handbook. pap. 2.50 (*0-87497-246-9*) Impress Hse.

— Baseball Play & Strategy. pap. 2.50 (*0-87497-244-2*) Impress Hse.

— Baseball Team & Field Management. pap. 2.50 (*0-87497-245-0*) Impress Hse.

— Basketball Play. pap. 2.50 (*0-87497-248-5*) Impress Hse.

Reeves, G. M., ed. The Geologist's Directory. vi, 538p. 1994. 41.75 (*1-897799-00-4*, Pub. by Geol Soc Pub Hse UK) AAPG.

Reeves, G. W., ed. Recent Developments in Clinical Immunology. (Research Monographs in Immunology: Vol. 6). 216p. 1984. 103.00 (*0-444-80554-0*, I-273-84) Elsevier.

Reeves, Gareth. T. S. Eliot: A Virgilian Poet. LC 88-23373. 192p. 1989. text ed. 39.95 (*0-312-02474-6*) St Martin.

***Reeves, Garland.** By the Fruit of Her Own Hands: The Life & Times of Julia Tutwiler. 1995. pap. write for info. (*1-878561-35-9*) Seacoast AL.

Reeves, Geoffrey, jt. auth. see Hunt, Albert.

Reeves, Geoffrey W. Communications & the 'Third World' LC 92-13310. (Studies in Culture & Communication). 496p. 1993. 55.00 (*0-415-04761-7*, A7902); pap. 17.95 (*0-415-04762-5*, A7906) Routledge.

Reeves, George. The New Idioms in Action. 1975. pap. 18. 95 (*0-8384-2652-2*, Newbury) Heinle & Heinle.

Reeves, George E. Mining Lease Handbook. 300p. 1992. student ed, pap. 135.00 (*0-929047-32-X*, ML) Rocky Mtn Mineral Law Found.

Reeves, Gordon. Lecture Notes on Immunology. 3rd ed. 226p. 1994. pap. write for info. (*0-632-03812-8*) Blackwell Sci.

Reeves, Gordon & Todd, I. Lecture Notes on Immunology. 2nd ed. 1991. pap. 29.95 (*0-632-02769-X*) Blackwell Sci.

Reeves, Greg. Judy Ford: World Champion Cowgirl. (Illus.). 46p. (J). (gr. 4-8). 1992. pap. 5.95 (*0-938349-88-0*) State House Pr.

Reeves, H. Clyde, ed. Measuring Fiscal Capacity. LC 85-30979. (Lincoln Institute of Land Policy Book Ser.). 221p. reprint ed. pap. 63.00 (*0-7837-5754-9*, 2045416) Bks Demand.

Reeves, H. Clyde & Ellsworth, Scott, eds. Funding Clean Water. LC 83-22202. (Lincoln Institute of Land Policy Book Ser.). 235p. reprint ed. pap. 67.00 (*0-7837-3271-6*, 2043290) Bks Demand.

— The Role of the State in Property Taxation. LC 82-48536. (Lincoln Institute of Land Policy Book Ser.). 231p. reprint ed. pap. 65.90 (*0-7837-3272-4*, 2043291) Bks Demand.

Reeves, Harriet R. Song & Dance Activities for Elementary Children's. 1984. 17.95 (*0-13-260613-5*, Parker Publishing Co) P-H.

— Song & Dance Activities for Elementary Children. LC 85-12029. 241p. 1985. pap. text ed. 21.95 (*0-13-822677-6*, Busn) P-H.

Reeves, Henry, jt. auth. see Shoaf, Mary J.

Reeves, Hershel C. Photo Guide for Appraising Surface Fuels in East Texas. (Illus.). 89p. (Orig.). 1988. 10.00 (*0-938361-04-X*) Austin Univ Forestry.

Reeves, Hubert. Evolution Stellaire et Nucleosynthese. (Cours & Documents de Mathematiques & de Physique Ser.). 114p. (Orig.). 1968. text ed. 79.00 (*0-677-50150-1*) Gordon & Breach.

— The Hour of Our Delight. (Illus.). 256p. (FRE.). (C). 1995. reprint ed. text ed. write for info. (*0-7167-2220-8*) W H Freeman.

— Nuclear Reactions in Stellar Surfaces & Their Relations with Stellar Evolution. (Illus.). 98p. 1971. text ed. 87.00 (*0-677-02960-8*); pap. text ed. 62.00 (*0-677-02965-9*) Gordon & Breach.

— Stellar Evolution & Nucleosynthesis. (Documents on Modern Physics Ser.). 114p. (Orig.). (C). 1968. text ed. 79.00 (*0-677-30150-2*) Gordon & Breach.

Reeves, I. S. The People, Art of Native Americans: Items from the Collection of Sara W. Reeves & I.S.K. Reeves V. (Illus.). 56p. (Orig.). 1992. pap. 15.00 (*0-918548-03-9*) Green APC.

Reeves, J. B. The Hymn As Literature. 1972. 59.95 (*0-8490-0378-4*) Gordon Pr.

Reeves, James. English Fables & Fairy Stories. 1993. 19.75 (*0-8446-6660-2*) Peter Smith.

— Mr. Horrox & the Gratch. LC 91-13326. (Illus.). 32p. (J). (gr. 1-6). 1991. 13.95 (*0-922984-08-5*) Wellington IL.

Reeves, James, ret. English Fables & Fairy Stories. (Oxford Myths & Legends Ser.). (Illus.). 240p. 1989. pap. 10.95 (*0-19-274137-3*) OUP.

Reeves, James H., jt. auth. see Ward, Charles R.

Reeves, James R. & Taylor, James C. Covert Actions. (Orig.). 1987. mass mkt. 5.95 (*0-345-33136-2*) Ballantine.

Reeves, Janet. The Apple a Day Cookbook. (Illus.). 256p. (Orig.). 1993. pap. 13.95 (*0-921556-32-2*, Pub. by Gynergy-Ragweed CN) InBook.

— One Potato, Two Potato: A Cookbook & More! 256p. (Orig.). 1994. pap. 13.95 (*0-920304-70-2*, Pub. by Gynergy-Ragweed CN) InBook.

***Reeves, Jeanne.** Where's That Recipe? A Simple Solution for Finding Your Favorite Recipes. 186p. (Orig.). 1995. pap. 9.95 (*0-9644072-0-5*) Canyon View.

— Where's That Recipe? A Simple Solution for Finding Your Favorite Recipes. 2nd rev. ed. Reeves, Don, ed. 176p. (Orig.). 1995. pap. 9.95 (*0-9644072-1-3*) Canyon View.

Reeves, Jesse S. The International Beginings of the Congo Free State. LC 78-63834. (Johns Hopkins University. Studies in the Social Sciences. Thirtieth Ser. 1912: 11-12). reprint ed. 11.50 (*0-404-61094-3*) AMS Pr.

— The Napoleonic Exiles in America: A Study in Diplomatic History, 1815-1819. LC 78-63910. (Johns Hopkins University. Studies in the Social Sciences. Thirtieth Ser. 1912: 9-10). reprint ed. 16.50 (*0-404-61162-1*) AMS Pr.

Reeves, Jim. The Songs of Jim Reeves. (Piano-Vocal-Guitar Personality Folio Ser.). (Illus.). 80p. 1985. pap. 12.95 (*0-88188-340-9*, 00358033) H Leonard.

Reeves, Jimmie L. & Campbell, Richard. Cracked Coverage: Television News, the Anti-Cocaine Crusade, & the Reagan Legacy. 360p. 1994. lib. bdg. 59.95 (*0-8223-1449-5*); pap. text ed. 19.95 (*0-8223-1491-6*) Duke.

Reeves, Joan. Summer's Fortune. 224p. (Orig.). 1993. pap. 2.95 (*1-56597-077-2*, Kismet) Meteor Pub.

Reeves, John. History of the English Law, from the Time of the Saxons, to the End of the Reign of Philip & Mary, 4 Vols. 2nd ed. 1969. reprint ed. 75.00 (*0-8377-2526-7*) Rothman.

— Reeves' History of the English Law from the Time of the Romans to the End of the Reign of Elizabeth, 5 vols., Set. Finlason, W. F. et al, eds. LC 80-84861. (Historical Writings in Law & Jurisprudence Ser.: No. 24, Bks.34-38). 2812p. 1981. reprint ed. lib. bdg. 240.00 (*0-89941-240-8*, 302480) W S Hein.

— The Rothschilds: Financial Rulers of Nations. 1975. 300. 00 (*0-87968-193-4*) Gordon Pr.

Reeves, John A. & Simon, J. Malcolm. Coaches' Collection of Soccer Drills. LC 80-84212. (Illus.). 160p. (Orig.). (C). 1981. pap. 13.95 (*0-918438-63-2*, PREE0063) Human Kinetics.

Reeves, John A., jt. auth. see Simon, J. Malcolm.

Reeves, John A., jt. ed. see Simon, J. Malcolm.

Reeves, John C. Jewish Lore in Manichaean Cosmogony: Studies in the "Book of Giants" Traditions. (Monographs of the Hebrew Union College: No. 14). 260p. 1992. 49. 95 (*0-87820-413-X*) Hebrew Union Coll Pr.

— Tracing the Threads: Studies in the Vitality of Jewish Pseudepigrapha. LC 94-25032. (SBL Early Judaism & Its Literature Ser.). 1994. pap. 19.95 (*1-55540-995-4*) Scholars Pr GA.

***Reeves, John C., ed.** Tracing the Threads: Studies in the Vitality of Jewish Pseudepigrapha. LC 94-25032. (SBL Early Judaism & Its Literature Ser.). 310p. 1994. 29.95 (*1-55540-994-6*, 063506) Scholars Pr GA.

Reeves, John R. & Maibach, Howard. Clinical Dermatology Illustrated: A Regional Approach. 2nd ed. (Illus.). 420p. 1991. pap. text ed. 39.00 (*0-8036-9883-6*) Davis Co.

Reeves, John T., comp. Good Words in Small Books. 24p. 1991. 1.00 (*1-882063-13-9*) Cottage Pr MA.

Reeves, John T., jt. ed. see Weir, E. Kenneth.

Reeves, Kari. My Billy Ray Cyrus Story: Some Gave Too Much. Courtney, Richard & Hines, Emily, eds. 163p. 1993. 18.95 (*0-9635026-3-8*) Eggman Pub.

Reeves, Kay, jt. auth. see Crawford, Barrie.

Reeves, Keith H. The Resurrection Narrative in Matthew: A Literary-Critical Examination. LC 93-36660. 124p. 1993. text ed. 59.95 (*0-7734-2384-2*, Mellen Biblical Pr) E Mellen.

Reeves, Linda. Get More Tail: A Guide to the Florida Lobster. rev. ed. (Illus.). (C). 1989. 3.95 (*0-9622619-0-4*) Sea Scripts.

— Get More Tail: Guide to the Florida Lobster. 3rd ed. (Illus.). 48p. 1990. 3.95 (*0-9622619-1-2*) Sea Scripts.

Reeves, M. Francis. Problems of Philosophy & Society: A Conversation with Plato. LC 88-2658. 146p. (Orig.). (C). 1988. pap. text ed. 17.00 (*0-8191-6912-9*) U Pr of Amer.

Reeves, Margaret. A Strange Bird on the Lagoon. 224p. (C). 1990. pap. 39.00 (*0-908175-95-7*, Pub. by Boolarong Pubns AT) St Mut.

— Training Schools for Delinquent Girls. 1992. lib. bdg. 79. 95 (*0-8490-5298-X*) Gordon Pr.

Reeves, Marie-Louise. A Collection of Victorian Poems, 1894-1895. 1991. 8.95 (*0-533-09373-2*) Vantage.

Reeves, Marjorie. The Crisis in Higher Education: Competence, Delight & the Common Good. 212p. 1988. 95.00 (*0-335-09530-5*, Open Univ Pr) Taylor & Francis.

— The Influence of Prophecy in the Later Middle Ages: A Study in Joachimism. (C). reprint ed. pap. text ed. 19.95 (*0-268-01170-2*) U of Notre Dame Pr.

— The Medieval Castle. (Then & There Ser.). 105p. (gr. 7-12). 1963. pap. text ed. 8.60 (*0-582-00381-4*, 78062) Longman.

— The Medieval Monastery: Then & There Ser. (Illus.). 90p. (Orig.). (gr. 7-12). 1980. reprint ed. pap. text ed. 8.60 (*0-582-00380-6*, 78064) Longman.

— The Medieval Town. (Then & There Ser.). (Illus.). 90p. (gr. 7-12). 1954. pap. text ed. 8.60 (*0-582-00385-7*, 78065) Longman.

— The Medieval Village. 2nd ed. (Then & There Ser.). (Illus.). 90p. (Orig.). (gr. 7-12). 1954. pap. text ed. 8.60 (*0-582-00386-5*, 78066) Longman.

— The Norman Conquest. (Then & There Ser.). (Illus.). 60p. (Orig.). (gr. 7-12). 1988. pap. text ed. 8.60 (*0-582-00384-9*, 78110) Longman.

— Why History? LC 81-111881. 159p. reprint ed. pap. 45.40 (*0-7837-1597-8*, 2041889) Bks Demand.

Reeves, Marjorie, ed. Prophetic Rome in the High Renaissance Period. (Oxford-Warburg Studies). (Illus.). 440p. 1992. 105.00 (*0-19-920173-0*) OUP.

Reeves, Marjorie & Gould, Warwick. Joachim of Fiore & the Myth of the Eternal Evangel in the Nineteenth Century. (Illus.). 264p. 1987. 74.00 (*0-19-826672-3*) OUP.

Reeves, Marjorie, ed. see Beacroft, Bernard.

Reeves, Marjorie, ed. see Chamberlain, E. R.

Reeves, Marjorie, ed. see Mack, Donald W.

Reeves, Marjorie, jt. auth. see Rosenthal, Miriam.

Reeves, Marjorie, ed. see Sylvester, David W.

Reeves, Marjorie, ed. see Turner, Derek.

Reeves, Marjorie, ed. see Williams, Ann.

Reeves-Marquardt, Dona, tr. see Sinner, Peter.

Reeves-Marquardt, Dona B., jt. ed. see Lich, Glen E.

Reeves, Martha & Bego, Mark. Dancing in the Street: Confessions of a Motown Diva. (Illus.). 304p. 1994. 22. 95 (*0-7868-6024-3*) Hyperion.

— Dancing in the Street: Confessions of a Mowtown Diva. (Illus.). 304p. 1995. pap. 12.95 (*0-7868-8094-5*) Hyperion.

Reeves, Maud P. Round about a Pound a Week. large type ed. 256p. 1993. 22.95 (*1-85695-030-1*, Pub. by ISIS UK) Transaction Pubs.

Reeves, Mildred. Old-Fashioned Love Story. 209p. 1974. 7.50 (*0-318-04130-8*) Prairie Pub.

Reeves, Mildred E. To Thee I Come. 220p. 1975. 7.50 (*0-686-12109-0*) Prairie Pub.

Reeves, Miriam. Felicianas of Louisiana. 1967. 13.95 (*0-87511-096-7*) Claitors.

Reeves, Miriam G. Governors of Louisiana. 3rd ed. Calhoun, James, ed. LC 72-89969. (Governors of the States Ser.). (Illus.). 128p. 1980. 17.95 (*0-911116-71-0*) Pelican.

Reeves, Mona R. I Had a Cat. LC 87-37608. (Illus.). 32p. (J). (ps-1). 1989. text ed. 13.95 (*0-02-775731-5*, Bradbury S&S) S&S Childrens.

— I Had a Cat. LC 93-45418. (Illus.). (J). 1995. pap. 4.95 (*0-689-71759-8*, Aladdin Paperbacks) S&S Childrens.

— The Spooky Eerie Night Noise. LC 89-447. (Illus.). 32p. (J). (ps-2). 1989. text ed. 13.95 (*0-02-775732-3*, Bradbury S&S) S&S Childrens.

Reeves, Nancy. Womankind: Beyond the Stereotypes. 2nd ed. LC 81-71348. 199p. 1982. lib. bdg. 41.95 (*0-202-30299-7*); pap. text ed. 21.95 (*0-202-30300-4*) Aldine de Gruyter.

***Reeves, Nicholas.** The Complete Tutankhamun: The King - The Tomb - The Royal Treasure. LC 90-70202. (Illus.). 224p. 1995. pap. 17.95 (*0-500-27810-5*) Thames Hudson.

— Into the Mummy's Tomb: The Real-Life Discovery of Tutankhamun's Treasures. (J). (gr. 4-7). 1993. pap. 6.95 (*0-590-45753-5*) Scholastic Inc.

— Official British Film Propaganda During the First World War. 304p. 1986. 49.95 (*0-7099-4225-7*, Pub. by Croom Helm UK) Routledge Chapman & Hall.

Reeves, Nicholas & Taylor, John H. Howard Carter Before Tutankhamun. LC 92-29416. (Illus.). 208p. 1993. 29.95 (*0-8109-3186-9*) Abrams.

Reeves, Nicholas, ed. see Brugsch, Emile & Maspero, Gaston.

Reeves, Nigel. Heinrich Heine: Poetry & Politics. 210p. 1994. pap. 24.95 (*1-870352-57-2*, Pub. by Libris UK) Paul & Co Pubs.

Reeves, Nigel, jt. auth. see Liston, David.

Reeves, Nigel, tr. see Von Kleist, Heinrich.

Reeves, P. Fusion of the Legal Profession: Are Two Legal Professions Necessary? (Legal & Social Policy Library). (Illus.). 128p. 1986. pap. 26.00 (*0-08-039218-0*, Pergamon Pr) Elsevier.

Reeves, Pamela. Ellis Island: Gateway to the American Dream. 1991. 15.99 (*0-517-05905-3*) Random Hse Value.

Reeves, Peter. Landlords & Governments in Uttar Pradesh. (Illus.). 350p. 1992. 29.95 (*0-19-562728-8*) OUP.

Reeves, Philip N. & Coile, Russell C., Jr. Introduction to Health Planning. 4th ed. LC 89-81230. (Illus.). xvii, 321p. 1993. reprint ed. text ed. 32.50 (*0-87815-059-5*) Info Resources. This widely recognized reference work & textbook has become a standard in its field. It has been adopted for use in graduate courses by more than 100 colleges & universities in the United States & abroad. In common with the

R

first three editions, this fourth edition provides the latest, most tested & proven techniques for the management of organizations & institutions such as health insurance plans, health maintenance organizations, hospitals, & government health departments that serve the health delivery & health financing needs of communities. It continues to provide cogent & timely instruction in methods of planning & operating proactive health programs that make use of the most effective & advanced tools & techniques available. The fourth edition departs in one major respect from the previous editions. Responding to the continuing turbulence within the United States health system, it features new chapters on methods & tools for predicting future developments, outcomes & problems. Price: $32.50, plus $3.50 shipping & handling. To order: Information Resources Press, 1110 North Glebe Road, Suite 550, Arlington, VA 22201. ***Publisher Provided Annotation.***

Reeves, R. A., jt. auth. see Dirksen, D. J.
Reeves, R. B., ed. Application of Walls to Landslide Control Problems. LC 82-70668. 133p. 1982. pap. 17.00 (*0-87262-302-5*) Am Soc Civil Eng.
Reeves, R. C., ed. see Lucretius.
Reeves, Randall R., jt. auth. see Leatherwood, Stephen P.
Reeves, Randall R., jt. ed. see Leatherwood, Stephen P.
Reeves, Randall R., jt. auth. see Leatherwood, Stephen.
Reeves, Randall R., et al. The Sierra Club Handbook of Seals & Sirenians. LC 92-946. (Illus.). 350p. (Orig.). 1992. pap. 18.00 (*0-87156-656-7*) Sierra.
Reeves, Richard. President Kennedy. (Illus.). 480p. 1993. 30.00 (*0-671-64879-9*) S&S Trade.
— President Kennedy: Profile of Power. (Illus.). 1994. pap. 15.00 (*0-671-89289-4*, Touchstone Bks) S&S Trade.
Reeves, Richard P., jt. ed. see DuBowy, Paul J.
***Reeves, Richard S., illus. & intro.** Royal Blood: Fifty Years of Classic Thoroughbreds. 284p. 1994. text ed. 75.00 (*0-939049-63-5*) Blood-Horse.
***Reeves, Richard S. & Bolus, Jim.** Royal Blood: Fifty Years of Classic Thoroughbreds. (Illus.). 288p. 1995. 75.00 (*0-8212-2207-4*) Bulfinch Pr.
***Reeves, Robert.** The Superpower Space Race: An Explosive Rivalry Through the Solar System. LC 94-28240. (Illus.). 360p. 1994. (*0-306-44768-1*, Plenum Pr) Plenum.
Reeves, Robert G. Flora of Central Texas. Orig. Title: Flora of South Central Texas. (C). 1977. reprint ed. pap. text ed. 17.75 (*0-934786-00-3*) G Davis.
Reeves, Robert N. The Ridiculous to the Delightful: Comic Characters in Sidney's New Arcadia. LC 73-91641. (LeBaron Russell Briggs Prize Honors Essays in English Ser.). 64p. 1974. pap. 2.50 (*0-674-76890-6*) HUP.
Reeves, Rosser. Reality in Advertising. 1961. 20.00 (*0-394-44228-8*) Knopf.
Reeves, Rosser, jt. auth. see Martin, Ray.
Reeves, Sally K. Legacy of a Century: Academy of the Sacred Heart in New Orleans. (Illus.). 200p. 1987. write for info. (*0-9618628-0-7*) Academy Sacred.
Reeves, Sally K., et al. Historic City Park: New Orleans. (Illus.). 256p. 1982. 24.95 (*0-9610062-0-X*) Friends City Park.
Reeves, Scott D. Creative Jazz Improvisation. (Illus.). 520p. 1988. 23.95 (*0-13-189671-7*) P-H.
— Creative Jazz Improvisation. 2nd ed. LC 94-10657. 332p. 1994. pap. text ed. 31.33 (*0-13-303280-9*) P-H Gen Ref & Trav.
Reeves-Smyth, Terence. Irish Gardens. (Appletree Pocket Guide Ser.). (Illus.). 96p. (Orig.). 1994. pap. 7.95 (*0-86281-374-3*, Pub. by Appletree Pr IE) Irish Bks Media.
Reeves, Stephen M. Wendover, Acme, & Virginia Point. LC 80-54382. 158p. 1981. 29.95 (*0-938794-01-9*) Red River Pub Co.
Reeves, Steve & Peterson, James A. Powerwalking. LC 81-18184. 1982. pap. write for info. (*0-672-52713-8*) Macmillan.
Reeves-Stevens, Garfield & Reeves-Stevens, Judith. Star Trek, No. 42: Memory Prime. 1991. mass mkt. 5.50 (*0-671-74359-7*) PB.
Reeves-Stevens, Garfield, jt. auth. see Reeves-Stevens, Judith.
Reeves-Stevens, Judith & Reeves-Stevens, Garfield. The Day of Descent. Ryan, Kevin, ed. (Alien Nation Ser.: No. 1). 416p. (Orig.). 1993. mass mkt. 4.99 (*0-671-73599-3*, Pocket Star Bks) PB.
— Prime Directive. Stern, Dave, ed. (Star Trek Ser.). 416p. (Orig.). 1991. reprint ed. mass mkt. 5.99 (*0-671-74466-6*) PB.
— Star Trek: Federation. Ryan, Kevin, ed. 1994. 22.00 (*0-671-89422-6*) PB.
— Star Trek: The Making of Deep Space Nine. Ryan, Kevin, ed. (Orig.). 1994. pap. 16.00 (*0-671-87430-6*) PB.
Reeves-Stevens, Judith, jt. auth. see Reeves-Stevens, Garfield.
Reeves, T. Zane. The Politics of the Peace Corps & Vista. LC 86-19194. (Illus.). 232p. 1988. 24.50 (*0-8173-0323-5*) U of Ala Pr.
Reeves, Thomas. Question of Character: Image & Reality in the Life of John F. Kennedy. 1991. 27.95 (*0-02-925965-7*) Free Pr.
Reeves, Thomas C. Gentleman Boss: The Life of Chester Alan Arthur. LC 91-71714. (Signature Ser.). (Illus.). 500p. 1991. 32.50 (*0-945707-03-7*) Amer Political.
— The Life & Times of Joe McCarthy. LC 79-3730. 1981. 19.95 (*0-8128-2337-0*, Scrbrough Hse) Madison Bks UPA.
— Life & Times of Joe McCarthy: A Biography. LC 83-42968. (Illus.). 848p. 1983. pap. 14.95 (*0-8128-6200-7*, Scrbrough Hse) Madison Bks UPA.
— A Question of Character: A Life of John F. Kennedy. (Illus.). 500p. 1992. pap. 13.95 (*1-55958-175-1*) Prima Pub.
Reeves, Thomas C., ed. John F. Kennedy: The Man, the Politician, the President. LC 89-33503. 178p. (C). 1990. pap. 11.50 (*0-89464-371-1*) Krieger.
— Mc Carthyism. 3rd ed. LC 88-13666. 154p. (C). 1989. pap. 10.50 (*0-89464-289-8*) Krieger.
Reeves, Thomas C., frwd. James Lloyd Breck: Apostle of the Wilderness. 194p. 1992. text ed. 22.00 (*1-881648-00-1*); pap. text ed. 12.95 (*1-881648-01-X*) Frontier Mission.
***Reeves, Tom.** Managing Effectively: Self Development Through Experience. 240p. 1994. pap. 29.95 (*0-7506-1924-4*) Buttrwrth-Heinemann.
Reeves, Trish. Returning the Question. LC 88-71364. (CSU Poetry Ser.: No. XXV). 62p. (Orig.). 1988. 12.00 (*0-914946-67-6*); pap. 6.00 (*0-914946-66-8*) Cleveland St Univ Poetry Ctr.
Reeves, W. Robert, tr. see Green, William C., ed. & tr.
Reeves, W. Robert, jt. tr. see Green, William C.
Reeves, William. The Bell of St. Patrick Called the Clog an Edachta. 1991. reprint ed. pap. 5.95 (*0-89979-055-0*) British Am Bks.
Reeves, William, ed. see Adamnan, Saint.
Reeves, William W. The Technology of Fluid Power. (Illus.). 320p. (C). 1987. text ed. 45.00 (*0-8359-7525-8*) P-H.
Refausse, Raymond, jt. ed. see Helferty, Seamus.
***Refences, Paul.** Neural Networks in the Capital Markets. 1995. text ed. 55.00 (*0-471-94364-9*) Wiley.
Reference Division Staff, ed. The Deluxe Reference Desk Set, 2 Vols. 1983. 37.95 (*0-395-35493-5*) HM.
— Webster's II New Riverside Desk Dictionary. LC 88-845. (Illus.). 1988. 8.25 (*0-395-48368-9*) HM.
Reference Division Staff, ed. see Cook, Claire K.
Reference Press Editors Staff. The Bay Area 500: Hoover's Guide to the Top San Francisco Area Companies, 1994-1995. 336p. 1994. 24.95 (*1-878753-52-5*) Ref Press.
— L. A. 500: Hoover's Guide to the Top Southern California Companies, 1994-1995. Date not set. 24.95 (*1-878753-53-3*) Ref Press.
Reference Press, Inc. Staff. Hoover's MasterList of Major U. S. Companies, 1993. 608p. (Orig.). 1993. lib. bdg. 49.95 (*1-878753-14-2*) Ref Press.
Reference Press, Inc. Staff, ed. The Texas Five Hundred: Hoover's Guide to the Top Texas Companies, 1994-1995. 300p. (Orig.). 1993. 24.95 (*1-878753-46-0*); pap. 14.95 (*1-878753-39-8*) Ref Press.
Reference Press, Inc. Staff & Publishers Group West Staff, eds. Hoover's Guide to the Book Business. 32p. (Orig.). 1993. pap. 4.95 (*1-878753-35-5*) Ref Press.
***Reference Press Staff, ed.** The American Almanac 1995-1996: Statistical Abstract of the United States. 1010p. 1995. 17.95 (*1-878753-89-4*) Ref Press.
— Fortune 500 Guide. 288p. 1995. 12.95 (*1-878753-94-0*) Ref Press.
— Hoover's Guide to the Top New York City Metro Area Companies 1995-1996. 336p. (Orig.). 1996. pap. 24.95 (*1-878753-59-2*) Ref Press.
— Hoover's Guide to the Top Texas 500 Companies. 300p. 1995. 24.95 (*1-878753-93-2*) Ref Press.
— Hoover's Handbook of American Companies 1996. 1080p. 1995. 29.95 (*1-878753-87-8*) Ref Press.
— Hoover's Handbook of Emerging Companies 1996. 432p. 1995. 29.95 (*1-878753-90-8*) Ref Press.
— Hoover's Masterlist of Major European Companies, 1995. 300p. 1995. lib. bdg. 79.95 (*1-878753-70-3*) Ref Press.
— Hoover's Masterlist of Major U. S. Companies, 1994-1995. 2nd ed. 672p. 1994. lib. bdg. 49.95 (*1-878753-56-8*) Ref Press.
— Hoover's Masterlist of Major U. S. Companies, 1995-1996. 3rd ed. 750p. 1995. lib. bdg. 69.95 (*1-878753-83-5*) Ref Press.
— Hoover's Masterlist of 2,500 of America's Largest & Fastest Growing Employers. 524p. 1995. pap. 19.95 (*1-878753-82-7*) Ref Press.
Reff, Daniel T. Disease, Depopulation, & Culture Change in Northwestern New Spain, 1518-1764. LC 90-52749. (Illus.). 416p. 1990. lib. bdg. 35.00 (*0-87480-355-1*) U of Utah Pr.
Reff, Theodore. Degas: The Artist's Mind. LC 87-11827. (Paperbacks in AA History Ser.). (Illus.). 352p. 1987. pap. 22.50 (*0-674-19543-4*) HUP.
— The Notebooks of Edgar Degas: A Catalogue of the Thirty-Eight Note-Books in the Bibliotheque Nationale & Other Collections., 2 vols. 2nd rev. ed. LC 84-82426. (Illus.). 167p. 1985. reprint ed. lib. bdg. 195.00 (*0-87817-304-8*) Hacker.
Reff, Theodore & Shoemaker, Innis H. Paul Cezanne: Two Sketchbooks. (Illus.). 244p. (Orig.). 1989. pap. 25.00 (*0-87633-080-4*) Phila Mus Art.
***Reff, Theodore & Valdes-Forain, Florence.** Jean-Louis Forain: The Impressionist Years: The Dixon Gallery & Gardens Collection. LC 95-6905. 1995. write for info. (*0-945064-00-4*) Dixon Gal.
Reffell, Terry, illus. Ronck's Hawaii Almanac. LC 84-8697. 192p. (Orig.). 1984. pap. 3.95 (*0-8248-0831-2*) UH Pr.
Reffin-Smith, Brian. Soft Computing: Art & Design. 192p. (C). 1986. pap. text ed. write for info. (*0-318-61094-9*) Addison-Wesley.
Reffo, G., et al. Nuclear Level Densities: Proceedings of the OECD Meeting. 350p. 1992. text ed. 95.00 (*981-02-1077-9*) World Scientific Pub.
Refi, James J. Fiber Optic Cable: A LightGuide. (Specialized Ser.). (Illus.). 208p. 1991. pap. 39.95 (*1-56016-043-8*) ABC TeleTraining.
Refioglu, H. I. Electronic Displays. LC 83-16753. 480p. 1983. 29.95 (*0-87942-169-X*, PC01628) Inst Electrical.
Refnes, Vera. Kinder Capers Songs: For Special Times & Special People. (Illus.). 23p. 1991. teacher ed 10.00 (*0-9627108-1-4*) Refhouse Pubns.
Refnes, Vera & Milhous, Enid. Kinder Capers. (Illus.). 311p. 1990. teacher ed 29.95 (*0-9627108-0-6*) Refhouse Pubns.
Reformed Church in America Staff. Rejoice in the Lord: A Hymn Companion to the Scriptures. Routley, Erik, ed. 608p. 1985. 14.99x (*0-8028-9009-1*) Eerdmans.
Refregier, Philippe, ed. see Javidi, Bahram.
Refsal, Harley. Woodcarving in the Scandinavian Style. LC 92-16979. (Illus.). 132p. 1992. pap. 12.95 (*0-8069-8633-6*) Sterling.
***Refshauge, Kathryn M. & Gass, Elizabeth M., eds.** Musculoskeletal Physiotherapy: Clinical Science & Practice. LC 94-40453. 1995. write for info. (*0-7506-1746-2*, Focal) Buttrwrth-Heinemann.
Refsing, Kirsten. The Ainu Language: The Morphology & Syntax of the Shizunai Dialect. 301p. 1986. 73.00x (*87-7288-020-1*) Coronet Bks.
Refsing, Kirsten, jt. auth. see Goodman, Roger.
Reftery, Larry, ed. Worship His Majesty. 32p. 1981. pap. 0.75 (*0-88144-056-6*) Christian Pub.
Refugee Women in Development Staff. Understanding Family Violence within U. S. Refugee Communities: A Training Manual. Richie, Beth, ed. 1988. 8.00 (*0-9620653-0-7*) Ref Women Dev.
Refugio County History Book Committee, ed. The History of Refugio County, Texas. (Illus.). 598p. 1985. 55.00 (*0-88107-030-0*) Curtis Media.
Rega, Alcides F. CA 2 Plus Pump of Plasma Membrane. Garrahan, Patricio J., ed. 184p. 1986. 102.00 (*0-8493-6253-9*, QH601, CRC Reprint) Franklin.
***Regal, Martin S.** Harold Pinter: A Question of Timing. 172p. 1995. 45.00 (*0-312-12476-7*) St Martin.
Regal, Phillip. The Anatomy of Judgment. 376p. 1989. text ed. 39.95 (*0-8166-1823-2*); pap. text ed. 14.95 (*0-8166-1824-0*) U of Minn Pr.
Regalado, Nancy, jt. auth. see Beaujour, Michel.
Regalado, Nancy F. Poetic Patterns in Rutebeuf: A Study in Noncourtly Poetic Modes of the Thirteenth Century. LC 70-104620. (Yale Romanitc Series, Second Ser.: No. 21). 384p. reprint ed. pap. 109.50 (*0-317-29720-1*, 2022033) Bks Demand.
Regalado, Nancy F., ed. see Yale French Studies Staff.
Regalbuto, Robert J. A Guide to Monastic Guest Houses. 2nd ed. LC 92-852. (Illus.). 175p. 1992. pap. 13.95 (*0-8192-1582-1*) Morehouse Pub.
***Regalia, Phillip.** Adaptive IIR Filtering in Signal Processing & Control. LC 94-30294. (Electrical Engineering & Electronics Ser.: 90). 576p. 1994. 150.00 (*0-8247-9289-0*) Dekker.
Regamey, Constantin, tr. Three Chapters from the Samadhirajasutra. 112p. 1984. reprint ed. lib. bdg. 19.50 (*0-88181-003-7*) Canon Pubns.
Regamey, Konstanty. The Bhadramayakara-Vyakarana. 1990. reprint ed. 19.00 (*81-208-0761-8*, Pub. by Motilal Banarsidass II) S Asia.
Regamey, R. H., ed. International Symposium on Pyrogenicity, Innocuity & Toxicity Test System for Biological Products. (Developments in Biological Standardization Ser.: Vol. 34). (Illus.). 1977. 30.50 (*3-8055-2676-8*) S Karger.
Regamey, R. H. & Horodniceanu, F., eds. European Society of Animal Cell Technology, General Meeting. (Developments in Biological Standardization Ser.: Vol. 42). (Illus.). 1979. pap. 48.00 (*3-8055-2989-9*) S Karger.
Regamey, R. H., ed. see International Association of Biological Standardization Staff.
Regamey, R. H., ed. see International Association of Biological Standardization Symposium Staff.
Regamey, R. H., ed. see International Association of Biological Standardization Staff.
Regamey, R. H., jt. ed. see International Association of Biological Standardization Staff.
Regamey, R. H., ed. see International Congress of Microbiological Standardization Staff.
Regamey, R. H., ed. see International Symposium on BCG Vaccine Staff.
Regamey, R. H., ed. see International Symposium on Enterobacterial Vaccines Staff.
Regamey, R. H., ed. see International Symposium on Smallpox Vaccine Staff.
Regamey, R. H., ed. see International Symposium on Standardization & Use of Vaccines in the Developing Countries Staff.
Regamey, R. H., ed. see Joint WHC-IABS Staff.
Regamey, R. H., ed. see Permanent Section of Microbiological Standardization, 31st Symposium, Omstotite of Child Health, Ondon, 1969.
Regamey, R. H., et al, eds. International Symposium on Brucellosis 2. (Developments in Biological Standardization Ser.: Vol. 31). (Illus.). 1976. 38.50 (*3-8055-2364-5*) S Karger.
— International Symposium on Vaccination of Man & Animals by the Non-Parenteral Route: Proceedings, Douglas 1975. (Developments in Biological Standardization Ser.: Vol. 33). (Illus.). 1976. 38.50 (*3-8055-2399-8*) S Karger.
— Joint OIE-IABS Symposium on Clostridial Products in Veterinary Medicine. (Developments in Biological Standardization Ser.: Vol. 32). 1976. 30.50 (*3-8055-2435-8*) S Karger.
Regan. Guide to Surviving Nursing School. (Notes Ser.). 1991. 14.95 (*0-87434-316-X*) Springhouse Pub.
— The Haunted Campground Mystery. (Ghost Twins Ser.: No. 06). 1995. pap. (*0-590-25242-9*) Scholastic Inc.
Regan, D., et al, eds. Systems Approach in Vision: Proceedings of a Workshop Held in Amsterdam, the Netherlands, 27-29 August 1984. (Illus.). 226p. 1986. 55.00 (*0-08-032033-3*, Pub. by PPL UK) Elsevier.
***Regan, D. M.** Human Brain Electrophysiology Evoked Potentials & Magnetic Fields in Science & Medicine. 864p. 1988. 160.00 (*0-8385-3962-9*) Appleton & Lange.
Regan, Dana. At My School: Paint Box Fun. (J). (ps-3). 1993. pap. 1.95 (*0-590-46291-1*) Scholastic Inc.
Regan, Dana, illus. Baby Boo! 12p. (J). (ps). 1992. 5.99 (*0-679-81544-9*) Random Bks Yng Read.
***Regan, David.** Experience the Mystery: Pastoral Possibilities for Christian Mystagogy. 160p. (Orig.). 1995. pap. text ed. 11.95 (*0-8146-2328-X*, Liturg Pr Bks) Liturgical Pr.
Regan, David, ed. The New City Republics: Municipal Intervention in Defence. (C). 1990. 35.00 (*0-907967-87-6*, Pub. by Inst Euro Def & Strat UK) St Mut.
Regan, David J. Mourning Glory: The Making of a Marine. 1980. 9.95 (*0-8159-6218-5*) Devin.
Regan, Dian C. The Class with the Summer Birthdays. (Illus.). 80p. (J). (gr. 2-4). 1991. 13.95 (*0-8050-1657-0*, Redfeather BYR) H Holt & Co.
— The Curse of the Trouble Dolls. LC 91-28572. (Illus.). 64p. (J). (gr. 2-4). 1992. 14.95 (*0-8050-1944-8*, Bks Young Read) H Holt & Co.
— The Curse of the Trouble Dolls. LC 91-28572. (Illus.). 64p. (J). (gr. 2-4). 1993. pap. 4.95 (*0-8050-2952-4*, Bks Young Read) H Holt & Co.
— Game of Survival. 144p. (Orig.). (J). 1989. pap. 2.75 (*0-380-75585-8*, Flare) Avon.
— Ghost Twins. (Mystery at Kickingbird Lake Ser.: No. 01). (J). (gr. 4-7). 1994. pap. 3.25 (*0-590-48253-X*) Scholastic Inc.
— The Initiation. 176p. (Orig.). (J). (gr. 5). 1993. pap. 3.50 (*0-380-76325-7*, Flare) Avon.
— I've Got Your Number. 144p. 1986. pap. 2.50 (*0-380-75082-1*, Flare) Avon.
— Jilly's Ghost. 144p. (Orig.). 1990. pap. 2.95 (*0-380-75831-8*, Flare) Avon.
— Liver Cookies. (J). (gr. 4-7). 1991. pap. 2.75 (*0-590-44337-2*) Scholastic Inc.
— The Missing Moose Mystery. (Ghost Twins Ser.: No. 4). (J). (gr. 4-7). 1995. pap. 3.25 (*0-590-48256-4*) Scholastic Inc.
— Monster of the Month lub. LC 94-3405. (J). 1994. 14.95 (*0-8050-3443-9*) H Holt & Co.
— Monsters in the Attic. LC 95-16174. (J). 1995. write for info. (*0-8050-3709-8*) H Holt & Co.
— My Zombie Valentine. (J). (gr. 4-7). 1993. pap. 2.95 (*0-590-46038-2*) Scholastic Inc.
— The Mystery of One Wish Pond. (Ghost Twins Ser.: No. 02). (J). (gr. 4-7). 1994. pap. 3.25 (*0-590-48254-8*) Scholastic Inc.
— The Mystery of the Disappearing Dogs. (Ghost Twins Ser.: No. 5). (J). (gr. 2-7). 1995. pap. 3.25 (*0-590-25241-0*) Scholastic Inc.
— The Mystery on Walrus Mountain. (Ghost Twin Book Ser.: No. 03). (J). (gr. 4-7). 1995. pap. 3.25 (*0-590-48255-6*) Scholastic Inc.
— The Peppermint Race. (J). 1994. 14.95 (*0-8050-2753-X*) H Holt & Co.
— The Perfect Age. 192p. 1987. pap. 2.50 (*0-380-75337-5*, Flare) Avon.
— Princess Nevermore. LC 94-30020. 1995. 14.95 (*0-590-45758-6*) Scholastic Inc.
— The Thirteen Hours of Halloween. LC 92-41207. (Illus.). (J). 1993. write for info. (*0-8075-7876-2*) A Whitman.
— Vampire Who Came for Christmas. (J). (gr. 4-7). 1994. pap. 2.95 (*0-590-47862-1*) Scholastic Inc.
Regan, Donald H. Duties of Preservation. (Working Papers on the Preservation of Species). 1988. 2.50 (*0-318-33310-4*, PS1) IPPP.
Regan, Donald T. For the Record: From Wall Street to Washington. (Illus.). 352p. 1988. 21.95 (*0-15-163966-3*) HarBrace.
— For the Record: From Wall Street to Washington. 1989. mass mkt. 4.95 (*0-312-91518-7*) St Martin.
***Regan, Edward V.** Infrastructure Investment for Tomorrow: A Financing Plan to Eliminate the Deferred Maintenance on the Nation's Roads. (Public Policy Brief Ser.: No. 16). (Illus.). 64p. (Orig.). 1994. pap. write for info. (*0-941276-04-X*, J Levy Econ Inst) Bard Coll Pubns.
Regan, Elizabeth A. & O'Connor, Bridget N. End-User Information Systems: Perspectives for Managers & Information Systems Professionals. LC 93-20214. (Illus.). 604p. (C). 1994. text ed. write for info. (*0-02-399163-1*) Macmillan.
***Regan, Frank & Spencer, Gary.** Championship Ballroom Dancing. (Illus.). 112p. 1994. 60.00 (*0-9642890-0-8*) EAB Pr.
Regan, Frank J. & Anandakrishnan, Satya M. Dynamics of Atmospheric Re-Entry. LC 92-33727. (Educ Ser.). 604p. 1993. 99.95 (*1-56347-048-9*) AIAA.
Regan, Frauke, tr. see Mendelssohn, Moses.
Regan, G. & Shapiro, D. The Healer's Hand Book. 112p. 1988. pap. 11.95 (*1-85230-022-1*) Element MA.
Regan, Gary. Bartender's Bible. 1991. 77.70 (*0-06-016734-3*, HarpT) HarpC.
— Bartender's Bible. 1993. mass mkt. 5.99 (*0-06-109220-7*, Harp PBks) HarpC.
— The Bartender's Bible: One Thousand & One Mixed Drinks & Everything You Need to Know to Set up Your Bar. LC 91-55104. (Illus.). 288p. 1991. 14.95 (*0-06-016722-X*, HarpT) HarpC.
***Regan, Gary & Regan, Mardee H.** The Book of Bourbon & Other Fine American Whiskeys. Estabrook, Barry, ed. (Illus.). 256p. 1995. 29.95 (*1-881527-89-1*) Chapters Pub.

R

An Asterisk (*) at the beginning of an entry indicates that the title is appearing in BIP for the first time.

***Regan, Geoffrey.** Blue on Blue: A History of Friendly Fire. LC 94-23280. 256p. (Orig.). 1995. pap. 12.50 (*0-380-77655-3*) Avon.
— The Book of Military Blunders. 192p. 1991. lib. bdg. 45.00 (*0-87436-668-2*) ABC-CLIO.
— Elizabethan England. (Living Through History Ser.). (Illus.). 64p. 1990. 19.95 (*0-7134-6094-6*, Pub. by Batsford UK) Trafalgar.
— Great Military Disasters: A History of Incompetence on the Battlefield. LC 87-33593. 320p. 1987. 22.50 (*0-87131-537-8*) M Evans.
— Guinness Book of Decisive Battles. 240p. 1992. 29.95 (*1-55859-431-0*) Abbeville Pr.
— Guinness Book of Military Anecdotes. 224p. 1992. 24.95 (*1-55859-441-8*) Abbeville Pr.
— Israel & the Arabs. rev. ed. (Cambridge Introduction to World History Topic Bks.). (Illus.). 48p. (C). 1990. pap. 8.75 (*0-521-37820-6*) Cambridge U Pr.
— Saladin & the Fall of Jerusalem. 192p. 1988. lib. bdg. 55.00 (*0-7099-4208-7*, Pub. by Croom Helm UK) Routledge Chapman & Hall.
— SNAFU: Great American Military Disasters. 296p. (Orig.). 1993. pap. 10.00 (*0-380-76755-4*) Avon.
***Regan, Helen B. & Brooks, Gwen H.** Out of Women's Experience: Creating Relational Experience. (Illus.). 144p. 1995. 38.00 (*0-8039-6233-9*); pap. 18.00 (*0-8039-6234-7*) Corwin Pr.
Regan, Helen B., et al. Teacher: A New Definition & Model for Development. 118p. (Orig.). 1992. pap. 21.95 (*1-56602-048-4*) Research Better.
Regan, Hilary & Torrance, Alan J., eds. Christ & Context: The Confrontation Between Gospel & Culture. 288p. 1993. pap. text ed. 24.95 (*0-567-29235-5*, Pub. by T & T Clark UK) Bks Intl VA.
Regan, James D., et al, eds. The Science of Photomedicine. LC 82-9072. (Photobiology Ser.). 680p. 1982. 125.00 (*0-306-40924-0*, Plenum Pr) Plenum.
Regan, Jane E. Reading Between the Lines. 128p. (Orig.). 1999. pap. text ed. 7.95 (*0-8146-2152-X*) Liturgical Pr.
Regan, Jennifer. Graywolf Annual Eight: The New Family. 1991. pap. 11.00 (*1-55597-152-0*) Graywolf.
Regan, Jennifer, ed. The Invisible Enemy: Alcohol & the Modern Short Story. LC 89-31690. (Short Fiction Ser.). 256p. 1989. pap. 9.50 (*1-55597-118-0*) Graywolf.
Regan, Jim. Winning at Slot Machines: A Guide to Making Money at the Most Popular of All Casino Games. 196p. 1995. pap. 5.95 (*0-8065-0973-2*, Citadel Pr) Carol Pub Group.
Regan, John. The Aged Client & the Law. 1990. text ed. 35.00 (*0-231-06978-2*) Col U Pr.
***Regan, John, et al.** Atlas of Endoscopic Spine Surgery. 1995. 145.00 (*0-942219-73-2*) Quality Med Pub.
Regan, John H. Memoirs, with Special Reference to Secession & the Civil War. (American Biography Ser.). 351p. 1991. reprint ed. lib. bdg. 79.00 (*0-7812-8322-1*) Rprt Serv.
Regan, John J. Tax, Estate & Financial Planning for the Elderly. 1982. Updates. ring bd. write for info. (*0-8205-1289-3*) Bender.
Regan, Judith, ed. see Becker, Audrey.
Regan, Judith, ed. see Braiker, Harriet B.
Regan, Judith, ed. see Coupland, Doug.
Regan, Judith, ed. see Kirn, Walter.
Regan, Judith, ed. see Lamb, Wally.
Regan, Judith, ed. see Limbaugh, Rush.
Regan, Judith, ed. see Louv, Richard.
Regan, Judith, ed. see Marcinko, David & Weisman, John.
Regan, Judith, ed. see Marcinko, Richard & Weisman, John.
Regan, Judith, ed. see Smilgus, Martha.
Regan, Judith, ed. see Steel, Dawn.
Regan, Judith, ed. see Stumbo, Bella.
Regan, Judith, ed. see Walther, Anne.
***Regan, Ken, et al.** The Bridges of Madison County: The Film. 128p. 1995. 22.95 (*0-446-51997-9*) Warner Bks.
Regan, Kevin. Twenty More Teen Prayer Services. LC 94-60339. 112p. (Orig.). 1994. pap. 9.95 (*0-89622-605-0*) Twenty-Third.
Regan, Laura, jt. auth. see Yolen, Jane.
Regan, Leo. Public Enemies. (Illus.). 114p. 1994. pap. 19.95 (*0-233-98830-0*, Pub. by A Deutsch UK) Trafalgar.
Regan, M. Joanna & Keiss, Isabelle. Tender Courage: Reflections on the Life & Spirit of Catherine Mcauley. 168p. (Orig.). pap. 7.95 (*0-8199-0917-3*, Frncscn Herld) Franciscan Pr.
Regan, Madelyn, jt. auth. see Simpson, Richard L.
Regan, Mardee H., jt. auth. see Leach, Robin.
Regan, Mardee H., jt. auth. see Regan, Gary.
Regan, Mariann S. Love Words: The Self & the Text in Medieval & Renaissance Poetry. LC 81-15126. 288p. 1982. 36.95 (*0-8014-1415-6*) Cornell U Pr.
Regan, Mary. A Family in France. LC 84-19392. (Families the World Over Ser.). (Illus.). 32p. (J). (gr. 2-5). 1985. lib. bdg. 13.50 (*0-8225-1651-9*, Lerner Publctns) Lerner Group.
Regan, Mary J. Echoes from the Past. (Robert Charles Billings Fund Publication Pamphlet Ser.: No. 7). (Illus.). 90p. 1927. 5.00 (*0-934552-15-0*) Boston Athenaeum.
***Regan, Michael.** American & European Furniture Price Guide. 1995. pap. 15.95 (*0-930625-46-3*) Antique Trader.
Regan, Milton C., Jr. Family Law & the Pursuit of Intimacy. LC 92-38948. 304p. 1993. 45.00 (*0-8147-7430-X*); pap. 20.00 (*0-8147-7457-1*) NYU Pr.
Regan, Nancy. The Institute of Chartered Financial Analysts: A Twenty-Five Year History. (Orig.). (C). write for info. (*0-935015-00-0*); pap. write for info. (*0-935015-01-9*) Inst Charter Finan Analysts.
Regan, Pat. Watercolor: A Painting Study Guide. (Illus.). 68p. pap. 12.95 (*0-9615826-0-X*) P Regan.
Regan, Patrick M. Organizing Societies for War: The Process & Consequences of Societal Militarization. LC 93-8621. 208p. 1994. text ed. 55.00 (*0-275-94670-3*, C4670, Praeger Pubs) Greenwood.
Regan, Peter. Touchstone. (Illus.). 208p. (J). (gr. 4-7). 1989. 13.95 (*0-947962-44-1*, Pub. by Childrens Pr IE) Irish Bks Media.
Regan, Peter F. & Schultze, Hans G. Education for the Health Professions: Policies for the 1980s. 93p. (Orig.). 1983. pap. text ed. 28.00x (*91-22-00627-3*, Pub. by Almqv & Wiksell SW) Coronet Bks.
***Regan, Priscilla M.** Rethinking Privacy: Social Values, Technological Change, & Public Policy. LC 94-49544. 1995. write for info. (*0-8078-2226-4*); pap. write for info. (*0-8078-4532-9*) U of NC Pr.
Regan, Richard J. The Moral Dimensions of Politics. 256p. 1986. pap. text ed. 15.95 (*0-19-503975-0*) OUP.
Regan, Richard J., ed. see Aquinas, Thomas.
Regan, Richard J., ed. see St. Thomas Aquinas.
Regan, Rick, illus. The Farmer, the Buffalo, & the Tiger: A Folktale from Vietnam. LC 93-21725. (Adventures in Storytelling Ser.). 32p. (J). (ps-3). 1993. lib. bdg. 12.90 (*0-516-05143-1*) Childrens.
— The Naughty Little Rabbit & Old Man Coyote: A Tewa Story from San Juan Pueblo. LC 92-8992. (Adventures in Storytelling Ser.). 24p. (J). (ps-3). 1992. lib. bdg. 12.90 (*0-516-05141-5*); pap. 4.95 (*0-516-45141-3*) Childrens.
Regan, Robert D., jt. ed. see Watson, Ken.
Regan, S. Kevin. Teen Prayer Services: Twenty Themes for Reflection. LC 92-81797. 80p. (Orig.). 1992. pap. 9.95 (*0-89622-520-8*) Twenty-Third.
Regan, Sandy. Home for Sale by Owner: The FSBO Guide. (Illus.). 1989. pap. 8.95 (*0-317-89466-8*) R & R Pub.
Regan, Stephen, ed. The Politics of Pleasure. LC 92-19298. (Ideas & Production Ser.). 1992. pap. 32.00 (*0-335-09759-6*, Open Univ Pr) Taylor & Francis.
Regan, Stephen & Treharne, Elaine, eds. The Year's Work in Critical & Cultural Theory Vol. I, 1991. 500p. (C). 1995. text ed. 90.00 (*0-391-03835-4*) Humanities.
— The Year's Work in English Studies, Vol. 72, 1991. LC 22-10024. 720p. (C). 1994. text ed. 140.00 (*0-391-03836-2*) Humanities.
— The Year's Work in English Studies, Vol. 73-1992. 1000p. (C). 1995. text ed. 140.00 (*0-391-03866-4*) Humanities.
Regan, Stephen D. In Bitter Tempest: The Biography of Admiral Frank Fletcher. LC 93-29772. (Illus.). 288p. 1994. text ed. 34.95 (*0-8138-0778-6*) Iowa St U Pr.
Regan, Sylvia. Zelda: Manuscript Edition. 1969. pap. 13.00 (*0-8222-1292-7*) Dramatists Play.
Regan, Tom. Animal Sacrifices: Religious Perspectives on the Use of Animals in Science. LC 85-22093. 288p. (C). 1988. pap. 18.95 (*0-87722-511-7*) Temple U Pr.
— The Case for Animal Rights. LC 83-1087. (C). 1983. pap. 14.00 (*0-520-05460-1*, CAL 741) U CA Pr.
— G. E. Moore: The Early Essays. LC 86-6007. 266p. 1986. 37.95 (*0-87722-442-0*) Temple U Pr.
— The Thee Generation: Reflections on the Coming Revolution. 176p. 1991. 24.95 (*0-87722-758-6*); pap. 16.95 (*0-87722-772-1*) Temple U Pr.
Regan, Tom, ed. Earthbound: Introductory Essays in Environmental Ethics. 3757p. (C). 1990. reprint ed. pap. text ed. 19.95 (*0-88133-568-1*) Waveland Pr.
— Just Business. (C). 1983. pap. text ed. write for info. (*0-07-554373-7*) McGraw.
— Matters of Life & Death. 3rd ed. LC 92-23158. 544p. (C). 1993. pap. text ed. write for info. (*0-07-051330-9*) McGraw.
Regan, Tom & McCarthy, Colman. The Struggle for Animal Rights. 208p. (Orig.). 1987. pap. 5.95 (*0-9602632-1-7*) ISAR Inc.
Regan, Tom & Singer, Peter. Animal Rights & Human Obligations. 2nd ed. 288p. 1989. pap. text ed. 25.60 (*0-13-036864-4*) P-H.
Regan, Tom & Van DeVeer, Donald, eds. And Justice for All: New Introductory Essays in Ethics & Public Policy. LC 81-23446. (Philosophy & Society Ser.). 320p. 1982. 52.25 (*0-8476-7059-7*); pap. 21.00 (*0-8476-7060-0*) Rowman.
Regan, Tom, ed. see Carter, William R.
Regan, Tom, jt. auth. see Linzey, Andrew.
Regan, Tom, jt. ed. see Linzey, Andrew.
Regan, Tom, jt. ed. see VanDeVeer, Donald.
Regani, Sarojini. Nizam - British Relations, 1724-1857. (C). 1989. 28.50 (*81-7022-195-1*, Pub. by Concept II) S Asia.
Regard, ed. see Chateaubriand, Rene.
Regard, Maurice, ed. see Chateaubriand, Francois-Rene de.
Regard, Maurice, jt. auth. see De Balzac, Honore.
Regard, Maurice, ed. see De Balzac, Honore.
Regard, Maurice, ed. see De Chateaubriand, Francois-Rene.
Regardie, et al. Psychology, Magic & Mysticism. 160p. (Orig.). 1994. pap. 12.95 (*1-56184-104-8*) New Falcon Pubns.
Regardie, Israel. The Art of True Healing. Allen, Marc, ed. LC 91-21732. (Classic Wisdom Collection). 96p. 1991. 9.95 (*0-931432-76-6*) New Wrld Lib.
— Complete Golden Dawn System of Magic. LC 83-81664. (Illus.). 1200p. 1991. reprint ed. 49.95 (*1-56184-037-8*) New Falcon Pubns.
— Complete Golden Dawn System of Magic: An Interpretation of Aleister Crowley. LC 83-81664. 1983. 49.95 (*0-941404-12-9*) New Falcon Pubns.
— Eye in the Triangle: An Interpretation of Aleister Crowley. rev. ed. LC 88-83355. 560p. 1993. reprint ed. pap. 17.95 (*1-56184-054-8*) New Falcon Pubns.
— A Garden of Pomegranates. LC 74-18984. (High Magick Ser.). (Illus.). 174p. 1970. pap. 8.95 (*0-87542-690-5*) Llewellyn Pubns.
— The Golden Dawn. 6th rev. ed. LC 86-15247. (Golden Dawn Ser.). (Illus.). 840p. 1986. pap. 24.95 (*0-87542-663-8*) Llewellyn Pubns.
— Healing Energy, Prayer, & Relaxation. rev. ed. LC 82-83292. 80p. 1982. pap. 9.95 (*1-56184-055-6*) New Falcon Pubns.
— Healing Energy Prayer & Relaxation. 150p. 1989. reprint ed. pap. 9.95 (*0-9622452-0-8*) Golden Dawn.
— Middle Pillar. rev. ed. LC 72-19899. (High Magick Ser.). (Illus.). 168p. 1970. pap. 6.95 (*0-87542-658-1*) Llewellyn Pubns.
— The One Year Manual: Twelve Steps to Spiritual Enlightenment. rev. ed. 96p. 1981. reprint ed. pap. 6.95 (*0-87728-489-X*) Weiser.
— The Philosopher's Stone: A Modern Comparative Approach to Alchemy from the Psychological & Magical Points of View. 204p. 1993. pap. 17.95 (*1-56459-282-0*) Kessinger Pub.
— Roll Away the Stone: An Introduction to Aleister Crowleys Essays on the Psychology of Hashish. 1994. pap. 12.95 (*0-87877-194-8*) Newcastle Pub.
— Tree of Life, a Study in Magic. LC 70-16403. 284p. 1972. reprint ed. pap. 12.95 (*0-87728-149-1*) Weiser.
— What You Should Know about the Golden Dawn. 6th rev. ed. LC 83-81663. (Illus.). 256p. 1993. pap. 12.95 (*1-56184-064-5*) New Falcon Pubns.
Regardie, Israel & Stephensen, P. R. The Legend of Aleister Crowley. LC 83-81836. 200p. 1983. reprint ed. pap. 12.95 (*0-941404-20-X*) New Falcon Pubns.
Regardz, Beth, jt. auth. see Schultz, Joseph.
Regazzi, John J. & Hines, Theodore C. A Guide to Indexed Periodicals in Religion. LC 75-22277. 328p. 1975. 25.00 (*0-8108-0868-4*) Scarecrow.
Regazzoni, P., jt. ed. see Aebi, M.
Regehr, Duncan. The Dragon's Eye: An Artist's View. (Illus.). 208p. 1994. 45.00 (*1-885203-03-9*) Jrny Editions.
Regehr, Lydia. Bible Riddles of Birds & Beasts & Creeping Things. (Illus.). 36p. (Orig.). (J). (gr. 7-12). 1982. pap. 1.25 (*0-89323-030-8*) Bible Memory.
Regeiro, Jose M. Spanish Drama of the Golden Age: A Catalogue of the Comedia Collection in the University of Pennsylvania Libraries. LC 75-172289. 106p. 1971. 70.00 (*0-89235-009-1*) Res Pubns CT.
Regel, L. L. & Sagdeev, R. Z. Materials Processing in Space, Vol. 1: Theory, Experiments, Technology. Bradley, J. E., tr. LC 89-7222. (Illus.). 248p. 1990. 69.50 (*0-306-11026-1*, Consultants) Plenum.
***Regel, Liya L. & Wilcox, William R., eds.** Materials Processing in High Gravity. LC 94-40006. 222p. 1995. 79.50 (*0-306-44862-9*, Plenum Pr) Plenum.
Regele, Michael B. Your Church & Its Mission: A Congregational Self-Study Program. 96p. (Orig.). 1989. 99.95 (*0-317-93394-9*) Church Information.
***Regelski, Michael.** Building Multimedia Applications with Visual Basic. (Illus.). 512p. (Orig.). 1995. pap. text ed. 39.99 (*0-7897-0139-1*) Que.
Regelski, Thomas A. Teaching General Music: Action Learning for Middle & Secondary Schools. LC 80-5561. (Illus.). 422p. 1981. text ed. 33.00 (*0-02-872070-9*) Schirmer Bks.
Regelson, Abraham, tr. The Deluxe Haggadah. 1961. ring bd. 40.00 (*0-914080-34-2*) Shulsinger Sales.
— The Haggadah-Kleinman. 1965. pap. 1.99 (*0-914080-33-4*) Shulsinger Sales.
Regelson, Lev, jt. auth. see Yakunin, Gleb.
Regelson, W., jt. ed. see Kalimi, M. Y.
Regen, Frank. Apuleius Philosophus Platonicus: Untersuchungen zur Apologie (De magia) und zu De Mundo. (Untersuchungen zur Antiken Literatur und Geschichte Ser.: Vol. 10). 123p. (C). 1971. 54.65 (*3-11-003678-9*) De Gruyter.
***Regenberg, Werner.** Captured American & British Tanks: Under the German Flag. (Illus.). 48p. 1993. pap. 8.95 (*0-88740-524-X*) Schiffer.
Regenberg, Werner & Scheibert, Horst. Captured Tanks under the German Flag - Russian Battle Tanks. LC 89-63355. (Illus.). 48p. 1989. pap. 6.95 (*0-88740-201-1*) Schiffer.
Regenbogen, L. S. & Eliahou, H. E., eds. Diseases Affecting the Eye & the Kidney. (Illus.). xviii, 458p. 1993. 358.50 (*3-8055-5660-8*) S Karger.
Regenbogen, Lucian S. & Coscas, Gabriel J., eds. Oculo-Auditory Syndromes. (Illus.). 368p. 1985. text ed. 86.50 (*0-89352-225-2*, Yr Bk Med Pubs) Mosby Yr Bk.
Regency Press, Ltd. Staff, ed. Secret of the Golden Hours. 112p. 1984. 40.00 (*0-7212-0656-5*, Pub. by Regency Press) St Mut.
— Simple South Indian Savoury Dishes for One & All. 48p. 1984. 25.00 (*0-7212-0604-2*, Pub. by Regency Press) St Mut.
Regency Press, Ltd. Staff, ed. see Roberts, Ursula.
Regency Press Staff. Earth Summit Ninety Two: The United Nations Conference on Environment & Development Rio de Janeiro 1992. 1992. pap. 39.95 (*0-9520469-0-3*, Pub. by Regency Press) St Mut.
— Healing Journeys by the Healer & the Sentinel. 144p. (C). 1991. pap. 22.00 (*0-7212-0856-8*, Pub. by Regency Press) St Mut.
Regenmortel. Structures of Antigens, Vol. I. 1992. 141.95 (*0-8493-8865-1*, QR186) CRC Pr.
Regens, J. Energy & the Western U. S. LC 82-18585. 195p. 1982. text ed. 49.95 (*0-275-90882-8*, C0882, Praeger Pubs) Greenwood.
***Regens, James L. & Gaddie, Ronald K.** The Economic Realities of Political Reform: Elections & the U.S. Senate. (Murphy Institute Studies in Political Economy: 4). (Illus.). 160p. (C). 1995. 39.95 (*0-521-47468-X*) Cambridge U Pr.
Regens, James L. & Rycroft, Robert W. The Acid Rain Controversy. LC 87-35769. (Series in Policy & Institutional Studies). (Illus.). 246p. (Orig.). 1988. pap. 19.95x (*0-8229-5404-4*) U of Pittsburgh Pr.
Regensburger, William, jt. auth. see Kimeldorf, Howard.
Regenstein, Carrie E., jt. auth. see Regenstein, Joe M.
Regenstein, Helen, jt. auth. see Miller, James E., Jr.
Regenstein, Joe M. & Regenstein, Carrie E. Food Protein Chemistry. LC 83-12320. (Food Science & Technology Ser.). 1984. text ed. 101.00 (*0-12-585820-5*) Acad Pr.
— An Introduction to Fish Science & Technology. (Illus.). 344p. 1991. text ed. 51.95 (*0-442-00500-8*) Chapman & Hall.
Regenstein, Lewis. How to Survive in America the Poisoned: What to Do about Radioactive & Toxic Contamination in Destroying Our Environment, Our Wildlife, Ourselves. LC 82-1813. (Illus.). 1982. 16.95 (*0-87491-486-8*); pap. 9.95 (*0-87491-838-3*) Acropolis.
Regenstein, Lewis G. Cleaning up America the Poisoned: How to Survive Our Polluted Society. 1993. pap. 14.95 (*0-87491-999-1*) Acropolis.
— Replenish the Earth: A History of Organized Religion's Treatment of Animals & Nature - Including the Bible's Message of Conservation & Kindness to Animals. 256p. (Orig.). 1991. pap. 14.95 (*0-8245-1075-5*) Crossroad NY.
Regensteiner, Else. The Art of Weaving. LC 86-61293. (Illus.). 192p. 1986. reprint ed. pap. 19.95 (*0-88740-079-5*) Schiffer.
— Geometric Design in Weaving. (Illus.). 160p. 1986. 29.50 (*0-671-61402-9*) P-H.
— Geometric Design in Weaving. LC 86-61294. (Illus.). 224p. 1986. 29.95 (*0-88740-078-7*) Schiffer.
— Weaver's Study Course: Sourcebook for Ideas & Techniques. LC 87-61437. (Illus.). 176p. 1987. pap. 19.95 (*0-88740-112-0*) Schiffer.
Regensteiner, Henry, ed. see Durrenmatt, Friedrich.
Regents, P. H. Endocrinology. 3rd ed. 64p. 1993. pap. 10.45 (*0-13-035502-X*) P-H.
— Orthopedics. 3rd ed. 130p. 1993. pap. 12.55 (*0-13-156845-0*) P-H.
Reger, Gary. Regionalism & Change in the Economy of Independent Delos. LC 93-22738. (Hellenistic Culture & Society Ser.: Vol. 14). 1994. 55.00 (*0-520-08460-8*) U CA Pr.
Reger, Janet & Clarke, Brian. Chastity in Focus. (Illus.). 128p. 1981. 30.00 (*0-7043-2151-3*, Pub. by Quartet UK) Charles River Bks.
Reger, Max. On the Theory of Modulation: Music Book Index. 50p. 1993. reprint ed. lib. bdg. 69.00 (*0-7812-9663-3*) Rprt Serv.
Reger, Zita, jt. ed. see Nelson, Keith E.
Reges, Stuart. Building Pascal Programs. (C). 1987. pap. text ed. 28.50 (*0-673-39243-0*) HarpCollege.
Regester, David. Basic Woodturning Techniques. (Illus.). 112p. (Orig.). 1993. pap. 14.95 (*1-55870-300-4*) Betterway Bks.
— Turning Boxes & Spindles: Step-by-Step. (Illus.). 110p. 1995. 29.95 (*0-7134-7240-5*, Pub. by Batsford UK) Trafalgar.
Regezi, Joseph & Sciubba, James. Oral Pathology: Clinical Pathologic Correlations. 2nd ed. LC 92-15452. (Illus.). 720p. 1993. text ed. 57.95 (*0-7216-3621-7*) Saunders.
Regge, Tullio, jt. auth. see Levi, Primo.
Reggia, J. A. & Tuhrim, S., eds. Computer-Assisted Medical Decision Making, Vol. 2. (Computers & Medicine Ser.). (Illus.). xix, 296p. 1985. 64.00 (*0-387-96136-4*) Spr-Verlag.
— Computer-Assisted Medical Decision Making I. (Computers & Medicine Ser.). (Illus.). 275p. 1985. 54.00 (*0-387-96104-6*) Spr-Verlag.
Reggia, J. A., jt. auth. see Peng, Y.
Reggiani, Aura, jt. auth. see Nijkamp, Peter.
Reggiani, Aura, jt. ed. see Nijkamp, Peter.
Reggiani, G. M., jt. ed. see Young, A. L.
Reggiani, L., ed. Hot-Electron Transport in Semiconductors. (Topics in Applied Physics Ser.: Vol. 58). (Illus.). 305p. 1985. 87.00 (*0-387-13321-6*) Spr-Verlag.
Reggie the Retiree, pseud. Laughs & Limericks on Aging. (Illus.). 96p. 1983. pap. 4.95 (*0-9609960-0-1*) Reggie the Retiree.
Reggs, Sandra K. Health Sciences Research I: Subject Analysis & Reference Guidebook with Bibliography. LC 84-45991. 150p. 1987. 37.50 (*0-88164-304-1*); pap. 34.50 (*0-88164-305-X*) ABBE Pubs Assn.
— Human Rights & Jurisprudence: Index of Modern Information. LC 88-47567. 150p. 1988. 39.50 (*0-88164-760-8*); pap. 34.50 (*0-88164-761-6*) ABBE Pubs Assn.
— Medical Reference Guidebook of Crime & Crime Research. LC 83-73537. 150p. 1985. 37.50 (*0-88164-140-5*); pap. 34.50 (*0-88164-141-3*) ABBE Pubs Assn.
Regguinti, Gordon. The Sacred Harvest: Ojibway Wild Rice Gathering. (We Are Still Here: Native Americans Today Ser.). (Illus.). 48p. (J). (gr. 3-6). 1992. lib. bdg. 19.95 (*0-8225-2650-6*, Lerner Publctns) Lerner Group.
— Sacred Harvest: Ojibway Wild Rice Gathering. (J). (gr. 4-7). 1992. pap. 6.95 (*0-8225-9620-2*, Lerner Publctns) Lerner Group.
Reghbati, H. & Lee, A. Y. Computer Graphics Hardware: Image Generation & Display. LC 88-70221. 375p. 1988. pap. 50.00 (*0-8186-0753-X*, 753) IEEE Comp Soc.
Reghbati, Hassan. VLSI Testing & Validation Techniques. LC 85-80876. 603p. 1985. pap. 7.95 (*0-8186-0668-1*, 668) IEEE Comp Soc.
— VLSI Testing & Validation Techniques. LC 85-80876. 603p. 1985. fiche 30.00 (*0-8186-4668-3*) IEEE Comp Soc.
Regian, J. Wesley & Shute, Valerie, eds. Cognitive Approaches to Automated Instruction. 264p. 1992. text ed. 59.95 (*0-8058-0992-9*) L Erlbaum Assocs.
Regier, Darrel A., jt. ed. see Robins, Lee N.
Regier, H., et al. Biohistory: The Interplay Between Human Society & the Biosphere. (Man & the Biosphere Ser.). 350p. 1992. 98.00 (*92-3-102747-6*, U6720) UNIPUB.

R

An Asterisk (*) at the beginning of an entry indicates that the title is appearing in BIP for the first time.

Regier, Kathleen J., comp. The Spiritual Image in Modern Art. LC 87-40127. (Illus.). 215p. (Orig.). (C). 1987. pap. 9.95 (*0-8356-0621-X*, Quest) Theos Pub Hse.

Regier, Mary H., et al. Biomedical Statistics with Computing. LC 82-2839. (Medical Computing Ser.). 112p. 1982. text ed. 120.00 (*0-471-10449-3*) Wiley.

— Biomedical Statistics with Computing. LC 82-2839. (Medical Computing Ser.: No. 6). (Illus.). 321p. reprint ed. pap. 91.50 (*0-8357-6041-3*, 2034234) Bks Demand.

Regier, Willis, ed. Masterpieces of American Indian Literature. (Illus.). 1994. 11.98 (*1-56731-035-4*, MJF Bks) Fine Comms.

Regina. Precious Moments: Book of Prayers. 1992. 15.95 (*0-88271-276-4*) Regina Pr.

Regina, Derieva. Otsutstvie. LC 92-46143. 122p. (Orig.). (RUS.). 1993. pap. 8.00 (*1-55779-053-1*) Hermitage.

Regina, Jocelyn. Wife-in-Law! Your Ex-Husband Married Her or Your Present Husband Divorced Her! 1984. pap. 14.95 (*0-914345-00-1*) Bereny Bear.

Regina, Karen & Rhodes, Gregory L., eds. Cincinnati: An Urban History Sourcebook, Bk. II. LC 87-72186. (Illus.). 88p. (Orig.). (YA). (gr. 7-8). 1988. pap. text ed. 6.95 (*0-911497-02-1*) Cinc Hist Soc.

— Cincinnati: An Urban History Sourcebook, Bk. 1. LC 87-72186. (Illus.). 88p. (Orig.). (J). (gr. 4-6). 1988. pap. text ed. 6.95 (*0-911497-01-3*) Cinc Hist Soc.

***Regina Press Staff.** Old Testament for Children. (J). (ps-3). Date not set. 1.95 (*0-88271-044-3*) Regina Pr.

— Precious Moments: My First Book of Prayers. 1991. 6.95 (*0-88271-275-6*); 6.95 (*0-88271-277-2*) Regina Pr.

***Regina Staff.** Precious Moments My Guardian Angel. (J). (ps-3). Date not set. 9.95 (*0-88271-288-8*) Regina Pr.

— Precious Moments Prayers for Boys & Girls. (J). (ps-3). Date not set. 3.95 (*0-88271-291-8*) Regina Pr.

Reginald, Jorge S. Smoking: Medical Subject Analysis & Research Guide with Bibliography. LC 84-45743. 150p. 1987. 44.50 (*0-88164-270-3*); pap. 39.50 (*0-88164-271-1*) ABBE Pubs Assn.

Reginald, R. Contemporary Science Fiction Authors. LC 74-16517. (Science Fiction Ser.). (Illus.). 358p. 1976. reprint ed. 26.95 (*0-405-06332-6*) Ayer.

Reginald, R., et al. Futurevisions: The New Golden Age of the Science Fiction Film. LC 85-20098. (Illus.). 192p. 1985. reprint ed. lib. bdg. 31.00x (*0-89370-681-7*) Borgo Pr.

Reginald, R. Science Fiction & Fantasy Literature Supplement 87. 1991. 140.00 (*0-8103-5511-6*) Gale.

Reginald, R. & Burgess, M. R. Cumulative Paperback Index, 1939-1959: A Comprehensive Bibliographic Guide to 14,000 Mass-Market Paperback Books of 33 Publishers Issued under 69 Imprints. xiii, 362p. (C). 1990. reprint ed. lib. bdg. 51.00x (*0-89370-022-3*) Borgo Pr.

Reginald, R. & Elliot, Jeffrey M. If J. F. K. Had Lived: A Political Scenario. LC 81-19516. (Borgo Political Scenarios Ser.: Vol. 1). 64p. 1982. lib. bdg. 20.00x (*0-89370-155-6*); pap. 10.00x (*0-89370-255-2*) Borgo Pr.

— Tempest in a Teapot: The Falkland Islands War. LC 83-8807. (Stokvis Studies in Historical Chronology & Thought: No. 3). (Illus.). 173p. 1983. lib. bdg. 29.00x (*0-89370-167-X*); pap. text ed. 19.00x (*0-89370-267-6*) Borgo Pr.

Reginald, R. & Melville, Douglas, eds. Dreamers of Dreams: An Anthology of Fantasy. LC 77-84280. (Lost Race & Adult Fantasy Ser.). (Illus.). 1978. lib. bdg. 44.95 (*0-405-11017-0*) Ayer.

— King Solomon's Children: Some Parodies of H. Rider Haggard. LC 77-84281. (Lost Race & Adult Fantasy Ser.). (Illus.). 1978. lib. bdg. 54.95 (*0-405-11018-9*) Ayer.

— Lost Race & Adult Fantasy Fiction Series, 69 bks., Set. (Illus.). 1978. lib. bdg. 2,018.00 (*0-405-10950-4*) Ayer.

— They: Three Parodies of H. Rider Haggard's She. LC 77-84277. (Lost Race & Adult Fantasy Ser.). (Illus.). 1978. lib. bdg. 54.95 (*0-405-11015-4*) Ayer.

— Worlds of Never: An Original Anthology. LC 77-84278. (Lost Race & Adult Fantasy Ser.). (Illus.). 1978. lib. bdg. 41.95 (*0-405-11016-2*) Ayer.

Reginald, R. & Menville, Douglas, eds. Ancestral Voices: An Anthology of Early Science Fiction. LC 74-16508. (Science Fiction Ser.). 1977. reprint ed. 23.95 (*0-405-06305-9*) Ayer.

— Ancient Haunting: An Orginal Anthology. LC 75-46269. (Supernatural & Occult Fiction Ser.). (Illus.). 1976. lib. bdg. 39.95 (*0-405-08163-4*) Ayer.

— The Boyhood Days of Guy Fawkes: Or, the Conspirators of Old London. LC 75-46257. (Supernatural & Occult Fiction Ser.). (Illus.). (YA). (gr. 7 up). 1976. reprint ed. lib. bdg. 20.95 (*0-405-08116-2*) Ayer.

— The Centenarian: Or, the Two Beringhelds. Slusser, George E., tr. LC 75-46250. (Supernatural & Occult Fiction Ser.). (Illus.). 1976. lib. bdg. 34.95 (*0-405-08110-3*) Ayer.

— Phantasmagoria: An Original Anthology. LC 75-46292. (Supernatural & Occult Fiction Ser.). 1976. lib. bdg. 34.95 (*0-405-08152-9*) Ayer.

— RIP: Five Stories of the Supernatural. LC 75-1539. (Supernatural & Occult Fiction Ser.). (Illus.). 1976. lib. bdg. 26.95 (*0-405-08425-0*) Ayer.

— The Spectre Bridegroom & Other Horrors: Original Anthology. LC 75-46305. (Supernatural & Occult Fiction Ser.). (Illus.). 1976. lib. bdg. 25.95 (*0-405-08165-0*) Ayer.

— Supernatural & Occult Fiction Series, 63 bks, Set. 1976. lib. bdg. 1,516.50 (*0-405-08107-3*) Ayer.

Reginald, R., ed. see Ainsworth, William H.

Reginald, R., ed. see Ames, Joseph B.

Reginald, R., ed. see Anderson, Olof W.

Reginald, R., ed. see Arlen, Michael.

Reginald, R., ed. see Arnold, Edwin L.

Reginald, R., ed. see Atkins, Frank.

Reginald, R., ed. see Barringer, Leslie.

Reginald, R., jt. ed. see Barron, Neil.

Reginald, R., ed. see Bennet, Robert A.

Reginald, R., ed. see Bennett, Gertrude B.

Reginald, R., ed. see Benson, Edward F.

Reginald, R., ed. see Blackwood, Algernon.

Reginald, R., ed. see Boothby, Guy.

Reginald, R., ed. see Bramah, Ernest.

Reginald, R., ed. see Bruce, Muriel.

Reginald, R., ed. see Burrage, Alfred M.

Reginald, R., ed. see Burton, Alice E.

Reginald, R., ed. see Campbell, Praed.

Reginald, R., ed. see Carew, Henry.

Reginald, R., ed. see Carnegie, James.

Reginald, R., ed. see Chambers, Robert W.

Reginald, R., ed. see Channing, Mark.

Reginald, R., ed. see Chester, George R.

Reginald, R., ed. see Clock, Herbert & Boetzel, Eric.

Reginald, R., ed. see Coblentz, Stanton A.

Reginald, R., ed. see Constantine, Murray.

Reginald, R., ed. see Cook, William W.

Reginald, R., ed. see Coppard, Alfred E.

Reginald, R., ed. see Cowan, Frank.

Reginald, R., ed. see Crawford, Francis M.

Reginald, R., ed. see Dalton.

Reginald, R., ed. see De Comeau, Alexander.

Reginald, R., ed. see De La Mare, Walter J.

Reginald, R., jt. auth. see Dikty, Thaddeus.

Reginald, R., ed. see Doughty, Francis W.

Reginald, R., ed. see Dunn, Allan J.

Reginald, R., ed. see Eddison, Eric R.

Reginald, R., jt. auth. see Elliot, Jeffrey M.

Reginald, R., ed. see Erckmann, Emile & Erckmann, Alexandre.

Reginald, R., ed. see Ewers, Hanns H.

Reginald, R., ed. see Fielding, Henry.

Reginald, R., ed. see Fleckenstein, Alfred C.

Reginald, R., ed. see Fyne, Neal.

Reginald, R., ed. see Gautier, Theophile.

Reginald, R., ed. see Gillmore, Inez H.

Reginald, R., ed. see Gompertz, Martin L.

Reginald, R., ed. see Green, Fitzhugh.

Reginald, R., ed. see Gregory, Jackson.

Reginald, R., ed. see Griffith, George.

Reginald, R., ed. see Guthrie, Thomas A.

Reginald, R., ed. see Hadley, George.

Reginald, R., ed. see Haggard, H. Rider.

Reginald, R., ed. see Haldane, Charlotte.

Reginald, R., jt. auth. see Hancer, Kevin B.

Reginald, R., ed. see Harris, Burland.

Reginald, R., ed. see Hartmann, Franz.

Reginald, R., ed. see Harvey, William F.

Reginald, R., ed. see Hecht, Ben.

Reginald, R., ed. see Heron-Allen, Edward.

Reginald, R., ed. see Hodder, William R.

Reginald, R., ed. see Holmes, Oliver Wendell.

Reginald, R., ed. see Housman, Clemence.

Reginald, R., ed. see Ingram, Eleanor M.

Reginald, R., ed. see James, Montague R.

Reginald, R., ed. see Keller, David H.

Reginald, R., ed. see Kingsmill, Hugh.

Reginald, R., ed. see Knowles, Vernon.

Reginald, R., ed. see Kummer, Frederic A.

Reginald, R., ed. see Large, E. C.

Reginald, R., ed. see Le Queux, William T.

Reginald, R., ed. see Leroux, Gaston.

Reginald, R., ed. see Lindsay, David.

Reginald, R., ed. see Linklater, Eric.

Reginald, R., ed. see London, Jack.

Reginald, R., ed. see Machen, Arthur.

Reginald, R., ed. see MacKay, Mary.

Reginald, R., ed. see Marrat, Florence.

Reginald, R., ed. see Marshall, Sidney J.

Reginald, R., ed. see McHugh, Vincent.

Reginald, R., jt. auth. see Menville, Douglas A.

Reginald, R., ed. see Merritt, Abraham.

Reginald, R., ed. see Moresby, Lily & Beck, Adams.

Reginald, R., ed. see Morris, Kenneth.

Reginald, R., ed. see Morris, William.

Reginald, R., ed. see Murray, G. G.

Reginald, R., ed. see Odell, Eric.

Reginald, R., ed. see O'Donnell, Elliot.

Reginald, R., ed. see Oliver, George.

Reginald, R., ed. see Owen, Frank.

Reginald, R., ed. see Paget, Violet.

Reginald, R., ed. see Paine, Albert B.

Reginald, R., ed. see Phillpotts, Eden.

Reginald, R., ed. see Potter, Margaret H.

Reginald, R., ed. see Powys, John C.

Reginald, R., ed. see Reynolds, George W.

Reginald, R., ed. see Rolfe, Frederick W., et al.

Reginald, R., ed. see Rosynyaine, J. H.

Reginald, R., ed. see Russell, William C.

Reginald, R., ed. see Savile, Frank.

Reginald, R., ed. see Scott, G. Firth.

Reginald, R., ed. see Sheldon-Williams, Miles.

Reginald, R., ed. see Sicard, Clara.

Reginald, R., ed. see Sinclair, Upton.

Reginald, R., ed. see Stewart, Mary L.

Reginald, R., ed. see Todd, Ruthven.

Reginald, R., ed. see Viereck, George S.

Reginald, R., ed. see Vivan, Charles E.

Reginald, R., ed. see Vivian, Charles E.

Reginald, R., ed. see Wakefield, Herbert R.

Reginald, R., ed. see Ward, Arthur S.

Reginald, R., ed. see Wells, H. G.

Reginald, R., ed. see Whiting, Sydney.

***Reginald, R., et al.** Futurevisions: The New Golden Age of the Science Fiction Film. (Illus.). 192p. 1985. pap. 21.00x (*0-89370-699-X*) Borgo Pr.

Reginald, Robert, ed. Science Fiction & Fantasy Literature: A Checklist from 1700 to 1974...with Contemporary Science Fiction Authors II, 2 vols. LC 76-46130. 1167p. 1979. 260.00 (*0-8103-1051-1*) Gale.

— Science Fiction & Fantasy Literature: Nineteen Seventy-Five to Nineteen Ninety-One Supplement, 2 vols. 1500p. 1992. 199.00 (*0-8103-1825-3*) Gale.

Reginald, Robert & Burgess, M. R., eds. Cumulative Paperback Index, Nineteen Thirty-Nine to Nineteen Fifty-Nine: A Comprehensive Bibliographic Guide to 14,000 Mass-Market Paperback Books of 33 Publishers Issued under 69 Imprints. LC 73-6866. 386p. 1973. 64.00 (*0-8103-1050-3*) Gale.

Reginald, Robert, jt. auth. see Elliot, Jeffrey M.

Reginald, Robert, jt. auth. see Mallett, Daryl F.

Reginato, Antonio J., jt. auth. see Schumacher, Ralph H.

Reginer, Victor, et al. Best Practices in Assisted Living: Innovations in Design, Management & Financing. (Illus.). 166p. (Orig.). (C). 1991. 18.00 (*1-881010-25-2*) USC Andrus Geron.

***Regini, Marino.** The Future of Labour Movements. (International Sociology Ser.: Vol. 43). (Illus.). 272p. 1992. pap. text ed. 22.95 (*0-8039-7977-0*) Sage.

— The Future of Labour Movements. (International Sociology Ser.: Vol. 43). (Illus.). 272p. (C). 1992. text ed. 55.00 (*0-8039-8761-7*) Sage.

— Uncertain Boundaries: The Social & Political Construction of European Economies. (Cambridge Studies in Comparative Politics Ser.). (Illus.). 192p. (C). 1995. 54.95 (*0-521-47371-3*) Cambridge U Pr.

Regini, Marino, jt. ed. see Lange, Peter.

Regional Kidney Disease Program, Education Department Staff. The Patient's Guide to Understandng Hemodialysis. rev. ed. 150p. 1986. reprint ed. ring bd. 20.00 (*1-56488-005-2*) Dialyrn.

— Principles & Practice of Hemodialysis. 214p. 1982. ring bd. 85.00 (*1-56488-000-1*) Dialyrn.

Regional Kidney Disease Program, Interstate Division Staff. Home Hemodialysis Training. 194p. 1980. ring bd. 25.00 (*1-56488-007-9*) Dialyrn.

Regional Laboratory for Educational Improvement of the Northeast & Islands Staff. What about Learning? 17p. 1993. pap. text ed. write for info. (*1-878234-05-6*) Reg Lab Educ IOT NE Isls.

Regional Plan Association Staff. A Framework for Transit Planning in the New York Region. (RPA Bulletin Ser.: No. 131). 130p. 1986. pap. 10.00 (*0-318-21808-9*) Regional Plan Assn.

— From Plan to Reality, 3 vols. in one. LC 73-14026. (Metropolitan America Ser.). (Illus.). 330p. 1974. reprint ed. 33.95 (*0-405-05437-8*) Ayer.

— Jamaica Center Nineteen Eighty-Seven: An Office Enterprise Zone. (RPA Bulletin Ser.: No. 132). 53p. 1986. 10.00 (*0-318-16370-5*) Regional Plan Assn.

— The Open Space Imperative I: Greenspaces & Greenways. (Illus.). 1987. pap. 5.00 (*0-938085-00-X*) Regional Plan Assn.

— The Open Space Imperative: II: Where the Pavement Ends. 1987. 5.00 (*0-938085-03-4*) Regional Plan Assn.

Regional Plan Association Staff, jt. auth. see Citizens Crime Commission of New York City Staff.

Regional Plan Association Staff, jt. auth. see Citizens Crime Commission of New York Staff.

Regional R. E. Centre (Midland) Westhi 11 College Staff, ed. Festivals, Pt. 1: Introduction - Teacher's Notes. (C). 1988. audio, text ed. 200.00 (*0-685-39399-2*, Pub. by S Thornes Pubs UK) St Mut.

Regional R. E. Centre (Midlands)-Westhi 11 College Staff, ed. Festivals, Pt. 3: Passover & Diwali - Teacher's Notes, 2 filmstrips, Set. (C). 1988. audio, text ed. 330.00 (*0-685-39398-4*, Pub. by S Thornes Pubs UK) St Mut.

Regional Research Conference on Differential Games & Control Theory Staff. Differential Games & Control Theory: Proceedings of a National Science Foundation-Conference Board of the Mathematical Sciences Regional Research Conference, Held at University of Rhode Island, Kingston, Rhode Island, June 4-8, 1973: the Invited Lectures & Contributed Papers. LC 74-21593. (Lecture Notes in Pure & Applied Mathematics Ser.: No. 10). 422p. reprint ed. pap. 120.30 (*0-7837-4774-8*, 2044529) Bks Demand.

Regis, Atticus, jt. auth. see Fisher, Stephen.

Regis, Ed. Great Mambo Chicken & the Transhuman Condition: Science Slightly Over the Edge. 1990. 18.22 (*0-201-09258-1*) Addison-Wesley.

— Great Mambo Chicken & the Transhuman Condition: Science Slightly Over the Edge. 288p. 1991. pap. 10.53 (*0-201-56751-2*) Addison-Wesley.

— Nano: The Emerging Science of Nanotechnology. LC 94-35378. 1995. 23.95 (*0-316-73858-1*) Little.

Regis, Edward. Who Got Einstein's Office? Eccentricity & Genius at the Institute for Advanced Study. LC 87-11568. (Illus.). 320p. 1987. 17.26 (*0-201-12065-8*) Addison-Wesley.

— Who Got Einstein's Office? Eccentricity & Genius at the Institute for Advanced Study. LC 87-11568. (Illus.). 320p. 1988. pap. 13.46 (*0-201-12278-2*) Addison-Wesley.

Regis, Edward, Jr., ed. Gewirth's Ethical Rationalism: Critical Essays with a Reply by Alan Gewirth. LC 83-17965. (C). 1984. pap. text ed. 12.50 (*0-226-70692-3*) U Ch Pr.

— Gewirth's Ethical Rationalism: Critical Essays with a Reply by Alan Gewirth. LC 83-17965. (C). 1984. lib. bdg. 30.00 (*0-226-70691-5*) U Ch Pr.

Regis, Emelina G. Dalawang Dula Ni Clarissa Sa Ecolohiya. 77p. (Orig.). (TAG.). 1993. pap. 5.75 (*971-10-0504-2*, Pub. by New Day Pub PH) Cellar.

Regis, Iester M., ed. see Dillon, Helen M.

Regis, Iester M., ed. see Edwards, Randi & Edwards, Stevie.

Regis, Louis-Marie. St. Thomas & Epistemology. (Aquinas Lectures). 1946. 10.00 (*0-87462-110-0*) Marquette.

Regis, Margaret, jt. auth. see Kimmett, Larry.

Regis, Pamela. Describing Early America: Bartram, Jefferson, Crevecoeur, & the Rhetoric of Natural History. LC 91-28145. 189p. 1992. lib. bdg. 30.00 (*0-87580-166-8*) N Ill U Pr.

Register, Alvaretta K. Bulloch County, Georgia Genealogical Source Material. 1985. 25.00 (*0-916369-00-5*) Magnolia Pr.

— State Census of North Carolina, 1784-1787. 2nd ed. LC 73-3664. 233p. 1993. reprint ed. 20.00 (*0-8063-0556-8*) Genealog Pub.

Register, Cheri. Are Those Kids Yours? American Families with Children Adopted from Other Countries. 250p. 1990. text ed. 22.95 (*0-02-925750-6*) Free Pr.

— Living with Chronic Illness: Days of Patience & Passion. 352p. 1987. 24.95 (*0-02-925730-1*) Free Pr.

Register, George. Basic Coin Collecting for Pathfinders: A Youth Enrichment Skill. (Illus.). 20p. (Orig.). 1987. pap. 5.00 (*0-936241-14-4*) Cheetah Pub.

— Basic Stamp Collecting for Pathfinders: A Youth Enrichment Skill. (Illus.). 20p. (Orig.). 1987. teacher ed 5.00 (*0-936241-13-6*) Cheetah Pub.

Register, James. Shadows of Old New Orleans. 1967. 12.50 (*0-87511-097-5*) Claitors.

Register, Jane. Blessed Assurance. 133p. (Orig.). 1993. pap. 12.95 (*1-880994-09-7*) Mt Olive Coll Pr.

— He's My Lord. 8p. 1993. 7.50 (*1-880994-27-5*) Mt Olive Coll Pr.

Register, L. B., tr. see Alvarez, A., et al.

Register, L. B., jt. ed. see Brunsken, E.

Register, Layton B., jt. tr. see Bruncken, Ernest.

Register, Layton B., tr. see Calisse, Carlo.

Register, Richard. Ecocity Berkeley: Building Cities for a Healthy Future. (Illus.). 140p. (Orig.). 1987. pap. 10.95 (*1-55643-009-4*) North Atlantic.

Regitz, Manfred & Maas, Gerhard. Diazo Compounds: Properties & Synthesis. 1987. text ed. 196.00 (*0-12-585840-X*) Acad Pr.

Reglar, Stephen, jt. auth. see Brugger, Bill.

Regler, David. Identifying Guide to Mushrooms. 1994. 6.98 (*0-7858-0048-4*) Bk Sales Inc.

Regler, M., et al. Data Analysis Techniques in High Energy Physics Experiments. (Illus.). 450p. (C). 1990. 120.00 (*0-521-34195-7*) Cambridge U Pr.

Regli, Robert B., jt. auth. see Swami Rama.

***Regli, Robert S.** Kona Kai Farms Guide to the Kona Coast: A Coffee Lover's Guide to the Vacation Pleasures of the Kona Coast & the Big Island of Hawaii. 225p. (Orig.). 1995. pap. 8.95 (*0-9646128-0-1*) Kona Kai Farms.

Reglin, Gary L. At Risk "Parent & Family" School Involvement: Strategies for Low Income Families & African-American Families of Unmotivated & Underachieving Students. LC 93-19838. 128p. (C). 1993. 31.95 (*0-398-05877-6*) C C Thomas.

— At Risk "Parent & Family" School Involvement: Strategies for Low Income Families & African-American Families Unmotivated & Underachieving Students. 128p. 1993. pap. 16.95 (*0-398-06340-0*) C C Thomas.

— Motivating Low-Achieving Students: A Special Focus on Unmotivated & Underachieving African American Students. 190p. 1993. pap. 29.95 (*0-398-06341-9*) C C Thomas.

— Motivating Low-Achieving Students: A Special Focus on Unmotivated & Underachieving African American Students. LC 92-46569. 190p. 1993. text ed. 45.95 (*0-398-05852-0*) C C Thomas.

Regling, Gunter, ed. Wolff's Law & Connective Tissue Regulation: Modern Interdisciplinary Comments on Wolff's Law of Connective Tissue Regulation & Rational Understanding of Common Clinical Problems. LC 93-20493. 1993. 121.55 (*3-11-013909-X*) De Gruyter.

Regmi, Mahesh C. Land Tenure & Taxation in Nepal. 1978. 150.00 (*0-7855-0247-5*, Pub. by Ratna Pustak Bhandar); 150.00 (*0-7855-0316-1*, Pub. by Ratna Pustak Bhandar) St Mut.

— Land Tenure & Taxation in Nepal: Mahesh Chandra Regmi, 4 vols. in 1. enl. rev. ed. 851p. (C). 1989. reprint ed. 350.00 (*0-89771-108-4*, Pub. by Ratna Pustak Bhandar) St Mut.

***Regmi, Murari P., ed.** The Himalayan Mind: A Nepalese Investigation. (Illus.). xiv, 240p. 1994. 20.00 (*81-85693-29-3*, Pub. by Nirala Pubns II) Nataraj Bks.

Regmi, R. R. The Dhimals Miraculour Migrants of Himalyan Anthropological Study of a Nepalese Ethnic Group. (C). 1991. text ed. 75.00 (*0-7855-0133-9*, Pub. by Ratna Pustak Bhandar) St Mut.

— Kathmandu, Patan & Bhaktapur: An Archaeological Anthropology of the Royal Cities of the Kathmandu Valley. (C). 1993. 36.00 (*0-7855-0187-8*, Pub. by Ratna Pustak Bhandar) St Mut.

Regmi, Rishikeshab R. Kathmandu, Patan & Bhaktapur: An Archaeological Anthropology of the Royal Cities of the Kathmandu Valley. 109p. 1993. 13.00 (*81-85693-30-7*, Pub. by Nirala Pubns II) Nataraj Bks.

Regnauld, B. The Foot. Elson, Reginald A., tr. (Illus.). 705p. 1986. 315.00 (*0-387-13222-8*) Spr-Verlag.

Regnault, Paule & Daniel, Rollin K. Aesthetic Plastic Surgery: Principles & Techniques. 800p. 1984. 230.00 (*0-316-73851-4*) Little.

Regner, Hermann, ed. Music for Children, 3 vols., 1. (Orff-Schulwerk Ser.). 1977. pap. 24.95 (*0-930448-12-X*, STAP012) Eur-Am Music.

— Music for Children, 3 vols., 2. (Orff-Schulwerk Ser.). 1977. pap. 39.95 (*0-930448-00-6*, STAP006) Eur-Am Music.

— Music for Children, 3 vols., 3. (Orff-Schulwerk Ser.). 1977. pap. 39.95 (*0-930448-08-1*, STAP008) Eur-Am Music.

Regnery, Alfred S., jt. auth. see Leighton, Richard J.

Regnery, Dorothy F. An Enduring Heritage: Historic Buildings of the San Francisco Peninsula. LC 76-14272. (Illus.). xiv, 124p. 1976. 27.50 (*0-8047-0918-1*) Stanford U Pr.

Regnery, Henry. The Cliff Dwellers: A History of a Chicago Cultural Institution. (Illus.). 86p. 1990. text ed. 20.00 (*0-924772-08-5*) CH Bookworks.

— Creative Chicago: From the Chap-Book to the University. LC 93-11130. 1993. 25.00 (*0-924772-24-7*) CH Bookworks.

— Memoirs of a Dissident Publisher. LC 78-22269. 260p. 1979. pap. 9.95 (*0-89526-802-7*) Regnery Pub.

Regnier, jt. ed. see Gooding.

Regnier, Adolphe. Lexique De la Langue De La Bruyere. Vol. III, No. 2. lxxi, 380p. 1970. reprint ed. write for info. (*0-318-71399-3*, Pub. by Georg Olms GW) Lubrecht & Cramer.

— Lexique de la Langue de Malherbe. Vol. V. lxxxvii, 680p. 1970. reprint ed. write for info. (*0-318-71400-0*, Pub. by Georg Olms GW) Lubrecht & Cramer.

Regnier, Gerard. Treasures of the Musee Picasso. (Tiny Folios Ser.). 1994. pap. 11.95 (*1-55859-836-7*) Abbeville Pr.

Regnier, John, ed. see Budreck, Frank.

Regnier, Philippe. Singapore, City State in South East Asia. 258p. (C). 1992. text ed. 39.00 (*0-8248-1406-1*); pap. text ed. 18.00 (*0-8248-1407-X*) UH Pr.

Regnier, Victor. Assisted Living Housing for the Elderly: Innovations in Design & Planning. LC 92-43118. 1993. text ed. 39.95 (*0-442-00702-7*) Van Nos Reinhold.

— Housing the Aged: Design Directives & Policy Considerations. Pynoos, Jon, ed. 517p. 1987. 65.00 (*0-444-01012-2*) P-H.

Regnier, Victor, et al. Assisted Living For the Aged & Frail: Innovations in Design, Management, & Financing. LC 93-38639. 271p. 1994. 35.00 (*0-231-08276-2*) Col U Pr.

Regnon, Theodore De. Etudes De Theologie Positive Sur la Sainte Trinite: Theories Grecques Des Processions Divines. LC 80-2363. (Troisieme Ser., II). reprint ed. 67.00 (*0-404-18915-6*) AMS Pr.

Regnot, Franz, tr. see Nachman of Breslov.

***Rego, Paul.** Single Envelope Printing. (Macintosh Insights Ser.). (Illus.). 12p. (Orig.). 1995. pap. 3.49 (*0-945876-08-4*) Insight Data.

Regoeczi, Erwin, ed. Iodine-Labeled Plasma Proteins, Vol. I. 240p. 1984. 102.00 (*0-8493-6556-2*, QP99, CRC Reprint) Franklin.

— Iodine-Labeled Plasma Proteins, Vol. 2. 1987. 86.00 (*0-8493-6555-4*, QP99, CRC Reprint) Franklin.

Regoli, Robert M. Criminal Justice. (Illus.). 696p. 1994. text ed. write for info. (*0-02-399181-X*) Macmillan.

Regoli, Robert M. & Hewitt, John D. Delinquency in Society: A Child-Centered Approach. 1991. text ed. write for info. (*0-07-051327-9*) McGraw.

— Delinquency in Society: A Child-Centered Approach. 2nd ed. LC 93-17346. 1993. Acid-free paper. text ed. write for info. (*0-07-051333-3*) McGraw.

Regoli, Robert M., et al. Juvenile Delinquency & Juvenile Justice. 448p. (C). 1985. text ed. write for info. (*0-07-554409-1*) McGraw.

***Regosin, Richard L.** Montaigne's Unruly Brood: Textual Engenderings, Monstrous Progeny, & the Challenge to Paternal Authority. LC 95-6077. 1996. write for info. (*0-520-20194-9*) U CA Pr.

Regosz, A., jt. ed. see Tomlinson, E.

Regrut, Brian. Stolen Identity. LC 93-20046. 300p. (Orig.). 1993. pap. 9.99 (*0-8308-1371-3*, 1371) InterVarsity.

— Venegeance Is Mine. LC 94-28133. 296p. (Orig.). 1994. pap. 9.99 (*0-8308-1372-1*, 1372) InterVarsity.

Regtien, P. P. Instrumentation Electronics. LC 92-11963. 1992. pap. text ed. 60.00 (*0-13-473562-5*) P-H.

Regueiro & Riechenberger. Spanish Drama of the Golden Age, Vols. 1-2. 85.00 (*0-87535-137-9*) Hispanic Soc.

Regueiro, Antonio M., tr. see Shigo, Alex L.

Regueiro, Helen. The Limits of Imagination: Wordsworth, Yeats & Stevens. LC 76-13663. 256p. 1976. 31.50 (*0-8014-0994-2*) Cornell U Pr.

Regueiro, Jose R., et al. Human T-Lymphocyte Activation Deficiencies. LC 93-39483. (Medical Intelligence Unit Ser.). 208p. 1994. 89.95 (*1-57059-020-6*) R G Landes.

Regueiro, M. Vocabulary of Iberian Languages: Vocabulario de las Lenguas Ibericas. 169p. (BAQ & SPA.). 1982. pap. 11.95 (*0-8288-1455-4*, S39893) Fr & Eur.

***Regueiro, Manuel P., ed.** Memorias del Primer Congreso del Presidio Politico Cubano. LC 94-70487. (Coleccion Cuba y Sus Jueces). 112p. 1994. pap. 13.00 (*0-614-00462-4*) Ediciones.

Reguis, Marie-Christine, tr. see Pontalis, J. B.

Regul, Lisa, ed. Steel Mirrors: A Prison Anthology. Date not set. pap. 20.00 (*0-934172-31-5*) WIM Pubns.

***Regula, deTraci.** Mysteries of Isis: Her Worship & Magick. (Llewellyn's World Religion & Magic Ser.). (Illus.). 320p. 1995. pap. 19.95 (*1-56718-560-6*) Llewellyn Pubns.

***Regulatory Compliance Assocs., Inc. Staff.** Compliance Training Service. 500p. 1995. 295.00 (*1-55738-712-5*) Probus Pub Co.

***Regulatory Impact Analysis Project, Inc. Staff.** Choices in Risk Assessment: The Role of Science Policy in the Environmental Risk Management Process. 300p. (Orig.). 1994. pap. write for info. (*0-9643747-1-4*) Regulatory Impact.

— Toward Common Sense: Understanding & Including Science Policy in the Environmental Risk Management Debate. 300p. (Orig.). 1994. pap. write for info. (*0-9643747-0-6*) Regulatory Impact.

Regulez, M., jt. auth. see Gardeazabal, J.

Regulska, Joanna & Kowalewski, Adam. Warsaw. (World Cities Ser.). 224p. 1994. text ed. 49.95 (*0-470-22014-7*) Halsted Pr.

Regulski, Jerzy, et al, eds. Decentralization & Local Government: A Danish-Polish Comparative Study in Political Systems. 200p. 1989. pap. 34.95 (*0-88738-730-6*) Transaction Pubs.

***Reh, ed.** Gender & Identity in Africa. (C). 1995. pap. text ed. 31.25 (*3-8258-2199-4*) Westview.

Reh, Jane. Hands-on BASIC Workbook for Kids Commodore 64. (Illus.). 350p. 14.95 (*0-317-12841-8*) P-H.

Rehaag, Godfrey. The Limited Company: Replacing the Victorian Steam Engine. 150p. 1994. 55.95 (*1-85628-682-7*, Pub. by Avebury Pub UK) Ashgate Pub Co.

Rehab Choice Incorporated Staff. Establishing Dysphagia Programs: A Speech-Language Pathologist's Guide. (Illus.). 96p. (Orig.). (C). 1993. pap. text ed. 39.95 (*0-937857-38-6*, 1521) Speech Bin.

Rehab Work Group Staff, jt. auth. see Enterprise Foundation Staff.

Rehacek, Z. & Sajdl, P. Ergot Alkaloids: Chemistry, Biological Effects, Biotechnology, Bioactive Molecules, No. 12. (Illus.). 370p. 1990. 159.00 (*0-444-98767-3*) Elsevier.

Rehahn, J. P. English-French-German Dictionary of Telecommunication Technology. 420p. 1992. 135.00 (*2-85608-048-0*, Pub. by La Maison Du Dict FR) IBD Ltd.

Rehahn, J. P. & Schafer, N. Dictionary of Optical Communications Technology (Optische Kommunikationstechnik) 155p. 1988. lib. bdg. 65.00 (*3-341-00330-4*, Pub. by Verlag Technik VEB) VCH Pubs.

***Rehahn, Jens P.** Optical Communication Engineering Dictionary in Four Languages: English-German-French-Russian. (ENG, FRE, GER & RUS.). 1992. 49.00 (*0-7859-8912-9*) Fr & Eur.

Rehahn, Jens P. & Schafer, N. Optical Communication Engineering Dictionary in Four Languages: English-German-French-Russian. 156p. (ENG, FRE, GER & RUS.). 1992. text ed. 50.00x (*3-86117-041-8*, Pub. by A Hatier GW) IBD Ltd.

Rehahn, Jens Peter. Technological Dictionary of Telecommunications: English - French - German. 480p. (ENG, FRE & GER.). 1992. lib. bdg. 275.00 (*0-7859-3657-2*, 3761170426) Fr & Eur.

Rehahn, Peter & Schafer, Natalja. Optical Communication Technology: Optische Kommunikationstechnik. 176p. (ENG, FRE, GER & RUS.). 1988. 95.00 (*0-8288-0874-0*, F18820) Fr & Eur.

Rehak, Theo. Practical Typecasting. (Illus.). 128p. 1993. 64.95 (*0-938768-33-6*) Oak Knoll.

***Rehart, Matthew J.** Writing Business Research Reports: A Guide to Scientific Writing. 201p. (C). 1993. pap. text ed. 18.95 (*0-9623744-6-6*) Pyrczak Pub.

Rehbein, Ed. Remembering God's Word. (Orig.). 1991. pap. 5.99 (*0-89900-359-1*) College Pr Pub.

Rehbein, Edna A., jt. auth. see Rojas, Sonia R.

Rehbein, Jochen, jt. auth. see Ehlich, Konrad.

Rehberg, Linda & Conway, Lois. Bread Machine Magic. 160p. (Orig.). 1992. pap. 10.95 (*0-312-06914-6*) St Martin.

— The Bread Machine Magic Book of Helpful Hints: Dozens of Problem-Solving Hints & Troubleshooting Techniques for Getting the Most Out of Your Bread Machine. (Illus.). 224p. (Orig.). 1993. pap. 10.95 (*0-312-09759-X*) St Martin.

***Rehbinder, Eckard.** Integration Through Law: Environmental Protection Policy. Stewart, Richard, ed. (European University Institute, Series A (Law): No. 2). xxiv, 351p. 1985. 119.25 (*3-11-010200-5*) De Gruyter.

Rehbinder, Eckard & Stewart, Richard. Environmental Protection Policy. 351p. (C). 1988. pap. text ed. 27.95 (*0-89925-396-2*) De Gruyter.

— Environmental Protection Policy. 351p. (C). 1988. pap. text ed. 27.95 (*3-11-011490-9*) De Gruyter.

— Integration Through Law: Environmental Protection Policy. (European University Institute, Series A (Law): No. 2). xxiv, 351p. 1985. 119.25 (*0-89925-112-9*) De Gruyter.

Rehbinder, Manfred. Einfuerung in die Rechtswissenschaft: Grundfragen, Grundlagen und Grundgedanken des Rechts. 254p. 1983. 24.60 (*3-11-009723-0*) De Gruyter.

Rehbinder, Manfred & Sonn, Ju-Chan, eds. Zur Rezeption des Deutschen Rechts in Korea. 111p. 1990. pap. 23.00 (*3-7890-1968-2*, Pub. by Nomos Verlags GW) Intl Bk Import.

Rehbinder, Manfred, jt. ed. see Becker, Jurgen.

Rehbock, Helmut, jt. auth. see Henne, Helmut.

Rehbock, Philip F. The Philosophical Naturalists: Themes in Early Nineteenth-Century British Biology. LC 83-47767. (Wisconsin Publications in the History of Science & Medicine: No. 3). (Illus.). 288p. 1983. text ed. 30.00 (*0-299-09430-8*) U of Wis Pr.

Rehbock, Philip F., ed. At Sea with the Scientifics: The Challenger Letters of Joseph Matkin. (Illus.). 424p. (C). 1993. text ed. 38.00 (*0-8248-1424-X*) UH Pr.

Rehbock, Philip F., jt. ed. see MacLeod, Roy M.

Rehbock, Philip F., jt. ed. see MacLeod, Roy.

Rehder, Alfred, jt. auth. see Wilson, Ernest.

Rehder, Denny & Fitch, Lucius W. The Shampoo King: F. W. Fitch & His Company. (Illus.). 160p. 1982. pap. 12.95 (*0-942240-05-7*) D Rehder.

Rehder, Harold A., contrib. Familiar Seashells of North America. (Illus.). 192p. 1988. pap. 8.00 (*0-394-75795-5*) Knopf.

Rehder, Harold A., jt. auth. see Audubon Society Staff.

Rehder, Robert. The Poetry of Wallace Stevens. 272p. 1988. text ed. 19.95 (*0-312-00860-0*) St Martin.

— Wordsworth & the Beginnings of Modern Poetry. 246p. 1981. 42.00 (*0-389-20209-6*, N6991) B&N Imports.

Reher, David S. Town & Country in Pre-Industrial Spain: Cuenca, 1540-1870. (Cambridge Studies in Population, Economy & Society in Past Time: No. 12). (Illus.). 345p. (C). 1990. 64.95 (*0-521-35292-4*) Cambridge U Pr.

Reher, David S. & Schofield, Roger S., eds. Old & New Methods in Historical Demography. LC 93-6635. (C). 1994. 59.00 (*0-19-828793-3*, Clarendon Pr) OUP.

Rehfeld, John E. The Leader's Alchemy: Blending the World's Best Management Skills to Outperform Your Competitors. LC 93-34342. 1994. text ed. 22.95 (*0-471-00836-2*) Wiley.

Rehfeldt, Phillip. Etudes for the Twenty-First-Century Clarinetist Anthology. (Editions for Clarinet Ser.). 1992. audio 50.00 (*0-933251-12-2*) Mill Creek Pubns.

— Getting the Most out of Clarinets. 1985. 11.00 (*0-933251-06-8*) Mill Creek Pubns.

— Guide to Playing Woodwind Instruments. 1988. 29.00 (*0-933251-09-2*) Mill Creek Pubns.

— Making & Adjusting Single Reeds. 1991. 11.00 (*0-933251-02-5*) Mill Creek Pubns.

— New Directions for Clarinet. rev. ed. (New Instrumentation Ser.: Vol. 4). 1993. pap. 35.00 (*0-520-03379-5*) U CA Pr.

— Research Materials in Music. (Music History Ser.). 98p. (C). 1990. pap. text ed. 20.00 (*0-933251-11-4*) Mill Creek Pubns.

— Study Materials for Clarinet, 3 vols., 1. (Clarinet Ser.). 1985. 11.00 (*0-933251-05-X*) Mill Creek Pubns.

— Study Materials for Clarinet, 3 vols., 2. (Clarinet Ser.). 1985. 14.00 (*0-933251-18-1*) Mill Creek Pubns.

— Study Materials for Clarinet, 3 vols., 3. (Clarinet Ser.). 1985. 17.50 (*0-933251-19-X*) Mill Creek Pubns.

Rehfeldt, Phillip, ed. Handbook for Flute Doubling. 1985. 11.50 (*0-933251-04-1*) Mill Creek Pubns.

— White's Edition for Clarinet & Piano, 1027. (Editions for Clarinet Ser.). 1983. 16.50 (*0-933251-03-3*) Mill Creek Pubns.

Rehfuss, John. The Job of the Public Manager. 305p. 1989. pap. 28.95 (*0-534-10921-7*) Intl Thomson.

Rehfuss, John A. Contracting out in Government: A Guide to Working with Outside Contractors to Supply Public Services. LC 88-30702. (Public Administration Ser.). 304p. 1989. 36.95 (*1-55542-137-7*) Jossey-Bass.

Rehg, James. Introduction to Robotics: A Systems Approach. (Illus.). 224p. (C). 1984. text ed. 68.00 (*0-13-495581-1*) P-H.

Rehg, James A. Computer Integrated Manufacturing. 460p. 1994. text ed. 52.00 (*0-13-463886-7*) P-H.

Rehg, Kenneth L. & Sohl, Damian G. Ponapean-English Dictionary. LC 79-19451. (PALI Language Texts, Micronesia Ser.). 278p. 1979. pap. text ed. 14.00 (*0-8248-0562-3*) UH Pr.

Rehg, Virgil R., jt. auth. see Lloyd, Russell F.

Rehg, William. Insight & Solidarity: The Discourse Ethics of Jurgen Habermas. LC 93-23800. (Philosophy, Social Theory, & the Rule of Law Ser.: No. 1). 1994. 35.00 (*0-520-08195-0*) U CA Pr.

Actually the ISBN reads (0-685-71902-2) U CA Pr.

***Rehkopf, Friedrich.** Griechisch-Deutsches Woerterbuch Zum Neuen Testament. 140p. (GER & GRE.). 1992. 75.00 (*0-7859-8412-7*, 3525501188) Fr & Eur.

Rehl, Beatrice, ed. see Picasso, Pablo, et al.

***Rehm.** To Give It Up. LC 95-15850. (New American Poetry Ser.). 80p. 1995. pap. text ed. 9.95 (*1-55713-212-7*) Sun & Moon CA.

Rehm, Donald S. The Myopia Myth: The Truth About Nearsightedness & How to Prevent It. LC 83-80453. (Illus.). 165p. 1983. reprint ed. pap. 12.50 (*0-9608476-0-X*) Intl Myopia.

Rehm, Ellen. Untersuchungen Zum Schmuck der Achameniden. (Altertumskunde des Vorderen Orients Ser.: Vol. 2). xii, 468p. (GER.). 1992. 81.00 (*3-927120-11-1*, Pub. by UGARIT GW) Eisenbrauns.

***Rehm, H. J. & Reed, G.** Biotechnology: A Multi-Volume Comprehensive Treatise, Bioprocessing, Vol. 3. 816p. 1994. 320.00 (*1-56081-153-6*) VCH Pubs.

— Biotechnology, a Comprehensive Treatise in Eight Volumes Vol. 2: Fundamentals of Biochemical Engineering. Brauer, H., ed. & intro. by. 819p. 1985. lib. bdg. 365.00 (*0-89573-042-1*); 260.00 (*0-685-10754-X*) VCH Pubs.

Rehm, H. J. & Reed, G., eds. Biotechnology, a Comprehensive Treatise in Eight Volumes: Biotransformations, Vol. 6a. 473p. 1984. lib. bdg. 365.00 (*0-89573-046-4*); 260.00 (*0-685-09700-5*) VCH Pubs.

— Biotechnology, a Comprehensive Treatise in Eight Volumes Vol. 3: Biomass, Microorganisms for Special Applications, Microbial Products I, Energy from Renewable Resources. (Illus.). 642p. 1982. lib. bdg. 365.00 (*0-89573-043-X*); 260.00 (*0-685-05699-6*) VCH Pubs.

— Biotechnology, a Comprehensive Treatise in Eight Volumes Vol. 4: Microbial Products II. 673p. 1986. lib. bdg. 365.00 (*0-89573-044-8*); 260.00 (*0-685-13857-7*) VCH Pubs.

— Biotechnology, a Comprehensive Treatise in Eight Volumes Vol. 5: Food & Feed Production with Microorganisms. 631p. 1983. lib. bdg. 365.00 (*0-89573-045-6*); 260.00 (*0-685-08185-0*) VCH Pubs.

— Biotechnology, a Comprehensive Treatise in Eight Volumes Vol. 7a: Enzyme Technology. 761p. 1987. lib. bdg. 365.00 (*0-89573-047-2*); 260.00 (*0-685-19526-0*) VCH Pubs.

— Biotechnology, a Comprehensive Treatise in Eight Volumes Vol. 8: Microbial Degradations. 744p. 1986. lib. bdg. 365.00 (*0-89573-048-0*); 260.00 (*0-685-11867-3*) VCH Pubs.

— Biotechnology, Vol. 4: Measuring, Modeling & Control. 2nd ed. 658p. 1991. lib. bdg. 365.00 (*1-56081-154-4*) VCH Pubs.

— Gene Technology, Vol. 7B. (Biotechnology: A Comprehensive Treatise in Eight Volumes). 587p. 1989. lib. bdg. 365.00 (*0-89573-561-X*); 260.00 (*0-685-55978-5*) VCH Pubs.

— Special Microbial Processes. (Biotechnology: A Comprehensive Treatise in Eight Volumes: Vol. 6B). 810p. 1989. lib. bdg. 365.00 (*0-89573-413-3*); 295.00 (*0-685-55979-3*) VCH Pubs.

Rehm, H. J., et al, eds. Biotechnology: A Multi-Volume Comprehensive Treatise, Vol. 1. 2nd ed. 641p. 1994. 320.00 (*1-56081-151-X*) VCH Pubs.

Rehm, J., jt. auth. see Winold, Allen.

***Rehm, Karl.** Left or Right? (J). (ps-2). 1994. pap. 4.95 (*0-395-69943-6*, Clarion Bks) HM.

Rehm, Lynn P., ed. Behavior Therapy for Depression: Present Status & Future Directions. 1980. text ed. 90.00 (*0-12-585880-9*) Acad Pr.

***Rehm, Margarete.** Lexikon Buch, Bibliothek, Neue Medien. 294p. (GER.). 1991. 195.00 (*0-7859-8447-X*, 3598108893) Fr & Eur.

— Lexikon Buch, Bibliothek, Neue Medien. 294p. (GER.). 1991. pap. text ed. 30.00 (*3-598-10851-6*) K G Saur.

Rehm, Mary T., jt. auth. see DePietro, Anne C.

Rehm, Pam. The Garment in Which No One Had Slept. (Poetry Ser.). 64p. (Orig.). 1993. pap. 8.00 (*0-930901-87-8*) Burning Deck.

— The Garment in Which No One Had Slept. deluxe ed. (Poetry Ser.). 64p. (Orig.). 1993. pap. 15.00 (*0-930901-88-6*) Burning Deck.

Rehm, Rush. Greek Tragic Theatre. 168p. (Orig.). 1992. 55.00 (*0-415-04831-1*) Routledge.

— Greek Tragic Theatre. (Theatre Production Studies). 184p. (Orig.). 1994. pap. 14.95 (*0-415-11894-8*, B4729) Routledge.

— Marriage to Death: The Conflation of Wedding & Funeral Rituals in Greek Tragedy. LC 93-39939. 1994. 29.95 (*0-691-03369-2*, Princeton U Pr) Princeton U Pr.

Rehm, S., ed. Multilingual Dictionary of Agronomic Plants. LC 94-19353. 1994. lib. bdg. 120.00 (*0-7923-2970-8*) Kluwer Ac.

Rehman, A. A., ed. see Taylor, Jeremy.

Rehman, Afzalur. Muhammad, the Blessings. 1991. pap. 16.95 (*1-56744-149-1*) Kazi Pubns.

Rehman, Fazlur. Islamic Methodology in History. 15.95 (*1-56744-102-5*) Kazi Pubns.

Rehman, M. M. Education, Work & Women: An Inquiry into Gender Bias. (C). 1993. 24.00 (*81-7169-251-6*, Commonwealth) S Asia.

Rehman, Sajjad ur. Management Theory & Library Education. LC 86-22736. (New Directions in Information Management Ser.: No. 14). 160p. 1987. text ed. 45.00 (*0-313-25288-2*, RMN/, Greenwood Pr) Greenwood.

***Rehman, Sharaf N.** You're Not Listening. 80p. (Orig.). (YA). Date not set. pap. 7.95 (*1-883120-06-3*) Northern St U.

Rehman, T., jt. auth. see Romero, C.

Rehman, Z. Payamber: The Messenger, Vol. I, II, III. 12.50 (*0-933511-96-5*) Kazi Pubns.

Rehmann, R. M., jt. ed. see Decker, K. M.

Rehmel, Judy. Complete Index to the Quilt Keys. LC 84-90562. 60p. (Orig.). 1984. pap. 2.00 (*0-913731-06-4*) J Rehmel.

— Key to One Thousand Applique Quilt Patterns. LC 84-90635. (Illus.). 240p. 1984. ring bd. 12.00 (*0-913731-07-2*) J Rehmel.

— So You Want to Write a Cookbook. LC 83-61899. (Illus.). 100p. 1983. pap. 6.95 (*0-915216-88-4*) Marathon Intl Bk.

— So, You Want to Write a Cookbook! (Illus.). 52p. 1982. pap. 5.00 (*0-913731-04-8*) J Rehmel.

Rehmel, Judy, jt. auth. see Schaffhausen, Suzanne.

Rehmus, Charles M. Professional Updating of Personnel-Industrial Relations Training. (Occasional Publication: No. 146). 11p. 1983. 1.00 (*0-318-04753-5*) U Hawaii.

Rehmus, Charles M., ed. Public Employment Labor Relations: An Overview of Eleven Nations. LC 74-22858. (Comparative Studies in Public Employment Labor Relations Ser.). 1974. 10.00 (*0-87736-025-1*); pap. 5.00 (*0-87736-026-X*) U of Mich Inst Labor.

Rehn, L. E., et al, eds. Processing & Characterization of Materials Using Ion Beams, Vol. 128. (Materials Research Society Symposium Proceedings Ser.). 1989. text ed. 52.00 (*1-55899-001-1*) Materials Res.

Rehn, Victor. ERATO & Japan's Dreams of Future Technology. 31p. (Orig.). (C). 1992. pap. text ed. 29.95 (*1-56806-019-X*) Diane Pub.

Rehnberg, Clas. The Organization of Public Health Care: An Economic Analysis of the Swedish Health Care System. (Linkoping Studies in Arts & Sciences: No. 58). 172p. (Orig.). 1991. pap. 55.00x (*91-7870-728-5*, Pub. by Almqv & Wiksell SW) Coronet Bks.

Rehnberg, Pete. Coast Adventures. (Illus.). 40p. 1992. pap. 6.95 (*1-878175-17-3*) F Amato Pubns.

Rehnborg, C. F. C. F. Rehnborg: A Collection of His Essays, Speeches, & Writings. Johnson, Lee, ed. (Illus.). 300p. (Orig.). 1985. pap. write for info. (*0-9606564-2-1*) C F Rehnborg.

Rehner. Infertility: Old Myths, New Meanings. (NFS Canada Ser.). Date not set. pap. 14.95 (*0-929005-06-6*, Pub. by Second Story Pr CN) InBook.

Rehnke, Mary A., ed. Creating Career Programs in a Liberal Arts Context. LC 85-644752. (New Directions for Higher Education Ser.: No. HE 57). 1987. 16.95 (*1-55542-962-9*) Jossey-Bass.

Rehnquist, William H. Grand Inquests: The Historic Impeachments of Justice Samuel Chase & President Andrew Johnson. 1992. 23.00 (*0-688-05142-1*) Morrow.

— Grand Inquests: The Historic Impeachments of Justice Samuel Chase & President Andrew Johnson. 1993. pap. 15.00 (*0-688-12839-4*, Quill) Morrow.

R

— The Supreme Court. LC 88-29737. 1989. 13.00 (0-688-08668-3, Quill) Morrow.

Rehof, Lars A. Guide to the Travaux Preparatories of the United Nations Convention on the Elimination of All Forms of Discrimination Against Women. LC 93-12629. (International Studies in Human Rights: Vol. 29). 408p. 1993. lib. bdg. 132.00 (0-7923-2222-3) Kluwer Ac.

Rehof, Lars A. & Gulmann, Claus, eds. Human Rights in Domestic Law & Development. (C). 1989. lib. bdg. 70.00 (90-247-3743-5) Kluwer Ac.

Rehon, Peter M. Obtaining a Writ of Attachment, Pts. 1 & 2: Summer 1992, Action Guide. Lester, Ellen C., ed. 98p. 1992. pap. text ed. 52.00 (0-88124-547-X, CP-11122) Cont Ed Bar-CA.

— Obtaining a Writ of Possession, Pts. 1 & 2: Summer 1992, Action Guide. Lester, Ellen & Graber, Suzanne E., eds. 70p. 1992. pap. text ed. 52.00 (0-88124-554-2, CP-11352) Cont Ed Bar-CA.

— Obtaining an Injunction, Pts. 1 & 2: Fall 1992, Action Guide. Tindel, Kay E., ed. 142p. 1992. pap. text ed. 52.00 (0-88124-566-6, CP-11571) Cont Ed Bar-CA.

Rehr, et al, eds. Professional Accountability for Social Work Practice. 1979. lib. bdg. 16.95 (0-88202-127-3) Watson Pub Intl.

Rehr, Helen, ed. Ethical Dilemmas in Health Care: A Professional Search for Solutions. 1978. pap. text ed. 7.95 (0-88202-124-9) Watson Pub Intl.

— Milestones in Social Work & Medicine. LC 82-18542. 1982. pap. 8.95 (0-317-04157-6, Prodist) Watson Pub Intl.

Rehr, Helen, jt. ed. see Mailick, Mildred.

Rehr, Helen, jt. ed. see Rosenberg, Gary.

Rehr, Paula B. Why Is Everyone Growing Up & I'm Still in the 8th Grade? Poems about School Life Today. (Illus.). 48p. 1980. pap. 3.50 (0-912048-10-7) Garrett Pk.

Rehr, Stuart, jt. auth. see Lee, Kaiman.

Rehrig, William H. The Heritage Encyclopedia of Band Music: Composers & Their Music, 2 vols., Set. Bierley, Paul E., ed. LC 91-73637. 1065p. 1991. 110.00 (0-918048-08-7) Integrity.

Rehva. International Dictionary of Heating, Ventilating & Air Conditioning. 482p. (DUT, ENG, FRE, GER, HUN, ITA, POL, RUS, SPA & SWE.). 1982. 295.00 (0-8288-0966-6, M15644) Fr & Eur.

Rehwaldt, Susan S., jt. auth. see Higgerson, Mary L.

Rehwinkel, Alfred M. Flood. 2nd ed. (Orig.). (YA). (gr. 10-12). 1957. pap. 11.99 (0-570-03183-4, 12-2103) Concordia.

Rei Shiratori, jt. ed. see Alexander, Herbert E.

Reia, Flora. Business Communications: Speaking & Writing Effectively. (Illus.). 250p. (C). 1987. pap. text ed. 13.95 (0-935920-47-1, Ntl Pubs Blck) P-H.

Reibel, Paula. A Morning Moon. large type ed. 608p. 1987. 23.95 (0-7089-8399-5, Charnwood) Ulverscroft.

Reiber. Frommer's Japan, 94-95. (Illus.). 1994. pap. 19.00 (0-671-86796-2, P-H Travel) P-H Gen Ref & Trav.

Reiber, Beth. Berlin. (Frommer's Walking Tours Ser.). (Illus.). 176p. 1993. pap. 12.00 (0-671-79837-5, P-H Travel) P-H Gen Ref & Trav.

— Tokyo, 1992-1993. (Frommer's Comprehensive Travel Guide Ser.). (Illus.). 288p. 1992. pap. 13.00 (0-13-333477-5, P-H Travel) P-H Gen Ref & Trav.

Reiber, Duke B., ed. The NASA Mars Conference, July Twenty-First to Twenty-Third, 1986. (Science & Technology Ser.: Vol. 71). (Illus.). 570p. 1988. lib. bdg. 50.00 (0-87703-293-9); pap. text ed. 30.00 (0-87703-294-7) Am Astronaut.

Reiber, Johan H. & Serruys, Patrick W., eds. Advances in Quantitative Coronary Arteriography. LC 92-20819. (Developments in Cardiovascular Medicine Ser.: Vol. 137). 1993. lib. bdg. 299.00 (0-7923-1863-3) Kluwer Ac.

— New Developments in Quantitative Coronary Arteriography. (Developments in Cardiovascular Medicine Ser.). (C). 1988. lib. bdg. 150.00 (0-89838-377-3) Kluwer Ac.

— Progress in Quantitative Coronary Arteriography. LC 94-13374. (Developments in Cardiovascular Medicine Ser.: Vol. 155). 432p. (C). 1994. lib. bdg. 177.00 (0-7923-2814-0) Kluwer Ac.

— Quantitative Coronary Arteriography. (Developments in Cardiovascular Medicine Ser.). (C). 1991. lib. bdg. 180.00 (0-7923-0913-8) Kluwer Ac.

— State of the Art in Quantitative Coronary Arteriography. (Developments in Cardiovascular Medicine Ser.). 1986. lib. bdg. 166.50 (0-89838-804-X) Kluwer Ac.

Reiber, Johan H. & Van Der Wall, Ernst E., eds. Cardiovascular Nuclear Medicine & MRI. (Developments in Cardiovascular Medicine Ser.). 384p. (C). 1992. lib. bdg. 162.50 (0-7923-1467-0) Kluwer Ac.

Reiber, R. W., ed. The Psychology of War & Peace: The Image of the Enemy. (Illus.). 275p. 1990. 42.50 (0-306-43543-8, Plenum Pr) Plenum.

Reiber, R. W., ed. see Vygotsky, L. S.

Reibetanz, John. The Lear World: A Study of King Lear in Its Dramatic Context. LC 76-54829. 154p. reprint ed. pap. 43.90 (0-8357-4028-5, 2036720) Bks Demand.

Reiblich, G. Kenneth. The Supreme Court of the United States, Summary of the October, 1980 Term. 1983. write for info. (0-318-58311-9) West Pub.

***Reibman, James, et al.** The Frederic Wertheim Collection. (Illus.). 101p. 1995. pap. 14.95 (0-916724-75-1, 475-1) Harvard Art Mus.

Reibsamen, Gary G. S. T. A. R. A Novel of Future Reality (Non-Fiction) (Illus.). 244p. (Orig.). 1993. pap. 27.77 (0-9638374-0-0) STAR NJ.

Reibstein, David J. Marketing Concepts, Strategies & Decisions. (Illus.). 704p. (C). 1985. student ed write for info. (0-13-487249-5) P-H.

Reibstein, Janet & Richards, Martin. Sexual Arrangements: Marriage & the Inevitability of Infidelity. LC 93-12151. 256p. 1993. text ed. 20.00 (0-684-19540-2, Scribners) S&S Trade.

Reibstein, Richard J., jt. auth. see Green, Ronald M.

***Reich.** The Government & Politics of the Middle East & North Africa. 3rd ed. Long, ed. (C). 1995. pap. text ed. 26.95 (0-8133-2126-3) Westview.

— Passion of Youth. 1994. pap. 10.95 (1-56924-929-6) Marlowe & Co.

Reich, A. R., et al, eds. Progress in HPLC, Vol. 3: Flow Through Radioactivity Detection in HPLC. 214p. 1988. 115.00 (90-6764-114-6, Pub. by VSP NE) Coronet Bks.

Reich, Adam, jt. photos see Galatis, Michael.

Reich, Alice & Steele, Thomas J., eds. Fraser Haps & Mishaps: The Diary of Mary E. Cozens. LC 90-62379. (Illus.). 101p. (Orig.). 1990. pap. 5.95 (0-944340-03-2) Regis Coll.

***Reich, Allen Z.** Marketing Management for the Hospitality Industry: A Strategic Approach. LC 94-47535. 1995. text ed. write for info. (0-471-31012-3) Wiley.

Reich, Andreas. Friedrich Schleiermacher Als Pfarrer an der Berliner Dreifaltigkeitskirche 1809-1834. (Schleiermacher-Archiv Ser.: Bd. 12). xiv, 568p. (GER.). (C). 1992. lib. bdg. 190.80 (3-11-013636-8) De Gruyter.

Reich, Asher. Long Distance. Barkan, Stanley H. & Alkaley-Gut, Karen, eds. (Review Israeli Writers Chapbook Ser.: No. 2). 48p. (ENG & HEB.). 1991. 15.00 (0-89304-381-8); 15.00 (0-89304-383-4); pap. 5.00 (0-89304-382-6); pap. 5.00 (0-89304-384-2) Cross-Cultrl NY.

Reich, Astrid, jt. ed. see Dittmar, Norbert.

***Reich, Bernard.** The Government & Politics of the Middle East & North Africa. 3rd ed. Long, David E., ed. LC 95-5652. (C). 1995. text ed. 67.50 (0-8133-2125-5) Westview.

— Historical Dictionary of Israel. LC 92-5324. (Asian Historical Dictionaries Ser.: No. 8). (Illus.). 421p. 1992. 47.50 (0-8108-2535-X) Scarecrow.

— Quest for Peace: United States-Israel Relations & the Arab-Israeli Conflict. LC 76-45940. 495p. reprint ed. pap. 141.10 (0-317-27280-2, 2024160) Bks Demand.

— Securing the Covenant: The United States - Israeli Relations after the Cold War. LC 94-37881. (Contibutions in Political Science Ser.: No. 351). 184p. 1995. pap. text ed. 15.95 (0-275-95121-9, Praeger Pubs) Greenwood.

— Securing the Covenant: United States - Israeli Relations after the Cold War. LC 94-37881. (Contributions in Political Science Ser.: Vol. 351). 192p. 1995. text ed. 55.00 (0-313-29540-9, Greenwood Pr) Greenwood.

— The United States & Israel: Influence in the Special Relationship. LC 83-24795. (Studies of Influence in International Relations). 254p. 1984. text ed. 31.95 (0-275-91247-7, C1247, Praeger Pubs) Greenwood.

***Reich, Bernard, ed.** The Arab-Israeli Conflict: An Historical Encyclopedia. LC 95-6684. 1996. text ed. write for info. (0-313-27374-X, Greenwood Pr) Greenwood.

— Political Leaders of the Contemporary Middle East & North Africa: A Biographical Dictionary. LC 89-7498. 592p. 1990. text ed. 89.50 (0-313-26213-6, RPC/, Greenwood Pr) Greenwood.

— The Powers & the Middle East: The Ultimate Strategic Arena. LC 86-21266. 361p. 1986. text ed. 49.95 (0-275-92304-5, C2304, Praeger Pubs) Greenwood.

Reich, Bernard & Kieval, Gershon R. Israel: Land of Tradition & Conflict. 2nd ed. LC 93-16314. (Profiles - Nations of Contemporary Middle East Ser.). 236p. (C). 1993. pap. text ed. 19.95 (0-8133-8223-8) Westview.

— Israel: Land of Tradition & Conflict. 2nd ed. LC 93-16314. (Profiles - Nations of Contemporary Middle East Ser.). 236p. 1993. text ed. 58.00 (0-8133-8222-X) Westview.

Reich, Bernard & Kieval, Gershon R., eds. Israel Faces the Future. LC 86-21278. (Illus.). 240p. 1986. text ed. 59.95 (0-275-92190-5, C2190, Praeger Pubs) Greenwood.

— Israeli National Security Policy: Political Actors & Perspectives. LC 87-36099. (Contributions in Political Science Ser.: No. 210). 251p. 1988. text ed. 55.00 (0-313-26196-2, RHS/, Greenwood Pr) Greenwood.

— Israeli Politics in the Nineteen Nineties: Key Domestic & Foreign Policy Factors. LC 91-3956. (Contributions in Political Science Ser.: No. 285). 208p. 1991. text ed. 49.95 (0-313-27349-9, RIA, Greenwood Pr) Greenwood.

Reich, Bernard, jt. auth. see Silverburg, Sanford R.

Reich, Bernard, ed. see Silverburg, Sanford R.

Reich, Carl M., jt. auth. see Barefoot, Robert R.

***Reich, Charles.** Opposing the System. 1995. 23.00 (0-517-59777-2) Random.

***Reich, David.** Designing & Building Applications for OS-2 Version 3. 1995. pap. text ed. 34.95 (0-471-11586-X) Wiley.

Reich, David E. Designing OS-2 Applications. 336p. 1993. pap. text ed. 34.95 (0-471-58889-X) Wiley.

Reich, David G. The Big Red Book of Fantasy Football, 1994. 225p. (Orig.). 1994. pap. text ed. 11.95 (0-9636703-2-8) RCR Ent.

Reich, David L., jt. auth. see Brooks, Jean S.

Reich, Deborah, jt. auth. see Gallup, Barbara.

Reich, Doris, ed. see Geier, Joan A.

Reich, Ellen J. Waiting: A Diary of Loss & Hope in Pregnancy. LC 91-8720. 132p. 1991. lib. bdg. 32.95 (1-56024-087-3); pap. 11.95 (0-918393-88-4) Haworth Pr.

Reich, Emil. Hungarian Literature: Historical & Critical Survey. LC 72-80503. 1972. reprint ed. 20.95 (0-405-08876-0) Ayer.

Reich, H., jt. auth. see Garry, R.

Reich, H. J., jt. auth. see Uexkull, J. R.

Reich, Hans H., jt. ed. see Reid, Euan.

Reich, Harry, jt. auth. see Hulka, Jaroslav F.

Reich, Hermann. Der Mimus. xii, 900p. 1974. reprint ed. write for info. (3-487-05109-5, Pub. by Georg Olms GW) Lubrecht & Cramer.

Reich, J. H., jt. auth. see de Girolamo, G.

***Reich, Jane C.** Adventures of Jocko & Gip. (We're Heroes Too! Ser.). (Illus.). 50p. (J). 1995. 9.95 (0-9636703-6-0) RCR Ent.

— The Gentle Way. Wilkeson, Ann, ed. (We're Heroes Too! Ser.). 250p. (Orig.). 1995. pap. 9.95 (0-9636703-3-6) RCR Ent.

— Tarnished Silver. 270p. 1993. text ed. 19.95 (0-9636703-0-1) RCR Ent.

Reich, Janet. Gus & the Green Thing. LC 92-33845. (J). 1993. 8.95 (0-8027-8252-3); lib. bdg. 9.85 (0-8027-8253-1) Walker & Co.

Reich, Jerome R. Colonial America. 3rd ed. LC 92-46073. 1993. pap. text ed. write for info. (0-13-088808-7) P-H.

Reich, Jon. Reich: The Nudes of Jon Reich. LC 90-91911. (Illus.). 130p. 1991. 59.95 (0-9627203-0-5) Predictable Pr.

Reich, Klaus. The Completeness of Kant's Table of Judgments. Kneller, Jane & Losonsky, Michael, trs. LC 91-38006. (Series in Philosophy). 160p. (C). 1992. 25.00 (0-8047-1934-9) Stanford U Pr.

Reich, Laurence. New Jersey Corporation Law & Practice. (National Corporation Law Ser.). 1992. ring bd. 126.00 (0-13-109257-X) Aspen Law.

Reich, Lee. A Northeast Gardener's Year. 1992. 19.23 (0-201-55050-4) Addison-Wesley.

— Northeast Gardener's Year. 1993. pap. 11.54 (0-201-62233-5) Addison-Wesley.

— Uncommon Fruits Worthy of Attention: A Gardener's Guide. LC 90-45118. (Illus.). 1991. 18.22 (0-201-52381-7) Addison-Wesley.

— Uncommon Fruits Worthy of Attention: A Gardener's Guide. 1992. pap. 9.62 (0-201-60820-0) Addison-Wesley.

Reich, Leo & Schindler, A. Polymerization by Organometallic Compounds. LC 65-14732. (Polymer Rev. Ser.: Vol.12). 750p. reprint ed. pap. 180.00 (0-317-08659-6, 2011965) Bks Demand.

Reich, Leo & Stivala, Salvatore S. Autoxidation of Hydrocarbons & Polyolefins: Kinetics & Mechanisms. LC 68-17424. (Illus.). 541p. reprint ed. pap. 154.20 (0-7837-0775-4, 2041089) Bks Demand.

Reich, Leonard S. The Making of American Industrial Research: Science & Business at GE & Bell, 1876-1926. (Studies in Economic History & Policy: The United States in the Twentieth Century). (Illus.). 309p. 1985. 54.95 (0-521-30529-2) Cambridge U Pr.

Reich, Mark & Youell, Judd. Estimating with Timberline Precision Version 5.2. 762p. 1994. pap. text ed. 43.95 (0-8273-6002-9) Delmar.

Reich, Max I. Sweet Singer of Israel: Unfinished Poems & Devotional Thoughts. LC 70-38312. (Biography Index Reprint Ser.). 1977. reprint ed. 17.95 (0-8369-8127-8) Ayer.

Reich, Menachem M. Amukah - The Hidden Valley. 150p. 1992. write for info. (1-56062-129-X) CIS Comm.

***Reich, Michael.** Racial Inequality: A Political-Economic Analysis. LC 80-8573. (Illus.). 358p. 1981. reprint ed. pap. 102.10 (0-7837-8181-4, 2047886) Bks Demand.

Reich, Michael R. Toxic Politics: Responsing to Chemical Disasters. LC 91-55054. 392p. 1991. 46.00 (0-8014-2434-8); pap. 16.95 (0-8014-9986-0) Cornell U Pr.

Reich, Michael R. & Marui, Eiji, eds. International Cooperation for Health: Problems, Prospects & Priorities. LC 88-35321. 425p. 1989. text ed. 59.95 (0-86569-189-4, Auburn Hse) Greenwood.

Reich, Michael R. & Okubo, Toshiteru, eds. Protecting Workers' Health in the Third World: National & International Strategies. LC 92-6991. 328p. 1992. text ed. 55.00 (0-86569-026-X, T026, Auburn Hse) Greenwood.

Reich, Michael R., jt. auth. see Bell, David E.

Reich, Nancy B. Clara Schumann: The Artist & the Woman. LC 84-45798. (Illus.). 352p. 1987. pap. 15.95 (0-8014-9388-9) Cornell U Pr.

Reich, Norbert, jt. auth. see Micklitz, Hans W.

Reich, Paul R. Hematology: Physiopathologic Basis for Clinical Practice. 2nd ed. (Physiopathology Ser.). 528p. 1984. 31.00 (0-316-73863-8) Little.

Reich, Paul R., jt. ed. see Robinson, Stephen H.

***Reich, Peter L.** Mexico's Hidden Revolution: The Catholic Church in Law & Politics since 1929. LC 95-16516. (Helen Kellogg Institute for International Studies). (C). 1996. text ed. 28.95 (0-268-01418-3) U of Notre Dame Pr.

— Statistical Abstract of the United States-Mexico Borderlands. (Statistical Abstract of Latin America Supplement Ser.: Vol. 9). 204p. 1984. lib. bdg. 45.00 (0-87903-243-X) UCLA Lat Am Ctr.

Reich, Philipp E. Aus Dem Leben des Buchhandlers. reprint ed. write for info. (0-318-71732-8, Pub. by Georg Olms GW) Lubrecht & Cramer.

Reich, Richard. House Without Windows. 1952. pap. 13.00 (0-8222-0538-6) Dramatists Play.

Reich, Robert. Public Management in a Democratic Society. 240p. 1989. pap. text ed. 32.00 (0-13-738881-0) P-H.

— The Resurgent Liberal & Other Unfashionable Prophecies. 1989. 19.95 (0-8129-1833-9, Times Bks) Random.

— Resurgent Liberal & Other Unfashionable Prophecies. LC 90-50146. 320p. 1991. pap. 12.95 (0-679-73152-0, Vin) Random.

Reich, Robert B. American Competitiveness & American Brains. (Philip Morris Lectures on Business & Society Ser.). 20p. 1993. pap. write for info. (1-884663-03-6) Baruch Coll Cty U.

— Tales of a New America: The Anxious Liberal's Guide to the Future. LC 87-45915. 304p. 1988. reprint ed. pap. 11.00 (0-394-75706-8, Vin) Random.

— The Work of Nations: Preparing Ourselves for 21st-Century Capitalism. 1991. 27.50 (0-394-58352-3) Knopf.

— The Work of Nations: Preparing Ourselves for 21st Century Capitalism. 1992. 12.00 (0-679-73615-8, Vin) Random.

Reich, Robert B., ed. The Power of Public Ideas. 265p. 1990. pap. 12.95 (0-674-69590-9) HUP.

***Reich, Ron.** Cerf-Volant Precision: Votre Guide Complet Pour le Pilotage de Cerfs-Volants Acrobatiques. Fosset, Raoul, tr. & intro. by. (Illus.). 184p. (Orig.). (FRE.). 1994. pap. 14.95 (0-9639010-3-6) Tutor Text.

— Kite Precision: Your Comprehensive Guide for Flying Controllable Kites. LC 93-61552. (Illus.). 180p. (Orig.). 1994. pap. 14.95 (0-9639010-2-8) Tutor Text.

Reich, Sheldon. Andrew Dasburg: His Life & Art. LC 85-48158. (Illus.). 144p. 1989. 45.00 (0-8387-5098-2) Bucknell U Pr.

— Francisco Zuniga: Sculptor. LC 80-18986. 153p. 1980. 35.00 (0-8165-0665-5) U of Ariz Pr.

— John Marin Drawings, Eighteen Eighty-Six to Nineteen Fifty-One: A Retrospective Exhibition Honoring John Marin's Centennial, Organized by the University of Utah Museum of Fine Arts. LC 79-83660. (Illus.). 120p. reprint ed. pap. 34.20 (0-8357-4381-0, 2037212) Bks Demand.

— Keith Crown Watercolors. LC 86-6955. (Illus.). 128p. 1986. text ed. 26.00 (0-8262-0606-9) U of Mo Pr.

Reich, Simon. The Fruits of Fascism: Postwar Prosperity in Historical Perspective. LC 90-55136. (Cornell Studies in Political Economy). 384p. 1990. 49.95 (0-8014-2440-2); pap. 16.95 (0-8014-9729-9) Cornell U Pr.

— The Reagan Administration, the Auto Producers, & the 1981 Agreement with Japan. (Pew Case Studies in International Affairs). 50p. (C). 1992. pap. text ed. 2.50 (1-56927-119-4) Geo U Inst Dplmcy.

— Restraining Trade to Invoke Investment: MITI & the Japanese Auto Producers. (Pew Case Studies in International Affairs). 50p. (C). 1992. pap. text ed. 2.50 (1-56927-150-X) Geo U Inst Dplmcy.

Reich, T. E., jt. auth. see Shoup, C. S.

***Reich, Tova.** The Jewish War: A Novel. 272p. 1995. 22.00 (0-679-43987-0) Pantheon.

— Master of the Return. 300p. 1988. 19.95 (0-15-157880-X) HarBrace.

Reich, Walter, ed. Origins of Terrorism: Psychologies, Ideologies, Theologies, States of Mind. (Woodrow Wilson Center Ser.). 304p. (C). 1990. pap. 17.95 (0-521-38589-X) Cambridge U Pr.

***Reich, Warren T., ed.** Encyclopedia of Bioethics. rev. ed. 1995. write for info. (0-02-897355-0) Macmillan.

— Encyclopedia of Bioethics, 4 vols., Set. LC 78-8821. 1978. 250.00 (0-02-926060-4) Free Pr.

— Encyclopedia of Bioethics, 2 vols., Set. LC 78-8821. 1982. text ed. 200.00 (0-02-925910-X) Macmillan.

***Reich, Wilhelm.** Beyond Psychology: Letters & Journals, 1934-1939. Higgins, Mary B., ed. & intro. by. LC 94-14721. 1994. 25.00 (0-374-11247-9) FS&G.

— Character Analysis. rev. ed. Carfagno, Vincent R., tr. 576p. 1980. pap. 18.00 (0-374-50980-8) FS&G.

— The Function of the Orgasm: Discovery of the Orgone, Vol. 1. rev. ed. 1986. pap. 18.00 (0-374-50204-8) FS&G.

— Funksiyon-e Orgazm: Kashf-e Energi-ye Orgon: The Function of the Orgasm: The Discovery of the Orgone. Simonian, Stephan, tr. & intro. by. LC 94-75384. (Illus.). 448p. (Orig.). (PER.). pap. 18.00 (0-936347-38-4) Iran Bks.

— Listen, Little Man! Manheim, Ralph, tr. (Illus.). 144p. 1974. pap. 11.00 (0-374-50401-6) FS&G.

— The Mass Psychology of Fascism. Carfagno, Vincent R., tr. 1980. pap. 18.00 (0-374-50884-4) FS&G.

— Passion of Youth: An Autobiography, 1897-1922. Higgins, Mary B. & Raphael, Chester M., eds. Schmitz, Philip & Tompkins, Jerri, trs. 240p. 1988. 17.95 (0-374-22995-3) FS&G.

Reich, Wilhelm, et al. On Wilhelm Reich & Orgonomy. DeMeo, James, ed. (Illus.). 176p. (Orig.). (C). 1994. pap. text ed. 20.00 (0-9621855-3-1) Natural Energy.

Reich, Willi. Alban Berg. Cardew, Cornelius, tr. (Music Ser.). (Illus.). 239p. 1982. reprint ed. lib. bdg. 32.50 (0-306-76136-X) Da Capo.

— Schoenberg: A Critical Biography. Black, Leo, tr. LC 81-1163. (Music Ser.). (Illus.). xi, 268p. 1981. reprint ed. lib. bdg. 35.00 (0-306-76104-1) Da Capo.

Reich, Willi, ed. see Webern, Anton.

Reich, William. Studies in Psychology. 2nd ed. 1991. pap. 14.00 (0-536-58075-8) Ginn Pr.

***Reichard.** Hubert Humphrey. 1995. 26.95 (0-8057-7777-6, Twayne) Macmillan.

— Professional Graphics Programming in X Windows. 1993. pap. 29.95 (1-55828-256-4) MIS Press.

Reichard & Johnson. X Windows. 1989. 24.95 (1-55828-016-2); 59.95 (1-55828-035-9) MIS Press.

Reichard, Birge D. & Siewers, Christiane M. The Small Group Trainer's Survival Guide. Rodenhauser, Paul, ed. 168p. (C). 1992. text ed. 42.00 (0-8039-4740-2); pap. text ed. 18.95 (0-8039-4757-7) Sage.

Reichard, Cary & Blackburn, Dennis. Music-Based Instruction for the Exceptional Child: Grades K-6. 1973. pap. 7.95 (0-89108-025-2, 7308) Love Pub Co.

Reichard, David C. Exploring CADKEY Three. 352p. 1989. boxed, pap. text ed. 62.00 (0-13-296112-1) P-H.

— Exploring CADKEY 1: Book-Disk Package. 384p. 1990. 115.00 (0-13-297235-2) P-H.

— Version Three Supplement to Exploring CADKEY. 176p. 1988. pap. text ed. 8.40 (0-13-296120-2) P-H.

An Asterisk (*) at the beginning of an entry indicates that the title is appearing in BIP for the first time.

Reichard, Gary W. Politics As Usual: The Age of Truman & Eisenhower. Franklin, John H. & Eisenstadt, A. S., eds. LC 87-20726. 222p. (C). 1988. pap. text ed. write for info. (*0-88295-856-9*) Harlan Davidson.

— The Reaffirmation of Republicanism: Eisenhower & the Eighty-third Congress. LC 75-1017. (Twentieth-Century America Ser.). 330p. reprint ed. pap. 94.10 (*0-8357-8607-2*, 2035004) Bks Demand.

Reichard, Gary W., jt. ed. see Bremner, Robert H.

Reichard, Gladys A. Analysis of Coeur d'Alene Indian Myths. LC 48-2411. (AFS Memoirs Ser.). 1972. reprint ed. 25.00 (*0-527-01093-6*) Periodicals Srv.

— Melanesian Design: A Study of Style in Wood & Tortoiseshell Carving. LC 70-82256. (Illus.). reprint ed. 95.00 (*0-404-50568-6*) AMS Pr.

— Navaho Grammar. LC 73-15404. (American Ethnological Society Publications: No. 21). reprint ed. 47.00 (*0-404-58171-4*) AMS Pr.

— Navaho Religion: A Study of Symbolism. LC 63-14455. (Bollingen Ser.: Vol. 18). 863p. reprint ed. 180.00 (*0-8357-9504-7*, 2014880) Bks Demand.

— Navajo Medicine Man Sand Paintings. (Illus.). 1977. reprint ed. pap. 11.95 (*0-486-23329-4*) Dover.

— Navajo Shepherd & Weaver. LC 68-25390. (Beautiful Rio Grande Classics Ser.). (Illus.). 280p. 1984. pap. 12.00 (*0-87380-143-1*) Rio Grande.

— Prayer: The Compulsive Word. LC 84-45512. (American Ethnological Society Monographs: No. 7). 1988. reprint ed. 24.50 (*0-404-62907-5*) AMS Pr.

— Social Life of the Navajo Indians. LC 76-82350. (Columbia Univ. Contributions to Anthropology Ser.: Vol. 7). reprint ed. 31.00 (*0-404-50557-0*) AMS Pr.

— Spider Woman: A Story of Navajo Weavers & Chanters. (Illus.). 344p. 1968. pap. 12.00 (*0-87380-160-1*) Rio Grande.

— Weaving a Navajo Blanket. LC 73-86437. (Illus.). 256p. 1974. reprint ed. 4.95 (*0-486-22992-0*) Dover.

Reichard, Gladys A. & La Farge, Oliver. Navaho Religion: A Study of Symbolism. (Bollingen Ser.: No. XVIII). 856p. (C). 1990. pap. text ed. 24.95 (*0-691-01906-1*) Princeton U Pr.

Reichard, John & Barnett, Alicia A., eds. The Healthcare Alliance & Network Sourcebook. 700p. 1994. pap. 195.00 (*1-881393-22-4*) Faulkner & Gray.

Reichard, John, jt. ed. see Vibbert, Spencer.

Reichard, Kevin. Advanced X Windows Application Programming. 2nd ed. 1994. Incl. CD-ROM. pap. 34.95 (*1-55851-344-2*) M&T Bks.

— Power Programming Motif. 2nd ed. 1993. pap. 29.95 (*1-55828-319-6*); disk 59.95 (*1-55828-322-6*) MIS Press.

— Teach Yourself ... UNIX. 2nd ed. 1992. pap. 22.95 (*1-55828-239-4*) MIS Press.

— UNIX Fundamentals: UNIX Basics. LC 94-30873. 1995. pap. 19.95 (*1-55828-362-5*) MIS Press.

— UNIX Fundamentals: Unix for DOS & Windows Users. 1995. pap. 19.95 (*1-55828-361-7*) MIS Press.

— Unix Shareware & Freeware. 1995. cd-rom, pap. 24.95 (*1-55828-382-X*) MIS Press.

— UNIX Systems Administrators Guide to X Windows with CD ROM. 1994. pap. 44.95 (*1-55828-347-1*) MIS Press.

— Using X: Troubleshooting X Windows, Mofit, Open Systems. 1992. pap. 29.95 (*1-55828-212-2*) MIS Press.

*__Reichard, Kevin & Johnson, Eric.__ Teach Yourself UNIX. 3rd ed. 450p. 1995. pap. text ed. 24.95 (*1-55828-418-4*) MIS Press.

— Unix in Plain English. 304p. 1994. pap. 14.95 (*1-55828-345-5*) H Holt & Co.

*__Reichard, Kevin & Johnson, Eric F.__ Advanced X Windows Applications Programming. LC 94-34030. 1994. 44.95 (*1-55828-344-7*) M&T Bks.

Reichard, Max. The Human Journey. 1991. 31.00 (*0-536-58129-0*) Ginn Pr.

Reichard, Richard W. From the Petition to the Strike: A History of Strikes in Germany, 1869-1914. LC 90-46469. (American University Studies: History: Ser. IX, Vol. 67). 336p. (C). 1991. text ed. 55.95 (*0-8204-0905-7*) P Lang Pubs.

Reichard, Sherwood M. & Filkens, James P., eds. The Reticuloendothelial System: A Comprehensive Treatise, Vol. 7A: Physiology. LC 79-25933. 436p. 1984. 105.00 (*0-306-41422-8*, Plenum Pr) Plenum.

Reichard, Sherwood M. & Filkins, James P., eds. The Reticuloendothelial System: A Comprehensive Treatise, Vol. 7B: Physiology. LC 79-25933. 558p. 1984. 115.00 (*0-306-41423-6*, Plenum Pr) Plenum.

Reichard, Suzanne, et al. Aging & Personality: A Study of Eighty-Seven Older Men. Stein, Leon, ed. LC 79-8680. (Growing Old Ser.). (Illus.). 1980. reprint ed. lib. bdg. 25.95 (*0-405-12797-9*) Ayer.

*__Reichardt, Charles S. & Rallis, Sharon F., eds.__ The Qualitative-Quantitative Debate: New Perspectives. LC 85-644749. (New Directions for Program Evaluation Ser.: No. 61). 98p. (Orig.). 1994. pap. 17.95 (*0-7879-9967-9*) Jossey-Bass.

Reichardt, Christian. Solvents & Solvent Effects in Organic Chemistry. 2nd enl. rev. ed. 534p. 1985. lib. bdg. 130.00 (*0-89573-684-5*) VCH Pubs.

Reichardt, E. Die Diatomeen der Altmuehl. (Bibliotheca Diatomologica Ser.: Vol. 6). (Illus.). 170p. 1985. lib. bdg. 39.00 (*3-7682-1411-7*) Lubrecht & Cramer.

*__Reichardt, Erwin.__ Iconographia Diatomologica: Annotated Diatom Micrographs, Vol. 1. (Iconographia Diatomologica, Annotated Diatom Micrographs, Taxonomy Ser.). (Illus.). 92p. 1994. 56.00 (*1-878762-69-9*) Koeltz Sci Bks.

*__Reichardt, Irwin & Lange-Bertalot, Horst.__ Die Diatomeen, Bacillariophyceae in Ehrenbergs Material von Cayenne, Guyana Gallica, 1843. (Iconographia Diatomologica, Annotated Diatom Micrographs, Taxonomy Ser.). (Illus.). x, 92p. 1994. 56.00 (*3-87429-371-8*) Koeltz Sci Bks.

Reichardt, Johann F., jt. ed. see Kunzen, Friedrich L.

Reichardt, L. Dictionary of Technical Acoustics. (FRE, GER, HUN, POL, RUS, SLO & SPA.). 1978. 20.50 (*0-685-92166-2*) Adlers Foreign Bks.

Reichardt, Louise. Songs. LC 80-22799. (Women Composers Ser.). 1980. 27.50 (*0-306-79552-3*) Da Capo.

Reichardt, Mary. A Web of Relationship: Women in the Short Fiction of Mary Wilkins Freeman. LC 91-32352. 208p. 1992. 30.00 (*0-87805-555-X*) U Pr of Miss.

Reichardt, Mary R., ed. The Uncollected Stories of Mary Wilkins Freeman. LC 91-48011. 350p. 1992. 40.00 (*0-87805-564-9*); pap. 16.95 (*0-87805-565-7*) U Pr of Miss.

Reichardt, Peg. Conceptbuilding: Developing Meaning Through Narratives & Discussion. LC 91-43896. 144p. 1992. pap. 24.00 (*0-930599-71-3*) Thinking Pubns.

Reichardt, W. Acoustics Dictionary. 109p. (DUT, ENG, FRE & GER.). 1983. 95.00 (*0-8288-0056-1*, M6245) Fr & Eur.

Reichardt, Werner E. & Poggio, Tomaso, eds. Theoretical Approaches in Neurobiology. (Illus.). 208p. 1980. 35.00 (*0-262-18100-2*) MIT Pr.

Reichart, Elisabeth. February Shadows. Hoffmeister, Donna L., tr. & comment by. (Orig.). 1989. pap. 13.95 (*0-929497-02-3*) Ariadne CA.

Reichart, John F. & Sturm, Steven R., eds. American Defense Policy. 5th ed. LC 81-48186. 874p. reprint ed. pap. 180.00 (*0-8357-6906-2*, 2037964) Bks Demand.

Reichart, Natalie, jt. auth. see Klopsteg, Paul E.

*__Reichblum, Charles.__ Knowledge in a Nutshell Vol. 1. 1994. pap. 4.50 (*0-312-95349-6*) St Martin.

Reiche, A. Berlin. Date not set. 25.00 (*0-06-018212-1*, HarpT); pap. 12.95 (*0-06-098112-1*) HarpC.

Reiche, Eric G. The Development of the S. A. in Nurnberg, 1922-34. (Illus.). 352p. 1986. 49.95 (*0-521-30638-8*) Cambridge U Pr.

Reiche, Hans. Maintenance Minimization for Competitive Advantage: A Life-Cycle Approach for Product Manufacturers & End-Users. LC 92-46257. 1994. text ed. 55.00 (*2-88124-589-7*) Gordon & Breach.

Reichel, Aaron. The Maverick Rabbi. Friedman, Robert S., ed. LC 82-9664. 361p. 12.95 (*0-89865-174-3*); pap. 8.95 (*0-89865-299-5*) Donning Co.

Reichel, Brian J., et al. Research Through Biotechnology: Institutional Impacts & Societal Concerns. (Bibliographies in Technology & Social Change Ser.: No. 1). 150p. (Orig.). (C). 1987. pap. 12.00 (*0-945271-00-X*) ISU-TSCP.

Reichel, Cara. A Stone Promise. Thatch, Nancy R., ed. LC 91-15059. (Books for Students by Students Ser.). (Illus.). 26p. (YA). (gr. 5 up). 1991. lib. bdg. 14.95 (*0-933849-35-4*) Landmark Edns.

Reichel-Dolmatoff, G. The Sacred Mountain of Colombia's Kogi Indians. LC 90-2138. (Iconography of Religions Ser.: Vol. IX, Pt. 2). (Illus.). 1990. pap. 34.50 (*90-04-09274-9*) E J Brill.

Reichel-Dolmatoff, Gerardo. Basketry As Metaphor: Arts & Crafts of the Desana Indians of the Northwest Amazon. LC 84-62891. (Occasional Papers of the Museum of Cultural History, Los Angeles: No. 5). (Illus.). 104p. (Orig.). 1985. pap. text ed. 18.00 (*0-930741-03-X*) UCLA Fowler Mus.

Reichel-Dolmatoff, Gerardo & De Reichel, Alicia D. People of Aritama. LC 60-14234. (Illus.). 1962. lib. bdg. 30.00 (*0-226-70791-1*) U Ch Pr.

Reichel, E., jt. auth. see Baumgartner, A.

Reichel, H. Structural Induction on Partial Algebras. 206p. (C). 1984. 85.00 (*0-685-36876-9*, Pub. by Collets) St Mut.

Reichel, Horst. Initial Computability, Algebraic Specifications, & Partial Algebras. (International Series of Monographs on Computer Science: No. 2). (Illus.). 224p. 1987. 59.95 (*0-19-853806-5*) OUP.

Reichel, Lothar, et al, eds. Numerical Linear Algebra: Proceedings of the Conference in Numerical Linear Algebra & Scientific Computation, Kent (Ohio), March 13-14, 1992. LC 93-8437. ix, 199p. 1993. lib. bdg. 79.95 (*3-11-013784-4*) De Gruyter.

Reichel, Mary & Ramey, Mary A., eds. Conceptual Frameworks for Bibliographic Education: Theory into Practice. 208p. 1987. lib. bdg. 27.50 (*0-87287-552-0*) Libs Unl.

Reichel, Philip L. Comparative Criminal Justice Systems: Topical Approach. LC 93-4493. 1993. text ed. 45.00 (*0-13-151937-9*) Prentice ESL.

Reichel, William. Clinical Aspects of Aging. 3rd ed. (Illus.). 680p. 1989. 78.00 (*0-683-07204-8*) Williams & Wilkins.

Reichel, William & Schechter, Mal, eds. The Geriatric Patient. (Illus.). 1978. 18.95 (*0-913800-09-0*) HP Pub Co.

Reichel, William, jt. auth. see Doukas, David J.

*__Reichel, William, et al, eds.__ Clinical Aspects of Aging. 4th ed. LC 94-26125. 1995. write for info. (*0-683-07209-9*) Williams & Wilkins.

Reichelt, Karl. Truth & Tradition in Chinese Buddhism. 1972. 59.95 (*0-8490-1234-1*) Gordon Pr.

Reichelt, Karl L. Truth & Tradition in Chinese Buddhism. (Illus.). 415p. 1990. reprint ed. pap. 30.00 (*957-9482-17-9*) Oriental Bk Store.

Reichelt, Marie H. Yes, There Is Life after Aerospace: Career Transition from Military Defense - Aerospace to Commercial Civilian Life. Franklin, Reece & Fischer, Joanne, eds. (Illus.). 132p. (Orig.). 1994. pap. 14.95 (*0-9639036-5-9*) ABP Assocs.

Reichelt, Richard. Heartland Blacksmiths: Conversations at the Forge. LC 88-4482. (Shawnee Bks.). (Illus.). 192p. (C). 1988. 29.95 (*0-8093-1475-4*); pap. 19.95 (*0-8093-1476-2*) S Ill U Pr.

Reichen, J., ed. see Falk Symposium Staff.

*__Reichenbach, B. A., tr.__ The Book on Happiness. 133p. 1995. pap. 10.95 (*0-915034-04-2*) Kober Pr.

Reichenbach, B. A., tr. see Bo Yin Ra.

Reichenbach, Bodo A., tr. see Bo Rin Ra.

Reichenbach, Bodo A., tr. see Bo Yin Ra.

Reichenbach, Bruce. Evil & a Good God. LC 82-71120. xviii, 198p. 1982. 30.00 (*0-8232-1080-4*); pap. 15.00 (*0-8232-1081-2*) Fordham.

Reichenbach, Bruce R. The Law of Karma: A Philosophical Study. LC 90-41032. 256p. (C). 1991. text ed. 38.00 (*0-8248-1352-9*) UH Pr.

*__Reichenbach, Bruce R. & Anderson, V. Elving.__ On Behalf of God: A Christian Ethic for Biology. (Studies in a Christian World View). 368p. (Orig.). 1995. pap. 22.99 (*0-8028-0727-5*) Eerdmans.

Reichenbach, Frank, ed. Greenberg's Guide to Ives Trains: O Gauge. (Illus.). 176p. 1992. 39.95 (*0-89778-124-4*, 10-7185) Greenberg Bks.

— Greenberg's Guide to Ives Trains, Vol. I: 1 & Wide Gauges & Accessories, 1901-1932. (Illus.). 176p. 1991. 39.95 (*0-89778-108-2*, 10-6785) Greenberg Bks.

Reichenbach, Hans. The Direction of Time. Reichenbach, Maria, ed. 350p. 1991. pap. 16.00 (*0-520-07414-9*) U CA Pr.

— Experience & Prediction: An Analysis of the Foundations & the Structure of Knowledge. (Midway Reprint Ser.). 421p. reprint ed. pap. 120.00 (*0-317-20696-6*, 2024063) Bks Demand.

— From Copernicus to Einstein. Winn, Ralph B., tr. (Illus.). 1980. reprint ed. 3.95 (*0-486-23940-3*) Dover.

— Philosophy of Space & Time. Reichenbach, Maria, tr. 1957. pap. text ed. 6.95 (*0-486-60443-8*) Dover.

— The Rise of Scientific Philosophy. 1951. pap. 12.00 (*0-520-01055-8*) U CA Pr.

Reichenbach, Heinrich G. Die Vollstandigste Naturgeschicte der Affen. LC 78-72725. reprint ed. 72.50 (*0-404-18298-4*) AMS Pr.

Reichenbach, Maria, ed. see Reichenbach, Hans.

Reichenbach, Maria, tr. see Reichenbach, Hans.

*__Reichenbach, Wendy A.__ Studying Density Using Salad Oil & Vinegar. Neidig, H. A., ed. (Modular Laboratory Program in Chemistry Ser.). 7p. (C). 1993. pap. text ed. 1.25x (*0-87540-393-X*) Chem Educ Res.

Reichenberg, Monte. Cheating Chet. (Illus.). 32p. (Orig.). (J). (ps-4). 1992. pap. 3.00 (*0-9640260-1-5*) MM & I Ink.

— It'll Feel Better When It Quits Hurtin' rev. ed. (Illus.). 52p. 1994. pap. 6.95 (*0-9640260-3-1*) MM & I Ink.

— It'll Feel Better When It Quits Hurtin' 2nd ed. 44p. 1993. pap. 4.95 (*0-9640260-0-7*) MM & I Ink.

— Sam, Old Kate & I. (Illus.). 32p. (Orig.). (J). (ps-4). 1994. pap. 3.00 (*0-9640260-2-3*) MM & I Ink.

Reichenberg, Neil. AIDS in the Workplace. (Monograph Ser.). 1989. 10.00 (*0-685-41304-7*) Intl Personnel Mgmt.

— Drug Testing in the Workplace: An Update. (Monograph Ser.). 1991. 10.00 (*0-685-41301-2*) Intl Personnel Mgmt.

— Employment Discrimination in the Workplace: The Impact of the 1988-89 Supreme Court Term. (Monograph Ser.). 1989. 10.00 (*0-685-41302-0*) Intl Personnel Mgmt.

— Fair Labor Standards Act Exemption. (Monograph Ser.). 1990. 10.00 (*0-685-41300-4*) Intl Personnel Mgmt.

— FLSA Exemptions: An Update. (Monograph Ser.). 1992. 10.00 (*0-685-69342-2*) Intl Personnel Mgmt.

— Smoking in the Workplace. (Monograph Ser.). 1991. 10.00 (*0-685-41303-9*) Intl Personnel Mgmt.

Reichenberg, Norman & Raphael, Alan J. Advanced Psychodiagnostic Interpretation of the Bender Gestalt Test: Adults & Children. LC 91-37456. 176p. 1992. text ed. 47.95 (*0-275-94163-9*, C4163, Praeger Pubs) Greenwood.

Reichenberg, Shaul. Procedure for Setting Aside Trumot & Ma'asrot. 1991. pap. 2.95 (*0-685-49071-8*) Feldheim.

Reichenberg-Ullman, Judyth, jt. auth. see Ullman, Robert W.

Reichenberger, Arnold G., ed. see De Vega, Lope.

Reichenburg, Louisette. Contribution a l'histoire de la "querelle des Bouffons" LC 76-43938. (Music & Theatre in France in the 17th & 18th Centuries Ser.). reprint ed. 32.50 (*0-404-60188-X*) AMS Pr.

Reichenfeld, Rob. Windsurfing: Step by Step to Success. (Illus.). 176p. 1993. pap. 22.95 (*1-85223-746-5*, Pub. by Crowood Pr UK) Trafalgar.

*__Reichenfeld, Rob & Bruechert, Anna.__ Snowboarding. LC 94-28366. (Outdoor Pursuits Ser.). (Illus.). 144p. (Orig.). 1995. pap. 12.95 (*0-87322-677-1*, PREI0677) Human Kinetics.

Reichenfeld, Rob & Bruechert, Anna M. Skiing: Step by Step to Success with Alpine Skiing, Snowboarding & Telemarking. (Illus.). 160p. 1993. pap. 22.95 (*1-85223-707-4*, Pub. by Crowood Pr UK) Trafalgar.

Reicher, Murray A. & Kellerhouse, Leland E. MRI of the Wrist & Hand. 224p. 1990. 98.50 (*0-88167-664-0*) Raven.

Reicher, Stephen, jt. auth. see Emler, Nicholas.

Reichert & Klersy. VW Beetle: An Illustrated History. (Illus.). 160p. 1987. 29.95 (*0-85429-591-7*, F591, Pub. by G T Foulis Ltd) Haynes Pubns.

*__Reichert, Amy.__ Bustop the Cat & Mrs. Lin. (Illus.). 48p. (Orig.). (J). (gr. 1-4). 1994. pap. 9.95 (*1-880812-12-6*) S Ink WA.

— A Home for Ernie. (Illus.). 48p. (Orig.). (J). (gr. 2-6). 1994. pap. 9.95 (*1-880812-11-8*) S Ink WA.

Reichert-Facilides, Fritz, et al, eds. International Insurance Contract Law: Proceedings of a Comparative Law Conference Held at the European University Institute, Florence, May 23-24, 1991. LC 92-40852. 1993. write for info. (*90-6544-676-1*) Kluwer Law Tax Pubs.

Reichert, Heinrich. Introduction to Neurobiology. (Illus.). 272p. (C). 1993. reprint ed. pap. text ed. 35.00 (*0-19-521010-7*) OUP.

— Introductory Neurobiology. Boyan, G. S., tr. LC 92-49145. (Illus.). 1992. write for info. (*0-86577-469-2*) Thieme Med Pubs.

Reichert, Herbert W. Basic Concepts in the Philosophy of Gottfried Keller. LC 49-11614. (North Carolina. University. Studies in the Germanic Languages & Literatures: No. 1). reprint ed. 27.00 (*0-404-50901-0*) AMS Pr.

Reichert, Herbert W. & Salinger, Herman, eds. Studies in Arthur Schnitzler. LC 63-62703. (North Carolina. University. Studies in the Germanic Languages & Literatures: No. 42). reprint ed. 27.00 (*0-404-50942-8*) AMS Pr.

Reichert, J., jt. ed. see Meyer, W. E.

Reichert, John. Making Sense of Literature. LC 77-24455. 1978. lib. bdg. 8.00 (*0-226-70769-5*) U Ch Pr.

— Milton's Wisdom: Nature & Scripture in Paradise Lost. LC 92-20087. 282p. (C). 1992. text ed. 39.50 (*0-472-10324-5*) U of Mich Pr.

Reichert, Johnathan F. A Modern Introduction to Mechanics. 544p. (C). 1990. text ed. write for info. (*0-13-596248-X*) P-H.

Reichert, K. H. & Geiselar, W., eds. Polymer Reaction Engineering. LC 89-22680. (Illus.). 437p. 1989. text ed. 120.00 (*0-89573-950-X*) VCH Pubs.

Reichert, Kathryn J. Nutrition for Recovery: A Patient's Guide. 1993. 29.95 (*0-8493-8652-7*, RC552) CRC Pr.

— Nutrition for Recovery: Eating Disorders. 1993. 49.95 (*0-8493-8651-9*, RC552) CRC Pr.

Reichert, Kurt L. Artificial Intelligence: Index of Modern Information. LC 88-47541. 150p. 1988. 39.50 (*0-88164-840-X*); pap. 34.50 (*0-88164-841-8*) ABBE Pubs Assn.

— Automation & Autoanalysis in Medicine: Research & Reference Guidebook. LC 83-45002. 150p. 1985. 39.50 (*0-88164-180-4*); 34.50 (*0-88164-181-2*) ABBE Pubs Assn.

— DNA & Recombinants: Index of Modern Information. LC 88-47965. 150p. 1988. 39.50 (*1-55914-042-9*); pap. 34.50 (*1-55914-043-7*) ABBE Pubs Assn.

— Gold-Studies & Uses in Science & Health: Subject Analysis with Reference Bibliography. LC 85-48103. 150p. 1987. 39.50 (*0-88164-478-1*); pap. 34.50 (*0-88164-479-X*) ABBE Pubs Assn.

Reichert, Marimargaret & Young, Jack H. Sterilization Technology for the Health Care Facility. LC 93-18193. 320p. 1993. 135.00 (*0-8342-0373-1*, 20373) Aspen Pub.

*__Reichert, Mickey Z.__ Beyond Ragnarok. (Renshai Chronicles Ser.: Vol. 1). 688p. 1995. 21.95 (*0-88677-658-9*) DAW Bks.

— By Chaos Cursed. (Bifrost Guardians Ser.: No. 5). 304p. (Orig.). 1991. mass mkt. 4.50 (*0-88677-474-8*) DAW Bks.

— Child of Thunder. (Last of the Renshai Trilogy Ser.: Bk. 3). 592p. (Orig.). 1993. mass mkt. 5.99 (*0-88677-549-3*) DAW Bks.

— Godslayer. (Bifrost Guardians Ser.: No. 1). (YA). (gr. 9-12). 1990. pap. 2.95 (*0-88677-207-9*) DAW Bks.

— Godslayer. (Bifrost Guardians Ser.: No. 1). 224p. 1987. reprint ed. pap. 3.99 (*0-88677-372-5*) DAW Bks.

— The Last of the Renshai. 592p. (Orig.). 1992. mass mkt. 5.99 (*0-88677-503-5*) DAW Bks.

— The Legend of Nightfall. 496p. (Orig.). 1993. mass mkt. 5.99 (*0-88677-587-6*) DAW Bks.

— Shadow Climber. (Bifrost Guardians Ser.: No. 2). 304p. (Orig.). 1988. reprint ed. mass mkt. 3.99 (*0-88677-284-2*) DAW Bks.

— Shadow's Realm. (Bifrost Guardians Ser.: No. 4). 304p. 1990. mass mkt. 4.50 (*0-88677-419-5*) DAW Bks.

— The Unknown Soldier. 320p. (Orig.). 1994. mass mkt. 4.99 (*0-88677-600-7*) DAW Bks.

— The Western Wizard. (Renshai Trilogy Ser.: Bk. 2). 592p. (Orig.). 1992. mass mkt. 5.99 (*0-88677-520-5*) DAW Bks.

Reichert, N. Greer, jt. auth. see Giammattei, Victor M.

Reichert, Nanci, jt. auth. see Giammattei, Victor.

Reichert, Richard. Sexuality & Dating. LC 81-51011. (Illus.). 95p. (gr. 10-11). 1981. teacher ed, pap. text ed. 9.00 (*0-88489-138-0*); student ed, pap. text ed. 2.50 (*0-88489-139-9*) St Marys.

— Sexuality & Dating. LC 81-51011. (Illus.). 111p. (YA). (gr. 10-11). 1981. pap. text ed. 5.50x (*0-88489-133-X*) St Marys.

— Simulation Games for Religious Education. LC 75-142. 106p. 1975. pap. 4.95 (*0-88489-060-0*) St Marys.

— Teaching Tips for Religion Teachers Grades 1-3. 128p. 1989. spiral bd. 9.95 (*0-87973-364-0*, 364) Our Sunday Visitor.

— Teaching Tips for Religion Teachers Grades 4-8. 160p. 1989. spiral bd. 9.95 (*0-87973-365-9*, 365) Our Sunday Visitor.

Reichert, U. Pharmacology of Topical Retinoids. Schaefer, H. et al, eds. (Journal: Skin Pharmacology: Vol. 6, Suppl. 1, 1993). (Illus.). vi, 84p. 1994. pap. 35.25 (*3-8055-5922-4*) S Karger.

Reichert, U. & Shroot, B., eds. Pharmacology of Retinoids in the Skin: 8th CIRD Symposium on Advances in Skin Pharmacology, Cannes, September 1988. (Pharmacology & the Skin Ser.: Vol. 3). (Illus.). x, 282p. 1989. 190.50 (*3-8055-4909-1*) S Karger.

Reichert, William O. Partisans of Freedom: A Study in American Anarchism. LC 76-10109. 1976. 26.00 (*0-87972-118-9*) Bowling Green Univ.

Reichert, William O. & Ludd, Steven O., eds. Outlook on Ohio. (Orig.). 1983. pap. 13.50 (*0-940390-04-3*) Comwealth Bks NJ.

Reicherts, Michael, jt. auth. see Perrez, Meinrad.

Reichgelt, Han. Knowledge Representation: An AI Perspective. Shadbolt, Nigel, ed. LC 90-14470. (Tutorial Monographs in Cognitive Science). 272p. (C). 1991. text ed. 49.50 (0-89391-590-4); pap. 29.95 (0-89391-779-6) Ablex Pub.

Reichhold, Jane. A Dictionary of Haiku. 320p. (Orig.). 1991. pap. 12.95 (0-944676-87-1) AHA Bks.

— A Gift of Tanka. (Illus.). 140p. (Orig.). 1990. pap. 7.00 (0-944676-56-1) AHA Bks.

— Tigers in a Tea Cup: Collected Haiku. rev. ed. (Illus.). 344p. 1988. pap. 12.95 (0-944676-07-3) AHA Bks.

— Wave of Mouth Stories. 184p. (Orig.). 1993. pap. 9.00 (0-944676-09-X) AHA Bks.

Reichhold, Jane & Higginson, William J., eds. Narrow Road to Renga: A Collection of Renga. 270p. (Orig.). 1989. pap. 12.95 (0-944676-19-7) AHA Bks.

Reichhold, Jane & Reichhold, Werner, eds. Wind Five-Folded. 230p. 1994. 12.00 (0-944676-21-9) AHA Bks.

Reichhold, Jane, jt. auth. see Walker, Bambi.

Reichhold, Werner. Bridge of Voices. (Illus.). 190p. (Orig.). (ENG, FRE, GER & ITA.). 1990. pap. 14.00 (0-944676-13-8) AHA Bks.

— Handshake: In the Spirit of Exchange. (Illus.). 125p. (Orig.). 1989. pap. 10.00 (0-944676-11-1) AHA Bks.

— Sensescapes. (Illus.). 65p. (Orig.). 1991. pap. 8.00 (0-944676-14-6) AHA Bks.

— Tidal Wave. (Illus.). 170p. (Orig.). 1989. pap. 14.00 (0-944676-12-X) AHA Bks.

Reichhold, Werner, jt. ed. see Reichhold, Jane.

Reichholf-Riehm, Helgard. Field Guide to Butterflies & Moths of Britain & Europe. (Illus.). 287p. 1992. pap. 22.95 (1-85223-593-4, Pub. by Crowood Pr UK) Trafalgar.

Reichl, Christopher A., tr. see Takayasu, Rokuro.

Reichl, H., ed. Micro Systems Technologies Ninety: First International Conference on Micro, Electro, Mechanic Systems & Components, Berlin, 10-13 September 1990. (Illus.). xv, 858p. 1990. 193.00 (0-387-53025-8) Spr-Verlag.

Reichl, Karl. Turkic Oral Epic Poetry: Tradition, Forms, Poetic Structure. LC 92-16726. (Albert Bates Lord Studies in Oral Tradition: Vol. 7). 408p. 1992. 60.00 (0-8240-7210-3, H01247) Garland.

Reichl, L. E. The Transition to Chaos: In Conservative Classical Systems: Quantum Manifestations. (Institute for Nonlinear Science Ser.). (Illus.). xv, 551p. 1994. 45.00 (0-387-97753-8) Spr-Verlag.

Reichl, L. E., jt. ed. see Horton, C. W., Jr.

Reichle, D. E. Dynamic Properties of Forest Ecosystems. (C). 1991. text ed. 910.00 (0-89771-648-5, Pub. by Intl Bk Distr II) St Mut.

Reichle, D. E., jt. ed. see Trabalka, J. R.

Reichle, Joe & Wacker, David, eds. Communicative Alternatives to Challenging Behavior: Integrating Functional Assessment & Intervention Strategies. LC 93-14787. 496p. 1993. boxed 44.00 (1-55766-082-4) P H Brookes.

Reichle, Joe, jt. ed. see Warren, Steven F.

Reichle, Joe, et al. Implementing Augmentative & Alternative Communication: Strategies for Learners with Severe Disabilities. LC 90-2139. 320p. (C). 1991. text ed. 46.00 (1-55766-044-1, 0441) P H Brookes.

Reichler, Arny. A Celebration in Times of War. Layne, Carol, ed. 30p. (Orig.). 1987. pap. 6.95 (0-933865-13-9) Doris Pubns.

Reichler, Joseph. Baseball's Great Moments, 1990 Edition. 1990. 7.98 (0-88365-754-6) Galahad Bks.

Reichler, Joseph L. Baseball Trade Register. 1984. 19.95 (0-02-603110-8) Macmillan.

— Great All Time Baseball Record. 1981. 19.95 (0-02-603100-0) Macmillan.

Reichler, Judith M. New York Child Support Handbook. 80p. 1992. 7.50 (0-929396-08-1) Natl Ctr Women & Family Law Inc.

Reichley, A. James. Conservatives in an Age of Change: The Nixon & Ford Administrations. LC 81-1672. 482p. 1981. 38.95 (0-8157-7380-3); pap. 16.95 (0-8157-7379-X) Brookings.

— The Life of the Parties: A History of American Political Parties. LC 92-12690. 1992. text ed. 29.95 (0-02-926025-6) Free Pr.

— Religion in American Public Life. LC 85-21312. 402p. 1985. 36.95 (0-8157-7378-1); pap. 16.95 (0-8157-7377-3) Brookings.

Reichley, A. James, ed. Elections American Style. LC 87-34156. 292p. 1987. 35.95 (0-8157-7382-X); pap. 15.95 (0-8157-7381-1) Brookings.

Reichley, David. Jasper & Sam. (Illus.). (J). (gr. 4-6). 1992. 14.95 (1-879260-04-2) Evanston Pub.

Reichley, James. The Art of Government. (Reprint Series in Sociology). (Illus.). 1972. reprint ed. lib. bdg. 26.50 (0-697-00222-5); reprint ed. pap. 9.95 (0-89197-664-7) Irvington.

Reichlin, jt. ed. see Bigazzi.

Reichlin, Seymour, ed. The Neurohypophysis: Psychological & Clinical Aspects. LC 84-4861. 240p. 1984. 65.00 (0-306-41642-5, Plenum Med Bk) Plenum.

— Somatostatin: Basic & Clinical Status. (Serono Symposia U. S. A. Ser.). (Illus.). 364p. 1987. 85.00 (0-306-42573-4, Plenum Pr) Plenum.

Reichlin, Seymour, jt. auth. see Martin, Joseph B.

***Reichlin, Seymour, et al, eds.** The Hypothalamus. fac. ed. LC 77-83691. (Association for Research in Nervous & Mental Disease Research Publications: No. 56). (Illus.). 502p. Date not set. pap. 143.10 (0-7837-7350-1, 2047159) Bks Demand.

Reichman, Barry. The Pre-Calculus & Calculus Workbook & Videotape. (Pre-Calculus Ser.). 100p. (J). (gr. 6-12). 1990. 225.00 (0-685-38398-9) Video Tutorial Serv.

Reichman, Harold. Reshimos Shiurim: Succah. Kuntz, Y., ed. (Notes on Jewish Talmud Ser.). 300p. (C). 1989. text ed. 10.00 (0-685-29013-1) Torah Study.

Reichman, Helmut. Cross Country Soaring. rev. ed. 172p. 1993. text ed. 39.50 (1-883813-01-8) Soaring Soc.

— Flying Sailplanes. 128p. 1980. text ed. 25.00 (1-883813-00-X) Soaring Soc.

Reichman, Henry. Censorship & Selection: Issues & Answers for Schools. rev. ed. LC 93-19711. 160p. 1993. pap. text ed. 18.00 (0-8389-0620-6) ALA.

— Censorship & Selection: Issues & Answers for Schools. LC 88-16815. 151p. reprint ed. pap. 43.10 (0-7837-6155-4, 2045877) Bks Demand.

Reichman, Henry F. Censorship & Selection: Issues & Answers for Schools. rev. ed. 172p. 1993. pap. text ed. 18.00 (0-87652-129-4, 021-00219) Am Assn Sch Admin.

Reichman, Lee & Hershfield, Earl, eds. Tuberculosis: A Comprehensive International Approach. LC 93-20307. (Lung Biology in Health & Disease Ser.: Vol. 66). 792p. 1993. 215.00 (0-8247-8852-4) Dekker.

Reichman, Louis & Cardinale, Gary. The Orange County Experience: A Pictorial History of Orange County California. (Illus.). 228p. 1987. pap. 23.95 (0-932967-07-8) Pacific Shoreline.

Reichman, Louis, et al. The Orange County Experience. 2nd ed. (Orange County Centennial Edition Ser.). (Illus.). 250p. 1989. pap. text ed. 27.95 (0-932967-13-2) Pacific Shoreline.

— U. S. History & Government Cornerstone Documents. 1992. pap. 29.15 (1-56226-094-4) CT Pub.

Reichman, O. J. Konza Prairie: A Tallgrass Natural History. LC 87-18903. (Illus.). xii, 228p. (C). 1988. 25.00 (0-7006-0307-7); pap. 12.95 (0-7006-0450-2) U Pr of KS.

Reichman, Rachel. Getting Computers to Talk Like You & Me: Discourse, Context, Focus & Semantics; an ATN Model. (Comput'l Models Ser.). (Illus.). 144p. 1985. 31.50 (0-262-18118-5, Bradford Bks) MIT Pr.

***Reichman, Rick.** Formatting Your Screenplay. 200p. (Orig.). 1994. pap. 14.95 (0-9641594-0-6) BookSmiths.

Reichman, Rosalie. Stranger in Your Bed. 226p. 1989. text ed. 16.50 (0-471-61124-7) Wiley.

Reichman, S., jt. auth. see Nijkamp, P.

Reichman, S., et al, eds. Superalloys 1988. LC 88-62071. (Illus.). 892p. 1988. 52.00 (0-87339-076-8, 338) Minerals Metals.

Reichman, Steven, jt. ed. see Tien, John K.

Reichman, Sylvia. Transitions. Stewart, David & Stewart, Lee, eds. LC 87-63157. 160p. (Orig.). 1987. pap. 9.95 (0-934426-15-5) NAPSAC Reprods.

***Reichman, William E. & Katz, Paul R., eds.** Psychiatric Care in the Nursing Home. (Illus.). 304p. 1995. 45.00 (0-19-508515-9) OUP.

Reichmanis, Elsa, jt. auth. see O'Donnell, James J.

Reichmanis, Elsa, et al, eds. Irradiation of Polymeric Materials: Processes, Mechanisms, & Applications. LC 93-22431. (ACS Symposium Ser.: No. 527). (Illus.). 388p. 1993. text ed. 89.95 (0-8412-2662-8) Am Chemical.

Reichmanis, Else, ed. Advances in Resist Technology & Processing VI. 629p. 1989. 86.00 (0-8194-0121-8, VOL. 1086) SPIE.

***Reichmann.** Philosophy of the Human Person. 1985. write for info. (0-8294-0504-6) Loyola Univ Pr.

Reichmann & Co. Staff. Die Mittelalterlichen Munzen. (Illus.). 151p. (ENG & GER.). 1977. 15.00 (0-915018-32-2) Attic Bks.

***Reichmann, Eberhard, ed.** Hoosier German Tales: Small & Tall. (Illus.). xx, 258p. 1991. pap. 8.00 (1-880788-00-4) MKGAC & IGHS.

Reichmann, Eberhard, ed. see Adams, Willi P.

Reichmann, Eberhard, tr. see Adams, Willi P.

Reichmann, Eberhard, tr. see Nix, Jacob.

Reichmann, Eberhard, jt. auth. see Probst, George T.

***Reichmann, Eberhard, et al, eds.** Emigration & Settlement Patterns of German Communities in North America. 290p. 1995. pap. 19.00 (1-880788-04-7) MKGAC & IGHS.

Reichmann, Felix. The Sources of Western Literacy: The Middle Eastern Civilizations. LC 79-8292. (Contributions in Librarianship & Information Science Ser.: No. 29). 274p. 1980. text ed. 55.00 (0-313-20948-0, RWL/, Greenwood Pr) Greenwood.

Reichmann, Rebecca, jt. auth. see Correa, Sonia.

Reichmeider, P. F., jt. auth. see Mavrommatis, P. D.

Reichmeider, Philip. The Equivalence of Some Combinatorial Matching Theorems. LC 84-11746. (Illus.). 127p. 1985. 15.50 (0-936428-09-0) Polygonal Pub.

Reichmeier, Betty, illus. Potty Time! Yellow Ladder Books for Toddlers Through 4 Years. (Learning Ladders Ser.). 10p. (J). 1988. vinyl bd. 7.00 (0-394-89403-0) Random Bks Yng Read.

Reichmuth, Stefan. Der Arabische Dialekt der Sukriyya Im Ostsudan. (Studien Zur Sprachwissenschaft Ser.: Vol. 2). 325p. 1983. write for info. (3-487-07457-5, Pub. by Georg Olms GW) Lubrecht & Cramer.

Reichow, Alan W., jt. auth. see Stoner, Michael W.

Reichs, Kathleen J., ed. Forensic Osteology: Advances in the Identification of Human Remains. (Illus.). 360p. (C). 1986. 69.95 (0-398-05226-3) C C Thomas.

— Forensic Osteology: Advances in the Identification of Human Remains. (Illus.). 360p. 1986. pap. 38.95 (0-398-06342-7) C C Thomas.

Reichsman, F., ed. Epidemiologic Studies in Psychosomatic Medicine. (Advances in Psychosomatic Medicine Ser.: Vol. 9). (Illus.). 1977. 45.75 (3-8055-2654-7) S Karger.

Reichstein, Andreas V. Rise of the Lone Star: The Making of Texas. Willson, Jeanne R., tr. LC 89-30386. (Illus.). 328p. 1989. 35.00 (0-89096-318-5) Tex A&M Univ Pr.

Reichter, Eric. Chemical Processing with a Basic Computer. (Illus.). 120p. 1982. pap. text ed. 14.95 (0-917410-05-X) Basic Sci Pr.

Reichwage, Randall J., ed. see McGrew, J. R., et al.

Reichwaye, Randall J., ed. see Moorhead, et al.

Reichwein, A. China & Europe. 1972. 59.95 (0-87968-853-X) Gordon Pr.

Reichwein, Jeffrey. Emergence of Native American Nationalism in the Columbia Plateau. LC 90-21298. (Evolution of North American Indians Ser.: Vol. 17). 416p. 1991. reprint ed. 30.00 (0-8240-2512-1) Garland.

Reicke, Bo. The New Testament Era: The World of the Bible from 500 B.C. to A.D. 100. LC 68-15864. 352p. 1974. pap. 12.00 (0-8006-1080-6, 1-1080, Fortress Pr) Augsburg Fortress.

Reicke, Bo I. The Disobedient Spirits & Christian Baptism: Study of First Peter, III-19 & Its Context. LC 79-8117. 288p. 1984. reprint ed. 41.50 (0-404-18430-8) AMS Pr.

Reicke, Bo I., ed. Epistles of James, Peter & Jude. LC 63-8221. (Anchor Bible Ser.: Vol. 37). 1964. pap. 28.00 (0-385-01374-4, Anchor NY) Doubleday.

Reid. Amstrad PC1512-1640 ADV Users Guide. 1989. pap. 64.95 (0-434-91998-5) Buttrwrth-Heinemann.

— Bed & Breakfast in America Cities. 1994. pap. 16.00 (0-671-88035-7, P-H Travel) P-H Gen Ref & Trav.

— Canada Remapped. 1994. per. 14.95 (0-88978-249-0, Pub. by Arsenal Pulp CN) InBook.

— Complete DSM-IV Training Program, Set. 1995. text ed., sl. 405.00 (0-87630-771-3); text ed., trans. 405.00 (0-87630-772-1) Brunner-Mazel.

— DSM-IV Training Guide. 1995. vhs 100.00 (0-87630-764-0); vhs 100.00 (0-87630-782-9) Brunner-Mazel.

— DSM-IV Training Guide, 2 tapes, Set. 1995. vhs 179.95 (0-87630-783-7) Brunner-Mazel.

— Hospitality Marketing Management. 3rd ed. 1993. text ed. 34.95 (0-442-01754-5) Van Nos Reinhold.

— The Retreat. Date not set. per. 8.95 (0-85449-102-3, Pub. by Gay Mens Pr UK) InBook.

— Social Work Practice with Groups: A Clinical Perspective. 384p. (C). 1991. text ed. 48.95 (0-534-14820-4) Brooks-Cole.

— Uncle Stephen. Date not set. per. 9.95 (0-85449-083-3, Pub. by Gay Mens Pr UK) InBook.

Reid, ed. Greek Orators: Lycurgus Hyperides. (Classical Texts Ser.: Vol. 2). 1991. write for info. (0-85668-306-X, Pub. by Aris & Phillips UK); pap. write for info. (0-85668-307-8, Pub. by Aris & Phillips UK) David Brown.

Reid & Campion. Adult Hydrotherapy. 1990. 42.95 (0-433-00088-0) Buttrwrth-Heinemann.

Reid & Mercer. Administrative Law & Practice. 3rd ed. 704p. Date not set. 137.00 (0-409-80933-0) Butterworth Legal Pubs.

***Reid & Wise.** DSM-IV Training Guide. 384p. 1995. 49.95 (0-87630-768-3) Brunner-Mazel.

Reid, jt. auth. see Connerton.

Reid, tr. see Neruda, Pablo.

Reid, ed. see Simms, W. G.

Reid, et al. Friendly Foreign Language Series, 8 bks., Set. (Illus.). (Orig.). (ENG & SPA.). 1992. pap. 42.00 (1-881791-01-7) In One EAR.

***Reid & Priest Staff.** Electric Power Purchasing Handbook. 2nd ed. 1994. pap. text ed. 59.95 (0-471-11268-2) Wiley.

Reid, A. H. Reid's Branson Instruction to Juries, 7 vols., Set. 3rd suppl. ed. 1966. 250.00 (0-672-84048-0) Michie Butterworth.

Reid, A. S., jt. auth. see Hazel, A. C.

Reid, Ace. Cowpokes Comin' Yore Way. 5th ed. (Illus.). 64p. (J). (gr. k up). 1985. reprint ed. pap. 5.95 (0-917207-05-X) Reid Ent.

— Cowpokes Cookbook & Cartoons. 12th ed. (Illus.). 64p. (J). (gr. 5 up). reprint ed. pap. 5.95 (0-917207-06-8) Reid Ent.

— Cowpokes Cow Country Cartoons. 14th ed. (Illus.). 56p. (J). (gr. 5 up). reprint ed. pap. 5.95 (0-917207-00-9) Reid Ent.

— Cowpokes Home Remedies. 7th ed. (Illus.). 56p. (J). (gr. k-5). reprint ed. pap. 5.95 (0-917207-07-6) Reid Ent.

— Cowpokes Ole Jake. (Illus.). 64p. 1987. pap. 5.95 (0-917207-11-4) Reid Ent.

— Cowpokes Rarin' to Go. 2nd ed. (Illus.). 74p. (J). (gr. 5 up). reprint ed. pap. 5.95 (0-917207-09-2) Reid Ent.

— Cowpokes Ride Again. 4th ed. (Illus.). 64p. (J). (gr. k up). 1985. reprint ed. pap. 5.95 (0-917207-08-4) Reid Ent.

— Cowpokes Tales & Cartoons. 2nd ed. (Illus.). 64p. (J). (gr. 5 up). reprint ed. pap. 5.95 (0-917207-10-6) Reid Ent.

— Cowpokes Wanted. 12th ed. (Illus.). 62p. (J). (gr. 5 up). reprint ed. pap. 5.95 (0-917207-02-5) Reid Ent.

— Draggin' S Ranch Cowpokes. 14th ed. (Illus.). 65p. (J). (gr. 5 up). reprint ed. pap. 5.95 (0-917207-04-1) Reid Ent.

— More Cowpokes. 14th ed. (Illus.). 60p. (J). (gr. 5 up). reprint ed. pap. 5.95 (0-917207-01-7) Reid Ent.

— On the Hunt. (Illus.). (Orig.). 1993. pap. 6.95 (1-879894-02-5) Laffing Cow.

Reid, Aileen. Beardsley. 112p. 1994. 14.98 (0-8317-6114-8) Smithmark.

— Theatre Posters. 1994. 14.98 (0-8317-8752-X) Smithmark.

Reid, Alan. The Regality of Kirriemuir. (Illus.). 1987. 75.00 (0-317-89978-3, Pub. by W Culross & Son Ltd UK) St Mut.

Reid, Alastair. An Alastair Reid Reader: Selected Prose & Poetry. LC 94-20521. (Bread Loaf Series of Contemporary Writers). 256p. 1994. text ed. 40.00 (0-87451-692-7); pap. 16.95 (0-87451-693-5) U Pr of New Eng.

— Weathering: Poems & Translations. LC 87-30048. 144p. 1988. pap. 8.95 (0-8203-0990-7) U of Ga Pr.

— Whereabouts: Notes on Being a Foreigner. 1990. reprint ed. pap. 10.00 (1-877727-10-5) White Pine.

Reid, Alastair, tr. see Neruda, Pablo.

Reid, Alastair, jt. auth. see Neruda, Pablo.

Reid, Alastair, tr. see Neruda, Pablo & Reid, Alastair.

Reid, Alastair, tr. see Pacheco, Jose E.

Reid, Alastair, tr. see Padilla, Heberto.

Reid, Alastair J., jt. ed. see Biagini, Eugenio F.

Reid, Andrew B., jt. auth. see Sexton, Michael J.

Reid, Ann C., ed. Population Change, Natural Resources & Regionalism. (Breaking New Ground Ser.: No. 1). 104p. 1986. pap. 15.00 (0-938549-00-6) Grey Towers Pr.

Reid, Annette. The Toll of Victory. LC 79-144169. (Short Story Index Reprint Ser.). 1977. reprint ed. 19.95 (0-8369-3784-8) Ayer.

Reid, Anthony. The Indonesian National Revolution 1945-1950. LC 86-22768. (Studies in Contemporary Southeast Asia). (Illus.). 205p. 1986. reprint ed. text ed. 59.75 (0-313-25376-5, REIN, Greenwood Pr) Greenwood.

— Southeast Asia in the Age of Commerce, 1450-1680, Vol. 1: The Lands Below the Winds. 291p. (C). 1990. reprint ed. pap. 15.00 (0-300-04750-9) Yale U Pr.

— Southeast Asia in the Age of Commerce, 1450-1680, Vol. 2: Expansion & Crisis. (Illus.). 392p. 1993. 35.00 (0-300-05412-2) Yale U Pr.

Reid, Anthony, ed. Southeast Asia in the Early Modern Era: Trade, Power, & Belief. LC 92-54969. (Asia East by South Ser.). (Illus.). 286p. 1993. 42.50 (0-8014-2848-3); pap. 15.95 (0-8014-8093-0) Cornell U Pr.

Reid, Anthony & Akira, Oki, eds. The Japanese Experience in Indonesia: Selected Memoirs of 1942-1945. LC 82-90736. (Monographs in International Studies, Southeast Asia Ser.: No. 72). (Illus.). 450p. 1985. pap. text ed. 20.00 (0-89680-132-2, Ohio U Ctr Intl) Ohio U Pr.

Reid, Anthony, jt. ed. see Li Tana.

Reid, Arch & Kaiser, C. H. Creekside to Gourmet Cooking: Ozark Hills to Texas Society. (Illus.). (Orig.). 1986. pap. 8.95 (0-9616178-0-2) K & R Pub.

Reid, Art. Fishing Southern Illinois. LC 86-3717. (Shawnee Bks.). (Illus.). 160p. (Orig.). 1986. 19.95 (0-8093-1294-8); pap. 14.95 (0-8093-1295-6) S Ill U Pr.

Reid, B., jt. auth. see Coppleson, M.

Reid, B. C. A Casebook on Patents. (Waterlow Practitioner's Library). (Illus.). 388p. 1988. pap. 60.00 (0-08-033087-8, Pergamon Pr) Elsevier.

— Confidentiality & the Law. (Waterlow Practitioner's Library). 224p. 1986. 49.00 (0-08-039236-9, Pergamon Pr) Elsevier.

Reid, B. L. Necessary Lives: Biographical Reflections. 176p. 1990. 22.95 (0-8262-0736-7) U of Mo Pr.

Reid, Barbara. Two by Two. LC 92-9013. (Illus.). 32p. (J). (gr. k-3). 1993. 14.95 (0-590-45869-8) Scholastic Inc.

Reid, Barbara V., jt. ed. see Whitehead, Tony L.

Reid, Benedict. A Spirit Loose in the World: The Extraordinary Journey of a Beloved Benedictine Abbot in Search of Man's Place in the World & His Relationship with His Creator. LC 93-61087. 320p. (Orig.). 1993. pap. 17.95 (1-879560-20-8) Harbor Hse West.

Reid, Benjamin F. Glory to the Spirit. 1991. per. 4.95 (0-87162-512-1, D3800) Warner Pr.

Reid, Bernard J. Overland to California with the Pioneer Line: The Gold Rush Diary of Bernard J. Reid. Gordon, Mary M., ed. LC 82-62450. (Illus.). 264p. 1983. 32.50 (0-8047-1192-5) Stanford U Pr.

— Overland to California with the Pioneer Line: The Gold Rush Diary of Bernard J. Reid. Gordon, Mary M., ed. (Illus.). 272p. 1990. reprint ed. pap. 14.95 (0-252-01424-3) U of Ill Pr.

Reid, Bernice D., ed. Tapestry, Vol. I: A Multicultural Volume. 200p. 1992. pap. 12.00 (0-9636974-0-4) Lamar HS.

Reid, Bernice D., et al, eds. Tapestry, Vol. II: A Multicultural Volume. 2nd ed. (Illus.). 253p. 1993. pap. 15.00 (0-9636974-1-2) Lamar HS.

Reid, Beryl, jt. auth. see Morris, Desmond.

Reid, Bethany. The Coyotes & My Mom. 48p. (Orig.). 1989. pap. 4.00 (0-944920-03-9) Bellowing Ark Pr.

Reid, Betsy, et al. Organizing a Conference on National Security. 1986. spiral bd. 7.50 (0-937115-00-2) Comm Natl Security.

Reid, Bill & Bringhurst, Robert. The Raven Steals the Light. (Illus.). 94p. 1988. pap. 18.95 (0-295-96667-X) U of Wash Pr.

— The Raven Steals the Light. limited ed. LC 84-47978. (Illus.). 94p. 1984. 200.00 (0-295-96194-5) U of Wash Pr.

Reid, Bill G. Five for the Land & Its People. (Illus.). 154p. 1989. 12.00 (0-911042-37-7) N Dak Inst.

Reid, Brian H. J. F. C. Fuller: Military Thinker. LC 87-9819. 297p. 1990. text ed. 19.95 (0-312-04208-6) St Martin.

Reid, Brian H. & White, John, eds. American Studies: Essays in Honour of Marcus Cunliffe. 320p. 1991. text ed. 65.00 (0-312-05305-3) St Martin.

Reid, Brian H., jt. ed. see Rous, W. E.

Reid, C. Courant: In Goettingen & New York. LC 76-17062. (Illus.). 1976. 49.00 (0-387-90194-9) Spr-Verlag.

— Hilbert-Courant. (Illus.). 610p. 1986. pap. 43.00 (0-387-96256-5) Spr-Verlag.

Reid, C. & Dyer, R. Allen. A Review of the Southern African Species of Cyrtanthus. Beauchamp, R. Mitchel, ed. (Illus.). 68p. (Orig.). 1984. pap. 12.00 (0-930653-00-9) Intl Bulb Soc.

Reid, C. E. Chemical Thermodynamics. 1990. text ed. write for info. (0-07-051769-X); write for info. (0-318-67328-2) McGraw.

Reid, C. N. Deformation Geometry for Material Scientists. LC 73-1716. 220p. 1974. 94.00 (0-08-017237-7, Pub. by Pergamon Repr UK) Franklin.

Reid, C. W. Reading Keyboard Music, 3 vols. Miner, Martha et al, eds. 1988. teacher ed 3.00 (0-9620268-4-0) Demibach Eds.

— Reading Keyboard Music, 3 vols. rev. ed. Miner, Martha et al, eds. 1988. 2.00 (0-9620268-5-9); 9.95 (0-9620268-6-7); 9.95 (0-9620268-7-5) Demibach Eds.

 An Asterisk (*) at the beginning of an entry indicates that the title is appearing in BIP for the first time.

— Reading Keyboard Music, 3 vols., Set. rev. ed. Miner, Martha et al, eds. 120p. 1988. pap. 18.00 (*0-9620268-3-2*) Demibach Eds.
— Reading Keyboard Music, 3 vols., Vol. I. rev. ed. Miner, Martha et al, eds. 44p. 1988. pap. 6.95 (*0-9620268-0-8*) Demibach Eds.
— Reading Keyboard Music, 3 vols., Vol. II. rev. ed. Miner, Martha et al, eds. 36p. 1988. pap. 6.95 (*0-9620268-1-6*) Demibach Eds.
— Reading Keyboard Music, 3 vols., Vol. III. rev. ed. Miner, Martha et al, eds. 40p. 1988. pap. 6.95 (*0-9620268-2-4*) Demibach Eds.
Reid-Campion, Margaret. Hydrotherapy in Paediatrics. 2nd ed. (Illus.). 256p. 1991. pap. 32.50 (*0-7506-0061-6*) Buttrwrth-Heinemann.
Reid, Carlton. Adventure Mountain Biking: Touring, Sport & Expeditions. (Illus.). 160p. 1991. 34.95 (*1-85223-388-5*, Pub. by Crowood Pr UK) Trafalgar.
Reid, Carol, jt. auth. see Cochran, Belinda.
Reid, Charles. Flower Painting in Watercolor. (Illus.). 144p. 1986. 29.95 (*0-8230-1849-0*, Watsn-Guptill) Watsn-Guptill.
— The Natural Way to Paint. LC 94-28590. (Illus.). 144p. 1994. 29.95 (*0-8230-3158-6*) Watsn-Guptill.
— Painting by Design: Getting to the Essence of Good Picture-Making. (Illus.). 144p. 1991. 29.95 (*0-8230-3587-5*, Watsn-Guptill) Watsn-Guptill.
— Painting What You Want to See. (Illus.). 144p. 1987. pap. 18.95 (*0-8230-3879-3*, Watsn-Guptill) Watsn-Guptill.
— Portrait Painting in Watercolor. (Illus.). 160p. 1989. 27.50 (*0-8230-4192-1*, Watsn-Guptill) Watsn-Guptill.
— Portraits & Figures in Watercolor. (Artist's Painting Library). (Illus.). 80p. 1984. pap. 8.95 (*0-8230-4096-8*, Watsn-Guptill) Watsn-Guptill.
— Pulling Your Paintings Together. (Illus.). 160p. 1991. pap. 18.95 (*0-8230-4448-3*, Watsn-Guptill) Watsn-Guptill.
Reid, Charles F. Education in the Territories & Outlying Possessions of the United States. LC 70-177186. (Columbia University. Teachers College. Contributions to Education Ser.: No. 825). reprint ed. 37.50 (*0-404-55825-9*) AMS Pr.
Reid, Charles F., III. Guide to Residential Financing. 3rd ed. Mascari, Claude J. et al, eds. LC 84-61252. 286p. 1984. 34.95 (*0-9603790-3-7*) PaineWebber Mortgage.
Reid, Charles R. Environment & Learning: The Prior Issues. LC 75-36526. 1977. 33.50 (*0-8386-1711-5*) Fairleigh Dickinson.
Reid, Charlotte. Poems for All Occasions: Feelings of Life. 32p. 1993. pap. 5.95 (*0-8059-3340-9*) Dorrance.
***Reid, Charlotte B.** Tiki: Spirit Unbroken. LC 94-90588. (Illus.). 144p. (Orig.). 1995. pap. 11.95 (*0-9643061-3-1*) Egret Press.
Reid, Christian. The Land of the Sun: Vistas Mexicanas. 1976. lib. bdg. 69.95 (*0-8490-0483-7*) Gordon Pr.
Reid, Christina. The Belle of the Belfast City & Did You Hear the One about the Irishman. (Methuen New Theatrescripts Ser.). 89p. (Orig.). (C). 1989. pap. 9.95 (*0-413-61480-8*, A0374, Pub. by Methuen UK) Heinemann.
Reid, Christine. How to Use Microsoft Excel, Ver. 4, Macintosh. Wolf, Charles R., ed. 95p. (Orig.). pap. text ed. 125.00 (*1-56562-014-3*) OneOnOne Comp Trng.
— How to Use Microsoft Word, Ver. 2.0, for Windows. Hargrave, Sally, ed. 98p. (Orig.). 1992. pap. text ed. 125.00 (*1-56562-011-9*) OneOnOne Comp Trng.
— How to Use Microsoft Word, Ver. 5.x, Macintosh: Macintosh Version 5.x. Young, Natalie B., ed. 99p. (Orig.). 1992. pap. text ed. 125.00 (*1-56562-005-4*) OneOnOne Comp Trng.
— How to Use OS-2 Ver. 2.x. Wolf, Charles R., ed. 95p. (Orig.). 1993. pap. text ed. 195.00 (*1-56562-031-3*) OneOnOne Comp Trng.
Reid, Christine, ed. see Hargrave, Sally.
Reid, Christine, ed. see Jonas, Jacqueline.
Reid, Christine, ed. see Manthei & Assoc. Staff.
Reid, Christine, ed. see Paulson, Deborah.
Reid, Christine, ed. see Wolf, Charles R.
Reid, Christine, ed. see Wolf, Charles.
Reid, Christine, ed. see Wolff, Charles R.
Reid, Christopher. Edmund Burke & the Practice of Political Writing. LC 85-22261. 256p. 1986. text ed. 35.00 (*0-312-23696-4*) St Martin.
— In the Echoey Tunnel. 96p. (Orig.). 1992. pap. 9.95 (*0-571-16254-1*) Faber & Faber.
Reid, Christopher E. & Passin, Thomas B. Signal Processing in C. 352p. 1992. disk 77.95 (*0-471-56955-0*) Wiley.
Reid, Christopher E., et al. Signal Processing in C. 352p. 1991. pap. text ed. 44.95 (*0-471-52713-0*) Wiley.
Reid, Christopher T. A Band in the Face: A Collection of Song-Poems. 1992. 8.95 (*0-533-09553-0*) Vantage.
Reid, Clara, et al. Seven Tutula Writers. (Illus.). 82p. (Orig.). 1989. 5.00 (*0-930773-15-2*) Black Heron Pr.
Reid, Clyde. Celebrate the Temporary. LC 73-160643. 1974. pap. 8.95 (*0-06-066816-4*, RD81) Harper SF.
Reid, Colin W. Open Secret. LC 86-63639. (Illus.). 92p. 1987. pap. 12.95 (*0-86140-240-5*, Pub. by Colin Smythe Ltd UK) Dufour.
Reid Connell, Donna. S. T. A. G. E. S. Primary. 1989. 16.50 (*0-88047-158-1*, 8911) DOK Pubs.
Reid, Constance. From Zero to Infinity. 4th ed. LC 92-60161. 200p. 1992. pap. 22.00 (*0-88385-505-4*) Math Assn.
— Jerzy Neyman-From Life. (Illus.). 320p. 1982. 48.00 (*0-387-90747-5*) Spr-Verlag.
— The Search for E. T. Bell: Also Known As John Taine. LC 93-78369. (MAA Spectrum Ser.). (Illus.). 384p. 1993. 38.00 (*0-88385-508-9*) Math Assn.
Reid, Cornelius L. Bel Canto: Principles & Practices. LC 76-368704. 1950. reprint ed. pap. 6.95 (*0-915282-01-7*) J Patelson Mus.
— A Dictionary of Vocal Terminology: An Analysis. LC 81-86074. xxi, 478p. 1983. 39.95 (*0-915282-07-0*) J Patelson Mus.
— The Free Voice: A Guide to Natural Singing. LC 65-18533. 1965. reprint ed. pap. 6.95 (*0-915282-02-X*) J Patelson Mus.
— Voice: Psyche & Soma. LC 74-30987. (Orig.). 1975. pap. 6.95 (*0-915282-00-3*) J Patelson Mus.
Reid, D. Kim, et al. A Cognitive Approach to Learning Disabilities. 2nd ed. LC 90-19787. 495p. 1991. text ed. 39.00 (*0-89079-421-9*, 1941) PRO-ED.
Reid, D. M., jt. ed. see Pharis, R. P.
Reid, Daniel. The Complete Book of Chinese Health & Healing. LC 93-26702. (Illus.). 464p. (Orig.). 1994. 27.50 (*0-87773-929-3*) Shambhala Pubns.
— The Complete Book of Chinese Health & Healing: Guarding the Three Treasures. LC 93-26702. 496p. 1994. pap. text ed. 17.00 (*1-57062-071-7*) Shambhala Pubns.
— Handbook - Healing Herbs. Date not set. pap. 12.00 (*1-57062-094-6*) Shambhala Pubns.
— A Handbook of Chinese Healing Herbs. 1995. pap. 15.00 (*1-57062-093-8*) Shambhala Pubns.
Reid, Daniel, jt. auth. see Longman, Tremper, III.

Reid, Daniel G., et al, eds. Concise Dictionary of Christianity in America. abr. ed. 350p. 1995. pap. 16.99 (*0-8308-1446-9*) InterVarsity. Now thousands of facts related to the 500-year history of Christianity in America are right at your fingertips. BASED ON THE CRITICALLY ACCLAIMED DICTIONARY OF CHRISTIANITY IN AMERICA, THIS CONCISE DICTIONARY INCLUDES HUNDREDS OF BRIEF, UP-TO-DATE & INFORMATIVE ENTRIES on denominations & traditions; missionaries & evangelists; beliefs & practices; colleges & seminaries; women & ethnic groups; theologians, educators & writers; lay & denominational leaders; mission societies & social welfare organizations; & historical events, movements & struggles. Praise for the DICTIONARY OF CHRISTIANITY IN AMERICA: "The single most important volume on religion in the U.S. during 1990... Warmly, wholeheartedly, & enthusiastically recommended."--ADRIS NEWSLETTER. Editors include DANIEL G. REID, reference book editor at InterVarsity Press; ROBERT D. LINDER, professor of history at Kansas State University; BRUCE L. SHELLEY, professor of church history at Denver Seminary; & HARRY S. STOUT, professor of American religious history at Yale University. The work was condensed by freelance editor CRAIG A. NOLL. To order contact: Baker & Taylor, Riverside, Spring Arbor, Ingram or write InterVarsity Press, P.O. Box 1400 Downers Grove, IL 60515. Phone: 800-843-7225, FAX: 708-887-2520.** ***Publisher Provided Annotation.

Reid, Daniel G., ed. see Stout, Harry S., et al.
Reid, Daniel P. Chinese Herbal Medicine. LC 86-17814. (Illus.). 180p. 1987. reprint ed. pap. 25.00 (*0-87773-398-8*) Shambhala Pubns.
— The Tao of Health, Sex, & Longevity: A Modern Practical Guide to the Ancient Way. 1989. pap. 14.00 (*0-671-64811-X*, Fireside) S&S Trade.
Reid, David. The Humanism of Milton's Paradise Lost. 224p. (C). 1993. text ed. 50.00 (*0-7486-0401-4*, Pub. by Edinburgh U Pr UK) Col U Pr.
— New Wine: The Cultural Shaping of Japanese Christianity. LC 91-7732. (Nanzan Studies in Asian Religions: Vol. 2). (Illus.). 250p. (C). 1991. pap. text ed. 20.00 (*0-89581-932-5*, Asian Human Pr) Jain Pub Co.
— Sustainable Development Introduction Guide. 1995. 20.00 (*1-85383-241-3*, Pub. by Erthscan Pubns UK) Island Pr.
Reid, David, ed. Sex, Death, & God in L. A. LC 93-38872. 1994. pap. 13.00 (*0-520-08640-6*) U CA Pr.
Reid, David & Jerald, John. The (Second) Best of Everything. 1987. 14.95 (*0-15-179950-4*, Harvest Bks); pap. 6.95 (*0-685-19152-4*, Harvest Bks) HarBrace.
Reid, David & Jerald, Jonathan. Pure Silver: The Second Best of Everything. 320p. 1988. pap. 10.95 (*0-15-679960-X*) HarBrace.
Reid, David A. The Sales Presentation Manual: Role Playing for Sales Effectiveness. Burvikovs, ed. 231p. (C). 1992. pap. text ed. 23.75 (*0-314-92681-X*) West Pub.
Reid, David C. Sports Injury Assessment & Rehabilitation. (Illus.). 1269p. 1992. text ed. 134.00 (*0-443-08662-1*) Churchill.
Reid, David P. What Are They Saying about the Prophets? LC 80-80869. (What Are They Saying about...Ser.). 112p. (Orig.). 1980. pap. 3.95 (*0-8091-2304-5*) Paulist Pr.
Reid, David T., ed. see Jacobs, Paul F.
Reid, Dee, ed. see Good, E. Perry.
Reid, Dennis. Edwin H. Holgate. No. 4. write for info. (*0-318-59858-2*, Pub. by Natl Gallery CN) U Ch Pr.
— How to Catch Salmon. (Illus.). 200p. (Orig.). 1995. pap. 12.95 (*1-55143-030-4*) Orca Bk Pubs.
***Reid, Dennis H., et al.** Staff Management in Human Services: Behavioral Research & Application. (Illus.). 248p. 1989. pap. 34.95 (*0-398-06343-5*) C C Thomas.
— Staff Management in Human Services: Behavioral Research & Application. (Illus.). 248p. (C). 1989. text ed. 59.95x (*0-398-05547-5*) C C Thomas.
Reid, Derek A. A Monograph of the Stipitate Steroid Fungi. (Illus.). 1965. pap. 96.00 (*3-7682-5418-6*) Lubrecht & Cramer.
Reid, Desmond A. Dana Meets the Cow Who Lost Its Moo. 32p. 1985. 5.95 (*0-912444-29-0*) DARE Bks.
Reid, Don. Yosemite Climbs: Big Walls. (Illus.). 200p. 1993. pap. 18.00 (*0-934641-54-4*) Chockstone Pr.
— Yosemite Climbs: Free Climbs. (Illus.). 420p. (Orig.). 1994. pap. 25.00 (*0-934641-59-5*) Chockstone Pr.
— Yosemite Select. (Illus.). 120p. 1994. pap. 13.95 (*0-934641-41-2*) Chockstone Pr.
***Reid, Don & Falkenstein, Chris.** Rock Climbs of Toulumne Meadows. 3rd ed. (Illus.). 192p. 1994. pap. 18.00 (*0-934641-47-1*) Chockstone Pr.
Reid, Donald. The Miners of Decazeville: A Genealogy of Deindustrialization. (Illus.). 336p. 1985. 37.00 (*0-674-57634-9*) HUP.
— Paris Sewers & Sewermen: Realities & Representations. LC 90-40617. (Illus.). 235p. 1991. 45.00 (*0-674-65462-5*, REIPAR) HUP.
— Paris Sewers & Sewermen: Realities & Representations. (Illus.). 235p. (C). 1993. pap. 15.95 (*0-674-65463-3*) HUP.
Reid, Donald M. Cairo University & the Making of Modern Egypt. (Cambridge Middle East Library: No. 23). (Illus.). 320p. (C). 1990. 64.95 (*0-521-36641-0*) Cambridge U Pr.
— Lawyers & Politics in the Arab World, 1880-1960. LC 80-71053. (Studies in Middle Eastern History: No. 5). 435p. (C). 1981. 40.00 (*0-88297-028-3*) Bibliotheca.
— The Odyssey of Farah Antun: A Syrian Christian's Quest for Secularism. LC 74-80598. (Studies in Middle Eastern History: No. 2). 1975. 25.00 (*0-88297-009-7*) Bibliotheca.
Reid, Dorothy E. Coach into Pumpkin. LC 71-144727. (Yale Series of Younger Poets: No. 20). reprint ed. 18.00 (*0-404-53820-7*) AMS Pr.
Reid, Dottlee D. Whispers in the Wind. LC 91-68089. 65p. 1992. pap. 5.95 (*1-55523-502-6*) Winston-Derek.
Reid, E. Biochemical Approaches to Cancer. LC 65-24229. 1965. 88.00 (*0-08-011493-8*, Pub. by Pergamon Repr UK) Franklin.
Reid, E., et al. Complete Set of Readers & Workbooks: Short Vowels, Long Vowels, & Digraphs, 30 vols., Set. (Start Reading Ser.: Sets A,B,C). 440p. (J). (ps-3). 1986. pap. text ed. 49.95 (*1-56422-045-1*) Start Reading.
— Digraph Readers, 5 vols., Set. (Start Reading Ser.: Set C). 40p. (J). (ps-3). 1986. pap. text ed. 9.95 (*1-56422-038-9*) Start Reading.
— Digraph Readers & Workbooks, 10 vols., Set. (Start Reading Ser.: Set C). 144p. (J). (ps-3). 1986. pap. text ed. 18.95 (*1-56422-044-3*); pap. text ed. 269.95 (*1-56422-048-6*) Start Reading.
— Digraph Workbooks, 5 vols., Set. (Start Reading Ser.: Set C). 104p. (J). (ps-3). 1986. pap. text ed. 9.95 (*1-56422-041-9*) Start Reading.
— Long Vowel Readers, 5 vols., Set. (Start Reading Ser.: Set B). 40p. (J). (ps-3). 1986. pap. text ed. 9.95 (*1-56422-037-0*) Start Reading.
— Long Vowel Readers & Workbooks, 10 vols., Set. (Start Reading Ser.: Set B). 164p. (J). (ps-3). 1986. pap. text ed. 18.95 (*1-56422-043-5*); pap. text ed. 269.95 (*1-56422-047-8*) Start Reading.
— Long Vowel Workbooks, 5 vols., Set. (Start Reading Ser.: Set B). 124p. (J). (ps-3). 1986. pap. text ed. 9.95 (*1-56422-040-0*) Start Reading.
— Mastery Workbook for Ann: Short "a" Sound. (Start Reading Ser.: No. A1). 12p. (J). (ps-3). 1986. student ed, pap. 1.99 (*1-56422-015-X*) Start Reading.
— Mastery Workbook for Get Set: Short "e" Sound. (Start Reading Ser.: No. A5). 16p. (J). (ps-3). 1986. student ed, pap. 1.99 (*1-56422-019-2*) Start Reading.
— Mastery Workbook for the Blue Boat: Long "o" Sound. (Start Reading Ser.: No. B2). 28p. (J). (ps-3). 1986. student ed, pap. 1.99 (*1-56422-023-0*) Start Reading.
— Mastery Workbook for the Brown Mule: Long "u" Sound. (Start Reading Ser.: No. B5). 16p. (J). (ps-3). 1986. student ed, pap. 1.99 (*1-56422-024-9*) Start Reading.
— Mastery Workbook for the Chimp: Ch Sound. (Start Reading Ser.: No. C3). 20p. (J). (ps-3). 1986. student ed, pap. 1.99 (*1-56422-027-3*) Start Reading.
— Mastery Workbook for the Green Jeep: Long "e" Sound. (Start Reading Ser.: No. B3). 28p. (J). (ps-3). 1986. student ed, pap. 1.99 (*1-56422-021-4*) Start Reading.
— Mastery Workbook for the Queen: Qu Sound. (Start Reading Ser.: No. C4). 20p. (J). (ps-3). 1986. student ed, pap. 1.99 (*1-56422-028-1*) Start Reading.
— Mastery Workbook for the Red Plane: Long "a" Sound. (Start Reading Ser.: No. B1). 32p. (J). (ps-3). 1986. student ed, pap. 1.99 (*1-56422-020-6*) Start Reading.
— Mastery Workbook for the Shark: SH Sound. (Start Reading Ser.: No. C2). 20p. (J). (ps-3). 1986. student ed, pap. 1.99 (*1-56422-026-5*) Start Reading.
— Mastery Workbook for the Thing: Th Sound. (Start Reading Ser.: No. C5). 20p. (J). (ps-3). 1986. student ed, pap. 1.99 (*1-56422-029-X*) Start Reading.
— Mastery Workbook for the Whale: Wh Sound. (Start Reading Ser.: No. C1). 24p. (J). (ps-3). 1986. student ed, pap. 1.99 (*1-56422-025-7*) Start Reading.
— Mastery Workbook for the White Bike: Long "i" Sound. (Start Reading Ser.: No. B4). 20p. (J). (ps-3). 1986. student ed, pap. 1.99 (*1-56422-022-2*) Start Reading.
— Mastery Workbook for Tip: Short "i" Sound. (Start Reading Ser.: No. A2). 20p. 1986. student ed, pap. 1.99 (*1-56422-017-6*) Start Reading.
— Mastery Workbook for Top Dog: Short "o" Sound. (Start Reading Ser.: No. A3). 24p. (J). (ps-3). 1986. student ed, pap. 1.99 (*1-56422-016-8*) Start Reading.
— Mastery Workbook for up & Up: Short "u" Sound. (Start Reading Ser.: No. A4). 20p. (J). (ps-3). 1986. student ed, pap. 1.99 (*1-56422-018-4*) Start Reading.
— Mastery Worksheets. (Start Reading Ser.: Set A). 72p. (J). (ps-3). 1989. 39.95 (*1-56422-032-X*) Start Reading.
— Mastery Worksheets. (Start Reading Ser.: Set B). 86p. (J). (ps-3). 1989. 39.95 (*1-56422-033-8*) Start Reading.
— Mastery Worksheets. (Start Reading Ser.: Set C). 73p. (J). (ps-3). 1989. 39.95 (*1-56422-034-6*) Start Reading.
— Short Vowel, Long Vowel, Digraph Readers & Workbooks, 450 vols., Set. (Start Reading Ser.: Sets A, B,C). 6600p. (J). (ps-3). 1986. pap. text ed. 649.95 (*1-56422-049-4*) Start Reading.
— Short Vowel Readers, 5 vols., Set. (Start Reading Ser.: Set A). 40p. (J). (ps-3). 1986. pap. text ed. 9.95 (*1-56422-036-2*) Start Reading.
— Short Vowel Readers & Workbooks, 10 vols., Set. (Start Reading Ser.: Set A). 132p. (J). (ps-3). 1986. pap. text ed. 18.95 (*1-56422-042-7*); pap. text ed. 269.95 (*1-56422-046-X*) Start Reading.
— Short Vowel Workbooks, 5 vols., Set. (Start Reading Ser.: Set A). 92p. (J). (ps-3). 1986. pap. text ed. 9.95 (*1-56422-039-7*) Start Reading.
— The Start Reading Series: Instructor's Manual. 36p. 1986. teacher ed 11.95 (*1-56422-030-3*) Start Reading.
— Start Reading with Ann: Short "A" Sound. (Start Reading Ser.: No. A1). 8p. (J). (ps-3). 1986. pap. text ed. 1.99 (*1-56422-000-1*) Start Reading.
— Start Reading with Get Set: Short "e" Sound. (Start Reading Ser.: No. A5). 8p. (J). (ps-3). 1986. pap. text ed. 1.99 (*1-56422-004-4*) Start Reading.
— Start Reading with Red Plane: Long "a" Sound. (Start Reading Ser.: No. B1). 8p. (J). (ps-3). 1986. pap. text ed. 1.99 (*1-56422-005-2*) Start Reading.
— Start Reading with the Blue Boat: Long "o" Sound. (Start Reading Ser.: No. B2). 8p. (J). (ps-3). 1986. pap. text ed. 1.99 (*1-56422-006-0*) Start Reading.
— Start Reading with the Brown Mule: Long "u" Sound. (Start Reading Ser.: No. B5). 8p. (J). (ps-3). 1986. pap. text ed. 1.99 (*1-56422-009-5*) Start Reading.
— Start Reading with the Chimp: Ch Sound. (Start Reading Ser.: No. C3). 8p. (J). (ps-3). 1986. pap. text ed. 1.99 (*1-56422-012-5*) Start Reading.
— Start Reading with the Green Jeep: Long "e" Sound. (Start Reading Ser.: No. B3). 8p. (J). (ps-3). 1986. pap. text ed. 1.99 (*1-56422-007-9*) Start Reading.
— Start Reading with the Queen: Qu Sound. (Start Reading Ser.: No. C4). 8p. (J). (ps-3). 1986. pap. text ed. 1.99 (*1-56422-013-3*) Start Reading.
— Start Reading with the Shark: Sh Sound. (Start Reading Ser.: No. C2). 8p. 1986. pap. text ed. 1.99 (*1-56422-011-7*) Start Reading.
— Start Reading with the Thing: Th Sound. (Start Reading Ser.: No. C5). 8p. (J). (ps-3). 1986. pap. text ed. 1.99 (*1-56422-010-9*) Start Reading.
— Start Reading with the Whale: Wh Sound. (Start Reading Ser.: No. C1). 8p. (J). (ps-3). 1986. pap. text ed. 1.99 (*1-56422-014-1*) Start Reading.
— Start Reading with the White Bike: Long "i" Sound. (Start Reading Ser.: No. B4). 8p. (J). (ps-3). 1986. pap. text ed. 1.99 (*1-56422-008-7*) Start Reading.
— Start Reading with Tip: Short "i" Sound. (Start Reading Ser.: No. A2). 8p. (J). (ps-3). 1986. pap. text ed. 1.99 (*1-56422-001-X*) Start Reading.
— Start Reading with Top Dog: Short "o" Sound. (Start Reading Ser.: No. A3). 8p. (J). (ps-3). 1986. pap. text ed. 1.99 (*1-56422-002-8*) Start Reading.
— Start Reading with up & Up: Short "u" Sound. (Start Reading Ser.: No. A4). 8p. (J). (ps-3). 1986. pap. text ed. 1.99 (*1-56422-003-6*) Start Reading.
Reid, E., et al, eds. Bioanalysis of Drugs & Metabolites: Especially Anti-Inflammatory & Cardiovascular. LC 88-22412. (Methodological Surveys in Biochemistry & Analysis Ser.: Vol. 18). (Illus.). 430p. 1988. 110.00 (*0-306-42996-9*, Plenum Pr) Plenum.
— Cells, Membranes, & Disease: Including Renal. LC 87-22060. (Methodological Surveys in Biochemistry & Analysis Ser.: Vol. 17). (Illus.). 506p. 1987. 125.00 (*0-306-42678-1*, Plenum Pr) Plenum.
***Reid, E. Lee.** Marketing Made Easy! Basics for Home Builders. (Illus.). (Orig.). Date not set. pap. write for info. (*0-86718-403-5*) Home Builder.
Reid, Ebenezer E. Chemistry Through the Language Barrier: How to Scan Chemical Articles in Foreign Languages with Emphasis on Russian & Japanese. LC 75-112360. 150p. reprint ed. pap. 42.80 (*0-317-09870-5*, 2003893) Bks Demand.
Reid, Ed. Green Felt Jungle. 19.95 (*0-8488-1457-6*) Amereon Ltd.
Reid, Ed & Demaris, Ovid. The Green Felt Jungle. 256p. 1991. reprint ed. lib. bdg. 26.95 (*0-89966-783-X*) Buccaneer Bks.
Reid, Elizabeth. Bilingual ABC: Spanish & English. (Illus.). 64p. (ENG & SPA.). (J). (gr. k-3). 1995. pap. text ed. 2.50 (*0-9627080-6-2*) In One EAR.
— Moms & Dads - Mamis y Papis: Bilingual Coloring Book. (Illus.). 64p. (ENG & SPA.). (J). (gr. 1-4). 1992. pap. 1.95 (*0-9627080-5-4*) In One EAR.
— Spanish Lingo for the Savvy Gringo: A Do-it-Yourself Guide to Learning the Language. 2nd rev. ed. LC 89-85923. (Illus.). 192p. 1994. reprint ed. per. 12.95 (*0-9627080-2-X*) In One EAR.

R

Reid, Elizabeth, ed. & tr. Bilingual Cooking: La Cocina Bilingue. (Illus.). 224p. (Orig.). (ENG & SPA.). 1992. pap. 12.95 (*0-9627080-3-8*) In One EAR.
— Bilingual Recipes: Recetas Bilingues. (Illus.). 64p. (Orig.). (ENG & SPA.). 1992. pap. 2.95 (*0-9627080-4-6*) In One EAR.
Reid, Elmer T. Practical Guide for Royal Arch Chapter Officers & Companions. rev. ed. (Illus.). x, 92p. 1980. reprint ed. pap. 6.95 (*0-88053-015-4*, M-063) Macoy Pub.
Reid, Eric, et al, eds. Bioactive Analytes, Including CNS Drugs, Peptides, & Enantiomers. LC 86-21204. (Methodological Surveys in Biochemistry & Analysis Ser.: Vol. 16). 436p. 1986. 105.00 (*0-306-42400-2*, Plenum Pr) Plenum.
— Biofluid & Tissue Analysis for Drugs, Including Hypolipidaemics. 434p. 1994. 180.00 (*0-85186-644-1*, R6644) CRC Pr.
Reid, Escott. On Duty: A Canadian at the Making of the United Nations, 1945 to 1946. LC 83-12021. 203p. reprint ed. pap. 57.90 (*0-7837-1342-8*, 2041490) Bks Demand.
— Radical Mandarin: The Memoirs of Escott Reid. 35.00 (*0-8020-5811-6*) U of Toronto Pr.
— Radical Mandarin: The Memoirs of Escott Reid. 432p. 1992. pap. 19.95 (*0-8020-7365-4*) U of Toronto Pr.
Reid, Esmond. Understanding Buildings: A Multidisciplinary Approach. (Illus.). 256p. 1988. pap. 18.50 (*0-262-68054-8*) MIT Pr.
Reid, Euan & Reich, Hans H., eds. Breaking the Boundaries: A Comparative Evaluation of the Pilot Projects Supported by the EC from 1986-89 on the Education of Children of Migrant Workers. 270p. 1992. 79.00 (*1-85359-134-3*, Pub. by Multilingual Matters UK); pap. 29.95 (*1-85359-133-5*, Pub. by Multilingual Matters UK) Taylor & Francis.
Reid, F. H. & Goldie, W., eds. Gold Plating Technology. 630p. 1974. 133.00 (*0-318-12538-2*) Am Electro Surface.
Reid, F. Lee. Do-It-Yourself Marketing. Tennyson, Dorris, ed. 96p. 1994. write for info. (*0-318-72823-0*) Home Builder.
— Marketing Made Easy. Tennyson, Dorris, ed. 96p. 1994. write for info. (*0-86718-428-0*) Home Builder.
Reid, Forrest. Illustrators of the Eighteen Sixties. LC 74-12539. 352p. 1975. reprint ed. pap. 6.95 (*0-486-23121-6*) Dover.
— Illustrators of the Eighteen Sixties: An Illustrated Survey of the Work of 58 British Artists. 12.00 (*0-8446-5237-7*) Peter Smith.
— Pender among the Residents. 1988. reprint ed. lib. bdg. 59.00 (*0-7812-0344-9*) Rprt Serv.
— Pender among the Residents. LC 70-131812. 1971. reprint ed. 39.00 (*0-403-00699-6*) Scholarly.
— Pirates of the Spring. LC 76-145255. 1971. reprint ed. 24.00 (*0-403-01170-1*) Scholarly.
— Private Road. LC 75-41225. reprint ed. 37.50 (*0-404-14587-6*) AMS Pr.
— W. B. Yeats: A Critical Study. LC 72-1317. (Studies in Irish Literature: No. 16). 1972. reprint ed. lib. bdg. 75.00 (*0-8383-1434-1*) M S G Haskell Hse.
— Walter De La Mare: A Critical Study. LC 73-131813. 1970. reprint ed. 39.00 (*0-403-00700-3*) Scholarly.
— Young Tom & the Retreat. large type ed. 420p. 1995. lib. bdg. 22.00 (*0-939495-85-6*) North Bks.
Reid, Francis. Designing for the Theatre. 111p. 1989. pap. 13.95 (*0-87830-045-7*, A3765, Theatre Arts Bks) Routledge Chapman & Hall.
— Discovering Stage Lighting. LC 92-43267. (Illus.). 224p. 1993. pap. 29.95 (*0-240-51345-2*, Focal) Buttrwrth-Heinemann.
— Sing a Song of Mother Goose. (J). 1991. pap. 3.95 (*0-590-41699-5*) Scholastic Inc.
— Sing a Song of Mother Goose. (J). 1993. pap. 19.95 (*0-590-71380-9*) Scholastic Inc.
— Stage Lighting Handbook. LC 76-8319. (Illus.). 1976. pap. 13.95 (*0-87830-988-8*, Theatre Arts Bks) Routledge Chapman & Hall.
— Stage Lighting Handbook. 1987. pap. 10.45 (*0-87830-156-9*) Routledge Chapman & Hall.
— Stage Lighting Handbook. 4th ed. 1992. pap. 16.95 (*0-87830-013-9*, Theatre Arts Bks) Routledge Chapman & Hall.
— The Staging Handbook. (Illus.). 1978. 14.95 (*0-87830-160-7*, Theatre Arts Bks) Routledge Chapman & Hall.
Reid, Frank, III. Nehemiah Plan, No. 1. 140p. (Orig.). 1993. pap. 8.99 (*1-56043-766-9*) Destiny Image.
Reid, Freda M., ed. Torrey Pines State Reserve: A Scientific Reserve of the Department of Parks & Recreation, State of California. 3rd rev. ed. LC 91-65594. (Illus.). 108p. 1991. student ed. pap. 4.00 (*0-9629917-0-8*) Torrey Pines.
Reid, G., ed. Problems in Movement Control. (Advances in Psychology Ser.: No. 74). 384p. 1991. 128.75 (*0-444-88093-3*, North Holland) Elsevier.
Reid, G. Edward. It's Your Money, Isn't It? LC 93-12429. 1993. pap. 8.95 (*0-8280-0726-8*) Review & Herald.
Reid, G. Mcg. A Revision of African Species of Labeo: Pieces, Cyprinidae & a Redefinition of the Genus. (Theses Zoologicae Ser.: Vol. 6). (Illus.). 322p. 1985. lib. bdg. 143.00 (*3-7682-1413-3*) Koeltz Sci Bks.
Reid, G. S. & Forrest, M. A. Australia's Commonwealth Parliament, 1901-1988. 1988. 24.95 (*0-522-84383-2*) Intl Spec Bk.
Reid, G. S. & Oliver, M. R. The Premiers of Western Australia 1890-1982. (Illus.). viii, 122p. 1983. 16.95 (*0-85564-214-9*, Pub. by Univ of West Austr Pr AT) Intl Spec Bk.
Reid, G. T., jt. ed. see Robinson, D. W.
Reid, Garnett. Defeating Doubt. 1982. pap. 1.95 (*0-89265-076-1*) Randall Hse.
— How to Grow in Grace. 1982. pap. 1.95 (*0-89265-077-X*) Randall Hse.
— How to Know God's Will. 1982. pap. 1.95 (*0-89265-078-8*) Randall Hse.
— How to Know You're Saved. 1982. pap. 1.95 (*0-89265-075-3*) Randall Hse.
Reid, Gary. Linear System Fundamentals: Continuous, Discrete & Modern. (McGraw-Hill Series in Electrical Engineering). (Illus.). 512p. 1983. text ed. write for info. (*0-07-051808-4*) McGraw.
Reid, Gavin. The Kinked Demand Curve Analysis of Oligopoly. 113p. 1981. 15.00 (*0-85224-390-1*, Pub. by Edinburgh U Pr UK) Col U Pr.
Reid, Gavin C. Small Business Enterprise: An Economic Analysis. LC 92-37256. 368p. 1993. 65.00 (*0-415-05681-0*, B0708, Routledge NY) Routledge.
Reid, Gavin C. & Jacobsen, Lowell R. The Small Entrepreneurial Firm. (David Hume Papers). 100p. 1988. pap. text ed. 19.95 (*0-08-036577-9*, Pub. by Aberdeen U Pr) Macmillan.
Reid, Gavin C., et al. Profiles in Small Business: A Competitive Strategy Approach. LC 93-23855. 1994. write for info. (*0-415-09828-9*) Routledge.
Reid, George H. Primer of Towing. 2nd rev. ed. (Illus.). 256p. 1992. pap. text ed. 17.00 (*0-87033-430-1*) Cornell Maritime.
— Shiphandling with Tugs. LC 86-47712. (Illus.). 279p. 1986. text ed. 18.00x (*0-87033-354-2*) Cornell Maritime.
Reid, George K. Pond Life. Zim, Herbert S., ed. (Golden Guide Ser.). (Illus.). (J). (gr. 7 up). 1967. pap. write for info. (*0-307-24017-7*) Western Pub.
***Reid, Gerry.** ASK for Success! 21 Ways to Enhance Your Image & Maximize Your Potential. 304p. (Orig.). 1994. pap. 16.95 (*0-9643260-0-0*) E Thomas & Sons.
***Reid, Gord.** The Dinosaur Provincial Park: Land of Vanished Dinosaurs. (Illus.). 64p. 1995. lib. bdg. 33.00 (*0-8095-4832-1*) Borgo Pr.
Reid, Gordon. Head-Smashed-in-Buffalo Jump. (Illus.). 48p. (Orig.). pap. 10.95 (*0-317-05895-9*, Pub. by Boston Mills Pr CN) Genl Dist Srvs.
Reid, Graeme T., ed. Fringe Pattern Analysis. 266p. 1989. 53.00 (*0-8194-0199-4*, VOL. 1163) SPIE.
Reid, Grant W. From Concept to Form in Landscape Design. LC 92-22661. 1993. pap. 39.95 (*0-442-01247-0*) Van Nos Reinhold.
— Landscape Graphics. (Illus.). 216p. 1987. pap. 19.95 (*0-8230-7331-9*, Whitney Lib) Watsn-Guptill.
Reid-Green, Marcia, ed. see Matrau, Henry.
Reid, Greg. Teen Satanism: Redeeming the Devil's Children. 32p. (Orig.). 1990. pap. 10.00 (*1-877858-04-8*, TS-RDC) Amer Focus Pub.
— Treasures from the Master's Heart. 107p. (Orig.). 1991. pap. 10.00 (*1-877858-39-0*, TFTMH) Amer Focus Pub.
Reid, H. Extra South. (Illus.). 144p. 1986. pap. 21.95 (*0-911868-53-4*, C53) Carstens Pubns.
Reid, H. W., ed. The Management & Health of Farmed Deer. (Current Topics in Veterinary Medicine & Animal Science Ser.). (C). 1988. lib. bdg. 90.00 (*0-89838-408-7*) Kluwer Ac.
Reid, Hal J. No More Curb Service. 1992. 13.95 (*0-533-09122-5*) Vantage.
Reid, Harry. Dear Country: A Quest for England. (Illus.). 224p. 1992. 29.95 (*1-85158-374-2*, Pub. by Mnstream UK) Trafalgar.
Reid, Harvey, jt. auth. see Kuhn, Terry.
Reid, Henrietta. Dark Usurper. large type ed. 1990. 17.95 (*0-7451-9812-0*, C0306, Atlantic Lrg Print); pap. 10.95 (*0-7927-0260-3*, Atlantic Lrg Print) Chivers N Amer.
— New Boss at Birchfields. large type ed. 1991. 21.95 (*0-7089-2524-3*) Ulverscroft.
Reid, Howard & Croucher, Michael. The Way of the Warrior: The Paradox of the Martial Arts. (Illus.). 240p. 1991. 27.50 (*0-87951-433-7*) Overlook Pr.
— The Way of the Warrior: The Paradox of the Martial Arts. (Illus.). 240p. 1995. pap. 17.95 (*0-87951-606-2*) Overlook Pr.
Reid, Hugh B. Sheet Metal Layout Simplified, 3 vols., Vol. 1. 1981. 19.50 (*0-685-77694-8*) H B Reid.
— Sheet Metal Layout Simplified, 3 vols., Vol. 2. 1981. 19.50 (*0-685-41577-5*) H B Reid.
— Sheet Metal Layout Simplified, 3 vols., Vol. 3. 1981. 19.50 (*0-685-41578-3*) H B Reid.
Reid, Ian. Rhumbs. Kaplan, Peter, ed. LC 75-10586. 1975. 1.50 (*0-915176-07-6*) Pourboire.
Reid, Ian, ed. The Place of Genre in Learning: Current Debates. 124p. (C). 1987. 39.00 (*0-7300-0247-0*, Pub. by Deakin Univ AT) St Mut.
Reid, Ian W., jt. ed. see Bertholf, Robert J.
Reid, Inez S. Together Black Women. 2nd ed. LC 73-83156. 348p. 1974. reprint ed. 29.95 (*0-89388-114-7*); reprint ed. pap. 19.95 (*0-89388-115-5*) Okpaku Communications.
Reid, Ira D. Negro Immigrant: His Background, Characteristics & Social Adjustment, 1899-1937. LC 68-58615. (Columbia University. Studies in the Social Sciences: No. 449). reprint ed. 20.00 (*0-404-51449-9*) AMS Pr.
— Negro Immigrant: His Background, Characteristics & Social Adjustment, 1899-1937. LC 69-18771. (American Immigration Collection Ser., No. 1). 1975. reprint ed. 19.95 (*0-405-00537-7*) Ayer.
Reid, Isaiah. Grace & Spiritual Growth. 1989. pap. 4.99 (*0-88019-253-4*) Schmul Pub Co.
Reid, Ivan. The Sociology of School & Education. 320p. 1986. pap. 23.00 (*1-85396-183-3*, Pub. by P Chapman Pub UK) Taylor & Francis.
Reid, Ivan & Stratta, Drica, eds. Sex Differences in Britain. 2nd ed. (Illus.). 1989. text ed. 64.95 (*0-566-05595-3*, Pub. by Gower UK); pap. text ed. 21.95 (*0-566-05804-9*, Pub. by Gower UK) Ashgate Pub Co.
Reid, J., jt. auth. see Katz, L.
Reid, J. B. A Complete Word & Phrase Concordance to the Poems & Songs of Robert Burns, Incorporating a Glossary of Scotch Words. (BCL1-PR English Literature Ser.). 568p. 1992. reprint ed. lib. bdg. 99.00 (*0-7812-7468-0*) Rprt Serv.
Reid, J. D. & Yang, K. H., eds. Crashworthiness & Occupant Protection in Transportation Systems. LC 89-46297. 319p. 1993. pap. 70.00 (*0-7918-1022-4*) ASME.
Reid, J. Gavin & Thompson, John M. Exercise Prescription for Fitness. (Illus.). 352p. (C). 1985. pap. text ed. write for info. (*0-13-294638-6*) P-H.
Reid, J. Gavin, jt. auth. see Hay, James G.
Reid, J. H. The Origins of the British Labour Party. LC 55-11709. 272p. reprint ed. pap. 77.60 (*0-317-39673-0*, 2055899) Bks Demand.
— Writing without Taboos: The New East German Literature. 268p. 1990. 54.95 (*0-85496-020-1*) Berg Pubs.
Reid, J. H., ed. see Boll, Heinrich.
Reid, J. Jefferson, ed. see Haury, Emil W.
Reid, J. K., jt. ed. see Duff, I. S.
Reid, J. L. Total Geostrophic South Pacific: Flow Patterns, Tracers & Transports. 1985. pap. 50.00 (*0-08-034011-3*, Pub. by PPL UK) Elsevier.
Reid, J. L., et al. Lecture Notes on Clinical Pharmacology. 4th ed. (Lecture Notes Ser.). (Illus.). 320p. 1992. pap. 32.95 (*0-632-03404-1*) Blackwell Sci.
Reid, J. M., et al. Fluid Gasification of Oil. (Research Bulletin Ser.: No. 16). iv, 48p. 1953. 5.00 (*0-317-56834-5*) Inst Gas Tech.
— Natural Gas Supplements by Cyclic-Regenerative Hydrogasification of Oils. (Research Bulletin Ser.: No. 28). iv, 78p. 1960. 5.00 (*0-685-18410-2*) Inst Gas Tech.
Reid, J. Norman & Dubin, Elliott. Federal Funds to Rural Areas: Fair Share? Right Mix? (New Alliances for Rural America Ser.). (Orig.). 1988. pap. text ed. 6.00 (*1-55877-019-4*) Natl Governor.
Reid, J. Norman, jt. ed. see Sears, David W.
Reid, J. S., ed. see Cicero.
Reid, J. S., et al. Rubber Dam in Clinical Practice. (Illus.). 1991. pap. text ed. 32.00 (*1-85097-011-4*) Quint Pub Co.
Reid, James. Edward Seago: The Landscape Art. 264p. 1992. 90.00 (*0-85667-402-8*) Sothebys Pubns.
— Memoirs of the Westminster Divines. 768p. 29.95 (*0-85151-357-3*) Banner of Truth.
***Reid, James & Apesteguia, Raul.** The Textile Art of Peru. De Lavalle, Jose A. & Gonzalez, Jose A., eds. Hare, Isabel, tr. (Illus.). 373p. (Orig.). 1993. text ed. 65.00 (*0-9647468-0-8*) Industrial Textil.
Reid, James D. The Telegraph in America: Its Founders, Promoters & Noted Men. LC 74-7493. (Telecommunications Ser.). (Illus.). 926p. 1974. reprint ed. 69.95 (*0-405-06056-4*) Ayer.
Reid, James H. Heinrich Boll: A German for His Time. LC 87-15783. 245p. 1988. 49.95 (*0-85496-533-5*) Berg Pubs.
— Narration & Description in the French Realist Novel: The Temporality of Lying & Forgetting. LC 92-39126. (Cambridge Studies in French: No. 44). 240p. (C). 1993. 59.95 (*0-521-42092-X*) Cambridge U Pr.
Reid, James J., ed. Tribalism & Society in Islamic Iran 1500-1629. (Studies in Near Eastern Culture & Society Ser.: Vol. 4). 215p. 1983. pap. 23.00 (*0-89003-124-X*) Undena Pubns.
Reid, James M. & Silleck, Anne. Better Business Letters: A Programmed Book to Develop Skill in Writing. 3rd ed. LC 84-24457. 208p. 1985. pap. write for info. (*0-201-06350-6*) Addison-Wesley.
Reid, James S., ed. see Cicero, M. Tullius.
Reid, James W. Textile Masterpieces of Ancient Peru. (Illus.). 80p. 1987. pap. 10.95 (*0-486-25246-9*) Dover.
Reid, Jamie. Easy Money. 1987. 17.95 (*0-8027-0999-0*) Walker & Co.
— Home on the Range. 319p. 1995. 24.95 (*1-85158-563-X*, Pub. by Mnstream UK) Trafalgar.
Reid, Jamie & Savage, Jon. Up They Rise! The Unfinished Works of Jamie Reid. (Illus.). 144p. (Orig.). 1987. pap. 14.95 (*0-571-14762-3*) Faber & Faber.
Reid, Jan. Deerinwater. LC 85-7933. 224p. 1985. 15.95 (*0-87719-024-0*, Lone Star Bks) Gulf Pub.
— The Improbable Rise of Redneck Rock. LC 76-30434. (Quality Paperbacks Ser.). 1977. pap. 6.95 (*0-306-80065-9*) Da Capo.
— Vain Glory. 375p. 1986. 15.95 (*0-940672-37-5*) Shearer Pub.
Reid, Jan, ed. see Sansom, Andrew.
Reid, Jane D. A Guide to Classical Subjects in the Arts. LC 92-35374. 1993. 195.00 (*0-19-504998-5*) OUP.
Reid, Jeffrey. Cat-Dependent No More! (Illus.). 96p. (Orig.). 1992. mass mkt. 5.99 (*0-449-90668-X*, Columbine) Fawcett.
Reid, Jennings B. Jesus: God's Emptiness, God's Fullness: The Christology of St. Paul. LC 90-36837. 160p. 1990. pap. 7.95 (*0-8091-3165-X*) Paulist Pr.
Reid, Jepson. Reid Jepson's Devotional Dictionary. Steele, M. B., ed. 202p. (Orig.). 1993. pap. 6.95 (*0-939497-31-X*) Promise Pub.
Reid, Jesse W. History of the Fourth Regiment of South Carolina Volunteers. (Illus.). 143p. 1975. reprint ed. 17.50 (*0-89029-028-8*) Morningside Bkshop.
Reid, Jill, jt. auth. see Brown, Cynthia.
Reid, Jim. Newnes DOS Programmers Pocket Book. (Illus.). 350p. 1993. write for info. (*0-318-72449-9*) Buttrwrth-Heinemann.
Reid, Joan A. Rocky Mountain Law Institute: Annual Institute. (Rocky Mountain Mineral Law Foundation Ser.). Annual Proceedings. write for info. (*0-8205-1600-7*) Bender.
Reid, Joan A., jt. auth. see Rocky Mountain Mineral Law Staff.
Reid, Joanie. Life Line: A Journal for Parents Grieving a Miscarriage, Stillbirth or Other Early Infant Death. LC 93-86825. 100p. 1994. 15.95 (*1-878526-30-8*) Pineapple MI.
Reid, JoAnne, et al. Small Group Learning in the Classroom. 96p. 1990. pap. text ed. 12.50 (*0-435-08542-5*, 08542) Heinemann.
Reid, Jody, ed. see Black, Angela K.
Reid, John. The Best Little Boy in the World. 1986. mass mkt. 4.95 (*0-345-34361-1*) Ballantine.
— The Best Little Boy in the World. 256p. 1993. pap. 9.00 (*0-345-38176-9*, Ballantine Trade) Ballantine.
— Living with Teenagers: A Survival Manual for Adults. LC 81-70265. 268p. (Orig.). 1983. pap. 7.95 (*0-9607234-0-4*) Ampersand Pub.
— The Magnificent Society & the Democracy Amendments: How to Free Your Congressmen from the Control of the Special Interests. LC 80-85474. 220p. 1981. 11.95 (*0-939428-00-8*); pap. 8.95 (*0-939428-01-6*) Pony X Pr.
Reid, John & Eaton, John. The Life of Andrew Jackson. Owsley, Frank L., Jr., ed. LC 74-2567. (Southern Historical Publications: No. 19). 536p. reprint ed. 152.80 (*0-8357-9619-1*, 2013215) Bks Demand.
Reid, John, jt. auth. see Metcalf, Michael.
Reid, John C. Bird Life in Wington: Practical Parables for Young People. (Illus.). 142p. (J). (gr. 1-4). 1990. reprint ed. pap. 7.99 (*0-8028-4062-0*) Eerdmans.
— God's Promises & My Needs. 80p. (Orig.). 1986. pap. 2.50 (*0-914733-06-0*) Desert Min.
— Living Words of Wisdom & Encouragement. deluxe ed. Roe, Earl O., ed. LC 86-25978. 176p. 1987. ring bd. 14.99 (*0-8307-1200-3*, 5111674) Regal.
— My Commitment. 60p. (Orig.). 1991. pap. text ed. 2.00 (*0-914733-14-1*) Desert Min.
— Parables from Nature: Earthly Stories with Heavenly Meanings. 2nd ed. (Illus.). 96p. (J). (gr. k-4). 1991. pap. 7.99 (*0-8028-4052-3*) Eerdmans.
Reid, John C., jt. ed. see Buckner, Phillip A.
Reid, John G. The Manchu Abdication & the Powers 1908-1912, an Episode in Pre-War Diplomacy. LC 73-896. (China Studies: from Confucius to Mao Ser.). (Illus.). xiii, 497p. 1973. reprint ed. 30.00 (*0-88355-090-3*) Hyperion Conn.
— Mount Allison University: A History, to 1963, Vol. 1. LC 84-175462. (Illus.). 441p. 1984. reprint ed. pap. 125.70 (*0-8357-3663-6*, 2036390) Bks Demand.
— Mount Allison University: A History, to 1963, Vol. 2: 1914-1963. LC 84-175462. (Illus.). 544p. 1984. reprint ed. Vol. 2, 1914-1963, 544p. pap. 155.10 (*0-8357-3664-4*, 2036390) Bks Demand.
Reid, John G., jt. ed. see Axelrod, Paul.
Reid, John K. The Authority of Scripture: A Study of the Reformation & Post-Reformation Understanding of the Bible. LC 79-8716. 286p. 1981. reprint ed. text ed. 59.75 (*0-313-22191-X*, REAS, Greenwood Pr) Greenwood.
Reid, John P. Chief Justice: The Judicial World of Charles Doe. LC 67-12102. (Illus.). 499p. 1967. 40.00 (*0-674-11400-0*) HUP.
— The Concept of Liberty in the Age of the American Revolution. LC 87-14971. viii, 224p. 1988. 25.95 (*0-226-70896-9*) U Ch Pr.
— The Concept of Representation in the Age of the American Revolution. LC 89-32139. 248p. 1989. 32.00 (*0-226-70898-5*) U Ch Pr.
— Constitutional History of the American Revolution. LC 94-39045. 176p. 1995. text ed. 29.95 (*0-299-14660-X*) U of Wis Pr.
— Constitutional History of the American Revolution. abr. ed. LC 94-39045. 176p. 1995. pap. text ed. 14.95 (*0-299-14664-2*) U of Wis Pr.
— Constitutional History of the American Revolution, Vol. 2: The Authority to Tax. LC 87-8256. 384p. (C). 1987. text ed. 27.50 (*0-299-11290-X*) U of Wis Pr.
— Constitutional History of the American Revolution, Vol. 3: The Authority to Legislate. LC 91-50326. 508p. (C). 1991. 35.00 (*0-299-13070-3*) U of Wis Pr.
— Constitutional History of the American Revolution, Vol. 4: The Authority of Law. LC 86-40058. 288p. (C). 1993. 35.00 (*0-299-13980-8*) U of Wis Pr.
— In a Defiant Stance: The Conditions of Law in Massachusetts Bay, the Irish Comparison, & the Coming of the American Revolution. LC 76-42453. 1977. 30.00 (*0-271-01240-4*) Pa St U Pr.
— In Defiance of the Law: The Standing-Army Controversy, the Two Constitutions, & the Coming of the American Revolution. LC 80-14002. (Studies in Legal History). 295p. reprint ed. pap. 84.10 (*0-7837-5236-9*, 2044970) Bks Demand.
— Law for the Elephant: Property & Social Behavior on the Overland Trail. LC 79-26989. 447p. reprint ed. pap. 127.40 (*0-7837-5287-3*, 2045041) Bks Demand.
Reid, John P., ed. The Briefs of the American Revolution. (School of Law Series in Anglo-American Legal History: Linden Studies in American Constitutional History). 176p. 1981. 55.00x (*0-8147-7384-2*) NYU Pr.
Reid, John P., jt. auth. see Nelson, William E.
Reid, John Philip. Constitutional History of the American Revolution, Vol. 1: The Authority of Rights. LC 86-40058. 1987. text ed. 27.50 (*0-299-10870-8*) U of Wis Pr.
***Reid, John Z.** Born to Win: A Poetic Biography of African-Americans. LC 95-68267. 64p. (YA). (gr. 6-12). 1995. 17.95 (*1-887214-01-1*); pap. 12.95 (*1-887214-02-X*) Caribbean TX.
Reid, Joseph, ed. Research in Labor Economics: New Approaches to Labor Unions, Suppl. 2. 350p. 1983. 73.25 (*0-89232-265-9*) Jai Pr.
Reid, Joseph L., ed. Antarctic Oceanology One. LC 78-151300. (Antarctic Research Ser.: Vol. 15). (Illus.). 343p. 1971. 28.50 (*0-87590-115-8*) Am Geophysical.
Reid, Joseph L., jt. ed. see Capurro, Luis R.

An Asterisk (*) at the beginning of an entry indicates that the title is appearing in BIP for the first time.

***Reid, Joy.** Learning Styles in the ESL EFL. 240p. 1995. pap. 20.95 (*0-8384-6158-1*) Heinle & Heinle.
— Process of Paragraph Writing. 2nd ed. 272p. 1994. pap. text ed. 19.25 (*0-13-101205-3*) P-H.
Reid, Joy M. Basic Writing. (Illus.). 208p. (C). 1987. pap. text ed. 17.50 (*0-13-069261-1*) P-H.
— The Process of Composition. (Illus.). 224p. (C). 1982. pap. text ed. write for info. (*0-13-723015-X*) P-H.
— Teaching ESL Writing. 352p. 1993. pap. text ed. 24.95 (*0-13-888215-0*) P-H.
Reid, Joy M. & Lindstrom, M. The Process of Paragraph Writing. (Illus.). 200p. (C). 1985. pap. text ed. 14.00 (*0-13-723529-1*) P-H.
Reid, Joyce M., ed. Classic Scottish Short Stories. 352p. 1990. pap. 12.95 (*0-19-282686-7*) OUP.
Reid, K. Relationship Between Numerical Computation & Programming Language. 378p. 1982. 43.75 (*0-444-86377-X*, North Holland) Elsevier.
Reid, K. B., jt. auth. see Law, S. K.
Reid, K. B., jt. auth. see Law, Susan K.
Reid, K. F. Properties & Reactions of Bonds in Organic Molecules. LC 79-365421. 570p. reprint ed. pap. 162.50 (*0-317-09882-9*, 2004551) Bks Demand.
Reid, Kathryn G. Preventing Child Sexual Abuse: A Curriculum for Children Ages Five Through Eight. (Illus.). 136p. (Orig.). 1994. pap. 11.95 (*0-8298-1016-1*) Pilgrim OH.
Reid, Kathryn G. & Fortune, Marie M. Preventing Child Sexual Abuse: A Curriculum for Children Ages 9-12. LC 89-33084. (Illus.). 96p. (Orig.). (YA). 1989. pap. 9.95 (*0-8298-0810-8*) Pilgrim OH.
Reid, Kaye, ed. see Sommers, Maxine S.
Reid, Kaye, ed. see Sommers, Maxine.
Reid, Ken. Disaffection from School. 230p. 1988. pap. text ed. 15.95 (*0-423-51550-0*) Routledge Chapman & Hall.
Reid, Ken, jt. ed. see Solomon, Goody.
Reid, Kenneth E. From Character Building to Social Treatment: The History of the Use of Groups in Social Work. LC 79-6567. xviii, 249p. 1981. text ed. 45.00 (*0-313-22016-6*, RCB/, Greenwood Pr) Greenwood.
***Reid, Kenneth G. & Gretton, George L.** An Introduction to the Scottish Law of Property. 1995. pap. text ed. write for info. (*0-406-10517-0*, UK) Butterworth Legal Pubs.
Reid, Kenneth S., tr. see Marias Aquilera, Julian.
Reid, Kevin, jt. auth. see Slaughter, Enos.
Reid, Kim. Teaching the Learning Disabled & Other Underachievers: A Cognitive-Developmental Approach. 612p. (C). 1988. text ed. 46.00 (*0-205-10522-X*, H05226) Allyn.
Reid, L. D., ed. Opioids, Bulimia, & Alcohol Abuse & Alcoholism. xi, 393p. 1990. 60.00 (*0-387-97242-0*) Spr-Verlag.
Reid, Larry, jt. auth. see White, Reggie.
Reid, Laura. Adventures in Creating Earrings. Smith, Monte, ed. LC 90-82647. (Illus.). 96p. 1990. per. 9.95 (*0-943604-28-1*) Eagles View.
— New Adventures in Beading Earrings. Smith, Monte, ed. (Illus.). 64p. (Orig.). 1989. per., pap. 8.95 (*0-943604-18-4*) Eagles View.
Reid, Lawrence A. An Ivatan Syntax. LC 68-64243. (Oceanic Linguistics Special Publication Ser.: No. 2). 168p. (Orig.). reprint ed. pap. 47.90 (*0-8357-8679-X*, 2056836) Bks Demand.
Reid, Legh W. The Elements of the Theory of Algebraic Numbers. LC 10-23524. 474p. reprint ed. pap. 135.10 (*0-317-08884-X*, 2020743) Bks Demand.
***Reid, Leonard.** Crimson Blue. 1995. 23.95 (*0-8062-5081-X*) Carlton.
Reid, Leonard N., ed. Proceedings of the Conference of the American Academy of Advertising, 1992. 1992. pap. 25.00 (*0-931030-15-3*) Am Acad Advert.
Reid, Lola M., jt. ed. see Zern, Mark A.
Reid, Loren. Finally It's Friday: School & Work in Mid-America, 1921-1933. LC 80-27453. (Illus.). 304p. 1981. 29.00 (*0-8262-0330-2*) U of Mo Pr.
— Hurry Home Wednesday: Growing Up in a Small Missouri Town, 1905-1921. LC 77-25401. (Illus.). 304p. 1978. text ed. 29.00 (*0-8262-0247-0*) U of Mo Pr.
— Professor on the Loose. LC 92-96967. (Illus.). vi, 334p. (Orig.). 1992. pap. 13.95 (*0-9634518-0-4*) Mortgage Ln.
— Speaking Well. 4th ed. (Illus.). 448p. (C). 1982. text ed. write for info. (*0-07-051784-3*) McGraw.
— Speech Teacher: A Random Narrative. LC 90-63139. (Illus.). 109p. (C). 1990. pap. 5.00 (*0-944811-05-1*) Speech Commun Assn.
Reid, Lorene. Thinking Skills Resource Book. 94p. 1990. pap. 12.95 (*0-936386-58-4*) Creative Learning.
Reid, Loretta G. Control & Communication in Programs. LC 82-6893. (Computer Science: Systems Programming Ser.: No. 13). 175p. reprint ed. pap. 49.90 (*0-685-20830-3*, 2070046) Bks Demand.
Reid, Lori. Chinese Horoscopes. rev. ed. (Illus.). 96p. 1994. pap. 6.95 (*0-7063-7222-0*, Pub. by Ward Lock UK) Sterling.
— Elements of Handreading. LC 94-37917. (Elements of Ser.). 1995. pap. text ed. 9.95 (*1-85230-576-2*) Element MA.
— Lovers' Horoscopes. rev. ed. (Family Matters Ser.). (Illus.). 96p. 1995. pap. 6.95 (*0-7063-7325-1*, Pub. by Ward Lock UK) Sterling.
— Palmistry. rev. ed. (Family Matters Ser.). (Illus.). 96p. (Orig.). 1995. pap. 6.95 (*0-7063-7323-5*, Pub. by Ward Lock UK) Sterling.
Reid, Louis A. A Study in Aesthetics. LC 70-114546. 415p. 1973. reprint ed. text ed. 65.00 (*0-8371-4794-8*, RESA, Greenwood Pr) Greenwood.
— Ways of Knowledge & Experience. 287p. 1961. 69.50 (*0-614-00166-8*) Elliots Bks.
Reid, Lydia J., jt. ed. see Backstrom, T. E.
Reid, Lynn. Fairy Rebel. braille ed. 146p. 1990. vinyl bd. 11.68 (*1-56956-228-8*, BR7890) W A T Braille.
Reid, Lynne M., jt. auth. see Legg, Merle A.
Reid, M. Undergraduate Algebraic Geometry. (London Mathematical Society Student Texts Ser.: No. 11). (Illus.). 120p. 1989. 12.95 (*0-318-32477-6*); pap. 18.95 (*0-521-35662-8*) Cambridge U Pr.
Reid, M., et al, eds. Mathematical Papers in Honor of Yuri Ivanovich Manin. 650p. (C). 1987. lib. bdg. 128.00 (*0-8223-0798-7*) Duke.
Reid, M. J. & Moran, J. M., eds. The Impact of VLBI on Astrophysics & Geophysics. (C). 1988. lib. bdg. 165.50 (*90-277-2704-X*) Kluwer Ac.
Reid, Malcolm. Prehistoric Houses in Britain. 1989. pap. 25.00 (*0-7478-0218-1*, Pub. by Shire UK) St Mut.
— The Shouting Signpainters: A Literary & Political Account of Quebec Revolutionary Nationalism. LC 75-158922. 320p. 1972. pap. 3.95 (*0-85345-283-0*) Monthly Rev.
Reid, Margaret, jt. auth. see Kenney, John.
Reid, Margaret, et al. Training Interventions. 3rd ed. 456p. (C). 1992. pap. text ed. 95.00 (*0-85292-480-1*, Pub. by IPM Hse UK) St Mut.
Reid, Margaret A. The Polemics of Poetry: The Harlem Renaissance & Sixties in Retrospect. LC 94-11768. (Studies in African & African-American Culture: Vol. 8). 1994. write for info. (*0-8204-2482-X*) P Lang Pubs.
***Reid, Margaret A. & Barrington, Harry.** Training Interventions: Managing Employee Development. 456p. (C). 1994. pap. 36.00x (*0-85292-566-2*, Pub. by IPM Hse UK) St Mut.
Reid, Margaret G. Consumers & the Market. 3rd ed. LC 75-39270. (Getting & Spending: the Consumer's Dilemma Ser.). (Illus.). 1976. reprint ed. 51.95 (*0-405-08042-5*) Ayer.
— Food for People. LC 75-26312. (World Food Supply Ser.). (Illus.). 1976. reprint ed. 54.95 (*0-405-07790-4*) Ayer.
Reid, Margarette S. The Button Box. LC 89-38566. (Illus.). 24p. (J). (ps-2). 1990. 13.99 (*0-525-44590-0*, DCB) Dutton Child Bks.
— The Button Box. (Illus.). 24p. (J). (ps-2). 1995. pap. 4.99 (*0-14-055495-5*, Puff Unicorn) Puffin Bks.
— La Caja de los Botones. LC 89-38566. (Illus.). 24p. (SPA.). (J). (ps-2). 1995. 14.99 (*0-525-45445-4*, DCB) Dutton Child Bks.
— La Caja de los Botones. (Illus.). 24p. (SPA.). (J). (ps-2). 1995. pap. 4.99 (*0-14-055642-7*, Puff Unicorn) Puffin Bks.
Reid, Margo, ed. Law & Accounting: Nineteenth-Century American Legal Cases. (Foundations in Accounting Ser.: No. 15). 295p. 1989. reprint ed. 10.00 (*0-8240-6130-6*) Garland.
Reid, Marion. A Plea for Woman. LC 88-61923. 98p. 1988. reprint ed. pap. 12.95 (*0-948275-56-1*) Dufour.
Reid, Mark. Namib. 1992. 15.95 (*0-533-09397-X*) Vantage.
Reid, Mark A. Redefining Black Film. 1993. 30.00 (*0-520-07901-9*); pap. 15.00 (*0-520-07902-7*) U CA Pr.
Reid, Martine. Indians of the Northwest. (J). (gr. 1-9). 1992. pap. 3.95 (*0-88388-112-8*) Bellerophon Bks.
Reid, Martine, ed. Yale French Studies, 84: Boundaries: Writing & Drawing. 17.00 (*0-300-05836-5*) Yale U Pr.
Reid, Mary. Anytime Parties for Children. (Illus.). 80p. (J). (gr. 1-5). 1987. student ed. 5.99 (*0-87403-290-3*, 2802) Standard Pub.
— How Have I Grown? LC 93-44811. (Illus.). (J). 1993. write for info. (*0-590-49757-X*); write for info. (*0-590-72911-X*) Scholastic Inc.
— Topatopa & Dressed for Danger, 2 bks. in 1. (Citrus County Mystery Collections: No. 1). 7.95 (*1-55748-187-3*) Barbour & Co.
Reid, Mary C. Come to the Desert with Me. LC 91-71036. 32p. (J). 1991. pap. 4.99 (*0-8066-2552-X*, 9-2552) Augsburg Fortress.
— Come to the Island With Me. LC 92-73012. (Discover Bks.). 32p. (J). 1992. pap. 4.99 (*0-8066-2632-1*, 9-2632) Augsburg Fortress.
— Come to the Mountain With Me. LC 92-73011. (Discover Bks.). 32p. (J). 1992. pap. 4.99 (*0-8066-2631-3*, 9-2631) Augsburg Fortress.
— Come to the Ocean with Me. LC 91-71035. 32p. (J). 1991. pap. 4.99 (*0-8066-2551-1*) Augsburg Fortress.
Reid, Mehry M. Gourmet Cooking Persian Style. LC 89-91992. (Illus.). 192p. 1989. 30.00 (*0-685-27245-1*) Ceresville Pub Co.
— Persian Calligraphic Designs. (International Design Library). (Illus.). 48p. (Orig.). 1995. pap. 5.95 (*0-88045-130-0*) Stemmer Hse.
— Persian Carpet Designs. (International Design Library). (Illus.). 48p. 1982. pap. 5.95 (*0-88045-005-3*) Stemmer Hse.
— Persian Ceramic Designs. (International Design Library). (Illus.). 48p. (Orig.). 1983. pap. 5.95 (*0-88045-024-X*) Stemmer Hse.
— Persian Etching Designs. (International Design Library). (Illus.). 48p. 1985. pap. 5.95 (*0-88045-061-4*) Stemmer Hse.
— Persian Textile Designs. (International Design Library). (Illus.). 48p. (Orig.). 1984. pap. 5.95 (*0-88045-027-4*) Stemmer Hse.
— Snake's Marble. 1995. 21.95 (*0-533-11387-3*) Vantage.
Reid, Michaela. Ask Sir James. large type ed. 524p. 1989. 17.95 (*0-7089-1966-9*) Ulverscroft.
Reid, Michelle. Coercion to Love. (Presents Ser.). 1993. mass mkt. 2.99 (*0-373-11597-0*, 1-11597-1) Harlequin Bks.
— The Dark Side of Desire. (Presents Ser.). 1993. pap. 2.89 (*0-373-11533-4*, 1-11533-6) Harlequin Bks.
— House of Glass Presents Plus. (Presents Ser.). 1994. mass mkt. 2.99 (*0-373-11615-2*, 1-11615-1) Harlequin Bks.
— Lost in Love. (Presents Ser.). 1994. mass mkt. 2.99 (*0-373-11665-9*, 1-11665-6) Harlequin Bks.
— Lost in Love. large type ed. (Traditional Romance Ser.). 1994. 17.95 (*0-263-13779-1*, Pub. by Mills & Boon Ltd UK) Chivers N Amer.
— No Way to Begin. large type ed. 285p. 1991. reprint ed. lib. bdg. 18.95 (*0-263-12697-8*, Pub. by Mills & Boon UK) Thorndike Pr.
— Passion Becomes You. (Presents Ser.). 1995. mass mkt. 3.25 (*0-373-11752-3*, 1-11752-2) Harlequin Bks.
— Passionate Scandal. 1994. mass mkt. 2.99 (*0-373-11695-0*, 1-11695-3) Harlequin Bks.
— Slave to Love. 1995. mass mkt. 3.25 (*0-373-11776-0*) Harlequin Bks.
***Reid, Mick, illus.** A Treasury of Stories for Eight Year Olds. LC 94-30241. (J). 1995. pap. 5.95 (*1-85697-545-2*, Kingfisher LKC) LKC.
***Reid, Miles.** Undergraduate Commutative Algebra. (London Mathematical Society Student Texts Ser.: No. 29). (Illus.). 128p. (C). 1993. write for info. (*0-521-45255-4*); pap. write for info. (*0-521-45889-7*) Cambridge U Pr.
Reid, Miles, tr. see Shafarevich, Igor R.
Reid, Mont, jt. ed. see Koutlas, Theodore C.
Reid, Monty. Crawlspace: New & Selected Poems. 122p. (Orig.). 1993. pap. 14.95 (*0-88784-539-8*, Pub. by Hse of Anansi Pr CN) Genl Dist Srvs.
Reid, Muriel F. Speak the Thought: How to Read & Speak in Public, with Bible-Lesson Applications. 2nd exp. ed. 64p. 1984. 7.00 (*0-915878-05-4*) Joseph Pub Co.
Reid, Nancy, ed. see Duncan, Mike.
Reid, Norma. Research Methods & Statistics in Health Care. LC 92-28523. (Illus.). 224p. 1993. pap. 29.95 (*0-632-03466-1*) Blackwell Sci.
Reid, Norma, ed. Ultramicrotomy. (Practical Methods in Electron Microscopy Ser.: Vol. 3, Pt. 2). 353p. 1975. pap. 17.75 (*0-444-10667-7*, North Holland) Elsevier.
Reid, Norman, jt. ed. see Sears, David.
Reid, P. C. Bien Hecho en America. 1991. pap. text ed. 12.95 (*0-07-104044-7*) McGraw.
Reid, P. C., et al, eds. Protozoa & Their Role in Marine Processes. (NATO ASI Series G: Ecological Sciences: Vol. 25). x, 506p. 1991. 198.00 (*0-387-18565-8*) Spr-Verlag.
Reid, P. Carey. Swimming in the Starry River. 384p. 1994. 19.95 (*0-7868-6005-7*) Hyperion.
Reid, P. Nelson & Popple, Philip R., eds. The Moral Purposes of Social Work. (Social Welfare Ser.). 230p. (C). 1992. pap. text ed. 18.95 (*0-8304-1246-8*) Nelson-Hall.
Reid, P. R. The Colditz Story. (Classics of World War II Ser.). 278p. reprint ed. write for info. (*0-8094-8733-0*); reprint ed. lib. bdg. write for info. (*0-8094-8734-9*) Time-Life.
Reid, Patrick, ed. Readings in Western Religious Thought: The Ancient World. 304p. (Orig.). 1987. pap. 19.95 (*0-8091-2850-0*) Paulist Pr.
***Reid, Patrick V., ed.** Readings in Western Religious Thought II: The Middle Ages Through the Reformation. 400p. (Orig.). (C). 1995. pap. 24.95 (*0-8091-3533-7*) Paulist Pr.
Reid, Paul E. The Orator: Guy Vander Jagt on the Hustings. LC 85-149387. 250p. 1984. 14.95 (*0-89803-149-4*) Green Hill.
Reid, Peter C. Well Made in America: Lessons from Harley-Davidson on Being the Best. 224p. 1990. text ed. 21.50 (*0-07-026500-3*) McGraw.
— Well Made in America: Lessons from Harley-Davidson on Being the Best. 1991. pap. text ed. 14.95 (*0-07-051801-7*) McGraw.
Reid, Peter L. Tenth-Century Latinity: Rather of Verona. LC 80-54672. (Humana Civilitas Ser.: Vol. 6). xiii, 52p. 1981. pap. 22.25 (*0-89003-070-7*) Undena Pubns.
Reid, Peter L., tr. The Complete Works of Rather of Verona. (Medieval & Renaissance Texts & Studies: Vol. 76). 1991. 40.00 (*0-86698-087-3*, MR76) MRTS.
***Reid-Pharr, Robert.** Alvin Ailey. Duberman, Martin, ed. (Lives of Notable Gay Men & Lesbians Ser.). (Illus.). 168p. (YA). (gr. 9 up). 1995. pap. 9.95 (*0-7910-2886-0*) Chelsea Hse.
— Alvin Ailey. Duberman, Martin, ed. (Lives of Notable Gay Men & Lesbians Ser.). (Illus.). 168p. (YA). (gr. 9 up). 1995. lib. bdg. 19.95 (*0-7910-2314-1*) Chelsea Hse.
Reid, Philip D., et al, eds. Tissue Printing: Tools for the Study of Anatomy, Histochemistry, & Gene Expression. (Illus.). 188p. 1992. spiral bd. 24.95 (*0-12-585970-8*) Acad Pr.
Reid, Philip E. & Park, Carol M. Carbohydrate Histochemistry of Epithelial Glycoproteins. (Progress in Histochemistry & Cytochemistry Ser.: Vol. 21-4). 170p. 1990. 95.00 (*0-685-48103-4*); pap. 110.00 (*0-89574-323-X*) G F Verlag.
Reid, Proctor R., ed. see National Academy of Engineering, Committee on Engineering as an International Enterprise Staff.
Reid, R. Problems of Russian Romanticism. 1986. text ed. 56.95 (*0-566-05029-3*) Ashgate Pub Co.
Reid, R. A., ed. see Demosthenes.
Reid, R. A., jt. ed. see Oberst, B. B.
***Reid, R. Dan & Riegel, Carl D.** Purchasing Practices of Large Foodservice Firms. Ketchum, Carol, ed. 76p. (Orig.). (C). 1989. pap. text ed. 20.00 (*0-945968-02-7*) Ctr Advanced Purchasing.
Reid, R. Mark. Your Pain, Their Gain: How to Survive Health Care Fraud - a Patient's Guide. 112p. 1994. pap. 9.95 (*1-884441-44-0*) Tyler Pr.
Reid, Ralph, ed. Directory of Australian Directories. 2nd rev. ed. 256p. 1991. pap. 55.00 (*0-909532-80-X*) D W Thorpe.
Reid, Randy, jt. auth. see Kaysing, Bill.
Reid, Richard. The Georgian House & Its Details. 1989. 29.95 (*0-900873-93-0*, Pub. by Bishopsgte Pr UK) Intl Spec Bk.
Reid, Richard, ed. Elecktra: A Play by Ezra Pound. 110p. 1989. text ed. 22.95 (*0-691-06778-3*) Princeton U Pr.
Reid, Richard J. The Battle of Tippecanoe. LC 89-155804. (Illus.). 66p. 1988. reprint ed. pap. write for info. (*1-877713-00-7*) R J Reid.
— The Fight for Middle Creek. LC 91-93267. (Illus.). 52p. (Orig.). 1992. pap. write for info. (*1-877713-03-1*) R J Reid.
— Fourth Indiana Cavalry Regiment: A History. (Illus.). 244p. 1994. pap. 14.95 (*1-877713-06-6*) R J Reid.
— The Met at Perryville. 2nd ed. (Illus.). 81p. (Orig.). reprint ed. pap. 5.95 (*0-317-94067-8*) R J Reid.
— Stones River Ran Red. LC 89-189682. (Illus.). 83p. (Orig.). 1986. reprint ed. pap. write for info. (*1-877713-02-3*) R J Reid.
— They Met at Perryville. LC 89-184018. (Illus.). 80p. (Orig.). 1992. reprint ed. pap. 5.95 (*1-877713-01-5*) R J Reid.
Reid, Richard J., ed. The Army That Buell Built. LC 94-92107. 78p. (Orig.). 1994. pap. write for info. (*1-877713-05-8*) R J Reid.
***Reid, Rob.** Children's Jutebox: A Subject Guide to Musical Recordings & Programming Ideas for Songsters. LC 95-6163. 195p. (Orig.). 1995. pap. text ed. 25.00x (*0-8389-0650-8*) ALA.
Reid, Robert. Hospitality Marketing Management. 2nd ed. (Illus.). 384p. (C). 1989. text ed. 44.95 (*0-442-27848-9*) Van Nos Reinhold.
— Hospitality Marketing Management. 2nd ed. (Illus.). 384p. (C). 1989. 20.95 (*0-442-31915-0*) Van Nos Reinhold.
— Introduction to Hospital Management. (Hospitality, Travel & Tourism Ser.). 1992. text ed. write for info. (*0-442-00856-2*) Van Nos Reinhold.
— A Treasury of the Sierra Nevada. LC 82-62811. (Illus.). 256p. (Orig.). 1983. 19.95 (*0-89997-032-X*); pap. 15.95 (*0-89997-023-0*) Wilderness Pr.
— Year One: An Intimate Look Inside Harvard Business School. 336p. 1995. reprint ed. pap. 11.00 (*0-380-72559-2*) Avon.
— Year One: Starting Out at Harvard Business School. 1994. 23.00 (*0-688-12817-3*) Morrow.
Reid, Robert & Scott, Howard. Change from Within: People Make the Difference. (Illus.). 224p. 1995. 23.95 (*0-941893-04-9*) CEEPress Bks.
Reid, Robert C., jt. auth. see Modell, Michael.
Reid, Robert C., et al. The Properties of Gases & Liquids. 4th ed. (Illus.). 741p. 1987. text ed. 74.50 (*0-07-051799-1*) McGraw.
Reid, Robert D., jt. auth. see MacDougall, Curtis D.
Reid, Robert F., III. And Then There Was Now. LC 80-82920. (Illus.). (Orig.). 1980. pap. 4.25 (*0-9603490-5-7*) Noble Hse.
Reid, Robert G. Evolutionary Theory: The Unfinished Synthesis. 416p. (C). 1985. 39.95 (*0-8014-1831-3*) Cornell U Pr.
***Reid, Robert H. & Guerrero, Eileen.** Corazon Aquino & the Brushfire Revolution. (Illus.). 248p. (C). 1995. 29.95 (*0-8071-1980-6*) La State U Pr.
Reid, Robert L. Mountains of the Great Blue Dream. 240p. 1991. 21.95 (*0-86547-467-2*, North Pt Pr) FS&G.
— Picturing Texas: The FSA-OWI Photographers in Texas, 1935-1943. LC 94-21684. (Illus.). 224p. 1995. 49.95 (*0-87611-140-1*) Tex St Hist Assn.
Reid, Robert L., ed. & tr. Always a River: The Ohio River & the American Experience. LC 90-25293. (Illus.). 270p. 1991. 35.00 (*0-253-34958-3*) Ind U Pr.
Reid, Robert L., ed. Back Home Again: Indiana in the Farm Security Administration Photographs, 1935-1943. LC 86-46377. (Illus.). 158p. 1987. 28.95 (*0-253-31133-0*); pap. 18.95 (*0-253-21246-4*) Ind U Pr.
— Picturing Minnesota, 1936-1943: Photographs from the Farm Security Administration. LC 89-13104. (Illus.). 200p. (Orig.). 1989. 35.95 (*0-87351-247-2*); pap. 19.95 (*0-87351-248-0*) Minn Hist.
***Reid, Robert L. & Rogers, Thomas E.** A Good Neighbor: The First Fifty Years at Crane 1941-1991. (Illus.). 118p. (Orig.). 1991. pap. write for info. (*0-9640288-1-6*) Univ So IN.
Reid, Robert L. & Viskochil, Larry A., eds. Chicago & Downstate: Illinois As Seen by the Farm Security Administration Photographers, 1936-1943. LC 88-27873. (Visions of Illinois Ser.). (Illus.). 216p. 1989. 29.95 (*0-252-01635-1*); pap. 19.95 (*0-252-06078-4*) U of Ill Pr.
Reid, Robert L., ed. see Conference on Systems Simulation, Economic Analysis - Solar Heating & Cooling Operational Results Staff.
Reid, Robert L., ed. see Haley, Margaret A.
Reid, Robert S. The Red Corvette. 256p. 1992. 18.95 (*0-88184-803-4*) Carroll & Graf.
— The Red Corvette. 256p. 1993. pap. 4.50 (*0-88184-990-1*) Carroll & Graf.
Reid, Robert W. Science Experiments for the Primary Grades. 1962. pap. 5.99 (*0-8224-6300-8*) Fearon Teach Aids.
Reid, Roddey. Families in Jeopardy: Regulating the Social Body in France, 1750-1910. LC 93-16664. 384p. (C). 1993. 39.50 (*0-8047-2224-2*) Stanford U Pr.
Reid, Roger H., jt. auth. see Merill, David W.
Reid, Rolland R. & McMannis, William J. Precambrian Geology of North Snowy Block, Beartooth Mountains, Montana. LC 74-28529. (Geological Society of America, Special Paper Ser.: No. 157). 188p. reprint ed. pap. 53.60 (*0-317-28367-7*, 2025470) Bks Demand.
***Reid, Ronald F.** American Rhetorical Discourse. 2nd rev. ed. 841p. (C). 1995. pap. text ed. 25.95x (*0-88133-839-7*) Waveland Pr.
— Edward Everett: Unionist Orator. LC 89-27281. (Critical Studies, Speeches & Sources: No. 7). 304p. 1990. text ed. 55.00 (*0-313-26164-4*, REE/, Greenwood Pr) Greenwood.

R

An Asterisk (*) at the beginning of an entry indicates that the title is appearing in BIP for the first time.

Reid, Ronald F., ed. Three Centuries of American Rhetorical Discourse: An Anthology & a Review. 758p. (C). 1988. text ed. 33.95 (0-88133-313-1); pap. text ed. 23.95 (0-88133-310-7) Waveland Pr.

Reid, S. Discovery (Blu) (Famous Lives Ser.). (Illus.). 144p. (J). (gr. 4 up). 1994. pap. 14.95 (0-7460-1872-X, Usborne) EDC.

— Invention & Discovery. (Illustrated Dictionaries Ser.). (Illus.). 128p. (J). (gr. 6 up). 1987. lib. bdg. 16.96 (0-88110-231-8); pap. 10.95 (0-86020-956-3) EDC.

— Inventors. (Famous Lives Ser.). (Illus.). 48p. (J). (gr. 4 up). 1994. lib. bdg. 14.96 (0-88110-698-4, Usborne); pap. 7.95 (0-7460-0705-1, Usborne) EDC.

— Memory Skills. (Superskills Ser.). (Illus.). 48p. (YA). (gr. 6-10). 1988. lib. bdg. 12.96 (0-88110-305-5); pap. 5.95 (0-7460-0162-2) EDC.

— Space Facts. (Facts & Lists Ser.). (Illus.). 48p. (J). (gr. 3-7). 1987. lib. bdg. 12.96 (0-88110-240-7); pap. 5.95 (0-7460-0024-3) EDC.

Reid, S. & Fara, P. Scientists. (Famous Lives Ser.). (Illus.). 48p. (J). (gr. 4 up). 1993. lib. bdg. 14.96 (0-88110-587-2); pap. 7.95 (0-7460-1009-5) EDC.

Reid, S. R., ed. Metal Forming & Impact Mechanics. (Illus.). 360p. 1985. 152.00 (0-08-031679-4, Pub. by PPL UK) Franklin.

Reid, S. W., ed. see Brown, Charles B.

Reid, S. W., ed. see Conrad, Joseph.

Reid, Sally H. Close Call. 320p. 1994. mass mkt. 4.50 (0-8217-4627-8) Zebra.

— Undertow. 320p. 1992. mass mkt. 4.50 (0-8217-3962-X) Zebra.

Reid, Samuel C., Jr. Scouting Expeditions of McCulloch's Texas Rangers: Or, the Summer & Fall Campaign of the Army of the United States in Mexico 1846. LC 72-126252. (Select Bibliographies Reprint Ser.). 1977. 20.95 (0-8369-5479-3) Ayer.

Reid, Sarah, ed. see Hopkins, Jeanne.

Reid, Saralou L. Mommakitty's Surprise: "Skyler" LC 88-60613. (Illus.). (J). (gr. k-3). write for info. (0-9620420-0-5); lib. bdg. write for info. (0-9620420-1-3); pap. write for info. (0-9620420-3-X) Surge Pub.

***Reid, Sheila.** Art Without Rejection. (Illus.). 242p. (Orig.). 1993. 39.00 (0-9646268-1-0); pap. 18.00 (0-9646268-0-2) Rush Eds.

Reid, Shirley W., illus. Roots & Blossoms: An Anthology of 13 African American Plays African & Caribbean Plays with a Critical Introduction & Bibliographies. 620p. (Orig.). (C). 1991. pap. 21.00 (0-911557-03-2) Bedford Publishers.

Reid, Stanley D., jt. ed. see Rosson, Philip J.

***Reid, Stephen.** The Prentice Hall Guide for College Writers. 3rd ed. LC 94-23222. 704p. (C). 1994. text ed. write for info. (0-13-073669-4) P-H.

— The Prentice Hall Guide for College Writers. 3rd ed. LC 94-32196. 598p. 1994. pap. text ed. write for info. (0-13-073677-5) P-H.

— Purpose & Process: A Reader for Writers. 640p. (C). 1990. pap. text ed. write for info. (0-13-742552-X) P-H.

Reid, Stephen, ed. Purpose & Process: A Reader for Writers. 2nd ed. LC 93-43888. 570p. 1994. pap. text ed. write for info. (0-13-742628-3) P-H.

Reid, Stephen A., jt. ed. see Kuespert, Jonathon G.

Reid, Stephen B. Enoch & Daniel: A Form Critical & Sociological Study of Historical Apocalypses. Endres, John & Christensen, Duane L., eds. LC 88-72056. (BIBAL Monograph Ser.: No. 2). 147p. 1989. pap. 12.95 (0-941037-07-X) BIBAL Pr.

— Experience & Tradition: A Primer in Black Biblical Hermeneutics. LC 90-43485. 1991. pap. 11.95 (0-687-12400-X) Abingdon.

Reid, Steven, jt. auth. see Schaefer, Charles E.

Reid, Struan. Bird World. (Young Readers' Nature Library). (Illus.). 64p. (J). (gr. 4-6). 1991. lib. bdg. 15.40 (1-56294-009-0) Millbrook Pr.

— Cultures & Civilizations. (Silk & Spice Routes Ser.). (Illus.). 48p. (J). (gr. 6 up). 1994. text ed. 15.95 (0-02-726315-0, New Dscvry Bks) Silver Burdett Pr.

— Exploration by Sea. LC 93-14693. (Silk & Spice Routes Ser.). (Illus.). 48p. (YA). (gr. 6 up). 1994. text ed. 15.95 (0-02-775801-X, New Dscvry Bks) Silver Burdett Pr.

— Inventions & Trade. (Silk & Spice Routes Ser.). (Illus.). 48p. (YA). (gr. 6 up). 1994. text ed. 15.95 (0-02-726316-9, New Dscvry Bks) Silver Burdett Pr.

Reid, Stuart. Eighteenth Century Highlanders. (Men-at-Arms Ser.). (Illus.). 48p. 1993. pap. 11.95 (1-85532-316-8, 9232, Pub. by Osprey UK) Stackpole.

— King George's Army Vol. 2: 1740-93. (Men-at-Arms Ser.). (Illus.). 48p. 1995. pap. 12.95 (1-85532-564-0, Pub. by Osprey UK) Stackpole.

— Wellington's Highlanders. (Men-at-Arms Ser.: No. 253). (Illus.). 48p. pap. 11.95 (1-85532-256-0, 9224, Pub. by Osprey UK) Stackpole.

Reid, Stuart J. A Sketch of the Life & Times of Sydney Smith. 1972. 59.95 (0-8490-1060-8) Gordon Pr.

Reid, Stuart J., ed. see Blount, Edward.

Reid, Sue, ed. see Woolf, Virginia.

Reid, Sue T. The Correctional System: An Introduction. 592p. (C). 1981. text ed. 46.75 (0-03-042331-7) HB Coll Pubs.

— Crime & Criminology. LC 90-5168. (Illus.). 590p. (C). 1991. text ed. 46.75 (0-03-035302-5, HV6025.R515) HB Coll Pubs.

— Crime & Criminology. 7th ed. (C). 1994. boxed write for info. (0-697-27463-2) Brown & Benchmark.

— Criminal Justice. 3rd ed. (Illus.). 752p. (C). 1993. text ed. write for info. (0-02-399173-9) Macmillan.

— Criminal Law. 2nd ed. (Illus.). 464p. (C). 1992. text ed. write for info. (0-02-399171-2) Macmillan.

— Criminal Law. 3rd ed. LC 94-12638. 560p. 1994. text ed. 57.00 (0-02-399211-5) P-H.

***Reid, Suzan.** Follow That Bus. (Illus.). 32p. (Orig.). (J). (gr. 1-4). 1993. pap. 4.95 (0-920501-88-5) Orca Bk Pubs.

***Reid, Suzanne.** Presenting Cynthia Voigt. (Young Adult Authors Ser.). 1995. lib. bdg. 20.95x (0-8057-8219-2, Twayne) Macmillan.

Reid, T. J. Fashion, Fun, & Feelings: A Lady Looks at Life. Porter, Carolyn, ed. LC 83-93566. (Illus.). 196p. (Orig.). 1994. pap. 14.95 (1-880522-48-9) Retail Res.

— What Mother Never Told Ya about Retail: A Small Store Survival Guide. 2nd rev. ed. Porter, Carolyn, ed. (Illus.). 119p. (C). 1994. pap. 29.95 (1-880522-24-1) Retail Res.

Reid, T. R. Congressional Odyssey: The Saga of a Senate Bill. LC 80-10108. (Illus.). 140p. (C). 1995. pap. text ed. write for info. (0-7167-1172-9) W H Freeman.

— Ski Japan! Calogeras, Meagan, ed. (Illus.). 320p. 1994. pap. 20.00 (4-7700-1680-8) Kodansha.

Reid, T. W. Charlotte Bronte. LC 75-130243. (English Biography Ser.: No. 31). 1970. reprint ed. lib. bdg. 75.00 (0-8383-1133-4) M S G Haskell Hse.

Reid, T. Wemyss. Life of the Right Honourable William Edward Forster, 2 vols. in 1. LC 73-108853. 1970. reprint ed. 57.50 (0-678-07763-0) Kelley.

Reid, Tanya, ed. see Oden, ViAnn.

Reid, Thomas. Complete Works. Hamilton, Sir William, ed. 1986. reprint ed. lib. bdg. 45.00 (0-935005-68-4) Lincoln-Rembrandt.

— Essays on the Active Powers of Man. (C). 1986. reprint ed. lib. bdg. 25.95 (0-935005-63-3); reprint ed. pap. text ed. 15.95 (0-935005-64-1) Lincoln-Rembrandt.

— Essays on the Intellectual Powers of Man. Woozley, A. D., ed. (C). 1986. reprint ed. lib. bdg. 25.95 (0-935005-15-3); reprint ed. pap. text ed. 15.95 (0-935005-14-5) Lincoln-Rembrandt.

— German Belt Buckles, 1847-1945: An Illustrated History. 3rd ed. McPherson, John C., ed. (Illus.). 192p. 1989. 24.95 (0-935856-05-6) Lancer.

— Inquiry & Essays. Beanblossom, Ronald & Lehrer, Keith, eds. LC 83-22864. (HPC Classics Ser.). lxii, 430p. (C). 1983. reprint ed. lib. bdg. 22.50 (0-915145-86-3); reprint ed. pap. text ed. 8.95 (0-915145-85-5) Hackett Pub.

— An Inquiry into the Human Mind. Duggan, Timothy, ed. LC 74-108880. 331p. reprint ed. pap. 94.40 (0-317-12999-6, 2016974) Bks Demand.

— Inquiry into the Human Mind on the Principle of Common Sense. 3rd ed. (C). 1986. reprint ed. lib. bdg. 19.95 (0-935005-30-7); reprint ed. pap. text ed. 12.95 (0-935005-32-3) Lincoln-Rembrandt.

— Philosophical Works: With Notes & Supplementary Dissertations by Sir William Hamilton, 2 vols., Set. 8th ed. 1983. reprint ed. 154.70 (3-487-01617-6, Pub. by Georg Olms GW) Lubrecht & Cramer.

— Practical Ethics. Haakonssen, Knud, ed. (Illus.). 544p. 1990. text ed. 69.50 (0-691-07350-3) Princeton U Pr.

Reid, Thomas M. The Boy Hunters. LC 68-23725. (Americans in Fiction Ser.). reprint ed. lib. bdg. 17.00 (0-8398-1750-9); reprint ed. pap. text ed. 4.95 (0-89197-685-X) Irvington.

— The Quadroon: or, Adventures in the Far West. LC 67-29278. (Americans in Fiction Ser.). (Illus.). 447p. reprint ed. lib. bdg. 36.00 (0-8398-1751-7); reprint ed. pap. text ed. 6.95 (0-89197-912-3) Irvington.

— The White Chief: A Legend of North Mexico. LC 68-23726. (Americans in Fiction Ser.). (Illus.). 401p. reprint ed. lib. bdg. 29.50 (0-8398-1752-5); reprint ed. pap. text ed. 5.95 (0-89197-975-1) Irvington.

Reid, Tom & Bowen, Barbara. Selecting Contract Types. 2nd rev. ed. Gibbs, Anne M. & Rumbaugh, Margaret, eds. 115p. 1990. pap. 37.45 (0-940343-01-0) Natl Contract Mgmt.

Reid, Tommy. Kingdom Now but Not Yet. 128p. 1988. pap. 6.95 (0-917595-18-1) Kingdom Pubs.

Reid, V. S. The Leopard. (Caribbean Writers Ser.). 1980. pap. 7.95 (0-435-98660-0) Heinemann.

Reid, Victor S. The Leopard. 159p. 1972. reprint ed. 15.00 (0-911860-08-8) Chatham Bkseller.

Reid, W. H., jt. auth. see Drazin, P. G.

Reid, W. H., tr. see Landau, L. D., et al.

Reid, W. Max. Mohawk Valley. 455p. 1993. reprint ed. lib. bdg. 99.00 (0-7812-5133-8) Rprt Serv.

— The Mohawk Valley: Its Legends & Its History. (Illus.). 468p. 1984. reprint ed. 25.00 (0-916346-32-3) Harbor Hill Bks.

— The Mohawk Valley - Its Legends & Its History. (Illus.). 455p. 1993. reprint ed. lib. bdg. 47.50 (0-8328-3188-3) Higginson Bk Co.

— Story of Old Fort Johnson. 455p. 1993. reprint ed. lib. bdg. 99.00 (0-7812-5132-X) Rprt Serv.

***Reid-Wallace, Carolynn, et al.** The New Promise of American Life. Alexander, Lamar & Finn, Chester E., Jr., eds. 400p. (Orig.). 1995. pap. text ed. 12.95 (1-55813-053-5) Hudson Instit IN.

Reid, Wallis. Verb & Noun Number in English: A Functional Explanation. (Linguistics Library). 384p. (C). 1991. pap. text ed. 24.95 (0-582-29158-5) Longman.

Reid, Walter & Myddelton, D. R. The Meaning of Company Accounts. 5th ed. 370p. 1992. text ed. 69.95 (0-566-07349-8, Pub. by Gower UK); pap. text ed. 33.95 (0-566-07350-1, Pub. by Gower UK) Ashgate Pub Co.

Reid, Walter V. & Miller, Kenton R. Keeping Options Alive: The Scientific Basis for Conserving Biodiversity. 100p. (Orig.). 1989. pap. 10.00 (0-915825-41-4) World Resources Inst.

Reid, Walter V. & Trexler, Mark C. Drowning the National Heritage: Climate Change & Coastal Biodiversity in the United States. large type ed. 48p. 1991. Large format. pap. 14.95 (0-915825-62-7, REDNP) World Resources Inst.

Reid, Whitelaw. American & English Studies, 2 Vols. LC 68-29240. (Essay Index Reprint Ser.). 1977. reprint ed. 41.95 (0-8369-0815-5) Ayer.

Reid, William. Authentic Records of Revivals Now in Progress in the United Kingdom. 486p. 1980. 17.50 (0-939464-33-0) Labyrinth Pr.

— Blood of Jesus. 1969. pap. 3.00 (0-914053-02-7) Liberty Bell Pr.

Reid, William, ed. Authentic Records of Revival, Now in Progress in the United Kingdom. (Revival Library). viii, 478p. 1980. reprint ed. lib. bdg. 17.50 (0-940033-17-8) R O Roberts.

Reid, William A. The Pursuit of Curriculum: Schooling and the Public Interest. LC 93-46339. 1994. 42.00 (0-89391-980-2); pap. 22.50 (1-56750-051-X) Ablex Pub.

***Reid, William D.** The Loyalists in Ontario: The Sons & Daughters of the American Loyalists of Upper Canada. 418p. 1994. 35.00 (0-614-03823-5, 4865) Genealog Pub.

— Marriage Notices of Ontario. 1985. 25.00 (0-912606-05-3) Hunterdon Hse.

Reid, William H. Treatment of Psychiatric Disorders. rev. ed. 1995. write for info. (0-87630-765-9) Brunner-Mazel.

— The Treatment of Psychiatric Disorders: Revised for the DSM-III-R. enl. rev. ed. LC 88-19468. 438p. 1989. 40.95 (0-87630-536-2) Brunner-Mazel.

Reid, William H., ed. Mathematical Problems in the Geophysical Sciences I: Geophysical Fluid Dynamics. LC 62-21481. (Lectures in Applied Mathematics: Vol. 13). 383p. 1971. 66.00 (0-8218-1113-4, LAM-13) Am Math.

— Mathematical Problems in the Geophysical Sciences, No. 2: Inverse Problems, Dynamo Theory & Tides. LC 62-21481. (Lectures in Applied Mathematics: Vol. 14). 370p. 1971. 62.00 (0-8218-1114-2, LAM-14) Am Math.

Reid, William H. & Wise, Michael G. DSM-III-R Training Guide: For Use with the American Psychiatric Association's Diagnostic & Statistical Manual of Mental Disorders. rev. ed. LC 88-35186. 288p. 1989. pap. 19.95 (0-87630-507-9) Brunner-Mazel.

— DSM-III-R Training Guide: For Use with the American Psychiatric Association's Diagnostic & Statistical Manual of Mental Disorders. 3rd rev. ed. LC 88-35186. 288p. 1989. 33.95 (0-87630-505-2) Brunner-Mazel.

— DSM-IV Training Guide. 384p. 1995. pap. 26.95 (0-87630-763-2) Brunner-Mazel.

Reid, William H., ed. see Lebovitz, Norman, et al.

Reid, William H., jt. auth. see Wise, Michael G.

Reid, William H., et al, eds. Unmasking the Psychopath: Antisocial Personality & Related Syndromes. (Professional Bks.). 1986. 34.95 (0-393-70025-9) Norton.

Reid, William J. Family Problem Solving. 360p. 1985. text ed. 35.50 (0-231-06056-4) Col U Pr.

— Task Strategies: An Empirical Approach to Clinical Social Work. (Illus.). 320p. 1992. text ed. 35.00 (0-231-07550-2) Col U Pr.

Reid, William J. & Epstein, Laura. Task-Centered Casework. LC 72-4931. 350p. (C). 1972. text ed. 34.00 (0-231-03466-0) Col U Pr.

— Task-Centered Practice. LC 76-28177. 1977. text ed. 33.50 (0-231-04072-5) Col U Pr.

Reid, William J. & Shyne, Ann W. Brief & Extended Casework. LC 70-79192. 1969. text ed. 35.50 (0-231-03219-6) Col U Pr.

Reid, William J. & Smith, Audrey D. Research in Social Work. LC 81-2885. 416p. 1981. text ed. 47.00 (0-231-04700-2) Col U Pr.

— Research in Social Work. 2nd ed. 360p. 1989. text ed. 37.00 (0-231-06420-9) Col U Pr.

Reid, William J., jt. ed. see Sherman, Edmund.

Reid, William J., jt. auth. see Smith, Audrey D.

Reid, William J., jt. ed. see Videka-Sherman, Lynn.

Reid, William T. Sturmian Theory for Ordinary Differential Equations. (Applied Mathematical Sciences Ser.: Vol. 31). 559p. 1981. pap. 69.00 (0-387-90542-1) Spr-Verlag.

Reidel, Arthur, ed. Fundamental Rock Climbing. 1973. pap. 1.75 (0-9601698-0-6) MIT Outing.

Reidel, Carl H., ed. New England Prospects: Critical Choices in a Time of Change. LC 81-51604. (Futures of New England Ser.). (Illus.). 220p. (C). 1982. pap. 13.95 (0-87451-220-4) U Pr of New Eng.

Reidel-Geubtner, Virginia, jt. auth. see Boushahla, Jo J.

Reidel, James, ed. see Kees, Weldon.

Reidel, Johannes, jt. auth. see Schafer, William.

Reidel, Marlene. From Egg to Bird. (Carolrhoda Start to Finish Bks.). (Illus.). 24p. (J). (ps-3). 1981. lib. bdg. 13.50 (0-87614-159-9, Carolrhoda) Lerner Group.

— From Egg to Butterfly. LC 81-204. (Carolrhoda Start to Finish Bks.). Orig. Title: Von der Raupe Zum Schmetterling. (Illus.). 24p. (J). (ps-3). 1981. lib. bdg. 13.50 (0-87614-153-X, Carolrhoda) Lerner Group.

— From Ice to Rain. (Carolrhoda Start to Finish Bks.). Orig. Title: Vom Eis Zum Regen. (Illus.). 24p. (J). (ps-3). 1981. lib. bdg. 13.50 (0-87614-157-2, Carolrhoda) Lerner Group.

Reidel, S. P. & Hooper, P. R., eds. Volcanism & Tectonism in the Columbia River Flood-Basalt Province. (Special Paper Ser.: No. 239). 400p. 1990. 52.50 (0-8137-2239-X) Geol Soc.

Reidelbach, Maria. Completely Mad: A History of the Comic Book & Magazine. 1991. 50.00 (0-316-73890-5) Little.

— Completely Mad: A Histroy of the Comic Book & Magazine. 1992. pap. 24.95 (0-316-73891-3) Little.

— Microsoft Access. 1993. pap. 8.95 (1-56243-115-3) DDC Pub.

— MicroSoft Works for Windows Quick Reference Guide. Berkemeyer, Kathy, ed. (DDC Quick Reference Guides Ser.). (Illus.). 255p. (Orig.). 1993. pap. text ed., spiral bd. 8.95 (1-56243-101-3, H-18) DDC Pub.

— Quick Reference Guide for Access 2.0 for Windows. 1994. pap. 8.95 (1-56243-193-5) DDC Pub.

— Simple WordPerfect for Busy People. 1992. pap. 10.95 (1-56243-080-7) DDC Pub.

Reidelbach, Maria, jt. auth. see Garfinkel, Nina.

Reidemeister, Kurt. Knot Theory. Boron, Leo F. et al, trs. LC 83-72870. Orig. Title: Knotentheorie. (Illus.). 143p. (C). 1983. pap. text ed. 20.00 (0-914351-00-1) BCS Assocs.

— Kombinatorische Topologie. 14.95 (0-8284-0076-8) Chelsea Pub.

Reidenbach, R. Eric & Grubbs, M. Ray. Developing New Banking Products: A Manager's Guide. (Illus.). 160p. 1986. 46.50 (0-13-204603-2) P-H.

Reidenbach, R. Eric & Robin, Donald P. Business Ethics: Where Profits Meet Value Systems. 1989. 24.95 (0-13-095639-2) P-H.

— Ethics & Profits: A Convergence of Corporate America's Economy. 224p. 1989. text ed. 36.73 (0-13-290214-1) P-H.

Reidenbach, R. Eric, jt. auth. see Grubbs, M. Ray.

***Reidenbach, R. Eric, et al.** The Value Driven Bank: Strategies for Total Market Satisfaction. 225p. 1995. 37.50 (1-55738-773-7) Probus Pub Co.

Reidenbaugh, Lowell. Thirty-Third Virginia Infantry. (Virginia Regimental Histories Ser.). (Illus.). 151p. 1987. 19.95 (0-930919-37-8) H E Howard.

— Twenty-Seventh Virginia Infantry. (Virginia Regimental Histories Ser.). (Illus.). 191p. 1993. 19.95 (1-56190-044-3) H E Howard.

Reidenberg, M. M. Clinical Pharmacology of Biotechnology. (International Congress Ser.: Vol. 944). 1991. 145.00 (0-444-81376-4) Elsevier.

Reidenberg, M. M., jt. ed. see Lemberger, L.

Reidenberg, Marcus S. & Erill, Sergio, eds. Drug-Protein Binding: Esteve Foundation Symposium I. LC 85-12479. (Clinical Pharmacology & Therapeutics Ser.: Vol. 6). 380p. 1985. 49.95 (0-275-90010-X, C0010, Praeger Pubs) Greenwood.

Reider. Sports Medicine: The School Age Athlete. (Illus.). 720p. 1990. text ed. 132.50 (0-7216-3039-1) Saunders.

Reider, Barbara. A Hooray Kind of Kid: A Child's Self-Esteem & How to Build It. MacLain, M., ed. (Illus.). 133p. (Orig.). 1988. pap. 8.95 (0-9621156-0-6) Sierra Hse Pub.

— Notes in the Lunchbox: How to Help Your Child Succeed at School. Reimer, Kathleen & Ritter, Mary, eds. (Illus.). 144p. (Orig.). 1993. pap. 9.95 (0-9621156-1-4) Sierra Hse Pub.

Reider, Barbara E., jt. auth. see Charbonneau, Manon P.

Reider, Harry R. The Complete Guide to Operational Auditing. 296p. 1993. text ed. 100.00 (0-471-59419-9) Wiley.

Reider, Joseph, tr. The Book of Wisdom. LC 53-5114. xi, 233p. 1957. text ed. 15.00 (0-685-46287-0, Ctr Judaic Studies) Eisenbrauns.

***Reider, Marge.** Return to Millboro. 208p. (Orig.). 1995. pap. 13.00 (0-931892-28-7) B Dolphin Pub.

Reiderer, P., et al, eds. Neuroprotection in Neurodegeneration. 1995. pap. 73.00 (0-387-82542-8) Spr-Verlag.

Reidesel, C. Alan & Clements, Douglas H. Coping with Computers in the Elementary & Middle Schools. (Illus.). 384p. (C). 1985. pap. text ed. 35.00 (0-13-172420-7) P-H.

***Reidhead, C. Ty.** The Pfunny Pharm. (Illus.). 225p. (Orig.). 1995. pap. text ed. 19.50 (1-56053-114-2) Hanley & Belfus.

Reidinger, Paul. The Best Man. LC 88-83328. 176p. 1989. reprint ed. pap. 7.95 (1-55583-149-4) Alyson Pubns.

— Good Boys. LC 93-48610. 272p. 1994. pap. 9.95 (0-452-27220-3, Plume) NAL-Dutton.

— Intimate Evil. 256p. 1989. 17.95 (1-55611-140-1) D I Fine.

Reidinger, Rudolf. Der Codex Vindobonensis 418: Seine Vorlage und Seine Schreiber. (C). 1989. pap. text ed. 70.00 (0-7923-0350-4) Kluwer Ac.

Reidl, John O. A Catalogue of Renaissance Philosophers. 192p. 10.00 (0-87462-433-9) Marquette.

Reidle, James, jt. auth. see Spielman, Patrick.

Reidler, W. & Torkar, K. M., eds. Balloon Technology & Observations. (Advances in Space Research Ser.: Vol. 14). 212p. 1993. pap. 195.00 (0-08-042473-2, Pergamon Pr) Elsevier.

Reidt, Wilford. John G. Lake: A Man Without Compromise. 188p. (Orig.). 1989. pap. 6.95 (0-89274-316-6) Harrison Hse.

Reidy & Wallace. Southern Sky. 1988. pap. text ed. 29.95 (0-04-300094-0, Pub. by Allen Unwin AT) Paul & Co Pubs.

Reidy, Carolyn, ed. see Davis, Burke.

Reidy, David & Wallace, Ken. The Solar System: Practical Guide. 1991. 29.95 (0-04-442288-1, Pub. by Allen Unwin AT); pap. 19.95 (0-04-442260-1, Pub. by Allen Unwin AT) Paul & Co Pubs.

***Reidy, Denis, ed.** The Italian Book 1465-1800. (The British Library Studies in the History of the Book). (Illus.). 424p. 1993. 120.00 (0-7123-0295-6, Pub. by Brit Library UK) U of Toronto Pr.

Reidy, Joseph P. From Slavery to Agrarian Capitalism in the Cotton Plantation South: Central Georgia, 1800-1880. LC 92-53620. (Fred W. Morrison Series in Southern Studies). xvi, 360p. (C). 1992. 45.00 (0-8078-2061-X) U of NC Pr.

Reidy, Robert W., jt. auth. see Jones, William L.

***Reidy, Roisin, comp.** Profile of the International Pump Industry: Market Prospects to 1988. 2nd ed. 280p. 1994. pap. 870.00 (1-85617-225-2, Pub. by Elsevier Applied Sci UK) Elsevier.

Reiersen, Johan R. Pathfinder for Norwegian Emigrants. LC 81-132209. (Norwegian-American Historical Association. Travel & Description Ser.: No. 9). 253p. reprint ed. pap. 72.20 (0-317-55772-6, 2029293) Bks Demand.

Reiersen, Olav, jt. auth. see Ansteinsson, John.

R

An Asterisk (*) at the beginning of an entry indicates that the title is appearing in BIP for the first time.

Reierson, Gary B. The Art in Preaching: The Intersection of Theology, Worship, & Preaching with the Arts. LC 87-34943. 176p. (Orig.). (C). 1988. lib. bdg. 43.50 (*0-8191-6882-3*); pap. 19.50 (*0-8191-6883-1*) U Pr of Amer.

Reierson, Gary B., jt. auth. see Campbell, Thomas C.

Reierson, Vicki, ed. see Horner, Jody.

Reierson, Vickie, ed. Start Your Business: A Beginner's Guide. LC 93-23582. 198p. 1993. pap. 8.95 (*1-55571-198-7*) Oasis Pr OR.

Reierson, Vickie, ed. see DeThomas, Art.

Reierson, Vickie, ed. see Ernst & Young Staff & Jenkins, Michael D.

Reierson, Vickie, ed. see Hanania, David.

Reierson, Vickie, ed. see Horner, Jody.

Reierson, Vickie, ed. see Jenkins, Michael D. & Warner, Jonathan H.

Reierson, Vickie, ed. see Jenkins, Michael D., et al.

Reierson, Vickie, ed. see Jenkins, Michael D. & Hipp, Rodney.

Reierson, Vickie, ed. see Jenkins, Michael D., et al.

Reierson, Vickie, ed. see Jenkins, Michael D. & Ernst & Young Staff.

Reierson, Vickie, ed. see Jenkins, Michael D.

Reierson, Vickie, ed. see Jenkins, Michael D. & Ernst & Young Staff.

Reierson, Vickie, ed. see Jenkins, Michael D. & PSI Research Staff.

Reierson, Vickie, ed. see Jenkins, Michael D.

Reierson, Vickie, ed. see Jenkins, Michael D. & PSI Research Staff.

Reierson, Vickie, ed. see Jenkins, Michael D. & Ernst & Young Staff.

Reierson, Vickie, ed. see Jenkins, Michael D.

Reierson, Vickie, ed. see Jenkins, Michael D. & Sniffen, Carl R.

Reierson, Vickie, ed. see Jenkins, Michael D. & Ernst & Young Staff.

Reierson, Vickie, ed. see Keup, Erwin J.

Reierson, Vickie, ed. see PSI Research Staff.

Reiese, U. Erich. Sea Anemones As a Hobby. (Illus.). 320p. 1993. 39.95 (*0-86622-539-0*, TT027) TFH Pubns.

Reiesen, DeLoss & Reiesen, Ruby. RCC, Vol. 19: Counseling & Marriage. 246p. 1989. write for info. (*0-8499-0501-X*) Word Inc.

Reiesen, Ruby, jt. auth. see Reiesen, DeLoss.

Reif. How to Reach & Teach ADD-ADHD Children: Practical Techniques & Strategies for Grades K-8. 256p. 1993. pap. 27.95 (*0-87628-413-6*) Ctr Appl Res.

Reif & Schlesinger. Cell Surface Antigen Thy-1: Immunology, Neurology & Therapeutic Applications. (Immunology Ser.: Vol. 45). 640p. 1989. 55.00 (*0-8247-7925-8*) Dekker.

Reif, Arnold E., ed. Immunity & Cancer in Man: An Introduction. LC 75-145. (Immunology Ser.: No. 3). (Illus.). 187p. reprint ed. pap. 53.30 (*0-7837-0652-9*, 2040991) Bks Demand.

Reif, Daniel K. Home Quick Planner: Reusable, Peel & Stick Furniture & Architectural Symbols. (Illus.). 18p. 1993. student ed 16.95 (*1-880301-03-2*) Gardeners.

Reif, Emil, jt. auth. see Moller, Torsten B.

Reif, Emil, ed. see Moller, Torsten B., et al.

Reif, Emil, jt. auth. see Moller, Torsten B.

Reif, Frederick. Fundamentals of Statistical & Thermal Physics. (Fundamentals of Physics Ser.). 1965. text ed. write for info. (*0-07-051800-9*) McGraw.

— Understanding Basic Mechanics. 1995. pap. text ed. write for info. (*0-471-10337-3*); student ed, pap. text ed. write for info. (*0-471-11624-6*) Wiley.

Reif, J. A., ed. see Tirkel, Eliezer.

Reif, J. H., ed. VLSI Algorithms & Architectures. (Lecture Notes in Computer Science Ser.: Vol. 319). x, 476p. 1988. pap. 49.00 (*0-387-96818-0*) Spr-Verlag.

***Reif, Jane.** Reflections on the Tibetan Terrier: A Collection of Writings from the Gazette. 2nd ed. (Illus.). 128p. 1995. 16.00 (*0-913337-25-0*) Southfarm Pr.

— The Tibetan Terrier Book. 2nd ed. (Illus.). 256p. (Orig.). 1996. 30.00 (*0-913337-28-5*) Southfarm Pr.

Reif, John H. Synthesis of Parallel Algorithms. 1993. 59.95 (*1-55860-135-X*) Morgan Kaufmann.

Reif, Joseph A. & Levinson, Hanna. Hebrew Basic Course. Swift, Lloyd B., ed. (Foreign Service Institute Basic Course Ser.). (Illus.). 586p. (C). 1989. reprint ed. write for info. (*0-16-004357-3*, S/N 044-000-00265-5) USGPO.

— Spoken Modern Hebrew. (Spoken Language Ser.). 590p. 1980. pap. 25.00 (*0-87950-683-0*); audio 180.00 (*0-87950-684-9*); audio 205.00 (*0-87950-685-7*) Spoken Lang Serv.

Reif, Joseph A., jt. ed. see Stern, A. Z.

Reif, Karlheinz, ed. Ten European Elections: Campaigns & Results of the 1979-81 First Direct Elections to the European Parliament. LC 84-18874. 232p. 1985. text ed. 55.95 (*0-566-00694-4*) Ashgate Pub Co.

Reif, Karlheinz & Melich, Anna. Euro-Barometer Thirty: Immigrants & Out-Groups in Western Europe, October-November 1988. LC 91-70507. 836p. 1991. write for info. (*0-89138-868-0*) ICPSR.

— Euro-Barometer Thirty-Two: The Single European Market, Drugs, Alcohol, & Cancer, November 1989. 2nd ed. LC 92-70498. 992p. 1992. write for info. (*0-89138-864-8*) ICPSR.

— Euro-Barometer Twenty-Nine: Environmental Problems & Cancer, March-April 1988. LC 90-85881. 472p. 1990. write for info. (*0-89138-869-9*) ICPSR.

— Euro-Barometer 31: European Elections, 1989; Pre-Election Survey, March-April, 1989. 536p. 1991. write for info. (*0-89138-866-4*) ICPSR.

— Euro-Barometer, 31A: European Elections, 1989: Post-Election Survey, June-July 1989. LC 93-78540. 864p. 1993. write for info. (*0-89138-862-1*) ICPSR.

Reif, Laura & Trager, Brahna, eds. International Perspectives on Long-Term Care. LC 85-8442. (Home Health Care Services Quarterly Ser.: Vol. 5, Nos. 3 & 4). 341p. 1985. text ed. 59.95 (*0-86656-400-4*); pap. text ed. 24.95 (*0-86656-445-4*) Haworth Pr.

Reif-Lehrer, Liane. Grant Application Writers Handbook. 3rd ed. (Health Science Ser.). 283p. (C). 1994. pap. text ed. 34.95 (*0-86720-874-0*) Jones & Bartlett.

— Writing a Successful Grant Application. 2nd rev. ed. 200p. 1989. pap. 25.00 (*0-86720-104-5*) Jones & Bartlett.

Reif, R., jt. auth. see Munchow, L.

Reif, Stefan C. Judaism & Hebrew Prayer: New Perspectives on Jewish Liturgical History. LC 92-1709. 300p. (C). 1993. 74.95 (*0-521-44087-4*) Cambridge U Pr.

Reif, Stefan C., ed. Published Material from the Cambridge Genizah Collections: A Bibliography, 1896-1980. 850p. (C). 1989. 175.00 (*0-521-33336-9*) Cambridge U Pr.

Reif, Stefan C., jt. ed. see Blau, Joshua.

Reif, Stefan C., jt. ed. see Emerton, J. A.

Reif, Wolf-Ernst, ed. see Schindewolf, Otto H.

***Reife, Abe & Freeman, Harold S., eds.** Environmental Chemistry of Dyes & Pigments. LC 95-6113. 1995. write for info. (*0-471-58927-6*) Wiley-Interscience.

Reifel, Michael, jt. ed. see McClelland, Bramlette.

Reifel, Toni & Woodward, Bette. Mama Cooks a Day Ahead. (Illus.). 260p. 1990. write for info. (*0-9628049-0-8*) Mama Cooks.

— Mama Cooks a Day Ahead. (Illus.). 260p. 1991. reprint ed. write for info. (*0-9628049-1-6*) Mama Cooks.

— Mama Cooks a Day Ahead. (Illus.). 260p. 1993. reprint ed. write for info. (*0-9628049-4-0*) Mama Cooks.

— Mama Cooks for Christmas. (Illus.). 190p. 1991. 7.95 (*0-9628049-2-4*) Mama Cooks.

— Mama Cooks with Kids in the Kitchen. Jamieson, Suzanne, ed. & illus. by. 108p. 1992. write for info. (*0-9628049-3-2*) Mama Cooks.

Reifen, David. The Juvenile Court in a Changing Society: Young Offenders in Israel. LC 73-178000. 280p. 1973. 27.95 (*0-8122-7649-3*) U of Pa Pr.

Reifer, Donald J. Managing Software Reuse. 400p. 1995. 46.95 (*0-471-57853-3*) Wiley.

— Software Management. 4th ed. LC 92-27322. 664p. 1993. text ed. 79.00 (*0-8186-3342-5*, 3342) IEEE Comp Soc.

Reifer, Donald J., jt. auth. see Marciniak, John J.

Reifer, Manfred. Hitler's Anti-Semitism. 1991. lib. bdg. 66.95 (*0-8490-4427-8*) Gordon Pr.

Reiff & Ament. Steps in Home Living. (gr. 7-9). 1984. text ed. 15.40 (*0-02-665750-3*) Bennett IL.

Reiff, D. D., ed. see Pressure Vessels & Piping Conference Staff.

Reiff, Dan & Lampson-Reiff, Kim. Eating Disorders: Nutrition Therapy in the Recovery Process. LC 91-31614. 350p. 1991. 110.00 (*0-8342-0253-0*) Aspen Pub.

Reiff, Daniel. Small Georgian Houses in England & Virginia: Origins & Development Through the 1750s. LC 83-40521. (Illus.). 352p. 1986. 85.00 (*0-87413-254-1*) U Delaware Pr.

***Reiff, David.** Slaughterhouse. 1995. 22.00 (*0-671-88118-3*) S&S Trade.

Reiff, Dora. The Beauty of His Presence. 9p. 1980. 0.20 (*0-89814-048-X*) Grace Publns.

Reiff, Henry B., jt. auth. see Gerber, Paul J.

Reiff, Henry B., jt. ed. see Gerber, Paul J.

Reiff, Janice L. Structuring the Past: The Use of Computers in History. (Illus.). 160p. 1991. pap. 8.00 (*0-87229-050-6*) Am Hist Assn.

Reiff, Judith. Learning Styles. (What Research Says to the Teacher Ser.). 40p. 1992. 3.95 (*0-8106-1092-2*) NEA.

Reiff, Judith, jt. auth. see Fortson, Laura R.

Reiff, Richard F. Living & Learning for International Interchange: A Sourcebook for Housing Personnel. 28p. 1986. pap. text ed. 9.00 (*0-912207-13-2*) NAFSA Washington.

Reiff, Robert & Scheerer, Martin. Memory & Hypnotic Age Regression: Developmental Aspects of Cognitive Function Explored Through Hypnosis. LC 59-13120. 253p. 1970. text ed. 35.00 (*0-8236-3340-3*) Intl Univs Pr.

Reiff, Sandra. Jacques Cousteau Finds the Lost Syntax. (By-Invitation-Only Ser.). 11p. 1992. pap. 6.00 (*1-882448-01-4*, Machiavellian) Mac-Kinations.

Reiff, Stephanie A. Secrets of Tut's Tomb & the Pyramids. LC 77-22770. (Great Unsolved Mysteries Ser.). (Illus.). (J). (gr. 4 up). 1983. reprint ed. lib. bdg. 21.36 (*0-8172-1051-2*) Raintree Steck-V.

Reiff, Tana. Beauty & the Business. LC 94-76141. (Working for Myself Ser.). 80p. 1994. pap. 4.50 (*1-56103-903-9*) Lake Pub Co.

— Caring. LC 94-79122. (That's Life Ser.: Bk. 6). 96p. 1994. pap. 4.95 (*1-56103-781-8*); audio 9.90 (*1-56103-791-5*) Lake Pub Co.

— Clean As a Whistle. LC 94-76147. (Working for Myself Ser.). 80p. 1994. pap. 4.50 (*1-56103-909-8*) Lake Pub Co.

— Cooking for a Crowd. LC 94-76146. (Working for Myself Ser.). 80p. 1994. pap. 4.50 (*1-56103-908-X*) Lake Pub Co.

— Crafting a Business. LC 94-76142. (Working for Myself Ser.). 80p. 1994. pap. 4.50 (*1-56103-904-7*) Lake Pub Co.

— Deals on Wheels. LC 94-79121. (That's Life Ser.: Bk. 5). 1994. pap. 4.95 (*1-56103-780-X*) Lake Pub Co.

— Deals on Wheels. (That's Life Ser.: Bk. 5). 1995. audio 9.90 (*1-56103-790-7*) Lake Pub Co.

— Emergency. LC 94-79117. (That's Life Ser.: Bk. 1). 96p. 1994. pap. 4.95 (*1-56103-776-1*); audio 9.90 (*1-56103-786-9*) Lake Pub Co.

— The Flower Man. LC 94-76148. (Working for Myself Ser.). 80p. 1994. pap. 4.50 (*1-56103-910-1*) Lake Pub Co.

— The Green Team. LC 94-76144. (Working for Myself Ser.). 80p. 1994. pap. 4.50 (*1-56103-906-3*) Lake Pub Co.

— Handy All Around. LC 94-76145. (Working for Myself Ser.). 80p. 1994. pap. 4.50 (*1-56103-907-1*) Lake Pub Co.

— In a Family Way. LC 94-79120. (That's Life Ser.: Bk. 4). 96p. 1995. pap. 4.95 (*1-56103-779-6*); audio 9.90 (*1-56103-789-3*) Lake Pub Co.

— Layoff. LC 94-79119. (That's Life Ser.: Bk. 3). 96p. 1994. pap. 4.95 (*1-56103-778-8*); audio 9.90 (*1-56103-788-5*) Lake Pub Co.

— Mr. & Ms. LC 94-79116. (That's Life Ser.: Bk. 8). 96p. 1994. pap. 4.95 (*1-56103-783-4*) Lake Pub Co.

— Mr. & Ms. LC 94-79116. (That's Life Ser.: Bk. 8). (YA). (gr. 6-12). 1994. audio 9.90 (*1-56103-793-1*) Lake Pub Co.

— One More for the Road. (That's Life Ser.: Bk. 2). (YA). (gr. 6-12). 1994. audio 9.90 (*1-56103-787-7*) Lake Pub Co.

— One More for the Road. LC 94-79118. (That's Life Ser.: Bk. 2). 96p. 1995. pap. 4.95 (*1-56103-777-X*) Lake Pub Co.

— Other People's Pets. LC 94-76143. (Working for Myself Ser.). 80p. 1994. pap. 4.50 (*1-56103-905-5*) Lake Pub Co.

— Tax Time. LC 94-79115. (That's Life Ser.: Bk. 7). 1994. audio 9.90 (*1-56103-792-3*) Lake Pub Co.

— Tax Time. LC 94-79115. (That's Life Ser.: Bk. 7). 96p. 1995. pap. 4.95 (*1-56103-782-6*) Lake Pub Co.

— That's Life Basic Set, 8 bks., Set. 1995. pap. 49.50 (*1-56103-775-3*) Lake Pub Co.

— That's Life Classroom Library, 24 bks., Set. 1995. teacher ed, pap. 106.50 (*1-56103-785-0*) Lake Pub Co.

— That's Life Curriculum Guide. 272p. 1995. pap. 29.70 (*1-56103-784-2*) Lake Pub Co.

— Working for Myself Basic Set, 10 Bks., Set. 1994. pap. 45.00 (*1-56103-900-4*) Lake Pub Co.

— Working for Myself Classroom Library, 36 bks., Set. 1994. pap. 121.00 (*1-56103-912-8*) Lake Pub Co.

— Working for Myself Curriculum Guide. 96p. 1994. pap. 19.50 (*1-56103-911-X*) Lake Pub Co.

— You Call, We Haul. LC 94-76140. (Working for Myself Ser.). 80p. 1994. pap. 4.50 (*1-56103-902-0*) Lake Pub Co.

— Your Kids & Mind. LC 94-76139. (Working for Myself Ser.). 80p. 1994. pap. 4.50 (*1-56103-901-2*) Lake Pub Co.

***Reiff, Tana & Clews, Vince.** That's Life DramaTapes Cassette Program, 8 bks., Set. 1995. teacher ed, audio 106.50 (*1-56103-794-X*) Lake Pub Co.

Reiffel, James, et al, eds. Psychosocial Aspects of Cardiovascular Disease. LC 79-27765. 365p. 1980. 12.50 (*0-930194-32-2*) Ctr Thanatology.

Reiffen, Hannelotte, ed. see Barth, Karl.

Reifferscheid, August, ed. Bibliotheca Patrum Latinorum Italica, 2 vols. in 1. 1033p. 1976. reprint ed. write for info. (*3-487-05966-5*, Pub. by Georg Olms GW) Lubrecht & Cramer.

Reifferscheid, Augustus, ed. see Suetonius, C.

Reifler, David M., ed. The American Society of Ophthalmic Plastic & Reconstructive Surgery (ASOPRS): The First Twenty-Five Years 1969-1994: With a Brief History of Ophthalmic Plastic Surgery, 2500 BC-1995 AD. LC 94-7908. (Illus.). 493p. 1994. 75.00 (*0-930405-64-1*) Norman SF.

Reifler, Sam. I, Ching. 1991. mass mkt. 9.95 (*0-553-35424-8*) Bantam.

Reifman, Betsy. One Hundred One Creative & Effective Ways to Meet Worthwhile Men. LC 81-90612. 52p. 1982. pap. 8.95 (*0-9607672-0-7*) Sunrise Pub Hse.

Reifner, Udo & Ford, Janet, eds. Banking for People: I. Social Banking & New Poverty, II. Consumer Debts & Unemployment in Europe, National Reports. xxxii, 673p. (C). 1992. lib. bdg. 169.25 (*3-11-012675-3*) De Gruyter.

Reifsnider, K., ed. Damage in Composite Materials - STP 775. 282p. 1982. 33.50 (*0-8031-0696-3*, 04-775000-30) ASTM.

Reifsnider, K. L. Fatigue of Composite Materials. (Composite Materials Ser.: Vol. 4). 520p. 1991. 179.50 (*0-444-70507-4*, CCS 4) Elsevier.

Reifsnider, K. L. & Hyer, M. W., eds. Proceedings of the Sixth Japan-U. S. Conference on Composite Materials. LC 92-85213. 875p. 1993. text ed. 195.00 (*1-56676-021-6*) Technomic.

Reifsnider, K. L. & Lauritis, K. N., eds. Fatigue of Filamentary Composite Materials- STP 636. 282p. 1977. 26.00 (*0-8031-0347-6*, 04-636000-33) ASTM.

Reifsnider, K. L., jt ed. see Noor, A. K.

Reifsnider, K. L., jt. ed. see Reddy, J. N.

Reifsnyder, William. Adventuring in the Alps: The Sierra Club Travel Guide to the Alpine Regions of France, Switzerland, Germany, Austria, Liechtenstein, Italy & Yugoslavia. LC 85-18471. 1986. pap. 10.95 (*0-87156-754-7*) Sierra.

Reifsnyder, William E. High Huts of the White Mountains. 2nd ed. (Illus.). 240p. 1993. pap. 10.95 (*1-878239-20-1*) AMC Books.

— Weathering the Wilderness: The Sierra Club Guide to Practical Meteorology. LC 79-20859. (Outdoor Activities Guides Ser.). (Illus.). 288p. 1980. pap. 12.00 (*0-87156-266-9*) Sierra.

Reifsynder, William E. & Lull, Howard W. Radiant Energy in Relation to Forests. LC 77-10239. (U. S. Department of Agriculture. Technical Bulletin Ser.: 1344). reprint ed. 39.50 (*0-404-16217-7*) AMS Pr.

Reig, Daniel. Arabic-French, French-Arabic Dictionary: Dictionnaire Arabe-Francais-Arabe. 1448p. (ARA & FRE.). 1983. 95.00 (*0-8288-0442-7*, F290) Fr & Eur.

— Dictionnaire Arabe-Francais. 1991. write for info. (*0-7859-8607-3*, 203451209X) Fr & Eur.

Reig, Osvaldo A., jt. ed. see Nevo, Eviatar.

Reig, Teddy & Berger, Edward. Reminiscing in Tempo: The Life & Times of a Jazz Hustler. LC 90-36355. (Studies in Jazz: No. 10). (Illus.). 238p. 1990. 29.50 (*0-8108-2326-8*) Scarecrow.

Reigart, John F. Lancasterian System of Instruction in the Schools of New York City. LC 72-89220. (American Education: Its Men, Institutions & Ideas, Ser. 1). 1975. reprint ed. 13.95 (*0-405-01459-7*) Ayer.

Reigate, Emily. An Illustrated Guide to Lace. (Illus.). 264p. 1986. 49.50 (*1-85149-003-5*) Antique Collect.

Reigber, Christoph, jt. ed. see Montag, Horst.

Reigel, Charles E., Jr. & Perkins, Edward A. Executive Typewriting. 2nd ed. (Illus.). 256p. (gr. 12 up). 1981. text ed. 24.95 (*0-07-051826-2*) McGraw.

Reigel, Donald H., jt. ed. see Rowley-Kelly, Fern L.

Reigel, Gregory F. Fellowship Park. LC 93-93798. 64p. 1994. pap. 7.95 (*1-56002-330-9*, Univ Edtns) Aegina Pr.

Reigelman, Milton M. The Midland: A Venture in Literary Regionalism. LC 75-28219. 154p. (Orig.). 1975. pap. text ed. 9.95x (*0-87745-054-4*) U of Iowa Pr.

Reigeluth, Charles M. Instructional Design Theories & Models: An Overview of Their Current Status. 512p. 1983. text ed. 34.50 (*0-89859-275-5*) L Erlbaum Assocs.

Reigeluth, Charles M., ed. Instructional Theories in Action: Lessons Illustrating Selected Theories & Models. 360p. (C). 1987. 29.95 (*0-89859-825-7*) L Erlbaum Assocs.

Reigeluth, Charles M. & Garfinkle, Robert J., eds. Systemic Change in Education. LC 93-36654. 184p. 1994. 34.95 (*0-87778-271-7*) Educ Tech Pubns.

Reigeluth, Charles M., jt. auth. see Young, M. Jean.

Reigeluth, Charles M., et al, eds. Comprehensive Systems Design: A New Educational Technology. (NATO ASI Series F: Computer & Systems Sciences, Special Programme AET: Vol. 95). ix, 437p. 1993. write for info. (*3-540-56677-5*) Spr-Verlag.

— Comprehensive Systems Design: A New Educational Technology. LC 93-11329. (NATO ASI Series F, Computer & Systems Sciences: Vol. 95). 1993. 98.00 (*0-387-56677-5*) Spr-Verlag.

Reigeluth, George, jt. auth. see Wolman, Harold.

Reiger, George. Heron Hill Chronicle. 144p. 1994. 19.95 (*1-55821-296-5*) Lyons & Burford.

— Wanderer on My Native Shore. 286p. 1991. pap. 14.95 (*1-55821-120-9*) Lyons & Burford.

Reiger, George, comp. The Best of Zane Grey, Outdoorsman: Hunting & Fishing Tales. LC 91-35932. (Classics of American Sport Ser.). (Illus.). 368p. 1992. pap. 16.95 (*0-8117-2599-5*) Stackpole.

Reiger, George W. The Birder's Journal: And Illustrated Lifelist. Baughman, Mel M., ed. (Illus.). 1989. 30.00 (*0-9623149-0-0*) Baughman Co.

Reiger, Hans C., comp. ASEAN Economic Co-operation: A Handbook. 240p. 1991. pap. 23.95 (*981-3035-66-8*, Pub. by Inst SE Asian Studies SI) Ashgate Pub Co.

Reiger, John F. American Sportsmen & the Origins of Conservation. LC 86-40093. (Illus.). 320p. 1986. reprint ed. pap. 13.95 (*0-8061-2021-5*) U of Okla Pr.

— Two Essays in Conservation History: "Gifford Pinchot with Rod & Reel" & "Trading Places: From Historian to Environmental Activist" (Pinchot Lecture Series). 63p. 1994. pap. 8.95 (*0-685-75416-2*) Grey Towers Pr.

Reiger, Kerreen. The Journey of the Daughters of Eve & Mary. 72p. 1988. pap. 2.25 (*0-88028-086-7*, 954) Forward Movement.

Reiger, Kurt E., jt. auth. see Shenkman, Richard.

Reigle, David. The Books of Kiu-Te in the Tibetan Buddhist Tantras. LC 83-60416. (Secret Doctrine Reference Ser.). (Illus.). 80p. (Orig.). 1983. pap. 6.00 (*0-913510-49-1*) Wizards.

Reigler, Timothy J. Of Other Worlds. 128p. 1992. pap. 4.95 (*0-9633459-0-7*) Top Shelf Pr.

Reigot, Betty P. A Book about Planets & Stars. (Illus.). 48p. (J). (gr. 2-5). 1988. pap. 3.95 (*0-590-40593-4*) Scholastic Inc.

Reigstad, Paul. Rolvaag: His Life & Art. LC 70-175804. (Illus.). xiv, 160p. 1972. 19.95 (*0-8032-0803-0*) U of Nebr Pr.

Reihecky, Janet. Carefulness. LC 89-71195. (Values to Live By Ser.). (Illus.). 32p. (ENG & SPA.). (J). (ps-2). 1990. lib. bdg. 21.36 (*0-89565-564-0*) Childs World.

— Cooperation. LC 89-48284. (Values to Live By Ser.). (Illus.). 32p. (ENG & SPA.). (J). (ps-2). 1990. lib. bdg. 21.36 (*0-89565-565-9*) Childs World.

***Reiher, Ruth, ed.** Sprache Im Konflikt: Zur Rolle der Sprache in Sozialen, Politischen und Militaerischen Auseinandersetzung. (Sprache, Politik, Oeffentlichkeit Ser.: No. 5). 480p. (GER.). (C). 1994. lib. bdg. 204.65 (*3-11-013958-8*) De Gruyter.

Reihmane, Laima. Advance: Painting, Graphic Art, Sculpture. (C). 1987. 135.00 (*0-685-22615-8*, Pub. by Collets UK) Pro-Am Music.

Reij. Water Harvesting for Plant Production: A Comprehensive Review of the Literature, Vol. I. (Technical Paper Ser.: No. 91). 134p. 1988. pap. 10.95 (*0-8213-1142-5*, 11142) World Bank.

Reijers, T. J. & Hsu, Kenneth J. Manual of Carbonate Sedimentology. 1986. text ed. 170.00 (*0-12-584840-4*); pap. text ed. 76.00 (*0-12-584841-2*) Acad Pr.

Reijinders, P. J. & Wolff, W. J., eds. Marine Mammals of the Wadden Sea: Final Report of the Section "Marine Mammals" of the Wadden Sea WorkinG Group. 64p. (C). 1982. text ed. 39.00 (*90-6191-057-9*, Pub. by A A Balkema NE) Ashgate Pub Co.

Reijinders, Peter J., ed. Seals, Fur Seals, Sea Lions & Walruses: An Action Plan for Their Conservation. 88p. (C). 1993. pap. text ed. 20.00 (*2-8317-0141-4*, Pub. by IUCN SZ) Island Pr.

R

Reijnders, Jan. Long Waves in Economic Development. (Illus.). 384p. 1990. text ed. 69.95 (*1-85278-339-7*, Pub. by E Elgar Pub UK) Ashgate Pub Co.
Reijnders, P., ed. Seals: An Action Plan for Their Conservation. 80p. write for info. (*2-8317-0044-2*, Pub. by IUCN SZ) Island Pr.
Reijnen, G. C. Utilization of Outer Space & International Law. 180p. 1981. 82.00 (*0-444-41965-9*) Elsevier.
Reijnen, G. C. & De Graaff, W. Pollution of Outer Space: Scientific, Policy & Legal Aspects. (C). 1989. lib. bdg. 88.00 (*90-247-3750-8*) Kluwer Ac.
Reijns, G. L. & Dagless, E. L., eds. Concurrent Languages in Distributed Systems-Hardware Supported Implementation: Proceedings of the WG 10.3 Workshop Held in Bristol, U. K., March 26-28, 1984. 164p. 1985. 48.75 (*0-444-87635-9*, North Holland) Elsevier.
Reijns, G. L. & Luo, J., eds. Transputing for Numerical & Neural Network Applications. LC 92-73167. (Transputer & Occam Engineering Ser.: Vol. 30). 264p. 1993. pap. 79.00 (*90-5199-100-2*) IOS Press.
Reijns, G. L., ed. see IFIP WG 10.3 Working Conference.
Reik, L. Lyme Disease & the Nervous System. (Illus.). 192p. 1991. text ed. 51.00 (*0-86577-394-7*) Thieme Med Pubs.
Reik, Theodor. Compulsions to Confess: On the Psycho Analysis of Crime & Punishment. LC 72-1146. (Essay Index Reprint Ser.). 1977. reprint ed. 36.95 (*0-8369-2856-3*) Ayer.
— Dogma & Compulsion. LC 72-9369. 332p. 1973. reprint ed. text ed. 65.00 (*0-8371-6577-6*, REDC, Greenwood Pr) Greenwood.
— Psychology of Sex Relations. LC 74-28525. 243p. 1975. reprint ed. text ed. 59.75 (*0-8371-7916-5*, RESR, Greenwood Pr) Greenwood.
— The Unknown Murderer. 1978. pap. text ed. 24.95 (*0-685-02648-5*, 26700) Intl Univs Pr.
Reik, Theodore. Ritual. 1976. pap. text ed. 24.95 (*0-8236-8269-2*, 025840) Intl Univs Pr.
Reikes, Ursula, comp. Quilted for Christmas. LC 93-44135. 120p. 1994. 21.95 (*1-56477-054-0*) That Patchwork.
Reikes, Ursula, ed. see Berg, Alice, et al.
Reikes, Ursula, ed. see Doak, Carol.
Reikes, Ursula, ed. see Greenberg, Lesly-Claire.
Reikes, Ursula, ed. see Hammond, Suzanne.
Reikes, Ursula, ed. see Hanson, Joan & Hickey, Mary.
Reikes, Ursula, ed. see Kime, Janet.
Reikes, Ursula, ed. see Martin, Nancy J.
Reikes, Ursula, ed. see McConnell, Donna.
Reikes, Ursula, ed. see Noble, Maurine.
Reikes, Ursula, ed. see Parrott, Iva J.
Reikes, Ursula, ed. see Robinson, Jackie.
Reikes, Ursula, ed. see Rolfe, Margaret.
Reikes, Ursula, ed. see Thomas, Donna L.
Reikes, Ursula, ed. see Wolff, Jackie & Aluna, Lori.
Reikes, Ursula G. Quilts for Baby: Easy As ABC. LC 93-28647. 1993. 9.95 (*1-56477-041-9*) That Patchwork.
Reikichi, Ueda. Netsuke Handbook of Ueda Reikichi. Bushell, Raymond, tr. LC 61-8139. (Illus.). 325p. 1961. 45.00 (*0-8048-0424-9*) C E Tuttle.
Reil, Theodor. Beitrage zur Kenntnis des Gewerbes im Hellenistischen Agypten. Finley, Moses, ed. LC 79-5001. (Ancient Economic History Ser.). (GER.). 1979. reprint ed. lib. bdg. 21.95 (*0-405-12390-6*) Ayer.
***Reiland, Robert.** The Fire & the Cloud. 1995. 18.95 (*0-8062-5056-9*) Carlton.
Reiland, Robert F. The Fire & the Cloud. 1991. 22.95 (*0-87949-328-3*) Ashley Bks.
Reiland, Susan. Statistics for Business & Economics. 5th ed. 352p. (C). 1991. pap. write for info. (*0-02-399226-3*) Dellen Pub.
— Statistics for Business & Economics. 6th ed. 352p. (C). 1994. pap. write for info. (*0-02-399207-7*) Dellen Pub.
— Statistics, Study Guide. 6th ed. 240p. (C). 1994. pap. write for info. (*0-02-399210-7*) Dellen Pub.
Reiley, Eldon H. Guidebook to Security Interests in Personal Property. 2nd ed. LC 85-16673. 1986. ring bd. 130.00 (*0-87632-481-2*) Clark Boardman Callaghan.
Reiley, H. Edward & Shry, Carroll L., Jr. Introductory Horticulture. 4th ed. 576p. 1991. teacher ed 16.00 (*0-8273-4513-5*); student ed 13.95 (*0-8273-4511-9*); text ed. 39.50 (*0-8273-4512-7*) Delmar.
— Introductory Horticulture. 5th ed. LC 95-15151. 1995. text ed. write for info. (*0-8273-6766-X*) Delmar.
Reiling, J. & Swellengrebel, J. L. A Handbook on the Gospel of Luke. LC 92-40061. (UBS Handbook Ser.). Orig. Title: Translator's Handbook on the Gospel of Mark. xv, 798p. 1993. reprint ed. 18.00 (*0-8267-0157-4*, 102675) Untd Bible Soc.
***Reill, Peter H. & Wilson, Ellen J.** Encyclopedia of the Enlightenment. LC 95-11962. 1996. write for info. (*0-8160-2989-X*) Facts on File.
Reilley, C. N. & Sawyer, Donald T. Experiments for Instrumental Methods. LC 78-24543. 420p. 1979. reprint ed. pap. text ed. 27.50 (*0-88275-816-0*) Krieger.
Reilley, Robert R., jt. auth. see Dillard, John M.
Reilley, Timothy A., ed. Raising Money Through an Institutionally Related Foundation. 83p. 1985. 24.00 (*0-89964-225-X*) Coun Adv & Supp Ed.
***Reilly.** Jim Harrison. 1995. text ed. 24.95 (*0-8057-3978-5*) Macmillan.
— Landscaping with Annuals. 1989. pap. 2.95 (*0-88266-539-1*) Storey Comm Inc.
— Landscaping with Bulbs. 1988. pap. 2.95 (*0-88266-498-0*) Storey Comm Inc.
— Practical Strategies in Outpatient Medicine. 2nd ed. (Illus.). 1328p. 1990. text ed. 138.00 (*0-7216-2821-4*) Saunders.
— Private Practice. 1984. 15.95 (*0-02-604410-2*) Macmillan.
— Starting Seeds Indoors. 1989. pap. 2.95 (*0-88266-519-7*) Storey Comm Inc.
Reilly & Salvatore, Dominick. Knowing & Writing: New Perspectives on Classical Questions. (C). 1991. text ed. 30.00 (*0-06-045352-4*) HarpCollege.
Reilly, jt. auth. see North.
Reilly, Abigail P., ed. The Communication Game: Perspectives on the Development of Speech, Language & Non-Verbal Communication Skills. (Pediatric Round Table Ser.: No. 4). 98p. 1980. 10.00 (*0-931562-05-8*) J & J Consumer Prods.
Reilly, Ann. Better Homes & Gardens Gardening Naturally: A Guide to Growing Chemical-Free Flowers, Vegetables. 1993. 24.95 (*0-696-00039-3*) Meredith Bks.
— Enjoying Roses. Goldenberg, Janet, ed. LC 92-70585. (Illus.). 350p. 1992. 24.95 (*0-89721-242-8*, UPC 05606) Ortho Info.
— Ortho's Guide to Enjoying Roses. LC 94-67705. (Illus.). 352p. 1995. pap. 19.95 (*0-89721-271-1*, UPC05607) Ortho Info.
— Portraits of Flowers: The Garden in Bloom. 1991. 14.99 (*0-517-05073-0*) Random Hse Value.
— The Rose. (Illus.). 152p. 1989. 22.99 (*0-517-68830-1*) Random Hse Value.
— Taylor's Pocket Guide to Annuals. Hughes, Amy, ed. LC 89-85031. (Taylor's Pocket Guide Ser.: Vol. 11). (Illus.). (Orig.). 1990. pap. 4.95 (*0-395-52244-7*) HM.
— Taylor's Pocket Guide to Flowering Shrubs. Hughes, Amy, ed. LC 89-85030. (Taylor's Pocket Guide Ser.: Vol. 7). (Illus.). (Orig.). 1990. pap. 4.95 (*0-395-52247-1*) HM.
— Taylor's Pocket Guide to Ground Covers for Shade. Hughes, Amy, ed. LC 89-85029. (Taylor's Pocket Guide Ser.: Vol. 10). (Illus.). (Orig.). 1990. pap. 4.95 (*0-395-52248-X*) HM.
— Taylor's Pocket Guide to Ground Covers for Sun. Whitman, Ann, ed. LC 89-85028. (Taylor's Pocket Guide Ser.: Vol. 9). (Illus.). (Orig.). 1990. pap. 4.95 (*0-395-52249-8*) HM.
— Taylor's Pocket Guide to Herbs & Edible Flowers. Hughes, Amy, ed. LC 89-85027. (Taylor's Pocket Guide Ser.: Vol. 8). (Illus.). 1990. pap. 5.95 (*0-395-52246-3*) HM.
— Taylor's Pocket Guide to Perennials for Shade. Whitman, Ann, ed. LC 88-46141. (Taylor's Pocket Guide Ser.: Vol. 1). (Illus.). (Orig.). 1989. pap. 5.95 (*0-395-51019-8*) HM.
— Taylor's Pocket Guide to Vegetables. Hughes, Amy, ed. LC 89-85026. (Taylor's Pocket Guide Ser.: Vol. 12). (Illus.). (Orig.). 1990. pap. 4.95 (*0-395-52245-5*) HM.
Reilly, Ann T., jt. ed. see LoPucki, Lynn M.
Reilly, Barbara A., jt. auth. see Reilly, Robert R.
Reilly, Bernard. The Treasure of the Vanquished: A Novel of Visigothic Spain. 256p. 1993. 19.95 (*0-938289-27-6*, 7332) Combined Bks.
***Reilly, Bernard F.** The Contest of Christian & Muslim Spain: 1031-1157. Lynch, John, ed. (History of Spain Ser.). (Illus.). 284p. 1995. pap. write for info. (*0-631-19964-0*) Blackwell Pubs.
— The Contest of Christian & Muslim Spain: 1031-1157. abr. ed. Lynch, John, ed. (History of Spain Ser.). (Illus.). 284p. (C). 1995. text ed. 49.95 (*0-631-16913-X*) Blackwell Pubs.
— The Kingdom of Leon-Castilla under King Alfonso VI, 1065-1109. (Illus.). 410p. 1988. text ed. 65.00 (*0-691-05515-7*) Princeton U Pr.
— The Kingdom of Leon-Castilla under Queen Urraca: 1109-1126. LC 81-47949. (Illus.). 392p. 1982. 62.50 (*0-691-05344-8*) Princeton U Pr.
— The Medieval Spains. LC 92-23379. (Cambridge Medieval Textbooks Ser.). 275p. (C). 1993. 59.95 (*0-521-39436-8*); pap. 18.95 (*0-521-39741-3*) Cambridge U Pr.
Reilly, C. Metal Contamination of Food. 231p. 1980. 66.75 (*0-85334-905-3*, Pub. by Elsevier Applied Sci UK) Elsevier.
— Metal Contamination of Food. 2nd ed. 284p. 1991. 110.00 (*1-85166-540-4*) Elsevier.
***Reilly, Catherine, comp.** Winged Words: An Anthology of Victorian Women's Poetry & Verse. 174p. 1995. pap. 19.95 (*1-870612-24-8*) Dufour.
Reilly, Catherine W. Late Victorian Poetry, 1880-1899: A Biobibliography. 416p. 1995. 120.00 (*0-7201-2001-2*, Mansell Pub) Cassell.
***Reilly, Charles A., ed.** New Paths to Democratic Development in Latin America: The Rise of NGO-Municipal Collaboration. LC 94-31381. 376p. 1995. pap. text ed. 29.95 (*1-55587-557-2*) Lynne Rienner.
Reilly, Charles H. McKim, Mead & White. LC 71-180028. (Illus.). 1972. reprint ed. 17.95 (*0-405-08877-9*) Ayer.
— Representative British Architects of the Present Day. LC 67-26774. (Essay Index Reprint Ser.). 1977. reprint ed. 15.95 (*0-8369-0818-X*) Ayer.
Reilly, Charlie. Ballads & Ballast: Traditional Ballads, "Negro" Spirituals, Ancient Myths, & a Few Folk Literature Masterpieces. LC 93-93624. (Illus.). 150p. (Orig.). 1993. pap. 14.50 (*0-9638132-0-X*) A James & Son.
Reilly, Charlie, ed. Conversations with Amiri Baraka. (Literary Conversations Ser.). 288p. 1994. 37.50 (*0-87805-686-6*); pap. 15.95 (*0-87805-687-4*) U Pr of Miss.
Reilly, Christopher. Making Your Marriage Work: Growing in Love after Falling in Love. LC 88-51813. (Orig.). 1989. pap. 7.95 (*0-89622-387-6*) Twenty-Third.
Reilly, Cyril A. & Reilly, Renee T., eds. A Gift of Irish Wisdom. LC 94-20129. 1995. 15.00 (*0-688-05292-4*) Hearst Bks.
Reilly, Daniel F. School Controversy Eighteen Ninety-One to Eighteen Ninety-Three. LC 76-89221. (American Education: Its Men, Institutions & Ideas, Ser. 1). 1975. reprint ed. 26.95 (*0-405-01460-0*) Ayer.
Reilly, David P., jt. auth. see Wei, William.
Reilly, Dawn, jt. auth. see Reilly, Michael.
Reilly, Dean F., ed. Advances in Investment Analysis & Portfolio Management, Vol. 1. 73.25 (*0-89232-354-X*) Jai Pr.
Reilly, Dorothy. Graduate Professional Education Through Outreach. 208p. 1990. 20.95 (*0-88737-488-3*) Natl League Nurse.
Reilly, Dorothy & Oermann, Marilyn. Behavioral Objectives: Evaluation in Nursing. 3rd ed. 278p. 1990. 22.95 (*0-88737-500-6*) Natl League Nurse.
Reilly, Dorothy E. & Oermann, Marilyn H. Clinical Teaching in Nursing Education. 528p. (C). 1992. pap. text ed. 28.95 (*0-88737-549-9*) Natl League Nurse.
Reilly, Ed & McMannus, Maggie. Monkees - A Manufactured Image: The Ultimate Reference Guide to Monkee Memories & Memorabilia. Schultheiss, Thomas, ed. (Rock & Roll Reference Ser.). (Illus.). 324p. 1993. reprint ed. 39.50 (*1-56075-032-4*) Popular Culture.
Reilly, Edward C. Understanding John Irving. Bruccoli, Matthew J., ed. LC 91-14616. (Understanding Contemporary American Literature Ser.). 165p. 1991. text ed. 34.95 (*0-87249-770-4*) U of SC Pr.
— Understanding John Irving. LC 91-14616. (Understanding Contemporary American Literature Ser.). 165p. (C). 1993. pap. text ed. 14.95 (*0-87249-880-8*) U of SC Pr.
— William Kennedy. (Twayne's United States Authors Ser.: No. 570). 152p. 1990. text ed. 21.95 (*0-8057-7611-7*, Pub. by Royal Botanic Garden UK) Macmillan.
Reilly, Edward R., tr. see Quantz, Johann J.
Reilly, Edward R., ed. see Quantz, Johann J.
Reilly, Edwin D. & Federighi, Francis D. Pascalgorithms. 700p. (C). 1987. IM avail. text ed. write for info. (*0-318-62601-2*) HM.
— VAX Assembly Language. (Illus.). 800p. 1990. Casebound, incl. instr's. manual. teacher ed, boxed write for info. (*0-02-399255-7*) Free Pr.
Reilly, Edwin D. & Frederighi, Francis D. Pascalorithms. LC 87-80569. (C). 1988. pap. 49.56 (*0-395-35739-X*) HM.
Reilly, Edwin D., Jr., jt. ed. see Ralston, Anthony.
Reilly, Edwin D.
Reilly, Elizabeth C. Dictionary of Colonial American Printers' Ornaments & Illustrations. LC 75-5023. (Illus.). xxxvi, 514p. 1975. 60.00 (*0-912296-06-2*, U Pr of Va) Am Antiquarian.
Reilly, Francis E. Charles Peirce's Theory of Scientific Method. LC 79-105527. (Orestes Brownson Series on Contemporary Thought & Affairs: No. 7). 208p. reprint ed. pap. 59.30 (*0-7837-0465-8*, 2040788) Bks Demand.
Reilly, Frank K. Investment Analysis & Portfolio Management. 3rd ed. (Illus.). 1026p. (C). 1989. text ed. 57.25 (*0-03-025498-1*) Dryden Pr.
— Investment Analysis & Portfolio Management. 4th ed. LC 93-26470. 980p. (C). 1994. text ed. 56.25 (*0-03-097052-0*) Dryden Pr.
— Investments. 3rd ed. (Illus.). 864p. (C). 1992. text ed. 57.25 (*0-03-032663-X*) Dryden Pr.
Reilly, Frank K., ed. High-Yield Bonds: Analysis & Risk Assessment. (Orig.). 1990. pap. text ed. 30.00 (*1-879087-02-2*) Assn I M&R.
Reilly, Frank K. & Leahigh, David. Investment Analysis & Portfolio Management. 4th ed. LC 93-26470. 459p. (C). 1993. student ed, pap. text ed. 21.00 (*0-03-097699-5*) Dryden Pr.
Reilly, George. Guide to Cruise Ship Jobs. rev. ed. LC 84-7698. 40p. 1994. pap. 5.95 (*0-87576-188-7*) Pilot Bks.
Reilly, Gladys B., jt. auth. see Bogue, Merwyn.
Reilly, H. Edward. Success with Rhododendrons & Azaleas. LC 91-23249. (Illus.). 314p. 1992. 29.95 (*0-88192-211-0*) Timber.
— Success with Rhododendrons & Azaleas. (Illus.). 314p. 1995. pap. 22.95 (*0-88192-331-1*) Timber.
Reilly, H. V. The Balloon to the Moon: Chronology of New Jersey's Distinguished Aviation History. Suplee, Carol, ed. (Illus.). 340p. (Orig.). 1992. pap. 29.95 (*0-9632295-0-8*) H V Pubs.
Reilly, Harold. Edgar Cayce Handbook for Health Through Drugless Therapy. 348p. 1988. pap. 14.95 (*0-87604-215-9*, 2073) ARE Pr.
Reilly, Helen. McKee of Centre Street. 299p. 1980. reprint ed. lib. bdg. 14.25 (*0-89968-214-6*, Lghtyr Pr) Buccaneer Bks.
Reilly, Hugh J., jt. auth. see Hyland, Terry L.
Reilly, I, tr. see Marussi, A.
Reilly, J., ed. Videoscope: (Incorporating Radical Software), Vol. 2. 1990. pap. text ed. 19.00 (*0-677-47075-4*) Gordon & Breach.
Reilly, J. Patrick. Electrical Stimulation & Electropathology. (Illus.). 450p. (C). 1992. 84.95 (*0-521-41791-0*) Cambridge U Pr.
Reilly, James. The Albumen & Salted Paper Book. LC 80-14340. (Extended Photo Media Ser.: No. 2). (Illus.). 1980. pap. text ed. 8.95 (*0-87992-014-9*) Light Impressions.
***Reilly, James F.** The Dove & the Eagle. Date not set. 13.95 (*0-533-11188-9*) Vantage.
Reilly, James M. Care & Identification of Nineteenth Century Photographic Prints (G-2S) LC 85-81727. (Illus.). 116p. (Orig.). 1986. pap. 29.95 (*0-87985-365-4*) Saunders Photo.
Reilly, James R., jt. auth. see Murphy, Helen M.
Reilly, Jane A. Public Librarian As Adult Learners' Advisor: An Innovation in Human Services. LC 80-27307. (Contributions in Librarianship & Information Science Ser.: No. 38). (Illus.). 184p. 1981. text ed. 45.00 (*0-313-22134-0*, REP/) Greenwood.
Reilly, Jill M. Mentorship: The Essential Guide for Schools & Business. LC 91-42116. (Illus.). 210p. 1992. pap. 15.00 (*0-910707-18-9*) Ohio Psych Pr.
Reilly, Jill M., jt. auth. see Featherstone, Bonnie D.
Reilly, Jim. Conrad. (Life & Works: Set II). (Illus.). 112p. (YA). (gr. 7 up). 1990. lib. bdg. 19.94 (*0-86593-021-X*); lib. bdg. 14.95 (*0-685-36351-1*) Rourke Corp.
— Eliot. (Life & Works: Set II). (Illus.). 112p. (YA). (gr. 7 up). 1990. lib. bdg. 19.94 (*0-86593-022-8*); lib. bdg. 14.95 (*0-685-36353-8*) Rourke Corp.
— Shadowtime: History & Representation in Hardy, Conrad & George Eliot. LC 92-16199. 208p. 1993. 45.00 (*0-415-08597-7*, B0372, Routledge NY) Routledge.
— Shadowtime: History & Representation in Hardy, Conrad & George Eliot. LC 92-16199. 1995. pap. 18.95 (*0-415-11893-X*, B4788) Routledge.
Reilly, Jim, et al. Life & Works, 6 bks., Set. (Illus.). 672p. (YA). (gr. 7 up). 1990. lib. bdg. 119.64 (*0-86593-015-5*); lib. bdg. 89.70 (*0-685-36350-3*) Rourke Corp.
Reilly, John. Agency Relationships in Real Estate. 2nd rev. ed. LC 94-8705. 235p. (C). 1994. pap. text ed. 25.95 (*0-7931-0787-3*, 1560-0802, Real Estate Ed) Dearborn Finan.
Reilly, John & Terrell, Thomas. Texas RE Agency. 260p. 1994. pap. 25.95 (*0-7931-0985-X*, 156005-01, Real Estate Ed) Dearborn Finan.
Reilly, John & Vitousek, Paige B. Questions & Answers to Help You Pass the Real Estate Exam. 4th rev. ed. 320p. (C). 1992. pap. text ed. 21.95 (*0-7931-0418-1*, 1970-04) Dearborn Finan.
Reilly, John C., Jr., comp. & intro. Operational Experience of Fast Battleships: World War 2, Korea & Vietnam. 2nd ed. (Illus.). 252p. 1989. per., pap. 14.00 (*0-16-002057-3*, S/N 008-046-00129-4) USGPO.
Reilly, John E. The Image of Poe in American Poetry. 1976. pap. 2.50 (*0-910556-05-9*) Enoch Pratt.
Reilly, John E., ed. John Henry Ingram's Poe Collection at the University of Virginia. 2nd ed. (C). 1994. pap. text ed. 30.00 (*0-8139-1552-X*) U Pr of Va.
Reilly, John H. Arthur Adamov. LC 74-2162. (Twayne's World Authors Ser.). 177p. (C). 1974. lib. bdg. 17.95 (*0-8057-2005-7*) Irvington.
Reilly, John H., ed. see Giraudoux, Jean.
***Reilly, John J.** Spengler's Future. 198p. Date not set. pap. 14.95 (*0-9639606-0-1*) Millennium.
Reilly, John M. & Anderson, Margot, eds. Economic Issues in Global Climate Change: Agriculture, Forestry, & Natural Resources. 460p. (C). 1992. pap. text ed. 63.50 (*0-8133-8435-4*) Westview.
Reilly, John M., jt. auth. see Edmonds, Jae.
***Reilly, John P.** Rapid Prototyping: Reengineering the Development Process. (Computer Science Ser.). 300p. 1996. pap. 42.95 (*0-442-01957-2*) Van Nos Reinhold.
Reilly, John W. Agency Relationships in California Real Estate. LC 87-4762. 1987. 7.95 (*0-88462-657-1*, 1560-10, Real Estate Ed) Dearborn Finan.
— Language of Real Estate. 4th ed. LC 93-8367. (Orig.). 1993. pap. 28.95 (*0-7931-0583-8*, 196101, Real Estate Ed) Dearborn Finan.
Reilly, Joseph J. Dear Prue's Husband, & Other People. LC 68-8487. (Essay Index Reprint Ser.). 1977. 21.95 (*0-8369-0816-3*) Ayer.
— Of Books & Men. LC 68-57336. (Essay Index Reprint Ser.). 1977. 23.95 (*0-8369-0817-1*) Ayer.
Reilly, Joseph P. Human Fulfillment. LC 83-71415. 421p. (C). 1983. 16.00 (*0-912987-00-6*); pap. 12.00 (*0-912987-01-4*) Bionomic.
Reilly, Judy S., jt. ed. see Emmorey, Karen.
***Reilly, Kay T.** The Bottlewasher. Ingram, tr. 200p. Date not set. pap. 8.95 (*1-56901-859-6*) NW Pub.
***Reilly, Kevin.** Readings in World Civilization, 2 vols., Vol. 1. 3rd ed. 352p. 1995. pap. text ed. 18.62 (*0-312-09647-X*) St Martin.
— Readings in World Civilization, 2 vols., Vol. 2. 3rd ed. 368p. 1995. pap. text ed. 18.62 (*0-312-09648-8*) St Martin.
— The West & the World: A History of Civilization, Vol. 1. 2nd ed. 384p. (C). 1990. pap. text ed. 40.50 (*0-06-045346-X*) HarpCollege.
— The West & the World: A History of Civilization, Vol. 2. 2nd ed. 432p. (C). 1989. pap. text ed. 39.00 (*0-06-045347-8*) HarpCollege.
Reilly, Kevin, ed. The Introductory History Course: Six Models. 162p. 1984. teacher ed 8.00 (*0-685-48048-8*) Am Hist Assn.
— World History. 3rd ed. LC 90-24443. (Selected Syllabi from American Colleges & Universities in History Ser.). 300p. (Orig.). 1991. pap. text ed. 16.95 (*1-55876-033-4*) Wiener Pubs Inc.
Reilly, Kevin, et al. Hurricane Treasure: One Thousand Fifteen Beach Sites, Locations Revealed. 1990. pap. 9.95 (*1-881777-02-2*) Pirate Express.
Reilly, Leo. How to Outnegotiate Anyone (Even a Car Dealer!) 144p. (Orig.). 1993. pap. 7.95 (*1-55850-283-1*) Adams Pubng.
Reilly, Lucille. The Hammered Dulcimer: A-Chording to Lucille Reilly. LC 90-39604. (Illus.). 170p. 1990. pap. 27.95 (*0-9613356-3-7*, SP-05) Shadrach.
— Striking Out & Winning! An Unabridged Guide for the Hammered Dulcimer. LC 84-199357. (Illus.). 170p. (Orig.). 1984. pap. 23.00 (*0-9613356-0-2*); audio 42.00 (*0-9613356-2-9*) Shadrach.
— Striking Out & Winning! An Unabridged Guide for the Hammered Dulcimer, 3 vols., Set. LC 84-199357. (Illus.). 170p. (Orig.). 1984. audio 23.00 (*0-9613356-1-0*) Shadrach.
Reilly, Maria. Now That I Am Old: Meditations on the Meaning of Life. LC 92-63179. 112p. (Orig.). 1994. pap. 7.95 (*0-89622-559-3*) Twenty-Third.
***Reilly, Mary A.** Achieving Reading & Writing Competence: A Companion Bk. 1: Narrative Text. 251p. (YA). (gr. 9-12). 1994. text ed. 14.95 (*1-886292-07-8*) CEO Sftware.

R

An Asterisk (*) at the beginning of an entry indicates that the title is appearing in BIP for the first time.

— Achieving Reading & Writing Competence: A Companion Bk. 2: Informational Text. 268p. (YA). (gr. 9-12). 1994. text ed. 14.95 (*1-886292-06-X*) CEO Sftware.

— Achieving Reading & Writing Competence: A Companion Bk. 3: Persuasive-Argumentative Text. 264p. (YA). (gr. 9-12). 1994. text ed. 14.95 (*1-886292-05-1*) CEO Sftware.

— Achieving Reading & Writing Competence: A Companion Bk. 4: Workplace Text. 306p. (YA). (gr. 9-12). 1994. text ed. 14.95 (*1-886292-04-3*) CEO Sftware.

Reilly, Mary E., jt. auth. see Luebke, Barbara.

Reilly, Mary J. Mexico. LC 90-22469. (Cultures of the World Ser.: Group 2: Latin America). (Illus.). 128p. (YA). (gr. 5-9). 1991. lib. bdg. 21.95 (*1-85435-385-3*) Marshall Cavendish.

Reilly, Mary L. & Olson, Lynn F. It's Time for Music: Songs & Lesson Outlines for Early Childhood Music. 80p. 1985. teacher ed 16.95 (*0-88284-339-7*, 2456) Alfred Pub.

Reilly, Matthew H. A Performance Monitor for Parallel Programs. 178p. 1990. text ed. 50.00 (*0-12-586330-6*) Acad Pr.

Reilly, Maureen E., jt. auth. see Fleishman, Edwin.

***Reilly, Michael.** Reilly of the White House. (American Autobiography Ser.). 248p. 1995. reprint ed. lib. bdg. 79.00 (*0-7812-8623-9*) Rprt Serv.

Reilly, Michael & Reilly, Dawn. The Bumper Sticker Book: Plus Games on the Go. (Illus.). 96p. (Orig.). 1992. pap. 5.95 (*0-930753-10-0*) Spect Ln Pr.

Reilly, Michael E., jt. auth. see Law, Gordon T., Jr.

Reilly, N. S., et al, eds. Civil War Maps: A Graphic Index to the Atlas to Accompany the Official Records of the Union & Confederate Armies. (Illus.). 68p. 1987. pap. 8.00 (*0-911028-36-6*) Newberry.

Reilly, Norman B. Quality: What Are They Talking About? LC 93-13457. 1994. text ed. 14.95 (*0-442-01635-2*) Van Nos Reinhold.

— Successful Systems Engineering for Engineers & Managers. LC 93-69. 1993. text ed. 54.95 (*0-442-01586-0*) Van Nos Reinhold.

Reilly, Pat. Paperweights: The Collector's Guide to Identifying, Enjoying, & Acquiring New & Vintage Paperweights. (Collector's Library). (Illus.). 80p. 1994. 12.98 (*1-56138-433-X*) Running Pr.

***Reilly, Patricia L.** A God Who Looks Like Me. LC 94-31514. 1995. 22.50 (*0-345-37519-X*) Ballantine.

Reilly, Patrick. Jonathan Swift: The Brave Desponder. LC 81-85639. 295p. 1982. 22.50 (*0-8093-1075-9*) S Ill U Pr.

— The Literature of Guilt: From "Gulliver" to Golding. LC 88-50164. 186p. 1988. text ed. 24.95 (*0-87745-215-6*) U of Iowa Pr.

— Lord of the Flies: Fathers & Sons. (Masterwork Studies). 170p. 1992. text ed. 22.95 (*0-8057-7999-X*, Twayne); pap. 12.95 (*0-8057-8049-1*, Twayne) Macmillan.

— Nineteen Eighty-Four: Past, Present & Future. (Masterwork Studies). 160p. 1989. text ed. 21.95 (*0-8057-8065-3*, Twayne); pap. 12.95 (*0-8057-8110-2*, Twayne) Macmillan.

— Tom Jones: Adventure & Providence. (Twayne's Masterworks Ser.: No. 72). 192p. 1991. text ed. 21.95 (*0-8057-9422-0*, Pub. by Royal Botanic Garden UK); pap. 12.95 (*0-8057-8143-9*, Pub. by Royal Botanic Garden UK) Macmillan.

Reilly, Paul & Rahtz, Sebastian, eds. Archaeology & the Information Age. (One World Archaeology Ser.: No. 20). (Illus.). 415p. 1992. 89.95 (*0-415-07858-X*, A8152) Routledge.

Reilly, Pauline. Echidna. (Picture Roo Bks.). (Illus.). 32p. (Orig.). (J). 1993. pap. 6.95 (*0-86417-285-0*, Pub. by Kangaroo Pr AT) Seven Hills Bk.

— Emu That Walks Toward Rain. 2nd ed. (Picture Roo Bks.). (Illus.). 32p. (Orig.). (J). (gr. 2-6). 1994. pap. 6.95 (*0-86417-571-X*, Pub. by Kangaroo Pr AT) Seven Hills Bk.

— Frillneck: An Australian Dragon. (Picture Roo Bks.). (Illus.). 32p. (Orig.). (J). 1993. pap. 6.95 (*0-86417-414-4*, Pub. by Kangaroo Pr AT) Seven Hills Bk.

— Galah. (Picture Roo Bks.). (Illus.). 32p. (Orig.). (J). 1993. pap. 6.95 (*0-86417-346-6*, Pub. by Kangaroo Pr AT) Seven Hills Bk.

— Kiwi. (Picture Roo Bks.). (Illus.). 32p. (Orig.). (J). 1993. pap. 6.95 (*0-86417-488-8*, Pub. by Kangaroo Pr AT) Seven Hills Bk.

— Koala. (Picture Roo Bks.). (Illus.). 32p. (Orig.). (J). 1993. pap. 6.95 (*0-86417-243-5*, Pub. by Kangaroo Pr AT) Seven Hills Bk.

— Kookaburra. 2nd ed. (Picture Roo Bks.). (Illus.). 32p. (J). (gr. 2-6). 1994. pap. 6.95 (*0-86417-528-0*, Pub. by Kangaroo Pr AT) Seven Hills Bk.

— The Lyrebird: A Natural History. 1988. pap. 19.95 (*0-86840-183-8*, Pub. by New South Wales Univ Pr AT) Intl Spec Bk.

— Lyrebird That Is Too Busy to Dance. (Picture Roo Bks.). (Illus.). 32p. (Orig.). (J). 1993. pap. 6.95 (*0-86417-086-6*, Pub. by Kangaroo Pr AT) Seven Hills Bk.

— The Penguin That Walks at Night. (Picture Roo Bks.). (Illus.). 32p. (Orig.). (J). 1993. pap. 6.95 (*0-86417-034-3*, Pub. by Kangaroo Pr AT) Seven Hills Bk.

— Penguins of the World. (Illus.). 184p. 1994. pap. 16.95 (*0-19-553547-2*) OUP.

— Platypus. (Picture Roo Bks.). (Illus.). 32p. (Orig.). (J). (gr. 2-6). 1994. pap. 6.95 (*0-86417-391-1*, Pub. by Kangaroo Pr AT) Seven Hills Bk.

— Sugar Glider. (Picture Roo Bks.). (Illus.). 32p. (J). (gr. 2-6). 1994. pap. 6.95 (*0-86417-590-6*, Pub. by Kangaroo Pr AT) Seven Hills Bk.

— Tasmanian Devil. (Picture Roo Bks.). (Illus.). 32p. (Orig.). (J). 1993. pap. 6.95 (*0-86417-207-9*, Pub. by Kangaroo Pr AT) Seven Hills Bk.

— Wombat. (Picture Roo Bks.). (Illus.). 32p. (Orig.). (J). 1993. pap. 6.95 (*0-86417-148-X*, Pub. by Kangaroo Pr AT) Seven Hills Bk.

Reilly, Philip. Genes & Your Fate: Understanding Your Genetic Heritage. 1994. text ed. 24.95 (*0-02-926045-0*) Macmillan.

Reilly, Philip R. The Surgical Solution: A History of Involuntary Sterilization in the United States. LC 90-5090. 208p. 1991. 24.50 (*0-8018-4096-1*) Johns Hopkins.

— To Do No Harm: A Journey Through Medical School. LC 86-26576. 309p. 1987. text ed. 49.95 (*0-86569-162-2*, Auburn Hse); pap. text ed. 16.95 (*0-86569-163-0*, Auburn Hse) Greenwood.

Reilly, R. Wedgwood, 2 vols., Set. LC 89-21609. 1989. 850.00 (*0-935859-85-3*, Stockton Pr) Groves Dictionaries.

Reilly, R. G., ed. Communication Failure in Dialogue & Discourse: Detection & Repair Processes. 404p. 1987. 81.50 (*0-444-70112-5*, North Holland) Elsevier.

Reilly, R. T. Irish Saints. 1992. 4.99 (*0-517-36833-1*) Random Hse Value.

Reilly, Raymond E. Human Performance in the Undersea Environment: An Annotated Bibliography. LC 76-135084. 90p. 1970. 15.00 (*0-403-04530-4*) Scholarly.

Reilly, Renee T., jt. ed. see Reilly, Cyril A.

Reilly, Richard L. Living with Pain: A New Approach to the Management of Chronic Pain. LC 93-6820. 160p. 1993. pap. 9.95 (*0-925190-64-0*) Fairview Press.

Reilly, Rick, jt. auth. see Barkley, Charles.

Reilly, Rick, jt. auth. see Gretzky, Wayne.

***Reilly, Robert.** Drug Comparison Handbook: Generic to Brand Brand to Generic. 2nd ed. 600p. (C). 1994. pap. text ed. 26.95 (*1-56930-016-X*) Skidmore Roth Pub.

Reilly, Robert, ed. The Transcendent Adventure: Studies of Religion in Science Fiction-Fantasy. LC 84-542. (Contributions to the Study of Science Fiction & Fantasy Ser.: No. 12). x, 266p. 1985. text ed. 59.95 (*0-313-23062-5*, RET/, Greenwood Pr) Greenwood.

***Reilly, Robert, et al.** The Pharmacy Tech: Basic Pharmacology & Calculations. (Illus.). 140p. (C). 1994. pap. text ed. 24.95 (*1-56930-005-4*) Skidmore Roth Pub.

Reilly, Robert M. American Socket Bayonets & Scabbards. LC 90-81582. (Illus.). 208p. 1990. 40.00 (*0-917218-45-0*) A Mowbray.

— United States Martial Flintlocks. LC 86-60684. (Illus.). 263p. 1986. 39.50 (*0-917218-21-3*) A Mowbray.

— United States Military Small Arms, 1816-1865. 1983. 39.95 (*0-88227-019-2*) Gun Room.

Reilly, Robert R. & Lewis, Ernest L. Educational Psychology. 624p. (C). 1983. pap. write for info. (*0-02-399250-6*) Macmillan.

Reilly, Robert R. & Reilly, Barbara A. MMPI-2 Tutorial Workbook. 1991. pap. text ed. 19.00 (*0-89079-267-4*, 1510) PRO-ED.

Reilly, Robert T. Handbook of Professional Tour Management. 2nd ed. 1990. text ed. 29.95 (*0-8273-3525-3*) Delmar.

— Handbook of Professional Tour Management: Instructor's Guide. 2nd ed. 1990. teacher ed 10.00 (*0-8273-3526-1*) Delmar.

— Public Relations in Action. 1981. 34.00 (*0-13-738526-9*) P-H.

— Public Relations in Action. 2nd ed. (Illus.). 480p. 1987. text ed. 65.00 (*0-13-738428-9*) P-H.

Reilly, Robin. Wedgwood Jasper. LC 94-60284. (Illus.). 408p. 1994. 60.00 (*0-500-01624-0*) Thames Hudson.

— Wedgwood the New Illustrated Dictionary. (Illus.). 1994. 89.50 (*1-85149-209-7*) Antique Collect.

Reilly, Robin & Savage, George. The Dictionary of Wedgwood. (Illus.). 414p. 1980. 79.50 (*0-902028-85-5*) Antique Collect.

Reilly, Robin L. Japan's Complete Fighting System: Shin Kage Ryu. LC 88-50069. (Illus.). 320p. 1989. 35.00 (*0-8048-1536-4*) C E Tuttle.

Reilly, Ronan G. & Sharkey, Noel E., eds. Connectionist Approaches to Natural Language Processing. 496p. 1992. text ed. 99.95 (*0-86377-179-3*) L Erlbaum Assocs.

Reilly, Rosemary M., ed. see American Institute of Certified Public Accountants Staff.

Reilly, Sarah C. Public Pension Plans: The State Regulatory Framework. 115p. write for info. (*0-318-60967-3*) Natl Coun Teach.

Reilly, Sidney. Britain's Master Spy: The Adventures of Sidney Reilly. 296p. 1986. pap. 3.95 (*0-88184-230-3*) Carroll & Graf.

Reilly, Stephen M., jt. ed. see Wainwright, Peter C.

Reilly, Susan S., jt. auth. see Goodall, Hillary.

Reilly, T., jt. auth. see Eston, R. G.

Reilly, T., et al, eds. Biomechanics & Medicine in Swimming. 400p. 1991. 89.95 (*0-419-15600-3*, A6115, E & FN Spon) Routledge Chapman & Hall.

— Physiology of Sports. (Illus.). 320p. 1990. 63.00 (*0-419-13580-4*, A4403, E & FN Spon); pap. 25.00 (*0-419-13590-1*, A4407, E & FN Spon) Routledge Chapman & Hall.

— Science & Football. 500p. 1988. text ed. 57.50 (*0-419-14360-2*, E & FN Spon) Routledge Chapman & Hall.

— Science & Football, No. 2. 2nd ed. 768p. 1992. 150.00 (*0-419-17850-3*, A9478, E & FN Spon) Chapman & Hall.

***Reilly, Thomas E. & Pollock, David W.** Effect of Seasonal & Long-Term Changes in Stress on Sources of Water to Wells. LC 94-49421. (Water-Supply Paper Ser.: Vol. 2445). 1995. write for info. (*0-615-00473-3*) US Geol Survey.

Reilly, Thomas E., jt. auth. see Appel, Charles A.

Reilly, Thomas P. Value Added Sales Management: A Manager's Guide to Creating the Value Added Sales Culture. 176p. (C). 1993. 24.95 (*0-944448-08-9*) Motivation Pr.

— Value Added Selling Techniques. LC 87-90744. 1987. 19.95 (*0-944448-07-0*) Motivation Pr.

Reilly, Tim, ed. see Lunde, Ken.

***Reilly, Tom.** Value Added Customer Service: Every Employee's Guide for Creating Satisfied Customers. LC 94-79761. 70p. (Orig.). (C). 1995. pap. 5.00 (*0-944448-10-0*) Motivation Pr.

— Value-Added Sales Management: A Guide for Salespeople & Their Managers. LC 92-43380. 192p. 1993. pap. 9.95 (*0-8092-3787-3*) Contemp Bks.

— Value-Added Selling Techniques: How to Sell More Profitably, Confidently, & Professionally. 1989. pap. 10.95 (*0-86553-205-2*) Congdon & Weed.

Reilly, Wayne E., ed. Sarah Jane Foster, Teacher of the Freedmen: A Diary & Letters. 240p. 1990. 35.00 (*0-8139-1284-9*); pap. 14.95 (*0-8139-1305-5*) U Pr of Va.

Reilly, William J. Marketing Investigations. Assael, Henry, ed. LC 78-251. (Century of Marketing Ser.). 1979. reprint ed. lib. bdg. 23.95 (*0-405-11176-2*) Ayer.

Reilly, William K., jt. auth. see Skinner, Samuel K.

Reily, Nancy. I Am at an Age. 1991. 18.95 (*1-878096-02-8*) Best E TX Pubs.

Reim, T., jt. auth. see Long, K.

Reiman, Donald H. Intervals of Inspiration: The Skeptical Tradition & the Psychology of Romanticism. 437p. 1988. write for info. (*0-913283-23-1*) Penkevill.

— Percy Bysshe Shelley. (Twayne's English Authors Ser.: No. 81). 1970. lib. bdg. 14.50 (*0-8057-1488-X*, Twayne) Macmillan.

— Percy Bysshe Shelley. (Twayne's English Authors Ser.: No. 81). 200p. 1989. text ed. 22.95 (*0-8057-6981-1*, Twayne) Macmillan.

— Romantic Texts & Contexts. 408p. 1988. text ed. 35.00 (*0-8262-0649-2*) U of Mo Pr.

— The Study of Modern Manuscripts: Public, Confidential & Private. LC 92-43641. 224p. (C). 1993. text ed. 29.95 (*0-8018-4590-4*) Johns Hopkins.

Reiman, Donald H., contrib. Shelley's Lost Notebook: Bodleian MSS Shelley Adds, Nos. e.15 & e.20. (Bodleian Shelley Manuscripts: Vol. VII). 665p. 1990. 175.00 (*0-8240-6983-8*) Garland.

Reiman, Donald H., ed. Peter Bell the Thrid Bound with the Triumph of Life. LC 83-49277. (Bodleian Shelley Manuscripts). 362p. 1986. lib. bdg. 91.00 (*0-8240-6261-2*) Garland.

Reiman, Donald H., ed. see Hayley, William.

Reiman, Donald H., jt. auth. see Shelley, Percy Bysshe.

Reiman, Donald H., ed. see Shelley, Percy Bysshe.

Reiman, Donald H., ed. see Wiffen, Jeremiah H.

Reiman, Jeffrey. Justice & Modern Moral Philosophy. 320p. (C). 1990. text ed. 35.00 (*0-300-04518-2*) Yale U Pr.

— Justice & Modern Moral Philosophy. 336p. (C). 1992. reprint ed. pap. text ed. 17.00 (*0-300-05234-0*) Yale U Pr.

— The Rich Get Richer & the Poor Get Prison: Ideology, Class & Criminal Justice. 3rd ed. 240p. (C). 1990. pap. write for info. (*0-02-399241-7*) Macmillan.

Reiman, Joey. Battery Book: Five Hundred Ways to Charge Yourself Up. LC 93-79668. 96p. 1993. pap. 5.95 (*1-56352-106-7*) Longstreet Pr Inc.

— Success - the Original Hand Book: Life's Five Greatest Secrets Are Right in Your Hand. LC 92-71789. 128p. 1992. 14.95 (*1-56352-044-3*) Longstreet Pr Inc.

Reiman, John & Bollis, Michael. Research on Measurement Procedures with Individuals with Hearing Impairments. pap. text ed. write for info. (*0-944232-04-3*) Teaching Res.

Reiman, Michael. The Birth of Stalinism: The U. S. S. R. on the Eve of the "Second Revolution" Saunders, George, tr. LC 85-45885. (Indiana-Michigan Series in Russian & East European Studies). 200p. 1987. 24.95 (*0-253-31196-9*) Ind U Pr.

Reiman, Michael, jt. auth. see Kaaz, Carsten.

Reiman, R. Combating Your Child's Cholesterol: A Pediatrician Shows You How. (Illus.). 290p. (C). 1993. 24.95 (*0-306-44468-2*, Plenum Pr) Plenum.

Reiman, Richard A. The New Deal & American Youth: Ideas & Ideals in a Depression Decade. LC 91-22124. 224p. 1992. 35.00 (*0-8203-1407-2*) U of Ga Pr.

Reiman, Robert, jt. auth. see Lovingood, Paul.

Reiman, Robert E., jt. ed. see Ross, Thomas E.

Reimann, B. Harvard Presentation Graphics. 350p. 1992. text ed. 49.33 (*0-13-382524-8*) P-H.

Reimann, Bernard C. Managing for Value: A Guide to Value-Based Strategic Management. 256p. 1987. 33.00 (*0-912841-26-5*) Planning Forum.

Reimann, Hobart A. The Pneumonias. LC 78-166458. (Illus.). 224p. 1971. 10.60 (*0-87527-119-7*) Green.

Reimann, K. U. Geology of Bangladesh. (Beitraege Zur Regionalen Geologie der Erde Ser.: Vol. 20). (Illus.). 160p. 1993. lib. bdg. 85.00 (*3-443-11020-7*, Pub. by Gebrueder Borntraeger GW) Lubrecht & Cramer.

Reimbert, A., jt. auth. see Reimbert, M.

Reimbert, M. & Reimbert, A. Silos: Theory & Practice. (Bulk Materials Handling Ser: Vol.1, No. 3). (Illus.). 251p. (C). 1976. text ed. 35.00 (*0-87849-014-0*, Pub. by Trans Tech GW) LPS Dist Ctr.

Reimel, J. Christopher. Image Processing & Optical Character Recognition: How They Work & How to Implement Them. LC 93-32942. 1993. 14.00 (*0-87051-142-4*) Am Inst CPA.

Reimensnyder, Barbara L. Powwowing in Union County: A Study of Pennsylvania German Folk Medicine in Context. LC 88-35082. (Immigrant Communities & Ethnic Minorities in the U. S. & Canada Ser.: No. 31). 1989. 55.00 (*0-404-19441-9*) AMS Pr.

***Reimer & Safarik.** Quotations on the Jays. 1994. per. 4.95 (*0-88978-273-3*, Pub. by Arsenal Pulp CN) InBook.

Reimer, jt. auth. see Safarik.

Reimer, A. James. The Paul Tillich & Emanuel Hirsch Debate: A Study in the Political Ramifications of Theology. LC 89-13568. (Toronto Studies in Theology: Vol. 42). 384p. 1989. lib. bdg. 109.95 (*0-88946-991-1*) E Mellen.

Reimer, A. James, ed. The Influence of the Frankfurt School on Contemporary Theology: Critical Theory & the Future of Religion: Dubrovnik Papers in Honour of Rudolf J. Siebert. LC 92-36327. (Toronto Studies in Theology: Vol. 64). 364p. 1992. text ed. 99.95 (*0-7734-9169-4*) E Mellen.

Reimer, Al. Mennonite Literary Voices: Past & Present. LC 93-70395. (C. H. Wedel Historical Ser.: Vol. 6). 75p. 1993. pap. 10.00 (*0-9630160-2-4*) Bethel Coll.

Reimer, Bennett. Philosophy of Music Education. 2nd ed. 240p. 1988. text ed. 45.33 (*0-13-663881-3*) P-H.

Reimer, Bennett & Evans, Edward. The Experience of Music. (Illus.). 384p. (C). 1973. lp 302.40 (*0-13-294892-3*); lp 129.95 (*0-686-76953-8*) P-H.

Reimer, Bennett & Smith, Ralph A., eds. The Arts, Education, & Aesthetic Knowing. (National Society for the Study of Education Publication Ser.). 288p. 1992. 27.50 (*0-226-60158-7*) U Ch Pr.

Reimer, Bennett & Wright, Jeffrey E., eds. On the Nature of Musical Experience. 327p. (C). 1992. text ed. 39.95 (*0-87081-248-3*) Univ Pr Colo.

***Reimer, Bo.** The Most Common of Practices: On Mass Media Use in Late Modernity. (Gothenburg Studies in Journalism & Mass Communications SEr.: No. 4). (Illus.). 250p. (Orig.). 1994. pap. 52.50x (*91-22-01622-8*, Pub. by Almqv & Wiksell SW) Coronet Bks.

Reimer-Bohner, Ute, tr. see Buchanan, Brian.

Reimer, C. Ground Water...Defined. Voytek, J., ed. 46p. 1985. 6.25 (*1-56034-021-5*, K214) Natl Water Well.

Reimer, C., ed. Governmental Affairs Survey. 61p. 1987. 6.25 (*1-56034-066-5*, K435) Natl Water Well.

— State Agencies Responsible for Water Well Contractor Licensing, Domestic Well Construction Standards & Well Records Collection. 29p. 1988. 6.25 (*1-56034-044-4*, K231) Natl Water Well.

Reimer, Carol J., jt. auth. see Reimer, Robert C.

Reimer, Charles W., jt. auth. see Patrick, Ruth.

Reimer, David J. The Oracles Against Babylon in Jeremiah 50-51: A Horror among the Nations. LC 92-29514. 340p. 1992. text ed. 99.95 (*0-7734-9821-4*) E Mellen.

Reimer, Everett. Futuros Alternativos. LC 76-14982. (Planning Ser.: No. S-4: Graduate Program in Planning). 110p. (Orig.). 1976. pap. text ed. 2.80 (*0-8477-2434-4*) U of PR Pr.

Reimer, G. C., tr. see Freytag, Gustav.

Reimer, Gail T., jt. ed. see Kates, Judith A.

***Reimer, James A.** Emanuel Hirsch und Paul Tillich: Theologie und Politik in Einer Zeit der Krise. xxi, 489p. (GER.). (C). 1995. lib. bdg. 152.30 (*3-11-012933-7*) De Gruyter.

Reimer, Jo, et al. Shopping & Traveling in Exotic Hong Kong. rev. ed. (Impact Guides Ser.). 247p. 1991. pap. 12.95 (*0-942710-43-6*) Impact VA.

— Shopping in Exotic Hong Kong: Your Passport to Asia's Most Incredible Shopping Bazaar. (Shopping in Exotic Places Ser.). (Illus.). 208p. (Orig.). 1989. pap. 10.95 (*0-942710-14-2*) Impact VA.

Reimer, Joseph, et al. Promoting Moral Growth: From Piaget to Kohlberg. 2nd ed. LC 82-20898. 285p. (C). 1990. reprint ed. pap. text ed. 16.95x (*0-88133-570-3*) Waveland Pr.

Reimer, Kathie. Thousand & One Ways to Help Your Child Walk with God. 1994. pap. 10.99 (*0-8423-4605-8*) Tyndale.

Reimer, Kathleen. One Thousand & One Ways to Introduce Your Child to God. 288p. 1992. pap. 10.99 (*0-8423-4757-7*) Tyndale.

Reimer, Kathleen, ed. see Reider, Barbara.

Reimer, Keith A., jt. auth. see Hackel, Donald B.

Reimer, L. Image Formation in Low-Voltage Scanning Electron Microscopy. LC 92-43451. (Tutorial Texts in Optical Engineering Ser.: Vol. TT 12). 1993. write for info. (*0-8194-1206-6*) SPIE.

Reimer, Larry, jt. auth. see Reimer, Sandy.

Reimer, Lawrence & Wagner, James. The Hospital Handbook: A Practical Guide to Hospital Visitation. LC 84-61207. 176p. (Orig.). 1988. pap. 10.95 (*0-8192-1470-1*) Morehouse Pub.

Reimer, Lawrence D. Living at the Edge of Faith. 96p. 1984. pap. 7.00 (*0-8170-1023-8*) Judson.

Reimer, Ludwig. Scanning Electron Microscopy. (Optical Sciences Ser.: Vol. 45). (Illus.). 480p. 1985. 84.00 (*0-387-13530-8*) Spr-Verlag.

— Transmission Electron Microscopy: Physics of Image Formation & Microanalysis. 3rd ed. LC 93-27996. (Optical Sciences Ser.: Vol. 36). 1993. 59.00 (*0-387-56849-2*) Spr-Verlag.

***Reimer, Ludwig, ed.** Energy-Filtering Transmission Electron Microscopy. LC 94-43581. (Series in Optical Sciences: Vol. 71). 1995. write for info. (*3-540-58479-X*) Spr-Verlag.

Reimer, Luetta & Reimer, Wilbert. Mathematicians Are People, Too: Stories from the Lives of Great Mathematicians. (Illus.). 143p. (Orig.). (J). (gr. 3-10). 1990. pap. 11.95 (*0-86651-509-7*, DS01032) Seymour Pubns.

— Mathematicians Are People, Too: Stories from the Lives of Great Mathematicians, Vol. 2. (Illus.). 150p. (Orig.). (J). (gr. 3 up). 1994. pap. 11.95 (*0-86651-823-1*, DS21326) Seymour Pubns.

Reimer, Luetta, jt. auth. see Reimer, Wilbert.

Reimer, Mavis. Such a Simple Little Tale: Critical Responses to L. M. Montgomery's Anne of Green Gables. LC 92-7392. (Children's Literature Association Ser.). 210p. 1992. 25.00 (*0-8108-2560-0*) Scarecrow.

R

***Reimer, Nadia H.** Colored Sand. 260p. (Orig.). 1995. pap. 8.95 (*0-7610-0158-1*) NW Pub.

Reimer, Neal. The Future of the Democratic Revolution: Toward a More Prophetic Politics. LC 84-8254. 320p. 1984. text ed. 65.00 (*0-275-91250-7*, C1250, Praeger Pubs) Greenwood.

Reimer, Pierce & Mills, Steven. Custom Fords. (Illus.). 152p. 1987. 29.95 (*0-85429-581-X*, F581, Pub. by G T Foulis Ltd) Haynes Pubns.

Reimer, Robert C. & Reimer, Carol J. Nazi-Retro Film: How German Narrative Cinema Remembers the Past. LC 92-18054. (Twayne's Filmmakers Ser.). 200p. 1992. text ed. 23.95 (*0-8057-9316-X*, Twayne); pap. 13.95 (*0-8057-9322-4*, Twayne) Macmillan.

Reimer, Sandy & Reimer, Larry. The Retreat Handbook. LC 86-21672. 192p. (Orig.). 1987. pap. 9.95 (*0-8192-1393-4*) Morehouse Pub.

Reimer, Sheldon & Hallfrisch, Judith, eds. Metabolic Effects of Dietary Fructose. 176p. 1987. 156.00 (*0-8493-6457-4*, QP702) CRC Pr.

Reimer, T., tr. see Devillers, Charles & Chaline, Jean.

Reimer, Thomas, tr. see Dvillers, C. & Chaline, Jean.

Reimer, Thomas, tr. see Enay, R.

Reimer-Torn, Susan, jt. auth. see Reynolds, Nancy.

Reimer, Wilbert & Reimer, Luetta. Historical Connections in Mathematics: Resources for Using History of Mathematics in the Classroom, No. 2. (Illus.). 120p. (Orig.). 1993. pap. text ed. 14.95 (*1-881431-38-X*, 2003) AIMS Educ Fnd.

— Historical Connections in Mathematics: Resources for Using History of Mathematics in the Classroom, Vol. 1. (Illus.). 103p. (Orig.). (J). (gr. 5-9). 1992. pap. text ed. 12.95 (*1-881431-35-5*, 2002) AIMS Educ Fnd.

— Historical Connections in Mathematics: Resources for Using History of Mathematics in the Classroom, Vol. 3. (Illus.). 120p. (Orig.). 1995. pap. 14.95 (*1-881431-49-5*) AIMS Educ Fnd.

Reimer, Wilbert, jt. auth. see Reimer, Luetta.

Reimers, David. The Immigrant Experience. (Peoples of North America Ser.). (Illus.). 112p. (YA). (gr. 5 up). 1989. 17.95 (*0-87754-881-1*) Chelsea Hse.

***Reimers, David M.** A Land of Immigrants. Stotsky, Sandra, ed. LC 95-13820. (Immigrant Experience Ser.). (J). 1995. write for info. (*0-7910-3361-9*) Chelsea Hse.

— A Land of Immigrants. Stotsky, Sandra, ed. LC 95-13820. (Immigrant Experience Ser.). (J). 1995. pap. write for info. (*0-7910-3373-2*) Chelsea Hse.

— Still the Golden Door: The Third World Comes to America. LC 84-29273. 320p. 1987. text ed. 45.00 (*0-231-05770-9*); pap. text ed. 18.00 (*0-231-05771-7*) Col U Pr.

— Still the Golden Door: The Third World Comes to America. 350p. 1992. text ed. 50.00 (*0-231-07680-0*); pap. text ed. 14.50 (*0-231-07681-9*) Col U Pr.

Reimers, David M., jt. auth. see Binder, Frederick M.

Reimers, David M., jt. auth. see Dinnerstein, Leonard.

Reimers, Henry L. The Abrams Story. 60p. 1977. 7.50 (*0-87770-181-4*) Ye Galleon.

— The Secret Saga of Five-Sack. 25p. 1975. pap. 4.95 (*0-87770-145-8*) Ye Galleon.

Reimers, P. Quality Assurance of Radioactive Waste Packages by Computerized Tomography. 80p. 1992. pap. 11.00 (*92-826-3365-9*, CD-NA-13879-EN-C, Pub. by Europ Com) UNIPUB.

Reimers, Sigurd & Treacher, Andy. Introducing User-Friendly Family Therapy. LC 94-10723. 240p. 1994. 59.95x (*0-415-07430-4*, B4450); pap. 18.95 (*0-415-07431-2*, B4454) Routledge.

Reimerth, Gudrun, tr. see Cohen, Donald.

Reimherr, Otto, ed. Quest for Faith, Quest for Freedom: Aspects of Pennsylvania's Religious Experience. LC 86-61790. (Illus.). 208p. 1987. 36.50 (*0-941664-26-0*) Susquehanna U Pr.

Reimold, Cheryl. Being a Boss. (Clear & Simple Ser.). (Orig.). 1995. pap. 8.95 (*0-440-50595-X*, Dell Trade Pbks) Dell.

— The Language of Business: A TAPPI Press Anthology of Published Papers 1980-1991. LC 92-3287. 175p. reprint ed. pap. 49.90 (*0-7837-1978-7*, 2042252) Bks Demand.

— The Woman's Guide to Staying Safe. write for info. (*0-318-58788-2*) S&S Trade.

***Reimonenq, Alden, et al.** Milking Black Bull: 11 Gay Black Poets. 168p. 1995. per. 12.00 (*0-614-04703-X*) Vega Pr.

— Milking Black Bull: 12 Gay Black Poets. LC 95-725. 168p. 1995. pap. 12.00 (*1-880729-11-3*) Vega Pr.

Reims, Gordon. Photographer's Guide to New England. (Yankee Books Travel Guide). (Illus.). 176p. (Orig.). 1991. pap. 10.95 (*0-89909-328-0*, 80-650-9) Yankee Bks.

Rein, David. Grammar Exercises: Part Two Intermediate ESL. Clark, Raymond C., ed. (Interplay ESL Ser.). (Illus.). 224p. (Orig.). (gr. 8 up). 1986. pap. text ed. 12.50 (*0-86647-014-X*) Pro Lingua.

— Vardis Fisher: Challenge to Evasion. 1992. lib. bdg. 79.95 (*0-8490-5475-3*) Gordon Pr.

Rein, Evgenii. Protiv Chasovoi Strelki. LC 91-14980. 128p. (Orig.). (RUS.). 1991. pap. 8.00 (*1-55779-033-7*) Hermitage.

Rein, Gustav A. Sir John Robert Seeley: A Study of the Historian. LC 82-18662. 155p. 1987. text ed. 25.00 (*0-89341-550-2*, Longwood Academic) Hollowbrook.

Rein-Hagen, Mark, jt. auth. see Weinberg, Robert.

Rein-Hagen, Mark, et al. Vampire: The Masquerade. 2nd ed. Wieck, Stephen, ed. (Vampire). (Illus.). 264p. 1993. 25.00 (*1-56504-029-5*, 2002) White Wolf.

Rein, Harry. The Primer on Medical Malpractice. 400p. 1988. student ed 100.00 (*1-55917-569-9*, 132B) Natl Prac Inst.

— The Primer on Soft Tissue Injuries. 272p. 1988. student ed 25.00 (*1-55917-566-4*, 131B) Natl Prac Inst.

— The Primer on Thermography. 275p. 1988. 85.00 (*1-55917-563-X*, 133B) Natl Prac Inst.

Rein, Horst, jt. ed. see Ruckpaul, Klaus.

***Rein, J. J.** The Industries of Japan: Together with an Account of Its Agriculture, Forestry, Arts & Commerce. fac. ed. (Illus.). 580p. (C). 1995. text ed. 449.00 (*0-7007-0351-9*, Pub. by Curzon Pr UK) Humanities.

Rein, Martin & Rainwater, Lee, eds. Public - Private Interplay in Social Protection. LC 86-11911. (Comparative Public Policy Analysis Ser.). 256p. 1986. 62.95 (*0-87332-383-1*); pap. 25.95 (*0-87332-498-6*) M E Sharpe.

Rein, Martin, jt. ed. see Atkinson, A. B.

Rein, Martin, jt. auth. see Marris, Peter.

Rein, Martin, jt. auth. see Schon, Donald A.

Rein, Martin, et al. Income Packaging in the Welfare State. (Illus.). 320p. 1987. 59.00 (*0-19-828482-9*) OUP.

Rein, Michelle. Elaborate Floral Designs. (Illus.). 52p. 1993. 10.95 (*0-936459-22-0*) Stained Glass.

Rein, Mildred. Dilemmas of Welfare Policy: Why Work Strategies Haven't Worked. LC 82-3726. 190p. 1982. text ed. 49.95 (*0-275-90883-6*, C0883, Praeger Pubs) Greenwood.

Rein, R. C. Treasury of Themes & Illustrations. (Illus.). 1983. pap. 9.50 (*0-317-17226-3*, 15N0386) Northwest Pub.

Rein, Raanan. The Franco-Peron Alliance: The Relations Between Spain & Argentina, 1946-1955. Grenzeback, Martha, tr. LC 92-35764. (Latin American Ser.). 344p. (C). 1993. text ed. 49.95 (*0-8229-3751-4*) U of Pittsburgh Pr.

Rein, Rachel, jt. auth. see Rein, Raelynne P.

Rein, Raelynne P. & Rein, Rachel. How to Develop Your Child's Gifts & Talents Through the Elementary Years: A Gifted & Talented Book. 144p. 1994. pap. 9.95 (*1-56565-165-0*) Lowell Hse Juvenile.

Reina & Muller. Surf Fishing with the Experts. 2nd ed. (With the Experts Ser.). (Illus.). 242p. Date not set. pap. 11.95 (*0-9625187-5-1*) Wavecrest Comns.

Reina, Jacqueline, ed. see Juusola, Detta.

Reina, Richard & Muller, William A. Partyboat Fishing with the Experts. (With the Experts Ser.). (Illus.). 269p. 1987. text ed. 14.95 (*0-9625187-1-9*) Wavecrest Comns.

— Surf Fishing with the Experts. (With the Experts Ser.). (Illus.). 242p. 1984. text ed. 14.95 (*0-9625187-0-0*) Wavecrest Comns.

Reina, Ruben & Kensinger, Kenneth, eds. The Gift of Birds: Featherworking of Native South American Peoples. (University Museum Monographs: Vol. 75). (Illus.). xxii, 266p. (C). 1991. 60.00 (*0-924171-11-1*); pap. 40.00 (*0-924171-12-X*) U PA Mus Pubns.

Reina, Ruben E. Parana: Social Boundaries in an Argentine City. LC 72-8265. (Latin American Monographs: No. 31). 446p. reprint ed. pap. 127.20 (*0-8357-7758-8*, 2036116) Bks Demand.

— Shadows: A Mayan Way of Knowing. 1984. 13.95 (*0-88282-008-7*) New Horizon NJ.

Reinach, A. Textes Grecs & Latines Relatifs a l'Histoire de la Peinture Ancienne. 429p. 1921. 40.00 (*0-89005-390-1*) Ares.

Reinach, Adolf. Samtliche Werke: Textcritical Edition in Two Volumes, Set. Schuhmann, Karl & Smith, Barry, eds. (Philosophia Resources Library Ser.). xviii, 848p. (GER.). 1989. 199.00 (*3-88405-015-X*) Philosophia Pr.

Reinach, Adolf, et al. Epistemology. Seifert, Josef & Crosby, John, eds. LC 81-6249. (Aletheia-an International Journal of Philosophy: Vol. 2). 272p. (Orig.). (C). 1982. pap. 15.00 (*0-86663-780-X*); 15.95 (*0-86663-778-8*) Ide Hse.

Reinach, Adolph J. Rapport Sur Les Fouilles de Koptos (Janvier-Fevrier 1910) (Illus.). 58p. (FRE.). reprint ed. pap. 25.00 (*0-933175-21-3*) Van Siclen Bks.

Reinach, Salomon. Repertoire de peintures du Moyen Age et de la renaissance (1280-1580), 6 Vols. 1974. 510.00 (*0-8115-0047-0*) Periodicals Srv.

— Repertoire des Vases Peints Grecs et Etrusques, 2 Vols. 1974. 120.00 (*0-685-13239-0*) Periodicals Srv.

Reinach, T. Jewish Coins. xvi, 92p. 1966. 15.00 (*0-89005-068-6*) Ares.

Reinach, Theodore. Mithradates Eupator, Koenig von Pontos: Mit Berichtigung und Nachtraegen Ins Deutsche Uebersetzt. Goetz, A., tr. 488p. (GER.). 1975. reprint ed. lib. bdg. 125.00 (*3-487-05585-6*, Pub. by Georg Olms GW) Lubrecht & Cramer.

— Textes d'Auteurs Grecs et Romains Relatifs au Judaisme. xx, 376p. 1983. reprint ed. write for info. (*3-487-00346-5*, Pub. by Georg Olms GW) Lubrecht & Cramer.

Reinacher, Eduard. Eine Bibliographie Seiner Werke. (Bibliographien Zur Deutschen Literature Ser.: Vol. 4). lii, 272p. 1984. write for info. (*3-487-07598-9*, Pub. by Georg Olms GW) Lubrecht & Cramer.

Reinagel, Wayne, see Adam Warlock, pseud..

Reinagel, Wayne A., see Adam Warlock, pseud..

Reinagle, Alexander. Four Sonatas; Andante, Theme & Variations; & Adagio for Piano. (Music Reprint Ser.). 100p. 1987. reprint ed. lib. bdg. 24.50 (*0-306-76254-4*) Da Capo.

Reinagle, Damon & DuBosque, Doug. Learn to Draw 3-D. (Draw! Bks.). (Illus.). 64p. (J). (gr. 3-8). 1992. pap. 7.95 (*0-939217-30-9*) Peel Prod.

Reinard, jt. auth. see Wolberg.

Reinard, John C. Foundations of Argument: Effective Communication for Critical Thinking. 512p. (C). 1991. pap. write for info. (*0-697-05338-5*) Brown & Benchmark.

— Introduction to Communication Research. 384p. 1994. boxed write for info. (*0-697-06458-1*) Brown & Benchmark.

Reinard, R. Douglas. More Sermons from the Mystery Box. 96p. (Orig.). 1992. pap. 7.95 (*0-687-27186-X*) Abingdon.

— Sermons from the Mystery Box. 1991. pap. 7.95 (*0-687-37534-7*) Abingdon.

Reinardt Schuhmann International Symposium on Innovative Technology & Reactor Design in Extraction Metallurgy Staff, et al. The Reinhardt Schuhmann International Syposium on Innovative Technology & Reactor Design in Extraction Metallurgy (1986: Colorado Springs, CO) Gaskell, D. R. et al, eds. LC 86-23469. (Illus.). 1080p. reprint ed. pap. 180.00 (*0-8357-5545-2*, 2035160) Bks Demand.

Reinarman, Craig. American States of Mind: Political Beliefs & Behavior among Private & Public Workers. LC 86-26752. 272p. reprint ed. pap. 77.60 (*0-7837-4550-8*, 2080341) Bks Demand.

***Reinartz, Dirk, photos.** Deathly Still: Pictures of Concentration Camps. (Illus.). 1995. 49.95 (*1-881616-44-4*, Pub. by Scalo Pubs) Dist Art Pubs.

Reinartz, Dirk, jt. auth. see Serra, Richard.

Reinartz, Kay F. Tukwila - Community at the Crossroads. (Illus.). 264p. (Orig.). 1991. 35.00 (*0-9629652-0-0*); pap. 18.00 (*0-9629652-1-9*) City Tukwila.

Reinarz, Robert C. Property & Liability Reinsurance Management: A Recognized Text on P. & L. Reinsurance. LC 68-59174. (C). 1969. 15.95 (*0-916910-01-6*) Mission Pub.

Reinarz, Robert C., et al. Reinsurance Practices, 2 vols. LC 90-84892. 459p. (C). 1990. pap. 26.00 (*0-89462-057-6*) IIA.

Reinaud, M., tr. see Abu al-Fida.

Reinbach, Salomon. Traite d'Epigraphie Grecque. xliv, 560p. reprint ed. write for info. (*0-318-71401-9*, Pub. by Georg Olms GW); reprint ed. write for info. (*0-318-72106-6*, Pub. by Georg Olms GW) Lubrecht & Cramer.

Reinberg, Alain. Clinical Chronopharmacology. 260p. 1990. 93.00 (*0-89116-943-1*) Hemisp Pub.

Reinberg, Alain, ed. see International Congress of Pharmacology Staff.

Reinberg, Alain, et al, eds. Annual Review of Chronopharmacology, Vol. 2. (Illus.). 334p. 1986. 108.00 (*0-08-034135-7*, Pub. by PPL UK) Elsevier.

— Night & Shift Work- Biological & Social Aspects: Proceedings of the 5th International Symposium on Night & Shift Work-Scientific Committee on Shift Work of the Permanent Commission & International Association on Occupational Health (PCIAIH, Rouen, 12-16 May 1980. (Illus.). 516p. 1981. 100.00 (*0-08-025516-7*, Pergamon Pr) Elsevier.

Reinberg, Alan R., jt. ed. see Bondur, James.

***Reinberg, Linda.** In the Field: The Language of the Vietnam War. fac. ed. LC 90-41550. 283p. 1991. reprint ed. pap. 80.70 (*0-7837-8127-X*, 2047934) Bks Demand.

Reinberg, Steven. First Aid & Safety for Day Care Provider's Instructor's Guide. (Illus.). 50p. (C). 1994. ring bd., sl. 110.00 (*1-884225-04-7*) Communs Skills.

Reinberg, Steven E., ed. see Paturas, James L. & Werdmann, Michael J.

Reinbold, Paul J., jt. auth. see Burgess, David R.

Reinbolt, Jacob C. Meeting Statutory Deadlines: Business Entities' Filing Requirements & Deadlines, Winter 1993, Action Guide, Pt. 7. Lester, Ellen, ed. (Meeting Statutory Deadlines Ser.). 90p. 1993. pap. text ed. 47.00 (*0-88124-603-4*, BU-11422) Cont Ed Bar-CA.

Reinburg, J. Hunter. Aerial Combat Escapades. Ebersole, Michael J., ed. 280p. 1988. pap. 12.95 (*0-9613218-2-2*) GCBA.

Reinburg, Peggy K. Arp Schnitger, Organ Builder: Catalyst for the Centuries. LC 81-47829. 188p. reprint ed. pap. 53.60 (*0-7837-3725-4*, 2057903) Bks Demand.

Reinckens, Sunnhild. Making Dolls. Maclean, Donald, tr. (Illus.). 56p. (GER.). (J). (ps-3). 1989. reprint ed. pap. 10.95 (*0-86315-093-4*, Pub. by Floris Bks UK) Gryphon Hse.

Reinders, Judy A. & Ross, Steven C. Understanding & Using Supercalc 4. 212p. (C). 1988. pap. text ed. 26.75 (*0-314-34291-5*) West Pub.

Reinders, Judy A., jt. auth. see Ross, Steven C.

Reinders, Robert C. End of an Era: New Orleans 1850-1860. 1964. 22.95 (*0-911116-18-4*) Pelican.

Reine, A. L. Distant Love. (Orig.). 1992. pap. 4.95 (*1-56333-056-3*) Masquerade.

Reineccius, Gary A. Sourcebook of Flavors. 2nd ed. 1992. text ed. 149.95 (*0-442-00376-5*) Chapman & Hall.

Reineccius, Gary A., jt. auth. see Heath, Henry B.

Reineccius, Gary A., jt. ed. see Risch, Sara J.

Reineck & Reineck Staff, illus. Karte & Fuhrer Zum Yosemite Valley. (GER.). 1992. 2.50 (*0-939666-61-8*) Yosemite Assn.

Reineck & Reineck Staff, tr. see Medley, Steven P.

Reineck & Reineck Staff, tr. see Shenk, Dean.

Reineck, H. E. & Singh, I. B. Depositional Sedimentary Environments-with Reference to Terrigenous Classics. (Illus.). 439p. 1992. 80.00 (*0-387-10189-6*) Spr-Verlag.

Reinecke, Hans P. Cents Frequency Period: Umrechnungstabellen fuer musikalische Akustik und Musikethnologie. (ENG & GER.). (C). 1970. 36.95 (*3-11-006397-2*) De Gruyter.

Reinecke, Herb. Whittling Simplified: Everything You Need to Know. LC 85-11136. (Illus.). 176p. (Orig.). 1985. pap. 11.95 (*0-930256-14-X*) Almar.

Reinecke, John A., jt. ed. see Dessler, Gary.

Reinecke, John A., et al. Introduction to Business. 6th ed. 750p. 1989. teacher ed write for info. (*0-318-63844-4*, H18351); 6.67 (*0-685-44204-7*, H20043); Instr's. manual, enrichment examples & lectures, resource file, test bank, transparencies. teacher ed. write for info. (*0-318-63845-2*, H18377); student ed 18.00 (*0-685-44205-5*, H25299); trans. write for info. (*0-318-63847-9*, H18401); boxed 46.00 (*0-205-11832-1*, H18328); write for info. (*0-685-21996-8*, H18369); write for info. (*0-318-63846-0*, H18393); write for info. (*0-685-21997-6*) Allyn.

Reinecke, John E. Language & Dialect in Hawaii: A Sociolinguistic History to 1935. Tsuzaki, Stanley M., ed. LC 88-14346. 254p. 1988. reprint ed. pap. text ed. 17.00 (*0-8248-1209-3*) UH Pr.

— A Man Must Stand Up: The Autobiography of a Gentle Activist. Beechert, Alice M. & Beechert, Edward D., eds. (Biography Monographs). 96p. (Orig.). 1993. pap. text ed. 12.95 (*0-8248-1517-3*) UH Pr.

Reinecke, John E., jt. auth. see Tsuzaki, Stanley M.

***Reinecke, M. F.** General Principles of Insurance. (Lawsa Student Text Ser.). 323p. 1989. pap. text ed. 64.00 (*0-409-05046-6*, SA) Butterworth Legal Pubs.

Reinecke, Manfred. Neurotensin. (Progress in Histochemistry & Cytochemistry Ser.: Vol. 16, No. 1). 175p. 1985. text ed. 65.00 (*0-89574-204-7*, Pub. by Gustav Fischer Verlag); 55.00 (*0-685-55844-4*, Pub. by Gustav Fischer Verlag) VCH Pubs.

Reinecke, Mark, jt. auth. see Freeman, Arthur.

Reinecke, Robert D., ed. Ophthalmology Annual, 1989. (Ophthalmology Annual Ser.). 384p. 1989. text ed. 121.50 (*0-88167-465-6*) Raven.

Reinecke, Robert D. & Farrell, Thomas A. Fundamentals of Ophthalmology: A Programmed Text. 1989. 12.50 (*0-317-94087-2*) Am Acad Ophthal.

Reinecke, Robert D., ed. see Ophthalmology Annual Staff.

***Reinecke, Thomas C.** To Know, Love & Serve God. (Illus.). 200p. (Orig.). 1994. pap. write for info. (*0-9643291-0-7*) Faith Hope & Love.

Reinehr, Frances G. Bloody Mary: Gentle Woman. LC 89-84199. (Illus.). 104p. 1989. pap. 6.95 (*0-934988-16-1*) Foun Bks.

Reinehr, Robert C. The Machine That Oils Itself: A Critical Look at the Mental Health Establishment. LC 75-23326. 264p. 1975. 28.95 (*0-88229-248-X*) Nelson-Hall.

Reinehr, Robert C., jt. auth. see Swartz, Jon D.

Reineke, R. K. Veterinary Helminthology. (Illus.). 1986. text ed. 52.95 (*0-409-11262-3*) Buttrwrth-Heinemann.

Reineker, P., jt. auth. see Kenkre, V. M.

Reineking, James. Logical Space. LC 74-82737. (Illus.). 90p. 1975. 25.00 (*0-8150-0703-5*) Oolp Pr.

***Reinelt, Gerhard.** The Traveling Salesman. LC 94-31562. (Lecture Notes in Computer Science: 840). 1994. 37.00 (*0-387-58334-3*) Spr-Verlag.

Reinelt, Janelle. After Brecht: British Epic Theater. LC 94-17613. (Theater -- Theory-Text-Performance Ser.). (Illus.). 212p. 1994. 39.50 (*0-472-10321-0*) U of Mich Pr.

Reinelt, Janelle, jt. ed. see Case, Sue-Ellen.

Reinelt, Janelle G. & Roach, Joseph R., eds. Critical Theory & Performance. (Theater: Theory - Text - Performance Ser.). (Illus.). 450p. (C). 1992. text ed. 49.50 (*0-472-09458-0*); pap. text ed. 18.95 (*0-472-06458-4*) U of Mich Pr.

Reinelt, Sabine. Magic of Character Doll. 1994. 29.95 (*0-87588-414-8*) Hobby Hse.

Reinen, David P. Guitar Tools: Guitar Study Course. 128p. 1992. student ed 19.95 (*0-9631942-0-8*) Driftwood Pubns.

Reiner, Ann C., jt. auth. see Carnevali, Doris L.

Reiner, Anne. Manual of Patient Care Standards. 1988. 235.00 (*0-87189-765-2*) Aspen Pub.

***Reiner, Annie.** The Naked I. 90p. (Orig.). 1994. pap. text ed. 9.95 (*1-881168-22-0*) Red Danceflr.

— The Potty Chronicles: A Story to Help Children Adjust to Toilet Training. LC 91-86. (Illus.). 32p. (J). (ps-2). 1991. 16.95 (*0-945354-36-3*); pap. 8.95 (*0-945354-35-5*) Magination Pr.

— Visit to the Art Galaxy. LC 91-16989. (Illus.). (J). (gr. 1 up). 1991. 15.95 (*0-671-74957-9*, Green Tiger S&S) S&S Childrens.

Reiner, Anton, jt. ed. see Smeets, Wilhelmus J.

Reiner, Beatrice S. & Kaufman, Irving. Character Disorders in Parents of Delinquents. LC 59-15631. 183p. reprint ed. pap. 52.20 (*0-317-07996-4*, 2019945) Bks Demand.

Reiner, Bradley K., ed. see Texas Medical Association Staff.

Reiner, Carl. All Kinds of Love. LC 92-35890. 1993. 18.95 (*1-55972-163-4*, Birch Ln Pr) Carol Pub Group.

— All Kinds of Love. large type ed. LC 93-4210. 1993. 24.95 (*0-7927-1656-6*, Curley Lrg Print); pap. 22.95 (*0-7927-1655-8*, Curley Lrg Print) Chivers N Amer.

— Continue Laughing: A Novel. LC 94-44308. 288p. 1995. 19.95 (*1-55972-273-8*, Birch Ln Pr) Carol Pub Group.

Reiner, David. Deluxe Anthology of Fiddle Styles. 1993. 7.95 (*0-87166-497-6*, 93647); audio 16.95 (*0-87166-499-2*, 93647); audio 9.98 (*0-87166-498-4*, 93647) Mel Bay.

Reiner, David & Anick, Peter. Old-Time Fiddling Across America. 1993. spiral bd. 12.95 (*0-87166-766-5*, 94205); audio 9.98 (*1-56222-641-X*, 94205) Mel Bay.

Reiner, E. & Pingree, D. Babylonian Planetary Omens, Pt. 2: The Venus Tablet. (Bibliotheca Mesopotamica Ser.: Vol. 2-1). 65p. (C). 1975. pap. text ed. 18.75 (*0-89003-010-3*) Undena Pubns.

Reiner, Eric L. Series Sixty-Two Exam Preparations. 184p. (Orig.). 1989. pap. text ed. 69.95 (*0-932889-10-7*) Examco Inc.

***Reiner, Erica.** Astral Magic in Babylonia. LC 95-76539. (Transactions Ser.: Vol. 85, Pt. 4). (Illus.). 80p. (C). 1995. pap. 20.00 (*0-87169-854-4*, T854-ree) Am Philos.

— Your Thwarts in Pieces, Your Mooring Rope Cut: Poetry from Babylonia & Assyria. Matejka, Ladislav, ed. (Michigan Studies in the Humanities: No. 5). (C). 1985. 10.00 (*0-936534-04-4*) Mich Studies Human.

Reiner, Erica, ed. Letters from Early Mesopotamia. Michalowski, Piotr, tr. LC 92-43832. (Writings from the Ancient World Ser.: No. 3). 160p. 1993. 29.95 (*1-55540-819-2*, 061503); pap. 19.95 (*1-55540-820-6*, 061503) Scholars Pr GA.

An Asterisk (*) at the beginning of an entry indicates that the title is appearing in BIP for the first time.

Reiner, Erica & Pingree, D. Babylonian Planetary Omens, Enuma Anu Enlil, Tablet 50-51. LC 79-67168. (Bibliotheca Mesopotamica Ser.: Vol. 2, Pt. 2). 100p. (Orig.). 1980. pap. 18.75 (0-89003-049-9) Undena Pubns.

Reiner, Erica, jt. ed. see Oppenheim, A. Leo.

Reiner, Erica, et al, eds. The Assyrian Dictionary of the Oriental Institute of the University of Chicago, 2 pts., Pt. 1 & 2. LC 56-58292. 1980. lib. bdg. 110.00 (0-918986-17-6) Orientl Inst Pr IT.

— The Assyrian Dictionary of the Oriental Institute of the University of Chicago, Vol. 13, Q. LC 56-58292. xxiv, 332p. 1982. text ed. 60.00 (0-918986-24-9) Orientl Inst Pr IT.

— The Assyrian Dictionary of the Oriental Institute of the University of Chicago, Vol. 15, S. LC 56-58292. xxiv, 428p. 1984. text ed. 65.00 (0-918986-40-0) Orientl Inst Pr IT.

— Assyrian Dictionary of the Oriental Institute of the University of Chicago, Vol. 17, S, Pt. 1. LC 56-58292. xxviii, 492p. 1989. 85.00 (0-918986-55-9) Orientl Inst Pr IT.

— Assyrian Dictionary of the Oriental Institute of the University of Chicago, Vol. 17, S, Pt. 2. LC 56-58292. xxiii, 453p. 1992. lib. bdg. 115.00 (0-918986-78-8) Orientl Inst Pr IT.

Reiner, Hans. Duty & Inclination. 1983. lib. bdg. 117.00 (90-247-2818-5) Kluwer Ac.

Reiner, I. Class Groups & Picard Groups of Group Rings & Orders. LC 76-10337. (CBMS Regional Conference Series in Mathematics: Vol. 26). 44p. 1986. reprint ed. 21.00 (0-8218-1676-4, CBMS/26C) Am Math.

Reiner, I., ed. Representation Theory of Finite Groups & Related Topics: Proceedings of the Symposia in Pure Mathematics-Madison, Wis.-1970. LC 79-165201. 178p. 1971. 41.00 (0-8218-1421-4, PSPUM-21) Am Math.

Reiner, I. & Roggenkamp, Klaus W., eds. Orders & Their Applications. (Lecture Notes in Mathematics Ser.: Vol. 1142). x, 306p. 1985. pap. 42.30 (0-387-15674-7) Spr-Verlag.

Reiner, Irving, jt. auth. see Curtis, Charles W.

Reiner, Larry. Minute of Silence. LC 90-34659. 268p. 1990. lib. bdg. 18.95 (0-9626148-0-7) Integra Pr.

Reiner, Laurence E. Methods & Materials of Residential Construction. (Illus.). 336p. 1981. text ed. 48.00 (0-13-578864-1) P-H.

***Reiner, M.** Dialogue & Instruction. Beun, R. J. & Baker, M., eds. (NATO ASI Ser.: Vol. 142). 368p. 1995. 90.00 (3-540-58834-5) Spr-Verlag.

Reiner, Martha, ed. see Kleinberg, Howard.

***Reiner, Miriam, et al.** Designing Intelligent Learning Environments: From Cognitive Analysis to Computer Implementation. (Cognition & Computing Ser.). 1995. write for info. (1-56750-104-4); pap. write for info. (1-56750-127-3) Ablex Pub.

Reiner, Robert. The Blue-Coated Worker: A Sociological Study of Police Unionism. LC 77-85695. (Cambridge Studies in Sociology: No. 10). 307p. reprint ed. pap. 87. 50 (0-8357-7329-9, 2030616) Bks Demand.

— Chief Constables: Bobbies, Bosses, or Bureaucrats? 400p. 1991. 39.00 (0-19-825622-1) OUP.

— The Politics of the Police. 2nd ed. 334p. 1993. 60.00 (0-8020-2942-6); pap. 19.95 (0-8020-7769-2) U of Toronto Pr.

Reiner, Thomas A. Trucking Terminal Impact & Community Response: Case Studies in the Philadelphia Region. (Discussion Paper Ser.: No. 86). 1975. pap. 10.00 (1-55869-127-8) Regional Sci Res Inst.

Reiner, Traudl. Yoga for Cats. 1990. pap. 6.95 (0-312-92438-0) St Martin.

Reiner, V. Quotients of Coexter Complexes & P-Partitions. LC 91-36297. 134p. 1992. 27.00 (0-8218-2525-9, MEMO 95/460) Am Math.

Reiner, Walter. Astrology for Cats. 1993. pap. 7.95 (0-425-13863-1) Berkley Pub.

***Reinerman, Alan J.** Austria & the Papacy in the Age of Metternich: Between Conflict & Cooperation, 1809-1830, Vol. 1. LC 79-774. reprint ed. pap. 75.30 (0-7837-9188-7, 2049888) Bks Demand.

— Austria & the Papacy in the Age of Metternich II, Vol. 2: Revolution & Reaction 1830-1838. LC 79-774. 429p. 1989. 49.95 (0-8132-0669-3) Cath U Pr.

Reiners, Kenneth G. Addicted to the Addict: From Codependency to Recovery. LC 87-50843. 64p. (Orig.). (YA). (gr. 9-12). 1987. pap. 5.50 (0-934104-06-9) Woodland.

— There's More to Life Than Pumpkins, Drugs & Other False Gods. LC 80-50424. 64p. (Orig.). 1980. pap. 5.50 (0-934104-03-4) Woodland.

Reinersmann, Elisabeth E., tr. see Lichter, Gerhard.

Reinerstsen, H., et al. Fish Farming Technology: Proceeding of the First International Conference, Trondheim, Norway, August 1993. (Illus.). 492p. (C). 1994. text ed. 115.00 (90-5410-326-4, Pub. by A A Balkema NE) Ashgate Pub Co.

Reinert, Al, jt. auth. see Winningham, Geoff.

Reinert, Andy & Burke, Bink. I'll Walk Again: Faith, Love, Laughter. LC 86-72724. (Illus.). 240p. (Orig.). 1986. pap. text ed. 14.50 (0-86516-183-6) Bolchazy-Carducci.

Reinert, Benedikt. Haqani als Dichter: Poetische Logik und Phantasie. (Studien zur Sprache, Geschichte und Kultur des Islamischen Orients: Vol. 4). viii, 120p. (GER.). (C). 1972. 46.95 (3-11-002481-0) De Gruyter.

Reinert, H. Robert & Huang, Allen. Children in Conflict: Educational Strategies for the Emotionally Disturbed & Behaviorally Disordered. 3rd ed. 320p. (C). 1987. pap. write for info. (0-675-20740-1, Merrill Pub Co) Macmillan.

Reinert, J., ed. Chloroplasts. (Results & Problems in Cell Differentiation Ser.: Vol. 10). (Illus.). 280p. 1980. 59.00 (0-387-10082-2) Spr-Verlag.

Reinert, J. & Bajaj, Y. P., eds. Applied & Fundamental Aspects of Plant Cell, Tissue, & Organ Culture. (Illus.). xviii, 803p. 1989. reprint ed. 148.00 (0-387-07677-8) Spr-Verlag.

Reinert, J. & Binding, H., eds. Differentiation of Protoplasts & of Transformed Plant Cells. (Results & Problems in Cell Differentiation Ser.: Vol. 12). (Illus.). 180p. 1986. 69.00 (0-387-16539-8) Spr-Verlag.

Reinert, Otto & Arnott, Peter D. Twenty-Three Plays: An Introductory Anthology. (C). 1987. pap. text ed. 20.50 (0-673-39234-1) HarpCollege.

***Reinert, Rita C.** Boots: Trailing the Appalachians. 80p. 1995. pap. 9.95 (0-9645648-0-7) Atir Pr.

Reinertsen, Donald G., jt. auth. see Smith, Preston G.

Reinertsen, Lauren. Clipart Book of Promotional & Program Artwork. 2nd ed. LC 74-84398. (Illus.). 64p. 1974. pap. 11.95 (0-87874-013-9) Galloway.

Reinertsen, R. E., jt. ed. see Bech, C.

Reinertson, Kristen E. The Holy City with Signs & Wonders. LC 86-90554. (Illus.). 157p. (Orig.). (C). 1989. text ed. 14.95 (0-9617564-6-2); pap. text ed. 9.95 (0-9617564-5-4) Skoglie Storevik Pubs.

Reines, Alvin J. Polydoxy: Explorations in a Philosophy of Liberal Religion. LC 87-2259. 219p. 1987. 29.95x (0-87975-399-4) Prometheus Bks.

Reines, Alvin J., jt. auth. see Abravanel, Isaac.

Reines, Frederick, ed. Cosmology, Fusion & Other Matters: George Gamow Memorial Volume. LC 77-159018. (Illus.). 334p. reprint ed. pap. 95.20 (0-8357-5503-7, 2035118) Bks Demand.

Reinfeld, Barbara K. Karel Havlicek. (East European Monographs: No. 98). 135p. 1982. text ed. 42.00 (0-914710-92-3) East Eur Quarterly.

Reinfeld, Fred. Be a Winner at Chess. 1986. pap. 3.95 (0-449-21257-2) Fawcett.

— Beginner's Guide to Winning Chess. 1994. pap. 13.95 (0-572-02022-8, Pub. by W Foulsham UK) Trans-Atl Phila.

— Beginner's Guide to Winning Chess. 1980. pap. 7.00 (0-87980-215-4) Wilshire.

— Chess Problems for Beginners. 1979. pap. 7.00 (0-87980-017-8) Wilshire.

— Colle's Chess Masterpieces. 106p. 1984. reprint ed. pap. 3.95 (0-486-24757-0) Dover.

— The Complete Book of Chess Stratagems. 188p. 1972. reprint ed. pap. 5.95 (0-486-20690-4) Dover.

— Complete Chess Course. LC 59-13043. 1959. 25.00 (0-385-00464-8) Doubleday.

— The Complete Chessplayer. 1981. pap. 2.50 (0-449-14101-2, GM) Fawcett.

— Great Brilliancy Prize Games of the Chess Masters. (Illus.). xv, 222p. 1995. pap. text ed. 8.95 (0-486-28614-2) Dover.

— How to Force Checkmate. (Illus.). 1947. pap. 3.50 (0-486-20439-1) Dover.

— How to Win at Checkers. 1977. pap. 5.00 (0-87980-068-2) Wilshire.

— Hypermodern Chess. 1948. pap. 6.95 (0-486-20448-0) Dover.

— Immortal Gamea of Capablanca. 1990. pap. 6.95 (0-486-26333-9) Dover.

— One Thousand One Brilliant Ways to Checkmate. (Illus.). 1969. reprint ed. pap. 10.00 (0-87980-110-7) Wilshire.

— One Thousand One Winning Chess Sacrifices & Combinations. 1969. reprint ed. pap. 10.00 (0-87980-111-5) Wilshire.

— Pony Express. LC 64-21330. (Illus.). 135p. 1973. pap. 6.00 (0-8032-5786-4, Bison Books) U of Nebr Pr.

— Win at Chess. 1945. pap. 3.50 (0-486-20438-3) Dover.

— Winning Chess Openings. (Illus.). 288p. 1973. pap. 13.95 (0-02-029760-2, Pub. by Gebrueder Borntraeger GW) Macmillan.

Reinfeld, Fred, ed. Chess Tactics for Beginners. 1975. pap. 7.00 (0-87980-019-4) Wilshire.

Reinfeld, Fred & Fine, Reuben, eds. A. Alekhine vs E. D. Bogolijubow: World's Chess Championship, 1934. pap. 4.95 (0-486-21813-9) Dover.

— Lasker's Greatest Chess Games, 1889-1914. 1965. pap. 5.95 (0-486-21450-8) Dover.

Reinfeld, Fred, jt. auth. see Chernev, Irving.

Reinfeld, Fred, jt. auth. see Hobson, Burton.

Reinfeld, Fred, jt. auth. see Horowitz, Al.

Reinfeld, Fred, jt. auth. see Horowitz, I. A.

Reinfeld, Fred, jt. auth. see Horowitz, Israel A.

Reinfeld, Fred, ed. see Mason, James.

Reinfeld, Fred, ed. see Spielmann, Rudolf.

Reinfeld, Fred, ed. see Znosko-Borovsky, Eugene.

Reinfeld, Linda. Language Poetry: Writing As Rescue. LC 91-24848. (Horizons in Theory & American Culture Ser.). 192p. 1992. text ed. 27.50 (0-8071-1698-X) La State U Pr.

Reinfeld, Nyles V. Community Recycling: System Design to Management. 240p. 1992. text ed. 62.00 (0-13-155789-0) P-H.

— Open Heart Surgery: A Second Chance. 192p. 1983. 22. 00 (0-13-637520-0); pap. 14.95 (0-13-637512-X) P-H.

Reinfeld, W. Vel. Index of Outreach Programs in Israel. 98p. 1989. pap. write for info. (0-9623723-0-7) AVI CHAI.

Reinforced Concrete Research Council Staff. Long Reinforced Concrete Columns. (Bulletin Ser.: No. 21). 250p. 1986. 30.00 (0-87262-537-0) Am Soc Civil Eng.

Reinfrank, Arno, jt. auth. see Reinfrank, Karin.

Reinfrank, Karin & Reinfrank, Arno. Berlin: Two Cities under Seven Flags: A Kaleidoscopic A-Z. 254p. 1987. 19.95 (0-85496-530-0) Berg Pubs.

Reinfrank, M., et al. Non-Monotonic Reasoning. (Lecture Notes in Computer Science Ser.: Vol. 346). xiv, 237p. 1989. pap. text ed. 37.00 (0-387-50701-9) Spr-Verlag.

Reingen, Peter H. & Woodside, Arch G., eds. Buyer-Seller Interactions: Empirical Research & Normative Issues. LC 81-855. (Proceedings Ser.). (Illus.). 189p. 1982. pap. text ed. 12.00 (0-87757-149-X) Am Mktg.

Reingold, Carmel B. Lovers. 1989. pap. 3.95 (1-55817-231-9, Pinnacle NY) Windsor NY.

Reingold, Carmel B., jt. auth. see Burke, David.

Reingold, Edward M. & Hansen, Wilfred J. Data Structures in Pascal. (C). 1987. text ed. 58.50 (0-673-39069-1) HarpCollege.

Reingold, Edward M., et al. Combinatorial Algorithms: Theory & Practice. 1977. text ed. write for info. (0-13-152447-X) P-H.

Reingold, Edwin. Chrysanthemums & Thorns: The Untold Story of Modern Japan. (Illus.). 384p. 1994. pap. 14.95 (0-312-10440-5) St Martin.

Reingold, Edwin M. Chrysanthemums & Thorns: The Untold Story of Modern Japan. (Illus.). 384p. 1992. 24. 95 (0-312-08160-X) St Martin.

Reingold, Ida H., jt. ed. see Reingold, Nathan.

***Reingold, Jacquelyn.** Girl Gone. Date not set. 4.75 (0-8222-1471-7) Dramatists Play.

Reingold, Nathan. Science, American Style. LC 90-9068. 414p. (C). 1991. text ed. 42.00 (0-8135-1660-9); pap. text ed. 18.00 (0-8135-1661-7) Rutgers U Pr.

Reingold, Nathan, ed. The Papers of Joseph Henry, Vol. 3: The Princeton Years, January 1836-1837. LC 72-2005. (Illus.). 585p. 1979. 49.95 (0-87474-174-2, REP3) Smithsonian.

— The Papers of Joseph Henry, Vol. 4: The Princeton Years, January 1838-1840. LC 72-2005. (Joseph Henry Papers). (Illus.). 475p. 1981. text ed. 49.95 (0-87474-792-9, REP4) Smithsonian.

— The Papers of Joseph Henry, Vol. 5: The Princeton Years, January 1841-December 1843. LC 72-2005. (Joseph Henry Papers). (Illus.). 500p. 1985. 49.95 (0-87474-793-7, REP5) Smithsonian.

— Science in Nineteenth-Century America: A Documentary History. LC 85-1021. xii, 340p. 1985. pap. text ed. 12.50 (0-226-70947-7) U Ch Pr.

Reingold, Nathan & Reingold, Ida H., eds. Science in America: A Documentary History, 1900-1939. LC 81-2584. 1981. 37.50 (0-226-70946-9) U Ch Pr.

Reingold, Nathan & Rothenberg, Marc, eds. Scientific Colonialism: A Cross-Cultural Comparison, Papers at a Conference at Melbourne, 1981. LC 85-43238. 264p. (Orig.). (C). 1986. pap. 37.00 (0-87474-785-6) Smithsonian.

Reingruber, Michael C. The Data Modeling Handbook: A Best Practice Approach to Building Quality Data Models. LC 94-12669. 1994. text ed. 49.95 (0-471-05290-6) Wiley.

Reinhard, Dale W. Simply Celebrating Children: Parties As Unique & Special As a Child. 140p. (J). 1991. 12.95 (0-9628888-0-X) Pressed Duck.

Reinhard, David W. The Republican Right since Nineteen Forty-Five. LC 82-40460. 304p. 1983. 30.00 (0-8131-1484-5) U Pr of Ky.

Reinhard, Donald K. Introduction to Integrated Circuit Engineering. LC 86-80842. 480p. (C). 1987. teacher ed 6.36 (0-395-37069-8) Williams & Wilkins.

Reinhard, Geoffrey G., jt. ed. see Schomer, Karine.

Reinhard, Herve. Differential Equations: Foundations & Applications. 1987. 60.00 (0-07-051841-6) McGraw.

Reinhard, John. Burning the Prairie. 96p. 1988. pap. 5.00 (0-89823-104-3) New Rivers Pr.

Reinhard, John R., tr. Medieval Pageant. LC 75-129969. (Studies in European Literature: No. 56). 1970. reprint ed. lib. bdg. 75.00 (0-8383-1166-0) M S G Haskell Hse.

Reinhard, Karl J., jt. auth. see Gregonis, Linda M.

Reinhard, Kenneth, jt. auth. see Lupton, Julia R.

Reinhard, Lisa A. The Nutmeg Adventure. (Illus.). 40p. (J). (ps-2). 1994. 9.95 (0-87935-099-7) Colonial Williamsburg.

Reinhard, Margaret, jt. auth. see Forester, Anne.

Reinhard, P. G., jt. auth. see Goeke, K.

Reinhard, Richard O. Human Factors in Pilot Performance. (Illus.). 352p. 1991. 32.95 (0-8306-7662-7, 3662, TAB-Aero) TAB Bks.

Reinhardsbrunn, V., ed. Recent Trends in Mathematics. 1985. 60.00 (0-317-46708-5, Pub. by Collets) St Mut.

Reinhardsbrunn, V., ed. see Collet's Holdings Ltd. Staff.

***Reinhardt.** Official Cat Codependents Handbook. 1995. pap. text ed. 9.95 (1-56906-019-3) R Sellers Prods.

Reinhardt, Al S. Jewish Communities of Russian Carpathia: From Early Settlement to WWI. LC 89-85091. 192p. (HEB.). 1989. pap. 12.50 (0-911437-75-4) Labyrinthos.

Reinhardt, Christoph A., ed. Alternatives to Animal Testing: New Ways in the Biomedical Sciences, Trends, & Progress. LC 93-44359. 1994. pap. 90.00 (1-56081-831-X) VCH Pubs.

Reinhardt, Curt. Brainwashed. 232p. 1993. pap. write for info. (0-9631949-2-5) Graphic Pub Williamsbrg.

Reinhardt, David P., jt. auth. see Kimbaall, Russell D.

Reinhardt, Dietrich & Schmidt, Eberhard, eds. Food Allergy. (Nestle Nutrition Workshop Ser.: Vol. 17). (Illus.). 320p. 1988. text ed. 65.50 (0-88167-438-9) Raven.

Reinhardt, Donald. Microbiology Laboratory: A Logical Approach. 112p. (C). 1992. pap. text ed. 11.95 (0-8403-8156-5) Kendall-Hunt.

Reinhardt, Ed & Rogers, Hal. How to Make Your Own Picture Frames. 3rd ed. (Illus.). 144p. 1989. pap. 14.95 (0-8230-2452-0, Watsn-Guptill) Watsn-Guptill.

Reinhardt, H. J. Analysis of Approximation Methods for Differential & Integral Equations. (Applied Mathematical Sciences Ser.: Vol. 57). (Illus.). xi, 398p. 1985. pap. 76.00 (0-387-96214-X) Spr-Verlag.

Reinhardt, H. W., ed. Testing During Concrete Construction: Proceedings of RILEM Colloquium, Darmstadt, 1990. (Illus.). 420p. 1991. 85.95 (0-442-31389-6) Chapman & Hall.

Reinhardt, H. W. & Bouvy, J. J., eds. Demountable Concrete Structures: A Challenge for Precast Concrete. (Illus.). 360p. (Orig.). 1985. pap. text ed. 57.50 (90-6275-182-2, Pub. by Delft U Pr NE) Coronet Bks.

Reinhardt, H. W. & Naaman, A. E., eds. High Performance Fiber Reinforced Cement Composites: Proceedings of the International RILEM-ACI Workshop. 576p. 1992. 74.95 (0-442-31615-1) Chapman & Hall.

Reinhardt, Hellmuth. Airborne Operations: A German Appraisal. (Center for Military History Publication German Report Series, DA Pam: Nos. 104-13 & 20-232). 64p. 1989. reprint ed. pap. 2.00 (0-16-001976-1, S/N 008-029-00174-8) USGPO.

Reinhardt, J. & Sigleo, W. R., eds. Paleosols & Weathering Through Geologic Time: Principles & Applications. (Special Paper Ser.: No. 216). (Illus.). 200p. 1988. pap. 13.00 (0-8137-2216-0) Geol Soc.

Reinhardt, J., jt. auth. see Greiner, W.

Reinhardt, J., jt. auth. see Muller, B.

***Reinhardt, Jennifer B.** The Giant's Toybox. (Illus.). 32p. (J). 1995. text ed. 13.95 (0-941711-20-X) Wyrick & Co.

Reinhardt, Joachim, jt. auth. see Greiner, Walter.

Reinhardt, Jon M. Foreign Policy & National Integration: The Case of Indonesia. LC 70-175548. (Monograph Ser.: No. 17). vi, 230p. 1971. 8.50 (0-938692-12-7) Yale U SE Asia.

Reinhardt, K. & Eyrich, K., eds. Sepsis. (Illus.). 410p. 1989. 113.00 (0-387-17763-9) Spr-Verlag.

Reinhardt, Karl. Poseidonios, 2 vols. viii, 895p. 1976. Bd. I: Poseidonios. write for info. (0-318-71005-6, Pub. by Georg Olms GW); Bd. II: Kosmos und Sympathie. write for info. (0-318-71006-4, Pub. by Georg Olms GW) Lubrecht & Cramer.

— Poseidonios, 2 vols., Set. viii, 895p. 1976. write for info. (3-487-06106-6, Pub. by Georg Olms GW) Lubrecht & Cramer.

Reinhardt, Kim, ed. Directory of Computers & Software Retailers, 1993. 814p. pap. 275.00 (0-685-65049-9, CSG Info Servs) Lebhar Friedman.

— Directory of Consumer Electronics, 1993. 136p. pap. 125. 00 (0-685-65050-2, CSG Info Servs) Lebhar Friedman.

— Directory of Value Added Resellers, 1993. 884p. pap. 275.00 (0-685-65052-9, CSG Info Servs) Lebhar Friedman.

Reinhardt, Klaus. Moscow: The Turning Point? 495p. 1992. 74.95 (0-85496-695-1) Berg Pubs.

Reinhardt, Kurt F. Germany: Two Thousand Years, 2 Vols. rev. ed. LC 60-53139. 1981. pap. 33.90 (0-685-05126-9, F Ungar Bks) Continuum.

— Germany: Two Thousand Years, 2 Vols, Vol. 1: The Rise & Fall of the Holy Empire. rev. ed. LC 60-53139. 1981. Vol.1: The Rise & Fall of the Holy Empire. pap. 16.95 (0-8044-6692-0, F Ungar Bks) Continuum.

— Germany: Two Thousand Years, 2 Vols, Vol. 2. rev. ed. LC 60-53139. 350p. 1992. Vol.2. pap. text ed. 19.95 (0-8044-1784-9, F Ungar Bks) Continuum.

Reinhardt, Lloyd, jt. ed. see Freadman, Richard.

Reinhardt, Madge. The Unclean Bird. LC 85-72901. 135p. 1986. pap. 6.95 (0-917162-10-2) Back Row Pr.

— The Voice of the Stranger. LC 81-65402. (Illus.). 477p. 1982. pap. 8.50 (0-917162-06-4) Back Row Pr.

— The Year of the Silence. LC 78-59573. 177p. 1978. pap. 5.50 (0-917162-08-0) Back Row Pr.

— You've Got to Ride the Subway. LC 76-4760. 278p. 1977. pap. 6.50 (0-917162-02-1) Back Row Pr.

Reinhardt, Mona. Programmer's Desk Reference for Your Commodore 64. write for info. (0-318-58214-7) P-H.

Reinhardt, Nola. Our Daily Bread: The Peasant Question & Family Farming in the Colombian Andes. 312p. 1988. 40.00 (0-520-06225-6) U CA Pr.

Reinhardt, Peter A. & Gordon, Judith G. Infectious & Medical Waste Management. (Illus.). 350p. 1990. 79.95 (0-87371-158-0, RA567) Lewis Pubs.

***Reinhardt, Peter A., et al, eds.** Pollution Prevention & Waste Minimization in Laboratories. 512p. 1995. 69.95 (0-87371-975-1, L975) Lewis Pubs.

Reinhardt, Robert. Telling Moments: Sixteen Gay Monologues. (Acting Ser.). 96p. 1994. pap. 8.95 (1-55783-163-7) Applause Theatre Bk Pubs.

Reinhardt, Robert M. & Hall, Alice G. Nubian History: America & Great Britain. LC 77-809029. (Illus.). 1978. pap. text ed. 5.50 (0-932218-07-5) Hall Pr.

Reinhardt, Steven G. Justice in the Sarladais, 1770-1790. LC 90-28831. (Illus.). 336p. 1991. text ed. 39.95 (0-8071-1587-8); pap. text ed. 16.95 (0-8071-1658-0) La State U Pr.

Reinhardt, Steven G., ed. The Sun King: Louis XIV & the New World. (Studies in Louisiana Culture: Vol. III). (Illus.). 344p. (Orig.). 1984. write for info. (0-916137-00-7); pap. write for info. (0-916137-01-5) L A Mus Foun.

Reinhardt, Steven G. & Cawthon, Elisabeth A., eds. Essays on the French Revolution: Paris & the Provinces. LC 91-22146. (Walter Prescott Webb Memorial Lectures: No. 25). 144p. 1992. 24.50 (0-89096-498-X) Tex A&M Univ Pr.

***Reinhardt, Thomas A., et al.** Ornamental Grasses: Design Ideas, Uses, & Varieties. LC 95-13522. Orig. Title: Ornamental Grass Gardening. (Illus.). 1995. pap. write for info. (1-56799-219-6, Friedman-Fairfax) M Friedman Pub Grp Inc.

Reinhardt, Uwe E., jt. ed. see Shortell, Stephen M.

Reinhardt, V. Untersuchungen Zum Sozialverhalten Des Rindes. (Tierhaltung Ser.: No. 10). (Illus.). 96p. (GER.). 1980. pap. 27.50 (0-8176-1138-X) Birkhauser.

R

***Reinhardt Werba Bowen Advisory Services Staff.** The Prudent Investor's Guide to Beating the Market. 275p. 1995. 30.00 (*0-7863-0365-4*) Irwin Prof Pubng.

Reinhardt, Werner, et al. Deutsche Fachsprache der Technik. (Studien Zu Sprache und Technik Ser.: Bd. 3). xi, 174p. (GER.). 1992. write for info. (*3-487-09608-0*, Pub. by Georg Olms GW) Lubrecht & Cramer.

Reinhardt, William G., jt. auth. see Hansen, Kenneth D.

Reinhardt, William W. The Legislative Council of the Punjab, 1987-1912. LC 73-162865. 160p. (Orig.). (C). 1972. pap. text ed. 5.00 (*0-685-59533-1*) Ctr Intl Stud Duke.

Reinhart, A. Kevin. Before Revelation: The Boundaries of Muslim Moral Thought. LC 94-13372. (SUNY Series in Middle Eastern Studies). 267p. 1995. text ed. 59.50 (*0-7914-2289-5*); pap. 19.95 (*0-7914-2290-9*) State U NY Pr.

Reinhart, B. L. Differential Geometry of Folitations: The Fundamental Integrability Problem, Set. (Ergebnisse der Mathematik Ser.: Folge 2, Vol. 99). 195p. 1983. 69.00 (*0-387-12269-9*) Spr-Verlag.

Reinhart, C., et al, eds. Irritation Testing of Skin & Mucous Membranes: Proceedings of a Workshop Held at the Karthhaus-Ittingen, near Frauenfeld, Switzerland, April 1984. (Illus.). 180p. 1985. pap. 41.00 (*0-08-032004-X*, Pub. by PPL UK) Elsevier.

Reinhart, Carlene, jt. auth. see Chalofsky, Neal E.

Reinhart, Carmen M., jt. ed. see Khan, Mohsin S.

Reinhart, Charles. You Can't Do That! Beatles Bootlegs & Novelty Records, 1963-1980. (Rock & Roll Reference Ser.: No. 5). (Illus.). 450p. 1989. reprint ed. 29.50 (*1-56075-009-X*) Popular Culture.

Reinhart, Cornell, ed. see Johnson, Isaac.

Reinhart, Dietrich, jt. auth. see Kwatera, Michael.

Reinhart, G. D., jt. ed. see Jameson, D. M.

Reinhart, J. R. The Power of Knowing Who I Am in Christ. LC 82-73254. 220p. 1983. pap. 8.95 (*0-918060-04-4*) Burn Hart.

Reinhart, Jo An, jt. auth. see Morgan, Sharon.

Reinhart, Johanna M., ed. Small Boat Design. (Illus.). 79p. 1983. pap. text ed. 12.00 (*0-89955-393-1*, Pub. by ICLARM PH) Intl Spec Bk.

Reinhart, K. & Eyrich, K., eds. Clinical Aspects of O2-Transport & Tissue Oxygenation. (Illus.). xiii, 511p. 1989. pap. 118.00 (*0-387-51470-8*, 3312) Spr-Verlag.

Reinhart, K., et al, eds. Sepsis: Current Perspectives in Pathophysiology & Therapy. LC 94-373. (Update in Intensive Care & Emergency Medicine Ser.: Vol. 18). 1994. 98.00 (*0-387-57349-6*) Spr-Verlag.

Reinhart, L. P., jt. auth. see Streeter, M. K.

Reinhart, Margaret. The Wilder Side of Providence: And Other True & False Tales. 80p. 1992. 11.00 (*0-8233-0479-5*) Golden Quill.

Reinhart, Marx, comp. & intro. Johann Hellwig: A Descriptive Bibliography. LC 92-42474. (Studies in German Literature, Linguistics & Culture). xxxviii, 158p. 1993. 65.00 (*1-879751-46-1*) Camden Hse.

Reinhart, Max. Johann Hellwig's "Die Nymphe Noris" (1650) A Critical Edition. 250p. 1994. 65.00 (*1-879751-63-1*) Camden Hse.

Reinhart, Melanie. Chiron & the Healing Journey: An Astrological & Psychological Perspective. 464p. 1990. pap. 12.00 (*0-14-019209-3*, Penguin Bks) Viking Penguin.

Reinhart, Peter. Brother Junipers Bread Book. 1991. 17.26 (*0-201-57076-9*) Addison-Wesley.

— Brother Juniper's Bread Book: Slow Rise as Method & Metaphor. (Illus.). 224p. 1993. pap. 10.58 (*0-201-62467-2*) Addison-Wesley.

— Sacramental Magic in a Smalltown Cafe. 1994. 19.23 (*0-201-62259-9*) Addison-Wesley.

Reinhart, Richard O. Basic Flight Physiology. 1992. 34.95 (*0-07-051823-8*) McGraw.

— Basic Flight Physiology. 248p. 1992. 34.95 (*0-8306-3890-3*, 4141) TAB Bks.

— FAA Medical Certification: Guidelines for Pilots. LC 91-31005. (Illus.). 212p. 1992. pap. 19.95 (*0-8138-1412-X*) Iowa St U Pr.

— Fit to Fly: A Pilot's Guide to Health & Safety. 1992. 24.95 (*0-07-051822-X*); pap. 15.95 (*0-07-051821-1*) McGraw.

— Fit to Fly: A Pilot's Guide to Health & Safety. (Illus.). 208p. 1992. 24.95 (*0-8306-2070-2*, 3682); pap. 15.95 (*0-8306-2059-1*, 3682) TAB Bks.

— The Pilot's Medical Manual of Certification & Health Maintenance. 2nd ed. 180p. reprint ed. pap. 19.95 (*0-317-93950-5*) FAPA Inc.

Reinhart, Robert C. A History of Shadows. 3rd ed. 317p. (Orig.). 1995. pap. 5.95 (*1-55583-604-6*, AlyCat) Alyson Pubns.

— Walk the Night: A Novel of Gays in the Holocaust. LC 94-29726. 222p. (Orig.). 1994. pap. 9.95 (*1-55583-267-9*) Alyson Pubns.

Reinhart, Rodney. Splinters on the Wind. (Illus.). 1985. 3.00 (*0-931081-01-7*) Operation DOME.

Reinhart, Susan H. & Fisher, Ira. Speaking & Social Interaction: Activities for Intermediate to Advanced ESL Students. (Illus.). 112p. (C). 1984. pap. text ed. 13.25 (*0-13-825787-6*) P-H.

Reinhart, Susan M. Testing Your Grammar. 1985. pap. text ed. 12.95x (*0-472-08054-7*) U of Mich Pr.

Reinhart, Susan M., jt. auth. see Madden, Carolyn G.

Reinhart, T. S., ed. see International SAMPE Technical Conference Staff.

***Reinhart, Theodore R., ed.** The Archaeology of Shirley Plantation. fac. ed. LC 84-15245. (Illus.). 238p. 1984. reprint ed. pap. 67.90 (*0-7837-7983-6*, 2047739) Bks Demand.

— A Cumulative Index to the Quarterly Bulletin of the Archeological Society of Virginia 1940-1990, No. 24. 208p. 1991. pap. 26.00 (*1-884626-10-6*) Archeolog Soc.

Reinhart, Theodore R. & Hodges, Mary E., eds. Early & Middle Archaic Research in Virginia: A Synthesis, No. 22. 311p. 1990. pap. 26.00 (*1-884626-08-4*) Archeolog Soc.

— Late Archaic & Early Woodland Research in Virginia: A Synthesis, No. 23. 275p. 1991. pap. 26.00 (*1-884626-09-2*) Archeolog Soc.

— Middle & Late Woodland Research in Virginia: A Synthesis, No. 29. 311p. 1992. pap. 25.00 (*1-884626-12-2*) Archeolog Soc.

Reinhart, Theodore R. & Pogue, Dennis J., eds. The Archaeology of Seventeenth Century Virginia: A Synthesis. (SP Ser.: No. 30). 402p. 1993. pap. 25.00 (*1-884626-13-0*) Archeolog Soc.

Reinhartz & Beach, Barbara. Secondary Education: A Focus on Curriculum. (C). 1992. text ed. 44.00 (*0-06-045361-3*) HarpCollege.

Reinhartz, Adele. The Word in the World: The Cosmological Tale in the Fourth Gospel. LC 92-38139. 156p. 1992. 39.95 (*1-55540-798-6*, 06 00 45); pap. 25.95 (*1-55540-799-4*) Scholars Pr GA.

Reinhartz, Dennis. Milovan Djilas: A Revolutionary As Writer. (East European Monographs: No. 89). 112p. 1981. text ed. 46.00 (*0-914710-83-4*) East Eur Quarterly.

Reinhartz, Dennis & Colley, Charles C., eds. The Mapping of the American Southwest. LC 86-22992. (Special Collections Publication of the University of Texas at Arlington Ser.). (Illus.). 112p. 1987. reprint ed. 24.50 (*0-89096-237-5*) Tex A&M Univ Pr.

Reinhartz, Dennis & Maizlish, Stephen E., eds. Essays on Walter Prescott Webb & the Teaching of History. LC 85-40047. (Walter Prescott Webb Memorial Lectures: No. 19). 116p. 1985. 17.50 (*0-89096-234-0*) Tex A&M Univ Pr.

Reinhartz, Dennis & Reinhartz, Judy. Geography Across the Curriculum. 96p. 1990. 10.95 (*0-8106-3070-2*) NEA.

Reinhartz, Dennis, jt. ed. see Palmer, Stanley.

Reinhartz, Dennis, jt. auth. see Reinhartz, Judy.

Reinhartz, Jehuda & Mosse, George L. The Impact of Western Nationalisms. (Illus.). 336p. (C). 1992. 69.95 (*0-8039-8766-8*) Sage.

Reinhartz, Judy, ed. Teacher Induction. 128p. 1989. 14.95 (*0-8106-3003-6*) NEA.

Reinhartz, Judy & Beach, Don M. Improving Middle School Instruction: A Research Based Self-Assesment System. 64p. 1983. 8.95 (*0-8106-1688-2*) NEA.

Reinhartz, Judy & Reinhartz, Dennis. Teach-Practice-Apply: The TPA Instruction Model, 7-12. 104p. 1988. 9.95 (*0-8106-1834-6*) NEA.

Reinhartz, Judy & Van Cleef, Daniel. Teach - Practice - Apply: The TPA Instructional Model, K-8. 112p. 1986. 10.95 (*0-8106-1830-3*) NEA.

Reinhartz, Judy, jt. auth. see Reinhartz, Dennis.

Reinharz, Jehuda. Chaim Weizmann: The Making of a Statesman, Vol. 2. (Illus.). 560p. 1993. 39.95 (*0-19-507215-4*) OUP.

— Chaim Weizmann: The Making of a Zionist Leader. LC 84-7898. (Illus.). 1987. pap. 15.95 (*0-19-505069-X*) OUP.

Reinharz, Jehuda, ed. Living with Antisemitism: Modern Jewish Responses. LC 86-40388. (Tauber Institute Ser.: No. 6). 510p. 1987. text ed. 50.00 (*0-87451-388-X*); pap. 24.95 (*0-87451-412-6*) U Pr of New Eng.

Reinharz, Jehuda & Schatzberg, Walter, eds. The Jewish Response to German Culture: From the Enlightenment to the Second World War. LC 85-14185. 378p. 1985. text ed. 45.00 (*0-87451-345-6*); pap. 19.95 (*0-87451-552-1*) U Pr of New Eng.

***Reinharz, Jehuda & Shapira, Anita, eds.** Essential Papers on Zionism. (Essential Papers on Jewish Studies Ser.). 750p. 1995. 75.00 (*0-8147-7448-2*); pap. 25.00 (*0-8147-7449-0*) NYU Pr.

Reinharz, Jehuda, jt. auth. see Mendes-Flohr, Paul R.

Reinharz, Jehuda, jt. ed. see Mendes-Flohr, Paul.

Reinharz, Shulamit. On Becoming a Social Scientist. 466p. (C). 1991. pap. 19.95 (*0-87855-968-X*) Transaction Pubs.

— On Becoming a Social Scientist. LC 79-83577. (Jossey-Bass Social & Behavioral Science Ser.). 442p. reprint ed. pap. 126.00 (*0-8357-6886-4*, 2037938) Bks Demand.

— Social Research Methods, Feminist Perspectives. (Athene Ser.). 1993. text ed. 50.01 (*0-08-032794-X*, Pub. by PPI UK); pap. text ed. 21.01 (*0-08-032793-1*, Pub. by PPI UK) Elsevier.

Reinharz, Shulamit & Davidman, Lynn. Feminist Methods in Social Research. 424p. 1992. pap. text ed. 21.00 (*0-19-507386-X*, 3474) OUP.

Reinharz, Shulamit & Rowles, Graham, eds. Qualitative Gerontology. 336p. (C). 1988. 36.95 (*0-8261-5230-9*) Springer Pub.

Reinharz, Shulamit, jt. ed. see Conrad, Peter.

Reinheimer, Joel. The Adventure of Squeek the Rabbit. (J). 1990. 6.95 (*0-533-08900-X*) Vantage.

Reinherz, E. L., et al, eds. Leukocyte Typing II: Human B Lymphocytes, Vol. 2. (Illus.). 530p. 1985. 146.00 (*0-387-96176-3*) Spr-Verlag.

— Leukocyte Typing II: Human Myeloid & Hematopoietic Cells, Vol. 3. (Illus.). xvi, 366p. 1985. 118.00 (*0-387-96177-1*) Spr-Verlag.

— Leukocyte Typing II: Human T Lymphocytes, Vol. 1. (Illus.). 575p. 1985. 146.00 (*0-387-96175-5*) Spr-Verlag.

Reinhold. Golden Age of August. 1978. 25.00 (*0-88866-585-7*); 17.95 (*0-88866-586-5*) Edgar Kent.

— Past & Present. 1972. 29.95 (*0-88866-508-3*); 24.95 (*0-88866-509-1*) Edgar Kent.

Reinhold, Bill, jt. auth. see Starlin, Jim.

***Reinhold, Gerd.** Soziologie-Lexikon. 2nd ed. 677p. (GER.). 1992. 85.00 (*0-614-00539-6*, 3486223402) Fr & Eur.

Reinhold, L. & Liwschitz, Y., eds. Progress in Phytochemistry, 1. LC 68-24347. reprint ed. pap. 160.00 (*0-317-29865-8*, 2016177) Bks Demand.

— Progress in Phytochemistry, 2. LC 68-24347. reprint ed. pap. 130.80 (*0-317-29866-6*) Bks Demand.

Reinhold, L., et al. Progress in Phytochemistry, Vol. 7. LC 68-24347. (Illus.). 410p. 1981. 105.00 (*0-08-026362-3*, Pergamon Pr) Elsevier.

Reinhold, L., et al, eds. Progress in Phytochemistry, 2 vols., 4. LC 68-24347. 1978. 128.00 (*0-08-021004-X*, Pub. by Pergamon Repr UK) Franklin.

— Progress in Phytochemistry, 2 vols., 5. LC 68-24347. 1978. 105.00 (*0-08-022645-0*, Pub. by Pergamon Repr UK) Franklin.

— Progress in Phytochemistry, Vol. 6. LC 68-24347. (Illus.). 1980. 105.00 (*0-08-024946-9*, Pergamon Pr) Elsevier.

Reinhold, Margaret. Watchers by the Pool. (Illus.). 192p. 1993. 18.95 (*0-7867-0009-2*) Carroll & Graf.

Reinhold, Meyer. Classica Americana: The Greek & Roman Heritage in the United States. LC 83-197790. 370p. 1984. 34.95 (*0-8143-1744-8*) Wayne St U Pr.

— From Republic to Principate: An Historical Commentary on Cassius Dio's Roman History, Books 49-52. LC 87-9498. (American Philological Association Philological Monographs). 1988. pap. 27.00 (*1-55540-246-1*) Scholars Pr GA.

Reinhold, Meyer, jt. ed. see Haase, Wolfgang.

Reinhold, Meyer, jt. auth. see Lewis, Naphtali.

***Reinhold, Michael.** Why Rush Limbaugh Is Wrong. LC 95-77891. 200p. 1995. 17.95 (*0-9647470-0-6*); pap. write for info. (*0-9647470-1-4*) Mighty Pen.

Reinhold, Roy A. The Day of the Lord: Prophecy Revealed. LC 86-51559. (Illus.). 216p. (Orig.). 1987. pap. 6.95 (*0-9616306-0-4*) Windstar Bks.

Reinhold, Ruth M. Sky Pioneering: Arizona in Aviation History. LC 81-11514. (Illus.). 232p. 1982. 27.50 (*0-8165-0737-6*); pap. 13.95 (*0-8165-0757-0*) U of Ariz Pr.

Reinhold, Timothy A., ed. see International Workshop on Wind Tunnel Modeling Criteria & Techniques in Civil Engineering Applications (1982: Gaithersburg, MD).

***Reinhold, Walter W.** Culture 2.0 Workbook: Interdisciplinary Lessons. rev. ed. 310p. 1992. pap. 45.00 (*0-9624372-4-7*) Cultural Rescs.

Reinholdt, Bill, jt. auth. see Andersen, Honey.

Reinholdt, Bill, jt. auth. see Anderson, Honey.

Reinholtz, Charles F., jt. auth. see Mabie, Hamilton H.

Reinhorn, Marc. Dictionnaire Laotien-Francais: Laotian - French Dictionary, 2 vols., Set. 2000p. (FRE & LAO.). 1970. 175.00 (*0-8288-6527-2*, M-6481) Fr & Eur.

Reinhoudt, D. N. Structure & Activity of Anti-Tumour Agents. 1982. lib. bdg. 103.00 (*90-247-2783-9*) Kluwer Ac.

***Reinicke, Wolfgang H.** Banking, Politics & Global Finance: American Commercial Banks & Regulatory Change, 1980-1990. (Studies in International Political Economy). 264p. 1995. 59.95 (*1-85898-176-X*, Pub. by E Elgar Pub UK) Ashgate Pub Co.

— Building a New Europe: The Challenge of System Transformation & Systemic Reform. 216p. (C). 1993. pap. 12.95 (*0-8157-7391-9*) Brookings.

Reinicke, Wolfgang H., jt. auth. see Heilemann, Ullrich.

Reinig, Christa. Idleness Is the Root of All Love. Mueller, Ilze, tr. LC 91-11708. 114p. 1991. 19.95 (*0-934971-22-6*); pap. 10.00 (*0-934971-21-8*) Calyx Bks.

Reiniger, Anne, et al. NYSPCC Professionals' Handbook Identifying & Reporting Child Abuse & Neglect. Charnizon, Marlene, ed. (Illus.). 80p. 1990. pap. text ed. 12.95 (*0-9628247-0-4*) NYSPCC.

Reiniger, P., jt. ed. see Zadrazil, F.

***Reinikka, Merle A.** A History of the Orchid. rev. ed. (Illus.). 325p. 1995. 29.95 (*0-88192-325-7*) Timber.

Reining, Conrad C. The Zande Scheme: An Anthropological Case Study of Development in Africa. LC 65-24665. (Northwestern University African Studies Ser.: No. 17). 285p. reprint ed. pap. 81.30 (*0-317-29802-X*, 2016721) Bks Demand.

Reining, Priscilla & Tinker, Irene, eds. Population: Dynamics, Ethics, & Policy. LC 75-4498. (AAAS Miscellaneous Publication Ser.: No. 75-5). 192p. reprint ed. pap. 54.80 (*0-7837-0062-8*, 2040309) Bks Demand.

Reinis, J. G. The Portrait Medallions of David D'Angers: Galerie des Contemporains. (Illus.). 576p. (ENG & FRE.). Date not set. text ed. 195.00 (*0-937370-01-0*) Polymath Pr.

Reinis, Stanislav & Goldman, Jerome M. The Chemistry of Behavior: A Molecular Approach to Neuronal Plasticity. LC 82-13294. 622p. 1982. 110.00 (*0-306-41161-X*, Plenum Pr) Plenum.

Reinisch, June M. Kinsey Institute New Report on Sex. 1994. pap. 7.99 (*0-312-95184-1*) St Martin.

Reinisch, June M., et al, eds. Masculinity-Femininity: Basic Perspectives. (Kinsey Institute Ser.). (Illus.). 384p. 1987. 35.00 (*0-19-504105-4*) OUP.

Reinisch, June M. & Beasley, Ruth. The Kinsey Institute New Report on Sex. 560p. 1991. pap. 14.95 (*0-312-06386-5*) St Martin.

Reinisch, K. & Thoma, M., eds. Large Scale Systems: Theory & Applications, 1989. (IFAC Proceedings Ser.: No. 9009). 580p. 1990. 270.00 (*0-08-035731-8*, Pergamon Pr) Elsevier.

Reinisch, Leonhard, ed. Theologians of Our Time. LC 64-17067. 1964. pap. 8.95 (*0-268-00378-5*) U of Notre Dame Pr.

Reinisch, Raymond, jt. ed. see Ostrowsky, Daniel B.

Reinitz, R. Tensions in American Puritanism. LC 70-100325. (Problems in American History Ser.). 208p. reprint ed. pap. 59.30 (*0-8357-9991-3*, 2019292) Bks Demand.

Reinitz, Richard. Irony & Consciousness: American Historiography & Reinhold Niebuhr's Vision. LC 77-92574. 232p. 1978. 34.50 (*0-8387-2062-5*) Bucknell U Pr.

Reinius, Trish. The Planet of Tears. (Illus.). 157p. 1985. reprint ed. pap. 8.00 (*0-932987-00-1*) Iris IO.

— Power of the White Wolf. (Illus.). 160p. 1985. pap. 8.00 (*0-932987-01-X*) Iris IO.

Reinke, W. A., jt. auth. see Grundy, F.

Reinke, William A., ed. Health Planning for Effective Management. (Illus.). 304p. 1988. 32.50 (*0-19-505337-0*) OUP.

Reinke, William A. & Williams, Kathleen N., eds. Health Planning: Qualitative Aspects & Quantitative Techniques. LC 79-189139. (Illus.). 360p. 1972. 12.00 (*0-912888-00-8*) Dept Intl Health.

Reinken, Gunter. Deer Farming: A Practical Guide to German Techniques. Meadowcroft, P., tr. (Illus.). 300p. 1990. 38.95 (*0-85236-206-4*, Pub. by Farming Pr UK) Diamond Farm Bk.

Reinker, Harry L., jt. auth. see Martinus, Norman.

Reinking, David, ed. Reading & Computers: Issues for Theory & Practice. (Computers & Education Ser.). 220p. (C). 1987. text ed. 24.95 (*0-8077-2866-7*) Tchrs Coll.

***Reinking, James A., et al.** Strategies for Successful Writing: A Rhetoric, Research Guide & Reader. 4th ed. LC 95-8296. 1995. pap. text ed. write for info. (*0-13-190802-2*) P-H.

— Strategies for Successful Writing: A Rhetoric, Research Guide & Reader. 4th ed. LC 95-8295. 1995. write for info. (*0-13-439860-2*) P-H.

Reinking, James A., jt. auth. see Hart, Andrew W.

Reinking, James A., et al. Improving College Writing: A Book of Exercises. 300p. (C). 1981. pap. text ed. 17.50 (*0-312-41060-3*) St Martin.

— Strategies for Successful Writing: A Rhetoric & Reader. 3rd ed. LC 92-17399. 562p. (C). 1992. pap. text ed. write for info. (*0-13-847583-0*) P-H.

— Strategies for Successful Writing: A Rhetoric, Reader & Handbook. 3rd ed. LC 92-11304. 704p. (C). 1992. pap. text ed. write for info. (*0-13-847591-1*) P-H.

Reinking, Victor, tr. see Schwab, Raymond.

Reinman, Jacob J. The Book of Esther. 124p. (C). Date not set. write for info. (*1-56062-247-4*); pap. write for info. (*1-56062-248-2*) CIS Comm.

— The Passover Haggadah. Marmorstein, Armohom, tr. LC 94-70476. (Illus.). 130p. 1994. 8.95 (*1-56062-251-2*); pap. 4.95 (*1-56062-252-0*) CIS Comm.

Reinman, Y. Y., ed. see Gold, Avner.

Reinman, Y. Y., ed. see Teichman, Avigail.

Reinmiller, Elinor C., jt. auth. see Chapman, Carl B.

***Reinmuth.** Regulation of Reciprocal Insurance Exchanges. (C). 1967. 10.50 (*0-256-00676-8*) Irwin.

***Reinmuth, Dean.** Tension-Free Golf: Unleashing Your Greatest Shots More Often. (Illus.). 240p. 1995. pap. 19.95 (*1-57243-039-7*) Triumph Bks.

Reinmuth, Howard S., Jr., ed. Early Stuart Studies: Essays in Honor of David Harris Willson. LC 71-139962. 283p. reprint ed. pap. 80.70 (*0-317-42209-X*, 2055900) Bks Demand.

Reino, Joseph. Stephen King: The First Decade, Carrie to Pet Sematary. (United States Authors Ser.: No. 531). 176p. 1988. text ed. 20.95 (*0-8057-7512-9*, Pub. by Royal Botanic Garden UK) Macmillan.

Reinoehl, Richard & Hanna, Thomas, eds. Computer Literacy in Human Services. LC 89-71738. (Computers in Human Services Ser.: Vol. 6, Nos. 1-4). 337p. 1990. text ed. 69.95 (*0-86656-866-2*) Haworth Pr.

Reinoehl, Richard & Mueller, B. Jeanne. Computer Literacy in Human Services Education. LC 90-34943. (Computers in Human Services Ser.: Vol. 7, Nos. 1-4). 381p. 1990. text ed. 69.95 (*0-86656-980-4*) Haworth Pr.

Reinold, E. Ultrasonics in Early Pregnancy: Diagnostic Scanning & Fetal Motor Activity. Keller, P. J., ed. (Contributions to Gynecology & Obstetrics Ser.: Vol. 1). 1976. 47.25 (*3-8055-2332-7*) S Karger.

Reinold, E., ed. Fortbildungstagung und Jahrestagung der Oesterreichischen Gesellschaft Fuer Gynaekologie und Geburtshilfe, Gmunden, Juni 1992. (Gynaekologische Rundschau Journal: Vol. 32, Suppl. 1). (Illus.). iv, 160p. 1992. pap. 45.00 (*3-8055-5725-6*) S Karger.

— Gitsch, E., Festschrift. (Journal: Gynaekologische Rundschau: Vol. 30, No. 4, 1990). (Illus.). xiv, 64p. 1991. pap. 29.75 (*3-8055-5393-5*) S Karger.

— Jahrestagung der Oesterreichischen Gesellschaft fuer Gyaekologie und Geburtshilfe, Krems, June 1980. (Gynaekologische Rundschau Journal: Vol. 20, Suppl. 2, 1981). (Illus.). xviii, 294p. 1981. pap. 53.00 (*3-8055-2191-X*) S Karger.

— Oesterreichische Gesellschaft fuer Gynaekologie & Geburtshilfe, Bayerische Gesellschaft fuer Geburtshilfe & Frauenheilkunde, Jahrestagung, Salzburg, June 1993. (Journal: Gynaekologische Geburtshilfliche Rundschau: Vol. 33, Suppl. 1, 1993). (Illus.). x, 354p. 1993. pap. 145.75 (*3-8055-5916-X*) S Karger.

— Oesterreichische Gesellschaft fuer Gynaekologie und Geburtshilfe, Jahrestagung, Bregenz, June 1994: Journal: Gynaekologisch-geburtshilfliche Rundschau, 1994, Vol. 34, Supp. 1. (Illus.). viii, 214p. 1994. pap. 89.00 (*3-8055-6108-3*) S Karger.

Reinold, E., jt. auth. see Gitsch, E.

Reinold, E., jt. ed. see Gitsch, E.

***Reinoso-Suarez, Fernando & Ajmone-Marsan, Cosimo, eds.** Cortical Integration: Basic, Archicortical, & Cortical Association Levels of Neural Integration. LC 84-17798. (International Brain Research Organization Monograph Ser.: No. 11). (Illus.). Date not set. reprint ed. pap. 129.40 (*0-7837-9555-6*, 2060304) Bks Demand.

Reinsch, Paul S. American Legislatures & Legislative Methods. LC 91-55447. (American State Ser.). 347p. 1991. reprint ed. lib. bdg. 61.00 (*0-912004-97-5*) W W Gaunt.

R

— Colonial Government, an Introduction to the Study of Colonial Institutions. LC 72-107829. (Select Bibliographies Reprint Ser.). 1977. 29.95 (0-8369-5221-9) Ayer.
— English Common Law in the Early American Colonies. 1976. lib. bdg. 200.00 (0-8490-1373-9) Gordon Pr.
— English Common Law in the Early American Colonies. LC 75-110969. (American Constitutional & Legal History Ser). 1970. reprint ed. lib. bdg. 16.95 (0-306-71910-X) Da Capo.
— Intellectual & Political Currents in the Far East. LC 79-165804. (Select Bibliographies Reprint Ser.). 1977. reprint ed. 26.95 (0-8369-5960-4) Ayer.
Reinschke, K. J. Multivariable Control - A Graph-theoretic Approach. (Lecture Notes in Control & Information Sciences Ser.: Vol. 108). 275p. 1988. pap. 43.00 (0-387-18899-1) Spr-Verlag.
Reinsel, Gregory C. Elements of Multivariate Time Series Analysis. LC 93-13954. (Series in Statistics). 1993. 49.95 (0-387-94063-4) Spr-Verlag.
— Elements of Multivariate Time Series Analysis. (Series in Statistics). (Illus.). 250p. 1993. write for info. (3-540-94063-4) Spr-Verlag.
Reinsel, Robert, ed. Managing Food Security in Unregulated Markets. LC 92-38150. 115p. (C). 1992. pap. text ed. 35.50 (0-8133-1704-5) Westview.
Reinsma, Carol. Friends Forever. (Really Reading! Bks.). (Illus.). 48p. (Orig.). (J). (gr. 1-3). 1993. pap. 4.49 (0-7847-0096-6, 24-03946) Standard Pub.
— The Picnic Caper. LC 93-29567. (Really Reading! Bks.). (Illus.). 48p. (Orig.). (J). (gr. k-3). 1994. pap. 4.49 (0-7847-0006-0, 24-03956) Standard Pub.
— A Place in the Palace. (Really Reading! Bks.). (Illus.). 48p. (Orig.). (J). (gr. 1-3). 1993. pap. 4.49 (0-7847-0095-8, 24-03945) Standard Pub.
— The Secret of the Ring in the Offering. (Really Reading! Bks.). (Illus.). 48p. (Orig.). (J). (gr. 1-3). 1993. pap. 4.49 (0-7847-0094-X, 24-03944) Standard Pub.
— The Shimmering Stone. (Really Reading! Bks.). (Illus.). 48p. (Orig.). (J). (gr. k-3). 1994. pap. 4.49 (0-7847-0007-9, 24-03957) Standard Pub.
Reinsma, Carol & Bruno, Bonnie. The Young Reader's Bible. Stortz, Diane, ed. (Illus.). 448p. (J). (ps-3). 1994. 17.99 (0-7847-0161-X, 24-03950) Standard Pub.
Reinsma, Luke M. Aelfric: An Annotated Bibliography. LC 85-45125. (Reference Library of the Humanities: Vol. 617). 328p. 1987. lib. bdg. 60.00 (0-8240-8665-1) Garland.
Reinsmith, Richard. A Body for Christmas. (Bodyguard Ser.). 240p. 1984. pap. 2.50 (0-8439-2071-8) Dorchester Pub Co.
— Body in Paradise. (Bodyguard Ser.). 240p. 1984. pap. 2.50 (0-8439-2106-4) Dorchester Pub Co.
— The Model Body. (Bodyguard Ser.). 240p. 1984. pap. 2.50 (0-8439-2087-4) Dorchester Pub Co.
— Nobody's Perfect. (Bodyguard Ser.). 256p. (Orig.). 1984. pap. 2.75 (0-8439-2137-4) Dorchester Pub Co.
— Somebody to Kill. (Bodyguard Ser.). 240p. (Orig.). 1984. pap. 2.50 (0-8439-2072-6) Dorchester Pub Co.
Reinsmith, William A. Archetypal Forms in Teaching: A Continuum. LC 91-44433. (Contributions to the Study of Education Ser.: No. 56). 232p. 1992. text ed. 47.95 (0-313-28405-9, RTG/, Greenwood Pr) Greenwood.
Reinstatler, Laura, ed. see Edie, Marge.
Reinstatler, Laura, ed. see Hopkins, Judy.
Reinstatler, Laura, ed. see Maison, Mary B.
Reinstatler, Laura, ed. see Parrott, Jo.
Reinstatler, Laura, ed. see Roberts, Barbara.
Reinstatler, Laura, ed. see Rozmyn, Mia.
Reinstatler, Laura, ed. see Swain, Gabrielle.
Reinstatler, Laura, ed. see Warehime, Retta.
Reinstatler, Laura M. Botanical Wreaths. Hoffman, Kerry, ed. LC 94-17052. (Illus.). 120p. (Orig.). 1994. pap. 21.95 (1-56477-056-7) That Patchwork.
Reinstedt, Randall A. Ghost Notes. LC 88-82533. (Illus.). 190p. 1991. pap. 9.95 (0-933818-09-2) Ghost Town.
— Ghostly Tales & Mysterious Happenings of Old Monterey. LC 79-110356. (Illus.). 64p. 1977. pap. 4.95 (0-933818-04-1) Ghost Town.
— Ghosts, Bandits & Legends of Old Monterey. LC 74-189524. (Illus.). 48p. 1974. reprint ed. pap. 4.50 (0-933818-00-9) Ghost Town.
— Incredible Ghosts of Old Monterey's Hotel Del Monte. LC 80-131190. (Illus.). 48p. 1980. pap. 3.95 (0-933818-07-6) Ghost Town.
— Incredible Ghosts of the Big Sur Coast. LC 82-164106. (Illus.). 52p. 1981. pap. 3.95 (0-933818-08-4) Ghost Town.
— The Monterey Peninsula: An Enchanted Land. Mosher, Jerry, ed. 128p. 1987. 29.95 (0-89781-199-2) Preferred Mktg.
— Monterey's Mother Lode. LC 79-110351. Orig. Title: Gold in the Santa Lucias. (Illus.). 104p. 1977. pap. 6.95 (0-933818-01-7) Ghost Town.
— Mysterious Sea Monsters of California's Central Coast. LC 80-114610. (Illus.). 74p. (Orig.). 1979. pap. 6.50 (0-933818-06-8) Ghost Town.
— One-Eyed Charley: The California Whip. Bergez, John, ed. LC 90-81382. (History & Happenings of California Ser.). (Illus.). 84p. (J). (gr. 3-6). 1990. pap. 8.95 (0-933818-77-7); boxed 12.95 (0-933818-23-8) Ghost Town.
— Otters, Octopuses, & Odd Creatures of the Deep. Bergez, John, ed. LC 87-82106. (History & Happenings of California Ser.). (Illus.). 64p. (J). (gr. 3-6). 1987. pap. 8.95 (0-933818-76-9); boxed 12.95 (0-933818-21-1) Ghost Town.
— Shipwrecks & Sea Monsters of California's Central Coast. LC 76-350548. (Illus.). 168p. 1975. pap. 7.95 (0-933818-02-5) Ghost Town.
— Stagecoach Santa. Bergez, John, ed. LC 86-81735. (History & Happenings of California Ser.). (Illus.). 48p. (J). (gr. 3-6). 1986. pap. 8.95 (0-933818-75-0); boxed 12.95 (0-933818-20-3) Ghost Town.
— The Strange Case of the Ghosts of the Robert Louis Stevenson House. Bergez, John, ed. LC 88-81933. (History & Happenings of California Ser.). (Illus.). 70p. (J). (gr. 3-6). 1988. pap. 8.95 (0-933818-78-5); boxed 12.95 (0-933818-22-X) Ghost Town.
— Tales & Treasures of California's Missions. Bergez, John, ed. LC 92-73253. (History & Happenings of California Ser.). (Illus.). 120p. (J). (gr. 3-6). 1992. pap. 10.95 (0-933818-79-3); boxed 13.95 (0-933818-24-6) Ghost Town.
— Tales & Treasures of the California Gold Rush. Bergez, John, ed. (History & Happenings of California Ser.). (Illus.). 112p. (J). (gr. 3-6). 1994. pap. 10.95 (0-933818-80-7); boxed 13.95 (0-933818-28-9) Ghost Town.
— Tales, Treasures, & Pirates of Old Monterey. LC 79-110354. (Illus.). 72p. 1976. pap. 5.95 (0-933818-03-3) Ghost Town.
— Where Have All the Sardines Gone? LC 79-101716. (Illus.). 168p. 1978. pap. 7.95 (0-933818-05-X) Ghost Town.
Reinstein, Alan, jt. auth. see Weinrich, Thomas R.
Reinstra, Marchiene V. Swallow's Nest: A Feminine Reading of the Psalms. 1992. pap. 18.95 (0-377-00248-8) Friendship Pr.
Reinthaler, Joan. Mathematics & Music: Some Intersections. 1990. 2.50 (0-940790-08-4) Mu Alpha Theta.
Reinties, J., jt. ed. see Fischer, R. E.
Reintjes, Afton E. How to Research "A Little Bit of Indian" 109p. 1989. 16.00 (0-940764-39-3) Genealog Inst.
— Scotch-Irish Sources of Research. 50p. 1986. 10.00 (0-940764-46-6) Genealog Inst.
— Tennessee Research. 50p. 1986. 12.00 (0-940764-45-8) Genealog Inst.
Reintjes, J. F., ed. Laser Wavefront Control. 1988. 48.00 (0-8194-0035-1, 1000) SPIE.
Reintjes, J. F., jt. auth. see Fisher, R. A.
Reintjes, J. F., jt. ed. see Fisher, R. A.
Reintjes, J. Francis. Numerical Control: Making a New Technology. (Oxford Series on Advanced Manufacturing: No. 9). (Illus.). 272p. (C). 1991. text ed. 39.95 (0-19-506772-X) OUP.
Reintjes, John F. Nonlinear Optical Parametric Processes in Liquids & Gases. LC 82-11603. 1984. text ed. 121.00 (0-12-585980-5) Acad Pr.
Reintjes, John W., ed. Improving Multiple Use of Coastal & Marine Resources. LC 83-71211. 96p. 1983. pap. 10.50 (0-913235-01-6) Am Fisheries Soc.
Reintzell, John F. The Police Officer's Guide to Survival, Health & Fitness. 152p. 1990. 34.95 (0-398-05711-7) C C Thomas.
— The Police Officer's Guide to Survival, Health & Fitness. 152p. 1990. pap. 19.95 (0-398-06344-3) C C Thomas.
Reinvang, Ivar. Aphasia & Brain Organization. LC 85-9545. (Applied Psycholinguistics & Communication Disorders Ser.). 208p. 1985. 49.50 (0-306-41975-0, Plenum Pr) Plenum.
Reinwein, D., jt. auth. see Beckers, C.
Reiquam, Steve W., ed. Solidarity & Poland: Impacts East & West. LC 87-29537. (Illus.). 72p. (Orig.). (C). 1988. lib. bdg. 20.25 (0-943875-05-6, Johns Hopkins); pap. text ed. 9.00 (0-943875-02-1, Johns Hopkins) W Wilson Ctr Pr.
Reiring, Janelle. Untitled, Black - White. (Illus.). 1978. pap. text ed. 4.95 (0-931706-03-3) L Lawler.
***Reis.** Through the Goddess: A Woman's Way of Healing. 240p. 1995. pap. text ed. 14.95 (0-8264-0856-7) Continuum.
Reis, A., ed. Economics & Management of Energy in Industry: Proceedings of the European Congress, Algarve, Portugal, 2-5 April 1984, 2 Vols., Set. 700p. 1985. 149.00 (0-08-030558-X, 310884, Pub. by Pergamon Repr UK) Franklin.
Reis, Augie. Painting Flowers with Augie. 48p. 1984. pap. 6.50 (1-56770-152-3) S Scheewe Pubns.
Reis, Barry, jt. auth. see Hall, Gary.
Reis, Bernard J. False Security: The Betrayal of the American Investor. LC 75-2663. (Wall Street & the Security Market Ser.). 1975. 33.95 (0-405-06987-1) Ayer.
Reis, Carlos A. Towards a Semiotics of Ideology. LC 92-21173. (Approaches to Semiotics Ser.: No. 109). vii, 163p. (C). 1993. lib. bdg. 90.80 (3-11-011829-7) Mouton.
Reis, Claire R. Composers in America. LC 77-4158. (Music Reprint Ser.: 1977). 1977. reprint ed. lib. bdg. 42.50 (0-306-70893-0) Da Capo.
Reis, Howard R. Personal Injury & Product Liability Litigation. LC 86-30250. 160p. 1986. write for info. (0-13-657602-8) P-H.
***Reis, Jaime, ed.** International Monetary Systems in Historical Perspective. LC 95-4171. 1995. write for info. (0-312-12540-2) St Martin.
Reis, Jim. Pieces of the Past. (Illus.). 200p. (Orig.). 1988. pap. 9.95 (0-9621043-0-2) KY Post.
— Pieces of the Past, Pt. II. (Illus.). 190p. (Orig.). 1991. pap. 9.95 (0-9624673-3-2) Picture This Bks.
***Reis, Joao J.** Slave Rebellion in Brazil: The Muslim Uprising of 1835 in Bahia. Brakel, Arthur, tr. (Studies in Atlantic History & Culture). (Illus.). 320p. 1995. reprint ed. pap. text ed. 15.95x (0-8018-5250-1) Johns Hopkins.
— Slave Rebellion in Brazil: The Muslim Uprising of 1853 in Bahia. Brakel, Arthur, tr. LC 92-27067. (Studies in Atlantic History & Culture). (Illus.). 320p. 1993. text ed. 45.00 (0-8018-4462-2) Johns Hopkins.
Reis, Joyce G., jt. auth. see Good, Julia P.
Reis, M. D., jt. ed. see Pinkerton, P. H.
Reis, Marion J., jt. tr. see Lemon, Lee T.
Reis Network Staff. Buying Foreclosures Before the Auction. (Home Study Book & Cassette Tapes Ser.). 62p. 1985. 69.95 (0-9616384-1-9) Reis Network.
REIS Network Staff. Computerized Bookkeeping Service, 3 cass., Set. (Make Money at Home with Your Personal Computer Ser.). 27p. (Orig.). 1989. student ed, audio 69.95 (1-878408-03-8) Reis Network.
— Computerized Diet & Meal Planning Service, 3 cass., Set. (Make Money at Home with Your Personal Computer Ser.). 23p. (Orig.). 1989. student ed, audio 69.95 (1-878408-01-1) Reis Network.
Reis Network Staff. On Line Shopping Center Service, 3 cass., Set. (Make Money at Home with Your Personal Computer Ser.). 24p. (Orig.). 1989. student ed, audio 69.95 (1-878408-02-X) Reis Network.
REIS Network Staff, et al. Computerized Tax Preparation Service, 3 cass., Set. (Make Money at Home with Your Personal Computer Ser.). 23p. (Orig.). 1989. student ed, audio 69.95 (1-878408-00-3) Reis Network.
Reis, Pat. Positive Parenting: A Survival Guide. (Illus.). 176p. (Orig.). (C). 1991. pap. 15.99 (1-85594-018-3, Pub. by Attic IE) InBook.
***Reis, Patricia.** Daughters of Saturn: From Father's Daughter to Creative Woman, Vol. 1. 286p. 1995. 24.95 (0-8264-0812-5) Continuum.
— Through the Goddess: A Woman's Way of Healing. 225p. 1991. 24.95 (0-8245-1343-6) Crossroad NY.
Reis, Richard. George MacDonald's Fiction: A Twentieth Century View. 1989. 8.95 (0-940652-32-3) Sunrise Bks.
Reis, Roberto. The Pearl Necklace: Toward an Archaeology of the Brazilian Transition Discourse. (Illus.). 192p. (C). 1992. lib. bdg. 24.95 (0-8130-1105-1) U Press Fla.
Reis, Roberto, intro. Toward Socio-Criticism: Selected Proceedings of the Conference "Luso Brazilian Literatures: a Socio-Critical Approach" LC 91-563. 325p. (Orig.). 1991. pap. text ed. 25.00x (0-87918-074-9) ASU Lat Am St.
Reis, Ronald A. Digital Electronics Through Project Analysis. 541p. (C). 1990. pap. write for info. (0-675-21141-7, Merrill Pub Co) Macmillan.
— Electronic Project Design & Fabrication. 3rd ed. LC 94-2996. 464p. (C). 1994. pap. write for info. (0-02-399293-X) Merrill.
— On Becoming an Electronics Technician: Securing Your High-Tech Future. LC 92-12595. 192p. (C). 1993. pap. write for info. (0-02-399231-X, Merrill Pub Co) Macmillan.
— Understanding Electronic & Computer Technology. (Illus.). 384p. 1990. text ed. 18.50 (0-911908-19-6) Tech Ed Pr.
Reis, Ronald A., jt. auth. see Webb, John W.
Reis, Sally M. & Renzulli, Joseph S. The Secondary Triad Model: A Practical Plan for Implementing Gifted Programs at the Junior & Senior High School Levels. 1985. pap. 16.95 (0-936386-33-9) Creative Learning.
Reis, Sally M., jt. auth. see Renzulli, Joseph S.
Reis, Sally M., jt. ed. see Renzulli, Joseph S.
***Reis, Sally M., et al.** Curriculum Compacting: The Complete Guide to Modifying the Regular Curriculum for High Ability Students. 1992. pap. 24.95 (0-936386-63-0) Creative Learning.
***Reis, Stuart.** King George's Army 1740-93 Vol. 1: Infantry. (Men-at-Arms Ser.). (Illus.). 48p. 1995. pap. 12.95 (1-85532-515-2, Pub. by Osprey UK) Stackpole.
Reisan, John. P.S. Your Shrink Is Dead. 1979. pap. 1.95 (0-8439-0687-1) Dorchester Pub Co.
Reisberg. Baby Rattlesnake. (Children's Book Press Ser.). 32p. (J). (gr. 3-4). 1990. 21.34 (0-8172-6749-2) Raintree Steck-V.
Reisberg, Barry. A Guide to Alzheimer's Disease: For Families, Spouses & Friends. LC 80-69717. 216p. (C). 1984. pap. 12.95 (0-02-926370-0) Free Pr.
Reisberg, Barry, ed. Alzheimer's Disease: The Standard Reference Book. 120p. (C). 1983. text ed. 80.00 (0-02-926230-5) Free Pr.
Reisberg, Dan, jt. auth. see Schwartz, Barry.
Reisberg, Daniel, ed. Auditory Imagery. 288p. 1991. text ed. 59.95 (0-8058-0556-7) L Erlbaum Assocs.
Reisberg, Liz A. Argentina: A Study of the Educational System & a Guide to the Placement of Students in Educational Institutions in the United States. (World Education Ser.). (Illus.). 150p. 1993. pap. text ed. 45.00 (0-929851-17-X) Am Assn Coll Registrars.
Reisberg, Sidney, jt. auth. see Cashman, Kevin.
Reisberg, Veg, illus. Elinda Who Danced in the Sky: An Eastern European Folktale from Estonia. LC 99-2247. 32p. (J). (gr. 1-7). 1990. 13.95 (0-89239-066-2) Childrens Book Pr.
Reisbick, Anna M., jt. ed. see Olson, Marie M.
Reisch, Michael, jt. auth. see Wenocur, Stanley.
Reischaue, jt. auth. see Fairbank.
Reischauer, A. K. Studies in Japanese Buddhism. LC 73-107769. reprint ed. 24.50 (0-404-05237-1) AMS Pr.
Reischauer, August. Studies in Japanese Buddhism. 1973. 250.00 (0-8490-1147-7) Gordon Pr.
Reischauer, Edwin O. Ennin's Travels in T'ang China. LC 55-6273. 357p. reprint ed. pap. 101.80 (0-317-11321-6, 2012367) Bks Demand.
— Japan: The Story of a Nation. rev. ed. (Illus.). 428p. (C). 1980. pap. text ed. 13.50 (0-685-02837-2, KnopfC) McGraw.
— Japan: The Story of a Nation. 4th ed. 1991. 29.45 (0-394-58527-5) Knopf.
— Japan: The Story of a Nation. 4th ed. 448p. (C). 1990. pap. text ed. write for info. (0-07-557074-2) McGraw.
— Japan: The Story of a Nation. LC 79-565893. 384p. reprint ed. pap. 109.50 (0-317-42005-4, 2026115) Bks Demand.
— The Japanese Today: Change & Continuity. LC 87-14904. (Illus.). 436p. 1988. 36.00 (0-674-47181-4); 25.00 (0-318-32782-1) Belknap Pr.
— Japanese Today: Change & Continuity. LC 87-14904. (Illus.). 436p. 1989. pap. text ed. 12.95 (0-674-47182-2) HUP.
Reischauer, Edwin O., tr. Ennin's Diary: The Record of a Pilgrimage to China in Search of the Law. LC 55-5553. (Illus.). 478p. reprint ed. pap. 136.30 (0-8357-9521-7, 2012366) Bks Demand.
Reischauer, Edwin O. & Craig, Albert M. Japan: Tradition & Transformation, 2 Vols. LC 77-77979. (Illus.). (C). 1989. pap. 34.76 (0-395-49696-9) HM.
***Reischauer, Edwin O. & Jansen, Marius B.** The Japanese Today: Change & Continuity. enl. ed. LC 94-31346. 471p. 1995. text ed. 14.95 (0-674-47184-9) Belknap Pr.
Reischauer, Haru M. Samurai & Silk: A Japanese & American Heritage. (Illus.). 400p. 1986. 35.00 (0-674-78800-1) Belknap Pr.
Reischauer, Robert D. Reforming School Finance. LC 73-1080. (Brookings Institution Studies in Social Experimentation). 199p. reprint ed. pap. 56.80 (0-317-26349-8, 2025401) Bks Demand.
Reischauer, Robert K. Japan, Government-Politics. LC 75-41226. reprint ed. 20.00 (0-404-14589-2) AMS Pr.
Reischauser, Haru M. Samurai & Silk: A Japanese & American Heritage. 400p. 1988. reprint ed. pap. text ed. 17.95 (0-674-78801-X) Belknap Pr.
Reische, Diana. Arafat & the Palestine Liberation Organization. LC 90-46868. (Illus.). 160p. (YA). (gr. 9-12). 1991. lib. bdg. 15.33 (0-531-11000-1) Watts.
— Electing a U. S. President. LC 91-32339. (Illus.). 144p. (YA). (gr. 7-12). 1992. lib. bdg. 15.33 (0-531-11043-5) Watts.
Reischl, Dennis, et al. Managing the Civilian Workforce: A Guide for the Military Manager. (Orig.). 1991. pap. text ed. 9.95 (0-936295-22-8) FPMI Comns.
***Reischl, Dennis K.** A Practical Guide to Interest Based Bargaining. 56p. (Orig.). 1994. pap. text ed. 9.95 (0-936295-47-3) FPMI Comns.
— Supervisor's Guide to Federal Labor Relations. 2nd ed. (Illus.). 120p. 1993. pap. text ed. 9.95 (0-936295-34-1) FPMI Comns.
— The Union Representative's Guide to Federal Labor Relations. (Illus.). 100p. (Orig.). 1988. pap. text ed. 9.95 (0-936295-05-8) FPMI Comns.
— Winning an Athletic Scholarship. 121p. (Orig.). (YA). (gr. 9-12). 1994. pap. text ed. 19.95 (0-936295-53-8) FPMI Comns.
Reischl, Dennis K. & Gilson, Robert J. Managing Leave & Attendance Problems: A Guide for the Federal Supervisor. 2nd ed. (Illus.). 96p. 1993. pap. text ed. 9.95 (0-936295-35-X) FPMI Comns.
— Managing Leave & Attendance Problems: A Guide for the Federal Supervisor. 3rd ed. 110p. 1994. pap. text ed. 9.95 (0-936295-54-6) FPMI Comns.
Reischl, Dennis K. & Smith, Ralph. The Federal Manager's Survival Guide: What You Need to Know about Managing Personnel. (Illus.). 142p. 1992. pap. 8.95 (0-936295-23-6) FPMI Comns.
Reischl, Dennis K. & Smith, Ralph R. The Federal Manager's Guide to Discipline. 2nd ed. (Illus.). 95p. 1991. pap. text ed. 9.95 (0-936295-19-8) FPMI Comns.
— Federal Manager's Guide to Preventing Sexual Harassment. 2nd ed. 65p. 1992. pap. text ed. 9.95 (0-936295-27-9) FPMI Comns.
— Sexual Harassment & the Federal Employee. 2nd ed. 52p. 1992. pap. text ed. 6.95 (0-936295-29-5) FPMI Comns.
Reischl, Dennis K. & Smith, Ralph R., eds. The Supervisor's Guide to Federal Labor Relations. 3rd ed. 131p. (Orig.). 1993. pap. text ed. 9.95 (0-936295-40-6) FPMI Comns.
Reischl, W. C., ed. see Hierosolymitanus, Cyrillus.
Reisdorf, Phyllis. Water, Water, Everywhere, So Many Drops to Drink. (Illus.). 52p. (Orig.). 1988. pap. 4.95 (0-317-93900-9) P Reisdorf.
Reisdorff, Earl J., et al. Pediatric Emergency Medicine. (Illus.). 1190p. 1992. text ed. 142.00 (0-7216-3281-5) Saunders.
Reisdorff, James J. Locomotive Sixty-Nine: From Alaska to Nebraska. (Illus.). 28p. 1984. pap. 1.50 (0-9609568-2-4) South Platte.
— North Platte Canteen. 2nd ed. (Illus.). 36p. 1986. pap. 6.95 (0-9609568-6-7) South Platte.
Reisdorff, James J., ed. see Barak, Anthony J.
Reisdorff, James J., ed. see Gschwind, Francis G.
Reisdorff, James J., jt. auth. see Mills, Rick W.
Reisdorff, James J., ed. see Stagner, Lloyd E.
Reise, K. Tidal Flat Ecology. (Ecological Studies: Vol. 54). (Illus.). 210p. 1985. 83.00 (0-387-15447-7) Spr-Verlag.
Reisel, Jerome, jt. auth. see Weschler, Irving R.
Reisel, Robert R. Elementary Theory of Metric Spaces: A Course in Constructing Mathematical Proofs. (Universitext Ser.). 120p. 1982. pap. 42.00 (0-387-90706-8) Spr-Verlag.
***Reisem, Richard.** Mr. Hope, Rochester, NY: America's First Municipal Victorian Cemetery. (Illus.). 128p. Date not set. 39.95 (0-9641706-3-9) Landmark Soc.
— 200 Years of Rochester Architecture & Gardens. (Illus.). 144p. 1994. 39.95 (0-9641706-1-2) Landmark Soc.
Reisen, Avraham. The Heart-Stirring Sermon. Leviant, Curt, ed. & tr. by. 224p. 1992. 23.95 (0-87951-436-1) Overlook Pr.
Reisen, Helmut. Debts, Deficits & Exchange Rates. 256p. 1994. 59.95 (1-85278-930-1, Pub. by E Elgar Pub UK) Ashgate Pub Co.
— Public Debt, External Competitiveness, & Fiscal Discipline in Developing Countries. LC 89-24746. (Studies in International Finance: No. 66). 1989. pap. text ed. 11.00 (0-88165-238-5) Princeton U Int Finan Econ.
Reisen, Helmut, jt. auth. see Fischer, Bernhard.

R

Reisenauer, Cindy, illus. How to Draw Creepy Creatures. (How to Draw Ser.). 32p. (J). 1991. 3.98 (*1-56156-019-7*); pap. 2.95 (*1-56156-064-2*) Kidsbks.

Reisenberger, John R., jt. auth. see Moran, Robert T.

Reisenfeld, Robin. The German Print Portfolio 1890-1930: Serial for Private Sphere. (Illus.). 160p. 1992. 80.00 (*0-85667-147-9*, Pub. by P Wilson Pubs) Sothebys Pubns.

— The German Print Portfolio 1890-1930: Serials for a Private Sphere. (Illus.). 158p. 1992. pap. 29.95 (*0-85667-417-6*) D & A Smart Museum.

Reiser. Handbook of Fisheries Engineering Techniques - Procedures. 1995. write for info. (*0-87371-544-6*) Lewis Pubs.

Reiser & Rosen. Medicine As a Human. 192p. 1984. 45.00 (*0-8391-2037-0*, 12037) Aspen Pub.

Reiser, A., ed. Photochemistry Seven: IUPAC Symposium on Photochemistry, Leuven, Belgium, 24-28 July, 1978, Seventh IUPAC Symposium. (IUPAC Symposium Ser.). 1979. 84.00 (*0-08-022358-3*, Pub. by Pergamon Repr UK) Franklin.

Reiser, Arnost. The Science & Technology of Resists. 409p. 1989. text ed. 107.00 (*0-471-85550-2*) Wiley.

Reiser, Bob, jt. auth. see Seeger, Pete.

Reiser, Carl, jt. auth. see Kaplan, Daniel I.

Reiser, David & Morris, Holly. Using WordPerfect Version 3 for the Mac. 2nd ed. (Illus.). 608p. 1993. pap. 29.95 (*1-56529-465-3*) Que.

— Using WordPerfect 2.1 for the Mac. 500p. (Orig.). 1992. pap. text ed. 24.95 (*0-88022-739-7*) Que.

Reiser, Dee & Dormer, Teresa. Best of Friends. LC 85-90457. 168p. (Orig.). 1985. pap. 9.95 (*0-9615950-5-1*) Best Friends.

Reiser, Dee, jt. auth. see Dormer, Teresa.

Reiser, Howard. Barry Sanders: Lion with a Quiet Roar. LC 93-19780. (Sports Stars Ser.). (Illus.). 48p. (J). (gr. 2-8). 1993. lib. bdg. 11.85 (*0-516-04377-3*); pap. 3.95 (*0-516-44377-1*) Childrens.

— Jackie Robinson: Baseball Pioneer. Rich, Mary P., ed. LC 91-28617. (First Bks.). (Illus.). 64p. (J). (gr. 3-5). 1992. lib. bdg. 13.93 (*0-531-20095-7*) Watts.

— Jim Abbott: All-American Pitches. LC 93-7424. (Sports Stars Ser.). 48p. (J). (gr. 2-8). 1993. lib. bdg. 11.85 (*0-516-04376-5*); pap. 3.95 (*0-516-44376-3*) Childrens.

— Ken Griffey, Jr. The Kid. LC 93-41054. (Sports Stars Ser.). (Illus.). 48p. (J). (gr. 2-8). 1994. lib. bdg. 11.85 (*0-516-04384-6*) Childrens.

— Ken Griffey Jr. The Kid. LC 93-41054. (Sports Stars Ser.). (J). (gr. 3-6). 1994. pap. 3.95 (*0-516-44384-4*) Childrens.

— Nolan Ryan: Strikeout King. LC 92-35741. (Sports Stars Ser.). (Illus.). 48p. (J). (gr. 2-8). 1993. lib. bdg. 11.85 (*0-516-04365-X*); pap. 3.95 (*0-516-44365-8*) Childrens.

— Patrick Ewing: Center of Attention. LC 94-14399. (Sports Stars Ser.). (Illus.). 48p. (J). (gr. 2-8). 1994. lib. bdg. 11.85 (*0-516-04388-9*); pap. 3.95 (*0-516-44388-7*) Childrens.

— Scottie Pippen: Prince of the Court. LC 92-42023. (Sports Stars Ser.). (Illus.). 48p. (J). (gr. 2-8). 1993. lib. bdg. 11.85 (*0-516-04366-8*); pap. 3.95 (*0-516-44366-6*) Childrens.

Reiser, J., jt. ed. see Fiechter, A.

Reiser, Jean-Marc. Les Copines. 135p. (FRE.). 1985. pap. 16.95 (*0-7859-4219-X*, 2070376362) Fr & Eur.

— Fous d'Amour. 107p. (FRE.). 1989. pap. 13.95 (*0-7859-4320-X*, 2070381552) Fr & Eur.

— Gros Degueulasse. (FRE.). 1985. pap. 11.95 (*0-7859-4235-1*) Fr & Eur.

— Mon Papa. (FRE.). 1976. pap. 10.95 (*0-7859-4067-7*) Fr & Eur.

— On Vit une Epoque Formidable. (FRE.). 1978. pap. 10.95 (*0-7859-4092-8*) Fr & Eur.

Reiser, Lynn. Any Kind of Dog. LC 91-12771. 24p. (J). (ps up). 1992. 14.00 (*0-688-10914-4*); lib. bdg. 13.93 (*0-688-10915-2*) Greenwillow.

— Any Kind of Dog. Cohn, Amy, ed. LC 91-12771. (Illus.). 24p. (J). (ps up). 1994. reprint ed. pap. 4.95 (*0-688-13572-2*, Mulberry) Morrow.

— Beach Feet. LC 95-12208. (Illus.). 32p. (J). 1996. write for info. (*0-688-14400-4*); lib. bdg. write for info. (*0-688-14401-2*) Greenwillow.

— Bedtime Cat. LC 90-30751. (Illus.). 24p. (J). (ps up). 1991. 13.95 (*0-688-10025-2*); lib. bdg. 13.88 (*0-688-10026-0*) Greenwillow.

— Cherry Pies & Lullabies. LC 95-2259. 1996. write for info. (*0-688-13391-6*); lib. bdg. write for info. (*0-688-13392-4*) Greenwillow.

— Christmas Counting. LC 91-32501. (Illus.). 32p. (J). (ps-4). 1992. 14.00 (*0-688-10676-5*); lib. bdg. 13.93 (*0-688-10677-3*) Greenwillow.

— Dog & Cat. LC 90-3553. (Illus.). 24p. (J). (ps up). 1991. 13.95 (*0-688-09892-4*); lib. bdg. 13.88 (*0-688-09893-2*) Greenwillow.

— Margaret & Margarita, Margarita y Margaret. LC 92-29012. 32p. (J). (ps up). 1993. 14.00 (*0-688-12239-6*); lib. bdg. 13.93 (*0-688-12240-X*) Greenwillow.

— Night Thunder & the Queen of the Wild Horses. LC 93-25734. (Illus.). 32p. (J). 1995. 15.00 (*0-688-11791-0*); lib. bdg. 14.93 (*0-688-11792-9*) Greenwillow.

— The Surprise Family. LC 93-16249. (Illus.). 32p. (J). (ps up). 1994. 14.00 (*0-688-11671-X*); lib. bdg. 13.93 (*0-688-11672-8*) Greenwillow.

— Tomorrow on Rocky Pond. LC 91-45801. (Illus.). 32p. (J). (ps up). 1993. 14.00 (*0-688-10672-2*); lib. bdg. 13.93 (*0-688-10673-0*) Greenwillow.

— Two Mice in Three Fables. LC 93-35935. 32p. (J). (ps up). 1995. 15.00 (*0-688-13389-4*); lib. bdg. 14.93 (*0-688-13390-8*) Greenwillow.

Reiser, M. & Rostoker, N., eds. Collective Methods of Acceleration. (Accelerators & Storage Rings Ser.: Vol. 2). 752p. 1979. text ed. 169.00 (*3-7186-0005-6*) Gordon & Breach.

Reiser, Martin. Handbook of Investigative Hypnosis. LC 79-53215. 1980. 24.95 (*0-934486-00-X*) LEHI Pub Co.

— Police Psychology: Collected Papers. LC 81-82247. 1982. 24.95 (*0-934486-01-8*) LEHI Pub Co.

— Programming in Oberon: Steps Beyond Pascal & Modula-2. (C). 1992. pap. text ed. 37.75 (*0-201-56543-9*) Addison-Wesley.

— Theory & Design of Charged Particle Beams. LC 93-33110. (Beam Physics & Accelerator Technology Ser.). 1994. text ed. 74.95 (*0-471-30616-9*) Wiley.

Reiser, Martin, et al, eds. Heavy Ion Inertial Fusion: AIP Conference Proceedings, No. 152. LC 86-73185. 638p. 1987. lib. bdg. 80.00 (*0-88318-352-8*) Am Inst Physics.

Reiser, Morton F. Memory in Mind & Brain: What Dream Imagery Reveals. 232p. 1994. pap. 14.00 (*0-300-06032-7*) Yale U Pr.

Reiser, Morton F., jt. auth. see Leigh, Hoyle.

Reiser, Oliver. Cosmic Humanism & World Unity. LC 73-86468. (World Institute Creative Findings Ser.). (Illus.). 286p. 1975. text ed. 77.00 (*0-677-03870-4*); pap. text ed. 41.00 (*0-677-03875-5*) Gordon & Breach.

Reiser, Robert A., jt. auth. see Dick, Walter.

Reiser, Robert S., jt. auth. see Seeger, Pete.

Reiser, Ron. Florida Passport. (Illus.). 36p. (Orig.). 1989. 3.95 (*0-9625515-0-3*) VJR Passports.

— Illinois Passport. (Illus.). 36p. (Orig.). 1990. 3.95 (*0-9625515-1-1*) VJR Passports.

Reiser, Ronald J. Indiana Passport. (Illus.). 36p. (Orig.). (YA). (gr. 9-12). 1991. 3.95 (*0-9625515-5-4*) VJR Passports.

— Kentucky Passport. (Illus.). 36p. (Orig.). (YA). (gr. 9-12). 1991. 3.95 (*0-9625515-9-7*) VJR Passports.

— Michigan Passport. (Illus.). 36p. (Orig.). (YA). (gr. 9-12). 1991. 3.95 (*0-9625515-7-0*) VJR Passports.

— North Carolina Passport. (Illus.). 36p. (Orig.). (YA). (gr. 9-12). 1991. 3.95 (*0-9625515-8-9*) VJR Passports.

— Ohio Passport. (Illus.). 36p. (Orig.). (YA). (gr. 9-12). 1991. 3.95 (*0-9625515-6-2*) VJR Passports.

Reiser, Sheldon. Metabolic Effects of Utilizable Dietary Carbohydrates. LC 82-10079. (Illus.). 358p. reprint ed. pap. 102.10 (*0-7837-0669-3*, 2041004) Bks Demand.

Reiser, Stanley J. Medicine & the Reign of Technology. LC 77-87389. (Illus.). 317p. (Orig.). 1981. pap. 21.95 (*0-521-28223-3*) Cambridge U Pr.

Reiser, Stanley J. & Anbar, Michael, eds. The Machine at the Bedside: Strategies for Using Technology in Patient Care. (Illus.). 336p. 1984. pap. 27.95 (*0-521-31832-7*) Cambridge U Pr.

Reiser, Stanley J., jt. ed. see Bulger, Ruth E.

Reiser, Stanley J., et al, eds. Divided Staffs, Divided Selves: A Case Approach to Mental Health Ethics. LC 86-28416. (Illus.). 160p. 1987. pap. 14.95 (*0-521-31890-4*) Cambridge U Pr.

Reiser, Stewart. The Israeli Arms Industry: Foreign Policy, Arms Transfers, & Military Doctrine of a Small State. LC 89-2205. 250p. 1989. 55.00 (*0-8419-1028-6*) Holmes & Meier.

Reiser, Sylvia. Sylvia's Songs. 52p. 1984. pap. 6.00 (*0-88734-900-5*) Players Pr.

Reiser, Virginia S. Favorite Poems in Large Print. large type ed. (General Ser.). 1993. 21.95 (*0-8161-3160-0*, Large Print Bks) Hall.

Reiser, Virginia S., ed. Best Loved Poems in Large Print. large type ed. (General Ser.). 1983. 21.95 (*0-8161-3575-4*, Large Print Bks) Hall.

Reiser, Walter A., Jr. A Comparison of the Federal Rules of Evidence with South Carolina Evidence Law. 4th ed. 99p. (Orig.). 1990. pap. text ed. 18.00 (*0-943856-28-0*, 402) SC Bar CLE.

Reiser, William. Forever Faithful: The Unfolding of God's Promise to Creation. 104p. (Orig.). 1993. 7.95 (*0-8146-5849-0*, M Glazier) Liturgical Pr.

— Looking for a God to Pray To: Christian Spirituality in Transition. LC 94-10552. 176p. 1994. pap. 9.95 (*0-8091-3480-2*) Paulist Pr.

— Renewing the Baptismal Promises. 141p. 1992. pap. 7.95 (*0-8146-6089-4*, Pueblo Bks) Liturgical Pr.

— Talking about Jesus Today: An Introduction to the Story Behind Our Faith. LC 92-33240. 240p. 1993. pap. 11.95 (*0-8091-3358-X*) Paulist Pr.

Reiser, William E. What Are They Saying about Dogma? LC 78-58955. (What Are They Saying about...Ser.). 1978. pap. 3.95 (*0-8091-2127-1*) Paulist Pr.

Reisfeld, Eric. Consumer Karate: A Guide to Economic Survival. 5.95 (*0-686-18908-6*) Meridian Ed.

Reisfeld, R., jt. ed. see Sell, Stewart.

Reisfeld, Ralph A. & Ferrone, Soldano, eds. Current Trends in Histocompatability, 2 vols. Incl. Vol. 1. Immunogenetic & Molecular Profiles. LC 80-18211. 570p. 1981. 110.00 (*0-306-40480-X*); Vol. 2. Biological & Clinical Concepts. LC 80-18211. 326p. 1981. 85.00 (*0-306-40481-8*); LC 80-18211. 1981. write for info. (*0-318-55317-1*, Plenum Pr) Plenum.

— Melanoma Antigens & Antibodies. LC 82-5288. 462p. 1982. 95.00 (*0-306-40852-X*, Plenum Pr) Plenum.

***Reisfeld, Randi.** American Gladiators: The Official Book. 1995. pap. 12.00 (*0-671-51966-2*) PB.

— The Bar - Bat Mitzvah Survival Guide. (Illus.). 144p. 1992. pap. 9.95 (*0-8065-1295-4*, Citadel Pr) Carol Pub Group.

— Johnny Depp. 1989. pap. 3.50 (*0-312-91629-9*) St Martin.

— Marky Mark & the Funky Bunch. 160p. (Orig.). 1992. pap. 7.00 (*0-380-77100-4*) Avon.

— Melrose Place. (J). 1994. mass mkt. 4.99 (*0-671-50584-X*) PB.

— Melrose Place: Meet the Stars of Today's Hottest New Show. Clancey, Lisa, ed. 192p. (J). (gr. 5 up). 1992. mass mkt. 4.50 (*0-671-79781-6*) PB.

— Young Stars. Clancy, Lisa, ed. 144p. (Orig.). (J). 1992. pap. 3.50 (*0-671-76987-1*) PB.

Reisfeld, Randi, jt. auth. see Preston-Gomez, Cheryl.

Reisgies, Teresa, jt. auth. see Salzman, Marian.

***Reish, Donald.** Marine Life of Southern California. 240p. (C). 1995. pap. text ed. 20.00 (*0-7872-1045-5*) Kendall-Hunt.

Reishus, Nancy B. Gone to the Dogs. (Orig.). 1981. lib. bdg. 6.95 (*0-938571-00-1*) Glorycliff Pub.

***Reisig, Michael.** Brothers of the Sword. 430p. 1995. pap. 12.95 (*1-56901-715-8*) NW Pub.

Reisig, W. A Primer in Petri Net Design. Muchnick, S. S. & Schnupp, P., eds. (Compass International Ser.). (Illus.). xiv, 120p. 1992. 49.00 (*0-387-52044-9*) Spr-Verlag.

Reisig, W., jt. ed. see Girault, C.

Reisiger, Hans. Johann Gottfried Herder: Sein Leben in Selbstzeugnissen, Briefen und Berichten. 352p. 1970. reprint ed. write for info. (*0-318-71943-6*, Pub. by Georg Olms GW) Lubrecht & Cramer.

Reisine, T. Molecular Biology of Neurotransmitter Receptors. (Molecular Biology Intelligence Unit Ser.). 1995. write for info. (*1-57059-059-1*) R G Landes.

Reising, Chris. Noedgelines. (Illus.). (Orig.). 1986. pap. 7.00 (*0-937061-00-X*) Earhart Pr.

Reising, Russell J. The Unusable Past: Theory & the Study of American Literature. 224p. 1986. text ed. 35.00 (*0-416-01311-2*, 9811); pap. text ed. 12.95 (*0-416-01321-X*, 9827) Routledge Chapman & Hall.

***Reisinger, Anette.** Radiocaesium in Pilzen. (Bibliotheca Mycologica Ser.: 155). (Illus.). 342p. (GER.). 1994. pap. 97.50 (*3-443-59057-8*) Lubrecht & Cramer.

Reisinger, Ernest C. The Carnal Christian: What Should We Think of the Carnal Christian? 75p. 1992. reprint ed. 1.95 (*0-85151-389-1*) Banner of Truth.

— Lord & Christ: The Implications of Lordship for Faith & Life. LC 94-33274. 198p. (Orig.). 1994. pap. 8.99 (*0-87552-388-9*) Presby & Reformed.

— Today's Evangelism: It's Message & Methods. 1982. pap. 5.99 (*0-87552-417-6*) Presby & Reformed.

Reisinger, John. Appointment You Will Keep. pap. 6.00 (*0-87377-125-7*) GAM Pubns.

***Reisinger, John E.** Maya - The Confessions of Gonzalo Guererro. 450p. 1995. pap. 12.95 (*1-56901-734-4*) NW Pub.

Reisinger, John G. But "I" Say unto You. 112p. (Orig.). 1989. pap. write for info. (*0-925703-04-4*) Crown MA.

— The Sovereignty of God in Providence. 40p. (Orig.). 1989. reprint ed. pap. write for info. (*0-925703-06-0*) Crown MA.

— Tablets of Stone. 120p. (Orig.). 1989. pap. write for info. (*0-925703-05-2*) Crown MA.

Reisinger, Steven M. Valuation of Privately-Owned Businesses. 155p. 1981. pap. 24.95 (*0-940694-00-X*) Acquisition Plan.

Reisinger, William M. Energy & the Soviet Bloc: Alliance Politics after Stalin. LC 91-55530. (Illus.). 208p. 1992. 37.95 (*0-8014-2657-X*) Cornell U Pr.

Reiskin, Allan B. Advances in Oral Radiology. LC 79-21095. (Postgraduate Dental Handbook Ser.: No. 12). (Illus.). 328p. reprint ed. pap. 93.50 (*0-8357-7600-X*, 2056922) Bks Demand.

Reisler, Jim. Black Writers - Black Baseball: An Anthology of Articles from Black Sportswriters Who Covered the Negro Leagues. 183p. 1994. lib. bdg. 21.95 (*0-7864-0002-1*) McFarland & Co.

Reisler, Mark. By the Sweat of Their Brow: Mexican Immigrant Labor in the United States, 1900-1940. LC 76-5329. 304p. (Orig.). 1976. text ed. 59.95 (*0-8371-8894-6*, RPE/, Greenwood Pr) Greenwood.

Reisman, A. & Kiley, M. Health Care Delivery Planning. (Studies in Operations Research). 384p. 1973. text ed. 105.00 (*0-677-04570-0*) Gordon & Breach.

Reisman, A., et al. Industrial Inventory Control. (Studies in Operations Research). 192p. (C). 1972. text ed. 132.00 (*0-677-04180-2*) Gordon & Breach.

Reisman, Albert F. Business Loan Workouts, 1988. (Commercial Law & Practice Course Handbook Ser.). 1073p. 1988. 17.50 (*0-685-69387-2*) PLI.

Reisman, Arnold. Management Science Knowledge: Its Creation, Generalization, & Consolidation. LC 91-44705. 324p. 1992. text ed. 57.95 (*0-89930-739-6*, RMK/, Quorum Bks) Greenwood.

Reisman, Arnold & Reisman, Ellen, eds. Welcome Tomorrow. LC 82-91107. (Illus.). 1982. pap. 6.95 (*0-686-39632-4*); 4.17 (*0-912269-00-6*) North Coast Pubs.

Reisman, Bernard. The Jewish Experiential Book: The Quest for Jewish Identity. 1979. 45.00 (*0-87068-688-7*) Ktav.

Reisman, Bernard & Rosen, Gladys. Single-Parent Families at Camp: The Essence of an Experience. LC 84-70480. 54p. 1984. pap. 2.50 (*0-87495-061-9*) Am Jewish Comm.

Reisman, Bill, jt. auth. see Whitemarsh, Darylann.

Reisman, Daniel & Durst, Sanford J. Buying & Selling Country Land. (Illus.). 1981. lib. bdg. 19.95 (*0-915262-40-1*) S J Durst.

Reisman, David. Alfred Marshall: Progress & Politics. LC 87-4811. 500p. 1987. text ed. 49.95 (*0-312-00773-6*) St Martin.

— The Economics of Alfred Marshall. LC 85-22321. 300p. 1986. text ed. 45.00 (*0-312-23430-9*) St Martin.

— Market & Health. LC 93-17299. 254p. 1993. text ed. 45.00 (*0-312-09981-9*) St Martin.

— Theories of Collective Action: Downs, Olson & Hirsch. LC 89-36477. 380p. 1990. text ed. 55.00 (*0-312-03595-0*) St Martin.

Reisman, David, ed. Economic Thought & Political Theory. LC 93-42898. (Recent Economic Thought Ser.). 256p. (C). 1994. lib. bdg. 89.95 (*0-7923-9433-X*) Kluwer Ac.

— The Political Economy of James Buchanan. LC 89-4435. (Economics Ser.: No. 10). 216p. 1990. 39.50 (*0-89096-430-0*) Tex A&M Univ Pr.

— Theories of the Mixed Economy, 10 vols. 1995. 895.00 (*1-85196-213-1*, Pub. by Pickering & Chatto UK) Ashgate Pub Co.

Reisman, David A. The Political Economy of Health Care. LC 93-10466. 267p. 1993. text ed. 69.95 (*0-312-09986-X*) St Martin.

Reisman, Ellen, jt. ed. see Reisman, Arnold.

Reisman, Fredricka K. Teaching Mathematics: Methods & Content for Grades K-8. 2nd ed. (Illus.). 512p. (C). 1987. reprint ed. text ed. 35.95 (*0-88133-259-3*) Waveland Pr.

Reisman, George. The Government Against the Economy. LC 79-83689. 225p. 1985. 14.95 (*0-89803-004-8*, Jameson Bks); pap. 14.95 (*0-915463-23-7*, Jameson Bks) Green Hill.

Reisman, H. B., ed. Economic Analysis of Fermentation Processes. (Biotechnologists & Microbiologists Ser.). 272p. 1988. 217.00 (*0-8493-6886-3*, TP156) CRC Pr.

Reisman, Jane, jt. auth. see Borman, Kathryn M.

Reisman, Jane, jt. auth. see Kohl, Jeanne.

Reisman, Jane, jt. auth. see Zeigler, Harmon.

Reisman, John, ed. Behavioral Disorders in Infants, Children, & Adolescents. 416p. 1986. text ed. 27.50 (*0-89859-887-7*) L Erlbaum Assocs.

Reisman, John M. Anatomy of Friendship. LC 79-12857. 1979. 19.95 (*0-89197-646-9*) Irvington.

— A History of Clinical Psychology. 2nd ed. 424p. 1991. 69.00 (*1-56032-041-9*); pap. 34.00 (*1-56032-188-1*) Hemisp Pub.

— A History of Clinical Psychology: Enlarged Edition of the Development of Clinical Psychology. LC 75-40102. 430p. 1983. reprint ed. pap. text ed. 19.95 (*0-8290-0873-X*) Irvington.

— Toward the Integration of Psychotherapy. LC 77-147236. (Wiley Series on Psychological Disorders). 169p. reprint ed. pap. 48.20 (*0-317-08444-5*, 2011884) Bks Demand.

Reisman, John M., ed. Behavior Disorders in Infants, Children, & Adolescents. 400p. (C). 1986. pap. text ed. write for info. (*0-07-553909-8*) McGraw.

Reisman, John M. & Ribordy, Shelia. Principles of Psychotherapy with Children. 2nd ed. LC 93-1430. (Scientific Foundations of Clinical & Counseling Psychology Ser.). 1993. text ed. 49.95 (*0-669-28055-0*) Free Pr.

Reisman, Judith & Eichel, Edward. Kinsey Sex & Fraud: The Indoctrination of a People. Muir, J. Gordon & Court, John H., eds. LC 90-62974. 256p. 1993. pap. 11.99 (*1-56384-057-X*) Huntington Hse.

Reisman, Judith A. Soft Porn Plays Hardball: Its Tragic Effects on Women, Children & the Family. LC 90-84932. (Illus.). 219p. (Orig.). 1991. 16.99 (*0-910311-92-7*); pap. 8.99 (*0-910311-65-X*) Huntington Hse.

Reisman, Judith A. & Eichel, Edward W. Kinsey, Sex & Fraud: The Indoctrination of a People. Muir, J. Gordon & Court, John H., eds. LC 90-62974. 256p. (C). 1990. 19.99 (*0-910311-20-X*) Huntington Hse.

Reisman, L., et al. The New Orleans Voter: A Handbook of Political Description, Vol. 2. Bd. with Republicanism in New Orleans. LC 56-3785. LC 56-3785. 1955. 11.00 (*0-930598-01-6*) Tulane Stud Pol.

Reisman, M. & Antoniou, C. The Laws of War: The Basic Legal Documents on International Armed Conflict. 1994. pap. 13.00 (*0-679-73712-X*, Vin) Random.

***Reisman, Rosemary M. & Canfield, Christopher J.** Contemporary Southern Women Fiction Writers. 237p. 1994. 32.50 (*0-8108-2832-4*) Scarecrow.

Reisman, Sorel, ed. Multimedia Computing: Preparing for the Twenty-First Century. 624p. (C). 1994. text ed. 59.95 (*1-878289-22-5*) Idea Group Pub.

Reisman, W. Michael. Systems of Control in International Adjudication & Arbitration: Breakdown & Repair. LC 91-33033. 188p. 1992. text ed. 31.95 (*0-8223-1202-6*) Duke.

Reisman, W. Michael & Baker, James. Regulating Covert Action: Practices, Contexts, & Policies of Covert Coercion Abroad in International & American Law. 256p. (C). 1992. text ed. 32.50 (*0-300-05059-3*) Yale U Pr.

Reisman, W. Michael & Schreiber, Aaron M. Jurisprudence: Understanding & Shaping Law. LC 87-11243. (Illus.). 640p. (C). 1987. text ed. 42.95 (*0-913275-00-X*) New Haven Pr.

Reisman, W. Michael & Westerman, Gayl L. Straight Baselines in International Maritime Boundary Delimitation. 210p. 1992. text ed. 59.95 (*0-312-06034-3*) St Martin.

Reisman, W. Michael & Weston, Burns H., eds. Toward World Order & Human Dignity: Essays in Honor of Myres S. McDougal. LC 75-36109. (Illus.). 1976. pap. 39.95 (*0-02-926290-9*) Free Pr.

Reisman, W. Michael & Willard, Andrew R., eds. International Incidents: The Law that Counts in World Politics. (Illus.). 304p. 1988. text ed. 45.00 (*0-691-07772-X*); pap. text ed. 13.95 (*0-691-02280-1*) Princeton U Pr.

Reisman, W. Michael, jt. auth. see McDougal, Myres S.

Reisman, William M. The Art of the Possible: Diplomatic Alternatives in the Middle East. LC 70-136196. 169p. reprint ed. pap. 48.20 (*0-8357-8806-7*, 2033383) Bks Demand.

Reismann, Herbert. Elastic Plates: Theory & Application. LC 88-2662. 381p. 1988. text ed. 99.95 (*0-471-85601-0*) Wiley.

Reismann, Herbert & Pawlik, Peter S. Elasticity: Theory & Applications. 446p. (C). 1991. reprint ed. lib. bdg. 68.50 (*0-89464-532-3*) Krieger.

R

An Asterisk (*) at the beginning of an entry indicates that the title is appearing in BIP for the first time.

Reismann, John M. Anatomy of Friendship. 1987. pap. text ed. 6.95 (*0-8290-2116-7*) Irvington.

Reisner, G. A. Excavations at Kerma, Pts. I-III. Hooton, E. A. & Bates, Natica I., eds. (Harvard African Studies: Vol. 5). 1972. lib. bdg. 130.00 (*0-527-01028-6*) Periodicals Srv.

— Excavations at Kerma, Pts. IV-V. Hooton, E. A. & Bates, Natica I., eds. (Harvard African Studies: Vol. 5). 1972. lib. bdg. 111.00 (*0-527-01029-4*) Periodicals Srv.

Reisner, Georgea. The Egyptian Conception of Immortality. ix, 85p. (Orig.). reprint ed. pap. 12.50 (*0-933175-22-1*) Van Siclen Bks.

Reisner, Helen, ed. Children with Epilepsy: A Parents' Guide. LC 87-51319. 314p. (Orig.). 1987. pap. 14.95 (*0-933149-19-0*) Woodbine House.

Reisner, Jack. The Last Hope. LC 83-61200. 288p. (Orig.). 1983. pap. 7.95 (*0-9611680-1-3*) Reisner Pub.

Reisner, Marc. Cadillac Desert: The American West & Its Disappearing Water. 592p. 1987. pap. 13.00 (*0-14-010432-1*, Penguin Bks) Viking Penguin.

— Cadillac Desert: The American West & Its Disappearing Water. rev. ed. (Illus.). 624p. 1993. pap. 14.95 (*0-14-017824-4*, Penguin Bks) Viking Penguin.

— Game Wars: The Undercover Pursuit of Wildlife Poachers. 304p. 1992. pap. 11.00 (*0-14-008768-0*, Penguin Bks) Viking Penguin.

Reisner, Marc & Bates, Sarah. Overtapped Oasis: Reform or Revolution for Western Water. LC 89-24459. (Illus.). 197p. (C). 1990. 31.95 (*0-933280-76-9*); pap. 17.95 (*0-933280-75-0*) Island Pr.

Reisner, Ralph & Gruson, Michael. Regulation of Foreign Banks: United States & International. 750p. 1993. boxed 125.00 (*0-88063-287-9*) Michie Butterworth.

— Regulation of Foreign Banks: United States & International. suppl. ed. 900p. 1993. 35.00 (*0-685-74147-8*) Butterworth Legal Pubs.

Reisner, Ralph & Slobogin, Christopher. Law & the Mental Health System: Civil & Criminal Aspects, Teacher's Manual to Accompany. 2nd ed. (American Casebook Ser.). 68p. (C). 1992. pap. text ed. write for info. (*0-314-01378-4*) West Pub.

— Law & the Mental Health System - Civil & Criminal Aspects, 1992 Supplement To. 2nd ed. (American Casebook Ser.). 73p. (C). 1992. pap. text ed. 8.00 (*0-314-01301-6*) West Pub.

— Law & the Mental Health System, Civil & Criminal Aspects: Civil & Criminal Aspects. 2nd ed. (American Casebook Ser.). 1117p. 1990. text ed. 52.50 (*0-314-73302-7*) West Pub.

Reisner, Ralph, et al. Administracao Da Divida De Paises Latino-Americanos: Aspectos Legais E Regulamentares. 1991. write for info. (*0-940602-05-9*) IADB.

Reisner, Ralph, et al, eds. Administracion De la Deuda De los Paises Latinoamericanos: Aspectos Juridicos y Reglamentarios. 1991. write for info. (*0-940602-50-4*) IADB.

— Latin American Sovereign Debt Management: Legal & Regulatory Aspects. (Illus.). 273p. (Orig.). 1990. pap. text ed. write for info. (*0-940602-33-4*) IADB.

***Reisner, Ralplh & Slobogin, Christopher.** Law & the Mental Health System Civil & Criminal Aspects: 1995 Supplement To. 2nd ed. (American Casebook Ser.). 190p. (C). 1994. pap. text ed. 12.00 (*0-314-05904-0*) West Pub.

Reisner, Robert G. Show Me the Good Parts: The Reader's Guide to Sex in Literature. 1964. pap. 2.45 (*0-8065-0049-2*, C262, Citadel Pr) Carol Pub Group.

Reisner, Robert G., ed. Bird: The Legend of Charlie Parker. LC 74-30084. (Roots of Jazz Ser.). (Illus.). 256p. 1975. reprint ed. lib. bdg. 29.50 (*0-306-70677-6*); reprint ed. pap. 12.95 (*0-306-80069-1*) Da Capo.

Reisner, Robert George. The Jazz Titans. LC 76-58559. (Roots of Jazz Ser.). 1977. reprint ed. lib. bdg. 25.00 (*0-306-70866-3*) Da Capo.

Reisner, Trudi. Ami Pro 3 Quick Reference. (Illus.). 192p. (Orig.). 1992. pap. 9.95 (*1-56529-113-1*) Que.

— Easy Word for Windows. 2nd ed. 1994. pap. 19.99 (*1-56529-808-X*) Que.

— Excel VisiRef. 1994. pap. 12.99 (*1-56529-739-3*) Que.

— Harvard Graphics 3 Quick Reference. (Quick Reference Ser.). (Illus.). 160p. (Orig.). 1992. pap. 9.95 (*0-88022-887-3*) Que.

— Quattro Pro Four Quick Reference. (Quick Reference Ser.). (Illus.). (Orig.). 1992. pap. 9.95 (*0-88022-939-X*) Que.

— Ten Minute Guide to Windows 95. 160p. 1995. 10.99 (*1-56761-515-5*) Alpha Bks IN.

— Windows 95: Sneak Preview. (Illus.). 200p. (Orig.). 1994. pap. text ed. 12.99 (*1-56761-538-4*) Alpha Bks IN.

— Word for Windows 2 Quick Reference. (Quick Reference Ser.). (Illus.). (Orig.). 1992. pap. 9.95 (*0-88022-950-0*) Que.

— WordPerfect Solutions. 608p. 1993. pap. text ed. 24.95 (*0-471-58935-7*) Wiley.

Reisner, Trudi & Acklen, Laura. Easy Windows 3.1. (Illus.). 246p. (Orig.). 1994. pap. 19.99 (*1-56529-865-9*) Que.

Reisner, Trudi, jt. auth. see Snyder, Jan.

***Reisner, Trudie.** Easy Ami Pro 3.1 for Windows. (Illus.). (Orig.). 1994. pap. 19.99 (*1-56529-996-5*) Que.

***Reisner, Trudy.** Easy Microsoft Office. 1994. pap. 24.99 (*0-7897-0013-1*) Que.

Reison, Dennis S., ed. Physician's Reference Guide to Cardiology. 935p. 1992. write for info. (*1-878212-00-1*) Prof & Tech Pub.

Reiss, Albert J., Jr. & Tonry, Michael H., eds. Communities & Crime. LC 80-642217. (Studies in Crime & Justice Ser.: Vol. 8). viii, 421p. (C). 1986. lib. bdg. 27.50 (*0-226-80802-5*) U Ch Pr.

— Communities & Crime. LC 80-642217. (Studies in Crime & Justice Ser.: Vol. 8). viii, 421p. (C). 1987. pap. text ed. 19.95 (*0-226-80798-3*) U Ch Pr.

Reiss, Albert J., Jr., ed. see National Research Council, Panel on the Understanding & Control of Violent Behavior Staff.

Reiss, Albert J., Jr., ed. see National Research Council, Panel on the Understanding & Control of violent Behavior Staff.

Reiss, Albert J., Jr., jt. ed. see Tonry, Michael H.

Reiss, Albert J., Jr., ed. see Wirth, Louis.

Reiss, Albert J., Jr., et al. Occupations & Social Status. Stein, Leon, ed. LC 77-70525. (Work Ser.). (Illus.). 1977. reprint ed. lib. bdg. 33.95 (*0-405-10193-7*) Ayer.

Reiss, Albrt J., Jr., ed. see National Research Council, Panel on the Understanding & Control of Violent Behavior Staff & Roth, Jeffrey A.

Reiss, Alvin H. Arts Management: A Guide to Finding Funds & Winning Audiences. 267p. 1992. 45.00 (*0-930807-32-4*, 600321) Fund Raising.

— Arts Management Reader. 704p. 1979. 65.00 (*0-8247-6850-7*) Dekker.

— Cash In! Funding & Promoting the Arts. LC 86-23040. (Illus.). 240p. (Orig.). 1986. 24.95 (*0-930452-62-3*); pap. 12.95 (*0-930452-59-3*) Theatre Comm.

— Don't Just Applaud, Send Money! The Most Successful Strategies for Funding & Marketing the Arts. (Illus.). 200p. (Orig.). 1995. pap. 15.95 (*1-55936-105-0*) Theatre Comm.

Reiss, Barry S. & Evans, Mary E. Pharmacological Aspects of Nursing Care. 4th ed. LC 92-49601. 766p. 1993. pap. text ed. 41.95 (*0-8273-4846-0*) Delmar.

— Pharmacological Aspects of Nursing Care: Computerized Testmaker & Testbank for DOS Compatible Computers. 4th ed. 1993. 49.95 (*0-685-70404-1*) Delmar.

— Pharmacological Aspects of Nursing Care: Instructor's Guide. 4th ed. 139p. 1993. 16.00 (*0-8273-5447-9*) Delmar.

Reiss, Barry S. & Melick, Mary E. Pharmacological Aspects of Nursing Care. 3rd ed. 640p. 1987. teacher ed 16.00 (*0-8273-3678-0*); pap. text ed. 41.95 (*0-8273-3677-2*) Delmar.

Reiss, Bob. Cruising Altitude. 1994. 23.00 (*0-671-77650-9*) S&S Trade.

— Last Spy. 1994. mass mkt. 5.99 (*0-312-95231-7*) St Martin.

— The Last Spy. large type ed. LC 93-22359. 1993. bds. 20. 95 (*1-56054-696-4*) Thorndike Pr.

Reiss, Carol. Experiments in Plant Physiology. LC 93-2239. (Illus.). 1993. pap. text ed. write for info. (*0-13-701285-3*) P-H.

Reiss, David. The Family's Construction of Reality. 440p. 1987. pap. 17.50 (*0-674-29416-5*) HUP.

Reiss, David, ed. Psychosocial Treatments. 104p. 1994. pap. text ed. 9.95 (*0-89862-298-0*, 2298) Guilford Pr.

Reiss, David, jt. ed. see Cole, Robert.

Reiss, David, et al, eds. Children & Violence. 144p. (Orig.). 1993. pap. text ed. 14.95 (*0-89862-588-2*) Guilford Pr.

Reiss, David S. M. A. S. H. The Exclusive Inside Story of the TV's Most Popular Show. rev. ed. LC 89-19743. 168p. 1983. pap. write for info. (*0-672-52762-6*) Macmillan.

Reiss, Diana. Camelot World: The Secrets of the Dolphins. 144p. (Orig.). (J). (gr. 7). 1991. pap. 2.95 (*0-380-76046-0*, Camelot) Avon.

Reiss, Donna, ed. see Bogger, Tommy L. & Wiggins, William B.

Reiss, E. Molecular Immunology of Mycotic & Actinomycotic Infections. 490p. 1986. 115.75 (*0-444-01039-4*) Elsevier.

Reiss, Edmund, et al, eds. Arthurian Legend & Literature: An Annotated Bibliography: Renaissance to Present, Vol. II. LC 83-47612. (Publications in Medieval Studies). 400p. lib. bdg. 54.00 (*0-8240-9122-1*) Garland.

Reiss, Edward. The Strategic Defense Initiative. (Studies in International Relations: No. 23). (Illus.). 280p. (C). 1992. 54.95 (*0-521-41097-5*) Cambridge U Pr.

Reiss, Elayne & Friedman, Rita. A-Choo. (Illus.). (J). (gr. k-1). 1990. 12.50 (*0-89796-864-6*) New Dimens Educ.

Reiss, Elayne & Friedman, Rita. A Buttonmat for Beautiful Buttons. (J). (gr. k-1). 1978. 12.50 (*0-89796-865-4*) New Dimens Educ.

— Exercise Expert. (J). (gr. k-1). 12.50 (*0-89796-866-2*) New Dimens Educ.

— Fantastic Funny Feet. (J). (gr. k-1). 12.50 (*0-89796-867-0*) New Dimens Educ.

— Hat Helpers Hullabaloo. (J). (gr. k-1). 12.50 (*0-89796-868-9*) New Dimens Educ.

— The Tale of Tall Toothbrush. (J). (gr. k-1). 1978. 12.50 (*0-89796-869-7*) New Dimens Educ.

Reiss, Ellen, ed. see Siegel, Eli.

***Reiss, Eric L.** The Complete Talking Machine: A Guide to the Restoration of Antique Phonographs. (Illus.). 184p. Date not set. reprint ed. pap. 19.95 (*1-886606-08-0*) Sonoran Pub.

Reiss, Fern. Taking Time off in Israel. LC 85-1225. (Illus.). 149p. 1985. pap. 9.95 (*0-915361-15-9*) Modan-Adama Bks.

***Reiss, Fred.** Gidget Must Die. 188p. (Orig.). 1995. pap. 14. 95 (*0-9623869-1-X*) F Reiss Comedy.

— Insult & Live! The Ultimate Abuse Guide. (Illus.). 375p. (Orig.). 1993. pap. 14.95 (*0-9623869-9-5*) F Reiss Comedy.

Reiss, Fred, ed. The Standard Guide to the Jewish & Civil Calendars: A Parallel Jewish & Civil Calender from 1899-2050. 160p. 1986. pap. text ed. 14.95 (*0-87441-428-8*) Behrman.

Reiss, Frederick. How To Abuse & Insult Everyone. (Illus.). 88p. (Orig.). (C). 1989. pap. 9.95 (*0-9623869-0-1*) F Reiss Comedy.

Reiss, H. Progress in Solid State Chemistry, Vol. 2. LC 63-11362. 1965. 188.00 (*0-08-011000-2*, Pub. by Pergamon Repr UK) Franklin.

— Radiative Transfer in Nontransparent, Dispersed Media. (Tracts in Modern Physics Ser.: Vol. 113). (Illus.). 200p. 1988. 73.00 (*0-387-18608-5*) Spr-Verlag.

Reiss, H., et al, eds. Progress in Solid State Chemistry, Vol. 1. 1964. 227.00 (*0-08-010246-8*, Pub. by Pergamon Repr UK) Franklin.

— Progress in Solid State Chemistry, Vol. 3. 1967. 216.00 (*0-08-011886-0*, Pub. by Pergamon Repr UK) Franklin.

— Progress in Solid State Chemistry, Vol. 5. 1971. 98.00 (*0-08-015846-3*, Pub. by Pergamon Repr UK) Franklin.

— Progress in Solid State Chemistry, Vol. 6. 1971. 98.00 (*0-08-016723-3*, Pub. by Pergamon Repr UK) Franklin.

— Progress in Solid State Chemistry, Vol. 7. 1972. 98.00 (*0-08-016916-3*, Pub. by Pergamon Repr UK) Franklin.

Reiss, H. S., ed. see Kant, Immanuel.

Reiss, Harriet M., jt. auth. see Reiss, Ira L.

Reiss, Ira L. & Lee, Gary R. Family Systems in America. 4th ed. 592p. (C). 1988. text ed. 33.25 (*0-03-071113-4*) HB Coll Pubs.

Reiss, Ira L. & Reiss, Harriet M. An End to Shame: Shaping Our Next Sexual Revolution. 287p. (C). 1990. 24.95 (*0-87975-635-7*) Prometheus Bks.

Reiss, James. The Breathers. LC 73-86610. (American Poetry Ser.: Vol. 4). 64p. 1974. pap. 2.95 (*0-912946-17-2*) Ecco Pr.

Reiss, Jill, ed. see Templeton, Michael.

Reiss, Johanna. The Journey Back. LC 76-12615. (Trophy Keypoint Bk.). 224p. (YA). (gr. 7 up). 1987. pap. 3.95 (*0-06-447042-3*, Trophy) HarpC Child Bks.

— The Journey Back. braille ed. 242p. 1992. Braille. vinyl bd. 19.36 (*1-56956-268-7*, BR8398) W A T Braille.

— The Upstairs Room. LC 77-187940. 196p. (YA). (gr. 7 up). 1972. 15.00 (*0-690-85127-8*) HarpC Child Bks.

— The Upstairs Room. LC 77-187940. 196p. (YA). (gr. 7 up). 1987. lib. bdg. 14.89 (*0-690-04702-9*, Crowell Jr Bks) HarpC Child Bks.

— The Upstairs Room. LC 77-187940. (Trophy Bk.). 208p. (YA). (gr. 7 up). 1990. pap. 3.95 (*0-06-440370-X*, Trophy) HarpC Child Bks.

— Upstairs Room. braille ed. 268p. 1992. vinyl bd. 21.44 (*1-56956-327-6*, BR8399) W A T Braille.

— The Upstairs Room. LC 77-187940. (Trophy Keypoint Bk.). 192p. (YA). (gr. 7 up). 1987. reprint ed. pap. 3.95 (*0-06-447043-1*, Trophy) HarpC Child Bks.

Reiss, John J. Colors. LC 69-13653. (Illus.). 32p. (J). (ps-2). 1982. text ed. 13.95 (*0-02-776130-4*, Bradbury S&S) S&S Childrens.

— Colors. LC 86-22189. (Illus.). 32p. (J). (ps-2). 1987. reprint ed. pap. 4.95 (*0-689-71119-0*, Aladdin Paperbacks) S&S Childrens.

— Numbers. LC 76-151313. (Illus.). 32p. (J). (ps-2). 1982. text ed. 13.95 (*0-02-776150-9*, Bradbury S&S) S&S Childrens.

— Numbers. LC 86-22243. (Illus.). 32p. (J). (ps-2). 1987. pap. 3.95 (*0-689-71120-4*, Aladdin Paperbacks) S&S Childrens.

— Shapes. LC 73-76545. (Illus.). 32p. (J). (ps-2). 1982. text ed. 13.95 (*0-02-776190-8*, Bradbury S&S) S&S Childrens.

— Shapes. LC 86-22164. (Illus.). 32p. (J). (ps-2). 1987. reprint ed. pap. 3.95 (*0-689-71121-2*, Aladdin Paperbacks) S&S Childrens.

Reiss, Kathryn. Dreadful Sorry. LC 92-38780. (J). (gr. 5-9). 1993. 16.95 (*0-15-224213-9*) HarBrace.

— The Glass House People. (J). 1992. 16.95 (*0-15-231040-1*, HB Juv Bks) HarBrace.

— Glass House People. (YA). (gr. 7 up). 1992. pap. 6.95 (*0-15-231041-X*, HB Juv Bks) HarBrace.

— Pale Phoenix. LC 93-32299. (J). (gr. 5 up). 1994. pap. write for info. (*0-15-200031-3*) HarBrace.

— Pale Phoenix. LC 93-32299. (J). (gr. 5 up). 1994. 10.95 (*0-15-200030-5*) HarBrace.

— Time Windows. 260p. (J). (gr. 5 up). 1991. 15.95 (*0-15-288205-7*, HB Juv Bks) HarBrace.

— Time Windows. (J). (gr. 4-7). 1994. pap. 3.50 (*0-590-46536-8*) Scholastic Inc.

Reiss, Leonard, jt. auth. see Weber, Christopher.

Reiss, Levi. Applying SQL in Business. 1992. text ed. write for info. (*0-07-051842-4*) McGraw.

— Open Computing Guide to Mosaic. 1994. pap. text ed. 19.95 (*0-07-882088-X*) Osborne-McGraw.

— Unix System Administration Guide. 1993. pap. text ed. 34.95 (*0-07-881951-2*) McGraw.

— Using Paradox for Windows. 1993. pap. text ed. write for info. (*0-07-052018-6*) McGraw.

— Using Paradox 4.0. 448p. 1993. text ed. write for info. (*0-07-051848-3*) McGraw.

Reiss, Levi & Radin, Joseph. XWindow Inside & Out. 650p. 1992. pap. text ed. 27.95 (*0-07-881796-X*) Osborne-McGraw.

***Reiss, Louis H.** The Engineering Aspects of Fractured Formations. (Illus.). 120p. (C). 1980. pap. text ed. 43.00 (*2-7108-0374-7*) Technip.

Reiss, Michael J. The Allometry of Growth & Reproduction. (Illus.). 168p. (C). 1989. 54.95 (*0-521-36091-9*) Cambridge U Pr.

— The Allometry of Growth & Reproduction. (Illus.). 182p. (C). 1991. pap. 22.95 (*0-521-42358-9*) Cambridge U Pr.

— Science Education for a Pluralist Society. LC 92-47138. (Developing Science & Technology Education Ser.). 1993. 75.00 (*0-335-15761-0*, Open Univ Pr); pap. 23.00 (*0-335-15760-2*, Open Univ Pr) Taylor & Francis.

Reiss, Michael J., jt. ed. see King, Anna S.

***Reiss, Mitchell.** Bridled Ambition: Why Countries Constrain Their Nuclear Capabilities. LC 95-2646. (Special Studies). 360p. 1995. text ed. 45.00 (*0-943875-72-2*); pap. 16.95 (*0-943875-71-4*) W Wilson Ctr Pr.

— Without the Bomb: The Politics of Nuclear Non-Proliferation. 368p. 1988. text ed. 47.50 (*0-231-06438-1*) Col U Pr.

— Without the Bomb: The Politics of Nuclear Nonproliferation. 337p. 1989. pap. text ed. 15.50 (*0-231-06439-X*) Col U Pr.

Reiss, Mitchell & Litwak, Robert S., eds. Nuclear Proliferation after the Cold War. (Woodrow Wilson Center Press Ser.). 320p. (C). 1994. text ed. 45.00 (*0-943875-64-1*); pap. text ed. 16.95 (*0-943875-57-9*) Johns Hopkins.

Reiss, Nira. Speech Acts Taxonomy As a Tool for Ethnographic Description: An Analysis Based on Videotapes of Continuous Behavior in Two New York Households. LC 86-8207. (Pragmatics & Beyond Ser.: VI-7). x, 153p. (Orig.). 1985. pap. 53.00x (*0-915027-93-3*) Benjamins North Am.

Reiss, R. Approximate Distributions of Order Statistics. (Series in Statistics). (Illus.). xii, 355p. 1989. 59.00 (*0-387-96851-2*) Spr-Verlag.

Reiss, R. D., jt. ed. see Husler, J.

Reiss, R. D., et al. A Course on Point Processes. Fienberg, Stephen E. et al, eds. LC 92-29587. (Series in Statistics). (Illus.). 264p. 1992. 54.95 (*0-387-97924-7*) Spr-Verlag.

***Reiss, Raymond F.** Red Wing Art Pottery: Including Pottery Made for Rumrill. LC 94-64711. Date not set. write for info. (*0-9642087-0-9*) Property IL.

Reiss, Richard F., ed. see Ojai Symposium Staff.

Reiss, Stephen. The Child Art of Peggy Somerville. (Illus.). 96p. 1992. 25.00 (*1-871569-17-6*) New Amsterdam Bks.

— The Reiss Rules for Two-Hour Monopoly: Fun, Fast, Unofficial Way to Play America's Favorite Board Game. LC 93-85455. (Illus.). 64p. (Orig.). (J). (gr. 1-12). 1994. pap. 6.95 (*0-9637853-3-8*) Prosprty Prtnrs.

***Reiss, Steven.** Handbook of Challenging Behavior: Mental Health Aspects of Mental Retardation. 301p. (C). 1994. text ed. 42.95 (*0-9642598-1-8*) IDS Pubng.

***Reiss, Steven P.** The Field Programming Environment: A Friendly Integrated Environment for Learning & Development. (International Series in Engineering & Computer Science, Natural Language Processing & Machine Translation). 312p. (C). 1994. lib. bdg. 89.95 (*0-7923-9537-9*) Kluwer Ac.

Reiss, Thomas H. Recognizing Planar Objects Using Invariant Image Features. LC 93-19397. 1993. 35.00 (*0-387-56713-5*) Spr-Verlag.

Reiss, Timothy J. The Discourse of Modernism. LC 81-15212. 416p. (Orig.). (C). 1985. 49.95 (*0-8014-1464-4*); pap. 17.95 (*0-8014-9336-6*) Cornell U Pr.

— The Meaning of Literature. LC 91-23344. 408p. 1992. 47. 50 (*0-8014-2646-4*); pap. 15.95 (*0-8014-9947-X*) Cornell U Pr.

— Tragedy & Truth: Studies in the Development of a Renaissance & Neoclassical Discourse. LC 80-10413. 344p. reprint ed. pap. 98.10 (*0-7837-4549-4*, 2080338) Bks Demand.

— The Uncertainty of Analysis: Problems in Truth, Meaning, & Culture. LC 88-47741. 312p. 1988. 36.95 (*0-8014-2162-4*) Cornell U Pr.

Reiss, W. & Linderman, F. B. Blackfeet Indians. 1977. lib. bdg. 75.95 (*0-8490-1513-8*) Gordon Pr.

***Reiss, Walt S.** Gettin' Where You're Goin' The Right Way is Better Than the Easy Way. 350p. 1995. 19.95 (*0-9643376-0-6*) W Reiss Bks.

Reisser, Anne N. All's Fair - Come Love, Call My Name. 368p. 1990. pap. 3.95 (*0-8439-2978-2*) Dorchester Pub Co.

— The Captive Love - the Face of Love, 2 vols. in 1. 368p. 1990. reprint ed. pap. 3.95 (*0-8439-2939-1*) Dorchester Pub Co.

— Deceptive Love - By Love Betrayed. 368p. 1990. pap. 3.95 (*0-8439-3008-X*) Dorchester Pub Co.

Reisser, Anne N., jt. auth. see McCue, Noelle B.

Reisser, Craig, tr. see Lichtenberger, Elisabeth.

Reisser, Linda, jt. auth. see Chickering, Arthur.

Reisser, Paul & Reisser, Teri. What You Need to Know about Menopause: Answers to the Questions Women Ask Most. 200p. 1994. pap. 8.99 (*0-89283-880-9*, Vine Bks) Servant.

Reisser, Teri, jt. auth. see Reisser, Paul.

Reisser, W., ed. Algae & Symbosis: Plants-Animals-Fungi-Viruses-Interactions Explored. (Illus.). 746p. 1992. lib. bdg. 199.00 (*0-948737-15-8*, Pub. by Biopress Ltd UK) Lubrecht & Cramer.

Reissiger, Friedrich A., jt. auth. see Kortsen, Bjarne.

Reissigl, H. & Schoenitzer, D. Transfusionsmedizin und Schock. (Handbuch der Infusionstherapie und Klinischen Ernaehrung Ser.: Band 3). xii, 256p. 1986. 100.00 (*3-8055-3744-1*) S Karger.

Reissigl, H. & Schonitzer, D. Die Bluttransfusion. (Illus.). x, 214p. 1986. 93.75 (*3-8055-4491-X*) S Karger.

Reissigl, H., et al, eds. Infusionstherapie bei Volumenmangel und bei rheologischen Indikationen. (Beitraege zur Infusionstherapie und Klinische Ernaehrung Ser.: Band 2). 1979. pap. 13.75 (*3-8055-3014-5*) S Karger.

Reissman, Leonard. Class in American Society. 1960. pap. 16.95 (*0-02-926270-4*) Free Pr.

— Urban Process. LC 64-20301. 1970. pap. text ed. 16.95 (*0-02-926300-X*) Free Pr.

***Reissman, Rose.** The Evolving Multicultural Classroom. LC 94-25103. 1994. 13.95 (*0-87120-233-6*) Assn Supervision.

Reissner, tr. see Borge, Tomas, et al.

Reissner, E., ed. see Applied Mathematics Symposium Staff, et al.

***Reissner, Eric.** Selected Works. (Math Ser.). 656p. 1995. 75.00 (*0-86720-968-2*) Jones & Bartlett.

Reissner, Eric, jt. auth. see Martin, William T.

Reissner, Will, jt. auth. see Frankel, Dave.

Reist, A., ed. see Held, E., et al.

Reist, A., et al, eds. Diabetes und Graviditaet. (Fortschritte der Geburtshilfe & Gynaekologie Ser.: Vol. 54). (Illus.). 1975. pap. 15.25 (*3-8055-2144-8*) S Karger.

R

Reist, Benjamin A. Processive Revelation. 208p. 1992. text ed. 25.00 (*0-664-21955-1*) Westminster John Knox.

— A Reading of Calvin's Institutes. 132p. (Orig.). 1991. pap. 7.99 (*0-664-25155-2*) Westminster John Knox.

Reist, Linnaeus L. The Colorful Landis Brothers: Founders of the Landis Valley Museum. Severs, Susan B., ed. & illus. by. LC 87-90447. 100p. (Orig.). (YA). (gr. 11-12). 1987. pap. write for info. (*0-9618501-0-8*) S R Severs.

Reist, Parker. Aerosol Science & Technology. 2nd ed. 1992. text ed. 59.00 (*0-07-051882-3*) McGraw.

Reistroffer, Mary. Conversations to Foster Parents from Mary Reistroffer, No. 3: Foster Parents & Social Workers - on the Job Together. LC 73-93881. 1974. pap. 7.00 (*0-87868-111-6*) Child Welfare.

Reiswig, Gary. Water Boy. 304p. 1993. 20.00 (*0-671-79506-6*) S&S Trade.

Reisz, Karel & Millar, Gavin. Technique of Film Editing. enl. ed. (Library of Communication Techniques Ser). (Illus.). 426p. 1974. pap. 39.95 (*0-240-50846-7*, Focal) Buttrwrth-Heinemann.

Reisz, Robert R. A Diapsid Reptile from the Pennsylvanian of Kansas. (Special Publication Ser.: No. 7). 74p. (Orig.). 1981. pap. 5.00 (*0-89338-011-3*) U of KS Mus Nat Hist.

— Pelycosauria. (Encyclopedia of Paleoherpetology Ser.: Pt. 17 A). 140p. 1986. pap. 110.00 (*3-437-30486-0*, Pub. by Gustav Fischer Verlag); 95.00 (*0-685-55845-2*, Pub. by Gustav Fischer Verlag) VCH Pubs.

***Reit, Seymour.** A Dog's Tale. LC 94-49332. (Bank Street Ready-to-Read Ser.). (Illus.). (J). 1996. text ed. write for info. (*0-553-09745-8*); pap. write for info. (*0-553-37577-6*) Bantam.

— Trains. (J). (ps-3). 1990. write for info. (*0-307-17869-2*, Golden Bks) Western Pub.

Reit, Seymour V. Behind Rebel Lines: The Incredible Story of Emma Edmonds, Civil War Spy. (Odyssey Ser.). 114p. (J). (gr. 3-7). 1991. pap. 5.00 (*0-15-200424-6*, Odyssey) HarBrace.

— Guns for General Washington: A Story of the American Revolution. (J). (gr. 4-7). 1992. pap. 4.95 (*0-15-232695-2*) HarBrace.

— Guns for General Washington: The Impossible Journey. 98p. (J). (gr. 3-7). 1990. 15.95 (*0-15-200466-1*, Gulliver Bks) HarBrace.

— Rebus Bears-Bank Street. (J). (ps-3). 1989. 3.99 (*0-553-34689-X*) Bantam.

— Sibling Rivalry. 208p. 1988. mass mkt. 5.99 (*0-345-35553-9*) Ballantine.

— Things That Go: A Traveling Alphabet. 1990. pap. 3.99 (*0-553-34849-3*) Bantam.

Reitan, Earl A. Politics, War, & Empire: The Rise of Britain to a World Power, 1688-1792. Eubank, Keith, ed. (European History Ser.). 200p. (C). 1994. pap. text ed. write for info. (*0-88295-899-2*) Harlan Davidson.

Reitan, Earl A., ed. & intro. The Best of the Gentleman's Magazine, 1731-1754. LC 87-1709. (Studies in British History: Vol. 4). (Illus.). 432p. 1987. lib. bdg. 109.95 (*0-88946-457-X*) E Mellen.

Reitan, Ralph M. Aphasia & Sensory-Perceptual Deficits in Children. 208p. (Orig.). 1985. pap. text ed. 32.00 (*0-934515-01-8*) Neuropsych Pr.

Reitan, Ralph M. & Davison, Leslie A., eds. Clinical Neuropsychology: Current Status & Applications. LC 66-40726. 417p. 1974. pap. 40.00 (*0-89116-367-0*) Hemisp Pub.

Reitan, Ralph M. & Wolfson, Deborah. The Halstead-Reitan Neuropsychological Test Battery: Theory & Clinical Interpretation. LC 85-71561. 486p. 1985. teacher ed write for info. (*0-934515-04-2*); text ed. 39.95 (*0-934515-02-6*) Neuropsych Pr.

— Neuroanatomy & Neuropathology: A Clinical Guide for Neuropsychologists. LC 85-61660. (Illus.). 353p. 1985. teacher ed write for info. (*0-934515-05-0*); text ed. 39.95 (*0-934515-03-4*) Neuropsych Pr.

— Traumatic Brain Injury: Pathophysiology & Neuropsychological Evaluation, Vol. 1. LC 86-60951. (Illus.). 425p. 1986. text ed. 59.95 (*0-934515-06-9*) Neuropsych Pr.

— Traumatic Brain Injury: Recovery & Rehabilitation, Vol. 2. LC 86-60952. (Illus.). 400p. 1987. text ed. 59.95 (*0-934515-07-7*) Neuropsych Pr.

Reitano, Joanne. The Tariff Question: Confronting Industrialism in the Gilded Age. LC 93-5313. 1994. 28.50 (*0-271-01035-5*) Pa St U Pr.

Reitci, Rita, ed. see Tozuks, Takako.

Reite, Martin & Field, Tiffany, eds. Psychobiology of Attachment. (Behavioral Biology Ser.). 1985. text ed. 81.00 (*0-12-586780-8*) Acad Pr.

Reite, Martin, et al. Concise Guide to Evaluation & Management of Sleep Disorders. LC 89-15117. (American Psychiatric Press Concise Guides Ser.). 175p. 1990. pap. text ed. 19.50 (*0-88048-334-2*) Am Psychiatric.

Reiten, Brent. Transient Sex. 60p. (Orig.). 1989. pap. 8.00 (*0-317-94038-4*) Scalding Pr.

Reiten, I. & Van Den Bergh, M. Two-Dimensional Tame & Maximal Orders of Finite Representation Type. LC 89-15024. (MEMO Ser.: Vol. 80/408). 72p. 1989. pap. 18.00 (*0-8218-2469-4*, MEMO 80/408) Am Math.

Reitenauer, Ronald L., ed. see Van Bogaert, Daniel A.

Reiter, Beth L. Coastal Georgia. LC 85-81036. (Golden Coast Book Ser.). (Illus.). 127p. 1985. 30.00 (*0-8203-1585-0*); pap. 15.00 (*0-8203-1586-9*) U of Ga Pr.

Reiter-Brandwein, Donna, ed. see Frishberg, Nancy.

Reiter, Clifford A. & Jones, William R. APL with a Mathematical Accent. 225p. (C). 1990. boxed, text ed. 41.75 (*0-534-12864-5*) Chapman & Hall.

Reiter, David P. The Snow in Us. (Illus.). 64p. (C). 1989. 39.00 (*0-9587972-3-4*, Pub. by Five Islands Pr AT) St Mut.

Reiter, Edith & Swerdlick, Harriet. Rainy Day Baseball Games. 24p. 1991. pap. 2.95 (*0-8431-2812-7*) Putnam Pub Group.

— Rainy Day Golf Games. 48p. 1985. bds. 2.95 (*0-8431-1433-9*) Putnam Pub Group.

Reiter, Edith, jt. auth. see Swerdlick, Harriet.

Reiter, Edward. Global Communication & Information Bibliography. LC 84-7223. (Collection of Bibliographic & Research Resources). 85p. 1984. 35.00 (*0-379-20849-0*) Oceana.

— Selective Bibliography on Oil & Gas. (Collection of Bibliographic & Research Resources). 29p. (Orig.). 1985. 35.00 (*0-379-20901-2*) Oceana.

Reiter, Elmar R. Atmospheric Transport Processes Pt. 1: Energy Transfers & Transformations. LC 76-603262. (DOE Critical Review Ser.). 253p. 1969. pap. 14.25 (*0-87079-396-9*, TID-24868); fiche 9.00 (*0-87079-397-7*) DOE.

— Atmospheric Transport Processes, Pt. 2: Chemical Tracers. LC 76-603262. (DOE Critical Review Ser.). 382p. 1971. pap. 17.50 (*0-87079-140-0*, TID-25314); fiche 9.00 (*0-87079-141-9*, TID-25314) DOE.

— Atmospheric Transport Processes, Pt. 3: Hydrodynamic Tracers. LC 76-603262. (DOE Critical Review Ser.). 216p. 1972. pap. 36.50 (*0-87079-142-7*, TID-25731); fiche 9.00 (*0-87079-143-5*, TID-25731) DOE.

— Atmospheric Transport Processes, Pt. 4: Radioactive Tracers. LC 76-603262. (DOE Critical Review Ser.). 615p. 1978. 23.50 (*0-87079-114-1*, TID-27114); fiche 9.00 (*0-87079-145-1*, TID-27114) DOE.

— Jet-Stream Meteorology. LC 63-13074. 529p. reprint ed. pap. 150.80 (*0-317-08097-0*, 2020153) Bks Demand.

— Jet Streams: How Do They Affect Our Weather? LC 78-25793. (Illus.). 189p. 1979. reprint ed. text ed. 35.00 (*0-313-20782-8*, REJS, Greenwood Pr) Greenwood.

Reiter, Ester. Making Fast Food: From the Frying Pan into the Fryer. pap. 17.95 (*0-7735-0947-X*, Pub. by McGill CN) U of Toronto Pr.

Reiter, Frank, tr. see Blundall, John, et al.

Reiter, G., et al, eds. Dynamics of Magnetic Fluctuations in High-Temperature Superconductors. (NATO ASI Series B, Physics: Vol. 246). (Illus.). 368p. 1991. 95.00 (*0-306-43810-0*, Plenum Pr) Plenum.

Reiter, H. Metaplectic Groups & Segal Algebra. (Lecture Notes in Mathematics Ser.: Vol. 1382). xi, 128p. 1989. pap. 26.50 (*0-387-51417-1*) Spr-Verlag.

Reiter, Henry H. Compendium of Abnormal Psychology. 2nd ed. 110p. 1980. pap. text ed. 10.00 (*0-9606044-0-5*) Psychometric.

Reiter, Joel, jt. auth. see Richard, Adrienne.

Reiter, John, ed. see Kolbisen, Irene M.

Reiter, Leon. Earthquake Hazard Analysis. 1991. text ed. 68.50 (*0-231-06534-5*) Col U Pr.

***Reiter, M., ed.** Dynamics of Business Cycles: Contributions to Economics. 215p. 1995. pap. 54.00 (*3-7908-0823-7*) Spr-Verlag.

Reiter, Mary J. Weaving a Life: The Story of Mary Meigs Atwater. Patterson, Veronica, ed. 208p. (Orig.). 1992. pap. 14.95 (*0-934026-77-7*) Interweave.

Reiter, Prosper, Jr. Profits, Dividends & the Law: Profits Available for Dividends from Standpoint of Law & Best Accounting Practice. LC 75-18481. (History of Accounting Ser.). (Illus.). 1979. reprint ed. 23.95 (*0-405-07563-4*) Ayer.

Reiter, R. Fields, Currents & Aerosols in the Lower Troposphere. Kothekar, V. S., tr. 736p. (ENG.). (C). 1986. text ed. 130.00 (*90-6191-469-8*, Pub. by A A Balkema NE) Ashgate Pub Co.

— Fields, Currents & Aerosols in the Lower Troposphere. (C). 1987. 44.00 (*0-8364-2123-X*, Pub. by Oxford IBH II) S Asia.

— Phenomena in Atmospheric & Environmental Electricity. LC 92-5574. (Developments in Atmospheric Science Ser.: Vol. 20). 1992. write for info. (*0-444-89286-9*) Elsevier.

— Pineal Gland Series, 3 vols., Set. 439.00 (*0-8493-5713-6*, CRC Reprint) Franklin.

Reiter, R. J. Melatonin. (Medical Intelligence Unit Ser.). write for info. (*1-57059-061-3*) R G Landes.

Reiter, R. J., ed. The Pineal & Reproduction. (Progress in Reproductive Biology & Medicine Ser.: Vol. 4). (Illus.). 1978. 95.25 (*3-8055-2815-9*) S Karger.

Reiter, R. J. & Follett, B. K., eds. Seasonal Reproduction in Higher Vertebrates. (Progress in Reproductive Biology & Medicine Ser.: Vol. 5). (Illus.). vi, 222p. 1980. 124.00 (*3-8055-0246-X*) S Karger.

Reiter, R. J., jt. ed. see Fraschini, F.

***Reiter, Russel J., ed.** The Pineal Gland. LC 84-4762. (Comprehensive Endocrinology Ser.). (Illus.). reprint ed. pap. 112.30 (*0-7837-9579-3*, 2060328) Bks Demand.

— Pineal Gland, Vol. I. 1981. 180.00 (*0-8493-5714-4*, QP188, CRC Reprint) Franklin.

— The Pineal Gland: Reproductive Effects, Vol. II. 240p. 1981. 129.95 (*0-8493-5716-0*, QP188, CRC Reprint) Franklin.

Reiter, Seymour. A Study of Shelley's Poetry. LC 67-22735. 1967. 20.00 (*0-8263-0085-5*) Lib Soc Sci.

Reiter, Stanley, ed. Studies in Mathematical Economics. LC 85-63770. (Studies in Mathematics: Vol. 25). 422p. 1986. 12.00 (*0-88385-127-X*) Math Assn.

***Reiter, Thomas.** Crossovers: Poems. LC 95-2450. 62p. 1995. 23.00 (*0-910055-19-X*); pap. 12.50 (*0-910055-20-3*) East Wash Univ.

— Time in the Air. Ellis, Ron, ed. 36p. (Orig.). 1990. pap. write for info. (*0-9624746-1-4*) Woodhenge.

Reiter, Tom. Basketball Inbound Attack. LC 93-12084. (Spalding Sports Library). (Illus.). 128p. (Orig.). 1993. pap. text ed. 12.95 (*0-940279-60-6*) Masters Pr IN.

— Basketball's Offensive Sets. (Spalding Sports Library). (Illus.). 128p. (Orig.). 1995. pap. 14.95 (*1-57028-038-X*, Spalding Sports) Masters Pr IN.

Reiter, Victoria, tr. see Conde, Maryse.

Reiter, William A. Aemilius Paullus, Conquerer of Greece. 160p. 1988. lib. bdg. 55.00 (*0-7099-4285-0*, Pub. by Croom Helm UK) Routledge Chapman & Hall.

Reith, Albrecht & Mayhew, Terry M., eds. Stereology & Morphometry in Election Microscopy: Some Problem & Their Solutions. (Ultrastructural Pathology Publication). 215p. 1988. 91.00 (*0-89116-623-8*) Hemisp Pub.

Reith, Charles. The Blind Eye of History: A Study of the Origins of the Present Police Era (With Intro. Added) LC 74-26636. (Criminology, Law Enforcement, & Social Problems Ser.: No. 203). (C). 1975. reprint ed. 25.00 (*0-87585-203-3*) Patterson Smith.

— Police Principles & the Problem of War. 1992. lib. bdg. 88.75 (*0-8490-5299-8*) Gordon Pr.

Reith, Charles, jt. auth. see Caldwell, Jack A.

Reith, Charles C. & Thomson, Bruce M., eds. Deserts As Dumps? The Disposal of Hazardous Materials in Arid Ecosystems. LC 92-16983. 347p. 1993. pap. 32.50 (*0-8263-1298-5*) U of NM Pr.

Reith, Gerry, ed. Neutron Gun. 2nd ed. (Illus.). 72p. 1987. pap. 4.95 (*0-911627-12-X*) Neither-Nor Pr.

Reith, H. B. Sonographie des Knochens: Experimentelle und Klinische Ergebnisse Zur Verlaufskontrolle Nach Frakturen und Spongiosatransplantationen. (Illus.). vi, 58p. 1994. pap. 25.75 (*3-8055-5965-8*) S Karger.

Reith, H. B., jt. ed. see Kozuschek, W.

Reith, Mary K., ed. see Zobel, Herbert L.

Reither, Joseph. The Development of Tactical Doctrines at AAFSAT & AAFTAC. (USAF Historical Studies: No. 13). 121p. 1944. pap. text ed. 21.95 (*0-89126-036-6*) MA-AH Pub.

— World History: A Brief Introduction. LC 65-17275. Orig. Title: World History at a Glance. (Illus.). 512p. 1973. reprint ed. pap. text ed. 12.95 (*0-07-051875-0*) McGraw.

Reither, Joseph, ed. Masterworks of History, 3 vols., 1. (Masterworks Ser.). (C). 1973. reprint ed. write for info. (*0-07-040810-6*) McGraw.

— Masterworks of History, 3 vols., 3. (Masterworks Ser.). (C). 1973. reprint ed. write for info. (*0-07-040812-2*) McGraw.

Reither, Joseph, jt. auth. see England, J. Merton.

Reithmaier, Larry. Computer Guide for Pilots. LC 78-94966. (Pilot Guides Ser.). pap. 1.00 (*0-8168-7200-7*, 27200, TAB-Aero) TAB Bks.

— Mach One: The Illustrated Guide to High-Speed Flight. LC 94-1421. 1994. pap. text ed. 19.95 (*0-07-052021-6*) TAB Bks.

— Standard Aircraft Handbook. 5th ed. 1991. pap. text ed. 12.95 (*0-07-157642-8*) McGraw.

— Standard Aircraft Handbook. 5th ed. (Illus.). 256p. 1991. vinyl bd. 11.95 (*0-8306-8634-7*, 3634, TAB-Aero) TAB Bks.

Reithmaier, Larry, ed. Standard Aircraft Handbook. 4th ed. (Illus.). 240p. 1987. 11.95 (*0-8306-8812-9*, 28512V, TAB-Aero) TAB Bks.

Reitlinger, Gerald. The Economics of Taste, 3 Vols. LC 82-80311. (Illus.). 1959p. 1982. reprint ed. 100.00 (*0-87817-288-2*) Hacker.

— The S. S. Alibi of a Nation, 1922-1945. (Quality Paperbacks Ser.). (Illus.). 534p. 1989. reprint ed. pap. 14.95 (*0-306-80351-8*) Da Capo.

Reitman, Alan, ed. Price of Liberty: Perspectives on Civil Liberties by Member of the A.C.L.U. (C). 1969. pap. text ed. 1.95 (*0-393-00505-4*) Norton.

Reitman, Edward. Exploring Parallel Processing. 1990. pap. 18.95 (*0-8306-3367-7*, Windcrest) TAB Bks.

Reitman, Jeffrey B. & Weisblatt, Harold. Checks, Drafts & Notes. 1983. write for info. (*0-8205-1074-2*) Bender.

Reitman, Jerry I., comp. Beyond Two Thousand: The Future of Direct Marketing: 28 of the World's Leading Experts Predict the Changes Which Will Impact You, Your Job, & Your Company. LC 93-42158. 1994. 34.95 (*0-8442-3450-8*, NTC Busn Bks) NTC Pub Grp.

***Reitman, Judith.** Stolen for Profit. 272p. 1995. pap. 12.00 (*0-8217-4951-X*) Kensington MI.

Reitman, Kearney, jt. auth. see Higgins, Frank.

Reitman, Robert, ed. see Janenko, Patricia.

Reitman, Sanford W. The Educational Messiah Complex: American Faith in the Culturally Redemptive Power of Schooling. 224p. 1992. pap. text ed. 19.95 (*1-880192-00-4*) Caddo Gap Pr.

Reitman, Walter. Artificial Intelligence Applications for Business. Ginzberg, Michael, ed. LC 83-26648. (Computer-Based Systems in Information Management Ser.). 360p. 1984. text ed. 65.00 (*0-89391-220-4*) Ablex Pub.

Reitmeister, Lewis A. If Tomorrow Comes: A Tale of Two Worlds. LC 74-154458. (Utopian Literature Ser.). (Illus.). 1976. reprint ed. 28.95 (*0-405-03540-3*) Ayer.

Reitner, J. & Keupp, H., eds. Fossil & Recent Sponges. (Illus.). 608p. 1991. 193.00 (*0-387-52509-2*) Spr-Verlag.

Reitsch, Arthur G., jt. auth. see Hanke, John E.

Reitsch, Hanna. The Sky My Kingdom: The Memoirs of the Famous German Test Pilot. 232p. 1991. 35.00 (*1-85367-093-6*) Stackpole.

Reitsma, Pieter & Verhoeven, Ludo, eds. Acquisition of Reading in Dutch: A State of the Art. (Studies on Language Acquisition). 160p. (Orig.). (C). 1989. pap. 46.15 (*90-6765-490-6*) Mouton.

Reitt, Barbara, ed. see Turner, Richard & Butcher, Thomas E.

Reittinger, Janice. Iowa's Complete Guide to Antique Shops & Malls. 164p. (Orig.). 1994. pap. 4.75 (*0-9640314-0-X*) DJs Pubng.

— Iowa's Complete Guide to Antique Shops & Malls. 197p. (Orig.). 1995. pap. 4.95 (*0-9640314-1-8*) DJs Pubng.

Reitwiesner, William A., jt. auth. see Roberts, Gary B.

Reitz, jt. auth. see Baumgartner.

Reitz, Allen B., ed. Inositol Phosphates & Derivatives: Synthesis, Biochemistry, & Therapeutic Potential. LC 91-17716. (Symposium Ser.: No. 463). (Illus.). 248p. 1991. 59.95 (*0-8412-2086-7*) Am Chemical.

Reitz, Charles R., ed. see Farnsworth, E. Allan, et al.

Reitz, Curtis R. Consumer Product Warranties under Federal & State Laws. 2nd ed. 286p. 1987. text ed. 83.00 (*0-8318-0484-X*, B484) Am Law Inst.

Reitz, Curtis R., jt. auth. see Honnold, John O.

Reitz, Deneys. Boer Commando: An Afrikaner Journal of the Boer War. 288p. 1993. reprint ed. pap. 12.95 (*0-9627613-3-8*) Sarpedon.

— Trilogy of Deneys Reitz, Commando - Trekking On - No Outspan: A Boer Journal of the Boer War. 971p. 1994. 45.00 (*1-879356-39-2*) Wolfe Pub Co.

***Reitz, Earl F.** American Gold Mettle: A Sentient Perspective of Ulysses Grant. 205p. 1994. 50.00 (*0-9627654-2-2*) Xenolith Pr.

Reitz, J. J. Reitz: Family History & Record Book of the Descendants of Johan Friedrich Reitz, the Pioneer, Who Landed at Philadelphia, Sept. 7, 1748. (Illus.). 288p. 1992. reprint ed. lib. bdg. 53.50 (*0-8328-2712-6*); reprint ed. pap. 43.50 (*0-8328-2713-4*) Higginson Bk Co.

— Reitz: Family History & Record Book of the Descendants of Johan Friedrich Reitz, the Pioneer, Who Landed at Philadelphia, Sept. 7, 1748. (Illus.). 289p. 1994. reprint ed. lib. bdg. 54.50 (*0-8328-4053-X*); reprint ed. pap. 44.50 (*0-8328-4054-8*) Higginson Bk Co.

Reitz, Jeffery G., jt. auth. see Lazardfeld, Paul.

Reitz, Jeffrey G., jt. auth. see Lazarsfeld, Paul F.

Reitz, John R., et al. Foundations of Electromagnetic Theory. 3rd ed. LC 78-18649. (Physics Ser.). (Illus.). 1979. write for info. (*0-201-06333-6*); text ed. 54.95 (*0-201-06332-8*) Addison-Wesley.

Reitz, Ken. The Baseball Listener's Guide. 90p. (Orig.). 1993. pap. 5.00 (*0-9627654-1-4*) Xenolith Pr.

— Satellite Television Source Book. (Illus.). 100p. (Orig.). 1991. pap. 20.00 (*0-9627654-0-6*) Xenolith Pr.

Reitz, M. Die Alge im System der Pflanzen: Nanochlorum Eucaryotum - Eine Alge mit Minimalen Eukaryotischen Kriterien. (Illus.). 273p. (GER.). 1986. lib. bdg. 55.35 (*3-437-30523-9*) Lubrecht & Cramer.

***Reitz, Mercedes M. & Reitz, Russell T.** The Black Wolves of Yellow Mountain. (Yellow Mountain Ser.). (Illus.). 198p. (Orig.). (J). (gr. 6-8). 1994. pap. 11.95 (*0-9625344-5-5*) Creative Multi-Media.

— The Dreadful Monsters of Yellow Mountain. (Yellow Mountain Ser.). (Illus.). 216p. (Orig.). (J). (gr. 5-7). 1991. text ed. 19.95 (*0-9625344-2-0*); pap. 9.95 (*0-9625344-3-9*) Creative Multi-Media.

***Reitz, Mercedes M., et al.** Trouble Double on Yellow Mountain. (Yellow Mountain Ser.). (Illus.). 184p. (Orig.). (J). (gr. 4-7). 1990. pap. 9.95 (*0-9625344-1-2*) Creative Multi-Media.

Reitz, Miriam & Watson, Kenneth W. Adoption & the Family System: Strategies for Treatment. LC 91-44266. 340p. 1992. lib. bdg. 30.00 (*0-89862-797-4*) Guilford Pr.

Reitz, Raymond L. Photography in Life Sciences: Index of Modern Authors & Subjects with Guide for Rapid Research. LC 90-56305. 160p. 1991. 44.50 (*1-55914-396-7*); pap. 39.50 (*1-55914-397-5*) ABBE Pubs Assn.

Reitz, Robert, ed. see Ask, Robert W.

Reitz, Rosetta. Menopause: A Positive Approach. 1979. pap. 11.95 (*0-14-005120-1*, Penguin Bks) Viking Penguin.

Reitz, Russell T., jt. auth. see Reitz, Mercedes M.

Reitz, Sandra A., jt. auth. see Livo, Norma J.

Reitzel, J. David, et al. Contemporary Business Law: Principles & Cases. rev. ed. 1344p. (C). 1990. Test Bank. 25.95 (*0-07-051908-0*) McGraw.

— Contemporary Business Law & the Legal Environment: Principles & Cases. 5th rev. ed. LC 93-37330. Orig. Title: Contemporary Business Law. 1994. text ed. write for info. (*0-07-051912-9*) McGraw.

Reitzel, Rick W. From the Flower to the Vein. Hilvosky, Judy, ed. LC 89-30725. 1991. pap. 13.95 (*0-87949-287-2*) Ashley Bks.

Reitzel, Robert. Adventures of a Greenhorn: An Autobiographical Novel. Erhardt, Jacob, tr. LC 91-28511. (New German-American Studies - Neue Deutsch-Amerikanische Studien: Vol. 3). 94p. (C). 1992. text ed. 35.95 (*0-8204-1330-5*) P Lang Pubs.

— Des Armen Teufel: Gesammelte Schriften, 3 vols., Set. 1975. lib. bdg. 600.00 (*0-685-57118-1*) Revisionist Pr.

Reitzenstein, Richard. Epigramm und Skolion. 296p. 1970. reprint ed. write for info. (*0-318-70820-5*, Pub. by Georg Olms GW) Lubrecht & Cramer.

— The Hellenistic Mystery-Religions. Steely, John E., tr. LC 77-12980. (Pittsburgh Theological Monographs: No. 15). Orig. Title: Die Hellenistischen Mysterienreligionen Nach Ihren Arundgedanken und Wirkungen. 1978. pap. text ed. 20.00 (*0-915138-20-4*) Pickwick.

— Verrianische Forschungen. Vol. I.4. vi, 116p. 1966. reprint ed. write for info. (*0-318-71212-1*, Pub. by Georg Olms GW) Lubrecht & Cramer.

Reitzer, Stefan, jt. ed. see Korn, Matthias.

Reitzes, Lisa, jt. auth. see Wright, Patricia.

Reitzes, Lisa B., jt. auth. see Wright, Patricia.

Reitzug, Ulrich C., jt. auth. see Kowalski, Theodore J.

Reizenstein, Milton. The Economic History of the Baltimore & Ohio Railroad. 1827-1853. LC 78-63858. (Johns Hopkins University. Studies in the Social Sciences. Thirtieth Ser. 1912: 7-8). reprint ed. 11.50 (*0-404-61114-1*) AMS Pr.

Reizenstein, P., jt. ed. see Mathe, G.

Reizenstein, Peter. Hematologic Stress Syndrome: The Biological Response to Disease. LC 83-4023. 204p. 1983. text ed. 55.00 (*0-275-91408-9*, C1408, Praeger Pubs) Greenwood.

Reizes, Haim. The Mechanics of Vehicle Collisions. (Illus.). 152p. 1973. 33.95 (*0-398-02639-4*) C C Thomas.

R

An Asterisk (*) at the beginning of an entry indicates that the title is appearing in BIP for the first time.

— The Mechanics of Vehicle Collisions. (Illus.). 152p. 1973. pap. 19.95 (0-398-06345-1) C C Thomas.

Reizes, J. A., ed. Transport Phenomena in Heat & Mass Transfer: Proceedings of the Fourth International Symposium on Transport Phenomena in Heat & Mass Transfer (ISTP-IV), Sydney, Australia, 14-19 July, 1991, Organized under the Auspices of the Pacific Center of Thermal-Fluid Engineering. LC 92-36403. 1992. write for info. (0-444-89851-4) Elsevier.

***Rejab, F. I.** The Crocodile & the Elephant. (Illus.). 40p. (J). 1995. 9.95 (983-9808-25-7, Pub. by Delta Edits II) Weatherhill.

— The Fiery Cave. (Illus.). 40p. (J). 1995. 9.95 (983-9808-29-X, Pub. by Delta Edits II) Weatherhill.

— The Hero of Indera Kayangan. (Illus.). 40p. 1995. 9.95 (983-9808-27-3, Pub. by Delta Edits II) Weatherhill.

— The Magic Frog. (Illus.). 40p. (J). 1995. 9.95 (983-9808-14-1, Pub. by Delta Edits II) Weatherhill.

— Mahsuri: The Legend of Langkawi. (Illus.). 40p. (J). 1995. 9.95 (983-9808-24-9, Pub. by Delta Edits II) Weatherhill.

— The Merchant's Two Daughters. (Illus.). 40p. (J). 1995. 9.95 (983-9808-23-0, Pub. by Delta Edits II) Weatherhill.

— The Mousedeer & the Tiger Cubs. (Illus.). 24p. (J). 1994. 9.95 (983-9808-15-X, Pub. by Delta Edits II) Weatherhill.

— The Prince of Mount Kinabalu. (Illus.). 40p. (J). 1995. 9.95 (983-9808-26-5, Pub. by Delta Edits II) Weatherhill.

— The Young Heroes. (Illus.). 40p. (J). 1995. 9.95 (983-9808-28-1, Pub. by Delta Edits II) Weatherhill.

Rejai, Hostafa & Phillips, Kay. Loyalists & Revolutionaries: Political Leaders Compared. LC 87-27888. (Illus.). 192p. 1988. text ed. 49.95 (0-275-92915-9, C2915, Praeger Pubs) Greenwood.

Rejai, Mostafa. Decline of Ideology? (Controversy Ser.). 325p. 1971. text ed. 12.95 (0-202-24094-0); pap. text ed. 6.95 (0-202-24095-9) Lieber-Atherton.

— Political Ideologies: A Comparative Approach. LC 90-26349. 216p. (C). 1991. 45.00 (0-87332-806-X) M E Sharpe.

— Political Ideologies: A Comparative Approach. 2nd ed. 264p. 1995. pap. text ed. 19.95 (1-56324-142-0) M E Sharpe.

Rejai, Mostafa & Phillips, Kay. Demythologizing an Elite: American Presidents in Empirical, Comparative, & Historical Perspective. LC 92-31840. 172p. 1993. text ed. 47.95 (0-275-94331-3, C4331, Praeger Pubs) Greenwood.

Rejali, Darius M. Torture & Modernity: Self, Society & State in Modern Iran. (Institutional Structures of Feeling Ser.). 289p. (C). 1993. text ed. 49.50 (0-8133-1660-X); pap. text ed. 23.50 (0-8133-1879-3) Westview.

Rejda, George E. Principles of Insurance. 3rd ed. (C). 1989. text ed. 37.50 (0-673-38409-8) HarpCollege.

— Principles of Risk Management & Insurance. 4th ed. (C). 1991. text ed. 48.00 (0-673-46541-1); 16.75 (0-673-46542-X) HarpCollege.

— Principles of Risk Management & Insurance. 5th ed. LC 94-17221. (C). 1994. 46.00 (0-673-99027-3) HarpCollege.

— Social Insurance & Economic Security. 2nd ed. (Illus.). 512p. (C). 1984. 33.00 (0-13-815845-2) P-H.

— Social Insurance & Economic Security. 5th ed. LC 93-11492. 1994. text ed. 64.00 (0-13-834359-4) P-H.

Rejda, L. J. & Neville, Kris. Industrial Motor Users' Handbook of Insulation for Rewinds. LC 76-26949. 408p. 1977. 73.50 (0-444-00191-3) Elsevier.

Rejebian, Gary P. Think Green! A Retailer's Environmental Idea Book. (Illus.). 50p. (Orig.). 1992. pap. 25.00 (1-885337-00-0) IL Retail Merchants.

Rejeski, W. Jack & Kenney, Elizabeth A. Fitness Motivation: Preventing Participant Dropout. LC 88-4584. (Illus.). 168p. 1988. pap. text ed. 18.00x (0-87322-928-2, BREJ0928) Human Kinetics.

Rejeski, Walker J., ed. see Martinek, Thomas J. & Crowe, Patricia B.

***Rejhon, Annalee C.** Ryan Rolant: The Medieval Welsh Version of the Song of Roland. LC 82-20031. (University of California Publications in Entomology: No. 113). 276p. (ENG & WEL.). 1984. pap. 78.70 (0-7837-8422-8, 2049224) Bks Demand.

Rejnis, Ruth. How to Buy a Home. (No Nonsense Guides Ser.). 96p. 1992. pap. 4.95 (0-681-41468-5) Longmeadow Pr.

— Squeeze Your Home for Cash. 224p. 1994. pap. 14.95 (0-7931-0991-4, 191325-01, Real Estate Ed) Dearborn Finan.

— You Can Buy a Home. 192p. 1992. pap. 7.95 (0-681-41405-7) Longmeadow Pr.

Rejnis, Ruth, jt. auth. see Janik, Carolyn.

Rejwan, Nissim. Nasserist Ideology: Its Exponents & Critics. 271p. 1974. boxed 34.95 (0-87855-162-X) Transaction Pubs.

— Nasserist Ideology: Its Exponents & Critics. LC 74-2116. (Shiloah Center for Middle Eastern & African Studies. The Monograph Ser.). 282p. reprint ed. pap. 80.40 (0-8357-8962-4, 2033583) Bks Demand.

Rekach, V. G. Manual of the Theory of Elasticity. 318p. 1979. 50.00 (0-317-46650-X, Pub. by Collets UK) Pro-Am Music.

Rekany, Ilonia. Dental Care & Health Factors: Subject Analysis Index with Research Bibliography. LC 85-47865. 150p. 1986. 39.50 (0-88164-404-8); pap. 34.50 (0-88164-405-6) ABBE Pubs Assn.

Rekany, Ilonia M. Chin & Mandible: Medical & Dental Subject Analysis with Reference Bibliography. LC 85-48096. 150p. 1987. 39.50 (0-88164-464-1); pap. 34.50 (0-88164-465-X) ABBE Pubs Assn.

— Dental Practice & Research: Index of Modern Information. LC 88-47950. 150p. 1990. 39.50 (1-55914-132-8); pap. 34.50 (1-55914-133-6) ABBE Pubs Assn.

Rekate, ed. Comprehensive Management of Spina Bifida. 1990. 99.95 (0-8493-0151-3, RJ496) CRC Pr.

Rekdal, Jan E., jt. ed. see Corrain, Ailbhe O.

Rekela, George R. Hakeem Olajuwon: Tower of Power. LC 92-38905. (Achievers Ser.). (J). (gr. 4-9). 1993. lib. bdg. 13.50 (0-8225-0518-5, Lerner Publctns); pap. 4.95 (0-8225-9637-7, Lerner Publctns) Lerner Group.

— State Champions: The Story of the Buhl Bulldogs' Rise to Glory in 1941 & 1942. (Orig.). 1991. pap. 5.95 (0-9619505-0-1) Milkees Pr.

Rekenthaler, Doug, Jr., ed. see DiGregorio, Ron.

Rekenthaler, Doug, Jr., ed. see Gipson, Melinda.

Rekenthaler, Doug, Jr., ed. see Schomisch, Jeff.

Rekers, George A. RCC Vol. 14: Counseling Families. 211p. 1988. write for info. (0-8499-0595-8) Word Inc.

***Rekers, George A., ed.** Handbook of Child & Adolescent Sexual Problems. LC 94-40653. (Series in Scientific Foundations of Clinical & Counseling Psychology). 1995. 45.00 (0-02-926317-4, M Kessler Bks) Free Pr.

Rekha Chowdhury. Ideology & Politics of Ruling Parties in India. 1991. 19.00 (81-7100-301-X, Pub. by Deep) S Asia.

Rekker, Roelof F. & Mannhold, Raimund. Calculation of Drug Lipophilicity: The Hydrophobic Fragmental Constant Approach. 115p. 1992. text ed. 78.00 (1-56081-214-1) VCH Pubs.

Reklaitis, G. V. Introduction to Material & Energy Balances. LC 82-23800. 683p. (C). 1983. Net. text ed. write for info. (0-471-04131-9) Wiley.

Reklaitis, G. V., ed. Large Scale Optimization: Annual Meeting of the American Institute of Chemical Engineers, 1982. 100p. 1983. write for info. (0-08-030270-X, Pergamon Pr) Elsevier.

Reklaitis, G. V. & Spriggs, H. D., eds. Computer-Aided Process Oprations: Proceedings of the 1st International Conference, Park City, UT, July 5-10, 1987. 720p. 1988. 218.00 (0-444-98925-0) Elsevier.

Reklaitis, G. V., jt. ed. see Squires, Robert G.

Reklaitis, G. V., et al. Engineering Optimization: Methods & Application. LC 83-3545. 684p. 1983. text ed. 95.00 (0-471-05579-4, Wiley-Interscience) Wiley.

Rektorys, Karel. The Method of Discretization in Time. 1982. lib. bdg. 154.50 (90-277-1342-1) Kluwer Ac.

— Survey of Applicable Mathematics, Set. 2nd rev. ed. (Mathematics & Its Applications Ser.). 1769p. 1994. lib. bdg. 482.00 (0-7923-0679-1) Kluwer Ac.

— Variational Methods in Mathematics, Science & Engineering. Basch, Michael, tr. 572p. 1980. lib. bdg. 80.50 (90-277-1060-0) Kluwer Ac.

Rekus. Complete Confined Spaces Handbook. 1995. write for info. (0-87371-487-3) Lewis Pubs.

Rela, Walter. Uruguayan Literature: A Selective Bibliographical Guide. LC 86-15989. 85p. 1987. pap. 5.00 (0-87918-060-9) ASU Lat Am St.

Rela, Walter, comp. A Bibliographical Guide to Spanish American Literature: Twentieth-Century Sources. LC 88-15443. (Bibliographies & Indexes in World Literature Ser.: No. 13). 400p. 1988. text ed. 65.00 (0-313-25861-9, RBG/, Greenwood Pr) Greenwood.

Rela, Walter, jt. auth. see Foster, David W.

Relander, Click. Drummers & Dreamers. (Illus.). 345p. (Orig.). 1986. reprint ed. pap. text ed. 9.95 (0-914019-09-0) NW Interpretive.

***Relative Value Studies Inc. Staff.** The McGraw-Hill Complete RBRVS. 300p. (Orig.). 1995. audio 189.95 (0-07-810183-2); pap. 89.95 (0-07-600780-4) Hlthcare Mgmt Grp.

Relative Value Studies, Inc. Staff. Relative Values for Dentists. 128p. 1992. 99.00 (0-685-71297-4, D7052) PennWell Bks.

— Relative Values for Physicians. 64p. 1985. write for info. (0-07-073965-X) McGraw.

— Relative Values for Physicians. 2nd ed. 544p. 1986. text ed. 150.00 (0-07-073969-2) McGraw.

— Relative Values for Physicians: 1994-1995. rev. ed. 900p. 1994. ring bd. 249.00 (0-07-600726-X) Hlthcare Mgmt Grp.

***Relative Value Studies Inc. Staff.** Relative Values for Physicians, 1995-1996. rev. ed. 900p. 1995. ring bd. 249.00 (0-07-600771-5) Hlthcare Mgmt Grp.

— RVP Fees, 2 bks., Set. rev. ed. 900p. 1995. audio 795.00 (0-07-810179-4) Hlthcare Mgmt Grp.

Relative Value Studies, Inc. Staff. RVP Fees: Primary Care. 1994. disk 99.95 (0-07-809883-1) Hlthcare Mgmt Grp.

Rele, J. R. Fertility Analysis Through Extension of Stable Population Concepts & Stochastic Model of Human Reproduction, Vol. 2. LC 76-5422. (Population Monograph Ser.: No. 11). 1976. reprint ed. text ed. 55.00 (0-8371-8826-1, REFA, Greenwood Pr) Greenwood.

Rele, J. R. & Kanitkar, Tara. Fertility & Family Planning in Greater Bombay. 217p. 1980. 22.95 (0-940500-87-6, Pub. by Popular Prakashan II) Asia Bk Corp.

Rele, V. G. Human Mind Power: Secrets of the Vedic Gods. 136p. 1983. reprint ed. pap. text ed. 5.95 (0-86590-231-3, Pub. by Taraporevala II) Apt Bks.

— The Mysterious Kundalini: The Physical Basis of Kundalini Yoga. 1991. lib. bdg. 69.95 (0-8490-4191-0) Gordon Pr.

Rele, Vasant G. The Mysterious Kundalini. 92p. (Orig.). 1985. reprint ed. spiral bd. 6.60 (0-7873-1032-8) Mokelumne.

Relei, Carolyn. Bird Designs Stained Glass Pattern Book. (Illus.). 64p. 1989. pap. 4.95 (0-486-25947-1) Dover.

— Decorative Doorways Stained Glass Pattern Book. 1990. pap. 4.95 (0-486-26494-7) Dover.

Re'lem, Dyob, pseud. High Bloodpressures, Heart Attack, Diagrams. rev. ed. LC 89-92415. (Illus.). 90p. 1989. pap. write for info. (0-9622463-2-8) B Melger.

— Hoge Bloeddruk, Hart Infarct, Grafieken. rev. ed. (Illus.). 90p. (DUT.). 1989. pap. write for info. (0-9622463-3-6) B Melger.

Re'lem, Dyob & Melger, Boyd A. Hoge Bloeddruk, Myocardiale Infarct, Grafieken. (Illus.). 69p. (Orig.). (DUT.). 1989. pap. write for info. (0-9622463-1-X) B Melger.

Re'lem, Dyob, see Boyd A. Melger, pseud..

Relethford, John H. Fundamentals of Biological Anthropology. LC 93-28692. 338p. (C). 1994. pap. 36.95 (1-55934-280-3) Mayfield Pub.

— The Human Species: An Introduction to Biological Anthropology. 2nd ed. LC 93-3659. (Illus.). 575p. (C). 1994. pap. 43.95 (1-55934-206-4) Mayfield Pub.

— Instructor's Manual for The Human Species: An Introduction to Biological Anthropology. 2nd ed. LC 93-3659. (C). 1994. teacher ed. pap. write for info. (1-55934-308-7) Mayfield Pub.

Relf, Diane, ed. The Role of Horticulture in Human Well-Being & Social Development. LC 91-19911. (Illus.). 1992. 49.95 (0-88192-209-9) Timber.

Relf, Pat. Hurry! Hurry! (Little Golden Sound Story Book Ser.). 24p. (J). (ps up). 1992. write for info. (0-307-74802-2, 64802) Western Pub.

Relf, Pat & Hanavan, Louise. Barnyard Mystery. (Little Golden Sound Story Book Ser.). 24p. (J). (ps up). 1992. write for info. (0-307-74801-4, 64801) Western Pub.

***Relf, Patricia.** The Magic School Bus Hops Home: A Book about Animal Habitats. LC 94-25969. (Illus.). 1995. 2.50 (0-590-48413-3) Scholastic Inc.

Relfe, Mary S. Cuando el Dinero Falla: When Your Money Fails. (SPA.). 5.50 (84-7228-732-7, 360121, Pub. by Edit Clie SP) TSELF.

— The New Money System. 271p. 1982. pap. 6.95 (0-9607986-1-7) League Prayer.

— When Your Money Fails. 234p. (Orig.). 1981. pap. text ed. 5.95 (0-9607986-0-9) League Prayer.

Relfe, Stewart. Nuevo Sistema Monetario: New Money System. (SPA.). 7.50 (84-7228-814-5, 220635, Pub. by Edit Clie SP) TSELF.

Relgis, Eugen. Max Nettlau, Rudolf Rocker, Han Ryner, Rodolfo Gonzalez Pacheco, Joseph Ishill & Other Essays in Anarchism, Humanism, Libertarianism & Freedom. (History of Anarchism Ser.). 1984. lib. bdg. 250.00 (0-8490-3234-2) Gordon Pr.

Relgis, Eugene. Muted Voices. 1972. reprint ed. lib. bdg. 250.00 (0-87968-001-6) Gordon Pr.

Reliability Analysis Center. Hybrid Microcircuit Reliability Data Compiled by IIT Research Institute, Chicago. 200p. 1976. pap. 92.00 (0-08-020535-6, Pub. by Pergamon Repr UK) Franklin.

Relief Society Staff, ed. Parenting from A to Z: An Encyclopedia for Latter-Day Saint Families. LC 90-39284. 275p. 1990. pap. 8.95 (0-87579-298-7) Deseret Bk.

Relier, J. P., ed. Twenty-First Journees Nationales de Neonatologie, 1991. (Progres en Neonatologie Ser.: Vol. 11). (Illus.). vi, 370p. 1991. pap. 148.00 (3-8055-5446-X) S Karger.

— XIXes Journees Nationales de Neonatologie, 1989. (Progres en Neonatologie Ser.: Vol. 9). (Illus.). 268p. 1989. pap. 106.50 (3-8055-5060-X) S Karger.

— XVIIes Journees Nationales de Neonatologie, 1987: Paris, Mai Ser. (Progres en Neonatologie Ser.: Vol. 7). vi, 382p. 1987. pap. 128.00 (3-8055-4652-1) S Karger.

— XXIes Journees Nationales de Neonatologie, 1990. (Progres en Neonatologie Ser.: Vol. 10). (Illus.). vi, 312p. 1990. pap. 126.50 (3-8055-5249-1) S Karger.

— XXIIes Journees Nationales De Neonatologie Paris, May 1992. (Progres en Neonatologie Ser.: Vol. 12). (Illus.). vi, 326p. 1992. pap. 156.00 (3-8055-5636-5) S Karger.

— XXIVemes Journees Nationales de Neonatologie 1994, No. 14. (Progres en Neonatologie Ser.: Vol. 14). (Illus.). iv, 256p. 1994. pap. 157.00 (3-8055-6015-X) S Karger.

Relier, J. P., jt. ed. see Minkowski, A.

Religious Education Office, Archdiocese of San Antonio Staff. Gifted, Growing, & Sharing: A Self-Directed Journal for Parish Lay Ministry Leaders. 95p. 1992. 6.25 (0-7829-0365-7, 22058) Tabor Pub.

***Religious Public Relations Council Staff.** How Shall They Hear? A Handbook for Religion Communicators. 5th ed. Slack, R. Thomas, ed. (Illus.). 150p. 1995. pap. 12.95 (0-9646110-0-7) Relig Public Rel Coun.

Religious Research Writers Group. Death with Understanding. LC 87-61427. 284p. (Orig.). 1987. pap. 12.50 (0-915151-10-3) Religious Res Pr.

Relihan, Constance C. Fashioning Authority: The Development of Elizabethan Novelistic Discourse. LC 93-32278. (Illus.). 192p. 1994. lib. bdg. 24.00 (0-87338-495-4) Kent St U Pr.

Relihan, Heather, tr. see Ait-El-Hadj, Smail.

Relihan, Joel C. Ancient Menippean Satire. LC 92-36271. 344p. (C). 1993. text ed. 47.50 (0-8018-4524-6) Johns Hopkins.

Relis, Nurie, jt. auth. see Jaffe, Hilde.

Reljic, L. & Radovanovic, D. Folk Embroidery in Yugoslavia. (Illus.). 176p. (C). 1988. text ed. 225.00 (0-685-40324-6, Pub. by Collets) St Mut.

Relkin, Donald B., jt. auth. see Miller, Donald E.

Rella, Franco. The Myth of the Other: Lacan, Foucault, Deleuze, Bataille. Moe, Nelson, tr. & intro. by. (Post Modern Positions Ser.: Vol. 7). (Illus.). 120p. (C). 1994. 29.95 (0-944624-20-0); pap. 11.95 (0-944624-21-9) Maisonneuve Pr.

Reller, John E., ed. The Diaries & Writing of Ann Morrison Reed, 1849-1921. 1978. 7.95 (0-910312-48-6) Calif Hist.

Reller, L. Barth, et al. Clinical Internal Medicine. 1979. 28.50 (0-316-73970-7) Little.

Reller, Theodore L., jt. ed. see Erickson, Donald A.

Relles, Daniel A., jt. auth. see Brelsford, William M.

Rellich, F. Perturbation Theory of Eigenvalue Problems. x, 128p. 1969. text ed. 121.00 (0-677-00680-2) Gordon & Breach.

Rellimeo. Within the Holy of Holies: Attitudes of Attainment. rev. ed. reprint ed. spiral bd. 4.95 (0-7873-0712-2) Mokelumne.

***Relling, William, Jr.** Deadly Vintage: A Jack Donne Mystery. LC 94-45904. 1995. 19.95 (0-8027-3262-3) Walker & Co.

— The Infinite Man. (Illus.). 1988. lib. bdg. 25.00 (0-910489-25-4) Scream Pr.

Relman, Arnold S. When More Is Less: The Paradox of American Health Care & How to Resolve It. 224p. 1993. 19.95 (0-393-03579-4) Norton.

Relman, Arnold S., ed. see Curran, William J.

Relman, Arnold S., ed. see Lister, John.

Relman, John P. Housing Discrimination Practice Manual. LC 91-37449. (Civil Rights Ser.). 1992. ring bd. 130.00 (0-87632-828-1) Clark Boardman Callaghan.

Relph, Anne K. & Wilson, Karen. How to Communicate with Difficult People: A Survival Guide. 96p. (Orig.). (C). 1990. pap. 12.00 (0-9624644-0-6) Enter Woman Enter.

Relph, Edward. The Modern Urban Landscape: 1880 to the Present. LC 87-3809. 288p. (Orig.). 1987. text ed. 42.00x (0-8018-3559-3); pap. text ed. 15.95 (0-8018-3560-7) Johns Hopkins.

— Rational Landscapes & Humanistic Geography. LC 81-10782. 232p. 1981. 58.50 (0-389-20237-1, N7033) B&N Imports.

Relph, Inge. Christmas Make & Bake. (Illus.). 48p. (J). (gr. 2-4). 1993. pap. 8.99 (0-7459-2505-7) Lion USA.

Relton, Frederic, jt. auth. see Overton, John H.

Relton, J., jt. auth. see Hohenadel, P.

Relton, V., jt. auth. see Hohenadel, P.

Relyea, Douglas B. Practical Application of SPC in the Flexible Packaging Industry. 176p. 1992. pap. text ed. 21.50 (0-527-91645-5, 916455) Qual Resc.

— Practical Application of SPC in the Wire & Cable Industry. (Illus.). 176p. 1990. pap. 21.50 (0-527-91643-9, 916439) Qual Resc.

Relyea, Harold C. Evolution & Organization of Intelligence Activities in the United States. 322p. 1988. pap. 32.80 (0-89412-156-1) Aegean Park Pr.

— Silencing Science: National Security Controls & Scientific Communication. LC 93-50697. (Information Management, Policies & Services Ser.). 248p. 1994. 42.50 (1-56750-096-X); pap. 24.50 (1-56750-097-8) Ablex Pub.

Relyea, Harold C., jt. ed. see Riley, Tom.

Relyea, Harold C., et al. The Presidency & Information Policy. 216p. (Orig.). 1981. 10.00 (0-938204-03-3); pap. 8.00 (0-938204-04-1) Ctr Study Presidency.

Remafedi, Gary, intro. Death by Denial: Preventing Suicide in Gay & Lesbian Teenagers. 205p. (Orig.). 1993. pap. 9.95 (1-55583-260-1) Alyson Pubns.

Remak, Joachim. The Gentle Critic: Theodor Fontane & German Politics, 1848-1898. LC 64-16920. 116p. reprint ed. pap. 33.10 (0-317-52008-3, 2027402) Bks Demand.

— The Nazi Years: A Documentary History. 178p. (C). 1990. reprint ed. pap. text ed. 9.95 (0-88133-527-4) Waveland Pr.

— The Origins for World War One, 1871-1914. 2nd ed. (Illus.). 170p. (C). Date not set. pap. text ed. write for info. (0-15-501438-2) HB Coll Pubs.

— A Very Civil War: The Swiss Sonderbund War of 1847. 221p. 1993. text ed. 26.50 (0-8133-1529-8) Westview.

Remak, Joachim, ed. Nazi Years: A Documentary History. LC 69-11359. 1969. pap. text ed. 5.95 (0-13-610535-1, S195, Spectrum Bks) P-H.

— War, Revolution & Peace: Essays in Honor of Charles B. Burdick. (Illus.). 298p. (C). 1987. lib. bdg. 50.00 (0-8191-6342-2) U Pr of Amer.

Remak, Robert. Anatomical & Microscopic Observations on the Structure of the Nervous System. (Fascimiles of Classical Medical-Science Theses Ser.). (Illus.). 58p. (LAT.). 1994. pap. 14.50 (0-685-71272-9) KABEL Pubs.

Remakus, Bernard L. Keystone. Costa, Gwen, ed. LC 89-17582. 441p. (Orig.). 1992. 22.95 (0-87949-294-5) Ashley Bks.

— The Malpractice Epidemic: A Layman's Guide to Medical Malpractice. O'Donnell, Cara, ed. LC 89-17582. 1990. 22.95 (0-87949-295-3) Ashley Bks.

Remaley, Alan, et al. Clinical Pathology. 1992. write for info. (0-89189-315-6) Am Soc Clinical.

***Remaley, William A. & Morning Star, Inc., Staff.** Marketbase-E, 1994-1995. 2nd ed. (C). 1994. pap. 35.95 (0-256-18117-9) Irwin.

Reman, Edward. The Norse Discoveries & Explorations in America. LC 76-1871. (Illus.). 201p. 1976. reprint ed. text ed. 38.50 (0-8371-8745-1, REND, Greenwood Pr) Greenwood.

Remand, B., jt. auth. see Ohta, M.

Remane, Adolf. Die Grundlagen des Natuerlichen Systems, der Vergleichenden Anatomie & der Phylogenetik. 2nd rev. ed. vi, 362p. 1956. reprint ed. 135.00 (3-87429-029-8) Koeltz Sci Bks.

Remane, Adolf & Schlieper, Carl. Biology of Brackish Water. 2nd ed. (Binnengewaesser Ser.: Vol. 25). (Illus.). 382p. 1971. lib. bdg. 57.50 (3-510-40034-8, Pub. by Schweizerbart'sche GW) Lubrecht & Cramer.

Remark, Robert. Anatomical & Microscopic Observations on the Structure of the Nervous System. fac. ed. (Fascimiles of Classical Medical-Science Theses Ser.). (Illus.). 50p. (ENG & LAT.). (C). 1994. pap. text ed. 19.50 (0-930329-66-X) KABEL Pubs.

Remarque. Drei Kameraden. 1957. 10.95 (0-442-22070-7) Heinle & Heinle.

R

Remarque, Erich M. All Quiet on the Western Front. 16.95 (*0-8488-1459-2*) Amereon Ltd.
— All Quiet on the Western Front. (Book Notes Ser.). (C). 1984. pap. 2.50 (*0-8120-3401-5*) Barron.
— All Quiet on the Western Front. 1987. mass mkt. 4.95 (*0-449-21394-3*, Crest) Fawcett.
— All Quiet on the Western Front. (YA). (gr. 7 up). 1929. 21.95 (*0-316-73992-8*) Little.
— All Quiet on the Western Front. 391p. 1981. reprint ed. lib. bdg. 21.95x (*0-89966-292-7*) Buccaneer Bks.
— The Black Obelisk. Lindley, Denver, tr. LC 57-8840. 440p. 1957. 19.95 (*0-15-113181-3*) HarBrace.
— Bobby Deerfield. 1978. pap. 1.95 (*0-449-23367-7*, Crest) Fawcett.
Remarque, Erich-Maria. Apres. (FRE.). 1977. pap. 11.95 (*0-7859-4087-1*) Fr & Eur.
— Les Camarades, 2 vols. 1976. pap. 11.95 (*0-7859-4070-7*); pap. 11.95 (*0-7859-4071-5*) Fr & Eur.
Remas, William A. What's Stopping You? Attitude Adjustment for the About-to-Be Entrepreneur. (Know How Now Ser.). 55p. 1995. pap. 5.00 (*0-9639557-0-5*) Know How Now.
Remaud, B., et al, eds. Topics in Atomic & Nuclear Collisions. (NATO ASI Series B, Physics: Vol. 321). (Illus.). 456p. (C). 1994. 125.00 (*0-306-44662-6*, Plenum Pr) Plenum.
Remaul, Catherine. Scenes of Childhood. 1994. pap. 12.95 (*0-533-10282-0*) Vantage.
Rembaum, A., ed. see Symposium on Biomedical Polymers Staff.
Rembaum, Alan & Selegny, Eric, eds. Charged & Reactive Polymers, Vol. 2: Polyelectrolytes & Their Applications. LC 74-34151. 350p. 1975. lib. bdg. 121.50 (*90-277-0561-5*) Kluwer Ac.
Rembaum, Alan & Tokes, Zoltan A., eds. Microspheres: Medical & Biological Applications. 272p. 1988. 204.00 (*0-8493-6571-6*, RS201) CRC Pr.
Rembe, N. S. Africa & the International Law of the Sea: A Study of the Contribution of the African States to the Third United Nations Conference on the Law of the Sea. (Series on Ocean Development: No. 6). 272p. 1980. lib. bdg. 91.50 (*90-286-0639-4*) Kluwer Ac.
Rember, John. Cheerleaders from Gomorrah: Tales from the Lycra Archipelago. 125p. 1994. 20.00 (*1-881090-03-5*); pap. 12.00 (*1-881090-06-X*) Confluence Pr.
— Coyote in the Mountains: And Other Stories. (Illus.). 102p. (Orig.). 1989. pap. 9.95 (*0-931659-05-1*) Limberlost Pr.
Rembold, ed. Robot Technology & Applications. (Manufacturing Engineering & Materials Processing Ser.: Vol. 34). 696p. 1990. 190.00 (*0-8247-8206-2*) Dekker.
Rembold, et al. Computer-Integrated Manufacturing Technology & Systems. (Manufacturing Engineering & Materials Processing Ser.: Vol. 16). 792p. 1985. 175.00 (*0-8247-7403-5*) Dekker.
Rembold, Kristen S. Coming into This World. 38p. (Orig.). 1992. pap. 3.00 (*1-880575-13-2*) Hot Pepper.
— Felicity. (First Novel Ser.). 192p. (Orig.). 1994. pap. 12.00 (*0-922811-19-9*) Mid-List.
Rembold, Ulrich. Computer Integrated Manufacturing & Engineering. (C). 1993. text ed. 59.25 (*0-201-56541-2*) Addison-Wesley.
Rembold, Ulrich & Dillman, R., eds. Computer-Aided Design & Manufacturing. 2nd rev. ed. (Symbolic Computation Ser.). (Illus.). 510p. 1986. 126.00 (*0-387-16321-2*) Spr-Verlag.
Rembold, Ulrich & Horman, K., eds. Languages for Sensor-Based Control in Robotics. (NATO ASI Series H: Vol. 29). x, 625p. 1987. 123.00 (*0-387-17665-9*) Spr-Verlag.
Rembold, Ulrich, jt. ed. see Dillman, R.
Rembold, Ulrich, ed. see IFAC-IFIP Symposium Staff.
Rembold, Ulrich, et al. Interface Technology for Computer Controlled Manufacturing Processes. (Manufacturing Engineering & Materials Processing Ser.: Vol. 9). (Illus.). 376p. 1983. 115.00 (*0-8247-1836-4*) Dekker.
Rembold, Ulrich, et al, eds. Computers in Manufacturing. (Manufacturing Engineering & Materials Processing Ser.: No. 1). (Illus.). 592p. 1977. 175.00 (*0-8247-1821-6*) Dekker.
***Remboldt.** Violence in Schools: The Enabling Factor. 1995. pap. text ed. 2.95 (*1-56246-096-X*) Johnsn Inst.
***Remboldt, Carol.** Good Intentions, Bad Results: Preventing Teenage Peer Enabling & Chemical Use: a Guide for Educators, Am I An Enabler? 1993. student ed, pap. write for info. (*1-56246-077-3*) Johnsn Inst.
Remboldt, Carole. Good Intentions, Bad Results: Preventing Teenage Peer Enabling & Chemical Use: a Guide for Educators. LC 93-21083. 106p. 1993. pap. 19.95 (*1-56246-076-5*, P308) Johnsn Inst.
— Good Intentions, Bad Results: Preventing Teenage Peer Enabling & Chemical Use: a Guide for Educators, How Chemical Use Becomes Chemical Dependence. 1993. student ed, pap. write for info. (*1-56246-081-1*) Johnsn Inst.
— Solving Violence Problems in Your School: Why a Systematic Approach Is Necessary. 52p. 1994. pap. 2.95 (*1-56246-095-1*, P336) Johnsn Inst.
— Violence in Schools: The Enabling Factor. 50p. 1994. pap. 2.95 (*0-615-00355-9*, P337) Johnsn Inst.
Rembrandt. Drawings of Rembrandt, 2 Vols, 1. Slive, Seymour, ed. (Illus.). pap. 14.95 (*0-486-21485-0*) Dover.
— Drawings of Rembrandt, 2 Vols, 2. Slive, Seymour, ed. (Illus.). pap. 14.95 (*0-486-21486-9*) Dover.
Rembrandt Research Project Staff. A Corpus of Rembrandt Paintings, Vol. III: 1635-1642. (C). 1990. lib. bdg. 625.00 (*90-247-3781-8*) Kluwer Ac.
Rembret, James A. Swift & the Dialectical Tradition. LC 87-14077. 280p. 1988. text ed. 39.95 (*0-312-01160-1*) St Martin.
Rembry, J. Control of Feral Cat Populations by Long Term Administration of Magestrol Acetate. 1978. 16.00 (*0-317-43827-1*) St Mut.
Remeika, Paul & Lindsay, Lowell. Geology of Anza-Borrego: Edge of Creation. 208p. (Orig.). 1992. per. 14.95 (*0-8403-8285-5*) Kendall-Hunt.
— Geology of Anza-Borrego: Edge of Creation. LC 92-33102. (Illus.). 208p. (Orig.). 1993. pap. 12.95 (*0-932653-17-0*) Sunbelt Pubns.
Remeis, Mot & Siemer, Thomas K. Cruise Missiles: A Drama about Nuclear First Strike Planning. 142p. (Orig.). (C). 1989. pap. 14.95 (*0-685-30774-3*) Abbeyhills O C.
***Remele, Patricia.** Money Freedom: Finding Your Inner Source of Wealth. Skidmore, Ken, ed. 242p. 1995. pap. 14.95 (*0-87604-333-3*, 422) ARE Pr.
***Remensnyder, Amy G.** Remembering Kings Past: Monastic Foundation Legends in Medieval Southern France. (Illus.). 376p. 1996. 49.95 (*0-8014-2954-4*) Cornell U Pr.
Rementsova, M. M. Brucellosis in Wild Animals. 1987. 35.00 (*81-7087-005-4*, Pub. by Oxford IBH II) S Asia.
Remeny, K. Combustion Stability. 176p. 1980. 89.75 (*0-569-08640-X*) St Mut.
Remenyi, Andrew. New Developments in Worker Rehabilitation: The Workcare Model in Australia. Swerissen, Hal & Thomas, Shane A., eds. (International Exchange of Experts & Information in Rehabilitation Ser.: No. 40). 102p. 1987. pap. 3.00 (*0-939986-54-X*) World Rehab Fund.
Remenyi, Dan & Dalby, James. The DBASE II & III. 336p. (C). 1986. text ed. 130.00 (*0-582-29676-5*, Pub. by Pitman Pubng UK) St Mut.
***Remenyi, Dan, et al.** A Guide to Measuring & Managing IT Benefits. 2nd ed. 340p. Date not set. text ed. 49.95 (*1-85554-378-8*) Blackwell Pubs.
***Remenyi, Joe, et al.** Aid Trade & Development: An Interpretive Essay. 1993. pap. 21.00 (*0-7300-1601-3*, SSS338, Pub. by Deakin Univ AT) St Mut.
Remenyi, K. Industrial Firing. 498p. (C). 1987. 378.00 (*0-569-09004-0*, Pub. by Collets) St Mut.
— The Theory of Grindability & the Comminution of Binary Mixtures. 144p. (C). 1974. 30.00x (*963-05-0231-3*) St Mut.
***Remer.** Legal Care for Your Software. 1995. disk 39.99 (*0-7821-1729-5*) Sybex.
Remer, Charles F. Foreign Investments in China. LC 67-24594. (C). 1968. 55.00 (*0-86527-067-8*) Fertig.
— A Study of Chinese Boycotts, with Special References to Their Economic Effectiveness. 1979. 28.95 (*0-405-10620-3*) Ayer.
Remer, Charles F. & Kawai, Saburo. Japanese Economics: A Guide to Japanese Reference & Research Materials. LC 78-5534. (University of Michigan Center for Japanese Studies Bibliographical Ser.: No. 5). 91p. 1978. reprint ed. text ed. 55.00 (*0-313-20435-7*, REJE) Greenwood.
Remer, Daniel & Dunaway, Robert. Legal Care for Your Software. rev. ed. 368p. 1993. pap. 39.95 (*0-9636256-0-8*) RDS Pub.
***Remer, Gary.** Humanism & the Rhetoric of Toleration. LC 95-9739. 1996. write for info. (*0-271-01480-6*) Pa St U Pr.
Remer, Jane. Changing Schools Through the Arts: How to Build on the Power of an Idea. LC 90-1293. 250p. 1990. pap. 14.95 (*0-915400-86-3*, 2150, ACA Bks) Am Council Arts.
Remer, John H., Jr. The New Bull Terrier. (Illus.). 1989. 25.95 (*0-87605-096-8*) Howell Bk.
***Remer, Nicolaus.** Laws of Life in Agriculture. Castelliz, K. et al, trs. (Illus.). 158p. 1995. pap. 12.95 (*0-938250-40-X*) Bio-Dynamic Farm.
Remer, Pam, jt. auth. see Worell, Judith.
Remers, William, jt. auth. see Delgado, Jaime N.
Remers, William A. The Chemistry of Antitumor Antibiotics, Vol. 1. LC 78-12436. 299p. reprint ed. pap. 85.30 (*0-317-09762-8*, 2017401) Bks Demand.
— The Chemistry of Antitumor Antibiotics, Vol. 2. 290p. 1988. text ed. 79.95 (*0-471-08180-9*) Wiley.
Remers, William A., ed. Antineoplastic Agents. LC 83-12411. 286p. 1990. reprint ed. lib. bdg. 75.00 (*0-471-08080-2*) Krieger.
Remes, jt. ed. see Mrazkova.
Remes, Vladimir, ed. see Macijauskas, Aleksandras.
Remesh, T., jt. auth. see Razkova, S.
Remfry, J., jt. auth. see Neville, P.
Remiasz, Stella V. Designing Bridal Veils, Headpieces & Hats. (Illus.). 136p. (Orig.). (C). 1992. pap. text ed. 15.95 (*0-9617414-1-4*) Hat Tree Studio.
— Hats, Design & Construction. 2nd ed. LC 86-82042. (Illus.). 160p. 1990. pap. text ed. 15.95 (*0-9617414-0-6*) Hat Tree Studio.
Remich, Daniel. History of Kennebunk, from Its Earliest Settlement to 1890, Including Biographical Sketches. (Illus.). 580p. 1992. reprint ed. lib. bdg. 55.00 (*0-8328-2526-3*) Higginson Bk Co.
Remick, Bill, ed. see Bailey, Dan E.
Remick, Daniel G., jt. ed. see Kunkel, Steven L.
Remick, Helen. Comparable Worth & Wages: Economic Equity for Women. (Occasional Publication: No. 149). 14p. 1984. 1.00 (*0-318-04754-3*) U Hawaii.
Remick, Helen, ed. Comparable Worth & Wage Discrimination: Technical Possibilities & Political Realities. (Women in the Political Economy Ser.). 320p. 1985. pap. 22.95 (*0-87722-385-8*) Temple U Pr.
Remick, Jack. The Stolen House. LC 79-91912. (Fiction Ser.). 168p. (Orig.). 1980. pap. 4.95 (*0-917530-13-6*) Pig Iron Pr.
— Terminal Weird. 160p. (Orig.). 1994. lib. bdg. 20.95 (*0-930773-33-0*); pap. 10.95 (*0-930773-34-9*) Black Heron Pr.
Remick, Oliver P. A Record of the Services of the Commissioned Officers & Enlisted Men of Kittery & Eliot, Maine, in the American Revolution. LC 86-60507. (Illus.). 235p. 1986. reprint ed. 25.00 (*0-89725-062-1*) Picton Pr.
Remick, Raymond M. & Frampton, Charles W. Pennsylvanian Orphans' Court Practice, 7 vols. 1980. Looseleaf updates avail. write for info. (*0-8205-1580-9*) Bender.
Remick, Sue, jt. auth. see Consumers' Checkbook Magazine Editors.
Remie, Cornelius H. & Lacroix, Jean-Michel, eds. Canada on the Threshold of the 21st Century: European Reflections upon the Future of Canada. Selected Papers of the First All-European Studies Conference, The Hague, The Netherlands, Oct 24-27, 1990. LC 91-20633. xx, 565p. 1991. 50.00x (*1-55619-124-3*) Benjamins North Am.
Remie, R., jt. auth. see Van Dongen, J. J.
Remillieux, J., et al, eds. Shim Eighty-Nine: Proceedings of the First International Symposium on Swift Heavy Ions in Matter, Caen, France, May 18-19, 1989: A Special Issue of the Journal Radiation Effects & Defects in Solids. x, 228p. 1989. pap. text ed. 310.00 (*0-677-25960-3*) Gordon & Breach.
Remine, Daniel, et al. Self-Help Groups & Human Service Agencies: How They Work Together. LC 83-48645. 109p. (Orig.). (C). 1984. pap. text ed. 6.95 (*0-87304-204-2*) Families Intl.
ReMine, Walter J. The Biotic Message: Evolution Versus Message Theory. LC 93-92637. 538p. (C). 1993. text ed. 44.95 (*0-9637999-0-8*) St Paul Sci.
ReMine, William H., et al. Manual of Upper Gastrointestinal Surgery. (Comprehensive Manuals of Surgical Specialties Ser.). (Illus.). xiv, 124p. 1985. 121.00 (*0-387-96148-8*) Spr-Verlag.
***Remington, ed.** Parliaments in Transition: The New Legislative Politics in the Former U. S. S. R. & Eastern Europe. (C). 1995. pap. text ed. 19.95 (*0-8133-2686-9*) Westview.
Remington, Bob, ed. The Challenge of Severe Mental Handicap: A Behavior Analytic Approach. (Clinical Psychology Ser.: No. 1837). 398p. 1991. text ed. 139.95 (*0-471-92503-9*) Wiley.
Remington, Dennis W. & Higa, Barbara W. Back to Health: A Comprehensive Medical & Nutritional YEAST Control Program. (Illus.). 256p. 1986. pap. 9.95 (*0-912547-03-0*, 801-224-9214) Vitality Hse Int Inc.
Remington, Dennis W., et al. How to Lower Your Fat Thermostat: The No-Diet Reprogramming Plan for Lifelong Weight Control. LC 83-80794. (Illus.). 256p. 1983. pap. 9.95 (*0-912547-01-4*) Vitality Hse Int Inc.
Remington, Douglas. The Answer to the Secret of Life. LC 87-206430. 125p. (Orig.). 1989. pap. 5.00 (*0-9624473-0-7*) Two Fortyeight.
— The Answer to the Secret of Life, I. 125p. (Orig.). 1989. write for info. (*0-318-65917-4*) Two Fortyeight.
— The Answer to the Secret of Life, II. LC 87-206430. 125p. (Orig.). 1989. write for info. (*0-9624473-2-3*) Two Fortyeight.
Remington, Frank J., jt. ed. see Ohlin, Lloyd E.
Remington, Frederic. Crooked Trails. LC 74-101820. (Short Story Index Reprint Ser.). 1898. 3.95 (*0-8369-3208-0*) Ayer.
— Crooked Trails. (Illus.). 226p. 1992. reprint ed. pap. 18.00 (*1-55613-566-1*) Heritage Bk.
— Crooked Trails. LC 72-104547. (Illus.). 1979. reprint ed. lib. bdg. 17.00 (*0-8398-1753-3*) Irvington.
— Frederic Remington: One Hundred Seventy-Three Drawings & Illustrations. Pitz, Henry C., ed. & intro. by. LC 78-158963. (Illus.). 160p. (Orig.). 1972. pap. 9.95 (*0-486-20714-5*) Dover.
— Frederic Remington: One Hundred Seventy-Three Drawings & Illustrations. (Orig.). 21.50 (*0-8446-4601-6*) Peter Smith.
— Frederic Remington's Own West. 1994. 9.98 (*0-88394-005-1*) Promntory Pr.
— John Ermine of the Yellowstone. LC 68-20020. (Americans in Fiction Ser.). (Illus.). reprint ed. lib. bdg. 19.50 (*0-8398-1754-1*); reprint ed. pap. text ed. 5.95 (*0-89197-810-0*) Irvington.
— On the Apache Indian Reservations & Artist Wanderings among the Cheyenne. (Illus.). 36p. 1974. (*0-318-51891-0*) Filter.
— On the Apache Indian Reservations & Artist Wanderings among the Cheyenne. (Wild & Woolly West Ser.: No. 30). (Illus.). 36p. 1974. pap. 3.00 (*0-910584-83-4*) Filter.
— Pony Tracks. 20.95 (*0-89190-780-7*, Am Repr) Amereon Ltd.
— Pony Tracks. (Golden West Ser.). (Illus.). 1977. pap. 1.25 (*0-8439-0457-7*) Dorchester Pub Co.
— Stories of Peace & War. LC 75-125237. (Short Story Index Reprint Ser.). 1977. 15.95 (*0-8369-3604-3*) Ayer.
— The Way of an Indian. LC 76-50438. 1976. 25.00 (*0-89436-000-0*) Memento.
Remington, Frederick. Frederick Remington: Selected Writings. 1992. 7.98 (*0-89009-441-1*) Bk Sales Inc.
— Pony Tracks. (Western Frontier Library: No. 19). (Illus.). 1975. reprint ed. 11.95 (*0-8061-1248-4*) U of Okla Pr.
Remington, J. S. Current Clinical Topics in Infectious Diseases, Vol. 13. 1993. 75.00 (*0-86542-278-8*) Blackwell Sci.
Remington, J. S. & Swartz, M. N., eds. Current Clinical Topics in Infectious Diseases, Vol. 14. (Illus.). 320p. 1994. 75.00 (*0-86542-359-8*) Blackwell Sci.
***Remington, Jack S. & Klein, Jerome O., eds.** Infectious Diseases of the Fetus & Newborn Infant. 4th ed. LC 94-23372. 1994. text ed. 185.00 (*0-7216-6782-1*) Saunders.
Remington, Jack S. & Swartz, Morton N., eds. Current Clinical Topics in Infectious Diseases, Vol. 10. (Illus.). 384p. (C). 1990. 75.00 (*0-86542-058-0*) Blackwell Sci.
— Current Clinical Topics in Infectious Diseases, Vol. 11. (Illus.). 384p. (C). 1991. 75.00 (*0-86542-109-9*) Blackwell Sci.
— Current Clinical Topics in Infectious Diseases, Vol. 12. (Illus.). 384p. (C). 1992. 75.00 (*0-86542-207-9*) Blackwell Sci.
Remington, Janet, ed. Endangered Wildlife & Habitats in Southern California. (Memoirs of the Natural History Foundation of Orange County Ser.: Vol. 3). (Illus.). 114p. (Orig.). 1990. pap. 10.00 (*1-879065-02-9*) Nat Hist Fndtn CA.
Remington, Jim & Remington, Leona. Avioanxiety Becomes Controlled: Now, Fly Without Fear. (Illus.). 160p. (Orig.). 1992. 9.95 (*1-879855-01-1*) Inner Marker.
— Avioanxiety Becomes Controlled or How to Fly Without Fear: Reducing Fear & Anxiety While Flying on a Commercial Jet Airliner. (Illus.). 180p. 1991. audio 49.95 (*1-879855-00-3*) Inner Marker.
***Remington, Kathleen.** Ten Secrets of Highly Successful Women. White, Tim, ed. & illus. by. 220p. 1994. pap. 59.95 (*1-887126-92-9*) Natl Bus Bur.
Remington, Leona, jt. auth. see Remington, Jim.
Remington, Michele G. & Burak, Carl. The Cradle Will Fall: One Woman's Story of Her Descent into Madness Following the Birth of Her Baby - & Her Remarkable, Inspiring Recovery. LC 94-71107. 240p. 1994. 21.95 (*1-55611-408-7*) D I Fine.
***Remington, R. Roger.** Lester Beall: Trailblazer of American Graphic Design. (Illus.). 320p. 1995. 60.00 (*0-393-73002-6*) Norton.
Remington, R. Roger & Hodik, Barbara. Nine Pioneers in American Graphic Design. (Illus.). 200p. 1989. 55.00 (*0-262-18133-9*) MIT Pr.
Remington, Richard & Schork, M. Anthony. Statistics with Applications to the Biological & Health Sciences. 2nd ed. (Illus.). 432p. (C). 1984. text ed. write for info. (*0-13-846171-6*) P-H.
Remington, Robin A. Warsaw Pact. 2nd ed. (C). 1929. pap. text ed. 29.95 (*0-8133-8122-3*) Westview.
Remington, Thomas, ed. Parliaments in Transition: New Legislation in the Former U. S. S. R. & Eastern Europe. 256p. (C). 1994. text ed. 54.95 (*0-8133-8814-7*) Westview.
Remington, Thomas, jt. auth. see Barghoorn, Frederick C.
***Remington, Thomas F.** Building Socialism in Bolshevik Russia: Ideology & Industrial Organization, 1917-1921. LC 84-3603. (Series in Russian & East European Studies: No. 6). 232p. 1984. pap. 66.20 (*0-7837-8543-7*, 2049358) Bks Demand.
— The Truth of Authority: Ideology & Communication in the Soviet Union. LC 88-4745. (Series in Russian & East European Studies). (Illus.). 270p. (Orig.). (C). 1988. 49.95 (*0-8229-3590-2*); pap. 19.95 (*0-8229-5408-7*) U of Pittsburgh Pr.
Remington, Thomas F., jt. ed. see Petrov, Nikolai.
Remini, Robert O., jt. auth. see Clark, James I.
Remini, Robert V. Andrew Jackson. 1969. reprint ed. pap. 7.00 (*0-06-080132-8*, P132, PL) HarpC.
— Andrew Jackson & the Bank War. (Essays in American History Ser.). (C). 1967. pap. text ed. 7.95 (*0-393-09757-9*) Norton.
— The Era of Good Feelings & the Age of Jackson, 1816-1841. LC 79-84211. (Goldentree Bibliographies Series in American History). (C). 1979. pap. text ed. write for info. (*0-88295-579-9*) Harlan Davidson.
— Henry Clay: Statesman for the Union. 880p. 1993. pap. 15.95 (*0-393-31088-4*) Norton.
— The Jacksonian Era. Franklin, John H. & Eisenstadt, Abraham, eds. (American History Ser.). 140p. (C). 1989. pap. text ed. write for info. (*0-88295-864-X*) Harlan Davidson.
— The Legacy of Andrew Jackson: Essays on Democracy, Indian Removal, & Slavery. LC 87-24137. (Walter Lynwood Fleming Lectures in Southern History). 117p. 1988. pap. text ed. 8.95 (*0-8071-1642-4*) La State U Pr.
— The Life of Andrew Jackson. (Illus.). 416p. 1990. pap. 12.95 (*0-14-013267-8*, Penguin Bks) Viking Penguin.
— Revolutionary Age of Andrew Jackson. 1987. pap. text ed. 13.00 (*0-06-132074-9*, Harp PBks) HarpC.
Remini, Robert V. & Rupp, Robert O. Andrew Jackson: A Bibliography. LC 90-41976. (Bibliographies of the Presidents of the United States Ser.: No. 7). 352p. 1990. text ed. 75.00 (*0-313-28165-3*, AP07, Greenwood Pr) Greenwood.
Remini, Susan, ed. The Rainbow Book of Adventures. (Illus.). 114p. (Orig.). 1983. pap. 7.95 (*0-932471-01-3*) Falsoft.
Remini, William C., ed. Evaluation of Current Developments in Municipal Waste Treatment: Proceedings. LC 77-10538. (ERDA Symposium Ser.). 130p. 1977. pap. 11.25 (*0-87079-201-6*, CONF-770108); fiche 9.00 (*0-87079-205-9*, CONF-770108) DOE.
Reminick, Joan, jt. auth. see Gianotti, Peter M.
Remizov, Aleksei. Rossiia V Pis'menakh: Tom 1. LC 79-91965. (Illus.). 232p. (RUS.). 1982. reprint ed. pap. 7.95 (*0-89830-013-4*) Russica Pubs.
Remizov, Aleksei M. The Clock. Cournos, John, tr. LC 76-23894. (Classics of Russian Literature Ser.). 1993. reprint ed. lib. bdg. 24.50 (*0-88355-509-3*) Hyperion Conn.
— Iveren. Raevsky-Hughes, Olga, ed. (Modern Russian Literature & Culture, Studies & Texts: Vol. 7). 400p. (Orig.). (RUS.). 1986. pap. 19.00 (*0-933884-35-4*) Berkeley Slavic.
— On a Field Azure. Scott, B., tr. LC 76-23896. (Classics of Russian Literature Ser.). 1977. reprint ed. pap. 10.00 (*0-88355-513-1*) Hyperion Conn.
— Tsar Maksimilian. 128p. (RUS.). 1988. reprint ed. pap. 8.00 (*0-933884-55-9*) Berkeley Slavic.

R

An Asterisk (*) at the beginning of an entry indicates that the title is appearing in BIP for the first time.

Remizov, Aleksel M. Fifth Pestilence with the History of the Tinkling Symbol & Sounding Brass: Ivan Semyonovich Stratilatov. Brown, Alec, tr. LC 76-23895. (Classics of Russian Literature Ser.). 1977. reprint ed. 15.00 (*0-88355-511-5*) Hyperion Conn.
***Remkiewicz.** Fiona Raps It Up. 1995. (*0-688-13146-8*) Lothrop.
Remkiewicz, Frank. Bone Stranger. LC 93-25214. (Illus.). (J). 1994. lib. bdg. 14.93 (*0-688-12042-3*) Lothrop.
— The Bone Stranger. LC 93-25214. (Illus.). (J). 1994. 15.00 (*0-688-12041-5*) Lothrop.
— GreedyAnna. LC 91-149230. (J). (ps-3). 1992. lib. bdg. 13.93 (*0-688-10295-6*); pap. 14.00 (*0-688-10294-8*) Lothrop.
— The Last Time I Saw Harris. LC 90-40263. (Illus.). 32p. (J). (gr. k up). 1991. 13.95 (*0-688-10291-3*); lib. bdg. 13.88 (*0-688-10292-1*) Lothrop.
— There's Only One Harris. LC 92-44163. (Illus.). (J). (gr. 3-6). 1993. write for info. (*0-688-11827-5*); lib. bdg. write for info. (*0-688-11828-3*) Lothrop.
Remlap, Tera. Private Time. LC 93-93871. 144p. (Orig.). 1994. pap. 9.00 (*1-56002-282-5*, Univ Edtns) Aegina Pr.
Remler, P. Ascomyceten auf Ericaceen in den Ostalpen. (Bibliotheca Mycologica Ser.: No. 68). (Illus.). (GER.). 1980. lib. bdg. 48.00 (*3-7682-1248-3*) Lubrecht & Cramer.
Remley, David. Bell Ranch: Cattle Ranching in the Southwest, 1824-1947. LC 92-23474. (Illus.). 409p. 1993. 42.50x (*0-8263-1399-X*) U of NM Pr.
Remley, Frederick M., frwd. Tomorrow's Television. (Illus.). 256p. 1982. pap. text ed. 30.00 (*0-940690-06-3*) Soc Motion Pic & TV Engrs.
Remley, Mary L. Women in Sport: An Annotated Bibliography. 178p. 1991. text ed. 35.00 (*0-8161-8977-3*, Hall Reference) Macmillan.
***Remley, Shawn E.** Song of a Nightingale. 120p. Date not set. pap. 7.95 (*0-7610-0251-0*) NW Pub.
Remley, Theodore P., Jr. ACA Legal Series, Vol. 1: Preparing for Court Appearances. 64p. (C). 1991. pap. text ed. 12.95 (*1-55620-077-3*) Am Coun Assn.
Remley, Theodore P., Jr., ed. see Arthur, Gibbs L., Jr. & Swanson, Carl D.
Remley, Theodore P., Jr., ed. see Bullis, Ronald K.
Remley, Theodore P., jt. ed. see Huey, Wayne C.
Remley, Theodore P., Jr., ed. see Mitchell, Robert W.
Remley, Theodore P., Jr., ed. see Salo, Mark M. & Shumate, Stephen.
Remley, Theodore P., Jr., ed. see Weikel, William J. & Hughes, Paula R.
Remling, John. Automotive Electricity. LC 86-11042. 444p. 1987. pap. text ed. 33.95 (*0-471-80508-4*) P-H.
— Basics. 2nd ed. 1989. text ed. 34.50 (*0-471-61651-6*) P-H.
— Brakes. 2nd ed. LC 82-2798. (Automotive Ser.). 328p. 1983. teacher ed write for info. (*0-471-03764-8*); pap. text ed. 34.95 (*0-471-09583-4*) P-H.
— Steering & Suspension. 2nd ed. (Automotive Ser.). 422p. 1983. pap. text ed. 34.95 (*0-471-87614-3*) P-H.
Remlinger-Trounstine, Connie. The Worst Christmas Ever. LC 94-14326. (Illus.). 128p. (J). (gr. 3-6). 1994. pap. 2.95 (*0-8167-3516-6*, Rainbow NJ) Troll Assocs.
***Remme, Camille.** Birds & Bees & Butterflies Too. (Illus.). 80p. (Orig.). Date not set. pap. 17.95 (*0-929950-10-0*) ME Pubns.
— Braid & Chevron Updated. (Illus.). 72p. (Orig.). Date not set. pap. 17.95 (*0-929950-09-7*) ME Pubns.
— Frogs & Flowers: Impressions of Ponds & Gardens Made into Quilts. Shimp, Mimi, ed. & illus. by. 96p. (Orig.). 1991. pap. 17.95 (*1-879844-03-6*) Boyd Pub.
— Modular Magic. Shimp, John, ed. & illus. by. 80p. (Orig.). 1992. pap. write for info. (*0-929950-07-0*) ME Pubns.
— Starburst Mosaic. (Illus.). (Orig.). Date not set. pap. 14.95 (*0-929950-12-7*) ME Pubns.
Remme, Tilman. Britain & Regional Cooperation in South-East Asia, 1945-49. LC 94-9183. 224p. 1994. 69.95x (*0-415-09753-3*, B4002) Routledge.
Remme, W. I., jt. ed. see Hjalmarson, A.
Remmel, Jeffrey B., jt. ed. see Clote, Peter.
Remmen, F. Fundamentals of Data Bases. (Illus.). 208p. (C). 1985. text ed. write for info. (*0-13-336090-3*) P-H.
Remmer, Karen L. Military Rule in Latin America. 208p. 1989. 39.95 (*0-04-445479-1*) Routledge Chapman & Hall.
— Party Competition in Argentina & Chile: Political Recruitment & Public Policy, 1890-1930. LC 84-13119. x, 296p. 1984. 25.00 (*0-8032-3871-1*) U of Nebr Pr.
Remmers, Hermann H. Anti-Democratic Attitudes in American Schools. LC 63-11565. 356p. reprint ed. 101.50 (*0-8357-9447-4*, 2015428) Bks Demand.
— Introduction to Opinion & Attitude Measurement. LC 74-138127. 437p. 1972. reprint ed. text ed. 65.00 (*0-8371-4166-4*, REOA, Greenwood Pr) Greenwood.
Remmert, H. Arctic Animal Ecology. (Illus.). 250p. 1980. pap. 54.00 (*0-387-10169-1*) Spr-Verlag.
— Ecology: A Textbook. (Illus.). 300p. 1980. 49.00 (*0-387-10059-8*) Spr-Verlag.
Remmert, H., et al, eds. The Mosaic-Cycle Concept of Ecosystems. (Ecological Studies: Vol. 85). (Illus.). 200p. 1991. 122.00 (*0-387-52502-5*) Spr-Verlag.
Remmert, Hermann, ed. Minimum Animal Populations. LC 93-34010. 1994. 88.00 (*0-387-56684-8*) Spr-Verlag.
Remmert, R. Theory of Complex Functions. Burckel, R. B., tr. (Graduate Texts in Mathematics Readings in Mathematics Ser.: Vol. 122). (Illus.). xix, 453p. 1995. 59.00 (*0-387-97195-5*) Spr-Verlag.
Remmert, R., jt. auth. see Grauert, H.
Remmes, Harold. Computers: New Opportunities for the Disabled. LC 84-1058. 31p. (Orig.). 1984. pap. 3.50 (*0-87576-114-3*) Pilot Bks.
— Lobbying for Your Cause. LC 85-28555. 48p. 1986. pap. 3.95 (*0-87576-123-2*) Pilot Bks.
Remmey, G. Bickley, Jr. Firing Ceramics. 220p. 1994. text ed. 67.00 (*981-02-1678-5*); pap. text ed. 41.00 (*981-02-1679-3*) World Scientific Pub.
Remmler, Karen, jt. ed. see Gilman, Sander L.
Remmling, Gunter W. South American Sociologists, A Directory. (Guides & Bibliographies Ser.). 57p. reprint ed. pap. 25.00 (*0-685-15616-8*, 2027326) Bks Demand.
Remmling, Gunter W. & Campbell, Robert B. Basic Sociology. (Quality Paperback Ser.: No. 229). 384p. 1976. reprint ed. pap. 7.95 (*0-8226-0229-6*) Littlefield.
Remnant, Mary. Early English Bowed Instruments. (Oxford Monographs on Music). (Illus.). 240p. 1987. 92.00 (*0-19-816134-4*) OUP.
Remnant, Mary, ed. Plays by Women, Vol. 5. (Methuen New Theatrescripts Ser.). 181p. 1988. pap. 11.95 (*0-413-41570-8*, A0221, Pub. by Methuen UK) Heinemann.
Remnant, Mary, intro. & sel. Plays by Women, Vol. 6. (Methuen New Theatrescripts Ser.). 126p. 1988. pap. 11.95 (*0-413-14080-6*, A0222, Pub. by Methuen UK) Heinemann.
Remnant, Peter, ed. see Leibniz, Gottfried W.
Remnet, Valerie L. Understanding Older Adults: An Experiential Approach to Learning. LC 86-45995. 256p. (Orig.). (C). 1989. pap. 34.95 (*0-669-14825-3*) Free Pr.
Remnick, David. Lenin's Tomb: The Last Days of the Soviet Empire. LC 92-56841. 512p. 1993. 25.00 (*0-679-42376-1*) Random.
— Lenin's Tomb: The Last Days of the Soviet Empire. 1994. pap. 14.00 (*0-679-75125-4*, Vin) Random.
Remocker, A. Jane & Storch, Elizabeth T. Action Speaks Louder: A Handbook of Structured Group Techniques. 5th ed. (Illus.). 190p. (Orig.). 1992. pap. text ed. 39.95 (*0-443-04364-7*) Churchill.
Remoissenet, M. Waves Called Solitons: Concepts & Experiments. LC 93-36462. 1994. 49.00 (*0-387-57000-4*) Spr-Verlag.
Remoissenet, M. & Peyrard, M., eds. Nonlinear Coherent Structures in Physics & Biology: Proceedings of the 7th Interdisciplinary Workshop Held at Dijon, France, 4-6 June 1991. (Lecture Notes in Physics Ser.: Vol. 393). xii, 398p. 1991. 70.00 (*0-387-54890-4*) Spr-Verlag.
Remole, Mary J. Mary Jane's Cookbook: From the Heart of America. (Illus.). 144p. (YA). (gr. 9-12). 1986. text ed. 8.95 (*0-317-90470-1*) Mary Janes Cookbook.
— Mary Jane's Cookbook: From the Heart of America. LC 92-37292. (Illus.). 160p. 1993. 5.98 (*0-8317-5762-0*) Smithmark.
Remond, A. & Izard, C. Electrophysiological Effects of Nicotine. 254p. 1980. 77.50 (*0-444-80183-9*, North Holland) Elsevier.
Remond, A., jt. ed. see Gevins, A. S.
Remond, Gabriel. Royer-Collard. Mayer, J. P., ed. LC 78-67377. (European Political Thought Ser.). (FRE.). 1980. reprint ed. lib. bdg. 17.95 (*0-405-11727-2*) Ayer.
Remondi, Anne, jt. ed. see Bricklin, Mark.
Remondino, Peter C. History of Circumcision, from the Earliest Times to the Present. LC 72-9675. (Physicians' & Students' Ready Reference Ser.). reprint ed. 47.50 (*0-404-57492-0*) AMS Pr.
Remp, Richard, jt. auth. see Etzioni, Amitai.
Rempe, Jennifer M., ed. see CTFA Staff.
Rempel, Gerhard. Hitler's Children: The Hitler Youth & the SS. LC 88-28036. (Illus.). xiv, 354p. (C). 1991. reprint ed. pap. 13.95 (*0-8078-4299-0*) U of NC Pr.
Rempel, John D. The Lord's Supper in Anabaptism: A Study in the Christology of Balthasar Hubmaier, Pilgram Marpeck, & Dirk Philips. (Studies in Anabaptist & Mennonite History: No. 33). 272p. 1993. 29.95 (*0-8361-3112-6*) Herald Pr.
Rempel, John I. Building with Wood & Other Aspects of Nineteenth Century Building in Central Canada. rev. ed. LC 81-116855. 470p. reprint ed. pap. 134.00 (*0-8357-7473-2*, 2026387) Bks Demand.
***Rempel, Richard, et al.** Collected Papers of Bertrand Russell Vol. 14: The No-Conscription Fellowship: Pacifism & Revolution 1916-18. 640p. 1995. 165.00x (*0-415-09410-0*, C0233) Routledge.
Rempel, Richard A. & Moran, Margaret, eds. The Collected Papers of Bertrand Russell, Vol. XIII: Prophesy & Dissent, 1914-1916. 774p. 1988. text ed. 150.00 (*0-04-920079-8*, A9421) Routledge Chapman & Hall.
Rempel, S. & Schulze, B. W. Index Theory of Elliptic Boundary Problems. 394p. 1982. text ed. 48.95 (*0-685-06229-5*) Birkhauser.
Rempel, Siegfried. The Care of Photographs. (Illus.). 192p. (Orig.). 1987. pap. 16.95 (*0-941130-48-7*) Lyons & Burford.
— Health Hazards for Photographers. (Illus.). 256p. 1992. pap. 16.95 (*1-55821-181-0*) Lyons & Burford.
Rempel, Valerie, et al, eds. Your Daughters Shall Prophesy: Women in Ministry in the Church. 222p. (Orig.). (C). 1992. pap. 11.50 (*0-921788-14-2*) Kindred Prods.
Rempel, William C. Delusions of a Dictator: The Mind of Marcos As Revealed in His Secret Diaries. 1993. 24.95 (*0-316-74015-2*) Little.
Rempp, P., ed. see International Symposium on Macromolecules Staff.
Remsberg, Charles. The Tactical Edge: Surviving High-Risk Patrol. LC 85-73162. (Illus.). 544p. (C). 1986. 39.95 (*0-935878-05-X*) Calibre Pr.
— Tactics for Criminal Patrol: Vehicle Stops, Drug Discovery & Officer Survival. (Illus.). 520p. 1995. text ed. 39.95 (*0-935878-12-2*) Calibre Pr.
Remsberg, Charles, jt. auth. see Gallagher, Richard.
***Remsberg, John E.** The Christ: A Critical Review & Analysis of the Evidence of His Existence. 437p. (C). 1994. 29.95 (*0-87975-924-0*) Prometheus Bks.
Remsburg, George J., jt. auth. see Remsburg, John E.
Remsburg, John E. & Remsburg, George J. Charley Reynolds: Soldier, Hunter, Scout & Guide. Carroll, John M., ed. 1985. 15.95 (*0-8488-0249-7*, J M C & Co) Amereon Ltd.
Remschmidt, H. & Schmidt, M. H., eds. Anorexia Nervosa. LC 90-4848. (Child & Youth Psychiatry: European Perspectives Ser.: Vol. 1). (Illus.). 270p. 1990. text ed. 64.00 (*0-88937-041-9*) Hogrefe & Huber Pubs.
— Developmental Psychopathology. LC 90-4957. (Child & Youth Psychiatry: European Perspectives Ser.: Vol. 2). (Illus.). 180p. 1992. text ed. 64.00 (*0-88937-051-6*) Hogrefe & Huber Pubs.
Remschmidt, H., jt. ed. see Schmidt, M.
Remsen, J. V., Jr. Community Ecology of Neotropical Kingfishers. LC 90-46525. (Publications in Zoology: Vol. 124). (Illus.). 128p. 1991. pap. 13.00 (*0-520-09673-8*) U CA Pr.
Remsen, J. V., Jr. & Traylor, Melvin A., Jr. Annotated List of the Birds of Bolivia. LC 89-61415. (Illus.). 1989. 15.00 (*0-931130-16-6*) Harrell Bks.
Remsen, Jim, jt. auth. see Petsonk, Judy.
Remter, Mary H., ed. see Ohio Genealogical Society (Hamilton Co. Chapter) Staff.
Remus, Harold. Pagan-Christian Conflict over Miracle in the Second Century. LC 83-6729. (Patristic Monograph: No. 10). xiii, 371p. 1983. pap. 11.00 (*0-915646-09-9*) N Amer Patristic Soc.
Remus, Tim. Boyd Coddington's How to Build Hot Rod Bodywork. (Power Pro Ser.). (Illus.). 160p. 1993. pap. 17.95 (*0-87938-798-X*) Motorbooks Intl.
— Boyd Coddington's How to Build Hot Rod Chassis. (Illus.). 160p. 1992. pap. 17.95 (*0-87938-626-6*) Motorbooks Intl.
— Custom Cars & Lead Sleds. (Illus.). 128p. 1990. pap. 19.95 (*0-87938-424-7*) Motorbooks Intl.
— Harley-Davidson: The Customs of Arlen Ness. (Illus.). 128p. 1994. pap. text ed. 19.95 (*0-9641358-0-9*) Wolfgang Prods.
— How to Customize Your Harley Davidson. (Illus.). 160p. 1992. pap. 19.95 (*0-87938-619-3*) Motorbooks Intl.
Remus, Timothy. America's Best Harley-Davidson Customs. LC 92-29760. 160p. 1993. pap. 19.95 (*0-87938-702-5*) Motorbooks Intl.
— Arlen Ness: Master Harley Customizer. (Illus.). 128p. 1990. pap. 19.95 (*0-87938-407-7*) Motorbooks Intl.
— Boyd Coddington's How to Build Hot Rod Engines & Drivelines. LC 92-43458. (MBI Ser.). (Illus.). 160p. 1993. pap. 17.95 (*0-87938-721-1*) Motorbooks Intl.
— Boyd Coddington's How to Paint Your Hot Rod. (Boyd Coddington How-to Ser.). (Illus.). 160p. 1994. pap. 17.95 (*0-87938-942-7*) Motorbooks Intl.
— Ford 'Thirty Two Deuce Hot Rods & Hi Boys. (Illus.). 128p. 1991. pap. 19.95 (*0-87938-542-1*) Motorbooks Intl.
— Harley-Davidson Customs. (Enthusiast Color Ser.). (Illus.). 96p. 1995. pap. 12.95 (*0-87938-989-3*) Motorbooks Intl.
— Hot Rod Detailing. LC 92-29759. (Illus.). 128p. 1993. pap. 14.95 (*0-87938-703-3*) Motorbooks Intl.
— Hot Rods by Boyd Coddington. (Illus.). 128p. 1992. pap. 19.95 (*0-87938-596-0*) Motorbooks Intl.
— How to Air Condition Your Car. LC 93-1775. 1993. 19.95 (*0-87938-765-3*) Motorbooks Intl.
— How to Build Ultimate American V-Twin Motorcycle. (Illus.). 144p. Date not set. pap. 19.95 (*0-9641358-2-5*) Wolfgang Prods.
— How to Custom Paint Your Harley-Davidson. (Illus.). 136p. 1994. pap. 17.95 (*0-87938-861-7*) Motorbooks Intl.
***Remus, Timothy S.** Harley-Davidson Sheet Metal Fabrication: Make & Modify Tanks, Fenders, Side Covers. 144p. (Orig.). 1995. 19.95 (*0-9641358-1-7*) Wolfgang Prods.
Remusat, Charles F. Histoire de la Philosophie en Angleterre depuis Bacon Jusqu'a Locke, 2 vols. viii, 836p. reprint ed. write for info. (*0-318-71402-7*, Pub. by Georg Olms GW) Lubrecht & Cramer.
Remusat, M. M. Pilgrimage of Fa Hian. (C). 1990. reprint ed. text ed. 31.50 (*0-685-50087-X*, Pub. by Mittal II) S Asia.
Remuzzi, G., ed. Renal Transplant Tolerance: Molecular Mechanisms of T Cell Regulation. (Journal: Experimental Nephrology: Vol. 1, No. 2, 1993). (Illus.). 76p. 1993. pap. 37.00 (*3-8055-5699-3*) S Karger.
Remuzzi, Giuseppe, jt. auth. see Ritz, Eberhard.
Remy, A. F. The Influence of India & Persia on the Poetry of Germany. 1976. lib. bdg. 59.95 (*0-8490-2059-X*) Gordon Pr.
Remy, Bob. Louisiana Sports Encyclopedia. 358p. (J). (gr. 4-10). 1977. pap. 10.95 (*0-88289-120-0*) Pelican.
Remy, Bob, jt. auth. see Mule, Marty.
***Remy, Carole.** Beauty of the Beast. (Orig.). 1995. pap. text ed. 5.95 (*1-56333-332-5*) Masquerade.
Remy, Dorothy, jt. auth. see Sacks, Karen B.
Remy, J. L., jt. ed. see Rusinowitch, Michael.
Remy, Jean-Pierre. La Vie d'Adrian Putney, Poete. (FRE.). 1979. pap. 10.95 (*0-7859-4119-3*) Fr & Eur.
Remy, M. Jules. Contributions of a Venerable Native to the Ancient History of the Hawaiian Islands. Alexander, W. D. & Brigham, William T., trs. (Illus.). 1979. pap. 3.95 (*0-89646-056-8*) Vistabooks.
***Remy, Michael H., et al.** Guide to the California Environmental Quality Act (CEQA) 8th ed. (Illus.). 880p. 1994. pap. 45.00 (*0-923956-40-9*) Solano Pr.
— Supplement to the Guide to the California Environmental Quality Act (CEQA) 1995. 280p. (Orig.). 1995. pap. text ed. 30.00 (*0-923956-36-0*); pap. text ed. 18.50 (*0-923956-39-5*) Solano Pr.
Remy, Richard C. Handbook of Basic Citizenship Competencies: Guidelines for Comparing Materials, Assessing Instruction & Setting Goals. Brandt, Ronald S., ed. LC 79-56888. 112p. (Orig.). 1980. pap. 4.75 (*0-87120-098-8*, 611-80196) Assn Supervision.
Remy, Richard C., jt. ed. see Merryfield, Merry M.
Remy, Richard C., jt. auth. see Patrick, John J.
Remys, Edmund. Hermann Hesse's "Das Glasperlenspiel" A Concealed Defense of the Mother World. (American University Studies: Germanic Languages & Literature: Ser. I, Vol. 19). 212p. (Orig.). (C). 1983. pap. text ed. 22.10 (*0-8204-0029-7*) P Lang Pubs.
Remz, Carol L. Remz-It! A Simple Method for Developing Inexpensive & Effective Training. (Remz-It! Training System Ser.: No. 1). 135p. 1987. 295.00 (*0-941999-01-7*) Human Resc.
Remz, Carol L. & Blumberg, Judith E. Remz-It! How to Easily Create Non-Computereze Documentation that End Users Love. (Remz-It! Training System Ser.: No. 2). 100p. 1987. 295.00 (*0-941999-02-5*) Human Resc.
Remzhin, Yu, jt. auth. see Rudomino, B.
Ren, D. L. Topics in Integral Geometry. 256p. 1994. text ed. 55.00 (*981-02-1101-5*); pap. text ed. 32.00 (*981-02-1107-4*) World Scientific Pub.
***Ren Jen Sun & Johnston, Richard H.** Regional Aquifer-System Analysis Program of the U.S. Geological Survey, 1978-1992. (U. S. Geological Survey Circular Ser.: Vol. 1099). 1994. write for info. (*0-615-00264-1*) USGPO.
Ren, Marah, ed. see Alexander, Skye.
Ren, Marah, ed. see Ford, Norman.
Ren, Marah, ed. see Konraad, Sandor.
Ren, Marah, ed. see Steiger, Brad.
Ren, Marah, ed. see Van Pelt, Tamise.
Ren, Z. D., jt. auth. see Rao, M. M.
***Rena B., Lewis & Donald H., Doorlag.** Teaching Special Students in the Mainstream. 4th ed. LC 94-3463. 1994. write for info. (*0-02-370502-7*, Merrill Pub Co) Macmillan.
Renahan, Doug. Goldilocks & Little Bear's Birthday. 1988. pap. 3.75 (*0-89137-050-1*) Quality Pubns.
— Little Bear & His Teddy Bear. 1989. 6.25 (*0-89137-060-9*) Quality Pubns.
— Little Bear Visits His Grandparents. (J). 1994. 6.25 (*0-89137-066-8*) Quality Pubns.
***Renaissance Society at Tucson Staff.** Body. 1993. pap. 27.50 (*0-941548-23-6*) Ren Soc U Chi.
Renaissance Symposium Staff. The Renaissance: A Reconsideration of the Theories & Interpretations of the Age, Proceedings of the Symposium, University of Wisconsin, 1959. Helton, Tinsley, ed. LC 80-21869. xiii, 160p. 1980. reprint ed. text ed. 49.75 (*0-313-22797-7*, SYRE) Greenwood.
Renal Resource Center Staff. Healthy Eating on a Renal Diet: A Cookbook for People with Kidney Disease. 183p. 1991. pap. 33.00 (*0-8036-9887-9*) Davis Co.
Renal Stone Research Symposium Staff. Urinary Calculi: Recent Advances in Aetiology, Stone Structure & Treatment, Proceedings of the Renal Stone Research Symposium, Madrid, Sept. 1972. Cifuentes Delatte, L. et al, eds. (Illus.). 1973. 104.00 (*3-8055-1618-5*) S Karger.
Renaldi, Thomas W. The Two Versions of Mariano Azuela's "Los De Abajo" A Comparative Study. 1978. lib. bdg. 250.00 (*0-8490-1396-8*) Gordon Pr.
Renan, Ary. Le Costume in France. (Illus.). 274p. 1984. reprint ed. pap. 25.00 (*0-87556-689-8*) Saifer.
Renan, Ernest. Averroes et l'Averroisme. xvi, 486p. 1987. reprint ed. write for info. (*3-487-07816-3*, Pub. by Georg Olms GW) Lubrecht & Cramer.
— Caliban. Vickery, Eleanor G., tr. LC 70-169928. (Shakespeare Society of New York. Publications: No. 9a). reprint ed. 27.50 (*0-404-54209-3*) AMS Pr.
— Histoire et Paroles; Oeuvres Diverses. (FRE.). 1984. pap. 36.95 (*0-7859-3404-9*) Fr & Eur.
— Histoires des Origines du Christianisme; Marc Aurele et la Fin du Monde. (FRE.). 1984. pap. 16.95 (*0-7859-3416-2*) Fr & Eur.
— Lectures on the Influence of the Institutions, Thought & Culture of Rome, on Christianity & the Development of the Catholic Church. Beard, Charles, tr. LC 77-27170. (Hibbert Lectures: 1880). reprint ed. 32.00 (*0-404-60402-1*) AMS Pr.
— The Life of Jesus. (Great Minds Ser.). 227p. (Orig.). 1991. pap. 11.95 (*0-87975-704-3*) Prometheus Bks.
— Oeuvres Completes, 10 tomes, Set. Psichari, ed. 175.00 (*0-685-34960-8*) Fr & Eur.
— La Reforme Intellectuelle et Morale de la France. (FRE.). 1990. pap. 24.95 (*0-7859-3333-6*, 2870273614) Fr & Eur.
— Souvenirs d'Enfance et de Jeunesse. (FRE.). 1992. pap. 8.95 (*0-7859-3173-2*, 2253061751) Fr & Eur.
— Vie de Jesus. (FRE.). 1974. pap. 11.95 (*0-7859-4034-0*) Fr & Eur.
— Vie de Jesus. (Folio Ser.: No. 618). (FRE.). 1974. pap. 9.95 (*2-07-036618-9*) Schoenhof.
Renard, Georges. Guilds in the Middle Ages. Terry, Dorothy, tr. LC 68-55330. (Reprints of Economic Classics Ser.). 1968. reprint ed. 27.50 (*0-678-00438-2*) Kelley.
Renard, John. All the King's Falcons: Rumi on Prophets & Revelation. LC 94-2307. 236p. (C). 1994. text ed. 57.50x (*0-7914-2221-6*); pap. text ed. 18.95x (*0-7914-2222-4*) State U NY Pr.
— In the Footsteps of Muhammad: Understanding the Islamic Experience. LC 92-11396. 184p. 1992. pap. 9.95 (*0-8091-3316-4*) Paulist Pr.
Renard, John & Schimmel, Annemarie B., trs. IBN Abbad of Ronda, Letters on the Sufi Path. (Classics of Western Spirituality Ser.: No. 49). 256p. 1986. 12.95 (*0-8091-0365-6*); pap. 9.95 (*0-8091-2730-X*) Paulist Pr.
Renard, Jules. L' Ecornifleur. (FRE.). 1980. pap. 10.95 (*0-7859-4128-2*) Fr & Eur.

R

— Histoires Naturelles, Nos Freres Farouches, Ragotte. (FRE.). 1984. pap. 15.95 (*0-7859-4207-6*) Fr & Eur.
— Journal: 1902-1905, Vol. 3. (FRE.). 1984. pap. 16.95 (*0-7859-3448-0*) Fr & Eur.
— Journal, 1887-1910. Guichard, Henri, ed. 1504p. (FRE.). 1960. lib. bdg. 125.00 (*0-7859-3783-8*, 2070104737) Fr & Eur.
— Journal, 1887-1910. (FRE.). 1990. pap. 48.95 (*0-7859-3031-0*) Fr & Eur.
— Journal, 1887-1910, 4 vols., Set. Guichard, Leon & Sigaux, Gilbert, eds. (Bibliotheque de la Pleiade Ser.). pap. 34.95 (*0-685-34964-0*) Fr & Eur.
— Journal, 1887-1910, 4 vols., Vol. 1: 1887-1895. Guichard, Leon & Sigaux, Gilbert, eds. (Bibliotheque de la Pleiade Ser.). Vol. 1, 1887-1895. pap. 18.95 (*0-7859-3185-6*, 2264006102) Fr & Eur.
— Journal, 1887-1910, 4 vols., Vol. 2: 1897-1901. Guichard, Leon & Sigaux, Gilbert, eds. (Bibliotheque de la Pleiade Ser.). Vol. 2, 1897-1901. pap. 16.95 (*0-7859-3186-4*, 2264006110) Fr & Eur.
— Journal, 1887-1910, 4 vols., Vol. 3: 1902-1905. Guichard, Leon & Sigaux, Gilbert, eds. (Bibliotheque de la Pleiade Ser.). Vol. 3, 1902-1905. pap. 16.95 (*0-685-67477-0*) Fr & Eur.
— Journal, 1887-1910, 4 vols., Vol. 4: 1906-1910. Guichard, Leon & Sigaux, Gilbert, eds. (Bibliotheque de la Pleiade Ser.). Vol. 4, 1906-1910. pap. 16.95 (*0-7859-3187-2*, 2264006358) Fr & Eur.
— Oeuvres, Vol. 1. Guichard, Leon, ed. 1120p. (FRE.). 1970. lib. bdg. 105.00 (*0-7859-3784-6*, 2070104745) Fr & Eur.
— Oeuvres, Vol. 2. Guichard, Leon, ed. (FRE.). 1971. 100.00 (*0-7859-3809-5*) Fr & Eur.
— Poil de Carotte. (FRE.). 1957. pap. 6.95 (*0-8288-6913-8*) Fr & Eur.
— Poil de Carotte. 90p. 1965. 6.95 (*0-685-61098-5*) Fr & Eur.
— Poil de Carotte. La Bigote. (Folio Ser.: No. 1090). (FRE.). pap. 9.95 (*2-07-037090-9*) Schoenhof.
— Poil de Carotte Suivi de la Bigote. (FRE.). 1979. pap. 11.95 (*0-7859-4114-2*) Fr & Eur.
Renard, Jules, tr. see Becquer, Gustavo.
Renard, Kenneth G., jt. ed. see Replogle, John A.
Renard, Louis. Fishes, Crayfishes, & Crabs: Louis Renard's Natural History of the Rarest Curiosities of the Seas of the Indies. Pietsch, Theodore W., ed. LC 93-49411. (Foundations of Natural History Ser.). (Illus.). 480p. 1995. text ed. 95.00x (*0-8018-4790-7*) Johns Hopkins.
Renard, M. & Binbenet, J. J., eds. Automatic Control & Optimization of Food Processes: Proceedings of the International Symposium on the Automatic Control & Optimization of Food Processes (ACOFOP), Paris, France, 12-13 Nov., 1986. 570p. 1989. 138.75 (*1-85166-139-5*) Elsevier.
Renard, P., et al. Sales & Distribution Guide to Thailand. (Southeast Asian Business Guides Ser.: No. 2). 144p. 1988. text ed. 55.00 (*0-08-035838-1*, Pub. by Pergamon Repr UK) Franklin.
Renard, Pierre. The Solar Revolution & the Prophet. (Testimonials Ser.). (Illus.). 193p. (Orig.). 1980. pap. 13.95 (*2-85566-135-8*, Pub. by Prosveta FR) Prosveta USA.
Renard, Vincent, jt. auth. see Acosta, Rodrigo.
Renardy, Michael & Rogers, Robert C. A First Graduate Course in Partial Differential Equations. LC 92-37449. (Texts in Applied Mathematics Ser.: Vol. 13). 1994. 42.00 (*0-387-97952-2*) Spr-Verlag.
Renardy, Yuriko Y., jt. auth. see Joseph, Daniel D.
Renart, Jean. The Romance of the Rose; Or Guillaume de Dole: The Late Medieval Resistance to the Renaissance. Terry, Patricia & Durling, Nancy V., eds. Durling, Nancy V., tr. LC 93-16414. (Middle Ages Ser.). 136p. (Orig.). (C). 1993. text ed. 24.95 (*0-8122-3111-2*); pap. text ed. 13.95 (*0-8122-1388-2*) U of Pa Pr.
***Renau, Lynn S.** Racing Around Kentucky. (Illus.). 218p. (Orig.). 1995. pap. 16.95 (*0-9646111-0-4*) L S Renau.
— Starting from Scratch. (Illus.). (Orig.). 1995. pap. write for info. (*0-9646111-1-2*) L S Renau.
***Renaud, Ary.** In Search of the Lost Sword: Journessy, No. 3. 350p. 1995. lib. bdg. 39.95 (*0-9645708-1-5*) Sea of Fanta Pubns.
— Journey to the Far Side of the Earth: Journessy, No. 2. 210p. 1994. lib. bdg. 29.95 (*0-9645708-0-7*) Sea of Fanta Pubns.
Renaud, Bertrand. Housing Reform in Socialist Economies. 69p. 1991. 7.95 (*0-8213-1829-2*, 11829) World Bank.
Renaud, Bertrand, jt. auth. see Bertaud, Alain.
Renaud, Frank. Trading with Mexico, No. YGB-170A: The Automobile & Auto Parts Industry. (Illus.). 112p. 1994. 1,500.00 (*0-685-74999-1*) BCC.
Renaud, Georges & Kahn, Victor. Art of the Checkmate. 1953. pap. 4.95 (*0-486-20106-6*) Dover.
Renaud, P. S. Applied Political Economic Modeling. (Studies in Contemporary Economics). (Illus.). xii, 246p. 1989. pap. 47.00 (*0-387-51597-6*, 3424) Spr-Verlag.
Renaud, Paul E. Introduction to Client - Server Systems: A Practical Guide for Systems Professionals. 352p. 1993. text ed. 52.00 (*0-471-57773-1*); pap. text ed. 34.95 (*0-471-57774-X*) Wiley.
Renaud, S., ed. see Inserm-International Symposium Staff.
Renauld, Christiane. Journey in a Shell. (Child's World Library). (Illus.). 32p. (J). (gr. 3-5). 1991. lib. bdg. 18.50 (*0-89565-752-X*) Childs World.
— The Magic Shoes. (Child's World Library). (Illus.). 32p. (J). (gr. 3-5). 1991. lib. bdg. 18.50 (*0-89565-753-8*) Childs World.
— A Pal for Martin. (Child's World Library). (Illus.). 32p. (J). (gr. 3-5). 1991. 18.50 (*0-89565-756-2*) Childs World.
— Tomorrow Will Be a Nice Day. (Child's World Library). (Illus.). 32p. (J). (gr. k-2). 1991. 18.50 (*0-89565-763-5*) Childs World.

Renault, B., et al, eds. Event Related Potential Investigations of Cognition. 360p. 1989. 115.50 (*0-444-87151-9*, North Holland) Elsevier.
Renault, Francois. Cardinal Lavigerie: Churchman & Missionary 1825-1892. O'Donohue, John, tr. LC 94-2304. 360p. (C). 1994. text ed. 60.00 (*0-485-11453-4*, Pub. by Athlone Pr UK) Humanities.
Renault, Mable. Avenue of Ghosts. 120p. (Orig.). 1988. pap. text ed. 10.00 (*0-685-28898-6*) Rivendell Hse Ltd.
— Queen Esther. 60p. (Orig.). 1988. pap. text ed. 6.00 (*0-685-28899-4*) Rivendell Hse Ltd.
Renault, Mary. The Bull from the Sea. 1975. pap. 7.00 (*0-394-71504-7*, Vin) Random.
— Charioteer. 1994. pap. 10.95 (*0-15-616768-9*) HarBrace.
— Fire from Heaven. 1977. pap. 8.95 (*0-394-72291-4*, Vin) Random.
— Kind Are Her Answers. 287p. 1976. reprint ed. lib. bdg. 24.95x (*0-89244-078-3*) Queens Hse-Focus Serv.
— The King Must Die. LC 86-46178. 352p. 1988. pap. 10.00 (*0-394-75104-3*, Publishers Media) Random.
— The Last of the Wine. 1975. pap. 8.95 (*0-394-71653-1*, Vin) Random.
— The Mask of Apollo. LC 86-46177. 384p. 1988. pap. 12.00 (*0-394-75105-1*, Vin) Random.
— Middle Mist. 21.95 (*0-685-71944-8*, Queens House) Amereon Ltd.
— The Nature of Alexander. LC 74-15152. 1979. pap. 11.00 (*0-394-73825-X*) Pantheon.
— North Face. 286p. 1976. reprint ed. lib. bdg. 21.95 (*0-88411-072-9*, Queens House) Amereon Ltd.
— The Persian Boy. LC 86-46179. 432p. 1988. pap. 12.00 (*0-394-75101-9*, Vin) Random.
— Promise of Love. 382p. 1976. reprint ed. lib. bdg. 24.95x (*0-89244-079-1*) Queens Hse-Focus Serv.
— Return to Night. 21.95 (*0-88411-073-7*, Aeonian Pr) Amereon Ltd.
Renaut, Alain, jt. auth. see Ferry, Luc.
***Renaut, R. W. & Last, W. M., eds.** Sedimentology & Geochemistry of Modern & Ancient Saline Lakes. (SEPM Special Publications: No. 50). (Illus.). 348p. 1994. text ed. 90.00 (*1-56576-014-X*) SEPM.
Renaux, Sigrid. The Turn of the Screw: A Semiotic Reading. LC 92-26035. (American University Studies: American Literature: Ser. XXIV, Vol. 46). 290p. 1992. 46.95 (*0-8204-2017-4*) P Lang Pubs.
Renave, Coleen, jt. auth. see Uhlman, Jerry.
Renay, Liz. My Face for the World to See. LC 74-156889. 1971. 7.95 (*0-8184-0058-7*) Carol Pub Group.
— My First Two Thousand Men. LC 91-38524. 1992. 21.95 (*0-942637-44-5*) Barricade Bks.
— Staying Young. 192p. 11.95 (*0-8184-0329-2*) Carol Pub Group.
Renberg, Dalia H. The Complete Family Guide to Jewish Holidays. LC 84-11008. (Illus.). (J). (gr. 4 up). 1985. pap. 22.95 (*0-915361-09-4*) Modan-Adama Bks.
— King Solomon & the Bee. LC 92-30411. (Illus.). 32p. (J). (ps-3). 1994. 15.00 (*0-06-022899-7*); lib. bdg. 14.89 (*0-06-022902-0*) HarpC Child Bks.
***Renberg, Werner.** All about Bond Funds. LC 94-40818. 1995. pap. text ed. 19.95 (*0-471-31195-2*) Wiley.
Renborg, B. A. International Drug Control: A Study of International Administration by & Through the League of Nations. (Studies in the Administration of International Law & Organization). 1941. reprint ed. 25.00 (*0-527-00885-0*) Periodicals Srv.
Renc, Bill, jt. auth. see Bansemer, Roger.
Rench, Cecile E., jt. auth. see Swift, Helen C.
Rench, Janice. Understanding Sexual Identity. (YA). 1992. pap. 4.95 (*0-8225-9602-4*, Lerner Publctns) Lerner Group.
Rench, Janice E. Family Violence: Coping with Modern Issues. 64p. (J). (gr. 4 up). 1991. lib. bdg. 17.50 (*0-8225-0047-7*, Lerner Publctns) Lerner Group.
— Teen Sexuality: Decisions & Choices. (Coping with Modern Problems Ser.). (Illus.). 72p. (YA). (gr. 6 up). 1988. lib. bdg. 15.95 (*0-8225-0041-8*, Lerner Publctns) Lerner Group.
— Understanding Sexual Identity: A Book for Gay Teens & Their Friends. (Coping with Modern Problems Ser.). 72p. (YA). (gr. 5 up). 1990. lib. bdg. 17.50 (*0-8225-0044-2*, Lerner Publctns) Lerner Group.
Rench, Janice E., jt. auth. see Terkel, Susan N.
***Rencher, Alvin C.** Methods of Multivariate Analysis Vol. 1: Basic Applications. (Series in Probability & Mathematics). 1995. text ed. 74.95 (*0-471-57152-0*) Wiley.
Rencis, J. J. & Brebbia, C. A., eds. Boundary Elements XV, 2 vols., Set. LC 93-71026. (BEM Ser.: Vol. 15). 1330p. 1993. 440.00 (*1-56252-161-6*) Computational Mech MA.
— Boundary Elements XV Vol. 1: Fluid Flow & Computational Aspects. (BEM Ser.: Vol. 15). 706p. 1993. 229.00 (*1-56252-197-7*) Computational Mech MA.
— Boundary Elements XV Vol. 2: Stress Analysis. LC 93-71026. (BEM Ser.: Vol. 15). 650p. 1993. 211.00 (*1-56252-198-5*) Computational Mech MA.
Rencis, J. J., jt. ed. see Brebbia, C. A.
Rencis, Joseph J. & Mullens, Robert L., eds. Structural Engineering & Microcomputers. 80p. 1987. 13.00 (*0-87262-585-0*) Am Soc Civil Eng.
Rencken, Robert H. Intervention Strategies for Sexual Abuse. 1989. 22.95 (*1-55620-057-9*) Am Coun Assn.
***Renckens, Hans.** A Bible of Your Own: Growing with the Scriptures. Forest-Flier, Nancy, tr. LC 94-45525. 125p. (Orig.). 1995. pap. 12.95 (*1-57075-007-6*) Orbis Bks.
Rencoret, Francisco J. New York City: The Edge of Enigma. (Illus.). 100p. (Orig.). 1992. pap. 19.95 (*1-878271-05-9*) Princeton Arch.
Rendahl, J. Stanley. Working with Older Adults. LC 84-80708. (Equipping Ser.). (Illus.). 130p. (Orig.). 1984. pap. 5.95 (*0-935797-08-4*) Harvest IL.

Rendal, Justine. Dancing Cat. 40p. (J). 1991. pap. 13.95 (*0-671-72637-4*, S&S Bks Young Read) S&S Childrens.
— The Girl Who Listened to Sinks. (J). (ps-6). 1993. pap. 14.00 (*0-671-77745-9*, S&S Bks Young Read) S&S Childrens.
— How a Computer Saved My Life. LC 95-2252. (Joanna Cotler Books). (Illus.). 192p. (J). (gr. 3 up). 1995. lib. bdg. 13.89 (*0-06-025408-4*) HarpC Child Bks.
— Very Personal Computer. LC 95-2252. (Joanna Cotler Books). (Illus.). 192p. (J). (gr. 3 up). 1995. 13.95 (*0-06-025404-1*) HarpC Child Bks.
Rendall, Carol W., jt. auth. see Kohl, Wilfred L.
Rendall, Doris L., jt. ed. see Tuohy, Donald R.
Rendall, Gerald H. Shakespeare: Handwriting & Spelling. LC 76-169107. (Studies in Shakespeare: No. 24). 1971. reprint ed. lib. bdg. 50.95 (*0-8383-1335-3*) M S G Haskell Hse.
Rendall, Ivan. Checkered Flag: Hundred Years of Auto Racing. 1993. 34.98 (*1-55521-961-6*) Bk Sales Inc.
— The Power & the Glory: A Century of Motor Racing. (Illus.). 240p. 1993. 34.95 (*0-563-36093-3*, BBC-Parkwest) Parkwest Pubns.
— The Power & the Glory: A Century of Motor Racing. (Illus.). 240p. 1994. pap. 24.95 (*0-563-36468-8*, BBC-Parkwest) Parkwest Pubns.
— Senna: A Tribute. (Illus.). 192p. 1995. 29.95 (*1-85793-517-9*, Pub. by Pavilion UK) Trafalgar.
Rendall, Jane. The Origins of Modern Feminism: Women in Britain, France & the United States, 1780-1860. 2nd rev. ed. LC 90-6672. (Illus.). 369p. (C). 1990. reprint ed. pap. text ed. 22.95 (*0-925065-39-0*) Lyceum IL.
— Women in an Industrializing Society: England 1750-1880. (Historical Association Studies). (Illus.). 96p. 1990. pap. text ed. 10.95 (*0-631-15303-9*) Blackwell Pubs.
Rendall, Jane, jt. auth. see Mendus, Susan.
Rendall, K. Norline. Just a Taste of Honey. (Quiet Time Books for Women). (J). 1975. pap. 3.99 (*0-8024-4494-6*) Moody.
Rendall, Stephen, tr. see Le Goff, Jacques.
Rendall, Steven. Distinguo: Reading Montaigne Differently. 180p. 1992. 39.95 (*0-19-815180-2*) OUP.
***Rendall, Steven, tr. & intro.** Astrea Pt. I: Honore d'Urfe. LC 94-32421. (Medieval & Renaissance Texts & Studies Ser.: 134). 416p. 1995. 30.00 (*0-86698-142-X*) MRTS.
Rendall, Steven, tr. see Steinert, Marlis.
Rendall, Steven F., tr. see De Certeau, Michel.
Rende, Michael L. Lonergan on Conversion: The Development of a Notion. 238p. (C). 1990. lib. bdg. 41.00 (*0-8191-7525-0*) U Pr of Amer.
Rendel, Peter. Understanding the Chakras: Discovering & Using the Energy of Your Seven Vital Force Centers. 128p. 1991. pap. 6.95 (*0-685-48204-9*, Pub. by Aquarian Pr UK) Thorsons SF.
Rendell. Crocodile Bind. large type ed. 1994. write for info. (*0-318-72285-2*) Thorndike Pr.
Rendell-Baker, Leslie, jt. auth. see Mushin, William W.
Rendell, D. A., jt. auth. see Hill, Roger.
Rendell, David. Fluorescence & Phosphorescence Spectroscopy. LC 87-8157. (Analytical Chemistry by Open Learning Ser.). 419p. 1987. pap. text ed. 67.95 (*0-471-91381-2*) Wiley.
Rendell, Doris L., jt. ed. see Tuohy, Donald R.
Rendell, Fred. Cook's First Voyage. (C). 1989. 50.00 (*1-85098-054-3*, Pub. by Jordanhill College UK) St Mut.
— Invaders. (C). 1989. 35.00 (*1-85098-138-8*, Pub. by Jordanhill College UK) St Mut.
— Mary Queen of Scots. (C). 1989. 35.00 (*1-85098-137-X*, Pub. by Jordanhill College UK) St Mut.
— River Crossing. (C). 1989. 35.00 (*1-85098-264-3*, Pub. by Jordanhill College UK) St Mut.
— Scottish Wars of Independence. (C). 1989. 50.00 (*1-85098-073-X*, Pub. by Jordanhill College UK) St Mut.
— Topic Study, How & Why? (C). 1989. 40.00 (*1-85098-055-1*, Pub. by Jordanhill College UK) St Mut.
— Volcano. (C). 1989. 35.00 (*1-85098-131-0*, Pub. by Jordanhill College UK) St Mut.
Rendell, Fred, ed. Alexander Mackenzie. (C). 1989. 30.00 (*1-85098-075-6*, Pub. by Jordanhill College UK) St Mut.
— Cattle Drive. (C). 1989. 35.00 (*1-85098-110-8*, Pub. by Jordanhill College UK) St Mut.
— Conquistador. (C). 1989. 30.00 (*1-85098-074-8*, Pub. by Jordanhill College UK) St Mut.
— Industrial Revolution. (C). 1989. 40.00 (*1-85098-052-7*, Pub. by Jordanhill College UK) St Mut.
— Into Hiding: Anne Frank. (C). 1989. 50.00 (*1-85098-166-3*, Pub. by Jordanhill College UK) St Mut.
— Making the Desert Bloom. (C). 1989. 65.00 (*1-85098-399-2*, Pub. by Jordanhill College UK) St Mut.
— People of the Seal. (C). 1989. 35.00 (*1-85098-129-9*, Pub. by Jordanhill College UK) St Mut.
— Plains Indians. (C). 1989. 35.00 (*1-85098-130-2*, Pub. by Jordanhill College UK) St Mut.
Rendell, Fred & Bell, Arnold. Balaclava Street. (C). 1989. 35.00 (*1-85098-072-1*, Pub. by Jordanhill College UK) St Mut.
— Bedouin. (C). 1989. 30.00 (*1-85098-069-1*, Pub. by Jordanhill College UK) St Mut.
— Doon the Watter. (C). 1989. 50.00 (*1-85098-079-9*, Pub. by Jordanhill College UK) St Mut.
— Drake. (C). 1989. 30.00 (*1-85098-071-3*, Pub. by Jordanhill College UK) St Mut.
— Earth, No. 11. (C). 1989. 30.00 (*1-85098-068-3*, Pub. by Jordanhill College UK) St Mut.
— Holiday Town. (C). 1989. 55.00 (*1-85098-086-1*, Pub. by Jordanhill College UK) St Mut.
— Mountain Village. (C). 1989. 30.00 (*1-85098-139-6*, Pub. by Jordanhill College UK) St Mut.
— North Sea Oil. (C). 1989. 45.00 (*1-85098-067-5*, Pub. by Jordanhill College UK) St Mut.
— Ports & Harbours. (C). 1989. 35.00 (*1-85098-308-9*, Pub. by Jordanhill College UK) St Mut.

— Raiders. (C). 1989. 45.00 (*1-85098-105-1*, Pub. by Jordanhill College UK) St Mut.
— Trans-Siberian Railway. (C). 1989. 30.00 (*1-85098-051-9*, Pub. by Jordanhill College UK) St Mut.
— Travel Agency. (C). 1989. 40.00 (*1-85098-077-2*, Pub. by Jordanhill College UK) St Mut.
— Waterways. (C). 1989. 75.00 (*1-85098-053-5*, Pub. by Jordanhill College UK) St Mut.
— Western Front. (C). 1989. 35.00 (*1-85098-065-9*, Pub. by Jordanhill College UK) St Mut.
Rendell, Fred & Bell, Arnold, eds. The Gold Rush. (C). 1989. 45.00 (*1-85098-066-7*, Pub. by Jordanhill College UK) St Mut.
— Tobacco Lords. (C). 1989. 60.00 (*1-85098-085-3*, Pub. by Jordanhill College UK) St Mut.
— Western Isle. (C). 1989. 35.00 (*0-685-52522-8*, Pub. by Jordanhill College UK) St Mut.
Rendell, Fred & Watterson, Tricia. Whale. (C). 1989. 750.00 (*1-85098-180-9*, Pub. by Jordanhill College UK) St Mut.
Rendell, Fred, jt. auth. see Bell, Arnold.
Rendell, Kenneth W. Forging History: The Detection of Fake Letters & Documents. (Illus.). 184p. 1994. 24.95 (*0-8061-2636-1*) U of Okla Pr.
— History Comes to Life: Collecting Historical Letters & Documents. LC 95-1984. 1995. write for info. (*0-8061-2764-3*) U of Okla Pr.
Rendell, Ruth, pseud. Anna's Book. LC 92-34309. 1993. 22.00 (*0-517-58796-3*, Harmony) Crown Pub Group.
Rendell, Ruth. The Best Man to Die. 208p. 1987. mass mkt. 4.95 (*0-345-34530-4*) Ballantine.
— The Best Man to Die. 18.95 (*0-89190-887-0*) Yestermorrow.
— Best Man to Die. 18.95 (*0-685-71740-2*) Yestermorrow.
— The Bridesmaid. 1989. 17.95 (*0-89296-388-3*) Mysterious Pr.
— The Bridesmaid. 1990. mass mkt. 4.95 (*0-445-40912-6*, Mysterious Paperbk) Warner Bks.
— The Bridesmaid. large type ed. 462p. 1990. reprint ed. pap. 11.95 (*0-89621-948-8*) Thorndike Pr.
— The Copper Peacock. large type ed. 1993. pap. 16.95 (*0-7927-1262-5*, Paragon Lrg Print) Chivers N Amer.
— Copper Peacock & Other Stories. 1991. 17.95 (*0-89296-465-0*) Mysterious Pr.
— The Copper Peacock & Other Stories. 192p. 1992. mass mkt. 4.99 (*0-446-40055-6*, Mysterious Paperbk) Warner Bks.
— The Copper Peacock & Other Stories. large type ed. 1992. 18.95 (*0-7927-1263-3*, Eagle Lrg Print) Chivers N Amer.
— The Crocodile Bird. LC 93-14734. 1993. 20.00 (*0-517-59576-1*, Crown) Crown Pub Group.
— Crocodile Bird. 1994. pap. 5.99 (*0-440-21865-9*) Dell.
— The Crocodile Bird. large type ed. LC 93-37403. 1994. 20.95 (*0-7862-0091-X*); pap. 13.95 (*0-7862-0092-8*) Thorndike Pr.
— Death Notes. (Chief Inspector Wexford Ser.). 224p. 1986. mass mkt. 5.99 (*0-345-34198-8*) Ballantine.
— Face of Trespass. 19.95 (*0-8488-0617-4*) Yestermorrow.
— From Doon with Death. (Chief Inspector Wexford Ser.). 160p. 1988. mass mkt. 4.95 (*0-345-34817-6*) Ballantine.
— Going Wrong. 304p. 1990. 18.95 (*0-89296-389-1*) Mysterious Pr.
— Going Wrong. 1991. mass mkt. 4.99 (*0-446-40028-9*, Mysterious Paperbk) Warner Bks.
— Going Wrong. large type ed. 1992. pap. 15.95 (*0-7927-0822-9*, Paragon Lrg Print) Chivers N Amer.
— A Guilty Thing Surprised. (Chief Inspector Wexford Ser.). 176p. 1987. mass mkt. 5.99 (*0-345-34811-7*) Ballantine.
— Heartstones. 1988. mass mkt. 4.95 (*0-345-34800-1*) Ballantine.
— House of Stairs. 1990. pap. 4.99 (*0-451-40211-1*, Onyx) NAL-Dutton.
— A Judgement in Stone. 19.95 (*0-89190-888-9*, Am Repr) Amereon Ltd.
— The Killing Doll. 288p. 1985. mass mkt. 4.95 (*0-345-31199-X*) Ballantine.
— Kissing the Gunner's Daughter. 384p. 1992. 19.95 (*0-89296-390-5*) Mysterious Pr.
— Kissing the Gunner's Daughter. 384p. 1993. mass mkt. 5.50 (*0-446-40334-2*, Mysterious Paperbk) Warner Bks.
— Live Flesh. 1987. mass mkt. 4.95 (*0-345-34485-5*) Ballantine.
— Master of the Moor. 1986. mass mkt. 4.95 (*0-345-34147-3*) Ballantine.
— Means of Evil. large type ed. LC 93-13793. 1993. 18.95 (*0-7927-1676-0*, Eagle Lrg Print); pap. 16.95 (*0-7927-1675-2*, Eagle Lrg Print) Chivers N Amer.
— Murder Being Once Done. 19.95 (*0-89190-372-0*, Am Repr) Amereon Ltd.
— No More Dying Then. 19.95 (*0-89190-373-9*, Am Repr) Amereon Ltd.
— Ruth Rendell's Suffolk. (Illus.). 144p. 1993. pap. 19.95 (*0-09-177587-6*, Pub. by Hutchnson UK) Trafalgar.
— The Secret House of Death. 240p. 1987. mass mkt. 5.99 (*0-345-34950-4*) Ballantine.
— The Secret House of Death. reprint ed. lib. bdg. 19.95 (*0-88411-144-X*, Aeonian Pr) Amereon Ltd.
— Simisola. 320p. 1995. 23.00 (*0-517-70073-5*, Crown) Crown Pub Group.
— Simisola: An Inspector Wexford Novel. large type ed. 1995. pap. 22.00 (*0-679-76502-6*) Random.
— Sins of the Fathers. 1994. reprint ed. lib. bdg. 29.95 (*1-56849-322-3*) Buccaneer Bks.
— Speaker of Mandarin. (Chief Inspector Wexford Ser.). 224p. 1984. mass mkt. 4.95 (*0-345-30274-5*) Ballantine.
— Talking to Strange Men. 1988. mass mkt. 4.99 (*0-345-35174-6*) Ballantine.
— To Fear a Painted Devil. 208p. 1987. mass mkt. 5.99 (*0-345-34951-2*) Ballantine.

R

An Asterisk (*) at the beginning of an entry indicates that the title is appearing in BIP for the first time.

— The Tree of Hands. LC 85-8148. 320p. 1986. mass mkt. 4.95 (*0-345-31200-7*) Ballantine.
— An Unkindness of Ravens. 1986. mass mkt. 4.95 (*0-345-32746-2*) Ballantine.
— Vanity Dies Hard. 18.95 (*0-89190-374-7*, Am Repr) Amereon Ltd.
— Vanity Dies Hard. 192p. 1987. mass mkt. 4.95 (*0-345-34952-0*) Ballantine.
— The Veiled One. 320p. 1989. mass mkt. 4.95 (*0-345-35994-1*) Ballantine.
— The Veiled One. large type ed. (General Ser.). 422p. 1989. lib. bdg. 19.95 (*0-8161-4804-X*, Large Print Bks) Hall.
— Wolf to the Slaughter. 224p. 1987. mass mkt. 4.95 (*0-345-34520-7*) Ballantine.
Rendell, Ruth, see Barbara Vine, pseud..
Rendell, Ruth, et al. Murder for Mother. 320p. (Orig.). 1994. pap. 4.99 (*0-451-18036-4*, Sig) NAL-Dutton.
***Rendell, Sharon.** Living with Big Cats: The Story of Jungle Larry, Safari Jane, & David Tetzlaff. LC 94-31632. (Illus.). 224p. 1994. 11.95 (*0-9642604-0-9*) Intl Zool Soc.
Render, Barry & Heizer, Jay. Principles of Operations Management: Building & Managing World Class Operations. LC 93-38560. 1994. text ed. write for info. (*0-205-15644-4*) Allyn.
Render, Barry & Stair, Ralph M., Jr. Quantitative Analysis for Management. 5th annot. ed. LC 93-24363. 1993. Annotated tchr's ed. teacher ed, text ed. write for info. (*0-205-15379-8*) Allyn.
Render, Barry, jt. auth. see Heizer, Jay.
Render, Barry, et al. Cases & Readings in Management Science. 2nd ed. 350p. 1990. teacher ed write for info. (*0-318-66342-2*, H23039); pap. text ed. 33.00 (*0-205-12302-3*, H23021) Allyn.
— Microcomputer Software for Management Science & Operations Management. 2nd ed. 1989. pap. 24.00 (*0-685-44218-7*); Apple. 3.5 hd 26.67 (*0-205-11969-7*) Allyn.
Render, Lorne E. The Mountains & the Sky. LC 75-27295. (Illus.). 224p. 1976. 35.00 (*0-295-95462-0*) U of Wash Pr.
***Render, Shirley.** No Place for a Lady: The Story of Canadian Women Pilots, 1928-1992. (Illus.). 389p. 1992. 39.95 (*0-9694264-2-9*) Peguis Pubs Ltd.
Render, Sylvia L., ed. The Short Fiction of Charles W. Chesnutt. LC 81-6314. 428p. (C). 1981. pap. 9.95 (*0-88258-092-2*) Howard U Pr.
Rendero, Thomasine, ed. see Albano, Charles.
Rendig, V. V., jt. ed. see Grunes, D. L.
Rendig, Victor V. Principles of Soil-Plant Interrelations. 1989. text ed. 44.00 (*0-07-051879-3*) McGraw.
Rendina, Dave. Eastern Treasure Hunter. 1978. pap. 10.00 (*0-686-14204-7*) D Rendina.
Rendle, Alfred B. The Classification of Flowering Plants, Vol. 1: Gymnosperms & Monocotyledons. 2nd ed. 428p. reprint ed. pap. 122.00 (*0-317-26387-0*, 2024529) Bks Demand.
— The Classification of Flowering Plants, Vol. 2: Dicotyledons. 2nd ed. 660p. reprint ed. pap. 180.00 (*0-685-10694-2*, 2024529) Bks Demand.
Rendle-Short, John. Reasonable Christianity. 1991. pap. 8.99 (*0-85234-289-6*, Pub. by Evangel Pr UK) Presby & Reformed.
Rendleman, Danny. Asylum. 1977. per. 3.00 (*0-88031-040-5*) Invisible-Red Hill.
— Victrola. 28p. (Orig.). 1994. pap. text ed. 6.00x (*1-56439-033-0*) Ridgeway.
Rendleman, Danny L. Signals to the Blind. LC 72-19183. 50p. 1972. 2.95 (*0-87886-015-0*, Greenfld Rev Pr) Greenfld Rev Lit.
— The Winter Rooms. LC 75-315873. 65p. 1975. 3.50 (*0-87886-061-4*, Greenfld Rev Pr) Greenfld Rev Lit.
***Rendleman, Doug.** Enforcement of Judgments & Liens in Virginia. 480p. 1994. 75.00 (*1-55834-158-7*) Michie Butterworth.
Rendleman, Doug, ed. Enforcement of Judgments & Liens in Virginia: With 1989 Cumulative Supplement. 433p. 1982. 55.00 (*0-87215-419-X*) Michie Butterworth.
— Enforcement of Judgments & Liens in Virginia: With 1989 Cumulative Supplement. suppl. ed. 433p. 1982. 22. 50 (*0-87473-293-X*) Michie Butterworth.
Rendleman, Doug, jt. auth. see Fiss, Owen M.
***Rendleman, Edith B.** All Anybody Ever Wanted of Me Was to Work: The Memoirs of Edith Bradley Rendleman. Adams, Jane, ed. & intro. by. LC 94-37252. (Shawnee Bks.). (Illus.). 232p. (C). 1996. 39.95 (*0-8093-1931-4*) S Ill U Pr.
***Rendler, Elaine.** In the Midst of the Assembly. Colombari, Bari, ed. 192p. (Orig.). 1994. pap. 9.95 (*0-915531-37-2*) OR Catholic.
***Rendoff, Patty.** An Exceptional Resource Guide for the Gifted: For Home Schooling & Or Supplementing Education. 75p. 1994. 14.95 (*0-9644479-1-6*) Diggies Do It All.
— Special Needs Resource Guide: For Home Schooling & Or Supplementing Education. 100p. 1994. 20.95 (*0-9644479-0-8*) Diggies Do It All.
Rendon, A. Perez, jt. auth. see Garcia, P. L.
***Rendon, Al.** Sights & Scenes of Texas: San Antonio. 64p. 1995. 7.95 (*0-88415-261-8*) Gulf Pub.
— Texas Sights & Scenes: San Antonio. (Illus.). 64p. 1995. pap. 7.95 (*0-88719-261-0*) Gulf Pub.
***Rendon, Al, photos.** San Antonio. LC 94-43910. (Texas Monthly Sights & Scenes Ser.). (Illus.). 64p. 1995. write for info. (*0-87719-261-8*, 9261) Gulf Pub.
***Rendon, Laura I. & Hope, Richard O.** Educating a New Majority: Transforming America's Educational System for Diversity. (Higher & Adult Education Ser.). 1995. 34.95 (*0-7879-0130-X*) Jossey-Bass.
Rendon, Marion B. & Kranz, Rachel. Straight Talk about Money. Ryan, Elizabeth A., ed. (Straight Talk Ser.). 128p. (YA). (gr. 7-12). 1992. lib. bdg. 16.95 (*0-8160-2612-2*) Facts on File.
Rendra, Willibordus S. The Struggles of the Naga Tribe. Lane, Max, tr. LC 79-16537. Orig. Title: Kisah Perjuangan Suku Naga. 1980. text ed. 29.95 (*0-312-76876-1*) St Martin.
Rendrell, Fred & Watterson, Tricia. Desperate Journey. (C). 1989. 550.00 (*1-85098-043-8*, Pub. by Jordanhill College UK) St Mut.
Rendsberg, Gary, jt. ed. see Gordon, Cyrus H.
Rendsburg, G. A. Diglossia in Ancient Hebrew. (American Oriental Ser.: Vol. 72). xxi, 233p. 1990. text ed. 26.00 (*0-940490-72-2*) Am Orient Soc.
Rendsburg, Gary, et al. The Bible World: Essays in Honor of Cyrus H. Gordon. 1981. 49.50 (*0-87068-758-1*) Ktav.
Rendsburg, Gary A. Linguistic Evidence for the Northern Origin of Selected Psalms. 143p. 1990. 24.95 (*1-55540-565-7*); pap. 14.95 (*1-55540-566-5*) Scholars Pr GA.
Rendsburg, Gary A., jt. ed. see Gordon, Cyrus H.
Rendtorff, Rolf. Canon & Theology: Overtures to an Old Testament Theology. Kohl, Margaret, ed. Kohl, Margeret, tr. LC 93-22408. (Overtures to Biblical Theology Ser.). 1993. Alk. paper. 16.00 (*0-8006-2665-6*, 1-2665, Fortress Pr) Augsburg Fortress.
— Old Testament: An Introduction. Bowden, John, tr. LC 85-47728. 320p. (GER.). 1991. pap. 17.00 (*0-8006-2544-7*, 1-2544, Fortress Pr) Augsburg Fortress.
Rene, E. Hands & How to Read Them. reprint ed. spiral bd. 6.60 (*0-7873-0713-0*) Mokelumne.
Rene-Jacques. Mont Saint-Michel. (Panorama Bks.). 62p. (FRE.). 3.95 (*0-685-23348-0*) Fr & Eur.
***Rene, R. M. & Stanonis, F. L.** Reflection Seismic Profiling of the Wabash Valley Fault System in the Illinois Basin. LC 94-44233. (U. S. Geological Survey Professional Papers: Vol. 1538-0). 1996. write for info. (*0-615-00573-X*) USGPO.
Rene, Wendy, ed. see Rochester, David, Jr.
Reneau, Don, tr. see Asendorf, Christoph.
Reneau, Don, tr. see Riesebrodt, Martin.
Reneau, Don, tr. see Sachs, Wolfgang.
Reneau, Jack & Reneau, Susan. Colorado's Biggest Bucks & Bulls. (Illus.). 1990. reprint ed. 19.95 (*0-9611376-0-6*) Colo Big Game.
***Reneau, Jack & Reneau, Susan, eds.** Boone & Crockett Club's Twenty-Second Big Game Awards, 1992-1994. (Illus.). 498p. 1995. 39.95 (*0-940864-22-3*) Boone & Crockett.
— Records of North American Big Game, 1993. 10th ed. (Illus.). 624p. 1993. 49.95 (*0-940864-20-7*) Boone & Crockett.
— Records of North American Whitetail Deer. 3rd ed. (Illus.). 319p. 1995. pap. 18.95 (*0-940864-24-X*) Boone & Crockett.
Reneau, Jack, jt. ed. see Nesbitt, W. H.
Reneau, Jack, jt. ed. see Sitton, Gary.
Reneau, Susan, jt. auth. see Reneau, Jack.
Reneau, Susan, jt. ed. see Reneau, Jack.
Reneau, Susan C. The Adventures of Moccasin Joe: The True Life Story of Sgt. George S. Howard. Strohm, Jack, ed. LC 91-73719. (Illus.). 224p. (Orig.). 1994. pap. 19.95 (*0-9611376-1-4*) Colo Big Game.
Reneau, Susan C., ed. see Gray, Prentiss N.
Reneaux, J. J. Cajun Folktales. 176p. (J). (gr. 5 up). 1992. 19.95 (*0-87483-283-7*); pap. 9.95 (*0-87483-282-9*) August Hse.
— Haunted Bayou, & Other Cajun Ghost Stories. LC 94-27774. (J). 1994. 19.95 (*0-87483-384-1*); pap. 9.95 (*0-87483-385-X*) August Hse.
— Why Alligator Hates Dog. LC 94-46965. (Illus.). (J). (ps-2). 1995. 15.95 (*0-87483-412-0*) August Hse.
Renee, see Andrea Lindsey, pseud..
Renee, Janina. Playful Magic. LC 93-44559. (Illus.). 240p. 1994. pap. 12.95 (*0-87542-678-6*) Llewellyn Pubns.
— Tarot Spells. LC 89-77199. (New Age Tarot Ser.). (Illus.). 288p. (Orig.). 1990. pap. 12.95 (*0-87542-670-0*) Llewellyn Pubns.
Renehan, Edward J., Jr. John Burroughs: An American Naturalist. 356p. 1992. 24.95 (*0-930031-59-8*) Chelsea Green Pub.
— The Secret Six: The True Tale of the Men Who Conspired with John Brown. 1995. 25.00 (*0-517-59028-X*, Crown) Crown Pub Group.
Renehan, Robert. Greek Textual Criticism: A Reader. LC 72-82297. (Loeb Classical Monographs). 160p. reprint ed. pap. 46.80 (*0-7837-2319-9*, 2057407) Bks Demand.
***Reneise, Tonyia.** Another Color of Love. 230p. 1995. pap. 8.95 (*1-56901-746-8*) NW Pub.
Reneke, et al. Structured Hereditary Systems. (Pure & Applied Mathematics Ser.: Vol. 107). 232p. 1987. 110.00 (*0-8247-7772-7*) Dekker.
Reneke, J. A. Calculator Enhancement for Multivariable Calculus. (Clemson Calculator Enhancement Ser.). 144p. (C). 1992. pap. text ed. 12.00 (*0-03-092731-5*) SCP.
— Calculator Enhancement for Multivariate Calculus. 94p. (C). 1990. pap. text ed. 8.00 (*0-15-505675-1*) HB Coll Pubs.
Renel, C. Contes de Madagascar, 3 vols., Set. LC 78-20146. (Collection de contes et de chansons populaires: Vols. 37-38, 46). reprint ed. 64.50 (*0-404-60436-6*) AMS Pr.
Renella, R. R. Microsurgery of the Temporo-Medical Region. (Illus.). 220p. 1989. 106.00 (*0-387-82144-9*) Spr-Verlag.
Renelt, Heinrich. Elliptic Systems & Quasiconformal Mappings. LC 87-25347. 146p. 1989. text ed. 98.00 (*0-471-91731-1*) Wiley.
Reneman, R. S. & Bollinger, A., eds. Serotonin & Microcirculation. (Mikrozirkulation in Forschung und Klinik; Progress in Applied Microcirculation Ser.: Vol. 10). (Illus.). x, 92p. 1986. pap. 53.00 (*3-8055-4163-5*) S Karger.
Reneman, Robert S. & Hoeks, Arnold P., eds. Doppler Ultrasound in the Diagnosis of Cerebrovascular Disease. LC 81-19854. (Ultrasound in Biomedicine Ser.: No. 5). (Illus.). 312p. reprint ed. pap. 89.00 (*0-8357-6097-9*, 2034235) Bks Demand.
Reneman, Robert S. & Strackee, Jan, eds. Data in Medicine. (Instrumentation & Techniques in Clinical Medicine Ser.: No. 1). 1979. lib. bdg. 107.50 (*90-247-2150-4*) Kluwer Ac.
Renes. Never Take Money from a Stranger. 144p. 1993. pap. text ed. 19.95 (*0-8403-8505-6*) Kendall-Hunt.
Renes, Robert M. & Ollila, Dale G. Independent Contracting: A Primer. (Going Independent Ser.). (Illus.). 270p. 1993. 34.95 (*1-883487-22-6*); pap. 24.95 (*1-883487-24-2*); ring bd. 29.95 (*1-883487-23-4*) Eagle Pr Ltd.
Renesch, John. Setting Goals. 3rd ed. 170p. 1983. 15.00 (*0-932654-08-8*) Context Pubns.
Renesch, John, ed. New Traditions in Business: Spirit & Leadership in the 21st Century. LC 92-52970. 272p. 1992. pap. 17.95 (*1-881052-03-6*) Berrett-Koehler.
— New Traditions in Business: Spirit & Leadership in the 21st Century. 256p. 1991. 24.75 (*0-9630390-0-8*) New Leaders.
Renesch, John, jt. ed. see Chawla, Sarita.
Renesse, Robert van, jt. auth. see Birman, Kenneth P.
Renetzky, Alvin. Listening to Myself. LC 78-50943. 1978. pap. 3.95 (*0-930946-02-2*) Newaves Pub.
Renewal in Education, Inc. Associates Staff. City of Magnificent Intentions: A History of the District of Columbia. rev. ed. (Illus.). 615p. 1993. text ed. 26.50 (*0-685-61095-0*) Intac.
***Renfer, Linda H., ed.** Daily Readings from Quaker Writings Ancient & Modern, Vol. II. 384p. 1995. 31.95 (*0-9620869-1-6*) Serenity Pr.
Renfer, Linda H., ed. & pref. Daily Readings from Quaker Writings Ancient & Modern, 2 Vol. Set. 400p. 1995. 31. 95 (*0-9620869-0-8*) Serenity Pr.
Renford, Beverly & Hendrickson, Linnea. Bibliographic Instruction: A Handbook. LC 80-12300. 192p. 1980. 29. 95 (*0-918212-24-3*) Neal-Schuman.
Renforth, William & Raveed, Sion. A Comparative Study of Multinational Corporation Joint International Business Ventures with Family Firm or Non-Family Firm Partners. Bruchey, Stuart, ed. LC 80-782. (Multinational Corporations Ser.). 1981. lib. bdg. 23.95 (*0-405-13395-2*) Ayer.
Renfree, Marilyn, jt. auth. see Tyndale-Biscoe, C. Hugh.
Renfrew, Charles. Rambling Through Life. (C). 1988. 39.00 (*0-85439-236-X*, Pub. by St Paul Pubns UK) St Mut.
Renfrew, Colin. Approaches to Social Archaeology. (Illus.). 440p. 1984. 40.00 (*0-674-04165-8*) HUP.
— Archaeology & Language: The Puzzle of Indo-European Origins. (Illus.). 325p. (C). 1990. pap. 19.95 (*0-521-38675-6*) Cambridge U Pr.
— Cycladic Spirit: Masterpieces from the Nicholas P. Goulandris Collection. (Illus.). 207p. 1991. 49.50 (*0-8109-3169-9*) Abrams.
— Investigations in Orkney. LC 80-510107. (Reports of the Research Committee of the Society of Antiquaries of London). (Illus.). 328p. reprint ed. pap. 93.50 (*0-7837-6402-2*, 2046118) Bks Demand.
Renfrew, Colin, ed. The Prehistory of Orkney: 4000 B.C. to 1000 A.D. (Illus.). 310p. 1987. pap. 15.00 (*0-85224-506-8*, Pub. by Edinburgh U Pr UK) Col U Pr.
Renfrew, Colin & Bahn, Paul. Archaeology: Theories, Methods & Practice. LC 90-70289. (Illus.). 544p. (C). 1991. pap. text ed. 34.95 (*0-500-27605-6*) Thames Hudson.
Renfrew, Colin & Wagstaff, Malcolm, eds. An Island Polity: The Archaeology of Exploitation in Melos. LC 81-7683. (Illus.). 350p. 1982. 99.95 (*0-521-23785-8*) Cambridge U Pr.
Renfrew, Colin & Zubrow, Ezra B., eds. The Ancient Mind: Elements of Cognitive Archaeology. (New Directions in Archaeology Ser.). (Illus.). 208p. (C). 1994. pap. 19.95 (*0-521-45620-7*) Cambridge U Pr.
— The Ancient Mind: Elements of Cognitive Archaeology. (New Directions in Archaeology Ser.). (Illus.). 208p. (C). 1994. 59.95 (*0-521-43488-2*) Cambridge U Pr.
Renfrew, Colin, jt. auth. see Daniel, Glyn.
Renfrew, Colin, jt. ed. see Hardy, D. A.
Renfrew, Colin, et al, eds. Excavations at Sitagroi, a Prehistoric Village in Northeast Greece, Vol. 1. LC 85-11928. (Monumenta Archaeologica Ser.: No. 13). (Illus.). 644p. 1986. text ed. 48.00 (*0-917956-51-6*) UCLA Arch.
Renfrew, Jane, ed. New Light on Early Farming. 1990. text ed. 59.00 (*0-685-47275-2*, Pub. by Edinburgh U Pr UK) Col U Pr.
Renfrew, Malcolm, jt. ed. see Ashbrook, Peter.
Renfrew, Malcolm M., ed. Safety in the Chemical Laboratory, Vol. 4. 1981. pap. 20.00 (*0-910362-06-8*) Chem Educ.
Renfrew, Mary, et al. Bestfeeding. LC 89-920. 1989. pap. 12.95 (*0-89087-571-5*) Celestial Arts.
Renfrew, Nita. Saddam Hussein. (Library of Biography). (Illus.). 128p. (J). (gr. 5 up). 1993. 18.95 (*0-7910-1776-1*, Am Art Analog) Chelsea Hse.
Renfrew, Tom, ed. see MacNeill, Carol.
Renfro, Anthony C. A Guide for a Single Man in Relationship to Women. 147p. 1984. pap. 9.99 (*0-9621521-2-9*) Renfro Pub.
— A Guide for a Single Woman in Relationship to Men. 151p. (Orig.). 1988. pap. 9.99 (*0-9621521-0-2*) Renfro Pub.
Renfro, Elizabeth. Basic Writing: Process & Product, Cases & Readings. 356p. (C). 1985. pap. text ed. 19.75 (*0-03-069773-5*) HB Coll Pubs.
— The Shasta Indians of California & Their Neighbors. Brown, Keven, ed. (Illus.). 126p. (Orig.). 1992. pap. 8.95 (*0-87961-221-5*) Naturegraph.
Renfro, Nancy. Bags Are Big: A Paper Bag Craft Book. Cromack, Celeste, ed. (Illus.). 78p. (J). (gr. 1-6). 1983. pap. 14.95 (*0-931044-10-3*) Renfro Studios.
— Puppet Shows Made Easy! Cromack, Celeste, ed. (Puppetry in Education Ser.). (Illus.). 96p. (Orig.). (J). (gr. 2-12). pap. 14.95 (*0-931044-13-8*) Renfro Studios.
— Puppetry Language & the Special Child: Discovering Alternate Languages. Cromack, Celeste, ed. (Puppetry in Education Ser.). (Illus.). 160p. (Orig.). (C). (ps-6). 1984. pap. 15.95 (*0-931044-12-X*) Renfro Studios.
Renfro, Nancy & Armstrong, Beverly. Make Amazing Puppets. (Holiday & Art Ser.). 32p. (J). (gr. 1-6). 1979. 3.95 (*0-88160-007-5*, LW 109) Learning Wks.
Renfro, Nancy & Frazier, Nancy. Imagination: At Play with Puppets & Creative Drama. Schwalb, Ann W., ed. (Puppetry in Education Ser.). (Illus.). 96p. (J). (gr. 1-6). 1987. 16.95 (*0-931044-16-2*) Renfro Studios.
Renfro, Nancy & Sullivan, Debbie. Puppets U. S. A. - Texas: Exploring Folklore, Music & Crafts with Puppets. Schwalb, Ann W. & Marion, Craig A., eds. (Puppetry in Education Ser.). (Illus.). 96p. (Orig.). (J). (gr. 1-6). 1985. pap. 15.95 (*0-931044-11-1*) Renfro Studios.
Renfro, Nancy, jt. auth. see Bissinger, Kristen.
Renfro, Nancy, jt. auth. see Champlin, Connie.
Renfro, Nancy, jt. auth. see Hunt, Tamara.
Renfro, Nancy, jt. auth. see Sullivan, Debbie.
Renfro, William L. Issues Management in Strategic Planning. LC 93-18244. 200p. 1993. text ed. 49.95 (*0-89930-785-X*, RIC/, Quorum Bks) Greenwood.
Renfroe, Earl W. Edgewise. LC 74-671. 512p. reprint ed. pap. 146.00 (*0-317-26699-3*, 2056006) Bks Demand.
Renfroe, Fred. Arabic-Ugaritic Lexical Studies. (Abhandlungen Zur Literatur Alt-Syrien-Palastinas Ser.: Vol. 5). xii, 198p. 1992. text ed. 49.00 (*3-927120-09-X*, Pub. by UGARIT GW) Eisenbrauns.
Renfroe, Walter J., Jr., tr. see Delbruck, Hans.
Renfrow, Cindy. Take a Thousand Eggs or More: A Translation of Medieval Recipes from Harleian MS. 279, Harleian MS. 4016, & Extracts of Ashmole MS. 1439, Laud MS. 553, & Douce MS. 55, with almost 100 Recipes Adapted for Modern Cookery, 2 vols., 1. (Illus.). (Orig.). 1991. pap. 13.00 (*0-9628598-1-8*) C Renfrow.
— Take a Thousand Eggs or More: A Translation of Medieval Recipes from Harleian MS. 279, Harleian MS. 4016, & Extracts of Ashmole MS. 1439, Laud MS. 553, & Douce MS. 55, with almost 100 Recipes Adapted for Modern Cookery, 2 vols., 2. (Illus.). (Orig.). 1991. pap. 13.00 (*0-9628598-2-6*) C Renfrow.
— Take a Thousand Eggs or More: A Translation of Medieval Recipes from Harleian MS. 279, Harleian MS. 4016, & Extracts of Ashmole MS. 1439, Laud MS. 553, & Douce MS. 55, with almost 100 Recipes Adapted for Modern Cookery, 2 vols., Set. (Illus.). (Orig.). 1991. pap. 25.00 (*0-9628598-0-X*) C Renfrow.
***Renfrow, Jan.** Cryptoverse! 16p. (Orig.). 1994. 4.95 (*0-9613072-8-5*) JANART-LOVE.
— For the Feeling Heart. (Illus.). 24p. (Orig.). 1989. pap. 8.95 (*0-9613072-3-4*) JANART-LOVE.
— Songs of Love. (Illus.). 32p. (Orig.). 1987. pap. 10.00 (*0-9613072-2-6*) JANART-LOVE.
— Stranger in the Wind. 28p. (Orig.). 1983. pap. 6.00 (*0-9613072-0-X*) JANART-LOVE.
— What Compassionate Men Need to Know About Women. 1991. pap. 7.00 (*0-9613072-5-0*) JANART-LOVE.
— Within & Beyond. (Illus.). 34p. (Orig.). 1993. pap. 10.00 (*0-9613072-7-7*) JANART-LOVE.
Rengachary, Setti S. & Wilkins, Robert H., eds. Principles of Neurosurgery. LC 93-10153. 1993. 95.00 (*1-56375-022-8*) Mosby Yr Bk.
Rengachary, Setti S., jt. ed. see Doty, James R.
Rengachary, Setti S., jt. auth. see Wilkins, Robert H.
Rengachary, Setti S., jt. ed. see Wilkins, Robert H.
Rengers, Christopher. Mary of the Americas: Our Lady of Guadalupe. LC 88-8155. 154p. (Orig.). 1988. pap. 8.95 (*0-8189-0543-3*) Alba.
— The Youngest Prophet: The Life of Jacinta Marto, Fatima Visionary. LC 85-30789. 144p. (Orig.). 1986. pap. 5.95 (*0-8189-0496-8*) Alba.
***Rengers, Niek, ed.** Engineering Geology of Quaternary Sediments: Proceedings of the Twenty-Year Jubilee Symposium of the INGEOKRING, Delft, Netherlands, June 1994. (Illus.). 146p. (C). 1994. text ed. 50.00 (*90-5410-398-1*, Pub. by A A Balkema NE) Ashgate Pub Co.
Rengger. Treaties & Alliances of the World. 5th ed. 1991. 120.00 (*0-582-05733-7*) Longman.
***Rengger, N. J.** Political Theory, Modernity & Postmodernity. 200p. (C). 1995. write for info. (*0-631-19158-5*); pap. write for info. (*0-631-19159-3*) Blackwell Pubs.
Rengger, N. J., jt. ed. see Baylis, John.
Renggli, Bernard J. & Blankenship, G. Wesley. The Development of a CNC Spur Gear Generating System. (Fall Technical Meeting Papers 88FTMS2). (Illus.). 19p. 1988. pap. text ed. 30.00 (*1-55589-522-0*) AGMA.
Rengier, John. By Hex. 1956. pap. 4.75 (*0-8222-0170-4*) Dramatists Play.
Rengo, F., jt. ed. see Vigorito, C.
Rengstorf, Karl, et al, eds. Die Mischna: Text, Ubersetzung und Ausfuhrliche Erklarung mit Eingehenden Gesschichtlichten und Sprachelichen Einleitungen und Textkritischen Anhangen. x, 188p. (Orig.). (GER.). (C). 1991. pap. text ed. 104.65 (*3-11-012464-5*, 147-91) De Gruyter.

Renich, Jill. Tener y Retener: To Have & to Hold. (SPA.). 5.25 (*84-7228-124-8*, 220868, Pub. by Edit Clie SP) TSELF.
Renich-Meyers, Jill. So You're a Teenage Girl. rev. ed. 144p. 1989. pap. 9.99 (*0-310-31801-7*) Zondervan.
***Renich, T. Elizabeth.** Word of Honor. (Shadowcreek Chronicles Ser.). 300p. (Orig.). 1994. pap. 8.99 (*1-883002-10-9*) Emerald WA.
Renick. Trust Me. 1994. pap. 2.99 (*0-06-108258-9*, PL) HarpC Child Bks.
Renick, Clay, jt. auth. see Kruppenbach, Jack.
Renick, Jeane. Always... 1993. mass mkt. 4.99 (*0-06-108141-8*, Harp PBks) HarpC.
— Always. 1994. pap. 2.99 (*0-06-108294-5*, Harp PBks) HarpC.
— Promises. 1994. mass mkt. 4.99 (*0-06-108140-X*, Harp PBks) HarpC.
— Trust Me. 1992. mass mkt. 4.50 (*0-06-108006-3*, Harp PBks) HarpC.
Renie, William A. Goldberg's Genetic & Metabolic Eye Disease. 2nd ed. 608p. 1986. 142.00 (*0-316-74016-0*, Little Med Div) Little.
Renier, Fernand G. Colloquial Dutch. 1986. pap. 13.95 (*0-7100-0785-X*, RKP) Routledge.
— Colloquial Dutch. (Colloquial Ser.). 1992. audio 29.95 (*0-415-07424-X*, A6896); audio 14.95 (*0-415-07423-1*, A6892) Routledge.
— Colloquial Dutch. 3rd ed. 256p. 1983. pap. 14.95 (*0-415-04039-6*) Routledge.
— Dutch-English - English-Dutch Dictionary. 1985. pap. 13.95 (*0-415-04610-6*) Routledge.
— Dutch-English, English-Dutch Dictionary. (DUT & ENG.). 39.50 (*0-87557-014-3*, 014-3) Saphrograph.
Renier, Fernand G., ed. Dutch-English & English-Dutch Dictionary. (DUT & ENG.). 1949. pap. 13.95 (*0-7100-9352-7*, RKP) Routledge.
Renier, Fernand G., tr. see Ciliga, Ante.
Renier, Fernand G., tr. see Ciliga, Anton.
Renier, G. J., tr. see Blok, Petrus J.
Reniewicz, Frank. For God, Country, & Polonia: One Hundred Years of the Orchard Lake Schools. LC 85-72080. (Illus.). 177p. 1985. 9.95 (*0-9615564-0-4*) Ctr Polish.
Reniker, S., jt. ed. see Maruyama, M.
Reniker, Sherry. GEO Frictions: (Open Meeting Bks.). 82p. 1991. pap. 7.00 (*0-87924-081-4*) Membrane Pr.
Reniker, Sherry, ed. World's Edge: An Anthology. 1991. pap. 12.00 (*0-87924-077-6*) Membrane Pr.
Renineke, jt. ed. see Rothstein, Erica L.
Rening, Linda J., jt. auth. see Carnes, Patrick J.
Reninger, H. W., jt. auth. see Knickerbocker, K. L.
Renino, Marjorie C., comp. The Guide to Genealogical Research for Westchester County. rev. ed. LC 88-151242. (Illus.). xviii, 228p. (Orig.). 1987. reprint ed. per. 35.00 (*0-9615866-0-5*) M Renino.
Renique, Gerardo, jt. auth. see Poole, Deborah.
Renirkens, Clement. Love with Your Eyes Open. Lucas, Marc & Lucas, Claudia, trs. LC 85-28669. 145p. (Orig.). 1986. pap. 7.95 (*0-8189-0491-7*) Alba.
Renish, Peggy. Home Educator's Guide for Washington State. LC 86-90511. 136p. 1986. pap. 5.50 (*0-9617607-0-2*) R & R Publish.
Renji, Alfred. A Diary on Information Theory. 192p. (C). 1984. 67.50x (*963-05-3876-8*, Pub. by Akad Kiado HU) St Mut.
Renjilian-Burgy, Joy. Justina: Homenaje a Justina Ruiz De Conde En Su Ochenta Cumpleanos. Gascon-Vera, Elena, ed. (Homenajes De ALDEEU Ser.). (Illus.). 224p. (ENG & SPA.). (C). 1992. pap. 25.00 (*0-9626630-1-8*) Spanish Profs Amer.
Renjilian-Burgy, Joy, jt. auth. see Valette, Rebecca M.
Renjun, Zou. Fundamentals of Pyrolysis in Petrochemical Technology. 1993. 110.00 (*0-8493-7760-9*) CRC Pr.
Renk, Erns. Spiegelungen: Gedichte. LC 86-7046. 291p. 1985. 29.50 (*0-317-39973-X*) KABEL Pubs.
Renk, Ernst. Spiegelungen. 291p. (GER.). 1985. text ed. 34.50 (*0-930329-40-6*) KABEL Pubs.
Renkawitz, R., ed. Tissue Specific Gene Expression. LC 89-16997. 221p. 1989. lib. bdg. 160.00 (*0-89573-886-4*) VCH Pubs.
Renkema, Barb. Fabric Foto Framers: Picture & Greeting Card Mats in Counted Cross-Stitch. 20p. 1986. 5.98 (*0-88290-314-4*) Horizon Utah.
Renkema, Guillermo. Credos y Confesiones I-bL-Alumno. (SPA.). 1989. 1.10 (*1-55955-014-7*) CITE MI.
— Credos y Confesiones I-C-Alumno. (SPA.). 1992. 1.50 (*1-55955-142-9*) CITE MI.
— Credos y Confesiones I-C-Maestro. (SPA.). 1992. 1.30 (*1-55955-143-7*) CITE MI.
— Credos y Confesiones I-Db-Alumno. (SPA.). 1989. 1.30 (*1-55955-012-0*) CITE MI.
— Credos y Confesiones I-Db-Maestro. (SPA.). 1989. 1.80 (*1-55955-013-9*) CITE MI.
— Credos y Confesiones II: C-Alumno. (SPA.). 1993. write for info. (*1-55955-165-8*) CITE MI.
— Credos y Confesiones II: C-Maestro. (SPA.). 1993. write for info. (*1-55955-166-6*) CITE MI.
— Credos y Confesiones II-bL-Alumno. (SPA.). 1993. 1.50 (*1-55955-158-5*) CITE MI.
— Credos y Confesiones II-bL-Maestro. (SPA.). 1993. 1.10 (*1-55955-159-3*) CITE MI.
— Credos y Confesiones II-Db-Alumno. (SPA.). 1993. 1.50 (*1-55955-156-9*) CITE MI.
— Credos y Confesiones II-Db-Maestro. (SPA.). 1993. 1.10 (*1-55955-157-7*) CITE MI.
— Credos y Confesions I-bL-Maestro. (SPA.). 1989. 1.30 (*1-55955-015-5*) CITE MI.
Renkema, Jan. Discourse Studies: An Introductory Textbook. LC 93-1453. ix, 224p. 1993. 53.00x (*1-55619-492-7*); pap. 22.95 (*1-55619-493-5*) Benjamins North Am.

Renken, Anthony L., jt. auth. see Karony, Stephenie.
Renken, Maxine. Bibliography of Henry Miller. LC 72-4735. (American Literature Ser.: No. 49). 1972. reprint ed. lib. bdg. 75.00 (*0-8383-1592-5*) M S G Haskell Hse.

Renkens, Jack H. Recruiting Realities: Educating the High School Student Athlete in the Recruiting Process. 110p. (Orig.). 1995. pap. 19.95x (*0-9647041-9-6*) Brookes & John. Student-athletes in all sports have dreams of continuing their athletic careers at the college level. A low cost publication has finally been developed that educates student athletes & their families in collegiate recruiting process. Whether the student athlete is being highly recruited or not recruited at all, RECRUITING REALITIES supplies detailed information that addresses every possible recruiting situation. It is a clear & direct guide essential to the aspirations of student athletes in all sports. "Renkens is at his best when discussing recruitment of student athletes. RECRUITING REALITIES is concise, informative & necessary... expertly organized & full of hard facts, helpful hints & a real eye-opener."--Michael Wilson, Director of Athletics, New Berlin, WI. "We think it is terrific! It is well written, easy for the layman to understand, contains great advice & should help any student athlete who is willing to put in time & effort to follow guidelines."--Duncan Stewart, Principal, Barre, MA. Introductory offer only $19.95. Call TOLL FREE 1-800-928-7848 or mail payment payable to: Brookes & John Publishing, 1807 North Brookfield Road, Oakham, MA 01068-9902.** ***Publisher Provided Annotation.

Renkes, Jim. The Quad-Cities & the People. LC 94-24648. (Illus.). 112p. (Orig.). 1994. pap. 14.95 (*1-56037-067-X*) Am Wrld Geog.
Renkewitz, Heinz. Hochmann von Hochenau, 1670-1721. Willoughby, William G., tr. (Monograph Ser.). 148p. (C). 1993. 30.00 (*0-936693-24-X*) Brethren Encyclopedia.
— Hochmann Von Hochenau (1670-1721) Willoughby, William G., tr. (Monograph Ser.). 1993. 30.00 (*0-614-06604-2*) Brethren Encyclopedia.
Renkin, Eugene M. & Michel, C. Charles, eds. Handbook of Physiology: Section 2, The Cardiovascular System, Vol. IV, Pts. 1 & 2: Microcirculation. (American Physiological Society Book). (Illus.). 1124p. 1988. 275.00 (*0-19-520666-5*) OUP.
Renkl, Margaret. The Marigold Poems. 28p. (Orig.). 1992. pap. 5.00 (*1-877801-25-9*) Still Waters.
Renko, Hal, et al. The Antagonists: A Complete Microworld Adventure for the IBM-PC. 128p. 1985. pap. write for info. (*0-201-16492-2*) Addison-Wesley.
Renkoski, Angela, ed. see Morgan, Bessie C.
Renkowitz, Marshall, jt. auth. see Okos, Martin R.
***Renn.** 1995 Wiley Bankruptcy Law Update. (Bankruptcy Practice Library). 1995. pap. text ed. 95.00 (*0-471-12043-X*, Pub. by Wiley Law Pubns) Wiley.
Renn, Dorothy L. Emotional Abuse of the Child. LC 87-92179. 1988. 16.95 (*0-87212-216-6*) Libra.
***Renn, Erin M.** The Breads, Cakes, Cookies, Sweets, & Special Food of a Midwest German Christmas. (Illus.). 76p. 1994. spiral bd. 10.95 (*1-57216-018-7*) Penfield.
Renn, Jurgen & Schulmann, Robert, eds. Albert Einstein - Mileva Maric: The Love Letters. Smith, Shawn, tr. (Illus.). 160p. 1992. 16.95 (*0-691-08760-1*) Princeton U Pr.
Renn, Jurgen, et al. Einstein in Context. (Science in Context Ser.: Vol. 6). (Illus.). 360p. (C). 1993. pap. 39.95 (*0-521-44834-4*) Cambridge U Pr.
Renn, Leslie D., jt. auth. see Lewis, Jerre G.
Renn, Ludwig. Warfare: The Relation of War to Society. Fitzgerald, Edward, tr. LC 79-160989. (Select Bibliographies Reprint Ser.). 1977. reprint ed. 23.95 (*0-8369-5857-8*) Ayer.
***Renn, Ortwin, ed.** Fairness & Competence in Citizen Participation: Evaluating Models for Environmental Discourse. (Technology, Risk, & Society Ser.). 400p. (C). 1995. lib. bdg. 99.50 (*0-7923-3517-1*); pap. text ed. 46.00 (*0-7923-3518-X*) Kluwer Ac.
Renn, Walter, et al. The Treatment of the Holocaust in Textbooks: The Federal Republic of Germany, Israel, the United States. (Holocaust Studies). 288p. 1987. text ed. 43.50 (*0-88033-955-1*) East Eur Quarterly.
Renna, Giani, jt. auth. see Shore, Donna.
Renna, Giani, jt. auth. see Tyler, Laura.
Rennard, Steven, jt. auth. see Linder, James.
Renne, Daisy L. My Mother's House. (Illus.). 16p. 1994. 5.95 (*0-8059-3553-3*) Dorrance.
Renne, Elisha P. Cloth That Does Not Die: The Meaning of Cloth in Bunu Social Life. LC 94-12014. (McLellan Book Ser.). (Illus.). 216p. (C). 1995. text ed. 40.00 (*0-295-97392-7*) U of Wash Pr.

Renneberg, Monkia & Walker, Mark. Science, Technology & National Socialism. LC 92-41633. (Illus.). 416p. (C). 1993. 59.95 (*0-521-40374-X*) Cambridge U Pr.
Renneberg, Robert C. Winchester Model 94. LC 90-63918. (Illus.). 208p. 1991. 34.95 (*0-87341-161-7*) Krause Pubns.
Renneisen, Robert. How to Be Treated Like a High Roller: Even Though You're Not One. 128p. 1992. pap. 7.95 (*0-8184-0556-2*, L Stuart) Carol Pub Group.
Renneker, Mark. Sick Surfers Ask the Surf Docs & Dr. Geoff. 1993. pap. 12.95 (*0-923521-26-7*) Bull Pub.
— Understanding Cancer. 4th ed. 1994. pap. 39.95 (*0-923521-29-1*) Bull Pub.
Rennell, Diane S., ed. Appendix Materials. rev. ed. (Service Technology Ser.). 52p. 1989. write for info. (*0-924635-02-9*); text ed. 90.00 (*0-924635-01-0*) Natl Spa Pool.
— Basic Pool & Spa Technology. rev. ed. (Service Technology Ser.). (Illus.). 390p. 1989. pap. text ed. 140.00 (*0-924635-00-2*); pap. text ed. 90.00 (*0-685-25190-X*) Natl Spa Pool.
Rennell, Francis J. British Military Administration of Occupied Territories in Africa During the Years of 1941-1947. 1970. reprint ed. text ed. 85.00 (*0-8371-4319-5*, REBM, Greenwood Pr) Greenwood.
Rennell, James, jt. auth. see Park, Mungo.
Rennels, Max R. The Art of Appreciation: A Cultural Awareness Perspective. 160p. 1992. per. 24.95 (*0-8403-7078-4*) Kendall-Hunt.
Rennenberg, H., et al, eds. Sulfur Nutrition & Sulfur Assimilation in Higher Plants: Fundamental Environmental & Agricultural Aspects. (Illus.). 276p. 1990. 89.00 (*90-5103-038-X*, Pub. by SPB Acad Pub NE) Koeltz Sci Bks.
Renner. Diccionario de Modismos y Lenguaje Coloquial: Espanol - Aleman. (GER & SPA.). 1991. write for info. (*0-7859-3704-8*, 8428318506) Fr & Eur.
Renner & Boucher. Removable Partial Dentures. 1987. text ed. 60.00 (*0-86715-189-7*, 1897) Quint Pub Co.
Renner, et al. Wirtschaftssprache German-English. 2nd ed. (ENG & GER.). 1970. 63.50 (*3-19-006201-3*) Adlers Foreign Bks.
Renner, Adrienne G., jt. auth. see Layman, Katie.
Renner, Adrienne G., jt. auth. see Layman, N. Kathryn.
Renner, Brian, jt. auth. see Weatherford, William H., Sr.
Renner, Bruce. The Language of Light Ambits. 53p. per. 8.00 (*0-934332-48-7*) LEpervier Pr.
— Song Made Out of a Pale Smoke. LC 81-15617. 51p. text ed. 9.95 (*0-934332-37-1*); pap. text ed. 4.95 (*0-934332-36-3*) LEpervier Pr.
— Wakefulness. LC 78-71828. 78p. (Orig.). 1978. pap. 3.75 (*0-934332-10-X*) LEpervier Pr.
Renner, D. Laser Diode Technology & Applications III, Vol. 1418. 1991. 77.00 (*0-8194-0508-6*) SPIE.
Renner, D., ed. Laser Diode Technology & Applications IV. 1992. 92.00 (*0-8194-0780-1*, 1634) SPIE.
Renner, Donald, et al. Microeconomics - Alternative Views. 1993. pap. text ed. 39.95 (*1-56226-160-6*) CT Pub.
Renner, E., ed. Micronutrients in Milk & Milk-Based Food Products. 314p. 1989. 86.50 (*1-85166-309-6*) Elsevier.
Renner, E. & El-Salam, M. H., eds. Application of Ultrafiltration in the Dairy Industry. 378p. 1991. 114.00 (*1-85166-531-5*) Elsevier.
Renner, Eric. The International Pinhole Photography Exhibition. Center for Contemporary Arts Staff, ed. (Illus.). 64p. (Orig.). 1989. pap. text ed. 18.00 (*0-929762-01-0*) CCA Santa Fe.
— Pinhole Photography: Rediscovering a Historic Technique. (Illus.). 192p. 1994. pap. 29.95 (*0-240-80231-4*, Focal) Buttrwrth-Heinemann.
Renner, Franz C. & Seemann, Max. Viennese Stained Glass Designs in Full Color. (Illus.). 32p. 1988. reprint ed. pap. 6.95 (*0-486-25590-5*) Dover.
Renner, Frederic G., jt. auth. see Yost, Karl.
Renner, G. K. Joplin: From Mining Town to Urban City. 1985. 19.95 (*0-89781-153-4*, 5122) Preferred Mktg.
Renner, Gail K. In Pursuit of Excellence: Missouri Southern State College, 1937-1992. LC 93-29631. 1993. write for info. (*0-89865-876-4*) Donning Co.
Renner, Ginger. Charles M. Russell: The Frederic G. Renner Collection. 80p. (Orig.). 1981. pap. 10.00 (*0-910407-09-6*) Phoenix Art.
***Renner, Ginger K.** Charlie Russell & the Ladies in His Life. 32p. Date not set. pap. 3.25 (*0-614-06138-5*) Falcon Pr MT.
Renner, Jeff. Northwest Marine Weather: From the Columbia River to Cape Scott, Including Puget Sound, the San Juan & Gulf Islands, & the Straits of Juan de Fuca, Georgia, Johnstone, & Queen Charlotte. 1993. write for info. (*0-89886-376-7*) Mountaineers.
— Northwest Mountain Weather: Understanding & Forecasting for the Backcountry User. LC 91-46559. (Illus.). 96p. (Orig.). 1992. pap. 10.95 (*0-89886-297-3*) Mountaineers.
Renner, Jeff & Kawaky, Joseph. Captain Jack's Almanac: Puget Sound Edition, 1993. (Illus.). 432p. (Orig.). 1993. pap. 11.95 (*1-878258-32-X*) Marine Trade.
Renner, John H. Healthsmarts: How to Spot the Quacks, Avoid the Nonsense & Get the Facts that Affect Your Health. Vaughn, Lewis, ed. 160p. (Orig.). 1990. pap. 12.95 (*0-9626145-0-5*) Health Facts Pub.
Renner, John H., ed. A Self-Administered Patient Education Audit for Family Practices. 19p. 1990. 10.00 (*0-9626145-1-3*) Health Facts Pub.
Renner, Karl. Wandlungen der Modernen Gesellschaft: Transformations of Modern Society. LC 74-25776. (European Sociology Ser.). 227p. 1975. reprint ed. 24.95 (*0-405-06530-2*) Ayer.
Renner, Louis L. Father Tom of the Arctic. LC 85-71951. (Illus.). 176p. (Orig.). 1985. 24.95 (*0-8323-0445-X*); pap. 10.95 (*0-8323-0443-3*) Binford Mort.

— The KNOM: Father Jim Poole Story. LC 85-71950. (Illus.). 184p. (Orig.). 1985. pap. 8.95 (*0-8323-0444-1*) Binford Mort.
Renner, M. J. & Rosenzweig, Mark R. Enriched & Impoverished Environments. (Recent Research in Psychology Ser.). (Illus.). 150p. 1987. pap. 40.00 (*0-387-96523-8*) Spr-Verlag.
Renner-McCaffrey, Jo & Leyshon, Anna H. Quality Assurance in Hospital Nutrition Services. 152p. 1988. 44.00 (*0-8342-0028-7*) Aspen Pub.
***Renner, Michael.** Budgeting for Disarmament: The Costs of War & Peace. 70p. (Orig.). 1994. pap. 5.00 (*1-878071-23-8*) Worldwatch Inst.
— Critical Juncture: The Future of Peacekeeping. 70p. (Orig.). 1993. pap. 5.00 (*1-878071-15-7*) Worldwatch Inst.
— Economic Adjustments after the Cold War: Strategies for Conversion. 1992. 59.95 (*1-85521-259-5*, Pub. by Dartmth Pub UK) Ashgate Pub Co.
— Jobs in a Sustainable Economy. 70p. (Orig.). 1991. pap. 5.00 (*1-878071-05-X*) Worldwatch Inst.
— National Security: The Economic & Environmental Dimension. 1989. pap. write for info. (*0-916468-90-9*) Worldwatch Inst.
— Rethinking the Role of the Automobile. (Papers). 72p. (Orig.). (C). 1988. pap. 5.00 (*0-916468-85-2*) Worldwatch Inst.
— Swords Into Plowshares: Converting to a Peace Economy. 70p. (Orig.). 1990. pap. 5.00 (*0-916468-97-6*) Worldwatch Inst.
Renner, P. Basic Hotel Front Office Procedures. 3rd ed. 1994. text ed. write for info. (*0-442-01612-3*) Van Nos Reinhold.
Renner, Peter & Quinlivan-Hall, David. In Search of Solutions: Sixty Ways to Guide Your Problem-Solving Group. 176p. 1993. pap. 12.95 (*0-89384-236-2*) Pfeiffer & Co.
Renner, Peter F. Basic Hotel Front Office Procedures. 3rd ed. LC 93-1587. 1993. text ed. 29.95 (*0-442-01611-5*) Van Nos Reinhold.
Renner, Richard R., ed. see Latin American Conference Staff.
Renner, Rick. The Dynamic Duo: The Holy Spirit & You. 1994. pap. 9.99 (*0-88419-362-4*, Creation Hse) Strang Comms Co.
— Seducing Spirits & Doctrines of Demons. MacKall, Phyllis, ed. (Orig.). 1988. 6.95 (*0-9621436-0-X*) R Renner Minst.
Renner, Robert, ed. QDT, 1993. (Illus.). 188p. (Orig.). 1993. pap. text ed. 54.00 (*0-86715-186-2*) Quint Pub Co.
Renner, Ron. Secrets to Decorating & Moving to Florida. LC 91-91378. (Orig.). 1991. pap. 12.95 (*0-9631435-0-6*) Renner FL.
***Renner, Rudiger.** Economic Terminology English-German, German-English. 4th ed. 543p. (ENG & GER.). 1992. 125.00 (*0-7859-6872-5*) Fr & Eur.
Renner, Rudiger & Tooth, J. English & German Legal Terminology. 526p. (ENG & GER.). 1971. 95.00 (*0-8288-6466-7*) Fr & Eur.
Renner, Rudiger, jt. auth. see Haensch, G.
Renner, Sandra L. & Winget, W. Gary. Fast Track Exporting: How Your Company Can Succeed in the Global Market. 250p. 1991. 29.95 (*0-8144-5009-1*) AMACOM.
Renner, Susanne, jt. auth. see Kubitzki, Klaus.
Renner, Susanne S. A History of Botanical Exploration in Amazonian Ecuador, 1739-1988. LC 92-5840. (Smithsonian Contributions to Botany Ser.: No. 82). 43p. reprint ed. pap. 25.00 (*0-7837-5166-4*, 2044895) Bks Demand.
— Systematic Studies in the Melastomataceae: Bellucia, Loreya & Macairea. LC 88-39155. (Memoirs Ser.: No. 50). (Illus.). 111p. 1989. pap. 24.00 (*0-89327-335-X*) NY Botanical.
Renner, Tari. Statistics Unraveled: A Practical Guide to Using Data in Decision Making. 198p. (Orig.). 1988. pap. text ed. 28.00 (*0-87326-934-9*) Intl City-Cnty Mgt.
Renner, Thomas C., jt. auth. see Cantalupo, Joseph.
Renner, Thomas C., jt. auth. see Giancana, Antoinette.
Renner, Thomas C., jt. auth. see Kirby, Cecil.
Renner, Thomas C., jt. auth. see Teresa, Vincent.
Renner, Thomas L., ed. see Michigan Intercollegiate Athletic Association Staff.
Rennert. Richard Scott. 1993. pap. 3.95 (*0-87067-780-2*, Melrose Sq) Holloway.
***Rennert, Amy.** Helen Mirren: Prime Suspect. (Illus.). 160p. (Orig.). 1995. pap. 15.95 (*0-912333-69-3*) KQED.
Rennert, Hal H. Eduard Moerike's Reading & the Reconstruction of His Extant Library. LC 83-49184. (American University Studies: Comparative Literature: Ser. III, Vol. 8). 230p. (C). 1985. 26.00 (*0-8204-0080-7*) P Lang Pubs.
Rennert, Hugo A. Life of Lope De Vega. LC 67-13337. 1972. reprint ed. 30.95 (*0-405-08878-7*) Ayer.
— Spanish Pastoral Romances. LC 67-29552. 1968. reprint ed. 25.00 (*0-8196-0214-0*) Biblo.
Rennert, Jack. One Hundred Posters of Buffalo Bill's Wild West. (Illus.). 1977. 19.95 (*0-88201-013-1*); pap. 8.95 (*0-88201-012-3*) Darien Hse.
— One Hundred Years of Bicycle Posters. (Illus.). 1977. pap. 7.95 (*0-685-85023-4*) Darien Hse.
— One Hundred Years of Circus Posters. (Illus.). pap. 7.95 (*0-380-00144-6*) Darien Hse.
— Posters of the Belle Epoque: The Wine Spectator Collection. LC 90-60771. (Illus.). 256p. 1990. 75.00 (*0-918076-75-7*) Rizzoli Intl.
Rennert, Jack & Terry, Walter. One Hundred Years of Dance Posters. (Illus.). 1977. pap. 7.95 (*0-88201-010-7*) Darien Hse.
Rennert, Maggie. I Love You. (Illus.). (J). (ps up). 1987. 9.95 (*0-915361-71-X*) Modan-Adama Bks.

R

An Asterisk (*) at the beginning of an entry indicates that the title is appearing in BIP for the first time.

Rennert, Owen M. & Chan, Wayiee, eds. Metabolism of Trace Metals in Man, Vol. I. 192p. 1984. 119.95 (0-8493-5798-5, QP534, CRC Reprint) Franklin.
— Metabolism of Trace Metals in Man, Vol. II. 1984. 144. 00 (0-8493-5799-3, QP534, CRC Reprint) Franklin.
***Rennert, R. S.** African American Answer Book: Science & Discovery. (Illus.). 64p. (YA). (gr. 5 up). 1995. 7.95 (0-7910-3207-8) Chelsea Hse.
— African-American Answer Book: Sports. (Illus.). 64p. (YA). (gr. 5 up). 1995. 7.95 (0-7910-3205-1); pap. 4.95 (0-7910-3208-6); pap. 4.95 (0-7910-3206-X) Chelsea Hse.
— African American Answer Book, Arts & Entertainment: 325 Questions Drawn from the Expertise of Harvard's Du Bois Institute. LC 94-29999. (Illus.). 64p. (YA). (gr. 5 up). 1995. 12.95 (0-7910-3201-9) Chelsea Hse.
— African American Answer Book, History: Three Hundred Twenty-Five Questions Drawn from the Expertise of Harvard's Du Bois Institute. LC 94-30202. 1995. pap. write for info. (0-7910-3210-8) Chelsea Hse.
— African American Answer Book, History: Three Hundred Twenty-Five Questions Drawn from the Expertise of Harvard's Du Bois Institute. LC 94-30202. (J). (gr. 1-8). 1995. write for info. (0-7910-3209-4) Chelsea Hse.
Rennert, Richard. Male Writers: Profiles of Great Black Americans. 1994. pap. 5.95 (0-7910-2062-2) Chelsea Hse.
— Pioneers of Discovery: Profiles of Great Black Americans. (J). 1994. pap. 5.95 (0-7910-2068-1) Chelsea Hse.
Rennert, Richard, ed. Book of Firsts: Leaders of America. LC 93-25878. (Profiles of Great Black Americans Ser.). (Illus.). (J). 1993. 13.95 (0-7910-2065-7, Am Art Analog); pap. write for info. (0-7910-2066-5, Am Art Analog) Chelsea Hse.
— Book of Firsts: Sports Heroes. LC 93-18437. (Profiles of Great Black Americans Ser.). (Illus.). (J). 1993. 13.95 (0-7910-2055-X, Am Art Analog); pap. 5.95 (0-7910-2056-8, Am Art Analog) Chelsea Hse.
— Civil Rights Leaders. LC 92-37655. (Profiles of Great Black Americans Ser.). (Illus.). (J). 1993. 13.95 (0-7910-2051-7, Am Art Analog); pap. 5.95 (0-7910-2052-5, Am Art Analog) Chelsea Hse.
— Female Leaders. (Profiles of Great Black Americans Ser.). (Illus.). 1993. 13.95 (0-7910-2057-6, Am Art Analog); pap. 5.95 (0-7910-2058-4, Am Art Analog) Chelsea Hse.
— Female Writers. LC 93-21673. (Profiles of Great Black Americans Ser.). (Illus.). (J). (gr. 6 up). 1993. 13.95 (0-7910-2063-0, Am Art Analog); pap. write for info. (0-7910-2064-9, Am Art Analog) Chelsea Hse.
— Jazz Stars. (Profiles of Great Black Americans Ser.). (Illus.). 1993. 13.95 (0-7910-2059-2, Am Art Analog); pap. 5.95 (0-7910-2060-6, Am Art Analog) Chelsea Hse.
— Male Writers. (Profiles of Great Black Americans Ser.). (Illus.). 1993. 13.95 (0-7910-2061-4, Am Art Analog) Chelsea Hse.
— Performing Artists. (Profiles of Great Black Americans Ser.). (Illus.). 1993. 13.95 (0-7910-2069-X, Am Art Analog); pap. write for info. (0-7910-2070-3, Am Art Analog) Chelsea Hse.
— Pioneers of Discovery. (Profiles of Great Black Americans Ser.). (Illus.). 1993. 13.95 (0-7910-2067-3, Am Art Analog) Chelsea Hse.
— Profiles of Great Black Americans, 10 vols., Set. (Illus.). 1993. write for info. (0-7910-2050-9, Am Art Analog) Chelsea Hse.
— Shapers of America. LC 92-39962. (Profiles of Great Black Americans Ser.). (J). 1993. 13.95 (0-7910-2053-3, Am Art Analog); pap. 5.95 (0-7910-2054-1, Am Art Analog) Chelsea Hse.
***Rennert, Richard S.** African American Answer Book, Arts & Entertainment: 325 Questions Drawn from the Expertise of Harvard's Du Bois Institute. LC 94-29999. (J). 1995. pap. write for info. (0-7910-3202-7) Chelsea Hse.
— African American Answer Book, Biography: Three Hundred Twenty-Five Questions Drawn from the Expertise of Harvard's Du Bois Institute. LC 94-30201. (J). 1995. write for info. (0-7910-3203-5) Chelsea Hse.
— African American Answer Book, Facts & Trivia: 325 Questions Drawn from the Experience of Harvard's Du Bois Institute. LC 94-30203. 1995. pap. write for info. (0-7910-3212-4) Chelsea Hse.
— Jesse Owens: Champion Athlete. (Junior Black Americans of Achievement Ser.). (Illus.). 80p. (J). (gr. 3-6). 1991. lib. bdg. 14.95 (0-7910-1570-X) Chelsea Hse.
— Julius Erving. (Black Americans of Achievement Ser.). (Illus.). (YA). (gr. 5 up). 1992. lib. bdg. 17.95 (0-7910-1125-9) Chelsea Hse.
***Rennert, Richard S., ed.** African American Answer Book, Facts & Trivia: 325 Questions Drawn from the Experience of Harvard's Du Bois Institute. LC 94-30203. (YA). (gr. 10 up). 1995. write for info. (0-7910-3211-6) Chelsea Hse.
Rennert, Rick. Jesse Owens: Champion Athlete. (Junior Black Americans of Achievement Ser.). (Illus.). 80p. (J). (gr. 3-6). 1992. pap. 4.95 (0-7910-1955-1) Chelsea Hse.
Renneville, ed. see Rimbaud, Arthur.
Rennhoff, Harley A. Get That Business Loan: Convince Your Banker to Say Yes. LC 87-2245. 160p. 1987. 14.95 (0-88289-602-4) Pelican.
Rennick, Penny, ed. Kuskokwim. (Alaska Geographic Ser.: Vol. 15, No. 4). (Illus.). 96p. (Orig.). 1989. pap. 17.95 (0-88240-187-4) Alaska Geog Soc.
***Rennick, Penny, et al, eds.** Aleutian Islands. (Alaska Geographic Ser.: Vol. 22, No. 2). (Illus.). 1995. pap. 19. 95 (1-56661-026-5) Alaska Geog Soc.
Rennick, Penny & Campbell, L. J. Alaska: The Great Land. (Alaska Geographic Ser.: Vol. 19, No. 2). (Illus.). 112p. 1992. pap. 18.95 (1-56661-002-8) Alaska Geog Soc.
***Rennick, Penny & Campbell, L. J., eds.** Fairbanks. (Alaska Geographic Ser.: Vol. 22, No. 1). (Illus.). 96p. 1995. pap. 19.95 (1-56661-025-7) Alaska Geog Soc.
— People of Alaska. (Alaska Geographic Ser.: Vol. 21, No. 3). (Illus.). 96p. 1994. pap. text ed. 19.95 (1-56661-022-2) Alaska Geog Soc.
Rennick, Penny, ed. see Alaska Geographic Society Staff.
Rennick, Penny, ed. see Alaska Geographic Staff.
Rennick, Penny, ed. see Alaska Geographic Staff & Campbell, L. J.
Rennick, Penny, ed. see Alaska Geographic Staff.
Rennick, Penny, jt. auth. see Campbell, L. J.
Rennick, Penny, jt. ed. see Campbell Staff, L. J.
Rennick, Penny, ed. see McDonald, Lucile.
***Rennick, Penny, et al.** World War II in Alaska. (Alaska Geographic Ser.: Vol. 22, No. 4). (Illus.). 96p. (Orig.). 1995. pap. 19.95 (1-56661-028-1) Alaska Geog Soc.
Rennick, Robert M. Kentucky Place Names. LC 87-31617. 400p. 1984. pap. 17.00 (0-8131-0179-4) U Pr of Ky.
Rennicke, Jeff. Colorado Mountain Ranges. LC 86-81754. (Colorado Geographic Ser.). (Illus.). 104p. 1986. 14.95 (0-934318-92-1); pap. 9.95 (0-934318-66-2) Falcon Pr MT.
— Colorado Wildlife. (Colorado Geographic Ser.). (Illus.). 160p. 1991. pap. 19.95 (1-56044-036-8) Falcon Pr MT.
— The Rivers of Colorado. LC 85-80606. (Illus.). 112p. (Orig.). 1985. 19.95 (0-934318-68-9); pap. 14.95 (0-934318-59-X) Falcon Pr MT.
— The Smoky Mountain Black Bear: Spirit of the Hills. Kemp, Steve, ed. (Illus.). 60p. (Orig.). 1991. pap. 7.95 (0-937207-04-7) GSMNH.
Rennicke, Jeff, ed. River Days: A Collection of Essays. LC 88-3821. (Illus.). 174p. 1988. 17.95 (1-55591-029-7) Fulcrum Pub.
Rennicke, Jeff & Simonson, Dorothy. Isle Royale: Moods, Magic & Mystique. (Illus.). 40p. (Orig.). 1989. pap. 7.95 (0-935289-01-1) Isle Royale Hist.
***Rennicke, Penny, et al, eds.** Mining in Alaska. (Alaska Geographic Ser.: Vol. 22, No. 3). (Illus.). 1995. pap. 19. 95 (1-56661-027-3) Alaska Geog Soc.
Rennie, A. R. & Oberthur, R. C. Practical Small Angle Neutron Scattering. 200p. 1993. 75.00 (0-85066-840-9) Taylor & Francis.
Rennie, A R., jt. ed. see Ottewill, R. H.
***Rennie, Bryan S.** Reconstructing Eliade: Making Sense of Religion. 320p. 1996. text ed. 59.50x (0-7914-2763-3); pap. 19.95x (0-7914-2764-1) State U NY Pr.
Rennie, Caroline & MacLean, Alair. Salvaging the Future: Waste-Based Production. LC 89-11209. (Illus.). 160p. 1989. pap. text ed. 20.00 (0-917582-37-3) Inst Local Self Re.
***Rennie, Cindy.** CC: Mail Administrator's Guide. 1995. 34. 99 (0-7821-1743-0) Sybex.
— CC: Mail Plain & Simple. LC 94-66853. 278p. 1994. pap. 16.99 (0-7821-1553-5) Sybex.
Rennie, David L., jt. auth. see Toukmanian, Shake G.
Rennie, Dorothy, jt. ed. see Isaacson, Martin.
Rennie, Dorothy A., jt. auth. see Isaacson, Martin J.
Rennie, Frank, jt. ed. see Bruce, George.
Rennie, Jeanne, jt. ed. see Holt, Daniel D.
Rennie, John C. Exportise: An International Trade Sourcebook for the Smaller Company Executive. 3rd ed. (Illus.). 260p. 1990. pap. text ed. 49.50 (0-912501-02-2) Small Bus Amer.
Rennie, John C., ed. Exportise: An International Trade Source Book for Smaller Company Executives. rev. ed. (Illus.). 237p. 1987. reprint ed. pap. 29.50 (0-912501-01-4) Small Bus Amer.
***Rennie, M. Michele.** Computer Contracts. 1994. disk, ring bd. 160.00 (0-421-49050-0) W W Gaunt.
***Rennie, Neil.** Far-Fetched Facts: The Literature of Travel & the Idea of the South Seas. 352p. 1995. 72.00 (0-19-811975-5) OUP.
Rennie, Robert, jt. auth. see Cusine, Douglas J.
Rennie, Susan, jt. auth. see Gearhart, Sally.
Rennie, William R., jt. ed. see Cruess, Richard L.
Rennie, Ysabel F. The Argentine Republic. LC 74-12767. (Illus.). 431p. 1975. reprint ed. text ed. 38.50 (0-8371-7739-1, REAR, Greenwood Pr) Greenwood.
Rennilson, Jay J. & Hale, W. N., Jr., eds. Review & Evaluation of Appearance: Method & Techniques, STP 914. LC 86-7999. (Special Technical Publication Ser.). (Illus.). 112p. 1986. text ed. 24.00 (0-8031-0480-4, 04-914000-36) ASTM.
Renninger, John P., ed. The Future Role of the United Nations in an Interdependent World. (C). 1990. lib. bdg. 102.00 (0-7923-0532-9) Kluwer Ac.
Renninger, K. Ann, jt. ed. see Cocking, Rodney R.
Renninger, K. Ann, et al, eds. The Role of Interest in Learning & Development. 368p. 1992. text ed. 69.95 (0-8058-0718-7) L Erlbaum Assocs.
Rennke, Helmut G., jt. auth. see Rose, Burton D.
Renny, Arnold J. Consumers' Data Book of Activities, Investigations, Satisfactions & Organizations: Index of New Information. 150p. 1994. 44.50 (0-7883-0130-6); pap. 39.50 (0-7883-0131-4) ABBE Pubs Assn.
Reno, Ben. If This Is Friday, It's English Muffins: or I Can't Stand Pubic Hair in the Bathtub. 1992. 12.95 (0-533-10135-2) Vantage.
Reno, Bill. Backlash. large type ed. (Nightingale Series Large Print Bks.). 295p. (Orig.). 1991. pap. 14.95 (0-8161-5172-5, Nightingale) Hall.
— The Black Coffin. large type ed. 304p. 1989. pap. 12.95 (0-8161-4778-7, Large Print Bks) Hall.
— Sundance. large type ed. LC 92-28127. (Nightingale Ser.). 336p. 1993. pap. 14.95 (0-8161-5630-1, Nightingale) Hall.
Reno, Carolyn. Almost...but Lost. pap. 0.25 (1-56632-013-5) Revival Lit.
Reno, Dawn. All That Glitters. 512p. 1993. mass mkt. 4.99 (1-55817-694-2, Pinnacle NY) Windsor NY.
***Reno, Dawn & Tiegs, Jacque.** Collecting Romance Novels. (Instant Expert Ser.). 120p. 1995. pap. 12.00 (0-9641509-5-6) Allian Pubng.
Reno, Dawn E. Advertising: Identification & Price Guide. 572p. (Orig.). 1993. pap. 15.00 (0-380-76884-4, Confident Collect) Avon.
— The Encyclopedia of Black Collectibles: A Value & Identification Guide. LC 95-11637. (Illus.). 328p. 1995. pap. 19.95 (0-87069-703-X, Wallace-Hmestead) Chilton.
— Native American Collectibles: Identification & Price Guide. 538p. (Orig.). 1994. pap. 17.00 (0-380-77069-5, Confident Collect) Avon.
Reno, Fred, jt. ed. see Burton, Richard D.
***Reno, Harley W., et al.** Pocket Guide to Lure Fishing for Trout in a Stream. (Illus.). 28p. 1995. spiral bd. 12.95 (1-886127-06-9) Greycliff Pub.
— Pocket Guide to Target - Field Archery. (Illus.). 28p. 1994. spiral bd. 12.95 (1-886127-01-8) Greycliff Pub.
— Pocket Guide to Walleye Fishing in Lakes. (Illus.). 28p. 1995. spiral bd. 12.95 (1-886127-08-5) Greycliff Pub.
Reno, J. Paul. Daniel Nash - Prevailing Prince of Prayer. 1989. pap. 1.99 (1-56632-089-5) Revival Lit.
— To Fight or Not to Fight. 1984. pap. 1.99 (1-56632-012-7) Revival Lit.
Reno, Jane W. The Hell with Politics: The Life & Writings of Jane Wood Reno. Hurchalla, George, ed. (Illus.). 192p. 1994. 18.95 (1-56145-092-8) Peachtree Pubs.
Reno, Janet. Ishmael Alone Survived. LC 89-45971. 176p. 1991. 32.50 (0-8387-5171-7) Bucknell U Pr.
***Reno, Liz & Devrais, Joanna.** Allergy-Free Eating. 400p. 1995. pap. 14.95 (0-89087-745-9) Celestial Arts.
Reno, Margarida F., et al. Spoken Portuguese, Bk. I. (ENG & POR.). 1978. audio 80.00 (0-87950-186-3); audio 70. 00 (0-87950-185-5) Spoken Lang Serv.
— Spoken Portuguese, Bk. I, Units 1-12. 218p. (ENG & POR.). 1978. Bk. I, units 1-12, 218 p. 10.00 (0-87950-180-4) Spoken Lang Serv.
— Spoken Portuguese, Bk. II, Units 13-30. 307p. (ENG & POR.). 1978. Bk. II, units 13-30, 307 p. 10.00 (0-87950-181-2) Spoken Lang Serv.
Reno, Ottie W. State of Ohio vs. Isaac Milton Smith, Murder. LC 90-55329. (Illus.). 376p. 1991. 24.95 (0-8453-4832-9, Cornwall Bks) Assoc Univ Prs.
Reno, R. R., jt. ed. see Radner, Ephraim.
***Reno, Robert C.** A Physics Review for the MCAT. 3rd ed. LC 94-73545. (Illus.). 116p. (Orig.). (C). 1995. pap. 17. 95 (0-916615-04-9) Bks of Sci.
— Radiation in Medicine. 2nd ed. LC 94-73544. (Illus.). 104p. (C). 1994. pap. text ed. 27.95 (0-916615-05-7) Bks of Sci.
Reno, Robert P. The Gothic Visions of Ann Radcliffe & Matthew G. Lewis. Varma, Devendra P., ed. LC 79-8473. (Gothic Studies & Dissertations). 1980. lib. bdg. 31.95 (0-405-12648-4) Ayer.
Reno, Ronald L. & McLane, Alvin R. Historic Archaeology of the Borealis Mine, Mineral County, Nevada. (Social Sciences Center Technical Report Ser.: No. 29). (Illus.). 102p. (C). 1987. spiral bd. 10.00 (0-945920-29-6) Desert Rsch Inst.
Reno, Ronald L. & Pippin, Lonnie C. An Archaeological Reconnaissance of the Groom Range, Lincoln County, Nevada. (Social Sciences Center Technical Report Ser.: No. 46). (Illus.). 270p. (Orig.). (C). 1986. pap. 25.00 (0-945920-46-6) Desert Rsch Inst.
— An Archaeological Reconnaissance of Yucca Flat, Nye County, Nevada. (Social Sciences Center Technical Report Ser.: No. 35). (Illus.). 211p. (Orig.). (C). 1985. pap. 20.00 (0-945920-35-0) Desert Rsch Inst.
— Archaeology of the Moody Dune Site, 26Ny4844, Tonopah Test Range, Nye County, Nevada. (Illus.). 30p. 1986. 2.50 (0-945920-48-2) Desert Rsch Inst.
Reno, Ronald L., jt. auth. see Ryan, Richard.
Reno, Ronald L., et al. Miscellaneous Data Recovery Studies at Yucca Mountain. (Illus.). 225p. 1989. 22.50 (0-945920-59-8) Desert Rsch Inst.
Reno, Russell R., Jr. & Simmons, Wilbur E. Maryland Real Estate Forms, 2 vols., Set. 900p. 1986. disk, ring bd. 229.00 (0-87189-281-2) Michie Butterworth.
***Reno, William.** Corruption & State Politics in Sierra Leone. (African Studies Ser.: 83). (Illus.). 228p. (C). 1995. write for info. (0-521-47179-6) Cambridge U Pr.
Renoir, Alain. A Key to Old Poems: Oral-Formulaic Rhetorical Context & the Interpretation of Traditional West-Germanic Poetry. LC 86-43040. 260p. 1988. 35.00 (0-271-00482-7) Pa St U Pr.
Renoir, Alain & Hernandez, Ann, eds. Approaches to Beowulfian Scansion: Four Essays by John Miles Foley, Winfred P. Lehmann, Robert Creed, & Dolores Warwick Frese. (Old English Colloquium Ser.: No. 1). 64p. 1985. reprint ed. pap. text ed. 15.00 (0-8191-4518-1) U Pr of Amer.
***Renoir, Jean.** Letters. Thompson, David & LoBianco, Lorraine, eds. (Illus.). 512p. 1995. 40.00 (0-571-17298-9) Faber & Faber.
— My Life & My Films. Denny, Norman, tr. (Quality Paperbacks Ser.). (Illus.). 287p. 1991. reprint ed. pap. 14. 95 (0-306-80457-3) Da Capo.
— Pierre-Auguste Renoir, Mon Pere. (FRE.). 1981. pap. 13. 95 (0-7859-4151-7) Fr & Eur.
— Renoir on Renoir. Volk, Carol, tr. (Cambridge Studies in Film). (Illus.). 421p. (C). 1990. pap. 17.95 (0-521-38593-8) Cambridge U Pr.
Renoir, Pierre A. Drawings of Renoir. Longstreet, Stephen, ed. (Master Draughtsman Ser.). (Illus.). (Orig.). 1965. 10.95 (0-87505-030-1); pap. 4.95 (0-87505-183-9) Borden.
Renoir, Pierre-Auguste. Renoir Lithographs: Thirty Two Works. LC 93-32998. 30p. 1993. pap. 3.95 (0-486-27884-0) Dover.
Renolds, Sallie, ed. see Mantis, Elizabeth M.
Renon, H., ed. Fluid Properties & Phase Equilibria for Chemical Process Design: Proceedings of the 4th International Conference, Helsingor, Denmark, May 11-16, 1986. 1000p. 1986. 318.00 (0-444-42724-4) Elsevier.
Renon, H., jt. auth. see Kehianian, H. V.
***Renorio, JoAnn M. & Nishida, Gordon M.** What's Bugging Me? Identifying & Controlling Household Pests in Hawaii. LC 95-10158. 1995. write for info. (0-8248-1742-7) UH Pr.
Renou. Vedic India. (C). pap. 19.95 (0-7007-0268-7, Pub. by Curzon Pr UK) Humanities.
Renou, Louis. Religions of Ancient India. 1972. 16.00 (0-8364-2614-2, Pub. by Munshiram Manoharial II) S Asia.
Renou, M., jt. ed. see Van Mens-Verhulst, Janneke.
Renou, Philippe. Dictionnaire du Diabetique. 320p. (FRE.). 1991. 79.95 (0-8288-9478-7) Fr & Eur.
Renouard, Antoine-Augustin. Annales de l'Imprimere des Alde, Ou Histoire des Trois Manuce et de Leurs Editions. 680p. (FRE.). 1991. reprint ed. 80.00 (0-938768-27-1) Oak Knoll.
Renouard, H. Fachworterbuch Neue Informationsdienste. 2nd enl. rev. ed. 400p. (ENG & GER.). 1993. 175.00 (0-7859-3719-6, F140270) Fr & Eur.
— Imprimeurs et Libraires Parisiens Du XVIe Siecle. Incl. Tome I. Abada Avril. 135.00 (0-685-35948-4); Tome II. Baaleu Banville. 165.00 (0-685-35949-2); write for info. (0-318-52031-1) Fr & Eur.
— Repertoire Des Imprimeurs Parisiens, Libraires, Foundeurs De Caracteres et Correcteurs De l'Imprimerie Depius l'Introduction De l'Imprimerie (1470) Jusqu'a la Fin Du Xvie Siecle. 61.95 (0-685-35952-2) Fr & Eur.
Renouf, Deane, ed. Behaviour of Pinnipeds. 424p. 1991. 130. 00 (0-412-30540-2, A4527) Chapman & Hall.
Renouf, Michael, jt. auth. see Norall, Christopher.
Renouf, Nicholas. Jean-Philippe Rameau, 1683-1764: A Tercentenary Tribute: An Exhibition of Instruments by French Makers, Contemporary Graphics, Printed Music & Books. 10p. (Orig.). 1983. pap. 1.50 (0-929530-03-9) Yale U Coll Musical Instruments.
— Musical Instruments in the Viennese Tradition, 1750-1850: An Exhibition of Instruments by Austrian Makers with Supplementary Exhibits of Contemporary Graphics, Printed Music & Books. (Illus.). 32p. (Orig.). 1981. pap. 4.00 (0-929530-02-0) Yale U Coll Musical Instruments.
— A Yankee Lyre: Musical Instruments by American Makers: An Exhibition of Instruments by 19th-Century American Makers with Supplementary Exhibits of Graphics, Books & Furniture. (Illus.). 62p. (Orig.). 1985. pap. 5.00 (0-929530-04-7) Yale U Coll Musical Instruments.
Renouf, Nicholas, jt. auth. see Rephann, Richard.
***Renouf, Norman.** Spain & Portugal by Rail. (Bradt Guides Ser.). (Illus.). 208p. 1994. 14.95 (1-56440-553-2) Globe Pequot.
Renouf, Peter L. Lectures on the Origin & Growth of Religion As Illustrated by the Religion of Ancient Egypt. 2nd ed. LC 77-27171. (Hibbert Lectures: 1879). reprint ed. 39.00 (0-404-60401-3) AMS Pr.
Renouil, Yves & Traversay, Yves de. Dictionnaire du Vin: Dictionary of Wine. (FRE.). 1962. 95.00 (0-8288-6809-3, M-6482) Fr & Eur.
Renouvin, Pierre. Forms of War Government in France. (Economic & Social History of the World War Ser.). 1927. 100.00 (0-685-69856-4) Elliots Bks.
— The Immediate Origins of the War. LC 68-9591. 1969. 49.50 (0-86527-101-1) Fertig.
Renov, M., jt. auth. see Gaines, J.
Renov, Michael. Hollywood's Wartime Woman: Representation & Ideology. LC 87-25546. (Studies in Cinema: No. 42). 285p. reprint ed. pap. 81.30 (0-8357-1813-1, 2070636) Bks Demand.
Renov, Michael, ed. Theorizing Documentary. (AFI Film Readers Ser.). 1992. 45.00 (0-415-90381-5, A5177, Routledge NY); pap. 14.95 (0-415-90382-3, A5181, Routledge NY) Routledge.
***Renov, Michael & Suderberg, Erika, eds.** Resolutions: Contemporary Video Practices. 512p. 1995. text ed. 59. 95 (0-8166-2327-9); pap. text ed. 21.95 (0-8166-2330-9) U of Minn Pr.
Renovare. Devotional Classics. LC 92-53912. 272p. 1993. pap. 15.00 (0-06-066966-7) Harper SF.
— Spiritual Formation Workbook. 96p. 1993. pap. 8.00 (0-06-066965-9) Harper SF.
Renowden, P., jt. auth. see Dixon, B. R.
Renquist, Thomas A. What Grace They Received: Worship Commemorations for 12 Ancient & Modern Saints. 1992. pap. 7.95 (1-55673-567-7, 9314) CSS OH.
Rensberger, Boyce. How the World Works: A Guide to Science's Greatest Discoveries. LC 86-33236. 384p. 1987. pap. 10.00 (0-688-07293-3, Quill) Morrow.
Rensberger, David. Johannine Faith & Liberating Community. LC 88-10052. 168p. 1988. pap. 16.99 (0-664-25041-6, Westminster) Westminster John Knox.
Rensberger, John M. Successions of Meniscomyine & Allomyine Rodents (Aplodontidae) in the Oligo-Miocene John Day Formation, Oregon. LC 83-1403. (Publications in Geological Sciences: Vol. 124). 176p. (C). 1983. pap. 27.50 (0-520-09668-1) U CA Pr.
***Rensberger, Susan.** A Multicultural Portrait of the Great Depression. (Perspectives Ser.). 80p. (J). (gr. 5-9). 1995. lib. bdg. write for info. (0-7614-0053-2, Benchmark NY) Marshall Cavendish.
Rensch, Bernhard. Biophilosophy. 1971. text ed. 55.00 (0-231-03299-4) Col U Pr.
— Biophilosophy. Sym, Cecilia, tr. LC 72-132692. 1971. 52. 50 (0-685-01146-1) Col U Pr.
— Homo Sapiens: From Man to DemiGod. LC 72-80482. (C). 1972. text ed. 49.00 (0-231-03683-3) Col U Pr.
Rensch, Calvin, jt. auth. see Oltrogge, David.

R

An Asterisk (*) at the beginning of an entry indicates that the title is appearing in BIP for the first time.

Rensch, Calvin R. An Etymological Dictionary of the Chinantec Languages: Studies in Chinantec Languages, Vol. 1. Merrifield, William R., ed. (Publications in Linguistics: No. 87). 140p. 1989. pap. 13.50 (0-88312-003-8); fiche 12.00 (0-88312-462-9) Summer Instit Ling.

Rensch, Calvin R., jt. ed. see Merrifield, William R.

Rensch, H. E. Historic Spots in California, 2 vols., Set. 1992. reprint ed. lib. bdg. 150.00 (0-7812-5077-3) Rprt Serv.

— Historic Spots in California: The Southern Counties, Vol. I. 1992. reprint ed. write for info. (0-318-69404-2) Rprt Serv.

— Historic Spots in California: Valley & Sierra Counties, Vol. II. 1992. reprint ed. write for info. (0-318-69405-0) Rprt Serv.

Rensch, Joseph R., ed. Papers of the Eighth International Conference on Liquefied Natural Gas: Los Angeles, U. S. A., June 15-19, 1986, 2 vols., Set. 768p. 1986. pap. 85.00 (0-910091-59-5) Inst Gas Tech.

Rensch, Roslyn. Harps & Harpists. LC 88-37609. (Illus.). 334p. 1989. 39.95 (0-253-34903-6) Ind U Pr.

Renschler, C. L., et al, eds. Novel Forms of Carbon. (Materials Research Society Symposium Proceedings Ser.: Vol. 270). 1992. text ed. 62.00 (1-55899-165-4) Materials Res.

— Novel Forms of Carbon: Materials Research Society Symposium Proceedings, Vol. 349, No. 2. 1994. text ed. 52.00 (1-55899-249-9) Materials Res.

Rensenbrink, John. The Greens & the Politics of Transformation. LC 90-92159. 305p. 1992. 22.95 (0-936810-21-1); pap. 14.95 (0-936810-20-3) R&E Miles.

— Poland Challenges a Divided World. LC 88-1393. 256p. 1988. text ed. 29.95 (0-8071-1446-4) La State U Pr.

Renshall, Michael & Walmsley, Keith, eds. Butterworths Company Law Guide. 2nd ed. 1990. U.K. pap. 47.00 (0-406-19702-4) Butterworth Legal Pubs.

Renshaw, Betty, jt. auth. see Hacker, Diana.

Renshaw, Betty B., et al. Values & Voices: A College Reader. 3rd ed. 372p. (C). 1986. pap. text ed. 20.75 (0-03-071039-1) HB Coll Pubs.

*Renshaw, Domeena. Seven Weeks to Better Sex. 1995. write for info. (0-615-00492-X) Random.

Renshaw, Domeena C. The Hyperactive Child. LC 73-86936. 304p. 1974. 25.95 (0-911012-76-1) Nelson-Hall.

— Incest: Understanding & Treatment. 1982. 38.95 (0-316-74031-4) Little.

— Seven Weeks to Better Sex. LC 94-18120. 1995. 22.00 (0-679-43546-8) Random.

Renshaw, Edward, ed. The Practical Forecasters' Almanac: 137 Reliable Indicators for Investors, Hedgers, & Speculators. 400p. 1992. 52.50 (1-55623-470-8) Irwin Prof Pubng.

Renshaw, Eric, ed. Modelling Biological Populations in Space & Time. (Cambridge Studies in Mathematical Biology: No. 11). 422p. (C). 1993. pap. 29.95 (0-521-44855-7) Cambridge U Pr.

Renshaw, G. T., ed. Market Liberalisation, Equity & Development. xiv, 181p. 1989. pap. 20.00 (92-2-106397-6) Intl Labour Office.

Renshaw, Geoffrey. Adjustment & Economic Performance in Industrialized Countries: A Synthesis. (Employment, Adjustment & Industrialization Ser.: No. 8). xiii, 110p. (Orig.). 1986. 32.00 (92-2-105509-4); pap. 24.00 (92-2-105510-8) Intl Labour Office.

Renshaw, Geoffrey, ed. Employment, Trade & North-South Co-Operation: (A WEP Study) xiv, 263p. (Orig.). 1981. pap. 22.00 (92-2-102531-4) Intl Labour Office.

Renshaw, Janet, jt. auth. see Lister, Ted.

Renshaw, Jeffrey H. The American Wind Symphony Commissioning Project: A Descriptive Catalog of Published Editions 1957-1991. LC 91-30220. (Music Reference Collection Ser.: No. 34). 408p. 1991. text ed. 65.00 (0-313-28146-7, RWY/, Greenwood Pr) Greenwood.

Renshaw, Joyce. Teaching Children to Read Art. Renshaw, Ken, ed. (Illus.). 115p. (Orig.). 1992. pap. 16.50 (0-9616620-8-5) Constellation Pr.

Renshaw, Joyce, jt. auth. see Renshaw, Ken.

*Renshaw, Ken & Renshaw, Joyce. Benefits of Brain-Based Art in Schools: A New Look at the Role of Art in Education. LC 94-21286. (Illus.). 115p. 1994. pap. 21.95 (0-614-04750-1) Constellation Pr.

Renshaw, Ken, ed. see Renshaw, Joyce.

Renshaw, Martin, jt. auth. see Barnes, Alan.

Renshaw, Patrick. American Labor & Consensus Capitalism, 1935-1990. LC 91-13034. 258p. 1992. text ed. 38.50 (0-87805-536-3); pap. text ed. 16.95 (0-87805-537-1) U Pr of Miss.

Renshaw, Paul. Marketing Plan Development Guide. (C). 1994. pap. text ed. 17.00 (0-13-037755-4) P-H.

Renshaw, Polly & Levens, Ann. Teacher's Guide for Uncle Noel's Fun Fables. (Illus.). 52p. 1991. student ed 5.95 (0-9630734-1-9) Aesop Systs.

Renshaw, R., jt. auth. see Lister, L.

Renshaw, Samuel, et al. Children's Sleep: A Series of Studies on the Influence of Motion Pictures. LC 76-124031. (Literature of Cinema Ser.). 1970. reprint ed. 21.95 (0-405-01631-X) Ayer.

Renshaw, Thomas S. Pediatric Orthopaedics. (Major Problems in Clinical Pediatrics Ser.). (Illus.). 3277p. 1986. text ed. 44.95 (0-7216-1179-6) Saunders.

Renshaw, Vernon, et al. Nebraska Population Projections: State, County, Region & Town 1975-2020. 232p. (Orig.). 1973. pap. 14.00 (1-55719-111-5) U NE CPAR.

*Renshon, Stanley A. The Clinton Presidency: Campaigning, Governing & the Psychology of Leadership. LC 94-27952. (C). 1994. pap. text ed. 19.95 (0-8133-1977-3) Westview.

— The Clinton Presidency: Campaigning, Governing & the Psychology of Leadership. LC 94-27952. (C). 1994. text ed. 64.95 (0-8133-1976-5) Westview.

— The Political Psychology of the Gulf War: Leaders, Publics, & the Process of Conflict. LC 92-34182. (Series in Policy & Institutional Studies). 408p. (C). 1993. text ed. 49.95 (0-8229-3744-1); pap. text ed. 16.95 (0-8229-5495-8) U of Pittsburgh Pr.

— The Psychological Assessment of Presidential Candidates. 400p. 1996. 34.95 (0-8147-7469-5) NYU Pr.

— Psychological Needs & Political Behavior: A Theory of Personality & Political Efficacy. LC 73-11735. 1974. pap. 22.95 (0-02-926320-4) Free Pr.

Rensi, Ray C. & Williams, H. David. Gold Fever: America's First Gold Rush. (Georgia Humanities Council Publications). (Illus.). 54p. 1988. pap. 9.95 (0-8203-1314-9) U of Ga Pr.

Rensin, David. Bob Book. 1991. mass mkt. 8.99 (0-440-50312-4) Dell.

Rensing, L. & Jaeger, N. I., eds. Temporal Order. (Synergetics Ser.: Vol. 29). (Illus.). ix, 325p. 1985. 73.00 (0-387-15274-1) Spr-Verlag.

Rensing, L. & Mackey, M. C., eds. Temporal Disorder in Human Oscillatory Systems. (Synergetics Ser.: Vol. 36). (Illus.). 270p. 1987. 70.00 (0-387-17765-5) Spr-Verlag.

Rensing, Ludger, ed. Oscillations & Morphogenesis. LC 92-29094. (Cellular Clocks Ser.: Vol. 5). 520p. 1992. 175.00 (0-8247-8765-X) Dekker.

Renske, C. Ek. Flora of the Guianas: Supplementary Series: Index of Guyana Plant Collectors, Fascicle 1. Gorts Van Rijn, A. R., ed. (Illus.). 85p. 1990. pap. text ed. 50.00 (1-878762-02-8) Koeltz Sci Bks.

— Flora of the Guianas: Supplementary Series: Index of Suriname Plant Collectors, Fascicle 2. Gorts Van Rijn, A. R., ed. (Illus.). 97p. 1991. pap. text ed. 50.00 (1-878762-26-5, 046325) Koeltz Sci Bks.

Renson, C. E. Oral Disease. (Illus.). 1980. lib. bdg. 32.00 (0-906141-04-4) Kluwer Ac.

Renstrom, Mary. Legislative Television Programming in the States. (State Legislative Reports: Vol. 17, No. 13). 16p. 1992. pap. text ed. 5.00 (1-55516-284-3, 7302-1713) Natl Conf State Legis.

— Public Information & Media Relations in State Legislatures. (State Legislative Reports: Vol. 17, No. 22). 29p. 1992. pap. text ed. 5.00 (1-55516-295-9, 7302-1722) Natl Conf State Legis.

Renstrom, Per A., ed. Clinical Practice of Sports Injury Prevention & Care. 2nd ed. LC 93-39208. (Encyclopedia of Sports Medicine Ser.: Vol. V). (Illus.). 748p. 1993. text ed. 79.00x (0-632-03785-7, BREN3785) Blackwell Sci.

— Sports Injuries: Basic Principles of Prevention & Care. 2nd ed. (Encyclopedia of Sports Medicine Ser.: Vol. IV). (Illus.). 504p. 1993. text ed. 59.00x (0-632-03331-2, BREN3331) Blackwell Sci.

Renstrom, Peter G. The American Law Dictionary. (Clio Dictionaries in Political Science Ser.). 308p. 1990. lib. bdg. 52.00 (0-87436-226-1) ABC-CLIO.

— Constitutional Law for Young Adults: A Handbook on the Bill of Rights & the Fourteenth Amendment. 413p. 1992. lib. bdg. 35.00 (0-87436-483-3) ABC-CLIO.

Renstrom, Peter G. & Rogers, Chester B. Electoral Politics Dictionary. 350p. 1989. lib. bdg. 49.50 (0-87436-517-1); pap. text ed. 20.50 (0-87436-518-X) ABC-CLIO.

Renstrom, Richard. Motorcycle Milestones, Vol. 1. LC 80-66669. (Illus.). 112p. 1980. 20.00 (0-936660-00-7) Classics Unltd.

*Rensvold, Sandy. A Ride on the Historical Virginia V. (J). (gr. 2-3). 1995. pap. text ed. 7.95 (0-9647088-0-9) Keeper Bks.

Rentel, Victor, et al. Psychophysiological Aspects of Reading & Learning. (Monographs in Psychobiology). 390p. 1985. text ed. 108.00 (2-88124-000-3); pap. text ed. 51.00 (2-88124-025-9) Gordon & Breach.

Rentell, Phili. Historic P & O - Orient Liners. (Illus.). 48p. 1990. 15.95 (0-946184-56-9, Kingfisher Pubns) Hallenbook.

Rentell, Philip. Historic White Star Liners. 48p. 1987. 15.95 (0-9512313-0-8, Pub. by Blue Water Pubns UK) Hallenbook.

Renteln, Alison D. International Human Rights: Universalism vs. Relativism. (Frontiers of Anthropology Ser.: Vol. 6). 208p. (C). 1990. text ed. 49.95 (0-8039-3505-6); pap. text ed. 24.00 (0-8039-3506-4) Sage.

Renteln, Alison D. & Dundes, Alan, eds. Folk Law: Essays in the Theory & Practice of Lex Non Scripta. LC 93-29340. (Reference Library of the Humanities: Vol. 1715). 1072p. 1994. 150.00 (0-8153-1314-4, H1715) Garland.

— Folk Law: Essays in the Theory & Practice of Lex Non Scripta. LC 94-812. 1994. pap. write for info. (0-299-14344-9) U of Wis Pr.

*Renteros, Exora. Pensar Es un Pecado. LC 93-74793. (Coleccion Caniqui). 198p. 1994. pap. 16.00 (0-89729-720-2) Ediciones.

Rentmeister, Jean. Marriage & Death Notices Extracted from the Genius of Liberty & Fayette Advertiser of Uniontown, Pa., 1805-1854. 52p. (Orig.). per. 8.50 (0-933227-41-8) Closson Pr.

Renton. Orthopedic Radiology: Pattern Recognition-Differential Diagnosis. 392p. 1989. 69.95 (0-8151-7231-1, Yr Bk Med Pubs) Mosby Yr Bk.

Renton, Alexander W., ed. see Burge, William.

Renton, Andrew. Technique Anglaise: Current Trends in British Art. LC 91-65285. (Illus.). 224p. (Orig.). 1991. pap. 19.95 (0-500-97396-2) Thames Hudson.

Renton, B. Andrew. Psyched on Bikes: The Bicycle Owner's Handbook. 184p. 1992. pap. 14.95 (0-8306-1987-9, 3668) TAB Bks.

Renton, Bruce A. Psyched on Bikes: The Bicycle Owner's Handbook. 1992. pap. 14.95 (0-07-052510-2) McGraw.

Renton, Jeanne, jt. auth. see Eble, Mary M.

Renton, Jeanne L., jt. auth. see Eble, Mary M.

Renton, John. Physical Geology. Pullins, ed. LC 93-11457. 500p. (C). 1994. pap. text ed. 44.50 (0-314-02514-6) West Pub.

Renton, N. E. Guide for Meetings. 5th ed. xxiii, 225p. 1990. pap. 19.50 (0-455-21004-7, Pub. by Law Bk Co) W W Gaunt.

— Guide for Voluntary Associations. 5th ed. xix, 237p. 1991. pap. 19.50 (0-455-21001-2, Pub. by Law Bk Co) W W Gaunt.

— Metaphorically Speaking: A Dictionary of 3,800 Picturesque Idiomatic Expressions. 1992. reprint ed. pap. 10.99 (0-446-39353-3) Warner Bks.

Renton, P. B. Electroweak Interactions. (Illus.). 480p. (C). 1990. pap. 47.95 (0-521-36692-5) Cambridge U Pr.

Renton, R., jt. auth. see MacDonald, J.

Renton, R. W. & MacDonald, J. A. Scottish Gaelic-English English-Scottish Gaelic Dictionary. 162p. (Orig.). 1994. pap. 8.95 (0-7818-0316-0) Hippocrene Bks.

*Rentoul, Annie R. Elves & Fairies. (Illus.). 74p. 1995. 16.95 (0-85091-543-0, Pub. by Lothian Pub AT) Seven Hills Bk.

Rentoul, J. N. Expanding Your Orchid Collection. 1990. pap. 34.95 (0-85091-364-0, Pub. by Lothian Pub AT) Intl Spec Bk.

— Growing Orchids: The Hybrid Story. (Growing Orchids Ser.). (Illus.). 200p. (Orig.). 1991. pap. 24.95 (0-88192-210-2) Timber.

— Growing Orchids: The Specialist Orchid Grower. (Growing Orchids Ser.). (Illus.). 208p. 1987. 34.95 (0-88192-085-1) Timber.

— Growing Orchids IV: The Australasian Families. (Growing Orchids Ser.). (Illus.). 224p. 1985. pap. 22.95 (0-88192-021-5) Timber.

*Rentoul, Jim. The Specialist Orchid Grower. (Illus.). 220p. (Orig.). 1995. pap. 24.95 (0-85091-280-6, Pub. by Lothian Pub AT) Seven Hills Bk.

Rentoul, Robert, jt. ed. see Dryden, Wendy.

Rentschler, Bill. Live Each New Day. 1991. pap. 8.95 (0-913617-14-8) Highlander Pr.

Rentschler, Bill, jt. auth. see Hale, Jon M.

Rentschler, Eric, ed. The Films of G. W. Pabst. (Films in Print Ser.). (Illus.). 350p. (C). 1990. text ed. 45.00 (0-8135-1533-5); pap. 17.95 (0-8135-1534-3) Rutgers U Pr.

— German Film & Literature: Adaptations & Transformations. (Illus.). 384p. 1986. lib. bdg. 45.00 (0-416-60331-9, 9885); pap. text ed. 18.95 (0-416-60341-6, 9866) Routledge Chapman & Hall.

— West German Filmmakers on Film: Visions & Voices. LC 87-14856. (Modern German Voices Ser.). 300p. 1988. 49.00 (0-8419-0984-9); pap. 22.50 (0-8419-0985-7) Holmes & Meier.

Rentschler, I. & Epstein, D. Beauty & the Brain. 250p. 1988. 69.00 (0-8176-1924-0) Birkhauser.

Rentschler, L. A. Jitters. 288p. 1994. pap. 12.95 (0-9640583-0-8) White Willow.

Renty, Ivan de. Lexique Quadrilingue Des Affaires. 702p. (ENG, FRE, GER & SPA.). 1977. 59.95 (0-8288-5497-1, M6483) Fr & Eur.

Rentz, Audrey L., ed. Student Affairs: A Profession's Heritage. 2nd ed. LC 94-19521. 718p. (C). 1995. pap. text ed. 44.50 (1-883485-06-1) Am Coll Personnel.

— Student Affairs: A Profession's Heritage. 28th ed. LC 94-19521. 718p. (C). 1995. lib. bdg. 61.00 (1-883485-05-3) Am Coll Personnel.

Rentz, Audrey L. & Saddlemire, Gerald L., eds. Student Affairs Functions in Higher Education. (Illus.). 344p. (C). 1988. pap. 44.95x (0-398-05480-0) C C Thomas.

Rentz, D. C. A Monograph of the Tettigoniidae of Australia, Vol. 1: The Tettigoniidae, with an Appendix by D. H. Colles. (Illus.). 384p. 1985. lib. bdg. 70.00 (0-685-25035-0) Lubrecht & Cramer.

— The Tettigoniidae, Vol. 1. 384p. 1985. text ed. 80.00 (0-643-03839-6, Pub. by CSIRO AT) Intl Spec Bk.

— Tettigoniidae of Australia, Vol. 2: The Austrosaginae, Zaprochilinae & Phasmodinae. (Illus.). 386p. 1993. text ed. 80.00 (0-643-05424-3, Pub. by CSIRO AT) Intl Spec Bk.

Rentz, David C. & Weissman, David B. Faunal Affinities, Systematics, & Bionomics of the Orthoptera of the California Channel Islands. LC 80-26399. (University of California Publications in Social Welfare: No. 94). (Illus.). 254p. reprint ed. pap. 72.40 (0-685-24000-2, 2031585) Bks Demand.

Rentz, John N. Bougainville & the Northern Solomons. (Elite Unit Ser.: No. 22). (Illus.). 166p. reprint ed. 32.50 (0-89839-137-7) Battery Pr.

— Marines in the Central Solomons. (Elite Unit Ser.: No. 24). (Illus.). 216p. 1989. reprint ed. 32.50 (0-89839-143-1) Battery Pr.

Rentz, Mark D. The Reader's Journal: Authentic Reading for Writers. 208p. (C). 1992. pap. text ed. 16.95 (0-13-755273-4) P-H.

Rentz, William F., jt. auth. see Kahl, Alfred L.

*Rentzch, H. German & English Electric Motor Handbook. (ENG & GER.). 1992. 85.00 (0-7859-8899-8) Fr & Eur.

Rentzel, Lori, jt. auth. see Davies, Bob.

Rentzepis, Peter M. & Capellos, Christos, eds. Advances in Chemical Reaction Dynamics. 1986. lib. bdg. 172.50 (90-277-2312-5) Kluwer Ac.

Rentzsch, H. German & English Electric Motor Handbook. 861p. 1992. 85.00 (3-590-80853-5, Pub. by Cornelsen) IBD Ltd.

Rentzsch, S. B. Electronics Terms: German & English. 861p. (GER.). 1992. 49.95 (0-8288-1377-9, M15121) Fr & Eur.

Renu, Ma, ed. see Dass, Baba Hari.

Renu, Phanishwar N. The Third Vow & Other Stories. Hansen, Kathryn, tr. 1986. 18.50 (81-7001-013-6, Pub. by Chanakya II) S Asia.

Renvoize, Jean. Incest: A Family Pattern. 224p. 1985. pap. 11.95 (0-7102-0681-X, RKP) Routledge.

— Innocence Destroyed: A Study of Child Sexual Abuse. LC 92-49994. 256p. 1993. 49.95 (0-415-06283-7, B0228, Routledge NY); pap. 15.95 (0-415-06284-5, B0232, Routledge NY) Routledge.

Renvoize, S. A., jt. auth. see Clayton, W. D.

Renwei, Zhao, jt. ed. see Griffin, Keith.

Renwick, A. & Swinburn, I. Basic Political Concepts. (C). 1987. 60.00 (0-09-170771-4, Pub. by S Thornes Pubs UK) St Mut.

*Renwick, Alan & Swinburn, Ian. Basic Political Concepts. 172p. (C). 1987. pap. 40.00x (0-7487-0394-2, Pub. by S Thornes Pubs UK) St Mut.

Renwick, David A. Paul, the Temple, & the Presence of God. 179p. 1991. 54.95 (1-55540-615-7) Scholars Pr GA.

Renwick, E. S. Thermostatic Incubator: Raising Chickens by Hand. 98p. 1883. pap. 25.00 (0-87556-756-8) Saifer.

Renwick, Ethel H. Real Food Cookbook. 2nd ed. LC 83-48080. 272p. 1983. reprint ed. pap. 4.95 (0-87983-346-7) Keats.

Renwick, George. A Fair Go for All: A Guide for Australians & Americans. LC 91-9628. (InterAct Ser.). 96p. (Orig.). 1991. pap. text ed. 11.95 (0-933662-96-3) Intercult Pr.

*Renwick, George, et al. Managing in Malaysia: Cultural Insights & Practical Guidelines for Americas. 108p. 1996. write for info. (1-877864-27-7) Intercult Pr.

Renwick, James. Life of David Rittenhouse. 1993. reprint ed. lib. bdg. 89.00 (0-7812-5822-7) Rprt Serv.

Renwick, John. Rhetoric & the Revolution. 160p. 1989. 35.00 (0-7486-0122-8, Pub. by Edinburgh U Pr UK) Col U Pr.

*Renwick, Neil. Japan's Alliance Politics & Defense Production. LC 95-577. 1995. write for info. (0-312-12675-1) St Martin.

Renwick, W. H., jt. ed. see Phillips, J. D.

Renwick, W. L. Burns As Others Saw Him. 52p. 1982. 30.00 (0-686-87372-6, 085411015, Pub. by Saltire Soc) St Mut.

Renwick, W. L., ed. see Spenser, Edmund.

*Renwick, W. M. The Accounting Equation. 1991. pap. 21.00 (0-409-49283-3, Austral) Butterworth Legal Pubs.

*Renwick, William. Analyzing Fugue: A Schenkerian Approach. LC 94-47622. (Harmonologia Ser.: No. 8). 1995. 54.00 (0-945193-52-1) Pendragon NY.

*Renwick, William H. & Rubenstein, James M. People, Places, & Environment: An Introduction to Geography. LC 94-25277. 1995. pap. text ed. write for info. (0-02-399311-1) P-H.

Renwick, William L. The Beginnings of English Literature to Skelton, Fifteen Nine. 1988. reprint ed. lib. bdg. 69.00 (0-7812-0190-X) Rprt Serv.

— Edmund Spenser: An Essay on Renaissance Poetry. (BCL1-PR English Literature Ser.). 198p. 1992. reprint ed. lib. bdg. 69.00 (0-7812-7228-9) Rprt Serv.

Renyi, A. A Diary of Information Theory. 192p. 1984. 150.00 (0-569-08839-9, Pub. by Collets UK) Pro-Am Music.

Renyi, Alfred. Dialoge Uber Mathematik. (Science & Civilization Ser.: No. 22). 123p. (GER.). 1980. 27.50 (0-8176-0308-5) Birkhauser.

— Foundations of Probability. LC 72-105221. 366p. 1970. 44.00 (0-8162-7114-3) Holden-Day.

— Tagebuch ueber die Informationstheorie. (Wissenschaft und Kultur Ser.: No. 34). 174p. 1980. 33.00 (0-8176-1006-5) Birkhauser.

Renyi, Judith. Going Public: Schooling for a Diverse Democracy. LC 92-56918. 304p. 1993. 25.00 (1-56584-083-6, Norton) New Press NY.

Renyi, Pierre & Amrouni, D. English - French Dictionary of Electronics & Electrical Engineering: Dictionnaire Anglais-Francais De l'Electronique et De l'Electrotechnique. 1122p. (ENG & FRE.). 1986. 125.00 (0-8288-0282-3, F12765) Fr & Eur.

*Renyi, Pierre & Amrouni, Dominique. Dictionary of Electronics & Electrical Engineering. (Illus.). 1130p. 1986. text ed. 143.00 (0-921137-01-X) Technip.

*Renyi-Vamos, F. & Balogh, F. Pyelonephritis. 190p. (C). 1979. 50.00x (963-05-1724-8) St Mut.

— Titles from the Hungarian Academy of Sciences. 1981. 65.00 (0-569-08544-6, Pub. by Collets UK) Pro-Am Music.

Renyong, Wu, et al, eds. Directory of Chinese Libraries. (World Books Reference Guide: No. 3). 500p. (CHI & ENG.). 1982. 84.00 (0-8103-4354-1) Gale.

*Renz, C. J., ed. Ruah 1995, Vol. 5. 28p. 1995. write for info. (1-883734-06-1) Power of Poetry.

Renz, Chris, ed. Ruah, 1993, Vol. 3. 44p. 1993. pap. 7.00 (1-883734-04-5) Power of Poetry.

*Renz, Loren, ed. Foundation Giving: Yearbook of Facts & Figures on Private, Corporate & Community Foundations. 1994. pap. text ed. 24.95 (0-87954-554-2) Foundation Ctr.

Renz, Loren, ed. see Foundation Center Staff.

Renz, Loren, ed. see Greenberg, Barbara R., et al.

Renz, Loren, ed. see Jacobs, Nancy F. & Sommers, Ira B.

Renz, Mary Anne, jt. auth. see Boyd, Stephen D.

Renz, Michael E. Practical Groundwater Hydrology. 1995. write for info. (0-87371-643-4) Lewis Pubs.

Renza, Louis A. A "White Heron" & the Question of Minor Literature. LC 84-40157. (Wisconsin Project on American Writers Ser.: No. 1). 256p. 1984. text ed. 25.00x (0-299-09960-1) U of Wis Pr.

— White Heron & the Question of Minor Literature. LC 84-40157. (Wisconsin Project on American Writers Ser.: No. 1). 256p. 1985. pap. text ed. 12.95 (0-299-09964-4) U of Wis Pr.

Renzetti, Claire, jt. ed. see Hamberger, L. Kevin.

Renzetti, Claire M. Violent Betrayal: Partner Abuse in Lesbian Relationships. 168p. (C). 1992. text ed. 52.00 (*0-8039-3888-8*); pap. text ed. 24.00 (*0-8039-3889-6*) Sage.

***Renzetti, Claire M. & Curran, Daniel J.** Women, Men & Society. 3rd ed. LC 94-31685. (LSMS Working Paper Ser.). 1994. pap. text ed. write for info. (*0-205-15619-3*) Allyn.

— Women, Men, & Society: The Sociology of Gender. 400p. 1989. pap. text ed. write for info. (*0-205-11898-4*, H18989); write for info. (*0-318-63896-7*, H24987) Allyn.

Renzetti, Claire M. & Lee, Raymond M. Researching Sensitive Topics. (Focus Editions Ser.: Vol. 152). (Illus.). 312p. (C). 1992. 49.95 (*0-8039-4844-1*); pap. 24.95 (*0-8039-4845-X*) Sage.

Renzetti, Claire M., jt. auth. see Curran, Daniel J.

Renzetti, Claire M., jt. ed. see Curran, Daniel J.

Renzglia, Karen S. Comparative Developmental Investigation of the Gametophyte Generation in the Metzgeriales (Hepatophyta) (Bryophytorum Bibliotheca Ser.: Vol. 24). (Illus.). 253p. (Orig.). 1982. text ed. 84.00 (*3-7682-1336-6*) Lubrecht & Cramer.

Renzi, Thomas C. H. G. Wells: Six Scientific Romances Adapted for Film. LC 92-19038. (Illus.). 249p. 1992. 29. 50 (*0-8108-2549-X*) Scarecrow.

Renzi, William A. & Roehrs, Mark D. Never Look Back: A History of World War II in the Pacific. LC 90-25884. 240p. 1991. 30.95 (*0-87332-808-6*) M E Sharpe.

Renzini, Alvio. Physical Processes in Red Giants. Iben, Icko, Jr., ed. xviii, 488p. 1981. lib. bdg. 117.00 (*90-277-1284-0*) Kluwer Ac.

Renzini, Alvio, jt. ed. see Chiosi, Cesare.

Renzini, Alvio, jt. ed. see Kron, Richard G.

Renzini, Alvio, jt. ed. see Maeder, Andre.

Renzo, D. J., ed. Ceramic Raw Materials. LC 87-22002. (Illus.). 890p. 1988. 96.00 (*0-8155-1143-4*) Noyes.

Renzo, Peter. Beyond the Gemstone Files. 1991. pap. 7.95 (*0-533-09097-0*) Vantage.

Renzoni, Aristeo, ed. see Fossi.

Renzoni, Tommy. Baccarat: Everything You Want to Know About Playing & Winning. abr. ed. 1977. reprint ed. pap. 4.95 (*0-8065-0603-2*, Citadel Pr) Carol Pub Group.

Renzsetti, Claire M., jt. auth. see Curran, Daniel J.

Renzulli, Joseph S. Action Information Message, Set. 1981. pap. 24.95 (*0-936386-27-4*) Creative Learning.

— The Enrichment Triad Model: A Guide for Developing Defensible Programs for the Gifted & Talented. (Illus.). 89p. 1977. pap. 9.95 (*0-936386-01-0*) Creative Learning.

— The Interest-A-Lyzer. 1977. pap. 28.95 (*0-936386-28-2*) Creative Learning.

— New Directions in Creativity-Mark 1. 1986. pap. 34.95 (*0-936386-40-1*) Creative Learning.

— New Directions in Creativity-Mark 2. 1986. pap. 34.95 (*0-936386-41-X*) Creative Learning.

— Schools for Talent Development: A Practical Plan for Total School Improvement. 1994. pap. 39.95 (*0-936386-65-7*) Creative Learning.

— Secondary Action Information Message, Set. 1987. pap. 24.95 (*0-936386-48-7*) Creative Learning.

Renzulli, Joseph S., ed. Systems & Models for Developing Programs for the Gifted & Talented. 1986. pap. text ed. 38.95 (*0-936386-44-4*) Creative Learning.

Renzulli, Joseph S. & Callahan, C. M. New Directions in Creativity-Mark 3. 1986. pap. 34.95 (*0-936386-42-8*) Creative Learning.

Renzulli, Joseph S. & Reis, Sally M. The Complete Triad Trainer's Inservice Manual. 140p. 1990. pap. 22.95 (*0-936386-57-6*) Creative Learning.

— The Schoolwide Enrichment Model: A Comprehensive Plan for Educational Excellence. 522p. (Orig.). 1985. pap. 42.95 (*0-936386-34-7*) Creative Learning.

Renzulli, Joseph S. & Reis, Sally M., eds. The Triad Reader. 218p. 1986. pap. 22.95 (*0-936386-35-5*) Creative Learning.

Renzulli, Joseph S. & Smith, Linda H. The Compactor, Set. 1978. pap. 19.95 (*0-936386-25-8*) Creative Learning.

— A Guidebook for Developing Individualized Educational Programs for Gifted & Talented Students. 51p. 1979. pap. 12.95 (*0-936386-13-4*) Creative Learning.

— Learning Styles Inventory: A Measure of Student Preference for Instructional Techniques. 1978. pap. 8.95 (*0-936386-14-2*) Creative Learning.

— The Strength-A-Lyzer. 1978. pap. 22.95 (*0-936386-24-X*) Creative Learning.

Renzulli, Joseph S., jt. ed. see Barbe, Walter B.

Renzulli, Joseph S., jt. auth. see Reis, Sally M.

Renzulli, Joseph S., et al. The Revolving Door Identification Model. (C). 1981. pap. 22.95 (*0-936386-16-9*) Creative Learning.

— Scales for Rating Behavioral Characteristics of Superior Students. 1977. pap. 8.95 (*0-936386-00-2*) Creative Learning.

Renzulli, L. Marx. Maryland: The Federalist Years. LC 70-149405. 354p. 1975. 39.50 (*0-8386-7903-X*) Fairleigh Dickinson.

Renzulli, M. J., et al. New Directions in Creativity-Mark A. 1986. pap. 34.95 (*0-936386-38-X*) Creative Learning.

Reo, Vincent. Finding Hot Horses. 135p. 1993. pap. 12.00 (*0-929387-96-1*) Bonus Books.

Reo, Vincent M. Workouts & Maidens. 200p. 1994. pap. 11. 95 (*1-56625-000-5*) Bonus Books.

Reohr, Janet R. Friendship: An Exploration of Structure & Process. LC 91-19930. 152p. 1991. 20.00 (*0-8240-7242-1*, SS431) Garland.

***Reorganized Church of Jesus Christ of Latter Day Saints, Board of Publication Staff.** Couples Who Care: An Essay to Use Resource to Create a Premarital Discussion Process for Engaged Couples in Your Congregation. LC 94-45060. 1994. 10.00 (*0-8309-0699-1*) Herald Hse.

Reouven, Rene. Diccionario de los Asesinos. 386p. (SPA.). 1976. pap. 24.95 (*0-8288-5595-1*, S50083) Fr & Eur.

— Dictionnaire des Assassins. rev. ed. 429p. (FRE.). 1986. 85.00 (*0-7859-4844-9*) Fr & Eur.

Repa, Barbara K. Your Rights in the Workplace. 2nd ed. 352p. 1993. pap. 15.95 (*0-87337-200-X*) Nolo Pr.

Repa, Barbara K., ed. see Lewis, Loida N. & Madlansacay, Len T.

Repa, Barbara K., jt. auth. see Petrocelli, William.

Repa, Barbara K., et al. Nolo's Law Form Kit: Hiring Child Care & Household Help. 1993. pap. 14.95 (*0-87337-229-8*) Nolo Pr.

Repacholi, M. H., et al, eds. Ultrasound: Medical Applications, Biological Effects, & Hazard Potential. 386p. 1987. 89.50 (*0-306-42411-8*, Plenum Pr) Plenum.

Repacholi, Michael H. & Benwell, Deirdre A., eds. Essentials of Medical Ultrasound. LC 80-85522. (Medical Methods Ser.). (Illus.). 352p. 1982. 89.50 (*0-89603-028-8*) Humana.

***Repak, Terry A.** Waiting on Washington: Central American Workers in the Nation's Capital. (Illus.). 240p. (Orig.). (C). 1995. lib. bdg. 49.95 (*1-56639-301-9*); pap. text ed. 16.95 (*1-56639-302-7*) Temple U Pr.

Repas, Bob. Contract Administration: A Guide for Stewards & Local Officers. LC 84-9857. 266p. 1984. pap. text ed. 28.00 (*0-87179-434-9*, 0434) BNA.

Repasky, Michael G. The Elite Corps. 1988. 7.95 (*0-685-21989-5*) Beatty.

Repass, Craig. Custer for President? LC 85-61362. (Source Custeriana Ser.: No. 12). (Illus.). 1985. 37.50 (*0-88342-064-3*) Old Army.

Repath, Ann, ed. see Schweitzer, Albert.

Repath, Austin. The Waterbearer. 208p. (Orig.). 1994. pap. 12.95 (*0-9697399-0-7*) Reed Pr.

***Repath, Derek J.** Fleur de Lis. LC 95-60770. 40p. 1996. 5.95 (*1-55523-745-2*) Winston-Derek.

***Repchuk, Caroline.** The Glitter Dragon. (Illus.). 32p. (J). 1995. 14.95 (*1-56924-838-9*) Marlowe & Co.

***Repenning, Charles A., et al.** Early Pleistocene (Latest Blancan-Earliest Irvingtonian) Froman Ferry Fauna & History of the Glenns Ferry Formation, Southwestern Idaho. (U. S. Geological Survey Bulletin Ser.: Vol. 2105). 1995. write for info. (*0-615-00199-8*) US Geol Survey.

Reperant, Dominique, photos. The Most Beautiful Villages of France. LC 90-70389. (Illus.). 220p. 1990. 40.00 (*0-500-54162-0*) Thames Hudson.

Repertory Theatre of St. Louis, Backers Volunteer Board Staff. Opening Night Entertaining, 2 vols., Set, Vols. 1-2. (Illus.). (Orig.). 1993. Set. pap. 16.95 (*0-9605504-1-0*) Repertory Theatre SL.

— Opening Night Entertaining, 2 vols., Vols. 1-2. (Illus.). 72p. (Orig.). 1993. Act I, 72p. write for info. (*0-318-72146-5*); Act III. write for info. (*0-318-72147-3*) Repertory Theatre SL.

Repetto-Alaia, Margherita, jt. ed. see Coppa, Frank J.

Repetto, Robert. Economic Equality & Fertility in Developing Countries. LC 78-20533. (Resources for the Future Ser.). 204p. 1979. text ed. 16.50 (*0-8018-2212-2*) Johns Hopkins.

— Forest for the Trees? Government Policies & the Misuse of Forest Resources. LC 88-50465. 120p. (Orig.). 1988. pap. 10.00 (*0-915825-25-2*) World Resources Inst.

— Jobs, Competitiveness & Environmental Regulation: What Are the Real Issues? LC 95-1197. 1995. write for info. (*1-56973-030-X*) World Resources Inst.

— Paying the Price: Pesticide Subsidies in Developing Countries. 40p. (Orig.). 1985. pap. text ed. 10.00 (*0-915825-12-0*) World Resources Inst.

— Promoting Environmentally Sound Economic Progress: What the North Can Do. 20p. 1990. Large format. pap. 12.95 (*0-915825-57-0*, REPEP) World Resources Inst.

— Skimming the Water: Rent-Seeking & the Performance of Public Irrigation Systems. LC 86-51517. 56p. (Orig.). 1986. pap. text ed. 10.00 (*0-915825-18-X*) World Resources Inst.

— World Enough & Time: Successful Strategies for Resource Management. LC 85-20180. 160p. 1986. text ed. 22.00 (*0-300-03648-5*); pap. 11.00 (*0-300-03649-3*) Yale U Pr.

Repetto, Robert, ed. The Global Possible: Resources, Development & the New Century. LC 85-8209. (World Resources Institute Book Ser.). 560p. 1985. 50.00 (*0-300-03382-6*) Yale U Pr.

Repetto, Robert & Gillis, Malcolm, eds. Public Policy & the Misuse of Forest Resources. 200p. 1988. pap. 37.95 (*0-521-33574-4*) Cambridge U Pr.

Repetto, Robert, jt. auth. see Cruz, Wilfrido.

Repetto, Robert, jt. auth. see Gillis, Malcolm.

Repetto, Robert, jt. auth. see Heaton, George.

Repetto, Robert, et al. Economic Development, Population Policy & Demographic Transition in the Republic of Korea. (East Asian Monographs: No. 93). 321p. (C). 1981. 25.00 (*0-674-23311-5*) HUP.

— Green Fees: How a Tax Shift Can Work for the Environment & the Economy. large type ed. 100p. 1992. Large format. pap. 14.95 (*0-915825-76-7*, REKCP) World Resources Inst.

— Wasting Assets: Natural Resources in the National Income Accounts. 120p. (Orig.). 1989. pap. text ed. 10. 00 (*0-915825-31-7*) World Resources Inst.

Repetto, Robert C. Economic Equality & Fertility in Developing Countries. LC 78-20533. 208p. reprint ed. pap. 59.30 (*0-685-23706-0*, 2032162) Bks Demand.

— Time in India's Development Programmes. LC 71-143230. (Economic Studies: No. 137). (Illus.). 249p. 1971. 16.50 (*0-674-89180-5*) HUP.

Rephann, Ricahrd T. A Catalogue of the Pedro Traversari Collection of Musical Instruments. Odiaga, Lola, tr. (Illus.). 146p. (Orig.). (ENG & SPA.). 1978. pap. 10.00 (*0-929530-01-2*) Yale U Coll Musical Instruments.

Rephann, Richard & Renouf, Nicholas. The Robyna Neilson Ketchum Collection of Bells. (Illus.). 28p. (Orig.). 1975. pap. 3.00 (*0-929530-00-4*) Yale U Coll Musical Instruments.

Rephann, Richard T. The Schambach-Kaston Collection of Musical Instruments. (Illus.). 88p. (Orig.). 1988. pap. 15. 00 (*0-929530-05-5*) Yale U Coll Musical Instruments.

Repic, Ed. Managing Engineers. (Illus.). (Orig.). 1981. pap. 25.00 (*0-939740-00-1*) Effect Mgmt.

Repin, I. E. Distant, Yet Familiar. 1982. 46.00 (*0-317-57247-4*, Pub. by Collets UK) St Mut.

Repine, J. E., jt. ed. see Cheronis, J. C.

***Repine, Jim.** Pacific Rim Fly Fishing: The Unrepentant Predator. (Illus.). 64p. 1995. pap. 24.95 (*1-57188-025-9*) F Amato Pubns.

Repington, Charles A. The First World War, 2 vols., Set. (Modern Revivals in Military History Ser.). 638p. 1992. 120.00 (*0-7512-0038-7*, Pub. by Gregg Revivals UK) Ashgate Pub Co.

***Repinski, Cynthia A.** The Univex Story. LC 91-71477. (Illus.). 272p. 1991. 34.95 (*0-931838-17-7*) Centennial Photo Serv.

Repishti, Sami, jt. ed. see Pippa, Arshi.

Repka, Joseph. Calculus with Analytic Geometry. (Illus.). 1344p. (C). 1993. text ed. write for info. (*0-697-06918-4*) Wm C Brown Pubs.

— Calculus with Analytic Geometry. (Illus.). 1344p. (C). 1993. Calculator View of Calculus Using the TI-81, TI-85. write for info. (*0-697-16777-1*); Calculator View of Calculus Using the Casio. write for info. (*0-697-16778-X*); Calculator View of Calculus Using the HP486. write for info. (*0-697-21296-3*) Wm C Brown Pubs.

— Calculus with Analytic Geometry. (Illus.). 1344p. (C). 1994. Solutions manual, Part 1. write for info. (*0-697-11365-5*); Solutions manual, Part 2. write for info. (*0-697-12197-6*) Wm C Brown Pubs.

— Single Variable Calculus. 880p. (C). 1993. text ed. write for info. (*0-697-15375-4*) Wm C Brown Pubs.

Replansky, Dennis. Truth-in-Lending & Regulation Z. LC 84-71018. (Illus.). xvi, 297p. 1984. 95.00 (*0-8318-0242-1*, B242) Am Law Inst.

Replansky, Dennis, jt. auth. see Schieber, Paul.

Replansky, Naomi. The Dangerous World: New & Selected Poems, 1934-1994. LC 94-15161. 96p. (Orig.). 1994. pap. 12.95 (*0-929968-34-4*) Another Chicago Pr.

— The Dangerous World: New & Selected Poems, 1934-1994. LC 94-15161. 96p. (Orig.). 1995. 22.00 (*0-929968-35-2*) Another Chicago Pr.

— Twenty-One Poems: Old & New. (Orig.). 1988. pap. 5.95 (*0-9619869-0-5*) Gingko Pr.

Replinger, Peter J., jt. auth. see Labbe, John T.

***Replogle, Elaine M.** Head Start As a Family Support Program: Renewing a Community Ethic. 96p. 1995. pap. text ed. 8.00 (*0-9630627-4-3*) Harvard Fam.

Replogle, John A. & Renard, Kenneth G., eds. Water Today & Tomorrow: Proceedings of a Specialty Conference Sponsored by the Irrigation & Drainage Division. 740p. 1984. 61.00 (*0-87262-408-0*) Am Soc Civil Eng.

Replogle, Michael A. Non-Motorized Vehicles in Asian Cities. (Technical Paper Ser.: No. 162). 80p. 1991. 6.95 (*0-8213-1963-9*, 11963) World Bank.

Replogle, Ron. Recovering the Social Contract. LC 87-33024. 256p. (C). 1989. 53.50 (*0-8476-7591-2*) Rowman.

REPOhistory Staff. Choice Histories: Framing Abortion: An Artists' Book by REPOhistory. 44p. 1992. 8.00 (*0-9636132-0-0*) REPOhistory.

Report of a Study Group. Toward Arab-Israeli Peace: Guidelines for American Policy. LC 88-70490. 49p. 1988. pap. 5.95 (*0-8157-7291-2*) Brookings.

***Report of the National Performance Review Staff & Gore, Al.** Creating a Government That Works Better & Costs Less. 1994. pap. write for info. (*0-929306-20-1*) Silicon Pr.

Report of the Price Statistics Review Committee. The Price Statistics of the Federal Government. (General Ser.: No. 73). 518p. 1961. reprint ed. 134.70 (*0-87014-072-8*) Natl Bur Econ Res.

Reporter. Reporter Reader. Ascoli, Max, ed. LC 74-93373. (Essay Index Reprint Ser.). 1977. 28.95 (*0-8369-1428-7*) Ayer.

***ReportSmith, Inc. Staff.** Primavera Project Planner for Windows: ReportSmith for Primavera. (Illus.). 406p. 1994. disk write for info. (*0-926282-83-2*) Primavera Syst.

Reposa, Carol. At the Border: Winter Lights. (Signature Ser.: Vol. 1). (Orig.). 1989. pap. 5.00 (*0-317-93651-4*) Pecan Grove.

Repp. The Mufti of Istanbul. 1991. 60.00 (*0-86372-041-2*, Pub. by Ithaca UK) Paul & Co Pubs.

— Radium Pool. 5.00 (*0-686-00478-7*); pap. 2.00 (*0-686-00479-5*) Fantasy Pub Co.

— Stellar Missiles. 5.00 (*0-686-00483-3*); pap. 2.00 (*0-686-00484-1*) Fantasy Pub Co.

Repp, Alan C. & Singh, Nirbhay N., eds. Current Perspectives in the Use of Nonaversive & Aversive Interventions for Persons with Developmental Disabilities. (Illus.). 300p. (C). 1990. write for info. (*0-318-66893-9*) Sycamore Pub.

Repp, Alan C., ed. see O'Neill, Robert, et al.

Repp, Arthur C., Sr. Luther's Catechism Comes to America: Theological Effects on the Issues of the Small Catechism Prepared in or for America Prior to 1850. LC 82-5453. (American Theological Library Association Monograph: No. 18). 329p. 1982. text ed. 32.50 (*0-8108-1546-X*) Scarecrow.

Repp, Gloria. His Best for God. (Illus.). 24p. (J). (gr. k-6). 1989. pap. text ed. 4.25 (*1-55976-150-4*) CEF Press.

— A Man for God's Plan. (Illus.). 24p. (J). (gr. k-6). 1991. 4.25 (*1-55976-155-5*) CEF Press.

— Night Flight. Sidwell, Mark, ed. (Light Line Ser.). 177p. (Orig.). (J). 1991. pap. 5.95 (*0-89084-563-8*) Bob Jones Univ Pr.

— Noodle Soup. LC 93-42417. (Illus.). (J). 1994. pap. 4.95 (*0-89084-582-4*) Bob Jones Univ Pr.

— Nothing Daunted: The Story of Isobel Kuhn. LC 94-15531. (Light Line Ser.). 1994. pap. 5.95 (*0-89084-753-3*) Bob Jones Univ Pr.

— A Question of Yams: A Missionary Story Based on True Events. Daniels, Karen, ed. (Light Line Ser.). (Illus.). 67p. (Orig.). (J). (gr. 2-4). 1992. pap. 5.95 (*0-89084-614-6*) Bob Jones Univ Pr.

— Secret of the Golden Cowrie. (Light Line Ser.). (Illus.). 199p. (Orig.). (J). (gr. 4-6). 1988. pap. 5.95 (*0-89084-459-3*) Bob Jones Univ Pr.

— The Stolen Years. (Light Line Ser.). 152p. (Orig.). (YA). (gr. 9-12). 1989. pap. 5.95 (*0-89084-481-X*) Bob Jones Univ Pr.

Repp, John. How We Live Now: Contemporary Multicultural Literature. LC 90-71626. 928p. (Orig.). (C). 1992. pap. text ed. 23.00 (*0-312-05191-3*); pap. text ed. 0.15 (*0-312-05256-1*) St Martin.

— Thirst Like This: Poems. 64p. 1990. 18.95 (*0-8262-0762-6*); pap. 9.95 (*0-8262-0765-0*) U of Mo Pr.

Repp, Philip C. Words & Images: Land Within the Maumee. (Illus.). 83p. (Orig.). 1990. pap. write for info. (*0-9623291-1-8*) Minnetrista.

Repp, T. O. Main Streets of the Northwest. LC 89-15467. (Illus.). 160p. (YA). (gr. 11). 1989. 19.95 (*0-87046-085-4*, Trans-Anglo) Interurban.

Repp, William. Complete Handbook of Business English. 1982. 29.50 (*0-13-160960-2*, Busn) P-H.

***Reppen, Joseph, ed.** Analysts at Work: Practice, Principles, & Techniques. LC 94-36490. 268p. 1995. pap. text ed. 30.00 (*1-56821-423-5*) Aronson.

— Analysts at Work: Practice, Principles & Techniques. LC 84-28207. (Advances in Psychoanalysis Ser.). 264p. reprint ed. pap. 75.30 (*0-8357-2739-4*, 2039848) Bks Demand.

Reppen, Joseph & Charney, Maurice, eds. The Psychoanalytic Study of Literature. LC 84-16791. 296p. reprint ed. pap. 84.40 (*0-8357-2737-8*, 2039846) Bks Demand.

Reppen, Joseph, jt. ed. see Charney, Maurice.

Reppert, Bertha. The Bride's Herbal. 182p. 1989. pap. 12.50 (*0-9617210-3-0*) Remembrance.

— Growing Your Herb Business. Balmuth, Deborah, ed. LC 93-36518. (Illus.). 192p. 1994. pap. 11.95 (*0-88266-612-6*, Storey Pub) Storey Comm Inc.

— Herbs for Weddings & Other Celebrations: A Treasury of Recipes, Gifts, & Decorations. Steege, Gwen, ed. LC 92-56147. (Illus.). 200p. 1994. 24.95 (*0-88266-866-8*, Garden Way Pub); pap. 16.95 (*0-88266-864-1*, Garden Way Pub) Storey Comm Inc.

— Herbs of the Zodiac. 68p. 1984. pap. 6.00 (*0-9617210-7-3*) Remembrance.

— Herbs with Confidence. LC 86-90486. (Illus.). 268p. (Orig.). 1986. pap. write for info. (*0-9617210-0-6*) Remembrance.

— A Heritage of Herbs: History, Early Gardening & Old Recipes. 192p. 1976. pap. 6.00 (*0-9617210-6-5*) Remembrance.

— Wreaths of All Sorts. 40p. 1987. pap. 6.50 (*0-9617210-1-4*) Remembrance.

Reppert, Bertha & Humphries, Pat. Potpourri: Recipes & Crafts. 40p. 1973. pap. 4.00 (*0-9617210-2-2*) Remembrance.

Reppert, Marjorie L. Guidance for Choosing a Career in the Visual Arts. 66p. 1992. pap. 7.95 (*0-9617210-4-9*) Remembrance.

Reppert, S., jt. auth. see Moore, R.

Reppert, Steven M., ed. Development of Circadian Rhythmicity & Photoperiodism in Mammals. LC 89-23095. (Research in Perinatal Medicine Ser.: No. IX). (Illus.). 1989. 102.50 (*0-916859-42-8*) Perinatology.

Repplier, Agnes. Americans & Others. LC 70-121503. (Essay Index Reprint Ser.). 1977. 23.95 (*0-8369-2025-2*) Ayer.

— Book of Famous Verse. LC 71-86802. (Granger Index Reprint Ser.). 1977. 18.95 (*0-8369-6086-6*) Ayer.

— Compromises. LC 78-98626. reprint ed. 27.50 (*0-404-05259-2*) AMS Pr.

— Compromises. (BCL1-PS American Literature Ser.). 277p. 1992. reprint ed. lib. bdg. 79.00 (*0-7812-6840-0*) Rprt Serv.

— Compromises. 1971. reprint ed. 8.00 (*0-403-00701-1*) Scholarly.

— Counter-Currents. LC 73-121504. (Essay Index Reprint Ser.). 1977. 23.95 (*0-8369-2026-0*) Ayer.

— Essays in Idleness. LC 70-121290. 1970. reprint ed. 27.50 (*0-404-05278-9*) AMS Pr.

— Essays in Idleness. (BCL1-PS American Literature Ser.). 224p. 1992. reprint ed. lib. bdg. 79.00 (*0-7812-6841-9*) Rprt Serv.

— Essays in Idleness. LC 70-131815. 1970. reprint ed. 8.00 (*0-403-00702-X*) Scholarly.

— Essays in Miniature. LC 70-112790. reprint ed. 27.50 (*0-404-05279-7*) AMS Pr.

— Essays in Miniature. (BCL1-PS American Literature Ser.). 217p. 1992. reprint ed. lib. bdg. 79.00 (*0-7812-6842-7*) Rprt Serv.

— Essays in Miniature. LC 74-131816. 1970. reprint ed. 8.00 (*0-403-00703-8*) Scholarly.

— A Happy Half-Century: And Other Essays. (BCL1-PS American Literature Ser.). 249p. 1992. reprint ed. lib. bdg. 79.00 (*0-7812-6843-5*) Rprt Serv.

— In Our Convent Days. (BCL1-PS American Literature Ser.). 256p. 1992. reprint ed. lib. bdg. 79.00 (*0-7812-6917-2*) Rprt Serv.

— In Our Convent Days. 1971. reprint ed. 8.00 (*0-403-00704-6*) Scholarly.

R

An Asterisk (*) at the beginning of an entry indicates that the title is appearing in BIP for the first time.

— Philadelphia, the Place & Its People. 1993. reprint ed. lib. bdg. 89.00 (0-7812-5823-5) Rprt Serv.
— Points of Friction. LC 77-121505. (Essay Index Reprint Ser.). 1977. 23.95 (0-8369-2027-9) Ayer.
— Times & Tendencies. LC 71-128297. (Essay Index Reprint Ser.). 1977. 21.95 (0-8369-2028-7) Ayer.
— Under Dispute. LC 75-167406. (Essay Index Reprint Ser.). 1977. reprint ed. 23.95 (0-8369-2668-4) Ayer.
***Repplier, Ted.** How to Get Started on Ocean Sailing. 81p. 1994. pap. 9.95 (0-9644143-0-9) Orion Pubns.
Reppucci, N. D. & Haugaard, J., eds. Prevention in Community Mental Health Practice. 1991. pap. 27.95 (0-914797-70-0) Brookline Bks.
Reppucci, N. Dickon, jt. auth. see Haugaard, Jeffrey J.
Reppucci, N. Dickon, et al, eds. Children, Mental Health, & the Law. LC 83-21116. (Sage Annual Reviews of Community Mental Health Ser.: No. 4). 312p. reprint ed. pap. 89.00 (0-8357-4847-2, 2037778) Bks Demand.
Reppy & Samuel. Community Property in the United States. 422p. (C). 1991. 45.50 (1-879581-00-0) Lupus Pubns.
— Community Property in the United States, 1994. 464p. Date not set. ring bd. 46.50 (1-879581-15-9) Lupus Pubns.
Reppy, Jessie M., jt. auth. see Shaffer-Koros, Carole.
***Reppy, John H.** Concurrent Programming in ML. 280p. (C). 1995. write for info. (0-521-48089-2) Cambridge U Pr.
Reppy, William A., Jr. Community Property in California: Cases, Statutes & Problems. 2nd ed. (Contemporary Legal Education Ser.). 443p. 1988. 38.00 (0-87473-375-8) Michie Butterworth.
Reprogle, Rod, et al. The Mother of All Car Books: How to Get More Fun & Profit Buying, Showing & Selling Vintage & Classic Cars. LC 91-58795. 270p. 1995. pap. 14.95 (0-911663-78-9) Duncliffs Intl.
Reps, John W. Cities of the Mississippi: Nineteenth-Century Images of Urban Development. LC 93-44630. (Illus.). 352p. 1994. 85.00 (0-8262-0939-4) U of Mo Pr.
— Cities on Stone: Nineteenth Century Lithograph Images of the Urban West. LC 76-12313. (Illus.). 99p. 1976. reprint ed. lib. bdg. 17.95 (0-88360-024-2); reprint ed. pap. 9.95 (0-88360-051-X) Amon Carter.
— The Forgotten Frontier: Urban Planning in the American West Before 1890. LC 81-10322. 184p. 1981. text ed. 27.00 (0-8262-0351-5); pap. 14.95 (0-8262-0352-3) U of Mo Pr.
— The Making of Urban America: A History of City Planning in the United States. (Illus.). 590p. 1991. text ed. 99.50 (0-691-04525-9); pap. text ed. 29.95 (0-691-00618-0) Princeton U Pr.
— Panoramas of Promise: Pacific Northwest Cities & Towns on Nineteenth-Century Lithographs. LC 84-13164. (Illus.). 93p. 1984. 18.75 (0-87422-016-5); pap. 10.95 (0-87422-017-3) Wash St U Pr.
— Saint Louis Illustrated: Nineteenth-Century Engravings & Lithographs of a Mississippi River Metropolis. LC 88-20914. (Illus.). 208p. 1989. 39.95 (0-8262-0698-0) U of Mo Pr.
— Town Planning in Frontier America. LC 68-20877. 336p. 1981. reprint ed. pap. 14.95 (0-8262-0316-7) U of Mo Pr.
— Views & Viewmakers of Urban America: Lithographs of Towns & Cities in the United States & Canada, Notes on the Artists & Publishers, & a Union Catalog of Their Work, 1825-1925. LC 83-6495. (Illus.). 588p. 1984. text ed. 89.50 (0-8262-0416-3) U of Mo Pr.
— Washington on View: The Nation's Capital since 1790. LC 90-46782. (Illus.). xi, 297p. (C). 1991. 55.00 (0-8078-1948-4) U of NC Pr.
Reps, Paul. Let Good Fortune Jump on You. (Illus.). 75p. 1990. reprint ed. pap. 7.95 (0-9620812-7-2) Good Karma.
— Zen Telegrams. (Illus.). 92p. (Orig.). 1995. pap. 11.95 (0-8048-2023-6) C E Tuttle.
Reps, Paul, ed. Zen Flesh, Zen Bones: A Collection of Zen & Pre-Zen Writings. 1961. mass mkt. 8.95 (0-385-08130-8, A233, Anchor NY) Doubleday.
Reps, Paul, jt. tr. see Senzaki, Nyogen.
Reps, T. W. & Teitelbaum, T. The Synthesizer Generator. (Texts & Monographs in Computer Science). (Illus.). xiii, 310p. 1988. 53.00 (0-387-96857-1) Spr-Verlag.
— The Synthesizer Generator: The Synthesizer Reference Manual, 2 vols., Set. (Texts & Monographs in Computer Science). (Illus.). 1989. 55.00 (0-387-97100-9) Spr-Verlag.
— The Synthesizer Generator Reference Manual. 3rd ed. (Texts & Monographs in Computer Science). (Illus.). viii, 165p. 1990. pap. 29.50 (0-387-96910-1) Spr-Verlag.
Repton, Humphry. The Art of Landscape Gardening. LC 76-51839. (Illus.). 1976. reprint ed. 25.00 (0-913728-20-9) Theophrastus.
Republic of China Staff. Laws, Ordinances, Regulations, & Rules Relating to the Judicial Administration of the Republic of China. LC 76-11420. (Studies in Chinese Government & Law). 364p. 1976. reprint ed. text ed. 65.00 (0-313-26957-2, U6957) Greenwood.
Republic of Egypt, Cabinet of the Grand Chamberlain Staff & Olson, David V. The Arab Republic of Egypt Military Decorations & Medals, 1953-1983. (Illus.). 50p. (Orig.). 1989. reprint ed. pap. 20.00 (0-929757-26-2) Regt QM.
Republic of Texas Press Staff, ed. see Adare, Sierra.
Repyev, Alexander, tr. see Frolov, K. V.
Repyev, Alexander, tr. see Logunov, A. A.
Requa, Barbara, et al. Applied Pharmacology for the Dental Hygienist. 2nd ed. (Illus.). 320p. 1989. pap. 34.95 (0-8016-4266-3) Mosby Yr Bk.
Requena, Yves. Character & Health. Felt, Robert L., ed. Bell, Carol, tr. (Illus.). 224p. (Orig.). 1989. pap. 16.95 (0-912111-23-2) Paradigm Publns.
— Terrains & Pathology in Acupuncture, Vol. 1. Felt, Robert L., ed. Ducharne, Allan, tr. (Illus.). 448p. 1986. 39.95 (0-912111-09-7) Paradigm Publns.
***Requena, Yves & Kenner, Dan.** Botanical Medicine: A European Professional Perspective. 250p. 35.00 (0-912111-48-8) Paradigm Publns.
Requicha, A. A., ed. Eurographics '86. 392p. 1986. 105.25 (0-444-70065-X, North Holland) Elsevier.
Requin, Jean & Stelmach, George E. Tutorials in Motor Neuroscience: Proceedings of the NATO Advanced Study Institute. 696p. (C). 1991. lib. bdg. 216.00 (0-7923-1385-2) Kluwer Ac.
Requin, Jean, ed. see International Symposium on Attention & Performance Staff.
Requin, Jean, jt. ed. see Kornblum, Sylvan.
Requin, Jean, jt. auth. see Stelmach, George E.
Rericha, Robert & Franke, Christopher. Killing Time - Vis-a-Vis Redivivus. 48p. 1990. pap. 5.00 (0-9601640-2-2) Deciduous.
Rericha, Vaclav. Harrap's Czech Phrase Book. 1991. pap. 4.00 (0-13-373986-4) P-H.
***Rerick, Rowland H.** State Centennial History of Ohio, Covering the Periods of Indian, French & British Dominion, the Territory Northwest, & the Hundred Years of Statehood. 425p. 1995. reprint ed. lib. bdg. 45.00 (0-8328-4616-3) Higginson Bk Co.
Res, Zannis & Motamen, Sima, eds. International Debt & Central Banking in the 1980s. LC 87-4300. 256p. 1987. text ed. 49.95 (0-312-00530-X) St Martin.
Resch, Barbara. A Place for Everyone. (Illus.). 28p. (J). (ps-3). 1991. 9.95 (1-56182-022-9) Atomium Bks.
Resch, Elyse, jt. auth. see Tribole, Evelyn.
Resch, H. & Beck, E. Arthroscopy of the Shoulder: Diagnosis & Therapy. Antoft, M. L. & Marschall, B., trs. (Illus.). 190p. 1992. 128.00 (0-387-82339-5) Spr-Verlag.
Resch, K. & Kirchner, H. Mechanics of Lymphocyte Activation. 714p. 1981. 136.50 (0-444-80376-9) Elsevier.
Resch, Kathleen & Robin, Marcy. Dark Shadows in the Afternoon. (Illus.). 112p. (Orig.). 1991. pap. 12.95 (0-685-50337-2) Image NY.
Resch, Kenneth E. & Schicker, Vicki D. Using Film in the High School Curriculum: A Practical Guide for Teachers & Librarians. LC 92-50316. (Illus.). 176p. 1992. pap. 27.50x (0-89950-750-6) McFarland & Co.
Resch, Margit, ed. Seltene Augenblicke: Interpretations of Poems by Hugo von Hofmannsthal. LC 88-62942. (Studies in German Literature, Linguistics & Culture: Vol. 40). (Illus.). 200p. 1989. 34.00 (0-938100-63-7) Camden Hse.
Resch, Robert P. Althusser & the Renewal of Marxist Social Theory. LC 91-3014. (C). 1992. 42.00 (0-520-06082-2) U CA Pr.
Resch, Tyler. Bennington's Battle Monument: Massive & Lofty. 64p. 1994. pap. 9.95 (1-884592-00-7) Beech Seal Pr.
— Deed of Gift: The Putnam Hospital Story. (Illus.). 154p. 1991. 24.95 (0-943741-01-7) Paradigm VT.
— Dorset: In the Shadow of the Marble Mountain. LC 89-25511. (Illus.). 416p. 1989. 30.00 (0-914659-44-8) Phoenix Pub.
— The Rutland Herald History: Bicentennial Chronicle. 1995. write for info. (0-9643308-2-2); lib. bdg. write for info. (0-9643308-3-0) Herald Assn.
***Resch, Tyler, ed.** The Bob Mitchell Years: An Anthology of Editorials by the Publisher of the Rutland Herald. 528p. 1994. write for info. (0-9643308-0-6) Herald Assn.
— The Bob Mitchell Years: An Anthology of Editorials by the Publisher of the Rutland Herald. 528p. 1994. pap. write for info. (0-9643308-1-4) Herald Assn.
Reschenthaler, Patricia. Postwar Readjustment in El Paso, Nineteen Forty-Five to Nineteen Fifty. (Southwestern Studies: No. 21). 1968. pap. 10.00 (0-87404-134-1) Tex Western.
Rescher, Nicholas. American Philosophy Today & Other Philosophical Studies. LC 94-16451. 188p. reprint ed. lib. bdg. 49.50 (0-8476-7935-7); reprint ed. pap. 19.95 (0-8476-7936-5) Rowman.
— Baffling Phenomena: And Other Studies in the Philosophy of Knowledge & Valuation. 188p. (C). 1990. lib. bdg. 46.50 (0-8476-7638-2) Rowman.
— Cognitive Economy: The Economic Dimension of the Theory of Knowledge. LC 89-5425. 178p. 1989. 49.95 (0-8229-3617-8) U of Pittsburgh Pr.
— The Development of Arabic Logic. LC 64-13361. 262p. reprint ed. pap. 74.70 (0-317-08129-2, 2015571) Bks Demand.
— Dialectics: A Controversy-Oriented Approach to the Theory of Knowledge. LC 77-9542. 128p. 1977. 39.50 (0-87395-372-X) State U NY Pr.
— Essays in the History of Philosophy. 379p. 1995. boxed, pap. 63.95 (1-85628-970-2, Pub. by Avebury Pub UK) Ashgate Pub Co.
— Ethical Idealism: An Inquiry into the Nature & Function of Ideals. 1987. pap. 12.00 (0-520-07888-8) U CA Pr.
— Forbidden Knowledge. (C). 1987. lib. bdg. 80.50 (90-277-2410-5) Kluwer Ac.
— G. W. Leibniz's Monadology: An Edition for Students. LC 90-24820. 480p. (C). 1991. 49.95 (0-8229-3670-4); pap. text ed. 22.50 (0-8229-5449-4) U of Pittsburgh Pr.
— Human Interests: Reflections on Philosophical Anthropology. LC 90-30349. (Series in Philosophy). 212p. 1990. 32.50 (0-8047-1811-3) Stanford U Pr.
— Induction. LC 80-52598. xii, 237p. 1981. 49.95 (0-8229-3431-0) U of Pittsburgh Pr.
— Induktion: Zur Rechtfertigung Induktiven Schliessens. Schaffner, Gerhard, tr. (Introductiones Ser.). 246p. (GER.). 1987. 46.00 (3-88405-051-6); pap. 36.00 (3-88405-078-8) Philosophia Pr.
— Introduction to Value Theory. LC 82-45292. (Nicholas Rescher Ser.). 200p. 1982. reprint ed. pap. 21.50 (0-8191-2474-5) U Pr of Amer.
— Leibniz: An Introduction to His Philosophy. (Modern Revivals in Philosophy Ser.). 176p. 1993. 49.95 (0-7512-0275-4, Pub. by Gregg Revivals UK) Ashgate Pub Co.
— The Logic of Decision & Action. LC 67-18272. 236p. reprint ed. pap. 67.30 (0-317-08258-2, 2010495) Bks Demand.
— Luck: The Brilliant Randomness of Everyday Life. 198p. Date not set. 19.00 (0-374-19428-9) FS&G.
— Many-Valued Logic. (Modern Revivals in Philosophy Ser.). 376p. 1993. 65.95 (0-7512-0274-6, Pub. by Gregg Revivals UK) Ashgate Pub Co.
— Metaphilosophical Inquiries. LC 93-5179. (System of Pragmatic Idealism Ser.: Vol. 3). 1994. 49.50 (0-691-07394-5) Princeton U Pr.
— Mid-Journey: An Unfinished Autobiography. LC 82-45083. (Illus.). 204p. (Orig.). 1983. lib. bdg. 50.00 (0-8191-2522-9) U Pr of Amer.
— Moral Absolute: An Essay on the Nature & Rationale of Morality. (Studies in Moral Philosophy: Vol. 2). 115p. (C). 1989. text ed. 29.00 (0-8204-0797-6) P Lang Pubs.
— Peirce's Philosophy of Science: Critical Studies in His Theory of Induction & Scientific Method. LC 77-82479. 1979. pap. text ed. 6.95 (0-268-01527-9) U of Notre Dame Pr.
— Philosophical Standardism: An Empiricist Approach to Philosophical Methodology. 224p. (C). 1994. 49.95 (0-8229-3790-5) U of Pittsburgh Pr.
— Pluralism: Against the Demand for Consensus. LC 93-18392. (Clarendon Library of Logic & Philosophy). (C). 1993. 29.95 (0-19-824062-7, Clarendon Pr) OUP.
— Pluralism: Against the Demand for Consensus. (Clarendon Library of Logic & Philosophy). (Illus.). 216p. 1995. reprint ed. pap. 16.95 (0-19-823601-8) OUP.
— Process Metaphysics: An Introduction to Process Philosophy. (SUNY Series in Philosophy). 160p. (C). 1996. text ed. 36.50x (0-7914-2817-6); pap. text ed. 12.95x (0-7914-2818-4) State U NY Pr.
— Rationality: A Philosophical Inquiry into the Nature & Rationale of Reason. (Clarendon Library of Logic & Philosophy). (Illus.). 248p. 1989. 49.95 (0-19-824435-5) OUP.
— Reason & Rationality in Natural Science: A Group of Essays. 228p. (Orig.). 1985. lib. bdg. 49.50 (0-8191-4763-X) U Pr of Amer.
— Risk: A Philosophical Introduction to the Theory of Risk Evaluation & Management. LC 82-21970. (Nicholas Rescher Ser.). 218p. (Orig.). 1983. pap. text ed. 23.00 (0-8191-2270-X) U Pr of Amer.
— Satisfying Reason: Studies in the Theory of Knowledge. LC 94-33491. (Episteme Ser.: Vol. 21). 256p. (C). 1995. lib. bdg. 99.00 (0-7923-3148-6) Kluwer Ac.
— Scientific Progress: A Philosophical Essay on the Economics of Research in Natural Science. LC 77-74544. 286p. 1977. 49.95 (0-8229-1128-0) U of Pittsburgh Pr.
— The Strife of Systems: An Essay on the Grounds & Implications of Philosophical Diversity. LC 84-21958. (Illus.). 295p. 1985. 49.95 (0-8229-3510-4) U of Pittsburgh Pr.
— Studies in the History of Arabic Logic. LC 63-17521. 108p. reprint ed. pap. 30.80 (0-317-08256-6, 2010499) Bks Demand.
— A System of Pragmatic Idealism, Vol. One: Human Knowledge in Idealistic Perspective. (Illus.). 367p. 1991. text ed. 49.50 (0-691-07391-0) Princeton U Pr.
— A System of Pragmatic Idealism, Vol. 2: The Validity of Values - A Normative Theory of Evaluative Rationality. 296p. 1993. text ed. 49.50 (0-691-07393-7) Princeton U Pr.
— Temporal Modalities in Arabic Logic. (Foundations of Language Supplementary Ser.: No. 2). 50p. 1966. lib. bdg. 36.50 (90-277-0083-4) Kluwer Ac.
— Unpopular Essays on Technological Progress. LC 79-21648. (Illus.). 132p. 1980. 49.95 (0-8229-3411-6) U of Pittsburgh Pr.
— Unselfishness: The Role of the Vicarious Affects in Moral Philosophy & Social Theory. LC 75-9123. 138p. 1975. 49.95 (0-8229-3308-X) U of Pittsburgh Pr.
— A Useful Inheritance: Evolutionary Aspects of the Theory of Knowledge. LC 89-27509. 148p. (C). 1990. lib. bdg. 43.50 (0-8476-7615-3) Rowman.
— Welfare: The Social Issues in Philosophical Perspective. LC 70-158184. 198p. reprint ed. pap. 56.50 (0-317-26659-4, 2025444) Bks Demand.
Rescher, Nicholas, ed. Aesthetic Factors in Natural Science. LC 89-35898. 110p. (C). 1990. lib. bdg. 37.50 (0-8191-7576-5) U Pr of Amer.
— Evolution, Cognition, & Realism: Studies in Evolutionary Epistemology. (CPS Publications in Philosophy of Science). 144p. (C). 1990. lib. bdg. 39.00 (0-8191-7754-7); pap. text ed. 19.00 (0-8191-7755-5) U Pr of Amer.
— Heritage of Logical Positivism. (CPS Publications in Philosophy of Science). 186p. (Orig.). 1985. pap. text ed. 23.00 (0-8191-4471-1) U Pr of Amer.
— Leibnizian Inquiries: A Group of Essays. LC 88-37059. (CPS Publications in Philosophy of Science). 196p. (Orig.). (C). 1989. lib. bdg. 37.00 (0-8191-7358-4, Ctr Philos Sci); pap. text ed. 19.50 (0-8191-7359-2, Ctr Philos Sci) U Pr of Amer.
— Scientific Inquiry in Philosophical Perspective. (CPS Publications in Philosophy of Science). (Illus.). 308p. (Orig.). 1987. pap. text ed. 26.00 (0-8191-5799-6, Ctr Philos Sci) U Pr of Amer.
Rescher, Nicholas, tr. see Al-Farabi.
Rescher, Nicholas, et al, eds. Essays in Honor of Carl G. Hempel: A Tribute on the Occasion of His Sixty-Fifth Birthday. (Synthese Library: No.24). 272p. 1969. pap. 22.00 (0-685-02824-0) Kluwer Ac.
Rescher, Nicolas. Ongoing Journey. (Illus.). 252p. (Orig.). (C). 1986. pap. text ed. 25.50 (0-8191-5591-8, Nicholas Rescher) U Pr of Amer.
Reschke, Angelika, et al. Voila: Glanzstucke Historischer Moden 1750-1960 (Masterpieces of Fashion 1750-1960) Hornsbostel, Wilhelm, ed. (Illus.). 192p. (GER.). 1991. 80.25 (3-7913-1117-4, Pub. by Prestel) TeNeues.
Reschke, Claus. Life As a Man: Contemporary Male-Female Relationships in the Novels of Max Frisch. LC 89-39785. (Studies in Modern German Literature: Vol. 34). 409p. (C). 1990. text ed. 72.95 (0-8204-1163-9) P Lang Pubs.
Reschke, H. & Schelle, H., eds. Dimensions of Project Management: Fundamentals, Techniques, Organization, Applications. (Illus.). xvii, 336p. 1990. pap. 77.00 (0-387-53157-2) Spr-Verlag.
Reschly, B. Supporting the Changing Family: A Guide to the Parent-to-Parent Model. 31p. 1979. pap. 10.95 (0-685-06046-2) High-Scope.
Reschovsky, Andrew, et al. State Tax Policy: Evaluating the Issues. (Illus.). 300p. 1983. pap. 15.00 (0-943142-04-0) St Local Inter.
Reschovsky, James, jt. auth. see Newman, Sandra.
Rescigno, A. & Boicelli, A., eds. Cerebral Blood Flow: Mathematical Models, Instrumentation, & Imaging Techniques. LC 88-25519. (NATO ASI Series A, Life Sciences: Vol. 153). (Illus.). 272p. 1988. 85.00 (0-306-43019-3, Plenum Pr) Plenum.
Rescigno, A. & Thakur, A. K., eds. New Trends in Pharmacokinetics. (NATO ASI Series A, Life Sciences: Vol. 221). (Illus.). 430p. 1992. 120.00 (0-306-44089-X, Plenum Pr) Plenum.
Rescigno, A., jt. ed. see Pecile, A.
Rescigno, Dolores. Behavior Modification in Business & Industry: A Selected Bibliography. (CPL Bibliographies Ser.: No. 140). 58p. 1984. 14.00 (0-86602-140-X) Coun Plan Librarians.
Rescigno, Federico, jt. auth. see Connell, Stanley W.
Resciniti, Angelo, et al. Super Bowl Excitement. 208p. (YA). (gr. 5 up). 1994. pap. 2.99 (0-87406-716-2) Willowisp Pr.
Rescorla, Leslie, et al, eds. Academic Instruction in Early Childhood: Challenge or Pressure? LC 85-644581. (New Directions for Child Development Ser.: No. CD). 1991. 17.95 (1-55542-769-3) Jossey-Bass.
Rescue American Red Cross Staff. American Red Cross CPR for the Professional Rescue. 32p. 1993. 100.00 (0-8016-7254-6); pap. 11.00 (0-8016-7067-5) Mosby Yr Bk.
Rescue Training Associates, Ltd. Staff, et al. Vehicle Rescue. (Illus.). 1975. teacher ed 7.95 (0-87618-611-8); pap. text ed. 35.00 (0-87618-137-X); pap. text ed. 24.95 (0-89303-118-6) P-H.
Rescue Training Association Staff. Action Guide for Emergency Service Personnel. 656p. 1985. pap. text ed. 39.00 (0-89303-301-4) P-H.
***Research & Education Association Staff.** Accounting Problem Solver. 1000p. 1995. text ed. 23.95 (0-89891-973-8) Res & Educ.
— ACT-American College Testing. 1000p. 1995. pap. text ed. 15.95 (0-87891-967-8) Res & Educ.
— Advanced Calculus Problem Solver. rev. ed. LC 81-52799. (Illus.). 1056p. 1994. pap. text ed. 29.95 (0-87891-533-8) Res & Educ.
— Advanced Placement Examination in Biology. rev. ed. LC 88-90702. (Illus.). 592p. 1994. pap. text ed. 15.95 (0-87891-652-0) Res & Educ.
— Advanced Placement Examination in Calculus AB. rev. ed. (Illus.). 416p. 1994. pap. text ed. 15.95 (0-87891-646-6) Res & Educ.
— Advanced Placement Examination in Calculus BC. rev. ed. (Illus.). 368p. 1994. pap. text ed. 15.95 (0-87891-647-4) Res & Educ.
— Advanced Placement Examination in Chemistry. rev. ed. (Illus.). 528p. 1994. pap. text ed. 16.95 (0-87891-648-2) Res & Educ.
— Advanced Placement Examination in Computer Science. rev. ed. (Illus.). 384p. 1994. pap. text ed. 14.95 (0-87891-882-5) Res & Educ.
— Advanced Placement Examination in Physics. rev. ed. (Illus.). 1994. pap. text ed. 16.95 (0-87891-881-7) Res & Educ.
— Advanced Placement Examination in Psychology. rev. ed. (Illus.). 336p. 1994. pap. text ed. 15.95 (0-87891-883-3) Res & Educ.
— Algebra & Trigonometry Problem Solver. rev. ed. LC 76-334. (Illus.). 924p. (C). 1994. pap. text ed. 23.95 (0-87891-508-7) Res & Educ.
— American History No. I. (CLEP Ser.). 400p. 1995. pap. text ed. 16.95 (0-87891-896-5) Res & Educ.
— Analysis & Interpretation of Literature. (CLEP Ser.). 368p. 1995. pap. text ed. 16.95 (0-87891-897-3) Res & Educ.
— AP Examination in English Literature & Composition. rev. ed. (Illus.). 368p. 1994. pap. text ed. 14.95 (0-87891-843-4) Res & Educ.
— AP Examination in European History. rev. ed. (Illus.). 640p. 1994. pap. text ed. 17.95 (0-87891-863-9) Res & Educ.
— AP Examination in U. S. History. rev. ed. (Illus.). 672p. 1994. pap. text ed. 17.95 (0-87891-844-2) Res & Educ.
— ASVAB: Armed Services Vocational Aptitude Battery Test. 600p. 1994. 16.95 (0-87891-895-7) Res & Educ.
— Automatic Control Systems-Robotic Problem Solver. rev. ed. LC 82-61485. (Illus.). 1088p. 1994. pap. text ed. 29.95 (0-87891-542-7) Res & Educ.
— Behavioral Genetics. LC 82-80748. (Illus.). 224p. (C). 1982. text ed. 13.30 (0-87891-537-0) Res & Educ.
— The Best Test Preparation for CLEP: General Examinations. 1008p. 1995. pap. text ed. 17.95 (0-87891-901-5) Res & Educ.

An Asterisk (*) at the beginning of an entry indicates that the title is appearing in BIP for the first time.

— Biology Builder for Standardized Tests. 512p. 1994. pap. text ed. 12.95 (*0-87891-940-6*) Res & Educ.

— Biology Problem Solver. rev. ed. LC 78-63610. (Illus.). 1088p. 1994. pap. text ed. 23.95 (*0-87891-514-1*) Res & Educ.

— Business, Accounting & Finance Problem Solver. rev. ed. LC 78-64582. (Illus.). 862p. 1994. pap. text ed. 23.95 (*0-87891-516-8*) Res & Educ.

— Calculus Problem Solver. rev. ed. LC 74-17899. (Illus.). 1088p. (C). 1994. pap. text ed. 23.95 (*0-87891-505-2*) Res & Educ.

— CDL - Truck & Bus Driver's Commercial License Examination. rev. ed. (Illus.). 336p. 1991. pap. text ed. 11.95 (*0-87891-871-X*) Res & Educ.

— Chemistry Builder for Standardized Tests. 544p. 1994. pap. text ed. 14.95 (*0-87891-939-2*) Res & Educ.

— Chemistry Problem Solver. rev. ed. LC 77-70335. (Illus.). 960p. 1994. pap. text ed. 23.95 (*0-87891-509-5*) Res & Educ.

— College Algebra. (CLEP Ser.). 368p. 1995. pap. text ed. 16.95 (*0-87891-898-1*) Res & Educ.

— Complex Variables Problem Solver. rev. ed. (Illus.). 928p. 1994. pap. text ed. 29.95 (*0-87891-604-0*) Res & Educ.

— Computer Science Problem Solver. rev. ed. LC 81-50900. (Illus.). 864p. (Orig.). (C). 1994. pap. text ed. 29.95 (*0-87891-525-7*) Res & Educ.

— Differential Equations Problem Solver. rev. ed. LC 78-63609. (Illus.). 1408p. 1994. pap. text ed. 29.95 (*0-87891-513-3*) Res & Educ.

— Economics Problem Solver. rev. ed. LC 80-53175. (Illus.). 1088p. (Orig.). (C). 1994. pap. text ed. 23.95 (*0-87891-524-9*) Res & Educ.

— Electric Circuits Problem Solver. rev. ed. LC 79-92401. (Illus.). 1176p. 1994. pap. text ed. 29.95 (*0-87891-517-6*) Res & Educ.

— Electrical Machines Problem Solver. rev. ed. LC 83-62280. (Illus.). 800p. 1994. pap. text ed. 29.95 (*0-87891-551-6*) Res & Educ.

— Electromagnetics Problem Solver. rev. ed. LC 83-62279. (Illus.). 1008p. 1994. 29.95 (*0-87891-550-8*) Res & Educ.

— Electronic Communications Problem Solver. rev. ed. LC 84-61814. (Illus.). 960p. 1994. pap. text ed. 29.95 (*0-87891-558-3*) Res & Educ.

— Electronics Problem Solver. rev. ed. LC 82-61484. (Illus.). 1310p. 1994. pap. text ed. 29.95 (*0-87891-543-5*) Res & Educ.

— ELM - CA State University Entry Level Mathematics Test. 1994. 16.95 (*0-87891-909-0*) Res & Educ.

— English Handbook of Grammar, Style, & Composition. rev. ed. LC 83-62275. (Illus.). 320p. 1994. pap. text ed. 16.95 (*0-87891-552-4*) Res & Educ.

— The Essential of Canadian History, Prehistory to 1867. 1994. 5.95 (*0-87891-916-3*) Res & Educ.

— The Essentials of Accounting, I. rev. ed. (Illus.). 96p. 1994. pap. text ed. 5.95 (*0-87891-667-9*) Res & Educ.

— The Essentials of Accounting, II. rev. ed. (Illus.). 80p. 1994. pap. text ed. 5.95 (*0-87891-672-5*) Res & Educ.

— The Essentials of Advanced Accounting I. rev. ed. (Illus.). 96p. 1994. pap. text ed. 5.95 (*0-87891-692-X*) Res & Educ.

— The Essentials of Advanced Accounting II. rev. ed. (Illus.). 128p. 1994. pap. text ed. 5.95 (*0-87891-905-8*) Res & Educ.

— The Essentials of Advanced Calculus I. rev. ed. (Illus.). 80p. 1994. pap. text ed. 5.95 (*0-87891-567-2*) Res & Educ.

— The Essentials of Advanced Calculus, II. rev. ed. (Illus.). 64p. 1994. pap. text ed. 5.95 (*0-87891-568-0*) Res & Educ.

— The Essentials of Algebra & Trigonometry, I. rev. ed. (Illus.). 96p. 1994. pap. text ed. 5.95 (*0-87891-569-9*) Res & Educ.

— The Essentials of Algebra & Trigonometry, II. rev. ed. (Illus.). 80p. 1994. pap. text ed. 5.95 (*0-87891-570-2*) Res & Educ.

— The Essentials of Anatomy & Physiology. 96p. 1994. pap. text ed. 5.95 (*0-87891-922-8*) Res & Educ.

— The Essentials of Ancient History 4,500 BC-500 AD. rev. ed. (Illus.). 96p. 1994. pap. text ed. 5.95 (*0-87891-704-7*) Res & Educ.

— The Essentials of Anthropology. rev. ed. (Illus.). 128p. 1994. pap. text ed. 5.95 (*0-87891-722-5*) Res & Educ.

— The Essentials of Automatic Control Systems - Robotics, I. rev. ed. (Illus.). 96p. 1994. pap. text ed. 5.95 (*0-87891-571-0*) Res & Educ.

— The Essentials of Automatic Control Systems - Robotics, II. rev. ed. (Illus.). 96p. 1994. pap. 5.95 (*0-87891-572-9*) Res & Educ.

— The Essentials of BASIC. rev. ed. (Illus.). 128p. 1994. pap. text ed. 5.95 (*0-87891-684-9*) Res & Educ.

— The Essentials of Biology, I. rev. ed. (Illus.). 64p. 1994. pap. text ed. 5.95 (*0-87891-573-7*) Res & Educ.

— The Essentials of Biology, II. rev. ed. (Illus.). 64p. 1994. pap. text ed. 5.95 (*0-87891-574-5*) Res & Educ.

— The Essentials of Boolean Algebra. rev. ed. (Illus.). 112p. 1994. pap. text ed. 5.95 (*0-87891-698-9*) Res & Educ.

— The Essentials of Business Law I. rev. ed. (Illus.). 128p. 1994. pap. text ed. 5.95 (*0-87891-690-3*) Res & Educ.

— The Essentials of Business Law II. rev. ed. (Illus.). 128p. 1994. pap. text ed. 5.95 (*0-87891-729-2*) Res & Educ.

— The Essentials of Business Statistics I. rev. ed. (Illus.). 112p. 1994. pap. text ed. 5.95 (*0-87891-841-8*) Res & Educ.

— The Essentials of Business Statistics II. rev. ed. (Illus.). 128p. 1994. pap. text ed. 5.95 (*0-87891-842-6*) Res & Educ.

— The Essentials of C Programming Language. rev. ed. (Illus.). 128p. 1994. pap. text ed. 5.95 (*0-87891-696-2*) Res & Educ.

— The Essentials of Calculus, I. rev. ed. (Illus.). 80p. 1994. pap. text ed. 5.95 (*0-87891-577-X*) Res & Educ.

— The Essentials of Calculus, II. rev. ed. (Illus.). 64p. 1994. pap. text ed. 5.95 (*0-87891-578-8*) Res & Educ.

— The Essentials of Calculus, III. rev. ed. (Illus.). 80p. 1994. pap. text ed. 5.95 (*0-87891-579-6*) Res & Educ.

— The Essentials of Canadian History, 1868 to Present. 1994. 5.95 (*0-87891-917-1*) Res & Educ.

— The Essentials of Chemistry. rev. ed. (Illus.). 96p. 1994. pap. text ed. 5.95 (*0-87891-580-X*) Res & Educ.

— The Essentials of COBOL I. rev. ed. (Illus.). 128p. 1994. pap. text ed. 5.95 (*0-87891-679-2*) Res & Educ.

— The Essentials of COBOL II. rev. ed. (Illus.). 112p. 1994. pap. text ed. 5.95 (*0-87891-680-6*) Res & Educ.

— The Essentials of Complex Variables I. rev. ed. (Illus.). 112p. 1994. pap. text ed. 5.95 (*0-87891-661-X*) Res & Educ.

— The Essentials of Complex Variables II. rev. ed. (Illus.). 112p. 1994. pap. text ed. 5.95 (*0-87891-662-8*) Res & Educ.

— The Essentials of Cost & Managerial Accounting I. rev. ed. (Illus.). 96p. 1994. pap. text ed. 5.95 (*0-87891-664-4*) Res & Educ.

— The Essentials of Cost & Managerial Accounting II. rev. ed. (Illus.). 96p. 1994. pap. text ed. 5.95 (*0-87891-668-7*) Res & Educ.

— The Essentials of Data Structures I. rev. ed. (Illus.). 112p. 1994. pap. text ed. 5.95 (*0-87891-728-4*) Res & Educ.

— The Essentials of Data Structures II. rev. ed. (Illus.). 112p. 1994. pap. text ed. 5.95 (*0-87891-837-X*) Res & Educ.

— The Essentials of Differential Equations, I. rev. ed. (Illus.). 96p. 1994. pap. text ed. 5.95 (*0-87891-581-8*) Res & Educ.

— The Essentials of Differential Equations, II. rev. ed. (Illus.). 96p. 1994. pap. text ed. 5.95 (*0-87891-582-6*) Res & Educ.

— The Essentials of Discrete Structures. rev. ed. (Illus.). 96p. 1994. pap. text ed. 5.95 (*0-87891-723-3*) Res & Educ.

— The Essentials of Electric Circuits, I. rev. ed. (Illus.). 64p. 1994. pap. text ed. 5.95 (*0-87891-585-0*) Res & Educ.

— The Essentials of Electric Circuits, II. rev. ed. (Illus.). 64p. 1994. pap. text ed. 5.95 (*0-87891-586-9*) Res & Educ.

— The Essentials of Electromagnetics, I. rev. ed. (Illus.). 80p. 1994. pap. text ed. 5.95 (*0-87891-587-7*) Res & Educ.

— The Essentials of Electromagnetics, II. rev. ed. (Illus.). 64p. 1994. pap. text ed. 5.95 (*0-87891-588-5*) Res & Educ.

— The Essentials of Electronic Communications I. rev. ed. (Illus.). 80p. 1994. pap. text ed. 5.95 (*0-87891-589-3*) Res & Educ.

— The Essentials of Electronic Communications II. rev. ed. (Illus.). 112p. 1994. pap. text ed. 5.95 (*0-87891-590-7*) Res & Educ.

— The Essentials of Electronics, I. rev. ed. (Illus.). 112p. 1994. pap. text ed. 5.95 (*0-87891-591-5*) Res & Educ.

— The Essentials of Electronics, II. rev. ed. (Illus.). 112p. 1994. pap. text ed. 5.95 (*0-87891-592-3*) Res & Educ.

— The Essentials of European History since 1935. rev. ed. (Illus.). 128p. 1994. pap. text ed. 5.95 (*0-87891-711-X*) Res & Educ.

— The Essentials of European History, 1450-1648. rev. ed. (Illus.). 96p. 1994. pap. text ed. 5.95 (*0-87891-706-3*) Res & Educ.

— The Essentials of European History, 1648-1789. rev. ed. (Illus.). 128p. 1994. pap. text ed. 5.95 (*0-87891-707-1*) Res & Educ.

— The Essentials of European History, 1789-1848. rev. ed. (Illus.). 96p. 1994. pap. text ed. 5.95 (*0-87891-708-X*) Res & Educ.

— The Essentials of European History, 1848-1914. rev. ed. (Illus.). 96p. 1994. pap. text ed. 5.95 (*0-87891-709-8*) Res & Educ.

— The Essentials of European History, 1914-1935. rev. ed. (Illus.). 128p. 1994. pap. text ed. 5.95 (*0-87891-710-1*) Res & Educ.

— The Essentials of Financial Management. rev. ed. (Illus.). 128p. 1994. pap. text ed. 5.95 (*0-87891-724-1*) Res & Educ.

— The Essentials of Finite & Discrete Math. rev. ed. (Illus.). 64p. 1994. pap. text ed. 5.95 (*0-87891-593-1*) Res & Educ.

— The Essentials of Fluid Mechanics - Dynamics, I. rev. ed. (Illus.). 80p. 1994. pap. text ed. 5.95 (*0-87891-594-X*) Res & Educ.

— The Essentials of Fluid Mechanics - Dynamics, II. rev. ed. (Illus.). 80p. 1994. pap. text ed. 5.95 (*0-87891-595-8*) Res & Educ.

— The Essentials of FORTRAN. rev. ed. (Illus.). 128p. 1994. pap. text ed. 5.95 (*0-87891-663-6*) Res & Educ.

— The Essentials of Fourier Analysis. rev. ed. (Illus.). 80p. 1994. pap. text ed. 5.95 (*0-87891-697-0*) Res & Educ.

— The Essentials of French. 96p. 1994. pap. text ed. 5.95 (*0-87891-926-0*) Res & Educ.

— The Essentials of Geometry, I. rev. ed. (Illus.). 80p. 1994. pap. text ed. 5.95 (*0-87891-606-7*) Res & Educ.

— The Essentials of Geometry II. rev. ed. (Illus.). 96p. 1994. pap. text ed. 5.95 (*0-87891-607-5*) Res & Educ.

— The Essentials of German. 96p. 1994. pap. text ed. 5.95 (*0-87891-927-9*) Res & Educ.

— The Essentials of Group Theory I. rev. ed. (Illus.). 112p. 1994. pap. text ed. 5.95 (*0-87891-686-5*) Res & Educ.

— The Essentials of Group-Theory II. rev. ed. (Illus.). 96p. 1994. pap. text ed. 5.95 (*0-87891-687-3*) Res & Educ.

— The Essentials of Heat Transfer, I. rev. ed. (Illus.). 80p. 1994. pap. text ed. 5.95 (*0-87891-608-3*) Res & Educ.

— The Essentials of Heat Transfer, II. rev. ed. (Illus.). 80p. 1994. pap. text ed. 5.95 (*0-87891-609-1*) Res & Educ.

— The Essentials of Intermediate Accounting I. rev. ed. (Illus.). 112p. 1994. pap. text ed. 5.95 (*0-87891-682-2*) Res & Educ.

— The Essentials of Intermediate Accounting II. rev. ed. (Illus.). 128p. 1994. pap. text ed. 5.95 (*0-87891-683-0*) Res & Educ.

— The Essentials of Italian. 96p. 1994. pap. text ed. 5.95 (*0-87891-929-5*) Res & Educ.

— The Essentials of La Place Transforms. rev. ed. (Illus.). 128p. 1994. pap. text ed. 5.95 (*0-87891-726-8*) Res & Educ.

— The Essentials of Linear Algebra. rev. ed. (Illus.). 96p. 1994. pap. text ed. 5.95 (*0-87891-610-5*) Res & Educ.

— The Essentials of Macroeconomics I. rev. ed. (Illus.). 96p. 1994. pap. text ed. 5.95 (*0-87891-700-4*) Res & Educ.

— The Essentials of Macroeconomics II. rev. ed. (Illus.). 96p. 1994. pap. text ed. 5.95 (*0-87891-719-5*) Res & Educ.

— The Essentials of Marketing Principles. rev. ed. (Illus.). 128p. 1994. pap. text ed. 5.95 (*0-87891-693-8*) Res & Educ.

— The Essentials of Mathematics for Engineers I. rev. ed. (Illus.). 96p. 1994. pap. text ed. 5.95 (*0-87891-858-2*) Res & Educ.

— The Essentials of Mathematics for Engineers II. rev. ed. (Illus.). 128p. 1994. pap. text ed. 5.95 (*0-87891-891-4*) Res & Educ.

— The Essentials of Mechanics, I. rev. ed. (Illus.). 96p. 1994. pap. text ed. 5.95 (*0-87891-611-3*) Res & Educ.

— The Essentials of Mechanics, II. rev. ed. (Illus.). 96p. 1994. pap. text ed. 5.95 (*0-87891-612-1*) Res & Educ.

— The Essentials of Mechanics III. rev. ed. (Illus.). 96p. 1994. pap. text ed. 5.95 (*0-87891-613-X*) Res & Educ.

— The Essentials of Medieval History, 500-1450 AD. rev. ed. (Illus.). 96p. 1994. pap. text ed. 5.95 (*0-87891-705-5*) Res & Educ.

— The Essentials of Microbiology. 96p. 1994. pap. text ed. 5.95 (*0-87891-924-4*) Res & Educ.

— The Essentials of Microeconomics. rev. ed. (Illus.). 128p. 1994. pap. text ed. 5.95 (*0-87891-660-1*) Res & Educ.

— The Essentials of Modern Algebra. rev. ed. (Illus.). 80p. 1994. pap. text ed. 5.95 (*0-87891-681-4*) Res & Educ.

— The Essentials of Money & Banking I. rev. ed. (Illus.). 112p. 1994. pap. text ed. 5.95 (*0-87891-691-1*) Res & Educ.

— The Essentials of Money & Banking II. rev. ed. (Illus.). 128p. 1994. pap. text ed. 5.95 (*0-87891-720-9*) Res & Educ.

— The Essentials of Numerical Analysis, I. rev. ed. (Illus.). 96p. 1994. pap. text ed. 5.95 (*0-87891-614-8*) Res & Educ.

— The Essentials of Numerical Analysis, II. rev. ed. (Illus.). 96p. 1994. pap. text ed. 5.95 (*0-87891-615-6*) Res & Educ.

— The Essentials of Organic Chemistry I. rev. ed. (Illus.). 128p. 1994. pap. text ed. 5.95 (*0-87891-616-4*) Res & Educ.

— The Essentials of Organic Chemistry, II. rev. ed. (Illus.). 128p. 1994. pap. text ed. 5.95 (*0-87891-617-2*) Res & Educ.

— The Essentials of PASCAL I. rev. ed. (Illus.). 80p. 1994. pap. text ed. 5.95 (*0-87891-694-6*) Res & Educ.

— The Essentials of PASCAL II. rev. ed. (Illus.). 96p. 1994. pap. text ed. 5.95 (*0-87891-718-7*) Res & Educ.

— The Essentials of Physical Chemistry, I. rev. ed. (Illus.). 128p. 1994. pap. text ed. 5.95 (*0-87891-620-2*) Res & Educ.

— The Essentials of Physical Chemistry, II. rev. ed. (Illus.). 128p. 1994. pap. text ed. 5.95 (*0-87891-621-0*) Res & Educ.

— The Essentials of Physics, I. rev. ed. (Illus.). 96p. 1994. pap. text ed. 5.95 (*0-87891-618-0*) Res & Educ.

— The Essentials of Physics, II. rev. ed. (Illus.). 80p. 1994. pap. text ed. 5.95 (*0-87891-619-9*) Res & Educ.

— The Essentials of PL-1 Programming. rev. ed. (Illus.). 112p. 1994. pap. text ed. 5.95 (*0-87891-695-4*) Res & Educ.

— The Essentials of Pre-Calculus. rev. ed. (Illus.). 128p. 1994. pap. text ed. 5.95 (*0-87891-877-9*) Res & Educ.

— The Essentials of Probability. rev. ed. (Illus.). 128p. 1994. pap. text ed. 5.95 (*0-87891-840-X*) Res & Educ.

— Essentials of Psychology, No. I. 96p. 1994. pap. text ed. 5.95 (*0-87891-930-9*) Res & Educ.

— Essentials of Psychology, No. II. 96p. 1994. pap. text ed. 5.95 (*0-87891-931-7*) Res & Educ.

— The Essentials of Real Variables. (Illus.). 96p. 1994. pap. text ed. 5.95 (*0-87891-921-X*) Res & Educ.

— The Essentials of Set Theory. rev. ed. (Illus.). 80p. 1994. pap. text ed. 5.95 (*0-87891-657-1*) Res & Educ.

— The Essentials of Spanish. 96p. 1994. pap. text ed. 5.95 (*0-87891-928-7*) Res & Educ.

— The Essentials of Statistics I. rev. ed. (Illus.). 112p. 1994. pap. text ed. 5.95 (*0-87891-658-X*) Res & Educ.

— The Essentials of Statistics II. rev. ed. (Illus.). 128p. 1994. pap. text ed. 5.95 (*0-87891-659-8*) Res & Educ.

— The Essentials of Strength of Materials I. rev. ed. (Illus.). 128p. 1994. pap. text ed. 5.95 (*0-87891-624-5*) Res & Educ.

— The Essentials of Strength of Materials II. rev. ed. (Illus.). 128p. 1994. pap. text ed. 5.95 (*0-87891-625-3*) Res & Educ.

— The Essentials of Thermodynamics I. rev. ed. (Illus.). 64p. 1994. pap. text ed. 5.95 (*0-87891-626-1*) Res & Educ.

— The Essentials of Thermodynamics II. rev. ed. (Illus.). 64p. 1994. pap. text ed. 5.95 (*0-87891-627-X*) Res & Educ.

— The Essentials of Topology. rev. ed. (Illus.). 112p. 1994. pap. text ed. 5.95 (*0-87891-685-7*) Res & Educ.

— The Essentials of Transport Phenomena I. rev. ed. (Illus.). 96p. 1994. pap. text ed. 5.95 (*0-87891-628-8*) Res & Educ.

— The Essentials of Transport Phenomena II. rev. ed. (Illus.). 112p. 1994. pap. text ed. 5.95 (*0-87891-629-6*) Res & Educ.

— The Essentials of U. S. History, 1500-1789. rev. ed. (Illus.). 96p. 1994. pap. text ed. 5.95 (*0-87891-712-8*) Res & Educ.

— The Essentials of U. S. History, 1789-1841. rev. ed. (Illus.). 112p. 1994. pap. text ed. 5.95 (*0-87891-713-6*) Res & Educ.

— The Essentials of U. S. History, 1841-1877. rev. ed. (Illus.). 96p. 1994. pap. text ed. 5.95 (*0-87891-714-4*) Res & Educ.

— The Essentials of U. S. History, 1877-1912. rev. ed. (Illus.). 96p. 1994. pap. text ed. 5.95 (*0-87891-715-2*) Res & Educ.

— The Essentials of U. S. History, 1912-1941. rev. ed. (Illus.). 128p. 1994. pap. text ed. 5.95 (*0-87891-716-0*) Res & Educ.

— The Essentials of Vector Analysis. rev. ed. (Illus.). 128p. 1994. pap. text ed. 5.95 (*0-87891-630-X*) Res & Educ.

— ExCET: Texas Education Certification. (Illus.). 336p. 1994. pap. text ed. 22.95 (*0-87891-971-6*) Res & Educ.

— FE - Fundamentals of Engineering Exam (EIT) rev. ed. (Illus.). 544p. 1994. pap. text ed. 21.95 (*0-87891-849-3*) Res & Educ.

— FE Review. 800p. 1994. pap. text ed. 24.95 (*0-87891-915-5*) Res & Educ.

— Finite & Discrete Math Problem Solver. rev. ed. LC 84-61815. (Illus.). 1032p. 1994. pap. text ed. 23.95 (*0-87891-559-1*) Res & Educ.

— Fluid Mechanics-Dynamics Problem Solver. rev. ed. LC 83-62278. (Illus.). 960p. 1994. pap. text ed. 29.95 (*0-87891-547-8*) Res & Educ.

— Freshman College Composition. (CLEP Ser.). 312p. 1995. pap. text ed. 16.95 (*0-87891-899-X*) Res & Educ.

— GED - General Educational Development Test, Canadian Edition. (Illus.). 1994. pap. text ed. 15.95 (*0-87891-918-X*) Res & Educ.

— GED - H.S. Equivalency Diploma Test. rev. ed. (Illus.). 912p. 1994. pap. text ed. 15.95 (*0-87891-869-8*) Res & Educ.

— General Examinations Review Book. (CLEP Ser.). 1008p. 1995. pap. text ed. 17.95 (*0-87891-900-7*) Res & Educ.

— Genetics Problem Solver. rev. ed. LC 85-62730. (Illus.). 640p. 1994. pap. text ed. 23.95 (*0-87891-560-5*) Res & Educ.

— Geometry Problem Solver. rev. ed. LC 77-70336. (Illus.). 942p. 1994. pap. text ed. 23.95 (*0-87891-510-9*) Res & Educ.

— GMAT. rev. ed. (Illus.). 816p. 1994. pap. text ed. 18.95 (*0-87891-730-6*) Res & Educ.

— GRE Biology Test Preparation. rev. ed. (Illus.). 736p. 1994. pap. text ed. 19.95 (*0-87891-602-4*) Res & Educ.

— GRE Chemistry Test Preparation. rev. ed. (Illus.). 480p. 1994. pap. text ed. 25.95 (*0-87891-600-8*) Res & Educ.

— GRE Computer Science Test Preparation. rev. ed. (Illus.). 272p. 1994. pap. text ed. 19.95 (*0-87891-847-7*) Res & Educ.

— GRE Economics Test Preparation. rev. ed. LC 88-90711. (Illus.). 672p. 1994. pap. text ed. 24.95 (*0-87891-632-6*) Res & Educ.

— GRE Engineering Test Preparation. rev. ed. (Illus.). 640p. 1994. pap. text ed. 24.95 (*0-87891-601-6*) Res & Educ.

— GRE General Test Preparation. rev. ed. (Illus.). 864p. 1994. pap. text ed. 18.95 (*0-87891-631-8*) Res & Educ.

— GRE Literature in English Test Preparation. rev. ed. (Illus.). 786p. 1994. pap. text ed. 25.95 (*0-87891-634-2*) Res & Educ.

— GRE Mathematics Test Preparation. rev. ed. (Illus.). 352p. 1994. pap. text ed. 24.95 (*0-87891-637-7*) Res & Educ.

— GRE Physics Test Preparation. rev. ed. (Illus.). 416p. 1994. pap. text ed. 25.95 (*0-87891-848-5*) Res & Educ.

— GRE Psychology Test Preparation. rev. ed. LC 86-60827. (Illus.). 592p. 1994. pap. text ed. 19.95 (*0-87891-599-0*) Res & Educ.

— Handbook & Guide for Comparing & Selecting Computer Languages. LC 84-61817. (Illus.). 128p. 1985. 8.95 (*0-87891-561-3*) Res & Educ.

— Handbook of Concrete Technology & Masonry Construction. LC 81-50761. (Illus.). 832p. (Orig.). 1981. 26.95 (*0-87891-528-1*) Res & Educ.

— Handbook of Economic Analysis. LC 81-86217. (Illus.). 224p. (Orig.). (C). 1982. pap. text ed. 13.30 (*0-87891-535-4*) Res & Educ.

— Handbook of Field Surveying. LC 83-61836. (Illus.). 317p. 1983. 19.85 (*0-87891-530-3*) Res & Educ.

— Handbook of Mathematical, Scientific, & Engineering Formulas, Tables, Functions, Graphs, Transforms. rev. ed. LC 80-52490. (Illus.). (Orig.). (C). 1993. 32.95 (*0-87891-521-4*) Res & Educ.

— Heat Transfer Problem Solver. rev. ed. LC 84-61813. (Illus.). 840p. 1994. pap. text ed. 29.95 (*0-87891-557-5*) Res & Educ.

— High School Algebra Tutor. rev. ed. LC 85-62004. (Illus.). 320p. 1994. pap. text ed. 13.95 (*0-87891-564-8*) Res & Educ.

— High School Biology Tutor. 352p. 1994. 12.95 (*0-87891-907-4*) Res & Educ.

— High School Chemistry Tutor. rev. ed. LC 86-63873. (Illus.). 360p. 1994. pap. text ed. 12.95 (*0-87891-596-6*) Res & Educ.

— High School Earth Science Tutor. 496p. 1995. pap. text ed. 13.95 (*0-87891-975-9*) Res & Educ.

— High School Geometry Tutor. rev. ed. LC 85-62003. (Illus.). 352p. 1994. pap. text ed. 12.95 (*0-87891-565-6*) Res & Educ.

— High School Physics Tutor. rev. ed. (Illus.). 288p. 1994. pap. text ed. 13.95 (*0-87891-597-4*) Res & Educ.

— High School Pre-Calculus Tutor. (YA). (gr. 9-12). 1994. 12.95 (*0-87891-910-4*) Res & Educ.

R

— High School Probability Tutor. 300p. 1994. pap. text ed. 13.95 (0-87891-958-9) Res & Educ.
— High School Trigonometry Tutor. rev. ed. LC 85-62002. (Illus.). 352p. 1994. pap. text ed. 12.95 (0-87891-566-4) Res & Educ.
— Human Aging. LC 82-80749. (Illus.). 544p. (Orig.). (C). 1982. pap. text ed. 14.95 (0-87891-536-2) Res & Educ.
— Human Growth & Development. (CLEP Ser.). 400p. 1995. pap. text ed. 16.95 (0-87891-902-3) Res & Educ.
— Introductory Sociology. (CLEP Ser.). 320p. 1995. pap. text ed. 16.95 (0-87891-903-1) Res & Educ.
— Linear Algebra Problem Solver. rev. ed. LC 79-92402. (Illus.). 1022p. 1994. pap. text ed. 29.95 (0-87891-518-4) Res & Educ.
— LSAT - Law School Admission Test. rev. ed. (Illus.). 688p. 1994. pap. text ed. 18.95 (0-87891-854-X) Res & Educ.
— Machine Design Problem Solver. rev. ed. (Illus.). 928p. 1994. pap. text ed. 29.95 (0-87891-605-9) Res & Educ.
— Math Builder for Standardized Tests. rev. ed. (Illus.). 368p. 1994. 13.95 (0-87891-876-0) Res & Educ.
— Mathematics for Engineers Problem Solver. rev. ed. (Illus.). 816p. 1994. pap. text ed. 29.95 (0-87891-838-8) Res & Educ.
— Max Notes - A Raisin in the Sun. (Illus.). 1994. pap. text ed. 3.95 (0-87891-945-7) Res & Educ.
— Max Notes - A Tale of Two Cities. (Illus.). 128p. 1994. pap. text ed. 3.95 (0-87891-949-X) Res & Educ.
— Max Notes - Gone with the Wind. (Illus.). 128p. 1994. pap. text ed. 3.95 (0-87891-955-4) Res & Educ.
— Max Notes - Hamlet. (Illus.). 128p. 1994. pap. text ed. 3.95 (0-87891-952-X) Res & Educ.
— Max Notes - Huckleberry Finn. (Illus.). 128p. 1994. pap. text ed. 3.95 (0-87891-953-8) Res & Educ.
— Max Notes - I Know Why the Caged Bird Sings. (Illus.). 128p. 1994. pap. text ed. 3.95 (0-87891-956-2) Res & Educ.
— Max Notes - Les Miserables. (Illus.). 128p. 1994. pap. text ed. 39.95 (0-87891-951-1) Res & Educ.
— Max Notes - Macbeth. (Illus.). 128p. 1994. pap. text ed. 3.95 (0-87891-944-9) Res & Educ.
— Max Notes - The Grapes of Wrath. (Illus.). 128p. 1994. pap. text ed. 3.95 (0-87891-947-3) Res & Educ.
— Max Notes - The Great Gatsby. (Illus.). 128p. 1994. pap. text ed. 3.95 (0-87891-942-2) Res & Educ.
— Max Notes - The Scarlet Letter. (Illus.). 128p. 1994. pap. text ed. 3.95 (0-87891-950-3) Res & Educ.
— Max Notes - To Kill a Mockingbird. (Illus.). 128p. 1994. pap. text ed. 3.95 (0-87891-946-5) Res & Educ.
— MCAT: Medical College Admission Test. rev. ed. (Illus.). 1008p. 1994. 39.95 (0-87891-872-8) Res & Educ.
— Mechanics Problem Solver. rev. ed. LC 79-92403. (Illus.). 1088p. 1994. pap. text ed. 29.95 (0-87891-519-2) Res & Educ.
— Modern Microelectronics: Circuit Design, IC Applications, Fabrication Technology, 2 vols., Set. 2nd ed. LC 81-50168. (Illus.). 1408p. 1981. 36.75 (0-87891-520-6) Res & Educ.
— NTE - Core Battery with Cassettes. rev. ed. (Illus.). 768p. 1994. pap. text ed. 19.95 (0-87891-851-5) Res & Educ.
— Numerical Analysis Problem Solver. rev. ed. LC 83-62277. (Illus.). 896p. 1994. pap. text ed. 29.95 (0-87891-549-4) Res & Educ.
— NYSTCE - The New York State Teacher Certification Exam. 592p. 1995. pap. text ed. 19.95 (0-87891-866-3) Res & Educ.
— Operations Research Problem Solver. rev. ed. LC 83-62276. (Illus.). 1068p. 1994. pap. text ed. 29.95 (0-87891-548-6) Res & Educ.
— Optics Problem Solver. rev. ed. LC 81-50899. 832p. 1994. 29.95 (0-87891-526-5) Res & Educ.
— Organic Chemistry Problem Solver. rev. ed. LC 77-19370. 1408p. 1994. pap. text ed. 29.95 (0-87891-512-5) Res & Educ.
— Physical Chemistry Problem Solver. rev. ed. LC 81-522778. (Illus.). 800p. 1994. pap. text ed. 29.95 (0-87891-532-X) Res & Educ.
— Physics Builder for Standardized Tests. 544p. 1994. pap. text ed. 12.95 (0-87891-941-4) Res & Educ.
— Physics Problem Solver. rev. ed. LC 76-332. (Illus.). 1200p. (C). 1994. pap. text ed. 23.95 (0-87891-507-9) Res & Educ.
— PPST - Pre-Professional Skills Test. 350p. 1995. pap. text ed. 14.95 (0-87891-867-1) Res & Educ.
— Pre-Calculus Problem Solver. rev. ed. LC 84-61812. (Illus.). 960p. 1994. pap. text ed. 23.95 (0-87891-556-7) Res & Educ.
— Principles of Marketing. (CLEP Ser.). 312p. 1995. pap. text ed. 16.95 (0-87891-904-X) Res & Educ.
— Psychology Problem Solver. rev. ed. LC 80-53174. (Illus.). 1056p. (Orig.). (C). 1994. pap. text ed. 23.95 (0-87891-523-0) Res & Educ.
— REA's Guide to Law Schools. (Illus.). 1994. 19.95 (0-87891-920-1) Res & Educ.
— REA's Guide to Medical & Dental Schools. rev. ed. (Illus.). 1994. 19.95 (0-87891-919-8) Res & Educ.
— REA's Literature Study Guides. 128p. 1994. pap. text ed. (0-87891-954-6) Res & Educ.
— SAT I Math Tutor. 325p. 1994. pap. text ed. 12.95 (0-87891-962-7) Res & Educ.
— SAT I Verbal Tutor. 256p. 1994. pap. text ed. 12.95 (0-87891-963-5) Res & Educ.
— SAT II American History & Social Studies. rev. ed. (Illus.). 508p. 1994. pap. text ed. 13.95 (0-87891-845-0) Res & Educ.
— SAT II Biology. rev. ed. (Illus.). 432p. 1994. pap. text ed. 13.95 (0-87891-644-X) Res & Educ.
— SAT II Chemistry. rev. ed. (Illus.). 368p. 1994. pap. text ed. 13.95 (0-87891-603-2) Res & Educ.
— SAT II French. 1994. pap. 13.95 (0-87891-969-4) Res & Educ.
— SAT II German. 1994. pap. 13.95 (0-87891-970-8) Res & Educ.
— SAT II Literature. rev. ed. (Illus.). 288p. 1994. pap. text ed. 13.95 (0-87891-846-9) Res & Educ.
— SAT II Math Level I. rev. ed. (Illus.). 336p. 1994. pap. text ed. 13.95 (0-87891-642-3) Res & Educ.
— SAT II Physics. rev. ed. (Illus.). 288p. 1994. pap. text ed. 13.95 (0-87891-870-1) Res & Educ.
— SAT II Spanish. 1994. pap. 13.95 (0-87891-968-6) Res & Educ.
— Sleep & Dream Research. LC 82-62130. (Illus.). 384p. 1988. 14.30 (0-87891-545-1) Res & Educ.
— Statistics Problem Solver. rev. ed. LC 78-64581. (Illus.). 1056p. 1994. pap. text ed. 23.95 (0-87891-515-X) Res & Educ.
— Strength of Materials & Mechanics of Solids Problem Solver. rev. ed. LC 80-83305. (Illus.). 1152p. (Orig.). (C). 1994. pap. text ed. 29.95 (0-87891-522-2) Res & Educ.
— TASP - Texas Academic Skills Program. rev. ed. 528p. 1994. pap. text ed. 16.95 (0-87891-893-0) Res & Educ.
— Theory of Linear Systems. LC 82-80746. (Illus.). 224p. (Orig.). (C). 1982. pap. text ed. 10.60 (0-87891-539-7) Res & Educ.
— Thermodynamics Problem Solver. rev. ed. LC 84-61810. (Illus.). 892p. 1994. pap. text ed. 29.95 (0-87891-555-9) Res & Educ.
— TOEFL. rev. ed. (Illus.). 720p. 1994. pap. text ed. 16.95 (0-87891-855-8); audio, pap. text ed. 29.95 (0-87891-850-7) Res & Educ.
— Topology Problem Solver. (Illus.). 1008p. 1994. pap. text ed. 29.95 (0-87891-925-2) Res & Educ.
— Transport Phenomena Problem Solver. rev. ed. LC 84-61816. (Illus.). 864p. 1994. pap. text ed. 29.95 (0-87891-562-1) Res & Educ.
— U. S. History Builder. 640p. 1994. pap. text ed. 14.95 (0-87891-961-9) Res & Educ.
— Vector Analysis Problem Solver. rev. ed. LC 84-61811. (Illus.). 1296p. 1994. pap. text ed. 29.95 (0-87891-554-0) Res & Educ.
— Verbal Builder for Standardized Tests. rev. ed. (Illus.). 368p. 1994. 12.95 (0-87891-875-2) Res & Educ.

Research & Education Association Staff, ed. Technical Design Graphics Problem Solver. rev. ed. LC 81-86648. (Illus.). 960p. (Orig.). 1994. 23.95 (0-87891-534-6) Res & Educ.

Research & Education Association Staff, jt. auth. see Giove, Frank C.

Research & Education Association Staff, jt. auth. see Segal, Mark A.

***Research & Education Staff.** Biology of Mental Disorders. 192p. 1994. pap. text ed. 14.95 (0-87891-960-0) Res & Educ.
— Chemical Engineering Handbook. 1500p. 1995. pap. text ed. 32.95 (0-87891-982-1) Res & Educ.
— Electrical Engineering Handbook. 1500p. 1995. pap. text ed. 32.95 (0-87891-981-3) Res & Educ.
— The Essentials of Astronomy. 100p. 1994. pap. text ed. 5.95 (0-87891-965-1) Res & Educ.
— The Essentials of College & University Writing. 100p. 1994. pap. text ed. 5.95 (0-87891-964-3) Res & Educ.
— Essentials of HIV-AIDS. 100p. 1994. pap. text ed. 5.95 (0-87891-984-8) Res & Educ.
— The Essentials of Molecular Structures of Life. 128p. 1995. pap. text ed. 5.95 (0-87891-983-X) Res & Educ.
— The Essentials of Sociology. 100p. 1995. pap. text ed. 5.95 (0-87891-966-X) Res & Educ.
— European History Builder for Admission & Standardized Tests. 544p. 1995. pap. text ed. 14.95 (0-87891-782-9) Res & Educ.
— GRE Sociology. 400p. 1995. pap. text ed. 24.95 (0-87891-999-6) Res & Educ.
— How to Create Catalogs That Sell. 208p. 1995. pap. text ed. 29.95 (0-87891-976-7) Res & Educ.
— How to Create Great Advertising by the Most Creative People in the Field. 208p. 1995. pap. text ed. 29.95 (0-87891-977-5) Res & Educ.
— How to Succeed in Business by Presidents of Successful Businesses. 208p. 1995. pap. text ed. 29.95 (0-87891-978-3) Res & Educ.
— MAT - The Miller Analogies Test. 256p. 1995. pap. text ed. 12.95 (0-87891-864-7) Res & Educ.
— Max Notes - Julius Caesar. 1500p. 1994. pap. text ed. 32.95 (0-87891-948-1) Res & Educ.
— Max Notes - The Odyssey. (Illus.). 100p. 1995. pap. text ed. 5.95 (0-87891-943-0) Res & Educ.
— Mechanical Engineering Handbook. 1536p. 1995. pap. text ed. 32.95 (0-87891-980-5) Res & Educ.
— MSAT - Multiple Subject Assessment for Teachers f. 400p. 1995. pap. text ed. 22.95 (0-87891-749-7) Res & Educ.
— NCLEX-RN. 600p. 1995. pap. text ed. 24.95 (0-87891-865-5) Res & Educ.
— Proven Successful Brochures & Methods for Direct Marketing. 208p. 1995. pap. text ed. 29.95 (0-87891-979-1) Res & Educ.
— The Republic. (Max Notes Ser.). (Illus.). 128p. 1995. pap. text ed. 3.95 (0-87891-987-2) Res & Educ.
— SAT II: English Language Proficiency Test. 336p. 1995. pap. text ed. 13.95 (0-87891-641-5) Res & Educ.
— Sat II Math Level IC: Math Level IC. 272p. 1995. pap. text ed. 13.95 (0-87891-750-0) Res & Educ.
— Top 75 Business Schools Directory. 352p. 1995. pap. text ed. 18.95 (0-87891-747-0) Res & Educ.

Research & Education Staff, jt. auth. see Conner, E.

Research & Information System for the Nonaligned & Other Developing Countries. Low Income Countries: Problems & Prospects. 100p. 1987. text ed. 12.50 (81-7027-101-0, Pub. by Radiant Pubs II) S Asia.

***Research & Policy Committee of the Committee for Economic Development.** Rebuilding Inner City Communities: An Emerging National Strategy Against Urban Decay. LC 95-1695. 1995. 18.00 (0-87186-120-8) Comm Econ Dev.
— U. S. Trade Policy Beyond the Uraguay Round: A Statement. LC 94-14783. 1994. 10.00 (0-87186-098-8) Comm Econ Dev.
— The United States in the New Global Economy: A Rallier of Nations. LC 92-34022. 90p. 1992. pap. 17.50 (0-87186-094-5) Comm Econ Dev.

***Research & Policy Committee of the Economic Development Committee, ed.** Who Will Pay for Your Retirement? The Looming Crisis: A Statement. LC 95-3345. 1995. 20.00 (0-87186-119-4) Comm Econ Dev.

Research & Reference Division Staff. Mass Media in India, Nineteen Eighty-One to Eighty-Three. 269p. 1984. 21.95 (0-318-37285-1) Asia Bk Corp.

Research & Technology Coordinating Committee (U. S.), jt. auth. see National Research Council (U. S.), Transportation Research Board Staff.

Research Alert Editors. Attracting the Affluent: The First Guide to America's Ultimate Market. LC 91-10939. 320p. 1991. boxed 49.95 (0-942061-23-3, Financial Sourcebks) Sourcebks.
— Future Vision: The 189 Most Important Trends of the 1990s. LC 90-49474. (Illus.). 248p. 1991. 21.95 (0-942061-17-9, Sourcebooks Trade); pap. 12.95 (0-942061-16-0, Sourcebooks Trade) Sourcebks.
— The Lifestyle Odyssey: The Facts Behind the Social, Personal & Cultural Changes Touching Each of Our Lives. LC 91-29738. (Illus.). 329p. 1992. pap. 15.95 (0-942061-36-5, Sourcebooks Trade) Sourcebks.

Research Associates Company Staff. Food for Sex: How to Improve Sex Through the Foods You Eat. LC 88-63835. 63p. (Orig.). 1989. reprint ed. pap. 9.95 (0-317-93479-1) Res Assocs Co.

Research Committee on the Study of Honolulu Residents. The Third Attitudinal Survey of Honolulu Residents, 1983. 170p. 1986. pap. text ed. 19.50 (0-8248-1054-6, Pub. by Inst Stat JA) UH Pr.

Research Committee on the Study of Honolulu Residents, comp. Honolulu Residents & Their Attitudes in Multi-Ethnic Perspective: Toward a Theory of the American National Character. 153p. 1980. pap. text ed. 10.00 (0-8248-0717-0) UH Pr.

Research Communications Ltd. Staff, ed. see Crane, Valerie, et al.

Research Conference on Geriatric Blindness & Severe Visual Impairment Staff. Proceedings of the Research Conference on Geriatric Blindness & Severe Visual Impairment, September, 7-8, 1967, Washington, D. C. Clark, Leslie L., ed. 91p. reprint ed. pap. 26.00 (0-7837-0134-9, 2040423) Bks Demand.

Research Conference on Structure & Property of Engineering Materials Staff. Materials Science Research: Proceedings of the Research Conference on Structure & Property of Engineering Materials, North Carolina State University, Raleigh, Nov. 16-18, 1964. Kriegel, W. Wurth & Palmour, Hayne, III, eds. LC 63-17645. (Illus.). 645p. reprint ed. pap. 180.00 (0-317-08351-1, 2019409) Bks Demand.

***Research Conference on Subjective Probability, Utility & Decision Making Staff.** Contributions to Decision Making. Caverni, Jean-Paul, ed. LC 95-2215. 1995. write for info. (0-444-82181-3) Elsevier.

Research Council for Complementary Medicine Staff. Complementary Medicine & the European Community. 160p. (Orig.). Date not set. pap. 23.95 (0-8464-4198-5) Beekman Pubs.

***Research Division Staff.** Financial Derivatives: New Instruments & Their Uses. 242p. 1993. per. 15.00 (0-9624159-1-X) FRB Atlanta.

Research Foundation of Jewish Emigration, Inc. Staff, ed. International Biographical Dictionary of Central European Emigres: 1933-1945, 3 Vols. Incl. Vol. 1. Politik, Wirtschaft, Offentliches Leben (In German) 933p. 1980. lib. bdg. 300.00 (3-598-10088-4); Set, Pt. 1, Pt. 2. Arts, Sciences & Literature, 2 pts. 1398p. 1983. Set, Pt. 1, 771p., Pt. 2, 627p. lib. bdg. 450.00 (3-598-10089-2); Vol. 3. Index. 301p. lib. bdg. 200.00 (3-598-10090-6); 2632p. (ENG & GER.). 1983. Set lib. bdg. 815.00 (3-598-10087-6) K G Saur.

Research Group on Living & Surviving Staff. Inhabiting the Earth as a Finite World. 1979. lib. bdg. 47.50 (0-89838-018-9) Kluwer Ac.

Research, Igos. Advanced Magick Quest Course, Bk. 4: Milanthros. 107p. 25.00 (1-57179-037-3) Intern Guild ASRS.

Research Inst. of Acupuncture & Moxibustion, China Staff. Chinese Therapeutical Methods of Acupuncture & Moxibustion. 18p. 1994. reprint ed. spiral bd. 2.75 (0-7873-1023-9) Mokelumne.

Research Institute for Peace & Security Staff. Asian Security 1987-1988: Asia 3. (Asia Ser.: No. 3). 212p. 1987. 28.75 (0-317-66310-0, Pergamon Pr) Elsevier.
— Asian Security 1991-1992. (Asia Seven Asian Security Ser.). 285p. 1991. 39.00 (0-08-041312-9, Pub. by Brasseys UK); pap. 20.00 (0-08-041316-1, Pub. by Brasseys UK) Brasseys Inc.

Research Institute for Peace & Security Staff, ed. Asian Security, 1985. 226p. 1985. 38.50 (0-08-031208-X, Pergamon Pr); pap. 19.95 (0-08-031209-8, Pergamon Pr) Elsevier.

Research Institute for Peace & Security, ed. Asian Security, 1986. (Asia Ser.: No. 2). 212p. 1986. 38.50 (0-08-033610-8, Pergamon Pr); pap. 19.95 (0-08-033611-6, Pergamon Pr) Elsevier.

Research Institute for Peace Studies Staff. Asian Security 1992-93. 250p. 1992. 45.00 (1-85753-042-X, Pub. by Brasseys UK) Brasseys Inc.
— Asian Security, 1993-94. Masataka, Kasaka & Bearman, Sidney, eds. 254p. 1993. 40.00 (1-85753-028-4, Pub. by Brasseys UK) Brasseys Inc.
— Asian Security, 1994-95. 256p. 1994. 40.00 (1-85753-074-8) Macmillan.

Research Institute for the Study of Man Staff. Testament: Life & Work of M. G. Smith 1921-1993. (InterAmericas Ser.: No. 3). 47p. (Orig.). 1994. 7.00 (0-9633741-3-3) RI Study of Man.

Research Institute of America, Inc. Staff. Employment Coordinator. write for info. (0-318-59234-7) Res Inst Am.
— Stock Market Values & Yields, 1993. rev. ed. 192p. 1993. pap. text ed. 19.50 (0-7811-0065-8) Res Inst Am.

Research Institute of America Staff. All States Tax Handbook 1994. rev. ed. 410p. 1993. pap. text ed. 30.00 (0-7811-0079-8) Res Inst Am.
— Masters Federal Tax Manual: 1992 Edition. 676p. 1992. pap. 25.00 (0-13-597089-X, J K Lasser) P-H Gen Ref & Trav.
— Stock Market Values, January 1, 1994. rev. ed. 195p. 1994. pap. text ed. 19.50 (0-7811-0083-6) Res Inst Am.

Research Institute on the Social Welfare Consequences of Migration & Residential Movement (1969: San Juan, PR). Migration & Social Welfare: Report. Easton, Joseph W., ed. LC 72-144344. 256p. reprint ed. pap. 73.00 (0-317-55739-4, 2029275) Bks Demand.

Research International Staff, ed. Freelancers of North America. 2nd ed. pap. 37.95 (0-911085-05-X) Author Aid.

Research Libraries of the New York Public Library & the Library of Congress MARC Tapes Staff. Bibliographic Guide to Government Publications - Foreign: 1990, 2 vols., Set. (Bibliographic Guides Ser.). 1600p. 1991. lib. bdg. 525.00 (0-8161-7139-4) G K Hall.
— Bibliographic Guide to Soviet & East European Studies: 1990, 3 vols., Set. (Bibliographic Guides Ser.). 2980p. 1991. lib. bdg. 580.00 (0-8161-7148-3) G K Hall.

Research Libraries of the New York Public Library & The Library of Congress Staff. Bibliographic Guide to North American History: 1990. (Bibliographic Guides Ser.). 740p. 1991. lib. bdg. 290.00 (0-8161-7145-9) G K Hall.

Research Libraries of the New York Public Library Staff & Library of Congress Staff. Bibliographic Guide to Conference Publications, 1991, 2 vols. (Bibliographic Guides Ser.). 1031p. 1992. text ed. 325.00 (0-8161-7156-4) G K Hall.
— Biblographic Guide to Psychology, 1991. (Bibliographic Guides Ser.). 154p. 1992. text ed. 185.00 (0-8161-7168-8) G K Hall.

Research Library of the New York Public Library & the Library of Congress MARC Tapes Staff. Bibliographic Guide to Government Publications - U. S. 1990, 2 vols., Set. (Bibliographic Guides Ser.). 1415p. 1991. lib. bdg. 475.00 (0-8161-7140-8) G K Hall.

***Research (Princeton-Williamsburg) Conference on Cerebrovascular Disease Staff.** Cerebrovascular Diseases: Fourteenth Research (Princeton-Williamsburg) Conference. Plum, Fred & Pulsinelli, William A., eds. LC 75-25125. (Illus.). Date not set. reprint ed. pap. 80.10 (0-7837-9527-0, 2060276) Bks Demand.

Research Publications, Inc. Staff. Goldsmiths' Kress Library of Economic Literature: A Consolidated Guide to the Microfilm Collection, 1976-1983, 7 vols., Set. write for info. (0-89235-077-6) Res Pubns CT.
— Goldsmiths' Kress Library of Economic Literature: A Consolidated Guide to the Microfilm Collection, 1976-1983, 7 vols., Vol. 1. 1976. 200.00 (0-89235-004-0) Res Pubns CT.
— Goldsmiths' Kress Library of Economic Literature: A Consolidated Guide to the Microfilm Collection, 1976-1983, 7 vols., Vol. 2. 1977. 200.00 (0-89235-143-8) Res Pubns CT.
— Goldsmiths' Kress Library of Economic Literature: A Consolidated Guide to the Microfilm Collection, 1976-1983, 7 vols., Vol. 3. 1978. 200.00 (0-89235-142-X) Res Pubns CT.
— Goldsmiths' Kress Library of Economic Literature: A Consolidated Guide to the Microfilm Collection, 1976-1983, 7 vols., Vol. 4. 1982. 200.00 (0-89235-036-9) Res Pubns CT.
— Goldsmiths' Kress Library of Economic Literature: A Consolidated Guide to the Microfilm Collection, 1976-1983, 7 vols., Vol. 5. 1983. 200.00 (0-89235-079-2) Res Pubns CT.
— Goldsmiths' Kress Library of Economic Literature: A Consolidated Guide to the Microfilm Collection, 1976-1983, 7 vols., Vol. 6. 1986. 200.00 (0-89235-102-0) Res Pubns CT.
— Goldsmiths' Kress Library of Economic Literature: A Consolidated Guide to the Microfilm Collection, 1976-1983, 7 vols., Vol. 7. 1987. 200.00 (0-89235-144-6) Res Pubns CT.

Research Publications, Inc. Staff, ed. American Fiction: Cumulative Author Index to the Microfilm Collection, 1901-1910. 217p. 1984. lib. bdg. 70.00 (0-89235-082-2) Res Pubns CT.
— American Poetry 1609-1870: A Guide to the Microfilm Collection. LC 82-7641. 592p. 1982. 105.00 (0-89235-039-3) Res Pubns CT.
— City Directories of the United States, Pre-1860 to 1901. 487p. 1984. 155.00 (0-89235-081-4) Res Pubns CT.
— Early British Fiction - Pre-1750: A Guide to the Microfilm Collection. LC 82-3864. 50p. 1982. 55.00 (0-89235-034-2) Res Pubns CT.
— The Eighteenth Century: Guide to the Microfilm Collection, Units 26-40. 850p. 1986. lib. bdg. 100.00 (0-89235-105-5) Res Pubns CT.
— The Eighteenth Century: Guide to the Microfilm Collection, Units 1-10, Set. 435p. 1984. lib. bdg. 100.00 (0-89235-083-0) Res Pubns CT.

R

An Asterisk (*) at the beginning of an entry indicates that the title is appearing in BIP for the first time.

— The Eighteenth Century: Guide to the Microfilm Collection, Units 11-25. 1200p. 1985. lib. bdg. 100.00 (*0-89235-101-2*) Res Pubns CT.
— The Eighteenth Century: Guide to the Microfilm Collection, Units 11-25, Set. 1200p. 1985. 100.00 (*0-318-59203-7*) Res Pubns CT.
— History of Photography: Bibliography & Reel Guide to the Microfilm Collection. LC 82-15002. 91p. 1982. text ed. 70.00 (*0-89235-058-X*) Res Pubns CT.
— Nineteenth-Century Legal Treatises: A Guide to the Microfiche Collections, Units 7-12. 268p. 1987. lib. bdg. 150.00 (*0-89235-123-3*) Res Pubns CT.
— Nineteenth-Century Legal Treatises: A Guide to the Microfilm Collections, Units 1-6. 363p. 1987. lib. bdg. 150.00 (*0-89235-118-7*) Res Pubns CT.
— Sex Research-Early Literature from Statistics to Erotica: Guide to the Microfilm Collection. 130p. 1983. 60.00 (*0-89235-075-X*) Res Pubns CT.

Research Publications, Inc. Staff & Budeit, Janice L., eds. Papers of William H. Seward: Guide & Index to the Microfilm Collection. 402p. 1983. 280.00 (*0-89235-073-3*) Res Pubns CT.

Research Publications, Inc. Staff & Del Cervo, Diane M., eds. The Faber Birren Collection of Books on Color. 65p. 1983. 60.00 (*0-89235-080-6*) Res Pubns CT.

Research Publications, Inc. Staff, ed. see Beers, Henry P.

Research Staff of the Russell Meerdink Company. Directory of Broodmare Buyers, 1990. Meerdink, Jan, ed. 225p. 1990. ring bd. 125.00 (*0-929346-07-6*) R Meerdink Co Ltd.
— Directory of Yearling Buyers, 1990. Meerdink, Jan, ed. 290p. 1990. ring bd. 125.00 (*0-929346-06-8*) R Meerdink Co Ltd.

Research Triangle Institute Staff. Approaches & Options for Integrating Students with Disabilities: A Decision Tool. 466p. 1993. teacher ed 25.00 (*0-944584-65-9*) Sopris.

Reseck. Scuba Safe & Simple. 1990. pap. 13.00 (*0-671-76502-7*, Fireside) S&S Trade.

Reseck, John, Jr. Marine Biology. rev. ed. (Illus.). 1979. text ed. 18.95 (*0-8359-4276-7*, Reston) P-H.
— Marine Biology. 2nd ed. (Illus.). 288p. 1988. text ed. 58. 00 (*0-8359-4454-9*) P-H.

Reseck, John. We Survived Yesterday. 1994. pap. 12.95 (*1-882180-18-6*) Griffin CA.

Resehtnyak, Y. G. Geometry IV: Nonregular Riemannian Geometry. Primrose, E., tr. (Encyclopaedia of Mathematical Sciences Ser.: Vol. 70). (Illus.). 270p. 1993. write for info. (*3-540-54701-0*) Spr-Verlag.

Resek, Carl, ed. The Progressives. (Orig.). (C). 1967. pap. write for info. (*0-672-60084-6*, AHSJ4, Bobbs) Macmillan.

Reselbach, Jennifer & Hathorn, Clay. The Pacific Rim, Vol. 1. Haupt, Jennifer, ed. WA Academy of Languages Staff, tr. LC 93-61377. (Illus.). 160p. (JPN.). (J). 1994. text ed. 49.95 (*0-9634100-1-6*) Wyndham Pubns.
— The Pacific Rim, Vol. 2. Haupt, Jennifer, ed. WA Academy of Languages Staff, tr. LC 93-61377. (Illus.). 160p. 1994. text ed. 49.95 (*0-9634100-2-4*) Wyndham Pubns.

***Resen, Sylvia.** Dreaming the Poem. 1994. pap. 9.95 (*0-9622847-8-5*) Red Wind Bks.

***Resendez, Carlos C.** Trade Liberalization in Mexico & the North American Free Trade Agreement. (Occasional Paper Ser.: No. 3). 36p. 1993. 7.00 (*0-614-01235-X*) LBJ Sch Pub Aff.

Resendiz, Daniel & Romo, Miguel P., eds. Soft-Ground Tunnelling: Failures & Displacements. 110p. (C). 1981. text ed. 70.00 (*90-6191-201-6*, Pub. by A A Balkema NE) Ashgate Pub Co.

Resener, Carl R. Kids on the Street. 1992. pap. 9.99 (*0-8054-5091-2*) Broadman.

Resenikoff, H. L. The Illusion of Reality. (Illus.). 385p. 1988. 60.00 (*0-387-96398-7*) Spr-Verlag.

***Reser, David W., comp.** Toward a New Beginning in Cooperative Cataloging: The History, Progress, & Future of the Cooperative Cataloging Council. LC 94-42740. 1994. write for info. (*0-8444-0867-0*) Lib Congress.

Resetarits, Paul. Using Cadkey 4.0: Instructor's Guide. 3rd ed. 1992. 15.00 (*0-8273-4946-7*) Delmar.

Resetarits, Paul & Bertoline, Gary. Using CADKey & Its Applications, Vols. 5-6. 36p. 1994. teacher ed 15.00 (*0-8273-5718-4*) Delmar.

***Resetarits, Paul J. & Bertoline, Gary.** Using CADKEY & Its Applications: Version 7. (Illus.). 640p. 1995. disk, pap. 39.95 (*0-8273-7009-1*) Delmar.

Resetarits, Paul J. & Bertoline, Gary R. Using CADKEY. 2nd ed. 400p. 1991. pap. text ed. 39.95 (*0-8273-3632-2*) Delmar.
— Using CADKEY & Its Applications Versions 5 & 6. 4th ed. LC 92-21484. 652p. 1994. pap. text ed. 39.95 (*0-8273-5607-2*) Delmar.
— Using Cadkey Light. 301p. 1992. pap. text ed. 39.95 (*0-8273-4735-9*) Delmar.

Resh, Howard M. Hydroponic Food Production: A Definitive Guide to Soilless Culture. 4th ed. LC 88-33748. (Illus.). 416p. 1989. text ed. 39.95 (*0-88007-171-0*) Woodbridge Pr.
— Hydroponic Home Food Gardens. LC 90-12143. (Illus.). 196p. (Orig.). 1990. pap. 12.95 (*0-88007-178-8*) Woodbridge Pr.
— Hydroponic Tomatoes for the Home Gardener. LC 93-18128. (Illus.). 142p. (Orig.). 1993. pap. 9.95 (*0-88007-199-0*) Woodbridge Pr.

Resh, Nura, jt. auth. see Dar, Yehezkel.

Resh, Vincent H. & Rosenberg, David M., eds. Ecology of Aquatic Insects. LC 83-21199. 638p. 1984. text ed. 59. 95 (*0-275-91248-5*, C1248, Praeger Pubs) Greenwood.

Resh, Vincent H., jt. ed. see Rosenberg, David M.

Reshetar, John S., Jr. The Soviet Polity: Government & Politics in the U. S. S. R. 3rd ed. 416p. (C). 1990. pap. text ed. 33.50 (*0-06-045398-2*) HarpCollege.
— The Ukrainian Revolution, 1917-1920: A Study in Nationalism. LC 72-4292. (World Affairs Ser.: National & International Viewpoints). 376p. 1980. reprint ed. 31. 95 (*0-405-04584-0*) Ayer.

Reshetar, John S., Jr., ed. see Meissner, Boris.

***Reshetniak, Iurii G.** Stability Theorems in Geometry and Analysis, 304. LC 94-33303. (Mathematics & Its Application Ser.). (ENG.). 1994. lib. bdg. 189.00 (*0-7923-3118-4*) Kluwer Ac.

Reshetnyak, Yuii G., jt. auth. see Gol'dshtein, V. M.

Reshetnyak, Yurii G., ed. Geometry IV: Non-Regular Riemannian Geometry. LC 93-13858. (Encyclopaedia of Mathematical Sciences Ser.: Vol. 70). 1993. 98.00 (*0-387-54701-0*) Spr-Verlag.

Reshetnyak, Yurii G., jt. auth. see Alexandrov, A. D.

Reshetov, D. N. & Portman, V. T., eds. Accuracy of Machine Tools. 304p. 1988. 68.00 (*0-7918-0004-0*, 800040) ASME Pr.

Reshetylo-Rothe, Daria A. Rilke & Russia: A Re-Evaluation. (Studies in Modern German Literature: Vol. 18). 357p. (C). 1989. text ed. 62.50 (*0-8204-0560-4*) P Lang Pubs.

Reshevsky, Sammy. Art of Positional Play. 1980. 14.00 (*0-679-14101-4*) McKay.

Reshtenyak, Y. Space Mappings with Bounded Distortion. McFaden, H., tr. LC 89-72. (MMONO Ser.: Vol. 73). 362p. 1989. 150.00 (*0-8218-4526-8*, MMONO-73) Am Math.

Resibois, Pierre & DeLeener, M. Classical Kinetic Theory of Fluids. LC 76-58852. 430p. reprint ed. pap. 122.60 (*0-317-55610-X*, 2056350) Bks Demand.

Resick, Matthew C., et al. Modern Administrative Practices in Physical Education & Athletics. 3rd ed. LC 78-67946. (Physical Education Ser.). (Illus.). 1979. text ed. 19.25 (*0-394-34893-1*) Random.

Resick, Patricia A. & Schnicke, Monica K. Cognitive Processing Therapy for Rape Victims: A Treatment Manual. (Interpersonal Violence Practice Ser.: Vol. 4). (Illus.). 174p. (C). 1993. text ed. 42.95 (*0-8039-4901-4*); pap. text ed. 18.95 (*0-8039-4902-2*) Sage.

***Residence Lighting Committee Staff.** Design Criteria for Lighting Interior Living Spaces. (Recommended Practice Ser.). 51p. 1995. pap. text ed. 40.00 (*0-87995-099-4*, RP-11-95) Illum Eng.

Residents of Stockbridge Staff. The Stockbridge Story: Seventeen Thirty-Nine to Nineteen Eighty-Nine. (Illus.). 1989. 25.00 (*0-685-27189-7*) Town Stockbridge.

Resing, Henry A., jt. ed. see Fraissard, Jacques P.

Resinger, H. & Gutierrez, J. M. Elsevier's Dictionary of Terrestrial Plant Ecology: English - Spanish, Spanish - English. 664p. (ENG & SPA.). 1992. 250.00 (*0-8288-9216-4*) Fr & Eur.

Resis, Albert, ed. see Chuev, Felix.

Reske, Charles F. MAC-V-SOG Command History Annex B 1971-1972: The Last Secret of the Vietnam War, 2 vols., Set. (Illus.). 350p. (Orig.). 1990. pap. 49.95 (*0-685-58844-0*, 09053) Alpha Pubns OH.
— MAC-V-SOG Command History Annex B 1971-1972: The Last Secret of the Vietnam War, 2 vols., Vol. 1. (Illus.). 350p. (Orig.). 1990. pap. 26.95 (*0-939427-60-5*) Alpha Pubns OH.
— MAC-V-SOG Command History Annex B 1971-1972: The Last Secret of the Vietnam War, 2 vols., Vol. 2. (Illus.). 350p. (Orig.). 1990. pap. 26.95 (*0-939427-61-3*) Alpha Pubns OH.
— MACV-SOG Command Histories (Annexes A, N & M) 1964-1966: First Secrets of the Vietnam War. LC 92-82789. (Illus.). 178p. (Orig.). 1992. pap. 19.95 (*0-939427-62-1*) Alpha Pubns OH.

Reskiewicz, A. Polish-English, English-Polish Dictionaries. (ENG & POL.). 1992. write for info. (*0-8288-7279-1*) Fr & Eur.

Reskin, Barbara. Women, Men, & Work. 128p. 1994. pap. 15.95 (*0-8039-9022-7*) Pine Forge.

Reskin, Barbara F. Sex Differences in the Professional Life Changes of Chemists. Zuckerman, Harriet & Merton, Robert K., eds. LC 79-9041. (Dissertations on Sociology Ser.). 1980. lib. bdg. 44.95 (*0-405-12987-4*) Ayer.

Reskin, Barbara F., ed. Sex Segregation in the Workplace: Trends, Explanations, Remedies. LC 84-8342. 323p. reprint ed. pap. 92.10 (*0-7837-5357-8*, 2045119) Bks Demand.

Reskin, Barbara F. & Roos, Patricia A. Job Queues, Gender Queues: Explaining Women's Inroads into Male Occupations. 368p. 1990. 39.95 (*0-87722-743-8*); pap. 22.95 (*0-87722-744-6*) Temple U Pr.

Reskin, Melvin A., jt. auth. see Rohan, Patrick J.

Resko, John. Reprieve: The Testament of John Resko. LC 75-17464. 285p. 1975. reprint ed. text ed. 59.75 (*0-8371-8311-1*, RERE, Greenwood Pr) Greenwood.

Resla, W. J. The Best of People & the Other Animals. abr. rev. ed. 200p. 1988. reprint ed. 14.00 (*0-318-35260-5*) Grant Dahlstrom.
— The Best of People & the Other Animals. Marshall, Elva, ed. 200p. 1988. reprint ed. 14.00 (*0-9620682-0-9*) W J Resla.

Resler, Michael, tr. see Hartmann Von Aue.

Resler, Michael, tr. see Stricker, Der.

Resmini, Ronald J. Rhode Island Practice: Tort Law & Personal Injury Practice, 2 vols. 1300p. 1990. boxed 165.00 (*0-88063-408-1*) Butterworth Legal Pubs.
— Rhode Island Practice: Tort Law & Personal Injury Practice. 1300p. 1994. boxed 165.00 (*0-614-05962-3*) Michie Butterworth.
— Rhode Island Practice: Tort Law & Personal Injury Practice, 2 vols. suppl. ed. 1300p. 1993. 37.00 (*0-685-74298-9*) Butterworth Legal Pubs.

Resmini, Ronald J., jt. auth. see Pope, Daniel C.

Resnick. CT G-U. 592p. 1991. 92.00 (*1-55664-350-0*) Mosby Yr Bk.
— Manual Complete Urology Asia. 1989. 10.95 (*0-316-74052-7*) Little.
— Manual Complete Urology ISE. 1989. 15.95 (*0-316-74053-5*) Little.
— Manual of Clinical Problems in Urology. 1989. 32.95 (*0-316-74054-3*) Little.
— Prostate Ultrasonography. (Illus.). 200p. (C). 1990. 69.50 (*1-55664-173-7*) Mosby Yr Bk.

Resnick & Chavez, Laura. Computer Companion: A User Friendly Guide to WordPerfect 5.1, Lotus 1- 2-3 2.3, Paradox 3.5, MSDOS 5.0. 368p. (C). 1992. pap. text ed. 22.95 (*0-8403-7947-1*) Kendall-Hunt.

Resnick & Page, Benjamin I. Reading & Reasoning. 352p. (C). 1984. pap. write for info. (*0-02-399320-0*) Macmillan.

Resnick, A., et al. Every Day's a Holiday. 1991. 22.99 (*0-8224-6372-5*) Fearon Teach Aids.

***Resnick, Abraham.** Bulgaria. LC 94-37948. (Enchantment of the World Ser.). 172p. (J). (gr. 5-9). 1995. lib. bdg. 20. 55 (*0-516-02631-3*) Childrens.
— The Commonwealth of Independent States. (Enchantment of the World Ser.). (Illus.). 128p. (J). (gr. 5-9). 1993. lib. bdg. 20.55 (*0-516-02613-5*) Childrens.
— The Holocaust. LC 91-441. (Overview Ser.). (Illus.). 112p. (J). (gr. 5-8). 1991. lib. bdg. 16.95 (*1-56006-124-3*) Lucent Bks.
— Money. (Lucent Overview Ser.). (Illus.). (J). (gr. 5-8). 1995. 16.95 (*1-56006-165-0*) Lucent Bks.
— Russia: A History to 1917. LC 83-7369. (Enchantment of the World Ser.). (Illus.). 128p. (J). (gr. 5-9). 1983. lib. bdg. 20.55 (*0-516-02785-9*) Childrens.
— The Union of Soviet Socialist Republics. LC 84-7602. (Enchantment of the World Ser.). (Illus.). 128p. (J). (gr. 5-9). 1985. lib. bdg. 20.55 (*0-516-02789-1*) Childrens.

Resnick, Alan N., jt. auth. see Weintraub, Benjamin.

Resnick, Alan N., et al. Bankruptcy Practice & Strategy. 1987. 175.00 (*0-88712-652-9*) Warren Gorham & Lamont.
— Bankruptcy Practice & Strategy, No. 1. suppl. ed. 1991. Supplemented annually. write for info. 64.00 (*0-685-56114-3*) Warren Gorham & Lamont.

Resnick, Barry P., jt. auth. see Capwell, Gerald K.

Resnick, D., ed. Electron-Beam, X-Ray, & Ion-Beam Technology: Submicrometer Lithographies IX. 1990. 62. 00 (*0-8194-0310-5*, VOL. 1263) SPIE.

Resnick, Daniel P. The White Terror & the Political Reaction After Waterloo. LC 66-18254. (Historical Studies: No. 77). 161p. 1966. 15.00 (*0-674-95190-5*) HUP.

Resnick, David M. Professional Ethics for Audiologists & Speech-Language Pathologists. LC 92-34723. (Illus.). 198p. (Orig.). (C). 1993. pap. text ed. 32.50x (*1-56593-087-8*) Singular Publishing.

Resnick, Donald. Diagnosis of Bone & Joint Disorders, 6 vols., Set. 3rd ed. LC 93-48321. (Illus.). 1994. text ed. 695.00 (*0-7216-5066-X*) Saunders.
— Essentials of Bone & Joint Imaging. (Illus.). 1392p. 1989. text ed. 199.00 (*0-7216-2215-1*) Saunders.

Resnick, Donald & Pak, Charles Y. Urolithiasis. (Illus.). 352p. 1990. text ed. 97.95 (*0-7216-2439-1*) Saunders.

Resnick, Donald & Pettersson, Holger, eds. Skeletal Radiology. (Nicer Series on Diagnostic Imaging). (Illus.). 674p. 1992. 52.00 (*1-873413-45-9*) Merit Pub Intl.

Resnick, Donald, jt. auth. see Kang.

***Resnick, Faye.** Nicole Brown Simpson: The Private Diary of a Life Interrupted. 1994. 14.95 (*0-7871-0339-X*) Dove Audio.

Resnick, Greg, ed. Natural for DB2 Developers Handbook. 560p. 1991. pap. 65.00 (*1-878960-06-7*) WH&O Intl.

Resnick, Hank. Positive Prevention: Successful Approaches to Preventing Youthful Drug & Alcohol Use. Quest National Center Staff et al, eds. 16p. (Orig.). 1985. pap. 1.50 (*0-87652-105-7*, 21-00154) Am Assn Sch Admin.

Resnick, Herman & Rino, J. Patti, eds. Change from Within: Humanizing Social Welfare Organizations. LC 80-13344. 344p. 1980. 29.95 (*0-87722-173-1*); pap. 19.95 (*0-87722-200-2*) Temple U Pr.

Resnick, Hy, ed. Electronic Tools for Social Work Practice & Education. (Computers in Human Services Ser.). (Illus.). 434p. 1994. lib. bdg. 59.95 (*1-56024-658-8*) Haworth Pr.

Resnick, Idrian. The Long Transition: Building Socialism in Tanzania. LC 80-8089. 416p. 1982. 18.50 (*0-85345-554-6*); pap. 10.00 (*0-85345-555-4*) Monthly Rev.

Resnick, Idrian N. Controlling Consulting: A Manual for Native American Governments & Organizations. 75p. 1990. reprint ed. pap. 10.00 (*0-9626861-1-5*) First Nations Finan.

Resnick, Irven M. Divine Power & Possibility in St. Peter Damian's De Divina Omnipotencia. LC 91-43923. (Studien und Texte zur Geistesgeschichte des Mittelalters Ser.: No. 31). 128p. 1992. 43.00 (*90-04-09572-1*) E J Brill.

Resnick, Irven M., tr. see Odo of Tournai.

Resnick, Jane. All about Seals, Sea Lions & Walruses. (Sea World All about Library). (Illus.). 32p. (J). (gr. 1-6). 1994. pap. 3.95 (*1-884506-13-5*) Third Story.
— All about Sharks. (Sea World All about Library). (Illus.). 32p. (Orig.). (J). (gr. 1-8). 1994. pap. 3.95 (*1-884506-10-0*) Third Story.
— All about Training Shamu. (Sea World All about Library). (Illus.). 32p. (Orig.). (J). (gr. 1-8). 1994. pap. 3.95 (*1-884506-11-9*) Third Story.
— Book of Baby Names: Classic & Contemporary Names for Your Baby. 1994. 5.98 (*0-8317-0668-6*) Smithmark.
— A Bouquet from the Kitchen. (Illus.). 64p. 1991. 5.95 (*0-681-41124-4*) Longmeadow Pr.
— Eyes on Nature: Fish. (Illus.). 32p. (J). 1992. pap. 4.95 (*1-56156-150-9*) Kidsbks.
— Goldilocks & the Three Bears. (J). 1986. 14.98 (*0-88705-151-0*) Joshua Morris.
— A Mother's Love. (Illus.). 96p. 1995. 5.98 (*0-8317-8088-6*) Smithmark.
— Original Fairy Tales from Brothers Grimm. (J). 1991. 12. 99 (*0-517-06577-0*) Random Hse Value.
— Shamu's Secrets of the Sea. (Shamu's Little Library). (Illus.). 12p. (J). (ps-00). 1994. 6.95 (*1-884506-03-8*) Third Story.

Resnick, Jane P. The Ant & the Dove. (Aesop's Fables Ser.). (Illus.). (J). 1992. bds. 3.25 (*0-8378-2523-7*) Gibson.
— Cherish the Cat. 96p. 1993. 5.99 (*0-681-41737-4*) Longmeadow Pr.
— Family. (Illus.). 96p. 1995. 5.98 (*0-8317-8057-6*) Smithmark.
— The Fox & the Crow. (Aesop's Fables Ser.). (Illus.). (J). 1992. bds. 3.25 (*0-8378-2525-3*) Gibson.

Resnick, Jane P. A Friend Makes All the Difference. (Illus.). 32p. 1984. 5.95 (*0-8378-2037-5*) Gibson.

Resnick, Jane P. The Lion & the Mouse. (Aesop's Fables Ser.). (Illus.). (J). 1992. bds. 3.25 (*0-8378-2526-1*) Gibson.
— The Tortoise & the Hare. (Aesop's Fables Ser.). (Illus.). (J). 1992. bds. 3.25 (*0-8378-2524-5*) Gibson.

Resnick, Jane P., ed. Love & Friendship. (Illus.). 80p. 1992. 5.95 (*0-681-41408-1*) Longmeadow Pr.

***Resnick, Jane P., ret.** Bible Stories: A Treasury for Young Readers. (Illus.). 1995. pap. 9.98 (*1-56138-485-2*) Running Pr.

Resnick, Kathleen. Kermit Learns Windows. (Muppet Computer Bks.). 48p. (Orig.). (J). (gr. 5 up). 1993. 9.95 (*1-55958-366-5*) Prima Pub.

Resnick, L. B., ed. The Nature of Intelligence. 364p. 1976. text ed. 69.95 (*0-89859-137-6*) L Erlbaum Assocs.

Resnick, Laibel. A Time to Weep. LC 93-72409. 200p. 1993. write for info. (*1-56062-211-3*); pap. write for info. (*1-56062-212-1*) CIS Comm.

Resnick, Laura. Sleight of Hand. 224p. (Orig.). 1993. pap. 2.95 (*1-56597-075-6*, Kismet) Meteor Pub.

Resnick, Laura & Klopfer, Leopold, eds. Toward the Thinking Curriculum: Current Cognitive Research. (Yearbook, 1989 Ser.). (Illus.). 221p. (Orig.). 1989. pap. 15.95 (*0-87120-156-9*, 610-89012) Assn Supervision.

Resnick, Lauren B. Education & Learning to Think. 72p. 1987. pap. text ed. 9.95 (*0-309-03785-9*) Natl Acad Pr.

Resnick, Lauren B., ed. Knowing, Learning & Instructions: Essays in Honor of Robert Glaser. 528p. (C). 1989. pap. 36.00 (*0-8058-0460-9*) L Erlbaum Assocs.

Resnick, Lauren B. & Ford, Wendy W. The Psychology of Mathematics for Instruction. LC 80-29106. 288p. 1981. text ed. 59.95 (*0-89859-029-9*) L Erlbaum Assocs.

Resnick, Lauren B. & Weaver, Phyllis A. Theory & Practice of Early Reading, Vol. 2. LC 79-23784. 368p. 1980. text ed. 79.95 (*0-89859-010-8*) L Erlbaum Assocs.

Resnick, Lauren B. & Weaver, Phyllis A., eds. Theory & Practice of Early Reading, Vol. 1. LC 79-22322. 416p. 1980. text ed. 79.95 (*0-89859-003-5*) L Erlbaum Assocs.
— Theory & Practice of Early Reading, Vol. 3. 400p. 1980. text ed. 79.95 (*0-89859-011-6*) L Erlbaum Assocs.

***Resnick, Lauren B & Wirt, John, eds.** Linking School at Work: Roles for Standards & Assessment. (Education Ser.). 1995. 45.00 (*0-7879-0165-2*) Jossey-Bass.

Resnick, Lauren B., et al, eds. Perspectives on Socially Shared Cognition. 444p. 1991. 40.00 (*1-55798-121-3*) Am Psychol.

Resnick, Martin I. & Novick, Andrew, eds. Urology Secrets: Questions You Will Be Asked on Rounds, in the OR, in the Clinic. (Secrets Ser.). (Illus.). 420p. (Orig.). 1994. pap. text ed. 31.95 (*1-56053-108-8*) Hanley & Belfus.

Resnick, Martin I. & Rifkin, Matthew D. Ultrasonography of the Urinary Tract. 3rd ed. (Illus.). 480p. 1991. 100.00 (*0-683-07222-6*) Williams & Wilkins.

Resnick, Martin I., jt. ed. see Cohen, Marc S.

Resnick, Martin I., jt. ed. see Kursh, Elroy D.

Resnick, Martin I., et al. Decision Making in Urology. 2nd ed. 264p. (C). 1990. 72.00 (*1-55664-266-0*) Mosby Yr Bk.

Resnick, Melvyn C. Introduccion a la Historia de la Lengua Espanola. LC 81-7209. 196p. (Orig.). (C). 1981. reprint ed. pap. text ed. 12.95 (*0-87840-083-4*) Georgetown U Pr.
— Phonological Variants & Dialect Identification in Latin American Spanish. LC 73-80498. (Janua Linguarum, Series Practica: No. 201). (Illus.). 484p. 1975. pap. text ed. 84.65 (*90-279-3227-1*) Mouton.

Resnick, Melvyn C., ed. Studies in Caribbean Spanish Dialectology. LC 88-4340. 256p. 1988. pap. 14.95 (*0-87840-098-2*) Georgetown U Pr.

Resnick, Michael. Turtles, Termites, & Traffic Jam: Explorations in Massively Parallel Microworlds. (Bradford Series in Complex Adaptive Systems). (Illus.). 192p. 1994. 24.95 (*0-262-18162-2*, Bradford Bks) MIT Pr.

Resnick, Michael A. & Vig, Baldev K., eds. Mechanisms of Chromosome Distribution & Aneuploidy. (Progress in Clinical & Biological Research Ser.). 416p. 1989. text ed. 172.95 (*0-471-56236-X*) Wiley.

Resnick, Mike. Bwana - Bully. 1991. mass mkt. 3.99 (*0-8125-1246-4*) Tor Bks.
— Eros at Zenith. 1984. 17.00 (*0-932096-32-8*) Phantasia Pr.
— Inferno. 288p. 1993. 20.95 (*0-312-85437-4*) Tor Bks.
— Inferno. 304p. 1995. mass mkt. 4.99 (*0-8125-2345-8*) Tor Bks.
— Ivory. 1989. mass mkt. 4.95 (*0-8125-0042-3*) Tor Bks.
— Lucifer Jones. 320p. (Orig.). 1992. mass mkt. 4.99 (*0-446-36319-7*, Aspect) Warner Bks.
— A Miracle of Rare Design. 256p. 1996. pap. write for info. (*0-614-05523-7*) Tor Bks.

R

An Asterisk (*) at the beginning of an entry indicates that the title is appearing in BIP for the first time.

— Oracle. 256p. (Orig.). 1992. mass mkt. 4.99 (0-441-58694-5) Ace Bks.

— The Oracle Trilogy, Bk. 3: Prophet. 256p. (Orig.). 1993. mass mkt. 4.99 (0-441-68329-0) Ace Bks.

— Paradise. 1990. mass mkt. 4.99 (0-8125-0716-9) Tor Bks.

— Purgatory. 320p. 1994. mass mkt. 4.99 (0-8125-3535-9) Tor Bks.

— Second Contact. 1990. pap. 3.95 (0-8125-1113-1) Tor Bks.

— Soothsayer. 1991. mass mkt. 4.99 (0-441-77285-4) Ace Bks.

— The Soul Eater. (Orig.). 1992. mass mkt. 4.99 (0-446-36318-9, Aspect) Warner Bks.

— Stalking the Unicorn. 320p. (Orig.). 1990. mass mkt. 3.95 (0-8125-0985-4) Tor Bks.

— Stalking the Wild Resnick. limited ed. (Boskone Bks.). (Illus.). viii, 216p. 1991. 15.00 (0-915368-45-5) New Eng SF Assoc.

— Stalking the Wild Resnick. limited ed. (Illus.). viii, 216p. 1991. boxed 30.00 (0-915368-96-X) New Eng SF Assoc.

— Through Darkest Resnick with Gun & Camera. 200p. 1990. 35.00 (0-9621725-1-0) Washington Sci Fiction.

— Will the Last Person to Leave the Planet... 368p. 1994. pap. 12.95 (0-312-89010-9) Orb NYC.

— Will the Last Person to Leave the Planet Please Shut off the Sun? 368p. 1992. 19.95 (0-312-85276-2) Tor Bks.

Resnick, Mike, ed. Alternate Kennedys. 416p. 1992. mass mkt. 4.99 (0-8125-1955-8) Tor Bks.

— Alternate Outlaws. 544p. (Orig.). (C). 1994. mass mkt. 4.99 (0-8125-3344-5) Tor Bks.

— Alternate Presidents. 1992. mass mkt. 4.99 (0-8125-1192-1) Tor Bks.

— Alternate Tyrants. 544p. (Orig.). 1996. pap. 5.99 (0-614-05546-6) Tor Bks.

— Alternate Warriors. 448p. (Orig.). 1993. mass mkt. 4.99 (0-8125-2346-6) Tor Bks.

— By Any Other Fame. 320p. 1994. 4.99 (0-88677-594-9) DAW Bks.

— More Whatdunits. 336p. (Orig.). 1993. mass mkt. 4.99 (0-88677-557-4) DAW Bks.

— Whatdunits. 320p. (Orig.). 1992. mass mkt. 4.99 (0-88677-533-7) DAW Bks.

Resnick, Mike & Dozois, Gardner, eds. Future Earths: Under African Skies. 320p. (Orig.). 1993. mass mkt. 4.99 (0-88677-544-2) DAW Bks.

— Future Earths: Under South American Skies. 320p. (Orig.). 1993. mass mkt. 4.99 (0-88677-581-7) DAW Bks.

Resnick, Mike & Greenberg, Martin H., eds. Aladdin: Master of the Lamp. 352p. (Orig.). 1992. mass mkt. 4.99 (0-88677-545-0) DAW Bks.

— Christmas Ghosts. 352p. 1993. mass mkt. 5.50 (0-88677-586-8) DAW Bks.

— Dinosaur Fantastic. 320p. (Orig.). 1993. mass mkt. 4.99 (0-88677-566-3) DAW Bks.

— Sherlock Holmes in Orbit. 320p. (Orig.). 1995. pap. 5.50 (0-88677-636-8) DAW Bks.

— Witch Fantastic. (Illus.). 352p. (Orig.). 1995. 4.99 (0-88677-640-6) DAW Bks.

Resnick, Mike & Nye, Jody L., eds. The Gods of War. 320p. 1992. mass mkt. 4.99 (0-671-72146-1) Baen Bks.

Resnick, Mike, ed. see Lake, Alexander.

Resnick, Mike, ed. see Neumann, Arthur H.

Resnick, Mike, et al, eds. Deals with the Devil. 304p. 1994. mass mkt. 4.99 (0-88677-623-6) DAW Bks.

Resnick, Paul. The Small Business Bible: The Make-or-Break Factors for Survival & Success. 230p. 1988. pap. text ed. 19.95 (0-471-62985-5) Wiley.

Resnick, Philip. The Masks of Proteus: Canadian Reflections on the State. 400p. (C). 1990. 44.95 (0-7735-0731-0, Pub. by McGill CN) U of Toronto Pr.

— Toward a Canada-Quebec Union. 160p. (Orig.). (C). 1991. pap. text ed. 17.95 (0-7735-0865-1, Pub. by McGill CN) U of Toronto Pr.

Resnick, Philip & Latouche, Daniel. Letters to a Quebecois Friend. 136p. (Orig.). (C). 1990. 34.95 (0-7735-0772-8, Pub. by McGill CN); pap. 14.95 (0-7735-0777-9, Pub. by McGill CN) U of Toronto Pr.

Resnick, R. Linda & Pechter, Kerry. A Big Splash in a Small Pond: Finding a Great Job in a Small, High-Growth Company. LC 93-5708. 1994. 11.00 (0-671-79807-3, Fireside) S&S Trade.

Resnick, Robert. Introduction to Special Relativity. LC 67-31211. 226p. 1968. Net. pap. text ed. write for info. (0-471-71725-8) Wiley.

Resnick, Robert & Halliday, David. Basic Concepts in Relativity. (Illus.). 224p. (Orig.). (C). 1992. pap. write for info. (0-02-399345-6) Macmillan.

— Basic Concepts in Relativity & Early Quantum Theory. 2nd ed. (Illus.). 352p. (C). 1992. pap. write for info. (0-02-399340-5) Macmillan.

Resnick, Robert, jt. auth. see Eisberg, Robert.

Resnick, Robert, jt. auth. see Halliday, David.

***Resnick, Robert J. & McEvoy, Kathleen, eds.** Attention-Deficit/Hyperactivity Disorder: Abstracts of the Psychological & Behavioral Literature, 1971-1994. (Bibliographies in Psychology Ser.: No. 14). 204p. 1994. 27.50 (1-55798-274-0) Am Psychol.

Resnick, Robert J., jt. ed. see Lowman, Rodney L.

***Resnick, Robert M.** National Survey of Education Reform. Elwell, Chris, ed. 30p. 1994. write for info. (0-88709-066-4) Simba Info Inc.

Resnick, Rosalind. Exploring the World of Online Services. LC 93-83101. 321p. 1993. pap. 17.95 (0-89588-798-3) Sybex.

— The Internet Business Guide: Riding the Information Superhighway. 464p. 1994. 25.00 (0-672-30530-5) Sams.

***Resnick, Rosalind, et al.** Interactive Publications Review, 1995: An Analysis of Newspapers & Magazines Online. 222p. 1995. write for info. (0-88709-081-8) Simba Info Inc.

Resnick, S. Adventures in Stochastic Processes. xii, 626p. 1994. 64.50 (0-8176-3591-2) Spr-Verlag.

— Extreme Values, Regular Variation, & Point Processes. (Applied Probability Ser.). 345p. 1987. 69.00 (0-387-96481-9) Spr-Verlag.

Resnick, Seymour. En Breve: A Concise Review of Spanish Grammar. 3rd ed. 1993. pap. 34.00 (0-15-500748-3) HarBrace.

— Essential French Grammar. (Orig.). 1963. pap. 3.95 (0-486-20419-7) Dover.

— Essential Spanish Grammar. (Orig.). 1963. pap. 3.50 (0-486-20780-3) Dover.

— Teach Yourself French: Essential Grammar. (Teach Yourself Ser.). 1992. 14.95 (0-8288-8326-2) Fr & Eur.

— Teach Yourself Spanish: Essential Grammar. (Teach Yourself Ser.). 1992. 12.95 (0-8288-8397-1) Fr & Eur.

Resnick, Seymour & Giuliano, William. En Breve: A Concise Review of Spanish Grammar. 2nd rev. ed. Vardy, Katherine L., ed. (Illus.). 320p. (C). 1990. pap. text ed. 25.50 (0-03-026388-3) HB Coll Pubs.

***Resnick, Seymour & Pasmantier, Jeanne.** Nueve Siglos de Literatura Espanola: Nine Centuries of Spanish Literature: A Dual-Language Anthology. unabridged ed. LC 94-19769. 480p. 1994. pap. text ed. 9.95 (0-486-28271-6) Dover.

Resnick, Stephen, jt. auth. see Wolff, Richard.

Resnick, Stephen A. & Wolff, Richard D. Knowledge & Class: A Marxian Critique of Political Economy. LC 86-32631. viii, 352p. 1989. pap. text ed. 14.95 (0-226-71023-8) U Ch Pr.

Resnick, Susan, tr. see Schwaller De Lubicz, Isha.

Resnick, Susan M. Bonsai: In Cooperation with the Brooklyn Botanic Garden. (Illus.). 144p. 1992. 35.00 (0-316-45630-6) Little.

Resnicow, Herb, jt. auth. see Seaver, Tom.

***Resnik, H. L., ed.** Suicidal Behaviors: Diagnosis & Management. LC 94-32435. 568p. 1995. pap. text ed. 30.00 (1-56821-263-1) Aronson.

Resnik, H. L., jt. auth. see Mitchell, Jeffrey.

Resnik, Hank. Activities & Assignments: Student Workbook. Barr, Linda, ed. (Skills for Adolescence Ser.). (Illus.). 178p. (YA). (gr. 6-8). 1988. student ed 4.85 (0-933419-26-0) Quest Intl.

Resnik, Hank, ed. Skills For Adolescence. (Illus.). 436p. 1985. student ed 4.85 (0-933419-05-8); student ed 4.85 (0-933419-09-0) Quest Intl.

— Youth & Drugs: Society's Mixed Messages. 174p. (Orig.). (C). 1994. pap. text ed. 40.00 (0-7881-0296-6) Diane Pub.

Resnik, Hank, ed. see Barr, Linda.

Resnik, Hank, jt. auth. see Schimmels, Cliff.

Resnik, Hank, et al. Actividades y Asignaciones: Cuaderno del Estudiante. Callejas, Juan et al, eds. Luobriel, Marta B. et al, trs. (Destrezas para la Adolescencia Ser.). (Illus.). (Orig.). (SPA.). (YA). (gr. 6-8). 1991. student ed 4.85 (1-56095-022-6) Quest Intl.

— Skills for Adolescence: Teachers Manual. rev. ed. Barr, Linda, ed. (Skills for Adolescence Ser.). (Illus.). 531p. 1988. 110.00 (0-933419-23-6) Quest Intl.

***Resnik, Jean.** Tales of Love & Death. 1995. 12.95 (0-8062-5242-1); 12.95 (0-8062-5339-8) Carlton.

Resnik, Judith. Managerial Judges. LC 83-117993. 74p. 1982. 7.50 (0-685-07251-7, R-3002-ICJ) Rand Corp.

Resnik, Judith, jt. auth. see Fiss, Owen M.

Resnik, Michael. Frege & the Philosophy of Mathematics. 240p. 1980. 32.50 (0-8014-1293-5) Cornell U Pr.

Resnik, Michael D. Choices: An Introduction to Decision Theory. LC 86-11307. 234p. 1987. text ed. 34.95 (0-8166-1439-3); pap. text ed. 14.95x (0-8166-1440-7) U of Minn Pr.

***Resnik, Michael D., ed.** Mathematical Objects & Mathematical Knowledge. (International Research Library of Philosophy). (Illus.). 500p. 1995. text ed. 129.95 (1-85521-638-8) Ashgate Pub Co.

Resnik, Muriel. Any Wednesday. 1966. pap. 4.75 (0-8222-0059-7) Dramatists Play.

Resnik, Robert, jt. ed. see Creasy, Robert K.

Resnik, Robert, jt. ed. see Hollingsworth, Dorothy R.

***Resnik, Salomon.** Mental Space. 135p. 1995. pap. text ed. 29.95 (1-85575-058-9) Brunner-Mazel.

— The Theatre of the Dream. LC 87-6538. 260p. (C). 1987. lib. bdg. 45.00 (0-422-61040-2, Pub. by Tavistock UK) Routledge Chapman & Hall.

Resnikoff, George J. & Lieberman, Gerald J. Tables of the Non-Central t-Distribution: Density Function, Cumulative Distribution Function & Percentage Points. LC 57-7832. x, 389p. 1957. 52.50 (0-8047-0492-9) Stanford U Pr.

Resnikoff, H. L. & Wells, R. O. Mathematics in Civilization. LC 72-83805. (Illus.). reprint ed. 29.50 (0-03-085035-5) Irvington.

Resnikoff, H. L. & Wells, R. O., Jr. Mathematics in Civilization. (Popular Science Ser.). 448p. 1984. reprint ed. pap. 11.95 (0-486-24674-4) Dover.

Resnikoff, Irene & Motzkin, Linda. Tall Tales Told in Biblical Hebrew. (Illus.). 144p. (Orig.). 1994. pap. 14.95 (0-939144-20-4) EKS Pub Co.

Resnikoff, Irene & Simon, Ethelyn. Teacher's Guide for the First Hebrew Primer. rev. ed. 64p. (Orig.). (C). 1992. pap. text ed. 8.95 (0-939144-17-4) EKS Pub Co.

Resnikoff, Irene, jt. auth. see Simon, Ethelyn.

Resnikoff, Marvin. The Next Nuclear Gamble: Transportation & Storage of Nuclear Waste. 378p. 1985. 34.95 (0-88738-095-6) Transaction Pubs.

Resor & Kutt, eds. The Medical Treatment of Epilepsy. (Neurological Disease & Therapy Ser.: Vol. 10). 760p. 1991. 215.00 (0-8247-8549-5) Dekker.

***Resource Center United Way of San Diego County Staff.** Directions 1995: Directory of Health & Human Care Services in San Diego County. 700p. 1994. 35.00 (0-9629793-3-3) United Way SD.

Resource Center, United Way Staff. Directions '94: Directory of Health & Human Care Services in San Diego County. 650p. 1993. 35.00 (0-9629793-2-5) United Way SD.

Resource Systems International Staff. Construction Materials I. 1982. pap. text ed. 15.00 (0-8359-0940-9, Reston) P-H.

— Mechanical Drawing: Geometric Construction. 1982. pap. text ed. 15.00 (0-8359-4306-2, Reston) P-H.

— Tanks, Vessels & Other Components. 1982. pap. text ed. 15.00 (0-8359-7538-X, Reston) P-H.

***Resources for Rehabilitation Organization.** A Woman's Guide to Coping with Disability. LC 94-21219. 1994. write for info. (0-929718-15-1) Resc Rehab.

Resources for Rehabilitation Staff. Living with Low Vision: A Resource Guide for People with Sight Loss. 3rd large type ed. 1993. pap. 35.00 (0-929718-09-7) Resc Rehab.

— Meeting the Needs of Employees with Disabilities. 1991. pap. 42.95 (0-929718-08-9) Resc Rehab.

— Rehabilitation Resource Manual: Vision. 3rd ed. 1990. pap. 39.95 (0-929718-05-4) Resc Rehab.

— Rehabilitation Resource Manual: Vision. 4th ed. 1993. pap. 39.95 (0-929718-10-0) Resc Rehab.

— Resources for Elders with Disabilities. 2nd large type ed. (Orig.). 1993. pap. 43.95 (0-929718-11-9) Resc Rehab.

— Resources for People with Disabilities & Chronic Conditions. 1991. pap. 44.95 (0-929718-06-2) Resc Rehab.

Resources for the Future, Inc. Staff. Agricultural Development in the Mekong Basin: Goals, Priorities, & Strategies: A Staff Study. LC 70-158820. 116p. reprint ed. pap. 33.10 (0-8357-5269-0, 2023810) Bks Demand.

— Design for a World Wide Study of Regional Development: Report to the United Nations on a Proposed Research-Training Program. LC 66-19959. 92p. reprint ed. pap. 26.30 (0-317-26476-1, 2023811) Bks Demand.

— Forest Credit in the United States: A Survey of Needs & Facilities; Report of a Committee Appointed by Resources for the Future, Inc. LC 58-8252. 176p. reprint ed. pap. 50.20 (0-317-27692-1, 2052105) Bks Demand.

— Publications of Resources for the Future, Inc., 12 vols., Set. reprint ed. write for info. (0-404-60325-4) AMS Pr.

— A Report on Planning, Policy Making & Research Activities. LC 61-14884. 46p. reprint ed. pap. 25.00 (0-317-27688-3, 2052106) Bks Demand.

— United States Energy Policies: An Agenda for Research. LC 68-28767. 166p. reprint ed. pap. 47.40 (0-317-26477-X, 2023812) Bks Demand.

Resources for the Future, Inc. Staff, jt. auth. see Farm Foundation Staff.

Resp, Richard A. In Pictures Hawaii Volcanoes: The Continuing Story. LC 92-71531. (Illus.). 48p. 1992. pap. 6.95 (0-88714-069-6) KC Pubns.

Respess, Kathryn. The Children of Israel: A Workbook Introduction to Ancient Israel. 124p. (YA). (gr. 9-12). 1984. student ed 22.00 (1-881678-08-3) CRIS.

Respighi, Elsa. Fifty Years of a Life in Music, 1905-1955: Cinquant Anni De Vita Nella Musica. Fontecchio, Giovanni & Johnson, Roger, trs. LC 93-27440. (Studies in the History & Interpretation of Music: Vol. 42). 348p. 1993. 99.95 (0-7734-9364-6) E Mellen.

Respiratory Nursing Society Staff, jt. auth. see American Nurses Association Staff.

Response Staff. Corporate Warrior. 240p. 1988. per. 21.95 (0-8403-4809-6) Kendall-Hunt.

Ress, David. The Burundi Ethnic Massacres, 1988. LC 91-45122. 136p. 1992. lib. bdg. 69.95 (0-7734-9878-8) E Mellen.

Ress, Georg, ed. Entwicklung des Europaischen Urheberrechts: Intellectual Property Rights & EC Law. 135p. (ENG, FRE & GER.). 1989. pap. 37.50 (3-7890-1817-1, Pub. by Nomos Verlags GW) Intl Bk Import.

Ress, Lisa. Flight Patterns. LC 84-19687. (Associated Writing Programs & Old Dominion University Series for Contemporary Poetry). 75p. 1985. 10.95 (0-8139-1053-6) U Pr of Va.

Ress, Lisa, et al. The Collected Works of C. G. Jung, No. 19: Bibliography of Jung's Writings. Adler, Gerhard et al, eds. Hull, R. F., tr. (Bollingen Ser.: No. 20). 366p. 1979. 35.00 (0-691-09893-X) Princeton U Pr.

Resseguie, Jacqueline, jt. auth. see Thompson, Stephen.

Resser, Linda C. & Epstein, Irwin. Professionalization & Activism in Social Work. 196p. 1990. text ed. 33.00 (0-231-06788-7) Col U Pr.

***Ressi, Michele.** Dictionnaire des Citations de l'Histoire de France. 800p. (FRE.). 1992. pap. 155.00 (0-7859-7880-1, 2268010171) Fr & Eur.

Ressich, John. Voices in the Wilderness. LC 79-152954. (Short Story Index Reprint Ser.). 1977. reprint ed. 19.95 (0-8369-3869-0) Ayer.

Ressler, Everett M., et al. Unaccompanied Children: Care & Protection in Wars, Natural Disasters & Refugee Movements. 432p. 1987. pap. 24.00 (0-19-504937-3) OUP.

Ressler, Martin E., et al. Lancaster County Churches in the Revolutionary War Era. Harrison, Matthew W., Jr., ed. LC 76-21210. (Illus.). 96p. 1976. pap. 5.00 (0-915010-11-9) Sutter House.

Ressler, Pauline. Poems for Praise & Power. 1978. pap. 5.05 (0-686-24053-7) Rod & Staff.

Ressler, Ralph. A World of Choice: Careers & You - Student Workbook. LC 77-4182. (Illus.). (YA). (gr. 9-12). 1978. pap. 14.95 (0-88280-050-7); teacher ed, pap. 19.95 (0-88280-051-5) ETC Pubns.

***Ressler, Robert.** Justice Is Served Vol. 1. 1994. 19.95 (0-312-11679-9, Pub. by Thomas Dunne Bks) St Martin.

Ressler, Robert K. & Schachtman, Thomas. Whoever Fights Monsters: A Brilliant FBI Detective's Career-Long War Against Serial Killers. 1993. mass mkt. 5.99 (0-312-95044-6) St Martin.

Ressler, Robert K. & Shachtman, Tom. Whoever Fights Monsters... A Brilliant FBI Detective's Career-Long War Against Serial Killers. (Illus.). 256p. 1992. 22.95 (0-312-07883-8, Pub. by Thomas Dunne Bks) St Martin.

Ressler, Robert K., et al, eds. Sexual Homicide: Patterns, Motives & Procedures for Investigation. 256p. 1988. text ed. 39.95 (0-669-16559-X) Free Pr.

Ressler, Sandy, jt. auth. see Libes, Don.

Ressler, Sanford. Perspectives on Electronic Publishing: Standards, Solutions, & More. LC 93-12696. 325p. 1993. pap. text ed. 39.00 (0-13-287491-1) P-H.

Ressler, Steve. Joseph Conrad: Consciousness & Integrity. 208p. 1988. 50.00x (0-8147-7405-9) NYU Pr.

Ressmeyer, Roger. Astronaut to Zodiac: A Young Stargazer's Alphabet. LC 92-9615. (Illus.). 32p. (J). (gr. k-6). 1992. 15.00 (0-517-58805-6); lib. bdg. 15.99 (0-517-58806-4) Crown Bks Yng Read.

Ressner, Ulla. The Hidden Hierarchy. 1987. text ed. 63.95 (0-566-05347-0, Pub. by Avebury Pub UK) Ashgate Pub Co.

Ressner, Ulla & Gunnarsson, Evy. Group Organized Work in the Automated Office. 130p. 1986. text ed. 57.00 (0-566-00767-3, Pub. by Avebury Pub UK) Ashgate Pub Co.

Rest, D., jt. auth. see Varshavsky, T.

Rest, Friedrich. Our Christian Symbols. LC 53-9923. (Illus.). 96p. 1954. pap. 5.95 (0-8298-0099-9) Pilgrim OH.

Rest, Friedrich O. A Month of Family Prayers. 72p. 1989. pap. 1.95 (0-8146-1840-5) Liturgical Pr.

— Prayers for Families of Today. 32p. 1989. pap. 1.95 (0-8146-1841-3) Liturgical Pr.

Rest, Gregory, jt. auth. see Salant, Stephen W.

Rest, Hillard C. How to Profit from Your Investment Personality: What You Need to Know to Identify Your Investment Personality & Increase Your Profits. Martin, Alice, ed. & illus. by. LC 90-84885. 224p. 1992. pap. 16.95 (1-879250-00-4) Hilmar Pub.

Rest, James R. Development in Judging Moral Issues. LC 79-22755. 327p. reprint ed. pap. 93.20 (0-318-39690-4, 2033285) Bks Demand.

— Moral Development: Advances in Research & Theory. LC 86-21708. 241p. 1986. text ed. 55.00 (0-275-92254-5, C2254, Praeger Pubs) Greenwood.

Rest, James R. & Narvaez, Darcia F., eds. Moral Development in the Professions: Psychology & Applied Ethics. 248p. 1994. text ed. 39.95 (0-8058-1538-4); pap. 19.95 (0-8058-1539-2) L Erlbaum Assocs.

***Rest, Richard F. & Morse, Stephen A.** Microbial Pathogenesis & Immune Response. Ades, Edwin W., ed. LC 94-25683. (Annals of the New York Academy of Sciences Ser.: Vol. 730). 1994. write for info. (0-89766-895-2); pap. 110.00 (0-89766-896-0) NY Acad Sci.

Rest, Stanley M., jt. auth. see Casciani, Joseph M.

Resta, Bart. Health & Wholeness. (Lifesearch Ser.). 64p. (Orig.). 1994. pap. 4.95 (0-687-77869-7) Abingdon.

***Resta, Bart & Harvill, Kitty.** Believe in Katie Lynn! Courtney, Richard & McCombs, Maryglenn, eds. LC 94-66209. (Illus.). 48p. (Orig.). (J). 1995. pap. 14.95 (1-886371-10-5) Eggman Pub.

Resta, R., jt. ed. see Baldereschi, A.

***Restad, Penne L.** Christmas in America: A History. (Illus.). 256p. 1995. 25.00 (0-19-509300-3) OUP.

Restagno, Enzo, jt. auth. see Carter, Elliott.

***Restaino, Joyce & Keenan, Judy.** New Jersey Property Tax Assessments: A Homeowner's Guided Tour to Understanding Assessments, Appeals, Revluations, & Reassessments. 2nd rev. ed. (Illus.). 50p. 1995. 12.95 (0-9628989-1-0) Milford Pr.

Restak. The Modular Brain. 256p. 1994. text ed. 22.00 (0-684-19544-5, Scribners) S&S Trade.

***Restak, Richard.** Brainscapes: An Introduction to What Neuroscience Has Learned about the Structure, Function & Abilities of the Brain. LC 95-14774. (Illus.). 192p. 1995. 19.95 (0-7868-6113-4) Hyperion.

— Receptors. 228p. 1995. pap. 12.95 (0-553-37441-9) Bantam.

Restak, Richard M. The Brain. 1988. mass mkt. 5.99 (0-446-35540-2) Warner Bks.

— The Brain Has a Mind of Its Own: Insights from a Practicing Neurologist. 192p. 1991. 18.00 (0-517-57483-7, Harmony) Crown Pub Group.

— The Brain Has a Mind of Its Own: Insights from a Practicing Neurologist. 1993. 12.00 (0-517-88080-6, Crown) Crown Pub Group.

— The Mind. braille ed. 807p. 1992. Braille. vinyl bd. 64.56 (1-56956-284-9, BR7768) W A T Braille.

— The Modular Brain: How New Discoveries in Neuroscience Are Answering Age-Old Questions about Memory, Free Will, Consciousness, & Personal Identity. 1995. pap. 14.00 (0-684-80126-4, Touchstone Bks) S&S Trade.

— Receptors. LC 93-20932. 1994. 23.95 (0-553-08198-5, Spectra) Bantam.

Restall, John & Hebbs, Donald. How to Make Wines with a Sparkle. (Illus.). 132p. (Orig.). 1993. reprint ed. pap. 10.95 (0-9619072-6-6) G W Kent.

— Making Sparkling Wines. 2nd ed. (Illus.). 144p. (Orig.). 1995. pap. 14.95x (1-85486-119-0, Pub. by Argus Books UK) Trans-Atl Phila.

Restany, Pierre. Bernard Stern. (Illus.). 200p. 1990. 60.00 (0-312-04923-4) St Martin.

— G. H. Rothe Master of the Mezzotint. Newell, Cam, ed. LC 83-81130. (Illus.). 271p. 1983. 60.00 (0-9611570-0-3); 60.00 (0-9611570-1-1) Hammer Gal.

R

— Yves Klein: Fire at the Heart of the Void. Ottmann, Klaus, ed. Loselle, Andrea, tr. (Journal of Contemporary Art Editions). (Illus.). 160p. (Orig.). (C). 1992. pap. 19.95 (*0-9634713-0-9*) Jrnl Contemp.

Restany, Pierre, ed. Dani Karavan. (Illus.). 159p. 1992. 70.00 (*3-7913-1237-5*, Pub. by Prestel) TeNeues.

Restany, Pierre, jt. auth. see Greene, Alison D.

ReSTAR (Oleksinsky-Oleksinsky) Staff. PC Food Service Spreadsheet Applications SD. 2nd ed. 96p. (C). 1988. per. 30.95 (*0-8403-4866-5*) Kendall-Hunt.

Restarick, Henry B. Sun Yat Sen, Liberator of China. LC 79-2837. (Illus.). 167p. 1985. reprint ed. 20.50 (*0-8305-0014-6*) Hyperion Conn.

Restaurant Business Inc. Menu Planning & Foods Merchandising. LC 73-163322. 1971. teacher ed 6.67 (*0-672-96094-X*, Bobbs); student ed 7.50 (*0-672-96093-1*, Bobbs) Macmillan.

Restelli, G. & Angeletti, G., eds. Physico-Chemical Behaviour of Atmospheric Pollutants. (C). 1990. lib. bdg. 232.00 (*0-7923-0700-3*) Kluwer Ac.

Restelli, G., jt. ed. see Angeletti, G.

Restelli, Giambattista, ed. Dimethylsulphide: Oceans, Atmosphere & Climate: Proceedings of the International Symposium Held in Belgirate, Italy, 13-15 October 1992. LC 93-30136. 412p. (C). 1993. lib. bdg. 136.00 (*0-7923-2490-0*) Kluwer Ac.

Rester, A. C., Jr. & Trombka, J. I., eds. High-Energy Radiation Background in Space. LC 89-83833. (AIP Conference Proceedings Ser.: No. 186). 520p. 1989. lib. bdg. 80.00 (*0-88318-386-2*) Am Inst Physics.

Restif de la Bretonne, Nicholas E. Nuits de Paris. (Folio Ser.: No. 1739). (FRE.). 1986. pap. 14.95 (*2-07-037739-3*) Schoenhof.

— La Vie De Mon Pere, 2 vols. in 1. iv, 291p. 1979. reprint ed. write for info. (*3-487-06844-3*, Pub. by Georg Olms GW) Lubrecht & Cramer.

Restif de la Bretonne, Nicolas. Monsieur Nicholas, Vol. 2. Testud, Jean-Yves, ed. (FRE.). 1989. lib. bdg. 170.00 (*0-7859-3888-5*) Fr & Eur.

Restifo, Robert A. Illustrated Key to the Mosquitoes of Ohio: Biological Notes, No. 17. (Illus.). 56p. 1982. 7.00 (*0-86727-092-6*) Ohio Bio Survey.

Restine, L. Nan. Women in Administration: Facilitators for Change. Herman, Jerry J. & Herman, Janice L., eds. (Road Maps to Success Ser.). 64p. 1993. pap. 15.00 (*0-8039-6059-X*) Corwin Pr.

Restivo, Sal. The Sociological Worldview. 224p. 1991. pap. 16.95 (*0-631-17781-7*) Blackwell Pubs.

Restivo, Sal, et al, eds. Math Worlds: Philosophical & Social Studies of Mathematics & Mathematics Education. LC 92-4252. (SUNY Series in Science, Technology & Society). 292p. (C). 1993. 59.50 (*0-7914-1329-2*); pap. 19.95 (*0-7914-1330-6*) State U NY Pr.

Restivo, Sal P. Mathematics in Society & History: Sociological Inquiries. LC 92-13695. (C). 1992. lib. bdg. 89.00 (*0-7923-1765-3*) Kluwer Ac.

— Science, Society, & Values: Toward a Sociology of Objectivity. LC 92-85310. 1993. write for info. (*0-934223-21-1*) Lehigh Univ Pr.

— The Social Relations of Physics, Mysticism & Mathematics. 1983. lib. bdg. 106.50 (*90-277-1536-X*) Kluwer Ac.

— The Social Relations of Physics, Mysticism & Mathematics. (Pallas Paperbacks Ser.). 1985. pap. text ed. 47.00 (*90-277-2084-3*) Kluwer Ac.

Restle, F., jt. ed. see Castellan, N. J., Jr.

Restle, F., et al, eds. Cognitive Theory, Vol. 1. LC 74-14293. 320p. 1975. text ed. 59.95 (*0-89859-436-7*) L Erlbaum Assocs.

Reston. Shermans March & Vietnam. 1985. 14.95 (*0-02-602300-8*) Macmillan.

Reston, James. Artillery of the Press. LC 67-11330. 128p. reprint ed. 36.50 (*0-8357-9150-5*, 2002159) Bks Demand.

— Deadline: A Memoir. LC 91-52679. (Illus.). 525p. 1991. 25.00 (*0-394-58558-5*) Random.

— Deadline: A Memoir. 1992. pap. 14.00 (*0-8129-2071-6*, Times Bks) Random.

Reston, James, Jr. Galileo: A Life. LC 93-29221. 288p. 1994. 25.00 (*0-06-016378-X*, HarpT) HarpC.

— Galileo: A Life. 336p. 1995. pap. 13.00 (*0-06-092607-4*, PL) HarpC.

Restout, Denise, tr. see Chambonnieres, Jacques C.

Restuccia, Frances L. Joyce & the Law of the Father. LC 88-39658. 208p. (C). 1989. text ed. 26.00 (*0-300-04444-5*) Yale U Pr.

Restuccia, Nancy. Hold It! How to Sew Bags, Totes, Duffels, Pouches, & More! LC 93-48333. 144p. 1994. pap. 17.95 (*0-8019-8494-7*) Chilton.

Restuccio, Jeffrey. Fitness the Dynamic Gardening Way: A Health & Wellness Lifestyle. Cornell, Philip, ed. (Illus.). 288p. 1992. pap. 12.95 (*1-880886-10-3*) Balance of Nature.

Resumil de Sanfilipo, Olga E. Criminologia General. 309p. 1992. 22.95 (*0-8477-3033-6*) U of PR Pr.

Resumil de Sanfilippo, Olga E. Derecho Procesal Penal, 2 Tomos. 400p. (SPA.). 1994. boxed 120.00 (*0-88063-691-2*, Equity Pub NH) Michie Butterworth.

Reswick, Irmtraud. Traditional Textiles of Tunisia & Related North African Weaving. (Illus.). 272p. 1985. pap. 24.95 (*0-295-96281-X*) U of Wash Pr.

Reswick, James B., jt. ed. see Hambrecht, F. Terry.

Resz, E. English-Hungarian & Hungarian-English Tourists Dictionary. 315p. (C). 1988. 315.00 (*0-569-19611-6*, Pub. by Collets) St Mut.

Resz, E., ed. English-Hungarian & Hungarian-English Tourists Dictionary. 9th ed. 315p. (C). 1988. 65.00 (*0-685-54136-3*, Pub. by Collets) St Mut.

Retail Advertising & Marketing Association Staff, ed. Excellence in Advertising: The Thirty-Ninth RAC Awards. (Illus.). 224p. 1992. 49.95 (*0-934590-43-5*) Retail Report.

Retail Partners, Inc., Staff. Eight Steps to Business Success: A Handbook for Independent Merchants. 105p. 1991. 14.95 (*0-9629238-0-X*) URA Pittsburgh.

***Retallack.** How to Do Things with Words. 1995. pap. text ed. 10.95 (*1-55713-213-5*) Sun & Moon CA.

Retallack, Greg J. Late Eocene & Oligocene Paleosols from Badlands National Park, South Dakota. LC 83-5675. (Geological Society of America, Special Paper Ser.: No. 193). 90p. reprint ed. pap. 25.70 (*0-7837-2685-6*, 2043062) Bks Demand.

Retallack, Gregory J. Miocene Paleosols & Ape Habitats in Pakistan & Kenya. (Oxford Monographs on Geology & Geophysics: No. 19). (Illus.). 352p. 1991. 75.00 (*0-19-506002-4*) OUP.

— Soils of the Past: An Introduction to Paleopedology. 300p. 1989. 100.00 (*0-04-551128-4*) Routledge Chapman & Hall.

Retallack, James, jt. ed. see Jones, Larry E.

Retallack, James N. Notables of the Right: The Conservative Party & Political Mobilization in Germany, 1876-1918. 224p. (C). 1988. text ed. 55.00 (*0-04-900038-1*) Routledge Chapman & Hall.

Retallack, James N., jt. ed. see Jones, Larry E.

***Retallack, Joan.** Afterrimages. 112p. 1995. 25.00x (*0-8195-2219-8*, Wesleyan Univ Pr); pap. 12.95 (*0-8195-1223-0*, Wesleyan Univ Pr) U Pr of New Eng.

— Circumstantial Evidence; Poems 1976-1983. LC 84-51705. 87p. (Orig.). 1985. pap. 6.00 (*0-911809-01-5*) Moon Lake Bks.

— Errata Suite. 63p. (Orig.). 1994. pap. 8.00 (*0-9619097-5-7*) Edge Bks.

Retallack, Joan, jt. contrib. see Cage, John.

Retallick, Martha J. Discovering America: Bicycle Adventures in All 50 States. LC 93-79530. 256p. (Orig.). 1993. pap. 15.95 (*0-9637803-0-1*) Lone Rider.

Retamar, Roberto F. Caliban & Other Essays. Baker, Edward, tr. 168p. (Orig.). 1989. text ed. 34.95 (*0-8166-1742-2*); pap. text ed. 14.95 (*0-8166-1743-0*) U of Minn Pr.

Retan. Bunnies, Bunnies, Bunnies. (J). 1995. pap. 7.95 (*0-671-88247-3*, S&S Bks Young Read) S&S Childrens.

Retan, Walter. Armies of Ants. LC 93-29782. (Hello Reader! Ser.: Level 4). (Illus.). 48p. (J). (ps-4). 1994. pap. 3.50 (*0-590-47616-5*, Cartwheel) Scholastic Inc.

— One Hundred & One Facts about Snakes & Reptiles. (J). (gr. 4-7). 1992. pap. 1.95 (*0-590-44891-9*) Scholastic Inc.

— Piggies Piggies Piggies. (J). (gr. 3 up). 1993. pap. 15.00 (*0-671-75244-8*, S&S Bks Young Read) S&S Childrens.

— The Story of Daniel Boone. (Illus.). 112p. (Orig.). (J). (gr. 2-5). 1992. pap. 3.25 (*0-440-40711-7*, YB) Dell.

Retan, Walter, ed. Bunnies, Bunnies, Bunnies. LC 90-41486. (Illus.). 96p. (J). (ps-2). 1991. pap. 14.95 (*0-671-73221-8*, S&S Bks Young Read) S&S Childrens.

Retat, Pierre. Le Dictionnaire de Bayle et la Lute Philosophique au 18e Siecle. 556p. (FRE.). 1972. pap. 45.00 (*0-7859-0731-9*, FA-410) Fr & Eur.

Retecki, Richard. Rainbow Dance Studio. Mycue, Edward, ed. (Took Modern Poetry in English Ser.: No. 8). (Illus.). 28p. (Orig.). 1993. pap. 3.00 (*1-879457-02-4*) Norton Coker Pr.

***Retention Marketing Staff.** Today in Western New York, 1995. 112p. 1994. pap. 9.95 (*0-9644538-0-0*) RMI Pub.

Rethati, L. Probabilistic Solutions in Geotechnics. (Developments in Geotechnical Engineering Ser.: Vol. 46). 250p. 1988. 117.25 (*0-444-98960-9*) Elsevier.

Rethati, L., jt. auth. see Kezdi, A.

Rethati, L., jt. ed. see Kezdi, A.

Retherford, J. R. Hilbert Space: Compact Operators & the Trace Theorem. (London Mathematical Society Student Texts Ser.: No. 27). 160p. (C). 1993. 47.95 (*0-521-41884-4*); pap. 21.95 (*0-521-42933-1*) Cambridge U Pr.

Retherford, Kristine S. Guide Applied: Production Characteristics of Language Impaired Children. LC 92-23583. 1992. pap. 39.00 (*0-930599-78-0*) Thinking Pubns.

— Guide to Analysis of Language Transcripts. 2nd rev. ed. LC 93-19445. 296p. (C). 1993. spiral bd. 35.00 (*0-930599-87-X*) Thinking Pubns.

Retherford, Robert D. The Changing Sex Differential in Mortality. LC 74-19808. (Studies in Demography & Urban Population). (Illus.). 139p. 1975. text ed. 45.00 (*0-8371-7848-7*, RSX/, Greenwood Pr) Greenwood.

Retherford, Robert D. & Alam, Iqbal. Comparison of Fertility Trends Estimated Alternatively from Birth Histories & Own Children. LC 85-13166. (Papers of the East-West Population Institute: No. 94). viii, 39p. 1985. pap. 3.00 (*0-86638-068-X*) EW Ctr HI.

Retherford, Robert D. & Choe, Minja K. Statistical Models for Causal Analysis. LC 93-23423. 258p. 1993. text ed. 49.95 (*0-471-55802-8*) Wiley.

Retherford, Robert D., jt. auth. see Levin, Michael J.

***Rethi, Lynn L. & Burns, Kristina L., comps.** A Comparison of Small Mines & Small Business: Health & Safety Barriers & Intervention Strategies. LC 94-25140. (Information Circular - Bureau of Mines Ser.). 1995. write for info. (*0-614-03330-6*) US Interior.

Rethorst. Welcome to. . . the Macintosh from Mystery to Mastery. 1993. pap. 19.95 (*1-55828-264-5*) MIS Press.

Rethorst, John. Teach Yourself WordPerfect 3.0 for Macintosh. 400p. 1994. pap. 21.95 (*1-55828-307-2*) H Holt & Co.

Rethwisch, David G., jt. ed. see Lewis, Kenrich M.

Reti, Ingrid. Echoes of Silence. 64p. (Orig.). 1989. pap. 6.95 (*0-939821-49-4*) HerBooks.

Reti, Irene, ed. Childless by Choice: An Anthology. 96p. 1992. pap. 9.95 (*0-939821-03-6*) HerBooks.

— Unleashing Feminism: A Critique of Lesbian Sadomasochism in the Gay Nineties. 160p. 1993. pap. 8.95 (*0-939821-04-4*) HerBooks.

Reti, Irene & Chase, Valerie, eds. Garden Variety Dykes: Lesbian Traditions in Gardening. 128p. 1994. 10.00 (*0-939821-05-2*) HerBooks.

***Reti, Irene & Chase, Valerie J., eds.** A Transported Life: Memories of Kindertransport: The Oral History of Thea Eden. (Illus.). 96p. (Orig.). 1995. pap. text ed. 9.00 (*0-939821-07-9*) HerBooks.

Reti, Irene & Sien, Shoney, eds. Cats (& Their Dykes) An Anthology. (Illus.). 160p. (Orig.). 1991. pap. 10.00 (*0-939821-47-8*) HerBooks.

Reti, Irene, et al, eds. The World Between Women. (Illus.). 126p. (Orig.). 1987. pap. 7.95 (*0-939821-27-3*) HerBooks.

Reti, Ladislao. Unknown Leonardo. (Illus.). 316p. 1990. pap. 34.98 (*0-8109-8101-7*) Abrams.

Reti, Ladislao, tr. see Da Vinci, Leonardo.

Reti, Richard. Masters of the Chessboard. Schwendemann, M. A., tr. 1976. reprint ed. pap. 7.95 (*0-486-23384-7*) Dover.

— Modern Ideas in Chess. pap. 4.95 (*0-486-20638-6*) Dover.

Reti, Richard & Golombek, H. Reti's Best Games of Chess. (Illus.). 173p. 1974. reprint ed. 4.95 (*0-486-21636-5*) Dover.

Reti, Rudolph. Thematic Patterns in Sonatas of Beethoven. (Music Reprint Ser.). 1992. 27.50 (*0-306-79714-3*) Da Capo.

Reti, Rudolph R. The Thematic Process in Music. LC 77-13622. 362p. 1978. reprint ed. text ed. 55.00 (*0-8371-9875-5*, RETH, Greenwood Pr) Greenwood.

— Tonality, Atonality, Pantonality: A Study of Some Trends in Twentieth Century Music. LC 78-6162. (Illus.). 166p. 1978. reprint ed. text ed. 38.50 (*0-313-20478-0*, RETO, Greenwood Pr) Greenwood.

Retian, Ralph M. Aphasia & Sensory-Perceptual Deficits in Adults. 173p. (Orig.). 1984. pap. text ed. 34.00 (*0-934515-00-X*) Neuropsych Pr.

Retif de la Bretonne, A. Monsieur Nicolas, Vol. 1. (FRE.). 1989. lib. bdg. 150.00 (*0-8288-3531-4*, F26670) Fr & Eur.

Retinger, J. Conrad & His Contemporaries. 1972. 59.95 (*0-87968-932-3*) Gordon Pr.

Retinger, Joseph. Conrad & His Contemporaries. LC 72-6504. (Studies in Conrad: No. 8). 156p. 1972. reprint ed. lib. bdg. 39.95 (*0-8383-1621-2*) M S G Haskell Hse.

Retino, Ernie & Kerner Rettino, Debbie. Solomon, the Supersonic Salamander: Choosing Good Friends. (Wisdom Ser.). 32p. (J). (ps-2). 1992. 7.99 (*0-8499-1017-X*) Word Inc.

***Retired Teachers of Pike County Staff.** Pike County, Georgia. (Illus.). 761p. 1989. 65.00 (*0-88107-153-6*) Curtis Media.

Retnakaran, Arthur, jt. ed. see Wright, James E.

Retowski, O. F. The Genoese-Tatar Coinage. Zander, R., tr. (Illus.). 62p. (Orig.). 1983. pap. 12.00 (*0-912671-05-X*) Russian Numis.

Retsinis, Joan M. It's OK Mom: The Nursing Home From a Sociological Perspective. LC 86-50614. 192p. (Orig.). 1986. 10.95 (*0-913292-14-1*) Tiresias Pr.

Retskin, Bill, ed. The Matchcover Collectors Resource Book & Price Guide. (Illus.). 272p. 1993. 24.95 (*0-318-63689-1*) Retskin Report.

Retso, Jan. Diathesis in the Semitic Languages: A Comparative Morphological Study. LC 89-39786. (Studies in Semitic Languages & Linguistics: Vol. XIV). xvii, 254p. 1989. text ed. 55.00 (*90-04-08818-0*) E J Brill.

***Rettenmund, Matthew.** Madonnica: The Woman & the Icon from A to Z. LC 94-48309. 1995. pap. 15.95 (*0-312-11782-5*) St Martin.

Retter, G. J. Matrix & Space-Phasor Theory of Electrical Machines. 412p. (C). 1987. 335.00 (*0-569-09003-2*, Pub. by Collets) St Mut.

***Retter, Gy.** Matrix & Space-Phasor Theory of Electrical Machines. 410p. (C). 1987. 150.00x (*963-05-4232-3*) St Mut.

Retterstol, N. & Dahl, A., eds. Functional Psychoses: Classification & Prognosis. (Journal: Psychopathology: Vpl. 29, No. 1-2, 1986). (Illus.). 92p. 1986. pap. 62.50 (*3-8055-4317-4*) S Karger.

Retterstol, N., et al. Functional Psychoses: Recent Follow-up Studies, 1991 - Psychopathology Journal, Vol. 24, No. 5. (Illus.). 92p. 1991. pap. 35.25 (*3-8055-5534-2*) S Karger.

Retterstol, Nils. Suicide: A European Perspective. (Illus.). 220p. (C). 1993. 54.95 (*0-521-42099-7*) Cambridge U Pr.

Rettger, J. F. The Development of Ablaut in the Strong Verbs of the East Midland Dialects of Middle English. (LD Ser.: No. 18). 1972. reprint ed. 16.00 (*0-527-00764-1*) Periodicals Srv.

***Rettie, Dwight F.** Our National Park System: Caring for America's Greatest Natural & Historic Treasures. LC 94-22632. 1995. write for info. (*0-252-02148-7*) U of Ill Pr.

Rettig, jt. auth. see Strickland.

Rettig, James. Distinguished Classics of Reference Publishing. 376p. 1992. 55.00 (*0-89774-640-6*) Oryx Pr.

Rettig, James, ed. see Block, Eleanor S. & Bracken, James K.

Rettig, James, ed. see Bracken, James K.

Rettig, James, ed. see Cates, Jo A.

Rettig, James, ed. see DeMiller, Anna L.

Rettig, John, tr. see Augustine, St.

Rettig, John, tr. see St. Augustine.

Rettig, John W., tr. see Augustine, St.

Rettig, Michael D., jt. auth. see Canady, Robert L.

Rettig, R., et al, eds. Salt & Hypertension. 385p. 1989. 99.00 (*0-387-50063-4*) Spr-Verlag.

Rettig, Rainer, tr. see Vanderlip, Sharon L.

Rettig, Richard A., ed. see Committee to Study the Use of Advisory Committees by the Food & Drug Administration Staff.

Rettig, Richard A., ed. see Institute of Medicine, Committee on Federal Regulation of Methadone Treatment.

Rettig, Rudi. Das Investitions und Finanzierungsverhalten Deutscher Grossunternehmen 1880-1911. Bruchey, Stuart, ed. LC 80-2827. (Dissertations in European Economic History Ser.). (Illus.). 1981. lib. bdg. 35.95 (*0-405-14019-3*) Ayer.

Rettig, S. The Discursive Social Psychology of Evidence: Symbolic Construction of Reality. LC 90-7911. (Illus.). 230p. 1990. 42.50 (*0-306-43701-5*, Plenum Pr) Plenum.

Rettig, Sam & French, Drucie. Sam's WIT: Water Interval Training for Fabulous People of Every Kind. large type ed. (Illus.). 118p. 1993. pap. 20.00 (*0-9637470-2-9*) DFC Seminars.

Rettig, Tom & Moody, Debby. Expert Advisor: dBASE III Plus. (Illus.). 400p. 1988. pap. 22.95 (*0-201-17197-X*) Addison-Wesley.

Rettinger, Michael. Acoustic Design, Vol. 1. 288p. 1977. 41.95 (*0-317-99711-4*) Peninsula CA.

— Handbook of Architecture & Noise Control: A Manual For Architects & Engineers. (Illus.). 272p. 1988. 32.95 (*0-8306-2686-7*, 2686) TAB Bks.

— Noise Control, Vol. 2. 400p. 1977. 51.95 (*0-932146-52-X*) Peninsula CA.

Rettino, Ernie & Kerner, Debby. Psalty in Alaska. 1991. 6.99 (*0-8499-0893-0*) Word Inc.

— Psalty in Australia. 1991. 6.99 (*0-8499-0897-3*) Word Inc.

— Psalty in Egypt. 1991. 6.99 (*0-8499-0894-9*) Word Inc.

— Psalty in the South Pacific. 1991. 6.99 (*0-8499-0895-7*) Word Inc.

— Psalty in the Soviet Circus. 1991. 6.99 (*0-8499-0892-2*) Word Inc.

— Psalty on Safari. 1991. 6.99 (*0-8499-0896-5*) Word Inc.

Rettino, Ernie & Kerner Rettino, Debbie. Solomon, the Supersonic Salamander: Telling the Truth. (Wisdom Ser.). 32p. (J). (ps-2). 1992. 7.99 (*0-8499-1018-8*) Word Inc.

Rettis, Richard A., ed. see Institute of Medicine, Committee for the Study of the Medicare ESRD Program Staff.

Rettke, Mari. Practical Data Communications. 256p. 1990. text ed. write for info. (*0-07-067667-4*) McGraw.

Retzer, Henry, tr. see Barth, R. Carl, ed.

Retzii, A. J. Observationes Botanicae: Six Fascicmles, 1779-1791. 1987. 160.00 (*0-317-89553-2*, Scientific) St Mut.

Retzinger, Suzanne M. Violent Emotions: Shame & Rage in Marital Quarrels. 256p. (C). 1991. 52.00 (*0-8039-4183-8*); pap. 24.00 (*0-8039-4184-6*) Sage.

Retzinger, Suzanne M., jt. auth. see Scheff, Thomas J.

***Retzlaff, Ewald.** Dictionary of Code Symbols for Cables & Insulated Cord According to UDE, CENELEC & IEC: German-English. 4th ed. 152p. (ENG & GER.). 1993. 49.95 (*0-7859-8693-6*, 380071860x) Fr & Eur.

Retzlaff, J. M. In Search. LC 89-81148. 62p. (Orig.). 1990. pap. 5.00 (*0-916383-95-4*) Aegina Pr.

Retzlaff, John, et al. Lens Implant Power Calculation: A Manual for Ophthalmologists & Biometrists. 3rd ed. LC 90-53345. 58p. 1990. 25.00 (*1-55642-186-9*) SLACK Inc.

Retzlaff, Nancy. Gods in the Making or How to Have Fun in the Galaxy. Roerden, Chris, ed. 78p. (Orig.). 1993. pap. 14.95 (*0-9635188-1-X*) Gemini Moon.

***Retzlaff, Paul D., ed.** Psychotherapy of the Personality Disorders: An MOMI-III-Based Approach. 1995. text ed. 38.95 (*0-205-15932-X*, Longwood Div) Allyn.

Reu, Johann M. The Augsburg Confession. LC 83-45650. reprint ed. 76.50 (*0-404-19859-7*) AMS Pr.

— Luther's German Bible. LC 83-45651. reprint ed. 75.00 (*0-404-19860-0*) AMS Pr.

— Thirty-Five Years of Luther Research. LC 79-13505. (Illus.). reprint ed. 36.50 (*0-404-05284-3*) AMS Pr.

Reubart, Dale. Anxiety & Musical Performance. LC 84-21422. (Music Ser.). 250p. 1985. 35.00 (*0-306-76253-6*) Da Capo.

Reuben. Dr. Reuben Mental First Aid Manual. 1982. 12.98 (*0-02-605730-1*) Macmillan.

Reuben, Carolyn. Antioxidants: Your Complete Guide. LC 93-49709. 1994. pap. write for info. (*1-55958-522-6*) Prima Pub.

— The Healthy Baby Book. LC 92-13548. 208p. (Orig.). 1992. 8.95 (*0-87477-679-1*) J P Tarcher.

Reuben, David. Everything You Always Wanted to Know about Nutrition. 1979. mass mkt. 4.50 (*0-380-44370-8*) Avon.

Reuben, David b., et al, eds. Geriatrics Review Syllabus Supplement: A Core Curriculum in Geriatric Medicine, 2 vols. LC 93-21369. 1994. 315.00 (*0-9624397-9-7*) Am Geriatrics.

— Geriatrics Review Syllabus Supplement: A Core Curriculum in Geriatric Medicine, 2 vols., Bk. I. LC 93-21369. 1994. write for info. (*0-9624397-7-0*) Am Geriatrics.

— Geriatrics Review Syllabus Supplement: A Core Curriculum in Geriatric Medicine, 2 vols., Bk. II. LC 93-21369. 1994. write for info. (*0-9624397-8-9*) Am Geriatrics.

Reuben, Davis. Recollections of Mississippi & Mississippians. (American Biography Ser.). 456p. 1991. reprint ed. lib. bdg. 89.00 (*0-7812-8100-8*) Rprt Serv.

***Reuben, Elaine & Hoffmann, Leonore, eds.** Unladylike & Unprofessional: Academic Women & Academic Unions. fac. ed. 63p. 1975. reprint ed. pap. 25.00 (*0-7837-8033-8*, 2047789) Bks Demand.

— Unladylike & Unprofessional: Academic Women & Academic Unions (MLA Commission on the Status of Women in the Profession) vi, 54p. (Orig.). 1975. pap. 10.00 (*0-87352-327-X*, B86) Modern Lang.

R

Reuben, Gabriel. Electricity Experiments for Children. (Illus.). 88p. (J). (gr. 5-9). pap. 2.95 (*0-486-22030-3*) Dover.

Reuben, Jacques, ed. see Berliner, Lawrence J.

Reuben, Jacques, jt. ed. see Berliner, Lawrence J.

Reuben, Robert. Materials in Marine Technology. LC 93-15462. 1994. 243.00 (*0-387-19789-3*) Spr-Verlag.

Reuben, Ruth, tr. see Sheldon, Charles M.

Reuben, S. Chess Openings: Your Choice. (Chess Ser.). (Illus.). 150p. 1985. 23.95 (*0-08-026895-1*, Pub. by PPL UK); pap. 17.90 (*0-08-026894-3*, Pub. by PPL UK) Elsevier.

Reuben, S., jt. auth. see Hartston, W. R.

Reuben, Shelly. Origin & Cause: A Crime Novel. 352p. 1994. text ed. 20.00 (*0-684-19702-2*, Scribners) S&S Trade.

Reuben, Steven C. Making Interfaith Marriage Work: A Nonjudgmental Guide to Coping with the Spiritual, Emotional, & Psychological Issues. LC 93-48111. 1994. write for info. (*1-55958-506-4*) Prima Pub.

— Raising Ethical Children: Ten Keys to Helping Your Children Become Moral & Caring. 275p. 1993. pap. 10.95 (*1-55958-360-6*) Prima Pub.

— Raising Jewish Children in a Contemporary World: The Modern Parent's Guide to Creating a Jewish Home. (Illus.). 300p. 1992. 18.95 (*1-55958-150-6*) Prima Pub.

— Raising Jewish Children in a Contemporary World: The Modern Parent's Guide to Creating a Jewish Home. 240p. 1993. pap. 12.95 (*1-55958-319-3*) Prima Pub.

Reuben, Willard. The Work of Michael R. Collings: An Annotated Bibliography & Guide. Clarke, Boden, ed. LC 93-340. (Bibliographies of Modern Authors Ser.: No. 22). 160p. Date not set. lib. bdg. write for info. (*0-8095-0501-0*); pap. write for info. (*0-8095-1501-6*) Borgo Pr.

Reubens, Beatrice G. The Hard-to-Employ: European Programs. LC 78-117018. (Illus.). 1970. text ed. 60.00 (*0-231-03388-5*) Col U Pr.

Reubens, Beatrice G., ed. Youth at Work: An International Survey. LC 83-8631. (Conservation of Human Resources Ser.: No. 22). 366p. (C). 1983. text ed. 76.50 (*0-86598-101-9*) Rowman.

Reubens, E. M. Chess - Trick & Treat. (Illus.). (Orig.). 1962. pap. 3.95 (*0-8283-1431-4*, 37, Intl Pocket Lib) Branden Pub Co.

Reubens, Peggy. Vocational Education for Immigrant & Minority Youth. 42p. 1983. 4.25 (*0-318-22240-X*, IN257) Ctr Educ Trng Employ.

Reuber, Grant L., jt. auth. see Caves, Richard E.

Reuchlin, Abelard. The True Authorship of the New Testament. 1979. pap. 4.00 (*0-930808-02-9*) Vector Assocs.

Reuchlin, Johann. Briefwechsel. 372p. (GER.). 1973. reprint ed. write for info. (*0-318-70505-2*, Pub. by Georg Olms GW) Lubrecht & Cramer.

— De Arte Cabalistica. Goodman, Martin & Goodman, Sarah, trs. LC 77-86231. (Janus Ser.). 384p. 1983. 20.00 (*0-913870-56-0*) Abaris Bks.

— On the Art of the Kabbalah (De Arte Cabalistica) Goodman, Martin & Goodman, Sarah, trs. LC 93-13872. (Illus.). xxix, 376p. (ENG & LAT.). 1993. pap. 15.00 (*0-8032-8946-4*, Bison Books) U of Nebr Pr.

Reucroff, Stephen, jt. ed. see Nath, Pran.

Reucroft, S., jt. ed. see Nath, Pran.

***Reudor.** The Doodled Family Haggadah. (Illus.). 80p. (J). 1995. 24.95 (*1-886611-22-X*) Atara Publ.

***Reuer, Barbara L. & Crowe, Barbara.** Best Practice in Music Therapy: Utilizing Group Percussion Strategies for Promoting Volunteerism in the Well Older Adult. 88p. (Orig.). 1995. pap. text ed. 25.00 (*1-879167-08-5*) SDSU Univ Ctr on Aging.

Reufenacht, Peter, jt. auth. see Bauer, Fred.

Reuijl, Jan C. On the Determination of Advertising Effectiveness: An Empirical Study of the German Cigarette Market. 1982. lib. bdg. 49.50 (*0-89838-125-8*) Kluwer Ac.

Reukauf, Diane & Trause, Mary Anne. Some Days Are Better Than Others: A Book About Breastfeeding. 1989. pap. text ed. 23.00 (*0-8359-7054-X*, Reston); pap. text ed. 9.95 (*0-686-96872-7*, Reston) P-H.

Reul, I. H., ed. see International Conference on Mechanics in Medicine & Biology Staff.

Reuland, Eric & Abraham, Werner, eds. Knowledge & Language, Vols. 1-2. LC 92-14226. 1993. lib. bdg. 143.00 (*0-7923-1789-0*) Kluwer Ac.

— Knowledge & Language, Vols. 1-2. LC 92-14226. 1993. lib. bdg. 124.00 (*0-7923-1790-4*) Kluwer Ac.

Reuland, Eric, jt. ed. see Koster, Jan.

Reuland, Eric J. & Ter Meulen, Alice G. The Representation of InDefiniteness. (Current Studies in Linguistics: Vol. 14). 360p. 1989. 40.00 (*0-262-18126-6*) MIT Pr.

Reuland, R., jt. ed. see Cassee, E.

Reulen, H. J., et al, eds. Brain Edema, No. VIII. (Acta Neurochirurgica - Supplementum Ser.: No. 51). (Illus.). xiii, 416p. 1991. 162.00 (*0-387-82240-2*) Spr-Verlag.

Reuling, Melly A., jt. auth. see Scott, James W.

Reum, Earl. Fund Raising for Student Councils. Lucas, Patricia, ed. (Orig.). (gr. 8-12). 1981. pap. text ed. 7.00 (*0-88210-118-8*) Natl Assn Principals.

— The Spirit of Student Council. Bruce, C., ed. (J). (gr. 7-9). 1981. pap. 7.00 (*0-88210-117-X*) Natl Assn Principals.

Reuman, Robert E. Walls: Physical & Psychological. LC 66-24444. (Orig.). 1966. pap. 3.00 (*0-87574-147-9*) Pendle Hill.

Reumann, John. Jesus in the Church's Gospels: Modern Scholarship & the Earliest Sources. LC 68-10983. 564p. 1973. pap. 15.00 (*0-8006-1091-1*, 1-1091, Fortress Pr) Augsburg Fortress.

— Variety & Unity in New Testament Thought. (Oxford Bible Ser.). (Illus.). 344p. 1991. 55.00 (*0-19-826201-9*); pap. 19.95 (*0-19-826204-3*) OUP.

Reumann, John H. Pentecost 2: Proclamation 5, Series B. 1994. pap. 4.50 (*0-8006-4191-4*, Fortress Pr) Augsburg Fortress.

— Stewardship & the Economy of God. fac. ed. LC 92-24696. (Library of Christian Stewardship). 171p. 1992. reprint ed. pap. 48.80 (*0-7837-7971-2*, 2047727) Bks Demand.

Reumann, John H., ed. The Promise & Practice of Biblical Theology. LC 91-18794. 232p. (Orig.). 1991. pap. 14.00 (*0-8006-2495-5*, 1-2495, Fortress Pr) Augsburg Fortress.

Reumann, John H., jt. ed. see Taylor, Walter F., Jr.

Reumaux, P., jt. auth. see Moenne-Loccoz, P.

Reummler, John, ed. see Crowdis, John.

Reummler, John, ed. see Longstreet, Roxanne.

Reunert, Theodore. Diamonds & Gold in South Africa. LC 72-3916. (Black Heritage Library Collection). 1977. reprint ed. 32.95 (*0-8369-9106-0*) Ayer.

Reunhold, Niebuhr. The Nature & Destiny of Man, Vol. I: Human Nature. 305p. (C). 1980. pap. write for info. (*0-02-387510-0*, Scribners) S&S Trade.

Reusch, Gary M., jt. auth. see Hartwig, Eric P.

Reusch, Peter. A Piece of Amber. Caroland, Mary, ed. LC 90-71000. 309p. 1991. pap. 8.95 (*1-55523-367-8*) Winston-Derek.

Reusch, William. An Introduction to Organic Chemistry. LC 76-50855. 1977. text ed. 37.95 (*0-8162-7161-5*) Holden-Day.

Reuschemeyer, Marilyn, et al. Soviet Emigre Artists. LC 84-23558. 184p. 1985. 49.95 (*0-87332-296-7*); pap. 25.95 (*0-87332-810-8*) M E Sharpe.

Reuscher, John A. Essays on the Metaphysical Foundation of Personal Identity. LC 80-6067. 111p. (C). 1981. lib. bdg. 44.00 (*0-8191-1471-5*) U Pr of Amer.

Reuschlein, Harold G. Jurisprudence: Its American Prophets; a Survey of Taught Jurisprudence. LC 70-158741. 527p. 1971. reprint ed. text ed. 79.50 (*0-8371-6180-0*, REJU, Greenwood Pr) Greenwood.

Reuschlein, Harold G. & Gregory, William A. The Law of Agency & Partnership: Student Edition. 2nd ed. (Hornbook Ser.). 683p. 1990. text ed. 34.50 (*0-314-56279-6*) West Pub.

Reuse, Ruth B., jt. auth. see O'Donnell, Joe.

Reush, Peter. The Thirteenth Floor. abr. ed. 200p. 1995. pap. 7.95 (*1-56901-506-6*) NW Pub.

Reusink, J. H., jt. ed. see Wardenier, J.

Reusner, Nicolas. Emblemata Partim Ethica, et Physica: Partim Vero Historica et Hieroglyphica. xxvi, 374p. (GER.). 1990. reprint ed. write for info. (*3-487-09407-X*, Pub. by Georg Olms GW) Lubrecht & Cramer.

Reuss, Carol, jt. auth. see Hiebert, Ray E.

Reuss, Edith A. Luz en la Oscuridad: A Glimpse of Sunshine. (SPA.). 3.25 (*84-7645-214-4*, 223255, Pub. by Edit Clie SP) TSELF.

Reuss, Frederick G. Fiscal Policy for Growth Without Inflation: The German Experiment. LC 63-17669. (Goucher College Ser.). 334p. reprint ed. pap. 95.20 (*0-317-28740-0*, 2020734) Bks Demand.

Reuss, Henry S. & Reuss, Margaret M. The Unknown South of France: A History Buff's Guide. LC 90-47384. (Illus.). (Orig.). 1991. pap. 12.95 (*1-55832-030-X*) Harvard Common Pr.

Reuss-Ianni, Elizabeth. Two Cultures of Policing: Street Cops & Management Cops. 145p. (C). 1993. pap. text ed. 18.95 (*1-56000-654-4*) Transaction Pubs.

Reuss, J. O. & Johnson, D. W. Acid Deposition & Acidification of Soils & Waters. (Ecological Studies: Vol. 59). (Illus.). viii, 119p. 1986. 60.00 (*0-387-96290-5*) Spr-Verlag.

Reuss, Jerry, jt. auth. see Whitburn, Joel.

Reuss, Luis, et al, eds. Regulation of Potassium Transport Across Biological Membranes. (Illus.). 512p. (C). 1990. text ed. 60.00 (*0-292-77043-X*) U of Tex Pr.

Reuss, M., jt. ed. see Heinzle, E.

Reuss, Margaret M., jt. auth. see Reuss, Henry S.

Reuss, Martin, ed. Water Resources Administration in the United States: Policy, Practice, & Emerging Issues. LC 93-7668. 300p. (C). 1993. 40.00 (*0-87013-333-0*) Mich St U Pr.

— Water Resources Administration in the United States Policy, Practice, & Emerging Issues. LC 93-7668. (Technical Publication Ser.: No. 92-3). (Illus.). 314p. 1993. 40.00 (*1-882132-19-X*, CIP) Am Water Resources.

Reuss, Martin, ed. see National Forum on Water Management Policy Staff.

Reuss, Matthias, et al, eds. Biochemical Engineering: Proceedings of 2nd International Symposium on Biochemical Engineering, Stuttgart. (Illus.). 472p. (Orig.). 1991. pap. text ed. 80.00 (*1-56081-319-9*, Pub. by Gustav Fischer Verlag) VCH Pubs.

Reuss, Monica, tr. see Misgeld, Dieter & Nicholson, Graeme, eds.

Reuss, Peter, tr. see Wachsmann, Konrad.

Reuss, Richard A. Songs of American Labor, Industrialization & the Urban Work Experience: A Discography. Lockwood, Yvonne, ed. (Program on Workers Culture Ser.). (Illus.). 109p. 1983. pap. 4.75 (*0-87736-344-7*) U of Mich Inst Labor.

Reuss, Suzanne, jt. auth. see Burkhart, Patrick J.

Reute, H., jt. auth. see Baker, P. F.

Reuten, Geert & Williams, Mike. Value Form & the State: The Tendencies of Accumulation & the Determination of Economic Policy in Capitalist Society. 320p. 1989. 75.00 (*0-415-00088-2*, A3585); pap. 21.95 (*0-415-03893-6*, A3589) Routledge.

Reutenauer. The Mathematics of Petri Nets. 150p. 1990. boxed 51.40 (*0-13-561887-8*) P-H.

Reutenauer, C., jt. auth. see Berstel, J.

Reutenauer, Christophe. Free Lie Algebras. LC 92-27318. (London Mathematical Society Monographs: New Series 7). 1993. 86.00 (*0-19-853679-8*, Clarendon Pr) OUP.

Reuter, Andreas, jt. auth. see Gray, Jim.

Reuter, Anna H., jt. auth. see Trahey, Jane.

Reuter, Bjarne. The Boys from St. Petri. 192p. (J). (gr. 6 up). 1994. 14.99 (*0-525-45121-8*, DCB) Dutton Child Bks.

— Buster, the Sheikh of Hope Street. braille ed. 150p. (J). 1994. text ed., vinyl bd. 12.00 (*1-56956-535-X*, BR9535) W A T Braille.

***Reuter, Christian.** Doing Business in the United States. 64p. (GER.). 1995. 30.00 (*0-86640-052-4*) German Am Chamber.

— Schelmuffsky. Wonderley, Wayne, tr. LC 62-62959. (North Carolina. University. Studies in the Germanic Languages & Literatures: No. 33). reprint ed. 27.00 (*0-404-50933-9*) AMS Pr.

Reuter, D. J. & Robinson, J. B., eds. Plant Analysis: An Interpretation Manual. (Illus.). 224p. 1987. pap. 69.95 (*0-909605-41-6*, Pub. by Inkata Pr AT) Intl Spec Bk.

Reuter, Edward B. Mulatto in the United States. LC 70-100495. (Studies in Black History & Culture: No. 54). 1970. 75.00 (*0-8383-1216-0*) M S G Haskell Hse.

— Mulatto in the United States. LC 69-16569. 417p. 1969. reprint ed. text ed. 52.50 (*0-8371-0938-8*, REM&, Negro U Pr) Greenwood.

Reuter, Eisabeth, jt. auth. see Becker, Antoinette.

Reuter, Frank, ed. see Greenberg, Michael A.

Reuter, Frank, jt. ed. see Orman, Mort.

Reuter, Frank, jt. auth. see Orman, Mort.

Reuter, Frank, ed. see Schwartz, Bob & Schwartz, Leah.

Reuter, Frank, ed. see Tanzer, Herbert.

Reuter, Frank, ed. see Van Buskirk, Kathleen, et al.

Reuter, Frank T. Trials & Triumphs: George Washington's Foreign Policy. LC 83-675. (A.M. Pate, Jr., Series on the American Presidency: No. 2). 250p. (C). 1983. 19.50 (*0-912646-70-5*); pap. 8.95 (*0-87565-038-4*) Tex Christian.

Reuter, Fritz. Seed-Time & Harvest; or, During My Apprenticeship. 292p. 1976. reprint ed. 45.00 (*0-86527-301-4*) Fertig.

— When the French Were Here. Bayerschmidt, Carl F., tr. 200p. 1984. 28.50 (*0-8386-3230-0*) Fairleigh Dickinson.

Reuter, H. Aseptic Packaging of Food. LC 89-50658. 284p. 1989. pap. 75.00 (*0-87762-694-4*) Technomic.

Reuter, Helmut, ed. Aseptic Processing of Foods. (Illus.). 313p. 1993. pap. 89.00 (*1-56676-058-5*, 760585) Technomic.

Reuter, Joachim, tr. see Steiner, Rudolf.

Reuter, Joe, tr. see Steiner, Rudolf.

Reuter, Laurel & Ratcliff, Carter. Peter Dean. (Illus.). 68p. (Orig.). 1989. pap. 15.00 (*0-943107-02-4*) ND Mus Art.

Reuter, Laurel, et al. Donald Anderson. (Illus.). 46p. (Orig.). 1987. pap. 12.00 (*0-943107-00-8*) ND Mus Art.

***Reuter, Laurel J.** Georgie Papageorge. (Illus.). 108p. (Orig.). 1995. pap. 29.95 (*0-943107-05-9*) ND Mus Art.

— JudyLand: The Art of Judy Onofrio. (Illus.). 66p. (Orig.). 1993. pap. 18.00 (*0-943107-03-2*) ND Mus Art.

***Reuter, Laurel J. & Constantine, Mildred.** Frontiers in Fiber: The Americans. (Illus.). 106p. (Orig.). 1988. pap. 18.00 (*0-943107-01-6*) ND Mus Art.

Reuter, M., jt. auth. see Dittrich, W.

***Reuter, Paul.** Introduction to the Law of Treaties. Mico, Jose & Haggenmacher, Peter, trs. LC 94-44908. (Publication of the Graduate Institute of International Studies, Geneva). (ENG & FRE.). 1994. write for info. (*0-7103-0502-8*, Pub. by Kegan Paul Intl UK) Routledge Chapman & Hall.

Reuter, Peter. Disorganized Crime: Illegal Markets & the Mafia. (Organization Studies: No. 3). 256p. 1985. pap. 10.95 (*0-262-68048-3*) MIT Pr.

Reuter, Peter, et al. Comparing Western European & North American Drug Policies: An International Conference Report. LC 93-28666. 1993. write for info. (*0-8330-1431-5*, MR-237-GMF/SF) Rand Corp.

Reuter, T. The Medieval Nobility: Studies in the Ruling Class of France & Germany from the 6th to the 12th Centuries. (Europe in the Middle Ages Ser.: Vol. 14). 376p. 1978. 89.75 (*0-444-85136-4*, North Holland) Elsevier.

Reuter, Theodore. The Minnesota House of Representatives & the Professionalization of Politics. LC 94-982. 244p. (Orig.). Date not set. lib. bdg. 47.50 (*0-8191-9451-4*); pap. 28.50 (*0-8191-9452-2*) U Pr of Amer.

Reuter, Timothy. Germany in the Early Middle Ages, 800-1056. 368p. (Orig.). (C). 1991. pap. text ed. 27.50 (*0-582-49034-0*, 78835) Longman.

Reuter, Timothy, ed. The Greatest Englishman: Essays on St. Boniface & the Church at Crediton. 140p. 1980. text ed. 22.95 (*0-85364-277-X*) Attic Pr.

— Warriors & Churchmen in the High Middle Ages: Essays Presented to Karl Leyser. LC 92-22268. 304p. 1992. boxed 55.00 (*1-85285-063-9*) Hambledon Press.

Reuter, Timothy, tr. & anno. The Annals of Fulda. LC 92-8388. (Ninth-Century Histories Ser.: Vol. 2). (ENG & LAT.). 1993. text ed. 59.95 (*0-7190-3457-4*); text ed. 19.95 (*0-7190-3458-2*) St Martin.

Reuter, Timothy, tr. see Fuhrmann, Horst.

Reuter, Timothy, ed. see Leyser, Karl.

Reuter, Timothy, tr. see Tellenbach, Gerd.

Reuter, Walter G. Surface Crack Growth: Models, Experiments, & Structures. Underwood, John H. & Newman, James C., Jr., eds. LC 89-49360. (Special Technical Publication (STP) Ser.: No. 1060). (Illus.). 425p. 1990. text ed. 88.00 (*0-8031-1284-X*, 04-010600-30) ASTM.

Reuterdahl, Arvid. Scientific Theism. 1926. 25.00 (*0-8159-6805-1*) Devin.

Reuters Staff. The Reuters Glossary: A Dictionary of International Economic & Financial Terms. 1989. pap. 12.95 (*0-582-04286-0*) Longman.

Reutershan, Joan. Clara Zetkin und Brot und Rosen: Literaturpolitische Konflikte zwischen Partei und Frauenbewegung in der deutschen Vorkriegssozialdemokratie. (New York University Ottendorfer Ser.: Vol. 20). 246p. (GER.). (C). 1985. text ed. 28.50 (*0-8204-0203-6*) P Lang Pubs.

Reuterwall, C., jt. ed. see Hogstedt, C.

Reuth, Ralf G. Goebbels. 1994. pap. 16.95 (*0-15-600139-X*) HarBrace.

Reuth, Ralf Georg. Goebbels. Winston, Krishna, tr. LC 93-15900. (ENG.). 1993. 27.95 (*0-15-136076-6*) HarBrace.

Reuther, Barbara M. & Fogler, Diane. Art Curriculum Activities Kit: Intermediate Level, Grades 5-8. (Illus.). 208p. 1988. pap. text ed. 24.95 (*0-13-047184-4*, Parker Publishing Co) P-H.

— Art Curriculum Activities Kit: Primary Level, Grades 1-4. (Illus.). 204p. 1988. pap. text ed. 24.95 (*0-13-047143-7*, Parker Publishing Co) P-H.

Reuther, David & Thorn, John, eds. The Armchair Mountaineer: The Triumphs & Tragedies of Ascent, from Fact & Fiction. (Illus.). 324p. 1989. reprint ed. pap. 12.95 (*0-89732-092-1*) Menasha Ridge.

Reuther, Ruth E. Meet at the Falls: The Story of the Pioneers. McCall, Jody, ed. (Series 2). (Illus.). (J). 1989. pap. text ed. write for info. (*0-9622632-1-4*) Wee-Chee-Taw.

Reuther, Ruth E. & Richardson, A. G. Meet Me at the Falls: Activities Book. (Series 1). (Illus.). (Orig.). 1989. pap. text ed. 5.98 (*0-9622632-0-6*) Wee-Chee-Taw.

Reuther, Walter, et al, eds. The Citrus Industry, Vol. IV: Crop Protection. LC 67-63041. 362p. 1978. 30.00 (*0-931876-24-9*, 4088) ANR Pubns CA.

— The Citrus Industry, Vol. V: Crop Protection, Postharvest Technology, & Early History of Citrus Research in California. LC 67-63041. (Illus.). 374p. 1989. 40.00 (*0-931876-87-7*, 3326) ANR Pubns CA.

Reutiman, Sherry, ed. see Engelmann, Barbara A. & Engelmann, Michael A.

Reutlinger, Shlomo. Techniques for Project Appraisal under Uncertainty. LC 74-94827. (World Bank Staff Occasional Papers: No. 10). (Illus.). 109p. (Orig.). reprint ed. pap. 31.10 (*0-7837-5385-3*, 2045149) Bks Demand.

Reutlinger, Shlomo & Selowsky, Marcelo. Malnutrition & Poverty: Magnitude & Policy Options. LC 76-17240. (World Bank Staff Occasional Papers: No. 23). 96p. reprint ed. pap. 27.40 (*0-7837-5384-5*, 2045148) Bks Demand.

Reutner, Friedrich. Turn Around: Strategies for Successful Restructuring. Corsi, Stephen E., tr. LC 93-4618. 272p. 1993. 59.95 (*0-631-19143-7*) Blackwell Pubs.

Reutov, O. Theoretical Principles of Organic Chemistry. MIR Publishers, tr. 500p. (C). 1975. text ed. 35.00 (*0-8464-0919-4*) Beekman Pubs.

Reutov, O. A., et al. CH-Acids. LC 77-30618. (Illus.). 1978. 104.00 (*0-08-021610-2*, Pub. by Pergamon Repr UK) Franklin.

Reutov, O. A., et al, eds. Ambident Anions. LC 83-10137. (Illus.). 352p. 1983. 95.00 (*0-306-10975-1*, Consultants) Plenum.

Reutter, E. Edmund, Jr. The Law of Public Education. 4th ed. 1015p. 1994. text ed. 48.00 (*1-56662-154-2*) Foundation Pr.

Reutter, E. Edmund. Schools & the Law. 5th ed. LC 81-80361. 126p. reprint ed. pap. 36.00 (*0-685-23754-0*, 2032797) Bks Demand.

Reutter, E. Edmund, Jr., et al. The Law of Public Education. 3rd ed. (University Miscellaneous Ser.). 929p. 1991. reprint ed. text ed. 35.00 (*0-88277-222-8*) Foundation Pr.

Reutter, Jeffrey M., jt. auth. see Kershner, Kelly.

Reutter, Klaus-Joachim, et al, eds. Tectonics of the Southern Central Andes: Structure & Evolution of an Active Continental Margin. LC 93-15961. 1994. 198.00 (*0-387-55232-4*) Spr-Verlag.

Reutter, M. On the Wings of the Zephyr. Date not set. 27.50 (*0-06-018233-4*, HarpT) HarpC.

Reutter, W., jt. ed. see Wieland, F.

Reutter, Werner, ed. Orotic Acid. 1981. lib. bdg. 55.50 (*0-85200-294-7*) Kluwer Ac.

Reutter, Werner, et al, eds. Modulation of Liver Cell Expression. (Falk Ser.: No. 43). 1987. lib. bdg. 177.50 (*0-85200-677-2*) Kluwer Ac.

Reutzel, D. Ray & Cooter, Robert B., Jr. Teaching Children to Read: From Basals to Books. (Illus.). 576p. (C). 1992. text ed. write for info. (*0-675-21287-1*) Macmillan.

Reuveni, Reuven. Novel Approaches to Integrated Pest Management. 1995. write for info. (*0-87371-881-X*) Lewis Pubs.

Reuver, H. A., jt. auth. see Hanken, A. F.

***Reuvid, Jonathan, ed.** The CBI European Business Handbook: The Essential Guide to Trading & Investment in the New Europe. 2nd ed. 680p. 1995. pap. 55.00 (*0-7494-1376-X*, Pub. by Kogan Pg UK) Cassell.

— Doing Business in South Africa. 330p. 1995. pap. 55.00 (*0-7494-1347-6*, Pub. by Kogan Pg UK) Cassell.

— Doing Business with North America. 320p. 1995. pap. 120.00 (*0-7494-1240-2*, Pub. by Kogan Pg UK) Cassell.

— The Regulation & Prevention of Economic Crime Internationally: A Handbook for Government Agencies, Financial Institutions, & Business Corporations. 250p. 1995. 70.00 (*0-7494-1539-8*, Pub. by Kogan Pg UK) Cassell.

— The Strategic Guide to International Trade. 350p. 1995. pap. 60.00 (*0-7494-1621-1*, Pub. by Kogan Pg UK) Cassell.

R

An Asterisk (*) at the beginning of an entry indicates that the title is appearing in BIP for the first time.

Rev. Bailey F. Davis. Lynchburg, Virginia, & Nelson County, Virginia: Wills, Deeds & Marriages, 1807-1831. 252p. 1985. reprint ed. 30.00 (*0-89308-289-9*) Southern Hist Pr.

Rev. Buller. Statistical Account of the Parish of St. Just-In-Penwith. (C). 1989. 80.00 (*0-907566-61-8*, Pub. by Dyllansow Truran UK) St Mut.

Rev. Frederick K. Jelly. Madonna: Mary in the Catholic Tradition. LC 86-61598. 210p. (Orig.). 1986. pap. 7.95 (*0-87973-536-8*, 536) Our Sunday Visitor.

Rev. William F. Maestri. Living Securely with Insecurity. LC 86-60328. 185p. (Orig.). 1986. pap. 6.95 (*0-87973-543-0*, 543) Our Sunday Visitor.

Rev. William Kramer. Evolution & Creation: A Catholic Understanding. LC 86-60907. 168p. (Orig.). 1986. pap. 6.95 (*0-87973-511-2*, 511) Our Sunday Visitor.

Revankar, Ratna G. The Indian Constitution: A Case Study of Backward Classes. LC 76-120067. 361p. 1975. 49.50 (*0-8386-7670-7*) Fairleigh Dickinson.

Revard, Carter C. An Eagle Nation. LC 93-12720. (Sun Tracks Ser.: Vol. 24). 123p. (Orig.). 1993. lib. bdg. 35.00 (*0-8165-1355-4*); pap. 14.95 (*0-8165-1403-8*) U of Ariz Pr.

***Revard, James M.** The Progressive Cavity Pump Handbook. LC 95-10764. 1995. write for info. (*0-87814-445-5*) PennWell Bks.

Revard, Stella P. The War in Heaven: Paradise Lost & the Tradition of Satan's Rebellion. LC 79-23297. 320p. 1980. 41.50 (*0-8014-1138-6*) Cornell U Pr.

Revard, Stella P., et al, eds. Acta Conventus Neo-Latini Guelpherbytani: Papers from the Sixth International Congress, 1985, at Wolfenbuttel. LC 88-11889. (Medieval & Renaissance Texts & Studies: Vol. 53). (Illus.). 720p. 1988. 60.00 (*0-86698-037-7*) MRTS.

Revault, Jacques. Designs & Patterns from North African Carpets & Textiles. Applebaum, Stanley, tr. (Illus.). 128p. (Orig.). 1973. pap. 8.95 (*0-486-22850-9*) Dover.

Reveal, Betsy, jt. auth. see Chase, Gordon.

Reveal, James L. Gentle Conquest: The Botanical Discovery of North America with Illustrations from the Library of Congress. LC 92-19205. (Library of Congress Ser.). 1992. 39.95 (*1-56373-002-2*) Fulcrum Pub.

Reveaux, Tony. Cool Mac Clip Art Plus, Incl. disk. 1993. Incl. high density disk. disk, pap. 24.95 (*0-672-48551-6*) Hayden.

Reveill, Ken, jt. auth. see Walters, Dennis A.

Revel, Alain & Riboud, Christophe. American Green Power. Tanner, Edward W., tr. LC 86-2706. 272p. 1987. text ed. 32.00 (*0-8018-2434-6*) Johns Hopkins.

Revel, Fleming. Night the Stars Sang. LC 91-11692. 1991. 17.99 (*0-8007-3021-6*) Revell.

Revel, J., et al, eds. Oeuvres de Pierre Curie. 643p. 1984. pap. text ed. write for info. (*2-903928-07-X*) Gordon & Breach.

Revel, J. P., et al, eds. The Science of Biological Specimen Preparation for Microscopy & Microanalysis. (Proceedings of the Pfefferkorn Conference Ser.: No. 2). (Illus.). x, 246p. 1984. text ed. 40.00 (*0-931288-32-0*) Scanning Microscopy.

Revel, Jean-Francois. Culture & Cuisine: A Journey Through the History of Food. Lane, Helen R., tr. (Quality Paperbacks Ser.). (Illus.). 300p. 1984. reprint ed. pap. 12.95 (*0-306-80222-8*) Da Capo.

— Democracy Against Itself: The Future of the Democratic Impulse. 300p. 1993. text ed. 24.95 (*0-02-926387-5*) Free Pr.

— The Flight from the Truth: The Reign of Deceit in the Age of Information. LC 89-43438. 448p. 1992. 24.50 (*0-394-57643-8*) Random.

Revel-Neher, Elisabeth. The Image of the Jew in Byzantine Art. Maizel, David, tr. (Studies in Antisemitism). (Illus.). 200p. 1992. 65.00 (*0-08-040655-6*, Pergamon Pr) Elsevier.

Revel, R., jt. auth. see Naterop, B. J.

Revelation Technologies Staff. Continuing Development in Advanced Revelation Training Manual. 200p. 1988. 50.00 (*0-923387-20-X*) Rev Tech Inc.

— Introduction to Development in Advanced Revelation Training Manual. 200p. 1988. 50.00 (*0-923387-18-8*) Rev Tech Inc.

— Introduction to Development in Advanced Revelation Training Manual (Instructor Manual) 150p. 1989. 100.00 (*0-923387-19-6*) Rev Tech Inc.

— Programming in Advanced Revelation Training Manual. 150p. 1990. 50.00 (*0-923387-22-6*) Rev Tech Inc.

— Programming in Advanced Revelation Training Manual (Instructor Manual) 75p. 1990. 100.00 (*0-923387-23-4*) Rev Tech Inc.

— SQL-I Training Manual. 90p. 1990. 50.00 (*0-923387-39-0*) Rev Tech Inc.

— Using Advanced Revelation Applications I Training Manual. 100p. 1989. 30.00 (*0-923387-26-9*) Rev Tech Inc.

— Using Advanced Revelation Applications I Training Manual (Instructor Manual) 75p. 1989. 60.00 (*0-923387-27-7*) Rev Tech Inc.

Reveles, Daniel. Enchiladas, Rice, & Beans. 256p. (Orig.). 1994. pap. 9.00 (*0-345-38426-1*, One World) Ballantine.

Reveley, Edith. A Pause for Breath. LC 82-22293. 210p. 1983. 15.95 (*0-87951-165-6*) Overlook Pr.

Reveley, James E. Vice-Versa. 128p. 7.95 (*0-89015-884-3*) Sunbelt Media.

Revelis, B. G. Greek-English Letterwriting. 9.00 (*0-685-09036-1*) Divry.

Revelis, B. O. Greek-English Guide to Letterwriting. 224p. (ENG & GRE.). 1960. pap. 19.95 (*0-8288-6838-7*, M-9440) Fr & Eur.

***Revell, Alex.** High in the Empty Blue. (Illus.). 456p. 1995. 49.95 (*0-9637110-3-2*) Flying Machines.

Revell, Don. The Broken Juke. Wilcox, Patricia, ed. LC 75-21920. (Iris Poets Ser.: Vol. 1). 55p. 1975. pap. 5.00 (*0-916078-00-0*) Iris Pr.

Revell, Donald. Beautiful Shirt. LC 94-20492. 80p. 1994. 22.50 (*0-8195-2216-3*, Wesleyan Univ Pr); pap. 10.95 (*0-8195-1219-2*, Wesleyan Univ Pr) U Pr of New Eng.

— Erasures. LC 92-12429. (Wesleyan Poetry Ser.). 58p. 1992. 22.50 (*0-8195-2203-1*, Wesleyan Univ Pr); pap. 10.95 (*0-8195-1206-0*, Wesleyan Univ Pr) U Pr of New Eng.

— The Gaza of Winter. LC 87-12523. (Contemporary Poetry Ser.). 80p. 1988. 14.00 (*0-8203-0988-5*); pap. 6.95 (*0-8203-0989-3*) U of Ga Pr.

— New Dark Ages. LC 89-49759. (Wesleyan Poetry Ser.). 72p. 1990. 22.50 (*0-8195-2184-1*, Wesleyan Univ Pr); pap. 10.95 (*0-8195-1186-2*, Wesleyan Univ Pr) U Pr of New Eng.

Revell, Donald, tr. see Apollinaire, Guillaume.

Revell, Dorothy. Healthy Oriental Cooking. abr. ed. 130p. 1995. pap. 7.95 (*1-56901-343-8*) NW Pub.

— Oriental Cooking for the Diabetic. (Illus.). 176p. (Orig.). 1981. pap. 9.95 (*0-87040-492-X*) Japan Pubns USA.

Revell, E. J. Hebrew Text with Palestinian Vocalization. LC 76-18746. (Near & Middle East Ser.: No. 7). 242p. reprint ed. pap. 69.00 (*0-317-10130-7*, 2051215) Bks Demand.

Revell, Elizabeth, ed. The Later Letters of Peter of Blois. (Auctores Britannici Medii Aevi British Academy Ser.: No. XIII). 424p. 1993. 115.00 (*0-19-726108-6*) OUP.

Revell, Fleming. Daniel & the Lions, Set. (J). (ps). 1991. pap. 10.99 (*0-8007-7116-8*) Revell.

***Revell, Glenda.** Glenda's Story. 1994. pap. 7.99 (*0-8474-1154-0*) Back to Bible.

Revell, Jack, ed. The Changing Face of European Banks & Securities Markets. LC 93-29483. 1994. text ed. 75.00 (*0-312-10645-9*) St Martin.

***Revell, Jeptha R.** The Partisan. 230p. 1995. pap. 8.95 (*1-56901-752-2*) NW Pub.

Revell, P. A. Pathology of Bone. (Illus.). 320p. 1985. 165.00 (*0-387-15418-3*) Spr-Verlag.

Revell, Peter. Quest in Modern American Poetry. (Critical Studies). 246p. 1981. 44.00 (*0-389-20238-X*, 07028) B&N Imports.

Revell, Richard A. & Slyn, Alan T. Kentucky Divorce: Practice Systems Library Manual. suppl. ed. 1992. Suppl. 1992. 120.00 (*0-318-11937-4*) Lawyers Cooperative.

— Kentucky Divorce: Practice Systems Library Manual. suppl. ed. 1993. Suppl. 1993. 75.00 (*0-317-03267-4*) Lawyers Cooperative.

Revell, Rod & Sweeney, Simon. In Print: Reading Business English. 128p. (C). 1993. pap. 11.95 (*0-521-38303-X*) Cambridge U Pr.

Revell, Roger. Songs for Camps & Reunions. 1986. pap. 5.00 (*0-8309-0447-6*) Herald Hse.

***Revell, Stephen, ed.** Capital Markets Forum Yearbook Vol. 1: 1993. (International Bar Association Ser.). 370p. (C). 1994. lib. bdg. 100.00 (*1-85966-066-5*, Pub. by Graham & Trotman UK) Kluwer Ac.

Revella, Andre, ed. see Taylor, Karen.

Revelle. The Global Environment: Securing a Sustainable Future. (Life Science Ser.). 496p. (C). 1992. boxed 47.50 (*0-86720-321-8*) Jones & Bartlett.

***Revelle, Jack, et al.** From Concept to Customer: Management 2000 Integrated Product Development. (Management Information Systems Ser.). 376p. 1994. text ed. 42.95 (*0-442-01892-4*) Van Nos Reinhold.

Revelle, Jack. Management Two Thousand Design Sourcebook: An Applications Guide to Achieving Customer. (Industrial Engineering Ser.). 1994. text ed. 42.95 (*0-442-01881-9*) Van Nos Reinhold.

Revelle, Jack B. Safety Training Methods: Practical Solutions for the Next Millenniu, Second Edition. LC 94-18137. 248p. 1980. text ed. 74.95 (*0-471-07761-5*) Wiley.

Revelle, Jack B. & Stephenson, Francis J., Jr. Safety Training Methods: Practical Solutions for the Next Millenniu, Second Edition. 2nd ed. LC 94-18137. 320p. 1995. text ed. 59.95 (*0-471-55230-5*) Wiley.

ReVelle, Jack B., jt. auth. see Moran, John W.

Revelle, Penelope & Johnson. Global Environment: Securing a Sustainable Future. (Life Science Ser.). 200p. 1992. teacher ed 10.00 (*0-86720-767-1*); student ed, pap. text ed. 12.50 (*0-86720-852-X*); trans. 50.00 (*0-86720-776-0*); disk 195.00 (*0-86720-768-X*) Jones & Bartlett.

Revelli, Claire. Baby & You. Zion, Claire, ed. 320p. (Orig.). 1993. pap. 8.00 (*0-671-77727-0*) PB.

Revelli, Clare. Color & You: A Guide to Determining Your Best Colors. rev. ed. (Illus.). 96p. 1994. reprint ed. pap. 7.99 (*0-9608092-3-6*) Revelli.

— Design & You: Your Guide to Decorating with Style. rev. ed. (Illus.). 96p. 1994. pap. 7.99 (*0-9608092-1-X*) Revelli.

— Style & You: Every Woman's Guide to Total Style. (Illus.). 96p. 1993. reprint ed. pap. 7.99 (*0-9608092-2-8*) Revelli.

Revelstroke, Simon & Corben, Richard. The Bodyssey. (Illus.). 64p. 1993. reprint ed. pap. 12.95 (*0-9623841-8-6*) Fantagor Pr.

***Revelt, Janet G.** Opening Doors: A Job Search Guide for Graduates. 1995. pap. 27.50 (*0-614-06592-5*) Graduate Group.

Revely, Edith. In Good Faith. LC 84-22677. 272p. 1985. 15.95 (*0-87951-992-4*) Overlook Pr.

Revenga, Ana, jt. ed. see Coricelli, Fabrizio.

Revenga, Luis & Lopez-Vidriero, M. L., eds. Tesoros De Espana, Ten Centuries of Spanish Books. (Illus.). 440p. (ENG & SPA.). 1985. pap. 19.95 (*84-398-4960-5*) NY Pub Lib.

Revenson, Tracey A., jt. ed. see Singer, Dorothy G.

Revenson, Tracey A., jt. auth. see Singer, Dorothy.

Reventlow, et al, eds. Justice & Righteousness: Biblical Themes & Their Influence. (JSOT Supplement Ser.: No. 137). 280p. (C). 1992. 35.00 (*1-85075-339-3*, Pub. by Sheffield Acad UK) CUP Services.

Reverand, Cedric D., II. Dryden's Final Poetic Mode: The Fables. LC 88-10768. 254p. (C). 1988. text ed. 33.95 (*0-8122-8121-7*) U of Pa Pr.

Reverand, Diane, ed. see Church, Connie.

Reverand, Diane, jt. ed. see Higginson, Dianne.

Reverby, Susan & Rosner, David, eds. Health Care in America: Essays in Social History. LC 79-14613. (Illus.). 288p. 1979. pap. 16.95 (*0-87722-171-5*) Temple U Pr.

Reverby, Susan, ed. see Grading of Nursing Schools Committee.

Reverby, Susan, ed. see Nutting, Adelaide M.

Reverby, Susan M. Ordered to Care: The Dilemma of American Nursing, 1850-1945. (Cambridge History of Medicine Ser.). (Illus.). 350p. 1987. pap. 16.95 (*0-521-33565-5*) Cambridge U Pr.

Reverby, Susan M., jt. ed. see Helly, Dorothy O.

***Reverchon, Alain & Ducamp, Marc.** Mathematical Software Tools in C. 1993. text ed. 35.00 (*0-471-93799-1*) Wiley.

— Mathematical Software Tools in C Plus Plus. 500p. (Orig.). 1993. pap. text ed. 44.95 (*0-471-93792-4*) Wiley.

— Mathematical Software Tools in C Plus Plus. 500p. (Orig.). 1993. disk, pap. 79.95 (*0-471-93798-3*) Wiley.

Reverdy, Pierre. Cette Emotion Appelee Poesie: Ecrits sur la Poesie. 288p. (FRE.). 1989. pap. 29.95 (*0-7859-1599-0*, 208060659X) Fr & Eur.

— Ferraille & Plein Verre, le Chant, des Morts, Buis Verts, Pierres Blanches. (Poesie Ser.). 256p. (FRE.). 1981. pap. 9.95 (*2-07-032207-6*) Schoenhof.

— Ferraille, Plein Verre, le Chant des Morts, Bois Verts, Pierres Blanches. (FRE.). 1981. pap. 10.95 (*0-8288-3869-0*, F105190) Fr & Eur.

— Flacques de Verre. (FRE.). 1984. pap. 10.95 (*0-7859-2984-3*) Fr & Eur.

— Lettres a Jean Rousselot (1949-1954) Avec: Rousselot, Jean. Pierre Reverdy Romancier, ou quand le Poete Se Dedouble. Rousselot, Jean, ed. 87p. 1973. 9.95 (*0-686-54722-5*) Fr & Eur.

— Le Livre de Mon Bord, Notes (1930-1936) 272p. (FRE.). 1989. pap. 18.95 (*0-686-54724-1*, 271521572X) Fr & Eur.

— Main-d'oeuvre: Poemes, 1913-1949. 548p. (FRE.). 1989. pap. 49.95 (*0-7859-1542-7*, 2715215819) Fr & Eur.

— Note Eternelle du Present: Ecrits sur l'Art (1923-1960) 288p. 16.95 (*0-686-54726-8*) Fr & Eur.

— Plupart du Temps, Vol. 1. (FRE.). 1970. pap. 10.95 (*0-8288-3870-4*, F121000) Fr & Eur.

— Plupart du Temps, Vol. 2. (FRE.). 1989. pap. 10.95 (*0-8288-3871-2*, F121001) Fr & Eur.

— Plupart du Temps, 1915-1922. (Poesie Ser.). Date not set. pap. 18.95 (*2-07-032532-6*) Schoenhof.

— Selected Poems. Rexroth, Kenneth, tr. LC 68-25548. 1969. 4.95 (*0-8112-0373-5*) New Directions.

— Selected Poems. Bree, Germaine, ed. Ashbery, John et al, trs. LC 90-72092. (French Poetry in Translation Ser.). 179p. 1991. 16.95 (*0-916390-47-0*); pap. 10.95 (*0-916390-46-2*) Wake Forest.

— Sources du Vent: Avec: La Balle au Bond. 256p. (FRE.). 1971. pap. 10.95 (*0-7859-1355-6*, 2070317919) Fr & Eur.

— Sources du Vent - Balle au Bond. (FRE.). 1971. pap. 10.95 (*0-8288-3872-0*, F121020) Fr & Eur.

— Sources du Vent. La Balle au Bond. (Poesie Ser.). 256p. (FRE.). 1971. pap. 9.95 (*2-07-031791-9*) Schoenhof.

— Le Voleur de Talan. 181p. 1967. 8.95 (*0-686-54733-0*) Fr & Eur.

Revere, Alan. Professional Goldsmithing: A Contemporary Guide to Traditional Jewelry Techniques. LC 90-35140. 1991. text ed. 62.95 (*0-442-23898-3*) Chapman & Hall.

Revere, Elizabeth. Cricket Moon. LC 92-5472. (Illus.). 80p. 1992. 7.95 (*0-918606-09-8*) Heidelberg Graph.

— Windows of Snow. LC 85-8722. 78p. 1985. pap. 5.95 (*0-918606-08-X*) Heidelberg Graph.

Revere, Glenn. All about Carpets: A Consumer Guide. (Illus.). 160p. 1988. 15.95 (*0-8306-0646-7*, 2646); pap. 9.95 (*0-8306-0446-4*, 2646) TAB Bks.

Revere, John, tr. see Magendie, Francois.

Revere, Lawrence. Playing Blackjack As a Business. (Illus.). 192p. 1995. pap. 14.95 (*0-8184-0064-1*, Citadel Pr) Carol Pub Group.

Revere, Virginia L. Applied Psychology for Criminal Justice Professionals. LC 81-16923. 300p. 1982. 36.95 (*0-911012-98-2*) Nelson-Hall.

Reverend Laurence Mancuso, tr. see Monks of New Skete Staff.

Reverend Mother Ruth. In Wisdom Thou Hast Made Them. Galanter, Patricia, ed. (Illus.). 141p. 1986. 15.95 (*0-937431-01-X*) Adams Bannister Cox.

Reverend William P. Steinhauser & Boyce, Laurie A. Reflections on Marriage. LC 84-71173. (Marriage & Marriage Preparation Ser.). (Illus.). 72p. (Orig.). 1984. 2.75 (*0-940679-00-0*) CCOC.

***Reverte.** La Table de Flandes: The Chess Master. 1995. pap. 16.95 (*0-679-76090-3*, Vin) Random.

Reves. Acute Revascularization of the Infarcted Heart. 112p. 1987. text ed. 41.95 (*0-8089-1870-2*, Grune) Saunders.

— Anesthesia Drug Handbook. 1991. 29.50 (*0-8151-7139-0*, Yr Bk Med Pubs) Mosby Yr Bk.

Reves, jt. auth. see Dirksen.

Revest, Patricia, jt. ed. see Longstaff, Alan.

Revesz, Akos G., jt. ed. see Walrafen, George E.

Revesz, G. E. Lambda-Calculus, Combinators & Functional Programming. (Cambridge Tracts in Theoretical Computer Science Ser.: No. 4). 200p. 1988. 39.95 (*0-521-34589-8*) Cambridge U Pr.

Revesz, Gabor, jt. auth. see Ehrlich, Eva.

Revesz, Geza. Introduction to the Psychology of Music. De Courcy, G., tr. LC 54-5937. (Illus.). 288p. reprint ed. pap. 82.10 (*0-317-09933-7*, 2010999) Bks Demand.

— Psychology of a Musical Prodigy. LC 70-114890. (Select Bibliographies Reprint Ser.). 1977. 19.95 (*0-8369-5294-4*) Ayer.

— Psychology of a Musical Prodigy. LC 78-100832. 180p. 1970. reprint ed. text ed. 49.75 (*0-8371-4004-8*, REMP, Greenwood Pr) Greenwood.

— The Psychology of a Musical Prodigy. LC 77-173178. (Illus.). 1972. reprint ed. 20.95 (*0-405-08879-5*) Ayer.

— The Psychology of a Musical Prodigy. 180p. 1990. reprint ed. lib. bdg. 59.00 (*0-7812-9002-3*) Rprt Serv.

Revesz, Gyorgy E. Introduction to Formal Languages. 1991. pap. 6.95 (*0-486-66697-2*) Dover.

Revesz, P. Random Walk in Random & Non-Random Environments. 348p. (C). 1990. text ed. 48.00 (*981-02-0237-7*) World Scientific Pub.

Revesz, P., ed. Limit Theorems in Probability & Statistics, 1. (Colloquia Mathematica Janos Bolyai Ser.: Vol. 36). 1985. write for info. (*0-444-86895-X*) Elsevier.

— Limit Theorems in Probability & Statistics, 2. (Colloquia Mathematica Janos Bolyai Ser.: Vol. 36). 1985. write for info. (*0-444-86896-8*) Elsevier.

— Limit Theorems in Probability & Statistics, Set. (Colloquia Mathematica Janos Bolyai Ser.: Vol. 36). 1985. 210.25 (*0-444-86764-3*) Elsevier.

Revesz, P., et al, eds. First Pannonian Symposium on Mathematical Statistics: Proceedings. (Lecture Notes in Statistics Ser.: Vol. 8). 308p. 1981. pap. 49.00 (*0-387-90583-9*) Spr-Verlag.

Revesz, Pal. Random Walks of Infinitely Many Particles. 220p. 1994. text ed. 58.00 (*981-02-1784-6*) World Scientific Pub.

***Revesz, Richard L. & Stewart, Richard B., eds.** Analyzing Superfund: Economics, Science, & Law. 260p. 1995. text ed. 39.00 (*0-915707-75-6*) Resources Future.

Revett, Nicholas, jt. auth. see Stuart, James.

***Revhaug, A.** Acute Catabolic State. 320p. 1995. 128.00 (*3-540-58445-5*) Spr-Verlag.

***Revhaug, A., ed.** Acute Catabolic State. LC 95-10442. (Update Intensive Care & Emergency Medicine Ser.: Vol. 21). 1995. write for info. (*0-387-58445-5*) Spr-Verlag.

Revi, A. C. Nineteenth Century Glass. rev. ed. LC 59-15032. (Illus.). 301p. 1981. reprint ed. 29.50 (*0-916838-43-9*) Schiffer.

Revi, Albert C. American Art Nouveau Glass. LC 68-18778. (Illus.). 476p. 1981. reprint ed. 40.00 (*0-916838-40-4*) Schiffer.

— American Cut & Engraved Glass. LC 65-22016. (Illus.). 498p. 1982. reprint ed. 35.00 (*0-916838-57-9*) Schiffer.

Revi, Aromar. Shelter in India. 1990. text ed. 27.95 (*0-7069-4937-4*, Pub. by Vikas II) S Asia.

Reviakina, I. A. Gorky: Life & Work. 216p. 1985. 35.00 (*0-317-92444-3*, Pub. by Collets UK) Pro-Am Music.

Revich, S. J. The Camel Boy. (Tales from the East Ser.). (Illus.). 158p. (J). (gr. 5-8). 1987. 9.95 (*0-935063-44-7*); pap. 7.95 (*0-935063-45-5*) CIS Comm.

— Ezra the Physician. (Tales from the East Ser.). (Illus.). 126p. (J). (gr. 5-7). 1988. 9.95 (*0-935063-63-3*); pap. 7.95 (*0-935063-64-1*) CIS Comm.

— Ibrahim the Magician. (Tales from the East Ser.). (Illus.). 126p. (J). (gr. 4-7). 1987. 9.95 (*0-935063-33-1*); pap. 7.95 (*0-935063-34-X*) CIS Comm.

— The Lion Tamer. 140p. (J). (ps-8). 1990. 10.95 (*0-685-47680-4*); pap. 7.95 (*1-56062-054-4*) CIS Comm.

— The Poet & the Thief. (Tales from the East Ser.). (Illus.). 158p. (J). (gr. 5-7). 1989. 10.95 (*0-935063-71-4*); pap. 7.95 (*0-935063-72-2*) CIS Comm.

— The Prince & the Scholar. LC 92-70596. 128p. 1992. 9.95 (*1-56062-111-7*); pap. write for info. (*1-56062-112-5*) CIS Comm.

Reviczky, Adam. Victorious Battles - Lost Wars, No. 349. 384p. 1992. text ed. 54.00 (*0-88033-246-8*) Col U Pr.

Revie, R. W., et al, eds. Materials Performance Maintenance: Proceedings of the International Symposium on Materials Performance Maintenance, Ottawa, Ontario, Canada, August 18-21, 1991. (Proceedings, Metallurgical Society of the Canadian Institute of Mining & Metallurgy Ser.: No. 25). (Illus.). 347p. 1991. text ed. 130.00 (*0-08-041441-9*, Pergamon Pr) Elsevier.

Revie, R. Winston, jt. auth. see Uhlig, Herbert H.

Revien, Leon. When Every Moment Counts, Count on Provision. 16p. 1987. pap. text ed. 4.95 (*0-940429-02-0*) M B Glass Assocs.

***Review for Religious Staff, ed.** Index: Topical & Author. 320p. (Orig.). (C). 1995. pap. text ed. 20.00 (*0-924768-04-5*) Review Relig.

Review of Personality & Social Psychology Staff. Review of Personality & Social Psychology, 5 vols., 2. Wheeler, Ladd, ed. LC 80-649712. 295p. pap. 84.10 (*0-8357-8404-5*, 2034677) Bks Demand.

— Review of Personality & Social Psychology, 5 vols., 3. Wheeler, Ladd, ed. LC 80-649712. 287p. pap. 81.80 (*0-8357-8405-3*, 2034677) Bks Demand.

— Review of Personality & Social Psychology, 5 vols., 4. Wheeler, Ladd, ed. LC 80-649712. 328p. pap. 93.50 (*0-8357-8406-1*, 2034677) Bks Demand.

— Review of Personality & Social Psychology, 5 vols., 5. Wheeler, Ladd, ed. LC 80-649712. 312p. pap. 89.00 (*0-8357-8407-X*, 2034677) Bks Demand.

— Review of Personality & Social Psychology, 5 vols., Vol. 1. Wheeler, Ladd, ed. LC 80-649712. 352p. pap. 100.40 (*0-8357-8403-7*, 2034677) Bks Demand.

Review of Politics Staff. Image of Man. Fitzsimons, M. A. et al, eds. LC 72-156710. (Essay Index Reprint Ser.). 1977. reprint ed. 30.95 (*0-8369-2369-3*) Ayer.

Revill, David. The Roaring Silence: A Biography of John Cage. (Illus.). 272p. 1992. 27.95 (1-55970-166-8) Arcade Pub Inc.

Revill, Don. Personnel Management in Polytechnic Libraries. 250p. 1987. text ed. 58.95 (0-566-05268-7, Pub. by Gower UK) Ashgate Pub Co.

Revill, Janie. Edgefield County, South Carolina, Records. 246p. 1984. 30.00 (0-89308-531-6) Southern Hist Pr.

— Original Index Book Showing the Revolutionary Claims Filed in South Carolina: Between August 20, 1783 & August 31, 1786. 387p. 1990. reprint ed. 25.00 (0-685-60360-1, 4875) Clearfield Co.

— Some South Carolina Genealogical Records. 456p. 1985. 35.00 (0-89308-539-1) Southern Hist Pr.

Revilla. Gramatica Espanola Moderna. rev. ed. (C). 1974. text ed. 19.95 (0-07-090830-3) McGraw.

***Revilla, Aurelio.** Industria Lactea Operaciones Cuantitativas. 245p. (C). 1994. 5.75 (1-885995-12-1) Escuela Agricola.

— Introduccion a la Microbiologia. 120p. (C). 1990. pap. text ed. 4.50 (1-885995-04-0) Escuela Agricola.

Revilla, Federico. Diccionario de Iconografia. 408p. 1990. pap. 32.95 (0-7859-6001-5, 8437609291) Fr & Eur.

Revilla, Linda A., et al, eds. Bearing Dreams, Shaping Visions: Asian Pacific American Perspectives. LC 93-1862. (Association for Asian American Studies Ser.). 284p. 1993. pap. 30.00 (0-87422-099-8) Wash St U Pr.

Revillard, J. P., jt. ed. see Brown, F.

Reville, Albert. The Life & Writings of Theodore Parker. 1972. 59.95 (0-8490-0525-6) Gordon Pr.

— The Native Religions of Mexico & Peru: Hibbert Lectures. Wicksteed, Phillip H., tr. LC 77-27167. 224p. (C). 1983. reprint ed. 45.00 (0-404-60405-6) AMS Pr.

Reville, Albert D. Lectures on the Origin & Growth of Religion As Illustrated by the Native Religions of Mexico & Peru. 1977. lib. bdg. 59.95 (0-8490-2140-5) Gordon Pr.

— Lectures on the Origin & Growth of Religion As Illustrated by the Native Religions of Mexico & Peru. LC 77-27167. (Hibbert Lectures: 1884). 45.00 (0-614-07017-1) AMS Pr.

Reville, Julie D. The Many Voices of Paws: A Workbook for Young Stutterers. (Illus.). 64p. (J). (ps-3). 1989. 25.00 (0-937857-11-4, 1568) Speech Bin.

Reville, Nicholas. Broadcasting: The New Law. 1991. U.K. pap. 30.00 (0-406-00137-5) Butterworth Legal Pubs.

Revillout, Eugene & Eisenlohr. Corpus Papyrorum Aegypti, 3 vols. in 1. xii, 67p. 1978. reprint ed. write for info. (3-487-06440-5, Pub. by Georg Olms GW) Lubrecht & Cramer.

Revis, Johan. Encounters with M. 210p. (Orig.). 1992. pap. 9.95 (0-9629956-0-6) Destel-Bergen.

Revision Conference Staff. Manual of the International Statistical Classification of Diseases, Injuries & Causes of Death: Proceedings of the Revision Conference, 8th, 2 vols. Set. 16.00 (0-686-09015-2) World Health.

— Manual of the International Statistical Classification of Diseases, Injuries & Causes of Death: Proceedings of the Revision Conference, 8th, 2 vols., 1. write for info. (92-4-154004-4) World Health.

— Manual of the International Statistical Classification of Diseases, Injuries & Causes of Death: Proceedings of the Revision Conference, 8th, 2 vols., Vol. 2. 1969. write for info. (92-4-154005-2) World Health.

ReVisions Plus, Inc. Staff, ed. see Sabotin, Katherine.

***Revitch, Eugene & Schlesinger, Louis B.** Sex Murder & Sex Aggression: Phenomenology, Psychopathology, Psychodynamics & Prognosis. (Illus.). 152p. 1989. pap. 24.95 (0-398-06346-X) C C Thomas.

— Sex Murder & Sex Aggression: Phenomenology, Psychopathology, Psychodynamics & Prognosis. (Illus.). 152p. (C). 1989. text ed. 39.95 (0-398-05556-4) C C Thomas.

Revitch, Eugene, jt. auth. see Schlesinger, Louis B.

Reviv, Hanoch. The Elders in Ancient Israel: A Study of a Biblical Institution. 222p. 1989. text ed. 22.00 (0-685-72506-5, Pub. by Magnes Press IS) Eisenbrauns.

***Revkin, Andrew.** The Burning Season: The Murder of Chico Mendes & the Fight for the Amazon Rain Forest. LC 94-30091. 1994. 10.95 (0-452-27405-2, Plume) NAL-Dutton.

— Death in the Rain Forest. 1990. write for info. (0-318-65605-1) HM.

Revkin, Andrew C. Global Warming: Understanding the Forecast. (Illus.). 180p. 1992. 19.98 (1-55859-310-1) Abbeville Pr.

Revland, Catherine, jt. auth. see Garey, Carol C.

Revoir. Respiratory Protection Handbook. 1995. write for info. (0-87371-281-1) Lewis Pubs.

Revoir, Trudie W. Legends & Traditions of Christmas. (Illus.). 112p. 1985. pap. 9.00 (0-8170-1082-3) Judson.

Revolutionary Communist Party, U. S. A. Staff. The Chicano Struggle & the Struggle for Socialism. 2nd ed. (Illus.). 1979. pap. 1.50 (0-89851-003-1) RCP Pubns.

— Cuba: The Evaporation of a Myth, from Anti-Imperialist Revolution to a Pawn of Social-Imperialism. 2nd ed. 1983. pap. 1.50 (0-89851-008-2) RCP Pubns.

— Revolution & Counter-Revolution: The Revisionist Coup in China & the Struggle in the Revolutionary Communist Party, U. S. A. 1978. pap. 4.95 (0-89851-016-3) RCP Pubns.

Revolutionary Communist Party, U. S A. Staff. New Programme & New Constitution of the Revolutionary Communist Party, U. S. A. 128p. (Orig.). (C). 1981. pap. 3.00 (0-89851-037-6) RCP Pubns.

Revonsuo, Antti & Kamppinen, Matti, eds. Consciousness in Philosophy & Cognitive Neuroscience. 312p. 1994. text ed. 49.95 (0-8058-1509-0) L Erlbaum Assocs.

***Revoyr, Jack.** Licensee Survival Guide. 182p. (Orig.). 1994. pap. 34.95 (0-9627106-2-8) Kent Communs.

— The New Complete "How to" Guide to Collegiate Licensing. 139p. (Orig.). 1990. pap. 25.00 (0-9627106-0-1) Kent Communs.

— A Primer on Licensing. 191p. (Orig.). 1994. pap. 34.95 (0-9627106-1-X) Kent Communs.

— A Primer on Licensing. 2nd ed. 246p. (Orig.). 1995. 37.95 (0-9627106-4-4); pap. 16.95 (0-9627106-5-2) Kent Communs.

Revsbach, N. P. & Sorensen, J., eds. Denitrification in Soil & Sediment. LC 91-7400. (FEMS Symposium Ser.: No. 56). (Illus.). 340p. 1990. 85.00 (0-306-43721-X, Plenum Pr) Plenum.

Revsine, Barbara, jt. auth. see Grunes, Barbara.

Revsine, Lawrence. Replacement Cost Accounting. (Contemporary Topics in Accounting Ser.). (Illus.). 224p. 1973. pap. text ed. write for info. (0-13-773630-4) P-H.

***Revue Fiduciaire Staff.** Dictionnaire Social 1992. 1992. 85.00 (0-7859-8141-1, 2-86521-191-6) Fr & Eur.

Revue Musicale Staff. Wagner et la France. LC 77-4006. (Music Reprint Ser.: 1977). (Illus.). 1977. reprint ed. lib. bdg. 32.50 (0-306-70889-2) Da Capo.

Revuelta, Gutierrez, tr. see Brown, Steven F., ed. & tr.

Revueltas, Jose. Los Dias Terrenales. Escalante, Evodio, ed. (Coleccion Archivos). 386p. (SPA.). (C). 1991. 34.95 (84-00-07113-1) U of Pittsburgh Pr.

— Human Mourning. 229p. 1989. text ed. 24.95 (0-8166-1809-7); pap. 9.95 (0-8166-1810-0) U of Minn Pr.

Revutsky, Valerian & Zinkewych, Osyp, eds. Les Kurbas: Collection of Works on Theatre, Essays by His Contemporaries, Documents (in Ukrainian) LC 89-62916. 1040p. 1989. 45.50 (0-914834-59-2) Smoloskyp.

Revuz, D. Markov Chains. rev. ed. (Mathematical Library: Vol. 11). 1984. 87.25 (0-444-86400-8, I-548-83, North Holland) Elsevier.

Revuz, D. & Yor, M. Continuous Martingales & Brownian Motion. (Grundlehren der Mathematischen Wissenschaften Ser.). (Illus.). 576p. 1990. 98.00 (0-387-52167-4) Spr-Verlag.

Revuz, Daniel & Yor, Marc. Continuous Martingales & Brownian Motion. LC 94-15097. (Grundlehren der Mathematischen Wissenschaften Ser.: Vol. 293). 1994. write for info. (0-387-57622-3) Spr-Verlag.

Revzan, David A. Wholesaling in Marketing Organization. Assael, Henry, ed. LC 78-256. (Century in Marketing Ser.). 1979. reprint ed. lib. bdg. 58.95 (0-405-11181-9) Ayer.

Revzin, ed. Biology of Non-Specific DNA Protein Interaction. 1990. 179.00 (0-8493-6177-X, QP624) CRC Pr.

Revzin, Arnold, ed. Footprinting of Nucleic Acid-Protein Complexes. (Separation, Detection, & Characterization of Biological Macromolecules Ser.). (Illus.). 193p. 1993. pap. 39.95 (0-12-586500-7) Acad Pr.

Rew, Alan, jt. ed. see Grillo, Ralph.

Rew, Lois J. God's Green Liniment. LC 81-84183. (Illus.). 204p. (Orig.). (J). (gr. 3-8). 1981. pap. 7.50 (0-938462-02-4) Green Leaf CA.

— Introduction to Technical Writing: Process & Practice. 2nd ed. LC 92-50047. (Illus.). 631p. (Orig.). (C). 1993. pap. text ed. 31.00 (0-312-06781-X) St Martin.

***Rew, Lynn.** Awareness in Healing. 1995. write for info. (0-8273-6397-4) Delmar.

Rew, Robert S., jt. ed. see Campbell, William C.

Rewald, John. Aristide Maillol: 1861-1944. LC 75-42576. (Illus.). 140p. 1975. pap. 9.95 (0-89207-000-5) S R Guggenheim.

— Cezanne: A Biography. (Illus.). 288p. 1986. 75.00 (0-8109-0775-5) Abrams.

— Cezanne & America: Dealers, Collectors, Artists, & Critics 1891-1921. (Bollingen Ser.). 352p. 1989. text ed. 65.00 (0-691-09960-X) Princeton U Pr.

— Cezanne (Paul) the Watercolors: A Catalogue Raisonne. (Illus.). 486p. 1984. boxed 200.00 (1-55660-167-0) A Wofsy Fine Arts.

— Degas's Complete Sculpture: A Catalogue Raisonne. rev. ed. (Illus.). 216p. 1990. 125.00 (1-55660-045-3) A Wofsy Fine Arts.

— The History of Impressionism. (Illus.). 672p. 1973. 55.00 (0-87070-360-9, 0-8109-6035-4); pap. 29.95 (0-87070-369-2, 0-8109-6036-2) Mus of Modern Art.

— History of Impressionism. 4th ed. 1990. 55.00 (0-8109-6035-4) Abrams.

— History of Impressionism. 4th rev. ed. 1990. pap. 29.95 (0-8109-6036-2) Abrams.

— Pissarro. (Library of Great Painters). (Illus.). 160p. 1963. 49.50 (0-8109-0413-6) Abrams.

— Pissarro. (Masters of Art Ser.). (Illus.). 128p. 1989. 22.95 (0-8109-1499-9) Abrams.

— Post-Impressionism: From Van Gogh to Gaugin. (Illus.). 592p. 1978. 60.00 (0-87070-532-6, 0-8109-6066-4) Mus of Modern Art.

— Seurat: A Biography. (Illus.). 240p. 1990. 75.00 (0-8109-3814-6) Abrams.

— Seurat: A Biography. (Illus.). 240p. 1992. pap. 34.98 (0-8109-8124-6, Abradale Pr) Abrams.

— Studies in Impressionism. Gordon, Irene & Weitzenhoffer, Frances, eds. (Illus.). 232p. 1986. 39.95 (0-8109-1617-7) Abrams.

— Studies in Post-Impressionism. (Illus.). 296p. 1986. 39.95 (0-8109-1632-0) Abrams.

Rewald, John, ed. Cezanne Letters. 5th rev. ed. LC 81-81716. (Illus.). 400p. 1985. lib. bdg. 60.00 (0-87817-276-9) Hacker.

Rewald, John & Near, Pinkney L. French Paintings: The Collection of Mr. & Mrs Paul Mellon in the Virginia Museum of Fine Arts. Cruger, George A., ed. LC 85-21707. (Illus.). 156p. 1985. 40.00 (0-917046-20-X, U of Wash Pr); pap. 22.50 (0-917046-19-6, U of Wash Pr) Va Mus Arts.

Rewald, John, ed. see Cezanne, Paul.

Rewald, John, ed. see Pissarro, Camille.

Rewald, John, jt. ed. see Pissarro, Camille.

Rewald, Sabine. Ninety Works from the Heinz Berggrun. 1994. pap. 24.95 (0-8109-2447-1) Abrams.

— Paul Klee: The Berggruen Klee Collection in the Metropolitan Museum of Art. (Illus.). 320p. 1988. 45.00 (0-87099-511-1, Abrams); pap. 25.00 (0-87099-513-8, Abrams) Metro Mus Art.

Rewald, Sabine, ed. The Romantic Vision of Caspar David Friedrich: Paintings & Drawings from the U.S.S.R. (Illus.). 120p. 1991. 24.50 (0-8109-6402-3, Abrams); pap. 18.75 (0-87099-603-7, Abrams) Metro Mus Art.

Rewald, Sabine, jt. auth. see Lieberman, William S.

Rewali, J. Paul Cezanne. 1972. 59.95 (0-8490-0807-7) Gordon Pr.

Rewes, Ralph. El Diario de un Cubanito. LC 87-82650. (Coleccion Caniqui Ser.). 180p. (Orig.). (SPA.). 1988. pap. 9.95 (0-89729-464-5) Ediciones.

Rewolinski, Leah. Geek Space Nine. (Star Wreck Ser.: No. 6). 1994. mass mkt. 3.99 (0-312-95223-6) St Martin.

— Space Fido Frontier Vol. 1. (Star Wreck Ser.: No. 07). 1994. pap. 4.50 (0-312-95362-3) St Martin.

— Star Wreck Four: Live Long & Profit. 1993. mass mkt. 4.50 (0-312-92985-4) St Martin.

— Star Wreck II: The Attack of the Jargonites. 1992. mass mkt. 3.99 (0-312-92737-1) St Martin.

— Star Wreck the Generation Gap. 1992. mass mkt. 3.99 (0-312-92802-5) St Martin.

— Star Wreck Three: Time Warped. 1992. mass mkt. 3.99 (0-312-92891-2) St Martin.

— Star Wreck V: The Undiscovered Nursing Home. 1993. mass mkt. 3.99 (0-312-95122-1) St Martin.

Rewt, Pauline, jt. ed. see Edwards, Paul.

Rex, Andrew F., jt. ed. see Leff, Harvey V.

Rex, Barbara. Saints & Innocents. 1972. 6.95 (0-393-08664-X) Norton.

Rex, D. F., ed. Climate of the Free Atmosphere. (World Survey of Climatology Ser.: Vol. 4). 450p. 1969. 174.50 (0-444-40703-0) Elsevier.

Rex, David & Roberts, Thomas, eds. Recording the Performance of U. S. Undergraduates at British Institutions: Guidelines Toward Standardized Reporting for Study Abroad. 9p. 1988. 9.00 (0-912207-22-1) NAFSA Washington.

Rex, Evelyn, ed. Foundations of Braille Literacy. Date not set. write for info. (0-89128-934-8) Am Foun Blind.

Rex, J., jt. ed. see Appleman, B. R.

Rex, J., jt. ed. see Drisko, R.

Rex, John. The Ghetto & the Underclass: Essays on Race & Social Policy. 235p. 1988. text ed. 49.95 (0-566-05651-8, Pub. by Avebury Pub UK) Ashgate Pub Co.

— Immigrant Association in Europe. (Studies in European Migration (EFS): Vol. 1). 1987. text ed. 54.95 (0-566-05474-4, Pub. by Avebury Pub UK) Ashgate Pub Co.

— Race & Ethnicity. LC 86-5197. (Concepts in Social Sciences Ser.). 160p. 1986. pap. 22.00 (0-335-15385-2, Open Univ Pr) Taylor & Francis.

— Race Relations in Sociological Theory. 180p. (Orig.). 1983. pap. 13.95 (0-7100-9299-7, RKP) Routledge.

***Rex, John & Drury, Beatrice, eds.** Ethnic Mobilisation in a Multi-Cultural Europe. (Research in Ethnic Relations Ser.). 178p. 1994. 57.95 (1-85628-573-1, Pub. by Avebury Pub UK) Ashgate Pub Co.

Rex, John & Mason, David S., eds. Theories of Race & Ethnic Relations. (Comparative Ethnic & Race Relations Ser.). (Illus.). 350p. 1988. pap. 19.95 (0-521-36939-8) Cambridge U Pr.

Rex-Johnson, Braiden. The Pike Place Market Cookbook: Recipes, Anecdotes, & Personalities from Seattle's Renowned Public Market. (Illus.). 280p. (Orig.). 1992. pap. 15.95 (0-912365-52-8) Sasquatch Bks.

***Rex-Johnson, Braiden & Wasson, David.** That's Fresh! Seasonal Recipes for Young Cooks. (Illus.). 32p. (Orig.). (J). (gr. 2 up). 1995. pap. 14.95 (1-57061-017-7) Sasquatch Bks.

Rex, Patricia. Bear Essentials. (J). (ps-00). 1988. pap. 9.99 (0-8224-0697-7) Fearon Teach Aids.

Rex, Percy F. The Prolific Pencil. Burrows, Fredrika A. & Sullwold, Stephen W., eds. LC 80-51482. (Illus.). 312p. 1980. 15.00 (0-88492-037-2) W S Sullwold.

Rex, Richard. Henry the Eighth & the English Reformation. LC 92-25105. (British History in Perspective Ser.). 1993. text ed. 39.95 (0-312-08665-2); pap. 16.95 (0-312-08664-4) St Martin.

— The Sins of Madame Eglentyne: And Other Essays on Chaucer. LC 94-48358. 208p. 1995. 35.00 (0-87413-567-2) U Delaware Pr.

— The Theology of John Fisher: A Study in the Intellectual Origins of the Counter-Reformation. 250p. (C). 1991. 69.95 (0-521-39177-6) Cambridge U Pr.

Rex, Richard, tr. see Garrisson, Janine.

Rex, Stefan. The Horror from the Grave. (Home Video Producer Ser.). (Illus.). 96p. (Orig.). 1987. pap. 14.95 (0-931145-11-2) Sandlight Pubns.

Rex, Stella Hay. Practical Hooked Rugs. (Illus.). 1975. 16.95 (0-89166-004-6); pap. 12.95 (0-89166-003-8) Cobblesmith.

Rexach, Nilda L. The Hispanic-American Cookbook. 224p. 1985. 12.00 (0-8184-0363-2) Carol Pub Group.

— The Hispanic Cookbook: Traditional & Modern Recipes in English & Spanish. 190p. 1995. pap. 9.95 (0-8065-1601-1, Citadel Pr) Carol Pub Group.

Rexach, Rosario. Dos Figuras Cubanas Y Una Sola Actitud: Felix Varela 1788-1853 - Jorge Manach 1898-1961. LC 90-86072. 258p. 1991. pap. 19.00 (0-89729-592-7) Ediciones.

— Rumbo al Punto Cierto. 1979. pap. 7.50 (84-499-2644-0) Edit Mensaje.

Rexer, F. The Urban Survival Arsenal: The Best Guns for Self-Preservation. 1986. lib. bdg. 79.95 (0-8490-3817-0) Gordon Pr.

***Rexer, Lyle & Klein, Rachel.** American Museum of Natural History: 125 Years of Expedition & Discovery. LC 95-6108. 1995. write for info. (0-8109-1965-6) Abrams.

Rexford, Eveoleen N., ed. A Developmental Approach to Problems of Acting Out. rev. ed. LC 77-17666. 223p. 1978. text ed. 32.50x (0-8236-1221-X) Intl Univs Pr.

Rexford, Eveoleen N., et al, eds. Infant Psychiatry: A New Synthesis. LC 75-2774. (Monographs of the Journal of the American Academy of Child Psychiatry: No. 2). (Illus.). 370p. reprint ed. pap. 105.50 (0-8357-8183-6, 2033866) Bks Demand.

Rexford, J. What Handwriting Indicates: An Analytical Graphology. 1991. lib. bdg. 79.95 (0-8490-4528-2) Gordon Pr.

Rexford, Janis, jt. auth. see Eisberg, George L.

Rexford, John. What Handwriting Indicates: An Analytical Graphology. 142p. 1972. reprint ed. spiral bd. 6.60 (0-7873-1082-4) Mokelumne.

Rexford, Kenneth B. Electrical Control for Machines. 3rd ed. 416p. 1987. teacher ed 14.00 (0-8273-2793-5); student ed 15.95 (0-8273-4880-0); text ed. 29.95 (0-8273-2792-7) Delmar.

— Electrical Control for Machines. 4th ed. 1991. text ed. 35.95 (0-8273-4868-1) Delmar.

— Electrical Control for Machines: Instructor's Guide. 4th ed. 105p. 1992. 14.00 (0-8273-4870-3) Delmar.

— Electrical Control for Machines: Student Manual. 4th ed. 120p. 1993. student ed 14.95 (0-685-66866-5) Delmar.

Rexine, John E. An Explorer of Realms of Art, Life, & Thought: A Survey of the Works of Philosopher & Theologian Constantine Cavarnos. LC 85-81278. (Illus.). 184p. 1985. 9.50 (0-914744-69-0); pap. 6.50 (0-914744-70-4) Inst Byzantine.

— Religion in Plato & Cicero. LC 68-28581. 72p. 1968. reprint ed. 45.00 (0-8371-0198-0, RERP, Greenwood Pr) Greenwood.

Rexroad, Eileen. Teaching Elementary School Music. 320p. (C). 1992. pap. text ed. write for info. (0-13-039983-3) P-H.

Rexroat, Cynthia. The Declining Economic Status of Black Children: Examining the Change. LC 93-44354. 1993. write for info. (1-880285-12-6); pap. write for info. (1-880285-11-8) Jt Ctr Pol Studies.

— The Declining Economic Status of Black Children: What Accounts for the Change? 90p. (C). 1991. lib. bdg. 38.00 (0-941410-95-1); pap. text ed. 12.50 (0-941410-96-X) Jt Ctr Pol Studies.

Rexroat, Stephen V. For Our Good: The Ten Commandments from a Positive Perspective. 106p. (Orig.). 1990. pap. 7.95 (0-942381-05-X) Sammamish Pr.

Rexrode, William F. Rexrode Art. (Illus.). 1966. 4.00 (0-87012-011-5) McClain.

Rexroth. Quarterly Review of Literature: The 1950s, Homestead Called Damascus, Vol. IX, No. 2. 1950. pap. 10.00 (0-317-05300-0) Quarterly Rev.

Rexroth, Kenneth. An Autobiographical Novel. rev. ed. Hamalian, Linda, ed. LC 91-4785. (Revived Modern Classics Ser.). 528p. 1991. pap. 14.95 (0-8112-1179-7, NDP725) New Directions.

— Beyond the Mountains. LC 51-9631. 192p. 1974. pap. 3.25 (0-8112-0552-5, NDP384) New Directions.

— A Bird in the Bush. LC 75-111860. (Essay Index Reprint Ser.). 1977. 21.95 (0-8369-1623-9) Ayer.

— Classics Revisited. LC 85-31088. (Revived Modern Classics Ser.). 256p. 1986. reprint ed. 23.95 (0-8112-0987-3); reprint ed. pap. 10.95 (0-8112-0988-1, NDP621) New Directions.

— The Collected Longer Poems. LC 68-25549. 1970. reprint ed. pap. 12.95 (0-8112-0177-5, NDP309) New Directions.

— Collected Shorter Poems. LC 66-17818. 1967. pap. 14.95 (0-8112-0178-3, NDP243) New Directions.

— Flower Wreath Hill: Later Poems - Combines "New Poems" & "The Morning Star" LC 91-18661. 176p. 1991. reprint ed. pap. 9.95 (0-8112-1178-9, NDP724) New Directions.

— More Classics Revisited. Morrow, Bradford, ed. LC 88-22789. (Revived Modern Classics Ser.). 160p. 1989. pap. 10.95 (0-8112-1083-9, NDP668) New Directions.

— One Hundred More Poems from the Chinese: Love & the Turning Year. LC 71-114845. (Orig.). 1970. 12.00 (0-8112-0369-7); pap. 9.95 (0-8112-0179-1, NDP308) New Directions.

— Selected Poems. Morrow, Bradford, ed. LC 84-9972. (Illus.). 160p. 1984. pap. 9.95 (0-8112-0917-2, NDP581) New Directions.

— Sky, Sea, Birds, Trees, Earth, House, Beast. 2nd ed. LC 76-134750. (Illus.). 30p. 1973. 17.50 (0-87775-044-0); pap. 7.95 (0-87775-048-3) Unicorn Pr.

— World Outside the Window: The Selected Essays of Kenneth Rexroth. Morrow, Bradford, ed. LC 86-28610. 352p. 1987. 24.95 (0-8112-1024-3); pap. 12.95 (0-8112-1025-1, NDP639) New Directions.

Rexroth, Kenneth, tr. One Hundred More Poems from the Japanese. LC 76-7486. (Illus.). 1976. 12.00 (0-8112-0618-1); pap. 9.95 (0-8112-0619-X, NDP420) New Directions.

— One Hundred Poems from the Chinese. LC 56-13351. (Orig.). 1956. pap. 8.95 (0-8112-0180-5, NDP192) New Directions.

— One Hundred Poems from the Japanese. LC 56-2557. (Orig.). (ENG & JPN.). 1955. 11.95 (0-8112-0371-9); pap. 8.95 (0-8112-0181-3, NDP147) New Directions.

— Poems from the Greek Anthology. (Illus.). 1962. pap. 8.95 (0-472-06063-5, 63, Ann Arbor Bks) U of Mich Pr.

An Asterisk (*) at the beginning of an entry indicates that the title is appearing in BIP for the first time.

Rexroth, Kenneth & Atsumi, Ikuko, trs. Women Poets of Japan. LC 77-1833. 192p. 1982. reprint ed. pap. 9.95 (*0-8112-0820-6*, NDP527) New Directions.

Rexroth, Kenneth & Chung Ling, trs. Women Poets of China. LC 72-6791. Orig. Title: The Orchid Boat. 160p. 1982. reprint ed. pap. 8.95 (*0-8112-0821-4*, NDP528) New Directions.

Rexroth, Kenneth, tr. see De L. Milosz, O. V.

Rexroth, Kenneth, tr. see Hamill, Sam, ed.

Rexroth, Kenneth, ed. see Li-Ching-Chao.

Rexroth, Kenneth, tr. see Reverdy, Pierre.

Rexroth, Kenneth, ed. see Shiraishi, Kazuko.

Rexroth, Kenneth, tr. see TuFu.

***Rexxxxx, Don J.** Modem Love: Step-by-Step Guide to Sex on the Information Highway. 1995. pap. text ed. 12.00 (*0-8217-4921-8*) Zebra.

Rey, Agapito, jt. ed. see Hammond, George P.

***Rey, Alain.** Essays on Terminology. Sager, Juan C., tr. LC 94-45807. (Translation Library: No. 9). xiii, 221p. 1995. lib. bdg. 69.00x (*1-55619-688-1*); pap. 24.95x (*1-55619-689-X*) Benjamins North Am.

— Le Petit Robert, Vol. 2. (FRE.). 1993. 185.00 (*0-685-01759-1*, F134381) Fr & Eur.

— Robert Dictionnaire des Expressions et Locutions. 1322p. (FRE.). 1989. pap. 31.95 (*0-7859-8058-X*, 2850361038) Fr & Eur.

— Robert Dictionnaire des Expressions et Locutions Figurees. 1036p. 1990. 75.00 (*0-7859-5651-4*, 2850360678) Fr & Eur.

— Robert Historical Dictionary of the French Language, 2 vols., Set. (FRE.). 1992. 350.00 (*0-8288-7321-6*, M1253) Fr & Eur.

Rey, Alfonso, ed. see De Quevedo, Francisco.

Rey, Anthony M. & Wieland, Ferdinand. Managing Service in Food & Beverage Operations. Paananen, Donna, ed. LC 85-12962. (Illus.). 395p. 1985. text ed. 57.95 (*0-86612-023-8*) Educ Inst Am Hotel.

Rey, Antonio B. Concierto de Primavera. (Romance Real Ser.). 180p. 1981. pap. 1.50 (*0-88025-001-1*) Roca Pub.

Rey, Bret. Gunsmoke in a Colorado Canyon. large type ed. (Linford Western Library). 240p. 1993. pap. 14.95 (*0-7089-7440-6*, Trailtree Bookshop) Ulverscroft.

— Marshal Without a Badge. large type ed. (Linford Western Library). 272p. 1993. pap. 14.95 (*0-7089-7362-0*, Linford) Ulverscroft.

— Trouble Valley. large type ed. (Linford Western Library). 1991. pap. 13.95 (*0-7089-7010-9*) Ulverscroft.

Rey, Brett. Runaway. large type ed. (Linford Western Library). 256p. 1992. pap. 14.95 (*0-7089-7151-2*, Trailtree Bookshop) Ulverscroft.

Rey, Charles. Monarch of All I Survey: Bechuanaland Diaries, 1929-1937. Parsons, Neil & Crowder, Michael, eds. LC 87-12570. (Illus.). 282p. 1988. text ed. 39.50 (*0-936508-22-1*) Barber Pr.

Rey-Debove, G. Dictionnaire des Anglicismes (Dictionary of Anglicisms) 1150p. (FRE.). 1990. 75.00 (*0-7859-4769-8*, M3259) Fr & Eur.

***Rey-Debove, Josette.** Robert Dictionnaire des Anglicismes. 1150p. (FRE.). 1988. 69.95 (*0-7859-7121-1*, 2850360279) Fr & Eur.

— Le Robert Methodique: Dictionnaire du Francais Actuel. 1617p. (FRE.). 1982. 85.00 (*0-7859-8057-1*, 2850360899) Fr & Eur.

Rey-Debove, Josette, ed. Recherches Sur les Systemes Significants: Symposium De Varsovie, 1968. (Approaches to Semiotics Ser.: No. 18). (Illus.). 1973. 140.00 (*90-279-2379-5*) Mouton.

Rey, Emmanuel. Colonies Franques De Syrie Aux Dix-Septieme & Dix-Huitieme Siecles. LC 75-168007. reprint ed. 55.00 (*0-404-05285-1*) AMS Pr.

Rey, F., jt. auth. see Estep, K. W.

Rey, Gar. Rand R. LC 92-61994. 200p. 1993. pap. 9.00 (*1-56002-206-X*, Univ Edtns) Aegina Pr.

***Rey, H. A.** The Adventures of Curious George, 3 Vols., Set. 1995. pap. 10.00 (*0-395-73518-1*) HM.

— Anybody at Home? (Illus.). 24p. (J). (gr. k-3). 1942. pap. 2.95 (*0-395-07045-7*, Sandpiper) HM.

— Cecily G. & the Nine Monkeys. (Illus.). 32p. (J). (gr. 1-3). 1974. 14.95 (*0-395-18430-4*) HM.

— Cecily G. & the Nine Monkeys. (Illus.). (J). (ps-3). 1989. pap. 3.95 (*0-395-50651-4*, Sandpiper) HM.

— Curious George. (Illus.). 56p. (J). (gr. k-3). 1973. 13.95 (*0-395-15993-8*) HM.

— Curious George. LC 93-40088. (J). 1994. pap. 19.95 (*0-395-69803-0*) HM.

— Curious George. (Illus.). 48p. (J). (gr. k-3). 1973. reprint ed. pap. 4.95 (*0-395-15023-X*, Sandpiper) HM.

— Curious George Gets a Medal. (Illus.). 48p. (J). (gr. k-3). 1957. 13.95 (*0-395-16973-9*) HM.

— Curious George Gets a Medal. LC 57-7206. (Illus.). 48p. (J). (gr. k-3). 1974. reprint ed. pap. 4.95 (*0-395-18559-9*, Sandpiper) HM.

— Curious George Learns the Alphabet. (Illus.). 72p. (J). (gr. k-3). 1963. 14.95 (*0-395-16031-6*) HM.

— Curious George Learns the Alphabet. LC 62-12261. (Illus.). 72p. (J). (gr. k-3). 1973. pap. 4.95 (*0-395-13718-7*, Sandpiper) HM.

— Curious George Paper Doll. (J). 1982. pap. 3.95 (*0-486-24386-9*) Dover.

— Curious George Rides a Bike. (Illus.). 48p. (J). (gr. k-3). 1952. 13.95 (*0-395-16964-X*) HM.

— Curious George Rides a Bike. 48p. (J). (gr. k-3). pap. 1.95 (*0-590-02045-5*) Scholastic Inc.

— Curious George Rides a Bike. (Illus.). 48p. (J). (gr. k-3). 1973. reprint ed. pap. 4.95 (*0-395-17444-9*, Sandpiper) HM.

— Curious George Takes a Job. (Illus.). 48p. (J). (gr. k-3). 1973. 13.95 (*0-395-15086-8*) HM.

— Curious George Takes a Job. (Illus.). 48p. (J). (gr. k-3). 1974. pap. 4.95 (*0-395-18649-8*, Sandpiper) HM.

— Feed the Animals. (Illus.). 24p. (J). (gr. k-3). 1944. pap. 2.25 (*0-395-07063-5*, Sandpiper) HM.

— Find the Constellations. rev. ed. (Illus.). 80p. (J). (gr. 3-7). 1976. 17.95 (*0-395-24509-5*) HM.

— Find the Constellations. rev. ed. (Illus.). 72p. (J). (gr. 3-7). 1976. pap. 8.95 (*0-395-24418-8*, Sandpiper) HM.

— Four Fold Our Books, 4 Vols. 1979. pap. 9.95 (*0-395-28659-X*) HM.

— Humpty Dumpty & Other Mother Goose Songs. (Illus.). 22p. (J). 1995. 9.95 (*0-694-00652-1*, Festival) HarpC Child Bks.

— Jorge el Curioso. (Illus.). (SPA.). (J). (gr. k-3). 1961. 13.95 (*0-395-17075-3*) HM.

— Jorge el Curioso. (Illus.). (SPA.). (J). (ps-3). 1976. pap. 5.95 (*0-395-24909-0*, Sandpiper) HM.

— See the Circus. (Illus.). (J). (gr. k-3). 1956. pap. 2.95 (*0-395-07068-6*, Sandpiper) HM.

— The Stars: A New Way to See Them. (J). (gr. 4 up). 1976. pap. 10.95 (*0-395-24830-2*) HM.

— The Stars: A New Way to See Them. 3rd ed. (Illus.). (J). (gr. 8 up). 1973. 17.95 (*0-395-08121-1*) HM.

— We Three Kings & Other Carols. (Illus.). 22p. (J). (ps up). 1994. reprint ed. 9.95 (*0-694-00661-0*, Festival) HarpC Child Bks.

— Where's My Baby? (Illus.). 24p. (J). (ps-3). 1943. pap. 2.95 (*0-395-07069-4*, Sandpiper) HM.

Rey, H. A. & Rey, Margaret. Curious George Goes to the Hospital. (Illus.). 48p. (J). (gr. 1-5). 1973. 14.95 (*0-395-18158-5*); pap. 4.95 (*0-395-07062-7*) HM.

Rey, H. A., jt. auth. see Rey, Margaret.

***Rey, Henri.** Universals of Psychoanalysis: In the Treatment of Psychotic & Borderline States. Magagna, Jeanne, ed. 319p. 1994. pap. 37.00 (*1-85343-370-5*) NYU Pr.

Rey, J. French Dictionary of the Difficulties of the English Version. 287p. pap. 25.00 (*2-7080-0066-7*) IBD Ltd.

Rey, J. J. Robust Statistical Methods. (Lecture Notes in Mathematics Ser.: Vol. 690). 1978. pap. 12.00 (*0-387-09091-6*) Spr-Verlag.

***Rey, Jean.** Dictionnaire Selectif et Commente des Difficultes de la Vers. 1973. write for info. (*0-7859-7927-1*, 2-7080-0066-7) Fr & Eur.

Rey, Jean, jt. auth. see Ballabriga, Angel.

Rey, Jean N. Video France - Optiques: La Vie Quotidienne. 80p. 1991. reprint ed. pap. 149.95 (*0-8442-1468-X*, Passport Bks) NTC Pub Grp.

— Video France - Panorama de la France. (Illus.). 80p. reprint ed. pap. 149.95 (*0-685-58865-3*, Natl Textbk) NTC Pub Grp.

— Video France - Profiles des Francaise. 80p. reprint ed. pap. 149.95 (*0-8442-1471-X*, Natl Textbk) NTC Pub Grp.

Rey, Jorge R. & Kain, Tim. A Guide to the Salt Marsh Impoundments of Florida. (Illus.). 1990. pap. write for info. (*0-9615224-3-7*) Fla Med Entom.

Rey, Louis, ed. Arctic Underwater Operations. 360p. 1985. lib. bdg. 115.50 (*0-86010-631-4*) G & T Inc.

Rey, Louis & Behrens, C., eds. Arctic Energy Resources: Proceedings of the Conference Held in Oslo, Norway, September 22-24, 1982. (Energy Research Ser.: Vol. 2). 366p. 1983. 105.25 (*0-444-42218-8*) Elsevier.

Rey, Louis, et al, eds. Unveiling the Arctic. (Illus.). 613p. 1985. 55.00 (*0-919034-09-8*) U of Alaska Pr.

Rey, Marcos. Memoirs of a Gigolo. 224p. 1987. pap. 7.95 (*0-380-75000-7*) Avon.

Rey, Margaret. Curious George & the Pizza. LC 85-2434. 32p. (J). (ps-2). 1985. 9.95 (*0-395-39039-7*); pap. 3.95 (*0-395-39033-8*) HM.

Rey, Margaret, ed. Curious George & the Dump Truck. (Illus.). 32p. (J). (ps-2). 1984. pap. 3.95 (*0-395-36629-1*) HM.

— Curious George at the Fire Station. LC 85-2471. 32p. (J). (ps-2). 1985. 9.95 (*0-395-39037-0*); pap. 3.95 (*0-395-39031-1*) HM.

— Curious George Goes to the Aquarium. (Illus.). 32p. (J). (ps-2). 1984. 9.95 (*0-395-36634-8*); pap. 3.95 (*0-395-36628-3*) HM.

— Curious George Visits the Zoo. LC 85-2415. 32p. (J). (ps-2). 1985. 9.95 (*0-395-39036-2*); pap. 3.95 (*0-395-39030-3*) HM.

Rey, Margaret & Rey, H. A. Curious George Flies a Kite. (Illus.). 80p. (J). (gr. k-3). 1973. 13.95 (*0-395-16965-8*) HM.

— Curious George Flies a Kite. (Illus.). (J). (gr. k-3). 1977. pap. 4.95 (*0-395-25937-1*) HM.

Rey, Margaret & Shalleck, Allan J. Curious George & the Dinosaur. (Illus.). 32p. (J). (ps-2). 1989. pap. 3.95 (*0-395-51936-5*) HM.

— Curious George & the Dinosaur. (Illus.). (J). (ps-3). 1990. audio, pap. 7.95 (*0-395-56484-0*, Clarion Bks) HM.

— Curious George & the Pizza. (Book & Cassette Favorites Ser.). (J). 1988. audio, pap. 7.95 (*0-395-48874-5*) HM.

— Curious George at the Fire Station. (Book & Cassette Favorites Ser.). (J). 1988. audio, pap. 7.95 (*0-395-48875-3*) HM.

— Curious George at the Railroad Station. (Illus.). 32p. (J). (ps-2). 1988. pap. 2.95 (*0-395-48657-2*) HM.

— Curious George Goes to School. (Illus.). 32p. (J). (ps-2). 1989. 9.95 (*0-395-51944-6*); pap. 3.95 (*0-395-51939-X*) HM.

— Curious George Goes to School, Incl. cass. (Illus.). (J). (ps-3). 1990. Bk. & cass. audio, pap. 7.95 (*0-395-56483-2*) HM.

— Curious George Goes to the Dentist. (Illus.). 32p. (J). (ps-2). 1989. 9.95 (*0-685-26499-8*) HM.

— Curious George Visits the Zoo. (Book & Cassette Package Ser.). (J). 1988. audio, pap. 7.95 (*0-395-48876-1*) HM.

Rey, Margaret & Shalleck, Allan J., eds. Curious George at the Airport. (Illus.). 32p. (J). (ps-2). 1987. pap. 2.95 (*0-395-45368-2*) HM.

— Curious George Plays Baseball. LC 86-10609. (Illus.). 32p. (J). (ps-2). 1986. 8.95 (*0-395-39041-9*); pap. 3.95 (*0-395-39035-4*) HM.

Rey, Margaret, jt. auth. see Rey, H. A.

Rey, Margret. Curious George & the Dinosaur. (J). (ps-3). 1989. 9.95 (*0-395-51942-X*) HM.

Rey, R. Poussin: Paintings. (Rhythem & Color One Ser.). 1970. 9.95 (*0-8288-9504-X*) Fr & Eur.

Rey, Robert. Manet. (CAL Art Ser.). (Illus.). 1988. 14.95 (*0-517-03722-X*, Crown) Crown Pub Group.

Rey-Rosa, Rodrigo. The Beggar's Knife. Bowles, Paul, tr. 112p. (Orig.). 1985. 12.95 (*0-87286-166-X*); pap. 5.95 (*0-87286-164-3*) City Lights.

— Dust on Her Tongue. 124p. (Orig.). 1992. pap. 7.95 (*0-87286-272-0*) City Lights.

***Rey, Roselyne.** The History of Pain. Wallace, Louise E. et al, trs. LC 94-31948. 1995. text ed. 39.95 (*0-674-39967-6*, REYHIS) HUP.

Rey, S. J., jt. auth. see Krauss, Lawrence M.

Rey, W. J. Introduction to Robust & Quasi-Robust Statistical Methods. (Universitext Ser.). (Illus.). 250p. 1983. pap. 42.00 (*0-387-12866-2*) Spr-Verlag.

Reybaud, Louis. Etudes Sur les Reformateurs Ou Socialistes Modernes, 2 vols. in one. Mayer, J. P., ed. LC 78-67379. (European Political Thought Ser.). (FRE.). 1980. reprint ed. lib. bdg. 68.95 (*0-405-11729-9*) Ayer.

Reybold, L. Earle, ed. Revolutions for Freedom: The Mass Media in Eastern & Central Europe. LC 91-19063. 250p. (Orig.). (C). 1991. pap. 10.95 (*0-943089-02-6*) U GA CFIMCTR.

Reybold, W. U. & Petersen, G. W. Soil Survey Techniques. 112p. 1987. 15.00 (*0-89118-783-9*) Soil Sci Soc Am.

Reyburn, Hugh Y. John Calvin: His Life, Letters & Work. LC 83-45630. reprint ed. 45.00 (*0-404-19847-3*) AMS Pr.

Reyburn, Stanley S. Escrows: Principles & Procedures. 2nd rev. ed. Anthony Schools Corporation Staff, ed. (Real Estate College-Level Ser.). (Illus.). 320p. (C). 1990. pap. text ed. 39.95 (*0-941833-34-8*) Anthony Schools.

— Real Estate Finance. 582p. (C). 1994. pap. text ed. 29.95 (*1-884811-00-0*) Felde Pubng.

— What a Wonderful World This Could Be. (Illus.). 28p. (Orig.). 1990. pap. 7.50 (*0-910147-87-6*) World Poetry Pr.

Reyburn, Wallace. Flushed with Pride: The Story of Thomas Crapper. (Illus.). 95p. 1993. pap. 8.95 (*1-85145-978-2*, Pub. by Pavilion UK) Trafalgar.

Reyburn, William D. A Handbook on Lamentations. LC 92-22755. (UBS Handbook Ser.). ix, 166p. 1992. 14.00 (*0-8267-0124-8*, 104975) Untd Bible Soc.

— A Handbook on the Book of Job. LC 92-12735. (UBS Handbook Ser.). (Illus.). ix, 806p. 1992. 16.00 (*0-8267-0117-5*, 104880) Untd Bible Soc.

Reyburn, William D., jt. auth. see Bratcher, Robert G.

Reychler, Luc, jt. ed. see Bauwens, Werner.

Reychler, Luc, jt. ed. see Rudney, Robert.

Reychman, J. Hungarian-Polish Comprehensive Dictionary. 2nd rev. ed. 1059p. (HUN & POL.). 1985. 75.00 (*0-8288-1064-8*, M 8566) Fr & Eur.

Reychman, Jan & Zajaczkowski, Ananiasz. Handbook of Ottoman-Turkish Diplomatics. rev. ed. Ehrenkreutz, Andrew S., tr. (Publications in Near & Middle East Studies: Ser. A, No. 7). (Illus.). 1968. 69.25 (*90-279-0513-4*) Mouton.

Reycroft-Hollingsworth, Dorothy, jt. auth. see Kreutner, A. Karen.

Reyder, Rimma. Jewish Ceremonial Designs. (International Design Library). (Illus.). 48p. 1987. pap. 5.95 (*0-88045-087-8*) Stemmer Hse.

Reyer, Carolyn, ed. see Monroe, Mark.

Reyer, Edward. Questions on Geologic Principles. Keller, Allen et al, trs. LC 79-89374. (Microform Publication: No. 9). (Illus.). 1979. 1.25 (*0-8137-6009-7*) Geol Soc.

Reyero, Carlos. The Key to Art from Romanticism to Impressionism. (Key to Art Bks.). (Illus.). 80p. (J). (gr. 8 up). 1990. lib. bdg. 21.50 (*0-8225-2058-3*, Lerner Publctns) Lerner Group.

Reyerson, Kathryn L. Society, Law & Trade in Medieval Montpellier. (Collected Studies Ser.: CS 475). 330p. 1995. 89.95 (*0-86078-460-6*, Pub. by Variorum UK) Ashgate Pub Co.

Reyerson, Kathryn L., jt. ed. see Chiat, Marilyn J.

Reyerson, Kathryn L., jt. ed. see Hanawalt, Barbara A.

Reyerson, Kathryn L., jt. ed. see MacLeish, Andrew.

Reyes, A. T. Archaic Cyprus: A Study of the Textual & Archaeological Evidence. LC 93-26237. (Oxford Monographs on Classical Archaeology). (Illus.). 320p. (C). 1994. 75.00 (*0-19-813227-1*, Clarendon Pr) OUP.

Reyes, Alfonso. Position of America & Other Essays. De Onis, Harriet, tr. LC 77-142690. (Essay Index Reprint Ser.). 1977. 19.95 (*0-8369-2067-8*) Ayer.

***Reyes, Alina.** The Butcher: A Novel. Watson, David, tr. 192p. 1994. 15.00 (*0-8021-1571-3*, Grove) Grove-Atltic.

Reyes, Ariel J. & Leary, William P., eds. Clinical Pharmacology & Therapeutic Uses of Diuretics. LC 88-11006. (Progress in Pharmacology Ser.: Vol. 6, No. 3). 319p. 1988. pap. text ed. 85.00 (*0-89574-267-5*, Pub. by Gustav Fischer Verlag); 70.00 (*0-685-44103-2*, Pub. by Gustav Fischer Verlag) VCH Pubs.

Reyes, Benito F. Conscious Dying: Psychology of Death & Guidebook to Liberation. LC 86-51403. 121p. (Orig.). (C). 1986. pap. text ed. 20.00 (*0-939375-15-X*) World Univ Amer. CONSCIOUS DYING, THE PSYCHOLOGY OF DEATH & GUIDE BOOK TO LIBERATION is principally & essentially a VADE MECUM guide to conscious dying. Its main objective is to help a person pass through the process of death without losing consciousness. CONSCIOUS DYING IS THE KEY THAT WILL UNLOCK THE DOOR TO IMMORTALITY. To prevent the loss of consciousness at the moment of death will bring about Spiritual Time-Binding, the ability to go through death consciously. The second section of this book, which is the GUIDEBOOK itself, is principally a set of guidelines which must be followed; a set of mantras, prayers & formulas which will be said, & read again & again; to bring about a kind of attitude which must be internalized & actualized by declaration, repeated assertion, & total acceptance. DR. BENITO F. REYES, A FULBRIGHT-SMITH-MUNDT & A FULBRIGHT HAYES PROFESSOR OF PHILOSOPHY & COMPARATIVE RELIGIONS. CO-FOUNDER OF WORLD UNIVERSITY OF AMERICA (OJAI), OJAI, CALIFORNIA. FIRST PRESIDENT OF THE UNIVERSITY OF THE CITY OF MANILA. TO ORDER: DOMINGA L. REYES, 107 N. VENTURA ST., OJAI, CA. 93023

Publisher Provided Annotation.

— Dialogues with God: Sonnet Psalms on the Significance of Being Human. LC 78-244706. 139p. 1969. reprint ed. pap. 10.00 (*0-939375-37-0*) World Univ Amer.

— Education for World Peace. 112p. 1971. pap. 7.50 (*0-939375-12-5*) World Univ Amer.

— The Essence of All Religions. 25p. 1983. pap. 3.00 (*0-939375-14-1*) World Univ Amer.

— The Eternal Christ: Sonnet Prayer for the Second Coming. 18p. 1977. pap. 5.50 (*0-939375-00-1*) World Univ Amer.

— Inspired Meditations in Upper Ojai. 177p. (Orig.). 1990. pap. 6.75 (*0-939375-17-6*) World Univ Amer.

— Inspired Meditations in Upper Ojai Treasured String of Pearls. 177p. 1990. write for info. (*0-318-69243-0*) World Univ Amer.

— Meditation: Cybernetics of Consciousness. Volz, Fred J., ed. 151p. 1978. pap. 15.00 (*0-939375-04-4*) World Univ Amer.

— Moments Without Self. 4th ed. LC 61-21760. 198p. 1986. reprint ed. 10.00 (*0-939375-36-2*) World Univ Amer.

— On World Peace. 24p. 1977. pap. text ed. 1.50 (*0-939375-10-9*) World Univ Amer.

— Our Father: Sonnet Symphony. 28p. (Orig.). 1994. pap. 3.00 (*0-939375-39-7*) World Univ Amer.

— The Practice of Conscious Dying: Off-Ramp to Liberation & Freeway to Conscious Immortality. 134p. (Orig.). 1990. pap. 6.75 (*0-939375-16-8*) World Univ Amer.

— The Process of Moral Choice. (Ethics 101 Ser.). 142p. 1970. pap. 7.50 (*0-939375-28-1*) World Univ Amer.

— Sonnet Adoration of the Avatar: The Splendor of the Sathya Sai. (Illus.). 300p. 1985. reprint ed. 45.00 (*0-939375-08-7*); reprint ed. pap. 25.00 (*0-939375-06-0*) World Univ Amer.

Reyes, Carlos. Nightmarks. LC 88-26747. 1990. 15.95 (*0-89924-060-7*); pap. 8.00 (*0-89924-059-3*) Lynx Hse.

— A Suitcase Full of Crows: Poems. LC 95-10394. 1995. write for info. (*1-878325-13-2*); write for info. (*1-878325-12-4*) Bluestem Press.

Reyes, Carmen S. Redaccion Comercial. 381p. 1992. pap. text ed. 12.95 (*0-8477-3679-2*) U of PR Pr.

Reyes, Dominga L. Meditations: Three Hundred Sixty-Five Days with Shai Sathya Baba. 1987. 7.50 (*0-939375-01-X*) World Univ Amer.

—The Story of Two Souls. 80p. 1984. pap. 5.50 (*0-939375-02-8*) World Univ Amer. THE STORY OF TWO SOULS is a short story dedicated to people interested in the life hereafter. The romantic part is fiction to make the story interesting; names & characters are fictional, but the description of the next world is from personal experience. The experiences can only be verified by people with an out-of-body experience (OOBE) or near-death experience (NDE). Dr. Arnold Toynbee, a historian of England when interviewed said, "I have only one problem about dying. I have had a good education as a physical being & quite successful, but I never had an education as a non- physical being. I will not know how to behave without a body." He was 80 years old then. The purpose of this book is to give all persons a glimpse of the next world & to eliminate the fear of death. Just read it & you will know how to live in a non-physical world. Dr. Dominga L. Reyes has been a teacher for over forty

R

years. She was the first administrator of the City University of Manila & Chairman of the Philosophy Department of the Philippine College of Commerce, & is the Co-Founder of the World University of America (OJAI). To order: Dominga L. Reyes, 107 N. Ventura St., OJAI, CA. 93023 ***Publisher Provided Annotation.***

Reyes, Felix O. Peregrinos de la Libertad. (Caribbean Collection). 245p. 1992. 29.95 (0-8477-0898-5) U of PR Pr.

Reyes, Felix O., ed. La Manigua En Paris: Correspondencia Diplomatica De Betances. 156p. (Orig.). (SPA.). 1984. pap. 6.00 (1-878483-09-9) Hunter Coll CEP.

Reyes, Francis. Fantastic Trucks: Customized Kings of the Road. 1994. 12.98 (0-681-45440-7) Longmeadow Pr.

Reyes, Fred, ed. see Fontoura, Marco.

Reyes, G. E., jt. auth. see Moerdijk, I.

Reyes-Garcia, Ismael. Actualidad del Quijote y Otros Ensayos. LC 83-21679. (UPREX, Ensayo Ser.: No. 66). 121p. (Orig.). (SPA.). 1984. pap. 3.00 (0-8477-0066-6) U of PR Pr.

Reyes, Gonzalo E., jt. auth. see MacNamara, John.

Reyes, Gracianus R. Death in the Cordilleras. 77p. (Orig.). (C). 1989. pap. 6.75 (971-10-0371-6, Pub. by New Day Pub PH) Cellar.

— The Moon & Bai Insiang & Other Stories. 108p. (Orig.). (C). 1990. pap. 8.75 (971-10-0276-0, Pub. by New Day Pub PH) Cellar.

— The Uncommitted. 90p. (Orig.). 1986. pap. 5.75 (971-10-0249-3, Pub. by New Day Pub PH) Cellar.

Reyes, Gracianus R. & Allego, Antonio M. Double Jeopardy: Fourteen Stories. 96p. (Orig.). (C). 1992. pap. 5.75 (971-10-0459-3, Pub. by New Day Pub PH) Cellar.

Reyes, Gregg, jt. auth. see Hindley, Judy.

Reyes-Guerra, Antonio. El Tratamiento de las Fracturas de la Mandibula los Maxilares el Cigoma. LC 77-551324. 193p. (SPA.). 1969. 25.00 (0-317-04088-X); pap. 20.00 (0-317-04089-8) Am Soc Ad Anesthesia Dentistry.

Reyes-Guerra, Antonio, ed. Modern Anesthesia in Dentistry. 343p. (C). 1977. pap. text ed. 35.00 (0-317-04087-1) Am Soc Ad Anesthesia Dentistry.

— Modern Pain Control in Dentistry. 354p. 1978. 15.00 (0-318-13134-X) Am Soc Ad Anesthesia Dentistry.

Reyes, J. A. Epistola a los Filipenses (Epistle to the Philipians) (SPA.). Date not set. 2.99 (0-945792-50-6, 498511) Editorial Unilit.

— Epistola a los Romanos (Epistle to the Romans) (SPA.). Date not set. 2.99 (0-945792-30-1, 498510) Editorial Unilit.

Reyes, Jorge, jt. auth. see Walton, Harold F.

Reyes, Jose S. Legislative History of America's Economic Policy Toward the Philippines. LC 23-11140. (Columbia University. Studies in the Social Sciences: No. 240). reprint ed. 20.00 (0-404-51240-2) AMS Pr.

Reyes, Jun C. Utos Ng Hari at Iba Pang Kuwento. (Illus.). 130p. (TAG.). 1981. pap. 7.50 (971-10-0221-3, Pub. by New Day Pub PH) Cellar.

Reyes, Jun Cruz. Tutubi, Tutubi, Wag Kang Magpahli Sa Mamang Salbahe. 196p. (Orig.). 1987. pap. 10.75 (971-10-0363-5, Pub. by New Day Pub PH) Cellar.

Reyes, Karen, ed. see Adleman, et al.

***Reyes, L. A.** A Partition Method for the Determination of Multiple DC Operating Points. 218p. (Orig.). 1994. pap. 52.50x (90-6275-974-2, Pub. by Delft U Pr NE) Coronet Bks.

Reyes Lagunes, I. & Poortinga, Ype H., eds. From a Different Perspective. vi, 390p. 1985. 34.00 (90-265-0672-4, Pub. by Swets Pub Serv NE) Taylor & Francis.

Reyes, Luis & Rubie, Peter, eds. Hispanics in Hollywood: An Encyclopedia of Film & Television. LC 93-40607. (Reference Library of the Humanities: Vol. 1761). (Illus.). 592p. 1994. 95.00 (0-8153-0827-2, H1761) Garland.

Reyes, Lynda A. The Textiles of the Southern Philippines. 170p. (C). 1992. text ed. 28.00 (971-542-005-2); pap. text ed. 18.00 (971-542-006-0) UH Pr.

Reyes, Narciso G. Lupang Tinubuan & Selected Works in English. 118p. (Orig.). (C). 1991. pap. 7.00 (971-10-0407-0, Pub. by New Day Pub PH) Cellar.

Reyes, Norman. Child of Two Worlds. (Illus.). 196p. 1995. 26.00x (0-89410-777-1); pap. 16.00x (0-89410-778-X) Three Continents.

***Reyes, Paulo J.** Health Care Reform or Redistribution of Cost? 1995. pap. 9.95 (0-533-11227-3) Vantage.

Reyes, Pedro, ed. Teachers & Their Workplace: Commitment, Performance, & Productivity. 320p. 1990. 46.00 (0-685-75359-X, 36885); pap. 23.95 (0-685-75360-3, 36893) Corwin Pr.

— Teachers & Their Workplace: Commitment, Performance, & Productivity. (Focus Editions Ser.: Vol. 122). (Illus.). 320p. (C). 1990. 49.95 (0-8039-3688-5); pap. 24.95 (0-8039-3689-3) Sage.

Reyes, Ray. The Ten Commandments for Teaching: A Teacher's View. 48p. 1991. 8.95 (0-8106-1539-8) NEA.

Reyes, Rebecca. Fajita Fiesta. (Illus.). 60p. 1985. pap. 3.57 (0-9622394-0-2) Fajita Fiesta.

Reyes, Reynaldo & Wilson, J. K. Rafaga: The Life Story of a Nicaraguan Miskito Comandante. Sloan, Tod, ed. LC 92-54141. (Illus.). 232p. 1992. 27.95 (0-8061-2453-9) U of Okla Pr.

Reyes, Rose. New Life for the Elderly: God's Vision to a Home Care Provider. 112p. (Orig.). 1994. pap. text ed. 8.00 (0-9636577-1-2) Trego-Hill.

Reyes, Sandra, tr. One More Stripe to the Tiger: A Selection of Contemporary Chilean Poetry & Fiction. LC 88-20945. 327p. (Orig.). 1989. 23.00 (1-55728-034-7); pap. 14.95 (1-55728-035-5) U of Ark Pr.

Reyes, Sandra, tr. see Parra, Nicanor.

Reyes, Saul T., jt. ed. see Urquidi, Victor L.

Reyes, Steve, jt. auth. see Featherston, David.

Reyes, Vinicio H. Bicultural-Bilingual Education for Latino Students. Cordasco, Francesco, ed. LC 77-90553. (Bilingual-Bicultural Education in the U. S. Ser.). 1978. lib. bdg. 36.95 (0-405-11092-8) Ayer.

Reyes, Z., jt. auth. see Cotts, D.

Reyfman, Irina. Vasilii Trediakovsky: The Fool of the "New" Russian Literature. LC 90-9682. (Illus.). 336p. 1991. 39.50 (0-8047-1824-5) Stanford U Pr.

Reyher, Becky. My Mother Is the Most Beautiful Woman in the World. (Illus.). 40p. (J). (gr. k-3). 1945. lib. bdg. 14.88 (0-688-51251-8) Lothrop.

Reyher, Paul. Masques Anglais. LC 64-14712. 1972. 36.95 (0-405-08880-9, Pub. by Blom Pubns UK) Ayer.

Reyhner, Jon, ed. Teaching American Indian Students. LC 92-54136. (Illus.). 344p. 1994. pap. 14.95 (0-8061-2674-4) U of Okla Pr.

Reyhner, Jon & Eder, Jeanne. A History of Indian Education. 1989. pap. 8.95 (0-89992-515-4) Coun India Ed.

Reyhner, Jon, ed. see Holland, Royce Q., et al.

Reyhons, Ken. Strategic Planning for the Real Estate Manager. 2nd rev. ed. Bettin, Christopher, ed. (Illus.). 125p. 1989. reprint ed. pap. 22.00 (0-913652-68-7) Realtors Natl.

— Strategic Planning for the Real Estate Manager. 3rd ed. Bettin, Christopher, ed. LC 93-4861. 1993. 22.00 (0-913652-78-4) Realtors Natl.

Reyhons, Ken & Godi, Art. Creative Listing Handbook: A Guide to Marketing Residential Real Estate. 2nd ed. Bettin, Christopher, ed. (Illus.). 272p. 1989. pap. 21.95 (0-913652-67-9, 111) Realtors Natl.

Reyhons, Ken, jt. auth. see Godi, Art.

Reyhons, Kenneth. Recruiting Sales Associates. 2nd ed. LC 86-63281. 153p. 1990. 22.00 (0-913652-62-8) Realtors Natl.

Reyle, U. & Rohrer, C., eds. Natural Language Parsing & Linguistic Theories. 1988. lib. bdg. 114.50 (1-55608-055-7) Kluwer Ac.

Reyles, Carlos. Castanets. Le Clerq, Jacques, tr. 1977. lib. bdg. 59.95 (0-8490-1583-9) Gordon Pr.

Reyman, A., tr. see Arnol'd, V. I. & Novikov, S. P., eds.

***Reyman, Jonathan.** The Gain Chichimeca: Essays on the Archaeology & Ethnohistory of North Meso America. (Worldwide Archaeology Series 12). 260p. 1995. 54.95 (1-85628-711-4, Pub. by Avebury Pub UK) Ashgate Pub Co.

Reyman, Jonathan E. Rediscovering Our Past: Essays on the History of American Archaeology. (Worldwide Archaeology Ser.: No. 2). 280p. 1992. 63.95 (1-85628-701-7, Pub. by Avebury Pub UK) Ashgate Pub Co.

Reyman, Randall. Jazz Band Builder. 1993. 5.95 (0-87166-373-2, 93831) Mel Bay.

— The Jazz Sax Primer. 1993. 5.95 (1-56222-090-X, 94530) Mel Bay.

— Jazz Trombone Primer. 1993. 5.95 (1-56222-398-4, 94652) Mel Bay.

— Jazz Trumpet Primer. 1993. 5.95 (1-56222-388-7, 94651) Mel Bay.

Reyman, Randall G. The Jazz Sax. (Building Excellence Ser.). 1993. 5.95 (0-685-64148-1, 94530) Mel Bay.

Reymann, John. The Roar, the Silence, the Grandeur. LC 90-70461. 85p. (Orig.). 1991. pap. 7.00 (1-56002-118-7) Aegina Pr.

Reyment, R. A., jt. ed. see Cubitt, J. M.

Reyment, Richard A. Morphometric Methods in Biostratigraphy. LC 79-41521. 1980. text ed. 106.00 (0-12-586980-0) Acad Pr.

— Multidimensional Palaeobiology. 416p. 1991. 180.00 (0-08-037231-7, Pergamon Pr); pap. 64.00 (0-08-041001-4, Pergamon Pr) Elsevier.

Reyment, Richard A. & Bengston, P., eds. Aspects of Mid-Cretaceous Regional Geology. LC 80-42379. 1981. text ed. 157.00 (0-12-587040-X) Acad Pr.

Reyment, Richard A. & Joreskog, K. G. Applied Factor Analysis in the Natural Sciences. 2nd ed. (Illus.). 250p. (C). 1993. 79.95 (0-521-41242-0) Cambridge U Pr.

Reyment, Richard A., jt. ed. see Cubitt, J. M.

Reymer & Gersin Associates Staff. Building Bridges with Cable: A Survey of Local Cable System Operators & MSO Executives. 130p. (Orig.). 1990. pap. 40.00 (0-89324-087-7) Natl Assn Broadcasters.

Reymert, Martin L., ed. Feelings & Emotions: The Wittenberg Symposium. LC 73-2986. (Classics in Psychology Ser.). 1974. reprint ed. 28.95 (0-405-05158-1) Ayer.

Reymes, William, tr. see Secchi, Nicolo.

Reymond. Catalogue Demotic Papyri in the Ashmolean Museum, Vol. 1: Embalmers Archives from Hawara. 1973. 85.00 (0-900416-08-4, Pub. by Aris & Phillips UK) David Brown.

Reymond, Arnold. History of the Sciences in Greco-Roman Antiquity. Bray, Ruth G. De, tr. LC 63-18046. 1963. 24.00 (0-8196-0128-4) Biblo.

Reymond, Henri & Mailick, Sidney. International Personnel Policies & Practices. 256p. 1985. text ed. 55.00 (0-275-90155-6, C0155, Praeger Pubs) Greenwood.

Reymond, Jean-Pierre. Metals: Born of Earth & Fire. LC 87-34596. (Illus.). 38p. (J). (gr. k-5). 1988. 5.95 (0-944589-19-7, 197) Young Discovery Lib.

Reymond, Lizelle. The Dedicated: A Biography of Nivedita. 380p. 1985. 10.95 (0-910261-16-4, Pub. by Samata Bks II) Lotus Light.

Reymond, P. Dictionary of Biblical Hebrew & Aramean. 1104p. (FRE & HEB.). 1991. 125.00 (0-8288-6920-0, 2204044636) Fr & Eur.

Reymond, Robert L. Jesus, Divine Messiah: The New Testament Witness. LC 89-35362. 1990. pap. 17.99 (0-87552-402-8) Presby & Reformed.

Reyn, J. W., tr. see Bulakh, B. M.

Reyna, Jose L., et al. Understanding Mexico: Historical Perspective & Future Potential. Blachman, Morris M. et al, eds. LC 85-62047. (Papers on International Issues: No. 7). 63p. (Orig.). 1985. pap. 5.00 (0-935082-09-3) Southern Ctr Intl Stud.

Reyna, Rene. El Sol Tiene Manchas. LC 92-71445. (Coleccion Caniqui Ser.). 177p. (Orig.). (SPA.). 1992. pap. 19.95 (0-89729-643-5) Ediciones.

***Reyna, Ruth, ed.** Dictionary of Oriental Philosophy. 419p. 1993. 57.50x (81-215-0118-0, Pub. by M Manoharial II) Coronet Bks.

Reyna, S. P. & Downs, R. E., eds. Studying War: Anthropological Perspectives. LC 93-32710. (War & Society Ser.: Vol. 2). 1993. text ed. 38.00 (2-88124-633-8); pap. text ed. 19.00 (2-88124-634-6) Gordon & Breach.

Reyna, S. P., jt. ed. see Downs, R. E.

Reyna, Stephen P. Wars without End: The Political Economy of a Precolonial African State. LC 89-40233. (Illus.). 222p. 1990. text ed. 35.00 (0-87451-505-X) U Pr of New Eng.

Reynal, Vicente. Civilizaciones de Occidente: Introduccion a las Humanidades. 4th ed. (Textbook Ser.). (Illus.). 470p. (Orig.). (SPA.). 1991. reprint ed. pap. text ed. 17.95 (1-56328-006-X) Edit Plaza Mayor.

— Introduccion a las Humanidades. LC 90-43241. 85p. (SPA.). 1990. pap. 4.75 (0-8477-2833-1) U of PR Pr.

Reynal, Vicente, ed. see Seneca, Lucius Annaeus.

Reynalds, Jeremy. Homeless in America: The Solution. LC 93-80788. 208p. 1994. 9.99 (1-56384-063-4) Huntington Hse.

Reynard, Alan M., jt. auth. see Smith, Cedric M.

Reynard, Elizabeth. The Mutinous Wind. (Illus.). 224p. 1985. reprint ed. pap. 7.95 (0-940160-29-3) Parnassus Imprints.

Reynard, K. W., jt. ed. see Barry, T., I.

Reynard, Keith W., ed. U. K. Materials Information Sources. 2nd ed. 432p. (C). 1992. pap. 42.95x (0-85072-293-4, Pub. by Design Council Bks UK) Ashgate Pub Co.

Reynard, Sue, ed. Fundamentals of Fourth Generation Management. (Illus.). 378p. (Orig.). 1993. write for info. (0-9622264-6-7) Joiner Assoc.

Reynard, Sue, ed. see Scholtes, Peter R., et al.

Reynard, Sue, ed. see Scholtes, Peter R.

Reynarowych, Z., tr. see Sachs, L.

Reynaud, Joyce. Samoyeds. (Illus.). 128p. 1980. 11.95 (0-86622-815-2, KW-072) TFH Pubns.

***Reynaud, Patricia.** Fiction et Failite: Economie et Metaphores dans Madame Bovary. (American University Studies, Series II, Romance Languages & Literature: Vol. 202). 233p. (FRE.). (C). 1994. text ed. 42.95 (0-8204-2047-6) P Lang Pubs.

Reyneke, Johan P., et al. Introduction to Orthognathic Surgery: A Color Atlas. Hacke, Gregory, ed. (Illus.). 125p. 1991. text ed. 55.00 (0-912791-84-5) Ishiyaku Euro.

Reynells, M. Louise, et al. The American Fur Trade: A Bibliography of Sources in English. (Stokvis Studies in Historical Chronology & Thought). 191p. Date not set. lib. bdg. write for info. (0-89370-333-8) Borgo Pr.

— The American Fur Trade: A Bibliography of Sources in English. (Stokvis Studies in Historical Chronology & Thought: No. 9). 191p. Date not set. pap. write for info. (0-89370-433-4) Borgo Pr.

Reyner, J. H. Gurdjieff in Action. 117p. 1982. 24.95 (0-04-294117-2) Routledge Chapman & Hall.

***Reynhout, Robert.** God's Wisdom for Handling Money. Simons, Cheryl, ed. 192p. (Orig.). 1995. pap. write for info. (0-9646412-0-8) R A Reynhout & Assocs.

Reyniak, J. Victor & Lauersen, Niels H., eds. Principles of Microsurgical Techniques in Infertility. LC 81-3045. 310p. 1982. 65.00 (0-306-40781-7, Plenum Med Bk) Plenum.

Reynierse, James H., ed. Current Issues in Animal Learning: A Colloquium. LC 78-98389. (Illus.). 402p. reprint ed. pap. 114.60 (0-8357-2944-3, 2039200) Bks Demand.

Reynold, ed. Anthology of Sinhalese Literature of the Twentieth Century. (C). 1994. pap. 19.95 (0-904404-53-6, Pub. by Curzon Pr UK) Humanities.

Reynold, C. S. Vertical Structure in Aquatic Environments & Its Impact on Tropical Likages & Nutrient Fluxes. Watanage, Y., ed. (Advances in Limnology Ser.: No. 35). (Illus.). 159p. 1992. pap. 60.00 (3-510-47036-2, Pub. by E Schweizerbartsche GW) Lubrecht & Cramer.

Reynold, Ralph, ed. see Purcell, Wayne.

Reynolds. Conference in Distributed Simulation, 1985. (Simulations Series of Bks.). 112p. 1985. 40.00 (0-685-66815-0, SS15-2) Soc Computer Sim.

— Governing America. (C). 1991. text ed. 53.50 (0-06-045393-1) HarpCollege.

— Governing America: Study Guide. (C). 1991. 19.50 (0-06-045394-X) HarpCollege.

— Hollywood Power Stats: The Essential Facts & Figures of the Motion Picture Industry 1995. 1995. pap. text ed. 18.95 (0-9638748-5-3) Cineview Pubng.

— Medical-Surgical SR Outline. 1993. 18.95 (0-944132-88-X) Skidmore Roth Pub.

— Multimedia Training: Developing Technology-Based Systems. 1995. 45.00 (0-07-912012-1) McGraw.

— Strength for the Storm: Spiritual Lessons from Chinese Preachers. 1988. pap. 4.95 (9971-972-62-X) OMF Bks.

— An Uncharted Journey. 5.00 (0-8065-0337-8, Citadel Pr) Carol Pub Group.

— Unit Operations & Processes in Environmental Engineering. 1982. text ed. 70.95 (0-8185-0493-5) PWS Pubs.

Reynolds & Michas. Principles of Economics, Macro: Personal Learning Aid. 4th ed. (Plaid Ser.). 1983. pap. 13.00 (0-87094-430-4) Irwin Prof Pubng.

Reynolds, jt. auth. see Abrams.

Reynolds, jt. auth. see Kirkpatrick.

Reynolds, jt. auth. see Richman.

Reynolds, A. G. Bilingualism, Multiculturalism, & Second Language Learning: The McGill Conference in Honour of Wallace E. Lambert. 288p. (C). 1991. text ed. 49.95 (0-8058-0694-6) L Erlbaum Assocs.

Reynolds, A. H. Cognac & Collard Greens. 138p. (Orig.). 1986. 7.00 (0-938887-00-9) Ngomas Gourd.

Reynolds, A. J. Turbulent Flows in Engineering. LC 73-8464. (Illus.). 478p. reprint ed. pap. 136.30 (0-317-11132-9, 2051617) Bks Demand.

Reynolds, A. L. Do Black Women Hate Black Men? 1994. 18.95 (0-8038-9360-4) Hastings.

***Reynolds, A. Wanjiku.** A Gathering of Hands. 172p. 1991. 10.00 (1-878065-00-9) Ngomas Gourd.

Reynolds, Alfred. Jesus Versus Christianity. 314p. (C). 1988. pap. 50.00 (0-946101-02-7, Cambridge Intl) St Mut.

Reynolds, Alice W. & Steckler, Del, eds. Practical Aspects of Blood Administration. LC 86-17470. 1986. text ed. 7.00 (0-915355-30-2) Am Assn Blood.

Reynolds, Althea C. & Brunetti, Argentina. Teatro, Prosa, Poesia. (Illus.). 160p. 1982. pap. text ed. 27.50 (0-915838-12-5) Anma Libri.

Reynolds, Angus. Building Multimedia Performance Support Systems. 1994. text ed., disk 45.00 (0-07-911684-1) McGraw.

— The Trainer's Dictionary: HRD Terms, Abbreviations, & Acronyms. 350p. 1993. pap. 19.95 (0-87425-219-9) Human Res Dev Pr.

Reynolds, Angus, ed. Technology Transfer: A Project Guide for International HRD. LC 83-12865. (Illus.). 145p. 1984. 21.00 (0-934634-68-8) Intl Human Res.

Reynolds, Angus & Anderson, Ronald H., eds. Selecting & Developing Media for Instruction. 3rd rev. ed. (Illus.). 288p. 1992. pap. 39.95 (0-442-00653-5) Van Nos Reinhold.

Reynolds, Angus & Nadler, Leonard. Global HRD Consultant's & Practitioner's Handbook. 477p. 1993. 49.95 (0-87425-180-X) Human Res Dev Pr.

Reynolds, Angus, jt. auth. see Marguardt, Michael.

Reynolds, Annette. Always & Forever: A Wedding Treasury. 1992. 7.98 (0-88486-060-4) Arrowood Pr.

— The Christmas Baby. (Board Bks.). (Illus.). 12p. (J). (ps-1). 1987. bds. 6.99 (0-7459-1368-7) Lion USA.

— The First Christmas Presents. (Board Bks.). (Illus.). 12p. (J). (ps-1). 1987. bds. 6.99 (0-7459-1369-5) Lion USA.

Reynolds, Annie & Gordon, Albert. Stage to Yosemite: Recollections of Wawona's Albert Gordon. Vocelka, Mary & Bentle, Jane, eds. (Illus.). 180p. (Orig.). 1994. pap. 19.95 (0-9639148-0-4) A L Reynolds.

Reynolds, Arlene, ed. The Civil War Memories of Elizabeth Bacon Custer: Reconstructed from Her Notes & Diaries. LC 94-1759. 1994. 24.95 (0-292-71168-9) U of Tex Pr.

Reynolds, Art. Logg'n Fever. (Illus.). 80p. 1982. pap. 2.95 (0-939116-07-3) Frontier OR.

***Reynolds, Audree.** High Acuity Nursing Care. (Outline Ser.). (Illus.). 300p. (C). 1994. pap. text ed. 16.95 (1-56930-028-3) Skidmore Roth Pub.

Reynolds, Audrey L. Explorations in Basic Writing. LC 92-50048. 261p. (C). 1993. pap. text ed. 16.00 (0-312-06664-3) St Martin.

Reynolds-Ball, E. A. Paris in Splendor, 2 vols., Set. 1976. lib. bdg. 200.00 (0-8490-2412-9) Gordon Pr.

Reynolds, Barbara. And Still We Rise. 1988. 14.95 (0-944347-02-9) USA Today Bks.

— The Concise Cambridge Italian Dictionary. 792p. (ITA.). 1975. pap. 14.00 (0-14-051064-8, Penguin Bks) Viking Penguin.

— Dorothy L. Sayers: Her Life & Soul. (Illus.). 416p. 1993. 25.95 (0-312-09787-5) St Martin.

— The Passionate Intellect: Dorothy L. Sayers' Encounter with Dante. LC 88-13930. 284p. 1989. 24.00x (0-87338-373-7) Kent St U Pr.

Reynolds, Barbara, tr. see Ariosto, Ludovico.

Reynolds, Barbara, tr. see Dante Alighieri.

Reynolds, Barbara A. Jesse Jackson: America's David. rev. ed. LC 85-80985. Orig. Title: Jesse Jackson-The Man, the Movement, the Myth. 489p. (Orig.). 1985. 17.95 (0-935707-00-X); pap. 11.95 (0-935707-01-8) JFJ Assocs.

Reynolds, Barrie & Stott, Margaret A. Material Anthropology: Contemporary Approaches to Material Culture. (Illus.). 242p. (Orig.). 1987. lib. bdg. 47.50 (0-8191-6543-3); pap. text ed. 22.00 (0-8191-6544-1) U Pr of Amer.

***Reynolds, Barry & Berryman, John.** Beyond Trout: A Flyfishing Guide. (Illus.). 176p. (Orig.). 1995. 23.00 (1-55566-155-6); pap. 16.95 (1-55566-156-4) Johnson Bks.

— Pike on the Fly: The Flyfishing Guide to Northerns, Tigers, & Muskies. LC 93-38057. (Illus.). 160p. (Orig.). 1993. pap. 16.95 (1-55566-113-0) Johnson Bks.

Reynolds, Beatrice. Proponents of Limited Monarchy in Sixteenth Century France. LC 68-58616. (Columbia University. Studies in the Social Sciences: No. 334). reprint ed. 22.50 (0-404-51334-4) AMS Pr.

Reynolds, Becky. Graveyard Cleaning-Off Day. 41p. 1991. pap. 2.50 (0-87129-001-4, G54) Dramatic Pub.

Reynolds, Ben, tr. see Kostov, Vladimir.

Reynolds, Ben, tr. see Le Roy-Ladurie, Emmanuel.

***Reynolds, Ben, et al.** Writing Instruction for Verbally Talented Youth: The Johns Hopkins Model. rev. ed. 204p. (YA). 1994. teacher ed, pap. text ed. 25.00 (1-881622-14-2) JHU Ctr Talent Youth.

R

An Asterisk (*) at the beginning of an entry indicates that the title is appearing in BIP for the first time.

Reynolds, Bertha C. Between Client & Community: A Study in Responsibility in Social Case Work. LC 82-81785. (NASW Classics Ser.). 128p. 1982. reprint ed. pap. text ed. 8.95 (0-87101-102-6) Natl Assn Soc Wkrs.
— Learning & Teaching in the Practice of Social Work. LC 65-18828. (NASW Classics Ser.). 390p. 1985. reprint ed. pap. 21.95 (0-87101-137-9) Natl Assn Soc Wkrs.
— Social Work & Social Living: Explorations in Philosophy & Practice. LC 75-29534. (NASW Classics Ser.). 176p. 1975. reprint ed. pap. 8.95 (0-87101-071-2) Natl Assn Soc Wkrs.
— Uncharted Journey: Fifty Years in Social Work by One of Its Great Teachers. LC 90-28265. 352p. 1991. reprint ed. 21.95 (0-87101-193-X) Natl Assn Soc Wkrs.
Reynolds, Bill. Bodybuilding for Beginners. (Illus.). 144p. (Orig.). 1983. pap. 11.95 (0-8092-5499-9) Contemp Bks.
— The Complete Weight Training Book. LC 75-32443. (Illus.). 222p. 1979. pap. 4.95 (0-89037-149-0) Anderson World.
— Fall River Dreams: A Team's Search for a Town's Soul. 384p. 1994. 22.95 (0-312-11271-8) St Martin.
— Lost Summer: The '67 Red Sox & the Impossible Dream. 328p. 1993. mass mkt. 5.50 (0-446-36427-4) Warner Bks.
— Mustangs: The Classic American Sports Car. 1993. 12.99 (0-517-07292-0) Random Hse Value.
— Weight Training for Beginners, Vol. 1. 1982. pap. 8.95 (0-8092-5728-9) Contemp Bks.
Reynolds, Bill & Jayde, Negrita. Sliced: State-of-the-Art Nutrition for Building Lean Body Mass. (Illus.). 256p. (Orig.). 1991. pap. 14.95 (0-8092-4116-1) Contemp Bks.
***Reynolds, Bill & Rand, Ritch.** The Cowboy Hat Book. LC 94-33734. (Illus.). 96p. 1995. pap. 17.95 (0-87905-659-2) Gibbs Smith Pub.
Reynolds, Bill & Vedral, Joyce L. Supercut: Nutrition for the Ultimate Physique. (Illus.). 320p. (Orig.). 1985. pap. 13.95 (0-8092-5387-9) Contemp Bks.
Reynolds, Bill, jt. auth. see Langer, Anja.
Reynolds, Bill, jt. auth. see McLish, Rachel.
Reynolds, Bill, jt. auth. see Napoli, Dede.
Reynolds, Bill, jt. auth. see Pirie, Lynne.
Reynolds, Bill, jt. auth. see Platz, Tom.
Reynolds, Bill, jt. auth. see Sprague, Ken.
Reynolds, Bill, ed. see Weider, Joe.
Reynolds, Bill, et al. Gold's Gym Complete Training & Nutrition Encyclopedia. (Illus.). 272p. 1992. pap. 14.95 (0-8092-3947-7) Contemp Bks.
— Gold's Gym Nutrition Bible. 224p. (Orig.). 1986. pap. 13.95 (0-8092-5188-4) Contemp Bks.
Reynolds, Billie I. Family Care Package. 1985. 5.00 (0-915807-01-7) Hidden Valley Bks.
— Planning Is the Key. 1983. 10.00 (0-915807-00-9) Hidden Valley Bks.
Reynolds, Blair. The Relationship of Calvin to Process Theology As Seen Through His Sermons. LC 93-32120. (Texts & Studies in Religion: Vol. 61). 112p. 1993. text ed. 59.95 (0-7734-9355-7) E Mellen.
— Toward a Process Pneumatology. LC 88-43326. 216p. 1990. 34.50 (0-941664-97-X) Susquehanna U Pr.
Reynolds, Blair, tr. see Benz, Ernst.
Reynolds, Blair, tr. see Calvin, Jean.
Reynolds, Blair, tr. see Descartes, Rene.
Reynolds, Blair, tr. see Heyer, Henri.
***Reynolds, Bob & Price Waterhouse, Staff.** Understanding Derivatives: What You Really Need to Know about the Wild-Card of Finance. (Illus.). 256p. 1995. 30.00 (0-273-61378-2, Pub. by Pitman Pub UK) Natl Bk Netwk.
Reynolds, Bonnie H. Space, Time & Crisis: The Theatre of Rene Marques. LC 87-61514. 181p. 1988. 20.00 (0-938972-13-8) Spanish Lit Pubns.
Reynolds, Bonnie J., jt. auth. see Choudhury, Bikram.
Reynolds, Brenda. Research Support & Federal Government Financing for Medicine with a Dictionary of Subjects, Research Index & Bibliography. Bartone, John C., ed. LC 83-70084. 141p. 1983. 34.50 (0-88164-038-7); pap. 29.50 (0-88164-039-5) ABBE Pubs Assn.
Reynolds, Brenda, et al. Psychological Improvements for Corporate Management with High Impact Foreign Words & Phrases. Bartone, J. C., ed. LC 83-70088. 142p. 1982. 24.50 (0-941864-38-3); pap. 19.50 (0-941864-39-1) ABBE Pubs Assn.
Reynolds, Brenda M. Curriculums in Health Sciences: Subject Analysis with Research Bibliography. LC 84-45650. 150p. 1985. 39.50 (0-88164-230-4); pap. 34.50 (0-88164-231-2) ABBE Pubs Assn.
— Human Abortion: Guide for Medicine, Science & Research. LC 83-46112. 147p. 1984. 37.50 (0-88164-158-8); pap. 34.50 (0-88164-159-6) ABBE Pubs Assn.
Reynolds, Brenda Mary. Personnel Management: Medical Subject Analysis & Research Guide. LC 83-45543. 130p. 1984. 37.50 (0-88164-102-2); pap. 34.50 (0-88164-103-0) ABBE Pubs Assn.
Reynolds, Brian. A Chance to Serve: Peer Ministers' Handbook. (Illus.). 84p. (Orig.). 1983. pap. 4.95 (0-88489-154-2); teacher ed, pap. 9.95 (0-88489-153-4) St Marys.
Reynolds, Bruce, ed. Chinese Economic Reform: How Far, How Fast? 233p. 1988. text ed. 53.00 (0-12-587045-0) Acad Pr.
Reynolds, Bruce L., ed. see Chinese Economic System Reform Research Institute Staff.
Reynolds, Bruce L., jt. ed. see Kim, Ilpyong J.
Reynolds, Bruford S. Becoming Self Sufficient with Dollars & Sense. 1977. pap. 3.95 (0-89036-070-7) Hawkes Pub Inc.
— How to Survive with Sprouting. 112p. 1970. pap. 4.95 (0-89036-028-6) Hawkes Pub Inc.
Reynolds, Burt. My Life. (Illus.). 352p. 1994. 22.95 (0-7868-6130-4) Hyperion.
Reynolds, Burt & Chadwick, Bruce. Seminole Seasons: Florida State's Rise to the National Title. 178p. 1994. 18.95 (0-87833-869-1); pap. 10.95 (0-87833-868-3) Taylor Pub.
Reynolds, C. E. Letters Plus: Communications on the Job. 136p. 1986. pap. text ed. 7.56 (0-07-052057-7) McGraw.
Reynolds, C. E. & Steedman, J. C. Examples of the Design of Reinforced Concrete Buildings to BS8110. 4th ed. (Illus.). 336p. 1992. pap. 69.95 (0-442-31417-5) Chapman & Hall.
— Examples of the Design of Reinforced Concrete Buildings to BS8110. 4th ed. (Illus.). 320p. 1991. 79.95 (0-419-16990-3, E & FN Spon); pap. write for info. (0-419-17000-6, E & FN Spon) Routledge Chapman & Hall.
— Reinforced Concrete Designer's Handbook. (Illus.). 500p. 1988. text ed. 95.00 (0-419-14530-3, E & FN Spon) Routledge Chapman & Hall.
Reynolds, C. S. The Ecology of Freshwater Photoplankton. LC 83-7211. (Cambridge Studies in Ecology). (Illus.). 300p. 1984. pap. 34.95 (0-521-28222-5) Cambridge U Pr.
Reynolds, C. W. & Wiltrout, R. H., eds. Functions of the Natural Immune System. LC 88-22488. (Illus.). 506p. 1989. 125.00 (0-306-42951-9, Plenum Pr) Plenum.
Reynolds, Carl L., jt. auth. see Phipps, Lloyd J.
Reynolds, Caroline. Dimensions in Professional Development. 4th ed. LC 92-18247. 1993. text ed. 34.95 (0-538-61416-1) S-W Pub.
Reynolds, Carolyn. The Book of Lovers: Men Who Excite Women, Women Who Excite Men. LC 91-46568. (Popular Astrology Ser.). 464p. 1992. pap. 14.95 (0-87542-289-6) Llewellyn Pubns.
— El Libro Para Amantes: Los Hombres Que Excitan a las Mujeres, las Mujeres Que Excitan a los Hombres. 480p. 1995. pap. 20.00 (1-56718-569-X) Llewellyn Pubns.
Reynolds, Catherine. The Highwayman. (Regency Romance Ser.). 1993. mass mkt. 2.99 (0-373-31209-1, 1-31209-9) Harlequin Bks.
Reynolds, Cecil R., ed. Cognitive Assessment: A Multidisciplinary Perspective. (Perspectives on Individual Differences Ser.). (Illus.). 265p. (C). 1994. 45.00 (0-306-44434-8, Plenum Pr) Plenum.
Reynolds, Cecil R. & Brown, Robert T., eds. Perspectives on Bias in Mental Testing. (Perspectives on Individual Differences Ser.). 594p. 1984. 80.00 (0-306-41529-1, Plenum Pr) Plenum.
Reynolds, Cecil R. & Fletcher-Janzen, E., eds. Handbook of Clinical Child Neuropsychology. LC 88-39536. (Critical Issues in Neuropsychology Ser.). (Illus.). 612p. 1989. 85.00 (0-306-42879-2, Plenum Pr) Plenum.
Reynolds, Cecil R. & Fletcher-Janzen, Elaine. Concise Encyclopedia of Special Education. 1215p. 1990. text ed. 135.00 (0-471-51527-2) Wiley.
Reynolds, Cecil R. & Kamphaus, Randy W., eds. Handbook of Psychological & Educational Assessment of Children: Intelligence & Achievement. LC 89-38018. 814p. 1990. lib. bdg. 75.00 (0-89862-391-X) Guilford Pr.
— Handbook of Psychological & Educational Assessment of Children: Personality Behavior & Context. LC 89-38018. 618p. 1990. lib. bdg. 65.00 (0-89862-392-8) Guilford Pr.
Reynolds, Cecil R. & Mann, Lester, eds. Encyclopedia of Special Education: Reference for the Education of the Handicapped & Other Exceptional Children & Adults, Vol. 3. LC 86-33975. iiiv, 1824p. 1987. text ed. 395.00 (0-471-82858-0) Wiley.
Reynolds, Cecil R. & Willson, Victor L., eds. Methodological & Statistical Advances in the Study of Individual Differences. LC 85-17042. (Perspectives on Individual Differences Ser.). 466p. 1985. 75.00 (0-306-41962-9, Plenum Pr) Plenum.
Reynolds, Cecil R., jt. ed. see Dean, R. S.
Reynolds, Cecil R., jt. auth. see Gutkin, Terry B.
Reynolds, Cecil R., jt. auth. see Kamphaus, Randy W.
Reynolds, Cecil R., et al. School Psychology: Essentials of Theory & Practice. LC 83-21918. 496p. (C). 1984. Net. text ed. write for info. (0-471-08327-5) Wiley.
Reynolds, Charles. The Politics of War: A Study of the Rationality of Violence. 256p. 1989. text ed. 45.00 (0-312-02022-8) St Martin.
— The World of States: An Introduction to Explanation & Theory. 304p. 1992. 64.95 (1-85278-133-5, Pub. by E Elgar Pub UK); pap. 22.95 (1-85278-134-3, Pub. by E Elgar Pub UK) Ashgate Pub Co.
Reynolds, Charles & Reynolds, Regina. One Hundred Years of Magic Posters. (Illus.). 1977. pap. 7.95 (0-685-85024-2) Darien Hse.
***Reynolds, Charles H., et al, eds.** Computer-Aided Molecular Design: Applications in Agrochemicals, Materials, & Pharmaceuticals. LC 95-2511. (Symposium Ser.: No. 589). (Illus.). 448p. 1995. 109.95 (0-8412-3160-5) Am Chemical.
Reynolds, Cheryl L. & Leininger, Madeleine. Madeleine Leininger: Cultural Care Diversity & Universality Theory. (Notes on Nursing Theories Ser.: Vol. 8). (Illus.). 64p. (C). 1993. text ed. 18.95 (0-8039-5097-7); pap. text ed. 8.95 (0-8039-5098-5) Sage.
Reynolds, Christopher. Hollywood Power Stats: The Essential Facts & Figures of the Motion Picture Industry. LC 93-73776. (Illus.). 208p. (Orig.). 1993. pap. 18.95 (0-9638748-4-5) Cineview Pubng.
— Public Health Law in Australia. 290p. 1995. pap. 39.00 (1-86287-158-2, Pub. by Federation Pr AU) W W Gaunt.
Reynolds, Christopher, ed. Beethoven Forum, Vol. 2. (Illus.). ix, 236p. 1993. 50.00 (0-8032-3909-2) U of Nebr Pr.
— Beethoven Forum 4. (Illus.). 320p. 1995. text ed. write for info. (0-8032-3916-5) U of Nebr Pr.
Reynolds, Christopher, et al, eds. Beethoven Forum, Vol. 1. (Illus.). xiv, 250p. 1992. 50.00 (0-8032-3906-8) U of Nebr Pr.
***Reynolds, Christopher A.** Papal Patronage & the Music of St. Peter's, 1380-1513. LC 94-5292. 410p. 1994. 60.00 (0-520-08212-5) U CA Pr.
Reynolds, Clark G. Admiral John H. Towers: The Struggle for Naval Air Supremacy. LC 91-14694. 576p. 1991. 39.95 (0-87021-031-9) Naval Inst Pr.
— Command of the Sea: The History & Strategy of Maritime Empires, 2 vols. LC 83-6129. 358p. 1983. reprint ed. Vol. 2 358p. text ed. 31.50 (0-89874-630-2) Krieger.
— Command of the Sea: The History & Strategy of Maritime Empires, No. 2. LC 83-6129. 1983. reprint ed. 31.50 (0-89874-629-9) Krieger.
— Command of the Sea: The History & Strategy of Maritime Empires, 2 vols., Set. LC 83-6129. 1983. reprint ed. text ed. 64.50 (0-89874-646-9) Krieger.
— The Fast Carriers: The Forging of an Air Navy. LC 91-39437. (Illus.). 576p. 1992. reprint ed. 32.95 (1-55750-701-5) Naval Inst Pr.
— The Fighting Lady: New Yorktown in the Pacific War. LC 86-61530. (Illus.). 364p. 1986. pap. 14.95 (0-933126-78-6) Pictorial Hist.
— History & the Sea: Essays on Maritime Strategies. Still, William N., Jr., ed. (Studies in Maritime History). 240p. 1989. text ed. 29.95 (0-87249-614-7) U of SC Pr.
— The Saga of Smokey Stover. LC 78-64485. 1978. 6.00 (0-937684-06-6) Tradd St Pr.
— War in the Pacific. 1990. 15.99 (0-517-69321-6) Random Hse Value.
Reynolds, Clark W. & Tello, Carlos, eds. U. S.-Mexico Relations: Economic & Social Aspects. LC 81-86450. xvi, 373p. 1983. reprint ed. 47.50 (0-8047-1163-1); reprint ed. pap. 16.95 (0-8047-1286-7) Stanford U Pr.
Reynolds, Clark W., et al, eds. The Dynamics of North American Trade & Investment: Canada, Mexico, & the United States. LC 90-41907. 300p. 1991. 42.50 (0-8047-1864-4) Stanford U Pr.
Reynolds, Clay. Franklin's Crossing. 688p. 1993. pap. 5.99 (0-451-17554-9, Sig) NAL-Dutton.
— Rage. 432p. 1994. 4.99 (0-451-40350-9, Sig) NAL-Dutton.
Reynolds, Clay, ed. & intro. Taking Stock: A Larry McMurtry Casebook. LC 88-43316. (Southwest Life & Letters Ser.). 448p. 1989. 26.95x (0-87074-291-4); pap. 15.95 (0-87074-261-2) SMU Press.
***Reynolds, Clay & Schein, Marie.** A Hundred Years of Heroes: A History of the Southwestern Exposition & Livestock Show. (Illus.). 352p. 1995. 19.95 (0-87565-145-3) Tex Christian.
Reynolds Cornell, Regine. Witnessing an Era: Georgette de Montenay & the Emblemes ou Devises Chrestiennes. LC 87-61487. (Illus.). 137p. 1987. lib. bdg. 19.95 (0-917786-53-X) Summa Pubns.
Reynolds-Cornell, Regine, tr. see Marguerite of Angouleme.
Reynolds, Craig, jt. auth. see Kiley, Martin D.
Reynolds, Craig J. Thai Radical Discourse: The Real Face of Thai Feudalism Today. (Studies on Southeast Asia: No. 3). (Illus.). 192p. (Orig.). (C). 1994. pap. text ed. 16.00 (0-87727-702-8) Cornell SE Asia.
— Thai Radical Discourse: The Real Face of Thai Feudalism Today. (Studies on Southeast Asia). (Illus.). 192p. (Orig.). reprint ed. pap. 54.80 (0-8357-3117-0, 2039375) Bks Demand.
Reynolds, Craig J., ed. see Cushman, Jennifer.
Reynolds, Cuyler. Hudson-Mohwawk Genealogical & Family Memoirs, 4 vols. (Illus.). 1847p. 1994. reprint ed. lib. bdg. 195.00 (0-8328-3991-4) Higginson Bk Co.
Reynolds, D. Chase. Old Masters of the West. LC 92-73119. (Illus.). 120p. (Orig.). 1993. pap. 14.95 (1-56626-002-7) Country Rds.
Reynolds, D. R. & Taylor, J. W., eds. The Fungal Holomorph: Mitotic, Meiotic & Pleomorphic Speciation in Fungal Systematics. 375p. 1993. text ed. 76.00 (0-85198-865-2) CAB Intl.
Reynolds, D. W. The Truth, the Whole Truth & Nothing But... A Police Officer's Guide to Testifying in Court. 90p. (C). 1990. text ed. 23.95x (0-398-05656-0) C C Thomas.
***Reynolds, D. William.** Powerbuilder Desktop: The Authorized Guide. 1995. disk 39.95 (0-201-40886-4) Addison-Wesley.
Reynolds, Dale, ed. see Fountain, Thomas E.
Reynolds, Dana. Be an Angel. 1994. 16.95 (0-671-89694-6) S&S Trade.
Reynolds, David. Britannia Overruled: British Policy & World Power in the 20th Century. (Studies in Modern History). (Illus.). 360p. (C). 1991. text ed. 66.50 (0-582-08427-X, 78924); pap. text ed. 28.50 (0-582-55276-1, 78925) Longman.
— The Creation of the Anglo-American Alliance, 1937-1941: A Study in Competitive Cooperation. LC 81-16503. 411p. reprint ed. pap. 117.20 (0-7837-6864-8, 2046693) Bks Demand.
— Handle with Care: Balanced Guidelines for Raising Today's Children. 298p. (Orig.). Date not set. pap. 9.95 (1-877917-11-7) Alpha Bible Pubns.
— Rich Relations: The American "Occupation" of Britain, 1942-1945. LC 94-13810. 1995. 30.00 (0-679-42161-0) Random.
Reynolds, David, ed. The Origins of the Cold War in Europe: International Perspectives. 352p. 1994. 27.50 (0-300-05892-6) Yale U Pr.
— Studying School Effectiveness. 216p. 1985. text ed. 44.00 (1-85000-023-9, Falmer Pr); pap. text ed. 25.00 (1-85000-024-7, Falmer Pr) Taylor & Francis.
Reynolds, David & Cuttance, Peter, eds. School Effectiveness: Research, Policy & Practice. (School Development Ser.). 208p. 1992. text ed. 65.00 (0-304-32295-4); pap. text ed. 24.95 (0-304-32276-8) Cassell.
Reynolds, David & Hargreaves, Andy. Education Policy: Controversies & Critiques. 250p. 1989. 75.00 (1-85000-482-X, Falmer Pr); pap. 33.00 (1-85000-483-8, Falmer Pr) Taylor & Francis.
Reynolds, David, ed. see Chapman, Judith, et al.
Reynolds, David, ed. see Dalin, Per.
Reynolds, David, jt. auth. see Dimbleby, David.
Reynolds, David, ed. see Ribbins, Peter & Whale, Elizabeth.
Reynolds, David, ed. see Scheerens, Jaap.
Reynolds, David, ed. see Wallace, Mike & McMahon, Agnes.
Reynolds, David, et al. Advances in School Effectiveness Research & Practice. LC 94-15705. 1994. text ed. 72.00 (0-08-042392-2, Pergamon Pr) Elsevier.
Reynolds, David, et al, eds. Allies at War: The Soviet, American, & British Experience, 1939-1945. LC 93-22957. (Franklin & Eleanor Roosevelt Institute Series on Diplomatic & Economic History: Vol. 7). 1994. text ed. 59.95 (0-312-10259-3) St Martin.
— The Comprehensive Experiment: A Comparison of the Selective & Non-Selective School Organization. (Education Policy Perspectives Ser.: Vol. 4). 188p. 1987. 55.00 (1-85000-210-X, Falmer Pr); pap. 33.00 (1-85000-211-8, Falmer Pr) Taylor & Francis.
Reynolds, David K. Constructive Living. 128p. 1984. pap. 9.50 (0-8248-0871-1) UH Pr.
— Even in Summer the Ice Doesn't Melt: Japan's Morita Therapy: Learn to Overcome Anxiety. LC 86-12260. 1986. 7.95 (0-688-06744-1, Quill) Morrow.
— Flowing Bridges, Quiet Waters: Japanese Psychotherapies, Morita & Naikan. LC 88-20100. (Transpersonal & Humanistic Psychology Ser.). 187p. 1989. 59.50 (0-88706-963-0); pap. 19.95 (0-88706-964-9) State U NY Pr.
— A Handbook for Constructive Living. LC 95-2360. 1995. write for info. (0-688-14226-5) Morrow.
— Playing Ball on Running Water: Living Morita Psychotherapy - The Japanese Way to Building a Better Life. LC 84-8399. 160p. 1984. pap. 7.95 (0-688-03913-8, Quill) Morrow.
— Pools of Lodging for the Moon: Strategy for a Positive Life-Style. 204p. 1992. pap. 7.00 (0-688-11278-1, Quill) Morrow.
— The Quiet Therapies: Japanese Pathways to Personal Growth. LC 80-17611. 144p. 1980. reprint ed. pap. 8.95 (0-8248-0801-0) UH Pr.
— Rainbow Rising from a Stream. LC 92-13871. 1992. pap. 8.00 (0-688-11967-0, Quill) Morrow.
— Reflections on the Tao te Ching: Practical Wisdom for Everyday Life. LC 92-1665. 1993. 15.00 (0-688-12258-2) Morrow.
— A Thousand Waves: A Sensible Life Style for Sensitive People. LC 89-14284. 192p. 1990. 17.95 (0-688-08157-6, Quill); pap. 6.95 (0-688-09434-1, Quill) Morrow.
— Water Bears No Scars. LC 87-7036. 192p. (Orig.). 1987. pap. 10.00 (0-688-07448-0, Quill) Morrow.
Reynolds, David K., ed. Plunging Through the Clouds: Constructive Living Currents. LC 91-45686. 199p. (C). 1993. 59.50 (0-7914-1313-6); pap. 19.95 (0-7914-1314-4) State U NY Pr.
Reynolds, David K. & Farberow, Norman L. Suicide: Inside & Out. LC 75-22661. 1976. pap. 14.00 (0-520-03506-2, CAL 370) U CA Pr.
Reynolds, David K., jt. ed. see Kalish, Richard A.
Reynolds, David K., tr. see Kora, Takehisa.
Reynolds, David S. Beneath the American Renaissance: The Subversive Imagination in the Age of Emerson & Melville. LC 87-40491. (Illus.). 640p. 1988. 40.00 (0-394-54448-X) Knopf.
— Beneath the American Renaissance: The Subversive Imagination in the Age of Emerson & Melville. LC 89-31146. (Illus.). 656p. 1989. pap. 19.50 (0-674-06565-4) HUP.
— Faith in Fiction: The Emergence of Religious Literature in America. LC 80-20885. 280p. (C). 1981. 50.00 (0-674-29172-7) HUP.
— Walt Whitman's America: A Cultural Biography. LC 94-12841. (Illus.). 671p. 1995. 35.00 (0-394-58023-0) Knopf.
Reynolds, David S., ed. see Lippard, George.
***Reynolds, Dee.** Symbolist Aesthetics & Early Abstract Art: Sites of Imaginary Space. (Cambridge Studies in French: No. 51). (Illus.). 320p. (C). 1995. 59.95 (0-521-42102-0) Cambridge U Pr.
Reynolds, Dee, jt. ed. see Florence, Penny.
Reynolds, Delicia & Taylor, John C. Troubleshooting Peachtree Complete Accounting Version 6. (Illus.). 400p. (Orig.). 1993. pap. write for info. (1-879656-04-3) Delicia AL.
— Using Peachtree Complete Accounting Version 6. (Illus.). 480p. (Orig.). 1993. pap. write for info. (1-879656-03-5) Delicia AL.
Reynolds, Dennis. Library Automation: Issues & Applications. 304p. 1985. 49.95 (0-8352-1489-3) Bowker.
Reynolds, Dennis J., ed. Citizen Rights & Access to Electronic Information: The 1991 LITA President's Program Presentations & Background Papers. LC 92-19782. 201p. 1992. pap. 22.00 (0-8389-7601-8) ALA.
Reynolds, Diana H., ed. Florida Senior Managers Handbook. 5th ed. 750p. 1993. Three ring binder. ring bd. 69.95 (0-932143-01-6) FL Ctr Public.
Reynolds, Dinah. Worcester Porcelain: Marshall Collection. (Illus.). 80p. 1995. pap. 17.95 (0-907849-75-X, 75XP, Pub. by Ashmolean Mus UK) A Schwartz & Co.
— Worcester Porcelain: Marshall Collection. (Illus.). 80p. 1995. 19.95 (1-85444-040-3, 75X, Pub. by Ashmolean Mus UK) A Schwartz & Co.

R

Reynolds, Don, Jr. How to Sharpen Your Competitive Edge. LC 93-31317. (Small Business Sourcebooks Ser.). 186p. 1993. 17.95 (0-942061-73-X); pap. 8.95 (0-942061-72-1) Sourcebks.

Reynolds, Dona & Older, Ricki. So Now You Own a Food Processor. (Illus.). 285p. 1984. pap. text ed. 10.95 (0-931955-00-9) East-West Pub.

Reynolds, Donald. The Nineteenth Century. (Cambridge Introduction to the History of Mankind Ser.). 144p. 1985. pap. 11.95 (0-521-29869-5) Cambridge U Pr.

Reynolds, Donald C. & Collins, Thomas C. Excitons: Their Properties & Uses. LC 80-1783. 1981. text ed. 81.00 (0-12-586580-5) Acad Pr.

Reynolds, Donald E. Editors Make War: Southern Newspapers in the Secession Crisis. LC 71-129050. 315p. reprint ed. pap. 89.80 (0-8357-3263-0, 2039484) Bks Demand.

— Professor Mayo's College: A History of East Texas State University. (Illus.). 212p. 1993. 24.95 (0-9637092-0-8) E TX St Univ.

Reynolds, Donald M. The Architecture of New York City: Histories & Views of Important Structures, Sites & Symbols. rev. ed. LC 94-5705. 1994. pap. text ed. 29.95 (0-471-01439-7) Wiley.

— Masters of American Sculpture: The Figurative Tradition. 1993. 67.50 (1-55859-276-8) Abbeville Pr.

— Nineteenth-Century Architecture. (Cambridge Introduction to Art Ser.). 1992. pap. 12.95 (0-521-35683-0) Cambridge U Pr.

Reynolds, Donald M., ed. see Wittkower, Rudolf.

Reynolds, Douglas R. China, Eighteen Ninety-Eight to Nineteen Twelve: The Xinzheng Revolution & Japan. (East Asian Monographs: No. 160). (Illus.). 332p. (C). 1993. text ed. 32.00 (0-674-11660-7) HUP.

***Reynolds, Dwight F.** Heroic Poets, Poetic Heroes: The Ethnography of Performance in an Arabic Oral Epic Tradition. (Myth & Poetics Ser.). (Illus.). 304p. 1995. 42.50x (0-8014-3174-3) Cornell U Pr.

— Heroic Poets, Poetic Heroes: The Ethnography of Performance in an Arabic Oral Epic Tradition. LC 94-44173. (Myth & Poetics Ser.). 1995. write for info. (0-8014-8225-9) Cornell U Pr.

Reynolds, E. Bruce. Thailand & Japan's Southern Advance, 1940-1945. LC 93-26125. 1994. text ed. 49.95 (0-312-10402-2) St Martin.

Reynolds, E. E. Life of St. Francis of Assisi. 128p. 1994. reprint ed. pap. 6.95 (0-940147-28-9) Source Bks CA.

— St. John Fisher. 328p. 1993. reprint ed. pap. 10.95 (0-940147-21-1) Source Bks CA.

Reynolds, E. L. Distribution of Subcutaneous Fat in Childhood & Adolescence. (SRCD Ser.: Vol. 15, No. 2). 1950. 16.00 (0-527-01551-2) Periodicals Srv.

Reynolds, Earle L. The Forbidden Voyage. LC 74-27390. (Illus.). 281p. 1975. reprint ed. text ed. 65.00 (0-8371-7906-8, REFV, Greenwood Pr) Greenwood.

Reynolds, Ed & Mixdorf, Marcia. Confidence in Writing: A Basic Text. 2nd ed. 350p. (C). 1990. pap. text ed. 20.00 (0-15-512987-2) HB Coll Pubs.

Reynolds, Edward. Evolution of the Human Pelvis in Relation to the Mechanics of the Erect Posture. (HU PMP Ser.: Vol. 11, No. 5). 1931. pap. 15.00 (0-527-01222-X) Periodicals Srv.

— The Exaltation of Christ, Vol. 2: The Works of Edward Reynolds (an Explication of Psalm 110) 480p. 1993. reprint ed. 29.95 (1-877611-62-X) Soli Deo Gloria.

— Stand the Storm: A History of the Atlantic Slave Trade. 192p. 1993. reprint ed. pap. 8.95 (1-56663-020-7) I R Dee.

— Treatise of the Passions & Faculties of the Soule of Man. LC 79-161935. (History of Psychology Ser.). 1971. 75.00 (0-8201-1095-7) Schol Facsimiles.

Reynolds, Edward H. & Trimble, Michael R., eds. The Bridge Between Neurology & Psychiatry. (Illus.). 400p. 1989. pap. text ed. 82.00 (0-443-03344-7) Churchill.

Reynolds, Edward H., jt. ed. see Trimble, Michael R.

Reynolds, Edward N., jt. auth. see Harris, Scott O.

Reynolds, Elaine, jt. auth. see Frazier, Kathy.

Reynolds, Eleanor. Guiding Young Children: A Child-Centered Approach. LC 89-12899. 311p. (C). 1990. pap. text ed. 27.95 (0-87484-925-X) Mayfield Pub.

Reynolds, Elisabeth B., ed. Income Security in Canada: Changing Needs, Changing Means. 230p. 1993. pap. 15.95 (0-88645-149-3, Pub. by Inst Res Pub CN) Ashgate Pub Co.

Reynolds, Erma. Bible People Quiz Book. (Quiz & Puzzle Bks.). 1979. pap. 4.99 (0-8010-7692-7) Baker Bk.

Reynolds, Ernest. Early Victorian Drama: 1830-1870. LC 65-16248. 1972. 21.95 (0-405-08881-7, Pub. by Blom Pubns UK) Ayer.

Reynolds, Ernest E. Thomas More & Erasmus. LC 65-26739. (Illus.). 278p. reprint ed. pap. 79.30 (0-7837-5582-1, 2045370) Bks Demand.

Reynolds-Feighn, A. J. The Effects of Deregulation on U. S. Air Networks. Batten, David F., ed. (Advances in Spatial & Network Economics Ser.). (Illus.). xiv, 131p. 1992. 64.00 (0-387-54758-4) Spr-Verlag.

***Reynolds, Fleur.** The House in New Orleans. (Black Lace Ser.). (Illus.). Date not set. pap. 5.95 (0-352-32951-3, London Bridge) Genl Dist Srvs.

— Odalisque. (Black Lace Ser.). Date not set. pap. 5.95 (0-352-32887-8, London Bridge) Genl Dist Srvs.

Reynolds, Floria. Women at War. LC 93-4889. (World War Two Ser.). (Illus.). 48p. (J). (gr. 5-9). 1993. 14.95 (1-56847-082-7) Thomson Lrning.

Reynolds, Francis E. Fairview Park, Bk. 2: Innocence Lost. Reynolds, Hazel A., ed. 212p. (Orig.). 1992. pap. 12.50 (0-9618116-1-7) Sarge Pubns.

Reynolds, Frank, jt. ed. see Burkhalter, Sheryl.

Reynolds, Frank E. & Capps, Donald, eds. The Biographical Process: Studies in the History & Psychology of Religion. (Religion & Reason, Method & Theory in the Study & Interpretation of Religion Ser.: No. 11). 1976. text ed. 75.40 (90-279-7522-1) Mouton.

Reynolds, Frank E. & Tracy, David, eds. Discourse & Practice. LC 91-18680. (SUNY Series, Toward a Comparative Philosophy of Religions). 316p. (C). 1992. 59.50 (0-7914-1023-4); pap. 19.95 (0-7914-1024-2) State U NY Pr.

— Myth & Philosophy. LC 89-48910. (SUNY Series, Toward a Comparative Philosophy of Religions). 382p. (C). 1990. 59.50 (0-7914-0417-X); pap. 19.95 (0-7914-0418-8) State U NY Pr.

— Religion & Practical Reason. (SUNY Series, Toward a Comparative Philosophy of Religions). 444p. (C). 1994. 64.50 (0-7914-2217-8); pap. 21.95 (0-7914-2218-6) State U NY Pr.

Reynolds, Frank E., jt. ed. see Lovin, Robin W.

***Reynolds, Frank J.** Capture the Flag, Set. 1994. pap. write for info. (1-886457-01-8) Intl Projects.

— Capture the Flag, Vol. I. abr. ed. 108p. 1995. pap. 35.00 (1-886457-04-2) Intl Projects.

— Capture the Flag, Vol. II. abr. ed. 170p. 1995. pap. 35.00 (1-886457-05-0) Intl Projects.

— Capture the Flag Vol. I. 108p. 1994. pap. 45.00 (1-886457-02-6) Intl Projects.

— Capture the Flag Vol. II. 170p. 1994. pap. 45.00 (1-886457-03-4) Intl Projects.

— Incoterms for Americans. 124p. 1993. pap. 37.00 (1-886457-00-X) Intl Projects.

Reynolds, Fred D. & Barksdale, Hiram C., eds. Marketing & the Quality of Life. LC 78-17765. (American Marketing Association, Proceedings Ser.). 88p. reprint ed. pap. 25.10 (0-317-20081-X, 2023362) Bks Demand.

Reynolds, Frederick. Life & Times of Frederick Reynolds, 2 Vols. in 1. 2nd ed. LC 74-88489. 1972. 39.95 (0-405-08882-5, Pub. by Blom Pubns UK) Ayer.

Reynolds, G., tr. see Birkmayer, W. & Riederer, P.

Reynolds, G. F. Some Principles of Elizabethan Staging. LC 78-130233. reprint ed. 22.50 (0-404-05286-X) AMS Pr.

Reynolds, Gail, jt. auth. see MacAdam, Don.

Reynolds, Gary A. American Bronze Sculpture: Eighteen Fifty to the Present. Sweeney, Mary S., ed. LC 84-22616. (Illus.). 72p. (Orig.). 1984. pap. 12.95 (0-932828-20-5) Newark Mus.

Reynolds, Gary A. & Wright, Beryl J. Against the Odds: African-American Artists & the Harmon Foundation. LC 89-27552. 298p. 1990. 40.00 (0-932828-21-3); pap. 20.00 (0-932828-22-1) Newark Mus.

— Against the Odds: African-American Artists & the Harmon Foundation. (Illus.). 256p. 1990. pap. 22.50 (0-295-96976-8) U of Wash Pr.

Reynolds, Gary D., jt. auth. see Fielding, John E.

Reynolds, George & Sjodahl, Janne M. Commentary on the Book of Mormon, 7 vols. 388p. Vol. 3, 388p., 1958. 9.95 (0-87747-041-3); Vol. 4, 451p., 1959. 9.95 (0-87747-042-1); Vol. 6, 246p., 1961. 9.95 (0-87747-044-8) Deseret Bk.

Reynolds, George, ed. see Sumeria Staff.

Reynolds, George E., tr. see Schnitzler, Arthur.

Reynolds, George G. Distribution of Power to Regulate Interstate Carriers Between the Nation & the States. LC 68-57578. (Columbia University. Studies in the Social Sciences: No. 295). reprint ed. 28.50 (0-404-51295-X) AMS Pr.

Reynolds, George O., et al. The New Physical Optics Notebook: Tutorials in Fourier Optics. Parrent, George B., Jr. & Thompson, Brian J., eds. LC 88-34527. (Illus.). 584p. (C). 1989. pap. text ed. 60.00 (0-8194-0130-7) SPIE.

Reynolds, George P. & Riecks, Donald. Introduction to Business Telecommunications. 2nd ed. 320p. (C). 1988. write for info. (0-675-20815-7, Merrill Pub Co) Macmillan.

Reynolds, George P., et al, eds. Foxfire Ten: Railroad Lore, Boarding Houses, Depression-Era Appalachia, Chairmaking, Whirligigs, Snakes Canes, & Gourd Art. LC 92-24634. 1993. 14.00 (0-385-42276-8, Anchor NY) Doubleday.

***Reynolds, George W.** Information Systems for Managers. 3rd ed. LC 94-37682. 500p. 1994. text ed. 62.00 (0-314-04597-X) West Pub.

— The Mysteries of London, 4 vols. in 2, 1. LC 79-8192. reprint ed. write for info. (0-404-62107-4) AMS Pr.

— The Mysteries of London, 4 vols. in 2, 2. LC 79-8192. reprint ed. write for info. (0-404-62108-2) AMS Pr.

— The Mysteries of London, 4 vols. in 2, Set. LC 79-8192. reprint ed. 84.50 (0-404-62106-6) AMS Pr.

— The Necromancer: A Romance. Reginald, R. & Menville, Douglas, eds. LC 75-46304. (Supernatural & Occult Fiction Ser.). (Illus.). 1976. reprint ed. lib. bdg. 23.95 (0-405-08164-2) Ayer.

Reynolds, Gil. The Fused Glass Handbook. LC 87-25114. (Illus.). 102p. 1990. pap. 18.95 (0-915807-02-5) Hidden Valley Bks.

Reynolds, Gilbert W. The Aloes of South Africa. 616p. (C). 1982. text ed. 135.00 (90-6191-230-X, Pub. by A A Balkema NE) Ashgate Pub Co.

***Reynolds, Glenn H.** Outer Space: Problems of Law. 2nd ed. (C). 1929. text ed. 68.00 (0-8133-1802-5) Westview.

Reynolds, Grace. The Thanksgiving Story Continues. Grace, Betse, ed. (Illus.). 80p. (Orig.). 1989. pap. 3.95 (1-878374-27-3) Pac Coast Pubs.

Reynolds, Graham. Catalogue of the Constable Collection. (Illus.). 264p. 1991. 55.00 (1-85177-042-9, Pub. by Victoria & Albert Mus UK) Trafalgar.

— Constable: The Natural Painter. (Illus.). 144p. 1977. reprint ed. pap. 5.95 (0-586-04401-9) Academy Chi Pubs.

— English Portrait Miniatures. rev. ed. (Illus.). 211p. (C). 1992. pap. 34.95 (0-521-33920-0) Cambridge U Pr.

— English Watercolors. (Illus.). 160p. (C). 1988. 35.00 (0-941533-43-3) New Amsterdam Bks.

— The Later Paintings & Drawings of John Constable, 2 vols., Set. LC 84-40186. (Studies in British Art). (Illus.). 880p. 1984. 250.00 (0-300-03151-3) Yale U Pr.

— Turner. (World of Art Ser.). (Illus.). 216p. 1985. pap. 12.95 (0-500-20083-1) Thames Hudson.

— Watercolors: A Concise History. (World of Art Ser.). (Illus.). 1986. pap. 12.95 (0-500-20109-9) Thames Hudson.

Reynolds, Gretchen, jt. auth. see Jones, Elizabeth.

Reynolds, H. T. Analysis of Nominal Data. 2nd ed. (Quantitative Applications in the Social Sciences Ser.: Vol. 7). 82p. 1984. 9.95 (0-8039-0653-6) Sage.

Reynolds, H. W. Dutch Houses in the Hudson Valley Before 1776. 467p. 1993. reprint ed. lib. bdg. 99.00 (0-7812-5303-9) Rprt Serv.

— Dutchess County Doorways, 1730-1830. 280p. 1993. reprint ed. lib. bdg. 79.00 (0-7812-5304-7) Rprt Serv.

Reynolds, Hanson S. & Warner, Joseph P. Massachusetts Probate Manual. rev. ed. LC 87-62744. (Illus.). 1988. ring bd. 95.00 (0-944490-06-9) Mass CLE.

Reynolds, Harold R. Fifty Ways to Get a Date Without Bars, Singles Clubs or Computers. Riddle, Florence K., ed. LC 84-62106. 64p. (Orig.). 1992. pap. 7.00 (0-9613987-2-8) Reliant Pub.

Reynolds, Harry W., jt. auth. see American Academy of Political.

Reynolds, Hazel A., ed. see Reynolds, Francis E.

Reynolds, Helen. The Economics of Prostitution. (Illus.). 218p. (C). 1985. 38.95x (0-398-05161-5) C C Thomas.

Reynolds, Helen, jt. auth. see Reynolds, Ivan G.

Reynolds, Helen A., jt. auth. see Nolds, Annrey.

Reynolds, Henry. Dispossession: Black Australians & White Invaders. (Illus.). 226p. (C). 1990. pap. text ed. 17.95 (0-04-370182-5) Routledge Chapman & Hall.

Reynolds, Hezekiah. Directions for House & Ship Painting. (AAS Facsimiles Ser.: No. 1). (Illus.). (Orig.). 1978. pap. 4.00 (0-912296-16-X, U Pr of Va) Am Antiquarian.

Reynolds, Horace. A Providence Episode in the Irish Literary Renaissance. 1929. 5.00 (0-685-67667-6) RI Hist Soc.

Reynolds, Howard, jt. auth. see Whiddon, N. Sue.

Reynolds, Hugh, ed. The Executive Branch of the U. S. Government: A Bibliography. LC 88-24704. (Bibliographies & Indexes in Law & Political Science Ser.: No. 11). 389p. 1988. text ed. 65.00 (0-313-26568-2, GEX/, Greenwood Pr) Greenwood.

Reynolds, I. James, jt. auth. see Goldstein, Robert H.

Reynolds, Ignatius A., jt. auth. see England, John.

Reynolds, Ivan G. & Reynolds, Helen. Treasure of Charter Oak: Growing up in the Masonic Home for Children, 1928-1938. LC 89-34633. (Illus.). 80p. (Orig.). 1989. pap. 7.95 (0-931832-34-9) Fithian Pr.

Reynolds, J. Craft of Programming. 1981. text ed. 38.00 (0-13-188862-5) P-H.

— Down under: Vanishing Cultures. (J). 1992. 16.95 (0-15-224182-5, HB Juv Bks); pap. 9.00 (0-15-224183-3, HB Juv Bks) HarBrace.

— Far North: Vanishing Cultures. (J). 1992. 16.95 (0-15-227178-3, HB Juv Bks); pap. 8.95 (0-15-227179-1, HB Juv Bks) HarBrace.

— Material & Energy Balances: A Self Instructional Problem Workbook. 240p. (C). 1992. pap. text ed. 50.00 (1-882767-07-1) ETS.

Reynolds, J., jt. auth. see Theodore, L.

Reynolds, J. A., jt. ed. see Henry, R. J.

Reynolds, J. F. Automotive Machine Shop. (C). 1985. text ed. 40.00 (0-8359-0346-X, Reston) P-H.

Reynolds, J. F., jt. auth. see Jamieson, Barrie G.

Reynolds, J. Frederick, ed. Rhetorical Memory & Delivery: Classical Concepts for Contemporary Composition. (Communications, Rhetoric & Public Address Ser.). 192p. 1993. text ed. 39.95 (0-8058-1292-X); pap. 19.95 (0-8058-1293-8) L Erlbaum Assocs.

Reynolds, J. M., jt. ed. see Hazelrigg, George.

Reynolds, Jack. Assessing Community Health Needs & Coverage Module 2: User's Guide. (Primary Health Care Management Advancement Programme (PHC MAP) Modules Ser.). 227p. 1993. pap. text ed. write for info. (1-882839-01-3) Aga Khan Fnd.

— Assessing Information Needs Module 1: User's Guide. (Primary Health Care Management Advancement Programme (PHC MAP) Modules Ser.). 54p. 1993. pap. text ed. write for info. (1-882839-00-5) Aga Khan Fnd.

— Cost Analysis Module 8: User's Guide. (Primary Health Care Management Advancement Programme (PHC MAP) Modules Ser.). 97p. 1993. pap. text ed. write for info. (1-882839-06-4) Aga Khan Fnd.

Reynolds, Jack & Stinson, Wayne. Sustainability Analysis Module 9: User's Guide. (Primary Health Care Management Advancement Programme (PHC MAP) Modules Ser.). 105p. 1993. pap. text ed. write for info. (1-882839-07-2) Aga Khan Fnd.

Reynolds, Jack, et al. Better Management - 100 Tips: Manager's Guide. (Primary Health Care Management Advancement Programme (PHC MAP) Modules Ser.). 64p. 1993. pap. text ed. write for info. (1-882839-17-X) Aga Khan Fnd.

Reynolds, Jacqueline, jt. auth. see Tanford, Charles.

Reynolds, Jaime, jt. auth. see Coutouvidis, John.

Reynolds, James. Top Secret. (J). 1987. 3.50 (0-553-15733-7) Bantam.

Reynolds, James A. Catholic Emancipation Crisis in Ireland, 1823-1829. LC 74-95134. 204p. 1970. reprint ed. text ed. 55.00 (0-8371-3141-3, RECE, Greenwood Pr) Greenwood.

Reynolds, James A. & Slaughter, James E. How to Plan Your Affordable Family Reunion. 52p. 1991. 10.00 (0-9630744-0-7) Portunity Pub.

Reynolds, James F., jt. auth. see Ludwig, John A.

Reynolds, James H. Computing in Psychology: An Introduction to Programming Methods & Concepts. (Illus.). 320p. 1987. pap. text ed. 36.40 (0-13-165812-3) P-H.

Reynolds, James J., ed. Modern Poetry for Children, Bk. 8. LC 30-10164. (Granger Poetry Library). (J). (gr. 4). 1979. reprint ed. 15.00 (0-89609-167-8) Roth Pub Inc.

Reynolds, James J., jt. auth. see Harshbarger, Ronald J.

Reynolds, Jan. Amazon: Vanishing Cultures. LC 92-21089. (Vanishing Cultures Ser.). (Illus.). (J). 1993. 16.95 (0-15-202831-5, HB Juv Bks); pap. 8.95 (0-15-202832-3, HB Juv Bks) HarBrace.

— Frozen Land: Vanishing Cultures. LC 92-30324. (J). 1993. 16.95 (0-15-238787-0); pap. 8.95 (0-15-238788-9) HarBrace.

— Himalaya Vanishing Cultures. 32p. (J). (gr. 2 up). 1991. 17.00 (0-15-234465-9); pap. 9.00 (0-15-234466-7) HarBrace.

— Inheritance: The History of Israel & Christianity Unveiled. (Illus.). 560p. 1990. 18.95 (0-944007-12-0) Sure Sellers.

— Mongolia: Vanishing Cultures. LC 93-1351. (Vanishing Cultures Ser.). (J). (gr. 6 up). 1994. 16.95 (0-15-255312-6); pap. 8.95 (0-15-255313-4) HarBrace.

— Sahara Vanishing Cultures. 30p. (J). (gr. 2 up). 1991. 16.95 (0-15-269959-7); pap. 8.95 (0-15-269958-9) HarBrace.

Reynolds, Jan, jt. auth. see Gillette, Ned.

Reynolds, Jane L. Sing to the Earth. 16p. (J). (gr. k-4). 1978. The Orange Book for First Chorus. 16p. write for info. (0-932320-01-5); The Yellow Book for Second Chorus. 20p. write for info. (0-932320-02-3); The Green Book for Third Chorus. 20p. write for info. (0-932320-03-1); The Blue Book for Fourth Chorus & Soloists. 24p. write for info. (0-932320-04-X); pap. write for info. (0-932320-00-7) Solar Studio.

— Skits for Seniors Only. 20p. 1980. The Yellow Book. write for info. (0-932320-06-6); The Green Book. write for info. (0-932320-07-4); The Orange Book. write for info. (0-932320-05-8) Solar Studio.

Reynolds, Janet, jt. auth. see Rob, Caroline.

Reynolds, Jean. Sentence Power. (C). 1991. pap. text ed. 20.75 (0-03-026333-6) HB Coll Pubs.

Reynolds, Jeanette & McCann, Annes, eds. Cased-Hole Logging. (Oil & Gas Production Ser.). (Illus.). 75p. (Orig.). (C). 1981. pap. text ed. 15.00 (0-88698-107-7, 3.30510) PETEX.

— Open-Hole Logging. (Oil & Gas Production Ser.). (Illus.). 87p. (Orig.). (C). 1981. pap. text ed. 15.00 (0-88698-108-5, 3.30410) PETEX.

Reynolds, Jeanie, ed. see Stanton, Bette L.

***Reynolds, Jeremy.** Christian Bashing: America's New National Pastime. 224p. 1995. pap. 10.99 (1-56384-084-7) Huntington Hse.

— The Walking Wounded: A Look at Faith Theology. LC 94-72827. 224p. 1995. pap. 10.99 (0-614-06757-X) Huntington Hse.

Reynolds, Jerry. What You Need to Know about Improving Basic English Skills. 1992. pap. 12.95 (0-8442-5285-9, Natl Textbk) NTC Pub Grp.

Reynolds, Jerry D., jt. auth. see Mueller, Lavonne.

Reynolds, Jerry D., et al. What You Need to Know about Improving Basic English Skills: Intermediate Through Advanced. 256p. (YA). 1993. pap. text ed. 15.95 (0-8442-5283-2, Natl Textbk) NTC Pub Grp.

— What You Need to Know about Improving Basic English Skills: Intermediate Through Advanced. annot. ed. 256p. (YA). 1993. teacher ed 19.95 (0-8442-5284-0, Natl Textbk) NTC Pub Grp.

Reynolds, Jim. Best of British Bikes. (Illus.). 160p. 1991. 27.95 (1-85260-033-0, Pub. by Thorsons UK) Motorbooks Intl.

— The Outer Path: Finding My Way in Tibet. Hallam, Kathleen, ed. LC 91-21086. (Illus.). 184p. (Orig.). 1992. pap. 10.95 (0-933271-06-9) Fair Oaks CA.

Reynolds, Jock. American Abstraction at the Addison. LC 91-71558. (Illus.). 96p. (Orig.). 1991. pap. 15.00 (1-879886-30-8) Addison Gallery.

Reynolds, Jock, ed. George B. Luks - Bronx Park, May 8, 1904. (Illus.). 96p. (Orig.). 1990. pap. 8.00 (1-879886-28-6) Addison Gallery.

Reynolds, Jock & Walker, Rebecca. House & Home: Spirits of the South. LC 94-70777. (Illus.). 100p. 1994. pap. 24.95 (1-879886-35-9) Addison Gallery.

Reynolds, Jock, jt. auth. see Keller, Andrea M.

Reynolds, Jock, ed. see Short, William & Seidenberg, Willa.

Reynolds, Joe. Out Front Leadership: Discovering, Developing, & Delivering Your Potential. 1993. 19.95 (0-9636391-0-2) Mott & Carlisle.

Reynolds, John. Case Method in Management Development: Guide for Effective Use. (Management Development Ser.: No. 17). vi, 264p. 1992. 24.00 (92-2-102363-X) Intl Labour Office.

— Golden Letters: The Tibetan Teachings of Garab Dorje, First Dzogchen Master. 1990. pap. 14.95 (0-88268-100-1) Station Hill Pr.

— Perfect Directions for All English Gold, Now Currant in This Kingdome. LC 77-7426. (English Experience Ser.: No. 886). 1977. reprint ed. lib. bdg. 20.00 (90-221-0886-4) Walter J Johnson.

— Self Liberation Through Seeing Everything in Its Nakedness. 1989. 29.95 (0-88268-058-7) Station Hill Pr.

— The Triumphs of God's Revenge Against the Crying & Execrable Sinne of Murther (1639), Bks. I-II, Vol. 1. Walmsley, Joan M., ed. LC 94-38864. 332p. 1995. text ed. 99.95 (0-7734-8992-4) E Mellen.

R

An Asterisk (*) at the beginning of an entry indicates that the title is appearing in BIP for the first time.

Reynolds, John, III & Odell, Daniel. Manatees & Dugongs. 192p. 1991. 24.95 (*0-8160-2436-7*) Facts on File.

Reynolds, John, ed. see Norbu, Namkhai.

Reynolds, John C., jt. ed. see Wootton, Lutian R.

Reynolds, John D. Fexible Benefits Handbook. LC 92-82081. 98.00 (*0-7913-1515-0*) Warren Gorham & Lamont.

— Flexible Benefits Handbook. 1993. text ed. 105.00 (*0-685-69670-7*, FLEX) Warren Gorham & Lamont.

Reynolds, John D. & Bischoff, Robin N. Health Insurance Answer Book. 3rd ed. Haffeman, JoAnne S., ed. 454p. 1990. 96.00 (*1-878375-18-0*) Panel Pubs.

Reynolds, John D., et al. Health Insurance Answer Book: 1992 Supplement. 200p. 1991. pap. text ed. 49.00 (*1-878375-56-3*) Panel Pubs.

Reynolds, John E. Readings in Natural Resource Economics. 199p. (C). 1974. text ed. 29.00 (*0-685-50581-2*) Irvington.

— Thames Ship Towage 1933-1992. (C). 1989. text ed. 70.00 (*1-85821-028-3*, Pub. by Pentland Pr UK) St Mut.

Reynolds, John F. Testing Democracy: Electoral Behavior & Progressive Reform in New Jersey, 1880-1920. LC 87-31947. (Illus.). xvii, 245p. (C). 1988. 49.95 (*0-8078-1789-9*) U of NC Pr.

Reynolds, John F., ed. Gellert, Christian Furchtegott Briefwechsel: Kritische Gesamtausgabe, 5 vols., Bd. III. xii, 560p. (GER.). (C). 1991. lib. bdg. 172.35 (*3-11-009886-5*) De Gruyter.

— Rhetoric, Cultural Studies, & Literacy: Selected Papers from the 1994 Conference of the Rhetoric Society of America. 216p. 1995. 39.95 (*0-8058-1608-9*) L Erlbaum Assocs.

— Rhetoric, Cultural Studies, & Literacy: Selected Papers from the 1994 Conference of the Rhetoric Society of America. 216p. 1995. pap. 19.95 (*0-8058-1609-7*) L Erlbaum Assocs.

Reynolds, John F., ed. see Gellart, Christian.

***Reynolds, John F., et al.** Writing & Reading Mental Health Records. 2nd ed. 125p. 1996. text ed. 25.00 (*0-8058-2001-9*); pap. 13.00 (*0-8058-2002-7*) L Erlbaum Assocs.

— Writing & Reading Mental Health Records: Issues & Analysis. (Illus.). 144p. 1992. 34.00 (*0-8039-4097-1*); pap. 15.95 (*0-8039-4098-X*) Sage.

***Reynolds, John F., et al, eds.** Professional Writing in Context: Lessons from Teaching & Consulting in Worlds of Work. 192p. 1995. 39.95 (*0-8058-1726-3*) L Erlbaum Assocs.

— Professional Writing in Context: Lessons from Teaching & Consulting in Worlds of Work. 192p. 1995. pap. 18.00 (*0-8058-1727-1*) L Erlbaum Assocs.

Reynolds, John H. The Letters of John Hamilton Reynolds. Jones, Leonidas M., ed. LC 72-90342. 122p. reprint ed. pap. 34.80 (*0-8357-3811-6*, 2036538) Bks Demand.

— Selected Prose. Jones, Leonidas M., ed. LC 66-15653. (Illus.). 502p. 1966. 45.00 (*0-674-79935-6*) HUP.

Reynolds, John J., jt. auth. see Dominicis, Maria C.

Reynolds, John M., ed. & frwd. The Golden Letters: The Tibetan Teachings of Garab Dorje, First Dzogchen Master. 150p. 1991. pap. 14.95 (*0-685-54672-1*) Station Hill Pr.

Reynolds, John M., tr. see Padmasambhava.

Reynolds, John S., jt. auth. see Stein, Benjamin J.

Reynolds, John T. From Scotland to America: The Descendants of William & Joanna Burns (1718-1987) LC 89-50772. 187p. 1989. lib. bdg. 24.95 (*0-9623150-0-1*); pap. 18.95 (*0-9623150-1-X*) W Burns Assn.

— The Porter Family: The Descendants of John Porter. 43p. 1991. pap. text ed. 7.50 (*0-9623150-2-8*) W Burns Assn.

Reynolds, Jonathan. Rubbers & Yanks Three Detroit Zero Top of the Seventh: Two Plays. 1976. pap. 4.75 (*0-8222-0974-8*) Dramatists Play.

***Reynolds, Joseph.** Materials Science & Engineering: A Self-Instructional Problem Workbook. 224p. 1994. pap. text ed. 50.00 (*1-882767-11-X*) ETS.

Reynolds, Joseph P., jt. auth. see Theodore, Louis.

Reynolds, Joseph P., et al. Hazardous Waste Incineration Calculations: Problems & Software. LC 09-111047. 249p. 1991. text ed. 74.95 (*0-471-50782-2*) Wiley.

Reynolds, Joshua. Discourses. 432p. 1992. 10.95 (*0-14-043278-7*, Penguin Classics) Viking Penguin.

— Letters by Joshua Reynolds. Hilles, Frederick W., ed. LC 75-41227. reprint ed. 45.00 (*0-404-14590-6*) AMS Pr.

Reynolds, Joshua & Malone, Edmond. The Works: To Which Is Prefixed an Account of the Life & Writings of the Author, 2 vols., Set. (Anglistica & Americana Ser.: No. 129). 1971. reprint ed. 180.70 (*0-685-66509-7*, 05103014, Pub. by Georg Olms GW) Lubrecht & Cramer.

Reynolds, Judith. Historic Properties: Preservation & the Valuation Process. 115p. 1982. 17.00 (*0-911780-56-4*) Appraisal Inst.

Reynolds, Judy, ed. & intro. Reference Services in the Humanities. LC 94-26131. (Reference Librarian Ser.: No. 47). 213p. 1994. lib. bdg. 39.95 (*1-56024-692-8*) Haworth Pr.

Reynolds, Julie, ed. see De Vegh, Elizabeth.

Reynolds, Julie, ed. see Dranow, Ralph.

Reynolds, Karen E., jt. auth. see Messick, Rosemary G.

Reynolds, Katherine. Abstracts of Wills of Cumberland Country, Virginia Will Book 1 & 2, 1749-1782. 104p. 1984. 17.50 (*0-89308-430-1*) Southern Hist Pr.

Reynolds, Katherine & Wiebvsch, John. Park City. (Illus.). 72p. 1984. 23.00 (*0-916873-50-1*) Weller Inst.

Reynolds, Kathy, ed. Marco Polo. LC 86-6678. (Stories Ser.). (Illus.). 32p. (J). (gr. 2-5). 1986. lib. bdg. 19.97 (*0-8172-2627-3*) Raintree Steck-V.

Reynolds, Kay. Robotech Art 1. limited ed. Carlton, Ardith, tr. LC 85-16291. (Illus.). 264p. (Orig.). 40.00 (*0-89865-462-9*, Starblaze) Donning Co.

— Robotech Art 1. rev. ed. Carlton, Ardith, tr. LC 85-16291. (Illus.). 264p. (Orig.). pap. 16.95 (*0-89865-412-2*, Starblaze) Donning Co.

— Robotech Art 2. (Illus.). 120p. 1987. pap. 12.95 (*0-89865-517-X*, Starblaze) Donning Co.

— Robotech Art 2. limited ed. (Illus.). 120p. 1987. Limited ed. boxed 40.00 (*0-89865-527-7*, Starblaze) Donning Co.

Reynolds, Kay, ed. Gate of Ivrel: Fever Dreams. (Gate of Ivrel Ser.). (Illus.). 64p. (Orig.). 1988. pap. 7.95 (*0-89865-556-0*, Starblaze) Donning Co.

Reynolds, Kay & Reynolds, Mike. Fortune's Friends: Hell Week. (Fortune's Friends Ser.: No. 1). (Illus.). 64p. (Orig.). 1987. 6.95 (*0-89865-469-6*, Starblaze) Donning Co.

Reynolds, Kay, ed. see Asprin, Robert.

Reynolds, Kay, ed. see Asprin, Robert & Foglio, Phil.

Reynolds, Kay, ed. see Asprin, Robert & Abbey, Lynn.

Reynolds, Kay, jt. auth. see Cherry, David A.

Reynolds, Kay, ed. see De Lint, Charles.

Reynolds, Kay, ed. see Doran, Colleen.

Reynolds, Kay, ed. see Ellison, Harlan.

Reynolds, Kay, ed. see Garrett, Randall.

Reynolds, Kay, ed. see Macek, Carl.

Reynolds, Kay, ed. see Pini, Wendy & Pini, Richard.

Reynolds, Kay, ed. see Pyle, Howard.

Reynolds, Kay, jt. auth. see Reynolds, Mike.

Reynolds, Kay, ed. see Smith, Phil & Fogilio, Phil.

Reynolds, Kay, ed. see Somtow, S. P.

Reynolds, Kay, ed. see Von Harbou, Thea.

Reynolds, Kay, ed. see Wagner, Matt.

Reynolds, Kay, ed. see Waldron, Lamar.

Reynolds, Kay, ed. see Weyland, M.

Reynolds, Kev. Kent. (Visitor's Guides Ser.). 256p. 1990. pap. 13.95 (*1-55650-263-X*) Hunter NJ.

Reynolds, Kevin & Price, Tim R. Rapu Nui: The Illustrated Story of the Epic Film. (Illus.). 160p. 1993. 29.95 (*1-55704-185-7*); pap. 16.95 (*1-55704-184-9*) Newmarket.

Reynolds, Kim. Children's Literature. 1990. 39.00 (*0-7463-0723-3*, Pub. by Northcote House UK) St Mut.

Reynolds, Kimberley. Girls Only? Gender & Popular Children's Fiction in Britian 1880-1910. (Illus.). 160p. 1990. 24.95 (*0-87722-737-3*) Temple U Pr.

Reynolds, Kimberley & Humble, Nicola. Victorian Heroines: Representations of Feminity in Nineteenth-Century Literature & Art. LC 93-27468. 1993. 45.00 (*0-8147-7361-3*); pap. 17.95 (*0-8147-7362-1*) NYU Pr.

Reynolds, Kimberly. Children's Literature. (Writers & Their Work Ser.). 96p. 1994. pap. text ed. 11.50 (*0-7463-0728-4*, Pub. by Northcote House UK) Trans-Atl Phila.

Reynolds, L. D., ed. see Sallust.

Reynolds, Larry, jt. ed. see Cox, Jeffrey.

Reynolds, Larry, et al. Autorobics. (Illus.). 52p. (Orig.). 1989. pap. 6.95 (*0-685-26250-2*) Autorobics.

Reynolds, Larry A. The Mudsock Scrapbook: A Pictorial Perspective of Fishers, Indiana the Early Years. LC 93-80648. 200p. 1993. 49.95 (*0-9639445-0-9*) Hoosier Cider.

Reynolds, Larry J. European Revolutions & the American Literary Renaissance. LC 88-3784. (C). 1988. text ed. 27.50 (*0-300-04242-6*) Yale U Pr.

Reynolds, Larry J., ed. see Fuller, Margaret.

Reynolds, Larry T. Interactionism: Exposition & Critique. 3rd ed. LC 92-73398. 320p. 1993. lib. bdg. 36.95 (*0-685-60898-0*); pap. text ed. 22.95 (*0-685-60899-9*) Gen Hall.

Reynolds, Larry T., jt. ed. see Herman, Nancy J.

Reynolds, Leah J. My Soliloquy. (Illus.). 43p. (Orig.). 1992. pap. 5.95 (*1-56411-022-2*) Untd Bros & Sis.

Reynolds, Leamon T. Love Em...& Leave Em. 184p. (Orig.). (C). 1989. pap. 6.95 (*1-877917-06-0*) Alpha Bible Pubns.

Reynolds, Leighton D. & Wilson, N. G. Scribes & Scholars: A Guide to the Transmission of Greek & Latin Literature. 3rd ed. (Illus.). 352p. 1991. 89.00 (*0-19-872145-5*); pap. 34.50 (*0-19-872146-3*) OUP.

Reynolds, Leighton D., ed. see Seneca, Lucius Annaeus.

Reynolds, Lily, jt. auth. see Jones, Mary G.

Reynolds, Linda & Simmonds, Doig. Presentation of Data in Science. 223p. 1981. lib. bdg. 84.00 (*90-247-2398-1*) Kluwer Ac.

— Presentation of Data in Science. 223p. 1982. pap. text ed. 51.50 (*90-247-3054-6*) Kluwer Ac.

Reynolds, Lloyd. Italic Calligraphy & Handwriting: Exercises & Text. pap. 5.95 (*0-8008-4284-7*) Taplinger.

— Macroeconomics: Analysis & Policy. 3rd ed. (C). 1979. 14.95 (*0-256-02173-2*) Irwin.

— My Dear Runemeister: A Voyage Through the Alphabet. LC 89-16400. (Illus.). 80p. (Orig.). 1990. reprint ed. pap. 9.95 (*0-87595-219-4*) Oregon Hist.

Reynolds, Lloyd G. The American Economy in Perspective. 2nd ed. 512p. (C). 1987. pap. text ed. write for info. (*0-07-052056-9*) McGraw.

— Image & Reality in Economic Development. LC 77-76312. 1977. 60.00 (*0-300-02088-0*) Yale U Pr.

— The Three Worlds of Economics. LC 71-151588. (Studies in Comparative Economics: No. 12). 358p. reprint ed. pap. 102.10 (*0-8357-8352-9*, 2033870) Bks Demand.

Reynolds, Lloyd G., ed. Agriculture in Development Theory. LC 74-20085. (Economic Growth Center, Yale University Publication Ser.). 522p. reprint ed. pap. 148.80 (*0-8357-8013-9*, 2033867) Bks Demand.

Reynolds, Lloyd G. & Shister, Joseph. Job Horizons: Study of Job Satisfaction & Labor Mobility. Stein, Leon, ed. LC 77-70526. (Work Ser.). (Illus.). 1977. reprint ed. lib. bdg. 19.95 (*0-405-10194-5*) Ayer.

Reynolds, Lloyd G. & Torruellas, Luz M. Wages, Productivity, & Industrialization in Puerto Rico. LC 65-12407. (Yale University, Economic Growth Center, Publications). 373p. reprint ed. pap. 106.40 (*0-317-29718-X*, 2022034) Bks Demand.

Reynolds, Lloyd G., et al. Labor Economics & Labor Relations. 10th ed. 624p. (C). 1990. text ed. write for info. (*0-13-517376-0*) P-H.

Reynolds, Lloyd J. Straight Impressions. LC 78-60187. (Illus.). 1979. 12.50 (*0-931474-06-X*) TBW Bks.

— Straight Impressions. LC 78-60187. (Illus.). 1984. pap. 5.95 (*0-931474-07-8*) TBW Bks.

Reynolds, Lois A., ed. see Pharmacists in Ophthalmic Practice, Inc. Staff.

***Reynolds, Lorin.** Scrimshander. 240p. Date not set. pap. 8.95 (*0-7610-0341-X*) NW Pub.

Reynolds, Lorna. Kate O'Brien: A Literary Portrait. LC 85-30612. 150p. 1986. 41.00 (*0-389-20613-X*, N8168) B&N Imports.

— Tasty Food for Hasty Folk. 144p. (C). 1990. pap. 11.99 (*1-85594-005-1*, Pub. by Attic IE) InBook.

Reynolds, Louis B. We Have Tomorrow. Woolsey, Raymond H., ed. 480p. 1984. 29.95 (*0-8280-0232-0*) Review & Herald.

Reynolds, Lura S., jt. auth. see Naylor, Phyllis R.

Reynolds, M. C., ed. Knowledge Base for the Beginning Teacher. 324p. 1989. text ed. 125.00 (*0-08-036767-4*, Pergamon Pr) Elsevier.

Reynolds, M. H. The History & Descendants of John & Sarah Reynolds (1630?- 1923), of Watertown, Mass., & Wethersfield, Stamford, & Greenwich, Connecticut. (Illus.). 509p. 1993. reprint ed. lib. bdg. 89.50 (*0-8328-3053-4*); reprint ed. pap. 79.50 (*0-8328-3054-2*) Higginson Bk Co.

— Reynolds: History & One Line of Descendants of Robert & Mary Reynolds (1630? - 1928) of Boston, with the Hyatt Family of Princeton, New Jersey. (Illus.). 92p. 1993. reprint ed. lib. bdg. 28.00 (*0-8328-3390-8*); reprint ed. pap. 18.00 (*0-8328-3391-6*) Higginson Bk Co.

Reynolds, M. H., comp. Reynolds: History & Some of the Descendants of Robert & Mary Reynolds (1630? - 1931) of Boston, Massachusetts. (Illus.). 236p. 1993. reprint ed. lib. bdg. 47.50 (*0-8328-3392-4*); reprint ed. pap. 37.50 (*0-8328-3393-2*) Higginson Bk Co.

Reynolds, M. Osborne, Jr. Local Government Law Handbook. LC 82-8573. (Hornbook Ser.). 860p. (C). 1993. reprint ed. text ed. 39.00 (*0-314-65452-6*) West Pub.

Reynolds, Mack. Brain World. 1978. pap. 1.75 (*0-8439-0595-6*) Dorchester Pub Co.

— Compounded Interests. LC 82-62697. (Boskone Bks.). (Illus.). xii, 164p. 1983. 13.00 (*0-915368-20-X*) New Eng SF Assoc.

— The Cosmic Eye. 1979. pap. 1.25 (*0-8439-0610-3*) Dorchester Pub Co.

— Earth Unaware. 1979. reprint ed. pap. 2.25 (*0-8439-0628-6*) Dorchester Pub Co.

— Trample an Empire Down. 1978. pap. 1.50 (*0-8439-0585-9*) Dorchester Pub Co.

Reynolds, Malvina. Magic Penny Big Book. (Illus.). (J). (ps-2). 1988. pap. text ed. 14.00 (*0-922053-19-7*) N Edge Res.

— Malvina Reynolds Songbook. 4th enl. ed. LC 74-20175. (Illus.). 112p. 1984. pap. 7.00 (*0-915620-07-3*) Schroder Music.

— Morningtown Ride. (Illus.). 20p. (J). (ps-4). 1984. 10.95 (*0-931793-00-9*) Turn the Page.

— Not in Ourselves, nor in Our Stars Either. 40p. 1975. pap. 1.00 (*0-915620-03-0*) Schroder Music.

— Tweedles & Foodles for Young Noodles. LC 73-80670. (Illus.). 42p. (J). (gr. k-4). 1961. pap. 5.75 (*0-915620-08-1*) Schroder Music.

Reynolds, Margaret, ed. Erotica: Women's Writing from Sappho to Margaret Atwood. 400p. 1992. pap. 12.00 (*0-449-90752-X*, Columbine) Fawcett.

— The Penguin Book of Lesbian Short Stories. 464p. 1994. 27.50 (*0-670-85425-5*, Viking) Viking Penguin.

— The Penguin Book of Lesbian Short Stories. LC 93-34061. 1999. write for info. (*0-670-84321-0*, Viking) Viking Penguin.

— The Penguin Book of Lesbian Short Stories. 464p. 1994. reprint ed. pap. 13.95 (*0-14-024018-7*, Penguin Bks) Viking Penguin.

Reynolds, Margaret, ed. see Browning, Elizabeth Barrett.

Reynolds, Margaret, jt. ed. see Leighton, Angela.

***Reynolds, Marianne C.** Reading Connections. LC 94-31933. 222p. (C). 1995. pap. 26.95 (*0-534-24456-4*) Intl Thomson.

— Reading for Understanding. 451p. (C). 1992. pap. 25.95 (*0-534-17064-1*) Intl Thomson.

— Reading for Understanding. 2nd ed. LC 94-31932. (Illus.). 466p. (C). 1995. pap. 26.95 (*0-534-23274-4*) Intl Thomson.

***Reynolds, Marigold.** The Odyssey, Vol. 1. 266p. (Orig.). 1995. pap. 15.95 (*0-614-06982-3*) Silver Fire.

— The Odyssey, Vol. 1. 266p. (Orig.). 1995. 19.95 (*0-9646831-0-5*) Silver Fire.

***Reynolds, Marilyn.** Beyond Dreams. (True-to-Life Series from Hamilton High). (Illus.). 192p. (Orig.). (YA). (gr. 7-13). 1995. 15.95 (*1-885356-00-5*); pap. 8.95 (*1-885356-01-3*) Morning Glory.

— Detour for Emmy. (Illus.). 256p. (Orig.). 1993. 15.95 (*0-930934-75-X*); pap. 9.95 (*0-930934-76-8*) Morning Glory.

— Telling. 186p. (Orig.). 1989. pap. 6.95 (*0-929848-01-2*) Peace Ventures Pr.

— Too Soon for Jeff. 224p. (Orig.). (YA). (gr. 7 up). 1994. 15.95 (*0-930934-90-3*); pap. 8.95 (*0-930934-91-1*) Morning Glory.

Reynolds, Marilyn M. Regional Transit Guide: San Francisco Bay Area. Kahn, Brenda, ed. (Illus.). 128p. (Orig.). 1989. pap. 3.95 (*0-9624272-0-9*) Metro Trans Comm.

— Regional Transit Guide 1991: San Francisco Bay Area. Kahn, Brenda, ed. (Illus.). 128p. 1990. pap. 3.95 (*0-9624272-1-7*) Metro Trans Comm.

***Reynolds, Marilynn.** Belle's Journey. (Illus.). 32p. (Orig.). (J). (gr. 1-4). 1994. pap. 6.95 (*1-55143-021-5*) Orca Bk Pubs.

— A Dog for a Friend. (Illus.). 32p. (J). (gr. 1-4). 1994. lib. bdg. 13.95 (*1-55143-018-5*) Orca Bk Pubs.

Reynolds, Mark. Haynes BSA A50 & A65 Twins Owners Workshop Manual, No. 155: '62-'73. 1979. 16.95 (*0-85696-155-8*) Haynes Pubns.

Reynolds, Mark, ed. Two-Year College English: Essays for A New Century. LC 93-46898. 241p. 1994. text ed. 19.95 (*0-8141-5541-3*) NCTE.

Reynolds, Mark & Rota, Gian-Carlo, eds. Science, Computers, & People: From the Tree of Mathematics, Stanislaw Ulam. (Illus.). 1986. 39.00 (*0-8176-3276-X*) Birkhauser.

Reynolds, Mark, jt. auth. see Gabbay, Dov M.

Reynolds, Mark J. America's Fastest Way to Become a Millionaire! The Magic Nine System. 150p. 1986. 4.95 (*0-915451-06-9*) New Start Pubns.

Reynolds, Martha, jt. auth. see Reynolds, Rick.

Reynolds, Martin, jt. auth. see Holt, Cedric.

Reynolds, Mary, et al. Pirandello: Annual Volume of Review of National Literature Essays on the Fiction & Plays of Luigi Pirandello, Nobel Laureate. Commemorative Volume. 1986. 23.00 (*0-918680-27-1*) Bagehot Council.

Reynolds, Mary T. Interdepartmental Committees in the National Administration, 1932-1936. LC 68-58618. (Columbia University. Studies in the Social Sciences: No. 450). reprint ed. 20.00 (*0-404-51450-2*) AMS Pr.

— Joyce & Dante: The Shaping Imagination. (Illus.). 400p. 1987. pap. text ed. 19.95 (*0-691-10198-1*) Princeton U Pr.

Reynolds, Mary T., ed. James Joyce: A Collection of Critical Essays. LC 92-16520. (New Century Views Ser.). 264p. 1992. pap. 12.95 (*0-13-512211-2*) P-H.

Reynolds, Maureen, ed. see Grimsdale, Annette.

Reynolds, Maureen, ed. see Kyte, Barbara & Greenberg, Kathy.

Reynolds, Maureen, ed. see Pappas, Lou S.

Reynolds, Maynard C. Categories & Variables in Special Education. (Augustana College Library Occasional Papers, Wallin Lecture: No. 9). 16p. 1968. pap. 0.50 (*0-910182-39-6*) Augustana Coll.

Reynolds, Maynard C., jt. ed. see Wang, Margaret C.

Reynolds, Merrill J., jt. auth. see Dott, Robert Henry.

Reynolds, Michael. A Coming of Wizards. (Illus.). 234p. (Orig.). 1989. pap. 12.95 (*0-9614010-3-6*) High Mesa Pr.

— Dead Ends. (Illus.). 304p. (Orig.). 1992. mass mkt. 4.99 (*0-446-36282-4*) Warner Bks.

— The Devil's Adjutant: Jochen Peiper, Panzer Leader. (Illus.). 320p. 1995. 27.50 (*1-885119-15-1*) Sarpedon.

— Earthship: How to Build Your Own, Vol. 1. (Illus.). 240p. 1990. 24.95 (*0-9626767-0-5*) Solar Survival.

— Earthship, Vol. II: Systems & Components. (Illus.). 230p. 1991. 24.95 (*0-9626767-1-3*) Solar Survival.

— Earthship, Vol. III: Evolution Beyond Economics. 250p. 1993. How to. 24.95 (*0-9626767-2-1*) Solar Survival.

— Group Work in Education & Training. Bell, Chris, ed. 160p. (Orig.). 1993. pap. text ed. 27.95 (*0-7494-1027-2*, Pub. by Kogan Page UK) Nichols Pub.

— The Young Hemingway. 281p. 1987. pap. 21.95 (*0-631-14787-X*) Blackwell Pubs.

Reynolds, Michael, comp. Hemingway: An Annotated Chronology. (Omni Chronology Ser.). 155p. 1991. lib. bdg. 54.00 (*1-55888-427-0*) Omnigraphics Inc.

Reynolds, Michael M. Guide to Theses & Dissertations: An International Annotated Bibliography of Bibliographies. LC 85-43094. 272p. 1986. 31.50 (*0-89774-149-8*) Oryx Pr.

Reynolds, Michael M., ed. Reader in the Academic Library. LC 71-112300. 378p. 1983. text ed. 65.00 (*0-313-24034-5*, ZRB/, Greenwood Pr) Greenwood.

Reynolds, Michael P. & King, Philip S. The Expert Witness & His Evidence. 2nd ed. LC 92-11007. (Illus.). 288p. 1992. 62.95 (*0-632-03389-4*) Blackwell Sci.

Reynolds, Michael S. Hemingway: The American Homecoming. LC 92-11662. 1992. pap. 24.95 (*0-631-18481-3*) Blackwell Pubs.

— Hemingway's Reading, Nineteen Ten to Nineteen Forty: Commentary & Inventory. LC 80-7549. 200p. 1981. 39.50 (*0-691-06447-4*) Princeton U Pr.

— The Sun Also Rises: A Novel of the Twenties. (Masterwork Studies: No. 16). 118p. 1988. text ed. 22.95 (*0-8057-7962-0*, Pub. by Royal Botanic Garden UK); pap. 12.95 (*0-8057-8015-7*, Pub. by Royal Botanic Garden UK) Macmillan.

***Reynolds, Mike & Martin-Nagy, Rebecca.** George Bireline. (Illus.). 20p. (Orig.). (YA). Date not set. pap. write for info. (*1-885449-01-1*) City Gallery Cntmprry Art.

Reynolds, Mike & Reynolds, Kay. Fortune's Friend: Lucky Lacey. (Fortune's Friends Ser.). (Illus.). 64p. (Orig.). 1988. pap. 9.95 (*0-89865-507-2*, Starblaze) Donning Co.

Reynolds, Mike, jt. auth. see Reynolds, Kay.

Reynolds, Moira. Coping with An Immigrant Parent. Rosen, Ruth, ed. (Coping Ser.). (YA). (gr. 7-12). 1992. 15.95 (*0-8239-1462-3*) Rosen Group.

Reynolds, Moira, jt. auth. see Strazzabosco, Gina.

Reynolds, Moira D. How Pasteur Changed History: The Story of Louis Pasteur & the Pasteur Institute. LC 94-2757. (Illus.). 151p. (Orig.). (YA). (gr. 8-12). 1994. pap. 14.95 (*1-881117-05-7*) McGuinn & McGuire.

— Margaret Sanger, Leader for Birth Control. Rahmas, Sigurd C., ed. (Outstanding Personalities Ser.: No. 93). 32p. (gr. 7-12). 1982. 4.95 (*0-87157-593-0*) SamHar Pr.

— Nine American Women of the Nineteenth Century: Leaders into the Twentieth. LC 87-43169. 167p. 1988. lib. bdg. 22.50x (*0-89950-325-X*) McFarland & Co.

R

An Asterisk (*) at the beginning of an entry indicates that the title is appearing in BIP for the first time.

— Women Advocates of Reproductive Rights: Eleven Who Led the Struggle in the United States & Great Britain. LC 93-41201. (Illus.). 179p. 1994. lib. bdg. 27.50 (0-89950-940-1) McFarland & Co.
— Women Champions of Human Rights: Eleven U. S. Leaders of the Twentieth Century. LC 91-52505. 168p. 1991. lib. bdg. 24.95x (0-89950-614-3) McFarland & Co.
Reynolds, Monica. Multiply Your Success with Real Estate Assistants: How to Hire, Train & Manage Your Assistant: Featuring 93 Ready-to-Use Forms. LC 93-32671. 208p. (Orig.). 1994. pap. 24.95 (0-7931-0776-8, 560888, Real Estate Ed); write for info. (0-7931-0775-X, Real Estate Ed) Dearborn Finan.
Reynolds, Morgan. How Much Government Does Texas Need? An Analysis of the Texas State Budget. 1989. pap. 10.00 (0-943802-41-5, 138) Natl Ctr Pol.
Reynolds, Morgan O. Crime & Punishment in Texas a 1993 Update. rev. ed. (Illus.). 28p. 1993. pap. 10.00 (0-943802-79-2, 175) Natl Ctr Pol.
— Crime in Texas. 1991. pap. 10.00 (0-943802-61-X, 158) Natl Ctr Pol.
— Crime Pays, but So Does Imprisonment. 1990. pap. 10.00 (0-943802-52-0, 149) Natl Ctr Pol.
— Economics of Labor. LC 94-18916. 1995. 32.95 (0-538-84434-5) S-W Pub.
— The History & Economics of Labor Unions. Pejovich, Steve & Dethloff, Henry, eds. (Series on Public Issues: No. 16). 18p. 1985. pap. 2.00 (0-86599-052-2) PERC.
— Using the Private Sector to Deter Crime. 42p. (Orig.). Date not set. pap. text ed. 10.00 (1-56808-015-8, 181) Natl Ctr Pol.
— Why Does Crime Pay? 1991. pap. 5.00 (0-943802-89-X, BG110) Natl Ctr Pol.
— Why Does Crime Pay? rev. ed. (Illus.). 15p. 1992. pap. 5.00 (1-56808-006-9, BG 123) Natl Ctr Pol.
Reynolds, Morgan O. & Caruth, W. W., III. Myths about Gun Control. 1992. pap. 10.00 (0-943802-99-7, 176) Natl Ctr Pol.
Reynolds, Morgan O. & Feulner, Edwin J., Jr., eds. W. H. Hutt: An Economist for the Long Run. LC 86-42794. 160p. 1986. pap. 7.95 (0-89526-797-7) Regnery Pub.
Reynolds, Myra. The Learned Lady in England 1650-1760. 1976. lib. bdg. 59.95 (0-8490-2136-7) Gordon Pr.
— The Learned Lady in England (1650-1760) 11.75 (0-8446-1382-7) Peter Smith.
— Treatment of Nature in English Poetry Between Pope & Wordsworth. LC 66-29468. 388p. 1966. reprint ed. 50.00 (0-87752-091-7) Gordian.
Reynolds, Myra, ed. see Finch, Anne K.
Reynolds, Nancy & Reimer-Torn, Susan. Dance Classics. LC 90-27665. (Illus.). 164p. 1991. pap. 14.95 (1-55652-106-5) A cappella Bks.
Reynolds, Nancy H. Older Volunteer Leaders in the Rural Community. LC 91-32211. (Studies on Elderly in America). 152p. 1992. 42.00 (0-8153-0528-1) Garland.
Reynolds, Nancy T. Adopting Your Child: Options, Answers, & Actions. (Reference Ser.). 1993. pap. 12.95 (0-88908-295-2) Self-Counsel Pr.
Reynolds-Naylor, Phyllis. Beetles Lightly Toasted. (J). (gr. k-6). 1989. reprint ed. pap. 3.50 (0-440-40143-7, YB) Dell.
— Night Cry. (J). (gr. 4-7). 1993. pap. 3.50 (0-440-40017-1, YB) Dell.
— The Witch's Sister. (J). (gr. k-6). 1993. pap. 3.50 (0-440-40028-7) Dell.
Reynolds, Neil B. & Manning, Ellis L., eds. Excursions in Science. LC 72-1237. (Essay Index Reprint Ser.). 1977. reprint ed. 22.95 (0-8369-2857-1) Ayer.
***Reynolds, Noel B. & Saxonhouse, Arlene W., eds.** Thomas Hobbes: Three Discourses: A Critical Modern Edition of Newly Identified Work of the Young Hobbes. LC 95-12724. 1995. write for info. (0-226-34545-9) U Ch Pr.
Reynolds, Noel B., jt. auth. see Bryner, Gary C.
Reynolds, O. & Baker, J. A Time to Train: Account of Experience Gained by RTB At IS Spencer Works. LC 66-28421. 1966. 106.00 (0-08-012146-2, Pub. by Pergamon Repr UK) Franklin.
Reynolds, Oliver. The Oslo Tram. 74p. (Orig.). 1991. pap. 8.95 (0-571-15258-9) Faber & Faber.
Reynolds, Ora E. The Social & Economic Status of College Students. LC 71-177189. (Columbia University. Teachers College. Contributions to Education Ser.: No. 272). reprint ed. 37.50 (0-404-55272-2) AMS Pr.
Reynolds, Osborne M., Jr. Local Government Law, 1993: Pocket Part. (Hornbook Ser.). 200p. 1993. pap. text ed. 12.50 (0-314-02256-2) West Pub.
Reynolds, Osborne M., Jr., jt. auth. see Kutner, Peter B.
Reynolds, P. A. An Introduction to International Relations. 3rd ed. LC 93-2567. (C). 1995. pap. text ed. 22.95 (0-582-21318-5, 76670) Longman.
Reynolds, P. K. The Banana: Its History & Cultivation. 1977. lib. bdg. 250.00 (0-8490-1474-3) Gordon Pr.
Reynolds, P. Preston. Watts Hospital of Durham, North Carolina, 1895-1976: Keeping the Doors Open. LC 91-77158. (Illus.). 133p. (Orig.). 1992. 24.95 (0-9631387-1-5); pap. 15.94 (0-9631387-0-7) Fund Adv Sci.
Reynolds, Pamela. Childhood in Crossroads: Cognition & Society in South Africa. (Illus.). 276p. (Orig.). reprint ed. pap. 78.70 (0-7837-5560-0, 2045335) Bks Demand.
— Dance, Civet Cat: Tonga Children & Labour in the Zambezi Valley. LC 89-22860. 208p. 1990. text ed. 24.95 (0-8214-0946-8) Ohio U Pr.
— Traditional Healers & Childhood in Zimbabwe. LC 94-47391. (Illus.). 320p. (C). 1995. text ed. 39.95 (0-8214-1121-7); pap. text ed. 17.95 (0-8214-1122-5) Ohio U Pr.
Reynolds, Pat. Tom's Friend. LC 93-170. (J). 1994. write for info. (0-383-03797-2) SRA Schl Grp.
Reynolds, Patrick & Shachtman, Tom. The Gilded Leaf: Triumph, Tragedy & Tobacco: Three Generations of the R. J. Reynolds Family & Fortune. (Illus.). 384p. 1989. 19.95 (0-316-74121-3) Little.
Reynolds, Patrick M. Big Apple Almanac. (Illus.). 112p. (Orig.). 1989. pap. 14.95 (0-932514-19-7) Red Rose Studio.
— Big Apple Almanac, No. 2. (Illus.). 112p. (Orig.). 1991. pap. 14.95 (0-932514-24-3) Red Rose Studio.
— Big Apple Almanac, No. 3. (Illus.). 112p. (Orig.). 1994. pap. 14.95 (0-932514-29-4) Red Rose Studio.
— The Book of Silly Lists. LC 92-38660. (J). 1993. 1.25 (0-89375-354-8) Troll Assocs.
— The Chicken War & Other Wild Stories about Texas: The Era of the Missions. (Texas Lore Ser.). (Illus.). 104p. (Orig.). 1995. pap. 6.95 (0-932514-30-8) Red Rose Studio.
— Colorful Characters of Pennsylvania: Pennsylvania Profiles, Vol. 12. (Illus.). 56p. (Orig.). 1987. pap. 3.75 (0-932514-17-0) Red Rose Studio.
— History & Mystery of Pennsylvania. (Pennsylvania Profiles Ser.: Vol. V). (Illus.). 56p. 1981. pap. 3.75 (0-932514-05-7) Red Rose Studio.
— It Started in Pennsylvania. (Pennsylvania Profiles Ser.: Vol. 14). (Illus.). 56p. (Orig.). 1990. pap. 3.75 (0-932514-22-7) Red Rose Studio.
— The Johnstown Flood & Other Stories about Pennsylvania. (Pennsylvania Profiles Ser.: Vol. 13). (Illus.). 56p. (Orig.). 1989. pap. 3.75 (0-932514-20-0) Red Rose Studio.
— Keystone Chronicles. (Pennsylvania Profiles Ser.: Vol. 15). (Illus.). 56p. (Orig.). 1991. pap. 3.75 (0-932514-25-1) Red Rose Studio.
— Lone Star Legacies. (Texas Lore Ser.: Vol. 8). (Illus.). 56p. (Orig.). 1990. pap. 3.75 (0-932514-23-5) Red Rose Studio.
— Pennsylvania Profiles, Vol. 10. (Illus.). 56p. 1986. pap. 3.75 (0-932514-14-6) Red Rose Studio.
— Pennsylvania Profiles, Vol. 11. (Illus.). 56p. 1987. pap. 3.75 (0-932514-16-2) Red Rose Studio.
— Pennsylvania Profiles Ser., Vol. 9. (Pennsylvania Profiles Ser.). (Illus.). 56p. (Orig.). 1985. pap. 3.75 (0-932514-12-X) Red Rose Studio.
— Pennsylvania's Hectic Heritage. (Pennsylvania Profiles Ser.: Vol. VI). (Illus.). 56p. (J). (gr. 7-12). 1982. pap. 3.75 (0-932514-06-5) Red Rose Studio.
— Scraping up Pennsylvania's Past. (Pennsylvania Profiles Ser.: Vol. 8). (Illus.). 56p. (Orig.). 1984. pap. 3.75 (0-932514-10-3) Red Rose Studio.
— Strange but True. 1978. pap. 3.75 (0-932514-00-6) Red Rose Studio.
— Texas' Action History. (Texas Lore Ser.: Vol. 7). (Illus.). 56p. (Orig.). 1990. pap. 3.75 (0-932514-21-9) Red Rose Studio.
— Texas Lore, Vol. 5. (Illus.). 56p. (Orig.). 1987. pap. 3.75 (0-932514-15-4) Red Rose Studio.
— Texas Lore, Vol. 9. (Illus.). 56p. (Orig.). 1991. pap. 3.75 (0-932514-26-X) Red Rose Studio.
— Texas Lore, Vols. 1, 2, 3, & 4. (Illus.). 228p. (Orig.). (YA). (gr. 8-12). 1992. pap. 12.95 (0-932514-27-8) Red Rose Studio.
— Texas Lore Ten. (Texas Lore Ser.). (Illus.). 56p. (Orig.). 1992. pap. 3.75 (0-932514-28-6) Red Rose Studio.
— Unusual Stories from Texas' History. (Texas Lore Ser.: Vol. 6). (Illus.). 56p. (Orig.). 1988. pap. 3.75 (0-932514-18-9) Red Rose Studio.
Reynolds, Paul D. Ethical Dilemmas & Social Science Research. LC 79-88110. (Jossey-Bass Social & Behavioral Science Ser.). 527p. reprint ed. pap. 150.20 (0-8357-6887-2, 2037939) Bks Demand.
— Primer in Theory Construction. 194p. (Orig.). (C). 1971. pap. write for info. (0-02-399600-5) Macmillan.
Reynolds, Paula B. & Andrus, Jenny G. Bay Area Baby: The Essential Guide to Local Resources for Pregnancy, Childbirth & Parenthood. LC 87-28445. (Illus.). 324p. (Orig.). 1991. pap. 14.95 (0-944296-05-X) Spirit Pr.
***Reynolds, Peter.** Dealing with Crime and Aggression at Work: A Handbook for Organizational Action. LC 94-34351. 1994. 18.95 (0-07-707932-9) McGraw.
— Practical Approaches to Teaching Shakespeare. Gill, Roma, ed. (Shakespeare Studies). 128p. 1992. pap. 11.95 (0-19-831954-1) OUP.
— Shakespeare: As You Like It. (Critical Studies). 128p. 1992. mass mkt. 5.95 (0-14-077145-X, Penguin Bks) Viking Penguin.
— Shakespeare: Text into Performance. (Critical Studies). 128p. 1992. mass mkt. 9.95 (0-14-077234-0, Penguin Bks) Viking Penguin.
Reynolds, Peter, ed. Novel Images: Literature in Performance. LC 92-24807. 224p. 1993. 49.95 (0-415-09102-0, B0017, Routledge NY); pap. 15.95 (0-415-09103-9, B0021, Routledge NY) Routledge.
Reynolds, Peter, jt. auth. see Phelan, Peter.
Reynolds, Peter C. On the Evolution of Human Behavior: The Argument from Animals to Man. LC 80-6056. 265p. 1981. pap. 16.00 (0-520-04416-9) U CA Pr.
— Stealing Fire: The Atomic Bomb as Symbolic Body. (Illus.). 304p. 1991. write for info. (0-9629261-0-8) Iconic Anthro.
Reynolds, Peter J. Political Economy: A Synthesis of Kaleckian & Post-Keynesian Economics. 256p. 1987. text ed. 45.00 (0-312-01328-0) St Martin.
Reynolds, Peter J., ed. On Clusters & Clustering: From Atoms to Fractals. LC 93-9513. (Random Materials & Processes Ser.). xiv, 444p. 1993. 80.00 (0-444-89022-X, North Holland) Elsevier.
Reynolds, Philip L. Marriage in the Western Church: The Christianization of Marriage During the Patristic Medieval Periods. LC 94-570. (Supplements to Vigiliae Christianae Ser.: Vol. 24). 1994. 108.75 (90-04-10022-9) E J Brill.
Reynolds, Phyllis C. & Dimon, Elizabeth F. Trees of Greater Portland. LC 92-19585. (Illus.). 216p. 1993. pap. 19.95 (0-88192-263-3) Timber.
Reynolds, Quentin. Amazing Mr. Doolittle: A Biography of Lieutenant General James H. Doolittle. LC 71-169434. (Literature & History of Aviation Ser.). 1976. reprint ed. 25.95 (0-405-03778-3) Ayer.
— Courtroom. LC 77-119943. (Select Bibliographies Reprint Ser.). 1977. 30.95 (0-8369-5386-X) Ayer.
— I, Willie Sutton. (Illus.). 283p. 1993. reprint ed. pap. 13.95 (0-306-80510-3) Da Capo.
— Quentin Reynolds. 24.95 (0-8488-1126-7) Amereon Ltd.
— The Wright Brothers. LC 50-11766. (Landmark Bks.). (Illus.). 160p. (J). (gr. 5-9). 1981. pap. 4.99 (0-394-84700-8) Random Bks Yng Read.
***Reynolds, R. & Ekstrom, Rosemary.** Concise Catholic Dictionary. LC 94-60980. 208p. 1994. pap. 9.95 (0-89622-622-0) Twenty-Third.
Reynolds, R. A. Computing for Architects. 2nd ed. LC 93-3314. 216p. 1993. pap. 49.95 (0-7506-1516-8, Butterwrth Archit) Buttrwrth-Heinemann.
— Introduction to International Relations. 200p. 1971. pap. 11.95 (0-582-48818-4) Schenkman Bks Inc.
Reynolds, R. C., Jr. & Walker, J. R., eds. Computer Applications to X-Ray Powder Diffraction Analysis of Clay Minerals. (CMS Workshop Lectures: Vol. 5). (Illus.). 171p. (Orig.). (C). 1993. pap. text ed. 15.00 (1-881208-06-0) Clay Minerals.
Reynolds, R. D. Ascomycete Systematics: The Luttrellian Concept. (Microbiology Ser.). (Illus.). 272p. 1981. 108.00 (0-387-90488-3) Spr-Verlag.
Reynolds, R. J., jt. intro. see Moore, Bob.
Reynolds, Ralph. Growing up Cowboy: Confessions of a Luna Kid. LC 91-71366. 192p. (Orig.). 1991. pap. 12.95 (1-55591-086-6) Fulcrum Pub.
— Making Full Proof of Our Ministry. 5th ed. 152p. (C). 1989. pap. 5.95 (1-877917-07-9) Alpha Bible Pubns.
Reynolds, Ralph, ed. see Bowers, Wendell.
Reynolds, Ralph D. John Hobbs 16??-1731: A Genealogy of the Hobbs Family of Ohio. 2nd ed. (Illus.). 400p. 1994. 29.00 (0-925861-01-4) Quaint Pub Co.
Reynolds, Ralph V. Alpha Bible Course, 6 vols. 2nd ed. 1728p. (C). 1987. pap. text ed. 124.95 (0-685-27256-7) Alpha Bible Pubns.
— Can a Believer Be Lost? 2nd ed. 118p. (C). 1986. pap. 5.50 (1-877917-00-1) Alpha Bible Pubns.
— The Cry of the Unborn. (Orig.). (C). 1989. pap. 5.95 (0-685-27250-8) Alpha Bible Pubns.
— The Cry of the Unborn: Understanding the Spiritual Birth Process. 125p. (Orig.). (YA). Date not set. pap. 5.95 (1-877917-09-5) Alpha Bible Pubns.
— Dear Pastor: If the Sheep Could Speak. 144p. (Orig.). (C). 1988. pap. 5.95 (1-877917-01-X) Alpha Bible Pubns.
— Dividing the Word of Truth. 193p. (YA). (gr. 9). Date not set. pap. 14.95 (1-877917-08-7) Alpha Bible Pubns.
— Dividing the Word of Truth. 9th ed. 193p. (C). 1987. pap. 14.95 (0-685-27252-4) Alpha Bible Pubns.
— If the Sheep Could Speak. 144p. (Orig.). (C). 1988. pap. 5.95 (0-685-27255-9) Alpha Bible Pubns.
— Living the Crucified Life. 118p. (Orig.). (C). 1987. pap. 5.50 (1-877917-02-8) Alpha Bible Pubns.
— Portraits of the Bride. 142p. (Orig.). (C). 1985. pap. 5.95 (0-685-27254-0) Alpha Bible Pubns.
— Truth Shall Triumph. 9th ed. 111p. 1983. pap. 3.99 (0-912315-07-5) Word Aflame.
— Unbroken Vows. 132p. (Orig.). (C). 1986. pap. 6.95 (0-685-27253-2) Alpha Bible Pubns.
— Usando Bien la Palabra De Verdad. Geissler, Darry & Geissler, Kimberly, eds. Crossley, Darry, tr. 220p. (Orig.). (SPA.). (YA). Date not set. pap. 14.95 (1-877917-12-5) Alpha Bible Pubns.
— Usando Bien la Palabra De Verdad. Geissler, Darry & Geissler, Kimberly, eds. Crossley, Darry, tr. (Dividing the World of Truth Ser.). 220p. (Orig.). (SPA.). (C). 1988. pap. 14.95 (0-685-27251-6) Alpha Bible Pubns.
Reynolds, Randy & Lynn, David. Codependency Confusion: Developing Healthy Relationships. (Recovery Discovery Ser.). 96p. 1992. pap. 4.99 (0-310-57361-0) Zondervan.
— Divorce Recovery: Putting Yourself Back Together Again. (Recovery Discovery Ser.). 96p. 1992. pap. 4.99 (0-310-57351-3) Zondervan.
— Stress Relief: Overcoming Exhaustion, Relapse, & Burnout. (Recovery Discovery Ser.). 96p. 1992. pap. 4.99 (0-310-57311-4) Zondervan.
***Reynolds, Randy & Moede, Paul.** Good News about Your Strong-Willed Child: Understanding & Raising the Child Who Opposes You. 200p. 1995. pap. 10.99 (0-310-48611-4) Zondervan.
Reynolds, Ray. California the Curious. (Illus.). 200p. (Orig.). 1989. pap. 12.95 (0-939919-25-7) Bear Flag Bks.
— Catspaw Utopia: Alfred K. Owen, the Adventurer of Topolobampo Bay, & the Last Grand Utopian Scheme. enl. rev. ed. LC 93-12180. (West Coast Studies: No. 4). (Illus.). 200p. Date not set. pap. write for info. (0-8095-3803-2) Borgo Pr.
— Catspaw Utopia: Alfred K. Owen, the Adventurer of Topolobampo Bay, & the Last Grand Utopian Scheme. 2nd enl. rev. ed. LC 93-12180. (West Coast Studies: No. 4). (Illus.). 200p. lib. bdg. write for info. (0-8095-2803-7) Borgo Pr.
Reynolds, Ray & Hill, Ed, eds. Puptent Poets: Soldier Verse of World War II. 122p. 1992. pap. 10.00 (0-9630288-0-4) Patchy Fog.
Reynolds, Ray, jt. auth. see Barlow, Ronald S.
Reynolds, Raymond J. Sharing My Notebook. 1980. 7.50 (0-87881-085-4) Mojave Bks.
***Reynolds, Rebecca A.** Bring Me the Ocean: Nature As Teacher, Messenger, & Intermediary. LC 94-61765. (Illus.). 120p. 1995. 21.95 (0-9641089-2-5) VanderWyk & Burnham.
Reynolds, Regina, jt. auth. see Reynolds, Charles.
Reynolds, Reginald. John Woolman & the Twentieth Century. (C). 1958. pap. 3.00 (0-87574-096-0) Pendle Hill.
Reynolds, Renny. The Art of the Party: Design Ideas for Successful Entertaining. (Illus.). 288p. 1992. 40.00 (0-670-83054-2, Viking Studio) Studio Bks.
Reynolds, Richard. The Foundation of Rhetoric. LC 45-7205. 1977. reprint ed. 50.00 (0-8201-1210-0) Schol Facsimiles.
— On Doctoring: Stories, Poems, Essays. 1995. 30.00 (0-684-80255-4) S&S Trade.
— On Doctoring Stories Poems & Essays. 1991. 29.95 (0-671-74015-6) S&S Trade.
— Super Heroes: A Modern Mythology. (Studies in Popular Culture Ser.). (Illus.). 134p. 1994. reprint ed. 35.00 (0-87805-693-9); reprint ed. pap. 13.95 (0-87805-694-7) U Pr of Miss.
Reynolds, Richard, ed. see Ireland, Patrick J.
Reynolds, Richard C. Stage Left: The Development of the American Social Drama in the Thirties. LC 85-52030. 205p. 1986. 22.50 (0-87875-311-7) Whitston Pub.
Reynolds, Richard C., et al. The Health of a Rural County: Perspectives & Problems. LC 75-35753. 203p. reprint ed. pap. 57.90 (0-7837-4946-5, 2044612) Bks Demand.
Reynolds, Richard D. The Ancient Art of Colima, Mexico. LC 88-92600. (Illus.). 96p. (Orig.). 1993. 18.95 (0-9618577-1-4) Squibob Pr.
— Cry for War: The Story of Suzan & Michael Carson. 368p. (Orig.). 1987. pap. 7.95 (0-9618577-2-2) Squibob Pr.
Reynolds, Richard D., ed. Squibob: An Early California Humorist. LC 89-61831. (Illus.). 256p. 1989. 15.95 (0-9618577-5-7); pap. 10.95 (0-9618577-6-5) Squibob Pr.
Reynolds, Rick & Reynolds, Martha. Dog Bites! 96p. (Orig.). 1992. pap. 8.95 (0-425-13511-X) Berkley Pub.
Reynolds, Rob. George Washington, Jesus Christ & Uncle Fred. LC 94-65020. 112p. (Orig.). 1994. pap. 11.95 (1-880222-18-3) Red-Apple Pub.
Reynolds, Robert. Thomas Wolfe: Memoir of a Friendship. LC 65-23163. 173p. reprint ed. pap. 49.40 (0-8357-7717-0, 2036074) Bks Demand.
Reynolds, Robert & Seslar, Patrick. Painting Nature's Peaceful Places. (Illus.). 144p. 1994. 27.95 (0-89134-511-6, 30518) North Light Bks.
Reynolds, Robert, jt. photos see Muench, David.
Reynolds, Robert C., jt. auth. see Moore, Duane M.
Reynolds, Robert L. Europe Emerges: Transition Toward an Industrial World-Wide Society, 600-1750. (Illus.). 544p. 1966. pap. 13.75 (0-299-02294-3) U of Wis Pr.
Reynolds, Robert W., photos. Oregon's National Forests. LC 89-81617. (Illus.). 84p. 1990. 26.50 (1-55868-016-0) Gr Arts Ctr Pub.
Reynolds, Roger. A Searcher's Path: A Composer's Ways. LC 87-82698. (I.S.A.M. Monographs: No. 25). 74p. (Orig.). 1988. audio 12.00 (0-914678-28-0) Inst Am Music.
Reynolds, Roger E. Law & Liturgy in the Latin Church, 5th-12th Centuries. LC 94-4774. (Collected Studies: Vol. CS457). 1994. 89.95 (0-86078-405-3, Pub. by Variorum UK) Ashgate Pub Co.
— The Ordinals of Christ from Their Origins to the Twelfth Century. (C). 1978. 110.00 (3-11-007058-8) De Gruyter.
Reynolds, Ron, jt. auth. see O'Morrow, Gerald.
Reynolds, Ron, jt. auth. see Rohn, Jim.
Reynolds, Ronald L. The Gift. LC 83-70419. 1983. write for info. (0-939490-03-X) Total Impact.
— The Magic of Goals. LC 83-71017. 1979. write for info. (0-939490-01-3) Total Impact.
Reynolds, Ronald L., jt. auth. see Rohn, E. James.
Reynolds, Ronald P. & O'Morrow, Gerald S. Problems, Issues & Concepts in Therapeutic Recreation. 304p. (C). 1985. text ed. 39.00 (0-13-717430-6) P-H.
Reynolds, Ronald P., jt. auth. see O'Morrow, Gerald S.
Reynolds, Ruth M. Campus in Bondage: A Nineteen Forty-Eight Microcosm of Puerto Rico in Bondage. Erazo, Blanca V., ed. (Illus.). 334p. (Orig.). 1989. pap. 12.00 (1-878483-00-5) Hunter Coll CEP.
Reynolds, Sharon E., ed. see Brown, Drollene P.
Reynolds, Sheri. Bitterroot Landing. LC 94-4915. 1994. write for info. (0-399-13994-X, Putnam) Putnam Pub Group.
— Bitterroot Landing. 240p. 1995. 19.95 (0-685-73076-X) Putnam Pub Group.
Reynolds, Sian. Brittanica's Typesetters: Women Compositors in Edwardian Edinburgh. (Edinburgh Education & Society Ser.). (Illus.). 160p. 1989. 37.50 (0-85224-634-X, Pub. by Edinburgh U Pr UK); pap. 15.00 (0-85224-652-8, Pub. by Edinburgh U Pr UK) Col U Pr.
Reynolds, Sian, ed. Women, State, & Revolution: Essays on Power & Gender in Europe Since 1789. LC 86-16074. (Illus.). 208p. 1987. lib. bdg. 27.50x (0-87023-552-4); pap. text ed. 14.95 (0-87023-553-2) U of Mass Pr.
Reynolds, Sian, tr. see Bramly, Serge.
Reynolds, Sian, tr. see Braudel, Fernand.
Reynolds, Sian, tr. see Le Roy-Ladurie, Emmanuel.
Reynolds, Simon. The Vision of Simeon Solomon. 183p. 1984. 45.00 (0-685-30068-4, Pub. by Catalpa Pr Ltd UK) Oak Knoll.
Reynolds, Simon & Albert, Bill. Blissed Out: The Apocalypse of Rock. LC 90-60291. 192p. (Orig.). 1990. pap. 15.95 (1-85242-199-1) Serpents Tail.
***Reynolds, Simon & Press, Joy.** The Sex Revolts: Gender, Rebellion, & Rock 'n' Roll. LC 94-30683. 428p. 1995. text ed. 24.95 (0-674-80272-1, REYSER) HUP.
Reynolds, Simon, jt. auth. see Toft, Brian.
***Reynolds, Stephen.** Beyond the Killing Tree: A Journey of Discovery. Graydon, Don, ed. (Illus.). 192p. 1995. 19.95 (0-945397-42-9) Epicenter Pr.

R

An Asterisk (*) at the beginning of an entry indicates that the title is appearing in BIP for the first time.

— Beyond the Killing Tree: A Wildlife Officer's Journey of Discovery from the Desert Southwest to the Alaska Bush. (Illus.). 192p. 1995. write for info. (*0-614-04392-1*) Epicenter Pr.

— The Christian Religious Tradition. 232p. (C). 1977. pap. 19.95 (*0-8221-0204-8*) Intl Thomson.

— Voyage of the New Hazard to the Northwest Coast, Hawaii & China, 1810-1813. 1970. 19.95 (*0-87770-076-1*) Ye Galleon.

Reynolds, Steve & Carver, H. E. The Murder of Che Guevara. LC 84-51288. (Mercenary Adventures Ser.). 160p. (Orig.). 1984. 9.95 (*0-918379-25-3*); pap. 6.95 (*0-317-11918-4*) Wild Geese.

— The U-One Hundred Sixty-Eight Incident. LC 84-51393. (Mercenary Adventures Ser.). 260p. (Orig.). 1985. 14.95 (*0-918379-01-6*); pap. 6.95 (*0-317-14780-3*) Wild Geese.

Reynolds, Steven, jt. auth. see Lomax, Ian S.

Reynolds, Steven, jt. auth. see Stewart, Chris.

Reynolds-Strauss, Karen & Gligor, Adrian. Romanian Fairy Tales. (Illus.). 85p. (Orig.). (J). (ps-6). 1992. pap. text ed. 11.95 (*0-9634797-0-9*) K Strauss & A Gligor.

Reynolds, Susan. Fiefs & Vassals: The Medieval Evidence Reinterpreted. 550p. 1994. 29.95 (*0-19-820458-2*) OUP.

— Ideas & Solidarities of the Medieval Laity: England & Western Europe. LC 95-1530. (Collected Studies Ser.: Vol. 495). 1995. 77.50 (*0-86078-485-1*, Pub. by Variorum UK) Ashgate Pub Co.

Reynolds, Susan L. Strandia. (Illus.). 240p. (YA). (gr. 9-12). 1991. 14.95 (*0-374-37274-8*) FS&G.

Reynolds, Terrence. The Coherence of Life Without God Before God: The Problem of Earthly Desires in the Later Theology of Dietrich Bonhoeffer. 190p. (C). 1989. lib. bdg. 39.00 (*0-8191-7237-5*) U Pr of Amer.

Reynolds, Terry. The Echocardiographer's Pocket Reference. 180p. Date not set. 34.95 (*0-9635767-0-4*) AZ Heart Inst.

— Seventy-Five Years of Progress. LC 83-11875. 200p. 1983. 16.50 (*0-8169-0231-3*) Am Inst Chem Eng.

Reynolds, Terry S., ed. The Engineer in America: A Historical Anthology from Technology & Culture. 380p. 1991. lib. bdg. 44.95 (*0-226-71031-9*); pap. text ed. 19.95 (*0-226-71032-7*) U Ch Pr.

Reynolds, Thomas H. & Flores, Arturo A. Foreign Law: Current Sources of Codes & Basic Legislation in Jurisdictions of the World, Vol. II, Western & Eastern Europe & the European Communities. LC 89-10223. (American Association of Law Libraries Publications Ser.: No. 33). 1160p. 1991. ring bd. 225.00 (*0-8377-0138-4*) Rothman.

— Foreign Law: Current Sources of Codes & Basic Legislation in Jurisdictions of the World, Vol. II, Western & Eastern Europe & the European Communities. LC 89-10223. (American Association of Law Libraries Publications Ser.: No. 33). x, 1366p. 1993. ring bd. 225.00 (*0-8377-0139-2*) Rothman.

Reynolds, Tim. Dawn Chorus. LC 80-24377. 42p. 1980. 4.00 (*0-87886-111-4*, Greenfld Rev Pr) Greenfld Rev Lit.

— Que. LC 76-155304. 1971. 25.00 (*0-912604-06-9*); pap. 3.50 (*0-912604-05-0*) Halty Ferguson.

Reynolds, Tonga & Cousins, Colleen C. Lwaano Lwanyika: Tonga Book of the Earth. (Illus.). 250p. 1994. pap. 19.95 (*1-870670-30-2*) Paul & Co Pubs.

Reynolds, Tony. Cities in Crisis. (World Issues Ser.). (Illus.). 48p. (J). (gr. 5 up). 1990. lib. bdg. 18.60 (*0-86592-118-0*); lib. bdg. 13.95 (*0-685-36376-7*) Rourke Corp.

Reynolds, Tony, et al. World Issues, 2 bks., Set. (Illus.). 336p. (J). (gr. 5 up). 1990. lib. bdg. 126.00 (*0-86592-095-8*); lib. bdg. 94.50 (*0-685-36375-9*) Rourke Corp.

Reynolds, Tulsi. The Little Cat Who Had No Name. LC 90-62915. (Illus.). 32p. 1990. 9.25 (*1-877675-04-0*) Midmarch Arts-WAN.

Reynolds, V. Finding Out about Child Development. (C). 1989. 55.00 (*0-85950-928-1*, Pub. by S Thornes Pubs UK) St Mut.

— A Practical Guide to Child Development - Teacher's Book. (C). 1988. 50.00 (*0-85950-525-1*, Pub. by S Thornes Pubs UK) St Mut.

***Reynolds, V. & Boyce, A. J., eds.** Human Populations: Diversity & Adaptation. 256p. 1995. 93.00 (*0-19-852294-0*) OUP.

Reynolds, V. & Wallis, G. A First Home Economics Course. (C). 1987. 45.00 (*0-85950-675-4*, Pub. by S Thornes Pubs UK) St Mut.

Reynolds, V. Paul, ed. see Haskell, Robert L.

Reynolds, Valrae. The Newark Museum Tibetan Buddhist Altar. VanDecker, Lori & Price, Mary S., eds. (Illus.). 32p. (Orig.). 1991. pap. 8.00 (*0-685-61611-8*) Newark Mus.

— Tibetan Buddhist Altar. LC 91-29588. 1991. pap. 8.00 (*0-932828-25-6*) Newark Mus.

Reynolds, Valrae & Heller, Amy. Catalogue of the Newark Tibetan Collection: Introduction, 5 vols., Set. 2nd ed. Sweeney, Mary S., tr. (Illus.). 84p. (Orig.). 1983. pap. (*0-932828-12-4*) Newark Mus.

— Catalogue of the Newark Tibetan Collection: Introduction, Vol. I. 2nd ed. Sweeney, Mary S., tr. (Illus.). 84p. (Orig.). 1983. pap. 12.50 (*0-932828-13-2*) Newark Mus.

Reynolds, Valrae, jt. contrib. see Pal, Pratapaditya.

Reynolds, Valrae, et al. The Newark Museum Tibetan Collection: Sculpture & Painting, Vol. III. 2nd rev. ed. (Illus.). 208p. 1987. pap. 20.00 (*0-932828-15-9*) Newark Mus.

Reynolds, Vernon, ed. Human Behavior & Adaptation. (Symposia of the Society for the Study of Human Biology Ser.: Vol. 18). 314p. 1978. 44.00 (*0-85066-137-4*) Taylor & Francis.

— The Sociobiology of Ethnocentrism: Evolutionary Dimensions of Xenophobia, Discrimination, Racism & Nationalism. 336p. 1986. 45.00 (*0-7099-4222-2*, Pub. by Croom Helm UK) Routledge Chapman & Hall.

Reynolds, Vernon & Kellett, John, eds. Mating & Marriage. (Biosocial Society Ser.: No. 3). (Illus.). 176p. 1991. 53.00 (*0-19-858406-7*) OUP.

Reynolds, Vernon & Tanner, Ralph. The Social Ecology of Religion. (Illus.). 304p. (C). 1995. 39.95 (*0-19-506973-0*); pap. text ed. 17.95 (*0-19-506974-9*) OUP.

Reynolds, Vernon, jt. ed. see Harre, Rom.

Reynolds, Vernon, jt. ed. see Jones, Eric L.

Reynolds, Vernon, jt. ed. see Landers, John.

Reynolds, Vernon, jt. auth. see Quiatt, Duane.

Reynolds, W. M. & Johnston, H. F., eds. Handbook of Depression in Children & Adolescents. (Issues in Clinical Child Psychology Ser.). (Illus.). 540p. (C). 1994. text ed. 85.00 (*0-306-44742-8*, Plenum Pr) Plenum.

Reynolds, Walter F. Dry Strength Additives. LC 79-67261. (Press Bks.). 188p. 1980. 28.00 (*0-89852-044-4*, 01-02-B044) TAPPI.

Reynolds, Walter F., ed. The Sizing of Paper. 2nd ed. 170p. reprint ed. pap. 44.20 (*0-8357-6343-9*, 2035615) Bks Demand.

— The Sizing of Paper. 2nd ed. 156p. 1989. 73.00 (*0-89852-051-7*, 0102B051) TAPPI.

Reynolds, Walter F., ed. see Technical Association of the Pulp & Paper Industry Staff.

Reynolds, William. The Theory of the Law of Evidence As Established in the United States & of the Conduct of the Examination of Witnesses. 3rd ed. xix, 206p. 1983. reprint ed. lib. bdg. 22.50 (*0-8377-1039-1*) Rothman.

***Reynolds, William & Trembley, Elizabeth.** It's a Print! Detective Fiction from Page to Screen. LC 94-70906. 235p. (C). 1994. 46.95 (*0-87972-661-X*) Bowling Green Univ.

— It's a Print! Detective Fiction from Page to Screen. LC 94-70906. 235p. (C). 1994. pap. text ed. 18.95 (*0-87972-662-8*) Bowling Green Univ.

Reynolds, William, jt. auth. see Henderson, Minnie.

Reynolds, William, jt. auth. see Mackay, Roderick.

Reynolds, William, jt. ed. see Pinar, William.

Reynolds, William, ed. see Splaver, Bernard.

Reynolds, William B. & Wasserstrom, Richard. Symposium: Looking at the Principles Behind Affirmative Action. (Working Papers on Civil Rights). 1988. 2.50 (*0-318-33315-5*, CR1) IPPP.

Reynolds, William C. & Perkins, Henry C. Engineering Thermodynamics. 2nd ed. (C). 1977. text ed. write for info. (*0-07-052046-1*) McGraw.

Reynolds, William H. & Warfield, Gerald. Common-Practice Harmony. 216p. (C). 1985. pap. 18.00 (*0-02-873170-0*) Schirmer Bks.

***Reynolds, William J. Drive-By: A Nebraska Mystery. Emmel, Gayle, ed. 330p. 1995. pap. 15.95 (*0-944287-14-X*) Ex Machina.**

Juvenile gangs have invaded the heartland. Cities like Minneapolis, Omaha & Des Moines are feeling the agony of children killing children. William J. Reynolds' writer-P.I. Nebraska, based in Omaha, takes on the gangs in DRIVE-BY. Reynolds brings his unique wit & sensitivity to the telling of this story. His sardonic sleuth has been appointed unofficial guardian angel of Darius LeClerc, a young man new to Omaha. When Darius is gunned down, Nebraska joins the boy's Uncle, Elmo Lammers, to find the killers. The backstreets through which the detective & his army buddy prowl for clues could be in a foreign country, teeming with fascinating, richly drawn people. The sense of the familiar suddenly grown alien should strike a chord with a public whose values have been challenged by the ruthlessness of young people with guns & an attitude. "In this sixth 'Nebraska' adventure, Reynolds once again reveals his delightful sense of humor as well as his ability to keep readers turning pages," writes William X. Kienzle, author of THE ROSARY MURDERS. For fans of Nebraska, DRIVE-BY is a landmark in the evolution of this intriguing character. For readers new to the series, it is a glorious introduction. ***Publisher Provided Annotation.***

— Sioux Falls: The City & The People. LC 94-28677. (Illus.). (Orig.). 1994. pap. 15.95 (*1-56037-070-X*) Am Wrld Geog.

Reynolds, William J. & Price, Milburn. A Survey of Christian Hymnody. rev. ed. LC 87-81996. (Illus.). 300p. 1987. pap. text ed. 24.95 (*0-916642-32-1*, 904) Hope Pub.

Reynolds, William L. Judicial Process in a Nutshell. 2nd ed. (Nutshell Ser.). 308p. 1991. pap. text ed. 16.00 (*0-314-88430-0*) West Pub.

Reynolds, William L., jt. auth. see Richman, William M.

Reynolds, William M. Reading Curriculum Theory: The Development of a New Hermeneutic. (American University Studies: Language: Ser. XIV, Vol. 19). 238p. (C). 1989. text ed. 30.95 (*0-8204-1001-2*) P Lang Pubs.

Reynolds, William M., ed. Internalizing Disorders in Children & Adolescents. (Series on Personality Processes: No. 1341). 352p. 1992. text ed. 59.95 (*0-471-50648-6*) Wiley.

Reynolds, William M., jt. auth. see Martusewicz, Rebecca A.

Reynolds, Woodson. And I Remember. LC 87-90716. (Illus.). 59p. 1987. pap. text ed. 12.50 (*0-318-23782-2*) Midnight Pubns.

Reynoldson, Fiona. Conflict & Change, 1650-1800. LC 92-20460. (Illustrated History of the World Ser.). (Illus.). 80p. (J). (gr. 2-6). 1993. 17.95 (*0-8160-2790-0*) Facts on File.

Reynoldson, George. Let's Reach for the Sun: Thirty Original Solar & Earth Sheltered Home Designs. rev. ed. (Illus.). 144p. 1981. pap. 12.95 (*0-9603570-1-7*) Space-Time WA.

Reynoldson, Ray W. Heat Treatment in Fluidized Bed Furnaces. LC 93-35827. 250p. 1993. 82.00 (*0-87170-485-4*) ASM.

Reynoldson, T. B. A Key to the British Species of Freshwater Triclads. 2nd ed. 1978. 35.00 (*0-900386-34-7*) St Mut.

Reynoldson, T. B. & Coates, K. A., eds. Aquatic Oligochaete Biology V: Proceedings of the 5th Symposium, Held in Tallinn, Estonia, 1991. LC 93-47117. (Developments in Hydrobiology Ser.). 328p. (C). 1994. lib. bdg. 185.50 (*0-7923-2686-5*) Kluwer Ac.

Reynosa, Larry, jt. auth. see Billingiere, Joseph.

Reys, Barbara. Elementary School Mathematics: What Parents Should Know about Estimation. (Illus.). 12p. 1982. pap. 1.25 (*0-87353-202-3*) NCTM.

— Elementary School Mathematics: What Parents Should Know about Problem Solving. (Illus.). 12p. 1982. pap. 1.25 (*0-87353-203-1*) NCTM.

Reys, Barbara J., et al. Developing Number Sense in the Middle Grades. Curcio, Frances, ed. LC 91-12623. (Curriculum & Evaluation Standards for School Mathematics Addenda Ser.). (Illus.). 56p. (Orig.). 1991. pap. 10.50 (*0-87353-322-4*) NCTM.

Reys, Georges, jt. ed. see Loewer, Barry.

Reys, Robert E. & Nohda, Nobuhiko, eds. Computational Alternatives for the 21st Century: Cross-Cultural Perspectives from Japan & the United States. LC 93-48037. (Illus.). 211p. (Orig.). 1994. pap. 13.00 (*0-87353-368-2*) NCTM.

Reys, Robert E., et al. Helping Children Learn Mathematics. 2nd ed. 272p. (C). 1989. pap. text ed. write for info. (*0-13-386426-X*) P-H.

— Helping Children Learn Mathematics. 3rd ed. 320p. (C). 1992. pap. 40.00 (*0-205-13142-5*) Allyn.

— Helping Children Learn Mathematics. 4th ed. LC 94-33394. 1994. pap. text ed. 44.00 (*0-205-16256-8*) Allyn.

Reyssat, Eric. Surfaces de Riemann. (Progress in Mathematics Ser.: No. 77). 256p. 1989. 49.50 (*0-8176-3441-X*) Birkhauser.

***Reza, Fazlollah M.** An Introduction to Information Theory. unabridged ed. LC 94-27222. (Illus.). 496p. 1994. pap. text ed. 12.95 (*0-486-68210-2*) Dover.

Reza, H. T. After the Storm, the Rainbow: The Church of the Nazarene in Cuba. 88p. 1994. pap. write for info. (*0-8341-1475-5*) Nazarene.

Reza-Vaez-Zadeh, jt. ed. see Downes, Patrick.

***Rezabek-Turner, Ellie.** A Bouquet of Night Flowers: Journey of a Soul Through Loss, Grief & Healing. (Illus.). 80p. (Orig.). 1995. pap. 12.00 (*0-9646595-3-0*) LinkaAges.

Rezak, R. & Lavoie, D. L., eds. Carbonate Microfabrics. LC 93-3272. (Frontiers in Sedimentary Geology Ser.). 1993. Acid-free paper. 79.00 (*0-387-94035-9*) Spr-Verlag.

Rezak, Richard & Henry, Vernon J., eds. Contributions on the Geological & Geophysical Oceanography of the Gulf of Mexico. LC 72-170029. (Texas A & M University Oceanographic Studies: No. 3). (Illus.). 319p. reprint ed. pap. 91.00 (*0-685-23793-1*, 2032890) Bks Demand.

Rezakovic, D. & Alpert, J. S., eds. Nitrate Therapy & Nitrate Tolerance: Current Concepts & Controversies. LC 92-49386. (Illus.). x, 548p. 1993. 232.00 (*3-8055-5669-1*) S Karger.

Rezanov, I. A. Catastrophes in the Earth's History. 168p. 1984. pap. 30.00 (*0-317-89619-9*) St Mut.

Rezanov, Nikolai P. The Rezanov Voyage to Nueva California in 1806. limited ed. 1988. 29.95 (*0-87770-448-1*) Ye Galleon.

***Rezau, Pierre.** Dictionnaire du Francais Parle. rev. ed. 382p. (FRE.). 1991. pap. 17.95 (*0-7859-7627-2*, 2020128683) Fr & Eur.

Rezazadeh, Reza. Iraq & Democracy: A Futuristic Perspective. LC 93-72961. 220p. 1994. 24.00 (*0-9629032-1-3*) Etarnalist.

— Technodemocratic Economic Theory: From Capitalism & Socialism to Democracy. LC 91-70823. 359p. (C). 1992. lib. bdg. 20.00 (*0-9629032-0-5*) Etarnalist.

Rezeau, Pierre. Dictionnaire du Francais Regional de Poitou-Charentes et de Vendee. 159p. (FRE.). 1990. 50.00 (*0-8288-9480-9*, 2862530972) Fr & Eur.

Rezen, Susan V. & Hausman, Carl. Coping with Hearing Loss: A Guide for Adults & Their Families. rev. ed. LC 92-36728. 1993. 17.95 (*0-942637-83-6*) Barricade Bks.

Rezende, Ricardo F. Rio Maria: Song of the Earth. abr. ed. Maloney, Linda, ed. & tr. by. LC 93-49654. 180p. 1994. reprint ed. pap. 14.95 (*0-88344-960-9*) Orbis Bks.

Rezendes, Paul. Tracking & the Art of Seeing: How to Read Animal Tracks & Signs. LC 92-10734. (Illus.). 320p. 1992. 29.95 (*0-944475-33-7*, Pub. by Camden Hse CN); pap. 19.95 (*0-944475-29-9*, Pub. by Camden Hse CN) Firefly Bks Ltd.

***Rezendes, Victor S.** Alternative-Fueled Vehicles: Progress Made in Accelerating Federal Purchases, but Benefits & Costs Remain Uncertain. (Illus.). 120p. (Orig.). (C). 1994. pap. text ed. 45.00x (*0-7881-1370-4*) Diane Pub.

— Electromagnetic Fields: Federal Efforts to Determine Health Effects Are Behind Schedule. (Illus.). 54p. (Orig.). (C). 1994. pap. text ed. 25.00 (*0-7881-1394-1*) Diane Pub.

— Geothermal Energy: Barriers to the Use of Geothermal Heat Pumps. (Illus.). 80p. (Orig.). (C). 1994. pap. text ed. 45.00 (*0-7881-1308-9*) Diane Pub.

Rezits, Joseph. Guitar Music in Print. LC 80-84548. 500p. (Orig.). 1983. pap. 95.00 (*0-8497-7802-6*, PM9) Kjos.

Rezk, A. M., ed. Heat & Fluid Flow in Power System Components. (Heat & Mass Transfer Ser.: Vol. 3). (Illus.). 300p. 1979. 127.00 (*0-08-024235-9*, Pub. by Pergamon Repr UK) Franklin.

Rezler, Agnes G. & Flaherty, Joseph A. The Interpersonal Dimension in Medical Education. (Medical Education Ser.: Vol. 6). 240p. 1985. 32.95 (*0-8261-4370-9*) Springer Pub.

Rezmer, Martin G., jt. auth. see Porter, Alan G.

Rezmerski, John C., ed. see Manfred, Frederick.

Rezneck, Samuel. Business Depressions & Financial Panics: Collected Essays in American Business & Economic History. LC 68-28644. 201p. 1969. text ed. 49.95 (*0-8371-1501-9*, REB/, Greenwood Pr) Greenwood.

Reznek, Lawrie. The Nature of Disease. (Studies in the Philosophy of Science). 301p. 1988. text ed. 37.50 (*0-7102-1082-5*, RKP) Routledge.

— Philosophical Defence of Psychiatry. (Philosophical Issues in Science Ser.). 255p. 1991. 45.00 (*0-415-03593-7*, A5393) Routledge.

Reznicek, Barbara. Journaling to Recovery. LC 88-83361. 120p. (Orig.). 1989. pap. 4.95 (*0-87029-219-6*, 20209-3) Abbey.

Reznicek, E. K. Hendrick Goltzius. Drawings Rediscovered 1962-1992: Supplement to "Die Zeichnungen von Hendrick Goltzius" Haverkamp-Begemann, Egbert & Allen, Elizabeth, eds. Gordenker, Emilie E., tr. LC 93-80160. (Illus.). 92p. 1993. reprint ed. pap. text ed. 75.00 (*0-9613754-1-8*) Mstr Draw Assn.

Reznicek, Rados, ed. Flow Visualization V: Proceedings of the Fifth International Symposium. 1064p. 1990. 172.00 (*0-89116-887-7*) Hemisp Pub.

— Physical Properties of Agricultural Materials & Products: Their Influence on Design & Performance of Agricultural Machines & Technologies. LC 66-55781. (Illus.). 1224p. 1987. 265.00 (*0-89116-677-7*) Hemisp Pub.

Reznick, B. Sum of Even Powers of Real Linear Forms. LC 91-44877. (MEMO Ser.). 155p. 1992. 29.00 (*0-8218-2523-2*, MEMO 96/463) Am Math.

Reznick, J. Steven, ed. Perspectives on Behavioral Inhibition. LC 89-32463. (John D. & Catherine T. MacArthur Foundation Series on Mental Health & Development). (Illus.). 392p. 1989. 32.95 (*0-226-71040-8*) U Ch Pr.

Reznick, Lawrence. Tools for Code Management: Using Make, Revision Control, Debuggers, Profilers an. 1994. pap. text ed. 30.00 (*0-13-100207-4*) P-H.

***Reznick, Leibel.** Bar Kokhba. 1995. write for info. (*1-56821-502-9*) Aronson.

— The Holy Temple Revisited. LC 89-27465. 224p. 1993. pap. 24.95 (*1-56821-067-1*) Aronson.

Reznick-Schuller, Hildegard M. Compare Ultrastructural Path: Selected Tumors in Man & Animals. 208p. 1989. 168.00 (*0-8493-5662-8*, RC269) CRC Pr.

***Reznicki, Jack.** Illustration Photography. 1987. pap. 18.95 (*0-8174-4011-9*) Watsn-Guptill.

Reznik, Gerd & Stinson, Sherman F., eds. Nasal Tumors in Animals & Man, 3 Vols., Vol. I. 296p. 1983. 168.00 (*0-8493-5577-X*, RC271, CRC Reprint) Franklin.

— Nasal Tumors in Animals & Man, 3 Vols., Vol. II. 288p. 1983. 155.00 (*0-8493-5578-8*, RC271, CRC Reprint) Franklin.

— Nasal Tumors in Animals & Man, 3 Vols., Vol. III. 280p. 1983. 143.00 (*0-8493-5579-6*, RC271, CRC Reprint) Franklin.

Reznik, Jack & Byrd, Ron. Badminton. 128p. (C). 1987. pap. 14.00 (*0-89787-604-0*) Gorsuch Scarisbrick.

Reznik, John W. & Grambeau, Rodney J. Official's Manual: Touch & Flag Football. (Illus.). 1978. pap. 9.95x (*0-918438-46-2*, PREZ0046) Human Kinetics.

Reznik, John W., et al. Racquetball for Men & Women. (Illus.). 1984. pap. 7.40 (*0-87563-246-7*) Stipes.

Reznik-Schuller, Hildegard M. Comparative Respiratory Tract Carcinogenesis, 2 Vols. 272p. 1983. Vol. I, 272p. 143.00 (*0-8493-5421-8*, RC280, CRC Reprint); Vol. II, 224p. 132.00 (*0-8493-5422-6*, RC280, CRC Reprint) Franklin.

Reznikoff, Charles. By the Waters of Manhattan. LC 86-50262. (Masterworks of Modern Jewish Writing Ser.). (Illus.). 264p. (C). 1986. reprint ed. pap. 9.95 (*0-910129-55-X*) Wiener Pubs Inc.

— Family Chronicle. LC 87-40102. (Masterworks of Modern Jewish Writing Ser.). 320p. 1988. reprint ed. 9.95 (*0-910129-73-8*); reprint ed. pap. 9.95 (*0-910129-74-6*) Wiener Pubs Inc.

— Poems Nineteen Eighteen to Nineteen Seventy-Five: The Complete Poems of Charles Reznikoff. LC 89-17816. 450p. (Orig.). (C). 1989. pap. 15.00 (*0-87685-790-X*) Black Sparrow.

— Poems, 1937-1975: The Complete Poems of Charles Reznikoff, Vol. 2. Cooney, Seamus, ed. LC 76-52383. 210p. 1978. 25.00 (*0-87685-301-7*) Black Sparrow.

— Testimony: The United States, 1885-1915, Vol. 1. Cooney, Seamus, ed. LC 78-7618. 280p. (Orig.). 1978. 25.00 (*0-87685-322-X*); pap. 10.00 (*0-87685-321-1*) Black Sparrow.

R

— Testimony: The United States, 1885-1915, Vol. 2. Cooney, Seamus, ed. LC 78-7618. 250p. (Orig.). 1979. 25.00 (*0-87685-333-5*); pap. 10.00 (*0-87685-332-7*) Black Sparrow.

— Testimony, the United States 1885-1890, Recitative. LC 65-15675. 1965. 10.00 (*0-685-79043-6*); 5.00 (*0-685-79044-4*) SPD-Small Pr Dist.

Reznikoff, Charles, tr. see Benjamin, Israel B.

Reznikoff, Natalie. Ognennaia Pamiat' Vospominaniia o Aleksee Remizove. (Modern Russian Literature & Culture, Studies & Texts: Vol. 4). (Illus.). 147p. (RUS.). 1980. pap. 8.50 (*0-933884-14-1*) Berkeley Slavic.

Reznikoff, S. C. Interior Graphic & Design Standards. (Illus.). 624p. 1986. 95.00 (*0-8230-7298-3*, Whitney Lib) Watsn-Guptill.

— Specifications for Commercial Interiors. rev. ed. 352p. 1989. 49.95 (*0-8230-4893-4*, Whitney Lib) Watsn-Guptill.

Reznikoff, W. S., jt. ed. see Miller, J. H.

Reznikoff, William, jt. ed. see Davies, Julian.

Reznikoff, William S. & Gold, Larry, eds. Maximizing Gene Expression. (Biotechnology Ser.). (Illus.). 375p. 1986. text ed. 28.00 (*0-409-90027-3*) Buttrwrth-Heinemann.

Reznikov, K. Y. Cell Proliferation & Cytogenesis in the Mouse Hippocampus. Beck, F. et al, eds. (Advances in Anatomy, Embryology & Cell Biology Ser.: Vol. 122). (Illus.). 96p. 1991. pap. 72.00 (*0-387-53689-2*) Spr-Verlag.

Reznikov, L. M., jt. auth. see Korenev, Boris G.

Rezoni, Tommy. Renzoni on Baccarat. LC 72-76844. 160p. 1974. 7.00 (*0-8184-0067-6*) Carol Pub Group.

***Rezun, Miron.** Europe & War in the Balkans: Toward a New Yugoslav Identity. LC 95-4289. 248p. 1995. text ed. 55.00 (*0-275-95238-X*, Praeger Pubs) Greenwood.

— Intrigue & War in Southwest Asia: The Struggle for Supremacy from Central Asia to Iraq. LC 91-16688. 168p. 1991. text ed. 49.95 (*0-275-94105-1*, C4105, Praeger Pubs) Greenwood.

— Saddam Hussein's Gulf Wars: Ambivalent Stakes in the Middle East. LC 92-4197. 164p. 1992. text ed. 45.00 (*0-275-94324-0*, C4324, Praeger Pubs) Greenwood.

Rezun, Miron, ed. The Impact of Nationalism in the U. S. S. R. The Collapse of an Empire? LC 92-4219. 208p. 1992. text ed. 42.95 (*0-275-94320-8*, C4320, Praeger Pubs) Greenwood.

Rezvan, Efim. Russian Ships in the Gulf 1899-1903. Naumkin, Vitaly, ed. 190p. 1994. 75.00 (*0-86372-155-9*, Pub. by Ithaca UK) Paul & Co Pubs.

Rezvan, Jerena B., ed. see Laskey, Carolyn T.

***Rezvani, Kate A.** Story Spinner: The Easy Way to Write a Story Outline. Lane, Jay, ed. LC 94-96237. (Illus.). 64p. 1995. pap. 19.95 (*0-9641318-4-6*) Lrning Circle.

Rezwin, Max. The Complete Book of Sick Jokes. (Illus.). 192p. 1984. pap. 4.95 (*0-8065-0761-6*, Citadel Pr) Carol Pub Group.

RFPR Staff. The Executive Crisis Manager: The Executive Planning Guide to Surviving Corporate Crisis. Newton, D. & Fons, R., eds. 154p. (C). 1987. student ed 150.00 (*0-9618792-0-3*) RFPR.

RGA Publishing Staff. Mystery of Pirate Island. (Amazing Mazes Story Ser.). 48p. (Orig.). (J). (gr. 1-4). 1993. pap. 2.95 (*0-8431-3536-0*) Price Stern.

***RH Value Publishing Staff.** The Book of Dinosaurs. 1995. pap. 8.99 (*0-517-12354-1*) Random.

— Brooklyn Botanic Garden. Date not set. pap. 12.99 (*0-517-12139-5*) Random.

— Cat Tails: Book of Days. 1995. pap. 12.99 (*0-517-12138-7*) Random.

— Clint Eastwood. 1995. pap. 9.99 (*0-517-12137-9*) Random.

— Easy to Make Salads. 1995. pap. 9.99 (*0-517-12147-6*) Random.

— Illustrated Cat's Life. (Illus.). Date not set. pap. 12.99 (*0-517-12136-0*) Random.

— The Kitchen Collection. 1995. pap. 12.99 (*0-517-12135-2*) Random.

— Times Atlas Second World War. 1995. pap. 29.99 (*0-517-12377-0*) Random.

Rha, Chokyun, ed. Theory, Determination & Control of Physical Properties of Food Materials. LC 74-76481. (Food Material Science Ser.: No. 1). xi, 315p. 1975. lib. bdg. 145.50 (*90-277-0468-6*) Kluwer Ac.

Rhawn, Heister G., jt. auth. see Sturm, Harry P.

Rhder, Ernest. Ibarguengoitia en Exelsior, 1968-1976: Una Bibliografia Anotada Con Introduccion Critica y Citas Memorables del Autor. LC 93-22214. (American University Studies, XXII: Latin American Literature: Vol. 23). 152p. (SPA.). (C). 1994. text ed. 40.95 (*0-8204-2195-2*) P Lang Pubs.

Rhea, jt. ed. see Dean, Jr.

Rhea, Buford, ed. The Future of the Sociological Classics. 224p. (C). 1982. text ed. 21.95 (*0-04-301136-5*) Routledge Chapman & Hall.

Rhea, D. L. How the Colt Navy .36 Revolver Was Gunsmithed & Fired in the Field During the Civil War: Techniques Learned from Civil War Vererans & Old-Time Gunsmiths. deluxe limited ed. 76p. 1985. Gold-stamped cloth, numbered edition, in dust jacket. 20.00 (*0-9627171-1-8*) Hera Pub.

Rhea, Gordon C. Battle of the Wilderness, May 5-6, 1864. LC 93-42110. (Illus.). 520p. 1994. 34.95 (*0-8071-1873-7*) La State U Pr.

Rhea, James T. & Vansonnenberg, Eric. Emergency Radiology. 256p. 1988. 72.95 (*0-316-74200-7*, Little Med Div) Little.

Rhea, John. The Department of the Air Force. (Know Your Government Ser.). (Illus.). 104p. (J). (gr. 5 up). 1990. 14.95 (*0-87754-834-X*) Chelsea Hse.

Rhea, Joseph C., et al. The Facts on File Dictionary of Health Care Management. (Illus.). 704p. 1988. 50.00 (*0-8160-1637-2*) Facts on File.

Rhea, Kathlyn. Mind Sense: Fine Tuning Your Intellect & Intuition--A Practical Workbook. 214p. 1988. pap. 12.95 (*0-89087-529-4*) Celestial Arts.

Rhea, Kathlyn & Rink, Cynthia. The Psychic Is You. LC 79-53023. 160p. 1990. pap. 8.95 (*0-89087-311-9*) Celestial Arts.

Rhea, Mildred. Henry & Bettie Homestead on the Prairie. LC 89-50582. 300p. 1990. 10.95 (*1-55523-229-9*) Winston-Derek.

***Rhea, Nicholas.** Constable on Call. large type ed. (Magna Large Print Ser.). 1994. 26.95 (*0-7505-0693-8*, Pub. by Magna Print Bks) Ulverscroft.

— Heartbeat of Yorkshire. 1993. pap. 15.95 (*0-7117-0605-0*, Pub. by Jarrold Pub UK) Seven Hills Bk.

Rhea, Randall W. HF Filter Design & Computer Simulation. (Illus.). 448p. 1994. 59.00 (*1-884932-25-8*) Noble Pubng.

— HF Filter Design & Computer Simulation. LC 95-1811. 1995. text ed. 60.00 (*0-07-052055-0*) McGraw.

— Oscillator Design & Computer Simulation. 2nd ed. (Illus.). 319p. Date not set. 64.00 (*1-884932-30-4*) Noble Pubng.

Rhea, Robert. The Dow Theory. 400p. 1991. reprint ed. lib. bdg. 31.95 (*0-89966-761-9*) Buccaneer Bks.

— The Dow Theory. LC 93-72199. 252p. (C). reprint ed. pap. text ed. 16.00 (*0-87034-110-3*) Fraser Pub Co.

Rhea, Robert A., jt. auth. see Parisher, Roy A.

***Rhead & Lawrence.** Robin Hood. (J). 1995. write for info. (*0-8050-3397-1*) H Holt & Co.

Rhead, Louis. Robin Hood. (Children's Classics Ser.). 1988. 12.99 (*0-517-67129-8*) Random Hse Value.

Rhead, Louis & Wheelwright, Rowland, illus. King Arthur & His Knights. (Children's Classics Ser.). 416p. (J). 1987. 12.99 (*0-517-61885-0*) Random Hse Value.

***Rhee, Helen C.** The Korean-American Experience: A Detailed Analysis of How Well Korean-Americans Adjust to Life in the United States. 1995. 16.95 (*0-533-11424-1*) Vantage.

Rhee, Hyun-Ku, et al. First-Order Partial Differential Equations: Theory & Application of Single Equations. (Illus.). 480p. 1986. text ed. 56.33 (*0-13-11828-2*) P-H.

Rhee, Jhoon. Chon-Ji of Tae Kwon Do Hyung. Alvarez, Roberto, tr. LC 74-120124. (Korean Arts Ser.). (Illus.). (ENG & SPA.). 1970. pap. text ed. 13.95 (*0-89750-000-8*, 102, Wehman) Ohara Pubns.

— Chung-Gun & Toi Gye of Tae Kwon Do Hyung. LC 76-163381. (Series 108). (Illus.). 1971. pap. text ed. 14.95 (*0-89750-003-2*) Ohara Pubns.

— Hwa-Rang & Chung-Mu of Tae Kwon Do Hyung. LC 77-163382. (Korean Arts Ser.). (Illus.). 1971. pap. text ed. 13.95 (*0-89750-004-0*, 109) Ohara Pubns.

— Tan-Gun & To-San of Tae Kwon Do Hyung. LC 71-150320. (Korean Arts Ser.). (Illus.). 1971. pap. text ed. 16.95 (*0-89750-001-6*, 106) Ohara Pubns.

— Won-Hyo & Yul-Kok of Tae Kwon Do Hyung. LC 70-157046. (Korean Arts Ser.). (Illus.). 1971. pap. text ed. 13.95 (*0-89750-002-4*, 107) Ohara Pubns.

Rhee, Jong-Chen. The State & Industry in South Korea: The Limits of the Authoritarian State. LC 93-43156. 224p. 1994. 65.00x (*0-415-11102-1*, B4408, Routledge NY) Routledge.

Rhee, Kyu H. Struggle for National Identity in the Third World. LC 83-80008. 233p. 1983. 16.50 (*0-930878-31-0*) Hollym Intl.

Rhee, Kyu-Ho. To the Young Korean Intellectuals. LC 81-84201. (Illus.). 197p. 1981. 14.95 (*0-930878-24-8*) Hollym Intl.

Rhee, Man Y. Cryptography & Secure Communications. 1993. text ed. 50.00 (*0-07-112502-7*) McGraw.

Rhee, Nami. Magic Spring. (Whitebird Bks.). (Illus.). 32p. (J). (ps-3). 1993. lib. bdg. 14.95 (*0-399-22420-3*, Putnam) Putnam Pub Group.

Rhee, S. C. & Chang, R. P. Pacific Basin Capital Markets Research. 1990. 95.00 (*0-444-88459-9*) Elsevier.

Rhee, S. G. Securities Markets & Systemic Risks in Dynamic Asian Economies. 95p. (Orig.). 1992. pap. 26.00 (*92-64-13638-X*) OECD.

Rhee, S. K., ed. see International Conference on Wear of Materials Staff.

Rhee, Song N., jt. ed. see Aikens, C. Melvin.

Rhee, Yung W., et al. Korea's Competitive Edge: Managing the Entry into World Markets. LC 84-47956. 173p. reprint ed. pap. 49.40 (*0-7837-4249-5*, 2043939) Bks Demand.

Rheede, R. Hortus Malabaricus, Set, Vols. 1-12. (C). 1988. Set. 4,000.00 (*0-685-22369-8*) St Mut.

Rhees, David J. Joseph Priestley: Enlightened Chemist: Catalogue to an Exhibit Celebrating the 250th Birthday of Joseph Priestley & the Inauguration of the Center for History of Chemistry. (BCHOC Publication Ser.: No. 1). (Illus.). 34p. (Orig.). 1983. pap. 5.00 (*0-941901-00-9*, QD22.P8 R53 1983) Chem Heritage Fnd.

Rhees, David J., jt. auth. see Heitmann, John A.

Rhees, R. Ward, jt. auth. see Van De Graaff, Kent M.

Rhees, R. Ward, jt. auth. see Van De Graaff, Kent.

Rhees, Rush, ed. Ludwig Wittgenstein: Personal Recollections. LC 79-28474. 246p. 1981. 53.50 (*0-8476-6253-5*) Rowman.

Rhees, Rush, ed. see Wittgenstein, Ludwig.

Rhees, William J. An Account of the Smithsonian Institution: Its Founder, Building, Operations, Etc. Cohen, I. Bernard, ed. LC 79-8404. (Three Centuries of Science in America Ser.). (Illus.). 1980. reprint ed. lib. bdg. 15.95 (*0-405-12582-8*) Ayer.

— The Smithsonian Institution: Documents Relative to Its History, 2 vols. Cohen, I. Bernard, ed. LC 79-8405. (Three Centuries of Science in America Ser.). (Illus.). 1980. lib. bdg. 86.00 (*0-686-65997-X*) Ayer.

— The Smithsonian Institution: Documents Relative to Its History, 2 vols., 1. Cohen, I. Bernard, ed. LC 79-8405. (Three Centuries of Science in America Ser.). (Illus.). 1980. 94.95 (*0-405-12597-6*) Ayer.

— The Smithsonian Institution: Documents Relative to Its History, 2 vols., 2. Cohen, I. Bernard, ed. LC 79-8405. (Three Centuries of Science in America Ser.). (Illus.). 1980. lib. bdg. 94.95 (*0-405-12599-2*) Ayer.

— The Smithsonian Institution: Documents Relative to Its History, 2 vols., Set. Cohen, I. Bernard, ed. LC 79-8405. (Three Centuries of Science in America Ser.). (Illus.). 1980. lib. bdg. 189.95 (*0-405-12583-6*) Ayer.

— William J. Rhees on James Smithson: An Original Anthology, 2 vols. in 1. Cohen, I. Bernard, ed. LC 79-7996. (Three Centuries of Science in America Ser.). (Illus.). 1980. lib. bdg. 25.95 (*0-405-12581-X*) Ayer.

Rheidt, Klaus. Altertumer von Pergamon, Die Stadtgrabung, Band XV-2: Teil 2: Die Byzantinische Wohnstadt. (Illus.). xviii, 253p. (GER.). (C). 1991. lib. bdg. 229.25 (*3-11-012621-4*) De Gruyter.

***Rheims, Bettina, photos.** Kim Harlow. (Illus.). 88p. 1995. pap. 20.00 (*3-929078-21-X*) Dist Art Pubs.

Rheims, Maurice. L' Art ou le Style Jules Verne, 1900. (Illus.). 424p. (FRE.). 1965. lib. bdg. 125.00 (*0-8288-3997-2*) Fr & Eur.

— Buffet's Complete Engravings, 1948-1980. (Illus.). 244p. 1983. 125.00 (*1-55660-046-1*) A Wofsy Fine Arts.

— Le Saint Office. (FRE.). 1985. pap. 17.95 (*0-7859-4230-0*) Fr & Eur.

Rhein, Bob, jt. auth. see Baer-Brown, Leslie.

Rhein, Donna E. The Handprinted Books of Leonard & Virginia Woolf at the Hogarth Press, 1917-1932. LC 85-14144. (Studies in Modern Literature: No. 52). 182p. reprint ed. pap. 51.90 (*0-8357-1694-5*, 2070519) Bks Demand.

Rhein, Phillip H. Albert Camus. (World Authors Ser.). 1969. lib. bdg. 16.95 (*0-8057-2196-7*, Twayne) Macmillan.

— Albert Camus. rev. ed. (World Authors Ser.: No. 69). 152p. 1989. text ed. 22.95 (*0-8057-8253-2*, Twayne) Macmillan.

— The Verbal & Visual Art of Alfred Kubin. (Studies in Austrian Literature, Culture, & Thought). (Illus.). 188p. 1989. 24.95 (*0-929497-01-5*) Ariadne CA.

***Rhein, Robert.** German Grammar Flipper No. 1. 39p. (YA). (gr. 6 up). 1994. 6.25 (*1-878383-31-0*) C Lee Pubns.

— German Grammar Flipper Vol. 2, No. 2. 49p. (GER.). (YA). (gr. 8 up). 1992. 6.25 (*1-878383-23-X*) C Lee Pubns.

Rheinboldt, Cornelie J., tr. see Burger, Dionys.

Rheinboldt, Werner C. Methods for Solving Systems of Nonlinear Equations. (CBMS-NSF Regional Conference Ser.: No. 14). ix, 104p. (Orig.). 1974. reprint ed. pap. text ed. 20.00 (*0-89871-011-1*) Soc Indus-Appl Math.

Rheinboldt, Werner C., jt. auth. see Ortega, James M.

Rheinbolt, W. C. Numerical Analysis of Parameterized Nonlinear Equations. LC 84-21974. (Lecture Notes in the Mathematical Sciences Ser.). 299p. 1986. pap. text ed. 92.95 (*0-471-88814-1*) Wiley.

Rheinfelder, Hans. Kultsprache und Profansprache In Den Romanischen Landern. (Bibliotheca Dell' "Archivum Romanicum", Ser.: No. 2-18). v, 481p. 1982. reprint ed. write for info. (*3-487-07236-X*, Pub. by Georg Olms GW) Lubrecht & Cramer.

Rheingold, A. L., ed. see Hudson Symposium, 9th, Plattsburgh, N.Y., Apr. 1976.

Rheingold, Harriet L. The Psychologist's Guide to an Academic Career. 216p. (Orig.). 1994. pap. text ed. 24.95 (*1-55798-227-9*) Am Psychol.

Rheingold, Howard. Tools for Thought: The History & Future of Mind-Extending Technology. (Illus.). 320p. 1986. 9.95 (*0-13-925108-1*) P-H.

— Virtual Community: Finding Connection in a Computerized World. 1993. 22.07 (*0-201-60870-7*) Addison-Wesley.

— The Virtual Community: Homesteading on the Electronic Frontier. LC 94-25495. 1994. pap. 13.00 (*0-06-097641-1*, PL) HarpC.

— Virtual Reality: The Revolutionary Technology of Computer-Generated Artificial Worlds - & How It Promises to Transform Society. 416p. 1992. pap. 12.00 (*0-671-77897-8*, Touchstone Bks) S&S Trade.

Rheingold, Howard, ed. The Millennium Whole Earth Catalog: Access to Tools & Ideas for the Twenty-First Century. LC 94-1125. (Illus.). 384p. 1994. pap. 30.00 (*0-06-251059-2*) Harper SF.

— The Millennium Whole Earth Catalog: Access to Tools & Ideas for the Twenty-First Century. LC 94-1125. (Illus.). 384p. 1994. 50.00 (*0-06-251141-6*) Harper SF.

Rheingold, Howard, jt. auth. see Harman, Willis.

Rheingold, Howard, jt. auth. see Laberge, Stephen.

Rheingold, Judith M. Gifted Button: Fashion Buttons into Great Gifts & Wearable Art. 1993. 16.00 (*0-688-11822-4*) Hearst Bks.

Rheingold, Paul D. New York Law of Product Liability. 1990. ring bd. 95.00 (*0-929179-49-8*) Transnatl Juris Pubns.

***Rheingold, Todd.** Dispelling the Myths: An Analysis of American Attitudes & Prejudice. 1993. 19.95 (*0-912526-75-0*) Believe Dream.

— Dispelling the Myths: An Analysis of American Attitudes & Prejudices. 1993. write for info. (*0-318-71676-3*) Believe Dream.

Rheinhardt, Emil A. Life of Eleanora Duse. LC 73-82841. 1972. 24.95 (*0-405-08883-3*, Pub. by Blom Pubns UK) Ayer.

Rheinhardt, Harrison-Simms. No China Doll: Enemy-in-Waiting. (Illus.). 308p. (Orig.). 1990. 25.00 (*0-9626181-1-X*); lib. bdg. 14.95 (*0-9626181-0-1*) Simms Pub.

Rheinheimer, G. Aquatic Microbiology. 4th ed. 363p. 1991. text ed. 99.95 (*0-471-92695-7*, Wiley-Liss) Wiley.

Rheinstein, Max. Marriage Stability, Divorce, & the Law. LC 79-169582. 496p. 1972. lib. bdg. 35.00 (*0-226-71773-9*) U Ch Pr.

Rheinstrom, Carroll. Psyching the Ads: The Case Book of Advertising; the Methods & Results of 180 Advertisements. LC 75-39271. (Getting & Spending: the Consumer's Dilemma Ser.). (Illus.). 1976. reprint ed. 31.95 (*0-405-08043-3*) Ayer.

Rhem, James, ed. Making Changes: Twenty-Seven Strategies from Recruitment & Retention. 110p. 1988. pap. 79.00 (*0-912150-05-X*) Magna Pubns.

Rhemick, John R. A New People of God: A Study in Salvationism. 261p. (C). 1993. write for info. (*1-883719-00-3*) Salvat Army Supp.

Rhemtulla, A., jt. ed. see Mura, R.

Rhenanus, Beatus. Briefwechsel. xxiv, 700p. (GER.). 1966. reprint ed. write for info. (*0-318-70506-0*, Pub. by Georg Olms GW) Lubrecht & Cramer.

— Briefwechsel. Horawitz, A. & Hartfelder, K., eds. xxiv, 700p. 1966. reprint ed. write for info. (*0-318-71276-8*, Pub. by Georg Olms GW) Lubrecht & Cramer.

Rhenman, Eric. Organization Theory for Long-Range Planning. LC 72-5724. 222p. reprint ed. pap. 63.30 (*0-8357-6246-7*, 2034236) Bks Demand.

Rhett, Anne & McLaughlin, J. Michael. Insiders' Guide to Charleston, S. C. 2nd ed. (Insiders' Guide Travel Ser.). 500p. pap. 12.95 (*0-912367-50-4*) Insiders Guide.

Rhett, Blanche S. Two Hundred Years of Charleston Cooking. 3rd ed. Gay, Lettie, ed. 289p. 1976. reprint ed. pap. 14.95 (*0-87249-348-2*) U of SC Pr.

Rhett, Robert, jt. auth. see Steele, John.

Rhetts, Paul, jt. auth. see Awalt, Barbe.

Rheuban, Joyce. Harry Langdon: The Comedian as Metteur-en-Scene. LC 81-65868. (Illus.). 248p. 1983. 35.00 (*0-8386-3111-8*) Fairleigh Dickinson.

Rheuban, Joyce, ed. see Fassbinder, Rainer W.

Rhiannon, Thea, ed. see Chaney, Casey.

Rhiannon, Thea, ed. see Parkel, Paula.

Rhie, Gene S., ed. Standard Korean-English Dictionary for Foreigners: Romanized. LC 85-80494. 394p. 1986. pap. 12.50 (*0-930878-49-3*) Hollym Intl.

Rhie, Gene S. & Jones, B. J., eds. Standard English-Korean & Korean-English Dictionary for Foreigners: Romanized. LC 90-86084. 452p. (Orig.). (ENG & KOR.). (C). 1992. pap. 18.50 (*0-930878-06-X*) Hollym Intl.

Rhie, Gene S., jt. ed. see Jones, B. J.

Rhie, Marilyn M. & Thurman, Robert A. Wisdom & Compassion: The Sacred Art of Tibet. (Illus.). 408p. 1991. 65.00 (*0-8109-3957-6*) Abrams.

Rhie, Schi-Zhin. Soon-Hee in America. LC 77-81780. (Illus.). 36p. (J). (gr. k-3). 1977. lib. bdg. 6.50 (*0-930878-00-0*) Hollym Intl.

Rhiel, Mary. The Discussive Construction of Authorial Subjectivity in West Re-Viewing Kleist: Kleist German Films. LC 90-22998. (Studies in Modern German Literature: Vol. 44). 168p. (C). 1991. text ed. 37.95 (*0-8204-1526-X*) P Lang Pubs.

Rhim, Johng S. & Dritschilo, Anatoly, eds. Neoplastic Transformation in Human Cell Culture: Mechanisms of Carcinogenesis. LC 91-35328. (Experimental Biology & Medicine Ser.). (Illus.). 408p. 1991. 99.50 (*0-89603-227-2*) Humana.

Rhind, David W. & Taylor, D. R., eds. Cartography Past, Present, & Future - a Festschrift for F. J. Ormeling: Published on Behalf of the International Cartographic Association. 196p. 1989. 110.00 (*1-85166-336-3*) Elsevier.

Rhind, Graham R. Building & Maintaining a European Direct Marketing Database. LC 94-174. 318p. 1994. 99.95 (*0-566-07471-0*, Pub. by Gower UK) Ashgate Pub Co.

Rhine, C. D., jt. ed. see Roberts, F. X.

Rhine, Edward E., jt. ed. see Hartjen, Clayton A.

Rhine, Edward E., et al. Paroling Authorities: Recent History & Current Practice. 220p. 1991. pap. 23.00 (*0-685-48361-4*, 313) Am Correctional.

Rhine, J. B. Extra-Sensory Perception. 1983. pap. 14.95 (*0-8283-1464-0*) Branden Pub Co.

Rhine, J. B., ed. Progress in Parapsychology. LC 76-140922. (Illus.). 313p. 1971. reprint ed. pap. 2.50 (*0-911106-03-0*) Parapsych Pr.

Rhine, J. B., et al. ESP after Sixty Years. 30.95 (*0-8283-1409-8*) Branden Pub Co.

— Parapsychology from Duke to FRNM. LC 65-28963. 121p. 1965. pap. 2.75 (*0-911106-00-6*) Parapsych Pr.

Rhine, Jeff M. & Tucker, Robert J. Modelling of Gas-Fired Furnaces & Boilers & Other Industrial Heating Processes. 444p. 1990. text ed. 70.00 (*0-07-707305-3*) McGraw.

Rhine, Joseph B. New Frontiers of the Mind: The Story of the Duke Experiments. LC 71-178080. (Illus.). 275p. 1972. reprint ed. text ed. 49.75 (*0-8371-6279-3*, RHNF, Greenwood Pr) Greenwood.

Rhine, Louisa. Hidden Channels of the Mind. (Collector's Library of the Unknown). 256p. 1990. reprint ed. write for info. (*0-8094-8050-6*); reprint ed. lib. bdg. write for info. (*0-8094-8051-4*) Time-Life.

Rhine, Louisa E. Manual for Introductory Experiments in Parapsychology. 2nd ed. LC 68-70901. 24p. 1977. 2.00 (*0-911106-01-4*) Parapsych Pr.

Rhine, Stan. Galloping Geese of the Rio Grande Southern. (Illus.). 62p. 1992. pap. 9.95 (*0-918654-40-8*) CO RR Mus.

Rhine, W. E., et al, eds. Synthesis & Processing of Ceramics: Scientific Issues. (Symposium Proceedings Ser.: Vol. 249). 1992. text ed. 59.00 (*1-55899-143-3*) Materials Res.

An Asterisk (*) at the beginning of an entry indicates that the title is appearing in BIP for the first time.

Rhine, W. Ray, ed. Making Schools More Effective: New Directions from Follow Through. LC 81-4901. (Educational Psychology Ser.). 1981. text ed. 55.00 (0-12-587060-4) Acad Pr.

***Rhinefort, Andrew.** Commercial Refrigeration. 206p. (C). 1994. 19.54 (1-56870-156-X) RonJon Pub.

Rhinehart, jt. auth. see NHC Staff.

***Rhinehart, Luke.** Long Voyage Back: A Novel. LC 82-23586. (Bluejacket Paperback Ser.). 408p. 1995. pap. 13.95 (1-55750-130-0) Naval Inst Pr.

Rhinehart, Marilyn D. A Way of Work & a Way of Life: Coal Mining in Thurber, Texas, 1888-1926. (Southwestern Studies: No. 9). 1992. 39.50 (0-89096-499-8) Tex A&M Univ Pr.

Rhinehart, Mary R. The Door. 352p. 1986. pap. 3.50 (0-8217-1895-9) Zebra.

— Miss Pinkerton. 256p. 1986. pap. 3.50 (0-8217-1847-9) Zebra.

Rhinehart, Russell, jt. auth. see Bethea, Robert M.

Rhinelander, Anthony L. Prince Michael Vorontsov: Viceroy to the Tsar. 304p. (C). 1990. text ed. 44.95 (0-7735-0747-7, Pub. by McGill CN) U of Toronto Pr.

Rhinelander, John B., et al, contribs. Building a Consensus Toward Space: Proceedings of the Air War College 1988 Space Issue Symposium. (Illus.). 138p. 1990. per., pap. 5.50 (0-16-020920-X, S/N 008-070-006) USGPO.

Rhinesmith, Stephen H. Bring Home the World: A Management Guide for Community Leaders of International Exchange Programs. 223p. 1986. pap. 9.95 (0-8027-7289-7) Walker & Co.

Rhinesmith, Steven H. A Manager's Guide to Globalization: Six Keys to Success in a Changing World. LC 92-19470. 264p. 1992. 28.00 (1-55623-904-1) Irwin Prof Pubng.

Rho, Mannque & Wilkinson, Denys, eds. Mesons in Nuclei, 3 vols., 1. 1979. 146.25 (0-444-85255-7, North Holland) Elsevier.

— Mesons in Nuclei, 3 vols., 2. 1979. 146.25 (0-444-85256-5, North Holland) Elsevier.

— Mesons in Nuclei, 3 vols., 3. 1979. 146.25 (0-444-85257-3, North Holland) Elsevier.

— Mesons in Nuclei, 3 vols., Set. 1979. 343.75 (0-444-85052-X, North Holland) Elsevier.

Rhoades, Alec G. & Brookshire, Janet L. Baking Ends Meet: Delicious Mouth Watering Meals & Recipes for Around Five Dollars. Hogue, Holly B., ed. (Illus.). 31p. (Orig.). (C). Date not set. student ed 4.99 (1-881571-00-9) Letters Etcetera.

Rhoades-Baum, Patrice, ed. see Bultema, Patrick.

Rhoades, Carol, tr. see Pagoldh, Susanne.

Rhoades, Chuck, jt. auth. see Cooperman, Carolyn.

Rhoades, Deb, jt. ed. see Weldon, Jay-Louise.

***Rhoades, Diane.** Garden Crafts for Kids: 50 Great Reasons to Get Your Hands Dirty. LC 94-37108. (Illus.). 144p. (J). 1995. 19.95 (0-8069-0998-6) Sterling.

Rhoades, Duane, comp. The Independent Monologue in Latin American Theater: A Primary Bibliography with Selective Secondary Sources. LC 85-12947. (Bibliographies & Indexes in World Literature Ser.: No. 5). xxvi, 242p. 1985. text ed. 59.95 (0-313-25080-4, RIN/) Greenwood.

Rhoades, Jacqueline, et al. Simple Cooperation in the Classroom. (Illus.). 165p. (Orig.). (J). (ps up). 1985. pap. 15.95 (0-933935-07-2) ITA Pubns.

Rhoades, Jacqueline & McCabe, Margaret E. The Cooperative Classroom: Social & Academic Activities. 151p. (Orig.). 1992. pap. 19.95 (1-879639-16-5) Natl Educ Serv.

— How to Stop Fighting with Your Kids. 39p. (Orig.). 1986. pap. 3.95 (0-933935-02-1) ITA Pubns.

Rhoades, Jacqueline, jt. auth. see McCabe, Margaret E.

Rhoades, Lawrence J. A History of the American Sociological Association: 1905-1980. 90p. 5.00 (0-317-36340-9) Am Sociological.

Rhoades, Lawrence J., ed. Cost Guide for Automatic Finishing Processes. LC 80-52614. 219p. reprint ed. pap. 62.50 (0-317-41902-1, 2026159) Bks Demand.

Rhoades, Nancy L. Croquet: An Annotated Bibliography from the Rendell Rhoades Croquet Collection. LC 92-12217. (Illus.). 244p. 1992. 29.50 (0-8108-2571-6) Scarecrow.

Rhoades, Randy. How to Solve Calculus Problems. rev. ed. (Illus.). 180p. (C). 1988. pap. text ed. 14.95 (0-944492-00-2) SW Res Grp Pubns.

— How to Solve Calculus Problems. 3rd rev. ed. (Illus.). 214p. (C). 1992. pap. text ed. 14.95 (0-944492-02-9) SW Res Grp Pubns.

— How to Solve Word Problems. (Illus.). 64p. (Orig.). (C). 1988. pap. text ed. 5.95 (0-944492-01-0) SW Res Grp Pubns.

Rhoades, Raphael H., ed. Therapy Through Hypnosis. 1976. pap. 5.00 (0-87980-162-X) Wilshire.

Rhoades, Robert E., jt. ed. see Moock, Joyce L.

Rhoades, Rodney A. & Pflanzer, Richard G. Human Physiology. 2nd ed. 992p. (C). 1992. text ed. 65.25 (0-03-072616-6) SCP.

***Rhoades, Rodney A. & Tanner, George A., eds.** Medical Physiology. LC 94-24639. 1995. 59.95 (0-316-74228-7) Little.

Rhoades, Roger A. Nickie: The Co-Dependent CAT. (Illus.). 48p. (Orig.). 1992. pap. 9.95 (0-9634617-0-2) R A Rhoades.

Rhoades, Ruby, jt. frwd. see Brubaker, Pamela.

Rhoades, Rufus V. & Lagner, Marshall J. Income Taxation of Foreign Related Transactions, 6 vols. 1971. Updates. lib. bdg. write for info. (0-8205-1337-7) Bender.

Rhoades, Sharon. Pattern from Proverbs Thirty-One. LC 85-14486. 158p. 1985. pap. 4.95 (0-87227-101-3) Reg Baptist.

Rhoades, Snowy. Diary of a Coastwatcher in the Solomons. 1982. pap. 5.00 (0-685-09256-9) Adm Nimitz Foun.

Rhoades, Weldon E. Flying MacArthur to Victory. LC 86-26105. (Military History Ser.: No. 1). (Illus.). 584p. 1987. 19.95 (0-89096-266-9) Tex A&M Univ Pr.

Rhoads, et al. Dental Laboratory Procedures: Fixed Partial Dentures, Vol. 2. 2nd ed. 528p. 1985. 89.00 (0-8016-4141-1) Mosby Yr Bk.

Rhoads, Ann F. & Klein, William M. The Vascular Flora of Pennsylvania: Annotated Checklist & Atlas. LC 92-85316. (Memoirs Ser.: Vol. 207). (Illus.). 600p. (C). 1993. 50.00 (0-87169-207-4, M207-RHA) Am Philos.

***Rhoads, B. Eric.** Blast from the Past. (Illus.). 300p. 1995. 75.00 (1-886745-06-4) Streamlne Pr.

Rhoads, David, jt. auth. see Michie, Donald.

Rhoads, Diana A. Shakespeare's Defense of Poetry: A Midsummer Night's Dream & the Tempest. 264p. (Orig.). 1986. lib. bdg. 58.50 (0-8191-4979-9); pap. text ed. 26.00 (0-8191-4980-2) U Pr of Amer.

Rhoads, Donald C. & Lutz, Richard A., eds. Skeletal Growth of Aquatic Organisms: Biological Records of Environmental Change. LC 79-25825. (Topics in Geobiology Ser.: Vol. I). (Illus.). 762p. 1980. 140.00 (0-306-40259-9, Plenum Pr) Plenum.

Rhoads, Dorothy. The Corn Grows Ripe. (J). 1994. 17.75 (0-8446-6756-0) Peter Smith.

— The Corn Grows Ripe. LC 92-24888. (J). (gr. 8-12). 1993. 4.99 (0-14-036313-0, Puffin) Puffin Bks.

Rhoads, Edward J. China's Republican Revolution: The Case of Kwangtung, 1895-1913. LC 74-84090. (East Asian Monographs: No. 81). 392p. 1975. 25.00 (0-674-11980-0) HUP.

Rhoads, Edward J., et al. Chinese Red Army, Nineteen Twenty-Seven to Nineteen Sixty-Three: An Annotated Bibliography. LC 65-1422. (East Asian Monographs: No. 16). 202p. 1964. pap. 11.00 (0-674-12500-2) HUP.

Rhoads, Ella, see Ella Higginson, pseud..

Rhoads, F. D. & Edwards, J. Law Office Guide to Small Computers. (General Publications). (Illus.). 431p. 1984. text ed. 95.00 (0-07-052091-7) Shepards-McGraw.

Rhoads, Gwen, ed. see Mitchell, Robert B., et al.

Rhoads, James L. The Hacker's Golf Guide: A Handbook for High-Handicappers. LC 90-84179. (Illus.). 332p. 1991. 19.95 (0-9627884-1-4) Cloverleaf Golf.

Rhoads, John K. Critical Issues in Social Theory. 352p. 1991. 45.00 (0-271-00709-5); pap. text ed. 15.95 (0-271-00753-2) Pa St U Pr.

***Rhoads, Loren, ed.** Death's Garden: Relationships with Graveyards. 180p. 1995. pap. 19.99 (0-9636794-1-4) Automatism Pr.

Rhoads, Loren & Jones, Mason, eds. Lend the Eye a Terrible Aspect: A Collection of Essays & Fiction. LC 93-72388. (Illus.). 165p. (Orig.). 1994. pap. 9.99 (0-9636794-0-6) Automatism Pr.

Rhoads, Robert A. Coming Out in College: The Struggle for a Queer Identity. LC 94-16454. 208p. 1994. text ed. 55.00 (0-89789-378-6) Greenwood.

— Coming Out in College: The Struggle for a Queer Identity. LC 94-16454. (Critical Studies in Education & Culture). 208p. 1994. pap. text ed. 15.95 (0-89789-421-9, Bergin & Garvey) Greenwood.

Rhoads, Robert A., jt. auth. see Tierney, William G.

Rhoads, Sam. The Sky Tonight: A Guided Tour of the Stars over Hawai'i. 1994. spiral bd. 29.95 (0-930897-75-7) Bishop Mus.

Rhoads, Samuel E. & Gearen, Michael V. Disciplined Programming Using Pascal. 560p. (C). 1989. pap. write for info. (0-697-06336-4) Wm C Brown Pubs.

Rhoads, Steven. The Economist's View of the World: Government, Markets, & Public Policy. 416p. 1985. pap. 18.95 (0-521-31764-9) Cambridge U Pr.

Rhoads, Steven E. Incomparable Worth: Pay Equity Meets the Market. (Illus.). 304p. (C). 1994. pap. 17.95 (0-521-47828-6) Cambridge U Pr.

Rhoads, Steven F. Incomparable Worth: Pay Equity Meets the Market. LC 92-39227. 396p. (C). 1993. 29.95 (0-521-44187-0) Cambridge U Pr.

Rhoda, Michael D. Bible Favorites Activity Book. Gress, Jonna, ed. (Illus.). 6p. (J). (ps-5). 1993. pap. 8.25 (0-944943-41-1, 22656-1) Current Inc.

— A Christmas Surprise! Gress, Jonna, ed. (Touchy-Feely Book Ser.). 10p. (J). (ps-1). 1994. write for info. (0-944943-43-8, CODE 23303-6) Current Inc.

Rhode. Mystery at Greycombe Farm. (Black Dagger Crime Ser.). 16.50 (0-86220-819-X, BD018, Black Dagger) Chivers N Amer.

Rhode & Swearengen, eds. Mechanical Testing for Deformation Model Development- STP 765. 478p. 1982. 51.50 (0-8031-0737-4, 04-765000-23) ASTM.

Rhode, David, jt. ed. see Madsen, David.

Rhode, Deborah L. Justice & Gender. LC 89-30854. 440p. 1989. 47.50 (0-674-49100-9) HUP.

— Justice & Gender. 440p. (C). 1991. pap. 17.95 (0-674-49101-7) HUP.

Rhode, Deborah L., ed. Theoretical Perspectives on Sexual Difference. 326p. (C). 1992. reprint ed. pap. text ed. 16.00 (0-300-05225-1) Yale U Pr.

Rhode, Deborah L. & Lawson, Annette, eds. The Politics of Pregnancy: Adolescent Sexuality & Public Policy. LC 92-38539. 400p. (C). 1993. text ed. 35.00 (0-300-05717-2) Yale U Pr.

***Rhode, Deborah L. & Luban, David.** Legal Ethics. 2nd ed. 1000p. 1995. text ed. 43.00 (1-56662-249-2) Foundation Pr.

Rhode, Deborah L. & Luban, David J. Legal Ethics Teacher's Manual. (University Casebook Ser.). 177p. 1991. pap. text ed. write for info. (0-88277-979-6) Foundation Pr.

Rhode, Deborah L., jt. auth. see Hazard, Geoffrey C., Jr.

Rhode, Deborah L., ed. see Hazard, Geoffrey C., Jr.

Rhode, Deborah L., jt. auth. see Luban, David J.

Rhode, Eric. A History of the Cinema: From Its Origins to 1970. (Quality Paperbacks Ser.). (Illus.). 684p. 1985. reprint ed. pap. 13.95 (0-306-80233-3) Da Capo.

— Psychotic Metaphysics. 342p. 1994. pap. 27.50 (1-85575-074-0, Pub. by Karnac Bks UK) Brunner-Mazel.

Rhode, Ginger, et al. The Tough Kid Book: Practical Classroom Management Strategies. (Tough Kid Ser.). (Illus.). 120p. 1993. teacher ed 19.50 (0-944584-54-3) Sopris.

***Rhode Island Historical Society Staff, ed.** The Early Records of the Town of Warwick (R. I.) 362p. 1993. lib. bdg. 39.50 (0-8328-3535-8) Higginson Bk Co.

Rhode, John. Death of an Author. large type ed. (Mystery Ser.). 1974. 16.95 (0-85456-247-8) Ulverscroft.

Rhode, John & Dickson, Carter. Fatal Descent. (Mystery Classics Ser.). 160p. 1987. reprint ed. pap. 5.95 (0-486-25409-7) Dover.

Rhode, Robert D. Setting in the American Short Story of Local Color, 1865-1900. (Studies in English Literature: No. 30). 190p. (Orig.). 1975. pap. text ed. 55.40 (90-279-3281-6) Mouton.

Rhode, Stephen J. & Ginsberg, Stephen P., eds. Ophthalmic Technology: A Guide for the Eye Care Assistant. (Illus.). 508p. 1987. pap. 46.50 (0-88167-276-9) Raven.

Rhode, U. & Bucher, T. Communications Receivers: Principles & Design. 1995. text ed. 64.95 (0-07-053608-2) McGraw.

Rhode, U. & Bucher, T. T. Communications Receivers: Principles & Design. 608p. 1988. text ed. 65.00 (0-07-053570-1) McGraw.

Rhode, William. Chewing Gum, Baling Wire & Guts: Story of the Gates Flying Circus. (Illus.). 194p. 1994. reprint ed. pap. write for info. (0-9632295-1-6) H V Pubs.

Rhodehamel, John & Schwartz, Thomas F. The Last Best Hope of Earth: Abraham Lincoln & the Promise of America. (Illus.). 80p. 1993. pap. 12.95 (0-87328-142-X) Huntington Lib.

***Rhoden, David & Grabowski, John.** Awesome Almanacs - New York. 1995. pap. 14.95 (1-880190-26-5) B&B Pub.

Rhoden, Nancy R., jt. auth. see Arras, John D.

Rhoderick, E. H. Metal-Semiconductor Contacts. (Monographs in Electrical & Electronic Engineering). (Illus.). 1978. text ed. 22.00 (0-19-859323-6) OUP.

Rhoderick, E. H., jt. auth. see Rose-Innes, A. C.

Rhoderick, George C., Jr. The Early History of Middletown, Maryland. LC 89-51152. (Illus.). 412p. 1989. 35.00 (0-9623594-9-1) Mddltwn Val Hist Soc.

Rhodes. Clinical Problems in Gastroenterology. 224p. 1994. pap. 39.95 (0-8151-7334-2, Yr Bk Med Pubs) Mosby Yr Bk.

— How to Identify Musical Instruments from Ancient to Modern Times. (Getting Started Ser.). 1990. 7.95 (0-685-32032-4, 85-44) Hansen Ed Mus.

— Organic Chemists Desk Reference. 1995. pap. (0-412-54100-9) Chapman & Hall.

— Preventing Substance Abuse. (Practitioner Guidebook Ser.). (C). 1992. pap. text ed. 25.95 (0-205-14463-2, H4463, Longwood Div) Allyn.

— A Short History of Clinical Midwifery. 1995. pap. 24.95 (1-898507-16-3, Focal) Buttrwrth-Heinemann.

Rhodes & Stone. The Language of the Earth. 350p. 1981. pap. 42.00 (0-08-025980-4, Pergamon Pr) Elsevier.

Rhodes, jt. auth. see Banker.

Rhodes, ed. see Thycydides.

Rhodes, A. & Fletcher, D. L. Principles of Industrial Microbiology. 1966. 140.00 (0-08-011906-9, Pub. by Pergamon Repr UK) Franklin.

Rhodes, Anthony. D'Annunzio: The Poet As Superman. 1960. 18.95 (0-8392-1022-1) Astor-Honor.

Rhodes, Arnold B. Mighty Acts of God. (Orig.). 1964. student ed, pap. 11.99 (0-8042-9010-5, John Knox) Westminster John Knox.

Rhodes, Benjamin D. The Anglo-American Winter War with Russia, 1918-1919: A Diplomatic & Military Tragicomedy. LC 87-23645. (Contributions in Military Studies: No. 71). 192p. 1988. text ed. 42.95 (0-313-26132-6, RHF/, Greenwood Pr) Greenwood.

Rhodes, Bennie. Christopher Columbus. LC 76-5788. (Sower Ser.). (Illus.). (J). (gr. 3-6). 1977. reprint ed. pap. 6.95 (0-915134-26-8) Mott Media.

Rhodes, Bob, ed. see Preble, Dave.

Rhodes, C. K., et al, eds. Excimer Lasers, Nineteen Eighty-Three: OSA, Lake Tahoe, Nevada. LC 83-71437. (AIP Conference Proceedings Ser., Subseries: Particle & Fields: No. 100, 3). 354p. 1983. lib. bdg. 36.50 (0-88318-199-1) Am Inst Physics.

***Rhodes, C. M.** The Dark Side of Civil Rights. 1995. 13.95 (0-8062-5191-3) Carlton.

Rhodes, Carol L. & Goldner, Norman S. Why Men & Women Don't Get Along. 1992. pap. 10.95 (0-9632309-6-4) Somerset MI.

Rhodes, Carolyn. Reciprocity, U. S. Trade Policy, & the GATT Regime. 256p. 1993. 32.50 (0-8014-2864-5) Cornell U Pr.

***Rhodes, Carolyn & Mazey, Sonia, eds.** The State of the European Union Vol. 3: Building a European Polity. 1995. lib. bdg. 49.95 (1-55587-605-6) Lynne Rienner.

Rhodes, Carolyn H., ed. American Notes & Queries Supplement, First Person Female American: A Selected & Annotated Bibliography of the Autobiographies of American Women Living after 1950, Vol. II. LC 77-93778. 453p. 1980. 28.50 (0-87875-140-8) Whitston Pub.

Rhodes, Cheryl, jt. auth. see Bove, Anthony.

Rhodes, Cheryl, jt. auth. see Bove, Tony.

Rhodes, Christopher, jt. ed. see Lund, Anders.

Rhodes, Clifford, ed. Authority in a Changing Society. LC 70-398288. 231p. reprint ed. pap. 65.90 (0-8357-5901-6, 2051277) Bks Demand.

Rhodes, Colin. Primitivism & Modern Art. LC 94-60286. (World of Art Ser.). (Illus.). 216p. (Orig.). 1995. pap. 14.95 (0-500-20276-1) Thames Hudson.

Rhodes, D. N., jt. ed. see Morton, I.

Rhodes, Daniel. Pottery Form. LC 76-301. 244p. 1976. 27.95 (0-8019-5935-7) Chilton.

Rhodes, Darrel R. Medical Graduates of Foreign Nations: Index of New Information Including Social & Professional Discrimination, Selection, Performance & Problems. 180p. 1993. 49.50 (1-55914-928-0); pap. 39.50 (1-55914-929-9) ABBE Pubs Assn.

Rhodes, David, jt. auth. see Wright, Mike.

***Rhodes, Dennis E.** Silent Printers: Anonymous Printing at Venice in the Sixteenth Century. (British Library Studies in the History of the Book). (Illus.). 304p. 1995. 120.00 (0-7123-0385-5) U of Toronto Pr.

***Rhodes, Dennis E., ed.** Bookbindings & Other Bibliophily. (Illus.). 368p. 1994. 125.00 (88-85033-26-1, Pub. by St Pauls Biblioq UK) Oak Knoll Pr.

Rhodes, Diane B., jt. auth. see Bell, George H.

Rhodes, Donald R. Introduction to Monopulse. LC 80-65818. (Illus.). 129p. reprint ed. pap. 36.80 (0-685-20804-4, 2030130) Bks Demand.

Rhodes, Donna M. Little Stories for Little Children: A Worship Resource. 128p. (Orig.). (J). (ps-6). 1995. pap. 7.95 (0-8361-9000-9) Herald Pr.

Rhodes, E. & Wield, D., eds. Implementing New Technologies. 320p. 1985. pap. 19.95 (0-631-14381-5) Blackwell Pubs.

Rhodes, E., jt. auth. see Lupas, L.

Rhodes, E. G. & Moslow, T. F. Marine Clastic Reservoirs: Examples & Analogues. Bouma, A. H., ed. (Frontiers in Sedimentary Geology Ser.). (Illus.). 360p. 1992. 109.00 (0-387-97788-0) Spr-Verlag.

Rhodes, E. W. Defensor's Liber Scintillarum. (EETS, OS Ser.: No. 93). 1972. reprint ed. 40.00 (0-527-00092-2) Periodicals Srv.

Rhodes, Edward. International Relations: Introductory Readings. 296p. (C). 1992. per. 29.95 (0-8403-8093-3) Kendall-Hunt.

— Power & Madness. 288p. 1991. pap. text ed. 16.00 (0-231-06821-2) Col U Pr.

— Power & Madness: The Logic of Nuclear Coercion. 350p. 1989. text ed. 43.50 (0-231-06820-4) Col U Pr.

Rhodes, Elizabeth. The Unrecognized Precursors of Montemayor's Diana. 280p. (C). 1992. text ed. 27.50 (0-8262-0818-5) U of Mo Pr.

Rhodes, Elvi. Summer Promise. large type ed. (Magna General Fiction Ser.). 389p. 1992. 21.95 (0-7505-0209-6) Ulverscroft.

Rhodes, Ernest L. Henslowe's Rose: The Stage & Staging. LC 73-80466. 348p. reprint ed. pap. 99.20 (0-7837-5778-6, 2045444) Bks Demand.

Rhodes, Erroll F., tr. see Aland, Kurt & Aland, Barbara.

Rhodes, Erroll F., tr. see Lapide, Phinn E.

Rhodes, Eugene G., jt. auth. see Moslow, Thomas F.

Rhodes, Eugene M. The Best Novels & Stories of Eugene Manlove Rhodes. Dearing, Frank V., ed. LC 87-12466. xxiv, 552p. 1987. reprint ed. pap. 14.95 (0-8032-8928-6) U of Nebr Pr.

Rhodes, F. M., ed. Power Up for the Recovery: Industrial Power Conference 1983. 104p. 1983. pap. text ed. 25.00 (0-317-02641-0, 100159) ASME.

Rhodes, Frank H. A Neglected Challenge: Minority Participation in Higher Education, No. 17. 13p. 1987. pap. 2.00 (0-685-66149-0) Acad Educ Dev.

Rhodes, Frank H., et al. Cornell Collects: A Celebration of American Art from the Collections of Alumni & Friends. LC 90-82601. (Illus.). 196p. (Orig.). (C). 1990. pap. 31.95 (0-8122-1507-9) U of Pa Pr.

— Fossils. (Golden Guide Ser.). (Illus.). (J). (gr. 6 up). 1962. lib. bdg. write for info. (0-307-63515-5); pap. write for info. (0-307-24411-3) Western Pub.

Rhodes, Frederick L. Beginnings of Telephony. LC 07-4694. (Telecommunications Ser.). (Illus.). 286p. 1974. reprint ed. 28.95 (0-405-06057-2) Ayer.

Rhodes, Gale. Crystallography Made Crystal Clear: A Guide for Users of Macromolecular Models. (Illus.). 202p. 1993. pap. text ed. 34.95 (0-12-587075-2) Acad Pr.

Rhodes, Geoffrey E., jt. auth. see Gullen, Harold V.

Rhodes, George F., Jr., ed. Advances in Econometrics, Vol. 6. 1987. 73.25 (0-89232-795-2) Jai Pr.

— Economic Inequality: Survey Methods & Measurements. (Advances in Econometrics Ser.: Vol. 4). 243p. 1985. 73.25 (0-89232-580-1) Jai Pr.

— Innovations in Quantitative Economics: Essays in Honor of Robert L. Basmann. (Advances in Econometrics Ser.: Vol. 5). 368p. 1986. 73.25 (0-89232-686-7) Jai Pr.

Rhodes, George F., jt. auth. see Basmann, R. L.

Rhodes, George F., jt. ed. see Basmann, R. L.

Rhodes, George F., Jr.

Rhodes, George S. Numbers-a-Minute Timing Copy for Ten-Key Adding & Calculating Machines. 36p. (Orig.). (C). 1980. pap. text ed. 4.85 (0-89420-219-7, 126000); audio 19.25 (0-89420-226-X, 126004) Natl Book.

— Three-Minute Timings for Typing. 2nd ed. Calhoun, Calfrey C., ed. 81p. 1983. pap. text ed. 4.85 (0-89420-228-6, 296951) Natl Book.

***Rhodes, Greg & Erardi, John.** Crosley Field: The Illustrated History of a Classic Ballpark. (Illus.). 1995. pap. 24.95 (0-9641402-1-7) Road West.

— The First Boys of Summer: The Eighteen Sixty-Nine Cincinnati Red Stockings Baseball's First Professional Team. (Illus.). 144p. (Orig.). 1994. pap. 13.95 (0-9641402-0-9) Road West.

Rhodes, Gregory L., jt. ed. see Regina, Karen.

Rhodes, Gwen R. The History of the South Carolina Army National Guard, 1670-1987. (Illus.). 400p. (C). 1988. 30.00 (0-9619911-0-0) SC Army Natl Guard.

Rhodes, H. T. The Satanic Mass. 256p. 1974. 7.95 (0-8065-0405-6, Citadel Pr) Carol Pub Group.

R

An Asterisk (*) at the beginning of an entry indicates that the title is appearing in BIP for the first time.

— The Satanic Mass. 254p. 1975. reprint ed. pap. 3.95 (0-8065-0484-6, Citadel Pr) Carol Pub Group.

Rhodes, Herbert. How to Identify Musical Instruments. LC 85-44. (Self Improvement Ser.). (Illus.). 96p. (Orig.). 1985. pap. text ed. 7.95 (0-8494-1721-X) Hansen Ed Mus.

Rhodes, Hodis, ed. Welfare Reform, No. 28. Incl. Vol. II. Income Maintenance Policy: An Analysis of Historical & Legislative Precedents. 145p. 1978. 2.00 (0-89940-622-X); Vol. III. Analyses of Contemporary Welfare Reform Issues. 98p. 1978. 3.00 (0-89940-623-8); Vol. IV. Family Independence Project: An Alternative Welfare Reform Approach. 130p. 1978. 2.00 (0-89940-624-6); (Policy Research Project Report Ser.). 1978. write for info. (0-318-57595-7) LBJ Sch Pub Aff.

Rhodes, Howard J. Rhodes Family in America: A Genealogy & History, from 1497 to the Present Day. (Illus.). 525p. 1992. reprint ed. lib. bdg. 89.00 (0-8328-2390-2); reprint ed. pap. 79.00 (0-8328-2391-0) Higginson Bk Co.

***Rhodes, J., ed.** Agricultural Science Policy in Transition: Executive Summary & Proceedings of a Workshop Sponsored by ARI, April 29-May 1, 1986, 2 vols., Set. 249p. Date not set. pap. 25.00 (0-614-04329-8) Agri Research Inst.

— Monoids & Semigroups Theory with Applications. 548p. (C). 1991. text ed. 113.00 (981-02-0117-6) World Scientific Pub.

Rhodes, J. & Spence, J., eds. Behavior of Thin-Walled Structures. (Illus.). x, 430p. 1984. 160.25 (0-85334-246-6, Pub. by Elsevier Applied Sci UK) Elsevier.

Rhodes, J. & Walker, A. C., eds. Developments in Thin-Walled Structures, Vol. 1. (Illus.). 290p. 1982. 93.75 (0-85334-123-0, Pub. by Elsevier Applied Sci UK) Elsevier.

— Developments in Thin-Walled Structures, Vol. 2. (Illus.). 244p. 1984. 79.25 (0-85334-247-4, I-520-83, Pub. by Elsevier Applied Sci UK) Elsevier.

— Developments in Thin-Walled Structures, Vol. 3. 290p. 1987. 88.25 (1-85166-076-3, Pub. by Elsevier Applied Sci UK) Elsevier.

Rhodes, Jack. Intercity Bus Lines of the Southwest: A Photographic History. LC 88-2207. (Centennial Series of the Association of Former Students: No. 29). (Illus.). 176p. 1988. 22.50 (0-89096-374-6) Tex A&M Univ Pr.

Rhodes, Jack W. Keats's Major Odes: An Annotated Bibliography of the Criticism. LC 83-16634. 224p. 1984. text ed. 45.00 (0-313-23809-X, RHK/, Greenwood Pr) Greenwood.

Rhodes, Jack W., jt. ed. see Evert, Walter H.

Rhodes, James F. History of the United States from the Compromise of 1850 to the End of the Roosevelt Administration, 9 vols., Set. rev. ed. (BCL1 - U. S. History Ser.). 1991. reprint ed. lib. bdg. 675.00 (0-7812-6039-6) Rprt Serv.

— Lectures on the American Civil War. LC 73-160990. (Select Bibliographies Reprint Ser.). 1977. reprint ed. 21.95 (0-8369-5858-6) Ayer.

Rhodes, James R. James R. Rhodes' Poems. LC 82-20374. (Lewiston Poetry Ser.). 112p. 1982. lib. bdg. 24.95 (0-88946-999-7) E Mellen.

— Little Vine. (Lewiston Poetry Ser.: Vol. 12). (Illus.). 84p. 1986. lib. bdg. 24.95 (0-88946-049-3) E Mellen.

Rhodes, Janis, jt. auth. see McClure, Nancee.

Rhodes, Jeanne. Fat to Fit Without Dieting: The No-Diet Eating Plan That Burns Off Excess Fat Forever. (Illus.). 288p. 1990. pap. 10.95 (0-8092-4158-7) Contemp Bks.

Rhodes, Jerry. Conceptual Toolmaking: Expert Systems of the Mind. (Developmental Management Ser.). 206p. (Orig.). 1994. 39.95 (0-631-17489-3); pap. 19.95 (0-631-19321-9) Blackwell Pubs.

Rhodes, Jewell P. Voodoo Dreams: A Novel of Marie Laveau. 496p. 1993. 22.95 (0-312-09869-3) St Martin.

— Voodoo Dreams: A Novel of Marie Laveau. 1995. pap. 13.00 (0-312-11931-3) St Martin.

Rhodes, Joan L., jt. auth. see Kutie, Rita C.

Rhodes, John. Kettering-Huntingdon Line. (C). 1985. 50.00 (0-85361-301-X) St Mut.

***Rhodes, John & Smith, Dean.** I Was There. 270p. 1995. 8.95 (0-7610-0435-1) NW Pub.

Rhodes, John D. Theory of Electrical Filters. LC 75-30767. 234p. reprint ed. pap. 66.70 (0-317-09071-2, 2022103) Bks Demand.

Rhodes, Judy C. The Hunter's Heart. LC 92-47025. 192p. (J). (gr. 5 up). 1993. lib. bdg. 14.95 (0-02-773935-X, Bradbury S&S) S&S Childrens.

— The Hunter's Heart. LC 92-47025. 160p. (J). (gr. 4-7). 1993. text ed. 14.95 (0-02-775935-0, Bradbury S&S) S&S Childrens.

— The King Boy. LC 91-2159. 160p. (J). (gr. 5-9). 1991. text ed. 14.95 (0-02-776115-0, Bradbury S&S) S&S Childrens.

Rhodes, Karen. Shining Tide. 320p. 1992. mass mkt. 3.99 (0-8217-3839-9) Zebra.

— Strings of Fortune. (Lucky in Love Ser.: No. 25). 320p. 1993. pap. 3.50 (0-8217-4111-X) Zebra.

***Rhodes, Katy, illus.** Bedtime Rhymes. (Carousel Ser.). (J). (ps-1). 1994. 7.95 (1-884628-10-9) Flying Frog.

— Nursery Rhymes. (Carousel Ser.). (J). (ps-1). 1994. 7.95 (1-884628-09-5) Flying Frog.

Rhodes, Lelia G. Jackson State University: The First Hundred Years, 1877-1977. LC 77-18107. (Illus.). 436p. reprint ed. pap. 124.30 (0-8357-4348-9, 2037151) Bks Demand.

Rhodes, Lisa. Understanding Personal Bankruptcy. (No Nonsense Financial Guide Ser.). 96p. 1993. pap. 4.95 (0-681-41741-2) Longmeadow Pr.

Rhodes, Lodis, contrib. Housing Low-Income Austinites: New Roles for the Austin Housing Authority in Meeting Changing Needs & New Community Demands. (Policy Research Project Report Ser.: No. 87). 122p. 1989. pap. 10.00 (0-89940-694-7) LBJ Sch Pub Aff.

— Runaways in Texas: A Statistical Estimate, 1985. (Special Project Report Ser.). 33p. 1985. 5.00 (0-89940-852-4) LBJ Sch Pub Aff.

— Teacher Retirement System of Texas: Survey of Annuitants & State Teacher Retirement Systems. (Policy Research Project Report Ser.: No. 79). 75p. 1987. 8.00 (0-89940-683-1) LBJ Sch Pub Aff.

Rhodes, Lodis, jt. contrib. see Grubb, W. Norton.

Rhodes, Lorna. Book of Children's Foods. 120p. 1992. pap. 10.95 (1-55788-047-6, HP Books) Berkley Pub.

— The Book of Salads. (Book of...Ser.). (Illus.). 120p. (Orig.). 1989. pap. 11.00 (0-89586-791-5, HP Books) Berkley Pub.

— Cookie Cookbook. 1994. 9.98 (0-681-45460-1) Longmeadow Pr.

— The Garlic Cookbook. LC 94-26735. 1994. 9.98 (0-8317-3885-5) Smithmark.

Rhodes, Lorna A. Emptying Beds: The Work of an Emergency Psychiatric Unit. LC 90-11161. (Comparative Studies of Health Systems & Medical Care: Vol. 27). (Illus.). 216p. 1991. 25.00 (0-520-07054-2) U CA Pr.

— Emptying Beds: The Work of an Emergency Psychiatric Unit. 1995. pap. 12.95 (0-520-20351-8) U CA Pr.

Rhodes, Lorne. Book of Fondues. Staub, Susan, ed. LC 87-15052. (Book of...Ser.). 120p. (Orig.). 1988. pap. 11.00 (0-89586-667-6, HP Books) Berkley Pub.

Rhodes, Lucien, jt. auth. see Little, Jeffrey B.

***Rhodes, Lynette.** The Roycroft Shops 1894-1915. (Illus.). 20p. 1975. pap. 8.95 (0-614-04814-1) Erie Art Mus.

Rhodes, Lynette I. American Folk Art: From the Traditional to the Naive. LC 79-104017. (Themes in Art Ser.). (Illus.). 116p. reprint ed. pap. 33.10 (0-8357-5368-9, 2022661) Bks Demand.

— Science Within Art. LC 79-93193. (Illus.). 72p. reprint ed. pap. 25.00 (0-317-10007-6, 2022660) Bks Demand.

Rhodes, Lynn K., ed. Literacy Assessment: A Handbook of Instruments. LC 92-1619. 181p. 1992. pap. text ed. 21.50 (0-435-08759-2, 08759) Heinemann.

Rhodes, Lynn K. & Dudley-Marling, Curt. Readers & Writers with a Difference: A Holistic Approach to Teaching Learning Disabled & Remedial Students. LC 87-23819. 329p. (Orig.). 1988. pap. text ed. 23.50 (0-435-08453-4) Heinemann.

Rhodes, Lynn K. & Shanklin, Nancy. Windows into Literacy: Assessing Learners K-Eight. LC 92-25297. 456p. (J). (gr. k-8). 1993. pap. text ed. 29.50 (0-435-08757-6, 08757) Heinemann.

Rhodes, Lynn N. Co-Creating: A Feminist Vision of Ministry. LC 87-10518. 132p. (C). 1987. pap. 11.99 (0-664-24032-1, Westminster) Westminster John Knox.

Rhodes, M. J., ed. Principles of Powder Technology. 439p. 1990. text ed. 168.00 (0-471-92422-9) Wiley.

Rhodes, M. J., jt. ed. see Charlwood, Barry V.

Rhodes, M. J., jt. ed. see Robins, R. J.

Rhodes, Mardi, ed. see Stessin, Nicolette.

Rhodes, Margaret L. Ethical Dilemmas in Social Work Practice. LC 91-17352. 216p. 1991. pap. 14.95 (0-87304-255-7) Families Intl.

— Ethical Dilemmas in Social Work Practice. 192p. 1986. pap. text ed. 12.95 (0-415-90157-X, RKP) Routledge.

***Rhodes, Mark, ed.** New York Actions & Remedies Vols. 1-5, 5 vols., Set. Incl. Vols. 1 & 2. New York Actions & Remedies Vols. 1 & 2: Tort Law. 1000p. 1991. ring bd. 170.00 (1-56257-164-8); Set. New York Actions & Remedies Vols. 3 & 4: Corporate & Commercial Law, 2 vols. 1300p. 1991. ring bd. 170.00 (0-88063-445-6); Vol. 5. New York Actions & Remedies Vol. 5: Family Law, Wills & Trusts. 500p. 1991. ring bd. 85.00 (1-56257-165-6); 1991. Set ring bd. 400.00 (1-56257-661-5) Michie Butterworth.

***Rhodes, Mark S.** The Handbook of Insurance Agency Law. Standard Publishing Corporation Staff, ed. 480p. 1994. text ed. 119.00 (0-923240-10-1) Stndrd Publishing.

— Insurance Laws Annotated: Federal & Model Acts. Standard Publishing Corporation Staff, ed. 342p. 1992. text ed. 117.00 (0-923240-04-7) Stndrd Publishing.

— The Law of Commercial Insurance. 1992. 124.00 (0-923240-00-4) Stndrd Publishing.

— Orfield's Criminal Procedure under the Federal Rules, 7 vols., Set. 2nd ed. LC 85-50534. 1985. 710.00 (0-685-59839-X) Clark Boardman Callaghan.

— Tort & Insurance Litigation Reference, 5 vols., Set. LC 92-71126. 1992. ring bd. 420.00 (0-685-59871-3) Clark Boardman Callaghan.

***Rhodes, Martha.** At the Gate, Vol. IV. Busa, Christopher, ed. LC 94-73949. (Provincetown Poets Ser.: IV). (Illus.). 72p. (Orig.). 1995. 35.00 (0-944854-19-2); pap. text ed. 10.00 (0-944854-18-4) Provincetown Arts.

Rhodes, Martha E. Food Protection Technology, No. II. (Illus.). 500p. 1990. 76.95 (0-87371-377-X, TX511) Lewis Pubs.

Rhodes, Michael, ed. The Presidency & the Political System. 609p. 1994. pap. 25.95 (0-87187-788-0) Congr Quarterly.

— The Presidency & the Political System. 4th ed. 609p. 1994. 39.95 (0-87187-786-4) Congr Quarterly.

Rhodes, Naomi. Twenty One Voices: The Art of Presenting the Performing Arts. Robins, Melinda, ed. (Illus.). 324p. (Orig.). 1990. pap. 27.00 (0-926517-09-0) Assn Perf Arts Presenters.

Rhodes, Neil. The Power of Eloquence & English Renaissance Literature. LC 92-14672. 1992. text ed. 49.95 (0-312-08421-8) St Martin.

— Symantec C Plus Plus Programming for the Macintosh. 2nd ed. 1994. pap. 40.00 (1-56686-155-1) Brady Compu Bks.

— Symantec Think C Plus Plus Macintosh Programming. 1993. pap. 39.95 (1-56686-049-0) Brady Compu Bks.

Rhodes, Neil, ed. see Donne, John.

Rhodes, Neil, jt. auth. see McKeehan, Julie.

***Rhodes, Norman.** Ibsen & the Greeks: Selected Works of Henrik Ibsen as Mediated by German & Scandinavian Culture. LC 94-24280. 208p. 1995. write for info. (0-8387-5298-5) Bucknell U Pr.

Rhodes, P. An Outline History of Medicine. 224p. (C). 1985. pap. text ed. 30.00 (0-407-00343-6) Buttrwrth-Heinemann.

Rhodes, P., ed. see International Conference on the Physics of Transition Metals Staff.

Rhodes, P. J. A Commentary on the Aristotelian Athenaion Politeia. (Illus.). 832p. 1993. reprint ed. pap. 42.00 (0-19-814942-5) OUP.

— The Greek City States: A Source Book. LC 86-3375. 286p. 1986. 34.95 (0-8061-2010-X); pap. 17.95 (0-8061-2013-4) U of Okla Pr.

***Rhodes, Paul C.** Decision Support Systems: Theory & Practice. 322p. Date not set. pap. 27.50 (1-872474-07-1, Pub. by Alfred Waller UK) Paul & Co Pubs.

Rhodes, Penny J. Racial Matching in Fostering: The Challenge to Social Work Practice. 225p. 1992. 59.95 (1-85628-264-3, Pub. by Avebury Pub UK) Ashgate Pub Co.

Rhodes, Peter C., tr. see Thoby-Marcelin, Philippe & Marcelin, Pierre.

Rhodes, Peter S., jt. auth. see Fincham, Robin.

Rhodes, R. & Henisch, Heinz K. Imperfections & Active Centers in Semiconductors. LC 63-18928. (International Series of Monographs on Semiconductors: Vol. 6). 1964. 157.00 (0-08-010186-0, Pub. by Pergamon Repr UK) Franklin.

Rhodes, R., jt. auth. see Sutherland, S.

Rhodes, R. A. Control & Power in Central-Local Government Relations. 208p. 1981. text ed. 58.00 (0-566-00333-3) Ashgate Pub Co.

***Rhodes, R. A. & Dunleavy, Patrick, eds.** Prime Minister, Cabinet, & Core Executive. LC 94-49141. 1995. write for info. (0-312-12616-6) St Martin.

Rhodes, R. A. & Wright, V., eds. Tensions in the Territorial Politics of Western Europe. (Illus.). 176p. 1988. text ed. 37.50 (0-7146-3329-1, Pub. by F Cass Pubs UK) Intl Spec Bk.

Rhodes, R. A., jt. ed. see Marsh, David.

Rhodes, R. Sanders, II. Paleoecology & Regional Paleoclimatic Implications of the Farmdalian Craigmile & Woodfordian Waubonsie Mammalian Local Faunas, Southwestern Iowa. (Reports of Investigations Ser.: No. 40). (Illus.). viii, 51p. (Orig.). 1984. pap. 5.00 (0-89792-103-8) Ill St Museum.

Rhodes, Raphael H. Hypnosis: Theory, Practice & Application. 1960. pap. 3.95 (0-8065-0117-0, Citadel Pr) Carol Pub Group.

— Hypnosis: Theory, Practice & Application. 192p. 1995. pap. 9.95 (0-8065-1119-2, Citadel Pr) Carol Pub Group.

Rhodes, Rhonda & Hartwell, Therese. Houston Parents' Grapevine: A Guide to Local Resources for Expectant Parents & Parents of Young Children. (Illus.). 504p. (Orig.). 1994. pap. 17.95 (0-9636321-2-4) Parenthd Res.

Rhodes, Rhonda, jt. auth. see Kupsh, Joyce.

***Rhodes, Richard.** Dark Sun: The Making of the Hydrogen Bomb. 1995. 32.50 (0-684-80400-X) S&S Trade.

— Eastern Ojibwa-Chippewa-Ottawa Dictionary. (Trends in Linguistics, Documentation Ser.: No. 3). liv, 626p. 1985. 144.65 (0-89925-114-5) Mouton.

— How to Write: Advice & Reflections. LC 94-45342. 1995. write for info. (0-688-14095-5) Morrow.

— The Inland Ground: An Evocation of the American Middle West. rev. ed. LC 91-26020. (Illus.). xvi, 328p. 1991. reprint ed. pap. 12.95 (0-7006-0499-5) U Pr of KS.

— The Inland Ground: An Evocation of the American Middle West. rev. ed. LC 91-26020. (Illus.). xvi, 328p. 1991. reprint ed. 25.00 (0-7006-0498-7) U Pr of KS.

— Making Love. 1993. pap. 10.00 (0-671-87072-6, Touchstone Bks) S&S Trade.

— Making Love: An Erotic Odyssey. LC 92-12467. 1992. 18.00 (0-671-78227-4) S&S Trade.

— The Making of the Atomic Bomb. (Illus.). 928p. 1988. pap. 14.95 (0-671-65719-4, Touchstone Bks) S&S Trade.

— The Making of the Atomic Bomb. 1995. pap. 16.00 (0-684-81378-5, Touchstone Bks) S&S Trade.

Rhodes, Richard, ed. see Serber, Robert.

Rhodes, Richard A. Eastern Ojibwa-Chippewa-Ottowa Dictionary. LC 92-37126. 1993. pap. 34.95 (3-11-013749-6) Mouton.

Rhodes, Rita M. Women & the Family in Post-Famine Ireland: Status & Opportunity in a Patriarchal Society. LC 92-836. (Modern European History Ser.). 384p. 1992. 95.00 (0-8153-0673-3) Garland.

Rhodes, Robert B., ed. Low Temperature Lubricant Rheology Measurement & Relevance to Engine Operation. LC 92-39198. (Special Technical Publication Ser.: No. 1143). (Illus.). 90p. 1993. 47.00 (0-8031-1438-9, 04-011430-12) ASTM.

Rhodes, Robert E., jt. ed. see Casey, Daniel J.

Rhodes, Robert H. All for the Union: The Civil War Diary & Letters of Elisha Hunt Rhodes. 1992. pap. 11.00 (0-679-73828-2, Vin) Random.

— General A. P. Hill. 1992. pap. 14.00 (0-679-73888-6, Vin) Random.

Rhodes, Robert H., ed. All for the Union: The Civil War Diary & Letters of Elisha Hunt Rhodes. (Illus.). 256p. 1991. 21.00 (0-517-58427-1, Orion Bks) Crown Pub Group.

Rhodes, Robert I. Imperialism & Underdevelopment: A Reader. LC 70-122736. (Illus.). 432p. reprint ed. pap. 123.20 (0-7837-6991-1, 2046803) Bks Demand.

Rhodes, Robert M., jt. ed. see Frank, James E.

Rhodes, Robert P. Health Care Politics, Policy, & Distributive Justice: The Ironic Triumph. LC 90-10364. (SUNY Series in Health Care Politics & Policy). 339p. (C). 1991. 64.50 (0-7914-0777-2); pap. 21.95 (0-7914-0778-0) State U NY Pr.

Rhodes-Roberts, Muriel, ed. Bacteria & Plants. (Society for Applied Bacteriology Symposium Ser.: No. 10). 1982. text ed. 93.00 (0-12-587080-9) Acad Pr.

***Rhodes, Robin F.** Architecture & Meaning on the Athenian Acropolis. (Illus.). 240p. (C). 1995. 60.00 (0-521-47024-2); pap. 16.95 (0-521-46981-3) Cambridge U Pr.

***Rhodes, Ron.** Angels Among Us. LC 94-22294. (Orig.). 1994. pap. 9.99 (1-56507-271-5) Harvest Hse.

— Christ before the Manger: The Life & Times of the Preincarnate Christ. LC 92-23993. 288p. 1992. pap. 13.99 (0-8010-7766-4) Baker Bk.

— The Counterfeit Christ of the New Age Movement. LC 90-43495. 256p. (Orig.). 1990. pap. 11.99 (0-8010-7757-5) Baker Bk.

— The Culting of America. LC 94-6868. 1994. pap. 11.99 (1-56507-186-7) Harvest Hse.

— New Age Movement. (Guide to Cults & Religious Movements Ser.). 64p. 1994. 4.99 (0-310-70431-6) Zondervan.

— Reasoning from the Scriptures with the Jehovah's Witnesses. LC 93-3488. 1993. pap. 11.99 (1-56507-106-9) Harvest Hse.

— When Servants Suffer: Finding Purpose in Pain. (Fisherman Bible Studyguide Ser.). 79p. (Orig.). 1989. 4.99 (0-87788-929-5) Shaw Pubs.

***Rhodes, Ron & Bodine, Marian M.** Reasoning from the Scriptures with the Mormons. (Orig.). 1995. pap. 11.99 (1-56507-328-2) Harvest Hse.

Rhodes, Royal, jt. auth. see McCarthy, George.

***Rhodes, Royal W.** The Lion & the Cross: Early Christianity in Victorian Novels. LC 94-26139. (Studies in Victorian Life & Literature). 1995. 49.50 (0-8142-0648-4) Ohio St U Pr.

Rhodes, Sammie J. The Best of Old Times Not Forgotten. LC 91-90544. 210p. 1991. pap. 11.95 (0-9630257-0-8) Cty Rhodes.

Rhodes, Sonya & Wilson, Josleen. Surviving Family Life: The Seven Crises of Living Together. 299p. 1986. reprint ed. pap. 11.95 (0-935005-06-4) Lincoln-Rembrandt.

Rhodes, Stuart, jt. auth. see Sutherland, Douglas.

Rhodes, Susan R. & Steers, Richard M. Managing Employee Absenteeism. (Managing Human Resources Ser.). (Illus.). 150p. (C). 1990. pap. text ed. 26.95 (0-201-51041-3) Addison-Wesley.

Rhodes, Terrel L., et al, eds. Applied Political Inquiry: Readings in Research Methodology. LC 83-14702. 300p. (C). 1983. pap. text ed. 26.50 (0-8191-3477-5) U Pr of Amer.

Rhodes, Timothy, jt. auth. see Czernecki, Stefan.

Rhodes, Tom. Stress Without Tears. (Illus.). 130p. (Orig.). 1990. 37.50 (0-9615234-1-7) Jacobs Pub.

— Stress Without Tears: A Primer on Aircraft-Stress Analysis Requiring No Advanced Mathematics. (Illus.). 123p. (Orig.). (C). 1994. pap. 40.00x (0-7881-1343-7) Diane Pub.

***Rhodes, V. James.** The Agricultural Marketing System. 4th ed. 496p. 1993. pap. write for info. (0-89787-130-8) Gorsuch Scarisbrick.

Rhodes, Warren A. Children Who Tell Lies. 20p. 1990. 2.95 (1-56456-027-9, 238) W Gladden Found.

Rhodes, Warren A., et al. Effects of Racism & Prejudice on Children. (Children in Turmoil Ser.). 20p. 1994. 2.95 (1-56456-086-4, 284) W Gladden Found.

Rhodes, Warren A. From the Jail House to the White House: A True Story. 20p. 1987. 2.95 (1-56456-012-0, 206) W Gladden Found.

Rhodes, Warren A. & Brown, Waln K., eds. Why Some Children Succeed Despite the Odds. LC 90-49203. 208p. 1991. text ed. 45.00 (0-275-93705-4, C3705, Praeger Pubs) Greenwood.

Rhodes, Warren A. & Hoey, Kim. Overcoming Childhood Misfortune: Children Who Beat the Odds. LC 93-19611. 168p. 1993. text ed. 45.00 (0-275-94081-0, Praeger Pubs) Greenwood.

Rhodes, William C. & Tracy, Michael L., eds. A Study of Child Variance, 2 vols. Incl. Vol. 2. Interventions. 700p. 1974. pap. 32.50 (0-472-08759-2); (Conceptual Project in Emotional Disturbance Ser.). (Illus.). 1974. reprint ed. Set pap. text ed. write for info. (0-318-56094-1) U of Mich Pr.

Rhodes, William H. Caxton's Book. LC 73-13263. (Classics of Science Fiction Ser.). 308p. 1974. reprint ed. 15.00 (0-88355-117-9); reprint ed. pap. 10.00 (0-88355-146-2) Hyperion Conn.

Rhodin, Johannes G. An Atlas of Histology. (Illus.). 1975. text ed. 45.00 (0-19-501944-X) OUP.

Rhodin, T. N. & Ertl, G., eds. Nature of the Surface Chemical Bond. 406p. 1979. 102.75 (0-444-85053-8, North Holland) Elsevier.

Rhodin, Thor N., ed. Physical Metallurgy of Stress Corrosion Fracture. LC 59-14890. (Metallurgical Society Conference Ser.: Vol. 4). 409p. reprint ed. pap. 116.60 (0-317-10921-9, 2000667) Bks Demand.

Rhodius, Apollonius. The Argonautica, Bk. III. xlviii, 160p. (GER.). 1989. reprint ed. 31.20 (3-487-04590-7, Pub. by Georg Olms GW) Lubrecht & Cramer.

— Argonautica Book III. Hunter, R. L., ed. (Cambridge Greek & Latin Classics Ser.). 300p. (C). 1989. 59.95 (0-521-32031-3); pap. 21.95 (0-521-31236-1) Cambridge U Pr.

An Asterisk (*) at the beginning of an entry indicates that the title is appearing in BIP for the first time.

— Scholia in Apollonium Rhodium Vetera. Wendel, Karl, ed. xxviii, 402p. (GER.). 1974. write for info. (*3-296-15400-0*, Pub. by Georg Olms GW) Lubrecht & Cramer.

Rhodius, H. & Darling, J. Walter Spies & Balinese Art. Stowell, John, ed. (Illus.). 1980. 40.00 (*90-6255-079-7*) IBD Ltd.

***Rhodus, Dennis.** Headfirst. (Read-along Radio Dramas Ser.). (J). (gr. 6-10). 1987. 35.00 (*1-878298-07-0*) Balance Pub.

Rhondda, Margaret H. Notes on the Way. LC 68-8488. (Essay Index Reprint Ser.). 1977. 19.95 (*0-8369-0822-8*) Ayer.

Rhone, Christine, jt. auth. see Michell, John.

Rhone, L. C. Total Auto Body Repair. LC 75-2551. (Illus.). 1976. 23.95 (*0-672-97659-5*, Bobbs) Macmillan.

— Total Auto Body Repair. LC 75-2551. 1978. teacher ed write for info. (*0-672-97137-2*, 2319); student ed write for info. (*0-672-97200-X*) Macmillan.

— Total Auto Body Repair. 21th ed. 1983. pap. 10.64 (*0-02-682130-3*) Macmillan.

— Total Auto Body Repair, No. 3. 1984. 39.96 (*0-02-682161-3*) Macmillan.

Rhone, L. C. & Yates, H. David. Total Auto Body Repair. 2nd ed. 464p. (C). 1982. teacher ed write for info. (*0-672-97969-1*); student ed write for info. (*0-672-97968-3*); text ed. write for info. (*0-672-97967-5*) Macmillan.

***Rhoner, Peter.** Industrial Hydraulic Control. 184p. (C). 1988. 54.00x (*0-471-53428-5*, Pub. by S Thornes Pubs UK) St Mut.

Rhoodie, Eschel M. Cultures in Conflict: A Global Survey of Ethnic, Racial, Linguistic, Religious & Nationalist Factors. LC 92-50946. 976p. 1995. lib. bdg. 95.00 (*0-89950-830-8*) McFarland & Co.

— Discrimination Against Women: A Global Survey of the Economic, Educational, Social & Political Status of Women. LC 89-42748. 630p. 1989. lib. bdg. 49.95x (*0-89950-448-5*) McFarland & Co.

***Rhoton, Dale.** How Much for the Man. Chiu, Peter, tr. 47p. (CHI.). 1988. 0.75 (*1-56582-070-3*) Christ Renew Min.

Rhoton, E. Un Barco Llamado Logos (The Logos Story) (SPA.). Date not set. 4.99 (*0-945792-49-2*, 498454) Editorial Unilit.

Rhoton, Elaine. Logos Story. rev. ed. (Illus.). 192p. reprint ed. pap. text ed. 5.99 (*0-9630908-4-4*) O M Lit.

Rhoton, Jared, tr. see Rinpoche, Deshung & Tenpa Nyima, Kunga.

Rhoton, Jared, tr. see Rinpoche, Deshung & Tenpay Nyima, Kunga.

Rhoton, Jessian L. The Magic Treble Tree. Vol. I. (Illus.). 48p. (J). 1989. lib. bdg. write for info. (*0-318-65826-7*) Happy Music Pub.

— The Magic Treble Tree. (All about the Magic of Music Ser.). (Illus.). 48p. (J). 1990. write for info. (*0-9624162-9-0*) Happy Music Pub.

Rhoton, John. All-in-One: Integrating Applications in V3.0. LC 92-27293. (All-in-One Ser.). (Illus.). 265p. 1992. pap. text ed. 52.95 (*1-55558-102-1*, EYJ850EDP, Digital DEC) Buttrwrth-Heinemann.

Rhu, Lawrence F. The Genesis of Tasso's Narrative Theory: English Translations of the Early Poetics & a Comparative Study of Their Significance. LC 92-45872. 192p. 1993. text ed. 28.95 (*0-8143-2118-6*); pap. 19.95 (*0-8143-2119-4*) Wayne St U Pr.

Rhuda, Charles A., ed. see American Institute of Certified Public Accountants Staff.

Rhue, Judith W., jt. auth. see Lynn, Steven J.

Rhue, Judith W., jt. ed. see Lynn, Steven J.

Rhue, Judith W., et al, eds. Handbook of Clinical Hypnosis. (Illus.). 772p. 1993. text ed. 59.95 (*1-55798-199-X*) Am Psychol.

Rhue, Morton. The Wave. 143p. (YA). (gr. 7 up). 1981. mass mkt. 4.50 (*0-440-99371-7*, LFL) Dell.

Rhunka, John C. Housing Justice in Small Claims Courts. LC 78-112816. (On Loan Through NCSC Library). 170p. 1979. pap. write for info. (*0-89656-031-7*, R-043) Natl Ctr St Courts.

***Rhymer.** Illustrated Atlas of the Bible. 1995. (*0-7858-0339-4*) Bk Sales Inc.

Rhymer, Joseph. The End of Time. 160p. (C). 1991. 39.00 (*0-85439-404-4*, Pub. by St Paul Pubns UK) St Mut.

— The Miracles of Jesus. 152p. (C). 1990. 45.00 (*0-85439-387-0*, Pub. by St Paul Pubns UK) St Mut.

***Rhymer, Joseph, tr.** The Psalms. 448p. 1992. 150.00 (*0-85439-474-5*, Pub. by St Paul Pubns UK) St Mut.

Rhyne & Golden. Seeking Scientific Explanations for Natural Phenomena. rev. ed. 94p. 1992. text ed. 15.95 (*0-88725-163-3*) Hunter Textbks.

Rhyne, Craig & Rhyne, Faith. Monthly Money: Allowance & Responsibility System for Kids & Teenagers. 44p. 1991. 19.95 (*1-882189-01-9*); 39.95 (*1-882189-00-0*) Monthly Money.

Rhyne, Elisabeth, jt. ed. see Otero, Maria.

Rhyne, Elisabeth H. Small Business, Banks, & SBA Loan Guarantees: Subsidizing the Weak or Bridging a Credit Gap? LC 87-36098. 188p. 1988. text ed. 55.00 (*0-89930-256-4*, RSB/, Quorum Bks) Greenwood.

Rhyne, Faith, jt. auth. see Rhyne, Craig.

Rhyne, J. J., ed. see American Institute of Physics.

Rhyne, Janie. The Gestalt Art Experience: Creative Process & Expressive Therapy. LC 84-60308. (Illus.). 224p. (C). 1984. reprint ed. pap. text ed. 18.95 (*0-9613309-0-2*) Magnolia St Pub.

— Gestalt Art Experience: Patterns that Connect. 2nd ed. LC 94-72915. (Illus.). 230p. (C). 1995. pap. text ed. write for info. (*0-9613309-6-1*) Magnolia St Pub.

Rhyne, Jennings J. Some Southern Cotton Mill Workers & Their Villages. Stein, Leon, ed. LC 77-70527. (Work Ser.). (Illus.). 1977. reprint ed. lib. bdg. 23.95 (*0-405-10195-3*) Ayer.

Rhyne, Nancy. Alice Flagg: The Ghost of the Hermitage. LC 89-28782. 256p. 1990. 19.95 (*0-88289-760-8*) Pelican.

— Carolina Seashells. (Illus.). 1989. pap. 6.95 (*0-87844-077-1*) Sandlapper Pub Co.

— Coastal Ghosts: Haunted Places from Wilmington, North Carolina to Savannah, Georgia. rev. ed. (Illus.). 188p. 1989. reprint ed. pap. 9.95 (*0-87844-049-6*) Sandlapper Pub Co.

— The Jack O'Lantern Ghost. (Illus.). 128p. (YA). (gr. 9-12). 1995. pap. text ed. 7.95 (*1-56554-132-4*) Pelican.

— More Tales of the South Carolina Low Country. LC 84-21710. 121p. 1984. pap. 5.95 (*0-89587-042-8*) Blair.

— Once upon a Time on a Plantation. LC 88-9896. 1988. 11.95 (*0-88289-702-0*) Pelican.

— Plantation Tales. 1989. pap. 8.95 (*0-87844-093-3*) Sandlapper Pub Co.

— The South Carolina Lizard Man. LC 92-17289. (Illus.). 128p. (J). (gr. 5-9). 1992. pap. 7.95 (*0-88289-907-4*) Pelican.

— Tales of the South Carolina Low Country. LC 82-9710. 112p. 1982. pap. 5.95 (*0-89587-027-4*) Blair.

— Touring the Coastal Georgia Backroads. LC 93-47130. (Touring the Backroads Ser.). (Illus.). (Orig.). 1994. pap. 14.95 (*0-89587-111-4*) Blair.

— Touring the Coastal South Carolina Backroads. LC 91-41378. (Touring the Backroads Ser.). (Illus.). 276p. (Orig.). 1992. pap. 14.95 (*0-89587-090-8*) Blair.

Rhyne, Tom, jt. ed. see Newman, Mike.

Rhyne, William R. Hazardous Materials Transportation Risk Analysis: Quantitative Approaches for Truck & Train. LC 93-38050. 1994. text ed. 49.95 (*0-442-01413-9*) Van Nos Reinhold.

Rhyner, Charles R., et al. Waste Management & Resource Recovery. 544p. 1995. 69.95 (*0-87371-572-1*, L572) Lewis Pubs.

Rhyner, Hans H. Ayurveda: The Gentle Health System. LC 93-43375. (Illus.). 128p. 1994. pap. 12.95 (*0-8069-0510-7*) Sterling.

Rhys Davids & Stede, William. Pali - English Dictionary. 753p. 1989. 95.00 (*0-8288-8479-X*) Fr & Eur.

Rhys Davids, C. A. Stories of the Buddha. 288p. 1989. pap. 6.95 (*0-486-26149-2*) Dover.

Rhys Davids, Caroline A. Buddhist Manual of Psychological Ethics. 1975. reprint ed. 24.00 (*0-8364-2573-1*, Pub. by Munshiram Manoharial II) S Asia.

Rhys, Ernest. Browning & His Poetry. LC 73-120992. (Poetry & Life Ser.). reprint ed. 27.50 (*0-404-52529-6*) AMS Pr.

— Lyric Poetry. LC 70-174315. (Channels of English Literature Ser.: No. 6). reprint ed. 43.50 (*0-404-07816-8*) AMS Pr.

— Modern English Essays, 5 Vols. reprint ed. write for info. (*0-318-50667-X*) AMS Pr.

— Modern English Essays, 5 Vols, 1. LC 73-174316. reprint ed. 12.00 (*0-404-08071-5*) AMS Pr.

— Modern English Essays, 5 Vols, 2. LC 73-174316. reprint ed. 12.00 (*0-404-08072-3*) AMS Pr.

— Modern English Essays, 5 Vols, 3. LC 73-174316. reprint ed. 12.00 (*0-404-08073-1*) AMS Pr.

— Modern English Essays, 5 Vols, 4. LC 73-174316. reprint ed. 12.00 (*0-404-08074-X*) AMS Pr.

— Modern English Essays, 5 Vols, 5. LC 73-174316. reprint ed. 12.00 (*0-404-08069-3*) AMS Pr.

— Modern English Essays, 5 Vols, Set. LC 73-174316. reprint ed. 60.00 (*0-404-08070-7*) AMS Pr.

— Rabindranath Tagore. LC 78-133286. (Studies in Asiatic Literature: No. 57). 1970. reprint ed. lib. bdg. 75.00 (*0-8383-1185-7*) M S G Haskell Hse.

Rhys, Ernest, comp. A Book of Nonsense. LC 83-45786. reprint ed. 27.50 (*0-404-20215-2*, PN6110) AMS Pr.

Rhys, Ernest, ed. Fairy Gold: A Book of Old English Fairy Tales. LC 77-114912. (Select Bibliographies Reprint Ser.). 1977. 21.95 (*0-8369-5317-7*) Ayer.

Rhys, Ernest, ed. see Shelley, Percy Bysshe.

Rhys, Horton. Theatrical Trip for a Wager. LC 73-81217. 1972. 24.95 (*0-405-08884-1*, Pub. by Blom Pubns UK) Ayer.

Rhys, J., jt. ed. see Evans, John G.

Rhys, Jean. After Leaving Mr. Mackenzie. 191p. 1990. pap. 8.95 (*0-88184-585-X*) Carroll & Graf.

— Good Morning, Midnight. (Shoreline Bks.). 1986. pap. 9.95 (*0-393-30394-2*) Norton.

— Jean Rhys: The Collected Short Stories. 1992. pap. 12.95 (*0-393-30625-9*) Norton.

— Left Bank, & Other Stories. LC 79-134976. (Short Story Index Reprint Ser.). 1977. 26.95 (*0-8369-3698-1*) Ayer.

— Letters, 1931-1966. Wyndham, Francis & Melly, Diana, eds. 320p. 1995. 12.95 (*0-14-018906-8*, Penguin Classics) Viking Penguin.

— My Day. LC 75-26592. 1975. pap. 3.00 (*0-685-64410-3*) SPD-Small Pr Dist.

— La Prisonniere de Sargasses. (FRE.). 1977. pap. 10.95 (*0-7859-4083-9*) Fr & Eur.

— Quai des Grand-Augustins. (FRE.). 1981. pap. 10.95 (*0-7859-4156-8*) Fr & Eur.

— Quartet. 1990. pap. 7.95 (*0-88184-538-8*) Carroll & Graf.

— Quartet. large type ed. LC 94-11346. 1994. reprint ed. 19.95 (*0-7927-2101-2*, Curley Lrg Print); reprint ed. pap. 18.95 (*0-7927-2100-4*, Curley Lrg Print) Chivers N Amer.

— Quatuor. (FRE.). 1982. pap. 10.95 (*0-7859-4166-5*) Fr & Eur.

— Sleep It Off Lady. 176p. 1995. 10.95 (*0-14-018345-0*, Penguin Classics) Viking Penguin.

— Smile Please: An Unfinished Autobiography. 176p. 1995. 9.95 (*0-14-018405-8*, Penguin Classics) Viking Penguin.

— Voyage dans les Tenebres. (FRE.). 1978. pap. 10.95 (*0-7859-4108-8*) Fr & Eur.

— Voyage in the Dark. 1994. pap. 6.95 (*0-393-31146-5*) Norton.

— Wide Sargasso Sea. 192p. 1992. pap. 8.95 (*0-393-30880-4*) Norton.

— Wide Sargasso Sea. large type ed. LC 93-35502. 1993. 19.95 (*0-7862-0073-1*) Thorndike Pr.

— Wide Sargasso Sea: Movie Tie-In Edition. 1993. pap. 8.95 (*0-393-31048-5*) Norton.

Rhys, Jean, tr. see Carco, Francis.

Rhys, John. Celtic Folklore, 2 vols., Set. 1973. lib. bdg. 500.00 (*0-87968-099-7*) Gordon Pr.

— Lectures on the Origin & Growth of Religion As Illustrated by Celtic Heathendom. LC 77-27165. (Hibbert Lectures: 1886). reprint ed. 67.50 (*0-404-60407-2*) AMS Pr.

Rhys, John & Evans, John G., eds. Series of Old Welsh Texts, 11 vols. in 14, Set. reprint ed. 600.00 (*0-404-60580-X*) AMS Pr.

— The Text of the Bruts from the Red Book of Hergest. LC 78-72662. (Series of Old Welsh Texts: Vol. 2). reprint ed. 62.50 (*0-404-60582-6*) AMS Pr.

— The Text of the Mabinogion from the Red Book of Hergest. LC 78-72663. (Series of Old Welsh Texts: Vol. 1). reprint ed. 52.50 (*0-404-60581-8*) AMS Pr.

Rhys, John & Jones, David B. Welsh People. LC 68-25263. (British History Ser.: No. 30). 1969. reprint ed. lib. bdg. 75.00 (*0-8383-0233-5*) M S G Haskell Hse.

Rhys, John & Morris Jones, John, eds. Eleucidarium. (Anecdota Oxoniensia Ser.: No. 6). 1988. reprint ed. 82.50 (*0-404-63956-9*) AMS Pr.

Rhys, John L. Celtic Folklore: Welsh & Manx, 2 vols. in 1. LC 72-80504. 1980. reprint ed. 53.95 (*0-405-08885-X*, Pub. by Blom Pubns UK) Ayer.

— England Is My Village. LC 72-152955. (Short Story Index Reprint Ser.). 1977. reprint ed. 18.95 (*0-8369-3870-4*) Ayer.

Rhys Jones, T. J. Teach Yourself Welsh. (Teach Yourself Ser.). 1992. 15.95 (*0-8288-8411-0*, 828884110); 45.00 (*0-8288-8413-7*) Fr & Eur.

Rhys-Jones, T. N., ed. Surface Stability. (Characterisation of High-Temperature Materials Ser.: No. 6). (Illus.). 296p. 1989. pap. text ed. 52.50 (*0-901462-61-6*, Pub. by Inst Materials UK) Ashgate Pub Co.

Rhys, Keidrych, ed. Wales: 1937-1940, Set. 310p. 1969. 55.00 (*0-7146-2217-6*, Pub. by F Cass Pubs UK) Intl Spec Bk.

Rhys, Natalie. Call Me Mistress: Memoirs of a Phone Sex Performer. LC 93-79544. 128p. (Orig.). 1993. pap. 7.50 (*0-9637672-0-8*) Miwok Pr.

RIA In-House Professional Staff. All States Tax Handbook. rev. ed. 400p. 1992. pap. text ed. 25.00 (*0-7811-0062-3*) Res Inst Am.

— All States Tax Handbook 1995. rev. ed. 410p. 1994. pap. text ed. 29.95 (*0-7811-0092-5*) Res Inst Am.

— California Income Tax Laws: 1993 Edition. rev. ed. 1000p. 1992. pap. text ed. 64.50 (*0-7811-0064-X*) Res Inst Am.

— The Complete Internal Revenue Code: January 1995 Edition. rev. ed. 2500p. 1995. pap. text ed. 34.50 (*0-7811-0098-4*) Res Inst Am.

RIA In-house Professional Staff. The Complete Internal Revenue Code January 1994 Edition. rev. ed. 2500p. 1994. pap. text ed. 33.50 (*0-7811-0084-4*) Res Inst Am.

***RIA In-House Professional Staff.** January 1, 1995 Stock Market Values. rev. ed. 200p. 1995. pap. text ed. 14.95 (*0-7811-0100-X*) Res Inst Am.

— Pension & Benefits Law, 1993. rev. ed. 2200p. 1993. pap. text ed. 55.00 (*0-7811-0068-2*) Res Inst Am.

— Pension & Benefits Law, 1994 Edition. rev. ed. 1712p. 1994. pap. text ed. 55.00 (*0-7811-0087-9*) Res Inst Am.

— Pension & Benefits Regulations, 1993. rev. ed. 2700p. 1993. pap. text ed. 75.00 (*0-7811-0069-0*) Res Inst Am.

— Pension & Benefits Regulations, 1994. 2880p. 1994. pap. text ed. 75.00 (*0-7811-0086-0*) Res Inst Am.

— Preambles to Pension & Benefits Regulations, 1993. rev. ed. 1400p. 1993. pap. text ed. 49.00 (*0-7811-0070-4*) Res Inst Am.

— Preambles to Pension & Benefits Regulations, 1994 Edution. rev. ed. 1504p. 1994. pap. 49.00 (*0-7811-0088-7*) Res Inst Am.

— RIA Federal Tax Handbook 1995. rev. ed. 765p. 1994. pap. text ed. 25.95 (*0-7811-0091-7*) Res Inst Am.

— RIA Federal Tax Regulations: January 1995 Edition, 4 vols., Set. rev. ed. 8000p. 1995. pap. text ed. 55.95 (*0-7811-0101-8*) Res Inst Am.

— RIA Federal Tax Regulations, 1993, 4 vols. Incl. RIA Federal Tax Regulations, 1993 Vol. I. rev. ed. 2300p. 1993. pap. (*0-318-69995-8*); RIA Federal Tax Regulations, 1993 Vol. II, 4 vols. rev. ed. 1850p. 1993. pap. (*0-318-69996-6*); RIA Federal Tax Regulations, 1993 Vol. III, 4 vols. rev. ed. 2000p. 1993. pap. (*0-318-69997-4*); RIA Federal Tax Regulations, 1993 Vol. IV, 4 vols. rev. ed. 2300p. 1993. pap. (*0-318-69998-2*); 52.00 (*0-7811-0067-4*) Res Inst Am.

***RIA Professional Staff.** Pension & Benefits Law (1995) rev. ed. 1456p. 1995. pap. text ed. 55.00 (*0-7811-0102-6*) Res Inst Am.

— Pension & Benefits Regulations (1995) rev. ed. 2912p. 1995. pap. text ed. 75.00 (*0-7811-0103-4*) Res Inst Am.

— Preambles to Pension & Benefits Regulations (1995) 1570p. 1995. pap. text ed. 49.00 (*0-7811-0104-2*) Res Inst Am.

RIA Staff. The Complete Internal Revenue Code: (January 1993 Edition) rev. ed. 2400p. 1993. pap. text ed. 32.00 (*0-7811-0074-7*) Res Inst Am.

— The Complete Internal Revenue Code: (Summer 1993 Edition) rev. ed. 2700p. 1993. pap. text ed. 32.00 (*0-7811-0075-5*) Res Inst Am.

— Corporation & Partnership Tax Return Guide, 1992. rev. ed. (Illus.). 134p. 1993. pap. text ed. 10.00 (*0-7811-0072-0*) Res Inst Am.

— Fiduciary Tax Return Guide, 1992. rev. ed. (Illus.). 140p. 1993. pap. text ed. 10.00 (*0-7811-0073-9*) Res Inst Am.

— Individual Tax Return Guide, 1992. rev. ed. (Illus.). 158p. 1993. pap. text ed. 10.00 (*0-7811-0071-2*) Res Inst Am.

— The RIA Complete Analysis of the Revenue Reconciliation Act of 1993. rev. ed. 800p. 1993. pap. text ed. 34.95 (*0-7811-0078-X*) Res Inst Am.

— RIA Federal Tax Handbook: (1994 Edition) rev. ed. 760p. 1993. pap. text ed. 24.00 (*0-7811-0077-1*) Res Inst Am.

— RIA Federal Tax Regulations: (July 1993 Edition), 4 vols., Set. rev. ed. 1993. pap. 54.00 (*0-7811-0076-3*) Res Inst Am.

— RIA Federal Tax Regulations: (July 1993 Edition), 4 vols., Vol. I. rev. ed. 2043p. 1993. pap. write for info. (*0-318-72168-6*) Res Inst Am.

— RIA Federal Tax Regulations: (July 1993 Edition), 4 vols., Vol. II. rev. ed. 1856p. 1993. pap. write for info. (*0-318-72169-4*) Res Inst Am.

— RIA Federal Tax Regulations: (July 1993 Edition), 4 vols., Vol. III. rev. ed. 1873p. 1993. pap. write for info. (*0-318-72170-8*) Res Inst Am.

— RIA Federal Tax Regulations: (July 1993 Edition), 4 vols., Vol. IV. rev. ed. 2096p. 1993. pap. write for info. (*0-318-72171-6*) Res Inst Am.

— RIA Federal Tax Regulations, January 1994, Vols. I-IV. 1994. pap. text ed. 54.00 (*0-7811-0085-2*) Res Inst Am.

Riach, Alan. Hugh MacDiarmid's Epic Poetry. 1991. text ed. 35.00 (*0-7486-0257-7*, Pub. by Edinburgh U Pr UK) Col U Pr.

Riach, Alan, ed. see MacDiarmid, Hugh.

Riad, Eva, jt. ed. see Kronholm, Tryggve.

Riad, S. & Baars, D. L., eds. Proceedings of the Fifth International Conference on Basement Tectonics. (Illus.). 350p. 1986. 37.50 (*0-317-43039-4*) Intl Basement.

Riahi-Belkaoui, Ahmed. Accounting in the Developing Countries. LC 93-50070. 232p. 1994. text ed. 65.00 (*0-89930-821-X*, Quorum Bks) Greenwood.

— The Cultural Shaping of Accounting. LC 94-45274. 176p. 1995. text ed. 55.00 (*0-89930-953-4*, Quorum Bks) Greenwood.

— Morality in Accounting. LC 92-7485. 224p. 1992. text ed. 55.00 (*0-89930-729-9*, BUN, Quorum Bks) Greenwood.

— The Nature & Consequences of the Multidivisional Structure. LC 94-32084. 208p. 1995. text ed. 59.95 (*0-89930-904-6*, Quorum Bks) Greenwood.

— Quality & Control: An Accounting Perspective. LC 92-34942. 240p. 1993. text ed. 65.00 (*0-89930-767-1*, BQC, Quorum Bks) Greenwood.

***Riahi-Belkaoui, Ahmed & Monti-Belkaoui, Janice.** Human Resource Valuation: A Guide to Strategies & Techniques. LC 94-39658. 192p. 1995. text ed. 55.00 (*0-89930-931-3*, Quorum Bks) Greenwood.

Riahi-Belkaoui, Ahmed & Pavlik, Ellen L. Accounting for Corporate Reputation. LC 92-8401. 272p. 1992. text ed. 59.95 (*0-89930-717-5*, BKK, Quorum Bks) Greenwood.

Riahi-Blekaoui, Ahmed. Organizational & Budgetary Slack. LC 93-30990. 144p. 1994. text ed. 49.95 (*0-89930-884-8*, Quorum Bks) Greenwood.

***Rial, Horacio V.** Frontera Sur. 1995. pap. 16.95 (*0-679-76339-2*, Vin) Random.

***Riales, Martha.** Tate County, Mississippi. (Illus.). 805p. 1991. 65.00 (*0-88107-190-0*) Curtis Media.

Riall, Lucy. The Italian Risorgimento: State, Society & National Unification. LC 93-33882. (Historical Connections Ser.). (Illus.). 120p. 1994. pap. 11.95 (*0-415-05775-2*, B2251) Routledge.

Rialp Staff. Diccionario de Cine. 912p. (SPA.). 1991. write for info. (*0-7859-5902-5*, 8432128252) Fr & Eur.

— Enciclopedia Sistematica Acta 2000, 9 vols., Set. 11th ed. 4500p. (SPA.). 1978. 295.00 (*0-8288-5229-4*, S50492) Fr & Eur.

— Gran Enciclopedia Rialp, 24 vols., Set. 21500p. (SPA.). 1976. 2,995.00 (*0-8288-5673-7*, S50493) Fr & Eur.

Rialp, Victoria. Children & Hazardous Work in the Philippines. (Child Labour Collection Ser.). v, 72p. 1993. pap. 12.00 (*92-2-106474-3*) Intl Labour Office.

Rian, Ide M. Wings of Prayer: One Hundred Meditations on Psalm 119. 1992. pap. 9.00 (*0-00-599345-8*) Harper SF.

Rian, Suzanne, jt. auth. see Bozich, Sally.

Riande, Evaristo, jt. auth. see Saiz, Enrique.

Riano, J. F. Critical & Biographical Notes on Early Spanish Music. LC 79-158958. (Music Ser.). 1971. reprint ed. lib. bdg. 29.50 (*0-306-70193-6*) Da Capo.

Riano, Pilar, ed. Women in Grassroots Communication: Effecting Global Social Change. (Communication & Human Values Ser.: Vol. 15). 332p. (C). 1994. text ed. 49.95 (*0-8039-4905-7*); pap. text ed. 24.00 (*0-8039-4906-5*) Sage.

RIAS Staff. Central Glasgow. 208p. (C). 1989. pap. 59.00 (*1-85158-200-2*, Pub. by Royal Inc Architects UK) St Mut.

— Fife. 208p. (C). 1990. pap. 70.00 (*1-85158-258-4*, Pub. by Royal Inc Architects UK) St Mut.

— Orkney. 104p. (C). 1991. pap. 75.00 (*1-873190-02-6*, Pub. by Royal Inc Architects UK) St Mut.

Riasanovsky & Watson. Readings in Russian History, Vol. II. 192p. (C). 1992. pap. text ed. 19.95 (*0-8403-7160-8*) Kendall-Hunt.

— Readings in Russian History, Vol. II. 192p. (C). 1992. pap. text ed. 19.95 (*0-8403-7758-4*) Kendall-Hunt.

Riasanovsky, Nicholas V. Collected Writings: 1947-1994. (Illus.). viii, 312p. (C). 1993. 39.95 (*1-884445-00-4*) C Schlacks Pub.

— The Emergence of Romanticism. 128p. 1992. 29.95 (*0-19-507341-X*) OUP.

— The Emergence of Romanticism. 128p. 1995. pap. 12.95 (*0-19-509646-0*) OUP.

— A History of Russia. 5th ed. (Illus.). 768p. (C). 1993. text ed. 38.00 (*0-19-507462-9*) OUP.
— The Image of Peter the Great in Russian History & Thought. 352p. 1992. pap. 18.95 (*0-19-507480-7*) OUP.
— Nicholas I & Official Nationality in Russia, 1825-1855. LC 59-11316. (Russian & East European Studies). 308p. reprint ed. pap. 87.80 (*0-7837-4750-0*, 2044497) Bks Demand.
Riasanovsky, V. A. Chinese Civil Law. LC 76-20214. (Studies in Chinese Government & Law). 310p. 1976. reprint ed. text ed. 55.00 (*0-313-26965-3*, U6965, Greenwood Pr) Greenwood.
Riase, Gwendolyn. How to Have the Wedding of Your Dreams on a Nightmare Budget: 150 Money-Saving Strategies to Slash Your Wedding Costs. (Illus.). 74p. 1992. pap. 16.95 (*0-9632446-4-7*) Applesauce.
Riaz, Fahmida A. Pakistan Literature & Society. 1986. 14.00 (*81-7050-021-4*, Pub. by Abhinav II) S Asia.
Riazanov, David. Karl Marx & Friedrich Engels: An Introduction to Their Lives. Kunitz, Joshua, tr. LC 73-8055. 237p. reprint ed. pap. 67.60 (*0-7837-6992-X*, 2046804) Bks Demand.
***Riaziat.** Introduction to Analog High-Speed Electronics & Optoelectronics. Date not set. text ed. 64.95 (*0-471-01582-2*) Wiley.
Riazuddin, Fayyazuddin. A Modern Introduction to Particle Physics. 676p. 1992. text ed. 78.00 (*981-02-1072-8*); pap. text ed. 44.00 (*981-02-1073-6*) World Scientific Pub.
— Quantum Mechanics. 504p. (C). 1990. text ed. 61.00 (*9971-5-0752-8*) World Scientific Pub.
Riba, Carles. Diccionari de Robotica. 2nd ed. 92p. 1991. 35.00 (*0-7859-6251-4*, 8476531443) Fr & Eur.
Riba, J. Illustrated Encyclopedia of Cacti & Other Succulents. 1993. 12.98 (*1-55521-878-4*) Bk Sales Inc.
Riba, Michelle, jt. ed. see Tasman, Allan.
Riba, Michelle B., jt. ed. see Oldham, John M.
Ribak, Charles E., ed. Inhibition in the Brain. LC 82-642121. 173p. 1987. pap. 24.00 (*0-930195-04-3*) Inst Mind Behavior.
Ribak, Charles E., et al, eds. The Dentate Gyrus & Its Role in Seizures. LC 92-18288. (Epilepsy Research, Supplement Ser.: No. 7). 1992. write for info. (*0-444-81447-7*) Elsevier.
***Ribak, Joseph, et al, eds.** Occupational Health in Aviation: Maintenance & Support Personnel. (Illus.). 238p. 1995. boxed 59.95 (*0-12-583560-4*) Acad Pr.
Ribakov, R. B. & Senkevich, A. N., eds. Indian Traditions Through the Ages. 1990. 22.50 (*81-202-0288-0*, Pub. by Ajanta II) S Asia.
Ribar, John. Bytes Windows Programmers Cookbook. 1994. cd-rom, pap. text ed. 34.95 (*0-07-882037-5*) Osborne-McGraw.
— C DiskTutor. 464p. 1992. 3.5 hd, pap. text ed. 39.95 (*0-07-881798-6*) Osborne-McGraw.
— FORTRAN Programming for Windows. 1993. pap. text ed. 29.95 (*0-07-881908-3*) Osborne-McGraw.
— Powerbuilder Construction Kit. 1994. pap. text ed. 24.95 (*0-07-882079-0*) Osborne-McGraw.
— Programming Primer a Guide to Programming Fundamentals. 1994. pap. text ed. 16.95 (*0-07-881999-7*) McGraw.
Ribaric, M. & Sustersic, L. Conservation Laws & Open Questions of Classical Electrodynamics. 348p. (C). 1990. text ed. 48.00 (*981-02-0151-6*) World Scientific Pub.
Ribaroff, Margaret, ed. see Rierden, Anne B.
***Ribas, Armando P.** Cuba Entre la Independencia y la Libertad. LC 94-71842. (Coleccion Cuba y sus Jueces). 91p. (Orig.). (SPA.). 1994. pap. 12.00 (*0-89729-745-8*) Ediciones.
Ribas, Oscar B. Uanga--Fetico: Romance Folclorico Angolano. 2nd ed. (B. E. Ser.: No. 69). (POR.). 1969. 22.00 (*0-8115-3019-1*) Periodicals Srv.
Ribaudo, Linda & Walker, Darlyne. Coming to America. LC 94-5511. (Today's World Ser.). (Illus.). 1994. write for info. (*1-56420-055-8*) New Readers.
— Teacher's Guide: Family Issues, Community Issues, Work Issues. LC 94-5516. (Today's World Ser.). 1994. 10.95 (*1-56420-067-1*) New Readers.
— Working Parents. LC 94-5504. (Today's World Ser.). 1994. write for info. (*1-56420-058-2*) New Readers.
Ribbans, Geoffrey. History & Fiction in Galdos's Narratives. LC 92-41137. 1993. 52.00 (*0-19-815881-5*, Clarendon Pr) OUP.
Ribbe, P. H., ed. Feldspar Mineralogy. 2nd ed. (Reviews in Mineralogy Ser.: Vol. 2). 362p. 1983. per. 9.00 (*0-939950-14-6*) Mineralogical Soc.
Ribbe, P. H., jt. ed. see Veblen, D. R.
Ribbe, Paul H., ed. see Kerrick, Derrill M.
Ribbe, Wolfgang, jt. ed. see Hansen, Reimer.
Ribbeck, O., ed. see Vergilius.
Ribbeck, Otto. Die Romische Tragodie Im Zeitalter der Republik. viii, 692p. 1968. reprint ed. write for info. (*0-318-71213-X*, Pub. by Georg Olms GW) Lubrecht & Cramer.
Ribbeck, Otto, ed. Scaenicae Romanorum Poesis Fragmenta, Bd. I: Tragicorum Fragmenta. ccxiv, 876p. 1978. reprint ed. write for info. (*0-318-71215-6*, Pub. by Georg Olms GW) Lubrecht & Cramer.
— Scaenicae Romanorum Poesis Fragmenta, Bd. II: Comicorum Fragmenta. ccxiv, 876p. 1978. reprint ed. write for info. (*0-318-71216-4*, Pub. by Georg Olms GW) Lubrecht & Cramer.
— Scaenicae Romanorum Poesis Fragmenta, 2 vols., Set. ccxiv, 876p. 1978. reprint ed. write for info. (*0-318-71214-8*, Pub. by Georg Olms GW) Lubrecht & Cramer.
Ribbeck, Otto, ed. see Vergilius.
Ribbel, Arthur. Yesterday in San Diego. LC 90-61926. (Illus.). (Orig.). 1990. pap. 8.95 (*0-9627384-0-9*) Rancho Pr CA.
***Ribbens, Jane.** Mothers & Their Children: A Feminist Sociology of Childrearing. 240p. 1995. 65.00 (*0-8039-8834-6*); pap. 22.95 (*0-8039-8835-4*) Sage.
Ribbens, K. A., jt. ed. see Carlson, D. S.
Ribbens, K. A., jt. ed. see Vig, P. S.
Ribbens, Katherine A., jt. ed. see McNamara, James A., Jr.
Ribbens, William B. Automotive Electronics. 3rd ed. 1988. pap. 17.95 (*0-672-27064-1*, Bobbs) Macmillan.
— Understanding Automotive Electronics. 4th ed. (Illus.). 380p. (Orig.). 1992. pap. 24.95 (*0-672-27358-6*) Sams.
Ribbing, C., ed. Hard Materials in Optics. 1990. 53.00 (*0-8194-0322-9*, VOL. 1275) SPIE.
Ribbins, Peter & Whale, Elizabeth. Improving Education: Promoting Quality in Schools. Reynolds, David & Hopkins, David, eds. (School Development Ser.). (Illus.). 176p. 1993. 75.00 (*0-304-32743-3*); pap. 30.00 (*0-304-32735-2*) Weidner & Sons.
Ribbins, Peter, jt. auth. see Greenfield, Thomas.
***Ribble, Ronald G.** Apples, Weeds, & Doggie Poo. (Illus.). 56p. (Orig.). 1995. pap. text ed. 7.95 (*0-614-07277-8*) Anderie Poetry.
Ribblett, David L. Nelly Custis: Child of Mount Vernon. LC 93-12419. 1993. pap. write for info. (*0-931917-23-9*) Mt Vernon Ladies.
Ribblett, David L., jt. auth. see Samford, Patricia.
Ribbon Art Publishing Company Staff. Old-Fashioned Ribbon Art: Ideas & Designs for Accessories & Decorations. 32p. 1986. pap. 2.95 (*0-486-25174-8*) Dover.
Ribbons, D. W., jt. ed. see Norris, John R.
Ribe, Helena, jt. auth. see Holt, Sharon L.
Ribe, Helena, et al. How Adjustment Programs Can Help the Poor: The World Bank Experience. (Discussion Paper Ser.: No. 71). 56p. 1990. 6.95 (*0-8213-1434-3*, 11434) World Bank.
Ribeiro. The Lizard's Smile. 320p. 1994. text ed. 21.00 (*0-689-12125-3*, Atheneum S&S) S&S Trade.
***Ribeiro, Aileen.** The Art of Dress: Fashion in England & France 1750 to 1820. LC 94-35347. 1995. write for info. (*0-300-06287-7*) Yale U Pr.
— Dress & Morality. LC 86-14839. 170p. 1986. 44.50 (*0-8419-1091-X*) Holmes & Meier.
— Fashion in the French Revolution. LC 88-21242. (Costume & Civilization Ser.). (Illus.). 144p. 1988. 49.95 (*0-8419-1197-5*) Holmes & Meier.
***Ribeiro, Alvaro & Basker, James G.** Tradition in Transition: Women Writers, Marginal Texts, & the Eighteenth-Century Canon. (Illus.). 320p. 1995. 56.00 (*0-19-818288-0*) OUP.
Ribeiro, Alvaro, ed. see Burney, Charles.
Ribeiro, Branca T. Coherence in Psychotic Discourse. LC 92-49156. (Oxford Studies in Sociolinguistics). 1994. 49.95 (*0-19-506597-2*); pap. 22.00 (*0-19-506615-4*) OUP.
Ribeiro e Sousa, L. M. & Grossman, N. F., eds. Eurock 93 - Safety & Environmental Issues in Rock Engineering: ISRM International Symposium, Lisbon, June 1993. (Illus.). 900p. (C). 1993. text ed. 150.00 (*90-5410-339-6*, Pub. by A A Balkema NE) Ashgate Pub Co.
Ribeiro, Edgard T. I Would Have Loved Him, If I Had Not Killed Him. Neves, Margaret A., tr. LC 94-6052. 1994. 18.95 (*0-312-11002-2*) St Martin.
Ribeiro, F. Ramoa, jt. auth. see NATO Advanced Study Institute Staff.
Ribeiro, Gustavo L. Transnational Capitalism & Hydropolitics in Argentina: The Yacyreta High Dam. LC 93-33426. (Center for Latin American Studies, University of Florida). (Illus.). 216p. (C). 1994. bds. 29.95 (*0-8130-1280-5*) U Press Fla.
Ribeiro, Leonidio. Brazilian Medical Contributions. 1976. lib. bdg. 69.95 (*0-8490-1548-0*) Gordon Pr.
Ribeiro, O. K. A Source Book of the Genus Phytophtora. (Illus.). 1978. lib. bdg. 45.00 (*3-7682-1200-9*) Lubrecht & Cramer.
Ribeiro, Stella C. Sambaqui: A Novel of Prehistory. Van der Heuvel, Claudia, tr. 144p. (POR.). 1987. pap. 3.95 (*0-380-89624-9*) Avon.
Ribeiro, Susan, ed. Arts from the Scholar's Studio Selected Oriental Masterpieces in Painting Lacquer, Glass, Ceramic, Wood, Metal & Stone. (Illus.). 287p. 1988. lib. bdg. 150.00 (*0-7103-0321-1*, Pub. by Kegan Paul Intl UK) Routledge Chapman & Hall.
Ribelin, William E. & Migaki, George, eds. Pathology of Fishes. LC 73-15261. (Illus.). 1016p. 1975. 75.00 (*0-299-06520-0*, 652) U of Wis Pr.
Riben, Marsha. The Dark Side of Adoption. 1988. 12.95 (*0-8187-0105-6*) Harlo Press.
Ribenboim, P. The Book of Prime Number Records. 385p. 1988. 49.80 (*0-387-96573-4*) Spr-Verlag.
— The Book of Prime Number Records. 2nd ed. xxiii, 479p. 1989. 49.80 (*0-387-97042-8*, 3007) Spr-Verlag.
— The Little Book of Big Primes. 304p. 1993. pap. 29.50 (*0-387-97508-X*) Spr-Verlag.
— Thirteen Lectures on Fermant's Last Theorem. 1994. 54.00 (*0-387-90432-8*) Spr-Verlag.
Ribenboim, Paulo. Catalan's Conjecture: Are Eight & Nine the Only Consecutive Powers? (Illus.). 364p. 1994. text ed. 64.95 (*0-12-587170-8*) Acad Pr.
— The New Book of Prime Number Records. 3rd rev. ed. LC 95-5441. 1995. write for info. (*0-387-94457-5*) Spr-Verlag.
Riber, Lorenzo, ed. see Fuenmayor, Antonio de.
Riber, Louise. Neria Production Notes. (Illus.). 15p. (Orig.). (C). 1992. pap. text ed. write for info. (*0-936731-26-5*) Devel Self Rel.
Ribera, Antonia. UFO Contact from Planet UMMO, Vol. II: The Incredible Truth. Stevens, Wendelle C., tr. (Factbooks Ser.). (Illus.). 384p. 1989. lib. bdg. 16.95 (*0-9608558-9-0*) UFO Photo.
Ribera, Antonio & Stevens, Wendelle C. UFO Contact from Planet UMMO, Vol. I: The Mystery of UMMO. White, Guilford L., tr. (Factbooks Ser.). (Illus.). 354p. 1986. lib. bdg. 15.95 (*0-9608558-5-8*) UFO Photo.
Ribera Chevremont, Evaristo. Canto De Mi Tierra. 97p. (C). 1971. 2.00 (*0-8477-3213-4*) U of PR Pr.
— Obra Poetica, 2 vols., Set. LC 76-41873. (Illus.). cii, 1665p. (Orig.). (SPA.). 1976. 30.00 (*0-8477-3218-5*); pap. 25.00 (*0-8477-3233-9*) U of PR Pr.
Ribera, Feliciano, jt. auth. see Meier, Matt S.
Ribera, Gilbert. Calculating for Business. 336p. (C). 1993. per., pap. text ed. 30.95 (*0-8403-8624-9*) Kendall-Hunt.
— Machine Calculation for Business & Personal Use. 220p. (C). 1994. pap. text ed., spiral bd. 23.95 (*0-8403-9483-7*) Kendall-Hunt.
Ribera, Gilbert J. Machine Calculation for Business & Personal Use. 2nd ed. LC 79-83523. 1979. pap. text ed. 18.95 (*0-8162-7180-1*); 5.00 (*0-8162-7181-X*) Holden-Day.
Ribera, Julian. Music in Ancient Arabia & Spain: Being La Musica De las Cantigas. LC 70-87614. (Music Ser.). 1970. reprint ed. lib. bdg. 45.00 (*0-306-71622-4*) Da Capo.
Ribera y Tarrago, Julian. Historia de la Musica Arabe Medieval y Su Influencia En la Espanola. LC 78-178587. reprint ed. 47.50 (*0-404-56664-2*) AMS Pr.
Ribera Y Tarrago, Julian. La Musica Andaluza Medieval En las Canciones De Trovadores, Troveros y Minnesinger, 3 vols. in 1. LC 71-178588. reprint ed. 57.50 (*0-404-56665-0*) AMS Pr.
Ribes-Inesta, E. & Bandura, A., eds. Analysis of Delinquency & Aggression. 256p. 1976. text ed. 49.95 (*0-89859-360-3*) L Erlbaum Assocs.
Ribes, Peter. More Parables & Fables. 144p. 1993. 28.00 (*0-85439-431-1*, Pub. by St Paul Pubns UK) St Mut.
— Parables & Fables for Modern Man. 184p. (C). 1990. text ed. 39.00 (*0-85439-325-0*, Pub. by St Paul Pubns UK) St Mut.
Ribet, K. Current Trends in Arithmetical Algebraic Geometry. LC 87-11506. (CONM Ser.: Vol. 67). 293p. 1990. reprint ed. pap. text ed. 38.00 (*0-8218-5074-1*, CONM-67) Am Math.
Ribeyre, Francis, jt. ed. see Boudou, Alain.
Ribeyro, Julio R. Marginal Voices: Selected Stories. Douglas, Dianne, tr. LC 92-30359. (Texas Pan American Ser.). 153p. (Orig.). (C). 1993. text ed. 27.50 (*0-292-77057-X*); pap. 11.95 (*0-292-77058-8*) U of Tex Pr.
Ribiere, Jean-Paul. Sudan the Passing of Time. 200p. 1994. 39.95 (*1-873938-79-9*, Pub. by Garnet Pubng Ltd UK) Paul & Co Pubs.
Ribil, Soltan & Kallai, Gabor. Winning with the English. (Batsford Chess Library). 192p. 1993. pap. 20.95 (*0-8050-2642-8*, Owl) H Holt & Co.
Ribman, Ronald. The Ceremony of Innocence. 1968. pap. 4.75 (*0-8222-0195-X*) Dramatists Play.
— Passing Through from Exotic Places. 1970. pap. 4.75 (*0-8222-0876-8*) Dramatists Play.
— The Rug Merchants of Chaos & Other Plays. LC 92-2568. 240p. 1992. 24.95 (*1-55936-050-X*); pap. 12.95 (*1-55936-049-6*) Theatre Comm.
Ribner, Irving & Huffman, Clifford C. Tudor & Stuart Drama. 2nd ed. LC 76-5215. (Goldentree Bibliographies Series in Language & Literature). (C). 1978. text ed. write for info. (*0-88295-572-1*); pap. text ed. write for info. (*0-88295-554-3*) Harlan Davidson.
Ribner, Jonathan P. Broken Tablets: The Cult of the Law in French Art from David to Delacroix. LC 92-23046. 1993. 50.00 (*0-520-07749-0*) U CA Pr.
Ribner, Richard. Living Without Fatigue. 160p. (Orig.). pap. 9.95 (*0-8159-6117-0*) Devin.
Riboli, E. & Delendi, M., eds. Autopsy in Epidemiology & Medical Research. (IARC Scientific Publications: No. 112). (Illus.). 308p. 1991. pap. 57.50 (*92-832-2112-5*) OUP.
Ribolini, Gabriele, jt. auth. see Leonardi, Leonardo.
Ribordy, Shelia, jt. auth. see Reisman, John M.
***Ribot, Jesse C., et al, eds.** Climate Variability, Climate Change & Social Vulnerability in the Semi-Arid Tropics. (Internationsl Hydrology Ser.). (Illus.). 270p. (C). 1995. write for info. (*0-521-48074-4*) Cambridge U Pr.
Ribot, Theodule A. Diseases of Memory. Smith, W. H. & Snell, M. M., trs. Bd. with Diseases of Personality. LC 77-72191.; Diseases of the Will. LC 77-72191. LC 77-72191. (Contributions to the History of Psychology Ser.: Vol. 1, Pt. C, Medical Psychology). 240p. 1977. reprint ed. Set text ed. 75.00 (*0-313-26940-8*, U6940, Greenwood Pr) Greenwood.
— Essay on the Creative Imagination. LC 73-2987. (Classics in Psychology Ser.). 1978. reprint ed. 26.95 (*0-405-05159-X*) Ayer.
— Heredity: A Psychological Study of Its Phenomena, Laws, Causes, & Consequences. LC 78-72821. (Brainedness, Handedness, & Mental Abilities Ser.). reprint ed. 40.00 (*0-404-60890-6*) AMS Pr.
Riboud, Christophe, jt. auth. see Revel, Alain.
Riboud, Jacques. The Case for a New ECU: Towards Another Monetary System. Harrison, Stephen, tr. LC 88-18641. 250p. 1989. text ed. 49.95 (*0-312-02124-0*) St Martin.
— The Mechanics of Money. 1980. text ed. 35.00 (*0-312-52455-2*) St Martin.
— A Stable External Currency for Europe. Harrison, Stephen, tr. 190p. 1991. text ed. 69.95 (*0-312-05363-0*) St Martin.
Riboud, Marc, photos. Angkor. LC 93-60222. (Illus.). 160p. 1993. 65.00 (*0-500-54182-5*) Thames Hudson.
Riboud, Michelle. Ivory Coast: 1960-1986. 28p. 1987. pap. 5.00 (*0-917616-99-5*) ICS Pr.
***Ribowsky, Mark.** A Complete History of the Negro Leagues, 1884 to 1955. (Illus.). 400p. 1995. 24.95 (*1-55972-283-5*, Birch Ln Pr) Carol Pub Group.
— Don't Look Back: Satchel Paige on the Shadows of Baseball. 1994. 23.00 (*0-671-77674-6*) S&S Trade.
Ribowsky, Mark & Feinberg, Bill. The Beach Boys. (Illus.). 240p. 1986. 17.45 (*0-671-53013-5*); pap. 7.95 (*0-671-54135-8*) S&S Trade.
Ribstein. Business Associations. 2nd ed. 1990. write for info. (*0-8205-0271-5*, 481); teacher ed write for info. (*0-8205-0276-6*); Documents Supplement. write for info. (*0-8205-0275-8*) Bender.
Ribstein, Larry E. & Keating, Robert R. Ribstein & Keating on Limited Liability Companies, 2 vols., Set. LC 92-36846. 1438p. 1993. text ed. 175.00 (*0-07-172409-5*) Shepards-McGraw.
Ribstein, Larry E., jt. auth. see Bromberg, Alan R.
Ribstein, Larry E., jt. auth. see Butler, Henry N.
Ribton-Turner, C. J. A History of Vagrants & Vagrancy, & Beggars & Begging. LC 75-129315. (Criminology, Law Enforcement, & Social Problems Ser.: No. 138). (Illus.). 780p. 1972. reprint ed. lib. bdg. 45.00 (*0-87585-138-X*) Patterson Smith.
Ribuffo, Leo P. The Old Christian Right: The Protestant Far Right from the Great Depression to the Cold War. LC 82-19687. 388p. (C). 1988. pap. 18.95 (*0-87722-598-2*) Temple U Pr.
— Right Center Left: Essays in American History. LC 91-5030. 325p. (C). 1992. text ed. 45.00 (*0-8135-1775-3*); pap. text ed. 16.95 (*0-8135-1776-1*) Rutgers U Pr.
Ribuoli, Patrizia & Robbiani, Marina. Frogs: Art, Legend, History. (Library of Collectibles). (Illus.). 112p. 1991. 14.95 (*0-8212-1876-X*) Bulfinch Pr.
Ribush, Nicholas, ed. see Perrin, Stuart.
Ribush, Nicholas, ed. see Yeshe, Lama T.
RIC Staff. Engineering Services Forms of Cost Analysis. 156p. (C). 1985. 60.00 (*0-85406-292-0*, Pub. by Surveyors Pubns) St Mut.
Rica, Amoros, jt. auth. see Merlin-Walch, Olivier.
Ricalton, James. James Ricalton's Photographs of China During the Boxer Rebellion: His Illustrated Travelogue of 1900. Lucas, Christopher, ed. LC 89-13574. (Studies in the Photographic Arts: Vol. 1). (Illus.). 344p. 1990. lib. bdg. 99.95 (*0-88946-508-8*) E Mellen.
***Rican, Rudolf.** History of the Unity of Brethren: A Protestant Hussite Church in Bohemia & Moravia. Crews, C. Daniel, tr. LC 92-62999. 446p. (Orig.). 1993. pap. 19.00 (*1-878422-05-7*) Moravian Ch in Amer.
Ricapito, J. V., ed. A Tri-Linear Edition of Lazarillo de Tormes of 1554, Burgos, Alcala de Henares, Amberes. xviii, 82p. 1987. 12.50 (*0-942260-91-0*) Hispanic Seminary.
Ricapito, Joseph, ed. Hispanic Studies in Honor of Joseph Silverman. 382p. 1989. 17.50 (*0-936388-46-3*) Juan de la Cuesta.
Ricapito, Joseph V., tr. see Valdes, Alfonso de.
Ricard, M., ed. International Diatom Symposium: Proceedings of the VIIIth, Paris 1984. (Illus.). 781p. 1986. lib. bdg. 278.00 (*3-87429-265-7*) Koeltz Sci Bks.
Ricard, Matthieu. The Life of Shabkar: The Autiobiography of a Tibetan Yogin. (Buddhist Studies Ser.). 705p. (C). 1994. text ed. 74.50x (*0-7914-1835-9*); pap. text ed. 24.95 (*0-7914-1836-7*) State U NY Pr.
— The Mystery of Animal Migration. LC 72-172577. 235p. reprint ed. pap. 67.00 (*0-317-28427-4*, 2051282) Bks Demand.
Ricard, Michel. Ouvrage Dedie a la Memoire du Professeur Henry Germain (1903-1989) (Illus.). 265p. 1991. 194.00 (*1-878762-16-8*) Koeltz Sci Bks.
Ricard, Raymond, ed. see Racine, Jean B.
Ricard, Rene. God with Revolver. 120p. (Orig.). 1989. 20.00 (*0-937815-31-4*); pap. 12.00 (*0-937815-30-6*) Hanuman Bks.
— Trusty Sarcophagus Co. Igliori, Paola & Zalopany, Michele, eds. 98p. (Orig.). 1990. English with French translations. pap. 25.00 (*0-9625119-1-9*) Inanout Pr.
— Trusty Sarcophagus Co. Igliori, Paola & Zalopany, Michele, eds. Ramaseder, Josef, tr. 100p. (Orig.). 1990. English with German Translations. pap. 25.00 (*0-9625119-3-5*) Inanout Pr.
— Trusty Sarcophagus Co. Igliori, Paola & Zalopany, Michele, eds. Diacono, Mario, tr. 100p. (Orig.). 1990. English with Italian Translations. pap. 25.00 (*0-9625119-4-3*) Inanout Pr.
— Trusty Sarcophagus Co. Igliori, Paola & Zalopany, Michele, eds. Lhardy, Patricia, tr. 100p. (Orig.). 1990. English with French Translations. pap. 25.00 (*0-9625119-2-7*) Inanout Pr.
— Trusty Sarcophagus Co. (Illus.). 100p. (Orig.). 1990. pap. 25.00 (*0-685-64744-7*) Petersburg Pr.
Ricard, Robert. The Spiritual Conquest of Mexico: An Essay on the Apostolate & the Evangelizing Methods of the Mendicant Orders in New Spain, 1523-1572. Simpson, Lesley B., tr. (Illus.). 435p. 1974. pap. 13.00 (*0-520-04784-2*) U CA Pr.
Ricard, Virginia B. Developing Intercultural Communication Skills. LC 92-11171. (Professional Practices in Adult Education & Human Resource Development Ser.). 198p. (Orig.). (C). 1993. lib. bdg. 19.50 (*0-89464-663-X*); pap. write for info. (*0-89464-815-2*) Krieger.
— Volunteer. LC 84-90642. (Illus.). 107p. 1985. pap. 12.95 (*0-9613508-0-6*) V B Ricard.
Ricard, Yann. Kiwi Power Menus: User's Manual. (Illus.). 8p. (Orig.). (C). 1992. disk 39.95 (*1-877777-03-X*) Kiwi Software.
— Kiwi Power Windows: User's Manual. (Illus.). 74p. (Orig.). (C). 1991. disk 79.95 (*1-877777-02-1*) Kiwi Software.
Ricard, Yann & Jones, Jill L. Kiwi Envelopes! Three User's Manual. rev. ed. (Illus.). 40p. (C). 1992. reprint ed. disk 49.95 (*1-877777-00-5*) Kiwi Software.

R

An Asterisk (*) at the beginning of an entry indicates that the title is appearing in BIP for the first time.

Ricardo-Campbell, Rita. The Economics & Politics of Health. LC 81-13377. xii, 379p. (C). 1985. reprint ed. pap. 13.95 (*0-8078-4140-4*) U of NC Pr.
— Food Safety Regulation: A Study of the Use & Limitations of Cost-Benefit Analysis. LC 74-14148. (AEI-Hoover Policy Studies: No. 12). 66p. reprint ed. pap. 25.00 (*0-317-29205-6*, 2022248) Bks Demand.
— Social Security: Promise & Reality. LC 77-83830. (Publication Ser.: No. 179). 368p. 1977. 6.38 (*0-8179-6791-5*) Hoover Inst Pr.
Ricardo-Campbell, Rita & Lazear, Edward P., eds. Issues in Contemporary Retirement. 427p. 1988. text ed. 14.38 (*0-8179-8701-0*) Hoover Inst Pr.
Ricardo-Campbell, Rita, et al. Health Care Policy: Today & Tomorrow. LC 94-10295. (Essays in Public Policy Ser.: No. 50). 1994. write for info. (*0-8179-5552-6*) Hoover Inst Pr.
Ricardo, Catherine. Database Systems: Principles, Design & Implementation. 592p. (C). 1990. write for info. (*0-02-399665-X*) Macmillan.
Ricardo, David. Minor Papers on the Currency Question, 1809-1823. 1979. 21.95 (*0-405-10624-6*) Ayer.
— Notes on Malthus's Measure of Value. Porta, Pier L., ed. 120p. (C). 1992. 34.95 (*0-521-40298-0*) Cambridge U Pr.
— On the Principles of Political Economy & Taxation. 597p. 1977. reprint ed. 96.20 (*3-487-06311-5*, Pub. by Georg Olms GW) Lubrecht & Cramer.
— The Principles of Political Economy & Taxation. 329p. 1911. pap. 6.95 (*0-460-87125-0*, Everyman's Classic Lib) C E Tuttle.
— Works & Correspondence: Index, Vol. 11. Sraffa, P. & Dobb, Maurice H., eds. 1973. 69.95 (*0-521-20039-3*) Cambridge U Pr.
— Works & Correspondence: Principles of Political Economy, Vol. 1. Sraffa, P., ed. 437p. 1981. pap. 29.95 (*0-521-28505-4*) Cambridge U Pr.
Ricardo, G. Amistad e Intimidad (Friendship & Intimacy) (SPA.). Date not set. 1.79 (*0-945792-70-0*, 498108) Editorial Unilit.
— La Excelencia En la Mujer (The Excellence in a Woman) (SPA.). Date not set. 1.79 (*0-945792-69-7*, 498107) Editorial Unilit.
Ricardo-Gil, Jose, ed. see Saloom, Barbara B.
*__Ricardo, Gloria.__ Amistad E Intimidad. 28p. 1992. pap. 1.00 (*1-885630-17-4*) HLM Producciones.
— Cuando la Mjuer Ora. (Estudio Biblico Para Mujeres Ser.). 72p. (Orig.). 1992. pap. 4.00 (*1-885630-29-8*) HLM Producciones.
— De Mujer A Mujer. 18p. 1992. pap. 1.00 (*1-885630-15-8*) HLM Producciones.
— La Mujer De Excelencia. 36p. 1992. pap. 1.00 (*1-885630-10-7*) HLM Producciones.
— La Mujer y Sus Emociones. (Estudio Biblico Para Mujeres Ser.). 76p. 1992. pap. 4.00 (*1-885630-23-9*) HLM Producciones.
— El Perfil De Una Mujer De Dios. 75p. 1994. pap. 4.00 (*1-885630-30-1*) HLM Producciones.
— Proverbios y la Mujer Moderna. (Estudio Biblico Para Mujeres Ser.). 76p. 1992. pap. 4.00 (*1-885630-26-3*) HLM Producciones.
— Sus Hijos, Barro En Sus Manos. 26p. 1992. pap. 1.00 (*1-885630-12-3*) HLM Producciones.
— Ten Mujeres Biblicas y Lecciones Actuales No. 1. (Estudio Biblico Para Mujeres Ser.). 50p. 1992. pap. 4.00 (*1-885630-21-2*) HLM Producciones.
— Ten Mujeres Biblicas y Lecciones Actuales No. 2. (Estudio Biblico Para Mujeres Ser.). 50p. 1992. pap. 4.00 (*1-885630-22-0*) HLM Producciones.
— La Verdadera Liberacion Femenina. 26p. 1993. pap. 1.00 (*1-885630-04-2*) HLM Producciones.
Ricardo, Gloria, jt. auth. see Ricardo, Victor.
Ricardo, Ilona, jt. auth. see Richter, Peyton.
Ricardo, J. El Salvador: A Memory of Home. (Orig.). 1992. pap. 4.95 (*0-910303-31-2*) Writers Pub Serv.
Ricardo, Jack. Death with Dignity. 160p. (Orig.). 1991. pap. 8.95 (*0-934411-34-4*, Banned Bks) Edward-William Austin.
— The Night G. A. A. Died. (Stonewall Inn Mysteries Ser.). 208p. 1993. 8.95 (*0-312-09353-5*) St Martin.
Ricardo, Jack, ed. Leathermen Speak Out: An Anthology on Leathersex, Vol. 1. 192p. (Orig.). 1991. pap. 14.95 (*0-943595-33-9*) Leyland Pubns.
— Leathermen Speak Out: An Anthology on Leathersex, Vol. 2. 192p. (Orig.). 1993. pap. 14.95 (*0-943595-40-1*) Leyland Pubns.
*__Ricardo, Maryann.__ The Complete Medical Marketing Handbook: A Guide for Physicians & Managers. 112p. 1994. student ed, ring bd. 49.95 (*1-57066-028-X*) Practice Mgmt Info.
*__Ricardo, Roger.__ Guantanamo: The Bay of Discord. (Illus.). 50p. 1995. pap. 7.95 (*1-875284-56-7*, Pub. by Ocean Pr AT) Talman.
Ricardo, V. Catore Reglas-Conflictos-Matrimonio (Fourteen Rules to Handle Conflict-Marriage) (SPA.). Date not set. 1.79 (*0-945792-68-9*, 498106) Editorial Unilit.
— La Oracion Que Da Resultado (Prayer That Produces Results) (SPA.). Date not set. 1.79 (*0-945792-67-0*, 498105) Editorial Unilit.
*__Ricardo, Victor.__ Catorce Reglas Para el Conflicto Matrimonial. 1992. pap. 1.00 (*1-885630-14-X*) HLM Producciones.
— Como Romper la Maldicion De la Pobreza. 30p. 1992. pap. 1.00 (*1-885630-16-6*) HLM Producciones.
— El Domino Del Creyente. 28p. 1992. pap. 1.00 (*1-885630-13-1*) HLM Producciones.
— El Joven y Su Sexualidad. 32p. 1992. pap. 1.00 (*1-885630-19-0*) HLM Producciones.
— Joyas Que Enriquecen la Familia. (Serie Mini Libros de Inspriacion Creaciones Victor Ricardo Ser.). 68p. 1995. pap. text ed. 1.50 (*0-614-06913-0*) HLM Producciones.
— Joyas Que Enriquecen la Vida. (Serie Mini Libros de Inspiracion Creaciones Victor Ricardo Ser.). 68p. 1994. pap. text ed. 1.50 (*1-885630-33-6*) HLM Producciones.
— Orando Para Lograr Resultados. 32p. 1992. pap. 1.00 (*1-885630-20-4*) HLM Producciones.
— La Persona Que Dios Usa. 32p. 1993. pap. 1.00 (*1-885630-05-0*) HLM Producciones.
— Poder En Tu Boca. 26p. 1992. pap. 1.00 (*1-885630-02-6*) HLM Producciones.
— Respuestas Biblicas A 10 Preguntas Actuales. (Estudio Biblico Ser.). 57p. 1992. pap. 4.00 (*1-885630-27-1*) HLM Producciones.
— Rompiendo Ataduras. 28p. 1992. pap. 1.00 (*1-885630-01-8*) HLM Producciones.
— El Secreto Para Cambiar Su Familia y Su Mundo. 26p. 1992. pap. text ed. 1.00 (*1-885630-09-3*) HLM Producciones.
— Seven Casas Que Jamas Aceptare: El Secreto Para Vivir En Perdon, Paz, Confianza, Fuerza, Victoria Abundancia y Salud. 30p. 1992. pap. 1.00 (*1-885630-00-X*) HLM Producciones.
— Usted Puede Ganar En la Vida. 26p. 1992. pap. 1.00 (*1-885630-11-5*) HLM Producciones.
*__Ricardo, Victor & Ricardo, Gloria.__ Como Complementarse y No Fastidiarse. 36p. 1993. pap. 1.00 (*1-885630-06-9*) HLM Producciones.
— Como Experimentar la Presencia De Dios. 35p. 1993. pap. 2.00 (*1-885630-08-5*) HLM Producciones.
— Conociendo a Dios: Dios Se Revela a Traves de Sus Nombres. 64p. 1994. pap. text ed. 4.00 (*1-885630-31-X*) HLM Producciones.
— Cuando Los Hijos Se Rebelan. 32p. 1993. pap. 1.00 (*1-885630-03-4*) HLM Producciones.
— Curso De Matrimonios: Una Aventura Amorosa Les Puede Suceder A Ustedes y A Su Conyuge. 66p. 1992. pap. 4.00 (*1-885630-24-7*) HLM Producciones.
— La Familia Feliz. 28p. 1992. pap. 1.00 (*1-885630-18-2*) HLM Producciones.
— Gocese en el Senor: Como el Poder del Gozo Puede Cambiar Su Mundo. 34p. 1995. pap. text ed. 1.00 (*1-885630-36-0*) HLM Producciones.
— Hagamos Fiesta! 34p. 1993. pap. 1.00 (*1-885630-07-7*) HLM Producciones.
— El Plan De Dios Para la Familia. (Estudio Biblico Para Padres Ser.). 98p. 1992. pap. 4.00 (*1-885630-25-5*) HLM Producciones.
— Verdades Que Transforman. (Estudio Biblico Ser.). 66p. 1992. pap. 4.00 (*1-885630-28-X*) HLM Producciones.
Ricardou, J. Le Nouveau Roman, Les Raison de l'Ensemble. (FRE.). 1990. pap. 16.95 (*0-7859-2718-2*) Fr & Eur.
Ricart Matas, Juan. Diccionario Biografico de la Musica. 2nd ed. 1144p. (SPA.). 1986. 150.00 (*0-7859-5124-5*) Fr & Eur.
Ricaud, B. C., et al, eds. Diseases of Sugarcane: Major Diseases. 410p. 1989. 128.25 (*0-444-42797-X*) Elsevier.
Ricaud, Lulu C. Crosland: Family of Edward & Ann Snead Crosland, 1740-1957. (Illus.). 546p. 1994. reprint ed. lib. bdg. 93.00 (*0-8328-4205-2*); reprint ed. pap. 83.00 (*0-8328-4206-0*) Higginson Bk Co.
— Crosland - Family of Edward & Ann Snead Crosland, 1740-1957. (Illus.). 546p. 1994. reprint ed. lib. bdg. 93.00 (*0-8328-4533-7*); reprint ed. pap. 83.00 (*0-8328-4534-5*) Higginson Bk Co.
— The Family of Edward & Ann Snead Crosland, 1740-1957. LC 87-4274. (Illus.). 656p. 1988. reprint ed. 30.00 (*0-87152-422-8*) Reprint.
Ricca, Franco & Lo Bue, Erberto. The Great Stupa of Gyantse: A Complete Tibetan Pantheon of the Fifteenth Century. (Illus.). 320p. 1994. 90.00 (*0-906026-30-X*) Weatherhill.
Ricca, Sergio. International Migration in Africa: Legal & Administrative Aspects. xii, 190p. (Orig.). 1989. 30.00 (*92-2-106502-2*); pap. 22.00 (*92-2-106501-4*) Intl Labour Office.
Riccaboni, Angelo, jt. auth. see Ghirri, Rosanna.
Riccardi, A. C. The Cretaceous System of Southern South America. (Memoir Ser.: No. 168). 168p. 1988. 18.00 (*0-8137-1168-1*) Geol Soc.
Riccardi, C., jt. ed. see Santoni, A.
Riccardi-Cubitt, Monique. The Art of the Cabinet. LC 92-80825. (Illus.). 224p. 1992. 60.00 (*0-500-23642-9*) Thames Hudson.
Riccardi, Margaret, ed. see Bruno, Michael.
Riccardi, Margaret B., ed. see Coats, Warren L., Jr., et al.
Riccardi, Margaret B., ed. see Giovannini, Alberto.
Riccardi, Margaret B., ed. see Larrain, Felipe & Velasco, Andres.
Riccardi, Margaret B., ed. see Mussa, Michael L.
Riccardi, Margaret B., ed. see Padoa-Schioppa, Tommaso.
Riccardi, Margaret B., ed. see Tavlas, George S.
Riccardi, Pietro. Saggio di una Bibliografia Euclidea, 4 pts. in 1. 260p. 1974. reprint ed. write for info. (*3-487-05407-8*, Pub. by Georg Olms GW) Lubrecht & Cramer.
Riccardi, Theodore, ed. A Nepali Version of the Vetalapancavimsati. (American Oriental Ser.: Vol. 54). 1971. pap. 17.50 (*0-940490-54-4*) Am Orient Soc.
Riccardi, V. M., ed. Optic Pathway Gliomas. (Journal: Neurofibromatosis, 1988: Vol. 1, No. 4). (Illus.). 60p. 1989. pap. 30.50 (*3-8055-4945-8*) S Karger.
Riccardi, Vincent M. Neurofibromatosis: Phenotype, Natural History, & Pathogenesis. 2nd rev. ed. (Illus.). 520p. 1992. text ed. 95.00 (*0-8018-4348-0*) Johns Hopkins.
*__Riccardo.__ Perspectives. 238p. 1993. 12.50 (*0-911541-26-8*) Gregory Pub.
— Wisdom of Love. 1995. write for info. (*0-614-04555-X*) Gregory Pub.
Riccardo, Edward. Perspectives. (Illus.). 243p. Date not set. pap. 12.95 (*0-911541-07-1*) Gregory Pub.
— The Wisdom of Love. 192p. (Orig.). 1985. pap. 9.95 (*0-911541-06-3*) Gregory Pub.
Riccardo, Renee, jt. auth. see Laster, Paul.
Riccardo, Thomas. Wedding Warnings: What Every Bride & Groom Must Know but Were Never Told until Now! Becka, Brenda, ed. 120p. (Orig.). Date not set. pap. text ed. write for info. (*0-9633972-0-6*) Club Wed Pubns.
*__Riccards.__ Ferocious Engine of Democracy: A History of the American Presidency, 2 vols., Set. 1995. 69.95 (*1-56833-052-9*) Madison Bks UPA.
*__Riccards, Michael P.__ The Ferocious Engine of Democracy: A History of the American Presidency; Vol. Two: From Theodore Roosevelt Through George Bush. 424p. 1995. lib. bdg. 57.50 (*0-8476-7999-3*) Rowman.
— The Ferocious Engine of Democracy: The American Presidency from 1789 to 1989: from the Origins Through McKinley, Vol. 1. 368p. (C). 1994. lib. bdg. 54.50 (*1-56833-041-3*) Rowman.
— The Ferocious Engine of Democracy: The American Presidency from 1789 to 1989: from the Origins Through McKinley, Vol. 2. 368p. 1994. lib. bdg. 54.50 (*1-56833-042-1*) Rowman.
— The Ferocious Engine of Democracy: The American Presidency from 1789 to 1989, Vol. 1: From the Origins Through Mckinley. 368p. (C). 1994. lib. bdg. 54.50 (*0-8476-7974-8*) Rowman.
— A Republic, If You Can Keep It: The Foundation of the American Presidency, 1700-1800. LC 86-29595. (Contributions in Political Science Ser.: No. 167). 242p. 1987. text ed. 55.00 (*0-313-25462-1*, RRE/, Greenwood Pr) Greenwood.
Riccella, Christopher J. Muhammad Ali. 1991. pap. 3.95 (*0-87067-574-5*, Melrose Sq) Holloway.
Riccero, Delores & Bingham, Joan. More Haunted Houses. Peters, Sally, ed. 336p. (Orig.). 1991. pap. 9.00 (*0-671-69585-1*) PB.
Ricchiardi, Sherry & Young, Virginia. Women on Deadline: A Collection of America's Best. LC 90-41648. (Illus.). 224p. 1991. 25.95 (*0-8138-1687-4*); pap. 14.95 (*0-8138-1688-2*) Iowa St U Pr.
Ricchini, John A. Construction Documentation. 2nd ed. (Construction Law Library). 280p. 1991. pap. text ed. 85.00 (*0-471-55334-4*) Wiley.
Ricchio, Paul P., jt. auth. see Buttram, Harold E.
Ricchio, Paul P., ed. see McDaniel, Ivan G.
Ricchiute, David N. Auditing. (C). 1991. text ed. write for info. (*0-538-81402-0*, AJ99CA) S-W Pub.
— Auditing. 4th ed. LC 94-28905. 256p. 1995. text ed. 63.95 (*0-538-83883-3*) S-W Pub.
Ricchiuti, Paul B. Ellen: Trial & Triumph on the American Frontier. LC 76-44051. 160p. (YA). (gr. 6 up). 1988. reprint ed. pap. 7.95 (*0-945460-03-1*) Upward Way.
— The End-of-the-World-Man & Other Stories. Woolsey, Raymond H., ed. 96p. (J). (gr. 8). 1989. pap. 6.95 (*0-8280-0458-7*) Review & Herald.
— Where's Moo Cow? Tig's Tale. LC 94-23758. (J). 1994. write for info. (*0-8280-0890-6*) Review & Herald.
Ricci. Mom's House - Dad's House. 1980. 12.95 (*0-02-602550-7*) Macmillan.
Ricci, ed. see Barros-Neto, Jose.
Ricci, ed. see Berlinger, Eli & Zirkel, Gene.
Ricci, ed. see Cleary, Joseph & Gleason, Walter.
Ricci, ed. see Goodman, Arthur & Hirsch, Lewis R.
Ricci, ed. see Hirsch, Lewis R. & Goodman, Arthur.
Ricci, ed. see Radel, Stanley R. & Navidi, Marjorie.
Ricci, ed. see Smith, Terry M.
Ricci, Benjamin. Experiments in the Physiology of Human Performance. LC 76-102701. 218p. reprint ed. pap. 62.20 (*0-318-34653-2*, 2056574) Bks Demand.
Ricci, C., et al, eds. Rotifer Symposium, No. V. (Developments in Hydrobiology Ser.). (C). 1990. lib. bdg. 239.00 (*0-7923-0413-6*) Kluwer Ac.
*__Ricci, Carla.__ Mary Magdalene & Many Others: Women Who Followed Jesus. 1994. pap. 15.00 (*0-8006-2718-0*, Fortress Pr) Augsburg Fortress.
Ricci, David. The Tragedy of Political Science. LC 84-3510. 352p. 1987. pap. 17.00 (*0-300-03760-0*, Y-631) Yale U Pr.
Ricci, David M. The Tragedy of Political Science: Politics, Scholarship, & Democracy. LC 84-3510. 352p. 1984. 42.00 (*0-300-03088-6*) Yale U Pr.
— The Transformation of American Politics: The New Washington & the Rise of Think Tanks. 320p. 1994. pap. 15.00 (*0-300-06123-4*) Yale U Pr.
— The Transformation of American Politics: The New Washington & the Rise of Washington Think Tanks. LC 92-36419. 280p. (C). 1993. text ed. 32.50 (*0-300-05340-1*) Yale U Pr.
Ricci, Elisa. Italian Lace Designs: Two Hundred Forty-Three Classic Examples. LC 93-16990. (Pictorial Archive Ser.). 1993. pap. 7.95 (*0-486-27588-4*) Dover.
Ricci, Franco. Difficult Games: A Reading of "I Racconti" by Italo Calvino. 200p. (C). 1990. text ed. 29.95 (*0-88920-990-1*, Pub. by Wilfrid Laurier CN) Humanities.
Ricci, G., ed. Decision Processes in Economics: Proceedings of the VI Italian Conference on Game Theory Held in Modena, Italy, October 9-10, 1989. (Lecture Notes in Economics & Mathematical Systems Ser.: Vol. 353). (Illus.). iii, 209p. 1991. pap. 37.00 (*0-387-53592-6*) Spr-Verlag.
*__Ricci, Giorgio, et al, eds.__ Therapeutic Selectivity & Risk-Benefit Assessment of Hypolipidemic Drugs. LC 81-40550. (Illus.). Date not set. reprint ed. pap. 100.10 (*0-7837-9541-6*, 2060290) Bks Demand.
Ricci, Isolina. Mom's House, Dad's House: Making Shared Custody Work. (Illus.). 288p. 1982. pap. 10.00 (*0-02-077710-8*) Macmillan.
Ricci, J. Elsevier's Banking Dictionary. 3rd enl. rev. ed. 360p. (DUT, ENG, FRE, GER, ITA, POR & SPA.). 1990. 250.00 (*0-8288-9259-8*, M7911) Fr & Eur.
Ricci, J., ed. Elsevier's Banking Dictionary. 3rd rev. ed. 360p. (DUT, ENG, FRE, GER, ITA, POR & SPA.). 1991. 143.00 (*0-444-88067-4*) Elsevier.
Ricci, James. Development of Gynaecological Surgery & Instruments. (Illus.). 594p. 1990. reprint ed. 165.00 (*0-930405-28-5*) Norman SF.
Ricci, John E. Hydrogen Ion Concentration. 1952. 80.00 (*0-691-07981-1*) Princeton U Pr.
Ricci, Julio. Falling Through the Cracks. Zlotchew, tr. 1989. 8.00 (*0-934834-25-3*) White Pine.
Ricci Lucchi, F., ed. see Mutti, E.
Ricci, Luigi. Un Avventura di Scaramuccia. LC 86-755124. (Italian Opera Ser., 1810-1840: Vol. 44). 312p. 1987. 40.00 (*0-8240-6593-X*) Garland.
— Chiara Di Rosembergh & Excerpts from Some Earlier Operas. LC 90-753306. (Italian Opera 1810-1840 Ser.: Vol. 42). 328p. 1991. 124.00 (*0-8240-6591-3*) Garland.
Ricci, Luigi, tr. see Machiavelli, Niccolo, et al.
Ricci, M. & Marone, G., eds. Progress in Clinical Immunology. (Monographs in Allergy: Vol. 18). (Illus.). x, 314p. 1983. 131.25 (*3-8055-3697-6*) S Karger.
Ricci, Mark, jt. auth. see Conway, Michael.
Ricci, Mark, jt. auth. see Vermilye, Jerry.
Ricci, Mark, et al. The Films of John Wayne. (Illus.). 288p. 1972. reprint ed. pap. 7.95 (*0-8065-0296-7*, Citadel Pr) Carol Pub Group.
Ricci, Matteo. The True Meaning of the Lord of Heaven. Malatesta, Edward J., ed. LC 84-80944. (Jesuit Primary Sources in English Translation Series I: No. 6). (Illus.). xiv, 485p. (CHI & ENG.). 1985. 39.00 (*0-912422-78-5*); 34.00 (*0-912422-77-7*) Inst Jesuit.
Ricci, Michael A. & Szabo, Joseph G. Was It Worth It? A Collection of International Cartoons about Columbus & His Trip to America. 112p. 1992. pap. 12.95 (*0-9631600-0-1*) WittyWrld ICM.
Ricci, Nino. Book of Saints. 1991. pap. 18.50 (*0-679-40118-0*) McKay.
Ricci, P. F. & Rowe, M., eds. Health & Environmental Risk Assessment: Workshop at Brookhaven National Laboratory, December 1981. LC 85-12309. (Illus.). 300p. 1985. 132.00 (*0-08-031578-X*, Pub. by Pergamon Repr UK) Franklin.
Ricci, Paolo F., ed. see Cox, L. A.
Ricci, Paolo F., et al. Technological Risk Assessment. 1984. lib. bdg. 106.50 (*90-247-2961-0*) Kluwer Ac.
Ricci, R., jt. ed. see Molinari, A.
Ricci, R. A., jt. auth. see Eliezer, S.
Ricci, R. A., jt. auth. see Faraggi, H.
Ricci, R. A., jt. ed. see Moretto, L. G.
Ricci, R. A., ed. see Winter School.
Ricci, Ralph V. Multiple Choice Questions in Preparation for the AP Biology Examination. 2nd ed. 115p. 1991. student ed 15.95 (*1-878621-12-2*) D & S Mktg Syst.
— Multiple Choice Questions in Preparation for the AP Biology Examination. 2nd ed. 71p. (YA). (gr. 11-12). 1991. teacher ed write for info. (*1-878621-13-0*) D & S Mktg Syst.
Ricci, Stefania & Maeder, Edward. Salvatore Ferragamo: Art of the Shoe 1896-1960. LC 91-34780. (Illus.). 250p. 1992. 45.00 (*0-8478-1496-3*) Rizzoli Intl.
*__Ricci, Stefano, et al.__ Ambulatory Phlebectomy: A Practical Guide for Treating Varicose Veins. 1995. write for info. (*0-8151-7045-9*) Mosby Yr Bk.
Ricci, Steven, jt. ed. see Noriega, Chon A.
Ricci, Susan C., jt. auth. see Stebbins, Theodore R., Jr.
Ricci, Vincent L., jt. auth. see Duffy, James P.
Ricciardi, Antonio. St. Maximilian Kolbe. Daughters of St. Paul, tr. LC 82-18316. (Illus.). 314p. 1982. pap. 7.95 (*0-8198-6837-X*) Pauline Bks.
Ricciardi, L. & Scott, A., eds. Biomathematics in Nineteen Eighty. (Mathematics Studies: Vol. 58). 298p. 1982. 77.00 (*0-444-86355-9*, North Holland) Elsevier.
Ricciardi, L. M. Diffusion Processes & Related Topics in Biology. LC 77-7464. (Lecture Notes in Biomathematics Ser.: Vol. 14). 1977. pap. 27.00 (*0-387-08146-1*) Spr-Verlag.
Ricciardi, Luigi M., ed. Biomathematics & Related Computational Problems. (C). 1988. lib. bdg. 212.00 (*90-277-2726-0*) Kluwer Ac.
Ricciardi, Mirella. Vanishing Amazon. (Illus.). 240p. 1991. 49.50 (*0-8109-3915-0*) Abrams.
Ricciardi, Sal. Running Microsoft FoxPro for MS-DOS. LC 93-19415. 486p. 1993. pap. 24.95 (*1-55615-556-5*) Microsoft.
Riccio, Barry D. Walter Lippmann: Odyssey of a Liberal. LC 92-37471. 376p. (C). 1993. text ed. 34.95 (*1-56000-096-1*) Transaction Pubs.
Riccio, D., jt. auth. see Bingham, J.
Riccio, David C., jt. auth. see Spear, Norman E.
Riccio, Dolores. Superfoods: Three Hundred Recipes for Foods That Heal Body & Mind. LC 92-36868. 320p. (Orig.). 1993. 26.95 (*0-446-51753-4*) Warner Bks.
— Superfoods for Women. 1996. write for info. (*0-446-51795-X*) Warner Bks.
Riccio, Peter. Italian Authors of Today. LC 75-128298. (Essay Index Reprint Ser.). 1977. 18.95 (*0-8369-1842-8*) Ayer.
*__Ricciotti, Hope & Connelly, Vincent.__ The Pregnancy Cookbook. LC 95-6383. 1995. pap. 14.00 (*0-393-31386-7*) Norton.
Ricciuti, E., jt. auth. see Albano, Lou.
Ricciuti, Ed. Fish of the Atlantic. (Illus.). 96p. pap. 7.95 (*0-88839-155-2*) Hancock House.
— Secrets of Potfishing. (Illus.). 74p. pap. 3.50 (*0-88839-085-8*) Hancock House.
Ricciuti, Edward. Amphibians. (Our Living World Ser.). (Illus.). 64p. (J). (gr. 4-8). 1993. lib. bdg. 16.95 (*1-56711-045-2*) Blackbirch.
— Birds. (Our Living World Ser.). (Illus.). 64p. (J). (gr. 4-8). 1993. lib. bdg. 16.95 (*1-56711-038-X*) Blackbirch.

R

— Birds. (Our Living World Ser.). (Illus.). 64p. (J). (gr. 4-8). 1993. 14.95 (1-56711-053-3) Blackbirch.
— Crustaceans. (Our Living World Ser.). (Illus.). 64p. (J). (gr. 4-8). 1994. lib. bdg. 16.95 (1-56711-046-0) Blackbirch.
— Fish. (Our Living World Ser.). (Illus.). 64p. (J). (gr. 4-8). 1993. lib. bdg. 16.95 (1-56711-041-X) Blackbirch.
— Fish. (Our Living World Ser.). (Illus.). 64p. (J). (gr. 4-8). 1993. 14.95 (1-56711-056-8) Blackbirch.
— The Our Living World Resource Guide & Reference. (Our Living World Ser.). (Illus.). 64p. (J). (gr. 4-8). 1994. lib. bdg. 16.95 (1-56711-057-6) Blackbirch.
— Patterns in Nature. (Our Living World Ser.). (Illus.). 64p. (J). (gr. 4-8). 1994. lib. bdg. 16.95 (1-56711-058-4) Blackbirch.
— Reptiles. (Our Living World Ser.). (Illus.). 64p. (J). (gr. 4-8). 1993. lib. bdg. 16.95 (1-56711-047-9) Blackbirch.
— Reptiles. (Our Living World Ser.). (Illus.). 64p. (J). (gr. 3-7). 1993. 14.95 (1-56711-063-0) Blackbirch.
— Secrets of Shellfishing. (Illus.). 70p. pap. 3.50 (0-88839-140-4) Hancock House.
— Wrestlemania. Emanuel, Tom, ed. (Illus.). 100p. (Orig.). 1986. pap. 5.95 (0-9616263-2-1) WWF Bks.

Ricciuti, Edward R. Bret "Hit Man" Hart. Glassman, Bruce, ed. (Face to Face Ser.). 25p. (Orig.). (J). (gr. 5 up). Date not set. text ed. 12.95 (1-56711-075-4, Topdog) Blackbirch.
— Bret "Hit Man" Hart. Glassman, Bruce, ed. (Face to Face Ser.). 25p. (Orig.). (J). (gr. 5 up). 1994. pap. text ed. 6.95 (1-56711-070-3) Blackbirch.
— Capybara. Glassman, Bruce, ed. LC 94-36827. (What on Earth Is...? Ser.). 32p. (J). 1995. lib. bdg. 12.95 (1-56711-097-5) Blackbirch.
— Exploring the New England Aquarium: Windows on the World of Water. LC 86-24192. (Illus.). 64p. 1991. pap. 9.95 (0-571-12971-4) Faber & Faber.
— Galago. Glassman, Bruce, ed. LC 94-40356. (What on Earth Is...? Ser.). (Illus.). 32p. (J). (gr. 2-5). 1995. lib. bdg. 12.95 (1-56711-101-7) Blackbirch.
— Hyrax. Glassman, Bruce, ed. LC 94-36411. (What on Earth Is...? Ser.). (Illus.). 32p. (J). (gr. 2-5). 1995. lib. bdg. 12.95 (1-56711-100-9) Blackbirch.
— Macho Man Randy Savage. Glassman, Bruce, ed. (Face to Face Ser.). 25p. (Orig.). (J). (gr. 5 up). Date not set. text ed. 12.95 (1-56711-077-0, Topdog) Blackbirch.
— Macho Man Randy Savage. Glassman, Bruce, ed. (Face to Face Ser.). 25p. (Orig.). (J). (gr. 5 up). 1994. pap. text ed. 6.95 (1-56711-072-X, Topdog) Blackbirch.
— Microorganisms: The Unseen World. LC 93-44544. (Our Living World Ser.). (Illus.). 64p. (J). (gr. 4-8). 1994. lib. bdg. 16.95 (1-56711-040-1) Blackbirch.
— Rainforest. (Biomes of the World Ser.). 64p. (J). (gr. 3-5). 1995. lib. bdg. write for info. (0-7614-0081-8, Benchmark NY) Marshall Cavendish.
— Rainforest, 4 bks., Set. LC 95-4021. (Biomes of the World Ser.). (J). (gr. 3-5). 1995. lib. bdg. write for info. (0-7614-0078-8, Benchmark NY) Marshall Cavendish.
— Razor Ramon. Glassman, Bruce, ed. (Face to Face Ser.). 25p. (Orig.). (YA). (gr. 5 up). text ed. 12.95 (1-56711-076-2, Topdog) Blackbirch.
— Razor Ramon. Glassman, Bruce, ed. (Face to Face Ser.). 25p. (Orig.). (YA). (gr. 5 up). 1994. pap. text ed. 6.95 (1-56711-071-1, Topdog) Blackbirch.
— Somalia: A Crisis of Famine & War. LC 93-15094. (Headliners Ser.). (Illus.). 64p. (J). (gr. 5-8). 1993. lib. bdg. 15.90 (1-56294-376-6); pap. 6.95 (1-56294-751-6) Millbrook Pr.
— The Steiner Brothers. Glassman, Bruce, ed. (Face to Face Ser.). 25p. (Orig.). (J). (gr. 5 up). Date not set. text ed. 12.95 (1-56711-078-9) Blackbirch.
— The Steiner Brothers. Glassman, Bruce, ed. (Face to Face Ser.). 25p. (Orig.). (J). (gr. 5 up). 1994. pap. text ed. 6.95 (1-56711-073-8) Blackbirch.
— The Undertaker. Glassman, Bruce, ed. (Face to Face Ser.). 25p. (Orig.). (J). (gr. 5 up). Date not set. text ed. 12.95 (1-56711-079-7, Topdog) Blackbirch.
— The Undertaker. Glassman, Bruce, ed. (Face to Face Ser.). 25p. (Orig.). (J). (gr. 5 up). 1994. pap. text ed. 6.95 (1-56711-074-6) Blackbirch.
— War in Yugoslavia: The Breakup of a Nation. LC 92-32126. (Headliners Ser.). (Illus.). 64p. (J). (gr. 5-8). 1993. lib. bdg. 15.90 (1-56294-375-8); pap. 6.95 (1-56294-750-8) Millbrook Pr.

Ricciuti, Gail A. & Mitchell, Rosemary C. Birthings & Blessings, II: More Liberating Worship Services for the Inclusive Church. LC 93-20569. 190p. (Orig.). 1993. pap. 13.95 (0-8245-1380-0) Crossroad NY.

Ricciuti, Gail A., jt. auth. see Mitchell, Rosemary C.

Ricciuti, Henry N., jt. auth. see Caldwell, Bettye M.

***Ricciuitti, Edward R.** Ocean. LC 95-4064. (Biomes of the World Ser.). 64p. (J). (gr. 3-5). 1995. lib. bdg. write for info. (0-7614-0079-6, Benchmark NY) Marshall Cavendish.

Ricco, Roger, et al. American Primitive: Discoveries in Folk Sculpture. LC 88-45341. (Illus.). 304p. 1988. 75.00 (0-394-54467-6) Knopf.

Riccoboni, Luigi. A General History of the Stage from Its Origin....with Two Essays: On the Art of Speaking in Public & a Comparison Between the Ancient & Modern Drama. LC 76-43937. (Music & Theatre in France in the 17th & 18th Centuries Ser.). reprint ed. 57.50 (0-404-60187-1) AMS Pr.

Riccomini, Donald R. & Rosenzweig, Philip M. Unexpected Japan: Why American Business Should Return to Its Own Traditional Values--& Not Imitate the Japanese. 144p. 1985. 12.95 (0-8027-0858-7) Walker & Co.

***Riccucci, Norma M.** Unsung Heroes: Federal Execucrats Making a Difference. LC 95-7073. 1995. 45.00 (0-87840-592-5); pap. 17.95 (0-87840-595-X) Georgetown U Pr.
— Women, Minorities & Unions in the Public Sector. LC 89-7481. (Contributions in Labor Studies: No. 28). 200p. 1990. text ed. 45.00 (0-313-26043-5, RWM, Quorum Bks) Greenwood.
— Women, Minorities & Unions in the Public Sector. braille ed. 555p. 1992. vinyl bd. 44.40 (1-56956-105-2, BR8758) W A T Braille.

Riccucci, Norma M., jt. auth. see Ban, Carolyn.

***Riccuiti, Edward R.** Chuckwalla. Glassman, Bruce, ed. LC 94-28248. (What on Earth Is...? Ser). 32p. (J). (gr. 2-5). 1994. lib. bdg. 12.95 (1-56711-089-4) Blackbirch.
— Guanaco. Glassman, Bruce, ed. LC 94-22523. (What on Earth Is...? Ser). 32p. (J). (gr. 2-5). 1994. lib. bdg. 12.95 (1-56711-095-9) Blackbirch.
— Pangolin. Glassman, Bruce, ed. LC 94-22517. (What on Earth Is...? Ser). 32p. (J). (gr. 2-5). 1994. lib. bdg. 12.95 (1-56711-090-8) Blackbirch.

Rice. Advanced Oxidation Processes. 1995. write for info. (0-87371-203-X) Lewis Pubs.
— Countdown! 1990. pap. 18.95 (0-8384-3379-0) Heinle & Heinle.
— Cry to Heaven. 1995. mass mkt. 6.99 (0-345-39693-6) Ballantine.
— Evidence: Common Law & Federal Rules of Evidence. 2nd ed. 1990. write for info. (0-8205-0344-4, 606); teacher ed write for info. (0-8205-0345-2) Bender.
— Evidence Law: Transcripts Supplement. 1987. write for info. (0-8205-0126-3, 232) Bender.
— Explorations. 1988. pap. 18.95 (0-8384-3355-3) Heinle & Heinle.
— Handbook of Home Health Nursing Procedures. 504p. 1995. spiral bd. 25.95 (0-8016-6946-4) Mosby Yr Bk.
— Inpatient Group Therapy. 1987. text ed. 26.95 (0-07-105351-4) McGraw.
— Instructor's Guide & Testbank for Medical Terminology with Human Anatomy. 3rd ed. (C). 1994. teacher ed, pap. text ed. 29.95 (0-8385-6272-8) Appleton & Lange.
— Manual of Home Health Nursing Procedures. 576p. 1994. 99.95 (0-8016-6945-6) Mosby Yr Bk.
— Medical Terminology with Human Anatomy. 3rd ed. (C). 1994. pap. text ed. 29.95 (0-8385-6268-X) Appleton & Lange.
— Understanding Customers. 2nd ed. 414p. 1995. pap. 32.95 (0-7506-2322-5, Focal) Buttrwrth-Heinemann.

Rice, jt. auth. see Bragger.

Rice, jt. ed. see Prigogine.

Rice, jt. auth. see Schofer.

Rice, et al. New Structural Design Guide to ACI Building Code. 3rd ed. 480p. 1985. write for info. (0-318-60873-1) Concrete Reinforcing.

Rice, A., jt. ed. see Lockley, M.

Rice, A. H. A Genealogical History of the Rice Family & Descendants of Deacon Edward Rice, Who Came from Berkhamstead, England, & Settled at Sudbury, Mass., in 1638. 387p. 1989. reprint ed. lib. bdg. 51.00 (0-8328-1018-5); reprint ed. pap. 41.00 (0-8328-1019-3) Higginson Bk Co.

Rice, Alan L., tr. see Langewiesche, Karl R.

Rice, Albert R. The Baroque Clarinet. (Early Music Ser.: No. 13). (Illus.). 216p. 1992. 79.00 (0-19-816188-3) OUP.

Rice, Alice C. Happiness Road. LC 68-58810. (Essay Index Reprint Ser.). 1977. 17.95 (0-8369-0123-1) Ayer.

Rice, Alice H. Lovey Mary. 18.95 (0-8488-1133-X) Amereon Ltd.
— Mr. Opp. 23.95 (0-8488-1132-1) Amereon Ltd.
— Mrs. Wiggs of the Cabbage Patch. 17.95 (0-89190-859-5, Am Repr) Amereon Ltd.
— Mrs. Wiggs of the Cabbage Patch. (J). 1992. reprint ed. lib. bdg. 19.95 (0-89968-273-1, Lghtyr Pr) Buccaneer Bks.
— My Pillow Book. 15.95 (0-8488-1134-8) Amereon Ltd.
— The Peninsula. 21.95 (0-89190-728-9, Am Repr) Amereon Ltd.
— Quin. 25.95 (0-8488-1135-6) Amereon Ltd.
— Romance of Billy-Goat Hill. 25.95 (0-8488-1136-4) Amereon Ltd.
— Sandy. 22.95 (0-8488-1137-2) Amereon Ltd.

Rice, Alison, tr. see Bulgakov, Mikhail.

Rice, Alison M. Teaching with Video: Techniques & Activities with Family Album, U. S. A. LC 92-5414. 1992. 12.95 (0-02-881250-6) Macmillan.

Rice, Allan L. Gothic Prepositional Compounds in Their Relation to the Greek Originals. (LD Ser.: No. 11). 1932. 16.00 (0-527-00757-9) Periodicals Srv.
— Swedish, A Practical Grammar. rev. ed. LC 58-13379. 110p. reprint ed. pap. 31.40 (0-685-16044-0, 2026950) Bks Demand.

Rice, Allen T., ed. Reminiscences of Abraham Lincoln. LC 72-13766. (Concordance Ser.: No. 37). 1971. reprint ed. lib. bdg. 69.95 (0-8383-1227-6) M S G Haskell Hse.

Rice, Ann. Farm Babies. LC 93-26192. (All Aboard Reading Ser.). (Illus.). 32p. (J). (ps-3). 1994. pap. 2.25 (0-448-40212-2, G&D) Putnam Pub Group.

Rice, Ann B. Angelwhisp. Goodman, Frances B., ed. (Illus.). 96p. 1993. 25.00 (0-89896-130-0, Post Oak Pr) Larksdale.

Rice, Ann S. Family Life Management. (C). 1986. teacher ed write for info. (0-318-60353-5) Macmillan.
— Family Life Management. 6th ed. 464p. (C). 1986. write for info. (0-02-399740-0) Macmillan.

Rice, Anne. Belinda. Rampling, Anne, ed. 512p. 1988. pap. text ed. 6.99 (0-515-09355-6) Jove Pubns.
— Cry to Heaven. 536p. 1988. mass mkt. 4.95 (1-55817-105-3, Pinnacle NY) Windsor NY.
— Interview with the Vampire. 1991. mass mkt. 6.99 (0-345-33766-2) Ballantine.
— Interview with the Vampire. 1994. mass mkt. 6.99 (0-345-90333-1) Ballantine.
— Interview with the Vampire. 1994. pap. 6.99 (0-345-90444-3) Ballantine.
— Interview with the Vampire. 320p. 1991. reprint ed. lib. bdg. 29.95 (0-89966-781-3) Buccaneer Bks.
— Lasher. 592p. 1994. pap. 14.00 (0-345-37764-8) Ballantine.
— Lasher. 1995. pap. 6.99 (0-345-39781-9) Ballantine.
— Memnock the Devil: The Vampire Chronicles. 368p. 1995. pap. 25.00 (0-679-44101-8) Random.
— The Queen of the Damned. 1994. mass mkt. 6.99 (0-345-90335-8) Ballantine.
— The Tale of the Body Thief. 1994. mass mkt. 6.99 (0-345-90336-6) Ballantine.
— Tale of the Body Thief. 1992. 6.99 (0-517-11710-X) Random Hse Value.
— Taltos. 480p. 1995. pap. 14.00 (0-345-39471-2) Ballantine.
— Taltos: Lives of the Mayfair Witches. deluxe ed. 467p. 1994. 150.00 (0-9631925-1-5) B E Trice.
— Taltos: Tales of the Mayfair Witches. LC 93-35693. 1994. 25.00 (0-679-42573-X) Knopf.
— Vampire Chronicles. 1993. pap. 27.96 (0-345-38540-3) Ballantine.
— The Vampire Lestat. 1994. mass mkt. 6.99 (0-345-90334-X) Ballantine.
— The Vampire Lestat. (Vampire Chronicles Ser.). 384p. 1991. 39.95 (1-56521-002-6) Innovative.

Rice, Anne, see A. N. Roquelaure, pseud..

***Rice, Anne, et al.** Practical Approaches to Usability Testing for Technical Documentation. Velotta, Christopher, ed. & intro. by. (Anthology Ser.). (Illus.). 105p. (Orig.). (C). 1995. pap. 45.00 (0-914548-81-6) Soc Tech Comm.

Rice, Anne O. Cry to Heaven. LC 81-19368. 1982. 25.00 (0-394-52351-2) Knopf.
— Cry to Heaven. 1991. pap. 12.00 (0-345-37370-7, Ballantine Trade) Ballantine.
— The Feast of All Saints. 1986. mass mkt. 6.99 (0-345-33453-1) Ballantine.
— The Feast of All Saints. 576p. 1992. pap. 14.00 (0-345-37604-8, Ballantine Trade) Ballantine.
— Feast of All Saints. 1985. mass mkt. 4.95 (0-449-21063-4) Fawcett.
— Interview with a Vampire. Date not set. pap. write for info. (0-394-25662-X) Knopf.
— Interview with the Vampire. 1976. 24.00 (0-394-49821-6) Knopf.
— Interview with the Vampire. 1986. pap. 17.00 (0-394-55617-8) Random.
— Interview with Vampire. Date not set. pap. 23.00 (0-394-26725-7) Knopf.
— Lasher. Date not set. pap. 22.00 (0-394-28021-0) Knopf.
— Lasher. LC 93-12246. 1993. 25.00 (0-679-41295-6) Knopf.
— The Mummy or Ramses the Damned. 1989. pap. 12.50 (0-345-36000-1, Ballantine Trade) Ballantine.
— The Mummy or Ramses the Damned. 416p. 1991. mass mkt. 6.99 (0-345-36994-7) Ballantine.
— The Queen of the Damned. LC 88-45310. (Vampire Chronicles Ser.: Bk. III). 432p. 1988. 25.00 (0-394-55823-5) Knopf.
— The Queen of the Damned. 512p. 1989. mass mkt. 6.99 (0-345-35152-5) Ballantine.
— Queen of the Damned. Date not set. pap. write for info. (0-394-25660-3) Knopf.
— The Tale of the Body Thief. LC 92-53085. (Vampire Chronicles Ser.). 428p. 1992. 23.50 (0-394-22317-9) Knopf.
— The Tale of the Body Thief. 1993. mass mkt. 6.99 (0-345-38475-X) Ballantine.
— The Tale of the Body Thief: The Vampire Chronicles. LC 92-5308. 1992. 24.00 (0-679-40528-3) Knopf.
— Vampire Chronicle, 4 vols., Set. 1989. Boxed set. boxed 20.97 (0-345-36422-8) Ballantine.
— The Vampire Lestat. LC 85-40123. (Chronicles of the Vampires Ser.: Bk. 2). 512p. 1985. 25.00 (0-394-53443-3) Knopf.
— The Vampire Lestat. 1986. mass mkt. 6.99 (0-345-31386-0) Ballantine.
— Vampire Lestat. Date not set. pap. write for info. (0-394-25661-1) Knopf.
— Witching Hour. Date not set. pap. write for info. (0-394-25663-8) Knopf.
— Witching Hour. 1990. 22.45 (0-394-58786-3) Knopf.
— The Witching Hour. 976p. 1991. pap. 14.00 (0-345-36789-8, Ballantine Trade) Ballantine.
— The Witching Hour. 1993. mass mkt. 6.99 (0-345-38446-6) Ballantine.

Rice, Anthony. Accounts Demystified: How to Understand & Use Company Accounts. 192p. (Orig.). 1993. pap. 45.00x (0-273-60154-7, Pub. by Pitman Pubng UK) St Mut.

Rice, Arnold M., et al. United States History from 1865. 20th ed. LC 90-56006. (HarperCollins College Outline Ser.). (Illus.). 320p. (Orig.). 1991. pap. 13.00 (0-06-467100-3, Harper Ref) HarpC.
— United States History to 1865. LC 90-56006. (HarperCollins College Outline Ser.). (Illus.). 320p. (Orig.). 1991. pap. 13.00 (0-06-467111-9, Harper Ref) HarpC.

Rice, Arnold S. The Ku Klux Klan in American Politics. LC 72-1152. (Southern Literature & History Ser.: No. 65). 1972. reprint ed. lib. bdg. 75.00 (0-8383-1427-9) M S G Haskell Hse.

Rice, B. Lewis. Mysore & Coorg from the Inscriptions. (Illus.). 256p. 1986. reprint ed. write for info. (0-8364-1700-3, Pub. by Manohar II) S Asia.

Rice, Bebe F. Class Trip. (YA). 1993. mass mkt. 3.50 (0-06-106731-8, Harp PBks) HarpC.
— Class Trip Vol. II. (YA). 1994. pap. 3.50 (0-06-106195-6) HarpC Child Bks.
— Love You to Death. (J). 1994. mass mkt. 3.50 (0-06-106184-0, Harp PBks) HarpC.

Rice, Bebe Faas. The Year the Wolves Came. 128p. (J). (gr. 3-7). 1994. 14.99 (0-525-45209-5) Dutton Child Bks.

Rice, Berkeley. Trafficking. 1991. mass mkt. 5.95 (0-312-92523-9) St Martin.

Rice, Bernard & Strange, Jerry. Algebra & Trigonometry with Applications. 4th ed. (Illus.). 552p. (C). 1989. student ed, disk write for info. (0-318-63833-9) Brooks-Cole.
— Ordinary Differential Equations with Applications. 2nd ed. LC 88-21725. (Illus.). 465p. (C). 1988. text ed. 59.95 (0-534-09906-8) Brooks-Cole.

Rice, Bernard J. & Strange, Jerry D. Ordinary Differential Equations with Applications. 3rd ed. LC 93-24600. 1994. text ed. 63.95 (0-534-21318-9) Brooks-Cole.
— Plane Trigonometry. 6th ed. 400p. 1992. text ed. 53.95 (0-534-92894-3) PWS Pubs.

Rice, Bernard J., et al. Finite Mathematics for College Students. 500p. (C). 1992. text ed. 62.95 (0-534-17172-9) Brooks-Cole.

Rice, Bob. Nursery & Landscape Weed Control Manual. 264p. 1987. pap. 19.95 (0-913702-42-0) Thomson Pubns.

Rice, Bradley R. Progressive Cities: The Commission Government Movement in America, 1901-1920. LC 77-8458. 180p. reprint ed. pap. 51.30 (0-7837-1013-5, 2041324) Bks Demand.

Rice, Bradley R., jt. ed. see Bernard, Richard M.

Rice, Bradley R., jt. auth. see Jackson, Harvey H.

Rice, Bradley R., ed. see McCarley, J. Britt, et al.

Rice, C. Colliver. Persian Women & Their Ways. 1976. lib. bdg. 59.95 (0-8490-2424-2) Gordon Pr.

Rice, C. David, jt. auth. see Foley, William E.

Rice, C. David, jt. ed. see McClure, Arthur F.

Rice, C. Duncan. The Rise & Fall of Black Slavery. LC 72-9149. (Illus.). xiv, 429p. 1976. pap. text ed. 14.95 (0-8071-0257-1) La State U Pr.

Rice, C. S. Rice. "We Sought the Wilderness" (Memoirs of Some Descendants of Dea. Edmund Rice) 257p. 1991. reprint ed. lib. bdg. 49.50 (0-8328-1975-1); reprint ed. pap. 39.50 (0-8328-1976-X) Higginson Bk Co.

Rice, Cale Y. Selected Plays & Poems. LC 27-16490. xviii, 786p. 1972. reprint ed. 79.00 (0-403-01174-4) Scholarly.

Rice, Cecil A. The Letters & Friendships of Sir Cecil Spring Rice, 2 vols, 1. Gwynn, Stephen L., ed. LC 73-110868. (Illus.). 1971. reprint ed. text ed. 45.00 (0-8371-4546-5, SPLF) Greenwood.
— The Letters & Friendships of Sir Cecil Spring Rice, 2 vols, Set. Gwynn, Stephen L., ed. LC 73-110868. (Illus.). 1971. reprint ed. text ed. 85.00 (0-8371-4545-7, SPLE) Greenwood.
— The Letters & Friendships of Sir Cecil Spring Rice, 2 vols, Vol. 2. Gwynn, Stephen L., ed. LC 73-110868. (Illus.). 1971. reprint ed. text ed. 45.00 (0-8371-4547-3, SPLG) Greenwood.
— The Letters & Friendships of Sir Cecil Spring Rice: A Record, 2 vols., Set. Gwynn, Stephen L., ed. LC 79-37912. (Select Bibliographies Reprint Ser.). 1977. reprint ed. 58.95 (0-8369-6750-X) Ayer.

Rice, Charles. No Exceptions. 1990. 5.00 (0-9627667-0-4, Z602) Human Life Intl.

***Rice, Charles D.** The Scots Abolitionists, 1833-1861. fac. ed. LC 81-3789. 235p. 1981. reprint ed. pap. 67.00 (0-7837-7818-X, 2047574) Bks Demand.

Rice, Charles E. The Supreme Court & Public Prayer: The Need for Restraint. LC 64-18392. 216p. reprint ed. pap. 61.60 (0-7837-0466-6, 2040789) Bks Demand.

Rice, Charles L. The Embodied Word: Preaching As Art & Liturgy. LC 90-21915. (Resources for Preaching Ser.). 144p. (Orig.). 1990. pap. 11.00 (0-8006-2453-X, 1-2453, Fortress Pr) Augsburg Fortress.

***Rice, Charles L., ed.** Elements of Pennsylvanian Stratigraphy, Central Appalachian Basin. LC 94-32979. (Special Papers-Geological Society of America Ser.: Vol. 294). 1994. pap. 40.00 (0-8137-2294-2) Geol Soc.

Rice, Charles L., jt. ed. see Lyons, Paul C.

Rice, Cheryl F., jt. auth. see Cerbus, Deborah P.

Rice, Chris. Consumer Behavior: Behavioral Aspects of Marketing. (CIM Student Ser.). 414p. 1993. pap. 27.00 (0-7506-0549-9) Buttrwrth-Heinemann.

Rice, Chris & Perkins, Spencer. More Than Equals: Racial Healing for the Sake of the Gospel. LC 93-7442. (Illus.). 244p. (Orig.). 1993. pap. 11.99 (0-8308-1318-7, 1318) InterVarsity.

***Rice, Chris & Rice, Melanie.** How Children Lived. LC 94-33412. (Illus.). 48p. (J). (gr. 2 up). 1995. 14.95 (1-56458-876-9) Dorling Kindersley.

***Rice, Christopher & Rice, Melanie.** My First Body Book. LC 94-40835. 48p. (J). 1995. 16.95 (1-56458-893-9, 5-70553) Dorling Kindersley.

Rice, Clyde. A Heaven in the Eye. LC 84-6238. (Illus.). 1990. reprint ed. pap. 10.95 (0-932576-84-2) Breitenbush Bks.
— Night Freight. LC 87-808. 144p. 1987. 17.95 (0-932576-50-8); pap. 7.95 (0-932576-57-5) Breitenbush Bks.
— Nordi's Gift. LC 90-1948. 460p. 1990. 21.95 (0-932576-77-X) Breitenbush Bks.

Rice, Colin, jt. auth. see Addleson, Lyall.

Rice, Condoleezza. The Soviet Union & the Czechoslovak Army, 1948-1983. LC 84-42566. 280p. 1984. text ed. 47.50x (0-691-06921-2) Princeton U Pr.
— The Soviet Union & the Czechoslovak Army, 1948-1983: Uncertain Allegiance. LC 84-42566. Date not set. reprint ed. pap. 90.70 (0-7837-9432-0, 2060174) Bks Demand.

Rice, Condoleezza, jt. auth. see Zelikow, Philip D.

Rice, Craig. The Big Midget Murders. 365p. pap. 6.95 (1-55882-112-0) Intl Polygonics.
— The Corpse Steps Out. LC 89-85720. 186p. 1989. reprint ed. pap. 7.95 (1-55882-022-1, Lib Crime Classics) Intl Polygonics.
— The Double Frame. 224p. 1992. reprint ed. 16.50 (0-86220-836-X, Black Dagger) Chivers N Amer.

R

An Asterisk (*) at the beginning of an entry indicates that the title is appearing in BIP for the first time.

— Eight Faces at Three. 256p. 1989. reprint ed. pap. 5.95 (1-55882-007-8, Lib Crime Classics) Intl Polygonics.
— Having Wonderful Crime. LC 92-70421. 310p. 1992. reprint ed. pap. 6.95 (1-55882-125-2, Lib Crime Classics) Intl Polygonics.
— Lucky Stiff. Date not set. pap. 6.95 (1-55882-136-8) Intl Polygonics.
— Marketing Planning Strategies: A Guide for the Small or Medium-Sized Company. 300p. 1984. 91.50 (0-85013-146-4) Dartnell Corp.
— The Right Murder. LC 90-84276. 311p. 1990. reprint ed. pap. 8.95 (1-55882-078-7) Intl Polygonics.
— Strategic Planning for the Small Business: Situations, Weapons, Objectives & Tactics. 300p. 1990. pap. 10.95 (1-55850-858-9) Adams Pubng.
— Trial by Fury. LC 91-70598. 255p. 1991. pap. 5.95 (1-55882-091-4, Lib Crime Classics) Intl Polygonics.
— The Wrong Murder. LC 90-80762. 311p. 1990. reprint ed. pap. 7.95 (1-55882-067-1) Intl Polygonics.
Rice, Craig, jt. auth. see Palmer, Stuart.
Rice, Craig S. Marketing Without a Marketing Budget. (Illus.). 320p. 1989. pap. 9.95 (1-55850-986-0) Adams Pubng.
Rice, Cy, jt. auth. see Wander, Chester.
Rice, D., jt. auth. see Bragger, J.
Rice, D. D. & Gluskoter, H. J. Economic Geology: U. S. Taylor, R. B. et al, eds. (DNAG, Geology of North America Ser.: Vol. P2). (Illus.). 630p. 1991. 80.00 (0-8137-5214-0) Geol Soc.
Rice, D. D., jt. ed. see Law, B. E.
Rice, D. S. The Wade Cup in the Cleveland Museum of Art. (Islamic Art Reprint Ser.: No. 2). (Illus.). 64p. (C). 1988. reprint ed. lib. bdg. 15.00 (0-939214-57-1) Mazda Pubs.
***Rice, Dale.** The Salivary Glands: Radiology, Surgery, Pathology, 2. Hanafee & Ward, eds. LC 94-30197. (Clinical Correlations in the Head & Neck Ser.: Vol. 2). (Illus.). 59p. 1994. 59.00 (0-86577-364-5) Thieme Med Pubs.
***Rice, Dale H. & Becker, Terry S.** The Salivary Glands: Radiology, Surgery, Pathology. (Clinical Correlations in the Head & Neck Ser.: Vol. 2). 1994. write for info. (3-13-755601-5) Thieme Med Pubs.
Rice, Dale H. & Schaefer, Steven D. Endoscopic Paranasal Sinus Surgery. 2nd ed. LC 92-17094. 272p. 1993. 126.00 (0-88167-946-1) Raven.
Rice, Dale W. & Wolman, Alan A. The Life History & Ecology of the Gray Whale (Eschrichteus Robustus) (ASM Special Publication Ser.: No 3). (Illus.). viii, 142p. 1971. pap. 6.00 (0-943612-02-0) Am Soc Mammalogists.
***Rice, Dan.** Bengal Cats: Everything about Purchase, Care, Nutrition, Breeding, Diseases, & Behavior. (Complete Pet Owner's Manual Ser.). (Illus.). 1995. write for info. (0-8120-9243-0) Barron.
Rice, Daniel F. Reinhold Niebuhr & John Dewey: An American Odyssey. LC 92-4270. (Illus.). 358p. 1993. 59.50 (0-7914-1345-4); pap. 19.95 (0-7914-1346-2) State U NY Pr.
Rice, Daniel M., ed. see Taylor, Phyllis.
Rice, Daniel R. The Clifford Years: The University of North Dakota, 1971-1992. (Illus.). 224p. 1992. pap. 10.00 (0-9608700-9-1) U NDak Pres.
Rice, Darcy. Island Secrets. 224p. (Orig.). 1991. pap. 2.95 (1-878702-71-8, Kismet) Meteor Pub.
— Love with Interest. 224p. (Orig.). 1991. pap. 2.75 (1-878702-24-6, Kismet) Meteor Pub.
***Rice, David.** Blood Guilt. 247p. 1995. pap. 12.95 (0-85640-531-0) Dufour.
— Give the Pig a Chance & Other Stories. 1995. pap. 9.00 (0-927534-54-1) Biling Rev-Pr.
— Shattered Vows: Priests Who Leave. LC 91-29569. 288p. 1992. pap. 9.95 (0-89243-507-0, Triumph Books) Liguori Pubns.
— Slavery Inconsistent with Justice & Good Policy. LC 70-82216. (Anti-Slavery Crusade in America Ser.). 1970. reprint ed. 11.95 (0-405-00655-1) Ayer.
Rice, David G. Dual-Career Marriage: Conflict & Treatment. LC 79-7179. 1979. text ed. 22.95 (0-02-926380-8) Free Pr.
Rice, David G. & Stambaugh, John E. Sources for the Study of Greek Religion. LC 79-18389. (Society of Biblical Literature Sources for Biblical Study Ser.: No. 14). 1979. pap. 14.95 (0-89130-347-2, 060314) Scholars Pr GA.
Rice, David G., jt. auth. see Rice, Joy K.
Rice, David L. Lock This Man Up. LC 77-91707. 67p. 1978. per. 3.50 (0-916418-14-6) Lotus.
Rice, David T. Art of the Byzantine Era. (World of Art Ser.). (Illus.). 288p. 1985. pap. 12.95 (0-500-20004-1) Thames Hudson.
— Islamic Painting. 185p. 1972. 15.00 (0-85224-112-7, Pub. by Edinburgh U Pr UK) Col U Pr.
Rice, Denis T. & Ortmeyer, Charles P. Securities Regulation Forms, 3 vols., Set. LC 88-17561. 1988. ring bd. 395.00 (0-87632-606-8) Clark Boardman Callaghan.
— Securities Regulation Forms, 3 vols., Set with forms on disk. (Securities Law Ser.). 1988. disk 495.00 (0-614-07308-1) Clark Boardman Callaghan.
Rice, Dennis G. English Porcelain Animals of the Nineteenth Century. (Illus.). 282p. 1989. 49.50 (1-85149-085-X) Antique Collect.
Rice, Dolores B., ed. see Council on Tall Buildings & Urban Habitats Staff.
Rice, Don, ed. Famous Nineteenth Century Faces. LC 91-70263. 128p. 1991. text ed. 12.50 (0-88108-082-9) Art Dir.
— The New Testament: A Pictorial Archive from Nineteenth-Century Sources. (Pictorial Archive Ser.). (Illus.). 192p. (Orig.). 1986. pap. 7.95 (0-486-25073-3) Dover.
***Rice, Don A.** Challenges Facing Distributors. 180p. 1994. pap. 31.00 (1-881154-11-4) Darco Pr.
— The Electrical Distributor: Purpose & Function. 224p. 1988. pap. 22.00 (1-881154-03-3) Darco Pr.
— Financial Transactions of the Wholesale Distributor. 146p. (C). 1994. reprint ed. pap. 21.00 (1-881154-04-1) Darco Pr.
— The Guidebook to Service Quality. 264p. 1993. pap. 20.00 (1-881154-25-4) Darco Pr.
— Planning & Managing for Greater Profit. 65p. 1989. teacher ed, pap. 14.00 (1-881154-08-4); student ed, pap. 14.00 (1-881154-09-2) Darco Pr.
— Planning & Managing for Greater Profit, No. 1 & 2. 1989. pap., vhs 300.00 (1-881154-07-6) Darco Pr.
— The Wholesale Distributor: Purpose & Function. 246p. 1990. pap. 19.00 (1-881154-01-7) Darco Pr.
Rice, Don A. & Rice, Sara V. Financial Freedom: How to Attain It. 166p. 1991. pap. 10.00 (1-881154-15-7) Darco Pr.
Rice, Don S., ed. Latin American Horizons: A Symposium at Dumbarton Oaks, 11th & 12th October, 1986. LC 92-14833. (Illus.). 382p. 1993. 30.00 (0-88402-207-2, RIHO, Dumbarton Rsch Lib) Dumbarton Oaks.
Rice, Don S., jt. ed. see Culbert, T. Patrick.
Rice, Don S., jt. ed. see Hanks, William F.
***Rice, Dona & La Bounty, Blanca.** Theme of the Month. 1995. pap. text ed. 14.95 (1-55734-509-0) Tchr Create Mat.
Rice, Donald. Asset Financial Set. 1990. 145.00 (0-316-74311-9) Little.
Rice, Donald & Schofer, Peter. Rhetorical Poetics: Theory & Practice of Figural & Symbolic Reading in Modern French Literature. LC 83-47768. 256p. 1983. text ed. 22.50 (0-299-09440-5) U of Wis Pr.
Rice, Donald, jt. auth. see Balas, Robert S.
Rice, Donald, jt. auth. see Bragger, Jeannette.
Rice, Donald E. The Rhetorical Uses of the Authorizing Figure: Fidel Castro & Jose Marti. LC 91-35027. 192p. 1992. text ed. 45.00 (0-275-94214-7, C4214, Praeger Pubs) Greenwood.
Rice, Donald E. & Fisher, Joseph. Selected Experiments in College Chemistry: Some Basic Concepts & Techniques. 288p. 1992. spiral bd. 19.96 (0-8403-7907-2) Kendall-Hunt.
Rice, Donald L., ed. The Agitator: A Collection of Diverse Opinions from America's Not So Popular Press. LC 74-178271. (Schism Anthology Ser.). 462p. reprint ed. pap. 131.70 (0-8357-5261-5, 2024188) Bks Demand.
Rice, Dorothy. Los Angeles with Love. (Illus.). 100p. (Orig.). 1984. pap. text ed. write for info. (0-918269-00-8) Glen Hse.
Rice, Dorothy, illus. & text. Israel with Love. LC 92-10106. 144p. 1992. 45.00 (0-918269-01-6) Glen Hse.
Rice, Dorothy P. Economic Costs of Alcohol & Drug Abuse in Mental Illness, 1985. (Illus.). 310p. 1990. per. 15.00 (0-16-025326-8, S/N 017-024-01413-2) USGPO.
Rice, Dudley D., ed. Oil & Gas Assessment: Methods & Applications. LC 86-14158. (AAPG Studies in Geology: No. 21). (Illus.). 275p. reprint ed. pap. 78.40 (0-7837-2598-1, 2042762) Bks Demand.
Rice, Dudley D. & Gautier, Donald L. Patterns of Sedimentation, Diagenesis, & Hydrocarbon Accumulation in Cretaceous Rocks of the Rocky Mountains. (Short Course Notes Ser.: No. 11). 310p. 1983. pap. 28.00 (0-918985-21-8) SEPM.
Rice, Dudley D., jt. auth. see Cappa, James A.
Rice, E. Lee, jt. auth. see Tver, David F.
Rice, E. P. A History of Kannada Literature. (Illus.). 128p. 1986. reprint ed. 14.00 (0-8364-1701-1, Pub. by Manohar II) S Asia.
***Rice, Earle, Jr.** The Battle of Britain. LC 95-16224. (Battles of World War II Ser.). (J). 1995. lib. bdg. write for info. (1-56006-414-5) Lucent Bks.
— The Battle of Midway. LC 95-12206. (Battles of World War II Ser.). (J). 1996. lib. bdg. write for info. (1-56006-415-3) Lucent Bks.
— The Cuban Revolution. (World History Ser.). (Illus.). 128p. (J). (gr. 5-9). 1995. lib. bdg. 16.95 (1-56006-275-4, 2754) Lucent Bks.
***Rice, Earle.** The Inchon Invasion. LC 95-11698. (Battles of the Twentieth Century Ser.). (J). 1996. lib. bdg. write for info. (1-56006-418-8) Lucent Bks.
Rice, Edward. Captain Sir Richard Francis Burton: The Secret Agent Who Made the Pilgrimage to Mecca, Discovered the Kama Sutra, & Brought the Arabian Nights to the West. 512p. 1990. text ed. 35.00 (0-684-19137-7, Scribners) S&S Trade.
— The Man in the Sycamore Tree: The Good Life & Hard Times of Thomas Merton. LC 84-22490. (Illus.). 192p. 1985. pap. 6.95 (0-15-656960-4, Harvest Bks) HarBrace.
Rice, Edward E. Mao's Way. LC 70-186116. (Center for Chinese Studies, UC Berkeley: No. 7). 600p. 1972. pap. 12.00 (0-520-02623-3) U CA Pr.
— Wars of the Third Kind: Conflict in Underdeveloped Countries. 186p. 1988. pap. 14.00 (0-520-07195-6) U CA Pr.
Rice, Edwin W. Sunday-School Movement, 1780-1917, & the American Sunday-School Union, 1817-1917. LC 70-165728. (American Education Ser., No. 2). (Illus.). 1977. reprint ed. 39.95 (0-405-03717-1) Ayer.
Rice, Ellen, ed. Revolution & Counter-Revolution. (Wolfson College Lectures). 240p. (C). 1991. text ed. 44.95 (0-631-17816-3) Blackwell Pubs.
Rice, Elmer. Court of Last Resort. (Lost Play Ser.). 1985. pap. 3.95 (0-912262-87-7) Proscenium.
— Dream Girl. 1950. pap. 4.75 (0-8222-0332-4) Dramatists Play.
— The Grand Tour: Manuscript Edition. 1952. pap. 13.00 (0-8222-0474-6) Dramatists Play.
— The Living Theatre. LC 71-138129. 306p. 1972. reprint ed. text ed. 55.00 (0-8371-4688-7, RILT, Greenwood Pr) Greenwood.
— The Winner. 1954. pap. 4.75 (0-8222-1263-3) Dramatists Play.
Rice, Elroy L. Allelopathy (Monograph) 2nd ed. LC 83-11782. (Physiological Ecology Ser.). 1983. text ed. 127.00 (0-12-587055-8) Acad Pr.
— Biological Control of Weeds & Plant Diseases: Advances in Applied Allelopathy. LC 94-23242. (Illus.). 439p. 1995. 55.00x (0-8061-2698-1) U of Okla Pr.
— Pest Control with Nature's Chemicals: Allelochemics & Pheromones in Gardening & Agriculture. LC 83-47838. (Illus.). 240p. 1983. 34.95 (0-8061-1853-9) U of Okla Pr.
Rice, Emanuel. Freud & Moses: The Long Journey Home. LC 89-77695. 266p. 1990. 64.50 (0-7914-0453-6); pap. 21.95 (0-7914-0454-4) State U NY Pr.
Rice, Emma. High Altitude Baking & Cooking. 1979. pap. 5.00 (0-936204-01-X) Jelm Mtn.
Rice, Eugene F., Jr. The Prefatory Epistles of Jacques Lefevre d'Etaples & Related Texts. LC 71-123577. 480p. (C). 1972. text ed. 74.00 (0-231-03163-7) Col U Pr.
— The Renaissance Idea of Wisdom. LC 72-12117. (Illus.). 220p. 1973. reprint ed. text ed. 35.00 (0-8371-6712-4, RIRI, Greenwood Pr) Greenwood.
— Saint Jerome in the Renaissance. LC 84-21324. (Symposia in Comparative History Ser.: No. 13). (Illus.). 304p. 1988. reprint ed. pap. text ed. 14.95 (0-8018-3747-2) Johns Hopkins.
Rice, Eugene F., Jr. & Grafton, Anthony. The Foundation of Early Modern Europe, 1460-1559. 2nd ed. LC 93-11535. (C). 1994. pap. text ed. 11.95 (0-393-96304-7) Norton.
Rice, Eugene F., Jr., jt. auth. see Mommsen, Theodor.
Rice-Evans, Catherine A. & Burdon, Roy H., eds. Free Radical Damage & Its Control. LC 93-40154. 1994. write for info. (0-444-89716-X) Elsevier.
Rice, Eve. Aren't You Coming Too? LC 86-33506. (Illus.). 32p. (J). (ps-3). 1988. 11.95 (0-688-06446-9); lib. bdg. 11.88 (0-688-06447-7) Greenwillow.
— At Grammy's House. LC 89-34617. (Illus.). 32p. (J). (ps up). 1990. 12.95 (0-688-08874-0); lib. bdg. 12.88 (0-688-08875-9) Greenwillow.
— Benny Bakes a Cake. LC 80-17313. (Illus.). 32p. (J). (gr. k-3). 1981. write for info. (0-688-80312-1); lib. bdg. write for info. (0-688-84312-3) Greenwillow.
— Benny Bakes a Cake. LC 80-17313. 32p. (J). (ps-3). 1993. 14.00 (0-688-11579-9); lib. bdg. 13.93 (0-688-11580-2) Greenwillow.
— Benny Bakes a Cake. LC 92-33053. (Illus.). 32p. (J). (ps up). 1993. pap. 4.95 (0-688-07814-1, Mulberry) Morrow.
— City Night. (Illus.). 24p. (J). (ps-1). 1987. 11.75 (0-688-06856-1); lib. bdg. 11.88 (0-688-06857-X) Greenwillow.
— Goodnight, Goodnight. LC 79-17253. (Illus.). (J). (ps-1). 1980. 13.95 (0-688-80254-0); lib. bdg. 13.88 (0-688-84254-2) Greenwillow.
— Goodnight, Goodnight. ALC Staff, ed. LC 79-17253. (Illus.). 32p. (J). (ps up). 1992. pap. 3.95 (0-688-11707-4, Mulberry) Morrow.
— Oh, Lewis! LC 92-24584. (Illus.). 32p. (J). (ps up). 1993. pap. 4.95 (0-688-11790-2, Mulberry) Morrow.
— Once in a Wood. LC 78-16294. (Illus.). 64p. (J). 1979. lib. bdg. 13.93 (0-688-84191-0) Greenwillow.
— Peter's Pockets. LC 87-15640. (Illus.). 32p. (J). (ps up). 1989. 16.95 (0-688-07241-0); lib. bdg. 14.88 (0-688-07242-9) Greenwillow.
— Sam Who Never Forgets. LC 76-30370. 32p. (J). (ps-3). 1977. lib. bdg. 13.88 (0-688-84088-4) Greenwillow.
— Sam Who Never Forgets. LC 76-30370. (Illus.). 32p. (J). (ps up). 1987. pap. 3.95 (0-688-07335-2, Mulberry) Morrow.
— What Sadie Sang. (J). (ps). 1983. 11.95 (0-688-02179-4) Greenwillow.
Rice, Eve, illus. & adapt. Once in a Wood: Ten Tales from Aesop. LC 92-24605. 64p. (J). (gr. 1 up). 1993. reprint ed. pap. 4.95 (0-688-12268-X, Mulberry) Morrow.
Rice, F. Philip. The Adolescent: Development, Relationships & Culture. 6th ed. 650p. 1989. text ed. 45.00 (0-205-12310-4, H23104) Allyn.
— The Adolescent: Development, Relationships, & Culture. 7th ed. LC 92-37109. 1992. text ed. write for info. (0-205-14125-0) Allyn.
— The Adolescent: Development, Relationships & Culture. 8th ed. 1995. text ed. 55.00 (0-205-18444-8, H84445) Allyn.
— Adult Development & Aging. 411p. 1985. teacher ed write for info. (0-318-61421-9) Allyn.
— Human Development: A Life Span Approach. (Illus.). 608p. (C). 1992. text ed. write for info. (0-02-399765-6); write for info. (0-318-69919-2) Macmillan.
— Human Development: A Lifespan Approach. 2nd ed. (Illus.). 680p. (C). 1994. text ed. write for info. (0-02-399772-9) Macmillan.
— Instructor's Manual for Intimate Relationships, Marriages, & Families. 2nd ed. (C). 1993. teacher ed, text ed. write for info. (1-55934-236-6) Mayfield Pub.
— Intimate Relationships, Marriages & Families. 2nd ed. LC 92-17315. 598p. (C). 1993. text ed. 49.95 (1-55934-084-3); student ed, pap. text ed. 15.95 (1-55934-221-8) Mayfield Pub.
Rice, Ferill J. & McMichael, LaVeria, eds. Caught in the Butterfly Net. 140p. 1992. pap. 19.95 (0-9632974-0-6) Fenton Art Glass.
Rice, Frances, jt. auth. see Rice, Wallace.
Rice, Frank A. Eastern Arabia: An Introduction to the Spoken Arabic of Palestine, Syria & Lebanon. 1953. pap. 20.00 (0-86685-049-X); audio 95.00 (0-685-02570-5) Intl Bk Ctr.
— Mines of Ouray (Colorado) County. rev. ed. Benham, Jack L., ed. (Illus.). 56p. (Orig.). 1980. reprint ed. pap. 3.50 (0-941026-05-1) Bear Creek Pub.
Rice, Frank A. & Sa'id, Majed. Eastern Arabic. LC 79-22782. 400p. 1979. pap. 14.95 (0-87840-021-4) Georgetown U Pr.
Rice, Frank A. & Sa'id, Majed F. Arabic: Eastern. 400p. 1979. audio 175.00 (0-88432-201-7, AFA450); 19.95 (0-685-73880-9) Audio-Forum.
Rice, Freddie. Fly Tying Illustrated: Salmon & Sea Trout Patterns. (Illus.). 160p. 1991. 45.00 (0-7134-6092-X, Pub. by Batsford UK) Trafalgar.
— Fly Tying Illustrated: Salmon & Sea Trout Patterns. (Illus.). 160p. 1992. pap. 24.95 (0-7134-6093-8, Pub. by Batsford UK) Trafalgar.
— Tying Trout Flies: Nymphs, Lures & Buzzers. (Illus.). 104p. 1994. 34.95 (0-7134-6582-4, Pub. by Batsford UK) Trafalgar.
***Rice, G. Wesley.** Pecans--A Grower's Perspective: Popular Varieties, Propagation, Culture, & More. (Illus.). 198p. 1994. 57.50 (0-614-00615-5); pap. 39.50 (0-89745-995-4) Sunflower U Pr.
Rice, Gene. One Kings: Nations under God. Holmgren, Fredrick C. & Knight, George A., eds. (International Theological Commentary Ser.). 192p. (Orig.). 1990. pap. 10.99 (0-8028-0492-6) Eerdmans.
Rice, Geoffrey W., ed. The Oxford History of New Zealand. 2nd ed. (Illus.). 776p. 1993. pap. 32.00 (0-19-558257-8) OUP.
Rice, George. How to Deal with Grief. (Christian Living Ser.). 39p. 1988. pap. 2.50 (0-8341-1251-5) Beacon Hill.
— My Adventures with Your Money. (Illus.). 332p. 1986. 25.00 (0-913814-75-X) Nevada Pubns.
Rice, George A., comp. Vital Records of Pepperell, Massachusetts, to the Year 1850. LC 84-16660. 323p. 1985. 20.00 (0-88082-008-X) New Eng Hist.
Rice, George G. My Adventures with Your Money. 1975. 10.00 (0-685-54481-8) Bookfinger.
Rice, George W. Hymns from a Woman's Heart. 55p. (Orig.). 1993. pap. 2.10 (0-8341-1461-5, 55707) Beacon Hill.
— Mary: A Mother Highly Favored. 56p. 1994. pap. 2.25 (0-8341-1524-7) Beacon Hill.
— Monica: A Prodigal's Praying Mother. 48p. 1989. pap. 1.95 (0-8341-1286-8) Beacon Hill.
— A Preacher Named Emma. 64p. Date not set. pap. 2.25 (0-8341-1564-6) Beacon Hill.
— Shipping Days of Old Boothbay (Maine) LC 84-61955. (Illus.). 463p. 1984. reprint ed. 45.00 (0-89725-054-0) Picton Pr.
Rice, Graham. Bedding Plants. (Royal Horticultural Society - Wisley Handbooks Ser.). (Illus.). 64p. 1993. pap. 5.95 (0-304-32025-0, Pub. by Cassell UK) Sterling.
— The Complete Book of Perennials. LC 95-13645. 1996. write for info. (0-89577-825-4) RD Assn.
— Hardy Perennials. (Illus.). 209p. 1995. 27.95 (0-88192-338-9) Timber.
— Plants for Problem Places. (Illus.). 184p. 1995. pap. 19.95 (0-88192-314-1) Timber.
***Rice, Graham & Sanecki, Kay N.** Gardening with Flowers. (Wisley Gardening Companion Ser.). (Illus.). 192p. 1995. 19.95 (0-304-34410-9, Pub. by Cassell UK) Sterling.
Rice, Graham & Strangman, Elizabeth. The Gardener's Guide to Growing Hellebores. (Illus.). 160p. 1993. 29.95 (0-88192-266-8) Timber.
Rice, Graham, jt. auth. see Lloyd, Christopher.
Rice, Grantland. The Duffer's Handbook of Golf. rev. ed. (Illus.). 165p. 1989. reprint ed. text ed. 28.00 (0-685-23291-3) Classics Golf.
Rice, Gregory E. & Brennecke, Shaun P., eds. Molecular Aspects of Placental & Fetal Autacoids. LC 92-48814. 1993. 219.00 (0-8493-6239-3, QP281) CRC Pr.
Rice, Harold S. & Knight, Raymond M. Technical Mathematics. 3rd ed. 1972. text ed. 35.95 (0-07-052200-6) McGraw.
— Technical Mathematics with Calculus. 3rd ed. (Illus.). 704p. (C). 1974. text ed. 42.95 (0-07-052205-7) McGraw.
Rice, Helen S. Always a Springtime. (Illus.). 96p. 1987. 13.99 (0-8007-1556-X) Revell.
— Blossoms of Friendship: Celebrate the Joy of Friendship with This Gift of Verse & Watercolors. LC 91-41049. 1992. 13.99 (0-8007-1664-7) Revell.
— A Book of Blessings. 2nd ed. (Illus.). 96p. 1995. text ed. 13.99 (0-8007-1714-7) Revell.
— A Book of Comfort: Deep Valleys & Still Waters. LC 93-38026. (Illus.). 96p. 1994. 13.99 (0-8007-1700-7) Revell.
— A Book of Prayer. (Illus.). 96p. 1995. 13.99 (0-8007-1707-4) Revell.
— A Book of Thanks. LC 93-3967. (Illus.). 96p. 1993. 13.99 (0-8007-1695-7) Revell.
— Celebrations of the Heart. LC 87-16272. (Illus.). 128p. 1987. 16.99 (0-8007-1553-5) Revell.
— Christmas Blessings. (Illus.). 128p. 1991. 16.99 (0-8007-1656-6) Revell.
— Daily Bouquets. 1990. 13.99 (0-8007-1637-X) Revell.
— Daily Pathways. 96p. 1989. 13.99 (0-8007-1625-6) Revell.
— Daily Reflections. 1990. 13.99 (0-8007-1642-6) Revell.
— Daily Steppingstones. LC 89-32210. 1989. 13.99 (0-8007-1616-7) Revell.
— Everyone Needs Someone: Poems of Love & Friendship. LC 78-11999. 80p. 1973. 13.99 (0-8007-1555-1) Revell.
— For Each New Day. abr. ed. (Illus.). 92p. 1995. 4.99 (0-8007-7143-5) Revell.
— From the Heart: A Daily Inspirational Calendar. (Illus.). 182p. 1993. pap. 9.99 (0-8007-7500-7) Revell.
— Gifts of Love. Ruehlmann, Virginia, ed. LC 92-23413. (Illus.). 96p. 1993. 13.99 (0-8007-1677-9) Revell.
— God Bless America. 128p. 1991. 16.99 (0-8007-1652-3) Revell.
— Heart Gifts. 2nd ed. LC 68-28438. (Illus.). 128p. 1988. 13.99 (0-8007-1520-9) Revell.

— Helen Steiner Rice New Testament & Psalms. (Illus.). 560p. 1994. 17.99 (0-8007-1703-1) Revell.

— Inspiration for Living. abr. ed. (Illus.). 92p. 1995. 4.99 (0-8007-7142-7) Revell.

— Joy for the Heart. LC 92-12413. 1992. 13.99 (0-8007-1674-4) Revell.

— Loving Promises. (Illus.). 128p. 1975. 13.95 (0-8007-0736-2) Revell.

— Loving Promises. (Illus.). 1988. 16.99 (0-8007-1600-0) Revell.

— Loving Promises. large type ed. (Illus.). 176p. 1975. 13.95 (0-8007-1333-8) Revell.

— Lovingly. LC 77-123061. 1987. 13.99 (0-8007-1521-7) Revell.

— A New Beginning. abr. ed. (Illus.). 92p. 1995. 4.99 (0-8007-7141-9) Revell.

— Poems of Faith. 1984. 14.95 (0-89952-086-3) Littlebrook.

— Precious Moments Caring Angels. Ruehlmann, Virginia, ed. LC 94-17006. (Illus.). 64p. 1994. 9.99 (0-8007-7139-7) Revell.

— Precious Moments Christmas Angels. Ruehlmann, Virginia, ed. LC 94-17018. (Illus.). 64p. 1994. 9.99 (0-8007-7140-0) Revell.

— Precious Moments of Inspiration. LC 93-12072. (Illus.). 64p. 1993. 11.99 (0-8007-1692-2) Revell.

— Precious Moments of Praise. LC 93-12070. (Illus.). 64p. 1993. 11.99 (0-8007-1693-0) Revell.

— The Priceless Gift of Christmas. 1990. 14.95 (0-89952-060-X) Littlebrook.

— Showers of Blessings. 1988. 13.99 (0-8007-1567-5) Revell.

— Somebody Loves You. LC 76-25559. (Illus.). 1988. 16.99 (0-8007-1601-9) Revell.

— Somebody Loves You. large type ed. (Illus.). 128p. 1992. 16.99 (0-8007-1670-1) Revell.

— Someone Cares: The Collected Poems of Helen Steiner Rice. LC 75-186538. 128p. 1972. 16.99 (0-8007-0524-6) Revell.

— The Story of the Christmas Guest. (Illus.). 34p. (J). 1991. reprint ed. pap. 9.95 (0-89966-842-9) Buccaneer Bks.

— Sunshine of Joy. 1988. 13.99 (0-8007-1568-3) Revell.

— Time for Reflection. abr. ed. (Illus.). 92p. 1995. 4.99 (0-8007-7144-3) Revell.

— To Mother with Love. large type ed. 1995. pap. 12.95 (0-8027-2690-9) Walker & Co.

— Wings of Encouragement. (Illus.). 96p. 1995. 15.99 (0-8007-1704-X) Revell.

Rice, Helen Steiner. Precious Moments of Meditation. Ruehlmann, Virginia J., ed. LC 93-6576. (Illus.). 64p. 1993. 11.99 (0-8007-1694-9) Revell.

— To Mother with Love. 1991. 13.99 (0-8007-1649-3) Revell.

Rice, Helen Steiner & Allen, Charles L. When You Lose a Loved One: Life Is Forever. LC 59-5995. 128p. 1979. pap. 6.99 (0-8007-5031-4) Revell.

Rice, Helen Steiner & Ruehlman, Virginia J. Daily Reflections. braille ed. 109p. 1992. vinyl bd. 8.72 (1-56956-050-1, BR8872) W A T Braille.

***Rice, Herbert W.** Toni Morrison & the American Tradition: A Rhetorical Reading. LC 94-34714. (American University Studies, Ser. 24, American Literature: Vol. 60). 1995. write for info. (0-8204-2679-2) P Lang Pubs.

Rice, Howard C., Jr. New Jersey Road Maps of the Eighteenth Century. (Illus.). 42p. 1981. pap. 10.00 (0-87811-024-0) Princeton Lib.

Rice, Howard C. Rudyard Kipling in New England. LC 72-6747. (English Biography Ser.: No. 31). 39p. 1972. reprint ed. lib. bdg. 50.95 (0-8383-1635-2) M S G Haskell Hse.

— Thomas Jefferson's Paris. LC 75-30203. (Illus.). 168p. reprint ed. pap. 47.90 (0-8357-3569-9, 2034649) Bks Demand.

Rice, Howard C., Jr. Thomas Jefferson's Paris. (Illus.). 166p. 1991. pap. text ed. 16.95 (0-691-00776-4) Princeton U Pr.

Rice, Howard C. & Brown, Anne S., eds. The American Campaigns of Rochambeau's Army, 1780-1783: The Journals of Clermont-Crevecoeur, Verger & Berthier, 2 vols., Vol. I, The Journals; Vol. II, Maps & Views. LC 71-166388. 1972. 275.00x (0-691-04610-7) Princeton U Pr.

Rice, Howard L. Reformed Spirituality: An Introduction for Believers. 192p. (Orig.). 1991. pap. 14.99 (0-664-25230-3) Westminster John Knox.

Rice, J. & Boisvert, R. F. Solving Elliptic Problems Using ELLPACK. (Computational Mathematics Ser.: Vol. 2). (Illus.). 350p. 1985. 54.00 (0-387-90910-9) Spr-Verlag.

Rice, J. & DeMillo, R. A., eds. Studies in Computer Science: In Honor of Samuel D. Conte. (Software Science & Engineering Ser.). (Illus.). 170p. 1994. 69.50 (0-306-44697-9) Plenum.

Rice, J. M. Public School System of the United States. LC 77-89224. (American Education: Its Men, Institutions & Ideas, Ser. 1). 1975. reprint ed. 26.95 (0-405-01461-9) Ayer.

— Scientific Management in Education. LC 70-89225. (American Education: Its Men, Institutions & Ideas, Ser. 1). 1975. reprint ed. 23.95 (0-405-01462-7) Ayer.

Rice, J. R., ed. Mathematical Aspects of Scientific Software. (IMA Volumes in Mathematics & Its Applications Ser.: Vol. 14). (Illus.). xi, 208p. 1988. 30.00 (0-387-96706-0) Spr-Verlag.

Rice, James. A Cajun Alphabet: Full-Color Edition. LC 90-39342. (Illus.). 64p. (J). (ps-8). 1991. 16.95 (0-88289-822-1) Pelican.

— Cajun Night Before Christmas Coloring Book. 32p. (J). (gr. k-4). 1976. pap. 2.75 (0-88289-138-3) Pelican.

— Christmas at the J-O. (Illus.). 32p. (J). (gr. 1-4). 1995. 14.95 (1-56554-087-5) Pelican.

— Cowboy Alphabet. 1982. pap. 10.95 (0-08-829427-7, Pergamon Pr) Elsevier.

— Cowboy Alphabet. 2nd ed. LC 88-33087. (Illus.). 40p. (gr. k-4). 1990. 14.95 (0-88289-726-8) Pelican.

— Cowboy Night Before Christmas. LC 90-7280. Orig. Title: Praire Night Before Christmas. (Illus.). 32p. (J). (ps-4). 1986. reprint ed. 12.95 (0-88289-811-6) Pelican.

— Cowboy Night Before Christmas Coloring Book. (Illus.). 32p. (Orig.). (J). (gr. 4-8). 1994. pap. 2.75 (1-56554-093-X) Pelican.

— Cowboy Rodeo. LC 91-34924. (Illus.). 32p. (J). 1992. 14.95 (0-88289-903-1) Pelican.

— Gaston Drills an Offshore Oil Well. LC 82-11240. (Gaston the Green-Nosed Alligator Ser.). (Illus.). 48p. (J). (gr. 1-6). 1982. 12.95 (0-88289-289-4) Pelican.

— Gaston Goes to Mardi Gras. LC 77-13302. (Illus.). 40p. (J). (gr. 1-6). 1977. 12.95 (0-88289-158-8) Pelican.

— Gaston Goes to Nashville. LC 85-6605. (Gaston the Green-Nosed Alligator Ser.). (Illus.). 32p. (J). (gr. 1-6). 1985. 12.95 (0-88289-477-3) Pelican.

— Gaston Goes to Texas. LC 78-12490. (Illus.). 32p. (J). (gr. 1-6). 1978. 12.95 (0-88289-204-5) Pelican.

— Gaston Goes to the Kentucky Derby. LC 94-2196. (Illus.). 32p. (J). (gr. 1-6). 1994. 14.95 (1-56554-065-4) Pelican.

— Gaston Lays an Offshore Pipeline. LC 79-20335. (Illus.). (J). (gr. 1-6). 1979. 12.95 (0-88289-177-4) Pelican.

— Gaston the Green-Nosed Alligator. (Illus.). 40p. (J). (gr. 1-6). 1974. 12.95 (0-88289-049-2) Pelican.

— Gaston the Green-Nosed Alligator Coloring Book. (Illus.). 32p. (Orig.). (J). (gr. 1-6). 1976. pap. 2.75 (0-88289-139-1) Pelican.

— Lyn & the Fuzzy. LC 75-19096. (Illus.). 40p. (J). (gr. 2-6). 1975. 12.95 (0-88289-087-5) Pelican.

— La Nochebuena South of the Border. Smith, Ana, tr. LC 93-13002. (Illus.). 32p. (ENG & SPA.). (J). (gr. k-3). 1993. 14.95 (0-88289-966-X) Pelican.

Rice, James, Jr. Teaching Library Use: A Guide for Library Instruction. LC 80-21337. (Contributions in Librarianship & Information Science Ser.: No. 37). (Illus.). 216p. 1981. text ed. 45.00 (0-313-21485-9, RTL/, Greenwood Pr) Greenwood.

Rice, James. Texas Alphabet. LC 87-31159. (Illus.). 132p. (J). (gr. k-5). 1988. 12.95 (0-88289-692-X) Pelican.

— Texas Jack at the Alamo. LC 88-31691. (Illus.). 40p. (J). 1989. 12.95 (0-88289-725-X) Pelican.

— Texas Night Before Christmas. LC 86-9445. (Illus.). 32p. (J). (gr. 1-6). 1986. 12.95 (0-88289-603-2) Pelican.

— Texas Night Before Christmas: Coloring Book. (Illus.). (J). 1989. pap. 2.75 (0-88289-727-6) Pelican.

Rice, James, illus. Cowboy Alphabet. 40p. (J). (gr. k-4). 1983. 11.95 (0-88289-427-7) Pelican.

Rice, James L. Freud's Russia: National Identity in the Evolution of Psychoanalysis. LC 92-31244. 210p. (C). 1993. text ed. 34.95 (1-56000-091-0) Transaction Pubs.

Rice, James O., jt. auth. see Rosaler, R. C.

Rice, Jane. The Key to Medical Terminology. (Illus.). 384p. 1986. pap. text ed. 21.95 (0-13-515032-9) P-H.

— Principles of Pharmacology for Medical Assisting. 2nd ed. LC 93-26739. 548p. 1994. pap. text ed. 25.95 (0-8273-5744-3) Delmar.

— Principles of Pharmacology for Medical Assisting: Instructor's Guide. 2nd ed. 89p. 1994. 12.00 (0-8273-6353-2) Delmar.

— Spellright: A Medical Word Book. 772p. (C). 1991. pap. text ed. 19.95 (0-8385-6290-6, A6290-9) Appleton & Lange.

Rice, Jane & Skelley, Esther G. Medications & Mathematics for the Nurse. 7th ed. LC 92-18283. 620p. 1993. 29.95 (0-8273-5119-4) Delmar.

— Medications & Mathematics for the Nurse: Instructor's Guide. 7th ed. 87p. 1994. 12.00 (0-8273-5120-8) Delmar.

Rice, Jayne. Bonnet House: The Life & Gift. (Illus.). 48p. (Orig.). 1990. pap. text ed. write for info. (0-9624757-1-8) Bonnet Hse.

— Reflections of a Legacy: The Bonnet House Story. Robinson, Jayne, ed. (Illus.). 152p. 1989. 35.00 (0-9624757-0-X) Bonnet Hse.

Rice, Jean & Henke, James. Friendly BASIC: Apple Version. (Illus.). 125p. 14.95 (0-317-13086-2) P-H.

— Friendly BASIC: For the Apple II, Apple IIplus, Apple IIe & Apple IIc. (C). 16.95 (0-8359-2103-4, Reston) P-H.

Rice, Jim & Hayhoe, Mike. Writing from Canada. LC 93-11687. (Figures in a Landscape Ser.). 1994. pap. write for info. (0-521-42305-8) Cambridge U Pr.

Rice, Jim, jt. auth. see Onword Press Development Staff.

Rice, Jim, jt. auth. see OnWord Press Development Team.

Rice, Joe, contrib. Metalworking: The Best of Projects in Metal 1990-1991, Bk. 2. (Illus.). 240p. (C). 1994. text ed. 32.00 (0-941653-17-X) Village Pr Pubns.

***Rice, Joe, ed. & intro.** Projects Six. (Illus.). 250p. Date not set. write for info. (0-941653-19-6) Village Pr Pubns.

Rice, Joe, jt. auth. see Allen, JoCindee.

Rice, Joe D., ed. The Best of Live Steam: Nineteen Sixty-Six to Nineteen Seventy-One, Vol. 1. LC 85-51037. (Illus.). 176p. 1985. 26.95 (0-914104-08-X) Wildwood Pubns MI.

— Projects Two. 200p. 1988. 24.95 (0-941653-01-3) Village Pr Pubns.

Rice, Joel M. Hatred for a Season. 46p. 1993. pap. 4.00 (1-883749-00-X) Dark Water.

— Questions in the Night. 158p. 1993. pap. 6.00 (1-883749-01-8) Dark Water.

Rice, John. Better Food for Hospital Patients: New Menus, Cooking, & Ward Service for Hospital Patients, 3 vols. (King Edward's Hospital Fund Ser.). 1975. 25.00 (0-8464-0191-6) Beekman Pubs.

— Mathematical Statistics & Data Analysis. LC 87-8047. 595p. (C). 1988. text ed. 63.95 (0-534-08247-5) Intl Thomson.

Rice, John, jt. auth. see Murray, Michael.

Rice, John A. Mathematical Statistics & Data Analysis. 2nd ed. 602p. 1995. text ed. 63.95 (0-534-20934-3) Intl Thomson.

Rice, John F., ed. HDTV: The Politics, Policies, & Economics of Tomorrow's Television. 250p. (Orig.). 1990. pap. text ed. 24.95 (0-941817-08-3) Union Sq Pr.

Rice, John R. Numerical Methods, Software, & Analysis. 2nd ed. (Illus.). 720p. 1992. text ed. 59.95 (0-12-587755-2) Acad Pr.

Rice, John R., jt. ed. see Houstis, Elias N.

Rice, Jonathan. Curiosities of Cricket. (Illus.). 1993. 29.95 (1-85145-929-4, Pub. by Pavilion UK) Trafalgar.

— Curiosities of Golf. (Illus.). 160p. 1995. 19.95 (1-85793-281-1, Pub. by Pavilion UK) Trafalgar.

— Encyclopedia of Antiques. 1991. 19.99 (0-517-06509-6) Random Hse Value.

— The Pavilion Book of Pavilions. (Illus.). 160p. 1992. pap. 22.95 (1-85145-873-5, Pub. by Pavilion UK) Trafalgar.

Rice, Jonathan & Ciabattoni, Francis. How to Survive & Profit from the Coming Currency Recall. LC 86-6215. 258p. 1988. 19.95 (0-945999-22-4) Independent Inst.

Rice, Jonathan, jt. auth. see Clarke, Roy.

Rice, Joseph. Irving: A Texas Odyssey-An Illustrated History. 144p. 1989. 29.95 (0-89781-300-6, 5312) Preferred Mktg.

***Rice, Joseph P.** The Gifted: Developing Total Talent. 2nd ed. (Illus.). 318p. 1985. pap. 29.95 (0-398-06347-8) C C Thomas.

— The Gifted: Developing Total Talent. 2nd ed. (Illus.). 318p. (C). 1985. 49.95 (0-398-04977-7) C C Thomas.

Rice, Josette, ed. see Elrick, Harold.

Rice, Josette, ed. see Hansen, Burdette.

Rice, Josette, jt. auth. see Knox, Dahk.

Rice, Joy K. & Rice, David G. Living Through Divorce: A Developmental Approach to Divorce Therapy. LC 85-27173. (Guilford Family Therapy Ser.). 303p. 1985. lib. bdg. 40.00 (0-89862-061-9) Guilford Pr.

***Rice, Judith A.** The Kindness Curriculum: Introducing Young Children to Loving Values. LC 95-7275. 122p. (Orig.). 1995. pap. 13.95 (1-884834-02-7) Redleaf Pr.

— Those Mean Nasty Dirty Downright Disgusting but... Invisible Germs. LC 89-34409. (Illus.). 32p. (Orig.). (J). (ps-3). 1989. pap. 7.95 (0-934140-46-4) Redleaf Pr.

Rice, Judith R. Learning Workplace Writing. LC 93-15880. 336p. 1994. pap. text ed. 32.40 (0-13-337437-8) P-H.

Rice, Julian. Black Elk's Story: Distinguishing Its Lakota Purpose. 184p. 1994. pap. 16.95 (0-8263-1497-X) U of NM Pr.

— Deer Women & Elk Men: The Lakota Narratives of Ella Deloria. LC 91-46077. 219p. 1992. 24.95x (0-8263-1362-0) U of NM Pr.

— Ella Deloria's Iron Hawk. LC 93-10515. 237p. 1993. 35.00x (0-8263-1435-X); pap. 15.95 (0-8263-1447-3) U of NM Pr.

— Lakota Storytelling: Black Elk, Ella Deloria, & Frank Fools Crow. (American University Studies: Regional Studies: Ser. XXI, Vol. 3). 252p. 1989. 36.50 (0-8204-0774-7) P Lang Pubs.

Rice, Julian, ed. Ella Deloria's The Buffalo People" LC 93-33519. 232p. 1994. 45.00x (0-8263-1506-2); pap. 22.50 (0-8263-1507-0) U of NM Pr.

Rice, June. One Writer's Voice. LC 94-60121. 250p. 1994. 15.95 (1-55523-680-4) Winston-Derek.

Rice, Keren. A Grammar of Slave. xliv, 1370p. (C). 1989. lib. bdg. 194.95 (0-89925-140-4) Mouton.

Rice, Keren, jt. ed. see Cook, Eung D.

Rice, Kym S. Early American Taverns: For the Entertainment of Friends & Strangers. (Illus.). 168p. (Orig.). 1983. text ed. 16.95 (0-9616415-0-9); pap. text ed. 12.95 (0-9616415-1-7) Fraunces Tavern.

Rice, Kym S., jt. auth. see Bernstein, Richard B.

Rice, Kym S., jt. ed. see Campbell, Edward D., Jr.

Rice, L., jt. ed. see Cope, L.

Rice, L. S., jt. auth. see Keyes, M. A.

Rice, Larry. Alaska Reflections. LC 93-11578. (Reflections of the Wilderness Ser.). (Illus.). 64p. (Orig.). 1993. pap. 11.99 (0-934802-04-1) ICS Bks.

— Baja to Patagonia: Latin American Adventures. (Illus.). 320p. (Orig.). 1993. pap. 15.95 (1-55591-113-7) Fulcrum Pub.

— Canoe Country Reflections. (Illus.). 64p. (Orig.). 1993. pap. 11.99 (0-934802-85-8) ICS Bks.

Rice, Larry M. Gathering Paradise: Alaska Wilderness Journeys. LC 89-29590. (Illus.). 303p. (Orig.). 1990. pap. 14.95 (1-55591-057-2) Fulcrum Pub.

Rice, Laura, ed. see Eberhardt, Isabelle.

Rice, Laura, tr. see Eberhardt, Isabelle.

Rice, Laura, jt. auth. see Rice, Robert P., Jr.

Rice, Laura N. & Greenberg, Leslie S., eds. Patterns of Change: Intensive Analysis of Psychotherapy Process. LC 82-15535. 308p. 1984. lib. bdg. 40.00 (0-89862-624-2) Guilford Pr.

Rice, Laura W. & Rice, Robert P., Jr. Practical Horticulture. 2nd ed. 480p. 1992. text ed. 63.00 (0-13-678806-8) P-H.

Rice, Lee M. & Vernam, Glenn R. They Saddled the West. LC 75-5734. (Illus.). 202p. reprint ed. pap. 57.60 (0-8357-4431-0, 2037262) Bks Demand.

Rice, Leland, intro. New Portfolios. (Illus.). 24p. 1976. 2.00 (0-915478-35-8) Galleries Coll.

Rice, Leland, photos. Up Against It! Photographs of the Berlin Wall. LC 91-295. (Illus.). 156p. 1991. 50.00 (0-8263-1291-8) U of NM Pr.

Rice, Leland D. & Steadman, David W., eds. Photographs of Moholy-Nagy from the William Larson Collection. 2nd ed. LC 75-4035. (Illus.). 64p. 1977. 8.50 (0-915478-08-0) Galleries Coll.

Rice, Leonard & White, Michael D. Engineering Aspects of Water Law. 216p. (C). 1991. reprint ed. lib. bdg. 44.50 (0-89464-548-X) Krieger.

Rice, Lesley O. VMS Systems Management. 352p. 1994. pap. text ed. 45.00 (0-13-948456-6) P-H.

Rice, Leslie, jt. auth. see Goodman, Nancy.

Rice, Lewis, ed. Naga Varmma's Karnataka Bhasha-Bhushana. (C). 1985. reprint ed. 12.00 (0-8364-2407-7, Pub. by Asian Educ Servs II) S Asia.

Rice-Licare, Jennifer & Delaney-McLoughlin, Katharine. Cocaine Solutions: Help for Cocaine Abusers & Their Families. LC 90-4843. (Addiction Treatment Ser.). 150p. 1990. 39.95 (1-56024-035-0); pap. text ed. 10.95 (0-918393-82-5) Haworth Pr.

Rice, Linda L. Southern Exposure. 1992. mass mkt. 4.99 (0-8041-0935-4) Ivy Books.

Rice, Louise. Soapsuds to Sunday School: A Living History of the Pioneer Housewife - In Celebration of the 1989 Washington State Centennial. (Illus.). 294p. 1993. reprint ed. pap. 14.95 (1-879354-04-7) State Assn DOTPOW.

Rice, Luanne. Blue Moon. 1994. mass mkt. 5.99 (0-553-56818-3) Bantam.

— Blue Moon. LC 92-50732. 320p. 1993. 21.00 (0-670-84301-6, Viking) Viking Penguin.

— Blue Moon. large type ed. LC 93-44120. 547p. 1994. lib. bdg. 21.95 (0-7862-0148-7) Thorndike Pr.

— Home Fires. LC 94-23911. 320p. 1995. 21.95 (0-553-09728-8) Bantam.

— Secrets of Paris. large type ed. (General Ser.). 393p. 1992. text ed. 20.95 (0-8161-5329-9) G K Hall.

Rice, Lyn P., illus. The Little Book of Famous Insults. (Gift Editions Ser.). 64p. 1993. 7.99 (0-88088-366-9) Peter Pauper.

Rice, Lynn. Our Pieceful Village. Rose, Sharon & White, Janet, eds. (Sampler Ser.). (Illus.). 48p. (Orig.). 1994. pap. 10.95 (1-56477-071-0) That Patchwork.

Rice, Lynn, ed. see Siebold, Bert A.

Rice, M. Handbook of Airfoil Sections for Light Aircraft. (Illus.). 143p. 1974. pap. 10.25 (0-87994-015-8) Aviat Pub.

Rice, M. A. & Sammes, A. J. Command & Control Support Systems in the Gulf War: Land Warfare: Brassey's Battlefield Weapons Systems & Technology. Vol. 13. 1994. 40.00 (1-85753-010-1) Macmillan.

— Command & Control Support Systems in the Gulf War: Land Warfare: Brassey's Battlefield Weapons Systems & Technology, Vol. 13. 1994. 25.00 (1-85753-015-2, Pub. by Brasseys UK) Brasseys Inc.

— Communications & Information Systems for Battlefield Command & Control. Lee, R. G. & Hartley, Frank, eds. (Brassey's Battlefield Weapons Systems & Technology Ser.: Vol. 5). 276p. 1989. 40.00 (0-08-036266-4, Pub. by Brasseys UK); 25.00 (0-08-036267-2, Pub. by Brasseys UK) Brasseys Inc.

Rice, M. E., et al. Violence in Institutions: Understanding, Prevention & Control. LC 89-11029. 304p. 1989. 39.00 (0-920887-47-3) Hogrefe & Huber Pubs.

Rice, M. S., ed. see Curtiss Aeroplane & Motor Corp.

***Rice, Mabel L., ed.** Toward a Genetics of Language. 375p. 1996. text ed. 75.00 (0-8058-1677-1); pap. 40.00 (0-8058-1678-X) L Erlbaum Assocs.

***Rice, Mabel L. & Wilcox, Kim A.** Building a Language-Focused Curriculum for the Preschool Classroom Vol. I: A Foundation for Lifelong Communication. LC 94-49085. 248p. 1995. pap. 32.00 (1-55766-177-4) P H Brookes.

Rice, Mabel L., jt. ed. see Watkins, Ruth V.

Rice, Madeleine H. Federal Street Pastor: The Life of William Ellery Channing. 16.95 (0-8084-0372-9) NCUP.

Rice, Margery S. Working Class Wives: Their Health & Conditions. (Illus.). 1990. pap. 15.95 (0-86068-153-X, Pub. by Virago Pr UK) Trafalgar.

Rice, Marian L. Herpes Genitalis: Medical Subject Analysis with Reference Bibliography. LC 88-47597. 150p. 1988. 39.50 (0-88164-508-7); pap. 34.50 (0-88164-509-5) ABBE Pubs Assn.

Rice, Marion, jt. auth. see De Vorsey, Louis, Jr.

Rice, Martha & Burns, Jane. Thinking-Writing: An Introduction to the Writing Process for Students of ESL. (Illus.). 200p. (C). 1985. pap. text ed. 18.00 (0-13-918244-6) P-H.

Rice, Martin P., tr. see Cizevskij, Dmitrij.

Rice, Mary E., jt. ed. see Harrison, Frederick W.

Rice, Mary K. Sintesis de Distancia e Immersion en Cuatro Obras de Antonio Buero Vallejo. LC 91-3802. (American University Studies: Romance Languages & Literature: Ser. II, Vol. 169). 112p. (C). 1992. text ed. 35.95 (0-8204-1555-3) P Lang Pubs.

Rice, Mary Kellogg, jt. auth. see Wada, Yoshiko.

Rice, Matthew. Traditional Houses of Rural Britain. (Illus.). 160p. 1992. 29.95 (1-55859-338-1, Cross Riv Pr) Abbeville Pr.

Rice, Max M. Your Rewards in Heaven. LC 80-68885. 160p. 1981. teacher ed 9.95 (0-685-00101-6); pap. 4.95 (0-89636-063-6) Accent CO.

Rice-Maximin, Edward. Accommodation & Resistance: The French Left, Indochina & the Cold War, 1944-1954. LC 86-4624. (Contributions to the Study of World History Ser.: No. 2). 186p. 1986. text ed. 45.00 (0-313-25355-2, RMX/, Greenwood Pr) Greenwood.

Rice-Maximin, Edward, jt. auth. see Buhle, Paul.

Rice, Melanie. The Complete Book of Children's Activities. LC 92-30859. (J). 1993. pap. 9.95 (1-85697-907-5, Kingfisher LKC) LKC.

Rice, Melanie, jt. auth. see Rice, Chris.

Rice, Melanie, jt. auth. see Rice, Christopher.

Rice, Michael. The Archaeology of the Arabian Gulf. LC 93-7006. 1994. write for info. (0-415-03268-7) Routledge.

— Egypt's Making: The Origins of Ancient Egypt 5000-2000 BC. (Illus.). 416p. 1990. 29.95 (0-415-05092-8, A4688) Routledge.

R

An Asterisk (*) at the beginning of an entry indicates that the title is appearing in BIP for the first time.

— Egypt's Making: The Origins of Ancient Egypt 5000-2000 BC. (Illus.). 320p. 1991. pap. 15.95 (*0-415-06454-6*, A5838) Routledge.
— False Inheritance: Israel in Palestine & the Search for a Solution. LC 93-28499. 232p. 1994. 34.00 (*0-7103-0473-0*, Pub. by Kegan Paul Intl UK) Routledge Chapman & Hall.
— The Golden Age of Ancient Egypt. 192p. (C). 1988. lib. bdg. 65.00 (*0-7103-0296-7*) Routledge Chapman & Hall.
— Public Television Issues of Purpose & Governance. 38p. 1981. pap. text ed. 9.50 (*0-8191-5878-X*, Aspen Inst for Humanistic Studies) U Pr of Amer.
Rice, Michael, jt. ed. see Al-Khalifa, Shaikh A.
Rice, Michael A. The Northern Quahog: The Biology of Mercenaria Mercenaria. Jaworski, Carole & Schwartz, Maria, eds. (Illus.). (Orig.). 1992. pap. text ed. write for info. (*0-938412-33-7*) Sea Grant Pubns.
Rice, Michael D. Asset Financing. 770p. 1989. 145.00 (*0-316-74313-5*) Little.
— Prentice-Hall Dictionary of Business, Finance & Law. LC 83-3022. 362p. 1983. 39.95 (*0-13-696583-0*) P-H.
Rice, Michael S., ed. see Dzik, Stanley J.
Rice, Millard M. This Was the Life - Excerpts from the Judgment Records of Frederick County, Maryland, 1748-1765. LC 79-84276. (C). 1979. 12.00 (*0-913186-08-2*) Monocacy.
— William Rice of Frederick County, Maryland, & Some of His Descendants. (Illus.). 1979. pap. 4.00 (*0-913186-09-0*) Monocacy.
Rice, Miriam C. How to Use Mushrooms for Color. rev. ed. (Illus.). 145p. 1980. pap. 14.95 (*0-916422-19-4*) Mad River.
Rice, Mitchell F. & Jones, Woodrow, Jr. Public Policy & the Black Hospital: From Slavery to Segregation to Integration. LC 93-4851. (Contributions in Afro-American & African Studies: No. 165). 176p. 1994. text ed. 49.95 (*0-313-26309-4*, RBP/, Greenwood Pr) Greenwood.
Rice, Mitchell F. & Jones, Woodrow, Jr., comps. Black American Health: An Annotated Bibliography. LC 86-25745. (Bibliographies & Indexes in Afro-American & African Studies: No. 17). 133p. 1987. text ed. 49.95 (*0-313-24887-7*, RBH/, Greenwood Pr) Greenwood.
— Health of Black Americans from Post-Reconstruction to Integration, 1871-1960: An Annotated Bibliography of Contemporary Sources. LC 89-78161. (Bibliographies & Indexes in Afro-American & African Studies: No. 26). 256p. 1990. text ed. 59.95 (*0-313-26314-0*, RHB/, Greenwood Pr) Greenwood.
Rice, Mitchell F. & Jones, Woodrow, Jr., eds. Contemporary Public Policy Perspectives & Black Americans: Issues in an Era of Retrenchment Politics. LC 84-717. (Contributions in Afro-American & African Studies: No. 77). (Illus.). xiii, 213p. 1984. text ed. 55.00 (*0-313-23711-5*, RIP/) Greenwood.
Rice, Mitchell F., jt. ed. see Jones, Woodrow, Jr.
***Rice, Molly.** Silent Masquerade. (Intrigue Ser.). 1995. pap. 3.50 (*0-373-22315-3*, 1-22315-5) Harlequin Bks.
— Unforgettable. 1995. mass mkt. 3.50 (*0-373-22348-X*) Harlequin Bks.
Rice, N. L., jt. auth. see Blanchard, Jonathan.
***Rice, Nicky.** Coming up to Midnight. 68p. 1994. pap. 14.95 (*1-870612-48-5*, Pub. by Enitha Pr UK) Dufour.
Rice, Otis K. Charleston & the Kanawha Valley (West Virginia) 136p. 1981. 19.95 (*0-89781-046-5*) Preferred Mktg.
— Frontier Kentucky. LC 93-7821. 160p. 1993. 16.00 (*0-8131-1840-9*) U Pr of Ky.
— The Hatfields & the McCoys. LC 82-1916. (Illus.). 168p. 1982. reprint ed. 18.00 (*0-8131-1459-4*) U Pr of Ky.
— West Virginia: The State & Its People. 4th ed. 1979. reprint ed. 10.00 (*0-87012-129-4*) McClain.
Rice, Otis K. & Brown, Stephen W. West Virginia: A History. 2nd ed. LC 93-17819. (Illus.). 376p. 1993. Alk. paper. 32.00 (*0-8131-1854-9*) U Pr of Ky.
Rice, P. C., ed. Teaching Anthropology. (Special Issues of the Anthropology & Education Quarterly Ser.: Vol. 16, No. 4). 1985. 7.50 (*0-317-66347-X*) Am Anthro Assn.
Rice, Pat. Love's First Surrender. 1984. pap. 3.75 (*0-8217-1328-0*) Zebra.
— Moonlight Mistress. 1985. pap. 3.95 (*0-8217-1637-9*) Zebra.
***Rice, Patricia.** Change & Conflict: Britain, Ireland & Europe from the Late 16th to the Early 18th Centuries. (Irish History in Perspective Ser.). (Illus.). 80p. 1994. pap. 10.95 (*0-521-46603-2*) Cambridge U Pr.
— Change & Conflict: Teachers Resource Book: Britain, Ireland & Europe from the Late 16th to the Early 18th Centuries. (Irish History in Perspective Ser.). (Illus.). 32p. 1995. teacher ed, pap. 10.95 (*0-521-46604-0*) Cambridge U Pr.
— Devil's Lady. 384p. (Orig.). 1992. pap. 4.99 (*0-451-40325-8*, Onyx) NAL-Dutton.
— The Genuine Article. 224p. (Orig.). 1994. pap. 3.99 (*0-451-18235-9*, Sig) NAL-Dutton.
— Indigo Moon. 416p. 1988. pap. 4.50 (*0-451-15184-4*, Sig) NAL-Dutton.
— Mad Maria's Daughter. (Signet Regency Romance Ser.). 224p. (Orig.). 1992. pap. 3.99 (*0-451-17079-2*, Sig) NAL-Dutton.
— Moon Dreams. (Historical Romance Ser.). 416p. (Orig.). 1991. pap. 4.95 (*0-451-40232-4*, Onyx) NAL-Dutton.
— Moonlight & Memories. 384p. (Orig.). 1993. pap. 4.99 (*0-451-40411-4*, Topaz) NAL-Dutton.
— Paper Roses. 384p. (Orig.). 1995. pap. 4.99 (*0-451-40469-6*, Topaz) NAL-Dutton.
— Paper Tiger. 384p. 1995. pap. 5.99 (*0-451-40608-7*) NAL-Dutton.
— Rebel Dreams. 384p. (Orig.). 1991. pap. 4.99 (*0-451-40272-3*, Onyx) NAL-Dutton.
— Shelter from the Storm. 384p. (Orig.). 1993. pap. 4.99 (*0-451-40358-4*, Onyx) NAL-Dutton.
— Texas Lily. 384p. (Orig.). 1994. pap. 4.99 (*0-451-40468-8*, Topaz) NAL-Dutton.
— Touched by Magic. 384p. (Orig.). 1992. pap. 4.99 (*0-451-40298-7*, Onyx) NAL-Dutton.
Rice, Patricia B., jt. auth. see Dorchak, Susan F.
Rice, Patricia O. & Ogburn, Joyce L., eds. Serials Partner Ship: Teamwork, Technology & Trends: Proceedings of the North American Serials Interest Group, Inc. Fourth Annual Conference. LC 89-28050. (Serials Librarian Ser.: Vol. 17, Nos. 3-4). (Illus.). 215p. 1990. text ed. 24.95 (*0-86656-991-X*) Haworth Pr.
Rice, Patricia O. & Robillard, Jane A., eds. The Future of Serials: Proceedings of the North American Serials Interest Group, Inc. (Serials Librarian Ser.). (Illus.). 247p. 1990. text ed. 29.95 (*1-56024-081-4*) Haworth Pr.
***Rice, Patty C.** Amber, Golden Gem of the Ages. rev. ed. 289p. 1988. pap. text ed. 19.95x (*0-917004-22-1*) Kosciuszko.
— Amber, Golden Gem of the Ages. rev. ed. 289p. (C). 1988. 29.95 (*0-917004-20-5*) Kosciuszko.
Rice, Paul. Timesource. (Illus.). 256p. (Orig.). 1989. 21.95 (*0-89815-312-3*); pap. 14.95 (*0-89815-311-5*) Ten Speed Pr.
Rice, Paul & Rice, Valeta. Aquarius: Through the Numbers. 64p. 1983. pap. 3.95 (*0-87728-575-6*) Weiser.
— Aries: Through the Numbers. 64p. 1983. pap. 3.95 (*0-87728-565-9*) Weiser.
— Cancer: Through the Numbers. 64p. 1983. pap. 3.95 (*0-87728-568-3*) Weiser.
— Capricorn: Through the Numbers. 64p. 1983. pap. 3.95 (*0-87728-574-8*) Weiser.
— Gemini: Through the Numbers. 64p. 1983. pap. 3.95 (*0-87728-567-5*) Weiser.
— Leo: Through the Numbers. 64p. 1983. pap. 3.95 (*0-87728-569-1*) Weiser.
— Libra: Through the Numbers. 64p. 1983. pap. 3.95 (*0-87728-571-3*) Weiser.
— Pisces: Through the Numbers. 64p. 1983. pap. 3.95 (*0-87728-576-4*) Weiser.
— Potential: The Name Analysis Book. 192p. (Orig.). 1987. pap. 8.95 (*0-87728-632-9*) Weiser.
— Sagittarius: Through the Numbers. 64p. 1983. pap. 3.95 (*0-87728-573-X*) Weiser.
— Scorpio: Through the Numbers. 64p. 1983. pap. 3.95 (*0-87728-572-1*) Weiser.
— Taurus: Through the Numbers. 64p. 1983. pap. 3.95 (*0-87728-566-7*) Weiser.
— Virgo: Through the Numbers. 64p. 1983. pap. 3.95 (*0-87728-570-5*) Weiser.
Rice, Paul F. Negotiating Your Contracts. 8p. (Orig.). 1988. 3.95 (*0-9620188-5-6*) Lifestyle Group.
— Selecting Your Accountant. 8p. (Orig.). 1988. 3.95 (*0-9620188-2-1*) Lifestyle Group.
— Selecting Your Financial Advisors: Keys to Choosing a Good Accountant, Lawyer, Securities Broker, Financial Planner & Other Sources of Financial Advice. 52p. (Orig.). 1988. pap. 7.95 (*0-318-23895-0*) Lifestyle Group.
— Selecting Your Lawyer. 8p. (Orig.). 1988. 3.95 (*0-9620188-1-3*) Lifestyle Group.
— Selecting Your Securities Broker & Financial Planner. 8p. (Orig.). 1988. 3.95 (*0-9620188-3-X*) Lifestyle Group.
Rice, Paul F. & Hoffman, Edward S. Structural Design Guide to AISC Specifications for Buildings. LC 75-40491. (Illus.). 368p. reprint ed. pap. 104.90 (*0-317-11089-6*, 2007877) Bks Demand.
Rice, Paul R. Attorney-Client Privileges in the U. S. 1993. ring bd. 105.00 (*0-317-05382-5*) Lawyers Cooperative.
Rice, Peggy, jt. auth. see McFarland, June.
***Rice, Peggy, et al, eds.** Carbonate Rocks I: Classifications-Dolomite-Dolomitization. (AAPG Reprint Ser.: No. 4). (Illus.). 237p. 1972. pap. 6.00 (*0-89181-528-7*) AAPG.
Rice, Peter, et al. Columbia Documents of Architecture & Theory, Vol. 1: D. (Illus.). 150p. (Orig.). 1992. pap. 20.00 (*0-9623829-5-7*) CUGSA.
Rice, Peter L. Far Country. (BattleTech Ser.). 288p. (Orig.). 1993. pap. 4.99 (*0-451-45291-7*, ROC) NAL-Dutton.
— Frost Death. Ippolito, Donna, ed. (Renegade Legion Ser.). (Illus.). 272p. (Orig.). 1991. pap. 7.95 (*1-55560-140-5*) FASA Corp.
Rice, Philip & Waugh, Patricia. Modern Literary Theory: A Reader. 200p. 1989. 49.50 (*0-7131-6596-0*, Pub. by E Arnold UK); pap. 15.95 (*0-7131-6541-3*, Pub. by E Arnold UK) Routledge Chapman & Hall.
Rice, Philip & Waugh, Patricia, eds. Modern Literary Theory: A Reader. 2nd ed. LC 92-19707. 1992. 17.95 (*0-340-57599-9*, Pub. by E Arnold UK) Routledge Chapman & Hall.
Rice, Philip A., jt. auth. see Schuylkill Roots Staff.
***Rice, Phillip A.** Church Records of the Bethany Evangelical Congregational Church (Formerly Bethany United Evangelical Church) 197p. 1994. pap. 22.95 (*1-55856-179-X*) Closson Pr.
— German Protestant Cemetery of Mahanoy City Located in Mahonoy Township, Schuylkill County, PA. 152p. 1995. pap. 16.95 (*1-55856-180-3*) Closson Pr.
— Index to the Obituaries As Found in the Pottsville Republican & Citizen Standard for the Year 1992. 82p. 1994. pap. text ed. 8.50 (*1-55856-200-1*) Closson Pr.
***Rice, Phillip A. & Dellock, Jean.** Church Records of St. David's Lutheran & Reformed Church at Hebe, Jordan Township, Northumberland County, PA. 74p. 1995. pap. 9.95 (*1-55856-181-1*) Closson Pr.
***Rice, Phillip A. & Dellock, Jean A.** Collected Church Records of Berks County, PA. 587p. 1995. pap. 49.95 (*1-55856-184-6*) Closson Pr.
— St. Paul's (White Church) Cemetery & Reformed Congregation Records (1874-1913) with Collected Cemeteries of Union Township & North Union Township, Schuylkill County, PA. 260p. 1994. pap. text ed. 24.95 (*1-55856-161-7*) Closson Pr.
Rice, Phillip A., jt. auth. see Schuylkill Roots Staff.
Rice, Phillip L. Stress & Health. 2nd ed. LC 91-36428. 448p. (C). 1992. pap. 27.95 (*0-534-17280-6*) Brooks-Cole.
Rice, Pierce. Man As Hero: The Human Figure in Western Art. (Classical America Series in Art & Architecture). (Illus.). 1987. pap. 12.95 (*0-393-30474-4*) Norton.
Rice, Prudence M. Macanche Island, El Peten, Guatemala: Excavations, Pottery, & Artifacts. LC 87-2040. (Illus.). 280p. (C). 1987. text ed. 37.95 (*0-8130-0838-7*) U Press Fla.
— Pottery Analysis: A Sourcebook. LC 86-24958. (Illus.). xxiv, 560p. (C). 1987. 50.00 (*0-226-71118-8*) U Ch Pr.
Rice, Prudence M., ed. Pots & Potters: Current Approaches in Ceramic Archaeology. (Monograph: No. 24). (Illus.). 255p. 1984. pap. 22.50 (*0-917956-44-3*) UCLA Arch.
Rice, R. Talking Turkey. (C). 1989. text ed. 29.95 (*0-948032-38-3*, Pub. by Rosters Ltd) St Mut.
Rice, R. P., et al. Fruit & Vegetable Production in Warm Climates. (Illus.). 496p. (Orig.). 1990. pap. text ed. 35.00 (*0-333-46850-3*, Pub. by Macmill Press UK) Scholium Intl.
Rice, Ralph S. & Rice, Terence R. California Family Tax Planning, 2 vols. 2nd ed. 1966. Updates. ring bd. write for info. (*0-8205-1184-6*, 184) Bender.
Rice, Ralph S. & Terence, R. Rice. Family Tax Planning, 2 vols., Set. 1960. ring bd. write for info. (*0-8205-1585-X*) Bender.
Rice, Richard. God's Foreknowledge & Man's Free Will. LC 85-13330. 128p. (Orig.). 1985. pap. 6.99 (*0-87123-845-4*) Bethany Hse.
— The Reign of God: An Introduction to Christian Theology from a Seventh-Day Adventist Perspective. LC 85-70344. 424p. 1985. text ed. 29.95 (*0-943872-90-1*) Andrews Univ Pr.
Rice, Richard A., jt. ed. see Campbell, Oscar J.
***Rice, Richard G. & Do, Duong D.** Applied Mathematics & Modeling for Chemical Engineers. 1994. text ed. 41.50 (*0-471-30377-1*) Wiley.
Rice, Rip G. Ozone Drinking Water Treatment Handbook. (Illus.). 450p. 1991. 69.95 (*0-87371-227-7*, T) Lewis Pubs.
Rice, Rip G., ed. First International Symposium on Ozone for Water & Wastewater Treatment. LC 74-28539. (Illus.). 1974. text ed. 15.00 (*0-918650-03-8*); text ed. 20.00 (*0-918650-04-6*) Pan Am Intl Ozone.
— Safe Drinking Water: The Impact of Chemicals on a Limited Resource. LC 84-25105. (Illus.). 280p. 1985. 153.00 (*0-9614032-0-9*, CRC Reprint) Franklin.
— Safe Drinking Water: The Impact of Chemicals on a Limited Resource. 275p. 1985. 34.95 (*0-317-01439-0*); 29.95 (*0-318-17815-X*) Intl Bottled Water.
Rice, Rip G. & Browning, Myron E., eds. Ozone: Analytical Aspects & Odor Control. LC 76-17611. (Illus.). 1976. text ed. 25.00 (*0-918650-09-7*) Pan Am Intl Ozone.
Rice, Rip G. & Cotruvo, Joseph A., eds. Ozone Chlorine-Dioxide Oxidation Products of Organic Materials. LC 78-53924. (Illus.). 1978. text ed. 50.00 (*0-918650-02-X*) Pan Am Intl Ozone.
Rice, Rip G., et al, eds. International Symposium on Ozone Technology, Second. LC 76-28267. (Illus.). 1976. text ed. 18.00 (*0-918650-07-0*); text ed. 23.00 (*0-918650-08-9*) Pan Am Intl Ozone.
Rice, Robert. The Last Pendragon. 340p. 1992. 19.95 (*0-8027-1180-4*) Walker & Co.
— The Last Pendragon. large type ed. 368p. 1992. reprint ed. lib. bdg. 17.95 (*1-56054-432-5*) Thorndike Pr.
Rice, Robert F., et al, eds. Firm Foundations: The First English Language Adult Literacy Series in the 20th Century with Bible-Content Lessons - Projected for the 21st Century. rev. ed. LC 89-80387. (Illus.). 80p. 1989. Tutors guide, 80 pp. teacher ed 3.00 (*1-877596-12-4*); Pre-reading, 32 pp. 3.00 (*1-877596-13-2*) Literacy & Evangelism.
— Firm Foundations: The First English Language Adult Literacy Series in the 20th Century with Bible-Content Lessons - Projected for the 21st Century, Bk. 1. rev. ed. LC 89-80387. (Illus.). 64p. 1989. Book 1, 64 pp. 3.00 (*1-877596-14-0*) Literacy & Evangelism.
— Firm Foundations: The First English Language Adult Literacy Series in the 20th Century with Bible-Content Lessons - Projected for the 21st Century, Bk. 2. rev. ed. LC 89-80387. (Illus.). 56p. 1989. Book 2, 56 pp. 3.00 (*1-877596-16-7*) Literacy & Evangelism.
— Firm Foundations: The First English Language Adult Literacy Series in the 20th Century with Bible-Content Lessons - Projected for the 21st Century, Bk. 3. rev. ed. LC 89-80387. (Illus.). 56p. 1989. Book 3, 56 pp. 3.00 (*1-877596-18-3*) Literacy & Evangelism.
— Firm Foundations: The First English Language Adult Literacy Series in the 20th Century with Bible-Content Lessons - Projected for the 21st Century, Set. rev. ed. LC 89-80387. (Illus.). 1989. 20.00 (*0-685-27867-0*) Literacy & Evangelism.
— Firm Foundations: The First English Language Adult Literacy Series in the 20th Century with Bible-Content Lessons - Projected for the 21st Century, Wkbk. 1. LC 89-80387. (Illus.). 56p. 1989. Wookbook 1, 56 pp. student ed 3.00 (*1-877596-15-9*) Literacy & Evangelism.
— Firm Foundations: The First English Language Adult Literacy Series in the 20th Century with Bible-Content Lessons - Projected for the 21st Century, Wkbk. 2. LC 89-80387. (Illus.). 56p. 1989. Wookbook 2, 56 pp. student ed 3.00 (*1-877596-17-5*) Literacy & Evangelism.
— Firm Foundations: The First English Language Adult Literacy Series in the 20th Century with Bible-Content Lessons - Projected for the 21st Century, Wkbk. 3. LC 89-80387. (Illus.). 56p. 1989. Wookbook 3, 56 pp. student ed 3.00 (*1-877596-19-1*) Literacy & Evangelism.
— Firm Foundations in Learning English: The First English Language Adult Literacy Series in the 20th Century with Bible-Content Lessons - Projected for the 21st Century, 8 bks. LC 89-80387. (Illus.). 456p. 1989. teacher ed 3.00 (*0-317-93584-4*) Literacy & Evangelism.
— Firm Foundations in Learning English: The First English Language Adult Literacy Series in the 20th Century with Bible-Content Lessons - Projected for the 21st Century, 8 bks. rev. ed. LC 89-80387. (Illus.). 32p. 1989. Pre-Reading, 32p. pap. 3.00 (*0-317-93580-1*) Literacy & Evangelism.
— Firm Foundations in Learning English: The First English Language Adult Literacy Series in the 20th Century with Bible-Content Lessons - Projected for the 21st Century, 8 bks., Bk. 1. rev. ed. LC 89-80387. (Illus.). 64p. 1989. pap. 3.00 (*0-317-93581-X*) Literacy & Evangelism.
— Firm Foundations in Learning English: The First English Language Adult Literacy Series in the 20th Century with Bible-Content Lessons - Projected for the 21st Century, 8 bks., Bk. 2. rev. ed. LC 89-80387. (Illus.). 56p. 1989. pap. 3.00 (*0-317-93582-8*) Literacy & Evangelism.
— Firm Foundations in Learning English: The First English Language Adult Literacy Series in the 20th Century with Bible-Content Lessons - Projected for the 21st Century, 8 bks., Bk. 3. rev. ed. LC 89-80387. (Illus.). 56p. 1989. pap. 3.00 (*0-317-93583-6*) Literacy & Evangelism.
— Firm Foundations in Learning English: The First English Language Adult Literacy Series in the 20th Century with Bible-Content Lessons - Projected for the 21st Century, 8 bks., No. 1. LC 89-80387. (Illus.). 456p. 1989. student ed 3.00 (*0-317-93585-2*) Literacy & Evangelism.
— Firm Foundations in Learning English: The First English Language Adult Literacy Series in the 20th Century with Bible-Content Lessons - Projected for the 21st Century, 8 bks., No. 2. LC 89-80387. (Illus.). 456p. 1989. student ed 3.00 (*0-317-93586-0*) Literacy & Evangelism.
— Firm Foundations in Learning English: The First English Language Adult Literacy Series in the 20th Century with Bible-Content Lessons - Projected for the 21st Century, 8 bks., No. 3. LC 89-80387. (Illus.). 456p. 1989. student ed 3.00 (*0-317-93587-9*) Literacy & Evangelism.
— Firm Foundations in Learning English: The First English Language Adult Literacy Series in the 20th Century with Bible-Content Lessons - Projected for the 21st Century, 8 bks., Set. rev. ed. LC 89-80387. (Illus.). 456p. 1989. pap. 20.00 (*1-877596-11-6*) Literacy & Evangelism.
Rice, Robert P., Jr. Thomson's English-Spanish - Spanish-English Illustrated Agricultural Dictionary. 160p. 1993. pap. 27.95 (*0-913702-56-0*) Thomson Pubns.
Rice, Robert P., Jr. & Rice, Laura. Practical Horticulture: A Guide to Growing Indoor & Outdoor Plants. (C). 1985. text ed. 57.00 (*0-8359-5771-3*, Reston) P-H.
— Practical Horticulture: A Guide to Growing Indoor & Outdoor Plants. (C). 1986. teacher ed write for info. (*0-8359-5772-1*, Reston) P-H.
Rice, Robert P., Jr., jt. auth. see Rice, Laura W.
Rice, Robyn. Home Health Nursing Practice: Concepts & Application. 316p. 1992. pap. 28.95 (*0-8016-4103-9*) Mosby Yr Bk.
Rice, Rodney R. One Hundred One Weapons for Women: Implement Weaponry. Jones, Lynn, ed. (Illus.). 128p. 1992. pap. 10.95 (*0-9632402-1-8*) RiJo Prods.
Rice, Ronald E. & Atkin, Charles K., eds. Public Communication Campaigns. 2nd ed. 416p. (C). 1989. text ed. 52.00 (*0-8039-3262-6*); pap. text ed. 24.00 (*0-8039-3263-4*) Sage.
Rice, Ronald E. & Paisley, William J., eds. Public Communication Campaigns. LC 81-2706. 328p. reprint ed. pap. 93.50 (*0-8357-4848-0*, 2037779) Bks Demand.
Rice, Ronald E., jt. auth. see Johnson, Bonnie M.
Rice, Ronald E., et al. The New Media: Communication, Research, & Technology. LC 84-3287. (Illus.). 352p. reprint ed. pap. 100.40 (*0-7837-4560-5*, 2044088) Bks Demand.
Rice, Ross R. Carl Hayden: Builder of the American West. LC 93-43763. 372p. (C). Date not set. lib. bdg. 48.50 (*0-8191-9399-2*) U Pr of Amer.
Rice, Russ. Joe B. Hall: My Own Kentucky Home. LC 81-52628. (College Sports Book Ser.). 1981. 12.95 (*0-87397-196-5*) Strode.
Rice, Russell. Adolph Rupp: Kentucky's Basketball Baron. (Illus.). 250p. 1994. 22.95 (*0-915611-98-8*) Sagamore Pub.
Rice, Ruth. English Teacher's Book of Instant Word Games. 256p. 1992. pap. 27.95 (*0-87628-303-2*) Ctr Appl Res.
Rice, S. El Hogar Cristiano: The Christian Home. (SPA.). 5.50 (*0-317-04314-5*, 220466, Pub. by Edit Clie SP) TSELF.
Rice, Sally, jt. ed. see Brettle, Jane.
Rice, Samuel O., ed. Fundamentals of Investment. LC 75-2664. (Wall Street & the Security Market Ser.). 1975. reprint ed. 34.95 (*0-405-06988-X*) Ayer.
Rice, Sara S., comp. Holiday Selections: For Readings & Recitations; Specially Adapted to Christmas, New Year... LC 72-39402. (Granger Index Reprint Ser.). 1977. reprint ed. 18.95 (*0-8369-6348-2*) Ayer.
Rice, Sara V., jt. auth. see Rice, Don A.
Rice, Sarah. He Included Me: The Autobiography of Sarah Rice. Westling, Louise, ed. LC 88-38690. (Illus.). 200p. 1989. 22.50 (*0-8203-1141-3*) U of Ga Pr.
— He Included Me: The Autobiography of Sarah Rice. Westling, Louise, ed. LC 88-38690. (Brown Thrasher Bks.). (Illus.). 200p. 1991. reprint ed. pap. 11.95 (*0-8203-1337-8*) U of Ga Pr.
Rice, Scott. Right Words, Right Places. 445p. (C). 1993. pap. 23.95 (*0-534-16038-7*) Intl Thomson.

R

Rice, Scott, comp. Bride of Dark & Stormy: Yet More of the Best (?) from the Bulwer-Lytton Contest. (Illus.). 144p. 1988. pap. 7.00 (*0-14-010304-X*, Penguin Bks) Viking Penguin.

— It Was a Dark & Stormy Night: The Best(?) from the Bulwer-Lytton Contest. (Illus.). 124p. (Orig.). 1984. pap. 7.00 (*0-14-007556-9*, Penguin Bks) Viking Penguin.

— It Was a Dark & Stormy Night: The Final Conflict: Yet More of the Best(?) from the Bulwer-Lytton Fiction Contest. 144p. (Orig.). 1992. pap. 8.00 (*0-14-015791-3*, Penguin Bks) Viking Penguin.

— Son of "It Was a Dark & Stormy Night" 160p. 1986. pap. 7.00 (*0-14-008839-3*, Penguin Bks) Viking Penguin.

Rice, Sean M. Did Ya See the Masked Man? LC 91-51083. (Orig.). 1985. pap. 5.00 (*0-88734-304-X*) Players Pr.

Rice, Shirley A., ed. Community: Birthplace of Popular Consent, a Salute to New York's Bicentennial Towns. LC 87-37925. (Illus.). 56p. (Orig.). 1988. pap. 2.50 (*1-55787-024-1*, NY70057) Hrt of the Lakes.

***Rice-Spearman, Lori & Larsen, Hal S.** The Rotation Manual for Clinical Laboratory Science. 181p. 1994. pap. 35.00 (*0-683-07259-5*) Williams & Wilkins.

— The Rotation Manual for Clinical Laboratory Science. 1994. write for info. (*0-683-04821-X*) Williams & Wilkins.

Rice, Stan. New & Selected Poems. 1992. pap. 22.50 (*0-679-41145-3*) McKay.

— Whiteboy. 1975. pap. 3.00 (*0-685-52155-9*) Mudra.

Rice, Stan & More, Alan S., eds. Collecting Assessments: An Operational Guide. 3rd ed. (GAP Report Ser.: No. 10). 20p. (C). 1994. reprint ed. pap. 14.50 (*0-944715-29-X*) CAI.

Rice, Stanley. Book Design: Systematic Aspects. LC 77-28186. (Illus.). 274p. 1978. 34.95 (*0-8352-1044-8*) Bowker.

— Book Design: Text Format Models. LC 77-26908. 215p. 1978. 34.95 (*0-8352-1045-6*) Bowker.

Rice, Stuart A., jt. ed. see Prigogine, Ilya.

Rice, Steve. Great Adventures Map: U. S. A. 1983. 2.95 (*0-912831-01-4*) Map Ink.

— Multi-Purpose Map: Texas. 1983. 2.95 (*0-912831-02-2*) Map Ink.

— Oklahoma Multi-Purpose Map. 1982. 2.95 (*0-912831-00-6*) Map Ink.

— Travel Adventures & Trivia Map: California. 1986. 2.95 (*0-912831-04-9*) Map Ink.

— Travel Adventures & Trivia Map: New Mexico - Arizona. 1985. 2.95 (*0-912831-03-0*) Map Ink.

Rice, Steve, ed. see Miami Herald Staff & El Nuevo Herald Staff.

Rice, Steven J. Introduction to Taxation. 3rd ed. LC 94-7200. (C). 1994. text ed. 55.95 (*0-538-84413-2*) S-W Pub.

— Introduction to Taxation. 4th ed. LC 95-11381. 1995. pap. 58.95 (*0-538-85528-2*) S-W Pub.

— An Introduction to Taxation, 1994. LC 93-22190. 1993. write for info. (*0-538-82890-0*) S-W Pub.

Rice, Stuart A. Farmers & Workers in American Politics. LC 78-82242. (Columbia University. Studies in the Social Sciences: No. 253). reprint ed. 20.00 (*0-404-51253-4*) AMS Pr.

Rice, Stuart A. & Freed, Karl F., eds. Statistical Mechanics: New Concepts, New Problems, New Applications. LC 72-85434. 434p. reprint ed. pap. 123.70 (*0-317-08081-4*, 2019965) Bks Demand.

Rice, Stuart A., jt. ed. see Prigogine, I.

Rice, Stuart A., jt. ed. see Prigogine, Ilya.

Rice, Stuart S., jt. ed. see Prigogine, I.

Rice, Susan. A Compound of Excelsior. (Illus.). 93p. (Orig.). 1992. pap. 10.95 (*0-938501-14-3*) Gasogene Pr.

Rice, Susan & Todd, Ginger. Travel Perspectives: A Guide to Becoming a Travel Agent. 300p. 1991. teacher ed 12.00 (*0-8273-4571-2*); ring bd. 43.95 (*0-8273-4570-4*) Delmar.

— Travel Perspectives Update One. 1991. ring bd. 6.00 (*0-8273-4569-0*) Delmar.

Rice, Susan, jt. auth. see Todd, Ginger.

Rice, Susan A. & Fish, Kevin J., eds. Anesthetic Toxicity. LC 93-39550. 320p. 1994. 98.00 (*0-7817-0202-X*) Raven.

Rice, Tamara T. Everyday Life in Byzantium. 1987. 17.95 (*0-88029-145-1*) Dorset Pr.

Rice, Ted, jt. auth. see Turner, Karla.

Rice, Terence R., jt. auth. see Rice, Ralph S.

Rice, Thomas A., et al, eds. Operative Surgery: Ophthalmic Surgery. 4th ed. (Rob & Smith's Operative Surgery Ser.). (Illus.). 456p. 1984. text ed. 150.00 (*0-407-00657-5*) Buttrwrth-Heinemann.

Rice, Thomas J., ed. English Fiction, Nineteen Hundred to Nineteen Fifty: A Guide to Information Sources, Vol. 1. LC 73-16989. (American Literature, English Literature, & World Literatures in English Information Guide Ser.: Vol. 20). 624p. 1979. 68.00 (*0-8103-1217-4*) Gale.

— English Fiction, Nineteen Hundred to Nineteen-Fifty: A Guide to Information Sources, Vol. 2. (American Literature, English Literature, & World Literatures in English Information Guide Ser.: Vol. 21). 656p. 1983. 68.00 (*0-8103-1505-X*) Gale.

***Rice, Tim & John, Elton.** Circle of Life Vol. 1. (Illus.). 48p. 1994. 9.95 (*0-7868-6148-7*) Hyperion.

Rice, Tim & Webber, Andrew L. Joseph & the Amazing Technicolor Dreamcoat. (Illus.). 32p. (J). (gr. k-3). 1993. pap. 11.95 (*1-85793-119-X*, Pub. by Pavilion UK) Trafalgar.

Rice, Timothy. May It Fill Your Soul: Experiencing Bulgarian Music. LC 93-34083. (Chicago Studies in Ethnomusicology). (C). 1994. lib. bdg. 65.00 (*0-226-71121-8*); pap. text ed. 24.95 (*0-226-71122-6*) U Ch Pr.

Rice, Tom. Beach Banquet. Swant, Dale, ed. (Illus.). 64p. (Orig.). 1983. pap. 2.95 (*0-943470-01-3*) Daisy Bks.

Rice, Tony. Ocean World. (Young Readers' Nature Library). (Illus.). 64p. (J). (gr. 4-6). 1991. lib. bdg. 15.40 (*1-56294-027-9*) Millbrook Pr.

Rice, Trudy T. St. Joseph's First One Hundred Years. 104p. 1991. write for info. (*0-929690-12-5*) Herit Pubs AZ.

Rice, Valeta, jt. auth. see Rice, Paul.

Rice, Wallace & Rice, Frances. The Humbler Poets: Second Series; a Collection of Newspaper & Periodical Verse, 1885-1910. LC 70-39395. (Granger Index Reprint Ser.). 1977. reprint ed. 23.95 (*0-8369-6349-0*) Ayer.

Rice, Wayne. Enjoy Your Middle Schooler. 144p. 1994. pap. 9.99 (*0-310-40581-5*) Zondervan.

— Great Ideas for Small Youth Groups. 256p. (Orig.). (J). (gr. 7-12). 1986. pap. 10.99 (*0-310-34891-9*, 10823P) Zondervan.

— Junior High Ministry. rev. ed. 1990. pap. 12.99 (*0-310-53361-9*) Zondervan.

— The Youth Specialties Clip Art Book. 240p. (Orig.). 1985. pap. 17.99 (*0-310-34911-7*, 10824P) Zondervan.

Rice, Wayne, comp. Hot Illustrations for Youth Talks: 100 Attention-Getting Stories, Parables, & Anecdotes. LC 93-30815. 1994. 12.99 (*0-310-40261-1*) Zondervan.

— The Youth Specialties Clip Art Book, Vol. II. 112p. (Orig.). 1987. pap. 17.99 (*0-310-39791-X*, 10828P) Zondervan.

Rice, Wayne, ed. Ideas Combo Edition 33-36, 4 bks. in 1. (Illus.). 192p. (Orig.). (YA). 1988. pap. 19.95 (*0-910125-33-3*) Youth Special.

— One Hundred Ten Tips, Time-Savers & Tricks of the Trade for Youth Workers. (Illus.). 72p. (Orig.). (YA). 1984. pap. 5.95 (*0-910125-04-X*) Youth Special.

Rice, Wayne & McLaughlin, Tim, eds. Ideas, 52 vols. (Ideas Library). (Illus.). (Orig.). pap. 199.95 (*0-910125-00-7*) Youth Special.

— Ideas Combo Edition 41-44, 4 bks. in 1. (Illus.). 200p. (Orig.). (YA). 1988. pap. 19.95 (*0-910125-35-X*) Youth Special.

— Ideas Combo Edition 45-48, 4 bks. in 1. (Illus.). 208p. (Orig.). (YA). 1992. pap. 19.95 (*0-910125-36-8*) Youth Special.

— Ideas Combo Edition 49-52, 4 bks. in 1. (Illus.). 192p. (Orig.). (YA). 1992. pap. 19.95 (*0-910125-37-6*) Youth Special.

Rice, Wayne & Thigpen, Paul, eds. Ideas Combo Edition 37-40, 4 bks. in 1. (Illus.). 200p. (Orig.). (YA). 1990. pap. 19.95 (*0-910125-34-1*) Youth Special.

Rice, Wayne & Yaconelli, Mike. Creative Activities for Small Youth Groups. Stamschror, Robert P., ed. (Creative Resources for Youth Ministry Ser.). (Illus.). 101p. (YA). (gr. 7-12). 1991. pap. 12.95 (*0-88489-264-6*) St Marys.

— Creative Communication & Discussion Activities. Stamschror, Robert P., ed. (Creative Resources for Youth Ministry Ser.). (Illus.). 96p. (YA). (gr. 7-12). 1991. pap. 12.95 (*0-88489-266-2*) St Marys.

— Creative Crowd-Breakers, Mixers & Games. Stamschror, Robert P., ed. (Creative Resources for Youth Ministry Ser.). (Illus.). 96p. 1991. pap. 12.95 (*0-88489-265-4*) St Marys.

— The Greatest Skits on Earth. 288p. (Orig.). (J). (gr. 3-7). 1986. pap. 10.99 (*0-310-35141-3*, 10775P) Zondervan.

— Greatest Skits on Earth, Vol. 2. 192p. 1987. pap. 10.99 (*0-310-35211-8*, 10776P) Zondervan.

— Holiday Ideas. rev. ed. 256p. 1989. pap. 12.99 (*0-310-51731-1*) Zondervan.

— Juegos para Cada Ocasion. Lazo, Julia A., tr. 192p. (Orig.). (SPA.). 1988. pap. 6.25 (*0-311-11047-9*) Casa Bautista.

— Play It: Great Games for Groups. 256p. 1986. pap. 10.99 (*0-310-35191-X*, 10799P) Zondervan.

Rice, Wayne & Yaconelli, Mike, eds. Ideas Combo Edition 1-4, 4 bks. in 1. (Illus.). 192p. (Orig.). (YA). 1979. pap. 19.95 (*0-910125-25-2*) Youth Special.

— Ideas Combo Edition 13-16, 4 bks. in 1. (Illus.). 208p. (Orig.). (YA). 1981. pap. 19.95 (*0-910125-28-7*) Youth Special.

— Ideas Combo Edition 17-20, 4 bks. in 1. (Illus.). 206p. (Orig.). (YA). 1981. pap. 19.95 (*0-910125-29-5*) Youth Special.

— Ideas Combo Edition 21-24, 4 bks. in 1. (Illus.). 200p. (Orig.). (YA). 1984. pap. 19.95 (*0-910125-30-9*) Youth Special.

— Ideas Combo Edition 25-28, 4 bks. in 1. (Illus.). 208p. (Orig.). (YA). 1985. pap. 19.95 (*0-910125-31-7*) Youth Special.

— Ideas Combo Edition 29-32, 4 bks. in 1. (Illus.). 200p. (Orig.). (YA). 1987. pap. 19.95 (*0-910125-32-5*) Youth Special.

— Ideas Combo Edition 5-8, 4 bks. in 1. (Illus.). 176p. (Orig.). (YA). 1984. pap. 19.95 (*0-910125-26-0*) Youth Special.

— Ideas Combo Edition 9-12, 4 bks. in 1. (Illus.). 180p. (Orig.). (YA). 1980. pap. 19.95 (*0-910125-27-9*) Youth Special.

— Play It Again! More Great Games for Groups. 240p. 1993. pap. 10.99 (*0-310-37291-7*) Zondervan.

Rice, Wayne, jt. auth. see Yaconelli, Mike.

Rice, William C., jt. auth. see Lovelace, Austin C.

Rice, William G. The Carillon in Literature. 1977. lib. bdg. 59.95 (*0-8490-1576-6*) Gordon Pr.

— Carillon Music & Singing Towers of the Old World & the New. 1977. lib. bdg. 59.95 (*0-8490-1577-4*) Gordon Pr.

— Carillons of Belgium & Holland. 1977. lib. bdg. 59.95 (*0-8490-1578-2*) Gordon Pr.

— Tale of Two Courts: Judicial Settlement of Controversies Between the States of the Swiss & American Federations. LC 67-20758. 149p. reprint ed. pap. 42.50 (*0-317-39658-7*, 2023718) Bks Demand.

***Ricekit, T. R.** Pennsylvania Pete. (Illus.). (Orig.). (YA). (gr. 7 up). 1995. lib. bdg. 15.00 (*0-88092-251-6*); pap. 7.00 (*0-88092-250-8*) Royal Fireworks.

Rich. Clinical Immunology: Principles & Practice. 2000p. 1995. 225.00 (*0-8016-7636-3*) Mosby Yr Bk.

Rich, A., ed. see Moore, G. R. & Pettigrew, G. W.

Rich, Adrienne. Adrienne Rich's Poetry & Prose. Gelpi, Barbara C. & Gelpi, Albert, eds. (Critical Editions Ser.). (C). 1993. pap. text ed. 8.95 (*0-393-96147-8*) Norton.

— An Atlas of the Difficult World: Poems 1988-1991. 64p. 1991. pap. 7.95 (*0-393-30831-6*) Norton.

— Blood, Bread & Poetry. 1994. pap. 9.95 (*0-393-31162-7*) Norton.

— Blood, Bread & Poetry: Selected Prose 1979-1985. 1986. 15.95 (*0-393-02376-1*) Norton.

— Collected Early Poems: 1950-1970. 464p. 1995. pap. 15.00 (*0-393-31385-9*) Norton.

— Collected Early Poems, 1950-1970. LC 92-13150. 416p. 1993. 27.50 (*0-393-03418-6*) Norton.

— Dark Fields of the Republic: Poems, 1991-1995. LC 95-2272. 1995. 22.00 (*0-393-03868-8*); pap. 10.00 (*0-393-31398-0*) Norton.

— Diving into the Wreck: Poems, 1971-1972. 1994. pap. 8.95 (*0-393-31163-5*) Norton.

— The Dream of a Common Language: Poems 1974-1977. 88p. 1993. pap. 8.95 (*0-393-31033-7*) Norton.

— The Fact of a Doorframe: Poems Selected & New, 1950-1984. 1984. 18.95 (*0-393-01905-5*) Norton.

— The Facts of a Doorframe: Poems Selected & New: 1950-1984. 360p. 1994. pap. 10.95 (*0-393-31075-2*) Norton.

— Of Woman Born: Motherhood As Experience & Institution. 352p. 1995. pap. 12.00 (*0-393-31284-4*, Norton Paperbks) Norton.

— Of Woman Born: Motherhood As Experience & Institution. 10th aniversary ed. 1986. 17.95 (*0-393-02379-6*) Norton.

— On Lies, Secrets & Silence: Selected Prose 1966-1978. 1980. pap. 8.95 (*0-393-00942-4*, N A Talese) Norton.

— On Lies, Secrets, & Silence: Selected Prose 1966-1978. 320p. 1995. pap. 11.00 (*0-393-31285-2*, Norton Paperbks) Norton.

— Sources. deluxe ed. LC 83-81462. (Illus.). 48p. (Orig.). 1983. 185.00 (*0-940592-15-0*); pap. 15.00 (*0-940592-16-9*) Heyeck Pr.

— Time's Power: Poems 1985-1988. 1989. pap. 9.95 (*0-393-30575-9*) Norton.

— What Is Found There: Notebooks On Poetry & Politics. LC 93-9912. 1993. 20.00 (*0-393-03565-4*) Norton.

— What Is Found There? Notebooks on Poetry & Politics. 320p. 1994. pap. 11.00 (*0-393-31246-1*) Norton.

— A Wild Patience Has Taken Me This Far: Poems 1978-1981. 1981. 12.95 (*0-393-01494-0*) Norton.

— A Wild Patience Has Taken Me This Far: Poems 1978-1981. 72p. 1993. pap. 8.95 (*0-393-31037-X*) Norton.

— Will to Change: Poems. LC 78-146842. 1971. pap. 7.95 (*0-393-04361-4*) Norton.

— Women & Honor: Some Notes on Lying. 16p. 1990. 3.95 (*0-939416-44-1*) Cleis Pr.

— Your Native Land, Your Life. 128p. 1993. pap. 8.95 (*0-393-31082-5*) Norton.

— Your Native Land, Your Life: Poems. 1986. pap. 8.95 (*0-393-30325-X*) Norton.

Rich, Adrienne, tr. see Alarcon, Francisco X.

Rich, Adrienne C. Change of World. LC 72-144754. (Yale Series of Younger Poets: No. 48). reprint ed. 18.00 (*0-404-53848-7*) AMS Pr.

***Rich, Alan.** American Pioneers. (20th Century Composers Ser.). (Illus.). 240p. (Orig.). (C). 1995. pap. 19.95 (*0-7148-3173-5*, Pub. by Phaidon Press UK) Chronicle Bks.

— Johann Sebastian Bach: Play by Play. LC 94-49113. 1995. 25.00 (*0-06-263547-6*, HarpT) HarpC.

— Ludwig van Beethoven: Play by Play. LC 94-49111. 1995. 25.00 (*0-06-263545-X*, HarpT) HarpC.

— Pyotr Ilyich Tchaikovsky: Play by Play. LC 95-1393. 1995. 25.00 (*0-06-263544-1*, HarpT) HarpC.

— Wolfgang Amadeus Mozart: Play by Play. LC 94-48625. (Newport Classic CD-B Presentation Ser.). 1995. cd-rom 25.00 (*0-06-263548-4*, HarpT) HarpC.

***Rich, Alexander.** How to Be Thin Forever. 70p. (Orig.). 1995. pap. write for info. (*1-885591-65-9*) Morris Pubng.

Rich, Andrew M. How to Survive & Succeed in a Small Financial Planning Practice. 1984. pap. text ed. 33.95 (*0-8359-2931-0*, Reston) P-H.

Rich, Andrew M. & Arowesty, Jill. The Expert's Guide to Managing & Marketing a Successful Financial Planning Practice. (Illus.). 368p. (C). 1988. text ed. 54.40 (*0-13-295155-X*) P-H.

Rich, Anne J. Instructor's Manual to Accompany Maher - Stickney - Weil, Managerial Accounting, 5th Ed. 5th ed. 199p. (C). 1994. pap. text ed. 28.00 (*0-03-098474-2*); pap. text ed. 28.00 (*0-03-006782-0*) Dryden Pr.

— Study Guide to Accompany Maher - Stickney - Weil, Managerial Accounting. 5th ed. 248p. (C). 1994. pap. text ed. 20.00 (*0-03-098476-9*) Dryden Pr.

***Rich, Annette.** Wildflower Embroidery. (Illus.). 104p. 1995. pap. 14.95 (*1-86351-141-5*, Pub. by S Milner AT) Sterling.

***Rich, Anthony.** Dictionnaire des Antiquites Romaines et Gracques. 740p. (FRE.). 1987. pap. 79.95 (*0-7859-8067-9*, 2851994255) Fr & Eur.

Rich, Avery E. Growing up Yankee. (Illus.). 140p. 1987. lib. bdg. 17.50 (*0-941216-37-3*); pap. 6.95 (*0-941216-39-X*) Cay-Bel.

— Potato Diseases. LC 82-24290. (Monograph). 1983. text ed. 91.00 (*0-12-587420-0*) Acad Pr.

Rich, Barnabe. Faultes, Faults, & Nothing Else but Faultes. LC 65-10396. 1978. reprint ed. 50.00 (*0-8201-1266-6*) Schol Facsimiles.

Rich, Barnaby. Newes from Virginia, the Lost Flocke Triumphant. LC 70-25514. (English Experience Ser.: No. 269). 16p. 1970. reprint ed. 15.00 (*90-221-0269-6*) Walter J Johnson.

— A Path-Way to Military Practice. LC 75-25920. (English Experience Ser.: No. 177). 88p. 1969. reprint ed. 11.50 (*90-221-0177-0*) Walter J Johnson.

Rich, Barnett. Review of Elementary Mathematics. (Schaum's Outline Ser.). (Orig.). 1977. pap. text ed. 11.95 (*0-07-052260-X*) McGraw.

— Schaum's Outline of Geometry. 2nd ed. (Outline Ser.). 272p. 1989. pap. text ed. 11.95 (*0-07-052246-4*) McGraw.

— Schaum's Outline of Theory & Problems of Elementary Algebra. 2nd rev. ed. LC 92-18533. 1993. pap. text ed. 11.95 (*0-07-052262-6*) McGraw.

Rich, Beatrice. ABCDEFGHIJKLMNOPQRSTUVWXYZ in English & French. LC 81-20838. (Illus.). 64p. (J). (gr. k-2). 1983. lib. bdg. 15.95 (*0-87460-353-6*) Lion Bks.

Rich, Ben R. & Janos, Leo. Skunk Works: A Personal Memoir from the U-2 to the Stealth Fighter. LC 94-8732. 1994. 24.95 (*0-316-74330-5*) Little.

Rich, Bennett M. The Presidents & Civil Disorder. LC 79-26839. (Institute for Government Research of the Brookings Institution, Studies in Administration Ser.: No. 42). x, 235p. 1980. reprint ed. text ed. 59.75 (*0-313-22299-1*, RIPD) Greenwood.

Rich, Bennett M. & Baum, Martha. The Aging: A Guide to Public Policy. LC 84-40228. (Contemporary Community Health Ser.). (Illus.). 288p. 1984. 19.95 (*0-8229-5364-1*) U of Pittsburgh Pr.

Rich, Beverly. Louis Pasteur: The Scientist Who Found the Cause of Infectious Disease & Invented Pasteurization. LC 88-24867. (People Who Have Helped the World Ser.). (Illus.). 64p. (J). (gr. 5-6). 1989. lib. bdg. 21.26 (*1-55532-839-3*) Gareth Stevens Inc.

Rich, Bill. Guitars of the Stars, Vol. 1: Rick Nielsen. (Illus.). 182p. 1994. 39.95 (*0-7935-3090-3*, HL00330103) H Leonard.

Rich, Bill & Nielsen, Rick. Guitars of the Stars: Rick Nielsen, Vol. 1. (Illus.). 180p. 1993. 39.95 (*0-9635279-0-8*) GOTS Pub.

Rich, Bruce. Mortgaging the Earth: The World Bank, Environmental Impoverishment, & the Crisis of Development. LC 93-3848. 1993. 29.00 (*0-8070-4704-X*) Beacon Pr.

— Mortgaging the Earth: The World Bank, Environmental Impoverishment, & the Crisis of Development. LC 93-3848. 384p. 1995. pap. 16.00 (*0-8070-4707-4*) Beacon Pr.

Rich, Buddy & Adler, Henry. Buddy Rich's Modern Interpretation of Snare Drum Rudiments. (Illus.). 100p. 1942. pap. 9.95 (*0-8256-1003-6*, AM36419) Music Sales.

Rich, C. B. Life, Times & Poetry of C. B. Rich. (Orig.). 1992. pap. 7.95 (*0-9633062-0-0*) Double Arrow.

— Memories from the Mountains. 200p. (Orig.). 1992. pap. 7.95 (*0-9633062-1-9*) Double Arrow.

Rich, Carole. Writing & Reporting News: A Coaching Method. 590p. (C). 1994. pap. 37.95 (*0-534-19074-X*) Intl Thomson.

Rich, Charles. Autobiography. LC 90-52664. 143p. (Orig.). 1991. pap. 5.95 (*0-932506-80-1*) St Bedes Pubns.

— The Embrace of the Soul: Reflections on the Song of Songs. LC 83-23066. 1984. pap. 3.95 (*0-932506-31-3*) St Bedes Pubns.

— Reflections. LC 86-17732. 131p. 1986. pap. 5.95 (*0-932506-49-6*) St Bedes Pubns.

Rich, Charles & Waters, Richard C. The Programmer's Apprentice. (ACM Press Frontier Ser.). (Illus.). 256p. (C). 1990. text ed. 37.75 (*0-201-52425-2*) Addison-Wesley.

Rich, Charles & Waters, Richard C., eds. Readings in Artificial Intelligence & Software Engineering. LC 86-18627. (Illus.). 624p. (Orig.). 1986. pap. text ed. 29.95 (*0-934613-12-5*) Morgan Kaufmann.

Rich, Chris. The Book of Paper Cutting: A Complete Guide to All the Techniques with More than 100 Project Ideas. LC 92-21536. 128p. 1994. pap. 12.95 (*0-8069-0286-8*) Sterling.

— The Book of Papercutting: A Complete Guide to All the Techniques with More Than 100 Project Ideas. LC 92-21536. (Illus.). 128p. (YA). (gr. 10-12). 1993. 24.95 (*0-8069-0285-X*) Sterling.

Rich, Chris, ed. see Kumiko, Murashima.

Rich, Clayton, et al, eds. From Pragmatism to Vision: Leadership & Values in Academic Health Ctrs. 150p. (Orig.). 1991. pap. 14.95 (*1-879694-02-6*) AAH Ctrs.

Rich, Cynthia. Desert Years: Undreaming the American Dream. LC 89-35667. 120p. (Orig.). 1989. pap. 7.95 (*0-933216-67-X*) Spinsters Ink.

Rich, Cynthia, jt. auth. see Macdonald, Barbara.

Rich, D. C. & Linge, Godfrey J., eds. The State & the Spatial Management of Industrial Change. 256p. (C). 1991. text ed. 74.00 (*0-415-03851-0*, A5125) Routledge.

Rich, Daniel, jt. ed. see Byren, John.

Rich, Daniel, jt. ed. see Byrne, John.

Rich, Daniel C. Degas. (Library of Great Painters). (Illus.). (Orig.). 1966. 49.50 (*0-8109-0067-X*) Abrams.

— Degas. (Masters of Art Ser.). (Illus.). (Orig.). 1985. 22.95 (*0-8109-0829-8*) Abrams.

— Henri Rousseau. LC 75-86436. (Museum of Modern Art Publications in Reprint). (Illus.). 1969. reprint ed. 17.95 (*0-405-01543-7*) Ayer.

Rich, Dave. Boulderides: The Mountain Biking Guide to Boulder, Colorado. (Fat Tire Guides Ser.). (Orig.). 1993. pap. 7.95 (*0-9634607-1-4*) Little Rose Pub.

— Denverides: The Mountain Bike Guide to Denver. (Fat Tire Guides Ser.). 62p. 1993. pap. 7.95 (*0-9634607-2-2*) Little Rose Pub.

— Tellurides: A Mountain Bike Guide to Telleride, Colorado. (Fat Tire Guides Ser.). 56p. 1992. pap. 9.95 (*0-9634607-0-6*) Little Rose Pub.

— Tellurides: A Mountain Biking Guide to Telluride Colorado. 1994. pap. 10.95 (*0-943727-18-9*) Wayfinder Pr.

An Asterisk (*) at the beginning of an entry indicates that the title is appearing in BIP for the first time.

***Rich, Dave & Swenson, Pete.** Trailside Repair Made Simple. 1995. pap. 5.95 (0-9634607-4-9) Little Rose Pub.

***Rich, David.** The Question to Everyone's Answer: How to Stay Motivated on a Daily Basis. 176p. 1994. boxed 24. 95 (0-8403-9849-2) Kendall-Hunt.

Rich, David C. The Industrial Geography of Australia. Thompson, Ian, ed. (Croom Helm Industrial Geography Ser.). 350p. 1987. 75.00 (0-7099-2214-0, Pub. by Croom Helm UK) Routledge Chapman & Hall.

Rich, David Z. Contemporary Economics: A Unifying Approach. LC 85-16762. 208p. 1985. text ed. 55.00 (0-275-92033-X, C2033, Praeger Pubs) Greenwood.

— The Dynamics of Knowledge: A Contemporary View. LC 87-36100. (Contributions in Philosophy Ser.: No. 36). 240p. 1988. text ed. 55.00 (0-313-26102-4, RDY/, Greenwood Pr) Greenwood.

— The Economic Theory of Growth & Development. LC 93-23474. 272p. 1994. text ed. 59.95 (0-275-94687-8, Praeger Pubs) Greenwood.

— The Economics of International Trade: An Independent View. LC 91-33600. 216p. 1992. text ed. 55.00 (0-89930-753-1, RIT, Quorum Bks) Greenwood.

— The Economics of Welfare: A Contemporary Analysis. LC 89-30899. 212p. 1989. text ed. 52.95 (0-275-93309-1, C3309, Praeger Pubs) Greenwood.

Rich, Deike, jt. auth. see Begg, Ean.

Rich, Diana, ed. see Jarvis, Frederick D.

Rich, Doris L. Amelia Earhart: A Biography. (Illus.). 1989. 24.95 (0-87474-836-4) Smithsonian.

— Queen Bess: Daredevil Aviator. LC 93-14785. (Illus.). 208p. 1993. 18.95 (1-56098-265-9) Smithsonian.

— Queen Bess: Daredevil Aviator. (Illus.). 172p. 1995. pap. 13.95 (1-56098-618-2) Smithsonian.

Rich, Dorothy. Helping Your Child Succeed in School: With Activities for Children Aged 5 Through 11. Martin, Margery, ed. (Illus.). 52p. (Orig.). (C). 1993. pap. text ed. 14.95x (1-56806-385-7) Diane Pub.

— MegaSkills: In School & Life - the Best Gift You Can Give Your Child. rev. ed. LC 92-14759. (Illus.). 368p. 1992. pap. 12.95 (0-395-63753-8) HM.

— Schools & Families: Issues & Actions. 128p. 1987. 11.95 (0-8106-0276-8) NEA.

— Teachers & Parents: An Adult-to-Adult Approach. 112p. 1987. 10.95 (0-8106-0277-6) NEA.

Rich, E., ed. Dictionary of Correspondences. LC 88-43279. 396p. 1988. 12.00 (0-87785-140-9) Swedenborg.

Rich, E. E., ed. Copy-Book of Letters Outward Etc. Begins 29 May, 1680, Ends 5 July, 1687. (Hudson's Bay Record Society Publications Ser.: Vol. 11). 1972. reprint ed. pap. 58.00 (0-8115-3185-6) Periodicals Srv.

— James Isham's Observations on Hudson's Bay, 1743, & Notes & Observations on a Book Entitled "A Voyage to Hudson Bay in the Dobbs Galley 1749" (Hudson's Bay Record Society Publications Ser.: Vol. 12). 1969. reprint ed. pap. 58.00 (0-8115-3186-4) Periodicals Srv.

— Journal of Occurrences in the Athabasca Department by George Simpson, 1820 & 1821, & Report. (Hudson's Bay Record Society Publication Ser.: Vol. 1). 1969. reprint ed. pap. 58.00 (0-8115-3175-9) Periodicals Srv.

— The Letters of John McLoughlin in from Fort Vancouver to the Governor & Committee: First Series 1825-1838. (Hudson's Bay Record Society Publications Ser.: Vol. 4). 1969. reprint ed. pap. 58.00 (0-8115-3178-3) Periodicals Srv.

— The Letters of John McLoughlin in from Fort Vancouver to the Governor & Committee: Second Series, 1839-1844. (Hudson's Bay Record Society Publications Ser.: Vol. 6). 1969. reprint ed. pap. 58.00 (0-8115-3180-5) Periodicals Srv.

— The Letters of John McLoughlin in from Fort Vancouver to the Governor & Committee: Third Series, 1844-1846. (Hudson's Bay Record Society Publications Ser.: Vol. 7). 1969. reprint ed. pap. 58.00 (0-8115-3181-3) Periodicals Srv.

— Minutes of the Hudson's Bay Company: 1679-1684, Pt. 1. (Hudson's Bay Record Society Publications Ser.: Vol. 8). 1974. reprint ed. pap. 58.00 (0-8115-3182-1) Periodicals Srv.

— Minutes of the Hudson's Bay Company, 1671-1674. (Hudson's Bay Record Society Publications Ser.: Vol. 5). 1974. reprint ed. pap. 58.00 (0-8115-3179-1) Periodicals Srv.

— Part of Dispatch from George Simpson, Esquire, Governor of Ruperts Land, to the Governor & Committee of the Hudson's Bay Company, London, March 1, 1829: Continued & Completed March 24 & June 5, 1829. (Hudson's Bay Record Society Publications Ser.: Vol. 10). 1974. reprint ed. pap. 58.00 (0-8115-3184-8) Periodicals Srv.

Rich, Elaine, ed. JTEC Panel Report on Machine Translation in Japan. (JTEC Panel Reports). vi, 142p. 1992. pap. write for info. (1-883712-17-3, JTEC) Intl Tech Res.

Rich, Elaine & Knight, Kevin. Artificial Intelligence. 2nd ed. (Artificial Intelligence Ser.). 1991. text ed. write for info. (0-07-052263-4) McGraw.

***Rich, Elaine S.** Mennonite Women: A Story of God's Faithfulness, 1683-1983. fac. ed. LC 82-15452. 260p. 1994. pap. 74.10 (0-7837-7328-5, 2047257) Bks Demand.

Rich, Elaine S., ed. Prayers for Everyday. LC 90-80749. 95p. 1990. pap. 6.95 (0-87303-137-7) Faith & Life.

Rich, Everett. The Heritage of Kansas. 1960. pap. 8.95 (0-686-14877-0) Flint Hills.

Rich, Everett, ed. The Heritage of Kansas. 1960. pap. 5.00 (0-686-00367-5) AG Pr.

Rich, Foster. Prayers from the Heart. 120p. 1994. 15.00 (0-06-062847-2) Harper SF.

Rich, Frank. Avenging Angel. 1993. mass mkt. 3.50 (0-373-63607-5, 1-63607-5) Harlequin Bks.

— Boris Aronson: Stage Design as Visual Metaphor. (Illus.). 24p. 1989. 8.00 (0-915171-14-7) Katonah Gal.

— Day of Judgment. (Jake Strait Ser.). 1994. mass mkt. 3.50 (0-373-63609-1, 1-63609-1) Harlequin Bks.

— The Devil Knocks. (Jake Strait Ser.). 1993. mass mkt. 3.50 (0-373-63608-3, 1-63608-3) Harlequin Bks.

— Twist of Cain. (Jake Strait Ser.). 1994. mass mkt. 4.99 (0-373-63610-5, 1-63610-9) Harlequin Bks.

Rich, Frederic C. The Ivy Club: Eighteen Seventy-Nine to Nineteen Seventy-Nine. Snyder, Jon R. & Scheuch, W. Allen, II, eds. (Illus.). 1979. 9.95 (0-934756-00-7) Ivy Club.

Rich, Fredrick J., ed. Geology of the Black Hills, South Dakota & Wyoming. 2nd ed. (Illus.). 304p. 1986. pap. 24.95 (0-913312-81-9) Am Geol.

Rich, G. Proceedings of the First Oxford-Waterloo Research Seminar, Vol. 2: Planning & Design in Britian & Canada. A Comparison of Education & Practice. (C). 1987. 40.00 (0-685-30252-0, Pub. by Oxford Polytechnic UK) St Mut.

Rich, G. K. Mountain of Mysteries. LC 89-51088. 93p. 1990. pap. 6.95 (1-55523-255-8) Winston-Derek.

Rich, George. Common Bible Questions of Our Day. (New Life Ser.). 24p. (Orig.). 1991. teacher ed 1.95 (0-87227-164-1); student ed, pap. text ed. 1.95 (0-87227-160-9) Reg Baptist.

— Famous Interviews with Jesus Christ. (New Life Ser.). 24p. (YA). (gr. 6 up). 1991. teacher ed 1.95 (0-87227-165-X); student ed, pap. text ed. 1.95 (0-87227-157-9) Reg Baptist.

— God Pursues a Priest. LC 86-10187. 64p. (Orig.). 1986. reprint ed. pap. 3.95 (0-87227-109-9) Reg Baptist.

— How to Have a Successful Marriage. (New Life Ser.). 16p. 1991. teacher ed, pap. 1.95 (0-87227-163-3, RBP5188) Reg Baptist.

— Important Things God Can Do for You. (New Life Ser.). 32p. 1991. student ed, pap. 1.95 (0-87227-158-7, RBP5195); teacher ed, pap. 1.95 (0-87227-166-8, RBP5194) Reg Baptist.

— The Professional Practice of Urban & Rural Planning in Canada. LC 92-41583. 172p. 1993. pap. 59.95 (0-7734-1942-X) E Mellen.

— What's Bothering You? (New Life Ser.). 24p. 1991. teacher ed 1.95 (0-87227-162-5); student ed, pap. text ed. 1.95 (0-87227-155-2) Reg Baptist.

— You Can Make the Right Decision. (New Life Ser.). 32p. 1992. student ed, pap. 1.95 (0-87227-159-5, RBP5199); teacher ed, pap. 1.95 (0-87227-168-4, RBP5198) Reg Baptist.

— Your Relationship to God. (New Life Ser.). 32p. 1992. student ed, pap. 1.95 (0-87227-156-0, RBP5197); teacher ed, pap. 1.95 (0-87227-167-6, RBP5196) Reg Baptist.

Rich, Guy J., jt. auth. see Smith, Tom W.

***Rich, Hilary.** How to Be a Great Catch. 256p. (Orig.). 1995. mass mkt. 4.99 (0-380-77841-6) Avon.

Rich, Ivan N. & Lappin, Terence R., eds. Molecular, Cellular, & Developmental Biology of Erythropoietin & Erythropoiesis. LC 94-10689. (Annals Ser.: Vol. 718). 376p. 1994. write for info. (0-89766-837-5); pap. 100.00 (0-89766-838-3) NY Acad Sci.

Rich, J. David. Myths of the Tribe: When Religion, Economics, Government & Ethics Converge. 296p. (C). 1993. 29.95 (0-87975-824-4) Prometheus Bks.

Rich, J. W., ed. see Dio, Cassius.

Rich, Jack C. Sculpture in Wood. (Illus.). 176p. 1992. reprint ed. pap. 9.95 (0-486-27109-9) Dover.

Rich, Jacqueline & Coltman, Virginia. Summary & Recommendations: Clean Water Act Section 404 Discharge of Dredged & Fill Materials & Section 401 Water Quality Certification Programs in Arizona. 200p. 1991. pap. text ed. 25.00 (1-884320-05-8) ASU Herberger Ctr.

***Rich, Jan G. & Hurlburt, David.** Free Trade with Mexico: What's in It for Texas? (Policy Report Ser.: No. 1). 80p. 1992. 10.00 (0-89940-310-7) LBJ Sch Pub Aff.

Rich, Jane K. & Blake, Nelson M., eds. A Lasting Spring: Jessie Catherine Kinsley, Daughter of the Oneida Community. LC 82-19200. (New York State Bks.). (Illus.). 300p. (Orig.). 1982. 39.00x (0-8156-0183-2); pap. 15.95 (0-8156-0176-X) Syracuse U Pr.

Rich, Jason. Celebrity Teen Talk: Exclusive Celebrity Interviews, Video Game Tips & Reviews. (Illus.). 224p. (Orig.). (YA). (gr. 4-12). 1991. pap. 6.95 (0-9625057-5-7) DMS ID.

— Civilization Strategies & Secrets. 2nd ed. LC 94-66850. 262p. 1994. 14.99 (0-7821-1585-3) Sybex.

— Def Leppard. (CD Bks.). (Illus.). 120p. 1994. pap. 7.99 (1-886894-11-6, MBS Paperbk) Mus Bk Servs.

— Green Day. (CD Book Ser.). (Illus.). 120p. (Orig.). 1995. pap. 7.99 (1-886894-24-8, MBS Paperbk) Mus Bk Servs.

— The Official Rocket Science Guide to Cadillac & Dinosaurs. 1995. pap. text ed. 18.95 (0-07-882134-7) Osborne-McGraw.

— Official Sega Genesis Game Gear Games & Strategies. 1994. pap. 10.95 (0-679-75810-0) Knopf.

— Super Nintendo Almanac. 1994. pap. 12.99 (1-56686-203-5) Brady Compu Bks.

— Super Street Fighter II Official Strategy Guide. 1994. pap. 9.99 (1-56686-196-9) Brady Compu Bks.

— Ultimate Unauthorized Nintendo Super NES Game Strategies. 1994. pap. 10.95 (0-679-75811-9) Knopf.

— Virtua Racing: Official Driver's Strategy Guide. (Orig.). 1994. pap. (1-56686-184-5) Brady Compu Bks.

— Virtua Racing: Official Driver's Strategy Guide. (Illus.). 96p. (Orig.). 1994. pap. 9.95 (0-614-06069-9) Brady Compu Bks.

***Rich, Jason & Brady Games Staff.** The Lion King Official Game Book. (Illus.). 112p. (Orig.). 1995. pap. text ed. 9.99 (1-56686-231-0) Brady Compu Bks.

Rich, Jason R. Civilization Strategies & Secrets. LC 93-83897. 235p. 1993. pap. 12.95 (0-7821-1293-5) Sybex.

— A Parent's Guide to Video Games: A Practical Guide to Selecting & Managing Home Video Games. Dekeles, Jon C., ed. (Illus.). 128p. (Orig.). 1991. pap. 4.95 (0-9625057-7-3) DMS ID.

Rich, Jillian, jt. auth. see Rawlins, George.

Rich, Jim & Bozek, Sandy. Photoshop in Black & White. (Illus.). 48p. 1993. pap. 18.00 (1-56609-117-9) Peachpit Pr.

***Rich, Jim & Bozek, Snady.** Photoshop in Black & White. 2nd ed. 48p. 1995. pap. 18.00 (1-56609-189-6) Peachpit Pr.

Rich, John, ed. The City in Late Antiquity. LC 91-36367. (Leicester-Nottingham Studies in Ancient Society). 256p. 1992. 59.95 (0-415-06855-X, A7464) Routledge.

***Rich, John & Shipley, Graham.** War & Society in the Greek World. (Leicester-Nottingham Studies in Ancient Society). (Illus.). 264p. 1995. pap. 16.95 (0-415-12166-3, C0202) Routledge.

— War & Society in the Roman World. (Leicester-Nottingham Studies in Ancient Society). 320p. 1995. pap. 17.95 (0-415-12167-1, C0218) Routledge.

Rich, John & Shipley, Graham, eds. War & Society in the Greek World. LC 92-29074. (Leicester-Nottingham Studies in Ancient Society: Vol. 4). 1993. write for info. (0-415-06643-3, Routledge NY) Routledge.

— War & Society in the Roman World. LC 92-36698. (Leicester-Nottingham Studies in Ancient Society: Vol. 5). 1993. write for info. (0-415-06644-1) Routledge.

Rich, John & Wallace-Hadrill, Andrew, eds. City & Country in the Ancient World. (Leicester-Nottingham Studies in Ancient Society). 304p. 1991. 55.00 (0-415-01974-5, A4866) Routledge.

— City & Country in the Ancient World. (Leicester-Nottingham Studies in Ancient Society). (Illus.). 320p. 1992. pap. 16.95 (0-415-08223-4, A7623) Routledge.

Rich, John M. Chief Seattle's Unanswered Challenge. 61p. 1977. reprint ed. pap. 7.50 (0-87770-072-9) Ye Galleon.

— Innovations in Education: Reformers & Their Critics. 6th ed. 336p. (C). 1991. pap. text ed. 29.00 (0-205-13299-5) Allyn.

Rich, John M. & DeVitis, Joseph L. Competition in Education. 214p. (C). 1992. text ed. 41.95x (0-398-05819-9) C C Thomas.

— Competition in Education. 214p. 1992. pap. 24.95 (0-398-06348-6) C C Thomas.

— Theories of Moral Development. 2nd ed. LC 94-21565. 164p. (C). 1994. 34.95 (0-398-05924-1) C C Thomas.

Rich, John Martin, jt. auth. see DeVitis, Joseph L.

Rich-Jones, W., ed. Vetus Registrum Sarisberiense, Alias Dictum Registrum S. Osmundi Episcopi, Register of St. Osmund, 2 vols., Set. (Rolls Ser.: No. 78). 1974. reprint ed. 160.00 (0-8115-1148-0) Periodicals Srv.

Rich, Judy B., et al. Accounting in Life & Health Insurance Companies. LC 86-83715. (FLMI Insurance Education Program Ser.). 1987. student ed, pap. text ed. 10.00 (0-915322-86-2) LOMA.

Rich, Kathleen. The Art of Speech: A Handbook of Elocution. 4th rev. ed. 108p. 1984. 25.00 (0-905418-38-7, Pub. by Gresham Bks UK) St Mut.

Rich, Kim. Johnny's Girl: A Daughter's Memoir of Growing up in Alaska's Underworld. LC 92-19973. 1993. 22.00 (0-688-11836-4) Morrow.

Rich, Laurence D., ed. see Harding, Vicki R. & Petkun, Lisa B.

Rich, Laurie A. When Pregnancy Isn't Perfect: A Layperson's Guide to Complications in Pregnancy. 496p. 1991. 19.95 (0-525-24961-3, Dutton) NAL-Dutton.

— When Pregnancy Isn't Perfect: A Layperson's Guide to Complications in Pregnancy. 368p. 1993. pap. 12.00 (0-452-26963-6, Plume) NAL-Dutton.

Rich, Liddy. Odyssey Book of Houseplants. 1990. pap. 19.95 (0-9625702-0-6) Plant Odyssey Pr.

Rich, Linda, jt. auth. see Fahey, David.

Rich, Linda G., et al. Neighborhood: A State of Mind. LC 81-5992. (Illus.). 152p. 1981. 30.00 (0-8018-2558-X); pap. 16.95 (0-8018-2559-8) Johns Hopkins.

Rich, Linvil G. Low-Maintenance, Mechanically-Simple Wastewater Treatment Systems. (Water Resources & Environmental Engineering Ser.). (Illus.). 1980. text ed. write for info. (0-07-052252-9) McGraw.

— Unit Operations of Sanitary Engineering. LC 61-15410. (C). pap. 20.00 (0-686-11818-9) Rich SC.

— Unit Processes of Sanitary Engineering. LC 63-14067. (C). pap. 20.00 (0-686-15000-7) Rich SC.

Rich, Louise D. The Coast of Maine: An Informal History & Guide. LC 93-30612. 400p. 1993. reprint ed. pap. 13.95 (0-89272-342-4) Down East.

— Innocence under the Elms. 286p. 1983. reprint ed. pap. 7.95 (0-940160-22-6) Parnassus Imprints.

— Start of the Trail. 19.95 (0-89190-726-2, Am Repr) Amereon Ltd.

— We Took to the Woods. 22.95 (0-89190-858-7, Am Repr) Amereon Ltd.

— We Took to the Woods. 250p. 1992. reprint ed. lib. bdg. 18.95 (0-89966-913-1) Buccaneer Bks.

— We Took to the Woods. (Illus.). 1975. reprint ed. pap. 10. 95 (0-89272-016-6) Down East.

Rich, M. Robert, et al, eds. Contemporary Southwest Art. 52p. 1988. 5.00 (0-942746-14-7) SUNYP R Gibson.

Rich, Malcolm C. & Brucar, Wayne E. The Central Panel System for Administrative Law Judges: A Survey of Seven States. LC 82-74139. 99p. 1983. text ed. 42.95 (0-313-27084-8, U7084, Greenwood Pr) Greenwood.

Rich, Maria F. Who's Who in Opera: An International Biographical Directory of Singers, Conductors, Directors, Designers & Administers. 1976. 12.95 (0-405-06652-X, 19119) Ayer.

Rich, Marion K. A Song for All Seasons: Harmony in the Inner Life. 100p. (Orig.). 1992. pap. 6.95 (0-8341-1446-1) Beacon Hill.

Rich, Martin, jt. auth. see Waye, Jerome.

Rich, Marvin A., ed. Leukemia Reviews International, 2 vols., Vol. 1. LC 88-659642. (Illus.). 367p. 1983. reprint ed. pap. 99.10 (0-7837-0620-0, 2040965) Bks Demand.

— Leukemia Reviews International, 2 vols., Vol. 2. LC 88-659642. (Illus.). 201p. 1984. reprint ed. pap. 57.30 (0-7837-0621-9) Bks Demand.

Rich, Marvin A. & Furmanski, Philip, eds. Biological Carcinogenesis. LC 82-4996. (Illus.). 320p. reprint ed. pap. 91.20 (0-7837-0886-6, 2041192) Bks Demand.

Rich, Marvin A., et al, eds. Breast Cancer: Origins, Detection, & Treatment. (Developments in Oncology Ser.). 1986. lib. bdg. 80.50 (0-89838-792-2) Kluwer Ac.

— Breast Cancer: Progress in Biology, Clinical Management & Prevention. (Developments in Oncology Ser.). (C). 1989. lib. bdg. 79.00 (0-7923-0507-8) Kluwer Ac.

— Breast Cancer: Scientific & Clinical Progress. (C). 1988. lib. bdg. 127.00 (0-89838-387-0) Kluwer Ac.

— Understanding Breast Cancer: Clinical & Laboratory Concepts. LC 83-18981. (Illus.). 415p. reprint ed. pap. 118.30 (0-7837-0673-1, 2041008) Bks Demand.

***Rich, Mary & Jose, Carol.** Evil Web: A True Story of Cult Abuse & Courage. 320p. Date not set. 22.95 (0-88282-139-3) New Horizon NJ.

Rich, Mary L. Bandit's Kiss. (Wildflower Ser.). 336p. (Orig.). 1993. mass mkt. 4.99 (1-55773-842-4) Diamond.

— Colorado Tempest. (Wildflower Ser.). 352p. (Orig.). 1992. mass mkt. 4.99 (1-55773-799-1) Diamond.

Rich, Mary P., ed. see Brown, Fern G.

Rich, Mary P., ed. see Reiser, Howard.

Rich, Mary P., ed. see Wolfe, Rinna E.

Rich, Meredith. Bare Essence. 320p. (Orig.). 1982. pap. 2.95 (0-449-12376-6, GM) Fawcett.

— Tender Offerings. LC 93-42074. 1994. 22.00 (0-671-78883-3) S&S Trade.

Rich, Michael J. Federal Policymaking & the Poor: National Goals, Local Choices, & Distributional Outcomes. LC 93-7298. (Illus.). 424p. (C). 1993. text ed. 39.50 (0-691-08652-4) Princeton U Pr.

Rich, Nelson G. & Gilligan, Lawrence G. The TI-85 Reference Guide. (Illus.). 112p. (Orig.). 1993. pap. 18.95 (0-9626661-6-5) Gilmar Pub.

Rich, Neysa. Florida Real Estate Closings. 450p. 1991. ring bd. 90.00 (0-409-27142-X, Equity Pub NH) Butterworth Legal Pubs.

— Florida Real Estate Closings. 450p. 1994. ring bd. 90.00 (0-614-05822-8) Michie Butterworth.

— Florida Real Estate Closings. suppl. ed. 1993. 40.00 (0-685-74288-1) Butterworth Legal Pubs.

Rich, Norman. Great Power Diplomacy, 1815-1914. 1992. pap. text ed. write for info. (0-07-052254-5) McGraw.

— Why the Crimean War? A Cautionary Tale. 1991. pap. text ed. write for info. (0-07-052255-3) McGraw.

— Why the Crimean War? A Cautionary Tale. LC 84-40593. (Illus.). 280p. 1985. text ed. 35.00 (0-87451-328-6) U Pr of New Eng.

Rich, Norman M., jt. auth. see Wind, Gary G.

Rich, P. J. Elixir of Empire: The English Public Schools, Ritualism, Freemasonry & Imperialism. 152p. (C). 1988. 70.00 (0-7212-0759-6, Pub. by Regency Press) St Mut.

Rich, P. V. New World Vultures with Old World Affinities. (Contributions to Vertebrate Evolution Ser.: Vol. 5). (Illus.). 1979. pap. 31.25 (3-8055-0280-X) S Karger.

Rich, P. V. & Van Tets, G. F., eds. Kadimakara: Extinct Vertebrates of Australia. (Illus.). 284p. 1991. 25.00 (0-691-08733-4) Princeton U Pr.

Rich, Pamela E. & Tussing, Arlon R. The National Park System in Alaska: An Economic Impact Study. LC 73-620004. (ISER Reports: No. 35). (Illus.). 88p. 1973. pap. 2.00 (0-88353-008-2) U Alaska Inst Res.

Rich, Paul B. Hope & Despair: English-Speaking Intellectuals & South African Politics 1896-1976. 224p. 1993. text ed. 69.50 (1-85043-489-1, Pub. by I B Tauris UK) St Martin.

Rich, Paul B., ed. The Dynamics of Change in Southern Africa. LC 93-45832. 1994. text ed. 59.95 (0-312-12120-2) St Martin.

Rich, Peggy B. & Whitehurst, Marion A. The People's Journal: Pickens, South Carolina, 1894-1903, Historical & Genealogical Abstracts. x, 398p. (Orig.). 1991. pap. 35.00 (1-55613-428-2) Heritage Bk.

***Rich, Peggy B. & Whitehurst, Marion A., comps.** The Pickens Sentinel Favorite Newspaper of Pickens County: Pickens Court House, South Carolina 1872-1893 Historical & Genealogical Abstracts. (Illus.). 755p. (Orig.). 1994. pap. text ed. 70.00 (1-55613-985-3) Heritage Bk.

Rich, Peggy B., et al. Alexander Families of Upper South Carolina. (Illus.). 1100p. 1988. 45.00 (0-9620691-0-8) Rich SC.

Rich, Penny. Pamper Your Partner. 1990. pap. 15.95 (0-671-69526-6) S&S Trade.

Rich Publishing Company Staff, ed. see Blakely, James, et al.

Rich, R. A., et al. Hydrothermal Uranium Deposits. (Developments in Economic Geology Ser.: Vol. 6). 264p. 1977. 74.50 (0-444-41551-3) Elsevier.

Rich, Richard, ed. Urban Service Distributions. (Orig.). (C). 1981. pap. 12.00 (0-918592-46-1) Pol Studies.

Rich, Richard C., jt. auth. see Manheim, Jarol B.

Rich, Robert F. Social Science Information & Public Policy Making. LC 79-92468. (Jossey-Bass Social & Behavioral Science Ser.). 231p. reprint ed. pap. 65.90 (0-8357-6888-0, 2037940) Bks Demand.

Rich, Russell R. Ensign to the Nations: A History of the LDS Church from 1846 to 1972. LC 72-91730. (Illus.). 680p. (C). 1972. pap. 14.95 (0-8425-0671-3) BYU Scholarly.

An Asterisk (*) at the beginning of an entry indicates that the title is appearing in BIP for the first time.

Rich, Ruth & D'Onofrio, Carol N. Decisions for Health. (Discover Ser.). (Illus.). 520p. (YA). (gr. 9-12). 1993. teacher ed 41.95 (*0-7854-0050-8*, 15192); text ed. 31.95 (*0-7854-0149-0*, 15191); audio 113.95 (*0-7854-0060-5*, 15190); Total tchr. support system. 221.95 (*0-7854-0051-6*, 15193) Am Guidance.

Rich, S. & Edwards, T. GCSE Technology. (C). 1990. teacher ed 110.00 (*0-7487-0025-0*, Pub. by S Thornes Pubs UK) St Mut.

Rich, Sandra L. & Tucker, Roy W. Oregon Corporation Law & Practice. (National Corporation Law Ser.). 1991. ring bd. 126.00 (*0-13-640129-5*) Aspen Law.

Rich, Sandra L., jt. auth. see Burton, Robert E.

***Rich, Scharlotte.** I Love My Mommy. (J). 1995. 9.99 (*0-88070-748-8*, Gold & Honey) Questar Pubs.

Rich, Sharon. Sweethearts: The Timeless Love Affair - On-Screen & Off - Between Jeanette MacDonald & Nelson Eddy. LC 94-71105. (Illus.). 400p. 1994. 23.95 (*1-55611-407-9*) D I Fine.

Rich, Sharon L. & Phillips, Ariel, eds. Women's Experience & Education. LC 84-81321. (Reprint Ser.: No. 17). 312p. (C). 1985. pap. 17.95 (*0-916690-19-9*) Harvard Educ Rev.

Rich, Shebnah. Truro-Cape Cod; Landmarks & Seamarks. (Illus.). 580p. 1989. reprint ed. lib. bdg. 58.00 (*0-8328-0916-0*, MA0203) Higginson Bk Co.

Rich, Sheila. Fun & Fitness: A Step-by-Step Guide. LC 89-27393. (Be the Best! Ser.). (Illus.). 64p. (J). (gr. 4-8). 1990. lib. bdg. 9.79 (*0-8167-1949-7*); pap. text ed. 2.95 (*0-8167-1950-0*) Troll Assocs.

Rich, Shellie, jt. auth. see Mancini, Stephen C.

Rich, Stanley R. & Gumpert, David E. Business Plans That Win: Lessons from the MIT Enterprise Forum. LC 84-48617. (Illus.). 224p. 1987. pap. 12.00 (*0-06-091391-6*, PL 1391, PL) HarpC.

Rich, Steven H., Sr. High Desert Testament: What We Had, How We Lost It, How We Can Get It Back, & a Vision of a World Beyond Bull. 56p. 1992. pap. text ed. 5.95 (*1-881753-00-X*) Buckskin Mtn.

Rich, Sue. Mistress of Sin. 1994. mass mkt. 5.50 (*0-671-79408-6*) PB.

— Rawhide & Roses. Tolley, Carolyn, ed. 272p. (Orig.). 1993. mass mkt. 4.99 (*0-671-75914-0*) PB.

— The Scarlet Temptress. 336p. (Orig.). 1991. mass mkt. 5.50 (*0-671-73625-6*) PB.

— Shadowed Vows. Tolley, Carolyn, ed. 272p. (Orig.). 1992. mass mkt. 5.50 (*0-671-73626-4*) PB.

— The Silver Witch. Tolley, Carolyn, ed. 320p. (Orig.). 1995. mass mkt. 5.99 (*0-671-79409-4*) PB.

Rich, Susan. Kline Guide to Packaging. Deitsch, Marian, ed. (Illus.). 324p. 1980. pap. 70.00 (*0-685-02813-5*) Kline.

Rich, Susan, ed. Directory of Cosmetic & Toiletry Ingredients. 2nd ed. 365p. 1982. pap. 985.00 (*0-686-84482-3*) Kline.

— Kline Guide to the Paint Industry. 6th ed. LC 81-84942. (Illus.). 200p. 1981. pap. 97.00 (*0-917148-01-0*) Kline.

— Profiles of U. S. Chemical Distributors. LC 81-83812. 265p. 1981. pap. 277.00 (*0-917148-77-0*) Kline.

Rich, Susan, jt. ed. see Curry, Susan.

***Rich, Susanna.** The Flexible Writer: A Basic Guide. 2nd ed. LC 94-28568. 1994. pap. text ed. 21.00 (*0-205-15934-6*) Allyn.

***Rich, Terry L.** Your Opportunities in Accounting. (Illus.). 8p. 1994. pap. 2.00 (*1-884241-00-X*) Energeia Pub.

Rich, Thomas P., jt. ed. see Hudson, C. Michael.

Rich, Tracey R., jt. auth. see Zanan, Arthur S.

Rich, Vera, jt. auth. see Blum, Jakub.

Rich, Vincent. The International Lead Trade. 192p. 1993. 150.00 (*1-85573-103-7*, Pub. by Woodhead Pubng UK) St Mut.

Rich, Virginia. The Baked Bean Supper Murders. 1984. mass mkt. 4.95 (*0-345-31252-X*) Ballantine.

— Crafts for Fun. (Illus.). 96p. 1986. pap. 6.00 (*0-8170-1090-4*) Judson.

— The Nantucket Diet Murders. 1986. mass mkt. 4.99 (*0-440-16264-5*) Dell.

Rich, Wesley. History of the U. S. Post Office to 1829. 1973. 300.00 (*0-8490-0363-6*) Gordon Pr.

Rich, Wilbur. Coleman Young & Detroit Politics: From Social Activist to Power Broker. LC 88-39480. (African American Life Ser.). 298p. (C). 1989. 29.95 (*0-8143-2093-7*) Wayne St U Pr.

Rich, Wiley D. Legal Responsibilities & Rights of Public Accountants. Brief, Richard P., ed. LC 80-1514. (Dimensions of Accounting Theory & Practice Ser.). 1980. reprint ed. lib. bdg. 28.95 (*0-405-13539-4*) Ayer.

Rich, Will B. Easy Gourmet Recipes. (Illus.). 196p. 1984. pap. 15.95 (*0-9612468-7-1*) W B Rich.

Rich, William D., et al. Sentencing by Mathematics: An Evaluation of the Early Attempts to Develop & Implement Sentencing Guidelines. 240p. 1982. pap. write for info. (*0-318-56906-X*, R-071) Natl Ctr St Courts.

***Rich, Ysrael.** Education & Instruction in the Heterogeneous Class. LC 92-44302. (Illus.). 192p. 1993. pap. 25.95 (*0-398-06349-4*) C C Thomas.

— Education & Instruction in the Heterogeneous Class. LC 92-44302. (Illus.). 192p. 1993. text ed. 41.95 (*0-398-05847-4*) C C Thomas.

Richabhchand. Integral Yoga of Sri Aurobindo. 2nd ed. 1979. 6.00 (*0-89744-939-8*); pap. 4.50 (*0-89744-940-1*) Auromere.

Richalet, J., et al. Identification des Processus par la Methode du Modele. (Theorie des Systemes Ser.). 378p. 1972. text ed. 320.00 (*0-677-50740-2*) Gordon & Breach.

Richalton, James. James Richalton's Photographic Travelogue of Imperial India. Lucas, Christopher J., ed. LC 90-46220. (Studies in the Photographic Arts: Vol. 2). (Illus.). 308p. 1990. lib. bdg. 99.95 (*0-88946-509-6*) E Mellen.

Richan, Willard C. Beyond Altruism: Social Welfare Policy in American Society. LC 86-29437. (Administration in Social Work Ser.: Supp. No. 3). 238p. 1987. 39.95 (*0-86656-633-3*) Haworth Pr.

— Lobbying for Social Change. (Social Administration Ser.). 255p. (C). 1991. text ed. 39.95 (*1-56024-079-2*); pap. text ed. 19.95 (*1-56024-074-1*) Haworth Pr.

Richan, Willard C., ed. see Professional Symposium on Human Services & Professional Responsibility (2nd: 1968: San Francisco).

Richard, jt. auth. see Exley, Helen.

Richard, jt. auth. see Kemp.

Richard, ed. see Rousseau, Jean-Jacques.

Richard, Abbe M. What Happened at Pontmain. 80p. 1971. 1.25 (*0-911988-07-6*) AMI Pr.

***Richard, Adrienne & Reiter, Joel.** Epilepsy. 1995. pap. 11.95 (*0-8027-7465-2*) Walker & Co.

Richard-Akers, Nancy. Lady Sarah's Charade. 1992. mass mkt. 3.99 (*0-380-76531-4*) Avon.

Richard, Alfred. Panama Canal in American National Consciousness, 1870-1990. LC 90-3045. (Foreign Economic Policy of the United States Ser.). 378p. 1990. reprint ed. 35.00 (*0-8240-7471-8*) Garland.

Richard, Alfred C. Censorship & Hollywood's Hispanic Image: An Interpretive Filmography, 1936-1955. LC 92-40161. (Bibliographies & Indexes in the Performing Arts Ser.: No. 14). 640p. 1993. text ed. 79.50 (*0-313-28842-9*, GR8842, Greenwood Pr) Greenwood.

— Contemporary Hollywood's Negative Hispanic Image: An Interpretive Filmography, 1956-1993. LC 94-10862. (Bibliographies & Indexes in the Performing Arts Ser.: No. 16). 680p. 1994. text ed. 79.50 (*0-313-28841-0*, Greenwood Pr) Greenwood.

Richard, Alfred C., Jr. The Hispanic Image on the Silver Screen: An Interpretive Filmography from Silents into Sound, 1898-1935. LC 92-8917. (Bibliographies & Indexes in the Performing Arts Ser.: No. 12). 608p. 1992. text ed. 69.50 (*0-313-27832-6*, RHJ, Greenwood Pr) Greenwood.

Richard, Alison F. Behavioral Variation: Case Study of a Malagasy Lemur. LC 76-19837. (Illus.). 213p. 1978. 37.50 (*0-8387-1965-1*) Bucknell U Pr.

— Primate Ecology & Social Organization. Head, J. J., ed. LC 80-66617. (Carolina Biology Readers Ser.: No. 108). (Illus.). 16p. (C). (gr. 10 up). 1982. pap. 2.75 (*0-89278-308-7*, 45-9708) Carolina Biological.

— Primates in Nature. LC 84-18802. (Illus.). 558p. (C). 1995. pap. text ed. write for info. (*0-7167-1647-X*) W H Freeman.

Richard-Amato, Patricia A. Exploring Themes: An Interactive Approach to Literature. LC 92-40536. (Illus.). 1993. text ed. 18.50 (*0-8013-0601-9*) Longman.

— Making It Happen: Interaction in the Second Language Classroom. 1988. pap. text ed. 39.90 (*0-8013-0027-4*, 75692) Longman.

— Reading in the Content Areas: An Interactive Approach for Advanced Students. (YA). 1990. pap. text ed. 20.50 (*0-8013-0247-1*, 75902) Longman.

Richard-Amato, Patricia A. & Snow, Marguerite A., eds. The Multicultural Classroom: Readings for Content-Area Teachers. 432p. (C). 1991. pap. text ed. 32.25 (*0-8013-0511-X*, 78405) Longman.

Richard, Carl J. The Founders & the Classics: Greece, Rome, & the American Enlightenment. LC 93-28468. 307p. (Orig.). 1994. text ed. 44.50 (*0-674-31425-5*) HUP.

— The Founders & the Classics: Greece, Rome, & the American Enlightenment. 312p. (Orig.). (C). 1995. pap. text ed. 15.95 (*0-674-31426-3*) HUP.

Richard Caves & Associates Staff. Industrial Efficiency in Six Nations. (Illus.). 520p. 1992. 52.50 (*0-262-03193-0*) MIT Pr.

Richard, Chait & Papirno, Ralph, eds. Compression Testing of Homogeneous Materials & Composites - STP 808. LC 82-73768. 294p. 1983. text ed. 40.00 (*0-8031-0248-8*, 04-808000-23) ASTM.

Richard, Christopher. Brazil. LC 90-22471. (Cultures of the World Ser.: Group 2: Latin America). (Illus.). 128p. (YA). (gr. 5-9). 1991. lib. bdg. 21.95 (*1-85435-382-9*) Marshall Cavendish.

Richard, Cleo J. Comprehensive Nephrology Nursing. (C). 1986. text ed. 27.75 (*0-673-39368-2*) HarpCollege.

Richard, Cliff. Which One's Cliff? (Illus.). 256p. 1993. pap. 7.95 (*0-340-53049-9*, Pub. by H & S UK) Trafalgar.

Richard, D., jt. auth. see Pouzet, M.

***Richard, David.** Gathering the Wind. 64p. (Orig.). 1994. pap. 5.00 (*0-9637547-3-4*) Arbor Hill Pr.

Richard, Dinah. Has Sex Education Failed Our Teenagers? A Research Report. 112p. (Orig.). 1990. pap. text ed. 7.95 (*0-929608-22-4*) Focus Family.

***Richard, Earl.** 1 & 2 Thessalonians. (Sacra Pagina Ser.: No. 11). (Orig.). 1995. pap. text ed. write for info. (*0-8146-5813-X*, M Glazier) Liturgical Pr.

— Jesus One & Many: The Christology Concept of New Testament Authors. 546p. 1988. 29.95 (*0-8146-5641-2*) Liturgical Pr.

— New Views on Luke & Acts. 196p. (Orig.). 1991. pap. 12.95 (*0-8146-5704-4*) Liturgical Pr.

***Richard Earl of Bradford.** Stately Secrets: Behind-the-Scene Stories from the Stately Homes of Britain. 211p. 1995. 23.95 (*0-86051-917-1*, Robson-Parkwest) Parkwest Pubns.

Richard, Ellis. Lassen Volcanic: The Story Behind the Scenery. LC 88-80120. (Illus.). 48p. 1988. pap. 6.95 (*0-88714-020-3*) KC Pubns.

Richard, Francoise. On Cat Mountain. LC 93-11408. (Illus.). 40p. (J). (ps-4). 1994. 15.95 (*0-399-22608-7*, Putnam) Putnam Pub Group.

Richard, Frederic M., jt. ed. see Tometsko, Andrew M.

Richard, Gail & Hanner, Mary A. LPR (Language Processing Remediation) & LPT (Language Processing Test) 1987. student ed, spiral bd. 86.90 (*1-55999-056-2*) LinguiSystems.

— LPT (Language Processing Test) 1985. 54.95 (*1-55999-054-6*) LinguiSystems.

— LPT (Language Processing Test) Examiner's Manual. 1985. 36.00 (*1-55999-055-4*) LinguiSystems.

Richard, Gail J. & Hanner, Mary A. LPR (Language Processing Remediation) 1987. student ed, spiral bd. 31.95 (*1-55999-053-8*) LinguiSystems.

Richard, Gisbert. Fluorescein Angiography. Blodi, Frederick C., tr. (Illus.). 231p. 1990. text ed. 97.00 (*0-86577-336-X*) Thieme Med Pubs.

Richard, Herman G. The Relation of Accelerated Normal & Retarded Puberty to the Height & Weight of School Children. (SRCD M: Vol. 2, No. 1). 1937. pap. 15.00 (*0-527-01494-X*) Periodicals Srv.

Richard, J. The Latin Kingdom of Jerusalem, 2 Pts., Set. (Europe in the Middle Ages Selected Studies: Vol. 11). 514p. 1978. 91.50 (*0-444-85092-9*, North Holland) Elsevier.

Richard, J. A. Student's Guide to Better Grades. 1976. pap. 3.00 (*0-87980-152-2*) Wilshire.

***Richard, J. E.** Board Compensation Committee Manual. (Illus.). 184p. 1995. 125.00 (*1-887434-00-3*) J Richard.

***Richard, J. E., et al.** Board of Director Compensation Guide. 184p. 1995. 95.00 (*1-887434-25-9*) J Richard.

Richard, J. L. & Thurston, J. R., eds. Diagnosis of Mycotoxicoses. (Current Topics in Veterinary Medicine & Animal Science Ser.). 1986. lib. bdg. 216.00 (*0-89838-751-5*) Kluwer Ac.

Richard, J. M., et al, eds. The Elementary Structure of Matter. (Proceedings in Physics Ser.: Vol. 26). (Illus.). 530p. 1988. 78.00 (*0-387-19013-9*) Spr-Verlag.

Richard, J. P. Onze Etudes sur la Poesie Moderne. (FRE.). 1981. pap. 18.95 (*0-7859-2686-0*) Fr & Eur.

— Poesie et Profondeur. (FRE.). 1976. pap. 14.95 (*0-7859-2673-9*) Fr & Eur.

Richard, Jack & Lowe, David. The City of Lace. (C). 1988. 60.00 (*0-685-30218-0*, Pub. by Lace Centre UK) St Mut.

Richard, Jacqueline. Save Your Marriage Ahead of Time: Pre-Marital Contracting for Today's Couples. LC 91-3131. 256p. 1991. 18.95 (*0-87131-628-5*) M Evans.

Richard, James W. The Confessional History of the Lutheran Church. LC 83-45672. reprint ed. 62.50 (*0-404-19861-9*) AMS Pr.

Richard, Jean. Le Comte de Tripoli Sous la Dynastie Toulousaine (1102-1187) LC 78-63365. (Crusades & Military Orders Ser.: Second Series). reprint ed. 47.50 (*0-404-17033-1*) AMS Pr.

— Croisades et Etats Latins d'Orient. 336p. 1992. 95.00 (*0-86078-340-5*, Pub. by Variorum UK) Ashgate Pub Co.

— Croises, Missionaires et Voyageurs: Perspectives Orientales du Monde Latin Medieval. (Collected Studies: No. CS182). 340p. (FRE.). (C). 1983. reprint ed. lib. bdg. 99.50 (*0-86078-130-5*, Pub. by Variorum UK) Ashgate Pub Co.

— Saint Louis: Crusader King of France. abr. ed. Lloyd, Simon, ed. Birrell, Jean, tr. (Illus.). 408p. (C). 1992. 69.95 (*0-521-38156-8*) Cambridge U Pr.

***Richard, Jean-Marc.** Dictionnaire des Expressions Paillardes et Libertines de la Litterature Francaise. 271p. (FRE.). 1993. pap. 49.95 (*0-7859-8053-9*, 2850183806) Fr & Eur.

***Richard, Jesse, et al.** First Hand: Personal Accounts of Breakthroughs in Facilitated Communications. (Movin' On Ser.). 64p. 1993. pap. 10.00 (*1-886928-03-7*) DRI Pr.

***Richard, John.** Dress Your Bear: Seven Bears to Cut Out & Dress. (Illus.). (J). (gr. 1 up). 1995. pap. 7.95 (*0-316-74442-5*) Little.

Richard, Judith, ed. see Highstein, Ellen.

Richard, Kevin, jt. auth. see Burdette, David.

Richard, L. Comprehensive Geography of the Chinese Empire & Dependencies. Kennelly, M., tr. 1978. reprint ed. 40.00 (*0-89986-339-6*) Oriental Bk Store.

Richard, Lena. New Orleans Cook Book. (Cookery Ser.). 160p. 1985. reprint ed. pap. 3.95 (*0-486-24819-4*) Dover.

Richard, Lionel. Encyclopedie de l'Expressionisme. 288p. (FRE.). 1977. 59.95 (*0-8288-5419-X*, M6485) Fr & Eur.

Richard, Lucien. What Are They Saying about the Theology of Suffering? LC 92-21583. (What Are They Saying about...Ser.). 176p. 1993. pap. 7.95 (*0-8091-3347-4*) Paulist Pr.

Richard, Margaret C., jt. ed. see Kohl, Lawrence F.

Richard, Mark. Fishboy: A Ghost's Story. LC 92-37196. 1993. pap. 19.95 (*0-385-42560-0*, N A Talese) Doubleday.

— Fishboy: A Ghost's Story. LC 93-46786. 1994. 9.95 (*0-385-42568-6*, Anchor NY) Doubleday.

— The Ice at the Bottom of the World. 1989. 16.95 (*0-394-56485-5*) Knopf.

— Ice at the Bottom of the World. 1991. mass mkt. 7.95 (*0-385-41544-3*, Anchor NY) Doubleday.

***Richard, Mary F., ed.** Deaths from the Delaware Gazette 1854-59, 61-64. (Delaware Genealogical Abstracts from Newspapers Ser.: Vol. 1). 314p. 1995. pap. text ed. 25.00 (*1-887061-06-1*) DE Geneal Soc.

Richard, Mary M. Before & after School Programs: A Start-Up & Administration Manual. 108p. (Orig.). (C). 1991. pap. text ed. 24.95 (*0-917505-05-0*) School Age.

Richard, Michel. Michel Richard's Home Cooking with a French Accent. 1993. 30.00 (*0-688-08494-X*) Morrow.

Richard, Michel P. Without Passport: The Life & Work of Paul Richard. (American University Studies: History: Ser. IX, Vol. 28). 281p. (C). 1987. text ed. 44.95 (*0-8204-0444-6*) P Lang Pubs.

Richard, Michel P. & Mann, John. Exploring Social Space: Participant's Manual. LC 72-88813. (C). 1973. pap. 13.95 (*0-02-926410-3*) Free Pr.

Richard, Nancy. Once upon a Rainbow. (Illus.). 31p. (Orig.). 1992. pap. 4.95 (*0-9631685-0-9*) N&R Enter.

Richard, Nancy, jt. auth. see Carll, Barbara.

Richard, Naomi N., ed. see Clark, Timothy, et al.

Richard, Naomi N., ed. see Lee, Sherman E.

Richard, Nathanael. Tragedy of Messalina: The Roman Emperesse. Skemp, A., ed. (Material for the Study of the Old English Drama Ser.: No. 1, Vol. 30). 1974. reprint ed. pap. 24.00 (*0-8115-0279-1*) Periodicals Srv.

Richard, Norma, jt. auth. see Britz, Joan.

Richard, Octavia, ed. Charlemagne Romances, No. 10: Four Sonnes of Aymon, 1 pts., Pt. 1. (EETS, ES Ser.: Nos. 44). 1972. reprint ed. 40.00 (*0-527-00253-4*) Periodicals Srv.

— Charlemagne Romances, No. 10: Four Sonnes of Aymon, 1 pts., Pt. 2. (EETS, ES Ser.: Nos. 44). 1972. reprint ed. 40.00 (*0-527-00254-2*) Periodicals Srv.

Richard of St. Victor. Richard of St. Victor's "Treatise on the Study of Wisdom That Men Call Benjamin" As Adapted in Middle English by the Author of "The Cloud of Unknowing" Together with "Treatise on Discretion of Spirits" & "Epistle on Discretion of Stirrings" Barnes, Dick, tr. LC 90-39519. (Studies in Mediaeval Literature: Vol. 7). 120p. 1990. lib. bdg. 59.95 (*0-88946-294-1*) E Mellen.

Richard of St. Victor, et al. Cell of Self-Knowledge. Gardner, E. G., ed. LC 66-25702. (Medieval Library). reprint ed. 42.00 (*0-8154-0188-4*) Cooper Sq.

***Richard, Pablo.** Apocalypse: Reconstruction of Hope. (Bible & Liberation Ser.). 150p. (Orig.). 1995. pap. 16.95 (*1-57075-043-2*) Orbis Bks.

— The Idols of Death & the God of Life: A Theology. Campbell, Barbara E. & Shepard, Bonnie, trs. LC 83-6788. 240p. (Orig.). reprint ed. pap. 68.40 (*0-8357-2689-4*, 2040225) Bks Demand.

Richard, Patrick, jt. ed. see Marton, L. L.

Richard, Patrick, jt. ed. see Stockli, Martin.

Richard, Paul. The Dollarplan: Spending & Savings Techniques for the 1990s. 122p. 1990. 24.95 (*0-685-34772-9*) Natl Ctr Fin Ed.

Richard, Paul E. Russia Survival Guide: The Definitive Guide to Doing Business & Traveling in Russia. 5th ed. 232p. 1994. pap. 18.50 (*1-880100-18-5*) Russian Info Srvs.

Richard, Paul S. The Dollarplan: A Financial Education Course. (Illus.). 1985. teacher ed 55.00 (*0-318-04706-3*) Natl Ctr Fin Ed.

— The Dollarplan: A Financial Education Course. (Illus.). 230p. 1994. ring bd. 24.00 (*0-935451-00-5*) Natl Ctr Fin Ed.

— Financial Education One Hundred One: The Student Dollar Plan. (Illus.). 1986. 15.00 (*0-317-47155-4*) Natl Ctr Fin Ed.

Richard, Pearl & Pearl, Mignon W., eds. America's Mountain. 2nd ed. (Illus.). 36p. 1990. reprint ed. pap. 3.50 (*0-936564-38-5*) Little London.

Richard, Philippe, jt. auth. see Urban, Ivan.

Richard, Poor, jt. auth. see Fawthrop, Paul B.

Richard, Ralph. All about Wills for Florida Residents. rev. ed. (Illus.). 1983. pap. 4.95 (*0-88251-078-9*) Trend Bk Div.

***Richard, Ramesh.** Scripture Sculpture: A Do-It-Yourself Manual for Biblical Preaching. LC 94-34615. 144p. 1995. pap. 10.99 (*0-8010-7774-5*) Baker Bk.

Richard, Reginald L. & Staley, Marlys J., eds. Burn Care & Rehabilitation: Principles & Practice. LC 93-8304. (Contemporary Perspectives in Rehabilitation Ser.: Vol. 12). (Illus.). 711p. (C). 1993. 90.00 (*0-8036-7361-2*) Davis Co.

Richard, Renaud, ed. see Icaza, Jorge.

Richard, Roy, ed. see Conrad, Chris.

Richard, S. Releasing Anger. 20p. 1985. pap. 1.55 (*0-89486-249-9*, 1420B) Hazelden.

Richard, Sandra C., jt. ed. see Gray, H. Peter.

Richard, Stephen. Directory of British Official Publications: A Guide to Sources. 2nd ed. LC 84-12559. 468p. 1984. 120.00 (*0-7201-1706-2*, Mansell Pub) Cassell.

Richard, Stephen A., jt. ed. see Yocom, Margaret R.

Richard, Sukey, et al, eds. NOLS Cookery. 2nd ed. LC 88-60635. (Illus.). 105p. 1988. pap. 5.95 (*1-882045-00-9*) NOLS.

Richard T. Ingram & Associates Staff. Governing Independent Colleges & Universities: A Handbook for Trustees, Chief Executives, & Other Campus Leaders. LC 93-19511. (Higher & Adult Education Ser.). 515p. 1993. 49.95 (*1-55542-567-4*) Jossey-Bass.

— Governing Public Colleges & Universities: A Handbook for Trustees, Chief Executives, & Other Campus Leaders. LC 93-19512. (Higher & Adult Education Ser.). 509p. (C). 1993. 49.95 (*1-55542-566-6*) Jossey-Bass.

Richard, Valliere T. Norman McLaren, Manipulator of Movement: The National Film Board Years, 1947-67. LC 80-53998. (Illus.). 128p. 1982. 28.50 (*0-87413-192-8*) U Delaware Pr.

Richard, Wesley. Guide-A-Write. (Illus.). 120p. 1982. pap. 5.95 (*0-933704-22-4*) Dawn Pr.

Richard, Willis J. An Introduction to Economics, Economists, & Economies. 114p. 1969. pap. text ed. 9.95 (*0-8290-1095-5*) Irvington.

Richard, Yann. Shiite Islam: Polity, Ideology & Creed. Nevill, Antonia, tr. LC 94-15820. (Studies in Social Discontinuity). 256p. (C). 1995. text ed. 54.95 (*1-55786-469-1*); pap. text ed. 21.95 (*1-55786-470-5*) Blackwell Pubs.

Richard, Yann, jt. auth. see Keddie, Nikki R.

Richardin, A. Dactylology: Conversing with the Deaf & Dumb. 1973. 59.95 (*0-87968-990-0*) Gordon Pr.

Richards. Behavioral Psychotherapy. 1990. 38.95 (*0-433-02526-3*) Buttrwrth-Heinemann.

— By the Cut of Your Clothes. Grad, Doug, ed. 224p. (Orig.). 1995. mass mkt. 4.99 (*0-671-87242-7*) PB.

R

— Invisibility. 1992. pap. 9.00 (*1-85538-168-0*) Thorsons SF.
— Let the Circle Be Unbroken: The Implications of African Spirituality in the Diaspora. 1994. per. 6.95 (*0-932415-25-3*) Red Sea Pr.
— Traditional Astrology & Jung's Psychology. 1992. write for info. (*0-86690-399-2*) Am Fed Astrologers.
Richards, ed. Document Forms for Orders of Official Appointment in the Mughal Empire: Translation Notes & Text. (Gibb Memorial New Ser.: Vol. 29). 1986. 65.00 (*0-906094-14-3*, Pub. by Aris & Phillips UK) David Brown.
Richards & Hildebrand. Prayers That Prevail for America. 261p. 1993. write for info. (*0-932081-34-7*) Victory Hse.
Richards, jt. auth. see Gough.
Richards, A. J. Plant Breeding Systems in Seed Plants. (Illus.). 320p. (C). 1986. text ed. 100.00 (*0-04-581020-6*); pap. text ed. 44.95 (*0-04-581021-4*) Routledge Chapman & Hall.
Richards, Adian J. Primula. (Illus.). 352p. 1993. 49.95 (*0-88192-228-5*) Timber.
Richards, Adrian F., ed. Marine Geotechnique: Proceedings. International Research Conference on Marine Geotechnique (1966: Allerton House) LC 67-27773. (Illus.). 335p. reprint ed. 95.50 (*0-8357-9688-4*, 2014936) Bks Demand.
— Vane Shear Strength Testing in the Field & Laboratory. LC 88-7684. (Special Technical Publication Ser.: No. STP 1014). (Illus.). 450p. 1988. text ed. 79.00 (*0-8031-1188-6*, 04-010140-38) ASTM.
Richards-Akers, Nancy. The Heart & the Heather. 384p. (Orig.). 1994. mass mkt. 4.50 (*0-380-77519-0*) Avon.
— The Heart & the Rose. 384p. (Orig.). 1995. mass mkt. 4.99 (*0-380-78001-1*) Avon.
— Lord Fortune's Prize. 224p. (Orig.). 1993. mass mkt. 3.99 (*0-380-77191-8*) Avon.
— Miss Wickham's Betrothal. 224p. (Orig.). 1992. mass mkt. 3.99 (*0-380-76532-2*) Avon.
***Richards, Alan.** Are You Thinking of Moving from the City to the Country. (Illus.). 205p. (Orig.). 1995. pap. text ed. 12.95 (*0-9643911-0-4*) A Richards.
— Birds of Prey: Hunters of the Sky. (Illus.). 144p. 1992. 16.98 (*1-56138-176-4*) Courage Bks.
— Development & Modes of Production in Marxian Economics (a Critical Evaluation) (In the Fundamentals of Pure & Applied Economics Ser.: Volume 12). 160p. 1986. pap. text ed. 44.00 (*3-7186-0332-2*) Gordon & Breach.
Richards, Alan & Waterbury, John. A Political Economy of the Middle East: State, Class, & Economic Development. 495p. (C). 1990. pap. text ed. 26.50 (*0-8133-0156-4*) Westview.
Richards, Albert G. The Secret Garden - One Hundred Floral Radiographs. (Illus.). 114p. 1991. 40.00 (*0-9628791-0-X*) Almar Ml.
Richards, Alison, jt. auth. see Morgan, Joan.
Richards, Alison, jt. ed. see Wolpert, Lewis.
Richards, Allan. How to Get a 4.0, Easily: One Hundred Twenty-Seven Ways to Get A's. 64p. 1993. pap. text ed. 7.95 (*0-9630737-0-2*) Vector NY.
Richards, Alun. Plays for Players. 367p. (C). 1975. text ed. 75.00 (*0-85088-290-7*, Pub. by Gomer Pr UK) St Mut.
Richards, Ann & Nobile, Peter. High Heels & Backwards. 1989. 18.95 (*0-318-42520-3*) S&S Trade.
Richards, Ann & Wanner, Glen. Bicycling Middle Tennessee: A Guide to Scenic Bicycle Rides in Nashville's Countryside. LC 93-86049. (Illus.). 192p. (Orig.). 1993. pap. 13.95 (*0-9637798-0-X*) Pennywell Pr.
— Bicycling Middle Tennessee: A Guide to Scenic Bicycle Rides in Nashville's Countryside. 2nd ed. (Orig.). 1994. pap. 14.95 (*0-9637798-1-8*) Pennywell Pr.
Richards, Ann L., jt. auth. see Wiehe, Vernon R.
Richards, Arlene K. & Richards, Arnold, eds. The Spectrum of Psychoanalysis: Essays in Honor of Martin S. Bergmann. 378p. 1994. text ed. 55.00 (*0-8236-4505-3*) Intl Univs Pr.
Richards, Arlene K. & Willis, Irene. How to Get It Together When Your Parents Are Coming Apart. 170p. (J). (gr. 5-12). 1986. reprint ed. pap. 9.95 (*0-9615349-0-7*, HQ536.R48) Willard Pr.
— What to Do If You or Someone You Know Is under 18 & Pregnant. LC 82-12698. (Illus.). 256p. 1983. 14.88 (*0-688-51961-X*) Lothrop.
— What to Do If You Or Someone You Know Is under 18 & Pregnant. LC 82-12698. (Illus.). 256p. (J). (gr. 7 up). 1983. pap. 8.95 (*0-688-01044-X*, Pub. by Beech Tree Bks) Morrow.
Richards, Arnold, jt. ed. see Richards, Arlene K.
Richards, Arnold D. & Willick, Martin S., eds. Psychoanalysis: The Science of Mental Conflict. (Essays in Honor of Chas Brenner Ser.). 439p. 1986. text ed. 49.95 (*0-88163-054-3*) Analytic Pr.
Richards, Arthur. The End: Year 2287. 200p. 1989. per. 10.95 (*0-89697-296-8*) Intl Univ Pr.
Richards, Audrey. Chisungu: A Girl's Initiation Ceremony among the Bemba. 224p. 1982. pap. 14.95 (*0-422-78070-7*, NO. 3665, Pub. by Tavistock UK) Routledge Chapman & Hall.
— Managing Volunteers for Results. 2nd ed. LC 79-87850. 1979. ring bd. 49.00 (*0-916664-10-4*) Datarex Corp.
Richards, Audrey I. Hunger & Work in a Savage Society. LC 84-22540. xvi, 238p. 1985. reprint ed. text ed. 55.00 (*0-313-24688-2*, RIHW, Greenwood Pr) Greenwood.
— Land, Labour & Diet in North. (Classics in African Anthropology Ser.). (C). 1995. text ed. 64.50 (*3-89473-689-5*); pap. text ed. 25.50 (*3-89473-876-6*) Westview.
— The Multicultural States of East Africa. LC 74-101260. (Centre for Developing-Area Studies, McGill University, Keith Callard Lectures: No. 3). 135p. reprint ed. pap. 38.50 (*0-7837-1160-3*, 2041689) Bks Demand.
Richards, Audrey I. & Kuper, Adam, eds. Councils in Action. LC 76-160101. (Cambridge Papers in Social Anthropology: No. 6). 222p. reprint ed. pap. 63.30 (*0-317-27985-8*, 2025594) Bks Demand.
Richards, B. P. & Foorner, P. K. The Role of Microscopy in Semiconductor Failure Analysis. (Royal Microscopical Society Microscopy Handbooks Ser.: No. 25). (Illus.). 104p. 1992. pap. 27.50 (*0-19-856432-5*) OUP.
***Richards, Barry.** Disciplines of Delight: The Psychoanalysis of Popular Culture. 200p. 1994. pap. 25.00 (*1-85343-325-X*) NYU Pr.
— Images of Freud. 223p. 1989. 29.95 (*0-312-04004-0*) St Martin.
Richards, Barry, ed. Crises of the Self: Further Essays on Psychoanalysis & Politics. 278p. 1989. 45.00 (*1-85343-095-1*) Col U Pr.
— Crises of the Self: Further Essays on Psychoanalysis & Politics. 278p. 1989. pap. 19.50 (*1-85343-094-3*) Col U Pr.
Richards, Barry, jt. auth. see Heny, Frank.
Richards, Barry, et al. Temporal Representation & Inference. (Cognitive Science Ser.). 370p. 1989. text ed. 52.00 (*0-12-587770-6*) Acad Pr.
Richards, Barry M. Thriving After Surviving. LC 88-84104. 128p. (Orig.). 1989. pap. 9.95 (*0-9622787-0-X*) Hartley Commns.
Richards, Bartlett, Jr. & Van Ackeren, Ruth. Bartlett Richards: Nebraska Sandhills Cattleman. LC 79-92129. (Illus.). 289p. (Orig.). 1980. 12.00 (*0-686-31143-4*) Nebraska Hist.
Richards, Benjamin B., ed. see Davis, Stephen C.
Richards, Bernard A. English Poetry of the Victorian Period, 1830-1890. (Literature in English Ser.). 304p. (Orig.). (C). 1988. pap. text ed. 25.50 (*0-582-49345-5*, 73584) Longman.
Richards, Beth, jt. auth. see Simmerman, Jim.
Richards, Betty W. & Kaneko, Anne. Japanese Plants: Know Them & Use Them. (Illus.). 224p. 1988. pap. 14.95 (*4-07-975121-4*, Pub. by Shufunomoto Co Ltd JA) C E Tuttle.
***Richards, Bradley W.** The Savage View: Charles Savage, Mormon Pioneer Photographer. Chapman, Jean, ed. LC 94-77983. (Illus.). 250p. 1995. 34.95 (*0-9621940-5-0*) C Mautz Pubng.
— The Savage View: Charles Savage, Mormon Pioneer Photographer. Chapman, Jean, ed. (Illus.). 250p. 1995. pap. 19.95 (*0-9621940-6-9*) C Mautz Pubng.
Richards, Brian, ed. see Canalos, David.
Richards, Brian J. Language Development & Individual Differences: A Study of Auxiliary Verb Learning. (Illus.). 250p. (C). 1990. 64.95 (*0-521-36253-9*) Cambridge U Pr.
Richards, Brian J., jt. ed. see Gallaway, Clare.
Richards, Bruce. Blind Date. (Freddy Krueger's Tales of Terror Ser.: No. 1). 164p. (YA). 1994. mass mkt. 3.99 (*0-8125-5168-0*) Tor Bks.
— Cat Scratch Fever. 224p. 1995. mass mkt. 3.99 (*0-8217-4981-1*) Windsor NY.
— Deadly Stakes. (Nightmare Club Ser.: No. 8). 224p. 1994. pap. 3.50 (*0-8217-4450-X*) Zebra.
— Fatal Games. (Freddy Krueger's Tales of Terror Ser.: No. 2). (J). (gr. 4-7). 1995. pap. 3.99 (*0-8125-5189-3*) Tor Bks.
— The Killing Game. 224p. 1994. mass mkt. 3.50 (*0-8217-4764-9*) Zebra.
— The Other Twin. 224p. 1995. pap. 3.99 (*0-8217-5054-2*) Zebra.
— Twice Burned: A New Elm Street Novel. (Freddy Krueger's Tales of Terror Ser.: No. 4). (Orig.). (YA). 1995. mass mkt. 3.99 (*0-8125-5192-3*) Tor Bks.
— Virtual Terror: A New Elm Street Novel. (Freddy Kruger's Tales of Terror Ser.: No. 3). 160p. (Orig.). (YA). 1995. mass mkt. 3.99 (*0-8125-5190-7*) Tor Bks.
Richards, C. Dialogue with the Masters. Arledge, G., ed. 54p. (Orig.). 1994. pap. text ed. 4.00 (*0-9625067-1-0*) Helpers Pr.
— The Helpers. Arledge, G., ed. 44p. (Orig.). 1989. 3.00 (*0-9625067-0-2*) Helpers Pr.
Richards, C., jt. ed. see Ford, J. M.
Richards, C. G., ed. Control of Mammal Pests. 250p. 1986. 125.00 (*0-85066-371-7*) Taylor & Francis.
Richards, Carl. Prey: Designing & Tying New Imitations. (Illus.). 144p. 1995. 24.95 (*1-55821-332-5*) Lyons & Burford.
Richards, Carl, jt. auth. see Swisher, Doug.
Richards, Caroline, jt. ed. see Lonergan, Anne.
Richards, Caroline C. Village Life in America, 1852-1872. 1977. lib. bdg. 59.95 (*0-8490-2798-5*) Gordon Pr.
— Village Life in America, 1852-1872: Diary of a School Girl. 225p. 1972. reprint ed. 22.50 (*0-87928-029-8*) Corner Hse.
Richards, Carolyn, ed. see Coleman, Richard.
Richards, Cathy, jt. ed. see Coker, Annabel.
Richards, Celia G. Jade Ecstasy. 1981. pap. 2.95 (*0-89083-790-2*) Zebra.
Richards, Ceri, tr. see Stuart-Smith, Stephen & Redden, Mary, eds.
Richards, CherylAnne, jt. auth. see Michrina, Barry P.
Richards, Cinda. Dillon's Promise. large type ed. LC 93-1348. 1993. 19.95 (*0-7927-1630-2*, Curley Lrg Print); pap. 17.95 (*0-7927-1629-9*, Curley Lrg Print) Chivers N Amer.
— One from the Heart. large type ed. (Linford Romance Library). 320p. 1994. pap. 14.95 (*0-7089-7521-6*, Linford) Ulverscroft.
— Such Rough Splendor. large type ed. 1994. 20.95 (*0-7927-2099-7*, Curley Lrg Print); pap. 19.95 (*0-7927-2098-9*, Curley Lrg Print) Chivers N Amer.
Richards, Clarice E. A Tenderfoot Bride: Tales from an Old Ranch. LC 88-14347. viii, 240p. 1988. 20.00 (*0-8032-3889-4*); pap. 7.95 (*0-8032-8930-8*) U of Nebr Pr.
Richards, Clay. Marble Jungle. 1961. 12.95 (*0-8392-1064-7*) Astor-Honor.
Richards, Colin. Sheriff Pat Garrett's Last Days. LC 85-25020. (Illus.). 96p. (Orig.). 1986. pap. 8.95 (*0-86534-079-X*) Sunstone Pr.
Richards, Colin, jt. ed. see Pearson, Michael P.
Richards, Connie L., ed. see Gilman, Charlotte P.
Richards, Craig E. Microcomputer Applications for Strategic Management in Education: A Case Study Approach. 127p. (C). 1989. pap. text ed. 22.95 (*0-582-28668-9*, 71684) Longman.
Richards, D. J., ed. see Lermontov.
Richards, D. J., tr. see Suetin, A. S.
Richards, Daniel, III. Statistical Exercises & Calculator Procedures. 120p. 1993. spiral bd. 12.95 (*0-8403-8410-6*) Kendall-Hunt.
Richards, Daniel L. Building & Managing Your Private Practice. 1990. 26.95 (*1-55620-071-4*) Am Coun Assn.
***Richards, David.** Masks of Difference: Cultural Representations in Literature, Anthropology & Art. (Cultural Margins Ser.: No. 2). (Illus.). 350p. (C). 1995. 59.95 (*0-521-44458-6*) Cambridge U Pr.
— Masks of Difference: Cultural Representations in Literature, Anthropology & Art. (Cultural Margins Ser.: No. 2). (Illus.). 350p. (C). 1995. pap. 18.95 (*0-521-47972-X*) Cambridge U Pr.
— Russian Rightists & the Revolution of Nineteen Hundred Five. LC 94-8850. (Cultural Margins Ser.: No. 2). (Illus.). 300p. (C). 1995. pap. 29.95 (*0-521-48386-7*) Cambridge U Pr.
Richards, David, ed. The Penguin Book of Russian Short Stories. 1981. pap. 11.00 (*0-14-004816-2*, Penguin Bks) Viking Penguin.
Richards, David, tr. see Bunin, Ivan.
Richards, David, jt. ed. see Schulte, Hans.
Richards, David A. Conscience & the Constitution: History, Theory, & the Law of the Reconstruction Amendments. LC 92-42895. 248p. (C). 1993. text ed. 35.00 (*0-691-03231-9*) Princeton U Pr.
— For Those Who Hunt the Wounded Down. 1994. pap. 14.95 (*0-7710-7464-6*, Pub. by McClelland & Stewart CN) Firefly Bks Ltd.
— Foundations of American Constitutionalism. 336p. 1989. 45.00 (*0-19-505939-5*) OUP.
— Sex, Drugs, Death & the Law: An Essay on Human Rights & Overcriminalization. LC 81-23392. (Philosophy & Society Ser.). 328p. 1982. 50.50 (*0-8476-7063-5*); pap. 21.00 (*0-8476-7525-4*) Rowman.
— Toleration & the Constitution. 368p. 1989. reprint ed. pap. 18.95 (*0-19-505947-6*) OUP.
Richards, David B. Goethe's Search for the Muse: Translation & Creativity. (German Language & Literature Monographs: No. 7). vi, 114p. 1979. 29.00x (*90-272-0967-7*) Benjamins North Am.
Richards, David G. The Hero's Quest for the Self: An Archetypal Approach to Hesse's Demian & Other Novels. LC 87-8167. (Illus.). 170p. (Orig.). (C). 1987. pap. text ed. 19.50 (*0-8191-6316-3*, Pub. by McMaster Colloquium) U Pr of Amer.
Richards, David H. Come to Stay. 96p. 1986. pap. 4.95 (*0-913152-25-0*) Folder Edns.
***Richards, David P.** How To Discover Your Personal Painting Style. LC 94-41902. 1995. write for info. (*0-89134-593-0*) North Light Bks.
Richards, David R. Tea: The Gentle Brew. 44p. 1985. pap. text ed. 9.95 (*0-9614431-0-3*) D R Richards.
Richards, Deborah D., ed. see Ibrahim, Zafar Y.
Richards, Debra D., ed. see Ibrahim, Zafar Y.
Richards, Dell. Lesbian Lists. 246p. (Orig.). 1990. pap. 8.95 (*1-55583-163-X*) Alyson Pubns.
— Superstars: Twelve Lesbians Who Changed the World. 256p. 1993. pap. 12.95 (*0-88184-955-3*) Carroll & Graf.
Richards, Delphene & Bishop, Carolyn, eds. Home Decorating Guide. LC 73-11786. (Family Circle Bks.). (Illus.). 128p. 1977. 12.95 (*0-405-09843-X*) Ayer.
***Richards, Denis.** The Hardest Victory: RAF Bomber Command in the Second World War. LC 94-36070. (Illus.). 384p. 1995. 29.95 (*0-393-03763-0*) Norton.
— An Illustrated History of Modern Europe. 7th ed. 1986. pap. text ed. 20.49 (*0-582-33204-4*, 72074) Longman.
— An Illustrated History of Modern Europe 1789-1974. (Illus.). 369p. (Orig.). (gr. 9-12). 1977. pap. text ed. 18.96 (*0-582-34106-X*) Longman.
Richards, Denise. Deadly Coincidence. 224p. (Orig.). 1991. pap. 2.75 (*1-878702-43-2*) Meteor Pub.
— A Family Affair. 224p. (Orig.). 1992. pap. 2.95 (*1-56597-034-9*, Kismet) Meteor Pub.
— Hannah's Hero. 224p. (Orig.). 1993. pap. 2.95 (*1-56597-062-4*) Meteor Pub.
— How to Open an Elegant Resale Boutique. 1977. pap. 5.50 (*0-9614714-1-7*) Pavillion Fashion.
— Searching for a New You. Media-Siegel Graphics, tr. LC 85-61014. (Illus.). 109p. 1985. pap. 7.95 (*0-9614714-0-9*) Pavillion Fashion.
Richards, Derek, jt. auth. see Percival, Ian C.
Richards, Diane. Angel in My Stocking. 100p. 1992. pap. 7.50 (*1-56770-254-6*) S Scheewe Pubns.
— Forever in My Heart. 100p. 1988. pap. 6.50 (*1-56770-188-4*) S Scheewe Pubns.
— Forever in My Heart Two. 100p. 1989. pap. 7.50 (*1-56770-205-8*) S Scheewe Pubns.
— Memories in My Heart. 100p. 1988. pap. 6.50 (*1-56770-189-2*) S Scheewe Pubns.
— Memories in Your Heart. 100p. 1991. pap. 7.50 (*1-56770-237-6*) S Scheewe Pubns.
***Richards, Dick.** Artful Work: Awakening Joy, Meaning, & Commitment in the Workplace. LC 94-46161. (Illus.). 160p. 1995. 25.00 (*1-881052-63-X*) Berrett-Koehler.
— South-East Asian Ceramics: Thai, Khmer, & Vietnamese from the Collection of the Art Gallery of South Australia, Adelaide. (Asia Collection). (Illus.). 150p. 1995. 65.00 (*967-65-3075-1*) OUP.
***Richards, Dick & Smyth, Susan.** Assessing Your Team: Seven Measures of Team Success Team Leader's Package. LC 94-65546. 32p. 1994. student ed, pap. 9.95 (*0-88390-420-9*) Pfeiffer & Co.
— Assessing Your Team: Seven Measures of Team Success Team Leader's Package. LC 94-65546. 72p. 1994. pap. 24.95 (*0-88390-437-3*) Pfeiffer & Co.
Richards, Dick, et al. Waste-to-Energy Commercial Facilities Profiles: Technical, Operational & Economic Perspectives. LC 89-70986. (Pollution Technology Review Ser.: No. 177). (Illus.). 423p. 1990. 58.00 (*0-8155-1226-0*) Noyes.
Richards, Dickinson W., jt. ed. see Fishman, Alfred P.
Richards, Don L. Twilight. 289p. (Orig.). 1992. pap. 24.95 (*0-9632478-0-8*) R T Partners.
***Richards, Donald M. & Ratsoy, Eugene W.** Introduction to the Economics of Canadian Education. 127p. (Orig.). (C). 1987. pap. text ed. 17.95x (*0-920490-66-2*) Temeron Bks.
Richards, Donald S., ed. Hypergeometric Functions on Domains of Positivity, Jack Polynomials, & Applications: (Proceedings of an AMS Special Session Held May 22-23, 1991 in Tampa, Florida) LC 92-26610. (Contemporary Mathematics Ser.: Vol. 138). 259p. 1992. 44.00 (*0-8218-5159-4*) Am Math.
Richards, Dorothy & Buyukmichi, Hope S. Beaversprite: My Years Building an Animal Sanctuary. 2nd ed. LC 77-24150. (Illus.). 192p. 1984. 14.95 (*0-932334-66-0*, NY73053); pap. 9.95 (*0-932334-67-9*, NY73054) Hrt of the Lakes.
Richards, Dorothy S. A Practical Guide to Selecting a Cat. (Illus.). 162p. 10.95 (*3-923880-35-9*, 16014) Tetra Pr.
— The World of Cats. (Fact Finders Ser.). (Illus.). 64p. (J). 1989. 7.99 (*0-517-69085-3*) Random Hse Value.
Richards, Douglas. I'm on the Way to a Brighter Day: A Collection of Poems. LC 83-73535. 1984. pap. 7.95 (*0-88396-202-0*) Blue Mtn Pr CO.
Richards, Dusty. From Hell to Breakfast. 1994. mass mkt. 3.99 (*0-671-87241-9*) PB.
— Noble's Way. LC 91-46114. (Novel of the West Ser.). 1992. 16.95 (*0-87131-669-2*) M Evans.
Richards, E. & Clough, Monica. Cromartie: Highland Life 1650-1914. 672p. 1989. text ed. 59.00 (*0-08-037732-7*, Pub. by Aberdeen U Pr) Macmillan.
Richards, E. J. & Mead, D. J., eds. Noise & Acoustic Fatigue in Aeronautics. LC 68-55813. (Illus.). 524p. reprint ed. pap. 149.40 (*0-317-11082-9*, 2016149) Bks Demand.
Richards, E. Randolph. Secretary in the Letters to Paul. (WissUNT Neuen Testament Ser.). 280p. (Orig.). 1990. pap. 67.50x (*3-16-145575-4*, Pub. by J C B Mohr GW) Coronet Bks.
Richards, Earl J., tr. see De Pizan, Christine.
Richards, Earl J., et al, eds. Reinterpreting Christine de Pizan. LC 90-45959. (Illus.). 296p. 1992. 40.00 (*0-8203-1307-6*) U of Ga Pr.
Richards, Edward P., III & Rathbun, Katharine C. Law & the Physician: A Practical Guide. LC 92-32594. 570p. 1993. pap. 37.95 (*0-316-74417-4*) Little.
— Medical Risk Management: Preventive Legal Strategies for Health Care Providers. LC 82-16346. 311p. 1982. 78.00 (*0-89443-840-9*) Aspen Pub.
Richards, Elizabeth. The Ravishers. 1992. write for info. (*0-9633891-0-6*) B S Richards.
Richards, Ellen H. Euthenics: the Science of Controllable Environment: A Plea for Better Conditions As a First Step Toward Higher Human Efficiency. Rosenkrantz, Barbara G., ed. LC 76-40639. (Public Health in America Ser.). (Illus.). 1977. reprint ed. lib. bdg. 19.95 (*0-405-09827-8*) Ayer.
Richards, Emilie. Bayou Midnight. 1994. 3.59 (*0-373-45168-7*) Silhouette.
— Duncan's Lady: (Heartbreakers, the Men of Midnight) (Intimate Moments Ser.). 1995. pap. 3.75 (*0-373-07625-8*, 1-07625-6) Silhouette.
— Fugitive. large type ed. (Sensation Ser.). 1994. 17.95 (*0-373-58846-1*, Silhouette Lrg Print); pap. 16.95 (*0-373-59068-7*, Silhouette Lrg Print) Chivers N Amer.
— Iain Ross's Woman. (Intimate Moments Ser.). 1995. mass mkt. 3.75 (*0-373-07644-4*, 1-07644-7) Silhouette.
— MacDougall's Darling. (Intimate Moments Ser.). 1995. mass mkt. 3.75 (*0-373-07655-X*, 1-07655-3) Silhouette.
— Runaway. large type ed. (Silhouette Sensation Ser.). 1993. 17.95 (*0-373-58826-7*, Silhouette Lrg Print); pap. 16.95 (*0-373-58918-2*, Silhouette Lrg Print) Chivers N Amer.
— The Trouble with Joe. 1994. mass mkt. 3.50 (*0-373-09873-1*, 5-09873-6) Silhouette.
— The Way Back Home. large type ed. (Silhouette Sensation Ser.). 1993. 17.95 (*0-373-58829-1*, Silhouette Lrg Print); pap. 16.95 (*0-373-58921-2*, Silhouette Lrg Print) Chivers N Amer.
Richards, Emlie. Somewhere Out There. (Silhouette Intimate Moments Ser.). 1993. mass mkt. 3.39 (*0-373-07498-0*, 5-07498-4) Silhouette.
Richards, Eric L. Law for Global Business. LC 93-48202. (Legal Studies in Business Ser.). (Illus.). 496p. (C). 1994. text ed. 64.95 (*0-256-11372-6*) Irwin.
Richards, Ernie, ed. see Weller, Robert.
***Richards, Ernie, et al.** Offa's Dyke Path North: Knighton to Prestatyn. (National Trail Guides Ser.). (Illus.). 168p. (Orig.). Date not set. pap. 19.95 (*1-85410-016-5*, London Bridge) Genl Dist Srvs.
— Offa's Dyke Path South. (National Travel Guide Ser.). (Illus.). 168p. (Orig.). Date not set. pap. 19.95 (*1-85410-017-3*, London Bridge) Genl Dist Srvs.
Richards, Ernie S., ed. see Weller, Robert F.
Richards, Ernst, jt. auth. see Hodgson, John.

R

Richards, Eugene. Americans We. (Illus.). 144p. 1994. 40.00 (0-89381-594-2) Aperture.

— Cocaine True, Cocaine Blue. (Illus.). 160p. 1994. 40.00 (0-89381-543-8) Aperture.

— Knife & Gun Club: Scenes from an Emergency Room. 1991. pap. 16.95 (0-87113-446-2) Grove-Atltic.

Richards, Eugene & Bird, Christiane. Below the Line: Living Poor in America. 224p. (Orig.). 1987. 132.00 (0-89043-062-4); pap. 20.00 (0-89043-061-6) Consumer Reports.

Richards, Evelleen. Vitamin C & Cancer: Medicine or Politics? LC 90-8795. 200p. 1991. text ed. 39.95 (0-312-05242-1) St Martin.

Richards, F., ed. Coastal Upwelling. (Coastal & Estuarine Sciences Ser.: Vol. 1). (Illus.). 529p. 1981. 29.00 (0-87590-250-2) Am Geophysical.

Richards, Francis A., ed. Coastal Upwelling Ecosystems Analysis Program. 1977. pap. 23.00 (0-08-021375-8, Pergamon Pr) Elsevier.

Richards, Francis A. & Armon, Cheryl. Beyond Formal Operations: Late Adolescent & Adult Cognitive Development. Commons, Michael L., ed. LC 83-21142. 494p. 1984. text ed. 55.00 (0-275-91139-X, C1139, Praeger Pubs) Greenwood.

***Richards, Frank.** Hello. LC 93-94130. 144p. (Orig.). 1995. pap. 8.00 (1-56002-389-9, Univ Edtns) Aegina Pr.

Richards, Frank F., jt. auth. see Baumgarten, Alexander.

Richards, Fred & Welch, I. David, eds. Sightings: Essays in Humanistic Psychology. LC 72-96552. 228p. (C). 1973. pap. 6.95 (0-88310-002-9) Publishers Consult.

Richards, Fred, jt. ed. see Welch, I. David.

Richards, G. Scattering Methods in Polymer Science. 2nd ed. 350p. 1992. text ed. write for info. (0-13-791567-5) P-H.

Richards, G. K., jt. auth. see Jones, R. N.

Richards, Gavin. Die Kinder. LC 92-80846. 192p. (Orig.). 1993. pap. 6.95 (0-563-36104-2, BBC-Parkwest) Parkwest Pubns.

Richards, George. Horoscope for Each Day of the Month. 143p. 1994. pap. 12.00 (0-89540-237-8, SB-237, Sun Bks) Sun Pub.

Richards, George C. Cicero. LC 79-109830. 298p. 1970. reprint ed. text ed. 55.00 (0-8371-4321-7, RCIC, Greenwood Pr) Greenwood.

Richards, Gerald T., jt. auth. see Hadley, Donald W.

Richards, Gertrude R., ed. see Davison, Ellen S.

Richards, Gertrude R., ed. see National Society of Colonial Dames of America in the Commonwealth of Virginia Staff.

Richards, Gillian & MacColl, Linda, eds. Dramatists Sourcebook, 1994-95. 312p. (Orig.). 1994. pap. 15.95 (1-55936-093-3) Theatre Comm.

Richards, Gillian, jt. ed. see Osborn, M. Elizabeth.

Richards, Glyn. The Philosophy of Gandhi: A Study of His Basic Ideas. 200p. 1981. 30.00 (0-7007-0150-8, Pub. by Curzon Pr UK) Humanities.

— The Philosophy of Gandhi: A Study of His Basic Ideas. LC 90-43207. 192p. (C). 1991. pap. 17.50 (0-391-03701-3) Humanities.

— A Source Book of Modern Hinduism. 222p. (C). 1985. text ed. 49.95 (0-7007-0173-7, Pub. by Curzon Pr UK) Humanities.

— Studies in Religion. LC 95-5584. 1995. write for info. (0-312-12676-X) St Martin.

— Towards a Theology of Religions. 208p. 1989. 55.00 (0-415-02450-1) Routledge.

Richards, Glyn, ed. A Source-Book of Modern Hinduism. 228p. (Orig.). (C). 1995. pap. 19.95 (0-7007-0317-9, Pub. by Curzon Pr UK) Humanities.

Richards, Graham. Human Evolution: An Introduction for the Behavioral Sciences. (Illus.). 448p. 1987. pap. text ed. 32.50 (0-7102-1381-6, RKP) Routledge.

— Mental Machinery: The Origins & Consequences of Psychological Ideas, 1600-1850. LC 92-1552. 416p. (C). 1992. text ed. 49.95 (0-8018-4544-0) Johns Hopkins.

— On Psychological Language: And the Physiomorphic Basis of Human Nature. (International Library of Psychology). 192p. 1990. 49.95 (0-415-01038-1, A3952) Routledge.

Richards, Grant. Memories of a Misspent Youth, Eighteen Seventy-Two to Eighteen Ninety-Six. LC 79-8073. reprint ed. 35.00 (0-404-18383-2) AMS Pr.

Richards, Gregory. Jim Thorpe: World's Greatest Athlete. LC 84-14240. (People of Distinction Ser.). (Illus.). 112p. (J). (gr. 4 up). 1984. lib. bdg. 14.40 (0-516-03207-0) Childrens.

Richards, Guy. Imperial Agent: The Goleniewski-Romanov Case. 1966. 9.95 (0-8159-5804-8) Devin.

— The Rescue of the Romanovs. LC 74-27953. (Illus.). 1975. 12.95 (0-8159-6717-9) Devin.

— The Salekov Kill. 256p. (Orig.). 1981. pap. 2.50 (0-449-14405-4, GM) Fawcett.

Richards, Guyon. The Chain of Life. 3rd ed. 232p. pap. 17. 95 (0-8464-4202-7) Beekman Pubs.

Richards, H. J. The Creed for Children. 28p. (Orig.). (YA). 1991. pap. 2.95 (0-8146-2037-X) Liturgical Pr.

— God's Diary: Some Excerpts. LC 90-71819. (Illus.). 128p. (Orig.). 1991. pap. 7.95 (0-89622-474-0, C54) Twenty-Third.

— The Mass for Children. 28p. (Orig.). (J). 1991. pap. 2.95 (0-8146-2038-8) Liturgical Pr.

Richards, H. M., Jr. Faith & Prayer. (Uplook Ser.). 32p. 1971. pap. 0.99 (0-8163-0071-2, 06010-3) Pacific Pr Pub Assn.

Richards, H. M. Weiser Family. (Illus.). 115p. 1992. reprint ed. lib. bdg. 28.50 (0-8328-2760-6); reprint ed. pap. 18. 50 (0-8328-2761-4) Higginson Bk Co.

Richards, Harold M. Practical Secrets of the Spiritual Life: How-To Revealed. LC 89-2198. 160p. (Orig.). 1989. pap. 9.00 (0-922615-05-5) Hampton Hill.

Richards, Henry J. Therapy of the Substance Abuse Syndromes. LC 92-48826. 496p. 1994. 60.00 (0-87668-539-4) Aronson.

Richards, Henry J., tr. see Bass, Nelson E.

Richards, Henry M. Revolutionary War: The Pennsylvania-German in the Revolutionary War, 1775-1783. (Illus.). 542p. 1991. reprint ed. 35.00 (0-685-48614-1, 4890) Genealog Pub.

Richards, Herbert. A Beginner's Guide to Tropical Fish. (Beginner's Guide Ser.). (Illus.). 64p. 1986. 3.95 (0-86622-704-0, T-108) TFH Pubns.

— Dog Breeding for Professionals. (Illus.). 1978. 17.95 (0-86622-655-9, H969) TFH Pubns.

— Dogs: Look & Learn. (Illus.). 64p. 1993. 7.95 (0-7938-0066-8, KD005) TFH Pubns.

— Puppies As a Hobby. (Illus.). 96p. 1993. pap. 7.95 (0-86622-413-0, TT010) TFH Pubns.

— Rottweilers. (Illus.). 80p. 1984. pap. text ed. 5.95 (0-86622-095-X, PB-132) TFH Pubns.

Richards, Horace G. Annotated Bibliography of Quaternary Shorelines (Second Supplement, 1970-1973) (Special Publication: No. 11). 214p. 1974. pap. 10.00 (0-910006-45-8) Acad Nat Sci Phila.

Richards, Horace G., comp. Catalogue of Invertebrate Fossil Types at the Academy of Natural Sciences of Philadelphia. (Special Publication: No. 8). 222p. (Orig.). 1968. pap. 7.00 (0-910006-36-9) Acad Nat Sci Phila.

Richards, Horace G. & Fairbridge, Rhodes W. Annotated Bibliography of Quaternary Shorelines (1945-1964) (Special Publication: No. 6). 280p. (Orig.). 1965. pap. 7.00 (0-910006-34-2) Acad Nat Sci Phila.

Richards, Horace G., et al. Annotated Bibliography of Quaternary Shorelines (Supplement, 1965-1969) (Special Publication: No. 10). 240p. 1970. lib. bdg. 9.00 (0-910006-37-7); pap. 7.00 (0-910006-44-X) Acad Nat Sci Phila.

Richards, Howard. Letters from Quebec: A Philosophy for Peace & Justice. LC 93-37945. 1994. 74.95 (1-883255-16-3); pap. 54.95 (1-883255-17-1) Intl Scholars.

Richards, Hubert. The Gospel According to St. Paul. 136p. (Orig.). 1991. pap. 9.95 (0-8146-2057-4) Liturgical Pr.

— The Gospel According to St. Paul. 136p. (Orig.). (C). 1988. 45.00 (0-85597-451-6, Pub. by McCrimmon Pub) St Mut.

— Some Catholic Prayers. 48p. (Orig.). 1992. pap. text ed. 3.95 (0-8146-2196-1) Liturgical Pr.

— Some Catholic Prayers. (Orig.). (C). 1993. 35.00 (0-85597-483-4, Pub. by McCrimmon Pub) St Mut.

— What Christians Believe. 72p. (Orig.). 1992. pap. text ed. 4.95 (0-8146-2198-8) Liturgical Pr.

— What Christians Believe. 72p. (Orig.). (C). 1993. 30.00 (0-85597-481-8, Pub. by McCrimmon Pub) St Mut.

— What Jesus Taught. 48p. (Orig.). 1992. pap. text ed. 3.95 (0-8146-2197-X) Liturgical Pr.

— What Jesus Taught. (Orig.). (C). 1993. 40.00 (0-85597-482-6, Pub. by McCrimmon Pub) St Mut.

Richards, Hubert J. The First Easter: What Really Happened? LC 85-51494. (What Really Happened? Ser.). 128p. 1986. reprint ed. pap. 5.95 (0-89622-282-9) Twenty-Third.

— Pilgrim to Rome. 216p. 1994. pap. 29.00 (0-85597-532-6) St Mut.

— Pilgrim to the Holy Land. 256p. 1993. 39.00 (0-85597-321-8) St Mut.

Richards, Hugh T. Through Los Alamos, 1945: Memoirs of a Nuclear Physicist. (Illus.). 106p. (Orig.). 1993. pap. 15. 00 (0-9637521-1-1) Arlington Pl.

Richards, Hylda M. Next Year Will Be Better. LC 84-24029. 230p. 1985. reprint ed. 19.50 (0-8032-3869-X) U of Nebr Pr.

Richards, I. & Youn, H. The Theory of Distribution: A Nontechnical Introduction. (Illus.). (C). 1990. 47.95 (0-521-37149-X) Cambridge U Pr.

Richards, I. A. Poetries: Their Media & Ends. LC 73-93947. (De Proprietatibus Litterarum, Ser. Major: No. 30). 256p. 1974. pap. text ed. 56.95 (90-279-3482-7) Mouton.

— Poetries & Sciences. LC 68-22862. (C). 1972. pap. text ed. 2.25 (0-393-00652-2) Norton.

— Richards on Rhetoric: Selected Essays, 1929-1974. Berthoff, Ann E., ed. (Illus.). 304p. (C). 1990. pap. text ed. 18.95 (0-19-506426-7) OUP.

— Science & Poetry. LC 74-6484. (Studies in Poetry: No. 38). 1974. lib. bdg. 75.00 (0-8383-1916-5) M S G Haskell Hse.

Richards, I. A., et al. Foundations of Aesthetics. LC 74-1364. (Studies in Philosophy: No. 40). 1974. lib. bdg. 75. 00 (0-8383-2046-5) M S G Haskell Hse.

Richards, I. G., et al. The Reclamation of Former Coal Mines & Steelworks. (Studies in Environmental Science: Vol. 56). 750p. 1993. 275.00 (0-444-81703-4) Elsevier.

Richards, Ian. How to Give a Professional Presentation. rev. ed. (C). 1988. pap. text ed. 14.00 (1-85333-087-6, Pub. by Graham & Trotman UK) Kluwer Ac.

— How to Use the Computer to Improve Your Business. (C). 1990. pap. text ed. 19.50 (1-85333-323-9, Pub. by Graham & Trotman UK) Kluwer Ac.

— How to Use the Computer to Improve Your Business. (C). 1990. lib. bdg. 32.00 (1-85333-324-7, Pub. by Graham & Trotman UK) Kluwer Ac.

***Richards, Ian & Youn, Heekyung.** The Theory of Distributions: A Nontechnical Introduction. (Illus.). 160p. (C). 1995. pap. 19.95 (0-521-55890-5) Cambridge U Pr.

Richards, Ivor A. Complementarities: Uncollected Essays. Russo, John P., ed. LC 76-19044. (Illus.). 317p. reprint ed. pap. 90.40 (0-7837-6087-6, 2059133) Bks Demand.

— Mencius on the Mind: Experiments in Multiple Definition. LC 79-2838. (Illus.). 1989. reprint ed. 23.50 (0-8305-0015-4) Hyperion Conn.

— Philosophy of Rhetoric. (YA). (gr. 9 up). 1965. pap. 7.95 (0-19-500715-8) OUP.

— Practical Criticism, a Study of Literary Judgment. LC 56-13740. 362p. 1956. pap. 12.00 (0-15-673626-8, Harvest Bks) HarBrace.

— Principles of Literary Criticism. LC 61-1440. 299p. 1961. pap. 7.95 (0-15-674592-5, Harvest Bks) HarBrace.

Richards, Ivor A., ed. see Coleridge, Samuel Taylor.

Richards, Ivor A., jt. auth. see Ogden, Charles K.

Richards, J. Longman Dictionary of Applied Linguistics. Date not set. pap. text ed. 22.95 (0-582-07244-1) Addison-Wesley.

Richards, J. A. Analysis of Periodically Time-Varying Systems. (Communications & Control Engineering Ser.). (Illus.). 173p. 1983. 89.00 (0-387-11689-3) Spr-Verlag.

— Remote Sensing: Digital Image Analysis. (Illus.). 320p. 1986. 69.00 (0-387-16007-8) Spr-Verlag.

— Remote Sensing Digital Image Analysis. 2nd enl. rev. ed. LC 94-29196. 330p. 1994. pap. text ed. 59.00 (0-387-58219-3) Spr-Verlag.

— Remote Sensing Image Analysis: An Introduction. 2nd ed. LC 94-29196. 1994. write for info. (3-540-58219-3) Spr-Verlag.

Richards, J. F., ed. Precious Metals in the Later Medieval & Early Modern Worlds. LC 82-73059. (Illus.). 502p. (C). 1983. 55.00 (0-89089-224-5) Carolina Acad Pr.

Richards, J. L., jt. auth. see Pour-El, M. B.

Richards, J. M. & Pevsner, Nikolaus, eds. The Anti-Rationalists. LC 72-95812. (Illus.). 216p. reprint ed. pap. 61.60 (0-8357-5630-0, 2014339) Bks Demand.

Richards, Jack. Error Analysis: Perspectives on Second Language Acquisition. (Applied Linguistics & Language Study Ser.). 1974. pap. text ed. 27.95 (0-582-55044-0, 74284) Longman.

Richards, Jack, ed. New Treasury of Basketball Drills from Top Coaches. LC 82-2156. 185p. 1982. 16.95 (0-13-615864-1, Parker Publishing Co) P-H.

Richards, Jack & Bycina, David. Person to Person: Communicative Speaking & Listening Skills, Bk. 2. 1985. teacher ed write for info. (0-318-59138-3); pap. 9.50 (0-19-434152-6) OUP.

— Person to Person: Communicative Speaking & Listening Skills, Bk. 2. 1985. audio 31.95 (0-19-434153-4) OUP.

Richards, Jack & Bycina, David, eds. Person to Person: Communicative Speaking & Listening Skills, Bk. 1. 1985. pap. 9.50 (0-19-434150-X) OUP.

— Person to Person: Communicative Speaking & Listening Skills, Bk. 1. 1985. 31.95 (0-19-434151-8) OUP.

— Person to Person: Communicative Speaking & Listening Skills, Bk. 1. 1985. teacher ed 7.95 (0-19-434154-2) OUP.

Richards, Jack & Hull, Jonathan. As I Was Saying: Conversation Tactics. (Illus.). (C). 1987. text ed. 19.74 (0-201-06433-2) Addison-Wesley.

Richards, Jack, jt. auth. see Lowe, David.

Richards, Jack, et al. Longman Dictionary of Applied Linguistics. 324p. 1985. pap. text ed. 25.95 (0-582-55708-9, 74434) Longman.

Richards, Jack C. The Context of Language Teaching. (Cambridge Language Teaching Library). 228p. 1985. 39.95 (0-521-26565-7); pap. 16.95 (0-521-31952-8) Cambridge U Pr.

— Interchange: English for International Communication Level 2: Video Activity Book. (Illus.). 80p. (C). 1995. pap. write for info. (0-521-46805-1) Cambridge U Pr.

— Interchange: English for International Communication Level 2: Video Teacher's Guide. (Illus.). 112p. (C). 1995. teacher ed, pap. write for info. (0-521-46804-3) Cambridge U Pr.

— Interchange Intro: English for International Communication. (Illus.). 144p. (C). 1994. pap. 5.50 (0-521-47185-0) Cambridge U Pr.

— Interchange Intro: English for International Communication. (Illus.). 144p. (C). 1994. pap. 9.95 (0-521-46744-6); pap. 29.95 (0-521-46741-1); pap. 10.95 (0-521-46740-3) Cambridge U Pr.

— Interchange Intro: English for International Communication. (Illus.). 144p. (C). 1994. pap. 5.95 (0-521-46743-8) Cambridge U Pr.

— Interchange Intro: English for International Communication. (Illus.). 144p. (C). 1995. pap. 13.95 (0-521-46742-X) Cambridge U Pr.

— Interchange Introduction - English for International Communication: Student Book B. 80p. (C). 1994. pap. 10.95 (0-521-47189-3) Cambridge U Pr.

— Interchange Introduction - English for International Communication: Student Book B. 80p. (C). 1994. pap. 5.50 (0-521-47186-9) Cambridge U Pr.

— Interchange Introduction - English for International Communication: Workbook A. 40p. (C). 1994. pap. 3.50 (0-521-47187-7) Cambridge U Pr.

— Interchange Introduction - English for International Communication: Workbook B. 40p. (C). 1994. pap. 3.50 (0-521-47188-5) Cambridge U Pr.

— The Language Teaching Matrix: Curriculum, Methodology, & Materials. (Language Teaching Library). (Illus.). 192p. (C). 1990. pap. 15.95 (0-521-38794-9) Cambridge U Pr.

Richards, Jack C. & Lockhart, Charles. Reflective Teaching in Second Language Classrooms. (Language Education Ser.). 256p. (C). 1994. 39.95 (0-521-45181-7); pap. 17.95 (0-521-45803-X) Cambridge U Pr.

Richards, Jack C. & Nunan, David, eds. Second Language Teacher Education. (Cambridge Language Teaching Library). (Illus.). 336p. (C). 1990. pap. 18.95 (0-521-38779-5) Cambridge U Pr.

Richards, Jack C. & Rodgers, Theodore S. Approaches & Methods in Language Teaching: A Description & Analysis. (Cambridge Language Teaching Library). (Illus.). 176p. 1986. 39.95 (0-521-32093-3); pap. 16.95 (0-521-31255-8) Cambridge U Pr.

Richards, Jack C. & Schmidt, Richard W. Language & Communication. (Applied Linguistics & Language Ser.). 276p. (Orig.). (C). 1983. pap. text ed. 27.95 (0-582-55034-3, 74279) Longman.

Richards, Jack C., jt. auth. see Homer.

Richards, Jack C., jt. auth. see Long, Michael H.

Richards, Jack C., et al. Interchange: English for International Communication, Level 2. (Illus.). (C). 1990. Student's bk. student ed, pap. 9.95 (0-521-37681-5); Student's cassette. student ed, pap. 16. 95 (0-521-37535-5); pap. 29.95 (0-521-37534-7) Cambridge U Pr.

— Interchange: English for International Communication, Level 2. (Illus.). (C). 1991. Wkbk. student ed, pap. 5.95 (0-521-37683-1) Cambridge U Pr.

— Interchange: English for International Communication, Level 2. (Illus.). (C). 1991. Tchr's. manual. teacher ed, pap. 13.95 (0-521-37682-3) Cambridge U Pr.

— Interchange: English for International Communication, Level 3. (Illus.). (C). 1991. pap. 9.95 (0-521-37684-X); pap. 16.95 (0-521-37537-1); pap. 29.95 (0-521-37536-3) Cambridge U Pr.

— Interchange: English for International Communication, Level 3. (Illus.). (C). 1991. student ed, pap. 5.95 (0-521-37686-6) Cambridge U Pr.

— Interchange: English for International Communication, Level 3. (Illus.). (C). 1992. teacher ed, pap. 13.95 (0-521-37685-8) Cambridge U Pr.

— Interchange: English for International Communication, Level 3. (Illus.). (C). 1993. student ed, pap. 11.95 (0-521-42222-1) Cambridge U Pr.

— Interchange: English for International Communication, Level 1, Level 1. (C). 1990. student ed, pap. 9.95 (0-521-35988-0); pap. 16.95 (0-521-35204-5); pap. 29.95 (0-521-35203-7) Cambridge U Pr.

— Interchange: English for International Communication, Level 1, Level 1. (C). 1990. student ed, pap. 5.95 (0-521-35990-2); teacher ed, pap. 13.95 (0-521-35989-9) Cambridge U Pr.

— Interchange: English for International Communication, Level 1, Level 1. (C). 1992. student ed, pap. 11.95 (0-521-42218-3) Cambridge U Pr.

Richards, James B. The Gospel of Peace: The Message of the Cross. 110p. (Orig.). 1990. pap. 5.00 (0-924748-04-4) Impact Ministries.

— Grace: The Power to Change. 88p. (Orig.). 1990. pap. 5.00 (0-924748-02-8) Impact Ministries.

— Grace the Power to Change. 2nd rev. ed. 1993. pap. 10. 00 (0-924748-07-9) Impact Ministries.

— Leadership That Builds People. 120p. (Orig.). 1990. pap. 5.00 (0-924748-03-6) Impact Ministries.

— Leadership That Builds People, Vol. 1. 143p. (Orig.). 1993. pap. 12.95 (0-924748-06-0) Impact Ministries.

— The Prayer Organizer. rev. ed. 114p. 1990. ring bd. 20.00 (0-924748-01-X) Impact Ministries.

Richards, James H. How to Die Young at the Oldest Possible Age. (Illus.). 88p. (Orig.). (C). 1991. pap. text ed. 9.95 (1-880047-01-2) Creative Des.

Richards, James L. Pascal. 2nd ed. 671p. (C). 1986. text ed. 40.00 (0-15-568160-5); teacher ed, pap. text ed. 3.50 (0-15-568161-3) Dryden Pr.

Richards, Jeanette. The Crofter's Cottage. large type ed. (Dales Romance Ser.). 201p. 1993. pap. 16.95 (1-85389-404-4, Medcom-Trainex) Ulverscroft.

— In Love's Image. (Rainbow Romances Ser.: No. 889). 160p. 1994. 14.95 (0-7090-4841-6, Hale-Parkwest) Parkwest Pubns.

— In Love's Image. large type ed. (Romance Library). 288p. 1995. pap. 14.95 (0-7089-7669-7, Linford) Ulverscroft.

Richards, Jef I. Deceptive Advertising: Behavioral Study of a Legal Concept. (Communication Ser.). 264p. (C). 1990. text ed. 49.95 (0-8058-0649-0) L Erlbaum Assocs.

Richards, Jeffrey. Fire Island: In Color. (Illus.). 144p. (Orig.). 1991. 40.00 (0-9628881-0-9); pap. 30.00 (0-9628881-1-7) KYX Pr.

— Happiest Days: The Public Schools in English Fiction. LC 87-36707. 327p. 1991. reprint ed. text ed. 24.95 (0-7190-2775-6, Pub. by Manchester Univ Pr UK) St Martin.

— Sex, Dissidence & Damnation: Minority Groups in the Middle Ages. 192p. 1991. 29.95 (0-415-03342-X, A5343) Routledge.

— Sex, Dissidence & Damnation: Minority Groups in the Middle Ages. 192p. 1995. pap. 15.95 (0-415-07147-X, C0428) Routledge.

— Swordsmen of the Screen: From Douglas Fairbanks to Michael York. (Cinema & Society Ser.). (Illus.). 312p. 1980. pap. 10.95 (0-7100-0681-0, RKP) Routledge.

Richards, Jeffrey & MacKenzie, John M. The Railway Station: A Social History. (Illus.). 480p. 1986. teacher ed write for info. (0-318-60820-0) OUP.

Richards, Jeffrey & MacKenzie, John M., eds. Imperialism & Juvenile Literature. LC 88-25009. (Studies in Imperialism). (Illus.). 240p. 1989. text ed. 59.95 (0-7190-2420-X, Pub. by Manchester Univ Pr UK) St Martin.

***Richards, Jeffrey H.** Mercy Otis Warren. (Twayne's United States Author Ser.). 1995. lib. bdg. 22.95x (0-8057-4003-1, Twayne) Macmillan.

— Theater Enough: American Culture & the Metaphor of the World Stage, 1607-1789. LC 90-47943. 359p. 1991. text ed. 36.95 (0-8223-1107-0) Duke.

Richards, Jeffrey J. Contemporary Christian Options of the World's End: The Eschatology of Lewis Sperry Chafer. LC 93-33936. (Illus.). 256p. 1993. text ed. 89.95 (0-7734-9391-3) E Mellen.

— The Cry at Salem. 80p. (Orig.). (C). 1992. pap. text ed. 8.50 (0-88252-153-5) Paladin Hse.

An Asterisk (*) at the beginning of an entry indicates that the title is appearing in BIP for the first time.

— The Promise of Dawn: The Eschatology of Lewis Sperry Chafer. 280p. (C). 1991. lib. bdg. 49.00 (0-8191-8196-X); pap. 25.00 (0-8191-8197-8) U Pr of Amer.

— Twenty-One Who Speak: Powerful Voices of Christianity from the First Through the Twentieth Centuries. 123p. (Orig.). (C). 1992. pap. text ed. 14.00 (0-88252-154-3) Paladin Hse.

Richards, Jerrold. Nuclear War & You: Before, During, After. LC 84-70562. 272p. (Orig.). 1984. pap. 8.95 (0-9613278-0-4) CFPR Pubns.

Richards, Joan. Mathematical Visions: The Pursuit of Geometry in Victorian England. 266p. 1988. text ed. 61.00 (0-12-587445-6) Acad Pr.

***Richards, Joanette.** A Summer of Innocence. (Rainbow Romances Ser.). 160p. 1995. 14.95 (0-7090-5497-1, 925) Parkwest Pubns.

Richards, Joanne & Standley, Marianne. One for the Books. (Illus.). 128p. (J). (gr. 4-6). 1984. pap. text ed. 8.95 (0-86530-023-2, IP 23-2) Incentive Pubns.

— Write Here. (Illus.). 80p. (J). (gr. 3-6). 1984. pap. text ed. 7.95 (0-86530-013-5, IP 13-5) Incentive Pubns.

Richards, Joanne & Standley, Marianne V. Dealing with Feelings. (Values & Feelings Ser.). 72p. (J). (gr. 3-7). 1982. 7.95 (0-88160-015-6, LW 118) Learning Wks.

Richards, Joanne, jt. auth. see Blankenhorn, Kathy.

Richards, Joanne, jt. auth. see Standley, Marianne.

Richards, Joe. Princess New York. LC 72-95162. (Illus.). 258p. 1989. reprint ed. pap. 12.95 (0-9622407-0-2) MM Dunedin FL.

Richards, John. Basic Bass. (Illus.). 32p. 1987. pap. 8.95 (0-7119-1075-8, AM64858) Music Sales.

— Hidden Country: Nature on Your Doorstep. LC 72-12745. (Illus.). 144p. (J). (gr. 5-8). 1973. lib. bdg. 22.95 (0-87599-195-5) S G Phillips.

— Legal Aspects of Introducing Products to the US Market. 478p. 1988. 100.00 (90-6544-292-8) Kluwer Law Tax Pubs.

— The Pigeon Factory. (Illus.). (Orig.). 1987. pap. 6.95 (0-932274-40-4) Cadmus Eds.

— Primulas of the British Isles. (Shire Natural History Ser.: No. 38). (Illus.). 24p. 1989. pap. text ed. 5.25 (0-7478-0020-0, Pub. by Shire Pubns UK) Lubrecht & Cramer.

— Time Management: A Manual for Trainers. Adair, John, ed. 255p. (C). 1989. ring bd. 285.00x (0-85171-088-3, Pub. by IPM Hse UK) St Mut.

Richards, John, jt. ed. see Gunton, Thomas.

Richards, John, jt. auth. see Vaillant, Janet.

Richards, John A. Remote Sensing Digital Image Analysis: An Introduction. 2nd ed. LC 93-10179. (Illus.). 344p. 1993. 119.00 (0-387-54840-8) Spr-Verlag.

Richards, John D. Uncreated Light. 32p. (Orig.). 1993. pap. 3.95 (1-881692-05-1) Trillium WV.

Richards, John F. The Mughal Empire. (New Cambridge History of India Ser.: I: 5). (Illus.). 256p. (C). 1993. 47.95 (0-521-25119-2) Cambridge U Pr.

— Power, Administration & Finance in Mughal India. (Collected Studies: Vol. 419). 336p. 1993. 89.95 (0-86078-366-9, Pub. by Variorum UK) Ashgate Pub Co.

Richards, John F., ed. The Imperial Monetary System of Mughal India. (Illus.). 392p. 1988. 29.95 (0-19-561953-6) OUP.

Richards, John F. & Tucker, Richard P., eds. World Deforestation in the Twentieth Century. LC 87-31953. (Duke Press Policy Studies). x, 321p. 1989. reprint ed. pap. text ed. 18.95 (0-8223-1013-9) Duke.

***Richards, John H.** Horizon Nine Keys Personality Identifier Version 3. 22p. 1994. 4.95 (1-885802-50-1) Horiz Nine Keys.

— The Illustrated Enneagram: An Animated Look at the Nine Enneagram Personalities. (Illus.). 44p. 1994. pap. 4.95 (1-885802-00-5) Horiz Nine Keys.

***Richards, John T.** The Fool of Love. (Mandrake Saga Ser.). (Illus.). 176p. (Orig.). 1995. pap. 8.00 (0-9605980-4-9) J T Richards.

— Luminous Sanity: Literary Criticism Written by John G. Neihardt. 1973. pap. 5.00 (0-9605980-0-6) J T Richards.

— Rawhide Laureate: John G. Neihardt, a Selected Annotated Bibliography. LC 83-10117. (Author Bibliographies Ser.: No. 65). 189p. 1983. 20.00 (0-8108-1640-7) Scarecrow.

— Sorrat: A History of the Neihardt Psychokinesis Experiments, 1961-1981. LC 81-18312. 356p. 1982. 27.50 (0-8108-1491-9) Scarecrow.

— A Voice Against the Wind: John G. Neihardt as Critic & Reviewer. (Illus.). 161p. (Orig.). 1986. pap. 6.00 (0-9605980-1-4) J T Richards.

— The Year of the Sorrats, Vol. I. (Mandrake Saga Ser.). (Illus.). 242p. (Orig.). 1994. pap. 8.00 (0-9605980-3-0) J T Richards.

— The Year of the Sorrats, Vol. 2. (Mandrake Saga Ser.). (Illus.). 175p. (Orig.). 1994. pap. 8.00 (0-9605980-2-2) J T Richards.

***Richards, Josiah B.** God of Our Fathers: Advice & Prayers of Our Nation's Founders. (Illus.). 304p. (Orig.). 1994. pap. 12.00 (0-9643679-1-2) Reading Bks.

***Richards, Josiah B., ed.** Historical Background & Sources for Parents & Teachers: For Use with Advice & Prayers of Our Nation's Founders. (Illus.). 288p. (Orig.). 1994. pap. 18.95 (0-9643679-2-0) Reading Bks.

Richards, Judith. After the Storm. 354p. 1987. 14.95 (0-934601-17-8) Peachtree Pubs.

— Summer Lightning. 272p. 1987. reprint ed. pap. 6.95 (0-934601-18-6) Peachtree Pubs.

Richards, Judith W. Fundamentals of Development Finance: A Practitioner's Guide. LC 82-18958. 224p. 1983. text ed. 55.00 (0-275-91062-8, C1062, Praeger Pubs) Greenwood.

Richards, Judy. Catering: Start & Run a Money-Making Business. 1994. pap. text ed. 17.95 (0-07-052272-3) McGraw.

Richards, Julian. English Heritage Book of Stonehenge. (Illus.). 144p. 1992. pap. 29.95 (0-7134-6142-X, Pub. by Batsford UK) Trafalgar.

Richards, K. S., ed. Biology of the Integument: Invertebrates, Vol. 1. (Illus.). 800p. 1984. 299.00 (0-387-13062-4) Spr-Verlag.

Richards, K. S., jt. auth. see Morris, D. L.

Richards, Karen B. & Fallon, Maureen O. Workbook for the Verbally Apraxic Adult. 144p. 1987. student ed 19.95 (0-88450-986-9, 7367) Commun Skill.

Richards, Karen K. & Leoter, John. Turning the Tide: How to Be an Advocate for the ADD - ADHD Child. LC 92-61264. 96p. (Orig.). 1992. pap. 8.95 (0-939644-88-6) Media Pub.

Richards, Keith. Rivers: Form & Process in Alluvial Channels. 272p. 1982. pap. 27.50 (0-416-74910-0, NO. 3739) Routledge Chapman & Hall.

— Tender Mercies: Inside the World of a Child Abuse Investigator. LC 91-50624. 280p. (Orig.). 1991. pap. 12.95 (1-879360-07-1) Noble Pr.

Richards, Keith, jt. ed. see Edge, Julian.

Richards, Keith S., ed. River Changes. 352p. 1987. text ed. 89.95 (0-631-14577-X) Blackwell Pubs.

Richards, Kelly F. Merry Christmas! LC 90-83243. (Wee Pudgy Board Bks.). (Illus.). 24p. (J). (ps-3). 1991. 2.50 (0-448-40125-8, G&D) Putnam Pub Group.

Richards, Kenneth & Richards, Laura. The Commedia dell'Arte: A Documentary History. (Illus.). 370p. 1989. text ed. 74.95 (0-631-19590-4) Blackwell Pubs.

Richards, Kenneth G. The Gettysburg Address. LC 91-43371. (Cornerstones of Freedom Ser.). (Illus.). 32p. (J). (gr. 3-6). 1992. lib. bdg. 12.30 (0-516-06654-4) Childrens.

— The Gettysburg Address. LC 91-43371. (Cornerstones of Freedom Ser.). (Illus.). 32p. (J). (gr. 3-6). 1993. pap. 3.95 (0-516-46654-2) Childrens.

Richards, Kent, ed. SBL, 1986: Seminar Papers. 1986. 22.95 (1-55540-044-2, 06 09 25) Scholars Pr GA.

— SBL, 1987: Seminar Papers. 1987. 22.95 (1-55540-200-3, 06 09 26) Scholars Pr GA.

— Society of Biblical Literature Nineteen Eighty-One: Seminar Papers. (Society of Biblical Literature Seminar Papers & Abstracts). 1981. pap. 22.95 (0-89130-548-3, 06-09-20) Scholars Pr GA.

Richards, Kent, ed. see Cook, James I.

Richards, Kent, ed. see Crossan, John D.

Richards, Kent D. Isaac I. Stevens: Young Man in a Hurry. LC 92-41393. (Washington State University Press Reprint Ser.). (Illus.). 484p. 1993. reprint ed. pap. 18.95 (0-87422-094-7) Wash St U Pr.

Richards, Kent H., ed. Society of Biblical Literature: Seminar Papers Nineteen Eighty-Three. (Society of Biblical Literature Seminar Papers & Abstracts). 490p. (C). 1983. pap. 22.95 (0-89130-607-2, 06 09 22) Scholars Pr GA.

Richards, Kent H., jt. auth. see Petersen, David L.

Richards, Larry. Bible Difficulties Solved: Answers to More Than 500 Baffling Questions from Genesis to Revelation. LC 92-598. 416p. 1993. 15.99 (0-8007-1681-7) Revell.

— Ciencia y Biblia, ? Se Contradicen? Science & Bible, Can We Believe. (SPA.). 3.25 (84-7228-378-X, 220160, Pub. by Edit Clie SP) TSELF.

— Como Entender el Antiguo Testamento: How to Understand the Old. (SPA.). 2.95 (84-7228-591-X, 220158, Pub. by Edit Clie SP) TSELF.

— God Hears You. 1993. text ed. 4.99 (0-310-96257-9) Zondervan.

— God's Promises for Women. 1995. 4.99 (0-310-96301-X) Zondervan.

— God's Promises for Women Daybreak. 1993. text ed. 7.99 (0-310-96203-X) Zondervan.

— International Children's Bible Handbook. 224p. 1989. write for info. (0-8499-0811-6) Word Inc.

— It Couldn't Just Happen. 191p. (J). (gr. 2-7). 1989. write for info. (0-8499-0715-2) Word Inc.

— Lo Que Todos Debemos Saber Sobre: What Everyone Should Know About. (SPA.). 2.95 (84-7228-448-4, 220552, Pub. by Edit Clie SP) TSELF.

— Promises for the Graduate. (For the Graduate Ser.). 128p. 1988. 6.99 (0-310-39430-9, 18304); 6.99 (0-310-39440-6) Zondervan.

— Promises for the Graduate. (For the Graduate Ser.). 128p. 1993. 6.99 (0-310-39700-6) Zondervan.

— Psicologia & la Biblia: Psychology & the Bible. (SPA.). 2.95 (84-7228-364-X, 220729, Pub. by Edit Clie SP) TSELF.

— Remarriage: A Healing Gift from God. 144p. 1990. pap. write for info. (0-8499-3250-5) Word Inc.

— Talkable Bible Stories: Helping Your Kids Apply God's Word to Their Lives. LC 91-12923. (Illus.). 256p. (J). (ps-3). 1994. reprint ed. pap. 9.99 (0-8007-5505-7) Revell.

— Teaching Youth. 155p. 1982. pap. 7.95 (0-8341-0776-7) Beacon Hill.

— The Three Hundred Sixty-Five Day Devotional Commentary. 1216p. 1990. text ed. 37.99 (0-89693-503-5) SP Pubns.

— Wisdom for the Graduate. (For the Graduate Ser.). 128p. 1993. 6.99 (0-310-39710-3) Zondervan.

Richards, Larry, ed. Canadian Center for Architecture: Building & Gardens. (Illus.). 156p. (Orig.). 1989. pap. 17.95x (0-262-68058-0) MIT Pr.

Richards, Larry & Richards, Sue. Three Hundred & Sixty Five Ways to Keep Your Love Alive 1995 Calendar. 1994. spiral bd. 7.99 (0-310-96356-7) Zondervan.

— Three Hundred Sixty Five Ways to Show Your Kids You Care 1995 Calendar. 1994. spiral bd. 7.99 (0-310-96355-9) Zondervan.

Richards, Larry, jt. ed. see Baraness, Marc.

Richards, Laura, jt. auth. see Richards, Kenneth.

Richards, Laura E. For Tommy & Other Stories. LC 79-110210. (Short Story Index Reprint Ser.). 1977. 19.95 (0-8369-3361-3) Ayer.

— Julia Ward Howe, 1819-1910, 2 vols., Set. (BCL1-PS American Literature Ser.). 1992. reprint ed. lib. bdg. 150.00 (0-7812-6745-5) Rprt Serv.

Richards, Laura E. & Elliott, Maude H. Julia Ward Howe, Eighteen Nineteen to Nineteen Ten. LC 90-47729. (Illus.). 826p. 1990. reprint ed. 39.95 (0-87797-196-X) Cherokee.

Richards, Laura E., ed. see Howe, Samuel G.

Richards, Laurence D. Constraint Theory: An Approach to Policy-Level Modeling. (Illus.). 424p. (C). 1984. lib. bdg. 63.00 (0-8191-3512-7); pap. text ed. 33.00 (0-8191-3513-5) U Pr of Amer.

Richards, Lawrence. Everyday Bible Insights. 1989. write for info. (0-8499-0707-1) Word Inc.

— Richard's Complete Bible Handbook. 1987. 9.99 (0-8499-3097-9) Word Inc.

Richards, Lawrence O. The Bible Reader's Companion. 936p. 1991. 36.99 (0-89693-039-4) SP Pubns.

— Children's Ministry: Nursing Faith Within the Family of God. 448p. 1988. pap. 24.99 (0-310-52071-1, 18215P) Zondervan.

— Christian Education: Modeling the Gift of New Life. 336p. 1988. pap. 18.99 (0-310-52081-9, 18216P) Zondervan.

— Creative Bible Teaching. LC 74-104830. (C). 1970. 18.99 (0-8024-1640-3) Moody.

— It Couldn't Just Happen: Fascinating Facts about God's World. (J). (gr. 4-7). 1994. pap. 14.99 (0-8499-3583-0) Word Inc.

— The New Testament Bible Background Commentary. LC 93-27863. 640p. 1994. 27.99 (0-89693-507-8, Victor Books) SP Pubns.

— Small Group Member's Commentary. 656p. 1992. pap. 18.99 (0-89693-055-6) SP Pubns.

— The Teacher's Commentary. 1200p. 1987. text ed. 36.99 (0-89693-810-7, Victor Books) SP Pubns.

— Youth Ministry. 1990. pap. 19.99 (0-310-32011-9) Zondervan.

— The Zondervan Expository Dictionary of Bible Words. 736p. 1991. 24.99 (0-310-57270-3) Zondervan.

Richards, Lawrence O., ed. The Revell Bible Dictionary. deluxe ed. LC 90-33022. (Illus.). 1168p. 1990. 39.99 (0-8007-1594-2) Revell.

— The Revell Concise Bible Dictionary. LC 91-21230. (Illus.). 672p. 1991. 14.99 (0-8007-1658-2) Revell.

Richards, Lawrence P. & Bock, Walter J. Functional Anatomy & Adaptive Evolution of the Feeding Apparatus in the Hawaiian Honeycreeper Genus Loxops (Drepanididae) 173p. 1973. 9.00 (0-685-06251-1) Am Ornithologists.

Richards, LeGrand. A Marvelous Work & a Wonder. LC 76-2237. xv, 424p. 1976. 9.95 (0-87747-161-4); pap. 4.95 (0-87579-171-9) Deseret Bk.

Richards, Leila. The Hills of Sidon: Journal of an American Doctor in Lebanon. 224p. 1988. 17.95 (1-55774-015-1) Modan-Adama Bks.

Richards, Lenore, jt. auth. see Treat, Nola.

Richards, Leo. My Obsession. 1994. 12.95 (0-533-11014-9) Vantage.

Richards, Leonard, jt. auth. see Graebner, William.

Richards, Leonard, jt. ed. see Graebner, William.

Richards, Leonard L. Gentlemen of Property & Standing: Anti-Abolition Mobs in Jacksonian America. 1971. pap. 9.95 (0-19-501351-4) OUP.

Richards, Leslie. Love's Deadly Silhouette, Vol. II. (Illus.). 1979. pap. 1.95 (0-89083-438-5) Zebra.

***Richards, Linda.** Reminiscences of Linda Richards. (American Autobiography Ser.). 121p. 1995. reprint ed. lib. bdg. 69.00 (0-7812-8624-7) Rprt Serv.

Richards, Linda M., jt. auth. see Niemeyer, Paul V.

Richards, Llyn & Jeffery, Peter. Best of Set: Discipline. (C). 1990. 59.00 (0-86431-000-5, Pub. by Aust Coun Educ Res AT) St Mut.

— Best of Set: Junior Classes. (C). 1992. 60.00 (0-86431-222-9, Pub. by Aust Coun Educ Res AT) St Mut.

Richards, Llyn, et al. Best of Set: Writing. (C). 1990. 70.00 (0-685-67426-6, Pub. by Aust Coun Educ Res AT) St Mut.

Richards, Louise E., jt. auth. see Pillsbury, Edmund P.

Richards, Lynn B., et al. The Vaginal Birth after Cesarean (VBAC) Experience: Birth Stories by Parents & Professionals. LC 87-15107. (Illus.). 304p. 1987. pap. text ed. 16.95 (0-89789-120-1, Bergin & Garvey) Greenwood.

Richards, Lynne & McGee, Howard. Introduction to Experimental Chemistry. 4th ed. (Illus.). 192p. 1987. 14.95 (0-89529-378-1) Avery Pub.

Richards, Lysander S. History of Marshfield, Massachusetts, Vol. 2: Old Historic Families. 247p. 1993. reprint ed. lib. bdg. 32.50 (0-8328-3142-5) Higginson Bk Co.

Richards, M. & Whitby-Strevens, C. BCPL-The Language & Its Compiler. LC 77-71098. (Illus.). 1981. pap. 17.95 (0-521-28681-6) Cambridge U Pr.

Richards, M. C. Imagine Inventing Yellow: New & Selected Poems. (Illus.). 192p. 1991. 24.95 (0-88268-102-8); pap. 12.95 (0-88268-127-3) Station Hill Pr.

Richards, M. Gregory. When Someone You Know Is Hurting: What You Can Do to Help. 256p. 1994. pap. 5.99 (0-06-104305-2) Zondervan.

Richards, M. J., jt. ed. see Szwilski, A. B.

Richards, M. P., ed. The Integration of the Child into a Social World. LC 73-82464. 320p. 1974. 59.95 (0-521-20306-6) Cambridge U Pr.

Richards, M. P., jt. ed. see Chart, T.

***Richards, Marcos.** Sexo y el Soltero. 40p. (YA). 1995. pap. text ed. 1.00 (1-885630-34-4) HLM Producciones.

Richards, Margaret. Key Issues in Child Sexual Abuse: Some Lessons from Cleveland & Other Inquiries. (C). 1988. 50.00 (0-902789-58-9, Pub. by Natl Inst Soc Work); 35.00 (0-7855-0095-2, Pub. by Natl Inst Soc Work) St Mut.

Richards, Margaret & Righton, Peter. Social Work Education in Conflict. 1979. 25.00 (0-317-05763-4, Pub. by Natl Inst Soc Work) St Mut.

Richards, Margaret, et al. Staff Supervision in Child Protection Work. (C). 1990. 95.00 (0-7855-0072-3, Pub. by Natl Inst Soc Work) St Mut.

Richards, Margaret, et al, eds. Staff Supervision in Child Protection Work. (Illus.). (C). 1989. 59.00 (0-685-40360-2, Pub. by Natl Inst Soc Work) St Mut.

— Staff Supervision in Child Protection Work. (C). 1990. 60.00 (0-902789-70-8, Pub. by Natl Inst Soc Work) St Mut.

Richards, Marion K. Ellen Glasgow's Development As a Novelist. LC 70-110957. (Studies in American Literature: No. 24). 1971. text ed. 65.40 (90-279-1606-3) Mouton.

Richards, Mark. The Cotswold Way. (C). 1988. pap. 45.00 (0-904110-93-1, Pub. by Thornhill Pr UK) St Mut.

— Through Welsh Border Country. (C). 1988. pap. 29.00 (0-904110-53-2, Pub. by Thornhill Pr UK) St Mut.

Richards, Mark B., jt. auth. see Abbey, Robert M.

Richards, Martin & Light, Paul C., eds. Children of Social Worlds. 336p. 1986. 38.00 (0-674-11622-4) HUP.

Richards, Martin, jt. auth. see Reibstein, Janet.

Richards, Marty, et al. Choosing a Nursing Home: A Guidebook for Families. LC 84-25651. (Illus.). 112p. (Orig.). 1985. pap. 9.95 (0-295-96221-6) U of Wash Pr.

Richards, Mary A. Amos Starr Cooke & Juliette Montague Cooke, Their Autobiographies Gleaned from their Journals & Letters. rev. ed. (Illus.). text ed. 19.95 (0-938851-03-9) Daughters of HI.

Richards, Mary B. Camping Out in the Yellowstone, 1882. rev. ed. Slaughter, William W., ed. (Illus.). 120p. 1994. pap. 10.95 (0-87480-449-3) U of Utah Pr.

Richards, Mary C. Centering in Poetry, Pottery, & the Person. 2nd ed. LC 88-38316. 187p. 1989. pap. 12.95 (0-8195-6200-9, Wesleyan Univ Pr) U Pr of New Eng.

— The Crossing Point: Selected Talks & Writings. LC 73-6010. (Illus.). 256p. 1973. pap. 15.95 (0-8195-6029-4, Wesleyan Univ Pr) U Pr of New Eng.

— Sweet Voices of Lahaina: Life Story of Maui's Fabulous Fardens. (Illus.). 91p. 1990. 15.95 (0-89610-170-3) Island Heritage.

— Toward Wholeness: Rudolf Steiner Education in America. LC 80-14905. 222p. 1980. pap. 13.95 (0-8195-6062-6, Wesleyan Univ Pr) U Pr of New Eng.

Richards, Mary C., tr. see Artaud, Antonin.

Richards, Mary D., ed. see Kaup, Donna L.

***Richards, Mary F., ed.** Delaware Genealogical Abstracts from Newspapers. 1995. text ed. write for info. (1-887061-05-3) DE Geneal Soc.

Richards, Mary F., jt. auth. see Hart, Matilda S.

Richards, Mary P. Texts & Their Traditions in the Medieval Library of Rochester Cathedral Priory. LC 87-72869. (Transactions Ser.: Vol. 78, Pt. 3). (Illus.). 212p. (C). 1988. pap. 20.00 (0-87169-783-1, T783-RIM) Am Philos.

Richards, Mary P., ed. Anglo-Saxon Manuscripts: Basic Readings. LC 94-12990. (Basic Readings in Anglo-Saxon England Ser.: Vol. 2). 424p. 1994. 62.00 (0-8153-0100-6, H1434) Garland.

Richards, Maryse H., jt. auth. see Larson, Reed.

Richards, Max D. Intermediate & Long-Term Credit for Small Corporations. Bruchey, Stuart & Carosso, Vincent P., eds. LC 78-18975. (Small Business Enterprise in America Ser.). (Illus.). 1979. lib. bdg. 25.95 (0-405-11478-8) Ayer.

***Richards, Maxwell J.** George & the Dragon. 340p. 1995. pap. 9.95 (1-56901-864-2) NW Pub.

Richards, Michael. The Church of Christ. (C). 1988. 39.00 (0-85439-203-3, Pub. by St Paul Pubns UK) St Mut.

— The Church Two Thousand One. (C). 1988. 65.00 (0-85439-202-5, Pub. by St Paul Pubns UK) St Mut.

— Nature & Necessity of Christ's Church. LC 83-2596. 142p. 1983. pap. 7.95 (0-8189-0458-5) Alba.

Richards, Michael, jt. ed. see French, David.

Richards, Michael, tr. see Rahner, Karl.

Richards, Michael, tr. see Rinpoche, Pabongka.

***Richards, Mildred P.** For Grandchildren: Stories, Letters, Etc. (Illus.). 74p. (Orig.). 1994. pap. 5.00 (0-9637521-2-X) Arlington Pl.

— Second Thoughts: More Poems. (Illus.). (Orig.). 1995. pap. 5.00 (0-9637521-3-8) Arlington Pl.

— Twigs: Poems by Mildred P. Richards. (Illus.). 53p. (Orig.). 1992. pap. 5.00 (0-9637521-0-3) Arlington Pl.

Richards, Mose, jt. auth. see Costeau, Jean-Michel.

Richards, Mose, jt. auth. see Cousteau, Jacques-Yves.

Richards, Mose, jt. auth. see Cousteau, Jean-Michel.

***Richards, Myron.** The Greatest Sound on Earth - Eine Kleine Alte Fahrt Mit Orchester. LC 94-66243. (Illus.). 128p. 1994. 20.00 (0-9622337-4-9) Perry Pub WA.

Richards, Nanci B. & Schneier, Betsy R. The Golden Horizons Retirement Guide: California Edition. (Orig.). 1988. pap. 19.95 (0-944261-01-9) Golden Horizons.

— The Golden Horizons Retirement Guide: Washington State Edition. LC 87-81652. (Orig.). 1987. pap. 18.95 (0-944261-00-0) Golden Horizons.

Richards, Nat. Otis Dunn-Manhunter. Young, Billie, ed. LC 73-83919. 150p. 1974. 21.95 (0-87949-018-7) Ashley Bks.

R

An Asterisk (*) at the beginning of an entry indicates that the title is appearing in BIP for the first time.

Richards, Norman. Dreamers & Doers: Inventors Who Changed the World. LC 81-21029. (Illus.). 168p. (YA). (gr. 5 up). 1984. lib. bdg. 13.95 (*0-689-30914-7*, Atheneum Bks Young) S&S Childrens.

— Monticello. LC 94-35654. (Cornerstones of Freedom Ser.). (Illus.). 32p. (J). (gr. 3-6). 1995. lib. bdg. 12.30 (*0-516-06695-1*) Childrens.

— The Story of the Alamo. LC 70-100698. (Cornerstones of Freedom Ser.). (Illus.). 32p. (J). (gr. 3-6). 1970. 12.30 (*0-516-04601-2*); pap. 3.95 (*0-516-44601-0*) Childrens.

— The Story of the Declaration of Independence. LC 68-24379. (Cornerstones of Freedom Ser.). (Illus.). 32p. (J). (gr. 3-6). 1968. pap. 3.95 (*0-516-44606-1*) Childrens.

— The Story of the Mayflower Compact. LC 67-22901. (Cornerstones of Freedom Ser.). (Illus.). 32p. (J). (gr. 3-6). 1967. pap. 3.95 (*0-516-44625-8*) Childrens.

Richards, Norvin. Humility. 240p. (C). 1992. 37.95 (*0-87722-927-9*) Temple U Pr.

Richards, P. B., ed. Recent Developments in Space Flight Mechanics. (Science & Technology Ser.: Vol. 9). 1966. 25.00 (*0-87703-037-5*) Univelt Inc.

Richards, P. G., ed. see Travers, Tony.

Richards, P. J., jt. ed. see Leonor, M. D.

Richards, P. J., jt. ed. see Van der Hoeven, R.

Richards, P. W. The Tropical Rain Forest: An Ecological Study. 2nd ed. LC 93-49019. (Illus.). 600p. (C). 1992. write for info. (*0-521-42054-7*); pap. write for info. (*0-521-42194-2*) Cambridge U Pr.

Richards, Pamela S. Scientific Information in Wartime: An Allied-German Rivalry, 1939-1945. LC 93-25050. (Contributions in Military Studies: No. 151). 192p. 1994. text ed. 49.95 (*0-313-29062-8*) Greenwood.

Richards, Patricia. Dark Knight. (Rainbow Romances Ser.). 160p. 1993. 14.95 (*0-7090-4900-5*, Hale-Parkwest) Parkwest Pubns.

Richards, Paul. The Unblessed. 384p. 1988. pap. 3.95 (*0-8217-2380-4*) Zebra.

Richards, Paul & Harris, Nicola, eds. African Environment: Problems & Perspectives. LC 76-371759. (African Environment: Special Report Ser.: Vol. 1). 131p. reprint ed. pap. 37.40 (*0-8357-5232-1*, 2055389) Bks Demand.

Richards, Paul, ed. see Krigger, John T.

Richards, Paul, jt. ed. see Simpson, David W.

Richards, Paul, et al. Indigenous Knowledge Systems for Agriculture & Rural Development: The CIKARD Inaugural Lectures. (Studies in Technology & Social Change: Vol. 13). 40p. (C). 1989. pap. 5.00 (*0-945271-18-2*) ISU-TSCP.

Richards, Paul B. & Bolger, Philip H., eds. Skylab & Pioneer Report: Proceedings of the 12th Goddard Memorial Symposium. (Science & Technology Ser.: Vol. 36). (Illus.). 160p. 1975. lib. bdg. 20.00 (*0-87703-071-5*, Pub. by Am Astro Soc) Univelt Inc.

Richards, Paul D. Critical Focus: The Black & White Photographs of Harvey Wilson Richards. 104p. (Orig.). 1987. pap. 12.95 (*0-9618725-0-0*) Estuary Pr.

Richards, Penny. Eden. (Calloway Corners Ser.). 1993. mass mkt. 3.50 (*0-373-83281-8*, 1-83281-5) Harlequin Bks.

— Passionate Kisses. (Crystal Creek Ser.). 1994. mass mkt. 3.99 (*0-373-82526-9*, 1-82526-4) Harlequin Bks.

— Unanswered Prayers. 1994. mass mkt. 3.99 (*0-373-82533-1*, 1-82533-0) Harlequin Bks.

— Where Dreams Have Been... (That Special Woman!) (Special Edition Ser.). 1995. mass mkt. 3.75 (*0-373-09949-5*, 1-09949-8) Silhouette.

Richards, Peter. Learning Medicine 1993. (Illus.). 108p. 1992. pap. text ed. 12.00 (*0-7279-0820-0*, BMJ Pubng Grp) Amer Coll Phys.

— Learning Medicine, 1994. 10th ed. 112p. 1993. pap. text ed. 12.00 (*0-685-72637-1*, BMJ Pubng Grp) Amer Coll Phys.

— Living Medicine: Planning a Career: Choosing a Specialty. (Illus.). 136p. (C). 1990. pap. 18.95 (*0-521-38628-4*) Cambridge U Pr.

— Living Medicine: Planning a Career: Choosing a Specialty. (Illus.). 136p. (C). 1990. 49.95 (*0-521-38478-8*) Cambridge U Pr.

Richards, Peter, jt. ed. see Paukert, Liba.

Richards, Phil & Banigan, John J. How to Abandon Ship. LC 88-18954. (Illus.). 160p. 1988. reprint ed. pap. 6.95 (*0-87033-388-7*) Cornell Maritime.

Richards, R. Clinical Pharmacology. LC 67-19416. 1968. 58.00 (*0-08-012369-4*, Pub. by Pergamon Repr UK) Franklin.

— A Slide Atlas of Strabismus Surgery. (Illus.). 240p. 1991. ring bd. 895.00 (*0-442-31557-0*) Chapman & Hall.

Richards, R. J. Solving Problems in Control: Dynamic Models & Single-Input Single-Ouput Linear Continuous Systems. LC 93-3396. (Solving Problems Ser.). 232p. 1993. pap. text ed. 44.95 (*0-470-22076-7*) Halsted Pr.

Richards, R. J. & Rajan, K. T., eds. Tissue Culture in Medical Research (II) Second International Symposium on Tissue Culture in Medical Research, 1-3 April 1980, Cardiff, Wales. LC 80-40939. (Illus.). 281p. 1980. 115.00 (*0-08-025924-3*, Pub. by Pergamon Repr UK) Franklin.

Richards, R. W. Brothers in Gray. Boart, Jeff, ed. (Alternative History Trilogy Ser.: Bk. II). (Illus.). 313p. 1993. pap. 12.95 (*0-9625502-1-3*) RoKarn Pubns.

— A Southern Yarn. Bogart, Jeffrey, ed. LC 89-92811. (Illus.). (Orig.). (YA). 1990. pap. 12.95 (*0-9625502-0-5*) RoKarn Pubns.

— Survival. Bogart, Jeff, ed. (Story of the New Southland Ser.: Bk. I). (Illus.). 252p. (YA). 1995. pap. text ed. 13.95 (*0-9625502-4-8*) RoKarn Pubns.

Richards, R. W., jt. auth. see Pethrick, R. A.

Richards, Ralph. All about Wills & Trusts for Florida Residents. 11th rev. ed. Diamond, Sandra F. & Valentine, Laurie W., eds. LC 64-25300. 1994. pap. text ed. 5.95 (*0-88251-085-1*) Trend Bk Div.

Richards, Rand. The Complete San Francisco Bay Area Sightseeing Guide. LC 94-25847. (Illus.). 224p. (Orig.). 1994. pap. 12.95 (*1-879367-02-5*) Hrtage Hse.

— Historic San Francisco: A Concise History & Guide. LC 91-70670. (Illus.). 320p. (Orig.). 1991. pap. 14.95 (*1-879367-00-9*) Hrtage Hse.

Richards, Ray, ed. see Thakur, Bhaktivinoda.

Richards, Raymond. Closing the Door to Destitution: The Shaping of the Social Security Acts of the United States & New Zealand. 1994. 42.50 (*0-271-01060-6*) Pa St U Pr.

— Closing the Door to Destitution: The Shaping of the Social Security Acts of the United States & New Zealand. LC 92-41698. 208p. (C). 1994. 42.50 (*0-271-01061-4*) Pa St U Pr.

Richards, Regina & Oppenheim, Gary S. Visual Skills Appraisal (VSA) 80p. 1984. 60.00 (*0-685-42805-2*, 453-0A); teacher ed 17.00 (*0-87879-453-0*); 15.00 (*0-685-42807-9*); 6.00 (*0-87879-454-9*); 8.00 (*0-87879-455-7*); 9.00 (*0-87879-456-5*); 9.00 (*0-87879-457-3*); 8.00 (*0-87879-458-1*); 10.00 (*0-685-42806-0*) Acad Therapy.

Richards, Regina & Smith, Jeralee A. Angling for Words-Memory Foundations for Reading: MFR Manual. (Angling for Words Ser.). 64p. 1983. 8.00 (*0-87879-369-0*); 8.00 (*0-685-53923-7*); 6.00 (*0-87879-371-2*); 8.00 (*0-87879-372-0*) Acad Therapy.

Richards, Regina G. Classroom Visual Activities (CVA) Brownell, Rick, ed. (Illus.). 80p. (Orig.). 1988. pap. text ed. 12.00 (*0-87879-657-6*) Acad Therapy.

— Learn: Playful Techniques to Accelerate Learning. LC 93-21956. 192p. (J). (gr. k-12). 1993. 22.00 (*0-913705-89-6*) Zephyr Pr AZ.

Richards, Rhys. American Whaling on the Chatham Grounds. (Illus.). 70p. 1971. 1.00 (*0-9607340-3-1*) Nantucket Hist Assn.

— Captain Simon Metcalfe, Pioneer Fur Trader on the Northwest Coast, 1787-1794. (Alaska History Ser.: No. 37). 1991. 18.00 (*0-919642-37-3*) Limestone Pr.

Richards, Rick, ed. Ski Pioneers: Ernie Blake, His Friends, & the Making of Taos Ski Valley. (Illus.). 1992. 39.95 (*1-56044-157-7*) Falcon Pr MT.

Richards, Robert C. & Lein, Laura, contribs. Texas Probation Officers' Attitudes & Alternatives to Incarceration. (Policy Research Project Report Ser.: No. 95). 90p. 1992. 9.00 (*0-89940-703-X*) LBJ Sch Pub Aff.

Richards, Robert D. Uninhabited, Robust, & Wide Open: Mr. Justice Brennan's Legacy to the First Amendment. LC 94-4973. 1994. pap. 35.00 (*0-9635752-4-4*) Pkway Pubs.

Richards, Robert H., et al. Textbook of Ore Dressing. 3rd rev. ed. LC 40-10540. 624p. reprint ed. pap. 177.90 (*0-317-29998-0*, 2051848) Bks Demand.

Richards, Robert J. Darwin & the Emergence of Evolutionary Theories of Mind & Behavior. LC 87-10891. (Science & Its Conceptual Foundations Ser.). (Illus.). 688p. 1989. pap. text ed. 17.95 (*0-226-71200-1*) U Ch Pr.

— The Meaning of Evolution: The Morphological Construction & Ideological Reconstruction of Darwin's Theory. LC 91-19017. (Science & Its Conceptual Foundations Ser.). (Illus.). 192p. 1992. lib. bdg. 22.50 (*0-226-71202-8*) U Ch Pr.

— The Meaning of Evolution: The Morphological Construction & Ideological Reconstruction of Darwin's Theory. LC 91-19017. (Science & Its Conceptual Foundations Ser.). (Illus.). xvi, 206p. (C). 1993. pap. text ed. 9.95 (*0-226-71203-6*) U Ch Pr.

Richards, Robert R. Alaska: Business & Industry. 1989. 34.95 (*0-89781-265-4*) Preferred Mktg.

Richards, Roberta & Z, Rachel. The Devil Next Door. LC 93-84894. 180p. (Orig.). Date not set. pap. 10.00 (*0-931104-38-6*) Sunflower Ink.

Richards, Ron. A Director's Method for Film & Television. 256p. 1992. pap. 34.95 (*0-240-80119-9*, Focal) Buttrwrth-Heinemann.

Richards, Ronald, comp. A Guide to Sources for the History of Western Australia. 1993. 45.00 (*1-875560-11-4*, Pub. by Univ of West Aust Pr AT) Intl Spec Bk.

***Richards, Ronald W., et al.** Building Partnerships: Educating Health Professionals for the Communities They Serve. (Health Ser.). 1995. 31.95 (*0-7879-0150-4*) Jossey-Bass.

Richards, Roosevelt. A Long Ways from Where I've Been: An African-American's Journey from the Jim Crow South to Chicago's Gold Coast. 1994. pap. 10.95 (*1-879360-35-7*) Noble Pr.

Richards, Roy. One Hundred One Science Surprises: Exciting Experiments with Everyday Materials. LC 92-32491. (Illus.). 104p. (J). 1993. 16.95 (*0-8069-8822-3*) Sterling.

— One Hundred One Science Surprises: Exciting Experiments with Everyday Materials. (Illus.). 104p. 1994. pap. 9.95 (*0-8069-8823-1*) Sterling.

— One Hundred-One Science Tricks: Fun Experiments with Everyday Materials. LC 91-13263. (Illus.). 104p. (J). (gr. 3-10). 1991. 16.95 (*0-8069-8388-4*) Sterling.

— One Hundred One Science Tricks: Fun Experiments with Everyday Materials. (Illus.). 104p. (J). (gr. 4-10). 1993. pap. 9.95 (*0-8069-8389-2*) Sterling.

Richards, Roy, ed. see Bennett, Matthew.

Richards, Ruth, ed. see Andreasen, Nancy C., et al.

Richards, Ruth M., jt. auth. see Israeli, Isaac.

Richards, S. A. & Fielden, P. S. Temperature Regulation. LC 73-77794. (Wykeham Science Ser.: No. 27). 212p. (C). 1973. pap. 18.00 (*0-8448-1335-4*, Crane Russak) Taylor & Francis.

Richards, S. J., jt. ed. see Dunnett, Stephen B.

Richards, Sandra. Rise of the English Actress. LC 91-37873. 352p. 1993. text ed. 39.95 (*0-312-07578-2*) St Martin.

Richards, Sara & Moore, Russell. The Woman: Eve Page. (Illus.). 100p. 1994. 39.50 (*1-883740-15-0*) Pebble Bch Pr Ltd.

***Richards, Scott.** Understanding Homosexuality. 140p. 1995. pap. 10.95 (*1-55517-173-7*) CFI Dist.

Richards, Scott, ed. see Adams, Sandy.

Richards, Scott, ed. see Eastman, Mark & Smith, Chuck.

Richards, Scott, ed. see Smith, Chuck.

Richards, Selena. Rebecca Goes Out. (Grandmother Days Ser.). (Illus.). 18p. (J). (ps). 1992. 3.50 (*1-56288-269-4*) Checkerboard.

— Rebecca Goes to the Country. (Grandmother Days Ser.). (Illus.). 18p. (J). (ps). 1992. 3.50 (*1-56288-270-8*) Checkerboard.

— Rebecca Goes to the Park. (Grandmother Days Ser.). (Illus.). 18p. (J). (ps). 1992. 3.50 (*1-56288-271-6*) Checkerboard.

— Rebecca's Rainy Day. (Grandmother Days Ser.). (Illus.). 18p. (J). (ps). 1992. 3.50 (*1-56288-272-4*) Checkerboard.

Richards, Shaun, jt. auth. see Cairns, David.

Richards, Stanley. The Most Popular Plays of the American Theatre. LC 79-65112. (Illus.). 1979. 24.95 (*0-8128-2682-5*, Scrbrough Hse) Madison Bks UPA.

Richards, Stephen P. Numbers at Work & at Play. (Illus.). 213p. (Orig.). (C). (gr. 10-12). 1987. pap. 8.95 (*0-9608224-2-9*) S P Richards.

Richards, Steve. Levitation: What It Is, How It Works, How to Do It. 160p. 1992. reprint ed. pap. 9.00 (*1-85538-089-7*, Pub. by Aquarian Pr UK) Thorsons SF.

Richards, Sue, jt. auth. see Metcalfe, Les.

Richards, Sue, jt. auth. see Richards, Larry.

Richards, Susan, jt. auth. see Ober, Stuart.

Richards, T. Military Jeeps, Nineteen Forty-One to Nineteen Forty-Five. 100p. 1985. pap. 17.95 (*0-946489-27-0*) Portrayal.

Richards, T. H. & Stanley, Philip E., eds. Stability Problems in Engineering Structures & Components. (Illus.). 428p. 1979. 113.50 (*0-85334-836-7*, Pub. by Elsevier Applied Sci UK) Elsevier.

Richards, T. H., jt. ed. see Gibbs, H. G.

Richards, Tad & Shestack, Melvin. The New Country Music Encyclopedia. LC 93-17689. 1993. pap. 14.00 (*0-671-78258-4*, Fireside) S&S Trade.

Richards, Tad, jt. auth. see Godfrey, Neale.

Richards, Terri, jt. auth. see Pendleton, Moses.

Richards, Tessa, ed. Medicine in Europe. 152p. 1992. pap. text ed. 25.00 (*0-7279-0319-5*, Pub. by British Med Jrnl UK) Amer Coll Phys.

Richards, Theodore W. & Behr, Gustavus E., Jr. The Electromotive Force of Iron under Varying Conditions, & the Effect of Occluded Hydrogen. LC 07-3935. (Carnegie Institution of Washington Publication Ser.: No. 61). 43p. reprint ed. pap. 25.00 (*0-317-29736-8*, 2015698) Bks Demand.

***Richards, Thomas.** At Work with Grotowski on Physical Actions. LC 94-23889. (ENG & ITA.). 1995. write for info. (*0-415-12491-3*); pap. write for info. (*0-415-12492-1*) Routledge.

— The Commodity Culture of Victorian England: Advertising & Spectacle, 1851-1914. LC 89-37035. 320p. 1990. 37.50 (*0-8047-1652-8*); pap. 12.95 (*0-8047-1901-2*) Stanford U Pr.

— The Imperial Archive: Knowledge & the Fantasy of Empire. 224p. 1993. 59.95 (*0-86091-400-3*, B0534, Pub. by Verso UK); pap. 17.95 (*0-86091-605-7*, B0538, Pub. by Verso UK) Routledge Chapman & Hall.

Richards, Thomas J. Clausalform Logic: An Introduction to the Logic of Computer Reasoning. (International Computer Science Ser.). (Illus.). (C). 1989. pap. text ed. 38.75 (*0-201-12920-5*) Addison-Wesley.

Richards, Tim, jt. auth. see Kaltenbach, Don.

Richards, Toni, et al. Prenatal & Obstetric Care in Los Angeles County, 1990. LC 93-20333. 1993. 9.00 (*0-8330-1343-2*, MR-182) Rand Corp.

Richards, V., ed. Current Cancer Immunology. (Progress in Experimental Tumor Research Ser.: Vol. 25). (Illus.). 1980. 116.00 (*3-8055-3033-1*) S Karger.

— Immunology of Cancer. (Progress in Experimental Tumor Research Ser.: Vol. 19). 416p. 1974. 118.50 (*3-8055-1762-9*) S Karger.

Richards, Vernon. Lessons of the Spanish Revolution. 3rd ed. 210p. (Orig.). (C). reprint ed. pap. 11.00 (*0-900384-23-9*) Left Bank.

— Protest Without Illusions. 168p. 1981. pap. 8.50 (*0-900384-19-0*) Left Bank.

Richards, Vernon, ed. Spain, 1936-39: Social Revolution & Counter-Revolution. (Centenary Ser.: Vol. 2). 270p. (Orig.). 1990. pap. 12.00 (*0-900384-54-9*) Left Bank.

— Why Work? Arguments for the Leisure Society. (Illus.). 210p. (Orig.). (C). 1983. pap. 10.00 (*0-900384-25-5*) Left Bank.

Richards, Vernon, tr. see Kropotkin, Peter.

Richards, Vernon, tr. see Leval, Gaston.

Richards, Vernon, ed. see Malatesta, Errico.

Richards, Vikki, jt. auth. see Kirkpatrick, Doug.

Richards, Vikki, ed. see Kirkpatrick, Douglas.

Richards, Vyvyan. Portrait of T. E. Lawrence. LC 75-22043. (English Biography Ser.: No. 31). 1975. lib. bdg. 75.00 (*0-8383-2093-7*) M S G Haskell Hse.

Richards, W. G. & Scott, P. R. Structure & Spectra of Molecules. LC 84-15333. 182p. 1985. text ed. 98.00 (*0-471-90577-1*) Wiley.

Richards, W. Graham. The Problems of Chemistry. (Illus.). 112p. (C). 1986. 17.95 (*0-19-219191-8*) OUP.

Richards, W. Graham, ed. Computer-Aided Molecular Design. (Illus.). 284p. 1989. text ed. 115.00 (*0-89573-738-8*) VCH Pubs.

***Richards, W. Graham & Scott, Peter.** Energy Levels in Atoms & Molecules. (Oxford Chemistry Primers Ser.: No. 26). (Illus.). 96p. (C). 1995. pap. text ed. 9.95 (*0-19-855804-X*) OUP.

Richards, W. Graham, jt. auth. see Grant, Guy H.

Richards, W. H., jt. ed. see Peters, W.

Richards, W. Wiley. The Bible & Christian Traditons: Keys to Understanding the Allegorical Subplot of Nietzsche's "Zarathrustra" LC 90-33111. (American University Studies: Ser. XII, Vol. 75). 425p. (C). 1990. text ed. 34.95 (*0-8204-1312-7*) P Lang Pubs.

— Winds of Doctrines: The Origin & Development of Southern Baptist Theology. 244p. 1991. 52.00 (*0-8191-8254-0*); pap. 31.50 (*0-8191-8255-9*) U Pr of Amer.

Richards, Wallace F., jt. auth. see McClendon, Dennis E.

Richards, Whitman. Vision Research for Flight Simulation: A Report on a Workshop on Simulation of Low-Level Flight. 109p. reprint ed. pap. 31.10 (*0-8357-7689-1*, 2036040) Bks Demand.

Richards, Whitman & Ullman, Shimon, eds. Image Understanding, 3 vols., Vol. 2. 368p. 1987. text ed. 75.00 (*0-89391-311-1*) Ablex Pub.

Richards, Whitman, jt. auth. see Ullman, Shimon.

Richards, Whitman, jt. ed. see Ullman, Shimon.

Richards, Whitman A., ed. Natural Computation: Selected Readings. 480p. (Orig.). 1988. pap. 27.50 (*0-262-68055-6*, Bradford Bks) MIT Pr.

Richards, Willard. Fear, Faith, Courage: A Love Story. (Illus.). 205p. (Orig.). 1993. pap. 18.95 (*0-9641104-0-7*) W Richards.

Richards, William, tr. see Mookini, Esther T.

Richards, William L. The Classification of the Greek Manuscripts of the Johannine Epistles. LC 77-23469. (Society of Biblical Literature. Dissertation Ser.: No. 35). 304p. reprint ed. pap. 86.70 (*0-7837-5456-6*, 2045221) Bks Demand.

Richardsen, Cailen, jt. auth. see Caldwell, Stevhan.

Richardson. Bathtime. (Can You Find Ser.: No. 4). (J). 1994. 2.95 (*0-671-89314-9*, Litl Simon S&S) S&S Childrens.

— Bedtime. (Can You Find Ser.: No. 3). (J). 1994. 2.95 (*0-671-89313-0*, Litl Simon S&S) S&S Childrens.

— The Birthday. (Can You Find Ser.: No. 2). (J). 1994. 2.95 (*0-671-89312-2*, Litl Simon S&S) S&S Childrens.

— Handbook of Human Blood Constituent. 1994. 179.95 (*0-8493-8664-0*) CRC Pr.

— Heidegger. 3rd ed. (Phaenomenologica Ser.: No. 13). 1974. lib. bdg. 99.00 (*90-247-0246-1*) Kluwer Ac.

— In the Garden. (Can You Find Ser.: No. 1). (J). (gr. k up). 1994. 2.95 (*0-671-89311-4*, Litl Simon S&S) S&S Childrens.

— Jobsmarts for Twentysomethings. 1995. pap. 13.00 (*0-679-75717-1*, Vin) Random.

— The Mathematics of Drugs & Solutions with Clinic. 208p. 1994. pap. 19.95 (*0-8016-7895-1*) Mosby Yr Bk.

— The Mathematics of Drugs & Solutions with Clinical Applications. (Illus.). 208p. 1990. pap. 19.95 (*0-8016-6049-1*) Mosby Yr Bk.

— MS-DOS Batch File Programming Including OS-2. 1988. pap. 17.95 (*0-318-32660-4*, 0-8306-9328-9) TAB Bks.

— Principles of Cell Adhesion. 1995. write for info. (*0-8493-4559-6*) CRC Pr.

— Still More Stories from Grandma's Attic. 1994. pap. (*0-7814-0087-2*, Lion) Chariot Family.

— Treasures from Grandma. 1994. pap. (*0-7814-0088-0*, Lion) Chariot Family.

Richardson, ed. X-Rays from Laser Plasmas. 332p. 1987. 59.00 (*0-89252-866-4*, 831) SPIE.

Richardson & Gunston. High Tech Warfare: Weapons of Operation Desert Storm. 1991. 17.99 (*0-517-06673-4*) Random Hse Value.

Richardson & Peacock. Coulson & Richardson's Chemical Engineering, Vol. 3. 3rd ed. (Chemical Engineering Technical Ser.: No. 3). 1994. text ed. 135.00 (*0-08-041002-2*, Pergamon Pr); pap. text ed. 46.00 (*0-08-041003-0*, Pergamon Pr) Elsevier.

Richardson & Reader. Analogue Electronics Circuit Analysis. 200p. 1992. boxed 30.00 (*0-13-026311-7*) P-H.

— Digital Electronics Circuit Analysis. 200p. 1995. text ed. 34.00 (*0-13-211210-8*) P-H.

Richardson & Sisler. Inorganic Chemistry. 720p. 1996. write for info. (*0-8016-6562-0*) Mosby Yr Bk.

***Richardson & Smith.** Crisis Management: A Work Book for Managers. Date not set. text ed. 45.00 (*0-471-95356-3*) Wiley.

— Low Temperature Techniques in Experimental Condensed Matter Physics. (Orig.). 1988. pap. 41.95 (*0-318-33228-0*, 15002) Addison-Wesley.

Richardson, jt. auth. see Hahn, Kevin A.

Richardson, jt. auth. see Spenser.

Richardson, jt. auth. see Swihart.

Richardson, A., jt. auth. see Carter, Geoffrey W.

Richardson, A. G., jt. auth. see Reuther, Ruth E.

***Richardson, Al, ed. & intro.** In Defence of the Russian Revolution: A Selection of Bolshevik Writings, 1917-1923. 1995. 40.00 (*1-899438-01-7*, Pub. by Porcupine Bks UK); pap. 19.50 (*1-899438-02-5*, Pub. by Porcupine Bks UK) Humanities.

Richardson, Alan. Corporate & Organizational Video. 1992. text ed. write for info. (*0-07-052334-7*) McGraw.

— Earth God Rising: The Return of the Male Mysteries. LC 90-45552. (Men's Spirituality Ser.). (Illus.). 224p. (Orig.). 1990. pap. 9.95 (*0-87542-672-7*) Llewellyn Pubns.

— Individual Differences in Imaging: Their Measurement, Origins, & Consequences. LC 93-28218. (Imagery & Human Development Ser.). 223p. 1994. text ed. 26.95 (*0-89503-116-7*); pap. 20.95 (*0-89503-117-5*) Baywood Pub.

— Literature, Education, & Romanticism: Reading As Social Practice, 1780-1832. LC 93-49343. (Cambridge Studies in Romanticism: No. 8). (Illus.). 373p. (C). 1995. 54.95 (*0-521-46276-2*) Cambridge U Pr.

R

An Asterisk (*) at the beginning of an entry indicates that the title is appearing in BIP for the first time.

— Magical Gateways. LC 92-17844. (New Age Ser.). (Illus.). 208p. 1992. pap. 4.95 (*0-87542-681-6*) Llewellyn Pubns.

— A Mental Theater: Poetic Drama & Consciousness in the Romantic Age. LC 87-10922. 170p. 1988. lib. bdg. 30.00 (*0-271-00612-9*) Pa St U Pr.

— Science, History & Faith. LC 86-22863. 216p. 1986. reprint ed. text ed. 55.00 (*0-313-25325-0*, RISHF, Greenwood Pr) Greenwood.

— Theological Wordbook of the Bible. 288p. 1962. pap. 12.00 (*0-02-089090-7*, Pub. by Gebrueder Borntraeger GW) Macmillan.

— Twentieth Century Magic & the Old Religion - Dion Fortune, Christine Hartley, Charles Seymour. LC 90-28621. (High Magick Ser.). 256p. 1991. pap. 12.95 (*0-87542-673-5*) Llewellyn Pubns.

Richardson, Alan & Bowden, John, eds. The Westminster Dictionary of Christian Theology. LC 83-14521. 632p. 1983. 32.00 (*0-664-21398-7*, Westminster) Westminster John Knox.

Richardson, Alan & Hughes, Geoff. Ancient Magicks for a New Age. LC 88-45185. (High Magick Ser.). (Illus.). 320p. (Orig.). 1989. pap. 12.95 (*0-87542-671-9*) Llewellyn Pubns.

Richardson, Alan, tr. see Erdman, Nikolai.

Richardson, Albert D. The Secret Service: The Field, the Dungeon, & the Escape. LC 77-173119. 1972. reprint ed. 39.95 (*0-405-08888-4*, Pub. by Blom Pubns UK) Ayer.

— The Secret Service, the Field, the Dungeon, & the Escape. LC 70-37315. (Black Heritage Library Collection). 1977. reprint ed. 39.95 (*0-8369-8952-X*) Ayer.

Richardson, Albert E. Georgian England: A Survey of Social Life, Trades, Industries & Art from 1700 to 1820. LC 67-23265. (Essay Index Reprint Ser.). 1977. 34.95 (*0-8369-0823-6*) Ayer.

— The Old Inns of England. LC 72-80704. (Illus.). 1972. reprint ed. lib. bdg. 18.95 (*0-405-08886-8*, Pub. by Blom Pubns UK) Ayer.

Richardson, Albert E. & Eberlein, H. Donaldson. English Inn Past & Present. LC 68-56499. (Illus.). 1972. reprint ed. 24.95 (*0-405-08887-6*, Pub. by Blom Pubns UK) Ayer.

Richardson, Alfred. Plants of Southernmost Texas. 298p. (Orig.). 1990. pap. text ed. 13.00 (*0-9627293-0-2*) Gorgas Sci Fndtn.

— Plants of the Rio Grande Delta. (Gorgas Science Foundation, Inc., Treasures of Nature Ser.). (Illus.). 440p. (Orig.). 1995. text ed. 45.00 (*0-292-77068-5*); pap. 24.95 (*0-292-77070-7*) U of Tex Pr.

Richardson, Alfred M. The Medieval Modes: Their Melody & Harmony for the Use of the Modern Composer. LC 78-66918. (Encore Music Editions Ser.). (Illus.). 1979. reprint ed. 16.00 (*0-88355-758-4*) Hyperion Conn.

Richardson, Alice M. Index to Stories of Hymns. LC 72-1690. reprint ed. 20.00 (*0-404-09911-4*) AMS Pr.

Richardson, Allen F. Careers Without College: Sports. Colton, Kitty, ed. LC 93-4488. 96p. (YA). (gr. 10-12). 1993. pap. 7.95 (*1-56079-250-7*) Petersons Guides.

Richardson, Alphyn P. Barnegat Ways. LC 79-166564. (Short Story Index Reprint Ser.). (Illus.). 1977. reprint ed. 19.95 (*0-8369-3994-8*) Ayer.

Richardson, Alphyn P. & Brief, Richard P., eds. The Influence of Accountants' Certificates on Commercial Credit. LC 80-1574. (Dimensions of Accounting Theory & Practice Ser.). 1980. reprint ed. lib. bdg. 17.95 (*0-405-13540-8*) Ayer.

Richardson, Andrea, ed. The Research Tradition at UCSF: Conversations with Dr. Leslie Latty Bennett. (Oral History Ser.). (Illus.). 200p. (Orig.). 1992. pap. 20.00 (*1-881525-00-7*) Univ Calif SF.

Richardson, Andrew. Interceptive Orthodontics. 2nd ed. (Illus.). 62p. 1989. pap. 20.00 (*0-904588-21-1*, Pub. by Brit Dental Assn UK) Ishiyaku Euro.

Richardson, Ann & Ritchie, Jane. Letting Go: Dilemmas for Parents Whose Son or Daughter Has a Mental Handicap. 112p. 1989. 80.00 (*0-335-15841-2*, Open Univ Pr); pap. 27.00 (*0-335-15840-4*, Open Univ Pr) Taylor & Francis.

Richardson, Anne, jt. ed. see Dick, John A.

Richardson, Anthony. One Man & His Dog. large type ed. 1965. 15.95 (*0-85456-577-9*) Ulverscroft.

Richardson, Arleen, jt. ed. see Fedoroff, Sergey.

Richardson, Arleigh D., 3rd, ed. see Alcott, Ron.

Richardson, Arlene Z. & Hannah, Sheila, eds. Introduction to Visual Resource Library Automation. (Visual Resources Association Guides). (Illus.). 178p. 1981. 17.00 (*0-938852-08-6*) Visual Resources Assn.

Richardson, Arlene Z. & Kuehn, Rosemary, eds. Guide to Copy Photography for Visual Resource Collections. (Visual Resources Association Guides). 122p. 1980. 10.00 (*0-938852-05-1*) Visual Resources Assn.

Richardson, Arleta. Andrew's Secret. Payne, Peggy & Yoder, Tamra, eds. (Illus.). 30p. (Orig.). (J). (gr. 1-3). 1989. pap. 3.00 (*0-89367-143-6*) Light & Life.

— At Home in North Branch. LC 88-9529. (Grandma's Attic Ser.). (J). (gr. 3-7). 1988. pap. 3.99 (*1-55513-312-6*, Chariot Bks) Chariot Family.

— A Day at the Fair. (Grandma's Attic Ser.). (Illus.). 32p. (J). (ps-3). 1995. 14.99 (*0-7814-0249-2*, Chariot Bks) Chariot Family.

— Eighteen & on Her Own. LC 85-29050. (Grandma's Attic Ser.). 173p. (J). (gr. 3-7). 1986. pap. 3.99 (*0-89191-512-5*, Chariot Bks) Chariot Family.

— The Grandma's Attic Cookbook. LC 93-3132. 1993. pap. 9.99 (*0-7814-0065-1*, Chariot Bks) Chariot Family.

— The Grandma's Attic Storybook. LC 92-33823. (J). 1993. pap. 9.99 (*0-7814-0070-8*, Chariot Bks) Chariot Family.

— A Heart for God in India. Payne, Peggy & Yoder, Tamra, eds. (Illus.). 52p. (Orig.). (J). (gr. 4-6). 1989. pap. 4.00 (*0-89367-144-4*) Light & Life.

— In Grandma's Attic. LC 74-75541. 112p. (Orig.). (J). (gr. 3-7). 1984. pap. 3.99 (*0-912692-32-4*, Chariot Bks) Chariot Family.

— In Grandma's Attic. (Orig.). (J). (gr. 4-7). 1994. pap. 4.99 (*0-7814-0085-6*) Cook.

— Letters from Grandma's Attic. (Grandma's Attic Collection Ser.). (Illus.). 24p. (J). (gr. 4-8). 1995. 14.99 (*0-7814-0229-8*) Chariot Family.

— Looking for Home. LC 92-46259. (Orphan Journey Ser.: Bk. 1). (J). 1993. pap. 4.99 (*0-7814-0921-7*, Chariot Bks) Chariot Family.

— More Stories from Grandma's. (J). (gr. 4-7). 1994. pap. 4.99 (*0-7814-0086-4*) Cook.

— More Stories from Grandma's Attic. LC 78-73125. (Illus.). (J). (gr. 3-7). 1979. pap. 3.99 (*0-89191-131-6*, Chariot Bks) Chariot Family.

— New Faces, New Friends. LC 88-34639. (Grandma's Attic Ser.). (J). (gr. 3-7). 1989. pap. 3.99 (*1-55513-985-X*, Chariot Bks) Chariot Family.

— Nineteen & Wedding Bells Ahead. LC 87-461. (Grandma's Attic Ser.). 156p. (J). (gr. 3-7). 1987. pap. 3.99 (*1-55513-061-5*, Chariot Bks) Chariot Family.

— Prairie Homestead. LC 94-27086. (Orphans' Journey Ser.: Vol. 3). (J). (gr. 1-8). 1994. write for info. (*0-7814-0091-0*) Chariot Family.

— Sixteen & Away from Home. LC 85-438. (Grandma's Attic Ser.). (J). (gr. 3-7). 1985. pap. 3.99 (*0-89191-933-3*, 59337, Chariot Bks) Chariot Family.

— Still More Stories from Grandma's Attic. (J). (gr. 3-7). 1980. pap. 3.99 (*0-89191-252-5*, Chariot Bks) Chariot Family.

— Stories from the Growing Years. LC 90-20123. (Grandma's Attic Ser.). (J). (gr. 3-7). 1991. pap. 3.99 (*1-55513-819-5*, 38190, Chariot Bks) Chariot Family.

— Treasures from Grandma. LC 84-12736. (Grandma's Attic Ser.). (J). (gr. 3-7). 1984. pap. 3.99 (*0-89191-934-1*, 59345, Chariot Bks) Chariot Family.

— Whistle-Stop West. LC 92-46260. (Orphan Journey Ser.: Bk. 2). (J). 1993. pap. 4.99 (*0-7814-0922-5*, Chariot Bks) Chariot Family.

Richardson, B., et al. Case Studies in Business Planning. 176p. (Orig.). 1989. pap. 26.50 (*0-273-03127-9*, Pub. by Pitman Pub Ltd UK); teacher ed 26.50 (*0-273-03128-7*, Pub. by Pitman Pub Ltd UK) Trans-Atl Phila.

Richardson, B. A. Defects & Deterioration in Buildings. (Illus.). 220p. 1991. 72.95 (*0-442-31302-0*) Chapman & Hall.

Richardson, Barbara L. & Wirtenberg, Jeana, eds. Sex Role Research: Measuring Social Change. LC 83-2426. 286p. 1983. text ed. 36.95 (*0-275-91063-6*, C1063, Praeger Pubs) Greenwood.

Richardson, Barrie & Castronovo Fusco, Mary A. The Plus Ten Percent Principle: How to Get Extraordinary Results from Ordinary People. Pechtimaldjian, Katharine, ed. LC 92-51045. 243p. 1993. 29.95 (*0-88390-371-7*); pap. 12.95 (*0-89384-221-4*) Pfeiffer & Co.

*__Richardson, Barry A.__ Remedial Treatment of Buildings. 2nd ed. LC 94-22800. (Illus.). 256p. 1995. pap. 37.95 (*0-7506-2158-3*) Buttrwrth-Heinemann.

— Wood Preservation. 2nd ed. LC 92-30664. 1993. write for info. (*0-419-17490-7*, E & FN Spon) Routledge Chapman & Hall.

Richardson, Ben & Foley, William A. Great Black Americans. LC 75-12841. (Illus.). 352p. (YA). (gr. 7 up). 1990. lib. bdg. 17.89 (*0-690-04791-6*, Crowell Jr Bks) HarpC Child Bks.

Richardson, Benjamin W., ed. see Pemberton, Robert.

Richardson, Bernard, jt. ed. see Lee, Courtland C.

Richardson, Bessie E. Old Age among the Ancient Greeks. LC 74-93775. (Illus.). reprint ed. 42.50 (*0-404-05289-4*) AMS Pr.

Richardson, Betty, ed. see Reed, Keith.

*__Richardson, Bill.__ Come into My Parlour: Cautionary Verses & Instructive Tales for the New Millennium. (Illus.). 144p. (Orig.). 1995. pap. 11.95 (*0-919591-85-X*, Pub. by Polestar Bk Pubs CN) Orca Bk Pubs.

— Queen of All the Dustballs: And Other Epics of Everyday Life. (Illus.). 96p. (Orig.). 1995. pap. 11.95 (*0-919591-98-1*, Pub. by Polestar Bk Pubs CN) Orca Bk Pubs.

Richardson, Bill & Richardson, Dana. Appaloosa Horse. 1979. pap. 7.00 (*0-87980-182-4*) Wilshire.

Richardson, Bill & Richardson, Roy. Business Planning: A Approach to Strategic Management. 288p. (Orig.). 1992. pap. 36.50 (*0-273-03720-X*, Pub. by Pitman Pub Ltd UK) Trans-Atl Phila.

Richardson, Bob, jt. auth. see Richardson, Peter.

Richardson, Bonham C. The Caribbean in the Wider World, 1492-1992: A Regional Geography. (Geography of the World Economy Ser.). (Illus.). 240p. (C). 1992. 54.95 (*0-521-35186-3*); pap. 18.95 (*0-521-35977-5*) Cambridge U Pr.

— Caribbean Migrants: Environment & Human Survival on St. Kitts & Nevis. LC 82-7078. (Illus.). 224p. (C). 1983. text ed. 31.00x (*0-87049-360-4*); pap. text ed. 17.95 (*0-87049-361-2*) U of Tenn Pr.

— Panama Money in Barbados, 1900-1920. LC 85-6127. (Illus.). 308p. 1986. text ed. 34.00x (*0-87049-477-5*) U of Tenn Pr.

Richardson, Boyce. People of Terra Nullius: Betrayal & Rebirth in Aborginal Canada. LC 94-11955. (Illus.). 408p. 1994. pap. 19.95 (*0-295-97391-9*) U of Wash Pr.

— Strangers Devour the Land. LC 90-26332. (Illus.). 386p. (Orig.). 1991. reprint ed. pap. 14.95 (*0-930031-40-7*) Chelsea Green Pub.

*__Richardson, Boyd.__ Danger Trail: Knife Thrower's Journey West. LC 95-4126. (J). 1995. write for info. (*1-55503-777-1*) Covenant Comms.

— Knife Thrower. Date not set. pap. 9.98 (*1-55503-696-1*, 01111620) Covenant Comms.

Richardson, Boyd C. Voices in the Wind. 1992. 6.95 (*0-685-56848-2*, 0111996) Covenant Comms.

Richardson, Bradley M. The Political Culture of Japan. (Center for Japanese Studies, UC Berkeley: No. 11). 1974. pap. 15.00 (*0-520-03049-4*) U CA Pr.

Richardson, Bradley M. & Flanagan, Scott C. Politics in Japan. (Comparative Politics Ser.). (C). 1987. pap. text ed. 18.75 (*0-673-39472-7*) HarpCollege.

Richardson, Bradley M., ed. see East Asian Studies Program-Ohio State University.

Richardson, Brenda. Brice Marden - Cold Mountain: The Way to Cold Mountain. LC 92-16791. 1992. 35.00 (*0-939594-30-7*); 25.00 (*0-940619-09-1*) Menil Found.

— Dr. Claribel & Miss Etta: The Cone Collection of the Baltimore Museum of Art. LC 85-70732. (Illus.). 204p. 1985. pap. 29.95 (*0-912298-58-8*) Baltimore Mus.

— Scott Burton. LC 86-22235. (Illus.). 92p. 1986. pap. 12.95 (*0-912298-61-8*) Baltimore Mus.

Richardson, Brenda, jt. auth. see Alston, John.

Richardson, Brenda L. Chesapeake Song. LC 93-26412. 371p. 1993. 19.95 (*1-56743-040-6*) Amistad Pr.

— Chesapeake Song. LC 93-26412. 371p. 1994. pap. 10.95 (*1-56743-063-5*) Amistad Pr.

Richardson, Brenda L., jt. auth. see Wade, Brenda.

Richardson, Brian. Print Culture in Renaissance Italy: The Editor & the Vernacular Text, 1470-1600. LC 93-30907. (Studies in Publishing & Printing History: No. 8). 256p. (C). 1994. 54.95 (*0-521-42032-6*) Cambridge U Pr.

Richardson, Brian, jt. auth. see Broome, Jon.

Richardson, Brian, ed. see Machavelli, Niccolo.

Richardson, Brian A. About Juvenile Violence & Its Prevention. (Family Forum Library Ser.). 16p. 1992. 1.95 (*1-56688-046-7*) Bur For At-Risk.

Richardson, Byron A., jt. auth. see Enloe, Stelle.

Richardson, C. Faith, tr. see Pettinato, Giovanni.

Richardson, C. James, jt. auth. see Himelfarb, Alexander.

Richardson, C. Joan, jt. ed. see Daeschner, C. William, Jr.

Richardson, Carl. Autopsy: An Element of Realism in Film Noir. LC 91-44181. (Illus.). 257p. 1992. 29.50 (*0-8108-2496-5*) Scarecrow.

Richardson, Carol B. Communications Skills for the Military Family. (Family Forum Library). 16p. 1994. 1.95 (*1-56688-167-6*) Bur For At-Risk.

— Effective Child Discipline for Successful Military Families. (Family Forum Library). 16p. 1994. 1.95 (*1-56688-168-4*) Bur For At-Risk.

— Loss & Change in the Military Family. (Family Forum Library Ser.). 16p. 1993. 1.95 (*1-56688-074-2*) Bur For At-Risk.

— The Single Military Parent. (Family Forum Library). 16p. 1994. 1.95 (*1-56688-166-8*) Bur For At-Risk.

— Stress & the Military Family. (Family Forum Library Ser.). 16p. 1993. 1.95 (*1-56688-070-X*) Bur For At-Risk.

— Successful Parenting for the Military Family. (Family Forum Library Ser.). 16p. 1993. 1.95 (*1-56688-073-4*) Bur For At-Risk.

Richardson, Carol P., jt. auth. see Atterbury, Betty W.

Richardson, Charles. From Churchill's Secret Circle to the BBC: A Biography of Lieutenant General Sir Ian Jacob, GBE, CB, DL. 250p. 1991. 49.00 (*0-08-037692-4*, Pub. by Brasseys UK) Brasseys Inc.

*__Richardson, Charles C., ed.__ Annual Review of Biochemistry, Vol. 64. 1995. lib. bdg. 49.00 (*0-8243-0864-6*) Annual Reviews.

Richardson, Charles C., et al, eds. Annual Review of Biochemistry, Vol. 53. LC 32-25093. (Illus.). 1984. text ed. 41.00 (*0-8243-0853-0*) Annual Reviews.

— Annual Review of Biochemistry, Vol. 54. LC 32-25093. (Illus.). (C). 1985. text ed. 41.00 (*0-8243-0854-9*) Annual Reviews.

— Annual Review of Biochemistry, Vol. 55. LC 32-25093. (Illus.). 1986. text ed. 41.00 (*0-8243-0855-7*) Annual Reviews.

— Annual Review of Biochemistry, Vol. 56. LC 32-25093. (Illus.). 1987. text ed. 41.00 (*0-8243-0856-5*) Annual Reviews.

— Annual Review of Biochemistry, Vol. 57. LC 32-25093. (Illus.). 1988. text ed. 41.00 (*0-8243-0857-3*) Annual Reviews.

— Annual Review of Biochemistry, Vol. 58. 1989. text ed. 41.00 (*0-8243-0858-1*) Annual Reviews.

— Annual Review of Biochemistry, Vol. 59. 1990. 41.00 (*0-8243-0859-X*) Annual Reviews.

— Annual Review of Biochemistry, Vol. 60. 1991. text ed. 41.00 (*0-8243-0860-3*) Annual Reviews.

— Annual Review of Biochemistry, Vol. 61. 1992. text ed. 46.00 (*0-8243-0861-1*) Annual Reviews.

— Annual Review of Biochemistry, Vol. 62. (Illus.). 1993. text ed. 46.00 (*0-8243-0862-X*) Annual Reviews.

— Annual Review of Biochemistry, Vol. 63. (Illus.). 1994. text ed. 49.00 (*0-8243-0863-8*) Annual Reviews.

Richardson, Charles F. American Literature. 2 vols. LC 79-122461. (American Literature Ser.: No. 49). 1970. reprint ed. lib. bdg. 89.95 (*0-8383-0901-1*) M S G Haskell Hse.

Richardson, Christine, jt. auth. see Barlow, Jeffrey.

Richardson, Christine, jt. auth. see Johnston, Jackie.

Richardson, Christine, tr. see Manetti, Giovanni.

*__Richardson, Christopher D., ed. & intro.__ Baculovirus Expression Protocols. LC 94-44674. (Methods in Molecular Biology Ser.: Vol. 39). (Illus.). 432p. 1995. 64.50 (*0-89603-272-8*) Humana.

Richardson, Chung, tr. see Perrolle, Pierre M., ed.

Richardson, Clement. National Cyclopedia of the Colored Race. 1973. 75.00 (*0-8490-0711-9*) Gordon Pr.

Richardson, Clinton D. Growth Company Guide to Investors, Deal Structures, & Legal Strategies: Practical Advice for Growing Companies & Private Company Investors. 302p. 1993. 29.95 (*0-89384-233-8*) Pfeiffer & Co.

Richardson, Clive. Driving: An Instructional Guide to Driving Singles & Pairs. Date not set. 27.50 (*0-7134-6946-3*, Pub. by Batsford UK) Trafalgar.

— The Fell Pony. 140p. 1990. 60.00 (*0-85131-511-9*, Pub. by J A Allen & Co UK) St Mut.

— The Hackney. 1993. 40.00 (*0-85131-613-1*, Pub. by J A Allen & Co UK) St Mut.

Richardson, Colin, jt. ed. see Burston, Paul.

Richardson, Constantine L. The United States & Argentina, 1945-47: A Case Study in Diplomatic Practice. 1993. 15.95 (*0-533-10495-5*) Vantage.

Richardson, Craig. Deep Woods. (Orig.). 1984. pap. 2.95 (*0-87067-825-6*, BH825) Holloway.

*__Richardson, Craug R. & Ziebart, Geoff C.__ Red Tape in America: Stories from the Front Line. 111p. 1995. 14.95 (*0-89195-059-1*) Heritage Found.

Richardson, Cyril C. Christianity of Ignatius of Antioch. LC 35-7948. reprint ed. 20.00 (*0-404-05297-5*) AMS Pr.

— The Church Through the Centuries. LC 72-6726. reprint ed. 34.50 (*0-404-10645-5*) AMS Pr.

Richardson, Cyril C., ed. Early Christian Fathers. (Library of Christian Classics: Vol. 1). 416p. (C). 1970. reprint ed. pap. 12.95 (*0-02-088980-1*, Pub. by Gebrueder Borntraeger GW) Macmillan.

Richardson, D. E. The Production of New Potato Varieties: Technological Advances. Jellis, G. J., ed. 300p. 1987. 84.95 (*0-521-32458-0*) Cambridge U Pr.

Richardson, D. M., jt. ed. see Davis, G. W.

Richardson, D. R., jt. auth. see Baron, Robert A.

Richardson, Dale. Plutonian Phoenix. 168p. 1974. 8.00 (*0-86690-145-0*, R1398-014) Am Fed Astrologers.

*__Richardson, Dan.__ Create Stereograms: Discover the World of 3D Illusion. 224p. 1994. disk, pap. 26.95 (*1-878739-75-1*) Waite Group Pr.

— Create Stereograms on Your PC. 200p. 1994. boxed, pap. 26.95 (*1-878739-98-0*) Waite Group Pr.

Richardson, Dan K. The Cost of Environmental Protection: Regulating Housing Development in the Coastal Zone. 219p. 1976. pap. text ed. 17.95 (*0-87855-614-1*) Transaction Pubs.

Richardson, Dana, jt. auth. see Richardson, Bill.

Richardson, Dana R., jt. auth. see Haidinger, Timothy P.

Richardson, Daphne, ed. see Blue, Lionel.

Richardson, Darcy. Rainforests. (Bertinetti Ser.). (Illus.). 128p. 1992. reprint ed. 14.98 (*0-8317-7342-1*) Smithmark.

— The South. (Bertinetti Ser.). 1992. 14.98 (*0-8317-7939-X*) Smithmark.

Richardson, David. Esperanto: Learning & Using the International Language. 1989. write for info. (*0-945742-00-2*) Esperanto League North Am.

— Esperanto: Learning & Using the International Language. 2nd ed. LC 88-9858. (Illus.). 368p. 1990. reprint ed. 14.95 (*0-939785-00-5*, ESP046); reprint ed. text ed. 13.45 (*0-685-45056-2*); reprint ed. 14.95 (*0-685-33260-8*) Esperanto League North Am.

— Puget Sounds: A Nostalgic Review of Radio & TV in the Great Northwest. LC 80-26557. 1981. 14.95 (*0-87564-636-0*) Orcas Pub.

Richardson, David, ed. Abolition & Its Aftermath: The Historical Context, 1790-1916. (Legacies of West Indian Slavery Ser.: No. 1). 224p. 1985. 35.00 (*0-7146-3261-9*, Pub. by F Cass Pubs UK) Intl Spec Bk.

Richardson, David, jt. auth. see Hapgood, David.

Richardson, David B. Pig War Islands: The San Juans of Northwest Washington. LC 70-149337. (Illus.). 416p. 1990. reprint ed. pap. 15.95 (*0-945742-04-5*) Orcas Pub.

Richardson, David J. The Star Dwarves Travesty. 256p. 1994. pap. 8.95 (*1-56901-298-9*) NW Pub.

Richardson, David W., et al, eds. Frozen Human Semen: A Royal College of Obstetricians & Gynaecologists Workshop in the Cryobiology of Human Semen & Its Role on Artificial Insemination by Donor, March 22 & 23, 1979. (Developments in Obstetrics & Gynecology Ser.: No. 4). 280p. 1980. lib. bdg. 99.00 (*90-247-2370-1*) Kluwer Ac.

Richardson, Dawn. Smoke. 112p. (YA). (gr. 9-12). 1985. 7.95 (*0-920806-73-2*, Pub. by Penumbra Pr CN) U of Toronto Pr.

Richardson, Debbie, et al. Language Quicktionary Instruction Manual: A QuickDraw Game for Vocabulary Growth. (J). (gr. 3-12). 1990. 29.95 (*1-55999-107-0*) LinguiSystems.

Richardson, Deborra A., jt. auth. see Hobson, Constance T.

Richardson, Delores. Can You Dig It? (Illus.). 20p. (J). (gr. 3-7). 1990. write for info. (*0-9619482-9-9*) Little Spirit.

Richardson, Derk. Two to Twenty Two Days in Thailand: The Itinerary Planner. (Two to Twenty-Two Days Ser.). (Illus.). 180p. 1993. pap. 10.95 (*1-56261-118-6*) John Muir.

— Two to Twenty-Two Days in Thailand: The Itinerary Planner 1993. rev. ed. (Two to Twenty-Two Days Ser.). (Illus.). 176p. 1992. pap. 9.95 (*1-56261-058-9*) John Muir.

Richardson, Diane. Women & AIDS. 160p. 1987. 29.95 (*0-415-90175-8*, A0762, Routledge NY); pap. 11.95 (*0-416-01751-7*, A0766, Routledge NY) Routledge.

— Women, Motherhood, & Childrearing. LC 92-19905. 1993. text ed. 35.00 (*0-312-08593-1*) St Martin.

Richardson, Diane & Robinson, Vicki, eds. Thinking Feminist: Key Concepts in Women's Studies. LC 92-28106. 368p. 1993. lib. bdg. 45.00 (*0-89862-989-6*); pap. text ed. 18.95 (*0-89862-160-7*) Guilford Pr.

Richardson, Dick. The Evolution of British Disarmament Policy in the 1920s. LC 89-30894. 256p. 1989. text ed. 45.00 (*0-312-03177-7*) St Martin.

R

Richardson, Dick & Rootes, Chris, eds. The Green Challenge: The Development of Green Parties in Europe. LC 94-15095. 1995. 59.95 (0-415-10649-4); pap. 16.95 (0-415-10650-8) Routledge.
Richardson, Dick, jt. ed. see Stone, Glyn.
Richardson, Dick, ed. see Tree, Christina, et al.
Richardson, Don. Acting Without Agony: An Alternative to the Method. 2nd ed. LC 93-24467. 1993. pap. text ed. 32.00 (0-205-15165-5) Allyn.
— Eternity in Their Hearts. rev. ed. LC 84-2036. 1984. pap. 7.99 (0-8307-0925-8, 5418111) Regal.
— Eyewitnesses: Dramatic Voices from the Gospels. LC 87-28762. 208p. (Orig.). 1988. pap. 7.99 (0-87788-250-9) Shaw Pubs.
— Lords of the Earth. LC 77-74534. 368p. 1977. pap. 7.99 (0-8307-0529-5, 5405718) Regal.
— Peace Child. LC 75-26356. (Illus.). 288p. 1975. reprint ed. 7.99 (0-8307-0415-9, 5403006) Regal.
Richardson, Donald. Ghosts of Love. limited ed. (Illus.). 1987. 2.00 (0-932616-18-6) New Poets Chestnut Hills.
— Great Zeus & All His Children. 156p. (C). 1993. pap. text ed. 10.75 (1-57074-091-7) Greyden Pr.
— Greek Mythology For Everyone: Legends of the Gods & Heroes. 1989. 4.99 (0-517-66561-1) Random Hse Value.
— Knocking Them Dead. (Illus.). 50p. 1982. pap. 3.95 (0-932616-13-5) New Poets Chestnut Hills.
— Men of Style. Date not set. pap. 4.99 (0-517-11236-1) Random Hse Value.
— Men of Style. 1992. 19.50 (0-679-41211-5, Villard Bks) Random.
— Stories of the Greeks & Romans: Introduction to Classical Mythology. (Illus.). (C). 1995. lib. bdg. 65.00 (0-89241-515-0) Caratzas.
— Stories of the Greeks & Romans: Introduction to Classical Mythology, 2 vols., Set. 2nd rev. ed. (Illus.). (C). 1995. pap. text ed. 42.50 (0-89241-549-5) Caratzas.
— Stories of the Greeks & Romans Vol. I: Introduction to Classical Mythology. 2nd rev. ed. (Illus.). (C). 1995. pap. text ed. 22.50 (0-89241-575-4) Caratzas.
— Stories of the Greeks & Romans Vol. II: Introduction to Classical Mythology. 2nd rev. ed. (Illus.). (C). 1995. pap. text ed. 22.50 (0-89241-576-2) Caratzas.
Richardson, Donald C. Croquet: The Art & Elegance of Playing the Game. (Illus.). 112p. 1988. 19.95 (0-517-56826-8, Harmony) Crown Pub Group.
Richardson, Donald V. & Caisse, Arthur J., Jr. Rotating Electric Machinery & Transformer Technology. 3rd ed. (Illus.). 672p. (C). 1986. text ed. 77.00 (0-8359-6747-6) P-H.
Richardson, Donna. Visual Paraphrasing of Poetry: A Sourcebook for Teachers & Readers. 222p. (Orig.). (C). 1992. lib. bdg. 47.50 (0-8191-8819-0); pap. text ed. 23.50 (0-8191-8820-4) U Pr of Amer.
Richardson, Donna, jt. auth. see Beaser, Richard S.
Richardson, Donna L., ed. Youth Information Resources: An Annotated Guide for Parents, Professionals, Students, Researchers & Concerned Citizens. LC 86-33492. (Bibliographies & Indexes in Sociology Ser.: No. 10). 371p. 1987. text ed. 75.00 (0-313-25304-8, WYI/) Greenwood.
Richardson, Dorothy. The Long Day: The Story of a New York Working Girl. 320p. (C). 1990. reprint ed. pap. text ed. 10.95 (0-8139-1289-X) U Pr of Va.
— Pilgrimage, Vol. 1: Pointed Roofs, Backwater, Honeycomb. 496p. 1989. reprint ed. pap. 12.50 (0-252-06076-8) U of Ill Pr.
— Quest of Simon Richardson. large type ed. (Illus.). 384p. 1987. 16.95 (0-7089-1714-3) Ulverscroft.
— Windows on Modernism: Selected Letters of Dorothy Richardson. Fromm, Gloria G., ed. LC 94-4170. (Illus.). 696p. 1995. 65.00 (0-8203-1659-8) U of Ga Pr.
Richardson, Dorothy & Ruta, Tina, eds. Arie Antiche English Translations. LC 90-62112. 150p. 1990. pap. text ed. 18.95 (1-55725-017-0) Paraclete MA.
Richardson, Dorothy L. Half-Seen Face. LC 78-24600. 1979. 6.95 (0-87233-047-8) Bauhan.
— The Invisible Giant. LC 86-1032. 75p. 1986. 10.95 (0-87233-085-0) Bauhan.
Richardson, Dorothy M. Backwater. 286p. 1977. reprint ed. lib. bdg. 13.85 (0-89966-154-8) Buccaneer Bks.
— Honeycomb. 286p. 1977. reprint ed. lib. bdg. 13.95 (0-89966-155-6) Buccaneer Bks.
Richardson, Dorsey. Constitutional Doctrines of Justice Oliver Wendell Holmes. LC 78-64115. (Johns Hopkins University. Studies in the Social Sciences. Thirtieth Ser. 1912: 3). reprint ed. 15.00 (0-404-61230-X) AMS Pr.
Richardson, Doug. AH-64 Apache. (Combat Aircraft Ser.). 1992. 9.99 (0-517-06739-0) Random Hse Value.
— F-16 Fighting Falcon. (Combat Aircraft Ser.). 1992. 9.99 (0-517-06737-4) Random Hse Value.
Richardson, Douglass B. Networking. LC 93-49881. 1994. text ed. 32.50 (0-471-31026-3); pap. text ed. 10.95 (0-471-31027-1) Wiley.
Richardson, Drew, ed. see Shreeves, Karl, et al.
Richardson, Drew, ed. see Wohlers, Bob, et al.
Richardson, E. History of Woonsocket, R. I. 264p. 1990. reprint ed. lib. bdg. 32.50 (0-8328-1630-2) Higginson Bk Co.
Richardson, E. Allen. East Comes West. LC 82-13247. 232p. 1984. pap. 12.95 (0-8298-0480-3) Pilgrim OH.
— Strangers in This Land: Pluralism & the Response to Diversity in the United States. LC 88-9634. (Illus.). 288p. (Orig.). 1988. pap. 12.95 (0-8298-0764-0) Pilgrim OH.
Richardson, E. M. We Keep a Light. large type ed. 1990. 21.95 (0-7089-2227-9) Ulverscroft.
Richardson, Edgar P., et al. Charles Willson Peale & His World. 1983. 39.95 (0-8109-1478-6) Abrams.
Richardson, Edward. Love Yourself. 64p. 1970. pap. 2.95 (0-89243-567-4) Liguori Pubns.
— Research Techniques for the Social Sciences Manual. LC 83-10749. 123p. 1983. pap. 5.00 (0-913480-58-4) Inter Am U Pr.
Richardson, Edward, illus. To See a World in a Grain of Sand. 96p. 1972. 9.50 (0-8378-1789-7) Gibson.
Richardson, Edward P., Jr. & DeGirolami, Umberto. Pathology of the Peripheral Nerve. LC 94-20440. (Major Problems in Pathology Ser.: No. 32). 176p. 1994. text ed. 55.00 (0-7216-3298-X) Saunders.
Richardson, Eileen, jt. auth. see Kemp, Nan.
Richardson, Elbert L., et al, eds. McKay's Modern Portuguese-English & English-Portuguese Dictionary. (Modern Dictionaries Ser.). (ENG & POR.). 1943. 12.95 (0-679-10077-6) McKay.
***Richardson, Eleanor M.** Andover: A Century of Change. LC 95-7906. 1995. write for info. (0-89865-938-8) Donning Co.
Richardson, Elisha R. An Atlas of Craniofacial Growth in Americans of African Descent. (Craniofacial Growth Ser.: Vol. 26). (Illus.). 1991. 75.00 (0-929921-22-4) UM CHGD.
Richardson, Elizabeth R., ed. A Bloomsbury Iconography. 372p. 1989. 40.00 (0-906795-63-X) Oak Knoll.
***Richardson, Elliot L., frwd.** Arthur Flemming Crusader at Large. 371p. 1992. 25.00 (0-9628363-2-X) Caring Pub.
Richardson, Elliot L., jt. frwd. see Fasulo, Linda M.
Richardson, Ellis. Book of Lessons & Fun Book, Level A: Beginner Sequence. rev. ed. (Linguistic Pattern Ser.). 21p. 1993. pap. text ed. 8.00 (1-56775-037-0) ISM Teach Systs.
— Book of Lessons & Fun Book, Level B: Beginner Sequence. rev. ed. (Linguistic Pattern Ser.). 21p. 1993. pap. text ed. 8.00 (1-56775-038-9) ISM Teach Systs.
— Book of Lessons & Fun Book, Level C: Beginner Sequence. rev. ed. (Linguistic Pattern Ser.). 21p. (J). 1993. pap. text ed. 8.00 (1-56775-039-7) ISM Teach Systs.
— Book of Lessons & Fun Book, Level D: Beginner Sequence. rev. ed. (Linguistic Pattern Ser.). 21p. 1993. pap. text ed. 8.00 (1-56775-040-0) ISM Teach Systs.
— Book of Lessons & Fun Book, Level 1: Introductory Sequence. rev. ed. (Linguistic Pattern Ser.). 33p. (-2). 1993. pap. text ed. 8.00 (1-56775-041-9) ISM Teach Systs.
— Book of Lessons & Fun Book, Level 2: Introductory Sequence. rev. ed. (Linguistic Pattern Ser.). 33p. 1993. pap. text ed. 8.00 (1-56775-042-7) ISM Teach Systs.
— Book of Lessons & Fun Book, Level 3: Introductory Sequence. rev. ed. (Linguistic Pattern Ser.). 33p. 1993. pap. text ed. 8.00 (1-56775-043-5) ISM Teach Systs.
— Book of Lessons & Fun Book, Level 4: Short Vowel I Sequence. rev. ed. (Linguistic Pattern Ser.). 33p. (J). (gr. 2-3). 1994. pap. text ed. 8.00 (1-56775-054-0) ISM Teach Systs.
— Book of Lessons & Fun Book, Level 5: Short Vowel I Sequence. rev. ed. (Linguistic Pattern Ser.). 33p. 1994. pap. text ed. 8.00 (1-56775-055-9) ISM Teach Systs.
— Book of Lessons & Fun Book, Level 6: Short Vowel I Sequence. rev. ed. (Linguistic Pattern Ser.). 33p. 1994. pap. text ed. 8.00 (1-56775-056-7) ISM Teach Systs.
— Book of Lessons & Fun Book, Level 7: Short Vowel I Sequence. rev. ed. (Linguistic Pattern Ser.). 33p. (J). (gr. 2-3). 1994. pap. text ed. 8.00 (1-56775-057-5) ISM Teach Systs.
— Book of Lessons, Level 1: Getting Ready Sequence. (Linguistic Pattern Ser.). (Illus.). 72p. (Orig.). 1989. student ed, pap. 7.00 (1-56775-000-1, GRIL1) ISM Teach Systs.
— Book of Lessons, Level 2: Getting Ready Sequence. (Linguistic Pattern Ser.). (Illus.). 72p. (Orig.). 1988. student ed, pap. 7.00 (1-56775-001-X, GRIIL5) ISM Teach Systs.
— Book of Lessons, Levels 8-11: Short Vowell II Sequence. (Linguistic Pattern Ser.). 44p. (Orig.). 1989. student ed, pap. 5.00 (1-56775-024-9, SVIIL1) ISM Teach Systs.
— Fun Book Answer Key, Levels 4-7: Short Vowel I Sequence. (Linguistic Pattern Ser.). 12p. (Orig.). 1992. teacher ed, pap. 5.00 (1-56775-023-0, SVIFBA8) ISM Teach Systs.
— Read Aloud, Bk. A: We Can Sing: Beginner Sequence. (Linguistic Pattern Ser.). (Illus.). 24p. (Orig.). 1988. pap. text ed. 4.00 (1-56775-005-2, BGSA3) ISM Teach Systs.
— Read Aloud, Bk. B: We May Ride Away: Beginner Sequence. (Linguistic Pattern Ser.). 20p. (Orig.). 1988. pap. text ed. 4.00 (1-56775-006-0, BGSB4) ISM Teach Systs.
— Read Aloud, Bk. C: We Can Try to Fly Away: Beginner Sequence. (Linguistic Pattern Ser.). 20p. (Orig.). 1988. pap. text ed. 4.00 (1-56775-007-9, BGSC5) ISM Teach Systs.
— Read Aloud, Bk. D: Flying on Wings: Beginner Sequence. (Linguistic Pattern Ser.). 24p. (Orig.). 1988. pap. text ed. 4.00 (1-56775-008-7, BGSD6) ISM Teach Systs.
— Read Aloud, Bk. 1: Of Seals & Jeeps & Steam That's Green: Introductory Sequence. (Linguistic Pattern Ser.). 28p. (Orig.). 1988. pap. text ed. 4.00 (1-56775-012-5, INS1-2) ISM Teach Systs.
— Read Aloud, Bk. 2: Reading Like Kings & Queens: Introductory Sequence. (Linguistic Pattern Ser.). 36p. (Orig.). 1988. pap. text ed. 4.00 (1-56775-013-3, INS2-3) ISM Teach Systs.
— Read Aloud, Bk. 3: Becoming Friends: Introductory Sequence. (Linguistic Pattern Ser.). 24p. (Orig.). 1988. pap. text ed. 4.00 (1-56775-014-1, INS3-5) ISM Teach Systs.
— Read Aloud, Bk. 4: Of Rams & Sacks & Tramps in Shacks: Short Vowel I Sequence. (Linguistic Pattern Ser.). 32p. (Orig.). 1988. pap. text ed. 4.00 (1-56775-018-4, SVIS4-3) ISM Teach Systs.
— Read Aloud, Bk. 5: The Battle of Trappers Pass: Short Vowel I Sequence. (Linguistic Pattern Ser.). 32p. (Orig.). 1988. pap. text ed. 4.00 (1-56775-019-2, SVIS5-4) ISM Teach Systs.
— Read Aloud, Bk. 6: Wiggles & Giggles: Short Vowel I Sequence. (Linguistic Pattern Ser.). 32p. (Orig.). 1988. pap. text ed. 4.00 (1-56775-020-6, SVIS6-5) ISM Teach Systs.
— Read Aloud, Bk. 7: Of Frocks & Frogs & Clogs in Bogs: Short Vowel I Sequence. (Linguistic Pattern Ser.). 32p. (Orig.). 1989. pap. text ed. 4.00 (1-56775-021-4, SVIS7-6) ISM Teach Systs.
— Read Aloud, Bk. 8: The Rainmaker of Cullmans Bluff: Short Vowel II Sequence. (Linguistic Pattern Ser.). 32p. (Orig.). 1990. pap. text ed. 4.00 (1-56775-025-7, SVIIS8-3) ISM Teach Systs.
— Read Aloud, Bk. 9: Misconduct & Mysteries: Short Vowel II Sequence. (Linguistic Pattern Ser.). 28p. (Orig.). 1990. pap. text ed. 4.00 (1-56775-026-5, SVIIS9-4) ISM Teach Systs.
Richardson, Ellis & DiBenedetto, Barbara. Book of Lessons, Levels 12-15: Long Vowel Sequence. (Linguistic Pattern Ser.). 44p. (Orig.). 1992. student ed, pap. 6.00 (1-56775-031-1, LVL1) ISM Teach Systs.
— Fun Book Answer Key for Levels 12-15: Long Vowel Sequence. (Linguistic Pattern Ser.). 12p. (Orig.). 1992. teacher ed, pap. 5.00 (1-56775-034-6, LV-FBA-8) ISM Teach Systs.
— Fun Book Answer Key, Levels 8-11: Short Vowel II Sequence. (Linguistic Pattern Ser.). 12p. (Orig.). 1992. teacher ed, pap. 5.00 (1-56775-029-X, SVIIFBA8) ISM Teach Systs.
— Fun Book, Levels 12-15: Long Vowel Sequence. (Linguistic Pattern Ser.). 64p. (Orig.). 1992. student ed, pap. 6.00 (1-56775-032-X, LVF2) ISM Teach Systs.
— Fun Book, Levels 8-11: Short Vowel Two Sequence. (Linguistic Pattern Ser.). 64p. (Orig.). 1989. student ed, pap. 6.00 (1-56775-035-4, SVII-F-2) ISM Teach Systs.
— Implementation Guide for Levels A-D: Beginner Sequence. (Linguistic Pattern Ser.). 52p. (Orig.). 1992. teacher ed, pap. 8.00 (1-56775-009-5, BGIG7) ISM Teach Systs.
— Implementation Guide for Levels I & II: Getting Ready Sequence. (Linguistic Pattern Ser.). 34p. (Orig.). 1989. teacher ed, pap. 8.00 (1-56775-002-8, GRIG9) ISM Teach Systs.
— Implementation Guide for Levels 1-3: Introductory Sequence. (Linguistic Pattern Ser.). 52p. (Orig.). 1992. teacher ed, pap. 8.00 (1-56775-015-X, INIG6) ISM Teach Systs.
— Implementation Guide for Levels 4-7: Short Vowel I Sequence. (Linguistic Pattern Ser.). 60p. (Orig.). 1992. teacher ed, pap. 8.00 (1-56775-022-2, SVIIG7) ISM Teach Systs.
— Implementation Guide for Levels 8-11: Short Vowel II Sequence. (Linguistic Pattern Ser.). 56p. (Orig.). 1992. teacher ed, pap. 8.00 (1-56775-030-3, SVIIIG7) ISM Teach Systs.
— Implementation Guide, Levels 12-15: Long Vowel Sequence. (Linguistic Pattern Ser.). 60p. (Orig.). 1992. teacher ed, pap. 8.00 (1-56775-033-8, LVIG7) ISM Teach Systs.
— The Integrated Skills Method (ISM) Manual: A Resource Guide for Teaching Reading. 150p. 1993. 25.00 (1-56775-036-2, TM-3) ISM Teach Systs.
— Read Aloud, Bk. 10: The Misfit: Short Vowel II Sequence. (Linguistic Pattern Ser.). 32p. (Orig.). 1991. pap. text ed. 4.00 (1-56775-027-3, SVIIS10-5) ISM Teach Systs.
— Read Aloud, Bk. 11: The Prom: Short Vowel II Sequence. (Linguistic Pattern Ser.). 32p. (Orig.). 1991. pap. text ed. 4.00 (1-56775-028-1, SVIIS11-6) ISM Teach Systs.
Richardson, Ellis & Freeman, Harold, Jr. Reading Progress Feedback System (RFFS) 86p. (Orig.). 1981. pap. 15.00 (0-939632-32-2) ILM.
Richardson, Elmo. David T. Mason: Forestry Advocate: His Role in the Application of Sustained Yield Management to Private & Public Forest Lands. LC 83-16533. (Illus.). xiii, 125p. 1983. pap. text ed. 8.00 (0-89030-044-5) Forest Hist Soc.
Richardson, Elmo, jt. auth. see Pach, Chester J., Jr.
Richardson Engineering Services, Inc. Staff. General Construction Estimating Standards: 1994, 3 vols., Set. 34th ed. (Illus.). 2438p. 1994. 227.00 (1-881386-09-0) Richardson Eng.
— General Construction Estimating Standards: 1994 - Masonry Metals Carpentry Doors Finishes Windows Specialties, Vol. 2. 34th ed. (Illus.). 754p. 1994. write for info. (1-881386-11-2) Richardson Eng.
— General Construction Estimating Standards: 1994 - Mechancial Electrical, Vol. 3. 34th ed. (Illus.). 762p. 1994. write for info. (1-881386-12-0) Richardson Eng.
— General Contruction Estimating Standards: 1994 - Sitework Piling Concrete, Vol. 1. 34th ed. (Illus.). 922p. 1994. write for info. (1-881386-10-4) Richardson Eng.
— Process Plant Construction Estimating Standards: 1994, 4 vols., Set. 33th ed. (Illus.). 4048p. 1994. 457.00 (1-881386-13-9) Richardson Eng.
— Process Plant Construction Estimating Standards: 1994 - Masonry, Metals, Carpentry, Doors, Finishes, Windows, Specialties, Vol. 2. 34th ed. (Illus.). 782p. 1994. write for info. (1-881386-15-5) Richardson Eng.
— Process Plant Construction Estimating Standards: 1994 - Mechanical & Electrical, Vol. 3. 34th ed. (Illus.). 1026p. 1994. write for info. (1-881386-16-3) Richardson Eng.
— Process Plant Construction Estimating Standards: 1994 - Process Equipment, Vol. 4. 34th ed. (Illus.). 1290p. 1994. write for info. (1-881386-17-1) Richardson Eng.
— Process Plant Construction Estimating Standards: 1994 - Sitework Piling Concrete, Vol. 1. 34th ed. (Illus.). 950p. 1994. write for info. (1-881386-14-7) Richardson Eng.
Richardson, Ernest C. Some Aspects of International Library Cooperation. 1977. lib. bdg. 75.00 (0-685-01972-1) Gordon Pr.
***Richardson, Ethel.** Howard - "The Lion & the Rose", the Great Howard Story: Norfolk Line, 957-1646; Suffolk Line, 1603-1917, 2 vols. in 1. (Illus.). 615p. 1994. reprint ed. write for info. (0-614-03918-5) Higginson Bk Co.
***Richardson, Evelyn.** Lady Alex's Gamble. (Regency Romance Ser.). 224p. (Orig.). 1995. pap. 3.99 (0-451-18340-1, Sig) NAL-Dutton.
— Seven Streets by Seven Streets. (Illus.). 156p. (Orig.). 1984. pap. write for info. (0-914110-15-2) Blyden Pr.
— The Willful Widow. 224p. 1994. 3.99 (0-451-17869-6, Sig) NAL-Dutton.
Richardson, Evelyn M. My Other Islands. large type ed. 1991. 21.95 (0-7089-2542-1) Ulverscroft.
Richardson, F. Breeding Cycles of Hawaiian Sea Birds. (BMB Ser.: No. 218). 1972. reprint ed. pap. 15.00 (0-527-02326-4) Periodicals Srv.
Richardson, F. Don. Life in the Past Lane. 80p. 1993. pap. 7.95 (0-8059-3346-8) Dorrance.
— Potpourri. LC 90-72112. 120p. 1991. 7.95 (1-55523-419-4) Winston-Derek.
Richardson, F. L. & Walker, Charles E. Human Relations in an Expanding Company: Manufacturing Departments, Endicott Plant of the International Business Machines Corporation. Stein, Leon, ed. (Work Ser.). (Illus.). 1977. reprint ed. lib. bdg. 19.95 (0-405-10196-1, 77-70528) Ayer.
Richardson, Florence.
Richardson, Francis, ed. see McGarvey, Tracy.
Richardson, Frank C. Kleist in France. LC 62-64205. (North Carolina. University. Studies in the Germanic Languages & Literatures: No. 35). reprint ed. 27.00 (0-404-50935-5) AMS Pr.
Richardson, Frank C., jt. auth. see Woolfolk, Robert I.
Richardson, Frank H. Solo para Muchachos. 112p. 1986. reprint ed. pap. 3.50 (0-311-46929-9) Casa Bautista.
Richardson, Franklin D. The Anguish of the Earth. LC 89-50183. 181p. (Orig.). 1990. pap. 5.95 (0-916383-92-X) Aegina Pr.
Richardson, Frederick. Big Big Book of Mother Goose: Favorite Rhymes Selected from the Original Volland Edition. 1987. 4.99 (0-517-64628-5) Random Hse Value.
Richardson, Frederick, illus. Great Children's Stories: Classic Volland Edition. LC 72-83891. 160p. (J). (ps-3). 1938. 12.95 (1-56288-040-3) Checkerboard.
— Mother Goose. LC 72-161577. 160p. (J). (ps-4). 1915. 12.95 (1-56288-254-6) Checkerboard.
— Mother Goose: The Original Volland Edition. 128p. (J). (gr. k up). 1985. 8.99 (0-517-43619-1) Random Hse Value.
Richardson, Freida. Madagascar's Miracle Story. LC 89-32335. (Illus.). 156p. (Orig.). (YA). 1989. pap. 6.99 (0-932581-47-1) Word Aflame.
Richardson, G. B. Information & Investment: A Study in the Working of the Competitive Economy. (Illus.). 294p. 1991. 49.95 (0-19-828728-3) OUP.
Richardson, G. J., et al. Worked Examples in Metalworking. 209p. 1985. pap. text ed. 29.40 (0-904357-77-5, Pub. by Inst Materials UK) Ashgate Pub Co.
Richardson, Gail. Saving Water from the Ground Up: A Pilot Study of Irrigation Scheduling on Four California Fields. LC 85-60576. 69p. reprint ed. pap. 25.00 (0-7837-0335-X, 2040654) Bks Demand.
— A Welcome for Every Child: How France Protects Maternal & Child Health - A New Frame of Reference for the United States. 62p. (Orig.). 1994. pap. text ed. 10.00 (1-57285-011-6) Nat Ctr Educ.
Richardson, Gail & Mueller-Beilschmidt, Peter. Managing Irrigation with Gypsum Blocks: A Step-by-Step Guide for Farmers. LC 88-38255. 36p. 1989. pap. 4.95 (0-918780-52-7) INFORM NY.
— Winning with Water: Soil-Moisture Monitoring for Efficient Irrigation. LC 88-8846. 192p. 1988. pap. 24.95 (0-918780-42-X) INFORM NY.
Richardson, Gale, ed. see Graves, Lawrence L., et al.
Richardson, Gale, jt. ed. see Hanna, Paul.
Richardson, Gale, ed. see Newlin, Deborah L.
Richardson, Gale, ed. see Sullivan, Jerry M.
Richardson, Gale T. Anderson Island Poetry. 14p. 1989. 5.00 (0-9614337-3-6) Poetry Unltd.
— Serenity, Courage & Wisdom. 2p. (J). (ps). 1989. 3.50 (0-9614337-2-8) Poetry Unltd.
— The Wall. 9p. (Orig.). 1989. pap. write for info. (0-9614337-1-X) Poetry Unltd.
— The Wings. (YA). (gr. 9-12). 1989. write for info. (0-9614337-4-4) Poetry Unltd.
Richardson, Gary, jt. auth. see Watt, Stephen.
Richardson, Gary A. American Drama from the Colonial Period Through World War I: A Critical History. LC 92-36497. (Twayne's Critical History of American Drama Ser.). 320p. 1993. text ed. 26.95 (0-8057-8956-1, Twayne) Macmillan.
Richardson, Gary H., ed. Standard Methods for the Examination of Dairy Products. 16th ed. 450p. 1992. 55.00 (0-87553-208-X); pap. 45.00 (0-87553-210-1) Am Pub Health.
Richardson, Gary L., et al. A Primer of Structured Program Design. 1980. pap. 15.00 (0-89433-110-8) Petrocelli.
***Richardson, Geneva & Genn, Hazel, eds.** Administrative Law & Government Action: The Courts & Alternative Mechanisms of Review. 320p. 1995. 65.00 (0-19-876276-3) OUP.
Richardson, Genevieve. No Good Men: Things Men Do That Make Women Crazy. (Illus.). 96p. (Orig.). 1990. pap. 6.95 (0-929923-26-X) Lowell Hse.
Richardson, George P. Feedback Thought in Social Science & Systems Theory. LC 90-22746. (Illus.). 380p. (C). 1991. text ed. 44.95 (0-8122-3053-1); pap. text ed. 20.95x (0-8122-1332-7) U of Pa Pr.

R

Richardson, George P. & Pugh, Alexander I., III, eds. Introduction to System Dynamics Modeling with Dynamo. LC 81-12371. 424p. (C). 1981. reprint ed. pap. text ed. 35.00 (*0-915299-24-0*, XINTRO) Prod Press.
***Richardson, Gillian.** Saskatchewan. LC 94-44842. (Hello Canada Ser.). (J). 1995. lib. bdg. write for info. (*0-8225-2760-X*) Lerner Group.
Richardson, Gladwell. Navajo Trader. Rulon, Philip R., ed. LC 86-11443. (Illus.). 217p. 1991. reprint ed. pap. 13.95 (*0-8165-1262-0*) U of Ariz Pr.
Richardson, Glenn & Felts, Michael. Health Enhancement Handbook. 310p. (Orig.). (C). 1990. pap. text ed. 18.95x (*0-89641-196-6*) American Pr.
Richardson, Glenn, jt. auth. see Bruess, Clint E.
Richardson, Gordon, jt. auth. see Dobereiner, Peter.
Richardson, Graham T. Illustrations. LC 85-735. 352p. 1985. 69.50 (*0-89603-070-9*); 44.50 (*0-89603-096-2*) Humana.
***Richardson, Gregory, et al.** Design, Operation, & Closure of Municipal Solid Waste Landfills: Seminar Publication. (Illus.). 86p. (Orig.). (C). 1994. pap. text ed. 50.00x (*0-7881-1419-0*) Diane Pub.
Richardson, H. Edward. Cassius Marcellus Clay: Firebrand of Freedom. LC 74-7882. (Illus.). 192p. 1987. 20.00 (*0-8131-1418-7*) U Pr of Ky.
Richardson, H. G., et al. The English Parliament in the Middle Ages. 560p. (C). 1981. text ed. 70.00 (*0-9506882-1-5*) Hambledon Press.
Richardson, H. G., ed. The Memoranda Roll for the Michaelmas Term of the 1st Year of the Reign of John, 1199-1200. Bd. with Fragments of the Originalia Roll of the 7th Year of Richard I, 1195-1196.; Liberate Roll of the Second Year of King John, 1200-1201.; Norman Roll of the Fifth Year of King John, 1203. (Pipe Roll Society London Ser.: No. 2, Vol. 21). 1969. reprint ed. (*0-8115-1308-4*) Periodicals Srv.
***Richardson, H. L.** The Devil's Eye. LC 95-15550. 1995. write for info. (*0-8499-3855-4*) Word Pub.
Richardson, Hamilton P. The Journal of the Federal Convention of 1787 Analyzed: The Acts & Proceedings Thereof Compared, & Their Precedents Cited. 244p. 1985. reprint ed. lib. bdg. 25.00 (*0-8377-1042-1*) Rothman.
***Richardson-Hawkins, Mary E.** AJ's World. (J). 1995. 7.95 (*0-533-11093-9*) Vantage.
Richardson, Helen, ed. see Weavers of Southern Australia Inc. Staff.
Richardson, Henry B. Outline of French Grammar with Vocabularies. rev. ed. (FRE.). 1950. text ed. 12.50 (*0-89197-327-3*) Irvington.
Richardson, Henry G. The English Jewry under Angevin Kings. LC 83-18539. ix, 313p. 1983. reprint ed. text ed. 65.00 (*0-313-24247-X*, RIEJ, Greenwood Pr) Greenwood.
Richardson, Henry H. The Getting of Wisdom. LC 92-45021. 1993. 25.00 (*1-56279-042-0*) Mercury Hse Inc.
— The Getting of Wisdom. (Virago Modern Classic Ser.). 256p. 1992. pap. 10.95 (*0-86068-179-3*, Pub. by Virago Pr UK) Trafalgar.
Richardson, Henry S. Practical Reasoning about Final Ends. (Cambridge Studies in Philosophy). 368p. (C). 1994. 54.95 (*0-521-46472-2*) Cambridge U Pr.
Richardson, Herbert, ed. Constitutional Issues in the Case of Rev. Moon: Amicus Briefs Presented to the United States Supreme Court. (Studies in Religion & Society: Vol. 10). 450p. 1989. 109.95 (*0-88946-873-7*) E Mellen.
— New Studies in Richard Wagner's "The Ring of the Nibelung" LC 91-38295. (Studies in the History & Interpretation of Music: Vol. 20). 200p. 1992. lib. bdg. 79.95 (*0-88946-445-6*) E Mellen.
— On the Problem of Surrogate Parenthood: Analyzing the Baby in Case. LC 87-24752. (Symposium Ser.: Vol. 25). 144p. 1987. lib. bdg. 69.95 (*0-88946-717-X*) E Mellen.
Richardson, Herbert, tr. see Anselm of Canterbury.
Richardson, Herbert, tr. see Anselm Of Canterbury.
Richardson, Herbert, tr. see Anselm of Canterbury.
Richardson, Herbert, ed. see Anselm Of Canterbury.
Richardson, Herbert, tr. see Hopkins, Jasper, ed.
Richardson, Herbert W. Nun, Witch, Playmate: The Americanization of Sex. 2nd ed. xii, 147p. 1977. reprint ed. lib. bdg. 69.95 (*0-88946-950-4*) E Mellen.
— Toward an American Theology. 182p. 1967. lib. bdg. 79.95 (*0-88946-028-0*) E Mellen.
Richardson, Herbert W., ed. New Religions & Mental Health: Understanding the Issues. (Symposium Ser.: Vol. 5). 240p. (Orig.). (C). 1980. lib. bdg. 89.95 (*0-88946-910-5*) E Mellen.
Richardson, Herbert W., jt. auth. see Bryant, M. Darrol.
Richardson, Herbert W., jt. ed. see Clark, Elizabeth.
***Richardson, Hester D.** Side-Lights on Maryland History, 2 Vols., Set. (Illus.). 990p. 1995. 85.00 (*0-8063-0296-8*) Genealog Pub.
Richardson, Hilary & Scarry, John. An Introduction to Irish High Crosses. (Illus.). 152p. 1990. pap. 19.95 (*0-85342-954-5*) Dufour.
Richardson, Horst. Indoor Soccer: A Guide for YMCA Coaches. 24p. 1982. pap. 2.00x (*0-88035-044-X*, 4413, YMCA USA) Human Kinetics.
Richardson, Howard & Berney, William. Dark of the Moon. LC 56-9611. (Orig.). 1966. pap. 6.95 (*0-87830-517-3*, Theatre Arts Bks) Routledge Chapman & Hall.
Richardson, Howard D., jt. auth. see Masters, Lowell F.
Richardson, Hugh. Ceremonies of the Lhasa Year. Aris, Michael, ed. (Illus.). 136p. (Orig.). 1994. pap. 24.95 (*0-906026-29-6*) Weatherhill.
***Richardson, Hugh & Snellgrove, David.** A Cultural History of Tibet. rev. ed. 1995. pap. 20.00 (*1-57062-102-0*) Shambhala Pubns.
Richardson, I. M. The Adventures of Eros & Psyche. LC 82-16057. (Illus.). 32p. (J). (gr. 4-8). 1983. lib. bdg. 11.79 (*0-89375-861-2*); pap. text ed. 2.95 (*0-89375-862-0*) Troll Assocs.
— The Adventures of Hercules. LC 82-16557. (Illus.). 32p. (J). (gr. 4-8). 1983. lib. bdg. 11.79 (*0-89375-865-5*); pap. text ed. 2.95 (*0-89375-866-3*) Troll Assocs.
— Demeter & Persephone: The Seasons of Time. LC 82-16023. (Illus.). 32p. (J). (gr. 4-8). 1983. lib. bdg. 11.79 (*0-89375-863-9*); pap. text ed. 2.95 (*0-89375-864-7*) Troll Assocs.
— Prometheus & the Story of Fire. LC 82-15979. (Illus.). 32p. (J). (gr. 4-8). 1983. lib. bdg. 11.79 (*0-89375-859-0*); pap. text ed. 2.95 (*0-89375-860-4*) Troll Assocs.
— Story of the Christmas Rose. LC 87-13817. (Illus.). 32p. (J). (gr. k-4). 1988. lib. bdg. 9.79 (*0-8167-1069-4*); pap. text ed. 2.50 (*0-8167-1070-8*) Troll Assocs.
Richardson, I. M., ed. see Dickens, Charles.
Richardson, I. M., ed. see Grahame, Kenneth.
Richardson, I. M., ed. see Grimm, Jacob & Grimm, Wilhelm K.
Richardson, I. W. & Neergaard, Ejler B. Physics for Biology & Medicine. LC 76-180711. (Illus.). 257p. reprint ed. pap. 73.30 (*0-685-44049-4*, 2030538) Bks Demand.
Richardson, Irvine. Linguistic Survey of the Northern Bantu Borderland, Vol. 2. LC 57-2700. 98p. reprint ed. pap. 28.00 (*0-8357-6967-4*, 2039027) Bks Demand.
Richardson, J. Roman Provincial Administration. 88p. 1984. reprint ed. 10.75 (*0-86292-128-7*, Pub. by Brstl Class Pr UK) Focus Info Gr.
— Thomas's Sitter. 1994. pap. 4.99 (*0-517-13309-1*) Random.
Richardson, J. & Moon, Jeremy. Unemployment in the U. K. Politics & Policies. 240p. 1985. pap. text ed. 72.95 (*0-566-00892-0*) Ashgate Pub Co.
Richardson, J., jt. ed. see Corlett, E. N.
Richardson, J. A. Falling Towers: The Trojan Imagination in The Waste Land, The Dunciad, & Speke Parott. LC 90-50984. 192p. 1992. 36.50 (*0-87413-419-6*) U Delaware Pr.
Richardson, J. David. The Case for Trade: A Modern Reconsideration. 175p. (Orig.). (C). 1995. pap. text ed. 17.95 (*0-88132-210-5*) Inst Intl Eco.
— Sizing Up U. S. Export Disincentives. LC 92-37854. 182p. 1993. pap. 21.95 (*0-88132-107-9*) Inst Intl Eco.
Richardson, J. David, jt. ed. see Arndt, Sven W.
Richardson, J. David, jt. auth. see Graham, Edward M.
Richardson, J. David, jt. auth. see Grossman, Gene M.
Richardson, J. David, jt. ed. see Hooper, Peter.
Richardson, J. F. A Selection of European Folk Dances, 5 vols., 1. 1965. pap. text ed. 4.20 (*0-08-010833-4*, Ed Skills Dallas) Elsevier.
— A Selection of European Folk Dances, 5 vols., 2. 1966. pap. text ed. 4.20 (*0-08-010842-3*) Elsevier.
— A Selection of European Folk Dances, 5 vols., 3. 1966. pap. text ed. 4.20 (*0-08-011926-3*) Elsevier.
— A Selection of European Folk Dances, 5 vols., 4. 1971. pap. text ed. 4.20 (*0-08-016190-1*) Elsevier.
— A Selection of European Folk Dances, 5 vols., Vol. 5. 1978. pap. text ed. 4.20 (*0-08-021589-0*, Pergamon Pr) Elsevier.
Richardson, J. F., jt. auth. see Coulson, J. M.
Richardson, J. F., jt. ed. see Coulson, J. M.
Richardson, J. G. Precast Concrete Production. 1977. pap. 50.00 (*0-7210-0912-3*, Pub. by C & CA UK) Scholium Intl.
— Supervision of Concrete Construction, Vol. 1. (Viewpoint Ser.). (Illus.). 220p. (C). 1987. text ed. 80.00 (*0-86310-012-0*, Pub. by Palladian) Scholium Intl.
— Supervision of Concrete Construction, Vol. 2. (Viewpoint Ser.). (Illus.). 210p. 1987. text ed. 70.00 (*0-86310-023-6*, Pub. by Palladian) Scholium Intl.
Richardson, J. J . & DeFries, Marjorie, eds. Intelligent Systems in Business: Integrating the Technology. LC 90-260. 344p. (C). 1990. text ed. 59.50 (*0-89391-550-5*) Ablex Pub.
Richardson, J. J., jt. auth. see Dudley, G. F.
Richardson, J. J., jt. auth. see Jordan, Grant.
Richardson, J. Jeffrey, ed. Artificial Intelligence in Maintenance. LC 85-15394. (Illus.). 485p. 1986. 48.00 (*0-8155-1042-X*) Noyes.
Richardson, J. Kenneth. An Assessment of the Performance of Automatic Sprinkler Systems. 1984. 4.35 (*0-318-03819-6*, TR84-2) Society Fire Protect.
Richardson, J. M. Astrological Symbolism in Spenser's "The Shepheardes Calender" The Cultural Background of a Literary Text. LC 88-8436. (Studies in Renaissance Literature: Vol. 1). (Illus.). 1989. 119.95 (*0-88946-144-9*) E Mellen.
Richardson, J. T. Principles of Catalyst Development. (Fundamental & Applied Catalysis Ser.). (Illus.). 280p. 1989. 59.50 (*0-306-43162-9*, Plenum Pr) Plenum.
Richardson, J. T., ed. Cognition & the Menstrual Cycle. (Contributions to Psychology & Medicine Ser.). (Illus.). xi, 216p. 1991. 65.00 (*0-387-97612-4*) Spr-Verlag.
Richardson, J. W. Boxtime Charterparty: An Industry Report. 1990. pap. 160.00 (*1-85044-285-1*) Lloyds London Pr.
Richardson, Jabez. Monitor of Freemasonry. 13.00 (*0-685-19491-4*) Powner.
Richardson, Jack. Gallows Humor. 1976. pap. 4.75 (*0-8222-0431-2*) Dramatists Play.
— Xmas in Las Vegas. 1966. pap. 4.75 (*0-8222-1282-X*) Dramatists Play.
Richardson, Jack, jt. auth. see Richardson, Wendy.
Richardson, Jacques, ed. Integrated Technology Transfer. LC 79-88170. 1979. 22.75 (*0-912338-19-9*); fiche 9.50 (*0-912338-20-2*) Lomond.
— Models of Reality: Shaping Thought & Action. LC 83-80819. 328p. 1984. 32.95 (*0-912338-35-0*); fiche 15.00 (*0-912338-36-9*) Lomond.
Richardson, Jacques G., ed. Managing the Ocean: Resources, Research, Law. LC 88-50823. 407p. 1985. 28.95 (*0-912338-49-0*); fiche 19.50 (*0-912338-50-4*) Lomond.
— Windows on Creativity & Invention. LC 86-83428. 344p. 1988. 34.75 (*0-912338-57-1*); fiche 15.75 (*0-912338-58-X*) Lomond.
Richardson, James. As If: Poems. LC 91-43330. (National Poetry Ser.). 96p. (Orig.). 1992. pap. 9.95 (*0-89255-171-2*) Persea Bks.
— The God Who Shows Up. LC 81-47889. 55p. (Orig.). 1981. pap. 4.00 (*0-914520-16-4*) Insight Pr.
— Narrative of a Mission to Central Africa: 1850-1851, 2 vols., Set. (Illus.). 704p. 1970. reprint ed. 95.00 (*0-7146-1848-9*, BHA-01848, Pub. by F Cass Pubs UK) Intl Spec Bk.
— Reservations: Poems. LC 76-45908. (Contemporary Poets Ser.). 75p. 1977. pap. 9.95 (*0-691-01334-9*) Princeton U Pr.
— Science Dictionary of Animals. LC 91-18826. (Science Dictionary Ser.). (Illus.). 48p. (YA). (gr. 3-7). 1992. lib. bdg. 11.59 (*0-8167-2521-7*); pap. 3.95 (*0-8167-2440-7*) Troll Assocs.
— Science Dictionary of Dinosaurs. LC 91-4110. (Science Dictionary Ser.). (Illus.). 48p. (YA). (gr. 3-7). 1992. lib. bdg. 11.59 (*0-8167-2522-5*); pap. 3.95 (*0-8167-2441-5*) Troll Assocs.
— Science Dictionary of Space. LC 91-16551. (Science Dictionary Ser.). (Illus.). 48p. (YA). (gr. 3-7). 1992. lib. bdg. 11.59 (*0-8167-2524-1*); pap. 3.95 (*0-8167-2443-1*) Troll Assocs.
— Science Dictionary of the Human Body. LC 91-19162. (Science Dictionary Ser.). (Illus.). 48p. (YA). (gr. 3-7). 1992. lib. bdg. 11.59 (*0-8167-2523-3*); pap. 3.95 (*0-8167-2442-3*) Troll Assocs.
— Travels in the Great Desert of Sahara, 1845-1846, 2 vols., Set. (Illus.). 1970. reprint ed. 95.00 (*0-7146-1850-0*, BHA-01850, Pub. by F Cass Pubs UK) Intl Spec Bk.
— Travels in the Great Sahara, Vol. 1. (C). 1988. 135.00 (*1-85077-192-8*, Darf Pubs Ltd) St Mut.
— Travels in the Great Sahara, Vol. 2. (C). 1988. 135.00 (*1-85077-193-6*, Darf Pubs Ltd) St Mut.
— Vanishing Lives: Style & Self in Tennyson, D. G. Rossetti, Swinburne, & Yeats. LC 87-25269. (Virginia Victorian Studies). 325p. 1988. 32.50 (*0-8139-1165-6*) U Pr of Va.
Richardson, James, ed. Debt Recovery in Europe. 165p. 1993. pap. 34.00 (*1-85431-242-1*, Pub. by Blackstone Pr UK) W W Gaunt.
Richardson, James B. The Jim Richardson Boat Book, 1985. (Illus.). pap. 12.95 (*0-9609772-2-8*) Ocean Wrld MD.
***Richardson, James B., III.** People of the Andes. LC 94-22754. (Exploring the Ancient World Ser.). (Illus.). 1994. write for info. (*0-89599-041-5*) Smithsonian Bks.
Richardson, James B., III, jt. ed. see Jacobs, Martina M.
Richardson, James H. Handbook for the Light Microscope: A User's Guide. LC 90-27389. (Illus.). 520p. 1991. 79.00 (*0-8155-1269-4*) Noyes.
— Optical Microscopy for the Materials Science. LC 79-179481. (Monographs & Textbooks in Material Science: Vol. 3). (Illus.). 702p. reprint ed. pap. 180.00 (*0-317-07850-X*, 2055017) Bks Demand.
Richardson, James L. Crisis Diplomacy: The Great Powers since the Mid-Nineteenth Century. LC 93-41564. (Cambridge Studies in International Relations: No. 35). (Illus.). 464p. (C). 1994. pap. 19.95 (*0-521-45987-7*) Cambridge U Pr.
— Crisis Diplomacy: The Great Powers since the Mid-Nineteenth Century. LC 93-41564. (Cambridge Studies in International Relations: No. 35). (Illus.). 464p. (C). 1994. 59.95 (*0-521-45392-5*) Cambridge U Pr.
— Germany & the Atlantic Alliance: The Interaction of Strategy & Politics. LC 66-13184. 414p. reprint ed. pap. 118.00 (*0-317-08193-4*, 2016545) Bks Demand.
Richardson, James L. & Leaver, Richard L., eds. Charting the Post-Cold War Order. LC 93-32736. (C). 1993. text ed. 52.50 (*0-8133-8753-1*); pap. text ed. 20.95 (*0-8133-2150-6*) Westview.
Richardson, James T., jt. ed. see Bromley, David G.
Richardson, James T., et al. Organized Miracles: A Study of a Contemporary, Youth, Communal, Fundamentalist Organization. LC 78-55937. 368p. 1979. 32.95 (*0-87855-284-7*) Transaction Pubs.
Richardson, James T., et al, eds. The Satanism Scare. (Social Institutions & Social Change Ser.). 326p. 1991. lib. bdg. 48.95 (*0-202-30378-0*); pap. text ed. 27.95 (*0-202-30379-9*) Aldine de Gruyter.
Richardson, James W., Jr., ed. Application & Performance of Structural Materials & Exterior Facades. LC 86-25910. 140p. 1986. pap. 18.00 (*0-87262-566-4*) Am Soc Civil Eng.
Richardson, Jan L. Sacred Journeys: A Woman's Book of Daily Prayer. 432p. 1995. pap. 12.95 (*0-8358-0709-6*) Upper Room Bks.
Richardson, Jane. Law & Status among the Kiowa Indians. LC 84-45509. (American Ethnological Society Monographs: No. 1). 1988. reprint ed. 23.50 (*0-404-62901-6*) AMS Pr.
— Virgin Princess: An Historic Novel of Mewar (Udaipur, India) - The World's Oldest Dynasty. LC 90-90395. 434p. (Orig.). 1991. pap. 15.95 (*1-879403-09-9*) Thistle Pub.
***Richardson, Janet C. & Bailey, Brad.** Unsung Heroes: Hope Encourage & Inspiration. (Illus.). 256p. 1995. 19.95 (*1-56796-117-7*) WRS Group.
Richardson, Janice K. & Iglarsh, Z. Annette. Clinical Orthopaedic Physical Therapy. LC 93-7209. (Illus.). 816p. 1993. text ed. 65.00 (*0-7216-3257-2*) Saunders.
***Richardson, Jean.** The Bear Who Went to the Ballet. (J). 1995. 14.95 (*0-7894-0318-8*, 5-70668) Dorling Kindersley.
— The Courage Seed. LC 93-20182. (Illus.). 76p. (J). (gr. 3-6). 1993. 14.95 (*0-89015-902-5*) Sunbelt Media.
— Dino, the Ding Bat Cat. LC 92-17736. (Illus.). 48p. (J). (gr. 1-3). 1992. 12.95 (*0-89015-869-X*) Sunbelt Media.
— Out of Step: The Twins Were So Alike...but So Different. LC 92-39666. (Illus.). 28p. (J). (ps-3). 1993. 12.95 (*0-8120-5790-2*); pap. 5.95 (*0-8120-1553-3*) Barron.
— Return of the Dingbat Cat. LC 94-37571. (Illus.). 1994. 12.95 (*0-89015-972-6*, Eakin Pr) Sunbelt Media.
— The Sleeping Beauty. (Illus.). 32p. (J). (ps-1). 1991. 14.95 (*1-55970-142-0*) Arcade Pub Inc.
— Tag-along Timothy Tours Alaska. Eakin, Edwin M., ed. (Illus.). 48p. (J). (gr. 2-3). 1989. 12.95 (*0-89015-706-5*) Sunbelt Media.
— Tag-along Timothy Tours Texas. (Illus.). (J). 1992. 10.95 (*0-89015-817-7*) Sunbelt Media.
— Thomas's Sitter. LC 90-13799. (Illus.). 32p. (J). (ps-1). 1991. lib. bdg. 13.95 (*0-02-776146-0*, Four Winds Pr) S&S Childrens.
Richardson, Jeanne L. A Bibliography of Selected Contemporary Rhode Island Authors. Schneider, Carolyn M., ed. 33p. 1984. pap. 2.00 (*0-917012-70-4*) RI Pubns Soc.
Richardson, Jeanne S. Here Lies Sioux Falls. (Illus.). 212p. 1992. 16.95 (*0-9632542-0-0*); pap. 12.95 (*0-9632542-1-9*) J S Richardson.
***Richardson, Jeffrey R.** Great Alaska Nature Factbook: A Guide to the State's Remarkable Animals, Plants, & Natural. 1994. pap. 14.95 (*0-88240-454-7*) Alaska Northwest.
Richardson, Jeremy, ed. Privatisation & Deregulation in Canada & Britain. (Illus.). 260p. 1990. text ed. 52.95 (*1-85521-066-5*, Pub. by Dartmth Pub UK) Ashgate Pub Co.
Richardson, Jeremy J., ed. Policy Styles in Western Europe. 224p. (C). 1982. text ed. 49.95 (*0-04-350062-5*) Routledge Chapman & Hall.
— Pressure Groups. LC 92-42267. (Readings in Politics & Government Ser.). 288p. 1993. Alk. paper. 48.00 (*0-19-878051-6*); Alk. paper. pap. 15.95 (*0-19-878052-4*) OUP.
Richardson, Jeremy J., jt. ed. see Mazey, Sonia.
Richardson, Jerry. Magic of Rapport. LC 87-63211. 1988. 14.95 (*0-916990-20-6*) META Pubns.
***Richardson, Jessica.** The Ring & I. McAlister, Jeffrey G. & Udd, Gary, eds. 225p. 1994. 16.95 (*0-9642398-0-9*) Jessica Richardson.
— The Ring & I. McAlister, Jeffrey G. & Udd, Gary, eds. 225p. 1994. pap. 12.95 (*0-9642398-1-7*) Jessica Richardson.
Richardson, Jim. Classic Car Restorer's Handbook: General Restoration Tips & Techniques for Owners & Restorers of Classic Automobiles. LC 94-19094. 176p. (Orig.). 1994. pap. 15.00 (*1-55788-194-4*, HP Books) Berkley Pub.
— Philippines. (World Bibliographical Ser.: Vol. 106). 374p. 1989. lib. bdg. 65.00 (*1-85109-077-0*) ABC-CLIO.
Richardson, Jim, photos. University of Colorado-Boulder. (Illus.). 112p. 1990. 39.00 (*0-916509-54-0*) Harmony Hse Pub LO.
— University of Nebraska - Then & Now. (Illus.). 112p. Date not set. 39.95 (*1-56469-008-3*) Harmony Hse Pub LO.
Richardson, Jim, jt. auth. see Leaver, Richard.
Richardson, Jimmy. A Dog Owner's Guide to Doberman Pinschers. (Illus.). 118p. 10.95 (*3-923880-36-7*, 16044) Tetra Pr.
Richardson, Joanna. Baudelaire: The Life of Charles Baudelaire. 624p. 1994. 35.00 (*0-312-11476-1*) St Martin.
Richardson, Joanna, ed. Letters from Lambeth: The Correspondence of the Reynolds Family with John Freeman Milward Dovaston 1808-1815. (Royal Society of Literature Ser.). (Illus.). 224p. 1982. 24.00 (*0-85115-150-7*) Boydell & Brewer.
Richardson, Joanna, tr. see Baudelaire, Charles P.
Richardson, Joe M. Christian Reconstruction: The American Missionary Association & Southern Blacks, 1861-1890. LC 85-13946. (Illus.). 352p. 1986. 30.00 (*0-8203-0816-1*) U of Ga Pr.
— History of Fisk University, Eighteen-Sixty Five to Nineteen Forty-Six. LC 79-9736. 240p. 1980. 24.50 (*0-8173-0015-5*) U of Ala Pr.
Richardson, Joe M., jt. auth. see Jones, Maxine D.
Richardson, Johanna, tr. see Verlaine, Paul M.
Richardson, John. Arctic Searching Expedition: A Journal of a Boat Voyage Through Rupert's Land & the Arctic Sea, in Search of the Discovery Ships under Command of Sir John Franklin, 2 Vols, Set. LC 68-55214. 1971. reprint ed. text ed. 75.00 (*0-8371-3858-2*, RIAS) Greenwood.
— Bad Mood Bear. (J). (ps). 1988. 6.95 (*0-8120-5871-2*) Barron.
— Clinical & Neuropsychological Aspects of Closed Head Injury. 360p. 1990. 69.95 (*0-86377-194-7*); pap. 32.50 (*0-86377-195-5*) L Erlbaum Assocs.
— Dictionary of the Persian Arabic: Arabic-English. (ARA, ENG & PER.). 1986. 150.00 (*0-8288-0546-6*, M 6600) Fr & Eur.
— Fauna Boreali-Americana, Pt. I. LC 73-17836. (Natural Sciences in America Ser.). (Illus.). 1974. 29.95 (*0-405-05759-8*) Ayer.
— Fauna Boreali-Americana: Zoology of the Northern Parts of British America, the Fish, Pt. 3. Sterling, Keir B., ed. LC 77-81088. (Biologists & Their World Ser.). (Illus.). 1978. reprint ed. lib. bdg. 34.95 (*0-405-10664-5*) Ayer.
— Giacometti: Sculpture. LC 93-77692. (Illus.). 10p. (Orig.). 1993. pap. 30.00 (*1-880154-04-8*) Gagosian Gallery.
Richardson, John, Jr. Government Information: Education & Research, 1928-1986. LC 86-27086. (Bibliographies & Indexes in Library & Information Science Ser.: No. 2). 203p. 1987. text ed. 49.95 (*0-313-25605-5*, RRV/, Greenwood Pr) Greenwood.
Richardson, John. Jack's Hat. (Illus.). 32p. (J). (gr. k-3). 1992. 16.95 (*0-09-174524-1*, Pub. by Hutchinson UK) Trafalgar.

R

An Asterisk (*) at the beginning of an entry indicates that the title is appearing in BIP for the first time.

— Manet. (Color Library). (Illus.). (C). 1994. reprint ed. pap. 14.95 (*0-7148-2755-X*, Pub. by Phaidon Press UK) Chronicle Bks.
— Manet. (Color Library). (Illus.). 128p. (C). 1994. reprint ed. 19.95 (*0-7148-3222-7*, Pub. by Phaidon Press UK) Chronicle Bks.
— Nietzsche's System. 320p. 1995. 35.00 (*0-19-509846-3*) OUP.
— The Polar Regions. LC 74-5869. reprint ed. 25.00 (*0-404-11676-0*) AMS Pr.
— Stories from the English Saints. 96p. 1993. 22.00 (*0-85439-455-9*, Pub. by St Paul Pubns UK) St Mut.
— Where's Jack? A Christmas Pop-up Book. (Illus.). 24p. (J). (ps-2). 1993. bds. 12.95 (*0-689-71713-X*, Aladdin Paperbacks) S&S Childrens.
Richardson, John, illus. Ten Bears in a Bed. LC 91-26501. 22p. (J). (ps-00). 1992. 13.95 (*1-56282-157-1*) Hyprn Child.
Richardson, John, Jr. & Ginsberg, Ralph B., eds. The Human Dimension of Foreign Policy: An American Perspective. LC 78-62597. (Annals Ser.: No. 442). 1979. 27.00 (*0-87761-234-X*); pap. 18.00 (*0-87761-235-8*) Am Acad Pol Soc Sci.
Richardson, John & McCully, Marilyn. A Life of Picasso: Volume I: 1881-1906. (Illus.). 548p. 1991. 44.50 (*0-394-53192-2*) Random.
Richardson, John & Swainson, William. Fauna Boreali-Americana: Pt. II, the Birds. Sterling, Keir B., ed. LC 73-17837. (Natural Sciences in America Ser.). (Illus.). 1974. reprint ed. lib. bdg. 54.95 (*0-405-05760-1*) Ayer.
Richardson, John, jt. auth. see Jain, Nalini.
Richardson, John, jt. ed. see Jaques, David.
Richardson, John, jt. ed. see Murray, Linda.
Richardson, John, et al. Fauna Boreali-Americana: Zoology of the Northern Parts of British America, the Fish, Pt. 4. Sterling, Keir B., ed. LC 77-81108. (Biologists & Their World Ser.). 1978. reprint ed. lib. bdg. 35.95 (*0-405-10692-0*) Ayer.
Richardson, John A. Art: The Way It Is. 3rd ed. (Illus.). 400p. (C). 1986. pap. text ed. 33.95 (*0-13-046533-X*) P-H.
— Art: The Way It Is. 4th ed. (Illus.). 416p. 1992. 49.50 (*0-8109-1911-7*) Abrams.
— Art: The Way It Is. 4th ed. 384p. 1991. pap. text ed. 45.95 (*0-13-040437-3*) P-H.
— Modern Art & Scientific Thought. LC 74-122914. (Illus.). 211p. reprint ed. pap. 60.20 (*0-317-10480-2*, 2014895) Bks Demand.
Richardson, John A., et al. Basic Design: Systems, Elements, Applications. (Illus.). 320p. (C). 1984. pap. text ed. write for info. (*0-13-060186-1*) P-H.
***Richardson, John E., ed.** Annual Editions: Business Ethics, 95-96. 7th rev. ed. (Illus.). 256p. (C). 1995. pap. text ed. 12.95x (*1-56134-347-1*) Dushkin Pub.
— Annual Editions: Marketing, 95-96. 17th rev. ed. (Illus.). 256p. (C). 1995. pap. text ed. 12.95x (*1-56134-362-5*) Dushkin Pub.
Richardson, John F., et al, eds. Proceedings: Papers from the Parasession on the Interplay of Phonology, Morphology & Syntax. LC 83-71958. 353p. 1983. pap. 8.00 (*0-914203-20-7*) Chicago Ling.
Richardson, John G. Formwork Construction & Practice. (Viewpoint Publication Ser.). (Illus.). 1978. pap. text ed. 60.00 (*0-7210-1058-X*, Pub. by C & CA UK) Scholium Intl.
— Quality in Precast Concrete: Design, Production & Supervision. (Concrete Design & Construction Ser.). 395p. 1991. text ed. 210.00 (*0-470-21685-9*) Wiley.
Richardson, John G., ed. Handbook of Theory & Research for the Sociology of Education. LC 85-931. (Illus.). 401p. 1986. text ed. 79.50 (*0-313-23529-5*, RHT/, Greenwood Pr) Greenwood.
Richardson, John H. Economic Disarmament: A Study of International Cooperation. LC 75-41228. reprint ed. 34.50 (*0-404-14591-4*) AMS Pr.
Richardson, John M., ed. Making It Happen: A Positive Guide to the Future. 232p. 1982. 9.95 (*0-685-05939-1*) Roundtable Pr.
Richardson, John R. What Happens After Death? Some Musing on -- Is God Through with a Person After Death? LC 81-52115. 1981. 6.95 (*0-686-79843-0*) St Thomas.
Richardson, John T., et al. Student Learning: Research on Education & Cognitive Psychology. 240p. 1987. 95.00 (*0-335-15601-0*, Open Univ Pr); pap. 39.00 (*0-335-15600-2*, Open Univ Pr) Taylor & Francis.
Richardson, John V., Jr. The Gospel of Scholarship: Pierce Butler & a Critique of American Librarianship. LC 91-45695. (Illus.). 366p. 1992. 42.50 (*0-8108-2499-X*) Scarecrow.
***Richardson, John V.** Knowledge-Based Systems in General Reference Work: Applications, Problems, & Progress. (Library & Information Science Ser.). (Illus.). 355p. 1995. boxed 49.95 (*0-12-588460-5*) Acad Pr.
Richardson, John V., Jr. & Davis, Jinnie Y., eds. Academic Librarianship: Past, Present, & Future - A Festschrift for David Kaser upon His 65th Birthday. 175p. 1989. lib. bdg. 32.50 (*0-87287-669-1*) Libs Unl.
Richardson, Jonathan. Explanatory Notes & Remarks on Milton's Paradise Lost. LC 77-174317. reprint ed. 55.00 (*0-404-05298-3*) AMS Pr.
— The Works: Consisting of: The Theory of Painting; Essay on the Art of Criticism, So Far As It Relates to Painting; The Science of a Connoisseur. (Anglistica & Americana Ser.: No. 37). xix, 346p. 1969. reprint ed. 76.70 (*0-685-66510-0*, 05102433, Pub. by Georg Olms GW) Lubrecht & Cramer.
Richardson, Jonothan L. Dimensions of Ecology. 1977. 29.95 (*0-19-502294-7*) OUP.
Richardson, Joseph E. & Schultz, Ronald C. Sourcecode for Object-Oriented Design Example. (C). 1992. 15.00 (*1-881974-02-2*) Berard Sftware.
Richardson, Joseph E., et al. A Complete Object-Oriented Design Example. (Illus.). 355p. (C). 1992. pap. text ed. 50.00 (*1-881974-01-4*) Berard Sftware.
Richardson, Joseph G. Long Life & How to Reach It. Rosenkrantz, Barbara G., ed. LC 76-40640. (Public Health in America Ser.). 1977. reprint ed. lib. bdg. 19.95 (*0-405-09828-6*) Ayer.
***Richardson, Joseph R. & Mitchell, Ginger.** Field Guide to Common Marine Algae of San Salvador Island, Bahamas. (Illus.). 89p. (Orig.). (C). 1994. pap. text ed. 10.00 (*0-935909-49-4*) Bahamian.
Richardson, Joy. Air. LC 91-42612. (Picture Science Ser.). (Illus.). 30p. (J). (gr. k-4). 1992. lib. bdg. 12.25 (*0-531-14201-9*) Watts.
— Airplanes. LC 93-42184. (Picture Science Ser.). (Illus.). (J). 1994. lib. bdg. 12.25 (*0-531-14324-4*) Watts.
— Airports. (Picture Science Ser.). (Illus.). 32p. (J). (gr. 2-4). 1994. lib. bdg. 12.25 (*0-531-14292-2*) Watts.
— Birds. LC 93-18558. (Picture Science Ser.). (Illus.). 32p. (J). (gr. 2-4). 1993. lib. bdg. 12.25 (*0-531-14262-0*) Watts.
— Bridges. LC 93-30058. (Picture Science Ser.). (Illus.). 32p. (J). (gr. 2-4). 1994. lib. bdg. 12.25 (*0-531-14289-2*) Watts.
— Cars. LC 93-42179. (Picture Science Ser.). (J). 1994. lib. bdg. 12.25 (*0-531-14325-2*) Watts.
— Day & Night. LC 92-31302. (Picture Science Ser.). (Illus.). 30p. (J). (gr. k-4). 1992. lib. bdg. 12.25 (*0-531-14139-X*) Watts.
— Fish. LC 92-32914. (Picture Science Ser.). (J). 1993. lib. bdg. 12.25 (*0-531-14255-8*) Watts.
— Flowers. LC 93-18653. (Picture Science Ser.). (Illus.). 32p. (J). (gr. 2-4). 1993. lib. bdg. 12.25 (*0-531-14274-4*) Watts.
— Heat. LC 92-14419. (Picture Science Ser.). (Illus.). (J). (gr. k-4). 1993. lib. bdg. 12.25 (*0-531-14239-6*) Watts.
— Insects. LC 92-32189. (Picture Science Ser.). (J). 1993. lib. bdg. 12.25 (*0-531-14248-5*) Watts.
— Inside the Museum: A Children's Guide to the Metropolitan Museum of Art. (Illus.). 72p. (J). 1993. pap. 12.95 (*0-8109-2561-3*) Abrams.
— Light. LC 92-14420. (Picture Science Ser.). (J). 1993. lib. bdg. 12.25 (*0-531-14240-X*) Watts.
— Mammals. LC 92-32913. (Picture Science Ser.). (J). 1993. lib. bdg. 12.25 (*0-531-14253-1*) Watts.
— Mollusks. LC 93-18542. (Picture Science Ser.). (Illus.). 32p. (J). (gr. 2-4). 1993. lib. bdg. 12.25 (*0-531-14263-9*) Watts.
— Reptiles. LC 92-32912. (Picture Science Ser.). (Illus.). 32p. (J). (gr. 2-4). 1993. lib. bdg. 12.25 (*0-531-14254-X*) Watts.
— Rocks & Soil. LC 91-42613. (Picture Science Ser.). (Illus.). 30p. (J). (gr. k-4). 1992. lib. bdg. 12.25 (*0-531-14206-X*) Watts.
— The Seasons. LC 91-29100. (Picture Science Ser.). (Illus.). 30p. (J). (gr. k-4). 1992. lib. bdg. 12.53 (*0-531-14158-6*) Watts.
— Ships. LC 93-49730. (Picture Science Ser.). (Illus.). (J). 1994. lib. bdg. 12.25 (*0-531-14326-0*) Watts.
— Skyscrapers. (Picture Science Ser.). (Illus.). 32p. (J). (gr. 2-4). 1994. lib. bdg. 12.25 (*0-531-14291-4*) Watts.
— Trains. LC 93-49731. (Picture Science Ser.). (Illus.). (J). 1994. lib. bdg. 12.25 (*0-531-14327-9*) Watts.
— Trees. LC 93-18652. (Picture Science Ser.). (Illus.). (J). (gr. 4 up). 1993. lib. bdg. 11.40 (*0-531-14273-6*) Watts.
— Tunnels. LC 93-30057. (Picture Science Ser.). (Illus.). 32p. (J). (gr. 2-4). 1994. lib. bdg. 12.25 (*0-531-14290-6*) Watts.
— The Water Cycle. LC 91-39572. (Picture Science Ser.). (Illus.). 30p. (J). (gr. k-4). 1992. lib. bdg. 12.25 (*0-531-14205-1*) Watts.
— The Weather. LC 91-43715. (Picture Science Ser.). (Illus.). 30p. (J). (gr. k-4). 1992. lib. bdg. 12.25 (*0-531-14164-0*) Watts.
Richardson, Joy O., jt. auth. see Faires, Virgil M.
Richardson, Judith B. Come to My Party. LC 91-16320. (Illus.). 32p. (J). (ps-1). 1993. text ed. 13.95 (*0-02-776147-9*, Mac Bks Young Read) S&S Childrens.
— David's Landing. LC 84-22084. (Illus.). 150p. (J). (gr. 3-7). 1984. write for info. (*0-9611374-1-X*) Woods Hole Hist.
— The Way Home. (J). (gr. k). 13.95 (*0-685-41406-X*) Macmillan.
— The Way Home. LC 93-25729. (Illus.). 32p. (J). (ps-1). 1994. reprint ed. pap. 3.95 (*0-689-71790-3*, Aladdin Paperbacks) S&S Childrens.
Richardson, Judith K., jt. auth. see Richardson, Lloyd I.
Richardson, Judy S. & Morgan, Raymond F. Reading to Learn in the Content Areas. 544p. (C). 1990. text ed. 45.95 (*0-534-11748-1*) Intl Thomson.
— Reading to Learn in the Content Areas. 2nd ed. 558p. 1994. text ed. 46.95 (*0-534-20328-0*) Intl Thomson.
Richardson, Julie, jt. ed. see Markandya, Anil.
Richardson, Justine. The Great British Art Search. (Illus.). 16p. (Orig.). (J). (gr. 2-6). 1993. student ed. pap. 2.50 (*0-685-70192-1*) Yale Ctr Brit Art.
Richardson, K. F., jt. auth. see Adlard, P. G.
Richardson, Karen L. A Spy for a Spy: A Mystery Jigsaw Puzzle. (BePuzzled Ser.). (C). 1989. 20.00 (*0-922242-44-5*) Lombard Mktg.
***Richardson, Katherine H. & Lee, Charles E.** Pawleys Island: Historically Speaking. (Illus.). 132p. 1994. 35.00 (*0-9643909-0-6*) Pawleys Islnd.
Richardson, Katherine W. The Salem Witchcraft Trials. LC 83-81118. (Illus.). 28p. (Orig.). 1988. pap. 5.95 (*0-88389-089-5*, Essx Institute) Peabody Essex Mus.
Richardson, Kathleen S., jt. auth. see Lowry, Thomas H.
Richardson, Kathy. Developing Number Concepts: Using Unifix Cubes. 1984. pap. text ed. 24.95 (*0-201-06117-1*) Addison-Wesley.
Richardson, Kay, jt. ed. see Meinho, Ulrike.
***Richardson, Keith.** Poetry & the Colonized Mind. 80p. 1995. 27.00 (*0-8095-4576-4*) Borgo Pr.
Richardson, Ken. Reich Star Rulebook. Bell, Simon, ed. & illus. by. (Reich Star Ser.). 246p. (Orig.). 1990. pap. 19.95 (*0-9627428-0-5*) Creative Encounters.
— Understanding Intelligence. 192p. 1990. 90.00 (*0-335-09398-1*, Open Univ Pr); pap. 32.00 (*0-335-09397-3*, Open Univ Pr) Taylor & Francis.
— Understanding Psychology. 160p. 1989. 80.00 (*0-335-09843-6*, Open Univ Pr); pap. 27.00 (*0-335-09842-8*, Open Univ Pr) Taylor & Francis.
Richardson, Ken & Sheldon, Sue, eds. Cognitive Development to Adolescence. 336p. 1988. 69.95 (*0-86377-087-8*); pap. text ed. 29.95 (*0-86377-088-6*) L Erlbaum Assocs.
Richardson-Koehler, Virginia, et al. School Children at Risk. 286p. 1989. 75.00 (*1-85000-514-1*, Falmer Pr); pap. 31.00 (*1-85000-515-X*, Falmer Pr) Taylor & Francis.
Richardson, Kristin K., ed. Total Quality Management in the Printing & Publishing Industry. 48p. 1992. 28.50 (*0-933505-23-X*) Graph Comm Assn.
Richardson, L., Jr. A New Topographical Dictionary of Ancient Rome. (Illus.). 480p. 1992. text ed. 65.00 (*0-8018-4300-6*) Johns Hopkins.
— Pompeii: An Architectural History. LC 87-17299. (Illus.). 448p. 1988. text ed. 65.00 (*0-8018-3533-X*) Johns Hopkins.
Richardson, Larry. Committed Aestheticism: The Poetic Theory & Practice of Gunter Eich. LC 83-48707. (American University Studies: Germanic Languages & Literature: Ser. I, Vol. 21). 248p. 1983. pap. text ed. 25.25 (*0-8204-0034-3*) P Lang Pubs.
Richardson, Larry A. Diets & Weight Loss. LC 93-93661. (Illus.). 192p. (Orig.). 1993. pap. 17.95 (*0-9636840-1-9*) L A Richardson.
— Sir Cadian Weight Management: Sir Cadian...It's about Time. LC 93-92672. (Illus.). 198p. (Orig.). 1993. pap. text ed. 20.00 (*0-9636840-0-0*) L A Richardson.
Richardson, Laurel. The Dynamics of Sex & Gender: A Sociological Perspective. 3rd ed. 294p. (C). 1989. pap. text ed. 27.50 (*0-06-045407-5*) HarpCollege.
— The New Other Woman: Contemporary Single Women in Affairs with Married Men. 288p. (C). 1987. text ed. 27.95 (*0-02-926890-7*); pap. 12.95 (*0-02-926891-5*) Free Pr.
— Writing Strategies: Reaching Diverse Audiences. (Qualitative Research Methods Ser.: Vol. 21). 88p. (C). 1990. 21.50 (*0-8039-3521-8*); pap. 9.50 (*0-8039-3522-6*) Sage.
Richardson, Laurel & Taylor, Verta, eds. Feminist Frontiers III. 1992. pap. text ed. write for info. (*0-07-052298-7*) McGraw.
Richardson, Laurel W. & Taylor, Verta. Feminist Frontiers. 480p. 1989. text ed. 18.95 (*0-394-37399-5*) Random.
Richardson, Lawrence, ed. Yale Classical Studies, Vol. 19. 292p. reprint ed. pap. 83.30 (*0-8357-8388-X*, 2033871) Bks Demand.
Richardson, Lee. Sophie's Surprise. 2nd ed. (Illus.). 28p. (J). (gr. 3-8). 1984. 16.95 (*0-9613476-0-0*) Shirlee.
Richardson, Lee, jt. ed. see Cateora, Philip R.
Richardson, Lee, ed. see Conference on Consumerism (1976: Baton Rouge, LA).
Richardson, Lenore H., ed. see Hennessey, D. L.
Richardson, Leonard T. Lexique De la Langue Des Oeuvres Burlesques De Scarron. lxv, 281p. 1976. reprint ed. write for info. (*3-487-05742-5*, Pub. by Georg Olms GW) Lubrecht & Cramer.
Richardson, Lewis. Come along with Me. (Poke & Look Bks.). (Illus.). 16p. (J). (ps-00). 1994. bds. 9.95 (*0-448-40188-6*, G&D) Putnam Pub Group.
Richardson, Lewis F. Arms & Insecurity: A Mathematical Study of the Causes & Origins of War. Rashevsky, Nicolas & Trucco, Ernesto, eds. LC 78-27901. 335p. reprint ed. pap. 95.50 (*0-8357-5745-5*, 2017006) Bks Demand.
— The Collected Works of Lewis Fry Richardson, 2 vols. Ashford, O. M. et al, eds. (Illus.). 500p. (C). 1993. Vol. 1, 500p. 150.00 (*0-521-38297-1*); Vol. 2, 500p. 150.00 (*0-521-38298-X*) Cambridge U Pr.
— Statistics of Deadly Quarrels. Wright, Quincy & Lienau, C. C., eds. (Illus.). 1960. 45.00 (*0-910286-10-8*) Boxwood.
Richardson, Linda. Bankers in the Selling Role: A Consultative Guide to Cross Selling Financial Services. 2nd ed. LC 84-11937. 177p. 1984. text ed. 55.00 (*0-471-81005-3*, Wiley-Interscience) Wiley.
— Bankers in the Selling Role: A Consultative Guide to Cross-Selling Financial Services. 2nd ed. 192p. 1992. pap. text ed. 22.50 (*0-471-57265-9*) Wiley.
— One Hundred One Tips for Selling Financial Services. LC 85-22705. 152p. 1986. text ed. 22.50 (*0-471-83457-2*) Wiley.
— Selling by Phone: How to Reach & Sell to Customers. 1994. pap. 12.95 (*0-07-052376-2*) McGraw.
— Stop Telling, Start Selling: Using Customer-Focused Dialogue to Close Sales. 1993. pap. text ed. 16.95 (*0-07-052368-1*) McGraw.
— Winning Group Sales Presentations. 144p. 1991. pap. 17.50 (*1-55623-690-5*) Irwin Prof Pubng.
— Winning Negotiation Strategies for Bankers. 150p. 1987. text ed. 45.00 (*0-87094-990-X*) Irwin Prof Pubng.
Richardson, Lloyd, tr. see Perrolle, Pierre M., ed.
Richardson, Lloyd I. & Richardson, Judith K. The Mathematics of Drugs & Solutions with Clinical Applications. 2nd rev. ed. (Illus.). 1979. pap. text ed. 19.95 (*0-07-052311-8*) McGraw.
— The Mathematics of Drugs & Solutions with Clinical Applications. 3rd ed. 192p. 1985. text ed. 24.95 (*0-07-052314-2*) McGraw.
Richardson, Lois A., jt. auth. see Richardson, Ron.
Richardson, Lou, ed. see Babawi, Sabri.
Richardson, Louvice F. & Callahan, Genevieve. How to Write for Homemakers. 2nd ed. LC 61-14205. 212p. reprint ed. pap. 60.50 (*0-317-28203-4*, 2022767) Bks Demand.
Richardson, Lynn. APLIC Sixteenth Annual Conference: Proceedings. LC 76-643241. (Annual Report, APLIC Ser.). 153p. (Orig.). 1984. pap. text ed. 15.00 (*0-317-07711-2*) APLIC Intl.
Richardson, Lynn S. Raising Kids Cheap in Greater Cleveland. LC 92-36375. 144p. 1992. pap. 7.95 (*0-9631738-1-2*) Gray & Co Pubs.
Richardson, M. D., jt. auth. see Evans, E. G.
Richardson, M. D., jt. ed. see Warnock, D. W.
Richardson, M. E., tr. see Koehler, Ludwig, et al.
Richardson, M. O., ed. Polymer Engineering Composites. (Illus.). 569p. 1977. 147.75 (*0-85334-722-0*, Pub. by Elsevier Applied Sci UK) Elsevier.
— Polymer Engineering Composites. (Applied Science Publishers Materials Science Ser.). (Illus.). 568p. 1977. 108.00 (*0-686-48248-4*, 0705) T-C Pubns CA.
Richardson, M. T. The Practical Horseshoer. LC 91-60936. (Illus.). 288p. 1991. reprint ed. pap. 10.95 (*1-55566-080-0*) Johnson Bks.
Richardson, M. T., comp. Practical Blacksmithing, 4 vols. in one. (Illus.). 1991. reprint ed. 14.99 (*0-517-25025-X*) Random Hse Value.
Richardson, M. T., ed. Practical Carriage Building, Set, Vols. I & II. (Illus.). 512p. 1994. reprint ed. Set. pap. 24.95 (*1-879335-50-6*) Astragal Pr.
Richardson, Margaret. Sir Edwin Lutyens: Drawings from the Collection of the Royal Institute of British Artifacts. (Illus.). 120p. 1995. pap. 35.00 (*1-85490-377-2*, Academy Edits) St Martin.
Richardson, Margaret, tr. see De Oliveira Setubal, Paulo.
Richardson, Margherita E. Teach Yourself Archery. rev. ed. (Illus.). 1980. pap. 4.95 (*0-679-12000-9*) McKay.
Richardson, Marilyn. We've Got to Do Something about Mother. 1991. pap. 8.95 (*0-9625755-0-X*) Unipress Brookings.
Richardson, Marilyn, ed. Maria W. Stewart, America's First Black Woman Political Writer: Essays & Speeches. LC 86-43048. (Blacks in the Diaspora Ser.). (Illus.). 160p. 1987. 25.00 (*0-253-36342-X*); pap. 8.95 (*0-253-20446-1*, MB-446) Ind U Pr.
Richardson, Marilyn, jt. ed. see Mikesell, Janice H.
Richardson, Marion, jt. ed. see Hutcheon, Linda.
Richardson, Martha. Francisco Jose De Goya: Spanish Painter. LC 93-2326. (Hispanics of Achievement Ser.). (Illus.). (J). (ps-3). 1994. write for info. (*0-7910-1799-0*, Am Art Analog); lib. bdg. 18.95 (*0-7910-1780-X*, Am Art Analog) Chelsea Hse.
Richardson, Martin J. Chess for Children. (J). (gr. 4-7). 1991. 13.00 (*0-08-041109-6*, Pub. by CHES UK) Macmillan.
Richardson, Marty, jt. auth. see Jorgenson, Karen.
Richardson, Mary. The Boy Jesus Goes A-Walking & Other Stories. (Illus.). 96p. 1988. pap. 2.95 (*0-8091-6575-9*) Paulist Pr.
— It Happened at Christmas & Other Stories. (Illus.). 96p. 1988. pap. 2.95 (*0-8091-6576-7*) Paulist Pr.
Richardson, Mary A., ed. Amino Acids in Psychiatric Disease. LC 89-18455. (Progress in Psychiatry Ser.). 250p. 1990. text ed. 25.00 (*0-88048-186-2*) Am Psychiatric.
***Richardson, Mary A. & Haugland, Gary, eds.** Use of Neuroleptics in Children. (Clinical Practice Ser.: No. 37). 256p. 1995. boxed 34.00 (*0-88048-475-6*, 8475) Am Psychiatric.
***Richardson, Mervyn.** Dictionary of Substances & Their Effects Vol. 5: I to M. 1000p. 1994. 325.00 (*0-85186-371-X*, R6371) CRC Pr.
Richardson, Mervyn, ed. Chemical Safety: International Reference Manual. LC 94-7950. 1994. 145.00 (*1-56081-815-8*) VCH Pubs.
— Ecotoxicology Monitoring. LC 93-3602. 1993. 110.00 (*1-56081-736-4*) VCH Pubs.
Richardson, Michael, et al. Early Childhood Programs: Organization & Administration. LC 92-60849. 250p. 1992. pap. text ed. 29.00 (*0-87762-881-5*) Technomic.
Richardson, Michael. Georges Bataille. LC 93-20940. 1994. 50.95 (*0-415-09841-6*, Routledge NY); pap. 14.95 (*0-415-09842-4*, Routledge NY) Routledge.
***Richardson, Michael, ed.** Dedalus Book of Surrealism Pt. I: Identity of Things. 2nd ed. (Anthology Ser.). 384p. 1995. pap. 14.95 (*0-7818-0347-0*, Pub. by Dedalus Bks UK) Hippocrene Bks.
— Dedalus Book of Surrealism Pt. II: Myth of the World. (Anthology Ser.). 320p. 1995. pap. 14.95 (*0-7818-0367-5*, Pub. by Dedalus Bks UK) Hippocrene Bks.
Richardson, Michael & Prickett, Robert. Publication Sources in Educational Leadership. LC 90-72122. 110p. 1991. 29.00 (*0-87762-789-4*) Technomic.
Richardson, Michael, ed. see Bataille, Georges.
Richardson, Michael, jt. ed. see Costello, Neil.
***Richardson, Michael, et al.** Managing School Indebtedness: The Complete Guide to School Bonding. LC 94-60934. 245p. 1994. text ed. 39.00 (*1-56676-180-8*) Technomic.
— The Organization of Public Education in South Carolina. 408p. 1992. per. 33.95 (*0-8403-8190-5*) Kendall-Hunt.
Richardson, Michael, et al, eds. Preparing to Study. 72p. 1979. pap. 20.00 (*0-335-00255-2*, Open Univ Pr) Taylor & Francis.
Richardson, Michael D., jt. auth. see Flanigan, Jackson L.

R

An Asterisk (*) at the beginning of an entry indicates that the title is appearing in BIP for the first time.

Richardson, Michael D., et al. School Principals & Change. LC 92-28436. (Source Books on Education: Vol. 33). 288p. 1993. 42.00 (0-8153-0383-1, SS783) Garland.

Richardson, Mike, ed. see Cailleteau, Thierry & Vatine, Olivier.

Richardson, Mike, tr. see Iwata, Kazuhisa.

***Richardson, Mike, et al, eds.** School Empowerment. LC 95-60051. 369p. 1995. text ed. 35.00 (1-56676-269-3) Technomic.

Richardson, Miles. Cry Lonesome & Other Accounts of the Anthropologist's Project. LC 89-26240. (Illus.). 170p. 1990. 59.50 (0-7914-0405-6); pap. 19.95 (0-7914-0406-4) State U NY Pr.

— San Pedro, Colombia: Small Town in a Developing Society. (Illus.). 99p. (C). 1986. reprint ed. pap. text ed. 7.95 (0-88133-252-6) Waveland Pr.

Richardson, Miles, ed. The Anthropologist As Word Shaman. (Anthropology & Humanism Quarterly Ser.: Vol. 5, No. 4). 1980. 7.50 (0-317-66357-7) Am Anthro Assn.

— Place: Experience & Symbol. LC 83-83212. (Geoscience & Man Ser.: Vol. 24). 80p. 1984. pap. 10.00 (0-938909-32-0) Geosci Pubns LSU.

Richardson, Minni. Alpha Hand: Transcription & Review: Second Semester Textbook & Cassette. (Alpha Hand Ser.). 148p. 1989. 15.00 (0-936862-47-5, AH-22); teacher ed 9.00 (0-936862-46-7, AH2-TM) DDC Pub.

Richardson, Nan & Chermayeff, Catherine. Wild Babies. LC 93-2330. (Illus.). 80p. 1994. 14.95 (0-8118-0477-1) Chronicle Bks.

Richardson, Nan, jt. auth. see Cherayeff, Catherine.

Richardson, Nan, jt. auth. see Umbra Editions Staff.

***Richardson, Nancy.** The Golden Globe. (Star Wars Junior Jedi Knights Ser.: No. 1). 128p. (Orig.). 1995. pap. 4.50 (1-57297-035-9) Blvd Books.

Richardson, Nancy A., jt. auth. see Karolyi, Bela.

Richardson, Neil R. Foreign Policy & Economic Dependence. LC 78-6451. 224p. reprint ed. pap. 63.90 (0-7837-1241-3, 2041378) Bks Demand.

Richardson, Nicholas, ed. see Homer.

Richardson, Nigel. Edith Cavell. (Profiles Ser.). (Illus.). 64p. (J). (gr. 5-9). 1991. 11.95 (0-237-60020-X, Pub. by Evans Bros Ltd UK) Trafalgar.

— J. F. Kennedy. (Profiles Ser.). (Illus.). 64p. (J). (gr. 5-9). 1991. 11.95 (0-237-60029-3, Pub. by Evans Bros Ltd UK) Trafalgar.

— Martin Luther King. (Profiles Ser.). (Illus.). 64p. (J). (gr. 5-9). 1991. 11.95 (0-237-60007-2, Pub. by Evans Bros Ltd UK) Trafalgar.

Richardson, Noel. Summer Delights: Cooking with Fresh Herbs. (Illus.). 128p. 1986. spiral bd. 9.95 (0-317-60787-1) Aris Bks.

Richardson, Norman & Stubbs, Thomas. Plants, Agriculture, & Human Society. LC 77-72644. 1978. pap. text ed. 26.95 (0-8053-8215-1) Benjamin-Cummings.

Richardson, P. & Granskou, D., eds. Anti-Judaism in Early Christianity Vol. 1: Paul & the Gospels. 240p. (C). 1986. pap. 19.95 (0-88920-167-6) Humanities.

Richardson, P. & Hurd, J. From Jesus to Paul: Studies in Honour of Francis Wright Beare. 256p. (C). 1984. pap. 18.50 (0-88920-138-2, Pub. by Wilfrid Laurier CN) Humanities.

Richardson, P. E., ed. see International Symposium on Electrochemistry in Mineral & Metal Processing Staff.

Richardson, P. E., jt. ed. see Woods, R.

***Richardson, P. H.** British Mining No. 44: Mining on Dartmoor & the Tamar Valley after 1913. 159p. 1990. 65.00x (0-901450-38-3, Pub. by Northern Mine Res UK) St Mut.

Richardson, P. J., ed. Archbold Criminal Pleading Evidence & Practice. 1,994th ed. 1993. 317.00 (0-421-47000-3, Pub. by Sweet & Maxwll) W W Gaunt.

Richardson, P. Mick. Flowering Plants: Magic in Bloom, No. 1. (Illus.). 1992. lib. bdg. 19.95 (0-685-52242-3) Chelsea Hse.

Richardson, Paul. Computers: Manager's Guide. (Primary Health Care Management Advancement Programme (PHC MAP) Modules Ser.). 76p. 1993. pap. text ed. write for info. (1-882839-20-X) Aga Khan Fnd.

Richardson, Paul E. Where in Moscow: The Ultimate Directory Including Maps, Telephone Lising, & Essential Good & Services. 4th ed. 260p. 1994. pap. 13.50 (1-880100-19-3) Russian Info Srvs.

— Where in St. Petersburg: The Ultimate Directory, including Maps, Telephone Listings & Essential Goods & Services. 2nd ed. (Illus.). 184p. 1994. pap. 13.50 (1-880100-13-4) Russian Info Srvs.

Richardson, Paul N. Introduction to Extrusion. (SPE Processing Ser.). (Illus.). 96p. 20.00 (0-686-48167-4, 1601) T-C Pubns CA.

Richardson, Pearl W. The Growth of Federal User Charges. (Illus.). 79p. (Orig.). (C). 1994. pap. text ed. 40.00 (0-7881-0653-8) Diane Pub.

Richardson, Peggy A., jt. auth. see Weinberg, Robert S.

Richardson, Peter & Richardson, Bob. Great Careers for People Interested in How Things Work, 6 vols., Vol. 5. LC 93-78076. (Career Connections Ser.: Vol. 5). (Illus.). 48p. (J). (gr. 6-9). 1993. 17.95 (0-8103-9389-1, 102107, UXL) Gale.

— Great Careers for People Interested in Math & Computers, 6 vols. LC 93-78079. (Career Connections Ser.: Vol. 1). (Illus.). 48p. (J). (gr. 6-9). 1993. 17.95 (0-8103-9385-9, 102103, UXL) Gale.

Richardson, Peter & Westerholm, Stephen, eds. Law in Religious Communities in the Roman Period: The Debate over Torah & Nomos in Post-Biblical Judaism & Early Christianity. 152p. (C). 1991. pap. 19.95 (0-88920-201-X, Pub. by Wilfrid Laurier CN) Humanities.

Richardson, Peter, jt. auth. see Wright, Patrick.

Richardson, Peter N., jt. auth. see Fischer, William B.

Richardson, Peter R. Cost Containment: The Ultimate Advantage. (Illus.). 304p. 1988. text ed. 35.00 (0-02-926432-4) Free Pr.

Richardson, Philip J. A History of English Ballroom Dancing: The Story of the Development of the Modern English Style. (Ballroom Dance Ser.). 1986. lib. bdg. 79.95 (0-8490-3477-9) Gordon Pr.

Richardson, Polly. Animal Poems. (J). (ps-3). 1992. 12.95 (0-8120-6283-3) Barron.

Richardson, R. Business Planning - an Approach to Strategic Management. 236p. (C). 1989. 145.00 (0-685-39854-4, Inst Pur & Supply) St Mut.

Richardson, R. A. Facial Wrinkles. reprint ed. spiral bd. 6.60 (0-7873-0714-9) Mokelumne.

— Healthy Eyes Without Glasses: Increasing the Strength of the Eyes & the Eye Muscles Without the Aid of Glasses. reprint ed. spiral bd. 8.80 (0-7873-0715-7) Mokelumne.

Richardson, R. C. The Debate on the English Revolution. 2nd ed. (Illus.). 400p. 1989. pap. 25.00 (0-415-01167-1) Routledge.

— The Study of History: A Bibliographical Guide. 112p. 1988. text ed. 69.95 (0-7190-1881-1, Pub. by Manchester Univ Pr UK) St Martin.

Richardson, R. C., ed. Images of Oliver Cromwell: Essays for & by Roger Howell. 288p. (C). 1993. text ed. 59.95 (0-7190-2503-6, Pub. by Manchester Univ Pr UK) St Martin.

— Town & Countryside in the English Revolution. LC 93-76. 288p. (C). 1993. text ed. 59.95 (0-7190-3462-0, Pub. by Manchester Univ Pr UK) St Martin.

Richardson, R. C. & James, T. B., eds. The Urban Experience: A Sourcebook of English, Scottish & Welsh Towns, 1450-1700. LC 82-62244. 192p. 1988. text ed. 100.00 (0-7190-0900-6, Pub. by Manchester Univ Pr UK) St Martin.

Richardson, R. C., jt. ed. see Taylor, Barry.

***Richardson, R. Dan.** Comintern Army: The International Brigades & the Spanish Civil War. fac. ed. LC 80-5182. 240p. 1994. pap. 68.40 (0-7837-7598-9, 2047351) Bks Demand.

Richardson, R. T. Activation to Acquisition: Functional Aspects of the Basal Forebrain Cholinergic System. (Illus.). 392p. 1991. 98.00 (0-8176-3467-3) Spr-Verlag.

— Chucker Jones' Adventures in Shadowland: What's It All about Chucker? Dobie, Bruce, ed. (Illus.). 32p. (Orig.). (J). (gr. k-8). 1994. pap. 1.95 (0-9643522-0-6) R T Richardson.

Richardson, Radford R. One Hundred One: The Best in Poetry & Lyrics for the Elderly, the Young at Heart, & for All Time. 1992. 14.95 (0-533-09532-8) Vantage.

Richardson, Ralph C., jt. ed. see Hahn, Kevin A.

Richardson, Ralph W. Historic Districts of America: New England. (Illus.). xvi, 182p. (Orig.). 1992. pap. 17.00 (1-55613-550-5) Heritage Bk.

— Historic Districts of America: The Mid-Atlantic. (Illus.). xviii, 309p. (Orig.). 1991. pap. 17.50 (1-55613-395-2) Heritage Bk.

— Historic Districts of America: The South. (Illus.). xvi, 223p. (Orig.). 1987. pap. text ed. 12.50 (1-55613-088-0) Heritage Bk.

— Historic Districts of America - the West. (Illus.). 311p. (Orig.). 1994. pap. text ed. 27.00 (1-55613-906-3) Heritage Bk.

Richardson, Rayman P. Evolving Ideas in Physical Science: Physical Science for Elementary Education Majors: Preliminary Edition. 124p. 1993. spiral bd. 22.95 (0-8403-8854-3) Kendall-Hunt.

Richardson, Recco. Teenagers Role in the Family Structure. Stokes, Tanya C., ed. 117p. (Orig.). 1991. pap. 8.00 (0-9627849-7-4) Temperance Pub Hse.

Richardson, Reed C. American Labor Unions: An Outline of Growth & Structure. 2nd ed. (ILR Bulletin Ser.: No. 30). 24p. 1970. pap. 3.00 (0-87546-238-3) ILR Pr.

— Collective Bargaining by Objectives: A Positive Approach. (Illus.). 1977. pap. 18.95 (0-685-03794-0) P-H.

Richardson, Richard C., Jr. & Bender, Louis W. Fostering Minority Access & Achievement in Higher Education: The Role of Urban Community Colleges & Universities. LC 87-45431. (Higher & Adult Education Ser.). 262p. 1987. 34.95x (1-55542-053-2) Jossey-Bass.

— Students in Urban Settings: Achieving the Baccalaureate Degree. Fife, Jonathan D., ed. LC 85-73509. (ASHE-ERIC Higher Education Report Ser.: No. 6, 1985). 90p. (Orig.). (C). 1985. pap. 10.00 (0-913317-25-X) GWU Schl E&HD.

Richardson, Richard C., Jr. & Skinner, Elizabeth F. Achieving Quality & Diversity: Universities in a Multicultural Society. (ACE-Oryx Series on Higher Education). 288p. 1991. 29.95 (0-02-897342-9, ACE-Oryx) Oryx Pr.

Richardson, Richard C., et al. Literacy in the Open-Access College. LC 83-11999. (Jossey-Bass Higher Education Ser.). 207p. reprint ed. pap. 59.00 (0-8357-4919-3, 2037849) Bks Demand.

Richardson, Richard W. Family Ties That Bind: A Self-Help Guide to Change Through Family of Origin Therapy. 2nd ed. (Psychology Ser.). 128p. 1987. pap. 8.95 (0-88908-655-9, 9527) Self-Counsel Pr.

***Richardson, Richard W. & Haralz, Jonas H.** Moving to the Market: The World Bank in Transition. LC 94-47640. (Policy Essay Ser.: Vol. 17). 1995. pap. 9.95 (1-56517-023-7) Overseas Dev Council.

Richardson, Robert. Charisma Factor: How to Develop Your Natural Leadership Ability. 1992. 19.95 (0-13-904368-3) P-H.

— The Lazarus Tree. (WWL Mystery Ser.). 1995. mass mkt. 3.99 (0-373-26166-7, 1-26166-8) Harlequin Bks.

— The Lazarus Tree. 208p. 1992. 17.95 (0-312-08232-0) St Martin.

— Sleeping in the Blood. large type ed. 348p. 1992. 21.95 (0-7505-0428-5) Ulverscroft.

Richardson, Robert, ed. see Mallet, Paul H.

Richardson, Robert, ed. see Potter, John.

Richardson, Robert, jt. ed. see Pratt, William.

Richardson, Robert C., jt. auth. see Bechtel, William.

***Richardson, Robert D., Jr.** Emerson: The Mind on Fire. LC 94-36008. 1995. 35.00 (0-520-08808-5) U CA Pr.

— Henry Thoreau: A Life of the Mind. LC 85-28845. (Illus.). 464p. 1986. 35.00 (0-520-05495-4); pap. 13.00 (0-520-06346-5) U CA Pr.

Richardson, Robert D. Myth & Literature in the American Renaissance. LC 77-22638. 317p. reprint ed. pap. 90.40 (0-8357-6684-5, 2056863) Bks Demand.

Richardson, Robert D., ed. see Faber, George S.

Richardson, Robert D., jt. auth. see Feldman, Burton.

Richardson, Robert D., ed. see Holbach, Paul H.

Richardson, Robert D., ed. see Jones, William.

Richardson, Robert D., ed. see Maurice, Thomas.

Richardson, Robert H., ed. Chesapeake Bay Decoys: The Men Who Made & Used Them. 240p. 1992. 40.00 (0-9631815-0-5) Decoy Mag.

***Richardson, Robert L.** Web Guide. 1995. 24.99 (0-7821-1726-0) Sybex.

Richardson, Robert M. Disassembled Handbook for the TRS-80 Model 1 & 3: Advanced Baudot Radio Teletype for the TRS-80 Model 1 & 3, Vol. 5. Blevins, T. F., ed. 205p. 1983. 22.00 (0-940972-06-9) Richcraft Eng.

— Disassembled Handbook for TRS-80, Vol. 3. Abear, Gerald J., ed. 236p. 1981. 20.00 (0-940972-03-4) Richcraft Eng.

— Synchronous Packet Radio Using the Software Approach: AX.25 Protocal, Vol. 2. Belvins, T. F., ed. 280p. 1984. 22.00 (0-940972-08-5) Richcraft Eng.

— Synchronous Packet Radio Using the Software Approach: Vancouver Protocol, Vol. 1. Blevins, T. F., ed. 223p. 1983. 22.00 (0-940972-07-7) Richcraft Eng.

***Richardson, Robert W.** Robert W. Richardson's Narrow Gauge News. LC 70-102682. (Colorado Rail Annual Ser.: No. 21). (Illus.). 303p. 1994. 44.95 (0-918654-21-1) CO RR Mus.

Richardson, Ron & Richardson, Lois A. Birth Order & You: How Your Sex & Position in the Family Affects Your Personality & Relationships. (Psychology Ser.). 280p. (Orig.). 1990. pap. text ed. 7.95 (0-88908-876-4) Self-Counsel Pr.

Richardson, Ronald K. Moral Imperium: Afro-Caribbeans & the Transformation of British Rule, 1776-1838. LC 86-3154. (Contributions in Comparative Colonial Studies: No. 22). 219p. 1987. text ed. 55.00 (0-313-24724-2, RMI/, Greenwood Pr) Greenwood.

Richardson, Ronnie. OS-2 Batch Files to Go. LC 93-31286. 1993. pap. text ed. 32.95 (0-07-052370-3, Windcrest) TAB Bks.

— OS-2 Batch Files to Go. LC 93-31286. 1994. text ed. 44.95 (0-07-052369-X, Windcrest) TAB Bks.

Richardson, Ronny. Batch File Hall of Fame. 1992. disk, pap. 34.95 (0-8306-3775-3, Windcrest) TAB Bks.

— Batch Files to Go: A Programmer's Library. 1992. pap. 34.95 (0-07-052347-9) McGraw.

— Batch Files to Go: A Programmer's Library. 352p. 1992. disk, pap. 34.95 (0-8306-3989-6, Windcrest) TAB Bks.

— Builder Lite: Developing Dynamic Batch Files. 1992. 44.95 (0-07-052362-2); pap. 32.95 (0-07-052363-0) McGraw.

— Builder Lite: Developing Dynamic Batch Files. (Illus.). 368p. 1992. 44.95 (0-8306-4175-0, 4248, Windcrest); pap. 32.95 (0-8306-4176-9, 4248, Windcrest) TAB Bks.

— Dr. Batch File's Ultimate Collection. 1992. 39.95 (0-07-052358-4); pap. 29.95 (0-07-052359-2) McGraw.

— Dr. Batch File's Ultimate Collection. LC 92-9172. (Illus.). 432p. 1992. 39.95 (0-8306-4112-2, 4220, Windcrest); pap. 29.95 (0-8306-4113-0, 4220, Windcrest) TAB Bks.

— MS-DOS Batch File Programming. 1993. pap. text ed. 32.95 (0-07-052366-5) McGraw.

— MS-DOS Batch File Programming. 1988. pap. 19.95 (0-8306-9328-9, Windcrest) TAB Bks.

— MS-DOS Batch File Programming. 1991. 24.95 (0-8306-6663-X) TAB Bks.

— MS-DOS Batch File Programming. 3rd ed. 384p. 1991. 36.95 (0-8306-2484-8, 3012, Windcrest); pap. 26.95 (0-8306-2483-X, Windcrest) TAB Bks.

— MS-DOS Batch File Programming. 4th ed. 1993. 39.95 (0-07-052371-1) McGraw.

— MS DOS Batch File Programming. 4th ed. LC 93-179. (Illus.). 400p. 1993. pap. 32.45 (0-8306-4315-X, Windcrest) TAB Bks.

— MS-DOS Batch File Utilities. 1991. 36.95 (0-07-157856-0); pap. 26.95 (0-07-157857-9) McGraw.

— MS-DOS Batch File Utilities. 384p. 1991. 36.95 (0-8306-2482-1, 3012, Windcrest); pap. 29.95 (0-8306-2481-3, Windcrest) TAB Bks.

— MS-DOS Utility Programs. 1991. 14.95 (0-8306-5384-8) TAB Bks.

— MS-DOS Utility Programs (five & one quarter) 1991. 14.95 (0-8306-5414-3); 14.95 (0-8306-5415-1); 14.95 (0-8306-5416-X); 14.95 (0-8306-5417-8); 14.95 (0-8306-5418-6); 14.95 (0-8306-5419-4); 14.95 (0-8306-5420-8); 14.95 (0-8306-5421-6); 14.95 (0-8306-5422-4); 14.95 (0-8306-5423-2); 14.95 (0-8306-5424-0); 14.95 (0-8306-5426-7); 14.95 (0-8306-5427-5); write for info. (0-8306-5444-5) TAB Bks.

— MS-DOS Utility Programs (three & one half) 1991. 14.95 (0-8306-5428-3); 14.95 (0-8306-5430-5); 14.95 (0-685-52274-1); 14.95 (0-8306-5431-3); 14.95 (0-8306-5432-1); 14.95 (0-8306-5433-X); 14.95 (0-8306-5434-8); 14.95 (0-8306-5435-6); 14.95 (0-8306-5436-4); 14.95 (0-8306-5437-2); 14.95 (0-8306-5438-0); 14.95 (0-8306-5439-9); 14.95 (0-8306-5440-2); 14.95 (0-8306-5441-0); 14.95 (0-8306-5442-9); 14.95 (0-8306-5443-7); write for info. (0-8306-5445-3) TAB Bks.

— The Ultimate Batch File Book! 1995. pap. text ed. 39.95 (0-07-912051-2) McGraw.

— The Ultimate Batch File Book! 1995. text ed. 49.95 (0-07-912050-4) McGraw.

— Writing DR DOS Batch Files. 432p. 1992. pap. 32.95 (0-8306-4244-7, 4289, Windcrest) TAB Bks.

— Writing Dr. DOS Batch Files. 1993. pap. 32.95 (0-07-052364-9) McGraw.

— Writing OS 2 REXX Programs. LC 94-913. 1994. pap. text ed. 39.95 (0-07-052372-X) McGraw.

— Writing VX-REXX Programs. LC 94-20646. 1994. 55.00 (0-07-911910-7); pap. 39.95 (0-07-911911-5) McGraw.

Richardson, Ros & McSeveney, Margaret. Teaching & Learning of Research & Reference Skills in Primary 4 & 7. (C). 1989. 80.00 (1-85098-169-8, Pub. by Jordanhill College UK) St Mut.

Richardson, Rosalie & Fox, Larry L. Hancock County, Indiana: A Pictorial History. LC 93-13530. 1993. write for info. (0-89865-869-1) Donning Co.

Richardson, Rosamond. Alfresco: Over One Hundred Recipes with Menus for Memorable Outdoor Meals. (Illus.). 1992. 35.00 (0-517-58482-4, C P Pubs) Crown Pub Group.

— Stalin's Shadow: Inside the Family of One of the World's Greatest Tyrants. 320p. 1993. 23.00 (0-312-10493-6, Pub. by Thomas Dunne Bks) St Martin.

***Richardson, Rosamond & Ward, James.** Yoga for Bears: A Little Primer on the Unbearable Rightness of Bending. LC 94-34777. 1994. 12.00 (0-06-251182-3) Harper SF.

Richardson, Roy, jt. auth. see Richardson, Bill.

Richardson, Rufus B., ed. see Aeschines.

Richardson, Rupert N. The College Man & Our Rural Civilization. Clayton, Lawrence R., ed. 1989. write for info. (0-910075-12-3) Hardin-Simmons.

— Comanche Barrier to South Plains Settlement. 1993. reprint ed. lib. bdg. 75.00 (0-7812-5948-7) Rprt Serv.

Richardson, Rupert N., et al. Along Texas Old Forts Trail. rev. ed. LC 90-38189. (Illus.). 112p. 1990. reprint ed. pap. 9.95 (0-929398-16-5) UNTX Pr.

— Texas: The Lone Star State. 4th ed. (Illus.). 464p. 1981. text ed. write for info. (0-13-912444-6) P-H.

— Texas: The Lone Star State. 6th ed. LC 92-16171. 480p. (C). 1992. pap. text ed. write for info. (0-13-912411-X) P-H.

Richardson, Ruth. Florencio Sanchez & the Argentine Theatre. 1974. 250.00 (0-87968-227-2) Gordon Pr.

— Tracks: Poems about People. LC 88-72339. (Illus.). 93p. (Orig.). 1989. pap. 7.00 (0-916383-73-3) Aegina Pr.

***Richardson, Ruth & Thorne, Robert.** The Builder Illustrations Index. (Illus.). 846p. 1995. 230.00 (0-907101-06-2, Pub. by Hutton Plus UK) Antique Collect.

Richardson, Ruth, tr. see Schlegel, Dorothea M.

Richardson, Ruth, ed. see Schlegel, Dorothea.

Richardson, Ruth D., ed. New Athenaeum - Neues Athenaeum, Vol. 3: 1992. 226p. 1993. 49.95 (0-7734-9274-7) E Mellen.

— Schleiermacher in Context: Papers from the 1988 International Symposium on Schleiermacher at Herrnhut, the German Democratic Republic. LC 91-3611. (Schleiermacher Studies & Translations: Vol. 6). (Illus.). 472p. 1991. lib. bdg. 109.95 (0-7734-9793-5) E Mellen.

Richardson, S., jt. ed. see Shackel, B.

Richardson, S. D. Forests & Forestry in China: Changing Patterns of Resource Development. LC 89-24514. (Illus.). 352p. 1990. text ed. 45.00 (1-55963-023-X); pap. 26.95 (1-55963-022-1) Island Pr.

Richardson, S. Fieldin. Pamela-Shamela. 1980. mass mkt. 5.95 (0-452-00856-5, Mer) NAL-Dutton.

Richardson, S. M., jt. ed. see Pearson, J. R.

Richardson, Samuel. The Apprentice's Vade Mecum: or Young Man's Pocket-Companion, 3 pts. LC 92-2483. (Augustan Reprints Ser.: No. 169-170 (1975)). reprint ed. 18.50 (0-404-70169-8, HD4885) AMS Pr.

— Clarissa. Sherburn, George, ed. LC 62-52256. (YA). (gr. 9 up). 1962. pap. 9.96 (0-395-05164-9, RivEd) HM.

— Clarissa: Or the History of a Young Lady. Ross, Angus, ed. (Classics Ser.). 1986. pap. 21.95 (0-14-043215-9, Penguin Classics) Viking Penguin.

— Clarissa: Or, The History of a Young Lady - Comprehending the Most Important Concerns of Private Life; with a New Introduction to the AMS Edition by Florian Stuber & A Bibliographic Note by O M Brack, Jr, 8 vols., Set. LC 90-368. reprint ed. 765.00 (0-404-64100-8) AMS Pr.

— A Collection of the Moral & Instructive Sentiments, Maxims, Cautions, & Reflections, Contained in the Histories of Pamela, Clarissa, & Sir Charles Grandison. LC 92-9738. (Clarissa Project Ser.: Vol. 11). 1992. 76.50 (0-404-64111-3) AMS Pr.

— A Collection of the Moral & Instructive Sentiments, Maxims, Cautions, & Reflexions, Contained in the Histories of Pamela, Clarissa, & Sir Charles Grandison. LC 80-22492. 1980. reprint ed. 75.00 (0-8201-1357-3) Schol Facsimiles.

— Correspondence of Samuel Richardson, 6 Vols, 1. Barbauld, Anna L., ed. LC 72-144675. reprint ed. write for info. (0-404-05301-7) AMS Pr.

R

— Correspondence of Samuel Richardson, 6 Vols, 2. Barbauld, Anna L., ed. LC 72-144675. reprint ed. write for info. (*0-404-05302-5*) AMS Pr.

— Correspondence of Samuel Richardson, 6 Vols, 3. Barbauld, Anna L., ed. LC 72-144675. reprint ed. write for info. (*0-404-05303-3*) AMS Pr.

— Correspondence of Samuel Richardson, 6 Vols, 4. Barbauld, Anna L., ed. LC 72-144675. reprint ed. write for info. (*0-404-05304-1*) AMS Pr.

— Correspondence of Samuel Richardson, 6 Vols, 5. Barbauld, Anna L., ed. LC 72-144675. reprint ed. write for info. (*0-404-05305-X*) AMS Pr.

— Correspondence of Samuel Richardson, 6 Vols, 6. Barbauld, Anna L., ed. LC 72-144675. reprint ed. write for info. (*0-404-05306-8*) AMS Pr.

— Correspondence of Samuel Richardson, 6 Vols, Set. Barbauld, Anna L., ed. LC 72-144675. reprint ed. write for info. (*0-404-05300-9*) AMS Pr.

— Letters & Passages Restored from the Original Manuscript of the History of Clarissa. LC 92-9737. (Clarissa Project Ser.: Vol. 10). 1992. 76.50 (*0-404-64110-5*) AMS Pr.

— Novels: Complete & Unabridged, 19 vols., Set. (BCL1-PR English Literature Ser.). 1992. reprint ed. lib. bdg. 1,425. 00 (*0-7812-7396-X*) Rprt Serv.

— Novels of Samuel Richardson, 19 Vols, Set. LC 75-114357. 1970. reprint ed. 1,282.50 (*0-404-05310-6*) AMS Pr.

— Pamela. 453p. (Orig.). 1991. pap. 7.95 (*0-460-87064-5*, Everyman's Classic Lib) C E Tuttle.

— Pamela. Duncan-Eaves, T. C. & Kimpel, B. D., eds. LC 71-134860. (Orig.). (C). 1971. pap. 9.96 (*0-395-11152-8*, RivEd) HM.

— Pamela: Or Virtue Rewarded. Sabor, Peter, ed. (English Library). 480p. 1981. mass mkt. 6.95 (*0-14-043140-3*, Penguin Classics) Viking Penguin.

Richardson, Scott. The Homeric Narrator. LC 89-38980. 296p. 1990. 29.95 (*0-8265-1236-4*) Vanderbilt U Pr.

Richardson, Selma K. Periodicals for School Media Programs. LC 77-25069. 419p. reprint ed. pap. 119.50 (*0-317-26568-7*, 2023952) Bks Demand.

Richardson, Selma K., ed. Magazines for Children: A Guide for Parents, Teachers, & Librarians. 2nd ed. LC 90-45152. (C). 1991. pap. text ed. 25.00 (*0-8389-0552-8*, 0552-8) ALA.

Richardson, Sheila. A Lakes Christmas. (Illus.). 176p. 1991. pap. 15.00 (*0-86299-921-9*) A Sutton Pub.

Richardson, Stephen C. Fluid Mechanics. (Illus.). 350p. (C). 1989. text ed. 59.50 (*0-89116-671-8*) Hemisp Pub.

Richardson, Steve, jt. auth. see Judson, Sheldon.

Richardson, Stewart, ed. see Bucholz, Barbara B. & Crane, Margaret.

Richardson, Stewart, ed. see Carr, Camilla.

Richardson, Stewart, ed. see Hanks, Stephen.

Richardson, Stewart, ed. see Hernon, Peter.

Richardson, Stewart, ed. see Midgley, Leslie.

Richardson, Stewart, ed. see Mitroff, Ian I. & Bennis, Warren.

Richardson, Stewart, ed. see O'Faolain, Sean.

Richardson, Stewart, ed. see Parrish, Richard.

Richardson, Stewart, ed. see Silverman, Chip.

***Richardson, Susan.** Bob Dylan. (Pop Culture Legends Ser.). (J). 1995. 18.95 (*0-7910-2335-4*) Chelsea Hse.

Richardson, Susan, jt. auth. see Travers, Peter.

Richardson, T. D. Modern Figure Skating. 1980. lib. bdg. 59. 95 (*0-8490-3126-5*) Gordon Pr.

Richardson, Terry. Composites: A Design Guide. LC 87-609. (Illus.). 384p. 1987. 34.95 (*0-8311-1173-9*) Indus Pr.

— A Guide to Metrics. LC 78-61695. (Illus.). 1978. pap. 12. 00 (*0-911168-38-9*) Prakken.

— Modern Industrial Plastics. LC 72-92621. 1974. 24.45 (*0-672-97657-9*, Bobbs) Macmillan.

Richardson, Terry L., jt. auth. see Toboldt, Bill.

Richardson, Theresa R. The Century of the Child: The Mental Hygiene Movement & Social Policy in the United States & Canada. LC 88-24894. 273p. 1989. 64. 50 (*0-7914-0020-4*); pap. 21.95 (*0-7914-0021-2*) State U NY Pr.

Richardson, Thomas J., ed. The Grandissimes: Centennial Essays. LC 81-13122. (Southern Quarterly Ser.). 100p. 1981. 16.00 (*0-87805-149-X*) U Pr of Miss.

Richardson, Thomas J., jt. auth. see Peck, Merton J.

Richardson, Tim, ed. see Wycoff, Joyce.

Richardson, Tony. Long-Distance Runner: A Memoir. 1993. 25.00 (*0-688-12101-2*) Morrow.

Richardson, Trevor. The Chair: From Artifact to Object. Beesch, Ruth K., ed. (Illus.). 40p. 1991. pap. text ed. 10. 00 (*0-9627541-2-9*) Weatherspoon.

Richardson, V. C. Diseases of Domestic Guinea Pigs. (Library of Veterinary Practice). (Illus.). 144p. 1992. pap. 39.95 (*0-632-03301-0*) Blackwell Sci.

Richardson, Valeria, ed. see Whitaker.

Richardson, Virginia. Retirement Counseling: A Handbook for Gerontology Practitioners. LC 92-48349. (Life Styles & Issues in Aging Ser.: Vol. 1). 224p. 1993. 31.95 (*0-8261-7020-X*) Springer Pub.

Richardson, Virginia, ed. Teacher Change & the Staff Development Process. 240p. (C). 1994. text ed. 40.00x (*0-8077-3361-X*); pap. text ed. 18.95 (*0-8077-3360-1*) Tchrs Coll.

Richardson, W. Christian Doctrine: The Faith... Once Delivered. LC 82-25598. (Bible College Textbooks Ser.). 448p. (Orig.). 1983. pap. 9.99 (*0-87239-610-X*, 88588) Standard Pub.

Richardson, W., jt. auth. see Morgan, Maurice.

Richardson, W. A., tr. see Sanchez-Albornoz, Nicolas.

Richardson, W. D., jt. ed. see Jessen, K. R.

***Richardson, W. John, et al.** Marine Mammals & Noise. (Illus.). 450p. 1995. boxed 64.95 (*0-12-588440-0*) Acad Pr.

Richardson, Wade. Reading & Variant in Petronius: Studies in the French Humanists & Their Manuscript Sources. 187p. 1993. 60.00 (*0-8020-2866-7*) U of Toronto Pr.

Richardson, Wally, et al. The Path to Illumination. LC 82-71211. (Illus.). 248p. (Orig.). 1982. pap. 9.95 (*0-87516-480-3*) DeVorss.

Richardson, Wally G. & Huett, Lenora. The Spiritual Value of Gem Stones. LC 79-54728. 168p. 1980. pap. 8.95 (*0-87516-383-1*) DeVorss.

Richardson, Walter C. Report of the Royal Commission of 1552, Set. LC 72-86893. 302p. 1974. 45.00 (*0-937058-08-4*) West Va U Pr.

Richardson, Wendy & Richardson, Jack. Animals: Through the Eyes of Artists. LC 90-34276. (Artists of the World Ser.). (Illus.). 48p. (J). (gr. 4 up). 1991. pap. 7.95 (*0-516-49281-0*) Childrens.

— Cities: Through the Eyes of Artists. LC 90-34277. (Artists of the World Ser.). 48p. (J). (gr. 4 up). 1991. lib. bdg. 15. 45 (*0-516-09282-0*); pap. 7.95 (*0-516-49282-9*) Childrens.

— Entertainers: Through the Eyes of Artists. LC 90-34278. (Artists of the World Ser.). 48p. (J). (gr. 4 up). 1991. lib. bdg. 15.45 (*0-516-09283-9*); pap. 7.95 (*0-516-49283-7*) Childrens.

— Families: Through the Eyes of Artists. LC 90-34279. (Artists of the World Ser.). (Illus.). 48p. (J). (gr. 4 up). 1991. lib. bdg. 15.45 (*0-516-09284-7*); pap. 7.95 (*0-516-49284-5*) Childrens.

— The Natural World: Through the Eyes of Artists. LC 90-34281. (Artists of the World Ser.). (Illus.). 48p. (J). (gr. 4 up). 1991. pap. 7.95 (*0-516-49285-3*) Childrens.

— Water: Through the Eyes of Artists. LC 90-34280. (Artists of the World Ser.). 48p. (J). (gr. 4 up). 1991. lib. bdg. 15.45 (*0-516-09286-3*); pap. 7.95 (*0-516-49286-1*) Childrens.

Richardson, William. Anecdotes of the Russian Empire. LC 68-27021. (Russia Through European Eyes Ser.). 1971. reprint ed. lib. bdg. 55.00 (*0-306-77025-3*) Da Capo.

— Anecdotes of the Russian Empire: In a Series of Letters, Written a Few Years Ago, from St. Petersburg. LC 79-115580. (Russia Observed, Series I). 1970. reprint ed. 26.95 (*0-405-03059-2*) Ayer.

— Essays on Shakespeare's Dramatic Character of Sir John Falstaff & on His Female Characters. LC 76-144676. reprint ed. 29.50 (*0-404-05307-6*) AMS Pr.

— Essays on Shakespeare's Dramatic Characters of Richard III, King Lear & Timon of Athens. LC 76-144676. reprint ed. 31.50 (*0-404-05308-4*) AMS Pr.

— Philosophical Analysis & Illustration of Some of Shakespeare's Remarkable Characters. rev. ed. LC 17-30453. 36.00 (*0-404-05309-2*) AMS Pr.

Richardson, William B. & Moore, Gary. Working in Horticulture. (Career Preparation for Agriculture-Agribusiness Ser.). (Illus.). 1980. text ed. 29.96 (*0-07-052285-5*) McGraw.

Richardson, William B., jt. auth. see Feldhusen, John F.

Richardson, William D. Melville's "Benito Cereno" An Interpretation, with an Annotated Text & a Concordance. LC 86-70369. 246p. (C). 1987. lib. bdg. 24.95 (*0-89089-274-1*) Carolina Acad Pr.

Richardson, William E. Paul among Friends & Enemies. (Anchor Ser.). 190p. 1992. pap. 4.99 (*0-8163-1084-X*) Pacific Pr Pub Assn.

Richardson, William F., tr. see Napier, John.

Richardson, William G., jt. auth. see Pritchett, Norman M.

Richardson, William H. Mexico Through Russian Eyes, 1806-1940. LC 87-17350. (Latin American Ser.). 296p. (C). 1988. 49.95 (*0-8229-3824-3*) U of Pittsburgh Pr.

Richardson, William J., jt. auth. see Muller, John P.

Richardson, William J., jt. ed. see Muller, John P.

***Richardson, Willie.** Reclaiming the Urban Family: How to Mobilize the Church As a Family Training Center. 192p. 1995. pap. 9.99 (*0-310-20008-3*) Zondervan.

Richardson, Willis. Plays & Pageants from the Life of the Negro. 1990. 25.00 (*0-87498-028-3*) Assoc Pubs DC.

— Plays & Pageants from the Life of the Negro. LC 93-27075. (Illus.). 400p. 1993. reprint ed. text ed. 40.00 (*0-87805-657-2*); reprint ed. pap. text ed. 17.95 (*0-87805-658-0*) U Pr of Miss.

Richardson, Wyman. The House on Nauset Marsh. (Illus.). 1980. reprint ed. pap. 7.95 (*0-85699-046-9*) Chatham Pr.

Richardus, Peter. Project Surveying: General Adjustment & Optimization Techniques with Applications to Engineering Surveying. 640p. (C). 1984. text ed. 150.00 (*90-6191-519-8*, Pub. by A A Balkema NE); pap. text ed. 85.00 (*90-6191-526-0*, Pub. by A A Balkema NE) Ashgate Pub Co.

Richardz, Klaus & Limbrunner, Alfred. World of Bats. (Illus.). 192p. 1993. 29.95 (*0-86622-540-4*, TS192) TFH Pubns.

Richarson, John. Bad Mood Bear & the Big Present. (Illus.). 32p. (J). (ps-1). 1994. 13.95 (*0-09-176169-7*, Pub. by Hutchnson UK) Trafalgar.

Richart, Robert W. Gyorgy Ligeti: A Bio-Bibliography. LC 90-14022. (Bio-Bibliographies in Music Ser.: No. 30). 200p. 1990. text ed. 49.95 (*0-313-25174-6*, RGL/, Greenwood Pr) Greenwood.

Richartz, G. Einfluss Exogener und Endogener Faktoren Fruchtkoerperentwicklung des Basiodiomyceten Pleurotus Ostreatus. (Bibliotheca Mycologica Ser.: Vol. 121). (Illus.). 166p. 1988. pap. text ed. 52.00 (*3-443-59022-5*) Lubrecht & Cramer.

Richarz, Monika, ed. Jewish Life in Germany: Memoirs from Three Centuries. Rosenfeld, Stella P. & Rosenfeld, Sidney, trs. LC 90-38733. (Modern Jewish Experience Ser.). (Illus.). 496p. 1991. 39.95 (*0-253-35024-7*) Ind U Pr.

Richarz, Sherrill. Understanding Children Through Observation. 222p. 1980. pap. text ed. 32.25 (*0-8299-0337-2*) West Pub.

Richcreek, John. Structure of Intelligent Justice. LC 87-71747. (Illus.). 650p. (Orig.). 1988. pap. 21.50 (*0-9600434-1-1*) Camda.

Riche. Picture Tests in Embryology. 1991. write for info. (*0-318-67213-8*) Mosby Yr Bk.

Riche, Pierre. The Carolingians: A Family Who Forged Europe. Allen, Michael I., tr. LC 91-303532. (Middle Ages Ser.). 424p. (Orig.). (C). 1993. text ed. 49.95 (*0-8122-3062-0*); pap. text ed. 19.95 (*0-8122-1342-4*) U of Pa Pr.

— Daily Life in the World of Charlemagne. McNamara, Jo Ann, tr. LC 78-53330. (Middle Ages Ser.). (Illus.). 352p. (C). 1978. pap. text ed. 20.95x (*0-8122-1096-4*) U of Pa Pr.

— Education & Culture in the Barbarian West: Sixth Through Eighth Centuries. Contreni, J. J., tr. LC 76-25249. (Illus.). 594p. 1978. pap. text ed. 14.95 (*0-87249-376-8*) U of SC Pr.

— Education et Culture dans l'Occident Medieval. (Collected Studies: Vol. 420). 304p. 1993. 89.95 (*0-86078-391-X*, Pub. by Variorum UK) Ashgate Pub Co.

Riche, Robert. What Are We Doing in Latin America? LC 90-53322. 208p. 1991. 22.00 (*1-877946-01-X*) Permanent Pr.

Riche, Robert, jt. auth. see Bauman, Lawrence.

Richeal, Kip. The Pittsburgh Pirates: Still Walking Tall. LC 92-63138. (Illus.). 275p. 1993. 19.95 (*0-915611-69-4*) Sagamore Pub.

— Welcome to the Big Ten: The 1993 Penn State Football Season. (Illus.). 250p. 1994. 19.95 (*0-685-73059-X*) Sagamore Pub.

— Welcome to the Big Ten: The 1993 Penn State Football Season. 1994. 19.95 (*1-57167-000-9*) Sagamore Pub.

Richeck, Margaret A. The World of Words. 1992. pap. text ed. write for info. (*0-318-68492-6*) HM.

Richecky, Janet. Excuse Me. (Manners Matter Ser.). (Illus.). 32p. (J). (ps-2). 1989. lib. bdg. 18.50 (*0-89565-539-X*) Childs World.

Richek, Margaret A. The World of Words. 2nd ed. 352p. 1988. write for info. (*0-318-63333-7*); pap. 23.56 (*0-685-44112-1*) HM.

Richel, Veronica C. The German Stage, Seventeen Sixty-Seven to Eighteen Hundred & Ninety: A Directory of Playwrights & Plays. LC 87-25155. (Bibliographies & Indexes in the Performing Arts Ser.: No. 7). 256p. 1988. text ed. 55.00 (*0-313-24990-3*, RGS/) Greenwood.

Richelet, Pierre. Dictionnaire Francois, 2 vols. in 1. 1128p. 1973. reprint ed. write for info. (*3-487-04587-7*, Pub. by Georg Olms GW) Lubrecht & Cramer.

Richelieu, Frank E. The Art of Being Yourself. LC 92-53722. 320p. (Orig.). 1992. pap. 12.95 (*0-917849-15-9*) Sci of Mind.

— Reincarnation: The Inheritance of a Soul. 32p. (Orig.). 1991. pap. 3.50 (*0-941992-25-X*) Los Arboles Pub.

Richelieu, Peter. A Soul's Journey. Orig. Title: From the Turret. (Illus.). 208p. 1989. pap. 9.95 (*0-85030-812-7*, Pub. by Aquarian Pr UK) Thorsons SF.

Richelle, M. & Lejeune, H. Time in Animal Behaviour. LC 79-40953. (Pergamon International Library Science Technology Engineering & Social Studies). (Illus.). 1980. 122.00 (*0-08-023754-1*, Pub. by Pergamon Repr UK) Franklin.

Richels, Richard, jt. auth. see Manne, Alan.

Richelson, Jeffrey, jt. ed. see Ball, Desmond.

Richelson, Jeffrey, ed. see National Security Archive Staff & Chadwyck-Healey Staff.

***Richelson, Jeffrey T.** A Century of Spies: Intelligence in the Twentieth Century. (Illus.). 544p. 1995. text ed. 25. 00 (*0-19-507391-6*) OUP.

— Social Choice Theory & Soviet National Security Decisionmaking. (CISA Working Paper Ser.: No. 37). 43p. (Orig.). Date not set. pap. 10.00 (*0-86682-048-5*) Ctr Intl Relations.

— The U. S. Intelligence Community. (C). 1995. pap. text ed. 24.95 (*0-8133-2376-2*) Westview.

— United States Strategic Reconnaissance: Photographic - Imaging Satellites. (CISA Working Paper Ser.: No. 38). 51p. (Orig.). Date not set. pap. 10.00 (*0-86682-050-7*) Ctr Intl Relations.

Richelson, Jeffrey T. & Ball, Desmond J. The Ties That Bind: Intelligence Co-operation Between the UKUSA Countries. (Illus.). 420p. 1986. text ed. 34.95 (*0-04-327092-1*) Routledge Chapman & Hall.

— The Ties That Bind: Intelligent Cooperation Between the Ukusa Countries. rev. ed. 420p. (C). 1990. text ed. 49.95 (*0-685-54061-8*); pap. text ed. 19.95 (*0-04-520009-2*) Routledge Chapman & Hall.

Richelson, Jeffrey T., ed. see National Security Archive Staff & Chadwyck-Healey Staff.

Richelson, Paul W., ed. The Permanent Collection of Twentieth Century Prints: Ohio University Gallery of Fine Art. LC 84-52582. (Illus.). 360p. (Orig.). 1985. pap. 14.95 (*0-933041-00-4*) Gallery Fine Art Ohio U.

Richelson, Paul W., ed. see Bunnell, Peter C.

***Richemont.** Magic Skateboard. LC 92-53010. (J). 1995. pap. text ed. 3.99 (*1-56402-449-0*) Candlewick Pr.

Richemont, Enid. The Glass Bird. LC 92-54585. 112p. (J). (gr. 3-6). 1993. 14.95 (*1-56402-195-5*) Candlewick Pr.

— The Magic Skateboard. LC 92-53010. (Illus.). 80p. (J), (gr. 3-6). 1993. 14.95 (*1-56402-132-7*) Candlewick Pr.

— The Time Tree. (J). (gr. 3-7). 1990. 12.95 (*0-316-74452-2*) Little.

Richens, A. & Woodford, F. Peter. Anticonvulsant Drugs & Enzyme Induction. (Institute for Research into Mental & Multiple Handicap Study Group Ser.: Vol. 9). 204p. 1976. 60.00 (*90-219-5002-2*, Excerpta Medica) Elsevier.

Richens, Calvin. Time Travelers & Other People. (Illus.). 69p. (Orig.). 1993. pap. 9.95 (*1-882892-01-1*) Creat Energies.

Richens, R. H. Elm. LC 82-17690. (Illus.). 325p. 1983. 99. 95 (*0-521-24916-3*) Cambridge U Pr.

Richer, ed. see Nerval, Gerard.

Richer, J. C., et al, eds. A Guide to IUPAC Nomenclature of Organic Compounds. (IUPAC Chemical Data Ser.). 224p. 1993. 39.95 (*0-632-03488-2*, Q) CRC Pr.

Richer, Jean. Sacred Geography of the Ancient Greeks: Astrological Symbolism in Art, Architecture, & Landscape. Rone, Christine, tr. LC 94-11960. (Series in Western Esoteric Traditions). (Illus.). 319p. (C). 1994. 59.50 (*0-7914-2023-X*); pap. text ed. 19.95 (*0-7914-2024-8*) State U NY Pr.

Richer, Mark, ed. AI Tools & Techniques. LC 88-21983. 384p. (C). 1989. text ed. write for info. (*0-89391-494-0*) Ablex Pub.

Richer, Paul. Artistic Anatomy. Hale, Robert B., ed. (Illus.). 256p. 1986. pap. 22.50 (*0-8230-0297-7*, Watsn-Guptill) Watsn-Guptill.

***Richer, Stephen & Weir, Lorna, eds.** Beyond Political Correctness: Toward the Inclusive University. 232p. 1995. pap. 17.95 (*0-8020-6010-2*) U of Toronto Pr.

Richer, Stephen, ed. see Barker, Arthur E.

Richerson, ed. Modern Ceramic Engineering: Properties, Processing, & Use in Design. 2nd ed. (Engineering Materials Ser.: Vol. 1). 872p. 1992. 165.00 (*0-8247-8634-3*) Dekker.

Richerson, D., ed. Ceramics Applications in Manufacturing. LC 88-63021. 250p. 1989. 42.00 (*0-87263-339-X*) SME.

Richerson, Peter J., jt. auth. see Boyd, Robert.

Richert & Feldhusen. Special Populations of Gifted Learners. Jenkins-Friedman et al, eds. 1991. pap. 10.00 (*0-89824-528-1*) Trillium Pr.

Richert, Donald, jt. auth. see Kelley, John L.

Richert, Emma B. Long, Long Ago in the Skokomish Valley. rev. ed. (Illus.). 84p. 1984. reprint ed. pap. text ed. 5.60 (*0-935693-04-1*) Mason Cty Hist.

Richert, R. & Blumen, A., eds. Disorder Effects on Relaxation Processes. LC 93-39077. 1994. 240.00 (*0-387-57327-5*) Spr-Verlag.

***Richert, Sandy, ed.** Cleveland As a Center of Regional American Art. 153p. (Orig.). (C). 1994. pap. 12.50 (*0-9639562-3-X*) Clevelnd Art.

***Riches.** Giraffes Have More Fun. 1994. pap. 5.99 (*0-517-13491-8*) Random Hse Value.

— Picture Tests in Histology. 128p. Date not set. 14.95 (*0-8151-7346-6*, Yr Bk Med Pubs) Mosby Yr Bk.

Riches, jt. auth. see Keenan, K.

Riches, B. E. Electric Circuit Theory. (Illus.). 288p. 1989. Comprises site license registration form, master disk for copying, backup disk & two copies of text. disk 270.00 (*0-7503-0080-9*); pap. 39.00 (*0-85274-041-7*) IOP Pub.

Riches, C., jt. auth. see Parker, C.

Riches, Colin & Morgan, Colin. Human Resource Management in Education. (Management in Education Ser.). 192p. 1990. 85.00 (*0-335-09251-9*, Open Univ Pr); pap. 27.00 (*0-335-09250-0*, Open Univ Pr) Taylor & Francis.

Riches, Collin. Developing Interviewing Skills in Education. 224p. 1988. lib. bdg. 35.00 (*0-415-00581-7*) Routledge.

Riches, Cromwell A. Unanimity Role & the League of Nations. LC 70-174318. reprint ed. 15.00 (*0-404-05330-0*) AMS Pr.

Riches, David. Northern Nomadic Hunter-Gatherer: A Humanistic Approach. (Studies in Anthropology). 1982. text ed. 80.00 (*0-12-587620-3*) Acad Pr.

Riches, Janice, jt. auth. see Woold, Emile.

Riches, John. Century of New Testament Study. LC 93-23575. 1993. pap. 17.00 (*1-56338-064-1*) TPI PA.

— The World of Jesus: First-Century Judaism in Crisis. (Understanding Jesus Today Ser.). 144p. (C). 1990. 32. 95 (*0-521-38505-9*); pap. 8.95 (*0-521-38676-4*) Cambridge U Pr.

Riches, John, ed. The Analogy of Beauty: The Theology of Hans Urs von Balthasar. 256p. 1986. 37.95 (*0-567-09351-4*, Pub. by T & T Clark UK) Bks Intl VA.

Riches, John, ed. see Best, Ernest.

Riches, John, ed. see Hubner, Hans.

Riches, John, ed. see Maddox, Robert.

Riches, John, ed. see Raisanen, Heikki.

Riches, John, tr. see Ritter, Gerhard.

Riches, John, ed. see Urs Von Balthasar, Hans.

Riches, John, ed. see Von Balthasar, Hans U.

Riches, John E., ed. see Wedderburn, A. J.

Riches, Judith. Giraffes Have More Fun. LC 91-21184. (Illus.). 32p. (J). (ps-3). 1992. 14.00 (*0-688-11042-8*, Tambourine Bks); lib. bdg. 13.93 (*0-688-11043-6*, Tambourine Bks) Morrow.

Riches, Naomi. Agricultural Revolution in Norfolk. 2nd ed. (Illus.). 194p. 1967. reprint ed. 32.00 (*0-7146-1356-8*, BHA-01356, Pub. by F Cass Pubs UK) Intl Spec Bk.

— Agricultural Revolution in Norfolk. LC 67-20814. (Reprints of Economic Classics Ser.). (Illus.). 1967. reprint ed. 29.50 (*0-678-05082-1*) Kelley.

Riches, Pierre. Back to Basics. (C). 1988. 39.00 (*0-85439-227-0*, Pub. by St Paul Pubns UK) St Mut.

— Back to Basics: Catholic Faith in Today's World. 176p. 1984. pap. 8.95 (*0-8245-0646-4*) Crossroad NY.

Richesin, L. Dale & Bouchard, Larry D., eds. Interpreting Disciples: Practical Theology in the Disciples of Christ. LC 86-30072. 278p. (Orig.). 1987. pap. text ed. 14.95 (*0-87565-072-4*) Tex Christian.

Richesin, L. Dale, jt. ed. see Mahan, Brian.

Richeson, Hawley, ed. see Sanchez, Ray.

Richeson, J. David, jt. auth. see Marino, Michael F., III.

Richeson, J. David, jt. auth. see Marino, Michael F., 3rd.

Richet, Charles. The Natural History of a Savant. Lodge, Oliver J., tr. LC 74-26288. (History, Philosophy & Sociology of Science Ser.). 1975. reprint ed. 23.95 (*0-405-06614-7*) Ayer.

— Thirty Years of Psychical Research: Being a Treatise on Metaphysics. De Brath, Stanley, tr. LC 75-7397. (Perspectives in Psychical Research Ser.). (Illus.). 1975. reprint ed. 54.95 (*0-405-07046-2*) Ayer.

Richet, Xavier. The Hungarian Model. Whitehouse, J. C., tr. (Cambridge Russian, Soviet & Post-Soviet Studies: No. 64). (Illus.). 211p. (C). 1989. 59.95 (*0-521-34314-3*) Cambridge U Pr.

Richetti, John J. Daniel Defoe. (English Authors Ser.: No. 453). 176p. 1987. text ed. 21.95 (*0-8057-6955-2*, Twayne) Macmillan.

— Philosophical Writing: Locke, Berkeley, Hume. 304p. (C). 1983. 37.50 (*0-674-66482-5*) HUP.

— Popular Fiction Before Richardson: Narrative Patterns, 1700-1739. LC 92-9979. 296p. 1992. pap. 24.95 (*0-19-811263-7*, Clarendon Pr) OUP.

Richetti, John J., et al, eds. The Columbia History of the British Novel. LC 92-35749. (C). 1994. 69.95 (*0-231-07858-7*) Col U Pr.

Richey, Charles R. Manual on Employment Discrimination & Civil Rights Actions in the Federal Courts, 1988 Replacement Edition. 630p. 1988. 80.00 (*0-685-28794-7*) Michie Butterworth.

— Manual on Employment Discrimination Law & Civil Rights Actions in the Federal Courts. LC 85-9640. 1985. ring bd. 100.00 (*0-87632-465-0*) Clark Boardman Callaghan.

— Manual on Employment Discrimination Law & Civil Rights Actions in the Federal Courts. 2nd ed. 1994. 140.00 (*0-318-72689-0*) Clark Boardman Callaghan.

Richey, Cheryl, jt. auth. see Gambrill, Eileen.

Richey, Cynthia. The Fashionable Miss Fonteyne. 320p. 1994. mass mkt. 3.99 (*0-8217-4754-1*) Zebra.

— The Heart's Gamble. 352p. 1992. mass mkt. 4.50 (*0-8217-3967-0*) Zebra.

— Love's Masquerade. 1990. 19.95 (*0-8027-1117-0*) Walker & Co.

— The Secret Scribbler. 288p. 1994. mass mkt. 3.99 (*0-8217-4572-7*) Zebra.

Richey, Cynthia K. Programming for Serving Children with Special Needs. LC 93-33365. (ALSC Program Support Publications). 19p. (Orig.). 1993. pap. text ed. 7.00 (*0-8389-5763-3*) ALA.

***Richey, D. Dean.** Activity Based Early Intervention: Strategies for Families, Caregivers, & Interventionists. 288p. 1995. 32.95 (*0-8273-6700-7*) Delmar.

Richey, David & Richey, Fred. Empowerment How to Stay a Knight. Bianchi, Susan & Richey, Josephine, eds. (Illus.). 304p. (Orig.). 1993. 19.95 (*0-930733-13-4*); pap. 14.95 (*0-930733-14-2*) Quality Groups Pub.

Richey, David L., jt. auth. see Forrest, Judith M.

Richey, Fern A. Readers & Doers of the Word...The Fun Way: Three Hundred Sixty-Five Days of Bible-Related Activities for Children. (Illus.). 320p. (Orig.). 1994. pap. 12.95 (*1-884898-02-5*) Eden Pubng NV.

Richey, Franklin D., jt. auth. see Wells, Alexander T.

Richey, Fred, jt. auth. see Richey, David.

Richey, George, jt. auth. see Cosgrave, Patrick.

Richey, Jim, ed. Fine Woodworking on More Proven Shop Tips. LC 89-40573. 96p. 1990. 9.95 (*0-942391-43-8*) Taunton.

— Fine Woodworking on Proven Shop Tips. LC 84-52095. (Illus.). 128p. (Orig.). 1985. pap. 9.95 (*0-918804-32-9*) Taunton.

Richey, Joseph. Riding the Big Earth: Poems 1980-86. (Collected Poems Ser.). 64p. 1987. pap. 5.95 (*0-915032-89-9*) Natl Poet Foun.

Richey, Joseph, ed. see Blue, Sharkmeat, pseud.

Richey, Joseph, ed. see Sikelianos, Eleni.

Richey, Josephine, ed. see Richey, David & Richey, Fred.

Richey, Louis R. & Brody, Lawrence. Comprehensive Deferred Compensation: A Complete Guide to Nonqualified Deferred Compensation. LC 89-61882. 234p. (C). 1989. pap. 32.95 (*0-87218-472-2*) Natl Underwriter.

Richey, Nancy, ed. see Young, Ross.

Richey, Paul, jt. auth. see Franks, Norman.

Richey, Peter P. Counseling--Guidance, Intervention, Skills, Management & Sex Infections. 150p. 1994. 44.50 (*0-7883-0146-2*); pap. 39.50 (*0-7883-0147-0*) ABBE Pubs Assn.

Richey, Rita. Designing Instruction for the Adult Learner: Theory & Practice for Employee Training. 224p. 1992. 69.00 (*0-7494-0477-9*, Pub. by Kogan Page Educ UK) Taylor & Francis.

Richey, Russell E. Early American Methodism: A Reconsideration. LC 91-4373. (Religion in North America Ser.). 160p. 1991. 25.00 (*0-253-35006-9*) Ind U Pr.

Richey, Russell E., jt. ed. see Mullin, Robert B.

Richey, Russell E., et al. Perspectives on American Methodism: Interpretive Essays. Schmidt, Jean M., ed. 384p. (Orig.). 1993. pap. 22.95 (*0-687-30782-1*) Abingdon.

Richey, Terry. The Marketer's Visual Tool Kit. 192p. 1994. 24.95 (*0-8144-0213-5*) AMACOM.

Richey, Virginia H. & Tuten-Puckett, Katharyn. Wordless - Almost Worldless Picture Books: A Guide. (Data Book Ser.). 125p. 1992. lib. bdg. 27.50 (*0-87287-878-3*) Libs Unl.

Richey, Virginia H., jt. auth. see Tuten-Puckett, Katharyn.

Richey, Will. Racism Is a Myth. Selph, Alexa, ed. 96p. (Orig.). 1994. pap. 8.95 (*0-87797-261-3*) Cherokee.

Richfield, Gloria, jt. auth. see Richfield, Lew.

***Richfield, Lew & Richfield, Gloria.** Together Forever: One Hundred & Twenty-Five Ways to Have a Vital & Romantic Marriage. LC 94-43296. 1995. write for info. (*0-385-31411-6*) Delacorte.

Richford, F. G. Common Sense Occultism. 1972. 69.95 (*0-87968-911-0*) Gordon Pr.

Richgeis, Donald J., jt. auth. see McGee, Lea M.

Richgels, Donald J., jt. auth. see McGee, Lea M.

***Richharia, M.** Satellite Communication Systems: Design Principles. 1995. text ed. 55.00 (*0-07-052374-6*) McGraw.

***Richie.** Japanese Tattoo. 1980. pap. 22.50 (*0-8348-0149-3*) Weatherhill.

Richie, Andrew. Major Taylor: The Extraordinary Career of a Champion Bicycle Racer. LC 87-70730. (Illus.). 304p. (Orig.). 1988. 19.95 (*0-933201-14-1*) Bicycle Books.

Richie, Anne T., ed. see Thackeray, William Makepeace.

Richie, Beth, ed. see Refugee Women in Development Staff.

Richie, Claude G. Kemal Ataturk, Father of the Turkish Republic. Rahmas, Sigurd C., ed. (Outstanding Personalities Ser.: No. 92). 32p. (gr. 7-12). 1982. 4.95 (*0-87157-592-2*) SamHar Pr.

***Richie, David.** Health & Medicine. LC 94-17793. (Life 100 Years Ago Ser.). (J). 1994. write for info. (*0-7910-2839-9*) Chelsea Hse.

Richie, David S. Memories & Meditations of a Workcamper. LC 73-84213. 36p. (Orig.). 1973. pap. 3.00 (*0-87574-190-8*) Pendle Hill.

Richie, Donald. Different People: Pictures of Some Japanese. LC 87-81681. 198p. 1988. pap. 16.95 (*0-87011-820-X*) Kodansha.

— The Films of Akira Kurosawa. rev. ed. (Illus.). 264p. (C). 1984. pap. 19.00 (*0-520-05191-2*) U CA Pr.

— Geisha, Gangster, Neighbor, Nun: Scenes from Japanese Lives. Orig. Title: Different People. 212p. 1991. pap. 7.95 (*4-7700-1526-7*) Kodansha.

— The Honorable Visitors. (Illus.). 160p. (Orig.). 1994. pap. 12.95 (*0-8048-1941-6*) C E Tuttle.

— The Inland Sea. Lancet, ed. 304p. 1993. pap. 9.00 (*4-7700-1751-0*) Kodansha.

— The Inland Sea. 1994. 20.50 (*0-8446-6723-4*) Peter Smith.

— Introducing Japan. Pockell & Katayama, eds. (Illus.). 72p. 1994. pap. 15.00 (*4-7700-1791-X*) Kodansha.

— Introducing Japan. (Illus.). Date not set. 24.00 (*0-87011-833-1*) Kodansha.

— Introducing Tokyo. LC 86-40436. (Introducing Japan - Introducing Kyoto Ser.). (Illus.). 88p. 1987. 24.00 (*0-87011-806-4*) Kodansha.

— Introducing Tokyo. Pockell & Katayama, eds. (Illus.). 80p. 1994. pap. 15.00 (*4-7700-1798-7*) Kodansha.

— Japanese Cinema: An Introduction. (Images of Asia Ser.). (Illus.). 116p. 1990. 12.95 (*0-19-584950-7*) OUP.

— A Lateral View: Essays on Culture & Style in Contemporary Japan. LC 91-47645. 248p. (Orig.). 1992. reprint ed. pap. 10.95 (*0-9628137-4-5*) Stone Bridge Pr.

— Ozu: His Life & Films. (Illus.). 1974. pap. 14.00 (*0-520-03277-2*) U CA Pr.

— A Taste of Japan. Tsuizaki & Pocknell, eds. (Illus.). 112p. 1993. pap. 13.00 (*4-7700-1707-3*) Kodansha.

— Tokyo Nights. 118p. 1994. pap. 9.95 (*0-8048-1923-8*) C E Tuttle.

— Zen Inklings: Some Stories, Fables, Parables & Sermons. 128p. (C). 1992. reprint ed. pap. 9.95 (*0-8348-0230-9*) Weatherhill.

Richie, Donald, ed. Rashomon. (Films in Print Ser.). 226p. (C). 1987. text ed. 35.00 (*0-8135-1179-8*); pap. text ed. 16.00 (*0-8135-1180-1*) Rutgers U Pr.

Richie, Donald, jt. auth. see Anderson, Joseph L.

Richie, Donald, jt. auth. see Buruma, Ian.

Richie, Donald, tr. see Kurosawa, Akira.

Richie, Donald A. U. S. Constitution. (Know Your Government Ser.). (Illus.). 120p. (J). (gr. 5 up). 1989. 14.95 (*0-87754-894-3*) Chelsea Hse.

— The Young Oxford Companion to the Congress of the United States. LC 93-6466. (J). (gr. 5 up). 1993. 35.00 (*0-19-507777-6*) OUP.

Richie, Jerome, jt. ed. see Garnick, Marc.

Richie, Jim, ed. Fine Woodworking on Proven Shop Tips. 1991. 18.50 (*0-8446-6440-5*) Peter Smith.

Richie, Lionel. Lionel Richie Songbook. (Illus.). 144p. 24.95 (*0-89524-220-6*); pap. text ed. 16.95 (*0-89524-248-6*, 9970) Cherry Lane.

Richie, Lloyd F. Table Top Lightning. 33p. 1992. 9.95 (*0-914119-26-5*) Tesla Bk Co.

***Richie, Nicholas D. & Alperin, Diane E.** Innovation & Change in the Human Services. (Illus.). 162p. 1992. pap. 19.95 (*0-398-06400-8*) C C Thomas.

— Innovation & Change in the Human Services. (Illus.). 162p. (C). 1992. text ed. 36.95x (*0-398-05763-X*) C C Thomas.

***Richie, Susan K.** Your Opportunities in the Fashion World. (Illus.). 8p. 1994. pap. 2.00 (*0-9626591-8-5*) Energeia Pub.

Richier, Maurice, ed. see De Nerval, Gerard.

Richir, M. Au-Dela Du Renversement Copernicien. (Phaenomenologica Ser.: No. 73). 1977. lib. bdg. 94.00 (*90-247-1903-8*) Kluwer Ac.

Richison, Marjorie W. Living Near to Nature's Heart: The History of the Pelican Lake Outing Club. 213p. 1992. 29.95 (*1-880458-00-4*) Kingswood.

Richiusa, Gordon F., ed. see Classic, Carl.

***Richler.** Jacob Two-Two & the Dinosaur. 1995. pap. 3.99 (*0-679-87042-3*) Random.

Richler, Binyamin. Hebrew Manuscripts: A Treasured Legacy. (Illus.). 1990. 29.95 (*0-87306-505-0*) Feldheim.

Richler, Binyamin & Brody, Robert. Hebrew Manuscripts: A Treasured Legacy. Shoshana, Abraham, ed. LC 89-64170. 166p. (C). 1990. 29.95 (*1-881255-05-0*) OFEQ Inst.

Richler, Daniel. Kicking Tomorrow. 1992. 20.50 (*0-679-41188-7*) Random.

Richler, Mordecai. The Apprenticeship of Duddy Kravitz. 320p. 1991. pap. 9.95 (*0-14-015296-2*, Penguin Bks) Viking Penguin.

— Jacob Two-Two Meets the Hooded Fang. (J). (gr. 4-7). 1994. pap. 3.50 (*0-679-85403-7*) Knopf Bks Yng Read.

— Jacob Two-Two Meets the Hooded Fang. (Illus.). 96p. (J). (gr. 2-7). 1994. pap. 3.50 (*0-685-71038-6*) Random Bks Yng Read.

— The Language of Signs. 1992. pap. 22.50 (*0-679-41246-8*) McKay.

— Oh Canada! Oh Quebec! 1992. 20.00 (*0-685-53593-2*) Knopf.

Richler, Mordecai, ed. Writers on World War Two: An Anthology. LC 92-50620. 1993. reprint ed. pap. 16.00 (*0-679-74234-4*, Vin) Random.

Richler, Mordechai. This Year in Jerusalem. LC 94-10455. 1994. 23.00 (*0-679-43610-3*) Knopf.

Richlin, Amy. The Garden of Priapus: Sexuality & Aggression in Roman Humor. rev. ed. 352p. 1992. pap. 16.95 (*0-19-506873-4*) OUP.

— Juvenal Satura Six. (Latin Commentaries Ser.). 107p. (Orig.). (C). 1986. pap. text ed. 6.00 (*0-929524-42-X*) Bryn Mawr Commentaries.

Richlin, Amy, ed. Pornography & Representation in Greece & Rome. (Illus.). 352p. (C). 1992. pap. text ed. 19.95 (*0-19-506723-1*) OUP.

Richlin, Amy, jt. ed. see Rabinowitz, Nancy S.

Richlin-Klonsky, Judith, jt. ed. see Schwartz, Rosalind.

***Richlin, Laurie, ed.** Preparing Faculty for the New Conceptions of Scholarship. LC 85-644763. (New Directions for Teaching & Learning Ser.: No. 54). 113p. 1993. pap. 16.95 (*1-55542-726-X*) Jossey-Bass.

***Richlin, Laurie & Manning, Brenda.** Improving a College/University Teaching Evaluation System: A Comprehensive, Developmental Curriculum for Faculty & Administrators. (Curriculum for Change Ser.). 250p. (C). 1995. 36.00 (*0-9645071-0-2*) Allnce Pub.

Richling, B., jt. ed. see Koos, W.

Richling, C. & Drewitz, I. Dictionary of Cable Engineering: English-German-French. 610p. (ENG, FRE & GER.). 1976. pap. 60.00 (*3-87097-072-3*) IBD Ltd.

Richling, Christel. Woerterbuch der Kabeltechnik. (ENG, FRE & GER.). 1976. pap. 95.00 (*0-8288-5775-X*, M6988) Fr & Eur.

Richman. Diagnostic Gastro Pathology. 1993. 250.00 (*0-685-65405-2*) Mosby Yr Bk.

Richman & Reynolds. Understanding Conflict of Laws. 1984. write for info. (*0-8205-0061-5*) Bender.

Richman, Barry M. & Farmer, Richard N. Leadership, Goals & Power in Higher Education: A Contingency & Open-Systems Approach to Effective Management. LC 74-9112. (Jossey-Bass Higher Education Ser.). 380p. reprint ed. pap. 108.30 (*0-317-20799-7*, 2023878) Bks Demand.

Richman, Beth & Hassol, Susan. Everyday Chemicals. 2nd ed. LC 89-51685. (Creating a Healthy World - 101 Practical Tips for Home & Work Ser.). (Illus.). 68p. 1989. pap. 3.95 (*0-9622492-4-6*) Windstar Foundation.

— Everyday Chemicals: Creating a Healthy World. Katzenberger, John, ed. (Illus.). 56p. 1989. write for info. (*0-318-65067-3*) Windstar Foundation.

Richman, Beth, jt. auth. see Hassol, Susan.

Richman, Brenda. From Disappointment to Joy: Studies in Ruth. 65p. (Orig.). 1993. pap. 3.95 (*0-943167-22-1*) Faith & Fellowship Pr.

Richman, Dan. From Aaron to Zoe: Fifteen Thousand Great Baby Names. LC 92-44632. 1993. pap. 11.95 (*0-316-74444-1*) Little.

Richman, Daniel A. James E. Carter: Thirty-Ninth President of the United States. Young, Richard G., ed. LC 88-24562. (Presidents of the United States Ser.). (Illus.). (J). (gr. 5-9). 1989. lib. bdg. 17.26 (*0-944483-24-0*) Garrett Ed Corp.

Richman, Darryl. Bock. (Classic Beer Style Ser.). (Illus.). 165p. (Orig.). 1994. pap. 11.95 (*0-937381-39-X*) Brewers Pubns.

Richman, David. Laughter, Pain, & Wonder: Shakespeare's Comedies & the Audience in the Theater. LC 89-40413. 200p. 1990. 36.50 (*0-87413-388-2*) U Delaware Pr.

Richman, Elizabeth. Be Jubilant, My Heart. LC 93-10926. 1993. 9.95 (*1-56233-039-X*) Star Song TN.

— Be Jubilant My Heart. 1994. pap. 7.99 (*1-56233-301-1*, Star Song Contemp) Star Song TN.

Richman, Ellen. Spotlight on Computer Literacy. (J). (gr. 6-8). 1984. pap. 14.00 (*0-07-480653-X*) McGraw.

Richman, Elliot. Honorable Manhood: Poems of Eros & Dust. LC 93-79281. 72p. (Orig.). 1994. pap. 8.95 (*1-878580-50-7*) Asylum Arts.

— The World Dancer. LC 93-71191. 112p. (Orig.). 1993. pap. 9.95 (*1-878580-44-2*) Asylum Arts.

Richman, Elliott. A Bucket of Nails. 20p. (Orig.). 1990. pap. 3.00 (*0-318-50052-3*) Samisdat.

— Retirement & Other Myths: Musings on the Leisurely Life with a Dash of Humor & Advice. LC 93-43072. 150p. 1994. pap. 9.95 (*1-56875-074-9*) R & E Pubs.

Richman, Fred, jt. auth. see Bridges, Douglas.

Richman, George J. History of Hancock County, Indiana. (Illus.). 815p. 1992. reprint ed. lib. bdg. 79.50 (*0-8328-2542-5*) Higginson Bk Co.

Richman, Harold. Truck Company Fireground Operations. 2nd ed. (Illus.). 200p. 1986. 38.00 (*0-87765-237-6*, FSP-76A) Natl Fire Prot.

Richman, Harold, jt. auth. see National Fire Protection Association Staff.

***Richman, Howard.** Fat & the Art of Focusing: Three Easy Non-Diet Steps to Permanently End the Yo-Yo Cycle. (Illus.). 150p. (Orig.). 1995. pap. 14.95 (*1-882060-76-8*) Sound Feelings.

— Story of a Bill: Legalizing Homeschooling in Pennsylvania. 152p. (Orig.). 1989. pap. 6.95 (*0-929446-01-1*) PA Homeschoolers.

— Stutter Control Drill: Mastering Elements of Fluent Speech. 12p. 1989. student ed 5.00 (*0-929060-75-X*) Sound Feelings.

Richman, Howard, ed. Guide to L. A. Music Teachers 1994: Your One-Stop Source for Finding Music Instruction in Every Category, from Accordion to Zither. 32p. (Orig.). 1994. pap. 5.95 (*1-882060-77-6*) Sound Feelings.

— Super Sight-Reading Secrets: An Innovative, Step-by-Step Program for Musical Keyboard Players of All Levels. 3rd rev. ed. LC 85-90522. 52p. (C). 1986. pap. 8.00 (*0-9615963-0-9*) Sound Feelings.

Richman, Howard B. & Richman, Susan P. The Three R's at Home. LC 88-90813. 228p. (Orig.). 1988. pap. 7.95 (*0-929446-00-3*) PA Homeschoolers.

Richman, Irving B. California under Spain & Mexico, 1535-1847. 1992. reprint ed. lib. bdg. 75.00 (*0-7812-5078-1*) Rprt Serv.

— From Discovery Through Kino: California under Spain & Mexico, 1535-1847. 75p. reprint ed. pap. 10.00 (*1-877959-00-6*) D Henson Bks.

— Rhode Island: A Study in Separatism. LC 72-3749. (American Commonwealths Ser.: No. 17). reprint ed. 42.50 (*0-404-57217-0*) AMS Pr.

Richman, Irwin, jt. ed. see Secor, Robert A.

Richman, J. William. Pureed Foods with Substance & Style. LC 93-43913. 1994. 49.00 (*0-8342-0554-8*) Aspen Pub.

***Richman, Jan.** Because the Brain Can Be Talked into Anything: Poems. LC 94-37532. 64p. 1995. text ed. 15.95 (*0-8071-1993-8*); pap. 8.95 (*0-8071-1994-6*) La State U Pr.

Richman, Jeanne, ed. see League of Women Voters of New York State Education Fund Staff.

Richman, John & Draycott, A. T., eds. Stone's Justices' Manual, 1993, 3 vols., Set. 7700p. 1993. 403.00 (*0-406-38627-7*) Butterworth Legal Pubs.

Richman, Jordan, ed. see Kule, Harvey.

Richman, Joseph. Family Therapy for Suicidal People. 224p. 1985. 30.95 (*0-8261-5010-1*) Springer Pub.

— Preventing Elderly Suicide: Overcoming Personal Despair, Professional Indifference, & Social Bias. LC 92-35995. (Death & Suicide Ser.: Vol. 11). 176p. 1993. 29.95 (*0-8261-7480-9*) Springer Pub.

Richman, Karin, tr. see Clahsen, Harald.

Richman, Larry L., ed. Prominent Men & Women of Provo, Utah. 188p. 1983. 10.95 (*0-941846-00-8*) Richman Pub.

— Tales of the Cakchiquels. 102p. 1984. 9.95 (*0-941846-01-6*) Richman Pub.

Richman, Linda. Listen to This. (Illus.). 294p. 1987. spiral bd. 29.00 (*0-9609160-2-4*) Mayer-Johnson.

— Stories about Me. (Illus.). 220p. 1989. spiral bd. 24.00 (*0-9609160-5-9*) Mayer-Johnson.

Richman, Linda G. Everybody's Doing It! (Illus.). 440p. (Orig.). 1992. spiral bd. 29.00 (*0-9609160-9-1*) Mayer-Johnson.

— Introduction to Kitchen Appliances. (Illus.). 144p. (Orig.). 1992. ring bd. 24.00 (*0-9609160-8-3*) Mayer-Johnson.

— Listen to These Nouns. (Illus.). 288p. (Orig.). 1994. spiral bd. 29.00 (*1-884135-01-3*) Mayer-Johnson.

— Listen to Verbs Those. (Illus.). 264p. (Orig.). 1994. spiral bd. 29.00 (*1-884135-02-1*) Mayer-Johnson.

— This is the One I Want. (Illus.). 172p. 1987. spiral bd. 24.00 (*0-9609160-3-2*) Mayer-Johnson.

***Richman, Marcella.** North Dakota...Where Food Is Love. 200p. 1994. pap. 10.95 (*0-9642215-0-0*) N Dakota Ckbook.

***Richman, Mina.** Words from the Heart & Mind. 1995. 8.95 (*0-8062-5155-7*) Carlton.

Richman, Nancy, jt. auth. see Glantz, Coralie H.

Richman, Naomi & Lansdown, Richard, eds. Problems of Preschool Children. LC 87-36538. 245p. 1988. text ed. 94.95 (*0-471-91460-6*) Wiley.

Richman, Naomi, jt. auth. see McGuire, Jacqueline.

Richman, Naomi, et al. Pre-School to School: A Behavioural Study. (Behavioral Development Monographs). 1982. text ed. 92.00 (*0-12-587940-7*) Acad Pr.

***Richman, Paul.** Diagnostic Cytopathology. 1994. vdisk 400.00 (*1-56815-031-8*) Image Premast.

Richman, Paula. Women, Branch Stories, & Religious Rhetoric in a Tamil Buddhist Text. LC 87-31551. (Foreign & Comparative Studies Program, South Asian Ser.: No. 12). 288p. (Orig.). (C). 1988. 19.00 (*0-915984-90-3*) Syracuse U Foreign Comp.

Richman, Paula, ed. Many Ramayanas: The Diversity of a Narrative Tradition in South Asia. LC 91-7273. 280p. 1991. 40.00 (*0-520-07281-2*); pap. 16.00 (*0-520-07589-7*) U CA Pr.

Richman, Robert J. Prolegomena to a Theory of Practical Reasoning. 1983. lib. bdg. 80.00 (*90-277-1548-3*) Kluwer Ac.

Richman, Sheldon. Separating School & State: How to Liberate America's Families. 150p. (Orig.). 1994. text ed. 22.95 (*0-9640447-1-4*); pap. text ed. 14.95 (*0-9640447-2-2*) Future of Freedom.

Richman, Sidney. Bernard Malamud. (United States Authors Ser.: No. 109). 1966. text ed. 19.95 (*0-8057-0472-8*, Twayne) Macmillan.

Richman, Stephen H. Conversational Spanish for Everyday Use. 304p. (C). 1994. per., pap. text ed. 36.95 (*0-8403-9510-8*) Kendall-Hunt.

Richman, Susan. Writing from Home: A Portfolio of Homeschooled Student Writing. (Illus.). 372p. (Orig.). 1990. 16.95 (*0-929446-02-X*); pap. 8.95 (*0-929446-03-8*) PA Homeschoolers.

Richman, Susan P., jt. auth. see Richman, Howard B.

***Richman, Ted.** The Oxford Gourmet Cookbook. LC 94-23174. 262p. (Orig.). 1994. 21.95 (*1-879094-36-3*) Momentum Bks.

Richman, William M. & Reynolds, William L. Understanding Conflict of Laws. 2nd ed. LC 92-45658. 1993. pap. write for info. (*0-8205-0062-3*) Bender.

Richmaw, Elliot. Blastin' Out of Abilene. 1988. 3.00 (*0-685-25017-2*) Windless Orchard.

Richmers, C. Mabel & Geiger, Wilhelm, trs. Culavamsa, 2 vols. (C). 1930. 38.00 (0-86013-013-4, Pub. by Pali Text) Wisdom MA.

Richmond. Cationic Surfactants: Organic Chemistry. (Surfactant Science Ser.: Vol. 34). 320p. 1990. 165.00 (0-8247-8381-6) Dekker.

— Decorative Painting. 1995. (0-7858-0320-3) Bk Sales Inc.

***Richmond & Cox.** The Web Developer's Guide. (Illus.). 800p. (Orig.). 1995. pap. 39.99 (0-614-07264-6) Sams.

Richmond & Gorham. Communication, Learning, & Affects. pap. 29.95 (0-8087-4699-5) Burgess MN Intl.

Richmond, jt. auth. see Clevely.

Richmond, jt. auth. see McCroskey.

Richmond, et al. Communication Problems of Children. pap. 29.95 (0-8087-7644-4) Burgess MN Intl.

Richmond, A. Readings in Race & Ethnic Relations. LC 78-161451. 1972. 144.00 (0-08-016213-4, Pub. by Pergamon Repr UK) Franklin.

Richmond-Abbott, Marie. Masculine & Feminine: Gender Roles Over the Life Cycle. 2nd ed. 1992. pap. text ed. write for info. (0-07-052357-6) McGraw.

Richmond, Al. Cowboys, Miners, Presidents & Kings: The Story of the Grand Canyon Railway. rev. ed. LC 89-80211. (Illus.). 230p. 1989. 19.95 (0-933269-03-X); pap. 14.95 (0-933269-02-1) Gd Canyon Railway.

— Rails to the Rim: Milepost Guide to the Grand Canyon Railway. rev. ed. LC 94-75686. (Illus.). 136p. 1994. pap. 6.95 (0-933269-32-3) Gd Canyon Railway.

Richmond, Alexander B. Narrative of the Condition of the Manufacturing Population: And the Proceedings of the Government Which Led to the State Trials in Scotland. LC 68-56571. (Reprints of Economic Classics Ser.). 1971. reprint ed. 37.50 (0-678-00676-8) Kelley.

Richmond, Allen E. Calculus for Electronics. 3rd ed. LC 81-23642. 512p. 1983. text ed. 39.95 (0-07-052353-3) McGraw.

Richmond, Allen E. & Hecht, Gary. Calculus for Electronics. 4th ed. 544p. (C). 1989. text ed. 34.95 (0-07-052355-X) McGraw.

Richmond, Amos. Handbook of Microalgal Mass Culture. 576p. 1986. 279.00 (0-8493-3240-0, SH389, CRC Reprint) Franklin.

Richmond, Arline L. Yenlo & the Mystic Brotherhood. reprint ed. spiral bd. 8.25 (0-7873-0716-5) Mokelumne.

Richmond, Ben, ed. see Coffin, Levi.

Richmond, Bert O. & Kicklighter, Richard. Children's Adaptive Behavior Scale. 32p. (Orig.). 1980. pap. 29.95 (0-89334-054-5); 24.95 (0-89334-055-3) Humanics Ltd.

Richmond, Bert O. & Kicklighter, Richard H. Children's Adaptive Behavior Report. 16p. (Orig.). 1982. pap. 1.00 (0-89334-030-8) Humanics Ltd.

— Children's Adaptive Behavior Scale: Administrator's Manual. rev. ed. 42p. (Orig.). (C). 1983. pap. 14.95 (0-89334-040-5) Humanics Ltd.

Richmond, C. R., ed. Health & Ecological Implications of Radioactively Contaminated Environments. (Proceedings Ser.: No. 12). 233p. (Orig.). 1991. pap. text ed. 25.00 (0-929600-14-2) NCRP Pubns.

Richmond, C. R., et al, eds. Mammalian Cells: Probes & Problems, Proceedings. LC 75-600009. (ERDA Symposium Ser.). 324p. 1975. pap. 16.00 (0-685-01478-9, CONF-731007); fiche 6.50 (0-87079-267-9, CONF-731007) DOE.

Richmond, C. W. & Vallette, H. F. A History of the County of Du Page, Illinois. 212p. 1994. reprint ed. lib. bdg. 29.50 (0-8328-4015-7) Higginson Bk Co.

Richmond, Carl. Twisted: One Drug Addict's Desperate Struggle for Recovery. LC 91-50641. 290p. 1991. pap. 11.95 (1-879360-08-X) Noble Pr.

Richmond, Carolyn, ed. see Clarin, Leopoldo A.

Richmond, Chandler S. Beyond the Spring: Cordelia Stanwood of Birdsacre. rev. ed. LC 88-83667. (Illus.). 176p. (Orig.). 1989. pap. 12.95 (0-932448-03-8) Latona Pr.

— Beyond the Spring: Cordelia Stanwood of Birdsacre. 2nd rev. ed. LC 88-83667. (Illus.). 176p. (Orig.). 1989. 24.95 (0-932448-02-X) Latona Pr.

Richmond, Clare. Hawaiian Heat. (American Romance Ser.). 1993. mass mkt. 3.39 (0-373-16476-9, 1-16476-3) Harlequin Bks.

***Richmond, Clint.** Selena. 1995. mass mkt. 5.99 (0-671-54522-1) PB.

Richmond, Colin. The Paston Family in the Fifteenth Century: The First Phase. (Illus.). 290p. (C). 1990. 69.95 (0-521-38502-4) Cambridge U Pr.

Richmond, Colin, jt. ed. see Rosenthal, Joel.

Richmond, Cricket & Valletti, Ginny. Secrets of Sizzlin' Sex: The Take Charge, Batteries-Not-Included, Adult Beducation Playshop of Sensual Satisfaction & 100 Percent Fat Free Fun, with or Without a Red Hot Lover, As Revealed by the Babes in Joyland. 192p. 1994. 14.95 (0-934061-23-8) Hourglass Bk.

Richmond, Don. Some Conversations with an Old Man & Other Poems & Songs. 67p. 1987. pap. write for info. (0-943909-02-3) Gibbs Assocs.

Richmond-Donahue, Dick & Richmond-Donahue, Leigh. Blindsided. 172p. (Orig.). 1993. pap. 10.95 (0-943975-03-4) Interdimens Sci.

Richmond-Donahue, Leigh, jt. auth. see Richmond-Donahue, Dick.

Richmond, Doug. How to Disappear Completely & Never Be Found. LC 94-17639. 1994. pap. 6.95 (0-8065-1559-7, Citadel Pr) Carol Pub Group.

Richmond, Douglas. Carlos Pellegrini & the Crisis of the Argentine Elites, 1880-1916. LC 88-34032. 206p. 1989. text ed. 49.95 (0-275-93288-5, C3288, Praeger Pubs) Greenwood.

Richmond, Douglas W. Venustiano Carranza's Nationalist Struggle, 1893-1920. LC 83-3652. (Illus.). 347p. reprint ed. pap. 98.90 (0-8357-2942-7, 2039198) Bks Demand.

Richmond, Douglas W., ed. Essays on the Mexican War. LC 86-5886. (Walter Prescott Webb Memorial Lectures: No. 20). (Illus.). 120p. 1986. 17.50 (0-89096-291-X) Tex A&M Univ Pr.

Richmond, Edmun B. A Comparative Survey of Seven Adult Functional Literacy Programs in Sub-Saharan Africa. (Illus.). 122p. (Orig.). (C). 1986. pap. text ed. 17.00 (0-8191-5521-7) U Pr of Amer.

***Richmond, Elmore, Jr.** The Power Pack - 101 Points to Social & Economic Justice. Miles, Linda B., ed. (Illus.). 300p. (Orig.). 1994. pap. text ed. 12.95 (1-886636-50-8) Victory Pubng.

***Richmond, Elmore, Jr. & Richmond, Mark A.** Youth Walk Through the Power Pack. 50p. 1994. pap. text ed. 2.50 (1-886636-51-6) Victory Pubng.

Richmond, Elmore, Jr., jt. auth. see Woodard, Michael D.

Richmond, Emma. Deliberate Provocation. large type ed. (Romance Ser.). 1992. 17.95 (0-263-13101-7, Pub. by Mills & Boon Ltd UK) Chivers N Amer.

— Deliberate Provocation: Presents Plus. (Presents Ser.). 1994. mass mkt. 2.99 (0-373-11624-1, 1011624-3) Harlequin Bks.

— A Family Closeness. (Romance Ser.). 1995. mass mkt. 2.99 (0-373-03374-5, 1-03374-5) Harlequin Bks.

— Fate of Happiness. large type ed. (Romance Ser.). 1993. 17.95 (0-263-13267-6, Pub. by Mills & Boon Ltd UK) Chivers N Amer.

— Fiery Attraction. large type ed. 1994. 17.95 (0-263-13661-2, Pub. by Mills & Boon Ltd UK) Chivers N Amer.

— The Gentle Trap. large type ed. 1990. reprint ed. lib. bdg. 18.95 (0-263-12273-5, Pub. by Mills & Boon UK) Thorndike Pr.

— Love of My Heart. (Romance Ser.). 1995. pap. 2.99 (0-373-03349-4, 1-03349-7) Harlequin Bks.

— More Than a Dream. (Presents Ser.). 1994. mass mkt. 2.99 (0-373-11669-1, 1-11669-8) Harlequin Bks.

— A Stranger's Trust. (Presents Ser.). 1993. mass mkt. 2.99 (0-373-11582-2, 1-11582-3) Harlequin Bks.

***Richmond, Emma, et al.** Christmas Journeys. 1995. pap. 4.99 (0-373-15271-X, 1-15271-9) Harlequin Bks.

Richmond, Farley, tr. see Thakur, Asaita.

Richmond, Farley P., et al, eds. Indian Theater: Traditions of Performance. LC 89-28699. (Illus.). 496p. 1990. text ed. 48.00 (0-8248-1190-9); pap. text ed. 24.95 (0-8248-1322-7) UH Pr.

Richmond, Frances J., jt. ed. see Peterson, Barry W.

Richmond, Frederick K. & Steketee, Martha W. State of the Child: A Profile of Pennsylvania's Children (A 1993 Factbook) (Illus.). 192p. (Orig.). 1993. pap. 20.00 (0-9637063-0-6) PA Ptnership.

— The State of the Child in Pennsylvania: A 1995 Kidscount Fact Book. 260p. 1995. pap. 29.00 (0-9645008-1-7) PA Ptnership.

Richmond, Gail L. Federal Tax Research: Guide to Materials & Techniques. 4th ed. (University Textbook Ser.). 189p. 1990. pap. text ed. 14.25 (0-88277-801-3) Foundation Pr.

Richmond, Gary. All God's Creatures. 1991. 8.99 (0-8499-3251-3) Word Inc.

— Backyard Safari. (J). (ps-3). 1990. write for info. (0-8499-0741-1) Word Inc.

— Barnaby Goes Wild, No. 7. (J). (gr. 1-5). 1991. text ed. 6.99 (0-8499-0914-7) Word Inc.

— The Divorce Decision. 215p. 1988. pap. write for info. (0-8499-3104-5) Word Inc.

— The Early Bird. 32p. (J). 1992. 7.99 (0-8499-0924-4) Word Inc.

— The Forgotten Friend. (J). (gr. 1-5). 1991. text ed. 6.99 (0-8499-0913-9) Word Inc.

— Henry & the Great Flood. 32p. (J). 1990. write for info. (0-8499-0745-4) Word Inc.

— Howard the Horrible Gets Even. 32p. (J). 1990. 6.99 (0-8499-0744-6) Word Inc.

— Life Is a Zoo - No Matter What Side of the Cage You're On. 200p. (Orig.). 1992. pap. 8.99 (0-89283-760-8, Vine Bks) Servant.

— Miss Otter Goes to the Movies. (J). 1990. 6.99 (0-8499-0743-8) Word Inc.

— Please Don't Feed the Bears. 1990. 12.99 (0-8499-0748-9); pap. write for info. (0-8499-3193-2) Word Inc.

— Prodigal Wolf. (J). 1990. 6.99 (0-8499-0746-2) Word Inc.

— A Scary Night at the Zoo. (J). 1990. write for info. (0-8499-0742-X) Word Inc.

— Successful Single Parenting. 258p. (Orig.). 1989. pap. 7.99 (0-89081-768-5) Harvest Hse.

— View from the Zoo. 206p. 1987. pap. write for info. (0-8499-3084-7) Word Inc.

— Zookeeper Looks at Bears. (Illus.). (J). (ps). 1991. lib. bdg. 3.99 (0-8499-0860-4) Word Inc.

— Zookeeper Looks at Big & Little Animals. (Illus.). (J). (ps). 1991. lib. bdg. 3.99 (0-8499-0887-6) Word Inc.

— Zookeeper Looks at Big Cats. (Illus.). (J). (ps). 1991. lib. bdg. 3.99 (0-8499-0862-0) Word Inc.

— Zookeeper Looks at Elephants. (Illus.). (J). (ps). 1991. lib. bdg. 3.99 (0-8499-0888-4) Word Inc.

— Zookeeper Looks at Monkeys. (J). 1991. pap. 3.99 (0-8499-0861-2) Word Inc.

— Zookeeper Looks at Mother & Baby Animals. (J). 1991. pap. 3.99 (0-8499-0863-9) Word Inc.

***Richmond, Gary & Bode, Lisa.** Ounce of Prevention: Divorce-Proofing Your Marriage. 220p. 1995. pap. 9.99 (0-89283-804-3, Vine Bks) Servant.

Richmond-Garza, Elizabeth M. Forgotten Cites - Sights: Interpretation & the Power of Classical Citation in Renaissance English Tragedy. LC 93-37795. (Renaissance & Baroque Studies & Texts: Vol. 13). 264p. (C). 1995. text ed. 44.95 (0-8204-2284-3) P Lang Pubs.

Richmond, Grace. The Cottage in the Wood. large type ed. (Linford Romance Library). 1991. pap. 13.95 (0-7089-7120-2) Ulverscroft.

— The Doctor's Secret. large type ed. LC 93-39311. 1994. 19.95 (0-7927-1911-5, Curley Lrg Print); pap. 17.95 (0-7927-1910-7, Curley Lrg Print) Chivers N Amer.

— Don't Cling to the Past. large type ed. (Linford Romance Library). 272p. 1988. pap. 11.95 (0-7089-6481-8, Trailtree Bookshop) Ulverscroft.

— Fugitive from Love. large type ed. (Linford Romance Library). 272p. 1992. pap. 14.95 (0-7089-7295-0, Trailtree Bookshop) Ulverscroft.

— The Love Race. large type ed. (Linford Romance Library). 304p. 1992. pap. 14.95 (0-7089-7276-4, Linford) Ulverscroft.

— Nurse to Doctor James. large type ed. (Linford Romance Library). 1989. pap. 11.95 (0-7089-6792-2, Linford) Ulverscroft.

— The Reluctant Heir. large type ed. (Linford Romance Library). 1990. pap. 12.95 (0-7089-6948-8, Trailtree Bookshop) Ulverscroft.

— The Touch of Your Hand. large type ed. LC 93-800. 1993. pap. 17.95 (0-7927-1622-1, Curley Lrg Print) Chivers N Amer.

— Vision of Love. large type ed. (Linford Romance Library). 272p. 1988. pap. 11.95 (0-7089-6549-0, Linford) Ulverscroft.

— Yesterday's Love. large type ed. (Linford Romance Library). 1991. pap. 13.95 (0-7089-7052-4) Ulverscroft.

Richmond, Grace S. Mrs. Red Pepper. 23.95 (0-89190-493-X, Am Repr) Amereon Ltd.

— Red Pepper Burns. reprint ed. lib. bdg. 19.95 (0-89190-491-3, Rivercity Pr) Amereon Ltd.

— Red Pepper's Patients. reprint ed. lib. bdg. 21.95 (0-89190-492-1, Rivercity Pr) Amereon Ltd.

Richmond, Graces S. Brotherly House. 1988. pap. 2.95 (0-345-35555-5, Ballantine Epiphany) Ballantine.

Richmond, H. I. Richmond Family Records, Vol. I: Maryland, Virginia, New England, Ireland & Somerset. 232p. 1994. reprint ed. lib. bdg. 47.00 (0-8328-4133-1); reprint ed. pap. 37.00 (0-8328-4134-X) Higginson Bk Co.

— Richmond Family Records, Vol. II: The Richmonds Alias Webb, of Wiltshire, England. 265p. 1994. reprint ed. lib. bdg. 52.00 (0-8328-4132-3); reprint ed. pap. 42.00 (0-685-75323-9) Higginson Bk Co.

— Richmond Family Records, Vol. III: The Richmonds of Wiltshire, England. 327p. 1994. reprint ed. lib. bdg. 59.50 (0-8328-4129-3); reprint ed. pap. 49.50 (0-8328-4130-7) Higginson Bk Co.

Richmond, H. M. Renaissance Landscapes: English Lyrics in a European Tradition. 1973. pap. text ed. 33.85 (90-279-2470-8) Mouton.

Richmond, Helen. Isaac Hull: A Forgotten American Hero. Anderson, Leslie J., ed. (Illus.). 78p. (Orig.). 1983. pap. text ed. 1.00 (0-913079-00-6) USS Constitution MFI.

Richmond, Herbert W. Sea Power in the Modern World. LC 72-4293. (World Affairs Ser.: National & International Viewpoints). 318p. 1972. reprint ed. 23.95 (0-405-04585-9) Ayer.

Richmond, Howard. Joy of Budgerigars. (Illus.). 96p. 1983. 9.95 (0-86622-082-8, PS-799) TFH Pubns.

— Joy of Cockatiels. (Illus.). 96p. 1984. 9.95 (0-87666-554-7, PS-797) TFH Pubns.

Richmond, Hugh M. John Milton's Drama of Paradise Lost. LC 91-30191. 80p. (C). 1992. text ed. 18.95 (0-8204-1719-X) P Lang Pubs.

— King Henry VIII. LC 93-28156. (Shakespeare in Performance Ser.). 1994. text ed. 49.95 (0-7190-3657-7, Pub. by Manchester Univ Pr UK) St Martin.

— King Richard III. (Shakespeare in Performance Ser.). 160p. 1991. text ed. 16.95 (0-7190-2724-1, Pub. by Manchester Univ Pr UK) St Martin.

Richmond, Hugh M., ed. Henry Fourth: Part One. LC 66-28232. 1967. pap. 2.05 (0-672-61092-2, Bobbs) Macmillan.

Richmond, I. A. Roman Britain. 1978. mass mkt. 5.95 (0-14-020315-X, Penguin Bks) Viking Penguin.

Richmond, Iain, jt. auth. see Cookson, John.

Richmond, Ian M., ed. Aspects of Internationalism: Language & Culture. (Papers of the Center for Research & Documentation on World Language Problems: No. 3). 162p. (C). 1992. lib. bdg. 36.50 (0-8191-8859-X) U Pr of Amer.

Richmond, J. A., jt. ed. see Martin, F. X.

Richmond, J. B. The Richmond Family, 1594-1896, & Pre-American Ancestry, 1040-1594. (Illus.). 633p. 1989. reprint ed. lib. bdg. 103.00 (0-8328-1022-3); reprint ed. pap. 95.00 (0-8328-1023-1) Higginson Bk Co.

Richmond, J. C. & DeWitt, D. P., eds. Applications of Radiation Thermometry- STP 895. LC 85-26709. (Illus.). 173p. 1985. text ed. 28.00 (0-8031-0445-6, 04-895000-40) ASTM.

Richmond, Jeff. Lobo a Go-Go. 60p. 1992. pap. 5.95 (1-56850-011-4) Chicago Plays.

Richmond, John. Chapters on Greek Fish-Lore. 89p. (Orig.). 1973. pap. text ed. 23.00 (3-515-00249-9) Coronet Bks.

— Egypt, Seventeen Ninety-Eight to Nineteen Fifty-Two: Her Advance Toward Modern Identity. LC 77-1969. 243p. 1977. text ed. 43.00 (0-231-04296-5) Col U Pr.

Richmond, Jonathan Y. & McKinney, Robert W., eds. Biosafety in Microbiological & Biomedical Laboratories. 3rd ed. 177p. (Orig.). (C). 1994. pap. text ed. 45.00 (0-7881-0548-5) Diane Pub.

Richmond, Joy S., comp. Medical Reference Works, 1679-1966: Supplement 2, 1969-1972. LC 67-30664. 1973. pap. 4.35 (0-8108-2440-X) Scarecrow.

— Medical Reference Works, 1679-1966: Supplement 3, 1973-1974. LC 67-30664. 89p. 1975. pap. 3.00 (0-8108-2441-8) Scarecrow.

Richmond, Julius B. Currents in American Medicine: A Developmental View of Medical Care & Education. LC 69-12733. (Commonwealth Fund Publications). 150p. 1969. 18.00 (0-674-18015-1) HUP.

Richmond, Julius B., jt. ed. see Cheung, Lilian W.

Richmond, Julius B., jt. ed. see Walker, Deborah K.

***Richmond, Katherine.** Herbal Pleasures. (Illus.). 128p. 1995. 14.98 (0-8317-4489-8) Smithmark.

Richmond, Kent D. & Middleton, David L. The Pastor & the Patient: A Practical Guidebook for Hospital Visitation. 144p. (Orig.). 1992. pap. 11.95 (0-687-30352-4) Abingdon.

Richmond, Lee. Fireflies: Selected Haiku. (New Poets Ser.: No. 3). (Illus.). 96p. (Orig.). 1989. pap. 7.50 (0-933806-56-6) Black Swan CT.

— Hazmat Emergency: Leader's Guide. 2nd ed. Massingham, Gordon, ed. 1992. pap. write for info. (0-318-69786-6) Detrick Lawrence.

Richmond, Leigh, jt. auth. see Richmond, Walter.

Richmond, Leslie, et al. Company Archives: A Survey of the Records of the Oldest 1000 Registered Companies. 400p. 1985. text ed. 99.95 (0-566-03547-2) Ashgate Pub Co.

Richmond, Lewis H., jt. ed. see Azima, Fern J.

Richmond, M. A. Bid the Vassal Soar: Interpretive Essays on the Life & Poetry of Phillis Wheatley & George Moses Horton. LC 73-85493. 1974. 14.95 (0-88258-001-9) Howard U Pr.

Richmond, M. H., jt. ed. see Clarke, P. H.

***Richmond, Mardi.** Eight Ways to Say No to Smoking. (Illus.). 6p. 1995. write for info. (1-56885-062-X) Journeyworks Pub.

***Richmond, Mardi, ed.** Caring for a Person with Memory Loss & Confusion. (Illus.). 32p. 1995. 3.95 (1-56885-059-X) Journeyworks Pub.

— Do I Want to Be a Teenage Parent? (Illus.). 16p. 1995. write for info. (1-56885-058-1) Journeyworks Pub.

— Sex, Teens & Abstinence. (Illus.). 16p. 1995. write for info. (1-56885-057-3) Journeyworks Pub.

Richmond, Marie L. Immigrant Adaptation & Family Structure Among Cubans in Miami, Florida. Cortes, Carlos E., ed. LC 79-6220. (Hispanics in the United States Ser.). (Illus.). 1981. lib. bdg. 23.95 (0-405-13168-2) Ayer.

Richmond, Mark A., jt. auth. see Richmond, Elmore, Jr.

Richmond, Marvin, jt. auth. see O'Toole, John.

Richmond, Mary. The Long View. (Russell Sage Foundation Reprint Ser.). (Illus.). 1971. reprint ed. lib. bdg. 34.00 (0-697-00209-8) Irvington.

Richmond, Mary E. Friendly Visiting among the Poor, a Handbook for Charity Workers. LC 69-16244. (Criminology, Law Enforcement, & Social Problems Ser.: No. 92). 1969. reprint ed. 18.00 (0-87585-092-8) Patterson Smith.

— Social Diagnosis. 512p. 1917. 45.00 (0-87154-703-1) Russell Sage.

— What Is Social Case Work: An Introductory Description. LC 70-137185. (Poverty U. S. A. Historical Record Ser.). 1977. reprint ed. 23.95 (0-405-03123-8) Ayer.

Richmond, Mary E. & Hall, Fred S. A Study of Nine & Eighty-Five Widows Known to Certain Charity Organization Societies in 1910. LC 74-3971. (Women in America Ser.). (Illus.). 84p. 1974. reprint ed. 16.95 (0-405-06119-6) Ayer.

Richmond, Mary L., ed. see Hurt, Peyton.

Richmond, Merle. Phyllis Wheatley. (American Women of Achievement Ser.). (Illus.). 112p. (Orig.). (YA). (gr. 5 up). 1988. 17.95 (1-55546-683-4); pap. 9.95 (0-7910-0218-7) Chelsea Hse.

***Richmond, Olney H.** Evolutionism Pt. 2: Temple Lectures. 2nd ed. McLaren-Owens, Lain, ed. & pref. by. (Astro-Cards Reprints Ser.). (Illus.). 111p. 1995. pap. text ed. 12.00 (1-885500-11-4, AR:9) Astro-Cards.

— The Mystic Test Book. (Orig.). 1983. pap. 9.95 (0-87877-064-X) Newcastle Pub.

— The Mystic Textbook: The Magic of the Cards. reprint ed. spiral bd. 9.90 (0-7873-0717-3) Mokelumne.

— Religion of the Stars: Temple Lectures. 5th ed. (Astro-Cards Reprints Ser.). 100p. 1994. pap. text ed. 10.00 (1-885500-05-X, AR2) Astro-Cards.

— Temple Lectures of the Order of the Magi. reprint ed. spiral bd. 8.80 (0-7873-0718-1) Mokelumne.

***Richmond, Pamela.** Bookbinding: A Manual of Techniques. (Illus.). 160p. 1995. pap. 24.95 (1-85223-886-0, Pub. by Crowood Pr UK) Trafalgar.

***Richmond, Patricia J.** Trail to Disaster. 1992. pap. 8.95 (0-87081-275-0) Univ Pr Colo.

Richmond, Paula A., ed. Directory of Greeting Card Sales Representatives, 1991-1992. rev. ed. 200p. 1991. pap. 50.00 (0-938369-11-3) Greeting Card Assn.

Richmond, Paula A. & Riviere, Nancy, eds. GCCN Talent Directory, Nineteen Ninety-One. rev. ed. 65p. 1991. pap. 25.00 (0-938369-09-1) Greeting Card Assn.

— The Greeting Card Industry Directory, 1991-1992. rev. ed. 175p. 1991. pap. 40.00 (0-938369-10-5) Greeting Card Assn.

***Richmond, Peter.** Ballpark. 1995. pap. text ed. 12.00 (0-684-80048-9, Fireside) S&S Trade.

— Ballpark: Camden Yards & the Building of an American Dream. (Illus.). 320p. 1993. 23.00 (0-671-74851-3) S&S Trade.

— Baseball: The Perfect Game. LC 91-34778. (Illus.). 128p. 1992. 29.95 (0-8478-1524-2) Rizzoli Intl.

Richmond, Robert. Kansas: A Land of Contrasts. 3rd ed. (Illus.). 372p. (C). 1989. text ed. write for info. (0-88273-245-5) Forum Pr IL.

***Richmond, Robert H., ed.** Proceedings of the Seventh International Coral Reef Symposium, 2 vols. Incl. Vol. 1. (Illus.). (C). 1994. (1-881629-01-5); Vol. 2. (Illus.). (C). 1994. (1-886129-02-9); 125.00 (1-881629-03-1) Univ Guam Pr.

Richmond, Robert W. Kansas: A Pictorial History. rev. ed. LC 92-13822. (Illus.). xii, 276p. 1992. 35.00 (0-7006-0543-6) U Pr of KS.
Richmond, Robert W., ed. A Souvenir Album of Topeka. (Illus.). 56p. 2.45 (0-686-79885-6, 64) Shawnee County Hist.
Richmond, Robert W. & Mardock, Robert W., eds. A Nation Moving West: Readings in the History of the American Frontier. LC 66-10446. 376p. reprint ed. pap. 107.20 (0-7837-6013-2, 2045824) Bks Demand.
Richmond, Robert W., jt. ed. see Ripley, John W.
Richmond, Robin. Animals in Art. LC 93-9766. (Story in a Picture Ser.). (Illus.). 48p. (J). (gr. 2-5). 1993. text ed. 15.95 (0-8249-8613-X, Ideals Child); lib. bdg. 16.00 (0-8249-8626-1, Ideals Child) Hambleton-Hill.
— Children in Art. LC 92-7184. (Story in a Picture Ser.). (Illus.). 48p. (J). (gr. 2-5). 1992. 15.95 (0-8249-8552-4, Ideals Child); lib. bdg. 16.00 (0-8249-8588-5, Ideals Child) Hambleton-Hill.
— Frida Kahlo in Mexico. LC 93-87358. (Painters & Places Ser.). (Illus.). 160p. 1994. 29.95 (1-56640-802-4) Pomegranate Calif.
— Introducing Michelangelo. (Illus.). 32p. (J). (gr. 2-5). 1992. 14.95 (0-316-74440-9) Little.
— Michelangelo & the Sistine Chapel. LC 95-14238. (Illus.). 1995. 17.99 (0-517-14194-9) Random Hse Value.
Richmond, Robyn L., ed. Interventions for Smokers: An International Perspective. LC 93-38968. 400p. 1994. 39.00 (0-683-07272-2) Williams & Wilkins.
Richmond, Roe. Blaze of Autumn. 1980. pap. 1.95 (0-8439-0841-6) Dorchester Pub Co.
— Crusade on the Chisholm. (Lashtrow Ser.). 192p. 1984. pap. 2.25 (0-8439-2148-X) Dorchester Pub Co.
— An End to Summer. 1980. pap. 2.25 (0-8439-0825-4) Dorchester Pub Co.
— Guns at Goliad. (Lashtrow Ser.: No. 4). 1980. pap. 1.75 (0-8439-0796-7) Dorchester Pub Co.
— Hell on a Holiday. (Lashtrow Ser.: No. 3). 208p. 1984. pap. 2.25 (0-8439-2171-4) Dorchester Pub Co.
— Kelleway's Luck. 240p. (Orig.). 1981. pap. 2.25 (0-8439-0969-2) Dorchester Pub Co.
— Lashtrow: Rio Grande Riptide. 192p. 1984. pap. 2.25 (0-8439-2110-2) Dorchester Pub Co.
— Legacy of a Gunfighter. 192p. 1986. pap. 2.50 (0-8439-2356-3) Dorchester Pub Co.
— Lifeline of Texas. (Lashtrow Ser.: No. 6). 1981. pap. 1.95 (0-8439-0892-0) Dorchester Pub Co.
— Nevada Queen High. (Lashtrow Ser.). 1985. pap. 2.25 (0-8439-2224-9) Dorchester Pub Co.
— Rio Grande Riptide. large type ed. (Linford Western Library). 368p. 1993. pap. 14.95 (0-7089-7359-0, Linford) Ulverscroft.
— Showdown at Fire Hill. (Orig.). 1979. pap. 1.95 (0-89083-560-8) Zebra.
— Staked Plains Rendezvous. (Lashtrow Ser.: No. 7). 208p. (Orig.). 1981. pap. 1.95 (0-8439-1019-4) Dorchester Pub Co.
— Wyoming Way. (Orig.). 1981. pap. 1.95 (0-8439-0926-9) Dorchester Pub Co.
Richmond, Sandra. Wheels for Walking. Kroupa, Melanie, ed. LC 85-70855. 196p. (YA). (gr. 6 up). 1985. 13.95 (0-316-74439-5, Joy St Bks) Little.
***Richmond, Scott.** Fishing in Oregon's Cascade Lakes. LC 94-70896. (Illus.). 214p. (Orig.). 1994. pap. 12.95 (0-916473-09-0) Flying Pencil.
— Fishing in Oregon's Deschutes River. LC 93-70651. (Illus.). 176p. (Orig.). 1993. pap. 12.95 (0-916473-08-2) Flying Pencil.
— The Pocket Gillie: Fly Fishing Essentials. 224p. 1992. pap. 14.95 (0-9633067-0-7) Four Rivers Pr.
Richmond, Steve. Aphrodite Rising. 66p. 1990. pap. 6.50 (0-9625349-2-7) Guerilla Poetics.
— Demon Notebook. 48p. (Orig.). 1988. pap. 6.95 (0-934953-21-X) Water Row Pr.
— Earth Rose. 249p. 1993. pap. 10.00 (1-883657-00-8) Earth Rose Pr.
— Five Point OL. Berlinski, Allen, ed. (Illus.). 32p. (Orig.). 1991. pap. 4.95 (0-941543-02-1) Sun Dog Pr.
— Hitler Painted Roses. (Illus.). 72p. 1994. pap. 11.00 (0-941543-05-6) Sun Dog Pr.
— Hitler Painted Roses. deluxe limited ed. (Illus.). 72p. 1994. pap. 20.00 (0-941543-06-4) Sun Dog Pr.
— Prospects. 40p. (Orig.). 1983. pap. 4.00 (0-935390-08-1) Wormwood Bks & Mag.
— Red Work, Black Widow. LC 76-15539. (Illus.). 1976. pap. 2.00 (0-916918-03-3) Duck Down.
— Santa Monica Poems. (Illus.). 48p. 1987. pap. 8.00 (0-941543-00-5) Sun Dog Pr.
— Wild Seed. LC 77-76903. 1977. pap. 5.00 (0-915016-13-3) Second Coming.
Richmond, Steven, jt. auth. see Greenblatt, Michael.
***Richmond, Susan.** Further Steps in Stagecraft. 80p. (Orig.). 1994. pap. 5.00 (0-88734-907-2) Empire Pub Srvs.
— A Junior Textbook of Stagecraft. 98p. (Orig.). 1994. pap. 5.00 (0-88734-906-4) Empire Pub Srvs.
— A Textbook of Stagecraft. 140p. (Orig.). 1994. pap. 5.00 (0-88734-908-0) Empire Pub Srvs.
***Richmond, Theo.** Konin: The Search for a Vanished Town & the Jews Who Lived There. (Illus.). 640p. 1995. 27.50 (0-679-43969-2) Pantheon.
Richmond, V. Nonverbal Communication in the Classroom. pap. 29.95 (0-8087-4698-7) Burgess MN Intl.
Richmond, Velma. The Popularity of Middle English Romance. LC 75-21576. 1975. 14.95 (0-87972-114-6) Bowling Green Univ.
Richmond, Velma B. Geoffrey Chaucer. (Literature & Life Ser.). 192p. 1992. 19.95 (0-8264-0545-2) Continuum.
***Richmond, Virginia P. & McCroskey, James C.** Communication: Apprehension, Avoidance, & Effectiveness. 4th ed. LC 94-21097. 1994. per. 16.00 (0-89787-354-8) Gorsuch Scarisbrick.
— Nonverbal Behavior in Interpersonal Relationships. 3rd ed. LC 94-32740. 1995. text ed. write for info. (0-205-15388-7) Allyn.
— Organizational Communication for Survival: Making Work, Work. 168p. (C). 1991. pap. text ed. write for info. (0-13-640079-5) P-H.
Richmond, Virginia P. & McCroskey, James C., eds. Power in the Classroom: Communication, Control, & Concern. (Communication Ser.). 224p. 1992. text ed. 45.00 (0-8058-1027-7) L Erlbaum Assocs.
Richmond, W., jt. auth. see Oakley, K.
Richmond, W. Edson. Ballads & Ballad Scholarship: An Annotated Bibliography. LC 84-48017. 328p. 1989. lib. bdg. 46.00 (0-8240-8932-4, H499) Garland.
Richmond, W. Edson, ed. see Wolford, Leah J.
Richmond, Walter & Richmond, Leigh. The Lost Millennium. rev. ed. xviii, 172p. 1986. pap. 7.00 (0-943975-00-X) Interdimens Sci.
Richmond, Winthrop E., ed. Studies in Folklore: In Honor of Distinguished Service Professor Stith Thompson. LC 72-163547. (Illus.). 270p. 1972. reprint ed. lib. bdg. 15.00 (0-8371-6208-4, RISF, Greenwood Pr) Greenwood.
Richmond, Yale. From Da to Yes: Understanding the East Europeans. (InterAct Ser.). 124p. (Orig.). (C). 1995. pap. 17.95 (1-877864-30-7) Intercult Pr.
— From Nyet to Da: Understanding the Russians. 2nd ed. LC 94-40331. 224p. 1995. 15.95 (1-877864-08-0) Intercult Pr.
— From Nyet to Da: Understanding the Russians. 2nd ed. 224p. 1995. write for info. (1-877864-41-2) Intercult Pr.
***Richmone, Anthony H.** Global Apartheid: Refugees, Racism & the New World Order. (Illus.). 256p. 1995. pap. text ed. 24.95 (0-19-541013-0) OUP.
Richnak, Barbara. A River Flows: The Life of Robert Lardin Fulton. LC 83-51605. (Illus.). 210p. (Orig.). 1984. pap. 9.95 (0-915933-00-4) Comstock NV Pub Co.
— Silver Hillside: The Life & Times of Virginia City. (Illus.). 200p. 1985. 29.95 (0-915933-01-2) Comstock NV Pub Co.
Richner, Hans & Phillips, Peter, eds. The Radiosonde Intercomparison SONDEX: Spring 1981, Payerne. (Contributions to Current Research in Geophysics Ser.: Vol. 11). 352p. 1984. text ed. 79.95 (3-7643-1614-4) Birkhauser.
Richo, David. How to Be an Adult. 1991. pap. 7.95 (0-8091-3223-0) Paulist Pr.
Richonne, Roc R. The Nobel Prize: A Drama-Comedy in Three Acts about Things-to-Come. 1994. 13.95 (0-533-10737-7) Vantage.
Richstad, Jim & Anderson, Michael H., eds. Crisis in International News: Policies & Prospects. LC 81-677. 480p. 1981. text ed. 53.50 (0-231-05254-5); pap. text ed. 22.50 (0-231-05255-3) Col U Pr.
Richstad, Jim & McMillan, Michael. Mass Communication & Journalism in the Pacific Islands: A Bibliography. LC 77-20695. 330p. reprint ed. pap. 94.10 (0-7837-3975-3, 2043805) Bks Demand.
Richstatter, Thomas. Before You Say 'I Do' Four Things to Remember When Planning Your Wedding Liturgy. 20p. 1989. 1.95 (0-86716-130-2) St Anthony Mess Pr.
— Liturgical Law Today: New Style, New Spirit. LC 77-3008. 271p. reprint ed. pap. 77.30 (0-317-28483-5, 2019104) Bks Demand.
Richsteig, E. Libanius: Index Nominum Propriorum. Vol. XII. 90p. 1963. reprint ed. write for info. (0-318-72041-8, Pub. by Georg Olms GW) Lubrecht & Cramer.
Richstein, Kelly & Sachsel, Nan, eds. Dark Orchid: Anthology of Erotica. (Illus.). 80p. (Orig.). 1993. pap. 8.75 (1-882300-02-5) Willo Trees.
Richt, Adrian, ed. see Dunn, Robert W.
Richtarik, Marilynn J. Acting Between the Lines: The Field Day Theatre Company & Irish Cultural Politics, 1980-84. (English Monographs). 320p. 1995. 55.00 (0-19-818247-3) OUP.
Richtel, Anne, jt. auth. see Bedford, Viola.
***Richter.** Windows 95: A Developer's Guide. 1995. disk, pap. text ed. 39.95 (1-55851-418-X) M&T Bks.
Richter-Addo, George B., jt. auth. see Legzdins, Peter.
Richter, Alan. Dictionary of Sexual Slang: Words, Phrases, & Idioms from AC - DC to Zig-Zag. LC 92-6316. 272p. 1993. text ed. 29.95 (0-471-54057-9) Wiley.
— The Language of Sexuality. LC 87-42520. 159p. 1987. lib. bdg. 21.95x (0-89950-245-8) McFarland & Co.
— Sexual Slang. 1994. pap. 10.00 (0-06-272504-1, HarpT) HarpC.
— Sexual Slang: A Compendium of Offbeat Words & Colorful Phrases, from Shakespeare to Today. 3rd ed. LC 94-34728. 1995. 12.00 (0-602-72504-6, PL) HarpC.
Richter, Allan D. Eve of the End. 1993. 10.95 (0-8062-4793-2) Carlton.
Richter, Anne. Arts & Crafts of Indonesia. LC 93-10290. (Illus.). 160p. 1994. 35.00 (0-8118-0454-2); pap. 22.95 (0-8118-0481-X) Chronicle Bks.
***Richter, Barbara.** Eat Like a Horse: And Lose Weight. (Illus.). 192p. (Orig.). 1994. pap. 11.95 (0-9641715-3-8) Airplane Bks.
***Richter, Benno.** Breitling Timepieces: 1884-Present. (Illus.). 176p. 1995. 49.98 (0-88740-864-8) Schiffer.
Richter-Bernburg, Lutz. Persian Medical Manuscripts at the University of California, Los Angeles. LC 77-94986. (Humana Civilitas Ser.: Vol. 4). (Illus.). xxi, 297p. 1978. 56.25 (0-89003-026-X) Undena Pubns.
Richter-Bernburg, Melanie, tr. see Von Westphalen, Joseph.
Richter, Bernd C. & Kreitler, Charles W. Geochemical Techniques for Identifying Sources of Ground-Water Salinization. 1993. 59.95 (1-56670-000-0, TD427) Lewis Pubs.
Richter, Bernice & Wenzel, Duane. The Museum of Science & Industry Basic List of Children's Science Books, 1973-1984. LC 85-18719. 167p. reprint ed. pap. 47.60 (0-7837-5917-7, 2045716) Bks Demand.
— The Museum of Science & Industry Basic List of Children's Science Books, 1986. LC 86-22320. 83p. reprint ed. pap. 25.00 (0-7837-5953-3, 2045753) Bks Demand.
— The Museum of Science & Industry Basic List of Children's Science Books, 1987. LC 87-641170. 85p. reprint ed. pap. 25.00 (0-7837-5954-1, 2045754) Bks Demand.
Richter, Bertina. Fort Miller, California, 1851-1865. (American University Studies: Regional Studies: Ser. XX, Vol. 2). 154p. (C). 1988. text ed. 27.00 (0-8204-0703-8) P Lang Pubs.
Richter, Betts. Something Special Within. 2nd ed. (Illus.). 48p. (J). (ps-5). 1982. reprint ed. pap. 6.95 (0-87516-488-9) DeVorss.
Richter, Betts & Jacobsen, Alice. Make It So! A Child's Book on Self-Direction Through Affirmations. 3rd ed. LC 79-84946. (Illus.). 55p. (J). (gr. k-4). 1988. reprint ed. pap. 7.95 (0-87516-599-0) DeVorss.
***Richter, Brigitte.** Precis de Bibliotheconomie. 5th rev. ed. ix, 298p. (FRE.). 1992. lib. bdg. 32.50 (3-598-11077-4) K G Saur.
Richter, C., et al, eds. Numerical Methods of Nonlinear Programming: Implementations. (Mathematical Research Ser.). 135p. 1991. text ed. 29.00 (3-05-500883-9, Pub. by Akademie GW) VCH Pubs.
Richter, Conrad. Awakening Land. 1966. 29.95 (0-394-41703-8) Knopf.
— Brothers of No Kin: And Other Stories. LC 72-10812. (Short Story Index Reprint Ser.). 1977. reprint ed. 24.95 (0-8369-4225-6) Ayer.
— Early Americana & Other Stories. 23.95 (0-89190-857-9, Am Repr) Amereon Ltd.
— The Fields. LC 90-20771. 158p. 1991. reprint ed. pap. 12.95 (0-8214-0979-4) Ohio U Pr.
— The Lady. 18.95 (0-89190-332-1, Am Repr) Amereon Ltd.
— The Lady. LC 84-20808. xviii, 191p. 1985. reprint ed. pap. 6.50 (0-8032-8918-9, Bison Books) U of Nebr Pr.
— Light in the Forest. (Illus.). 1953. 23.00 (0-394-43314-9) Knopf.
— Light in the Forest. (YA). 1994. pap. 3.99 (0-449-70437-8) Fawcett.
— The Light in the Forest. 19.95 (0-89190-333-X, Am Repr) Amereon Ltd.
— The Light in the Forest. 1991. lib. bdg. 21.95 (1-56849-064-X) Buccaneer Bks.
— The Rawhide Knot & Other Stories. LC 84-20799. xii, 207p. 1985. reprint ed. pap. 6.50 (0-8032-8916-2, Bison Books) U of Nebr Pr.
— Sea of Grass. 1937. 13.95 (0-394-44397-7) Knopf.
— The Sea of Grass. LC 92-5181. 149p. (C). 1992. reprint ed. pap. 9.95 (0-8214-1026-1) Ohio U Pr.
— The Town. 1981. lib. bdg. 17.95 (0-89967-048-2) Harmony Raine.
— The Town. LC 90-20736. 297p. 1991. reprint ed. pap. 14.95 (0-8214-0980-8) Ohio U Pr.
— The Trees. 1940. 18.95 (0-394-44951-7) Knopf.
— The Trees. LC 90-19936. 167p. 1991. reprint ed. pap. 12.95 (0-8214-0978-6) Ohio U Pr.
Richter, D. Metabolism of the Nervous System. LC 57-13324. 1957. 252.00 (0-08-009062-1, Pub. by Pergamon Repr UK) Franklin.
Richter, D., ed. Biochemical Factors Concerned in the Functional Activity of the Nervous System. LC 75-80290. 1969. pap. 103.00 (0-08-013311-8, Pub. by Pergamon Repr UK) Franklin.
Richter, D. & Springer, Timothy A., eds. Polymer Motion in Dense Systems. (Proceedings in Physics Ser.: Vol. 29). (Illus.). 305p. 1988. 70.00 (0-387-19167-4) Spr-Verlag.
Richter, D., et al, eds. Advanced Psychosomatic Research in Obstetrics & Gynecology. (Illus.). xv, 262p. 1991. pap. 98.00 (0-387-52500-9) Spr-Verlag.
— Dynamics of Disordered Materials. (Proceedings in Physics Ser.: Vol. 37). (Illus.). 320p. 1989. 64.00 (0-387-50942-9, 2789) Spr-Verlag.
Richter, D. K. Origin & Diagenesis of Devonian & Permotriassic Dolomites in the Eifel Mountains (Germany) Text in German with English Summary. (Contributions to Sedimentology Ser.: No. 2). (Illus.). 101p. 1974. pap. text ed. 30.95 (3-510-57002-2) Lubrecht & Cramer.
Richter, Daniel K. The Ordeal of the Longhouse: The Peoples of the Iroquois League in the Era of European Colonization. LC 92-53621. (Institute of Early American History & Culture Ser.). (Illus.). xviii, 436p. (C). 1992. 45.00 (0-8078-2060-1); pap. 17.95 (0-8078-4394-6) U of NC Pr.
Richter, Daniel K. & Merrell, James H., eds. Beyond the Covenant Chain: The Iroquois & Their Neighbors in Indian North America, 1600-1800. (Iroquois Bks.). (Illus.). 288p. 1987. text ed. 29.95 (0-8156-2416-6) Syracuse U Pr.
Richter, Darrel, jt. auth. see Fahle, Michael L.
Richter, David. Collectors Guide to Tootsietoys. 1991. pap. 16.95 (0-89145-442-X) Collector Bks.
Richter, David H. The Borzoi Book of Short Fiction. 1438p. 1983. pap. text ed. write for info. (0-07-554363-X) McGraw.
— Falling into Theory: Conflicting Views on Reading Literature. 320p. 1993. pap. text ed. 9.50 (0-312-08122-7) St Martin.
— Forms of the Novella: Ten Short Novels. 833p. 1981. pap. text ed. write for info. (0-07-553585-8) McGraw.
Richter, David H., ed. The Critical Tradition: Classic Texts & Contemporary Trends. LC 88-70423. 1436p. (C). 1989. pap. text ed. 42.00 (0-312-00344-7, Bedford Bks) St Martin.
Richter, Detlev. Lacquered Boxes. LC 89-84171. (Illus.). 216p. 1989. 69.95 (0-88740-197-X) Schiffer.
Richter, Dietmar, ed. Lipmann Symposium: Energy, Regulation & Biosynthesis in Molecular Biology. 698p. (C). 1974. 138.50 (3-11-004976-7) De Gruyter.
Richter, Don, jt. ed. see Wyckoff, D. Campbell.
Richter, Donald. Chemical Soldiers: British Gas Warfare in World War I. LC 92-12329. (Modern War Studies). (Illus.). xii, 284p. 1992. 35.00 (0-7006-0544-4) U Pr of KS.
— Chemical Soldiers: British Gas Warfare in World War One. (Illus.). 286p. 1994. 43.50 (0-85052-388-5, Pub. by L Cooper Bks UK) Trans-Atl Phila.
— Where the Sun Stood Still. LC 92-61189. 432p. 1992. text ed. 19.95 (0-9611696-3-X) Toucan Pub.
***Richter, Donald H., et al.** Guide to the Volcanoes of the Western Wrangell Mountains, ALaska: Wrangell-St. Elias National Park & Preserve, 2072. (Bulletin Ser.). 1994. write for info. (0-615-00181-5) US Geol Survey.
Richter, E. & Feyerabend, T. Normal Lymph Node Topography: A CT-Atlas. (Illus.). 120p. 1990. 140.00 (0-387-52549-1) Spr-Verlag.
***Richter, Eberhardt.** Woerterbuch Tibetisch-Deutsch. 3rd ed. 444p. (GER & TIB.). 1992. 115.00 (0-7859-8301-5, 3324002745) Fr & Eur.
Richter, Eileen, jt. auth. see Montgomery, Patricia.
Richter, Eileen W. & Montgomery, Patricia C. The Sensorimotor Performance Analysis. (Illus.). 135p. (C). 1989. pap. 30.00 (0-685-27007-6) PDP Pr.
Richter, Elisabeth, jt. ed. see Opitz, Helmut.
Richter, Ernst, et al. Imaging Anatomy of the Newborn. (Illus.). 296p. 1991. text ed. 175.00 (0-683-07274-9) Williams & Wilkins.
Richter, Erwin W. The Original Non Cookbook Environmentally Safe Laboratory Guide Using Cheap Chemicals for Beginning Chemistry Students. 128p. (C). 1990. spiral bd. 19.95 (0-8403-6140-8) Kendall-Hunt.
Richter, Eugene. Co-Operative Stores, Their History, Organization, & Management. LC 76-47885. reprint ed. 14.50 (0-404-60088-3) AMS Pr.
Richter, Eva, tr. see Neumann, Eckhard.
Richter, Franz A., tr. see Holm, Bill.
Richter, G. German-English - English-German Dictionary of Optics, Photography & Video. 429p. 1993. 110.00 (3-88955-063-0) IBD Ltd.
— German-English--English-German Dictionary of Optics, Photography & 429p. (ENG & GER.). 1993. write for info. (0-7859-8773-8) Fr & Eur.
Richter, G. & Schonfelder, A., eds. Sacramentarium Fuldense Saeculi X. (Henry Bradshaw Society Publication Ser.: No. CI (101)). 1970. 50.00 (0-907077-19-6) Boydell & Brewer.
Richter, G. M. The Portraits of the Greeks. Smith, R. R., ed. LC 83-73222. (Illus.). 272p. 1984. 49.95 (0-8014-1683-3) Cornell U Pr.
Richter, George. The Consciousness of Earth. 195p. (Orig.). 1989. pap. 10.00 (0-9622662-0-5) Gaia Pr.
— Evolving Order: Critical Path to Human Survival. LC 94-61712. (Illus.). 260p. 1995. pap. 12.95 (0-9643542-0-9) Yin-Yang Bks.
***Richter, Gerhard.** The Daily Practice of Painting: Writings 1960-1993. Obrist, Hans-Ulrich, ed. Britt, David, tr. LC 95-9818. 272p. (ENG & GER.). 1995. pap. 19.95 (0-262-68084-X) MIT Pr.
— Theodoros Dukas Laskaris: Der Naturliche Zusammenhang: Ein Zeugnis vom Stand der Byzantinischen Philosophie in der Mitte des 13. Jahrhunderts. viii, 258p. (Orig.). (GER.). 1989. pap. 54.00 (90-256-0944-9, Pub. by A M Hakkert NE) Benjamins North Am.
Richter, Gernot, jt. auth. see Durchholz, Reiner.
***Richter, Gert.** Lexikon der Kunstmotive: Antike und Christliche Welt. 319p. (GER.). 1993. 29.95 (0-7859-8689-8, 357200554x) Fr & Eur.
Richter, Gisela. A Handbook of Greek Art. 9th ed. (Quality Paperbacks Ser.). (Illus.). 431p. 1987. pap. text ed. 22.50 (0-306-80298-8) Da Capo.
— Handbook of Greek Art: A Survey of the Visual Arts of Ancient Greece. (Illus.). 328p. (C). 1994. reprint ed. pap. 19.95 (0-7148-2496-8, Pub. by Phaidon Press UK) Chronicle Bks.
Richter, Gisela M. Archaic Gravestones of Attica. (Illus.). 184p. 1988. reprint ed. 55.00 (0-86516-211-5); reprint ed. pap. text ed. 30.00 (0-86516-189-5) Bolchazy-Carducci.
— Catalogue of the Greek & Roman Antiquities in the Dumbarton Oaks Collection. LC 56-10351. (Illus.). 77p. 1956. 20.00 (0-88402-002-9) Dumbarton Oaks.
— Handbook of Greek Art: A Survey of the Visual Arts of Ancient Greece. rev. ed. Henig, Martin, ed. (Illus.). 320p. (C). 1995. pap. 19.95 (0-7148-2301-5, Pub. by Phaidon Press UK) Chronicle Bks.
— Korai: Archaic Greek Maidens: A Study of the Development of the Kore Type in Greek Sculpture. LC 87-80026. (Illus.). xii, 327p. 1988. reprint ed. lib. bdg. 100.00 (0-87817-318-8) Hacker.
— Kouroi: Archaic Greek Youths: A Study of the Development of the Kouros Type in Greek Sculpture. LC 87-80047. (Illus.). xvi, 365p. 1988. reprint ed. lib. bdg. 100.00 (0-87817-317-X) Hacker.
Richter, Goetz W., ed. International Review of Experimental Pathology, Vol. 29. 241p. 1986. text ed. 125.00 (0-12-364929-3) Acad Pr.
Richter, Goetz W. & Epstein, M. A. International Review of Experimental Pathology, Vol. 26. (Serial Publication Ser.). 1984. text ed. 148.00 (0-12-364926-9) Acad Pr.

Richter, Goetz W. & Epstein, M. A., eds. International Review of Experimental Pathology, Vol. 27. 246p. 1985. text ed. 142.00 (0-12-364927-7) Acad Pr.

— International Review of Experimental Pathology, Vol. 28. (Serial Publication Ser.). 1986. text ed. 134.00 (0-12-364928-5) Acad Pr.

Richter, Goetz W. & Solez, Kim, eds. International Review of Experimental Pathology, Vol. 30: Kidney Disease. 759p. 1988. text ed. 119.00 (0-12-364930-7) Acad Pr.

— International Review of Experimental Pathology, Vol. 32: Molecular Cell Pathology. (Illus.). 285p. 1991. text ed. 91.00 (0-12-364932-3) Acad Pr.

Richter, Goetz W., et al, eds. International Review of Experimental Pathology, Vol. 31: Transition Metal Toxicity. 195p. 1990. text ed. 94.00 (0-12-364931-5) Acad Pr.

— International Review of Experimental Pathology, Vol. 33: Progress in Hodgkins Disease. (Illus.). 368p. 1992. text ed. 95.00 (0-12-366833-6) Acad Pr.

Richter, Gottfried. Art & Human Consciousness. Frohlich, Margaret, tr. (Illus.). 300p. (Orig.). 1985. 30.00 (0-88010-108-3) Anthroposophic.

Richter, Gregory C., tr. see Rank, Otto.

***Richter, Gunter & Burian, Peter K.** Magic Lantern Guide to Nikon N70 - F70. Ohlig, Hayley, tr. (Magic Lantern Guide Ser.). (Illus.). 176p. (Orig.). (C). 1995. pap. 19.95 (1-883403-19-7, Silver Pixel Pr) Saunders Photo.

Richter, Gunter, jt. auth. see Burian, Peter K.

Richter, H., jt. ed. see Kittler, M.

Richter, H. J., ed. Thermodynamics & the Design, Analysis, & Improvement of Energy Systems 1993. LC 93-73595. 435p. Date not set. pap. 80.00 (0-7918-1042-9) ASME.

***Richter, H. P. & Schwan, W. C.** Wiring Simplified: Based on 1993 Code. 37th rev. ed. 175p. 1992. pap. 5.50 (0-9603294-5-5) Park Pub.

— Wiring Simplified: Based on 1996 Code. 38th rev. ed. 1995. pap. write for info. (0-9603294-6-3) Park Pub.

Richter, Hans. The Struggle for the Film: Towards a Socially Responsible Cinema. Romhild, Jurgen, ed. Brewster, Ben, tr. LC 85-10848. 176p. 1986. text ed. 29.95 (0-312-76875-3) St Martin.

— The World Between the Ox & the Swine: Dada Drawings by Hans Richter. (Illus.). 1971. 2.00 (0-911517-43-X) Mus of Art RI.

Richter, Hans-Joachim. Complete Book of Dwarf Cichlids. Charlton, William, tr. (Illus.). 208p. (C). 1988. lib. bdg. 29.95 (0-86622-701-6, TS-121) TFH Pubns.

— Gouramis & Other Anabantoids. Hirschhorn, Howard, tr. 224p. 1988. lib. bdg. 21.95 (0-86622-941-8, PS-874) TFH Pubns.

Richter, Hans P. Friedrich. (J). (gr. 6 up). 1992. 17.75 (0-8446-6573-8) Peter Smith.

— Friedrich. (Novels Ser.). (J). (gr. 5-9). 1987. pap. 4.99 (0-14-032205-1, Puffin) Puffin Bks.

— I Was There. (Novels Ser.). (J). (gr. 5-9). 1987. pap. 4.99 (0-14-032206-X, Puffin) Puffin Bks.

Richter, Harvena. Writing to Survive: The Private Notebooks on Conrad Richter. LC 87-34237. 289p. reprint ed. pap. 82.40 (0-7837-5851-0, 2045570) Bks Demand.

Richter-Heinrich, E. & Miller, Norman E. Biofeedback: Basic Problems in Clinical Applications. 141p. 1983. 51.50 (0-444-86345-1, I-122-82, North Holland) Elsevier.

Richter, Heinz. British Intervention in Greece from Varkiza to Civil War. 1985. 35.95 (0-85036-301-2, Pub. by Merlin Pr UK) Humanities.

Richter, Helmut, jt. ed. see Gibbon, Dafydd.

Richter, Herbert P. Practical Electrical Wiring: Residential, Farm & Industrial. 8th ed. 1972. text ed. 12.50 (0-07-052385-1) McGraw.

Richter, Herbert P. & Schwan, W. Creighton. Practical Electrical Wiring: Residential, Farm, & Industrial. 16th ed. LC 92-35995. 1993. text ed. 35.00 (0-07-052394-0) McGraw.

Richter, Horst E. All Mighty: A Study of the "God Complex" in Western Man. Van Heurck, Jan, tr. LC 83-81701. 304p. 1984. 19.95 (0-89793-028-2) Hunter Hse.

Richter, Ida. Compassion. 1973. pap. 2.95 (0-686-16723-6) Malcolm Hse.

Richter, Irma A., ed. see Da Vinci, Leonardo.

Richter, Irving. Labor's Struggles, 1945-1950: A Participant's View. (Illus.). 176p. (C). 1994. 54.95 (0-521-41412-1) Cambridge U Pr.

Richter, James G. Khrushchev's Double Bind: International Pressures & Domestic Coalition Politics. LC 93-48702. 263p. 1994. text ed. 45.00x (0-8018-4814-8) Johns Hopkins.

Richter, Jared H. Norway: Eighteen Seventy-One to Eighteen Seventy-Five Issue Skilling Denominations, Shaded Posthorn. (Illus.). 50p. (Orig.). 1984. pap. text ed. 5.00 (0-936493-07-0) Scand Philatelic.

Richter, Jared H., ed. see Berntsen, Arnstein.

Richter, Jared H., ed. see Gellein, Per.

Richter, Jared H., ed. see Thune-Larsen, D.

Richter, Jay. Where Credit Was Due: The Creation of the National Consumer Cooperative Bank. Thompson, David et al, eds. LC 84-73292. (Orig.). 1985. pap. 5.95 (0-910440-00-X) NCBA.

Richter, Jean P. Army-Chaplain Schmelzle's Journey to Flaetz & Life of Quintus Fixlein. Carlyle, Thomas, tr. (Studies in German Literature, Linguistics & Culture: Vol. 57). 240p. 1991. 59.00 (0-938100-89-0) Camden Hse.

Richter, Jean P., ed. see Da Vinci, Leonardo.

Richter, Jean-Paul, ed. see Da Vinci, Leonardo.

Richter, Jeffrey. Advanced Windows NT. 1993. pap. 39.95 (1-55615-567-0) Microsoft.

— Advanced Windows Programming: The Developer's Guide to the Win32 API for Windows NT & Windows 95. 1995. cd-rom, pap. 44.95 (1-55615-677-4) Microsoft.

Richter, Jeffrey M. Windows 3.1: A Developer's Guide. 2nd ed. LC 92-16517. 1992. 39.95 (1-55851-276-4) M&T Bks.

Richter, Joachim B. Hans Ferdinand Massmann: Altdeutscher Patriotismus im 19. Jahrhundert. (Quellen und Forschungen zur Sprach und Kulturgeschichte der Germanischen Voelker Ser.: NF Band 100, 224). xiv, 482p. (GER.). (C). 1992. lib. bdg. 175.40 (3-11-012910-8) De Gruyter.

Richter, Joachim F. Antique Enamels for Collectors. LC 90-61804. (Illus.). 176p. 1990. 59.95 (0-88740-261-5) Schiffer.

Richter, Jochen H. Die Knozeption Des "Neuen Menschen" In Ernst Barlachs Dramatischen Schaffen. LC 92-8238. (American University Studies: Germanic Languages & Literature: Ser. I, Vol. 95). 274p. (C). 1992. text ed. 38.95 (0-8204-1552-9) P Lang Pubs.

Richter, Joel, jt. auth. see Gelfand, David.

Richter, Joel E., ed. Ambulatory Esophageal pH Monitoring: Practical Approach & Clinical Applications. LC 90-7056. (Illus.). 248p. 1991. text ed. 63.00 (0-89640-208-8) Igaku-Shoin.

Richter, John, tr. see Say, Jean-Baptiste.

***Richter, John H., ed.** Topical Time, Vol. 12-13. 2nd ed. (Illus.). 44p. Date not set. reprint ed. pap. text ed. 7.00 (0-935991-26-3) Am Topical Assn.

Richter, John T. & Richter, Vera M. Nature, the Healer. reprint ed. spiral bd. 13.75 (0-7873-0719-X) Mokelumne.

***Richter, Judith.** Vaccination Against Pregnancy: Miracle or Menace? 128p. 1996. 55.00 (1-85649-281-8, Pub. by Zed Books UK) Humanities.

— Vaccination Against Pregnancy: Miracle Or Menance? 128p. (C). 1996. pap. 17.50 (1-85649-282-6, Pub. by Zed Books UK) Humanities.

Richter, Judy. Pony Talk: A Complete Learning Guide for Young Riders. 1993. 22.00 (0-87605-849-7) Howell Bk.

Richter, Julius. History of Protestant Missions in the Near East. LC 79-133822. reprint ed. 54.50 (0-404-05331-9) AMS Pr.

Richter, Karen, jt. auth. see Sandor, Bela I.

Richter, Klemens. The Meaning of the Sacramental Symbols: Answers to Today's Questions. Maloney, Linda M., tr. 132p. 1990. pap. 9.95 (0-8146-1882-0) Liturgical Pr.

Richter, Konrad. Wipe Your Feet, Santa Claus. LC 85-7246. (Illus.). 24p. (J). (gr. k-2). 1985. 14.95 (1-55858-016-6) North-South Bks NYC.

Richter, L. Training Needs: Assessment & Monitoring. viii, 83p. (Orig.). 1990. pap. 14.00 (92-2-105458-6) Intl Labour Office.

Richter, L., jt. auth. see Mason, W.

Richter, L., jt. ed. see Van Spronsen, C. J.

Richter, L. A. Thermal Power Plants & Environmental Control. 312p. 1984. 45.00 (0-317-46749-2, Pub. by Collets UK) Pro-Am Music.

Richter, Leibold. Guillelmi de Ockham: Expositio in Libros Physicorum, Bks. I-III. (Opera Philosophica Ser.: Vol. IV). 1985. 71.00 (0-318-35494-2) Franciscan Inst.

Richter, Linda K. Land Reform & Tourism Development: Policy Making in the Philippines. 240p. 1982. 22.95 (0-87073-413-X); pap. 13.95 (0-87073-414-8) Schenkman Bks Inc.

— Politics of Tourism in Asia. LC 88-27698. (Illus.). 280p. 1989. text ed. 24.00 (0-8248-1140-2) UH Pr.

Richter, Lydia. Beloved Kathe Kruse Yesterday & Today. 112p. 1991. pap. 12.95 (0-87588-210-2) Hobby Hse.

— Bru Dolls: Magnificent French Dolls. (Illus.). 104p. 1989. 29.95 (0-87588-357-5) Hobby Hse.

— China, Parian & Bisque German Dolls. 1993. 39.95 (0-87588-411-3) Hobby Hse.

— Collecting Antique Dolls. (Illus.). 124p. (Orig.). 1989. pap. 12.95 (0-87588-362-1) Hobby Hse.

Richter, Lydia & Schmelcher, Karin. Heubach Character Dolls & Figurines. (Illus.). 144p. 1992. 29.95 (0-87588-393-1) Hobby Hse.

Richter, M. M., jt. ed. see Muller, G. H.

Richter, M. M., et al, eds. Computation & Proof Theory, Pt. 2. (Lecture Notes in Mathematics Ser.: Vol. 1104). viii, 475p. 1984. pap. 53.80 (0-387-13901-X) Spr-Verlag.

Richter, Marcel K., jt. auth. see McFadden, Daniel.

Richter, Marga. Blackberry Vines & Winter Fruit for Orchestra. (Illus.). 1978. pap. 15.00 (0-8258-0063-3, 0-5073) Fischer Inc NY.

Richter, Maurice N., Jr. The Autonomy of Science: An Historical Comparative Analysis. LC 80-23534. 188p. 1981. text ed. 18.95 (0-87073-381-8); pap. text ed. 11.95 (0-87073-382-6) Schenkman Bks Inc.

— Science As a Cultural Process. 160p. 1972. pap. text ed. 11.95 (0-87073-073-8) Schenkman Bks Inc.

— Society: A Macroscopic View. 122p. 1980. pap. text ed. 11.95 (0-87073-804-6) Schenkman Bks Inc.

— Technology & Social Complexity. LC 82-5683. 120p. 1983. 64.50 (0-87395-644-3); pap. 21.95 (0-87395-645-1) State U NY Pr.

***Richter, Melvin.** The History of Political & Social Concepts: A Critical Introduction. 224p. 1995. text ed. 39.95 (0-19-508826-3) OUP.

Richter, Melvin, tr. see Montesquieu.

***Richter, Michael.** The Formation of the Medieval West: Studies in the Oral Culture of the Barbarians. LC 94-29797. 1995. write for info. (1-85182-153-8); write for info. (0-312-12402-3) Intl Spec Bk.

Richter, Michael, ed. see Hennig, John.

Richter, N., jt. auth. see Hoegner, W.

Richter, Nora. Austernpilz (Polyporaceae) Kochbuch: Ueber 100 Gerichte und Zubereitungstips mit Austernpilzen. (Illus.). 72p. (GER.). 1984. pap. 7.50 (0-318-19268-3) Lubrecht & Cramer.

— Champignon Kochbuch: Ueber 100 Gerichte und Zubereitungstips fuer Frische Kulturchampignons. (Illus.). 72p. (GER.). 1984. pap. text ed. 7.50 (3-923090-00-5) Lubrecht & Cramer.

— Die Schoensten Gerichte. (Illus.). 128p. (GER.). 1984. pap. text ed. 7.95 (3-923090-12-9) Lubrecht & Cramer.

Richter, O. & Sondgerath, D. Parameter Estimation in Ecology: The Link Between Data & Models. LC 89-25070. 218p. 1990. text ed. 140.00 (0-89573-917-8); 120.00 (0-685-56123-2) VCH Pubs.

Richter, O. G., jt. auth. see Huchtmeier, W. K.

Richter, P., jt. auth. see La Fauci, H. M.

Richter, P. H., jt. auth. see Peitgen, Heinz-Otto.

Richter, Patricia & Duvivier, Roger. Midlife, Madness, or Menopause: Does Anyone Know What's Normal? 250p. 1995. 9.95 (1-56561-059-8) Chronimed.

Richter, Paul, jt. auth. see Charcot, J. M.

Richter, Paul, jt. ed. see Schwadron, Terry.

Richter, Peter H., jt. ed. see Peitgen, Heinz-Otto.

Richter, Peyton. Funkaphilic Faust: And Other Pre-Millennial Verse. LC 93-90848. (Illus.). 50p. (Orig.). 1993. pap. 9.95 (0-9638954-0-0) Athenas Owl.

— Rhyming Through Georgia: Vintage Verse from the Empire State of the South. LC 94-78289. (Illus.). 52p. (Orig.). 1994. pap. 9.95 (0-9638954-1-9) Athenas Owl.

Richter, Peyton & Ricardo, Ilona. Voltaire. (World Authors Ser.: No. 583). 192p. 1980. text ed. 22.95 (0-8057-6425-9, Pub. by Royal Botanic Garden UK) Macmillan.

Richter, Peyton E. & Fogg, Walter L. Philosophy Looks to the Future: Confrontation, Commitment & Utopia. 2nd ed. 576p. (C). 1985. reprint ed. pap. text ed. 26.95 (0-88133-185-6) Waveland Pr.

Richter, R., ed. Graphs & Algorithms. LC 89-216. (CONM Ser.: Vol. 89). 1991. pap. 30.00 (0-8218-5095-4, CONM-89) Am Math.

Richter, R., jt. auth. see Assonyi, Cs.

Richter, Robert. Something in Vallarta. LC 90-53330. 1991. 22.00 (1-877946-09-5) Permanent Pr.

— Windfall Journal. (Illus.). 83p. 1980. pap. 4.00 (0-936204-10-9) Jelm Mtn.

Richter, Robert F. SEC Accounting & Reporting Manual, 2 vols. ring bd. 330.00 (0-685-69600-6, SAPM) Warren Gorham & Lamont.

Richter, Roland, tr. see Pflaum, Hans G.

Richter, Rudolf, jt. ed. see Furubotn, Eirik G.

Richter, Rudolf, jt. ed. see Haller, Max.

Richter, S., jt. auth. see Forcese, D.

Richter, Sandor, ed. The Transition from Command to Market Economies in East-Central Europe: The Vienna Institute for Comparative Economic Studies, Yearbook IV. 321p. (C). 1992. pap. text ed. 50.00 (0-8133-8559-8) Westview.

Richter, Sandor, jt. ed. see Marrese, Michael.

Richter, Scott E., et al. Securities Litigation: Forms & Analysis, 2 vols. 1989. ring bd. 250.00 (0-685-44956-4) Clark Boardman Callaghan.

Richter, Simon. Laocoon's Body & the Aesthetics of Pain: Winckelmann, Lessing, Herder, Moritz, Goethe. LC 92-13152. (Kritik: German Literary Theory & Cultural Studies). (Illus.). 231p. (C). 1992. text ed. 29.95 (0-8143-2404-5) Wayne St U Pr.

Richter, Stephen B. & Fields, Scott J. Winning Lottery Combinations, Vol. 1: Guaranteed Number Sets for All Pick 5, 6 & 7 Games. 137p. (Orig.). 1990. pap. 19.95 (0-9625318-0-4) Over Horizon.

Richter, Susan, jt. auth. see Kaare, Christian.

Richter, Vera M. Mrs. Richter's Cook-Less Book with Scientific Food Chart. 15th ed. reprint ed. spiral bd. 3.30 (0-7873-0720-3) Mokelumne.

Richter, Vera M., jt. auth. see Richter, John T.

Richter, Walter, jt. auth. see Herring, Charles, Jr.

Richter, Will, ed. see Schwartz, Eduard.

Richter, William L. The Army in Texas during Reconstruction, 1865-1870. LC 86-30056. (Military History Ser.: No. 3). 280p. 1987. 32.50 (0-89096-282-0) Tex A&M Univ Pr.

— Overreached on All Sides: The Freedmen's Bureau Administrators in Texas, 1865-1868. 448p. 1991. 49.50 (0-89096-473-4) Tex A&M Univ Pr.

— Transportation in America. (ABC-CLIO Companions Ser.). 300p. 1995. 55.00 (0-87436-789-1) ABC-CLIO.

Richter, William L. & Reagan, Charles E., eds. The Landon Lectures: Perspectives from the First Twenty Years. LC 87-81227. (Illus.). 361p. 1987. 25.00 (0-9616658-1-5) Friends Lib KSU.

Richter, William L., jt. auth. see Smith, Ronald D.

Richter, William L., et al, eds. Combating Corruption - Encouraging Ethics. 350p. 1990. 29.95 (0-936678-14-3) Am Soc Pub Admin.

Richterich, R. & Colombo, Jean-Pierre, eds. Klinische Chemie. Theorie, Praxis, Interpretation, 4: Vollstaendig neu bearbeitete Auflage. (Illus.). 1978. 65.75 (3-8055-2796-9) S Karger.

Richterich, Roland & Colombo, J. P. Clinical Chemistry: Theory, Practice, & Interpretation. LC 80-40286. (Illus.). 790p. reprint ed. pap. 180.00 (0-685-20605-X, 2030539) Bks Demand.

Richtmyer, R. D. Principles of Advanced Mathematical Physics, Vol. 1. (Texts & Monographs in Physics). (Illus.). 1985. 69.00 (0-387-08873-3) Spr-Verlag.

— Principles of Advanced Mathematical Physics, Vol. II. (Texts & Monographs in Physics). (Illus.). 350p. 1986. 65.00 (0-387-10772-X) Spr-Verlag.

Richtmyer, Robert D. & Morton, K. W. Difference Methods for Initial-Value Problems. 2nd ed. 420p. (C). 1994. reprint ed. lib. bdg. 49.50 (0-89464-763-6) Krieger.

Richtmyer, Robert D., jt. auth. see Ramsay, Arlan.

Richwine, Lynda R. Miracle in Bethlehem. 1969. 4.25 (0-685-68589-6, MC-21) Lillenas.

Ricigliano. Melody & Harmony in Contemporary Songwriting. 1978. 20.00 (0-935058-01-X); student ed 8.50 (0-935058-02-8) Donato Music.

— Popular & Jazz Harmony. 1967. 11.95 (0-935058-03-6) Donato Music.

Ricigliano, Lorraine. Austin Clarke: A Reference Guide. LC 92-42514. (Reference Publications in Literature). 180p. 1993. text ed. 45.00 (0-8161-7384-2, Hall Reference) Macmillan.

***Rick.** Reflexology Workout. 1995. write for info. (0-517-88485-2) Random Hse Value.

Rick, Abbott, tr. see Prevelakis, Pandelis.

Rick, John W. Heat-Altered Cherts of the Lower Illinois Valley. LC 80-102085. (Prehistoric Records Ser.: No. 2). (Illus.). 83p. 1978. 12.00 (0-942118-06-5); pap. 8.00 (0-942118-07-3) Ctr Amer Arche.

— Prehistoric Hunters of the High Andes. LC 79-28090. (Studies in Archaeology). 1980. text ed. 55.00 (0-12-587760-9) Acad Pr.

Rick, Shoshana. Of Milk & Honey. 56p. 1992. pap. 6.95 (965-229-086-6, Pub. by Gefen Pub Hse IS) Gefen Bks.

Rick, Stephanie. The Reflexology Workout: Hand & Foot Massage for Super Health & Rejuvenation. (Illus.). 1986. 12.00 (0-517-56176-X, Harmony) Crown Pub Group.

Rickabaugh, Marilyn. Wounded Lovers. Eaton, Dave & Flessing, Greg, eds. 20p. 1988. 34.95 (0-317-90947-9); vhs 29.95 (0-317-90948-7) Flessing & Flessing.

Rickaby, Glenys, jt. auth. see McConville, James.

Rickaby, Joseph J. Free Will & Four English Philosophers. LC 74-84333. (Essay Index Reprint Ser.). 1977. 17.95 (0-8369-1103-2) Ayer.

Rickard. Australia: A Cultural History. (Present & the Past Ser.). (Illus.). 309p. (Orig.). (C). 1988. pap. text ed. 29.50 (0-582-49330-7, 73580) Longman.

Rickard, Alan. A Book of Sonnets. pap. 7.00 (0-936128-17-8) De Young Pr.

— Collected Works of Alan Rickard. 24.49 (0-936128-50-X) De Young Pr.

— Green River Poems & Stories. (Australian Collection). pap. 7.00 (0-936128-14-3) De Young Pr.

— A Mountain Winter & Other Poems. (Australian Collection). 1984. pap. 7.00 (0-936128-12-7) De Young Pr.

— Snakes. 1991. pap. 7.00 (0-936128-26-7) De Young Pr.

— The Song of Joy & Other Poems. (Australian Collection). pap. 7.00 (0-936128-13-5) De Young Pr.

— A Story of Lebanon & Other Poems & Stories. (Australian Collection). pap. 7.00 (0-936128-15-1) De Young Pr.

Rickard, Arelene D., ed. see Rickard, Glen L.

Rickard, Clinton. Fighting Tuscarora: The Autobiography of Chief Clinton Rickard. Graymont, Barbara, ed. LC 73-8208. (York State Book Ser.). 252p. reprint ed. pap. 71.90 (0-8357-4965-7, 2037898) Bks Demand.

Rickard, Cole. Riders of the White Hell. large type ed. (Linford Western Library). 240p. 1993. pap. 14.95 (0-7089-7363-9, Linford) Ulverscroft.

Rickard, David, ed. see Royal Swedish Academy of Sciences Staff.

Rickard, G. Silver. (Spotlight on Resources Ser.). (Illus.). 48p. (J). (gr. 5 up). 1985. 12.95 (0-685-58323-6); lib. bdg. 17.27 (0-86592-273-X) Rourke Corp.

Rickard, Garth, jt. auth. see Cox, Heather.

Rickard, Glen L. Saint or Slaver. Rickard, Arelene D., ed. (Orig.). 1991. pap. 10.95 (0-9627012-0-3) G L Rickard Pub.

Rickard, Graham. Bioenergy. LC 91-9259. (Alternative Energy Ser.). (Illus.). 32p. (J). (gr. 4-6). 1991. lib. bdg. 17.27 (0-8368-0707-3) Gareth Stevens Inc.

— Bricks. LC 93-6833. (Resources Ser.). (Illus.). 32p. (J). (gr. 3-6). 1993. 13.95 (1-56847-046-0) Thomson Lrning.

— Building Homes. (Houses & Homes Ser.). (Illus.). 32p. (J). (gr. 2-5). 1989. 15.95 (0-8225-2129-6, Lerner Publctns) Lerner Group.

— Geothermal Energy. (Alternative Energy Ser.). (Illus.). 32p. (J). (gr. 4-6). 1991. lib. bdg. 17.27 (0-8368-0708-1) Gareth Stevens Inc.

— Homes in Space. (Houses & Homes Ser.). (Illus.). 32p. (J). (gr. 2-5). 1989. 13.50 (0-8225-2125-3, Lerner Publctns) Lerner Group.

— Mobile Homes. (Houses & Homes Ser.). (Illus.). 32p. (J). (gr. 2-5). 1989. 13.50 (0-8225-2130-X, Lerner Publctns) Lerner Group.

— Oil. LC 93-18304. (Resources Ser.). 32p. (J). (gr. 3-5). 1993. 13.95 (1-56847-045-2) Thomson Lrning.

— Solar Energy. (Alternative Energy Ser.). (Illus.). 32p. (J). (gr. 4-6). 1991. lib. bdg. 17.27 (0-8368-0709-X) Gareth Stevens Inc.

— Water Energy. (Alternative Energy Ser.). (Illus.). 32p. (J). (gr. 4-6). 1991. lib. bdg. 17.27 (0-8368-0710-3) Gareth Stevens Inc.

— Wind Energy. (Alternative Energy Ser.). (Illus.). 32p. (J). (gr. 4-6). 1991. lib. bdg. 17.27 (0-8368-0711-1) Gareth Stevens Inc.

Rickard, Graham, jt. auth. see Houghton, Graham.

Rickard, Henry C., ed. Behavioral Intervention in Human Problems. LC 76-112398. 434p. 1972. 181.00 (0-08-016327-0, Pub. by Pergamon Repr UK) Franklin.

Rickard, Jacqueline. Complete Premarital Contracting: Loving Communication for Today's Couples. 1993. 8.95 (0-87131-739-7) M Evans.

Rickard, John. Longer-Term Issues Conference Papers. 400p. 1991. 102.95 (1-85628-254-6, Pub. by Avebury Pub UK) Ashgate Pub Co.

Rickard, John S. Irishness & (Post) Modernism. (Buckness Review Ser., Vol. 38: No. 1). (Illus.). 232p. 1994. 22.00 (0-8387-5271-3) Bucknell U Pr.

R

An Asterisk (*) at the beginning of an entry indicates that the title is appearing in BIP for the first time.

Rickard, M. J., ed. Basement Tectonics Nine - Australia & Other Regions: Proceedings of the Ninth International Conference on Basement Tectonics, Held in Canberra, Australia, July, 1990. 272p. (C). 1992. lib. bdg. 109.50 (0-7923-1559-6) Kluwer Ac.

Rickard, Michael & Barnett, Masami D. Laboratory Exercises in Microbiology. 160p. 1993. spiral bd. 11.16 (0-8403-8514-5) Kendall-Hunt.

***Rickard, O'Ryan.** A Just Verdict: The Life of Caroline Bartlett Crane. 1994. 30.00 (0-932826-26-1); pap. 15.00 (0-932826-27-X) New Issues MI.

Rickard, P., ed. see Harmer, Lewis.

Rickard, Peter. The French Language in the Seventeenth Century: Contemporary Opinion in France. 563p. (ENG & FRE.). (C). 1992. text ed. 79.00 (0-85991-353-8, DS Brewer) Boydell & Brewer.

— A History of the French Language. 2nd ed. 192p. 1989. pap. text ed. 18.95 (0-04-445295-0) Routledge Chapman & Hall.

Rickard, Philip & Bennett, Henry. Hawaiian Heirloom Jewelry: A Lasting Remembrance. 128p. 1992. 35.00 (0-9635062-9-3); pap. 22.95 (0-9635062-8-5) HI Heirloom.

Rickard, Scott T., jt. auth. see Clement, Linda M.

Rickard, Stanley. With All Purity: What You Need to Know about Sexual Ethics. rev. ed. LC 89-29357. 30p. 1989. pap. text ed. 1.95 (0-87227-139-0, RBP5123) Reg Baptist.

Rickard, T. A. Across the San Juan Mountains. Benham, Jack L., ed. (Illus.). 178p. (Orig.). 1980. reprint ed. pap. 8.95 (0-941026-03-5) Bear Creek Pub.

Rickard, Thomas A. Man & Metals: A History of Mining in Relation to the Development of Civilization, 2 vols. in 1. LC 74-358. (Gold Ser.: Vol. 16). (Illus.). 1974. reprint ed. 81.95 (0-405-05919-1) Ayer.

Rickard, W. H., et al, eds. Shrub-Steppe: Balance & Change in a Semi-Arid Terrestrial Ecosystems. (Developments in Agricultural & Managed-Forest Ecology Ser.: No. 20). 284p. 1988. 141.00 (0-444-42990-5) Elsevier.

Rickards, Barrie, jt. ed. see Palmer, Douglas.

Rickards, Barrie, ed. see Whittington, H. B.

Rickards, G. K., jt. auth. see Jones, R. N.

***Rickards, Guy.** Hartmann, Hindemith, & Henze. (20th Century Composers Ser.). (Illus.). 240p. (Orig.). (C). 1995. pap. 19.95 (0-7148-3174-3, Pub. by Phaidon Press UK) Chronicle Bks.

Rickards, Robert & Lein, Laura. Policy Issues & Community Life in Texas: State Tax Issues, Child Care, Crime & Justice, & Hazardous Materials. (Special Project Report Ser.). 80p. 1989. 7.00 (0-89940-868-0) LBJ Sch Pub Aff.

— Vocational Education in Japan & Texas. (Policy Research Project Report Ser.: No. 100). 123p. 1992. 12.00 (0-89940-708-0) LBJ Sch Pub Aff.

Rickards, Robert, jt. auth. see Lein, Laura.

Rickards, Robert, et al. Sentencing Research in Texas: A Survey of Issues Relevant to Local Criminal Justice. (Special Project Report Ser.). 42p. 1991. 9.00 (0-89940-870-2) LBJ Sch Pub Aff.

Rickards, Robert C. Managing the Metropolis in Japan & Texas: Sister City Relationships, Municipal Finance, & Urban Economic Development Projects. (Policy Research Project Report Ser.: No. 94). 100p. 1991. 9.00 (0-89940-702-1) LBJ Sch Pub Aff.

— Socioeconomic & Political Influences on Industrial Production Decisions in East German Provinces. (Working Paper Ser.: No. 44). 36p. 1988. 5.00 (0-317-90566-X) LBJ Sch Pub Aff.

Rickards, Teresa. Dicionario Cambridge de Fisica. 256p. 1988. 39.95 (0-7859-5812-6) Fr & Eur.

— How to Win As a Mature Student. 136p. 1992. pap. 20.00 (0-7494-0677-1, Pub. by Kogan Page Educ UK) Taylor & Francis.

Rickards, Tudor. Creativity & Problem Solving at Work. 256p. 1990. pap. text ed. 25.95 (0-566-02891-3, Pub. by Gower UK) Ashgate Pub Co.

Rickart, C. E. Natural Functions Algebras. (Universitext Ser.). 240p. 1979. pap. 48.00 (0-387-90449-2) Spr-Verlag.

Rickart, Charles E. General Theory of Banach Algebras. LC 74-143. 406p. 1974. reprint ed. 41.50 (0-88275-091-7) Krieger.

— Structuralism & Structures. LC 94-28563. (Series in Pure Mathematics: Vol. 21). 230p. 1995. text ed. 48.00 (981-02-1860-5) World Scientific Pub.

Rickart, Eric A. Reproduction, Growth, & Development in Two Species of Cloud Forest Peromyscus from Southern Mexico. (Occasional Papers: No. 67). 22p. 1977. pap. 1.00 (0-317-04907-0) U of KS Mus Nat Hist.

Rickart, Paul A., ed. The Sporting News Record Book, 1925. 100p. 1988. reprint ed. pap. 3.50 (0-944786-20-0) Horton Pub.

— The Sporting News Record Book, 1926. 100p. 1988. reprint ed. pap. 3.50 (0-944786-06-5) Horton Pub.

— The Sporting News Record Book, 1927. 100p. 1988. reprint ed. pap. 3.50 (0-944786-07-3) Horton Pub.

— The Sporting News Record Book, 1928. 100p. 1988. reprint ed. pap. 3.50 (0-944786-08-1) Horton Pub.

Ricke, Helmut & Thor, Lars, eds. Swedish Glass Factories: Production Catalogues 1915-1960: Orrefors, Kosta, Elme, Eda, Stroembergshyttan. (Illus.). 442p. 1989. 185.00 (3-7913-0804-1, Pub. by Prestel) TeNeues.

Ricke, Herbert, et al. Ausgrabungen von Khor Dehmit bis Bet el-Wali. LC 68-15933. (Oriental Institute Nubian Expedition Publications: Vol. 2). (Illus.). 1968. lib. bdg. 30.00 (0-226-62366-1, OINE2) U Ch Pr.

— Beit El-Wali Temple of Ramesses Second. LC 67-18437. (Oriental Institute Nubian Expedition Publications: Vol. 1). (Illus.). 1967. lib. bdg. 30.00 (0-226-62365-3, OINE1) U Ch Pr.

Rickel, Annette U. Teen Pregnancy & Parenting. 225p. 1989. 41.00 (0-89116-808-7); pap. 26.00 (0-89116-908-3) Hemisp Pub.

Rickel, Annette U. & Allen, La Rue. Preventing Maladjustment from Infancy Through Adolescence. (Developmental Clinical Psychology & Psychiatry Ser.: Vol. 11). 160p. 1987. text ed. 37.00 (0-8039-2868-8); pap. text ed. 16.95 (0-8039-2869-6) Sage.

Rickel, Annette U., et al, eds. Social & Psychological Problems of Women: Prevention & Crisis Intervention. LC 83-18423. (Clinical & Community Psychology Ser.). 352p. 1984. text ed. 44.00 (0-89116-330-1) Hemisp Pub.

Rickel, Boyer. Arreboles. LC 91-7634. (Wesleyan New Poets Ser.). 64p. 1991. 22.50 (0-8195-2197-3, Wesleyan Univ Pr); pap. 10.95 (0-8195-1199-4, Wesleyan Univ Pr) U Pr of New Eng.

Rickels, Curtis E. The Three Ring Circus. 289p. 1992. pap. write for info. (0-9637087-0-8) Sunrise Track.

Rickels, Karl, jt. auth. see Freeman, Ellen W.

Rickels, Laurence A. Aberrations of Mourning: Writing on German Crypts. LC 87-18958. 418p. 1988. 39.95 (0-8143-1826-6) Wayne St U Pr.

— The Case of California. LC 90-49952. (Parallax). 192p. 1991. text ed. 45.00 (0-8018-4138-0); pap. text ed. 14.95x (0-8018-4139-9) Johns Hopkins.

Rickels, Laurence A., ed. Looking after Nietzsche. LC 89-4579. (SUNY Series, Intersections). 265p. 1989. 64.50 (0-7914-0156-1); pap. 21.95 (0-7914-0157-X) State U NY Pr.

Rickels, Milton. George Washington Harris. LC 65-24244. (Twayne's United States Authors Ser.). 1965. lib. bdg. 17.95 (0-89197-770-8); pap. 4.95 (0-8290-0009-7) Irvington.

— George Washington Harris. (Twayne's United States Authors Ser.). 1965. pap. 13.95 (0-8084-0144-0, T91) NCUP.

Ricken, A. Vademecum fuer Pilzfreunde: Taschenbuch Zur Bequemen Bestimmung Aller in Mittel-Europa Vorkommenden Ansehnlichen Pilzkoerper. 1969. reprint ed. 24.00 (3-7682-0603-3) Lubrecht & Cramer.

— Vademekum fuer Pilzfreunde. (GER.). 1969. 69.95 (0-8288-6618-X, M-7137) Fr & Eur.

Ricken, Friedo. Philosophy of the Ancients. Watkins, Eric, tr. LC 90-70852. 232p. (C). 1991. text ed. 29.95 (0-268-01587-2); pap. text ed. 14.95 (0-268-01588-0) U of Notre Dame Pr.

Ricken, Robert. Love Me When I'm Most Unlovable, Vol. II. 32p. (J). (gr. 6-9). 1987. pap. 4.00 (0-88210-198-6) Natl Assn Principals.

***Ricken, Robert & Anolic, Ari-zev.** The R-A Guide to Nassau County School Districts. (Orig.). 1995. pap. 14.95 (0-8062-5283-9) Carlton.

Ricken, Ulrich. Linguistics, Anthropology & Philosophy in the French Enlightenment: A Contribution to the History of the Relationship Between Language Theory & Ideology. Norton, Robert W., tr. LC 93-9651. (History of Linguistic Thought Ser.). 304p. 1993. 79.95 (0-415-07679-X, B2253) Routledge.

Ricken, Werner. Seidmentation as a Three-Component System: Organic Carbon, Carbonate, Noncarbonate. LC 93-34945. (Lecture Notes in Earth Sciences Ser.: Vol. 51). 1993. 59.00 (0-387-57386-0) Spr-Verlag.

Rickenbacher, J., et al. Applied Anatomy of the Back. Wilson, R. R. & Winstanley, D. P., trs. LC 85-9937. (Illus.). 425p. 1985. 587.00 (0-387-15132-X) Spr-Verlag.

Rickenbacker, Edward V. Rickenbacker. (Airlines History Project Ser.). (Illus.). reprint ed. 57.50 (0-404-19332-3) AMS Pr.

Rickenbacker, William F., jt. auth. see Bridges, Linda.

Rickenbaker, Michael. Breaking into Prison. 176p. (Orig.). 1993. pap. 7.95 (1-882673-00-X) Spirit & Truth.

Ricker, jt. auth. see DeWolf.

***Ricker, Elizabeth M.** Seppala - Alaskan Dog Driver. deluxe ed. 296p. 1995. 40.00 (0-614-04553-3) Donald R Hoflin.

Ricker, John F. Yuraq Janka: Guide to the Peruvian Andes - Cordilleras Blanca & Rosko. LC 77-82861. (Illus.). 180p. 1977. pap. 15.00 (0-930410-05-X) Amer Alpine Club.

Ricker, R. E. & Jones, R. H., eds. Environmental Effects on Advanced Materials. (Illus.). 315p. 1990. 94.00 (0-87339-126-8, 413) Minerals Metals.

Ricker, Robert S. & Pitkin, Ron. Soul Search: Hope for Twenty-First Century Living from Ecclesiastes. rev. ed. LC 85-21594. (Bible Commentary for Laymen Ser.). 168p. 1985. pap. 5.99 (0-8307-1100-7, S393118) Regal.

Rickerby, D. S. & Matthews, A., eds. Advanced Surface Coatings: A Handbook of Surface Engineering. 320p. 1991. 145.00 (0-412-02541-8, A4219, Blackie & Son-Chapman NY) Routledge Chapman & Hall.

Rickerby, Laura. Ulysses S. Grant & the Strategy of Victory. (History of the Civil War Ser.). (Illus.). 160p. (J). (gr. 5 up). 1990. lib. bdg. 12.95 (0-382-09944-3); pap. 7.95 (0-382-24053-7) Silver Burdett Pr.

Rickerson, Jeff. Real Estate Investors Master Guide to Real Estate Wealth & Success. Rickerson, Robert B., ed. LC 84-62753. 285p. 1985. 30.00 (0-933001-00-2); pap. 25.00 (0-317-17995-0) Intl Inst Fin Res.

Rickerson, Robert B., ed. see Rickerson, Jeff.

Rickerson, Wayne. Are We One Yet? Guide to a Growing Marriage. Schmid, Donna, ed. 64p. 1989. teacher ed 3.99 (0-87403-625-9, 3163); pap. 4.99 (0-87403-623-2, 3153) Standard Pub.

— Newly Married. (Family Ministry Ser.). 96p. 1986. pap. 19.95 (0-89191-967-8, 24836) Cook.

— This Is the Thanks I Get? A Guide to Raising Teenagers. 1988. 5.99 (0-87403-406-X, 3152) Standard Pub.

— What Should I Do Now? A Guide to Raising Children. 1988. 5.99 (0-87403-405-1, 3151) Standard Pub.

Rickert, Blandine M. Introduction a l'Etude de la Stylistique Francaise. LC 93-14526. 208p. (FRE.). 1993. pap. 29.95 (0-7734-1964-0) E Mellen.

Rickert, Corinne H. The Case of John Darrell: Minister & Exorcist. LC 62-62828. (University of Florida Humanities Monographs: No. 9). 76p. reprint ed. pap. 25.00 (0-7837-5006-4, 2044673) Bks Demand.

Rickert, Douglas E., ed. Toxicity of Nitroaromatic Compounds. LC 84-8937. (Chemical Industry Institute of Toxicology Ser.). (Illus.). 295p. 1985. 89.00 (0-89116-304-2) Hemisp Pub.

Rickert, E., jt. auth. see Manly, John M.

Rickert, Edith. Chaucer's World. Olson, Clair C. & Crow, Martin M., eds. LC 48-6059. (Illus.). 498p. reprint ed. pap. 142.00 (0-685-20584-3, 2030715) Bks Demand.

— Early English Romances in Verse, 2 vols. 1972. 200.00 (0-8490-0071-8) Gordon Pr.

Rickert, Edith, ed. The Romance of Emare. (EETS, ES Ser.: Vol. 99). 1974. reprint ed. 32.00 (0-8115-3407-3) Periodicals Srv.

Rickert, Edith & Paton, Jessie, eds. American Lyrics. LC 72-8289. (Granger Index Reprint Ser.). 1977. reprint ed. 37.95 (0-8369-6393-8) Ayer.

Rickert, Edith, jt. auth. see Manly, John M.

Rickert, Heinrich. The Limits of Concept Formation in Natural Science: A Logical Introduction to the Historical Sciences. abr. ed. Oakes, Guy, ed. & tr. by. (Texts in German Philosophy Ser.). 304p. 1986. pap. 24.95 (0-521-31015-6) Cambridge U Pr.

***Rickert, Vaughn I., ed.** Adolescent Nutrition: Assessment & Management. LC 95-7376. (Series in Clinical Nutrition). 1995. write for info. (0-412-05661-5) Chapman & Hall.

Rickert, William & Bloomquist, Jane. Resources in Theatre & Disability. LC 88-5545. 208p. (Orig.). (C). 1988. lib. bdg. 47.00 (0-8191-5748-1, Assn Theatre & Disabilty); pap. text ed. 25.00 (0-8191-5749-X, Assn Theatre & Disabilty) U Pr of Amer.

Rickes, Persis, jt. auth. see Kacmarczyk, Ronald H.

Ricketson, Anna & Ricketson, Walton, eds. Daniel Ricketson & His Friends: Letter, Poems, Sketches, Etc. LC 80-2513. (Thoreau Ser.). (Illus.). 440p. reprint ed. 67.50 (0-404-19061-8) AMS Pr.

Ricketson, Jean C., jt. auth. see Ricketson, William F.

***Ricketson, S.** Intellectual Property: Cases & Materials & Commentary. 1100p. 1994. pap. 147.00 (0-409-30265-1, Austral) Butterworth Legal Pubs.

Ricketson, Staniforth. The Law of Intellectual Property. clxxv, 1201p. 1984. 150.00 (0-455-20417-9, Pub. by Law Bk Co); pap. 130.00 (0-455-20553-1, Pub. by Law Bk Co) W W Gaunt.

Ricketson, Susan C. Dilemma of Love: Healing Co-dependent Relationships at Different Stages of Life. 192p. 1989. 9.95 (1-55874-051-1) Health Comm.

Ricketson, Walton, jt. ed. see Ricketson, Anna.

Ricketson, William F. & Ricketson, Jean C. Overview of Western Civilization: A Guide, Vol. I. 196p. (Orig.). (C). 1984. pap. text ed. 22.00 (0-8191-3968-8) U Pr of Amer.

Ricketson, William F., jt. auth. see Wilson, Jerome D.

Rickett, A. A., tr. see Wang Kuo-wei.

Rickett, Adele A., ed. Chinese Approaches to Literature from Confucius to Liang Chi-Chao. LC 77-7311. 282p. reprint ed. pap. 80.40 (0-8357-6055-3, 2034650) Bks Demand.

Rickett, Arthur. Vagabond in Literature. LC 68-8489. (Essay Index Reprint Ser.). 1977. reprint ed. 19.95 (0-8369-0825-2) Ayer.

Rickett, Frances. Doctors' Affairs. 1990. mass mkt. 4.50 (1-55817-413-3, Pinnacle NY) Windsor NY.

Rickett, H. W., intro. Tiny Folios: Wildflowers of America. LC 92-40132. 456p. 1993. 10.95 (1-55859-564-3) Abbeville Pr.

Rickett, H. W., ed. see Colden, J.

Rickett, Harold. The Northeastern States. LC 66-17920. (Wild Flowers of the United States Ser.: Vol. 1, 2 Pts.). (Illus.). 559p. 1966. text ed. 65.00 (0-89327-274-4) NY Botanical.

Rickett, Harold W. Central Mountain & Plains States. LC 66-17920. (Wild Flowers of the United States Ser.: Vol. 6, 3 Pts.). (Illus.). 784p. 1973. text ed. 92.00 (0-89327-287-6) NY Botanical.

— The Northwestern States. LC 66-17920. (World Flowers of the United States Ser.: Vol. 5, 2 Pts.). (Illus.). 666p. 1971. text ed. 85.00 (0-89327-284-1) NY Botanical.

— The Southeastern States. (Wild Flowers of the United States Ser.: Vol. 2). (Illus.). 688p. 1976. text ed. 85.00 (0-89327-277-9) NY Botanical.

— The Southwestern States. (Wild Flowers of the United States Ser.: Vol. 4). (Illus.). 801p. 1970. text ed. 92.00 (0-89327-280-9) NY Botanical.

— Wild Flowers of the United States, Vol. 1: Northeastern States. (Illus.). 559p. 1966. 60.00 (0-685-63143-5) NY Botanical.

— Wild Flowers of the United States, Vol. 2: Southeastern States. (Illus.). 688p. 1967. 90.00 (0-685-63144-3) NY Botanical.

— Wild Flowers of the United States, Vol. 4: Southwestern States. (Illus.). 801p. 1970. 99.00 (0-685-63145-1) NY Botanical.

— Wild Flowers of the United States, Vol. 5: Northwestern States. (Illus.). 666p. 1971. 90.00 (0-685-63146-X) NY Botanical.

— Wild Flowers of the United States, Vol. 6: Central Mountains & Plains. (Illus.). 784p. 1973. 99.00 (0-685-63147-8) NY Botanical.

Rickett, Richard. Music & Musicians in Vienna. (Illus.). 27.00 (3-85367-019-9) IBD Ltd.

Rickett, W. Allyn. Guanzi: Political, Economic, & Philosophical Essays from Early China-a Study & Translation. LC 84-15094. (Library of Asian Translations). 500p. 1985. 70.00 (0-691-06605-1) Princeton U Pr.

Rickett, W. Allyn, tr. see Kuan, Chung.

Ricketts, Alan. Dorothy Livesay: An Annotated Bibliography. 76p. (C). 1983. pap. text ed. 9.00 (0-920763-57-X, Pub. by ECW Press CN) Genl Dist Srvs.

Ricketts, Carl E. El Lobo & Spanish Gold: A Texas Maverick in Mexico. LC 74-77508. (Illus.). 210p. 1974. 11.50 (0-89052-006-2) Madrona Pr.

Ricketts, David & Guasti, Carol A., eds. Family Circle Busy Cooks Book. 320p. 1988. 19.95 (0-933585-09-8) Family Circle Bks.

Ricketts, David & McQuillan, Susan. Simply Healthful Fish: Delicious New Low-Fat Recipes. LC 92-39978. (Simply Healthful Ser.). (Illus.). 96p. (Orig.). 1993. pap. 9.95 (1-881527-05-0) Chapters Pub.

— Simply Healthful Pizzas & Calzones: Delicious New Low-Fat Recipes. LC 93-45013. (Simply Healthful Ser.). (Illus.). 96p. (Orig.). 1994. pap. 9.95 (1-881527-34-4) Chapters Pub.

Ricketts, David, ed. see Family Circle Editors.

Ricketts, David, jt. auth. see Family Circle Editors.

Ricketts, Donald & Gray, Jack. Managerial Accounting. 2nd ed. (C). 1991. write for info. (0-395-43362-2) HM Soft Schl Col Div.

Ricketts, Donald & Sorkin, Horton L. Quantitative Techniques for Internal Auditing. Holman, Richard, ed. (Research Reports: No. 27). (Illus.). 106p. (C). 1983. pap. text ed. 33.00 (0-89413-108-7) Inst Inter Aud.

Ricketts, Edward F., jt. auth. see Steinbeck, John.

Ricketts, Edward F., et al. Between Pacific Tides. 5th ed. LC 83-40620. (Illus.). 680p. (C). 1985. 55.00 (0-8047-1229-8); pap. 19.95 (0-8047-2068-1) Stanford U Pr.

Ricketts, Jennifer, ed. see Macduff, Nancy.

Ricketts, L. W. Fundamentals of Nuclear Hardening of Electronic Equipment. 586p. 1986. reprint ed. text ed. 67.50 (0-89874-941-7) Krieger.

Ricketts, Mac L. Mircea Eliade: The Romanian Roots, 1907-1945, 2 vols., Set. (East European Monographs: No. 248). 1500p. 1988. text ed. 240.00 (0-88033-145-3) East Eur Quarterly.

Ricketts, Mac L., tr. see Eliade, Mircea.

Ricketts, Mac Linscott, tr. see Stanescu, Gabriel, ed.

Ricketts, Marijane, ed. see Writers' League of Washington Staff.

Ricketts, Marijane G. Is It the Onions Making Life Pungent? Cameron, Dana, ed. (Orig.). (YA). (gr. 7 up). 1987. reprint ed. pap. 7.50 (0-9618223-0-9) M G Ricketts.

Ricketts, Marijane G. & Van den Broek, Gonny, eds. The Poets of Ellicott Street. 48p. (Orig.). 1989. pap. 5.00 (0-9618223-1-7) M G Ricketts.

***Ricketts, Mark.** Book of the Twilight Graphic Novel. (Illus.). 144p. 1994. 13.95 (0-941613-63-1) Stabur Pr.

Ricketts, Mark, jt. ed. see Bendis, Brian.

Ricketts, Martin. The Economics of Business Enterprise. 2nd ed. 400p. 1994. pap. text ed. 38.00 (0-13-302688-4) P-H.

— Neoclassical Microeconomics, 2 vols., Set. 372p. 1989. text ed. 229.95 (1-85278-115-7, Pub. by E Elgar Pub UK) Ashgate Pub Co.

— The New Industrial Economics: An Introduction to Modern Theories of the Firm. LC 86-27918. 320p. 1987. text ed. 39.95 (0-312-00458-3) St Martin.

Ricketts, Max & Bien, Edwin. The Great Anxiety Escape. (Illus.). 224p. (Orig.). 1990. pap. 9.95 (0-9626205-0-5) Matulungin Pub.

Ricketts, Mitchell S. Bobcat Trapper's Guide. (Illus.). 116p. (Orig.). 1987. pap. 10.95 (0-9617720-0-X) Elk River Pr.

— Muskrat Trapper's Guide. LC 88-81827. (Illus.). 182p. (Orig.). 1988. pap. 13.95 (0-9617720-1-8) Elk River Pr.

Ricketts, R. Allan & Norton, Richard J., eds. National Security: Case Studies in Policy Making & Implementation, Vol. I. (Illus.). (C). 1994. teacher ed, pap. write for info. (1-884733-02-6) Naval War Coll.

Ricketts, Robert, tr. see Hayashi, Ryoichi.

Ricketts, Robert M. The Reappearing American. 360p. 1993. text ed. 21.95 (0-9635961-0-1) Wright & Co.

Ricketts, Sarah, jt. auth. see Bubna, Donald.

Ricketts, Sarah J. A Window on Eternity: The Life & Poetry of Jane Hess Merchant. LC 82-16276. (Abingdon Classics Ser.). 336p. 1992. pap. 5.95 (0-687-45602-9) Abingdon.

Ricketts, Thomas C., III, jt. ed. see Gesler, Wilbert.

Ricketts, Thomas C., et al, eds. Geographic Methods for Health Services Research: A Focus on the Rural-Urban Continuum. 396p. (Orig.). 1994. lib. bdg. 54.00 (0-8191-9532-4); pap. text ed. 36.50 (0-8191-9533-2) U Pr of Amer.

Ricketts, Viva L., jt. auth. see Pisano, Beverly.

Ricketts, Wendell. Lesbians & Gay Men As Foster Parents. (Orig.). 1991. pap. write for info. (0-939561-09-3) Univ South ME.

Ricketts, Wendell, et al, eds. Intimate Relationships: Some Social Work Perspectives on Love. LC 87-19729. (Journal of Social Work & Human Sexuality: Vol. 5, No. 2). 140p. 1987. text ed. 24.95 (0-86656-712-7) Haworth Pr.

Rickey, Alfred J. Voyage to Destiny. 226p. (Orig.). 1989. pap. 8.95 (0-9623077-0-X) Aldarob Enterprises.

Rickey, Carrie, jt. auth. see Friis-Hansen, Dana.

Rickey, Don, Jr. Forty Miles a Day on Beans & Hay: The Enlisted Soldier Fighting the Indian Wars. LC 62-9952. (Illus.). 1963. reprint ed. pap. 14.95 (0-8061-1113-5) U of Okla Pr.

***Rickey, George.** Constructivism: Origins & Evolution. rev. ed. (Illus.). 306p. 1995. 25.00 (0-8076-1381-9) Braziller.

Rickey, Mary E. Rhyme & Meaning in Crashaw. LC 72-5491. (Studies in Poetry: No. 38). 1972. reprint ed. lib. bdg. 45.95 (0-8383-1603-4) M S G Haskell Hse.

Rickey, V. F., jt. ed. see Srzednicki, Jan T.

R

An Asterisk (*) at the beginning of an entry indicates that the title is appearing in BIP for the first time.

Rickford, John R. Dimensions of a Creole Continuum: History, Texts, & Linguistic Analysis of Guyanese Creole. LC 87-10065. (Illus.). 368p. 1987. 45.00 (*0-8047-1377-4*) Stanford U Pr.

Rickgarn, Ralph L. V. Perspectives on College Student Suicide. LC 94-41. (Death, Value, & Meaning Ser.). 262p. 1994. text ed. 25.95 (*0-89503-153-1*); pap. 19.45 (*0-89503-154-X*) Baywood Pub.

Rickheit, G. & Strohner, H., eds. Inferences in Text Processing: Advances in Psychology, Vol. 29. 360p. 1985. 105.25 (*0-444-87828-9*, North Holland) Elsevier.

Rickheit, Gert & Bock, Michael, eds. Psycholinguistic Studies in Language Processing. (Research in Text Theory Ser.: Vol. 7). viii, 305p. 1983. 112.35 (*3-11-008994-7*) De Gruyter.

Ricking, Myrl. Personnel Utilization in Libraries: A Systems Approach. LC 74-8688. 168p. reprint ed. pap. 47.90 (*0-317-26570-9*, 2023953) Bks Demand.

Ricklefs, M. C. A History of Modern Indonesia since c. 1300. 2nd ed. LC 92-85217. (Illus.). 380p. (C). 1993. 45.00 (*0-8047-2194-7*); pap. 15.95 (*0-8047-2195-5*) Stanford U Pr.

Ricklefs, Merle. War, Culture & Economy in Java: 1677-1726. 224p. 1993. pap. text ed. 24.95 (*1-86373-380-9*, Pub. by Allen Unwin AT) Paul & Co Pubs.

Ricklefs, Robert E. Ecology. 3rd ed. 832p. (C). 1995. text ed. write for info. (*0-7167-2077-9*) W H Freeman.

— The Economy of Nature: A Textbook in Basic Ecology. 3rd ed. LC 92-39616. (C). 1995. pap. text ed. write for info. (*0-7167-2409-X*) W H Freeman.

Ricklefs, Robert E., ed. Audubon Conservation Report No. 6: Report of the Advisory Panel on the California Condor. (Audubon Conservation Report Ser.). (Illus.). 1978. pap. 3.00 (*0-930698-04-5*) Natl Audubon.

***Ricklefs, Robert E. & Finch, Caleb E.** Aging: A Natural History. LC 95-2334. 1995. text ed. write for info. (*0-7167-5056-2*) W H Freeman.

Ricklefs, Robert E. & Schluter, Dolph, eds. Species Diversity in Ecological Communities: Historical & Geographical Perspectives. LC 93-16747. (Illus.). 454p. 1993. Acid-free paper. lib. bdg. 98.00 (*0-226-71822-0*); Acid-free paper. pap. text ed. 32.50 (*0-226-71823-9*) U Ch Pr.

Ricklefs, Roger, ed. see Stevenson, Robert Louis.

Ricklen, Neil. Baby's Big & Little. (J). 1990. 4.95 (*0-671-69542-8*) S&S Trade.

— Baby's Colors. (J). 1990. 4.95 (*0-671-69539-8*) S&S Trade.

— Baby's Day. (J). 1994. 4.95 (*0-671-89110-3*, Litl Simon S&S) S&S Childrens.

— Baby's Good Morning: A Super Chubby Board Book. (J). (ps). 1992. pap. 4.95 (*0-671-76084-X*, Litl Simon S&S) S&S Childrens.

— Baby's Good Night: A Super Chubby Board Book. (J). (ps). 1992. pap. 4.95 (*0-671-76085-8*, Litl Simon S&S) S&S Childrens.

— Baby's Neighborhood. (J). 1994. 4.95 (*0-671-89111-1*, Litl Simon S&S) S&S Childrens.

— Baby's Playtime. (J). 1994. 4.95 (*0-671-89113-8*, Litl Simon S&S) S&S Childrens.

— Baby's School: A Super Chubby Board Book. (J). (ps). 1992. pap. 4.95 (*0-671-76086-6*, Litl Simon S&S) S&S Childrens.

— Baby's Year. (J). 1994. 4.95 (*0-671-89112-X*, Litl Simon S&S) S&S Childrens.

— Baby's Zoo: A Super Chubby Board Book. (J). (ps). 1992. pap. 4.95 (*0-671-76087-4*, Litl Simon S&S) S&S Childrens.

— Baby's 1-2-3. (J). 1990. 4.95 (*0-671-69541-X*) S&S Trade.

— First Word Books: ABC. (J). (ps). 1994. pap. 5.95 (*0-671-86725-3*, Litl Simon S&S) S&S Childrens.

— First Word Books: Colors. (J). (ps). 1994. pap. 5.95 (*0-671-86726-1*, Litl Simon S&S) S&S Childrens.

— First Word Books: Opposites. (J). (ps). 1994. pap. 5.95 (*0-671-86728-8*, Litl Simon S&S) S&S Childrens.

— First Word Books: 1-2-3. (J). (ps). 1994. pap. 5.95 (*0-671-86727-X*, Litl Simon S&S) S&S Childrens.

Ricklen, Neil, illus. My Clothes: Mi Ropa. LC 93-27162. (Spanish English Board Bks.). 14p. (ENG & SPA.). (J). (ps-00). 1994. pap. 3.95 (*0-689-71773-3*, Aladdin Paperbacks) S&S Childrens.

— My Colors: Mis Colores. LC 93-27195. (Spanish English Board Bks.). 14p. (ENG & SPA.). (J). (ps-00). 1994. pap. 3.95 (*0-689-71772-5*, Aladdin Paperbacks) S&S Childrens.

— My Family: Mi Familia. LC 93-30661. (Spanish English Board Bks.). 14p. (ENG & SPA.). (J). (ps-00). 1994. pap. 3.95 (*0-689-71771-7*, Aladdin Paperbacks) S&S Childrens.

— My Numbers: Mis Numeros. LC 93-27165. (Spanish English Board Bks.). 14p. (ENG & SPA.). (J). (ps-00). 1994. pap. 3.95 (*0-689-71770-9*, Aladdin Paperbacks) S&S Childrens.

Ricklen, Neil, photos. Baby Inside. (Super Chubby Photo Board Bks.). (Illus.). 24p. (J). (ps). 1991. boxed, pap. 4.95 (*0-671-73878-X*, Litl Simon S&S) S&S Childrens.

— Baby Outside. (Super Chubby Photo Board Bks.). (Illus.). 24p. (J). (ps). 1991. boxed, pap. 4.95 (*0-671-73879-8*, Litl Simon S&S) S&S Childrens.

— Baby's ABC. (Super Chubby Photo Board Bks.). (Illus.). 24p. (J). 1990. boxed 4.95 (*0-671-69540-1*, Litl Simon S&S) S&S Childrens.

— Baby's Birthday. (Super Chubby Photo Board Bks.). (Illus.). 24p. (J). (ps). 1991. boxed, pap. 4.95 (*0-671-73880-1*, Litl Simon S&S) S&S Childrens.

— Baby's Christmas. (Super Chubby Photo Board Bks.). (Illus.). 24p. (J). (ps). 1991. boxed, pap. 4.95 (*0-671-73881-X*, Litl Simon S&S) S&S Childrens.

Ricklin, Neil. Baby's Clothes. (J). 1986. 4.95 (*0-671-62075-4*) S&S Trade.

— Baby's Friends. (J). 1986. 4.95 (*0-671-62076-2*) S&S Trade.

— Baby's Home. 1986. 4.95 (*0-671-62077-0*) S&S Trade.

— Baby's Toys. (J). 1986. 4.95 (*0-671-62078-9*) S&S Trade.

Ricklin, Neil, photos. Daddy & Me. (Super Chubby Photo Board Bks.). (Illus.). 28p. (J). (ps). 1988. 4.95 (*0-671-64537-4*, Litl Simon S&S) S&S Childrens.

— Grandma & Me. (Super Chubby Photo Board Bks.). (Illus.). 28p. (J). (ps-00). 1988. 4.95 (*0-671-64540-4*, S&S Bks Young Read) S&S Childrens.

— Grandpa & Me. (Super Chubby Photo Board Bks.). (Illus.). 28p. (J). (ps-00). 1988. 4.95 (*0-671-64539-0*, S&S Bks Young Read) S&S Childrens.

— Mommy & Me. (Super Chubby Photo Board Bks.). (Illus.). 28p. (J). (ps-00). 1988. 4.95 (*0-671-64538-2*, Litl Simon S&S) S&S Childrens.

Rickman. Handbook of Incineration of Hazardous Wastes. 1991. 268.00 (*0-8493-0557-8*, QD96) CRC Pr.

Rickman, jt. auth. see Goetsch, David L.

Rickman, Colleen B. & Rickman, John J. Shaken & Stirred: A Complete Drink Recipe Guide. (Orig.). 1992. pap. write for info. (*0-9632889-0-3*) Rabbit Eye.

Rickman, David. California Missions Coloring Book. (Illus.). (J). (gr. k-3). 1992. pap. 2.95 (*0-486-27346-6*) Dover.

— Cowboys of the Old West Coloring Book. (Illus.). (J). (gr. k-3). 1985. pap. 2.95 (*0-486-25001-6*) Dover.

— Plains Indians Coloring Book. (Illus.). (J). (gr. 4-7). 1983. pap. 2.95 (*0-486-24470-9*) Dover.

Rickman, Geoffrey. Roman Granaries & Store Buildings. LC 76-116843. 397p. reprint ed. pap. 113.20 (*0-317-10131-5*, 2013245) Bks Demand.

Rickman, H. P. Dilthey Today: A Critical Appraisal of the Contemporary Relevance of His Work. LC 87-31779. (Contributions in Philosophy Ser.: No. 35). 224p. 1988. text ed. 49.95 (*0-313-25933-X*, RDT/, Greenwood Pr) Greenwood.

Rickman, H. P., ed. The Adventure of Reason: The Uses of Philosophy in Sociology. LC 83-5622. (Contributions in Sociology Ser.: No. 46). xi, 172p. 1983. text ed. 49.95 (*0-313-23871-5*, RAR/, Greenwood Pr) Greenwood.

Rickman, John J., jt. auth. see Rickman, Colleen B.

Rickman, Jon T. & Hubbard, Dean L. The Electronic Campus: A Case History of the First Comprehensive High-Access Academic Computing Network at a Public University. LC 92-93868. (Illus.). 105p. (Orig.). (C). 1992. pap. 14.95 (*0-9633819-9-7*) Prescott Pub.

***Rickman, Phil.** Candlenight. 480p. Date not set. pap. text ed. 5.99 (*0-515-11715-3*) Jove Pubns.

— Curfew. LC 93-13721. Orig. Title: Crybbe. 496p. 1993. 23.95 (*0-399-13861-7*, Putnam) Putnam Pub Group.

Rickman, Seppo. Quasiregular Mappings. LC 93-4824. (Ergebnisse der Mathematik und Ihrer Grenzgebiete Ser.: Vol. 3). 1993. 89.00 (*0-387-56648-1*) Spr-Verlag.

Rickmers, A. D. & Todd, H. N. Statistics: An Introduction. 1967. text ed. write for info. (*0-07-052616-8*) McGraw.

Rickmers, C. Mabel. The Chronology of Indian History. 420p. reprint ed. text ed. 27.50 (*0-685-13325-7*) Coronet Bks.

Rickmers, C. Mabel, tr. Culavamsa: Being the More Recent Part of Mahavamsa, 2 vols., Set. (C). 1992. reprint ed. text ed. 42.00 (*81-206-0430-X*, Pub. by Asian Educ Servs II) S Asia.

Rickover, H. G. How the Battleship Maine Was Destroyed. LC 94-7345. (Illus.). 208p. 1995. 29.95 (*1-55750-717-1*) Naval Inst Pr.

Rickover, Robert M. Fitness Without Stress: A Guide to the Alexander Technique. (Positive Change Guide Ser.). 144p. 1988. lib. bdg. 14.95 (*0-943920-32-9*); pap. 9.95 (*1-55552-037-5*) Metamorphous Pr.

Ricks, Beatrice, comp. William Faulkner: A Bibliography of Secondary Works. LC 80-15251. (Author Bibliographies Ser.: No. 49). 684p. 1981. lib. bdg. 49.50 (*0-8108-1323-8*) Scarecrow.

Ricks, Betty, jt. auth. see McAfee, Bruce.

***Ricks, Betty R.** Contemporary Supervision: Managing People & Technology. 1994. pap. 39.95 (*0-07-052648-6*) McGraw.

Ricks, Betty R. & Gow, Kay F. Business Communication: Systems & Applications. LC 86-26747. 479p. 1987. text ed. 34.50 (*0-471-81824-0*) P-H.

Ricks, Betty R., jt. auth. see Daughtrey, Anne S.

Ricks, Chip. Exploring the New Testament: The Four Gospels. 194p. 1991. teacher ed. 18.99 (*1-56322-040-7*); pap. text ed. 12.99 (*1-56322-039-3*) V Hensley.

***Ricks, Christopher.** Beckett's Dying Words. 224p. 1995. pap. 12.95 (*0-19-282407-4*) OUP.

— Beckett's Dying Words: The Clarendon Lectures, 1990. LC 92-47234. 224p. (C). 1993. 28.00 (*0-19-812358-2*) OUP.

— The Faber Book of America. 1993. pap. 14.95 (*0-571-19826-0*) Faber & Faber.

— Faber Book of America. 1993. pap. 14.95 (*0-685-67237-9*) Faber & Faber.

— The Force of Poetry. 464p. 1995. pap. 15.95 (*0-19-818326-7*) OUP.

— Keats & Embarrassment. 1984. reprint ed. pap. 17.95 (*0-19-812829-0*) OUP.

— New Oxford Book of Victorian Verse. (Oxford Poets Ser.). 688p. 1990. pap. 14.95 (*0-19-282778-2*) OUP.

Ricks, Christopher, ed. A. E. Housman: A Collection of Critical Essays. (Twentieth Century Views Ser.). 1968. 12.95 (*0-13-395913-9*, Spectrum Bks); pap. 1.95 (*0-13-395905-8*, STC83, Spectrum Bks) P-H.

— English Drama to Seventeen Ten. LC 87-47748. (New History of Literature Ser.). 450p. 1987. 39.50 (*0-87226-127-1*) P Bedrick Bks.

— English Drama to 1710. (Penguin History of Literature Ser.). 480p. 1994. 12.00 (*0-14-017753-1*, Penguin Bks) Viking Penguin.

— English Poetry & Prose, Fifteen Forty to Sixteen Seventy Four. LC 86-14031. (New History of Literature Ser.). 472p. 1987. 39.50 (*0-87226-126-3*) P Bedrick Bks.

— English Poetry & Prose 1540-1674. (Penguin History of Literature Ser.). 480p. 1994. 12.00 (*0-14-017752-3*, Penguin Bks) Viking Penguin.

— The New Oxford Book of Victorian Verse: (Illus.). 698p. 1987. 30.00 (*0-19-214154-6*) OUP.

Ricks, Christopher & Day, Aidan, eds. Tennyson, No. XVI. (Tennyson Archive Ser.). 316p. 1989. reprint ed. 163.00 (*0-8240-4215-8*) Garland.

— Tennyson, No. XVII. (Tennyson Archive Ser.). 318p. 1989. reprint ed. 163.00 (*0-8240-4216-6*) Garland.

— Tennyson, No. XVIII. (Tennyson Archive Ser.). 336p. 1989. reprint ed. 163.00 (*0-8240-4217-4*) Garland.

— Tennyson, No. XIX. (Tennyson Archive Ser.). 328p. 1989. reprint ed. 163.00 (*0-8240-4218-2*) Garland.

— Tennyson, No. XX. (Tennyson Archive Ser.). 312p. 1989. reprint ed. 163.00 (*0-8240-4219-0*) Garland.

— Tennyson, No. XXI. (Tennyson Archive Ser.). 320p. 1989. reprint ed. 163.00 (*0-8240-4220-4*) Garland.

— Tennyson, No. XXII. (Tennyson Archive Ser.). 336p. 1989. reprint ed. 163.00 (*0-8240-4221-2*) Garland.

— Tennyson, No. XXIII. (Tennyson Archive Ser.). 304p. 1989. reprint ed. 163.00 (*0-8240-4222-0*) Garland.

— The Tennyson Archive: The Manuscripts at the Victoria & Albert Museum, the Robert H. Taylor Collection of Princeton University, & the Alderman Library of the University of Virginia. LC 92-16236. (Tennyson Archive Ser.: Vol. 30). 316p. 1992. 163.00 (*0-8240-4229-8*) Garland.

— Tennyson, the Manuscripts in the Minor Collections & the Indexes for the Tennyson Archive. LC 92-36298. 192p. 1993. 110.00 (*0-8240-4230-1*) Garland.

Ricks, Christopher & Michaels, Leonard, eds. The State of the Language, 1990 Edition. 600p. 1989. 40.00 (*0-520-05906-9*) U CA Pr.

Ricks, Christopher & Vance, William L., eds. The Faber Book of America. 624p. 1992. 24.95 (*0-571-14405-5*) Faber & Faber.

Ricks, Christopher, ed. see Milton, John.

Ricks, Christopher, ed. see Tennyson, Alfred.

Ricks, David. Byzantine Heroic Poetry. 192p. (ENG & GRE.). (C). 1990. text ed. 45.00 (*0-89241-498-7*) Caratzas.

— Origins of Psychopathology: Problems in Research & Public Policy. Dohrenwenwend, Barbara S., ed. LC 82-14638. (Illus.). 304p. 1983. 49.95 (*0-521-25298-9*) Cambridge U Pr.

— The Shade of Homer: A Study in Modern Greek Poetry. (C). 1990. 54.95 (*0-521-36663-1*) Cambridge U Pr.

Ricks, David, jt. auth. see Beaton, Roderick.

Ricks, David, jt. ed. see Lee, Simon.

Ricks, David A. Blunders in International Business. LC 92-33483. 192p. 1993. 16.95 (*1-55786-414-4*) Blackwell Pubs.

Ricks, David A., jt. ed. see Arpan, Jeffrey S.

Ricks, David A., jt. auth. see Punnett, Betty J.

Ricks, David F. & Dohrenwend, Barbara S., eds. Origins of Psychopathology: Problems in Research & Public Policy. LC 82-14638. 295p. reprint ed. pap. 84.10 (*0-318-34662-1*, 2031717) Bks Demand.

Ricks, Day, ed. The Tennyson Archive, Vol. 11: The Manuscripts at Trinity College, Cambridge: Miscellaneous Manuscripts & Notebooks 13-17. LC 88-16352. 318p. 1988. 163.00 (*0-8240-4210-7*) Garland.

— The Tennyson Archive, Vol. 12: The Manuscripts at Trinity College, Cambridge: Notebooks 18-25. LC 88-16352. 360p. 1988. 163.00 (*0-8240-4211-5*) Garland.

— The Tennyson Archive, Vol. 13: The Manuscripts at Trinity College, Cambridge: Notebooks 26-29. LC 88-16352. 334p. 1988. 163.00 (*0-8240-4212-3*) Garland.

— The Tennyson Archive, Vol. 14: The Manuscripts at Trinity College, Cambridge: Notebooks 30-36. LC 88-16352. 424p. 1988. 163.00 (*0-8240-4213-1*) Garland.

— The Tennyson Archive, Vol. 15: The Manuscripts at Trinity College, Cambridge: Notebooks 37-40 & Miscellaneous Manuscripts. LC 88-16352. 356p. 1988. 163.00 (*0-8240-4214-X*) Garland.

Ricks, Delthia T., et al. Hysterectomy & You. (Illus.). 1994. pap. 3.60 (*0-318-37516-8*) Budlong.

Ricks, Don M. Winning the Paper Wars: An Executive's Guide to Crystal Clear Communications. 225p. 1990. text ed. 25.00 (*1-55623-371-5*) Irwin Prof Pubng.

Ricks, Eldin. Combination Reference. 78p. 1979. pap. 6.95 (*0-87747-038-3*) Deseret Bk.

Ricks, Gary, jt. auth. see Crispin-Little, Jan.

Ricks, George R. Some Aspects of the Religious Music of the United States Negro. Dorson, Richard M., ed. LC 77-70621. (International Folklore Ser.). 1979. reprint ed. lib. bdg. 40.95 (*0-405-10123-6*) Ayer.

Ricks, Howard, et al, comps. Ricks: History & Genealogy of the Ricks Family of America, Descendants of Isaac Ricks, born in England, 1638, & His Wife Kathren, & Allied Families. rev. ed. (Illus.). 767p. 1994. reprint ed. lib. bdg. 119.00 (*0-8328-4088-2*); reprint ed. pap. 109.00 (*0-8328-4089-0*) Higginson Bk Co.

Ricks, J. Brent. Kachinas: Spirit Beings of the Hopi. LC 92-8363. (Illus.). 200p. 1993. 50.00 (*0-936755-21-0*) Avanyu Pub.

Ricks, Jay & Wiley, Richard E. The Cable Communication Policy Act of 1984. 1985. 35.00 (*0-317-29482-2*, #CO3360) HarBrace.

Ricks, Lucille. A Buffalo Soldier's Legacy: "Ready & Forward" 3rd ed. (Illus.). 126p. 1993. pap. 12.00 (*0-929757-99-8*) Regt QM.

Ricks, Melvin. Alaska Bibliography: An Introductory Guide to Alaskan Historical Literature. LC 77-80570. 288p. 1977. 20.00 (*0-8323-0292-9*) Binford Mort.

Ricks, R. C. & Fry, S. A., eds. The Medical Basis for Radiation Accident Preparedness. 548p. 1991. 175.00 (*0-444-01585-X*) P-H.

Ricks, Shirley S., ed. see Nibley, Hugh.

Ricks, Stephen D., ed. Western Language Literature on Pre-Islamic Central Arabia: An Annotated Bibliography. (Bibliographic Ser.: No. 8). 163p. (Orig.). 1991. pap. text ed. 10.00 (*0-933017-01-4*) Am Inst Islamic.

Ricks, Stephen D. & Welch, John W., eds. The Allegory of the Olive Tree. LC 93-36632. 624p. 1994. 28.95 (*0-87579-767-9*) Deseret Bk.

Ricks, Stephen D., jt. ed. see Brinner, William M.

Ricks, Stephen D., jt. ed. see Hamblin, William J.

Ricks, Stephen D., jt. ed. see Lundquist, John M.

Ricks, Stephen D., jt. auth. see Parry, Donald W.

Ricks, Stephen D., jt. auth. see Peterson, Daniel C.

Ricks, Thomas, jt. auth. see Armajani, Yahya.

Ricks, Thomas M., ed. Critical Perspectives on Modern Persian Literature. LC 81-51656. (Critical Perspectives Ser.). (Illus.). 540p. 1984. 40.00 (*0-914478-95-8*) Three Continents.

Ricks, Truett A., et al. Principles of Security. 3rd ed. LC 93-71748. (Illus.). 462p. (C). 1993. pap. text ed. write for info. (*0-87084-746-5*) Anderson Pub Co.

— Principles of Security: An Introduction. 2nd ed. LC 87-12159. (Criminal Justice Studies). 1988. 23.95 (*0-87084-745-7*) Anderson Pub Co.

***Rickson, R. J., ed.** Conserving Soil Resources: European Perspectives. 450p. 1994. 85.00x (*0-85198-948-9*) CAB Intl.

***Rickson, Richard, ed.** Asian & Australasian Companies: A Guide to Sources of Information. 334p. 1994. 94.95 (*0-900246-61-8*) CBD Res.

Rickwood, D., ed. Centrifugation. 2nd ed. (Practical Approach Ser.). 368p. 1984. pap. 46.00 (*0-904147-55-X*, IRL Pr) OUP.

— Iodinated Density Gradient Media. (Practical Approach Ser.). 254p. 1983. pap. 39.00 (*0-904147-51-7*, IRL Pr) OUP.

— Preparative Centrifugation: A Practical Approach. (Practical Approach Ser.: Vol. 113). (Illus.). 420p. 1993. 88.00 (*0-19-963208-1*, IRL Pr); pap. 48.00 (*0-19-963211-1*, IRL Pr) OUP.

Rickwood, D. & Hames, B. D., eds. Gel Electrophoresis of Nucleic Acids: A Practical Approach. 2nd ed. (Practical Approach Ser.). (Illus.). 336p. 1990. pap. 44.00 (*0-19-963083-6*, IRL Pr) OUP.

Rickwood, D., jt. ed. see Dealtry, G. B.

Rickwood, D., jt. ed. see Hames, B. D.

Rickwood, D., et al. Centrifugation: Essential Data. LC 94-4642. (Essential Data Ser.). 1994. pap. text ed. 19.95 (*0-471-94271-5*) Wiley.

Rickwood, David, jt. ed. see Chambers, J. A.

Rickwood, Edgell. Calendar of Modern Letters, 3 vols., Set. Garman, D., ed. 1966. reprint ed. 195.00 (*0-7146-2104-8*, Pub. by F Cass Pubs UK) Intl Spec Bk.

Rickword, Edgell. Rimbaud: The Boy & the Poet. LC 72-163208. (Studies in French Literature: No. 45). 1971. reprint ed. lib. bdg. 75.00 (*0-8383-1309-4*) M S G Haskell Hse.

Ricles, James M., ed. Annual Technical Session Proceedings, 1993. 434p. (Orig.). 1993. pap. 50.00 (*1-879749-54-8*) Structural Stability.

— Is Your Structure Suitably Braced? 257p. (Orig.). 1993. pap. 50.00 (*1-879749-55-6*) Structural Stability.

— SSRC Fiftieth Anniversary Conference Proceedings, 1994: SSRC - Link Between Research & Practice. 407p. 1994. text ed. 50.00 (*1-879749-56-4*) Structural Stability.

Rico & Mano. American Mosaic: Multicultural Readings in Context. 1991. write for info. (*0-318-69200-7*, 3-46985) HM Soft Schl Col Div.

Rico, A. G. & Boieau, J., eds. International Symposium on Food Toxicology: Proceedings of the International Symposium on Food Toxicology, France, October 1983. Vol. 1, No. 2. 164p. 1984. write for info. (*0-318-65446-6*) Taylor & Francis.

Rico, Andre G. Advances in Veterinary Science & Comparative Medicine: Experimental & Comparative Toxicology, Vol. 31. 1987. text ed. 106.00 (*0-12-039231-3*) Acad Pr.

— Drug Residues in Animals. (Veterinary Science & Comparative Medicine Ser.). 1986. text ed. 99.00 (*0-12-587970-9*) Acad Pr.

Rico, Armando. Three Coffins for Nino Lencho. 332p. 1987. lib. bdg. 12.00 (*1-879219-01-8*) Veracruz Pubs.

Rico, Armando B. Asinano. 155p. (ENG & SPA.). 1990. lib. bdg. 9.50 (*1-879219-00-X*) Veracruz Pubs.

— Asinano: A Bilingual Word Guide of the English & Spanish Language. 2nd rev. ed. 270p. (ENG & SPA.). 1995. pap. text ed. 18.00 (*1-879219-07-7*) Veracruz Pubs.

— Hay Roca en Tu Coca. (Illus.). 47p. (Orig.). (SPA.). (YA). 1992. pap. 2.75 (*1-879219-05-0*) Veracruz Pubs.

— Later with the Latex: AIDS. 44p. (Orig.). (YA). 1992. pap. 2.95 (*1-879219-06-9*) Veracruz Pubs.

— School Adventures: Aventuras Escolares. 27p. (Orig.). (J). 1989. pap. text ed. 4.95 (*1-879219-04-2*) Veracruz Pubs.

— A Sound Mind in a Sound Body. 23p. (Orig.). (YA). 1990. pap. 16.00 (*1-879219-03-4*) Veracruz Pubs.

— There's a Rock in Your Coke. 47p. (Orig.). (YA). 1987. pap. 2.50 (*1-879219-02-6*) Veracruz Pubs.

Rico, Barbara. American Mosaic: Multicultural Readings in Context. (C). 1991. write for info. (*0-395-53690-1*) HM Soft Schl Col Div.

Rico, Carlos, jt. ed. see Coatsworth, John H.

Rico, Carlos, jt. ed. see Middlebrook, Kevin J.

Rico, Diana. Kovacsland; A Biography of Ernie Kovacs. 1990. 19.95 (*0-15-147294-7*) HarBrace.

— Kovacsland: A Biography of Ernie Kovacs. 1991. pap. 10.95 (*0-15-647250-3*, Harvest Bks) HarBrace.

Rico, Don, ed. see Hurst, Walter E.

R

Rico, Donato, jt. auth. see Hurst, Walter E.

Rico, Gabriele L. Pain & Possibility. 288p. 1991. pap. 12.95 (*0-87477-571-X*) J P Tarcher.

— Writing the Natural Way: Using Right-Brain Techniques to Release Your Expressive Powers. LC 81-126. (Illus.). 288p. 1983. pap. 13.95 (*0-87477-236-2*) J P Tarcher.

Rico, Gabriele L., jt. auth. see Guth, Hans P.

Ricoeur, Paul. The Conflict of Interpretations: Essays on Hermeneutics. LC 73-91311. (Studies in Phenomenology & Existential Philosophy). 512p. 1974. pap. 19.95 (*0-8101-0529-2*) Northwestern U Pr.

— Essays on Biblical Interpretation. Mudge, Lewis S., ed. LC 80-8052. 192p. (Orig.). reprint ed. pap. 54.80 (*0-685-24168-8*, 2033045) Bks Demand.

— Fallible Man: Philosophy of the Will. rev. ed. LC 65-16280. l, 146p. 1986. 35.00 (*0-8232-1150-9*); pap. 17.50 (*0-8232-1151-7*) Fordham.

— Figuring the Sacred: Religion, Narrative & Imagination. Pellauer, David, tr. LC 95-5454. 1995. write for info. (*0-8006-2894-2*, Fortress Pr) Augsburg Fortress.

— Freedom & Nature: The Voluntary & the Involuntary. Kohak, E. V., tr. (Studies in Phenomenology & Existential Philosophy). 498p. 1966. 42.95 (*0-8101-0208-0*); pap. 19.95 (*0-8101-0534-9*) Northwestern U Pr.

— Freud & Philosophy: An Essay on Interpretation. Savage, Denis, tr. LC 70-89907. (Terry Lecture Ser.). 1977. pap. 19.00 (*0-300-02189-5*) Yale U Pr.

— From Text to Action. Blamey, Kathleen & Thompson, John B., trs. (Studies in Phenomenology & Existential Philosophy). 346p. (Orig.). 1991. 45.95 (*0-8101-0978-6*); pap. 17.95 (*0-8101-0992-1*) Northwestern U Pr.

— Hermeneutics & the Human Sciences. Thompson, John B., ed. LC 80-41546. 280p. 1981. pap. 29.95 (*0-521-28002-8*) Cambridge U Pr.

— History & Truth. Kelbley, C. A., tr. (Studies in Phenomenology & Existential Philosophy). 333p. 1965. 39.95 (*0-8101-0207-2*); pap. 19.95 (*0-8101-0598-5*) Northwestern U Pr.

— Husserl: An Analysis of His Phenomenology. Ballard, Edward G & Embree, Lester, trs. (Studies in Phenomenology & Existential Philosophy). 238p. 1967. pap. 15.95 (*0-8101-0530-6*) Northwestern U Pr.

— Interpretation Theory: Discourse & the Surplus of Meaning. LC 76-29604. 108p. (C). 1976. pap. 8.00 (*0-912646-59-4*) Tex Christian.

— Lectures on Ideology & Utopia. Taylor, George, ed. LC 86-6813. 384p. 1988. text ed. 52.50 (*0-231-06048-3*); pap. text ed. 15.50 (*0-231-06049-1*) Col U Pr.

— Main Trends in Philosophy. LC 79-14080. (Main Trends in the Social & Human Sciences Ser.). 469p. (C). 1979. pap. 26.50 (*0-8419-0506-1*) Holmes & Meier.

— Oneself As Another. Blamey, Kathleen, tr. LC 92-107. 384p. (C). 1992. 29.95 (*0-226-71328-8*) U Ch Pr.

— Oneself as Another. Blarney, Kathleen, tr. 1994. pap. 14.95 (*0-226-71329-6*) U Ch Pr.

— The Reality of the Historical Past. LC 84-60012. (Aquinas Lectures). 51p. 1984. 10.00 (*0-87462-152-6*) Marquette.

— A Ricoeur Reader: Reflection & Imagination. Valdes, Mario J., ed. 516p. 1991. 60.00 (*0-8020-5880-9*); pap. 24.95 (*0-8020-6814-6*) U of Toronto Pr.

— The Rule of Metaphor: Multi-Disciplinary Studies of the Creation of Meaning in Language. Czerny, Robert, tr. 1977. pap. 22.50 (*0-8020-6447-7*) U of Toronto Pr.

— The Rule of Metaphor: Multi-Disciplinary Studies of the Creation of Meaning in Language. Czerny, Robert et al, trs. LC 77-5514. 394p. reprint ed. pap. 112.30 (*0-8357-8313-8*, 2034022) Bks Demand.

— Symbolism of Evil. Buchanan, Emerson, tr. LC 67-11506. 1969. reprint ed. pap. 18.00x (*0-8070-1567-9*, BPA18) Beacon Pr.

— Time & Narrative, Vol. 1. Blamey, Kathleen & Pellauer, David, trs. LC 83-17995. 286p. 1990. pap. 13.95 (*0-226-71332-6*) U Ch Pr.

— Time & Narrative, Vol. 2. McLaughlin, Kathleen & Pellauer, David, trs. viii, 208p. 1986. lib. bdg. 25.00 (*0-226-71333-4*) U Ch Pr.

— Time & Narrative, Vol. 2. Blamey, Kathleen & Pellauer, David, trs. LC 83-17995. 216p. 1990. pap. 13.95 (*0-226-71334-2*) U Ch Pr.

— Time & Narrative, Vol. 3. Blamey, Kathleen & Pellauer, David, trs. 362p. 1988. lib. bdg. 29.95 (*0-226-71335-0*) U Ch Pr.

— Time & Narrative, Vol. 3. Blamey, Kathleen & Pellauer, David, trs. LC 83-17995. vi, 356p. 1990. pap. 14.95 (*0-226-71336-9*) U Ch Pr.

Ricoeur, Paul, jt. auth. see MacIntyre, Alasdair.

Ricoifi, T., jt. auth. see Scholz, J.

Ricon, Amado, jt. auth. see Davis, Thomas B.

Riconda, M. A., ed. Finding: Products & Services for the Information Profession. rev. ed. 152p. 1995. per. 24.95 (*0-935912-52-5*) LDA Pubs.

— Finding - Great Lakes: Products & Services for Librarians & Information Professionals. 172p. 1995. per. 39.95 (*0-935912-58-4*) LDA Pubs.

— Finding - Mid-Atlantic (Delaware, Maryland, District of Columbia, Virginia) Products & Services for Librarians & Information Professionals. 172p. 1995. per. 39.95 (*0-935912-57-6*) LDA Pubs.

— Finding - New Jersey, Pennsylvania: Products & Services for the Information Industry. 160p. 1992. 19.95 (*0-935912-56-8*) LDA Pubs.

— Finding - Northeast: Products & Services for Librarians & Information Professionals. 172p. 1995. per. 24.95 (*0-935912-55-X*) LDA Pubs.

Ricord, F. W., ed. History of Union County, New Jersey. 556p. 1992. reprint ed. lib. bdg. 66.00 (*0-685-59667-2*) Higginson Bk Co.

***Ricord, Frederick W.** dGeneral Index to the Documents Relating to the Colonial History of the State of New Jersey: First Series, in Ten Volumes. 198p. 1994. 22.50 (*0-614-03824-3*, 4895) Genealog Pub.

***Ricordi, Camillo, ed.** Methods in Cell Transplantation. 745p. 1995. student ed, ring bd. 295.00 (*1-57059-189-X*) R G Landes.

— Pancreatic Islet Cell Transplantation. 470p. 1992. 165.00 (*1-879702-08-8*) R G Landes.

Ricouard, M. J. Formwork for Concrete Construction. rev. ed. (Illus.). 195p. (C). 1983. text ed. 65.00 (*0-333-29360-6*, Pub. by Macmill Press UK) Scholium Intl.

Ricouart, Janine. Ecriture Feminine et Violence: Une Etude de Marguerite Duras. LC 91-65035. 222p. (FRE.). 1991. lib. bdg. 32.95 (*0-917786-82-3*) Summa Pubns.

Ricour, Maribeth. Chic Shopper's Guide to Paris. 1991. pap. 16.95 (*0-312-04575-1*) St Martin.

Ricour, Pierre. Lexique Anglais-Francais de la Banque et de la Monnaie: English - French Lexicon of Banking & Finance. 40p. (ENG & FRE.). 1974. pap. 9.95 (*0-8288-6311-3*, M-6486) Fr & Eur.

Ricoy, M. A. & Volakis, J. L. Electromagnetic Scattering from Two-Dimensional Thick Material Junctions. (University of Michigan Report Ser.: No. 025921-14-T). 178p. reprint ed. pap. 50.80 (*0-8357-2933-8*, 2039174) Bks Demand.

Ricquier, W. J. & Heong, Stanley Y. Breaches of Trust in Singapore & Malaysia. 98p. 1984. pap. 40.00 (*0-406-18115-2*) Butterworth Legal Pubs.

RICS Books Staff. The Mundic Problem: A Guidance Note Recommended Sampling, Examination & Classification Procedure for Suspect Concrete Building Materials in Devon & Cornwall. 1993. pap. 90.00 (*0-85406-586-5*, Pub. by R-I-C-S Bks UK) St Mut.

RICS Energy Efficience Office Staff. Energy Appraisal of Existing Buildings: A Handbook for Surveyors. 86p. 1993. 80.00 (*0-85406-561-X*, Pub. by R-I-C-S Bks UK) St Mut.

RICS Insurance Services Staff. Caveat Surveyor. (C). 1986. text ed. 75.00 (*0-85406-306-4*, Pub. by R-I-C-S Bks UK) St Mut.

— Caveat Surveyor Eleven. (C). 1989. text ed. 75.00 (*0-85406-425-7*, Pub. by R-I-C-S Bks UK) St Mut.

RICS Staff. Cost Management in Engineering Construction Projects: Guidance Notes. (C). 1992. pap. text ed. 90.00 (*0-85406-524-5*, Pub. by R-I-C-S Bks UK) St Mut.

— Directory of Planning & Development Consultants. 80p. (C). 1989. text ed. 85.00 (*0-85406-424-9*, Pub. by Surveyors Pubns) St Mut.

— Directory of Research & Development: Activities in the U. K. in Land Survey & Related Fields. 100p. (C). 1987. text ed. 65.00 (*0-85406-356-0*, Pub. by Surveyors Pubns) St Mut.

— Guidance Notes on the Valuation of Assets. 174p. (C). 1989. text ed. 125.00 (*0-85406-423-0*, Pub. by Surveyors Pubns) St Mut.

— A Guide to Life Cycle Costing for Construction. (C). 1986. text ed. 35.00 (*0-85406-322-6*, Pub. by Surveyors Pubns) St Mut.

— Guidelines for the Preparation of Hydrographic Surveys for Dredging. (C). 1984. text ed. 50.00 (*0-85406-232-7*, Pub. by Surveyors Pubns) St Mut.

— Guidelines for the Preparation of Specifications for Hydrographic Surveys. (C). 1984. text ed. 35.00 (*0-85406-185-1*, Pub. by Surveyors Pubns) St Mut.

— Housing the Nation, Vols. 1 & 2. (C). 1992. pap. text ed. 125.00 (*0-85406-510-5*, Pub. by R-I-C-S Bks UK) St Mut.

— The Making of Planning Applications. (C). 1991. text ed. 90.00 (*0-85406-497-4*, Pub. by R-I-C-S Bks UK) St Mut.

— Property Insurance: Some Points to Consider in Relation to the Proper Cover of Risks. (C). 1985. text ed. 39.00 (*0-85406-288-2*, Pub. by Surveyors Pubns) St Mut.

— Putting the Estate Agents Act 1979 & Its Order & Regulations into Practice. (C). 1991. pap. text ed. 90.00 (*0-85406-503-2*, Pub. by R-I-C-S Bks UK) St Mut.

— QS-2000 the Future Role of the Chartered Quantity Surveyor. (C). 1991. pap. text ed. 90.00 (*0-85406-495-8*, Pub. by R-I-C-S Bks UK) St Mut.

— Refurbishment & Alteration Work. (C). 1983. text ed. 29.00 (*0-85406-181-9*, Pub. by Surveyors Pubns) St Mut.

— RICS Directory of International Practices. 120p. (C). 1986. text ed. 75.00 (*0-685-40841-8*, Pub. by Surveyors Pubns) St Mut.

— Shaping Britain for the Twenty-First Century. (C). 1991. pap. text ed. 125.00 (*0-85406-501-6*, Pub. by R-I-C-S Bks UK) St Mut.

— Specification for Mapping at Scales Between 1: 1,000 & 1: 10,000. (C). 1988. text ed. 90.00 (*0-85406-375-7*, Pub. by Surveyors Pubns) St Mut.

— Terms & Conditions of Contract for Land Surveying Services. (C). 1989. text ed. 59.00 (*0-85406-418-4*, Pub. by Surveyors Pubns) St Mut.

RICS Staff, ed. Specification for Surveys of Land, Buildings & Utility Services at Scales of L: 500 & Larger. (C). 1986. text ed. 49.00 (*0-85406-297-1*, Pub. by Surveyors Pubns) St Mut.

RICS Staff & Building Design Partnership Staff. A Study of Quantity Surveying & Client Demand. (C). 1984. text ed. 80.00 (*0-685-40842-6*, Pub. by Surveyors Pubns) St Mut.

RICS Staff & Building Employers Confederation Staff. SMM7 - The Standard Method of Measurement of Building Works. 190p. (C). 1988. text ed. 125.00 (*0-85406-360-9*, Pub. by R-I-C-S Bks UK) St Mut.

— SMM7 Measurement Code. (C). 1988. pap. text ed. 75.00 (*0-85406-361-7*, Pub. by R-I-C-S Bks UK) St Mut.

RICS Staff, jt. auth. see ISVA Staff.

Rictman, Phil. Curfew. Orig. Title: Crybbe. 640p. 1994. reprint ed. pap. text ed. 5.99 (*0-425-14334-1*) Berkley Pub.

Ricucci, Betsy, jt. auth. see Ricucci, Gary.

Ricucci, Gary & Ricucci, Betsy. Love That Lasts: Making a Magnificent Marriage. Somerville, Greg, ed. 176p. 1992. pap. 8.00 (*1-881039-02-1*) People of Destiny.

Ridall, Kathryn. Channeling: How to Reach Out to Your Spirit Guides. 1988. mass mkt. 5.99 (*0-553-27181-4*) Bantam.

Ridcon, G. T. History of the Millingas & Millanges, Milliken, Millikin, Family of Saxony & Normandy. 882p. 1994. reprint ed. lib. bdg. 116.00 (*0-8328-3863-2*); reprint ed. pap. 106.00 (*0-8328-3864-0*) Higginson Bk Co.

Ridd, J. E., jt. auth. see Nicholson, A. S.

Ridd, Mark, tr. see Buarque, Cristovam.

Ridd, Merrill K., jt. auth. see Manson, Gary A.

Ridd, S. E., ed. Virginia's Breeding Birds: An Atlas Workbook. 228p. (Orig.). 1989. student ed write for info. (*0-9624527-0-X*) VA Soc Ornithology.

***Ridd, Stephen, et al, eds.** Julius Caesar in Gaul & Britain. LC 94-28699. (History Eyewitness Ser.). (J). (gr. 1-8). 1995. lib. bdg. write for info. (*0-8114-8283-9*) Raintree Steck-V.

Riddall, J. G. The Law of Trusts. 4th ed. 436p. 1992. U. K. pap. 46.00 (*0-406-51840-8*) Butterworth Legal Pubs.

— Riddall: Introduction to Land Law. 4th ed. 1988. pap. 40.00 (*0-406-64845-X*) Butterworth Legal Pubs.

— Riddall: Introduction to Land Law. 5th ed. 592p. 1993. pap. 75.00 (*0-406-00589-3*, U.K.) Butterworth Legal Pubs.

— Riddall: Jurisprudence. 1991. pap. 22.00 (*0-406-60064-3*) Butterworth Legal Pubs.

Riddel, Frank S., jt. auth. see Coffey, William E.

Riddel, Joseph N. Clairvoyant Eye: The Poetry & Poetics of Wallace Stevens. LC 91-15505. 308p. 1991. pap. text ed. 12.95 (*0-8071-0716-6*) La State U Pr.

— Inverted Bell: Modernism & the Counterpoetics of William Carlos Williams. LC 91-14721. 308p. 1991. pap. text ed. 12.95 (*0-8071-1697-1*) La State U Pr.

— Purloined Letters: Originality & Repetition in American Literature. Bauerlain, Mark, ed. LC 94-30483. (Horizons in Theory & American Culture Ser.). 232p. (C). 1995. text ed. 30.00 (*0-8071-1872-9*) La State U Pr.

Riddel, Roger C., et al. Manufacturing Africa: Performance & Prospects of Seven Countries in Sub-Saharan Africa. 419p. 1990. pap. 30.00 (*0-435-08050-4*, 08050) Heinemann.

Riddell, jt. auth. see Levin.

Riddell, C. Avian Histopathology. (Illus.). (Orig.). 1987. pap. text ed. 26.00 (*0-915538-03-2*) AAAP PA.

Riddell, Carol, jt. auth. see Coulson, Margaret.

Riddell, Chris. The Trouble with Elephants. LC 87-24963. (Trophy Picture Bk.). (Illus.). 32p. (J). (ps-2). 1990. reprint ed. pap. 6.95 (*0-06-443170-3*, Trophy) HarpC Child Bks.

Riddell-Dixon, Elizabeth. Canada & the International Seabed: Domestic Determinants & External Constraints. 240p. (C). 1989. text ed. 55.00 (*0-7735-0694-2*, Pub. by McGill CN) U of Toronto Pr.

Riddell, Edwina. My First Animal Word Book. (Illus.). 32p. (J). (ps). 1989. 9.95 (*0-8120-6127-6*) Barron.

— My First Ballet Class. LC 92-24450. (Illus.). 32p. (J). (ps-2). 1993. 10.95 (*0-8120-6296-5*); pap. 5.95 (*0-8120-1674-2*) Barron.

— My First Day at Preschool. (Illus.). 32p. (J). (ps). 1992. 9.95 (*0-8120-6261-2*) Barron.

— One Hundred First Words. (Illus.). 32p. (J). (ps). 1988. 8.95 (*0-8120-5786-4*) Barron.

— One Hundred First Words. 32p. (J). (ps). 1992. pap. 4.95 (*0-8120-4888-1*) Barron.

Riddell, Edwina, jt. auth. see Smallman, Clare.

Riddell, Francis A., jt. auth. see Meighan, Clement W.

Riddell, Frank G., jt. ed. see Lambert, Joseph B.

Riddell, George A. More Things That Matter. LC 79-128299. (Essay Index Reprint Ser.). 1977. 21.95 (*0-8369-1843-6*) Ayer.

— Some Things That Matter. LC 74-37793. (Essay Index Reprint Ser). 1977. reprint ed. 20.95 (*0-8369-2620-X*) Ayer.

Riddell, James & Dickerman, Carol. Country Profiles of the Land Tenure: Africa 1986. (LTC Research Paper Ser.: No. 127). 237p. (Orig.). (C). 1986. pap. text ed. 12.00 (*0-317-65863-8*) U of Wis Land.

Riddell, James, jt. auth. see Fortmann, Louise.

Riddell, James, ed. see Plato.

***Riddell, James A. & Stewart, Stanley.** Jonson's Spenser: Evidence & Historical Criticism. LC 95-11767. (Duquesne Studies: Language & Literature: Vol. 18). (Illus.). 290p. (C). 1995. text ed. 48.00 (*0-8207-0263-3*) Duquesne.

Riddell, John, ed. Founding the Communist International: Proceedings & Documents of the First Congress - March 1919. Cantrick, Bob & Dees, Robert, trs. LC 87-70239. (Communist International in Lenin's Time Ser.: Vol. 3). 432p. (Orig.). 1987. lib. bdg. 65.00 (*0-913460-96-6*); pap. 27.95 (*0-913460-97-4*) Pathfinder NY.

— The German Revolution & The Debate on Soviet Power Documents: 1918-1919. Cantrick, Bob et al, trs. LC 86-60845. (Communist International in Lenin's Time Ser.: Vol. 2). 560p. (Orig.). 1986. lib. bdg. 75.00 (*0-937091-00-6*); pap. 31.95 (*0-937091-01-4*) Pathfinder NY.

— Lenin's Struggle for a Revolutionary International: Documents: 1907-1916, the Preparatory Years. 2nd ed. Eardley, Kenneth et al, trs. LC 84-61519. 624p. 1986. lib. bdg. 75.00 (*0-913460-94-X*); pap. 32.95 (*0-913460-95-8*) Pathfinder NY.

— To See the Dawn: Baku, Nineteen Twenty - First Congress of the Peoples of the East. LC 93-85321. (Communist International in Lenin's Time Ser.). (Illus.). 344p. (Orig.). 1993. lib. bdg. 55.00 (*0-87348-768-0*); pap. 19.95 (*0-87348-769-9*) Pathfinder NY.

— Workers of the World & Oppressed Peoples Unite! Proceedings & Documents of the Second Congress, 1920, 2 vols., 1. LC 91-66263. (Illus.). 1200p. (C). 1991. lib. bdg. 85.00 (*0-937091-09-X*); pap. 35.95 (*0-937091-08-1*) Pathfinder NY.

— Workers of the World & Oppressed Peoples Unite! Proceedings & Documents of the Second Congress, 1920, 2 vols., 2. LC 91-66263. (Illus.). 1200p. (C). 1991. lib. bdg. 85.00 (*0-937091-11-1*); pap. 35.95 (*0-937091-10-3*) Pathfinder NY.

— Workers of the World & Oppressed Peoples Unite! Proceedings & Documents of the Second Congress, 1920, 2 vols., Set. LC 91-66263. (Illus.). 1200p. (C). 1991. lib. bdg. 160.00 (*0-937091-07-3*); pap. 65.00 (*0-937091-06-5*) Pathfinder NY.

Riddell, John, ed. see Trotsky, Leon & Marx, Karl.

Riddell, Peter. The Thatcher Era: And Its Legacy. 2nd ed. 284p. (C). 1992. pap. text ed. 21.95 (*0-631-18268-3*) Blackwell Pubs.

Riddell, R. H., ed. Dysplasia & Cancer in Colitis: Proceedings of the Symposium Held June 1-4, 1989, Baltimore, MD. 296p. 1991. 155.00 (*0-444-01570-1*) P-H.

Riddell, Robert. Ecodevelopment. 1981. text ed. 35.00 (*0-312-22585-7*) St Martin.

Riddell, Robert H., ed. Pathology of Drug-Induced & Toxic Diseases. LC 82-4230. (Illus.). 696p. reprint ed. pap. 180.00 (*0-7837-2584-1*, 2042745) Bks Demand.

Riddell, Roger, jt. auth. see Robinson, Mark.

Riddell, Roger C. Foreign Aid Reconsidered. LC 87-2949. (Johns Hopkins Studies in Development). 319p. reprint ed. pap. 91.00 (*0-7837-4488-9*, 2044265) Bks Demand.

Riddell, Ruth. Ice Warrior. LC 91-29506. 144p. (J). (gr. 4-7). 1992. text ed. 13.95 (*0-689-31710-7*, Atheneum Bks Young) S&S Childrens.

Riddell, Sheila. Dated Chinese Antiquities, 600-1650: Six Hundred to Sixteen Fifty. (Illus.). 256p. 1979. 39.95 (*0-571-09753-7*) Faber & Faber.

Riddell, Sheila & Brown, Sally, eds. Special Education Needs Policy in the 1990s: Warnock in the Market Place. LC 94-8490. 240p. 1994. 69.95x (*0-415-09758-4*, B3594); pap. 25.00x (*0-415-09759-2*, B3598) Routledge.

Riddell, Sheila I. Gender & the Politics of the Curriculum. LC 91-37174. 256p. 1992. 69.95 (*0-415-04813-3*, A5973) Routledge.

Riddell, Stephen. Motivation & Compensation. 200p. 1994. write for info. (*0-936840-14-5*) Tech Marketing.

Riddell, Stephen M. Selling Genius: Achieving Extraordinary Sales Results with Ordinary People. LC 94-60402. viii, 182p. 1994. write for info. (*0-936840-17-X*) Tech Marketing.

Riddell, Tom, et al. Economics: A Tool for Understanding Society. 3rd ed. LC 86-14043. (Economics Ser.). (Illus.). 600p. (C). 1987. pap. text ed. 37.75 (*0-201-06368-9*) Addison-Wesley.

— Economics: A Tool for Understanding Society. 4th ed. (Illus.). 640p. (C). 1991. pap. text ed. 41.95 (*0-201-50905-9*) Addison-Wesley.

Riddell, Walter A. Rise of Ecclesiastical Control in Quebec. (Columbia University. Studies in the Social Sciences: No. 174). reprint ed. 22.50 (*0-404-51174-0*) AMS Pr.

Riddell, William A. Regina: From Pile O' Bones to Queen. 1980. 24.95 (*0-89781-029-5*, 5040) Preferred Mktg.

***Ridder, Dale R.** Manual for Army Cooks. 1995. reprint ed. pap. write for info. (*1-885591-73-X*) Morris Pubng.

Ridder, Herman. Membership in the Reformed Church. 1980. pap. 1.95 (*0-686-23484-7*) Rose Pub MI.

Ridder-Patrick, Jane. A Handbook of Medical Astrology. (Illus.). 192p. (Orig.). 1991. pap. 9.95 (*0-14-019214-X*, Arkana) Viking Penguin.

Ridderbos, Herman. Redemptive History & the New Testament Scriptures. De Jongste, H. & Graffin, Richard B., Jr., trs. LC 87-32875. Orig. Title: The Authority of the New Testament Scriptures. 110p. (DUT.). 1988. pap. 6.99 (*0-87552-416-8*) Presby & Reformed.

Ridderbos, Herman N. Coming of the Kingdom. LC 62-15429. 1962. pap. 15.99 (*0-87552-408-7*) Presby & Reformed.

— Paul. DeWitt, J. Richard, tr. 587p. 1975. 34.99 (*0-8028-3438-8*) Eerdmans.

Ridderbos, N. H. Die Psalmen: Stilistische Verfahren und Aufbau mit besonderer Beruecksichtigung von Ps. 1-41. Mittring, Karl E., tr. (Beiheft 117 zur Zeitschrift fuer die Alttestamentliche Wissenschaft Ser.). 305p. (C). 1972. 110.00 (*3-11-001834-9*) De Gruyter.

Ridderikhoff, J. Methods in Medicine. (C). 1989. lib. bdg. 99.00 (*1-55608-080-8*) Kluwer Ac.

Riddervold, Hans O. Easily Missed Fractures & Corner Signs in Radiology. (Illus.). 416p. 1991. 150.00 (*0-87993-502-2*) Futura Pub.

Riddick, Barbara. Toys & Play for the Handicapped Child. (Illus.). 224p. 1982. pap. 27.50 (*0-7099-0292-1*, Pub. by Croom Helm UK) Routledge Chapman & Hall.

Riddick, Floyd M. & Butcher, Miriam H. Riddick's Rules of Procedure: A Modern Guide to Faster & More Efficient Meetings. LC 90-24274. 240p. 1991. reprint ed. pap. 14.95 (*0-8191-8064-5*) Madison Bks UPA.

Riddick, Glenda & Weir, Mary. The Growing Years: A Study Guide for the Television Course. 5th ed. 1991. pap. text ed. write for info. (*0-07-052891-8*) McGraw.

— A Time to Grow: A Study Guide for the Televised Course. 1992. pap. text ed. write for info. (*0-07-052892-6*) McGraw.

R

Riddick, John F., comp. Glimpses of India: An Annotated Bibliography of Published Personal Writings by Englishmen, 1608-1947. LC 88-37582. (Bibliographies & Indexes in World History Ser.: No. 15). 215p. 1989. text ed. 49.95 (*0-313-25661-6*, RGI/) Greenwood.
— A Guide to Indian Manuscripts. LC 93-4771. (Reference Guides to Archival & Manuscript Sources in World History Ser.: No. 2). 296p. 1993. text ed. 65.00 (*0-313-27501-7*, RGA/, Greenwood Pr) Greenwood.
Riddick, Ruth. The Right to Choose. (C). 1989. 40.00 (*0-946211-85-X*, Pub. by Attic Pr IE) St Mut.
Riddick, Sarah. Pioneer Studio Pottery: Milner-White Collection. (Illus.). 176p. (C). 1990. pap. 35.00 (*0-85331-581-7*, Pub. by Lund Humphries UK) Antique Collect.
— Pioneer Studio Pottery: Milner-White Collection. (Illus.). 176p. 1990. 60.00 (*0-85331-590-6*, Pub. by Lund Humphries UK) Antique Collect.
Riddick, Tut A. If You Ain't Dyin' Get Up: An Ozzie Scrapbook. 56p. 1992. pap. 10.00 (*1-883172-00-4*) Heart Press.
Riddick, Walter E. & Stewart, Eva M. Workbook for Program Evaluation in the Human Services. 196p. (Orig.). 1981. pap. text ed. 23.50 (*0-8191-1783-8*) U Pr of Amer.
Riddick, William. Charrette Processes: A Tool in Urban Planning. LC 74-14257. (Illus.). 110p. 1971. pap. 7.50 (*0-87387-041-7*) Shumway.
***Ridding, John.** Fuchsias. (Illus.). 1995. 8.00 (*0-00-412958-X*, HarpT) HarpC.
Ridding, Laura, ed. Travels of Macarius: Extracts from the Diary of the Travels of Macarius, Patriarch of Antioch. LC 77-115577. (Russia Observed Ser.). 1971. reprint ed. 15.95 (*0-405-03089-4*) Ayer.
Riddle. Analysis of Geological Materials. 480p. 1993. 165.00 (*0-8247-9132-0*) Dekker.
Riddle, Alfy. Applications of Electrical Engineering with Mathematica. (C). 1995. text ed. 39.75 (*0-201-53477-0*) Addison-Wesley.
***Riddle, Dan.** Crossword Review of Anatomy & Physiology. (Illus.). 348p. (C). 1995. student ed 15.00 (*1-886855-03-X*) Tavenner Pub.
Riddle, Donald H. The Truman Committee: A Study in Congressional Responsibility. LC 63-16306. 217p. reprint ed. pap. 61.90 (*0-317-08280-9*, 2050638) Bks Demand.
Riddle, Donald W. Congressman Abraham Lincoln. LC 79-11614. 280p. 1979. reprint ed. text ed. 59.75 (*0-8371-9307-9*, RIAL, Greenwood Pr) Greenwood.
Riddle, Dorothy I. Service-Led Growth: The Role of the Service Sector in World Development. LC 85-16743. 304p. 1985. text ed. 79.50 (*0-275-92041-0*, C2041, Praeger Pubs) Greenwood.
— Service-Led Growth: The Role of the Service Sector in World Development. LC 85-16743. 304p. 1987. pap. text ed. 16.95 (*0-275-92728-8*, B2728, Praeger Pubs) Greenwood.
Riddle, Douglas F. Analytic Geometry. 5th ed. 445p. (C). 1992. text ed. 55.95 (*0-534-17274-1*) PWS Pubs.
— Calculus & Analytic Geometry. alternate ed. 1110p. (C). 1984. text ed. 78.95 (*0-534-01198-5*) PWS Pubs.
— Calculus & Analytic Geometry. 4th ed. 1172p. (C). 1984. text ed. 78.95 (*0-534-01468-2*) PWS Pubs.
— Programming in PASCAL. 528p. (C). 1991. pap. write for info. (*0-02-399815-6*) Dellen Pub.
Riddle, Florence K., ed. see Reynolds, Harold R.
Riddle, Gordon. The Kestrel. 1989. pap. 25.00 (*0-685-71515-9*, Pub. by Shire UK) St Mut.
Riddle, Grant. Amputees & Devotees. 1989. 29.95 (*0-8290-1824-7*) Irvington.
Riddle, Ian. Shipbuilding Credit. (Bangor Occasional Papers in Economics: No. 20). xiv, 87p. 1983. pap. 28.50 (*0-7083-0843-0*, Pub. by U of Wales UK) Bks Intl VA.
Riddle, J. H. British & American Plans for International Currency Stabilization. (Occasional Papers: No. 16). 48p. 1943. reprint ed. 20.00 (*0-87014-331-X*); reprint ed. mic. film 20.00 (*0-685-61247-3*) Natl Bur Econ Res.
Riddle, Jeff C. The Indian History of the Modoc War. LC 74-78125. (Primary Source Book Ser.). (Illus.). 292p. 1975. reprint ed. 16.95 (*0-913522-03-1*); reprint ed. pap. 10.95 (*0-913522-04-X*) Urion Pr CA.
Riddle, Jesse L. The Guide to Free & Discount Travel. 110p. 1992. pap. 17.95 (*0-9626583-2-4*) Carriage Group.
— The Guide to Free & Discount Travel. 132p. 1993. pap. 7.95 (*1-56901-067-6*) NW Pub.
— A Simple Guide to Courier Travel: How to Fly Free Or at Discounted Prices to Cities Around the World. 50p. (Orig.). 1989. pap. text ed. 9.95 (*0-9626583-0-8*) Carriage Group.
— A Simple Guide to Courier Travel: How to Fly Free or at Discounted Prices to Cities Around the World. 2nd ed. 72p. 1991. pap. 14.95 (*0-9626583-1-6*) Carriage Group.
Riddle, John . Contraception & Abortion from the Ancient World to the Renaissance. 1994. pap. 16.95 (*0-674-16876-3*) HUP.
Riddle, John. Writing & Selling Information the Mail Order Way. LC 84-20659. 30p. 1994. pap. 5.95 (*0-87576-185-2*) Pilot Bks.
Riddle, John I. The Six-Year Rural High School: A Comparative Study of Small & Large Units in Alabama. LC 70-177191. (Columbia University. Teachers College. Contributions to Education Ser.: No. 737). reprint ed. 37.50 (*0-404-55737-6*) AMS Pr.
Riddle, John M. Contraception & Abortion from the Ancient World to the Renaissance. (Illus.). 245p. (C). 1992. 45.00 (*0-674-16875-5*) HUP.
— Quid Pro Quo: Studies in the History of Drugs. (Collected Studies: Vol. CS367). 320p. 1992. 89.95 (*0-86078-319-7*, Pub. by Variorum UK) Ashgate Pub Co.
Riddle, John T. Mama & Papa's Baker's Dozen. 1985. 4.95 (*0-932298-47-8*) Tri-State Pr Corp.
Riddle, Katharine P., jt. auth. see Taylor, Clara Mae.
***Riddle, Kelly E.** Private Investigating Made Easy: How to Conduct Investigations Using Public Records. (Illus.). 136p. (Orig.). 1994. pap. 12.95 (*1-881825-05-1*) Hist Pubns TX.
Riddle, Lenora. A Guide to Junior Showmanship. 2nd ed. (Training Bks.). (Illus.). 1994. write for info. (*0-87714-128-2*) Denlingers.
Riddle, Marilyn R. Large Print Innovative Cookbook. large type ed. (Illus.). 64p. (Orig.). 1984. pap. 7.00 (*0-9603748-3-3*) Sandpiper OR.
— Poems from the Oregon Sea Coast. large type ed. (Illus.). 24p. 1979. pap. 7.00 (*0-9603748-0-9*) Sandpiper OR.
— Unicorns for Everyone. large type ed. (Illus.). 24p. (Orig.). (J). 1980. pap. 7.00 (*0-9603748-1-7*) Sandpiper OR.
— Walk with Me: Prayers & Meditations. large type ed. (Illus.). 40p. (Orig.). 1982. pap. 7.00 (*0-9603748-2-5*) Sandpiper OR.
Riddle, Marilyn R., ed. Otherwhere... One Step Beyond: Anthology. large type ed. (Illus.). 48p. (Orig.). 1988. pap. 7.00 (*0-9603748-5-X*) Sandpiper OR.
— Physically Challenged Can-Do: Anthology. large type ed. 84p. (Orig.). 1989. pap. 8.00 (*0-9603748-6-8*) Sandpiper OR.
Riddle, Maxwell. Dogs Through History. Denlinger, William W. & Rathman, R. Annabel, eds. LC 87-533. (Other Dog Bks.). (Illus.). 192p. 1987. 19.95 (*0-87714-124-X*) Denlingers.
— The New Complete Brittany. LC 87-3891. (Illus.). 304p. 1987. 25.95 (*0-87605-090-9*) Howell Bk.
— The New Complete Shetland Sheepdog. (Illus.). 256p. 1992. 25.95 (*0-87605-333-9*) Howell Bk.
— Puppies. (Illus.). 80p. 1984. pap. text ed. 5.95 (*0-86622-211-1*, PB-123) TFH Pubns.
Riddle, Maxwell & Harris, Beth J. The New Complete Alaskan Malamute. Zingler, Marcy, ed. 256p. 1990. 25.95 (*0-87605-008-9*) Howell Bk.
Riddle, Michael R., jt. auth. see Clark, Michael B.
Riddle, Pauline, jt. auth. see Andrews, Mildred.
***Riddle, Peter.** Tips & Tricks for Toy Train Operators. 80p. 1994. 11.95 (*0-89778-395-6*, 10-7935) Greenberg Bks.
Riddle, Peter H. Greenberg's Guide to Lionel Trains, 1901-1942: Accessories, Vol. 3. 160p. 1993. text ed. 49.95 (*0-89778-318-2*, 10-7330HB) Greenberg Bks.
— Greenberg's Wiring Your Lionel Layout: A Primer for Lionel Train Enthusiasts. (Illus.). 80p. 1992. pap. 9.95 (*0-89778-206-2*, 10-7555) Greenberg Bks.
— Greenberg's Wiring Your Lionel Layout, Vol. 2: Intermediate Techniques. (Illus.). 80p. 1993. pap. 12.95 (*0-89778-372-7*, 10-7560) Greenberg Bks.
— Trains from Grandfather's Attic. (Illus.). 144p. 1991. pap. text ed. 22.95 (*0-89778-215-1*, 10-7585) Greenberg Bks.
Riddle, Ronald. Flying Dragons, Flowing Streams: Music in the Life of San Francisco's Chinese. LC 82-12005. (Contributions in Intercultural & Comparative Studies: No. 7). xiv, 349p. 1983. text ed. 59.95 (*0-313-23682-8*, RIF/, Greenwood Pr) Greenwood.
Riddle, Roz. The City Cat: How to Live Healthily & Happily with Your Indoor Pet. 1987. mass mkt. 4.99 (*0-449-21022-7*, Crest) Fawcett.
Riddle, S., et al. Practice Exercises in Basic English. large type ed. (J). (gr. 3-9). 1983. reprint ed. Grade 4, 18 pt. 34.00 (*0-317-03357-3*, J-21340-00); reprint ed. Grade 5, 18 pt. 34.00 (*0-317-03358-1*, J-21350-00); reprint ed. Grade 6, 18pt. 34.00 (*0-317-03359-X*, J-21360-00); reprint ed. Grade 7, 18pt. 28.16 (*0-317-03360-3*, 4-21370-00) Am Printing Hse.
Riddle, Thomas W. The Old Radicalism: John R. Rogers & the Populist Movement in Washington. LC 91-15137. (Modern American History Ser.). 336p. 1991. 76.00 (*0-8240-1896-6*) Garland.
Riddle, Tohby. A Most Unusual Dog. LC 93-38184. (Illus.). 32p. (J). (gr. 1 up). 1994. lib. bdg. 18.60 (*0-8368-1088-0*) Gareth Stevens Inc.
Riddlebaugh, Mary Jane. Millions & Illions. (Illus.). (J). (gr. 4-8). 1990. pap. 9.95 (*1-878347-16-0*) NL Assocs.
Riddleberger, Patrick W. Eighteen Sixty-Six: The Critical Year Revisited. (Illus.). 308p. 1984. reprint ed. pap. text ed. 25.50 (*0-8191-4239-5*) U Pr of Amer.
— George Washington Julian: Radical Republican. 344p. 1966. 5.00 (*1-885323-22-0*) IN Hist Bureau.
***Riddles, Libby & Gill, Shelley.** Danger - the Dogyard Cat. (Illus.). 36p. (J). (gr. 1-6). Date not set. 13.95 (*0-934007-09-8*); pap. 8.95 (*0-934007-20-9*) Paws Four Pub.
Riddles, Libby & Jones, Tim. Race Across Alaska: First Woman to Win the Iditarod Tells Her Story. LC 87-25273. (Illus.). 240p. (Orig.). 1988. pap. 14.95 (*0-8117-2253-8*) Stackpole.
Riddlesperger, James, jt. ed. see Jackson, Donald.
***Riddlesperger, James W. & Jackson, Donald W., eds.** Presidential Leadership & Civil Rights Policy. LC 95-5268. (Contributions in Political Science Ser.: Vol. 356). 208p. 1995. text ed. 55.00 (*0-313-29624-3*, Greenwood Pr) Greenwood.
Riddoch, J., jt. auth. see Humphreys, Glyn W.
Riddoch, Jane & Lennon, Sheila, eds. The Use of Single Case Research Designs in Rehabilitation Studies: Special Issue of Physiotherapy Theory & Practice, No. 712. 80p. 1991. text ed. 19.95 (*0-86377-164-5*) L Erlbaum Assocs.
Riddoch, M. Jane, ed. Neglect & the Peripheral Dyslexias: A Special Issue of Cognitive Neuropsychology. 344p. 1991. text ed. 69.95 (*0-86377-162-9*) L Erlbaum Assocs.
Riddoch, M. Jane, jt. ed. see Humphreys, Glyn W.
Riddoch, Mark. What's the Verdict? LC 93-24237. 1993. 4.25 (*1-56420-000-0*) New Readers.
Riddy, Felicity, ed. Regionalism in Late-Medieval Manuscripts & Texts: Essays Celebrating the Publication of a Linguistic Atlas of Late Medieval England. (York Manuscripts Conferences: II). 224p. (C). 1991. text ed. 79.00 (*0-85991-311-2*) Boydell & Brewer.
Riddy, Felicity, jt. ed. see Alexander, Michael.
Riddy, Felicity, jt. ed. see Carley, James P.
Ride, Sally. Voyager: An Adventure to the Edge of the Solar System. LC 91-32495. (Face to Face with Science Ser.). (Illus.). 36p. (J). (gr. 2-6). 1992. 14.00 (*0-517-58157-4*); lib. bdg. 14.99 (*0-517-58158-2*) Crown Bks Yng Read.
Ride, Sally & Okie, Susan. To Space & Back. LC 85-23757. (Illus.). 96p. (J). (gr. 1 up). 1989. pap. 12.95 (*0-688-09112-1*, Pub. by Beech Tree Bks) Morrow.
— To Space & Back. LC 85-23757. (Illus.). 96p. (J). (gr. 1 up). 1989. reprint ed. 16.95 (*0-688-06159-1*) Lothrop.
Ride, Sally K. & O'Shaughnessy, Tam. Third Planet. LC 92-40609. (Illus.). 48p. (J). (gr. 3-7). 1994. 15.00 (*0-517-59361-0*); lib. bdg. 15.99 (*0-517-59362-9*) Crown Bks Yng Read.
Ride, W. D. & Younes, T., eds. Biological Nomenclature Today. (International Union of Biological Sciences Monograph Ser.: No. 2). 76p. 1987. pap. 24.00 (*1-85221-016-8*, IRL Pr) OUP.
Ride, W. D., jt. ed. see Groves, R. H.
Rideal, C. F. Charles Dickens' Heroines. LC 74-7273. (Studies in Dickens: No. 52). 1974. lib. bdg. 75.00 (*0-8383-1987-4*) M S G Haskell Hse.
Rideal, Eric K., jt. auth. see Davies, John T.
Rideal, Liz. Double Take. (Illus.). 48p. 1991. pap. 14.95 (*0-9515642-5-0*) Antique Collect.
Rideau, S. Noel. Uncle Noel's Fun Fables Program. (Illus.). 80p. 1991. student ed 8.95 (*0-9630734-0-0*) Aesop Systs.
Rideau, Wilbert. Life Sentences. 1992. pap. 15.00 (*0-8129-2048-1*, Times Bks) Random.
Ridefort, Gerard, jt. auth. see Miller, David.
Ridefort, Gerard, jt. auth. see Myatt, Frederick.
***Rideiksaar, Rein.** Falling in Old Age: Its Prevention & Treatment. 2nd ed. (Illus.). 320p. 1995. write for info. (*0-8261-5291-0*) Springer Pub.
Rideman, Peter. Confession of Faith. LC 74-115840. 304p. 1970. 13.00 (*0-87486-202-7*) Plough.
— Rechenschaft. 240p. 1988. reprint ed. 8.00 (*0-685-56528-9*) Plough.
Riden, K., jt. auth. see Wilson, P.
Ridenhour, David E. I Was There: Good Friday Tenebrae Service. Sherer, Michael L., ed. (Orig.). 1988. pap. 1.60 (*1-55673-021-7*, 8808) CSS OH.
***Ridenour.** The Secret War. 1995. pap. 6.95 (*0-929408-13-6*) Amer Eagle Pubns Inc.
Ridenour, Crea. Ocupate en Ensenar. 48p. 1986. reprint ed. pap. 1.95 (*0-311-11031-2*) Casa Bautista.
Ridenour, David A. & Almasi, David. Nicaragua's Continuing Revolution, 1977-1990: A Chronology. LC 90-61757. pap. 20.00 (*0-930095-12-X*) Signal Bks.
Ridenour, Fritz. Como Ser Cristiano En Iglesia: How to Be a Christian. (SPA.). 2.95 (*84-7228-159-0*, 220170, Pub. by Edit Clie SP) TSELF.
— Como Ser Cristiano En un Mundo No: How to Be a Christian. (SPA.). 3.25 (*84-7228-147-7*, 220172, Pub. by Edit Clie SP) TSELF.
— Como Ser Cristiano Sin Ser Religioso (How to Be a Christian Without Being Religious) rev. ed. (SPA.). 1986. 4.50 (*0-685-74919-3*, 490231) Editorial Unilit.
— Cual Es la Diferencia? So What's the Difference? (SPA.). 5.50 (*84-7228-307-0*, 220222, Pub. by Edit Clie SP) TSELF.
— How to Be a Christian & Still Enjoy Life: A LifeTouch Experience in Philippians. Beckwith, Mary, ed. LC 88-11395. 192p. (Orig.). 1988. pap. 7.99 (*0-8307-1218-6*, 5419173) Regal.
— How to Be a Christian Without Being Religious. 166p. (YA). 1991. 5.99 (*0-8307-1026-4*, S182104); teacher ed 14.99 (*0-8307-1511-8*, SH215) Regal.
— How to Be a Christian Without Being Religious. 2nd ed. 176p. 1984. reprint ed. pap. 7.99 (*0-8307-0982-7*) Regal.
— Si Yo Fuera... It's Your Move. (SPA.). 3.95 (*84-7228-180-9*, 220840, Pub. by Edit Clie SP) TSELF.
— So What's the Difference? rev. ed. LC 67-31426. 1979. 7.99 (*0-8307-0721-2*, 5414008) Regal.
— Todo Depende... The Other Side of Morality. (SPA.). 5.50 (*84-7228-217-1*, 220883, Pub. by Edit Clie SP) TSELF.
Ridenour, Fritz, jt. auth. see Smith, Michael W.
Ridenour, James M. The National Parks Compromised: Pork Barrel Politics & Americas Treasures. 256p. 1994. 14.99 (*1-57034-003-X*) ICS Bks.
Ridenour, John N. The Town That Left America. 100p. (Orig.). 1989. pap. 19.95 (*0-9624226-0-6*) J N Ridenour.
Ridenour, Nina. Mental Health in the United States: A Fifty-Year History. LC 61-11630. 158p. reprint ed. pap. 45.10 (*0-7837-4707-1*, 2059057) Bks Demand.
Ridenour, Richard I., jt. ed. see Kaslow, Florence W.
***Ridenour, Ron.** Backfire: The CIA's Biggest Burn. 179p. 1991. pap. 9.95 (*0-9624975-1-7*) Infoservicios.
— Cuba at the Crossroads. 193p. 1994. pap. 9.95 (*0-9624975-7-6*) Infoservicios.
Rideout, Darryl C., jt. ed. see Chou, Ting-Chao.
Rideout, Edward, jt. auth. see Isacson, Orjan.
Rideout, G. Bradley: Andestors & Descendants of Morris A. Bradley. (Illus.). 176p. 1991. reprint ed. lib. bdg. 38.00 (*0-8328-2101-2*); reprint ed. pap. 28.00 (*0-8328-2102-0*) Higginson Bk Co.
Rideout, R. W. The Right to Membership of a Trade Union. LC 75-17201. (Univ. of London Legal Ser.: No. 5). 243p. 1975. reprint ed. text ed. 59.75 (*0-8371-8295-6*, RIMTU, Greenwood Pr) Greenwood.
Rideout, R. W. & Hepple, Bob A. Current Legal Problems 1992 Vol. 45, Pt. 2: Collected Papers. 304p. 1993. 49.95 (*0-19-825722-8*) OUP.
Rideout, Ralph, ed. see Timmons, Jonathan P.
Rideout, Walter B. The Radical Novel in the U. S., 1900-1954: Some Interrelations of Literature & Society. 360p. 1992. text ed. 29.00 (*0-231-08076-X*, Mrngside); pap. 13.95 (*0-231-08077-8*, Mrngside) Col U Pr.
Rideout, Walter B., ed. Sherwood Anderson: A Collection of Critical Essays. (Twentieth Century Views Ser.). 192p. 1974. 12.95 (*0-13-036558-0*, Spectrum Bks); pap. 2.45 (*0-13-036533-5*, Spectrum Bks) P-H.
Rideout, Walter B., jt. auth. see Robinson, James K.
Rider, Anne. A Safe Place. LC 73-22656. 192p. 1974. 6.95 (*0-672-51992-5*, Bobbs) Macmillan.
Rider, Bevan. A More Expeditious Conveyance. 160p. 1990. 50.00 (*0-85131-394-9*, Pub. by J A Allen & Co UK) St Mut.
Rider, Carl. How to Improve Your Psychic Power: A Practical Guide to Developing Your Natural Clairvoyant Abilities. 192p. 1989. pap. 6.95 (*0-8065-1146-X*, Citadel Pr) Carol Pub Group.
***Rider, Charles H.** EDGAR Filer Hanbook: A Guide for Electronic Filing with SEC. 5th ed. LC 94-29188. 1994. ring bd. 110.00 (*0-13-340746-2*) Aspen Law.
— TSO - E CLISTs: The Complete Tutorial & Desk Reference. 1992. pap. 34.95 (*0-89435-407-8*) Wiley.
— TSO - E CLISTs: The Complete Tutorial & Desk Reference. 1993. text ed. 39.95 (*0-471-58809-1*, GD4078) Wiley.
Rider, Christine. An Introduction to Economic History. LC 92-18279. (C). 1994. text ed. write for info. (*0-8013-0858-5*) Longman.
Rider, Christine, jt. ed. see Knell, Mark.
Rider, D. Adventures with Bernard Shaw. LC 74-1152. (Studies in Shaw Ser.: No. 92). 1974. lib. bdg. 40.95 (*0-8383-2023-6*) M S G Haskell Hse.
***Rider, D., ed.** Jane's Airports Equipment & Services, 95-96. 1995. 250.00 (*0-7106-1269-9*) Janes Info Group.
Rider, David. Jewellery Making: A Manual of Techniques. (Illus.). 160p. 1994. pap. 29.95 (*1-85223-813-5*, Pub. by Crowood Pr UK) Trafalgar.
Rider, David, jt. auth. see Salussolia, Barry.
Rider, Debra, jt. auth. see Blacke, Terry L.
Rider, Donald G. The Desktop Guide to Unfair Labor Practices. 264p. (Orig.). 1990. pap. text ed. 25.00 (*0-936295-16-3*) FPMI Comns.
— Effective Writing for Feds. (Illus.). 96p. 1992. pap. 9.95 (*0-936295-25-2*) FPMI Comns.
Rider, Frederick. The Dialectic of Selfhood in Montaigne. 128p. 1973. 19.50 (*0-8047-0830-4*) Stanford U Pr.
— The Dialectic of Selfhood in Montaigne. fac. ed. LC 72-91679. 111p. 1973. reprint ed. pap. 30.00 (*0-7837-7917-8*, 2047673) Bks Demand.
Rider, Fremont. Rider's California: A Guidebook for Travelers. 1992. reprint ed. lib. bdg. 75.00 (*0-7812-5079-X*) Rprt Serv.
Rider, G. Ghosts of Door County Wisconsin. (Illus.). 186p. 1992. pap. 9.95 (*1-878488-41-4*) Quixote Pr IA.
Rider, Gail, jt. auth. see Faimann, Don.
Rider, Hope S. Valour Fore & Aft. LC 76-17516. (Illus.). 280p. 1987. 17.00 (*0-934943-12-5*) Thirteen Colonies Pr.
***Rider, Janine.** Memory, Our Muse: An Interdisciplinary Study of Memory for Teachers of Writing. 250p. 1995. text ed. 50.00 (*0-8058-1980-0*); pap. 25.00 (*0-8058-1981-9*) L Erlbaum Assocs.
Rider, Jeff, tr. see Zink, Michel.
Rider, Joanne. First Grade Valentines. LC 92-35388. (First Grade Is the Best! Ser.). (Illus.). 32p. (J). (gr. k-2). 1992. lib. bdg. 9.79 (*0-8167-3004-0*); pap. text ed. 2.95 (*0-8167-3005-9*) Troll Assocs.
Rider, Leslie, jt. auth. see Herz, Martin F.
Rider Montgomery, Elizabeth. Alexander Graham Bell: Man of Sound. (Discovery Biographies Ser.). (Illus.). 80p. (J). (gr. 2-6). 1993. reprint ed. lib. bdg. 12.95 (*0-7910-1423-1*) Chelsea Hse.
Rider, Pamela, ed. see Senseman, Laurence A.
Rider, Paul R. & Fischer, Carl H. Mathematics of Investment. (C). 1951. text ed. 9.95 (*0-914004-02-6*) Ulrich.
***Rider, Peter.** Studies in History & Museums. (Canadian Museum of Civilization Murcury Ser.). 272p. 1994. pap. text ed. 24.95 (*0-660-14022-5*) U Ch Pr.
Rider, Raymond A. The Fearings & the Fearing Tavern with the Bumpus Family. (Illus.). 1977. 10.00 (*0-88492-021-6*) W S Sullwold.
Rider, Robert L. Alto Before the Dawn. LC 91-74091. (Illus.). 409p. 1992. 29.95 (*0-9634116-0-8*) Dawn Pub Co.
Rider, Robin E., comp. A Bibliography of Early Modern Algebra, Fifteen Hundred to Eighteen Hundred. LC 81-51030. (Berkeley Papers in History of Science: No. 7). 150p. (Orig.). 1982. pap. 8.00 (*0-918102-08-1*) U Cal Hist Sci Tech.
Rider, Robin E. & Lowood, Henry E., comps. Guide to Sources in Northern California for History of Science & Technology. LC 85-51383. (Berkeley Papers in History of Science: No. 10). (Illus.). 193p. (Orig.). 1985. pap. text ed. 12.00 (*0-918102-12-X*) U Cal Hist Sci Tech.
Rider, Rowland & Paulsen, Deirdre. The Roll Away Saloon: Cowboy Tales of the Arizona Strip. (Western Experience Ser.). 114p. 1985. pap. 12.95 (*0-87421-124-7*) Utah St U Pr.
***Rider, Stephen.** Queen: These Are the Days of Our Lives; the Essential Queen Biography. 1993. pap. 10.00 (*1-898141-20-7*, Pub. by Castle Communs UK) Viking Penguin.
— Queen: These Are the Days of Our Lives: The Essential Queen Biography. (Illus.). 240p. 1993. pap. 10.00 (*0-685-72583-9*, Pub. by Castle Communs UK) Viking Penguin.
Rider, Tracy, ed. see Bennett, Geraldine M.

R

An Asterisk (*) at the beginning of an entry indicates that the title is appearing in BIP for the first time.

Rider, William. An Historical & Critical Account of the Lives & Writings of the Living Authors of Great-Britain. LC 92-24818. (Augustan Reprints Ser.: No. 163 (1974)). reprint ed. 12.00 (*0-404-70163-9*, PR443) AMS Pr.

Ridett, Anthea, tr. see Chadefaud, Catherine & Coblence, Jean-Michel.

Ridge, Antonia. By Special Request. large type ed. 235p. 1981. 12.00 (*0-7089-0573-0*) Ulverscroft.

— For Love of a Rose. 254p. 1972. pap. 10.95 (*0-571-10118-6*) Faber & Faber.

— The Man Who Painted Roses: The Story of Pierre-Joseph Redoute. large type ed. 1976. 15.95 (*0-85456-496-9*) Ulverscroft.

— The Thirteenth Child. large type ed. 1978. 15.95 (*0-7089-0181-6*) Ulverscroft.

***Ridge, Ben.** Reproduce Almost Anything: Basic Silicone Mold Making. (Illus.). 44p. 1992. 39.95 (*0-9634267-0-2*); vhs write for info. (*0-614-00826-3*) Cherokee Access.

Ridge, Bill, Jr. The Geometric Approach to Golf: A New Concept of Golf. (Illus.). 136p. 1991. 7.95 (*0-9622532-0-0*) Lauschen Co.

Ridge, C. H., ed. Index to Wills Proved in the Prerogative Court of Canterbury, Vol. 10: 1676-1685. (British Record Society Index Library Ser.: Vols. 71-72). 1969. reprint ed. 85.00 (*0-8115-1512-5*) Periodicals Srv.

Ridge, Delores F., ed. see Matanah.

Ridge, Delores F., ed. see Matanah, pseud.

Ridge, Don E. Take a Lap: The Story of Don Sprinkle's Rainier Beach Athletic Club Ramblers & Seattle Ramblers. LC 88-92594. (Illus.). 240p. (Orig.). 1989. pap. text ed. 19.50 (*0-9621608-0-6*) D E Ridge.

Ridge, Dorothy K. Nursing Home or Board & Care: Making the Right Choice. LC 93-7797. 150p. (Orig.). 1993. pap. 9.95 (*0-938179-31-4*) Mills Sanderson.

Ridge, George R. Joris-Karl Huysmaus. 123p. 1968. 49.50 (*0-685-63211-3*) Elliots Bks.

***Ridge, Irene.** Plant Physiology: Biology: Form & Function. (Illus.). 372p. 1991. pap. 52.50 (*0-340-53186-X*, Pub. by Hodder & Stoughton Ltd UK) Lubrecht & Cramer.

Ridge, J. D. Annotated Bibliographies of Mineral Deposits in Africa Asia (Exclusive of the U. S. S. R.) & Australasia. 545p. 1976. 223.00 (*0-08-020459-7*, Pub. by Pergamon Repr UK) Franklin.

Ridge, J. D., et al. Geology & Metallogeny of Copper Deposits. Friedrich, G. H. et al, eds. (Illus.). 620p. 1986. 139.00 (*0-387-16101-5*) Spr-Verlag.

Ridge, J. D., ed. Ore Deposits of the United States, 1933-1967, 2 vols., Set. LC 68-24170. 1800p. 1968. 10.00 (*0-89520-008-2*) SMM&E Inc.

Ridge, John D. Annotated Bibliographies of Mineral Deposits in the Western Hemisphere: Includes 1974 Supplementary References. LC 72-178773. (Geological Society of America, Memoir Ser.: No. 131). 705p. reprint ed. pap. 180.00 (*0-8357-5491-X*, 2025459) Bks Demand.

— Selected Bibliographies of Hydrothermal & Magmatic Mineral Deposits. LC 59-1279. (Geological Society of America, Memoir Ser.: No. 75). 209p. reprint ed. pap. 59.60 (*0-317-10309-1*, 2004397) Bks Demand.

Ridge, John D., ed. Genesis of Ore Deposits: Proceedings of the Symposium of the International Association, 5th Quadrennial, Snowbird, Utah, 1978. (Illus.). 807p. 1980. text ed. 110.00 (*3-510-65094-8*, Pub. by E Schweizerbartsche GW) Lubrecht & Cramer.

— Ore Deposits of the United States, 1933-1967: The Graton-Sales Volume, Vol. 1. LC 68-24170. (Rocky Mountain Fund Ser.). (Illus.). 1023p. reprint ed. pap. 180.00 (*0-7837-9171-2*, 2049871) Bks Demand.

Ridge, John R. Life & Adventures of Joaquin Murieta, the Celebrated California Bandit. (Western Frontier Library: No. 4). (Illus.). 1986. reprint ed. pap. 11.95 (*0-8061-1429-0*) U of Okla Pr.

Ridge, M. & Billington, R. A., eds. America's Frontier Story: A Documentary History of Westward Expansion. LC 79-28118. 680p. 1980. reprint ed. pap. text ed. 28.50 (*0-89874-090-8*) Krieger.

Ridge, Martin. Ignatius Donnelly: Portrait of a Politician. LC 90-28170. (Illus.). xvi, 428p. 1991. reprint ed. pap. 17.50 (*0-87351-262-6*, Borealis Book) Minn Hist.

— The New Bilingualism: An American Dilemma. 272p. 1982. 34.95 (*0-88474-104-4*) Transaction Pubs.

Ridge, Martin, intro. Frederick Jackson Turner: Wisconsin's Historian of the Frontier. (Illus.). 71p. 1993. reprint ed. pap. 6.95 (*0-87020-246-4*) State Hist Soc Wis.

Ridge, Martin, jt. auth. see Billington, Ray A.

Ridge, Martin, et al. Writing the History of the American West. (Illus.). 109p. 1991. pap. 12.95 (*0-944026-31-1*) Am Antiquarian.

Ridge, Millie. Nostradamus: An Illustrated Guide to His Predictions. (Illus.). 80p. 1993. 9.98 (*0-8317-6447-3*) Smithmark.

Ridge, Peter. Sound Blaster Official Book, Second Edition. 2nd ed. 1994. pap. text ed. 34.95 (*0-07-882000-6*) Osborne-McGraw.

***Ridge, Peter M.** The Book of SCSI: A Guide for Adventurers. LC 94-44670. 450p. 1995. pap. 34.95 (*1-886411-02-6*) No Starch Pr.

***Ridge, Rohn D., ed.** Ore Deposits of the United States, 1933-1967: The Graton-Sales Volume, Vol. 2. LC 68-24170. (Rocky Mountain Fund Ser.). (Illus.). 895p. reprint ed. pap. 180.00 (*0-7837-9172-0*, 2049871) Bks Demand.

Ridge, Warren J. Value Analysis for Better Management. LC 75-96142. 207p. reprint ed. pap. 59.00 (*0-317-09939-6*, 2050439) Bks Demand.

Ridgefield Garden Club Coloring Book Committee Staff. Ridgefield to Color & Keep. Willis, Lillian, ed. (Illus.). 44p. (Orig.). 1988. pap. 3.75 (*0-317-91201-1*) Ridgefield Garden Club.

Ridgell, Reilly. Bending to the Trade Winds: Stories of the Peace Corps Experience in Micronesia. (Illus.). vi, 102p. (Orig.). (C). 1991. pap. 9.95 (*1-881629-00-7*) Univ Guam Pr.

— Pacific Nations & Territories. LC 88-70787. (Illus.). 112p. 1995. student ed, pap. 8.95 (*1-57306-002-X*) Bess Pr.

— Pacific Nations & Territories. 3rd rev. ed. LC 88-70787. (Illus.). 184p. 1995. 29.95 (*1-57306-001-1*) Bess Pr.

Ridgely, Beverly S. & Eglaus, Gustavs E. Supplement to Birds of the World in Philately. (Illus.). 62p. 1986. pap. text ed. 6.00 (*0-935991-00-X*) Am Topical Assn.

Ridgely, Frances S. The Condell Collection of Oriental Art. (Handbook of Collections: No. 1). (Illus.). 64p. 1963. pap. 1.25 (*0-89792-025-2*) Ill St Museum.

Ridgely, Frances S., jt. auth. see Holtz, Frederick C.

Ridgely, J. V. Nineteenth-Century Southern Literature. LC 79-4011. (New Perspectives on the South Ser.). 144p. 1980. 16.00 (*0-8131-0301-0*) U Pr of Ky.

Ridgely, Joseph V. John Pendleton Kennedy. (Twayne's United States Authors Ser.). 1966. pap. 13.95 (*0-8084-0190-4*, T102) NCUP.

— William Gilmore Simms. (Twayne's United States Authors Ser.). 1962. pap. 13.95 (*0-8084-0327-3*, T28) NCUP.

Ridgely, Joseph V., ed. see Simms, William G.

Ridgely-Nevitt, Cedric. American Steamships on the Atlantic. LC 78-66835. 360p. 1981. 85.00 (*0-87413-140-5*) U Delaware Pr.

Ridgely, Robert S. & Gwynne, John A., Jr. A Guide to the Birds of Panama, with Costa Rica, Nicaragua, & Honduras. enl. ed. (Illus.). 608p. (C). 1992. pap. text ed. 32.50 (*0-691-02512-6*) Princeton U Pr.

— A Guide to the Birds of Panama, with Costa Rica, Nicaragua, & Honduras. 2nd enl. ed. (Illus.). 608p. (C). 1992. text ed. 60.00 (*0-691-08529-3*) Princeton U Pr.

Ridgely, Robert S. & Tudor, Guy. Birds of South America, Vol. I: The Oscine Passerines. (Illus.). 562p. 1989. 70.00 (*0-292-70756-8*); 12.50 (*0-292-70777-0*) U of Tex Pr.

Ridgely, Roberta, ed. see Szekely, Deborah.

***Ridgeon, Bob.** The Economics of Pig Production. 275p. 1993. text ed. 34.95 (*0-85236-269-2*, Pub. by Farming Pr UK) Diamond Farm Bk.

Ridgeway, jt. auth. see Parkhouse.

Ridgeway, C. L., ed. Gender, Interaction & Inequality. (Illus.). ix, 247p. 1991. 54.00 (*0-387-97578-0*) Spr-Verlag.

Ridgeway, Christopher & Wallace, Brian. Empowering Change: The Role of People Management. 160p. 1993. pap. 175.00 (*0-85292-548-4*, Pub. by IPM Hse UK) St Mut.

Ridgeway, Donald G. The Healthy Peasant Gourmet. LC 82-90747. (Illus.). 220p. 1983. 12.95 (*0-910361-01-0*); pap. 7.95 (*0-910361-00-2*) Earth Basics.

***Ridgeway, Georgia.** Life: Devotional Poems: A Guide to an Overcoming Life. 75p. (Orig.). 1995. pap. write for info. (*1-885591-55-1*) Morris Pubng.

Ridgeway, James. Blood in the Face: The Ku Klux Klan, Aryan Nations, Nazi Skinheads, & the Rise of a New White Culture. (Illus.). 208p. 1991. pap. 19.95 (*1-56025-003-8*) Thunders Mouth.

— Haiti Files: Decoding the Crisis. 1994. pap. 10.00 (*0-9621259-7-0*) Essential Info Inc.

— March to War. LC 91-11607. 244p. 1991. pap. 9.95 (*0-941423-61-1*) FWEW.

Ridgeway, James, ed. Cast a Cold Eye: American Opinion Writing, 1990-91. LC 91-10124. 200p. 1991. 25.00 (*0-941423-55-7*); pap. 12.95 (*0-941423-54-9*) FWEW.

Ridgeway, James, jt. ed. see Udovicki, Jasminda.

Ridgeway, James, ed. see Udovicki, Karolina.

Ridgeway, Jaqueline. Louise Bogan. (United States Authors Ser.: No. 461). 160p. 1984. lib. bdg. 19.95 (*0-8057-7401-7*, Twayne) Macmillan.

Ridgeway, John. Flood Tide. large type ed. 1991. 23.95 (*0-7089-8620-X*, Trail West Pubs) Ulverscroft.

Ridgeway, Judy. The Vegetarian Gourmet. (Illus.). 176p. 1981. 14.95 (*0-13-941492-4*, Spectrum Bks) P-H.

Ridgeway, Rick. The Last Step: The American Ascent of K2. LC 80-19395. (Illus.). 352p. 1980. 25.00 (*0-89886-007-5*) Mountaineers.

Ridgeway, Roy. Asthma, the Natural Way. (Natural Way Ser.). 1994. pap. 5.95 (*1-85230-492-8*) Element MA.

Ridgeway, Sam H. & Harrison, Richard J., eds. Handbook of Marine Mammals Vol. 1: The Walrus, Sea Lions, Fur Seals & Sea Otter. LC 80-42010. 1981. text ed. 128.00 (*0-12-588501-6*) Acad Pr.

— Handbook of Marine Mammals Vol. 2: Seals. LC 80-42010. 1981. text ed. 128.00 (*0-12-588502-4*) Acad Pr.

Ridgeway, Trish, ed. Improving Teaching & Training in Libraries. LC 91-75413. (Studies in Library & Information Science: No. 2). 1992. 34.50 (*0-404-64002-8*) AMS Pr.

Ridgeway, Trish, jt. auth. see Rader, Hannelore B.

Ridgeway, William. Dramas & Dramatic Dances of Non-European Races. LC 63-23187. (Illus.). 1972. reprint ed. 33.95 (*0-405-08889-2*, Pub. by Blom Pubns UK) Ayer.

— The Origin & Influence of the Thoroughbred Horse. LC 73-174446. (Illus.). 1972. reprint ed. 30.95 (*0-405-08890-6*, Pub. by Blom Pubns UK) Ayer.

— Origin of Tragedy. LC 65-19621. (Illus.). 1972. 23.95 (*0-405-08891-4*, Pub. by Blom Pubns UK) Ayer.

Ridgewell, Jenny. A Taste of Japan. LC 93-14148. (Food Around the World Ser.). (Illus.). 48p. (J). (gr. 3-5). 1993. 14.95 (*1-56847-097-5*) Thomson Lrning.

Ridgley, Dianne & Hadley, Marji. Prairie People: Cloth Dolls to Make & Cherish. LC 93-49406. (Illus.). 100p. 1994. 21.95 (*1-56477-053-2*) That Patchwork.

Ridgley, Robert S. The Birds of South America: The Suboscine Passerines, Vol. 2. (Illus.). 940p. (C). 1994. 85.00 (*0-292-77063-4*) U of Tex Pr.

Ridgway. Hard Capsules: Development - Technology. 1987. 75.95 (*0-85369-159-2*, Pub. by Pharmaceutical Pr UK) Rittenhouse.

Ridgway, et al. Behavior-Modifying Chemicals for Insect Management. 760p. 1990. 250.00 (*0-8247-8156-2*) Dekker.

Ridgway, B. The Archaic Style in Greek Sculpture. 2nd rev. ed. (Illus.). xxviii, 497p. (C). 1993. pap. text ed. 55.00 (*0-89005-516-5*) Ares.

Ridgway, Brunhilde S. Classical Collection: Sculpture. LC 72-79496. 225p. 1973. 10.00 (*0-686-05424-5*) Mus of Art RI.

Ridgway, Brunilde, et al, eds. Ancient Anatolia: Aspects of Change & Cultural Development. LC 86-40059. (Studies in Classics). (Illus.). 144p. 1986. text ed. 35.00 (*0-299-10620-9*) U of Wis Pr.

Ridgway, Brunilde S. Hellenistic Sculpture I: The Styles of Ca. 331-200 B. C. LC 89-40266. (Studies in Classics). (Illus.). 288p. (C). 1990. text ed. 40.00 (*0-299-11820-7*) U of Wis Pr.

— Roman Copies of Greek Sculpture: The Problem of the Originals. (Jerome Lecture Ser.: No. 15). 304p. (C). 1984. text ed. 49.50 (*0-472-10038-6*) U of Mich Pr.

Ridgway, Brunilde S., jt. auth. see Eiseman, Cynthia J.

Ridgway, David. The First Western Greeks. (Illus.). 224p. (C). 1993. 54.95 (*0-521-30882-8*); pap. 18.95 (*0-521-42164-0*) Cambridge U Pr.

Ridgway, Donald P. Introduction to Vascular Scanning: A Guide for the Complete Beginner. LC 91-4864. 344p. (Orig.). 1992. pap. 57.50 (*0-941022-21-8*) Appleton Davies.

— Introduction to Vascular Scanning: A Guide for the Complete Beginner. 2nd ed. (Orig.). 1995. pap. 57.50 (*0-941022-39-0*) Appleton Davies.

Ridgway, George J., ed. see Wright, James E., et al.

Ridgway, George S., ed. see Wourms, John P., et al.

Ridgway, James, ed. see Peterson, B.

Ridgway, John. Flood Tide. (Illus.). 224p. 1989. 29.95 (*0-340-32027-3*, Pub. by H & S UK) Trafalgar.

Ridgway, John L. Scientific Illustration. (Illus.). xiv, 173p. 1938. 27.50 (*0-8047-0996-3*) Stanford U Pr.

Ridgway, Judith. Successful Media Relations: A Practitioner's Guide. LC 84-6128. 214p. 1984. text ed. 54.95 (*0-566-02469-1*) Ashgate Pub Co.

Ridgway, Matthew B. The Korean War. (Quality Paperbacks Ser.). (Illus.). 360p. 1986. pap. 13.95 (*0-306-80267-8*) Da Capo.

Ridgway, Peggi. Jump-Start Your Job Search. LC 92-93451. (Illus.). 112p. (Orig.). 1994. pap. text ed. 14.95 (*0-9635836-0-3*) Wordpictures.

Ridgway, Philip, jt. auth. see Sanders, Tim.

Ridgway, Rick. Three Squirt Dog. 176p. (Orig.). 1994. pap. 12.95 (*0-312-11079-0*) St Martin.

Ridgway, Robert. Ornithology: United States Geological Exploration of the Fortieth Parallel. LC 73-17839. (Natural Sciences in America Ser.: Pt. 3). (Illus.). 370p. 1974. reprint ed. 28.95 (*0-405-05761-X*) Ayer.

Ridgway, Ronald S. Voltaire & Sensibility. LC 72-94539. 308p. reprint ed. pap. 87.80 (*0-317-29412-1*, 2023845) Bks Demand.

Ridgway, Roy. The Unborn Child: How to Recognize & Overcome Pre-Natal Trauma. 160p. 1987. text ed. 36.95 (*0-7045-3089-9*, Pub. by Avebury Pub UK); pap. text ed. 15.50 (*0-7045-0511-8*, Pub. by Avebury Pub UK) Ashgate Pub Co.

Ridgway, S. H. & Harrison, R., eds. Handbook of Marine Mammals Vol. 5: The Dolphins. (Illus.). 416p. 1994. boxed 89.00 (*0-12-588505-9*) Acad Pr.

Ridgway, Sam H. Dolphin Doctor. 1988. pap. 3.95 (*0-449-21622-5*) Fawcett.

Ridgway, Sam H. & Harrison, Richard J., eds. Handbook of Marine Mammals Vol. 3. 1985. text ed. 128.00 (*0-12-588503-2*) Acad Pr.

— Handbook of Marine Mammals Vol. 4: River Dolphins & the Larger Toothed Whales. 442p. 1989. text ed. 128.00 (*0-12-588504-0*) Acad Pr.

Ridgway, Whitman H., jt. auth. see Melusky, Joseph A.

Ridgwell, Jenny. The Book of Cocktails. LC 86-81042. 128p. 1986. pap. 10.95 (*0-89586-483-5*) Price Stern.

— A Taste of Italy. LC 93-25200. (Food Around the World Ser.). (Illus.). 48p. (J). (gr. 3-5). 1993. 14.95 (*1-56847-098-3*) Thomson Lrning.

Ridick, Joyce. Treasures in Earthen Vessels: The Vows. (C). 1988. 39.00 (*0-685-22287-X*, Pub. by St Paul Pubns UK) St Mut.

***Ridilla, Paul.** Born to Build: A Parent's Guide to Academic Alternatives. LC 94-21564. 1994. 16.95 (*0-912524-93-6*) Busn News.

Riding, Alan. Distant Neighbors: A Portrait of the Mexicans. 1985. pap. 4.95 (*0-394-74015-7*) Random.

— Distant Neighbors: A Portrait of the Mexicans. 352p. 1989. pap. 11.00 (*0-679-72441-9*, Vin) Random.

Riding Jackson, Laura. First Awakenings: The Early Poems of Laura Riding. Friedmann, Elizabeth et al, eds. LC 92-8585. 320p. 1992. 29.95 (*0-89255-179-8*) Persea Bks.

— Four Unposted Letters to Catherine. LC 93-3467. 80p. 1993. 15.00 (*0-89255-192-5*) Persea Bks.

— The Poems of Laura Riding. 420p. (C). 1985. reprint ed. pap. 14.95 (*0-89255-087-2*) Persea Bks.

— Selected Poems: In Five Sets. 96p. 1993. reprint ed. pap. 9.95 (*0-89255-189-5*) Persea Bks.

— The Word "Woman" & Other Related Writings. Clark, Alan J., ed. 196p. (Orig.). 1993. 19.95 (*0-89255-184-4*); pap. 9.95 (*0-89255-185-2*) Persea Bks.

Riding, Laura. Modernistic Poetry. reprint ed. lib. bdg. 79.00 (*0-7812-0321-X*) Rprt Serv.

— A Pamphlet Against Anthologies. (BCL1-PR English Literature Ser.). 192p. 1992. reprint ed. lib. bdg. 69.00 (*0-7812-7082-0*) Rprt Serv.

— Progress of Stories: A New, Enlarged Edition with Commentary by Laura (Riding) Jackson. 414p. 1994. reprint ed. pap. 15.00 (*0-89255-203-4*) Persea Bks.

— A Survey of Modernist Poetry. (BCL1-PR English Literature Ser.). 295p. 1992. reprint ed. lib. bdg. 79.00 (*0-7812-7073-1*) Rprt Serv.

Riding, R., ed. Calcareous Algae & Stromatolites. (Illus.). 544p. 1990. 148.00 (*0-387-52373-1*) Spr-Verlag.

Riding, Richard & Butterfield, Susan. Assessment & Examination in the Secondary School. 256p. 1990. 55.00 (*0-415-03108-7*, A4318) Routledge.

Riding, Robvert, jt. ed. see Leadbeater, Barry S.

***Ridinger.** Gay & Lesbian Movement. 1995. text ed. 40.00 (*0-8161-7373-7*) G K Hall.

Ridinger, Robert B. African Archaeology: A Selected Bibliography. (G. K. Hall Reference Ser.). 550p. 1993. text ed. 55.00 (*0-8161-9086-0*, Hall Reference) Macmillan.

— The Peace Corps: An Annotated Bibliography. 300p. (C). 1989. text ed. 35.00 (*0-8161-8912-9*, Hall Reference) Macmillan.

Ridinger, Robert B., comp. The Homosexual & Society: An Annotated Bibliography. LC 90-31738. (Bibliographies & Indexes in Sociology Ser.: No. 18). 456p. 1990. text ed. 65.00 (*0-313-25357-9*, RHO, Greenwood Pr) Greenwood.

Ridinger, Robert B., jt. auth. see Gravel, Pierre B.

Ridings, Donald, jt. auth. see Dungan, Christopher.

Ridings, Eugene. Business Interest Groups in Nineteenth Century Brazil. LC 93-32152. (Latin American Studies: Vol. 78). 304p. (C). 1994. 59.95 (*0-521-45485-9*) Cambridge U Pr.

Ridings, Jean E., tr. see Lilie, Ralph-J.

Ridings, K. C. Facing the Brokenness: Meditations for Parents of Sexually Abused Children. 196p. (Orig.). 1991. pap. 9.95 (*0-8361-3573-3*) Herald Pr.

Ridington, Dick. Macro Engineer: A 1-2-3 Macro Developer's Toolkit-2 Disks Included. 1990. pap. 79.95 (*0-13-543331-2*) P-H.

Ridington, Jillian & Ridington, Robin. People of the Longhouse: How the Iroquoian Tribes Lived. (How They Lived Ser.). (Illus.). 48p. (J). (gr. 3-7). 1992. pap. 7.95 (*1-55054-221-4*, Pub. by Groundwood-Douglas & McIntyre CN) Firefly Bks Ltd.

Ridington, Jillian, jt. auth. see Ridington, Robin.

Ridington, Richard W. Inside Lotus 1-2-3 Macros. 1989. pap. 24.95 (*0-13-463522-1*) P-H.

— More Hidden Power of Lotus 1-2-3: Advanced Macro Applications. 1986. pap. 19.95 (*0-89303-673-0*); disk 49.95 (*0-89303-675-7*) P-H.

Ridington, Richard W., jt. auth. see Poor, Alfred.

Ridington, Robin. Little Bit Know Something: Stories in a Language of Anthropology. LC 89-48164. (Illus.). 299p. (Orig.). (C). 1990. text ed. 29.95 (*0-87745-268-7*); pap. 12.95x (*0-87745-286-5*) U of Iowa Pr.

— Trail to Heaven: Knowledge & Narrative in a Northern Native Community. LC 88-17098. (Illus.). 317p. 1988. reprint ed. text ed. 33.95x (*0-87745-212-1*) U of Iowa Pr.

— Trail to Heaven: Knowledge & Narrative in a Northern Native Community. LC 88-17098. (Illus.). 317p. 1992. reprint ed. pap. 11.95x (*0-87745-391-8*) U of Iowa Pr.

Ridington, Robin & Ridington, Jillian. People of the Trail: How the Northern Forest Indians Lived. (How They Lived Ser.). (Illus.). 40p. (J). (gr. 3-7). 1992. pap. 7.95 (*0-88894-412-8*, Pub. by Groundwood-Douglas & McIntyre CN) Firefly Bks Ltd.

Ridington, Robin, jt. auth. see Ridington, Jillian.

Ridjanovic, Midhat, tr. see Dizdarevic, Zlatko.

Ridker, Ronald G. Population & Development: The Search for Selective Interventions. LC 76-16806. (Resources for the Future Ser.). (Illus.). 488p. 1977. 45.00 (*0-8018-1884-2*) Johns Hopkins.

— The World Bank's Role in Human Resource Development in Sub-Saharan Africa: Education, Training & Technical Assistance. LC 94-20212. (Operations Evaluation Study Ser.). 1994. write for info. (*0-8213-2864-6*) World Bank.

Ridker, Ronald G., ed. Changing Resource Problems of the Fourth World. LC 75-42978. (Resources for the Future Working Paper Ser.: Pd-1). (Illus.). 162p. 1976. pap. 8.00 (*0-8018-1847-8*) Johns Hopkins.

— Changing Resource Problems of the Fourth World. LC 75-42978. (RFF Working Paper Ser.: No. PD-1). 161p. reprint ed. pap. 45.90 (*0-685-20406-5*, 2030213) Bks Demand.

Ridker, Ronald G. & Watson, William D., Jr. To Choose a Future. LC 79-3643. (Resources for the Future Ser.). 1980. 37.00 (*0-8018-2354-4*) Johns Hopkins.

Ridky, Jill & Sheldon, George F. Managing in Academics: A Health Center Model. LC 93-23854. 1993. 30.00 (*0-942219-11-2*) Quality Med Pub.

Ridl, Jack. After School. 1988. pap. 1.50 (*0-318-37519-2*) Samisdat.

— The Same Ghost. LC 84-73042. 68p. (Orig.). 1984. pap. 5.00 (*0-936014-13-X*) Dawn Valley.

Ridl, Julie, jt. auth. see West, Larry.

Ridler, Anne. A Matter of Life & Deth Death. (C). 1990. 60.00 (*0-906887-07-0*, Pub. by Greville Pr UK) St Mut.

Ridler, George E. & Shockley, Robert J. School Administrator's Budget Handbook: A Step-by-Step Guide for Preparing & Managing Your School Budget. 288p. 1989. text ed. 49.95 (*0-13-793332-0*) P-H.

Ridler, Philip, ed. Pocket Guide: Fortran. (C). 1981. pap. text ed. 30.00 (*0-273-01683-0*, Pub. by Pitman Pubng UK) St Mut.

Ridless, Glenn. Little Treasures. (Petites Ser.). (Illus.). 80p. 1991. 4.95 (*0-88088-733-8*) Peter Pauper.

***Ridley, Aaron.** Music, Value, & the Passions. (Illus.). 216p. 1995. 27.95x (*0-8014-3035-6*) Cornell U Pr.

R

An Asterisk (*) at the beginning of an entry indicates that the title is appearing in BIP for the first time.

Ridley, Aaron, ed. Arguing about Art: Topics in Contemporary Philosophical Aesthetics. LC 94-14036. 1994. pap. text ed. write for info. (0-07-046191-0) McGraw.

Ridley, Aaron, jt. auth. see Neill, Alex.

Ridley, Alison & Garfield, Curtis F. As Ancient Is This Hostelry: The Story of the Wayside Inn. (Illus.). 338p. (Orig.). (YA). (gr. 7 up). 1989. reprint ed. pap. 15.00 (0-9621976-0-2) Porcupine Enter.

— The Story of the Lygon Arms. (Illus.). 240p. (C). 1992. pap. 17.50 (0-9621976-1-0) Porcupine Enter.

Ridley, B. K. Quantum Processes in Semiconductors. 3rd ed. LC 93-9153. 1993. 52.50 (0-19-851752-1, Clarendon Pr); pap. 26.50 (0-19-851751-3, Clarendon Pr) OUP.

— Time, Space & Things. 3rd ed. (Canto Book Ser.). (Illus.). 200p. (C). 1995. pap. 9.95 (0-521-48486-3) Cambridge U Pr.

Ridley, C. M., et al. A Colour Atlas of Diseases of the Vulva. (Medical Atlas Ser.: No. 8). (Illus.). 128p. 1993. 132.00 (0-412-36520-0) Chapman & Hall.

***Ridley, Charles R.** Overcoming Unintentional Racism in Counseling & Therapy: A Practitioner's Guide to International Action. (Multicultural Aspects of Counseling Ser.: Vol. 5). 120p. 1994. 36.00 (0-8039-4869-7); pap. 16.95 (0-8039-4870-0) Sage.

Ridley, Chas, ed. see Brooks, Jennifer.

Ridley, Clarence H., et al. Computer Software Agreements. 1987. Supplemented annually, write for info. 175.00 (0-88712-750-9) Warren Gorham & Lamont.

— Computer Software Agreements: Forms & Commentary with Forms on Disk. rev. ed. 1993. disk, ring bd. 175.00 (0-685-69655-3, PLS) Warren Gorham & Lamont.

Ridley, Clifford. How to Grow Your Own Groceries for One Hundred Dollars a Year. 128p. 1974. pap. 3.95 (0-89036-029-4) Hawkes Pub Inc.

Ridley, D. S. The Pathogenesis of Leprosy & Related Diseases. 250p. 1988. 200.00 (0-7236-1031-2, Pub. by John Wright UK) Buttrwrth-Heinemann.

***Ridley, Dale S. & Walther, Bill.** Creating Responsible Learners: The Role of a Positive Classroom. (Psychology in the Classroom Ser.). 132p. (Orig.). 1996. pap. 17.95 (1-55798-295-3) Am Psychol.

Ridley, Edgar J. An African Answer: The Key to Global Productivity. LC 92-14518. 100p. (Orig.). 1992. 24.95 (0-86543-358-5); pap. 8.95 (0-86543-359-3) Africa World.

Ridley, Elizabeth. Throwing Roses. LC 92-34344. 1993. 22.00 (1-877946-29-X) Permanent Pr.

***Ridley, Elizabeth & O'Reilly, Tim.** What You Need to Know about Internet Marketing. 160p. 1995. 19.95 (1-56592-105-4) OReilly & Assocs.

Ridley, F. A. The Assassins: A Study of the Cult of the Assassins in Persia & Islam. (Islam Ser.). 1980. lib. bdg. 59.95 (0-8490-3077-3) Gordon Pr.

Ridley, F. F., ed. Government & Administration in Western Europe. LC 79-13518. 1979. text ed. 29.95 (0-312-34113-X) St Martin.

Ridley, Francis A. The Jesuits: A Study in Counter-Reformation. LC 83-45595. reprint ed. 35.00 (0-404-19888-0) AMS Pr.

— The Papacy & Fascism: The Crisis of the 20th Century. LC 72-180422. (Studies in Fascism: Ideology & Practice). reprint ed. 45.00 (0-404-56156-X) AMS Pr.

Ridley, H. N. Species: Book on Medicinal Plants. 449p. (C). 1983. reprint ed. 195.00 (81-7089-015-2, Pub. by Intl Bk Distr II) St Mut.

Ridley, Henry. The Flora of the Malay Peninsula, 5 vols. 1967. 250.00 (90-6123-260-0) Lubrecht & Cramer.

Ridley, Henry N. The Dispersal of Plants Throughout the World. (Illus.). 744p. 1990. reprint ed. 175.00 (0-685-61648-7, 043826) Koeltz Sci Bks.

Ridley, Hugh. Images of Imperial Rule. LC 82-25547. 250p. 1983. text ed. 25.00 (0-312-40926-5) St Martin.

— Mann: "Buddenbrooks" (Landmarks of World Literature Ser.). 1987. pap. 10.95 (0-521-31697-9) Cambridge U Pr.

— Mann: "Buddenbrooks" (Landmarks of World Literature Ser.). 1987. 29.95 (0-521-32813-6) Cambridge U Pr.

— The Problematic Bourgeois: Twentieth-Century Criticism on Thomas Mann's "Buddenbrooks" & "The Magic Mountain" 200p. 1994. 52.95 (1-879751-87-9) Camden Hse.

Ridley, J., jt. auth. see Crowe, M.

Ridley, Jack. Fifteen Million Southern Baptists Deceived. 1994. 12.95 (0-8062-4958-7) Carlton.

***Ridley, Jane.** Young Disraeli, 1804-1846. LC 94-25543. 1995. 35.00 (0-517-58643-6) Crown Pub Group.

Ridley, Jasper. Elizabeth I: The Shrewdness of Virtue. LC 88-29255. 391p. 1989. reprint ed. pap. 11.95 (0-88064-110-X) Fromm Intl Pub.

— The Law of Carriage of Goods by Land, Sea & Air. Whitehead, Geoffrey, ed. (C). 1982. pap. 110.00 (0-317-92375-7, Scientific) St Mut.

— The Tudor Age. LC 90-6884. (Illus.). 384p. 1990. 40.00 (0-87951-405-1) Overlook Pr.

Ridley, Jessica. The Decorated Doll House: How to Design & Create Miniature Interiors. (Illus.). 128p. 1990. 34.95 (0-8021-1232-3) Grove-Atltic.

— Finishing Touches: A Do-It-Yourself Guide to the Art of the Painted Finish. (Illus.). 214p. 1988. text ed. 27.50 (0-684-19025-7, Scribners) S&S Trade.

Ridley, Jo A., jt. auth. see Kennedy, Arthur R.

Ridley, John, ed. Safety at Work. 4th ed. LC 93-46862. 800p. 1994. 199.00 (0-7506-0746-7) Buttrwrth-Heinemann.

Ridley, Ken, jt. auth. see Morrison, Keith.

Ridley, M. Animal Behavior. 2nd ed. 1994. pap. write for info. (0-632-03833-0) Blackwell Sci.

— Animal Behaviour. 1986. pap. 29.95 (0-632-01416-4) Blackwell Sci.

Ridley, M. R. Keats' Craftsmanship: A Study in Poetic Development. LC 63-14696. (Illus.). 328p. reprint ed. 93.50 (0-8357-9707-4, 2011437) Bks Demand.

Ridley, M. R., ed. see Shakespeare, William.

***Ridley, Mark.** Animal Behavior: An Introduction to Behavioral Mechanisms, Development, & Ecology. 2nd ed. (Illus.). 223p. 1994. pap. (0-86542-390-3) Blackwell Sci.

— Evolution. (Illus.). 544p. 1993. 42.95 (0-86542-226-5) Blackwell Sci.

— The Problems of Evolution. LC 84-27300. (Illus.). 160p. 1985. 20.95 (0-19-219194-2) OUP.

Ridley, Mark, ed. see Darwin, Charles.

Ridley, Mark, jt. auth. see Dawkins, Richard.

Ridley, Mark, jt. ed. see Dawkins, Richard.

Ridley, Matt. The Red Queen: Sex & the Evolution of Human Nature. (Illus.). 416p. 1994. text ed. 25.00 (0-02-603340-2) Macmillan.

— The Red Queen: Sex & the Evolution of Human Nature. 416p. 1995. pap. 12.95 (0-14-024548-0, Penguin Bks) Viking Penguin.

Ridley, Maurice R. Keats' Craftsmanship: A Study in Poetic Development. (BCL1-PR English Literature Ser.). 312p. 1992. reprint ed. lib. bdg. 89.00 (0-7812-7574-1) Rprt Serv.

— Studies in Three Literatures: English, Latin & Greek Contrasts & Comparisons. LC 78-42. 1977p. 1978. reprint ed. text ed. 49.75 (0-313-20189-7, RISTL, Greenwood Pr) Greenwood.

Ridley, Michael. The Art of World Religions: Buddhism. (Illus.). 184p. 1978. 49.95 (0-7137-0886-7) Asia Bk Corp.

Ridley, Norman, jt. auth. see Pilling, John.

***Ridley, Pauline.** Modern Art. (Art & Artists Ser.). (Illus.). 48p. (YA). 1995. 16.95 (1-56847-356-7) Thomson Lrning.

***Ridley, Philip.** Apocalyptica. 96p. 1995. pap. 11.95 (0-413-68870-4, A0702) Heinemann.

— The Fastest Clock in the Universe. 83p. 1992. pap. 9.95 (0-413-67140-2, A0654, Pub. by Methuen UK) Heinemann.

— Ghost from a Perfect Place. 96p. 1995. pap. 11.95 (0-413-68860-7, Pub. by Methuen UK) Heinemann.

— Pitchfork Disney. (Methuen New Theatrescripts Ser.). 84p. (Orig.). 1991. pap. 11.95 (0-413-65670-5, AO583, Pub. by Methuen UK) Heinemann.

Ridley, Ronald T. The Eagle & the Spade: Archaeology in Rome During the Napoleonic Era, 1809-1814. (Illus.). 352p. (C). 1992. 89.95 (0-521-40191-7) Cambridge U Pr.

Ridley, RuthAnn. Every Marriage Is Different. (Tapestry Collection Ser.). 96p. (Orig.). 1993. pap. 5.99 (1-56476-051-0, Victor Books) SP Pubns.

Ridley, Sarah, jt. auth. see Merrill, Linda.

Ridley, Steve. Perspectives in Motion & Stillness: Inspired Commentary on T'ai Chi & Meditation. 2nd rev. ed. (Illus.). 97p. (Orig.). 1991. pap. 9.95 (0-9620812-6-4) Good Karma.

Ridley, W. N., jt. auth. see Picott, R.

Ridlington, Sandra S., jt. ed. see Good, James W.

Ridlon, Florence V. A Fallen Angel: The Status Insularity of the Female Alcoholic. LC 86-47992. 184p. 1988. 30.00 (0-8387-5115-6) Bucknell U Pr.

***Ridlon, G. T.** History of the Ancient Ryedales & Their Descendants in Normandy, Great Britain, Ireland, & America from 860 to 1884 Comprising the Genealogy & Biography, for about 1000 Years., of the Families of Riddell, Riddle, Ridlon, Ridley, Etc. (Illus.). 801p. 1994. pap. text ed. 46.00 (0-7884-0011-8) Heritage Bk.

— History of the Ancient Ryedales & Their Descendants in Normandy, Great Britain, Ireland, & America from 860-1914, Comprising the Family of Riddell, Riddle, Ridlon, Ridley, Etc. (Illus.). 796p. 1989. reprint ed. lib. bdg. 127.00 (0-8328-1024-X); reprint ed. pap. 119.00 (0-8328-1025-8) Higginson Bk Co.

— Saco Valley Settlements & Families. LC 84-60097. (Illus.). 1392p. 1984. reprint ed. 85.00 (0-89725-045-1) Picton Pr.

Ridlon, G. T., ed. see Gowdy, M. M.

Ridlon, Marci. Lightning Strikes Twice. 1984. write for info. (0-394-84088-7) Random.

Ridolfi, Carlo. The Life of Tintoretto. Enggass, Catherine & Enggass, Robert, trs. LC 83-23829. 112p. 1984. 28.50 (0-271-00369-3) Pa St U Pr.

Ridolfi, Ray. Shiatsu. (Tuttle Alternative Health Ser.). (Illus.). 128p. (Orig.). 1993. pap. 12.95 (0-8048-1834-7) C E Tuttle.

Ridolphi, Margaret, jt. auth. see Driscoll, Susan.

Ridout, Lucy, jt. auth. see Gray, Paul.

Ridout, Ronald. Activity Picture Dictionary. (Illus.). 48p. (J). (gr. 1 up). 1987. 9.95 (0-8120-5844-5) Barron.

Ridout, Samuel. The Church & Its Order According to Scripture. 1915. reprint ed. pap. 4.99 (0-87213-711-2) Loizeaux.

— Lectures on the Tabernacle. (Illus.). 1973. reprint ed. 16.99 (0-87213-715-5) Loizeaux.

***Ridpath, I.** Stars & Planets. 1994. pap. 16.00 (0-00-219979-3, Pub. by HarpC UK) HarpC.

Ridpath, Ian. Astronomy. (American Nature Guide Ser.). 1992. 9.98 (0-8317-6969-6) Smithmark.

— Atlas of Stars & Planets. LC 92-32463. 80p. (YA). (gr. 5-10). 1993. 16.95 (0-8160-2926-1) Facts on File.

— Space. LC 92-53096. (World Around Us Ser.). (Illus.). 48p. (J). (gr. 3-8). 1992. pap. 5.95 (1-85697-814-1, Kingfisher LKC) LKC.

Ridpath, Ian, ed. Norton's 2000.0 Star Atlas & Reference Handbook. 18th ed. 1989. text ed. 49.95 (0-470-21460-0) Halsted Pr.

Ridpath, Ian & Murtagh, Terence. A Comet Called Halley. LC 85-18981. 48p. reprint ed. pap. 25.00 (0-685-16368-7, 2027290) Bks Demand.

Ridpath, Ian & Tirion, Wil. The Monthly Sky Guide. 3rd ed. (Illus.). 64p. (C). 1993. pap. 14.95 (0-521-44865-4) Cambridge U Pr.

Ridpath, John. World War One: A Comprehensive History. (Illus.). 530p. 1992. reprint ed. text ed. 59.95 (1-877767-80-8) Univ Publng Hse.

Ridpath, John C. History of the United States: Prepared for Schools. LC 74-15750. (Popular Culture in America Ser.). 390p. 1975. reprint ed. 36.95 (0-405-06384-9) Ayer.

Ridpath, John C., ed. see Taylor, William.

Ridpath, M. G. & Corbett, L. K., eds. Ecology of the Wet Dry Tropics. 334p. (C). 1985. text ed. 80.00 (0-9596208-3-4, Pub. by Surrey Beatty & Sons AT) St Mut.

***Ridpath, Michael.** Free to Trade: A Novel of Suspense. LC 94-34508. 1994. 23.00 (0-06-017630-X, HarpT) HarpC.

Ridsdale, R. E. Electric Circuits. 2nd ed. 736p. 1984. text ed. 40.95 (0-07-052948-5) McGraw.

Ridsdill-Smith, T. James, jt. ed. see Bailey, Winston J.

Ridyard, Susan J. The Royal Saints of Anglo-Saxon England: A Study of West Saxon & East Anglian Cults. (Cambridge Studies in Medieval Life & Thought: No. 9). 376p. 1989. 79.95 (0-521-30772-4) Cambridge U Pr.

Ridyard, Susan J., jt. auth. see King, Edward B.

Ridzon, Leonard & Walters, Charles, Jr. The Carbon Connection. LC 90-61305. 112p. 1990. pap. 12.00 (0-911311-24-6) Halcyon Hse.

***Ridzon, Leonard & Walters, Charles.** The Carbon Cycle. LC 94-70735. 143p. 1994. 15.00 (0-911311-46-7) Halcyon Hse.

Rie, K. T., ed. Low Cycle Fatigue & Elastoplastic Behaviour of Materials. 750p. 1987. 167.50 (1-85166-143-3) Elsevier.

Rie, K. T., et al, eds. Low Cycle Fatigue & Elasto-Plastic Behaviour of Materials, No. 3. LC 92-22435. 1992. write for info. (1-85166-893-4, Pub. by Elsevier Applied Sci UK) Elsevier.

Riebel, Linda. Understanding Eating Disorders. 222p. 1988. 17.95 (0-685-18892-2); pap. 52.50 (0-942028-35-X) R D Anderson.

Rieben, L. & Perfetti, C. A., eds. Learning to Read: Basic Research & Its Implications. 224p. (C). 1991. text ed. 49.95 (0-8058-0564-8) L Erlbaum Assocs.

Riebenstahl, Horst. The First Panzer Division - A Pictorial History, 1935-1945. LC 90-62980. (Illus.). 226p. 1991. 29.95 (0-88740-283-6) Schiffer.

***Rieber, Alfred J.** Merchants & Entrepreneurs in Imperial Russia. fac. ed. LC 80-28554. (Illus.). 490p. 1982. reprint ed. pap. 139.70 (0-7837-8058-3, 2047811) Bks Demand.

— Merchants & Entrepreneurs in Imperial Russia. LC 80-28554. (Illus.). xxvi, 464p. (C). 1991. reprint ed. 49.95 (0-8078-1481-4); reprint ed. pap. 17.95 (0-8078-4305-9) U of NC Pr.

Rieber, Alfred J. & Rubinstein, Alvin Z., eds. Perestroika at the Crossroads. LC 90-8633. 400p. (C). 1991. 67.95 (0-87332-741-1); pap. text ed. 25.95 (0-87332-742-X) M E Sharpe.

Rieber, Hans, jt. auth. see Kuhn-Schnyder, Emil.

***Rieber, J.** Books of Magic: Bindings. Kahan, Bob, ed. (Illus.). 112p. 1995. pap. 12.95 (1-56389-187-5, Vertigo) DC Comics.

Rieber, J. E. & Lamb, V. R. Pogo User's Manual, General Aids to Graphic Programming. LC 70-131898. 191p. 1970. 25.00 (0-403-04531-2) Scholarly.

Rieber, Lloyd. Computers, Graphics, & Learning. 304p. 1994. pap. write for info. (0-697-14894-7) Brown & Benchmark.

Rieber, Ney. A Resource for the Study of Islam. 227p. 1993. pap. text ed. 9.95 (1-56794-045-5, C-2326) Star Bible.

Rieber, R. W., ed. Foundations of Neuropsychology: An Historical Reader. LC 78-72822. 1987. 32.50 (0-404-60891-4) AMS Pr.

— Handedness & Mental Abilities: An Historical Reader. LC 78-72823. 1987. 32.50 (0-404-60892-2) AMS Pr.

— Milestones in the History of Forensic Psychology & Psychiatry: A Book of Readings. (Historical Foundations of Forensic Psychiatry & Psychology Ser.). 250p. 1980. reprint ed. lib. bdg. 27.50 (0-306-76072-X) Da Capo.

Rieber, R. W. & Salzinger, Kurt, eds. The Roots of American Psychology: Historical Influences & Implications for the Future, Vol. 291. (Annals Ser.). 394p. 1977. 22.00 (0-89072-037-1) NY Acad Sci.

Rieber, R. W., ed. see Goldstein, Kurt.

Rieber, R. W., jt. auth. see Vetter, H. J.

Rieber, Robert W. Advances in Forensic Psychology & Psychiatry, Vol. 1. (Advances in Forensic Psych & Psychiatry Ser.). 200p. 1984. text ed. 55.00 (0-89391-191-7) Ablex Pub.

— Advances in Forensic Psychology & Psychiatry, Vol. 2. (Advances in Forensic Psych. & Psychiatry Ser.). 224p. 1987. text ed. 55.00 (0-89391-291-3) Ablex Pub.

Rieber, Robert W., ed. Communication Disorders. LC 80-18394. (Applied Psycholinguistics & Communication Disorders Ser.). 366p. 1981. 65.00 (0-306-40527-X, Plenum Pr) Plenum.

— Dialogues on the Psychology of Language & Thought: Conversations with Noam Chomsky, Charles Osgood, Jean Piaget, Ulric Neisser, & Marcel Kinsbourne. LC 82-42850. (Cognition & Language Ser.). 174p. 1983. 42.50 (0-306-41185-7, Plenum Pr) Plenum.

— The Individual, Communication & Society: Essays in Memory of Gregory Bateson. (Studies in Emotion & Social Interaction). (Illus.). 368p. (C). 1990. 69.95 (0-521-26741-2) Cambridge U Pr.

Rieber, Robert W. & Vetter, Harold J., eds. The Psychological Foundations of Criminal Justice: Historical Perspectives on Forensic Psychology, Vol. 1. LC 78-18781. (Illus.). (C). 1978. 20.00x (0-89444-009-8) John Jay Pr.

— The Psychological Foundations of Criminal Justice: Historical Perspectives on Forensic Psychology, Vol. 1. LC 78-18781. (Illus.). (C). 1978. pap. 20.00x (0-89444-012-8) John Jay Pr.

Rieber, Robert W., jt. ed. see Aaronson, Doris.

Rieber, Robert W., jt. ed. see Adler, Helmut E.

Rieber, Robert W., jt. auth. see Mercier, Charles.

Rieber, Robert W., jt. ed. see Vetter, Harold J.

Riebesell, M., jt. ed. see Hausen, P.

Riebeth, Carolyn R. J. H. Sharp among the Crow Indians 1902-1910: Personal Memories of His Life & Friendships on the Crow Reservation in Montana. LC 84-51553. (Montana & the West Ser.: Vol. 2). (Illus.). 178p. (Orig.). (C). 1985. 65.00 (0-912783-01-X) Upton Sons.

Riebling, Barbara, jt. ed. see Easterlin, Nancy.

Riebling, Mark. Wedge: The Secret War Between the FBI & CIA. LC 93-43703. 1994. 27.50 (0-679-41471-1) Knopf.

***Riebold, T. W., et al.** Large Animal Anesthesia: Principles & Techniques. 2nd ed. LC 94-24471. (Illus.). 312p. 1995. 39.95 (0-8138-0774-3) Iowa St U Pr.

Riebold, Thomas W., et al. Large Animal Anesthesia: Principles & Techniques. LC 81-15609. 162p. reprint ed. pap. 46.20 (0-7837-2174-9, 2042512) Bks Demand.

Riebsame, William E., et al. Drought & Natural Resource Management in the United States: Impacts & Implications of the 1987-1989 Drought. 174p. (C). 1990. pap. text ed. 51.00 (0-8133-8026-X) Westview.

Riech, Emil. Hungarian Literature: An Historical & Critical Survey. 1977. lib. bdg. 69.95 (0-8490-2028-X) Gordon Pr.

Riechel, Rosemarie. Improving Telephone Information & Reference Service in Public Libraries. LC 87-14998. ix, 123p. (C). 1987. 27.50 (0-208-02156-6, Lib Prof Pubns); pap. 21.00 (0-208-02157-4, Lib Prof Pubns) Shoe String.

— Personnel Needs & Changing Reference Service. LC 89-8091. 119p. (C). 1989. lib. bdg. 29.50 (0-208-02226-0, Lib Prof Pubns); pap. text ed. 22.50 (0-208-02227-9, Lib Prof Pubns) Shoe String.

— Public Library Services to Business. LC 94-7018. 131p. 1994. pap. 39.95 (1-55570-168-X) Neal-Schuman.

— Reference Services for Children & Young Adults. LC 91-31973. xvi, 219p. (C). 1991. lib. bdg. 36.00 (0-208-02290-2, Lib Prof Pubns) Shoe String.

Riechenberger, jt. auth. see Regueiro.

Riechers, A. Full Length Roof Framer. (Illus.). 116p. 1993. reprint ed. lib. bdg. 14.95 (0-89966-907-7) Buccaneer Bks.

Riechert, Traugott. Stereotactic Brain Operations: Methods, Clinical Aspects, Indications. (Illus.). 387p. 1980. text ed. 106.00 (0-317-68966-5) Hogrefe & Huber Pubs.

Rieck, G. Tungsten & Its Compounds. LC 66-24897. 1967. 61.00 (0-08-011975-1, Pub. by Pergamon Repr UK) Franklin.

Rieck, Sondra & Rutledge, Carol. Move & Match Colors with Busy Bear. 22p. (J). (ps-00). 1990. 9.95 (0-9634376-0-7) Woodville Pr.

Rieck, Sondra & Stippel, Lori. Learn Basic Concepts with Cuddles Clown. 24p. (J). (ps-00). 1990. 9.95 (0-9634082-0-8) Woodville Pr.

Riecken, E. O., et al, eds. Intestinal & Pancreatic Adaptation: Adaptational Response & Repair Mechanisms in the Entero Pancreatic System - Journal: Digestion, Vol. 46, Suppl. 2, 1990. (Illus.). vi, 478p. 1990. pap. 136.00 (3-8055-5314-5) S Karger.

Riecken, Nancy. Andrew's Own Place. LC 92-22953. (Illus.). (J). 1993. 14.95 (0-395-64723-1) HM.

***Riecken, Ted & Court, Deborah, eds.** Dilemmas in Educational Change. 106p. (Orig.). (C). 1993. pap. text ed. 17.95x (1-55059-053-7) Temeron Bks.

Riecker, R. E., ed. Rio Grande Rift: Tectonics & Magmatism. (Special Publications). (Illus.). 438p. 1979. 25.00 (0-87590-214-6) Am Geophysical.

Riecks, Donald, jt. auth. see Reynolds, George P.

Ried, Glenda E., jt. auth. see Gaylord, Gloria L.

Ried, J. L., ed. Pre-Harvest Sprouting in Cereals 1992. LC 93-71502. (Illus.). xiv, 480p. 1993. pap. 89.00 (0-913250-81-3, BEF 2345) Am Assn Cereal Chem.

Riede, Anne M. BASIC Computer Literacy. (Illus.). 244p. 1984. 10.95 (0-931983-01-0) Basic Comp Lit.

— Coach's Clipboards. (Illus.). 306p. (Orig.). (J). (gr. 5-8). 1986. 10.95 (0-931983-02-9, BCLTXT-3) Basic Comp Lit.

Riede, D. Critical Essays on Gabriel Rossetti. (Critical Essays on British Literature Ser.). 250p. 1992. text ed. 45.00 (0-8161-8863-7, Hall Reference) Macmillan.

Riede, David. Dante Gabriel Rossetti Revisited. (Twayne's English Author Ser.). 160p. 1992. text ed. 24.95 (0-8057-7027-5, Twayne) Macmillan.

Riede, David G. Dante Gabriel Rossetti & the Limits of Victorian Vision. LC 82-22099. (Illus.). 288p. 1983. 36.95 (0-8014-1552-7) Cornell U Pr.

— Matthew Arnold & the Betrayal of Language. LC 87-13693. (Virginia Victorian Studies). 253p. reprint ed. pap. 72.20 (0-7837-4347-5, 2044057) Bks Demand.

— Oracles & Hierophants: Constructions of Romantic Authority. LC 91-55074. 288p. 1991. 38.95 (0-8014-2626-X) Cornell U Pr.

Riedel, David. The Birds Here Sing at Night. pap. 5.00 (0-318-04289-4) Latitudes Pr.

Riedel, David T. Rhode Island Practice, Vol. 3: Wills, Trusts & Gifts. suppl. ed. 1993. ring bd. 40.00 (0-685-74272-5) Butterworth Legal Pubs.

— Rhode Island Practice, Vol. 3: Wills, Trusts & Gifts, Vol. 3. 700p. 1994. boxed 125.00 (0-88063-724-2) Michie Butterworth.

Riedel, Erwin. Allgemeine und Anorganische Chemie: Ein Lehrbuch fuer Studenten mit Nebenfach Chemie. 3rd ed. (Illus.). x, 346p. (GER.). 1985. pap. text ed. 37.70x (3-11-010269-2) De Gruyter.

R

Riedel, F. Carl. Crime & Punishment in the Old French Romances. LC 39-8313. reprint ed. 20.00 (*0-404-05333-5*) AMS Pr.

Riedel, H. Fracture at High Temperatures. (Materials Research & Engineering Ser.). (Illus.). 370p. 1987. 97.00 (*0-387-17271-8*) Spr-Verlag.

Riedel, Hermann. Originalmusik und Musikbearbeitung. 259p. 1971. 24.00 (*3-8059-0813-X*) Theodore Front.

***Riedel, Ingrid.** Taboo in Folktales. Whitcher, Douglas & Siegenthaler, Marie, trs. (Pychology Ser.). 208p. 1995. 19.95 (*0-88064-211-4*); pap. 12.95 (*0-88064-212-2*) Fromm Intl Pub.

Riedel, James. The Industrialization of Hong Kong. 168p. 1974. pap. text ed. 33.50 (*3-16-335381-9*) Coronet Bks.

— Myths & Reality of External Constraints on Development. (Thames Essays Ser.: No. 47). 100p. 1987. pap. text ed. 22.95 (*0-566-05336-5*, Pub. by Avebury Pub UK) Ashgate Pub Co.

Riedel, James, jt. auth. see Onis, Ziya.

Riedel, James, jt. ed. see Pearson, Charles.

Riedel, Manfred. Between Tradition & Revolution: The Hegelian Transformation of Political Philosophy. LC 83-20885. 210p. 1984. 74.95 (*0-521-25644-5*) Cambridge U Pr.

Riedel, Marc. Stranger Violence: A Theoretical Inquiry. LC 92-432. (Current Issues in Criminal Justice Ser.: Vol. 1). 208p. 1993. 31.00 (*0-8153-0094-8*, SS753) Garland.

Riedel-Michel, Madeleine. Spiritual Healing: As a Complement to the Art of Medicine. 216p. (C). 1988. 35.00 (*0-7212-0753-7*, Pub. by Regency Press) St Mut.

Riedel, Nicolai. Internationale Gunter-Kunert-Bibliographie. (Bibliographien Zur Deutschen Literature Ser.: Vol. 5). 584p. 1987. write for info. (*3-487-07950-X*, Pub. by Georg Olms GW) Lubrecht & Cramer.

— Untersuchungen Zur Geschichte der Internationalen Rezeption Uwe Johnsons. (Germanistische Texte und Studien Ser.: Vol. 21). xiii, 672p. 1985. write for info. (*3-487-07624-1*, Pub. by Georg Olms GW) Lubrecht & Cramer.

Riedel, W. R., jt. ed. see Funnell, B. M.

Riedel, Walter E., ed. The Old World & the New: Literary Perspectives of German-Speaking Canadians. LC 85-135731. 199p. reprint ed. pap. 56.80 (*0-8357-6388-9*, 2035743) Bks Demand.

Riedel, Wolfgang. Electroless Nickel Plating. 328p. 1992. 109.00 (*0-904477-12-6*, 6231R) ASM.

Riedemann, Peter. Love Is Like Fire: The Confession of an Anabaptist Prisoner: Written at Gmunden, Upper Austria, Between 1529 & 1532. Hutterian Brethren, tr. LC 93-4668. 80p. (Orig.). 1993. pap. 6.00 (*0-87486-058-X*) Plough.

Rieder, Davylu, ed. see Roberts, Imelda R.

Rieder, Helmut. Robust Asymptotic Statistics. LC 94-1070. (Series in Statistics). 416p. 1994. 49.00 (*0-387-94262-9*) Spr-Verlag.

Rieder, Ines. Feminism & Eastern Europe. (LIP Pamphlets Ser.). 24p. (Orig.). (C). 1989. pap. 5.99 (*1-85594-017-5*, Pub. by Attic IE) InBook.

Rieder, Ines, ed. Cosmopolis: Urban Stories by Women. 192p. (C). 1990. pap. 15.99 (*1-85594-013-2*, Pub. by Attic IE) InBook.

Rieder, Ines, ed. & tr. Cosmopolis: Urban Stories by Women. 200p. (Orig.). 1990. 24.95 (*0-939416-36-0*); pap. 9.95 (*0-939416-37-9*) Cleis Pr.

Rieder, Ines, tr. see Galgoczi, Erzsebet.

Rieder, Ines, tr. see Savier, Monika & Fiochetto, Rosanna, eds.

Rieder, Jonathan. Canarsie: The Jews & Italians of Brooklyn Against Liberalism. LC 84-15660. (Illus.). 328p. 1985. 37.50 (*0-674-09360-7*) HUP.

— Canarsie: The Jews & Italians of Brooklyn Against Liberalism. 328p. 1987. pap. 13.95 (*0-674-09361-5*) HUP.

Rieder, Marge. Mission to Millboro. LC 93-6003. (Illus.). 208p. 1993. pap. 13.00 (*0-931892-59-7*) B Dolphin Pub.

Rieder, William. France, Seventeen Hundred to Eighteen Hundred. LC 83-6230. (Guides to European Decorative Arts Ser.: No. 3). 48p. (Orig.). 1984. pap. 3.50 (*0-87633-052-9*) Phila Mus Art.

Rieder, William G. & Busby, Henry R. Introductory Engineering Modeling. LC 90-4319. 360p. (C). 1990. reprint ed. 49.50 (*0-89464-461-0*) Krieger.

Riederer, P. & Przuntek, H., eds. MAO-B-Inhibitor Selegiline (R-(-)-Deprenyl) (Journal of Neural Transmission Ser.: Suppl. 25). (Illus.). 220p. 1987. pap. 58.00 (*0-387-82009-4*) Spr-Verlag.

Riederer, P. & Wesemann, W., eds. Pathobiology & Clinics of Basal Ganglia Disorders. (Journal of Nonprofit & Public Sector Marketing: Suppl. 38). (Illus.). 155p. 1993. pap. 60.00 (*0-387-82425-1*) Spr-Verlag.

Riederer, P. & Youdim, M. B., eds. Amine Oxidases & Their Impact on Neurobiology. (Journal of Neural Transmission Ser.: Suppl. 32). xii, 491p. 1990. pap. 155.00 (*0-387-82239-9*) Spr-Verlag.

— Iron in Central Nervous System Disorders: With Contributions by Numerous Experts. (Key Topics in Brain Research Ser.). (Illus.). 208p. 1994. pap. 67.00 (*0-387-82520-7*) Spr-Verlag.

Riederer, P., jt. ed. see Beckmann, H.

Riederer, P., jt. auth. see Birkmayer, W.

Riederer, P., et al. An Introduction to Neurotransmission in Health & Disease. (Illus.). 416p. 1990. 98.00 (*0-19-261431-2*) OUP.

Riedesel, C. Alan. Teaching Elementary School Mathematics. 5th ed. 416p. (C). 1989. Casebound. text ed. write for info. (*0-13-892472-4*) P-H.

Riedesel, C. Alan, jt. auth. see Schwartz, James E.

Riedesel, Fredericka. Letters & Journals Relating to the War of the American Revolution, & the Capture of the German Troops at Saratoga. LC 67-29035. (Eyewitness Accounts of the American Revolution Ser., No. 1). 1968. reprint ed. 19.95 (*0-405-01120-2*) Ayer.

Riedesel, Friedrich A. Memoirs & Letters & Journals of Major-General Riedesel, During His Residence in America, 2 vols., 1. Stone, William L., tr. LC 79-77109. (Eyewitness Accounts of the American Revolution Ser., No. 1). (Illus.). 1969. reprint ed. 15.95 (*0-405-01173-3*) Ayer.

— Memoirs & Letters & Journals of Major-General Riedesel, During His Residence in America, 2 vols., 2. Stone, William L., tr. LC 79-77109. (Eyewitness Accounts of the American Revolution Ser., No. 1). (Illus.). 1969. reprint ed. 15.95 (*0-405-01174-1*) Ayer.

— Memoirs & Letters & Journals of Major-General Riedesel, During His Residence in America, 2 vols., Set. Stone, William L., tr. LC 79-77109. (Eyewitness Accounts of the American Revolution Ser., No. 1). (Illus.). 1969. reprint ed. 34.95 (*0-405-01172-5*) Ayer.

Riediger. Microsurgical Tissue Transplantation. 243p. 1989. text ed. 56.00 (*0-86715-219-2*) Quint Pub Co.

Riediger, Carsten. Paul Wunderlich's Graphic Work, 1948-1982. 456p. (GER.). 1983. 150.00 (*1-55660-115-8*) A Wofsy Fine Arts.

Riedijk, Willem, ed. Appropriate Technology in Industrialized Countries. (Illus.). 372p. (Orig.). 1989. pap. 42.50 (*90-6275-284-5*, Pub. by Delft U Pr NE) Coronet Bks.

***Riedinger, Edward A.** Where in the World to Learn: A Guide to Library & Information Science for International. LC 94-42728. (Educators' Reference Collection). 176p. 1995. text ed. 55.00 (*0-313-28703-1*, Greenwood Pr) Greenwood.

***Riedinger, Jeffrey M.** Agrarian Reform in the Philippines: Democratic Transitions & Redistributive Reform. LC 94-44005. 386p. 1995. 45.00x (*0-8047-2530-6*) Stanford U Pr.

Riedinger, Jeffrey M., jt. auth. see Prosterman, Roy L.

Riedinger-Johnson, Noel, ed. see Foster, Jeanne R.

Riedinger, Rudolf, ed. Acta Conciliorum Oecumenicorum Series Secunda, Pars Prima: Concilium Universale Constantinopolitanum Concilii Actiones I-IX. xiv, 513p. (C). 1990. pap. 400.00 (*3-11-011758-4*) De Gruyter.

— Acta Conciliorum Oecumenicorum Sub Auspiciis Academiae Scientiarum Bavaricae Edita Series Secunda, Volumen Secundum, Pars Tertia: Index Verborum Graecorum Quae un Actis Synodi Lateranensis a.649 et in Actis Concilii Oecumenici Sexti Continentur. viii, 258p. (GRE & LAT.). (C). 1995. pap. text ed. 229.25 (*3-11-014538-3*) De Gruyter.

— Concilium Universale Constantinopolitanum Concilii Actiones XII-XVIII, Epistulae, Indices. (Acta Conciliorum Oecumenicorum Series Secunda, Volumen Secundum, Pars Secunda). xxxiv, 962p. (GRE & LAT.). (C). 1992. lib. bdg. 380.80 (*3-11-012935-3*) De Gruyter.

Riedjik, W. Appropriate Technology for Developing Countries. 3rd ed. Riedjik, W, ed. 368p. (Orig.). 1987. pap. text ed. 32.50 (*90-6275-085-0*, Pub. by Delft U Pr NE) Coronet Bks.

— Technology for Liberation. 250p. (Orig.). 1986. pap. text ed. 29.50 (*90-6275-244-6*, Pub. by Delft U Pr NE) Coronet Bks.

Riedjik, W, ed. see Riedjik, W.

Riedl, Clare. Grosseteste: On Light. (Medieval Philosophical Texts in Translation Ser.). pap. 5.00 (*0-87462-201-8*) Marquette.

Riedl, F. A History of Hungarian Literature. 1973. 69.95 (*0-8490-0330-X*) Gordon Pr.

***Riedl, Joan.** The Integrated Technology Classroom: Building Self-Reliant Learners. LC 94-42727. 1995. pap. 35.95 (*0-205-16157-X*, Longwood Div) Allyn.

Riedl, John C., tr. see Giles Of Rome.

Riedl, John O. University in Process. LC 65-19126. (Aquinas Lectures). 1965. 10.00 (*0-87462-130-5*) Marquette.

Riedl, M. J., jt. ed. see Hale, R. R.

Riedl, O. & Zachar, D., eds. Forest Amelioration. (Developments in Agricultural & Managed-Forest Ecology Ser.: Vol. 14). 630p. 1984. 169.25 (*0-444-99613-3*) Elsevier.

Riedl, Richard. Die Industrie Osterreichs Wahrend des Krieges. (Wirtschafts-Und Sozialgeschichte des Weltkrieges (Osterreichische Und Ungarische Serie)). (GER.). 1932. 125.00 (*0-317-27476-7*) Elliots Bks.

Riedl, Rupert. Biology of Knowledge: The Evolutionary Basis of Reason. 252p. 1984. text ed. 110.00 (*0-471-10309-8*, Wiley-Interscience) Wiley.

— Order in Living Organisms: A Systems Analysis of Evolution. Jefferies, R. P., tr. LC 77-28245. (Illus.). 333p. reprint ed. pap. 95.00 (*0-685-20724-2*, 2030513) Bks Demand.

Riedler-Berger, et al. Life & Language: The Urban College Experience. 128p. 1992. pap. text ed. 19.95 (*0-8403-7505-0*) Kendall-Hunt.

Riedler, W., ed. Scientific Ballooning: Proceedings of a Symposium of the 21st Plenary Meeting of the Committee on Space Research, Innsbruck, Austria, May 29-June 10 1978. LC 78-41182. (Illus.). 226p. 1979. 76.00 (*0-08-023420-8*, Pergamon Pr) Elsevier.

Riedler, W. & Friedrich, M., eds. Scientific Ballooning-II. (Advances in Space Research Ser.: Vol. 1, No. 11). (Illus.). 274p. 1981. pap. 42.00 (*0-08-028390-X*, Pergamon Pr) Elsevier.

Riedler, W. & Torkar, K., eds. Scientific Ballooning: Proceedings of Symposium 7 of the COSPAR Twenty-Fifth Plenary Meeting Held in Graz, Austria, 25 June -7 July 1984, No. IV. (Illus.). 140p. 1985. pap. 54.00 (*0-08-032753-2*, Pub. by PPL UK) Elsevier.

Riedley, Mary P. And Where Were You, Dr. Spock? 1990. pap. 9.95 (*0-925928-08-9*) Tiny Thought.

Riedling, K. Ellipsometry for Industrial Applications. (Illus.). 99p. 1988. pap. 39.00 (*0-387-82040-X*) Spr-Verlag.

Riedlsperger, Max E. Lingering Shadow of Nazism. (East European Monographs: No. 42). 214p. 1978. text ed. 43.50 (*0-914710-35-4*) East Eur Quarterly.

Riedman, Marianne. The Pinnipeds: Seals, Sea Lions, & Walruses. 1990. 40.00 (*0-520-06497-6*) U CA Pr.

— The Pinnipeds: Seals, Sea Lions, & Walruses. (Illus.). 462p. 1991. reprint ed. pap. 22.00 (*0-520-06498-4*) U CA Pr.

— Sea Otters. (Monterey Bay Aquarium Natural History Book Ser.). (Illus.). 80p. 1990. pap. 9.95 (*1-878244-03-5*) Monterey Bay Aquarium.

Riedman, Sarah R. & Barish, Wendy. The Good Looks Skin Book. (Just for Teens Ser.). (Illus.). 144p. (J). (gr. 10 up). 1983. 9.29 (*0-685-06727-0*) S&S Trade.

Riedmann, Agnes. Science That Colonizes: A Critique of Fertility Studies in Africa. LC 92-26098. 256p. 1993. 34.95 (*1-56639-042-7*) Temple U Pr.

— The Story of Adamsville. 115p. (C). 1980. pap. 8.95 (*0-534-00823-2*) Intl Thomson.

Riedmann, Agnes, jt. auth. see Lamanna, Mary A.

Riedner, Michael. Mercedes Benz W196. (Illus.). 326p. 1990. 49.95 (*0-85429-717-0*, Pub. by J H Haynes & Co UK) Motorbooks Intl.

Riedner, Ulrich. Pea Soup Andersen's Scandinavian-American Cookbook. Rain, Patricia, ed. LC 88-70661. 180p. 1988. 9.95 (*0-89087-523-5*) Celestial Arts.

Riedwyl, H., jt. auth. see Flury, Bernhard.

Riedy, Mark. Airbrush Techniques: Liquids. (Graphic Workbook Ser.). 1988. 9.95 (*0-89134-241-9*, 30056) North Light Bks.

— Airbrush Techniques: Textured Surfaces. (Graphic Workbook Ser.). 1988. 9.95 (*0-89134-239-7*, 30054) North Light Bks.

— Airbrush Techniques: Transparent-Translucent Objects. (Graphic Workbook Ser.). 1988. 9.95 (*0-89134-240-0*, 30055) North Light Bks.

Rief, jt. auth. see Barbieri.

Rief, Linda. Seeking Diversity: Language Arts with Adolescents. LC 91-34800. 299p. (Orig.). 1991. pap. text ed. 21.00 (*0-435-08598-0*, 08598) Heinemann.

— Seeking Diversity: Language Arts with Adolescents. 299p. (Orig.). 1992. 28.95 (*0-435-08724-X*, 08724) Heinemann.

***Rief, Linda & Barbieri, Muareen, eds.** All That Matters: What Is It We Value in School & Beyond? LC 95-6643. 1995. pap. text ed. write for info. (*0-435-08848-3*) Heinemann.

***Riefe, Barbara.** For Love of Two Eagles. 384p. 1996. mass mkt. write for info. (*0-614-05509-1*) Forge NYC.

— Love of Two Eagles. 384p. 1995. 22.95 (*0-312-85703-9*) Tor Bks.

— The Woman Who Fell from the Sky. 336p. 1994. 22.95 (*0-312-85446-3*) Forge NYC.

— The Woman Who Fell from the Sky. 384p. 1995. mass mkt. 5.99 (*0-8125-2377-6*) Forge NYC.

Riefe, Robert H. Moscow, Havana, & National Liberation in Latin America: Three Decades of Guerillas & Terrorists. 118p. pap. 16.95 (*0-935501-33-9*) U Miami N-S Ctr.

Riefenberg, Jennifer & Wuest, William J. A Personal Computer Program & Spreadsheet for Calculating the Practical Coal Mine Roof Rating. 1994. write for info. (*0-318-72570-3*) US Interior.

Riefenstahl, L., et al. Film Anthology (Amsterdam 1927) Frita & Gordon, R., eds. 1976. lib. bdg. 200.00 (*0-8490-1809-9*) Gordon Pr.

Riefenstahl, L., et al, eds. Internationaler Tonfilm & Almanach of 1931. 1976. lib. bdg. 99.95 (*0-8490-2063-8*) Gordon Pr.

Riefenstahl, Leni. Leni Riefenstahl: A Memoir. (Illus.). 688p. 1993. 35.00 (*0-312-09843-X*) St Martin.

— Leni Riefenstahl: A Memoir. 1995. pap. 16.00 (*0-312-11926-7*) St Martin.

— Olympia. (Illus.). 288p. 1994. 50.00 (*0-312-11371-4*) St Martin.

Rieff, David. Exile. 1994. pap. 11.00 (*0-671-88627-4*, Litl Simon S&S) S&S Childrens.

— The Exile: Cuba in the Heart of Miami. LC 93-12141. 240p. 1993. 21.00 (*0-671-77604-5*) S&S Trade.

— Los Angeles: Capital of the Third World. (Illus.). 288p. 1992. pap. 12.00 (*0-671-79210-5*, Touchstone Bks) S&S Trade.

Rieff, David, ed. Humanities in Review, Vol. 1. LC 82-4589. 246p. reprint ed. pap. 70.20 (*0-318-34781-4*, 2031642) Bks Demand.

Rieff, Philip. The Feeling Intellect: Selected Writings. 416p. 1989. lib. bdg. 60.00 (*0-226-71641-4*) U Ch Pr.

— The Feeling Intellect: Selected Writings. 416p. 1990. pap. text ed. 19.95 (*0-226-71642-2*) U Ch Pr.

— Fellow Teachers: Of Culture & Its Second Death, with a New Preface. LC 84-8910. (Illus.). xxviii, 244p. 1985. reprint ed. pap. 7.95 (*0-226-71644-9*) U Ch Pr.

— Fellow Teachers: Of Culture & Its Second Death, with a New Preface. LC 84-8910. (Illus.). xxviii, 244p. 1985. reprint ed. lib. bdg. 20.00 (*0-226-71643-0*) U Ch Pr.

— Triumph of the Therapeutic: Uses of Faith after Freud. xviii, 274p. (C). 1987. reprint ed. pap. text ed. 13.95 (*0-226-71646-5*) U Ch Pr.

Rieff, Phillip. Freud: The Mind of the Moralist. 3rd ed. LC 78-69967. 1979. pap. text ed. 19.95 (*0-226-71639-2*, P777) U Ch Pr.

Rieffel, Alexis. The Role of the Paris Club in Managing Debt Problems. LC 85-23294. (Essays in International Finance Ser.: No. 161). 1985. pap. text ed. 8.00 (*0-88165-068-4*) Princeton U Int Finan Econ.

Rieffel, Marc A. Deformation Quantization for Actions of Rd. LC 93-6114. (Memoirs Ser.: No. 506). 116p. 1993. pap. 29.00 (*0-8218-2575-5*) Am Math.

Riefler-Bonham, Phyllis, tr. see Huber, Michael.

Riefler-Bonham, Phyllis M., tr. see Henniges, Heiner & Shell, Bob.

Riefler-Bonham, Phyllis M., tr. see Shell, Bob & Hunecke, Richard.

Riefler-Bonham, Phyllis M., tr. see Shell, Bob & Henniges, Heiner.

Riefler, S., jt. auth. see Finn, J. L.

Riefling, Darrin, jt. auth. see Riefling, Vern.

Riefling, Vern & Riefling, Darrin. Marriage Healed! God's Powerful Plan for Restoring Your Marriage. Werner, Loren, ed. LC 91-61077. (Illus.). 200p. (Orig.). 1991. pap. 8.95 (*1-879706-54-7*) Paper Chase.

Riefling, W., ed. see Black, Donald.

Riefling, W., ed. see Urquhart, Sharon C.

Riefling, Werner, ed. see Green Group Staff & Morgan, Barbara.

Riefling, Werner, ed. see Skinner, Patricia.

Riefling, Werner A., ed. see Urquhart, Sharon C.

Riefstahl, Elizabeth. Ancient Egyptian Glass & Glazes in the Brooklyn Museum. LC 68-57359. (Wilbour Monographs: No. 1). (Illus.). 1968. 15.00 (*0-913696-04-8*) Bklyn Mus.

Riegel, Barbara J. & Ehrenreich, Donna. Psychological Aspects of Critical Care Nursing. 352p. 1989. 55.00 (*0-87189-799-7*, 89799) Aspen Pub.

Riegel, Barbara J., et al, eds. Dreifus' Pacemaker Therapy: An Interprofessional Approach. LC 85-28239. (Illus.). 293p. 1986. pap. text ed. 35.00 (*0-8036-7330-2*) Davis Co.

Riegel, C. Fundamentals of Atmospheric Dynamics & Thermodynamics. 340p. 1992. text ed. 59.00 (*9971-978-86-5*); pap. text ed. 33.00 (*9971-978-87-3*) World Scientific Pub.

Riegel, Carl D., jt. auth. see Reid, R. Dan.

Riegel, E. B., comp. Gems of Thought for Fraternal Speakers in Poetry & Prose. rev. ed. viii, 183p. 1984. reprint ed. text ed. 7.50 (*0-88053-309-9*, S-71) Macoy Pub.

Riegel, E. C. Flight from Inflation: The Monetary Alternative. MacCallum, Spencer H. & Morton, George, eds. LC 76-25381. (Illus.). 1978. 10.00 (*0-9600300-9-3*); pap. 6.00 (*0-9600300-8-5*) Heather Foun.

— The New Approach to Freedom. rev. ed. MacCallum, Spencer H., ed. LC 76-24987. (Illus.). 1976. 14.95 (*0-9600300-7-7*) Heather Foun.

Riegel, Garland T. The American Species of Dacnusinae Hymenoptera-Braconidae. (Novitates Arthropodae Ser.). (Illus.). 200p. (Orig.). 1982. pap. 11.00 (*0-916170-19-5*) J-B Pub.

Riegel, Ilse L., jt. ed. see Boutwell, Roswell K.

Riegel, K. F., ed. The Development of Dialectical Operations: Journal: Human Development, Vol. 18, Nos. 1 & 2. (Illus.). vii, 241p. 1975. 30.50 (*3-8055-2225-8*) S Karger.

— Intelligence: Alternative Views of a Paradigm. (Journal: Human Development: Vol. 16, No. 1-2). 132p. 1974. reprint ed. pap. 13.00 (*3-8055-1710-6*) S Karger.

Riegel, Lynn, jt. auth. see Lazur, Carole.

Riegel, Martin P. California's Maritime Heritage. LC 87-62442. (California Heritage Ser.: Vol. I). (Illus.). 88p. (Orig.). (C). 1987. 15.00 (*0-944871-01-1*); pap. 9.00 (*0-944871-00-3*) Riegel Pub.

— Ghost Ports of the Pacific, Vol. I: California. LC 89-90772. (Illus.). 52p. (Orig.). (YA). 1989. 11.00 (*0-944871-18-6*); pap. 4.95 (*0-944871-19-4*) Riegel Pub.

— Ghost Ports of the Pacific, Vol. II: Oregon. LC 89-90772. (Illus.). 52p. (Orig.). (YA). 1989. 11.00 (*0-944871-20-8*); pap. 4.95 (*0-944871-21-6*) Riegel Pub.

— Ghost Ports of the Pacific, Vol. III: Washington. LC 89-90772. (Illus.). 52p. (Orig.). (YA). 1989. 11.00 (*0-944871-22-4*); pap. 4.95 (*0-944871-23-2*) Riegel Pub.

— Historic Ships of California. LC 88-60111. (California Heritage Ser.: Vol. III). (Illus.). 105p. (Orig.). 1988. 16.00 (*0-944871-05-4*); pap. 9.95 (*0-944871-04-6*) Riegel Pub.

— Historic Ships of Hawaii. LC 88-92776. (Illus.). 44p. (Orig.). (YA). 1988. 11.00 (*0-944871-12-7*); pap. 4.95 (*0-944871-13-5*) Riegel Pub.

— Historic Ships of Oregon. LC 88-92771. (Illus.). 48p. (Orig.). (YA). 1988. 11.00 (*0-944871-14-3*); pap. 4.95 (*0-944871-15-1*) Riegel Pub.

— Historic Ships of Washington. LC 88-63929. (Illus.). 52p. (Orig.). (YA). 1988. 11.00 (*0-944871-16-X*); pap. 4.95 (*0-944871-17-8*) Riegel Pub.

— A Ship Lovers Guide to California. LC 88-60110. (California Heritage Ser.: Vol. II). (Illus.). 168p. (Orig.). 1988. 16.00 (*0-944871-03-8*); pap. 9.95 (*0-944871-02-X*) Riegel Pub.

— Ship Lovers Guide to the Pacific Northwest. (Illus.). 110p. (Orig.). 1990. 15.95 (*0-944871-30-5*); pap. 9.95 (*0-944871-31-3*) Riegel Pub.

— A Ship Lovers Guide to the Pacific Northwest, Vol. 1: Oregon. (Illus.). 52p. (Orig.). 1989. 11.00 (*0-944871-24-0*); pap. 4.95 (*0-944871-25-9*) Riegel Pub.

— A Ship Lovers Guide to the Pacific Northwest, Vol. 2: Washington. (Illus.). 52p. (Orig.). 1989. 11.00 (*0-944871-26-7*); pap. 4.95 (*0-944871-27-5*) Riegel Pub.

— The Ships of Catalina Island. LC 88-61279. (California Heritage Ser.: Vol. IV). (Illus.). 88p. (Orig.). 1988. 14.00 (*0-944871-07-0*); pap. 9.95 (*0-944871-06-2*) Riegel Pub.

— The Ships of the California Gold Rush. LC 88-92421. (Illus.). 48p. (Orig.). (YA). 1988. 11.00 (*0-944871-11-9*); pap. 4.95 (*0-685-24979-4*) Riegel Pub.

— The Ships of the Orange Coast. LC 88-92522. (Illus.). 40p. (Orig.). (YA). (gr. 9 up). 1988. lib. bdg. 11.00 (*0-944871-08-9*); pap. 4.75 (*0-944871-09-7*) Riegel Pub.

Riegel, Mayburt S. Early Ohioans Residences from the Land Grant Records. 1994. reprint ed. 9.00 (*0-935057-73-0*) OH Genealogical.

R

An Asterisk (*) at the beginning of an entry indicates that the title is appearing in BIP for the first time.

Riegel, Oscar W. Mobilizing for Chaos: The Story of the New Propaganda. LC 72-4677. (International Propaganda & Communications Ser.). 231p. 1972. reprint ed. 20.95 (0-405-04761-4) Ayer.

Riegel, Robert E. American Feminists. LC 80-13163. (Illus.). 223p. 1980. reprint ed. text ed. 59.75 (0-313-22434-X, RIAF, Greenwood Pr) Greenwood.

— American Women: A Story of Social Change. LC 78-99327. 376p. 1975. 35.00 (0-8386-7615-4) Fairleigh Dickinson.

— The Story of the Western Railroads: From 1852 Through the Reign of the Giants. LC 26-9772. xviii, 345p. 1964. pap. 11.95 (0-8032-5159-9) U of Nebr Pr.

Riegelman. Studying a Study & Testing a Test: How to Read the Medical Literature, No. 2. 1989. 29.95 (0-316-74524-3) Little.

Riegelman, R. & Schoth, S. The Measures of Medicine: Benefits, Harms & Costs. 320p. 1994. disk, pap. 39.95 (0-86542-280-X) Blackwell Sci.

Riegelman, R. K., jt. auth. see Hirsch, R. P.

Riegelman, Richard K. Minimizing Medical Mistakes. 1991. 31.95 (0-316-74523-5) Little.

— Preventing Crime Package. 1988. 350.00 (0-316-74522-7) Little.

— Studying a Study & Testing a Test: How to Read the Medical Literature. 1981. pap. 19.50 (0-316-74518-9) Little.

Riegelman, Richard K. & Povar, Gail. Putting Prevention into Practice: Problem Solving in Clinical Prevention. 432p. 1988. 32.95 (0-316-74519-7, Little Med Div) Little.

— A Teacher's Guide for Putting Prevention into Practice. 68p. 1988. pap. text ed. write for info. (0-316-74520-0, Little Med Div) Little.

Rieger, Branimir, ed. Dionysus in Literature: Essays on Literary Madness. LC 93-74076. 233p. 1994. text ed. 34.95 (0-87972-649-0); pap. text ed. 15.95 (0-87972-650-4) Bowling Green Univ.

Rieger, Catherine. Waltz in the Shadows. 208p. (Orig.). 1993. pap. 4.50 (0-515-11254-2) Jove Pubns.

Rieger, Edythe. Science Adventures in Children's Play. rev. ed. 1978. 2.50 (0-936426-09-8) Play Schs.

Rieger, Erwin. Up Is the Mountain & Other Views. LC 73-89240. (Illus.). 200p. 1973. 12.95 (0-8323-0235-X) Binford Mort.

Rieger, Fritz, jt. ed. see Wong-Rieger, Durhane.

Rieger, H. Multilingual Dictionary for Mechanics, Salesmen & Engineers in Metal-Working. 519p. (ENG, FRE, GER, ITA, POR & SPA.). 1981. 75.00 (0-8288-0607-1, M 15547) Fr & Eur.

Rieger, Hans C., jt. ed. see Langhammer, Rolf J.

Rieger, Heinz. The Alternating Current Circuit. (Siemens Programmed Insturction Ser.: 13). 68p. reprint ed. pap. 25.00 (0-8357-5330-1, 2052103) Bks Demand.

— Alternating Voltage & Current. (Siemens Programmed Instruction Ser.: No. 12). 80p. reprint ed. pap. 25.00 (0-8357-5331-X, 2052089) Bks Demand.

— The Magnetic Circuit. (Siemens Programmed Instruction Ser.: 4). 69p. reprint ed. pap. 25.00 (0-317-26181-9, 2052081) Bks Demand.

— Power & Energy in Alternating-Current Circuits. (Siemens Programmed Instruction Ser.: No. 14). 68p. reprint ed. pap. 25.00 (0-317-27750-2, 2052090) Bks Demand.

Rieger, Ingo. Zoo Animals. (Mini Fact Finders Ser.). 64p. 1991. pap. 4.95 (0-8120-4449-5) Barron.

Rieger, James & Mathews, Boots. Dining In - Kansas City. rev. ed. (Dining in Ser.). 188p. 1983. pap. 8.95 (0-89716-127-0) P B Pubng.

Rieger, James H., ed. see Shelley, Mary Wollstonecraft.

Rieger, Martin M., ed. Surfactants in Cosmetics. LC 84-28718. (Surfactant Science Ser.: No. 16). (Illus.). 498p. reprint ed. pap. 142.00 (0-7837-4775-6, 2044530) Bks Demand.

Rieger, N. F. Unbalance Response & Balancing of Flexible Rotors in Bearings. LC 72-92595. (Flexible Rotor-Bearing System Dynamics Ser.: Vol. 2). (Illus.). 33p. reprint ed. pap. 25.00 (0-317-11118-3, 2012305) Bks Demand.

Rieger, N. F., ed. Rotordynamics Two Problems in Turbomachinery. (CISM International Centre for Mechanical Sciences Ser.: Vol. 297). (Illus.). viii, 586p. 1989. pap. 93.00 (0-387-82091-4) Spr-Verlag.

Rieger, Neville F., jt. ed. see Eshleman, Ronald L.

Rieger, Paula. Biotherapy: A Comprehensive Overview. (Nursing Ser.). 500p. 1994. pap. 49.95 (0-86720-707-8) Jones & Bartlett.

Rieger, Paula T., jt. auth. see Rumsey, Kimberly A.

Rieger, Philip H. Electrochemistry. 2nd ed. LC 93-25837. 483p. 1993. 59.95 (0-412-04391-2) Chapman & Hall.

Rieger, R. English & Spanish Dictionary of Genetics, Classical & Molecular Cytogenetics: Diccionario de Genetica y Citogenetica Clasica y Molecular. 538p. (ENG & SPA.). 1982. pap. 85.00 (0-8288-0952-6, S3212) Fr & Eur.

Rieger, R., et al. Glossary of Genetics: Classical & Molecular. 5th ed. (Illus.). vii, 546p. 1991. pap. 39.00 (0-387-52054-6) Spr-Verlag.

— Glossary of Genetics & Cytogenetics. 4th rev. ed. LC 76-16183. (Illus.). 1976. pap. 25.00 (3-540-07668-9) Spr-Verlag.

Riegert, jt. auth. see Bruscher.

Riegert, Evelyn, ed. see Mohr-Stephens, Judy.

Riegert, Lillian, jt. auth. see Kunath, Anne.

***Riegert, Ray.** Hidden Coast of California: The Adventurer's Guide. LC 94-61741. (Hidden Travel Ser.). (Illus.). 468p. (Orig.). 1995. pap. 14.95 (1-56975-027-0) Ulysses Pr.

— Hidden Coast of California: The Adventurer's Guide. 4th ed. Henriques, Leslie, ed. LC 93-60277. (Hidden Travel Guide Ser.). (Illus.). 480p. (Orig.). 1993. pap. 14.95 (0-915233-81-9) Ulysses Pr.

— Hidden Hawaii: The Adventurer's Guide. 8th ed. Van Young, Sayre, ed. LC 94-60462. (Hidden Travel Ser.). (Illus.). 468p. 1994. pap. 15.95 (1-56975-018-1) Ulysses Pr.

— Hidden Maui: The Adventurer's Guide. LC 95-60714. (Hidden Travel Ser.). (Illus.). 204p. (Orig.). 1995. pap. 12.95 (1-56975-035-1) Ulysses Pr.

— Hidden San Francisco & Northern California: The Adventurer's Guide. 6th ed. LC 94-60056. (Hidden Travel Guide Ser.). (Illus.). 468p. 1994. pap. 14.95 (1-56975-007-6) Ulysses Pr.

— Hidden Southern California: The Adventurer's Guide. 4th ed. LC 94-60054. (Hidden Travel Guide Ser.). Orig. Title: Hidden Los Angeles & Southern California: The Adventurer's Guide. (Illus.). 528p. 1994. pap. 14.95 (1-56975-006-8) Ulysses Pr.

— Ultimate California. 3rd ed. Kahn, Judith, ed. LC 93-60071. (Ultimate Guidebook Ser.). (Illus.). 528p. (Orig.). 1993. pap. 14.95 (0-915233-79-7) Ulysses Pr.

***Riegert, Ray & Henriques, Leslie, eds.** Know Your Body: The Atlas of Anatomy. (Illus.). 156p. 1995. pap. 11.95 (1-56975-021-1) Ulysses Pr.

Riegert, Ray, ed. see Farewell, Susan, et al.

Riegert, Ray, ed. see Ritz, Stacy.

Riegert, Ray, ed. see Ritz, Stacy & Olmstead, Marty.

Riegert, Ray, ed. see Vayda, William.

Riegger, Hal. The Camas Prairie: Idaho's Railroad on Stilts. Pacific Fast Mail Staff, ed. (Illus.). 160p. 1986. 32.50 (0-915713-13-6) Pac Fast Mail.

***Riegger, Michael.** More Management for Results: A "How to" Workbook for Improving the Management of Your Veterinary Practice. 300p. 1995. pap. 59.95 (0-929870-32-8) Advanstar Commns.

Riegger, Michael H. Management for Results: A "How to" Workbook for Improving the Management of Your Veterinary Practice. 200p. 1992. pap. 59.95 (0-929870-06-9) Advanstar Commns.

Riegl, Alois. Problems of Style: Foundations for a History of Ornament. Kain, Evelyn, tr. (Illus.). 384p. 1993. text ed. 49.50 (0-691-04087-7) Princeton U Pr.

Riegler, Gordon A. The Socialization of the New England Clergy Eighteen Hundred to Eighteen Sixty. LC 79-13027. (Perspectives in American History Ser.: No. 37). 187p. 1980. reprint ed. lib. bdg. 29.50 (0-87991-361-4) Porcupine Pr.

Riegler, Guenter R. & Blandford, Roger D., eds. The Galactic Center: AIP Conference Proceedings, No. 83, California Institute of Technology, Jan. 7-8, 1982. LC 82-71635. 216p. 1982. 30.25 (0-88318-182-7) Am Inst Physics.

Riehart, T. Engineered Materials Handbook: Composites, Vol. 1. 960p. 118.00 (0-318-23466-1) T-C Pubns CA.

***Riehecky.** I'm Sorry. 1989. pap. 3.95 (0-516-46246-6) Childrens.

Riehecky, J. Jack & Jill's Adventure in Alphabet Town. LC 91-20541. (Read Around Alphabet Town Ser.). (Illus.). 32p. (J). (ps-2). 1992. lib. bdg. 11.85 (0-516-05410-4) Childrens.

— Little Lady's Adventure in Alphabet Town. LC 91-20542. (Read Around Alphabet Town Ser.). (Illus.). 32p. (J). (ps-2). 1992. lib. bdg. 11.85 (0-516-05412-0) Childrens.

Riehecky, Janet. After You. (Manners Matter Ser.). (Illus.). 32p. (J). (ps-2). 1989. lib. bdg. 18.50 (0-89565-538-1) Childs World.

— Allosaurus. LC 80-1693. (Illus.). 32p. (ENG & SPA.). (J). (ps-2). 1988. text ed. 21.36 (1-56766-134-3) Childs World.

— Allosaurus. LC 88-1693. (Dinosaurs Bks.). (Illus.). 32p. (ENG & SPA.). (J). (ps-2). 1988. lib. bdg. 21.36 (0-89565-421-0) Childs World.

— Anatosaurus. (Dinosaurs Bks.). (Illus.). 32p. (ENG & SPA.). (J). (ps-2). 1989. lib. bdg. 21.36 (0-89565-545-4) Childs World.

— Ankylosaurus. (Dinosaur Bks.). (Illus.). 32p. (ENG & SPA.). (J). (ps-2). 1990. lib. bdg. 21.36 (1-56766-126-2) Childs World.

— Ankylosaurus. (Dinosaur Bks.). (Illus.). 32p. (ENG & SPA.). (J). (ps-2). 1990. lib. bdg. 21.36 (0-89565-621-3) Childs World.

— Apatosaurus. LC 88-1694. (Dinosaur Bks.). (Illus.). 32p. (ENG & SPA.). (J). (ps-2). 1988. lib. bdg. 21.36 (1-56766-131-9) Childs World.

— Apatosaurus. LC 88-1694. (Dinosaurs Bks.). (Illus.). 32p. (ENG & SPA.). (J). (ps-2). 1988. lib. bdg. 21.36 (0-89565-423-7) Childs World.

— Baryonyx. (Dinosaur Bks.). (Illus.). 32p. (ENG & SPA.). (J). (ps-2). 1990. lib. bdg. 21.36 (1-56766-132-7) Childs World.

— Baryonyx. (Dinosaur Bks.). (Illus.). 32p. (ENG & SPA.). (J). (ps-2). 1990. lib. bdg. 21.36 (0-89565-622-1) Childs World.

— Brachiosaurus. LC 89-22069. (Dinosaurs Bks.). (Illus.). 32p. (ENG & SPA.). (J). 1989. lib. bdg. 21.36 (0-89565-542-X); pap. text ed. 21.36 (1-56766-135-1) Childs World.

— Carolina Herrera: International Fashion Designer. LC 90-28886. (Picture-Story Biographies Ser.). (Illus.). 32p. (J). (gr. 2-4). 1991. lib. bdg. 11.85 (0-516-04178-9); pap. 3.95 (0-516-44178-7) Childrens.

— Cinco de Mayo. LC 93-13249. (Circle the Year with Holidays Ser.). (Illus.). 32p. (J). (ps-2). 1993. lib. bdg. 12.30 (0-516-00681-9); pap. 3.95 (0-516-40681-7) Childrens.

— Coelophysis. (Dinosaur Bks.). (Illus.). 32p. (ENG & SPA.). (J). (ps-2). 1990. lib. bdg. 21.36 (1-56766-136-X) Childs World.

— Coelophysis. (Dinosaur Bks.). (Illus.). 32p. (ENG & SPA.). (J). (ps-2). 1990. lib. bdg. 21.36 (0-89565-623-X) Childs World.

— Compsognathus. (Dinosaur Bks.). (Illus.). 32p. (ENG & SPA.). (J). (ps-2). 1990. lib. bdg. 21.36 (1-56766-133-5) Childs World.

— Compsognathus. (Dinosaur Bks.). (Illus.). 32p. (ENG & SPA.). (J). (ps-2). 1990. lib. bdg. 21.36 (0-89565-624-8) Childs World.

— Cooperation. LC 89-48284. (Values to Live By Ser.). (Illus.). 32p. (ENG & SPA.). (J). (ps-2). 1990. lib. bdg. 14.95 (0-89565-947-6) Childs World.

— Deinonychus. (Dinosaur Bks.). (Illus.). 32p. (ENG & SPA.). (J). (ps-2). 1990. lib. bdg. 21.36 (1-56766-127-0) Childs World.

— Deinonychus. (Dinosaur Bks.). (Illus.). 32p. (ENG & SPA.). (J). (ps-2). 1990. lib. bdg. 21.36 (0-89565-625-6) Childs World.

— Dinosaur Relatives. (Dinosaur Bks.). (Illus.). 32p. (ENG & SPA.). (J). (ps-2). 1990. lib. bdg. 21.36 (1-56766-125-4) Childs World.

— Dinosaur Relatives. (Dinosaur Bks.). (Illus.). 32p. (ENG & SPA.). (J). (ps-2). 1990. lib. bdg. 21.36 (0-89565-626-4) Childs World.

— Diplodocus. (Dinosaur Bks.). (Illus.). 32p. (ENG & SPA.). (J). (ps-2). 1990. lib. bdg. 21.36 (1-56766-140-8) Childs World.

— Diplodocus. (Dinosaur Bks.). (Illus.). 32p. (ENG & SPA.). (J). (ps-2). 1990. lib. bdg. 21.36 (0-89565-627-2) Childs World.

— Discovering Dinosaurs. (Dinosaur Bks.). (Illus.). 32p. (ENG & SPA.). (J). (ps-2). 1990. pap. text ed. 21.36 (1-56766-137-8) Childs World.

— Discovering Dinosaurs. (Dinosaur Bks.). (Illus.). 32p. (ENG & SPA.). (J). (ps-2). 1990. lib. bdg. 21.36 (0-89565-620-5) Childs World.

— Good Sportsmanship. (Values to Live By Ser.). (Illus.). 32p. (ENG & SPA.). (J). (ps-2). 1990. pap. text ed. 21.36 (0-89565-949-2) Childs World.

— Good Sportsmanship. LC 89-29663. (Values to Live By Ser.). (Illus.). 32p. (ENG & SPA.). (J). (ps-2). 1990. lib. bdg. 21.36 (0-89565-563-2) Childs World.

— Hypsilophodon. (Dinosaur Bks.). (Illus.). 32p. (ENG & SPA.). (J). (ps-2). 1990. lib. bdg. 14.95 (1-56766-128-9) Childs World.

— Hypsilophodon. (Dinosaur Bks.). (Illus.). 32p. (ENG & SPA.). (J). (ps-2). 1990. lib. bdg. 21.36 (0-89565-628-0) Childs World.

— Iguanodon. LC 89-15850. (Dinosaur Bks.). (Illus.). 32p. (ENG & SPA.). (J). (ps-2). 1989. lib. bdg. 14.95 (1-56766-143-2) Childs World.

— Iguanodon. LC 89-15850. (Dinosaurs Bks.). (Illus.). 32p. (ENG & SPA.). (J). (ps-2). 1989. lib. bdg. 21.36 (0-89565-544-6) Childs World.

— I'm Sorry. (Manners Matter Ser.). (J). (ps-2). 1989. lib. bdg. 18.50 (0-89565-389-3) Childs World.

— Irish Americans. LC 94-12604. (Cultures of America Ser.). 1994. 19.95 (1-85435-783-2) Marshall Cavendish.

— Japanese Boys' Festival. LC 93-47639. (Circle the Year with Holidays Ser.). (Illus.). 32p. (J). (ps-2). 1994. lib. bdg. 12.30 (0-516-00695-9); pap. 3.95 (0-516-40695-7) Childrens.

— Kwanzaa. LC 93-17076. (Circle the Year with Holidays Ser.). (Illus.). 32p. (J). (ps-2). 1993. lib. bdg. 12.30 (0-516-00686-X); pap. 3.95 (0-516-40686-8) Childrens.

— Maiasaura. LC 89-22076. (Dinosaurs Bks.). (Illus.). 32p. (ENG & SPA.). (J). (ps-2). 1989. lib. bdg. 21.36 (0-89565-543-8) Childs World.

— Maiasaura. LC 93-49059. (Dinosaurs Ser.). (Illus.). (ENG & SPA.). (J). (ps-2). 1994. lib. bdg. 21.36 (1-56766-147-5) Childs World.

— May I? LC 88-16838. (Manners Matter Ser.). (Illus.). 32p. (J). (ps-2). 1989. lib. bdg. 18.50 (0-89565-388-5) Childs World.

— The Mystery of the Missing Money. LC 94-928. (Red Door Detective Club Ser.: Bk. 1). 1995. lib. bdg. 12.95 (1-56674-087-8) Forest Hse.

— The Mystery of the UFO. LC 94-929. (Red Door Detective Club Ser.: Bk. 2). (Illus.). 1995. lib. bdg. 12.95 (1-56674-088-6) Forest Hse.

— Oviraptor. (Dinosaur Bks.). (Illus.). 32p. (ENG & SPA.). (J). (ps-2). 1990. lib. bdg. 21.36 (0-89565-631-0) Childs World.

— Oviraptor. (Dinosaur Bks.). (Illus.). 32p. (ENG & SPA.). (J). (ps-2). 1990. lib. bdg. 21.36 (1-56766-146-7) Childs World.

— Pachycephalosaurus. (Dinosaur Bks.). (Illus.). 32p. (ENG & SPA.). (J). (ps-2). 1990. lib. bdg. 21.36 (0-89565-632-9) Childs World.

— Pachycephalosaurus. (Dinosaur Bks.). (Illus.). 32p. (ENG & SPA.). (J). (ps-2). 1990. pap. 21.36 (1-56766-129-7) Childs World.

— Parasaurolophus. (Dinosaur Bks.). (Illus.). 32p. (ENG & SPA.). (J). (ps-2). 1990. lib. bdg. 21.36 (1-56766-130-0) Childs World.

— Parasaurolophus. (Dinosaur Bks.). (Illus.). 32p. (ENG & SPA.). (J). (ps-2). 1990. lib. bdg. 21.36 (0-89565-633-7) Childs World.

— Please. LC 88-16841. (Manners Matter Ser.). (Illus.). 32p. (J). (ps-2). 1989. lib. bdg. 18.50 (0-89565-386-9) Childs World.

— Protoceratops. (Dinosaur Bks.). (Illus.). 32p. (ENG & SPA.). (J). (ps-2). 1990. lib. bdg. 21.36 (0-89565-634-5) Childs World.

— Robots: Here They Come! LC 90-30634. (Discovery World Ser.). (Illus.). 32p. (J). (ps-2). 1990. lib. bdg. 21.36 (0-89565-577-2) Childs World.

— St. Patrick's Day. LC 93-47640. (Circle the Year with Holidays Ser.). (Illus.). 32p. (J). (ps-2). 1994. lib. bdg. 12.30 (0-516-00696-7); pap. 3.95 (0-516-40696-5) Childrens.

— Saltasaurus. (Dinosaur Bks.). (Illus.). 32p. (ENG & SPA.). (J). (ps-2). 1990. lib. bdg. 21.36 (1-56766-138-6) Childs World.

— Saltasaurus. (Dinosaur Bks.). (Illus.). 32p. (ENG & SPA.). (J). (ps-2). 1990. lib. bdg. 21.36 (0-89565-635-3) Childs World.

— Saving the Forests: A Rabbit's Story. LC 89-28122. (Discovery World Ser.). (Illus.). 32p. (J). (ps-2). 1990. lib. bdg. 21.36 (0-89565-561-6) Childs World.

— Sharing. LC 87-26811. (Values to Live By Ser.). (Illus.). 32p. (ENG & SPA.). (J). (ps-2). 1988. lib. bdg. 21.36 (0-89565-416-4) Childs World.

— Snow: When Will It Fall? LC 89-28084. (Discovery World Ser.). (Illus.). 32p. (J). (ps-2). 1990. lib. bdg. 21.36 (0-89565-560-8) Childs World.

— Stegosaurus. LC 88-15347. (Dinosaurs Bks.). (Illus.). 32p. (ENG & SPA.). (J). (ps-2). 1988. lib. bdg. 21.36 (0-89565-385-0) Childs World.

— Thank-You. LC 88-16840. (Manners Matter Ser.). (Illus.). 32p. (J). (ps-2). 1989. lib. bdg. 18.50 (0-89565-387-7) Childs World.

— Triceratops. LC 88-508. (Dinosaurs Bks.). (Illus.). 32p. (ENG & SPA.). (J). (ps-2). 1988. lib. bdg. 21.36 (0-89565-422-9) Childs World.

— Triceratops. LC 88-508. (Dinosaur Bks.). (Illus.). 32p. (ENG & SPA.). (J). (ps-2). 1988. lib. bdg. 21.36 (1-56766-122-X) Childs World.

— Troodon. (Dinosaur Bks.). (Illus.). 32p. (ENG & SPA.). (J). (ps-2). 1990. lib. bdg. 21.36 (0-89565-636-1) Childs World.

— Troodon. (Dinosaur Bks.). (Illus.). 32p. (ENG & SPA.). (J). (ps-2). 1990. lib. bdg. 14.95 (1-56766-139-4) Childs World.

— Tyrannosaurus. LC 88-1692. (Dinosaur Bks.). (Illus.). 32p. (ENG & SPA.). (J). (ps-2). 1988. lib. bdg. 21.36 (1-56766-123-8) Childs World.

— Tyrannosaurus. LC 88-1692. (Dinosaurs Bks.). (Illus.). 32p. (ENG & SPA.). (J). (ps-2). 1988. lib. bdg. 21.36 (0-89565-424-5) Childs World.

— Walrus' Adventure in Alphabet Town. LC 92-1330. (Read Around Alphabet Town Ser.). (Illus.). 32p. (J). (ps-2). 1992. lib. bdg. 11.85 (0-516-05423-6) Childrens.

— What Plants Give Us: The Gift of Life. LC 90-30374. (Discovery World Ser.). (Illus.). 32p. (J). (ps-2). 1990. lib. bdg. 21.36 (0-89565-570-5) Childs World.

Riehecky, Janet, tr. Ali Baba & the Forty Thieves: A Classic Tale. LC 88-36871. (Illus.). 32p. (J). (gr. 1-4). 1988. lib. bdg. 19.93 (0-89565-485-7) Childs World.

— The Old Sandman: A Classic Tale. LC 88-36793. (Illus.). 32p. (J). (gr. 1-4). 1988. lib. bdg. 19.93 (0-89565-461-X) Childs World.

— Sinbad the Sailor: A Classic Tale. LC 88-36872. (Illus.). 32p. (J). (gr. k-3). 1988. lib. bdg. 13.95 (0-685-56048-1) Childs World.

— Sinbad the Sailor: A Classic Tale. LC 88-36872. (Illus.). 32p. (J). (gr. k-3). 1988. lib. bdg. 19.95 (0-89565-472-5) Childs World.

— Till Eulenspiegel's Merry Pranks: A Classic Tale. LC 88-36794. (Illus.). 32p. (J). (gr. k-3). 1988. lib. bdg. 19.95 (0-89565-475-X) Childs World.

— The Vain Little Mouse: A Classic Tale. LC 88-35214. (Illus.). 32p. (J). (gr. 1-4). 1988. lib. bdg. 19.95 (0-89565-464-4) Childs World.

Riehecky, Janet, tr. see Andersen, Hans Christian.

Riehecky, Janet, tr. see Carroll, Lewis.

Riehecky, Janet, tr. see Grimm, Jacob & Grimm, Wilhelm K.

Riehecky, Janet, jt. auth. see Pemberton, Nancy.

Riehecky, Janet, tr. see Perrault, Charles.

Riehl, C. Luise. Family Nursing. (Illus.). 384p. (C). 1974. text ed. 23.20 (0-02-663760-X) Bennett IL.

***Riehl, Dan.** Desktop Guide to Programmer's Tools. (News 3X-400 Technical Reference Ser.). 200p. (Orig.). 1995. pap. 34.95 (1-882419-14-6, Duke Pr) Duke Commns Intl.

— News 3X - 400's Power Tools for the AS-400, Vol. I. 700p. 1995. pap. 99.00 (1-882419-25-1, Duke Pr) Duke Commns Intl.

***Riehl, Dan & Dick, Frederick, eds.** News 3X-400's Power Tools for the AS - 400 Vol. 2. 700p. (Orig.). 1995. pap. 129.00 (1-882419-08-1, Duke Pr) Duke Commns Intl.

Riehl, Dan, jt. auth. see Bianchi, Jeff.

Riehl, Dan, jt. auth. see Meyers, Bryan.

Riehl Foundation Staff. An Hour with Jesus. LC 94-65655. 120p. 1994. pap. 2.00 (1-877678-27-9) Riehle Found.

Riehl, H., et al. The Jet Stream. (Meteorological Monograph Ser.: Vol. 2, No. 7). (Illus.). 100p. (Orig.). 1954. pap. 17.00 (0-933876-02-5) Am Meteorological.

Riehl, Heinz. Foreign Exchange & Money Markets: Managing Foreign & Domestic Currency Operations. 3rd ed. 1993. text ed. 49.95 (0-07-052672-9) McGraw.

Riehl, Heinz & Rodriguez, Rita M. Foreign Exchange & Money Markets: Managing Foreign & Domestic Currency Operations. 2nd ed. (Illus.). 416p. 1983. text ed. 50.00 (0-07-052671-0) McGraw.

Riehl, Rudiger & Baensch, Hans. Aquarium Atlas. (Illus.). 994p. 39.95 (3-88244-050-3, 16050) Tetra Pr.

Riehl-Sisca, Joan P. Conceptual Models for Nursing Practice. 3rd ed. 502p. (C). 1988. pap. text ed. 34.95 (0-8385-1210-0, A1210-2) Appleton & Lange.

Riehl, Wilhelm H. The Natural History of the German People. Diephouse, David, ed. & tr. by. LC 89-12900. (Studies in German Thought & History: Vol. 13). 392p. 1990. lib. bdg. 99.95 (0-88946-789-7) E Mellen.

Riehle Foundation Staff, comp. A Man Named Father Jozo: His Story, His Talks, & the Production of the Film A Call to Holiness. LC 89-62822. (Illus.). 80p. (Orig.). 1989. pap. 4.50 (1-877678-06-6) Riehle Found.

Riehle Foundation Staff, ed. The Gold Book of Prayers. LC 88-61907. 96p. (Orig.). 1988. pap. 3.00 (0-9618840-4-5) Riehle Found.

An Asterisk (*) at the beginning of an entry indicates that the title is appearing in BIP for the first time.

— In Testimony: Priestly Reflections on Medjugorje. LC 92-64150. 144p. (Orig.). 1992. pap. 3.00 (*1-877678-21-X*) Riehle Found.

Riehle Foundation Staff, ed. see Laurentin, Rene.

Riehle Foundation Staff, ed. see O'Brien, Bartholomew J.

Riehle, Ginger, ed. see Marlette, Jerry.

Riehle, Ginger, ed. see McLellan, Dave & Warrick, Bill.

Riehle, Ginger, ed. see McLellan, David P. & Warrick, Bill.

Riehle, Kathleen A. What Smart People Do When Losing Their Jobs. 192p. 1991. text ed. 42.50 (*0-471-55081-7*); pap. text ed. 10.95 (*0-471-55082-5*) Wiley.

Riehle, Wolfgang. Shakespeare, Plautus & the Humanist Tradition. (Illus.). 316p. 1991. 90.00 (*0-85991-305-8*) Boydell & Brewer.

Riehm, C. R., jt. ed. see Hambleton, I.

Riehm, H., ed. Malignant Neoplasms in Childhood & Adolescence. (Monographs in Pediatrics: Vol. 18). (Illus.). viii, 396p. 1986. 120.00 (*3-8055-4206-2*) S Karger.

Riehn, Richard K. Eighteen Hundred Twelve: Napoleon's Russian Campaign. 525p. 1991. pap. text ed. 19.95 (*0-471-54302-0*) Wiley.

— French Imperial Army, 1813, 1814 & Waterloo. 1959. pap. 8.00 (*0-912364-01-7*) Imrie-Risley.

— French Infantry & Artillery, 1795-1812. 1963. pap. 5.00 (*0-912364-02-5*) Imrie-Risley.

Rieke, Alison. The Senses of Nonsense. LC 92-10292. 295p. 1992. text ed. 26.95 (*0-87745-384-5*) U of Iowa Pr.

Rieke, G. H. Detection of Light: From the Ultraviolet to the Submillimeter. (Illus.). 300p. (C). 1995. 59.95 (*0-521-41028-2*) Cambridge U Pr.

Rieke, H. H. & Chilingarian, G. V. Compaction of Argillaceous Sediments. LC 74-190682. (Developments in Sedimentology Ser.: Vol. 16). 424p. 1974. 107.75 (*0-444-41054-6*) Elsevier.

Rieke, Mark L., jt. ed. see Conn, Steven R.

Rieke, P. C., et al, eds. Materials Synthesis Utilizing Biological Processes: Materials Research Society Symposium Proceedings, Vol. 174. 1990. text ed. 33.00 (*1-55899-062-3*) Materials Res.

Rieke, Richard & Sillars, Malcolm O. Argumentation & Critical Decision Making. 3rd ed. LC 92-28490. (C). 1992. 27.75 (*0-673-46490-3*) HarpCollege.

— Argumentation & the Decision Making Process. 2nd ed. (C). 1989. pap. text ed. 23.25 (*0-673-15905-1*) HarpCollege.

Rieke, Richard D. & Stutman, Randall K. Communication in Legal Advocacy. (Studies in Communication Processes). 255p. 1989. text ed. 29.95 (*0-87249-639-2*) U of SC Pr.

— Communication in Legal Advocacy. (Studies in Communication Processes). 255p. (C). 1992. pap. text ed. 21.95 (*0-87249-681-3*) U of SC Pr.

Rieke, Susan. Small Indulgences. LC 89-17928. (Target Poetry Ser.). 64p. (Orig.). 1990. pap. 6.50 (*0-933532-72-5*) BkMk.

Riekehof, Lottie. Talk to the Deaf: A Manual of Approximately 1,000 Signs Used by the Deaf of North America. LC 63-17975. (Illus.). 154p. (J). (gr. k up). 1963. teacher ed 8.95 (*0-88243-612-0*, 02-0612) Gospel Pub.

Riekehof, Lottie L. The Joy of Signing. 2nd ed. LC 86-80173. (Illus.). 352p. 1987. teacher ed 17.95 (*0-88243-520-5*, 02-0520) Gospel Pub.
The best-selling sign language book is now offering more than ever. The new THE JOY OF SIGNING, SECOND EDITION provides a 15-page Appendix showing the most effective way to add signs from the American Sign Language to spoken English, & it includes these significant features: Information on which words are spoken without requiring the addition of a sign; the use of space & directionality in providing a visual picture; pluralization; tense; incorporating numbers; regularity & continuity; showing the difference between nouns & verbs where the actual sign formation is identical; indicating the difference between a statement, a command, & a question when identical signs are used; an introduction to the use of classifiers. THE JOY OF SIGNING, SECOND EDITION has approximately 1,500 signs with many of the signs updated to current usage. The "Suggested References" & the "Organizations Serving the Deaf" sections have been revised to offer more current resources. With over 1,000,000 copies in print, this best-seller combines with THE JOY OF SIGNING PUZZLE BOOK (0-88243-676-7, $2.95) to make learning the art & ministry of sign language even more enjoyable. Written by Dr. Lottie L. Riekehof, professor of sign communication at Gallaudet University in Washington, DC. Order your copy of THE JOY OF SIGNING, SECOND EDITION from your local bookstore or Gospel Publishing House, 1445 Boonville Ave., Springfield, MO 65802; 800-641-4310
Publisher Provided Annotation.

Riekehof, Lottie L., jt. auth. see Hillebrand, Linda L.

Rieken, Bill. Adventures in UNIX Network Application. 464p. 1992. pap. text ed. 44.95 (*0-471-52858-7*) Wiley.

Rieken, Bill & Weiman, Lyle. Adventures in UNIX Network Applications Programming. (Illus.). 464p. 1992. text ed. 39.95 (*0-471-52859-5*) Wiley.

Rieker, Hans-Ulrich. Yoga of Light: The Classic Esoteric Handbook of Kundalini Yoga. Becherer, Elsy, tr. LC 79-167868. (Illus.). 202p. 1974. pap. 14.95 (*0-913922-07-2*) Dawn Horse Pr.

Rieker, Hans-Urlich. The Yoga of Light: Hatha-Yoga-Pradipika with a Commentary by Hans-Urlich Rieker. 208p. 1990. pap. 12.95 (*0-04-440600-2*) Routledge Chapman & Hall.

Rieker, Jane, jt. auth. see Clytus, John.

Rieker, Patricia P. & Carmen, Elaine H., eds. The Gender Gap in Psychotherapy. LC 84-11511. 392p. 1984. 65.00 (*0-306-41657-3*, Plenum Pr) Plenum.

Riekerk, Marjon. Como Dar A Los Ninos Una Ventaja Emocional: Spanish Translation. 1989. pap. 2.00 (*0-913937-37-1*) Rational Isl.

— How to Give Children an Emotional Head Start. 1988. pap. 2.00 (*0-913937-33-9*) Rational Isl.

— How to Give Children an Emotional Head Start: Arabic Translation. 1992. pap. 2.00 (*0-913937-67-3*) Rational Isl.

Riekes, Linda. Young Consumers. 2nd ed. Ackerly, Sally M., ed. (Law in Action Ser.). (Illus.). 124p. (J). (gr. 5-9). 1980. pap. text ed. 24.50 (*0-8299-1021-2*); teacher ed, pap. text ed. 24.50 (*0-8299-1022-0*) West Pub.

Riekes, Linda & Ackerly, Sally M. Courts & Trials. Olsen, Harry, ed. (Law in Action Series, Lessons in Law for Young People). (Illus.). 165p. (gr. 5-9). 1980. student ed, pap. text ed. 24.50 (*0-8299-1027-1*) West Pub.

— Courts & Trials. 2nd ed. Olsen, Harry, ed. (Law in Action Series, Lessons in Law for Young People). (Illus.). 165p. (gr. 5-9). 1980. teacher ed write for info. (*0-8299-1028-X*) West Pub.

— Juvenile Problems & Law. 2nd ed. (Law in Action Ser.). (Illus.). 133p. 1980. pap. text ed. 24.50 (*0-8299-1026-3*) West Pub.

— Lawmaking. 2nd ed. (Law in Action Ser.). (Illus.). 142p. (J). (gr. 5-9). 1980. pap. text ed. 24.50 (*0-8299-1023-9*); teacher ed, pap. text ed. 24.50 (*0-8299-1024-7*) West Pub.

***Riekes, Linda, et al.** Citizenship Through Sports & Law. 2nd ed. LC 94-32063. 1994. pap. text ed. write for info. (*0-314-01180-3*) West Pub.

— Citizenship Through Sports & Law. 2nd ed. LC 94-32063. 1994. pap. write for info. (*0-314-40118-0*) West Pub.

Riekse, Robert & Holstege, Henry. Christian Guide to Parent Care. 1992. pap. 9.99 (*0-8423-0544-0*) Tyndale.

***Riel.** Object-Oriented Design Through Aeuristics. 1995. pap. 33.50 (*0-201-63385-X*) Addison-Wesley.

Riel, Louis. The Queen vs Louis Riel. LC 73-91562. (Social History of Canada Ser.: No. 19). 419p. reprint ed. pap. 119.50 (*0-7837-0377-5*, 2040697) Bks Demand.

Riel, Marquita, jt. auth. see Lowenthal, David.

Riel, Steven. How to Dream. (Amherst Writers & Artists Chapbook Ser.). 36p. (Orig.). 1993. pap. 8.00 (*0-941895-10-6*) Amherst Wri Art.

Riela, A. R., jt. auth. see Roach, E. S.

Riela, Anthony R., jt. ed. see Roach, E. S.

Rieland, Randy. The New Professionals: Baseball in the '70s. (World of Baseball Ser.). (Illus.). 192p. 1989. write for info. (*0-924588-05-5*) Redefinition Inc.

***Rieley, James B.** Total Quality Management in Higher Education. 52p. (Orig.). (C). 1994. pap. text ed. 25.00x (*0-7881-1293-7*) Diane Pub.

Rielly, E. J. The Furrow's Edge. (Haiku Ser.: No. 19). (Orig.). 1987. 3.50 (*1-55780-097-9*) Juniper Pr WI.

Rielly, Edward J. The Breaking of Glass Horses & Other Poems. 40p. 1988. pap. 4.50 (*0-9613465-9-0*) Great Elm.

Rielly, Edward J., ed. Approaches to Teaching Swift's Gulliver's Travels. LC 88-13148. (Approaches to Teaching World Literature Ser.: No. 18). ix, 148p. 1988. text ed. 37.50 (*0-87352-511-6*, AP18C); pap. 18.00x (*0-87352-512-4*, AP18P) Modern Lang.

***Riely, Elizabeth.** The Chef's Companion: A Concise Dictionary of Culinary Terms. (Hospitality, Travel & Tourism Ser.). 224p. 1995. pap. 19.95 (*0-442-02002-3*) Van Nos Reinhold.

— The Chef's Companion: A Dictionary of Culinary Terms. (Professional Bks.). (Illus.). 160p. (C). 1986. text ed. 29.95 (*0-442-27846-2*) Van Nos Reinhold.

— A Feast of Fruits. LC 92-46080. 288p. 1993. text ed. 25.00 (*0-02-601961-2*) Macmillan.

Riely, John & Pillsbury, Edmund P. Rowlandson Drawings from the Paul Mellon Collection. LC 77-85174. (Illus.). 93p. (Orig.). 1977. pap. 10.00 (*0-930606-05-1*) Yale Ctr Brit Art.

Riely, Phyllis E., jt. ed. see Gall, Lorraine S.

Riely, Sara J., ed. Connecting Arizona: The Natural Yellow Pages. (Illus.). 120p. (Orig.). 1989. pap. 3.69 (*0-685-29362-9*) Hampshire Group.

Rieman, Barbara & Rieman, Roy. Where in America's Past Is Carmen Sandiego. (Illus.). (Orig.). 1992. pap. 14.95 (*0-672-48527-3*) Hayden.

— Where in the U. S. A. Is Carmen Sandiego Book. (Illus.). (Orig.). 1992. pap. 14.95 (*0-672-48528-1*) Hayden.

— Where in the World Is Carmen Sandiego? Book. (Illus.). (Orig.). 1992. pap. 14.95 (*0-672-48525-7*) Hayden.

— Where in Time Is Carmen Sandiego? Book. (Illus.). (Orig.). 1992. pap. 14.95 (*0-672-48524-9*) Hayden.

Rieman, Dwight W. Strategies in Social Work Consultation: From Theory to Practice in the Mental Health Field. 208p. (C). 1992. pap. text ed. 39.95 (*0-8013-0394-X*, 78173) Longman.

Rieman, Roy, jt. auth. see Rieman, Barbara.

***Rieman, Timothy D.** Shaker: The Art of Craftmanship: the Mount Lebanon Collection. LC 94-36405. 1995. write for info. (*0-88397-109-7*) Art Srvc Intl.

Rieman, Timothy D. & Burks, Jean M. The Complete Book of Shaker Furniture. LC 92-47357. 1993. 75.00 (*0-8109-3841-3*) Abrams.

Rieman, Timothy D., jt. auth. see Muller, Charles R.

Rieman, W. & Walton, H. Ion Exchange in Analytical Chemistry. LC 74-105870. 1970. 128.00 (*0-08-015511-1*, Pub. by Pergamon Repr UK) Franklin.

Riemann. Riemann, Musiklexikon. 108p. (GER.). 1967. 350.00 (*0-8288-6690-2*, M-7602) Fr & Eur.

Riemann, B. & Sondergaard, M., eds. Carbon Dynamics in Eutrophic, Temperate Lakes. 296p. 1987. 84.75 (*0-444-42736-8*) Elsevier.

Riemann, Bernhard. Gesammelte Mathematische Werke, Wissenschaftlicher Nachlass & Nachtrage: Collected Papers. 888p. (GER.). 1990. 133.00 (*0-387-50033-2*) Spr-Verlag.

Riemann, Gottfried, ed. see Schinkel, Karl F.

Riemann, H. P. & Burridge, M. J. Impact of Diseases on Livestock Products in Tropics. (Developments in Animal & Veterinary Science Ser.: Vol. 15). 1984. 113.00 (*0-444-42326-5*) Elsevier.

Riemann, Hans & Bryan, Frank L., eds. Food-Borne Infections & Intoxication. 2nd ed. LC 79-14935. (Food Science & Technology Ser.). 1979. text ed. 130.00 (*0-12-588360-9*) Acad Pr.

Riemann, Hugo. Dictionary of Music. LC 75-125060. (Music Ser.). 1970. reprint ed. lib. bdg. 95.00 (*0-306-70025-5*) Da Capo.

— History of Music Theory, 2 Vols., Set. rev. ed. Haggh, Raymond, tr. LC 73-20223. (Music Ser.). 435p. 1974. reprint ed. lib. bdg. 47.50 (*0-306-70637-7*) Da Capo.

— Opern-Handbuch. LC 80-2295. reprint ed. 75.00 (*0-404-18864-8*) AMS Pr.

Riemann, Hugo, jt. auth. see Mickelsen, William C.

Riemann, Othon. Etudes sur la Langue et la Grammaire de Tite-Live. 326p. 1974. reprint ed. write for info. (*3-487-05226-1*, Pub. by Georg Olms GW) Lubrecht & Cramer.

Riemann, R., jt. ed. see Bjornsen, P. K.

***Riemenschneider, Faye.** An End to Freedom. 1995. 13.95 (*0-8062-5273-1*) Carlton.

Riemer, Andrew. The Habsburg Cafe. 279p. (Orig.). 1994. pap. 12.00 (*0-207-17414-8*, IntlDept) HarpC.

— The Habsburg Cafe. (Orig.). 1995. 22.00 (*0-8446-6867-2*) Peter Smith.

Riemer, David R. The Prisoners of Welfare: Liberating America's Poor from Unemployment & Low Wages. LC 88-3296. 219p. 1988. text ed. 55.00 (*0-275-92705-9*, C2705, Praeger Pubs) Greenwood.

***Riemer, David W.** Phonics in Your Face. (Illus.). 80p. 1995. pap. 9.00 (*0-8059-3718-8*) Dorrance.

Riemer, Donald N. Introduction to Freshwater Vegetation. rev. ed. LC 92-38624. 218p. (C). 1993. reprint ed. lib. bdg. 49.50 (*0-89464-820-9*) Krieger.

Riemer, E., ed. see Dore, Ian.

Riemer, George A. Oregon State Bar Desk Reference: A Guide to the Regulatory Programs of the Oregon State Bar. LC 90-62857. (Illus.). 856p. 1990. 80.00 (*1-879049-00-7*) Oregon St Bar.

***Riemer, Jack.** Wrestling with Angel. Date not set. pap. write for info. (*0-8052-1035-0*) Schocken.

Riemer, Jack, ed. Jewish Reflections on Death. LC 74-18242. 192p. 1987. pap. 10.00 (*0-8052-0516-0*) Schocken.

— Wrestling with the Angel: Jewish Insights on Death & Mourning. 432p. 1995. 25.00 (*0-8052-4129-9*) Schocken.

Riemer, Jack & Stampfer, Nathaniel, eds. So That Your Values Live On: Ethical Wills & How to Prepare Them. LC 91-28039. 272p. 1991. 23.95 (*1-879045-07-9*) Jewish Lights.

— So That Your Values Live On: Ethical Wills & How to Prepare Them. 272p. 1993. pap. 16.95 (*1-879045-34-6*) Jewish Lights.

Riemer, James D. From Satire to Subversion: The Fantasies of James Branch Cabell. LC 89-1903. (Contributions to the Study of Science Fiction & Fantasy Ser.: No. 38). 128p. 1989. text ed. 42.95 (*0-313-25569-5*, RNT, Greenwood Pr) Greenwood.

Riemer, Judith, jt. auth. see Dreifuss, Gustav.

Riemer, Neal. Karl Marx & Prophetic Politics. LC 86-30242. 177p. 1987. text ed. 55.00 (*0-275-92543-9*, C2543, Praeger Pubs); pap. 12.95 (*0-275-92635-4*, B2635, Praeger Pubs) Greenwood.

Riemer, Neal & Simon, Douglas. The New World of Politics: An Introduction to Political Science. 2nd ed. (Illus.). 580p. (C). 1991. pap. text ed. 30.75 (*0-939693-15-1*) Collegiate Pr.

Riemer, Neal & Thompson, Kenneth, eds. New Thinking & Developments in International Politics: Opportunities & Dangers, Vol. III. (Miller Center Series on a World in Change). 206p. (C). 1991. lib. bdg. 41.00 (*0-8191-8308-3*); pap. text ed. 21.50 (*0-8191-8309-1*) U Pr of Amer.

Riemer, Pierce & Mills, Steve. Ford Based Kit Cars. (Illus.). 29.95 (*0-85429-623-9*, F623, Pub. by G T Foulis Ltd) Haynes Pubns.

Riemer, Ruth, jt. auth. see Bloom, Leonard.

Riemer, Seth D. National Biases in French & English Drama. LC 90-44653. (Studies in Comparative Literature). 184p. 1990. reprint ed. 15.00 (*0-8240-5471-7*) Garland.

Riemers, Leo, jt. auth. see Kutsch, Karl J.

Riemersma, R. A. & Oliver, M. F., eds. Catecholamines in the Non-Ischaemic & Ischaemic Myocardium: Proceedings of the Sixth Argenteuil Symposiym, Waterloo, Belgium, 1981. (Argenteuil Symposia Ser.: Vol. 6). 260p. 1982. 134.00 (*0-444-80439-0*) Elsevier.

Riemsdyk, H. V., ed. see Borer, H.

Rienecker, Fritz. Lexicon of the Bible: Lexikon Zur Bibel. 10th ed. 968p. (GER.). 1985. 95.00 (*0-8288-2311-1*, M7192) Fr & Eur.

Rienecker, Fritz & Rogers, Cleon L. Linguistic Key to the Greek New Testament. 912p. (C). 1982. 34.99 (*0-310-32050-X*, 6277) Zondervan.

Rienhoff, O. & Schneider, B., eds. Expert Systems & Decision Support in Medicine. (Lecture Notes in Medical Informatics Ser.: Vol. 36). xii, 591p. 1988. pap. 103.00 (*0-387-50317-X*) Spr-Verlag.

Rienhoff, O., ed. see O'Moore, R. R., et al.

Rienits, Rex & Rienits, Thea. The Voyages of Columbus. (Illus.). 152p. 1990. 12.99 (*0-517-69039-X*) Random Hse Value.

Rienits, Thea, jt. auth. see Rienits, Rex.

Rienitz, Andrea. Diccionari Catala-Alemany, Alemany-Catala. 288p. 1990. pap. 11.95 (*0-7859-6036-8*, 8440461976) Fr & Eur.

Rienow, Nonie. Unbottled Scotch. 1987. pap. 10.95 (*0-940168-06-5*) Boxwood.

Rienstra, Ellen W., jt. auth. see Wilson, Callie C.

Rienstra, Marchiene. The Swallow's Nest: A Feminine Paraphrase of the Psalms for Women. 270p. (Orig.). 1992. pap. 18.99 (*0-8028-0624-4*) Eerdmans.

Rienzi, Leonard P. Narcotics Trial Manual for New York State. ring bd. 19.95 (*0-930137-78-7*) Looseleaf Law.

Rienzo, Patricia G. Nursing Care of the Person Who Smokes. 224p. 1992. 31.95 (*0-8261-7620-8*) Springer Pub.

Riepe, Dale. Objectivity & Subjectivism in the Philosophy of Science with Special Reference to India. 232p. 1986. 27.50 (*0-8364-1655-4*, Pub. by KP Bagchi IA) S Asia.

Riepe, Dale, ed. Asian Philosophy Today. 322p. 1981. text ed. 91.00 (*0-677-15490-9*) Gordon & Breach.

Riepe, Dale, et al, eds. Philosophy & Revolutionary Theory, Vol. 1. (Philosophical Currents Ser.: Vol. 32). 253p. (Orig.). (C). 1989. pap. 30.00 (*90-6032-278-9*, Pub. by Gruner NE) Benjamins North Am.

Riepe, Dale M. The Naturalistic Tradition in Indian Thought. LC 82-9185. xii, 308p. 1982. reprint ed. text ed. 59.75 (*0-313-23622-4*, RINA, Greenwood Pr) Greenwood.

Riepl, Wolfgang. Das Nachrichtenwesen Des Altertums Mit Besonderer Rucksicht Auf die Romer. xiv, 478p. 1972. reprint ed. write for info. (*3-487-04218-5*, Pub. by Georg Olms GW) Lubrecht & Cramer.

Rieppel, Oliver C. Fundamentals of Comparative Biology. 250p. 1988. 41.00 (*0-8176-1956-9*) Birkhauser.

— The Phylogeny of Anguinomorph Lizards. 88p. 1980. pap. text ed. 47.00 (*0-8176-1224-6*) Birkhauser.

Rieppel, Olivier, jt. ed. see Grande, Lance.

Rier, David C. The Lotus Guide to HAL: Techniques for Experienced 1-2-3 Users. (Illus.). 188p. 1987. pap. 19.95 (*0-201-16827-8*) Addison-Wesley.

Rier, David C. & Fine, Edmund S. Orchestrating 1-2-3: Notes for Advanced Users. LC 84-20436. 1985. pap. write for info. (*0-201-16901-0*) Addison-Wesley.

Riera, Carme. Mirror Images: Carma Riera's Joc de Miralls. De la Torre, Cristina, tr. LC 93-9535. (Catalan Studies: Vol. 9). 182p. 1993. 29.95 (*0-8204-2077-8*) P Lang Pubs.

Riera, Carmen. Te Dejo el Mar. Cotoner, Luisa, tr. & intro. by. (Nueva Austral Ser.: Vol. 211). (SPA.). 1991. pap. text ed. 24.95x (*84-239-7211-9*) Elliots Bks.

Riera, Emilio L., jt. auth. see Horvath, Juan.

Riera, Marti. The Cabbie. Metz, Bernd, ed. Lisle, Jeff, tr. (Illus.). 80p. 1987. pap. 10.95 (*0-87416-042-1*) Catalan Communs.

***Riera, Michael.** Uncommon Sense for Parents with Teenagers. 300p. 1995. pap. 12.95 (*0-89087-749-1*) Celestial Arts.

Rierden, Anne B. Reshaping the Supreme Court: New Justices, New Directions. Ribaroff, Margaret, ed. LC 87-25958. (Impact Ser.). (Illus.). 128p. (YA). (gr. 7-12). 1988. lib. bdg. 14.42 (*0-531-10512-1*) Watts.

Rierson, Judy & Claiborne, Mary. Extending Thinking Abilities via a Nature Trail, the Planetarum, an Airport, the Zoo, the Museum. (Illus.). 40p. 1981. pap. text ed. 4.95 (*0-914634-88-7*, 8112) DOK Pubs.

— Extending Thinking Abilities Via Legends & Ghost Tales, Greek Mythology, the Cemetery, Your City's Past. (Illus.). 40p. (Orig.). 1981. pap. text ed. 4.95 (*0-914634-89-5*, 8113) DOK Pubs.

Ries, Al & Trout, Jack. Bottom-up Marketing. 240p. 1989. text ed. 22.95 (*0-07-052733-4*); audio 9.95 (*0-07-052734-2*) McGraw.

— Bottom-up Marketing. 240p. 1990. pap. 11.95 (*0-452-26418-9*, Plume) NAL-Dutton.

— Horse Sense: How to Pull Ahead on the Business Track. 240p. 1992. reprint ed. pap. 10.00 (*0-452-26764-1*, Plume) NAL-Dutton.

— Horse Sense: The Key to Success is Finding a Horse to Ride. 256p. 1991. text ed. 19.95 (*0-07-052735-0*) McGraw.

— Marketing Warfare. (Illus.). 224p. 1986. text ed. 24.95 (*0-07-052730-X*) McGraw.

— Marketing Warfare. LC 86-8635. 228p. 1986. pap. 11.00 (*0-452-25861-8*, Plume) NAL-Dutton.

— Positioning: The Battle for Your Mind. 1985. text ed. 24.95 (*0-07-065264-3*) McGraw.

— Positioning: The Battle for Your Mind. 224p. 1987. mass mkt. 5.99 (*0-446-34794-9*) Warner Bks.

— The Twenty-Two Immutable Laws of Marketing: Violate Them at Your Own Risk! (Illus.). 160p. 1994. reprint ed. pap. 12.00 (*0-88730-666-7*) Harper Busn.

R

An Asterisk (*) at the beginning of an entry indicates that the title is appearing in BIP for the first time.

Ries, Arthur. The Pulsar Mission. 228p. 1988. pap. 8.95 (*0-89697-306-9*) Intl Univ Pr.

Ries, C. Ueberblick ueber die Ackerunkrautvegetation Oesterreichs und Ihre Entwicklung in Neuerer Zeit. (Dissertationes Botanicae Ser.: Vol. 187). (Illus.). 188p. (GER.). 1992. pap. text ed. 84.00 (*3-443-64099-0*, Pub. by Cramer-Borntraeger GW) Lubrecht & Cramer.

***Ries, Christine, ed.** Capital Controls in Emerging. (Political Economy of Global Interdependence Ser.). (C). 1995. text ed. 49.95 (*0-8133-8907-0*) Westview.

Ries, Estelle H. The Ingenuity of Man. LC 75-8726. (Illus.). 333p. 1975. reprint ed. text ed. 59.75 (*0-8371-8041-4*, RIIM, Greenwood Pr) Greenwood.

Ries, Ferdinand, jt. auth. see Wegeler, Franz.

Ries, Frank W. The Dance Theatre of Jean Cocteau. LC 85-19078. (Theater & Dramatic Studies: No. 33). 260p. reprint ed. pap. 74.10 (*0-8357-1994-4*, 2070661) Bks Demand.

***Ries, Joanne B. & Leukefeld, Karl G.** Applying for Research Funding: Getting Started & Being Funded. 252p. 1994. 38.00 (*0-8039-5364-X*); pap. 18.95 (*0-8039-5365-8*) Sage.

Ries, John C. The Management of Defence: Organization & Control of the United States Armed Services. LC 64-18122. 247p. reprint ed. pap. 70.40 (*0-317-08302-3*, 2004661) Bks Demand.

***Ries, Judith.** Ed O'Kelley: The Man Who Murdered. LC 94-67428. (Illus.). 120p. (Orig.). 1995. pap. 12.95 (*0-934426-61-9*) NAPSAC Reprods.

***Ries, Julien.** Origins of Religions. 160p. 1994. 39.99 (*0-8028-3767-0*) Eerdmans.

Ries, Karl & Ring, Hans. The Legion Condor: A History of the Luftwaffe in the Spanish Civil War 1936-1939. rev. ed. Johnston, David, tr. LC 91-62741. (Illus.). 288p. 1992. 37.50 (*0-88740-339-5*) Schiffer.

***Ries, Kernell G., III.** Estimation of Low-Flow Duration Discharges in Massachusetts. 1994. write for info. (*0-615-00031-2*) US Geol Survey.

Ries, Linda A. Guide to Photographs at the Pennsylvania State Archives. 229p. 1992. 9.95 (*0-89271-049-7*) Pa Hist & Mus.

Ries, Marcella L. I'll See You Through: Messages for the Journey. (Illus.). 52p. (Orig.). 1990. pap. 6.50 (*0-9624543-0-3*) HeartSong Pub.

Ries, Paula & Stone, Anne J., eds. The American Woman, 1992-1993. 560p. 1992. 24.95 (*0-393-03110-1*) Norton.

Ries, Pauls & Stone, Anne J., eds. The American Woman, 1992-1993. 560p. 1992. pap. 12.95 (*0-393-30871-5*) Norton.

Ries, Raul. From Fury to Freedom. LC 85-82383. 160p. (Orig.). 1986. pap. 5.99 (*0-89081-537-2*) Harvest Hse.

Ries, Raul A. Hear What the Spirit Is Saying: A Practical Approach to the Seven Churches of Revelation. LC 93-78422. 156p. (Orig.). 1993. pap. 6.95 (*0-9637117-0-9*) Logos Media.

Ries, Russel, ed. see Anderson, Jack R.

Ries, Sharon. My Husband My Maker. LC 87-81661. (Orig.). 1989. pap. 6.99 (*0-89081-603-4*) Harvest Hse.

Ries, Tomas. Cold Will: The Defence of Finland. (Illus.). 394p. 1988. 52.00 (*0-08-033592-6*, Pub. by Brasseys UK) Brasseys Inc.

Ries, Tommy & Skorve, Johnny. Investigating Kola: A Study of Military Bases Using Satellite Photographs. 83p. 1987. 44.00 (*0-08-034755-X*, Pub. by Brasseys UK) Brasseys Inc.

Riesbeck, C. K., jt. ed. see Kolodner, J. L.

Riesbeck, Christopher K. & Schank, Roger C. Inside Case-Based Reasoning. 448p. 1989. 79.95 (*0-89859-767-6*) L Erlbaum Assocs.

Riesbeck, Christopher K., jt. auth. see Schank, Roger C.

Riesch, Craig. U. S. M1 Carbines: Wartime Production: Wartime Production. (For Collectors Only Ser.). (Illus.). 124p. (Orig.). 1994. pap. 15.95 (*1-882391-03-9*) N Cape Pubns.

Riesch, Craig, jt. auth. see Poyer, Joe.

Riese, A., ed. Geographi Latini Minores. xlviii, 175p. 1964. reprint ed. write for info. (*0-318-71125-7*, Pub. by Georg Olms GW) Lubrecht & Cramer.

Riese, Alexander, ed. see Varro, Terentius.

Riese, Erika, jt. auth. see Pfeiffer, Ehrenfried.

Riese, Hans P., jt. auth. see Krane, Susan.

Riese, Herthe. Heal the Hurt Child: An Approach Through Educational Therapy with Special Reference to the Extremely Deprived Negro Child. LC 62-19623. 639p. reprint ed. pap. 180.00 (*0-317-20697-4*, 2024064) Bks Demand.

Riese, Randall. All about Bette: Her Life A to Z. 512p. 1993. 35.00 (*0-8092-4111-0*) Contemp Bks.

— Her Name Is Barbara Vol. 1. 1994. pap. 6.99 (*0-312-95391-7*) St Martin.

— Her Name is Barbra: An Intimate Portrait of the Real Barbra Streisand. LC 93-2521. (Illus.). 448p. 1993. 22.50 (*1-55972-203-7*, Birch Ln Pr) Carol Pub Group.

— The Unabridged James Dean: His Life & Legacy from A to Z. LC 94-6989. 1994. 15.99 (*0-517-10081-9*, Pub. by Wings Bks) Random Hse Value.

— Unabridged Marilyn: Her Life. 1990. 7.99 (*0-517-69619-3*) Random Hse Value.

Riesebrodt, Martin. Pious Passion: The Emergence of Modern Fundamentalism in the United States & Iran. Reneau, Don, tr. LC 92-32233. (Comparative Studies in Religion & Society: Vol. 6). 1993. 40.00 (*0-520-07463-7*) U CA Pr.

Riesel, Hans. Prime Numbers & Computer Method for Factorization. (Progress in Mathematics Ser.: No. 57). 1987. 62.50 (*0-8176-3291-3*) Birkhauser.

— Prime Numbers & Computer Methods for Factorization. 2nd ed. LC 94-27688. xvi, 464p. 1994. 69.50 (*0-8176-3743-5*) Birkhauser.

Rieselbach, Helen F. Conrad's Rebels: The Psychology of Revolution in the Novels from Nostromo to Victory. LC 84-23917. (Studies in Modern Literature: No. 42). 162p. reprint ed. pap. 46.20 (*0-8357-1600-7*, 2070572) Bks Demand.

Rieselbach, L. Congressional Reform: The Changing Modern Congress. 232p. 1993. pap. text ed. 20.95 (*0-87187-838-0*) Congr Quarterly.

Rieselbach, Leroy, ed. Legislative Reform. 272p. (C). 1978. pap. 12.00 (*0-918592-21-6*) Pol Studies.

***Rieselbach, Leroy N.** Congressional Politics: The Evolving Legislative System. 2nd ed. (Transforming American Politics Ser.). (C). 1995. text ed. 75.00 (*0-8133-2399-1*); pap. text ed. 29.95 (*0-8133-2458-0*) Westview.

— Roots of Isolationism: Congressional Voting & Presidential Leadership in Foreign Policy. (Orig.). (C). 1966. write for info. (*0-672-51169-X*, Bobbs) Macmillan.

Rieselbach, Leroy N., ed. Legislative Reform: The Policy Impact. 272p. 1985. reprint ed. lib. bdg. 42.00 (*0-8191-5157-2*, Pol Studies) U Pr of Amer.

Rieselbach, Leroy N., jt. auth. see Unekis, Joseph K.

Rieselbach, Richard E. & Garnick, Marc B., eds. Cancer & the Kidney. LC 81-8277. (Illus.). 949p. reprint ed. pap. 180.00 (*0-8357-7654-9*, 2056980) Bks Demand.

Riesen, A. H. & Thompson, R. F. Advances in Psychobiology, Vol. 3. LC 70-178148. 509p. reprint ed. 145.10 (*0-8357-9831-3*, 2015177) Bks Demand.

Riesen, Janet & Grall, Eloise. He's Your Father Now! Facts, Figures & Fantasies. LC 92-81067. (Illus.). 65p. (Orig.). 1992. pap. 5.95 (*0-9626993-2-2*) Armadillo Niche.

— Mama, Your Slip is Showing! A How-It-Is Prescription Guide for Caregivers on Aging. 36p. (Orig.). 1990. pap. 5.95 (*0-9626993-0-6*) Armadillo Niche.

Riesen, Janet, see Mancebo, pseud..

Riesenberg, Felix. Cape Horn. LC 94-11744. (Illus.). xvi, 500p. 1994. reprint ed. 39.95 (*1-881987-04-3*) Ox Bow.

— Pacific Ocean. LC 79-128300. (Essay Index Reprint Ser.). 1977. 23.95 (*0-8369-2125-9*) Ayer.

— Yankee Skippers to the Rescue. LC 78-93374. (Essay Index Reprint Ser.). 1977. 23.95 (*0-8369-1313-2*) Ayer.

Riesenberg, Peter. Citizenship in the Western Tradition Plato to Rousseau. LC 91-45807. 348p. (C). 1994. pap. text ed. 14.95 (*0-8078-4459-4*) U of NC Pr.

Riesenberg, Peter, jt. ed. see Agresto, John.

Riesenberg, Peter, jt. auth. see Mundy, John H.

***Riesenberger, John R.** Global Challenge: Building the New World Enterprise. 1994. 26.95 (*0-07-709002-0*) McGraw.

Riesener, Ingrid. Der Stamm 'Abad in Alten Testament. (Beiheft zur Zeitschrift fuer die Alttestamentliche Wissenschaft Ser.: Vol. 149). (C). 1979. 165.40 (*3-11-007260-2*) De Gruyter.

Riesenfeld, Richard F., jt. ed. see Barnhill, Robert E.

Riesenfeld, Stefan A. Creditors' Remedies & Debtors' Protection: Cases & Materials. 4th ed. (American Casebook Ser.). 514p. 1992. reprint ed. text ed. 43.50 (*0-314-30130-5*) West Pub.

— Creditors' Remedies & Debtors' Protection, 1990 Supplement. 4th ed. (American Casebook Ser.). 92p. 1990. pap. text ed. 10.50 (*0-314-76484-4*) West Pub.

Riesenfeld, Stefan A., ed. Parliamentary Participation in the Making & Operation of Treaties: A Comparative Study. LC 93-13382. (Current Legal Issues in International & Comparative Law Ser.). 612p. (C). 1994. lib. bdg. 197.50 (*0-7923-1735-1*) Kluwer Ac.

Riesenfeld, Stefan A., jt. ed. see Krueger, Robert B.

Rieser, A., et al, eds. Environmental Decisionmaking in a Transboundary Region. (Lecture Notes on Coastal & Estuarine Studies: Vol. 20). xiii, 209p. 1987. pap. 40.00 (*0-387-96446-0*) Spr-Verlag.

Rieser, Allan. Boy Meets Family: Manuscript Edition. 1990. pap. 13.00 (*0-8222-0141-0*) Dramatists Play.

Rieser, H., jt. ed. see Petofi, J. S.

Rieser, Max. Analysis of Poetic Thinking. Schueller, Herbert M., tr. LC 69-11535. (Criticism Monograph Ser.: No. 1). 170p. reprint ed. pap. 48.50 (*0-7837-3641-X*, 2043509) Bks Demand.

Riesgo, Rodolfo. Cuba: El Movimiento Obrero y Su Entorno Socio-Politico. (Realidades Ser.). 250p. (Orig.). (SPA.). 1985. pap. 10.00 (*0-917049-02-0*) Saeta.

Riesman, David. Abundance for What. rev. ed. 656p. (C). 1993. pap. 24.95 (*1-56000-599-8*) Transaction Pubs.

— Constraint & Variety in American Education. LC 56-13482. (Landmark Edition Ser.). 175p. reprint ed. pap. 49.90 (*0-8357-2945-1*, 2039201) Bks Demand.

— On Higher Education: The Academic Enterprise in an Era of Rising Student Consumerism. LC 80-8007. (Carnegie Council Ser.). 459p. reprint ed. pap. 130.90 (*0-8357-4690-9*, 2052345) Bks Demand.

— Thorstein Veblen. rev. ed. 287p. (C). 1994. pap. 21.95 (*1-56000-776-1*) Transaction Pubs.

Riesman, David & Glazer, Nathan. Faces in the Crowd: Individual Studies in Character & Politics. Coser, Lewis A. & Powell, Walter W., eds. LC 79-7015. (Perennial Works in Sociology Ser.). 1980. reprint ed. lib. bdg. 59.95 (*0-405-12114-8*) Ayer.

Riesman, David, jt. auth. see Grant, Gerald.

Riesman, David, jt. auth. see Jencks, Christopher.

Riesman, David, jt. auth. see McLaughlin, Judith B.

Riesman, David, et al. Lonely Crowd: A Study of the Changing American Character. abr. ed. (Studies in National Policy: No. 3). (C). 1961. reprint ed. pap. 15.00 (*0-300-00193-2*, Y41) Yale U Pr.

Riesman, Paul. First Find Your Child a Good Mother: The Construction of Self in Two African Communities. LC 91-18209. (Illus.). 260p. (C). 1992. text ed. 40.00 (*0-8135-1767-2*); pap. text ed. 15.00 (*0-8135-1768-0*) Rutgers U Pr.

Riesner, Dieter, jt. auth. see Schweik, Robert C.

Riesner, Rainer, jt. auth. see Betz, Otto.

***Riesner, Trudi.** Easy 123 Release 5 for Windows. 1994. pap. 19.99 (*1-56529-999-X*) Que.

Riess, Curt, ed. They Were There. LC 70-134127. (Essay Index Reprint Ser.). 1977. 37.95 (*0-8369-2029-5*) Ayer.

Riess, Jean G., jt. auth. see International Conference on Phosphorus Chemistry Staff.

***Riess, Jonathan.** Luca Signorelli: The San Brizio Chapel, Orvieto. (Great Fresco Cycles of the Renaissance Ser.). (Illus.). 104p. 1995. 25.00 (*0-8076-1312-6*) Braziller.

Riess, Jonathan B. Political Ideals in Medieval Italian Art: The Frescoes in the Palazzo dei Priori, Perugia, 1297. LC 81-12950. (Studies in the Fine Arts: Iconography: No. 1). (Illus.). 201p. reprint ed. pap. 57.30 (*0-8357-1238-9*, 2070252) Bks Demand.

— Renaissance Antichrist: Luca Signorelli's Orvieto Frescoes. (C). Date not set. 55.00 (*0-691-04086-9*) Princeton U Pr.

Riess, R. Dean, jt. auth. see Johnson, Lee W.

Riess, Steven A. City Games: The Evolution of American Urban Society & the Rise of Sports. (Sport & Society Ser.). (Illus.). 368p. 1991. pap. 13.95 (*0-252-06216-7*) U of Ill Pr.

— Sport in the Industrial Age, 1850-1920. Franklin, John H. & Eisenstadt, A. S., eds. (American History Ser.). 150p. (C). 1995. pap. text ed. 11.95 (*0-88295-916-6*) Harlan Davidson.

— Touching Base: Professional Baseball & American Culture in the Progressive Era. LC 79-6570. (Contributions in American Studies: No. 48). (Illus.). xv, 268p. 1980. text ed. 38.50 (*0-313-20671-6*, RTB/, Greenwood Pr) Greenwood.

Riess, Steven A., ed. The American Sporting Experience: A Historical Anthology of Sport in America. LC 84-7188. (Illus.). 400p. (Orig.). 1984. pap. 25.00x (*0-88011-210-7*, PRIE0210) Human Kinetics.

Riess, Suzanne B. & Baum, Willa K., eds. Catalogue of the Regional Oral History Office: 1954-1979. (Illus.). 119p. (Orig.). (C). 1980. pap. text ed. 6.50 (*0-9604164-0-4*) U CA Region Oral Hist.

Riesser, J. The German Great Banks & Their Concentration in Connection with the Economic Development of Germany. Wilkins, Mira, ed. LC 76-29741. (European Business Ser.). (Illus.). 1977. reprint ed. lib. bdg. 74.95 (*0-405-09758-1*) Ayer.

Riessman, Catherine K. Divorce Talk: Women & Men Make Sense of Personal Relationships. LC 89-36065. 264p. (Orig.). (C). 1990. text ed. 40.00 (*0-8135-1502-5*); pap. text ed. 15.00 (*0-8135-1503-3*) Rutgers U Pr.

— Narrative Analysis. (Qualitative Research Methods Ser.: Vol. 30). (Illus.). 96p. (C). 1993. text ed. 21.50 (*0-8039-4753-4*); pap. text ed. 9.50 (*0-8039-4754-2*) Sage.

Riessman, Catherine K., ed. Qualitative Studies in Social Work Research. (Illus.). 256p. (C). 1993. text ed. 45.00 (*0-8039-5451-4*); pap. text ed. 21.95 (*0-8039-5452-2*) Sage.

***Riessman, Frank & Carroll, David.** Self-Help in the Human Services: Policy & Practice. LC 94-38982. (Health-Social & Behavioral Sciences Ser.). 240p. 1995. 25.95 (*0-7879-0066-4*) Jossey-Bass.

Riessman, Frank, jt. auth. see Gartner, Alan.

Riessman, Frank, jt. ed. see Gartner, Alan.

Riessmann, F., et al. Essays on New Careers: Social Implications for Adult Educators. LC 74-127038. (Notes & Essays Ser.: No. 65). (C). 1970. pap. text ed. 2.50 (*0-87060-029-X*, NES 65) Syracuse U Cont Ed.

Riester, Albert E. & Kraft, Irvin A., eds. Child Group Psychotherapy: Future Tense. LC 86-10486. 1986. 37.50 (*0-8236-0765-8*, BN#00765) Intl Univs Pr.

***Riestra, J. A.** A Generalized Taylor's Formula for Functions of Several Variables & Certain of Its Applications. LC 95-11955. (Pitman Research Notes in Mathematics Ser.). 1995. write for info. (*0-615-00681-7*) Wiley.

Riestra, Miguel A. Fundamentos Filosoficos de la Educacion. 2nd ed. 320p. (SPA.). 1985. pap. 9.00 (*0-8477-2747-5*) U of PR Pr.

Riesz, C. H., et al. Improvement of Nickel Cracking Catalysts. (Research Bulletin Ser.: No. 20). iv, 28p. 1952. 3.50 (*0-317-56864-7*) Inst Gas Tech.

— Pilot Plant Catalytic Gasification of Hydrocarbons. (Research Bulletin Ser.: No. 6). viii, 44p. 1953. 5.00 (*0-317-56792-6*) Inst Gas Tech.

— Sulfur Poisoning of Nickel Catalysts. (Research Bulletin Ser.: No. 10). iv, 23p. 1951. 2.50 (*0-317-56798-5*) Inst Gas Tech.

Riesz, Marcel. Clifford Numbers & Spinors: With Riesz's Private Lectures to E. Folke Bolinder & a Historical Review by Pertti Lounesto. Bolinder, E. Folke & Lounesto, Pertti, eds. LC 93-1381. (Fundamental Theories of Physics Ser.: Vol. 54). 256p. (C). 1993. lib. bdg. 98.50 (*0-7923-2299-1*) Kluwer Ac.

Rietbergen, Simon, ed. The Earthscan Reader in Tropical Forestry. 328p. 1994. pap. 39.95 (*1-85383-127-1*) St Lucie Pr.

Rietchec, Robert & Korn, Daniel. Sunday Mass: What Part Do You Play? 32p. 1985. pap. 1.50 (*0-89243-235-7*) Liguori Pubns.

Rietema, K. Dynamics of Fine Powders. (Handling & Processing of Solids Ser.). 1991. 98.75 (*1-85166-594-3*) Elsevier.

Rieter, Russel J., ed. The Pineal Gland: Extra-Reproductive Effects, Vol. III. 248p. 1982. 129.95 (*0-8493-5717-9*, QP188, CRC Reprint) Franklin.

Rieth, A. Suesswasserflora von Mitteleuropa. Vol. 4: Xanthophyceae, Part 2. Pascher, A. et al, eds. (Illus.). 147p. (GER.). 1978. lib. bdg. 44.50 (*3-437-30304-X*) Lubrecht & Cramer.

***Rieth, Elizabeth & Johmann, Carol.** Playground Investigations. 120p. (J). (gr. 3-6). Date not set. 12.95 (*0-88160-242-6*, LW337) Learning Wks.

Rieth, Hamburg, ed. Proceedings: International Symposium on Bifonazole, Kopenhagen, June 1984. (Journal: Dermatologica: Vol. 169, Suppl. 1). iv, 148p. 1985. pap. 37.00 (*3-8055-4021-3*) S Karger.

Rieth, Otto. Die Kunst Menanders in Den "Adelphen" Des Terenz. Gaiser, Konrad, ed. xii, 160p. 1964. write for info. (*0-318-70821-3*, Pub. by Georg Olms GW) Lubrecht & Cramer.

Riethmueller, G., et al, eds. Genes & Antigenes in Cancer Cells: The Monocolonal Antibody Approach. (Beitraege zur Onkologie, Contributions to Oncology Ser.: Vol. 19). (Illus.). x, 192p. 1984. 50.50 (*3-8055-3843-X*) S Karger.

Riethmueller, Richard H. Walt Whitman & the Germans. 1972. 59.95 (*0-8490-1273-2*) Gordon Pr.

Rietman, Ed. Experiments in Artificial Neural Networks. (Advanced Technology Ser.). (Illus.). 160p. 1988. 24.95 (*0-8306-0237-2*, 3037); pap. 16.95 (*0-8306-9337-8*) TAB Bks.

Rietman, Eddward. Genesis Redux: Experiments Creating Artificial Life. 1994. pap. text ed. 29.95 (*0-07-052737-7*) McGraw.

Rietman, Edward. Creating Artificial Life: Computer Modeling Experiments. (Illus.). 256p. 1992. pap. 29.95 (*0-8306-4150-5*, 3719, Windcrest) TAB Bks.

— Exploring Parallel Processing. 1990. pap. text ed. 18.95 (*0-07-156077-7*) McGraw.

— Genesis Redux: Experiments Creating Artificial Life. LC 93-1149. 1993. pap. text ed. 29.95 (*0-8306-4503-9*, Windcrest) TAB Bks.

Rietman, Kearney. Language from Nine to Five: Developing Business Communication Skills. (Illus.). 192p. (C). 1985. pap. text ed. 12.00 (*0-13-523051-9*) P-H.

Rietmann, kearney. Upgrading & Fixing MACs for Dummies. 1994. pap. 19.95 (*1-56884-189-2*) IDG Bks.

Rietschel & Spencer. Methods for Cutaneous Investigation. (Cosmetic Science & Technology Ser.: Vol. 9). 248p. 1990. 115.00 (*0-8247-8264-X*) Dekker.

***Rietschel, Robert L. & Fowler, Joseph F., Jr., eds.** Fisher's Contact Dermatitis. 4th ed. LC 94-26917. 1995. write for info. (*0-683-07282-X*) Williams & Wilkins.

***Rietti, J. C.** Military Annals of Mississippi: Military Organizations Which Entered the Service of the Confederate States of America, from the State of Mississippi. LC 75-45377. 196p. 1995. reprint ed. 25.00 (*0-87152-218-7*) Reprint.

Rietti, Mario. Money & Banking in Latin America. LC 79-4157. 316p. 1979. text ed. 65.00 (*0-275-90412-1*, C0412, Praeger Pubs) Greenwood.

Rietveld, A. C. & Van Hout, R. Statistical Techniques for the Study of Language & Language Behaviour. LC 92-35677. 1993. 44.65 (*3-11-013663-5*) Mouton.

***Rietveld, M. T., ed.** Active Experiments in Space Plasmas. (Advances in Space Research (RJ) Ser.: Vol. 15). 156p. 1995. pap. 94.00 (*0-08-042620-4*) Elsevier.

Rietveld, P., jt. auth. see Nijkamp, Peter.

Rietveld, Piet, jt. auth. see Nijkamp, Peter.

Rietz, Helen L. & Manning, Marilyn. The One-Step Guide to Workshops. LC 93-13299. 324p. 1993. 40.00 (*1-55623-938-6*) Irwin Prof Pubng.

Rietz, Julius, ed. see Mendelssohn, Felix.

Rietz, Sandra A., jt. auth. see Livo, Norma J.

Rieu, C., jt. ed. see Cureton, W.

Rieu, Charles. Catalogus Codicum Manuscriptorum Orientalium Qui in Murso Britannico Asservantur: Supplement to the Catalogue of the Arabic Manuscripts in the British Museum. xv, 935p. reprint ed. write for info. (*0-318-71497-3*, Pub. by Georg Olms GW) Lubrecht & Cramer.

— Supplement to the Catalogue of the Arabic Manuscripts in the British Museum. xvi, 935p. reprint ed. write for info. (*0-318-71556-2*, Pub. by Georg Olms GW) Lubrecht & Cramer.

Rieu, D. C., tr. see Homer.

Rieu, Emil V., tr. see Appollonius of Rhodes.

Rieu, Emil V., tr. see Homer.

Rieul, Roland. Escape into Espionage: The True Story of a French Patriot in World War Two. 1987. 15.95 (*0-8027-0959-1*) Walker & Co.

— Escape into Espionage: The True Story of a French Patriot in World War Two. (Illus.). 224p. 1989. reprint ed. mass mkt. 4.50 (*0-380-70551-6*) Avon.

Riew, C. Keith & Gillham, John K., eds. Rubber-Modified Thermoset Resins. LC 84-21566. (Advances in Chemistry Ser.: No. 208). 374p. 1984. lib. bdg. 96.95 (*0-8412-0828-X*) Am Chemical.

— Rubber-Modified Thermoset Resins: Based on a Symposium Sponsored by the Division of Polymeric Materials Science & Engineering at the 186th Meeting of the American Chemical Society, Washington, DC, August 28-September 2, 1983. LC 84-21566. (Advances in Chemistry Ser.: No. 208). 384p. reprint ed. pap. 109.50 (*0-7837-1962-0*, 2052440) Bks Demand.

Riew, C. Keith & Kinloch, Anthony J., eds. Toughened Plastics, No. 1: Science & Engineering. LC 92-34578. (Advances in Chemistry Ser.: Vol. 233). (Illus.). 589p. 1992. 139.95 (*0-8412-2500-1*) Am Chemical.

Riewolt, Otto. Designer Offices. LC 94-17070. (Illus.). 240p. 1994. 60.00 (*0-86565-149-3*) Vendome.

Riezler, Kurt. Uber Finanzen und Monopole Im Alten Griechenland: Zur Theorie und Geschichte der antiken Stadtwirtschaft. Finley, Moses, ed. LC 79-5002. (Ancient Economic History Ser.). (GER.). 1979. reprint ed. lib. bdg. 15.95 (*0-405-12391-4*) Ayer.

Riezman, Raymond G., jt. ed. see Neuefeind, Wilhelm.

Rifaat, Ahmed M. International Aggression: A Study of the Legal Concept. (Its Development & Definition in International Law Ser.). 359p. 1979. pap. 45.00x (*91-22-00298-7*, Pub. by Almqv & Wiksell SW) Coronet Bks.

An Asterisk (*) at the beginning of an entry indicates that the title is appearing in BIP for the first time.

Rifa'at 'Ali Abou-El-Haj. Formation of the Modern State: The Ottoman Empire, Sixteenth to Eighteenth Centuries. LC 91-2049. (SUNY Series in the Social & Economic History of the Middle East). 155p. (C). 1992. 57.50 (*0-7914-0893-0*); pap. 18.95 (*0-7914-0894-9*) State U NY Pr.

Rifaat, Alifa. Distant View of a Minaret. Johnson-Davis, Denys, tr. 116p. 1993. 12.95 (*0-7043-2401-6*, Pub. by Quartet UK) Interlink Pub.

— Distant View of a Minaret & Other Stories. (African Writers Ser.). x, 116p. (C). 1987. reprint ed. pap. 9.95 (*0-435-90912-6*) Heinemann.

Rifai, Nader & Warnick, G. Russell. Methods for Clinical Laboratory Measurement of Lipid & Lipoprotein Risk Factors. 147p. 1991. 30.00 (*0-915274-59-0*) Am Assn Clinical Chem.

Rifai, Nader & Warnick, G. Russell, eds. Laboratory Measurement of Lipids, Lipoproteins & Apolipoproteins. LC 94-16802. 317p. 1994. 50.00 (*0-915274-74-4*, 630) Am Assn Clinical Chem.

Rifas, Leonard. Food First Comic. Goldenman, Gretta, ed. 24p. (Orig.). (J). (gr. 7-12). 1982. pap. 1.00 (*0-935028-11-0*) Inst Food & Develop.

Rifbjerg, Klaus. Anna, I, Anna. Taylor, Alexander, tr. LC 82-5140. 250p. (Orig.). 1982. pap. 10.95 (*0-915306-30-1*) Curbstone.

— War. Murray, Steven T. & Nunnally, Tiina, trs. (International Poetry Ser.: No. 3). 80p. (Orig.). 1995. pap. 12.00 (*0-940242-66-4*) Fjord Pr.

— War. Murray, Steven T. & Nunnally, Tiina, trs. (International Poetry Ser.: No. 3). 80p. 1995. 24.00 (*0-940242-67-2*) Fjord Pr.

— Witness to the Future. Murray, Steve, tr. LC 87-17359. 217p. (Orig.). 1987. 17.95 (*0-940242-21-4*); pap. 8.95 (*0-940242-18-4*) Fjord Pr.

Rife, Carl B. Bumper Sticker Religion: Seven Messages Unstuck from Bumper Stickers. 1992. pap. 4.75 (*1-55673-600-2*, 9320) CSS OH.

Rife, Carl B. & Bishop, Carolyn. The Church Is You & I. 1984. 2.00 (*0-89536-658-4*, 0394) CSS OH.

Rife, Ellouise A. The House at Stonehaven. 1983. pap. 2.50 (*0-8217-1239-X*) Zebra.

— The House at Windridge. 1981. pap. 2.25 (*0-89083-740-6*) Zebra.

Rife, Janet M. Injured Mind, Shattered Dreams: Brian's Recovery from a Severe Head Injury. LC 93-43284. 1993. pap. 17.95 (*0-914797-95-6*) Brookline Bks.

Rife, Janet W. Germans & German-Russians in Nebraska: A Research Guide to Nebraska Ethnic Studies. Welsch, Roger, ed. (Nebraska Ethnic Resource Ser.). 238p. (Orig.). (C). 1980. pap. text ed. 10.00 (*0-938932-01-2*) U Nebr CFGPS.

Rife, Joanne. Bicycling Country Roads: From San Jose to Santa Barbara. rev. ed. LC 81-52672. (Illus.). 124p. 1991. pap. 9.95 (*0-934136-45-9*) Western Tanager.

Rife, Joe, jt. auth. see Schulman, Karen.

***Rife, John C., ed.** Employment of the Elderly: An Annotated Bibliography. LC 94-39775. (Bibliographies & Indexes in Gerontology Ser.: Vol. 23). 152p. 1995. text ed. 59.95 (*0-313-29191-8*, Greenwood Pr) Greenwood.

Rife, William. Essentials of Chemistry. 560p. (C). 1992. pap. text ed. 45.25 (*0-03-030337-0*) SCP.

Rifelj, Carol D. Word & Figure: The Language of Nineteenth-Century French Poetry. LC 87-1504. 206p. 1987. 42.50 (*0-8142-0422-8*) Ohio St U Pr.

Rifelj, Carol D., jt. auth. see Knox, Edward C.

Riff, Michael. The Face of Survival: Jewish Life in Eastern Europe Past & Present. (Illus.). 224p. 1993. 35.00 (*0-85303-220-3*) NYU Pr.

Riffard, Pierre. Dictionnaire de l'Esoterisme. 396p. 1993. pap. 36.95 (*0-7859-5620-4*, 2228886548) Fr & Eur.

Riffaterre, Hermine, jt. ed. see Caws, Mary A.

Riffaterre, Michael. Fictional Truth. LC 89-45491. (Parallax). 144p. 1990. text ed. 30.00x (*0-8018-3933-5*); pap. text ed. 12.95x (*0-8018-3934-3*) Johns Hopkins.

— Semiotics of Poetry. LC 78-3245. (Advances in Semiotics Ser.). 224p. 1978. pap. 14.95 (*0-253-20332-5*, MB-332) Ind U Pr.

— Style des Pleiades de Gobineau. 239p. 1957. 23.95 (*0-8288-7498-0*) Fr & Eur.

— Text Production. Lyons, Therese, tr. LC 82-25509. 336p. 1985. text ed. 34.50 (*0-231-05334-7*) Col U Pr.

Riffe, Andrew L., IV, jt. ed. see Reddy, Anne W.

Riffe, Daniel, jt. auth. see Sneed, Don.

Riffel, Herman. Dream Interpretation. 182p. (Orig.). 1993. pap. 8.99 (*1-56043-122-9*) Destiny Image.

— Dreams: Wisdom Within. 144p. 1990. text ed. 14.99 (*1-56043-007-9*) Destiny Image.

Riffel, Paul. Reading Maps. LC 79-13628. (Illus.). (YA). (gr. 7 up). 1973. spiral bd. 8.95 (*0-8331-1300-3*) Hubbard Sci.

Riffenburgh, Bean. NFL: Official History of Pro Football. 1990. 24.99 (*0-517-02891-3*) Random Hse Value.

Riffenburgh, Beau. The Myth of the Explorer. LC 94-9382. (Illus.). 240p. 1994. pap. 11.95 (*0-19-285299-X*) OUP.

— The Myth of the Explorer. (Polar Research Ser.). (Illus.). 224p. 1993. text ed. 59.00 (*1-85293-260-0*, Pub. by Pinter Pubs UK) St Martin.

Riffer, Jeffey K. Sports & Recreational Injuries. 623p. 1985. text ed. 95.00 (*0-07-052828-4*) Shepards-McGraw.

Riffert, George R. Great Pyramid Proof of God. 1932. 8.00 (*0-685-08804-9*) Destiny.

Riffig, T. T. A Sharper Edge. 154p. (Orig.). 1989. pap. text ed. 5.95 (*0-9621755-0-1*) Metahomin Pub.

***Riffle, Dave.** The Greatest Hammerless Repeating Shotgun Ever Built: The Model 12 - 1912-1964. (Illus.). 300p. 1994. write for info. (*0-9644281-0-5*) D Riffles.

Riffle, Judy S., jt. ed. see Salamone, J. C.

Rifi, M. R. & Covitz, Frank H. Introduction to Organic Electrochemistry. LC 72-97484. (Techniques & Applications in Organic Synthesis Ser.). 429p. reprint ed. pap. 122.30 (*0-685-15825-X*, 2027812) Bks Demand.

Rifkah, Eve. Quilted Songs. LC 87-63214. 12p. (Orig.). 1987. pap. text ed. 3.00 (*0-938885-01-4*) Shu Pub.

Rifken, Blume J. Silhouettes in America, 1790-1840: A Collectors' Guide. (Illus.). 128p. (Orig.). 1987. pap. 12.95 (*0-943741-00-9*) Paradigm VT.

Rifkin. Biology & Physiology of the Osteoclast. 1992. 173.00 (*0-8493-5437-4*, QP88) CRC Pr.

***Rifkin, Adrian.** Street Noises: Studies in Parisian Pleasure, 1900-1940. (Illus.). 272p. 1995. text ed. 18.95 (*0-7190-4589-4*, Pub. by Manchester Univ Pr UK) St Martin.

Rifkin, Benjamin. Semiotics of Narration in Film & Prose Fiction: Case Studies of Scarecrow & My Friend Ivan Lapshin. LC 92-25032. (Russian & East European Studies in Aesthetics & the Philosophy of Culture: Vol. 2). (Illus.). 250p. (C). 1994. text ed. 59.95 (*0-8204-1995-8*) P Lang Pubs.

Rifkin, Benjamin, tr. see Amman, Jost & Sachs, Hans.

Rifkin, Danial B. & Klagsbrun, Michael, eds. Angiogenesis: Mechanisms & Pathobiology. (Current Communications in Molecular Biology Ser.). (Illus.). 200p. 1987. pap. 30.00 (*0-87969-300-2*) Cold Spring Harbor.

Rifkin, Don. A Brief Period of Time & Two Eggs Scrambled Soft. 1989. pap. 4.75 (*0-8222-0151-8*) Dramatists Play.

— The Delusion of Angels. 1987. pap. 4.75 (*0-8222-0298-0*) Dramatists Play.

Rifkin, Ellen, ed. see Morgan, Fiona.

Rifkin, Harold & Raskin, Philip, eds. Diabetes Mellitus, Vol. 5. (Illus.). 391p. 1980. text ed. 22.95 (*0-87619-747-0*) P-H.

Rifkin, Jeremy. Beyond Beef: The Rise & Fall of the Cattle Culture. LC 91-32285. 368p. 1993. pap. 12.95 (*0-452-26952-0*, Plume) NAL-Dutton.

— Biosphere Politics: A New Consciousness for a New Century. 1991. 20.00 (*0-517-57746-1*, Crown) Crown Pub Group.

— Declaration of a Heretic. 150p. 1985. pap. 8.95 (*0-7102-0710-7*, RKP) Routledge.

— The End of Work: The Decline of the Global Labor Force & the Dawn of the Post-Market Era. LC 94-12394. 352p. 1994. 24.95 (*0-87477-779-8*, J P T-Putnam) Putnam Pub Group.

— Time Wars: The Primary Conflict in Human History. 1989. pap. 11.00 (*0-671-67158-8*, Touchstone Bks) S&S Trade.

Rifkin, Jeremy & Rossen, John, eds. How to Commit Revolution American Style: Bicentennial Declaration. LC 72-86167. 209p. 1973. 7.95 (*0-8184-0041-2*) Carol Pub Group.

Rifkin, Joshua, et al. The New Grove North European Baroque Masters. (New Grove Composer Biography Ser.). (Illus.). 1985. pap. 9.95 (*0-393-30099-4*) Norton.

Rifkin, Lori, jt. auth. see Obermeyer, Vera.

Rifkin, Mark. The Nez Perce Indians. LC 93-12221. (Junior Library of American Indians). (Illus.). 80p. (J). (gr. 3-7). 1993. lib. bdg. 14.95 (*0-7910-1668-4*, Am Art Analog); pap. 6.95 (*0-7910-1992-6*, Am Art Analog) Chelsea Hse.

Rifkin, Mark, jt. auth. see Strasser, Todd.

Rifkin, Matthew D. Diagnostic Imaging of the Lower Genitourinary Tract. (Illus.). 352p. 1985. text ed. 108.50 (*0-88167-045-6*) Raven.

— Ultrasound of the Prostate. (Illus.). 304p. 1988. text ed. 110.50 (*0-88167-434-6*) Raven.

Rifkin, Matthew D. & Waldroup, Larry. Pocket Atlas of Normal Ultrasound Anatomy. (Illus.). 72p. 1985. pap. text ed. 15.95 (*0-88167-163-0*) Raven.

Rifkin, Matthew D., jt. auth. see Resnick, Martin I.

Rifkin, Morris W., jt. auth. see Zoubek, Charles E.

Rifkin, Ned. Made in Philadelphia VI. (Illus.). 38p. 1984. pap. 7.00 (*0-88454-035-9*) U of Pa Contemp Art.

Rifkin, Paul. The God Letters. 240p. (Orig.). 1986. mass mkt. 5.95 (*0-446-38319-8*) Warner Bks.

Rifkin, Shepard. King Fisher's Road. 160p. 1979. pap. 1.50 (*0-449-14236-1*, GM) Fawcett.

— King Fisher's Road. large type ed. (Western Ser.). 1976. 15.95 (*0-85456-497-7*) Ulverscroft.

Rifkind, ed. Drug Treatment of Hyperlipidemia. (Fundamental & Clinical Cardiology Ser.: Vol. 1). 280p. 1991. 99.75 (*0-8247-8512-6*) Dekker.

***Rifkind, Basil M., ed.** Lowering Cholesterol in High-Risk Individuals & Populations. LC 94-45081. (Fundamental & Clinical Cardiology Ser.: Vol. 24). 1995. write for info. (*0-8247-9412-5*) Dekker.

Rifkind, Carole. Field Guide to American Architecture. (Illus.). 1980. pap. 24.95 (*0-452-26269-0*, Z5224, Plume) NAL-Dutton.

Rifkind, Carole, ed. Tourism & Communities: Process, Problems, & Solutions, Vol. 1. (Livability Digest Ser.: No. 1). 46p. 1981. pap. 6.00 (*0-317-44277-5*) Partners Livable.

Rifkind Center Staff. Bibliography of German Expressionism: Catalog of the Library of the Robert Gore Rifkind Center for German Expressionist Studies at the Los Angeles County Museum of Art. 500p. (C). 1990. lib. bdg. 165.00 (*0-8161-0494-8*) G K Hall.

Rifkind, Lawrence, jt. auth. see Harper, Loretta.

Rifkind, Marion, tr. see Anderson, Rickie W.

Rifkind, R. A., ed. The Pharmacology of Cell Differentiation: Proceedings of the Esteve Foundation Symposium V, Son Vida, Mallorca, 12-15 October, 1992. LC 93-3366. (International Congress Ser.: Vol. 1016). 316p. 1993. 140.00 (*0-444-89680-5*, Excerpta Medica) Elsevier.

Rifkind, Simon H., et al. The Basic Equities of the Palestine Problem. Davis, Moshe, ed. LC 77-70736. (America & the Holy Land Ser.). 1977. reprint ed. lib. bdg. 19.95 (*0-405-10279-8*) Ayer.

Rifking, Lawrence & Harper, Loretta F. Sexual Harassment in the Workplace: Men & Women in Labor. 224p. (C). 1993. per. 22.95 (*0-8403-8650-8*) Kendall-Hunt.

Riforgiato, Leonard R. Missionary of Moderation: Henry Melchior Muhlenberg & the Lutheran Church in English America. LC 78-75203. 256p. 1970. 36.50 (*0-8387-2379-9*) Bucknell U Pr.

Riga, Alan T. & Neag, Micheal, eds. Materials Characterization by Thermomechanical Analysis, STP 1136. (Special Technical Publication Ser.). (Illus.). 200p. 1991. text ed. 61.00 (*0-8031-1434-6*, 04-011360-50) ASTM.

Riga, Carla L., jt. auth. see Federici, Carla.

Rigal, Jean, ed. Minor Surgical Procedures in Remote Areas. (Medecins Sans Frontieres - Hatier Ser.). 172p. 1989. vinyl bd. 23.95 (*2-218-02163-3*) Hatier Pub.

— Tecnicas Medico-Quirurgicas en Situaciones de Aislamiento. (Medecins Sand Frontieres - Hatier Ser.). 172p. (SPA.). 1989. vinyl bd. 23.95 (*2-218-02165-X*) Hatier Pub.

— Tecnicas Quirurgicas de Base. (Medesins Sans Frontieres - Hatier Ser.). 207p. (SPA.). 1992. vinyl bd. 23.95 (*2-218-02346-6*) Hatier Pub.

***Rigall, Mary O. & Morris, David J., Jr.** Guidelines for Making Presentations. LC 94-21103. 1994. 7.00 (*0-87757-250-X*) Am Mktg.

Rigamer, Anna, ed. Airport Planning, Operation, & Management (TRR 1423) (Transportation Research Record Ser.). (Illus.). 68p. 1994. pap. text ed. 22.00 (*0-309-05570-9*) Natl Res Coun.

— Field Performance of Subsurface Drainage (TRR 1425) (Transportation Research Record Ser.). (Illus.). 72p. 1994. pap. text ed. 24.00 (*0-309-05572-5*) Natl Res Coun.

— Lightweight Artificial & Waste Materials for Embankments over Soft Soils (TRR 1422) (Transportation Research Record Ser.). (Illus.). 80p. 1994. pap. text ed. 24.00 (*0-309-05569-5*) Natl Res Coun.

***Rigante, Elodia.** Italian Immigrant Cooking. LC 94-62213. 200p. 1995. 29.95 (*1-885440-02-2*) First Glance.

Riganti, R., jt. ed. see Bellomo, N.

Rigard, John M. Medieval Framlingham. 160p. (C). 1986. 30.00 (*0-85115-432-8*) Boydell & Brewer.

Rigas, Basil & Spiro, Howard M. Clinical Gastroenterology: Companion Handbook. 4th ed. (Illus.). 384p. 1995. pap. text ed. 27.50 (*0-07-003341-2*) Hlth Prof Div.

Rigas, Doganis, jt. auth. see Bergstrand, Simon.

Rigau, Jorge. Puerto Rico Nineteen Hundred: Turn-of-the-Century Architecture in the Hispanic Caribbean 1890-1930. LC 91-11264. (Illus.). 232p. 1992. 50.00 (*0-8478-1400-9*); pap. text ed. 35.00 (*0-8478-1430-0*) Rizzoli Intl.

Rigau, Jorge, jt. auth. see Stout, Nancy.

Rigaud, M. A., ed. Advances in Refractories for the Metallurgical Industries: Proceedings of the International Symposium, Winnipeg, August 1987. (CIM Ser.: No. 4). (Illus.). 327p. 1988. Delegates. 26.25 (*0-08-035881-0*, Pergamon Pr); 45.00 (*0-08-035880-2*, Pergamon Pr) Elsevier.

Rigaud, Milo. Secrets of Voodoo. Cross, Robert B., tr. (Illus.). 256p. 1985. reprint ed. pap. 12.95 (*0-87286-171-6*) City Lights.

— Ve-Ve Diagrammes Rituels du Voudou. 583p. (ENG, FRE & SPA.). 1992. pap. 59.95 (*0-8288-0000-6*, S10043) Fr & Eur.

Rigaud, Stephen J. Correspondence of Scientific Men of the Seventeenth Century: Including Letters of Barrow, Flamsteed, Wallis, & Newton, Printed from the Originals in the Collection of the Right Honourable the Earl of Macclesfield, 2 vols., Set. 1965. reprint ed. 180.70 (*0-685-66511-9*, 05101097, Pub. by Georg Olms GW) Lubrecht & Cramer.

Rigaudias-Weiss, Hilde. Las Enquetes Ouvrieres En France Entre 1830 et 1848: The Working Class Surveys in France Between 1830 & 1848. LC 74-25777. (European Sociology Ser.). 270p. 1975. reprint ed. 26.95 (*0-405-06531-0*) Ayer.

Rigaudis, Marc. Ito-san. Kirkup, James, tr. 135p. 1991. 29.00 (*0-7206-0818-X*, Pub. by P Owen Ltd UK) Dufour.

Rigauer, Bero. Sport & Work. Guttmann, Allen, ed. LC 81-793. 110p. (ENG.). 1981. text ed. 31.50 (*0-231-05200-6*) Col U Pr.

Rigault, Andre & Charbonneau, Rene, eds. Proceedings of the Seventh International Congress of the Phonetic Sciences, Montreal, 22-28 August 1971-Actes Du Septieme Congres International Des Sciences Phonetiques. (Janua Linguarum, Series Major: No. 57). (Illus.). 1972. 346.15 (*90-279-2311-6*) Mouton.

Rigaut de Barbezieux. Le Canzoni: Testi E Commento a Cura Di Mauro Braccini. LC 80-2188. reprint ed. 26.00 (*0-404-19017-0*) AMS Pr.

— Liriche Di Rigaut De Berbezilh, a Cura Di Alberto Varvaro. LC 80-2187. reprint ed. 39.50 (*0-404-19018-9*) AMS Pr.

Rigaut, J. P., jt. ed. see Mary, J. Y.

***Rigbey, Liz.** Total Eclipse. Grose, Bill, ed. 480p. 1995. 22.00 (*0-671-79579-1*) PB.

Rigbey, Loz, comp. The Archers Quizbook. 128p. 1990. pap. 3.95 (*0-563-20709-4*, Pub. by BBC UK) Parkwest Pubns.

Rigby, Andrew. Initiation & Initiative: An Exploration into the Life & Ideas of Dimitrije Mitrinovic. 217p. 1984. text ed. 42.00 (*0-88033-056-2*) East Eur Quarterly.

— Living the Intifada. 240p. (C). 1991. text ed. 55.00 (*1-85649-039-4*, Pub. by Zed Books UK); pap. 19.95 (*1-85649-040-8*, Pub. by Zed Books UK) Humanities.

Rigby, Bev, jt. auth. see Rigby, Geoff.

Rigby, D. Sue & Hanson, Robert N. Production Typing Projects. 1980. text ed. 10.12 (*0-07-052836-5*) McGraw.

Rigby, D. Sue, jt. auth. see Hanson, Robert N.

Rigby, Dick, jt. auth. see Breen, Ann.

Rigby, Elizabeth. Letters from the Shores of the Baltic. LC 73-115533. (Russia Observed, Series I). 1970. reprint ed. 33.95 (*0-405-03023-1*) Ayer.

Rigby, Geoff & Rigby, Bev. Colour Your Garden with Australian Natives. (Illus.). 128p. 1993. 29.95 (*0-86417-492-6*, Pub. by Kangaroo Pr AT) Seven Hills Bk.

Rigby, Graeme, ed. see Heslop, Harold.

Rigby, Gwynneth, jt. ed. see Shattock, Michael.

Rigby, Ida K. An Alle Kunstler-War-Revolution-Weimar: German Expressionist Prints, Drawings, Posters & Periodicals from the Robert Gore Rifkind Foundation. LC 83-60977. (Illus.). 118p. 1987. pap. 18.75 (*0-916304-62-0*) SDSU Press.

Rigby, Ida K., intro. Inner Visions: German Prints from the Age of Expressionism. (Illus.). 150p. 1992. pap. 24.95 (*0-295-97190-8*) U of Wash Pr.

Rigby, J. Keith & Hamblin, W. K., eds. Recognition of Ancient Sedimentary Environments. LC 72-194231. (Society of Economic Paleontologists & Mineralogists, Special Publication Ser.: No. 16). 350p. reprint ed. pap. 99.80 (*0-317-27126-1*, 2024741) Bks Demand.

Rigby, J. Keith, Jr., jt. ed. see Fassett, James E.

Rigby, J. Keith, jt. auth. see Petersen, Morris.

Rigby, Jennifer A. Outdoor Science Education in Orange County, California: A Comprehensive Directory of Facilities & Programs. 35p. 1992. 7.95 (*1-881150-00-3*) Acorn Grp.

Rigby, John P., ed. Public Transport Planning in Shire Counties: An Evaluation of the Public Transport Plan As an Aid to Transport Policy Making. (C). 1980. 29.00 (*0-685-30297-0*, Pub. by Oxford Polytechnic UK) St Mut.

Rigby, Julie. Career Portraits: Sports. LC 94-15315. (J). 1994. 12.95 (*0-8442-4361-2*, VGM Career Bks) NTC Pub Grp.

Rigby, Malcolm. Meteorological Abstracts & Bibliography: Cumulative Geographic Index, Vol. 1-10 (1950-1959), 3 vols., Set. 412p. (Orig.). 1963. pap. 210.00 (*0-933876-93-9*) Am Meteorological.

— Meteorological & Geoastrophysical Abstracts: Cumulative Author Index, 1970-1975, Vols. 21-26. 647p. 1978. text ed. 205.00 (*0-933876-94-7*) Am Meteorological.

Rigby, Malcolm, ed. Meteorological Abstracts & Bibliography: Cumulative Index, Authors-A-K, Vol. 1-10 (1950-1959), 3 vols., Set. 839p. (Orig.). 1963. pap. write for info. (*0-933876-91-2*) Am Meteorological.

— Meteorological Abstracts & Bibliography: Cumulative Index, Authors-L-Z (1950-1959), 3 vols., Set. 1724p. (Orig.). 1963. pap. write for info. (*0-933876-92-0*) Am Meteorological.

Rigby, Mike, ed. see Borgia, Anthony.

Rigby, Peter. Cattle, Capitalism & Class: Ilparakuyo Maasai Transformations. (Illus.). 272p. (C). 1992. 39.95 (*0-87722-954-6*); pap. 18.95 (*1-56639-204-7*) Temple U Pr.

Rigby, Peter, jt. auth. see Norris, Mark.

Rigby, Peter W. Genetic Engineering, Vol. 5. (Serial Publication Ser.). 1986. text ed. 46.00 (*0-12-270305-7*) Acad Pr.

Rigby, Peter W., ed. Genetic Engineering, Vol. 6. (Serial Publication Ser.). 183p. 1988. pap. text ed. 46.00 (*0-12-270306-5*) Acad Pr.

— Genetic Engineering, Vol. 7. (Serial Publication Ser.). 127p. 1988. text ed. 46.00 (*0-12-270307-3*) Acad Pr.

Rigby, Rodney. Hello, This Is Your Penguin Speaking. LC 91-39501. (Illus.). 32p. (J). (ps-2). 1992. lib. bdg. 13.89 (*1-56282-232-2*) Hyprn Child.

— The Night the Moon Fell Asleep. LC 92-45928. (Illus.). 32p. (J). (ps-3). 1993. 13.95 (*1-56282-334-5*); lib. bdg. 13.89 (*1-56282-335-3*) Hyprn Child.

— There's a Building on Sixth Avenue. LC 91-23097. (Illus.). 32p. (J). (ps-3). 1992. lib. bdg. 13.89 (*1-56282-156-3*) Hyprn Child.

Rigby, S. H. Engels & the Formation of Marxism: History, Dialectics & Revolution. 320p. 1992. text ed. 69.95 (*0-7190-3530-9*, Pub. by Manchester Univ Pr UK) St Martin.

— English Society in the Later Middle Ages: Class, Status, & Gender. LC 94-43981. 1995. write for info. (*0-312-12544-5*) St Martin.

— Marxism & History: A Critical Introduction. 250p. 1987. text ed. 45.00 (*0-312-00921-6*) St Martin.

— Marxism & History: A Critical Introduction. LC 87-9723. 320p. 1990. text ed. 22.95 (*0-7190-2268-1*, Pub. by Manchester Univ Pr UK) St Martin.

Rigby, Stephen, tr. see Bessieres, Albert.

Rigby, Susan. Caves. LC 91-45082. (Our Planet Ser.). (Illus.). 32p. (J). (gr. 4-6). 1993. lib. bdg. 11.59 (*0-8167-2749-X*); pap. text ed. 3.95 (*0-8167-2750-3*) Troll Assocs.

Rigby, T. H. Changing Soviet System: Mono-Organisational Socialism from Its Origins to Gorbachev's Restructuring. 288p. 1990. 63.95 (*1-85278-304-4*, Pub. by E Elgar Pub UK) Ashgate Pub Co.

— Political Elites in the USSR: Central Leaders & Local Cadres from Lenin to Gorbachev. 320p. 1990. text ed. 64.95 (*1-85278-303-6*, Pub. by E Elgar Pub UK) Ashgate Pub Co.

Rigby, T. H., jt. ed. see Miller, John D.

Rigby, T. H., et al, eds. Authority, Power & Policy in the U. S. S. R. Essays Dedicated to Leonard Schapiro. 207p. 1985. pap. 10.95 (*0-312-06135-8*) St Martin.

Rigby, Thomas H. Lenin's Government: Sovnarkom, Nineteen Seventeen to Nineteen Twenty-Two. LC 78-18754. (Soviet & East European Studies). 336p. reprint ed. pap. 95.80 (*0-318-34663-X*, 2031718) Bks Demand.

Rigby, Valery, jt. auth. see Stead, I. M.

Rigby, William H. Computer Interfacing: A Practical Approach to Data Acquisition & Control. 256p. 1994. text ed. 59.00 (*0-13-288374-0*) P-H.

Rigden, B. & Henry, L., eds. Water Quality & Management for Recreation & Tourism: Proceedings of IAWPRC Conference, Brisbane, Australia, 10-15 July 1988. (Water Science & Technology Ser.: No. 21). (Illus.). 318p. 1989. pap. 115.00 (0-08-037383-6, Pergamon Pr) Elsevier.

Rigden, Diana W. & Waugh, Susan S. The Shape of This Century: Readings from the Disciplines. 738p. (C). 1990. pap. text ed. 15.00 (0-685-45686-2); pap. text ed. 4.50 (0-15-580841-9) HB Coll Pubs.

Rigden, John S. Physics & the Sound of Music. 2nd ed. LC 84-10401. 353p. 1985. Net. text ed. write for info. (0-471-87412-4) Wiley.

Rigden, John S., jt. ed. see Brown, Laurie M.

Rigdon, Charles. Palace of Mirrors. LC 86-46395. 288p. 1987. 17.95 (1-55611-025-1) D I Fine.

Rigdon, Elizabeth H. Never a Day Off: Surviving Single Parenthood. 60p. 1991. pap. 2.50 (0-8341-1376-7) Beacon Hill.

Rigdon, Susan M. The Culture Facade: Art, Science, & Politics in the Work of Oscar Lewis. LC 87-19063. (Illus.). 352p. 1988. 27.95 (0-252-01495-2) U of Ill Pr.

Rige, Hillary, ed. see United Feature Syndicate II Staff.

Rigelhof, R., jt. ed. see Herz, C.

Rigelhof, T. F. The Education of J. J. Pass: A Novel. 200p. (C). 1989. 69.00 (0-907839-02-9, Pub. by Brynmill Pr Ltd UK); pap. text ed. 35.00 (0-907839-03-7, Pub. by Brynmill Pr Ltd UK) St Mut.

— Je T'aime Cowboy. 1993. pap. 13.95 (0-86492-144-6, Pub. by Goose Ln Edits CN) InBook.

Rigell, Elizabeth W., jt. auth. see Rigell, Joseph S.

Rigell, Joseph S. & Rigell, Elizabeth W. Fired Again & Again, Praise the Lord! 550p. 1992. pap. write for info. (0-9632253-0-8) Afikomen.

***Rigelsford, Adrian, et al.** Are You Being Served? The Inside Story of Britain's Funniest - & Public Television's Favorite - Comedy Series. (Illus.). 240p. (Orig.). 1995. pap. 14.95 (0-912333-04-9) KQED.

Riger, Robert, ed. Man in Sport. (Illus.). 1967. pap. 3.50 (0-912298-10-3) Baltimore Mus.

Riger, Roger P. One Frog Can Make a Difference. 1994. pap. 8.00 (0-671-88065-9) PB.

Riger, Stephanie, jt. auth. see Gordon, Margaret T.

Rigg, A. G. Editing Medieval Texts: Papers Given at the Twelfth Annual Conference on Editorial Problems, University of Toronto, 5-6 November, 1976. LC 88-47820. (Conference on Editorial Problems Ser.: No. 12). 1987. 37.50 (0-404-63662-4) AMS Pr.

— A History of Anglo-Latin Literature, 1066-1422. 425p. (C). 1993. 95.00 (0-521-41594-2) Cambridge U Pr.

Rigg, A. G., ed. see Langland, William.

Rigg, Diana, comp. No Turn Unstoned: The Worst Ever Theatrical Reviews. LC 91-11430. (Illus.). 192p. 1991. reprint ed. pap. 13.95 (1-879505-03-7) Silman James Pr.

Rigg, J. A., jt. ed. see Bliss, Anne M.

Rigg, Jennifer. Pencarnan. LC 76-45573. 1977. 8.95 (0-672-52288-8, Bobbs) Macmillan.

Rigg, Jonathan. Southeast Asia. LC 94-20444. (Country Fact Files Ser.). (J). 1995. lib. bdg. write for info. (0-8114-2788-9) Raintree Steck-V.

Rigg, Lucy. Baby's Christmas. (Little Christmas Treasure Bks.). (J). 1990. 2.95 (0-8378-1883-4) Gibson.

— Little Christmas Treasure Books: Christmas Joys. (Illus.). (J). (gr. 2 up). 1989. 2.95 (0-8378-1870-2) Gibson.

— Wedding Memories. (Illus.). 64p. Date not set. 21.00 (0-614-01771-8) Gibson.

— Welcome Baby. (Illus.). 1992. 18.50 (0-8378-4154-2) Gibson.

— We're Having a Party. (Tiny Touch Bks.). (Illus.). 1994. 7.50 (0-8378-7624-9) Gibson.

Rigg, Pat & Enright, D. S., eds. Children & ESL: Integrating Perspectives. 171p. 1986. 12.50 (0-939791-24-2) Tchrs Eng Spkrs.

Rigg, Pat, et al. Approaches to Adult ESL Literacy Instruction. Crandall, Joann & Peyton, Joy K., eds. LC 93-30665. (Language in Education Ser.: Vol. 82). 98p. (Orig.). 1993. pap. text ed. 13.50 (0-937354-82-1) Delta Systems.

Rigg, Peter W. Words of Still Waters. 68p. 1980. pap. 4.00 (0-910477-00-0) LoonBooks.

Rigg, Robert B. Red China's Fighting Hordes: A Realistic Account of the Chinese Communist Army by a U. S. Army Officer. LC 70-138177. (Illus.). 378p. 1971. reprint ed. text ed. 35.00 (0-8371-5634-3, RIRC, Greenwood Pr) Greenwood.

Riggar, T. F. Stress Burnout: An Annotated Bibliography. LC 84-5447. 319p. 1985. 19.95 (0-8093-1186-0) S Ill U Pr.

Riggar, T. F. & Matkin, R. E. Handbook for Management of Human Service Agencies. LC 85-26120. 184p. (Orig.). 1986. pap. text ed. 15.95 (0-8093-1285-9) S Ill U Pr.

Riggar, T. F. & Wolf, Arnold W. Applied Rehabilitation Counseling. LC 86-21923. (Series on Rehabilitation). 424p. 1986. pap. 33.95 (0-8261-5370-4) Springer Pub.

Riggar, T. F., jt. auth. see Crimando, William.

Riggar, T. F., jt. auth. see Matkin, Ralph E.

Riggenbach, Heidi & Samuda, Virginia. Grammar Dimensions: Form, Meaning, & Use, Bk. 2. 1993. pap. 20.95 (0-8384-3969-1) Heinle & Heinle.

— Grammar Dimensions: Form, Meaning, & Use, Bk. 2. 1993. teacher ed, pap. 7.95 (0-8384-4128-9) Heinle & Heinle.

Rigger, T. F., jt. auth. see Crimando, William.

***Riggers, Maxine.** Fabulous Friends. (Illus.). 126p. (J). (ps-2). 1994. teacher ed, pap. 12.95 (0-614-01620-7, MM 1986) Evan-Moor Corp.

— Whimsical Wishes. (Illus.). 126p. (J). (ps-2). 1994. teacher ed, pap. 12.95 (1-878279-64-5, MM 1985) Evan-Moor Corp.

Riggin, Judith M. John Wayne: A Bio-Bibliography. LC 91-35218. (Popular Culture Bio-Bibliographies Ser.). 160p. 1992. text ed. 39.95 (0-313-22308-4, RJW/, Greenwood Pr) Greenwood.

***Riggin Waugh, Debra.** Ex-Lover Weird Shit: A Collection of Short Fiction, Poetry, & Cartoons by Lesbians & Gay Men. 152p. 1994. pap. 10.95 (0-9642803-3-7) TOOTS.

Riggins & Harold, Stephen, eds. Beyond Goffman: Studies on Communication, Institution, & Social Interaction. (Approaches to Semiotics Ser.: No. 96). viii, 456p. (C). 1990. lib. bdg. 136.95 (3-11-012208-1) Mouton.

Riggins, J. H. Lest We Forget, or Character Gems Gleaned from South Arkansas. 224p. 1978. reprint ed. 20.00 (0-89308-072-1) Southern Hist Pr.

Riggins, John & Winter, Jack. Gameplan: The Language & Strategy of Pro Football. rev. ed. Halsey, Alexandra, ed. LC 84-40402. (Illus.). 240p. 1984. reprint ed. pap. 12.95 (0-915643-08-1) Santa Barb Pr.

Riggins, Robert E., et al, eds. Watershed Planning & Analysis in Action. 596p. 1990. pap. text ed. 50.00 (0-87262-767-5) Am Soc Civil Eng.

Riggins, Stephen H., ed. Ethnic Minority Media: An International Perspective. (Communication & Human Values Ser.: Vol. 10). (Illus.). 304p. (C). 1992. 49.95 (0-8039-4723-2); pap. 24.00 (0-8039-4724-0) Sage.

— The Socialness of Things: Essays on the Socio-Semiotics of Objects. (Approaches to Semiotics Ser.: No. 115). 490p. (C). 1994. lib. bdg. 175.40 (3-11-014133-7, 226-94) Mouton.

Riggins, William, tr. see Steiner, Rudolf.

Riggio. Introduction to Industrial-Organizational Psychology. (C). 1990. text ed. 64.50 (0-673-38188-9) HarpCollege.

Riggio, Anita. Beware the Brindlebeast. LC 93-70875. (Illus.). 32p. (J). (ps-1). 1994. 14.95 (1-56397-133-X) Boyds Mills Pr.

— A Moon in My Teacup. (Illus.). 32p. (J). (ps-3). 1993. lib. bdg. 14.95 (1-56397-008-2) Boyds Mills Pr.

Riggio, John J., jt. auth. see Dorfman, Mark H.

Riggio, Milla C. The Play of Wisdom: Its Texts & Contexts. LC 86-47840. (Studies in the Middle Ages: No. 14). 32.50 (0-404-61444-2) AMS Pr.

Riggio, Milla Cozart, ed. The Wisdom Symposium: Papers from the Trinity College Medieval Festival. LC 85-48070. (Studies in the Middle Ages: No. 11). (Illus.). 1986. 32.50 (0-404-61441-8) AMS Pr.

***Riggio, Ronald E.** Introduction to Industrial-Organization Psychology. 2nd ed. LC 95-10149. 1995. write for info. (0-673-46908-5) HarpCollege.

Riggio, Thomas P., ed. see Dreiser, Theodore.

Riggio, Thomas P., ed. see Eastman, Yvette.

Riggle, H. M. Beyond the Tomb. 288p. 5.00 (0-686-29100-X) Faith Pub Hse.

— Christian Baptism, Feet Washing & the Lord's Supper. 264p. 5.00 (0-686-29105-0) Faith Pub Hse.

— The Christian Church: Its Rise & Progress. 488p. 6.00 (0-686-29144-1) Faith Pub Hse.

— Jesus Is Coming Again. 111p. pap. 1.50 (0-686-29123-9) Faith Pub Hse.

— The Kingdom of God & the One Thousand Years Reign. 160p. pap. 2.00 (0-686-29153-0) Faith Pub Hse.

— The Sabbath & the Lord's Day. 160p. pap. 1.50 (0-686-29165-4) Faith Pub Hse.

— The Two Works of Grace. 56p. pap. 0.40 (0-686-29168-9); pap. 1.00 (0-686-29169-7) Faith Pub Hse.

Riggle, H. M., jt. comp. see Speck, S. L.

Riggle, H. M., jt. auth. see Speck, Von S.

Riggle, H. M., jt. auth. see Warner, D. S.

Riggle, Judith, jt. auth. see Barstow, Barbara.

Riggs. A Low-Budget Program for Multi-Ethnic Gifted Students. 1989. pap. 9.99 (0-89824-133-2) Trillium Pr.

Riggs, jt. ed. see Zimmie.

Riggs, A. R. & Velk, Tom, eds. Canadian-American Free Trade (The Sequel) Historical, Political & Economic Dimensions. 113p. 1989. pap. text ed. 18.00 (0-88645-073-X, Pub. by Inst Res Pub CN) Ashgate Pub Co.

***Riggs, Angela.** Voices of the Prairie. (Orig.). Date not set. pap. 12.00 (0-9634190-0-5) Cottonwood OR.

Riggs, Ann, jt. ed. see Mott, Sarah.

***Riggs, Anne & Farmer, Bev.** Current Trends in Biology. Olejnik, Irena, ed. 128p. (C). 1994. 150.00x (0-7478-1580-1, Pub. by S Thornes Pubs UK) St Mut.

Riggs, Anne, jt. auth. see Gibb, Heather.

Riggs, B. Lawrence & Melton, L. Joseph, III, eds. Osteoporosis: Etiology, Diagnosis & Management. (Illus.). 520p. 1988. text ed. 121.50 (0-88167-350-1) Raven.

— Osteoporosis: Etiology, Diagnosis & Management. 2nd ed. LC 95-7020. 1995. write for info. (0-7817-0275-5) Raven.

Riggs-Bergesen, Catherine. Candle Therapy. (Illus.). 153p. (Orig.). 1992. pap. 16.95 (0-9640440-1-3) Other Worldly.

***Riggs, Bob.** Make Room for Maki. 150p. (Orig.). (J). (gr. 6-9). 1995. pap. 5.95 (1-886747-02-4) Ward Hill Pr.

Riggs, Brett H., jt. ed. see Duggan, Betty J.

Riggs, C. E., Sr. One, Two or Three??? LC 89-60398. (Illus.). 320p. (Orig.). 1989. pap. 8.95 (0-938991-39-6) Colonial Pr AL.

Riggs, Charles H. Criminal Asylum in Anglo-Saxon Law. LC 63-63598. (University of Florida Monographs: Social Sciences: No. 18). 67p. reprint ed. pap. 25.00 (0-7837-5001-3, 2044668) Bks Demand.

Riggs, Charles T., tr. see Kritoboulos.

Riggs, Charlie. Learning to Walk with God. 208p. (Orig.). 1990. pap. 7.95 (0-89066-082-4) World Wide Pubs.

***Riggs, Claude E.** Flood Brothers. 270p. 1993. pap. text ed. write for info. (0-9631958-0-8) C E Riggs.

***Riggs, D. Randy.** Flat-Out Racing: An Insider's Look at the World of Stock Car Racing. LC 94-34798. 1995. write for info. (1-56799-165-3, MetroBooks) M Friedman Pub Grp Inc.

Riggs, David. Ben Jonson: A Life. (Illus.). 416p. 1989. pap. 16.95 (0-674-06626-X) HUP.

— Shakespeare's Heroical Histories: Henry VI & Its Literary Tradition. LC 75-152701. 206p. 1994. reprint ed. pap. 58.80 (0-7837-4183-9, 2059033) Bks Demand.

Riggs, David F. East of Gettysburg: Custer vs. Stuart. rev. ed. LC 85-61163. (Illus.). 1985. pap. 5.95 (0-88342-208-5) Old Army.

— Seventh Virginia Infantry. (Virginia Regimental Histories Ser.). (Illus.). 107p. 1982. 19.95 (0-930919-02-5) H E Howard.

— Thirteenth Virginia Infantry. (Virginia Regimental Histories Ser.). (Illus.). 158p. 1988. 19.95 (0-930919-65-3) H E Howard.

Riggs, Donald E. Library Communication: The Language of Leadership. LC 91-34565. (Illus.). 188p. (C). 1992. pap. text ed. 30.00 (0-8389-0581-1) ALA.

Riggs, Donald E., ed. Library Leadership: Visualizing the Future. LC 81-2174. 168p. 1982. 31.95 (0-912700-64-5) Oryx Pr.

Riggs, Donald E., intro. Creativity, Innovation & Entrepreneurship in Libraries. LC 89-33071. (Journal of Library Administration: Vol. 10, Nos. 2-3). (Illus.). 233p. 1989. text ed. 39.95 (0-86656-940-5) Haworth Pr.

Riggs, Donald E. & Sabine, Gordon A., eds. Libraries in the Nineties: What the Leaders Expect. (Illus.). 224p. 1988. pap. 27.50 (0-89774-532-9) Oryx Pr.

Riggs, Donald E. & Tarin, Patricia A. Cultural Diversity in Libraries. 200p. 1993. 39.95 (1-55570-139-6) Neal-Schuman.

Riggs, Donald E., jt. ed. see Aluri, Rao.

Riggs, Doug. Keelhauled. 1991. 19.95 (0-915160-85-4) Seven Seas.

Riggs, E. H. & Riggs, H. E. Hynes: Our Pioneer Ancestors, being a Record of Available Information as to the Hynes, Chenault, Dunn, McKee, Anderson, Talylor, Finley, Letcher & Houston Families in the Direct Line of Ancestry of Samuel B. & Ellen M. Anderson Hynes. (Illus.). 207p. 1991. reprint ed. lib. bdg. 42.00 (0-8328-1921-2); reprint ed. pap. 32.00 (0-8328-1922-0) Higginson Bk Co.

Riggs, Fred W. Frontiers of Development Administration: American Society for Public Administration. LC 70-134010. (Comparative Administration Group Ser.). 647p. reprint ed. pap. 180.00 (0-317-42136-0, 2026214) Bks Demand.

Riggs, H. C. Streamflow Characteristics: Developments in Water Science, No. 22. 250p. 1985. 79.50 (0-444-42480-6) Elsevier.

Riggs, H. C., jt. ed. see Wolman, M. G.

Riggs, H. E. Riggs: Our Pioneer Ancestors, Being a Record of Available Information As to the Riggs, Baldridge, Agnew, Earle, Kirkpatrick, Vreeland & Allied Families in the Ancestry of Samuel Agnew Riggs & Catherine Doane Earle Riggs. (Illus.). 230p. 1993. reprint ed. lib. bdg. 47.00 (0-8328-3736-9); reprint ed. pap. 37.00 (0-8328-3737-7) Higginson Bk Co.

Riggs, H. E., jt. auth. see Riggs, E. H.

Riggs, Henry E. Financial & Cost Analysis for Engineering & Technology Management. LC 93-42806. (Series in Engineering & Technology Management). 1994. text ed. 64.95 (0-471-57415-5) Wiley.

— Managing High Technology Companies. 2nd ed. 1991. text ed. write for info. (0-442-00813-9) Van Nos Reinhold.

Riggs, J. B. Riggs Family of Maryland: A Genealogical & Historical Record Including Several of the Families in England. (Illus.). 534p. 1993. reprint ed. lib. bdg. 91.00 (0-8328-3734-2); reprint ed. pap. 81.00 (0-8328-3735-0) Higginson Bk Co.

***Riggs, J. Rosemary.** Materials & Components of Interior Architecture. 4th ed. LC 95-7025. 1995. pap. text ed. 42.00 (0-13-186842-X) P-H.

— Materials & Components of Interior Design. 3rd ed. 224p. 1992. pap. text ed. 52.00 (0-13-571324-2) P-H.

Riggs, James. Production Systems: Planning, Analysis, & Control. 4th ed. (Illus.). 745p. (C). 1992. reprint ed. text ed. 50.95x (0-88133-658-0) Waveland Pr.

Riggs, James B. An Introduction to Numerical Methods for Chemical Engineers. 2nd ed. (Illus.). 472p. (C). 1994. text ed. 65.00 (0-89672-334-8) Tex Tech Univ Pr.

Riggs, James L. Essentials of Engineering Economics. (Industrial Engineering & Management Science Ser.). (Illus.). 528p. 1982. text ed. write for info. (0-07-052864-0) McGraw.

— Productive Supervision. (Illus.). 432p. (C). 1985. pap. text ed. write for info. (0-13-725151-3) P-H.

Riggs, James L. & Felix, Glenn H. Productivity by Objectives. (Illus.). 272p. (C). 1983. 33.95 (0-13-725374-5, Busn) P-H.

Riggs, James L. & West, Thomas. Engineering Economics. 3rd ed. 1986. text ed. write for info. (0-07-052873-X) McGraw.

— Essentials of Engineering Economics. 2nd ed. 1986. text ed. write for info. (0-07-052872-1) McGraw.

Riggs, James L., et al. Industrial Organization & Management. 6th ed. (Illus.). 1979. text ed. write for info. (0-07-052854-3); write for info. (0-07-052855-1) McGraw.

Riggs, Jennifer. Under the Sea Activity Book. (J). (ps-3). 1993. pap. 1.95 (0-590-46297-0) Scholastic Inc.

***Riggs, Jennifer, tr.** Paintings. LC 94-49433. (First Discovery Art Bks.). (Illus.). (ENG & FRE.). (J). 1995. 11.95 (0-590-55201-5, Cartwheel) Scholastic Inc.

— Portraits. LC 94-49121. (A First Discovery Art Book). (Illus.). (ENG & FRE.). (J). 1995. 11.95 (0-590-55200-7, Cartwheel) Scholastic Inc.

Riggs, John. A Dragon Lives Forever. large type ed. LC 92-40988. (Cloak & Dagger Ser.). 350p. 1993. reprint ed. lib. bdg. 19.95 (1-56054-605-0) Thorndike Pr.

Riggs, John B. Guide to Manuscripts in the Eleutharian Mills Historical Library, Supplement Containing Acessions for Years 1966 through 1975. 293p. 1978. 15.00 (0-914650-15-7) Hagley Museum.

Riggs, John H. Respiratory Facts. LC 88-2057. (Illus.). 327p. (C). 1988. text ed. 18.95 (0-8036-7333-7) Davis Co.

***Riggs, John R.** Cold Hearts & Gentle People. LC 94-25441. 1994. 17.95 (1-56980-021-9) Barricade Bks.

— Cold Hearts & Gentle People. large type ed. 1995. 19.95 (0-7862-0317-X) Thorndike Pr.

— Dead Letter. LC 91-28339. 1992. 15.95 (0-942637-40-2) Barricade Bks.

— Dead Letter. 208p. 1994. pap. 4.50 (0-515-11280-1) Jove Pubns.

— A Dragon Lives Forever. LC 92-17748. (Garth Ryland Mystery Ser.). 1992. pap. 17.95 (0-942637-78-X) Barricade Bks.

— A Dragon Lives Forever. 224p. 1994. reprint ed. pap. text ed. 4.50 (0-425-14301-5, Prime Crime) Berkley Pub.

— The Last Laugh. 192p. 1993. pap. 3.99 (0-515-11134-1) Jove Pubns.

— The Last Laugh. large type ed. LC 92-21006. 1992. 19.95 (0-7927-1394-X, Curley Lrg Print); pap. 17.95 (0-7927-1393-1, Curley Lrg Print) Chivers N Amer.

— The Last Laugh. large type ed. LC 94-28268. 1995. write for info. (0-7862-0318-8) Thorndike Pr.

— Let Sleeping Dogs Lie. 1993. pap. 4.50 (0-515-11211-9) Jove Pubns.

— One Man's Poison. LC 90-35745. (Garth Ryland Mystery Ser.). 1991. 17.95 (0-942637-31-3, Dembner NY) Barricade Bks.

— One Man's Poison. large type ed. LC 92-11659. 315p. 1992. reprint ed. lib. bdg. 16.95 (1-56054-424-4) Thorndike Pr.

— One Man's Poison, No. 4. 208p. 1993. pap. 3.99 (0-515-11078-7) Jove Pubns.

— Wolf in Sheep's Clothing. 192p. (Orig.). 1993. pap. 3.99 (0-515-11016-7) Jove Pubns.

— Wolf in Sheep's Clothing: A Garth Ryland Mystery. LC 89-30968. 1989. 16.95 (0-942637-16-X, Dembner NY) Barricade Bks.

Riggs, Karen B. The Preppy Chef. rev. ed. LC 82-960707. (Illus.). 229p. 1982. reprint ed. 7.00 (0-686-39718-5) Riggs.

Riggs, Larry W. Moliere & Plurality: Decomposition on the Classicist Self. LC 89-31588. (Sociocriticism: Literature, Society & History Ser.: Vol. 1). 276p. (C). 1989. text ed. 44.95 (0-685-46923-9) P Lang Pubs.

— Resistance to Culture in Moliere, Laclos, Flaubert, & Camus: A Post-Modernist Approach. LC 92-32474. (Studies in French Literature: Vol. 13). 228p. 1992. text ed. 89.95 (0-7734-9159-7) E Mellen.

Riggs, Lawrence B., ed. Prevention & Treatment of Osteoporosis: An International Symposium Held During the XIIth European Congress of Rheumatology, Budapest, Hungary, 30 June-6 July 1991. LC 92-48734. 50p. 1993. 19.90 (0-88937-098-2); write for info. (3-456-82311-8) Hogrefe & Huber Pubs.

Riggs, Leland S., jt. auth. see Halpin, Daniel W.

Riggs, Lou E., jt. auth. see Epstein, Alan.

Riggs, Lynne E., tr. see Ashihara, Yoshinobu.

Riggs, Marcia Y. Awake, Arise, & Act: A Womanist Call for Black Liberation. LC 94-23378. 168p. (Orig.). 1994. pap. 12.95 (0-8298-1009-9) Pilgrim OH.

Riggs, Maribeth. Natural Child Care: A Complete Guide to Safe & Effective Herbal Remedies & Holistic Health Strategies for Infants & Children. (Illus.). 288p. 1988. pap. 13.95 (0-517-56831-4, Harmony) Crown Pub Group.

— The Scented Bath: A Gift of Luxury from Nature's Garden. LC 90-50444. (Illus.). 64p. 1991. 12.95 (0-670-83172-7, Viking Studio) Studio Bks.

— The Scented Woman: Create Your Own Signature Perfume from Essential Oils. (Illus.). 64p. 1992. 13.00 (0-670-84117-X, Viking Studio) Studio Bks.

— The Woman's Home Remedy Kit: Simple Recipes for Treating Common Health Conditions. LC 95-14004. 1995. pap. 12.00 (0-671-89806-X) PB.

Riggs, Olen L., Jr. & Locke, Carl E. Anodic Protection: Theory & Practice in the Prevention of Corrosion. LC 80-20412. 298p. 1981. 85.00 (0-306-40597-0, Plenum Pr) Plenum.

***Riggs, Paula D.** The Bachelor Party. (Intimate Moments Ser.). 1995. mass mkt. 3.75 (0-373-07656-8, 1-07656-1) Silhouette.

— Firebrand. (Silhouette Intimate Moments Ser.). 1993. mass mkt. 3.39 (0-373-07481-6, 5-07481-0) Silhouette.

— Her Secret, His Child. 1995. mass mkt. 3.75 (0-373-07667-3, 1-07667-8) Silhouette.

— Murdock's Family. (Desire Ser.). 1994. mass mkt. 2.99 (0-373-05898-5, 1-05898-1) Silhouette.

— Once upon a Wedding: Romantic Traditions. (Silhouette Intimate Moments Ser.). 1993. mass mkt. 3.50 (0-373-07524-3, 5-07524-7) Silhouette.

— Rough Passage. large type ed. (Desire Ser.). 1993. 17.95 (0-373-58839-9, Silhouette Lrg Print); pap. 16.95 (0-373-58931-X, Silhouette Lrg Print) Chivers N Amer.

Riggs, Peter J. Whys & Ways of Science: Introducing Philosophical & Sociological Theories of Science. (Orig.). (C). 1995. pap. text ed. 19.95 (0-522-84471-5) Intl Spec Bk.

Riggs, R. D. Print Reading for Machine Shop. (Illus.). 164p. 1981. spiral bd. 15.96 (0-8269-1870-0) Am Technical.

Riggs, Ralph M. The Spirit Himself. rev. ed. 210p. 1977. 5.50 (0-88243-590-6, 02-0590) Gospel Pub.

An Asterisk (*) at the beginning of an entry indicates that the title is appearing in BIP for the first time.

***Riggs, Robert.** Twelve Steps to a Never Union Company. 74p. (Orig.). 1995. pap. 19.95 (0-9645296-0-2) Fam Busn Bks.

Riggs, Robert D. & Wrather, J. Allen, eds. Biology & Management of the Soybean Cyst Nematode. LC 92-70943. (Illus.). 186p. (Orig.). 1992. pap. 26.00 (0-89054-125-6) Am Phytopathol Soc.

Riggs, Robert E. Politics in the United Nations: A Study of United States Influence in the General Assembly. LC 83-20164. vi, 207p. 1984. reprint ed. text ed. 55.00 (0-313-24298-4, RIP0, Greenwood Pr) Greenwood.

Riggs, Robert E. & Plano, Jack C. The United Nations: International Organization & World Politics. 399p. (C). 1988. pap. 32.95 (0-534-10804-0) Intl Thomson.

— The United Nations: International Organization & World Politics. 2nd ed. 364p. (C). 1994. pap. 33.95 (0-534-19704-3) Intl Thomson.

***Riggs, Robert O., et al.** Sexual Harassment in Higher Education: From Conflict to Community. Fife, Jonathan D., ed. & frwd. by. (ASHE-ERIC Higher Education Report Ser.: No. 2). 89p. (Orig.). 1993. pap. 18.00x (1-878380-23-0) GWU Schl E&HD.

Riggs, Rollin, jt. auth. see Riggs, Ryan.

Riggs, Ryan & Riggs, Rollin. Memphis! The Insider's Guide to the Coolest City on Earth. LC 91-50887. (Illus.). 160p. (Orig.). 1996. pap. 9.95 (0-914457-48-9) Mustang Pub.

Riggs, S. R., jt. ed. see Burnett, W. C.

Riggs, Seth. Singing for the Stars: A Complete Program for Training Your Voice. rev. ed. Carratello, John, ed. (Illus.). 150p. (Orig.). 1985. audio 45.00 (0-88284-472-5, 2535); audio 35.00 (0-88284-340-0, 2200) Alfred Pub.

— Singing for the Stars: A Complete Program for Training Your Voice. 5th rev. ed. Carratello, John, ed. (Illus.). 164p. (Orig.). 1992. cd-rom 40.00 (0-88284-528-4, 3379) Alfred Pub.

Riggs, Stephen R. A Dakota-English Dictionary. 2nd ed. 680p. 1992. reprint ed. pap. 24.95 (0-87351-282-0, Borealis Book) Minn Hist.

— Dakota Grammar, Texts & Ethnography. LC 74-7998. reprint ed. 49.50 (0-404-11891-7) AMS Pr.

— Mary & I: Forty Years with the Sioux. 412p. 1971. 22.50 (0-87928-019-0) Corner Hse.

— Tah-Koo Wah-Kan: Or, The Gospel among the Dakotas. LC 78-38460. (Religion in America, Ser. 2). 534p. 1972. reprint ed. 36.95 (0-405-04081-4) Ayer.

Riggs, Susan A. Twenty-First Virginia Infantry. (Virginia Regimental Histories Ser.). (Illus.). 105p. 1991. 19.95 (1-56190-013-3) H E Howard.

Riggs, Timothy A., jt. auth. see Grad, Bonnie L.

Riggs, Webster, Jr. Pediatric Chest Roentgenology: Recognizing the Abnormal. LC 76-19337. (Illus.). 320p. 1979. 31.80 (0-87527-144-8) Green.

Riggs, William F., jt. ed. see Malhotra, Deepak.

Righetti, A., jt. ed. see Donath, A.

***Righetti, Georgio.** Capillary Electrophoresis in Analytical Biotechnology. 400p. 1995. write for info. (0-8493-7825-7, 7825) CRC Pr.

Righetti, Maggie. Crocheting in Plain English. (Illus.). 258p. 1988. pap. 14.95 (0-312-01412-0) St Martin.

— Sweater Design in Plain English. (Illus.). 352p. (Orig.). 1990. pap. 14.95 (0-312-05164-6) St Martin.

Righetti, P. G. Immobilized pH Gradients: Theory & Methodology. (Laboratory Techniques in Biochemistry & Molecular Biology Ser.: Vol. 20). 408p. 1990. 215.75 (0-444-81301-2); pap. 48.00 (0-444-81315-2) Elsevier.

— Isoelectric Focusing: Theory, Methodology & Applications. (Laboratory Techniques in Biochemistry & Molecular Biology Ser.: Vol. 11). 386p. 1983. pap. 26.50 (0-444-80467-6, I-104-83) Elsevier.

Righi-Belkaoui, Ahmed. Handbook of Cost Accounting Theory & Techniques. LC 90-45142. 400p. 1991. text ed. 85.00 (0-89930-583-0, BTQ, Quorum Bks) Greenwood.

— The New Foundations of Management Accounting. LC 91-36667. 192p. 1992. text ed. 45.00 (0-89930-700-0, BKJ/, Quorum Bks) Greenwood.

Righi, Francois. Francois Righi. 186p. 1994. pap. 45.00 (2-908257-06-8, Pub. by F R A C FR) Dist Art Pubs.

Righini, jt. ed. see Soares.

Righini, G. C. Glasses for Optoelectronics, Vol. 1513. 1991. 85.00 (0-8194-0622-8) SPIE.

Righini, Giancarlo C., ed. Glasses for Optoelectronics. 337p. 1989. 77.00 (0-8194-0164-1, VOL. 1128) SPIE.

Right Associates Staff. Lessons Learned: Dispelling the Myths of Downsizing. 84p. (Orig.). 1992. pap. 25.00 (0-9628438-1-4) Right Assocs.

— Severance: A Comprehensive Survey of Canadian Severance Practices. 121p. (Orig.). pap. 250.00 (0-9628438-2-2) Right Assocs.

Right, Zack. Everyone's Guide to Opening Doors by Telephone. 2nd ed. 352p. 1981. 24.95 (0-9604554-0-X) Talmud Pr.

— Selling to Consumers: Complete Training Book. 350p. (Orig.). (C). 1984. pap. 18.00 (0-9604554-1-8) Talmud Pr.

Righter, Carroll. Astrology & You. 1989. pap. 5.00 (0-87980-422-X) Wilshire.

Righter, Evie. The Best of Mexico: A Cookbook. LC 92-19622. (Illus.). 96p. 1992. 14.95 (0-00-255148-9) Collins SF.

Righter, Evie, ed. The Best of France: A Cookbook. (Best of Ser.). 96p. 1992. 14.95 (0-00-255086-5) Collins SF.

— The Best of Italy: A Cookbook. (Best of Ser.). 96p. 1992. 14.95 (0-00-255085-7) Collins SF.

Righter, Evie & Saacs, Alicia. The Best of Spain: A Cookbook. LC 92-36631. (Illus.). 1993. 14.95 (0-00-255207-8) Collins SF.

Righter, Evie & Young, Grace. The Best of China: A Cookbook. LC 92-17592. 1992. 14.95 (0-00-255149-7) Collins SF.

— The Best of Thailand: A Cookbook. LC 92-37715. (Illus.). 1993. 14.95 (0-00-255206-X) Collins SF.

Righter, Robert, jt. auth. see Andrews, Robert.

Righter, Robert W. Crucible for Conservation: The Creation of Grand Teton National Park. LC 81-69792. 1982. pap. 9.95 (0-87081-132-0) Univ Pr Colo.

Righter, Robert W., ed. A Teton Country Anthology. (Illus.). 210p. 1990. pap. 12.50 (0-911797-73-4) R Rinehart.

Righter, Ron. Flex: The Total Offense. 64p. (Orig.). 1984. pap. 8.95 (0-932741-99-1) Championship Bks & Vid Prodns.

***Righter, Rosemary.** Utopia Lost: The United Nations & World Order. LC 94-33886. 421p. (C). 1995. 29.95x (0-87078-358-0) TCFP-PPP.

— Utopia Lost: The United Nations & World Order. LC 94-33886. 421p. 1995. pap. 12.00 (0-87078-359-9) TCFP-PPP.

Righter, William. The Myth of Theory. LC 93-30388. 256p. (C). 1994. 49.95 (0-521-44544-2) Cambridge U Pr.

***Rightmire, Craig T., et al, eds.** Coalbed Methane Resources of the United States. (AAPG Studies in Geology: No. 17). (Illus.). viii, 378p. 1984. pap. 33.00 (0-89181-023-4) AAPG.

Rightmire, G. P. The Evolution of "Homo Erectus" Comparative Anatomical Studies of an Extinct Human Species. (Illus.). 260p. (C). 1993. pap. 27.95 (0-521-44998-7) Cambridge U Pr.

Rightmire, G. Philip. The Evolution of "Homo Erectus" Comparative Anatomical Studies of an Extinct Human Species. (Illus.). 250p. (C). 1990. 54.95 (0-521-30880-1) Cambridge U Pr.

Rightmire, R. David. Sacraments & the Salvation Army: Pneumatological Foundations. LC 90-21325. (Studies in Evangelicalism: No. 10). 341p. 1990. 42.50 (0-8108-2396-9) Scarecrow.

Righton, Peter, jt. auth. see Richards, Margaret.

Rights, Douglas L. The American Indian in North Carolina. LC 57-9277. (Illus.). 298p. 1988. reprint ed. pap. 14.95 (0-89587-066-5) Blair.

***Rights, Lucille R.** A Portrait of St. Lucie County, Florida. LC 94-32009. (Illus.). 1994. write for info. (0-89865-917-5) Donning Co.

Rights, Mollie. Beastly Neighbors: All About Wild Things in the City or Why Earwigs Make Good Mothers. (Brown Paper School Bks.). (Illus.). 128p. (Orig.). (J). (gr. 3 up). 1981. pap. 9.95 (0-316-74577-4) Little.

Rights, Mollie, jt. auth. see George, Jerry.

Rights, R., jt. auth. see Ketzner, R.

***Rightson, Keith & Levine, David.** Poverty & Piety in an English Village: Terling, 1525-1700. rev. ed. (Illus.). 250p. 1995. pap. 24.00 (0-19-820321-7) OUP.

Rigling. Rigid-Flex Printed Wiring Design for Production & Readiness. (Electrical Engineering & Electronics Ser.: Vol. 47). 296p. 1988. 125.00 (0-8247-7707-7) Dekker.

Rigmaiden, Paul. God Loves Us All. (Illus.). 32p. (Orig.). (J). (gr. k-4). 1988. pap. 5.00 (0-9621598-0-8) DADA Pubns.

Rigmant, Vladimir, jt. auth. see Gordon, Yefim.

Rignall, John. Realist Fiction & the Problem of Vision. LC 91-47726. 240p. 1992. 69.95 (0-415-06383-3, A7973) Routledge.

***Rignell, Gosta.** The Peshitta to the Book of Job: Critically Investigated with Introduction, Translation, Commentary & Summary. 382p. (Orig.). 1994. pap. 68.50x (91-88034-24-0, Pub. by Almqv & Wiksell SW) Coronet Bks.

Rignell, L. G. The Old Testament in Syriac According to the Peshitta Version, Pt. II, Fasc. 1a: Job. LC 78-339247. xix, 55p. 1993. reprint ed. 40.00 (90-04-06342-0) E J Brill.

Rignell, R. How to Survive & Inland Revenue Investigation. 1990. 80.00 (0-7463-0614-8, Pub. by Northcote UK) St Mut.

Rigney, Ann. The Rhetoric of Historical Representation: Three Narrative Histories of The French Revolution. 240p. (C). 1991. 54.95 (0-521-38152-5) Cambridge U Pr.

Rigney, Ann & Fokkema, Douwe, eds. Cultural Participation: Trends since the Middle Ages. LC 93-1451. (Utrecht Publications in General & Comparative Literature: Vol. 31). ix, 261p. 1993. 47.00x (1-55619-430-7) Benjamins North Am.

Rigney, Barbara. The Voices of Toni Morrison. 192p. 1991. 39.50 (0-8142-0554-2) Ohio St U Pr.

— The Voices of Toni Morrison. 192p. (C). 1994. pap. 12.50 (0-8142-0555-0) Ohio St U Pr.

Rigney, Barbara H. Lilith's Daughters: Women & Religion in Contemporary Fiction. LC 81-70012. 136p. 1982. 22.50 (0-299-08960-6) U of Wis Pr.

— Madness & Sexual Politics in the Feminist Novel: Studies in Bronte, Woolf, Lessing & Atwood. LC 78-53291. 158p. 1978. 26.50 (0-299-07710-1) U of Wis Pr.

— Madness & Sexual Politics in the Feminist Novel: Studies in Bronte, Woolf, Lessing & Atwood. LC 78-53291. 158p. 1980. pap. 10.50 (0-299-07714-4) U of Wis Pr.

— Margaret Atwood: A Critical Inquiry. LC 87-1370. (Women Writers Ser.). (C). 1987. pap. 19.50 (0-389-20743-8, N8301) B&N Imports.

Rigney, David A., ed. see American Society for Metals Staff.

Rigney, David A., ed. see ASM Materials Science Seminar (1980: Pittsburgh, PA) Staff.

Rigney, Francis J. A Beginner's Book of Magic. (Illus.). (J). (gr. 6 up). 1963. 9.95 (0-8159-5103-5) Devin.

Rigney, Francis J., jt. auth. see Murray, William D.

***Rigney, H. M.** Australian Business Taxation. 430p. 1990. pap. 69.00 (0-409-30159-0, Austral) Butterworth Legal Pubs.

Rigo, J. M., jt. ed. see Rollin, A. L.

Rigo, J. M., et al, eds. Reflective Cracking in Pavements: State of the Art & Design Recommendations. LC 93-7255. (RILEM Proceedings Ser.: No. 20). 1993. write for info. (0-419-18220-9, E & FN Spon) Routledge Chapman & Hall.

Rigobello, L., jt. auth. see Andrioli, G.

Rigobon, Roberto, jt. ed. see Hausmann, Ricardo.

Rigole, M. & Desjardins, D. Panama Travel Guide. (Illus.). 176p. (Orig.). 1994. pap. 14.95 (2-921444-47-X, Pub. by Editions Ulysse CN) Ulysses Travel.

Rigoni, Francine, et al. Des Roses Blanches pour Danielle, & Autres Histoires. (Serie Rouge). (Illus.). 64p. (C). 1994. pap. 5.50 (0-521-44981-2) Cambridge U Pr.

Rigoni, Orlando. Drove Rider. 1992. 13.95 (0-7451-4543-4, Gunsmoke) Chivers N Amer.

— Six-Gun Song. (Gunsmoke Western Ser.). 1992. 13.95 (0-7451-4519-1, Gunsmoke) Chivers N Amer.

Rigopoulos, Antonio. Life & Teachings of Sai Baba of Shirdi. LC 91-40880. (SUNY Series in Religious Studies). 494p. (C). 1993. 59.50 (0-7914-1267-9); pap. 19.95 (0-7914-1268-7) State U NY Pr.

Rigor, Benjamin M., jt. ed. see Schurr, Avital.

Rigos, Sarah A., tr. see Averoff-Tossizza, Evangelos.

Rigsbee, David. Your Heart Will Fly Away. LC 92-80447. 80p. (Orig.). 1992. pap. 10.95 (0-912292-97-0) The Smith.

***Rigsbee, Ed.** The Art of Partnering. 192p. 1994. 24.95 (0-8403-9343-1) Kendall-Hunt.

Rigsby, David. The Hopper Light. (Poetry Ser.). 56p. (Orig.). (C). 1988. pap. 8.00 (0-934332-45-2) LEpervier Pr.

Rigsby, Gregory U. Alexander Crummell: Pioneer in Nineteenth-Century Pan-African Thought. LC 86-15034. (Contributions in Afro-American & African Studies: No. 101). 249p. 1987. text ed. 55.00 (0-313-25570-9, RYC/, Greenwood Pr) Greenwood.

Rigsby, Lee, jt. auth. see Pruett, James.

Rigsby, Leo C., jt. auth. see McDill, Edward L.

Rigsby, Olga, tr. see Rivera, Guadalupe & Colle, Marie-Pierre.

Rigter, H. & Crabbe, J. C. Alcohol Tolerance & Dependence. 456p. 1981. 134.50 (0-444-80212-6) Elsevier.

Rigutini, G. & Bulle, O. Italian-German, German-Italian Dictionary. (GER & ITA.). 1992. reprint ed. 195.00 (0-8288-9425-6) Fr & Eur.

***Rigutini, Giuseppe.** Italian-German--German-Italian Dictionary. (GER & ITA.). Date not set. 175.00 (0-7859-8868-8) Fr & Eur.

Rigzin, Tsepak. Tibetan-English Dictionary of Buddhist Terminology. (ENG & TIB.). 1987. 95.00 (0-8288-2319-7, F 140705) Fr & Eur.

Riha, J. Contribution to the Analysis of the Hydrological Cycle & of the Water Consumption Cycle. 112p. 1982. 49.00 (0-317-89618-0, Pub. by Collets UK) Pro-Am Music.

Riha, Susanne. Animals in Winter. (Illus.). 32p. (J). (gr. 1-5). 1989. lib. bdg. 19.95 (0-87614-355-9, Carolrhoda) Lerner Group.

Riha, Thomas. A Russian European: Paul Miliukov in Russian Politics. LC 68-27582. 391p. reprint ed. pap. 111.50 (0-317-55789-0, 2029312) Bks Demand.

Riha, Thomas, ed. Readings in Russian Civilization, 3 vols. rev. ed. Incl. Vol. 1. Russia Before Peter the Great, 900-1700. LC 69-14825. 1969. pap. text ed. 12.95 (0-226-71853-0); Vol. 2. Imperial Russia, 1700-1917. LC 69-14825. 1969. pap. text ed. 10.95 (0-226-71855-7); Vol. 3. Soviet Russia, 1917-Present. LC 69-14825. 1969. pap. text ed. 15.95 (0-226-71857-3); LC 69-14825. 1969. write for info. (0-318-56069-0) U Ch Pr.

Rihaldi, Enrico. Seed of the Divine Fruit. LC 86-91340. 1987. 18.95 (0-87212-200-X) Libra.

Rihani, Ameen F. Maker of Modern Arabia. LC 83-1485. (Illus.). xvii, 370p. 1983. reprint ed. text ed. 89.50 (0-313-23854-5, RIMA, Greenwood Pr) Greenwood.

Rihoit, Catherine. Les Abimes du Coeur. (FRE.). 1984. pap. 13.95 (0-7859-4206-8) Fr & Eur.

— Le Bal des Debutantes. (FRE.). 1982. pap. 11.95 (0-7859-4168-1) Fr & Eur.

— La Favorite. (FRE.). 1985. pap. 10.95 (0-7859-4231-9) Fr & Eur.

Rihova & Vetvicka. Immunological Disorders in Mice. 1990. 167.00 (0-8493-5635-0, QR188) CRC Pr.

Riikonen, Nancy. Industrial Wastewater Source Control: An Inspection Guide: The City of San Diego. LC 91-66930. 300p. (Orig.). 1991. pap. text ed. 45.00 (0-87762-855-6) Technomic.

Riiley, Judith Merkle. The Oracle Glass. LC 93-4665. 1994. 22.95 (0-670-85054-3, Penguin Bks) Viking Penguin.

Riis, Jacob. Making of an American, 1902. (Illus.). 443p. 1992. pap. 35.00 (0-87556-121-7) Saifer.

Riis, Jacob A. The Battle with the Slum. LC 69-16245. (Criminology, Law Enforcement, & Social Problems Ser.: No. 77). (Illus.). 1969. reprint ed. 14.00 (0-87585-077-4) Patterson Smith.

— The Battle with the Slum: A Ten Years War Rewritten. (Illus.). 1972. reprint ed. 14.00 (0-8290-0653-2) Irvington.

— Children of the Poor. LC 73-137186. (Poverty U. S. A.). 1971. reprint ed. 25.95 (0-405-03124-6) Ayer.

— Children of the Tenements. LC 75-122732. (Short Story Index Reprint Ser.). (Illus.). 1977. 23.95 (0-8369-3565-9) Ayer.

— Children of the Tenements. LC 70-104549. (Illus.). reprint ed. lib. bdg. 19.00 (0-8398-1757-6) Irvington.

— How the Other Half Lives. (Illus.). 1971. pap. 9.95 (0-486-22012-5) Dover.

— How the Other Half Lives. (Illus.). 304p. 1972. reprint ed. 24.00 (0-87928-033-6) Corner Hse.

— Nibsy's Christmas. LC 71-90590. (Short Story Index Reprint Ser.). 1977. 15.95 (0-8369-3073-8) Ayer.

— Out of Mulberry Street. LC 74-104550. 279p. reprint ed. lib. bdg. 29.75 (0-8398-1758-4) Irvington.

— Ten Years' War: An Account of the Battle with the Slum in New York. LC 70-103655. (Select Bibliographies Reprint Ser.). 1977. 29.95 (0-8369-5155-7) Ayer.

— Theodore Roosevelt, the Citizen. LC 71-101270. reprint ed. 34.50 (0-404-05335-1) AMS Pr.

— Theodore Roosevelt, the Citizen. (History - United States Ser.). 471p. 1992. reprint ed. lib. bdg. 99.00 (0-7812-6220-8) Rprt Serv.

— Theodore Roosevelt, the Citizen. LC 77-108531. 1970. reprint ed. 15.00 (0-403-00224-9) Scholarly.

Riis, Ole, jt. ed. see Pettersson, Thorleif.

Riis, P. M. Dynamic Biochemistry of Animal Production. (World Animal Science Ser.: Vol. 3A). 502p. 1983. 161.75 (0-444-42052-5, I-311-83) Elsevier.

Riis, S. M. Karl Marx: Master of Fraud. 1962. 5.95 (0-8315-0042-5) Speller.

Riis, Thomas, ed. see Aiken, George L. & Howard, George C.

Riis, Thomas L. Just Before Jazz: Black Musical Theater in New York, 1890 to 1915. (Illus.). 336p. 1989. 29.95 (0-87474-788-0) Smithsonian.

— Just Before Jazz: Black Musical Theater in New York, 1890 to 1915. LC 88-56098. (Illus.). 336p. 1994. pap. 15.95 (1-56098-501-1) Smithsonian.

— More Than Just Minstrel Shows: The Rise of Black Musical Theatre at the Turn of the Century. LC 92-72055. (I.S.A.M. Monographs: No. 33). (Illus.). 72p. (Orig.). (C). 1992. pap. 15.00 (0-914678-36-1) Inst Am Music.

Riiff, Ger. Long Lonely Highway: A 1950's Elvis Scrapbook. Schultheiss, Thomas, ed. (Rock & Roll Remembrances Ser.). (Illus.). 200p. 1988. reprint ed. 28.50 (0-87650-237-0) Popular Culture.

Rijff, Ger J. Elvis Fire in the Sun. 1991. 18.95 (1-56182-036-9) Atomium Bks.

Rijff, Ger J. & Van Gestel, Jan. Elvis, the Cool King. (Illus.). 104p. 1991. 17.95 (1-56182-008-3) Atomium Bks.

Rijk, A. G. Agricultural Mechanization Policy & Strategy. 283p. 1989. text ed. 39.75 (92-833-1111-6, 0208, Pub. by APO JA) Qual Resc.

Rijk, P. P. van, ed. Nuclear Techniques in Diagnostic Medicine. 1986. lib. bdg. 265.00 (0-89838-744-2) Kluwer Ac.

Rijkens, R. & Miracle, G. E. European Regulation of Advertising: Supranational Regulation of Advertising in the European Economic Community. 416p. 1986. 65.00 (0-444-87972-2, North Holland) Elsevier.

Rijkens, Rein. European Advertising Strategies: The Profiles & Policies of Multinational Companies Operating in Europe. 176p. 1992. text ed. 55.00 (0-304-31796-9) Cassell.

— European Advertising Strategies: The Profiles & Policies of Multinational Companies Operating in Europe. 176p. 1993. pap. text ed. 24.95 (0-304-32813-8) Cassell.

Rijksbaron, A. Temporal & Causal Conjunctions in Ancient Greek. xvi, 240p. 1976. pap. 44.00 (90-256-0674-1, Pub. by A M Hakkert NE) Benjamins North Am.

Rijksbaron, A., et al, eds. In the Footsteps of Raphael Kuhner: Proceedings of the International Colloquium in Commemoration of the 150th Anniversary of the Publication of Raphael Kuhner's 'Ausfuhrliche Grammatik der griechischen Sprache', Two. Theil: Syntaxe. 392p. (Orig.). (C). 1988. pap. 85.00 (90-70265-90-7, Pub. by Gieben NE) Benjamins North Am.

Rijksbaron, Albert. Aristotle, Verb Meaning & Functional Grammar: Towards a New Typology of States of Affairs. vi, 54p. (Orig.). 1989. pap. 16.00 (90-5063-039-1, Pub. by Gieben NE) Benjamins North Am.

— Grammatical Observations on Euripides' Bacchae. (Amsterdam Studies in Greek Philology Ser.: Vol. 1). x, 217p. 1990. 41.00 (90-5063-041-3, Pub. by Gieben NE) Benjamins North Am.

— The Syntax & Semantics of the Verb in Classical Greek: An Introduction. 2nd ed. 199p. (C). 1994. 27.00 (90-70265-36-2, Pub. by Gieben NE) Benjamins North Am.

Rijlaarsdam, J. C., jt. ed. see Beylsmit, J. J.

Rijnberk, A. & Greidanus, Wimersma, eds. Comparative Pathophysiology of Regulatory Peptides. (Frontiers of Hormone Research Ser.: Vol. 17). (Illus.). viii, 236p. 1987. 170.50 (3-8055-4621-1) S Karger.

Rijnberk, A., ed. see Hazewinkel, H. A., et al.

***Rijnberk, Adam & De Vries, H. W., eds.** Medical History & Physical Examination in Companion Animals. Belshaw, B. E., tr. LC 94-29947. Orig. Title: Anamnese en Lichamelijk Onderzoek bij Gezelschapsdieren. 1994. lib. bdg. 169.00 (0-7923-3037-4) Kluwer Ac.

Rijnsdorp, jt. auth. see IFAC-IFIP Symposium Staff.

Rijnsdorp, J. E. Integrated Process Control & Automation. (Process Measurement & Control Ser.: No. 2). 424p. 1991. 168.50 (0-444-88128-X); pap. 48.50 (0-444-89097-1) Elsevier.

Rijnsdorp, J. E., ed. see IFAC-IFIP-IEA-IFORS Symposium Staff & Johannsen, G.

Rijnsdorp, J. E., ed. see IFAC Symposium Staff.

Rijnsdorp, J. E., et al, eds. Dynamics & Control of Chemical Reactors, Distillation Columns & Batch Processes: Selected Papers from the IFAC Symposium, Maastricht, The Netherlands, 21-23 August 1989. LC 90-32048. (IFAC Proceedings Ser.: No. IFPS 9007). 352p. 1990. 175.00 (0-08-037038-1, Pergamon Pr) Elsevier.

Rijnvos, C. J. A New Approach to the Theory of International Trade. 1976. pap. text ed. 40.50 (90-247-1851-1) Kluwer Ac.

R

Rijsdijk, Jan F. & Laming, Peter B. Physical & Related Properties of One Hundred Forty Five Timbers: Information for Practice. LC 94-12287. 392p. (C). 1994. lib. bdg. 105.00 (*0-7923-2875-2*) Kluwer Ac.

Rijsterborgh, H., ed. Echocardiology: Developments in Cardiovascular Medicine, No. 13. 504p. 1981. lib. bdg. 140.00 (*90-247-2491-0*) Kluwer Ac.

Rikard-Bell, Belinda, ed. The Largest Island: Modern Australian Short Stories. 150p. (C). 1990. 39.00 (*0-7316-5222-3*, Pub. by Pascoe Pub AT) St Mut.

Rike, Jennifer L., jt. ed. see Jeanrond, Werner C.

Rikel, James E., jt. auth. see McMurtrie, W. Hogin.

Riker. Morning Rain. 1991. mass mkt. 4.50 (*0-06-104050-9*, Harp PBks) HarpC.

Riker, A. J., jt. ed. see Kozlowski, Theodore T.

Riker, Audrey. Finding My Way. (gr. 9-12). 1979. student ed 4.36 (*0-02-663800-2*); teacher ed 5.32 (*0-02-663790-1*); pap. 9.72 (*0-02-663780-4*) Bennett IL.

— Married & Single Life. (gr. 9-12). 1984. text ed. 19.40 (*0-02-665040-1*) Bennett IL.

— Me: Understanding Myself & Others. 1977. 11.96 (*0-02-665070-3*); teacher ed 10.00 (*0-02-665080-0*); student ed 5.80 (*0-02-665090-8*) Bennett IL.

Riker, Dorothy, comp. Genealogical Sources. 456p. 1979. 16.00 (*0-87195-075-8*) Ind Hist Soc.

— Index to Indiana Source Book, Vols. 1-3. 406p. 1983. 25.00 (*0-87195-072-3*) Ind Hist Soc.

***Riker, Dorothy L.** Indiana Election Returns, 1816-1851. 493p. 1960. 6.00 (*1-885323-17-4*) IN Hist Bureau.

— Messages & Papers of David Wallace, 1837-1840. 501p. 1963. 6.00 (*1-885323-20-4*) IN Hist Bureau.

— Messages & Papers Relating to the Administration of James Brown Ray, Governor of Indiana, 1825-1831. 1954. 6.00 (*1-885323-13-1*) IN Hist Bureau.

— Messages & Papers Relating to the Administration of Noah Noble, Governor of Indiana, 1831-1837. 1958. 4.50 (*1-885323-15-8*) IN Hist Bureau.

***Riker, H. Jay.** Seals, the Warrior Breed: Purple Heart. (Orig.). 1994. mass mkt. 5.50 (*0-380-76969-7*) Avon.

— SEALs, the Warrior Breed: Silver Star. 400p. (Orig.). 1993. mass mkt. 4.99 (*0-380-76967-0*) Avon.

Riker, Harold C. & Myers, Jane. Retirement Counseling: A Handbook for Action. (Death Education, Aging & Health Care Ser.). 1989. 58.00 (*0-89116-628-9*) Hemisp Pub.

Riker, James. Annals of Newtown, of Queens County, New York, Containing Its History from Its Settlement, Together with Many Interesting Facts Concerning the Adjacent Towns, with Genealogies. (Illus.). 437p. 1992. reprint ed. lib. bdg. write for info. (*0-8328-2341-4*) Higginson Bk Co.

Riker, John. Human Excellence & an Ecological Conception of the Psyche. LC 90-34437. 239p. (C). 1991. 64.50 (*0-7914-0518-4*); pap. 21.95 (*0-7914-0519-2*) State U NY Pr.

Riker, L. Tears of Jade. 1993. mass mkt. 4.99 (*0-06-108047-0*, Harp PBks) HarpC.

Riker, L. S. Full Clip. 1992. mass mkt. 3.99 (*0-312-92848-3*) St Martin.

— Kill Crazy. 1993. mass mkt. 3.99 (*0-312-92906-4*) St Martin.

— Swagtown. 1992. mass mkt. 3.99 (*0-312-92694-4*) St Martin.

***Riker, Leigh.** Just One of Those Things. 1994. pap. 4.99 (*0-06-108194-9*, Harp PBks) HarpC.

— Oh, Susannah. 1994. pap. 4.99 (*0-06-108195-7*, Harp PBks) HarpC.

— Unforgettable. 1993. mass mkt. 4.99 (*0-06-108019-5*, Harp PBks) HarpC.

Riker, Paula. Going to the Dogs & Other Creatures. 64p. 1990. 9.50 (*0-8233-0463-9*) Golden Quill.

Riker, T. W. Making of Roumania: A Study of an International Problem, 1856-1866. LC 70-135830. (Eastern Europe Collection Ser.). 1971. reprint ed. 35.95 (*0-405-02772-9*) Ayer.

Riker, Tom. City & Suburban Gardens: Frontyards, Backyards, Terraces, Rooftops & Window Boxes. LC 76-58532. (Illus.). 1977. 12.95 (*0-685-03790-8*) P-H.

Riker, William H. Agenda Formation. 300p. 1993. text ed. 44.50 (*0-472-10381-4*) U of Mich Pr.

— The Art of Political Manipulation. LC 85-22248. 192p. 1986. pap. 12.00 (*0-300-03592-6*, Y-587) Yale U Pr.

— The Development of American Federalism. (C). 1987. lib. bdg. 55.00 (*0-89838-225-4*) Kluwer Ac.

— Liberalism Against Populism: A Confrontation Between the Theory of Democracy & the Theory of Social Choice. 311p. (C). 1988. reprint ed. pap. text ed. 18.95 (*0-88133-367-0*) Waveland Pr.

— Soldiers of the States. Kohn, Richard H., ed. LC 78-22394. (American Military Experience Ser.). 1980. reprint ed. lib. bdg. 15.95 (*0-405-11870-8*) Ayer.

— Theory of Political Coalitions. 1962. 59.50x (*0-685-26647-8*) Elliots Bks.

— The Theory of Political Coalitions. LC 84-684. xii, 300p. (C). 1984. reprint ed. text ed. 69.50 (*0-313-24299-2*, RITH, Greenwood Pr) Greenwood.

Rikert, Richard, ed. see American Institute of Certified Public Accountants Staff.

Rikhje, Indar Jit. The Sinai Blunder. 200p. 1978. 25.50 (*0-937722-19-7*) Intl Peace.

Rikhof, Herwi. The Concept of Church: A Methodological Inquiry into the Use of Metaphors in Ecclesiology. LC 80-84751. xvi, 304p. 1981. 35.00 (*0-915762-11-0*) Patmos Pr.

Rikhya, Ravi. Militarization of Mother India. 1990. 23.50 (*81-7001-060-8*, Pub. by Chanakya II) S Asia.

Rikhye, Indar J. Military Advisor to the Secretary-General: United Nations Peacekeeping & the Congo Crisis. 350p. 1993. text ed. 55.00 (*0-312-06737-2*) St Martin.

— Sinai Blunder: Withdrawal of the United Nations Emergency Force Leading to the Six-Day War of June, 1967. 240p. 1980. 35.00 (*0-7146-3136-1*, Pub. by F Cass Pubs UK) Intl Spec Bk.

Rikhye, Indar J., et al. The Thin Blue Line: International Peacekeeping & Its Future. LC 74-79977. 387p. reprint ed. pap. 110.30 (*0-8357-8348-0*, 2033874) Bks Demand.

Rikihisa, Yasuko, jt. auth. see Carter, Gordon R.

Rikitake, Tsuneji. Earthquake Forecasting. 1983. lib. bdg. 117.00 (*90-277-1218-2*) Kluwer Ac.

— Earthquake Prediction. (Developments in Solid Earth Geophysics Ser.: Vol. 9). 358p. 1976. 102.75 (*0-444-41373-1*) Elsevier.

— Magnetic & Electromagnetic Shielding. 1987. lib. bdg. 136.50 (*90-277-2406-7*) Kluwer Ac.

Rikitake, Tsuneji, ed. Current Research in Earthquake Prediction, Vol. 1. (Developments in Earth & Planetary Sciences Ser.: No. 2). 400p. 1981. lib. bdg. 90.00 (*90-277-1133-X*) Kluwer Ac.

Rikitake, Tsuneji & Honkura, Yoshimori. Solid Earth Geomagnetism. 1986. lib. bdg. 145.50 (*90-277-2120-3*) Kluwer Ac.

Rikitake, Tsuneji, et al. Applied Mathematics for Earth Scientists. 1987. lib. bdg. 162.50 (*90-277-1796-6*) Kluwer Ac.

Rikkers, Renate. Seniors on the Move. LC 85-24846. (Illus.). 256p. 1986. spiral bd. 27.00 (*0-87322-040-4*, BRIK0040) Human Kinetics.

Rikkert, W. E., jt. ed. see Jacobs, R.

Rikki. Illusions of the Children of Og. (Story of Og & Man Ser.: Part 3). 216p. 1983. pap. 10.00 (*0-910149-05-4*) Msng Link AZ.

— Mysteries of the Children of Og. (Story of Og & Man Ser.: Part 2). 216p. (Orig.). 1983. pap. 10.00 (*0-910149-03-8*) Msng Link AZ.

— Secrets of the Children of Og. (Story of Og & Man Ser.: Part 1). (Illus.). 220p. (Orig.). 1982. pap. 10.00 (*0-910149-01-1*) Msng Link AZ.

— The Story of Og & Man, 3 vols., Set. (Story of Og & Man Ser.). (Illus.). 662p. 1983. pap. 29.95 (*0-910149-06-2*) Msng Link AZ.

Rikles, C. D., ed. see Menendez Pidal, Ramon.

Riklis, E., ed. Photobiology: The Science & Its Applications. (Basic Life Sciences Ser.). (Illus.). 1182p. 1991. 185.00 (*0-306-43830-5*, Plenum Pr) Plenum.

Riklis, Emmanuel, ed. Frontiers of Radiation Biology: Proceedings of the 21st Annual Meeting. LC 90-11985. 712p. 1990. lib. bdg. 175.00 (*0-89573-867-8*) VCH Pubs.

Rikoon, J. Sanford. Threshing in the Midwest, 1820-1940: A Study of Traditional Culture & Technological Change. LC 87-45407. (Midwestern History & Culture Ser.). (Illus.). 230p. 1988. 35.00 (*0-253-36047-1*) Ind U Pr.

***Rikoon, J. Sanford, ed.** Rachel Calof's Story: Jewish Homesteader on the Great Plains. LC 95-5742. 1995. write for info. (*0-253-32942-6*) Ind U Pr.

Rikoon, J. Sanford & Austin, Judith, eds. Interpreting Local Culture & History. LC 86-34281. (Illus.). 200p. (Orig.). (C). 1991. pap. text ed. 14.95 (*0-931406-06-4*) U of Idaho Pr.

Rikoon, J. Sanford, jt. auth. see Petersen, Keith.

Rikys, Bodel. Red Bear's Fun with Shapes. LC 91-46997. (Illus.). 32p. (J). (ps-00). 1993. 10.99 (*0-8037-1317-7*) Dial Bks Young.

Riland, George. The New Steinerbooks Dictionary of the Paranormal. 370p. 1980. pap. 7.00 (*0-89345-225-4*, Steinerbks) Garber Comm.

— The New Steinerbooks Dictionary of the Paranormal, Vol. 5. LC 79-93353. 370p. 1980. lib. bdg. 10.00 (*0-89345-028-6*, Spir Sci Lib) Garber Comm.

Riland, George Henry. Dear Love, Letters from Henry. 190p. (Orig.). 1989. 5.95 (*0-924694-10-6*) Capricornis.

RILEM International Symposium Staff. Testing & Test Methods of Fibre Cement Composites: RILEM Symposium held April 5-7, 1978. Swamy, R. N., ed. (Illus.). 555p. reprint ed. pap. 158.20 (*0-317-08289-2*, 2019629) Bks Demand.

RILEM Technical Committee 51-ALC Staff, jt. auth. see RILEM Technical Committee 78-MCA Staff.

RILEM Technical Committee 78-MCA Staff & RILEM Technical Committee 51-ALC Staff. Autoclaved Aerated Concrete: Properties, Testing, & Design: RILEM Recommended Practices. LC 93-6890. 1993. Alk. paper. write for info. (*0-419-17960-7*, E & FN Spon) Routledge Chapman & Hall.

Riles, Wilson & Heizman, Jessie. Countdown to Retirement for Educators. 240p. 1985. pap. 9.95 (*0-944223-00-1*, BoothMark Bks) Moonlght Pr.

***Riley.** Conversation with Anne Rice. write for info. (*0-345-39636-7*) Ballantine.

— Cut-Out. 1993. per. 14.95 (*1-55050-053-8*, Pub. by Coteau Bks CN) InBook.

— Dandy, Day & the Devil. (Orig.). 50.00 (*0-8488-1580-7*); pap. 15.95 (*0-8488-1595-5*) Amereon Ltd.

— Patrick Duffy. 1987. pap. 3.50 (*0-312-90449-5*) St Martin.

— Using Modula-2. 1987. pap. 47.95 (*0-87835-236-8*) PWS Pubs.

— Using Modula 2. 1987. pap. 12.95 (*0-87835-237-6*) PWS Pubs.

Riley, jt. auth. see Giarratano.

Riley, Alan J., et al, eds. Sexual Pharmacology. (Illus.). 248p. 1994. 67.50 (*0-19-262283-8*) OUP.

***Riley, Alice C.** Slumber Boat. (Illus.). 24p. (J). (ps). 1995. 14.95 (*0-9642944-2-7*) Starry Night.

***Riley, Annabel.** The Beginning. (Mini Pop-up Bible Stories Ser.). (Illus.). 8p. (J). 1994. 4.99 (*0-7814-1521-7*) Chariot Family.

Riley, Anne. Help Me. LC 90-82929. (My First Prayers Ser.). (Illus.). 10p. (J). 1990. text ed. 3.99 (*0-8066-2495-7*, 9-2495) Augsburg Fortress.

— I'm Sorry. LC 90-82927. (My First Prayers Ser.). (Illus.). 10p. (J). 1990. text ed. 3.99 (*0-8066-2494-9*, 9-2494) Augsburg Fortress.

— Please God. LC 90-82930. (My First Prayers Ser.). (Illus.). 10p. (J). 1990. text ed. 3.99 (*0-8066-2496-5*, 9-2496) Augsburg Fortress.

— Thank You. LC 90-82928. (My First Prayers Ser.). (Illus.). 10p. (J). 1990. text ed. 3.99 (*0-8066-2493-0*, 9-2493) Augsburg Fortress.

Riley, Anne W. & Zaccaro, Stephen J., eds. Occupational Stress & Organizational Effectiveness. LC 86-25250. 287p. 1987. text ed. 59.95 (*0-275-92281-2*, C2281, Praeger Pubs) Greenwood.

Riley, Anne W., jt. ed. see Frederiksen, Lee W.

Riley, Basil, jt. auth. see Bohm, David.

Riley, Bernard W. & Brokensha, David. The Mbeere in Kenya, Vol. I: Changing Rural Ecology. LC 88-12108. (Illus.). 384p. (Orig.). (C). 1988. lib. bdg. 55.00 (*0-8191-6997-8*, Inst Dev Anthro); pap. text ed. 29.00 (*0-8191-6998-6*, Inst Dev Anthro) U Pr of Amer.

Riley, Betty. A Veil Too Thin: Reincarnation Out of Control. LC 84-50090. 96p. 1984. pap. 2.95 (*0-911842-37-3*) Valley Sun.

Riley, Bob. Doug Hall: The Spectacle of Image. (Illus.). 1987. 8.00 (*0-910663-48-3*) ICA Inc.

— Evaluation of Therapeutic Recreation Through Quality Assurance. LC 87-50299. 103p. 1987. text ed. 16.95 (*0-910251-18-5*) Venture Pub PA.

Riley, Bob, ed. Quality Management: Applications for Therapeutic Recreation. LC 91-66102. 242p. (C). 1991. text ed. 23.95 (*0-910251-47-9*) Venture Pub PA.

Riley, Bruce T. The Psychology of Religious Experience in Its Personal & Institutional Dimensions. (American University Studies: Theology & Religion: Ser. VII, Vol. 49). 361p. (C). 1988. text ed. 47.70 (*0-8204-0862-X*) P Lang Pubs.

Riley, C. J. The Encyclopedia of Trains & Locomotives. LC 94-1826. 1994. 19.98 (*1-56799-087-8*, MetroBooks) M Friedman Pub Grp Inc.

Riley, Caroline L. The Newsom Papers. 150p. 1988. 35.00 (*0-9621609-0-3*) C L Riley.

***Riley, Carroll L.** Rio Del Norte: People of the Upper Rio Grande from Earliest Times to the Pueblo Revolt. (Illus.). 336p. (C). 1995. text ed. 29.95 (*0-87480-466-3*) U of Utah Pr.

Riley, Carroll L., ed. see Bandelier, Adolph F.

Riley, Charles A., II. Color Codes: Modern Theories of Color in Philosophy, Painting & Architecture, Literature, Music, & Psychology. LC 94-9733. (Illus.). 376p. 1995. 39.95 (*0-87451-671-4*) U Pr of New Eng.

***Riley, Charles A., 2nd.** Jaime Franco: New Paintings. (Illus.). 12p. (Orig.). 1994. pap. 5.00 (*0-9626731-6-1*) Yoshii Gallery.

— Small Business, Big Politics: What Entrepreneurs Need to Know to Use Their Growing Political Power. 256p. 1995. 21.95 (*1-56079-474-7*, Petersons Pacesetter) Petersons Guides.

Riley, Charles M. Our Mineral Resources: An Elementary Textbook in Economic Geology. LC 76-57669. (Illus.). 348p. 1977. reprint ed. lib. bdg. 25.50 (*0-88275-530-7*) Krieger.

Riley, Charles V. Nine Annual Reports on the Noxious, Beneficial & Other Insects of the State of Missouri, 1869-1877: With a General Index & Supplement, 10 vols. in three. Sterling, Keir B., ed. LC 77-81105. (Biologists & Their World Ser.). 1979. reprint ed. lib. bdg. 145.95 (*0-405-10745-5*) Ayer.

***Riley, Christopher, et al, eds.** Releasing Resources to Achieve Health Gain. 1995. 79.95 (*1-85775-018-7*) Scovill Paterson.

Riley, Christopher M. Pharmaceutical & Biomedical Applications of Liquid Chromatography. Lough, W. John et al, eds. LC 94-20192. (Progress in Pharmacology & Clinical Pharmacology Ser.: No. 1). 1994. 150.00 (*0-08-041009-X*, Pergamon Pr) Elsevier.

Riley, Clay. Programming On-Line Help with C Plus Plus. (Advanced Computer Book Ser.). (Illus.). 416p. (Orig.). 1993. disk 24.95 (*1-55622-333-1*) Wordware Pub.

***Riley, Cole.** Dark Blood Moon. 256p. 1995. 5.95 (*0-87067-746-2*) Holloway.

— The Devil to Pay. 217p. (Orig.). 1994. pap. 3.95 (*0-87067-742-X*) Holloway.

— The Killing Kind. (Orig.). 1990. pap. 3.50 (*0-87067-548-6*) Holloway.

— Rough Trade. (Orig.). 1988. pap. 3.50 (*0-87067-835-3*) Holloway.

Riley, Corwin E. Selling's My Game: Riley's the Name. (Illus.). 96p. 1988. 6.95 (*0-9621048-0-9*) Corray Pub Co.

Riley, Dan. Dan Riley School for a Girl: An Adventure in Home Schooling. 1994. 21.95 (*0-395-68719-5*) HM.

Riley, Dan, ed. The Dodgers Reader. 1992. pap. 9.95 (*0-395-58778-6*) HM.

— The Red Sox Reader. enl. rev. ed. (Illus.). 304p. 1991. pap. 9.95 (*0-395-58776-X*) HM.

— The Red Sox Reader Thirty Years of Musings on Baseball's Most Amusing Team. LC 87-50180. (Illus.). 240p. (Orig.). 1987. pap. 9.95 (*0-941913-00-7*) Ventura Arts.

Riley, Dan, jt. ed. see Fulk, David.

Riley, Dan, jt. ed. see Weinberger, Miro.

Riley, Daniel P., ed. Strength Training by the Experts. 2nd ed. LC 81-85627. (Illus.). 256p. (Orig.). 1982. pap. 15.95 (*0-88011-041-4*, PRIL0041) Human Kinetics.

Riley, David D. Using Pascal: An Introduction to Computer Science I. 608p. 1987. pap. 46.95 (*0-87835-234-1*); teacher ed. pap. 12.95 (*0-87835-235-X*) PWS Pubs.

Riley, David D., jt. auth. see Headington, Mark R.

Riley, David L., Sr. Business. LC 89-91725. (Illus.). 60p. (Orig.). 1989. pap. 12.50 (*0-9618976-3-5*) EBI.

— Loci, Memory-Minute: How to Improve Your Memory Fast. LC 87-90689. (Illus.). 75p. (Orig.). 1987. pap. 10.00 (*0-9618976-0-0*) EBI.

— Some-One Died! What Is Life? (Illus.). 200p. (Orig.). 1988. pap. 12.00 (*0-9618976-1-9*) EBI.

***Riley, Dawn & Flanagan, Cynthia.** Taking the Helm. LC 94-47989. 1995. 24.95 (*0-316-74550-2*) Little.

Riley, Denise. Am I That Name? Feminism & the Category of "Women" in History: Feminism & the Category of Women in History. LC 88-21640. vi, 126p. (Orig.). 1989. pap. text ed. 12.95 (*0-8166-1731-7*) U of Minn Pr.

Riley, Dennis D. Controlling the Federal Bureaucracy. LC 86-14469. 216p. 1987. 32.95 (*0-87722-455-2*) Temple U Pr.

— Controlling the Federal Bureaucracy. 216p. 1990. pap. 14.95 (*0-87722-704-7*) Temple U Pr.

— Public Personnel Administration. (C). 1993. 58.00 (*0-06-500074-9*) HarpCollege.

Riley, Derrick, jt. auth. see Kennedy, David.

***Riley, Diana.** Perinatal Mental Health. 1994. 24.75 (*1-870905-78-4*, Radcliffe Med Pr) Scovill Paterson.

Riley, Dick & McAllister, Pam, eds. The New Bedside, Bathtub & Armchair Companion to Agatha Christie. 200p. 1986. pap. text ed. 14.95 (*0-8044-6725-0*, F Ungar Bks) Continuum.

Riley, Don & Selvig, Dick. High & Dry. rev. ed. Tyson Enterprises Co. Staff, ed. LC 80-7787. 360p. 1987. reprint ed. pap. 9.95 (*0-9618032-1-5*) Tyson Enter.

Riley, Don, jt. auth. see Rudensky, Morris R.

Riley, Don, jt. auth. see Selvig, Dick.

Riley, Donald P., et al. Parent-Child Communication. LC 77-13652. (Workshop Models for Family Life Education Ser.). 154p. 1977. spiral bd. 17.95 (*0-87304-157-7*) Families Intl.

Riley, Dorothy W. The Blackburn Affair. 25p. (YA). (gr. 4-12). 1986. pap. write for info. (*1-880234-04-1*) Winbush Pub.

— Family Reunion. 25p. (YA). 1986. pap. write for info. (*1-880234-02-5*) Winbush Pub.

— It's up to You. 25p. (YA). (gr. 4-12). 1986. pap. write for info. (*1-880234-03-3*) Winbush Pub.

— My Soul Looks Back, 'Less I Forget. 332p. (YA). 1991. write for info. (*1-880234-06-8*); pap. write for info. (*1-880234-00-9*) Winbush Pub.

— My Soul Looks Back, 'Less I Forget, Vol. 2. 332p. (YA). 1992. pap. write for info. (*1-880234-01-7*) Winbush Pub.

***Riley, Dorothy W., ed.** My Soul Looks Back, 'Less I Forget. rev. ed. 512p. 1995. pap. 14.00 (*0-06-272057-0*, Harper Ref) HarpC.

Riley, Dorothy W. & Riley, Tiaudra. Dorothy Mae's Cornbread. 25p. (YA). 1992. pap. write for info. (*1-880234-05-X*) Winbush Pub.

Riley, Dorothy W., ed. see Blakey, Scott.

Riley, Dru, ed. see Manns, William, et al.

Riley, E. B., jt. auth. see Ray, Sidney H.

Riley, E. Baxter. Among Papuan Headhunters. LC 75-35155. (Illus.). 344p. 1983. reprint ed. 52.50 (*0-404-14170-6*) AMS Pr.

Riley, E. C. Cervantes's Theory of the Novel. Lathrop, Thomas et al, eds. (Documentacion Cervantina Ser.: No. 13). 244p. Date not set. pap. 12.00 (*0-936388-56-0*) Juan de la Cuesta.

— Don Quixote. Rawson, Claude, ed. LC 85-11179. (Unwin Critical Library). 192p. 1986. text ed. 44.95 (*0-04-800009-4*) Routledge Chapman & Hall.

Riley, E. C., jt. ed. see Avalle-Arce, J. B.

Riley, E. C., ed. see Cervantes Saavedra, Miguel de.

Riley, Edward. Riley's Flute Melodies, 2vols. in 1. Hitchcock, H. Wiley, ed. & intro. by. LC 72-14213. (Earlier American Music Ser.: Vol. 18). 200p. 1973. reprint ed. lib. bdg. 27.50 (*0-306-70565-6*) Da Capo.

Riley, Edward M. Starting America: The Story of Independence Hall. rev. ed. (Illus.). 64p. (YA). 1990. reprint ed. pap. text ed. 4.95 (*0-939631-23-7*) Thomas Publications.

Riley, Edward P. & Vorhees, Charles V., eds. Handbook of Behavioral Teratology. LC 86-20517. 542p. 1986. 90.00 (*0-306-42246-8*, Plenum Pr) Plenum.

Riley, Eileen. Major Political Events in South Africa, 1948-1990. 256p. 1991. 29.95 (*0-8160-2310-7*) Facts on File.

Riley, Elizabeth, comp. Love Poems. LC 68-58827. (Granger Index Reprint Ser.). 1977. 15.95 (*0-8369-6040-8*) Ayer.

Riley, Erin. California Real Estate Law. 1991. pap. 32.95 (*0-915799-85-5*) Rockwell WA.

Riley, Eugene W. & Acuna, Victor E. Transmission Systems: Engineering Seminar II. 2nd ed. LC 76-15104. (ABC of the Telephone Ser.: Vol. 8). (Illus.). 68p. (C). 1984. pap. text ed. 13.95 (*1-56016-007-1*) ABC TeleTraining.

— Understanding Transmission: Engineering Seminar I. 2nd ed. LC 73-85629. (ABC of the Telephone Ser.: Vol. 7). (Illus.). 60p. (C). 1988. pap. text ed. 13.95 (*1-56016-006-3*) ABC TeleTraining.

Riley, Eugenia. Angel Flame. 1990. mass mkt. 4.95 (*0-446-34938-0*) Warner Bks.

— Ecstasy's Triumph. 1983. pap. 3.50 (*0-685-07869-8*) Zebra.

— Rogue's Mistress. 400p. (Orig.). 1991. mass mkt. 4.50 (*0-380-76474-1*) Avon.

— Taming Kate. 384p. (Orig.). 1992. mass mkt. 4.50 (*0-380-76475-X*) Avon.

— Tempest in Time. 448p. (Orig.). 1993. pap. 4.50 (*0-8439-3377-1*) Dorchester Pub Co.

— Timeswept Bride. 416p. (Orig.). 1995. mass mkt. 5.50 (*0-380-77157-8*) Avon.

— A Tryst in Time. 448p. (Orig.). 1992. pap. 4.50 (*0-8439-3198-1*) Dorchester Pub Co.

— A Tryst in Time. 448p. (Orig.). 1995. mass mkt. 4.99 (*0-505-52052-4*) Dorchester Pub Co.

Riley, F. J., ed. Electronic Assembly. (International Trends in Manufacturing Technology Ser.). (Illus.). 450p. 1987. 87.00 (0-387-17441-9) Spr-Verlag.

Riley, F. L. Biblical Allegorism. 1991. lib. bdg. 79.95 (0-8490-5008-1) Gordon Pr.

— Biblical Allegorism: A Key to the Mysteries of the Kingdom of God. 1991. lib. bdg. 89.95 (0-87700-983-X) Revisionist Pr.

Riley, F. L., ed. The Bible of Bibles: A Source Book of Religions Demonstrating the Unity of the Sacred Books of the World. 1991. lib. bdg. 250.00 (0-87700-960-0) Revisionist Pr.

— Progress in Nitrogen Ceramics. 1983. lib. bdg. 215.00 (90-247-2828-2) Kluwer Ac.

— Second European Symposium on Engineering Ceramics: Proceedings of the Second European Symposium on Engineering Ceramics Held in London, 23-24 Nov., 1987. 286p. 1989. 86.50 (1-85166-295-2) Elsevier.

— Third European Symposium on Engineering Ceramics: Proceedings Held in London, England, U. K., 28-29 Nov., 1989. 212p. 1991. 112.00 (1-85166-555-2) Elsevier.

Riley, Frank, jt. auth. see Clifton, Mark.

Riley, Frank, jt. auth. see Eshelman, Byron E.

Riley, Frank L. The Bible of Bibles. reprint ed. spiral bd. 15.40 (0-7873-0355-0) Mokelumne.

— Biblical Allegorism. reprint ed. spiral bd. 9.35 (0-7873-0724-6) Mokelumne.

Riley, Franklin L. School History of Mississippi. LC 76-68. (Illus.). 448p. 1976. reprint ed. 17.50 (0-87152-219-5) Reprint.

Riley, Franklin L., ed. General Robert E. Lee After Appomattox. LC 72-37353. (Select Bibliographies Reprint Ser.). 1977. reprint ed. 23.95 (0-8369-6700-3) Ayer.

Riley, Gary, jt. auth. see Giarratano, Joseph C.

Riley, Gary L. & Baldridge, Victor J., eds. Governing Academic Organizations: New Problems, New Perspectives. LC 76-56995. (C). 1977. 35.75 (0-8211-1715-7); text ed. write for info. (0-685-03219-1) McCutchan.

***Riley, Gay.** The Pocket Personal Trainer: A Total Nutrition & Fitness Planner for Busy People. Rodriguez, Patricia, ed. 290p. 1994. pap. text ed. 9.95 (0-9642204-0-7) Lipo-Visuals.

***Riley, George R.** Worship Space Sound Systems: A Guide to Better Sound in Your Parish. (Orig.). 1994. pap. text ed. 10.95 (1-56929-017-2) Pastoral Pr.

Riley, Gillian. The Dutch Table: Gastronomy in the Golden Age of the Netherlands. LC 93-87359. (Painters & Food Ser.). (Illus.). 96p. 1994. 19.95 (1-56640-978-0) Pomegranate Calif.

— Impressionist Picnics. LC 93-84102. (Painters & Food Ser.). (Illus.). 96p. 1993. 19.95 (1-56640-580-7) Pomegranate Calif.

— Renaissance Recipes. LC 93-84099. (Painters & Food Ser.). (Illus.). 96p. 1993. 19.95 (1-56640-577-7) Pomegranate Calif.

Riley, Glenda. Divorce: An American Tradition. (Illus.). 288p. 1991. 24.95 (0-19-506123-3) OUP.

— Divorce: An American Tradition. (Illus.). 280p. 1992. pap. 11.95 (0-19-507912-4) OUP.

— The Female Frontier: A Comparative View of Women on the Prairie & the Plains. LC 87-32447. (Illus.). xii, 292p. 1988. pap. 12.95 (0-7006-0424-3) U Pr of KS.

— Frontierswomen: The Iowa Experience. LC 94-5444. 212p. (C). 1994. pap. 8.95 (0-8138-1469-3) Iowa St U Pr.

— Inventing the American Woman: An Inclusive History, Early America to 1877, Vol. I. 2nd rev. ed. (Illus.). 168p. (C). 1995. pap. text ed. 16.95 (0-88295-922-0) Harlan Davidson.

— Inventing the American Woman: An Inclusive History, 1877 to the Present, Vol. II. 2nd rev. ed. (Illus.). 176p. (C). 1995. pap. text ed. 16.95 (0-88295-923-9) Harlan Davidson.

— The Life & Legacy of Annie Oakley. LC 94-10260. (Oklahoma Western Biographies Ser.: Vol. 7). (Illus.). 272p. 1994. 24.95 (0-8061-2656-6) U of Okla Pr.

— A Place to Grow: Women in the American West. 325p. 1992. pap. text ed. write for info. (0-88295-886-0) Harlan Davidson.

— Women & Indians on the Frontier, 1825-1915. LC 84-13235. (Illus.). 352p. 1984. pap. 16.95 (0-8263-0780-9) U of NM Pr.

Riley, Glyndon D. & Riley, Jeanna. Oral Motor Assessment & Treatment: Improving Syllable Production. 64p. (Orig.). 1985. pap. text ed. 69.00 (0-685-12077-5, 2983) PRO-ED.

***Riley, Gregory J.** Resurrection Reconsidered: Thomas & John in Controversy. 1995. pap. 15.00 (0-8006-2846-2, Fortress Pr) Augsburg Fortress.

Riley, H. T., tr. see De Hoveden, Roger.

Riley, H. T., tr. see Ingulf, Abbot.

Riley, Harold. The First Gospel. 220p. 1992. 25.00 (0-86554-409-3, MUP/H332) Mercer Univ Pr.

— The Making of Mark: An Exploration. LC 89-37902. 275p. (C). 1989. 25.00 (0-86554-359-3, MUP/H297) Mercer Univ Pr.

— Preface to Luke. 130p. 1993. text ed. 25.00 (0-86554-419-0, MUP/H337) Mercer Univ Pr.

Riley, Harold, jt. auth. see Orchard, Bernard.

Riley, Harvey. The Mule. (Illus.). 107p. 1897. reprint ed. pap. 5.00 (0-318-12504-8) Am Donkey.

Riley, Helen. The Bat in the Cave. LC 89-4469. (Animal Habitats Ser.). (Illus.). 32p. (J). (gr. 4-6). 1989. lib. bdg. 17.27 (0-8368-0112-1) Gareth Stevens Inc.

— Frogs & Toads. LC 92-41476. (Weird & Wonderful Ser.). 32p. (J). (gr. 2-5). 1993. 14.95 (1-56847-007-X) Thomson Lrning.

— Frogs & Toads. (Weird & Wonderful Ser.). (Illus.). 32p. (J). (gr. 2-5). 1995. reprint ed. pap. 5.95 (1-56847-302-8) Thomson Lrning.

Riley, Henry T., ed. Munimenta Gildhallae Londoniensis: Liber Albus, Liber Custumarum, et Liber Horn, 3 vols., Set. Incl. Vol. 1. Liber Albus. 1974. (0-8115-1015-8); Vol. 2, Pts. 1 & 2. Liber Custumarum, with Extracts from the Cottonian Ms Claudius D II. 1974. (0-8115-1016-6); Vol. 3. Transcript of the Anglo-Norman Passages in Liber Albus, Glossaries, Appendices, & Index. 1974. (0-8115-1017-4); (Rolls Ser.: No. 12). 1974. reprint ed. 190.00 (0-685-09995-4) Periodicals Srv.

Riley, Herbert J., et al. Current Trends in Grades & Grading Practices in Undergraduate Higher Education: The Results of the 1992 AACRAO Survey. 76p. (C). 1994. pap. text ed. 18.00 (0-929851-20-X) Am Assn Coll Registrars.

Riley, Herbert P. & Majumdar, Shyamal K. The Aloineae: A Biosystematic Survey. LC 77-92927. (Illus.). 192p. 1980. 28.00 (0-8131-1376-8) U Pr of Ky.

Riley, Hugh M. Christian Initiation: A Comparative Study of the Interpretation of the Baptismal Liturgy in the Mystagogical Writing of Cyril of Jerusalem, John Chrysostom, Theodore of Mopsuetia, & Ambrose of Milan. LC 74-11191. (Catholic University of America Studies in Christian Antiquity: No. 17). 515p. reprint ed. pap. 146.80 (0-317-27922-X, 2025126) Bks Demand.

Riley, Hugh M., ed. see Auer, Johann.

Riley, J., jt. auth. see DiSilvestro, J.

Riley, J. L. What Matters: No Expanding Universe, No Big Bang. (Illus.). 227p. 1993. lib. bdg. 29.00 (0-9636842-0-5); pap. 19.00 (0-9636842-1-3) J L Riley.

***Riley, J. P.** Soldiers of the Queen: The History of the Queen's Regiment 1966-1992. 832p. 1990. 180.00 (0-948251-65-4, Pub. by Picton UK) St Mut.

Riley, J. T., jt. ed. see Vourvopoulos, G.

Riley, Jack. Designing Quality & Balance into Your Life, Work & Play: A Self-Test Workbook That Shows You Where You Are Now & Guides You Where You'd Like To Be. 128p. (Orig.). 1987. pap. 6.95 (0-89997-077-X) Wilderness Pr.

***Riley, Jame A., et al, eds.** Once upon a Midnight... New Dark Verse. (Unnameable Poetry Works Ser.). (Illus.). 96p. (Orig.). 1995. pap. 10.95 (0-934227-16-0) Unnameable Pr.

Riley, James. Biographical Encyclopedia of the Negro Leagues. (Illus.). 1280p. 1994. 39.50 (0-7867-0065-3) Carroll & Graf.

Riley, James, jt. auth. see Leonard, Buck.

***Riley, James, et al.** Helping Children with Mathematics. 144p. (Orig.). (J). (gr. 3-5). 1995. pap. 12.95 (0-673-36155-1) GdYrBks.

— Helping Your Child with Mathematics. (Illus.). 144p. (Orig.). (J). (ps-2). 1993. pap. 12.95 (0-673-36061-X) GdYrBks.

— Stand Up Math: 180 Challenging Problems for Kids, Budding Genius Level, Ages 8-10. (Illus.). 184p. (Orig.). 1994. spiral bd. 9.95 (0-673-36144-6) GdYrBks.

— Stand Up Math: 180 Challenging Problems for Kids, Genius Level, Ages 9-11. (Illus.). 184p. (Orig.). 1994. spiral bd. 9.95 (0-673-36145-4) GdYrBks.

— Stand Up Math: 180 Challenging Problems for Kids, Super Genius Level, Ages 10 Up. (Illus.). 184p. (Orig.). 1994. spiral bd. 9.95 (0-673-36146-2) GdYrBks.

Riley, James A. Dandy, Day & the Devil. LC 87-90021. (Illus.). 153p. (Orig.). 1987. 49.95 (0-9614023-3-4); pap. 12.95 (0-9614023-2-6) TK Pubs.

— Negro World Series of 1942. (Orig.). 1989. pap. write for info. (0-9614023-4-2) TK Pubs.

— Too Dark for the Hall. (Illus.). 175p. (Orig.). 1991. pap. 15.95 (0-9614023-6-9) TK Pubs.

Riley, James A., ed. Black Baseball Journal, Vol. 1, No. 1. (Illus.). 64p. (Orig.). (YA). 1990. pap. 6.95 (0-9614023-5-0) TK Pubs.

Riley, James A. & Speer, Renwick W. The Hundred Years of Chet Hoff. 30p. (Orig.). 1991. pap. 10.00 (0-9614023-7-7) TK Pubs.

Riley, James C. The Eighteenth-Century Campaign to Avoid Disease. LC 86-22036. 323p. 1987. text ed. 35.00 (0-312-00238-6) St Martin.

— International Government Finance & the Amsterdam Capital Market, 1740-1815. LC 79-152. 379p. reprint ed. pap. 108.10 (0-685-20567-3, 2030617) Bks Demand.

— Population Thought in the Age of the Demographic Revolution. LC 83-70312. 224p. 1985. lib. bdg. 24.75 (0-89089-257-1) Carolina Acad Pr.

— The Seven Years War & the Old Regime in France: The Economic & Financial Toll. 256p. 1987. text ed. 45.00x (0-691-05488-6) Princeton U Pr.

— Sickness, Recovery, & Death: A History & Forecast of Ill Health. LC 88-51148. (Illus.). 288p. 1989. text ed. 36.95 (0-87745-233-4) U of Iowa Pr.

Riley, James W. The Best of James Whitcomb Riley. Manlove, Donald C., ed. LC 82-47958. (Illus.). 224p. 1982. 17.95 (0-253-10610-9); pap. 8.95 (0-253-20299-X, MB-299) Ind U Pr.

— Book of Joyous Children. LC 79-98085. (Granger Index Reprint Ser.). 1977. 20.95 (0-8369-6087-4) Ayer.

— The Boss Girl: A Christmas Story, & Other Sketches. LC 76-160948. (Short Story Index Reprint Ser.). 1977. reprint ed. 20.95 (0-8369-3927-1) Ayer.

— A Child-World. LC 76-39403. (Granger Index Reprint Ser.). 1977. reprint ed. 22.95 (0-8369-6350-4) Ayer.

— Complete Poems. 1992. reprint ed. lib. bdg. 35.95 (0-89968-289-8, Lghtyr Pr) Buccaneer Bks.

— The Complete Poetical Works of James Whitcomb Riley. LC 92-28235. 1993. 35.00 (0-253-34989-3); pap. 17.95 (0-253-20777-0, MB-777) Ind U Pr.

— The Complete Works of James Whitcomb Riley, 6 vols., Set. LC 74-153347. (Illus.). reprint ed. 435.00 (0-404-05340-8) AMS Pr.

— Letters of James Whitcomb Riley. Phelps, William L., ed. LC 78-153348. reprint ed. 49.50 (0-404-05336-X) AMS Pr.

— Letters of James Whitcomb Riley. (American Biography Ser.). 349p. 1991. reprint ed. lib. bdg. 79.00 (0-7812-8323-X) Rprt Serv.

— Little Orphan Annie & Other Poems. 80p. 1994. pap. text ed. 1.00 (0-486-28260-0) Dover.

Riley, James W. Love Letters of a Bachelor Poet. 1972. 59.95 (0-8490-0564-7) Gordon Pr.

Riley, James W. Riley Child-Rhymes. LC 74-121933. (Granger Index Reprint Ser.). 1977. 22.95 (0-8369-6174-9) Ayer.

— Riley Child Rhymes with Hoosier Pictures. (Illus.). 188p. (J). reprint ed. 18.95 (1-878208-17-9) Guild Pr IN.

— When the Frost Is on the Pumpkin. 1993. pap. 8.95 (0-87923-988-3) Godine.

Riley, James W., jt. auth. see Schachle, Ted.

Riley, Jan. The Bells: Donald Lipski. Robinson, Victoria, ed. (Illus.). 36p. 1991. pap. 60.00x (0-917562-59-3) Contemp Arts.

— The Bells: Donald Lipski. limited ed. Robinson, Victoria, ed. (Illus.). 36p. 1991. 300.00x (0-685-59430-0) Contemp Arts.

Riley, Jan & Burnham, Michael. Mechanika. (Illus.). 58p. (Orig.). 1991. pap. 20.00 (0-917562-57-7) Contemp Arts.

Riley, Jan, ed. see Rubinstein, Meyer R. & Schwabsky, Barry.

Riley, Jana. The Tarot Book: Basic Instruction for Reading Cards. (Illus.). 224p. (Orig.). 1992. pap. 11.95 (0-87728-723-6) Weiser.

— Tarot Dictionary & Compendium. 1995. pap. 14.95 (0-87728-821-6) Weiser.

Riley, Jane & Carlson, Mary. Help for Parents of Gifted & Talented Children. (Illus.). 64p. (J). (gr. k-6). 1984. student ed 5.95 (0-86653-190-4, GA 539) Good Apple.

Riley, Janeway. Us...& Our Good Stuff. (Illus.). 176p. (J). 1993. 19.95 (0-9637378-1-3) Janeway Riley.

***Riley, Jannelle M.** Laurel Quarberg: Treading Water. (Illus.). 8p. (Orig.). 1994. pap. 8.00 (1-885163-01-0) Virginia Beach Ctr.

Riley, Jeanna, jt. auth. see Riley, Glyndon D.

Riley, Jeni, ed. The National Curriculum & the Primary School: Spring Board or Straightjacket? (Bedford Way Ser.). 160p. 1992. pap. 24.95 (0-7494-0642-9, Pub. by Kogan Page Educ UK) Taylor & Francis.

Riley, Jo Ann, jt. auth. see McDonnell, Betty.

Riley, Joan. The Unbelonging. rev. ed. 160p. 1993. pap. 10.95 (0-7043-3959-5, Pub. by Womens Pr UK) Interlink Pub.

***Riley, Joanne M.** Crossing Without Daughters: Poems by Joanne Mokosh Riley. Bixby, Robert, ed. 34p. 1994. pap. text ed. 6.00 (1-882983-16-5) March Street Pr.

— Pacing the Moon. LC 85-4159. 72p. 1985. pap. 5.95 (0-941608-04-2) Chantry Pr.

***Riley, Jocelyn.** America Fever: A Resource Guide. 114p. 1995. 20.00 (1-877933-50-3) Her Own Words.

— Belle Case la Follette 1859-1931: A Resource Guide. 114p. 1995. 20.00 (1-877933-05-8) Her Own Words.

— Ethel Kvalheim, Rosemaler: A Resource Guide. 114p. 1995. 20.00 (1-877933-24-4) Her Own Words.

— Her Mother Before Her: Winnebago Women's Stories of Their Mothers & Grandmothers: A Resource Guide. 114p. 1995. 20.00 (1-877933-21-X) Her Own Words.

— The Literature of Quilts: A Resource Guide. 114p. 1995. 20.00 (1-877933-09-0) Her Own Words.

— The Literature of the Prairie: A Resource Guide. 114p. 1995. 20.00 (1-877933-14-7) Her Own Words.

— Mountain Wolf Woman 1884-1960: A Resource Guide. 114p. 1995. 20.00 (1-877933-12-0) Her Own Words.

— Norwegian Pioneer Women: A Resource Guide. 114p. 1995. 20.00 (1-877933-16-3) Her Own Words.

— Only My Mouth Is Smiling. LC 81-18688. 224p. (J). (gr. 7-9). 1982. 12.95 (0-688-01087-3) Morrow Jr Bks.

— Pioneer Women's Diaries: A Resource Guide. 114p. 1995. 20.00 (1-877933-07-4) Her Own Words.

— Seventy-Five Activities for Celebrating Seventy-Five Years of Votes for Women: A Resource Guide. 150p. 1995. 20.00 (1-877933-55-4) Her Own Words.

— Sisters & Friends: A Resource Guide. 114p. 1995. 20.00 (1-877933-45-7) Her Own Words.

— Votes for Women?! A Resource Guide. 114p. 1995. 20.00 (1-877933-10-4) Her Own Words.

— Winnebago Songs & Stories: A Resource Guide. 114p. 1995. 20.00 (1-877933-19-8) Her Own Words.

— Women in Construction: A Resource Guide. 114p. 1995. 20.00 (0-614-05258-0) Her Own Words.

— Women in Policing: A Resource Guide. 114p. 1995. 20.00 (1-877933-53-8) Her Own Words.

— Zona Gale: Her Life & Writings: A Resource Guide. 114p. 1995. 20.00 (1-877933-08-2) Her Own Words.

Riley, Joe G. Tennessee Criminal Law Update, 1988-1989. (Criminal Law Update Ser.). 60p. 1989. pap. text ed. 24.00 (0-925773-04-2) M Lee Smith.

Riley, Joe S. Bio Chemistry. reprint ed. spiral bd. 3.30 (0-7873-0721-1) Mokelumne.

— Correspondence Course in Zone Therapy, Reflex Technique & Hook Work. 13p. 1959. reprint ed. spiral bd. 9.35 (0-7873-1179-0) Mokelumne.

— Great Herbal Remedies. reprint ed. 3.85 (0-685-71656-2) Mokelumne.

— Iridology Simplified. reprint ed. spiral bd. 3.30 (0-7873-0722-X) Mokelumne.

Riley, Joe S. & Daglish, W. E. Zone Reflex Plus Translation Diet: Hydro-Therapy & Swedish Massage. 78p. 1961. reprint ed. spiral bd. 13.75 (0-7873-1124-3) Mokelumne.

Riley, Joe S., et al. Numerology & Vibration. reprint ed. spiral bd. 4.40 (0-7873-0726-2) Mokelumne.

Riley, John G. The Anatomy of Bad Debts. ix, 99p. 1987. pap. 19.50 (0-455-20726-7, Pub. by Law Bk Co) W W Gaunt.

Riley, John G., jt. auth. see Hirshleifer, Jack.

Riley, John H., Jr. Advanced Programming & Data Structures Using Pascal. 592p. (C). 1990. text ed. 55.95 (0-534-92035-7) PWS Pubs.

Riley, John J. A History of the American Soft Drink Industry: Bottled Carbonated Beverages, 1807-1957. LC 72-5071. (Technology & Society Ser.). (Illus.). 366p. 1975. reprint ed. 24.95 (0-405-04721-5) Ayer.

Riley, John P., ed. Chemical Oceanography, Vol. 9. 320p. 1989. text ed. 129.00 (0-12-588609-8) Acad Pr.

Riley, John P., et al, eds. Chemical Oceanography Vol. 10: SEAREX: the Sea-Air Exchange Program. 404p. 1989. text ed. 126.00 (0-12-588610-1) Acad Pr.

Riley, John W., Jr. & Johnson, Marilyn E. Aging & Society, Vol. 2: Aging & the Professions. Riley, Matilda W. et al, eds. LC 68-54406. 410p. 1969. 55.00 (0-87154-719-8) Russell Sage.

Riley, John W., Jr., jt. ed. see Riley, Matilda W.

Riley, Judith C. Ancient Peruvian Textiles. (Illus.). 15p. 1980. pap. 3.50 (0-940744-28-7) Chrysler Museum.

***Riley, Judith M.** The Oracle Glass. 528p. 1995. pap. 12.50 (0-449-91006-7) Fawcett.

Riley, Julia A. Making Mailbox Memories: Global Pen Friends for Grownups & Kids. LC 94-76206. 314p. 1994. pap. 20.00 (1-885291-01-9) Kindred Spirit.

Riley, K., jt. auth. see Motta, J.

Riley, K., et al. Small Millets. (C). 1989. 50.00 (81-204-0434-3) S Asia.

Riley, K. F. Problems for Physics Students: With Hints & Answers. LC 82-4575. 100p. 1982. pap. 27.95 (0-521-27073-1) Cambridge U Pr.

***Riley, Kana, ed.** See Us Hear Us: Voices of Breast Cancer. 128p. (Orig.). 1994. pap. 10.00 (0-9644254-0-8) NH Breast Cancer.

***Riley, Karl.** Tracing EMFs in Building Wiring & Grounding. (Illus.). 126p. (Orig.). 1995. pap. 27.50 (0-9646790-0-0) Magnetic Sci.

Riley, Katheryn A. & Nuttall, Desmond L., eds. Measuring Quality - Education Indicators: United Kingdom & International Perspectives. LC 94-2854. 176p. 1994. 75.00 (0-7507-0260-5, Falmer Pr); pap. 26.00 (0-7507-0261-3, Falmer Pr) Taylor & Francis.

Riley, Kathleen A., et al. Developing an Individualized Behavior Management Plan. 1994. 2.95 (1-56456-087-2, 285) W Gladden Found.

Riley, Kathryn. Quality & Equality: Promoting Opportunities in Schools. Sayer, John, ed. (Educational Management Ser.). (Illus.). 160p. 1994. 70.00 (0-304-32687-9); pap. 19.95 (0-304-32688-7) Cassell.

Riley, Kathryn, jt. auth. see Parker, Frank.

***Riley, Kathryn, et al.** Revising Technical & Business Writing: Principles & Applications. 153p. 1992. pap. text ed. write for info. (0-9644636-0-1) Parlay Enter.

Riley, Kelly. Celebrate Easter. (Celebrate Ser.). (Illus.). 144p. (J). (gr. k-6). 1987. pap. 11.95 (0-86653-385-0, SS 842, Shining Star Pubns) Good Apple.

Riley, Kenneth, et al, eds. Advances in Small Millets. (Illus.). 575p. (C). 1994. text ed. 70.00 (1-881570-07-X) Intl Sci Pub.

***Riley, Kevin J. & Hoffman, Bruce.** Domestic Terrorism: A National Assessment of State & Local Preparedness. LC 94-47133. (Orig.). 1995. pap. text ed. 13.00 (7-88301-627-X) Rand Corp.

***Riley, Kevin J. & Hoffman, Bruce R.** Domestic Terrorism: A National Assessment of State & Local Preparedness. LC 94-47133. (Orig.). 1995. write for info. (0-8330-1627-X) Rand Corp.

Riley, Kevin W. Street Gangs & the Schools: A Blueprint for Intervention. LC 91-60198. (Fastback Ser.: No. 321). (Orig.). 1991. pap. 1.25 (0-87367-321-2) Phi Delta Kappa.

Riley, L. A. Spiritual War Behind Prison Bars. 1992. 10.00 (0-533-09630-8) Vantage.

Riley, Laura. The Coastal Cook of West Marin: Kitchen Conversations & Recipes. (Illus.). 240p. (Orig.). 1991. pap. text ed. 12.95 (0-9628426-0-5) Riley & Co.

Riley, Laura & Riley, William. Guide to the National Wildlife Refuges. LC 92-19254. 1993. text ed. 40.00 (0-02-603440-9); pap. 16.00 (0-02-063660-1, Pub. by Gebrueder Borntraeger GW) Macmillan.

Riley, Lew. Where Was the Sexual Revolution When I Needed It? LC 92-56436. 68p. (Orig.). 1992. pap. 6.00 (0-88734-204-3) Players Pr.

Riley, Linda C. Aquarium: Bringing the Seas Inside. LC 93-16341. (Illus.). (J). (gr. 3 up). 1995. text ed. 17.95 (0-7167-6509-8, Sci Am Yng Rdrs) W H Freeman.

— Elephants Swim. LC 94-42185. (Illus.). (J). 1995. write for info. (0-395-73654-4) Ticknor & Flds Bks Yng Read.

***Riley, Linnea A., illus.** The Twelve Days of Christmas. LC 95-14362. (J). 1995. 15.00 (0-689-80275-7, S&S Bks Young Read) S&S Childrens.

Riley, Lynn M. Shelter Hill: An Analysis of Faunal Remains & Artifacts from a Marin County Shellmound (04-MRN-14) xiv, 206p. (C). 1985. reprint ed. pap. text ed. 17.50 (1-55567-014-8) Coyote Press.

Riley, M. J., ed. Management Information Systems. 2nd ed. 425p. 1981. pap. text ed. 23.95 (0-8162-7190-9) Holden-Day.

Riley, Margaret C. Whole Language Discovery Activities for the Primary Grades. 1992. pap. text ed. 27.95 (0-87628-616-3) Ctr Appl Res.

Riley, Margaret C. & Taylor, Donna L. Year Round Creative Thinking Activities for the Primary Classroom. 272p. 1990. pap. 22.95 (0-87628-985-5) P-H.

Riley, Maria. In God's Image. (Illus.). 32p. 1985. 2.95 (0-934134-21-9) Sheed & Ward MO.

R

— Wisdom Seeks Her Way: Liberating the Power of Women's Spirituality. 86p. (Orig.). 1987. pap. text ed. 5.95 (*0-934255-04-0*) Center Concern.
— Women Connecting: Facilitator's Guide. 40p. 1994. pap. 15.00 (*0-934255-11-3*) Center Concern.
— Women Connecting: Participant's Workbooks. (Illus.). 21p. (Orig.). 1994. pap. 3.50 (*0-934255-12-1*) Center Concern.
— Women Faithful for the Future. (Illus.). 32p. 1987. 2.95 (*1-55612-103-2*) Sheed & Ward MO.
Riley, Maria & Sylvester, Nancy. Trouble & Beauty: Women Encounter Catholic Social Teaching. 64p. (Orig.). 1991. pap. text ed. 3.95 (*0-934255-10-5*) Center Concern.
Riley, Marilyn A., ed. see Citation Directories, Ltd., Inc. Staff.
Riley, Marilyn A., ed. see Citation Directories, Ltd. Inc. Staff.
Riley, Marjorie. The Wife of Riley, Vol. I. 2nd ed. Riley, Wyman, ed. LC 88-886235. (Illus.). 173p. reprint ed. 16. 95 (*0-9623624-0-9*) Levee Hse Bks.
Riley, Martha, jt. auth. see Rathlev, Mary.
Riley, Martin. Boggart's Sandwich. (Illus.). 95p. (J). (gr. 7-9). 1992. pap. 3.95 (*0-563-20871-6*, BBC-Parkwest) Parkwest Pubns.
Riley, Mary. Corporate Healing: Solutions to the Impact of the Addictive Personality in the Workplace. 1990. pap. 8.95 (*1-55874-058-9*) Health Comm.
Riley, Mary A. & Beltran, Mary J. Clinical Nursing Interventions with Critical Elements. LC 85-20360. 385p. 1986. pap. text ed. 26.95 (*0-8273-4338-8*) Delmar.
Riley, Mary Ann K. Nursing Care of the Client with Ear, Nose & Throat Disorders. 368p. (C). 1987. 38.95 (*0-8261-5700-9*) Springer Pub.
Riley, Matilda W., ed. Social Change & the Life Course, Set, Vols. 1 & 2. (American Sociological Association Presidential Ser.). 560p. 1988. Set. 74.95 (*0-8039-3432-7*); Set. pap. 34.90 (*0-8039-3433-5*) Sage.
— Sociological Lives, Vol. 2: Social Change & the Life Course. (American Sociological Association Presidential Ser.). 192p. (C). 1988. text ed. 38.00 (*0-8039-3285-5*); pap. text ed. 18.50 (*0-8039-3286-3*) Sage.
Riley, Matilda W. & Foner, Anne. Aging & Society, Vol. 1: An Inventory of Research Findings. LC 68-54406. 636p. 1968. 55.00 (*0-87154-718-X*) Russell Sage.
Riley, Matilda W. & Riley, John W., Jr., eds. The Quality of Aging: Strategies for Interventions. (Annals Ser.: Vol. 503). 1989. 26.00 (*0-685-31242-9*); pap. 17.00 (*0-685-31243-7*) Sage.
Riley, Matilda W., jt. ed. see Merton, Robert K.
Riley, Matilda W., ed. see Riley, John W., Jr. & Johnson, Marilyn E.
Riley, Matilda W., et al. Aging & Society, Vol. 3: A Sociology of Age Stratification. LC 68-54406. 652p. 1972. 55.00 (*0-87154-720-1*) Russell Sage.
Riley, Matilda W., et al, eds. Age & Structural Lag: Changes in Work, Family, Retirement, & Other Structures. LC 93-46344. 1994. text ed. 42.50 (*0-471-01678-0*, Wiley-Interscience) Wiley.
— The Aging Dimension: Perspectives in Behavioral Medicine. 208p. 1987. text ed. 39.95 (*0-89859-927-X*) L Erlbaum Assocs.
— Aging in Society: Selected Reviews of Recent Research. 288p. (C). 1983. text ed. 59.95 (*0-89859-267-4*) L Erlbaum Assocs.
— AIDS in an Aging Society: What We Need to Know. 240p. 1989. 28.95 (*0-8261-7060-9*) Springer Pub.
— Social Change & the Life Course. LC 87-37658. (American Sociological Association Presidential Ser.). 368p. 1988. pap. 104.90 (*0-7837-8966-1*, 2049747) Bks Demand.
— Social Structures & Human Lives, Vol. 1: Social Change & the Life Course. (American Sociological Association Presidential Ser.). 368p. (C). 1988. text ed. 48.00 (*0-8039-3287-1*); pap. text ed. 21.50 (*0-8039-3288-X*) Sage.
Riley, Maurice W. The History of the Viola, Vol. I. LC 79-66348. 400p. 1980. 29.50 (*0-9603150-0-4*); pap. 24.50 (*0-9603150-1-2*) M W Riley.
— The History of the Viola, Vol. I. rev. ed. (Illus.). 400p. 1993. pap. 24.50 (*0-9603150-5-5*) M W Riley.
— The History of the Viola, Vol. I. 2nd rev. ed. (Illus.). 400p. 1993. 29.50 (*0-9603150-4-7*) M W Riley.
— The History of the Viola, Vol. II. (Illus.). 400p. 1991. 29. 50 (*0-9603150-2-0*); pap. 24.50 (*0-9603150-3-9*) M W Riley.
Riley, Michael. Human Resource Management: A Guide to Personnel Management in the Hotel & Catering Industry. 300p. 1991. pap. 22.95 (*0-7506-0140-X*) Buttrwrth-Heinemann.
— Managing People in the Hotel & Catering Industry. (Illus.). 224p. 1995. 24.95 (*0-7506-2289-X*, Focal) Buttrwrth-Heinemann.
Riley, Michael, jt. auth. see Palmer, James.
Riley, Michael H. Estate Administration in Massachusetts: A Handbook with Forms. 2nd ed. LC 93-39830. 420p. 1994. ring bd. 95.00 (*0-250-40726-4*) Michie Butterworth.
***Riley, Mildred.** Journey's End. 256p. 1995. pap. 4.99 (*0-8217-0102-9*) Zebra.
— Journey's End. 1995. pap. 4.99 (*0-7860-0102-X*, Pinnacle NY) Windsor NY.
Riley, Mildred E. Akayna, Sachem's Daughter. 1992. pap. 4.75 (*1-878634-07-0*) Odyssey Bks.
— Yamilla. 1990. pap. 4.75 (*1-878634-01-1*) Odyssey Bks.
Riley, Mona, jt. auth. see Sargent, Brad.
Riley, Monica, jt. ed. see Drlica, Karl.
***Riley, Natoma.** Natoma's Low Fat Home-Style Cooking. 260p. 1994. spiral bd., pap. 14.95 (*1-886246-00-9*) Alpha LifeSpan.
Riley, Noel. Tea Caddies. (Antique Pocket Guides Ser.). (Illus.). 64p. (Orig.). 1985. pap. 6.95 (*0-911403-25-6*) Seven Hills Bk.
Riley, P. A., jt. ed. see Spearman, R. I.
***Riley, Pat.** The Winner Within. 272p. 1994. pap. 12.00 (*0-425-14175-6*) Berkley Pub.
— The Winner Within: A Life Plan for Team Players. 224p. 1993. 22.95 (*0-399-13839-0*) Putnam Pub Group.
Riley, Pat, jt. auth. see Borst, Bill.
***Riley, Patricia, ed.** Growing Up Native American. 336p. 1995. pap. 11.00 (*0-380-72417-0*) Avon.
Riley, Patricia, intro. Growing up Native American: An Anthology. LC 92-46484. 1993. 23.00 (*0-688-11850-X*) Morrow.
Riley, Patrick. The General Will Before Rousseau: The Transformation of the Divine into the Civic. (Studies in Moral, Political, & Legal Philosophy). 272p. 1986. pap. 14.95 (*0-691-02292-5*) Princeton U Pr.
— Will & Political Legitimacy: A Critical Exposition of Social Contract Theory in Hobbes, Locke, Rousseau, Kant, & Hegel. 294p. 1982. 37.00 (*0-674-95316-9*) HUP.
— The X-Rated Videotape Guide V: Over 1000 Reviews of 1994 Adult Movies. LC 94-42854. (Illus.). 600p. 1995. pap. 21.95 (*0-87975-950-X*) Prometheus Bks.
— The X-Rated Videotape Star Index 1994. (Illus.). 526p. (Orig.). 1994. pap. 22.95 (*0-87975-916-X*) Prometheus Bks.
Riley, Patrick, ed. Essays on Political Philosophy. (Library of the History of Ideas: Vol. VI). 320p. 1992. text ed. 65. 00 (*1-878822-08-X*) Univ Rochester Pr.
Riley, Patrick & Shaw, Russell, eds. Anti-Catholicism in the Media: An Examination of Whether Elite News Organizations Are Biased Against the Church. LC 92-61550. 256p. (C). 1993. text ed. 16.95 (*0-87973-551-1*, 551) Our Sunday Visitor.
Riley, Patrick, ed. see Bossuet, Jacques.
Riley, Patrick, ed. see Fenelon, Francois.
Riley, Patrick, ed. see Leibniz, Gottfried W.
Riley, Patrick, tr. see Malebranche, Nicolas.
Riley, Patrick, jt. auth. see Rimmer, Robert H.
***Riley, Paul.** Flower Painting: How to Paint Free & Vibrant Watercolours. 1994. pap. 22.50 (*1-870586-10-7*, Pub. by D Porteous Edits UK) Seven Hills Bk.
Riley, Paul, jt. auth. see Dix, Mark.
Riley, Peter. Life Science: Groundwork in Biology. (Illus.). 160p. 1988. text ed. 50.00 (*0-7175-0865-X*, Pub. by S Thornes Pubs UK) St Mut.
— Looking at Microscopes. (Looking at Science Ser.). (Illus.). 48p. (J). (gr. 5-8). 1985. 19.95 (*0-7134-4632-3*, Pub. by Batsford UK) Trafalgar.
Riley, Phil M., jt. auth. see Cousins, Frank.
***Riley, Philip.** Mummys Curse: Universal Filmscripts Classic Horror Films, Vol. 11. 1994. pap. 19.95 (*1-882127-35-8*) Magicimage Filmbooks.
— Wolf Man. LC 93-32968. 1993. pap. 19.95 (*1-882127-21-8*) Magicimage Filmbooks.
Riley, Philip B., jt. ed. see Fallon, Timothy P.
Riley, Philip F., jt. auth. see Harding, Edith.
Riley, Philip F., et al. The Global Experience, Vol. 1: Readings in World History to 1500. 2nd ed. 336p. (C). 1991. pap. text ed. write for info. (*0-13-356981-0*) P-H.
— The Global Experience, Vol. 2: Readings in World History Since 1500. 2nd ed. 368p. (C). 1991. pap. text ed. write for info. (*0-13-356999-3*) P-H.
Riley, Philip J. A Blind Bargain. LC 88-90745. (Ackerman Archives Ser.: Vol. 2). (Illus.). 208p. 1988. 24.95 (*1-882127-00-5*) Magicimage Filmbooks.
— A Blind Bargain. (Ackerman Archives Ser.). (Illus.). 1991. 24.95 (*0-929127-00-5*) Magicimage Filmbooks.
— A Blind Bargain. deluxe limited ed. (Ackerman Archives Ser.). (Illus.). 1991. boxed 49.00 (*0-685-50114-0*) Magicimage Filmbooks.
— Phantom of the Opera. 1994. pap. 24.95 (*0-685-71917-0*) Magicimage Filmbooks.
Riley, Philip J., ed. The Bride of Frankenstein: The Original Shooting Script. LC 89-92189. (Universal Filmscript Series: Classic Horror Films: Vol. 2). (Illus.). 176p. (Orig.). 1989. pap. 19.95 (*1-882127-06-4*) Magicimage Filmbooks.
— The Bride of Frankenstein: The Original Shooting Script. limited ed. LC 89-92189. (Universal Filmscript Series: Classic Horror Films: Vol. 2). (Illus.). 176p. (Orig.). 1989. 60.00 (*0-685-44928-9*) Magicimage Filmbooks.
— Frankenstein: The Original Shooting Script. LC 89-92191. (Universal Filmscript Series: Classic Horror Films: Vol. 1). (Illus.). 176p. (Orig.). 1989. pap. 19.95 (*1-882127-05-6*) Magicimage Filmbooks.
— The Mummy: The Original Shooting Script. LC 89-92187. (Universal Filmscript Series: Classic Horror Films: Vol. 8). (Illus.). 170p. 1989. pap. 19.95 (*1-882127-07-2*) Magicimage Filmbooks.
Riley, Philip J. & Turner, George. Dracula: The Original 1931 Shooting Script. LC 90-61035. (Universal Filmscript Series: Classic Horror Films). (Illus.). 256p. (Orig.). 1990. pap. 19.95 (*1-882127-09-9*) Magicimage Filmbooks.
Riley, Philip J., ed. see Mank, Gregory W.
Riley, Philip J., jt. auth. see Miller, Patsy R.
Riley, Philip J., ed. see Skotak, Robert.
Riley, R. Getting a Job in Europe. (Starting Out Ser.). 1990. pap. 35.00 (*0-7463-0653-9*, Pub. by Northcote UK) St Mut.
Riley, R., ed. Essential Guide to Banking Course Supervision. (C). 1989. 50.00 (*0-85297-250-4*, Pub. by Inst Bankers UK) St Mut.
Riley, R. C. Belgium. (World Bibliographical Ser.: Vol. 104). 300p. 1989. lib. bdg. 70.00 (*1-85109-099-1*) ABC-CLIO.
Riley, R. C. & Ashworth, Gregory. Benelux: An Economic Geography of Belgium, the Netherlands, & Luxembourg. LC 74-84586. (Illus.). 258p. 1975. 30.00 (*0-8419-0174-0*) Holmes & Meier.
Riley, Ralph & Lewis, K. R., eds. Chromosome Manipulation & Plant Genetics: The Contributions to a Symposium Held During the Tenth International Botanical Congress, Edinburgh, 1964. LC 66-71193. 134p. reprint ed. pap. 38.20 (*0-317-28828-8*, 2020701) Bks Demand.
Riley, Robert. Matthew Barney. (Illus.). 52p. 1992. pap. text ed. 14.95 (*0-918471-23-0*) San Fran MOMA.
***Riley, Robert J.** Unionism, International Trade, & Trade Policy. rev. ed. LC 94-35675. (Foreign Economic Policy of the United States Ser.). (Illus.). 208p. 1995. 56.00 (*0-8153-1993-2*) Garland.
Riley, Robert Q. Alternative Cars in the Twenty-First Century: A New Personal Transportation Paradigm. 400p. 1994. 39.00 (*1-56091-519-6*, R139) Soc Auto Engineers.
Riley, Robert T., jt. auth. see Lorenzi, Nancy M.
Riley, Robyn, jt. auth. see Wood, Carl.
Riley, Roger S., et al. Clinical Applications of Flow Cytometry. (Illus.). 928p. 1993. 125.00 (*0-89640-200-2*) Igaku-Shoin.
***Riley, Sam G.** Biographical Dictionary of American Newspaper Columnists. LC 95-7185. 1995. text ed. write for info. (*0-313-29192-6*, Greenwood Pr) Greenwood.
— Gr8 Pl8s. (Orig.). 1991. pap. 6.95 (*0-942257-25-1*) New Chapter Pr.
— Index to Southern Periodicals. LC 85-27232. (Historical Guides to the World's Periodicals & Newspapers Ser.). 468p. 1986. text ed. 59.95 (*0-313-24515-0*, RII/, Greenwood Pr) Greenwood.
— Magazines of the American South. LC 85-8012. (Historical Guides to the World's Periodicals & Newspapers Ser.). 359p. 1986. text ed. 59.95 (*0-313-24337-9*, RPA/, Greenwood Pr) Greenwood.
Riley, Sam G., ed. American Magazine Journalists, 1741-1850, Vol. 73. (Dictionary of Literary Biography Ser.: Vol. 73). 430p. 1988. pap. 128.00 (*0-8103-4551-X*, 006541-M99348) Gale.
— American Magazine Journalists, 1850-1900, Vol. 79. (Dictionary of Literary Biography Ser.: Vol. 79). 387p. 1988. pap. 128.00 (*0-8103-4557-9*, 006547-M99348) Gale.
— The Best of the Rest: Non-Syndicated Newspaper Columnists Select Their Best Work. LC 92-36610. (Contributions to the Study of Mass Media & Communications Ser.: No. 39). 368p. 1993. text ed. 49. 95 (*0-313-28508-X*, RBC, Greenwood Pr) Greenwood.
— Consumer Magazines of the British Isles. LC 92-19876. (Historical Guides to the World's Periodicals & Newspapers Ser.). 336p. 1993. text ed. 79.50 (*0-313-28562-4*, RUZ, Greenwood Pr) Greenwood.
— Corporate Magazines of the United States: Historical Guides to the World's Periodicals & Newspapers. LC 91-33481. 296p. 1992. text ed. 79.50 (*0-313-27569-6*, RCG, Greenwood Pr) Greenwood.
— Dictionary of Literary Biography, Vol. 91: American Magazine Journalists, 1900-1960, Vol. 91. LC 89-48356. (First Ser.). (Illus.). 416p. 1990. text ed. 128.00 (*0-8103-4571-4*, 006559) Gale.
Riley, Sam G. & Selnow, Gary W., eds. Regional Interest Magazines of the United States: Historical Guides to the World's Periodicals & Newspapers. LC 90-36739. 432p. 1990. text ed. 99.50 (*0-313-26840-1*, RRI, Greenwood Pr) Greenwood.
Riley, Sandra. The Captain's Ladies. 384p. 1985. reprint ed. pap. 3.75 (*0-8439-2258-3*) Dorchester Pub Co.
Riley, Shannon. Hillbilly Blues. (Illus.). 50p. (Orig.). 1991. pap. 4.95 (*0-929560-05-1*) Southern Rose Prodns.
Riley, Shawn S. Borrowed Blood: Victory over Leukemia. 118p. (Orig.). 1991. pap. 10.95 (*0-936635-06-1*) Lion Pr & Vid.
***Riley, Shirley & Malchiodi, Cathy A.** Integrative Approaches to Family Art Therapy. LC 94-72843. (Illus.). 262p. (Orig.). (C). 1994. pap. text ed. 29.95 (*0-9613309-5-3*) Magnolia St Pub.
Riley, Shirley E. On the Real Side. (Illus.). 56p. 1989. pap. 6.50 (*0-936073-05-5*) Gumbs & Thomas.
Riley-Smith, Jonathan. Atlas of the Crusades. (Cultural Atlas Ser.). (Illus.). 192p. 1990. 40.00 (*0-8160-2186-4*) Facts on File.
— The Crusades: A Short History. 332p. (C). 1990. reprint ed. pap. 14.95 (*0-300-04700-2*) Yale U Pr.
— The First Crusade & the Idea of Crusading. LC 86-1608. (Middle Ages Ser.). 229p. (C). 1986. reprint ed. pap. text ed. 19.95 (*0-8122-1363-7*) U of Pa Pr.
Riley, Stan. Don't Be Denied God's Power. 184p. 1994. pap. 10.00 (*0-939513-79-X*) Joy Pub SJC.
Riley, Stanley. Learning Process Skills. 128p. (Orig.). 1991. pap. text ed. 15.00 (*0-87879-946-X*) Acad Therapy.
— Riley Inventory of Basic Learning Skills (RIBLS) 64p. 1991. pap. text ed. 17.00 (*0-87879-932-X*); student ed, vinyl bd. 50.00 (*0-87879-931-1*); student ed, vinyl bd. 50.00 (*0-87879-935-4*); 20.00 (*0-87879-933-8*); 20.00 (*0-87879-938-9*); 10.00 (*0-87879-934-6*); 10.00 (*0-87879-939-7*) Acad Therapy.
Riley, Stephen, jt. auth. see Parfitt, Trevor.
Riley, Stephen P., ed. The Politics of Global Debt. LC 93-14. (International Political Economy Ser.). 300p. 1993. text ed. 69.95 (*0-312-09636-4*) St Martin.
Riley, Stephen T., frwd. Collecting for Clio: An Exhibition of Representative Materials from the Holdings of the Massachusetts Historical Society. (Illus.). 73p. 1969. pap. 7.50 (*0-934909-02-4*) Mass Hist Soc.
Riley, Stephen T. & Hanson, Edward W., eds. The Papers of Robert Treat Paine, Vols. 1-2: Collections of the Massachusetts Historical Society, Vol. 87. 1992. Vol. 1. 50.00 (*0-934909-30-X*) Mass Hist Soc.
— The Papers of Robert Treat Paine, Vols. 1-2: Collections of the Massachusetts Historical Society, Vol. 88. 1992. Vol. 2. 50.00 (*0-934909-33-4*) Mass Hist Soc.
Riley, Sue. Afraid. LC 77-15627. (What Does It Mean? Ser.). (Illus.). 32p. (J). (ps-2). 1978. lib. bdg. 18.50 (*0-89565-011-8*) Childs World.
— Angry. LC 77-16791. (What Does It Mean? Ser.). (Illus.). (J). (ps-2). 1978. lib. bdg. 18.50 (*0-89565-014-2*) Childs World.
— Help! LC 77-16030. (What Does It Mean? Ser.). (Illus.). (J). (ps-2). 1978. lib. bdg. 18.50 (*0-89565-012-6*) Childs World.
— Sharing. LC 77-16293. (What Does It Mean? Ser.). (Illus.). (J). (ps-2). 1978. lib. bdg. 18.50 (*0-89565-015-0*) Childs World.
— Sorry. LC 77-16811. (What Does It Mean? Ser.). (Illus.). (J). (ps-2). 1978. lib. bdg. 18.50 (*0-89565-013-4*) Childs World.
— Success. LC 77-20992. (What Does It Mean? Ser.). (Illus.). (J). (ps-2). 1978. lib. bdg. 18.50 (*0-89565-016-9*) Childs World.
Riley, Sue S. How to Generate Values in Young Children: Integrity, Honesty, Individuality, Self-Confidence & Wisdom. LC 79-65310. 94p. 1984. pap. text ed. 4.50 (*0-912674-88-1*, NAEYC #202) Natl Assn Child Ed.
Riley, Susan L. & Colby, Peter W. Practical Government Budgeting: A Workbook for Public Managers. LC 89-26374. (SUNY Series in Public Administration). 138p. 1990. pap. 16.95 (*0-7914-0392-0*) State U NY Pr.
Riley, T. The Amazing World of Dinosaurs. (Illus.). 80p. (J). (gr. 2-6). 1991. 4.99 (*0-517-63993-9*) Random Hse Value.
Riley, Terence. Frank Lloyd Wright: Architect. 1994. 60.00 (*0-8109-6122-9*) Abrams.
— The International Style: Exhibition Fifteen & the Museum of Modern Art, Catalogue 3. Perrella, Stephen, ed. (Illus.). 224p. (Orig.). 1992. pap. 29.95 (*0-9623829-6-5*) CUGSA.
— International Style: Exhibition Fifteen at the Museum of Modern Art. (Illus.). 224p. (Orig.). 1992. pap. 29.95 (*0-8478-1560-9*) Rizzoli Intl.
Riley, Terence, ed. Frank Lloyd Wright: Architect. (Illus.). 336p. 1994. 60.00 (*0-87070-642-X*); pap. 29.95 (*0-87070-643-8*) Mus of Modern Art.
***Riley, Terrence.** Ship's Doctor. LC 95-8186. (Illus.). 312p. 1995. 29.95 (*1-55750-721-X*) Naval Inst Pr.
Riley, Thomas A. Germany's Poet-Anarchist: The Life & Work of John Henry Mackay. (Illus.). 336p. 1972. 250. 00 (*0-87700-101-4*) Revisionist Pr.
Riley, Thomas J. Noteven, the Mouse: A Christmas Story. LC 82-61683. (Illus.). 32p. (Orig.). 1982. pap. 4.95 (*0-933050-13-5*) New Eng Pr VT.
Riley, Thomas N., et al. Stereoisomerism in Pharmaceuticals: New Directions in Drug Discovery & Development (Seminar Notes) 194p. 1991. 75.00 (*0-87762-840-8*) Technomic.
Riley, Tiaudra, jt. auth. see Riley, Dorothy W.
Riley, Tim. Hard Rain: A Dylan Commentary. LC 92-50619. 1993. pap. 13.00 (*0-679-74527-0*, Vin) Random.
— Tell Me Why: Beatles. 1989. pap. 13.00 (*0-679-72198-3*, Vin) Random.
Riley, Tom. Proving Punitive Damages: The Complete Handbook. LC 81-2062. 347p. 1981. 37.50 (*0-13-731778-6*, Busn) P-H.
Riley, Tom & Relyea, Harold C., eds. Freedom of Information Trends in the Information Age. 180p. 1983. text ed. 30.00 (*0-7146-3221-X*, Pub. by F Cass Pubs UK) Intl Spec Bk.
Riley, Tom & Tomlinson, Colin. Principles of Electroanalytical Methods. James, Arthur M., ed. (Analytical Chemistry by Open Learning Ser.). 283p. 1987. pap. text ed. 49.95 (*0-471-91330-8*) Wiley.
Riley, Tom, et al. Polarography & Other Voltametric Methods. (Analytical Chemistry by Open Learning Ser.). 283p. 1987. pap. text ed. 57.95 (*0-471-91395-2*) Wiley.
Riley, V., ed. see International Pigment Cell Conference Staff.
Riley, Vera & Gass, Saul I. Linear Programming & Associated Techniques: A Comprehensive Bibliography on Linear, Nonlinear & Dynamic Programming. rev. ed. LC 58-3589. 623p. reprint ed. pap. 177.60 (*0-317-10665-1*, 2010406) Bks Demand.
Riley, Vernon, ed. see International Pigment Cell Conference Staff.
Riley, W. F., jt. ed. see Thompson, D. O.
Riley, W. Willshire. Sequel to Riley's Narrative. 1979. reprint ed. lib. bdg. 49.00 (*0-403-00317-2*) Scholarly.
***Riley, Wanda S.** Where Memories Meet: A Romantic & Spiritual Thriller. 160p. (Orig.). 1993. pap. 15.95 (*1-880222-21-3*) Red-Apple Pub.
Riley, William. The Bible Group: An Owner's Manual. 154p. 1989. pap. 22.00 (*0-86217-098-2*, Pub. by Veritas IE) St Mut.
— Tale of Two Testaments. LC 85-50692. 160p. (C). 1985. pap. 5.95 (*0-89622-240-3*) Twenty-Third.
— The Tale of Two Testaments. 150p. 1989. pap. 22.00 (*0-86217-180-6*, Pub. by Veritas IE) St Mut.
Riley, William, jt. auth. see McCarthy, Carmel.
Riley, William, jt. auth. see Riley, Laura.
***Riley, William B.** The Antievolution Pamphlets of William Bell Riley. Trollinger, William V., Jr., ed. & intro. by. LC 94-43258. (Creationism in Twentieth-Century America Ser.: Vol. 4). 1995. write for info. (*0-8153-1801-4*) Garland.
Riley, William B. & Montgomery, Austin. IBM VM - CMS Magnetic Tape. 1986. pap. write for info. (*0-07-052922-1*) McGraw.
Riley, William F. Engineering Mechanics Statics with Software, IBM 3.5. 1993. Net. text ed. write for info. (*0-471-59286-2*) Wiley.
Riley, William F. & Sturges, Leroy D. Engineering Mechanics: Dynamics. 592p. 1993. Net. text ed. write for info. (*0-471-51242-7*) Wiley.

R

An Asterisk (*) at the beginning of an entry indicates that the title is appearing in BIP for the first time.

— Engineering Mechanics: Statics. 600p. 1993. Net. text ed. write for info. (*0-471-51241-9*) Wiley.

Riley, William F. & Zachary, Loren W. Introduction to Mechanics of Materials. LC 88-21587. 747p. 1989. Net. text ed. write for info. (*0-471-84933-2*) Wiley.

Riley, William F., jt. auth. see Dally, James W.

Riley, Wyman, ed. see Riley, Marjorie.

Riling, Ray. Guns & Shooting: A Bibliography. (Illus.). 1981. 75.00 (*0-9603094-3-8*) Ray Riling.

— The Powder Flask Book. 496p. 1992. 70.00 (*1-884849-04-0*) R&R Bks.

Rilke, Clara, ed. see Rilke, Rainer Maria.

Rilke, Franco, ed. Cervical Neoplasia. (Journal: Applied Pathology: Vol. 5, No. 1). (Illus.). 76p. 1987. pap. 38.50 (*3-8055-4605-X*) S Karger.

Rilke, Maria R. Duino Elergies. Oswald, David, tr. 128p. 1995. 14.95 (*3-85630-535-1*, Pub. by Daimon Verlag SZ) Atrium Pubs.

***Rilke, Rainer.** Ahead of All Parting: The Selected Poetry & Prose of Rainer Maria Rilke. 1995. 18.00 (*0-679-60161-9*) Random.

Rilke, Rainer M. The Book of Fresh Beginnings: Selected Poems of Rainer Maria Rilke. Young, David, tr. & intro. by. (Field Translation Ser.: No. 20). 99p. 1994. 22.95 (*0-932440-68-1*) Oberlin Coll Pr.

— The Book of Fresh Beginnings: Selected Poems of Rainer Maria Rilke. Young, David, tr. & intro. by. (Field Translation Ser.: No. 20). 99p. 1994. pap. 12.95 (*0-932440-67-3*) Oberlin Coll Pr.

— The Book of Images. Snow, Edward, tr. 288p. 1991. 25.00 (*0-86547-468-0*, North Pt Pr) FS&G.

— Book of Images. Snow, Edward, tr. 1994. pap. 12.00 (*0-86547-477-X*, North Pt Pr) FS&G.

— Duino Elegies. MacIntyre, C. F., tr. 1961. pap. 10.00 (*0-520-01073-6*) U CA Pr.

— The Duino Elegies. Jaeger, Sharon A., tr. LC 91-3842. 91p. (Orig.). 1991. pap. 9.95 (*0-937584-15-0*) Sachem Pr.

— Duino Elegies. Mitchell, Stephen, tr. LC 92-50121. (Pocket Classics Ser.). 104p. 1992. reprint ed. pap. 6.00 (*0-87773-852-1*) Shambhala Pubns.

— Duino Elegies: The Sonnets to Orpheus. Hunter, Robert, tr. (Illus.). 1993. pap. 19.95 (*0-938493-21-3*) Hulogosi Inc.

— Dunio Elegies. David, Young, tr. 104p. 1992. pap. 8.95 (*0-393-30931-2*) Norton.

— Last Poems. limited ed. Mitchell, Stephen, tr. (Illus.). 75p. (ENG & GER.). 1989. 95.00 (*0-942067-01-0*) Okeanos Pr.

— Letters to a Young Poet. Allen, Marc, ed. Burnham, Joan M., tr. LC 91-42157. (Classic Wisdom Collection). 128p. 1992. 12.95 (*0-931432-94-4*) New Wrld Lib.

— Letters to a Young Poet. Mitchell, Stephen, tr. 128p. 1986. pap. 9.00 (*0-394-74104-8*, Vin) Random.

— Letters to a Young Poet. 128p. 1991. reprint ed. lib. bdg. 14.95 (*0-89966-767-8*) Buccaneer Bks.

— Letters to a Young Poet. Mitchell, Stephen, tr. LC 93-20169. (Pocket Classics Ser.). 112p. 1993. reprint ed. pap. 6.00 (*0-87773-946-3*) Shambhala Pubns.

— The Notebooks of Malte Laurids Brigge. Mitchell, Stephen, tr. LC 90-50272. (Vintage International Ser.). 304p. 1990. pap. 12.00 (*0-679-73245-4*, Vin) Random.

— The Notebooks of Malte Laurids Brigge. Norton, M. D., tr. 240p. 1992. pap. 9.95 (*0-393-30881-2*) Norton.

— Oeuvres en Prose. deluxe ed. 1280p. (FRE.). 1992. 150.00 (*0-7859-0966-4*, 2070112551) Fr & Eur.

— Roses & the Windows. 1978. 12.50 (*0-915308-21-5*) Graywolf.

— Selected Poems. MacIntyre, C. F., tr. (C). 1940. pap. 8.00 (*0-520-01070-1*) U CA Pr.

— Selected Poems of Rainer Maria Rilke. 1981. pap. 14.00 (*0-06-090727-4*, PL) HarpC.

— Selected Poetry of Rainer Maria Rilke. Mitchell, Stephen, ed. (Illus.). 315p. 1982. 25.00 (*0-394-52434-9*) Random.

— The Selected Poetry of Rainer Maria Rilke. Mitchell, Stephen, tr. (International Ser.). 1989. pap. 12.00 (*0-679-72201-7*, Vin) Random.

— Sonnets to Orpheus. MacIntyre, C. F., tr. (C). 1960. pap. 10.00 (*0-520-01069-8*) U CA Pr.

— Sonnets to Orpheus. Norton, M. D., tr. 160p. 1992. pap. 7.95 (*0-393-30932-0*) Norton.

— The Sonnets to Orpheus. Wadden, Paul, tr. 77p. (Orig.). 1989. pap. 8.00 (*0-933704-78-X*) Dawn Pr.

— The Sonnets to Orpheus. Mitchell, Stephen, tr. (Orig.). 1986. 13.95 (*0-685-43056-1*, Touchstone Bks) S&S Trade.

— The Sonnets to Orpheus. Mitchell, Stephen, tr. & intro. by. LC 92-50444. (Pocket Classics Ser.). 128p. (Orig.). reprint ed. pap. 6.00 (*0-87773-874-2*) Shambhala Pubns.

— Stories of God. Norton, M. D., tr. 144p. 1992. pap. 8.95 (*0-393-30882-0*) Norton.

— Translations from the Poetry. Norton, M. D., tr. 256p. 1993. pap. 9.95 (*0-393-31038-8*) Norton.

— Two Stories of Prague: King Bohush & The Siblings. Esterhammer, Angela, tr. & intro. by. LC 93-35912. (Illus.). 151p. (C). 1994. 18.95 (*0-87451-661-7*) U Pr of New Eng.

— Uncollected Poems. Snow, Edward, tr. LC 94-24438. 280p. 1995. 21.00 (*0-86547-482-6*, North Pt Pr) FS&G.

Rilke, Rainer M. & Poulin, A., Jr. Duino Elegies & the Sonnets to Orpheus. 1977. pap. 12.95 (*0-395-25058-7*) HM.

Rilke, Rainer Maria. The Best of Rilke: Seventy-Two Form-True Verse Translations with Facing Originals, Commentary, & Compact Biography. LC 88-40345. 213p. 1989. pap. 12.95 (*0-87451-461-4*) U Pr of New Eng.

— The Complete French Poems of Rainer Maria Rilke. Poulin, A., Jr., tr. & pref. by. LC 86-81786. 383p. (Orig.). 1986. pap. 14.00 (*0-915308-83-5*) Graywolf.

— Duino Elegies. Hunter, Robert, tr. LC 87-4256. (Illus.). 130p. (ENG.). 1987. 13.95 (*0-938493-06-X*) Hulogosi Inc.

— Ewald Tragy. Halpert, Inge D., ed. LC 61-7867. (Orig.). (GER.). 1961. pap. text ed. 4.95 (*0-89197-155-6*) Irvington.

— Geschichten Vom Lieben Gott. Wunderlich, Eva C., ed. (Illus.). 1957. 29.50 (*0-8057-5272-2*) Irvington.

— Letters on Cezanne. Rilke, Clara, ed. Agee, Joel, tr. LC 85-16014. 98p. 1985. pap. 7.95 (*0-88064-107-X*) Fromm Intl Pub.

— Letters to a Young Poet. Norton, M. D., tr. 128p. 1993. pap. 6.95 (*0-393-31039-6*) Norton.

— New Poems: The Other Part (1908) Snow, Edward, tr. LC 86-62835. 240p. 1990. pap. 12.00 (*0-86547-416-8*, North Pt Pr) FS&G.

— Poems from the Book of Hours. Deutsch, Babette, tr. & intro. by. LC 42-21208. 64p. 1975. pap. 4.95 (*0-8112-0595-9*, NDP408) New Directions.

— Possibility of Being: Selected Poems. Leishman, J. B., tr. LC 77-4656. 1977. pap. 6.95 (*0-8112-0651-3*, NDP436) New Directions.

— Rainer Maria Rilke: Aspects of His Mind & Poetry. Rose, William & Houston, G. Craig, eds. LC 73-114098. (Illus.). 189p. 1970. reprint ed. 45.00 (*0-87752-092-5*) Gordian.

— Rilke: Between Roots Selected Poems Rendered from German By Rika Lesser. Lesser, Rika, tr. LC 85-43204. (Lockert Library of Poetry in Translation). 75p. 1986. pap. 9.95 (*0-691-01429-9*) Princeton U Pr.

— Rodin. LC 74-6405. (Studies in French Literature: No. 45). 1974. lib. bdg. 75.00 (*0-8383-1913-0*) M S G Haskell Hse.

— Shadows on the Sundial. Barkan, Stanley H., ed. Krapf, Norbert, tr. (Review Chapbook Ser.: No. 21: Swiss (German) Poetry 1). (Illus.). 48p. (ENG & GER.). 1992. 15.00 (*0-89304-895-X*); pap. 5.00 (*0-89304-896-8*) Cross-Cultrl NY.

— Sonnets to Orpheus. Young, David, tr. LC 87-6146. (Wesleyan Poetry in Translation Ser.). 134p. (ENG & GER.). 1987. pap. 12.95 (*0-8195-6165-7*, Wesleyan Univ Pr) U Pr of New Eng.

— The Sonnets to Orpheus. Pitchford, Kenneth, tr. LC 81-84492. (Illus.). 68p. (Orig.). 1983. pap. 10.00 (*0-938266-01-2*) Purchase Pr.

— The Unknown Rilke. enl. ed. Wright, Franz, tr. & intro. by. (Field Translation Ser.: No. 17). 175p. (Orig.). 1990. pap. 12.95 (*0-932440-56-8*) Oberlin Coll Pr.

— Where Silence Reigns: Selected Prose. LC 78-9079. 1978. pap. 8.95 (*0-8112-0697-1*, NDP464) New Directions.

Rillema, James A., ed. Actions of Prolactin on Molecular Processes. 256p. 1987. 198.00 (*0-8493-5376-9*, QP572) CRC Pr.

Rillera, Mary J. Adoption Encounter: Hurt, Transition, Healing. 171p. (Orig.). 1991. pap. 15.95 (*0-941770-05-2*) Pure CA.

— The Adoption Searchbook: Techniques for Tracing People. 15.95 (*0-941770-02-8*) Triadoption Lib.

— The Adoption Searchbook: Techniques for Tracing People. 3rd rev. ed. 210p. 1991. reprint ed. pap. 18.95 (*0-910143-00-5*) Pure CA.

— The Family Book: Keepsake of Family Records for Children with Multiple Parents. 112p. (Orig.). 1991. pap. 13.95 (*0-910143-04-8*) Pure CA.

— The Reunion Book, Vol. 1. 216p. (Orig.). 1991. pap. 17.95 (*0-910143-05-6*) Pure CA.

— The Search & Support Directory. 216p. (Orig.). 1991. pap. 19.95 (*0-910143-01-3*) Pure CA.

Rillera, Mary J., ed. A Poem Is Where the Heart Is: A Chronicle of Verse. 226p. (Orig.). 1991. pap. 15.95 (*0-910143-03-X*) Pure CA.

Rillera, Mary J. & Kaplan, Sharon. Cooperative Adoption: A Handbook. 158p. 1985. pap. 14.95 (*0-941770-03-6*) Triadoption Lib.

— Cooperative Adoption: A Handbook. 2nd ed. 158p. 1991. pap. 14.95 (*0-685-54343-9*) Pure CA.

Rilliet, Albert. Calvin & Servetus: The Reformer's Share in the Trial of Michael Servetus Historically Ascertained. Tweedie, W. K., tr. LC 83-45631. reprint ed. 31.50 (*0-404-19848-1*) AMS Pr.

Rillo. Finders Keepers. 32p. (Orig.). 1992. pap. 9.00 (*1-880516-04-7*) Left Hand Bks.

— Hymns. 32p. (Orig.). 1991. pap. 9.00 (*1-880516-00-4*) Left Hand Bks.

— Wolf's Clothing. 80p. 1994. 25.00 (*1-880516-15-2*) Left Hand Bks.

— Wolf's Clothing. 80p. 1994. pap. 9.00 (*1-880516-12-8*) Left Hand Bks.

Rillo, Thomas J. Outdoor Education: Beyond the Classroom Walls. LC 85-61789. (Fastback Ser.: No. 232). 50p. 1985. pap. 1.25 (*0-87367-232-1*) Phi Delta Kappa.

Riloba, Fortunato, jt. tr. see Schmidt, J. J.

Rim, Jong-Joo, see Hailji, pseud..

Rima, A., jt. ed. see Van Wissen, L. J.

Rima, Ingrid, ed. The Joan Robinson Legacy. LC 90-28932. 296p. 1991. 62.95 (*0-87332-611-3*) M E Sharpe.

Rima, Ingrid H. Development of Economic Analysis. 5th ed. 592p. (C). 1991. text ed. 54.95 (*0-256-08631-1*) Irwin.

— Labor Markets in a Global Economy: A Macroeconomic Perspective. (Illus.). 388p. 1995. 64.95 (*0-87332-737-3*); pap. 24.95 (*0-87332-738-1*) M E Sharpe.

Rima, Ingrid H., ed. Measurement, Quantification & Economic Analysis: Numeracy in Economics. LC 94-14956. 1995. write for info. (*0-415-08915-8*) Routledge.

— The Political Economy of Global Restructuring: Economic Organization & Production, Vol. 1. (New Dimensions in Political Economy Ser.). 256p. 1993. 59.95 (*1-85278-638-8*, Pub. by E Elgar Pub UK) Ashgate Pub Co.

— The Political Economy of Global Restructuring: Trade & Finance, Vol. 2. (New Dimensions in Political Economy Ser.). 256p. 1993. 59.95 (*1-85278-808-9*, Pub. by E Elgar Pub UK) Ashgate Pub Co.

***Rimanelli, Giose.** Alien Cantica: An American Journey (1964-1993) Bonaffini, Luigi, ed. & tr. by. LC 94-37736. (Southern Italian & Italian-American Culture Ser.: Vol. 7). 1995. write for info. (*0-8204-2650-4*) P Lang Pubs.

Rimanelli, Giose & Atchity, Kenneth J., eds. Italian Literature: Roots & Branches: Essays in Honor of Thomas Goddard Bergin. LC 75-18182. 471p. reprint ed. pap. 134.30 (*0-8357-8189-5*, 2033875) Bks Demand.

Rimanelli, Goise. Benedetta in Guysterland. 249p. 1993. pap. 13.00 (*0-920717-88-8*) Guernica Editions.

Rimanelli, Marco & Lynn, Sheryl, eds. The Eighteen Ninety-One New Orleans Lynchings & U. S.-Italian Relations: A Look Back. LC 91-32335. (Studies in Southern Italian & Italian-American Culture: Vol. 2). 425p. (C). 1992. text ed. 59.95 (*0-8204-1672-X*) P Lang Pubs.

Rimanoczy, Richard S., jt. auth. see Wilkie, Leighton A.

***Rimaschewskaja, Emilja.** Deutsch-Russiches, Russiches-Deutsches Woerterbuch. 2nd ed. 935p. (GER & RUS.). 1991. 69.95 (*0-7859-8547-6*, 3894511109) Fr & Eur.

***Rimbali, Paul.** Boulangerie. LC 94-5372. 1995. 20.00 (*0-02-600865-3*) Macmillan.

***Rimbaud & Sloate.** Illuminations: Bilingual Edition. Date not set. per. 10.00 (*0-920717-04-7*) Guernica Editions.

Rimbaud, Arthur. Complete Works. Schmidt, Paul, tr. 1976. pap. 13.00 (*0-06-090490-9*, CN490, PL) HarpC.

— Complete Works with Selected Letters. Fowlie, Wallace, tr. LC 66-13885. 1967. reprint ed. pap. 13.95 (*0-226-71973-1*, P288) U Ch Pr.

— Correspondance 1888-1891. 228p. (FRE.). 1965. pap. 18.95 (*0-7859-1303-3*, 2070254364) Fr & Eur.

— Les Illuminations. Incl. Saison en Enfer. (*0-318-52030-3*); (Poesie Ser.). 7.50 (*0-685-34966-7*) Schoenhof.

— Illuminations. Varese, Louise, tr. LC 56-13365. (ENG & FRE.). (C). 1957. pap. 9.95 (*0-8112-0184-8*, NDP56) New Directions.

— Illuminations: Coloured Plates. Osmond, Nick, ed. (French Poets Ser.). 186p. (FRE.). (C). 1976. pap. 12.50 (*0-485-12710-5*, Pub. by Athlone Pr UK) Humanities.

— Lettres de la Vie Litteraire. (Imaginaire Ser.). (FRE.). 1990. pap. 11.95 (*2-07-072009-8*) Schoenhof.

— Lettres de sa Vie Litteraire, 1870-1875. 236p. (FRE.). 1931. pap. 10.95 (*0-7859-1302-5*, 2070254356) Fr & Eur.

— Lettres du Voyant: 13 et 15 Mai 1871. Schaeffer, Gerard, ed. 195p. (FRE.). 1975. pap. 49.95 (*0-7859-5380-9*) Fr & Eur.

— Oeuvres Completes. Adam, Antoine, ed. 1312p. (FRE.). 1972. lib. bdg. 105.00 (*0-7859-3785-4*, 2070104761) Fr & Eur.

— Oeuvres Completes. deluxe ed. Renneville & Moquet, eds. (Pleiade Ser.). (FRE.). 1946. 68.95 (*2-07-010476-1*) Schoenhof.

— Oeuvres Poetiques, 2 tomes, Set. (Illus.). 87.50 (*0-685-34968-3*) Fr & Eur.

— Oeuvres, Vol. 1: Poesies. pap. 3.95 (*0-7859-2992-4*) Fr & Eur.

— Oeuvres, Vol. 2: Une Saison en Enfer; Verse Nouveaux. (FRE.). 1989. pap. 10.95 (*0-7859-2993-2*) Fr & Eur.

— Oeuvres, Vol. 3: Illuminations - Correspondence, 1873-1891. (FRE.). 1989. pap. 10.95 (*0-7859-2995-9*) Fr & Eur.

— Poesies. (FRE.). 1984. pap. 10.95 (*0-7859-3122-8*) Fr & Eur.

— Poesies: Avec: une Saison en Enfer, Illuminations. Forestier, Louis, ed. 157p. (FRE.). 1992. pap. 8.95 (*0-7859-1493-5*, 2277231533) Fr & Eur.

— Poesies: Edition Critique. 232p. (FRE.). 1966. pap. 24.95 (*0-7859-5381-7*) Fr & Eur.

— Poesies; Une Saison en enfer; Illuminations. (Poesie Ser.). 318p. (FRE.). 1981. pap. 9.95 (*2-07-031955-5*) Schoenhof.

— Rimbaud: Collected Poems. 384p. 1987. pap. 10.95 (*0-14-042064-9*, Penguin Classics) Viking Penguin.

— Season in Hell. Varese, Louise, tr. Bd. with Drunken Boat. LC 61-14900. LC 61-14900. (ENG & FRE.). Set pap. 6.95 (*0-8112-0185-6*, NDP97) New Directions.

— A Season in Hell. Peschel, Enid R., tr. Bd. with Illuminations. Illus.). (ENG & FRE.). 1974. Set pap. 8.95 (*0-19-501760-9*) OUP.

— A Season in Hell & Illuminations: Bi-Lingual Edition. Mathieu, Bertrand, tr. 300p. (ENG & FRE.). 1991. 25.00 (*0-918526-88-4*); pap. 12.50 (*0-918526-89-2*) BOA Edns.

Rimbaud, Arthur & Verlaine, Paul. A Lover's Cock & Other Gay Poems. Murat, J. & Gunn, W., trs. (Illus.). 64p. (Orig.). 1979. lib. bdg. 25.00 (*0-917342-69-0*) Gay Sunshine.

Rimbaud, Jean N. Four Poems by Rimbaud: The Problem of Translation. Belitt, Ben, tr. LC 77-11475. reprint ed. 12.50 (*0-404-16337-8*) AMS Pr.

— Oeuvres de Arthur Rimbaud. Berrichon, Paterne, ed. LC 77-11477. reprint ed. 28.50 (*0-404-16338-6*) AMS Pr.

— Prose Poems from Les Illuminations of Arthur Rimbaud. Rootham, Helen, tr. LC 77-11478. reprint ed. 13.50 (*0-404-16339-4*) AMS Pr.

Rimbault, Edward. The Rounds, Catches & Canons of England: A Collection of Specimens of the Sixteenth, Seventeenth, & Eighteenth Centuries Adopted to Modern Use. LC 76-21067. (Music Reprint Ser.). 208p. 1976. 35.00 (*0-306-70823-X*) Da Capo.

Rimbault, Edward F. The Early English Organ Builders & Their Work. 1977. lib. bdg. 75.00 (*0-8490-1740-8*) Gordon Pr.

— The Early English Organ Builders & Their Works: Fifteenth Century to the Great Rebellion. LC 74-24201. reprint ed. 31.50 (*0-404-12819-X*) AMS Pr.

Rimbault, Edward F., ed. The Old Cheque-Book: or Book of Rememberance of the Chapel Royal from 1561 to 1744. LC 65-23407. (Music Ser.). 1966. reprint ed. lib. bdg. 35.00 (*0-306-70911-2*) Da Capo.

Rimbault, Edward F., jt. auth. see Hopkins, Edward J.

Rimbault, Edward F., ed. see North, Roger.

Rimbeaux, B. C., jt. auth. see Cassidy, John.

Rimberg, John. The Motion Picture in the Soviet Union, 1918-1952: A Sociological Analysis. LC 72-559. (Dissertations on Film Ser.). 238p. 1974. reprint ed. 19.95 (*0-405-04102-0*) Ayer.

Rimboi, N. R, jt. auth. see Kirk, F. W.

Rime, Bernard, jt. ed. see Feldman, Robert S.

Rimenhild, jt. auth. see Horn.

Rimer, J. Thomas. Modern Japanese Fiction & Its Traditions: An Introduction. LC 78-51188. 327p. reprint ed. pap. 93.20 (*0-8357-4287-3*, 2037086) Bks Demand.

— Pilgrimages: Aspects of Japanese Literature & Culture. LC 88-21621. (Illus.). 168p. (C). 1988. text ed. 17.00 (*0-8248-1148-8*) UH Pr.

— A Reader's Guide to Japanese Literature. 212p. (Orig.). 1991. reprint ed. pap. 6.95 (*4-7700-1477-5*) Kodansha.

Rimer, J. Thomas, ed. Culture & Identity: Japanese Intellectuals during the Interwar Years. (Illus.). 316p. (C). 1990. text ed. 45.00 (*0-691-05570-X*) Princeton U Pr.

— A Hidden Fire: Russian & Japanese Cultural Encounters, 1868-1926. LC 94-38116. 312p. 1995. 45.00 (*0-8047-2513-6*) Stanford U Pr.

— Mask & Sword: Two Plays for the Contemporary Japanese Theater. (Modern Asian Literature Ser.). (Illus.). 1980. text ed. 43.00 (*0-231-04932-3*) Col U Pr.

Rimer, J. Thomas, tr. The Way of Acting: The Theatre Writings of Tadashi Suzuki. LC 86-5894. (Illus.). 188p. 1986. pap. 9.95 (*0-930452-56-9*) Theatre Comm.

Rimer, J. Thomas & Masakazu, Yamazaki, trs. On the Art of the No Drama: The Major Treatises of Zeami. LC 83-42573. (Library of Asian Translations). (Illus.). 370p. 1984. pap. 19.95 (*0-691-10154-X*) Princeton U Pr.

Rimer, J. Thomas, ed. see Ogai, Mori.

Rimer, J. Thomas, tr. see Ogai, Mori.

Rimer, J. Thomas, ed. see Ogai, Mori.

Rimer, J. Thomas, jt. ed. see Schlant, Ernestine.

Rimer, J. Thomas, jt. auth. see Takashina, Shuji.

Rimer, Robert A. & Connolly, Michael A. HIV Positive: Working the System. LC 92-30659. 236p. (Orig.). 1993. pap. 12.95 (*1-55583-208-3*) Alyson Pubs.

***Rimer, Thomas, ed.** Kyoto Encounters. (Illus.). 112p. 1995. pap. 19.95 (*0-8348-0309-7*) Weatherhill.

Rimer, Thomas, et al. Shisendo: Hall of the Poetry Immortals. (Illus.). 224p. (Orig.). 1991. pap. 29.95 (*0-8348-0241-4*) Weatherhill.

Rimington, Anthony. Technology & Transition: A Survey of Biotechnology in Russia, Ukraine & the Baltic States. LC 92-20948. 384p. 1992. text ed. 79.50 (*0-89930-804-X*, Q804, Quorum Bks) Greenwood.

Rimini, E., jt. ed. see Boyd, I. W.

Rimini, E., ed. see Tenth International Conference on Ion Implantation Technology Staff.

***Rimini, Emanuele.** Ion Implantation: Basics to Device Fabrication. (International Series in Engineering & Computer Science, Natural Language Processing & Machine Translation). 408p. (C). 1994. lib. bdg. 120.00 (*0-7923-9520-4*) Kluwer Ac.

Rimkunas, Richard, jt. auth. see Phillips, Warren R.

Rimler, George W. & Humphreys, Neil J. Small Business: Developing the Winning Management Team. LC 79-54848. 190p. reprint ed. pap. 54.20 (*0-317-26901-1*, 2023562) Bks Demand.

Rimler, George W., jt. auth. see Newcomb, Donald L.

Rimler, Marlene. Don't Marry Be Happy. 78p. (Orig.). 1993. pap. 7.95 (*1-56245-034-4*) Great Quotations.

— Love Streams: The Language of Lovers & Dreamers. 64p. 1993. 5.95 (*1-56245-078-6*) Great Quotations.

— To A Very Special Husband. 64p. 1993. text ed. 5.95 (*1-56245-042-5*) Great Quotations.

— Women on Men. 168p. (Orig.). 1993. pap. 5.95 (*1-56245-040-9*) Great Quotations.

Rimler, Walter. A Gershwin Companion: A Critical Inventory & Discography, 1916-1984. 500p. 1991. lib. bdg. 55.00 (*1-56075-019-7*) Popular Culture.

— Not Fade Away: A Comparison of Two Generations of Composers of Contemporary Popular Music. (Illus.). 240p. 1983. 40.00 (*0-87650-159-5*) Popular Culture.

Rimlinger, Frank S. Pregroups & Bass-Serre Theory. LC 86-32112. (Memoirs of the American Mathematical Society Ser.: Vol. 361). 73p. 1987. 16.00 (*0-8218-2421-X*, MEMO/65/361C) Am Math.

Rimm, Martin. The Pornographer's Handbook: How to Exploit Women, Dupe Men, & Make Lots of Money. (Illus.). 67p. (Orig.). 1995. pap. 5.95 (*0-9625476-5-4*) Carnegie.

***Rimm, Sylvia.** Why Bright Kids Get Poor Grades & What You Can Do about It. 1995. 23.00 (*0-517-70062-X*, Crown) Crown Pub Group.

Rimm, Sylvia B. Gifted Kids Have Feelings Too: And Other Not-So-Fictitious Stories for & about Teenagers. LC 90-81442. (Illus.). 162p. (Orig.). (YA). (gr. 6-12). 1990. pap. text ed. 15.00 (*0-937891-06-1*) Apple Pub Wisc.

— How to Parent So Children Will Learn. LC 89-84190. (Illus.). 279p. (Orig.). 1989. pap. text ed. 15.00 (*0-937891-02-9*) Apple Pub Wisc.

— Keys to Parenting the Gifted Child. LC 94-6105. (Parenting Keys Ser.). 208p. (Orig.). 1994. pap. 5.95 (*0-8120-1820-6*) Barron.

— Sylvia Rimm on Raising Kids. (Illus.). 244p. (Orig.). 1992. pap. 15.00 (*0-937891-09-6*) Apple Pub Wisc.

R

Rimm, Sylvia B. & Priest, Christine. Gifted Kids Have Feelings Too: And Other Not-So-Fictitious Stories for & about Teenagers. LC 90-81442. (Illus.). 162p. (Orig.). (YA). (gr. 6-12). 1990. pap. text ed. 15.00 (0-937891-07-X) Apple Pub Wisc.

Rimm, Sylvia B., jt. auth. see Davis, Gary A.

Rimm, Sylvia B., et al. Guidebook - Underachievement Syndrome: Causes & Cures. LC 88-83204. 370p. 1989. pap. text ed. 35.00 (0-937891-01-0, SR101) Apple Pub Wisc.

***Rimmer.** Return to Planet Internet. 1995. pap. text ed. 24. 95 (0-07-053021-1) McGraw.

— Staying Poor: Ghana's Political Economy 1950-1990. 256p. 1995. 76.00 (0-08-041032-4, Focal) Buttrwrth-Heinemann.

— Windows & OS/2 Bitmapped Graphics. 2nd ed. 1996. disk, pap. text ed. 38.95 (0-07-911903-4) McGraw.

Rimmer, Alfred. Ancient Stone Crosses of England. 1991. lib. bdg. 79.95 (0-8490-4965-2) Gordon Pr.

— Ancient Stone Crosses of England. reprint ed. spiral bd. 8.25 (0-7873-0727-0) Mokelumne.

Rimmer, Christine. Born Innocent. (Silhouette Special Edition Ser.). 1993. mass mkt. 3.50 (0-373-09833-2, 5-09833-0) Silhouette.

— Cat's Cradle. (Desire Ser.). 1995. mass mkt. 3.25 (0-373-05940-X, 1-05940-1) Silhouette.

— Conterfeit Bride. (Silhouette Desire Ser.). 1993. mass mkt. 2.99 (0-373-05812-8, 5-05812-8) Silhouette.

— For the Baby's Sake: (That Special Woman!) (Special Edition Ser.). 1994. mass mkt. 3.50 (0-373-09925-8, 1-09925-8) Silhouette.

— Hard Luck Lady. large type ed. (Silhouette Desire Ser.). 1994. 17.95 (0-373-58850-X, Silhouette Lrg Print); pap. 16.95 (0-373-59072-5, Silhouette Lrg Print) Chivers N Amer.

— A Home for the Hunter. (Special Edition Ser.). 1994. mass mkt. 3.50 (0-373-09908-8, 1-09908-4) Harlequin Bks.

— Man of the Mountain. 1994. mass mkt. 3.50 (0-373-09886-3) Silhouette.

— Sweetbriar Summit. 1994. mass mkt. 3.50 (0-373-09896-0, 1-09896-1) Harlequin Bks.

— Wagered Woman. 1993. mass mkt. 3.39 (0-373-09794-8, 5-09794-4) Silhouette.

Rimmer, D. L., jt. ed. see Syers, J. K.

Rimmer, David. Album. 1981. pap. 4.75 (0-8222-0013-9) Dramatists Play.

Rimmer, Douglas, ed. Action in Africa: The Experience of People Involved in Government, Business & Aid. LC 93-38558. 192p. 1994. pap. 19.95 (0-435-08098-9) Heinemann.

— Rural Transformation in Tropical Africa. LC 88-5256. 196p. 1988. lib. bdg. 29.95 (0-8214-0895-X) Ohio U Pr.

Rimmer, Douglas, jt. auth. see Kirk-Greene, Anthony.

Rimmer, Harry. La Llave del Problema: Answers to Key Bible Questions. (SPA.). 5.50 (84-7228-004-7, 220542, Pub. by Edit Clie SP) TSELF.

Rimmer, James D. Fitness & Rehabilitation Programs for Special Populations. 344p. (C). 1994. boxed write for info. (0-697-11619-0) Brown & Benchmark.

Rimmer, Joan. Irish Harp. 1984. pap. 7.95 (0-85342-151-X) Dufour.

Rimmer, Robert. The Immoral Reverend. LC 85-43080. 356p. 1985. 25.95 (0-87975-299-8) Prometheus Bks.

Rimmer, Robert, ed. see Butler, Jerry.

Rimmer, Robert H. The Byrdwhistle Option. LC 82-81709. 409p. 1982. 26.95 (0-87975-184-3) Prometheus Bks.

— The Harrad Experiment. rev. ed. 324p. (C). 1990. reprint ed. pap. 16.95 (0-87975-623-3) Prometheus Bks.

— Let's Really Make Love: Sex, the Family, & Education in the Twenty-First Century. LC 95-2877. 300p. 1995. pap. 16.95 (0-87975-964-X) Prometheus Bks.

— The Resurrection of Anne Hutchinson. LC 86-25472. 419p. 1986. 26.95 (0-87975-370-6) Prometheus Bks.

— X-Rated Videotape Guide, 3 vols., Set. 1993. pap. 49.95 (0-87975-835-X) Prometheus Bks.

— X-Rated Videotape Guide, Vol. 1. 654p. 1993. pap. 18.95 (0-87975-799-X) Prometheus Bks.

— The X-Rated Videotape Guide II: More Than 1200 New Reviews & Ratings. (Illus.). 625p. 1991. pap. 18.95 (0-87975-673-X) Prometheus Bks.

Rimmer, Robert H. & Riley, Patrick. The X-Rated Videotape Guide, Vol. 3. LC 92-42911. (Illus.). 573p. (C). 1993. pap. 18.95 (0-87975-818-X) Prometheus Bks.

— The X-Rated Videotape Guide IV. (Illus.). 628p. 1994. pap. 19.95 (0-87975-897-X) Prometheus Bks.

Rimmer, Russell. Income Distribution in a Corporate Economy. (New Directions in Modern Economics Ser.). 256p. 1993. 69.95 (1-85278-695-7, Pub. by E Elgar Pub UK) Ashgate Pub Co.

Rimmer, Russell J. Generic Bifurications for Involutary Area Preserving Maps. LC 82-20615. (Memoirs Ser.: No. 41/272). 165p. 1982. pap. 19.00 (0-8218-2272-1, MEMO 41/272) Am Math.

***Rimmer, Steve.** Advanced Multimedia Programming. 1994. pap. 39.95 (0-07-911898-4, Windcrest) TAB Bks.

— Bit-Mapped Graphics. 1990. 38.95 (0-07-155670-2); pap. text ed. 26.95 (0-07-155681-8) McGraw.

— Bit-Mapped Graphics. 1992. pap. 26.95 (0-07-052998-1) McGraw.

— Bit-Mapped Graphics. (Illus.). 512p. 1990. pap. 26.95 (0-8306-3558-0, 3558, Windcrest) TAB Bks.

— Bit-Mapped Graphics. 1991. 5.25 hd 24.95 (0-8306-6750-4); 3.5 hd 24.95 (0-8306-6751-2) TAB Bks.

— Bit-Mapped Graphics. 2nd ed. 1992. 38.95 (0-07-052997-3) McGraw.

— Bit-Mapped Graphics. 2nd ed. (Illus.). 496p. 1992. 38.95 (0-8306-4209-9, 4266, Windcrest); pap. 26.95 (0-8306-4208-0, 4266, Windcrest) TAB Bks.

— Canned Code for DOS & Windows. 1994. pap. text ed. 29.95 (0-07-053003-3) McGraw.

— Constructing Windows Dialogs. 1994. pap. text ed. 34.95 (0-07-053009-2) McGraw.

— Corel Draw It! 552p. 1993. pap. (0-201-62637-3) Addison-Wesley.

— Graphic File Toolkit: Converting & Using Graphic Files. 1992. pap. 29.95 (0-201-60846-4) Addison-Wesley.

— Graphical User Interface Programming. 448p. 1991. 39.95 (0-8306-2475-9, Windcrest); pap. 24.95 (0-8306-2472-4, Windcrest) TAB Bks.

— Mondo Internet. LC 94-27583. 1994. 36.95 (0-07-053014-9); pap. text ed. 24.95 (0-07-053015-7) McGraw.

— Multimedia Programming for Windows. 1993. text ed. 49. 95 (0-07-053005-X) McGraw.

— Multimedia Programming for Windows. 1993. pap. text ed. 39.95 (0-07-053006-8) McGraw.

— Multimedia Programming for Windows with CD Rom. 1993. 49.95 (0-8306-4538-1, Windcrest); pap. 39.95 (0-8306-4539-X, Windcrest) TAB Bks.

— Super VGA Graphics: Programming Secrets. 1993. 49.95 (0-07-052999-X); pap. 36.95 (0-07-053000-9) McGraw.

— Super VGA Graphics: Programming Secrets. LC 92-38282. 1993. 44.95 (0-8306-4427-X, Windcrest); pap. 34.45 (0-8306-4428-8, Windcrest) TAB Bks.

— Supercharged Bit-Mapped Graphics. 1992. 38.95 (0-07-052976-0); pap. 26.95 (0-07-052979-5) McGraw.

— Supercharged Bit-Mapped Graphics. 664p. 1992. pap. 34. 95 (0-8306-3788-5, 4102, Windcrest) TAB Bks.

— Windows Bit-Mapped Graphics. 1993. 38.95 (0-07-052995-7); pap. 26.95 (0-07-052996-5) McGraw.

— Windows Bitmapped Graphics. (Illus.). 448p. 1992. 38.95 (0-8306-4207-2, 4265, Windcrest); pap. 26.95 (0-8306-4206-4, 4265, Windcrest) TAB Bks.

— Windows Graphics & Prepass. 1993. pap. write for info. (0-201-62205-X) Addison-Wesley.

Rimmer, Steve & Cooke, LeRoy. Canned Code for DOS & Windows. LC 93-34624. 1994. disk 39.95 (0-8306-4511-X, Windcrest); disk, pap. 29.95 (0-8306-4512-8, Windcrest) TAB Bks.

Rimmer, William. Art Anatomy. pap. 8.95 (0-486-20908-3) Dover.

Rimmerman, Craig A. The Presidency by Plebiscite: The Reagan-Bush Era in Institutional Perspective. LC 92-27254. 164p. (C). 1992. text ed. 50.00 (0-8133-8333-1) Westview.

Rimmington, Pat. The Adobes of Twentynine Palms. LC 88-51614. (Illus.). 144p. (Orig.). 1988. pap. 12.00 (0-9617961-3-8) Desert Moon Pr.

Rimmon-Kenan, Shlomith. Narrative Fiction: Contemporary Poetics. LC 82-18859. 173p. 1983. pap. 13.95 (0-416-74230-0, NO. 3817) Routledge Chapman & Hall.

Rimmon-Kenan, Shlomith, ed. Discourse in Psychoanalysis & Literature. 208p. (Orig.). 1987. pap. 13.95 (0-416-00452-0, A0394) Routledge Chapman & Hall.

Rimner, I. Movies - FX. (Great Bks.). (Illus.). 48p. (J). (gr. 3-8). 1989. 13.95 (0-685-58294-9); lib. bdg. 18.60 (0-86592-453-8) Rourke Corp.

Rimo Publications Staff, et al. Sepia Tones (7 Short Stories) 2nd ed. 1986. 11.50 (0-918680-32-8) Bagehot Council.

Rimoin, David L., ed. International Nomenclature of Constitutional Diseases of Bone With Bibliography. Vol. 15, No. 10. 1979. write for info. (0-318-54283-8) March of Dimes.

Rimoin, David L., jt. ed. see Emery, Alan E.

Rimoldi, Eleanor, jt. auth. see Rimoldi, Max.

Rimoldi, Max & Rimoldi, Eleanor. Hahalis & the Labour of Love: A Social Movement on Buka Island. 312p. 1992. 65.00 (0-85496-704-4) Berg Pubs.

Rimon, S. G. Fluids & Applied Mathematics. 1983. pap. 54. 00 (0-08-030531-8, Pergamon Pr) Elsevier.

Rimpoche, L., jt. tr. see Hopkins, J.

Rimrott, F. P. Introductory Orbit Dynamics. (Fundamentals & Advances in the Engineering Sciences Ser.). x, 193p. (C). 1989. 56.00 (3-528-06344-0, Pub. by Vieweg & Sohn GW) Ballen Bkslr.

Rimrott, F. P., jt. auth. see Tabarrok, B.

Rimrott, Friedrich P. & Schwaighofer, J., eds. Mechanics of the Solid State. LC 68-110059. 292p. reprint ed. pap. 83. 30 (0-317-08758-4, 2014383) Bks Demand.

Rimsa. Modular Systems Approach to Introductory Chemistry. 4th ed. 210p. 1986. pap. text ed. 21.95 (0-88725-138-2) Hunter Textbks.

Rimselis, Victor, ed. The Providential Path: Archbishop George Matulaitis, 1871-1927. (Illus.). 47p. 1977. pap. write for info. (0-933820-03-8) Marian Fathers.

Rimselis, Victor, intro. Constitutions of the Marian Clerics under the Title of the Immaculate Conception of the Most Blessed Virgin Mary. 121p. 1991. pap. write for info. (0-933820-07-0) Marian Fathers.

Rimselis, Viktoras, ed. Apvaizdos Skirtuoju Keliu. (Illus.). 47p. (LIT.). 1977. pap. write for info. (0-933820-02-X) Marian Fathers.

Rimsky-Korsakov, Nicholas. Principles of Orchestration: General Overview: Getting the Sounds in Your Head. 2nd rev. ed. (Rimsky-Korsakov Ser.: Vol. 1). (Illus.). 341p. (C). 1989. pap. text ed. 34.95 (0-939067-73-0) Alexander Pub.

Rimsky-Korsakov, Nikolai. Scheherazade in Full Score. 240p. 1984. pap. 9.95 (0-486-24734-1) Dover.

Rimsky-Korsakov, Nikolay. Principles of Orchestration. 1922. pap. text ed. 11.95 (0-486-21266-1) Dover.

Rimstidt, J. Donald, jt. auth. see Craig, James R.

Rinaldi, Angelo. Les Dames de France. (FRE.). 1980. pap. 11.95 (0-7859-4131-2) Fr & Eur.

— La Derniere Fete de l'Empire. (FRE.). 1984. pap. 11.95 (0-7859-4212-2) Fr & Eur.

— L' Education de l'Oubli. (FRE.). 1979. pap. 11.95 (0-7859-4089-8) Fr & Eur.

— Les Jardins du Consulat. 280p. (FRE.). 1986. pap. 11.95 (0-7859-4253-X, 2070377717) Fr & Eur.

— La Maison des Atlantes. (FRE.). 1973. pap. 15.95 (0-7859-4013-8) Fr & Eur.

Rinaldi, Ann. A Break with Charity: A Story about the Salem Witch Trials. LC 92-8858. (YA). 1992. 16.95 (0-15-200353-3, Gulliver Bks) HarBrace.

— Break with Charity: A Story about the Salem Witch Trials. LC 92-8858. (J). (gr. 4-7). 1994. pap. 5.00 (0-15-200101-8, HB Juv Bks) HarBrace.

— Broken Days. LC 94-17665. (Quilt Trilogy Ser.: Vol. 2). (J). 1995. 13.95 (0-590-46053-6) Scholastic Inc.

— The Fifth of March. (YA). 1993. pap. 3.95 (0-15-227517-7, HB Juv Bks) HarBrace.

— Fifth of March: A Story of the Boston Massacre. (YA). 1993. 10.95 (0-15-200343-6) HarBrace.

— Finishing Becca: A Story of Peggy Shippen & Benedict Arnold. (J). 1994. 10.95 (0-15-200880-2); pap. 3.95 (0-15-200879-9) HarBrace.

— In My Father's House. LC 91-46839. 304p. (YA). (gr. 7 up). 1993. 13.95 (0-590-44730-0) Scholastic Inc.

— In My Father's House. (YA). 1994. pap. 3.95 (0-590-44731-9) Scholastic Inc.

— Last Silk Dress. 1990. mass mkt. 3.99 (0-553-28315-4) Bantam.

— A Ride into Morning: The Story of Tempe Wick. Grove, Karen, ed. 289p. (YA). (gr. 7 up). 1991. 15.95 (0-15-200573-0, Gulliver Bks) HarBrace.

— A Ride into Morning: The Story of Tempe Wick. LC 90-49481. 368p. (YA). (gr. 7 up). 1995. pap. 5.00 (0-15-200673-7) HarBrace.

— The Secret of Sarah Revere. LC 95-5570. (J). 1995. write for info. (0-15-200393-2, Gulliver Bks); pap. write for info. (0-15-200392-4, Gulliver Bks) HarBrace.

— A Stitch in Time. (Quilt Trilogy Ser.). 304p. (YA). (gr. 7 up). 1994. 13.95 (0-590-46055-2, Scholastic Hardcover) Scholastic Inc.

— A Stitch in Time. LC 93-8964. (Quilt Trilogy Ser.: Vol. 1). (J). 1995. 3.99 (0-590-46056-0) Scholastic Inc.

— Time Enough for Drums. 249p. (J). 1989. pap. 2.50 (0-8167-1269-7) Troll Assocs.

— Wolf by the Ears. (J). 1991. 13.95 (0-590-43413-6, Scholastic Hardcover) Scholastic Inc.

— Wolf by the Ears. (YA). 1993. pap. 3.50 (0-590-43412-8) Scholastic Inc.

Rinaldi, Fiori. Drug Offences in Australia: Sentencing. xxv, 247p. 1986. pap. 48.50 (0-455-20649-X, Pub. by Law Bk Co) W W Gaunt.

Rinaldi, Fiori & Gillies, Peter. Narcotic Offences. xxx, 444p. 1991. 87.50 (0-455-21025-X, Pub. by Law Bk Co) W W Gaunt.

Rinaldi, Giacomo. A History & Interpretation of the Logic of Hegel. LC 92-12222. (Studies in the History of Philosophy: Vol. 26). 512p. 1992. lib. bdg. 119.95 (0-7734-9509-6) E Mellen.

Rinaldi, Maura. Kraak Porclain. (Illus.). 298p. 1989. 147.50 (1-870076-09-5, Pub. by Bamboo Pub UK) Antique Collect.

***Rinaldi, Maura & Eng-Lee Seok Chee.** Ceramics in Scholarly Taste. (Illus.). 152p. (C). Date not set. pap. 34. 95 (981-00-4395-3) Heian Intl.

Rinaldi, Nicholas. The Luftwaffe in Chaos. 83p. 1985. 10.00 (0-685-14614-6) Negative Capability Pr.

Rinaldi, Peter M. By Love Compelled: The Life of Fr. Philip Rinaldi. (Illus.). 228p. (Orig.). 1973. pap. 6.95 (0-89944-032-0) Don Bosco Multimedia.

— In Verdant Pastures: From a Pastor's Diary. LC 85-72837. 228p. (Orig.). 1985. 11.95 (0-685-13214-5) Don Bosco Multimedia.

— Man with a Dream: The Story of St. John Bosco. (Illus.). 166p. 1978. pap. 2.50 (0-89944-035-5) Don Bosco Multimedia.

Rinaldi, S., ed. Environmental Systems Analysis & Management. 828p. 1982. 107.75 (0-444-86406-7, I-257-82, North Holland) Elsevier.

Rinaldo, John B., jt. auth. see Martin, Paul S.

Rinaldo, Peter M. The Eastmans from Lockport, New York. (Illus.). 136p. (C). 1992. 40.00 (0-9622123-5-0) DorPete Pr.

— The Five-Day Weekend: A Proposal for Calendar & Work Schedule Change. LC 89-50030. 122p. (C). 1989. 14.95 (0-9622123-2-6); pap. 6.95 (0-9622123-3-4) DorPete Pr.

— Full Employment: Is It Possible? LC 94-70583. 136p. 1994. 14.95 (0-9622123-8-5) DorPete Pr.

— The Jacksons from Bermuda: John Richard Jackson Branch. (Illus.). 144p. 1992. 20.00 (0-9622123-4-2) DorPete Pr.

— The Rinaldos from Poland: A Family History. LC 84-71243. (Illus.). 436p. (C). 1984. 40.00 (0-9622123-0-X) DorPete Pr.

— The Trouts from London: William Trout Branch. LC 88-71508. (Illus.). 658p. (C). 1989. 45.00 (0-9622123-1-8) DorPete Pr.

— Trying to Change the World. LC 91-90387. 161p. (C). 1992. 14.95 (0-9622123-6-9) DorPete Pr.

— Unnecessary Wars? Causes & Effects of U. S. Wars from the American Revolution to Vietman. 161p. 1993. 14.95 (0-614-04200-3) DorPete Pr.

— Unnecessary Wars? Causes & Effects of United States Wars from the Revolution to Vietnam. LC 93-70883. (Illus.). 168p. (C). 1993. 14.95 (0-9622123-7-7) DorPete Pr.

Rinard, jt. ed. see Meyers, W.

Rinard, Judith E. Along a Rocky Shore. (Books for Young Explorers Ser.: Set 17, No. 1). (Illus.). (J). (gr. k-4). 1990. lib. bdg. 16.95 (0-87044-823-4) Natl Geog.

— Along a Rocky Shore, Set. (Books for Young Explorers Ser.: Set 17, No. 1). (Illus.). (J). (gr. k-4). 1990. 13.95 (0-87044-822-6) Natl Geog.

Rinard, Judith E. Zoos Without Cages. LC 79-3243. (Books for World Explorers Series 2: No. 3). (Illus.). 104p. (J). (gr. 3-8). 1981. 8.95 (0-87044-335-6); lib. bdg. 12.50 (0-87044-340-2) Natl Geog.

Rinard, Judy. Amazing Animals of the Sea. Crump, Donald J., ed. LC 80-8796. (Books for World Explorers Series 3: No. 1). (Illus.). 104p. (J). (gr. 3-8). 1981. 8.95 (0-87044-382-8); lib. bdg. 12.50 (0-87044-387-9) Natl Geog.

***Rinard, Julie & National Geographic Staff.** National Geographic Amazing Monkeys. (J). (ps-3). 1994. 16.00 (0-87044-596-0) Natl Geog.

Rinbochay, Khetsun S. Tantric Practice in Nying-Ma. Hopkins, Jeffery & Klein, Anne, eds. LC 86-3762. 238p. (Orig.). 1983. pap. 14.95 (0-937938-14-9) Snow Lion Pubns.

Rinbochay, Lati. Mind in Tibetan Buddhism. Napper, Elizabeth, ed. LC 86-3799. 172p. (Orig.). (C). 1980. lib. bdg. 10.95 (0-937938-02-5) Snow Lion Pubns.

Rinbochay, Lati & Hopkins, Jeffrey. Death, Intermediate State & Rebirth. 86p. 1981. pap. 9.95 (0-937938-00-9) Snow Lion Pubns.

Rinck, Margaret. Christian Men Who Hate Women. 208p. 1990. pap. 9.99 (0-310-51751-6) Zondervan.

Rinck, P. A. Magnetic Resonance in Medicine. 3rd ed. 1993. 70.00 (0-632-03781-4) Blackwell Sci.

Rincon, Carlos, jt. auth. see Eich, Dieter.

***Rincon Garcia, W.** Ayuntamientos de Espana. (Illus.). 416p. (SPA.). 1993. 295.00x (84-239-5279-7) Elliots Bks.

Rincover, Arnold. How to Use Sensory Extinction. (Teaching the Autistic Ser.). 34p. 1981. pap. 8.00 (0-89079-062-0, 1036) PRO-ED.

— The Parent-Child Connection: Your Guide to Baby & Child Behavior in the First Six Years. 208p. 1990. pap. 8.95 (0-671-68164-8) PB.

— The Parenting Challenge: Your Child's Behavior From 6-12. Peters, Sally, ed. 256p. (Orig.). 1991. pap. 9.00 (0-671-68163-X) PB.

Rind, B. Interactive Video Course for the SAT, 1990. student ed 20.00 (1-56321-045-2); student ed, digital audio 220.00 (1-56321-041-X); student ed, vhs 125.95 (1-56321-042-8); student ed, digital audio 200.00 (1-56321-043-6); student ed, digital audio 125.00 (1-56321-044-4) Acad Pr.

Rind, Bruce & Marasa, Paul, eds. The SAT Video Course. 1993. student ed 109.95 (1-57004-010-9); student ed, audio 129.95 (1-57004-007-9); vhs 99.95 (1-57004-008-7); vhs 99.95 (1-57004-011-7) L Erlbaum Assocs.

— The SAT Video Course, Set. 1993. lib. bdg. 169.95 (1-57004-006-0); pap. text ed. 149.95 (1-57004-009-5) L Erlbaum Assocs.

***Rind, Sherry.** Fall Out the Door. LC 94-71362. 72p. (Orig.). 1994. pap. 12.00 (1-881090-09-4) Confluence Pr.

— The Hawk in the Back Yard. 1985. pap. 8.00 (0-938078-20-8) Anhinga Pr.

Rinden, David. Directions: From the Word of God. 62p. 1992. pap. 3.95 (0-943167-15-9) Faith & Fellowship Pr.

— Living Faith: Studies in James. 75p. (Orig.). 1993. pap. 3.95 (0-943167-25-6) Faith & Fellowship Pr.

Rinden, David, ed. see Foss, Allen J.

Rinden, David, jt. auth. see Olsen, Warren.

Rinden, David, jt. ed. see Olsen, Warren.

Rinden, Gracia. The Life in Jesus: Twelve Studies in John 12-21. annot. ed. 116p. (Orig.). 1992. pap. 3.95 (0-943167-10-8) Faith & Fellowship Pr.

— Triumphant Christian Living. 37p. (Orig.). 1991. pap. 3.95 (0-943167-13-2) Faith & Fellowship Pr.

— The Truth in Jesus: Twelve Studies in John 1-11. annot. ed. 116p. (Orig.). 1992. pap. 3.95 (0-943167-09-4) Faith & Fellowship Pr.

Rinden, Robert & Witke, Roxane. The Red Flag Waves: A Guide to the Hung-Ch'i p'iao-p'iao Collection. LC 68-65796. (China Research Monographs: No. 3). 159p. 1968. pap. 2.00 (0-912966-04-1) IEAS.

Rinder, Larry & Estrin, Jerry, eds. Self Evidence. (Illus.). (C). 1989. write for info. (0-937335-05-3) LA Contemp Exhib.

Rinder, Lawrence, jt. auth. see Merrill, Kathleen.

Rinder, Lenore. A Big Mistake. LC 94-7028. (Illus.). 32p. (J). (ps up). 1994. lib. bdg. 18.60 (0-8368-0674-3) Gareth Stevens Inc.

Rinder, Walter. World I Used to Know. LC 89-81211. 1990. pap. 7.95 (0-89087-596-0) Celestial Arts.

Rinderer, Thomas E. Bee Genetics & Breeding. 1986. text ed. 116.00 (0-12-588920-8) Acad Pr.

Rinderknecht, Carol. A Checklist of American Imprints for 1839: Items 53806-59415. LC 64-11784. 291p. 1988. 42. 50 (0-8108-2124-9) Scarecrow.

— A Checklist of American Imprints, 1830-1839, Title Index, 2 vols. LC 64-11784. 830p. 1989. Vol. I, A-L, Vol. II, M-Z. 87.50 (0-8108-2208-3) Scarecrow.

Rinderknecht, Carol, comp. A Checklist of American Imprints for 1835: Items 29894-35601. LC 64-11784. 547p. 1985. 47.50 (0-8108-1828-0) Scarecrow.

— A Checklist of American Imprints for 1836: Items 35602-42652. LC 64-11784. 617p. 1986. 55.00 (0-8108-1839-6) Scarecrow.

— A Checklist of American Imprints for 1837: Items 42653-48672. LC 64-11784. 514p. 1986. 45.00 (0-8108-1841-8) Scarecrow.

— A Checklist of American Imprints for 1838: Items 48673-53805. LC 64-11784. 261p. 1988. 39.50 (0-8108-2123-0) Scarecrow.

— A Checklist of American Imprints, 1830-1839: Author Index. LC 64-11784. 177p. 1989. 29.50 (0-8108-2252-0) Scarecrow.

Rinderknecht, Carol & Bruntjen, Scott. A Checklist of American Imprints for 1834: Items 22796-29893. LC 64-11784. 646p. 1982. reprint ed. 45.00 (0-8108-1487-0) Scarecrow.

— A Checklist of American Imprints for 1844: Items 44-1 - 44-6827. LC 64-11784. 524p. 1993. 62.50 (0-8108-2654-2) Scarecrow.

Rinderknecht, Carol & Bruntjeu, Scott, eds. A Checklist of American Imprints 1843: Items 43-1 - 43-5454. LC 64-11784. 500p. 1992. 52.50 (0-8108-2653-4) Scarecrow.

Rinderknecht, Carol & Bruntjev, Scott, eds. A Checklist of American Imprints for 1842: Items 42-1 - 42-5379. LC 64-11784. 428p. 1992. 52.50 (0-8108-2533-3) Scarecrow.

Rinderle, Walter & Norling, Bernard. The Nazi Impact on a German Village. LC 92-10030. (Illus.). 296p. (C). 1993. text ed. 33.00 (0-8131-1794-1) U Pr of Ky.

Rindfleisch, Daniel H. OS & VS Job Control Language & Utility Programs. 2nd ed. (Illus.). 384p. (C). 1986. text ed. 69.00 (0-13-642901-7) P-H.

***Rindfleisch, Jan.** Coming Across: Art by Recent Immigrants. 64p. 1994. pap. 10.00 (1-886215-00-6) Euphrat Mus.

***Rindfleisch, Norval.** The Season of Letting Go. 144p. (Orig.). 1995. pap. 10.50 (0-9645843-7-9) Claritas Imprints.

Rindge, Ronald L., et al. Ceramic Art of the Mailbu Potteries, 1926-1932. LC 88-62053. (Malibu Lagoon Museum Ser.). (Illus.). 136p. 1994. pap. 35.00 (0-295-97372-2) U of Wash Pr.

Rindisbacher, Hans J. The Smell of Books: A Cultural-Historical Study of Olfactory Perception in Literature. 300p. (C). 1992. text ed. 47.50 (0-472-10383-0) U of Mich Pr.

Rindler, Michael E. The Challenge of Hospital Governance: How to Become an Exemplary Board. 183p. 1992. 34.95 (1-55648-086-5, 196627) AHPI.

— Managing a Hospital Turnaround: From Crisis to Profitability in Three Challenging Years. LC 87-61937. 245p. 1987. text ed. 38.00 (0-931028-95-7, 0302, Pluribus) Health Admin Pr.

— Putting Patients & Profits into Perspective. LC 86-63226. 228p. 1987. text ed. 35.00 (0-931028-80-9, 0303, Pluribus) Health Admin Pr.

Rindler, Wolfgang. Essential Relativity. rev. ed. (Texts & Monographs in Physics). (Illus.). 284p. 1993. pap. 49.00 (0-387-10090-3) Spr-Verlag.

— Introduction to Special Relativity. 2nd ed. (Illus.). 184p. (C). 1991. 59.00 (0-19-853953-3); pap. text ed. 29.95 (0-19-853952-5) OUP.

Rindler, Wolfgang, jt. auth. see Penrose, Roger.

***Rindo.** Secrets Men Keep. 1995. pap. text ed. 9.95 (0-89823-163-9) New Rivers Pr.

Rindo, Ronald J. Suburban Metaphysics: A Collection of Stories. 1990. pap. 7.95 (0-89823-114-0) New Rivers Pr.

Rindone, William R. Dusty Days & Distant Drums. LC 84-81865. (Illus.). 316p. 37.50 (0-9614007-3-0) Game Flds Pr.

— Dusty Days & Distant Drums. deluxe limited ed. LC 84-81865. (Illus.). 316p. 95.00 (0-317-14041-8) Game Flds Pr.

Rine, D. C., ed. Computer Science & Multiple Valued Logic: Theory & Applications. rev. ed. 642p. 1984. 100.00 (0-444-86882-8, North Holland) Elsevier.

***Rine, David C., ed.** Object-Oriented Systems & Applications (Readings In) LC 94-10044. 256p. 1994. text ed. 42.00 (0-8186-6222-0, BP06222) IEEE Comp Soc.

— Readings in Object-Oriented Systems & Applications. LC 94-10044. 1994. write for info. (0-8186-6221-2); pap. write for info. (0-8186-6220-4) IEEE Comp Soc.

Rinear, Bernie. Moose Creek Charlie & the Quick Freeze: A Tall, Tall Tale by Bernie Rinear. (Illus.). 14p. (Orig.). 1982. pap. 2.00 (1-878654-49-7) Lit Coun AK.

Rinear, Charles E. The Sexually Transmitted Diseases. LC 85-42732. 224p. 1986. lib. bdg. 27.50x (0-89950-185-0) McFarland & Co.

Rinear, David L. The Temple of Momus: Mitchell's Olympic Theatre. LC 85-22077. (Illus.). 237p. 1987. 29.50 (0-8108-1850-7) Scarecrow.

***Rinear, Sheila.** We're Doing Cinderella. 24p. (Orig.). (YA). (gr. 6-11). 1993. pap. 3.00 (1-57514-127-2) Encore Perform Pub.

Rinearson, Peter. Word Processing Power with Microsoft Word. 3rd ed. 512p. (Orig.). 1989. 21.95 (1-55615-126-8) Microsoft.

Rinebold, Albert, jt. auth. see Rinebold, Analo T.

Rinebold, Albert F. Aware Tribe: Relating the Ancient Wisdom of the Seneca Indian Wolf Clan Present Day Living. (Illus.). 150p. (Orig.). 1989. pap. 15.00 (0-9626135-0-9) Aware Tribe.

Rinebold, Albert F. & Rinebold, Analo T. Amber Wolf Enters Fifth World & (History Wolf Clan Teaching Lodge) Amber Wolf's Aware Tribe for Kids. LC 92-97452. (Illus.). (Orig.). 1993. pap. 11.50 (0-9626135-3-3) Aware Tribe.

Rinebold, Albert F., ed. see Nitsch, Twylah H.

Rinebold, Analo T. & Rinebold, Albert. Aware Tribe for Kids: Growing up among Native Americans. 50p. (Orig.). (YA). 1994. pap. 10.00 (0-9626135-4-1) Aware Tribe.

Rinebold, Analo T., jt. auth. see Rinebold, Albert F.

Rinefort, Foster C., ed. Readings in Cost Benefit-Cost Control. 88p. 1985. 10.00 (0-939874-68-7) ASSE.

Rinehart, Alice D. Mortals in the Immortal Profession: An Oral History of Teaching. LC 82-17200. 410p. 1983. pap. text ed. 19.95 (0-8290-1049-1) Irvington.

Rinehart, Carroll A., jt. auth. see Marsh, Mary V.

Rinehart, Constance, ed. Library Technical Services: A Selected, Annotated Bibliography. LC 76-27130. 248p. 1976. text ed. 42.95 (0-8371-9286-2, MAB/, Greenwood Pr) Greenwood.

Rinehart, Dean, et al. Mammoth Lakes Sierra: A Handbook for Roadside & Trail. 6th ed. Smith, Genny, ed. LC 93-1250. (Illus.). 232p. 1993. pap. 13.95 (0-931378-13-3) Genny Smith Bks.

Rinehart, Frederick R., ed. Chronicles of Colorado. 2nd ed. LC 83-62747. (Illus.). 1993. pap. 14.95 (1-879373-65-3) R Rinehart.

Rinehart, Gray. Quality Education. (Illus.). 329p. 1993. pap. 21.95 (0-87389-184-8, ASQC Qual Pr) Irwin Prof Pubng.

Rinehart, J. S. Geysers & Geothermal Energy. (Illus.). 223p. 1980. 54.00 (0-387-90489-1) Spr-Verlag.

Rinehart, James R. & Lee, Jackson F. American Education & the Dynamics of Choice. LC 90-21312. 184p. 1991. text ed. 49.95 (0-275-93823-9, C3823, Praeger Pubs) Greenwood.

Rinehart, James R., jt. ed. see Hektoen, Faith H.

Rinehart, Janice. How to Use Lotus 1-2-3 Rel. 2.3. Hannum, Karen, ed. 90p. (Orig.). 1991. pap. text ed. 125.00 (0-917792-92-0) OneOnOne Comp Trng.

Rinehart, Janice, ed. see August, B. Alan.

Rinehart, Janice, ed. see Sehr, Barbara.

Rinehart, Janice S., ed. see Menges, Patricia A.

Rinehart, John S. A Guide to Geyser Gazing. (Illus.). (Orig.). 1976. pap. 1.40 (0-913270-61-X) HyperDynamics.

— Stress Transients in Solids. 240p. (C). 1975. pap. 8.95 (0-913270-48-2) HyperDynamics.

Rinehart, Julia R., jt. auth. see Heise, Jon O.

Rinehart, Kimberly R. The Greatest Gift of All. (Illus.). 70p. (J). 1987. 12.95 (0-942865-02-2) It Takes Two.

Rinehart, Martin, jt. auth. see Simpson, Alan.

Rinehart, Martin L. Building dBase IV 2.0 Applications: A Hands-on Programming Guide. LC 93-35644. 1993. pap. 34.95 (0-201-62634-9) Addison-Wesley.

— Client/Server dBASE Programming: Building Mission-Critical SBase Systems. 1994. pap. 39.95 (0-201-40640-3) Addison-Wesley.

— Learn dBASE for Windows Programming: A Hands on Guide to Object-Oriented Database, set. 1994. disk, pap. 39.95 (0-201-60836-7) Addison-Wesley.

***Rinehart, Mary.** My Story. (American Autobiography Ser.). 570p. 1995. reprint ed. lib. bdg. 109.00 (0-7812-8625-5) Rprt Serv.

Rinehart, Mary Anne & Sutton, Tom. Musculoskeletal Trauma. LC 87-954. 285p. 1987. 56.00 (0-87189-624-9) Aspen Pub.

Rinehart, Mary R. After House. 21.95 (0-8488-1140-2) Amereon Ltd.

— After House. 1989. mass mkt. 3.99 (0-8217-4242-6) Zebra.

— Album. 1988. pap. 3.50 (0-8217-2334-0) Zebra.

— Alibi for Isabel. reprint ed. lib. bdg. 21.95 (0-89190-326-7, Rivercity Pr) Amereon Ltd.

— Alibi for Isabel & Other Stories. 1989. pap. 3.50 (0-8217-2764-8) Zebra.

— Alibi for Isabel & Other Stories. large type ed. LC 93-33293. 316p. 1993. lib. bdg. 19.95 (1-56054-464-3) Thorndike Pr.

— Amazing Interlude. 22.95 (0-8488-0311-6) Amereon Ltd.

— Bat. 1989. pap. 3.50 (0-8217-2627-7) Zebra.

— Best of Tish. 19.95 (0-8488-0188-1) Amereon Ltd.

— Case of Jennie Brice. pap. 2.95 (0-8217-2193-3) Zebra.

— Case of Jenny Brice. 13.95 (0-8488-1460-6) Amereon Ltd.

— Case of Jenny Brice. 1976. lib. bdg. 14.95 (0-89968-182-4, Lghtyr Pr) Buccaneer Bks.

— Circular Staircase. 1976. lib. bdg. 19.95 (0-89968-181-6, Lghtyr Pr) Buccaneer Bks.

— Circular Staircase. 1985. pap. 3.50 (0-8217-1723-5); pap. 3.95 (0-8217-3528-4) Zebra.

— Confession--Sight Unseen. 1989. pap. 3.50 (0-8217-2707-9) Zebra.

— Dangerous Days. 25.95 (0-8488-0312-4) Amereon Ltd.

— Episode of Wandering Knife. 1990. pap. 3.50 (0-8217-2874-1) Zebra.

— The Frightened Wife. 256p. 1988. pap. 3.50 (0-8217-2489-4) Zebra.

— The Frightened Wife & Other Murder Stories. large type ed. (All-Time Favorites Ser.). 380p. 1993. reprint ed. lib. bdg. 19.95 (1-56054-465-1) Thorndike Pr.

Rinehart, Mary R., et al. Golf Tales: Classic Stories from the Nineteenth Hole. LC 91-50140. (Illus.). 96p. 1991. 14.95 (0-670-83629-X, Viking Studio) Studio Bks.

Rinehart, Mary R. Haunted Lady. 1991. pap. 3.95 (0-8217-3680-9) Zebra.

— K. reprint ed. lib. bdg. 25.95 (0-8488-0313-2, Rivercity Pr) Amereon Ltd.

— K. 1992. reprint ed. lib. bdg. 19.95 (0-89968-275-8, Lghtyr Pr) Buccaneer Bks.

— Light in the Window. 1986. mass mkt. 3.99 (0-8217-4021-0) Zebra.

— Lost Ecstasy. 1986. pap. 3.50 (0-8217-1791-X) Zebra.

— The Man in Lower Ten. 1976. lib. bdg. 16.95 (0-89968-180-8, Lghtyr Pr) Buccaneer Bks.

— Man in Lower Ten. 19.95 (0-8488-0839-8) Amereon Ltd.

— Man in Lower Ten. 1990. pap. 3.50 (0-8217-3104-1) Zebra.

— Miss Pinkerton. reprint ed. lib. bdg. 22.95 (0-89190-327-5, Rivercity Pr) Amereon Ltd.

— More Tish. reprint ed. lib. bdg. 21.95 (0-89190-328-3, Rivercity Pr) Amereon Ltd.

— My Story. Baxter, Annette K., ed. LC 79-8806. (Signal Lives Ser.). (Illus.). 1980. reprint ed. lib. bdg. 69.95 (0-405-12852-5) Ayer.

— My Story. 1993. reprint ed. lib. bdg. 89.00 (0-7812-5824-3) Rprt Serv.

— A Poor Wise Man. 25.95 (0-8488-0314-0) Amereon Ltd.

— The Red Lamp. 336p. 1987. pap. 3.50 (0-8217-2017-1) Zebra.

— Red Lamp. 22.95 (0-8488-1139-9) Amereon Ltd.

— The State vs. Elinor Norton. 288p. 1988. pap. 3.50 (0-8217-2412-6) Zebra.

— State vs. Elinor Norton. 19.95 (0-8488-0618-2) Amereon Ltd.

— Swimming Pool. 1985. pap. 3.50 (0-8217-1686-7) Zebra.

— Through Glacier Park in 1915. LC 83-60777. 1983. 12.50 (0-911797-00-9); pap. 4.95 (0-911797-06-8) R Rinehart.

— Tish. reprint ed. lib. bdg. 24.95 (0-89190-329-1, Rivercity Pr) Amereon Ltd.

— Tish Returns. 22.95 (0-8488-0713-8) Amereon Ltd.

— The Wall. 352p. 1989. mass mkt. 3.99 (0-8217-4017-2) Zebra.

— When a Man Marries. 22.95 (0-8488-0315-9) Amereon Ltd.

— Window At the White Cat. 1990. mass mkt. 3.99 (0-8217-4246-9) Zebra.

— Window at the White Cat. 22.95 (0-8488-0316-7) Amereon Ltd.

— The Window at the White Cat. 1992. reprint ed. lib. bdg. 19.95 (0-89968-274-X, Lghtyr Pr) Buccaneer Bks.

— The Yellow Room. 352p. 1988. pap. 3.50 (0-8217-3493-8) Zebra.

Rinehart, Mary Roberts. The Man in Lower Ten. large type ed. 314p. 1992. reprint ed. bds. 19.95 (1-56054-463-5) Thorndike Pr.

Rinehart, Nanci W. Client or Patient? Power & Related Concepts in Health Care. Hacke, Gregory, ed. 341p. 1991. pap. 27.50 (0-912791-70-5) Ishiyaku Euro.

Rinehart, Paula. Cleavers Don't Live Here Anymore: Making the Transformation from Sixties Idealism. 1993. pap. 8.99 (0-8024-1597-0) Moody.

— Never Too Small for God. 56p. (J). (gr. 2-6). 1989. pap. 5.00 (0-89109-270-6) NavPress.

— One of a Kind. 64p. (J). (gr. 2-6). 1989. pap. 5.00 (0-89109-269-2) NavPress.

— Perfect Every Time: When Doing It All Leaves You with Nothing. LC 92-31969. 204p. (Orig.). 1992. pap. 10.00 (0-89109-708-2) NavPress.

— Stuck Like Glue. 48p. (J). (gr. 2-6). 1988. pap. 5.00 (0-89109-268-4) NavPress.

Rinehart, Paula, jt. auth. see Rinehart, Stacy.

Rinehart, Robert, ed. Finland & the United States: Diplomatic Relations Through Seventy Years. LC 92-33887. (Illus.). 154p. (Orig.). (C). 1993. pap. text ed. 12.00 (0-934742-63-4) Geo U Inst Dplmcy.

— Under the North Star: Reflections of Finland. 136p. (C). 1929. pap. text ed. 38.50 (0-8133-1303-1) Westview.

Rinehart, Ronald E. Radar for Meteorologists. (Illus.). 218p. (Orig.). (C). 1990. pap. text ed. 15.95 (0-9608700-5-9) U NDak Pres.

— Radar for Meteorologists. 2nd ed. 334p. (Orig.). (C). 1991. pap. text ed. 25.00 (0-9608700-7-5) U NDak Pres.

Rinehart, Rose A. The Treasure Hunters. 1994. 11.95 (0-8062-4967-6) Carlton.

Rinehart, Stacy. Alternativas. (SPA.). Date not set. pap. 6.99 (0-88113-111-3) Edit Betania.

Rinehart, Stacy & Rinehart, Paula. Choices: Finding God's Way in Dating, Sex, Singleness & Marriage. LC 82-62071. 170p. 1983. pap. 5.00 (0-89109-494-6) NavPress.

Rinehart, Stephen H., ed. see Freund, Norman C.

Rinehart, Sue T. Gender Consciousness & Politics. (Perspectives on Gender Ser.). (Illus.). 240p. 1992. 49.95 (0-415-90684-9, A8174, Routledge NY); pap. 16.95 (0-415-90685-7, A9553, Routledge NY) Routledge.

Rinehart, Theodore R., jt. ed. see Wittkofski, J. Mark.

***Rinehart, William.** How to Clear the Juvenile Criminal. 240p. (Orig.). Date not set. pap. 8.95 (0-7610-0190-5) NW Pub.

— How to Clear Your Criminal Record: A Step-by-Step Guide. LC 94-70389. 160p. (Orig.). 1994. pap. 12.00 (0-918751-41-1, 37) J O Flores.

Rinehold, Connie. Letters from a Stranger. 1993. mass mkt. 4.99 (0-440-21402-5) Dell.

— Veil of Tears. (American Romance Ser.: No. 380). 1991. pap. 2.95 (0-373-16380-0) Harlequin Bks.

***Rinehold, Cornie.** Unspoken Vows. 1995. pap. 4.99 (0-440-21358-4) Dell.

Rinella, Bernard B. Illinois Domestic Relations Forms. 620p. 1994. disk, ring bd. 159.00 (0-87189-797-0) Michie Butterworth.

Rinella, Bernard B. & Rinella, Richard A. Illinois Domestic Relations Forms. suppl. ed. 1993. ring bd. 85.00 (0-562-57353-4) Butterworth Legal Pubs.

Rinella, Jack. The Master's Manual: A Handbook of Erotic Dominance. Bean, Joseph, ed. LC 93-74629. 200p. (Orig.). 1994. pap. 14.95 (1-881943-03-8) Daedalus Pub.

Rinella, Joseph F., et al. Persistence of the DDT Pesticide in the Yakima River Basin, Washington. (Illus.). 1993. write for info. (0-318-70232-0) US Geol Survey.

***Rinella, Richard A.** Illinois Criminal Procedure, 2 vols., Set. 2nd suppl. ed. Ruebner, Ralph, ed. 800p. 1994. ring bd. 170.00 (0-250-40731-0) Michie Butterworth.

Rinella, Richard A., jt. auth. see Rinella, Bernard B.

Rinere, Elissa. New Law & Life: Sixty Practical Questions & Answers on the New Code of Canon Law. 103p. (Orig.). 1985. pap. 3.00 (0-943616-28-X) Canon Law Soc.

Rines, Edward. Old Historic Churches in America. 373p. 1993. reprint ed. lib. bdg. 89.00 (0-7812-5225-3) Rprt Serv.

Rines, Frank M. Landscape Drawing with Pencil. LC 91-43733. 112p. 1992. pap. 9.95 (0-8069-8546-1) Sterling.

Rines, J. E. & Hargraves, P. E. The Chaetoceros Ehrenberg (Bacillariophyceae) Flora of Narragansett Bay, Rhode Island, U. S. A. (Bibliotheca Phycologica Ser.: Vol. 79). (Illus.). 196p. 1988. pap. text ed. 78.00 (3-443-60006-9) Lubrecht & Cramer.

Riney, Bobye J., jt. auth. see Rubin, Rose M.

Riney, Deborah. The Good Health Journal. 112p. 1993. pap. 10.95 (0-9635454-0-X) DER Prods.

Riney, Hal, jt. auth. see Cederwall, Sandraline.

Riney-Kehrberg, Pamela. Rooted in Dust: Surviving Drought & Depression in Southwestern Kansas. LC 94-11032. (Rural America Ser.). (Illus.). 264p. 1994. 25.00 (0-7006-0644-0) U Pr of KS.

Riney, Larry. Technical Writing for Industry. 288p. 1989. boxed 29.00 (0-13-901828-X) P-H.

Ring, et al. The Early Virtuoso. 64p. (gr. 3-12). 1974. pap. text ed. 9.95 (0-87487-631-1) Summy-Birchard.

Ring, A. M. & Ostrin, S. L., eds. Review Questions in Anatomic Pathology. LC 83-73100. (Illus.). 432p. (Orig.). 1985. pap. text ed. 37.00 (0-931890-18-7, Yr Bk Med Pubs) Mosby Yr Bk.

Ring, Alfred A. & Dasso, Jerome. Real Estate Principles & Practices. 9th ed. (Illus.). 752p. 1981. student ed 29.95 (0-685-03905-6) P-H.

— Real Estate Principles & Practices. 10th ed. 768p. (C). 1985. 45.95 (0-13-765983-0) P-H.

Ring, Alfred A., jt. auth. see Boykin, James H.

Ring, Alfred A., jt. auth. see Dasso, Jerome.

Ring, Anne M. Read Easy: Large Print Libraries for Older Adults. 84p. (Orig.). 1991. ring bd. 19.95 (1-878866-13-3) CAREsource Prog.

Ring, B. Albert. The Neglected Cause of Stroke: Occlusion of the Smaller Intracranial Arteries & Their Diagnosis by Cerebral Angiography. LC 68-55659. (Illus.). 220p. 1969. 10.20 (0-87527-066-2) Green.

Ring, Betty. Girlhood Embroidery: American Samplers & Pictorial Needlework, 1650-1850, Vol. 1. LC 93-6735. 1993. write for info. (0-06-794129-X) Knopf.

— Samples & Pictorial. (Illus.). 1993. pap. 125.00 (0-394-55009-9) Knopf.

Ring, Betty J., jt. ed. see Plasa, Carl.

Ring, C. L. The Biology of Enterprise. LC 78-70432. 1979. 12.95 (0-87212-121-6) Libra.

Ring, Daniel F., ed. Studies in Creative Partnership: Federal Aid to Public Libraries During the New Deal. LC 80-15762. 154p. 1980. 20.00 (0-8108-1319-X) Scarecrow.

Ring Danzig, Sheila. Conduct a National Radio Talk Show Tour Without Leaving Your Home or Office...Without Paying a Cent for Air Time. Danzig, William, ed. (How to Make People Buy Whatever You're Selling Whether They Know They Need It or Not Ser.). 11p. (Orig.). 1989. 49.00 (0-9624333-5-7); spiral bd. 39.95 (0-9624333-6-5) Natl Success.

***Ring, David.** Macroeconomics Financial Markets & the International Sector: Readings, Cases & Problems. 376p. (C). 1993. 21.95 (0-256-03462-1) Irwin.

Ring, David & Gilbert, Lela. Just As I Am: The Life of David Ring As Told to Lela Gilbert. 1993. 14.99 (0-8024-1731-0) Moody.

Ring, Elizabeth. Assistance Dogs: In Special Service. LC 93-735. (Good Dogs! Ser.). (Illus.). 32p. (J). (gr. 2-4). 1993. lib. bdg. 13.90 (1-56294-290-5) Millbrook Pr.

— Companion Dogs: More Than Best Friends. (Good Dogs! Ser.). (Illus.). 32p. (J). (gr. 2-4). 1994. 13.90 (1-56294-293-X) Millbrook Pr.

— Detector Dogs: Hot on the Scent. LC 93-7275. (Good Dogs! Ser.). (Illus.). 32p. (J). (gr. 2-4). 1993. lib. bdg. 13.90 (1-56294-289-1) Millbrook Pr.

— Henry David Thoreau: In Step with Nature. LC 92-11559. (Gateway Greens Ser.). (Illus.). 48p. (J). (gr. 2-4). 1993. lib. bdg. 13.40 (1-56294-258-1); pap. 5.95 (1-56294-795-8) Millbrook Pr.

— Lucky Mouse. LC 94-46948. (Illus.). 32p. (J). (gr. k-3). 1995. 15.40 (1-56294-344-8) Millbrook Pr.

— Maine in the Making of the Nation 1783-1870. (Illus.). 384p. 1991. pap. text ed. write for info. (0-933858-13-2) Kennebec River.

— Night Flier. (J). (ps-3). 1994. 14.95 (1-56294-738-9) Millbrook Pr.

— Night Flier. LC 93-40115. (Illus.). 32p. (J). (gr. k-3). 1994. lib. bdg. 15.40 (1-56294-467-3) Millbrook Pr.

— Patrol Dogs: Keeping the Peace. (Good Dogs! Ser.). (Illus.). 32p. (J). (gr. 2-4). 1994. 13.90 (1-56294-291-3) Millbrook Pr.

— Performing Dogs: Stars of Stage, Screen, & Television. LC 93-41964. (Good Dogs! Ser.). (Illus.). 32p. (J). (gr. 2-4). 1994. lib. bdg. 13.90 (1-56294-296-4) Millbrook Pr.

— Rachel Carson: Caring for the Earth. (J). (gr. 4-7). 1992. pap. 5.00 (0-395-64730-4) HM.

— Rachel Carson: Caring for the Earth. LC 91-37644. (Gateway Green Biography Ser.). (Illus.). 48p. (J). (gr. 2-4). 1992. lib. bdg. 13.40 (1-56294-056-2); pap. 5.95 (1-56294-798-2) Millbrook Pr.

— Ranch & Farm Dogs: Herders & Guards. LC 93-41529. (Good Dogs! Ser.). (Illus.). 32p. (J). (gr. 2-4). 1994. lib. bdg. 13.90 (1-56294-295-6) Millbrook Pr.

— A Reference List of Manuscripts Relating to the History of Maine (1938) (Illus.). 970p. 1992. reprint ed. lib. bdg. 89.00 (0-8328-2519-0) Higginson Bk Co.

— Search-&-Rescue Dogs: Expert Trackers & Trailers. LC 93-42278. (Good Dogs! Ser.). (Illus.). 32p. (J). (gr. 2-4). 1994. lib. bdg. 13.90 (1-56294-294-8) Millbrook Pr.

— Sled Dogs: Arctic Athletes. (Good Dogs! Ser.). (Illus.). 32p. (J). (gr. 2-4). 1994. lib. bdg. 13.90 (1-56294-292-1) Millbrook Pr.

— Some Stuff. LC 94-26196. (Illus.). 32p. (J). (gr. k-3). 1995. lib. bdg. 15.90 (1-56294-466-5) Millbrook Pr.

— Tiger Lilies & Other Beastly Plants. LC 84-7499. (Illus.). 32p. (J). (gr. 3 up). 1985. 9.95 (0-8027-6540-8) Walker & Co.

***Ring, Elliot.** Ben's Revolution. 170p. Date not set. pap. 7.95 (0-7610-0225-1) NW Pub.

Ring, Frances. A Western Harvest: Gatherings of an Editor. LC 90-13882. (Illus.). 192p. (Orig.). 1991. pap. 9.95 (0-936784-87-3) J Daniel.

Ring, Frances, ed. Champions in the Sun. (Illus.). 112p. 1984. lib. bdg. 6.95 (0-910312-47-8) Calif Hist.

Ring, Frances K. Against the Current. 160p. (Orig.). 1987. pap. 6.95 (0-88739-015-3) Creat Arts Bk.

R

— Against the Current: As I Remember F. Scott Fitzgerald. LC 84-47682. (Illus.). 160p. (C). 1985. 14.95 (*0-88739-001-3*) Creat Arts Bk.

Ring, Francis J. & Phillips, Barbara, eds. Recent Advances in Medical Thermology. LC 84-3366. 723p. 1984. 135.00 (*0-306-41672-7*, Plenum Pr) Plenum.

Ring, Gerhard. Werberecht der Rechtsanwalte. 269p. 1990. pap. 37.50 (*3-7890-1907-0*, Pub. by Nomos Verlags GW) Intl Bk Import.

Ring, Grete. A Century of French Painting: Fourteen Hundred to Fifteen Hundred. LC 79-83857. (Illus.). 1979. reprint ed. lib. bdg. 50.00 (*0-87817-249-1*) Hacker.

Ring, Hans, jt. auth. see Ries, Karl.

Ring, Harry. Socialism & Individual Freedom. 22p. 1982. reprint ed. 2.50 (*0-87348-393-6*) Pathfinder NY.

Ring, J. & Burg, G., eds. New Trends in Allergy. (Illus.). 350p. 1981. pap. 69.00 (*0-387-10346-5*) Spr-Verlag.

Ring, J. & Przybilla, B., eds. New Trends in Allergy, No. III. (Illus.). 568p. 1991. 182.00 (*0-387-52993-4*) Spr-Verlag.

Ring, J., jt. ed. see Manno, V.

Ring, Jennifer. Modern Political Theory & Contemporary Feminism: A Dialectical Analysis. LC 90-46118. (SUNY Series in Feminist Political Theory). 229p. (C). 1991. 59.50 (*0-7914-0753-5*); pap. 19.95 (*0-7914-0754-3*) State U NY Pr.

Ring, Jim. Advertising on Trial: Managing Your Agency for Effective Results. (Financial Times Management Ser.). 224p. 1993. 77.50x (*0-273-03970-9*, Pub. by Pitman Pub Ltd UK) Trans-Atl Phila.

Ring, Kenneth. Life at Death: A Scientific Investigation of the Near-Death Experience. LC 82-5427. 310p. (Orig.). 1982. pap. 8.95 (*0-688-01253-1*, Quill) Morrow.

— Omega Project: Near Death Experiences, UFO Encounters, & Mind at Large. 1992. 20.00 (*0-688-10729-X*) Morrow.

— Omega Project: Near-Death Experiences, UFO Encounters, & Mind at Large. 1993. pap. 12.00 (*0-688-12846-7*, Quill) Morrow.

Ring, Kenneth & Kubler-Ross, Elizabeth. Heading Toward Omega: In Search of the Meaning of the Near-Death Experience. LC 85-62560. 348p. 1985. pap. 8.95 (*0-688-06268-7*, Quill) Morrow.

Ring, Layton, jt. auth. see Dolmetsch, Rudolph.

Ring, Layton, ed. see Dolmetsch, Rudolph & Ring, Layton.

Ring, Malvin E. Dentistry: An Illustrated History. (Illus.). 320p. 1985. 75.00 (*0-8109-1100-0*) Abrams.

— Dentistry: An Illustrated History. (Illus.). 320p. 1992. pap. 39.98 (*0-8109-8116-5*, Abradale Pr) Abrams.

— Dentistry: An Illustrated History. (Illus.). 1985. 34.95 (*0-8016-4146-2*) Mosby Yr Bk.

Ring, Merrill. Beginning with the Pre-Socratics. LC 86-63292. 166p. (C). 1987. pap. text ed. 18.95 (*0-87484-791-5*) Mayfield Pub.

Ring, Nancy C. Doctrine Within the Dialectic of Subjectivity & Objectivity: A Critical Study of the Positions of Paul Tillich & Bernard Lonergan. LC 91-625. 304p. 1991. lib. bdg. 99.95 (*0-7734-9948-2*) E Mellen.

Ring, P. & Schuck, P. The Nuclear Many-Body Problem. (Texts & Monographs in Physics). (Illus.). 800p. 1990. 59.00 (*0-387-09820-8*) Spr-Verlag.

***Ring, Terry.** Fundamentals of Ceramic Powder Processing. LC 95-15418. (Illus.). 480p. 1995. boxed write for info. (*0-12-588930-5*) Acad Pr.

***Ring Theory Conference Staff.** Ring Theory: Proceedings of the Oklahoma Conference, 1st, University of Oklahoma. fac. ed. McDonald, Bernard R. et al, eds. LC 73-90768. (Lecture Notes in Pure & Applied Mathematics Ser.: No. 7). 315p. 1994. pap. 89.80 (*0-7837-7717-5*, 2047479) Bks Demand.

— Ring Theory II: Proceedings of the Ring Theory Conference, 2nd, University of Oklahoma, 1975. McDonald, Bernard R. & Morris, Robert A., eds. LC 76-55134. (Lecture Notes in Pure & Applies Mathematics Ser.: Vol. 26). 315p. reprint ed. pap. 89.80 (*0-317-08349-X*, 2017693) Bks Demand.

Ring, Thomasina. Dreamcatcher. 368p. (Orig.). 1992. pap. 4.50 (*0-8439-3284-8*) Dorchester Pub Co.

— Time-Spun Rapture. 368p. (Orig.). 1994. mass mkt., pap. text ed. 4.99 (*0-505-51971-2*) Dorchester Pub Co.

— Time-Spun Treasure. 400p. (Orig.). 1992. pap. 4.50 (*0-8439-3334-8*) Dorchester Pub Co.

— Time-Spun Treasure. 400p. (Orig.). 1995. mass mkt. 4.99 (*0-505-52044-3*) Dorchester Pub Co.

***Ring, Tony & Clark, John.** Tax Warranties & Indemnities. 2nd ed. 180p. 1990. boxed 120.00 (*0-614-05553-9*, UK) Butterworth Legal Pubs.

— Tax Warranties & Indemnities (with Precedents) 2nd ed. 1990. U. K. 120.00 (*0-406-51166-7*) Butterworth Legal Pubs.

Ring, Trudy. Careers in Finance. 150p. 1993. 16.95 (*0-8442-4186-5*, VGM Career Bks); pap. 12.95 (*0-8442-4187-3*, VGM Career Bks) NTC Pub Grp.

Ringbom, Hakan. The Role of the First Language in Foreign Language Learning. 1987. 69.00 (*0-905028-81-3*); pap. 24.95 (*0-905028-80-5*) Taylor & Francis.

Ringbom, Nils-Eric. Jean Sibelius: A Master & His Work. De Courcy, G. I., tr. LC 77-14425. (Illus.). 196p. 1978. reprint ed. text ed. 49.75 (*0-8371-9842-2*, RIJS, Greenwood Pr) Greenwood.

Ringe, Buzz, jt. auth. see Hart, Gene.

Ringe, Dagmar, tr. see Tietze, Lutz & Eicher, Theophil.

Ringe, Donald A. Charles Brockden Brown. (Twayne's United States Authors Ser.). 1966. pap. 13.95x (*0-8084-0071-1*, T98) NCUP.

— Charles Brockden Brown. rev. ed. (Twayne's United States Authors Ser.). 226p. 1991. text ed. 22.95 (*0-8057-7606-0*, TUSAS 98, Twayne) Macmillan.

— James Fenimore Cooper. (United States Authors Ser.: No. 11). 176p. 1988. text ed. 20.95 (*0-8057-7527-7*, Pub. by Royal Botanic Garden UK) Macmillan.

— James Fenimore Cooper. (Twayne's United States Authors Ser.). 1962. pap. 13.95 (*0-8084-0168-8*, T11) NCUP.

Ringe, Donald A., Jr. On Calculating the Factor of Chance in Language Comparison. LC 92-70402. (Transactions Ser.: Vol. 82, Pt. 1). 110p. (C). 1992. pap. 16.00 (*0-87169-821-8*, T821-RID) Am Philos.

Ringe, Donald A., ed. see Cooper, James Fenimore.

Ringe, Sharon H., jt. ed. see Newsom, Carol A.

Ringe, Sharon H., tr. see Tamez, Elsa.

Ringeissen, J., jt. ed. see Grosmann, M.

Ringel, C. M. Tame Algebras & Integral Quadratic Forms. (Lecture Notes in Mathematics Ser.: Vol. 1099). xiii, 376p. 1985. pap. 46.20 (*0-387-13905-2*) Spr-Verlag.

Ringel, C. M., jt. auth. see Michler, G. O.

Ringel, Claus M., jt. auth. see Dlab, Vlastimil.

***Ringel, Faye.** New England's Gothic Literature: History & Folklore of the Supernatural from the Seventeenth Through the Twentieth Centuries. LC 94-34973. 272p. 1995. text ed. 89.95 (*0-7734-9047-7*) E Mellen.

Ringel, G. Map Color Theorem. LC 73-17986. (Grundlehren der Mathematischen Wissenschaften Ser.: Vol. 209). (Illus.). 220p. 1974. 74.00 (*0-387-06548-2*) Spr-Verlag.

Ringel, Gerhard, jt. ed. see Hartsfield, Nora.

Ringel, Harvey. History of the National Association of Teachers of Singing. (Illus.). 354p. (Orig.). 1990. pap. 33.00 (*0-932761-01-1*) NATS.

Ringel, Joseph. Marine Motifs on Ancients Coins. 1984. lib. bdg. 22.50 (*0-685-73697-0*) Numismatic Fine Arts.

***Ringel, S. A., et al.** Large Area Wafer Growth & Processing for Electronic & Photonic Devices - State-of-the-Art Program on Compound Semiconductors XX. 336p. 1995. pap. 42.00 (*1-56677-075-0*, PV 94-18) Electrochem Soc.

Ringel, William E. & Pellis, Mark. Searches & Seizures, Arrests & Confessions, 3 vols., Set. 2nd ed. LC 79-22482. (Criminal Law Ser.). 1980. ring bd. 375.00 (*0-87632-079-5*) Clark Boardman Callaghan.

Ringelberg, Joop. Diel Vertical Migration of Zooplankton. Proceedings of an International Symposium in the Netherlands. (Advances in Limnology Ser.: No. 39). (Illus.). 222p. 1993. pap. text ed. 63.75 (*3-510-47040-0*, Pub. by E Schweizerbartsche GW) Lubrecht & Cramer.

Ringelblum, Emmanuel. Notes from the Warsaw Ghetto: The Journal of Emmanuel Ringelblum. Sloan, Jacob, ed. & tr. by. LC 74-10147. 389p. 1974. reprint ed. pap. 16.00 (*0-8052-0460-1*) Schocken.

— Polish-Jewish Relations During the Second World War. Allon, Dafna et al, trs. LC 76-1394. 330p. 1976. 40.00 (*0-86527-155-0*) Fertig.

— Polish-Jewish Relations During the Second World War. annot. ed. Krakowski, Shmuel, ed. Allon, Dafna et al, trs. 671p. 1992. reprint ed. pap. 19.95 (*0-8101-0963-8*) Northwestern U Pr.

Ringelheim, Joan, comp. A Catalogue of Audio & Video Collections of Holocaust Testimony. 2nd ed. LC 91-43368. (Bibliographies & Indexes in World History Ser.: No. 23). 209p. 1992. text ed. 72.50 (*0-313-28221-8*, RAV/, Greenwood Pr) Greenwood.

***Ringelstein, E. B., ed.** Eighth International Symposium on Cerebral Hemodynamics, Muenster, September 1994: Abstracts. (Journal: Cerebrovascular Diseases Ser.: Vol. 4, Suppl. 3, 1994). xxii, 26p. 1994. pap. 19.25 (*3-8055-6065-6*) S Karger.

Ringen, Catherine O. Vowel Harmony: Theoretical Implications. LC 88-16514. (Outstanding Dissertations in Linguistics Ser.). 160p. 1988. 15.00 (*0-8240-5195-5*) Garland.

Ringen, Stein. Democracy, Science, & the Civic Spirit: An Inaugural Lecture Delivered Before the University of Oxford on 27 October, 1992. LC 93-18200. 1993. pap. 4.50 (*0-19-951359-7*, Clarendon Pr) OUP.

Ringen, Stein, jt. auth. see Wallace, Claire.

Ringenbach, Paul T. Tramps & Reformers, 1873-1916: The Discovery of Unemployment in New York. LC 77-175610. (Contributions in American History Ser.: No. 27). (Illus.). 224p. 1973. text ed. 59.95 (*0-8371-6266-1*, RAT/, Greenwood Pr) Greenwood.

***Ringenberg, Lawrence A.** A Portrait of 2. (Illus.). 42p. (YA). (gr. 10-12). Date not set. reprint ed. pap. write for info. (*0-87353-414-X*) NCTM.

Ringer, Alexander. Early Romantic Era Between Revolutions: 1789 & 1848. 400p. (C). 1990. pap. write for info. (*0-318-65464-4*) P-H.

— Early Romantic Era Between Revolutions: 1789 & 1848. 1990. pap. text ed. 12.30 (*0-13-222332-5*, 680106) P-H.

Ringer, Alexander L. Arnold Schoenberg: The Composer As Jew. (Illus.). 288p. 1990. 58.00 (*0-19-315466-8*) OUP.

Ringer, Benjamin B. We the People & Others: Duality & America's Treatment of Its Racial Minorities. 1178p. 1985. pap. text ed. 28.50 (*0-422-60160-8*, 9677, Pub. by Tavistock UK) Routledge Chapman & Hall.

— We the People & Others: Duality & America's Treatment of the Racial Minorities. 1165p. 1983. 75.00 (*0-422-78180-0*, NO. 3734, Pub. by Tavistock UK) Routledge Chapman & Hall.

Ringer, Benjamin B. & Lawless, Elinor R. Race, Ethnicity & Society. 256p. 1989. 35.00 (*0-415-90034-4*, A1587, Routledge NY); pap. 14.95 (*0-415-90035-2*, A1591, Routledge NY) Routledge.

Ringer, Bruce. Cycle Touring in New Zealand. LC 89-38348. (Illus.). 320p. (Orig.). 1989. pap. 14.95 (*0-89886-182-9*) Mountaineers.

— New Zealand by Bike. 2nd ed. (Illus.). 320p. 1994. pap. 16.95 (*0-89886-409-7*) Mountaineers.

Ringer, Francis. Becoming People of the Way: Intentional Christianity. LC 91-13301. (Kaleidoscope Ser.). 144p. (Orig.). 1991. teacher ed, pap. 9.95 (*0-8298-0879-5*); vhs 29.95 (*0-8298-0881-7*) Pilgrim OH.

Ringer, Fritz. Fields of Knowledge: French Academic Culture in Comparative Perspective, 1890-1920. 336p. (C). 1992. 19.95 (*0-521-40118-6*) Cambridge U Pr.

Ringer, Fritz K. The Decline of the German Mandarins: The German Academic Community, 1890-1933. LC 90-50315. 548p. 1990. pap. 25.00 (*0-8195-6235-1*, Wesleyan Univ Pr) U Pr of New Eng.

Ringer, Gordon, tr. see Marcel, Gabriel.

Ringer, R. Jeffrey, ed. Queer Words, Queer Images: Communication & the Construction of Homosexuality. 400p. (C). 1994. text ed. 50.00 (*0-8147-7440-7*); pap. text ed. 17.95 (*0-8147-7441-5*) NYU Pr.

Ringer, Robert J. Looking Out for Number One. 352p. 1991. mass mkt. 4.95 (*0-449-21010-3*, Crest) Fawcett.

— Million Dollar Habits. 320p. 1990. mass mkt. 5.95 (*0-449-21878-3*, Crest) Fawcett.

— Million Dollar Habits. LC 89-29399. 224p. 1990. 19.99 (*0-922066-29-9*, Wynwood Pr) Revell.

— Restoring the American Dream. 1980. pap. 2.95 (*0-449-24314-1*, Crest) Fawcett.

— Winning Through Intimidation. 304p. 1991. mass mkt. 5.95 (*0-449-20786-2*, Crest) Fawcett.

Ringer, Virginia, tr. see Marcel, Gabriel.

Ringerbach, Paul T. & Melly, Peter J. The Battle for An Loc. 102p. 1993. reprint ed. pap. 12.50x (*0-923135-59-6*) Dalley Bk Service.

Ringers, Joseph, Jr. Creating Interagency Projects: School & Community Agencies. 56p. (Orig.). 1977. pap. 3.95 (*0-930388-01-1*) Comm Collaborators.

Ringertz, Hans, jt. auth. see Pettersson, H.

Ringertz, Olof, et al. Sport Medicine: Pathology. LC 73-10369. (Sport Medicine Ser.: Vol. 3). 1973. 29.00 (*0-8422-7141-4*) Irvington.

Ringger, Carolyn. Reaching Toward Heaven. 1992. 9.95 (*1-55503-382-2*, 01111027) Covenant Comms.

Ringgold, Faith. Aunt Harriet's Underground in the Sky. LC 92-20072. (Illus.). 32p. (J). (ps-4). 1993. 16.00 (*0-517-58767-X*); lib. bdg. 17.99 (*0-517-58768-8*) Crown Bks Yng Read.

— Award Puzzles: The Coretta Scott King Collection - Tar Beach. (Illus.). 1993. 6.95 (*0-938971-92-1*) JTG Nashville.

— Dinner at Aunt Connie's House. LC 92-54871. (Illus.). 32p. (J). (gr. k-4). 1993. 14.95 (*1-56282-425-2*); lib. bdg. 14.89 (*1-56282-426-0*) Hyprn Child.

— Tar Beach. LC 90-40410. (Illus.). 32p. (J). (ps-3). 1991. 16.00 (*0-517-58030-6*); lib. bdg. 16.99 (*0-517-58031-4*) Crown Bks Yng Read.

— Tar Beach. (Book & Doll Packages Ser.). (Illus.). 32p. (J). (ps-4). 1994. 16.00 (*0-517-59961-9*) Crown Bks Yng Read.

— We Flew over the Bridge: The Memoirs of Faith Ringgold. LC 95-12988. (Illus.). 304p. 1995. 35.00 (*0-8212-2071-3*) Bulfinch Pr.

Ringgold, Gene. Complete Films of Bette Davis. 1990. pap. 15.95 (*0-8065-1177-X*, Citadel Pr) Carol Pub Group.

— The Complete Films of Rita Hayworth: The Legend & Career of a Love Goddess. (Illus.). 256p. 1992. pap. 15.95 (*0-8065-1260-1*, Citadel Pr) Carol Pub Group.

Ringgold, Gene & Bodeen, Dewitt. Chevalier: The Films & Career of Maurice Chevalier. (Illus.). 256p. 1973. 12.00 (*0-8065-0354-8*, Citadel Pr); pap. 7.95 (*0-8065-0483-8*, Citadel Pr) Carol Pub Group.

Ringgold, Gene & Bodeen, DeWitt. The Complete Films of Cecil B. Demille. (Illus.). 386p. 1985. reprint ed. pap. 12.95 (*0-8065-0956-2*, Citadel Pr) Carol Pub Group.

— Films of Cecil B. DeMille. 1969. 10.00 (*0-8065-0216-9*, Citadel Pr); pap. 6.95 (*0-8065-0207-X*, Citadel Pr) Carol Pub Group.

Ringgold, Gene & McCarthy, Clifford. The Films of Frank Sinatra. (Citadel Film Ser.). 1989. pap. 14.95 (*0-685-28303-8*, Citadel Pr) Carol Pub Group.

Ringgold, Nicolette P. Out of the Corner of My Eye: Living with Vision Loss in Later Life. large type ed. LC 91-3352. 120p. 1991. 14.95 (*0-89128-193-2*); audio 19.95 (*0-89128-211-4*) Am Foun Blind.

Ringgren, Helmer. The Faith of Qumram: Theology of the Dead Sea Scrolls. 324p. 1995. pap. 17.95 (*0-8245-1258-8*) Crossroad NY.

Ringgren, Helmer, jt. ed. see Botterweck, G. Johannes.

Ringheim, Karin. At Risk of Homelessness: The Roles of Income & Rent. LC 90-34290. 280p. 1990. text ed. 55.00 (*0-275-93582-5*, C3582, Praeger Pubs) Greenwood.

***Ringhofer, Kevin B. & Harding, Martha E.** Coaches Guide to Drugs & Sport. LC 95-16965. 160p. (Orig.). 1996. pap. 17.95 (*0-87322-715-8*, PRIN0715) Human Kinetics.

Ringholtz, Rae C. Diggings & Doings in Park City. 1977. reprint ed. 7.95 (*0-914740-16-4*) Western Epics.

Ringholz, Raye C. Park City Trails. LC 84-60807. (Illus.). 104p. 1984. pap. 6.50 (*0-915272-26-1*) Wasatch Pubs.

Ringis, Rita. Thai Temples & Temple Murals. (Illus.). 196p. 1990. 45.00 (*0-19-588933-9*) OUP.

Ringl & Dasso, Jerome. Real Estate Principles & Practices. 8th ed. Incl. Illinois Supplement. 1977. pap. 7.95 (*0-13-765867-2*); Florida Supplement. 1977. pap. 7.95 (*0-13-765875-3*); Texas Supplement. 1977. pap. 7.95 (*0-13-765883-4*); 1977. Set pap. write for info. (*0-318-54926-3*) P-H.

Ringland, Elinor. Alzheimer's Disease from Care to Caring. rev. ed. LC 85-81657. (Illus.). 115p. 1988. pap. 8.00 (*0-9613775-3-4*) Healthcare Pr.

Ringle, Martin H., jt. ed. see Lehnert, Wendy G.

Ringle, William M. & Smith-Stark, Thomas C. A Concordance to the Inscriptions of Palenque, Chiapas, 2 vols. (Publication Ser.: No. 62). Date not set. write for info. (*0-939238-92-6*) Tulane MARI.

— A Concordance to the Inscriptions of Palenque, Chiapas, Maxico. LC 92-12571. 1994. write for info. (*0-939238-93-4*) Tulane MARI.

Ringleb, Al H., et al. Managing in the Legal Environment. 2nd ed. Fenton, ed. LC 92-30982. 700p. (C). 1993. text ed. 65.75 (*0-314-01165-X*) West Pub.

Ringleben, Joachim. Aneignung: Die Spekulative Theologie Soren Kierkegaards. 509p. 1983. 123.10 (*3-11-008878-9*) De Gruyter.

— Hegels Theorie der Suende: Die Subjektivitaets-Logishe Umformung Eines Theologischen Begriffs. (Theologische Bibliothek Toepelmann Ser.: Vol. 31). 93.85 (*3-11-006650-5*) De Gruyter.

Ringleben, Joachim, ed. Christentumsgeschichte und Wahrheitsbewusstsein: Studien zur Theologie Emanuel Hirschs. (Theologische Bibliothek Toepelmann Ser.: Vol. 50). vii, 254p. (GER.). (C). 1991. lib. bdg. 86.15 (*3-11-012700-8*) De Gruyter.

Ringleben, Joachim, jt. ed. see Meckenstock, Gunter.

Ringler, Lenore H. & Weber, Carol K. A Language-Thinking Approach to Reading: Diagnosis & Teaching. 442p. (C). 1984. text ed. 29.50 (*0-15-550060-0*) HB Coll Pubs.

Ringler, R., jt. auth. see Cassidy, F. J.

Ringler, Richard N., jt. ed. see Rothstein, Eric.

Ringler, Susan J., ed. see Ringler, William A., Jr.

Ringler, William A. Bibliography & Index of English Verse Printed, 1476-1558. 448p. 1989. text ed. 200.00 (*0-7201-1892-1*, Mansell Pub) Cassell.

Ringler, William A., Jr. Index of English Verse in Manuscript, 1501-1558. Rudick, Michael & Ringler, Susan J., eds. 344p. 1992. text ed. 190.00 (*0-7201-2099-3*, Mansell Pub) Cassell.

Ringler, William A., jt. intro. see Fox, Denton.

Ringling Bros. & Barnum & Bailey Combined Shows, Inc. Staff. Animals of the Circus. Self, Kathy A., ed. LC 90-62395. (Orig.). (J). 1990. pap. 3.50 (*1-878163-01-9*) Ringling Bros.

— Circus Days Cookbook. Self, Kathy A., ed. LC 90-62393. (Orig.). (J). 1990. pap. 13.00 (*1-878163-00-0*) Ringling Bros.

Ringlstetter, Maria, tr. see Perkins, Anne.

Ringnalda, Don. Fighting & Writing the Vietnam War. LC 94-16059. 224p. 1994. text ed. 37.50 (*0-87805-730-7*) U Pr of Miss.

Ringnalda, Lisa, jt. auth. see Strom, Kay.

***Ringney.** Network Planning & Management: Your Personal Consultant. 1995. pap. text ed. 24.95 (*1-56276-309-1*) Ziff-Davis.

Ringo, Betty, ed. see Paull, Susan G.

Ringoir, S., et al, eds. Uremic Toxins. LC 87-25936. (Illus.). 308p. 1987. 85.00 (*0-306-42771-0*, Plenum Pr) Plenum.

Ringold, Fran, ed. Australia. 160p. 1993. pap. 6.95 (*0-685-65045-6*) Art & Human Council Tulsa.

— Awards Eighth. 144p. 1991. pap. 6.95 (*0-317-60728-6*) Art & Human Council Tulsa.

— Awards Eleventh. 148p. 1989. 6.50 (*0-685-34258-1*) Art & Human Council Tulsa.

— Awards Fifteen. 160p. 1993. pap. 6.90 (*0-685-62356-4*) Art & Human Council Tulsa.

— Awards Fourteenth. 160p. 1992. pap. 6.90 (*0-685-62340-8*) Art & Human Council Tulsa.

— Awards Ninth. 152p. 1987. pap. 5.50 (*0-685-45298-0*) Art & Human Council Tulsa.

— Awards Seventh. 107p. 1985. pap. 5.50 (*0-317-60726-X*) Art & Human Council Tulsa.

— Awards Sixteenth. 168p. 1994. pap. 6.95 (*0-614-03086-2*) Art & Human Council Tulsa.

— Awards Sixth. 119p. 1984. pap. 5.50 (*0-317-60711-1*) Art & Human Council Tulsa.

— Awards Tenth. 152p. 1988. 5.50 (*0-685-45299-9*) Art & Human Council Tulsa.

— Awards Third. (Nimrod Ser.). 109p. (Orig.). 1981. pap. text ed. 5.50 (*0-942374-06-1*) Art & Human Council Tulsa.

— Awards Thirteenth. 160p. 1991. 6.90 (*0-933031-54-8*) Art & Human Council Tulsa.

— Awards Twelfth. 160p. 1990. pap. 6.90 (*0-685-37855-1*) Art & Human Council Tulsa.

— China Today. 132p. 1986. pap. 5.50 (*0-317-60731-6*) Art & Human Council Tulsa.

— From the Soviets. 160p. 1990. pap. 6.90 (*0-933031-52-1*) Art & Human Council Tulsa.

— India: A Wealth of Diversity. 160p. 1988. pap. 5.50 (*0-318-32886-0*) Art & Human Council Tulsa.

— Making Language: Thirty-Fifth Anniversary Issue. 144p. 1992. pap. 6.90 (*0-685-62341-6*) Art & Human Council Tulsa.

— Nimrod: Awards XVI. (Orig.). 1994. pap. 6.95 (*0-571-78005-9*) Coun Oak Bks.

— Nimrod: Clap Hands & Sing: Writers of Age. 160p. (Orig.). 1991. pap. 6.95 (*0-933031-53-X*) Coun Oak Bks.

— Nimrod: O' Canada. (Illus.). 149p. (Orig.). 1994. pap. 6.95 (*0-933031-96-3*) Coun Oak Bks.

— Nimrod: Points North: The Arctic Circle. 1995. pap. 6.95 (*1-57178-005-X*) Coun Oak Bks.

— O, Canada. 160p. 1994. pap. 6.95 (*0-685-66039-7*) Art & Human Council Tulsa.

— Oklahoma Indian Markings. 160p. 1989. 6.95 (*0-685-45300-6*) Art & Human Council Tulsa.

— Thirty-Three. 146p. 1987. pap. 5.50 (*0-318-32887-9*) Art & Human Council Tulsa.

— Tulsa-Tbilisi. 168p. 1985. pap. 5.50 (*0-317-60730-8*) Art & Human Council Tulsa.

Ringold, Fran, et al, eds. Arabic Literature: Then & Now. (Nimrod Ser.). (Illus.). 149p. (C). 1981. pap. text ed. 5.50 (*0-942374-07-X*) Art & Human Council Tulsa.

Ringold, Francine, ed. Awards Fourth. (Nimrod Ser.). (Illus.). 112p. (Orig.). 1982. pap. 5.50 (*0-942374-09-6*) Art & Human Council Tulsa.

R

An Asterisk (*) at the beginning of an entry indicates that the title is appearing in BIP for the first time.

— Frontiers: Land, Space, & Mind. (Nimrod Ser.). 96p. 1982. pap. text ed. 5.50 (*0-942374-08-8*) Art & Human Council Tulsa.

Ringold, Francine & Rugh, Madeline M. Making Your Own Mark: A Drawing & Writing Guide for Senior Citizens. LC 89-85837. (Illus.). 102p. 1990. pap. 14.95 (*0-9624297-0-8*) Coun Oak Bks.

Ringold, Jeannette K., tr. see Minco, Marga.

Ringold, May S. The Role of the State Legislatures in the Confederacy. LC 66-27607. 149p. reprint ed. pap. 42.50 (*0-318-34872-1*, 2031051) Bks Demand.

Ringquist, Evan J. Environmental Protection at the State Level: Politics & Progress in Controlling Pollution. LC 93-12298. (Bureaucracies, Public Administration & Public Policy Ser.). 256p. (C). 1993. 57.95 (*1-56324-203-6*); pap. text ed. 25.95 (*1-56324-204-4*) M E Sharpe.

Ringrose, David R. Transportation & Economic Stagnation in Spain, 1750-1850. LC 78-101131. 213p. reprint ed. pap. 60.80 (*0-317-20423-8*, 2023441) Bks Demand.

Ringrose, Hyacinthe. The Inns of Court: An Historical Description of the Inns of Court & Chancery of England. (Illus.). iv, 183p. 1983. reprint ed. lib. bdg. 22.50 (*0-8377-1040-5*) Rothman.

Ringrose, Hyacinthe, ed. Marriage & Divorce Laws of the World. 270p. 1988. reprint ed. lib. bdg. 32.50 (*0-8377-2540-2*) Rothman.

Ringrose, John R., jt. auth. see Kadison, Richard V.

Ringrose, John R., jt. ed. see Kadison, Richard V.

Ringrose, Linda, jt. auth. see Rathbun, Linda.

Ringrose, Marjorie & Lerner, Adam, eds. Reimagining the Nation. LC 92-47424. 1993. 85.00 (*0-335-19150-9*, Open Univ Pr) Taylor & Francis.

***Ringrose-Voase, A. J. & Humphreys, G. S., eds.** Soil Micromorphology: Studies in Managment & Genesis. LC 94-21731. (Development in Soil Science Ser.: 22). 1994. write for info. (*0-444-89792-5*) Elsevier.

Rings, Lana, jt. auth. see Clausing, Gerhard.

Rings, Roy W., et al. The Owlet Moths of Ohio (Order Lepidoptera Family Noctuidae) LC 91-62768. (Bulletin New Ser.: Vol. 9, No. 2). (Illus.). 200p. 1992. 20.00 (*0-86727-110-8*) Ohio Bio Survey.

Ringskog, Klas, jt. auth. see Idelovitch, Emanuel.

Ringsrud, jt. auth. see Linne, Jean J.

Ringsrud, Karen M. Urinalysis & Body Fluids. 284p. 1994. pap. 31.95 (*0-8016-7043-8*) Mosby Yr Bk.

Ringstad, M. Adventures on Library Shelves. LC 68-16398. (Illus.). 48p. (J). (gr. 2 up). 1967. ring bd. 12.35 (*0-87783-001-0*) Oddo.

Ringstad, Muriel. Eye of the Changer. LC 83-7121. (Illus.). 96p. (Orig.). (J). (gr. 4 up). 1984. pap. 9.95 (*0-88240-251-X*) Alaska Northwest.

Ringsven, Mary K. Gerontology & Leadership Skills - Nurses. 1991. text ed. 28.95 (*0-8273-3450-8*) Delmar.

Ringsven, Mary K. & Bond, Donna. Gerontology & Leadership for Nurses: Instructor's Guide. 1991. 12.00 (*0-8273-3451-6*) Delmar.

Ringuest, Jeffery L. Multiobjective Optimization: Behavioral & Computational Considerations. 192p. (C). 1992. lib. bdg. 67.50 (*0-7923-9236-1*) Kluwer Ac.

Ringwald, Donald C. Steamboats for Rondout: Passenger Service Between New York & Rondout Creek, 1829-1863. LC 81-51099. (Illus.). 145p. 1981. 17.00 (*0-913423-00-9*) Steamship Hist Soc.

Ringwald, Lydia E. Blessings in Disguise. 36p. (Orig.). 1989. pap. 8.00 (*0-685-29073-5*) Creative Realities.

Ringwald, Richard. Means Heavy Construction Handbook: A Practical Guide to Estimating & Accounting Methods. 1993. pap. 69.95 (*0-87629-283-X*, 67148) R S Means.

Ringwood, A. E. Origin of the Earth & Moon. (Illus.). 1979. 73.00 (*0-387-90369-0*) Spr-Verlag.

Rinhart, Floyd & Rinhart, Marion. America's Centennial Celebration. LC 75-38859. (Illus.). 1976. pap. 4.95 (*0-914042-08-4*) Laura Bks.

Rinhart, Marion, jt. auth. see Rinhart, Floyd.

Rini, Joel. Motives for Lingustic Change in the Formation of the Spanish Object Pronouns. Lathrop, Thomas et al, eds. (Estudios Linguisticos Ser.). 152p. 1992. pap. 12.00 (*0-936388-52-8*) Juan de la Cuesta.

Rini, Kristiana S., jt. auth. see Woods, Paul.

Rini, Lisa, jt. auth. see Werner, Peter H.

Rini, Suzanne M. Beyond Abortion: A Chronicle of Fetal Experimentation. LC 92-82133. 197p. 1993. reprint ed. pap. 10.00 (*0-89555-487-9*) TAN Bks Pubs.

Rini, William A. The NYIF Vest-Pocket Guide to Stock Brokerage Math. LC 92-15201. 1992. 13.95 (*0-13-847690-X*) P-H.

Rinjiro, Shirata, jt. auth. see Stevens, John.

Rink, Cynthia, jt. auth. see Rhea, Kathlyn.

Rink, David R., jt. auth. see Kaminski, Peter F.

Rink, Glenn, et al. A Guide to Salt River Canyon: Natural History & River Running. Hauk, Rose, ed. (Illus.). 72p. (Orig.). 1990. pap. 15.00 (*0-685-30084-6*) Worldwide Explorations.

Rink, Henry W., jt. auth. see Gallo, Joseph D.

Rink, Hinrich J. Danish Greenland: Its People & Its Products. LC 74-5870. (Illus.). reprint ed. 64.50 (*0-404-11677-9*) AMS Pr.

— The Eskimo Tribes, 2 vols. in 1. LC 74-5871. reprint ed. 72.50 (*0-404-11678-7*) AMS Pr.

— Tales & Traditions of the Eskimo, with a Sketch of Their Habits, Religion, Language & Other Peculiarities. LC 74-5872. (Illus.). reprint ed. 67.50 (*0-404-11681-7*) AMS Pr.

***Rink, John, ed.** The Practice of Performance: Studies in Musical Interpretation. (Illus.). 304p. (C). 1995. write for info. (*0-521-45374-7*) Cambridge U Pr.

Rink, John & Samson, Jim, eds. Chopin Studies 2, No. 2. (Illus.). 300p. (C). 1995. 64.95 (*0-521-41647-7*) Cambridge U Pr.

Rink, Judith. Teaching Physical Education for Learning. 2nd ed. 336p. 1992. 31.95 (*0-8016-6744-5*) Mosby Yr Bk.

Rink, Oliver A. Holland on the Hudson: An Economic & Social History of Dutch New York. LC 86-2317. (Illus.). 288p. 1986. 39.95 (*0-8014-1866-6*); pap. 13.95 (*0-8014-9585-7*) Cornell U Pr.

Rink, Richard A. Programming with MacIntosh & Think Pascal. 2nd ed. 1995. pap. text ed. 47.00 (*0-13-093873-4*) P-H.

Rinke, Hans. Woerterbuch der Seeschiffahrt: Dictionary of Merchant Shipping, Vol. 1. 2nd ed. (ENG & GER.). 1975. 59.95 (*0-8288-5967-1*, M6958) Fr & Eur.

— Woerterbuch der Seeschiffahrt: Dictionary of Merchant Shipping, Vol. 2. 2nd ed. (ENG & GER.). 59.95 (*3-19-006295-1*, M-6957) Fr & Eur.

Rinke, Lynn T. & Wilson, Alexis A., eds. Outcome Measures in Home Care: Research, Vol. I. 250p. (Orig.). 1987. pap. 22.95 (*0-88737-378-X*) Natl League Nurse.

Rinke, Wolf J. Make It a Winning Life: Success Strategies for Life, Love & Business. LC 91-75609. 283p. 1992. 24.95 (*0-9627913-8-5*) Achvmnt Pubs.

— The Winning Foodservice Manager: Strategies for Doing More with Less. 2nd ed. LC 90-84599. 261p. 1990. reprint ed. text ed. 32.50 (*0-9627913-9-3*) Achvmnt Pubs.

Rinkel, Herbert J., et al. Food Allergy. (Illus.). 512p. 1950. 77.95 (*0-398-04167-9*) C C Thomas.

***Rinker Enterprises, Inc. Staff.** Garage Sale Manual & Price Guide. (Illus.). 160p. (Orig.). 1995. pap. 12.95 (*0-930625-37-4*, Antique Trdr Bks) Antique Trader.

Rinker, Harry, Jr. & Heistand, Robert. World War II Collectibles. LC 92-54942. (Collector's Library). (Illus.). 80p. 1994. 12.98 (*1-56138-217-5*) Courage Bks.

***Rinker, Harry L.** Hopalong Cassidy: King of the Cowboy Merchandisers. (Illus.). 160p. (Orig.). 1995. pap. 29.95 (*0-88740-765-X*) Schiffer.

— The Old Raging Erie...There Have Been Several Changes: A Postcard History of the Erie & Other New York State Canals, 1895-1915. (Illus.). 96p. (Orig.). 1984. pap. 12.00 (*0-9613675-0-4*) Canal Captains.

***Rinker, Harry L., Jr.** Price Guide to Flea Market Treasures. 3rd ed. 304p. 1995. pap. 19.95 (*0-87069-719-6*) Chilton.

Rinker, Harry L. Schuylkill Navigation: A Photographic History. LC 90-85567. (Illus.). 96p. 1991. pap. 16.00 (*0-9613675-2-0*) Canal Captains.

— Warman's Americana & Collectibles. 7th ed. 608p. 1995. pap. 16.95 (*0-87069-742-0*) Chilton.

— Warman's Antiques & Collectibles Price Guide 1995. 29th ed. 864p. 1995. pap. 14.95 (*0-87069-734-X*) Chilton.

Rinker, Harry L., Jr., ed. Warman's Americana & Collectibles. 6th ed. (Illus.). 608p. 1993. pap. 15.95 (*0-87069-684-X*) Chilton.

Rinker, Harry L., jt. auth. see Morykan, Dana G.

Rinker, Rosalind. Como Celebrar el Culto Familiar: How to Have Family Prayers. (SPA.). 4.95 (*84-7228-488-3*, 220163, Pub. by Edit Clie SP) TSELF.

— Como Testificar Con Eficacia: You Can Witness with Confidence. (SPA.). 4.95 (*84-7228-188-4*, 220177, Pub. by Edit Clie SP) TSELF.

— Compartiendo el Amor De Dios: Sharing God's Love. (SPA.). 4.25 (*84-7228-385-2*, 220181, Pub. by Edit Clie SP) TSELF.

— Learning Conversational Prayer. 48p. (Orig.). 1992. pap. text ed. 3.95 (*0-8146-2036-1*) Liturgical Pr.

— Transmitiendo Amor Por Medio Oracion: Communicating Love Thru Prayer. (SPA.). 4.25 (*84-7228-191-4*, 220897, Pub. by Edit Clie SP) TSELF.

— Tratamiento de Shock: Praying Together. (SPA.). 3.25 (*84-7228-179-5*, 220904, Pub. by Edit Clie SP) TSELF.

— You Can Witness with Confidence. LC 91-72627. 72p. 1991. reprint ed. pap. 7.95 (*0-940232-44-8*) Seedsowers.

Rinker, Wesley S. It's How You Throw the Game. (Illus.). 96p. 1988. pap. 9.95 (*0-9620890-1-X*) Cent FL Sports Expo.

— It's How You Throw the Game! (Illus.). 93p. (Orig.). 1990. pap. 9.95 (*0-9620890-0-1*) Cent FL Sports Expo.

***Rinkevich, Thomas E.** A KWIC Concordance to Lucretius' De Rerum Natura, 2 Vols., Set. LC 93-85190. v, 1030p. (LAT.). 1995. 90.00 (*0-9644790-1-X*) Nonce NE.

— A KWIC Concordance to Lucretius' De Rerum Natura, Vol. 1. LC 93-85190. v, 482p. (LAT.). Date not set. 45.00 (*0-9644790-0-1*) Nonce NE.

— A KWIC Concordance to Lucretius' De Rerum Natura, Vol. 2. 548p. (LAT.). 1995. 45.00 (*0-9644790-2-8*) Nonce NE.

Rinkieviczus, K. W. Channeling: Communicating with the Unseen. (Illus.). 48p. (Orig.). 1987. pap. 3.95 (*0-940137-00-3*) Prism Pubns ME.

Rinkle, Max & Denber, H. C. Chemical Concepts of Psychosis. (Illus.). 1958. 24.95 (*0-8392-1012-4*) Astor-Honor.

Rinkoff, Barbara. The Remarkable Ramsey. (Illus.). (J). (gr. 2-6). 15.25 (*0-8446-6195-3*) Peter Smith.

Rinkwich, Randy. While Beyond the Forest. Barkan, Stanley H., ed. (Review Chapbook Ser.: No. 24: Yiddish Poetry 1). 40p. (ENG & YID.). 1991. 15.00 (*0-89304-762-7*); 15.00 (*0-89304-764-3*); pap. 5.00 (*0-89304-763-5*); pap. 5.00 (*0-89304-765-1*) Cross-Cultrl NY.

Rinn, Joseph A. Sixty Years of Psychical Research. 618p. 3.00 (*0-318-17121-X*) Atheist Assn.

Rinn, Ludwig A. The Polychromatic Layering Technique. (Illus.). 110p. 1990. text ed. 82.00 (*0-86715-225-7*) Quint Pub Co.

Rinn, Roger C. & Markle, Allan. Positive Parenting. (Illus.). 1986. pap. text ed. 8.95 (*0-89147-052-2*) CAS.

Rinne, David. The Bronze Statue of a Youth. (Illus.). 30p. (Orig.). 1975. pap. 5.95 (*0-89236-043-7*) J P Getty Trust.

Rinne, U. K., et al. Parkinson's Disease: Current Progress, Problems & Management. 402p. 1980. 108.25 (*0-444-80263-0*) Elsevier.

***Rinnen, Henri.** Dictionnaire Francais-Luxembourgeois. 1170p. (FRE.). 1988. 95.00 (*0-7859-8664-2*, 287963007x) Fr & Eur.

Rinnooy-Kan, A. H., ed. New Challenges for Management Research. (Advanced Series in Management: Vol. 9). 1985. 61.75 (*0-444-87709-6*) Elsevier.

Rinnooy-Kan, A. H., jt. auth. see Kan, A. H.

Rino, J. Patti, jt. ed. see Resnick, Herman.

***Rinpoche, Akong T.** Taming the Tiger: Tibetan Teachings on Right Conduct, Mindfulness & Universal Compassion. (Illus.). 208p. 1996. pap. 12.95 (*0-89281-569-8*) Inner Tradit.

Rinpoche, Bokar. Chenrezig, Lord of Love: Principles & Methods of Deity Meditation. Jorgensen, Dan, ed. Buchet, Christiane, tr. & intro. by. LC 91-73587. (Illus.). 112p. (Orig.). 1991. pap. text ed. 11.95 (*0-9630371-0-2*) ClearPoint.

— Death & the Art of Dying in Tibetan Buddhism. Buchet, Christiane, tr. LC 93-74661. (Illus.). 144p. (Orig.). 1993. pap. text ed. 14.95 (*0-9630371-2-9*) ClearPoint.

— Meditation: Advice to Beginners. Pessereau, Jennifer, ed. LC 92-75390. (Illus.). 160p. (Orig.). 1993. pap. 14.95 (*0-9630371-1-0*) ClearPoint.

— Profound Wisdom of the Heart Sutra: And Other Teachings. Buchet, Christiane, tr. (Illus.). 96p. (Orig.). 1994. pap. text ed. 10.95 (*0-9630371-3-7*) ClearPoint.

Rinpoche, Chagdud T. Lord of the Dance: Autobiography of Chagdud Tulku. LC 92-22341. 248p. (Orig.). 1993. pap. 16.95 (*1-881847-00-4*) Chagdud Gonpa-Padma.

***Rinpoche, Dagyab.** Buddhist Symbols in Tibetan Culture. Walshe, Maurice, tr. (Illus.). 160p. (Orig.). 1995. pap. 14.95 (*0-614-07220-4*) Wisdom MA.

***Rinpoche, Deshung & Tenpa Nyima, Kunga.** The Three Levels of Spiritual Rinpoche: An Oral Commentary on the Three Visions (Nang Sum) of Ngorchen Konchong Lhundrub. Scott, Victoria R, ed. Rhoton, Jared, tr. LC 95-1490. (Illus.). 620p. (ENG & TIB.). 1995. 39.95 (*0-86171-101-7*) Wisdom MA.

***Rinpoche, Deshung & Tenpay Nyima, Kunga.** The Three Levels of Spiritual Rinpoche: An Oral Commentary on the Three Visions (Nang Sum) of Ngorchen Konchong Lhundrub. Scott, Victoria R, ed. Rhoton, Jared, tr. LC 95-1490. (Illus.). 620p. (ENG & TIB.). 1995. pap. 24.95 (*0-86171-069-X*) Wisdom MA.

Rinpoche, Dilgo K. Enlightened Courage: An Explanation of Atish's Seven Point Mind Training. Padmakara Translation Group, tr. LC 93-28462. (ENG.). 1993. pap. 12.95 (*1-55939-023-9*) Snow Lion Pubns.

Rinpoche, Dudjom. The Nyingma School of Tibetan Buddhism, 2 vols. Dorje, Gyurme, ed. LC 89-4053. (Illus.). 1500p. 1991. 240.00 (*0-86171-047-9*) Wisdom MA.

Rinpoche, Gyatrul. Ancient Wisdom: Nyingma Teachings on Dream Yoga, Meditation & Transformation. Wallace, B. Alan & Khandro, Sangye, trs. LC 93-13992. 1993. pap. 14.95 (*1-55939-018-2*) Snow Lion Pubns.

Rinpoche, Gyutrul. The Secret Oral Teachings on Generating the Deity. Khandro, Sangye, tr. (Illus.). 164p. 1992. pap. 25.00 (*957-638-105-3*, PRE015, Pub. by SMC Pub CC) Oriental Bk Store.

***Rinpoche, Kalu.** Esoteric Buddhism: Vajrayana Practices. Buchet, Christiane, tr. (Illus.). 200p. (Orig.). 1995. pap. text ed. 15.00 (*0-9630371-6-1*) ClearPoint.

— Excellent Buddhism: An Exemplary Life. Buchet, Christiane, tr. (Illus.). 200p. (Orig.). 1995. pap. text ed. 15.00 (*0-9630371-4-5*) ClearPoint.

— The Gem Ornament of Manifold Oral Instructions. 2nd ed. Clark, Nancy J. & Parke, Caroline M., eds. LC 87-20650. (Illus.). 204p. 1987. reprint ed. pap. 12.95 (*0-937938-59-9*) Snow Lion Pubns.

— Profound Buddhism: From Hinayana to Vajrayana. Buchet, Christiane, tr. (Illus.). 200p. (Orig.). 1995. pap. text ed. 15.00 (*0-9630371-5-3*) ClearPoint.

***Rinpoche, Khamtul.** Dzog Chen Meditation. Sparham, Gareth, tr. (C). 1994. text ed. 14.00 (*81-7030-407-5*, Pub. by Sri Satguru Pubns II) S Asia.

Rinpoche, Khenpo P. Ceaseless Echoes of the Great Silence: A Commentary on the Heart Sutra Prajnaparamito. Taylor, Phyllis & Kaye, Joan, eds. Rinpoche, Khenpo T., tr. (Illus.). 102p. (Orig.). (C). 1993. pap. text ed. write for info. (*1-880975-01-7*) Skydancer Pr.

Rinpoche, Khenpo T., tr. see Rinpoche, Khenpo P.

Rinpoche, Lama K., jt. auth. see Carnahan, Sumner.

***Rinpoche, Nyshul K.** Natural Great Perfection: Dzogchen Teachings & Vajra Songs. Das, Surya, ed. LC 95-15875. 1995. write for info. (*1-55939-049-2*) Snow Lion Pubns.

Rinpoche, Pabongka. Liberation in the Palm of Your Hand: A Concise Discourse on the Stages of the Path to Enlightenment. Rinpoche, Trijang, ed. Richards, Michael, tr. LC 91-10134. (Illus.). 980p. (Orig.). 1991. 37.50 (*0-86171-031-2*) Wisdom MA.

Rinpoche, Patrul. The Heart Treasure of the Enlightened Ones. LC 91-52593. 240p. (Orig.). 1993. pap. 15.00 (*0-87773-493-3*) Shambhala Pubns.

— The Words of My Perfect Teacher: Kunzang Lama'i Shelung. Association Padmakara Staff, tr. LC 93-37175. (Sacred Literature Ser.). 1994. 30.00 (*0-06-066449-5*) Harper SF.

Rinpoche, Sogyal. Glimpse after Glimpse: Daily Reflections on Living & Dying. Gaffney, Patrick, ed. 384p. 1995. pap. 12.00 (*0-06-251126-2*) Harper SF.

— Meditation. (Little Book of Wisdom Ser.). 96p. 1994. pap. 8.00 (*0-06-251114-9*) Harper SF.

— The Tibetan Way of Living & Dying. LC 90-56214. 1992. 24.00 (*0-06-250793-1*) Harper SF.

Rinpoche, Trijang, ed. see Rinpoche, Pabongka.

***Rinpoche, Tulka T.** The Practice of Dzogchen: Writings of Longchen Rabjampa. Talbott, Harold, ed. LC 88-39545. 482p. 1989. 22.95 (*1-55939-041-7*) Snow Lion Pubns.

Rinpoche, Zopa, ed. see Gyatso, Losang K.

Rinpoche, Zopa, jt. auth. see Yeshe, Lama T.

Rinschler, Geri, ed. Cranbrook Reflections: A Culinary Collection. (Illus.). 208p. 1991. 19.95 (*0-9628714-0-0*) Cranbrook Hse.

Rinse, Jacobus. The Rinse Formula. (Good Health Guide Ser.). 32p. (Orig.). 1988. pap. 1.95 (*0-87983-465-X*) Keats.

Rinsey, Mills. Original AC, Ace & Cobra. (Full Color Restoration Guides Ser.). (Illus.). 96p. 1990. 29.95 (*1-870979-14-1*, Pub. by Bay View Bks UK) Motorbooks Intl.

***Rinsky, Lee A.** Teaching Word Recognition Skills. 5th rev. ed. 1993. pap. text ed. 27.00 (*0-89787-535-4*) Gorsuch Scarisbrick.

Rinsky, Lee Ann, jt. auth. see Wassman, Rose.

Rinsland, Henry D. Analysis of Completion Sentences & Arithmetical Problems As Items for Intelligence Tests. LC 73-177192. (Columbia University. Teachers College. Contributions to Education Ser.: No. 666). reprint ed. 37.50 (*0-404-55666-3*) AMS Pr.

Rinsley, Donald B. Borderline & Other Self Disorders. LC 81-20538. 336p. 1982. 40.00 (*0-87668-447-9*) Aronson.

— Developmental Pathogenesis & Treatment of Borderline & Narcissistic Personalities. LC 89-17506. 192p. 1989. 27.50 (*0-87668-828-8*) Aronson.

— Treatment of the Severely Disturbed Adolescent. LC 80-66922. 368p. 1983. 45.00 (*0-87668-415-0*) Aronson.

— Treatment of the Severely Disturbed Adolescent. LC 80-66922. 364p. 1994. pap. 35.00 (*1-56821-222-4*) Aronson.

Rinsley, Donald B., jt. ed. see Grotstein, James S.

Rintala, J., et al, eds. Industrial Wastewaters '89-Nairobi: Proceedings of the First IAWPRC East African Regional Conference on Industrial Wastewaters, held in Nairobi, Kenya, 25-28 October 1989. (Water Science & Technology Ser.). (Illus.). 120p. 1991. pap. 68.00 (*0-08-041139-8*, Pergamon Pr) Elsevier.

Rintala, Marvin. The Constitution of Silence: Essays on Generational Themes. LC 78-20018. (Contributions in Political Science Ser.: No. 25). 95p. 1979. text ed. 49.95 (*0-313-20723-2*, RCS/, Greenwood Pr) Greenwood.

— Lloyd George & Churchill: How Friendship Changed Politics. LC 94-27342. 1994. 27.95 (*1-56833-031-6*) Madison Bks UPA.

Rintelmann, William F., ed. Hearing Assessment. 2nd ed. (Illus.). 885p. (C). 1991. write for info. (*0-205-13537-4*) Allyn.

Rintoul. Ontario Estate Administration: A Guide for Legal Secretaries & Law Clerks. 2nd ed. 184p. 1991. student ed, spiral bd. 29.95 (*0-409-90632-8*); spiral bd. 43.00 (*0-409-90377-9*) Butterworth Legal Pubs.

— The Solicitor's Guide to Estate Practice in Ontario. 2nd ed. 288p. 1990. 65.00 (*0-409-89336-6*) Butterworth Legal Pubs.

Rintoul, M. C. Dictionary of Real People & Places in Fiction. LC 92-46092. 1993. 125.00 (*0-415-05999-2*, A6963) Routledge.

***Rintoul, R. F., ed.** Farquharson's Textbook of Operative Surgery. 8th ed. LC 94-43499. 714p. 1994. 135.00 (*0-443-04712-X*) Churchill.

Rintoul, William. Drilling Through Time: Seventy-Five Years with California's Division of Oil & Gas. Hodgson, Susan F., ed. LC 90-81141. (Illus.). 200p. 1990. 10.00 (*0-9627124-0-X*) CA Div Oil Gas.

Rinvolucri, Mario. Anatomy of a Church: Greek Orthodoxy Today. LC 66-30071. 192p. reprint ed. pap. 54.80 (*0-7837-0468-2*, 2040791) Bks Demand.

— Grammar Games: A Resource Book for Teachers. (Illus.). 128p. 1985. pap. 14.95 (*0-521-27773-6*) Cambridge U Pr.

Rinvolucri, Mario, jt. auth. see Davis, Paul.

Rinvolucri, Mario, jt. auth. see Morgan, John.

Rinvolucri, Mario, tr. see Spatharis, Sotiris.

Rinzema, J. The Sexual Revolution: Challenge & Response. Smedes, Lewis B., tr. LC 73-14712. 107p. reprint ed. pap. 30.50 (*0-317-09741-5*, 2012849) Bks Demand.

Rinzler, Alan. Computerland Guide to Local Area Networks. 1991. pap. 18.95 (*0-9627212-0-4*) Computer CA.

Rinzler, Alan & Gancher, David, eds. The ComputerLand Guide to Local Area Networks. 2nd ed. (Illus.). 177p. (Orig.). 1992. pap. 18.95 (*0-9627212-2-0*) Computer CA.

Rinzler, Alan, jt. ed. see Brinton, William M.

Rinzler, Alan, ed. see Melnick, Ben.

Rinzler, Alan, jt. ed. see Ray, Michael.

Rinzler, Carol. Complete Book of Herbs, Spices & Condiments. 224p. 1990. 19.95 (*0-8160-2008-6*) Facts on File.

Rinzler, Carol A. Are You at Risk? 1993. mass mkt. 5.99 (*0-345-38013-4*) Ballantine.

— The Complete Book of Herbs, Spices, & Condiments: From Garden to Kitchen to Medicine Chest. (Illus.). 208p. (Orig.). 1991. pap. 12.00 (*0-8050-1618-X*, Owl) H Holt & Co.

— The Dictionary of Medical Folklore. 1980. pap. 2.75 (*0-345-28791-6*) Ballantine.

— Estrogen & Breast Cancer: A Warning to Women. LC 92-43809. 256p. 1993. text ed. 22.00 (*0-02-603491-3*) Macmillan.

— Feed A Cold, Starve a Fever: A Dictionary of Medical Folklore. 320p. 1991. 21.95 (*0-8160-2394-8*) Facts on File.

— Feed a Cold, Starve a Fever: A Dictionary of Medical Folklore. 1993. mass mkt. 4.99 (*0-345-38012-6*) Ballantine.

Rinzler, Carol Ann. Are You at Risk? 1991. 21.95 (*0-8160-2266-6*) Facts on File.

R

Rinzler, Paul E. Jazz Arranging & Performance Practice: A Guide for Small Ensembles. (Illus.). 178p. 1989. 22.50 (*0-8108-2257-1*) Scarecrow.

Rinzler, Susan, jt. ed. see Mair, Nancy.

Rio, Carmen D. Jorge Luis Borges y la Ficcion: El Conocimiento Como Invencion. LC 82-84262. (Coleccion Polymita Ser.). 192p. (Orig.). (SPA.). 1983. pap. text ed. 12.95 (*0-89729-325-8*) Ediciones.

Rio, Michel. Parrot's Perch. Hafrey, Leigh, tr. LC 85-744. 96p. 1985. 10.95 (*0-15-170964-5*) HarBrace.

Rioja, Jose A. Dictionary of Symbols & Myths: Diccionario de Simbolos y Mitos. 3rd ed. 436p. (SPA.). 1988. pap. 29.95 (*0-7859-4965-8*) Fr & Eur.

Riolo, et al. An Atlas of Craniofacial Growth. (Craniofacial Growth Ser.: Vol. 2). (Illus.). 379p. 1979. reprint ed. 55.00 (*0-929921-01-1*) UM CHGD.

Riolo, Al & Greenberg, Ellen. The New-Idea Success Book: Starting a Money-Making Business. 180p. 1988. pap. 12.95 (*0-8306-3013-9*, 30013, Liberty Hse) TAB Bks.

Riolo, Robert. Forty-Two Sure Ways to Become an Unsuccessful Actor. (Illus.). 37p. (Orig.). 1988. pap. 4.95 (*0-9620323-0-1*) WOW Enter.

***Riols, Noreen.** To Live Again. LC 95-7540. (House of Annanbrae Ser.: Bk. 2). 320p. (Orig.). 1995. pap. 9.99 (*0-89107-844-4*) Crossway Bks.

— Where Hope Shines Through. LC 94-4323. (House of Annanbrae Ser.). 320p. (Orig.). 1994. pap. 9.99 (*0-89107-790-1*) Crossway Bks.

Rion, Rosana, jt. auth. see Mott, Brian.

Rionero, S., ed. Waves & Stability in Continuous Media. 444p. (C). 1991. text ed. 118.00 (*981-02-0554-6*) World Scientific Pub.

***Rionero, S. & Ruggeri, T.** Waves Stability in Continuous Media: Proceedings of the 7th International Conference. 448p. 1994. text ed. 112.00 (*981-02-1878-8*) World Scientific Pub.

Rionero, S., jt. auth. see Flavin, M. N.

Rionero, S., jt. auth. see Galdi, Giovanni P.

Riopedre, Jorge A. Cubanacan (Decimas Cubanas) LC 79-90276. (Coleccion Espejo de Paciencia Ser.). (Illus.). 1979. pap. 3.50 (*0-89729-238-3*) Ediciones.

Riopel, James L. Organismal Biology: A Laboratory Introduction. 208p. (C). 1993. pap. text ed. 18.25 (*0-8403-8339-8*) Kendall-Hunt.

Riopel, Jim. Organismal Biology: A Laboratory Introduction. 208p. (C). 1994. spiral bd. 15.40 (*0-8403-9157-9*) Kendall-Hunt.

Riordan, Barbara, jt. auth. see Riordan, Lee A.

***Riordan, Colin.** Contemporary German Writers. 200p. 1995. 14.95 (*0-7083-1289-6*, Pub. by Univ Wales Pr UK) Paul & Co Pubs.

Riordan, Colin, ed. see Schneider, Peter.

Riordan, Cornelius. Girls & Boys in School: Together or Separate? 200p. (C). 1989. text ed. 35.00 (*0-8077-2993-0*) Tchrs Coll.

Riordan, Daniel, jt. auth. see Pauley, Steven E.

Riordan, Francis E. Concept of Love in the French Catholic Literary Revival. LC 76-94183. (Catholic University of America. Studies in Romance Languages & Literatures: No. 42). reprint ed. 37.50 (*0-404-50342-X*) AMS Pr.

Riordan, Hugh D. Medical Mavericks, Vol. 1. LC 88-63321. 102p. (Orig.). 1988. pap. 7.95 (*0-942333-07-1*) Bio-Comns Pr.

— Medical Mavericks, Vol. 2. LC 88-63321. 120p. (Orig.). 1989. pap. 7.95 (*0-942333-09-8*) Bio-Comns Pr.

Riordan, J. Russian Folk Tale Reader. 128p. (C). 1990. 39.00 (*0-569-09176-4*, Pub. by Collets) St Mut.

Riordan, James. Eastern Europe. (Countries Ser.). (Illus.). 48p. (J). (gr. 5 up). 1987. lib. bdg. 14.95 (*0-382-09468-9*) Silver Burdett Pr.

— Favorite Stories of the Ballet. LC 84-42778. (Illus.). 128p. (J). (gr. 4 up). 14.95 (*1-56288-252-X*) Checkerboard.

— My G-r-r-r-reat Uncle Tiger. LC 95-13109. (Illus.). (J). 1995. write for info. (*1-56145-110-X*) Peachtree Pubs.

— Russia & the Commonwealth of Independent States. (Countries Ser.). (Illus.). 48p. (J). (gr. 5 up). 1992. lib. bdg. 14.95 (*0-382-24378-1*) Silver Burdett Pr.

— Sport in Soviet Society. LC 76-9729. (Cambridge Russian, Soviet & Post-Soviet Studies: No. 22). (Illus.). 1980. pap. 24.95 (*0-521-28023-0*) Cambridge U Pr.

— Stone: The Controversies, Excesses, & Exploits of a Radical Filmmaker. (Illus.). 640p. 1995. 24.95 (*0-7868-6026-X*) Hyperion.

— The Sun Maiden & the Crescent Moon: Siberian Folk Tales. LC 90-42586. (International Folk Tale Ser.). 224p. 1991. 24.95 (*0-940793-66-0*); pap. 11.95 (*0-940793-65-2*) Interlink Pub.

— Tales from the Arabian Nights. LC 84-62456. (Illus.). 128p. (J). (gr. 4 up). 1985. 14.95 (*1-56288-258-9*) Checkerboard.

— Tales of King Arthur. LC 81-86152. (Illus.). 128p. (J). (gr. 4-7). 1982. 14.95 (*1-56288-251-1*) Checkerboard.

Riordan, James, ed. Soviet Education: The Gifted & the Handicapped. 240p. (C). 1988. lib. bdg. 55.00 (*0-415-00574-4*) Routledge.

— Soviet Social Reality in the Mirror of Glasnost. LC 91-44871. 188p. 1992. text ed. 65.00 (*0-312-07901-X*) St Martin.

— Soviet Youth Culture. LC 88-13487. (Illus.). 158p. 1989. 29.95 (*0-253-35423-4*) Ind U Pr.

— Sport Under Communism: A Comparative Study. 1978. 24.95 (*0-7735-0505-9*, Pub. by McGill CN) U of Toronto Pr.

— Sport under Communism: A Comparative Study. 1982. pap. 19.95 (*0-7735-0533-4*, Pub. by McGill CN) U of Toronto Pr.

Riordan, James, teller. Korean Folk Tales. (Myths & Legends Ser.). (Illus.). 128p. 1994. pap. 10.95 (*0-19-274160-8*) OUP.

Riordan, James, tr. Russian Gypsy Tales. LC 92-7316. (International Folk Tale Ser.). (Illus.). 160p. 1992. 24.95 (*1-56656-100-0*); pap. 11.95 (*0-940793-97-0*) Interlink Pub.

Riordan, James & Bridger, Sue, eds. Dear Comrade Editor: Readers' Letters to the Soviet Press under Perestroika. Bridger, Sue & Riordan, Jim, trs. LC 91-20441. (Illus.). 256p. (Orig.). 1992. text ed. 35.00 (*0-253-34990-7*); pap. text ed. 12.95 (*0-253-20696-0*, MB-696) Ind U Pr.

Riordan, James & Lewis, Brenda R. An Illustrated Treasury of Myths & Legends. (Illus.). 152p. (J). (gr. 7 up). 1991. 12.95 (*0-87226-349-5*) P Bedrick Bks.

Riordan, James & Prochnicky, Jerry. Break on Through: The Life & Death of Jim Morrison. (Illus.). 400p. 1991. 20.00 (*0-688-08829-5*) Morrow.

— Break on Through: The Life & Death of Jim Morrison. (Illus.). 544p. 1992. pap. 10.00 (*0-688-11915-8*, Quill) Morrow.

Riordan, James, jt. ed. see Kon, Igor.

Riordan, James F., et al, eds. Methods in Enzymology, Vol. 158: Metallobiochemistry, Pt. A. 464p. 1988. text ed. 99.00 (*0-12-182059-9*) Acad Pr.

Riordan, Jan. Breastfeeding & Human Lactation Student Study Guide. 168p. (C). 1993. pap. text ed. 14.95 (*0-86720-632-2*) Jones & Bartlett.

Riordan, Jan & Auerbach, Kathleen G. Breastfeeding & Human Lactation. (Nursing-Health Science Ser.). 600p. (C). 1993. boxed 82.50 (*0-86720-343-9*) Jones & Bartlett.

***Riordan, Jan, et al.** Amamantamiento y Lactacion. (Nursing Ser.). 300p. Date not set. pap. 29.95 (*0-86720-721-3*) Jones & Bartlett.

Riordan, Janice. A Practical Guide to Breastfeeding. 400p. 1991. pap. 19.95 (*0-86720-448-6*) Jones & Bartlett.

Riordan, Jim, tr. see Mikulsky, K.

Riordan, Jim, tr. see Riordan, James & Bridger, Sue, eds.

Riordan, John. An Introduction to Combinatorial Analysis. LC 80-337. 260p. (C). 1980. reprint ed. 39.50 (*0-691-08262-6*); reprint ed. pap. 19.95 (*0-691-02365-4*) Princeton U Pr.

Riordan, John, ed. Proceedings of the Art Symposium, October 30-November 1, 1980. 106p. (Orig.). 1982. spiral bd. 5.00 (*0-942746-01-5*) SUNYP R Gibson.

Riordan, John & Cotliar, William. Complying with FDA Good Manufacturing Requirements: How to Develop Your GMP - QA Manual. 252p. 1991. 175.00 (*0-910275-53-X*, GMP1-113); student ed, disk 275.00 (*0-685-59181-6*, GMP3-113); disk 175.00 (*0-685-59180-8*, GMP2-113) Assn Adv Med Instrn.

Riordan, John & Whitmore, Bob. Living with Dementia. LC 88-27359. (Living with Ser.). 128p. 1991. text ed. 24.95 (*0-7190-2515-X*, Pub. by Manchester Univ Pr UK) St Martin.

— Living with Dementia. (Living with Ser.). (Illus.). 144p. (C). 1992. text ed. 14.95 (*0-7190-2516-8*, Pub. by Manchester Univ Pr UK) St Martin.

Riordan, John C. The Art Collection at Potsdam. (Illus.). 118p. (Orig.). 1982. pap. 10.00 (*0-942746-04-X*) SUNYP R Gibson.

Riordan, John J. AIDS - STD Barriers: Benefits & Risks. 112p. 1993. 39.95 (*1-56167-110-X*) Noble Hse MD.

Riordan, John J. & Cotliar, William. How to Develop Your GMP QC Manual. 253p. pap. write for info. (*0-914176-20-X*) Wash Busn Info.

Riordan, Lee A. & Riordan, Barbara. College Bred or a Four Year Loaf. LC 87-60675. 264p. (Orig.). 1987. lib. bdg. 9.95 (*0-9618266-1-4*); pap. 6.95 (*0-9618266-0-6*) L Riordan.

Riordan, M. Lepton & Photon Interaction at High Energies. 556p. (C). 1990. pap. 48.00 (*981-02-0216-4*) World Scientific Pub.

Riordan, Mary, et al, eds. Michigan's Masterpieces: Art from Public Collections. (Illus.). 96p. 1987. pap. 11.95 (*0-8143-1973-4*) Wayne St U Pr.

Riordan, Mary M. Lillian Hellman: A Bibliography, 1926-1978. LC 80-16147. (Author Bibliographies Ser.: No. 50). 244p. 1980. 25.00 (*0-8108-1320-3*) Scarecrow.

***Riordan, Maurice.** A Word from the Loki. 64p. (Orig.). 1995. pap. 9.95 (*0-571-17364-0*) Faber & Faber.

Riordan, Michael. The Hunting of the Quark: A True Story of Modern Physics. LC 87-16530. (Touchstone Book Ser.). (Illus.). 400p. reprint ed. pap. 114.00 (*0-7837-3745-9*, AU00433) Bks Demand.

Riordan, Michael & Schramm, David. The Shadows of Creation: Dark Matter & the Structure of the Universe. (Illus.). 224p. 1995. text ed. write for info. (*0-7167-2157-0*) W H Freeman.

Riordan, Michael & Schramm, David N. Shadow of Creation: Dark Matters & the Structure of the Universe. LC 90-241997. 1995. pap. text ed. write for info. (*0-7167-2366-2*) W H Freeman.

Riordan, Michael, jt. auth. see Anderson, Bruce.

***Riordan, Mihcael.** The Day after Midnight: The Effects of Nuclear War. LC 82-9538. (Illus.). reprint ed. pap. 40.80 (*0-7837-9010-4*, AU00462) Bks Demand.

***Riordan, P. H., ed.** Geology of Asbestos Deposits: Sponsored by Industrial Minerals Division of SME-AIME, Society of Economic Geologists. fac. ed. LC 80-52898. (Illus.). 126p. 1981. reprint ed. pap. 36.00 (*0-7837-7858-9*, 2047617) Bks Demand.

Riordan, Patrick. The Practical Philosophy of Oswald Schwemmer. 128p. (Orig.). (C). 1991. lib. bdg. 40.00 (*0-8191-8180-3*); pap. text ed. 18.50 (*0-8191-8181-1*) U Pr of Amer.

***Riordan, Pauline & Bourget, Paul G.** World Weather Extremes. (Illus.). 77p. (Orig.). (C). 1994. pap. text ed. 45.00x (*0-7881-1537-5*) Diane Pub.

Riordan, Richard J., jt. auth. see Matheny, Kenneth B.

Riordan, Stephen J., IV. Government Advanced Open Water Diver Instructor Manual. 16p. 1994. pap. text ed. write for info. (*1-880229-18-8*) Concept Sys.

Riordan, Timothy M. Lesser Bird of Paradise: Selected Poems: 1979-1989. 115p. (Orig.). 1990. pap. 19.95 (*0-9625817-0-4*) In Hse Bks.

— Portfolio Breeches: A Poem. 21p. (Orig.). 1988. pap. 10.00 (*0-9625817-1-2*) In Hse Bks.

Riordan, William. Plunkitt of Tammany Hall. 1993. reprint ed. lib. bdg. 14.95 (*1-56849-215-4*) Buccaneer Bks.

Riordan, William I. Plunkitt of Tammany Hall. 101p. reprint ed. lib. bdg. 15.95 (*0-88411-977-7*, Aeonian Pr) Amereon Ltd.

Riordan, William L. Plunkitt of Tammany Hall. (C). 1963. pap. 3.50 (*0-525-48228-8*, Dutton) NAL-Dutton.

— Plunkitt of Tammany Hall: A Series of Very Plain Talks On Very Practical Politics. McDonald, Terrence J., ed. LC 92-72221. (Books in American History). 160p. (C). 1993. text ed. 35.00 (*0-312-09666-6*, Bedford Bks) St Martin.

— Plunkitt of Tammany Hall: A Series of Very Plain Talks On Very Practical Politics. McDonald, Terrence J., ed. LC 92-72221. (Books in American History). 160p. (C). 1993. pap. text ed. 6.00 (*0-312-08444-7*, Bedford Bks) St Martin.

— Plunkitt Tammy. 1991. pap. 7.00 (*0-452-01094-2*, Mer) NAL-Dutton.

Riordon, P. H. & Hollister, V. F., intros. Geology of Asbestos Deposits. LC 80-52898. (Illus.). 118p. (Orig.). 1981. pap. 5.00 (*0-89520-277-8*) SMM&E Inc.

Riordon, William L. Honest Graft: The World of George Washington Plunkitt. Bd. with Aka Plunkitt of Tammany Hall. (Illus.). 183p. (Orig.). (C). 1993. Net. Set pap. text ed. 7.96 (*1-881089-06-1*) Brandywine Press.

Rios, Alberto. Five Indiscretions. LC 84-52616. 98p. (Orig.). 1985. 14.95 (*0-935296-57-3*) Sheep Meadow.

— The Lime Orchard Woman. LC 88-18534. 94p. (Orig.). 1988. pap. 10.95 (*0-935296-77-8*) Sheep Meadow.

— Teodoro Luna's Two Kisses. 96p. 1992. pap. 9.95 (*0-393-30809-X*) Norton.

— Whispering to Fool the Wind. LC 82-3269. 72p. (C). 1982. pap. 10.95 (*0-935296-31-X*) Sheep Meadow.

Rios, Alberto A. The Iguana Killer: Twelve Stories of the Heart. (Illus.). 144p. 1984. 14.95 (*0-933188-28-5*); pap. 7.95 (*0-933188-29-3*) Blue Moon Pr.

— Pig Cookies & Other Stories. LC 94-22103. 1995. pap. text ed. 10.95 (*0-8118-0745-2*) Chronicle Bks.

Rios, Alicia & March, Lourdes. The Heritage of Spanish Cooking. LC 92-53633. 1992. 45.00 (*0-679-41628-5*) Random.

Rios, Antonio, jt. auth. see Castillo, Pedro.

Rios, Beatriz G., tr. see Fulbrook, Mary.

Rios-Bustamante, Antonio. Latinos in Hollywood. (Illus.). 120p. 1990. 35.00 (*0-685-47547-6*) Floricanto Pr.

— Mexican Los Angeles: A Narrative & Pictorial History. (Illus.). 250p. 1990. 35.00 (*0-915745-19-4*) Floricanto Pr.

Rios-Bustamante, Antonio, jt. auth. see Arroyo, Luis L.

Rios-Bustamante, Antonio, ed. see Harris, Robert L., Jr.

Rios-Bustamanter, Antonio, ed. see Wilson, Terry P.

***Rios, Eduardo E.** Life of Fray Antonio Margil: O. F. M. Lutenegger, Benedict, tr. 1959. 25.00 (*0-614-05573-3*) AAFH.

***Rios, Francisco A., ed.** Teacher Thinking in Multicultural Contexts. (Social Context of Education Ser.). 320p. 1996. text ed. 59.50x (*0-7914-2881-8*); pap. 19.95x (*0-7914-2882-6*) State U NY Pr.

***Rios, Guillermo.** Murphy Came to Stay. 1995. 14.95 (*0-8062-5213-8*) Carlton.

Rios, Juan G., I. Change: The Overhauling of the United States, As Seen by a Taxpayer. 1994. 15.95 (*0-533-10755-5*) Vantage.

Rios, Julian. Larva: Midsummer Night's Babel. Francis, Richard A. & Levine, Suzanne J., trs. LC 90-3773. (Illus.). 600p. 1990. 27.50 (*0-916583-66-X*) Dalkey Arch.

***Rios, Julian & Kitaj.** Kitaj: Pictures & Conversations. (Illus.). 288p. 1995. pap. 29.95 (*1-55921-148-2*) Moyer Bell.

Rios, M. S. & Sastre, A., eds. Dairy Products in Human Health & Nutrition: Proceedings of the First World Congress, Madrid, Spain, June 1993. (Illus.). 700p. (C). 1993. text ed. 99.00 (*90-5410-359-0*, Pub. by A A Balkema NE) Ashgate Pub Co.

Rios, Manual C., jt. auth. see Lamb, F. Bruce.

Rios, Manuel. Economics I. 5th ed. 1992. 16.00 (*0-536-58270-X*) Ginn Pr.

— Economics II. 4th ed. 1992. 15.00 (*0-536-58266-1*) Ginn Pr.

Rios, Sixto, et al, eds. Decision Theory & Decision Analysis: Trends & Challenges. LC 94-15768. 312p. (C). 1994. lib. bdg. 89.95 (*0-7923-9466-6*) Kluwer Ac.

***Rios, Stevie.** Playing for Keeps. 256p. 1995. pap. 10.99 (*1-883061-07-5*) Rising NY.

Rios, Victor, Jr. The Best Football in Texas! 1994. pap. 12.95 (*0-533-10851-9*) Vantage.

***Riosley, Lane.** A Night at the Hotel Pyramid. 57p. (Orig.). 1993. pap. 4.00 (*1-57514-115-9*, 1151) Encore Perform Pub.

***Riosley, Lane & Byars, Rebecca L.** Shakespeare's Clowns. 28p. (Orig.). 1994. pap. 3.00 (*1-57514-122-1*, 1078) Encore Perform Pub.

Riotte, J. C. Annotated List of Ontario Lepidoptera. 1994. pap. 19.95 (*0-88854-397-2*, Pub. by Royal Ont Mus CN) U of Toronto Pr.

Riotte, Louise. Astrological Gardening: The Ancient Wisdom of Successful Planting & Harvesting by the Stars. LC 89-11987. (Illus.). 224p. 1989. pap. 11.95 (*0-88266-561-8*, Garden Way Pub) Storey Comm Inc.

— Astrological Gardening: The Ancient Wisdom of Successful Planting & Harvesting by the Stars. LC 94-24541. (Illus.). 1994. 6.99 (*0-517-12272-3*) Random Hse Value.

— Carrots Love Tomatoes: Secrets of Companion Planting for Successful Gardening. LC 81-2379. (Illus.). 224p. 1975. pap. 9.95 (*0-88266-064-0*) Storey Comm Inc.

— The Complete Guide to Growing Berries & Grapes. LC 92-34629. (Illus.). 160p. 1993. reprint ed. pap. 9.95 (*0-87833-825-X*) Taylor Pub.

— The Complete Guide to Growing Nuts. LC 93-3709. (Illus.). 168p. 1993. reprint ed. pap. 9.95 (*0-87833-836-5*) Taylor Pub.

— In Nature's Hands: An Organic Gardening Potpourri, from Armadillos to Zucchini. LC 91-46772. (Illus.). 232p. 1992. pap. 13.95 (*0-87833-787-3*) Taylor Pub.

— Planetary Planting. (American Gardening Ser.: No. 13). 352p. 1982. pap. 9.95 (*0-917086-38-4*) ACS Pubns.

— Roses Love Garlic: Secrets of Companion Planting with Flowers. LC 83-1464. (Illus.). 240p. (Orig.). 1983. pap. 9.95 (*0-88266-331-3*, Garden Way Pub) Storey Comm Inc.

— Sleeping with a Sunflower: A Treasury of Old-Time Gardening Lore. LC 94-13129. (Illus.). (Orig.). 1994. pap. 6.99 (*0-517-11847-5*, Pub. by Wings Bks) Random.

— Sleeping with a Sunflower: A Treasury of Old-Time Gardening Lore. Burns, Deborah, ed. LC 87-45008. (Illus.). 224p. (Orig.). 1987. pap. 9.95 (*0-88266-502-2*, Garden Way Pub) Storey Comm Inc.

— Successful Small Food Gardens. (Illus.). 200p. 1993. 21.95 (*0-88266-816-1*, Garden Way Pub); pap. 11.95 (*0-88266-815-3*, Garden Way Pub) Storey Comm Inc.

***Rioux, Frank & Foster, Judith C.** Paper Chromatography of Selected Transition - Metal Cations. Neidig, H. A., ed. (Modular Laboratory Program in Chemistry Ser.). 12p. (C). 1989. pap. text ed. 1.25x (*0-87540-373-5*) Chem Educ Res.

Rioux, J. William & Berla, Nancy. Innovations in Parent & Family Involvement. 400p. 1993. 39.95 (*1-883001-03-X*) Eye On Educ.

Rioux, Jean-Pierre. The Fourth Republic, 1944-1958. Rogers, Godfrey, tr. (History of Modern France Ser.: No. 7). (Illus.). 548p. (C). 1989. pap. 19.95 (*0-521-38916-X*) Cambridge U Pr.

Rip, A., ed. see Bottcher, C. J., et al.

***Rip, Arie, et al.** Managing Technology in Society: The Approach of the CTA. 300p. 1995. 64.95 (*1-85567-307-X*); pap. 29.95 (*1-85567-318-5*) St Martin.

***Rip, Arie, et al, eds.** Managing Technology in Society. LC 95-3879. 1995. write for info. (*1-85567-339-8*, Pub. by Pinter Pubs UK); pap. write for info. (*1-85567-340-1*, Pub. by Pinter Pubs UK) St Martin.

Ripa, Cesare. Baroque & Rococo Pictorial Imagery: The 1758-60 Hertel Edition of Ripa's Iconologia. 1991. pap. 13.95 (*0-486-26595-1*) Dover.

Ripa, Cesare, pseud. Iconologia. Mandowsky, E., ed. (Illus.). vii, 528p. 1970. reprint ed. write for info. (*3-487-02342-3*, Pub. by Georg Olms GW) Lubrecht & Cramer.

Ripa, Louis W., jt. auth. see Mellberg, James R.

Ripa, Matteo. Memoirs of Father Ripa. LC 75-36239. reprint ed. 32.50 (*0-404-14487-X*) AMS Pr.

Ripamonti, Aldo, jt. auth. see Marshall, Norman F.

Ripellino, Angelo M. Magic Prague. Marinelli, David N., tr. 1993. 35.00 (*0-520-07352-5*) U CA Pr.

Riper, Guernsey V., Jr. Knute Rockne: Young Athlete. LC 86-10791. (Childhood of Famous Americans Ser.). (Illus.). 192p. (J). (gr. 2-6). 1986. reprint ed. pap. 3.95 (*0-02-042110-9*, Mac Bks Young Read) S&S Childrens.

***Riper, Jack Van.** Off the Wall: A Graduate Course in Deer Hunting. LC 94-72441. (Illus.). 128p. 1994. pap. 12.95 (*0-9643001-0-9*) Chippewa Advent.

Ripich, Danielle, ed. Handbook of Geriatric Communication Disorders. LC 90-74311. 494p. 1991. text ed. 39.00 (*0-89079-423-5*, 1944) PRO-ED.

Ripich, Danielle N. & Craighead, Nancy A., eds. School Discourse Problems. 2nd ed. LC 93-36789. (School-Age Children Ser.). 352p. (Orig.). 1994. 47.50 (*1-56593-096-7*, 0400) Singular Publishing.

Ripich, Danielle N. & Spinelli, Francesca M., eds. School Discourse Problems. (Illus.). 292p. (Orig.). (C). 1991. reprint ed. pap. text ed. 29.50 (*1-879105-20-9*, A060) Singular Publishing.

Ripin, Edwin M. Early Keyboard Instruments. (New Grove Musical Instrument Ser.). 1989. 25.00 (*0-393-02554-3*) Norton.

— Early Keyboard Instruments. (New Grove Musical Instrument Ser.). 1989. pap. 14.95 (*0-393-30515-5*) Norton.

Ripin, Kevin, ed. see Carey, Diane.

Ripin, Rowena, tr. see Buhler, Charlotte M.

Ripinsky-Naxon, Michael. The Nature of Shamanism: Substance & Function of a Religious Metaphor. LC 92-5415. 289p. 1993. 59.50 (*0-7914-1385-3*); pap. 19.95 (*0-7914-1386-1*) State U NY Pr.

Ripka, Georges, jt. auth. see Blaizot, Jean-Paul.

Ripka, L. V. Plumbing Installation & Design. 2nd ed. (Illus.). 375p. 1987. 27.96 (*0-8269-0606-0*) Am Technical.

***Ripka, L.V.** Plumbing. LC 94-23444. 1994. 31.95 (*0-8269-0612-5*) Am Technical.

***Ripken, Cal, Jr.** Count Me In. (Illus.). 40p. (J). (gr. 3-7). 1995. 14.95 (*0-87833-915-9*) Taylor Pub.

Ripko, Olena & Ovsychuk, Volodimir. The Lvov Picture Gallery. 1982. 40.00 (*0-317-14253-4*, Pub. by Collets UK) Pro-Am Music.

Ripley, Alexandra. Charleston. 560p. 1982. mass mkt. 4.95 (*0-380-57729-1*) Avon.

— Charleston. 560p. 1991. mass mkt. 6.50 (*0-446-36000-7*) Warner Bks.

— From Field of Gold. large type ed. LC 94-47560. 1995. 23.95 (*0-7838-1237-X*) Hall.

— From Fields of Gold. 480p. 1994. 24.95 (*0-446-51406-3*) Warner Bks.

— From Fields of Gold. 480p. 1996. mass mkt. 6.50 (*0-446-60249-3*, Warner Vision) Warner Bks.

R

An Asterisk (*) at the beginning of an entry indicates that the title is appearing in BIP for the first time.

— New Orleans Legacy. 496p. 1988. mass mkt. 5.99 (*0-446-34210-6*) Warner Bks.
— On Leaving Charleston. 576p. 1991. mass mkt. 6.50 (*0-446-36001-5*) Warner Bks.
— Scarlett: The Sequel to Margaret Mitchell's Gone with the Wind. 896p. 1992. mass mkt. 6.99 (*0-446-36325-1*) Warner Bks.
— Scarlett: The Sequel to Margaret Mitchell's Gone with the Wind. 1992. pap. 6.99 (*0-446-78168-1*) Warner Bks.
— Scarlett: The Sequel to Margaret Mitchell's Gone with the Wind. deluxe limited ed. 1992. 100.00 (*0-446-51718-6*) Warner Bks.
— Scarlett: The Sequel to Margaret Mitchell's Gone with the Wind. large type ed. (General Ser.). 1184p. 1992. 27.95 (*0-8161-5527-5*, Large Print Bks); pap. 21.95 (*0-8161-5528-3*, Large Print Bks) Hall.
— The Time Returns. 400p. 1996. mass mkt. 6.50 (*0-446-60258-2*) Warner Bks.
Ripley, Ann. Mulch. 224p. 1994. 19.95 (*0-312-11029-4*, Pub. by Thomas Dunne Bks) St Martin.
***Ripley, B. D. & Hjort, N. L.** Pattern Recognition & Neural Networks. (Illus.). 500p. (C). 1994. write for info. (*0-521-46086-7*) Cambridge U Pr.
Ripley, B. D., jt. auth. see Venables, W. N.
Ripley, Brian D. Spatial Statistics. LC 80-26104. (Probability & Mathematical Statistics Ser.). 252p. 1981. text ed. 99.95 (*0-471-08367-4*) Wiley.
— Statistical Inference for Spatial Processes. 1991. pap. 22.95 (*0-521-42420-8*) Cambridge U Pr.
— Stochastic Simulation. LC 86-15728. (Probabilbity & Mathematical Statistics Ser.). 237p. 1987. text ed. 74.95 (*0-471-81884-4*) Wiley.
Ripley, Brian J. & McHugh, John. John Maclean. Howell, David, ed. (Lives of the Left Ser.). 148p. 1989. text ed. 39.95 (*0-7190-2180-4*, Pub. by Manchester Univ Pr UK); text ed. 19.95 (*0-7190-2181-2*, Pub. by Manchester Univ Pr UK) St Martin.
Ripley, C. Peter. Richard Nixon. (World Leaders - Past & Present Ser.). (Illus.). 112p. (YA). (gr. 5 up). 1988. lib. bdg. 17.95 (*0-87754-585-5*) Chelsea Hse.
— Slaves & Freedmen in Civil War Louisiana. fac. ed. LC 75-18043. 253p. 1976. reprint ed. pap. 72.20 (*0-7837-7819-8*, 2047575) Bks Demand.
Ripley, C. Peter, ed. The Black Abolitionist Papers, Vol. IV: The United States, 1847-1858. LC 84-13131. (Illus.). xxxvi, 444p. (C). 1991. 50.00 (*0-8078-1974-3*) U of NC Pr.
— Black Abolitionist Papers, Vol. V: The United States, 1859-1865. LC 84-13131. (Illus.). xxviii, 436p. (C). 1992. 50.00 (*0-8078-2007-5*) U of NC Pr.
Ripley, C. Peter, et al, eds. The Black Abolitionist Papers, Vol. I: The British Isles, 1830-1865. LC 84-13131. (Illus.). xxx, 609p. 1985. 50.00 (*0-8078-1625-6*) U of NC Pr.
— The Black Abolitionist Papers, Vol. II: Canada, 1830-1865. LC 84-13131. (Illus.). xviii, 560p. 1987. 50.00 (*0-8078-1698-1*) U of NC Pr.
— The Black Abolitionist Papers, Vol. III: The United States, 1830-1846. LC 84-13131. (Illus.). xxx, 522p. (C). 1991. 50.00 (*0-8078-1926-3*) U of NC Pr.
— Witness for Freedom: African-American Voices on Race, Slavery, & Emancipation. LC 92-21591. (Illus.). xxvi, 306p. (C). 1993. 29.95 (*0-8078-2072-5*); pap. 10.95 (*0-8078-4404-7*) U of NC Pr.
***Ripley, Casey, Jr., ed.** The Media & the Public. LC 94-19621. 1994. 15.00 (*0-8242-0856-0*) Wilson.
Ripley, Catherine. Two Dozen Dinosaurs: A First Book of Dinosaur Facts & Mysteries, Games & Fun. (Illus.). 32p. (J). (gr. k up). 1992. pap. 7.95 (*0-920775-55-1*, Pub. by Greey dePencier CN) Firefly Bks Ltd.
Ripley, Clements & Ripley, Katharine B. Cities of Fear: And Other Adventure Stories. (Illus.). 380p. (Orig.). 1990. pap. 13.95 (*0-9626696-0-1*) W Ripley.
Ripley, Dillon S. A Naturalist's Adventure in Nepal: Search for the Spiny Babbler. 317p. (C). 1978. 90.00 (*0-89771-109-2*, Pub. by Ratna Pustak Bhandar) St Mut.
Ripley, Dorothy. Winter Barn. LC 93-32420. (Pictureback Ser.). (Illus.). 32p. (Orig.). (J). (ps-1). 1994. pap. 2.50 (*0-679-84472-4*) Random Bks Yng Read.
Ripley-Duggan, Edward, ed. Book Arts Collections: A Representative Selection. LC 88-15286. (Special Collections Ser.: Vol. 4, No. 1). 123p. 1989. text ed. 29.95 (*0-86656-594-9*) Haworth Pr.
Ripley, E., jt. auth. see Barrots, W.
Ripley, E. A. & Redmann, R. E. Energy Exchange in Ecosystems. write for info. (*0-318-56694-X*) Elsevier.
***Ripley, Earle A. & Redman, Robert E.** Environmental Effects of Mining. 300p. 1995. 59.95 (*1-884015-76-X*) St Lucie Pr.
Ripley, Edward H. Vermont General. Eisenschiml, Otto, ed. (Illus.). 1959. 12.50 (*0-8159-7101-X*) Devin.
Ripley, Eliza. Social Life in Old New Orleans: Being Recollections of My Girlhood. LC 75-1867. (Leisure Class in America Ser.). (Illus.). 1975. reprint ed. 26.95 (*0-405-06933-2*) Ayer.
Ripley Entertainment Inc. Ripley's Believe It Or Not: Wild Animals. 1992. pap. 3.50 (*0-8125-1289-8*) Tor Bks.
Ripley, Francis J. Mary, Mother of the Church: What Recent Popes Have Said about the Blessed Mother's Role in the Church. 1973. reprint ed. pap. 3.00 (*0-89555-094-6*) TAN Bks Pubs.
Ripley, George. The Compound of Alchemy. 87p. 1992. reprint ed. pap. 9.95 (*1-56459-077-1*) Kessinger Pub.
— The Compound of Alchymy. LC 77-7423. (English Experience Ser.: No. 887). 1977. reprint ed. lib. bdg. 35.00 (*90-221-0887-2*) Walter J Johnson.
— Five Preparations of the Philosopher's Mercury. reprint ed. pap. 2.95 (*1-55818-158-X*) Holmes Pub.
— The Marrow of Alchemy. Holmes, Jefferson D., ed. 1994. reprint ed. pap. 6.95 (*1-55818-281-0*) Holmes Pub.
— Sixty Aphorisms of Alchemy. 1994. pap. text ed. 4.95 (*1-55818-286-1*, Pub. by Alchemical Pr) Holmes Pub.
Ripley, Jill, ed. see Hunger, Bill.
Ripley, John W., comp. The Prairie Star: Journal of Kansas First Literary Society (1857) 140p. pap. 5.95 (*0-916934-02-0*) Shawnee County Hist.
Ripley, John W. & Richmond, Robert W., eds. The Santa Fe in Topeka. (Illus.). 1979. pap. 6.95 (*0-685-96284-9*) Shawnee County Hist.
Ripley, Jonathan G., jt. auth. see Greene, Michael.
Ripley, Joseph M., Jr. The Practices & Policies Regarding Broadcasting of Opinions About Controversial Issues by Radio & Television Stations in the United States. Sterling, Christopher H., ed. LC 78-21734. (Dissertations in Broadcasting Ser.). 1980. lib. bdg. 20.95 (*0-405-11771-X*) Ayer.
***Ripley, Karen.** Alchemist of Time, Bk. 3. (Orig.). 1994. pap. 4.99 (*0-345-38118-1*, Del Rey Discovery) Ballantine.
— The Persistence of Memory: Book One of the Slow World. 1993. mass mkt. 4.99 (*0-345-38120-3*, Del Rey) Ballantine.
— Warden of Horses, Bk. 2: The Slow World. 1994. mass mkt. 5.99 (*0-345-38119-X*, Del Rey) Ballantine.
***Ripley, Katharine B.** Sand in My Shoes. rev. ed. 332p. 1995. pap. 13.95 (*1-878086-40-5*) Down Home NC.
Ripley, Katharine B., jt. auth. see Ripley, Clements.
Ripley, M. M., tr. see Gautier, Theophile.
Ripley, Marie, jt. auth. see Ripley, Robert.
Ripley, Marie J., jt. auth. see Ripley, Robert E.
Ripley, Marie J., jt. auth. see Ripley, Robert.
***Ripley, Mike.** Angel City. 1995. 18.95 (*0-312-11742-6*) St Martin.
Ripley, R. Study Guide For Real Estate License Examinations. (Orig.). pap. 3.95 (*0-13-858753-1*, Reward) P-H.
Ripley, Randall B. American National Government & Public Policy. LC 73-10574. (Illus.). (Orig.). (C). 1974. pap. text ed. 9.95 (*0-02-926540-1*) Free Pr.
— Congress: Process & Policy. 4th ed. (Illus.). (C). 1988. text ed. 26.95 (*0-393-95617-2*) Norton.
— Policy Analysis in Political Science. LC 84-22607. (Illus.). 245p. 1984. 20.95 (*0-8304-1058-9*) Nelson-Hall.
— The Politics of Economic & Human Resource Development. LC 79-173977. (Policy Analysis Ser.). (C). 1972. write for info. (*0-672-51479-6*, Bobbs) Macmillan.
Ripley, Randall B. & Franklin, Grace A. Congress, the Bureaucracy, & Public Policy. 5th ed. LC 90-2022. 264p. (C). 1991. pap. 23.95 (*0-534-14454-3*) Intl Thomson.
Ripley, Randall B. & Franklin, Grace A., eds. Policy-Making in the Federal Executive Branch. LC 74-33093. (Illus.). 1975. 27.95 (*0-02-926490-1*) Free Pr.
Ripley, Randall B. & Lindsay, James M., eds. Congress Resurgent: Foreign & Domestic Policy on Capitol Hill. LC 93-16033. (Mershon Center Series on International Security & Foreign Policy). 350p. (C). 1993. text ed. 54.50 (*0-472-09533-1*); pap. text ed. 18.95 (*0-472-06533-5*) U of Mich Pr.
Ripley, Randall B. & Slotnick, Elliot E. Readings in American Government & Politics. 2nd ed. 592p. (C). 1993. pap. 26.95 (*0-534-16170-7*) Intl Thomson.
Ripley, Randall B., jt. auth. see Franklin, Grace A.
Ripley, Richard. The Ridgerunner. (Orig.). 1987. pap. 10.95 (*0-9603566-4-9*) Backeddy Bks.
***Ripley, Robert & Ripley, Marie.** Your Child's Ages & Stages. 290p. 1994. pap. 8.95 (*1-56901-647-X*) NW Pub.
***Ripley, Robert & Ripley, Marie J.** Guiding the Child. 330p. 1995. pap. 10.95 (*0-7610-0146-8*) NW Pub.
Ripley, Robert E. & Ripley, Marie J. How to Manage It All--Yourself, Your Company, Others. LC 88-71797. (Illus.). 290p. (C). 1988. 19.95 (*0-9621133-0-1*); lib. bdg. 19.95 (*0-685-22207-1*); pap. 10.95 (*0-9621133-1-X*); pap. text ed. 10.95 (*0-685-22208-X*) Carefree Pr.
— Managing Yourself, Your Company & Others. (Illus.). 250p. (Orig.). (C). 1988. 19.95 (*0-317-91381-6*); lib. bdg. 19.95 (*0-317-91382-4*); pap. 12.95 (*0-317-91383-2*) Carefree Pr.
— Organizational Empowerment: The Balancing Act: Fourteen Wonders of the World of Empowerment. LC 93-70692. (Illus.). 186p. 1993. pap. 21.95 (*0-9621133-6-0*, B001) Carefree Pr.
— Personal Empowerment - Taking Control of Your Life: Side-Roads & Main-Roads: A Trip for Discovering Your Personal Empowerment. LC 93-70693. (Illus.). 129p. 1993. pap. 19.95 (*0-9621133-2-8*, B006) Carefree Pr.
— Self-Managing Teams: Understanding Your Role As a Member Or a Leader. LC 93-70695. (Illus.). 100p. 1993. pap. 12.95 (*0-9621133-5-2*, WB011) Carefree Pr.
— Taking Control of Your Career & Quality Lifestyle: Taking Control of Your Ship on the Career Sea of Life. LC 93-70694. (Illus.). 191p. 1993. pap. 19.95 (*0-9621133-3-6*, B009) Carefree Pr.
— Training Adults: Life Long Learning. (Illus.). 180p. 1993. pap. 19.95 (*0-9621133-7-9*, WB011) Carefree Pr.
— What Next? Understanding Your Child at Each Age & Stage. LC 93-70691. (Illus.). 186p. 1993. pap. 19.95 (*0-9621133-4-4*, B010) Carefree Pr.
Ripley, Robert L. Amazing Records. (Ripley's Believe It Or Not! Ser.). (Illus.). 48p. (J). (gr. 3-6). 1992. lib. bdg. 12.95 (*1-56065-124-5*) Capstone Pr.
— Clothing. (Ripley's Believe It Or Not! Ser.). (Illus.). 48p. (J). (gr. 3-6). Date not set. lib. bdg. 12.95 (*1-56065-131-8*) Capstone Pr.
— Incredible Journeys. (Ripley's Believe It Or Not! Ser.). (Illus.). 48p. (J). (gr. 3-6). Date not set. lib. bdg. 12.95 (*1-56065-129-6*) Capstone Pr.
— Inventions. (Ripley's Believe It Or Not! Ser.). (Illus.). 48p. (J). (gr. 3-6). Date not set. lib. bdg. 12.95 (*1-56065-125-3*) Capstone Pr.
— Literature. (Ripley's Believe It Or Not! Ser.). (Illus.). 48p. (J). (gr. 3-6). 1992. lib. bdg. 12.95 (*1-56065-130-X*) Capstone Pr.
— Math & Science Facts. (Ripley's Believe It Or Not! Ser.). (Illus.). 48p. (J). (gr. 3-6). 1992. lib. bdg. 12.95 (*1-56065-128-8*) Capstone Pr.
— The Psychic & Supernatural. (Ripley's Believe It Or Not! Ser.). (Illus.). 48p. (J). (gr. 3-6). 1992. lib. bdg. 12.95 (*1-56065-127-X*) Capstone Pr.
— Puzzles. (Ripley's Believe It Or Not! Ser.). (Illus.). 48p. (J). (gr. 3-6). Date not set. lib. bdg. 12.95 (*1-56065-126-1*) Capstone Pr.
Ripley, S. Dillon. Cabinets, Lost & Found. (Connecticut Academy of Arts & Sciences Ser., Trans.: Vol. 46). 1975. pap. 29.50 (*0-685-22883-5*) Elliots Bks.
— Rails of the World: A Monograph of the Family Rallidae. LC 83-81671. (Illus.). 32p. 1984. 39.95 (*0-87474-804-6*, RIRW) Smithsonian.
— A Synopsis of the Birds of India & Pakistan: Together with Those of Nepal, Bhutan, Bangladesh, & Sri Lanka. 2nd ed. (Illus.). 680p. 1988. 35.00 (*0-19-562164-6*) OUP.
Ripley, S. Dillon, intro. Fire of Life: The Smithsonian Book of the Sun. (Illus.). 264p. 1981. 24.95 (*0-393-80006-7*) Norton.
Ripley, S. Dillon, jt. auth. see Ali, Salim.
Ripley, Sidney & Beenler, Bruce M. Rails of the World: A Compilation of New Information, 1975-1983 (Aves Hallidae) LC 84-600393. (Smithsonian Contribution to Zoology Ser.: No. 417). 32p. reprint ed. pap. 25.00 (*0-317-41853-X*, 2026178) Bks Demand.
Ripley Staff. Fun & Games. (Ripley's Believe It or Not! Mind Teasers Ser.). (Illus.). 48p. (J). (gr. 3-6). 1991. 11.95 (*1-56065-062-1*) Capstone Pr.
— Hours, Days & Years. (Ripley's Believe It or Not! Mind Teasers Ser.). (Illus.). 48p. (J). (gr. 3-6). 1991. 11.95 (*1-56065-065-6*) Capstone Pr.
Ripley, Steven M. The First Day Cover Manual: A Guide for the Intermediate Collector, Vol. 1. (Illus.). 100p. (Orig.). 1995. pap. write for info. (*1-879390-04-3*) Am First Day.
Ripley, Theresa, jt. auth. see Loughary, Jack.
Ripley, Theresa M., jt. auth. see Loughary, John W.
Ripley, Tim. Desert Storm Land Power. (Desert Storm Ser.). (Illus.). 64p. pap. 11.95 (*1-85532-177-7*, 9542, Pub. by Osprey UK) Stackpole.
Ripley, Tim, jt. auth. see Gunston, Bill.
Ripley, Tom. Bombs Gone: Modern Aircraft Ordinance in Action. (Illus.). 96p. 1994. pap. 17.95 (*1-872004-99-7*) Voyageur Pr.
— Security Forces in Northern Ireland 1969-92. (Elite Ser.: No. 44). (Illus.). 64p. pap. 12.95 (*1-85532-278-1*, 9459, Pub. by Osprey UK) Stackpole.
***Ripley, W. L.** Storm Front. LC 94-21891. 1995. 22.50 (*0-8050-3601-6*) H Holt & Co.
Ripley, Warren, ed. Siege Train: Journal of a Confederate Artilleryman in the Defense of Charleston. 386p. 1986. 24.95 (*0-87249-491-8*) U of SC Pr.
Ripley, William. Main Street & Wall Street. LC 72-93640. 1973. reprint ed. text ed. 20.00 (*0-914348-07-8*) Scholars Bk.
Ripley, William E., jt. auth. see Roedel, Phil M.
Ripley, William Z. Financial History of Virginia 1609-1776. LC 78-127449. (Columbia Studies in the Social Sciences: No. 10). reprint ed. 24.50 (*0-404-51010-8*) AMS Pr.
— Main Street & Wall Street. LC 73-2531. (Big Business; Economic Power in a Free Society Ser.). 1973. reprint ed. 26.95 (*0-405-05109-3*) Ayer.
— Railroads: Finance & Organization. Bruchey, Stuart, ed. LC 80-1699. (Railroads Ser.). (Illus.). 1981. reprint ed. lib. bdg. 60.95 (*0-405-13823-7*) Ayer.
— Railroads: Rates & Regulation. LC 73-2532. (Big Business; Economic Power in a Free Society Ser.). 1973. reprint ed. 42.95 (*0-405-05110-7*) Ayer.
Ripling, E., jt. auth. see Polakowski, N. H.
Riplinger, G. A. New Age Bible Versions: An Exhaustive Documentation of the Message, Men, & Manuscripts Moving Mankind to the Antichrist's One World Religion. 5th ed. LC 93-92561. 696p. 1993. pap. 14.95 (*0-9635845-0-2*) A V Pubns.
***Riplinger, Gail.** Which Bible Is God's Word? 150p. (Orig.). 1994. pap. 8.95 (*1-879366-81-9*) Hearthstone OK.
Ripman, Barbara. Basic Dressage. (Crowood Equestrian Guides Ser.). (Illus.). 96p. 1992. pap. 17.95 (*1-85223-535-7*, Pub. by Crowood Pr UK) Trafalgar.
— Basic Training. (Crowood Equestrian Guides Ser.). (Illus.). 96p. 1992. pap. 17.95 (*1-85223-534-9*, Pub. by Crowood Pr UK) Trafalgar.
Ripoll, Angeles S. Las Traducciones de Shakespeare en Espana: El Ejemplo de Othello. Editorial Arcos, Inc. Staff, ed. (Coleccion Interdisciplinar Ser.: No. 2). (Illus.). 302p. (SPA.). (C). 1988. lib. bdg. 25.00 (*0-937509-03-5*) Edit Arcos.
Ripoll, Carlos. Archivo Jose Marti: Repertorio Critico, Medio Siglo de Estudios Martianos. 1971. 14.50 (*0-88303-010-1*); pap. 11.50 (*0-685-73214-2*) E Torres & Sons.
— Conciencia Intelectual de America: Antologia del Ensayo Hispanoamericano. 3rd rev. ed. 1974. 9.50 (*0-88303-150-7*) E Torres & Sons.
— Escritos Desconocidos de Jose Marti. 1971. 10.50 (*0-88303-001-2*) E Torres & Sons.
— Harnessing the Intellectuals: Censoring Writers & Artists in Today's Cuba. 1985. 3.00 (*0-317-90494-9*) Cuban Amer Natl Fndtn.
— The Heresy of Words in Cuba. LC 85-20672. (Perspectives on Freedom Ser.: No. 4). 75p. 1985. 10.25 (*0-932088-07-4*) Freedom Hse.
— Jose Marti, Letras y Huellas Desconocidas. 1976. 10.95 (*0-88303-024-1*); pap. 6.50 (*0-685-73013-1*) E Torres & Sons.
— Jose Marti, the United States, & the Marxist Interpretaton of Cuban History. 95p. 1984. pap. 11.95 (*0-87855-976-0*) Transaction Pubs.
— Patria: El Periodico de Jose Marti, Registro General, 1892-1895. 1971. 9.95 (*0-88303-011-X*); pap. 6.95 (*0-685-73215-0*) E Torres & Sons.
Ripoll, Jamie. How Our Senses Work. (Invisible World Ser.). (Illus.). 32p. (J). (gr. 4 up). 1994. lib. bdg. 14.95 (*0-7910-2128-9*, Am Art Analog) Chelsea Hse.
Ripoll, Roger, ed. see Zola, Emile.
Riposa & Dersch. City of Angels. 224p. (C). 1992. pap. text ed. 24.95 (*0-8403-8061-5*) Kendall-Hunt.
Riposa, Gerry, jt. auth. see Andranovich, Gregory D.

Riposo, Joe. Jazz Improvisation: A Whole-Brain Approach. 3rd ed. (Illus.). 240p. (Orig.). 1992. audio, pap. 24.95 (*0-9623694-0-3*) JR Pubs.
An exciting new book that explores the concept Hemisphericity (Right-Left brain) & opens new avenues for learning Improvisation. Most interesting is the identification & analysis of the mental processing of performance through the four quadrants of the brain. The process used to teach or learn this creativity process is clearly labeled throughout the book. With the introduction of each new concept, the reader is reminded of the specialized function of the four quadrants of the brain. A holistic approach will teach the basic concepts of improvisation & is reinforced by practice material which has been designed to produce experiences involving the mental cognitive shift. Cassette with original tunes has been designed for experiencing the mental shift & enabling improvisation with a recorded rhythm section by Jamey Aebersold. The mental shift helps convert left brain information into right brain usable knowledge. The ultimate goal of the book is to develop musicians who can use both hemispheres equally well. This book will expose students to an experience that leads to the development of the four quadrants of the brain & learn to access information from each quadrant to make a musical response. ***Publisher Provided Annotation.***

Ripp, B. E., ed. Controlled Atmosphere & Fumigation in Grain Storages: Proceedings of an International Symposium Held from 11-12 April, 1983, in Perth, Western Australia. (Developments in Agricultural Engineering Ser.: No. 5). 798p. 1984. 161.75 (*0-444-42417-2*) Elsevier.
Ripp, Bart. South Sound Restaurant Guide. (Illus.). 64p. (Orig.). 1992. pap. text ed. 6.95 (*0-9633035-0-3*) Morn News Trib.
Ripp, Victor. Turgenev's Russia: From Notes of a Hunter to Fathers & Sons. 256p. 1980. 34.95 (*0-8014-1294-3*) Cornell U Pr.
Rippa, S. Alexander. Education in a Free Society: An American History. 7th ed. 434p. (C). 1992. pap. text ed. 33.95 (*0-8013-0606-X*, 78539) Longman.
Rippe. The Polar Fat-Free & Fit Forever Program. Date not set. pap. 2.50 (*0-671-88881-1*, Fireside) S&S Trade.
Rippe, James, jt. auth. see Kashiwa, Anne.
Rippe, James M. The Exercise Exchange Program: The Unique System That Allows You to Design Your Own Diet & Workout Every Day for a Lifetime of Good Health. (Illus.). 384p. 1993. pap. 12.00 (*0-671-79453-1*, Fireside) S&S Trade.
— Manual ICU Asia, No. 2. 1989. 10.95 (*0-316-74714-9*) Little.
— Manual ICU ISE. 2nd ed. 1989. 15.95 (*0-316-74713-0*) Little.
— Manual ICU Medicine. 2nd ed. 1989. 31.95 (*0-316-74712-2*) Little.
Rippe, James M. & Csete, Marie. Manual of Intensive Care Medicine. (Spiral Manual Ser.). 465p. 1983. spiral bd. 22.50 (*0-316-74708-4*) Little.
***Rippe, James M. & Curley, Frederick J., eds.** Procedures & Techniques in Intensive Care Medicine. LC 94-29395. 1994. 59.95 (*0-316-74721-1*) Little.
Rippe, James M. & Ward, Carol A. The Rockport Walking Program. 1989. pap. 12.95 (*0-318-42596-3*) P-H.
Rippe, James M., jt. auth. see Alpert, Joseph S.
Rippe, James M., jt. auth. see Ward, Ann.
Rippee, Nicki E., jt. auth. see Thomas, David O.
Rippeleau, Bruce E., jt. auth. see Funk, Robert E.
Rippen, Andrew & Knappert, Jan, eds. Textual Sources for the Study of Islam. Knappert, Jan, tr. (Textual Sources for the Study of Religion Ser.). (Illus.). xii, 212p. 1990. pap. text ed. 14.95 (*0-226-72063-2*) U Ch Pr.
Ripper, Charles L., jt. auth. see Niehaus, Theodore F.
Rippere, Vicky & Williams, Ruth, eds. Wounded Healers: Mental Health Workers' Experiences of Depression. LC 84-29118. 192p. 1987. text ed. 49.95 (*0-471-90746-4*); pap. text ed. 54.95 (*0-471-90592-5*) Wiley.
Rippeteau, Bruce E., jt. auth. see Funk, Robert E.
Rippey, J. Fred, ed. see Ugarte, Manuel.

R

*Rippey, John. Drug Abuse in America: An Historical Perspective. 36p. 1994. pap. 39.50 (1-884937-12-8) Manisses Communs.

Rippey, Robert M. The Evaluation of Teaching in Medical Schools. LC 80-19891. (Medical Education Ser.). 176p. 1981. 23.95 (0-8261-3440-8) Springer Pub.

Rippier, Jo S. Goodnight, Morning. 126p. 1977. 19.95 (0-901072-54-0, Pub. by Colin Smythe Ltd UK) Dufour.

— Short Stories of Sean O'Faolain. 1976. 26.00 (0-901072-30-3, Pub. by Colin Smythe Ltd UK) Dufour.

Rippin, Andrew. Muslims: Their Religious Beliefs & Practices, Vol. 1, The Formative Period. 1990. 45.00 (0-415-04518-5, A1662); pap. 13.95 (0-415-04519-3, A4179) Routledge.

Rippin, D. W. & Hughes, R. R., eds. Computer Applications in Chemical Engineering: Proceedings of the 12th Symposium of the European Federation of Chemical Engineering, Montreaux, April 1979. 639p. 1981. pap. 160.00 (0-08-025022-X, Pergamon Pr) Elsevier.

Rippinger, Joel. The Benedictine Order in the United States: An Interpretive History. 299p. (Orig.). 1990. pap. text ed. 19.95 (0-8146-1817-0) Liturgical Pr.

Ripple, G. Gary. Campus Pursuit: How to Make the Most of the College Visit & Interview. 5th ed. 32p. 1993. 4.00 (0-945981-78-3) Octameron Assocs.

— Do-It Write: How to Prepare a Great College Application. 5th ed. 32p. 1993. 4.00 (0-945981-77-5) Octameron Assocs.

Ripple, Jeff. Big Cypress Swamp & the Ten Thousand Islands: Eastern America's Last Great Wilderness. LC 92-6025. (Illus.). 137p. 1992. 24.95 (0-87249-842-5) U of SC Pr.

— The Florida Keys: Images of Paradise. LC 94-29896. (Illus.). 1995. 19.95 (0-89658-262-0) Voyageur Pr.

Ripple, Kenneth F. Constitutional Litigation. (Contemporary Litigation Ser.). 696p. 1984. 50.00 (0-87215-754-7) Michie Butterworth.

Ripple, Paula. Growing Strong at Broken Places. LC 86-71124. 184p. (Orig.). 1986. pap. 7.95 (0-87793-341-3) Ave Maria.

— Growing Strong at Broken Places. large type ed. LC 92-38594. (General Ser.). 269p. (Orig.). 1993. 18.95 (0-8161-5683-2) G K Hall.

*Ripple, William J., ed. Fundamentals of GIS: A Compendium. 248p. 1989. pap. 52.00 (0-614-06096-6, L332) Am Congrs Survey.

— Geographic Information Systems for Resource Management. 288p. 1986. pap. 52.00 (0-614-06097-4, L331) Am Congrs Survey.

Rippley. Of German Ways. 1992. pap. 9.00 (0-06-092380-6) HarpC.

Rippley, La Vern J. The Whoopee John Wilfahrt Old Time Dance Band: The German-Bohemian Roots of the Whoopee John Wilfahrt Dance Band. (Illus.). 22p. (Orig.). 1992. pap. write for info. (0-9622931-1-3) St Olaf German.

Rippley, La Vern J. & Schmeissner, Rainer. German Place Names in Minnesota. (Illus.). 106p. (ENG & GER.). 1989. 9.95 (0-9622931-0-5) St Olaf German.

*Rippley, LaVern J. & Paulson, Robert J. German-Bohemians: The Quiet Immigrants. (Illus.). 1995. write for info. (0-9622931-4-8) St Olaf German.

Rippley, LaVern J., tr. see Adams, Willi P.

Rippley, LaVern J., ed. see German-Bohemian Heritage Society Staff.

Rippley, Vern, ed. see Roba, William, et al.

Rippon & Fromtling, eds. Cutaneous Antifungal Agents: Selected Compounds in Clinical Practice & Development. (Basic & Clinical Dermatology Ser.: Vol. 7). 488p. 1993. 185.00 (0-8247-9055-3) Dekker.

Rippon, Hugh. Discovering English Folk Dance. 1989. pap. 25.00 (0-7478-0210-6, Pub. by Shire UK) St Mut.

— Discovering English Folk Dance. (C). 1989. pap. 25.00x (0-7478-0225-4, Pub. by Shire UK) St Mut.

— Discovering English Folk Dance. enl. rev. ed. 1993. reprint ed. pap. 6.95 (0-913714-58-5) Legacy Books.

Rippon, John W. Medical Mycology: The Pathogenic Fungi & Pathogenic Actinomytes. 3rd ed. (Illus.). 736p. 1988. text ed. 115.00 (0-7216-2444-8) Saunders.

Rippon, Michelle & Meyers, Walter E. Combining Sentences. 201p. (C). 1979. pap. text ed. 2.00 (0-15-512251-7) HB Coll Pubs.

Rippon, W. B., jt. auth. see Jamieson, A. M.

Ripps, David L. An Implementation Guide to Real-Time Programming. (Yourdon Press Computing Ser.). (Illus.). 262p. (C). 1989. text ed. 65.00 (0-13-451873-X, Yourdon) P-H.

Ripps, Susan. Passion for More: American Wives Reveal the Affairs that Make, or Break, Their Marriages. 1993. mass mkt. 4.99 (0-312-95049-7) St Martin.

— Sisters. 1995. pap. text ed. 12.00 (0-8217-4927-7) Windsor NY.

— Sisters: Devoted or Divided. 320p. 1994. 22.50 (0-8217-4679-0) Zebra.

Rippy, J. Fred. British Investment in Latin America: 1822-1949. Wilkins, Mira, ed. LC 76-29755. (European Business Ser.). 1977. reprint ed. lib. bdg. 23.95 (0-405-09771-9) Ayer.

— The Capitalists & Columbia. Bruchey, Stuart & Bruchey, Eleanor, eds. LC 76-5031. (American Business Abroad Ser.). (Illus.). 1976. reprint ed. 26.95 (0-405-09298-9) Ayer.

Rippy, J. Fred, tr. see Henao, Jesus M. & Arrubla, Gerardo.

Rippy, James F. Joel R. Poinsett, Versatile American. (History - United States Ser.). 257p. 1993. reprint ed. lib. bdg. 79.00 (0-7812-4826-4) Rprt Serv.

— Rivalry of the United States & Great Britain over Latin America. (BCL1 - U. S. History Ser.). 322p. 1991. reprint ed. lib. bdg. 89.00 (0-7812-6047-7) Rprt Serv.

— United States & Mexico. rev. ed. LC 73-137281. reprint ed. 29.00 (0-404-05337-8) AMS Pr.

Rippy, R. & Allan, Phillip F.

Rippy, Susan, jt. auth. see Brinkerhoff, Donna.

Rips, Lance J. The Psychology of Proof: Deductive Reasoning in Human Thinking. LC 93-5811. 416p. 1993. 47.50 (0-262-18153-3, Bradford Bks) MIT Pr.

RIPS Staff. Asian Security, 1988-89. (Asian Security Ser.: No. 4). (Illus.). 200p. 1988. 31.95 (0-08-036263-X, Pergamon Pr); pap. 19.95 (0-08-036703-8, Pergamon Pr) Elsevier.

— Asian Security, 1990-91. (Asian Security Ser.: No. 6). 250p. 1990. 39.00 (0-08-040709-9, Pub. by Brasseys UK) Brasseys Inc.

Ripslinger, Jon. Triangle. (YA). (gr. 7 up). 1994. 10.95 (0-15-200048-8); pap. 3.95 (0-15-200049-6) HarBrace.

Riquelme, John P. Harmony of Dissonances: T. S. Eliot, Romanticism, & Imagination. LC 90-4796. 368p. 1990. text ed. 42.50x (0-8018-4058-9) Johns Hopkins.

Riquelme, John P., ed. see Senn, Fritz.

Riquer, Martin D., jt. intro. see Menendez Pidal, Ramon.

Riquer, Martin de, ed. see Luque Faxardo, Francisco de.

Riquier, Aline. The Cotton in Your T-Shirt. (Young Discovery Library). (Illus.). 40p. (J). (gr. k-5). 1993. lib. bdg. 9.95 (1-56674-058-4, HTS Bks) Forest Hse.

— The Cotton in Your T-Shirt. Bogard, Vicki, tr. LC 91-45786. (Illus.). 38p. (J). (gr. k-5). 1992. 5.95 (0-944589-40-5) Young Discovery Lib.

Ririe, Robert L. Doin' Dutch Oven: Inside & Out. 130p. (Orig.). 1990. pap. 8.98 (0-88290-368-3) Horizon Utah.

— Let's Cook Dutch! A Complete Guide for the Dutch Oven Chef. LC 79-89360. (Illus.). 104p. 1979. pap. 7.98 (0-88290-120-6) Horizon Utah.

Risatti, Howard. New Music Vocabulary: A Guide to Notational Signs for Contemporary Music. LC 73-81565. 235p. reprint ed. pap. 67.00 (0-7837-5743-3, 2045404) Bks Demand.

— Post-Modern Perspectives: Issues in Contemporary Art. 352p. 1989. pap. text ed. 35.40 (0-13-688607-8) P-H.

Risberg, Debra, contrib. Olive Branch: Photographs & Texts by Cedric Chatterley, 1987-1993. (Illus.). 32p. 1994. 10.00 (0-945558-22-8) ISU Univ Galls.

Risbrudt, Christopher D., jt. ed. see Royer, Jack P.

Risbud, Subhash H., jt. ed. see Bergeron, Clifton G.

Risby, Bonnie, jt. auth. see Risby, Robby.

*Risby, Robby & Risby, Bonnie. M. A. P. S. Bk. 1: Map Activities for Primary Students. Draze, Dianne & Conroy, Sonsie, eds. (M. A. P. S. Ser.). (Illus.). 32p. (gr. 2-3). 1994. teacher ed 7.95 (1-883055-01-6, 93) Dandy Lion.

— M. A. P. S. Bk. 2: Map Activities for Primary Students. Draze, Dianne & Conroy, Sonsie, eds. (Map Activities for Primary Students Ser.). (Illus.). 32p. (J). (gr. 2-4). 1994. teacher ed 7.95 (1-883055-02-4, 94) Dandy Lion.

Risby, Terence H., ed. Ultratrace Metal Analysis in Biological Sciences. LC 78-31903. (Advances in Chemistry Ser.: No. 172). 1979. 43.95 (0-8412-0416-0) Am Chemical.

Risch, Ernest. Retail Merchandising. 2nd ed. 592p. (C). 1990. write for info. (0-675-21277-4, Merrill Pub Co) Macmillan.

Risch, Franz X. Pseudo-Basilius: Adversus Eunomium IV-V: Einleitung, Ubersetzung und Kommentar. LC 91-37162. (Supplements to Vigiliae Christianae Ser.: Vol. 16). 234p. 1992. 57.25 (90-04-09558-6) E J Brill.

Risch, S. Craig, ed. Central Nervous System Peptide Mechanisms in Stress & Depression. LC 90-14503. (Progress in Psychiatry Ser.: No. 30). 190p. 1991. text ed. 27.00 (0-88048-249-4) Am Psychiatric.

Risch, Sara J. & Hotchkiss, Joseph H., eds. Food & Packaging Interactions II. LC 91-31831. (Illus.). 265p. 1991. pap. 59.95 (0-8412-2122-7) Am Chemical.

*Risch, Sara J. & Reineccius, Gary A., eds. Encapsulation & Controlled Release of Food Ingredients. LC 95-2512. (ACS Symposium Ser.: No. 590). (Illus.). 224p. 1995. 64.95 (0-8412-3164-8) Am Chemical.

— Flavor Encapsulation. LC 88-10422. (ACS Symposium Ser.: No. 370). (Illus.). viii, 212p. 1988. 59.95 (0-8412-1482-4) Am Chemical.

Risch, Tore, jt. ed. see Litwin, Witold.

*Rischel, Jergen. Minor Mlabri: A Hunter-Gatherer Language of Northern Indochina. 350p. 1995. 98.00 (87-7289-294-3, Pub. by Mus Tusculanum DK) Paul & Co Pubs.

Rischer & Easton. Focus on Human Biology. LC 93-34610. (C). 1992. text ed. 38.00 (0-06-045416-4) HarpCollege.

— Focus on Human Biology. LC 93-34610. (C). 1992. 16.25 (0-06-500417-5) HarpCollege.

— Focus on Human Biology. 2nd ed. LC 93-34610. (C). 1994. Study guide. student ed 15.00 (0-06-501982-2) HarpCollege.

Rischer, Carl E. & Easton, Thomas A. Focus on Human Biology. 2nd ed. LC 93-34610. 591p. (C). 1994. pap. 38.00 (0-06-501796-X) HarpCollege.

*Rischer, Marti. Next Time. 300p. 1995. pap. 8.95 (1-56901-689-5) NW Pub.

Rischin, Moses. Immigration & the American Tradition. (AHS Ser: No. 79). 512p. 1976. pap. 9.95 (0-672-60130-3, Bobbs) Macmillan.

— The Promised City: New York's Jews, 1870-1914. (Illus.). 342p. 1976. pap. 14.95 (0-674-71501-2) HUP.

Rischin, Moses, ed. & intro. The Jews of North America. LC 87-10110. 280p. 1987. 39.95 (0-8143-1890-8); pap. 16.95 (0-8143-1891-6) Wayne St U Pr.

Rischin, Moses, ed. The Jews of the West: The Metropolitan Years. (Illus.). 156p. 1975. pap. 5.95 (0-943376-10-6) Magnes Mus.

— Modern Jewish Experience, 59 vols., Set. 1975. 1,630.50 (0-405-06690-2) Ayer.

— Yiddish Tales. Frank, Helena, tr. LC 74-29531. (Modern Jewish Experience Ser.). 1975. reprint ed. 52.95 (0-405-06755-0) Ayer.

Rischin, Moses & Asher, Raphael, intros. The Jewish Legacy & the German Conscience. (Illus.). 350p. 1991. 27.95 (0-943376-47-5); pap. 17.95 (0-943376-48-3) Magnes Mus.

Rischin, Moses, jt. ed. see Brinner, William M.

Rischin, Moses, ed. see Hapgood, Hutchins.

Rischin, Moses, jt. ed. see Livingston, John.

Riscuta, Dorutu H. Become Rich & Loved. Elletro Productions Staff, ed. LC 93-12862. 120p. (Orig.). 1993. pap. 6.95 (1-56875-040-4) R & E Pubs.

Risden, E. L. Songs of the City: Poems of Jazz & Blues. Hassan, Syed K., ed. (Wabash Chapbook Ser.). (Orig.). (C). 1989. pap. text ed. 2.00 (0-9622821-0-3) Demosthenes Pr.

— Through a Glass Darkly. LC 95-8693. 68p. 1995. pap. 12.95 (0-7734-2731-7, Mellen Poetry Pr) E Mellen.

Risden, E. L., tr. & intro. Beowulf: A Student's Edition. xxii, 99p. (C). Date not set. pap. text ed. 6.50 (0-87875-455-5) Whitston Pub.

Risden, Edward L. Beasts of Time: Apocalyptic Beowulf. LC 93-37320. (Studies in the Humanities: Vol. 8). 165p. (C). 1994. text ed. 41.95 (0-8204-2334-3) P Lang Pubs.

Rise, Elmer. Love among the Ruins. 1963. pap. 13.00 (0-8222-0917-9) Dramatists Play.

*Rise, Eric W. The Martinsville Seven: Race, Rape, & Capital Punishment. 256p. (C). 1995. 27.95 (0-8139-1567-8) U Pr of Va.

Rise, Eric W., jt. auth. see Hall, Kermit L.

Risebero, Bill. Fantastic Form. (Illus.). 192p. 1992. 30.00 (1-56131-057-3) New Amsterdam Bks.

— Modern Architecture & Design: An Alternative History. (Illus.). 256p. 1985. reprint ed. 32.00 (0-262-18108-8); reprint ed. pap. 16.50 (0-262-68046-7) MIT Pr.

— The Story of Western Architecture. (Illus.). 269p. (C). 1985. reprint ed. pap. 16.50 (0-262-68047-5) MIT Pr.

Riseborough, Donald J., ed. Canada & the French. LC 74-75155. 274p. reprint ed. pap. 78.10 (0-8357-7989-0, 2022901) Bks Demand.

Riseborough, George, jt. auth. see Bates, Inge.

Riseborough, P. A. & Walter, M. Management in Health Care. (Illus.). 323p. 1988. pap. 50.00 (0-7236-0862-8, Pub. by John Wright UK) Buttrwrth-Heinemann.

Riseden, Elizabeth I. Frontier Dynasty. (Orig.). 1982. pap. 3.50 (0-89083-935-2) Zebra.

Riseman, Edward M., jt. ed. see Hanson, Allen R.

Riseman, Tom. Understanding the I Ching: The History & Use of the World's Most Ancient System of Divination. 1990. pap. 5.95 (0-85030-985-9, Pub. by Aquarian Pr UK) Thorsons SF.

Risenhoover, C. C. White Heat. LC 91-77072. 362p. 1992. 20.00 (0-9627509-3-X) Baskerville.

Riser, Constance N. Klee. (Masters of Art Ser.). 1988. 19.99 (0-517-64792-3) Random Hse Value.

*Riser, Martin O. The Sternberg Family of Fossil-Hunters. LC 94-48127. (Illus.). 520p. 1995. text ed. 119.95 (0-7734-8985-1) E Mellen.

Riser, Mel, jt. auth. see Shroeder, Rick.

Riser, Robert R., jt. auth. see Bailes, Gordon L.

Riser-Roberts, Eve. In Situ-On-Site Bioremediation of Refined Oils & Fuels. 1992. 59.95 (0-87371-832-1, TD879) Smoley.

— Remediation of Petroleum Contaminated Soils. 1995. write for info. (0-87371-858-5) Lewis Pubs.

Rishabchand. Sri Aurobindo: His Life Unique. (Illus.). 427p. 1981. 18.75 (0-89071-326-X, Pub. by SAA II); pap. 15.00 (0-89071-325-1, Pub. by SAA II) Aurobindo Assn.

Rishabhchand. The Integral Yoga of Sri Aurobindo. 473p. 1974. pap. 4.75 (0-89071-281-6) Aurobindo Assn.

— Sri Aurobindo: His Life Unique. 427p. (Orig.). 1982. pap. 14.95 (0-89744-147-8) Auromere.

Rishbeth, H., ed. EISCAT Science: Results from the First Year's Operation of the European Incoherent Scatter Radar: Papers from the EISCAT Workshop, Aussois, France, 5-8 September 1983. 184p. 1984. pap. 73.00 (0-08-031440-6, Pergamon Pr) Elsevier.

Rishbeth, H., jt. ed. see Thomas, L.

Rishe, Naphtali. Database Design: The Semantic Modeling Approach. 528p. 1992. text ed. 45.00 (0-07-052955-8) McGraw.

Rishel, Jonas. The Indian Physician. 132p. 1980. 7.00 (0-88215-048-0) Friends Ohio St U Lib.

Rishel, Joseph F. Founding Families of Pittsburgh: The Evolution of a Regional Elite, 1760-1910. LC 89-39006. 256p. 1990. 49.95 (0-8229-3633-X) U of Pittsburgh Pr.

Rishel, Joseph F., ed. American Cities & Towns: Historical Perspectives. LC 92-20597. 264p. (C). 1992. text ed. 39.50x (0-8207-0239-0) Duquesne.

Rishel, Joseph J. The Henry P. McIlhenny Collection: An Illustrated History. LC 87-29196. (Illus.). 149p. (Orig.). 1987. pap. 5.00 (0-87633-073-1) Phila Mus Art.

— The Henry P. McIlhenny Collection: Nineteenth Century French & English Masterpieces. rev. ed. LC 84-80751. (Illus.). 118p. (Orig.). pap. 20.00 (0-939802-21-X) High Mus Art.

Rishel, R. W., jt. auth. see Fleming, Wendall H.

Rishel, Virginia. Wheels to Adventure: Bill Rishel's Western Routes. (Illus.). 160p. 1983. write for info. (0-318-57240-0); pap. 9.95 (0-935704-16-7) Howe Brothers.

Rishell, Lyle. Where the Wind Blows Free. 230p. 1993. 19.95 (0-913969-63-X, G Mason Univ Pr) Univ Pub Assocs.

— With a Black Platoon in Combat: A Year in Korea. LC 92-27918. (Military History Ser.: No. 29). 1993. 24.50 (0-89096-526-9) Tex A&M Univ Pr.

*Risher, Howard & Fay, Charles, eds. The Performance Inperative: Strategies for Enhancing Workforce Effectiveness. (Management Ser.). 480p. 1995. 33.95 (0-7879-0085-0) Jossey-Bass.

Rishikesh, S. Ancient & Medieval Nepal. (C). 1990. 65.00 (0-89771-058-4, Pub. by Ratna Pustak Bhandar) St Mut.

Rishmawi, Mona A., ed. see International Commission of Jurists.

Risho, Ray. Risho's Registry. 130p. (Orig.). 1985. pap. 5.00 (0-939872-03-X) MRP.

Rishord, Norman K. Insights on American History, Vol. I. 292p. (C). 1988. pap. text ed. 16.75 (0-15-541445-3) HB Coll Pubs.

— Insights on American History, Vol. II. 292p. (C). 1988. pap. text ed. 16.75 (0-15-541446-1) HB Coll Pubs.

Rising, Catharine. Darkness at Heart: Fathers & Sons in Conrad. LC 89-29432. (Contributions to the Study of World Literature Ser.: No. 37). 224p. 1990. text ed. 55.00 (0-313-26880-0, RDH/, Greenwood Pr) Greenwood.

*Rising, David. Great Careers for People Interested in Film, Video, & Photography, Vol.1. (Career Connections, Series 2: Communications, the Arts, & Entrepreneurship). 48p. 1994. 17.95 (0-8103-9968-7, UXL) Gale.

Rising, David P. Switch Reference in Koasati Discourse. LC 92-80355. xii, 90p. 1992. pap. 8.00 (0-88312-813-6); fiche 8.00 (0-88312-859-4) Summer Instit Ling.

Rising, Elmer. The Pen Renderings of Elmer Rising: New England in Black & White. LC 85-1463. (Illus.). 112p. 1985. 75.00 (0-9614380-0-2) FER Pub Co.

Rising, Trudy & Williams, Peter. Light Magic: And Other Science Activities about Energy. (Illus.). 64p. (J). (gr. 3-7). 1994. lib. bdg. 16.95 (1-895688-15-9, Pub. by Greey dePencier CN) Firefly Bks Ltd.

Risjord, Norman K. America: A History of the United States, 2 vols. (Illus.). (C). 1985. text ed. write for info. (0-13-024340-X) P-H.

— America: A History of the United States, 2 vols., Vol. I. (Illus.). 368p. (C). 1985. pap. text ed. write for info. (0-13-024324-8) P-H.

— America: The Glorious Republic, 2 vols. 2nd ed. (Illus.). 450p. (C). 1987. To 1877, 450 pgs. pap. text ed. write for info. (0-13-025156-9); Since 1865, 400 pgs. pap. text ed. write for info. (0-13-025198-4) P-H.

— Chesapeake Politics, Seventeen Eighty One to Eighteen Hundred. LC 78-7996. 1978. text ed. 74.00 (0-231-04328-7) Col U Pr.

— The Colonists. (Representative Americans Ser.: Vol. 1). 253p. (C). 1981. pap. text ed. 13.50 (0-669-02831-2) Heath.

— Jefferson's America: 1760-1815. (Illus.). 336p. 1991. 34.95 (0-945612-24-9); pap. 18.95 (0-945612-25-7) Madison Hse.

— The Revolutionary Generation. (Representative Americans Ser.: Vol. 2). 257p. (C). 1980. pap. text ed. 13.50 (0-669-02710-3) Heath.

— Thomas Jefferson. LC 94-6614. (American Profiles Ser.). 1994. 28.95 (0-945612-38-9); pap. 13.95 (0-945612-39-7) Madison Hse.

Risk, Clifford, tr. see Todorov, I. T.

Risk Insurance Management Society Staff. A Guide to Risk Management Department Annual Reports. 12p. 1983. pap. 3.50 (0-937802-05-0) RMSP.

Risk, J. C. The History of the Order of the Bath & Its Insignia. 1972. 26.00 (0-685-51511-7) S J Durst.

Risk, Louise B. House on the Hudson. 300p. 1993. pap. write for info. (0-9633934-0-5) L B Risk.

Risk Management Committee Staff. Risk Management for Newspapers. rev. ed. 40p. 1989. pap. 49.95 (1-877888-10-9) Intl Newspaper.

Risk, R. T. Four Private Presses. (Illus.). 60p. 1993. 45.00 (0-930126-43-2) Typographeum.

— Why Potocki? (Illus.). 60p. 1981. 50.00x (0-930126-07-6) Typographeum.

Riska, Elianne & Wegar, Katarina, eds. Gender, Work & Medicine: Women & the Medical Division of Labour. (International Sociology Ser.: Vol. 44). (Illus.). 224p. (C). 1993. text ed. 55.00 (0-8039-8902-4); pap. text ed. 19.95 (0-8039-8903-2) Sage.

Riska, Elianne, jt. auth. see Ettore, Elizabeth.

Riska, P. O., ed. Topics in Theoretical Physics. (Liperi Summer School of Theoretical Physics Ser.: Vol. 2). 416p. 1969. text ed. 309.00 (0-677-13240-9) Gordon & Breach.

*Riske, Bernadine. Chick-A-Dee-Dee-Dee & Ollie Owl View People. LC 94-96365. (Illus.). 16p. (Orig.). (J). 1994. pap. 7.95 (1-885981-00-7) Brisk Pubng.

— Dee-Dee Chickadee Goes to School. LC 95-96426. (Illus.). 20p. (Orig.). (J). (gr. 2-9). 1995. pap. 7.95 (1-885981-04-X) Brisk Pubng.

— Dee-Dee Chickadee Visits Neighbors. LC 94-92383. (Illus.). 20p. (Orig.). (J). (gr. 1-9). 1994. pap. 7.95 (1-885981-01-5) Brisk Pubng.

— Foxy Fox Sells Magic Berries. LC 94-96447. (Illus.). 20p. (Orig.). (J). (gr. 2-10). 1995. pap. 7.95 (1-885981-03-1) Brisk Pubng.

Riske, Milt. Those Magnificent Cowgirls. LC 83-71805. (Illus.). 130p. 1984. pap. 15.00 (0-913701-00-9) Wyoming Pub.

*Riske, S. Bernadine. Billy Goose Bombs Bullies. (Illus.). 20p. (Orig.). (J). (gr. 2 up). Date not set. pap. 7.95 (1-885981-09-0, Brisk Pubns) Brisk Pubng.

— Cheeky & the Grapevine. (Illus.). 20p. (Orig.). (J). (gr. 1-9). 1995. pap. 7.95 (1-885981-06-6, Brisk Pubns) Brisk Pubng.

— Dee-Dee Chickadee Gets Lost. LC 95-94019. (Illus.). 20p. (Orig.). (J). (gr. 2 up). 1995. pap. 7.95 (1-885981-05-8, Brisk Pubns) Brisk Pubng.

— Dolly Duck Plants Corn. (Illus.). (Orig.). (J). (gr. 2 up). 1995. pap. 7.95 (1-885981-08-2, Brisk Pubns) Brisk Pubng.

An Asterisk (*) at the beginning of an entry indicates that the title is appearing in BIP for the first time.

— Foxy Fox & Tom Turkey. (Illus.). (Orig.). (J). (gr. 1-9). 1995. pap. 7.95 (*1-885981-07-4*, Brisk Pubns) Brisk Pubng.
— The Musical Tree. LC 94-96424. (Illus.). 20p. (Orig.). (J). (gr. 2 up). 1994. pap. 7.95 (*1-885981-02-3*) Brisk Pubng.
Risken, H. The Fokker-Planck Equation: Methods of Solution & Applications. 2nd ed. Haken, H., ed. (Synergetics Ser.: Vol. 18). (Illus.). xiv, 472p. 1992. reprint ed. pap. 69.00 (*0-387-50498-2*) Spr-Verlag.
Riskin & McKenna. Practice Development: Creating the Marketing Mindset. 224p. 1989. pap. 63.00 (*0-409-80636-6*) Butterworth Legal Pubs.
***Riskin, Karen.** In Their Own Words: A Sexual Abuse Workbook for Teenage Girls. (Orig.). 1995. pap. text ed. 10.95 (*0-87868-596-0*) Child Welfare.
Riskin, Leonard L. Transcript & Simulation Materials: To Accompany Tape II: Mediation, the Red Devil Dog Lease, Instructor's Manual with A. (Dispute Resolution & Lawyers Videotape Ser.). 68p. (C). 1992. pap. text ed. write for info. (*0-314-01009-2*) West Pub.
— Transcript & Simulation Materials, Tape II: Transaction Negotiation the Carton Contract, Instructor's Manual with A. (Dispute Resolution & Lawyers Videotape Ser.). 47p. (C). 1992. pap. text ed. write for info. (*0-314-01008-4*) West Pub.
— Transcript & Simulation Materials to Accompany Tape I: Dispute Negotiation Thompson vs. Decker, a Medical Malpractice Claim, Instructor's Manual with A. (Dispute Resolution & Lawyers Videotape Ser.). 78p. (C). 1992. pap. text ed. write for info. (*0-314-01007-6*) West Pub.
— Transcript & Simulation Materials to Accompany Tape IV: Overview of ADR: The Roark vs. Daily Bugle Libel Claim, Instructor's Manual with A. (Dispute Resolution & Lawyers Videotape Ser.). 74p. (C). 1992. pap. text ed. write for info. (*0-314-01010-6*) West Pub.
Riskin, Leonard L. & Westbrook, James E. Dispute Resolution & Lawyers. (American Casebook Ser.). 468p. 1987. text ed. 31.50 (*0-314-36473-0*) West Pub.
— Dispute Resolution & Lawyers. abr. ed. (American Casebook Ser.). 223p. (C). 1987. pap. text ed. 19.50 (*0-314-68963-X*) West Pub.
— Dispute Resolution & Lawyers: 1993 Supplement to Abridged Edition. (American Casebook Ser.). 117p. 1992. pap. text ed. 9.00 (*0-314-01921-9*) West Pub.
— Dispute Resolution & Lawyers: 1993 Supplement to Hardcover Edition. (American Casebook Ser.). 276p. 1992. pap. text ed. 14.50 (*0-314-01920-0*) West Pub.
***Riskin, M.** The Barf Book. 96p. 1994. pap. 5.95 (*0-88032-449-X*) Ivory Tower Pub.
— Confessions from the Bathroom. 1991. pap. 5.95 (*0-88032-402-3*) Ivory Tower Pub.
— Once upon a Mattress - Life in Bed. 96p. 1994. pap. 5.95 (*0-88032-459-7*) Ivory Tower Pub.
Riskin, Marty, et al. Games You Can Play in Bed. 1994. pap. 5.95 (*0-88032-448-1*) Ivory Tower Pub.
***Riskin, Michael.** Stop in the Name of Love: Ejaculation Control for Life. 103p. (Orig.). 1994. pap. 14.95 (*0-9619609-1-4*) Choice Fullerton.
Riskin, Robert D. Between Opportunities: A Survival Guide for Job Seekers & Career Changers. 332p. (Orig.). 1992. pap. 14.95 (*0-9633781-0-4*) Aar Dee Aar Pub.
Riskin, Shlomo. The Wife's Role in Initiating Divorce in Jewish Law & the Agunah Problem: A Halakhic Solution. 1989. 19.95 (*0-88125-122-4*); pap. 11.95 (*0-88125-132-1*) Ktav.
Riskind, David H., jt. auth. see Burleson, Bob.
Riskind, Mary. Apple Is My Sign. 160p. (J). (gr. 5-9). 1993. pap. 4.95 (*0-395-65747-4*) HM.
Risko, Victoria, jt. auth. see Mohan, Maden.
Risler, J. J. Mathematical Methods for CAD. (Illus.). 200p. (C). 1993. 79.95 (*0-521-43100-X*) Cambridge U Pr.
Risley, jt. auth. see Hart.
Risley, E. H. Risley: Family History. (Illus.). 318p. 1990. reprint ed. lib. bdg. 59.00 (*0-8328-1618-3*); reprint ed. pap. 51.00 (*0-8328-1619-1*) Higginson Bk Co.
***Risley, H. H.** Gazetteer of Sikhim. (C). 1993. 22.00x (*81-85557-05-5*, Pub. by Low Price II) S Asia.
Risley, John S. & Geballe, Ronald, eds. Electronic & Atomic Collisions: Abstracts of Papers of the 9th International Conference on the Physics of Electronic & Atomic Collisions, 2 vols., Set. LC 75-15451. 1198p. 1975. pap. 50.00 (*0-295-95456-6*) U of Wash Pr.
— The Physics of Electronic & Atomic Collisions: Invited Lectures, Review Papers & Progress Reports of the Ninth International Conference on the Physics of Electronic & Atomic Collisions. LC 75-39962. 916p. 1976. 50.00 (*0-295-95455-8*) U of Wash Pr.
Risley, John S. & Redisch, Edward F., eds. Computers in Physics Instruction: Abstracts of Contributed Papers. 237p. (Orig.). (C). 1988. pap. text ed. 25.00 (*0-317-90354-3*) NCSU Physics.
Risley, John S., jt. auth. see Redish, Edward W.
Risley, Michael S. Chromosome Structure & Function. LC 85-17808. (VNR Advanced Cell Biology Ser.). (Illus.). 256p. 1986. 46.95 (*0-442-27638-9*) Van Nos Reinhold.
Risley, Robert L. Death with Dignity: A New Law Permitting Physician Aid-in-Dying. 109p. (Orig.). (C). 1989. pap. 6.00 (*0-9606030-8-5*) Hemlock Soc.
Risley, S., jt. auth. see Adams, A.
Risley, Teena, jt. auth. see McCollum, Susan.
Risley, Theodore G., ed. Wabash County, Illinois. (Illus.). 828p. 1994. reprint ed. lib. bdg. 85.00 (*0-8328-3986-8*) Higginson Bk Co.
Risley, Todd R., jt. auth. see Hart, Betty M.
Rismann, Daniel. Homo Solutus: A Seminalytical Programme. (Illus.). (Orig.). 1991. pap. 8.95 (*0-9629347-0-4*) PlasticMeans.
***Risner, Phyllis B., et al, eds.** Setting the PACE: Managing Transition to Patient-Centered Care. LC 94-43730. 1995. pap. write for info. (*1-56793-024-7*) Health Admin Pr.
Riso, Don R. Discovery Your Personality Type: The New Enneagram Questionnaire. 128p. 1994. pap. 6.95 (*0-395-71092-8*) HM.
— Enneagram Transformations: Releases & Affirmations for Healing Your Personality Type. LC 92-28727. 120p. 1993. pap. 5.95 (*0-395-65786-5*) HM.
— Personality Types. 1995. pap. 9.95 (*0-395-53518-2*) HM.
— Understanding the Enneagram: The Practical Guide to Personality Types. (Illus.). 224p. 1990. pap. 10.95 (*0-395-52148-3*) HM.
Risom, Ole. I Am a Kitten. (Golden Sturdy Bks.). (Illus.). 26p. (J). (ps). 1993. bds. 3.95 (*0-307-12169-0*, 12169, Golden Pr) Western Pub.
Rison, Alton D. Guide to Pass the TAAS. 2nd ed. 1993. pap. 25.00 (*0-9635870-1-3*) Sunbelt Theatre.
— How to Teach Black Children. (Illus.). 251p. 1992. pap. 25.00 (*0-9635870-0-5*) Sunbelt Theatre.
Rison, Robert. Elevated Dining: Cuisine Art of Healing with Vegetables, Vitamins Minerals & Gems. Allen, Chris, ed. (Illus.). 88p. (Orig.). 1993. pap. 16.95 (*0-9625706-3-X*) ECLAT Bks.
— The Living Information: Subconscious Mind & Power. (Illus.). 61p. (Orig.). (C). 1988. pap. 7.95 (*0-9625706-0-5*) ECLAT Bks.
Rispin, Karen. Ambush at Amboseli. LC 93-37801. (Anika Scott Ser.). (J). 1994. 4.99 (*0-8423-1295-1*) Tyndale.
— Anika's Mountain. LC 93-31345. (Anika Scott Ser.: No. 3). (Illus.). (J). 1994. pap. 4.99 (*0-8423-1219-6*) Tyndale.
— Sabrina the Schemer. LC 93-39634. (J). 1994. 4.99 (*0-8423-1296-X*) Tyndale.
— Tianna, the Terrible. LC 92-19294. (Anika Scott Ser.: No. 2). (J). 1992. 4.99 (*0-8423-2031-8*) Tyndale.
Rispler-Chaim, Vardit. Islamic Medical Ethics in the Twentieth Century. LC 92-47108. (Social, Economic & Political Studies of the Middle East: Vol. 46). vii, 149p. 1993. 51.50 (*90-04-09608-6*) E J Brill.
***Riss-Fang, Josephine, et al, eds.** World Guide to Libary & Information Science Education. 2nd ed. (IFLA: vol. 72/73). 600p. 1995. write for info. (*3-598-21799-4*) K G Saur.
Riss Fang, Josephine & Songe, Alice. World Guide to Library, Archival, & Information Science Associations. 3rd ed. (IFLA Publication Ser.: Vol. 52/53). 430p. 1990. lib. bdg. 95.00 (*3-598-10814-1*) K G Saur.
Riss, Richard M. A Survey of Twentieth Century Revival Movements in North America. 208p. 1988. pap. 9.95 (*0-913573-72-8*) Hendrickson MA.
Rissanen, J. Stochastic Complexity in Statistical Inquiry Theory. (Series in Computer Science: Vol. 15). 188p. (C). 1989. text ed. 55.00 (*9971-5-0859-1*); pap. text ed. 33.00 (*981-02-0311-X*) World Scientific Pub.
Rissanen, Matti, et al, eds. Early English in the Computer Age: Explorations Through the Helsinki Corpus. LC 93-27036. (Topics in English Linguistics Ser.: No. 11). x, 296p. (C). 1993. lib. bdg. 129.25 (*3-11-013739-9*) Mouton.
— History of Englishes: New Methods & Interpretations in Historical Linguistics. LC 92-31358. (Topics in English Linguistics Ser.: Vol. 10). (Illus.). xi, 799p. (C). 1992. lib. bdg. 229.25 (*3-11-013216-8*) Mouton.
Risse, Guenter B. Hospital Life in Enlightenment Scotland: Care & Teaching at the Royal Infirmary of Edinburgh. (Cambridge History of Medicine Ser.). (Illus.). 430p. 1986. 74.95 (*0-521-30518-7*) Cambridge U Pr.
Risse, Gunter B., tr. see Rothschuh, Karl E.
Risse, Joseph, jt. auth. see Wilson, J. A.
Risse, Joseph A., ed. Study Guide for the Associate CET Test. 4th ed. 72p. 1989. pap. 10.00 (*0-317-04954-2*) Intl Soc Cert Elect.
Risse, Joseph A., jt. auth. see Wilson, Sam.
Risse-Kappen, Thomas. Structure & Process in Superpower Arms Control: Lessons from INF. (CISA Working Paper Ser.: No. 69). 41p. (Orig.). Date not set. pap. 10.00 (*0-86682-085-X*) Ctr Intl Relations.
***Risse-Kappen, Thomas, ed.** Bringing Transnational Relations Back In: Non-State Actors, Domestic Structures & International Institutions. (Studies in International Relations: No. 42). 270p. (C). Date not set. write for info. (*0-521-48183-X*) Cambridge U Pr.
— Bringing Transnational Relations Back In: Non-State Actors, Domestic Structures & International Institutions. (Studies in International Relations: No. 42). 270p. (C). 1995. pap. write for info. (*0-521-48441-3*) Cambridge U Pr.
Risse-Kappen, Thomas, jt. auth. see Lebow, Richard N.
Risse, W., ed. Complutenses Discalceati - Collegii Complutensis Disputationes in Aristotelis Dialecticam Et Philosophiam Naturalem. vii, 338p. 1977. reprint ed. write for info. (*3-487-06240-2*, Pub. by Georg Olms GW) Lubrecht & Cramer.
— Conimbricenses - Commentarii Collegii Conimbricensis... in Universam Dialecticam Aristotelis, 2 vols. in 1. 38p. 1976. reprint ed. write for info. (*3-487-05906-1*, Pub. by Georg Olms GW) Lubrecht & Cramer.
Risse, Wilhelm. Bibliographia Logica, 4 vols., Pt. 1: Verzeichnis der Druckschriften Zur Logik mi. (Studien und Materialien Zur Geschichte der Philosophie Ser.: Vol. 1). 293p. 1979. write for info. (*3-487-04532-X*, Pub. by Georg Olms GW) Lubrecht & Cramer.
— Bibliographia Logica, 4 vols., Pt. 2: Verzeichnis der Druckschriften Zur Logik mi. (Studien und Materialien Zur Geschichte der Philosophie Ser.: Vol. 1). 494p. 1979. write for info. (*3-487-04531-1*, Pub. by Georg Olms GW) Lubrecht & Cramer.
— Bibliographia Logica, 4 vols., Pt. 3: Verzeichnis der Zeitschriftenartikel Zur Lo. (Studien und Materialien Zur Geschichte der Philosophie Ser.: Vol. 1). 412p. 1979. write for info. (*3-487-06960-1*, Pub. by Georg Olms GW) Lubrecht & Cramer.
— Bibliographia Logica, 4 vols., Pt. 4: Verzeichnis der Handschriften Zur Logik. (Studien und Materialien Zur Geschichte der Philosophie Ser.: Vol. 1). 390p. 1979. write for info. (*3-487-06961-X*, Pub. by Georg Olms GW) Lubrecht & Cramer.
Risseeuw, Carla. Gender Transformation, Power & Resistance among Women in Sri Lanka. (C). 1991. 34.00 (*81-85425-68-X*, Pub. by Manohar II) S Asia.
Rissel, Hilda. Three Plays by Moreto & Their Adaptation in France. LC 93-40940. 1994. write for info. (*0-8204-2364-5*) P Lang Pubs.
Risselada, Max, ed. Raumplan Versus Plan Libre: Adolf Loos & Le Corbusier, 1919-1930. LC 88-60972. (Illus.). 136p. 1988. pap. 29.95 (*0-8478-1000-3*) Rizzoli Intl.
Risselada, Rodie. Imperatives & Other Directive Expressions in Latin: A Study in the Pragmatics of a Dead Language. (Amsterdam Studies in Classical Philology Ser.: Vol. 2). xii, 349p. 1993. 71.00 (*90-5063-206-8*, Pub. by Gieben NE) Benjamins North Am.
Risser, Joy. OJT Traffic Clerk Resource Materials. 2nd ed. (Gregg Office Job Training Program Ser.). (Illus.). 112p. (gr. 11-12). 1981. pap. text ed. 9.88 (*0-07-052960-4*) McGraw.
Risser, Paul G., ed. Long-Term Ecological Research: An International Perspective. (Scientific Committee on Problems of the Environment Ser.: No. 1409). 294p. 1991. text ed. 225.00 (*0-471-93005-9*) Wiley.
Risser, Paul G. & Cornelison, Kathy D. Man & the Biosphere. LC 79-4953. (Illus.). 109p. 1979. pap. 12.95 (*0-8061-1610-2*) U of Okla Pr.
Risser, Rita. Stay Out of Court: The Manager's Guide to Preventing Employee Lawsuits. LC 93-6799. 1993. write for info. (*0-13-845561-9*); pap. write for info. (*0-13-845553-8*) P-H.
Rissik, Dee. Women in Society: South Africa. LC 92-12374. 1992. 22.95 (*1-85435-504-X*) Marshall Cavendish.
***Rissinger, Matt & Yates, Philip.** Biggest Joke Book in the World. LC 94-45605. (Illus.). 192p. (YA). 1995. 16.95 (*0-8069-0852-1*) Sterling.
— Great Book of Zany Jokes. LC 93-39189. (J). 1994. 13.95 (*0-8069-0470-4*) Sterling.
— Great Book of Zany Jokes. (Illus.). 96p. (J). 1995. pap. 3.95 (*0-8069-0471-2*) Sterling.
***Rissler, Jane & Mellon, Marget.** The Ecological Risks of Engineered Crops. (Illus.). 192p. (C). 1995. 35.00 (*0-262-18171-1*); pap. 16.95 (*0-262-68085-8*) MIT Pr.
Rissman, Paul & Chitalwala, Y. M. Harappan Civilization & Oriyo Timbo. 1990. 30.00 (*81-204-0484-X*, Pub. by Oxford IBH II) S Asia.
Rissman, Rainey. Cost Control Using Lotus 1-2-3. (Illus.). 112p. 1992. disk, pap. 15.95 (*1-55622-218-1*) Wordware Pub.
Risso, Giuseppe. Cospaia. Asselin, Claudette, tr. LC 78-70626. (Illus.). 1979. pap. 7.95 (*0-915570-14-9*) Oolp Pr.
Risso, Mario. Safari Grammar. 1989. pap. 5.95 (*0-8442-5466-5*, Natl Textbk) NTC Pub Grp.
— Safari Punctuation. 1989. pap. 5.95 (*0-8442-5467-3*, Natl Textbk) NTC Pub Grp.
Risso, Mario & Grathwohl, J. David. To Will? Or To Trust? That Is the Question. (Illus.). 160p. (Orig.). 1992. pap. text ed. 19.95 (*0-917035-01-1*) Chicken Little.
Risso, Mario & Risso, Nancy. Funny-Fax. (Illus.). 112p. (Orig.). 1992. pap. 9.95 (*0-917035-24-0*) Chicken Little.
Risso, Mario, jt. auth. see Collis, Harry.
Risso, Nancy, jt. auth. see Risso, Mario.
***Risso, Patricia.** Merchants & Faith: Muslim Commerce & Culture in the Indian Ocean. LC 94-42937. (New Perspectives on Asian History Ser.). (C). 1995. text ed. 48.50 (*0-8133-1682-0*); pap. text ed. 15.95 (*0-8133-8911-9*) Westview.
Rissover, F. & Birch, D. Mass Media & the Popular Arts. 3rd ed. 496p. 1983. text ed. write for info. (*0-07-052956-6*) McGraw.
Rist, Charles. History of Monetary & Credit Theory from John Law to the Present Day. LC 66-21371. (Reprints of Economic Classics Ser.). 1966. reprint ed. 45.00 (*0-678-00161-8*) Kelley.
Rist, Darrell Y. Heartlands: A Gay Man's Odyssey Across America. LC 93-16026. 496p. 1993. reprint ed. pap. 13.00 (*0-452-27037-5*, Plume) NAL-Dutton.
Rist, John M. Augustine: Ancient Thought Baptized. LC 93-32394. 360p. (C). 1994. 59.95 (*0-521-46084-0*) Cambridge U Pr.
— Epicurus: An Introduction. LC 70-177939. 199p. reprint ed. pap. 56.80 (*0-317-26381-1*, 2024523) Bks Demand.
— The Mind of Aristotle: A Study in Philosophical Growth. (Phoenix Supplementary Volumes Ser.). 361p. 1989. 60.00 (*0-8020-2692-3*) U of Toronto Pr.
— Plotinus: The Road to Reality. 1977. 39.50 (*0-521-06085-0*) Cambridge U Pr.
— Stoic Philosophy. LC 79-85736. 1977. pap. 22.95 (*0-521-29201-8*) Cambridge U Pr.
Rist, Ray C. The Invisible Children: School Integration in American Society. LC 77-24554. 301p. reprint ed. pap. 86.40 (*0-7837-2320-2*, 2057408) Bks Demand.
***Rist, Ray C., abr.** Policy Evaluation. LC 94-32281. (Reference Collection: International Library of Comparative Public Policy: Vol. 3). 1995. write for info. (*1-85278-946-8*, Pub. by E Elgar Pub UK) Ashgate Pub Co.
Rist, Ray C., ed. The Democratic Imagination: Dialogues on the Work of Irving Louis Horowitz. 475p. (C). 1994. 49.95 (*1-56000-174-7*) Transaction Pubs.
— Policy Issues for the Nineteen Nineties. (Policy Studies Review Annual: Vol. 9). 800p. 1988. 49.95 (*0-88738-265-7*) Transaction Pubs.
— Policy Studies Review Annual, Vol. 6. 776p. 1982. text ed. 69.95 (*0-8039-1875-5*) Transaction Pubs.
— Policy Studies Review Annual, Vol. 7. 700p. (C). 1985. text ed. 69.95 (*0-88738-008-5*) Transaction Pubs.
— Policy Studies Review Annual, Vol. 8. 726p. 1987. text ed. 79.95 (*0-88738-116-2*); pap. 34.95 (*0-88738-673-3*) Transaction Pubs.
— Pornography Controversy: Changing Moral Standards in American Life. LC 73-92813. (Social Policy Ser.). 290p. 1974. pap. 18.95 (*0-87855-587-0*) Transaction Pubs.
— Program Evaluation & the Management of Government. 378p. 1989. 39.95 (*0-88738-297-5*) Transaction Pubs.
— Restructuring American Education: Innovations & Alternatives. LC 75-186712. 250p. 1972. 34.95x (*0-87855-037-2*); pap. text ed. 18.95x (*0-87855-533-1*) Transaction Pubs.
Rist, Ray C. & Anson, Ronald J., eds. Education, Social Science, & the Judicial Process. LC 77-962. 154p. reprint ed. pap. 43.90 (*0-685-20395-6*, 2030180) Bks Demand.
Rist, Ray C., ed. see Fine, Doris.
Ristad, Eloise. A Soprano on Her Head: Right-side-up Reflections on Life-& Other Performances. LC 81-23369. 201p. (Orig.). 1982. 14.00 (*0-911226-20-6*); pap. 10.50 (*0-911226-21-4*) Real People.
Ristad, Eric S. The Language Complexity Game. Bobrow, Daniel G. et al, eds. (Artificial Intelligence Ser.). (Illus.). 150p. 1993. 30.00 (*0-262-18147-9*) MIT Pr.
***Ristad, Eric S., ed.** Language Computations. LC 94-28045. (DIMACS Series in Discrete Mathematics & Theoretical Computer Science: 17). 198p. 1994. 60.00 (*0-8218-6608-7*) Am Math.
Ristaino, Marcia R. China's Art of Revolution: The Mobilization of Discontent, 1927-1928. LC 87-470. xv, 274p. (C). 1987. 50.50 (*0-8223-0718-9*) Duke.
Ristau, Bruno A. International Judicial Assistance: Civil & Commercial, 6 vols. rev. ed. LC 84-63137. 900p. 1990. IJA: Civil & Commercial (vols. 1-2, including 1989 supplement). 220.00 (*0-935328-30-0*); IJA: Crimninal (vols. 3-6). 440.00 (*0-935328-60-2*) Intl Law Inst.
— International Judicial Assistance: Civil & Commercial, 6 vols., Set, Vols. 1-6. rev. suppl. ed. LC 84-63137. 900p. 1990. Set, vols. 1-6. 595.00 (*0-935328-61-0*) Intl Law Inst.
Ristau, Carolyn, ed. Cognitive Ethology: The Minds of Other Animals Essays in Honor of Donald R. Griffin. (Comparative Cognition & Neuroscience Ser.). 344p. 1990. text ed. 69.95 (*0-8058-0251-7*); pap. 29.95 (*0-8058-0252-5*) L Erlbaum Assocs.
Ristau, Harland. From Another Landscape. (Juniper Bk. Ser.: No. 38). 1981. 5.00 (*1-55780-037-5*) Juniper Pr WI.
Ristau, Karen M. & Rogus, Joseph F. Leadership of & on Behalf of Catholic Schools. (National Congress Catholic Schools for the 21st Century Ser.). 45p. (Orig.). 1991. pap. 2.50 (*1-55833-067-4*) Natl Cath Educ.
Riste & Nokleby. Norway Nineteen-Forty to Nineteen Forty-Five: The Resistance Movement. (Tanum of Norway Tokens Ser). (C). 1986. pap. 20.00 (*82-518-0164-8*, N488) Vanous.
Riste, Olav, ed. Western Security: The Formative Years. LC 85-7795. 410p. 1985. text ed. 56.00 (*0-231-06168-4*) Col U Pr.
Riste, T., ed. Phase Transitions & Relaxation in Systems with Competing Energy Scales: Proceedings of the NATO Advance Study Institute, Geilo, Norway, 13-23 April 1993. LC 93-31136. (NATO Advanced Science Institutes Series C: Mathematical & Physical Sciences). 464p. (C). 1993. lib. bdg. 164.00 (*0-7923-2504-4*) Kluwer Ac.
Riste, T. & Sherrington, D., eds. Phase Transitions in Soft Condensed Matter. (NATO ASI Series B, Physics: Vol. 211). (Illus.). 402p. 1990. 105.00 (*0-306-43394-X*, Plenum Pr) Plenum.
— Spontaneous Formation of Space-Time Structures & Criticality. 464p. (C). 1991. lib. bdg. 145.00 (*0-7923-1452-2*) Kluwer Ac.
Riste, T., jt. ed. see Pynn, Roger.
Ristelhueber, Rene. History of the Balkan Peoples. Spector, Sherman D., ed. & tr. by. LC 78-147184. (Illus.). 470p. 1978. reprint ed. 47.50 (*0-8290-0176-X*); reprint ed. pap. text ed. 19.95 (*0-8290-0177-8*) Irvington.
Ristenen, Elaine K., tr. see Popov, A. A.
Ristenin, Les. The Knives of Finland. 96p. 1990. pap. 14.95 (*0-9626839-0-6*) Suomi Shop.
Rister, Carl C. Comanche Bondage. LC 89-4943. (Illus.). 211p. 1989. pap. 7.50 (*0-8032-8934-0*, Bison Books) U of Nebr Pr.
— Fort Griffin on the Texas Frontier. LC 86-50127. (Illus.). 232p. (Orig.). 1986. pap. 10.95 (*0-8061-1981-0*) U of Okla Pr.
— Land Hunger: David L. Payne & the Oklahoma Boomers. LC 75-118. (Mid-American Frontier Ser.). (Illus.). 1975. reprint ed. 23.95 (*0-405-06884-0*) Ayer.
Rister, M. Edward, et al, eds. Rice Economics Research & Extension Programs at Texas A & M University. (Illus.). 65p. (Orig.). (C). 1993. pap. text ed. 40.00 (*1-56806-452-7*) Diane Pub.
Ristic, Ljubisa, ed. Sensor Technology & Devices. LC 94-2361. 524p. 1994. 98.00 (*0-89006-532-2*) Artech Hse.
Ristic, Mihailo, et al. Design, Dynamics & Control of Industrial Robots. 200p. 1992. write for info. (*0-13-200957-9*) P-H.
Ristic, Miodrag. Diseases of Cattle in the Tropics. 1981. lib. bdg. 183.00 (*90-247-2399-X*) Kluwer Ac.
— Diseases of Cattle in the Tropics. 1981. pap. text ed. 84.00 (*90-247-2495-3*) Kluwer Ac.
Ristic, Miodrag, ed. Babesiosis of Domestic Animals & Man, Vol. I. 176p. 1988. 152.00 (*0-8493-4908-7*, QR201, CRC Reprint) Franklin.
Ristic, Miodrag, jt. ed. see Woldehiwet, Zerai.
Ristic, Miodrag, et al, eds. Malaria & Babesiosis. (New Perspectives in Clinical Microbiology Ser.). 1984. lib. bdg. 148.00 (*0-89838-675-6*) Kluwer Ac.

R

Ristich, Alberta. Color Me Love. Satchell, Alexis, ed. LC 84-91395. (Illus.). 50p. (Orig.). 1984. pap. 6.25 (*0-931841-01-1*) Satchells Pub.

Ristinen, Robert A., jt. auth. see Kraushaar, Jack J.

Ristiniemi, Jari. Experiential Dialectics: An Inquiry into the Epistemological Status & the Methodological Role of the Experiential Core in Paul Tillich's Systematic Thought. (Studia Philosophiae Religionis: No. 14). 215p. (Orig.). 1987. pap. text ed. 41.00x (*91-22-00983-3*, Pub. by Almqv & Wiksell SW) Coronet Bks.

Ristori, Adelaide. Memoirs & Artistic Studies. LC 74-81977. (Illus.). 1972. 24.95 (*0-405-08892-2*, Pub. by Blom Pubns UK) Ayer.

Ristori, Al. Fishing for Bluefish. 4th rev. ed. Barrett, Linda, ed. (Fisherman Library). (Illus.). 176p. 1995. reprint ed. 14.95 (*0-923155-03-1*) Fisherman Lib.

Ristori, Bridget. Patients in My Care. large type ed. (Non-Fiction Ser.). 1971. 15.95 (*0-85456-089-0*) Ulverscroft.

Ristovic, Aleksandar. Some Other Wine & Light. Simic, Charles, tr. LC 89-60744. 1989. 10.00 (*0-910350-11-6*) Charioteer.

Ristow, James. Off-Road Emergency Repair & Survival. (Illus.). 160p. (Orig.). 1989. pap. 9.95 (*0-945465-26-2*) John Muir.

Ristow, Kate S. & Comeaux, Maureen N. Harvest: A Faithful Approach to Life Issues for Junior High People. (Illus.). 167p. (J). (gr. 6-8). 1984. pap. 24.50 (*0-940634-20-1*) Puissance Pubns.

Ristow, Walter W. American Maps & Mapmakers: Commercial Cartography in the 19th Century. LC 84-25798. (Illus.). 489p. 1985. 65.00 (*0-8143-1768-5*) Wayne St U Pr.

— Emergence of Maps in Libraries. 358p. 1980. 100.00x (*0-7201-1620-1*) Elliots Bks.

Ristow, William, ed. San Francisco Bar Book. LC 81-66873. (Illus.). 128p. 1981. pap. 3.95 (*0-913192-03-1*) SF Bay Guardian.

— San Francisco Free & Easy. rev. ed. LC 80-66932. (Illus.). 352p. 1980. pap. 5.95 (*0-913192-02-3*) SF Bay Guardian.

Ristuccia, Angela M. & Cunha, Burke A., eds. Antimicrobial Therapy. (Handbook of Therapeutic Drug Monitoring Ser.). 636p. 1984. text ed. 159.00 (*0-89004-826-6*) Raven.

Risvold, Floyd E. The Minnesota Territory in Postmarks, Letters & History. (Illus.). 344p. 1985. 65.00 (*0-916675-01-7*) Collectors Club IL.

***Rita, Baron F.** Breast Cancer: What Every Woman Should Know. LC 94-32852. 1995. 23.00 (*0-688-12069-5*) Hearst Bks.

Rita, Corinne J., jt. auth. see Gallagher, Bernard J., III.

Rita, Emilio S. Preparandose Para Triunfar. (SPA.). 25.00 (*0-536-57965-2*) Ginn Pr.

Ritajananda. Swami Turiyananda. pap. 1.95 (*0-87481-438-3*, Pub. by Ramakrishna Math II) Vedanta Pr.

Ritajananda, Swami. Swami Turiyananda. (Illus.). pap. 1.95 (*0-87481-473-1*) Vedanta Pr.

Ritamary, Sister, ed. see Sister Formation Conferences Staff.

Ritcey, G. M. Tailings Management: Problems & Solutions in the Mining Industry. (Process Metallurgy Ser.: No. 6). 1000p. 1989. 202.75 (*0-444-87374-0*) Elsevier.

Ritcey, G. M. & Ashbrook, A. W. Solvent Extraction: Principles & Applications to Process Metallurgy, Pt. 2. (Process Metallurgy Ser.: Vol. 1, Pt. 2). 738p. 1979. 151.50 (*0-444-41771-0*) Elsevier.

Ritcey, G. M., et al. Solvent Extraction: Principles & Applications to Process Metallurgy, Pt. 1. (Process Metallurgy Ser.: Vol. 1, Pt. 1). 362p. 1984. 113.00 (*0-444-41770-2*) Elsevier.

Ritch. Biology: Laboratory Manual. 608p. 1989. spiral bd. 27.50 (*0-8403-5394-4*) Kendall-Hunt.

Ritch, et al. The Glaucomas. (Illus.). 1472p. 1989. text ed. 199.00 (*0-8016-4116-0*) Mosby Yr Bk.

— The Glaucomas, Vol. 2. 1800p. 1995. 259.00 (*0-8016-7702-5*) Mosby Yr Bk.

Ritch, Barbara A. & Ficke, Mary M. A History of Aphrodisiacs & Related Subjects: Yesterday & Today. Dinin, Denise, ed. (Illus.). 200p. (Orig.). 1985. pap. 9.95 (*0-9614846-0-8*) Gems N Gold Pub.

Ritch, Barbara F. Coal Camp Kids, Coming up Hard & Making It. 352p. 1991. 29.95 (*0-942407-12-1*) Father & Son.

Ritch, David, jt. auth. see Kobayashi, Jane.

Ritch, Ronald. Bones of Molech. Graves, Helen, ed. LC 86-51078. 240p. (J). 1987. pap. 9.95 (*1-55523-061-X*) Winston-Derek.

Ritchard, D. B. Begin Chess. 1987. pap. 3.95 (*0-451-16518-7*, Sig) NAL-Dutton.

Ritchard, Dan & Moloney, Kathleen. Ventriloquism for the Total Dummy. LC 87-40186. 96p. 1987. pap. 7.95 (*0-394-75638-X*, Villard Bks) Random.

Ritchart, Ronald E. Making Numbers Make Sense: A Sourcebook for Developing Numeracy in Grades K-8. 1993. pap. 15.00 (*0-201-81749-7*) Addison-Wesley.

Ritchason, Jack. Little Herb Encyclopedia. 1984. pap. 5.95 (*0-913923-18-4*) Woodland UT.

— Little Herb Encyclopedia. 2nd ed. 1994. pap. 9.95 (*0-913923-89-3*) Woodland UT.

— La Pequena Enciclopedia de Hierbas (Little Herb Encyclopedia) 159p. (SPA.). pap. 6.95 (*0-913923-94-X*) Woodland UT.

— Vitamin & Health Encyclopedia. 129p. 1986. pap. 7.95 (*0-913923-92-3*) Woodland UT.

Ritchason, Verlyn, ed. Cook Right to Eat Right. 191p. 1987. spiral bd. 14.95 (*0-913923-03-6*) Woodland UT.

Ritche, Adrian C. French for Administration, Business & Commerce: An English-French Glossary. 241p. 1994. 29.95 (*0-7083-1199-7*, Pub. by U of Wales UK); pap. 16.00 (*0-7083-1178-4*, Pub. by U of Wales UK) Bks Intl VA.

Ritcher, Paul O. White Grubs & Their Allies: A Study of North American Scarabaeoid Larvae. LC 66-63008. (Illus.). 216p. 1966. 27.95x (*0-87071-054-0*) Oreg St U Pr.

Ritcheson, Charles R. Aftermath of Revolution: British Policy Toward the United States, 1783-1795. LC 77-86328. 519p. reprint ed. pap. 148.00 (*0-8357-8793-1*, 2033426) Bks Demand.

— British Politics & the American Revolution. LC 81-1808. (Illus.). xv, 320p. 1981. reprint ed. text ed. 59.75 (*0-313-22953-8*, RIBP, Greenwood Pr) Greenwood.

Ritchey, David, ed. A Guide to the Baltimore Stage in the Eighteenth Century: A History & Day Book Calendar. LC 81-13461. (Illus.). viii, 342p. 1982. text ed. 95.00 (*0-313-22589-3*, RBS/, Greenwood Pr) Greenwood.

Ritchey, Fern A. Bible Puzzles, Quizzes & Word Search: The Fun Way. (Illus.). 64p. (Orig.). 1994. pap. 3.95 (*1-884898-03-3*) Eden Pubng NV.

***Ritchey, Jamilah.** Catlin. 160p. 1995. pap. 7.95 (*1-56901-874-X*) NW Pub.

Ritchey, Lee W. & Blankenhorn, James C. High Speed PCB Design. 110p. (C). 1992. text ed. 299.95 (*1-882812-04-2*) SMT Plus.

Ritchey, Wendy, jt. auth. see Isaacs, Susan.

Ritchie, A. C. Newspaper French: A Vocabulary of Administrative & Commercial Idiom. viii, 164p. 1990. 21.00 (*0-7083-1060-5*, Pub. by U of Wales UK); pap. 15.00 (*0-7083-1059-1*, Pub. by U of Wales UK) Bks Intl VA.

Ritchie, Andrew C. Abstract Painting & Sculpture in America. LC 70-86432. (Museum of Modern Art Publications in Reprint). (Illus.). 1969. reprint ed. 24.95 (*0-405-01544-5*) Ayer.

— Edouard Vuillard. LC 79-86445. (Museum of Modern Art Publications in Reprint). (Illus.). 1969. reprint ed. 15.95 (*0-405-01545-3*) Ayer.

— English Painters, Hogarth to Constable. LC 68-57337. (Essay Index Reprint Ser.). 1977. 12.95 (*0-8369-0124-X*) Ayer.

— Sculpture of the Twentieth Century. LC 78-169311. (Museum of Modern Art Publications in Reprint). (Illus.). 288p. 1972. reprint ed. 42.95 (*0-405-01570-4*) Ayer.

Ritchie, Andrew C., ed. see Haftmann, Werner, et al.

Ritchie, Andrew C., jt. auth. see Museum of Modern Art Library Staff.

Ritchie, Ann & Breeze, David. Invaders of Scotland. 64p. 1991. pap. 11.95 (*0-11-494136-X*, HM136X) UNIPUB.

***Ritchie, Anna.** Prehistoric Orkney. (Historic Scotland Ser.). (Illus.). 128p. 1995. pap. 29.95 (*0-7134-7593-5*, Pub. by Batsford UK) Trafalgar.

Ritchie, Anna, jt. auth. see Ritchie, Graham.

Ritchie, Anne I. Blackstick Papers. LC 71-76911. (Essay Index Reprint Ser.). 1977. 21.95 (*0-8369-0027-8*) Ayer.

— From the Porch. LC 70-152208. (Essay Index Reprint Ser.). (Illus.). 1977. reprint ed. 20.95 (*0-8369-2252-2*) Ayer.

— Madame de Sevigne. LC 77-37716. reprint ed. 29.50 (*0-404-56809-2*) AMS Pr.

— Records of Tennyson, Ruskin & Browning. LC 70-172549. 1972. reprint ed. 24.95 (*0-405-08893-0*, Pub. by Blom Pubns UK) Ayer.

— The Works of Miss Thackeray, 15 vols., Set. LC 70-37717. reprint ed. 525.00 (*0-404-56810-6*) AMS Pr.

Ritchie, Antonia F., jt. auth. see Sirna, Anne L.

Ritchie, Bill. A Dad Who Loves You: Experience the Joy of a Perfect Father. Halliday, Steve, ed. 154p. (Orig.). 1992. pap. 8.99 (*0-88070-549-3*, Multnomah Bks) Questar Pubs.

Ritchie, Bill H., Jr. The Art of Selling Art: Between Production & Livelihood. 252p. (C). 1991. pap. 19.95 (*1-56235-117-6*) Ritchies Perfect Pr.

— Ghosts in the New Machine: Between Virtue & Reality. (Perfect Studios Ser.). 252p. 1995. pap. 19.95 (*1-56235-172-9*) Ritchies Perfect Pr.

— Reinventing Arts Studios: Between Tradition & Technology. (Perfect Studios Ser.). 252p. (C). 1994. pap. 19.95 (*1-56235-162-1*) Ritchies Perfect Pr.

Ritchie, Branson W., et al, eds. Avian Medicine: Principles & Application. LC 93-60501. (Illus.). 1384p. (C). 1994. text ed. 175.00 (*0-9636996-0-1*) Wingers Pub.

— Avian Medicine: Principles & Application. 1384p. (C). 1994. cd-rom 175.00 (*0-9636996-2-8*) Wingers Pub.

Ritchie, Calvin D., jt. ed. see Coetzee, J. F.

Ritchie, Carson. Q-Ships: Britain's Secret Weapon Against the U-Boats, 1914-1918. 236p. 1994. 48.00 (*0-86138-011-8*, Pub. by T Dalton UK) St Mut.

Ritchie, Carson I. Frontier Parish: An Account of the Society for the Propagation of the Gospel & the Anglican Church in America, Drawn from the Records of the Bishop of London. LC 75-3564. 210p. 1976. 18.50 (*0-8386-1735-2*) Fairleigh Dickinson.

— Rock Art of Africa. LC 76-24614. (Illus.). 157p. 1978. 25.00 (*0-87982-024-1*) Art Alliance.

— Rock Art of Africa. 25.00 (*0-8453-1753-9*, Cornwall Bks) Assoc Univ Prs.

Ritchie, Charles. Diplomatic Passport: More Undiplomatic Diaries. 200p. 1986. pap. 4.95 (*0-7715-9258-2*, Pub. by Stoddart Pubng CN) Genl Dist Srvs.

— Gemini G. E. L. Recent Prints & Sculpture. LC 94-19078. 1994. write for info. (*0-89468-123-0*) Natl Gallery Art.

— The Siren Years: A Canadian Diplomat Abroad. 216p. 1987. pap. 4.95 (*0-7715-9269-8*, Pub. by Stoddart Pubng CN) Genl Dist Srvs.

Ritchie, Charles M. The Nineteen Eighties: Prints from the Collection of Joshua P. Smith. Fine, Ruth E., ed. LC 89-14053. (Illus.). 136p. (Orig.). 1989. 19.95 (*0-89468-142-7*) Natl Gallery Art.

Ritchie, Daniel E., ed. Edmund Burke: Appraisals & Applications. 294p. (C). 1990. 37.95 (*0-88738-328-9*) Transaction Pubs.

Ritchie, David. Encyclopedia of Earthquakes & Volcanoes. (Illus.). 288p. 1994. 40.00 (*0-8160-2659-9*) Facts on File.

— Shipwrecks: An Encyclopedia of the World's Worst Disasters at Sea. LC 95-15664. 1996. write for info. (*0-8160-3163-0*) Facts on File.

— UFO: The Definitive Guide to Unidentified Flying Objects & Related Phenomena. LC 93-31037. (Illus.). 272p. 1994. 40.00 (*0-8160-2894-X*) Facts on File.

***Ritchie, David & Ritchie, Deborah.** Connecticut: Off the Beaten Path: A Guide to Unique Places. 2nd ed. LC 94-22267. (Voyager Ser.). 160p. 1995. 9.95 (*1-56440-519-2*) Globe Pequot.

Ritchie, David G. Natural Rights. LC 79-1640. 1985. reprint ed. 27.25 (*0-88355-943-9*) Hyperion Conn.

— Principles of State Interference. LC 70-94282. (Select Bibliographies Reprint Ser.). 1977. 21.95 (*0-8369-5060-7*) Ayer.

Ritchie, Deborah, jt. auth. see Ritchie, David.

Ritchie, Dennis M., jt. auth. see Kernighan, Brian W.

Ritchie, Don. North Toronto. (Illus.). 160p. 35.00 (*1-55046-011-0*, Pub. by Boston Mills Pr CN) Genl Dist Srvs.

***Ritchie, Donald, et al.** The Young Oxford Companion to the U. S. Government, 3 vols., Set. (Illus.). 912p. (J). 1995. lib. bdg. 105.00 (*0-19-509737-8*) OUP.

***Ritchie, Donald A.** Doing Oral History. (Twayne's Oral History Ser.). (Illus.). 288p. 1994. text ed. 26.95x (*0-8057-9124-8*, Twayne); pap. 14.95 (*0-8057-9128-0*, Twayne) Macmillan.

— James M. Landis: Dean of the Regulators. LC 80-12828. 276p. 1980. 32.00 (*0-674-47171-7*) HUP.

— Press Gallery: Congress & the Washington Correspondents. LC 90-43676. (Illus.). 293p. 1991. 36.00 (*0-674-70375-8*, RITPRE) HUP.

— Press Gallery: Congress & the Washington Correspondents. (Illus.). 312p. 1992. pap. 15.95 (*0-674-70376-6*) HUP.

— The Senate. (Know Your Government Ser.). (Illus.). 96p. (J). (gr. 5 up). 1988. lib. bdg. 14.95 (*1-55546-121-2*) Chelsea Hse.

Ritchie, Donald A., ed. see Gluck, Sherna B.

Ritchie, Donald A., jt. auth. see Manning, Diane.

Ritchie, Donald D. & Carola, Robert. Biology. 2nd ed. LC 82-11318. (Biology Ser.). (Illus.). 672p. (C). 1983. teacher ed write for info. (*0-201-06357-3*); text ed. write for info. (*0-201-06356-5*); student ed write for info. (*0-201-06358-1*); sl. write for info. (*0-201-06393-X*); write for info. (*0-201-06359-X*) Addison-Wesley.

Ritchie, Donald J. Ball Lightning: A Collection of Soviet Research in English Translation. LC 61-15177. 70p. reprint ed. pap. 25.00 (*0-8357-5950-4*, 2024707) Bks Demand.

Ritchie, Elisavietta. Flying Time: Stories & Half-Stories. LC 92-37103. 1992. pap. 12.00 (*0-930095-14-6*) Signal Bks.

— Flying Time: Stories & Half-Stories. LC 93-40936. 1993. 16.00 (*0-930095-31-6*) Signal Bks.

— Raking the Snow. LC 81-86642. 55p. 1982. pap. 7.00 (*0-931846-21-8*) Wash Writers Pub.

— Tightening the Circle over Eel Country. LC 74-17130. 110p. 1974. pap. 3.95 (*0-87491-390-X*) Signal Bks.

Ritchie, Elisavietta, ed. Finding the Name. 144p. 1983. pap. 5.95 (*0-9612158-0-1*) Wineberry Pr.

— A Wound-up Cat & Other Bedtime Stories. pap. write for info. (*1-895450-14-4*) Signal Bks.

Ritchie, Ethel M., ed. see Fairburn, William A.

Ritchie, Evelyn. Hickory Sled. 64p. 1989. pap. 5.95 (*0-932616-24-0*) New Poets Chestnut Hills.

Ritchie, Everett J., jt. auth. see Hehner, Nels E.

Ritchie, Fern J., jt. auth. see Ritchie, Ralph W.

Ritchie, G. S. No Day to Long - An Hydrographer's Tale. 247p. (C). 1989. text ed. 50.00 (*1-872795-63-3*, Pub. by Pentland Pr UK) St Mut.

Ritchie, George. Regreso del Futuro: Return from Tomorrow. (SPA.). 4.25 (*84-7228-535-9*, 220752, Pub. by Edit Clie SP) TSELF.

Ritchie, George & Stauffer, George B. Organ Technique: Modern & Early. 336p. 1991. text ed. 59.33 (*0-13-639873-1*) P-H.

Ritchie, George G., Jr. My Life after Dying. 1991. pap. 9.95 (*1-878901-25-7*) Hampton Roads Pub Co.

Ritchie, George G. Return from Tomorrow-Spire. LC 77-27543. 1988. pap. 3.99 (*0-8007-8412-X*) Revell.

Ritchie, George G. & Sherrill, Elizabeth. Return from Tomorrow. LC 77-27543. 1987. reprint ed. pap. 7.99 (*0-8007-9067-7*) Chosen Bks.

Ritchie, Gordon J. Transistor Circuit Techniques. 2nd ed. 1987. pap. 34.95 (*0-278-00034-7*) Chapman & Hall.

— Transistor Circuit Techniques: Discrete & Integrated. 3rd ed. LC 92-44028. (Tutorial Guides in Electronic Engineering Ser.: Vol. 1). 1993. write for info. (*0-412-46470-5*) Chapman & Hall.

Ritchie, Gordon J., et al. Principles & Practice of General Surgery: Essentials of Practice. (Illus.). 1200p. (C). 1994. text ed. 165.00 (*0-397-51114-0*, Lippincott Medical) Lippincott.

Ritchie, Graeme D. Computational Grammar: An Artificial Intelligence Approach to Linguistic Description. (Harvester Studies in Cognitive Science: No. 15). 254p. 1980. 42.00 (*0-389-20048-4*, N6819) B&N Imports.

Ritchie, Graeme D., et al. Computational Morphology Practical Mechanisms for the English Lexicon. (ACL-MIT Press Ser.). (Illus.). 304p. 1991. 40.00 (*0-262-18146-0*) MIT Pr.

Ritchie, Graham & Ritchie, Anna. Scotland: Archaeology & Early History. (Illus.). 208p. 1992. pap. 25.00 (*0-7486-0291-7*, Pub. by Edinburgh U Pr UK) Col U Pr.

Ritchie, H. D. & Hardcastle, J. D. Isolated Organ Perfusion. (Illus.). 1973. 17.95 (*0-8464-0534-2*) Beekman Pubs.

Ritchie, Harland D. Livestock Judging & Evaluation Manual. (Illus.). x, 205p. 1983. reprint ed. pap. 6.50 (*0-87013-152-4*) Mich St U Pr.

Ritchie, Henry & Durkee, Cornelius. A Name Index to the Eighteen Seventy-Eight History of Saratoga Co., New York. 84p. 1979. 10.00 (*0-932334-24-5*, NY46006) Hrt of the Lakes.

Ritchie, Ian. Well Connected Architecture. (Academy Educational Ser.). (Illus.). 144p. (Orig.). 1994. pap. 30.00 (*1-85490-292-X*, Academy Edits) St Martin.

Ritchie, Ingrid & Martin, Stephen J. Healthy Home Kit. 1994. pap. 19.95 (*0-7931-0898-5*, 19132101) Dearborn Finan.

Ritchie, J. B. & Thompson, Paul. Organization & People: Readings, Exercises & Cases in Organizational Behavior. 4th ed. Fenton, ed. 463p. (C). 1988. pap. text ed. 46.00 (*0-314-65672-3*) West Pub.

Ritchie, J. C. Past & Present Vegetation of the Far Northwest Canada. 272p. (C). 1984. 37.50 (*0-8020-2523-4*) U of Toronto Pr.

— Post-Glacial Vegetation of Canada. (Illus.). 240p. 1987. 94.95 (*0-521-30868-2*) Cambridge U Pr.

Ritchie, J. Douglas. Lachlan Macquarie: A Biography. 332p. 1986. pap. 24.95 (*0-522-84369-7*) Intl Spec Bk.

Ritchie, J. M., ed. see Al-Amin, Shaykh & Mazru'i, Ali A.

Ritchie, J. M., jt. auth. see Hawksworth, D. L.

Ritchie, J. M., tr. see Raabe, Paul, ed.

Ritchie, J. M., et al, eds. Control of Membrane Function: Short-Term & Long-Term. (Progress in Cell Research Ser.). 340p. 1990. 143.75 (*0-444-81125-7*) Elsevier.

Ritchie, J. Murdoch, jt. ed. see Waxman, Stephen G.

Ritchie, J. N., jt. auth. see Ritchie, W. F.

Ritchie, J. R. & Goeldner, Charles R. Travel, Tourism, & Hospitality Research: A Handbook for Managers & Researchers. 2nd ed. 512p. 1994. text ed. 59.95 (*0-471-58248-4*) Wiley.

Ritchie, J. R. & Hawkins, D., eds. World Travel & Tourism Review, Vol. 3. 320p. 1993. text ed. 170.00 (*0-85198-853-9*) CAB Intl.

— World Travel & Tourism Review, Vol. 2: Indicators, Trends, & Issues. 320p. 1992. text ed. 170.00 (*0-85198-771-0*) CAB Intl.

Ritchie, Jack. Tiger Island. 2nd ed. 1987. 4.95 (*0-932310-09-5*) U of Wis-Stevens Point.

Ritchie, James. Folkpsalms Intro Pak. 1993. 19.95 (*0-687-13257-6*) Abingdon.

— Over on the Lonesome Side. 192p. 1991. 19.95 (*0-8027-4118-5*) Walker & Co.

Ritchie, James A. Kerrigan. LC 93-8065. 1993. 19.95 (*0-8027-1276-2*) Walker & Co.

— Kerrigan. large type ed. LC 93-45624. 1994. bds. 17.95 (*0-7862-0164-9*) Thorndike Pr.

— The Last Free Range. 1995. write for info. (*0-8027-4150-9*) Walker & Co.

— Over on the Lonesome Side. large type ed. 284p. 1992. reprint ed. lib. bdg. 15.95 (*1-56054-341-8*) Thorndike Pr.

— The Payback. 172p. 1992. 19.95 (*0-8027-1233-9*) Walker & Co.

***Ritchie, James L., ed.** Thallium--201 Myocardial Imaging. fac. ed. LC 78-3004. (Illus.). 166p. Date not set. pap. 47.40 (*0-7837-7357-9*, 2047166) Bks Demand.

Ritchie, Jane, jt. auth. see Richardson, Ann.

Ritchie, Jean. The Dulcimer Book. (Illus.). 1963. pap. 9.95 (*0-8256-0016-2*, 000016, Oak) Music Sales.

— Jean Ritchie Celebration of Life: Her Songs...Her Poems. 128p. Date not set. pap. 9.95 (*0-8256-9676-3*) Music Sales.

— Singing Family of the Cumberlands. LC 88-17337. 264p. 1988. 25.00 (*0-8131-1679-1*); pap. 15.00 (*0-8131-0186-7*) U Pr of Ky.

Ritchie, Jean, ed. Jean Ritchie's Dulcimer People. (Illus.). pap. 11.95 (*0-8256-0142-8*, Oak) Music Sales.

***Ritchie, Jean & MacKenzie, Drew.** Kiss of Death: True Cases of Fatal Attraction. (Illus.). 301p. (Orig.). 1994. pap. 17.95 (*1-85479-934-7*, Pub. by Picador UK) Trans-Atl Phila.

Ritchie, Jim. Shocco Tales: Southern Fried Sagas. 1991. 17.95 (*1-879034-07-7*) MS River Pub.

Ritchie, John. Feasts of Jehovah. LC 82-182. 80p. 1982. reprint ed. pap. 5.99 (*0-8254-3613-3*) Kregel.

— Five Hundred Bible Subjects. 1993. reprint ed. pap. 6.99 (*0-88019-301-8*) Schmul Pub Co.

— Five Hundred Children's Sermon Outlines. LC 86-27396. 128p. 1987. reprint ed. pap. 5.99 (*0-8254-3623-0*) Kregel.

— Five Hundred Evangelistic Sermon Outlines. LC 86-27200. 128p. 1987. reprint ed. pap. 5.99 (*0-8254-3619-2*) Kregel.

— Five Hundred Gospel Sermon Illustrations. LC 86-27201. 152p. 1987. pap. 5.99 (*0-8254-3620-6*) Kregel.

— Five Hundred Gospel Sermon Outlines. LC 86-27760. 128p. 1987. reprint ed. pap. 5.99 (*0-8254-3621-4*) Kregel.

— Five Hundred Sermon Outlines on Basic Bible Truths. LC 86-27541. 128p. 1987. reprint ed. pap. 5.99 (*0-8254-3618-4*) Kregel.

— Five Hundred Sermon Outlines on the Christian Life. LC 86-27759. 128p. 1987. reprint ed. pap. 5.99 (*0-8254-3622-2*) Kregel.

— From Egypt to Canaan. LC 82-220. 104p. (C). 1982. reprint ed. pap. 5.99 (*0-8254-3614-1*) Kregel.

— The Tabernacle in the Wilderness. LC 82-178. 120p. (C). 1982. reprint ed. pap. 5.99 (*0-8254-3616-8*) Kregel.

— El Tabernaculo en el Desierto. Orig. Title: The Tabernacle in the Wilderness. (Illus.). 144p. (SPA.). 1987. pap. 5.99 (*0-8254-1616-7*) Kregel.

Ritchie, John, ed. Australian Dictionary of Biography, 1940-1980, Vol. 13: A-De. 626p. 1993. lib. bdg. 59.95 (*0-522-84512-6*) Intl Spec Bk.

Ritchie, John, III, et al. Cases & Materials on Decedents' Estates & Trusts. 8th ed. (University Casebook Ser.). 1424p. 1993. text ed. 46.95 (*1-56662-066-X*) Foundation Pr.

— Decedents' Estates & Trusts: Teacher's Manual to Accompany Cases & Materials. 7th ed. (University Casebook Ser.). 194p. 1988. pap. text ed. write for info. (*0-88277-676-2*) Foundation Pr.

***Ritchie, John C., Jr.** Fundamental Analysis: A Back-to-Basics Investment Guide to Selecting Quality Stocks. rev. ed. 375p. 1995. 24.95 (*1-55738-866-0*) Probus Pub Co.

— The Fundamentals of Fundamental Analysis. 364p. 1992. pap. 21.95 (*1-55738-473-8*) Probus Pub Co.

Ritchie, John C., Jr., jt. auth. see Phillips, Herbert E.

***Ritchie, Judy.** Stamp-a-Christmas Book & Kit. (Illus.). 96p. 1995. pap. 25.00 (*0-88363-895-9*) H L Levin.

***Ritchie, Karen.** Marketing to Generation X: Strategies for a New Era. 1995. 25.00 (*0-02-926545-2*) Free Pr.

***Ritchie, L. Carol, ed.** My First Year in Television. (First Year Career Ser.). (J). 1995. write for info. (*0-8027-1293-2*) Walker & Co.

— My First Year in Television. (First Year Career Ser.). (J). 1995. pap. write for info. (*0-8027-7424-5*) Walker & Co.

Ritchie, L. David. Information. (Communication Concepts Ser.: Vol. 2). 120p. (C). 1991. text ed. 24.00 (*0-8039-3904-3*); pap. text ed. 10.95 (*0-8039-3905-1*) Sage.

Ritchie, Leo. Reminiscences of Woodland Stalking. 174p. (C). 1989. 49.00 (*0-7223-2290-9*, Pub. by A H S Ltd UK) St Mut.

Ritchie, Lewis A. Naval Occasions, & Some Traits of the Sailorman. LC 70-130070. (Short Story Index Reprint Ser.). 1977. 23.95 (*0-8369-3651-5*) Ayer.

— Navy Eternal. LC 72-134977. (Short Story Index Reprint Ser.). 1977. 19.95 (*0-8369-3706-6*) Ayer.

Ritchie, Lewis A., ed. The Shipbuilding Industry: A Guide to Historical Records. LC 92-9472. (Studies in British Business Archives). 1992. text ed. 59.95 (*0-7190-3805-7*, Pub. by Manchester Univ Pr UK) St Martin.

Ritchie, M. Women's Studies: A Checklist of Bibliographies. 128p. 1980. text ed. 50.00 (*0-7201-0918-3*) Weidner & Sons.

Ritchie, Maureen, jt. auth. see Carter, Sarah.

***Ritchie, Michael.** Please Stand By. 280p. 1995. pap. 15.95 (*0-87951-615-1*) Overlook Pr.

— Please Stand By: The Prehistory of Television. (Illus.). 280p. 1994. 23.95 (*0-87951-546-5*) Overlook Pr.

Ritchie, Mildred H., ed. see Handy, Isaac W.

Ritchie, N. G. Brochs of Scotland. 1989. pap. 25.00 (*0-85263-928-7*, Pub. by Shire UK) St Mut.

Ritchie, Neil, jt. ed. see Chaney, Edwards.

Ritchie-Noakes, Nancy. Old Docks. 1989. pap. 25.00 (*0-85263-893-0*, Pub. by Shire UK) St Mut.

Ritchie, Norm. Murky Deep. (Advanced Dungeons & Dragons, Second Edition; Al-Qadim Ser.). (Illus.). 1993. pap. 6.95 (*1-56076-574-7*) TSR Inc.

***Ritchie, Patricia T.** Index to the 1880 Rockingham County, Virginia Census. iv, 178p. 1990. lib. bdg. 35.00x (*0-8095-8174-4*); pap. 14.00x (*0-8095-8609-6*) Borgo Pr.

Ritchie, Paul. Saint Honey & Oh David, Are You There? 124p. 1968. 12.95 (*0-910278-45-8*) Boulevard.

Ritchie, R., jt. auth. see Galletly, G.

Ritchie, R. O. & Lankford, J., eds. Workshop on Small Fatigue Cracks: Proceedings of the Second Engineering Foundation International Conference. LC 86-19175. (Illus.). 677p. reprint ed. pap. 180.00 (*0-318-39700-5*, 2052268) Bks Demand.

Ritchie, Ralph W. All That's Practical about Wood: Stoves, As a Fuel, Heating. (Illus.). 136p. (Orig.). 1992. pap. 9.95 (*0-939656-11-6*) Ritchie Unltd.

— Earthquake Handbook for Active Senior Citizens. (Emergency Procedures Ser.). 1994. pap. 7.50 (*0-939656-16-7*) Ritchie Unltd.

— Emergency Procedures for Country Living. (Emergency Procedures Ser.). 76p. (Orig.). 1993. pap. 19.95 (*0-939656-13-2*) Ritchie Unltd.

— Emergency Procedures for the Small Business & Shop. LC 95-92212. 90p. (Orig.). 1995. pap. 19.95 (*0-939656-19-1*) Ritchie Unltd.

— Emergency Procedures for Urban Living. (Emergency Procedures Ser.). 93p. (Orig.). 1993. pap. 19.95 (*0-939656-14-0*) Ritchie Unltd.

— First Aid for Disaster Stress Trauma Victims: A Guide & Self-Help Manual for the Lay Person Treating Disaster Stress Trauma Victims. LC 95-92032. (Emergency Procedures Ser.). 81p. (Orig.). 1995. pap. 11.95 (*0-939656-18-3*) Ritchie Unltd.

— Free Heat: How to Conserve, Recover & Re-Use Heat over & Over. (Illus.). 152p. (Orig.). 1993. pap. 11.95 (*0-939656-12-4*) Ritchie Unltd.

— How to Find & Benefit from a "Passive Solor Collector" As a Space Heater. Orig. Title: Solar Space Heating for Free Heat. (Illus.). 64p. (Orig.). 1993. pap. 14.95 (*0-939656-15-9*) Ritchie Unltd.

— How to Lift & Move Almost Anything: For Almost Anyone Who Finds the Need to Move Heavy, Bulky, or Massive Objects. 2nd ed. (Illus.). 64p. 1991. pap. 9.95 (*0-939656-10-8*) Ritchie Unltd.

— How to Make the Best Use of Fuels for Heating: A Guide to Efficient Combustion in Kilns & Furnaces. LC 95-92031. (Energy Conservation Ser.). (Illus.). 69p. (Orig.). 1994. pap. 9.95 (*0-939656-17-5*) Ritchie Unltd.

— Solar Energy Owner's Guide, No. 1. (Energy & Ecology "Do It" Bks.). (Illus.). 100p. (Orig.). 1981. pap. 6.00 (*0-939656-07-8*) Ritchie Unltd.

— Understanding & Using Burners. LC 81-90072. (Energy Conservation in the Crafts - Craft Monograph Ser.: No. 4). (Illus.). 60p. (Orig.). 1981. pap. 6.00 (*0-939656-03-5*) Ritchie Unltd.

— User's Fuel Handbook. LC 81-90075. (Energy Conservation in the Crafts - Craft Monograph Ser.: No. 7). (Illus.). (Orig.). 1981. pap. 6.00 (*0-939656-06-X*) Ritchie Unltd.

Ritchie, Ralph W. & Ritchie, Fern J. Electric Kiln Handbook, Vol. 6. LC 81-90074. (Energy Conservation in the Crafts - Craft Monograph Ser.). (Illus.). 60p. (Orig.). 1981. pap. 6.00 (*0-939656-05-1*) Ritchie Unltd.

— What? A Touch of Humor for Those Who Need or Wear Hearing Aids. (Illus.). 60p. (Orig.). 1992. pap. 9.95 (*0-939656-08-6*) Ritchie Unltd.

Ritchie, Rita. Mountain Gorillas in Danger. LC 91-10831. (Animal World Ser.). (Illus.). 32p. (J). (gr. 2-3). 1991. lib. bdg. 17.27 (*0-8368-0447-3*) Gareth Stevens Inc.

Ritchie, Rita, adapt. The Emperor's New Clothes. (Golden Sound Story Book - Classics Ser.). 20p. (J). (ps up). 1992. write for info. (*0-307-74704-2*) Western Pub.

— The Princess & the Pea. (Golden Sound Story Book - Classics Ser.). 20p. (J). (ps up). 1992. write for info. (*0-307-74702-6*, 64702) Western Pub.

Ritchie, Rob, jt. auth. see Ataie, Iraj J.

Ritchie, Robert C. Captain Kidd & the War Against the Pirates. 320p. 1989. reprint ed. pap. text ed. 14.95 (*0-674-09502-2*) HUP.

— The Duke's Province 1664-1691: A Study of New York Politics & Society. fac. ed. LC 77-681. 318p. 1977. reprint ed. pap. 90.70 (*0-7837-8057-5*, 2047810) Bks Demand.

Ritchie, Robert F., ed. Automated Immunoanalysis, 2 pts., Pt. 1. LC 77-28836. (Clinical & Biochemical Analysis Ser.: No. 7). (Illus.). 349p. reprint ed. pap. 94.30 (*0-7837-0817-3*, 2041132) Bks Demand.

— Automated Immunoanalysis, 2 pts., Pt. 2. LC 77-28836. (Clinical & Biochemical Analysis Ser.: No. 7). (Illus.). 303p. reprint ed. pap. 86.40 (*0-7837-0818-1*) Bks Demand.

Ritchie, Robert L. The Normans in Scotland. LC 80-2216. reprint ed. 57.50 (*0-404-18783-8*) AMS Pr.

Ritchie, Robert W. The Hell-Roarin' Forty-Niners. 1992. reprint ed. lib. bdg. 75.00 (*0-7812-5080-3*) Rprt Serv.

***Ritchie, Ron.** Primary Design & Technology: A Process for Learning. 192p. 1995. pap. text ed. 23.00x (*1-85346-340-X*, Pub. by D Fulton UK) Taylor & Francis.

Ritchie, Ron, ed. Profiling in Primary Schools: A Handbook for Teachers. 176p. 1992. spiral bd. 40.00 (*0-304-32450-7*) Cassell.

Ritchie, Ron, jt. auth. see Ollerenshaw, Chris.

***Ritchie, Roy.** Standard Guide to Razors. 1995. pap. 9.95 (*0-89145-658-9*) Collector Bks.

Ritchie, Sheila, ed. Modern Library Practice: A Manual & Textbook. 1982. 60.00 (*0-9505828-5-9*, Pub. by Elm Pubns UK) St Mut.

Ritchie, Sheri & Lavranos, Destini. Goodnight Little Reindeer. (Illus.). 2p. (J). (ps-00). 1993. 14.95 (*0-9638393-1-4*) Bedtime Bks.

Ritchie, Sheri, jt. auth. see Lavranos, Destini.

***Ritchie, Tony.** Dry Fly-Fishing for Trout. (Illus.). 80p. 1994. 25.95 (*0-86417-622-8*) Seven Hills Bk.

— Finding Feeding Trout. (Illus.). 48p. (Orig.). 1995. pap. 13.95 (*0-86417-632-5*) Seven Hills Bk.

Ritchie, Tori, ed. see Hizer, Cynthia.

Ritchie, Tori, ed. see Worthington, Diane R.

Ritchie, Tori, ed. see Worthington, Diane R. & Williams, Chuck.

Ritchie, W. & Stern, V., eds. Telecommunications Local Networks. 500p. 1992. 79.95 (*0-442-30883-3*) Chapman & Hall.

Ritchie, W. F. & Ritchie, J. N. Celtic Warriors. 1989. pap. 25.00 (*0-85263-714-4*, Pub. by Shire UK) St Mut.

Ritchie, Wallace. Advice to Violin Students. 110p. 1991. reprint ed. lib. bdg. 69.00 (*0-7812-9353-7*) Rprt Serv.

— Chats with Violinists. 112p. 1991. reprint ed. lib. bdg. 69.00 (*0-7812-9361-8*) Rprt Serv.

Ritchie, Ward. A Concise Account of Ward Ritchie: His Printing & His Books. (Illus.). ix, 55p. 1984. 30.00 (*0-87093-183-0*) Dawsons.

— Fine Printers: The New Generation in Southern California. (Illus.). 1988. pap. 15.00 (*0-929722-22-1*) CA State Library Fndtn.

— Fine Printing: The Los Angeles Tradition. LC 86-600279. 65p. 1987. 20.00 (*0-8444-0541-8*) Lib Congress.

— Growing up with Lawrence Clark Powell. 18p. 1987. pap. 3.95 (*0-929722-15-9*) CA State Library Fndtn.

— Jake Zeitlin. (Santa Susana Press Ser.). 1978. pap. 15.00 (*0-937048-20-8*) CSUN.

— The Mystique of Printing: A Half Century of Books Designed by Ward Ritchie. 30p. 1984. pap. 2.50 (*0-929722-00-0*) CA State Library Fndtn.

— Of Book Men & Printers - A Gathering of Memories. 189p. 1989. 50.00 (*0-87093-275-6*) Dawsons.

Ritchie, Ward, ed. see Powell, Lawrence C.

Ritchie, William. Surveying & Mapping for Field Scientists. 180p. 1988. pap. text ed. 49.95 (*0-470-20846-5*) Wiley.

Ritchie, William A. The Archaeology of New York State. LC 94-12299. 357p. 1994. pap. 25.00 (*0-935796-52-5*) Purple Mnt Pr.

Ritchie, William C., ed. Second Language Acquisition Research: Issues & Implications. (Perspectives in Neurolinguistics & Psycholinguistics Ser.). 1978. text ed. 54.00 (*0-12-589550-X*) Acad Pr.

***Ritchie, William C. & Bhatia, Tej K., eds.** Handbook of Language Acquisition Vol. 2: Second Language Acquisition. (Illus.). 588p. 1995. boxed write for info. (*0-12-589042-7*) Acad Pr.

Ritchie, William C. & Slack, Lee L. The Nature & Study of Language: A Course Manual. 2nd ed. 116p. (C). 1994. 22.95 (*0-8403-9232-X*) Kendall-Hunt.

Ritchik, Yu, jt. auth. see Zlydnev, V.

Ritchin, Fred. In Our Own Image: The Coming Revolution in Photography: How Computer Technology Is Changing Our View of the World. (Writers & Artists on Photography Ser.). (Illus.). 158p. (C). 1990. 35.00 (*0-89381-398-2*); pap. 15.95 (*0-89381-399-0*) Aperture.

Ritchin, Fred, jt. ed. see Naggar, Carole.

Ritchings, Joan D. Eva the Fair. LC 81-48147. (Illus.). 700p. 1982. 65.00 (*0-9608078-0-2*) Gray Moose.

— Welcome, Jesus! 20p. 1988. pap. 5.00 (*0-9608078-1-0*) Gray Moose.

***Ritchken.** Derivative Markets. (C). 1995. text ed. 63.50 (*0-673-46017-7*) HarpCollege.

Ritchken, Peter H. Options: Theory, Strategy, & Applications. (C). 1987. pap. text ed. 39.50 (*0-673-18307-6*) HarpCollege.

Ritchken, Peter H., et al. Portfolio Risk Management: A Computer Simulation for Stock & Options. (Illus.). (C). 1989. pap. text ed. 41.95 (*0-201-06498-7*) Addison-Wesley.

Ritchre, Elisavietta, ed. The Dolphin's Arc: Poems on Endangered Creatures of the Sea. LC 89-60251. (SCOP Ser.: No. 12). 166p. 1989. pap. 10.95 (*0-930526-11-2*) Signal Bks.

Ritenbaugh & Meyskens, Jr. Analysis of Dietary Associations of Vitamin A with Cancer. 1989. pap. 4.95 (*0-87983-456-0*) Keats.

Ritenour. Computer Applications in Diagnostic Radiology Institutions. 1985. 16.95 (*0-8016-1331-0*) Mosby Yr Bk.

— Computer Applications in Diagnostic Radiology Study. 1985. spiral bd. 19.95 (*0-8016-1351-5*) Mosby Yr Bk.

— Principles of Magnetic Resonance Imaging Instructo. 1985. spiral bd. 13.95 (*0-8016-4535-2*) Mosby Yr Bk.

— Principles of Magnetic Resonance Imaging, Lessons. 1985. 358.10 (*0-8016-4525-5*) Mosby Yr Bk.

— Principles of Magnetic Resonance Imaging-Student W. 1985. spiral bd. 13.95 (*0-8016-4532-8*) Mosby Yr Bk.

— Radiation Protection & Biology, Lesson 1 - What Is... 1985. 150.00 (*0-8016-4001-6*) Mosby Yr Bk.

— Radiation Protection & Biology, Lesson 2 - Radiation. 1985. 150.00 (*0-8016-4002-4*) Mosby Yr Bk.

— Radiation Protection & Biology, Lesson 3 - Principle. 1985. 150.00 (*0-8016-4003-2*) Mosby Yr Bk.

— Radiation Protection & Biology, Lesson 4 - Rad Prote... 1985. 150.00 (*0-8016-4004-0*) Mosby Yr Bk.

— Radiation Protection & Biology, Lesson 5 - Protection. 1985. 150.00 (*0-8016-4005-9*) Mosby Yr Bk.

— Radiation Protection & Biology Student Workbook. 1985. spiral bd. 16.95 (*0-8016-4013-X*) Mosby Yr Bk.

Ritenour, E. Russell, jt. auth. see Statkiewicz, Mary A.

Riter, Gerhard. The Corrupting Influence of Power. Pick, F. W., tr. LC 79-1641. 1980. reprint ed. 20.00 (*0-88355-944-7*) Hyperion Conn.

Riter, J. R. Exercises in Chemical Physics. 328p. 1972. text ed. 207.00 (*0-677-02350-2*) Gordon & Breach.

***Riter, Tim.** Deep Down: Getting Beyond Surface Christianity. LC 95-13606. 1995. pap. write for info. (*0-8423-1797-X*) Tyndale.

Ritger, Dick. Dick Ritger Academy: Coaches-Instructors' Manual. (Illus.). 68p. (C). 1987. write for info. (*0-318-63408-2*) R Ritger.

Ritger, Dick & Allen, George. The Complete Guide to Bowling Spares: The Encyclopedia of Spares. LC 78-68659. (Encyclopedia of Bowling Instruction Ser.: Vol. 3). (Illus.). 240p. (C). 1979. 17.95 (*0-933554-04-4*); pap. 12.95 (*0-933554-05-2*) Tech Ed Pub.

Ritger, Dick, jt. auth. see Allen, George.

Ritger, Paul D. & Rose, Nicholas J. Differential Equations with Applications. (International Series in Pure & Applied Physics). 1968. text ed. write for info. (*0-07-052945-0*) McGraw.

Ritholz, Jules & London, Barry. Tax Return Preparer's Liability. LC 85-147123. 25.00 (*0-13-885252-9*) P-H.

Ritholz, Sophie. Children's Behavior. 1966. 16.95 (*0-317-18406-7*) NCUP.

Ritley, M. R., jt. auth. see Borsch, Frederick H.

Ritman, Erik L., et al. Imaging Physiological Functions: Experience with the Dynamic Spatial Reconstructor. LC 84-18242. 318p. 1985. text ed. 69.50 (*0-275-91322-8*, C1322, Praeger Pubs) Greenwood.

Ritmeyer, Kathleen & Ritmeyer, Leen. Temple Mount: Reconstructing Herod's Temple Mount in Jerusalem. (Illus.). 30p. (Orig.). (C). 1990. pap. text ed. 7.95 (*0-9613089-1-5*) Biblical Arch Soc.

Ritmeyer, Leen, jt. auth. see Ritmeyer, Kathleen.

Ritner, Gary. Father's Liberation Ethics: A Holistic Ethical Advocacy for Active Nurturant Fathering. 306p. (Orig.). (C). 1992. lib. bdg. 46.00 (*0-8191-8465-9*); pap. text ed. 24.50 (*0-8191-8466-7*) U Pr of Amer.

Ritner, George. Bankruptcy, How to Avoid It, How to Use It. write for info. (*0-686-22992-4*) G Ritner.

Ritner, Robert K. The Mechanics of Ancient Egyptian Magical Practice. LC 92-61830. (Studies in Ancient Oriental Civilization: No. 54). (Illus.). xviii, 322p. 1992. pap. 45.00 (*0-918986-75-3*) Orientl Inst Pr IT.

Ritschel, W. A. Antacids & Other Drugs in Gastrointestinal Diseases. LC 84-6049. (Illus.). 189p. 1984. pap. text ed. 24.50 (*0-914768-42-5*) Drug Intell Pubns.

— Graphic Approach to Clinical Pharmacokinetics. 2nd ed. (Illus.). 89p. 1984. pap. text ed. 45.00 (*84-499-7575-1*) Drug Intell Pubns.

Ritschel, Wolfgang. GerontoKinetics. (Illus.). 225p. 1989. pap. 29.50 (*0-936923-15-6*) Telford Pr.

— GerontoKinetics: PharmacoKinetics of Drugs in the Elderly. 225p. 1989. 45.00 (*0-685-44558-5*); pap. write for info. (*0-936923-16-4*) Telford Pr.

Ritschel, Wolfgang A. Handbook of Basic Pharmacokinetics, Including Clinical Applications. 4th ed. LC 91-38402. (Illus.). 544p. 1994. pap. text ed. 36.00 (*0-914768-50-6*) Drug Intell Pubns.

Ritscher, Angelika V., tr. see Aeppli, Willi.

Ritschl, A. Prices & Production. (Contributions to Economics Ser.). (Illus.). v, 132p. 1989. pap. 27.90 (*0-387-50916-X*) Spr-Verlag.

Ritschl, Albrecht B. Three Essays. Hefner, Phillip, tr. & intro. by. LC 72-75654. 309p. reprint ed. pap. 88.10 (*0-685-15486-6*, 2026887) Bks Demand.

Ritschl, Dietrich, ed. see Barth, Karl.

Ritschl, Friedrich. Opuscula Philologica, 5 vols., Set. lxxxiv, 4122p. 1978. reprint ed. write for info. (*3-487-06642-4*, Pub. by Georg Olms GW) Lubrecht & Cramer.

Ritsema, jt. auth. see Karche.

Ritsema, jt. auth. see Karcher.

Ritsema, Robert Allen. A History of ASTA-First 25 Years. 4.00 (*0-318-18110-X*) Am String Tchrs.

Ritson, Christopher & Harvey, David, eds. The Common Agricultural Policy & the World Economy: Essays in Honour of Professor John Ashton. 340p. (C). 1991. text ed. 57.00 (*0-85198-688-9*) CAB Intl.

Ritson, Christopher, et al. The Food Consumer. LC 86-4092. 262p. 1987. text ed. 159.95 (*0-471-90984-X*) Wiley.

Ritson, Joseph. Ancient Songs & Ballads. 1972. 59.95 (*0-87968-631-6*) Gordon Pr.

— Cursory Criticism on the Edition of Shakespeare: Published by Edmond Malone Together with a Letter to the Rev. Richard Farmer, D.D. Relative to the Edition of Shakespeare, Published in 1790. 156p. 1970. reprint ed. 25.00 (*0-7146-2516-7*, Pub. by F Cass Pubs UK) Intl Spec Bk.

— Cursory Criticisms on the Edition of Shakespeare. Bd. with Letter to the Rev. Richard Farmer, D.D. Master of Emanuel College, Cambridge. LC 76-174322. LC 76-174322. reprint ed. 34.50 (*0-404-05338-6*) AMS Pr.

— Fairy Tales, Legends & Romances, Illustrating Shakespeare & Other Early English Writers. LC 70-174323. reprint ed. 52.50 (*0-404-05339-4*) AMS Pr.

— Remarks, Critical & Illustrative, on the Text & Notes of the Last Edition of Shakspeare. LC 73-174324. reprint ed. 32.50 (*0-404-05348-3*) AMS Pr.

— Scottish Songs, 2 vols. in 1. 2nd ed. LC 77-144573. reprint ed. 74.50 (*0-404-08688-8*) AMS Pr.

Ritson, Joseph & Malone, Edmond. Cursory Criticisms on the Edition of Shakespeare Published by Edmond Malone, & a Letter to the Rev. Richard Farmer. LC 70-96366. (Eighteenth Century Shakespeare Ser.: No. 20). 1970. reprint ed. 29.50 (*0-678-05132-1*) Kelley.

Ritson, Phil & Andrisani, John. Golf Your Way: A Comprehensive Instruction Manual by the Creator of the Bestselling "Video Encyclopedia of Golf" LC 92-52562. (Illus.). 288p. 1993. reprint ed. pap. 15.00 (*0-06-092436-5*, PL) HarpC.

Ritson, Robert J., jt. auth. see Hart, James E.

Ritsos, Yannis. Erotica. Friar, Kimon, tr. LC 82-17018. 96p. 1982. 13.50 (*0-937584-05-3*); pap. 6.95 (*0-937584-06-1*) Sachem Pr.

— Exile & Return. Keeley, Edmund, tr. (Selected Poems, 1967-1974 Ser.). 199p. 1985. pap. 8.50 (*0-88001-018-5*) Ecco Pr.

— The Fourth Dimension. Green, Peter & Bardsley, Beverly, trs. LC 92-27141. (Modern Greek Studies). (Illus.). 304p. (C). 1993. text ed. 45.00 (*0-691-06940-9*); pap. text ed. 14.95 (*0-691-02465-0*) Princeton U Pr.

— Monovasia & the Women of Monemvasia. Friar, Kimon & Myrsiades, Kostas, trs. LC 87-62280. 67p. 1988. 20.00 (*0-932963-04-8*) Nostos Bks.

— Scripture of the Blind. Friar, Kimon & Myrsiades, Kostas, trs. LC 78-14319. 277p. 1979. 42.50 (*0-8142-0298-5*) Ohio St U Pr.

— Yannis Ritsos: Selected Poems 1938-1988. Friar, Kimon & Myrsiades, Kostas, eds. Myrsiades, Kostas, tr. 1989. 30.00 (*0-918526-66-3*); pap. 15.00 (*0-918526-67-1*) BOA Edns.

Ritstein, Charles. Executive Guide to Computer Viruses. (Illus.). 60p. (Orig.). (C). 1993. pap. 32.95 (*1-56806-251-6*) Diane Pub.

Ritt, Joseph F. Integration in Finite Terms: Liouville's Theory of Elementary. LC 48-2225. 110p. reprint ed. pap. 31.40 (*0-317-08490-9*, 2050137) Bks Demand.

Ritt, Lawrence, jt. ed. see Bauer, Carol.

Ritt, Lawrence G., jt. ed. see Keller, Peter A.

Ritt, Michael J., Jr., ed. see Hill, Napoleon.

Ritt, Michael J., Jr., jt. auth. see Landers, Kirk.

Ritt, Morey, ed. Four-Hand Piano Music by Nineteenth-Century Masters. 1980. pap. 11.95 (*0-486-23860-1*) Dover.

Ritt, Nikolaus. Quantity Adjustment: Vowel Lengthening & Shortening in Early Middle English. (Studies in Linguistics: Supplementary Volumes). (Illus.). 224p. (C). 1995. 49.95 (*0-521-46232-0*) Cambridge U Pr.

Rittaler, Jan B., jt. auth. see Schmidt, Ingo L.

Rittberger, Volker, ed. International Regimes in East-West Politics. 256p. 1990. text ed. 49.00 (*0-86187-868-X*, Pub. by Pinter Pubs UK) St Martin.

Rittberger, Volker & Mayer, Peter, eds. Regime Theory & International Relations. (Illus.). 456p. 1993. 58.00 (*0-19-827783-0*) OUP.

Rittberger, Volker, ed. see Adcock, Fleur.

Rittelmeyer, Friedrich. Reincarnation. 164p. 1990. pap. 12.95 (*0-86315-515-4*, 1304, Pub. by Floris Books UK) Anthroposophic.

Rittenberg, Larry E. & Schwieger, Bradley J. Auditing. LC 93-72825. 1153p. (C). 1994. text ed. 68.00 (*0-03-029919-5*) Dryden Pr.

— Solutions Manual to Accompany Auditing. 644p. (C). 1993. 33.25 (*0-03-029918-7*) Dryden Pr.

R

Rittenberg, Larry E., et al. Audit & Control of End-User Computing. 188p. 1990. 45.00 (*0-89413-205-9*) Inst Inter Aud.

Rittenberg, Libby, jt. ed. see Katz, Bernard S.

***Rittenberg, Sidney & Bennett, Amanda.** The Man Who Stay Behind. LC 94-41606. 1995. pap. write for info. (*0-8248-1682-X*, Kolowalu Bk) UH Pr.

— The Man Who Stayed Behind. LC 93-6541. (Illus.). 512p. 1993. 25.00 (*0-671-73595-0*) S&S Trade.

Rittenberg, Stephen. Ethnicity, Nationalism, & the Pakhtuns: The Independence Movement in India's North-West Frontier Province. LC 84-70181. (Illus.). 286p. 1987. lib. bdg. 29.95 (*0-89089-277-6*) Carolina Acad Pr.

Rittenburg, J. H., ed. Development & Application of Immunoassay for Food Analysis. (Applied Food Science Ser.). 258p. 1990. 75.75 (*1-85166-403-3*) Elsevier.

***Rittenhouse.** CPT 1995. 1994. pap. text ed. 41.95 (*0-89970-651-7*) AMA.

— Ornamental & Figural Nutcrackers. 144p. 1992. pap. 16.95 (*0-89145-518-3*) Collector Bks.

Rittenhouse, Ardis, jt. auth. see Rittenhouse, Rohn.

***Rittenhouse, Caroline S., ed.** Like Good Steel: The China Letters of Margaret Bailey Speer, North China, 1925-1943. LC 94-26488. 1994. write for info. (*1-882275-05-5*) Rnd Table Pr.

***Rittenhouse, Don & Rittenhouse, Jane.** You Are the Light of the World. (Illus.). 24p. (J). (ps-5). Date not set. pap. 4.00 (*0-9646494-0-3*) Memor-Eyes.

Rittenhouse, J. D. Maverick Tales: True Stories of Early Texas. 20.95 (*0-89190-867-6*, Am Repr) Amereon Ltd.

Rittenhouse, Jack D. A Guide Book to Highway Sixty-Six. LC 89-4807. (Illus.). 131p. 1989. reprint ed. pap. 7.95 (*0-8263-1148-2*) U of NM Pr.

— Trail of Commerce & Conquest: A Brief History of the Road to Santa Fe. (Illus.). 30p. (Orig.). 1987. pap. 1.95 (*0-938463-03-9*) Western Bks.

Rittenhouse, Jane, jt. auth. see Rittenhouse, Don.

Rittenhouse, Jessie B. Younger American Poets. LC 68-16971. (Essay Index Reprint Ser.). 1977. 23.95 (*0-8369-0826-0*) Ayer.

Rittenhouse, Jessie B., ed. Little Book of American Poets, Seventeen Eighty-Seven to Nineteen Hundred. LC 74-149110. (Granger Index Reprint Ser.). 1977. 29.95 (*0-8369-6235-4*) Ayer.

— Little Book of Modern British Verse. LC 78-149111. (Granger Index Reprint Ser.). 1977. 21.95 (*0-8369-6236-2*) Ayer.

— Little Book of Modern Verse. LC 71-149112. (Granger Index Reprint Ser.). 1977. 18.95 (*0-8369-6237-0*) Ayer.

— Second Book of Modern Verse. LC 75-149113. (Granger Index Reprint Ser.). 1977. 18.95 (*0-8369-6238-9*) Ayer.

— Third Book of Modern Verse. LC 79-149114. (Granger Index Reprint Ser.). 1977. 23.95 (*0-8369-6239-7*) Ayer.

Rittenhouse, Jessie B., jt. comp. see Scollard, Clinton.

Rittenhouse, Jessie B., jt. ed. see Scollard, Clinton.

Rittenhouse, Jonathan & Rose, Courtice G., eds. Journal of History & Politics (Journal d'Histoire et de Politique) Regionalism & Theory, Vol. IX, 1991. 176p. 1992. 79.95 (*0-685-56668-4*) E Mellen.

Rittenhouse, Mignon. Amazing Nellie Bly. LC 74-148227. (Biography Index Reprint Ser.). 1977. 20.95 (*0-8369-8074-3*) Ayer.

***Rittenhouse, Norman & Jeremiah.** Gods in the Making: The New Solar System. 2nd ed. (Illus.). 307p. 1995. reprint ed. pap. 14.95 (*0-9639053-2-5*) Univ Truth Pr.

***Rittenhouse, Rohn & Rittenhouse, Ardis.** When Time Stood Still. 210p. (Orig.). Date not set. pap. 8.95 (*0-7610-0365-7*) NW Pub.

Rittenhouse, Stan. For Fear of the Jews. LC 81-68608. (Illus.). 258p. 1982. 11.00 (*0-9609260-0-3*) Exhorters.

***Ritter.** Fifty-Two Opening Talks for Children. (J). 1995. pap. 7.99 (*0-570-04688-2*) Concordia.

— Lively Art of Theatre. pap. 25.95 (*0-8087-4686-3*) Burgess MN Intl.

— Neuroanatomy & Physiology of Abdominal Vagal Afferents. 1992. 103.95 (*0-8493-8881-3*, QM471) CRC Pr.

Ritter, Adolf M., jt. ed. see Heil, Gunther.

Ritter, Alan, ed. see Rousseau, Jean-Jacques.

Ritter, Alexander, ed. Supplement Series - Materialien und Dokumente, 9 vols., Set. 760p. 1993. reprint ed. write for info. (*3-487-09316-2*, Pub. by Georg Olms GW) Lubrecht & Cramer.

***Ritter, Archibald R. & Kirk, John M., eds.** Cuba in the International System: Normalization & Integration. LC 95-1328. (International Political Economy Ser.). 1995. write for info. (*0-312-12653-0*) St Martin.

Ritter, Archibald R. & Pollock, David H., eds. Latin American Prospects for the 1980's: Equity, Democratization & Development. LC 82-18039. 344p. 1983. text ed. 59.95 (*0-275-91064-4*, C1064, Praeger Pubs) Greenwood.

Ritter, Archibald R., et al, eds. Latin America in the Year Two Thousand: Reactivating Growth, Improving Equity, Sustaining Democracy. LC 91-22939. 280p. 1992. text ed. 55.00 (*0-275-93747-X*, C3747, Praeger Pubs) Greenwood.

Ritter, Beverly L. Computer-Compatible Machine Shorthand for Expanding Careers: Basic Theory, Vol. I. (Computer-Compatible Machine Shorthand for Expanding Careers Ser.). 204p. (C). 1986. student ed 5.00 (*0-938643-05-3*); teacher ed 20.00 (*0-938643-00-2*) Stenotype Educ.

— Computer-Compatible Machine Shorthand for Expanding Careers: Basic Theory, Vol. I. rev. ed. (Computer-Compatible Machine Shorthand for Expanding Careers Ser.). 204p. (C). 1986. pap. text ed. 24.00 (*0-938643-01-0*) Stenotype Educ.

— Professional Dictionary. (Computer-Compatible Machine Shorthand for Expanding Careers Ser.). 270p. (Orig.). 1987. pap. text ed. 27.00 (*0-938643-12-6*) Stenotype Educ.

Ritter, Beverly L., ed. Computer-Compatible Machine Shorthand for Expanding Careers: Student Dictionary. rev. ed. 216p. (C). 1986. pap. text ed. 16.00 (*0-938643-02-9*) Stenotype Educ.

Ritter, Beverly L. & Davis, Kim C. Vocabulary Sampler. rev. ed. (Computer-Compatible Machine Shorthand for Expanding Careers Ser.). 116p. (C). 1986. teacher ed 10.00 (*0-938643-08-8*); pap. text ed. 14.00 (*0-938643-06-1*) Stenotype Educ.

Ritter, Beverly L. & LaBorde, Michael. Reporter on the Job, Vol. III. (Computer-Compatible Machine Shorthand for Expanding Careers Ser.). 166p. (C). 1986. teacher ed 15.00 (*0-938643-11-8*) Stenotype Educ.

— Reporter on the Job, Vol. III. rev. ed. (Computer-Compatible Machine Shorthand for Expanding Careers Ser.). 166p. (C). 1986. pap. text ed. 27.00 (*0-938643-09-6*) Stenotype Educ.

Ritter, Beverly L. & Sharber, Steven W. Reverse Dictionary. (Computer-Compatible Machine Shorthand for Expanding Careers Ser.). 225p. (Orig.). 1987. pap. text ed. 24.00 (*0-938643-13-4*) Stenotype Educ.

Ritter, Beverly L., ed. see Floyd, Sally & Mathias, Dot.

Ritter, Beverly L., ed. see Mathias, Dot & Floyd, Sally.

Ritter, Charles & Wakelyn, Jon L. American Legislative Leaders, 1850-1910, Vol. 2. Broussard, James H. et al, eds. LC 88-24734. 1156p. 1989. text ed. 155.00 (*0-313-23943-6*, BLL02, Greenwood Pr) Greenwood.

Ritter, Constantin. Bibliographies on Plato. LC 78-66617. (Ancient Philosophy Ser.). 906p. 1980. lib. bdg. 29.00 (*0-8240-9590-1*) Garland.

— Neue Untersuchungen Uber Platon. LC 75-13289. (History of Ideas in Ancient Greece Ser.). (GER.). 1976. reprint ed. 31.95 (*0-405-07332-1*) Ayer.

— Platon: Sein Leben, Seine Schriften, Seine Lehre, 2 vols., 1. LC 75-13291. (History of Ideas in Ancient Greece Ser.). (GER.). 1976. reprint ed. 51.95 (*0-405-07334-8*) Ayer.

— Platon: Sein Leben, Seine Schriften, Seine Lehre, 2 vols., 2. LC 75-13291. (History of Ideas in Ancient Greece Ser.). (GER.). 1976. reprint ed. 51.95 (*0-405-07335-6*) Ayer.

— Platon: Sein Leben, Seine Schriften, Seine Lehre, 2 vols., Set. LC 75-13291. (History of Ideas in Ancient Greece Ser.). (GER.). 1976. reprint ed. 101.95 (*0-405-07333-X*) Ayer.

— Die Quintilianischen Declamationen. xii, 275p. 1967. reprint ed. write for info. (*0-318-71217-2*, Pub. by Georg Olms GW) Lubrecht & Cramer.

Ritter, Dale F. Process Geomorphology. 2nd ed. 592p. (C). 1985. text ed. write for info. (*0-697-05047-5*) Wm C Brown Pubs.

Ritter, Dale F. & Kochel, R. Craig. Process Geomorphology. 3rd ed. 560p. (C). 1994. pap. text ed. write for info. (*0-697-07632-6*) Wm C Brown Pubs.

Ritter, Darlene M. The Letters of Louise Ritter from 1893-1925. (Illus.). 178p. (Orig.). (C). 1980. pap. 10.00 (*0-9609372-0-X*) Siegenthaler-Ritter.

***Ritter, Dorothea.** Venice in Old Photographs Vol. 1: 1841-1920. (Illus.). 208p. 1994. 35.00 (*0-8212-2127-2*) Bulfinch Pr.

Ritter, Dwight. Cross-Selling Financial Services. LC 87-37282. 220p. 1988. text ed. 55.00 (*0-471-63275-9*) Wiley.

***Ritter, Dwight S.** Cross-Selling Toolkit: The Complete Guide to Cross-Selling Financial Products & Services. 250p. 1994. 24.95 (*1-55738-717-6*) Probus Pub Co.

— Relationship Banking: Cross Selling the Banks Products & Services to Meet Your Customers. 1993. 32.50 (*1-55738-381-2*) Probus Pub Co.

Ritter, E. A. Shaka Zula. (Nonfiction Ser.). 416p. 1985. pap. 11.00 (*0-14-004826-X*, Penguin Bks) Viking Penguin.

— Shaka Zulu: The Rise of the Zulu Empire. 412p. 1990. 35.00 (*0-947898-99-9*, 5588) Stackpole.

Ritter, Ed, jt. auth. see Biasiotto, Judd.

Ritter, Eldon. Know Your Monthly Payments, Before You Buy, Borrow or Lend. 317p. 1992. pap. text ed. 14.95 (*0-934739-06-4*) Pussywillow Pub.

Ritter, Ellen M., jt. ed. see Arntzen, Charles J.

Ritter, Ernst, jt. ed. see International Council on Archives Staff.

Ritter, Erwin F. Johann Baptist von Alxinger & the Austrian Enlightenment. (European University Studies: German Language & Literature: Ser. 1, Vol. 34). 176p. 1970. pap. 14.30 (*3-261-00033-3*) P Lang Pubs.

Ritter, Fanny R., ed. see Schumann, Robert.

Ritter, Frank N. & Fritsch, Michael H. Atlas of Paranasal Sinus Surgery. LC 91-7018. (Illus.). 296p. 1992. 110.00 (*0-89640-194-4*) Igaku-Shoin.

Ritter, G. X., ed. Information Processing 'Eighty-Nine: Proceedings of the IFIP 11th World Computer Congress, San Francisco, CA, 28 Aug. to 1 Sept., 1989. (IFIP Congress Ser.: No. 11). 1230p. 1989. 151.50 (*0-444-88015-1*, North Holland) Elsevier.

Ritter, Gerhard. Frederick the Great: A Historical Profile. Paret, Peter, tr. & intro. by. 268p. 1968. pap. 12.00 (*0-520-02775-2*) U CA Pr.

— German Resistance. Clark, R. T., tr. LC 74-124253. (Select Bibliographies Reprint Ser.). 1977. 29.95 (*0-8369-5441-6*) Ayer.

— Luther: His Life & Work. Riches, John, tr. LC 78-2717. 256p. 1978. reprint ed. text ed. 35.00 (*0-313-20347-4*, RILU, Greenwood Pr) Greenwood.

Ritter, Gerhard & Hart, B. Liddell. The Schlieffen Plan, Critique of a Myth. LC 78-9962. (Illus.). 195p. 1979. reprint ed. text ed. 35.00 (*0-313-20757-7*, RISCH, Greenwood Pr) Greenwood.

Ritter, Harry. Alaska's History: The People, Land, & Events of the North Country. LC 92-38364. (Illus.). 144p. 1993. pap. 10.95 (*0-88240-432-6*) Alaska Northwest.

— Dictionary of Concepts in History. LC 85-27305. (Reference Sources for the Social Sciences & Humanities Ser.: No. 3). 511p. 1986. text ed. 75.00 (*0-313-22700-4*, RCH/, Greenwood Pr) Greenwood.

Ritter, Hartien & Bell, Carol, eds. First Families of Ohio Roster. 2nd ed. 1989. 17.00 (*0-935057-58-7*) OH Genealogical.

Ritter, Hartien S. History of the Ohio Genealogical Society, 1959-1984. 1984. 2.50 (*0-935057-09-9*) OH Genealogical.

Ritter, Helge, et al. Neural Networks: An Introduction to the Neural Information Process of Self-Organized Networks. (Computation & Neural Systems Ser.). 300p. (C). 1992. text ed. 46.25 (*0-201-55443-7*, Adv Bk Prog); pap. text ed. 29.25 (*0-201-55442-9*, Adv Bk Prog) Addison-Wesley.

Ritter, Irene. Cobbler Crusade. LC 92-12019. (Illus.). 144p. (Orig.). 1992. pap. 9.95 (*1-55561-044-7*) Fisher Bks.

— Dolce Memories: An American Rediscovery of Italian Desserts. LC 94-37123. 1995. 12.95 (*1-55561-070-6*) Fisher Bks.

Ritter, J. Representation Theory & Number Theory in Connection with the Local Langlands Conjecture. LC 88-39030. (CONM Ser.: Vol. 86). 266p. 1992. pap. 36.00 (*0-8218-5093-8*, CONM-86) Am Math.

Ritter, Jim, tr. see Cartan, Elie.

Ritter, John E., ed. Erosion of Ceramic Materials. 220p. 1992. text ed. 74.00 (*0-87849-637-8*, Pub. by Trans Tech GW) LPS Dist Ctr.

Ritter, Judith, jt. ed. see Wholey, Mary L.

Ritter, Jurgen, jt. ed. see Frey, Gerhard.

Ritter, K. Comparative Geography of Palestine & the Sinaitic Peninsula, 4 Vols, Set, Vol. 1. LC 68-26367. (Reference Ser.: No. 44). 721p. 1969. reprint ed. Set. lib. bdg. 159.95 (*0-8383-0180-0*) M S G Haskell Hse.

Ritter, K., jt. ed. see Korte, B.

Ritter, Karl. Comparative Geography. LC 77-174325. reprint ed. 39.50 (*0-404-05349-1*) AMS Pr.

— The Comparative Geography of Palestine, 4 vols., Set. 1865. 65.00 (*0-403-03564-3*) Scholarly.

— Comparative Geography of Palestine & the Sinaitic Peninsula, 4 vols. Gage, William L., tr. LC 69-10151. 1969. reprint ed. Set. text ed. 195.00 (*0-8371-9946-8*, RISP) Greenwood.

— Comparative Geography of Palestine & the Sinaitic Peninsula, 4 vols., 1. Gage, William L., tr. LC 69-10151. 1971. reprint ed. lib. bdg. 19.50 (*0-685-02003-7*) Greenwood.

— The Comparative Geography of Palestine & the Sinaitic Peninsula, 4 vols., Set. LC 69-10151. (Illus.). 1969. text ed. 65.00 (*0-8371-0638-9*, RISP, Greenwood Pr) Greenwood.

— Comparative Geography of Palestine & the Sinaitic Peninsula, 4 vols., Vol. 2. Gage, William L., tr. LC 69-10151. 1969. reprint ed. text ed. 65.00 (*0-8371-0838-1*, RISB) Greenwood.

— Comparative Geography of Palestine & the Sinaitic Peninsula, 4 vols., Vol. 3. Gage, William L., tr. LC 69-10151. 1969. reprint ed. text ed. 65.00 (*0-8371-0839-X*, RISC) Greenwood.

— Comparative Geography of Palestine & the Sinaitic Peninsula, 4 vols., Vol. 4. Gage, William L., tr. LC 69-10151. 1969. reprint ed. text ed. 65.00 (*0-8371-0840-3*, RISD) Greenwood.

Ritter, Kathleen, jt. auth. see O'Neill, Craig.

Ritter, Kurt & Henry, David. Ronald Reagan: The Great Communicator. LC 91-28148. (Great American Orators: Critical Studies, Speeches & Sources: No. 13). 224p. 1992. text ed. 45.00 (*0-313-26069-9*, HRR/, Greenwood Pr) Greenwood.

Ritter, Lawrence S. The Glory of Their Times: The Story of the Early Days of Baseball Told by the Men Who Played It. (Illus.). 384p. 1992. pap. 10.00 (*0-688-11273-0*, Quill) Morrow.

— Lost Ballparks: A Celebration of Baseball's Legendary Fields. (Illus.). 224p. 1994. pap. 16.95 (*0-14-023422-5*) Studio Bks.

— Lost Ballparks: A Celebration of Baseballs' Legendary Fields. (Illus.). 224p. 1992. 30.00 (*0-670-83811-X*, Viking) Viking Penguin.

— The Negro Leagues. LC 94-17512. (Illus.). 40p. (J). (gr. 2 up). 1995. 15.00 (*0-688-13316-9*); lib. bdg. 14.93 (*0-688-13317-7*) Morrow Jr Bks.

Ritter, Lawrence S. & Honig, Donald. Image of Their Greatness: An Illustrated History of Baseball from 1900 to the Present. 448p. 1992. pap. 15.00 (*0-517-58728-9*, Crown) Crown Pub Group.

— The Image of Their Greatness: An Illustrated History of Baseball from 1900 to the Present. rev. ed. (Illus.). 1984. 24.95 (*0-517-55422-4*, Crown) Crown Pub Group.

Ritter, Lawrence S. & Silber, William L. Money. rev. ed. LC 83-45252. 316p. 1984. pap. text ed. 15.00 (*0-465-04722-X*) Basic.

— Principles of Money, Banking & Financial Markets. 6th ed. LC 88-47759. 672p. 1988. teacher ed write for info. (*0-465-06352-7*) Basic.

— Principles of Money, Banking, & Financial Markets. 8th ed. LC 93-14741. (C). 1993. 64.50 (*0-465-06367-5*) Basic.

Ritter, Lennart, et al. EEC Competition Law: A Practitioners' Guide. 1200p. 1991. 185.00 (*90-6544-465-3*) Kluwer Law Tax Pubs.

Ritter, M. & Crisp, N. The Thymus: In Focus. (In Focus Ser.). (Illus.). 80p. (C). 1992. pap. text ed. 13.95 (*0-19-963144-1*, IRL Pr) OUP.

Ritter, M. A., jt. ed. see Kendall, M. D.

Ritter, Mark, tr. see Beck, Ulrich & Beck-Gernsheim, Elisabeth.

Ritter, Mark, tr. see Beck, Ulrick.

Ritter, Mark A., tr. see Beck, Ulrich.

Ritter, Marnie. Embroidery My Way: For Fabric & Canvas. (Illus.). 82p. (Orig.). 1993. pap. text ed. write for info. (*0-9635593-1-1*) Marnies Crewel.

— Marnie Ritter's Canvas Patterns Bk. 2. 109p. 1992. pap. text ed. 27.95 (*0-9635593-0-3*) Marnies Crewel.

— Marnie Ritter's Canvas Patterns Bk. 2. 101p. 1994. pap. text ed. 28.00 (*0-9635593-2-X*) Marnies Crewel.

Ritter, Mary, ed. see Reider, Barbara.

Ritter, Mary A. & Ladyman, Heather M., eds. Monoclonal Antibodies: Production, Engineering & Clinical Application. (Postgraduate Medical Science Ser.: No. 3). (Illus.). 500p. (C). 1995. 110.00 (*0-521-47354-3*) Cambridge U Pr.

— Monoclonal Antibodies: Production, Engineering & Clinical Application. (Postgraduate Medical Science Ser.: No. 2). (Illus.). 500p. (C). 1995. pap. 39.95 (*0-521-42503-4*) Cambridge U Pr.

Ritter, Merrill A. & Albohm, Marjorie J. Your Injury: A Common Sense Guide to Sports Injuries. (Illus.). 188p. 1987. spiral bd. write for info. (*0-697-14824-6*) Brown & Benchmark.

— Your Injury: A Common Sense Guide to Sports Injuries. LC 94-16249. (Illus.). 192p. 1994. reprint ed. pap. 14.95 (*1-57028-011-8*) Masters Pr IN.

Ritter, Merrill A. & Gosling, Craig. The Knee: A Guide to the Examination & Diagnosis of Ligament Injuries. (Illus.). 32p. 1979. spiral bd. 11.95x (*0-398-03901-1*) C C Thomas.

Ritter, Naomi. Art As Spectacle: Images of the Entertainer since Romanticism. LC 89-4844. (Illus.). 360p. 1989. text ed. 35.00 (*0-8262-0719-7*) U of Mo Pr.

Ritter, O. & Fattorusso, V. Atlas der Elektrokardiographie. 5th ed. 1976. 39.25 (*3-8055-2416-1*) S Karger.

Ritter, Otto, jt. auth. see Fattorusso, V.

Ritter, Paul. Concrete Fit for People. LC 79-40711. 1981. 57.00 (*0-08-024671-0*, Pub. by Pergamon Repr UK) Franklin.

— Educreation: Education for Creation, Growth & Change. 2nd ed. 1979. 184.00 (*0-08-021475-4*, Pub. by Pergamon Repr UK) Franklin.

Ritter, Robert. Problems in Engineering Drawing Using CADKEY. 224p. 1992. pap. 19.95 (*0-8273-5212-3*) Delmar.

Ritter, Robert C., et al, eds. Feeding Behavior: Neural & Humoral Controls. 357p. 1986. text ed. 99.00 (*0-12-589060-5*) Acad Pr.

Ritter, Thomas J. Say No to Circumcision! Retaining His Birthright. (Illus.). 128p. 1992. pap. 10.95 (*0-9630482-0-1*) Hourglass Bk.

Ritter, Ulrich. Grundwortschatz Wirtschaftswissenschaftlicher. 5th ed. 272p. (ENG & GER.). 1991. lib. bdg. 39.95 (*0-8288-3891-7*, M15083) Fr & Eur.

Ritter, Ulrich & Zinn, K. G. Grundwortschatz Wirtschaftswissenschaftlicher Begriffe. 4th ed. 231p. (ENG & GER.). 1987. 29.95 (*0-8288-0101-0*, M15083) Fr & Eur.

Ritter, W., jt. auth. see Gaillard, A. W.

Ritter-Walker, E., jt. ed. see Wurtman, R. J.

Ritter, William F., ed. Irrigation & Drainage. LC 91-21084. 821p. 1991. pap. text ed. 62.00 (*0-87262-811-6*) Am Soc Civil Eng.

Ritter, Zofia. Kuchina Amerykanska: American Cooking. (Illus.). 137p. (Orig.). (POL.). 1989. reprint ed. pap. 8.95 (*0-9617846-0-1*) Scorpio IL.

Ritterband, Paul & Kosmin, Barry A., eds. Contemporary Jewish Philanthropy in America. 250p. (C). 1991. lib. bdg. 52.00 (*0-8476-7647-1*) Rowman.

Ritterband, Paul & Wechsler, Harold S. Jewish Learning in American Universities: The First Century. LC 93-48233. (Modern Jewish Experience Ser.). 1994. 35.00 (*0-253-35039-5*) Ind U Pr.

Rittereiser, Robert & Geelan, John. Margin Regulations & Practices. 2nd ed. LC 83-11367. 1983. reprint ed. 29.95 (*0-13-557041-7*) NY Inst Finance.

Ritterman, Michele. Using Hypnosis in Family Therapy. LC 83-48162. (Jossey-Bass Social & Behavioral Science Ser.). 375p. reprint ed. pap. 106.90 (*0-7837-6525-8*, 2045637) Bks Demand.

Ritterman, Michelle. Hope under Siege: State Terror vs. Family Support in Chile. Tick, Edward, ed. (Frontiers in Psychotherapy Ser.). 304p. 1991. text ed. 45.00 (*0-89391-758-3*); pap. text ed. 19.95 (*0-89391-801-6*) Ablex Pub.

Rittershausen, Brian & Rittershausen, Wilma. Orchid Growing Illustrated. (Illus.). 160p. 1985. 29.95 (*0-7137-1365-8*, Pub. by Blandford Pr UK) Sterling.

— Orchids in Color. (Illus.). 176p. 1984. pap. 16.95 (*0-7137-1394-1*, Pub. by Blandford Pr UK) Sterling.

— Popular Orchids. 224p. 1982. 40.00 (*0-7223-0940-6*, Pub. by A H S Ltd UK) St Mut.

Rittershausen, Wilma, jt. auth. see Rittershausen, Brian.

Ritterskamp, James J. Purchasing Manager's Desk Book of Purchasing Law. 470p. 1987. 59.95 (*0-13-742115-X*, Busn) P-H.

— Purchasing Manager's Desk Book of Purchasing Law Supplement. 210p. 1990. pap. text ed. 35.00 (*0-13-739210-9*) P-H.

Ritterspoon, Gabor T., jt. ed. see Lampert, Nick.

Rittersporn, G. T. Simplifications Staliniennes et Complications Sovietiques. 384p. 1988. pap. text ed. 71.00 (*2-88124-223-5*) Gordon & Breach.

Ritthaler, Shelly. Dinosaurs Alive! 96p. (Orig.). (J). (gr. 2 up). 1994. pap. 3.50 (*0-380-77323-6*, Camelot Young) Avon.

— Dinosaurs for Lunch. 80p. (Orig.). (J). (gr. 2). 1993. pap. 3.50 (*0-380-76796-1*, Camelot Young) Avon.

— Dinosaurs Wild! 96p. (Orig.). (J). 1994. pap. 3.50 (*0-380-77322-8*, Camelot Young) Avon.

An Asterisk (*) at the beginning of an entry indicates that the title is appearing in BIP for the first time.

— The Ginger Jar. LC 90-91540. 92p. (Orig.). 1990. pap. 10.95 (*0-9625745-1-1*) Raven Creek Pr.

Ritti, R. Richard. The Ropes to Skip & the Ropes to Know: Studies in Organizational Behavior. 4th ed. 312p. 1993. Net. pap. text ed. write for info. (*0-471-58593-9*) Wiley.

Ritti, R. Richard & Funkhouser, G. Ray. Ropes to Skip & the Ropes to Know: Studies in Organizational Behavior. 3rd ed. LC 86-13330. 271p. 1987. Net. pap. text ed. write for info. (*0-471-81789-9*) Wiley.

Rittig, Falk R., jt. auth. see Ory, Robert L.

***Rittle, Nancy.** Mockery of Commitment. 210p. 1995. pap. 8.95 (*1-56901-739-5*) NW Pub.

Rittman, Bruce E., et al. In Situ Bioremediation. 2nd ed. LC 94-3867. (Illus.). 260p. 1994. 54.00 (*0-8155-1348-8*) Noyes.

Rittman, Sandra & Gonzalez, Jean. Effective Business Communication. 560p. (C). 1991. pap. 44.95 (*0-534-92557-X*) Intl Thomson.

Rittmayer, Jane F. Life, Time. 127p. reprint ed. pap. 36.20 (*0-317-26230-0*, 2055572) Bks Demand.

Rittmueller, Jean, jt. auth. see Koch, John T.

Rittner, jt. auth. see Ma.

Rittner, C. & Schneider, P. M., eds. Advances in Forensic Haemogenetics 4: 14th Congress of the International Society of Forensic Haemogenetics (Internationale Gesellschaft fur Forensische Hamogenetik e.V.) Mainz, September 18-21, 1991. (Illus.). 480p. 1992. pap. 68.00 (*0-387-55194-8*) Spr-Verlag.

Rittner, C., et al, eds. Proceedings of the Sixth Complement Genetics Workshop & Conference, Mainz, July 1989. (Illus.). vi, 142p. 1990. reprint ed. 104.00 (*3-8055-5342-0*) S Karger.

Rittner, Carol & Myers, Sondra. Courage to Care: Rescuers of Jews During the Holocaust. 176p. 1989. 35.00x (*0-8147-7397-4*); pap. 19.50 (*0-8147-7406-7*) NYU Pr.

Rittner, Carol & Roth, John K., eds. Different Voices: Women & the Holocaust. LC 92-28233. (Illus.). 384p. 1993. 25.95 (*1-55778-503-1*, Athena); pap. 18.95 (*1-55778-504-X*, Athena) Paragon Hse.

Rittner, Carol A. & Roth, John K., eds. Memory Offended: The Auschwitz Convent Controversy. LC 90-47333. 312p. 1991. text ed. 55.00 (*0-275-93606-6*, C3606, Praeger Pubs); pap. text ed. 17.95 (*0-275-93848-4*, B3848, Praeger Pubs) Greenwood.

Rittner, Debra, tr. see Kalechofsky, Roberta, ed.

Rittner, Don. EcoLinking: Everyone's Guide to Online Environmental Information. (Illus.). 368p. 1992. pap. 18.95 (*0-938151-35-5*) Peachpit Pr.

— Hello, Goodbye: Disappearing Artifacts & Landscapes of the Hudson & Mohawk Valley. (Illus.). 36p. (Orig.). 1989. pap. 21.00 (*0-685-29024-7*) Hardcopy News.

— Student's Online Sourcebook. 1993. pap. 19.95 (*1-56686-091-1*) Brady Compu Bks.

— USENET Starter Kit for Macintosh. (Illus.). 350p. (Orig.). 1995. pap. text ed. 25.00 (*1-56830-130-8*) Alpha Bks IN.

— The Whole Earth Online Almanac. LC 93-1950. 1993. pap. 32.95 (*1-56686-090-3*) Brady Compu Bks.

***Rittner, Roger.** Toltec's Tomb. (Read-along Radio Dramas Ser.). (YA). (gr. 6-11). Date not set. 35.00 (*0-614-04288-7*) Balance Pub.

— Traffic Incident. (Read-along Radio Dramas Ser.). (YA). (gr. 6-11). 1982. 35.00 (*1-878298-10-0*) Balance Pub.

Rittof, David J., jt. auth. see Baird, John E., Jr.

Ritton, Arthur S. Teach Yourself Arabic. (Teach Yourself Ser.). 1979. pap. 9.95 (*0-679-10164-0*) McKay.

Ritts, Blaine, jt. auth. see Leathers, Park.

***Ritts, Herb.** Africa Vol. 1. (Illus.). 136p. 1994. 75.00 (*0-8212-2121-3*) Bulfinch Pr.

— Duo. 64p. 1991. 45.00 (*0-944092-17-9*) Twin Palms Pub.

— Duo. limited ed. 64p. 1991. 150.00 (*0-944092-18-7*) Twin Palms Pub.

— Men - Women. (Illus.). 208p. 1989. 65.00 (*0-944092-11-X*) Twin Palms Pub.

— Notorious. LC 92-53227. (Illus.). 168p. 1992. 75.00 (*0-8212-1911-1*) Bulfinch Pr.

Ritts, Herb, photos. Herb Ritts: Pictures. (Illus.). 144p. 1988. 65.00 (*0-944092-01-2*) Twin Palms Pub.

Ritvo, Edward, jt. auth. see Katz, Illana.

Ritvo, Harriet. The Animal Estate: The English & Other Creatures in the Victorian Age. LC 87-11848. (Illus.). 368p. 1987. text ed. 38.00 (*0-674-03706-5*) HUP.

— The Animal Estate: The English & Other Creatures in the Victorian Age. (Illus.). 368p. 1989. reprint ed. pap. text ed. 12.95 (*0-674-03707-3*) HUP.

Ritvo, Harriet, jt. ed. see Arac, Jonathan.

Ritvo, Harriet, et al. An English Arcadia: Landscape & Architecture in Britain & America: Papers Delivered at a Huntington Symposium. LC 92-30971. (Illus.). 180p. (Orig.). 1992. pap. 20.00 (*0-87328-139-X*) Huntington Lib.

Ritvo, Ken & Kearsley, Greg. Desktop Publishing. rev. ed. LC 86-722. (Illus.). 216p. (Orig.). 1986. pap. 19.95 (*0-935749-10-1*) Park Row Pr.

Ritvo, Lucille B. Darwin's Influence on Freud: A Tale of Two Sciences. LC 89-16672. 272p. (C). 1990. text ed. 35.00 (*0-300-04131-4*) Yale U Pr.

— Darwin's Influence on Freud: A Tale of Two Sciences. 272p. (C). 1992. reprint ed. pap. text ed. 17.00 (*0-300-05262-6*) Yale U Pr.

Ritvo, Roger A., jt. ed. see Hokenstad, Merl C., Jr.

Ritvo, Roger A., ed. see Sargent, Alice G.

Ritvo, Roger A., et al, eds. Managing in the Age of Change: Essential Skills to Manage Today's Diverse Workplace. LC 94-9331. 324p. 1994. text ed. 25.00 (*0-7863-0303-4*) Irwin Prof Pubng.

Ritz, David. Barbells & Saxophones. 1990. 18.95 (*1-55611-158-4*) D I Fine.

— Blue Notes under a Green Felt Hat. 320p. 1989. 18.95 (*1-55611-130-4*) D I Fine.

— Divided Soul: The Life of Marvin Gaye. (Quality Paperbacks Ser.). (Illus.). 367p. 1991. reprint ed. pap. 13.95 (*0-306-80443-3*) Da Capo.

— Family Blood. 1991. 19.95 (*1-55611-176-2*) D I Fine.

— Family Blood. 448p. 1993. mass mkt. 4.99 (*0-8217-4058-X*) Zebra.

— Passion Flowers. LC 91-58659. 384p. 1992. 21.95 (*1-55611-283-1*) D I Fine.

— Passion Flowers. 1994. mass mkt. 4.99 (*0-312-95180-9*) St Martin.

— Ray Charles: Musician. LC 93-30224. (Great Achievers: Lives of the Physically Challenged Ser.). (Illus.). (J). 1994. 18.95 (*0-7910-2080-0*, Am Art Analog); pap. write for info. (*0-7910-2093-2*, Am Art Analog) Chelsea Hse.

— Take It Off, Take It All Off! LC 92-54987. 1993. 21.95 (*1-55611-366-8*) D I Fine.

Ritz, David, jt. auth. see Charles, Ray.

Ritz, David, jt. auth. see James, Etta.

Ritz, David, jt. auth. see Wexler, Jerry.

Ritz, E., ed. Issues in Gloerulonephritis & Renin System. (Contributions to Nephrology Ser.: Vol. 43). (Illus.). viii, 204p. 1984. 105.75 (*3-8055-3912-6*) S Karger.

Ritz, E. & Massry, S. G., eds. Pathophysiology of Renal Disease. (Contributions to Nephrology Ser.: Vol. 33). (Illus.). viii, 276p. 1982. pap. 125.75 (*3-8055-3534-1*) S Karger.

Ritz, E. & Schaefer, K., eds. Drug Therapy in Dialysis Patients. (Journal: Blood Purification: Vol. 3, Nos. 1-3, 1985). (Illus.). 168p. 1986. pap. 89.75 (*3-8055-4288-7*) S Karger.

Ritz, E., ed. see Heidelberg Seminars in Nephrology Staff.

***Ritz, Eberhard.** Mineral Metabolism. (Current Opinion in Nephrology & Hypertension Ser.). (Illus.). 480p. (Orig.). 1994. pap. text ed. 49.95 (*1-85922-615-9*) Current Science.

Ritz, Eberhard & Remuzzi, Giuseppe. Mineral Metabolism, Renal Pathophysiology. (Current Opinion in Nephrology & Hypertension Ser.). (Illus.). 170p. (Orig.). 1993. pap. 49.95 (*1-85922-004-5*) Current Science.

Ritz, George C. Total Engineering Project Management. (Engineering & Technology Management Ser.). 352p. 1990. text ed. 55.00 (*0-07-052966-3*) McGraw.

Ritz, George J. Total Construction Project Management. LC 93-27856. 1994. text ed. 49.00 (*0-07-052986-8*) McGraw.

Ritz, John, et al. Exploring Production Systems. (Illus.). 1991. teacher ed 13.81 (*0-87192-239-8*); text ed. 39.95 (*0-87192-205-3*) Delmar.

***Ritz, K., et al, eds.** Beyond the Biomass: Compositional & Functional Analysis of Soil Microbial Communities. 1994. text ed. 95.00 (*0-471-95096-3*) Wiley.

***Ritz, Norton D.** You & Your Blood: A Few Answers to Your Questions. 1995. pap. 10.95 (*0-533-11326-1*) Vantage.

Ritz, Paul S., ed. see Helms, Philip W.

Ritz, Richard E. An Architect Looks at Downtown Portland. 102p. 1991. pap. 19.95 (*0-9629661-1-8*) Greenhills.

— History of the Whitman College Campus & Its Buildings. 128p. 1992. 24.95 (*0-9632955-0-0*); 50.00 (*0-9632955-2-7*); pap. 15.95 (*0-9632955-1-9*) Whitman Coll.

Ritz, Stacy. Disney World & Beyond: The Ultimate Family Guidebook. 2nd ed. Riegert, Ray & Henriques, Leslie, eds. LC 93-60477. (Ultimate Guidebook Ser.). (Illus.). 300p. (Orig.). 1993. pap. 10.95 (*0-915233-92-4*) Ulysses Pr.

— Disney World & Beyond: The Ultimate Family Guidebook. 3rd ed. LC 95-60712. (Ultimate Travel Ser.). (Illus.). 312p. (Orig.). 1995. pap. 12.95 (*1-56975-042-4*) Ulysses Pr.

— Hidden Carolinas: The Adventurer's Guide. LC 94-61740. (Hidden Travel Ser.). (Illus.). 475p. (Orig.). 1995. pap. 14.95 (*1-56975-028-9*) Ulysses Pr.

— The New Key to Belize. Pearlman, Joanna, ed. LC 93-60746. (New Key Ser.). (Illus.). 228p. (Orig.). 1993. pap. 13.95 (*0-915233-93-2*) Ulysses Pr.

— The New Key to Belize. 2nd ed. LC 95-60710. (New Key Travel Ser.). (Illus.). 252p. (Orig.). 1995. pap. 14.95 (*1-56975-034-3*) Ulysses Pr.

Ritz, Stacy & Leslie, Candace. Hidden Florida: The Adventurer's Guide. 4th ed. Kahn, Judith, ed. LC 94-60465. (Hidden Travel Ser.). (Illus.). 528p. 1994. pap. 14.95 (*1-56975-020-3*) Ulysses Pr.

Ritz, Stacy & Olmstead, Marty. Florida's Gold Coast: The Ultimate Guidebook. Henriques, Leslie & Riegert, Ray, eds. LC 91-65702. (Ultimate Guidebook Ser.). (Illus.). 204p. 1992. pap. 8.95 (*0-915233-45-2*) Ulysses Pr.

Ritz, Stacy & Wade, Judy. Disneyland & Beyond: The Ultimate Family Guidebook. 2nd ed. LC 94-60058. (Ultimate Guidebook Ser.). (Illus.). 240p. 1994. pap. 9.95 (*1-56975-011-4*) Ulysses Pr.

Ritz, Stacy, jt. auth. see Harris, Richard.

Ritz, Susan. The Civil Rights Act of Nineteen Ninety-One: Its Impact on Employment Discrimination Litigation. (Litigation & Administrative Practice Ser.). 304p. 1992. pap. text ed. 70.00 (*0-685-56924-1*, H4-5127) PLI.

Ritz, Wilfred J. Rewriting the History of the Judiciary Act of 1789: Exposing Myths, Challenging Premises & Using New Evidence. Holt, Wythe & LaRue, L. H., eds. LC 89-37863. 288p. 1990. 32.95 (*0-8061-2239-0*) U of Okla Pr.

Ritz, Wilfred J., comp. American Judicial Proceedings First Printed Before 1801: An Analytical Bibliography. LC 83-18605. (Illus.). xlviii, 364p. 1984. text ed. 59.95 (*0-313-24057-4*, RAJ/, Greenwood Pr) Greenwood.

Ritzel, G., ed. Alkohol, Tabak und Drogen im Leben des jungen Mannes. (Sozialmedizinische und Paedagogische Jugendkunde Ser.: Band 14). (Illus.). 1976. 39.25 (*3-8055-2381-5*) S Karger.

Ritzel, G., ed. see Biener, K.

Ritzel, G., ed. see Mueller, Hans R.

Ritzel, Wolfgang. Immanuel Kant: Eine Biographie. xiv, 738p. (GER.). 1985. 161.55 (*3-11-010634-5*) De Gruyter.

Ritzen, Martin, ed. see Karolinska Institute Nobel Conference Staff.

Ritzenberg, Edna. The Pinballs: A Study Guide. (Novel-Ties Ser.). 1984. student ed, teacher ed 15.95 (*0-88122-090-6*) Lrn Links.

Ritzenburg, Edna. Sadako & the Thousand Paper Cranes: A Study Guide. (Novel-Ties Ser.). 1984. student ed, teacher ed 15.95 (*0-88122-062-0*) Lrn Links.

Ritzenthaler, Mary L., et al. Archives & Manuscripts: Administration of Photographic Collections. (Basic Manual Ser.). 176p. 1984. pap. text ed. 23.00 (*0-931828-61-9*) Soc Am Archivists.

Ritzenthaler, Mary L. Preserving Archives & Manuscripts. (Archival Fundamentals Ser.). 228p. 1993. 25.00 (*0-931828-94-5*) Soc Am Archivists.

Ritzenthaler, Pat, jt. auth. see Ritzenthaler, Robert.

Ritzenthaler, Robert & Ritzenthaler, Pat. The Woodland Indians of the Western Great Lakes. (Illus.). 160p. (C). 1991. reprint ed. pap. text ed. 9.50 (*0-88133-548-7*) Waveland Pr.

Ritzer, George. Classic Theory in Sociology. 1992. text ed. write for info. (*0-07-052972-8*) McGraw.

— Contemporary Sociological Theory. 3rd ed. 1992. text ed. write for info. (*0-07-052973-6*) McGraw.

— Expressing America: A Critique of the Global Credit Card Society. LC 94-38142. 1995. pap. write for info. (*0-8039-9044-8*) Pine Forge.

— Frontiers of Sociological Theory. 1991. pap. text ed. 20.50 (*0-231-07079-9*) Col U Pr.

— Frontiers of Sociological Theory: The New Synthesis. 320p. 1990. text ed. 52.00 (*0-231-07078-0*) Col U Pr.

— The McDonaldization of Society: An Investigation into the Changing Character of Contemporary Social Life. LC 92-17450. 240p. (Orig.). (C). 1992. pap. 13.95 (*0-8039-9000-6*) Pine Forge.

— Metatheorizing in Sociology. (Social Issues Ser.). 448p. 1991. text ed. 49.95 (*0-669-25008-2*) Free Pr.

— Social Problems. 2nd ed. (Illus.). 608p. (C). 1986. pap. text ed. write for info. (*0-07-554947-6*) McGraw.

— Sociological Beginnings for Beginners: On the Origins of Key Ideas in Sociology. LC 93-23915. 1993. pap. text ed. write for info. (*0-07-052974-4*) McGraw.

— Sociological Theory. 3rd ed. 1992. text ed. write for info. (*0-07-052971-X*) McGraw.

Ritzer, George, ed. Metatheorizing: A Coming of Age. (Key Issues in Sociological Theory Ser.: Vol. 6). (Illus.). 200p. (C). 1992. 48.00 (*0-8039-3990-6*); pap. 22.95 (*0-8039-3991-4*) Sage.

Ritzer, George & Trice, Harrison M. An Occupation in Conflict: A Study of the Personnel Manager. LC 76-627591. 140p. 1969. 5.00 (*0-87546-033-X*) ILR Pr.

Ritzer, George & Walczak, David. Working: Conflict & Change. 3rd ed. (Illus.). 448p. 1986. text ed. write for info. (*0-13-967589-2*) P-H.

Ritzer, George, jt. ed. see Calhoun, Craig.

Ritzer, George, jt. auth. see Vera, Hernan.

***Ritzer, Mariann.** An Evening on Mildred Street. 28p. 1995. pap. 6.00 (*0-9644333-0-3*) CrossplusRds.

Ritzman, Larry P., jt. auth. see Krajewski, Lee J.

Ritzman, Larry P., et al, eds. Disaggregation: Problems in Manufacturing & Service Organizations. 1979. lib. bdg. 96.00 (*0-89838-003-0*) Kluwer Ac.

Ritzman, Marlene, jt. auth. see Moffet, Stanley N.

Ritzmann, Carolyn T. Concentric Circles of Concern Study Guide. LC 88-36738. (Orig.). 1989. pap. 3.99 (*0-8054-6260-0*) Broadman.

Riu y Riu, M. Manual de Historia de Espana Vol. 2: Edad Media (711-1500) 644p. 1989. 125.00x (*84-239-5092-1*) Elliots Bks.

Riumin, A. A. Decorative Metal-Work of the Urals: Eighteenth to Nineteenth Centuries. 205p. 1982. 180.00 (*0-317-61253-0*, Pub. by Collets UK) Pro-Am Music.

Rius. Cuba for Beginners. (Documentary Comic Bks.). (Illus.). 1981. 6.95 (*0-906495-29-6*) Writers & Readers.

— Devilishness. (Diabluras: Un Libro de Todos Los Diablos Ser.). 70p. 1987. pap. 9.00 (*0-910309-50-7*, 5438) Am Atheist.

— Mao for Beginners. 1993. pap. 9.95 (*0-906386-07-1*) Writers & Readers.

— Marx for Beginners. LC 78-20422. 1989. pap. 11.00 (*0-679-72512-1*) McKay.

— The Myth of the Virgin of Guadalupe. Orig. Title: El Mito Guadalupano. 69p. 1988. pap. 9.00 (*0-910309-52-3*, 5439) Am Atheist.

Rius, Jorge. The Communist Manifesto in Cartoon Form. 3rd ed. Edelson, Morris, tr. (Illus.). reprint ed. pap. 1.50 (*0-9600306-1-1*) Quixote.

Rius, Maria & Parramon, J. M. The City. (Let's Discover Ser.). (J). (ps). 1986. 6.95 (*0-8120-5748-1*); pap. 3.95 (*0-8120-3700-6*) Barron.

— The Countryside. (Let's Discover Ser.). (J). (ps). 1986. 6.95 (*0-8120-5749-X*); pap. 6.95 (*0-8120-3701-4*) Barron.

— The Mountains. (Let's Discover Ser.). (J). (ps). 1986. 6.95 (*0-8120-5746-5*); 6.95 (*0-8120-3698-0*) Barron.

— The Seaside. (Let's Discover Ser.). (J). (ps). 1986. 6.95 (*0-8120-5747-3*); pap. 6.95 (*0-8120-3699-9*) Barron.

Rius, Maria & Parramon, Josep M. El Campo (Countryside) (Let's Discover Ser.). (Illus.). 32p. (SPA.). (J). (ps-1). 1986. pap. 6.95 (*0-8120-3750-2*) Barron.

— La Ciudad (City) (Let's Discover Ser.). 32p. (SPA.). (J). (ps-1). 1986. pap. 6.95 (*0-8120-3753-7*) Barron.

— El Mar (Seaside) (Let's Discover Ser.). 32p. (SPA.). (J). (ps). 1987. pap. 6.95 (*0-8120-3751-0*) Barron.

— La Montana (Mountains) (Let's Discover Ser.). 32p. (SPA.). (J). (ps-1). 1987. pap. 6.95 (*0-8120-3752-9*) Barron.

Rius, Maria, jt. auth. see Parramon, J. M.

RIUS Staff & Del Rio, Eduardo. Cuba for Beginners. LC 70-108717. 1993. reprint ed. lib. bdg. 40.00 (*0-87348-193-3*); reprint ed. pap. 12.95 (*0-87348-128-3*) Pathfinder NY.

Riuvolucci, Frank. Grammar in Action, Again: Awareness Activities for Language Learning. 2nd ed. 176p. 1991. pap. text ed. 19.50 (*0-13-362450-1*) P-H.

Riva, Alessandro & Motta, Pietro M., eds. Ultrastructure of the Extraparietal Glands of the Digestive Tract. (Electron Microscopy in Biology & Medicine Ser.). (C). 1989. lib. bdg. 164.50 (*0-7923-0303-2*) Kluwer Ac.

Riva, Alessandro, et al, eds. Ultrastructure of Male Urogenital Glands: Prostrate, Semial Vesicles, Urethral, & Bulbourethral Glands. LC 94-11636. (Electron Microscopy in Biology & Medicine Ser.: EMBM 11). 224p. (C). 1994. lib. bdg. 175.00 (*0-7923-2800-0*) Kluwer Ac.

***Riva, Anna.** Art of Domination. 32p. (Orig.). 1995. pap. text ed. 3.95 (*0-943832-23-3*) Intl Imports.

— Black & White Magic. 64p. (Orig.). 1994. pap. 4.50 (*0-943832-22-5*) Intl Imports.

— Candle Burning Magic. 96p. 1980. pap. 4.50 (*0-943832-06-3*) Intl Imports.

— Devotions to the Saints. 112p. 1982. pap. 4.50 (*0-943832-08-X*) Intl Imports.

— Enchantments. 180p. (Orig.). 1995. pap. text ed. 5.95 (*0-614-01211-2*) Intl Imports.

— Enchantments. 180p. (Orig.). 1995. pap. 5.95 (*0-943832-21-7*) Intl Imports.

— Golden Secrets of Mystic Oils Revised. 176p. (Orig.). 1990. pap. 5.95 (*0-943832-16-0*) Intl Imports.

— How to Conduct a Seance. rev. ed. 20p. 1994. pap. 2.95 (*0-943832-20-9*) Intl Imports.

— Magic with Incense & Powders. 128p. (Orig.). 1985. pap. 4.50 (*0-943832-11-X*) Intl Imports.

— Modern Herbal Spellbook. (Illus.). 64p. 1974. pap. 4.50 (*0-943832-03-9*) Intl Imports.

— Modern Witchcraft Spellbook. (Illus.). 64p. (Orig.). 1973. pap. 4.50 (*0-943832-02-0*) Intl Imports.

— Powers of the Psalms. 128p. (Orig.). 1982. pap. 4.50 (*0-943832-07-1*) Intl Imports.

— Secrets of Magical Seals. (Illus.). 64p. 1975. pap. 4.50 (*0-943832-04-7*) Intl Imports.

— Six Lessons in Crystal Gazing. 28p. (Orig.). 1993. pap. text ed. 2.95 (*0-943832-18-7*) Intl Imports.

— Spellcraft, Hexcraft & Witchcraft. (Illus.). 64p. 1977. pap. 4.50 (*0-943832-00-4*) Intl Imports.

— Voodoo Handbook of Cult Secrets. (Illus.). 48p. 1974. pap. 3.95 (*0-943832-01-2*) Intl Imports.

— Your Lucky Number Forever. 108p. (Orig.). 1993. pap. text ed. 4.95 (*0-943832-17-9*) Intl Imports.

Riva, Anna, et al, eds. Prayer Book. 128p. (Orig.). 1984. pap. 4.50 (*0-943832-09-8*) Intl Imports.

Riva, Douglas. Far from the Maddening Crowd. 1990. pap. 14.95 (*0-943748-30-5*) Ekay Music.

Riva, Emma & Hearse, David J. The Developing Myocardium. (Illus.). 144p. 1991. 30.00 (*0-87993-513-8*) Futura Pub.

Riva, Joseph P., Jr. Exploration Opportunities in Latin America. 288p. 1992. 64.95 (*0-87814-371-8*, P4502) PennWell Bks.

Riva, Joseph P. Petroleum Exploration Opportunities in the Former Soviet Union. LC 94-201. 316p. 1994. 64.95 (*0-87814-414-5*, P4524) PennWell Bks.

Riva, Maria. Marlene Dietrich. 800p. 1994. pap. 14.00 (*0-345-38645-0*, Ballantine Trade) Ballantine.

— Marlene Dietrich. 1994. pap. 9.99 (*0-517-13075-0*) Random.

Riva, Maria E. Marlene Dietrich. 1993. 29.00 (*0-679-42209-9*) Random.

— Marlene Dietrich. 1993. 29.00 (*0-679-74670-6*) Random.

Riva, Peter & Hitchcock, Barbara. Sightseeing: A Space Panorama. LC 85-40347. (Illus.). 120p. 1985. 24.95 (*0-394-54243-6*) Knopf.

Rivadue, Barry. Alice Faye: A Bio-Bibliography. LC 89-25631. (Bibliographies & Indexes in the Performing Arts Ser.: No. 10). 240p. 1990. text ed. 42.95 (*0-313-26525-9*, RVA/, Greenwood Pr) Greenwood.

— Lee Remick: A Bio-Bibliography. LC 95-12421. (Bio-Biographies in the Performing Arts Ser.: Vol. 64). 256p. 1995. text ed. 49.95 (*0-313-28447-4*, Greenwood Pr) Greenwood.

— Mary Martin: A Bio-Bibliography. LC 91-16233. (Bio-Bibliographies in the Performing Arts Ser.: No. 18). 272p. 1991. text ed. 39.95 (*0-313-27345-6*, RMF, Greenwood Pr) Greenwood.

***Rivage-Seul, D. Michael & Rivage-Seul, Marguerite K.** Imagining a New Earth Order: Changing Paradigms. LC 95-3341. 1995. text ed. write for info. (*0-275-95201-0*, Praeger Pubs) Greenwood.

Rivage-Seul, Marguerite K., jt. auth. see Rivage-Seul, D. Michael.

Rivail, Hippolytel., see Allan Kardec, pseud..

Rivail, J. L., ed. Modelling of Molecular Structures & Properties: Proceedings of the 44th International Meeting of Physical Chemistry & Biophysics, Organized by the Division de Chimie Physique of the Societe Francaise de Chimie, Nancy, France, 11-15 September, 1989. (Studies in Physical & Theoretical Chemistry: No. 71). 788p. 1990. 269.25 (*0-444-88714-8*) Elsevier.

Rivail, Jean-Louis, jt. ed. see Bernardi, Francesco.

Rival. Combinatorics & Ordered Sets. LC 86-8006. (Contemporary Mathematics Ser.: Vol. 57). 285p. 1986. pap. text ed. 38.00 (*0-8218-5051-2*, CONM-57) Am Math.

***Rival, Andre.** Self Images: 100 Women. 152p. 1995. 49.95 (*3-905514-45-1*) Dist Art Pubs.

Rival, Ivan. Algorithms & Order. (C). 1988. lib. bdg. 165.50 (*0-7923-0007-6*) Kluwer Ac.

Rival, Ivan, ed. Graphs & Order: The Role of Graphs in the Theory of Ordered Sets & Its Applications. 1985. lib. bdg. 217.50 (*90-277-1943-8*) Kluwer Ac.

— Ordered Sets. 1982. lib. bdg. 229.50 (*90-277-1396-0*) Kluwer Ac.

Rivard, David. Torque. LC 88-2167. (Poetry Ser.). 61p. (Orig.). 1988. 19.95 (*0-8229-3595-3*); pap. 10.95 (*0-8229-5410-9*) U of Pittsburgh Pr.

Rivard, Denis, ed. Ozone Layer Dictionary. (Orig.). 1993. pap. 48.05 (*0-660-58897-8*, Pub. by Canada Commun Grp CN) Accents Pubns.

Rivard, Paul E. Lion: The History of an Eighteen Forty-Six Locomotive Engine in Maine. (Business & Technology Ser.). (Illus.). 64p. 1987. pap. text ed. 7.50 (*0-913764-19-1*, Univ Pub Assocs) Maine St Mus.

Rivas, jt. auth. see Toseland.

Rivas, Alfredo M., ed. see Pietri, Pedro.

Rivas, Ana M. Asentamientos Indigenas en el Valle de la Laguna. 197p. 1987. 8.50 (*0-685-75379-4*) UPLAAP.

Rivas, Bob, jt. auth. see Toseland, Ronald.

Rivas De Jara, Orquidea, ed. see Aleshire, Daniel O.

Rivas de Jara, Orquidea, tr. see Aleshire, Daniel O.

Rivas, Duque de. Don Alvaro O la Fuerza del Sino. Ruiz Silva, Carlos, ed. (Nueva Austral Ser.: Vol. 162). (SPA.). 1991. pap. text ed. 17.95 (*84-239-1962-5*) Elliots Bks.

Rivas, Edelberto T., jt. ed. see Flora, Jan L.

Rivas, Jose G., tr. see Torrey, R. A.

Rivas, Yolanda, tr. see Rogovin, Janice.

Rivasseau, Vincent. From Perturbative to Constructive Renormalization. Anderson, Philip W. et al, eds. (Physics Ser.). (Illus.). 337p. 1991. text ed. 52.50 (*0-691-08530-7*) Princeton U Pr.

***Rivasseau, Vincent, ed.** Constructive Physics: Results in Field Theory, Statistical Mechanics & Condensed Matter Physics: Proceedings of the Conference Held at Palaiseau, France 25-27 July 1994. LC 95-12155. (Lecture Notes in Physics Ser.: Vol. 446). 1995. write for info. (*3-540-59190-7*) Spr-Verlag.

Rive, Richard. Advance, Retreat: Selected Short Stories. 131p. 1989. 19.95 (*0-312-03689-2*) St Martin.

— Advance, Retreat: Selected Short Stories. (Illus.). 128p. 1990. pap. 10.95 (*0-312-04772-X*) St Martin.

— Emergency Continued. 1991. 18.95 (*0-930523-87-3*); pap. 10.95 (*0-930523-88-1*) Readers Intl.

— Writing Black: An Author's Notebook. 240p. 1990. 14.95 (*0-908396-40-6*, Pub. by D Philip SA) Interlink Pub.

Rive, Richard & Couzens, Tim. Seme: The Founder of the ANC. LC 91-78313. 100p. 1992. 29.95 (*0-86543-312-7*); pap. 9.95 (*0-86543-313-5*) Africa World.

Rive, Richard, ed. see Schreiner, Olive.

Rivele, Stephen J., jt. auth. see Ramsey, Edwin P.

Rivelles, V. O., jt. auth. see Peboli, O. J.

Rivelli, Pauline & Levin, Robert, eds. Giants of Black Music. LC 79-27194. (Quality Paperbacks Ser.). 1980. reprint ed. pap. 7.95 (*0-306-80119-1*) Da Capo.

— Giants of Rock Music. LC 81-9685. (Quality Paperbacks Ser.). (Illus.). 125p. 1981. reprint ed. pap. 7.95 (*0-306-80148-5*) Da Capo.

Rivello, Robert M. Theory & Analysis of Flight Structures. LC 68-25662. (C). 1968. text ed. write for info. (*0-07-052985-X*) McGraw.

River, Chatham. Animal Antics ABC's. (Fun with Words Ser.). 48p. (J). 1990. 4.99 (*0-517-68881-6*) Random Hse Value.

— Animal Fun: A-Z Activity Books. 32p. (J). 1989. 3.50 (*0-517-68796-8*) Random Hse Value.

— Around the House. (Fun with Words Ser.). 48p. 1990. 4.99 (*0-517-68880-8*) Random Hse Value.

— Make a Pinocchio String Puppet. (Make a Model Ser.). (J). 1990. 4.99 (*0-517-69513-8*) Random Hse Value.

River Junction Poets. Poems of the River Junction: Anthology, 1991. Schmidt, Rosemary J., ed. 1991. 10.00 (*0-9628611-5-4*) Blue Denim.

River Oaks Garden Club Staff, ed. A Garden Book for Houston & the Gulf Coast. 4th ed. 448p. 1989. 27.50 (*0-88415-350-9*) Gulf Pub.

Rivera, jt. auth. see Tapia, Alejandro.

Rivera, A. Ramon & Gruenbaum, Thelma. To Music & Children with Love! Reflections for Parents & Teachers. 133p. (C). 1979. pap. 6.95 (*0-936190-03-5*) ExPressAll.

***Rivera, Andres.** La Revolucion es un Sueno Eterno. 1995. 12.50 (*0-679-76335-X*, Vin) Random.

***Rivera, Angel Q.** Workers' Struggle in Puerto Rico: A Documentary History. Belfrage, Cedric, tr. LC 76-40343. reprint ed. pap. 67.30 (*0-7837-9615-3*, 2060372) Bks Demand.

***Rivera-Batiz, Francisco L.** Reinventing Urban Education: Multiculturalism & the Social Context of Schooling. 300p. (C). 1994. pap. write for info. (*0-9638459-0-X*) IUME Pr.

Rivera-Batiz, Francisco L. & Rivera-Batiz, Luis. International Finance & Open Economy Macroeconomics. 2nd ed. (Illus.). 699p. (C). 1994. text ed. write for info. (*0-02-400581-9*) Macmillan.

Rivera-Batiz, Francisco L., et al, eds. U. S. Immigration Policy Reform in the 1980s: A Preliminary Assessment. LC 90-7377. 160p. 1991. text ed. 42.95 (*0-275-93620-1*, C3620, Praeger Pubs) Greenwood.

Rivera-Batiz, Luis, jt. auth. see Rivera-Batiz, Francisco L.

***Rivera, Beatriz.** African Passions. LC 94-36017. 168p. (Orig.). 1995. pap. 19.95 (*1-55885-135-6*) Arte Publico.

***Rivera, Benito V.** German Music Theory in the Early 17th Century: The Treatises of Johannes Lippius. 264p. (C). 1995. reprint ed. text ed. 39.00 (*1-878822-60-8*) Univ Rochester Pr.

Rivera, Benito V., tr. see Burmeister, Joachim.

Rivera, Benito V., jt. ed. see Mathiesen, Thomas J.

Rivera, Carlos & Eastman, P. D., trs. Are You My Mother? (Spanish Beginner Bks.: No. 4). (ENG & SPA.). (J). (gr. 2-4). 1967. 8.95 (*0-394-81596-3*) Random Bks Yng Read.

Rivera, Carlos, tr. see Dr. Seuss.

Rivera, Carlos, tr. see Palmer, Helen.

***Rivera, Catherine, ed.** CL Programming: An Introduction. (FastStart Ser.). (Illus.). 185p. (Orig.). 1994. pap. 59.00 (*1-884322-31-X*) Comp Applicatns.

Rivera, Charlene, ed. Communicative Competence Approaches to Language Proficiency Assessment: Research & Application. 150p. 1984. 74.00 (*0-905028-22-8*, Pub. by Multilingual Matters UK); pap. 25.00 (*0-905028-21-X*, Pub. by Multilingual Matters UK) Taylor & Francis.

— An Ethnographic-Sociolinguistic Approach to Language Assessment. 140p. 1983. 69.00 (*0-905028-20-1*, Pub. by Multilingual Matters UK); pap. 24.00 (*0-905028-19-8*, Pub. by Multilingual Matters UK) Taylor & Francis.

Rivera, Christine. Excel for Windows Insider. 1994. pap. 26.95 (*0-471-30432-8*) Wiley.

— Excel 4 for Windows Insider. 544p. 1992. pap. text ed. 26.95 (*0-471-57987-4*) Wiley.

— Signature: Wiley Command Reference. 352p. 1992. pap. text ed. 12.95 (*0-471-55818-4*) Wiley.

Rivera, David T. Love of an Eagle. 1994. 10.00 (*0-533-10778-4*) Vantage.

Rivera De Figueroa, Carmen A. Architecture for the Tropics: A Bibliographical Synthesis (from the Beginnings to 1972) LC 77-26261. (Illus.). 203p. 1980. pap. 12.00 (*0-8477-2107-8*) U of PR Pr.

Rivera de Hernandez, Hilda. Biologia Moderna: Serie de Modulos Para Laboratorio Primer Semestre. 2nd rev. ed. 265p. (C). 1991. 19.95 (*1-881375-07-2*) Libreria Univ.

— Biologia Moderna: Serie de Modulos Para Laboratorio Segundo Semestre. 291p. (C). 1991. 19.95 (*1-881375-08-0*) Libreria Univ.

Rivera De Otero, Consuelo. Mass Communication Services: An Analysis (Puerto Rican Government: Radio, Television, & Community Education) LC 76-2025. 153p. (Orig.). 1976. pap. 5.00 (*0-8477-2731-9*) U of PR Pr.

***Rivera, Diana.** Bird Language. LC 93-30723. 114p. 1994. 10.00 (*0-927534-41-X*) Biling Rev-Pr.

Rivera, Diane M., jt. auth. see Smith, Deborah D.

Rivera, Diego. My Art, My Life: An Autobiography (with Gladys March) (Illus.). 224p. 1992. reprint ed. pap. 6.95 (*0-486-26938-8*) Dover.

Rivera, Edward. Family Installments: Memories of Growing up Hispanic. 300p. 1983. pap. 11.95 (*0-14-006726-4*, Penguin Bks) Viking Penguin.

Rivera, Elena, ed. The Wait. 40p. 1994. 12.00 (*0-9632085-4-3*) Em Pr.

Rivera, Feliciano, jt. ed. see Meier, Matt S.

Rivera, Felix, et al, eds. Julida de Burgos (1914-1953) (Puerto Rican Bibliographies Ser.). 25p. (C). 1986. reprint ed. pap. 1.00 (*1-878483-41-2*) Hunter Coll CEP.

***Rivera, Felix G. & Erlich, John L., eds.** Community Organizing in a Diverse Society. 2nd ed. LC 94-26040. 1995. pap. text ed. write for info. (*0-205-15620-7*) Allyn.

Rivera, Fernando L. Personalidades del Pesebre. (Illus.). (Orig.). (SPA.). 1992. pap. 9.99 (*0-8272-2943-7*) Chalice Pr.

Rivera, Francisco P. & Hurtado, Mario. Introduccion a la Literatura Espanola. (C). (gr. 11-12). 1976. pap. text ed. 9.95 (*0-88345-437-8*) Prentice ESL.

Rivera, Francisco P., et al. Introductionn a la Literatura Espanola. 1987. pap. text ed. 21.30 (*0-13-477225-3*) Prentice ESL.

Rivera, Frank. Construcciones. LC 79-92418. (Senda Poetica Ser.). 55p. (Orig.). (SPA.). 1979. pap. 3.95 (*0-918454-19-0*) Senda Nueva.

— Cuentos Cubanos. LC 92-73682. (Coleccion Caniqui Ser.). (Illus.). 75p. (Orig.). (SPA.). 1992. pap. 9.95 (*0-89729-653-2*) Ediciones.

***Rivera, G. & Colle, M. P.** Las Fiestas de Frida. 1994. 35.00 (*0-517-70044-1*, Crown) Crown Pub Group.

Rivera, Garcia I. Dictionary of Legal Terms. 704p. (ENG & SPA.). 1985. 75.00 (*0-8288-7956-7*, F36820) Fr & Eur.

Rivera, Gladys, ed. see De Mena, Juan.

***Rivera Gonzalez, Melitina.** Mi Diccionario: Primera Coleccion de Palabras-Educacion Primaria, Primer Ciclo. (Illus.). 223p. (SPA.). 1992. pap. 49.50 (*84-207-4697-5*) Elliots Bks.

— Mi Diccionario, 2: Educacion Primaria, 8-12 Anos. (Illus.). 479p. (SPA.). 1993. pap. 69.50 (*84-207-5003-4*) Elliots Bks.

Rivera, Guadalupe & Colle, Marie-Pierre. Frida's Fiestas: Recipes & Recollections of Life with Frida Kahlo. Krabbenhoft, Kenneth & Rigsby, Olga, trs. LC 93-19284. (Illus.). 1994. 35.00 (*0-517-59235-5*, C P Pubs) Crown Pub Group.

Rivera, Guadalupe, jt. auth. see Miller, Carol.

Rivera, Guillermo, tr. see Cano, Fray A.

Rivera, Guillermo, tr. see De Avendano y Loyola, Fray A.

Rivera, Hector J. Introduccion a la Moneda y la Banca. LC 76-967. 292p. 1975. pap. 5.00 (*0-8477-2625-8*) U of PR Pr.

Rivera, Ignacio. Diccionario de Terminos Juridicos. 2nd ed. 1987. write for info. (*0-318-62483-4*) Equity Pubng NH.

— Eficiencia en el Bufete. (SPA.). 1987. write for info. (*0-318-62484-2*) Equity Pubng NH.

— Manual para la Secretaria Legal. (SPA.). 1987. 16.00 (*0-685-19453-1*) Equity Pubng NH.

— Manual Paralegal. 1987. 20.00 (*0-685-19454-X*) Equity Pubng NH.

Rivera, Illeana, jt. auth. see Colon, Doris E.

Rivera, J. Cilia Ciliated Epithelium Ciliary Activity. LC 61-14245. 1962. 79.00 (*0-08-009623-9*, Pub. by Pergamon Repr UK) Franklin.

Rivera, Jose. Marisol. 1994. 4.75 (*0-8222-1374-5*) Dramatists Play.

Rivera, Juan M. Letters to Jesus. 128p. (Orig.). 1990. pap. 9.99 (*0-8272-2121-5*) Chalice Pr.

— Poemas de la Nieve Negra. LC 84-62597. (Serie de Poesia Guampara: No. 3). 96p. (Orig.). (SPA.). 1985. pap. text ed. 5.95 (*0-910235-09-0*) Prisma Bks.

Rivera, Louis R. Who Pays the Cost. (Illus.). 40p. (Orig.). 1977. pap. 2.00 (*0-917886-03-8*) Shamal Bks.

Rivera, Louis R., ed. see Ismaili, Rashidah, et al.

Rivera, Louis R., ed. see Killens, John O.

Rivera, Louis R., et al. Poets in Motion. (Illus.). (Orig.). 1976. pap. text ed. 3.00 (*0-917886-00-3*) Shamal Bks.

Rivera-Lugo, Carlos, jt. auth. see Garcia-Passalacqua, Juan M.

Rivera, Luis M. Complete Works of Luis Munoz Rivera, 9 vols., Set. (Puerto Rico Ser.). 1979. lib. bdg. 1,350.00 (*0-8490-2896-5*) Gordon Pr.

Rivera, Luis N. A Violent Evangelism: The Political & Religious Conquest of the Americas. Herrera, Marina, tr. 352p. (Orig.). 1992. pap. 19.99 (*0-664-25367-9*) Westminster John Knox.

Rivera, Mario. Facing Unresolved Conflicts. LC 92-64448. 224p. (Orig.). 1992. pap. 8.95 (*0-89221-230-6*) New Leaf.

Rivera, Mario A. Decision & Structure: U. S. Refugee Policy & the Mariel Crisis. 278p. (C). 1991. lib. bdg. 42.00 (*0-8191-8389-X*) U Pr of Amer.

Rivera, Mario E. Emotional Freedom. LC 92-81732. 128p. (Orig.). 1992. pap. 5.95 (*0-89221-225-X*) New Leaf.

Rivera, Mark A. & Jacquart, Joanne. Touched by the Father's Hand. 138p. (Orig.). 1991. pap. 9.95 (*0-9625097-2-8*) Stonecrest FL.

Rivera, Mary, tr. see Maguire, Majorie R. & Maguire, Daniel.

Rivera-Medina, Eduardo & Ramirez, Rafael L. Del Canaveral a la Fabrica: Cambio Social en Puerto Rico. LC 85-80187. (Huracan Academia Ser.). 152p. (SPA.). 1985. pap. 7.25 (*0-940238-78-0*) Ediciones Huracan.

Rivera, Miquela. Minority Career Book. 1991. pap. 9.95 (*1-55850-012-X*) Adams Pubng.

Rivera, Monte, jt. ed. see Jennings, James.

***Rivera, Nilda R. & Betancourt, Luz.** Disenos de Bordados: Para Bebe's. rev. ed. (Illus.). 60p. (SPA.). 1995. pap. text ed. write for info. (*1-879185-04-0*) Lubnir.

— Disenos de Letras. rev. ed. (Illus.). 60p. (SPA.). 1995. pap. text ed. write for info. (*1-879185-03-2*) Lubnir.

***Rivera, Nilda Rosa.** Programacion Estructurada, 4 Vol. Set, Vol. 1. (Illus.). 133p. (SPA.). (C). 1994. pap. text ed. write for info. (*1-879185-02-4*) CompuConsultants.

— Programacion Estructurada y Cobol, 4 vol. set. rev. ed. (Programacion Estructurada Ser.). (Illus.). 133p. (SPA.). 1994. pap. text ed. 19.95 (*1-879185-01-6*) CompuConsultants.

Rivera, Oswald. Fire & Rain: A Novel of Vietnam. LC 90-34078. 185p. 1990. 17.95 (*0-941423-41-7*) FWEW.

— Puerto Rican Cuisine in America: Nuyorican & Bodega Recipes. LC 92-41478. (Illus.). 300p. (Orig.). 1993. pap. 16.95 (*0-941423-84-0*) FWEW.

Rivera, Pedro A. Manos a la Obra: The Story Behind Operation Bootstrap. 25p. 1986. pap. 7.00 (*1-878483-18-8*) Hunter Coll CEP.

Rivera, Ralph & Nieto, Sonia, eds. The Education of Latino Students in Massachusetts: Issues, Research, & Policy Implications. LC 93-32148. 278p. (Orig.). 1994. pap. 17.95x (*0-87023-895-7*) U of Mass Pr.

Rivera Ramos, Efren. Pequeno Canto a los Mios (Poemario) LC 87-25562. 72p. 1987. pap. 5.00 (*0-8477-3236-3*) U of PR Pr.

Rivera, Rhonda, jt. auth. see Whaley, Douglas J.

***Rivera, Rick P.** A Fabricated Mexican. LC 94-33576. 160p. (Orig.). 1995. pap. 9.95 (*1-55885-130-5*) Arte Publico.

Rivera, Robert, jt. ed. see Cawley, Joan.

Rivera-Rodas, Oscar. El Metateatro y la Dramatica de Vargas Llosa: Hacia una Poetica del Espectador. LC 92-33765. (Purdue University Monographs in Romance Languages: Vol. 41). vii, 213p. 1992. 65.00x (*1-55619-310-6*); pap. 27.95x (*1-55619-311-4*) Benjamins North Am.

***Rivera, Sergio.** Neusa: 9,000 Anos de Presencia Humana en el Parmo. (Illus.). 144p. (SPA.). 1992. pap. 8.50 (*1-877812-28-5*) UPLAAP.

Rivera, Tomas. The Harvest - La Cosecha. Olivares, Julian, ed. & tr. by. LC 88-37945. 128p. (Orig.). 1990. pap. 9.50 (*0-934770-94-8*) Arte Publico.

— The Searchers: Collected Poetry. Olivares, Julian, ed. 1990. 7.00 (*1-55885-018-X*) Arte Publico.

— This Migrant Earth. Hinojosa, Rolando, tr. LC 85-73354. 160p. (Orig.). 1986. pap. 9.00 (*0-934770-55-7*) Arte Publico.

— Y No Se lo Trago la Tierra - And the Earth Did Not Devour Him. 3rd ed. Vigil, Evangelina, tr. LC 87-70275. 206p. (ENG & SPA.). 1991. 10.00 (*0-934770-72-7*) Arte Publico.

Rivera, Tulio D. Hechos y Legitimidades Cubanas: Un Planteamento. LC 86-82313. (Coleccion Cuba y Sus Jueces Ser.). 96p. (Orig.). (SPA.). 1987. pap. 6.00 (*0-89729-418-1*) Ediciones.

Rivera, W. M. Planning Adult Learning: Issues, Practices & Directions. 180p. (C). 1986. 33.00 (*0-7099-4224-9*, Pub. by Croom Helm UK) Routledge Chapman & Hall.

Rivera, W. M., ed. Agricultural Extension Worldwide: Factors for Success. (International Perspectives on Adult & Continuing Education Ser.). 272p. 1986. 35.00 (*0-7099-4238-9*, Pub. by Croom Helm UK) Routledge Chapman & Hall.

Rivera, William M., jt. ed. see Charters, Alexander N.

Rivere, Richard, ed. Loyalty & Security in a Democratic State. LC 75-54570. (Great Contemporary Issues Ser.). 1977. lib. bdg. 27.95 (*0-405-09864-2*) Ayer.

Rivero, Albert J. The Plays of Henry Fielding: A Critical Study of His Dramatic Career. LC 88-35304. 170p. 1989. text ed. 28.50 (*0-8139-1228-8*) U Pr of Va.

Rivero, Andres. Recuerdos. LC 80-66235. (Short Stories in Spanish Ser.). 80p. 1980. pap. 4.00 (*0-933648-02-2*) Cruzada Span Pubns.

— Somos Como Somos. LC 81-70535. (Short Stories in Spanish Ser.). 52p. (Orig.). 1982. pap. 3.00 (*0-933648-04-9*) Cruzada Span Pubns.

— Sorpresivamente. LC 01-67366. (Short Stories in Spanish Ser.). 80p. 1981. pap. 4.00 (*0-933648-03-0*) Cruzada Span Pubns.

Rivero, Eliana S., jt. ed. see Rebolledo, Tey D.

Rivero, N. M. Sosnosky: A Novella. 1992. 10.00 (*0-533-09648-0*) Vantage.

Rivero-Potter, Alicia. Autor-Lector: Huidobro, Borges, Fuentes y Sarduy. LC 90-37640. (Latin American Literature & Culture Ser.). 184p. (SPA.). (C). 1990. text ed. 29.95 (*0-8143-2226-3*) Wayne St U Pr.

Riverol, A. R. Live from Atlantic City: The History of the Miss America Pageant Before, After & in Spite of Television. LC 92-81612. (Illus.). (C). 1992. text ed. 24.95 (*0-87972-557-5*); pap. text ed. 12.95 (*0-87972-558-3*) Bowling Green Univ.

Riveros, F., jt. auth. see Skerman, P. J.

Riveros, Luis A., jt. ed. see Paredes, Ricardo.

Rivers, jt. auth. see Silverthistle.

Rivers, Alice, jt. auth. see Jenness, Aylette.

Rivers, Caryl. More Joy Than Rage: Crossing Generations with the New Feminism. LC 91-50373. 250p. 1991. 22.95 (*0-87451-562-9*) U Pr of New Eng.

Rivers, Christopher. Face Value: Physiognomical Thought & the Legible Body in Marivaux, Lavatar, Balzac, Gautier & Zola. LC 94-14586. (Illus.). 288p. 1994. 54.50 (*0-299-14390-2*); pap. 24.95 (*0-299-14394-5*) U of Wis Pr.

Rivers, Clayton P. Alcohol & Human Behavior: Theory, Research, & Practice. LC 93-33821. 1993. pap. text ed. write for info. (*0-13-019878-1*) P-H.

***Rivers, Dan.** Addiction & Sigmund Freud: Freud's Psychology Applied to Addiction. 350p. (Orig.). 1995. pap. 29.95 (*0-9644355-2-7*) Mercie Pub.

Rivers, David A., ed. see Bingelis, Tony.

Rivers, Diana. Daughters of the Great Star. 400p. (Orig.). 1992. pap. 9.95 (*1-55583-314-4*, Lace MA) Alyson Pubns.

— The Hadra. 350p. (Orig.). 1995. pap. 9.95 (*1-55583-319-5*, Lace MA) Alyson Pubns.

— Journey to Zelindar: The Personal Account of Sair of Semasi. 301p. 1992. reprint ed. pap. 9.95 (*1-55583-305-5*, Lace MA) Alyson Pubns.

Rivers, Earl, jt. tr. see Wydeville, A.

Rivers, Elias. Muses & Masks: Some Classical Genres of Spanish Poetry. Lathrop, Thomas et al, eds. (U. California, Irvine, Hispanic Studies: No. 1). 120p. 1992. 15.50 (*0-936388-53-6*) Juan de la Cuesta.

Rivers, Elias, ed. Things Done with Words: Speech Acts in Hispanic Drama. 158p. 1986. 15.00 (*0-936388-26-9*) Juan de la Cuesta.

Rivers, Elias, ed. see Lincoln, Victoria.

Rivers, Elias L. Quixotic Scriptures: Essays on the Texuality of Hispanic Literature. LC 82-49300. 176p. 1984. 25.00 (*0-253-34761-0*) Ind U Pr.

Rivers, Elias L., ed. Garcilaso de la Vega: Obras Completas con Comentario, Edicion Critica. 544p. 1974. 42.50 (*0-8142-0183-0*) Ohio St U Pr.

— Renaissance & Baroque Poetry of Spain. 351p. (C). 1988. reprint ed. pap. text ed. 13.95x (*0-88133-363-8*) Waveland Pr.

Rivers, Elias L., ed. see Alonso, Damaso.

***Rivers, Francine.** As Sure As the Dawn. LC 95-1034. (Mark of the Lion Ser.). 1995. 9.99 (*0-8423-3976-0*) Tyndale.

— An Echo in the Darkness. LC 94-5909. (Mark of the Lion Ser.: No. 2). 464p. 1994. pap. 11.99 (*0-8423-1307-9*) Tyndale.

— Redeeming Love. large type ed. LC 93-13563. 1993. 21.95 (*0-8161-5823-1*, Large Print Bks) Hall.

— A Voice in the Wind. LC 93-16608. 1993. 9.99 (*0-8423-7750-6*) Tyndale.

***Rivers, Glenn.** Those Who Love the Game. (Trophy Nonfiction Bk.). (Illus.). 240p. (YA). (gr. 5 up). 1995. pap. 4.95 (*0-06-446174-2*, Trophy) HarpC Child Bks.

Rivers, Glenn & Brooks, Bruce. Those Who Love the Game: Glenn "Doc" Rivers on Life in NBA & Elsewhere. (Illus.). 176p. (YA). (gr. 6 up). 1994. 15.95 (*0-8050-2822-6*, Bks Young Read) H Holt & Co.

Rivers, Gloria. Eight Keys to Cosmic Consciousness. Cramer, Owen et al, eds. (Illus.). 32p. (Orig.). 1984. pap. 6.00 (*0-918341-00-0*) Temple Pubns.

Rivers, Isabel. Classical & Christian Ideas in English Renaissance Poetry. 1979. pap. text ed. 15.95 (*0-04-807003-3*) Routledge Chapman & Hall.

— Reason, Grace & Sentiment: A Study of the Language of Religion & Ethics in England, 1660-1780, Vol. 1: Whichcote to Wesley. (Studies in Eighteenth-Century English Literature & Thought: No. 8). 320p. (C). 1991. 59.95 (*0-521-38340-4*) Cambridge U Pr.

Rivers, Isabell. Classical & Christian Ideas in English Renaissance Poetry: A Student's Guide. 2nd ed. LC 94-12710. 240p. 1995. 59.00x (*0-415-10646-X*, B7069); pap. 16.95x (*0-415-10647-8*, B7073) Routledge.

Rivers, J. E. Proust & the Art of Love: The Aesthetics of Sexuality in the Life, Times & Art of Marcel Proust. LC 80-2403. 440p. 1983. pap. text ed. 17.00 (*0-231-05037-2*) Col U Pr.

Rivers, J. E. & Nicol, Charles, eds. Nabokov's Fifth Arc: Nabokov & Others on His Life's Work. LC 81-14764. 333p. (C). 1982. text ed. 30.00 (*0-292-75522-8*) U of Tex Pr.

Rivers, J. W. The Place of Understanding: A Poem. 72p. (Orig.). 1994. pap. 14.95 (*0-936044-06-3*) Pikestaff Pr.

R

— Proud & on My Feet: Poems by J. W. Rivers. LC 82-4768. (Contemporary Poetry Ser.). 88p. 1983. pap. 7.95 (*0-8203-0633-9*) U of Ga Pr.

— When the Owl Cries, Indians Die. LC 85-47624. 112p. 1986. 14.95 (*0-8453-4509-5*) VA Ctr Creative Arts.

Rivers, Joan. Having a Baby Can Be a Scream. 192p. 1978. pap. 3.50 (*0-380-00292-2*) Avon.

— Still Talking. 328p. 1992. mass mkt. 5.99 (*0-380-71992-4*) Avon.

— Still Talking. LC 90-53477. 288p. 1991. 21.00 (*0-394-57991-7*) Random.

Rivers, Kathryn, jt. auth. see Trent, Carolyn.

Rivers, Kenneth T. Transmutations: Understanding Literary & Pictorial Caricature. 330p. (Orig.). (C). 1991. lib. bdg. 49.00 (*0-8191-8328-8*); pap. text ed. 28.00 (*0-8191-8329-6*) U Pr of Amer.

Rivers, Larry. Some American History: Slavery: The Black Man & the Man. LC 72-153088. 50p. (Orig.). (YA). 1971. pap. text ed. 8.95 (*0-318-42723-0*) Inst for the Arts.

Rivers, Larry & Brightman, Carol. Larry River's Drawings & Digressions. (Illus.). 264p. 1988. 75.00 (*0-517-53430-4*, C P Pubs) Crown Pub Group.

Rivers, Larry & Weinstein, Arnold. What Did I Do? The Unauthorized Autobiography. LC 92-52554. (Illus.). 512p. 1993. reprint ed. pap. 15.00 (*0-06-099509-2*, A Asher Bks) HarpC.

Rivers, Larry, jt. auth. see Wolf, Steven.

Rivers, Laura, ed. Pigtails & Froglegs: A Family Cookbook from Neiman Marcus. (Illus.). 256p. 1993. 19.95 (*0-15-261697-7*) Neiman-InCircle.

— Pigtails & Frogles: A Family Cookbook from Neiman Marcus. (Illus.). 1993. 19.95 (*0-9629473-1-8*) Neiman-InCircle.

Rivers, Linda. Through Her Eyes. 128p. 1990. pap. 7.95 (*0-941831-40-X*) Beyond Words Pub.

***Rivers, Mark.** Taggard Point: Shapes, Bk. 2. 208p. (Orig.). (YA). 1995. pap. text ed. 3.99 (*0-425-14726-6*) Berkley Pub.

— Taggard Point: The Clown, Bk. 4. 176p. (Orig.). 1995. pap. 3.99 (*0-425-15016-X*) Berkley Pub.

— Taggard Point Bk. 1: The Forever House. 176p. (Orig.). 1995. pap. text ed. 3.99 (*0-425-14567-0*) Berkley Pub.

— Taggard Point Bk. 3: When the Dead Scream. 176p. (Orig.). (YA). 1995. pap. text ed. 3.99 (*0-425-14880-7*) Berkley Pub.

Rivers, Michele. Time for Tea: Conversations with English Women. LC 93-42375. 1995. 22.00 (*0-517-59219-3*, Crown) Crown Pub Group.

***Rivers, Nikki.** Daddy's Little Matchmaker. (American Romance Ser.). 1995. mass mkt. 3.50 (*0-373-16592-7*, 1-16592-7) Harlequin Bks.

— Seducing Spencer. (American Romance Ser.). 1994. mass mkt. 3.50 (*0-373-16550-1*, 1-16550-5) Harlequin Bks.

Rivers, P. Clayton, ed. Nebraska Symposium on Motivation, 1986: Alcohol & Addictive Behavior. LC 53-11655. (Nebraska Symposium on Motivation Ser.: Vol. 34). xx, 346p. 1987. 29.95 (*0-8032-3880-0*); pap. 15.95 (*0-8032-8925-1*) U of Nebr Pr.

Rivers, R. J. Path Integral Methods in Quantum Field Theory. (Cambridge Monographs on Mathematical Physics). 300p. 1988. pap. 34.95 (*0-521-36870-7*) Cambridge U Pr.

Rivers, R. W. On-Scene Traffic Accident Investigators' Manual. (Illus.). 200p. 1981. 49.95 (*0-398-04121-0*) C C Thomas.

— On-Scene Traffic Accident Investigators' Manual. (Illus.). 200p. 1981. pap. 29.95 (*0-398-06401-6*) C C Thomas.

— Traffic Accident Field Measurements & Scale Diagrams Manual. (Illus.). 154p. 1983. spiral bd. 31.95 (*0-398-04845-2*) C C Thomas.

— Traffic Accident Investigation: A Training & Reference Manual. 584p. (C). 1988. pap. text ed. 40.00 (*1-884566-03-0*) Inst Police Tech.

— Traffic Accident Investigators' Book of Formulae & Tables. (Illus.). 160p. 1981. spiral bd. 38.95 (*0-398-04537-2*) C C Thomas.

— Traffic Accident Investigators' Handbook. (Illus.). 336p. 1980. 59.95 (*0-398-03917-8*) C C Thomas.

— Traffic Accident Investigators' Handbook. (Illus.). 336p. 1980. pap. 34.95 (*0-398-06402-4*) C C Thomas.

— Traffic Accident Investigator's Manual: A Levels 1 & 2 Reference, Training & Investigation Manual. 2nd ed. LC 94-40334. Orig. Title: On-Scene Traffic Accident Investigator's Manual. (Illus.). 238p. (C). 1995. text ed. 59.95x (*0-398-05967-5*); pap. text ed. 34.95x (*0-398-05968-3*) C C Thomas.

Rivers, Richard A., jt. auth. see Anderson, Donald T.

Rivers, Theodore J. Contra Technologiam: The Crisis of Value in a Technological Age. 128p. (C). 1993. lib. bdg. 29.50 (*0-8191-9090-X*) U Pr of Amer.

Rivers, Theodore J., intro. Laws of the Salian & Ripuarian Franks. LC 85-48002. (Studies in the Middle Ages). 1986. 42.50 (*0-404-61438-8*) AMS Pr.

Rivers, Thomas. The Rose Amateur's Guide. (Old Roses Ser.). 1979. 15.00 (*0-685-01528-9*) E M Coleman Ent.

Rivers, Thomas E. My Sixty Years in Recreation Working for Life Enrichment: An Autobiography: a Story of the Leisure Movement in the Twentieth Century. Douglass, Paul, ed. LC 83-61662. (Illus.). 108p. reprint ed. pap. 30.80 (*0-7837-1548-X*, 2041836) Bks Demand.

Rivers, Tony, et al. The Name of the Room: A History of the British House & Home. (Illus.). 192p. 1994. 22.95 (*0-563-36321-5*, BBC-Parkwest) Parkwest Pubns.

Rivers, W. H. The Todas, 2 vols., Set. 1990. reprint ed. 78.00 (*81-7033-014-9*, Pub. by Rawat II) S Asia.

Rivers, W. Napoleon, ed. see Dumas, Alexandre.

Rivers, Wilga. Teaching French. 412p. (C). 1988. 180.00 (*0-8442-1265-2*, Pub. by S Thornes Pubs UK) St Mut.

— Teaching Languages in College. 448p. 1992. pap. 29.95 (*0-8442-9364-4*, NTC Busn Bks) NTC Pub Grp.

Rivers, Wilga, et al. Teaching Spanish. 412p. (C). 1988. 170.00 (*0-8442-7605-7*, Pub. by S Thornes Pubs UK) St Mut.

Rivers, Wilga, et al, eds. Teaching German. 412p. (C). 1988. 160.00 (*0-8442-2401-4*, Pub. by S Thornes Pubs UK) St Mut.

Rivers, Wilga M. Communicating Naturally in a Second Language: Theory & Practice in Language Teaching. LC 82-23620. (Cambridge Language Teaching Library). 243p. 1983. 39.95 (*0-521-25401-9*); pap. 16.95 (*0-521-27417-6*) Cambridge U Pr.

— Opportunities in Foreign Language Careers. LC 92-15588. 1993. 13.95 (*0-8442-4042-7*, VGM Career Bks); pap. 10.95 (*0-8442-4043-5*, VGM Career Bks) NTC Pub Grp.

— Teaching Foreign Language Skills. rev. ed. LC 80-24993. (C). 1981. reprint ed. pap. text ed. 24.95 (*0-226-72097-7*) U Ch Pr.

Rivers, Wilga M., ed. Interactive Language Teaching. (Illus.). 224p. 1987. pap. 16.95 (*0-521-31108-X*) Cambridge U Pr.

— Interactive Language Teaching. (Illus.). 224p. 1987. 44.95 (*0-521-32216-2*) Cambridge U Pr.

Rivers, Wilga M. & Temperley, Mary S. A Practical Guide to the Teaching of English As a Second or Foreign Language. 1978. pap. 14.95 (*0-19-502210-6*) OUP.

Rivers, William. Issues & Images: An Argument Reader. (Illus.). 880p. (Orig.). (C). 1993. pap. text ed. write for info. (*0-03-055157-9*) HB Coll Pubs.

— Issues & Images: An Argument Reader. (Illus.). 880p. (Orig.). (C). 1993. Instructor's manual. teacher ed, pap. text ed. 4.00 (*0-03-096599-3*) HB Coll Pubs.

Rivers, William, et al, eds. Aspen Handbook on the Media, 1977-1979 Edition. 6.95 (*0-686-25999-8*) Aspen Inst Human.

Rivers, William E. Business Reports: Samples from the "Real World" (Illus.). 272p. 1981. pap. text ed. write for info. (*0-13-107656-6*) P-H.

Rivers, William H. Kinship & Social Organization; Together with the Genealogical Method of Anthropological Enquiry. LC 68-108214. (London School of Economics. Monographs on Social Anthropology: No. 34). 124p. reprint ed. pap. 35.40 (*0-685-23916-0*, 2032985) Bks Demand.

— Medicine, Magic & Religion. LC 76-44784. reprint ed. 32.50 (*0-404-15967-2*) AMS Pr.

— Social Organization. LC 76-44785. reprint ed. 22.50 (*0-404-15968-0*) AMS Pr.

Rivers, William L. Free-Lancer & Staff Writer: Newspaper Features & Magazine Articles. 5th ed. 283p. (C). 1992. pap. 36.95 (*0-534-15996-6*) Intl Thomson.

— The Opinionmakers. LC 83-18529. 270p. 1983. reprint ed. text ed. 55.00 (*0-313-24251-8*, RIOP, Greenwood Pr) Greenwood.

Rivers, William L. & Harrington, Susan L. Finding Facts: Research Writing Across the Curriculum. 2nd ed. (Illus.). 256p. 1987. pap. text ed. write for info. (*0-13-316845-X*) P-H.

Rivers, William L. & Mathews, Cleve. Ethics for the Media. 320p. 1988. pap. text ed. write for info. (*0-13-290560-4*) P-H.

***Rivers, William L. & Rodriguez, Alison W.** Understanding Grammar. LC 94-27634. 1994. pap. text ed. write for info. (*0-205-14633-3*) Allyn.

Rivers, William L., jt. auth. see Garvey, Daniel.

***Riverside.** Don't Forget the Rubber Ducky! The Ultimate Book of Lists for Parents of Young Children. 1995. pap. 12.00 (*0-671-51125-4*) PB.

Riverside Mothers' Playgroup Staff. Entertain Me! Zion, Claire, ed. LC 93-6983. 224p. (Orig.). 1993. pap. 8.00 (*0-671-74536-0*) PB.

Riverson, John, et al. Rural Roads in Sub-Saharan Africa: Lessons from World Bank Experience. (Technical Paper Ser.). 62p. 1991. pap. 6.95 (*0-8213-1869-1*; 11869); pap. 6.95 (*0-8213-2064-5*) World Bank.

***Riverson, John D. & Carapetis, Steve.** Intermediate Means of Transport in Sub-Saharan Africa: Its Potential for Improving Rural Travel & Transport. (Technical Paper Ser.: No. 161). 38p. (FRE.). 1991. 6.95 (*0-8213-2281-8*, 12281) World Bank.

— Intermediate Means of Transport in Sub-Saharan Africa: Its Potential for Improving Rural Travel & Transport. (Technical Paper Ser.: No. 161). 38p. 1991. 6.95 (*0-8213-1951-5*, 11951) World Bank.

Riverson, L. Kwabena. Telecommunications Development: The Case of Africa. 130p. (C). Date not set. lib. bdg. 34.00 (*0-8191-9315-1*) U Pr of Amer.

Riverview School Staff. Second Chance: A Guide to Post-Secondary Options for Young Adults with Severe Learning Disabilities. 224p. 1993. 15.95 (*0-9635773-0-1*) Riverview Sch.

Rives, David. Walk Yourself Thin. 1990. 19.95 (*1-878143-00-X*); pap. 12.95 (*1-878143-01-8*) Moon River.

Rives, David A. Dying for a Smoke. 176p. 1991. 19.95 (*1-878143-06-9*) Moon River.

Rives, Hallie E. Smoking Flax. LC 72-2026. (Black Heritage Library Collection). 1977. reprint ed. 26.95 (*0-8369-9057-9*) Ayer.

Rives, Hallie E. & Forbush, Gabrielle E. John Book. (Biography Index Reprint Ser.). 1977. reprint ed. 22.95 (*0-8369-8107-3*) Ayer.

***Rives, J. B.** Religion & Authority in Roman Carthage: From Augustus to Constantine. (Illus.). 352p. 1995. text ed. 55.00 (*0-19-814083-5*) OUP.

Rives, Margaret R. Blue Ridge Parkway: The Story Behind the Scenery. LC 82-82578. (Illus.). 48p. (Orig.). 1982. pap. 6.95 (*0-916122-81-6*) KC Pubns.

Rives, Norfleet W., Jr. & Serow, William J. Introduction to Applied Demography: Data Sources & Estimation Techniques. (Quantitative Applications in the Social Sciences Ser.: Vol. 39). 96p. (C). 1984. pap. text ed. 9.95 (*0-8039-2134-9*) Sage.

Rives, William C. History of the Life & Times of James Madison, 3 Vols, Set. LC 76-126253. (Select Bibliographies Reprint Ser.). 1977. reprint ed. 108.95 (*0-8369-5480-7*) Ayer.

Rivest, Ronald, et al, eds. Computational Learning Theory Proceedings of the 2nd Annual Workshop: Proceedings. 450p. (Orig.). (C). 1989. pap. 19.95 (*1-55860-086-8*) Morgan Kaufmann.

Rivet, A. L. & Smith, Colin. The Place-Names of Roman Britain. LC 79-21616. (Illus.). 584p. 1980. 190.00x (*0-691-03953-4*) Princeton U Pr.

Rivet, Mary M. Influence of the Spanish Mystics on the Works of Saint Francis De Sales. LC 79-115355. (Catholic University of America. Studies in Romance Languages & Literatures: No. 22). reprint ed. 37.50 (*0-404-50322-5*) AMS Pr.

Rivett, Kenneth, ed. Australia & the Non-White Migrant. 327p. 1975. 34.95 (*0-522-84078-7*) Intl Spec Bk.

Rivett, Patrick. The Craft of Decision Modelling. LC 93-10008. 300p. 1994. text ed. 49.95 (*0-471-93962-5*) Wiley.

— Model Building for Decision Analysis. LC 79-40739. (Illus.). 184p. reprint ed. pap. 52.50 (*0-8357-4687-9*, 2052342) Bks Demand.

Rivett, Patrick & Ackoff, Russell L. A Manager's Guide to Operational Research. LC 63-14115. (Illus.). 117p. reprint ed. pap. 33.40 (*0-7837-6394-8*, 2046107) Bks Demand.

Rivette, David A. Guidebook for California Seniors: Answers to Legal & Financial Problems of California Senior Citizens. 208p. (Orig.). 1989. pap. text ed. 15.00 (*0-929913-00-0*) Darcal Pubns.

Rivier, Catherine, jt. ed. see Tache, Yvette.

Rivier, Laurent & Crozier, Alan, eds. Principles & Practice of Plant Hormone Analysis, Vol. 1. (Biological Techniques Ser.). 1987. text ed. 94.00 (*0-12-198375-7*) Acad Pr.

— Principles & Practice of Plant Hormone Analysis, Vol. 2. (Biological Techniques Ser.). 1987. text ed. 94.00 (*0-12-198376-5*) Acad Pr.

Riviera Publications Staff. Children's Directory. Nelson, Elizabeth, ed. 1989. 4.95 (*0-317-93658-1*) Riviera Pubns.

— Orange County Children's Directory. Nelson, Elizabeth A., ed. 110p. 1990. pap. 4.95 (*1-877609-01-3*) Riviera Pubns.

— San Diego Children's Directory. Nelson, Elizabeth, ed. 96p. 1990. pap. text ed. 3.95 (*1-877609-03-X*) Riviera Pubns.

Riviere. Handbook Comparative Pharmacokinetics & Residues: Pesticides & Environmental Contaminants - Animals. 1995. write for info. (*0-8493-3213-3*) CRC Pr.

Riviere, Bill. The Open Canoe. (Illus.). 288p. 1985. pap. 12.95 (*0-316-74768-8*) Little.

Riviere, Bill & Elman, Robert. Gunner's Bible. 3rd rev. ed. LC 82-45489. (Illus.). 192p. 1985. pap. 12.00 (*0-385-18291-0*, Outdoor Bible) Doubleday.

Riviere, Claude. Guinea: The Mobilization of a People. Adloff, Richard & Thompson, Virginia, trs. LC 76-50262. (Africa in the Modern World Ser). (Illus.). 272p. 1977. 31.50 (*0-8014-0904-7*) Cornell U Pr.

Riviere, J. Recueil de contes populaires de la Kabylie du Djurdjura. LC 78-20113. (Collection de contes et de chansons populaires: Vol. 4). reprint ed. 21.50 (*0-404-60354-8*) AMS Pr.

Riviere, J. C. Surface Analytical Techniques. (Monographs on the Physics & Chemistry of Materials). (Illus.). 720p. 1990. 175.00 (*0-19-851370-4*) OUP.

Riviere, J. Edmond, et al, eds. Handbook of Comparative Pharmacokinetics & Tissue Residues of Veterinary Antimicrobial Drugs. 1045p. 1991. 321.95 (*0-8493-3211-7*) CRC Pr.

Riviere, Jacques, jt. auth. see Proust, Marcel.

Riviere, Jean R. El Arte de la China. (Summa Artis Ser.: Vol. 20). 600p. 1989. 295.00x (*84-239-5220-7*) Elliots Bks.

— El Arte de la India. (Summa Artis Ser.: Vol. 19). 600p. 1989. 295.00x (*84-239-5219-3*) Elliots Bks.

***Riviere, Jim.** Stop Worrying & Eat Your Vegetables. 1996. write for info. (*0-614-05602-0*) WRS Group.

Riviere, Joan, tr. see Freud, Sigmund.

Riviere, Joan, jt. ed. see Klein, Melanie.

Riviere, Nancy, ed. Greeting Card Creative Network Talent Directory: 1990 Issue. (Illus.). 60p. 1990. pap. text ed. 25.00 (*0-938369-07-5*) Greeting Card Assn.

— Greeting Card Industry Directory: 1990 Supplement, Set. rev. ed. 30p. 1990. pap. 40.00 (*0-938369-08-3*) Greeting Card Assn.

Riviere, Nancy & Farley, Patricia, eds. Artists & Writers Market List, 1991: Greeting Card Creative Network's Artists & Writers' Market List. 50p. 1991. pap. 25.00 (*0-938369-12-1*) Greeting Card Assn.

Riviere, Nancy, jt. ed. see Albertson, Mila.

Riviere, Nancy, jt. ed. see Jones, Patricia.

Riviere, Nancy, jt. ed. see Richmond, Paula A.

***Riviere, Peter.** Absent-Minded Imperialism: Britain & the Expansion of Empire in Nineteenth-Century Brazil. 224p. 1995. text ed. 59.50 (*1-85043-913-3*) St Martin.

— Individual & Society in Guiana: A Comparative Study of AmerIndian Social Organization. (Cambridge Studies in Social & Cultural Anthropology: No. 51). 136p. 1984. pap. 16.95 (*0-521-26997-0*) Cambridge U Pr.

***Riviere, William.** Eros & Psyche. 246p. 1995. pap. 10.95 (*0-340-60967-2*, Pub. by H & S UK) Trafalgar.

Riviere, William, jt. auth. see Bean, L. L., Staff.

Riviere, Yves. Pierre Courtin. L'Oeuvre Grave 1944-1972. 240p. 1973. 50.00 (*0-915346-18-4*) A Wofsy Fine Arts.

— Soulages: Etchings & Lithographs, 1952-1973. 146p. (FRE.). 1974. 175.00 (*1-55660-152-2*) A Wofsy Fine Arts.

Rivierre. Dictionnaire Paici-Francais, Suivi d'un Lexique Francais-Paici. 372p. (FRE.). 1984. 39.95 (*0-8288-1628-X*, F37540) Fr & Eur.

Rivington, Charles A. Samuel Pepys & the London Booksellers. (C). 1989. pap. 39.00 (*1-85072-113-0*, Pub. by W Sessions UK) St Mut.

Rivington, Charles A., jt. auth. see Sessions, William, Ltd. Staff.

Rivinus, E. F. & Youssef, E. M. Spencer Baird of the Smithsonian. LC 92-6897. (Illus.). 232p. (C). 1992. text ed. 29.95 (*1-56098-155-5*) Smithsonian.

Rivinus, Edward F. Jim Thorpe. (Raintree-Rivilo American Indian Stories Ser.). (Illus.). 32p. (J). (gr. 3-6). 1990. lib. bdg. 19.97 (*0-8172-3403-9*); pap. 4.95 (*0-8114-4094-X*) Raintree Steck-V.

Rivinus, T. M., ed. Children of Chemically Dependent Parents: Multiperspectives from the Cutting Edge. LC 90-15181. 384p. 1991. 45.95 (*0-87630-595-8*) Brunner-Mazel.

Rivinus, Timothy M., intro. Alcoholism Chemical Dependency & the College Student. LC 88-9443. (Journal of College Student Psychotherapy: Vol. 2, Nos. 3-4). (Illus.). 257p. (Orig.). 1988. text ed. 49.95 (*0-86656-734-8*); pap. text ed. 14.95 (*0-86656-812-3*) Haworth Pr.

Rivkin, Allen & Kerr, Laura. Farmer's Daughter. adapted ed. 1962. pap. 4.75 (*0-8222-0386-3*) Dramatists Play.

Rivkin, Arnold. Nation-Building in Africa: Problems & Prospects. Morrow, John H., ed. LC 74-96028. 320p. reprint ed. pap. 91.20 (*0-7837-5681-X*, 2059109) Bks Demand.

Rivkin, Bernard. Patenting & Marketing Your Invention. (Illus.). 264p. 1986. text ed. 49.95 (*0-442-27824-1*) Van Nos Reinhold.

Rivkin, C. L. Thermodynamic Properties of Gases: A Handbook. 4th rev. ed. 300p. 1988. 110.00 (*0-89116-750-1*) Hemisp Pub.

Rivkin, Francine V., jt. auth. see Houseworth, Steven D.

Rivkin, Jack L., jt. auth. see Doerflinger, Thomas M.

Rivkin, Mary, jt. ed. see Fein, Greta.

Rivkin, Mary S., jt. auth. see Harlan, Jean D.

Rivkin, Y. The Metallurgy of Soviet High Speed Diesels. Jones, Steven, ed. 101p. (Orig.). 1984. pap. text ed. 75.00 (*1-55831-041-X*) Delphic Associates.

Rivlin. David Ben Gurion Album. 1987. 24.95 (*0-915361-76-0*) Modan-Adama Bks.

Rivlin, Alice & Cox, Carol. Understanding Economic Policy: A Citizen's Handbook. 1990. 5.95 (*0-89959-417-4*, 896) LWVUS.

Rivlin, Alice M. Reviving the American Dream: The Economy, the States, & the Federal Government. 196p. (C). 1993. 15.95 (*0-8157-7476-1*); pap. 9.95 (*0-8157-7483-4*) Brookings.

— Systematic Thinking for Social Action. LC 74-161600. 150p. 1971. 26.95 (*0-8157-7478-8*); pap. 9.95 (*0-8157-7477-X*) Brookings.

Rivlin, Alice M., ed. Economic Choices 1984. LC 84-71381. 171p. 1984. 22.95 (*0-8157-7488-5*); pap. 8.95 (*0-8157-7487-7*) Brookings.

Rivlin, Alice M. & Timpane, P. Michael, eds. Planned Variation in Education: Should We Give Up or Try Harder? LC 75-5151. (Brookings Institution Studies in Social Experimentation). 198p. reprint ed. pap. 56.50 (*0-317-26352-8*, 2025402) Bks Demand.

Rivlin, Alice M. & Wiener, Joshua M. Caring for the Disabled Elderly: Who Will Pay? LC 88-10528. 318p. 1988. pap. 16.95 (*0-8157-7497-4*) Brookings.

Rivlin, Alice M., jt. ed. see Bosworth, Barry P.

Rivlin, Benjamin, ed. Ralph Bunche: The Man & His Times. LC 89-24666. (Illus.). 279p. (C). 1989. 36.50 (*0-8419-1145-2*) Holmes & Meier.

Rivlin, Benjamin & Gordenker, Leon, eds. The Challenging Role of the U. N. Secretary-General: Making "the Most Impossible Job in the World" Possible. LC 92-34949. 320p. 1993. text ed. 59.95 (*0-275-94466-2*, C4466, Praeger Pubs) Greenwood.

Rivlin, Elizabeth. Elmo's Little Glowworm. LC 93-38193. (Illus.). 16p. (J). (ps-1). 1994. pap. 5.99 (*0-679-85402-9*) Random Bks Yng Read.

Rivlin, Gary. Drive-By. 1995. 25.00 (*0-8050-2921-4*) H Holt & Co.

— Fire on the Prairie: Chicago's Harold Washington & the Politics of Race. (Illus.). 464p. 1993. pap. 14.95 (*0-8050-2698-3*, Owl) H Holt & Co.

***Rivlin, Gershon.** Haganah Highlights. (Orig.). 1994. pap. 14.95 (*0-930832-05-1*) Herzl Pr.

***Rivlin, Gideon.** Guide to Organizing an International Scientific Conference. (Illus.). viii, 70p. 1995. pap. 35.00 (*3-8055-6151-2*) S Karger.

Rivlin, Joseph. The Dyeing of Textile Fibers: Theory & Practice. (Illus.). 220p. 1992. 49.95 (*0-9633133-0-4*) J Rivlin Assocs.

Rivlin, Michael E. Handbook of Drug Therapy in Reproductive Endocrinology & Infertility. 1990. 32.95 (*0-316-74772-6*) Little.

— Manual of Gynecology ISE, No. 3. 1990. 15.95 (*0-316-74773-4*) Little.

Rivlin, Michael E., et al. Manual of Clinical Problems in Obstetrics & Gynecology: With Annotated Key References. 2nd ed. 448p. 1986. 22.50 (*0-316-74769-6*, Little Med Div) Little.

Rivlin, Michel E. & Martin, Rick W., eds. Manual of Clinical Problems in Obstetrics & Gynecology. 4th ed. LC 93-35803. 1994. 29.95 (*0-316-74777-7*) Little.

Rivlin, Paul. The Dynamics of Economic Policymaking in Egypt. LC 85-12190. 220p. 1985. text ed. 49.95 (*0-275-90156-4*, C0156, Praeger Pubs) Greenwood.

R

An Asterisk (*) at the beginning of an entry indicates that the title is appearing in BIP for the first time.

— The Israeli Economy. 183p. (C). 1992. pap. text ed. 49.00 (*0-8133-7653-X*) Westview.

Rivlin, R. S., ed. see American Society of Mechanical Engineers, Applied Mechanics Division Staff.

Rivlin, Robert & Gravelle, Karen. Deciphering the Senses. 1985. pap. 7.95 (*0-317-31522-6*, Touchstone Bks) S&S Trade.

Rivlin, Theodore J. Chebyshev Polynomials: From Approximation Theory to Algebra & Number Theory. 2nd ed. 249p. 1990. text ed. 91.95 (*0-471-62896-4*) Wiley.

— An Introduction to the Approximation of Functions. 160p. (C). 1981. reprint ed. pap. 4.95 (*0-486-64069-8*) Dover.

Rivoira, Giovanni T. Lombardic Architecture: Its Origin, Development & Derivatives, 2 vols. Rushforth, G. McN., tr. LC 73-76789. (Illus.). 1975. reprint ed. 75.00 (*0-87817-137-1*) Hacker.

***Rivoirard, Jacques.** Introduction to Disjunctive Kriging & Non-Linear Geostatistics. (Spatial Information Systems Ser.). (Illus.). 192p. 1994. text ed. 45.00 (*0-19-874180-4*) OUP.

Rivoire, Jeanne L., jt. ed. see Kidd, Aline H.

Rivolier, J., et al, eds. Man in the Antarctic. 200p. 1988. 90.00 (*0-85066-280-X*) Taylor & Francis.

Rivolta, Barbara C., ed. Media Listings for Passau County. 1988. write for info. (*0-318-66959-5*) Poetry Ctr PCCC.

Rix, Alan. Intermittent Diplomat: The Japan & Batavia Diaries of W. Macmahon Ball. 1988. 39.95 (*0-522-84359-X*) Intl Spec Bk.

Rix, Alan G. Japan's Economic Aid: Policy-Making & Politics. 1980. text ed. 39.95 (*0-312-44063-4*) St Martin.

— Japan's Foreign Aid Challenge: Policy Reform & Aid Leadership. LC 92-38840. (Nissan Institute Japanese Studies). 240p. 1993. 59.95 (*0-415-09010-5*, B0691, Routledge NY) Routledge.

Rix, Brian. Tour de Farce. (Illus.). 320p. 1993. 45.00 (*0-340-52265-8*, Pub. by H & S UK) Trafalgar.

Rix, David, jt. tr. see King, Donald.

Rix, Diana & Rix-Paxson, Monica. Complete Garage Sale Kit: Everything You Need to Make Money At Your Next Garage Sale. LC 94-8046. 1994. pap. 7.95 (*1-57071-000-7*) Sourcebks.

— Fabulous Money Making Garage Sale Kit. LC 93-16693. 1993. pap. 12.95 (*0-942061-52-7*) Sourcebks.

Rix, G. S. History & Genealogy of the Eastman Family of America: Containing Biographical Sketches & Genealogy of Both Males & Females. (Illus.). 1000p. 1989. reprint ed. lib. bdg. 158.00 (*0-8328-0510-6*); reprint ed. pap. 150.00 (*0-8328-0511-4*) Higginson Bk Co.

Rix, Herbert. Tent & Testament: Camping Tour in Palestine with Some Notes on Scriptural Sites. Davis, Moshe, ed. LC 77-70737. (America & the Holy Land Ser.). (Illus.). 1977. reprint ed. lib. bdg. 33.95 (*0-405-10280-1*) Ayer.

Rix, Herbert D. Martin Luther: The Man & the Image. 335p. 1983. text ed. 37.50 (*0-8290-0554-4*) Irvington.

Rix, J. & Schlechtendahl, E. G., eds. Interfaces in Industrial Systems for Production & Engineering: Proceedings of the IFIP TC5-WG5.10 Working Conference, Darmstadt, Germany, March 1993. LC 93-4732. (IFIP Transactions B: Applications in Technology Ser.: Vol. B-10). 1993. write for info. (*0-444-81496-5*, North Holland) Elsevier.

Rix, Jonathan. Some Hope. 228p. 1994. pap. 15.95 (*0-233-98834-3*, Pub. by A Deutsch UK) Trafalgar.

Rix, Judy, intro. Welcome Home to Lenexa. (Illus.). 96p. 1993. write for info. (*0-9638542-0-8*) Geo Graphics.

Rix, K. J., jt. ed. see Mortimer, A. M.

Rix, Martyn. Art in Nature: Classic Botanical Prints from the Eighteenth to the Twentieth Century. LC 91-52766. (Illus.). 304p. 1991. 75.00 (*0-8478-1401-7*) Rizzoli Intl.

— Art of Botanical Illustrations. 1990. 85.00 (*0-685-33410-4*); pap. 29.99 (*0-517-69628-2*) Random Hse Value.

— The Art of the Plant World: The Great Botanical Illustrators & Their Work. deluxe ed. LC 80-14274. (Illus.). 224p. 1982. 175.00 (*0-87951-139-7*) Overlook Pr.

Rix, Martyn & Phillips, Roger. The Random House Book of Vegetables. LC 93-13857. 1994. 25.00 (*0-679-75024-X*) Random.

Rix, Martyn, jt. auth. see Phillips, Roger.

Rix-Paxson, Monica, jt. auth. see Rix, Diana.

Rix, Sara E. American Woman, 1990-91: A Status Report. 1990. 10.95 (*0-393-02840-2*) Norton.

— Older Workers. (Choices & Challenges: An Older Adult Reference Ser.). 243p. 1990. lib. bdg. 45.00 (*0-87436-259-8*) ABC-CLIO.

Rix, Sara E., ed. The American Woman, 1990-91: A Status Report. 420p. 1990. 13.50 (*0-685-55242-X*) SLA.

Rix, Sara E. & Fisher, Paul. Retirement-Age Policy: An International Perspective. (Policy Studies on Social Policy). (Illus.). 176p. 1982. 56.00 (*0-08-028840-5*, K110, L115, Pergamon Pr) Elsevier.

Rix, Sara E., jt. auth. see Sheppard, Harold L.

Rixen, Gail. Pictures of Three Seasons: A Collection of Poems. 1991. pap. 6.00 (*0-89823-126-4*) New Rivers Pr.

Rixford, Elizabeth M. Families Directly Descended from All the Royal Families in Europe (495 to 1932) & Mayflower Descendants. (Illus.). 190p. 1992. reprint ed. pap. 28.00 (*0-685-60336-9*, 9401) Clearfield Co.

— Three Hundred Colonial Ancestors & War Service: Their Part in Making American History from 495 to 1934, Incl. Supplements I-II. (Illus.). 425p. 1991. reprint ed. Incl. Supplement I, Supplement II & Supplement II Concluded. pap. 35.00 (*0-685-60335-0*, 9400) Clearfield Co.

Rixford, Ellen. Three-Dimensional Illustration: Designing with Paper, Clay, Casts, Wood, Assemblage, Plastics, Fabric, Metal, & Food. LC 92-11619. (Illus.). 176p. 1992. 55.00 (*0-8230-5367-9*, Watsn-Guptill) Watsn-Guptill.

Rixom, M. R. & Mailvaganam, N. P. Chemical Admixtures for Concrete. 275p. 1986. text ed. 47.50 (*0-419-12630-9*, 9571, E & FN Spon) Routledge Chapman & Hall.

Rixon, Angela. World of Dogs. 96p. 1994. 12.98 (*0-8317-9322-8*) Smithmark.

— World of Horses. 96p. 1994. 12.98 (*0-8317-9323-6*) Smithmark.

Rizack, Martin A., ed. Handbook of Adverse Drug Interactions. 121p. (Orig.). 1995. pap. 16.00 (*0-318-03363-1*) Med Letter.

Rizer, Arden, Jr. The American Spiritualist Ministry. American Spiritualist Assembly Directors, ed. 240p. (Orig.). 1987. pap. 20.00 (*0-939795-30-2*) Amer Spirit.

— American Spiritualist Psychology. 24p. 1987. pap. 9.00 (*0-939795-20-5*) Amer Spirit.

— I Am the Power. (Illus.). 87p. (Orig.). (J). (gr. 7-12). 1992. pap. 10.00 (*0-939795-46-9*) Amer Spirit.

— A Metasciences Textbook. A.S.A. Educations & Research Staff, ed. (Orig.). 1987. pap. 23.50 (*0-939795-32-9*) Amer Spirit.

— Paths of Attainment. 82p. 1987. pap. 18.00 (*0-939795-13-2*) Amer Spirit.

— Spiritual Magic: Yi King Numerology. 180p. (Orig.). 1987. pap. 18.00 (*0-939795-29-9*) Amer Spirit.

Rizer, Arden, Jr., pref. Catalogue of Numbers, Vol. 4: Sexuality, Courtship, Marriage. (Orig.). pap. 20.00 (*0-939795-38-8*) Amer Spirit.

Rizer, Arden C., Jr. Astral Projection (Out of Body Experience) A. S. A. Staff, ed. 25p. 1991. pap. 6.92 (*0-939795-41-8*) Amer Spirit.

Rizicka, ed. Eicosanoids & the Skin. 1990. 144.00 (*0-8493-6032-3*, RL96) CRC Pr.

Rizik, Peter, ed. Conference on Applied Defense, 1992. 166p. 1992. 60.00 (*1-56555-005-6*) Soc Computer Sim.

Rizk, A., et al, eds. Hypertext: Concepts, Systems & Applications: Proceedings of the First European Conference on Hypertext, INRIA, France, November 1990. (Series on Electronic Publishing: No. 5). (Illus.). 383p. (C). 1991. 64.95 (*0-521-40517-3*) Cambridge U Pr.

Rizk, Abdel-Fattah M. Naturally Occurring Pyrrolizidine Alkaloids. (Illus.). 224p. 1990. 179.00 (*0-8493-4650-9*, QP801) CRC Pr.

— Poisonous Plant Contamination of Edible Plants. (Illus.). 192p. 1990. 133.00 (*0-8493-6369-1*, RA1250) CRC Pr.

Rizk, Beatriz J. El Nuevo Teatro Latinoamericano: Una Lectura Historica. (Towards a Social History of Hispanic & Luso-Brazilian Literature Ser.). 144p. (Orig.). (SPA.). (C). 1987. pap. 9.95 (*0-910235-25-2*) Prisma Bks.

Riznichenko, Yu V. Problems of Seismology: Selected Papers. (Illus.). xvii, 445p. 1992. 200.00 (*0-387-54230-2*) Spr-Verlag.

Rizo, Alberto, ed. see Binzen, Susanna C., et al.

***Rizo, Luis, illus.** Plants of the Desert. LC 95-10768. (Incredible World of Plants Ser.). (J). 1996. write for info. (*0-7910-3466-6*); pap. write for info. (*0-7910-3472-0*) Chelsea Hse.

Rizopolous, Nicholas, ed. Sea Changes: American Foreign Policy in a World Transformed. 400p. 1990. pap. 14.95 (*0-87609-087-0*) Coun Foreign.

Rizos, C., jt. auth. see Brunner, F. K.

Rizuto, Chuck & Stoddard, Roy T. Flyfishing the San Juan. (Illus.). 112p. (Orig.). 1988. pap. 19.95 (*0-945458-00-2*) Three Rivs Pubs.

Rizvi & Mital. Experimental Methods in Food Engineering. 1991. pap. 49.95 (*0-442-00886-4*) Chapman & Hall.

Rizvi, jt. auth. see Rao.

Rizvi, jt. ed. see Rao.

Rizvi, Br. Balti: A Scheduled Tribe of Jammu & Kashmir. 1993. 14.00 (*81-212-0402-X*, Pub. by Gian Publng Hse II) S Asia.

Rizvi, Fazal. Administrative Leadership & the Democratic Community As a Social Ideal. 119p. (C). 1986. 48.00 (*0-7300-0417-1*, Pub. by Deakin Univ AT) St Mut.

— Ethnicity, Class & Multicultural Education. 102p. (C). 1986. 51.00 (*0-7300-0401-5*, Pub. by Deakin Univ AT) St Mut.

— Multiculturalism As an Educational Policy. 120p. (C). 1985. 56.00 (*0-7300-0118-0*, Pub. by Deakin Univ AT) St Mut.

Rizvi, Fazal, jt. ed. see Gunew, Sneja.

Rizvi, Gowher. South Asia in a Changing International Order. LC 92-40699. 180p. 1993. 28.95 (*0-8039-9467-2*) Sage.

Rizvi, Hasan-Askari. The Military & Politics in Pakistan. 367p. 1989. text ed. 30.00 (*81-220-0084-3*, Pub. by Konark Pubs Pvt Ltd II) Advent Bks Div.

Rizvi, M. Haseeb, ed. Modern Statistical Selection: Proceedings of the Conference "Statistical Ranking & Selection--Three Decades of Development", University of California at Santa Barbara, December 1984, Part I. LC 86-71924. (Mathematical & Management Sciences Ser.: Vol. 13). 1986. 110.00 (*0-935950-13-3*) Am Sciences Pr.

— Modern Statistical Selection: Proceedings of the Conference "Statistical Ranking & Selection--Three Decades of Development", University of California at Santa Barbara, December 1984, Part II. LC 86-71924. (Mathematical & Management Sciences Ser.: Vol.14). 1987. 110.00 (*0-935950-14-1*) Am Sciences Pr.

Rizvi, S. A. A History of Sufism in India, Vol. 1. 467p. 1975. 34.95 (*0-318-37182-0*) Asia Bk Corp.

— Wonder That Was India, Vol. II. (C). 1993. 14.00 (*0-8364-2889-7*, Pub. by Rupa II) S Asia.

***Rizvi, S. H. & Roy, Shivani.** In Search of Roots: A Study in Ethnogenesis. (C). 1994. 18.50x (*81-7018-760-5*, Pub. by BR Pub II) S Asia.

Rizvi, S. H., jt. auth. see Roy, Shibani.

Rizvi, S. J. & Rizvi, V. Allelopathy: Basic & Applied Aspects. 450p. 1991. 109.95 (*0-412-39400-6*) Chapman & Hall.

Rizvi, S. N. Learning English Through Arabic. 384p. 1992. lib. bdg. 60.00 (*81-209-0505-9*, Pub. by Pitambar Pub II) St Mut.

— Medical Anthropology of the Jaunsaris. (C). 1991. text ed. 16.00 (*81-7211-012-X*, Pub. by Northern Bk Ctr II) S Asia.

— The Shompen. (Andaman & Nicobar Island Tribes Ser.). (C). 1990. 7.50 (*81-7046-075-1*, Pub. by Seagull Bks II) S Asia.

Rizvi, S. N., jt. auth. see Fuste, J. M.

Rizvi, S. N., et al. The Art of Composition, Vol. 1. 202p. 1990. pap. 30.00 (*81-209-0772-8*, Pub. by Pitambar Pub II) St Mut.

— The Art of Comprehension, Vol. 2. 122p. 1990. pap. 30.00 (*81-209-0767-1*, Pub. by Pitambar Pub II) St Mut.

Rizvi, S. S. Islamic Philosophy of Education. 19.95 (*1-56744-103-3*) Kazi Pubns.

Rizvi, S. T., jt. auth. see Jain, Subodh K.

Rizvi, Saiyid A. History of Sufism in India, 2 vols. 1986. write for info. (*0-318-63156-3*, Pub. by Munshiram Manoharial II) S Asia.

— History of Sufism in India, 2 vols. (Illus.). 1983. 62.50x (*0-685-13690-6*) Coronet Bks.

— History of Sufism in India Vol. 1: Early Sufism & Its History, 2 vols. 1986. 44.00 (*81-215-0039-7*, Pub. by Munshiram Manoharial II) S Asia.

— History of Sufism in India Vol. 2: From Sixteenth Century to Modern Times, 2 vols. 1986. 44.00 (*81-215-0040-0*, Pub. by Munshiram Manoharial II) S Asia.

— Muslim Revivalist Movements in Northern India: In the Sixteenth & Seventeenth Centuries. 1993. reprint ed. 42.00 (*81-215-0590-9*, Pub. by Munshiram Manoharial II) S Asia.

— Socio Intellectual History of the Isna Ashari Shi'is in India, 7th to 19th Century AD, Set, Vols. 1 & 2. 1986. Set. 78.50 (*81-215-0004-4*, Pub. by Munshiram Manoharial II) S Asia.

Rizvi, Saiyid A. & Flynn, Vincent J. Fathpur-Sikri. (Illus.). 175p. (C). 1981. text ed. 45.00 (*0-86590-041-8*, Pub. by Taraporevala II) Apt Bks.

Rizvi, Syed A. Muslim Tradition in Psychotherapy & Modern Trends. 25.50 (*1-56744-160-2*) Kazi Pubns.

Rizvi, Syed S. Elements of Islamic Studies. Husnain, Syed T., ed. LC 89-51359. 100p. 1989. pap. 4.95 (*0-940368-99-4*, 84) Tahrike Tarsile Quran.

Rizvi, V., jt. auth. see Rizvi, S. J.

Rizwani, R. H., ed. see Al-Sadr, Ayatullah B.

Rizwani, Raza H. Qur'an Made Easy. rev. ed. 130p. 1983. reprint ed. pap. 6.00 (*0-941724-09-3*) Islamic Seminary.

Rizwani, Raza H., ed. see Sadr, Muhammad B. & Murtaza, Mutahhery.

Rizzardi, Fran, jt. auth. see Abrahams, D. Mark.

Rizzardi, V. Understanding MAP: Manufacturing Automation Protocol. 264p. 1988. 42.00 (*0-87263-302-0*) SME.

Rizzarelli, E. & Theophanides, Theophile M., eds. Chemistry & Properties of Biomolecular Systems. 248p. (C). 1991. lib. bdg. 97.00 (*0-7923-1393-3*) Kluwer Ac.

***Rizzatti, Lorella, illus.** Duckling. LC 94-66666. (Animal Shape Board Bks.). 6p. (J). (ps-1). 1995. bds. 3.99 (*0-679-87060-1*) Random Bks Yng Read.

— Fish. LC 94-66668. (Animal Shape Board Bks.). 6p. (J). (ps-1). 1995. bds. 3.99 (*0-679-87062-8*) Random Bks Yng Read.

— Rabbit. LC 94-66669. (Animal Shape Board Bks.). 6p. (J). (ps-1). 1995. bds. 3.99 (*0-679-87059-8*) Random Bks Yng Read.

— Raccoon. LC 94-66667. (Animal Shape Board Bks.). 6p. (J). (ps-1). 1995. bds. 3.99 (*0-679-87061-X*) Random Bks Yng Read.

Rizzi, Bruno. The Bureaucratization of the World. Westoby, Adam, tr. 272p. (C). 1985. 19.95 (*0-02-927140-1*) Free Pr.

Rizzi, Cesare. Candrakirti. (C). 1988. 11.00 (*81-208-0401-5*, Pub. by Motilal Banarsidass II) S Asia.

Rizzi, James. Three-D Constructions. (Illus.). 119p. 1988. 50.00 (*0-936598-02-6*) J Szoke Graphics.

Rizzi, Joseph N. Joe's War: The Memoirs of a Doughboy. Baumgartner, Richard A., ed. & intro. by. (Illus.). 170p. 1983. 11.95 (*0-9604770-1-2*) RMR Bks.

Rizzi, Luigi, jt. ed. see Belletti, Adriana.

Rizzi, Marcia S. Some Pictures from My Life: A Diary. LC 72-87034. (Illus.). 64p. (Orig.). 1972. pap. 3.25 (*0-87810-022-9*) Times Change.

Rizzi, Peter A. Microwave Engineering. (Illus.). 512p. (C). 1987. text ed. 76.00 (*0-13-586702-9*) P-H.

Rizzi, R. & Visentin, M., eds. Pain Therapy. 552p. 1983. 116.00 (*0-444-80452-8*) Elsevier.

Rizzi, Timothy. Nightstalker. LC 91-58662. 430p. 1992. 21.95 (*1-55611-290-4*) D I Fine.

— The Phalanx Dragon. LC 93-74476. (Illus.). 432p. 1994. 21.95 (*1-55611-391-9*) D I Fine.

— Strike of the Cobra. LC 92-54980. 1993. 21.95 (*1-55611-359-5*) D I Fine.

— Strike of the Cobra. 480p. 1994. reprint ed. mass mkt., pap. text ed. 5.99 (*0-8439-3630-4*) Dorchester Pub Co.

Rizzini, Carlos T., jt. auth. see Mors, Walter B.

***Rizzo.** Laser Techniques in Chemistry. (Techniques of Chemistry Ser.). Date not set. text ed. 125.00 (*0-471-59769-4*) Wiley.

Rizzo, Ann-Marie & Mendez, Carmen. The Integration of Women in Management: A Guide for Human Resources & Management Development Specialists. LC 90-8422. 224p. 1990. text ed. 55.00 (*0-89930-475-3*, RON, Quorum Bks) Greenwood.

Rizzo, Betty. Companions Without Vows: Relationships among Eighteenth-Century British Women. LC 92-45141. (Illus.). 432p. 1994. 55.00 (*0-8203-1541-9*) U of Ga Pr.

— Priorities: A Handbook for Basic Writing. 426p. (C). 1984. pap. 16.25 (*0-06-045427-X*) HarpCollege.

— The Writer's Studio: Exercises for Grammar, Proofreading & Composition. 2nd ed. 528p. (C). 1990. pap. text ed. 21.00 (*0-06-045426-1*) HarpCollege.

Rizzo, Betty & Mahony, Robert, eds. The Annotated Letters of Christopher Smart. 144p. (C). 1991. 24.50 (*0-8093-1609-9*) S Ill U Pr.

Rizzo, Betty, ed. see Scott, Sarah.

***Rizzo, Cindy, et al, eds.** All the Ways Home: Parenting & Children in the Lesbian & Gay Communities - A Collection of Short Fiction. 200p. (Orig.). 1995. pap. 10.95 (*0-934678-65-0*) New Victoria Pubs.

— All the Ways Home: Parenting & Children in the Lesbian & Gay Communities - A Collection of Short Fiction. 200p. 1995. 19.95 (*0-934678-68-5*) New Victoria Pubs.

Rizzo, David. Freeway Alternates: A Guide to Commuting in Los Angeles & Orange Counties. LC 90-83235. (Illus.). (Orig.). 1990. pap. 10.95 (*0-935182-45-4*) Gem Guides Bk.

***Rizzo, Diurny.** Magia Hecha en Casa. 1994. pap. 5.95 (*0-942272-38-2*) Original Pubns.

Rizzo, Fran, jt. auth. see Lorey, Dean.

Rizzo, Ilde. The Hidden Debt. (C). 1990. lib. bdg. 75.50 (*0-7923-0610-4*) Kluwer Ac.

Rizzo, Ilde, jt. ed. see Peacock, Alan.

Rizzo, Janis, jt. ed. see Banks, Carolyn.

Rizzo, Jeff, jt. auth. see Landes, William-Alan.

Rizzo, John. How Macs Work. 1993. pap. 24.95 (*1-56276-146-3*) Ziff-Davis.

— MacUser Guide to Connectivity. (Guide to...Ser.). (Illus.). 380p. (Orig.). 1992. pap. 27.95 (*1-56276-056-4*) Ziff-Davis.

Rizzo, John A., jt. ed. see Sato, Ryuzo.

Rizzo, John R. Management for Librarians: Fundamentals & Issues. LC 79-8950. (Contributions in Librarianship & Information Science Ser.: No. 33). (Illus.). xvii, 339p. 1980. text ed. 49.95 (*0-313-21990-7*, RML/, Greenwood Pr) Greenwood.

Rizzo, Joseph V., jt. auth. see Suran, Bernard G.

Rizzo, Joyce A. Underground Storage Tank Management: A Practical Guide. 4th ed. (Illus.). 420p. 1991. pap. 79.00 (*0-86587-271-6*) Gov Insts.

Rizzo, Kay. Love's Tender Prelude. LC 94-5442. 1994. pap. 11.95 (*0-8163-1219-2*) Pacific Pr Pub Assn.

— Winter's Silent Song. LC 94-7118. 1994. pap. 11.95 (*0-8163-1220-6*) Pacific Pr Pub Assn.

Rizzo, Kay D. Claims upon My Heart. LC 92-43931. 1993. pap. 10.95 (*0-8163-1133-1*) Pacific Pr Pub Assn.

— Flee My Father's House. LC 92-33707. 1993. pap. 10.95 (*0-8163-1134-X*) Pacific Pr Pub Assn.

— Gospel in the Grocery Store. Wheeler, Penny E., ed. 96p. (YA). (gr. 7 up). 1989. pap. 4.95 (*0-8280-0446-3*) Review & Herald.

— Love's Cherished Refrain. LC 94-27523. (Chloe Celeste Chronicles: 4). 1994. pap. 11.95 (*0-8163-1222-2*) Pacific Pr Pub Assn.

— She Said No: But He Crossed the Line Between Passion & Violence. LC 93-28923. 1994. pap. 10.95 (*0-8163-1179-X*) Pacific Pr Pub Assn.

— Silence of My Love. LC 92-43132. 1993. pap. 10.95 (*0-8163-1135-8*) Pacific Pr Pub Assn.

— Someone to Love Me. Wheeler, Gerald, ed. (Banner Ser.). 96p. (Orig.). 1987. pap. 6.95 (*0-8280-0365-3*) Review & Herald.

— Still My Aching Heart. LC 92-43699. 1993. pap. 10.95 (*0-8163-1136-6*) Pacific Pr Pub Assn.

— Up Against the Wall. Wheeler, Penny, ed. 96p. 1989. pap. 6.95 (*0-8280-0485-4*) Review & Herald.

Rizzo, Kay D., jt. auth. see Huston, Todd.

Rizzo, Kay D., jt. auth. see Johnson, Terry.

Rizzo, Leo. Automotive Cylinder Boring. LC 79-730978. 1979. student ed 5.00 (*0-8064-0131-1*, 433); audio 159.00 (*0-8064-0132-X*) Bergwall.

— CNC Lathe. 1985. student ed 8.00 (*0-8064-0255-5*, 519); audio 369.00 (*0-8064-0256-3*) Bergwall.

— Digital Codes & Numbering Systems. (Series 870). (Orig.). 1983. student ed, pap. 6.00 (*0-8064-0355-1*, 870); audio 159.00 (*0-8064-0356-X*) Bergwall.

— The Drill Press Explained. LC 81-730687. 1982. student ed 7.00 (*0-8064-0249-0*, 516); audio 219.00 (*0-8064-0250-4*) Bergwall.

— The Four Cycle Diesel Engine. LC 79-730763. 1978. student ed 5.00 (*0-8064-0189-3*, 470); audio 189.00 (*0-8064-0190-7*) Bergwall.

— The Horizontal Surface Grinder. LC 81-730686. 1982. student ed 7.00 (*0-8064-0251-2*, 517); 219.00 (*0-8064-0252-0*) Bergwall.

— Lathe Cutting Explained. LC 79-730988. 1979. student ed 5.00 (*0-8064-0243-1*, 513); audio 189.00 (*0-8064-0244-X*) Bergwall.

— The Lathe Explained. LC 72-737347. 1971. student ed 6.00 (*0-8064-0219-9*, 501); audio 329.00 (*0-8064-0220-2*) Bergwall.

— Measuring Tools Explained. LC 73-732668. 1972. student ed 6.00 (*0-8064-0223-7*, 503); audio 329.00 (*0-8064-0224-5*) Bergwall.

— Milling Machine Explained. LC 73-732667. 1984. student ed 6.00 (*0-8064-0221-0*, 502); audio 319.00 (*0-8064-0222-9*) Bergwall.

— Pneumatics Explained. LC 84-730253. 1984. student ed 11.00 (*0-8064-0038-2*, 530); audio 259.00 (*0-8064-0037-4*) Bergwall.

— Sheet Metal Machinery. LC 82-730275. 1982. student ed 7.00 (*0-8064-0253-9*, 518); audio 419.00 (*0-8064-0254-7*) Bergwall.

— The Vertical Milling Machine Explained. LC 79-731074. (Orig.). 1978. student ed 6.00 (*0-8064-0241-5*, 512); audio 319.00 (*0-8064-0242-3*) Bergwall.

Rizzo, Margaret, jt. auth. see Jweid, Rosann.

Rizzo, Mario J., jt. ed. see Cowan, Robin.

Rizzo, Mario J., jt. auth. see O'Driscoll, Gerald P., Jr.

Rizzo, Michael R. How to Make Profits with Service Contracts. LC 86-47590. 320p. 1987. 65.00 (*0-8144-5807-6*) AMACOM.

Rizzo, N. D., jt. ed. see Gray, W.

Rizzo, P. A., jt. ed. see Morocutti, C.

Rizzo, Philip A. Cambridge Brick Details. LC 83-63460. 128p. 1984. 13.95 (*0-9613164-0-3*) Rotunda Bks.

Rizzo, Raymond. The Voice As an Instrument. 2nd ed. LC 77-9433. 288p. (C). 1978. pap. write for info. (*0-02-401850-3*) Macmillan.

Rizzo, Rebecca, ed. Campfire Thrillers. LC 94-4279. (East Woods Book Ser.). 192p. 1994. pap. 9.95 (*1-56440-371-8*) Globe Pequot.

Rizzo, Stephen R., Jr. & Trudeau, Michael D., eds. Clinical Administration in Audiology & Speech-Language Pathology. LC 93-25798. (Illus.). 320p. (Orig.). (C). 1993. pap. text ed. 59.95 (*1-56593-088-6*) Singular Publishing.

***Rizzo, Susan & Thompson, Sue.** From the Heart of Harvest Cafe. (Illus.). 114p. (Orig.). 1994. pap. text ed. 10.00 (*0-9645715-0-1*) Voyager Enter.

***Rizzo, Thomas.** Speaking with Impact. 144p. 1994. per., pap. text ed. 16.95 (*0-7872-0261-4*) Kendall-Hunt.

Rizzo, Thomas A. Friendship Development among Children in School. Wallat, Cynthia, ed. LC 88-24053. (Language & Learning for Human Service Professions Ser.: Vol. 6). 208p. (C). 1988. text ed. 35.00 (*0-89391-503-3*); pap. text ed. 22.50 (*0-89391-548-3*) Ablex Pub.

Rizzoli. Sotheby's Art at Auction: The Art Market Review 1992-93. 1994. 65.00 (*0-8478-5755-7*) Rizzoli Intl.

Rizzoli, P. M. Botany Dictionary: Dizionario Di Botanica. 528p. (ITA.). 1984. 75.00 (*0-8288-1245-4*, M15663) Fr & Eur.

***Rizzolo, Florence.** Logan County, Colorado War Book. (Illus.). 128p. 1992. 34.95 (*0-88107-213-3*) Curtis Media.

Rizzolo, Mary A., ed. Interactive Video: Expanding Horizons in Nursing. 200p. (C). 1994. 29.95 (*0-937126-27-6*) Am Journal Nurse.

Rizzoni, G., et al, eds. Transportation Systems - 1992. (DSC Ser.: Vol. 44). 464p. 1992. 72.50 (*0-7918-1119-0*, G00763) ASME.

Rizzoni, Giorgio. A Practical Introduction to Electronic Instrumentation. 176p. (C). 1994. spiral bd. 17.56 (*0-8403-9035-1*) Kendall-Hunt.

— Principles & Applications of Electrical Engineering. 768p. (C). 1993. text ed. 66.95 (*0-256-07827-0*) Irwin.

Rizzotti, Michel A. God, Myth, & Metaphor: The Profane Reality of the Goddess. LC 91-91489. 224p. (Orig.). 1992. pap. 14.95 (*0-9630980-3-9*) Northshore.

***Rizzuto & Ferdegmini.** ICEC 15th International Cryogenic Engineering Conference. 912p. 1995. pap. 190.00 (*0-7506-2160-5*, Focal) Buttrwrth-Heinemann.

Rizzuto, Ana-Maria. The Birth of the Living God: A Psychoanalytic Study. LC 78-10475. (Illus.). 246p. 1981. pap. text ed. 12.95 (*0-226-72102-7*) U Ch Pr.

Rizzuto, Anthony. Camus' Imperial Vision. LC 81-1370. 160p. 1981. 15.00 (*0-8093-1002-3*) S Ill U Pr.

Rizzuto, Charlz, tr. see Balbin, Julius.

Rizzuto, James. How to Prepare for SAT II: Mathematics Level I. 6th ed. (SAT II: Subject Test Preparation Manuals Ser.). 1994. pap. 11.95 (*0-8120-1814-1*) Barron.

Rizzuto, James J. Barron's How to Prepare for the College Board Achievement Test - CBAT: Mathematics Level I. 5th ed. Dodge, Howard, ed. 400p. 1990. pap. 10.95 (*0-8120-4396-0*) Barron.

Rizzuto, Jim. Modern Hawaiian Gamefishing. LC 76-58414. 265p. (Orig.). 1977. pap. 9.95 (*0-8248-0481-3*) UH Pr.

Rizzuto, Phil & Horton, Tom. The October Twelve. 240p. 1994. 19.95 (*0-312-85621-0*) Forge NYC.

— The October Twelve. 320p. 1995. mass mkt. 5.99 (*0-8125-3480-8*) Forge NYC.

RMG Consultants, Inc. Staff. Plans & Recommendations for Linking Automated Systems in Long Island Libraries. 84p. 1991. pap. 10.00 (*0-938435-21-3*) LI Lib Resources.

***RMT/Jones & Neuse, Inc. Staff.** Guidelines for Safe Process Operations & Maintenance. LC 94-46233. 1995. 130.00 (*0-8169-0627-0*, G-29) Am Inst Chem Eng.

Ro, Chung-Hyun. Public Administration & the Korean Transformation: Concepts, Policies, & Value Conflicts. LC 93-3592. (Library of Management for Development). (Illus.). 224p. 1993. 35.00 (*1-56549-023-1*); pap. 24.95 (*1-56549-022-3*) Kumarian Pr.

Ro, Sen-cuo. Programming the I386 I486: Real Mode, Protected Mode, & Virtual-8086 Mode. 1993. text ed. 44.95 (*0-442-01377-9*) Van Nos Reinhold.

Roa, Annia. Peter Pelican-Pedro Pelicano. LC 64-22715. (Illus.). (ENG & SPA.). (J). (gr. k-4). 1974. 9.95 (*0-87208-006-4*) Island Pr Pubs.

Roa, Anthony. Favorite Animals Masks: Six Punch-Out Designs. (Illus.). (J). (gr. k-3). 1993. pap. 2.95 (*0-486-27654-6*) Dover.

— Wild Animals Masks: Six Punch-Out Designs. (Illus.). (J). (gr. k-3). 1993. pap. 2.95 (*0-486-27653-8*) Dover.

Roa, Michael. Environmental Science Activities Kit. LC 93-12227. (Illus.). 320p. 1993. spiral bd. 27.95 (*0-87628-304-0*) Ctr Appl Res.

Roa, Michael & Tinkelenberg, Donnell. Biology Teacher's Instant Vocabulary Kit with Ready to Use Crossword Puzzles & Word Searches. 368p. 1990. pap. text ed. 29.95 (*0-13-083841-1*) P-H.

Roa, Michael & Tonkelenberg, Donnell. Biology Teacher's Instant Vocabulary Kit: With Ready-to-Use Crosswords & Wordsearches for Grades 7-12. 212p. 1990. 24.95 (*0-87628-189-7*) P-H.

Roach & Leddy. Basic College Chemistry. 1991. 22.00 (*0-536-58063-4*) Ginn Pr.

Roach & Williams. Troubleshooting Grammar Problems in Writing. 2nd ed. 256p. 1992. per. 19.95 (*0-8403-7337-6*) Kendall-Hunt.

Roach, jt. ed. see Wood.

Roach, Abby M. Some Successful Marriages. LC 76-152956. (Short Story Index Reprint Ser.). (Illus.). 1977. reprint ed. 21.95 (*0-8369-3871-2*) Ayer.

Roach, Carol A. & Wyatt, Nancy J. Successful Listening. 141p. (C). 1989. pap. text ed. 12.00 (*0-06-045439-3*) HarpCollege.

Roach, Catharyn & Moore, JoAnne. Teaching Library Skills in Grades K Through 6: A How-to-Do-It Manual for School & Public Librarians. (How-to-Do-It Ser.). 157p. 1993. 32.50 (*1-55570-126-4*) Neal-Schuman.

Roach, Colleen, ed. Communication & Culture in War & Peace. (Communication & Human Values Ser.: Vol. 11). (Illus.). 216p. (C). 1993. text ed. 49.95 (*0-8039-5062-4*); pap. text ed. 24.00 (*0-8039-5063-2*) Sage.

Roach, Donald W. Complete Secondary Choral Music Guide. 304p. 1990. pap. text ed. 29.95 (*0-13-162538-1*) P-H.

Roach, Dudley, intro. National Conference on Bulk Materials Handling, 1993. (National Conference Publication Ser.: No. 93-8). (Illus.). 279p. (Orig.). 1993. pap. text ed. 72.00 (*0-85825-578-2*, Pub. by Inst Engrs Aust-EA Bks AT) Accents Pubns.

***Roach, E. S. & Riela, A. R.** Pediatric Cerebrovascular Disorders. 2nd ed. (Illus.). 480p. 1995. write for info. (*0-87993-622-3*) Futura Pub.

Roach, E. S. & Riela, Anthony R., eds. Pediatric Cerebrovascular Disorders. (Illus.). 272p. (C). 1988. 45.00 (*0-87993-322-4*) Futura Pub.

Roach, Eloise, tr. see Jimenez, Juan R.

Roach, G. Aspects of Nonlinear Scattering Theory. LC 93-19958. (Pitman Monographs & Surveys in Pure & Applied Mathematics). 1993. write for info. (*0-582-09230-2*, Pub. by Longman UK) Longman.

Roach, G. F. Green's Functions. 2nd ed. LC 81-10017. 320p. 1982. pap. 29.95 (*0-521-28288-8*) Cambridge U Pr.

***Roach, G. F. & McBride, A., eds.** Recent Developments in Evolution Equations. (Pitman Research Notes in Mathematics Ser.). 1995. write for info. (*0-615-00303-6*) Wiley.

Roach, Gary, et al. Pro-Mo's Secrets for Finding Walleyes. (Illus.). 112p. (Orig.). 1988. pap. write for info. (*0-318-64036-8*) Fishing Pro-Mos Inc.

— Pro-Mo's Secrets to Jigging Walleyes. (Illus.). 112p. (Orig.). 1988. pap. write for info. (*0-318-64037-6*) Fishing Pro-Mos Inc.

— Pro-Mo's Secrets to Rigging Walleyes. (Illus.). 112p. (Orig.). 1988. pap. write for info. (*0-318-64035-X*) Fishing Pro-Mos Inc.

Roach, Gerry. Colorado's Fourteeners: From Hikes to Climbs. LC 91-58671. (Illus.). 272p. (Orig.). 1992. pap. 15.95 (*1-55591-103-X*) Fulcrum Pub.

— Colorado's Indian Peaks Wilderness Area: Classic Hikes & Climbs. LC 88-31471. (Fulcrum's Guide Ser.). (Illus.). 240p. 1989. pap. 14.95 (*1-55591-041-6*) Fulcrum Pub.

— Flatiron Classics: A Guide to Easy Climbs & Trails in Boulder's Flatirons. LC 86-29449. (Fulcrum's Guide Ser.). (Illus.). 316p. 1987. pap. 14.95 (*1-55591-017-3*) Fulcrum Pub.

— Rocky Mountain National Park: Classic Hikes & Climbs. LC 88-16307. (Fulcrum's Guide Ser.). 1988. pap. 14.95 (*1-55591-033-5*) Fulcrum Pub.

***Roach, Hannah B.** Taxables in the City of Philadelphia. (Special Publication Ser.: No. 4). 41p. 1990. reprint ed. pap. 6.00 (*1-887099-03-4*) Geneal Soc Pa.

***Roach, Hannah B., comp.** The Pennsylvania Militia in 1777. (Special Publication Ser.: No. 1). 80p. 1994. reprint ed. pap. 5.00 (*1-887099-00-X*) Geneal Soc Pa.

Roach, Harry. Gettysburg - Hour-by-Hour: An Account of the Battle. (Illus.). 76p. (C). 1993. pap. text ed. 7.95 (*0-939631-50-4*) Thomas Publications.

Roach, Helen P. History of Speech Education at Columbia College, 1754-1940. LC 70-177194. (Columbia University. Teachers College. Contributions to Education Ser.: No. 963). reprint ed. 37.50 (*0-404-55963-8*) AMS Pr.

Roach, Hildred. Black American Music: Past & Present. 2nd ed. LC 82-25860. 390p. (C). 1992. 52.50 (*0-89464-580-3*); pap. 42.50 (*0-89464-766-0*) Krieger.

— Black American Music: Past & Present. 2nd ed. LC 82-25860. 390p. 1994. pap. 42.50 (*0-89464-865-9*) Krieger.

***Roach, J. Ashley & Smith, Robert W.** International Law Studies 1994: Excessive Maritime Claims. Vol. 66. 1994. write for info. (*0-615-00080-0*) Naval War Coll.

Roach, James R. India Two Thousand: The Next Fifteen Years. LC 85-63423. 228p. (C). 1986. 33.00 (*0-913215-11-2*) Riverdale Co.

***Roach, Jerry V.** The Gathering Storm. (Illus.). 288p. (Orig.). 1994. pap. 16.95 (*0-943639-20-4*) Anchor Pub Co.

— A New & Living Way. (Illus.). 123p. (Orig.). 1993. pap. text ed. 11.95 (*0-943639-16-6*) Anchor Pub Co.

Roach, John. Secondary Education in England, 1870-1902: Public Activity & Private Enterprise. 320p. 1991. 85.00 (*0-415-03572-4*, A5695) Routledge.

— Surprizing Adventures of John Roach, Mariner of Whitehaven. 2nd ed. 864p. 1986. reprint ed. pap. 8.00 (*0-913129-14-3*) La Tienda.

Roach, John, ed. A Bibliography of Modern History. LC 67-11528. 412p. reprint ed. pap. 117.50 (*0-8357-7197-0*, 2051466) Bks Demand.

Roach, John C. Williamsburg: An Artist's Sketchbook. (Illus.). 50p. 1994. pap. 9.50 (*1-884824-05-6*) Tryon Pubng.

Roach, John C. & Martin, Tyrone G. USS Constitution - "Old Ironsides" An Artist's Sketchbook. 56p. 1994. pap. 9.50 (*1-884824-04-8*) Tryon Pubng.

***Roach, Jonathan.** Allison's Happy Summer. 1995. 8.95 (*0-8062-5264-2*) Carlton.

Roach, Joseph E. The Canadian Law of Mortgages of Land. 592p. 1993. text ed. 95.00 (*0-409-90349-3*) Butterworth Legal Pubs.

Roach, Joseph R. The Player's Passion: Studies in the Science of Acting. LC 84-40059. (Illus.). 256p. 1986. 38.50 (*0-87413-265-7*) U Delaware Pr.

— The Player's Passion: Studies in the Science of Acting. (Theater: Theory - Text - Performance Ser.). 256p. (C). 1993. reprint ed. pap. text ed. 14.95 (*0-472-08244-2*) U of Mich Pr.

Roach, Joseph R., jt. ed. see Reinelt, Janelle G.

Roach, Joyce, jt. auth. see Linck, Ernestine S.

Roach, Joyce G. C. L. Sonnichsen. LC 79-53653. (Western Writers Ser.: No. 40). (Illus.). 48p. (Orig.). 1979. pap. 3.95 (*0-88430-064-1*) Boise St U W Writ Ser.

— The Cowgirls. rev. ed. LC 90-39339. (Illus.). 256p. 1990. reprint ed. pap. 15.95 (*0-929398-15-7*) UNTX Pr.

Roach, Joyce G., ed. This Place of Memory: A Texas Perspective. LC 92-6890. (Illus.). 161p. (Orig.). 1992. pap. 15.95 (*0-929398-32-7*) UNTX Pr.

Roach, Joyce G., jt. ed. see Alter, Judy.

Roach, Lee S., jt. auth. see Ludwig, William B.

Roach, Margaret. Burpee Groundcovers. (Burpee American Gardening Ser.). (Illus.). 96p. 1993. pap. 9.00 (*0-671-84647-7*, P-H Gardening) P-H Gen Ref & Trav.

Roach, Margaret, jt. auth. see Druse, Ken.

Roach, Margaret J. I Love You, Charles Henry: Cats & Dogs in My Life. Moore, Susan & Craft, Page, eds. (Illus.). (J). (gr. 1-6). 1994. pap. 13.50 (*1-882666-02-X*) M Roach & Assocs.

— Mac & His Dog, Sir John. (Illus.). (Orig.). (J). (gr. k-8). 1993. Spanish ed., Mac y Su Perro, Don Juan. pap. 13.50 (*1-882666-01-1*); English ed. pap. 13.50 (*1-882666-00-3*) M Roach & Assocs.

***Roach, Marilynne K.** Day to Day in Salem: The Life Behind the Witchcraft Trials. LC 94-32383. (J). 1995. 15.95 (*0-395-69704-2*) Ticknor & Fields.

— Encounters with the Invisible World Being Ten Tales of Ghosts, Witches & the Devil Himself in New England. 16.95 (*0-89190-874-9*, Am Repr) Amereon Ltd.

***Roach, Martin.** The Prodigy: Electronic Punks: The Official Story. (Illus.). 176p. Date not set. pap. 9.95 (*1-897783-04-3*, MR55592) Omnibus NY.

Roach, Paul, ed. see Castro, Fred.

Roach, Penelope. Political Socialization in the New Nations of Africa. LC 66-24873. (Columbia University, Center for Education in Asia, Publications). 41p. reprint ed. pap. 25.00 (*0-317-41857-2*, 2026058) Bks Demand.

***Roach, Peter.** Complete Book of Pet Care. (Illus.). 272p. 1995. 17.95 (*0-87605-484-X*) Howell Bk.

Roach, Peter, ed. Computing in Linguistics & Phonetics: Introductory Readings. (Illus.). 128p. 1992. pap. text ed. 35.00 (*0-12-589340-X*) Acad Pr.

Roach, Susan. Bread Dough Creations. (Illus.). 68p. 1994. pap. 7.95 (*1-86351-102-4*, Pub. by S Milner AT) Sterling.

Roach, Thomas R. Newsprint: Canadian Supply & American Demand. LC 94-6940. (Issues Ser.). 1994. pap. 6.95 (*0-89030-050-X*) Forest Hist Soc.

Roach, Thomas R., jt. auth. see Gillis, Peter.

Roach, William, ed. The First Continuation: Redaction of Manuscripts A L P R S, Vol. 3, Pt. 1. (Continuations of the Old French Perceval of Chretien de Troyes). 1952. 12.00 (*0-87169-997-4*, AP3A-ROW) Am Philos.

— The First Continuation: Redaction of Manuscripts T V D, Vol. 1. (Continuations of the Old French Perceval of Chretien de Troyes). 1949. 12.00 (*0-87169-999-0*, AP10-ROW) Am Philos.

Roach, William, jt. ed. see Ivy, Robert H., Jr.

Roach, William F., Jr., et al. Medical Records & the Law. 2nd ed. 368p. 1994. 49.00 (*0-8342-0317-0*, 20317) Aspen Pub.

Roache, Catharine S. Old Children of God. (Illus.). 16p. 1973. 2.00 (*0-685-02261-7*) Hermosa.

— What Are Forests For? 44p. 1971. 2.00 (*0-913478-01-6*) Hermosa.

Roache, Gordon. A Halifax ABC. (Illus.). 32p. 1987. pap. 14.95 (*0-88776-183-6*, U of Toronto Pr) Tundra Bks.

***Roache, James D.** Five Eighty Worst. 210p. 1995. pap. 8.95 (*0-7610-0323-1*) NW Pub.

Roache, James D. Seven Days with the Wizard. abr. ed. 156p. 1994. pap. 7.95 (*1-56901-464-7*) NW Pub.

— Windsong. Van Treese, James B., ed. 334p. (Orig.). 1994. pap. 9.95 (*1-56901-106-0*) NW Pub.

Roache, L. D., tr. see Plattard, Jean.

Roache, Patrick J. Computational Fluid Dynamics. rev. ed. vii, 446p. 1976. 26.50 (*0-913478-05-9*) Hermosa.

Roache-Selk, Evelyn. From the Womb of Earth: An Appreciation of Yoruba Bronze Art. LC 78-56919. (Illus.). 1978. pap. text ed. 15.00 (*0-8191-0521-X*) U Pr of Amer.

Roadarmel, Paul. Beach House Seven. 320p. 1988. pap. 4.50 (*0-373-97077-3*) Harlequin Bks.

Roades, M. T. Cervantes & Mark Twain. 1972. 59.95 (*0-87968-830-0*) Gordon Pr.

Roads & Transportation Association of Canada, Project Committee on Bridge Hydraulics. Guide to Bridge Hydraulics. Neill, C. R., ed. LC 72-95811. 203p. reprint ed. pap. 57.90 (*0-685-15895-0*, 2056117) Bks Demand.

***Roads, C. H.** The British Soldiers Firearm, 1850-1864. (Illus.). 336p. 1994. reprint ed. 53.00 (*1-884849-13-X*) R&R Bks.

Roads, Curtis, ed. The Music Machine: Selected Readings from Computer Music Journal. (Illus.). 740p. 1992. reprint ed. 26.50 (*0-262-68078-5*) MIT Pr.

Roads, Curtis, et al. The Computer Music Tutorial. LC 94-19027. 1995. 60.00x (*0-262-18158-4*); pap. 39.95x (*0-262-68082-3*) MIT Pr.

Roads, Michael J. Journey into Nature: A Spiritual Adventure. Lipsett, Suzanne, ed. LC 89-80727. 228p. 1990. pap. 10.95 (*0-915811-19-7*) H J Kramer Inc.

— Journey into Oneness: A Spiritual Odyssey. Carleton, Nancy, ed. LC 93-38394. 252p. 1994. pap. 10.95 (*0-915811-54-5*) H J Kramer Inc.

— Simple Is Powerful: Anecdotes for a Complex World. Ober, Doris, ed. LC 91-52848. 216p. 1992. pap. 10.95 (*0-915811-35-9*) H J Kramer Inc.

— Talking with Nature: Sharing the Energies & Spirit of Trees, Plants, Birds & Earth. Armstrong, Gregory, ed. (Illus.). 156p. (Orig.). 1987. pap. 9.95 (*0-915811-06-5*) H J Kramer Inc.

Roads, Samuel, Jr. The History & Traditions of Marblehead. rev. ed. (Illus.). 595p. 1989. reprint ed. lib. bdg. 60.00 (*0-8328-0842-3*, MA0111) Higginson Bk Co.

Roadstrum, William H. Being Successful As an Engineer. LC 77-27435. 246p. (C). 1988. pap. text ed. 13.50x (*0-910554-24-2*) Engineering.

Roadstrum, William H. & Wolaver, Dan H. Electrical Engineering: For All Engineers. 2nd ed. LC 93-23818. 714p. 1993. Net. text ed. 75.95 (*0-471-51043-2*) Wiley.

Roaf, Caroline & Bines, Hazel, eds. Needs, Rights & Opportunities. (Education & Alienation Ser.). 250p. 1989. 55.00 (*1-85000-516-8*, Falmer Pr); pap. 28.00 (*1-85000-517-6*, Falmer Pr) Taylor & Francis.

Roaf, John, jt. auth. see Kalman, Harold.

Roaf, Michael & Postgate, Nicholas. Cultural Atlas of Mesopotamia & the Ancient Near East. (Cultural Atlas Ser.). (Illus.). 240p. 1990. 45.00 (*0-8160-2218-6*) Facts on File.

Roaf, R., jt. ed. see Ghista, Dhanjoo N.

Roaf, Susan & Hancock, Mary. Energy Efficient Building: A Design Guide. 293p. 1992. text ed. 89.95 (*0-470-21952-1*) Halsted Pr.

Roaf, Susan, jt. auth. see Beamon, Sylvia.

Roah, Kathy, ed. see Hilbert, Donna, et al.

Roake, Margaret. Essays in Kentish History. Whyman, John, ed. (Illus.). 315p. 1973. 30.00 (*0-7146-2956-1*, Pub. by F Cass Pubs UK) Intl Spec Bk.

Roalf, Peggy. Cats. LC 91-73829. (Looking at Paintings Ser.). (Illus.). 48p. (J). (gr. 3-7). 1992. lib. bdg. 14.89 (*1-56282-092-3*); pap. 6.95 (*1-56282-091-5*) Hyprn Child.

— Children. LC 92-52982. (Looking at Paintings Ser.). (Illus.). 48p. (Orig.). (J). (gr. 3-7). 1993. lib. bdg. 14.89 (*1-56282-308-6*); pap. 6.95 (*1-56282-309-4*) Hyprn Child.

— Circus. LC 92-52983. (Looking at Paintings Ser.). (Illus.). 48p. (Orig.). (J). (gr. 3-7). 1993. lib. bdg. 14.89 (*1-56282-304-3*); pap. 6.95 (*1-56282-305-1*) Hyprn Child.

— Dancers. LC 91-73827. (Looking at Paintings Ser.). (Illus.). 48p. (J). (gr. 3-7). 1992. lib. bdg. 14.89 (*1-56282-090-7*); pap. 6.95 (*1-56282-089-3*) Hyprn Child.

— Dogs. LC 93-10585. (Looking at Paintings Ser.). (Illus.). (J). (gr. 3-7). 1993. lib. bdg. 14.89 (*1-56282-531-3*) Hyprn Child.

— Dogs. LC 93-20585. (Looking at Paintings Ser.). (Illus.). 48p. (J). (gr. 3-7). 1993. lib. bdg. 14.89 (*1-56282-530-5*); pap. 6.95 (*0-685-70878-0*) Hyprn Ppbks.

— Families. LC 91-73830. (Looking at Paintings Ser.). (Illus.). 48p. (J). (gr. 3-7). 1992. lib. bdg. 14.89 (*1-56282-088-5*); pap. 6.95 (*1-56282-087-7*) Hyprn Child.

— Flowers. LC 92-72015. (Looking at Paintings Ser.). (Illus.). 48p. (J). (gr. 3-7). 1993. lib. bdg. 14.89 (*1-56282-359-0*); pap. 6.95 (*1-56282-358-2*) Hyprn Child.

— Horses. LC 92-52979. (Looking at Paintings Ser.). (Illus.). 48p. (Orig.). (J). (gr. 3-7). 1992. lib. bdg. 14.89 (*1-56282-306-X*); pap. 6.95 (*1-56282-307-8*) Hyprn Child.

— Landscapes. LC 92-52980. (Looking at Paintings Ser.). (Illus.). 48p. (Orig.). (J). (gr. 3-7). 1992. lib. bdg. 14.89 (*1-56282-302-7*); pap. 6.95 (*1-56282-303-5*) Hyprn Child.

— Musicians. LC 93-15555. (Looking at Paintings Ser.). (Illus.). 48p. (J). (gr. 3-7). 1993. lib. bdg. 14.89 (*1-56282-533-X*); pap. 6.95 (*1-56282-532-1*) Hyprn Child.

— Seascapes. LC 91-73828. (Looking at Paintings Ser.). (Illus.). 48p. (J). (gr. 3-7). 1992. lib. bdg. 14.89 (*1-56282-094-X*); pap. 6.95 (*1-56282-093-1*) Hyprn Child.

— Self-Portraits. LC 92-72042. (Looking at Paintings Ser.). (Illus.). 48p. (J). (gr. 3-7). 1993. lib. bdg. 14.89 (*1-56282-357-4*); pap. 6.95 (*1-56282-356-6*) Hyprn Child.

Roalman, Arthur R. Investor Relations That Work. LC 80-65707. 287p. reprint ed. pap. 81.80 (*0-317-20405-X*, 2023504) Bks Demand.

Roalson, Louise, ed. Notably Norwegian: Recipes, Festivals, Folk Arts. LC 82-81569. (Illus.). 88p. 1982. pap. 7.95 (*0-941016-05-6*) Penfield.

Roan, jt. auth. see Kaiser.

Roan, Carol. Clues to American Dance. (Clues to American Arts Ser.). (Illus.). 80p. (Orig.). 1993. pap. 7.95 (*0-913515-83-3*, Starrhill) Elliott & Clark.

— Speak Easy: A Guide to Successful Performances, Presentations, Speeches, & Lectures. 80p. (Orig.). 1995. pap. 8.95 (*1-57359-000-2*, Starrhill) Elliott & Clark.

Roan, Sharon. Ozone Crisis: The Fifteen Year Evolution of a Sudden Global Emergency. 270p. 1989. text ed. 18.95 (*0-471-61985-X*) Wiley.

— Ozone Crisis: The Fifteen Year Evolution of a Sudden Global Emergency. 270p. 1990. pap. text ed. 9.95 (*0-471-52823-4*) Wiley.

— Postpartum Depression. 1993. write for info. (*0-471-54678-X*) Wiley.

Roane, M. K., et al. Chestnut Blight, Other Endothia Diseases, & the Genus Endothia. (Monograph Ser.). (Illus.). 53p. 1986. 15.00 (*0-89054-073-X*) Am Phytopathol Soc.

Roane, Martha K., jt. ed. see Coyier, Duane L.

R

RoAne, Susan. How to Work a Room. 224p. 1989. pap. 10.99 (*0-446-39065-8*) Warner Bks.
— How to Work a Room: A Guide to Successfully Managing the Mingling. LC 88-26388. (Illus.). 224p. 1988. 14.95 (*0-944007-06-6*) Sure Sellers.
— The Secrets of Savvy Networking: How to Make the Best Connections for Business & Personal Success. 224p. (Orig.). 1993. 11.99 (*0-446-39410-6*) Warner Bks.
Roankin, Myron, ed. see Wolkinson, Benjamin W. & Block, Richard N.
Roanoke Bar Association, jt. auth. see Virginia Law Foundation Committee on Continuing Legal Education.
***Roaring, Elena D.** Upgrading Technological Capabilities of Small Industry. 168p. 1991. pap. text ed. 15.00 (*92-833-2107-3*, 321073, Pub. by APO JA) Qual Resc.
***Roark, Carol.** Fort Worth's Legendary Landmarks: Eighty Buildings. (Illus.). 264p. 1995. 42.50 (*0-87565-143-7*) Tex Christian.
Roark, Carol E., et al. Catalogue of the Amon Carter Museum Photography Collection. LC 92-36173. (Illus.). 720p. 1993. 95.00 (*0-88360-063-3*) Amon Carter.
Roark, James L. Masters Without Slaves. (C). 1978. pap. text ed. 9.95 (*0-393-00901-7*) Norton.
Roark, James L., jt. auth. see Johnson, Michael P.
Roark, James L., jt. ed. see Johnson, Michael P.
Roark, Kelley. The Connecticut Outdoor Activity Guide. LC 93-47044. (Outdoor Activity Guide Ser.). (Illus.). 120p. (Orig.). 1994. pap. 9.95 (*1-56626-046-9*) Country Rds.
Roark, Kelley, ed. Land for Housing: Developing a Research Agenda. (Monograph Ser.: No. 85-3). 81p. reprint ed. pap. 25.00 (*0-7837-2172-2*, 2042497) Bks Demand.
***Roarke.** Blood River: The War for the Northwest Territory. 1995. mass mkt. 4.99 (*0-312-95420-4*) St Martin.
***Roarke, Mike.** Shadows on the Longhouse Vol. 1. 1994. pap. 4.99 (*0-312-95322-4*) St Martin.
— Silent Drums: The First Frontier Series, Bk. 2. 1994. mass mkt. 4.99 (*0-312-95224-4*) St Martin.
— Thunder in the East. 1993. mass mkt. 4.50 (*0-312-95192-2*) St Martin.
Roarty, Robert Sean, ed. see Ruttenber, Tim, pseud.
Roat, Ronald C. Close Softly the Doors. (First Stuart Mallory Mystery Ser.). 160p. 1993. pap. 12.95 (*0-934257-96-5*) Story Line.
— Close Softly the Doors: A Mystery. 2nd ed. (First Stuart Mallory Mystery Ser.). 148p. 1991. 18.95 (*0-934257-48-5*) Story Line.
— A Still & Icy Silence. (First Stuart Mallory Mystery Ser.). 325p. 1993. 21.95 (*0-934257-94-9*) Story Line.
Roath, S. & Corn, M., eds. Adult T-Cell Leukemia in Japan. (Hematology Reviews & Communications Ser.: Vol. 3, No. 4). 102p. 1990. pap. text ed. 139.00 (*3-7186-4933-0*) Gordon & Breach.
— Current Approaches to Bone Marrow Histopathology. (Hematology Reviews & Communications Ser.: Vol. 3, Nos. 2-3). 114p. 1989. pap. text ed. 158.00 (*3-7186-4974-8*) Gordon & Breach.
— Hematology Reviews & Communications, Vol. 3, No. 1. 88p. 1989. pap. text ed. 113.00 (*3-7186-4935-7*) Gordon & Breach.
Roath, S., ed. see Mauri, C.
Roath, Stuart, ed. Raynaud's: A Guide for Health Professionals. (Illus.). 160p. 1990. pap. 22.95 (*0-412-33680-4*, A4442) Chapman & Hall.
Roath, Stuart & Huisman, Titus H., eds. Current Views on Thalassaemia: With Special Reference to Its Mediterranean Presence. LC 92-1571. 1992. text ed. 58.00 (*3-7186-5262-5*) Gordon & Breach.
Roazen, Paul. Brother Animal: The Story of Freud & Tausk. 224p. (C). 1990. pap. 21.95 (*0-88738-851-5*) Transaction Pubs.
— Encountering Freud: The Politics & Histories of Psychoanalysis. 405p. 1989. 39.95 (*0-88738-295-9*) Transaction Pubs.
— Erik H. Erikson: The Power & Limits of a Vision. LC 76-10496. 1976. 15.95 (*0-02-926450-2*) Free Pr.
— Erik H. Erikson: The Power & Limits of a Vision. 235p. 1986. pap. 14.95 (*0-02-927170-3*) Free Pr.
— Freud: Political & Social Thought. (Psychoanalysis: Examined & Re-Examined Ser.). xii, 332p. 1986. reprint ed. lib. bdg. 35.00 (*0-306-76294-3*) Da Capo.
— Freud & His Followers. (Illus.). 643p. 1992. reprint ed. pap. 17.95 (*0-306-80472-7*) Da Capo.
— Helene Deutsch: A Psychoanalyst's Life. 384p. 1985. 19.95 (*0-671-25028-0*) S&S Trade.
— Helene Deutsch: A Psychoanalyst's Life. 384p. (C). 1991. pap. 21.95 (*1-56000-552-1*) Transaction Pubs.
— How Freud Worked: First-Hand Accounts of Patients. 1995. 30.00 (*1-56821-556-8*) Aronson.
— Meeting Freud's Family. LC 93-22734. (Illus.). 232p. 1993. 29.95 (*0-87023-873-6*) U of Mass Pr.
Roazen, Paul, ed. Sigmund Freud. (Series in Science). vi, 186p. 1987. reprint ed. pap. 9.95 (*0-306-80292-9*) Da Capo.
Roazen, Paul & Swerdloff, Bluma. Heresy: Sandor Rado & the Psychoanalytic Movement. LC 94-21882. 232p. 1995. 35.00 (*1-56821-321-2*) Aronson.
Roazen, Paul, ed. see Deutsch, Helene.
Roazen, Paul, ed. see Hartz, Louis.
Roazen, Paul, ed. see Tausk, Victor.
Rob, Caroline & Reynolds, Janet. The Caregiver's Guide: Helping Older Friends & Relatives with Health & Safety Concerns. 320p. 1992. pap. 12.95 (*0-395-58780-8*) HM.
Rob, Charles G. & Hinshaw, J. Raymond. Specialty Board Review: General Surgery. 4th ed. 203p. 1991. pap. text ed. 42.95 (*0-8385-8638-4*, A-8638-7) Appleton & Lange.
Rob, Peter. Big Blue BASIC: Programming the IBM PC & Compatibles. 2nd ed. 591p. (C). 1988. pap. 41.95 (*0-534-08706-X*) Boyd & Fraser.
— Identifying & Solving Statistical Problems with Microstat-II, Version 2.5. 462p. (C). 1991. pap. 44.95 (*0-534-14790-9*) Intl Thomson.
***Rob, Peter & Coronel, Carlos.** Database Systems: Design, Implementation, & Management. 2nd ed. LC 94-40216. 1995. write for info. (*0-7895-0052-3*) Boyd & Fraser.
— Database Systems: Implementation & Management. 643p. (C). 1993. text ed. 51.95 (*0-534-17052-8*) Boyd & Fraser.
***Roba, William, et al.** Hans Reimer Claussen, 1804-1894: A Sketch of His Life - Eine Lebensskinzize. Rippley, Vern, ed. (Illus.). (GER.). 1994. pap. 6.00 (*0-614-04594-0*) Hesperian Pr.
Roback, A. A. A Dictionary of International Slurs. LC 76-5696. (Maledicta Press Publications Ser.: Vol. 5). (C). 1979. reprint ed. pap. 15.00 (*0-916500-05-5*) Maledicta.
— The Story of Yiddish Literature. 1972. 300.00 (*0-87968-084-9*) Gordon Pr.
Roback, A. A., ed. The Albert Schweitzer Jubilee Book. LC 79-97392. (Illus.). 508p. 1971. reprint ed. text ed. 65.00 (*0-8371-2670-3*, ASJB, Greenwood Pr) Greenwood.
Roback, Abraham A. History of Psychology & Psychiatry. LC 71-88929. 422p. 1969. reprint ed. text ed. 65.00 (*0-8371-2104-3*, ROHP, Greenwood Pr) Greenwood.
— The Psychology of Character: With a Survey of Temperament. LC 73-2988. (Classics in Psychology Ser.). 1974. reprint ed. 37.95 (*0-405-05160-3*) Ayer.
Roback, C. W. The Mysteries of Astrology & the Wonders of Magic. reprint ed. spiral bd. 9.35 (*0-7873-0728-9*) Mokelumne.
Roback, Howard B., ed. Helping Patients & Their Families Cope with Medical Problems: A Guide to Therapeutic Group Work in Clinical Settings. LC 83-49267. (Joint Publication in the Jossey-Bass Social & Behavioral Science Series & the Jossey-Bass Health Ser.). 589p. reprint ed. pap. 167.90 (*0-7837-2522-1*, 2042681) Bks Demand.
Roback, Jennifer. A Matter of Choice: A Critique of Comparable Worth by a Skeptical Feminist - A Twentieth Century Fund Paper. 53p. (Orig.). (C). 1986. pap. text ed. 7.00 (*0-87078-172-3*) TCFP-PPP.
Roback, Selwyn S. Adults of the Subfamily Tanypodinae (Pelopiinae) in North America (Diptera: Chironomidae) (Monograph: No. 17). (Illus.). 410p. (Orig.). 1971. pap. 8.00 (*0-910006-25-3*) Acad Nat Sci Phila.
Robaer, Ken, pseud. Apples of Gold. (Orig.). 1985. pap. text ed. 14.95 (*0-937957-00-3*) B Roberts.
Robaire, Bernard, ed. The Male Germ Cell: Spermatogonium to Fertilization. LC 91-38987. (Annals Ser.: Vol. 637). 510p. 1992. pap. 106.00 (*0-89766-710-7*, QL696) NY Acad Sci.
Robalto, Matilde A. Redaccion y Eshilo. 6th ed. Marle, Inc. Staff, ed. 400p. Date not set. pap. write for info. (*0-9627933-0-2*) A L Matilde.
***Robards, A. W. & Wilson, A. J., eds.** Procedures in Electron Microscopy. pap. text ed. write for info. (*0-471-92853-4*) Wiley.
Robards, Anthony W., ed. Botanical Microscopy, 1985. (Illus.). 378p. 1986. 32.50 (*0-19-854587-8*) OUP.
Robards, Anthony W., jt. ed. see Bald, W. B.
Robards, Anthony W., jt. ed. see Betts, W. B.
Robards, Anthony W., et al, eds. Low Temperature Methods in Biological Electron Microscopy. (Practical Methods in Electron Microscopy Ser.: Vol. 10). 550p. 1986. 181.75 (*0-444-80685-7*); pap. 54.00 (*0-444-80684-9*) Elsevier.
***Robards, Brooks & Kaplan, Jim.** Sweet & Sour: One Woman's Chinese Adventure, One Man's Chinese Fortune. 200p. (Orig.). 1995. pap. 14.95 (*0-9645250-0-3*) Smmrst Pr.
Robards, K., et al. Principles & Practice of Modern Chromatography. (Illus.). 512p. 1994. text ed. 55.00 (*0-12-589570-4*) Acad Pr.
Robards, Karen. Amanda Rose. 432p. 1984. mass mkt. 5.99 (*0-446-30617-7*) Warner Bks.
— Dark of the Moon. 416p. 1988. mass mkt. 5.99 (*0-380-75437-1*) Avon.
— Desire in the Sun. 400p. 1988. mass mkt. 5.99 (*0-380-75554-8*) Avon.
— Forbidden Love. 384p. 1994. pap. 4.99 (*0-8439-3592-8*) Dorchester Pub Co.
— Green Eyes. 400p. (Orig.). 1993. lib. bdg. 20.00 (*0-7278-4390-7*) Severn Hse.
— Green Eyes. 400p. (Orig.). 1995. reprint ed. mass mkt. 5.99 (*0-380-75889-X*) Avon.
— Hunter's Moon. LC 95-8856. 1996. write for info. (*0-385-31036-6*) Delacorte.
— Island Flame. 352p. (Orig.). 1993. pap. 4.99 (*0-8439-3414-X*) Dorchester Pub Co.
— Island Flame. 352p. (Orig.). 1995. mass mkt., pap. 5.99 (*0-8349-3844-8*) Dorchester Pub Co.
— Loving Julia. 384p. 1986. mass mkt. 4.99 (*0-446-30057-8*) Warner Bks.
— Maggy's Child. LC 93-23792. 1994. 19.95 (*0-385-31205-9*) Delacorte.
— Maggy's Child. 1994. pap. 5.99 (*0-440-20830-0*) Dell.
— Maggy's Child. large type ed. LC 93-47353. 1994. 25.95 (*1-56895-057-8*) Wheeler Pub.
— Morning Song. 400p. 1995. reprint ed. mass mkt. 5.99 (*0-380-75888-1*) Avon.
— Night Magic. 384p. 1988. mass mkt. 5.50 (*0-446-35391-4*) Warner Bks.
— Night Magic. large type ed. LC 93-32210. 1993. 21.95 (*0-7927-1873-9*, Eagle Lrg Print) Chivers N Amer.
— Nobody's Angel. 1992. mass mkt. 5.99 (*0-440-20828-9*) Dell.
— Nobody's Angel. large type ed. 575p. 1992. reprint ed. lib. bdg. 20.95 (*1-56054-449-X*) Thorndike Pr.
— One Summer. 1993. mass mkt. 5.99 (*0-440-20829-7*) Dell.
— One Summer. large type ed. LC 93-12459. 1993. 23.95 (*0-7927-1609-4*, Eagle Lrg Print) Chivers N Amer.
— One Summer. large type ed. 1994. pap. 21.95 (*0-7927-1608-6*, Paragon Lrg Print) Chivers N Amer.
— Sea Fire. 416p. 1991. pap. 4.95 (*0-8439-3121-3*) Dorchester Pub Co.
— This Side of Heaven. 448p. 1991. mass mkt. 4.99 (*0-440-20827-0*) Dell.
— Tiger's Eye. 400p. (Orig.). 1989. mass mkt. 5.99 (*0-380-75555-6*) Avon.
— To Love a Man. 384p. 1988. mass mkt. 5.50 (*0-446-35350-7*) Warner Bks.
— Walking after Midnight. 1995. 21.95 (*0-385-31034-X*) Delacorte.
— Walking After Midnight. large type ed. LC 94-38992. 545p. 1995. 22.95 (*0-7838-1178-0*) Hall.
— Wild Orchids. 384p. 1986. mass mkt. 5.50 (*0-446-32692-5*) Warner Bks.
Robards, Martin F. Running a Team for Disabled Children & Their Families. (Clinics in Developmental Medicine Ser.: No. 130). (Illus.). 150p. (C). 1994. 44.95 (*0-521-45517-0*) Cambridge U Pr.
Robards, Terry. The New York Times Book of Wine. 480p. 1977. pap. 8.95 (*0-380-01720-2*) Avon.
Robare, Lorie, jt. illus. see Gerrity, Peg.
Robart, Rose. The Cake That Mack Ate. LC 86-47709. (Joy Street Bks.). (Illus.). (J). (ps-3). 1987. 14.95 (*0-316-74890-0*) Little.
— The Cake That Mack Ate. (Illus.). (J). (ps-3). 1991. mass mkt. 4.95 (*0-316-74891-9*) Little.
Robarts, Sadie, jt. auth. see Stamp, Paddy.
Robartson, Linda. The Complete Kwanzaa Celebration Book. 52p. 1993. pap. 9.95 (*0-9639026-9-5*) Creat Acrylic.
Robaton, John, jt. auth. see Smith, Harris.
Robaut, Alfred. L' Oeuvre Complet de Eugene Delacroix: Peintures, Dessins, Gravures Lithographies. LC 78-75310. (Graphic Arts, Painting & Sculpture Ser.). 1969. lib. bdg. 85.00 (*0-306-71628-3*) Da Capo.
***Robb.** Lady Chapel. 1995. mass mkt. 5.50 (*0-312-95460-3*) St Martin.
Robb, Amanda, ed. Encyclopedia of American Family Names. Date not set. 45.00 (*0-06-270075-8*, Harper Ref) HarpC.
Robb, Beverly. Collectible Golfing Novelties. LC 92-60627. (Illus.). 160p. (Orig.). 1992. pap. 29.95 (*0-88740-423-5*) Schiffer.
Robb, Bob. Hunting Wild Boar in California. LC 89-92684. (Illus.). 160p. (Orig.). 1989. pap. text ed. 14.95 (*0-936513-09-8*) Larsens Outdoor.
***Robb, Brian J.** River Phoenix: A Short Life. 1995. pap. 15.00 (*0-06-095132-X*, PL) HarpC.
Robb, Candace. The Lady Chapel. (Owen Archer Mystery Ser.). 304p. 1994. 20.95 (*0-312-11409-5*) St Martin.
***Robb, Candace M.** Apothecary Rose Vol. 1. 1994. pap. 4.50 (*0-312-95360-7*) St Martin.
***Robb, Carol S.** Equal Value: An Ethical Approach to Economics & Sex. 240p. (C). 1996. 25.00 (*0-8070-6504-8*) Beacon Pr.
Robb, Carol S. & Casebolt, Carl J., eds. Covenant for a New Creation: Ethics, Religion, & Public Policy. LC 90-27013. 1991. pap. 17.95 (*0-88344-740-1*) Orbis Bks.
Robb, Carol S., jt. ed. see Deats, Paul.
Robb, Carol S., ed. see Harrison, Beverly W.
Robb, D. A. & Pierpoint, S. Metals & Micronutrients: Uptake & Utilization by Plants. 1983. text ed. 117.00 (*0-12-589580-1*) Acad Pr.
Robb, Dale. Love & Living Together. LC 77-15242. 110p. (Orig.). reprint ed. pap. 31.40 (*0-685-15405-X*, 2027180) Bks Demand.
Robb, David. God's Fiction: Symbolism & Allegory in the Works of George MacDonald. 1989. 8.95 (*0-940652-36-6*) Sunrise Bks.
Robb, Dorian, pseud. Travel Careers & How to Get Started. 74p. (Orig.). (C). 1989. pap. 9.95 (*0-9622910-0-5*) Gar Pub Co.
***Robb, Frank T. & Place, Allen R., eds.** Archaea: A Laboratory Manual: Thermophiles. (Illus.). 264p. (C). 1995. pap. 65.00 (*0-87969-440-8*) Cold Spring Harbor.
***Robb, Frank T., et al, eds.** Archaea: A Laboratory Manual. 1048p. (C). 1995. 375.00 (*0-87969-397-5*) Cold Spring Harbor.
Robb, George. White-Collar Crime in Modern England: Financial Fraud & Business Morality, 1845-1929. 264p. (C). 1992. 59.95 (*0-521-41234-X*) Cambridge U Pr.
***Robb, Graham.** Balzac: A Biography. (Illus.). 521p. 1994. 57.50x (*0-330-33237-6*, Pub. by Pan Books UK) Trans-Atl Phila.
— Balzac: A Biography. (Illus.). 572p. 1995. pap. 15.00 (*0-393-31387-5*, Norton Paperbks) Norton.
— Balzac: A Life. LC 94-18614. 1994. 35.00 (*0-393-03679-0*) Norton.
Robb, Gwenda & Smith, Elaine. Concise Dictionary of Australian Artists. Smith, Robert, ed. 288p. (Orig.). 1993. pap. 24.95 (*0-522-84478-2*) Intl Spec Bk.

Robb, I. D., ed. Microemulsions. LC 81-17766. 268p. (C). 1982. 65.00 (*0-306-40834-1*, Plenum Pr) Plenum.
Robb, I. M. Jolly Roger. LC 90-70460. 151p. (Orig.). 1991. pap. 4.95 (*1-56002-117-9*) Aegina Pr.
Robb, James, ed. see Gracia, Jorge J.
Robb, James, ed. see Parr, Roger P.
Robb, James H. Man As Infinite Spirit. LC 74-76084. (Aquinas Lectures). 1974. 10.00 (*0-87462-139-9*) Marquette.
— St. Thomas Aquinas: Questions on the Soul. LC 84-61636. (Medieval Philosophical Texts in Translation Ser.). 1984. 25.00 (*0-87462-226-3*) Marquette.
Robb, James W. Patterns of Image & Structure in the Essays of Alfonso Reyes. LC 70-94192. (Catholic University of America. Studies in Romance Languages & Literatures: No. 56). 1969. reprint ed. 37.50 (*0-404-50356-X*) AMS Pr.
Robb, Jay. The Fat Burning Diet: Accessing Unlimited Energy for a Lifetime. 138p. (Orig.). 1994. pap. 9.95 (*0-9620608-1-X*) Loving Hlth Pubns.
***Robb, Jean M.** Secrets of a Small Town. 175p. 1995. pap. 7.95 (*0-7610-0141-7*) NW Pub.
Robb, John D. Focus! The Power of People Group Thinking. 101p. 1989. 5.95 (*0-912552-66-2*) MARC.
— Lawyers' Quest I - Twelve Notions about Lawyers: An Introduction to Discipleship. (Lawyers' Quest Ser.). 82p. (Orig.). (C). 1986. pap. text ed. 8.00 (*0-944561-09-8*) Chr Legal.
Robb, John S. Streaks of Squatter Life & Far-West Scenes. LC 62-7018. 1978. reprint ed. 50.00 (*0-8201-1038-8*) Schol Facsimiles.
Robb, Kevin. Literacy & Paideia in Ancient Greece. (Illus.). 320p. 1994. 45.00 (*0-19-505905-0*) OUP.
Robb, Kevin, ed. Language & Thought in Early Greek Philosophy. (Monist Library of Philosophy). 288p. 1983. 29.95 (*0-914417-01-0*); pap. 12.95 (*0-914417-05-3*) Hegeler Inst.
Robb, Laura. Whole Language, Whole Learners: Creating a Literature-Centered Classroom. (Illus.). 480p. 1994. 30.00 (*0-688-11957-3*); 19.95 (*0-688-11956-5*) Morrow.
Robb, Laura, comp. Music and Drum: Voices of War and Peace, Hope and Dreams. LC 92-39312. (J). 1994. write for info. (*0-399-22024-0*, Philomel Bks) Putnam Pub Group.
Robb, Louis. Dictionary of Modern Business. (ENG & SPA.). 1960. 35.00 (*0-910136-00-9*) Anderson Kramer.
Robb, Louis A. Dictionary of Legal Terms (Diccionario de Terminos Lagales) Spanish-English, English-Spanish. (ENG & SPA.). 1976. pap. 15.00 (*968-18-0384-1*) Intl Lang.
— Engineers' Dictionary. 664p. (ENG & SPA.). 1981. 125.00 (*0-8288-0670-5*, S31339) Fr & Eur.
— Engineers' Dictionary, Spanish-English & English-Spanish. 2nd ed. LC 49-50261. 680p. reprint ed. pap. 180.00 (*0-685-16201-X*, 2056291) Bks Demand.
— Spanish-English, English-Spanish Dictionary of Legal Terms: Diccionario de Terminos Legales Espanol-Ingles-Espanol. 12th ed. 228p. (ENG & SPA.). 1982. pap. 49.95 (*0-8288-0405-2*, S28548) Fr & Eur.
Robb, Margaret D. Dynamics of Motor-Skill Acquisition. (Illus.). 192p. 1972. pap. text ed. 15.95 (*0-685-03846-7*) P-H.
Robb, Marianne, ed. see Anderson, Marianne & Greenwood, Betty.
Robb, Mary M., ed. see Austin, Gilbert.
Robb, N. A. William of Orange: Personal Portrait, 2 vols. Incl. Vol. 2. Later Years, 1674-1702. LC 73-89359. 580p. 1966. (*0-685-23146-1*); LC 73-89359. (Illus.). write for info. (*0-318-55858-0*) St Martin.
Robb, P. G. Evolution of British Policy Towards Indian Politics, 1880-1920: Essays on Colonial Attitudes, Imperial Strategies, & Bihar. (C). 1992. text ed. 32.00 (*81-7304-001-X*, Pub. by Manohar II) S Asia.
Robb, Peter, ed. Dalit Movements & the Meanings of Labour in India. (SOAS Studies on South Asia). 375p. 1994. 21.00 (*0-19-563213-3*) OUP.
— Rural India: Land, Power & Society under British Rule. (Oxford India Paperbacks Ser.). 324p. 1993. pap. 12.95 (*0-19-563186-2*) OUP.
— Society & Ideology: Essays in South Asian History Presented to Professor K. A. Ballhatchet. (SOAS Studies on South Asia). 276p. 1993. 24.00 (*0-19-563214-1*) OUP.

An Asterisk (*) at the beginning of an entry indicates that the title is appearing in BIP for the first time.

Robb, Peter, jt. ed. see Arnold, David.

Robb, Peter G. The Evolution of British Policy Towards Indian Politics, 1880-1920. 400p. (C). 1992. 39.00 (*0-913215-67-8*) Riverdale Co.

Robb, Phyllis J. Cooking for Hyperactive & Allergic Children. LC 79-55878. (Orig.). 1980. lib. bdg. 12.95 (*0-935316-01-9*); pap. 7.95 (*0-935316-00-0*) Cedar Creek IN.

Robb, R., jt. auth. see Boddington, C.

Robb, R. I., ed. see Heindel, Max.

Robb, R. I., ed. see Proclus.

Robb, R. I., ed. see Westcott, W. Wynn.

***Robb, Richard A.** Three Dimensional Biomedical Imaging: Principles & Practice. LC 94-38015. 1994. 145.00 (*1-56081-570-1*) VCH Pubs.

Robb, Richard I., ed. The Secret Doctrine of H. P. Blavatsky: First International Symposium, July 1984. 112p. 1984. pap. 6.00 (*0-913510-52-1*) Wizards.

Robb, Richard M. Ophthalmology for the Pediatric Practitioner. (Clinical Pediatrics Ser.). 1981. 31.50 (*0-316-74894-3*) Little.

Robb, Robert A. Three-Dimensional Biomedical Imaging, Vol. I. 184p. 1985. 85.00 (*0-8493-5264-9*, RC78, CRC Reprint) Franklin.

— Three-Dimensional Biomedical Imaging, Vol. II, incl. poster. 160p. 1985. Vol. II, 160 p. 85.00 (*0-8493-5265-7*, CRC Reprint) Franklin.

Robb, Robert L. Robert L. Robb's Bible Heritage Cookbook: A Gourmet Guide to Cooking with the Bible. LC 78-59914. (Illus.). 14.95 (*0-917182-08-1*) Triumph Pub.

Robb, Scott H. Television-Radio Age Communications Coursebook. 1981. 29.00 (*0-686-12160-0*); ring bd. 16.50 (*0-686-12159-7*) CRI.

Robb-Smith, A. H. & Taylor, G. B. Lymph-Node Biopsy: A Diagnostic Atlas. (Illus.). 1981. text ed. 125.00 (*0-19-520247-3*) OUP.

Robb, Stewart, tr. see Nostradamus.

Robb, Theodore K., jt. ed. see Rotberg, Robert I.

Robb, Thomas B. Growing Up: Pastoral Nurture for the Later Years. LC 91-7735. 160p. (Orig.). 1991. lib. bdg. 39.95 (*1-56024-072-5*); pap. text ed. 12.95 (*1-56024-073-3*) Haworth Pr.

Robb, Tom. Art Course. 1990. 15.99 (*0-517-05380-2*) Random Hse Value.

— Start Now in Watercolour. (Illus.). 96p. Date not set. 14.95 (*1-85410-206-0*, London Bridge) Genl Dist Srvs.

Robb, William, jt. auth. see Hamilton, Douglas M.

Robbe-Grillet, Alain. Angelique. 1994. pap. 13.95 (*0-7145-4197-4*) Riverrun NY.

— Annee Derniere a Marienbad: Cine-roman. 176p. (FRE.). 1961. pap. 19.95 (*0-7859-1512-5*, 2707303119) Fr & Eur.

— La Belle Captive. (Illus.). (FRE.). 1976. 95.00 (*0-7859-5558-5*) Fr & Eur.

— Dans le Labyrinthe. 224p. (FRE.). 1959. pap. 19.95 (*0-7859-1507-9*) Fr & Eur.

— The Erasers. Howard, Richard, tr. 256p. 1989. pap. 12.95 (*0-8021-5086-1*) Grove-Atltic.

— For a New Novel. LC 72-128301. (Essay Index Reprint Ser.). 1977. 19.95 (*0-8369-1844-4*) Ayer.

— For a New Novel. Howard, Richard, tr. 175p. 1989. pap. 12.95 (*0-8101-0821-6*) Northwestern U Pr.

— Glissements Progressifs du Plaisir. (Illus.). 224p. (FRE.). 1974. pap. 24.95 (*0-7859-1502-8*, 2707300020) Fr & Eur.

— Gommes. 264p. (FRE.). 1953. pap. 19.95 (*0-7859-1511-7*, 2707302562) Fr & Eur.

— L' Immortelle. 312p. 1975. 9.95 (*0-686-54744-6*) Fr & Eur.

— Immortelle: Cine-roman. 212p. (FRE.). 1963. pap. 19.95 (*0-7859-1610-5*, 270730350X) Fr & Eur.

— Instantanees: Roman. 112p. (FRE.). 1962. pap. 13.95 (*0-7859-1608-3*, 270730087X) Fr & Eur.

— La Jalousie. Bree, Germaine & Schoenfeld, Eric, eds. 129p. (FRE.). (C). 1990. pap. text ed. 7.50 (*0-88133-475-8*) Waveland Pr.

— Jalousie: Roman. 224p. (FRE.). 1957. pap. 24.95 (*0-7859-1504-4*, 2707300543) Fr & Eur.

— Jealousy & In the Labyrinth. Howard, Richard, tr. 320p. (Orig.). 1989. pap. 10.95 (*0-8021-5106-X*) Grove-Atltic.

— La Maison de Rendez-Vous & Djinn. Howard, Richard et al, trs. 288p. (Orig.). 1987. pap. 10.95 (*0-8021-3017-8*) Grove-Atltic.

— Maison Des Rendez-Vous: Roman. 192p. (FRE.). 1980. pap. 13.95 (*0-7859-1514-1*, 2707303151) Fr & Eur.

— Pour un Nouveau Roman: Critique litteraire. 144p. (FRE.). 1963. pap. 17.95 (*0-7859-1505-2*, 2707300624) Fr & Eur.

— Project for a Revolution in New York. Howard, Richard, tr. 184p. 1991. pap. 3.95 (*0-8021-5043-8*) Grove-Atltic.

— Projet Pour une Revolution a New York. 20.50 (*0-685-37077-1*) Fr & Eur.

— Recollections of the Golden Triangle. Underwood, J. A., tr. Orig. Title: Souvenirs due triangle d'or. 160p. (C). 1986. reprint ed. pap. 6.95 (*0-8021-5200-7*) Grove-Atltic.

— Le Rendezvous. Walker, David, ed. 176p. 1987. pap. 9.95 (*0-423-51520-9*, A3862) Routledge Chapman & Hall.

— Robbe-Grillet: Dans le Labyrinthe. Meakin, David, ed. (Bristol French Texts Ser.). 144p. (FRE.). 1992. 12.95 (*0-631-13019-5*, Pub. by Brstl Class Pr UK) Focus Info Gr.

— Souvenirs du Triangle d'Or. (FRE.). 1985. pap. 16.95 (*0-7859-2700-X*, 2020086123) Fr & Eur.

— Topologie d'une Cite Fantome. 204p. (FRE.). 1976. pap. 20.95 (*0-7859-1506-0*, 2707300713) Fr & Eur.

— The Voyeur. Howard, Richard, tr. 224p. 1989. pap. 9.95 (*0-8021-3165-4*) Grove-Atltic.

— Voyeur: Roman. 256p. (FRE.). 1955. pap. 24.95 (*0-7859-1510-9*, 2707302430) Fr & Eur.

Robbe-Grillet, Alain & Ionesco, I. Temple aux Miroirs. 50.00 (*0-686-54740-3*) Fr & Eur.

Robbe-Grillet, Alain & Magritte, Rene. La Belle Captive: A Novel. Stoltzfus, Ben, tr. LC 94-17127. 1995. 35.00 (*0-520-05916-6*) U CA Pr.

Robbe-Grillet, Alain, jt. auth. see Praeger, Michele.

Robbe-Grillet, Lenard. Le Rendez-Vous. (FRE.). (C). 1981. pap. text ed. 25.00 (*0-03-056248-1*) HB Coll Pubs.

Robbe, Mary Ann F. The Working Mothers Survival Kit: How to Maintain Sanity While Balancing Career, Home, & Family. (Illus.). 110p. (Orig.). 1990. student ed 9.95 (*0-9624357-1-6*) Quailhill Pr.

Robbelen, G., et al. Oil Crops of the World. 560p. 1989. text ed. 50.00 (*0-07-053081-5*) McGraw.

Robben, Antonius C. Sons of the Sea Goddess: Economic Practice & Discursive Conflict in Brazil. 360p. 1989. text ed. 37.00 (*0-231-06842-5*) Col U Pr.

— Sons of the Sea Goddess: Economic Practice & Discursive Conflict in Brazil. 328p. (C). 1992. pap. text ed. 17.50 (*0-231-06843-3*) Col U Pr.

Robben, Antonius C., jt. ed. see Nordstrom, Carolyn.

Robbennolt, Roger. Tales of Gletha, the Goatlady. LC 91-71004. (Illus.). 160p. (Orig.). 1991. pap. 9.95 (*0-939516-14-4*) Forest Peace.

— Tales of Hermit Uncle John. LC 92-83892. (Illus.). 200p. (Orig.). 1993. pap. 9.95 (*0-939516-17-9*) Forest Peace.

— Tales of Tony Great Turtle. (Illus.). 160p. (Orig.). 1994. pap. 9.95 (*0-939516-27-6*) Forest Peace.

Robberson, Donald L. & Saunders, Grady F., eds. Perspectives on Genes & the Molecular Biology of Cancer. (M. D. Anderson Symposium on Fundamental Cancer Research Ser.: Vol. 35). (Illus.). 348p. 1983. text ed. 115.00 (*0-89004-771-5*) Raven.

Robbiani, Marina, jt. auth. see Ribuoli, Patrizia.

Robbiano, Lorenzo, jt. ed. see Eisenbud, David.

Robbie, Dorothy. Ribbon with Gold. (Lost Play Ser.). 1977. pap. 1.25 (*0-912262-41-9*) Proscenium.

Robbie, Dorothy & Hand, Desmond. Alice in Wonderland. (Adaptation Ser.). (J). (gr. k up). 1970. pap. 1.50 (*0-912262-19-2*) Proscenium.

Robbillard, Jean & Conley, Edgar, eds. Industrial Applications for Optical Data Processing & Holography. 1992. 85.00 (*0-8493-0139-4*, TA1542) CRC Pr.

Robbin, Joel W. Matrix Algebra Using MINImal MATlab. LC 93-39372. 540p. 1994. text ed. 59.95 (*1-56881-024-5*) AK Peters.

Robbin, Sallie. A Lighted Candle in Her Heart. 200p. 1985. 9.95 (*0-930061-15-2*) Interspace Bks.

Robbins. The Adventurers. 1993. pap. 6.99 (*0-671-87482-9*) PB.

— Air. (J). 1996. 16.95 (*0-8050-2292-9*) H Holt & Co.

— The Betsy. 1993. mass mkt. 5.99 (*0-671-87483-7*) PB.

— California Girls Paper Dolls. 1990. pap. 5.95 (*0-913035-57-2*) Eclipse Bks.

— Descent from Xanadu. 1993. mass mkt. 5.99 (*0-671-87485-3*) PB.

— The Dream Merchants. 1993. mass mkt. 5.99 (*0-671-87486-1*) PB.

— Dreams Die First. 1993. mass mkt. 5.99 (*0-671-87487-X*) PB.

— Earth: The Elements II. (J). 1995. 16.95 (*0-8050-2294-5*) H Holt & Co.

— Fire. (J). 1996. write for info. (*0-8050-2293-7*) H Holt & Co.

— Goodbye, Janette. 1993. mass mkt. 5.99 (*0-671-87488-8*) PB.

— The Lonely Lady. Date not set. mass mkt. 5.99 (*0-671-87490-X*) PB.

— Paper Dolls from the Comics. (Illus.). 1990. pap. 4.95 (*0-913035-20-3*) Eclipse Bks.

— Seventy-Nine Park Avenue. 1993. mass mkt. 5.99 (*0-671-87496-9*) PB.

— Spellbinder. 1993. mass mkt. 5.99 (*0-671-87495-0*) PB.

— The Storyteller. 1994. mass mkt. 5.99 (*0-671-87522-1*) PB.

— Water: The Elements. (J). 1994. 16.95 (*0-8050-2257-0*, Bks Young Read) H Holt & Co.

— Where Love Has Gone. 1994. mass mkt. 5.99 (*0-671-87498-5*) PB.

Robbins & Bernstein, eds. Three-Dimensional Imaging & Remote Sensing Imaging. 1988. 38.00 (*0-89252-937-7*, 902) SPIE.

Robbins & Stevens. American Experiences: Readings in Social & Political History. 17.75 (*0-536-58310-2*) Ginn Pr.

Robbins, jt. auth. see Evans, C. H.

Robbins, jt. ed. see McAllister.

Robbins & Robbins Staff. Mastering Nintendo Video Games. 1990. pap. 9.95 (*0-672-48491-9*, Bobbs) Macmillan.

Robbins, Alan. Cut & Construct Your Own Brontosaurus. 32p. 1988. pap. 7.95 (*0-345-35557-1*) Ballantine.

— Final Run. (Illus.). 8p. (C). 1991. 20.00 (*0-922242-29-1*) Lombard Mktg.

— Heading for Trouble: Adventure Mystery for Kids Ages 8-12. (Illus.). 20p. (J). (gr. 5-7). 1992. 14.00 (*0-922242-34-8*) Lombard Mktg.

— Last Chill & Testament: A Mystery Jigsaw Puzzle. (BePuzzled Ser.). (Orig.). (C). 1993. 20.00 (*0-922242-52-6*) Lombard Mktg.

— Murder on the Rocks: A Mystery Jigsaw Puzzle Thriller. (BePuzzled Ser.). (Orig.). 1994. 20.00 (*0-922242-62-3*) Lombard Mktg.

— Purrceptive Detective. (YA). (gr. 7 up). 1994. 20.00 (*0-922242-71-2*) Bepuzzled.

— Puzzicles. 1988. pap. 3.95 (*0-345-35271-8*) Ballantine.

— Sonata for a Spy. (Illus.). 8p. (C). 1991. 19.95 (*0-922242-23-2*) Lombard Mktg.

— To Kill a Boss: A Mystery Jigsaw Puzzle Thriller. (BePuzzled Ser.). (Orig.). (YA). (gr. 7 up). 1994. 20.00 (*0-922242-60-7*) Bepuzzled.

— To Kill a Lawyer: A Mystery Jigsaw Puzzle. (BePuzzled Ser.). (YA). (gr. 7 up). 1993. 20.00 (*0-922242-54-2*) Bepuzzled.

Robbins, Aldona. The ABCs of Social Security: Basic Questions & Answers about the Retirement Program. (Illus.). 37p. (Orig.). 1988. pap. 5.95 (*0-922623-00-7*) IRET.

Robbins, Aldona & Robbins, Gary. The Bush Savings Plan. 1990. pap. 10.00 (*0-943802-55-5*, 152) Natl Ctr Pol.

— Capital, Taxes & Growth. (Illus.). 45p. (C). 1992. pap. 10.00 (*0-943802-72-5*, 169) Natl Ctr Pol.

— The Case for IRAs. 1991. pap. 10.00 (*0-943802-66-0*, 163) Natl Ctr Pol.

— Paying People Not to Work: The Economic Cost of the Social Security Retirement Earnings Limit. 1989. pap. 10.00 (*0-943802-45-8*, 142) Natl Ctr Pol.

— A Strategy for Growth. (Illus.). 21p. (C). 1992. pap. 10.00 (*0-943802-73-3*, 170) Natl Ctr Pol.

— Why Bush Lost the Election: Ten Lessons for the Clinton Administration. (Illus.). 24p. 1993. pap. 5.00 (*1-56808-007-7*, BG 120) Natl Ctr Pol.

Robbins, Aldona, jt. auth. see Robbins, Gary.

Robbins, Allan & Miller, Wilhelm. Circuit Analysis: Theory & Practice. LC 94-10022. (Illus.). 1120p. 1995. 58.95 (*0-8273-5414-2*) Delmar.

Robbins, Allan H., et al. Introduction to Troubleshooting Microprocessor Based Systems. (Illus.). 448p. (C). 1987. text ed. 28.95 (*0-8359-3249-4*) P-H.

***Robbins, Allen.** The Glenmore Haunting. 1993. 20.00 (*0-922242-32-1*) Bepuzzled.

— Swim at Your Own Risk: Adventure Mystery for Kids Ages 8-12. (Spider Tales Ser.). (Orig.). (J). (gr. 3-7). 1995. 14.00 (*0-922242-76-3*) Bepuzzled.

Robbins, Andrea. The Fires of Oakheath. (Orig.). 1981. pap. 2.95 (*0-89083-867-4*) Zebra.

Robbins, Ann R. Twenty-Five Vegetables Anyone Can Grow. 1974. pap. 5.95 (*0-486-23029-5*) Dover.

— Twenty-Five Vegetables Anyone Can Grow. (Illus.). 11.25 (*0-8446-5080-3*) Peter Smith.

Robbins, Anthony. Awaken the Giant Within: How to Take Immediate Control of Your Mental, Emotional, Physical, & Financial Destiny. LC 92-30041. 1992. pap. 12.00 (*0-671-79154-0*, Fireside) S&S Trade.

— Giant Steps: Small Changes to Make a Big Difference: Daily Lessons in Self-Mastery. 1994. pap. 9.00 (*0-685-71043-2*, Fireside) S&S Trade.

— Notes from a Friend: A Quick & Simple Guide to Taking Control of Your Life. 1995. pap. 7.95 (*0-684-80056-X*, Fireside) S&S Trade.

— On the Tropic of Time: Poems. LC 95-8286. 1995. write for info. (*0-89924-092-5*); pap. write for info. (*0-89924-091-7*) Lynx Hse.

— Unlimited Power. 1987. pap. 12.00 (*0-449-90280-3*) Fawcett.

Robbins, Arnold. Korn Shell Reference. 20p. (Orig.). (C). 1991. pap. 4.50 (*0-916151-50-6*) Specialized Sys.

— Korn Shell Reference. rev. ed. 28p. (Orig.). (C). 1995. pap. text ed. 4.50 (*0-916151-72-7*) Specialized Sys.

Robbins, Arnold D., et al. Gawk Manual. (Illus.). 186p. 1993. pap. 20.00 (*1-882114-25-6*) Free Software.

Robbins, Arthur. The Artist As Therapist. LC 86-10466. 226p. 1987. 42.95 (*0-89885-322-2*); pap. 22.95 (*0-89885-439-3*) Human Sci Pr.

— Between Therapists: The Processing of Transference - Countertransference Material. 227p. (C). 1988. 38.95 (*0-89885-373-7*) Human Sci Pr.

— A Multi-Modal Approach to Creative Art Therapy. 250p. 1994. pap. 23.00x (*1-85302-262-4*, Pub. by J Kingsley Pubs UK) Taylor & Francis.

Robbins, Arthur, et al. Expressive Therapy: A Creative Arts Approach to Depth-Oriented Treatment. LC 80-13005. 319p. 1980. 45.95 (*0-87705-101-1*); pap. 21.95 (*0-89885-279-X*) Human Sci Pr.

Robbins, Barbara H. Just for Fun: Nature Stories in Sign Language. (Illus.). 112p. (Orig.). (J). (gr. k-12). 1992. pap. 12.95 (*0-9630060-0-2*) Robbinspring.

— Just for Fun - Nature Stories in Sign Language. 2nd rev. ed. (Illus.). (J). (gr. k-12). 1995. pap. write for info. (*0-9630060-3-7*) Robbinspring.

— Wolf Country - A Mystery in Progress. (Illus.). (J). (gr. k-12). 1995. pap. write for info. (*0-9630060-2-9*) Robbinspring.

***Robbins, Barbara H. & Stahl, Kathryn M.** Awful Abigail & Why She Changed. (Illus.). 58p. (J). (gr. k-12). 1995. pap. 6.50 (*0-9630060-1-0*) Robbinspring.

Robbins, Beverly. Definite Article in English Transformations. 1968. pap. text ed. 56.95 (*90-279-0082-5*) Mouton.

Robbins, Bonnie N. Nap-Time Tales. (J). 1992. 7.95 (*0-533-10232-4*) Vantage.

Robbins, Bruce. Secular Vocations: Intellectuals, Professionalism, Culture. 256p. 1993. 59.95 (*0-86091-430-5*, B0526, Pub. by Verso UK); pap. 18.95 (*0-86091-630-8*, B0530, Pub. by Verso UK) Routledge Chapman & Hall.

— The Servant's Hand: English Fiction from Below. LC 85-14955. 256p. 1986. text ed. 37.50 (*0-231-05966-3*) Col U Pr.

— The Servant's Hand: English Fiction from Below. LC 93-7141. 280p. (C). 1993. pap. text ed. 15.95 (*0-8223-1397-9*) Duke.

Robbins, Bruce, ed. Intellectuals: Aesthetics, Politics, Academics. (Cultural Politics Ser.). 408p. (Orig.). 1990. text ed. 39.95x (*0-8166-1830-5*); pap. text ed. 14.95 (*0-8166-1831-3*) U of Minn Pr.

— The Phantom Public Sphere. LC 92-28619. (Cultural Politics Ser.: Vol. 5). 336p. (C). 1993. text ed. 49.95 (*0-8166-2124-1*); pap. 18.95 (*0-8166-2126-8*) U of Minn Pr.

Robbins, C. R. Chemical & Physical Behavior of Human Hair. (Illus.). 330p. 1988. 79.00 (*0-387-96660-9*) Spr-Verlag.

Robbins, Carol & Robbins, Clive. Music for the Hearing Impaired & Other Special Groups: A Resource Manual & Curriculum Guide. (Illus.). 480p. 1980. spiral bd., pap. 24.95 (*0-918812-11-9*, ST 027) MMB Music.

Robbins, Carol T., jt. auth. see Wolff, Herbert.

Robbins, Carol T., et al. Removing Regulatory Barriers to Affordable Housing: How States & Localities Are Moving Ahead. 84p. (Orig.). (C). 1993. pap. text ed. 30.00 (*0-7881-0068-8*) Diane Pub.

Robbins, Carroll, ed. see Rutstein, Nathan.

Robbins, Casey, jt. ed. see Cabarga, Leslie.

Robbins, Casey, jt. ed. see Robbins, Trina.

Robbins, Ceila, ed. see Cross, Wilbur.

Robbins, Ceila D., ed. see Blodgett, Richard.

Robbins, Ceila D., ed. see Evans, Glen.

Robbins, Ceila D., ed. see Filson, Brent.

Robbins, Ceila D., ed. see Harrington, Melissa.

Robbins, Ceila D., ed. see Hubbard, Ian.

Robbins, Ceila D., jt. auth. see Lurdang, Laurence.

Robbins, Ceila D., ed. see Naleid, James C.

Robbins, Ceila D., jt. auth. see Spector, Robert.

Robbins, Ceila D., ed. see Yenne, William P.

Robbins, Cella D., ed. see Blodgett, Richard.

Robbins, Chandler S., et al. Birds of North America. rev. ed. (Golden Field Guide Ser.). (Illus.). 360p. 1983. write for info. (*0-307-37002-X*); pap. 11.95 (*0-307-33656-5*) Western Pub.

Robbins, Charles E. Attorney's Master Guide to Expediting Top Dollar Case Settlements. 1975. 69.50 (*0-13-050526-9*) Exec Reports.

— How to Make Dramatic Use of Witnesses to Win in Court. 1979. 69.50 (*0-13-418194-8*) Exec Reports.

Robbins, Charles J., ed. see Cannon, Thomas H.

Robbins, Charles L. R. Madison Mitchell: His Life & Decoys. (Illus.). 1988. 24.95 (*0-9620028-0-1*) C L Robbins.

— Teachers in Germany in the Sixteenth Century: Conditions in Protestant Elementary & Secondary Schools. LC 74-177195. (Columbia University. Teachers College. Contributions to Education Ser.: No. 52). reprint ed. 37.50 (*0-404-55052-5*) AMS Pr.

Robbins, Charles T. Wildlife Feeding & Nutrition. 2nd ed. (Animal Feeding & Nutrition Ser.). (Illus.). 352p. 1992. reprint ed. text ed. 79.95 (*0-12-589382-5*) Acad Pr.

— Wildlife Feeding & Nutrition. 2nd ed. (Animal Feeding & Nutrition Ser.). (Illus.). 347p. 1994. pap. text ed. 59.95 (*0-12-589383-3*) Acad Pr.

Robbins, Charles T., jt. auth. see Palo, R. Thomas.

Robbins, Christopher. The Earl of Wharton & Whig Party Politics, 1679-1715. LC 91-43272. (Studies in British History: Vol. 29). (Illus.). 484p. 1992. lib. bdg. 109.95 (*0-7734-9462-6*) E Mellen.

— Thorsons Introductory Guide to Herbalism. 1994. pap. 9.00 (*0-7225-2791-8*) Thorsons SF.

Robbins, Christopher, jt. auth. see Polunin, Miriam.

Robbins, Clarence R. Chemical & Physical Behavior of Human Hair. LC 93-38111. 1994. 69.00 (*0-387-94191-6*) Spr-Verlag.

Robbins, Clive, jt. auth. see Nordoff, Paul.

Robbins, Clive, jt. auth. see Robbins, Carol.

Robbins, Coy D. Indiana Negro Registers, 1852-1865. 185p. (Orig.). 1994. pap. text ed. 30.00 (*1-55613-940-3*) Heritage Bk.

***Robbins, D. V. Embarrassed by the Light: A Terminal-Death Experience. (Illus.). 144p. 1995. pap. 8.95 (*0-9644907-5-7*) Raven Hse.**

This book is a riotous parody on near-death experiences. It spoofs the ultimate metaphysical journey, revealing for the first time ever, how it feels to be terminally dead. Buzzy Boedecker is a fatally deceased Insurance Salesman who met his untimely & tragic demise while amusing himself in a hot shower. As his senses leave him forever, a strange thing happens. He discovers the power of astral channeling & uses this ancient & mysterious form of communication to tell his story...through his cousin Franny Tyler! The team of Boedecker & Tyler have joined together to take their readers on this ultimate metaphysical journey. EMBARRASSED BY THE LIGHT documents this journey. REVIEWS: "...a riveting account of what can happen to the irreversibly deceased...It almost makes me want to kill myself."--Lois Blake, Cooking with Garlic magazine. "Folks just don't want to be on life support anymore!"--Rhonda Reef, Critical Care Nurse, St. Elvis Hospital. Order from Baker & Taylor (800-775-1100), Koen (800-257-8481), Ingram & for fulfillment sales from Twin Peaks (800-637-2256). Raven House, L.L.C., 1201 Waterfront Drive, #301, Virginia Beach, VA 23451. (805) 491-8356.

Publisher Provided Annotation.

R

— Life & Love in the Paradise Lounge: Favorite Lines of the Barstool Buzzards. LC 93-70916. (Illus.). 112p. (Orig.). 1993. pap. 6.95 (1-56790-115-8) Cool Hand Comms.

Robbins, D. W. Robbins. 221p. 1991. reprint ed. lib. bdg. 44.50 (0-8328-2027-X); reprint ed. pap. 34.50 (0-8328-2028-8) Higginson Bk Co.

Robbins, Daniel. Beyond Minimalism, George Waterman Collection. LC 78-105670. (Illus.). 1969. 2.00 (0-911517-21-9) Mus of Art RI.

— Edward Koren: Prints & Drawings, 1959-1981. Littlefield, Thomson, ed. LC 82-61087. (Illus.). 56p. (Orig.). 1982. pap. 10.00 (0-910763-00-3) U Albany Art Mus.

— Joaquin Torres-Garcia, 1874-1949. LC 74-130023. (Illus.). 1970. 4.50 (0-911517-23-5) Mus of Art RI.

— Mountain Artisans - Appalachia. (Illus.). 1970. 3.00 (0-911517-28-6) Mus of Art RI.

— Vintage Racing Machine: Cars from the Collection of George Waterman Jr. (Illus.). 1970. 5.00 (0-911517-41-3) Mus of Art RI.

Robbins, Daniel & Downing, George, eds. Herbert & Nannette Rothschild Collection. LC 66-29131. (Illus.). 1966. 7.50 (0-911517-22-7) Mus of Art RI.

Robbins, Daniel & Seitz, William, eds. Exchange Exhibition, Exhibition Exchange. LC 67-19406. (Illus.). 1967. 5.00 (0-911517-18-9) Mus of Art RI.

Robbins, David. Anaheim Run. (Endworld Ser.: No. 13). 192p. (Orig.). 1988. pap. 2.95 (0-8439-2698-8) Dorchester Pub Co.

— Anaheim Run & Seattle Run, 2 vols. in 1. (Endworld Ser.). 384p. 1991. pap. 4.50 (0-8439-3189-2) Dorchester Pub Co.

— Armageddon Run. (Endworld Ser.: No. 7). 256p. (Orig.). 1987. pap. 2.95 (0-8439-2527-2) Dorchester Pub Co.

— Atlanta Run. (Endworld Ser.: No. 17). 192p. 1989. pap. 2.95 (0-8439-2816-6) Dorchester Pub Co.

— Atlanta Run - Memphis Run, 2 vols. in 1. (Endworld Double Edition Ser.). 384p. 1992. pap. 4.50 (0-8439-3299-6) Dorchester Pub Co.

— Boston Run. (Endworld Ser.: No. 21). 192p. (Orig.). 1990. pap. 2.95 (0-8439-2952-9) Dorchester Pub Co.

— Boston Run - Green Bay Run, 2 vols. in 1. (Endworld Double Ser.). 384p. 1993. pap. 4.50 (0-8439-3392-5) Dorchester Pub Co.

— Capital Run - New York Run, 2 vols. in 1. (Endworld Ser.). 432p. 1991. pap. 4.50 (0-8439-3173-6) Dorchester Pub Co.

— Chicago Run. (Endworld Ser.: No. 27). 192p. (Orig.). 1991. pap. 3.50 (0-8439-3145-0) Dorchester Pub Co.

— Cincinnati Run; Dallas Run, 2 vols. in 1. (Endworld Double Edition Ser.). 384p. 1992. pap. 4.50 (0-8439-3359-3) Dorchester Pub Co.

— Citadel Run. (Endworld Ser.: No. 6). 256p. (Orig.). 1987. pap. 2.95 (0-8439-2507-8) Dorchester Pub Co.

— Crusher Strike. (Blade Ser.: No. 6). 192p. (Orig.). 1990. pap. 2.95 (0-8439-2909-X) Dorchester Pub Co.

— Dakota Run. (Endworld Ser.: No. 5). 256p. (Orig.). 1987. pap. 2.95 (0-8439-2473-X) Dorchester Pub Co.

— Dallas Run. (Endworld Ser.: No. 20). 192p. (Orig.). 1990. pap. 2.95 (0-8439-2938-3) Dorchester Pub Co.

— Dead Zone Strike. (Blade Ser.: No. 10). 192p. (Orig.). 1990. pap. 2.95 (0-8439-3013-6) Dorchester Pub Co.

— Death Master Strike. (Blade Ser.: No. 12). 192p. (Orig.). 1991. pap. 3.50 (0-8439-3116-7) Dorchester Pub Co.

— Denver Run. (Endworld Ser.: No. 8). 256p. (Orig.). 1987. pap. 2.95 (0-8439-2548-5) Dorchester Pub Co.

— Devil Strike. (Blade Ser.: No. 8). 192p. (Orig.). 1990. pap. 2.95 (0-8439-2964-2) Dorchester Pub Co.

— First Strike. (Blade Ser.: No. 1). 192p. (Orig.). 1989. pap. 2.95 (0-8439-2760-7) Dorchester Pub Co.

— First Strike - Outlands Strike. (Blade Ser.). 384p. 1992. pap. 4.50 (0-8439-3257-0) Dorchester Pub Co.

— The Fox Run. (Endworld Ser.: No. 1). 256p. 1992. pap. 3.50 (0-8439-3105-1) Dorchester Pub Co.

— Green Bay Run. (Endworld Ser.: No. 22). 192p. (Orig.). 1990. pap. 2.95 (0-8439-2979-0) Dorchester Pub Co.

— Hell-O-Ween. 368p. (Orig.). 1992. pap. 4.50 (0-8439-3335-6) Dorchester Pub Co.

— Houston Run. (Endworld Ser.: No. 12). 192p. (Orig.). 1988. pap. 2.95 (0-8439-2672-4) Dorchester Pub Co.

— Kalispell Run. (Endworld Ser.: No. 4). 256p. (Orig.). 1987. pap. 2.95 (0-8439-2449-7) Dorchester Pub Co.

— L. A. Strike. (Blade Ser.: No. 9). 192p. (Orig.). 1990. pap. 2.95 (0-8439-2987-1) Dorchester Pub Co.

— L.A. Strike - Dead Zone Strike. (Blade Double Edition Ser.). 384p. 1993. pap. 4.50 (0-8439-3446-8) Dorchester Pub Co.

— Liberty Run. (Endworld Ser.: No. 11). 192p. (Orig.). 1988. pap. 2.95 (0-8439-2644-9) Dorchester Pub Co.

— Liberty Run - Houston Run, 2 vols. in 1. (Endworld Ser.). 384p. 1991. pap. 4.50 (0-8439-3180-9) Dorchester Pub Co.

— Madman Run. (Endworld Ser.: No. 26). 192p. (Orig.). 1991. pap. 3.50 (0-8439-3124-8) Dorchester Pub Co.

— Memphis Run. (Endworld Ser.: No. 18). 192p. (Orig.). 1989. pap. 2.95 (0-8439-2868-9) Dorchester Pub Co.

— Miami Run. (Endworld Ser.: No. 16). 192p. pap. 2.95 (0-8439-2786-0) Dorchester Pub Co.

— Nevada Run. (Endworld Ser.: No. 15). 192p. pap. 2.95 (0-8439-2749-6) Dorchester Pub Co.

— Nevada Run & Miami Run, 2 vols. in 1. (Endworld Ser.). 384p. 1991. pap. 4.50 (0-8439-3202-3) Dorchester Pub Co.

— New Orleans Run. (Endworld Ser.: No. 24). 192p. (Orig.). 1991. pap. 2.95 (0-8439-3054-3) Dorchester Pub Co.

— New York Run. (Endworld Ser.: No. 10). 208p. (Orig.). 1988. pap. 2.95 (0-8439-2606-6) Dorchester Pub Co.

— Outlands Strike. (Blade Ser.: No. 2). 192p. pap. 2.95 (0-8439-2774-7) Dorchester Pub Co.

— Pirate Strike; Crusher Strike, 2 vols. in 1. (Blade Double Edition Ser.). 368p. 1992. pap. 4.50 (0-8439-3371-2) Dorchester Pub Co.

— Prank Night. 368p. (Orig.). 1994. mass mkt., pap. text ed. 4.50 (0-8439-3676-2) Dorchester Pub Co.

— Quest Strike. (Blade Ser.: No. 11). 192p. (Orig.). 1991. pap. 2.95 (0-8439-3085-3) Dorchester Pub Co.

— Return of the Virginian. 1994. mass mkt. 4.99 (0-553-56321-1) Bantam.

— The Return of the Virginian. large type ed. LC 94-10669. 535p. 1994. 18.95 (0-8161-5997-1) Hall.

— Seattle Run. (Endworld Ser.: No. 14). 192p. (Orig.). 1989. pap. 2.95 (0-8439-2725-9) Dorchester Pub Co.

— Spartan Run. (Endworld Ser.: No. 25). 192p. (Orig.). 1991. pap. 3.50 (0-8439-3080-2) Dorchester Pub Co.

— Spartan Run - Madman Run. (Endworld Double Edition Ser.). 384p. 1993. pap. 4.50 (0-8439-3484-0) Dorchester Pub Co.

— Spectre. 368p. pap. 3.95 (0-8439-2681-3) Dorchester Pub Co.

— Spook Night. 368p. (Orig.). 1995. mass mkt., pap. 4.99 (0-8439-3845-5) Dorchester Pub Co.

— Terror Strike. (Blade Ser.: No. 7). 192p. (Orig.). 1990. pap. 2.95 (0-8439-2956-1) Dorchester Pub Co.

— Terror Strike - Devil Strike, 2 vols. in 1. (Blade Double Edition Ser.). 368p. 1993. pap. 4.50 (0-8439-3407-7) Dorchester Pub Co.

— Thief River Falls Run. (Endworld Ser.: No. 2). 256p. 1992. pap. 3.50 (0-8439-3106-X) Dorchester Pub Co.

— Twin Cities Run. (Endworld Ser.: No. 3). 256p. (Orig.). 1986. pap. 2.95 (0-8439-2418-7) Dorchester Pub Co.

— Vampire Strike. (Blade Ser.: No. 3). 192p. 1989. pap. 2.95 (0-8439-2803-4) Dorchester Pub Co.

— Vampire Strike - Pipeline Strike, 2 vols. in 1. (Blade Double Edition Ser.). 384p. 1992. pap. 4.50 (0-8439-3310-0) Dorchester Pub Co.

— Vengeance Strike. (Blade Ser.: No. 13). 192p. (Orig.). 1991. pap. 3.50 (0-8439-3132-9) Dorchester Pub Co.

— The Wereling. 336p. 1986. pap. 3.50 (0-8439-2343-1) Dorchester Pub Co.

— The Wrath. 368p. (Orig.). 1988. pap. 3.95 (0-8439-2629-5) Dorchester Pub Co.

— Yellowstone Run. (Endworld Ser.: No. 23). 192p. (Orig.). 1990. pap. 2.95 (0-8439-3000-4) Dorchester Pub Co.

— Yellowstone Run - New Orleans Run. (Endworld Double Ser.). 384p. 1993. pap. 4.50 (0-8439-3418-2) Dorchester Pub Co.

Robbins, David, jt. auth. see Brown, Richard.

Robbins, David, et al, eds. Rethinking Social Inequality. 272p. 1982. text ed. 68.95 (0-566-00557-3) Ashgate Pub Co.

Robbins, David C., jt. ed. see Leslie, R. D.

***Robbins, David E.** Securities Arbitration Procedure Manual. 300p. 1994. ring bd. 125.00 (0-614-05963-1) Michie Butterworth.

— Securities Arbitration Procedure Manual, 1990-1993. 300p. 1990. ring bd. 125.00 (0-88063-345-X) Butterworth Legal Pubs.

— Securities Arbitration Procedure Manual, 1990-1993. suppl. ed. 1994. ring bd. 63.00 (0-614-03168-0) Butterworth Legal Pubs.

Robbins, Dennis & Sweatt, Jeremy, eds. Big Road Exit Guide, 1993. (Eastern Edition Ser.). (Illus.). 188p. (Orig.). 1993. pap. 9.95 (1-880477-01-7) Inter Am Pub.

Robbins, Derek. The Rise of Independent Study: The Politics & the Philosophy of an Educational Innovation, 1970-1987. 160p. 1988. 95.00 (0-335-15848-X, Open Univ Pr) Taylor & Francis.

Robbins, Diana, ed. Community Care - Findings from Department of Health Funded Research, 1988-92. 300p. 1993. pap. 45.00 (0-11-321567-3, HM15673, Pub. by HMSO UK) UNIPUB.

Robbins, Don. The Preservation of Food by Irradiation. 128p. (C). 1991. 320.00 (1-85271-149-3, Pub. by IBC Tech Srvs UK) St Mut.

Robbins, Doren. Sympathetic Manifesto: Poems. LC 87-42791. 91p. (Orig.). 1987. pap. 7.95 (0-912288-26-4) Perivale Pr.

Robbins, Duffy. Going the Distance: How to Build Your Faith for the Long Haul. 176p. 1991. pap. 8.99 (0-310-54051-8) Zondervan.

— Have I Got News for You! 112p. (YA). 1994. pap. 7.99 (0-310-37461-8) Zondervan.

— The Ministry of Nurture: Helping Teenagers to Grow Spiritually. 192p. 1990. pap. 12.99 (0-310-52581-0) Zondervan.

— Nuts & Bolts: Youth Ministry Between the Meetings. 192p. 1991. pap. 12.99 (0-310-52571-3) Zondervan.

— Youth Ministry That Works. 144p. 1991. pap. 8.99 (0-89693-918-9) SP Pubns.

Robbins, Duffy, ed. Hot Talks: A Youth Speaker's Sourcebook. 240p. (Orig.). 1987. pap. 12.99 (0-310-34841-2, 11392P) Zondervan.

Robbins, Ed, ed. see Spillane, Mickey.

Robbins, Edward. Why Architects Draw. 303p. 1994. 42.50 (0-262-18157-6) MIT Pr.

Robbins, Edward M. The Gospel of Morris. LC 92-59950. 117p. 1993. 7.95 (1-55523-574-3) Winston-Derek.

— Poems for Ecumencity. 59p. 1985. 7.95 (0-89697-236-4) Intl Univ Pr.

Robbins, Edwin C. Railway Conductors. LC 76-127435. (Columbia University. Studies in the Social Sciences: No. 148). reprint ed. 32.50 (0-404-51148-1) AMS Pr.

Robbins, Fern. Eastern Cowgirl Fern Goes West. (Eastern Cowgirl Fern Ser.). (Illus.). 64p. 1994. pap. 7.95 (0-9634541-0-2) F Robbins ECF.

Robbins, Florence G. Educational Sociology: A Study in Child Youth, School & Community. LC 72-94592. 529p. 1970. reprint ed. text ed. 75.00 (0-8371-2573-1, ROES, Greenwood Pr) Greenwood.

Robbins, Fred, jt. auth. see Schlessinger, Nathan.

Robbins, Gary. Taxing Capital Gains. 1989. pap. 10.00 (0-943802-46-6, 143) Natl Ctr Pol.

Robbins, Gary & Robbins, Aldona. Federal Budget Issue: Jerry Brown's Tax Plan. (Illus.). 15p. (C). 1992. pap. 5.00 (0-943802-96-2, BG117) Natl Ctr Pol.

— Federal Budget Issue: The Clinton Economic Plan. 1992. pap. 5.00 (1-56808-003-4, BG120) Natl Ctr Pol.

— Federal Budget Issue: The Perot Economic Plan. 1992. pap. 5.00 (1-56808-005-0, BG122) Natl Ctr Pol.

— Forecasting the Effects of the Clinton Plan. (Illus.). 38p. (Orig.). Date not set. pap. text ed. 10.00 (1-56808-044-1) Natl Ctr Pol.

— If the Budget Summit Was a Success, Why Is the Five-Year Deficit Heading Toward One Trillion Dollars? 1991. pap. 5.00 (0-943802-88-1, BG109) Natl Ctr Pol.

— President Clinton's Economic Plan. (Illus.). 23p. 1993. pap. text ed. 4.00 (1-56808-008-5, BG 125) Natl Ctr Pol.

— A Pro-Growth Budget Strategy: Vision for the 1990s. 1990. pap. 10.00 (0-943802-57-1, 154) Natl Ctr Pol.

— Tax Fairness: Myths & Reality. 1991. pap. 10.00 (0-943802-63-6, 160) Natl Ctr Pol.

— Taxes, Deficits & the Current Recession. 1991. pap. 10.00 (0-943802-59-8, 156) Natl Ctr Pol.

— What a Canadian-Style Health Care System Would Cost U. S. Employers & Employees. 1990. pap. 10.00 (0-943802-48-2, 145) Natl Ctr Pol.

— Will the New Budget Package Create a Recession? 1990. pap. 5.00 (0-943802-87-3, BG108) Natl Ctr Pol.

Robbins, Gary, jt. auth. see Robbins, Aldona.

Robbins, Gary, et al. How Our Health Care System Works. (Illus.). 44p. (Orig.). 1993. pap. 10.00 (1-56808-000-X, 177) Natl Ctr Pol.

— Immigration Solution. 1992. pap. 10.00 (0-943802-75-X, 172) Natl Ctr Pol.

— Inefficiency in the U. S. Health Care System: What Can We Do. 26p. (Orig.). Date not set. pap. text ed. 10.00 (1-56808-016-6, 182) Natl Ctr Pol.

Robbins, George. International Political Relations. 200p. (Orig.). (C). 1993. pap. text ed. 30.00 (1-878045-47-4) Whittier Pubns.

— Political Psychology. 228p. (Orig.). (C). 1993. pap. text ed. 30.00 (1-878045-48-2) Whittier Pubns.

Robbins, Guy F. Clio Chirugica: The Breast. rev. ed. (Surgery Ser.). (Illus.). 300p. (Orig.). 1987. pap. 35.00 (0-941432-13-0) R G Landes.

Robbins, Guy L. And in the Seventh Day. (American University Studies: Ser. VII, Vol. 36). 242p. (C). 1995. pap. text ed. 32.95 (0-8204-0504-3) P Lang Pubs.

Robbins, Gwen, et al. A Wellness Way of Life. 2nd ed. 496p. 1994. pap. write for info. (0-697-12659-5) Brown & Benchmark.

Robbins, H. Bryan, jt. auth. see Yates, Keith D.

***Robbins, Harold.** The Carpetbaggers. 624p. 1995. 10.95 (1-56865-130-9, GuildAmerica) Dblday Bk Music.

— Carpetbaggers. 1993. mass mkt. 5.99 (0-671-87484-5) PB.

— The Carpetbaggers. 1993. reprint ed. lib. bdg. 39.95x (1-56849-141-7) Buccaneer Bks.

— Harold Robbins: Three Complete Novels. 1994. pap. 12.99 (0-517-10071-1) Random Hse Value.

— Never Leave Me. 224p. 1978. mass mkt. 4.99 (0-380-00179-9) Avon.

— Never Love a Stranger. 1993. mass mkt. 5.99 (0-671-87492-6) PB.

— Piranha. 1986. write for info. (0-318-60976-2) S&S Trade.

— Piranhas. 1991. 21.95 (0-685-50250-3) S&S Trade.

— Piranhas. 1992. pap. 5.99 (0-671-87494-2) S&S Trade.

— The Piranhas. large type ed. 1992. 18.95 (0-7927-1114-9, E0033, Eagle Lrg Print) Chivers N Amer.

— The Piranhas. large type ed. 1992. pap. 15.95 (0-7927-1113-0, Paragon Lrg Print) Chivers N Amer.

— Pirate. 1993. mass mkt. 5.99 (0-671-87493-4) PB.

— El Precio del Placer. 256p. (SPA.). 1992. pap. 3.95 (1-56780-155-2) La Costa Pr.

— Raiders. 1995. 23.00 (0-671-87289-3) S&S Trade.

— Stiletto. large type ed. 272p. 1983. 23.95 (0-7089-8101-1, Trail West Pubs) Ulverscroft.

— A Stone for Danny Fisher. 1994. mass mkt. 5.99 (0-671-87497-7) PB.

Robbins, Harvey. How to Speak & Listen Effectively. (AMA Worksmart Ser.). 120p. (Orig.). 1993. pap. 10.95 (0-8144-7793-3) AMACOM.

— Turf Wars: Moving from Competition to Collaboration. 252p. 1992. pap. text ed. 9.95 (1-880416-68-9) NW Pub.

***Robbins, Harvey & Finley, Michael.** Why Teams Don't Work: What Went Wrong & How to Make It Right. LC 95-3270. 240p. 1995. 20.95 (1-56079-497-6, Petersons Pacesetter) Petersons Guides.

Robbins, Harvey B. Betrayal: Michael Dukakis & the Struggle to Save Historic Prowse Farm. (Illus.). 112p. 1988. 12.95 (0-89803-161-3) Green Hill.

Robbins, Hayes, ed. see Gompers, Samuel.

Robbins, Herbert, jt. auth. see Courant, Richard.

***Robbins, Ina.** From My Heart to Your Heart. LC 94-19538. (J). 1994. pap. 4.95 (0-8091-6619-4) Paulist Pr.

Robbins, Ira A. Test Your Rock IQ: The Sixties - Folk Rock & Acid Rock, Bubblegum & Woodstock, 250 Mindbenders from Rock's Glory Decade. LC 93-13673. (Illus.). 1993. 7.95 (0-316-74898-6) Little.

— Test Your Rock IQ: The '70s - Disco & Funk, Metal & Punk, 250 Mindbenders from Rock's Lost Decade. LC 93-4414. (Illus.). 1993. 7.95 (0-316-74907-9) Little.

— The Trouser Press Record Guide. 4th ed. 800p. 1991. pap. 20.00 (0-02-036361-3, Pub. by Gebrueder Borntraeger GW) Macmillan.

Robbins, Ira A., ed. The New Trouser Press Record Guide. rev. ed. 516p. 1985. 24.95 (0-684-18377-3, Scribners); pap. 13.95 (0-684-18378-1, Scribners) S&S Trade.

Robbins, Ira P. Habeas Corpus Checklists, 1 vol. (Criminal Law Ser.). 1993. 75.00 (0-87632-906-7) Clark Boardman Callaghan.

— Post-Conviction Remedies: Cases & Materials. LC 82-2557. (American Casebook Ser.). 506p. 1982. text ed. 37.00 (0-314-64851-8) West Pub.

— Prisoners & the Law, 4 vols., Set. LC 85-16678. (Civil Rights Ser.). 1985. ring bd. 450.00 (0-87632-478-2) Clark Boardman Callaghan.

Robbins, Ireene. Easy Art Projects for Every Month of the School Year. 572p. 1990. pap. 24.95 (0-13-223744-X) P-H.

***Robbins, J.** May All Be Fed. Date not set. pap. 4.98 (0-8317-4371-9) Smithmark.

***Robbins, J. & Moscrop, J. E.** Caring for the Dying Patient & the Family. 3rd ed. 304p. 1995. pap. 47.75 (1-56593-328-1, 0658) Singular Publishing.

Robbins, J., ed. see Braverman, L. E.

Robbins, J., jt. ed. see Kankey, R.

Robbins, J. Albert, ed. American Literary Scholarship: An Annual, 1968. LC 65-19450. xiv, 335p. 1970. 48.00 (0-8223-0235-7) Duke.

— American Literary Scholarship: An Annual, 1969. LC 65-19450. xiv, 385p. 1971. 48.00 (0-8223-0248-9) Duke.

— American Literary Scholarship: An Annual, 1970. LC 65-19450. xii, 434p. 1972. 48.00 (0-8223-0270-5) Duke.

— American Literary Scholarship: An Annual, 1971. LC 65-19450. xiv, 418p. 1973. 48.00 (0-8223-0293-4) Duke.

— American Literary Scholarship: An Annual, 1972. LC 65-19450. xvi, 448p. 1974. 48.00 (0-8223-0324-8) Duke.

— American Literary Scholarship: An Annual, 1976. LC 65-19450. xv, 490p. 1978. 48.00 (0-8223-0406-6) Duke.

— American Literary Scholarship: An Annual, 1978. LC 65-19450. xviii, 528p. 1980. 48.00 (0-8223-0443-0) Duke.

— American Literary Scholarship: An Annual, 1985. LC 65-19450. 536p. (C). 1987. 48.00 (0-8223-0720-0) Duke.

— American Literary Scholarship: An Annual, 1988. 616p. (C). 1990. lib. bdg. 48.00 (0-8223-1033-3) Duke.

— American Literary Scholarship, 1980. LC 65-1950. xix, 625p. 1982. 48.00 (0-8223-0464-3) Duke.

— American Literary Scholarship, 1984. LC 65-19450. 613p. 1986. text ed. 48.00 (0-8223-0666-2) Duke.

Robbins, J. H. Knowing Herself: Women Tell Their Stories in Psychotherapy. LC 89-26727. (Illus.). 320p. 1990. 21.95 (0-306-43430-X, Plenum Insight) Plenum.

Robbins, Jack A., ed. The Complete Poetry of John Reed. LC 82-21915. 102p. (Orig.). 1983. lib. bdg. 40.50 (0-8191-2931-3) U Pr of Amer.

Robbins, James G. & Jones, Barbara S. Effective Communication for Today's Manager. LC 74-79216. (Illus.). 174p. 1989. pap. 28.95 (0-912016-36-1) Lebhar Friedman.

Robbins, James M., jt. ed. see Kirmayer, Laurence J.

Robbins, Jan C. Public Schools As Public Forums: Use of Schools by Non-School Publics. LC 90-60217. (Fastback Ser.: NO. 302). 40p. (Orig.). (C). 1990. pap. 1.25 (0-87367-302-6) Phi Delta Kappa.

— Student Press & the Hazelwood Decision. LC 88-61691. (Fastback Ser.: No. 274). 42p. (Orig.). (C). 1988. pap. 1.25 (0-87367-274-7) Phi Delta Kappa.

— Voluntary Religious Activities in Public Schools: Policy Guidelines. LC 86-63881. (Fastback Ser.: No. 253). 50p. 1987. pap. 1.25 (0-87367-253-4) Phi Delta Kappa.

Robbins, Jane & Zweizig, Douglas L. Are We There Yet? Evaluating Library Collections, Reference Services, Programs & Personnel. 152p. 1988. pap. 8.00 (0-936442-12-3) U Wis Sch Lib.

Robbins, Jane, et al. Evaluation Strategies & Techniques for Public Library Children's Services: A Sourcebook. 302p. 1990. pap. 18.00 (0-936442-14-X) U Wis Sch Lib.

Robbins, Jane B., ed. see Urban Libraries Council Staff.

Robbins, Jeffrey M., ed. Primary Care Podiatry. LC 93-17926. 1994. text ed. 60.00 (0-7216-4363-9) Saunders.

***Robbins, Jenni L., ed.** Quality Program: Quality Plan Manual. (Illus.). (C). Date not set. ring bd. 175.00 (1-56395-040-5) Am Assn Blood.

— Quality Program: Self-Assessment Manual. (Illus.). (C). Date not set. ring bd. 175.00 (1-56395-039-1) Am Assn Blood.

Robbins, Jerome. Jerome Robbins Broadway. 1990. pap. 12.95 (0-88188-829-X, HL 00490156) H Leonard.

Robbins, Jerry K. Carevision: The Why & How of Christian Caregiving. LC 93-23840. 176p. 1993. pap. 13.00 (0-8170-1195-1) Judson.

Robbins, Jerry K., ed. see Luther, Martin.

Robbins, Jill. Prodigal Son - Elder Brother: Interpretation & Alterity in Augustine, Petrarch, Kafka, Levinas. LC 90-19722. (Religion & Postmodernism Ser.). 184p. 1991. 24.95 (0-226-72110-8) U Ch Pr.

Robbins, Jim. Crappie! 1991. 21.95 (1-879034-02-6) MS River Pub.

— Last Refuge: The Environmental Showdown in the American West. LC 94-6630. 288p. 1994. pap. 12.00 (0-06-258548-7) HarpC West.

— Last Refuge: The Environmental Showdown in Yellowstone & the American West. LC 93-9426. 285p. 1993. 23.00 (0-688-11178-5) Morrow.

Robbins, Joan H. & Siegel, Rachel J., eds. Women Changing Therapy: New Assessments, Values, & Strategies in Feminist Therapy. LC 83-12643. (Women & Therapy Ser.: Vol. 2, Nos. 2-3). 240p. 1983. text ed. 39.95 (0-86656-239-7); pap. text ed. 14.95 (0-86656-240-0) Haworth Pr.

— Women Changing Therapy: New Assessments, Values & Strategies in Feminist Therapy. LC 84-19276. 240p. 1985. pap. text ed. 14.95 (0-918393-07-8) Harrington Pk.

Robbins, Joel. High Performance Futures Trading: Power Lessons from the Masters. rev. ed. 1994. 47.50 (1-55738-571-8) Probus Pub Co.

Robbins, John. May All Be Fed: Diet for a New World. LC 92-12596. 1992. 23.00 (0-688-11625-6) Morrow.

— May All Be Fed: Diet for a New World. 416p. 1993. reprint ed. pap. 12.00 (0-380-71901-0) Avon.

R

An Asterisk (*) at the beginning of an entry indicates that the title is appearing in BIP for the first time.

Robbins, John & Macy, Joanna R. Diet for a New America: How Your Food Choices Affect Your Health, Happiness & the Future of Life on Earth. LC 87-61157. (Illus.). 432p. 1987. pap. 13.95 (0-913299-54-5) Stillpoint.

Robbins, John & Mortifee, Ann. In Search of Balance: Discovering Harmony in a Changing World. Carleton, Nancy, ed. LC 90-50860. 132p. 1991. pap. 9.95 (0-915811-31-6) H J Kramer Inc.

Robbins, John B., et al, eds. Bacterial Vaccines. LC 86-9523. 589p. 1987. text ed. 115.00 (0-275-92157-3, C2157, Praeger Pubs) Greenwood.

Robbins, John W. Cornelius Van Til: The Man & the Myth. 42p. (Orig.). 1986. pap. 2.45 (0-940931-15-X) Trinity Found.

Robbins, John W., ed. & intro. Gordon H. Clark: Personal Recollections. 150p. (Orig.). 1989. pap. 6.95 (0-940931-27-3) Trinity Found.

Robbins, John W. & Spangler, Mark, eds. A Man of Principle: Essays in Honor of Hans F. Sennholz. (C). 1992. text ed. 30.00 (0-9631818-0-7) Grove City Coll.

Robbins, John W., ed. see Augustine, Aurelius & Clark, Gordon H.

Robbins, John W., ed. see Bonar, Horatius.

Robbins, John W., ed. see Bordwine, James E.

Robbins, John W., ed. see Carranza, Elihu.

Robbins, John W., ed. see Clark, Gordon H.

Robbins, John W., ed. see Crampton, W. Gary.

Robbins, John W., ed. see Hodge, Charles.

Robbins, John W., ed. see Hoeksema, Herman.

Robbins, Johnny. You Can Be a Country Music Songwriter. (Illus.). 84p. 1982. pap. 4.95 (0-9609748-0-6) Green Block.

Robbins, Judd. El ABC del 123 Version 3. 261p. 1993. pap. text ed. 24.95 (968-6346-75-9, Pub. by Ventura Ediciones MX) Computer & Tech.

— Amazing Windows Games. LC 93-85587. 155p. 1993. disk, pap. 19.99 (0-7821-1361-3) Sybex.

— Fun with Fractals. LC 92-83715. 220p. 1992. 19.95 (0-7821-1126-2) Sybex.

— Lotus 1-2-3 Release 2.3 & 2.4 for DOS Instant Reference. 2nd ed. LC 92-81524. 277p. 1992. pap. 9.95 (0-7821-1132-7) Sybex.

— Lotus 123: Step by Step. 1990. pap. 24.95 (0-672-22712-6, Bobbs) Michie Butterworth.

— Lotus 123 Version 2.3. 235p. 1992. pap. text ed. write for info. (968-6346-43-0, Pub. by Ventura Ediciones MX) Computer & Tech.

— Mastering DOS 6.2: Special Edition. LC 93-86583. 1016p. 1993. 29.99 (0-7821-1442-3) Sybex.

— WordPerfect 5.1 Step by Step. 1990. pap. 24.95 (0-672-22711-8, Bobbs) Macmillan.

Robbins, Judd & Braly, Ken. Expert dBASE: An Advanced Textbook for dBASE Programmers. 264p. (Orig.). (C). 1985. pap. 25.00 (0-9614937-0-4) Present Dynam.

Robbins, Juliette, jt. auth. see Collins, Brad.

Robbins, K. A. & Robbins, S. The Cray X-MP - Model 24. (Lecture Notes in Computer Science Ser.: Vol. 374). iv, 165p. 1989. pap. 22.00 (0-387-97089-4, 3132) Spr-Verlag.

Robbins, Kay A., jt. auth. see Gonzales, Mario J.

Robbins, Keith. Appeasement. (Historical Association Studies). 96p. 1990. pap. text ed. 9.95 (0-631-16013-2) Blackwell Pubs.

— Bibliography of Writings on British History 1914-1989. 1200p. 1995. 125.00 (0-19-822496-6) OUP.

— Churchill. 1993. pap. text ed. 19.95 (0-685-72550-2, 79372) Longman.

— The Eclipse of a Great Power: Modern Britain, 1870-1975. LC 81-18608. (Illus.). 304p. (C). 1983. pap. text ed. 27.50 (0-582-48972-5, 73420) Longman.

— The Eclipse of a Great Power: Modern Britain, 1870-1992. LC 94-841. (Foundations of Modern British Ser.). (C). 1995. pap. text ed. 28.50 (0-582-09611-1, 76706, Pub. by Longman UK) Longman.

— The Eclipse of a Great Power: Modern Britain, 1870-1992. 2nd ed. LC 94-841. (Foundations of Modern Britain Ser.). (C). 1994. text ed. 63.95 (0-582-09612-X, 76707, Pub. by Longman UK) Longman.

— The First World War. (Illus.). 208p. 1985. pap. 13.95 (0-19-289149-9) OUP.

— History, Religion, & Identity in Modern Britain. LC 93-17978. 312p. 1993. boxed 60.00 (1-85285-101-5) Hambledon Press.

— Nineteenth-Century Britain: Integration & Diversity. 212p. 1995. pap. 19.95 (0-19-820585-6) OUP.

— Politicians, Diplomacy & War in Modern British History. LC 94-2354. 336p. 1994. 60.00 (1-85285-111-2) Hambledon Press.

Robbins, Keith, ed. The Blackwell Biographical Dictionary of British Political Life in the Twentieth Century. 360p. 1990. 83.95 (0-631-15768-9) Blackwell Pubs.

— Protestant Evangelicalism: Britain, Ireland, Germany & America c.1750-c.1950. (Studies in Church History). 400p. 1990. 59.95 (0-631-17818-X) Blackwell Pubs.

Robbins, Keith, jt. ed. see Collins, Bruce.

Robbins, Ken. Bridges. (Illus.). (J). 1991. lib. bdg. 13.89 (0-8037-0930-7) Dial Bks Young.

— Make Me a Peanut Butter Sandwich & a Glass of Milk. (Illus.). (J). (ps up). 1992. 14.95 (0-590-43550-7, 023, Scholastic Hardcover) Scholastic Inc.

Robbins, Ken, photos & text. Power Machines. LC 92-30649. (Illus.). 32p. (J). (gr. k-3). 1993. 15.95 (0-8050-1410-1, Bks Young Read) H Holt & Co.

Robbins, Kenn. Buttermilk Bottoms: A Novel. LC 87-4997. 268p. reprint ed. pap. 76.40 (0-7837-1625-7, 2041918) Bks Demand.

Robbins, Kenneth. The Baptism of Howie Cobb. LC 94-13788. 1994. 13.50 (0-929925-28-9) Univ SD Pr.

— A Good & Dandy World. 1980. pap. 1.75 (0-686-38380-X) Eldridge Pub.

Robbins, L. The Business of Writing & Speaking: A Managerial Communication Manual. 224p. 1985. text ed. write for info. (0-07-053089-0) McGraw.

Robbins, L. Pearne. One Shahapton Stirring Ashes. rev. ed. (Illus.). 135p. 1993. pap. 8.00 (1-883501-00-8) R Lodges Pub.

***Robbins, Lawrence & Lang, Susan S.** Headache Help: A Complete Guide to Understanding Headaches & the Medicines That Relieve Them. LC 94-43494. 224p. 1995. 10.95 (0-395-70751-X) HM.

Robbins, Lawrence D. Management of Headache & Headache Medications. LC 93-19226. 217p. 1994. 49.00 (0-387-94040-5) Spr-Verlag.

Robbins, Lawrence H. Stones Bones & Ancient Cities. 1990. 18.95 (0-312-04431-3) St Martin.

— Stones, Bones, & Ancient Cities: Great Discoveries in Archaeology & the Search for Human. 1992. pap. 10.95 (0-312-07848-X) St Martin.

— Stones, Bones, & Ancient Cities: Great Discoveries in Archaeology & the Search for Human Origins. (Illus.). 304p. 1992. 10.95 (0-685-52431-0) St Martin.

***Robbins, Lillian W.** Light on the Shore. LC 94-61604. 168p. (Orig.). 1995. 9.95 (1-884570-18-6) Research Triangle.

Robbins, Lionel, ed. see Wicksell, Knut.

Robbins, Lionel C. Economic Planning & International Order. LC 72-4294. (World Affairs Ser.: National & International Viewpoints). 348p. 1972. reprint ed. 23.95 (0-405-04586-7) Ayer.

— Great Depression. LC 75-150198. (Select Bibliographies Reprint Ser.). 1977. reprint ed. 25.95 (0-8369-5711-3) Ayer.

Robbins, Louise M. Footprints: Collection, Analysis & Interpretation. (Illus.). 244p. 1985. 46.95 (0-398-05138-0) C C Thomas.

— Footprints: Collection, Analysis & Interpretation. (Illus.). 244p. 1985. pap. 29.95 (0-398-06403-2) C C Thomas.

Robbins, M. S. Amelie. 1986. pap. 5.00 (0-941240-07-X) Ommation Pr.

Robbins, Manuel. Fluorescence: Gems & Minerals under Ultraviolet Light. LC 93-77811. (Illus.). 374p. 1994. 40.00 (0-945005-13-X) Geoscience Pr.

Robbins, Manuel A. The Collector's Book of Fluorescent Minerals. 320p. 1983. text ed. 69.95 (0-442-27506-4) Chapman & Hall.

***Robbins, Marc L. & McIver, D. W.** Precision-Guided Logistics: Flexible Support for the Force-Projection Army's High-Technology Weapons. LC 94-30295. 1994. write for info. (0-8330-1574-5, MR437A) Rand Corp.

Robbins, Margaret. AppWare: A Developers Guide. 1994. Incl. diskette. pap. 39.95 (1-55851-403-1) M&T Bks.

Robbins, Margaret, jt. auth. see Tittel, Ed.

Robbins, Mari L. Dicey's Song: A Literature Unit. (Literature Units Ser.). (Illus.). 48p. (Orig.). 1993. student ed, pap. 6.95 (1-55734-422-1) Tchr Create Mat.

— Dragonwings: A Literature Unit. (Literature Units Ser.). (Illus.). 48p. 1993. student ed 6.95 (1-55734-429-9) Tchr Create Mat.

— Literature Unit: I Heard the Owl Call My Name. Cain, Janet, ed. (Illus.). 48p. (Orig.). 1994. student ed, pap. 6.95 (1-55734-520-1) Tchr Create Mat.

— Literature Unit: Sounder. Cain, Janet, ed. (Illus.). 48p. (Orig.). 1994. student ed, pap. 6.95 (1-55734-530-9) Tchr Create Mat.

— The Red Pony: A Literature Unit. (Literature Units Ser.). (Illus.). 48p. (Orig.). (J). (gr. 6-8). 1993. student ed, pap. 6.95 (1-55734-443-4) Tchr Create Mat.

***Robbins, Mari Lu & Bruce, Kathy.** Literature Unit: The Golden Goblet. (Literature Units Ser.). 1995. pap. text ed. 6.95 (1-55734-442-6) Tchr Create Mat.

***Robbins, Mari Lu & Herweck, Dona.** Native Americans. (Interdisciplinary Units Ser.). (Illus.). 1994. 14.95 (1-55734-607-0) Tchr Create Mat.

Robbins, Maria P. Blue Ribbon Cookies. 144p. 1988. 11.95 (0-312-01738-3); pap. 7.95 (0-312-01739-1) St Martin.

— Blue-Ribbon Pies. (Illus.). 128p. 1987. pap. 7.95 (0-312-00569-5) St Martin.

— Cookies for Christmas: Fifty of the Best Cookie Recipes for Holiday Gift Giving, Decorating, & Eating. (Illus.). 144p. (Orig.). 1993. pap. 6.95 (0-312-09775-1) St Martin.

— Puss in Books: A Collection of Great Cat Quotations. LC 94-4579. 1994. 17.95 (0-525-93827-3, Dutton) NAL-Dutton.

Robbins, Maria P., ed. A Gardener's Bouquet of Quotations. LC 93-18688. (Illus.). 288p. 1993. 18.00 (0-525-93669-6, Dutton) NAL-Dutton.

Robbins, Maria P., jt. auth. see Fischer, Leah L.

Robbins, Maria P., jt. auth. see Fisher, Leah.

Robbins, Mark. Angles of Incidence. LC 92-29640. (Illus.). 80p. (Orig.). 1992. pap. 19.95 (1-878271-67-9) Princeton Arch.

Robbins, Mark B. & Easterla, David A. Birds of Missouri: Their Distribution & Abundance. (Illus.). 416p. (C). 1991. text ed. 59.95 (0-8262-0791-X) U of Mo Pr.

Robbins, Martha A. Midlife Women & Death of Mother: A Study of Psychhistorical & Spiritual Transformation. LC 89-13610. (American University Studies: Psychology: Ser. VIII, Vol. 8). 335p. (C). 1990. text ed. 48.95 (0-8204-1220-1) P Lang Pubs.

Robbins, Martin. A Year with Two Winters. 65p. (Orig.). 1984. pap. 10.00 (0-932662-55-2) St Andrews NC.

***Robbins, Meyera.** Great Food for Great Kids Recipes: Quick & Easy Recipes for a Healthy Family. 300p. 1994. pap. write for info. (0-614-04591-6) Great Kids.

Robbins, Michael. Experiences of Schizophrenia: An Integration of the Personal, Scientific, & Therapeutic. LC 92-48311. 550p. 1993. lib. bdg. 45.00 (0-89862-997-7) Guilford Pr.

Robbins, Michael D. The Tapestry of the Gods: Psychological Transformation & the Seven Rays, 2 vols., Set. (Orig.). 1988. pap. write for info. (0-9621869-2-9) Univ Seven Rays Pub.

— The Tapestry of the Gods: Psychological Transformation & the Seven Rays, 2 vols., Vol. I. 400p. (Orig.). 1988. pap. write for info. (0-9621869-0-2) Univ Seven Rays Pub.

— The Tapestry of the Gods: Psychological Transformation & the Seven Rays, 2 vols., Vol. II. 400p. (Orig.). 1988. pap. write for info. (0-9621869-1-0) Univ Seven Rays Pub.

Robbins, Michael J., jt. auth. see Olson, Gail A.

Robbins, Morgan. Morgan Robbins' Tarot. 32p. 1983. 12.00 (0-88079-028-8) US Games Syst.

Robbins, Nancy, ed. Fan Fare. (Illus.). 324p. reprint ed. 14.50 (0-9612176-0-X) Rochester Philharmonic.

Robbins, Naomi C., jt. auth. see Herstein, Sheila R.

Robbins, Neal. Contemporary Chinese Fiction: Four Short Stories. 225p. (Orig.). (CHI.). 1986. pap. text ed. 10.95 (0-88710-140-2) Yale Far Eastern Pubns.

— The Crimson Fish. (Illus.). 58p. (Orig.). (J). (gr. 1 up). Date not set. pap. 4.00 (1-884993-02-8) Koldarana.

— The Island of the Three Sapphires. (Illus.). 98p. (J). (gr. 6 up). Date not set. pap. 4.00 (1-884993-04-4) Koldarana.

— Kana of the Snow Capped Mountains. (Illus.). 77p. (Orig.). (J). (gr. 1 up). 1992. pap. 4.00 (1-884993-01-X) Koldarana.

— The Neglected Princess. 72p. (J). 1992. pap. 4.00 (1-884993-00-1) Koldarana.

— The Star Locusts. (Illus.). 142p. (YA). 1995. pap. 5.00 (1-884993-05-2) Koldarana.

Robbins, Neal E. Ronald W. Reagan: Fortieth President of the United States. Young, Richard G., ed. LC 89-39955. (Presidents of the United States Ser.). (Illus.). 128p. (J). (gr. 5-9). 1990. lib. bdg. 17.26 (0-944483-66-6) Garrett Ed Corp.

— Rutherford B. Hayes: Nineteenth President of the United States. Young, Richard G., ed. LC 88-24565. (Presidents of the United States Ser.). (Illus.). (J). (gr. 5-9). 1989. lib. bdg. 17.26 (0-944483-23-2) Garrett Ed Corp.

***Robbins, Ocean & Solomon, Sol.** Choices for Our Future: A Generation Rising for Life on Earth. LC 94-29060. (Illus.). 192p. (Orig.). 1994. pap. 9.95 (1-57067-002-1) Book Pub Co.

Robbins, Pam. How to Plan & Implement a Peer Coaching Program. LC 91-27082. 69p. 1991. pap. 6.95 (0-87120-184-4, 611-91149) Assn Supervision.

***Robbins, Pam & Alvy, Harvey B.** The Principal's Companion: Strategies & Hints to Make the Job Easier. (Illus.). 304p. 1995. 59.95 (0-8039-6196-0); pap. 29.95 (0-8039-6197-9) Corwin Pr.

Robbins, Paul R. Designer Drugs. LC 94-16314. (Drug Library). (Illus.). 112p. (YA). (gr. 6 up). 1995. lib. bdg. 17.95 (0-89490-488-4) Enslow Pubs.

— Marijuana: A Short Course Updated for the Eighties. LC 75-22753. 80p. 1983. pap. 9.95 (0-8283-1856-5) Branden Pub Co.

— The Psychology of Dreams. LC 87-29889. 184p. 1988. lib. bdg. 24.95 (0-89950-270-9) McFarland & Co.

— Understanding Depression. LC 92-56685. 200p. 1993. lib. bdg. 21.95 (0-89950-878-2) McFarland & Co.

***Robbins, Paula I.** Nights of Summer, Nights of Autumn. (Illus.). 195p. (C). 1992. pap. 12.95 (0-9632975-0-3) Finnish Amer.

— Nights of Summer, Nights of Autumn: Self-Care for Bodyworkers. 195p. (Orig.). (C). 1992. spiral bd. 12.95 (0-9632875-0-8) Finnish Amer.

Robbins, Phillip, jt. auth. see Beatty, Patricia.

Robbins, Phillips W., jt. ed. see Das, Rathindra C.

Robbins, Phillips W., jt. ed. see Ginsberg, Victor.

Robbins, R. H., ed. see Browne, Thomas.

Robbins, R. J. & Melmed, Schlomo, eds. Acromegaly: A Century of Scientific & Clinical Progress. LC 87-13016. (Serono Symposia U. S. A. Ser.). (Illus.). 302p. 1987. 75.00 (0-306-42618-8, Plenum Pr) Plenum.

***Robbins, R. Laurie.** Field & Laboratory Biology for Elementary Teaching Majors. 256p. (C). 1994. 26.36 (0-8403-9648-1) Kendall-Hunt.

Robbins, R. O. What the Righteous Desire to See: The Revelation Revealed & the Prophets Dictionary. LC 88-81268. (E.T.M.'s Systematic Theology Ser.). 470p. 1988. ring bd. 39.95 (1-882074-99-8) ETM.

Robbins, R. Robert, jt. auth. see Hemenway, Mary K.

Robbins, R. Robert, jt. auth. see Jefferys, William H.

***Robbins, R. Robert, et al.** Discovering Astronomy & Activities Kit. 3rd ed. 1994. text ed. write for info. (0-471-11667-X) Wiley.

Robbins, Rae G. The Bloomsbury Group: A Selective Bibliography. 219p. 1978. 17.00 (0-685-04148-4) Price Guide.

Robbins, Ray & Nichols, Larry. The California Peace Officer: The Basic Training Course, 3 vols., Set. 2nd ed. LC 91-66585. (Illus.). 1018p. (Orig.). (C). 1992. pap. text ed. 0.75 (0-8211-1520-0) McCutchan.

Robbins, Ray K. Criminal Investigation Procedures. LC 93-77666. 350p. (C). 1993. text ed. 38.00 (0-8211-1752-1) McCutchan.

— The Florida Law Enforcement Officer: The Basic Recruit Training Course. LC 91-66586. (Illus.). 269p. (C). 1992. pap. text ed. 25.00 (0-8211-1727-0) McCutchan.

Robbins, Ray K., et al. The Texas Peace Officer, 2 vols. 3rd ed. LC 89-63475. 707p. 1990. 46.00 (0-8211-1723-8) McCutchan.

***Robbins, Rebecca.** An Irresistible Pursuit. 2403p. (Orig.). 1995. mass mkt. 3.99 (0-380-77671-5) Avon.

— Lucky in Love. 224p. (Orig.). 1994. mass mkt. 3.99 (0-380-77485-2) Avon.

— The Mischievous Maid. 256p. (Orig.). 1993. mass mkt. 3.99 (0-380-77336-8) Avon.

— An Unusual Inheritance. 224p. (Orig.). 1994. mass mkt. 3.99 (0-380-77670-7) Avon.

Robbins, Richard. The Invisible Wedding: Poems. LC 83-16930. (Breakthrough Ser.: No. 44). 80p. 1984. pap. 10.95 (0-8262-0438-4) U of Mo Pr.

— London Underground. (Illus.). 32p. (Orig.). 1989. pap. 4.00 (0-9628094-0-3) Pearl Edit.

Robbins, Richard, jt. ed. see Powell, Walter W.

Robbins, Richard G., Jr. Famine in Russia, Eighteen Ninety-One to Eighteen Ninety-Two: The Imperial Government Responds to a Crisis. LC 74-8528. (Studies of the Russian Institute of Columbia University). 1975. text ed. 42.00 (0-231-03836-4) Col U Pr.

— The Tsar's Viceroys: Russian Provincial Governors in the Last Years of the Empire. LC 87-47700. 328p. 1987. 39.95 (0-8014-2046-6) Cornell U Pr.

Robbins, Richard H. Cultural Anthropology: A Problem-Based Approach. (Orig.). (C). 1993. teacher ed write for info. (0-318-69541-3); pap. 25.00 (0-87581-375-5) Peacock Pubs.

Robbins, Richard J., jt. ed. see Olefsky, Jerrold M.

Robbins, Richard L. The Automated Law Firm: A Complete Guide to Software & Systems. 254p. 1989. ring bd. 75.00 (0-13-051038-6) P-H.

— The Automated Law Firm: A Complete Guide to Software & Systems. 2nd ed. 590p. 1992. ring bd. 110.00 (0-13-291352-6) Aspen Law.

***Robbins, Robert, et al.** Discovering Astronomy. 3rd ed. LC 94-5244. 1994. text ed. 50.95 (0-471-58437-1) Wiley.

Robbins, Robert K. Evolution, Comparative Morphology, & Identification of the Eumaeine Butterfly Genus Rekoa Kaye (Lycaenidae: Theclinae) LC 89-600292. (Smithsonian Contributions to Zoology Ser.: No. 498). 68p. reprint ed. pap. 25.00 (0-7837-0269-8, 2040578) Bks Demand.

Robbins, Robin. Looking at Nature. (Illus.). 48p. (J). (gr. 7-9). 1992. 13.95 (0-563-34498-9, BBC-Parkwest); pap. 7.50 (0-563-34499-7, BBC-Parkwest) Parkwest Pubns.

Robbins, Roland. Mantracking, Introduction to the Step-by-Step Method. Anderson, Elizabeth et al, eds. LC 77-77680. (Illus.). 1977. pap. 24.00 (0-9603392-0-5) Search & Rescue.

Robbins, Roland W. Discovery at Walden. (Illus.). 1970. reprint ed. pap. 3.00 (0-912130-02-4) Thoreau Found.

— Pilgrim John Alden's Progress: Archaeological Excavations in Duxbury. 1969. 3.00 (0-940628-28-7) Pilgrim Soc.

Robbins, Ronald. The Rhythmic Cycle of Change. LC 88-25446. 306p. (Orig.). 1989. pap. 24.95 (0-9620928-1-9) Neshama Pubns.

— Rhythmic Integration. 1990. pap. 13.95 (0-88268-099-4) Station Hill Pr.

Robbins, Ronald E., jt. auth. see Katz, Bernard.

Robbins, Rossell H., jt. auth. see Brown, Carleton.

Robbins, Roy M. Our Landed Heritage: The Public Domain, 1776-1970. LC 75-3569. (Illus.). 517p. reprint ed. 147.40 (0-8357-9712-0, 2019116) Bks Demand.

Robbins, Royal. Advanced Rockcraft. (Illus.). 1990. 4.95 (0-910856-56-7) La Siesta.

— Basic Rockcraft. (Illus.). 1989. 3.95 (0-910856-34-6) La Siesta.

Robbins, Russell H. Encyclopedia of Witchcraft & Demonology. 1988. 8.99 (0-517-36245-7) Random Hse Value.

Robbins, Ruth. Baboushka & the Three Kings. LC 60-15036. (Illus.). 32p. (J). (ps-3). 1986. pap. 5.95 (0-395-42647-2) HM.

Robbins, S., jt. auth. see Robbins, K. A.

***Robbins, Sally F.** Porches: Structure & Design. LC 95-12221. 1995. write for info. (1-56799-208-0, Friedman-Fairfax) M Friedman Pub Grp Inc.

Robbins, Samuel D., Jr. Wisconsin Birdlife: Population & Distribution Past & Present. LC 90-50095. 720p. 1991. 75.00 (0-299-10260-2) U of Wis Pr.

Robbins, Sandra. Big Annie: An American Tall Tale. (See-More's Stories Ser.). (Illus.). 32p. (Orig.). (J). (ps-4). 1993. pap. 4.95 (1-882601-09-2); audio, pap. 9.98 (1-882601-03-3) See-Mores Wrkshop.

— The Firefly Star: A Hispanic Folk Tale. (Illus.). 32p. (Orig.). (J). (gr. k-4). 1995. audio, pap. 11.95 (1-882601-21-1); pap. 6.95 (1-882601-23-8) See-Mores Wrkshop.

— The Growing Rock: A Native American Tale. (See-More's Stories Ser.). (Illus.). 32p. (Orig.). (J). (ps-4). 1993. audio, pap. 9.98 (1-882601-15-7); pap. 4.95 (1-882601-16-5) See-Mores Wrkshop.

— How the Turtle Got Its Shell: An African Tale. (See-More's Stories Ser.). (Illus.). 32p. (Orig.). (J). (ps-4). 1993. pap. 4.95 (1-882601-10-6); audio, pap. 9.98 (1-882601-04-1) See-Mores Wrkshop.

— Lumpy Bumpy Pumpkin: A Halloween Tale. (See-More's Stories Ser.). (Illus.). 32p. (Orig.). (J). (ps-4). 1993. audio, pap. 9.98 (1-882601-18-1); pap. 4.95 (1-882601-19-X) See-Mores Wrkshop.

— Ring Around a Rainbow: A Health Adventure. (See-More's Stories Ser.). (Illus.). 32p. (Orig.). (J). (gr. k-5). 1993. pap. 4.95 (1-882601-08-4); digital audio 9.98 (1-882601-05-X) See-Mores Wrkshop.

— See-More's Stories: A Series of Six Read-Aloud Books & Read-Along/Move-Along Tapes. (See-More's Stories Ser.). (Illus.). 32p. (Orig.). (J). (ps-4). 1993. audio, pap. 54.95 (1-882601-22-X) See-Mores Wrkshop.

— Tobias Turkey: A Thanksgiving Tale. (See-More's Stories Ser.). (Illus.). 32p. (Orig.). (J). (ps-3). 1993. pap. 4.95 (1-882601-07-6); audio, pap. 9.98 (1-882601-06-8) See-Mores Wrkshop.

Robbins, Sara. Baby M Case: A Collection of the Complete Trial Transcripts, 6 vols. LC 88-80607. 1988. lib. bdg. 475.00 (0-89941-637-3, 305470) W S Hein.

— Crushed for Better Wine. 1979. reprint ed. 7.00 (0-87516-373-4) DeVorss.

R

— Surrogate Parenting: An Annotated Review of the Literature. LC 84-1824. (CompuBibs Ser.: No. 3). 40p. 1984. pap. 10.00 (0-914791-04-4) Vantage Info.

— Today: A Primer on the Philosophic Path. 4th ed. 1979. pap. 5.00 (0-87516-283-5) DeVorss.

Robbins, Sara, jt. auth. see Levy, Charlotte L.

Robbins, Sarah F. & Yentsch, Clarice. Sea Is All about Us: A Guide to Marine Environments of Cape Ann & Other Northern New England Waters. 1973. pap. 10.95 (0-87577-046-0, Peabody Museum) Peabody Essex Mus.

Robbins, Scott, jt. auth. see Duston, Robert L.

Robbins, Serena. Isle of Rapture. large type ed. (Romance Ser.). 592p. 1984. 15.95 (0-7089-1145-5) Ulverscroft.

***Robbins, Shawn.** Shawn Robbins' Prophecies for the End of Time. 240p. (Orig.). 1995. mass mkt. 4.99 (0-380-77694-4) Avon.

Robbins, Stanley. Patologia Estructural y Funcional. 4th ed. 1990. text ed. 99.00 (0-07-104001-3) McGraw.

***Robbins, Stanley L., et al.** Pocket Companion to Pathologic Basis of Disease. 5th ed. 624p. 1995. pap. text ed. 22.95 (0-7216-5742-7) Saunders.

Robbins, Stephen P. Essentials of Organizational Behavior. 4th ed. LC 93-26322. 1993. pap. text ed. 30.67 (0-13-300096-6) P-H.

— Organizational Behavior: Concepts, Controversies, & Applications. 6th ed. LC 92-11991. 752p. (C). 1992. text ed. write for info. (0-13-644667-1) P-H.

— Organizational Behavior: Concepts, Controversies, & Applications. 7th ed. LC 94-46765. 1995. text ed. 64.00 (0-13-192519-9) P-H.

— Personnel: The Management of Human Resources. 2nd ed. (Illus.). 544p. 1982. text ed. write for info. (0-13-657825-X) P-H.

— Training in Interpersonal Skills: Tips for Managing People at Work. 256p. (C). 1988. pap. text ed. write for info. (0-13-926817-0) P-H.

***Robbins, Stephen P. & Decenzo, David A.** Foundations of Management: Essential Concepts & Applications. LC 94-22360. 1994. pap. text ed. 46.67 (0-13-304270-7) P-H.

***Robbins, Stephen P. & O'Neil, Sharon L.** Supervision Today! LC 94-25500. 608p. 1994. pap. text ed. 51.00 (0-13-876848-X) P-H.

Robbins, Stephen P., jt. auth. see De Cenzo, David A.

Robbins, Stephen P., jt. auth. see DeCenzo, David A.

Robbins, Stephen P., jt. auth. see Wright, Penny L.

Robbins, Sterling. Auyana: Those Who Held onto Home. LC 81-2707. (Anthropological Studies in the Eastern Highlands of New Guinea: No. 6). (Illus.). 274p. 1982. 40.00 (0-295-95788-3) U of Wash Pr.

Robbins, Susan, et al. Academic Productivity in Social Work Education. 1985. 3.95 (0-318-35321-0) Coun Soc Wk Ed.

Robbins, Thomas. Another Roadside Attraction. 1990. pap. 10.00 (0-553-34948-1) Bantam.

— Another Roadside Attraction. 1991. mass mkt. 5.99 (0-553-29205-6) Bantam.

— Cults, Converts, & Charisma: The Sociology of New Religious Movements. 288p. (C). 1988. text ed. 45.00 (0-8039-8158-9); pap. text ed. 22.50 (0-8039-8159-7) Sage.

— Even Cowgirls Get the Blues. 1984. mass mkt. 5.99 (0-553-26611-X) Bantam.

— Even Cowgirls Get the Blues. 1990. pap. 10.95 (0-553-34949-X) Bantam.

— Jitterbug Perfume. 1985. mass mkt. 5.99 (0-553-26844-9) Bantam.

— Jitterbug Perfume. 1990. pap. 10.95 (0-553-34898-1) Bantam.

— Skinny Legs & All. 1991. mass mkt. 5.99 (0-553-28969-1) Bantam.

— Still Life with Woodpecker. 288p. (Orig.). 1984. mass mkt. 5.99 (0-553-27093-1, Bantam Classics) Bantam.

— Still Life with Woodpecker. (Orig.). 1990. pap. 10.95 (0-553-34897-3) Bantam.

Robbins, Thomas & Anthony, Dick. In Gods We Trust: New Patterns of Religious Pluralism in America. 2nd rev. ed. 500p. 1989. pap. 24.95 (0-88738-800-0) Transaction Pubs.

Robbins, Thomas & Robertson, Roland, eds. Church-State Relations: Tensions & Transitions. 380p. 1986. 39.95x (0-88738-108-1) Transaction Pubs.

Robbins, Thomas, et al, eds. Cults, Culture & the Law: Perspectives on New Religious Movements. (American Academy of Religion, Studies in Religion: No. 36). (C). 1985. pap. 14.95 (0-89130-833-4, 01 00 36) Scholars Pr GA.

Robbins, Tom. Half Asleep in Frog Pajamas. LC 94-11549. 1994. 23.95 (0-553-07625-6) Bantam.

— Half Asleep in Frog Pajamas. large type ed. LC 94-48493. 1995. pap. 21.95 (1-56895-091-8) Wheeler Pub.

Robbins, Trina. Catswalk: The Growing of a Girl. (Illus.). 83p. (Orig.). (YA). (gr. 3-6). 1990. pap. 17.95 (0-89087-608-8) Celestial Arts.

— A Century of Women Cartoonists. Schreiner, Dave, ed. (Illus.). 176p. 1993. pap. 16.95 (0-87816-200-3) Kitchen Sink.

— A Century of Women Cartoonists. Schreiner, Dave, ed. (Illus.). 176p. 1993. 24.95 (0-87816-201-1) Kitchen Sink.

— A Century of Women Cartoonists. deluxe limited ed. Schreiner, Dave, ed. (Illus.). 176p. 1993. 39.95 (0-87816-206-2) Kitchen Sink.

Robbins, Trina & Robbins, Casey, eds. Travel & Vacation Advertising Cuts from the Twenties & Thirties. LC 94-13334. (Pictorial Archive Ser.). 1994. pap. write for info. (0-486-28199-X) Dover.

Robbins, Vernon K. Jesus the Teacher: A Socio-Rhetorical Interpretation of Mark. LC 91-42381. 280p. 1992. pap. 19.00 (0-8006-2595-1, 1-2595, Fortress Pr) Augsburg Fortress.

— New Boundaries in Old Territory: Forms & Social Rhetoric in Mark, Vol. 3. LC 93-21579. (Emory Studies in Early Christianity: Vol. 3). 270p. (C). 1994. text ed. 39.95 (0-8204-1911-7) P Lang Pubs.

Robbins, Vernon K., ed. Ancient Quotes & Anecdotes: From Crib to Crypt. LC 88-12583. (Foundations & Facets: Reference Ser.). 512p. 1989. 29.95 (0-944344-02-X); pap. 21.95 (0-944344-03-8) Polebridge Pr.

— Semeia 64: The Rhetoric of Pronouncement. (Semeia Ser.). 301p. 1994. pap. 19.95 (0-614-01355-0, 062064) Scholars Pr GA.

Robbins, Vernon K., jt. auth. see Mack, Burton L.

Robbins, Vesta O. No Coward Soul. LC 74-7399. 119p. reprint ed. pap. 34.00 (0-685-15331-2, 2026660) Bks Demand.

Robbins, Warren & Elisofon, Eliot. Tribute to Africa: The Photography & Collection of Eliot Elisofon. (Illus.). 1974. 9.00 (0-686-25967-X) Mus African Art.

Robbins, Wendy H., jt. auth. see Options, Inc. Staff.

***Robbins, Wilfred W.** Ethnobotany of the Tewa Indians. (Bureau of American Ethnology Bulletins Ser.). 124p. 1995. lib. bdg. 79.00 (0-7812-4055-7) Rprt Serv.

Robbins, William. Newman Brothers: An Essay in Comparative Intellectual Biography. LC 66-4976. (Illus.). 214p. 1966. 23.50 (0-674-62200-6) HUP.

Robbins, William G. American Forestry: A History of National, State, & Private Cooperation. LC 84-28122. xvi, 344p. 1985. 35.00 (0-8032-3872-X) U of Nebr Pr.

— Colony & Empire: The Capitalist Transformation of the American West. LC 94-11029. (Development of Western Resources Ser.). 274p. (Orig.). (C). 1995. 29.95x (0-7006-0645-9) U Pr of KS.

— Colony & Empire: The Capitalist Transformation of the American West. LC 94-11029. (Development of Western Resources Ser.). (Orig.). (C). 1995. pap. 14.95 (0-7006-0750-1) U Pr of KS.

— Hard Times in Paradise: Coos Bay, Oregon, 1850-1986. (Illus.). 208p. 1988. 30.00 (0-295-96616-5); pap. 16.95 (0-295-96617-3) U of Wash Pr.

Robbins, William G., et al, eds. Regionalism & the Pacific Northwest. LC 83-2416. 256p. 1983. 24.95 (0-87071-337-X); pap. 15.95 (0-87071-338-8) Oreg St U Pr.

Robboy, Anita, jt. auth. see Ginsburg, Edward M.

Robboy, Howard, jt. auth. see Clark, Candace.

Robe, jt. auth. see Harben, Peter W.

Robe, Rosebud Y. Tonweya & the Eagles. LC 78-72470. (Illus.). 118p. (J). (gr. 2-6). 1992. 14.00 (0-8037-8973-4); lib. bdg. 13.89 (0-8037-8974-2) Dial Bks Young.

Robe, Stanley. Hispanic Folktales from New Mexico: Narratives from the R. D. Jameson Collection. LC 76-52036. (University of California Publications, Folklore Studies: No. 30). 234p. reprint ed. pap. 66.70 (0-317-29029-0, 2021209) Bks Demand.

Robe, Stanley L., ed. Hispanic Legends from New Mexico: Narratives from the R. D. Jameson Collection. LC 79-64490. (University of California Publications Folklore & Mythology Studies: No. 31). 560p. reprint ed. pap. 159.60 (0-317-29564-0, 2021210) Bks Demand.

Robeck, Cecil M., Jr. Prophecy in Carthage: Perpetua, Tertullian, & Cyprian. LC 92-28622. 344p. (Orig.). 1992. 29.95 (0-8298-0924-4) Pilgrim OH.

Robeck, M. C. & Wallace, R. R., eds. Psychology of Reading: An Interdisciplinary Approach. 2nd ed. 456p. (C). 1990. text ed. 89.95 (0-8058-0373-4); pap. 32.50 (0-8058-0374-2) L Erlbaum Assocs.

Robeck, Mildred C. & Wallace, Randall R. The Psychology of Reading: An Interdisciplinary Approach. 2nd ed. 154p. 1990. teacher ed, pap. write for info. (0-8058-0885-X) L Erlbaum Assocs.

Robeck, Nesta D., pref. Music of the Italian Renaissance. LC 69-12689. (Music Ser.). 1969. reprint ed. lib. bdg. 25.00 (0-306-71232-6) Da Capo.

***Robek, Mary F., et al.** Information & Records Management: Document-Based Information Systems. 4th ed. LC 94-31467. 1995. write for info. (0-02-801793-5) Glencoe.

Robel, tr. see Bakhtine.

Robel, Nicole. Sam & Violet's Get Well Book. 1985. pap. 2.50 (0-380-89821-7, Camelot) Avon.

Robenek, Horst. Ultrastructure, Membrane & Cell Interactions. Severs, Nicholas J., ed. 1992. 196.00 (0-8493-5505-2, RC692) CRC Pr.

Robens, E., ed. see Conference on Vacuum Microbalance Techniques (9th: 1970: Berlin, Germany).

Robens, Erich, jt. auth. see Mikhail, Raouf S.

Robequain, Charles. The Economic Development of French Indo-China. Ward, Isabel A., tr. LC 71-179238. reprint ed. 38.50 (0-404-54864-4) AMS Pr.

— Malaya, Indonesia, Borneo & the Philippines: A Geographical, Economic, & Political Description of Malaya, the East Indies, the Philippines. Laborde, E. D., tr. LC 75-30078. reprint ed. 37.00 (0-404-59555-3) AMS Pr.

Roberage, Pierre R., jt. ed. see Trethewey, Kenneth R.

Roberdeau, Thomas. Michael Strogoff: A Film Script. 106p. (Orig.). 1995. pap. 10.95 (1-55713-098-1) Sun & Moon CA.

Roberfroid, M. B. & Preat, V., eds. Experimental Hepatocarcinogenesis. LC 87-35725. (Illus.). 332p. 1988. 85.00 (0-306-42797-4, Plenum Pr) Plenum.

Roberg, Alex, jt. ed. see Ottensoser, Max.

Roberg, Robert. The Outsider. (Folk Literature Ser.). 32p. (Orig.). 1993. pap. 4.95 (1-878781-12-X) Free River Pr.

Roberg, Roy R. Police Management & Organizational Behavior: A Contingency Approach. (Criminal Justice Ser.). (Illus.). 348p. 1979. text ed. 56.50 (0-8299-0275-9); teacher ed, pap. text ed. write for info. (0-314-44225-1) West Pub.

Roberg, Roy R. & Kuykendall, Jack. Police & Society. LC 92-35788. 484p. 1993. text ed. 39.95 (0-534-19872-4) Intl Thomson.

— Police Organization & Management: Behavior, Theory, & Processes. LC 89-1037. 520p. (C). 1990. text ed. 43.95 (0-534-11802-X) Intl Thomson.

Roberg, Roy R. & Webb, Vincent J. Critical Issues in Corrections: Problems, Trends, & Prospects. 380p. (C). 1981. pap. text ed. 48.75 (0-8299-0405-0) West Pub.

Roberge, Gaston. Mediation: The Action of the Media in Our Society. 1980. 24.00 (0-8364-0604-4, Pub. by Manohar II) S Asia.

— Subject of Cinema. (C). 1990. 22.50 (0-685-49100-5, Pub. by Seagull Bks II) S Asia.

— Ways of Film Studies: Film Theory & the Interpretation of Film. (C). 1992. 26.00 (81-202-0348-8, Pub. by Ajanta II) S Asia.

***Roberge, James.** Data Structures in C++ A Laboratory Course. 285p. (C). 1995. 3.5 hd, pap. text ed. write for info. (0-669-34947-X); 5.25 hd, pap. text ed. write for info. (0-669-34948-8) Heath.

— Data Structures in Pascal: A Laboratory Course. 284p. (C). 1994. 3.5 hd, pap. text ed. write for info. (0-669-29524-8); 5.25 hd, pap. text ed. write for info. (0-669-29525-6) Heath.

***Roberge, James & Smith, George.** Introduction to Programming in C++ A Laboratory Course. 285p. (C). 1995. text ed., 3.5 hd write for info. (0-669-34945-3); text ed., 5.25 hd write for info. (0-669-34946-1) Heath.

Roberge, James K. Operational Amplifiers: Theory & Practice. LC 75-2309. 678p. (C). 1975. text ed. 70.95 (0-471-72585-4) Krieger.

Roberge, James K., jt. auth. see Wedlock, Bruce D.

Roberge, Marc-Andre. Ferruccio Busoni: A Bio-Bibliography. LC 90-22927. (Bio-Bibliographies in Music Ser.: No. 34). 432p. 1991. text ed. 65.00 (0-313-25587-3, RFB, Greenwood Pr) Greenwood.

***Roberge, P. R., et al, eds.** Computers in Corrosion Control. (Illus.). 128p. 1994. 60.00 (1-877914-72-X) NACE Intl.

Roberge, Paul T., ed. see Mel'cuk, Igor A.

Roberge, Yves. The Syntactic Recoverability of Null Arguments. 224p. (C). 1990. text ed. 49.95 (0-7735-0732-9, Pub. by McGill CN) U of Toronto Pr.

Robergs & Roberts. Fundamental Principles of Exercise Physiology. 608p. 1994. 46.95 (0-8016-7907-9) Mosby Yr Bk.

Roberson, C. W. & Driscoll, C. F., eds. Non-Neutral Plasma Physics. LC 88-72275. (AIP Conference Proceedings Ser.: No. 175). 311p. 1988. lib. bdg. 65.00 (0-88318-375-7) Am Inst Physics.

Roberson, Cliff. Aviation: A Complete Legal Guide. 210p. 1987. 19.95 (0-8306-9414-5, 2414) TAB Bks.

— Avoiding Probate: Tamper-Proof Estate Planning. (Illus.). 240p. 1989. 29.95 (0-8306-9174-X, Liberty Hse); pap. 14.95 (0-8306-3074-0, Liberty Hse) TAB Bks.

— The Businessperson's Legal Advisor. 2nd ed. (Illus.). 352p. 1990. pap. 19.95 (0-8306-3547-5, 3547) TAB Bks.

— The Complete Book of Business Forms & Agreements. LC 93-24204. 1993. 3.5 hd 79.95 (0-07-911611-6) McGraw.

— Criminal Justice, Introduction to. 500p. 1993. pap. 34.95 (0-942728-58-0) Copperhouse.

— Criminal Law, California. 3rd rev. ed. LC 88-72096. 175p. 1993. pap. 24.95 (0-942728-56-4) Copperhouse.

— Hire Right - Fire Right: A Manager's Guide to Employment Practices That Avoid Lawsuits. 1992. text ed. 39.95 (0-07-053114-5); pap. text ed. 16.95 (0-07-053115-3) McGraw.

— McGraw Hill Personal Tax Advisor. 2nd ed. 224p. 1992. text ed. 27.95 (0-07-053112-9); pap. text ed. 12.95 (0-07-053113-7) McGraw.

— McGraw Hill Small Business Tax Advisor. 2nd ed. 256p. 1992. text ed. 29.95 (0-07-053111-0); pap. text ed. 14.95 (0-07-053110-2) McGraw.

— The Personal Tax Advisor: Understanding the New Tax Law. LC 86-27850. 1987. pap. 12.95 (0-8306-3134-8, Liberty Hse) TAB Bks.

— Preventing Employee Misconduct: A Self-Defense Manual for Business. LC 85-45518. 160p. 1986. text ed. 29.95 (0-669-11868-0) Free Pr.

— The Small Business Tax Advisor: Understanding the New Tax Law. (Orig.). 1987. pap. text ed. 12.95 (0-07-155640-0) McGraw.

— The Small Business Tax Advisor: Understanding the New Tax Law. 176p. (Orig.). 1987. pap. 12.95 (0-8306-3024-4, 30024, Liberty Hse) TAB Bks.

— Vietnam Medic: What Am I Doing Here? (Illus.). 200p. (Orig.). Date not set. pap. 6.95 (0-9647256-0-6) CSR Indus.

Roberson, Cliff, jt. auth. see Futrell, Max.

Roberson, Cliff, jt. auth. see Masters, Ruth.

Roberson, D. D. Labyrinth of the Minotaur. LC 94-60484. (Illus.). 64p. (Orig.). 1994. pap. 12.95 (1-56664-067-9) WorldComm.

Roberson, Don. Rare Birds of the West Coast of North America. LC 80-51054. (Illus.). 548p. 1980. 24.95 (0-9605352-0-9) Woodcock.

Roberson, E. Wayne, ed. Educational Accountability Through Evaluation. LC 72-155346. 128p. 1971. pap. 14.95 (0-87778-017-X) Educ Tech Pubns.

***Roberson, Ed.** Voices Cast Out to Talk Us In. LC 95-1031. (Iowa Poetry Prize). 182p. (Orig.). 1995. pap. 10.95 (0-87745-510-4) U of Iowa Pr.

Roberson, Elizabeth W. Weep Not for Me Dear Mother. (Illus.). 168p. 1993. 19.95 (1-878853-18-X) Venture Pr FL.

***Roberson, Erriel D.** The Maafa & Beyond: Remembrance, Ancestral Connections & Nation Building for the African Global Community. LC 94-74578. 160p. (Orig.). Date not set. pap. 15.00 (0-9644932-0-9) Kujichagulia Pr.

Roberson, Frances, jt. auth. see Hazelip, Linda.

Roberson, Glenda F. & Johnson, Mary A., eds. Leaders in Education: Their Views on Controversial Issues. LC 88-19918. (Illus.). 228p. (Orig.). (C). 1988. pap. text ed. 22.50 (0-8191-7123-9) U Pr of Amer.

Roberson, Gloria G., jt. auth. see Schroeder, Carol F.

Roberson, J. Conrad, jt. auth. see Mills, Terry, III.

Roberson, James T., jt. auth. see Harris, Forrest E., Sr.

Roberson, Jennifer. Daughter of the Lion. (Chronicles of the Cheysuli Ser.: Bk. 6). 384p. (Orig.). 1989. mass mkt. 4.99 (0-88677-324-5) DAW Bks.

— Flight of the Raven. (Chronicles of the Cheysuli Ser.: Bk. 7). 384p. 1990. mass mkt. 4.99 (0-88677-422-5) DAW Bks.

— Lady of the Forest. 608p. 1995. pap. 12.00 (0-8217-4891-2) Kensington MI.

— Lady of the Forest. 608p. 1992. 22.00 (0-8217-3919-0) Zebra.

— Lady of the Forest. 768p. 1993. mass mkt. 5.99 (0-8217-4284-1) Zebra.

— Legacy of the Sword. (Chronicles of the Cheysuli Ser.: Bk. III). (Orig.). 1986. mass mkt. 4.99 (0-88677-316-4) DAW Bks.

— A Pride of Princes. (Chronicles of the Cheysuli Ser.: Bk. 5). 464p. (Orig.). 1988. pap. 5.99 (0-88677-261-3) DAW Bks.

— Shapechangers. (Chronicles of the Cheysuli Ser.: Bk. 1). (Orig.). 1984. mass mkt. 4.99 (0-88677-140-4) DAW Bks.

— The Song of Homana. (Chronicles of the Cheysuli Ser.: Bk. 2). 352p. 1985. mass mkt. 4.99 (0-88677-434-9) DAW Bks.

— Sword-Breaker. (Novels of Tiger & Del: No. 4). 464p. 1991. mass mkt. 5.99 (0-88677-476-4) DAW Bks.

— Sword Dancer, Bk. 1. 1986. mass mkt. 5.50 (0-88677-376-8) DAW Bks.

— Sword-Maker. (Novels of Tiger & Del Ser.: No. 3). 1989. mass mkt. 5.99 (0-88677-379-2) DAW Bks.

— Sword-Singer, Bk. 2. 384p. 1988. mass mkt. 4.99 (0-88677-447-0) DAW Bks.

— A Tapestry of Lions. (Chronicles of the Cheysuli Ser.: Bk. 8). 464p. (Orig.). 1992. mass mkt. 5.99 (0-88677-524-8) DAW Bks.

— Track of the White Wolf. (Chronicles of the Cheysuli Ser.: Bk. 4). 1987. mass mkt. 4.99 (0-88677-193-5) DAW Bks.

***Roberson, John A. & Crowe, Clayton T.** Engineering Fluid Mechanics. 5th ed. LC 95-11617. 1994. text ed. write for info. (0-471-12474-5) Wiley.

Roberson, John R. Transforming Russia, 1682-1991. LC 92-1377. (Illus.). 192p. (YA). (gr. 5 up). 1992. lib. bdg. 15.95 (0-689-31495-7, Atheneum Bks Young) S&S Childrens.

Roberson, Lee. Are You Tired of Living? 208p. 1986. pap. 4.95 (0-931117-06-2) Univ Pub.

— Fireworks Don't Last. 265p. 1987. pap. 6.95 (0-931117-07-0) Univ Pub.

— Start the Fire. 385p. 1986. pap. 7.95 (0-931117-04-6) Univ Pub.

Roberson, Mary-Russell. Guide to the National Zoological Park. Lumpkin, Susan, eds. LC 89-80422. (Illus.). 56p. (Orig.). 1989. pap. 3.95 (0-9622062-0-2) Friends Natl Zoo.

Roberson, Maxine. Chosen to Walk. LC 88-35643. (Orig.). 1988. pap. 4.00 (0-915541-41-6) Star Bks Inc.

Roberson, Nancy, jt. auth. see Walker, Pam.

Roberson, Pamela, jt. auth. see Bangs, Richard.

Roberson, R. E. & Schwertassek, R. Dynamics of Multibody Systems. (Illus.). 480p. 1988. 104.00 (0-387-17447-8) Spr-Verlag.

Roberson, Ruth H., ed. North Carolina Quilts. LC 88-10598. (Illus.). xviii, 214p. (C). 1988. 19.95 (0-8078-1811-9) U of NC Pr.

Roberson, Sheila F. & Drawe, Lynn, intros. Deer-Proof Fencing. (Illus.). 41p. (Orig.). 1985. pap. 1.50 (0-912229-10-1) CK Wildlife Res.

Roberson, Sheila F., jt. ed. see Beasom, Sam L.

Roberson, Susan L. Emerson in His Sermons: A Man-Made Self. 240p. 1994. 39.95 (0-8262-0983-1) U of Mo Pr.

Roberson, Virginia L. Careers in Graphic Arts. rev. ed. (Careers in Depth Ser.). (Illus.). (YA). (gr. 7-12). 1993. lib. bdg. 14.95 (0-8239-1349-X); pap. 9.95 (0-8239-1715-0) Rosen Group.

Roberson, Whitney. The Mass: Remembering Our Story. (Catholic Home Library). (Illus.). 128p. 1989. 4.95 (1-55944-002-3) Franciscan Comns.

Roberson, William. The Ironic Space: Philosophy & Form in the Nineteenth Century Novel. LC 93-20208. (American University Studies: Vol. 46). 128p. (C). 1994. text ed. 47.95 (0-8204-1927-3) P Lang Pubs.

Roberson, William H. George Washington Cable: An Annotated Bibliography. LC 82-3201. (Author Bibliographies Ser.: No. 62). 269p. 1982. 24.00 (0-8108-1537-0) Scarecrow.

— James Wright: An Annotated Bibliography. LC 95-1504. (Author Bibliographies Ser.: No. 94). 1995. write for info. (0-8108-3000-0) Scarecrow.

— Robert Bly: A Primary & Secondary Bibliography. Lee, Barbara, ed. LC 86-939. (Author Bibliographies Ser.: No. 75). 419p. 1986. 39.50 (0-8108-1879-5) Scarecrow.

Roberson, William H. & Battenfeld, Robert L. Walter M. Miller, Jr. A Bio-Bibliography. LC 92-7335. (Bio-Bibliographies in American Literature Ser.: No. 3). 192p. 1992. text ed. 42.95 (0-313-27651-X, RWA, Greenwood Pr) Greenwood.

***Roberson-Williams, Judy.** So, You Want to Learn How to Double Dutch? How to Jump, Judge & Make Adjustments. (Illus.). 72p. 1994. pap. 8.00 (0-8059-3606-8) Dorrance.

R

An Asterisk (*) at the beginning of an entry indicates that the title is appearing in BIP for the first time.

Roberston, A. T. Imagenes Verbales En el N. T. Word Pictures in the N. T., 6 vols., I. (SPA.). 29.95 (*0-317-06115-1*, 223281, Pub. by Edit Clie SP) TSELF.
— Imagenes Verbales En el N. T. Word Pictures in the N. T., 6 vols., II. (SPA.). 29.95 (*84-7645-325-6*, 223350, Pub. by Edit Clie SP) TSELF.
— Imagenes Verbales En el N. T. Word Pictures in the N. T., 6 vols., III. (SPA.). 29.95 (*84-7645-347-7*, 223446, Pub. by Edit Clie SP) TSELF.
— Imagenes Verbales En el N. T. Word Pictures in the N. T., 6 vols., IV. (SPA.). 29.95 (*84-7645-382-5*, 223353, Pub. by Edit Clie SP) TSELF.
— Imagenes Verbales En el N. T. Word Pictures in the N. T., 6 vols., V. (SPA.). 29.95 (*84-7645-400-7*, 223470, Pub. by Edit Clie SP) TSELF.
— Imagenes Verbales En el N. T. Word Pictures in the N. T., 6 vols., VI. (SPA.). 29.95 (*84-7645-414-7*, 223505, Pub. by Edit Clie SP) TSELF.
Roberston, Merle G. & Benson, Elizabeth P., eds. Fourth Palenque Round Table, Nineteen Eighty. LC 85-61556. (Palenque Round Table Ser.: Vol. VI). (Illus.). 290p. (Orig.). 1985. pap. 55.00 (*0-934051-03-8*) Pre-Columbian Art.
Roberston, Ronald, ed. Talcott Parsons: Theorist of Modernity. (Theory, Culture & Society Ser.). 272p. (C). 1991. 55.00 (*0-8039-8513-4*); pap. 19.95 (*0-8039-8514-2*) Sage.
Robert. Consultaton in Hematoloty-Oncology. Date not set. 24.95 (*1-55009-014-3*) Mosby Yr Bk.
— Express Train to Trouble: A Miss Mallard Mystery. Date not set. pap. 5.95 (*0-671-66297-X*) S&S Trade.
— 5-Minute Massage: Quick & Simple Exercises to Reduce Tension & Stress. LC 95-12946. Orig. Title: Stressbusters Five Minute Massage. (Illus.). 96p. 1995. pap. 12.95 (*0-8069-4200-2*) Sterling.
— Robert's Rules of Order. pap. 3.99 (*0-8007-8610-6*) Revell.
Robert, A. Advanced Calculus for Users. 366p. 1989. 59.00 (*0-444-87324-4*, North Holland) Elsevier.
Robert, A. M. & Robert, L., eds. Biology & Pathology of Elastic Tissues. (Frontiers of Matrix Biology Ser.: Vol. 8). (Illus.). viii, 232p. 1980. 99.25 (*3-8055-3078-1*) S Karger.
Robert, Adolphe & Cougny, Gaston. Dictionnaire des Parlementaires Francais Comprenant Tous les Membres des Assemblees Francaises et Tous les Ministres Francais depuis le Ler Mai 1789 Jusqu'au Ler Mai 1889, 5 vols. xvi, 3189p. reprint ed. write for info. (*0-318-71403-5*, Pub. by Georg Olms GW) Lubrecht & Cramer.
Robert, Adrian. The Awful Mess Mystery. LC 84-8724. (Illus.). 48p. (J). (gr. 2-4). 1985. lib. bdg. 10.89 (*0-8167-0402-3*); pap. text ed. 3.50 (*0-8167-0403-1*) Troll Assocs.
— Ellen Ross, Private Detective. LC 84-8744. (Illus.). 48p. (J). (gr. 2-4). 1985. lib. bdg. 10.89 (*0-8167-0414-7*); pap. text ed. 3.50 (*0-8167-0415-5*) Troll Assocs.
— My Grandma, the Witch. LC 84-8742. (Illus.). 48p. (J). (gr. 2-4). 1985. lib. bdg. 10.89 (*0-8167-0422-8*); pap. text ed. 3.50 (*0-8167-0423-6*) Troll Assocs.
— Secret of the Haunted Chimney. LC 84-8763. (Illus.). 48p. (J). (gr. 2-4). 1985. lib. bdg. 10.89 (*0-8167-0408-2*); pap. text ed. 3.50 (*0-8167-0409-0*) Troll Assocs.
— Secret of the Old Barn. LC 84-8743. (Illus.). 48p. (J). (gr. 2-4). 1985. lib. bdg. 10.89 (*0-8167-0412-0*); pap. text ed. 3.50 (*0-8167-0413-9*) Troll Assocs.
Robert, Alain. Non-Standard Analysis. 2nd ed. LC 87-27925. 156p. 1988. text ed. 94.95 (*0-471-91703-6*) Wiley.
***Robert, Art.** Easy Adding & Subtracting Tables (for Little Learners) The New Learning Tool. (Illus.). (J). 1995. text ed. 9.95 (*1-887252-04-5*) Kids Success Learn.
Robert, B. P. & Silverman, Stephen. Defending Animals' Rights Is the Right Thing to Do. 1991. pap. 11.95 (*1-56171-044-X*) Sure Sellers.
Robert, Barbara, ed. see International Colloquium of Dermo-Chemistry on Aging of Skin Staff.
Robert Bentley Inc. Staff. BMW 5-Series Service Manual: 1982-1988. (Illus.). 59.95 (*0-8376-0318-8*) Bentley.
Robert Bentley, Inc. Staff. Toyota Pickup, 4Runner Service Manual: 1978-1988 Including Gasoline, Diesel, & Turbo Diesel, 4-cylinder & 6-cylinder Engines. (Orig.). 39.95 (*0-8376-0258-0*) Bentley.
— Volkswagen Cabriolet, Scirocco Service Manual: 1985-1993, Including 16V. 49.95 (*0-8376-0362-5*) Bentley.
Robert Bentley Publishers Staff. Volkswagen Fox Service Manual, 1987-1993: Including GL, GL Sport, & Wagon. 1993. pap. 39.95 (*0-8376-0363-3*) Bentley.
Robert, Bently. Volvo 240 Service Manual 1983 Through 1993. 1993. 49.95 (*0-8376-0285-8*) Bentley.
Robert, Carl. Archaeologische Hermeneutik: Anleitung Zur Deutung Klassischer Bildwerke. LC 75-10652. (Ancient Religion & Mythology Ser.). (Illus.). (GER.). 1976. reprint ed. 32.95 (*0-405-07276-7*) Ayer.
— Bild und Lied: Archaologische Beitrage Zur Geschichte der Griechischen Heldensage. LC 75-10653. (Ancient Religion & Mythology Ser.). (Illus.). (GER.). 1976. reprint ed. 18.95 (*0-405-07277-5*) Ayer.
Robert, Carl, ed. see Eratosthenes.
Robert, Carse. The Young Mariners. 9.95 (*0-911660-20-8*) Yankee Peddler.
Robert, Cavett, jt. auth. see McCants, Louise.
Robert, Charles, ed. Manipulated Man: The Power of Man Over Man, Its Risks & Its Limits. European Studies. Strasbourg, September 24-29, 1973. Frank, C. P., tr. LC 77-24330. (Pittsburgh Theological Monographs: No. 16). 1977. pap. 8.00 (*0-915138-21-2*) Pickwick.
Robert, Charles, et al. Intrapersonal Communication Processes. 150p. (Orig.). (C). 1987. pap. text ed. 15.00 (*0-89787-327-0*) Gorsuch Scarisbrick.
Robert, Charles E. Negro Civilization in the South. LC 70-173614. (Black Heritage Library Collection). 1977. reprint ed. 17.95 (*0-8369-8906-6*) Ayer.
Robert, Christian P. The Bayesian Choice: A Decision-Theoretic Motivation. LC 94-10781. (Texts in Statistics Ser.). 1994. 49.00 (*0-387-94296-3*) Spr-Verlag.
Robert, Craig. Combat Medic: Vietnam. 288p. 1991. mass mkt. 4.95 (*0-671-73691-4*) PB.
Robert Crown Center for Health Education, Womens Auxiliary Staff. An Invitation to Dine. (Illus.). 254p. 1977. 10.95 (*0-9613700-0-9*) R Crown Ctr.
Robert, E. B. Footnotes Not in the Book. 2nd ed. 1969. 4.50 (*0-87511-664-7*); pap. 4.50 (*0-87511-665-5*) Claitors.
Robert, Emile A., Jr., jt. auth. see Glacel, Barbara P.
Robert, F. Discrete Iterations. Rokne, J., tr. (Computational Mathematics Ser.: Vol. 6). (Illus.). 195p. 1986. 64.00 (*0-387-13623-1*) Spr-Verlag.
Robert Gore Rifkind Center for German Expressionist Studies Staff. German Expressionist Prints & Drawings, 2 vols. (Illus.). 1076p. 1989. 300.00 (*3-7913-0959-5*, Pub. by Prestel) TeNeues.
— German Expressionist Prints & Drawings, 2 vols., Vol. 1. (Illus.). 846p. 1989. 268.00 (*3-7913-0974-9*, Pub. by Prestel) TeNeues.
Robert Haber & Co., Staff, intro. Gods, Beasts & Men: Images from Antiquity. LC 91-66769. (Illus.). 48p. 1991. pap. 15.00 (*0-935037-43-8*) G Peters Gallery.
Robert, Harvey. George Washington Swept Here. 32p. (J). (gr. 2 up). 1975. 35.00 (*0-317-03601-7*) I E Clark.
— George Washington Swept Here. 32p. (J). (gr. 2 up). 1975. pap. 3.00 (*0-88680-068-4*); Director's Production Script. pap. 10.00 (*0-88680-069-2*) I E Clark.
Robert, Henry M. Parliamentary Law. 610p. (C). 1975. lib. bdg. 46.50 (*0-8290-0874-8*) Irvington.
— Parliamentary Practice: An Introduction to Parliamentary Law. 209p. (C). 1975. 15.95 (*0-8290-0875-6*) Irvington.
— Robert's Rules of Order. Vixman, Rachel, ed. 1984. pap. 3.99 (*0-515-09032-8*) Jove Pubns.
— Robert's Rules of Order. rev. ed. 19.95 (*0-89190-990-7*, Am Repr) Amereon Ltd.
— Robert's Rules of Order. rev. ed. 1989. pap. 3.99 (*0-425-11690-5*) Berkley Pub.
— Robert's Rules of Order. rev. ed. 160p. 1993. pap. 8.95 (*0-425-13928-X*) Berkley Pub.
— Robert's Rules of Order. 1993. reprint ed. lib. bdg. 18.95 (*1-56849-216-2*) Buccaneer Bks.
— Robert's Rules of Order Revised. 1971. reprint ed. pap. 6.45 (*0-688-05306-8*, Quill) Morrow.
Robert, Henry M., III & Evans, William J., eds. Robert's Rules of Order. 9th ed. LC 21-8. 1991. 27.50 (*0-06-275002-X*, Harper Ref); pap. 15.00 (*0-06-276051-3*, Harper Ref) HarpC.
Robert, Henry M., III, et al. Robert's Rules of Order. rev. ed. 1981. 16.95 (*0-673-15472-6*) Scott F.
Robert Herrick Memorial Conference, University of Michigan Staff. Trust to Good Versus: Herrick Tercentenary Essays, Dearborn, 1974. Rollin, Roger B. & Patrick, J. Max, eds. LC 77-74547. 297p. reprint ed. pap. 84.70 (*0-7837-2147-1*, 2042433) Bks Demand.
Robert, J. & Tran, D. K., eds. Modelling & Simulation of Electrical Machines & Power Systems: Proceedings of the Second International Symposium, Quebec City, Canada, 24-25 Aug. 1987. 344p. 1988. 87.25 (*0-444-70392-6*, North Holland) Elsevier.
Robert, J., jt. ed. see Buyse, H.
Robert, J., jt. auth. see Le Doeuff, R.
***Robert, J. L., ed.** Micronic Integrated Sensors: Proceedings of Symposium B on New Materials, Physics & Technologies for Micronic Integrated Sensors, E-MRS Spring Conference, Strasbourg, France, 28-30 May 1991. (European Materials Research Society Symposia Proceedings Ser.: 23). x, 274p. 1992. 151.50 (*0-444-89417-9*) Elsevier.
Robert, J-M. Genetique. (De la Biologie a la Clinique Ser.). (Illus.). 452p. (FRE.). 1983. lib. bdg. 37.00 (*0-318-04484-6*) S M P F Inc.
Robert, Jacques, jt. ed. see Anghileri, Leopold J.
Robert, Jean. Dictionnaire de Proverbes & Dictons. 45.00 (*0-317-45633-4*) Fr & Eur.
— Dictionnaire des Citations du Monde Entier. 45.00 (*0-317-45621-0*) Fr & Eur.
— Dictionnaire des Difficultes du Francais. 45.00 (*0-317-45622-9*) Fr & Eur.
— Dictionnaire des Expressions & Locutions Figurees. 45.00 (*0-317-45624-5*) Fr & Eur.
— Dictionnaire des Idees par le Mots. 45.00 (*0-317-45630-X*) Fr & Eur.
— Dictionnaire des Structures du Vocabulaire Savant. 45.00 (*0-317-45634-2*) Fr & Eur.
— Dictionnaire des Synonymes. 45.00 (*0-317-45635-0*) Fr & Eur.
— Dictionnaire Etymologique. 45.00 (*0-317-45625-3*) Fr & Eur.
— Grand Robert Vert, 9 vols. 995.00 (*0-317-45638-5*) Fr & Eur.
— Robert & Signorelly. French-Italian. 3008p. (FRE & ITA.). 1981. 175.00 (*0-8288-4675-8*, M9403) Fr & Eur.
Robert, Jean, jt. auth. see Mongredien, Georges.
Robert, Jean, jt. auth. see Quinton.
Robert, Joseph C. Ethyl: A History of the Corporation & the People Who Made It. LC 83-6620. (Illus.). 467p. reprint ed. pap. 133.10 (*0-7837-4226-6*, 2043913) Bks Demand.
— Road from Monticello: A Study of the Virginia Slavery Debate of 1832. LC 70-109912. (Duke University. Trinity College Historical Society. Historical Papers: No. 24). reprint ed. 30.00 (*0-404-51774-9*) AMS Pr.
— The Tobacco Kingdom. 1938. 11.75 (*0-8446-1386-X*) Peter Smith.
Robert, K. Q., ed. see Symposium on Cotton Dust: Sampling, Monitoring, & Control Staff.
Robert Koch Gallery, Inc. Staff, ed. Lloyd Ullberg: A Structuralist's Overview, Catalogue. (Illus.). 16p. 1988. 10.00 (*0-929196-00-7*) R Koch Gallery.
Robert, L. Les Gladiateurs dans l'Orient Grec. (Illus.). 372p. reprint ed. lib. bdg. 67.50 (*0-685-13622-1*, Pub. by A M Hakkert SP) Coronet Bks.
Robert, L., ed. Adipose Tissue. (Frontiers of Matrix Biology Ser.: Vol. 2). (Illus.). 200p. 1976. 73.00 (*3-8055-2223-1*) S Karger.
— Studies on the Biology & Pathology of the Skin. (Frontiers of Matrix Biology Ser.: Vol. 4). (Illus.). 220p. 1977. 109.00 (*3-8055-2666-0*) S Karger.
Robert, L., ed. see Garrone, R.
Robert, L., ed. see International Colloquium of Dermo-Chemistry on Aging of Skin Staff.
Robert, L., ed. see International Colloquium, Paris Staff.
Robert, L., jt. ed. see Robert, A. M.
Robert, L., et al, eds. Burkitt Lymphoma, Hemostasis & Intercellular Matrix: Barbara Robert Memorial. (Frontiers of Matrix Biology Ser.: Vol. 3). (Illus.). 1976. 143.25 (*3-8055-2326-2*) S Karger.
— Methods of Connective Tissue Research. (Frontiers of Matrix Biology Ser.: Vol. 10). (Illus.). xiv, 250p. 1985. 131.25 (*3-8055-3899-5*) S Karger.
Robert L. Humphrey, J. D., & Associates Staff. Paradigm Shift: Teach the Universal Values. LC 83-83386. (Illus.). 100p. 1984. pap. 7.95 (*0-915761-00-9*) Life Values Pr.
Robert, Ladislas & Hornebeck, William, eds. Elastin & Elastases, Vol. II. 272p. 1989. 204.00 (*0-8493-6429-9*, QP552) CRC Pr.
Robert, Louis. Noms Indigenes Dans L'Asie-Mineure Greco-Romaine: Premiere Partie. (Bibliotheque Archeologique Et Historique De L'Institut Francais D'Archeologie D'Istanbul Ser.: No. XIII). 659p. (FRE.). 1991. pap. 90.00 (*0-685-50578-2*, Pub. by A M Hakkert SP) Benjamins North Am.
Robert, Louis, ed. Le Martyre de Pionios, Pretre de Smyrne. LC 93-24110. 152p. 1994. 35.00x (*0-88402-217-X*) Dumbarton Oaks.
Robert, M., ed. see Cavalli-Sforza, L. L. & Feldman, M. W.
Robert, Marc. Managing Conflict from the Inside Out. LC 81-70980. 150p. 1982. text ed. 24.95 (*0-89384-065-3*) Pfeiffer & Co.
Robert, Martin, jt. auth. see Parrott, Thomas M.
Robert, Michel. The Essence of Leadership: Strategy, Innovation & Decisiveness. LC 91-17356. 136p. 1991. text ed. 39.95 (*0-89930-655-1*, REJ, Quorum Bks) Greenwood.
— New Product Strategy Pure & Simple: How Winning Companies Outpace Their Competitors. LC 95-11855. 1995. write for info. (*0-07-053132-3*) McGraw.
— The Strategist CEO: How Visionary Executives Build Organizations. LC 87-10945. 160p. 1988. text ed. 45.00 (*0-89930-268-8*, RST/, Quorum Bks) Greenwood.
— Strategy Pure & Simple: How Winning CEOs Outthink Their Competition. 1992. text ed. 22.95 (*0-07-053131-5*) McGraw.
Robert of Orkney. St. Magnus. MacDonald, Iain, ed. (Celtic Saints Ser.). 62p. 1994. pap. 5.95 (*0-86315-164-7*, Pub. by Floris Books UK) Anthroposophic.
Robert of Thornton. Morte Arthure: An Alliterative Poem of the Fourteenth Century. Banks, Mary M., ed. LC 71-178545. reprint ed. 21.50 (*0-404-56648-0*) AMS Pr.
***Robert Oxley Training & Consulting Staff.** How to Increase Your Sales Immediately. 1994. audio 34.95 (*0-8403-9785-2*) Kendall-Hunt.
Robert, P. C., et al, eds. Proceedings of Soil Specific Crop Management: A Workshop on Research & Development Issues, April 14-16, 1992, Sheraton Airport Inn, Minneapolis, MN. LC 93-21790. 1993. write for info. (*0-89118-116-4*) Soil Sci Soc Am.
Robert Parker & Associates Book Staff, ed. see Haverstock, Henry W.
Robert, Paul. French & Dutch Dictionary: Dictionnaire Robert et Van Dale Francais-Neerlandais-Francais. 1410p. (DUT & FRE.). 1988. 95.00 (*0-8288-0454-0*, F20210) Fr & Eur.
— Le Micro-Robert, Dictionnaire du Francais Primordial. (FRE.). 1988. 49.95 (*0-8288-1949-1*, M6487) Fr & Eur.
— Organic Metamorphism & Geothermal History. (C). 1987. lib. bdg. 154.50 (*90-277-2500-4*); pap. text ed. 88.00 (*90-277-2501-2*) Kluwer Ac.
— Petit Robert, Vol. 1. 2467p. (FRE.). 1993. 135.00 (*0-8288-1951-3*, F134380) Fr & Eur.
Robert, Paul, et al. Micro Robert en Poche: Dictionnaire du Francais Primordial. 1210p. (FRE.). 1988. pap. 29.95 (*0-8288-1948-3*, M4519) Fr & Eur.
— Le Nouveau Micro Robert. 1376p. (FRE.). 1988. 69.95 (*0-8288-1947-5*, M4457) Fr & Eur.
Robert, Philippe, et al, eds. Proceedings of the Eighteenth Collegium Internationale Neuro-Psychopharmacologicum Congress, 2 vols., Set. LC 92-17141. 1440p. 1992. 157.50 (*0-88167-943-7*) Raven.
Robert, Phillippe. Electrical & Magnetic Properties of Materials. (Materials Library). 475p. 1988. text ed. 79.00 (*0-89006-262-5*) Artech Hse.
***Robert R. Nathan Associates, Inc., Staff.** Private & Public Sector Costs of Proposed Legislation Calling for Additional Benefits for Employees - Family & Medical Leave, Occupational Risk, Mandated Health Benefit Insurance, & Mandatory Advance Notification Legislation. 216p. 1988. pap. 20.00x (*0-614-06167-9*, 2010-PP-4040) EPF.
***Robert Staff.** Dictionnaire des Grandes Oeuvres de la Litterature Francaise. 720p. (FRE.). 1992. 85.00 (*0-7859-8060-1*, 2850361968) Fr & Eur.
— Shogakukan-Robert, Grand Dictionnaire Francais Japonais. 2597p. (FRE & JPN.). 1989. 795.00 (*0-7859-8701-0*, 409515201x) Fr & Eur.
Robert Taylor Elementary School Students. A Day in the Desert. 24p. (J). (ps-2). 1994. 5.99 (*0-87406-686-7*) Willowisp Pr.
Robert Tilton Ministries Staff. El Poder para Crear Prosperidad. 133p. (SPA.). 1989. pap. write for info. (*0-318-64838-5*) Abbasons.
Robert, Ulysse. Bullaire Du Pape Calixte the Second, 2 vols. in 1. (Illus.). c, 931p. 1979. reprint ed. write for info. (*3-487-06765-X*, Pub. by Georg Olms GW) Lubrecht & Cramer.
Robert, Yves. The Impact of Vector & Parallel Architectures on the Gaussian Elimination Algorithm. (Algorithms & Architecture for Advanced Ser.). 194p. 1991. text ed. 70.95 (*0-470-21703-0*) Wiley.
Roberta, Egan, pseud. High Jinks with This Ring. (Illus.). 300p. 1988. 19.95 (*0-9619233-0-X*) Four Leaf Clover.
Robertazzi, T. G. Computer Networks & Computer Systems: Queueing Theory & Performance Evaluation. Gerla, M. et al, eds. (Telecommunications Networks & Computer Systems Ser.). (Illus.). 328p. 1990. text ed. 49.50 (*0-387-97393-1*) Spr-Verlag.
Robertazzi, Thomas, ed. Performance Evaluation of High Speed Switching Fabrics & Networks: ATM, Broadband ISDN, & MAN Technology. LC 92-44950. (Illus.). 480p. 1993. text ed. 69.95 (*0-7803-0436-5*, PC03335) Inst Electrical.
Robertazzi, Thomas G. Computer Networks & Systems: Queuing Theory & Performance Evaluation. 2nd ed. LC 93-36469. 1994. 54.00 (*0-387-94170-3*) Spr-Verlag.
Robertfroid. Free Radicals & Oxidation Phenomena in Biological Systems. 288p. 1995. 115.00 (*0-8247-9587-3*) Dekker.
Roberti, L., jt. ed. see Chiabo, M.
Roberti, Luciana, jt. auth. see Chiabo, Maria.
Roberti, Luciana, jt. ed. see Chiabo, Maria.
Roberti, Mark. The Fall of Hong Kong: China's Triumph - Britain's Betrayal. LC 94-9891. 1994. text ed. 24.95 (*0-471-02621-2*) Wiley.
Roberti, Paolo, jt. ed. see Baldassarri, Mario.
Robertie, Bill. Advanced Backgammon, Vol. 1: Positional Play. 288p. 1993. pap. 30.00 (*1-880604-02-7*) Gammon Pr.
— Advanced Backgammon, Vol. 2: Technical Play. 288p. 1993. pap. 30.00 (*1-880604-03-5*) Gammon Pr.
— Backgammon for Winners. LC 93-70982. (Illus.). 80p. (Orig.). 1993. pap. 6.95 (*0-940685-42-6*) Cardoza Pub.
— Backgammon for Winners. 2nd ed. (Illus.). 160p. (Orig.). 1995. pap. 9.95 (*0-940685-58-2*) Cardoza Pub.
— Beginning Chess Play. LC 94-70604. (Illus.). 144p. 1994. pap. 8.95 (*0-940685-50-7*) Cardoza Pub.
— Winning Chess Openings. LC 94-70603. (Illus.). 144p. 1994. pap. 8.95 (*0-940685-51-5*) Cardoza Pub.
Robertiello, Richard C. & Hoguet, Diana. The WASP Mystique. LC 87-46024. 207p. 1987. pap. 6.95 (*1-55611-109-6*) D I Fine.
Robertiello, Richard C. & Schoenewolf, Gerald. One Hundred One Common Therapeutic Blunders: Countertransference & Conterresistance in Psychotherapy. LC 87-1406. 304p. 1992. reprint ed. pap. 30.00x (*0-87668-384-7*) Aronson.
Robertin, Hector & Bratton, Joseph C. Computers, Video Games & Your Child's Development. LC 83-62878. (Illus.). 120p. 1984. pap. 9.95 (*0-912921-02-1*) Pau Hana Pr.
Roberto, Calasso. The Marriage of Cadmus Harmony Tent Card. 1994. pap. write for info. (*0-394-25870-3*) Random.
Roberto, D. The Love of Mary. LC 83-51545. 240p. 1985. reprint ed. pap. 7.00 (*0-89555-235-3*) TAN Bks Pubs.
Roberto, Eduardo L., jt. auth. see Kotler, Philip.
Roberto, J. B., et al, eds. Advanced Photon & Particle Techniques for the Characterization of Defects in Solids, Vol. 41. LC 85-5061. (Materials Research Society Symposium Proceedings Ser.). 1985. text ed. 43.00 (*0-931837-06-5*) Materials Res.
Roberto, Jerry T., jt. auth. see Heindel, Lee E.
***Roberto, John.** Leadership. 176p. 1990. 14.95 (*0-89944-150-5*) Don Bosco Multimedia.
— Planning a Youth Ministry: A Step by Step Manual. 80p. 1994. 7.95 (*0-89944-302-8*) Don Bosco Multimedia.
— Volunteer Leadership: Empowering Volunteers for Youth Ministry. 80p. 1994. 7.95 (*0-89944-303-6*) Don Bosco Multimedia.
***Roberto, John, ed.** Early Adolescent Ministry. 260p. 1991. 14.95 (*0-89944-207-2*) Don Bosco Multimedia.
— Family Rituals & Celebrations. 154p. 1992. 6.95 (*0-89944-224-2*) Don Bosco Multimedia.
— Foundations of Leadership. 233p. 1992. 19.95 (*0-89944-156-4*) Don Bosco Multimedia.
— Growing in Faith. (Catholic Family Sourcebook). 150p. 1990. 12.95 (*0-89944-155-6*) Don Bosco Multimedia.
— Guide to Christian Faith. 72p. 1991. 4.95 (*0-89944-160-2*) Don Bosco Multimedia.
— Guide to Understanding Youth. 80p. 1991. 4.95 (*0-89944-157-2*) Don Bosco Multimedia.
— Guide to Youth Ministry Programming. 72p. 1991. 4.95 (*0-89944-158-0*) Don Bosco Multimedia.
— Rituals for Sharing Faith: A Resource for Parish Ministers. 238p. 1992. 14.95 (*0-89944-223-4*) Don Bosco Multimedia.
***Roberto, John & Bright, Thomas.** Creating a Partnership in Faith: A Parish Planning Guide. 25p. 1992. 3.95 (*0-89944-262-5*) Don Bosco Multimedia.
***Roberto, John & Bright, Thomas, eds.** Faith & Families: A Parish Program for Parenting in Faith Growth. 118p. 1992. 13.95 (*0-89944-252-8*) Don Bosco Multimedia.
***Roberto, John & Ekstrom, Reynolds R., eds.** Evangelization. (Access Guide to Youth Ministry Ser.). 144p. (Orig.). 1995. pap. 14.95 (*0-89944-321-4*, 321-4) Don Bosco Multimedia.
Roberto, John, jt. ed. see Bright, Thomas.

R

Roberto, John, jt. auth. see Kehrwald, Leif.
Roberto, John, jt. auth. see Reed, Sharon.
Roberto, Karen A. The Elderly Caregiver: Research & Practice. (Focus Editions Ser.: Vol. 160). (Illus.). 240p. (C). 1993. text ed. 49.95 (*0-8039-5020-9*); pap. text ed. 24.95 (*0-8039-5021-7*) Sage.
***Roberto, Karen A., ed. & intro.** Older Women with Chronic Pain. (Journal of Women & Aging Ser.). (Illus.). 1994. pap. 9.95 (*1-56023-061-4*) Haworth Pr.
— Older Women with Chronic Pain. (Journal of Women & Aging Ser.). (Illus.). 128p. 1994. lib. bdg. 29.95 (*1-56024-706-1*) Haworth Pr.
Roberto, Laura G. Transgenerational Family Therapies. LC 92-1530. (Guilford Family Therapy Ser.). 219p. 1992. lib. bdg. 26.95 (*0-89862-107-0*) Guilford Pr.
Roberto, Vito, ed. Intelligent Perceptual Systems: New Directions in Computational Perception. LC 93-33441. (Lecture Notes in Computer Science, Lecture Notes in Artificial Intelligence Ser.: Vol. 745). 1993. 54.00 (*0-387-57379-8*) Spr-Verlag.
Roberton, Arthur. Listen for Success: A Guide to Effective Listening. 216p. 1993. text ed. 17.00 (*1-55623-830-4*) Irwin Prof Pubng.
Roberton, N. R., ed. Textbook of Neonatology. 2nd ed. (Illus.). 1329p. 1992. text ed. 275.00 (*0-443-04088-5*) Churchill.
Roberton, Reginald S., jt. ed. see Young, William C.
***Roberts.** Baby-Sitting Is a Dangerous Job. (J). 1996. pap. 3.95 (*0-689-80657-4*, Mac Bks Young Read) S&S Childrens.
— Biomechanics: Problem Solving for Functional Activity. (Illus.). 194p. 1991. 25.95 (*0-8016-4047-4*) Mosby Yr Bk.
— City of Sokrates. 1984. pap. 13.95 (*0-7102-1102-3*, RKP) Routledge.
— Collector's Encyclopedia of Hull Pottery. 1990. 19.95 (*0-89145-149-8*) Collector Bks.
— Complete Pec Asia. 3rd ed. 1989. 10.95 (*0-316-74991-5*) Little.
— Difficult Problems in Adult Cardiac Surgery, Vol. 2. 1991. 85.00 (*0-8151-7305-9*, Yr Bk Med Pubs) Mosby Yr Bk.
— Faces of Mathematics. 3rd ed. (C). 1994. student ed, text ed. write for info. (*0-06-502129-0*) HarpCollege.
— Fish Pathology. 2nd ed. 448p. 1989. text ed. 195.00 (*0-7020-1314-5*) Saunders.
— Flat Processing of Steel. (Manufacturing Engineering & Materials Processing Ser.: Vol. 24). 928p. 1988. 215.00 (*0-8247-7780-8*) Dekker.
— For the Love of the Rockies. 1989. pap. 6.95 (*0-9620621-1-1*) Earth Images.
— Fun with Sun Prints & Box Cameras. (J). 1981. 8.95 (*0-679-20629-9*) McKay.
— General Chemistry in the Lab. 3rd ed. (C). 1995. pap. text ed. write for info. (*0-7167-2120-1*) W H Freeman.
— Instructor's Manual for General Chemistry in the Lab. 3rd ed. (C). 1995. pap. text ed. write for info. (*0-7167-2212-7*) W H Freeman.
— Make It So: Leadership for the Next Generation. 1995. 22.00 (*0-671-52097-0*) PB.
— Manual of Complete Pediatrics ISE, No. 3. 1989. 15.95 (*0-316-74992-3*) Little.
— Myocardial Protection in Cardiac Surgery. (Cardiothoracic Surgery Ser.: Vol. 3). 640p. 1987. 210.00 (*0-8247-7638-0*) Dekker.
— Orthopedics in Infancy & Childhood. 2nd ed. 1990. 160.00 (*0-7506-1030-1*) Buttrwrth-Heinemann.
— Professional Liability: Guidelines in Obstetrics & Gynecology. 1991. 275.00 (*0-8016-3357-5*) Mosby Yr Bk.
— Quality Assurance in Research & Development. (Industrial Engineering Ser.: Vol. 8). 152p. 1983. 65.00 (*0-8247-7071-4*) Dekker.
— A Rich Man's Secret: An Amazing Formula for Success. LC 95-6490. 208p. 1995. pap. text ed. 9.95 (*1-56718-580-0*) Llewellyn Pubns.
— Roberts on Competition-Antitrust: Canada & the United States. 608p. 1992. 150.00 (*0-409-80890-3*) Butterworth Legal Pubs.
— Separates General Chemistry in the Lab. 3rd ed. (C). 1995. 2.95 (*0-7167-2259-3*) W H Freeman.
— Social Laws of the Qoran Considered & Compared with Those of the Hebrew & Other: Ancient Codes. LC 89-27402. 1990. pap. 15.00 (*0-7007-0204-0*, Pub. by Curzon Pr UK) Humanities.
— Survey of Applications of Simulation to Health Care. 112p. 1981. 36.00 (*0-685-66788-X*, SS10-1) Soc Computer Sim.
— Truth, the Way, the Life. 1995. pap. text ed. 19.95 (*1-56085-077-9*) Signature Bks.
— World's Weirdest Sea Creatures. 1994. pap. 2.25 (*0-8167-3689-8*) Troll Assocs.
Roberts & Dyer. Notes on Prosthetic Dentistry. 1989. pap. 39.95 (*0-7236-1235-8*, Pub. by John Wright UK) Buttrwrth-Heinemann.
Roberts & Khalaf. Friedel-Crafts Alkylation Chemistry: A Century of Discovery. (Studies in Organic Chemistry: Vol. 10). 800p. 1984. 250.00 (*0-8247-6433-1*) Dekker.
Roberts & Monroe, eds. Simulation Applications in Business Management & MIS. 124p. 1993. pap. 50.00 (*1-56555-023-4*, MC93-3) Soc Computer Sim.
Roberts & Olson, Charles L. American Experiences, 2 vols., I. 3rd ed. (C). 1993. text ed. 28.50 (*0-673-46736-8*) HarpCollege.
— American Experiences, 2 vols., II. 3rd ed. (C). 1993. text ed. 28.50 (*0-673-46737-6*) HarpCollege.
Roberts, jt. auth. see Beaumariage.
Roberts, jt. auth. see Becker.
Roberts, jt. auth. see Hickman.
Roberts, jt. auth. see Robergs.
Roberts, jt. auth. see Schmidt.
Roberts, jt. auth. see Veidenheimer.
Roberts, et al. A Clinician's Guide to Fungal Disease. LC 84-14932. (Infectious Diseases & Antimicrobial Agents Ser.: Vol. 5). (Illus.). 264p. 1984. 110.00 (*0-8247-7190-7*) Dekker.
— Hot Mix Asphalt Materials, Mixture Design & Construction. 490p. 1991. text ed. 45.00 (*0-914313-01-0*) Natl Asphalt Pavement.
— Mirrors of Mind: An Introduction to Humanities. 300p. 1985. pap. text ed. 23.95 (*0-88725-041-6*) Hunter Textbks.
— Mirrors of Mind: Commitment & Creativity in the Twentieth Century. 320p. 1991. text ed. 28.95 (*0-88725-158-7*) Hunter Textbks.
Roberts, A. & Donaldson, J., eds. Ante-Nicene Fathers, Vol. 1: Apostolic Fathers. (EArly Church Fathers Ser.). 1950. 29.99 (*0-8028-8087-8*) Eerdmans.
— Ante-Nicene Fathers, Vol. 10: Original Supplement. (EArly Church Fathers Ser.). 1950. 29.99 (*0-8028-8096-7*) Eerdmans.
— Ante-Nicene Fathers, Vol. 2: Second Century. (EArly Church Fathers Ser.). 1950. 29.99 (*0-8028-8088-6*) Eerdmans.
— Ante-Nicene Fathers, Vol. 3: Latin Christianity. (EArly Church Fathers Ser.). 1950. 29.99 (*0-8028-8089-4*) Eerdmans.
— Ante-Nicene Fathers, Vol. 9: Bibliography, Synopsis, Index. (EArly Church Fathers Ser.). 1950. 29.99 (*0-8028-8095-9*) Eerdmans.
— Ante-Nicene Fathers, Vols. 4-6: Third Century, 3 vols., 4. (EArly Church Fathers Ser.). 1951. 29.99 (*0-8028-8090-8*) Eerdmans.
— Ante-Nicene Fathers, Vols. 4-6: Third Century, 3 vols., 5. (EArly Church Fathers Ser.). 1951. write for info. (*0-8028-8091-6*) Eerdmans.
— Ante-Nicene Fathers, Vols. 4-6: Third Century, 3 vols., 6. (EArly Church Fathers Ser.). 1951. write for info. (*0-8028-8092-4*) Eerdmans.
— Ante-Nicene Fathers, Vols. 7-8: Third & Fourth Centuries, 2 vols., 7. (EArly Church Fathers Ser.). 1951. 29.99 (*0-8028-8093-2*) Eerdmans.
— Ante-Nicene Fathers, Vols. 7-8: Third & Fourth Centuries, 2 vols., 8. (EArly Church Fathers Ser.). 1951. write for info. (*0-8028-8094-0*) Eerdmans.
— The Early Church Fathers: Ante-Nicene Fathers, 10 vols., Set. 1951. 275.00 (*0-8028-8097-5*) Eerdmans.
Roberts, A. B. Applied Geotechnology: A Text for Students & Engineers on Rock Excavation & Related Topics. (Illus.). 416p. 1981. text ed. 138.00 (*0-08-024015-1*, Pub. by Pergamon Repr UK) Franklin.
Roberts, A. B., jt. ed. see Sporn, Michael B.
Roberts, A. D., ed. Frontiers of Tribology: Proceedings of the International Conference on Frontiers of Tribology, Stratford-upon-Avon, U. K. 15-17 April 1991. (Illus.). 354p. 1992. 90.00 (*0-7503-0190-2*) IOP Pub.
Roberts, A. Hood. Statistical Linguistic Analysis of American English. (Janua Linguarum, Series Practica: No. 8). 1965. text ed. 89.25 (*90-279-0627-0*) Mouton.
***Roberts, A. J.** A One-Dimensional Introduction to Continuum Mechanics. LC 94-30315. 170p. 1994. text ed. 28.00 (*981-02-1913-X*) World Scientific Pub.
Roberts, A. M., et al, eds. The Geometry of Normal Faults. (Geological Society Special Publications: No. 56). (Illus.). 264p. 1991. 115.00 (*0-903317-59-1*, Pub. by Geol Soc Pub Hse UK) AAPG.
Roberts, A. W. Breeze for a Bargeman. 144p. 1994. pap. 22.00 (*0-86138-007-X*, Pub. by T Dalton UK) St Mut.
Roberts, A. Wayne. Elementary Linear Algebra. 2nd ed. 1985. teacher ed 9.95 (*0-8053-8306-9*); text ed. 34.95 (*0-8053-8305-0*) Addison-Wesley.
— Faces of Mathematics. 3rd ed. LC 94-2399. (C). 1994. 53.00 (*0-06-501069-8*) HarpC.
Roberts, A. Wayne & Varberg, Dale E. Faces of Mathematics: An Introductory Course for College Students. 2nd ed. 492p. (C). 1989. text ed. 53.50 (*0-06-045471-7*) HarpCollege.
Roberts, Ada Lou. Sourdough Breads & Coffee Cakes from Lane Farm: Worth 104 Recipes. (Cookery, Wine, Nutrition Ser.). 192p. 1983. reprint ed. pap. 4.50 (*0-486-24529-2*) Dover.
Roberts, Adam. Civil Resistance in the East European & Soviet Revolutions. (Einstein Institution Monograph Ser.). 43p. 1991. 3.00 (*1-880813-04-1*) A Einstein Inst.
Roberts, Adam & Guelff, Richard, eds. Documents on the Laws of War. 2nd ed. (Illus.). 528p. 1989. pap. 34.50 (*0-19-825657-4*) OUP.
Roberts, Adam & Kingsbury, Benedict. Presiding over a Divided World: Changing UN Roles, 1945-1993. LC 94-4467. (International Peace Academy Occasional Paper Ser.). 95p. 1994. pap. text ed. 9.95 (*1-55587-519-X*) Lynne Rienner.
Roberts, Adam & Kingsbury, Benedict, eds. United Nations, Divided World: The U. N.'s Roles in International Relations. 2nd ed. 396p. 1994. 68.00 (*0-19-827906-X*); pap. 19.95 (*0-19-827926-4*) OUP.
Roberts, Adam, et al. Academic Freedom under Israeli Military Occupation: Report of WUS-ICJ Mission of Enquiry into Higher Education in the West Bank & Gaza. 87p. reprint ed. pap. 25.00 (*0-8357-5028-0*, 2027734) Bks Demand.

Roberts, Adrian C. Arthur Schnitzler & Politics. (Studies in Austrian Literature, Culture, & Thought. Translation Ser.). 214p. 1989. 29.00 (*0-929497-06-6*); pap. 23.00 (*0-929497-14-7*) Ariadne CA.

Roberts, Alan. The Self-Managing Environment. 189p. 1980. 29.00 (*0-8476-6211-X*) Rowman.
Roberts, Alan & Bush, B. M., eds. Neurones Without Impulses. LC 79-42572. (Society for Experimental Biology Seminar Ser.: No. 6). (Illus.). 250p. 1981. 89.95 (*0-521-23364-X*); pap. 32.95 (*0-521-29935-7*) Cambridge U Pr.
Roberts, Alan, et al. Computer Shorthand Theory & Transcription. 2nd ed. 368p. (C). 1990. pap. text ed. write for info. (*0-13-173105-X*) P-H.
Roberts, Alasdair. Out to Play: The Middle Years of Childhood. 175p. 1980. text ed. 13.00 (*0-08-025719-4*, Pergamon Pr); pap. text ed. 13.00 (*0-08-025718-6*, Pergamon Pr) Elsevier.
Roberts, Albert. Battered Women & Their Families: Intervention Strategies & Treatment Programs. LC 83-20022. (Social Work Ser.: Vol. 1). 224p. 1984. 25.95 (*0-8261-4590-6*) Springer Pub.
Roberts, Albert F. Geotechnology: An Introductory Text for Students & Engineers. LC 76-45440. 1977. 148.00 (*0-08-019602-0*, Pub. by Pergamon Repr UK) Franklin.
Roberts, Albert R. Crisis Intervention Handbook: Assessment, Treatment & Research. 341p. (C). 1990. text ed. 49.95 (*0-534-12510-7*) Brooks-Cole.
— Helping Crime Victims: Research, Policy, & Practice. 256p. 1990. text ed. 46.00 (*0-8039-3468-8*); pap. text ed. 22.95 (*0-8039-3469-6*) Sage.
— Social Work in Juvenile & Criminal Justice Settings. (Illus.). 412p. 1983. pap. 29.95 (*0-398-06404-0*) C C Thomas.
— Social Work in Juvenile & Criminal Justice Settings. (Illus.). 412p. (C). 1983. 49.95x (*0-398-04862-2*) C C Thomas.
Roberts, Albert R., ed. Critical Issues in Crime & Justice. 328p. (C). 1994. text ed. 48.00 (*0-8039-5497-2*); pap. text ed. 22.95 (*0-8039-5498-0*) Sage.
— Helping Battered Women: New Perspectives & Remedies. (Illus.). 256p. (C). 1995. 49.95 (*0-19-509586-3*); pap. text ed. 24.00 (*0-19-509587-1*) OUP.
***Roberts, Alexander & Donaldson, James, eds.** The Ante-Nicene Fathers, 10 vols., Set. 1994. 299.00 (*1-56563-082-3*) Hendrickson MA.
Roberts, Alexander, jt. tr. see Donaldson, James.
Roberts, Alexander, tr. see Jahangir.
***Roberts, Alexander, et al.** Early Church Fathers, 38 vols., Set. 1994. 1,100.00 (*1-56563-081-5*) Hendrickson MA.
Roberts, Alexnder, tr. see Origen, et al.
Roberts, Alfred R. Robert H. Montgomery: A Pioneer Leader of American Accounting. LC 75-31805. (Research Monograph: No. 63). 358p. 1975. spiral bd. 35.00 (*0-88406-095-0*) GA St U Busn Pr.
— Selected Papers of Earle C. King. Brief, Richard P., ed. LC 80-1464. (Dimensions of Accounting Theory & Practice Ser.). 1980. lib. bdg. 25.95 (*0-405-13486-X*) Ayer.
Roberts, Alina. Prairie Summer. (Great Escapes Ser.). 1994. pap. 1.99 (*0-373-83274-5*, 1-83274-0) Harlequin Bks.
Roberts, Alison J. Fun with Fitness. Hayes, Dympna, ed. (Fun with Ser.). (Illus.). 32p. (J). (gr. 2). 1987. lib. bdg. 14.97 (*0-88625-167-2*); pap. 2.95 (*0-88625-157-5*) Durkin Hayes Pub.
Roberts, Allan. Fossils. LC 82-23521. (New True Bks.). (Illus.). 48p. (J). (gr. k-4). 1983. lib. bdg. 12.90 (*0-516-01678-4*); pap. 4.95 (*0-516-41678-2*) Childrens.
Roberts, Allen. Robert Francis Kennedy: The Biography of a Compulsive Politician. 1984. 19.95 (*0-8283-1890-5*) Branden Pub Co.
Roberts, Allen D., jt. auth. see Sillitoe, Linda.
Roberts, Allen E. Craft & Its Symbols. 8th ed. LC 73-89493. (Illus.). xii, 90p. 1993. reprint ed. text ed. 8.75 (*0-88053-058-8*, M 321) Macoy Pub.
— The Diamond Years. (History of Babcock Lodge Ser.: No. 322). (Illus.). 316p. 1987. 12.50 (*0-935633-04-9*) Anchor Comm.
— La Francmasoneria y Sus Simbolos. Callejas, Roger F., tr. 188p. (SPA.). 1986. 9.50 (*0-88053-084-7*, M 330) Macoy Pub.
— Freemasonry in American History. (Illus.). xxx, 462p. 1985. text ed. 19.50 (*0-88053-078-2*, M 317) Macoy Pub.
— G. Washington; Master Mason. LC 76-16296. (Illus.). xiv, 208p. 1976. 11.50 (*0-88053-060-X*, M-323) Macoy Pub.
— House Undivided: The Story of Freemasonry & the Civil War. xx, 356p. 1982. reprint ed. 22.95 (*0-88053-056-1*, M 319) Macoy Pub.
— How to Conduct a Leadership Seminar. 12p. 1993. pap. 3.00 (*0-88053-013-8*, M 057) Macoy Pub.
— Key to Freemasonry's Growth. LC 76-107026. 188p. 1988. reprint ed. text ed. 7.50 (*0-88053-057-X*, M320) Macoy Pub.
— The Mystic Tie. xvi, 296p. 1991. 14.00 (*0-88053-086-3*, M331) Macoy Pub.
— The Search for Leadership. 236p. 1987. 15.95 (*0-935633-05-7*) Anchor Comm.
— Seekers of Truth. (History of the Philalethes Society Ser.). (Illus.). 218p. 1988. 17.95 (*0-935633-06-5*) Anchor Comm.
Roberts, Allen E. & Hunt, Bruce H. Brother Truman: The Masonic Life & Philosophy of Harry S. Truman. (Illus.). 314p. 1986. 17.95 (*0-935633-01-4*) Anchor Comm.
***Roberts, Allen F.** Animals in African Art: From the Familiar to the Marvelous. LC 94-73442. (Illus.). 192p. 1995. pap. 32.00 (*0-945802-17-X*) Museum African.
— Animals in African Art: From the Familiar to the Marvelous. (Illus.). 176p. 1995. 65.00 (*3-7913-1455-6*, Pub. by Prestel) TeNeues.
— Threshold: African Art on the Verge. (Illus.). 96p. 1994. pap. 19.95 (*3-7913-1369-X*) Mus African Art.
Roberts, Allen F. & Maurer, Evan M., eds. The Rising of a New Moon: A Century of Tabwa Art. LC 87-401130. (Illus.). 304p. 1985. pap. 39.95 (*0-295-96447-2*) U of Wash Pr.
Roberts, Allen F., jt. auth. see Maurer, Evan M.
Roberts, Allene. The Curiosity Club: Kids' Nature Activity Book. 192p. (J). 1992. pap. text ed. 14.95 (*0-471-55589-4*) Wiley.
Roberts, Alma, ed. New Breezes: An Anthology of African American Literary Voices. 51p. 1993. pap. 7.95 (*0-9638191-0-0*) New Breezes.
Roberts, Alton O., ed. see Geno, Marie G. & Schegerin, Barbara M.
Roberts, Alvin. Tavern Tales. LC 91-77387. 78p. 1993. pap. 7.00 (*1-56002-143-8*) Aegina Pr.
***Roberts, Andrew.** Eminent Churchillians. 368p. 1995. 27.50 (*0-684-80403-4*) S&S Trade.
— A History of Zambia. LC 76-40923. (Illus.). 288p. (C). 1976. 39.50 (*0-8419-0291-7*, Africana); pap. 25.00 (*0-8419-0490-1*, Africana) Holmes & Meier.
Roberts, Andrew, ed. The Colonial Moment in Africa: Essays on the Movement of Minds & Materials, 1900-1940. (Illus.). 304p. (C). 1990. pap. 21.95 (*0-521-38674-8*) Cambridge U Pr.
— The Colonial Moment in Africa: Essays on the Movement of Minds & Materials, 1900-1940. (Illus.). 304p. (C). 1990. 69.95 (*0-521-39090-7*) Cambridge U Pr.
Roberts, Andrew D. A History of the Bemba: Political Growth & Change in North-Eastern Zambia Before 1900. LC 73-5813. 454p. 1974. 35.00 (*0-299-06450-6*) U of Wis Pr.
***Roberts, Anita.** The Last Chance Cafe: And Other Stories. 176p. (Orig.). 1993. pap. 12.95 (*0-919591-80-9*, Pub. by Polestar Bk Pubs CN) Orca Bk Pubs.
Roberts, Anita B. & Sporn, Michael B. The Retinoids, Vol. 1. 1984. text ed. 106.00 (*0-12-658101-0*) Acad Pr.
— The Retinoids, Vol. 2. 1984. text ed. 107.00 (*0-12-658102-9*) Acad Pr.
Roberts, Ann. Growing Vegetables in Alaska: & Other Far North Climates. (Illus.). 265p. 1986. 19.95 (*0-918270-08-1*) That New Pub.
Roberts, Ann, ed. The Children's Treasury of Animal Stories. (Illus.). 192p. (J). (ps-5). 1993. 18.95 (*1-55013-504-X*, Pub. by Key Porter Bks CN) Natl Bk Netwk.
Roberts, Ann R. Mr. Rockefeller's Roads: The Untold Story of Acadia's Carriage Roads & Their Creator. LC 90-84029. (Illus.). 184p. 1990. 24.95 (*0-89272-295-9*); pap. 14.95 (*0-89272-296-7*) Down East.
Roberts, Ann V. Louisa Elliott. 800p. 1990. mass mkt. 5.95 (*0-380-70991-0*) Avon.
— Morning's Gate. 640p. 1993. reprint ed. mass mkt. 5.99 (*0-380-70992-9*) Avon.
— Morning's Gate: A Novel. 620p. 1992. 22.00 (*0-688-11074-6*) Morrow.
Roberts, Anne F. & Blandy, Susan G. Public Relations for Librarians: Getting It All, Saving It All, Sharing It All. 200p. 1989. lib. bdg. 24.50 (*0-87287-684-5*) Libs Unl.
Roberts, Anne F. & Cockrell, Marcia W., eds. Historic Albany: Its Churches & Synagogues. (Illus.). 415p. (Orig.). 1986. pap. 15.00 (*0-941237-00-1*) Libr Commns Servs.
Roberts, Anne F., ed. see Burkett, Lucille F.
Roberts, Anne F., ed. see Findlay, Lois P.
Roberts, Annie L., jt. auth. see Ziga, Charles J.
Roberts, Anthony, tr. see Patin, Sylvie.
Roberts, Arch E. Rakkasan! The 187th Regimental Combat Team. (Airborne Ser.: No. 8). (Illus.). 1978. 25.00 (*0-89839-008-7*) Battery Pr.
Roberts, Archibald. Peace. 1972. 10.00 (*0-913558-03-6*) Educator Pubns.
Roberts, Archibald E. America in Crisis Survival Portfolio. 100p. 1992. pap. 14.95 (*0-934120-23-4*) Comm Restore Const.
— Emerging Struggle for State Sovereignty. 300p. 1979. 9.95 (*0-318-13711-9*); pap. 5.95 (*0-318-13712-7*) Comm Restore Const.
— The Most Secret Science. LC 84-70100. (Illus.). 200p. 1984. pap. 12.00 (*0-934120-08-0*) Betsy Ross Pr.
— The Most Secret Science. 1984. pap. write for info. (*0-318-61784-6*) Comm Restore Const.
— Peace: By the Wonderful People Who Brought You Korea & Viet Nam. 377p. 1972. 6.95 (*0-318-13713-5*, Betsy Ross Pr) Comm Restore Const.
— The Republic: Decline & Future Promise. 1975. write for info. (*0-318-61783-8*, Betsy Ross Pr) Comm Restore Const.
— Victory Denied. 300p. 1966. pap. 2.00 (*0-318-13714-3*, Betsy Ross Pr) Comm Restore Const.
Roberts, Ardell, jt. auth. see Johnson, Maeve.
***Roberts, Art.** Easy Multiplying & Dividing Tables (for Young Readers) The New Learning Tool. (Illus.). (J). 1995. text ed. 9.95 (*1-887252-05-3*) Kids Success Learn.
Roberts, Arthur & Prentice, Richard. Programming for Numerical Control Machines. 2nd ed. (Illus.). 1978. text ed. 40.95 (*0-07-053156-0*) McGraw.
Roberts, Arthur, jt. auth. see Raistrick, Arthur.
Roberts, Arthur C. Litigating Head Trauma Cases. (Personal Injury Library). (Illus.). 710p. 1991. 138.00 (*0-471-55324-7*) Wiley.
— Litigating Head Trauma Cases. suppl. ed. (Personal Injury Library). (Illus.). 176p. 1991. ring bd. 65.00 (*0-471-59150-5*) Wiley.
Roberts, Arthur C., et al. Litigating Head Trauma Cases: 1992 Supplement. (Illus.). 160p. 1992. 55.00 (*0-471-57042-7*) Wiley.
Roberts, Arthur D. & Cawelti, Gordon. Redefining General Education in the American High School. LC 84-71655. 160p. (Orig.). 1984. pap. text ed. 8.50 (*0-87120-126-7*, 611-84332) Assn Supervision.
Roberts, Arthur D. & Lapidge, S. Manufacturing Processes. 1977. text ed. write for info. (*0-07-053159-5*) McGraw.
Roberts, Arthur J., ed. Coronary Artery Surgery: Application of New Technologies. LC 82-23905. (Illus.). 495p. reprint ed. pap. 141.10 (*0-8357-7630-1*, 2056953) Bks Demand.

An Asterisk (*) at the beginning of an entry indicates that the title is appearing in BIP for the first time.

Roberts, Arthur J., jt. ed. see Adams, Ann S.

Roberts, Arthur O. The Association of Evangelical Friends. 1975. pap. 3.50 (*0-913342-04-1*) Barclay Pr.

— Listen to the Lord. LC 74-84371. 1974. 7.95 (*0-317-59618-7*) Barclay Pr.

— Move over, Elijah. LC 67-24903. 161p. 1967. 7.95 (*0-913342-11-4*) Barclay Pr.

— Sunrise & Shadow. LC 84-62861. 112p. (Orig.). 1985. pap. 7.95 (*0-913342-48-3*) Barclay Pr.

Roberts, Arthur O., ed. Faith & Practice: A Book of Christian Discipline. LC 87-73151. 114p. 1987. pap. 4.95 (*0-913342-62-9*) Barclay Pr.

Roberts, Arthur O., jt. ed. see Oliver, John W.

Roberts, Arthur R. Incredible Interlude at Tahoe. 212p. 1977. pap. 2.50 (*0-87881-066-8*) Mojave Bks.

Roberts, Arthur W., jt. ed. see Roberts, Nancy L.

Roberts, Aubrey C. & Wallis, James F. Concepts of Accounting Theory. (Orig.). 1979. pap. 9.98 (*0-89894-013-3*) Advocate Pub Group.

Roberts, Audrey. Bibliography of Commissions of Enquiry & Other Government-Sponsored Reports on the Commonwealth Caribbean, 1900-1975. (Bibliography & Reference Ser.: No. 14). 89p. (Orig.). 1985. pap. 17.50 (*0-917617-06-1*) SALALM.

Roberts, Audrey, jt. ed. see Thompson, Irene.

Roberts, August C. & Stevens, Wendelle C. UFO Photographs Around the World, Vol. 2. (Factbooks Ser.). (Illus.). 286p. 1987. lib. bdg. 16.95 (*0-934269-01-7*) UFO Photo.

Roberts, August C., jt. auth. see Stevens, Wendelle C.

Roberts, Augustine. Centered on Christ: An Introduction to Monastic Profession. rev. ed. LC 93-7100. 1993. pap. 12.95 (*0-932506-99-2*) St Bedes Pubns.

Roberts, B. A., ed. see Proctor, J.

Roberts, B. E., ed. Standard Hematology Practice. 264p. 1991. 110.00 (*0-632-02623-5*) Blackwell Sci.

Roberts, B. H. The Life of John Taylor. 11.95 (*0-88494-106-X*) Bookcraft Inc.

— A New Witness for God. 122p. 1987. text ed. 8.95 (*0-9622545-4-1*) Pulsipher Pub.

— A Scrap Book, Vol. I. (Illus.). 529p. 1989. 54.95 (*0-9622545-9-2*) Pulsipher Pub.

— Seventy's Course in Theology. 1000p. (C). 1995. 49.95 (*0-910523-16-9*) Grandin Bk Co.

— Studies of the Book of Mormon. 2nd ed. Madsen, Brigham, ed. LC 92-22758. (Illus.). 409p. 1992. reprint ed. pap. 14.95 (*1-56085-027-2*) Signature Bks.

— The Truth, the Way, the Life: An Elementary Treatise on Theology. Larson, Stan, ed. LC 94-14856. (Illus.). 800p. 1994. text ed. 28.95 (*1-56085-074-4*) Signature Bks.

Roberts, B. H., intro. History of the Church, 7 vols. Incl. Vol. 4 (1839-1842). 620p. 1976. 15.95 (*0-87747-077-4*); Vol. 5 (1842-1843). 563p. 1980. 15.95 (*0-87747-078-2*); Vol. 6 (1843-1844). 641p. 1980. 15.95 (*0-87747-079-0*); Vol. 7 (period 2, The Apostolic Interregnum). 640p. 1980. 15.95 (*0-87747-080-4*); Index. 15.95 (*0-87747-291-2*) Deseret Bk.

Roberts, B. M., jt. auth. see Billington, N. S.

Roberts, B. T. Holiness Teachings. pap. 8.99 (*0-88019-190-2*) Schmul Pub Co.

— Ordaining Women. rev. ed. 106p. 1992. reprint ed. pap. 5.95 (*0-89367-176-2*) Light & Life.

***Roberts, Barbara.** Decoupage Quilts. Reinstatler, Laura, ed. (Illus.). 48p. (Orig.). 1995. pap. 12.95 (*1-56477-111-3*, B228) That Patchwork.

— Whence They Came: Deportation from Canada, 1900-1935. 246p. 1988. pap. 25.00 (*0-7766-0163-6*, Pub. by Univ Ottawa Pr CN) Paul & Co Pubs.

Roberts, Barbara, jt. auth. see Jaffe, Charlotte.

***Roberts, Barry J. & Upton, Kevin.** The Complete Facilitator: A Guide. (Illus.). 96p. (Orig.). 1994. pap. 29.95 (*0-9646972-0-3*) Howick Assocs.

Roberts, Barry S., jt. auth. see Mann, Richard A.

Roberts, Benjamin C. Labour in the Tropical Territories of the Commonwealth. LC 64-25334. 444p. reprint ed. 126.60 (*0-8357-9110-6*, 2017925) Bks Demand.

Roberts, Bennett, jt. auth. see Myers, Diana.

Roberts, Bernadette. The Experience of No-Self: A Contemplative Journey. rev. ed. 213p. 1993. pap. 14.95 (*0-7914-1694-1*) State U NY Pr.

— The Path to No-Self: Life at the Center. LC 91-30833. 214p. (Orig.). 1991. 39.50 (*0-7914-1141-9*); pap. 14.95 (*0-7914-1142-7*) State U NY Pr.

— What Is Self? A Study of the Spiritual Journey in Terms of Consciousness. LC 89-91249. 216p. (Orig.). 1989. pap. 13.00 (*0-9623993-0-2*) M Goens Pub.

Roberts, Bethany. Cat Parade! LC 93-26726. (J). 1995. write for info. (*0-395-67893-5*, Clarion Bks) HM.

— Gramps & the Fire Dragon. LC 94-43097. (Illus.). (J). 1996. write for info. (*0-395-69849-9*, Clarion Bks) HM.

— Halloween Mice! LC 93-17192. (Illus.). (J). 1994. 12.95 (*0-395-67064-0*, Clarion Bks) HM.

— Monster Manners: A Guide to Monster Etiquette. LC 94-23219. (Illus.). (J). 1996. write for info. (*0-395-69850-2*, Clarion Bks) HM.

— The Two O'Clock Secret. Grant, Christy, ed. LC 92-6405. (Illus.). 32p. (J). (ps-2). 1993. 13.95 (*0-8075-8159-3*) A Whitman.

— Waiting-for-Christmas Stories. LC 93-11480. (Illus.). (J). 1994. 13.95 (*0-395-67324-0*) HM.

Roberts, Bette B. Anne Rice. LC 93-40509. (Twayne's United States Author Ser.: No. 644). 192p. 1994. text ed. 22.95x (*0-8057-3961-0*, Twayne) Macmillan.

— The Gothic Romance: Its Appeal to Women Writers & Readers in Late Eighteenth-Century England. Varma, Devendra P., ed. LC 79-8474. (Gothic Studies & Dissertations). 1980. lib. bdg. 31.95 (*0-405-12658-1*) Ayer.

Roberts, Bill. Stories on the Orift. LC 87-63108. (Illus.). 220p. 1988. pap. 8.00 (*0-944100-02-3*) Pirogue Pub.

Roberts, Bob. Coasting Bargemaster. 168p. 1994. pap. 24.00 (*0-904623-95-5*) St Mut.

— Last of the Sailormen. (Illus.). 166p. 1985. pap. 15.00 (*0-87556-766-5*) Saifer.

— Last of the Sailormen. (Illus.). 149p. 1986. pap. 12.95 (*0-85036-342-X*, Pub. by Seafarer Bks UK) Sheridan.

— Rough & Tumble. 144p. (C). 1988. 60.00 (*0-685-24326-5*, Pub. by T Dalton UK) St Mut.

— Rough & Tumble. 144p. 1994. pap. 22.00 (*0-904623-96-3*, Pub. by T Dalton UK) St Mut.

Roberts, Bob, Sr. Sixty Second Sermons. 225p. 1988. pap. 6.95 (*0-9620462-0-5*) Christian Fndtns Faith Inc.

Roberts, Bob. A Slice of Suffolk. 112p. 1994. pap. 22.00 (*0-86138-020-7*, Pub. by T Dalton UK) St Mut.

Roberts, Bobby & Moneyhon, Carl. Portraits of Conflict: A Photographic History of Arkansas in the Civil War. LC 87-5869. (Illus.). 250p. 1987. pap. 30.00 (*0-938626-84-1*) U of Ark Pr.

— Portraits of Conflict: A Photographic History of Mississippi in the Civil War. LC 92-21637. (Illus.). 424p. (C). 1993. 70.00 (*1-55728-260-9*) U of Ark Pr.

Roberts, Bobby, jt. auth. see Moneyhon, Carl.

***Roberts, Bonita K. & Schlueter, Linda L.** Legal Research Guide: Patterns & Practice. 2nd ed. 157p. 1990. pap. 18.00 (*0-87473-641-2*) Michie Butterworth.

Roberts, Brad. The New Democracies: Global Change & U. S. Policy. 240p. 1990. 24.95 (*0-262-18137-1*) MIT Pr.

— Securing Democratic Transitions. (Significant Issues Ser.: Vol. 12, No. 1). 58p. (Orig.). 1990. pap. text ed. 1.00 (*0-89206-155-3*) CSI Studies.

Roberts, Brad, ed. Biological Weapons: Weapons of the Future? LC 92-47356. (Significant Issues Ser.: Vol. 15, No. 1). 1993. pap. 15.00 (*0-89206-210-X*) CSI Studies.

— Chemical Disarmament & U. S. Security. 158p. (C). 1992. pap. text ed. 46.00 (*0-8133-8577-6*) Westview.

— Chemical Warfare Policy: Beyond the Binary Production Decision. (Significant Issues Ser.: Vol. 9, No. 3). 50p. (Orig.). (C). 1987. pap. 1.00 (*0-89206-103-0*) CSI Studies.

— The Chemical Weapons Convention: Implementation Ideas. LC 92-43724. (Significant Issues Ser.). 48p. 1993. pap. text ed. 8.95 (*0-89206-207-X*) CSI Studies.

— The New Democracies: Global Change & U. S. Policy. 240p. 1990. pap. 14.95 (*0-262-68062-9*) MIT Pr.

— Ratifying the Chemical Weapons Convention. LC 94-17403. (Signficant Issues Ser.). 112p. (Orig.). (gr. 13). 1994. pap. 13.50 (*0-89206-264-9*) CSI Studies.

— U. S. Foreign Policy after the Cold War. (Illus.). 310p. 1992. 31.50 (*0-262-18148-7*); pap. 18.00 (*0-262-68074-2*) MIT Pr.

— U. S. Security in an Uncertain Era. (Illus.). 350p. 1993. 30.00 (*0-262-18155-X*); pap. 17.00 (*0-262-68080-7*) MIT Pr.

— Weapons Proliferation in the 1990s. (Washington Quarterly Reader Ser.). (Illus.). 450p. 1995. pap. 18.00x (*0-262-68086-6*) MIT Pr.

Roberts, Brad & Belyaeva, Nina, eds. After Perestroika: Democracy in the Soviet Union. (Significant Issues Ser.). 130p. (Orig.). 1991. pap. text ed. 6.95 (*0-89206-173-1*) CSI Studies.

Roberts, Brad, jt. ed. see Laqueur, Walter.

Roberts, Brandon. Competition Across the Atlantic: The States Face Europe '92. Hurley, Larry, ed. (Illus.). 48p. 1991. pap. text ed. 15.00 (*1-55516-805-1*, 3909) Natl Conf State Legis.

Roberts, Brandon D. Investment Across the Atlantic: New Competition & Challenges for States. 48p. 1992. pap. text ed. 15.00 (*1-55516-806-X*, 3911) Natl Conf State Legis.

Roberts, Brenda. The Companion Guide to Roberts' Ultimate Encyclopedia of Hull Pottery. (Illus.). 308p. 1992. 24.95 (*0-9632136-1-X*) Cntry Side Antiques.

— Roberts' Ultimate Encyclopedia of Hull Pottery. LC 91-68348. (Illus.). 340p. 1992. 41.95 (*0-9632136-0-1*) Cntry Side Antiques.

Roberts, Brenda C. Sticks & Stones, Bobbie Bones. (J). (gr. 4-7). 1993. pap. 2.95 (*0-590-46518-X*) Scholastic Inc.

Roberts, Brian. Land Care Manual. 1992. pap. 24.95 (*0-86840-053-X*, Pub. by New South Wales Univ Pr AT) Intl Spec Bk.

Roberts, Brian & Schwadel, Richard. L. A. Shortcuts: The Guidebook for Drivers Who Hate to Wait. Graham, Dennis, ed. LC 88-64173. (Illus.). 216p. (Orig.). 1989. pap. 14.95 (*0-926055-00-3*) Red Car Pr.

Roberts, Brigham H. The Autobiography of B. H. Roberts. Bergera, Gary J., ed. LC 90-39781. 266p. 1991. pap. 12.95 (*1-56085-005-1*) Signature Bks.

— Mormon Doctrine of Deity: The Roberts-Van der Donckt Discussion. 296p. 1975. 16.98 (*0-88290-058-7*) Horizon Utah.

Roberts, Bruce. Plantation Homes of the James River. LC 89-39204. (Illus.). xii, 116p. (C). 1990. 29.95 (*0-8078-1879-8*); pap. 16.95 (*0-8078-4278-8*) U of NC Pr.

— The Project Manual. 31.50 (*0-317-59581-4*) Constr Ind Pr.

Roberts, Bruce, photos. Ghosts & Specters of the Old South. LC 73-20909. (Illus.). 93p. (J). (gr. 3 up). 1984. reprint ed. pap. 8.95 (*0-87844-058-5*) Sandlapper Pub Co.

Roberts, Bruce & Feiner, Susan, eds. Radical Economics. (Recent Economic Thought Ser.). 272p. (C). 1991. lib. bdg. 63.00 (*0-7923-9178-0*) Kluwer Ac.

Roberts, Bruce & Jones, Ray. American Country Stores. LC 91-12279. (Illus.). 128p. 1991. 19.95 (*0-87106-228-3*) Globe Pequot.

Roberts, Bruce & Jones, Ray, photos. Western Lighthouses: Olympic Peninsula to San Diego. LC 92-32521. (Illus.). 128p. (Orig.). 1993. pap. 19.95 (*1-56440-133-2*) Globe Pequot.

Roberts, Bruce, jt. auth. see Jones, Ray.

Roberts, Bruce B., jt. auth. see Thorsheim, Howard I.

Roberts, Bruce R. Water Management in Desert Environments: A Comparative Analysis. LC 93-12681. (Lecture Notes in Earth Sciences Ser.: Vol. 48). 1993. Acid-free paper. 89.00 (*0-387-56562-0*) Spr-Verlag.

***Roberts, Bryan.** Cities of Peasants Further Explored. 2nd ed. 256p. 1994. pap. 16.95 (*0-340-60478-6*, B4020, Pub. by E Arnold UK) Routledge Chapman & Hall.

Roberts, Bryan R. Cities of Peasants: The Political Economy of Urbanization in the Third World. LC 79-87589. (Explorations in Urban Analysis Ser.: No. 1). 215p. reprint ed. pap. 61.30 (*0-8357-8505-X*, 2034786) Bks Demand.

— Organizing Strangers: Poor Families in Guatemala City. LC 72-3513. (Texas Pan-American Ser.). 378p. reprint ed. pap. 107.80 (*0-8357-7759-6*, 2036117) Bks Demand.

Roberts, Brynley. Edward Llwyd: The Making of a Scientist. 21p. 1980. pap. 2.00 (*0-7083-0747-7*, Pub. by U of Wales UK) Bks Intl VA.

Roberts, Brynley F. Studies on Middle Welsh Literature. LC 91-36558. (Welsh Studies: Vol. 5). 160p. 1992. lib. bdg. 69.95 (*0-7734-9641-6*) E Mellen.

Roberts, Butch. How to Survive the Move to Florida. Fries, Robert K., ed. (Illus.). (Orig.). 1987. pap. text ed. write for info. (*0-937957-02-X*) B Roberts.

Roberts, Butch, jt. auth. see Ell, Johnny J.

Roberts, Calvin G., jt. auth. see Roberts, Susan A.

***Roberts, Carey.** Pray God to Die. 320p. 1994. mass mkt. 4.99 (*0-380-72259-3*) Avon.

— Pray God to Die: A Detective Anne Fitzhugh Mystery. 384p. 1993. text ed. 21.00 (*0-684-19562-3*, Scribners) S&S Trade.

Roberts, Carey & Seely, Rebecca. Tidewater Dynasty: The Lees of Stratford Hall. LC 80-8758. 1981. 19.95 (*0-15-190294-1*) HarBrace.

— Tidewater Dynasty: The Lees of Stratford Hall. LC 80-8758. 456p. 1983. pap. 10.95 (*0-15-690336-9*, Harvest Bks) HarBrace.

Roberts, Carl E. Through Starving Russia: Being the Record of a Journey to Moscow & the Volga Provinces in August & September 1921. LC 75-39060. (Russian Studies: Perspectives on the Revolution). (Illus.). xv, 165p. 1977. reprint ed. 20.35 (*0-88355-440-2*) Hyperion Conn.

Roberts, Carla A., ed. see Smith, Jaune Quick to See, et al.

Roberts, Carol. Timothy Findley: An Annotated Bibliography. 150p. (C). 1990. text ed. 30.00 (*1-55022-112-4*, Pub. by ECW Press CN) Genl Dist Srvs.

— Timothy Findley: Stories from a Life. (Illus.). 180p. 1994. pap. 9.95 (*1-55022-195-7*, Pub. by ECW Pr CN) InBook.

— Timothy Findley: Stories from a Life. (Illus.). 180p. 1994. pap. write for info. (*1-55022-185-X*, Pub. by ECW Pr CN) InBook.

Roberts, Carol A. & Burke, Sharon O. Nursing Research: A Quantitative & Qualitative Approach. 400p. 1989. boxed 40.00 (*0-86720-415-X*) Jones & Bartlett.

Roberts, Carol E., ed. see Grin, Oliver D. & Bouwman, Dorothy L.

Roberts, Carol E., jt. auth. see Wiley, D. Eugene.

Roberts, Carolyn C. & Beck, Eugene C. Marketing in Small & Rural Hospitals. LC 89-15003. 151p. (Orig.). 1989. 35.00 (*1-55648-036-9*, 136105) AHPI.

Roberts, Cary M. Separate Peace Notes. 1965. pap. 3.75 (*0-8220-1183-2*) Cliffs.

Roberts, Casey. Shenanigans. (Superromance Ser.). 1993. mass mkt. 3.39 (*0-373-70547-6*, 1-70547-4) Harlequin Bks.

Roberts, Catherine. Science, Animals & Evolution: Reflections on Some Unrealized Potentials of Biology & Medicine. LC 79-52322. (Contributions in Philosophy Ser.: No. 14). 221p. 1980. text ed. 49.95 (*0-313-21479-4*, RSA/, Greenwood Pr) Greenwood.

— Scientific Conscience: Reflections on the Modern Biologist & Humanism. 1974. 22.95 (*0-8464-0819-8*) Beekman Pubs.

Roberts, Catherine M. Women & Rape. 224p. 1989. pap. 15.00 (*0-8147-7412-1*) NYU Pr.

Roberts, Catherine W., ed. Library of Congress Subject Headings, Significant Changes, 1974-1988. 74p. 1988. pap. text ed. 7.50 (*0-936996-33-1*) Soldier Creek.

Roberts, Celia, et al. Language & Discrimination: A Study of Communication in Ethnic Workplaces. (Applied Linguistics & Language Study Ser.). 288p. (Orig.). (C). 1992. pap. text ed. 18.95 (*0-582-55265-6*, 78652) Longman.

Roberts, Challon O. & Roberts, William P. Partners in Intimacy: Living Christian Marriage Today. 176p. 1988. pap. 11.95 (*0-8091-3006-8*) Paulist Pr.

Roberts, Chalmers M. How Did I Get Here So Fast? Rhetorical Questions & Available Answers from a Long & Happy Life. LC 91-50080. 176p. 1991. 14.95 (*0-446-51651-1*) Warner Bks.

— How Did I Get Here So Fast: Rhetorical Questions & Available Answers from a Long & Happy Life. large type ed. LC 92-17743. (General Ser.). 176p. 1992. lib. bdg. 17.95 (*0-8161-5543-7*); pap. 14.95 (*0-8161-5544-5*) G K Hall.

— In the Shadow of Power: The Story of the Washington Post. Gold, Jane, ed. LC 89-10274. 544p. (Orig.). 1989. pap. 16.95 (*0-932020-71-2*) Seven Locks Pr.

Roberts, Charles. New Card Games for You to Play. 160p. 1995. pap. 7.95 (*0-572-01381-7*, Pub. by Foulsham UK) Atrium Pubs.

— An Olive Branch for the Conquered. 64p. 1990. pap. 6.95 (*0-932616-31-3*) New Poets Chestnut Hills.

Roberts, Charles, ed. see Witt, Bill.

Roberts, Charles, jt. auth. see Zazarine, Paul.

Roberts, Charles G. By the Marshes of Minas. LC 74-178456. (Short Story Index Reprint Ser.). 1977. reprint ed. 21.95 (*0-8369-4057-1*) Ayer.

— Earth's Enigmas. LC 72-94742. (Short Story Index Reprint Ser.). 1977. 20.95 (*0-8369-3122-X*) Ayer.

— The Kindred of the Wild: A Book of Animal Life. 1977. 26.95 (*0-8369-4253-1*, 6062) Ayer.

— Selected Poetry & Critical Prose. LC 73-91558. (Literature of Canada, Poetry & Prose in Reprint Ser.: No. 9). 366p. reprint ed. pap. 104.40 (*0-317-27000-1*, 2023662) Bks Demand.

Roberts, Charles S. B&O Great Photos: A Portfolio. LC 94-94110. (Illus.). 208p. 1994. 40.00 (*0-934118-21-3*) Barnard Roberts.

— Sand Patch: Clash of Titans (B&O-PRR) LC 93-90583. (Cumberland to Connellsville & Branches 1837-1993 Ser.). (Illus.). 224p. 1993. 50.00 (*0-934118-20-5*) Barnard Roberts.

— West End: B & O Cumberland to Grafton 1848-1991. LC 91-74019. (Illus.). 224p. 1991. 50.00 (*0-934118-18-3*) Barnard Roberts.

Roberts, Charles S., ed. see Harwood, Herbert H., Jr.

Roberts, Charles S., jt. auth. see Hollis, Jeffrey R.

Roberts, Charles V. & Watson, Kittie W., eds. Intrapersonal Communication Processes: Original Essays. (Illus.). 580p. (C). 1989. 39.95 (*0-89787-336-X*) SPECTRA Inc.

Roberts, Charles W. & Hirsch, Mary, eds. Treasures of Iowa. (Illus.). 76p. (Orig.). 1987. pap. 4.95 (*0-317-61645-5*) Mid Am Pub.

***Roberts, Charlotte & Manchester, Keith.** The Archaeology of Disease. 2nd ed. LC 95-15961. (Illus.). 256p. 1995. 39.95 (*0-8014-3220-0*) Cornell U Pr.

Roberts, Chris. Newnes Z80 Pocket Book. 185p. 1992. 24.95 (*0-7506-0308-9*) Buttrwrth-Heinemann.

— Pow Wow Country. (Illus.). 128p. 1992. pap. 17.95 (*1-56037-025-4*) Am Wrld Geog.

***Roberts, Chris, ed.** Idle Worship: How Pop Empowers the Weak, Rewards the Faithful & Succors the Needy. 208p. (Orig.). 1995. pap. 10.95 (*0-571-19870-8*) Faber & Faber.

Roberts, Clayton. History of England: Sixteen Eighty-Eight to the Present, Vol. II. 3rd ed. 496p. (C). 1990. pap. text ed. write for info. (*0-13-390410-5*) P-H.

— The Logic of Historical Explanation. 1995. 45.00 (*0-271-01442-3*); pap. 17.95 (*0-271-01443-1*) Pa St U Pr.

— Schemes & Undertakings: A Study of English Politics in the Seventeenth Century. LC 85-25572. 347p. 1985. 47.50 (*0-8142-0377-9*); pap. 25.00 (*0-8142-0402-3*) Ohio St U Pr.

Roberts, Clayton & Roberts, David. History of England, Vol. I: Prehistory to 1714. 3rd ed. 464p. (C). 1990. pap. text ed. write for info. (*0-13-390394-X*) P-H.

Roberts, Cokie & Sono, Ayako. Democracy & Discontent: Questions Facing the Political Process of Japan & the United States. 140p. write for info. (*0-9635265-0-2*) U MT Mansfld.

Roberts, Colin. Chiens Perdue s.c.-La Cle'sur la Porte, Cesbron-Cardinal: Critical Monographs in English. 64p. 1993. pap. 32.00 (*0-85261-249-4*, Pub. by Univ of Glasgow UK) St Mut.

Roberts, Colin H. & Skeat, T. C. The Birth of the Codex. (Illus.). 96p. 1987. pap. 29.95 (*0-19-726061-6*) OUP.

Roberts, Cory, ed. Harmonization Whys & Wherefores. 136p. (C). 1985. 45.00 (*0-85292-348-1*, Pub. by IPM Hse UK) St Mut.

Roberts, Craig. Kill Zone - A Sniper Looks at Dealey Plaza. (Illus.). 252p. (Orig.). 1994. pap. 11.95 (*0-9639062-0-8*) Consol Pr Intl.

— Police Sniper. Tobias, Eric, ed. 320p. (Orig.). 1993. mass mkt. 5.99 (*0-671-79459-0*) PB.

Roberts, Craig & Appel, Allen. Hellhound. 352p. (Orig.). 1994. mass mkt. 4.99 (*0-380-76783-X*) Avon.

***Roberts, Craig & Armstrong, John.** JFK - The Dead Witnesses. (Illus.). 187p. (Orig.). 1995. pap. text ed. 11.95 (*0-9639062-3-2*) Consol Pr Intl.

Roberts, Craig & Sasser, Charles W. The Walking Dead: A Marine's Story of Vietnam. 1989. pap. 3.95 (*0-671-65777-1*) PB.

Roberts, Craig, jt. auth. see Sasser, Charles W.

***Roberts, Cynthia.** An End to Summer. 1994. lib. bdg. 22.00 (*0-7278-4667-1*) Severn Hse.

— Hunters & the Hunted. 1994. 22.00 (*0-7278-4601-9*) Severn Hse.

— Parents' Guide to the Delaware Valley. LC 88-15021. 272p. (Orig.). 1989. pap. 12.95 (*0-940159-04-X*) Camino Bks.

— The Running Tide. large type ed. (Romance Suspense Ser.). 624p. 1989. 17.95 (*0-7089-1998-7*) Ulverscroft.

— The Savage Shore. 448p. 1993. lib. bdg. 22.00 (*0-7278-4477-6*) Severn Hse.

— The Storms of Fate. 288p. 1992. lib. bdg. 19.00 (*0-7278-4337-0*) Severn Hse.

Roberts, Cynthia S. The Storms of Fate. large type ed. (Romance Ser.). 592p. 1993. 21.95 (*0-7089-2940-0*) Ulverscroft.

— Upon Stormy Downs. large type ed. (Romance Suspense Ser.). 1990. 21.95 (*0-7089-2256-2*) Ulverscroft.

— A Wind from the Sea. large type ed. (Romance Suspense Ser.). 1991. 21.95 (*0-7089-2351-8*) Ulverscroft.

Roberts, D., jt. auth. see Duncan, R. M.

Roberts, D. F., ed. Human Variation & Natural Selection. (Symposia of the Society for the Study of Human Biology Ser.: Vol. 13). 220p. 1975. 36.00 (*0-85066-080-7*) Taylor & Francis.

Roberts, D. F. & Chester, Robert, eds. Molecular Genetics in Medicine: Advances, Applications & Ethical Implications. LC 90-9249. (Illus.). 250p. 1991. text ed. 75.00 (*0-312-06133-1*) St Martin.

Roberts, D. F. & De Stefano, G. F., eds. Genetic Variation & Its Maintenance. (Society for the Study of Human Biology Symposium Ser.: No. 27). (Illus.). 304p. 1986. 64.95 (*0-521-33257-5*) Cambridge U Pr.

Roberts, D. F. & Sunderland, Eric, eds. Genetic Variation in Britain. (Symposia of the Society for the Study of Human Biology Ser.: Vol. 12). 314p. 1973. 36.00 (0-85066-062-9) Taylor & Francis.
Roberts, D. F., jt. ed. see Barron, S. L.
Roberts, D. F., tr. see Bernal, J. E.
Roberts, D. F., jt. ed. see Bittles, A. H.
Roberts, D. F., jt. ed. see Collins, K. J.
Roberts, D. F., jt. ed. see Hill, Allan G.
Roberts, D. F., et al, eds. Isolation, Migration & Health. (Society for the Study of Human Biology Symposium Ser.: No. 33). (Illus.). 300p. (C). 1992. 74.95 (0-521-41912-3) Cambridge U Pr.
Roberts, D. J., jt. auth. see Spurgeon, C. J.
Roberts, D. Jeanne. Taking Care of Caregivers: For Families & Others Who Care for People with Alzheimer's Disease & Other Forms of Dementia. (Illus.). 200p. (Orig.). 1991. pap. 14.95 (0-923521-09-7) Bull Pub.
Roberts, D. W., jt. auth. see Roberts, Dan W.
Roberts, Daffyd R., tr. see Serres, Michel, ed.
Roberts, Dan. Durez City Bonanza. large type ed. 1992. 19. 95 (0-7927-1204-8, Curley Lrg Print) Chivers N Amer.
Roberts, Darrell, ed. Human Factors. LC 91-75708. (Quality Instruction Materials Ser.). 272p. 1991. 44.00 (0-929355-18-0, M1591) Am Soc Ag Eng.
***Roberts, Dave.** Developing for the Internet with Winsock. 1995. pap. 39.99 (1-883577-42-X) Coriolis Grp.
— Elvis Presley. (CD Bks.). (Illus.). 120p. 1994. pap. 7.99 (1-886894-15-9, MBS Paperbk) Mus Bk Servs.
— PC Game Programming Explorer. 1994. pap. 34.95 (1-883577-07-1) Coriolis Grp.
— Pipe & Excavation Contracting. 400p. (Orig.). 1987. pap. 23.50 (0-934041-22-9) Craftsman.
Roberts, Dave, jt. auth. see Walker, Robin.
Roberts, David. Art & Enlightenment: Aesthetic Theory after Adorno. LC 90-35508. (Modern German Culture & Literature Ser.). xx, 250p. 1991. 35.00 (0-8032-3897-5) U of Nebr Pr.
— The Ba'th & the Creation of Modern Syria. LC 86-17745. 256p. 1987. text ed. 39.95 (0-312-06948-0) St Martin.
— David Roberts - The Early Climbs: Deborah & the Mountain of My Fear. LC 90-28126. (Illus.). 368p. 1991. pap. 16.95 (0-89886-270-1) Mountaineers.
— From an Antique Island. 1994. pap. 9.99 (0-517-11550-6) Random Hse Value.
— Jean Stafford: A Biography. 1988. 24.95 (0-316-74998-2) Little.
— The Ladies: Female Patronage of Restoration Drama. (Oxford English Monographs). 200p. 1989. 55.00 (0-19-811743-4) OUP.
— Moments of Doubt & Other Mountaineering Writings of David Roberts. LC 86-16357. 256p. (Orig.). 1986. pap. 12.95 (0-89886-118-7) Mountaineers.
— Once They Moved Like the Wind: Cochise, Geronimo, & the End of the Indian Wars. LC 93-7112. (Illus.). 320p. 1993. 24.00 (0-671-70221-1) S&S Trade.
— Once They Moved Like the Wind: Cochise, Geronimo, & the End of the Indian Wars. 1994. pap. 14.00 (0-671-88556-1, Fireside) S&S Trade.
Roberts, David & Thomson, Philip, eds. The Modern German Historical Novel: Paradigms, Problems, Perspectives. LC 89-18380. (Berg European Studies Ser.). 240p. 1991. 59.95 (0-85496-667-6) Berg Pubs.
Roberts, David, tr. see Boudroit, Jean.
Roberts, David, jt. auth. see Roberts, Clayton.
Roberts, David, jt. auth. see Washburn, Bradford.
***Roberts, David D.** Nothing but History: Reconstruction & Extremity after Metaphysics. LC 94-43786. 1995. 40.00 (0-520-20080-2) U CA Pr.
Roberts, David D. & Mecham, Robert P., eds. Cell Surface & Extracellular Glycoconjugates: Structure & Function. (Biology of Extracellular Matrix Ser.). (Illus.). 314p. 1993. text ed. 79.95 (0-12-589630-1) Acad Pr.
Roberts, David E. Psychotherapy & a Christian View of Man. LC 88-21391. 162p. 1990. reprint ed. text ed. 49. 75 (0-313-25326-9, RPSY, Greenwood Pr) Greenwood.
***Roberts, David L.** Sage Street: A Collection of Stories. LC 91-66153. 108p. (Orig.). (YA). 1991. pap. 6.95 (0-914767-20-8) Skyline West Pr.
Roberts, David L. & Roberts, Philip J. Wyoming Almanac. LC 86-80500. (Illus.). 376p. (Orig.). 1989. pap. text ed. 11.95 (0-914767-16-X) Skyline West Pr.
Roberts, David W., ed. see Allen, Timothy F. & Hoekstra, Thomas W.
Roberts, Debbie. Rejoice: A Biblical Study of the Dance. 212p. 1987. pap. 7.99 (0-938612-02-6) Revival Press.
— The Super Studio: The Guide to a Successful Dance Studio! (Illus.). 160p. (Orig.). 1992. pap. 14.95 (1-879260-07-7) Evanston Pub.
Roberts-DeGennaro, Maria & Weil, Marie, eds. Diversity & Development in Community Practice. LC 93-39428. (Journal of Community Practice). (Illus.). 144p. 1994. lib. bdg. 29.95 (1-56024-611-1); pap. text ed. 12.95 (1-56024-612-X) Haworth Pr.
Roberts, Delno, ed. see Halbert, D. S.
Roberts, Dennis. Islam: A Concise Introduction. LC 81-47845. 224p. 1982. pap. 7.95 (0-06-066880-6, CN 4026) Harper SF.
Roberts, Dennis C., ed. Designing Campus Activities to Foster a Sense of Community. LC 85-644751. (New Directions for Student Services Ser.: No. SS 48). 1989. 16.95 (1-55542-857-6) Jossey-Bass.
Roberts, Dennis L., 2nd, ed. Planning Urban Education: New Techniques to Transform Learning in the City. LC 73-160895. 384p. 1972. 34.95 (0-87778-024-2) Educ Tech Pubns.
Roberts, Dennis M. Data Analysis for the Social Sciences. 352p. (C). 1992. pap. text ed. 41.95 (0-8403-7583-2) Kendall-Hunt.
— Minitab: An Introduction for Business. 172p. 1992. spiral bd. 18.95 (0-8403-7447-X) Kendall-Hunt.
Roberts, Denton L. Able & Equal: A Gentle Path to Peace. 162p. 1987. 15.95 (0-9613559-0-5); pap. 9.95 (0-9613559-9-9) Human Esteem Pub.
Roberts, Derek. British Longcase Clocks. LC 89-64089. (Illus.). 400p. 1989. 95.00 (0-88740-230-5) Schiffer.
— British Skeleton Clocks. 272p. 1987. 79.50 (1-85149-059-0) Antique Collect.
— Carriage & Other Traveling Clocks. (Illus.). 368p. 1993. 99.99 (0-88740-454-5) Schiffer.
— Collector's Guide to Clocks. 1992. 12.98 (1-55521-778-8) Bk Sales Inc.
— Continental & American Skeleton Clocks. LC 89-62600. (Illus.). 288p. 1989. 79.95 (0-88740-182-1) Schiffer.
Roberts, Derrick P. & Smith, Nigel L. Radiographic Imaging: A Practical Approach. (Illus.). 368p. (Orig.). 1988. pap. write for info. (0-443-03061-8) Churchill.
— Radiographic Imaging: A Practical Approach. LC 94-4029. (Orig.). 1994. 52.00 (0-443-04397-3) Churchill.
Roberts, Diane. Faulkner & Southern Womanhood. LC 93-9957. 256p. (C). 1994. 35.00 (0-8203-1567-2) U of Ga Pr.
— For Women Only: Accept No Substitutes. Harlan, Roberta & Hamilton, Vivian, eds. (Illus.). 87p. (Orig.). 1995. pap. 7.00 (1-879619-12-1) East Hill Church.
— The Myth of Aunt Jemima: Representations of Race & Religion. LC 93-50574. 240p. 1994. 55.00 (0-415-04918-0, B4241, Routledge NY); pap. 15.95 (0-415-04919-9, B4245, Routledge NY) Routledge.
Roberts, Diane & Schroeder, Bonnie. Calc - Spreadsheet Planner: Lab Pack. (Illus.). 199.95 (1-56177-095-7, L394-3); 199.95 (1-56177-047-7, L194-3); disk 8.95 (1-56177-094-9, D394-3); Apple II 8.95 (1-56177-046-9, D194-3) CES Compu-Tech.
— Computer Applications: Calc - Spread Sheet Planner: Course Code S94-3. (Illus.). 81p. (gr. 8). 1989. reprint ed. pap. text ed. 8.95 (0-917531-56-6) CES Compu-Tech.
Roberts, Diane, jt. auth. see Hobbs, Betty C.
Roberts, Diane, jt. auth. see Mossman, Marilyn.
Roberts, Diane, et al. Calc - Spreadsheet Planner: Lab Pack. (Illus.). 1990. student ed, teacher ed 179.95 (1-56177-145-7, L494-3) CES Compu-Tech.
***Roberts, Diane, et al, eds.** Practical Food Microbiology. (Public Health Laboratory Service Publication Ser.). (Illus.). 250p. (C). Date not set. 49.95 (0-521-55196-X) Cambridge U Pr.
Roberts, Diane H. Down the Dirt Road. 47p. (Orig.). 1986. pap. 5.00 (0-932662-63-3) St Andrews NC.
Roberts, Dick. American Railroads: The Case for Nationalization. LC 80-80795. (Illus.). 1980. lib. bdg. 35. 00 (0-87348-601-3); pap. 11.95 (0-87348-600-5) Pathfinder NY.
Roberts-Dominguez, Jan. The Mustard Book. LC 93-19559. (Illus.). 160p. 1993. text ed. 20.00 (0-02-603641-X) Macmillan.
— Sandwich Cuisine - Oregon Style. Battrick, Craig J., ed. LC 90-82414. (Illus.). 188p. 1991. pap. 15.95 (0-9626441-0-2) Drift Creek Pr.
Roberts, Don. Prayers for the Young Child. 1981. pap. 7.99 (0-570-04051-5, 56-1717) Concordia.
— Rap to Live By. 1993. 8.95 (1-878901-55-9) Hampton Roads Pub Co.
— Two Hundred Twenty-two BASIC Computer Programs for Home, School & Office. 288p. 1984. 18.95 (0-86668-039-X) ARCsoft.
***Roberts, Don & Boyle, Dierdre, eds.** Mediamobiles: Views from the Road. fac. ed. LC 79-18488. (Public Library Reporter: No. 19). 126p. 1994. pap. 36.00 (0-7837-7321-8, 2047248) Bks Demand.
Roberts, Don D. Existential Graphs of Charles S. Peirce. LC 73-85776. (Approaches to Semiotics Ser.: Vol. 27). (Illus.). 168p. 1973. text ed. 41.55 (90-279-2523-2) Mouton.
Roberts, Don W. Renters' Revenge: (A Landlord's Nightmare) LC 91-65693. (Illus.). 112p. (Orig.). 1991. pap. 6.95 (0-9629979-0-0) Tower Pub GA.
Roberts, Donald. Grace: God's Special Gift. (J). (gr. 1-4). 1982. pap. 3.99 (0-570-04060-4, 56-1363) Concordia.
Roberts, Donald L. The Practicing Church. LC 01-67318. 100p. (Orig.). 1981. pap. 2.99 (0-87509-303-5) Chr Pubns.
Roberts, Donald L., ed. Remedies, Potions & Razzmatazz. (Illus.). 510p. (Orig.). 1991. reprint ed. pap. 15.95 (0-9628676-0-8) Nostalgia CA.
Roberts, Donovan. Stubborn Ounces - Just Scales. 1992. pap. 14.95 (1-55673-417-4, 7900) CSS OH.
Roberts, Doreen. Only a Dream Away. (Silhouette Intimate Moments Ser.). 1993. mass mkt. 3.50 (0-373-07513-8, 5-07513-0) Silhouette.
— So Little Time. (Intimate Moments Ser.). 1995. mass mkt. 3.75 (0-373-07653-3, 1-07653-8) Silhouette.
— Where There's Smoke. 1994. 3.50 (0-373-07567-7) Silhouette.
Roberts, Doris L., jt. ed. see Krout, Anne M.
Roberts, Dorothy. Women, Pregnancy & Substance Abuse. (Law & Pregnancy Ser.). 21p. (Orig.). (C). 1991. pap. 15. 00 (1-877966-09-6) Ctr Women Policy.
Roberts, Duane F. How to Lease Office Space Profitably. rev. ed. 1981. 42.95 (0-686-46409-5) Inst Real Estate.
— Marketing & Leasing of Office Space. rev. ed. (Illus.). 448p. 1986. 44.95 (0-912104-86-4, 952) Inst Real Estate.
Roberts, E. Vegetable Materia Medica of India & Ceylon. 437p. (C). 1984. 60.00 (0-685-22358-2, Scientific) St Mut.
Roberts, E., et al, eds. GABA in Nervous System Function. 1975. 39.50 (0-7204-7567-8, North Holland) Elsevier.
Roberts, E. C. English, Indiana: Memories of Main Street. LC 91-6301. (Illus.). 160p. 1991. 17.95 (0-253-35032-8) Ind U Pr.
Roberts, E. H., ed. Viability of Seeds. LC 73-39736. (Illus.). 448p. (C). 1972. 39.95 (0-8156-5033-7) Syracuse U Pr.
Roberts, E. Kirk. Principles of Physical Chemistry. (C). 1984. pap. text ed. 51.00 (0-205-08011-1, H80112); teacher ed 7.00 (0-685-07782-9, H80120) P-H.
Roberts, E. M. A Flying Fighter: An American Above the Lines in France. 352p. 1989. pap. 19.95 (0-947898-98-0) Stackpole.
Roberts, E. Stanton, ed. Reprints of Welsh Manuscripts, 7 vols., Set. Incl. Vol. 1. Llanstephan, Ms. 6. LC 78-72656. 24.50 (0-404-18241-0); Vol. 2. Peniarth, Ms. 67. LC 78-72656. 24.50 (0-404-18242-9); Vol. 3. Peniarth, Ms. 57. LC 78-72656. 24.50 (0-404-18243-7); Vol. 4. Peniarth, Ms. 76. LC 78-72656. 24.50 (0-404-18244-5); Vol. 5. Peniarth, Ms. 53. LC 78-72656. 24.50 (0-404-18245-3); Vol. 6. Peniarth, Ms. 49. LC 78-72656. 24.50 (0-404-18246-1); Vol. 7. Gwyneddon, Ms. 3. LC 78-72656. 24.50 (0-404-18247-X); LC 78-72656. (Celtic Language & Literature Ser.: Goidelic & Brythonic). reprint ed. 171.50 (0-404-18240-2) AMS Pr.
Roberts, Earl J. Unpublished Activities of World War II. LC 87-61783. (Illus.). 341p. 1988. 13.55 (0-317-89751-9) Scanly Pr.
Roberts, Eddie, ed. see Briggs, Frank M., Sr.
***Roberts, Edgar V.** Writing about Literature. 8th ed. LC 94-27498. 368p. 1994. pap. text ed. write for info. (0-13-097585-0) P-H.
— Writing about Literature. 8th ed. LC 94-30182. 256p. 1994. pap. text ed. write for info. (0-13-097593-1) P-H.
— Writing Themes about Literature. 7th ed. 400p. 1990. pap. text ed. 18.67 (0-13-971052-3) P-H.
— Writing Themes about Literature, Brief Edition. 7th ed. 240p. (C). 1990. pap. text ed. write for info. (0-13-971060-4) P-H.
Roberts, Edgar V. & Jacobs, Henry E. Fiction: An Introduction to Reading & Writing. 3rd ed. 832p. (C). 1991. pap. text ed. write for info. (0-13-319260-1) P-H.
— Literature: An Introduction to Reading & Writing. 4th ed. LC 94-20463. 1724p. 1994. text ed. write for info. (0-13-097510-9) P-H.
Roberts, Edgar V., ed. see Fielding, Henry.
Roberts, Edgar V., ed. see Gay, John.
Roberts, Edmund B. & Onishenko, Gary. Fundamentals of Men's Fashion Design: A Guide to Casual Clothes. 2nd ed. (Illus.). 300p. (C). 1985. text ed. 23.50 (0-685-57963-8) Fairchild.
Roberts, Edward, et al, eds. Biomedical Innovation. (Illus.). 368p. 1982. 40.00 (0-262-18103-7) MIT Pr.
Roberts, Edward B. Entrepreneurs in High Technology: Lessons from MIT & Beyond. (Illus.). 400p. 1991. 30.00 (0-19-506704-5) OUP.
Roberts, Edward B., ed. Generating Technological Innovation. (Executive Bookshelf-Sloan Managament Review Ser.). (Illus.). 316p. 1987. 25.00 (0-19-505023-1) OUP.
— Managerial Applications of System Dynamics. 562p. (C). reprint ed. pap. text ed. 25.00 (0-915299-59-3) Prod Press.
Roberts, Edward F. Ireland in America. LC 74-22756. (Labor Movement in Fiction & Non-Fiction Ser.). 1976. reprint ed. 39.50 (0-404-58509-4) AMS Pr.
Roberts, Edwards. The City of Denver, 1888. Jones, William R., ed. (Illus.). 24p. 1977. reprint ed. pap. 3.95 (0-89646-006-1) Vistabooks.
Roberts, Elaine & Templeton, Betty. Home Care Services. (Skills for Caring Ser.). (Illus.). 48p. 1992. spiral bd., pap. 12.00 (0-443-04623-9) Churchill.
Roberts, Elda M. The Stubborn Fisherman. 2nd ed. LC 86-71820. (Illus.). 234p. 1987. 20.95 (0-9617139-1-7); pap. 12.95 (0-9617139-0-9) Creighton Pub.
Roberts, Elfed V., et al. Historical Dictionary of Hong Kong & Macau. LC 92-20816. (Asian Historical Dictionaries Ser.: No. 10). (Illus.). 406p. 1992. 49.50 (0-8108-2574-0) Scarecrow.
Roberts, Elizabeth. Earth Prayers from Around the World. 1991. pap. 15.00 (0-06-250746-X) Harper SF.
— Georgia, Armenia, & Azerbaijan. LC 92-2242. (Former Soviet States Ser.). (Illus.). 32p. (J). (gr. 4-6). 1992. lib. bdg. 15.40 (1-56294-309-X) Millbrook Pr.
— Speech Communication: One Hundred Course Manual. 160p. (C). 1992. spiral bd. 12.95 (0-8403-7033-4) Kendall-Hunt.
— Women & Families: An Oral History, 1940-1970. (Family, Sexuality & Social Relations in Past Times Ser.). (Illus.). 272p. 1995. 54.95 (0-631-19612-9); pap. 21.95 (0-631-19613-7) Blackwell Pubs.
Roberts, Elizabeth & Amidon, Elias, eds. Earth Prayers: From Around the Word, 365 Prayers, Poems, & Invocations for Honoring the Earth. rev. ed. 480p. 1993. 22.00 (0-06-250888-1) Harper SF.
— Honoring the Earth: A Journal of New Earth Prayers. 256p. 1993. 16.00 (0-06-250738-9) Harper SF.
Roberts, Elizabeth, jt. ed. see Amidon, Elias.
Roberts, Elizabeth, tr. see Rost, Yuri.
Roberts, Elizabeth M. The Great Meadow. LC 76-12120. 1980. reprint ed. 27.50 (0-404-15235-X) AMS Pr.
— The Great Meadow. (Southern Classics Ser.). 356p. 1992. reprint ed. pap. 10.95 (1-879941-07-4) J S Sanders.
— The Haunted Mirror. LC 76-2121. reprint ed. 39.50 (0-404-15236-8) AMS Pr.
— Not by Strange Gods. LC 76-12119. reprint ed. 39.50 (0-404-15237-6) AMS Pr.
Roberts, Elizabeth Madox. Black Is My Truelove's Hair. Hardwick, Elizabeth, ed. LC 76-51675. (Rediscovered Fiction by American Women Ser.). 1977. reprint ed. lib. bdg. 33.95 (0-405-10053-1) Ayer.
Roberts, Ellis A. Sequential Data in Biological Experiments: An Introduction for Research Workers. (Illus.). 184p. 1991. 67.50 (0-412-41410-4, A6307) Chapman & Hall.
Roberts, Ellis H. New York: The Planting & the Growth of the Empire State, 2 vols. LC 72-3763. (American Commonwealths Ser.: Nos. 8-9). reprint ed. 76.50 (0-404-57221-9) AMS Pr.
— New York: The Planting & the Growth of the Empire State, 2 vols., Set. 1993. reprint ed. lib. bdg. 99.00 (0-7812-5197-4) Rprt Serv.
Roberts, Ellis W. Along the Susquehanna. 128p. 1980. 7.95 (0-686-28856-4) Colwyn-Tangno.
— The Breaker Whistle Blows: Mining Disasters & Labor Leaders in the Anthracite Region. LC 85-147902. (Illus.). 166p. 1984. 12.95 (0-917445-01-5) Anthracite.
Roberts, Ellwood. Biographical Annals of Montgomery County, Pennsylvania, 2 vols., Set. (Illus.). 1994. reprint ed. lib. bdg. 110.00 (0-8328-4009-2) Higginson Bk Co.
Roberts, Eric. Thinking Recursively. 179p. 1986. Net. pap. text ed. write for info. (0-471-81652-3) Wiley.
— Welzenbach's Climbs. LC 81-80502. (Illus.). 270p. 1981. 14.95 (0-89886-018-0) Mountaineers.
Roberts, Eric S. The Art & Science of C: An Introduction to Computer Science. LC 94-16744. (Illus.). 700p. (C). 1995. pap. text ed. 45.25 (0-201-54322-2) Addison-Wesley.
Roberts, Ernest H. Treasures from Near Eastern Looms. LC 81-68474. (Illus.). 1981. pap. 10.00 (0-916606-02-3) Bowdoin Coll.
Roberts, Eugene, et al, eds. GABA in Nervous System Function. LC 74-21983. 576p. 1976. 86.00 (0-89004-043-5) Raven.
Roberts, Evan, jt. auth. see Penn-Lewis, Jessie.
Roberts, F., et al. Reliability of Computer & Communication Networks. LC 91-9953. (DIMACS Ser.: Vol. 5). 259p. 1991. 45.00 (0-8218-6592-7, DIMACS-5) Am Math.
Roberts, F. Barry. Confusion to Confidence: Informed Parenting. (Illus.). 210p. 1988. 16.95 (0-9620695-0-7) F B Roberts.
Roberts, F. M. Tales of a Dakota Pilot, the Way It Was, 1929-1937. (Illus.). 112p. 1991. pap. 8.95 (0-912746-09-2) F M Roberts.
Roberts, F. W., ed. see Lawrence, D. H.
Roberts, F. Warren, ed. see Lawrence, D. H.
***Roberts, F. X. & Rhine, C. D., eds.** James A. Michener: A Checklist of His Works, with a Selected, Annotated Bibliography. LC 94-42118. (Bibliographies & Indexes in American Literature Ser.: No.20). 152p. 1995. text ed. 49.95 (0-313-29453-4, Greenwood Pr) Greenwood.
Roberts, Fitzmahan & Associates Staff, jt. auth. see Developmental Research.
Roberts, Frances J. Angel in the Fire. 1979. pap. 4.25 (0-932814-31-X) Kings Farspan.
— Christmas Reflections. 1982. pap. 3.25 (0-932814-28-X) Kings Farspan.
— Come Away, My Beloved. 1970. 13.50 (0-932814-01-8); pap. 8.95 (0-932814-02-6) Kings Farspan.
— Come Away, My Beloved. deluxe ed. 1970. 9.95 (0-932814-05-0) Kings Farspan.
— Dialogues with God. 1968. 9.50 (0-932814-07-7); pap. 6.50 (0-932814-08-5) Kings Farspan.
— Launch out! 1964. 3.25 (0-932814-21-2) Kings Farspan.
— Learn to Reign. 1963. 3.25 (0-932814-22-0) Kings Farspan.
— Listen to the Silence. 1964. 3.25 (0-932814-23-9) Kings Farspan.
— Living Water. 1965. 3.25 (0-932814-20-4) Kings Farspan.
— Lovest Thou Me? 1967. 3.25 (0-932814-19-0) Kings Farspan.
— Make Haste, My Beloved. 1978. 10.25 (0-932814-25-5); pap. 7.50 (0-932814-26-3) Kings Farspan.
— On the Highroad of Surrender. 1973. 10.25 (0-932814-14-X); pap. 7.50 (0-932814-15-8) Kings Farspan.
— Progress of Another Pilgrim. 1970. 10.25 (0-932814-10-7); pap. 7.50 (0-932814-11-5) Kings Farspan.
— Sounding of the Trumpet. 1966. 3.25 (0-932814-24-7) Kings Farspan.
— When the Latch Is Lifted. 1970. 4.25 (0-932814-18-2) Kings Farspan.
***Roberts, Frank, Jr.** Archeological Remains in the Whitewater District, Eastern Arizona. (Bureau of American Ethnology Bulletins Ser.). 276p. 1995. lib. bdg. 89.00 (0-7812-4121-9); lib. bdg. 79.00 (0-7812-4126-X) Rprt Serv.
Roberts, Frank. Is God Limited? 1993. 8.95 (0-8062-4561-1) Carlton.
***Roberts, Frank, Jr.** River Basin Survey Papers, No. 25. (Bureau of American Ethnology Bulletins Ser.). 447p. 1995. lib. bdg. 109.00 (0-7812-4182-0) Rprt Serv.
— River Basin Surveys Papers, Nos. 9-14. (Bureau of American Ethnology Bulletins Ser.). 392p. 1995. lib. bdg. write for info. (0-7812-4169-3) Rprt Serv.
— River Basin Surveys Papers, Nos. 15-20. (Bureau of American Ethnology Bulletins Ser.). 337p. 1995. lib. bdg. 99.00 (0-7812-4176-6) Rprt Serv.
— River Basin Surveys Papers, Nos. 21-24. (Bureau of American Ethnology Bulletins Ser.). 337p. 1995. lib. bdg. 99.00 (0-7812-4179-0) Rprt Serv.
— River Basin Surveys Papers, Nos. 26-32. (Bureau of American Ethnology Bulletins Ser.). 344p. 1995. lib. bdg. 99.00 (0-7812-4185-5) Rprt Serv.
— River Basin Surveys Papers, Nos. 33-38. (Bureau of American Ethnology Bulletins Ser.). 405p. 1995. lib. bdg. 109.00 (0-7812-4189-8) Rprt Serv.
— Ruins at Kiatuthlanna, Eastern Arizona. (Bureau of American Ethnology Bulletins Ser.). 195p. 1995. lib. bdg. 79.00 (0-7812-4100-6) Rprt Serv.
— Shabik'eshchee Village: A Late Basket Maker Site in the Chaco Canyon, New Mexico. (Bureau of American Ethnology Bulletins Ser.). 164p. 1995. lib. bdg. 79.00 (0-7812-4092-1) Rprt Serv.
***Roberts, Frank, Jr., ed.** Early Pueblo Ruins in the Piedra District, Southwestern Colorado. (Bureau of American Ethnology Bulletins Ser.). 190p. 1995. lib. bdg. 79.00 (0-7812-4096-4) Rprt Serv.

R

An Asterisk (*) at the beginning of an entry indicates that the title is appearing in BIP for the first time.

Roberts, Frank, ed. Obituaries for the London Times, 1961-1970. 951p. 1977. text ed. 235.00 (*0-313-28138-6*, ROK/, Greenwood Pr) Greenwood.
— Songs of Joyful Praise. 1975. pap. 2.00 (*0-88027-060-8*) Firm Foun Pub.
***Roberts, Frank, Jr., ed.** Village of the Great Kivas on the Zuni Reservation, New Mexico. (Bureau of American Ethnology Bulletins Ser.). 197p. 1995. lib. bdg. 79.00 (*0-7812-4111-1*) Rprt Serv.
Roberts, Frank C., ed. Obituaries from the London Times, 1971-1975. 647p. 1978. text ed. 175.00 (*0-313-28137-8*, ROG/, Greenwood Pr) Greenwood.
— Obituaries from The Times, 1951-1960. 896p. 1979. text ed. 195.00 (*0-313-28136-X*, ROE/, Greenwood Pr) Greenwood.
Roberts, Frank H. Ceramic Sequence in the Chaco Canyon, New Mexico, & Its Relation to the Cultures of the San Juan Basin. LC 91-20404. (Evolution of North American Indians Ser.). 350p. 1991. 30.00 (*0-8240-2513-X*) Garland.
Roberts, Fred M. Darkroom Logbook for Photographers. 94p. 1973. pap. 9.50 (*0-912746-04-1*) F M Roberts.
— Guide to the Ricoh Hi-Color 35 & Marine Capsule. (Illus.). (Orig.). 1972. pap. 4.50 (*0-912746-05-X*) F M Roberts.
— Living With a Hearing Problem: Coping Strategies & Devices for the Hearing Impaired. (Illus.). 184p. 1990. pap. 16.95 (*0-912746-10-6*) F M Roberts.
Roberts, Fred S. Applied Combinatorics. (Illus.). 672p. (C). 1984. text ed. 56.00 (*0-685-07641-5*) P-H.
— Graph Theory & Its Applications to Problems of Society. LC 78-6277. (CBMS-NSF Regional Conference Ser.: No. 29). v, 122p. (Orig.). 1978. pap. text ed. 25.50 (*0-89871-026-X*) Soc Indus-Appl Math.
Roberts, Fred S., ed. Applications of Combinatorics & Graph Theory to the Biological & Social Sciences. (IMA Volumes in Mathematics & Its Applications Ser.: Vol. 17). (Illus.). ix, 345p. 1989. 42.00 (*0-387-97046-0*, 2990) Spr-Verlag.
Roberts, Fred S., et al, eds. Applications of Discrete Mathematics. LC 87-51542. (Proceedings in Applied Mathematics Ser.: No. 33). x, 230p. 1988. 40.75 (*0-89871-219-X*) Soc Indus-Appl Math.
Roberts, Fulton. Disney's Aladdin: Jasmine's Magic Charm. (Golden Book & Necklace Ser.). (Illus.). 32p. (J). 1994. write for info. (*0-307-16154-4*, Golden Bks) Western Pub.
Roberts, G. & Cary, R. Tool Steels. 4th ed. 820p. 1980. 160.00 (*0-87170-096-4*) ASM.
Roberts, G., jt. auth. see Roberts, R.
Roberts, G. C., ed. see Burgen, A. S.
Roberts, G. C., jt. auth. see Burgen, A. S.
Roberts, G. C., jt. ed. see Burgen, A. S.
Roberts, G. G. & Pitt, C. W., eds. Langmuir-Blodgett Films, 1982. (Thin Films Science & Technology Ser.: Vol. 3). 330p. 1983. 102.75 (*0-444-42173-4*) Elsevier.
Roberts, G. Humphreys, tr. see Brod, Max.
Roberts, G. N., jt. ed. see Pourzanjani, M. M.
Roberts, Gail, jt. auth. see Carothers, Steven.
Roberts, Gail C. & Guttormson, Lorraine. A Leader's Guide to You & Your Family, You & School, You & Stress. 64p. (Orig.). 1990. teacher ed. 6.95 (*0-915793-27-X*) Free Spirit Pub.
— You & School: A Survival Guide for Adolescence. Wallner, Rosemary, ed. (Self-Help for Kids Ser.). 120p. (Orig.). (YA). (gr. 4-8). 1990. pap. 8.95 (*0-915793-25-3*) Free Spirit Pub.
— You & Stress: A Survival Guide for Adolescence. Wallner, Rosemary, ed. (Self-Help for Kids Ser.). 128p. (Orig.). (YA). (gr. 4-8). 1990. pap. 8.95 (*0-915793-26-1*) Free Spirit Pub.
— You & Your Family: A Survival Guide for Adolescence. Espeland, Pamela, ed. (Self-Help for Kids Ser.). 112p. (Orig.). (YA). (gr. 4-8). 1990. pap. 8.95 (*0-915793-24-5*) Free Spirit Pub.
Roberts, Gareth. The Faerie Queene. (Open Guides to Literature Ser.). 144p. 1992. 75.00 (*0-335-09036-2*, Open Univ Pr); pap. 22.00 (*0-335-09037-0*, Open Univ Pr) Taylor & Francis.
— The Mirror of Alchemy: Alchemical Ideas & Images in Manuscripts & Books from Antiquity to the 17th Century. (Illus.). 128p. 1995. 55.00 (*0-8020-0710-4*); pap. 24.95 (*0-8020-7660-2*) U of Toronto Pr.
— The Romance of Crime. (Dr. Who Ser.). (Illus.). Date not set. pap. 5.95 (*0-426-20435-2*, London Bridge) Genl Dist Srvs.
***Roberts, Gareth W. & Polak, Julia M., eds.** Molecular Neuropathology. (Postgraduate Medical Science Ser.: No. 4). (Illus.). 190p. (C). 1995. pap. write for info. (*0-521-42558-1*) Cambridge U Pr.
***Roberts, Gary B.** Ancestors of American Presidents: First Definitive Edition. 1995. 35.00 (*0-936124-19-9*) C Boyer.
— Notable Kin. 300p. Date not set. write for info. (*0-936124-17-2*) C Boyer.
— The Royal Descents of Five Hundred Immigrants: To the American Colonies or the United States. 700p. 1993. 45.00 (*0-8063-1395-1*) Genealog Pub.
Roberts, Gary B., intro. & sel. Rhode Island Families, Genealogies of, from the New England Historical & Genealogical Register, 2 vols., Set. 1989. 95.00 (*0-8063-1218-1*, 4883) Genealog Pub.
Roberts, Gary B. & Reitwiesner, William A. American Ancestors & Cousins of the Princess of Wales. LC 84-81095. (Illus.). 194p. 1984. 14.95 (*0-8063-1085-5*) Genealog Pub.
Roberts, Gary L. Death Comes for the Chief Justice: The Slough-Rynerson Quarrel & Political Violence in New Mexico. (Illus.). 288p. 1990. 24.95 (*0-87081-212-2*) Univ Pr Colo.
Roberts, Gary L., jt. ed. see Henderson, Harold P.
Roberts, Gary R., jt. auth. see Weiler, Paul C.
Roberts, Garyn G. A Cent a Story: The Best from Ten Detective Aces. LC 86-70384. 197p. 1986. 22.95 (*0-87972-353-X*); pap. 10.95 (*0-87972-354-8*) Bowling Green Univ.
— Dick Tracy & American Culture: Morality & Mythology, Text & Context. LC 92-56687. (Illus.). 350p. 1993. lib. bdg. 45.00 (*0-89950-880-4*) McFarland & Co.
Roberts, Garyn G., et al, eds. Old Sleuth's Freaky Female Detectives. LC 89-85966. (Dime Novels Ser.). 118p. 1990. 31.95 (*0-87972-475-7*) Bowling Green Univ.
Roberts, Gemma. Unamuno: Coincidencias y Afinidades Kierkegaardianas. LC 86-60967. 144p. 1986. pap. 30.00 (*0-89295-041-2*) Society Sp & Sp-Am.
Roberts, Gemma, ed. Analisis Existencial de Abaddon, el Exterminador de Ernesto Sabato. 98p. 1990. pap. 15.00 (*0-89295-061-7*) Society Sp & Sp-Am.
Roberts, Gene, Jr., jt. auth. see Nelson, Jack.
Roberts, Geoffrey. Party Politics in Germany. (New Germany Ser.). 220p. 1993. write for info. (*1-85567-029-1*, Pub. by Pinter Pubs UK) St Martin.
— The Soviet Union & the Origins of Second World War: Russo-German Relations & the Road to War. LC 94-46862. (Making of the Twentieth Century Ser.). 1995. write for info. (*0-312-12603-4*) St Martin.
— The Unholy Alliance: Stalin's Pact with Hitler. LC 89-15456. 314p. 1990. 39.95 (*0-253-35117-0*) Ind U Pr.
Roberts, Geoffrey & Edwards, Alistair. A New Dictionary of Political Analysis. LC 91-26692. 192p. 1991. pap. 15.95 (*0-340-52860-5*, A6837, Pub. by E Arnold UK) Routledge Chapman & Hall.
***Roberts, George.** Dire Wolf: And Other Fearful & Fanciful Works by Sculptor George Roberts. Jacobson, Robert, ed. LC 95-7063. 152p. (Orig.). 1995. pap. 25.00 (*0-89301-182-7*) U of Idaho Pr.
— Night Visits to a Wolf's Howl. 1979. 12.50 (*0-933114-03-6*); pap. 3.50 (*0-933114-02-8*) Oyster Pr.
— Scrut. LC 82-81349. 64p. 1983. pap. 4.00 (*0-930100-10-7*) Holy Cow.
Roberts, George & Roberts, Jan. Discover Historic California. rev. ed. Ping, April G. & Nordhues, Robin, eds. LC 94-76113. (Illus.). 560p. 1994. pap. 12.95 (*0-935182-74-8*) Gem Guides Bk.
Roberts, George, tr. see Evdokimov, F. E.
Roberts, George, ed. see Yonge, Walter.
Roberts, George C. Paul M. Butler: Hoosier Politician & National Political Leader. LC 87-6275. (Illus.). 210p. (Orig.). (C). 1987. pap. text ed. 22.50 (*0-8191-6296-5*) U Pr of Amer.
Roberts, George O. The Anguish of Third World Independence: The Sierra Leone Experience. LC 81-48679. (Illus.). (Orig.). 1982. pap. text ed. 34.50 (*0-8191-2396-X*) U Pr of Amer.
Roberts, George S. Historic Towns of the Connecticut River Valley. (Illus.). 494p. 1992. reprint ed. pap. 30.00 (*1-55613-614-5*) Heritage Bk.
— Old Schenectady (N. Y.) (Illus.). 292p. 1994. reprint ed. lib. bdg. 35.00 (*0-8328-4352-0*) Higginson Bk Co.
***Roberts, George W., ed.** Quality Planning, Control & Improvement in Research & Development. LC 94-39690. (Quality & Reliability Ser.: Vol. 44). 356p. 1994. 99.75 (*0-8247-9585-7*) Dekker.
Roberts, Gerald. Gerard Manley Hopkins: A Literary Life. LC 93-15981. 1994. text ed. 39.95 (*0-312-10174-0*) St Martin.
Roberts, Gerald, ed. Gerard Manley Hopkins. 448p. 1987. 88.50 (*0-7102-0414-0*, 04140, RKP) Routledge.
Roberts, Gillian. Caught Dead in Philadelphia. 1988. mass mkt. 4.95 (*0-345-35340-4*) Ballantine.
— How I Spent My Summer Vacation. LC 94-9394. 240p. 1994. 20.00 (*0-345-38595-0*) Ballantine.
— How I Spent My Summer Vacation. 1995. pap. 5.99 (*0-345-38594-2*) Ballantine.
— I'd Rather Be in Philadelphia. LC 91-58641. 224p. 1992. 17.50 (*0-345-37781-8*, Ballantine Trade) Ballantine.
— I'd Rather Be in Philadelphia. 1993. mass mkt. 4.99 (*0-345-37782-6*) Ballantine.
— In the Dead of Summer. LC 95-7627. 224p. 1995. 21.00 (*0-345-39136-5*) Ballantine.
— Philly Stakes. 1990. mass mkt. 4.99 (*0-345-36266-7*) Ballantine.
Roberts, Gillian & Foster, Alan D. With Friends Like These... LC 92-97480. 256p. 1994. mass mkt. 4.99 (*0-345-37784-2*) Ballantine.
Roberts, Glenda S. Staying on the Line: Blue-Collar Women in Contemporary Japan. LC 93-27346. 1994. text ed. 36.00 (*0-8248-1531-9*); pap. text ed. 16.95 (*0-8248-1579-3*) UH Pr.
Roberts, Gloria A. A Family Planning Library Manual. 5th enl. rev. ed. LC 93-84534. (Illus.). 148p. (Orig.). 1994. pap. text ed. 15.00 (*0-934586-72-1*) Plan Parent.
Roberts, Gloria A., comp. Small Library in Family Planning. 5th ed. LC 93-85194. 40p. 1993. pap. write for info. (*0-934586-74-8*) Plan Parent.
Roberts, Glyn. The Most Powerful Man in the World: Sir Henry Deterding. 1981. lib. bdg. 75.00 (*0-686-71632-9*) Revisionist Pr.
— The Most Powerful Man in the World: The Life of Sir Henri Deterding. LC 75-6484. (History & Politics of Oil Ser.). 448p. 1976. reprint ed. 27.50 (*0-88355-301-5*) Hyperion Conn.
Roberts, Glyn C., ed. Motivation in Sport & Exercise. LC 91-22864. (Illus.). 288p. (Orig.). 1992. text ed. 34.00x (*0-87322-345-4*, BROB0345) Human Kinetics.
— Motivation in Sport & Exercise. LC 91-22864. (Illus.). 288p. 1992. pap. text ed. write for info. (*0-87322-876-6*, BROB0876) Human Kinetics.
Roberts, Glyn C., ed. see North American Society for the Psychology of Sport & Physical Activity Staff.
Roberts, Glyn C., et al. Learning Experiences in Sport Psychology. LC 85-24845. 152p. 1986. spiral bd. 22.00x (*0-87322-042-0*, BROB0042) Human Kinetics.
— Social Science of Play, Games & Sport: Learning Experiences. LC 79-89695. 110p. reprint ed. pap. 31.40 (*0-317-55492-1*, 2029532) Bks Demand.
Roberts, Godfrey, ed. Population Policy: Contemporary Issues. LC 89-36160. 240p. 1990. text ed. 55.00 (*0-275-93039-4*, C3039, Praeger Pubs) Greenwood.
***Roberts-Goodson, R. Bruce.** Spray: The Ultimate Cruising Boat. (Illus.). 224p. 1995. 29.95 (*0-924486-87-2*) Sheridan.
Roberts, Gordon, jt. auth. see Viscione, Jerry A.
Roberts, Gordon C., ed. NMR of Macromolecules: A Practical Approach. LC 93-17466. (Practical Approach Ser.: Vol. 134). (Illus.). 320p. 1993. 88.00 (*0-19-963225-1*, IRL Pr); pap. 48.00 (*0-19-963224-3*, IRL Pr) OUP.
***Roberts, Gordon W. & Lu, Albert K.** Analog Signal Generation for Built-in-Self-Test of Mixed-Signal Integrated Circuits. LC 95-989. (International Engineering & Computer Science Ser., Vol. 312; Analog Circuits & Signal Processing: 312). 136p. (C). 1995. lib. bdg. 75.00 (*0-7923-9564-6*) Kluwer Ac.
Roberts, Grace S., tr. see Hunt, Gladys.
Roberts, Graeme, comp. Computerised Reservations System Words & Phrases. (Illus.). 150p. 1991. pap. 24.95 (*1-875114-19-X*, Blckstone AT) W W Gaunt.
Roberts-Gray, Cynthia, jt. ed. see Conrad, Kendon J.
Roberts, Gregory & Roberts, Mark E. American Ancestors of Stephen. (Illus.). write for info. (*0-9616192-1-X*) Roberts CA.
Roberts, Gwyneth, jt. ed. see Griffiths, Aled.
Roberts, H. Forest Insects in Nigeria. 1969. 45.00 (*0-85074-006-1*) St Mut.
— Homeopathic Medicine: Principles & Art of Cure. 1974. lib. bdg. 250.00 (*0-685-51361-0*) Revisionist Pr.
— Nostradamus: Prophesies. 15.00 (*0-685-22062-1*) Wehman.
Roberts, H., jt. auth. see Wallis, W.
Roberts, H. E., et al, eds. Reports on the Iconclass Workshop, November 1987 at Santa Monica, CA: A Special Issue of the Journal Visual Resources. x, 70p. 1988. text ed. 24.00 (*2-88124-371-1*) Gordon & Breach.
— Visual Resources, Vol. IV, No. 3: A Special Issue of the Journal Visual Resources. viii, 90p. 1987. text ed. 37.00 (*2-88124-370-3*) Gordon & Breach.
Roberts, H. H., jt. ed. see Doyle, L. J.
Roberts, H. J. Aspartame (NutraSweet) Is It Safe? LC 89-81086. 328p. 1992. pap. 11.95 (*0-914783-58-0*) Charles.
— Aspartame (NutraSweet) Is It Safe? LC 89-81086. 328p. 1990. text ed. 19.95 (*0-914783-37-8*) Charles.
— Defense Against Alzheimer's Disease: A Rational Blueprint for Prevention. LC 93-86995. (Illus.). 236p. 1995. 27.95 (*1-884243-00-2*) Sunshine Sentinel.
— Is Vasectomy Safe? Medical, Public Health, & Legal Implications. (Illus.). 1978. 16.95 (*0-933064-00-4*) Sunshine Acad.
— Is Vasectomy Worth the Risk? A Physician's Case Against Vasectomania. LC 92-64348. (Illus.). 125p. 1993. pap. 16.95 (*0-9633260-2-3*); digital audio 19.95 (*0-9633260-3-1*) Sunshine Sentinel.
— The Medical Risks of Vitamin E "Therapy" 137p. 1994. audio 19.95 (*0-9633260-5-8*) Sunshine Sentinel.
— Sweet'ner Dearest: Bittersweet Vignettes about Aspartame (NutraSweet) LC 92-64347. (Illus.). 300p. 1992. pap. 19.95 (*0-9633260-1-5*); audio 19.95 (*0-9633260-0-7*) Sunshine Sentinel.
— Vitamin E: Is It Safe? LC 93-85653. (Illus.). 130p. 1994. pap. 17.95 (*0-9633260-8-2*) Sunshine Sentinel.
— West Palm Beach: Centennial Reflections: Including "The Social Event of the Century" LC 94-68705. (Illus.). 300p. 1994. 25.95 (*1-884243-02-9*) Sunshine Sentinel.
Roberts, Hadley B. Birds of East Central Idaho. (Illus.). 128p. (Orig.). (C). 1993. pap. text ed. 9.95 (*0-9634903-0-3*) H B Roberts.
Roberts, Harold R., jt. ed. see High, Katherine A.
Roberts, Harold S. Roberts' Dictionary of Industrial Relations. rev. ed. 615p. reprint ed. pap. 175.30 (*0-685-15905-1*, 2026798) Bks Demand.
Roberts, Harry. The Basic Essentials of Backpacking. LC 88-34802. (Basic Essentials Ser.). (Illus.). 72p. (Orig.). 1989. pap. 5.99 (*0-934802-44-0*) ICS Bks.
— The Basic Essentials of Canoe Paddling. Todd, Thomas, ed. LC 90-25773. (Basic Essentials Ser.). (Illus.). 72p. (Orig.). 1992. pap. 5.99 (*0-934802-68-8*) ICS Bks.
— Movin' Out: Equipment & Technique for Hikers. rev. ed. LC 78-26618. (Illus.). 160p. 1979. pap. 9.95 (*0-913276-29-4*) Stone Wall Pr.
Roberts, Harry, ed. see Goll, John.
Roberts, Harry H. Field Guidebook to the Reefs & Geology of Grand Cayman Island, B.W.I. (Third International Symposium on Coral Reefs Ser.). (Illus.). 44p. 1977. pap. 4.00 (*0-932981-39-9*) Univ Miami A R C.
***Roberts, Harry V.** Academic Initiatives in Total Quality for Higher Education. 1995. 45.00 (*0-87389-326-3*) ASQC Qual Pr.
— Data Analysis for Managers with MINITAB 7.0. 2nd ed. 510p. 1991. text ed., 3.5 hd 47.50 (*0-89426-193-2*); boxed, 5.25 hd 47.50 (*0-89426-192-4*) Boyd & Fraser.
Roberts, Harry V. & Sergesketter, Bernard F. Quality Is Personal: A Foundation for Total Quality Management. LC 93-21723. 192p. 1993. text ed. 29.95 (*0-02-926626-2*); pap. 19.95 (*0-02-926625-4*) Free Pr.
Roberts, Harry V., jt. auth. see Wallis, W. Allen.
Roberts, Hayden. Community Development: Learning & Action. LC 78-12986. (Canadian University Paperbooks Ser.: No. 224). 219p. reprint ed. pap. 62.50 (*0-685-15925-6*, 2056125) Bks Demand.
Roberts, Helen. The Acrylic Watercolor Book. (Illus.). 32p. 1986. pap. 8.95 (*0-941284-35-2*) J Shaw Studio.
— Destiny of the Soul. rev. ed. Loehr, Franklin, ed. LC 83-82485. Orig. Title: The Soul That Sinneth--It Shall Die. 1987. pap. 10.50 (*0-915151-13-8*) Religious Res Pr.
— Karma, the Great Teacher. rev. ed. LC 93-85317. 328p. (Orig.). 1993. pap. 12.50 (*0-915151-19-7*) Religious Res Pr.
— Women, Health, & Reproduction. 208p. (Orig.). 1981. pap. 13.95 (*0-7100-0703-5*, RKP) Routledge.
— Women's Health Matters. 1991. 69.95 (*0-415-06685-9*, A6521); pap. 18.95 (*0-415-04891-5*, A6525) Routledge.
Roberts, Helen, ed. Doing Feminist Research. 224p. (Orig.). 1981. pap. 13.95 (*0-7100-0772-8*, RKP) Routledge.
— Women's Health Counts. 192p. 1990. pap. 18.95 (*0-415-04890-7*, A4575) Routledge.
Roberts, Helen, ed. see Church of Religious Research, Inc. Staff.
Roberts, Helen, ed. see Pinkston, Isabel H.
Roberts, Helen H. Ancient Hawaiian Music. (BMB Ser.). 1972. reprint ed. pap. 60.00 (*0-527-02132-6*) Periodicals Srv.
— Basketry of the San Carlos Apache Indians. LC 72-10331. (American Museum of Natural History Anthropological Papers: Vol. XXXI, Pt. II). (Illus.). 104p. 1985. reprint ed. pap. 10.00 (*0-87380-147-4*) Rio Grande.
Roberts, Helen R., et al. Teaching in the Multicultural Classroom. (Survival Skills for Scholars Ser.: Vol. 12). 128p. 1994. 27.50 (*0-8039-5613-4*); pap. 12.95 (*0-8039-5614-2*) Sage.
Roberts, Helene E. Art History Through the Camera's Lens. 1995. text ed. 60.00 (*2-88124-642-7*); pap. text ed. 24.95 (*2-88124-643-5*) Gordon & Breach.
— Iconographic Index to Old Testament Paintings Represented in Photographs & Slides of Paintings in the Visual Collections, Fine Arts Library, Harvard University. (Illus.). 224p. 1987. 54.00 (*0-8240-8345-8*) Garland.
Roberts, Helene E. & Hall, Rachael. Iconographic Index to Narrative New Testament Subjects in the Italian School: Represented in Photographs & Slides of Paintings in the Visual Collections, Fine Arts Library, Harvard University. 266p. 1992. 58.00 (*0-8240-4385-5*, H1154) Garland.
***Roberts, Henry.** Complete Prophecies of Nostradamus. 1994. 20.00 (*0-517-59092-1*, Crown) Crown Pub Group.
Roberts, Henry C., tr. The Complete Prophecies of Nostradamus. (Illus.). 352p. 1983. 15.00 (*0-517-54956-5*, Crown) Crown Pub Group.
Roberts, Henry H. Occupational Hazards. 1981. pap. 2.50 (*0-8439-0904-8*) Dorchester Pub Co.
Roberts, Henry L. Rumania: Political Problems of an Agrarian State. 1951. 89.50 (*0-685-45660-9*) Elliots Bks.
Roberts, Henry M. Robert's Rules of Order: Classic Man. 1988. 5.99 (*0-517-25920-6*) Random Hse Value.
Roberts, Herbert A. Sensations "As If -" 1976. 9.95 (*0-685-76571-7*) Formur Intl.
Roberts, Herrell B. The Inner World of the Black Juvenile Delinquent: Three Case Studies. 168p. 1987. text ed. 29.95 (*0-89859-895-8*) L Erlbaum Assocs.
Roberts, Hildegarde W., ed. Classical Rome Comes Alive. LC 92-13233. (Illus.). 200p. (Orig.). 1992. pap. text ed. 23.50 (*0-87287-915-1*) Teacher Ideas Pr.
Roberts, Howard. Chord Directory. (Illus.). 108p. write for info. (*0-318-69299-6*) Playback Mus Pub.
— Howard Roberts Guitar Manual: Chord Melody. 56p. 1972. pap. 9.95 (*0-89915-002-0*) Playback Mus Pub.
— Plectrum Picking. (Illus.). write for info. (*0-89915-025-X*) Playback Mus Pub.
— Super Chops: Jazz Guitar Technique in 20 Weeks. LC 79-88145. (Howard Roberts Guitar Manuals Ser.). (Illus.). 87p. 1978. pap. text ed. 12.95 (*0-89915-010-1*) Playback Mus Pub.
— Super Chops for Jazz Guitar. pap. 10.95 (*0-685-75236-4*) Cherry Lane.
— Super Solos. pap. 9.95 (*0-685-75237-2*) Cherry Lane.
Roberts, Howard, comp. The Electric Bach. (Illus.). write for info. (*0-89915-008-X*) Playback Mus Pub.
Roberts, Howard & Eschete, Ron. Super Solos. (Howard Roberts Guitar Manuals Ser.). (Illus.). 48p. 1977. pap. text ed. 9.95 (*0-89915-011-X*) Playback Mus Pub.
Roberts, Howard & Grebb, Bob. Sightreading. (Howard Roberts Guitar Manuals Ser.). (Illus.). 63p. 1972. pap. text ed. 9.95 (*0-89915-003-9*) Playback Mus Pub.
Roberts, Howard & Hagberg, Garry. The Jazz Improviser: Technique, Musicianship, Theory, Performance. Palmer, Evie, ed. (Illus.). 328p. 1992. write for info. (*0-89915-047-0*) Playback Mus Pub.
— The Praxis System: Guitar Compendium, Vol. 1: Technique, Improvisation, Musicianship & Theory. (Illus.). 163p. (C). 1989. 35.00 (*3-89221-019-5*, Pub. by Advance Mus GW); pap. text ed. 19.95 (*0-317-04756-6*, Pub. by Advance Mus GW) Playback Mus Pub.
— The Praxis System: Guitar Compendium, Vol. 2: Technique, Improvisation, Musicianship & Theory. (Illus.). 237p. 1989. 40.00 (*3-89221-021-7*, Pub. by Advance Mus GW); pap. text ed. 19.95 (*0-317-04626-8*, Pub. by Advance Mus GW) Playback Mus Pub.
— The Praxis System: Guitar Compendium, Vol. 3: Technique, Improvisation, Musicianship & Theory. (Illus.). 227p. 1989. 40.00 (*3-89221-020-9*, Pub. by Advance Mus GW); pap. text ed. 24.95 (*0-317-04757-4*, Pub. by Advance Mus GW) Playback Mus Pub.
Roberts, Howard & Marshall, Jack, eds. Instant Blues. (Howard Roberts Guitar Manuals Ser.). (Illus.). 40p. 1973. pap. text ed. 5.95 (*0-89915-006-3*) Playback Mus Pub.
Roberts, Howard & Stewart, James. The Howard Roberts Guitar Book. (Howard Roberts Guitar Manuals Ser.). (Orig.). 1971. pap. 9.95 (*0-89915-000-4*) Playback Mus Pub.

Roberts, Howard, et al. The Accelerator: The Theory-Fingerboard Connection. (Howard Roberts Guitar Manuals Ser.). 207p. (Orig.). 1980. pap. 16.95 (*0-89915-014-4*) Playback Mus Pub.

Roberts, Howard M. & Hagberg, Garry. Style & Craft - The Alchemy of Unique Style. pap. 7.95 (*0-89915-012-8*) Cherry Lane.

Roberts, Howard R., ed. Food Safety. LC 80-25335. 352p. reprint ed. pap. 101.20 (*0-685-20444-8*, 2056457) Bks Demand.

Roberts, Howard W. Approaching the Third Millennium: The Church's Ethical Challenge. LC 92-25109. 192p. 1992. pap. 10.95 (*1-880837-04-8*) Smyth & Helwys.

— Doc. LC 86-90702. (Illus.). 176p. 1987. 11.95 (*0-9617971-0-X*) Circuit Writer.

— Doc. 176p. 1987. 12.95 (*0-317-56840-X*) McClain.

— Pastoral Care Through Worship. 220p. (Orig.). 1995. pap. 12.95 (*1-880837-74-9*) Smyth & Helwys.

— Sins That Crucify. 112p. (Orig.). 1994. pap. 10.95 (*1-880837-84-6*) Smyth & Helwys.

Roberts, Ian, jt. ed. see Battye, Adrian.

Roberts, Ian G. Verbs & Diachronic Syntax: A Comparative History of English & French. (Studies in Natural Language & Linguistic Theory). 372p. (C). 1993. lib. bdg. 134.00 (*0-7923-1705-X*) Kluwer Ac.

— Verbs & Diachronic Syntax: A Comparative History of English & French. (Studies in Natural Language & Linguistic Theory). 388p. (C). 1993. pap. text ed. 39.00 (*0-7923-2495-1*) Kluwer Ac.

Roberts, Ian P. Craft, Class, & Control: The Sociology of a Shipbuilding Community. 224p. 1993. text ed. 50.00 (*0-7486-0395-6*, Pub. by Edinburgh U Pr UK) Col U Pr.

Roberts, Ian W. Nicholas the First & the Russian Intervention in Hungary. LC 90-34608. 310p. 1991. text ed. 49.95 (*0-312-04897-1*) St Martin.

Roberts, Imelda R. J. O. B. S. - Job Opportunities & Business Series: The Employment Guide to the Washington, D.C. Metropolitan Area. Rieder, Davylu, ed. (Illus.). 319p. (Orig.). (C). 1989. pap. 17.95 (*0-929936-00-0*) JSI Network.

Roberts, Irene. Golden Rain. (Inflation Fighter Ser.). 144p. 1982. reprint ed. pap. 1.50 (*0-8439-1083-6*) Dorchester Pub Co.

Roberts, Isaac P. Autobiography of a Farm Boy. (American Biography Ser.). 207p. 1991. reprint ed. lib. bdg. 69.00 (*0-7812-8324-8*) Rprt Serv.

Roberts, Ivanka, tr. see Maniguet, Xavier.

Roberts, J. & Whitehouse, D. G. Practical Plant Physiology. LC 75-46566. 171p. reprint ed. pap. 48.80 (*0-317-27666-2*, 2025213) Bks Demand.

Roberts, J. A., ed. China Through Western Eyes: The Nineteenth Century: A Reader in History. 125p. 1991. text ed. 16.00 (*0-86299-828-X*) A Sutton Pub.

— Indirect Imaging: Measurement & Processing. LC 83-26348. 464p. 1984. 99.95 (*0-521-26282-8*) Cambridge U Pr.

Roberts, J. A. & Pembrey, M. E. Introduction to Medical Genetics. 8th ed. (Illus.). 400p. 1985. pap. 29.95 (*0-19-261409-6*) OUP.

Roberts, J. B. & Spanos, P. D. Random Vibration & Statistical Linearization. 407p. 1990. text ed. 74.95 (*0-471-91699-4*) Wiley.

Roberts, J. B., jt. ed. see Casciati, F.

Roberts, J. C., ed. Paper Chemistry. 288p. 1991. 127.50 (*0-412-02511-6*, A4216, Blackie & Son-Chapman NY) Routledge Chapman & Hall.

Roberts, J. C., jt. auth. see Lynch, M.

Roberts, J. D., tr. see Otero, Corazon.

Roberts, J. Deotis. Black Theology in Dialogue. LC 86-15665. 132p. (Orig.). 1987. pap. 13.99 (*0-664-24022-4*, Westminster) Westminster John Knox.

— Liberation & Reconciliation: A Black Theology. rev. ed. LC 93-38133. 150p. 1994. reprint ed. pap. 16.95 (*0-88344-951-X*) Orbis Bks.

— A Philosophical Introduction to Theology. LC 90-24500. 192p. (Orig.). (C). 1991. pap. 15.95 (*1-56338-006-4*) TPI PA.

— The Prophethood of Black Believers: An African-American Political Theology for Ministry. LC 93-32901. 192p. (Orig.). 1994. pap. 14.99 (*0-664-25488-8*) Westminster John Knox.

Roberts, J. H. Angle Modulation: The Theory of System Assessment. LC 78-317398. (IEE Telecommunications Ser.: Vol. 5). (Illus.). 294p. reprint ed. pap. 83.80 (*0-8357-5478-2*, 2032253) Bks Demand.

— My Wife, the Politician: (A Three-Act Play) 137p. 1993. pap. 17.95 (*0-614-05273-4*) Sunshine Sentinel.

Roberts, J. Hatcher, jt. auth. see Wijeyaratne, P.

Roberts, J. J. Nahum, Habakkuk, & Zephaniah. (Old Testament Library). 224p. 1991. text ed. 21.00 (*0-664-21937-3*) Westminster John Knox.

Roberts, J. J., jt. ed. see Goedicke, Hans.

Roberts, J. J., et al. Concrete Masonry Designer's Handbook. (Viewpoint Ser.). (Illus.). 1983. 90.00 (*0-86310-013-9*, Pub. by Palladian); pap. 75.00 (*0-86310-008-2*, Pub. by Palladian) Scholium Intl.

Roberts, J. J, et al. Handbook on BS 5628: The Structural use of Reinforced & Prestressed Masonry, Pt. 2. (Illus.). 207p. 1987. text ed. 75.00 (*0-86310-020-1*, Pub. by Palladian) Scholium Intl.

Roberts, J. L., III, et al, eds. Arator's De Actibus Apostolorum. Makowski, John F. et al, trs. LC 87-9661. (American Academy of Religion, Classics in Religious Studies). 100p. 1988. 19.95 (*1-55540-133-3*, 01-05-06) Scholars Pr GA.

Roberts, J. M. Antiquity Unveiled: The Heathen Origins of Christianity. 1992. lib. bdg. 89.00 (*0-8490-8747-3*) Gordon Pr.

— A Concise History of the World. (Illus.). 616p. 1995. 30.00 (*0-19-521151-0*) OUP.

— Europe, 1880-1945. 2nd ed. (General History of Europe Ser.). 631p. (C). 1989. pap. text ed. 25.95 (*0-582-49414-1*, 73612) Longman.

— The French Revolution. 1978. pap. text ed. 14.95 (*0-19-289069-7*) OUP.

— The Pelican History of the World. 1056p. 1984. pap. 11.95 (*0-14-022101-8*, Penguin Bks) Viking Penguin.

— The Pelican History of the World. rev. ed. 1056p. 1988. pap. 11.95 (*0-14-022785-7*, Penguin Bks) Viking Penguin.

— The Penguin History of the World. rev. ed. (Illus.). 1152p. 1995. pap. 16.95 (*0-14-015495-7*, Penguin Bks) Viking Penguin.

— Without Sanction. 320p. (Orig.). 1993. pap. 8.95 (*1-55583-215-6*) Alyson Pubns.

Roberts, J. M., ed. History of the World. (Illus.). 992p. 1993. 45.00 (*0-19-521043-3*) OUP.

Roberts, J. M., jt. auth. see Miller, Patrick D.

Roberts, J. R. Ambush Moon. (Gunsmith Ser.: No. 148). 192p. (Orig.). 1994. pap. 3.99 (*0-515-11358-1*) Jove Pubns.

— Blind Justice. (Gunsmith Ser.: No. 147). 192p. (Orig.). 1994. pap. 3.99 (*0-515-11340-9*) Jove Pubns.

— The Caliente Gold Robbery. (Gunsmith Ser.: No. 128). 192p. (Orig.). 1992. pap. 3.99 (*0-515-10903-7*) Jove Pubns.

— Dakota Guns. (Gunsmith Ser.: No. 136). 192p. (Orig.). 1994. pap. text ed. 3.99 (*0-515-11507-X*) Jove Pubns.

— Deadly Gold. (Gunsmith Ser.: No. 138). 192p. (Orig.). 1993. pap. 3.99 (*0-515-11121-X*) Jove Pubns.

— The Empty Gun. (Gunsmith Ser.: No. 161). 192p. (Orig.). 1995. pap. text ed. 3.99 (*0-515-11614-9*) Jove Pubns.

— Gila River Crossing. (Gunsmith Ser.: No. 143). 1993. pap. 3.99 (*0-515-11240-2*) Jove Pubns.

— Golden Gate Killers. (Gunsmith Ser.: No. 129). 192p. (Orig.). 1992. pap. 3.99 (*0-515-10931-2*) Jove Pubns.

— The Great Riverboat Race. (Gunsmith Ser.: No. 132). 192p. (Orig.). 1992. pap. 3.99 (*0-515-10999-1*) Jove Pubns.

— The Gunsmith: Champion with a Gun, No. 151. (Gunsmith Ser.: No. 151). 192p. (Orig.). 1994. pap. text ed. 3.99 (*0-515-11409-X*) Jove Pubns.

— The Gunsmith: Lethal Ladies, No. 152. 192p. (Orig.). 1994. pap. text ed. 3.99 (*0-515-11437-5*) Jove Pubns.

— The Gunsmith: Night of the Wolf. (Gunsmith Ser.: No. 150). 192p. (Orig.). 1994. pap. 3.99 (*0-515-11393-X*) Jove Pubns.

— The Gunsmith: Spanish Gold. (Gunsmith Ser.: No. 149). 192p. (Orig.). 1994. pap. 3.99 (*0-515-11377-8*) Jove Pubns.

— The Gunsmith: Tolliver's Deputies, No. 153. 192p. (Orig.). 1994. pap. text ed. 3.99 (*0-515-11456-1*) Jove Pubns.

— The Gunsmith No. 154: Orphan Train, No. 154. 192p. (Orig.). 1994. pap. text ed. 3.99 (*0-515-11478-2*) Jove Pubns.

— The Gunsmith No. 158: The Ransom. 192p. (Orig.). 1995. pap. text ed. 3.99 (*0-515-11553-3*) Jove Pubns.

— The Gunsmith No. 159: The Huntsville Trip. 192p. (Orig.). 1995. pap. text ed. 3.99 (*0-515-11571-1*) Jove Pubns.

— The Gunsmith No. 160: The Ten Year Hunt. 192p. (Orig.). 1995. pap. text ed. 3.99 (*0-515-11593-2*) Jove Pubns.

— The Gunsmith No. 163: The Wild Women of Glitter Gulch. 192p. (Orig.). Date not set. pap. text ed. 4.99 (*0-515-11656-4*) Jove Pubns.

— The Gunsmith No. 164: The Omaha Heat. 192p. (Orig.). 1995. pap. text ed. 3.99 (*0-515-11688-2*) Jove Pubns.

— The Gunsmith No. 165: The Denver Ripper. 192p. (Orig.). 1995. pap. text ed. 3.99 (*0-614-05265-3*) Jove Pubns.

— Gunsmith Giant: Life & Times of Clint Adams, No. 2. 288p. (Orig.). Date not set. pap. 4.99 (*0-515-11728-5*) Jove Pubns.

— Gunsmith Giant Edition, No. 1: Trouble in Tombstone. 1993. pap. 4.50 (*0-515-11212-7*) Jove Pubns.

— Gunsmith, No. 1: Macklin's Women. pap. 3.99 (*0-515-10145-1*) Jove Pubns.

— Gunsmith, No. 121: The Deadly Derringer. 1992. pap. 3.50 (*0-515-10755-7*) Jove Pubns.

— Gunsmith, No. 139: Vigilante Hunt. 192p. (Orig.). 1993. pap. 3.99 (*0-515-11138-4*) Jove Pubns.

— Gunsmith, No. 140: Samurai Hunt. 192p. (Orig.). 1993. pap. 3.99 (*0-515-11168-6*) Jove Pubns.

— Gunsmith, No. 141: Gambler's Blood. 192p. (Orig.). 1993. pap. 3.99 (*0-515-11196-1*) Jove Pubns.

— Gunsmith, No. 142: Wyoming Justice. 1993. pap. 3.99 (*0-515-11218-6*) Jove Pubns.

— Gunsmith, No. 145: Gillett's Rangers. 192p. 1994. pap. 3.99 (*0-515-11285-2*) Jove Pubns.

— Last Bounty. (Gunsmith Ser.: No. 135). 192p. (Orig.). 1993. pap. 3.99 (*0-515-11063-9*) Jove Pubns.

— The Last Great Scout. (Gunsmith Ser.: No. 162). 192p. (Orig.). 1995. pap. text ed. 3.99 (*0-515-11635-1*) Jove Pubns.

— The Magician. (Gunsmith Ser.: No. 155). 192p. (Orig.). 1994. pap. text ed. 3.99 (*0-515-11495-2*) Jove Pubns.

— Nevada Guns. (Gunsmith Ser.: No. 137). 192p. (Orig.). 1993. pap. 3.99 (*0-515-11105-8*) Jove Pubns.

— Outlaw Women. (Gunsmith Ser.: No. 134). 192p. (Orig.). 1993. pap. 3.99 (*0-515-11045-0*) Jove Pubns.

— Return to Deadwood. (Gunsmith Ser.: No. 146). 192p. (Orig.). 1994. pap. 3.99 (*0-515-11315-8*) Jove Pubns.

— The Road to Testimony. (Gunsmith Ser.: No. 130). 192p. (Orig.). 1992. pap. 3.99 (*0-515-10957-6*) Jove Pubns.

— Seminole Vengeance. (Gunsmith Ser.: No. 157). 192p. (Orig.). 1995. pap. text ed. 3.99 (*0-515-11530-4*) Jove Pubns.

— Two Guns for Justice. (Gunsmith Ser.: No. 133). 192p. (Orig.). 1993. pap. 3.99 (*0-515-11020-5*) Jove Pubns.

— Valley Massacre. (Gunsmith Ser.: No. 136). 192p. (Orig.). 1993. pap. 3.99 (*0-515-11084-1*) Jove Pubns.

— The Witness. (Gunsmith Ser.: No. 131). 192p. (Orig.). 1992. pap. 3.99 (*0-515-10982-7*) Jove Pubns.

— The Wolf Teacher. (Gunsmith Ser.: No. 166). 192p. (Orig.). 1995. pap. 3.99 (*0-515-11732-3*) Jove Pubns.

Roberts, J. S., pseud. Nineteen Thirty-Three: The Devil Comes to Henry County. limited ed. Long, Robert, ed. (Illus.). 571p. 1989. 29.95 (*0-938650-48-3*) Thinkers Pr.

Roberts, J. T., ed. Structural Materials in Nuclear Power Systems. LC 81-1883. (Modern Perspectives in Energy Ser.). 500p. 1981. 89.50 (*0-306-40669-1*, Plenum Pr) Plenum.

Roberts, J. W. The Letter of James. LC 76-51637. 1984. 12.95 (*0-915547-35-X*) Abilene Christ U.

— The Letters of John. 1984. 12.95 (*0-915547-37-6*) Abilene Christ U.

— Looking Within: The Misleading Tendencies of Looking Backward Made Manifest. LC 78-154459. (Utopian Literature Ser.). 1976. reprint ed. 24.95 (*0-405-03541-1*) Ayer.

— Richard Boleslavsky: His Life & Work in the Theatre. LC 81-16411. (Theater & Dramatic Studies: No. 7). (Illus.). 298p. reprint ed. pap. 85.00 (*0-8357-1250-8*, 2070279) Bks Demand.

***Roberts, Jack.** Construction Surveying: Layout & Dimension Control. LC 94-28591. 372p. 1994. pap. text ed. 45.95 (*0-8273-5723-0*) Delmar.

— Dian Fossey. LC 94-6841. (Importance of Ser.). (Illus.). 128p. (J). (gr. 5-9). 1995. 16.95 (*1-56006-068-9*) Lucent Bks.

— Nelson Mandela: Determined to Be Free. LC 94-21519. (Gateway Biographies Ser.). (Illus.). 48p. (J). (gr. 2-4). 1994. lib. bdg. 13.40 (*1-56294-558-0*) Millbrook Pr.

— Rock Climb Primer: To Be Read Before Your First Climb & Then Afterwards. (Outdoor Sports Primer Ser.). (Illus.). 160p. 1995. pap. write for info. (*1-879415-04-6*) Mtn n Air Bks.

***Roberts, Jack L.** Booker T. Washington: Educator & Leader. LC 94-21484. (Gateway Civil Rights Ser.). (Illus.). 32p. (J). (gr. 2-4). 1995. 13.40 (*1-56294-487-8*) Millbrook Pr.

— The Importance of Oskar Schindler. LC 95-11712. (Importance of Ser.). (J). 1996. lib. bdg. write for info. (*1-56006-079-4*) Lucent Bks.

— Ruth Bader Ginsburg: Supreme Court Justice. LC 93-39015. (Gateway Biographies Ser.). (Illus.). 48p. (J). (gr. 2-4). 1994. lib. bdg. 13.40 (*1-56294-497-5*); pap. 6.95 (*1-56294-744-3*) Millbrook Pr.

Roberts, Jackie, ed. see Rose, Tui.

Roberts, James. Absalom, Absalom! Notes. 1982. pap. 3.75 (*0-8220-0110-1*) Cliffs.

— As I Lay Dying Notes. 1969. pap. 3.95 (*0-8220-0210-8*) Cliffs.

— The Bear Notes. 86p. (Orig.). 1986. pap. text ed. 4.50 (*0-8220-0222-1*) Cliffs.

— Bud's Easy Note Taking Kit. 44p. (C). 1989. pap. text ed. write for info. (*0-9609436-5-X*) Lawrence Hse.

— The Counter-Revolution in France, 1787-1830. LC 89-70226. 134p. 1990. text ed. 45.00 (*0-312-04568-9*) St Martin.

— Go Down, Moses Notes. 102p. (Orig.). (C). 1985. pap. text ed. 4.50 (*0-8220-0537-9*) Cliffs.

— The Revelation of John. LC 73-20857. 1984. 12.95 (*0-915547-38-4*) Abilene Christ U.

Roberts, James, jt. auth. see Taylor, Meril.

Roberts, James A. Just What Is EIR? 1991. write for info. (*0-9630515-0-4*) Global Env Mgmt.

***Roberts, James A., ed.** New York in the Revolution As Colony & State: These Records Were Discovered, Arranged & Classified 1895, 1896-1897 & 1898. 534p. 1993. reprint ed. lib. bdg. 53.50 (*1-56012-127-0*, 124) Kinship Rhinebeck.

Roberts, James D. Black Theology Today: Liberation & Contextualization. LC 83-17246. (Toronto Studies in Theology: Vol. 12). 218p. 1984. lib. bdg. 99.95 (*0-88946-755-2*) E Mellen.

Roberts, James L. Adventures of Huckleberry Finn Notes. 1971. pap. 3.95 (*0-8220-0606-5*) Cliffs.

— American Notes. (Orig.). 1965. pap. 4.50 (*0-8220-0164-0*) Cliffs.

— Crime & Punishment Notes. 1982. pap. 3.95 (*0-8220-0328-7*) Cliffs.

— Daisy Miller & the Turn of the Screw Notes. 1965. pap. 4.25 (*0-8220-0355-4*) Cliffs.

— Death of a Salesman Notes. 1982. pap. 3.75 (*0-8220-0382-1*) Cliffs.

— Dr. Jekyll & Mr. Hyde Notes. 60p. (Orig.). (C). 1984. pap. 4.25 (*0-8220-0408-9*) Cliffs.

— Farewell to Arms Notes. 1982. pap. 3.75 (*0-8220-0461-5*) Cliffs.

— Glass Menagerie & the Streetcar Named Desire Notes. 1965. pap. 3.95 (*0-8220-0533-6*) Cliffs.

— Grapes of Wrath Notes. 1965. pap. 3.75 (*0-8220-0542-5*) Cliffs.

— Light in August Notes. 1968. pap. 3.75 (*0-8220-0744-4*) Cliffs.

— Madame Bovary Notes. 1964. pap. 3.95 (*0-8220-0780-0*) Cliffs.

— Moby Dick Notes. 1966. pap. 3.95 (*0-8220-0852-1*) Cliffs.

— Notes from the Underground Notes. 1970. pap. 3.95 (*0-8220-0900-5*) Cliffs.

— Of Mice & Men Notes. 1966. pap. 3.75 (*0-8220-0939-0*) Cliffs.

— Portrait of a Lady Notes. 1965. pap. 3.50 (*0-8220-1066-6*) Cliffs.

— Sound & the Fury Notes. 1992. pap. 3.95 (*0-8220-1219-7*) Cliffs.

— Three Musketeers Notes. 86p. (Orig.). 1989. pap. text ed. 3.95 (*0-8220-1300-2*) Cliffs.

— The Unvanquished Notes. 87p. (Orig.). (C). 1980. pap. text ed. 4.50 (*0-8220-1316-9*) Cliffs.

Roberts, James L., jt. auth. see Allen, L. David.

Roberts, James L., jt. auth. see Calandra, Denis M.

Roberts, James L., jt. auth. see Fisher, Jeffrey.

***Roberts, James P., ed.** Dark Iowa, Bright Iowa. vi, 158p. 1994. pap. 8.95 (*0-9636544-1-1*) White Hawk.

Roberts, James R. & Hedges, Jerris R. Clinical Procedures in Emergency Medicine. (Illus.). 1184p. 1991. text ed. 175.00 (*0-7216-7611-1*) Saunders.

Roberts, James T., ed. Clinical Management of the Airway. LC 93-12115. (Illus.). 512p. 1994. text ed. 72.50 (*0-7216-3670-5*) Saunders.

Roberts, Jan. Beverly Hills International Party Planner. 1994. 29.95 (*0-9634398-9-8*); pap. 19.95 (*0-9634398-4-7*) J Roberts Pubns.

Roberts, Jan, jt. auth. see Roberts, George.

***Roberts, Jane.** Adventures in Consciousness. 1994. lib. bdg. 24.95x (*1-56849-496-3*) Buccaneer Bks.

— Adventures in Consciousness: An Introduction to Aspect Psychology. 1978. 7.95 (*0-13-013953-X*) P-H.

— The Coming of Seth. (Orig.). 1993. reprint ed. lib. bdg. 21.95 (*1-56849-243-X*) Buccaneer Bks.

— Dialogues of the Soul & Mortal Self in Time. 1979. pap. 4.95 (*0-685-03831-9*) P-H.

— A Dictionary of Michelangelo's Watermarks. 49p. (Orig.). 1988. pap. 5.95 (*0-685-60732-1*) Natl Gallery Art.

— Emir's Education in the Proper Use of Magical Powers. (Illus.). 138p. (J). (gr. 3 up). 1984. reprint ed. pap. 8.95 (*0-913299-08-1*) Stillpoint.

— The Further Education of Oversoul Seven. 198p. 1984. pap. 6.95 (*0-685-07788-8*) P-H.

— How to Develop Your ESP Power. 2nd ed. LC 66-17331. 264p. 1993. pap. 12.95 (*0-8119-0379-6*) LIFETIME.

— The Individual & the Nature of Mass Events. (Seth Book Ser.). 320p. (Orig.). 1995. reprint ed. 15.95 (*1-878424-21-1*) Amber-Allen Pub.

— The Magical Approach: Seth Speaks about the Art of Creative Living. (Seth Book Ser.). 144p. 1995. 12.95 (*1-878424-09-2*) Amber-Allen Pub.

— The Nature of Personal Reality. 1993. reprint ed. lib. bdg. 21.95 (*1-56849-244-8*) Buccaneer Bks.

— The Nature of Personal Reality: A Seth Book: Specific, Practical Techniques for Solving Everyday Problems & Enriching the Life You Know. 544p. 1994. reprint ed. pap. 17.95 (*1-878424-06-8*) Amber-Allen Pub.

— The Oversoul Seven Trilogy: The Education of Oversoul Seven; The Further Education of Oversoul Seven; Oversoul Seven & the Museum of Time. 1995. pap. 19.95 (*1-878424-17-3*) Amber-Allen Pub.

— The Seth Material. 1993. reprint ed. lib. bdg. 25.95x (*1-56849-185-9*) Buccaneer Bks.

— Seth Speaks: A Seth Book: The Eternal Validity of the Soul. 512p. 1994. reprint ed. pap. 15.95 (*1-878424-07-6*) Amber-Allen Pub.

— World View of Paul Cezanne. 1994. lib. bdg. 24.95x (*1-56849-495-5*) Buccaneer Bks.

Roberts, Jane & Roberts, Richard. A Seth Reader. 336p. (Orig.). 1993. pap. 15.95 (*0-942380-15-0*) Vernal Equinox.

Roberts, Jane, et al. Privatising Electricity: The Politics of Power. 256p. 1991. text ed. 55.00 (*1-85293-180-9*, Pub. by Pinter Pubs UK) St Martin.

Roberts, Jane W., jt. auth. see Roberts, Kenneth D.

Roberts, Janice & Johnson, Joy. Thank You for Coming. (Illus.). 48p. 1994. pap. 5.50 (*1-56123-071-5*) Centering Corp.

Roberts, Janine. Tales & Transformation: Stories in Families & Family Therapy. 220p. (C). 1994. 27.00 (*0-393-70174-3*) Norton.

Roberts, Janine, jt. auth. see Imber-Black, Evan.

***Roberts, Jason.** Director Demystified. 500p. 1995. pap. 39.95 (*1-56609-170-5*) Peachpit Pr.

Roberts, Jason C. How to Lose Your Ex-Wife (Financially) Forever: Gain Financial Freedom from Your Ex, Escape the Bondage of Excessive Child Support & Alimony. Jorgensen, Ron, ed. LC 90-61343. (Illus.). 182p. (Orig.). 1990. per. 17.95 (*0-922507-05-8*) Liberty UT.

Roberts, Jeanie, jt. auth. see Roberts, Royston M.

Roberts, Jeanne A. The Shakespearean Wild: Geography, Genus & Gender. LC 90-13037. (Illus.). x, 214p. 1991. 35.00 (*0-8032-3899-1*) U of Nebr Pr.

— The Shakespearean Wild: Geography, Genus, & Gender. (Illus.). 214p. 1991. reprint ed. pap. 12.00 (*0-8032-8950-2*, Bison Books) U of Nebr Pr.

— Shakespeare's English Comedy: "The Merry Wives of Windsor" in Context. LC 78-24239. xx, 169p. 1979. 20.00 (*0-8032-3851-7*) U of Nebr Pr.

Roberts, Jeanne A., jt. auth. see McManaway, James G.

Roberts, Jeff & Davis, Frank. Using the Dataease Query Language. 1988. pap. 21.95 (*0-916515-50-8*) Mercury Hse Inc.

Roberts, Jeff & Pines, Malcolm, eds. The Practice of Group Analysis. (International Library of Group Psychotherapy & Group Process). (Illus.). 208p. 1991. 55.00 (*0-415-05219-X*, A6126, Tavistock); pap. 16.95 (*0-415-04484-7*, A6130, Tavistock) Routledge.

Roberts, Jennifer, jt. tr. see Blanco, Walter.

Roberts, Jennifer D. Norman Bel Geddes: An Exhibition of Theatrical & Industrial Designs. (Illus.). 60p. 1979. pap. 10.00 (*0-87959-092-0*) U of Tex H Ransom Ctr.

Roberts, Jennifer T. Accountability in Athenian Government. LC 81-69827. 288p. 1982. text ed. 35.00 (*0-299-08680-1*) U of Wis Pr.

— Athens on Trial: The Antidemocratic Tradition in Western Thought. LC 93-24553. 1994. 29.95 (*0-691-05697-8*) Princeton U Pr.

Roberts, Jenny. Introduction to the Bible. 1991. 12.98 (*1-55521-751-6*) Bk Sales Inc.

An Asterisk (*) at the beginning of an entry indicates that the title is appearing in BIP for the first time.

Roberts, Jeremy K. Differential Diagnosis in Neuropsychiatry. LC 83-23289. 377p. 1984. text ed. 206.95 (*0-471-90402-3*, Wiley-Interscience) Wiley.

Roberts, Jerry. Dianne Feinstein: Never Let Them See You Cry. 224p. 1994. 20.00 (*0-06-258508-8*) HarpC West.

— Robert Mitchum: A Bio-Bibliography. LC 92-23784. (Bio-Bibliographies in the Performing Arts Ser.: No. 32). 448p. 1992. text ed. 47.95 (*0-313-27547-5*, RRM, Greenwood Pr) Greenwood.

Roberts, Jerry & Gaydos, Steven, eds. Movie Talk from the Front Lines: Filmmakers Discuss Their Works with the Los Angeles Film Critics Association. (Illus.). 352p. 1995. lib. bdg. 37.50 (*0-7864-0005-6*) McFarland & Co.

Roberts, Jerry, jt. auth. see Marshall, John.

Roberts, Jill, ed. Pennsylvania German Fraktur & Printed Broadsides: A Guide to the Collections in the Library of Congress. LC 88-600044. 48p. 1988. 9.95 (*0-8444-0600-7*) Lib Congress.

Roberts, Jim. Strutters Complete Guide to Clown Makeup. LC 89-39206. (Illus.). 96p. (Orig.). 1991. pap. 18.95 (*0-941599-10-8*, Empire Pub Srvs) Piccadilly Bks.

— Strutter's Complete Guide to Clown Makeup. LC 90-52814. (Illus.). 1991. 30.00 (*0-88734-607-3*) Players Pr.

***Roberts, Jim, Jr.** Warren County Running: An In-Depth Race History. (Illus.). 144p. (Orig.). 1995. pap. 13.00 (*0-9645729-2-3*, 500) J W Roberts.

Roberts, Jim & Scheck, Joann. Bible Pop-O-Rama Books, 2 vols. Incl. Brightest Star. 1978. 5.99 (*0-8066-1601-6*, 10-0915); (Illus.). 12p. (J). (gr. 3 up). 1978. write for info. (*0-318-50943-1*, Augsburg) Augsburg Fortress.

Roberts, Jo. Internal Gravity Waves in the Ocean. LC 74-78969. (Marine Science Ser.: No. 2). (Illus.). 289p. reprint ed. pap. 82.40 (*0-7837-0773-8*, 2041087) Bks Demand.

Roberts, Jo-Anna. Alligator & the Toothfairy. (Illus.). 56p. (J). (ps-2). 1991. 11.50 (*1-879212-00-5*) Desert Star Intl.

Roberts, Joan, jt. auth. see Hickman, Dwayne.

Roberts, Joan D. Caring for Those with Alzheimer's: A Pastoral Approach. LC 90-26574. 94p. (Orig.). 1991. pap. 4.95 (*0-8189-0593-X*) Alba.

***Roberts, Joan I.** Feminism & Nursing: An Historical Perspective on Power, Status, & Political Activism. LC 94-33756. 400p. 1995. pap. text ed. 24.95 (*0-275-95120-0*, Praeger Pubs) Greenwood.

***Roberts, Joan I. & Group, Thetis M.** Feminism & Nursing: An Historical Perspective on Power, Status & Political Activism. LC 94-33756. 400p. 1995. text ed. 65.00 (*0-275-94916-8*, Praeger Pubs) Greenwood.

Roberts, Joan L., jt. ed. see Harbert, Anita S.

***Roberts, JoAnn.** Art & Illusion: a Guide to Crossdressing Vol. 1: Face & Hair. 3rd ed. (Illus.). 40p. 1994. pap. 15.00 (*1-880715-05-8*) Creat Des Srvs.

— Art & Illusion: a Guide to Crossdressing Vol. 2: Fashion & Style. 3rd ed. (Illus.). 40p. 1994. pap. 15.00 (*1-880715-08-2*) Creat Des Srvs.

— Coping with Crossdressing. 2nd ed. 80p. (Orig.). 1992. pap. 12.00 (*1-880715-10-4*) Creat Des Srvs.

— Coping with Crossdressing. 3rd rev. ed. 84p. (Orig.). 1995. pap. 12.00 (*1-880715-12-0*) Creat Des Srvs.

— Sacred Cows Make the Best Hamburger. 99p. 1993. pap. 12.00 (*1-880715-13-9*) Creat Des Srvs.

Roberts, JoAnn, ed. Who's Who & Resource Guide, 1994. 84p. 1993. pap. 10.00 (*1-880715-14-7*) Creat Des Srvs.

Roberts, JoAnn, ed. see Van Maris, Delia.

Roberts, John. The Aircraft Carrier Intrepid. LC 82-81105. (Anatomy of the Ship Ser.). (Illus.). 96p. 1982. 36.95 (*0-87021-901-4*) Naval Inst Pr.

— Amele. 400p. 1987. 72.50 (*0-7099-4254-0*, Pub. by Croom Helm UK) Routledge Chapman & Hall.

— The Battleship Dreadnought. (Anatomy of the Ship Ser.). (Illus.). 256p. 1993. 36.95 (*1-55750-057-6*) Naval Inst Pr.

— The Boating Book: A Practical Guide to Safe Pleasure Boating-Sail & Power. 1991. 39.95 (*0-393-03342-2*) Norton.

— A Guide to River Trout Flies. (Illus.). 240p. 1991. 45.00 (*1-85223-167-X*, Pub. by Crowood Pr UK) Trafalgar.

— The Gulf, Integration, & OPEC: Overseas Downstream Activities. 20p. 1988. pap. 10.00 (*0-918714-14-1*) Intl Res Ctr Energy.

— Noise Control in the Built Environment. 352p. 1989. text ed. 69.95 (*0-566-09001-5*) Ashgate Pub Co.

— Ondina: A Narrative Poem. (Illus.). 136p. 1986. 18.00 (*0-9615617-0-X*); pap. 12.00 (*0-9615617-1-8*) Cloud Ridge Pr.

— OPEC & Non-OPEC Relations. 20p. 1989. pap. 10.00 (*0-918714-18-4*) Intl Res Ctr Energy.

— Selected Errors: Writings on Art & Politics, 1981-90. 292p. (C). 1993. text ed. 66.50 (*0-7453-0498-2*); pap. text ed. 18.95 (*0-7453-0497-4*) Westview.

— To Rise a Trout. (Illus.). 224p. (Orig.). 1989. pap. 24.95 (*0-88317-151-1*) Stoeger Pub Co.

— Trout on a Nymph. (Illus.). 192p. 1992. 45.00 (*1-85223-340-0*, Pub. by Crowood Pr UK) Trafalgar.

— A War for Oil? Energy Issues & the Gulf War of 1991. 20p. 1991. pap. 10.00 (*0-918714-28-1*) Intl Res Ctr Energy.

— Warship, Vol. V. LC 78-55455. (Illus.). 288p. 1982. 39.95 (*0-87021-980-4*) Naval Inst Pr.

Roberts, John, ed. Art Has No History! Critical Essays on Contemporary Art. LC 94-4882. 1994. write for info. (*0-86091-627-8*, Pub. by Verso UK); pap. write for info. (*0-86091-457-7*, Pub. by Verso UK) Routledge Chapman & Hall.

— Escaping Prison Myths: Selected Topics in the History of Federal Corrections. 270p. (Orig.). 1994. lib. bdg. 58.50 (*1-879383-27-6*); pap. text ed. 24.50 (*1-879383-28-4*) Am Univ Pr.

— Reinhard Keiser, Vol. 1. (Handel Sources Ser.). 1987. 35.00 (*0-8240-6475-5*) Garland.

— Reinhard Keiser, Vol. 2. (Handel Sources Ser.). 1986. 30.00 (*0-8240-6476-3*) Garland.

— Reinhard Keiser, Vol. 3. (Handel Sources Ser.). 1987. 30.00 (*0-8240-6477-1*) Garland.

— Warship, Vol. III. LC 78-55455. (Illus.). 288p. 1981. 39.95 (*0-87021-977-4*) Naval Inst Pr.

— Warship, Vol. IV. LC 78-55455. (Illus.). 286p. 1981. 39.95 (*0-87021-979-0*) Naval Inst Pr.

— Warship, Vol. VII. LC 78-55455. (Illus.). 288p. 1984. 39.95 (*0-87021-982-0*) Naval Inst Pr.

— Warship 1995. (Illus.). 256p. 1995. 41.95 (*0-85177-654-X*) Naval Inst Pr.

Roberts, John & Mann, Maria. Choosing Your Boat. 1986. 19.95 (*0-393-03315-5*) Norton.

Roberts, John & Roberts, Nedra P. Excellence in English. (J). 1987. pap. text ed. 12.00 (*0-8013-0134-3*, 75798) Longman.

Roberts, John, jt. auth. see Milgrom, Paul.

***Roberts, John, et al, eds.** Travel Sickness: The Need for a Sustainable Transport Policy for Britain. 384p. Date not set. pap. write for info. (*0-85315-748-0*, Pub. by Lawrence & Wishart UK) Humanities.

Roberts, John A., jt. auth. see Kirby, Ronald E.

Roberts, John D. The Right Place at the Right Time. (Illus.). 299p. 1990. 24.95 (*0-8412-1766-1*) Am Chemical.

Roberts, John G. Mitsui: Three Centuries of Japanese Business. 1988. 35.00 (*0-8348-0080-2*) Weatherhill.

Roberts, John H. Giovanni Bononcini. (Handel Sources Ser.). 456p. 1986. 35.00 (*0-8240-6482-8*) Garland.

— Steffani & Others: Bononcini & Miscellaneous Sources, Vol. 9. (Handel Sources Ser.). 362p. 1987. 30.00 (*0-8240-6483-6*) Garland.

Roberts, John H., ed. Gasparini & Porta. (Handel Sources Ser.). 264p. 1987. 30.00 (*0-8240-6478-X*) Garland.

Roberts, John H., jt. auth. see Ryskind, Morrie.

Roberts, John H., et al, eds. Duke Mathematical Journal: Index 1-22. 60p. 1957. pap. 8.00 (*0-8223-0629-8*) Duke.

Roberts, John M. Cloak of Illusion. 288p. (Orig.). 1985. 2.95 (*0-8125-5202-4*) Tor Bks.

— Conan & the Amazon. 288p. (Orig.). 1995. mass mkt. 4.99 (*0-8125-2493-4*) Tor Bks.

— Conan & the Manhunters. 320p. 1994. mass mkt. 4.99 (*0-8125-2489-6*) Tor Bks.

— Conan & the Treasure of Python. (Orig.). 1993. pap. 7.99 (*0-8125-1415-7*) Tor Bks.

— Conan & the Treasure of Python. 288p. (Orig.). 1994. mass mkt. 4.99 (*0-8125-5000-5*) Tor Bks.

— Queens of Land & Sea. 320p. (Orig.). 1994. mass mkt. 4.99 (*0-8125-2307-5*) Tor Bks.

— The Sacrilege: An SPQR Mystery. 224p. (Orig.). 1992. mass mkt. 4.50 (*0-380-76627-2*) Avon.

— SPQR. 224p. 1990. mass mkt. 3.99 (*0-380-75993-4*) Avon.

— SPQR Two: The Catiline Conspiracy. 224p. 1991. pap. 3.50 (*0-380-75995-0*) Avon.

— Stormlands No. 1: The Islander. 1990. pap. 3.95 (*0-8125-0627-8*) Tor Bks.

— The Temple of the Muses: An SPQR Mystery. 224p. (Orig.). 1992. mass mkt. 4.50 (*0-380-76629-9*) Avon.

— Zuni Daily Life. Bd. with Zuni Kin Terms. LC 67-2866. 145p. LC 67-2866. (Monographs). 174p. 1965. reprint ed. Set pap. 15.00x (*0-87536-810-7*) HRAFP.

Roberts, John M., jt. auth. see Nutini, Hugo G.

Roberts, John Mack, jt. ed. see Weinberg, Scott.

Roberts, John Maddox. A Typical American Town. 256p. 1994. 20.95 (*0-312-11359-5*, Pub. by Thomas Dunne Bks) St Martin.

Roberts, John R. George Herbert: An Annotated Bibliography of Modern Criticism, 1905-1984. rev. ed. LC 87-19095. 456p. 1988. text ed. 42.00 (*0-8262-0487-2*) U of Mo Pr.

— John Donne: An Annotated Bibliography of Modern Criticism, 1912-1967. LC 72-913760. 336p. 1973. text ed. 37.50 (*0-8262-0136-9*) U of Mo Pr.

— John Donne: An Annotated Bibliography of Modern Criticism, 1912-1967. LC 82-1849. 448p. 1982. 44.00 (*0-8262-0364-7*) U of Mo Pr.

— Richard Crashaw: An Annotated Bibliography of Criticism, 1632-1980. LC 84-52264. 488p. 1985. text ed. 45.00 (*0-8262-0468-6*) U of Mo Pr.

Roberts, John R., ed. New Perspectives on the Life & Art of Richard Crashaw. LC 84-52264. (Illus.). 248p. 1990. text ed. 32.50 (*0-8262-0739-1*) U of Mo Pr.

— New Perspectives on the Seventeenth-Century English Religious Lyric. (Illus.). 336p. (C). 1994. text ed. 47.50 (*0-8262-0909-2*) U of Mo Pr.

Roberts, John S. Black Music of Two Worlds. LC 74-6472. 282p. (C). 1982. reprint ed. pap. 12.95 (*0-9614458-0-7*) Original Music.

— The Latin Tinge: The Impact of Latin American Music on the United States. LC 78-26543. (Illus.). 246p. 1985. pap. 12.95 (*0-9614458-1-5*) Original Music.

— The Life & Explorations of David Livingston. 1988. reprint ed. lib. bdg. 75.00 (*0-7812-0204-3*) Rprt Serv.

Roberts, John T. Seasons: Kalidasa's Ritusamhara. LC 89-82402. (Monograph Ser.: No. 25). 180p. 1990. pap. 10.00 (*0-939252-22-8*) ASU Ctr Asian.

Roberts, John T., tr. The Homely Touch: Folk Poetry of Old India. (Indo-Aryan Languages & Literature Ser.). 80p. (Orig.). (C). 1986. lib. bdg. 12.00 (*0-939214-32-6*); pap. text ed. 7.95 (*0-939214-33-4*) Mazda Pubs.

Roberts, John W. From Trickster to Badman: The Black Folk Hero in Slavery & Freedom. LC 88-20804. 234p. (C). 1989. reprint ed. pap. text ed. 16.95 (*0-8122-1333-5*) U of Pa Pr.

Roberts, John W., ed. see Das, Jagannath.

Roberts, Jon, jt. auth. see Weir, Cyril.

Roberts, Jon H. Darwinism & the Divine in America: Protestant Intellectuals & Organic Evolution, 1859-1900. LC 87-40374. (History of American Thought & Culture Ser.). 368p. (C). 1988. text ed. 26.75 (*0-299-11590-9*) U of Wis Pr.

Roberts, Jonathan M. Antiquity Unveiled: Ancient Voices from the Spirit Realms. reprint ed. spiral bd. 27.50 (*0-7873-0729-7*) Mokelumne.

— Decision-Making During International Crises. LC 88-3233. 250p. 1988. text ed. 45.00 (*0-312-01872-X*) St Martin.

Roberts, Jonathan N. & Spearman, Gretta, eds. There Was No Jesus: The Teacher of the New Testament Was Apollonius of Tyana. reprint ed. spiral bd. 13.75 (*0-7873-0730-0*) Mokelumne.

Roberts, Joseph. Goldfish. (Illus.). 80p. 1989. pap. 5.95 (*0-86622-147-6*, PB-112) TFH Pubns.

— The Lure of the Integers. LC 91-62053. (MAA Spectrum Ser.). 300p. 1992. pap. 33.00 (*0-88385-502-X*) Math Assn.

Roberts, Josephine A., ed. Poems of Lady Mary Wroth. LC 82-20843. (Illus.). 304p. (C). 1992. pap. text ed. 14.95 (*0-8071-1799-4*) La State U Pr.

Roberts, Josephine A., ed. see Wroth, Mary.

Roberts, Judy G. Easy to Make Inlay Wood Projects - Intarsia. 250p. 1993. pap. 19.95 (*1-56523-023-X*) Fox Chapel Pub.

— Fine Line Design: Circus & Clowns. Booher, Jerry, ed. (Design Book Ser.: No. 7). (Illus.). 37p. 1995. pap. 14.95 (*1-883083-06-0*) Roberts Studio.

— Fine Line Design: General. (Design Book Ser.: No. 1). 32p. 1992. pap. 14.95 (*1-883083-00-1*) Roberts Studio.

— Fine Line Design: Great Outdoors. (Design Book Ser.: No. 3). 35p. 1992. pap. 14.95 (*1-883083-02-8*) Roberts Studio.

— Fine Line Design: Pets & People. Booher, Jerry, ed. (Design Book Ser.: No. 6). (Illus.). 37p. 1994. pap. 14.95 (*1-883083-05-2*) Roberts Studio.

— Fine Line Design: Rural America. Booher, Jerry, ed. (Design Book Ser.: No. 5). (Illus.). 37p. 1993. pap. 14.95 (*1-883083-04-4*) Roberts Studio.

— Fine Line Design: Sports Book. Booher, Jerry, ed. (Design Book Ser.: No. 4). (Illus.). 42p. 1993. pap. 14.95 (*1-883083-03-6*) Roberts Studio.

— Fine Line Design: Western - South Western. (Design Book Ser.: No. 2). 37p. 1992. pap. 16.95 (*1-883083-01-X*) Roberts Studio.

Roberts, Judy G., jt. auth. see Booher, Jerry.

Roberts, Julian. The Logic of Reflection: German Philosophy in the Twentieth Century. 256p. (C). 1992. text ed. 32.00 (*0-300-05207-3*) Yale U Pr.

Roberts, Julian L., Jr., jt. auth. see Ifft, James B.

Roberts, Julian V. & Mohr, Renate M., eds. Sexual Assault in Canada: A Decade of Legal & Social Change. 384p. (C). 1994. 50.00 (*0-8020-5928-7*); pap. 19.95 (*0-8020-6868-5*) U of Toronto Pr.

Roberts, June C. Born in the Spring: A Collection of Spring Wildflowers. LC 75-36979. (Illus.). 160p. 1976. reprint ed. pap. 21.95 (*0-8214-0226-9*) Ohio U Pr.

— Season of Promise: Wild Plants in Winter, Northeastern United States. (Illus.). 336p. (C). 1992. 49.95 (*0-8214-1022-9*); pap. 24.95 (*0-8214-1023-7*) Ohio U Pr.

Roberts, K. & Tarkington, B. Collectors Whatnot. LC 77-96944. 1969. 4.50 (*0-87282-089-0*) Am Life Foun.

Roberts, K. B. & Tomlinson, J. D. The Fabric of the Body: European Traditions of Anatomical Illustration. (Illus.). 872p. 1992. 125.00 (*0-19-261198-4*) OUP.

Roberts, K. F., ed. Advanced Technology in Water Management. 257p. 1991. text ed. 76.00 (*0-7277-1638-7*, Pub. by T Telford UK) Am Soc Civil Eng.

Roberts, Karen. Night Magic. large type ed. 1994. pap. 20.95 (*0-7927-1872-0*, Paragon Lrg Print) Chivers N Amer.

***Roberts, Karen & Wilson, Mark, eds.** Policy Choices: NAFTA & Michigan's Future. 230p. 1996. pap. 21.95 (*0-87013-415-9*) Mich St U Pr.

Roberts, Karlene & Hunt, David M. Organizational Behavior. 800p. (C). 1991. text ed. 58.95 (*0-534-92249-X*) Intl Thomson.

Roberts, Karlene H. New Challenges to Understanding Organizations. LC 92-22771. (Illus.). 256p. (Orig.). (C). 1993. pap. write for info. (*0-02-402052-4*) Macmillan.

Roberts, Karlene H., et al. Developing an Interdisciplinary Science of Organizations. LC 78-62568. (Jossey-Bass Social & Behavioral Science Ser.). 191p. reprint ed. pap. 54.50 (*0-8357-6889-9*, 2037941) Bks Demand.

Roberts, Katherine E. Persistence & Change in Personality Patterns. (SRCD M: Vol. 8, No. 3). 1943. 21.00 (*0-527-01528-8*) Periodicals Srv.

Roberts, Katherine J. Fair Ladies: Sir Philip Sydney's Female Characters. LC 93-20209. (Renaissance & Baroque Studies & Texts: Vol. 9). 136p. 1993. 42.95 (*0-8204-2145-6*) P Lang Pubs.

Roberts, Keith. Anita. (Illus.). 195p. 1990. reprint ed. 20.25 (*0-913896-27-6*) Owlswick Pr.

— Bruegel. (Color Library). (Illus.). 128p. (C). 1994. reprint ed. pap. 14.95 (*0-7148-2239-6*, Pub. by Phaidon Press UK) Chronicle Bks.

— Bruegel. (Color Library). (Illus.). 128p. (C). 1994. reprint ed. 19.95 (*0-7148-3206-5*, Pub. by Phaidon Press UK) Chronicle Bks.

— Degas. (Color Library). (Illus.). 128p. (C). 1994. reprint ed. pap. text ed. 14.95 (*0-7148-2757-6*, Pub. by Phaidon Press UK) Chronicle Bks.

— Degas. (Color Library). (Illus.). 128p. (C). 1994. reprint ed. 19.95 (*0-7148-3212-X*, Pub. by Phaidon Press UK) Chronicle Bks.

— Soldiers of the English Civil War, Vol. 1: Infantry. (Elite Ser.: No. 25). (Illus.). 64p. pap. 12.95 (*0-85045-903-6*, 9425, Pub. by Osprey UK) Stackpole.

Roberts, Keith & Michels, Leo. Introductory Mathematics for Industry Science, & Technology. LC 85-7714. (Mathematics Ser.). 315p. (C). 1986. pap. 49.95 (*0-534-05148-0*) Brooks-Cole.

— Mathematics for Health Sciences. LC 81-12234. (Mathematics Ser.). 423p. (C). 1982. pap. 42.95 (*0-8185-0478-1*) Brooks-Cole.

Roberts, Keith A. Religion in Sociological Perspective. 2nd ed. 400p. (C). 1990. text ed. 42.95 (*0-534-12102-0*) Intl Thomson.

— Religion in Sociological Perspective. 3rd ed. 465p. 1995. text ed. 42.95 (*0-534-20466-X*) Intl Thomson.

***Roberts, Keli.** Keli Roberts' Fitness Hollywood: The Trainer to the Stars Shares Her Body-Shaping Secrets. 1994. 24.95 (*1-56530-147-1*) Summit TX.

***Roberts, Kelsey.** Handsome As Sin. 1995. pap. 3.50 (*0-373-22349-8*, 1-22349-4) Harlequin Bks.

— Legal Tender. (Intrigue Ser.). 1993. mass mkt. 2.99 (*0-373-22248-3*, 1-22248-8) Harlequin Bks.

— Stolen Memories. (Intrigue Ser.). 1994. mass mkt. 2.99 (*0-373-22276-9*) Harlequin Bks.

— Things Remembered. 1994. mass mkt. 2.99 (*0-373-22294-7*, 1-22294-2) Harlequin Bks.

— Undying Laughter. (Intrigue Ser.). 1995. mass mkt. 3.50 (*0-373-22334-X*, 1-22334-6) Harlequin Bks.

— Unlawfully Wedded. (Intrigue Ser.). 1995. mass mkt. 3.50 (*0-373-22330-7*, 1-22330-4) Harlequin Bks.

— Unspoken Confessions. (Intrigue Ser.). 1995. mass mkt. 3.50 (*0-373-22326-9*, 1-22326-2) Harlequin Bks.

Roberts, Ken. The Hollywood Principle: How to Use the "Magic" of Movies to Make Your Dreams Come True. LC 91-90145. (Illus.). 256p. (Orig.). (C). 1991. pap. text ed. 17.95 (*0-9629127-7-8*) Four Star Pub.

— A Rich Man's Secret: An Amazing Formula for Success. LC 95-6490. 1995. write for info. (*1-56718-588-6*) Llewellyn Pubns.

— Stephanie Kaye. (Degrassi Book Ser.). (YA). 1995. pap. 4.95 (*1-55028-109-7*); bds. 16.95 (*1-55028-111-9*) Formac Dist Ltd.

— Youth & Employment in Modern Britain. (Oxford Modern Britain Ser.). (Illus.). 144p. 1995. text ed. 39.95 (*0-19-827965-5*) OUP.

Roberts, Ken, jt. auth. see Castellarin, Loretta.

Roberts, Ken, jt. ed. see Kidd, Alan J.

Roberts, Kenneth. Arundel. 1986. pap. 3.95 (*0-449-21305-6*) Fawcett.

— Arundel. (Illus.). 496p. (YA). (gr. 10-12). 1995. reprint ed. pap. 15.95 (*0-89272-364-5*) Down East.

— The Battle of Cowpens. 15.95 (*0-89190-967-2*, Am Repr) Amereon Ltd.

— The Battle of Cowpens. 111p. 1981. pap. 3.50 (*0-915992-05-1*) Eastern Acorn.

— Captain Caution. 224p. 1982. pap. 2.95 (*0-449-24509-8*, Crest) Fawcett.

— Guidelines for Marketing a Community Pharmacy. 38p. (Orig.). 1983. pap. 12.00 (*0-910769-16-8*) Am Coll Apothecaries.

— The Kenneth Roberts Reader. 460p. 1976. reprint ed. lib. bdg. 23.95 (*0-89190-444-1*, Rivercity Pr) Amereon Ltd.

— Leisure. 2nd ed. LC 80-42055. (Aspects of Modern Sociology: the Social Structure of Modern Britain Ser.). 146p. reprint ed. pap. 41.70 (*0-317-27725-1*, 2025223) Bks Demand.

— The Lively Lady: A Chronicle of Arundel. large type ed. LC 94-15064. 405p. 1994. 20.95 (*0-8161-5996-3*) Hall.

— The Lively Lady: Chronicle of Arundel, of Privateering, & of the Circular Prison on Dartmoor. large type ed. 1994. write for info. (*0-318-72724-2*) Hall.

— Mary, the Perfect Prayer Partner. LC 89-64274. 134p. (Orig.). 1990. pap. 4.95 (*0-87973-451-5*, 451) Our Sunday Visitor.

— Northwest Passage. 1986. mass mkt. 4.95 (*0-449-21383-8*) Fawcett.

— The Northwest Passage. 1983. write for info. (*0-318-56616-8*) Haas Ent NH.

— Oliver Wiswell. 1983. mass mkt. 4.95 (*0-449-21193-2*) Fawcett.

— School Leavers & Their Prospects: Youth & the Labor Market in the 1980's. 169p. 1984. pap. 25.00 (*0-335-10418-5*, Open Univ Pr) Taylor & Francis.

— Up on the Mountain. LC 92-64000. 220p. (Orig.). 1992. pap. 8.95 (*1-55725-053-7*) Paraclete MA.

— The Working Class. LC 77-26300. (Aspects of Modern Sociology Ser.). 216p. reprint ed. pap. 61.60 (*0-317-27663-8*, 2025212) Bks Demand.

— Youth & Leisure. (Leisure & Recreation Studies: No. 3). 240p. 1985. pap. text ed. 18.95 (*0-04-301204-3*) Routledge Chapman & Hall.

Roberts, Kenneth, jt. auth. see Huffman, D. C.

Roberts, Kenneth A. & Sharpels, Win, Jr. A Primer for Film-Making: A Complete Guide to 16 & 35mm Film Production. 560p. (C). 1971. pap. write for info. (*0-02-402070-2*) Macmillan.

Roberts, Kenneth B. Manual of Clinical Problems in Pediatrics. 2nd ed. 1985. spiral bd. 22.50 (*0-316-74990-7*) Little.

***Roberts, Kenneth B., ed.** Manual of Clinical Problems in Pediatrics: With Annotated Key References. 4th ed. LC 94-22643. (Illus.). 1994. 28.95 (*0-316-75006-9*) Little.

Roberts, Kenneth B., jt. auth. see Davis, Roger L.

Roberts, Kenneth B., jt. auth. see Huffman, D. C.

Roberts, Kenneth D. Agrarian Structure & Labor Migration in Rural Mexico. (Research Report Ser.: No. 30). 46p. (Orig.). (C). 1981. ring bd. 5.00 (*0-935391-29-0*, RR-30) UCSD Ctr US-Mex.

— The Contributions of Joseph Ives to Connecticut Clock Technology, 1810-1862. 2nd rev. ed. (Illus.). 388p. 1988. 40.00 (*0-913602-65-5*) K Roberts.

— Introduction to Rule Collecting. (Illus.). 22p. (Orig.). 1982. pap. text ed. 3.00 (*0-913602-52-3*) K Roberts.

R

— Scottish & English Spiers-Norris Metal Planes. 2nd rev. ed. (Illus.). 100p. 1991. pap. text ed. 15.00 (*0-913602-69-8*) K Roberts.
— Some 19th Century English Woodworking Tools. rev. ed. (Illus.). 500p. 1991. 42.50 (*0-913602-68-X*) K Roberts.
— The Stanley Combination Plane. rev. ed. (Illus.). 80p. 1989. pap. 8.50 (*0-9618088-3-7*) Astragal Pr.
— Tools for the Trades & Crafts. 1976. 25.00 (*0-913602-18-3*) K Roberts.
— Wooden Planes in Nineteenth Century America, Vol. II. (Illus.). 472p. 1983. 40.00 (*0-913602-59-0*) K Roberts.
Roberts, Kenneth D., ed. Belcher Brothers & Co.'s Eighteen Sixty Price List of Boxwood & Ivory Rules. (Illus.). 40p. 1982. reprint ed. pap. text ed. 5.00 (*1-879335-06-9*) Astragal Pr.
— The Carpenter's Slide Rule: Its History & Use. 32p. (Orig.). 1982. pap. text ed. 4.00 (*1-879335-16-6*) Astragal Pr.
— John Rabone & Sons Eighteen Ninety-Two Catalogue of Rules, Tapes, Spirit Levels, etc. (Illus.). 96p. 1982. reprint ed. pap. 16.95 (*1-879335-15-8*) Astragal Pr.
— Lufkin Measuring Instruments, 1888-1940: Excerpts from Trade Catalogues. (Illus.). 72p. 1983. pap. text ed. 6.50 (*1-879335-11-5*) Astragal Pr.
Roberts, Kenneth D. & Roberts, Jane W. Planemakers & Other Edge Tool Enterprises in New York State in the Nineteenth Century. 2nd rev. ed. (Illus.). 244p. 1989. reprint ed. pap. text ed. 30.00 (*0-913602-66-3*) K Roberts.
***Roberts, Kenneth D. & Taylor, Snowden.** Eli Terry & the Connecticut Shelf Clock. 2nd rev. ed. (Illus.). 384p. 1994. 40.00 (*0-913602-71-X*) K Roberts.
— Forestville Clockmakers. (Illus.). 177p. (Orig.). 1992. pap. 24.00 (*0-913602-67-1*) K Roberts.
— Jonathan Clark Brown & the Forestville Manufacturing Co. (Illus.). 120p. 1988. pap. 18.75 (*0-913602-64-7*) K Roberts.
Roberts, Kenneth H. & Sharples, Win, Jr. Primer for Film-Making: A Complete Guide to 16mm & 35mm Film Production. LC 70-91620. (Illus.). 1971. pap. 17.55 (*0-672-63582-8*) Pegasus.
Roberts, Kenneth J. The Evangelizers. Waters, Anna M., ed. (Illus.). 100p. (Orig.). 1984. pap. text ed. 3.50 (*0-9610984-2-2*) PAX Tapes.
— Mary, the Perfect Prayer Partner. Waters, Anna Marie, ed. LC 83-61151. (Illus.). 128p. (Orig.). 1983. pap. 3.95 (*0-9610984-1-4*) PAX Tapes.
— Playboy to Priest. LC 78-169145. 304p. 1974. reprint ed. pap. 5.95 (*0-87973-782-4*) Our Sunday Visitor.
— Pray It Again, Sam. Ruskin, Anna Marie, ed. LC 83-61243. 116p. (Orig.). 1983. pap. 3.95 (*0-9610984-0-6*) PAX Tapes.
— Pray it Again, Sam. LC 91-61272. 112p. (Orig.). 1991. pap. 4.95 (*0-87973-461-2*, 461) Our Sunday Visitor.
— The Rest of the Week. LC 73-87984. 191p. 1988. reprint ed. pap. text ed. 5.95 (*0-318-37581-8*) PAX Tapes.
— You Better Believe It. LC 77-84944. (Illus.). 1977. pap. 6.95 (*0-87973-750-6*) Our Sunday Visitor.
Roberts, Kenneth L. Why Europe Leaves Home: a True Account of the Reasons Which Cause Central Europeans to Overrun America. Grob, Gerald, ed. LC 76-46100. (Anti-Movements in America Ser.). 1977. reprint ed. lib. bdg. 34.95 (*0-405-09971-1*) Ayer.
Roberts, Kim. The Wishbone Galaxy. LC 94-4232. 1994. 10.00 (*0-931846-45-5*) Wash Writers Pub.
Roberts, L., jt. ed. see Crouch, M. A.
Roberts, L. E., et al. Power Generation & the Environment. (Science, Technology, & Society Ser.: No. 6). (Illus.). 224p. 1990. 49.95 (*0-19-858338-9*) OUP.
Roberts, L. R., jt. ed. see Skalny, J. P.
Roberts, L. W., jt. auth. see Dodds, John H.
Roberts, L. W., et al. Vascular Differentiation & Plant Growth Regulators. (Wood Science Ser.). (Illus.). x, 154p. 1988. 111.00 (*0-387-18989-0*) Spr-Verlag.
Roberts, Lamar, jt. auth. see Penfield, Wilder.
Roberts, Larenda. Dallas Uncovered. LC 94-11345. 1994. 12.95 (*1-55622-378-1*, Rep of TX Pr) Wordware Pub.
Roberts, Larry. Underwater World of Sport Diving. 240p. 1991. pap. 15.95 (*0-8016-4130-6*) Mosby Yr Bk.
Roberts, Larry S., jt. auth. see Hickman, Cleveland P., Jr.
***Roberts, Larry S., et al.** Foundations of Parasitology. 5th ed. 736p. (C). 1995. text ed. write for info. (*0-697-26071-2*) Wm C Brown Pubs.
Roberts, Launey F., Jr., ed. Individualizing Instruction in Educational Administration: A Performance-Based Worktext. 256p. 1976. pap. text ed. 8.25 (*0-8422-0531-4*) Irvington.
Roberts, Laura, jt. auth. see Kirby, Colleen.
***Roberts, Laura V.** First Thessalonians 5:21: The Resurrection, the Jews, & the Hebrew Calendar. 2nd expanded large type ed. LC 94-76999. (Illus.). 176p. 1994. spiral bd. 14.95 (*0-9632387-6-0*) LVI Pubns.
Roberts, Laurance. The Bernard Berenson Collection of Oriental Art at Villa I Tatti. LC 91-71550. (Illus.). 112p. 1991. 50.00 (*1-55595-060-4*) Hudson Hills.
Roberts, Lawrence C. The Gospel Truth. (Illus.). 48p. 1994. pap. 9.95 (*0-8059-3459-6*) Dorrance.
Roberts, Lawrence D. How Reference Works: Explanatory Models for Indexicals, Descriptions, & Opacity. LC 92-31942. (SUNY Series, Scientific Studies in Natural & Artificial Intelligence). 202p. (C). 1993. 57.50 (*0-7914-1575-9*); pap. 18.95 (*0-7914-1576-7*) State U NY Pr.
Roberts, Lawrence D., ed. Approaches to Nature in the Middle Ages. LC 82-8264. (Medieval & Renaissance Texts & Studies: Vol. 16). (Illus.). 1982. 20.00 (*0-86698-051-2*) MRTS.
Roberts, Lee. The Policy Environment of Management Development Institutions in Anglophone Africa: Problems & Prospects for Reform. (EDI Policy Seminar Report Ser.: No. 26). 60p. 1990. 6.95 (*0-8213-1613-3*, 11613) World Bank.
Roberts, Leigh. Built to Last. (Superromance Ser.). 1993. mass mkt. 3.39 (*0-373-70543-3*, 1-70543-3) Harlequin Bks.
Roberts, Leigh M., ed. see Symposium on Comprehensive Mental Health Staff.
Roberts, Leigh M., et al, eds. Comprehensive Mental Health: The Challenge of Evaluation. (Illus.). 350p. 1968. 30.00 (*0-299-05000-9*) U of Wis Pr.
Roberts, Lemuel. Memoirs of Captain Lemuel Roberts. Decker, Peter, ed. LC 70-79945. (Eyewitness Accounts of the American Revolution Ser., No. 1). 1969. reprint ed. 15.95 (*0-405-01175-X*) Ayer.
Roberts, Len. Black Wings. (National Poetry Ser.: 1988). 64p. 1989. pap. 9.95 (*0-89255-141-0*) Persea Bks.
— Counting the Black Angels: Poems. LC 93-30476. 96p. 1994. pap. 12.95 (*0-252-06381-3*) U of Ill Pr.
— Dangerous Angels. LC 93-12261. 64p. (Orig.). 1993. pap. 9.95 (*0-914278-61-4*) Copper Beech.
— Learning about the Heart. 28p. 1992. pap. 5.00 (*1-878851-03-9*) Silverfish Rev Pr.
— Sweet Ones: Poems. LC 87-63529. (Lakes & Prairies Ser.). 72p. (Orig.). 1988. pap. 6.95 (*0-915943-24-7*) Milkweed Ed.
Roberts, Len, tr. see Csoori, Sandor.
Roberts, Leonard W. South from Hell-fer-Sartin: Kentucky Mountain Folk Tales. LC 87-30039. 296p. 1988. 28.00 (*0-8131-1637-6*); pap. 14.95 (*0-8131-0175-1*) U Pr of Ky.
— Up Cutshin & Down Greasy. LC 87-29600. 176p. 1988. 22.00 (*0-8131-1638-4*) U Pr of Ky.
Roberts, Les. The Cleveland Connection. LC 92-42606. 1993. 19.95 (*0-312-08746-2*, Pub. by Thomas Dunne Bks) St Martin.
— Deep Shaker. 1991. 17.95 (*0-312-05855-1*) St Martin.
— The Lake Effect. 352p. 1994. 21.95 (*0-312-11537-7*, Pub. by Thomas Dunne Bks) St Martin.
— The Lemon Chicken Jones. 288p. 1993. 20.95 (*0-312-10490-1*, Pub. by Thomas Dunne Bks) St Martin.
Roberts, Leslie. Cancer Today: Origins, Prevention & Treatment. LC 84-19031. (Illus.). 144p. reprint ed. pap. 41.10 (*0-8357-6647-0*, 2035314) Bks Demand.
— The Mackenzie. LC 73-20906. 276p. 1974. reprint ed. text ed. 59.75 (*0-8371-5864-8*, ROMR, Greenwood Pr) Greenwood.
Roberts, Lewes. The Marchants Mapp of Commerce. LC 74-80203. (English Experience Ser.: No. 689). 468p. 1974. reprint ed. 126.00 (*90-221-0689-6*) Walter J Johnson.
***Roberts, Lewis, ed.** Innovation & Environmental Risk. 1994. text ed. 69.95 (*0-471-94762-8*) Wiley.
Roberts, Lewis & Wheale, Albert, eds. Innovation & Environmental Risk. 1992. text ed. 57.95 (*1-85293-156-6*, Pub. by Pinter Pubs Ltd UK) CRC Pr.
***Roberts, Lewis E.** The By-Name Index to the Centennial History of Arkansas. 1994. pap. 28.50 (*0-941765-97-0*) Arkansas Res.
— The By-Name Index to the Centennial History of Arkansas. 2nd ed. 260p. 1994. 38.50 (*0-941765-96-2*) Arkansas Res.
***Roberts, Libby.** Survival Skills. (All Action Ser.). (Illus.). 48p. (J). (gr. 4 up). 1993. 17.50 (*0-8225-2481-3*, Lerner Publctns) Lerner Group.
Roberts, Linleigh J. Let Us Make Man. 168p. (Orig.). (C). 1988. pap. 9.95 (*0-85151-525-8*) Banner of Truth.
Roberts, Lois J. San Miguel Island: Santa Barbara's Fourth Island West. LC 91-73715. 224p. 1992. pap. 9.95 (*0-9630370-0-5*) Cal Rim.
Roberts, Lon. Process Reengineering: The Key to Achieving Break-Through Success. LC 93-45524. 1994. write for info. (*0-87389-274-7*) ASQC Qual Pr.
Roberts, Lora. Murder in a Nice Neighborhood. (Northern California Mysteries Ser.). (Orig.). 1994. mass mkt. 4.99 (*0-449-14891-2*, GM) Fawcett.
— Murder in the Marketplace. 1995. mass mkt. 5.50 (*0-449-14890-4*) Fawcett.
Roberts, Lorin W. Cytodifferentiation in Plants: Xylogenesis as a Model System. LC 75-10041. (Developmental & Cell Biology Ser.). 174p. reprint ed. pap. 49.60 (*0-317-26380-3*, 2024522) Bks Demand.
Roberts, Lorin W., jt. auth. see Dodds, John H.
Roberts, Louis. The Theological Aesthetics of Hans Urs von Balthasar. 1987. 36.95 (*0-8132-0634-0*) Cath U Pr.
— The Theological Aesthetics of Hans Urs von Balthasar. LC 86-28321. 272p. Date not set. reprint ed. pap. 77.60 (*0-7837-9118-6*, 2049919) Bks Demand.
Roberts, Louis F. Italian Greyhounds. 1990. 11.95 (*0-86622-770-9*, KW188) TFH Pubns.
Roberts, Lydia J. The Dona Elena Project. 113p. 1963. pap. 3.00 (*0-8477-2420-4*) U of PR Pr.
Roberts, Lydia J. & Stefani, Rosa L. Patterns of Living in Puerto Rican Families. LC 74-14247. (Puerto Rican Experience Ser.). (Illus.). 440p. 1975. reprint ed. 35.95 (*0-405-06233-8*) Ayer.
Roberts, Lynda. Mitt Magic: Fingerplays for Finger Puppets. (Illus.). (Orig.). (ps-1). 1986. pap. 9.95 (*0-87659-111-X*) Gryphon Hse.
Roberts, Lynn, ed. see Wilson, Theodore A.
Roberts, Lynn S. & Turner, Eric. English Silver: Masterpieces by Omar Ramsden from the Campbell Collection. 60p. 1992. pap. 15.00 (*0-9632870-0-1*) D A Hanks.
Roberts, Lynn S., jt. auth. see Wardropper, Ian.
Roberts, M. Mishnah-Nezikin: Bava Basra. Danziger, Y., ed. (ArtScroll Mishnah Ser.). (Illus.). 240p. 1986. 22.95 (*0-89906-293-8*) Mesorah Pubns.
— Mishnah-Nezikin: Sanhedrin. Danzinger, Y., ed. (ArtScroll Mishnah Ser.). (Illus.). 206p. 1987. 22.95 (*0-89906-295-4*) Mesorah Pubns.
Roberts, M. & Arem, T. Z. Mishnah-Nashim: Gittin-Kiddushin. (ArtScroll Mishnah Ser.). (Illus.). 314p. 1986. 22.95 (*0-89906-283-0*) Mesorah Pubns.
Roberts, M, ed. see Grimmer, Glenna.
Roberts, M., ed. see Kahrimanis, Leola.
Roberts, M., ed. see Kerr, Rita.
Roberts, M., ed. see Liles, Maurine W.
Roberts, M., ed. see Pamplin, Laurel J.
Roberts, M. I. Managing a Shoot. (Illus.). 112p. 1990. 24.95 (*0-948253-43-6*, Pub. by Sportsmans Pr UK) Trafalgar.
Roberts, M. L. World's Weirdest Bugs & Other Creepy Crawlies. LC 94-18027. (Illus.). 32p. (J). (ps-2). 1994. lib. bdg. 11.89 (*0-8167-3536-0*, Whistlstop); pap. 2.25 (*0-8167-3537-9*, Whistlstop) Troll Assocs.
— World's Weirdest Reptiles. LC 93-8493. (Illus.). 32p. (J). (gr. 2-9). 1993. lib. bdg. 11.89 (*0-8167-3229-9*); pap. 2.95 (*0-8167-3221-3*) Troll Assocs.
— World's Weirdest Underwater Creatures. LC 93-21053. (J). 1993. lib. bdg. 11.89 (*0-8167-3230-2*); pap. 2.95 (*0-8167-3222-1*) Troll Assocs.
***Roberts, M. L., ed. & illus.** World's Weirdest Birds. LC 95-17781. 32p. (J). (gr. k-3). 1995. lib. bdg. 12.50 (*0-8167-3733-9*, Whistlstop); pap. 2.50 (*0-8167-3734-7*, Whistlstop) Troll Assocs.
Roberts, M. S. Genealogy of the Descendants of John Kirk, 1660-1705. Cope, G., ed. (Illus.). 729p. reprint ed. lib. bdg. 107.50 (*0-8328-0735-4*); reprint ed. pap. 99.50 (*0-8328-0736-2*) Higginson Bk Co.
***Roberts, M. Susan.** Living Without Procrastination: How to Stop Postponing Your Life. 195p. (Orig.). 1995. text ed. 24.95 (*1-57224-027-X*); pap. 12.95 (*1-57224-026-1*) New Harbinger.
Roberts, Madge T. Star of Destiny: The Private Life of Sam & Margaret Houston. LC 92-31587. 464p. 1993. 29.50 (*0-929398-51-3*) UNTX Pr.

***Roberts, Malcolm B. The Wit & Wisdom of Wally Hickel. 2nd ed. LC 94-93929. (Illus.). 240p. 1995. reprint ed. text ed. 24.95 (*0-9644316-1-0*); reprint ed. pap. text ed. 14.95 (*0-9644316-0-2*) Searchers Pr.**
Quips & quotes from one of America's boldest & most interesting thinkers, former US Interior Secretary Walter J. Hickel. Fired by President Richard Nixon for defending America's youth during the Vietnam era, twice governor of Alaska, Hickel became known for his colorful expressions: "If I leave the cabinet (he told 60 Minutes), I'll go with an arrow in my heart, not a bullet in my back." Later: "A true environmentalist is a caveman without a match." His phrases, dubbed "Hickelisms" by the AP, were collected over 25 years by Roberts. Subjects range from optimism about the "inexhaustible earth" & the future of humanity, to practical ways to protect the environment, build a culture & beat poverty. PAUL HARVEY writes: "Wally Hickel...is able to reduce complex considerations to shirt-sleeve English...a treasure trove for researchers & constructive bedtime reading for us all." MIKE DOOGAN, Anchorage Daily News: "There's a gem on nearly every page." You'll laugh, you'll be challenged, you'll discover 400 timeless quotes for speeches & writing. Order from: Searchers Press, 2001 Churchill, Anchorage, AK 99517; 907-258-1167. ***Publisher Provided Annotation.***

***Roberts, Marc.** Neue Lexikon der Esoterik. 461p. (GER.). 1993. 75.00 (*0-7859-8426-7*, 3552045015) Fr & Eur.
Roberts, Marc J. & Bluhm, Jeremy S. The Choices of Power: Utilities Face the Environmental Challenge. LC 80-20729. 468p. reprint ed. pap. 133.40 (*0-7837-4110-3*, 2057933) Bks Demand.
Roberts, Margaret. Pioneer California: Tales of Explorers, Indians, & Settlers. LC 81-22543. (Illus.). 296p. (J). (gr. 6 up). 1982. 12.95 (*0-914598-42-2*) Bear Flag Bks.
— Pot-Pourri Making. LC 94-5873. (Illus.). 96p. 1994. pap. 10.95 (*0-8117-2590-1*) Stackpole.
— Summer Cooking with Herbs. LC 94-8636. (Illus.). 104p. 1994. pap. 10.95 (*0-8117-3070-0*) Stackpole.
— Winter Cooking with Herbs. LC 94-9077. (Illus.). 96p. 1994. pap. 10.95 (*0-8117-3096-4*) Stackpole.
Roberts, Margaret C. Trial Psychology: Communication & Persuasion in the Courtroom. 490p. 1987. boxed 95.00 (*0-409-25105-4*) Michie Butterworth.
Roberts, Marie & Ormsby-Lennon, Hugh, eds. Secret Texts: The Literature of Secret Societies. LC 91-13789. (Studies in Cultural History: No. 1). 1992. 45.00 (*0-404-64251-9*) AMS Pr.
Roberts, Marie E. Gothic Immortals: The Fiction of the Brotherhood of the Rosy Cross. 256p. 1990. 35.00 (*0-415-02368-8*, A3721) Routledge.
Roberts, Marie M. The Artist's Design: Probing the Hidden Order. (Illus.). 208p. (Orig.). 1993. pap. 54.00 (*0-9639758-0-3*) Fradema Pr.
***Roberts, Marie M. & Mizuta, Tamae.** Controversies in the History of British Feminism, 6 vols., Set. (History of British Feminism Ser.). 1995. boxed 720.00 (*0-415-11873-5*, C0434, Pub. by Thoemmes Pr UK) Routledge.
***Roberts, Marie M. & Mizuta, Tamae, eds.** Perspectives on the History of British Feminism, 6 vols., Set. (History of British Feminism Ser.). 2301p. 1994. boxed 695.00 (*0-415-10352-5*, B4783, Pub. by Thoemmes Pr UK) Routledge.
Roberts, Marie M. & Porter, Roy, eds. Literature & Medicine During the Eighteenth Century. LC 92-23538. (Wellcome Institute Series in the History of Medicine). (Illus.). 304p. 1993. 74.50 (*0-415-07082-1*, A9942) Routledge.
Roberts, Marie M. & Zephaniah, Benjamin, eds. Out of the Night: Writings from Death Row. (Illus.). 192p. 1994. 45.00 (*1-873797-10-9*, Pub. by New Clarion UK); pap. 17.95 (*1-873797-09-5*, Pub. by New Clarion UK) Paul & Co Pubs.
Roberts, Marilyn M., et al. Women in the Judiciary: A Symposium for Women Judges. LC 83-22047. 116p. 1983. pap. 7.00 (*0-89656-072-4*, R-084) Natl Ctr St Courts.
Roberts, Marion. Living in a Man-Made World: Gender Assumptions in Modern Housing Design. (Illus.). 192p. 1991. 39.95 (*0-415-05747-7*, A5114); pap. 14.95 (*0-415-03237-7*, A5118) Routledge.
— Mediation in Family Disputes: A Guide to Practice. (Community Care Practice Handbook Ser.). 120p. 1988. pap. text ed. 19.95 (*0-7045-0585-1*, Pub. by Gower UK) Ashgate Pub Co.
Roberts, Marion, jt. auth. see Davies, Gwynn.
Roberts, Mark. CC, OT, Vol. 11: Ezra-Nehemiah. 1993. 21.99 (*0-8499-0416-1*) Word Inc.
— SEAL Team Combat Missions: Search & Destroy. 1994. pap. 4.99 (*1-56171-328-7*) Sure Sellers.
***Roberts, Mark & Watson, Jim.** Navy Seals: Shoot & Scoot. 290p. 1995. pap. 5.50 (*1-56171-386-4*) Sure Sellers.
Roberts, Mark E. War Drums. 256p. 1993. pap. 3.50 (*0-8217-4268-X*) Zebra.
Roberts, Mark E., jt. auth. see Roberts, Gregory.
Roberts, Mark K. Gallow Riders. 240p. 1986. pap. 2.50 (*0-8217-1934-3*) Zebra.
— Jakarta Coup. (Soldier for Hire Ser.: No. 8). (Orig.). 1983. pap. 2.50 (*0-8217-1225-X*) Zebra.
— Prairie Fire. 288p. 1993. pap. 3.50 (*0-8217-4167-5*) Zebra.
— Soldier for Hire, No. 1: Commando Squad. 1982. pap. 2.50 (*0-8217-1094-X*) Zebra.
— Soldier for Hire, No. 7: Pathet Vengeance. 1983. pap. 2.50 (*0-8217-1140-7*) Zebra.
— Thunder Hooves. 256p. 1993. pap. 3.50 (*0-8217-4071-7*) Zebra.
— Warrior Outlaws. 256p. 1993. pap. 3.50 (*0-8217-4374-0*) Zebra.
Roberts, Mark K. & Andrews, Patrick. Apache Gold. 336p. 1986. pap. 2.95 (*0-8217-1899-1*) Zebra.
Roberts, Mark S., tr. see Lyotard, Jean-Francois.
Roberts, Mark S., ed. see Lyotard, Jean-Francois.
Roberts, Marta. Tumbleweeds. LC 74-22805. reprint ed. 37.50 (*0-404-58461-6*) AMS Pr.
Roberts, Martha D., jt. auth. see Roberts, Mervin F.
Roberts, Martha G. Honeymaid: The Story of Silver Dollar Tabor. 1977. pap. 3.95 (*0-87315-064-3*) Golden Bell.
Roberts, Martin. Italian Renaissance. (Longman Origin Ser.). 1992. pap. text ed. 10.64 (*0-582-08252-8*) Longman.
— Machines & Liberty, a Portrait of Europe 1789-1914. (Portrait of Europe Ser.). (Illus.). 1972. pap. 16.95 (*0-19-913040-X*) OUP.
— Michel Tournier: "Bricolage" & Cultural Mythology. (Stanford French & Italian Studies: No. 79). 192p. 1995. pap. 46.50 (*0-915838-95-8*) Anma Libri.
— The New Barbarism? A Portrait of Europe 1900-1973. (Portrait of Europe Ser.). (Illus.). 1975. pap. 16.95 (*0-19-913225-9*) OUP.
Roberts, Martin M., tr. see Taibo, Paco I., 2nd.
Roberts, Marvin L. & Stuckey, Ronald L. Bibliography of Theses & Dissertations on Ohio Floristics & Vegetation in Ohio Colleges & Universities. (Informative Circular Ser.: No. 7). 1974. 2.00 (*0-86727-074-8*) Ohio Bio Survey.
Roberts, Mary. The Creeper. LC 93-134. (J). 1994. write for info. (*0-383-03684-4*) SRA Schl Grp.
Roberts, Mary, jt. ed. see Johnson, Susan.
Roberts, Mary, ed. see Scherer, Bonnie L.
Roberts, Mary J. Tangled Vines. LC 86-21683. 252p. 1987. 16.95 (*0-916515-16-8*) Mercury Hse Inc.
Roberts, Mary Jo. Write with Your Ears. (Illus.). 158p. 1983. student ed 14.95 (*0-913609-01-3*); pap. 19.95 (*0-913609-00-5*) Hse of Tomorrow.
Roberts, Mary K. & Bergner, Raymond M., eds. Advances in Descriptive Psychology, Vol. VI: Clinical Topics: Adolescent-Family Problems, Bulimia, Chronic Mental Illness, & Mania. 316p. (C). 1991. 70.00 (*0-9625661-1-X*) Descriptive Psych Pr.
Roberts, Mary L. Civilization Without Sexes: Reconstructing Gender in Postwar France, 1917-1927. LC 93-26899. (Women in Culture & Society Ser.). 1994. lib. bdg. 48.00 (*0-226-72121-3*); pap. text ed. 18.95 (*0-226-72122-1*) U Ch Pr.
Roberts, Mary L. & Berger, Paul. Direct Marketing Management. 440p. 1989. text ed. 65.00 (*0-13-214784-X*) P-H.
***Roberts, Mary N., et al.** African Masterworks in the Detroit Institute of Arts. LC 95-6169. (Illus.). 192p. 1995. 34.95 (*1-56098-602-6*) Smithsonian.
Roberts, Marylyle. Chanting the Morning Star. Tolley, Carolyn, ed. 320p. (Orig.). 1993. mass mkt. 5.50 (*0-671-74563-8*, Pocket Star Bks) PB.

Roberts, Matis. Mishnah-Kodashim, Vol. 1B: Menachos. Kempler, Naftoli & Danziger, Yehezkel, eds. (ArtScroll Mishnah Ser.). 302p. 1989. 22.95 (*0-89906-303-9*) Mesorah Pubns.

Roberts, Matt & Etherington, Don. Bookbinding & the Conservation of Books: A Dictionary of Descriptive Terminology. LC 81-607974. (Illus.). x, 296p. 1982. 27.00 (*0-8444-0366-0*, 030-000-00126-5) Lib Congress.

Roberts, Matthew W. Export Processing Zones in Jamaica & Mauritius: Evolution of an Export-Oriented Development Model. LC 92-30975. 200p. 1992. text ed. 79.95 (*0-7734-9837-0*) E Mellen.

— The Impact of the World Bank & IMF on Political Developments in Sub-Saharan Africa: Examples from Ghana & Kenya. (Graduate Student Term Paper Ser.). 33p. 1986. pap. text ed. 2.00 (*0-941934-50-0*) Indiana Africa.

Roberts, Maurice. The Thought of God. 232p. 1993. pap. 7.95 (*0-85151-658-0*) Banner of Truth.

Roberts, Maxine B., comp. The Cousin Finder Directory: A Related Line Locating Aid, Vol. 1. 146p. (Orig.). 1985. pap. text ed. 10.00 (*0-9616192-0-1*) Roberts CA.

Roberts, Maxine B., ed. The Cousin Finder Directory: A Related Line Locating Aid, Vol. 2. (Orig.). 1988. pap. text ed. write for info. (*0-9616192-2-8*) Roberts CA.

Roberts, Meg-Lynn. An Alluring Lady. 1992. mass mkt. 3.99 (*0-8217-3757-0*) Zebra.

— Christmas Escapade. 320p. 1994. mass mkt. 3.99 (*0-8217-4787-8*) Zebra.

— A Midnight Masquerade. 320p. 1993. mass mkt. 3.99 (*0-8217-4336-8*) Zebra.

— A Perfect Match. 320p. 1993. mass mkt. 3.99 (*0-8217-4140-3*) Zebra.

Roberts, Melissa, ed. see Baker, Charlotte.

Roberts, Melissa, ed. see Beverley, Mary F.

Roberts, Melissa, ed. see Bradshaw, Thomas I. & Clark, Marsha.

Roberts, Melissa, ed. see Carson, Geraldine P.

Roberts, Melissa, ed. see Charles, H. Robert.

Roberts, Melissa, ed. see Clendenin, Mary J.

Roberts, Melissa, ed. see Donaly, E. Brice.

Roberts, Melissa, ed. see Ebeling, Jean.

Roberts, Melissa, ed. see Gurasich, Marjorie A.

Roberts, Melissa, ed. see Harman, Betty & Meador, Nancy.

Roberts, Melissa, ed. see Hart, Jan S.

Roberts, Melissa, ed. see Kerr, Rita.

Roberts, Melissa, ed. see Machado, Manuel A., Jr.

Roberts, Melissa, ed. see Matthews, Billie P. & Chichester, A. Lee.

Roberts, Melissa, ed. see O'Neal, Bill.

Roberts, Melissa, ed. see Parnell, Ben.

Roberts, Melissa, ed. see Sharpe, George.

Roberts, Melissa, ed. see Swendson, Patsy.

Roberts, Melissa, ed. see Swift, Roy.

Roberts, Melissa, ed. see Townsend, Tom.

Roberts, Melissa, ed. see Wade, Mary D.

Roberts, Melissa, ed. see Westmoreland, Ronald P.

Roberts, Melissa, ed. see Wiggs, Susan.

Roberts, Melissa, ed. see Wilkins, Frederick.

Roberts, Mervin F. All about Breeding Budgerigars. (Illus.). 96p. 1989. 9.95 (*0-86622-997-3*, PS-804) TFH Pubns.

— All about Breeding Lovebirds. (Illus.). 96p. 1983. 9.95 (*0-86622-695-8*, PS-800) TFH Pubns.

— All about Chameleons & Anoles. (Illus.). 80p. 1989. 9.95 (*0-86622-795-4*, PS-310) TFH Pubns.

— All about Ferrets. (Illus.). 1977. 29.95 (*0-87666-914-3*, PS-754) TFH Pubns.

— All about Land Hermit Crabs. (Illus.). 96p. 1989. pap. 9.95 (*0-86622-793-8*, PS-767) TFH Pubns.

— A Complete Introduction to Hamsters. (Illus.). 128p. 1987. pap. 5.95 (*0-86622-282-0*) TFH Pubns.

— A Complete Introduction to Snakes. (Complete Introduction to...Ser.). (Illus.). 128p. (Orig.). 1987. pap. 5.95 (*0-86622-352-5*, CO-023S) TFH Pubns.

— Pearlmakers: The Tidemarsh Guide to Clams, Oysters, Mussels & Scallops. LC 84-50701. (Tidemarsh Guides Ser.). (Illus.). 168p. 1984. 6.95 (*0-917941-00-4*) M Roberts.

— Snakes. 1985. pap. 5.95 (*0-86622-784-9*) TFH Pubns.

— Snakes. (Illus.). 80p. 1990. pap. text ed. 5.95 (*0-86622-861-6*, PB-126) TFH Pubns.

— Starting Right with Rabbits. (Illus.). 128p. 1983. 9.95 (*0-87666-814-7*, PS-796) TFH Pubns.

— Terrariums for Your New Pet. (Illus.). 64p. (Orig.). 1990. pap. 5.95 (*0-86622-525-0*, TU-017) TFH Pubns.

— The Tidemarsh Guide. LC 79-63522. (Tidemarsh Guides Ser.). (Illus.). 240p. 1985. 5.95 (*0-933614-19-5*) M Roberts.

— The Tidemarsh Guide to Fishes. LC 85-90364. (Tidemarsh Guides Ser.). (Illus.). 370p. (Orig.). 1985. 10.95 (*0-9615047-0-6*) M Roberts.

— Zebra Finches. (Illus.). 1981. 9.95 (*0-86622-762-8*, KW-055) TFH Pubns.

Roberts, Mervin F. & Roberts, Martha D. All about Iguanas. (Orig.). 1976. 9.95 (*0-86622-747-4*, PS-311) TFH Pubns.

Roberts, Michael. The Age of Liberty: Sweden 1719-1772. 185p. 1986. 49.95 (*0-521-32092-5*) Cambridge U Pr.

— Blackjack: You & Me Against the Dealer. 150p. 1991. pap. 12.95 (*0-9630817-2-1*) Emery-Oakes.

— British Diplomacy & Swedish Politics, 1758-1773. LC 80-11499. (Nordic Ser.: No. 1). 553p. reprint ed. pap. 157.70 (*0-7837-2925-1*, 2057529) Bks Demand.

— The Early Vasas: A History of Sweden, 1523-1611. LC 68-10332. 524p. reprint ed. pap. 149.40 (*0-317-09282-0*, 2022468) Bks Demand.

— Fresh from the Freezer. LC 90-5750. 384p. 1990. 19.95 (*0-688-08543-1*) Morrow.

— From Oxenstierna to Charles Twelfth: Four Studies in Swedish History. 214p. (C). 1991. 49.95 (*0-521-40014-7*) Cambridge U Pr.

— Gustavus Adolphus. 2nd ed. (Profiles in Power Ser.). 216p. (C). 1992. text ed. 49.50 (*0-582-09001-6*, 79385); pap. text ed. 21.95 (*0-582-09000-8*, 79384) Longman.

— An Illustrated Directory of the United States Airforce. (Illus.). 260p. 1989. 14.99 (*0-517-67335-5*) Random Hse Value.

— Illustrated Directory of the U.S. Navy. 1990. 19.99 (*0-517-69711-4*) Random Hse Value.

— Make-Ahead Gourmet. 1993. 20.00 (*0-688-12413-5*) Morrow.

— Modern Mind. LC 68-29241. (Essay Index Reprint Ser.). 1977. reprint ed. 19.95 (*0-8369-0827-9*) Ayer.

— Poetry & the Cult of the Martyrs: The Liber Peristephanon on Prudentius. (Recentiores: Later Latin Texts & Contexts Ser.). 180p. 1993. text ed. 37.50 (*0-472-10449-7*) U of Mich Pr.

— The Swedish Imperial Experience, 1560-1718. LC 78-58799. 166p. 1984. pap. 19.95 (*0-521-27889-9*) Cambridge U Pr.

— T. E. Hulme. LC 72-169106. (English Biography Ser.: No. 31). 1971. reprint ed. lib. bdg. 59.95 (*0-8383-1342-6*) M S G Haskell Hse.

— What's for Dinner? LC 92-1492. 1993. 22.00 (*0-688-08544-X*) Morrow.

— Whig Party, 1807-1812. 453p. 1965. 45.00 (*0-7146-1512-9*, Pub. by F Cass Pubs UK) Intl Spec Bk.

Roberts, Michael, ed. The Faber Book of Modern Verse. rev. ed. 432p. (C). 1982. pap. 12.95 (*0-571-18017-5*) Faber & Faber.

— New Country: Prose & Poetry by the Authors of New Signatures. LC 78-178457. (Short Story Index Reprint Ser.). 1977. reprint ed. 20.95 (*0-8369-4058-X*) Ayer.

Roberts, Michael, ed. & tr. Swedish Diplomats at Cromwell's Court. (Royal Historical Society: Camden Fourth Ser.: No. 36). 336p. 1989. 30.00 (*0-86193-117-3*) Boydell & Brewer.

Roberts, Michael & Wallander, Jan L., eds. Family Issues in Pediatric Psychology. 288p. 1992. pap. text ed. 29.95 (*0-8058-0854-X*) L Erlbaum Assocs.

Roberts, Michael, tr. see Ahnlund, Nils G.

Roberts, Michael, jt. auth. see Konstan, David.

Roberts, Michael, et al, eds. Readings in Pediatric Psychology. LC 93-7736. (Illus.). 388p. (C). 1993. pap. 34.50 (*0-306-44423-2*, Plenum Pr) Plenum.

Roberts, Michael C. & Walker, C. Eugene, eds. Casebook of Child & Pediatric Psychology. 468p. 1989. lib. bdg. 45.00 (*0-89862-739-7*) Guilford Pr.

Roberts, Michael C., jt. auth. see Hidore, John J.

Roberts, Michael C., jt. auth. see Walker, C. Eugene.

Roberts, Michael C., et al, eds. Publishing Child-Oriented Articles in Psychology: A Compendium of Publication Outlets. LC 82-45067. 178p. (Orig.). (C). 1982. lib. bdg. 52.50 (*0-8191-2660-8*); pap. text ed. 20.50 (*0-8191-2661-6*) U Pr of Amer.

Roberts, Michael J. The Jeweled Style: Poetry & Poetics in Late Antiquity. LC 88-47941. (Illus.). 192p. 1989. 28.95 (*0-8014-2265-5*) Cornell U Pr.

— The Spiders of Great Britain & Ireland, 3 vols. (Illus.). 1985. Vol. I, 229 pgs. write for info. (*0-318-64516-5*); Vol. II, 204 pgs. write for info. (*0-318-64517-3*); Vol. III, plates. write for info. (*0-318-64518-1*) Lubrecht & Cramer.

— The Spiders of Great Britain & Ireland, 3 vols., Set. (Illus.). 1985. 400.00 (*90-04-07658-1*) Lubrecht & Cramer.

***Roberts, Michael L. & Cusimano, Gregory S.** Alabama Tort Law Handbook. suppl. ed. 1065p. 1994. 90.00 (*0-87473-581-5*) Michie Butterworth.

Roberts, Michele. Daughters of the House. LC 92-45713. 1993. 18.00 (*0-688-04610-X*) Morrow.

— Daughters of the House. 224p. 1994. reprint ed. pap. 10.00 (*0-380-72139-2*) Avon.

— The Visitation. 1984. pap. 8.95 (*0-7043-3909-9*, Pub. by Womens Pr UK) Interlink Pub.

Roberts, Michele S., ed. see Palmer Memorial Episcopal Churchwomen, Houston, Texas Staff.

Roberts, Michelle. How to Draw Cars & Trucks & Other Vehicles. (Illus.). (J). (gr. k-3). 1994. pap. 2.50 (*0-486-28114-0*) Dover.

— How to Draw Dinosaurs. LC 94-40101. (J). 1995. pap. write for info. (*0-486-28460-3*) Dover.

Roberts, Miles, et al, eds. The Biology & Management of Australasian Carnivorous Marsupials. (Illus.). 158p. 1993. pap. text ed. 20.00 (*0-9638408-1-9*) C & RC Nat Zool.

Roberts, Millard F. History of Remsen. 2nd ed. LC 84-52801. 453p. 1985. 15.00 (*0-317-19605-7*) Licht Pubns.

— Narrative History of Remsen, N. Y. 397p. 1993. reprint ed. lib. bdg. 42.50 (*0-8328-2884-X*) Higginson Bk Co.

Roberts, Mirvin F. Turtles. 1989. 9.95 (*0-86622-834-9*, KW-051) TFH Pubns.

Roberts, Morgan J. Classical Deities & Heroes. LC 94-10307. (Myths of the World Ser.). 1994. write for info. (*1-56799-089-4*, Friedman-Fairfax) M Friedman Pub Grp Inc.

— Norse Gods & Heroes. LC 94-10323. (Myths of the World Ser.). 1994. write for info. (*1-56799-090-8*) M Friedman Pub Grp Inc.

Roberts, Morley. Blue Peter: Sea Yarns. LC 71-178458. (Short Story Index Reprint Ser.). 1977. reprint ed. 20.95 (*0-8369-4059-8*) Ayer.

Roberts, Morris. Henry James' Criticism. LC 65-26463. (Studies in Henry James: No. 17). 1969. reprint ed. lib. bdg. 75.00 (*0-8383-0614-4*) M S G Haskell Hse.

Roberts, Morton S., ed. Astronomy & Astrophysics. LC 85-13380. (AAAS Publication Ser.: No. 84-5). (Illus.). 407p. reprint ed. pap. 116.00 (*0-7837-6742-0*, 2046370) Bks Demand.

Roberts, Moss, ed. Chinese Fairy Tales & Fantasies. (Fairy Tale & Folklore Library). (Illus.). 1980. pap. 14.00 (*0-394-73994-9*) Pantheon.

Roberts, Moss, tr. see Guanzhong, Luo.

Roberts, Moss, tr. see Mao Tse-Tung.

Roberts, Myrna L., ed. see Roberts, Myrna P.

***Roberts, Myrna P.** Recipes from My Mom's Kitchen. Roberts, Myrna L., ed. 150p. (Orig.). 1990. pap. 12.95 (*0-9627075-0-3*) Conch Shell Pubns.

Roberts, N., ed. see Hardy, Deborah, et al.

Roberts, N. H., et al. Fault Tree Handbook. (Illus.). 1981. pap. 9.00 (*0-16-005582-2*, 052-010-02012-9) USGPO.

Roberts, Nadine. Who Said Sweet Sixteen. 1987. pap. 2.50 (*0-449-70301-0*) Fawcett.

Roberts, Nancy. America's Most Haunted Places. (Illus.). 95p. (J). (gr. 4 up). 1987. reprint ed. pap. 8.95 (*0-87844-074-7*) Sandlapper Pub Co.

— Animal Ghost Stories. (American Storytelling Ser.). 128p. (YA). (gr. 6 up). 1995. 14.95 (*0-87483-401-5*) August Hse.

— Blackbeard & Other Pirates of the Atlantic Coast. LC 93-698. 1993. 9.95 (*0-89587-098-3*) Blair.

— Civil War Ghost Stories & Legends. LC 92-10411. (Illus.). 192p. 1992. text ed. 19.95 (*0-87249-851-4*); pap. 9.95 (*0-87249-852-2*) U of SC Pr.

— Ghosts of the Carolinas. 116p. 1988. reprint ed. 17.95 (*0-87249-586-8*); reprint ed. pap. 9.95 (*0-87249-587-6*) U of SC Pr.

— Ghosts of the Southern Mountains & Appalachia. rev. ed. (Illus.). 156p. 1989. reprint ed. 17.95 (*0-87249-597-3*); reprint ed. pap. 9.95 (*0-87249-598-1*) U of SC Pr.

— The Gold Seekers: Gold, Ghosts & Legends from Carolina to California. (Illus.). 283p. 1989. pap. 9.95 (*0-87249-658-9*) U of SC Pr.

— Haunted Houses: Tales from 30 American Homes. LC 87-20598. (Illus.). 181p. 1988. 19.95 (*0-87106-775-7*); pap. 12.95 (*0-87106-768-4*) Globe Pequot.

— North Carolina Ghosts & Legends. LC 91-14469. (Illus.). 133p. 1991. reprint ed. pap. 9.95 (*0-87249-765-8*) U of SC Pr.

— Recognitions: Images of a Woman Artist. LC 88-51097. 96p. (Orig.). 1989. 25.00 (*0-944072-02-X*); pap. 15.95 (*0-944072-03-8*) Zoland Bks.

— Recognitions: Images of a Woman Artist. limited ed. LC 88-51097. 96p. (Orig.). 1989. 50.00 (*0-944072-05-4*) Zoland Bks.

— South Carolina Ghosts: From the Mountains to the Coast. (Illus.). 152p. 1983. 17.95 (*0-87249-428-4*); pap. 9.95 (*0-87249-429-2*) U of SC Pr.

— Southern Ghosts. (Illus.). 72p. (J). (gr. 4 up). 1987. reprint ed. pap. 8.95 (*0-87844-075-5*) Sandlapper Pub Co.

— This Haunted Southland: Where Ghosts Still Roam. 152p. 1988. reprint ed. 17.95 (*0-87249-588-4*); reprint ed. pap. 9.95 (*0-87249-589-2*) U of SC Pr.

— Women & Other Bodies of Water. 150p. 1987. 14.00 (*0-937872-38-5*) Dragon Gate.

Roberts, Nancy, et al. Integrating Computers into the Elementary & Middle School. (Illus.). 240p. 1988. pap. text ed. 26.00 (*0-13-468794-9*) P-H.

— Introduction to Computer Simulation: Systems Dynamics Modeling Approach. LC 94-63. 570p. 1994. reprint ed. 35.00 (*1-56327-052-8*) Prod Press.

— Introduction to Computer Simulation: The System Dynamics Approach. (Illus.). 1983. text ed. 21.56 (*0-201-06414-6*) Addison-Wesley.

Roberts, Nancy L. American Peace Writers, Editors, & Periodicals: A Dictionary. LC 90-23169. 408p. 1991. text ed. 69.50 (*0-313-26842-8*, RPB, Greenwood Pr) Greenwood.

— Dorothy Day & the Catholic Worker. LC 84-8492. 226p. 1985. 49.50 (*0-87395-938-8*); pap. 16.95 (*0-87395-939-6*) State U NY Pr.

Roberts, Nancy L. & Roberts, Arthur W., eds. As Ever, Gene: The Letters of Eugene O'Neill to George Jean Nathan. LC 86-45800. (Illus.). 248p. 1987. 42.50 (*0-8386-3303-X*) Fairleigh Dickinson.

Roberts, Nancy N., tr. see Samman, Ghada.

Roberts, Naurice. Andrew Young: Freedom Fighter. rev. ed. LC 83-7633. (Picture-Story Biographies Ser.). (Illus.). 32p. (J). (gr. 2-5). 1990. lib. bdg. 11.85 (*0-516-03450-2*); pap. 3.95 (*0-516-43450-0*) Childrens.

— Barbara Jordan: The Great Lady from Texas. rev. ed. LC 83-23169. (Picture-Story Biographies Ser.). (Illus.). 32p. (J). (gr. 2-5). 1990. lib. bdg. 11.85 (*0-516-03511-8*); pap. 3.95 (*0-516-43511-6*) Childrens.

— Cesar Chavez & La Causa. LC 85-27980. (Picture Story Biographies Ser.). (Illus.). 32p. (J). (gr. 2-4). 1986. lib. bdg. 11.85 (*0-516-03484-7*); pap. 3.95 (*0-516-43484-5*) Childrens.

— Cesar Chavez y la Causa. (Spanish Picture-Story Biographies Ser.). 32p. (J). (gr. 2-5). 1986. pap. 3.95 (*0-516-53484-X*) Childrens.

— Harold Washington: Mayor with a Vision. LC 87-7247. (Picture-Story Biographies Ser.). (Illus.). 32p. (J). (gr. 2-4). 1988. lib. bdg. 11.85 (*0-516-03657-2*); pap. 3.95 (*0-516-43657-0*) Childrens.

— Henry Cisneros: A Leader for the Future. rev. ed. LC 91-2330. (Picture-Story Biographies Ser.). 32p. (J). (gr. 2-4). 1991. lib. bdg. 11.85 (*0-516-04175-4*); pap. 3.95 (*0-516-44175-2*) Childrens.

— Henry Cisneros: Alcalde Mexico-Americano. LC 85-29057. (Spanish Picture-Story Biographies Ser.). 32p. (J). (gr. 2-5). 1987. pap. 3.95 (*0-516-53485-8*) Childrens.

Roberts, Ned. Muzzle-Loading Caplock Rifle. 1991. 30.00 (*0-935632-96-4*) Wolfe Pub Co.

Roberts, Nedra P. The Play's the Thing: An Introduction to Drama. 417p. (Orig.). (gr. 9-12). 1981. pap. text ed. 10.50 (*0-88334-141-7*) Longman.

Roberts, Nedra P., jt. auth. see Roberts, John.

Roberts, Neil. The Changing Global Environment. LC 92-35490. 1993. 64.95 (*1-55786-271-0*); pap. 34.95 (*1-55786-272-9*) Blackwell Pubs.

— The Holocene: An Environmental History. (Illus.). 320p. 1989. pap. 19.95 (*0-631-16178-3*) Blackwell Pubs.

Roberts, Neil, jt. ed. see Butlin, Robin A.

Roberts, Nickie. Whores in History. (Illus.). 384p. 1992. 28.00 (*0-246-13234-5*, Pub. by HarpC UK) HarpC.

— Whores in History. (Illus.). 384p. 1993. pap. 12.00 (*0-586-20029-0*, Pub. by HarpC UK) HarpC.

Roberts, Nigel, ed. Agricultural Extension in Africa. (Symposium Ser.). 114p. 1989. 11.95 (*0-8213-1195-6*, BK1195) World Bank.

Roberts, Nora. All the Possibilities. 1992. mass mkt. 3.59 (*0-373-51015-2*, 5-51015-1) Harlequin Bks.

— The Art of Deception. (NR Flowers Ser.: No. 27). 1993. mass mkt. 3.59 (*0-373-51027-6*, 1-51027-0) Silhouette.

— Blithe Images. (NR Flowers Ser.: No. 38). 1993. mass mkt. 3.59 (*0-373-51038-1*, 1-51038-7) Silhouette.

— Born in Fire. 416p. (Orig.). 1994. pap. text ed. 5.99 (*0-515-11469-3*) Jove Pubns.

— Born in Fire. large type ed. LC 94-41311. 506p. 1995. 22.95 (*0-7862-0373-0*) Thorndike Pr.

— Born in Ice. 384p. (Orig.). 1995. pap. text ed. 5.99 (*0-515-11675-0*) Jove Pubns.

— Boundary Lines. (NR Flowers Ser.: No. 47). 1994. mass mkt. 3.59 (*0-373-51047-0*, 1-51047-8) Silhouette.

— Brazen Virtue. 1988. 5.99 (*0-553-27283-7*) Bantam.

— Captivated. 1992. mass mkt. 3.39 (*0-373-09768-9*, 5-09768-8) Silhouette.

— Captivated. large type ed. LC 93-620. 1993. pap. 17.95 (*1-56054-714-6*) Thorndike Pr.

— Carnal Innocence. 1992. 5.99 (*0-553-29597-7*) Bantam.

— Charmed. large type ed. LC 93-613. 1993. pap. 16.95 (*1-56054-716-2*) Thorndike Pr.

— Command Performance. (NR Flowers Ser.: No. 37). 1993. mass mkt. 3.59 (*0-373-51037-3*, 1-51037-9) Silhouette.

— Convincing Alex. 1994. mass mkt. 3.50 (*0-373-09872-3*, 5-09872-8) Silhouette.

— Dance of Dreams. (NR Flowers Ser.: No. 8). 1992. mass mkt. 3.59 (*0-373-51008-X*, 5-51008-6) Harlequin Bks.

— Dance to the Piper. 1994. pap. 4.99 (*1-55166-007-5*, 1-66007-5, Mira Bks) Harlequin Bks.

— Divine Evil. 1992. mass mkt. 5.99 (*0-553-29490-3*) Bantam.

— Divine Evil. large type ed. 24.95 (*1-56895-118-3*) Wheeler Pub.

— Dual Image. (Language of Love Ser.: No. 29). 1993. mass mkt. 3.59 (*0-373-51029-2*, 1-51029-6) Silhouette.

— Entranced. large type ed. LC 93-618. 1993. pap. 17.95 (*1-56054-715-4*) Thorndike Pr.

— Falling for Rachel. 1993. mass mkt. 3.39 (*0-373-09810-3*, 5-09810-8) Silhouette.

— For Now, Forever. (NR Flowers Ser.: No. 19). 1992. mass mkt. 3.59 (*0-373-51019-5*, 5-51019-3) Harlequin Bks.

— For the Love of Lilah. (Special Edition Ser.: No. 685). 1991. mass mkt. 3.25 (*0-373-09685-2*) Harlequin Bks.

— For the Love of Lilah. large type ed. LC 92-42102. (Nightingale Ser.). 1993. write for info. (*0-8161-5725-1*) G K Hall.

— Gabriel's Angel. (Language of Love Ser.: No. 32). 1993. mass mkt. 3.59 (*0-373-51032-2*, 1-51032-2) Silhouette.

— Gabriel's Angel. large type ed. (Sensation Ser.). 1993. 17.95 (*0-373-58806-2*, Silhouette Lrg Print); pap. 16.95 (*0-373-58906-9*, Silhouette Lrg Print) Chivers N Amer.

— Genuine Lies. 1991. mass mkt. 5.99 (*0-553-29078-9*) Bantam.

— Hidden Riches. LC 93-37425. 400p. 1994. 21.95 (*0-399-13948-6*, Putnam) Putnam Pub Group.

— Hidden Riches. 480p. 1995. mass mkt. 5.99 (*0-515-11606-8*) Jove Pubns.

— Hidden Riches. large type ed. LC 94-25466. 648p. 1994. lib. bdg. 22.95 (*0-7862-0272-6*) Thorndike Pr.

— Honest Illusions. 512p. 1993. mass mkt. 5.99 (*0-515-11097-3*) Jove Pubns.

— Hot Ice. 288p. (Orig.). 1987. mass mkt. 5.99 (*0-553-26461-3*) Bantam.

— Hot Ice. large type ed. (General Ser.). 446p. (Orig.). 1988. lib. bdg. 18.95 (*0-8161-4489-3*) G K Hall.

— Last Honest Man. 1995. pap. 4.99 (*1-55166-020-2*, Mira Bks) Harlequin Bks.

— Lessons Learned. (NR Flowers Ser.: No. 25). 1993. mass mkt. 3.59 (*0-373-51025-X*, 1-51025-4) Silhouette.

— Local Hero. (NR Flowers Ser.: No. 48). 1994. mass mkt. 3.59 (*0-373-51048-9*, 1-51048-6) Silhouette.

— Loving Jack. (Language of Love Ser.: No. 42). 1994. mass mkt. 3.59 (*0-373-51042-X*, 1-51042-9) Silhouette.

— Luring a Lady. large type ed. (Silhouette Special Edition Ser.). 1994. 17.95 (*0-373-58894-1*, Silhouette Lrg Print) Chivers N Amer.

— Mind over Matter. (NR Flowers Ser.: No. 45). 1994. mass mkt. 3.59 (*0-373-51045-4*, 1-51045-2) Silhouette.

— Night Moves. (NR Flowers Ser.: No. 7). 1992. mass mkt. 3.59 (*0-373-51007-1*, 5-51007-8) Harlequin Bks.

— Night Shadow. large type ed. 329p. 1991. reprint ed. lib. bdg. 18.95 (*1-56054-175-X*) Thorndike Pr.

— Night Smoke. 1994. mass mkt. 3.50 (*0-373-07595-2*, 1-07595-1) Harlequin Bks.

— Nightshade: American Hero, Night Tales. (Silhouette Intimate Moments Ser.). 1993. mass mkt. 3.50 (*0-373-07529-4*, 5-07529-6) Silhouette.

— One Man's Art. (NR Flowers Ser.: No. 17). 1992. mass mkt. 3.59 (*0-373-51017-9*, 5-51017-7) Harlequin Bks.

— One Summer. (Language of Love Ser.: No. 31). 1993. mass mkt. 3.59 (*0-373-51031-4*, 1-51031-8) Silhouette.

— The Playboy Prince. (NR Flowers Ser.: No. 39). 1994. mass mkt. 3.59 (*0-373-51039-X*, 1-51039-5) Silhouette.

— The Pride of Jared Mackade. 1995. pap. 3.75 (*0-373-24000-7*, 1-24000-1) Silhouette.

— Private Scandals. 512p. 1994. mass mkt. 5.99 (*0-515-11400-6*) Jove Pubns.

R

An Asterisk (*) at the beginning of an entry indicates that the title is appearing in BIP for the first time.

— Private Scandals. LC 92-39607. 352p. 1993. 19.95 (0-399-13828-5, Putnam) Putnam Pub Group.
— Private Scandals. large type ed. LC 93-30905. 1994. bds. 21.95 (0-7862-0040-5) Thorndike Pr.
— Public Secrets. 1990. mass mkt. 5.99 (0-553-28578-5) Bantam.
— Public Secrets. large type ed. LC 93-44106. 1994. 24.95 (1-56895-055-1) Wheeler Pub.
— Reflections. (NR Flowers Ser.: No. 6). 1992. mass mkt. 3.59 (0-373-51006-3, 5-51006-0) Harlequin Bks.
— The Return of Rafe Mackade: (Heartbreakers) (Intimate Moments Ser.). 1995. mass mkt. 3.75 (0-373-07631-2, 1-07631-4) Silhouette.
— The Right Path. (NR Flowers Ser.: No. 26). 1993. mass mkt. 3.59 (0-373-51026-8, 1-51026-2) Silhouette.
— Sacred Sins. 304p. (Orig.). 1987. mass mkt. 5.99 (0-553-26574-1) Bantam.
— Second Nature. (Language of Love Ser.: No. 30). 1993. mass mkt. 3.59 (0-373-51030-6, 5-51030-0) Silhouette.
— Skin Deep. 1995. pap. 4.99 (1-55166-050-4, 1-66050-5, Mira Bks) Harlequin Bks.
— Summer Desserts. (NR Flowers Ser.: No. 23). 1993. mass mkt. 3.59 (0-373-51023-3, 5-51023-5) Silhouette.
— Suzanna's Surrender. large type ed. LC 93-32760. 1994. write for info. (0-8161-5872-X) G K Hall.
— Sweet Revenge. 1989. 5.99 (0-553-27859-2) Bantam.
— Tempting Fate. (NR Flowers Ser.: No. 13). 1992. mass mkt. 3.59 (0-373-51013-6) Silhouette.
— This Magic Moment. (NR Flowers Ser.: No. 24). 1993. mass mkt. 3.59 (0-373-51024-1, 5-51024-3) Silhouette.
— Treasures Lost, Treasures Found. (NR Flowers Ser.: No. 40). 1994. mass mkt. 3.59 (0-373-51040-3, 1-51040-3) Silhouette.
— True Betrayals. LC 94-39229. 400p. 1995. 21.95 (0-399-14059-X, Putnam) Putnam Pub Group.
— Unfinished Business. (Intimate Moments Ser.: No. 433). 1992. mass mkt. 3.39 (0-373-07433-6, 5-07433-1) Harlequin Bks.
— Unfinished Business. large type ed. (Popular Ser.). 294p. 1993. reprint ed. pap. 16.95 (1-56054-634-4) Thorndike Pr.
— Untamed. (NR Flowers Ser.: No. 28). 1993. mass mkt. 3.59 (0-373-51028-4, 1-51028-8) Silhouette.
— Without a Trace. large type ed. (Special Edition Ser.). 1993. 17.95 (0-373-58817-8, Silhouette Lrg Print); pap. 16.95 (0-373-58917-4, Silhouette Lrg Print) Chivers N Amer.

Roberts, Nora, et al. Historical Christmas Stories 1990. braille ed. 518p. 1992. vinyl bd. 41.44 (1-56956-062-5, BR8732) W A T Braille.
— Jingle Bells, Wedding Bells: All I Want for Christmas; A Very Merry Step-Christmas; Jack's Ornament; The Forever Gift. 1994. mass mkt. 4.99 (0-373-48331-7, 1-48331-2) Harlequin Bks.

Roberts, Norma. Masterpieces of Impressionism & European Modernism from the Columbus Museum of Art, Columbia Museum of Art & TG Concepts, Inc. LC 92-83841. (Illus.). 1993. pap. 29.95 (0-685-72344-5) Columbus Mus Art.

Roberts, Norma, ed. The Quest for Self-Expression: Painting in Moscow & Leningrad, 1965-1990. LC 90-81953. (Illus.). 192p. (Orig.). 1990. pap. 29.95x (0-918881-25-0) Columbus Mus Art.

Roberts, Norma, ed. see Griffith, Dennison W.
Roberts, Norma, ed. see Keny, James M. & Maciejunes, Nannette V.
Roberts, Norma, ed. see Schwindler, Gary.
Roberts, Norma J., ed. see Bishop, Budd H.
Roberts, Norma J., ed. see Brettel, Richard & Selz, Peter.
Roberts, Norma J., ed. see Columbus Museum of Art Staff.
Roberts, Norma J., ed. see Davis, Susan L.
Roberts, Norma J., ed. see Maciejunes, Nannette V., et al.
Roberts, Norma J., ed. see Maciejunes, Nannette V.
Roberts, Norma J., jt. ed. see Maciejunes, Nannette.
Roberts, Norma J., ed. see Robertson, Jean.
Roberts, Norma J., ed. see Rosen, Steven W. & Fergus-Jean, John.

Roberts, Norman C. Baja California Plant Field Guide. (Illus.). 324p. (Orig.). (C). 1989. 22.95 (0-9603144-1-5) Nat Hist Pub Co.

Roberts, O. M. Texas. Evans, Clement A., ed. (Confederate Military History Extended Edition Ser.: Vol. XV). (Illus.). 713p. 1989. reprint ed. 50.00 (1-56837-034-2) Broadfoot.

Roberts, Oran. Description of Texas: Its Advantages & Resources. 1993. reprint ed. lib. bdg. 75.00 (0-7812-5898-7) Rprt Serv.

Roberts, P. West Indians & Their Language. 224p. 1988. 59.95 (0-521-35136-7); pap. 16.50 (0-521-35955-4) Cambridge U Pr.

Roberts, P., ed. see Goorney, Howard.

Roberts, P. A. Neuroanatomy. (Oklahoma Notes Ser.). (Illus.). ix, 84p. (C). 1989. pap. 11.95 (0-387-96335-9) Spr-Verlag.
— Neuroanatomy. (Oklahoma Notes Ser.). (Illus.). xi, 100p. 1991. pap. 13.95 (0-387-97477-6) Spr-Verlag.
— Neuroanatomy. 3rd ed. (Oklahoma Notes Ser.). (Illus.). 128p. 1992. 13.95 (0-387-97777-5) Spr-Verlag.

Roberts, P. C. Modelling Large Systems. 120p. 1978. 31.00 (0-85066-170-6) Taylor & Francis.

Roberts, P. H., ed. see European Geophysical Society Staff.
Roberts, P. J., ed. see Workshop on Biochemistry of the Dementias Staff.

Roberts, P. J., et al, eds. Glutamate: Transmitter in the Central Nervous System. LC 80-42300. (Wiley-Interscience Publication Ser.). 250p. reprint ed. pap. 71.30 (0-317-27739-1, 2052093) Bks Demand.

Roberts, P. L., ed. see Gould, Glenn.
Roberts, P. V., jt. ed. see McCarty, Perry L.

***Roberts, Palmer W.** Winds of the World & the Many Cloud Forms. 1995. 10.95 (0-533-11198-6) Vantage.

Roberts, Pam. MicroStation for AutoCAD Users Tablet Menu. 1992. disk, pap. 99.95 (0-934605-33-5, OnWord Pr) High Mtn.

Roberts, Pam, jt. auth. see Gibson, Robin.

Roberts, Pamela. Teaching the Child Rider. 1987. 7.50 (0-87556-302-3) Saifer.
— Teaching the Child Rider. 102p. (C). 1990. pap. 21.00 (0-85131-195-4, Pub. by J A Allen & Co UK) St Mut.

Roberts, Pasco. Book of Florida Gardening. LC 62-52630. (Orig.). 1962. pap. 3.95 (0-8200-0402-2) Great Outdoors.

Roberts, Pat. Projects for Kids. (Illus.). 74p. 1991. write for info. (0-937769-16-9) Mark Inc CA.

Roberts, Patricia. Variations: Knitting Patterns for More Than Fifty Seasonal Designs. 1992. 29.95 (0-8021-1490-3) Grove-Atltic.

Roberts, Patricia, ed. Parenting Alone. 1980. pap. 6.50 (0-8309-0297-X) Herald Hse.

Roberts, Patricia, jt. auth. see Kelly, Thomas L.

Roberts, Patricia, et al. Gender Positive! A Teachers' & Librarians' Guide to Nonstereotyped Children's Literature, K-8. LC 92-56686. 206p. 1993. pap. 24.95 (0-89950-816-2) McFarland & Co.

Roberts, Patricia L. Alphabet: A Handbook of ABC Books & Book Extensions for the Elementary Classroom. 2nd ed. LC 93-42444. 1994. 32.50 (0-8108-2823-5) Scarecrow.
— Alphabet Books As a Key to Language Patterns. LC 87-3216. ix, 263p. 1988. 36.00 (0-208-02151-5, Lib Prof Pubns) Shoe String.
— Counting Books Are More Than Numbers: An Annotated Action Bibliography. x, 264p. (C). 1989. lib. bdg. 36.00 (0-208-02216-3, Lib Prof Pubns) Shoe String.
— A Green Dinosaur Day: A Guide for Developing Thematic Units in Literature-Based Instruction, K-6. LC 92-26441. (Illus.). 284p. 1992. pap. 33.95 (0-205-14007-6, Longwood Div) Allyn.

Roberts, Patricia L. & Cecil, Nancy L. Developing Multicultural Awareness Through Children's Literature: A Guide for Teachers & Librarians, Grades K-8. 224p. 1993. pap. 24.95 (0-89950-879-0) McFarland & Co.
— Teaching Peace Through Children's Literature: A Guide for Teachers & Librarians, K-6. (Illus.). 150p. Date not set. pap. text ed. 23.00 (1-56308-188-1) Teacher Ideas Pr.

Roberts, Patricia L., jt. auth. see Cecil, Nancy L.
Roberts, Patricia L., jt. auth. see Cecil, Nancy.
Roberts, Patricia L., jt. auth. see Kellough, Richard D.

Roberts, Paul. An American Fuhrer: Lyndon LaRouche & the Politics of Paranoia. 208p. 1988. 16.95 (0-312-02161-5, Pub. by Thomas Dunne Bks) St Martin.
— Becoming Mr. Nobody: The Philosophy & Poetry of John Cowper Powys. 52p. (C). 1992. reprint ed. pap. 13.00x (0-946650-37-3) Borgo Pr.

Roberts, Paul, ed. Becoming Mr. Nobody: The Philosophy & Poetry of John Cowper Powys. 52p. (C). 1992. reprint ed. lib. bdg. 25.00x (0-8095-6768-7) Borgo Pr.

Roberts, Paul & Willmore, Chris. Role of Forensic Science Evidence in Criminal Proceedings. (Research Study Ser.: No. 11). 196p. 1993. pap. 45.00 (0-11-341064-6, HM10646, Pub. by HMSO UK) UNIPUB.

Roberts, Paul C. Alienation & the Soviet Economy: The Collapse of the Socialist Era. 2nd ed. LC 90-5046. (Independent Institute Ser.). 152p. 1991. 29.95 (0-8419-1247-5); pap. 14.95 (0-8419-1248-3) Holmes & Meier.
— Marx's Theory of Exchange. LC 83-19136. 144p. 1983. text ed. 49.95 (0-275-91065-2, C1065, Praeger Pubs) Greenwood.
— The Supply-Side Revolution: An Insider's Account of Policymaking in Washington. (Illus.). 328p. 1984. 37.00 (0-674-85620-1) HUP.
— The Supply-Side Revolution: An Insider's Account of Policymaking in Washington. 328p. 1986. pap. text ed. 10.95 (0-674-85621-X) HUP.

Roberts, Paul C. & LaFollette, Karen. Meltdown: Inside the Soviet Economy. 152p. 1990. 19.95 (0-932790-79-8); pap. 9.95 (0-932790-80-1) Cato Inst.

***Roberts, Paul C. & Stratton, Lawrence M., Jr.** Redrawing the Color Line: How the Civil Rights Movement Destroyed Liberalism. 192p. 1995. 19.95 (0-89526-462-5) Regnery Pub.

Roberts, Paul H. An Introduction to Magnetohydrodynamics. LC 67-88253. 274p. reprint ed. pap. 78.10 (0-317-08669-3, 2055320) Bks Demand.

Roberts, Paul M. Review Text in United States History. 2nd ed. (YA). (gr. 7-9). 1989. pap. text ed. 13.33 (0-87720-857-3) AMSCO Sch.

Roberts, Paul V., et al, eds. Adsorption Techniques in Drinking Water Treatment, Vol. 3. (Journal of Environmental Pathology, Toxicology & Oncology Ser.: Vol. 7, No. 7/8, 1987). 438p. 43.50 (0-685-34725-7) Chem-Orbital.

***Roberts, Paul W.** In Search of the Birth of Jesus. 1995. 24.95 (1-57322-012-4) Riverhead Bks.
— Palace of Fears. LC 93-25413. 1994. 23.00 (0-679-43077-6) Random.

Roberts, Paul W., ed. Useful Procedures in Medical Practice. LC 85-4534. (Illus.). 632p. reprint ed. pap. 180.00 (0-7837-1495-5, 2057191) Bks Demand.

Roberts, Paula. Women, Poverty, & Child Support. (Illus.). 166p. (Orig.). 1986. pap. 15.00 (0-941077-15-2, 41,980) NCLS Inc.

Roberts, Paula, jt. auth. see Junior League of Galveston County, Inc. Staff.

Roberts, Paulette & Whaley, Jeanette. Seeds for Progress. LC 89-52122. (Illus.). 140p. (J). 1990. pap. 12.95 (1-55523-309-0) Winston-Derek.

Roberts, Peggy. Heart's Desire. 512p. 1994. mass mkt. 4.99 (0-8217-4780-0) Zebra.
— Just in Time. 480p. 1993. mass mkt. 4.50 (0-8217-4188-8) Zebra.
— Mrs. Perfect. 1992. mass mkt. 4.50 (0-8217-3789-9) Zebra.
— Whispers at Midnight. 352p. 1994. mass mkt. 4.50 (0-8217-4529-8) Zebra.

Roberts, Peggy, ed. The Source: The Greater Boston Theatre Resource Guide. rev. ed. 448p. 1994. pap. 16.95 (0-9624740-2-9) StageSource.

Roberts, Perri L. Masolino da Panicale. LC 93-6826. (Studies in the History of Art). 1994. 105.00 (0-19-817509-4, Clarendon Pr) OUP.

Roberts, Peter. Anthracite Coal Communities: A Study of the Demography, the Social, Educational & Moral Life of the Anthracite Regions. LC 75-129410. (American Immigration Collection Ser. 2). (Illus.). 1970. reprint ed. 26.95 (0-405-00564-4) Ayer.
— Birdwatchers Guide to the Sydney Region. (Illus.). 204p. (Orig.). 1994. pap. 15.95 (0-86417-565-5, Pub. by Kangaroo Pr AT) Seven Hills Bk.
— George Costakis, a Russian Life in Art. LC 94-26229. (Illus.). 224p. 1994. 35.00 (0-8076-1366-5) Braziller.
— Granny's Incredible Edibles Cookbook. LC 94-76784. (Illus.). 160p. (Orig.). 1994. pap. 8.95 (0-9641565-5-5) Goldtree Pr.
— New Immigration: A Study of the Industrial & Social Life of Southeastern Europeans in America. LC 79-129411. (American Immigration Collection, Ser. 2). (Illus.). 1970. reprint ed. 26.95 (0-405-00565-2) Ayer.
— The New Immigration: A Study of the Industrial & Social Life of Southeastern Europeans in America. LC 78-145490. (American Immigration Library). xxii, 418p. 1971. reprint ed. lib. bdg. 44.95 (0-89198-023-7) Ozer.
— OJ: 101 Theories, Conspiracies & Alibis. 160p. (Orig.). 1995. pap. 9.95 (0-9641565-9-8) Goldtree Pr.
— Shakespeare & the Moral Curriculum: Rethinking the Secondary School Shakespeare Syllabus. LC 91-66911. 266p. (Orig.). 1992. pap. text ed. 17.95 (0-9631311-0-9) Pripet Pr.

Roberts, Peter, ed. The Best of Plays & Players, Vol. 2. (Illus.). 272p. 1989. pap. 25.95 (0-413-53720-X, A0494, Pub. by Methuen UK) Heinemann.
— The Best of Plays & Players: 1969-1983, Vol. 2. (Illus.). 272p. 1989. 31.95 (0-413-62150-2, A0391, Pub. by Methuen UK) Heinemann.
— The Best of Plays & Players, Vol. 1: 1953-1968. (Illus.). 253p. 1988. 29.95 (0-413-52960-6, A0022) Heinemann.

Roberts, Peter, jt. ed. see Fletcher, Anthony.
Roberts, Peter, tr. see Thrangu, Kenchen.

Roberts, Peter, et al, eds. Metropolitan Renaissance: New Life for Old City Regions. 366p. 1993. 69.95 (1-85628-383-6, Pub. by Avebury Pub UK) Ashgate Pub Co.

Roberts, Peter D. Modernism in Russian Piano Music: Skriabin, Prokofiev, & Their Russian Contemporaries, 2 vols. LC 91-32124. (Russian Music Studies). 1992. 89.95 (0-253-34992-3) Ind U Pr.

Roberts, Phil, ed. Readings in Wyoming History: Issues in the History of the Equality State. (Wyoming History Ser.). 120p. (Orig.). 1994. pap. 6.95 (0-914767-22-4) Skyline West Pr.

Roberts, Phil, jt. auth. see Sullivan, Jim.

***Roberts, Phil, et al.** Wyoming Almanac. 3rd rev. ed. LC 94-66659. 460p. (Orig.). (YA). 1994. pap. 11.95 (0-914767-21-6) Skyline West Pr.

Roberts, Philip, comp. Bond on File. (Methuen Writer-Files Ser.). 96p. (C). 1985. pap. 9.95 (0-413-54040-5, A0034) Heinemann.

Roberts, Philip, jt. auth. see Hay, Malcolm.

Roberts, Philip D. How Poetry Works. 256p. 1986. mass mkt. 6.95 (0-14-022584-6, Penguin Bks) Viking Penguin.

Roberts, Philip J. Valuation of Development Land in Hong Kong. LC 76-369546. 97p. reprint ed. pap. 27.70 (0-317-27920-3, 2025128) Bks Demand.

Roberts, Philip J., jt. auth. see Roberts, David L.

Roberts, Philip J., et al. Wyoming Almanac. 2nd ed. 376p. (Orig.). 1990. pap. 11.95 (0-914767-19-4) Skyline West Pr.

Roberts, Philip M. The Gift of Tongues: An Evaluation. LC 91-70592. 50p. 1991. pap. 4.95 (0-944788-96-3) IBRI.

Roberts, Philip S. & Thomason, Ivan J. Sugarbeet Pest Management: Nematodes. (Illus.). 30p. 1981. pap. text ed. 3.00 (0-931876-52-4, 3272) ANR Pubns CA.

Roberts, R. Molecular Basis of Cardiology. (Molecular Basis of Clinical Medicine Ser.). (Illus.). 480p. 1993. pap. 39.95 (0-86542-196-X) Blackwell Sci.
— A Ragged Schooling. 1988. text ed. 12.95 (0-7190-2453-6, Pub. by Manchester Univ Pr UK) St Martin.

Roberts, R. & Roberts, G. To Fight Better. 1989. pap. 6.95 (0-946616-58-2) OMF Bks.

Roberts, R., jt. auth. see Laidlaw, L.
Roberts, R., jt. auth. see Majapuria, M.

Roberts, R. E. Henrik Ibsen: A Critical Study. LC 73-21628. (Studies in Ibsen: No. 63). 1974. lib. bdg. 75.00 (0-8383-1834-7) M S G Haskell Hse.

Roberts, R. G. The Structure of the Proton: Deep Inelastic Scattering. (Monographs on Mathematical Physics). 192p. (C). 1993. pap. 27.95 (0-521-44944-8) Cambridge U Pr.

Roberts, R. H. & Good, J. M., eds. The Recovery of Rhetoric: Persuasive Discourse & Disciplinarity in the Human Sciences. LC 92-39541. (Knowledge, Disciplinarity & Beyond Ser.). 278p. (C). 1993. lib. bdg. 45.00 (0-8139-1455-8); pap. text ed. 17.95 (0-8139-1456-6) U Pr of Va.

Roberts, R. J., jt. auth. see Bromage, N.
Roberts, R. J., ed. see Qualben, Lois.
Roberts, R. M., jt. ed. see Stewart, I. A.

Roberts, R. Phillip. Continuity & Change: London Calvinistic Baptists & the Evangelical Revival, 1760-1820. 282p. 1989. lib. bdg. 30.00 (0-940033-30-5) R O Roberts.

***Roberts, Rachel.** Library Development in Central & Eastern Europe - from Assistance to Cooperation. 139p. 1994. pap. 25.00 (92-826-2657-1, CDNA15660ENC, Pub. by Europ Com) UNIPUB.

Roberts, Rachel, ed. see Merchanthouse, Don C.

Roberts, Ralph. Auction Action! A Survival Companion for Any Auction Goer. (Illus.). 192p. 1986. pap. 12.95 (0-8306-2752-9, NO. 2752) TAB Bks.
— Auction Action: A Survival Companion for Any Auction Goer. 1986. pap. 12.95 (0-07-156628-7) McGraw.
— E. Y. Ponder: High Sheriff of the Kingdom of Madison. (Illus.). (Orig.). 1993. pap. 7.95 (1-56664-043-1) WorldComm.
— Excursion into the Endless Caves. (Illus.). 96p. (Orig.). 1993. pap. 9.95 (1-56664-025-3) WorldComm.
— First Book of Microsoft Publisher. 1991. pap. 18.95 (0-672-27399-3) Alpha Bks IN.
— How to Get Published: And Published & Published. Hall, Kathryn, ed. (Illus.). 208p. (Orig.). 1994. pap. 12.95 (1-56664-003-2) WorldComm.
— In Plain English: The Internet. Hall, Kathryn, ed. (Illus.). 144p. Date not set. pap. text ed. 9.95 (1-56664-077-6) WorldComm.
— Leo White: Rocket Man. (Illus.). (Orig.). 1994. pap. 7.95 (1-56664-042-3) WorldComm.
— Lord Rifkin's Risk. 64p. 1994. pap. 10.00 (1-56664-046-6) WorldComm.
— The Pepsi Challenge: From 12 Full Ounces to a New Generation, 100 Years of Pepsi History. Hall, Kathryn, ed. (Illus.). 320p. 1994. pap. text ed. 14.95 (1-57090-008-6) Alexander Bks.
— The Power of Turbo Prolog: The Natural Language of Artificial Intelligence. (Illus.). 256p. 1987. 22.95 (0-8306-0782-X, 2782); pap. 14.95 (0-8306-2782-0) TAB Bks.
— Using Novell Netware Lite: Networking for Everybody. 1992. pap. 20.00 (0-679-74298-0) Random.
— Veteran's Guide to Benefits. 1989. pap. 5.99 (0-451-16017-7, Sig) NAL-Dutton.

Roberts, Ralph, ed. see Boone, Don.
Roberts, Ralph, jt. auth. see Graham, Elizabeth C.
Roberts, Ralph, jt. auth. see Hall, Betty L.
Roberts, Ralph, ed. see Harris, Robert E.

Roberts, Ralph G. Tick Creek Cave: An Archaic Site in the Gasconade River Valley of Missouri. Bray, Robert T., ed. (Missouri Archaeologist Ser.: Vol. 27, No. 2). (Illus.). 52p. (Orig.). 1965. pap. 2.00 (0-943414-44-X) MO Arch Soc.

Roberts, Randy. Jack Dempsey: The Manassa Mauler. LC 83-27514. (Illus.). 344p. 1984. pap. 9.95 (0-8071-1161-9) La State U Pr.
— Papa Jack: Jack Johnson & the Era of White Hopes. LC 82-49017. 1985. 24.95 (0-02-926640-8); pap. 14.95 (0-02-926900-8) Free Pr.

Roberts, Randy & Olson, James. Winning Is the Only Thing: Sports in America since 1945. LC 89-1689. (Illus.). 208p. 1989. 38.95 (0-8018-3830-4) Johns Hopkins.
— Winning Is the Only Thing: Sports in America since 1945. LC 89-1689. (American Moment Ser.). (Illus.). 208p. 1991. reprint ed. pap. 12.95 (0-8018-4240-9) Johns Hopkins.

***Roberts, Randy & Olson, James S.** John Wayne: American. 1995. 27.50 (0-02-923837-4) Free Pr.

Roberts, Randy, jt. auth. see Garrison, J. Gregory.
Roberts, Randy, jt. auth. see Olson, James S.

Roberts, Ransom. How to Have a Happier Year: Take a Number (Nonsense Numerology) LC 81-90709. (Illus.). 128p. (Orig.). 1982. pap. 5.95 (0-9607834-0-7) Uptown Bks.

Roberts, Ray. Bentley Specials & Special Bentleys. (Illus.). 496p. 1991. 150.00 (0-85429-699-9, Pub. by G T Foulis Ltd) Haynes Pubns.
— John Updike: A Biographical Checklist. Date not set. 12.50 (0-89679-011-8); pap. text ed. 4.50 (0-89679-010-X) Moretus Pr.
— Paper Airplanes from Around the World, Vol. I. 3rd enl. rev. ed. (Illus.). 240p. (J). (gr. 6 up). 1992. reprint ed. lib. bdg. 19.95 (0-929995-00-7) AIR Burbank.

Roberts, Ray, ed. see Goebel, Julius, Jr.

Roberts, Rebecca E., intro. Still Life with Conversation: A Poetry Play. 80p. (Orig.). 1993. pap. 9.95 (1-56439-027-6) Ridgeway.

Roberts, Rhia, jt. auth. see Mather, Nancy.

Roberts, Richard. From Eden to Eros: Origins of the Put down of Women. (Illus.). 167p. (Orig.). 1985. pap. 8.95 (0-942380-05-3) Vernal Equinox.
— The Original Tarot & You. 210p. (Orig.). 1987. pap. 8.95 (0-317-61776-1) Vernal Equinox.
— Save the Whales! (Illus.). (Orig.). 1991. pap. 10.95 (0-942380-12-6) Vernal Equinox.
— Tales for Jung Folk: Original Fairytales for Persons of All Ages Dramatizing C. G. Jung's Archetypes of the Collective Unconscious. (Illus.). 120p. (Orig.). 1983. lib. bdg. 15.95 (0-942380-02-9); pap. 9.95 (0-942380-01-0) Vernal Equinox.
— The Wind & The Wizard, 2 vols. (Illus.). 1990. 18.95 (0-685-22209-8); pap. 15.95 (0-685-74023-4) Vernal Equinox.
— The Wind & The Wizard, 2 vols., Vol. 1. (Illus.). 256p. 1990. 19.95 (0-942380-08-8); 15.95 (0-942380-07-X) Vernal Equinox.
— The Wind & The Wizard, 2 vols., Vol. 2. (Illus.). 180p. 1990. 19.95 (0-942380-10-X); 15.95 (0-685-74024-2) Vernal Equinox.

R

An Asterisk (*) at the beginning of an entry indicates that the title is appearing in BIP for the first time.

Roberts, Richard, ed. International Financial Centers Series, 4 vols. 2200p. 1994. 623.95 (*1-85278-758-9*, Pub. by E Elgar Pub UK) Ashgate Pub Co.

***Roberts, Richard & Kynaston, David, eds.** The Bank of England 1694-1994: Money, Power, & Influence. 230p. 1995. 35.00 (*0-19-828952-9*) OUP.

Roberts, Richard, jt. auth. see Campbell, Joseph.

Roberts, Richard, jt. ed. see Isaacman, Allen.

Roberts, Richard, jt. auth. see Mann, Kristin.

Roberts, Richard, jt. auth. see Roberts, Jane.

Roberts, Richard A. Custer's Last Battle. (Custer Monograph: No. 4). 60p. 1978. pap. 8.00 (*0-940696-01-0*) Monroe County Lib.

— An Introduction to Applied Probability. (Illus.). 500p. (C). 1992. text ed. 64.50 (*0-201-05552-X*) Addison-Wesley.

Roberts, Richard A. & Mullis, Clifford T. Digital Signal Processing. (Electrical Engineering Ser.). (Illus.). 650p. (C). 1987. text ed. 67.95 (*0-201-16350-0*) Addison-Wesley.

Roberts, Richard A., jt. auth. see Gabel, Robert A.

Roberts, Richard B., ed. Studies in Macromolecular Biosynthesis. (Illus.). 702p. 1964. 29.00 (*0-87279-635-3*, 624) Carnegie Inst.

Roberts, Richard B., et al. Studies of Biosynthesis in Escherichia Coli. (Illus.). 521p. 1958. pap. 22.00 (*0-87279-618-3*, 607) Carnegie Inst.

Roberts, Richard C. & Sadler, Richard W. Ogden: Junction City. rev. ed. LC 85-7540. 288p. 1985. 25.95 (*0-89781-154-2*) Preferred Mktg.

Roberts, Richard C., jt. auth. see Sadler, Richard W.

Roberts, Richard D. Flightrivia. (Illus.). 6p. 1991. 14.95 (*1-880580-02-0*) Strebor.

— Jetrivia. (Illus.). 6p. 1990. 11.95 (*1-880580-00-4*) Strebor.

Roberts, Richard E. Henrik Ibsen: A Critical Study. 1972. 59.95 (*0-8490-0292-3*) Gordon Pr.

Roberts, Richard H. Hope & Its Hieroglyph: Critical Decipherment of Ernst Bloch's Principle of Hope. 325p. 1990. 20.95 (*1-55540-369-7*); pap. 13.95 (*1-55540-370-0*) Scholars Pr GA.

— A Theology on Its Way? Essays on Karl Barth. 256p. 1991. text ed. 37.95 (*0-567-09585-1*, Pub. by T & T Clark UK) Bks Intl VA.

***Roberts, Richard H., ed.** Religion & the Transformations of Capitalism: Comparative Approaches. LC 94-28913. 464p. 1995. 89.95x (*0-415-11917-0*, B4332) Routledge.

Roberts, Richard H., ed. see Ewald, William P., et al.

Roberts, Richard J., jt. ed. see Linn, Stuart M.

Roberts, Richard J., et al, eds. Nucleases, Monograph 25. 2nd ed. (Illus.). 300p. (C). 1994. pap. 75.00 (*0-87969-426-2*) Cold Spring Harbor.

Roberts, Richard L. Warriors, Merchants, & Slaves: The State & the Economy in the Middle Niger Valley, 1700-1914. LC 86-23138. 305p. 1987. 42.50 (*0-8047-1378-2*) Stanford U Pr.

Roberts, Richard L., jt. ed. see Miers, Suzanne.

Roberts, Richard L., et al. Freeze Fracture Images of Cells & Tissues. (Illus.). 416p. 1991. 75.00 (*0-19-505228-5*) OUP.

Roberts, Richard O. Revival. rev. ed. 159p. (C). 1991. reprint ed. pap. 7.95 (*0-940033-36-4*) R O Roberts.

— Revival. 2nd rev. ed. 159p. (C). 1991. reprint ed. lib. bdg. 12.95 (*0-940033-37-2*) R O Roberts.

— Revival Literature: An Annotated Bibliography with Biographical & Historical Notices. xxxii, 575p. 1987. lib. bdg. 60.00 (*0-940033-27-5*) R O Roberts.

— Sanctify the Congregation: A Call to the Solemn Assembly & to Corporate Repentance. LC 93-80173. xiv, 338p. (Orig.). 1994. pap. text ed. 18.95 (*0-926474-10-3*) Intl Awakening Pr.

— Whitefield in Print: A Bibliographic Record. xlii, 765p. 1988. lib. bdg. 75.00 (*0-940033-28-3*) R O Roberts.

Roberts, Richard O., ed. Salvation in Full Color: Twenty Sermons by Great Awakening Preachers. LC 93-80172. xxii, 362p. (Orig.). 1994. pap. text ed. 17.95 (*0-926474-12-X*) Intl Awakening Pr.

Roberts, Richard O., ed. see Lewis, et al.

Roberts, Richard O., ed. see Orr, J. Edwin.

***Roberts, Robert.** Classic Slum: Salford Life. 1990. pap. 10.95 (*0-14-013624-X*, Penguin Bks) Viking Penguin.

— The Classic Slum: Salford Life in the First Quarter of the Century. 272p. 1973. pap. 7.95 (*0-14-021692-8*, Penguin Bks) Viking Penguin.

— Roberts' Guide for Butlers & Household Staff. LC 93-19131. 168p. 1988. reprint ed. pap. 8.95 (*1-55709-120-X*) Applewood.

— The Social Laws of the Qoran: Considered & Compared with Those of the Hebrew & Other Ancient Codes. LC 89-27402. 136p. 1990. pap. 15.00 (*0-391-03661-0*) Humanities.

Roberts, Robert, ed. Coronary Heart Disease & Risk Factors. (Clinical Cardiovascular Therapeutics Ser.: Vol. 3). (Illus.). 360p. 1991. 59.00 (*0-87993-375-5*) Futura Pub.

Roberts, Robert, jt. ed. see Suzuki, Shosuke.

Roberts, Robert, et al. A Primer of Molecular Biology. LC 92-14601. (Current Topics in Cardiology Ser.). 1992. write for info. (*0-444-01657-0*) Elsevier.

Roberts, Robert B. New York's Forts in the Revolution. LC 77-74395. 500p. 1979. 38.50 (*0-8386-2063-9*) Fairleigh Dickinson.

Roberts, Robert B., ed. Encyclopedia of Historic Forts: The Military, Pioneeer, & Trading Posts of the United States. (Illus.). 480p. 1987. 105.00 (*0-02-926880-X*) Macmillan.

Roberts, Robert C. Taking the Word to Heart: Self & Other in an Age of Therapies. LC 92-34333. 1993. pap. 14.99 (*0-8028-0659-7*) Eerdmans.

Roberts, Robert C., jt. ed. see Kruschwitz, Robert B.

Roberts, Robert J., jt. auth. see Leff, Richard D.

Roberts, Robert N. White House Ethics: The History of the Politics of Conflict of Interest Regulation. LC 87-24962. (Contributions in Political Science Ser.: No. 204). 224p. 1988. text ed. 55.00 (*0-313-25934-8*, RWH/, Greenwood Pr) Greenwood.

Roberts, Robert W., ed. The Unwed Mother. LC 80-20554. (Readers in Social Problems). viii, 270p. 1980. reprint ed. text ed. 59.75 (*0-313-22677-6*, ROUM, Greenwood Pr) Greenwood.

Roberts, Robert W. & Northen, Helen. Theories for Social Work with Groups. LC 76-4967. 400p. 1976. text ed. 38.00 (*0-231-03885-2*) Col U Pr.

Roberts, Robert W., jt. ed. see Taylor, Samuel H.

Roberts, Robin. A New Species: Gender & Science in Science Fiction. LC 92-25385. (Illus.). 200p. (C). 1993. 29.95 (*0-252-01983-0*); pap. 12.95 (*0-252-06284-1*) U of Ill Pr.

Roberts, Robin, jt. auth. see Lieberman-Cline, Nancy.

Roberts, Roger L., ed. see Julian of Norwich.

Roberts, Ron E. Social Problems. 310p. 1978. pap. 12.95 (*0-8016-4143-8*) Schenkman Bks Inc.

Roberts, Ron E. & Brintnall, Douglas. Reinventing Inequality. 339p. 1983. text ed. 22.95 (*0-87073-793-7*); pap. text ed. 13.95 (*0-87073-794-5*) Schenkman Bks Inc.

Roberts, Ron E., jt. auth. see Keefe, Thomas.

Roberts, Ronald. Iowa's Ethnic Roots. 192p. (C). 1993. pap. text ed. 21.95 (*0-8403-8421-1*) Kendall-Hunt.

— John L. Lewis: Hard Labor & Wild Justice. 240p. (C). 1994. per. 23.96 (*0-8403-9297-4*) Kendall-Hunt.

Roberts, Ronald, jt. auth. see Muir, J. E.

Roberts, Ronald J. & Shepherd, C. Jonathan. Handbook of Trout & Salmon Diseases. 1978. 90.00 (*0-685-63425-6*) St Mut.

Roberts, Ronald R. Ditches of Edison County. 1993. pap. 7.00 (*0-452-27256-4*, Plume) NAL-Dutton.

— The Ditches of Edison County. LC 93-37206. 1993. write for info. (*0-525-27256-9*, Plume) NAL-Dutton.

Roberts, Ronald S. Clarence Thomas & the Tough Love Crowd: Counterfeit Heroes & Unhappy Truths. 304p. 1994. 24.95 (*0-8147-7454-7*) NYU Pr.

Roberts, Roy R. Life in the Pressure Cooker: Studies in James. pap. 5.99 (*0-88469-033-4*) BMH Bks.

Roberts, Royston M. Serendipity: Accidental Discoveries in Science. 270p. 1989. pap. text ed. 14.95 (*0-471-60203-5*) Wiley.

— Serendipity: Accidental Discoveries in Science. 270p. 1989. text ed. 22.95 (*0-471-50658-3*) Wiley.

***Roberts, Royston M. & Roberts, Jeanie.** Lucky Science: Accidental Discoveries from Gravity to Velcro, with Experiments. 1994. pap. text ed. 10.95 (*0-471-00954-7*) Wiley.

Roberts, Royston M., et al. Modern Experimental Organic Chemistry. 4th ed. 804p. (C). 1985. text ed. 47.00 (*0-03-063018-5*) SCP.

— Modern Experimental Organic Chemistry. 4th ed. 832p. (C). 1985. teacher ed, pap. text ed. 15.00 (*0-03-063019-3*) SCP.

— Modern Experimental Organic Chemistry. 4th ed. 832p. (C). 1985. pap. text ed. 50.75 (*0-03-006954-8*) SCP.

Roberts, Rozella. Mind Assassins. large type ed. 201p. (Orig.). 1992. pap. 9.95 (*0-9633452-0-6*) Roxanne Unltd.

Roberts, Rozella, jt. auth. see Chiaverini, Evelyn.

Roberts, Russell. All about Blue Crabs: And How to Catch Them. 88p. 1993. pap. 8.95 (*1-882418-07-7*) Centenn Pubns.

— Choice: A Fable of Free Trade & Protectionism. 1993. pap. 11.95 (*0-13-083008-9*) P-H.

— Discover the Hidden New Jersey. (Illus.). 300p. (C). 1995. pap. 18.95 (*0-8135-2252-8*) Rutgers U Pr.

Roberts, Russell & Youmans, Richard. Down the Jersey Shore: A Historical Tour. LC 92-44337. (Illus.). 275p. (C). 1993. text ed. 29.95 (*0-8135-1995-0*); pap. 12.95 (*0-8135-1996-9*) Rutgers U Pr.

Roberts, Russell D. The Choice: A Fable of Free Trade & Protectionism. LC 93-44899. 1994. text ed. 64.00 (*0-13-288341-4*) P-H.

Roberts, Ruth, jt. auth. see Walsh, John.

Roberts, S. PC-XT-AT-386 Hardware Reference: Concise Explanations of Hardware Elements, with Illustrations. (Info Compact Ser.). (Illus.). 100p. (C). 1991. pap. 5.00 (*0-911827-07-2*) Elcomp.

— PC-XT-AT-386 Technical Pocket Reference, Pt. 2: Important Information, Tables, Technical Data. (Info Compact Ser.). (Illus.). 100p. (C). 1991. pap. 5.00 (*0-911827-08-0*) Elcomp.

— Windows 3 Pocket Reference: Concise Explanations of All Windows 3 Commands, Illustrated with Examples. (Info Compact Ser.). (Illus.). 100p. (C). 1991. pap. 5.00 (*0-911827-06-4*) Elcomp.

Roberts, S., ed. Law & the Family in Africa. 1977. 33.85 (*90-279-7663-5*) Mouton.

Roberts, S., jt. auth. see Hawthorn, P.

Roberts, S., et al, eds. Mechanisms, Regulation & Special Functions of Protein Synthesis in the Brain. (Developments in Neuro-Science Ser.: Vol. 2). 1978. 107.25 (*0-444-80030-1*) Elsevier.

Roberts, S. C. Doctor Watson. 32p. 1977. reprint ed. lib. bdg. 20.00 (*0-910278-63-6*) Boulevard.

— Holmes & Watson: A Miscellany. 144p. 1994. reprint ed. pap. 8.00 (*1-883402-96-4*) S&S Trade.

Roberts, S. C., ed. see Piozzi, Hester L.

Roberts, S. C., ed. see Piozzi, Hesther L.

Roberts, S. D. Forth Applications: Ready to Run Programs. (Illus.). 149p. (Orig.). 1990. pap. 9.95 (*0-911827-00-5*, 61) Elcomp.

— Forth Quick Start: Introduction to Forth. (Illus.). 59p. (Orig.). 1990. pap. 5.00 (*0-911827-01-3*, 65) Elcomp.

— The Great Book of Batch Jobs: Introduction to Batch Programming on PC - XT - AT. (Illus.). 98p. (Orig.). 1990. pap. 9.95 (*0-911827-05-6*, 71) Elcomp.

Roberts, S. D., ed. FORTH - FORTH-83 Quick Start Introduction: FORTH-83 Tutorial. (Illus.). 58p. (Orig.). (C). 1989. pap. 5.00 (*0-685-33373-6*, 65) Elcomp.

Roberts, S. Lowell. Back to Buck Lake. LC 93-71649. 304p. (YA). (gr. 7 up). 1993. 14.95 (*0-9636894-0-1*) Estrn Itascan.

Roberts, S. M. & Price, B. J., eds. Medicinal Chemistry: The Role of Organic Synthesis in Drug Research. 1985. pap. text ed. 61.00 (*0-12-589731-6*) Acad Pr.

Roberts, S. M. & Scheinmann, F., eds. Chemistry, Biochemistry & Pharmacology of Prostanoids. 1979. 175.00 (*0-08-023799-1*, Pub. by Pergamon Repr UK) Franklin.

— New Synthetic Routes to Prostaglandins & Thromboxanes. LC 81-68962. 1982. text ed. 138.00 (*0-12-589620-4*) Acad Pr.

Roberts, S. M., jt. ed. see Ganellin, C. R.

Roberts, S. M., et al. Introduction to Biocatalysis Using Enzymes & Microorganisms. (Illus.). 240p. (C). 1995. 49.95 (*0-521-43070-4*); pap. 19.95 (*0-521-43685-0*) Cambridge U Pr.

Roberts, Sally. The Attic Pyxis. 366p. 1978. 50.00 (*0-89005-210-7*) Ares.

Roberts, Sam. Games for the Atari. 1982. pap. 7.95 (*0-936200-36-7*) Blue Cat.

— Tricks for VICs. 1984. 9.95 (*3-88963-176-2*) Blue Cat.

— Who We Are: A Portrait of America. 1995. pap. 13.00 (*0-8129-2526-2*, Times Bks) Random.

— Who We Are: A Portrait of America Today Based on the Latest United States Census. LC 92-56842. 240p. 1994. 18.00 (*0-8129-2192-5*, Times Bks) Random.

Roberts, Sam D. How to Program Your Atari in 6502 Machine Language. 106p. 1982. 9.95 (*0-936200-37-5*) Blue Cat.

— Statistics on the IBM: Introduction, Practial Applications, Ready to Run Programs. (Illus.). 200p. 1985. pap. 12.95 (*3-88963-047-2*) Elcomp.

— UNIX, XENIX & VENIX: Introduction, Applications Tips & Tricks. (Illus.). 206p. 1985. pap. 12.95 (*3-88963-064-2*) Elcomp.

— UNIXV Pocket Reference. (Info Compact Ser.). 88p. 1992. pap. 5.00 (*0-911827-14-5*) Elcomp.

Roberts, Samuel J. Survival or Hegemony? The Foundations of Israeli Foreign Policy. LC 73-8134. (Studies in International Affairs: No. 20). 175p. reprint ed. pap. 49.90 (*0-317-41684-7*, 2025852) Bks Demand.

Roberts, Samuel R., III. Existence, Faith & Responsibility: Carl Michalson's Christian Ethics. (Contemporary Existentialism Ser.: Vol. 2). 280p. (C). 1989. text ed. 57.95 (*0-8204-0875-1*) P Lang Pubs.

Roberts, Sarah. The Adventures of Big Bird in Dinosaur Days. LC 83-61891. (Sesame Street Mini-Storybooks Ser.). (Illus.). 32p. (J). (ps-3). 1984. pap. 1.50 (*0-394-85926-X*) Random Bks Yng Read.

— Bert & the Missing Mop Mix-Up. LC 82-22971. (Sesame Street Start-to-Read Bks.). (Illus.). 40p. (J). (gr. k-2). 1983. 4.95 (*0-394-85752-6*) Random Bks Yng Read.

— Don't Cry, Big Bird. LC 81-4075. (Sesame Street Start-to-Read Bks.). (Illus.). 40p. (J). (gr. k-2). 1981. 4.95 (*0-394-84868-3*) Random Bks Yng Read.

— Don't Cry, Big Bird. LC 81-4075. (Sesame Street Start-to-Read Bks.). (Illus.). 40p. (J). (ps-3). 1993. pap. 2.99 (*0-679-83950-X*) Random Bks Yng Read.

— Ernie's Big Mess. LC 81-2464. (Sesame Street Start-to-Read Bks.). (Illus.). 40p. (J). (ps-3). 1992. 4.95 (*0-394-84847-0*); pap. 2.99 (*0-679-82398-0*) Random Bks Yng Read.

— I Want to Go Home. LC 84-11725. (Sesame Street Start-to-Read Bks.). (Illus.). 40p. (J). (ps-3). 1985. 4.95 (*0-394-87027-1*) Random Bks Yng Read.

— Nobody Cares about Me! LC 81-15913. (Sesame Street Start-to-Read Bks.). (Illus.). 40p. (J). (ps-3). 1992. reprint ed. pap. 2.99 (*0-679-82399-9*) Random Bks Yng Read.

***Roberts, Scott.** Fitness Walking. (Illus.). (Orig.). 1995. pap. 14.95 (*1-57028-034-7*) Masters Pr IN.

— Health Wellness: An Introductory Approach. 2nd ed. 350p. 1992. pap. 18.95 (*0-945483-22-8*) E Bowers Pub.

Roberts, Scott, et al. Strength & Weight Training for Young Athletes: A Safe, Scientific Approach to Weight Training That Puts Young Athletes Ahead of the Game. 208p. 1994. pap. 13.95 (*0-8092-3697-4*) Contemp Bks.

Roberts, Shane. The Art & Science of Making Money: Earning, Investing, & Sweeping Your Way to Greater Personal Wealth. LC 92-61032. 288p. 1993. 22.95 (*0-9633122-9-4*) McMahon Pub.

Roberts, Sharee D. Creative Machine Art. 1991. pap. 24.95 (*0-89145-986-3*) Collector Bks.

***Roberts, Sharon L.** Friendship. LC 86-9641. (Values to Live By Ser.). (Illus.). 32p. (ENG & SPA.). (J). (ps-2). 1986. lib. bdg. 14.95 (*0-89565-936-0*) Childs World.

— Friendship. LC 86-9641. (Values to Live By Ser.). (Illus.). 32p. (ENG & SPA.). (J). (ps-2). 1986. lib. bdg. 21.36 (*0-89565-350-8*) Childs World.

— Somebody Lives Inside: The Holy Spirit. (Concept Books for Children). (Illus.). 24p. (Orig.). (J). (gr. k-4). 1986. pap. 3.99 (*0-570-08530-6*, 56-1557) Concordia.

Roberts, Sheila, ed. Still the Frame Holds: Essays on Women Poets & Writers. LC 87-823. (I. O. Evans Studies in the Philosophy & Criticism of Literature: No. 10). 216p. 1993. 31.00x (*0-89370-304-4*); pap. 21.00x (*0-89370-404-0*) Borgo Pr.

Roberts, Shelly. The Dyke Detector: How to Tell the Real Lesbians from Ordinary People. LC 92-61205. (Illus.). 96p. (Orig.). 1992. pap. 7.95 (*0-9628595-6-7*) Paradigm San Diego.

— Hey Mom, Guess What! One Hundred Fifty Ways to Tell Your Mother: One Hundred Fifty Ways to Tell Your Mother. LC 93-84467. (Illus.). 160p. 1993. pap. 8.95 (*0-9628595-9-1*) Paradigm San Diego.

— Make News & Make Noise! How to Get Publicity for Your Book. LC 93-87210. 64p. (Orig.). 1994. pap. 5.95 (*1-882587-03-0*) Paradigm San Diego.

— Weighing in on the Butch-Fem Scale. (Illus.). 160p. (Orig.). 1995. pap. text ed. 9.95 (*0-614-03301-2*) Paradigm San Diego.

Roberts, Sherry. Maud's House. 200p. 1994. 18.00 (*0-918949-32-7*) Papier-Mache Press.

— Maud's House. 200p. 1994. pap. 11.00 (*0-918949-28-9*) Papier-Mache Press.

Roberts, Sherry, jt. auth. see Thompson, Deanna L.

Roberts, Shirley. Charles Hotham: A Biography. (Illus.). 201p. 1985. 29.95 (*0-522-84287-9*) Intl Spec Bk.

— Sophia Jex-Blake: A Woman Pioneer in Nineteenth Century Medical Reform. LC 93-14890. (Wellcome Institute Series in the History of Medicine). (Illus.). 192p. 1994. 59.95 (*0-415-08753-8*, B0865) Routledge.

Roberts, Sidney I., et al. Annotated Tax Forms. write for info. (*0-318-57361-X*) P-H.

Roberts, Sidney I. U. S. Tax Conventions, 16 vols., Set. (Roberts & Holland Collection). 1986. ring bd. 1,950.00 (*0-89941-379-X*, 303850) W S Hein.

Roberts, Simon. Solar Electricity: A Practical Guide to Designing & Installing Small Photovoltaic Systems. 448p. 1992. pap. text ed. 43.00 (*0-13-825068-5*) P-H.

— Solar Electricity: A Practical Guide to Small Photovoltaic Systems. 448p. 1991. boxed 35.00 (*0-13-826314-0*) P-H.

Roberts, Simon, jt. auth. see Comaroff, John L.

Roberts, Sonia. The Right Way to Keep Birds. large type ed. (Illus.). 160p. 1989. reprint ed. lib. bdg. 17.95 (*1-85089-300-4*, Pub. by ISIS UK) Transaction Pubs.

***Roberts Staff.** The Boer War Afrikaaners P. O. W. Roll. (C). 1993. 295.00x (*1-873058-16-0*, Pub. by Roberts UK) St Mut.

— British South Africa Company's Medal: The 1890 Mashonsland Medal. (C). 1989. 95.00x (*1-873058-45-4*, Pub. by Roberts UK) St Mut.

— British South Africa Company's Medal: The 1893 Metabeleland Medal. (C). 1989. 95.00x (*1-873058-50-0*, Pub. by Roberts UK) St Mut.

— British South Africa Company's Medal: The 1896 Rhodesia Medal. (C). 1989. 95.00x (*1-873058-55-1*, Pub. by Roberts UK) St Mut.

— British South Africa Company's Medal: The 1897 Mashonsland Medal. (C). 1989. 95.00x (*1-873058-60-8*, Pub. by Roberts UK) St Mut.

— British South Africa Company's Medal Complete Roll. (C). 1989. 360.00x (*1-873058-40-3*, Pub. by Roberts UK) St Mut.

— The Cape Cooper Company Limited Medal for the Defence of O'Kiep. (C). 1989. 90.00x (*1-873058-30-6*, Pub. by Roberts UK) St Mut.

— Cape of Good Hope Medal 1880-1897. (C). 1993. 90.00x (*1-873058-25-X*, Pub. by Roberts UK) St Mut.

— Colonial Auxiliary Forces Long Service Medal. (C). 1989. 90.00x (*1-873058-56-X*, Pub. by Roberts UK) St Mut.

— Decorations Awarded to Natal, Cape Colony & Union Defence Forces 1877-1961. (C). 1989. 90.00x (*1-873058-51-9*, Pub. by Roberts UK) St Mut.

— Defenders of Mafeking. (C). 1993. 90.00x (*1-873058-06-3*, Pub. by Roberts UK) St Mut.

— The Efficiency Decoration-The Union of South Africa. (C). 1989. 90.00x (*1-873058-70-5*, Pub. by Roberts UK) St Mut.

— Etonians Who Served in the Boer War. (C). 1989. 90.00x (*1-873058-21-7*, Pub. by Roberts UK) St Mut.

— The Jameson Raiders 1896. (C). 1989. 95.00x (*1-873058-85-3*, Pub. by Roberts UK) St Mut.

— Kings Commendations-Union Forces 1939-1945. (C). 1989. 90.00x (*1-873058-80-2*, Pub. by Roberts UK) St Mut.

— The Matabele Rebellion 1896. (C). 1989. 95.00x (*1-873058-05-5*, Pub. by Roberts UK) St Mut.

— Die Medaljerol. (C). 1989. 125.00x (*1-873058-01-2*, Pub. by Roberts UK) St Mut.

— Medals for Gallantry & Distinguished Conduct Award to Natal, Cape Colony & Union Defence Forces 1877-1961. (C). 1989. 95.00x (*1-873058-95-0*, Pub. by Roberts UK) St Mut.

— The Officers, Men & Women of the Australian Imperial Forces Vol. 6. (C). 1989. 125.00 (*1-873058-66-7*, Pub. by Roberts UK) St Mut.

— The Officers, Men & Women of the Merchant Navy & Mercantile Fleet Auxiliary Vol. 5. (C). 1989. 125.00 (*1-873058-41-1*, Pub. by Roberts UK) St Mut.

— The Officers, Men & Women of the New Zealand Expeditionary Forces Vol. 8. (C). 1989. 125.00 (*1-873058-76-4*, Pub. by Roberts UK) St Mut.

— The Officers, Men & Women of the South African Forces Vol. 7. (C). 1989. 125.00 (*1-873058-71-3*, Pub. by Roberts UK) St Mut.

— Officers Who Died in the Service of British, Indian & East African Regiments & Corps 1914-1919, Vol. 1. (C). 1989. 125.00 (*1-873058-26-8*, Pub. by Roberts UK) St Mut.

— Officers Who Died in the Service of The Royal Navy, Royal Naval Reserve, Royal Naval Volunteer Reserve, Royal Marines, Royal Marines Reserve, Royal Navy Air Service & Royal Air Force Vol. 2. (C). 1989. 125.00 (*1-873058-31-4*, Pub. by Roberts UK) St Mut.

— Roll of Honour South Africa 1939-1945 European, Natives & Coloured. (C). 1993. 95.00x (*1-873058-86-1*, Pub. by Roberts UK) St Mut.

— South African Mounted Irregular Forces 1899-1902: A Multinational Force in the Boer War. (C). 1993. 90.00x (*1-873058-65-9*, Pub. by Roberts UK) St Mut.

— South African War Medal 1877-89 the Medal Roll. (C). 1989. 90.00 (*1-873058-20-9*, Pub. by Roberts UK) St Mut.

— South Africa's Roll of Honour 1914-1918. (C). 1989. 95.00x (*1-873058-75-6*, Pub. by Roberts UK) St Mut.

R

An Asterisk (*) at the beginning of an entry indicates that the title is appearing in BIP for the first time.

— The Transport Medal Roll. (C). 1989. 95.00x (*1-873058-15-2*, Pub. by Roberts UK) St Mut.

— The Zulu Rebellion 1906. rev. ed. (C). 1989. 90.00x (*1-873058-00-4*, Pub. by Roberts UK) St Mut.

***Roberts Staff, ed.** Defenders of Kimberley. (C). 1989. 90.00x (*1-873058-35-7*, Pub. by Roberts UK) St Mut.

— Female Officers, Nurses, Enlisted Women & Civilians Vol. 9. (C). 1989. 125.00 (*1-873058-81-0*, Pub. by Roberts UK) St Mut.

— Non-Commissioned Officers & Men of the Royal Navy & Commonwealth & Colonial Revies Who Died in Service 1914-1919 Vol. 4. (C). 1989. 125.00 (*0-614-03380-2*, Pub. by Roberts UK) St Mut.

— Officers Who Died in the Service of Commonwealth & Colonial Regiments & Corps Vol. 3. (C). 1989. 125.00 (*1-873058-36-5*, Pub. by Roberts UK) St Mut.

— Orders of Chivalry, Foreign Decorations & Awards to Natal, Cape Colony & Union Defence Forces. (C). 1989. 90.00x (*1-873058-90-X*, Pub. by Roberts UK) St Mut.

Roberts, Stanley. The Beginner's Guide to Winning Blackjack. (Illus.). (Orig.). 1983. pap. text ed. 10.00 (*0-89746-014-6*) Gambling Times.

— Gambling Times Guide to Blackjack. (Illus.). (Orig.). 1983. pap. text ed. 5.95 (*0-685-01828-8*) Carol Pub Group.

— Gambling Times Guide to Blackjack, 1990. (Illus.). (Orig.). 1984. pap. text ed. 9.95 (*0-89746-015-4*) Gambling Times.

Roberts, Stephanie, jt. auth. see Diamond, Lynn.

Roberts, Stephen. The House That Hitler Built. 1975. 250.00 (*0-87968-338-4*) Gordon Pr.

— Radical Politicians & Poets in Early Victorian Britain: The Voices of Six Chartist Leaders. LC 93-50810. (Studies in British History: Vol. 27). 160p. 1994. text ed. 69.95 (*0-7734-9126-0*) E Mellen.

***Roberts, Stephen A.** Financial Management for Library & Information Services. 2nd ed. 250p. 1996. 50.00 (*1-85739-089-X*) Bowker-Saur.

Roberts, Stephen H. Population Problems of the Pacific. LC 71-99884. reprint ed. 55.00 (*0-404-00599-3*) AMS Pr.

Roberts, Stephen R. Pelt Songs: The Steel-Belted Radial Round-Up Poems. 16p. 1993. pap. 5.00 (*1-885710-06-2*) Geekspeak Unique.

— A Slash of Waking. Sherman, Alana, ed. 20p. (Orig.). 1995. pap. text ed. 5.95 (*0-939689-19-7*) Alms Hse Pr.

Roberts, Stephen S., jt. auth. see Bauer, K. Jack.

Roberts, Stephen S., ed. see Ropp, Theodore.

Roberts, Stephen S., jt. auth. see Stone, Jack L.

***Roberts, Steve, ed.** Telecommunications. (Spicers European Union Policy Briefings Ser.). 228p. 1995. 150.00 (*1-56159-140-8*, Stockton Pr) Groves Dictionaries.

Roberts, Steven K. The Complete Guide to Microsystem Management. 192p. (C). 1984. 26.00 (*0-13-160556-9*) P-H.

— Computing Across America: The Bicycle Odyssey of a High-Tech Nomad. (Illus.). 368p. 1988. 14.95 (*0-938734-25-3*); pap. 9.95 (*0-938734-18-0*) Learned Info.

— Creative Design with Microcomputers. (Illus.). 400p. 1984. 16.95 (*0-13-189317-3*) P-H.

— Industrial Design with Microcomputers. (Illus.). 416p. (C). 1982. 41.00 (*0-13-459461-4*) P-H.

Roberts, Sue N. Ginny Doll Encyclopedia. 1994. 29.95 (*0-87588-419-9*) Hobby Hse.

Roberts, Susan, ed. see Iowa Dietetic Association Staff.

Roberts, Susan A. & Roberts, Calvin G. A History of New Mexico. rev. ed. (Illus.). 400p. (J). (gr. 6-9). 1991. text ed. 48.50 (*0-8263-1264-0*) U of NM Pr.

— New Mexico. LC 87-30086. (Illus.). 220p. 1989. pap. 16.95 (*0-8263-1145-8*) U of NM Pr.

Roberts, Suzanne. Farewell to Alexandria. large type ed. LC 92-46982. 1993. 19.95 (*0-7927-1574-8*, Curley Lrg Print); pap. 17.95 (*0-7927-1573-X*, Curley Lrg Print) Chivers N Amer.

Roberts, Sydney. Holmes & Watson: A Miscellany. LC 78-157958. 137p. 1972. reprint ed. text ed. 35.00 (*0-8371-6172-X*, ROHW, Greenwood Pr) Greenwood.

Roberts, T., jt. ed. see Narayanan, R.

Roberts, T., jt. ed. see Potier, R.

Roberts, T. A. Adventures in Conservation: Painting the Cows & Other Tales. LC 88-63984. 176p. 1989. pap. 12.95 (*0-913276-53-7*) Stone Wall Pr.

— Beyond Saru. Chirich, Nancy, ed. 264p. (Orig.). 1993. pap. 12.95 (*0-912761-38-5*) Cliffhanger Pr.

Roberts, T. A. & Sutherland, Stuart R., eds. Religion, Reason & the Self. vi, 173p. 1989. 35.00 (*0-7083-1042-7*, Pub. by U of Wales UK) Bks Intl VA.

***Roberts, T. D.** Understanding Balance: The Mechanics of Posture & Locomotive. 360p. 1995. pap. 47.99 (*1-56593-416-4*, 1082) Singular Publishing.

Roberts, T. R. Radiochromatography: The Chromatography & Electrophoresis of Radiolabelled Compounds. (Journal of Chromatography Library: Vol. 14). 174p. 1978. 77.00 (*0-444-41656-0*) Elsevier.

Roberts, T. R., jt. ed. see Hutson, D. H.

***Roberts, Ted.** For Men Only: The Corageous Fight for Healthy Sexuality. Harlan, Roberta, ed. (Illus.). 132p. (Orig.). 1993. pap. 7.00 (*1-879619-09-1*) East Hill Church.

Roberts, Ted E. Practical Radio Promotions. (Electronic Media Guide Ser.). 92p. 1992. pap. 15.95 (*0-240-80090-7*, Focal) Buttrwrth-Heinemann.

Roberts, Terence A. & Skinner, Frederick A., eds. Food Microbiology: Advances & Prospects. (Society for Applied Bacteriology Symposium Ser.: Vol. II). 1983. text ed. 119.00 (*0-12-589670-0*) Acad Pr.

Roberts, Terence A., et al, eds. Psychrotrophic Microorganisms in Spoilage & Pathogenicity. LC 81-67902. 552p. 1982. text ed. 138.00 (*0-12-589720-0*) Acad Pr.

***Roberts, Teresa N.** Digging up the Bones. 70p. (Orig.). 1994. pap. 7.00 (*0-944920-12-8*) Bellowing Ark Pr.

Roberts, Terry. Self & Community in the Fiction of Elizabeth Spencer. LC 93-26078. (Southern Literary Studies). 176p. 1994. text ed. 29.95 (*0-8071-1879-6*) La State U Pr.

Roberts, Thom. Atlantic Free Balloon Race. (J). (gr. 3-7). 1986. pap. 2.50 (*0-380-89868-3*, Camelot) Avon.

— Summerdog. (Illus.). 128p. (Orig.). (J). (gr. 1 up). 1978. pap. 2.25 (*0-380-01950-7*, Camelot) Avon.

Roberts, Thomas, jt. ed. see Kramutschke, Eleanor.

Roberts, Thomas, jt. ed. see Rex, David.

Roberts, Thomas G., ed. GSA Cincinnati Eighty-One Field Trip Guidebooks, 3 Vols. Incl. Vol. I, Stratigraphy, Sedimentology. (Illus.). 258p. (Orig.). 1981. pap. 38.00 (*0-913312-57-6*); Vol. II, Economic Geology, Structure. (Illus.). 150p. (Orig.). 1981. pap. 29.00 (*0-913312-58-4*); Vol. III, Geomorphology, Hydrogeology, Geoarcheology, Engineering Geology. (Illus.). 163p. (Orig.). 1981. pap. 29.00 (*0-913312-59-2*); 1981. Set. write for info. (*0-913312-60-6*) Am Geol.

Roberts, Thomas J. An Aesthetics of Junk Fiction. LC 89-4911. 288p. 1990. 30.00 (*0-8203-1149-9*) U of Ga Pr.

Roberts, Thomas P. Prayers for God's People. Sherer, Michael L., ed. (Orig.). 1988. pap. 5.95 (*1-55673-025-X*, 8810) CSS OH.

Roberts, Thomas W. A Systems Perspective of Parenting: The Individual, the Family, & the Social Network. LC 93-41870. 1994. pap. 35.95 (*0-534-15546-4*) Brooks-Cole.

Roberts, Tim, jt. ed. see Parker, Colin.

Roberts, Tom. Friends & Villains. large type ed. (Non-Fiction Ser.). (Illus.). 384p. 1989. 17.95 (*0-7089-2045-4*) Ulverscroft.

— Friends & Villains: An Autobiography. (Illus.). 192p. 1988. 22.95 (*0-340-41150-3*, Pub. by H & S UK) Trafalgar.

— Goldilocks. LC 93-6679. (Illus.). (J). (ps-6). 1993. Incl. cassette. audio 9.95 (*0-88708-322-6*, Picture Book Studio) S&S Childrens.

— Goldilocks & the Three Bears. (Illus.). 32p. (J). (gr. k up). 1991. pap. 14.95 (*0-88708-146-0*, Rabbit); pap. 19.95 (*0-88708-147-9*, Rabbit) S&S Childrens.

— I Dream of War. Winkler, Chris, ed. (Illus.). 6p. 1988. pap. text ed. 0.50 (*0-929611-06-3*) Plutonium Pr.

— Red Riding Hood. LC 93-12152. (Illus.). (J). (ps-6). 1993. Incl. cassette. 9.95 (*0-88708-320-X*, Rabbit) S&S Childrens.

— The Three Billy Goats Gruff. LC 89-32138. (Illus.). 32p. (J). (gr. 1 up). 1991. 19.95 (*0-88708-118-5*, Rabbit); pap. 14.95 (*0-88708-117-7*, Rabbit) S&S Childrens.

— The Three Billy Goats Gruff. LC 93-6678. (J). (ps-6). 1993. 9.95 (*0-88708-319-6*, Picture Book Studio) S&S Childrens.

— The Three Little Pigs. LC 89-70097. (Illus.). 32p. (J). (ps up). 1991. pap. 14.95 (*0-88708-132-0*, Rabbit); pap. 19.95 (*0-88708-133-9*, Rabbit) S&S Childrens.

— The Three Little Pigs. (Illus.). 64p. (J). 1993. reprint ed. 9.95 (*0-88708-299-8*, Rabbit) S&S Childrens.

Roberts, Tom & DeWitt, James L. Racquetball: Learning the Fundamentals. 160p. (C). 1992. per. 10.95 (*0-8403-7617-0*) Kendall-Hunt.

Roberts, Tom J. The Birds of Pakistan Vol. 1: Regional Studies & Non-Passeriformes. (Illus.). 666p. 1991. 85.00 (*0-19-577404-3*, 8452) OUP.

— The Birds of Pakistan Vol. 2. (Illus.). 682p. 1992. 85.00 (*0-19-577405-1*) OUP.

Roberts, Tris. Expectation Technique. 265p. (C). 1990. 64.00 (*0-85131-555-0*, Pub. by J A Allen & Co UK) St Mut.

Roberts, Tristan D. Neurophysiology of Postural Mechanisms. 2nd ed. LC 77-30548. (Illus.). 430p. reprint ed. pap. 122.60 (*0-685-23603-X*, 2056318) Bks Demand.

Roberts, Tyson R. The Freshwater Fishes of Western Borneo (Kalimantan Barat, Indonesia) LC 88-70981. (Memoirs of the California Academy of Sciences Ser.: No. 14). (Illus.). 1989. 20.00 (*0-940228-21-1*) Calif Acad Sci.

— An Ichthyological Survey of the Fly River in Papua New Guinea: With Descriptions of New Species. LC 78-606184. (Smithsonian Contributions to Zoology Ser.: No. 281). 78p. reprint ed. pap. 25.00 (*0-317-30002-4*, 2051859) Bks Demand.

Roberts, Ursula. Living in Two Worlds: The Autobiography of Ursula Roberts. Regency Press, Ltd. Staff, ed. 200p. 1984. 39.00 (*0-7212-0629-8*, Pub. by Regency Press) St Mut.

— The Mystery of the Human Aura. rev. ed. 64p. 1984. reprint ed. pap. 3.95 (*0-87728-331-1*) Weiser.

— Reminiscences: A Lifetime of Spiritualism. 115p. 1985. 35.00 (*0-7212-0726-X*, Pub. by Regency Press) St Mut.

Roberts, V. L. Product Standard Index. 2nd ed. 1977. 219.00 (*0-08-022123-8*, Pub. by Pergamon Repr UK) Franklin.

Roberts, Verne L. Machine Guarding: A Historical Perspective. LC 80-84798. (Illus.). 282p. 1980. text ed. 39.95 (*0-938830-00-7*) Inst Product.

***Roberts, Victoria.** Cattitudes. LC 95-10252. (Illus.). 1995. pap. 15.00 (*0-679-42361-3*) Random.

Roberts, Victoria, illus. Tell Me Another One: The Woman's Guide to Men's Classic Lines. LC 93-21913. 1994. 7.99 (*0-440-50552-6*) Dell.

Roberts, Victoria S. A Pleasure of Flowers. LC 76-47181. (Illus.). (Orig.). 1977. pap. 5.95 (*0-89407-001-0*) Strawberry Hill.

Roberts, Virginia C. With Their Own Blood: A Saga of Southwestern Pioneers. LC 91-15195. (Illus.). 288p. 1991. 24.95 (*0-87565-090-2*) Tex Christian.

Roberts, W. The Caribbean. 1976. lib. bdg. 59.95 (*0-8490-1574-X*) Gordon Pr.

— Marat in England. 1972. 69.95 (*0-8490-0583-3*) Gordon Pr.

Roberts, W. Adolphe. French in the West Indies. LC 70-147313. (Illus.). 1971. reprint ed. 53.50 (*0-8154-0377-1*) Cooper Sq.

Roberts, W. Dayton. Patching God's Garment: Environment & Mission in the 21st Century. 180p. 1994. pap. 13.95 (*0-912552-85-9*) MARC.

Roberts, W. G. Rental Management Made Easy. (Illus.). 150p. 1992. pap. 14.95 (*0-9629979-1-9*) Tower Pub GA.

Roberts, W. H., III & Cordell, Robert J., eds. Problems of Petroleum Migration. LC 80-80879. (AAPG Studies in Geology: No. 10). (Illus.). 283p. reprint ed. pap. 80.70 (*0-7837-2597-3*, 2042761) Bks Demand.

Roberts, W. R., jt. auth. see Head, Barclay V.

Roberts, W. Rhys, ed. see Dionysius Of Halicarnassus.

Roberts, Wade, ed. see Koike, Kazuo.

Roberts, Wally. Happy Shoes. (C). 1990. 23.00 (*0-947333-13-4*, Pub. by Pascoe Pub AT) St Mut.

Roberts, Walter A. Mayor Harding of New York. LC 73-18602. reprint ed. 42.50 (*0-404-11412-1*) AMS Pr.

— The Mind Reader: A Mystery. LC 73-18600. reprint ed. 42.50 (*0-404-11410-5*) AMS Pr.

— The Moralist. LC 73-18601. reprint ed. 42.50 (*0-404-11411-3*) AMS Pr.

— Royal Street, a Novel of Old New Orleans. LC 73-18605. reprint ed. 42.50 (*0-404-11415-6*) AMS Pr.

— The Strange Career of Bishop Sterling. LC 73-18603. reprint ed. 21.50 (*0-404-11413-X*) AMS Pr.

— The Top-Floor Killer. LC 73-18604. reprint ed. 42.50 (*0-404-11414-8*) AMS Pr.

— U. S. Navy Fights. (Essay Index Reprint Ser.). 1977. 23.95 (*0-8369-2068-6*) Ayer.

Roberts, Walter O. & Friedman, Edward J. Living with the Changed World Climate. 38p. (Orig.). 1982. pap. text ed. 10.50 (*0-8191-5884-4*, Aspen Inst for Humanistic Studies) U Pr of Amer.

Roberts, Walter R. Tito, Mihailovic, & the Allies. LC 87-5357. (Illus.). xxi, 406p. 1987. pap. text ed. 21.95 (*0-8223-0773-1*) Duke.

Roberts, Warren. A Bibliography of D. H. Lawrence. 2nd ed. LC 81-10149. 644p. reprint ed. pap. 180.00 (*0-8357-7181-4*, 2024582) Bks Demand.

— Jacques-Louis David, Revolutionary Artist: Art, Politics, & the French Revolution. xiv, 310p. 1992. pap. 17.95 (*0-8078-4350-4*) U of NC Pr.

— Jane Austen & the French Revolution. 240p. (C). 1995. pap. 25.00 (*0-485-12110-7*, Pub. by Athlone Pr UK) Humanities.

— Morality & Social Class in Eighteenth Century French Literature & Painting. LC 74-187951. (Toronto University Romance Ser.: No. 25). (Illus.). 204p. reprint ed. pap. 58.20 (*0-317-10544-2*, 2020514) Bks Demand.

Roberts, Warren, jt. auth. see Moore, Harry T.

Roberts, Warren E. Log Buildings of Southern Indiana. LC 85-51209. (Illus.). 231p. (Orig.). 1984. pap. 10.00 (*0-915305-00-3*) Trickster Pr.

— The Tale of the Kind & the Unkind Girls: AA-Th 480 & Related Tales. LC 93-27257. (Classics in Folklore Ser.). 164p. (C). 1994. reprint ed. pap. text ed. 16.95 (*0-8143-2490-8*) Wayne St U Pr.

— Viewpoints on Folklife: Looking at the Overlooked. Bronner, Simon J., ed. LC 87-22710. (American Material Culture & Folklife Ser.). (Illus.). 350p. reprint ed. pap. 94.40 (*0-8357-1849-2*, 2070758) Bks Demand.

Roberts, Wayne, jt. auth. see Ehring, George.

Roberts, Wes, jt. auth. see Wright, Norm.

Roberts, Wes, jt. auth. see Wright, Norman.

Roberts, Wess. Leadership Secrets of Attila the Hun. LC 88-27739. 128p. 1990. pap. 10.99 (*0-446-39106-9*) Warner Bks.

— Leadership Secrets of Attila the Hun. 86p. 1987. reprint ed. 7.95 (*0-9617442-1-9*) Peregrine Pub.

— Leadership Secrets of Attila the Hun: A Metaphorical Primer. LC 86-62559. 86p. 1986. reprint ed. 14.95 (*0-9617442-0-0*) Peregrine Pub.

— Straight A's Never Made Anybody Rich: Lessons in Personal Achievement. LC 90-55940. 208p. 1992. reprint ed. pap. 9.00 (*0-06-092303-2*, PL) HarpC.

— Victory Secrets of Attila the Hun. 1994. pap. 11.95 (*0-440-50591-7*) Dell.

Roberts, William. An Account of the First Discovery, & Natural History of Florida: A Facsimile Reproduction of the 1763 Edition with an Introduction & Index by Robert L. Gold. LC 76-1971. 189p. reprint ed. pap. 53.90 (*0-7837-0598-0*, 2040946) Bks Demand.

— The Earlier History of English Bookselling. 1972. 59.95 (*0-8490-0064-5*) Gordon Pr.

— Prophet in Exile: Joseph Mazzini in England, 1837-1868. (Studies in Modern European History). 153p. (C). 1989. text ed. 37.50 (*0-8204-1051-9*) P Lang Pubs.

— A Treatise on the Construction of the Statutes, 13 Eliz. C.5. & 27 Eliz. C.4. Relating to Voluntary & Fraudulent Conveyances, & on the Nature & Force of Different Considerations to Support Deeds & Other Legal Instruments, in the Courts of Law & Equity. 2nd ed. xv, 667p. 1979. reprint ed. lib. bdg. 35.00 (*0-8377-1028-6*) Rothman.

Roberts, William C. Cardiology, 1993. Willerson, James T. et al, eds. LC 93-71211. (Illus.). 490p. 1993. 95.00 (*0-7506-9451-3*) Buttrwrth-Heinemann.

— Cardiology 1995. (Illus.). 528p. 1995. 69.00 (*0-87993-617-7*) Futura Pub.

Roberts, William C., ed. Adult Congenital Heart Disease. LC 86-11565. (Illus.). 752p. 1987. text ed. 85.00 (*0-8036-7420-1*) Davis Co.

Roberts, William C., ed. see American Federation of Labor Staff.

Roberts, William C., jt. comp. see Coppa, Frank J.

Roberts, William C., jt. auth. see Sammartino, Peter.

Roberts, William C., et al, eds. Cardiology, 1992. (Illus.). 1992. 95.00 (*0-7506-9318-5*) Buttrwrth-Heinemann.

Roberts, William F., Jr. How to Save Money on Just about Everything. 2nd ed. 244p. 1993. pap. 12.95 (*0-9629498-1-7*) Strebor Pubns.

Roberts, William H. About Language: A Reader for Writers. 2nd ed. 1989. teacher ed write for info. (*0-318-63334-5*) HM.

Roberts, William H., jt. auth. see Rome, Edwin P.

Roberts, William L. Cold Rolling of Steel. (Manufacturing Engineering & Materials Processing Ser.: Vol. 2). (Illus.). 808p. 1978. 199.00 (*0-8247-6780-2*) Dekker.

— Encyclopedia of Minerals. 2nd ed. 1989. text ed. 115.00 (*0-442-27681-8*) Chapman & Hall.

— Hot Rolling of Steel. (Manufacturing Engineering & Materials Processing Ser.: Vol. 10). (Illus.). 1024p. 1983. 215.00 (*0-8247-1345-1*) Dekker.

Roberts, William P., ed. Divorce & Remarriage: Religious & Psychological Perspectives. LC 89-63115. 224p. (Orig.). (C). 1990. pap. 13.95 (*1-55612-231-4*) Sheed & Ward MO.

Roberts, William P., jt. auth. see Roberts, Challon O.

Roberts, William R. Greek Rhetoric & Literary Criticism. LC 63-10296. (Our Debt to Greece & Rome Ser.). reprint ed. 44.00 (*0-8154-0194-9*) Cooper Sq.

Roberts, William R., ed. New Interpretations in Naval History: Selected Papers from the Ninth Naval History Symposium. LC 91-25528. 384p. 1991. 32.95 (*1-55750-724-4*) Naval Inst Pr.

Roberts, William R., tr. & comment. Dionysius of Halicarnassus, on Literary Composition. xiii, 358p. 1910. write for info. (*0-318-70914-7*, Pub. by Georg Olms GW) Lubrecht & Cramer.

Roberts, William R., tr. see Dionysius of Halicarnassus.

Roberts, William R., jt. ed. see Hagan, Kenneth J.

Roberts, William W., jt. auth. see Johnson, Ivan C.

Roberts, Williams C. Cardiology 1986. (Illus.). 444p. 1986. text ed. 80.00 (*0-914316-52-4*, Yorke Med Bks) Buttrwrth-Heinemann.

Roberts, Willo D. The Absolutely True Story of My Visit to Yellowstone with the Terrible Rupes. LC 94-14436. (J). (gr. 3-7). 1994. text ed. 14.95 (*0-689-31939-8*, Mac Bks Young Read) S&S Childrens.

— Baby-Sitting Is a Dangerous Job. 144p. (J). 1987. mass mkt. 3.99 (*0-449-70177-8*, Juniper) Fawcett.

— Baby-Sitting Is a Dangerous Job. LC 84-20445. 168p. (J). (gr. 4-6). 1985. text ed. 14.95 (*0-689-31100-1*, Atheneum Bks Young) S&S Childrens.

— Caught! LC 93-14422. 160p. (J). (gr. 3-7). 1994. text ed. 14.95 (*0-689-31903-7*, Atheneum Bks Young) S&S Childrens.

— Don't Hurt Laurie! LC 76-46569. (Illus.). 176p. (J). (gr. 4-6). 1977. text ed. 14.95 (*0-689-30571-0*, Atheneum Bks Young) S&S Childrens.

— Don't Hurt Laurie! 2nd ed. LC 87-21742. (Illus.). 176p. (J). (gr. 3-7). 1988. reprint ed. pap. 3.95 (*0-689-71206-5*, Aladdin Paperbacks) S&S Childrens.

— Eddie & the Fairy Godpuppy. LC 83-15678. (Illus.). 136p. (J). (gr. 3-5). 1984. text ed. 13.95 (*0-689-31021-8*, Atheneum Bks Young) S&S Childrens.

— Eddie & the Fairy Godpuppy. LC 91-28003. (Illus.). 128p. (J). (gr. 3-7). 1992. reprint ed. pap. 3.95 (*0-689-71602-8*, Aladdin Paperbacks) S&S Childrens.

— Expendable. 18.95 (*0-89190-855-2*, Am Repr) Amereon Ltd.

— The Girl with the Silver Eyes. 208p. (J). (gr. 3-7). 1991. pap. 3.50 (*0-590-44248-1*) Scholastic Inc.

— The Girl with the Silver Eyes. LC 80-12391. 192p. (J). (gr. 4-7). 1980. text ed. 14.95 (*0-689-30786-1*, Atheneum Bks Young) S&S Childrens.

— Inherit the Darkness. reprint ed. lib. bdg. 19.95 (*0-89190-865-X*, Rivercity Pr) Amereon Ltd.

— Jo & the Bandit. LC 91-4100. 192p. (J). (gr. 4-7). 1992. text ed. 14.95 (*0-689-31745-X*, Atheneum Bks Young) S&S Childrens.

— The Magic Book. LC 85-20056. 156p. (J). (gr. 3-7). 1986. text ed. 13.95 (*0-689-31120-6*, Atheneum Bks Young) S&S Childrens.

— The Magic Book. LC 88-19360. 160p. (J). (gr. 2-6). 1988. reprint ed. pap. 3.95 (*0-689-71284-7*, Aladdin Paperbacks) S&S Childrens.

— Megan's Island. LC 87-17505. 192p. (J). (gr. 3-7). 1988. text ed. 14.95 (*0-689-31397-7*, Atheneum Bks Young) S&S Childrens.

— Megan's Island. LC 89-18457. 192p. (J). (gr. 4-7). 1990. pap. 3.95 (*0-689-71387-8*, Aladdin Paperbacks) S&S Childrens.

— The Minden Curse. LC 89-18336. 224p. (J). (gr. 4-7). 1990. pap. 3.95 (*0-689-71378-9*, Aladdin Paperbacks) S&S Childrens.

— More Minden Curses. LC 90-31674. 240p. (J). (gr. 3-7). 1990. reprint ed. pap. 3.95 (*0-689-71412-2*, Aladdin Paperbacks) S&S Childrens.

— Nightmare. LC 89-7038. 224p. (J). (gr. 5-9). 1989. text ed. 14.95 (*0-689-31551-1*, Atheneum Bks Young) S&S Childrens.

— Nightmare. LC 91-26831. 224p. (YA). (gr. 7 up). 1992. reprint ed. pap. 3.95 (*0-02-044938-0*, Collier Bks Young) S&S Childrens.

— No Monsters in the Closet. LC 91-46059. 128p. (J). (gr. 3-7). 1992. reprint ed. pap. 3.95 (*0-689-71577-3*, Aladdin Paperbacks) S&S Childrens.

— The Pet-Sitting Peril. LC 82-13757. 192p. (J). (gr. 4-6). 1983. text ed. 14.95 (*0-689-30963-5*, Atheneum Bks Young) S&S Childrens.

— The Pet-Sitting Peril. 2nd ed. LC 89-77696. 176p. (J). (gr. 3-7). 1990. reprint ed. pap. 3.95 (*0-689-71427-0*, Aladdin Paperbacks) S&S Childrens.

— Scared Stiff. LC 90-37732. 192p. (J). (gr. 3-7). 1991. text ed. 14.95 (*0-689-31692-5*, Atheneum Bks Young) S&S Childrens.

— Sugar Isn't Everything: A Support Book, in Fiction Form, for the Young Diabetic. LC 86-17275. 208p. (J). (gr. 4 up). 1987. lib. bdg. 14.95 (*0-689-31316-0*, Atheneum Bks Young) S&S Childrens.
— Sugar Isn't Everything: A Support Book, in Fiction Form, for the Young Diabetic. LC 88-3358. 192p. (J). (gr. 3-7). 1988. pap. 3.95 (*0-689-71225-1*, Aladdin Paperbacks) S&S Childrens.
— To Grandmother's House We Go. LC 89-34972. 192p. (J). (gr. 3-7). 1990. lib. bdg. 14.95 (*0-689-31594-5*, Atheneum Bks Young) S&S Childrens.
— To Grandmother's House We Go. LC 94-466. (J). 1994. pap. 3.95 (*0-689-71838-1*, Aladdin Paperbacks) S&S Childrens.
— To Share a Dream. (Historical Ser.). (Orig.). 1994. mass mkt. 3.99 (*0-373-28831-X*, 1-28831-5) Harlequin Bks.
— The View from the Cherry Tree. LC 75-6759. 192p. (YA). (gr. 5 up). 1975. text ed. 15.95 (*0-689-30483-8*, Atheneum Bks Young) S&S Childrens.
— The View from the Cherry Tree. 2nd ed. LC 93-31170. 192p. (J). (gr. 3-7). 1994. reprint ed. pap. 3.95 (*0-689-71784-9*, Aladdin Paperbacks) S&S Childrens.
— What Are We Going to Do about David? LC 92-4726. 176p. (J). (gr. 3-7). 1993. text ed. 14.95 (*0-689-31793-X*, Atheneum Bks Young) S&S Childrens.
— What Could Go Wrong? LC 88-27484. 176p. (J). (gr. 3-7). 1989. text ed. 13.95 (*0-689-31438-8*, Atheneum Bks Young) S&S Childrens.
— What Could Go Wrong? LC 92-26177. 176p. (J). (gr. 3-6). 1993. reprint ed. pap. 3.95 (*0-689-71690-7*, Aladdin Paperbacks) S&S Childrens.
Roberts, Zack, jt. auth. see Joyer, Mike.
Robertshaw, et al. Reading First. 2nd ed. 1990. pap. 19.95 (*0-8384-3384-7*) Heinle & Heinle.
Robertshaw, Gregory A. Understanding Antennas for Radar, Communication & Avionics. (Illus.). 336p. 1987. text ed. 74.95 (*0-442-27772-5*) Van Nos Reinhold.
Robertshaw, H., jt. auth. see Abercrombie, G.
Robertshaw, Joseph E. & Mecca, Stephen J. Problem Solving: A System Approach. 1991. 3.00 (*0-89433-119-1*) Petrocelli.
Robertshaw, Joseph E., jt. auth. see Mecca, Stephen J.
***Robertshaw, Paul.** The Crown Court in Action. (Illus.). 230p. 1995. text ed. 59.95 (*1-85521-430-X*) Ashgate Pub Co.
— Rethinking Legal Need: The Case of Criminal Justice. 259p. 1991. text ed. 59.95 (*1-85521-207-2*, Pub. by Dartmth Pub UK) Ashgate Pub Co.
Robertshaw, Peter, ed. A History of African Archaeology. LC 89-26733. (Illus.). 378p. (Orig.). (C). 1990. pap. 30.00 (*0-435-08041-5*) Heinemann.
***Robertshaw, Stuart.** Dear Dr. Humor: A Collection of Humorous Stories for All Occasions. 155p. (Orig.). 1995. pap. 10.00 (*0-9645793-0-8*) NAHI.
***Robertson.** Big Catch: A Practical Introduction. (C). 1995. pap. text ed. 17.95 (*0-8133-2522-6*) Westview.
— Bridge to College Success. 1991. pap. 22.95 (*0-8384-2907-6*); teacher ed, pap. 8.95 (*0-8384-2908-4*) Heinle & Heinle.
— Bridge to College Success. 1991. audio 25.00 (*0-8384-3007-4*) Heinle & Heinle.
— Bridge to College Success. 1991. vhs 10.00 (*0-8384-3006-6*) Heinle & Heinle.
— Bridge to College Success, 2 vols., Set. 1991. vhs 75.00 (*0-8384-3009-0*) Heinle & Heinle.
— Denmark Vesey. Date not set. pap. write for info. (*0-679-44288-X*) Random Hse Value.
— Diccionario Ingles-Espanol, Espanol-Ingles. 894p. (ENG & SPA.). 12.25 (*84-303-0107-0*, S-50396); pap. 49.95 (*84-303-0108-9*, S-50397) Fr & Eur.
— Handbook of Histology. 1991. write for info. (*0-8151-7408-X*, Yr Bk Med Pubs) Mosby Yr Bk.
— Little Book of Love. 1995. (*0-7858-0294-0*) Bk Sales Inc.
— New International Commentary on the Old Testament Nahum, Habakkuk, & Zephaniah. 1994. (*0-8028-2532-X*) Eerdmans.
— Pesticide Bioassays with Arthropods. 1991. 110.00 (*0-8493-6463-9*, QH545) CRC Pr.
— Simple Program Design. 188p. 1991. 14.00 (*0-87835-709-2*) Boyd & Fraser.
— Sopena Robertson English-Spanish, Spanish-English Dictionary: Robertson Diccionario Ingles-Espanol-Ingles. 900p. (ENG & SPA.). 1984. 35.00 (*0-8288-2327-8*, S50396) Fr & Eur.
— Violence in Your Workplace. 1995. pap. 11.95 (*0-285-63153-5*, Pub. by Souvenir UK) Atrium Pubs.
Robertson & Estes. Textbook of Family Practice. 1991. write for info. (*0-8151-7407-1*, Yr Bk Med Pubs) Mosby Yr Bk.
***Robertson & Taeusch.** Surfactant Therapy for Lung Disease. (Lung Biology in Health & Disease Ser.). 772p. 1995. write for info. (*0-8247-9502-4*) Dekker.
Robertson, jt. ed. see Timms, Edward.
Robertson, A. Maps & Mapping: Down to Earth Ser. (Illus.). (C). 1980. 40.00 (*0-09-139811-8*, Pub. by S Thornes Pubs UK) St Mut.
— Selection Experiments in Laboratory & Domestic Animals. 245p. (Orig.). 1980. pap. text ed. 34.00 (*0-85198-461-4*) CAB Intl.
Robertson, A., jt. auth. see Coe, W. R.
Robertson, A. F. Beyond the Family: The Social Organization of Human Reproduction. LC 91-9381. 250p. 1991. 45.00 (*0-520-07518-8*); pap. 15.00 (*0-520-07721-0*) U CA Pr.
— Community of Strangers. (C). 1979. pap. text ed. 19.95 (*0-85967-715-X*, Pub. by Scolar Pr UK) Ashgate Pub Co.
Robertson, A. F., ed. Fire Standards & Safety - STP 614. 343p. 1977. 27.75 (*0-8031-0352-2*, 04-614000-31) ASTM.
Robertson, A. F., jt. ed. see Friedland, Roger.
Robertson, A. H. Human Rights in the World: An Introduction to the Study of the International Protection of Human Rights. 3rd rev. ed. LC 89-36489. 320p. 1990. text ed. 49.95 (*0-7190-2278-9*, Pub. by Manchester Univ Pr UK) St Martin.
Robertson, A. H., ed. European Yearbook, Vol. 24. 1978. lib. bdg. 164.50 (*90-247-2043-5*) Kluwer Ac.
— European Yearbook - Annuaire Europeen (1979), Vol. 27. 710p. 1981. lib. bdg. 234.50 (*90-247-2458-9*) Kluwer Ac.
— European Yearbook-Annuaire Europeen, Vol. XXV. 1979. lib. bdg. 196.00 (*90-247-2161-X*) Kluwer Ac.
— European Yearbook-Annuaire Europeen, Vol. XXVI. 696p. (ENG & FRE.). 1980. lib. bdg. 215.00 (*90-247-2298-5*) Kluwer Ac.
***Robertson, A. H. & Merrills, J. G.** Human Rights in Europe: A Study of the European Convention on Human Rights. 3rd ed. 448p. 1995. text ed. 29.95 (*0-7190-4613-0*, Pub. by Manchester Univ Pr UK) St Martin.
— Human Rights in the World: An Introduction to the Study of the International Protection of Human Rights. 3rd ed. 320p. (C). 1992. text ed. 19.95 (*0-7190-3886-3*, Pub. by Manchester Univ Pr UK) St Martin.
Robertson, A. H., et al, eds. The Geology & Tectonics of the Oman Region. (Geological Society Special Publications: No. 49). (Illus.). 864p. (C). 1990. 160.00 (*0-903317-46-X*, Pub. by Geol Soc Pub Hse UK) AAPG.
Robertson, A. Haeworth. Social Security: What Every Taxpayer Should Know. LC 92-80166. (Illus.). xxvi, 326p. 1992. lib. bdg. 40.00 (*0-9632345-4-4*) Retire Policy.
— Social Security: What Every Taxpayer Should Know. 1992. pap. 14.95 (*0-9632345-5-2*) Retire Policy.
Robertson, A. J., ed. The Laws of the Kings of England from Edmund to Henry I. LC 80-2210. reprint ed. 57.50 (*0-404-18784-6*) AMS Pr.
Robertson, A. M., jt. auth. see Hobson, Peter N.
Robertson, A. T. Una Armonia De los Cuatro Evangelios. Patterson, W. F., tr. Orig. Title: Harmony of the Four Gospels. 259p. (SPA.). 1986. reprint ed. pap. 7.25 (*0-311-04302-X*) Casa Bautista.
— Estudios en el Nuevo Testamento. Hale, Sara A., tr. Orig. Title: Studies in the New Testament. 224p. (SPA.). 1987. reprint ed. pap. 5.60 (*0-311-03629-5*) Casa Bautista.
— Estudios En el Nuevo Testamento: Studies on the New Testament. (SPA.). 5.25 (*84-7645-229-2*, 223298, Pub. by Edit Clie SP) TSELF.
— A Harmony of the Gospels. 1932. 19.00 (*0-06-066890-3*) Harper SF.
— Word Pictures in the New Testament, 6 vols. 1982. 125.00 (*0-8010-7710-9*) Baker Bk.
***Robertson, Adele C.** The Orchard: A Memoir. LC 95-17187. 1995. write for info. (*0-8050-4092-7*) H Holt & Co.
Robertson, Agnes. The Chestnut Tree. 90p. 1987. pap. 6.00 (*0-940584-13-1*) Gull Bks.
— The Me Inside of Me. 72p. 1987. pap. 6.00 (*0-940584-14-X*) Gull Bks.
Robertson, Agnes J. Anglo-Saxon Charters. LC 85-81803. (Cambridge Studies in English Legal History). 580p. 1986. reprint ed. 128.00 (*0-912004-51-7*) W W Gaunt.
Robertson, Alden. Wild Horse Gatherers. 95p. 1978. 6.95 (*0-684-15591-5*) Lahontan Images.
Robertson, Alec. Dvorak: Music Book Index. 234p. 1993. reprint ed. lib. bdg. 79.00 (*0-7812-9596-3*) Rprt Serv.
— Requiem: Music of Mourning & Consolation. LC 75-32462. 300p. 1976. reprint ed. text ed. 35.00 (*0-8371-8552-1*, RORE, Greenwood Pr) Greenwood.
Robertson, Alex & Osborne, Avril, eds. Planning to Care: Social Policy & the Quality of Life. (Studies in Social Policy & Welfare: Vol. XXII). 152p. 1985. text ed. 52.00 (*0-566-00849-1*) Ashgate Pub Co.
Robertson, Alistair, jt. ed. see Alongi, Daniel.
Robertson, Allen & Hutera, Donald, eds. The Dance Handbook. (Monograph Ser.). 278p. 1990. text ed. 25.00 (*0-8161-9095-X*, Hall Reference); pap. 16.95 (*0-8161-1829-9*, Hall Reference) Macmillan.
Robertson, Allen B. John Wesley's Nova Scotia Businessmen: Halifax Methodist Merchants. LC 94-15262. (American University Studies: Vol. 163). 1995. write for info. (*0-8204-2484-6*) P Lang Pubs.
Robertson, Andrew, ed. see Lawrence, D. H.
Robertson, Andrew, jt. ed. see Scavia, Donald.
Robertson, Andrew C. The Military Investor's Handbook. LC 85-70435. 179p. 1985. pap. 9.95 (*0-935871-00-4*) Global Man.
***Robertson, Andrew W.** The Language of Democracy: Political Rhetoric in the United States & Britain, 1790-1900. (Illus.). 240p. 1995. 32.50x (*0-8014-2899-8*) Cornell U Pr.
Robertson, Anne W. The Service Books of the Royal Abbey of Saint-Denis: Images of Ritual & Music in the Middle Ages. (Oxford Monographs on Music). (Illus.). 608p. 1991. 125.00 (*0-19-315254-1*) OUP.
Robertson, Archibald. Archibald Robertson, Lieutenant-General Royal Engineers. LC 70-140879. (Eyewitness Accounts of the American Revolution Ser., No. 1). 1971. reprint ed. 20.95 (*0-405-01224-1*) Ayer.
— Morals in World History. LC 74-6354. (World History Ser.: No. 48). (C). 1974. lib. bdg. 49.95 (*0-8383-1918-1*) M S G Haskell Hse.
Robertson, Archibald & Plummer, Alfred. Corinthians One: Critical & Exegetical Commentary. Driver, Samuel R. & Briggs, Charles A., eds. (International Critical Commentary Ser.). 496p. 1914. 36.95 (*0-567-05027-0*, Pub. by T & T Clark UK) Bks Intl VA.
Robertson, Archibald T. Grammar of the Greek New Testament in the Light of Historical Research. (C). 1947. 59.99 (*0-8054-1308-1*) Broadman.
— That Old-Time Religion. LC 78-24159. 282p. 1979. reprint ed. text ed. 59.75 (*0-313-20823-9*, ROOT, Greenwood Pr) Greenwood.
Robertson, Arlene. The Moon in Your Life. LC 84-71623. 245p. 1986. 16.95 (*0-86690-283-X*, R2604-014) Am Fed Astrologers.
Robertson, Arlene, ed. see Linares, Enrique.
Robertson, Arlene, ed. see Merriman, Raymond.
Robertson, Arlene, ed. see Sandbach, John.
Robertson, Arlene, ed. see Starck, Marcia.
Robertson, Arthur. Matthew. (Everyman's Bible Commentary Ser.). (Orig.). 1983. pap. 7.99 (*0-8024-0233-X*) Moody.
Robertson, Arthur H. Characterization in the Conflict of Laws. LC 40-10604. (Harvard Studies in the Conflict of Laws: Vol. 4). xxix, 301p. 1978. reprint ed. lib. bdg. 45.00 (*0-89941-129-0*, 301350) W S Hein.
Robertson, Arthur K. & Proctor, William. The Four Hour Day. LC 93-8365. 1994. 17.00 (*0-688-10359-6*) Morrow.
Robertson, B., et al, eds. Experimental & Clinical Aspects of Surfactant Replacement. (Journal: Biology of the Neonate: Vol. 61, Suppl. 1, 1992). (Illus.). vi, 66p. 1992. pap. 21.00 (*3-8055-5644-6*) S Karger.
Robertson, Barbara, jt. auth. see Whyte, Hamish.
Robertson, Ben. Red Hills & Cotton: An Upcountry Memory. (Southern Classics Ser.). 341p. 1991. reprint ed. pap. 12.95 (*0-87249-306-7*) U of SC Pr.
Robertson, Bengt D., et al. Pulmonary Surfactant. 1984. 224.75 (*0-444-80553-2*) Elsevier.
Robertson, Bengt D., et al, eds. Pulmonary Surfactant: From Molecular Biology to Clinical Practice. LC 92-48791. 1992. write for info. (*0-444-89475-6*, Pub. by Elsevier Applied Sci UK) Elsevier.
Robertson, Betty B. Bible-Teaching Ideas That Work. (Illus.). 56p. 1989. pap. 5.95 (*0-8341-1313-9*) Beacon Hill.
— TLC for Aging Parents: A Practical Guide. 103p. (Orig.). 1992. per. 8.95 (*0-8341-1456-9*, 85018) Beacon Hill.
Robertson, Beverly. Nursing Assistant: A Basic Study Guide. 1991. pap. 9.95 (*1-880246-00-7*) First Class Bks.
— Nursing Assistant: A Basic Study Guide. 2nd ed. (Illus.). 184p. 1993. pap. 11.95 (*1-880246-05-8*) First Class Bks.
— Study Guide for Nursing Assistants: Covers the New Obra Regulations with Thirty Two Flash Cards. 1992. pap. 11.95 (*1-880246-01-5*) First Class Bks.
Robertson, Bill. How to Play Better Golf. (Illus.). 160p. 1992. pap. 14.95 (*0-7063-6995-5*, Pub. by Ward Lock UK) Sterling.
Robertson-Boudreaux, Jane. Personal Transformation Through the Right Use of Ritual. (Illus.). 100p. (Orig.). 1990. student ed, spiral bd. 16.95 (*1-879203-01-4*) Metagnosis.
Robertson-Boudreaux, Jane, ed. see Hughes, Deborah L.
Robertson-Boudreaux, Jane, jt. auth. see Hughes, Deborah.
Robertson, Bozena-Eva. Alcohol Disabilities Primer: A Guide to Physical & Psychological Disabilities Caused by Alcohol Use. LC 93-22609. 208p. 1993. 39.95 (*0-8493-8966-6*, RC565, CRC Reprint) Franklin.
Robertson, Brenda. Studies in Ruth. (Bible Study Ser.). (Illus.). 32p. 1988. pap. 4.50 (*0-8309-0523-5*) Herald Hse.
Robertson, Brian. Brian Robertson's Favorite Texas Tales. LC 92-17115. (Illus.). 112p. (J). (gr. 4-7). 1992. 12.95 (*0-89015-862-2*) Sunbelt Media.
— Wild Horse Desert. (Illus.). 336p. 1985. 13.95 (*0-935071-00-8*) New Santander.
Robertson, Bridget M. Angels in Africa: A Memoir of Colonial Nursing. 200p. 1993. text ed. 39.50 (*1-85043-527-8*, Pub. by I B Tauris UK) St Martin.
Robertson, Bruce. Designing with Letters: Imaginative Alphabets & Creative Ways to Use Them. (Lettering Workbooks Ser.). (Illus.). 80p. 1989. pap. 8.95 (*0-8230-1328-6*, Watsn-Guptill) Watsn-Guptill.
— How to Draw Charts & Diagrams. (Illus.). 160p. 1988. 24.95 (*0-89134-242-7*, 30041) North Light Bks.
— Marsden Hartley. LC 93-46820. 1994. write for info. (*0-8109-3416-7*) Abrams.
— Reckoning with Winslow Homer: His Late Paintings & Their Influence. LC 90-31989. 212p. 1990. 40.00 (*0-940717-02-6*); pap. 29.95 (*0-940717-03-4*) Cleveland Mus Art.
— Representing America: The Ken Trevey Collection of American Realist Prints. LC 94-48298. (Illus.). 68p. (C). 1995. pap. 19.95 (*0-942006-26-7*) U of CA Art.
— You Can Draw. (Illus.). 192p. 1986. 22.95 (*0-13-972621-7*) P-H.
Robertson, Bruce & Pinkus, Sue. Let's All Draw Dinosaurs, Pterodactyls & Other Prehistoric Creatures. (Illus.). 144p. (J). (gr. 3-7). 1991. pap. 9.95 (*0-8230-2706-6*, Watsn-Guptill) Watsn-Guptill.
Robertson, Bruce, jt. auth. see White, Anthony.
Robertson, Bruce, jt. auth. see White, Antony.
Robertson, Bruce, jt. auth. see White, Tony.
***Robertson, Bruce C.** Ram Mohan Ray: The Father of Modern India. (Illus.). 200p. 1995. 19.95 (*0-19-563417-9*) OUP.
Robertson, Bryan. Elisabeth Frink: Sculpture & Drawings, 1950-1990. LC 90-60050. (Illus.). 80p. 1990. 32.95 (*0-940979-12-8*); pap. 21.95 (*0-940979-13-6*) Natl Museum Women.
Robertson, Bryan & Hughes, Robert, intros. Lee Krasner: Collages. (Illus.). 63p. 1986. pap. 20.00 (*0-944680-16-X*) R Miller Gal.
Robertson, C. C. On the Track of the Exodus. LC 89-82327. (Illus.). 120p. 1990. reprint ed. pap. 7.00 (*0-934666-40-7*) Artisan Sales.
Robertson, C. Grant, et al. Humanism & Technology & Other Essays. LC 68-22099. (Essay Index Reprint Ser.). 1977. 17.95 (*0-8369-0553-9*) Ayer.
Robertson, C. N. Oneida Community Profiles. (Illus.). 1977. 35.00x (*0-8156-0140-9*) Syracuse U Pr.
Robertson, C. P., et al. Nitrogen Cycling in Ecosystems of Latin America & the Caribbean. 1982. 65.00 (*0-686-38400-8*) Kluwer Ac.
Robertson, Carleton J. Robby's Revelry. Vernon, Sidney, ed. (Illus.). (Orig.). pap. 7.00 (*0-943150-12-4*) Rovern Pr.
Robertson, Carol. Health Visiting in Practice. 2nd ed. (Illus.). 1991p. 1991. pap. text ed. 39.00 (*0-443-04137-7*) Churchill.
— Portuguese Cooking: The Authentic & Robust Cuisine of Portugal. (Illus.). 166p. (Orig.). 1993. 24.95 (*1-55643-158-9*) North Atlantic.
Robertson, Carol E., ed. Musical Repercussions of Fourteen Ninety-Two: Encounters in Text & Performance. LC 92-6895. (Illus.). 496p. (C). 1993. text ed. 62.00 (*1-56098-183-0*) Smithsonian.
Robertson, Carolyn, jt. auth. see Robertson, James.
Robertson, Carolyn, et al. Anatomy & Physiology Laboratory Manual. rev. ed. 256p. (C). 1994. pap. text ed., spiral bd. 24.95 (*0-8403-9466-7*) Kendall-Hunt.
Robertson, Carolyn C., et al. Anatomy & Physiology Laboratory Manual. 2nd ed. 256p. 1991. spiral bd. 23.95 (*0-8403-6755-4*) Kendall-Hunt.
Robertson, Charles B. How to Deal on an Automobile. 90p. (Orig.). 1988. pap. write for info. (*0-318-64785-0*) Blue Mountain Pub.
— How To Deal on An Automobile. 2nd rev. ed. 96p. (Orig.). 1990. pap. 7.95 (*0-9622155-1-1*) Blue Mountain Pub.
Robertson, Charles H. & Merrill, Jo Lynne. Texas Family Law Trial Guide, 1 vol. 1983. Updates available. ring bd. write for info. (*0-8205-1767-4*) Bender.
Robertson, Charles K. South Africa. 128p. 1986. pap. 3.95 (*0-88144-072-8*) Christian Pub.
Robertson, Charles L. The International Herald Tribune: The First Hundred Years. (Illus.). 380p. 1987. text ed. 47.00 (*0-231-06562-0*) Col U Pr.
Robertson, Charles T., II & Haman, Edward A. How to File for Divorce in Georgia. LC 93-86526. 140p. (Orig.). 1993. pap. 19.95 (*0-913825-79-4*) Sphinx Pub FL.
Robertson, Cheryl D., ed. see Kaufman, Betty R.
Robertson, Chimp. POW-MIA: America's Missing Men. 304p. 1995. 19.95 (*0-914984-64-0*) Starburst.
Robertson, Claire & Berger, Iris, eds. Women & Class in Africa. LC 85-17568. 300p. (C). 1986. 55.00 (*0-8419-0979-2*); pap. 19.95 (*0-8419-1187-8*) Holmes & Meier.
Robertson, Claire C. Sharing the Same Bowl: A Socioeconomic History of Women & Class in Accra, Ghana. LC 89-20660. (Illus.). 320p. 1990. lib. bdg. 37.50 (*0-472-09444-0*); pap. 14.95 (*0-472-06444-4*) U of Mich Pr.
Robertson, Clara H. Kansas Territorial Settlers of 1860 Who Were Born in Tennessee, Virginia, North Carolina & South Carolina. (Illus.). 215p. 1990. reprint ed. 25.00 (*0-685-60374-1*, 4970) Clearfield Co.
Robertson, Clare. Il Grand Cardinale: Alessandro Farnese, Patron of the Arts. (Illus.). 256p. (C). 1992. text ed. 45.00 (*0-300-05045-3*) Yale U Pr.
Robertson, Colin. The Green Diamonds. large type ed. (Mystery Ser.). 1976. 16.95 (*0-85456-415-2*) Ulverscroft.
Robertson, Colin & Little, Keith, eds. A Manual of Accident & Emergency Resuscitation. LC 83-1290. (Wiley-Medical Publication Ser.). (Illus.). 191p. reprint ed. pap. 54.50 (*0-8357-3927-9*, 2036662) Bks Demand.
Robertson, Colin & Redmond, Anthony D. The Management of Major Trauma. (Oxford Handbooks in Emergency Medicine Ser.). (Illus.). 208p. 1991. pap. 24.95 (*0-19-261824-5*) OUP.
Robertson, Colin, jt. auth. see Dymond, Bill.
Robertson, Colin E. & Redmond, Anthony D. The Management of Major Trauma. (Hardbooks in Emergency Medicine Ser.: Vol. 9). (Illus.). 208p. 1994. 59.95 (*0-19-262448-2*); pap. 24.95 (*0-19-262447-4*) OUP.
Robertson, Constance N. Oneida Community: The Breakup, 1876 - 1881. LC 72-38405. (New York State Bks.). (Illus.). 330p. 1972. 35.00x (*0-8156-0086-0*) Syracuse U Pr.
Robertson, Constance N., ed. Oneida Community: An Autobiography, 1851-1876. LC 75-115417. (New York State Bks.). (Illus.). 1981. pap. 16.95 (*0-8156-0166-2*) Syracuse U Pr.
Robertson, D. B., ed. Power & Empowerment in Higher Education: Studies in Honor of Louis Smith. LC 77-76333. 167p. reprint ed. pap. 47.60 (*0-7837-5792-1*, 2045458) Bks Demand.
Robertson, D. B., ed. see Neibuhr, Reinhold.
Robertson, D. J., jt. auth. see Hunter, Lawrence C.
Robertson, D. R., jt. auth. see Allan, Gerald R.
Robertson, D. Ross & Glynn, Peter W. Field Guidebook to the Reefs of San Blas Island, Panama. (Third International Symposium on Coral Reefs Ser.). (Illus.). 16p. 1977. pap. 2.00 (*0-932981-42-9*) Univ Miami A R C.
Robertson, D. W., Jr. Essays in Medieval Culture. LC 79-3228. (Illus.). 1980. 72.50 (*0-691-06429-6*) Princeton U Pr.
— Literature of Medieval England. LC 75-95827. (C). 1970. text ed. write for info. (*0-07-053158-7*) McGraw.
— Preface to Chaucer: Studies in Medieval Perspective. (Illus.). 1962. pap. 27.95 (*0-691-01294-6*) Princeton U Pr.
Robertson, Dan & Taylor, Ron. Huntin' Humor I. (Illus.). 96p. 1990. 3.95 (*0-9627332-0-2*) DRT-Ink.
Robertson, Darrel M. The Chicago Revival, Eighteen Seventy-Six: Society & Revivalism in a Nineteenth-Century City. LC 88-34865. (Studies in Evangelicalism: No. 9). 239p. 1989. 25.00 (*0-8108-2181-8*) Scarecrow.

R

Robertson, David. GATT Rules for Emergency Protection. (Thames Essays of the Trade Policy Research Center Ser.). 136p. 1993. text ed. 42.50 (0-472-10421-7) U of Mich Pr.
— A Guide to Modern Defense & Strategy. 335p. 1987. 65.00 (0-946653-37-2, 070608-99584, Pub. by Europa UK) Gale.
— Sly & Able: A Political Biography of James F. Byrnes. LC 93-19329. 1994. 29.95 (0-393-03367-8) Norton.
— West of Eden: A History of Art & Literature of Yosemite. (Illus.). 1984. 15.95 (0-939666-40-5); pap. 9.95 (0-939666-41-3) Yosemite Assn.
— West of Eden: A History of the Art & Literature of Yosemite. LC 83-51539. (Illus.). 200p. 1984. 14.95 (0-89997-035-4); pap. 9.95 (0-89997-043-5) Wilderness Pr.
Robertson, David & Berrey, Henry. Yosemite As We Saw It - A Centennial Collection of Early Writings & Art. LC 89-28251. (Illus.). 104p. 1990. 34.95 (0-939666-53-7) Yosemite Assn.
Robertson, David, jt. auth. see Cuthbertson, Ian M.
Robertson, David, jt. auth. see Davis, Richard.
Robertson, David, jt. ed. see Freeman, Michael.
Robertson, David, et al. Eco-Logic: Logic-Based Approaches to Ecological Modelling. (Logic Programming - Ehud T. Shapiro Ser.). (Illus.). 250p. 1991. 37.50 (0-262-18143-6) MIT Pr.
Robertson, David A., et al. Ecce Agnus Dei: Sacrificial Imagery of Christ 1350-1750 from the Collection of Loyola University. 1994. pap. 15.00 (1-884936-00-8) Loyola U Chicago.
Robertson, David B. A Theory of Party Competition. LC 74-23542. 220p. reprint ed. pap. 62.70 (0-685-20753-6, 2030394) Bks Demand.
Robertson, David B., et al. The Development of American Public Policy: The Structure of Policy Restraint. (C). 1989. pap. text ed. 26.00 (0-673-39881-1) HarpCollege.
Robertson, David P., jt. auth. see Lowstuter, Clude C.
Robertson, David P., jt. auth. see Lowstuter, Clyde C.
Robertson, David W. & Meyer, Robin, eds. The Correspondence Between Leon Green & Charles McCormick, 1927-1962. x, 222p. 1988. 27.50 (0-8377-1046-4) Rothman.
Robertson, David W., Jr., et al. Torts: Cases & Materials. (American Casebook Ser.). 932p. 1991. reprint ed. text ed. 43.50 (0-314-50709-4) West Pub.
Robertson, David W., et al. Torts Cases & Materials on, Teachers Manual to Accompany. (American Casebook Ser.). 201p. 1989. pap. text ed. write for info. (0-314-55687-7) West Pub.
Robertson, Davies. Murther & Walking Spirits. large type ed. LC 92-17880. (General Ser.). 480p. 1992. lib. bdg. 22.95 (0-8161-5466-X); pap. 16.95 (0-8161-5467-8) G K Hall.
Robertson, Debbie. Blast off with Book Reports. 64p. (J). (gr. 3-8). 1985. student ed 7.95 (0-86653-327-3, GA 682) Good Apple.
Robertson, Debbie & Barry, Patricia. Super Kids Publishing Company. 300p. 1989. pap. text ed. 25.00 (0-87287-704-3) Libs Unl.
Robertson, Debra. Portraying Persons with Disabilities: An Annotated Bibliography of Fiction for Children & Teenagers. (Serving Special Needs Ser.). 482p. 1992. 39.95 (0-8352-3023-6) Bowker.
Robertson, Dede & Sherrill, John. My God Will Supply: A Fascinating Story of God's Provision with Practical Lessons for Trust. (Illus.). 172p. (Orig.). 1979. pap. 5.99 (0-8007-9121-5) Chosen Bks.
Robertson, Denise. Anxious Heart. 1993. mass mkt. 4.99 (0-06-108082-9, Harp PBks) HarpC.
— The Beloved People. large type ed. 671p. 1994. 19.95 (0-7505-0615-6, Pub. by Magna Print Bks) Ulverscroft.
— None to Make You Cry. 1991. mass mkt. 4.99 (0-06-104041-X, Harp PBks) HarpC.
— Remember the Moment. 1992. mass mkt. 4.99 (0-06-104065-7, Harp PBks) HarpC.
— Remember the Moment. large type ed. 485p. 1993. 21.95 (0-7505-0271-1) Ulverscroft.
— Stars Burn On. 1992. mass mkt. 4.99 (0-06-108011-X, Harp PBks) HarpC.
— The Stars Burn On. large type ed. (Magna General Fiction Ser.). 575p. 1992. 21.95 (0-7505-0300-9) Ulverscroft.
— Strength for the Morning. large type ed. (Magna Large Print Ser.). 1994. 24.95 (0-7505-0616-4, Pub. by Magna Print Bks) Ulverscroft.
— Towards Jerusalem. large type ed. (Magna Large Print Ser.). 1994. 24.95 (0-7505-0617-2, Pub. by Magna Print Bks) Ulverscroft.
Robertson, Denise A. A Year of Winter. large type ed. (Dales General Fiction Ser.). 376p. 1993. pap. 16.95 (1-85389-400-1, Dales) Ulverscroft.
Robertson, Dennis H. Banking Policy & the Price Level: An Essay in the Theory of the Trade Cycle. rev. ed. LC 50-3461. (Reprints of Economic Classics Ser.). 1989. reprint ed. 25.00 (0-678-00675-X) Kelley.
— Economic Commentaries. LC 79-1589. 1981. reprint ed. 18.75 (0-88355-894-7) Hyperion Conn.
— Essays in Monetary Theory. LC 78-20487. 1988. 25.00 (0-88355-864-5) Hyperion Conn.
— Robertson on Economic Policy. Dennison, S. R. & Presley, John R., eds. LC 91-44082. 240p. 1992. text ed. 69.95 (0-312-07913-3) St Martin.
Robertson, Don. Barb. 164p. 1988. 14.95 (0-939738-93-7) Zubal Inc.
— The Forest of Arden. 354p. 1986. 17.95 (0-685-17070-5) Zubal Inc.
— Harv. 170p. 1985. 11.95 (0-939738-69-4) Zubal Inc.
— The Ideal, Genuine Man. deluxe ed. 1987. 50.00 (0-318-23786-5) Philtrum Pr.
— The Ideal, Genuine Man. limited ed. 1987. 25.00 (0-318-23785-7) Philtrum Pr.
— Praise the Human Season. 544p. 1983. pap. 3.95 (0-345-29528-5) Ballantine.
Robertson, Donald. Mexican Manuscript Painting of the Early Colonial Period: The Metropolitan Schools. LC 94-12120. 234p. (Orig.). 1994. pap. 29.50x (0-8061-2675-2) U of Okla Pr.
***Robertson, Donald B.** Encyclopedia of Western Railroad History: Oregon & Washington, Vol. III. LC 86-9611. (Illus.). 340p. 1995. 34.95 (0-87004-366-8) Caxton.
— Encyclopedia of Western Railroad History: The Desert States. LC 86-9611. (Illus.). 336p. reprint ed. pap. 95.80 (0-7837-7138-X, 2059165) Bks Demand.
Robertson, Donald R. Dear You. 212p. 1989. write for info. (0-8499-0677-6) Word Inc.
Robertson, Donald R., jt. auth. see Robertson, Douglas F.
Robertson, Donald W., jt. auth. see Murray, Thomas J.
Robertson, Dougal. Survive the Savage Sea. (Illus.). 224p. 1994. pap. 14.95 (0-924486-73-2) Sheridan.
— Survive the Savage Sea. large type ed. (Non-Fiction Ser.). 448p. 1986. 15.95 (0-7089-1409-8) Ulverscroft.
Robertson, Dougal, ed. see Greenwald, Michael.
Robertson, Douglas, ed. Manual of Transportation Engineering Studies. 5th ed. LC 93-13519. 1994. text ed. 65.00 (0-13-097569-9) P-H.
Robertson, Douglas F. Using Microcomputer Applications: A Computer Lab Manual with PC-TypePlus, PC-CalcPlus, & PC-FilePlus. 250p. (C). 1990. Incl. software. student ed, disk 17.50 (0-15-594511-4) Dryden Pr.
Robertson, Douglas F. & Robertson, Donald R. Instructor's Manual & Test Bank to Accompany Microcomputer Applications & Programming, & Using Microcomputer Applications. 272p. (C). 1992. pap. text ed. 12.00 (0-15-500703-3) Dryden Pr.
— Microcomputer Applications & Programming: A Complete Computer Course with dBASE IV & Basic. 900p. (C). 1992. text ed. 37.25 (0-15-558372-7) Dryden Pr.
— Microcomputer Applications & Programming with dBASE III PLUS. 750p. (C). 1992. text ed. 37.25 (0-15-558371-9) Dryden Pr.
— Using Microcomputer Applications: A Computer Lab Manual with DOS, WordPerfect, VPPlannerPlus & dBASE III Plus. (C). 1990. pap. text ed. 24.00 (0-15-594510-6) Dryden Pr.
— Using Microcomputer Applications: A Computer Lab Manual with DOS, WordPerfect, VPPlannerPlus & dBASE III Plus. 250p. (C). 1990. disk 26.75 (0-15-594515-7) HB Coll Pubs.
— Using Microcomputer Applications: A Computer Lab Manual with DOS, WordPerfect 5.1, Lotus 1-2-3, & dBASE IV. 475p. (C). 1992. teacher ed 10.75 (0-685-70051-8); pap. text ed. 27.00 (0-15-594509-2) Dryden Pr.
— Using Microcomputer Applications: A Computer Lab Manual with DOS, WordPerfect 5.1, Lotus 1-2-3, & dBASE IV. 2nd ed. LC 92-72685. 592p. (C). 1992. pap. text ed. 25.50 (0-15-500765-3) Dryden Pr.
Robertson, Douglas L. Self-Directed Growth. LC 87-72746. xxiv, 213p. (C). 1988. pap. text ed. 18.95 (0-915202-75-1) Accel Devel.
***Robertson, Duncan.** The Medieval Saints' Lives: Spiritual Renewal & Old French Literature. (Edward C. Armstrong Monographs on Medieval Literature: No. 8). 267p. (Orig.). 1995. pap. 24.95x (0-917058-90-9) French Forum.
Robertson, Durant W. Chaucer's London. LC 68-30920. (New Dimension in History Ser.: Historical Cities). 256p. reprint ed. pap. 73.00 (0-317-09555-2, 2013409) Bks Demand.
— Essays in Medieval Culture. LC 80-13130. (Illus.). Date not set. reprint ed. pap. 121.70 (0-7837-9433-9, 2060175) Bks Demand.
Robertson, E. Arnot. Ordinary Families. (Virago Modern Classic Ser.). 331p. 1992. pap. 10.95 (0-86068-281-1, Pub. by Virago Pr UK) Trafalgar.
Robertson, E. Bruce. Art of Paul Sandby. LC 85-40260. (Illus.). 112p. (Orig.). 1985. pap. 12.95 (0-930606-47-7) Yale Ctr Brit Art.
Robertson, E. F. & Campbell, C. M., eds. Proceedings of Groups-St. Andrews, 1985. (London Mathematical Society Lecture Note Ser.: Series 121). (Illus.). 368p. 1987. pap. 54.95 (0-521-33854-9) Cambridge U Pr.
Robertson, E. F., jt. auth. see Blyth, T. S.
Robertson, E. F., jt. ed. see Campbell, C. M.
Robertson, E. S., ed. see Birrell, Augustine.
Robertson, Ed. The Fugitive Recaptured: The Thirtieth Anniversary Companion to a Television Classic. (Illus.). 208p. (Orig.). 1993. pap. 17.95 (0-938817-34-5) Pomegranate Pr.
— Maverick: Legend of the West. (Illus.). 208p. (Orig.). 1994. pap. 17.95 (0-938817-35-3) Pomegranate Pr.
— This Is Jim Rockford: The Rockford Files. (Illus.). 176p. (Orig.). 1995. pap. 17.95 (0-938817-36-1) Pomegranate Pr.
Robertson, Edna C. Handbook of the Collections: Museum of Fine Arts: 1917-1974. (Illus.). 1974. pap. 6.95 (0-89013-081-7) Museum NM Pr.
Robertson, Edna W. Fundamentals of Document Examination. (Illus.). 500p. 1991. 50.95 (0-8304-1238-7) Nelson-Hall.
Robertson, Edward D., Jr. Personal Autonomy & Substituted Judgment: Legal Issues in Medical Decisions for Incompetent Patients. (Orig.). 1991. pap. 5.99 (0-685-50296-1) Diocesan Pr.
Robertson, Edwin. The Biblical Bases of Healing. (C). 1990. pap. 35.00 (0-85305-287-5, Pub. by J Arthur Ltd UK) St Mut.
— Bonhoeffer's Legacy: The Christian Way in a World Without Religion. 240p. 1991. pap. 8.95 (0-02-036372-9, Collier S&S) S&S Trade.
— Shame & Sacrifice: The Life & Martyrdom of Dietrich Bonhoeffer. 288p. 1989. pap. 7.95 (0-02-036371-0, Pub. by Gebrueder Borntraeger GW) Macmillan.
Robertson, Edwin, tr. see Lange, Ernst.
Robertson, Edwin H., tr. see Lochman, Jan M.
Robertson, Elizabeth. Early English Devotional Prose & the Female Audience. LC 89-24836. 240p. 1990. text ed. 32.00x (0-87049-641-7) U of Tenn Pr.
Robertson, Elizabeth, ed. Chaucer's Religious Tales. (Chaucer Studies: Vol. XV). 224p. 1990. 79.00 (0-85991-302-3) Boydell & Brewer.
Robertson, Elizabeth J., et al, eds. Cell-Cell Signaling in Vertebrate Development. LC 93-7463. (Illus.). 269p. 1993. text ed. 79.00 (0-12-590370-7) Acad Pr.
Robertson, Ellen H. Magic Menu. (Illus.). (Orig.). 1954. pap. 2.00 (0-87505-136-7) Borden.
Robertson, Esmonde M., jt. ed. see Boyce, Robert.
Robertson, Everett, ed. Puppet Scripts for Use at Church. LC 78-72843. 1979. pap. 7.99 (0-8054-7516-8) Broadman.
— Puppet Scripts for Use at Church, No. 2. LC 78-72843. (J). (gr. k up). 1980. 7.99 (0-8054-7519-2) Broadman.
— Using Puppetry in the Church. LC 78-72842. 1979. pap. 7.99 (0-8054-7517-6) Broadman.
Robertson, F. E. A Practical Treatise on Organ - Building, 2 vols. (Illus.). 370p. 1997. reprint ed. Text & Atlas. pap. 75.00 (0-913746-04-5) Organ Lit.
Robertson, Fiona. Legitimate Histories: Scott, Gothic, & the Authorities of Fiction. LC 93-27024. (Oxford English Monographs). 336p. 1994. 55.00 (0-19-811224-6, Clarendon Pr) OUP.
Robertson, Fiona, ed. see Sir Walter Scott.
Robertson, Fleur. Little Book of Thoughtful Moments. 1994. 4.98 (1-55521-992-6) Bk Sales Inc.
Robertson, Florence H. Shadow Land: Stories of the South. LC 72-3188. (Black Heritage Library Collection). 1977. reprint ed. 19.95 (0-8369-9077-3) Ayer.
Robertson, Foster. The Wood Path. LC 75-1439. 40p. (Orig.). 1975. pap. 2.00 (0-914476-36-X) Thorp Springs.
Robertson, Frank C. A Ram in the Thicket: The Story of a Roaming Homesteader Family on the Mormon Frontier. (Idaho Yesterdays Ser.). 350p. (C). 1995. reprint ed. pap. 15.95 (0-89301-173-8) U of Idaho Pr.
— Sheriff's Deputy. large type ed. (Linford Western Library). 352p. 1985. pap. 11.95 (0-7089-6191-6, Trailtree Bookshop) Ulverscroft.
— Squatter's Rights. large type ed. (Linford Western Library). 352p. 1985. pap. 11.95 (0-7089-6184-3, Trailtree Bookshop) Ulverscroft.
— Trouble at Topaz. large type ed. (Western Ser.). 1975. 15.95 (0-85456-324-5) Ulverscroft.
***Robertson, G. C.** Butterworths Student Companions Industrial Law. 2nd ed. 104p. 1994. pap. 18.00 (0-409-30864-1, Austral) Butterworth Legal Pubs.
Robertson, G. Croom, ed. see Grote, George.
Robertson, G. Leo. Happiness & Many Things: Reflections on Happiness. 32p. 1987. pap. 3.50 (0-9618775-1-0) G L Robertson.
— Loving Is Many Things: Reflections on Love. 32p. 1987. pap. 3.50 (0-9618775-0-2) G L Robertson.
Robertson, Geoffrey. Obscenity: An Account of Censorship Laws & Their Enforcement in England & Wales. (Law in Context Ser.). xviii, 364p. 1979. 40.50 (0-297-77213-9) Rothman.
Robertson, George. Port. 4th ed. (Illus.). 208p. 1993. 24.95 (0-571-16541-9); pap. 14.95 (0-571-16542-7) Faber & Faber.
Robertson, George & Charteris, Henry. De Vita et Morte Roberti Rollok. Lee, John, ed. LC 77-172040. (Bannatyne Club, Edinburgh. Publications: No. 16). reprint ed. 30.00 (0-404-52716-7) AMS Pr.
Robertson, George, jt. auth. see Kuske, Albrecht.
Robertson, George, et al. Travellers' Tales: Narratives of Home & Displacement. LC 93-23698. (Futures, New Perspectives for Cultural Analysis Ser.). 272p. 1994. 59.95x (0-415-07015-5, B3895); pap. 16.95 (0-415-07016-3, B3899) Routledge.
Robertson, George C. Elements of Psychology. Davids, C. A., ed. LC 78-72820. (Brainedness, Handedness, & Mental Abilities Ser.). reprint ed. 24.50 (0-404-60889-2) AMS Pr.
— Hobbes. LC 70-137283. reprint ed. 22.50 (0-404-05359-9) AMS Pr.
— Hobbes. 1910. reprint ed. 7.00 (0-403-00251-6) Scholarly.
Robertson, Georgia D. The Harvest of Hate. viii, 586p. 1986. 22.00 (0-930046-08-0) CSUF Oral Hist.
Robertson, Gordon. A House Divided: Meech Lake, Senate Reform & the Canadian Union. 98p. 1989. pap. text ed. 17.95 (0-88645-096-9, Pub. by Inst Res Pub CN) Ashgate Pub Co.
Robertson, Gordon L. Food Packaging: Principles & Practice. LC 92-25591. (Packaging & Converting Technology: Vol. 6). 688p. 1992. 180.00 (0-8247-8749-8) Dekker.
Robertson, Grace. Grace Robertson: Photojournalist of the 50's. (Illus.). 128p. 1990. pap. 39.95 (1-85381-089-4, Pub. by Virago Pr UK) Trafalgar.
Robertson, Graham, jt. auth. see Dell, Susanne.
Robertson, Harry S. Statistical Thermophysics. LC 92-17052. 592p. 1992. text ed. 84.00 (0-13-845603-8) P-H.
Robertson, Harry S., jt. ed. see Pardo, William B.
Robertson, Heard, jt. auth. see Cashin, Edward J.
Robertson, Hector M. Aspects of the Rise of Economic Individualism: A Criticism of Max Weber & His School. LC 73-17059. (Reprints of Economic Classics Ser.). 1973. reprint ed. 35.00 (0-678-00867-1) Kelley.
— South Africa: Economic & Political Aspects. LC 57-8817. (Duke University, Commonwealth-Studies Center, Publication Ser.: No. 2). 204p. reprint ed. pap. 58.20 (0-317-20422-X, 2023442) Bks Demand.
Robertson Hodges, Deborah. Etiquette: An Annotated Bibliography of Literature Published in English in the United States, 1900 through 1987. LC 89-42724. 192p. 1989. lib. bdg. 49.95x (0-89950-429-9) McFarland & Co.
Robertson, Howard W. To the Fierce Guard in the Assyrian Saloon. Trusky, Tom, ed. LC 86-71904. (Ahsahta Press Modern & Contemporary Poets of the West Ser.). 65p. (Orig.). 1987. pap. 6.95 (0-916272-33-8) Ahsahta Pr.
Robertson, Hugh D., et al, eds. Plant Infectious Agents: Viruses, Viroids, Virusoids & Satellites. (Current Communications in Molecular Biology Ser.). 230p. 1983. pap. text ed. 28.00 (0-87969-159-X) Cold Spring Harbor.
Robertson, Ian. Austria. 3rd rev. ed. (Blue Guides Ser.). (Illus.). 428p. 1992. pap. 22.95 (0-393-30836-7) Norton.
— Blue Guide: Ireland. 6th ed. (Illus.). 404p. 1992. pap. 22.50 (0-393-30841-3) Norton.
— Blue Guide: Paris & Versailles. 8th ed. (Illus.). 294p. 1992. pap. 19.95 (0-393-30889-8) Norton.
— Blue Guide: Switzerland. 5th ed. (Illus.). 384p. 1992. pap. 21.95 (0-393-30890-1) Norton.
— Blue Guide: Spain. 6th ed. 508p. 1993. pap. 23.00 (0-393-31053-1) Norton.
— Blue Guides Vol. 3: Cyprus. 1991. pap. 18.95 (0-393-30730-1) Norton.
— France. 2nd ed. (Blue Guides Ser.). 1988. pap. 29.95 (0-393-30366-7) Norton.
— MS DOS 6.0 Step by Step. (Step by Step Ser.). (Illus.). 300p. 1993. pap. 22.95 (0-7506-1726-8) Buttrwrth-Heinemann.
— NEWNES PC Pocket Book. 368p. 1994. 19.95 (0-7506-1778-0) Buttrwrth-Heinemann.
— Paris & Versailles. 7th ed. (Illus.). 1990. pap. 18.95 (0-685-28289-9) Norton.
— Portugal. 3rd ed. (Blue Guides Ser.). (Illus.). 1988. pap. 19.95 (0-393-30477-9) Norton.
— Portugal: A Traveller's Guide. (Illus.). 224p. 1993. pap. 24.95 (0-7195-5207-9, Pub. by John Murray UK) Trafalgar.
— Society: A Brief Introduction. xvii, 416p. (Orig.). (C). 1989. text ed. 37.95x (0-87901-548-9); pap. 33.95x (0-87901-412-1); student ed, pap. 11.95x (0-87901-415-6) Worth.
— Sociology. 3rd ed. 715p. (C). 1987. text ed. 49.95x (0-87901-245-5); student ed, pap. 11.95x (0-87901-246-3); 20.95 (0-87901-330-3) Worth.
Robertson, Ian, ed. Audio-Visual Equipment: A Technician's & User's Handbook. (Illus.). 180p. 1991. text ed. 59.95 (0-7506-0021-7) Buttrwrth-Heinemann.
— MMIC Design. (IEE Circuits & Systems Ser.: No. 7). 520p. 1995. boxed 95.00 (0-85296-816-7) Inst Elect Eng.
— Rugby World Cup '95: In Association with Scottish Life. (Illus.). 192p. 1995. 35.00 (0-340-64953-4, Pub. by H & S UK) Trafalgar.
Robertson, Ian & McKee, Michael. Social Problems. 2nd ed. 494p. 1980. text ed. write for info. (0-07-553583-1) McGraw.
Robertson, Ian & Whitten, Phillip, eds. Race & Politics in South Africa. LC 76-50334. 274p. 1978. text ed. 32.95 (0-87855-137-9) Transaction Pubs.
Robertson, Ian, jt. auth. see Heather, Nick H.
Robertson, Ian, jt. auth. see Rothery, Brian.
***Robertson, Ian M., et al, eds.** Microstructure of Irradiated Materials: 1994 MRS Fall Meeting, Boston, MA, Vol. 373. (MRS Symposium Proceedings Ser.: Vol. 373). 569p. 1995. 71.00 (1-55899-275-8, 373N) Materials Res.
Robertson, Ian W., tr. see Barth, Karl.
Robertson, Ina. France. 3rd ed. (Blue Guide Ser.). 1994. pap. 29.95 (0-393-31055-8) Norton.
Robertson, Irvine. What the Cults Believe. rev. ed. pap. 7.99 (0-8024-9414-5) Moody.
Robertson, Isabel. Jehanne. 341p. (C). 1990. 79.00 (1-85634-979-9, Pub. by Excalibur UK) St Mut.
***Robertson, Ivan T. & Cooper, Dominic.** The Psychology of Personnel Selection: A Quality Approach. LC 95-7748. (Essential Business Psychology Ser.). 1995. write for info. (0-415-13081-6); pap. write for info. (0-415-10326-6) Routledge.
Robertson, Ivan T. & Smith, Mike. Motivation & Job Design: Theory, Research & Practice. 176p. (C). 1985. 51.00 (0-85292-346-5) St Mut.
Robertson, Ivan T., jt. ed. see Cooper, C. L.
Robertson, Ivan T., jt. ed. see Cooper, Carey L.
Robertson, Ivan T., jt. auth. see Cooper, Cary L.
Robertson, Ivan T., jt. ed. see Cooper, Cary L.
Robertson, Ivan T., et al, eds. Motivation: Strategy, Theory & Practice. 200p. (C). 1992. pap. 75.00 (0-85292-488-7, Pub. by IPM Hse UK) St Mut.
Robertson, J. Modern Humanists Reconsidered. 1972. 59.95 (0-8490-0649-X) Gordon Pr.
Robertson, J., jt. auth. see Harpp, D. N.
Robertson, J. A. List of Documents in Spanish Archives Relating to the History of the United States. (Carnegie Institute Ser.: Vol. 19). 1910. 32.00 (0-527-00699-8) Periodicals Srv.
Robertson, J. D. A Glossary of Dialect & Archaic Words Used in the County of Gloucester. Moreton, ed. (English Dialect Society Publications Ser.: No. 61). 1969. reprint ed. pap. 25.00 (0-8115-0481-6) Periodicals Srv.
Robertson, J. Daniel, jt. auth. see Delavigne, Kenneth T.
Robertson, J. G. & Tango, W. J., eds. Very High Angular Resolution Imaging: Proceedings of the 158th Symposium of the International Astronomical Union Held at the Women's College, University of Sydney, Australia, 11-15 January 1993. LC 93-23649. 524p. (C). 1994. lib. bdg. 145.00 (0-7923-2632-6); pap. text ed. 71.00 (0-7923-2633-4) Kluwer Ac.

Robertson, J. I., jt. ed. see Janssen, Herwig.
Robertson, J. Logie, ed. see Campbell, Thomas.
Robertson, J. M. Christ & Krishna. 1972. 59.95 (*0-87968-422-4*) Gordon Pr.
— Collected Works. 1973. 400.00 (*0-87968-896-3*) Gordon Pr.
— Forensic Examination of Fibres. 200p. 1992. text ed. 99.00 (*0-13-325309-0*) P-H.
Robertson, J. M., ed. Courses of Study: Clues to the Independent Study of Important Subjects. 1977. lib. bdg. 59.95 (*0-8490-1680-0*) Gordon Pr.
Robertson, J. M. & Wislicenus, G. F., eds. Cavitation State of Knowledge: Presented at the ASME Fluids Engineering & Applied Mechanics Conference, Northwestern University, Evanston, Ill., June 16-18, 1969. LC 73-173121. 247p. reprint ed. pap. 70.40 (*0-317-29952-2*, 2051713) Bks Demand.
Robertson, J. M., ed. see American Society of Mechanical Engineers Staff.
Robertson, J. M., jt. auth. see Dummer, Geoffrey W.
Robertson, J. M., jt. ed. see Dummer, Geoffrey W.
Robertson, J. N., tr. see Orthodox Eastern Church Staff.
Robertson, Jack. CCL: Cajun & Creole Cookbook. 96p. 1994. 10.98 (*0-8317-1306-2*) Smithmark.
Robertson, Jack C. Auditing. 7th ed. LC 92-16451. 1152p. (C). 1992. text ed. 68.95 (*0-256-10318-6*) Irwin.
Robertson, Jack S. Twentieth-Century Artists on Art: An Index to Artists Writings, Statements, & Interviews. (Visual Arts Ser.). 350p. 1985. lib. bdg. 40.00 (*0-8161-8714-2*, Hall Reference) Macmillan.
Robertson, James. Any Fool Can Be a Dairy Farmer. 176p. 1989. reprint ed. pap. 8.95 (*0-85236-195-5*, Pub. by Farming Pr UK) Diamond Farm Bk.
— Any Fool Can Be a Pig Farmer. 156p. 1989. reprint ed. pap. 8.95 (*0-85236-196-3*, Pub. by Farming Pr UK) Diamond Farm Bk.
— Future Wealth: A New Economics for the 21st Century. LC 90-831. (TOES Bks.). 190p. (Orig.). 1990. pap. 14.50 (*0-942850-25-4*) Intermediate Tech.
— The Hidden Cinema: British Film Censorship in Action. (Cinema & Society Ser.). 200p. 1993. pap. 18.95 (*0-415-09034-2*, B0329) Routledge.
— Sales: The Mind's Side: What They Never Taught You in Sales Training. 224p. (Orig.). 1990. pap. 12.95 (*1-55552-006-5*) Metamorphous Pr.
— The Sane Alternative: A Choice of Futures. 3rd ed. 152p. (Orig.). 1983. pap. 4.95 (*0-936106-00-X*) River Basin.
Robertson, James, ed. Hospitals & Children. 160p. 1963. text ed. 25.00 (*0-8236-2360-2*) Intl Univs Pr.
Robertson, James & Robertson, Carolyn. The Small Towns Book: Show Me the Way to Go Home. LC 76-23813. 208p. reprint ed. pap. 59.30 (*0-317-29958-1*, 2051722) Bks Demand.
Robertson, James & Robertson, Joyce. Separation & the Very Young. 245p. 1989. 45.00 (*1-85343-097-8*); pap. 19.50 (*1-85343-096-X*) Col U Pr.
Robertson, James & Robertson, Suzanne. Complete Systems Analysis: The Workbook, the Textbook, the Answers, 2 vols. LC 93-44616. 532p. 1994. 70.00 (*0-932633-25-0*) Dorset Hse Pub Co.
Robertson, James, ed. see Miller, Joaquin.
Robertson, James A., ed. Louisiana Under the Rule of Spain, France & the United States 1785-1807, 2 vols, Set. LC 72-102254. (Select Bibliographies Reprint Ser.). 1977. 68.95 (*0-8369-5139-5*) Ayer.
Robertson, James A., tr. see Gentlemen of Elvias.
Robertson, James B., jt. ed. see Johnston, William R.
Robertson, James B., tr. see Von Schlegel, Frederick.
Robertson, James C. The Casablanca Man: The Career of Michael Curtiz. LC 92-33281. (Illus.). 224p. 1993. 25.00 (*0-415-06804-5*, B0722, Routledge NY) Routledge.
— The Hidden Cinema: British Film Censorship in Action, 1913-1972. (Cinema & Society Ser.). 208p. 1989. 58.00 (*0-415-03291-1*) Routledge.
— Introduction to Fire Prevention. 3rd ed. 412p. (C). 1989. text ed. write for info. (*0-02-402230-6*) Macmillan.
— Introduction to Fire Prevention. 4th ed. LC 94-205423. 320p. 1995. 39.75 (*0-02-402241-1*) P-H.
Robertson, James C. & Sheppard, J. B., eds. Materials for the History of Thomas Becket, 7 vols., Set. (Rolls Ser.: No. 67). 1969. reprint ed. 560.00 (*0-8115-1135-9*) Periodicals Srv.
Robertson, James C., ed. see Bargrave, John.
Robertson, James C., jt. auth. see Jacob, Naomi.
***Robertson, James D.** A Beer Drinkers Guide to Australia & New Zealand. (Illus.). 80p. 1994. per. 9.95 (*0-9635332-6-6*) Bosak Pub.
— A Beer Drinkers Guide to Southern Germany. (Illus.). 96p. 1994. per. 9.95 (*0-9635332-3-1*) Bosak Pub.
— The Beer Log. (Illus.). 408p. ring bd. 37.50 (*0-9635332-0-7*) Bosak Pub.
— The Beer Log. (Illus.). 384p. 1995. pap. 39.75 (*0-9635332-5-8*) Bosak Pub.
— The Beer Log 1993 Update. (Illus.). 182p. 1994. ring bd. 16.00 (*0-9635332-1-5*) Bosak Pub.
— The Beer Log 1994 Update. (Illus.). Date not set. ring bd. 16.00 (*0-9635332-2-3*) Bosak Pub.
Robertson, James E. The Birth of Humanity Being. LC 74-79179. 114p. 1974. 5.90 (*0-9600756-1-5*); pap. 3.90 (*0-9600756-2-3*) J E Robertson.
Robertson, James I., Jr. Civil War! America Becomes One Nation. LC 91-19177. (Illus.). 192p. (J). (gr. 5-9). 1992. lib. bdg. 16.99 (*0-394-92996-9*) Knopf Bks Yng Read.
— Civil War Sites in Virginia: A Tour Guide. LC 81-7426. (Illus.). 108p. 1982. pap. 6.95 (*0-8139-0907-4*) U Pr of Va.
— Civil War Virginia: Battleground for a Nation. (Illus.). 197p. (C). 1993. pap. text ed. 8.95 (*0-8139-1457-4*) U Pr of Va.
***Robertson, James I.** Common Soldier of the Civil War. (Civil-Structural Inspection Ser.). 52p. (Orig.). 1994. pap. 3.95 (*0-915992-65-5*) Eastern Acorn.
— Eighteenth Virginia Infantry. (Virginia Regimental Histories Ser.). (Illus.). 96p. 1984. 19.95 (*0-930919-07-6*) H E Howard.
— Fourth Virginia Infantry. (Virginia Regimental Histories Ser.). (Illus.). 87p. 1982. 19.95 (*0-930919-00-9*) H E Howard.
Robertson, James I., Jr. General A. P. Hill: The Story of a Confederate Warrior. LC 86-31365. (Illus.). 1987. 30.00 (*0-394-55257-1*) Random.
— Jackson & Lee: Legends in Grey. (Illus.). 180p. 1995. 29.95 (*1-55853-333-8*) Rutledge Hill Pr.
— Soldiers Blue & Gray. Connelly, Thomas L., ed. (American Military History Ser.). 288p. 1988. 24.95 (*0-87249-572-8*) U of SC Pr.
— The Stonewall Brigade. LC 63-9648. (Illus.). xiii, 272p. 1963. pap. 11.95 (*0-8071-0396-9*) La State U Pr.
Robertson, James I., Jr., ed. An Index Guide to the Southern Historical Society Papers 1876-1959, 2 vols. LC 79-24910. 1980. 140.00 (*0-527-75516-8*) Kraus Intl.
— The Medical & Surgical History of the Civil War, 15 vols., Set. Orig. Title: The Medical & Surgical History of the War of the Rebellion. (Illus.). 1992. reprint ed. 1,400.00 (*0-916107-86-8*) Broadfoot.
— The Medical & Surgical History of the Civil War Index, 3 vols., Set. 1400p. 1992. 400.00 (*0-916107-95-7*) Broadfoot.
Robertson, James I., ed. Medical & Surgical History of the Civil War, Vol. 1. (Illus.). 729p. 1990. reprint ed. 125.00 (*1-56837-092-X*) Broadfoot.
— Medical & Surgical History of the Civil War, Vol. 10. (Illus.). 552p. 1991. reprint ed. 125.00 (*1-56837-101-2*) Broadfoot.
— Medical & Surgical History of the Civil War, Vol. 11. (Illus.). 426p. 1992. reprint ed. 125.00 (*1-56837-102-0*) Broadfoot.
— Medical & Surgical History of the Civil War, Vol. 12. (Illus.). 560p. 1992. reprint ed. 125.00 (*1-56837-103-9*) Broadfoot.
— Medical & Surgical History of the Civil War, Vol. 2. (Illus.). 365p. 1991. reprint ed. 125.00 (*1-56837-093-8*) Broadfoot.
— Medical & Surgical History of the Civil War, Vol. 3. (Illus.). 482p. 1991. reprint ed. 125.00 (*1-56837-094-6*) Broadfoot.
— Medical & Surgical History of the Civil War, Vol. 4. (Illus.). 360p. 1991. reprint ed. 125.00 (*1-56837-095-4*) Broadfoot.
— Medical & Surgical History of the Civil War, Vol. 5. (Illus.). 480p. 1991. reprint ed. 125.00 (*1-56837-096-2*) Broadfoot.
— Medical & Surgical History of the Civil War, Vol. 6. (Illus.). 486p. 1991. reprint ed. 125.00 (*1-56837-097-0*) Broadfoot.
— Medical & Surgical History of the Civil War, Vol. 7. (Illus.). 266p. 1991. reprint ed. 125.00 (*1-56837-098-9*) Broadfoot.
— Medical & Surgical History of the Civil War, Vol. 8. (Illus.). 384p. 1991. reprint ed. 125.00 (*1-56837-099-7*) Broadfoot.
— Medical & Surgical History of the Civil War, Vol. 9. (Illus.). 472p. 1991. reprint ed. 125.00 (*1-56837-100-4*) Broadfoot.
Robertson, James I., Jr., ed. Proceedings of the Advisory Council of the State of Virginia, April 21-June 19, 1861. LC 76-27470. (Illus.). xxiv, 182p. 1977. 15.00 (*0-88490-007-X*) VA State Lib.
Robertson, James I., Jr., ed. see Casler, John O.
Robertson, James I., ed. see Howard, McHenry.
Robertson, James I., Jr., ed. see Longstreet, James.
Robertson, James I., Jr., et al, eds. The Southern Historical Society Papers, 55 vols., Set. (Illus.). 1992. reprint ed. 1,700.00 (*0-916107-98-1*) Broadfoot.
— The Southern Historical Society Papers Index, 3 vols., Set. 1768p. 1992. 150.00 (*0-916107-99-X*) Broadfoot.
Robertson, James L. In Scottish Fields. LC 73-144469. reprint ed. 39.50 (*0-404-08525-3*) AMS Pr.
Robertson, James O. American Myth, American Reality. (American Century Ser.). 406p. 1982. pap. 12.95 (*0-8090-0152-7*) Hill & Wang.
— America's Business. 288p. 1986. pap. 7.95 (*0-8090-0164-0*) Hill & Wang.
Robertson, James R. A Kentuckian at the Court of the Tsars. (Illus.). 286p. 1989. reprint ed. 12.50 (*0-935680-23-3*) Kentucke Imprints.
— Petitions of the Early Inhabitants of Kentucky to the General Assembly of Virginia, 1769 to 1792. LC 74-146415. (First American Frontier Ser.). 1971. reprint ed. 30.95 (*0-405-02879-2*) Ayer.
— Petitions of the Early Inhabitants of Kentucky to the General Assembly of Virginia, 1769 to 1792. 292p. 1981. reprint ed. 25.00 (*0-89308-206-6*) Southern Hist Pr.
Robertson, James S., ed. Compartmental Distribution of Radiotracers. 208p. 1983. 119.95 (*0-8493-6010-2*, R895, CRC Reprint) Franklin.
Robertson, James W., jt. auth. see Alhashim, Dhia D.
Robertson, Jane & Pinkus, Sue. Let's All Draw Cats, Dogs & Other Animals. (Illus.). 144p. (J). (gr. 3-7). 1991. pap. 9.95 (*0-8230-2705-8*, Watsn-Guptill) Watsn-Guptill.
— Let's All Draw Monsters, Ghosts, Ghouls & Demons. (Illus.). 144p. (J). (gr. 3-7). 1991. pap. 9.95 (*0-8230-2707-4*, Watsn-Guptill) Watsn-Guptill.
Robertson, Janet. Colorado Traveler: Day Hikes on the Colorado Trail. (American Traveler Ser.). (Illus.). 48p. 1991. pap. 4.95 (*1-55838-116-3*) R H Pub.
— The Magnificent Mountain Women: Adventures in the Colorado Rockies. LC 89-14717. (Illus.). xxiv, 274p. 1990. pap. 10.95 (*0-8032-8933-2*, Bison Books) U of Nebr Pr.
— The Magnificent Mountain Women: Adventures in the Colorado Rockies. LC 89-14717. (Illus.). 274p. 1990. 25.00 (*0-8032-3892-4*) U of Nebr Pr.
— Oscar's Spots. LC 93-22199. (Illus.). 32p. (J). (ps-2). 1993. lib. bdg. 13.95 (*0-8167-3133-0*); pap. 3.95 (*0-8167-3134-9*) BrdgeWater.
Robertson, Jean. Modern Sculpture. Roberts, Norma J., ed. LC 86-73072. (Illus.). 32p. pap. 3.50 (*0-918881-17-X*) Columbus Mus Art.
Robertson, Jeanie. Thoughts in Rhyme. 128p. (Orig.). 1992. pap. 9.95 (*0-9632312-0-0*) Thoughts Rhyme.
Robertson, Jeanne. Humor: The Magic of Genie: Seven Potions for Developing a Sense of Humor. (Illus.). 232p. 1990. 14.95 (*0-9607256-9-5*) Rich Pub Co.
Robertson, Jeffrey D. Psychiatric Malpractice: Liability of Mental Health Professionals. LC 87-28059. 575p. 1988. text ed. 135.00 (*0-471-84098-X*) Wiley.
Robertson, Jeffrey D. & Keavy, William. Plastic Surgery Malpractice & Damages. (Medico-Legal Library). 476p. 1990. text ed. 138.00 (*0-471-60831-9*) Wiley.
Robertson, Jennifer. Native & Newcomer: Making & Remaking a Japanese City. LC 90-27918. (Illus.). 224p. 1991. 30.00 (*0-520-07296-0*) U CA Pr.
— Native & Newcomer: Making & Remaking a Japanese City. (Illus.). 252p. (C). 1994. pap. 15.00 (*0-520-08655-4*) U CA Pr.
Robertson, Jenny. Enciclopedia de Historias Biblicas. LaValle, Maria T., tr. (Illus.). 272p. (SPA.). (J). (gr. 3-5). 1984. 17.00 (*0-311-03671-6*) Casa Bautista.
Robertson, Jenny, tr. see Alfeyeva, Valeria.
Robertson, Jim. TeleVisionaries: In Their Own Words, Public Television's Founders Tell How It All Began. LC 92-62246. (Illus.). 280p. 1992. 29.95 (*0-9627974-8-0*) Tabby Hse Bks.
Robertson, Jo, ed. see Benzel, David.
Robertson, Jo, ed. see Finn, Tony.
Robertson, Jo, ed. see Kjellander, Mike.
Robertson, Jo, ed. see Klarich, Tony.
Robertson, Jo, ed. see McMillan, Kent.
Robertson, Jo, ed. see Scarpa, Ron & Dorner, Terrence.
Robertson, Jo, ed. see Waterski Magazine Staff.
Robertson, Joan, jt. auth. see Graeme, E.
Robertson, Joan F., jt. ed. see Bengtson, Vern L.
Robertson, Joanne, jt. auth. see Scott, James.
Robertson, Joe E. Life Without a Mercedes. Davis, Irving, ed. 200p. 1994. 24.95 (*0-9640753-1-8*) Tchrs Press.
Robertson, Joe E. & Ninotschka, Rose. A Jewel of a Grandmother - Una Voya de Abuelita. 290p. (SPA.). 1994. 24.95 (*0-9640753-2-6*) Tchrs Press.
Robertson, John. Art & Music of John Lennon. 1991. 17.95 (*1-55972-076-X*, Birch Ln Pr) Carol Pub Group.
— Art & Music of John Lennon. 232p. 1993. pap. 12.95 (*0-8065-1438-8*, Citadel Pr) Carol Pub Group.
— Complete Guide to the Music of Elvis Presley. (Illus.). (Orig.). 1995. pap. 7.95 (*0-7119-3549-1*, OP47376, Pub. by Omnibus Press UK) Omnibus NY.
— Complete Guide to the Music of Jimi Hendrix. (Illus.). 128p. (Orig.). 1995. pap. 7.95 (*0-7119-4304-4*, OP 47738, Pub. by Omnibus Press UK) Omnibus NY.
— Complete Guide to the Music of The Beatles. (Illus.). (Orig.). 1995. pap. 7.95 (*0-7119-3548-3*, OP 47368, Pub. by Omnibus Press UK) Omnibus NY.
— Morrissey: In His Own Words. (Illus.). 96p. 1988. pap. 15.95 (*0-7119-1547-4*, OP44874) Omnibus NY.
— Neil Young: A Visual Documentary. 1994. 19.95 (*0-7119-3816-4*, OP47568) Omnibus NY.
— Seven Hundred Seventy-Seven Baseball Trivia Teasers: A Quiz for Die-Hard Fans. 1992. pap. 10.00 (*0-533-10128-X*) Vantage.
***Robertson, John, ed.** A Union for Empire: Political Thought & the British Union of 1707. 336p. (C). 1995. 59.95 (*0-521-43113-1*) Cambridge U Pr.
Robertson, John & McCarthy, John. Australian War Strategy, Nineteen Thirty-Nine to Nineteen Forty-Five: A Documentary History. 612p. 1985. text ed. 49.95 (*0-7022-1924-X*, Pub. by Univ Queensland Pr AT) Intl Spec Bk.
Robertson, John, tr. see Haich, Elisabeth.
Robertson, John, jt. auth. see Rutherford, Brett.
Robertson, John A. Children of Choice: Freedom & the New Reproductive Technologies. LC 93-35880. 1994. 29.95 (*0-691-03353-6*) Princeton U Pr.
***Robertson, John C., Jr.** The Loss & Recovery of Transcendence: The Will to Power & the Light of Heaven. LC 95-5874. (Princeton Theological Monograph: Vol. 39). 1995. 14.00 (*1-55635-027-9*) Pickwick.
Robertson, John C. Mixed Company. LC 77-107735. (Essay Index Reprint Ser.). 1977. 20.95 (*0-8369-1533-X*) Ayer.
***Robertson, John G.** Baseball's Greatest Controversies: Rhubarbs, Hoaxes, Blown Calls, Ruthian Myths, Managers' Miscues & Front-Office Flops. LC 94-48265. 192p. 1995. lib. bdg. 22.50 (*0-7864-0107-9*) McFarland & Co.
— Essays & Addresses on Literature. LC 68-26471. (Essay Index Reprint Ser.). 1977. reprint ed. 20.95 (*0-8369-0828-7*) Ayer.
— Goethe. LC 74-16295. (Studies in Goethe: No. 61). 1974. lib. bdg. 75.00 (*0-8383-2036-8*) M S G Haskell Hse.
— Goethe & the Twentieth Century. LC 72-3678. (Studies in German Literature: No. 13). 1972. reprint ed. lib. bdg. 35.95 (*0-8383-1581-X*) M S G Haskell Hse.
— The Life & Work of Goethe. LC 72-8646. (Studies in German Literature: No. 13). 1973. reprint ed. lib. bdg. 75.00 (*0-8383-1671-9*) M S G Haskell Hse.
— The Life & Work of Goethe, 1749-1832. LC 79-179536. (Select Bibliographies Reprint Ser.). 1977. reprint ed. 23.95 (*0-8369-6665-1*) Ayer.
— Robertson's Words for a Modern Age: A Cross Reference of Latin & Greek Combining Elements. deluxe ed. 266p. 1991. 35.00 (*0-9630919-0-5*); 25.00 (*0-9630919-1-3*) Sr Scribe.
Robertson, John G., ed. Lessing's Dramatic Theory. LC 63-14713. (Illus.). 1972. 36.95 (*0-405-08894-9*) Ayer.
Robertson, John H. William Ernest Henley. 1972. 59.95 (*0-8490-1303-8*) Gordon Pr.
Robertson, John J. Gift of Tongues. (Discovery Ser.). 30p. 1987. pap. 0.79 (*0-8163-0729-6*) Pacific Pr Pub Assn.
Robertson, John M. Baconian Heresy. LC 74-109660. (Select Bibliographies Reprint Ser.). 1977. 35.95 (*0-8369-5269-3*) Ayer.
— The Baconian Heresy, a Confutation. (BCL1-PR English Literature Ser.). 612p. 1992. reprint ed. lib. bdg. 109.00 (*0-7812-7290-4*) Rprt Serv.
— Croce As Shakespearean Critic. (Studies in Shakespeare: No. 24). 1978. lib. bdg. 23.95 (*0-8383-1810-X*) M S G Haskell Hse.
— Did Shakespeare Write "Titus Andronicus"? LC 77-39875. reprint ed. 31.50 (*0-404-05361-0*) AMS Pr.
— The Genuine in Shakespeare. LC 72-3656. (Studies in Shakespeare: No. 24). 1972. reprint ed. lib. bdg. 49.95 (*0-8383-1568-2*) M S G Haskell Hse.
— Introduction to the Study of the Shakespeare Canon. LC 70-109659. (Select Bibliographies Reprint Ser.). 1977. 34.95 (*0-8369-5268-5*) Ayer.
— Modern Humanists Reconsidered. LC 72-3443. (English Literature Ser.: No. 33). 1972. reprint ed. lib. bdg. 49.95 (*0-8383-1556-9*) M S G Haskell Hse.
— Montaigne & Shakespeare & Other Essays on Cognate Questions. LC 68-24914. (Studies in Comparative Literature: No. 35). 1969. reprint ed. lib. bdg. 49.95 (*0-8383-0234-3*) M S G Haskell Hse.
— Montaigne & Shakespeare, & Other Essays on Cognate Questions. (BCL1-PR English Literature Ser.). 358p. 1992. reprint ed. lib. bdg. 89.00 (*0-7812-7291-2*) Rprt Serv.
— Perdonado. Lumpuy, Luis B., tr. Orig. Title: Pardoned. (Illus.). 64p. (SPA.). 1985. pap. 0.95 (*0-8297-0909-6*) Life Pubs Intl.
— The Problems of the Shakespeare Sonnets. LC 72-8700. (Studies in Shakespeare: No. 24). 1973. reprint ed. lib. bdg. 75.00 (*0-8383-1676-X*) M S G Haskell Hse.
— Shakespeare & Chapman: A Thesis of Chapman's Authorship of a Lover's Complaint, & His Origination of Timon of Athens. (BCL1-PR English Literature Ser.). 302p. 1992. reprint ed. lib. bdg. 89.00 (*0-7812-7293-9*) Rprt Serv.
— A Short History of Freethought, Ancient & Modern. LC 74-169215. (Atheist Viewpoint Ser.). 464p. 1972. reprint ed. 29.95 (*0-405-03804-6*) Ayer.
Robertson, John P. Letters on South America Comprising Travels on the Banks of the Parana & the Rio De la Plata, 3 vols., Set. LC 70-128428. reprint ed. 145.00 (*0-404-05380-7*) AMS Pr.
Robertson, John P. & Robertson, W. P. Letters on Paraguay Comprising an Account of a Four Years' Residence in That Republic, under the Government of the Dictator Francia, 3 Vols, Set. 2nd ed. LC 74-128429. reprint ed. 155.00 (*0-404-05390-4*) AMS Pr.
Robertson, John S. Engineering Math with Mathematica. 1993. text ed. write for info. (*0-07-053171-4*) McGraw.
— The History of Tense - Aspect - Mood - Voice in the Mayan Verbal Complex. 261p. (C). 1992. text ed. 35.00 (*0-292-72075-0*) U of Tex Pr.
Robertson, John W. Edgar Allan Poe. LC 71-117583. (Studies in Poe: No. 23). 1970. reprint ed. lib. bdg. 59.95 (*0-8383-1016-8*) M S G Haskell Hse.
Robertson, Jon, ed. The Man with Nine Lives: A Search for Evidence of Reincarnation. 304p. 1994. pap. 12.95 (*0-87604-325-2*) ARE Pr.
Robertson, Jon, ed. see Brown, Frederick S.
Robertson, Jon, ed. see Ehrhardt, Thomas.
Robertson, Jon, ed. see Gershom, Yonassan.
Robertson, Jon, ed. see Gould, Katherine T.
Robertson, Jon, ed. see Howard, Jane M.
Robertson, Jon, ed. see Lazur, Carole & Riegel, Lynn.
Robertson, Jon, ed. see McClure, Michael.
Robertson, Jon, ed. see Murphy, Marie.
Robertson, Jon H. & Clark, W. Craig, eds. Lasers in Neurosurgery. (Foundations in Neurological Surgery Ser.). (C). 1988. lib. bdg. 100.00 (*0-89838-966-6*) Kluwer Ac.
Robertson, Joseph, ed. Concilia Scotiae, 2 Vols. LC 77-39875. (Bannatyne Club, Edinburgh. Publications: No. 113). reprint ed. 65.00 (*0-404-52866-X*) AMS Pr.
— Inuentaires De la Royne Descosse Douairiere De France. LC 78-172847. (Bannatyne Club, Edinburgh. Publications: No. 111). reprint ed. 37.50 (*0-404-52865-1*) AMS Pr.
— Liber Collegii Nostre Domine: Registrum Ecclesie B. V. Marie et S. Anne Infra Muros Civitatis Glasguensis. LC 71-168165. (Maitland Club, Glasgow. Publications: No. 65). reprint ed. 40.00 (*0-404-53073-7*) AMS Pr.
Robertson, Joseph, jt. ed. see Innes, Cosmos.
Robertson, Joseph E. Mama Jewells. 214p. 1994. pap. 12.95 (*0-9640753-0-X*) Tchrs Press.
Robertson, Joseph F. The Magic of Film Editing. (Illus.). 352p. (Orig.). 1984. pap. 16.50 (*0-8306-1267-X*, 1267P) TAB Bks.
Robertson, Joyce, jt. auth. see Robertson, James.
Robertson, K. G. Nineteen Ninety-Two: The Security Implications. (C). 1990. 35.00 (*0-907967-11-6*, Pub. by Inst Euro Def & Strat UK) St Mut.
Robertson, Karen, jt. ed. see Levin, Carole.

R

Robertson, Karen A. Get Ready: A Step-by-Step Handbook for Preparedness & Personal Survival in the 1990's. 175p. 1989. pap. 10.00 (0-9623177-1-3) Paragon Dallas.
Robertson, Kayo. Signs along the River: Learning to Read the Natural Landscape. 1986. pap. 5.95 (0-911797-22-X) R Rinehart.
Robertson, Keith. Henry Reed, Inc. (Illus.). 240p. (J). (gr. 4-6). 1989. pap. 4.99 (0-14-034144-7, Puffin) Puffin Bks.
— Henry Reed's Baby-Sitting Service. 208p. (J). (gr. 4-6). 1989. pap. 4.99 (0-14-034146-3, Puffin) Puffin Bks.
— Henry Reed's Journey. (Illus.). 224p. (J). (gr. 4-6). 1989. pap. 4.99 (0-14-034145-5, Puffin) Puffin Bks.
Robertson, Kell. Bear Crossing. Jacobsen, Steven, ed. & illus. by. 33p. 1990. pap. text ed. 4.00 (0-9625349-0-0) Guerilla Poetics.
Robertson, Kell, et al. Five Card Stud. 1978. pap. 3.00 (0-916918-09-2) Duck Down.
Robertson, Kent A. Pedestrian Malls & Skywalks: Traffic Separation Strategies in American Downtown. LC 94-8723. 1994. 51.95 (1-85628-687-8, Pub. by Avebury Pub UK) Ashgate Pub Co.
Robertson, Kevin. The Last Days of Steam Around London. LC 89-36193. (Last Days of Steam Ser.). (Illus.). 192p. 1989. 22.00 (0-86299-502-7) A Sutton Pub.
— Last Days of Steam in Berkshire. LC 89-36180. (Last Days of Steam Ser.). (Illus.). 168p. 1989. 22.00 (0-86299-395-4) A Sutton Pub.
— Leader: Steam's Last Chance. LC 89-36196. (Illus.). 192p. 1989. 24.00 (0-86299-376-8) A Sutton Pub.
— Locomotives Between the Wars. (Illus.). 160p. 1991. 30. 00 (0-86299-914-6) A Sutton Pub.
Robertson, Kevin & Abbott, David. GWR: The Badminton Line. (Illus.). 252p. 1989. 22.00 (0-86299-459-4) A Sutton Pub.
Robertson, Kirk. Ar-Ti-Facts. Gordon, Coco, ed. 20p. (Orig.). 1985. pap. 12.00 (0-931956-17-X) Water Mark.
— CETA & the Arts in Santa Barbara. (Illus.). 1978. pap. 3.00 (0-916918-10-6) Duck Down.
— Drinking Beer at Twenty-Two Below. 1976. 2.50 (0-917554-04-3) Maelstrom.
— Driving to Vegas: New & Selected Poems 1969-87. (Sun Lizard, Desert Southwest Bk.). 296p. (Orig.). 1989. 25. 00 (0-933313-09-8); pap. 14.95 (0-933313-10-1) SUN Gemini Pr.
— Origins, Initiations. (Illus.). 1980. 45.00 (0-918824-19-2) Turkey Pr.
— Reasons & Methods: Poems by Kirk Robertson, with Constellations, Typoglifs by Karl Kempton. (Illus.). 20p. (Orig.). (C). 1981. pap. 2.50 (0-916918-15-7) Duck Down.
— Two Weeks Off. (Illus.). 48p. (Orig.). 1984. pap. 5.00 (0-912449-11-X) Floating Island.
— Under the Weight of the Sky. LC 77-23446. 1978. pap. 2.50 (0-916156-22-2) Cherry Valley.
Robertson, Kirk, ed. New Works: An Anthology of Ten Contemporary Poets. LC 81-65314. (Windriver Ser.). (Illus.). (Orig.). (C). 1981. pap. 5.95 (0-916918-13-0) Duck Down.
Robertson, Kirk & Barker, David. High Fallon, Southern Comfort. 1980. 3.00 (0-917554-11-6) Maelstrom.
Robertson, Kirk, ed. see Allen, Jo Harvey.
Robertson, Kirk, ed. see Bennett, John.
Robertson, Kirk, ed. see Fox, William L.
Robertson, Kirk, ed. see Haslam, Gerald.
Robertson, Kirk, ed. see Hogan, Michael.
Robertson, Kirk, ed. see Krapt, Norbert.
Robertson, Kirk, ed. see Masarik, Al.
Robertson, Kirk, ed. see Matte, Robert, Jr.
Robertson, Kirk, ed. see Northsun, Nila & Sagel, Jim.
Robertson, Kirk, ed. see Short, Gary.
Robertson, Kirk, ed. see Wagner, D. R.
Robertson, Kirk, jt. auth. see Weidman, Phil.
Robertson, L. R., ed. see Minns, Michael L.
Robertson, LaRae C. You Can Be a Doctrine & Covenants Expert in Five Minutes a Day. LC 79-89352. 1984. reprint ed. pap. 9.98 (0-88290-128-1) Horizon Utah.
Robertson, Laura P. Robertson, Purcell, & Related Families. (Illus.). 242p. 1993. reprint ed. lib. bdg. 48.00 (0-8328-3394-0); reprint ed. pap. 38.00 (0-8328-3395-9) Higginson Bk Co.
Robertson, Laurel. Laurel's Kitchen Bread Book. 1985. pap. 19.95 (0-394-72434-8) Random.
— The Laurel's Kitchen Bread Book. 1994. 27.00 (0-8446-6748-X) Peter Smith.
Robertson, Laurel, et al. Laurel's Kitchen Recipes. 1993. pap. 10.95 (0-89815-537-1) Ten Speed Pr.
— The New Laurel's Kitchen. 2nd ed. LC 86-14330. (Illus.). 512p. 1986. 27.95 (0-89815-167-8); pap. 24.95 (0-89815-166-X) Ten Speed Pr.
Robertson, Laurie. Fraction Fun Through Cooperative Learning. (Illus.). 94p. 1992. pap. text ed. 19.00 (1-879097-15-X) Kagan Cooperative.
Robertson, Laurie & Kagan, Spencer. Co-op Across the Curriculum. (Illus.). 150p. 1992. pap. text ed. 20.00 (1-879097-12-5) Kagan Cooperative.
Robertson, Laurie S. The Night Sea Sky. Iddings, Kathleen, ed. (Illus.). 29p. (Orig.). 1988. pap. text ed. 6.00 (0-931721-09-1) La Jolla Poets.
Robertson, Lawrence D. Year of the Goddess. 1990. pap. 12.95 (0-85030-859-3, Pub. by Aquarian Pr UK) Thorsons SF.
Robertson, Lee. Field Guide to Reality & Other Poems. 133p. (Orig.). 1989. pap. 15.00 (0-685-26247-2) Thermopylae.
— Mind Like a Mirror. Lansford, Kim D., ed. LC 92-61739. (Illus.). (Orig.). Date not set. pap. 15.00 (0-9623377-8-1) Thermopylae.
Robertson, Leon. Injury Epidemiology. (Illus.). 272p. 1992. 34.95 (0-19-506956-0) OUP.
Robertson, Leon S., jt. auth. see Mazur, Allan.
Robertson, Leroy J., ed. Hymns from the Crossroads. (Illus.). 51p. 1965. pap. 8.50 (0-8258-0137-0, 0-4516) Fischer Inc NY.
Robertson, Lesley A. Student's Guide to Program Design. (Illus.). 188p. 1992. pap. 24.95 (0-7506-0495-6) Buttrwrth-Heinemann.
***Robertson, Linda.** The Complete Kwanzaa Celebration Book. rev. ed. LC 94-92261. (Illus.). 80p. 1994. pap. 9.95 (0-9639026-8-7) Creat Acrylic.
Robertson, Linda R. Discovery: Reading, Writing & Thinking in the Academic Disciplines. 576p. (C). 1989. text ed. 22.75 (0-03-007313-8) HB Coll Pubs.
Robertson, Lisa. The Apothecary. 1991. pap. 4.00 (0-921331-16-9) SPD-Small Pr Dist.
Robertson, Lorie L., jt. auth. see Sherman, Ed.
Robertson, Lucretia, jt. auth. see Lang, Donna.
Robertson, Lynn C., jt. ed. see Knapp, Terry.
Robertson, Lynne N. Productivity in Foodservice. LC 90-46631. (Illus.). 96p. 1991. reprint ed. pap. text ed. 12.95 (0-8138-0784-0) Iowa St U Pr.
— Purchasing for Foodservice. 2nd ed. LC 94-5798. 104p. 1994. pap. 14.95 (0-8138-1463-4) Iowa St U Pr.
Robertson, M. J. Directory of World Futures & Options Markets. 656p. 1990. boxed 125.00 (0-13-217951-2) P-H.
Robertson, M. J. & Greenblatt, M., eds. Homelessness: A National Perspective. (Topics in Social Psychiatry Ser.). (Illus.). 290p. 1992. 45.00 (0-306-43789-9, Plenum Pr) Plenum.
***Robertson, Malcolm H.** Psychotherapy Education & Training: An Integrative Perspective. 122p. 1995. text ed. 25.00 (0-8236-5402-8) Intl Univs Pr.
Robertson, Malcolm H., jt. auth. see Woody, Robert H.
Robertson, Marc. Eighth House. 80p. 1976. 8.00 (0-86690-146-9, R1401-014) Am Fed Astrologers.
— Engine of Destiny. 98p. 1976. 8.50 (0-86690-147-7, R1402-014) Am Fed Astrologers.
— Not a Sign in the Sky, but a Living Person. 32p. 1975. 6.00 (0-86690-219-8, R1403-014) Am Fed Astrologers.
— Sex, Mind & Habit Compatibility. 56p. 1975. 6.00 (0-86690-148-5, R1404-014) Am Fed Astrologers.
— Time out of Mind. 44p. 1972. 6.00 (0-86690-220-1, R1405-014) Am Fed Astrologers.
— Transit of Saturn. 74p. 1976. 9.00 (0-86690-149-3, R1406-014) Am Fed Astrologers.
Robertson, Martha. Night-Scented Stock in Bloom? (C). 1989. pap. text ed. 49.00 (1-85821-035-6, Pub. by Pentland Pr UK) St Mut.
Robertson, Martha B. Mexican Indian Manuscript Painting: A Catalog of the Tulane University Collection. (Illus.). 20p. (Orig.). 1991. pap. 7.50 (0-87409-100-4) Tulane Univ.
Robertson, Martha O., jt. ed. see Klaus, Marshall H.
Robertson, Martin. The Art of Vase-Painting in Classical Athens. (Illus.). 364p. (C). 1992. 94.95 (0-521-33010-6) Cambridge U Pr.
— The Art of Vase-Painting in Classical Athens. (Illus.). 364p. (C). 1994. pap. 34.95 (0-521-33881-6) Cambridge U Pr.
— History of Greek Art, 2 vols, Set. LC 73-79317. 1976. 180.00 (0-521-20277-9) Cambridge U Pr.
Robertson, Martyn, et al, eds. Toward the Twenty-First Century: The Challenges for Small Business. (U. K. Enterprise Management & Research Association Ser.). 295p. 1992. 88.00 (0-9519230-0-5, Pub. by P Chapman UK) Taylor & Francis.
Robertson, Mary D., ed. Lucy Breckinridge of Grove Hill: The Journal of a Virginia Girl, 1862-1864. rev. ed. LC 93-46329. (Women's Diaries & Letters of the Nineteenth-Century South Ser.). (Illus.). 230p. (C). 1994. reprint ed. pap. text ed. 14.95 (0-87249-999-5) U of SC Pr.
Robertson, Mary D., ed. see Breckinridge, Lucy.
Robertson, Mary D., ed. see Heyward, Pauline D.
Robertson, Mary E. Family Life. large type ed. (Americana Ser.). 37p. 1988. lib. bdg. 7.95 (0-89621-137-1) Thorndike Pr.
— Meditations for Working Men. (Illus.). 72p. (Orig.). 1988. pap. 5.00 (0-9620614-2-5) Spirit Connect.
— Meditations for Working Women. rev. ed. (Illus.). 64p. 1988. reprint ed. spiral bd., pap. 5.00 (0-9620614-5-X) Spirit Connect.
Robertson, Mary E., ed. see Golliday, Mary.
Robertson, Matra. Starving in the Silences: An Exploration of Anorexia Nervosa. LC 92-16188. 125p. (C). 1992. pap. text ed. 14.95 (0-8147-7435-0) NYU Pr.
Robertson, Merle G. The Sculpture of Palenque: The Early Buildings of the Palace & the Wall Paintings, Vol. II. LC 82-341. (Illus.). 305p. 1985. 175.00x (0-691-03568-7) Princeton U Pr.
— The Sculpture of Palenque, Vol. IV: The Cross Group, the North Group, the Olvidado, & Other Pieces. (Illus.). 228p. 1991. text ed. 175.00 (0-691-03572-5) Princeton U Pr.
Robertson, Merle G., ed. Sixth Palenque Round Table, Nineteen Eighty-Six. LC 90-12171. (Illus.). 368p. 1990. 68.50 (0-8061-2277-3) U of Okla Pr.
Robertson, Merle G. & Fields, Virginia M., eds. Fifth Palenque Round Table, 1983. LC 85-60786. (Palenque Round Table Ser.: Vol. VII). (Illus.). 290p. (Orig.). 1985. pap. 48.00 (0-934051-00-3) Pre-Columbian Art.
Robertson, Michael. South African Human Rights & Labour Law Yearbook, Vol. 1: 1990. (Illus.). 480p. 1991. pap. 39.95 (0-19-570596-3) OUP.
Robertson, Michael, ed. Human Rights for South Africans. (Contemporary South African Debates Ser.). 264p. 1991. pap. text ed. 12.95 (0-19-570632-3) OUP.
Robertson, Michael, tr. see Moller, Torsten B., et al.
Robertson, Michael, jt. auth. see Wiggerhaus, Rolf.
Robertson, Michael, tr. see Wiggershaus, Rolf.
Robertson, Michael J., jt. auth. see Dennis, Marshall W.
Robertson, Morgan. Down to the Sea. LC 71-101289. (Short Story Index Reprint Ser.). 1977. 20.95 (0-8369-3226-9) Ayer.
— Futility: or the Wreck of the Titan. 120p. 1991. reprint ed. lib. bdg. 25.95 (0-89966-821-6) Buccaneer Bks.
— Futility, Wreck of the Titan. 13.95 (0-8488-1461-4) Amereon Ltd.
— Land Ho! LC 76-101290. (Short Story Index Reprint Ser.). 1977. 23.95 (0-8369-3227-7) Ayer.
— Spun-Yarn. LC 76-98592. (Short Story Index Reprint Ser.). 1977. 19.95 (0-8369-3166-1) Ayer.
— Three Laws & the Golden Rule. LC 70-86152. (Short Story Index Reprint Ser.). 1977. 20.95 (0-8369-3058-4) Ayer.
— Where Angels Fear to Tread, & Other Tales of the Sea. LC 79-122733. (Short Story Index Reprint Ser.). 1977. 19.95 (0-8369-3566-7) Ayer.
— Wreck of the Titan. LC 71-132125. (Short Story Index Reprint Ser.). 1977. 27.95 (0-8369-3682-5) Ayer.
Robertson, Nan. Getting Better. Congdon, Thomas, ed. LC 87-31153. 320p. 1988. 17.95 (0-688-06869-3) Morrow.
— The Girls in the Balcony: Women, Men & the New York Times. LC 91-52692. 274p. 1992. 21.50 (0-394-58452-X) Random.
— The Girls in the Balcony: Women, Men, & "The New York Times" (Illus.). 288p. 1993. pap. 10.00 (0-449-90793-7, Columbine) Fawcett.
Robertson, Narelle. Australian Cattle Dogs. (Illus.). 192p. 1990. lib. bdg. 11.95 (0-86622-568-4, KW198) TFH Pubns.
— Australian Cattle Dogs. 1994. 11.95 (0-7938-1085-X) TFH Pubns.
Robertson, Neil & Seymour, Paul, eds. Graph Structure Theory: Proceedings of the Joint Summer Research Conference on Graph Minors, Held June 22-July 5, 1991 at the University of Washington, Seattle, With Support from the National Science Foundation & the Office of Naval Research. LC 93-18553. (Contemporary Mathematics Ser.: Vol. 147). 688p. 1993. 81.00 (0-8218-5160-8) Am Math.
Robertson, Noel. Festivals & Legends: The Formation of Greek Cities in the Light of Public Ritual. (Phoenix Supplementary Volumes Ser.: No. XXXI). 336p. 1992. 75.00 (0-8020-5988-0) U of Toronto Pr.
Robertson, Noel, ed. The Archaeology of Cyprus: Recent Developments. LC 75-34930. 232p. 1976. 24.00 (0-8155-5039-1, NP) Noyes.
Robertson, Noel, jt. auth. see Blaxter, Kenneth.
Robertson, O. H., et al. Endocrines & Aging. 232p. 1972. text ed. 46.50 (0-8422-7029-9) Irvington.
Robertson, O. Palmer. The Books of Nahum, Habakkuk, & Zephaniah. (New International Commentary on the Old Testament Ser.). 384p. (C). 1990. 29.99 (0-8028-2374-2) Eerdmans.
— The Christ of the Covenants. 1981. pap. 9.99 (0-87552-418-4) Presby & Reformed.
— The Final Word. 150p. 1993. pap. 7.95 (0-85151-659-9) Banner of Truth.
— Jonah: A Study in Compassion. 64p. 1990. pap. 3.95 (0-85151-575-4) Banner of Truth.
Robertson, Olga J. The Men in My Life. Steele, M. B., ed. (Illus.). 160p. (Orig.). 1992. pap. 6.95 (0-939497-30-1) Promise Pub.
Robertson, P. A. The Pheasant. 1989. pap. 25.00 (0-85263-950-3, Pub. by Shire UK) St Mut.
— Poplars of the British Isles. 1989. pap. 25.00 (0-7478-0093-6, Pub. by Shire UK) St Mut.
Robertson, P. J. Criticism & Creativity. 84p. (C). 1989. 60. 00 (0-907839-22-3, Pub. by Brynmill Pr Ltd UK) St Mut.
— The Leavises on Fiction: A Historic Partnership. LC 80-5099. 172p. 1981. text ed. 29.95 (0-312-47731-7) St Martin.
Robertson, Pamela, ed. Charles Rennie Mackintosh: The Architectural Papers. (Illus.). 240p. 1991. 35.00x (0-262-18142-8) MIT Pr.
***Robertson, Pat.** Collected Works of Pat Robertson. 1994. 14.98 (0-88486-106-6) Arrowood Pr.
— Inspirational Writings of Pat Robertson. 1989. 12.98 (0-88486-029-9) Arrowood Pr.
— Inspirational Writings of Pat Robertson. 1991. 12.98 (0-88486-052-3, Inspirational Pr) Arrowood Pr.
— My Prayer for You. LC 77-8607. 1988. pap. 5.99 (0-8007-5264-3) Revell.
— New World Order. 1992. pap. 5.99 (0-8499-3394-3) Word Inc.
— Proclamadlo Desde las Azoteas: Shout from the House Tops. (SPA.). 6.95 (84-7228-354-2, 360592, Pub. by Edit Clie SP) TSELF.
— Secret Kingdom. large type ed. (Large Print Inspirational Ser.). 352p. 1986. pap. 14.95 (0-8027-2534-1) Walker & Co.
— Secret Kingdom: Your Path to Peace, Love, & Financial Security. 1992. 17.99 (0-8499-1004-8) Word Inc.
— Secret Kingdom: Your Path to Peace, Love, & Financial Security. 1994. pap. 5.99 (0-8499-3567-9) Word Inc.
— Turning Tide: The Fall of Liberalism & the Rise of Common Sense. 1993. 19.99 (0-8499-0972-4) Word Inc.
Robertson, Pat & Buckingham, Jamie. The Autobiography of Pat Robertson: Shout It from the Housetops! rev. ed. LC 72-76591. 275p. (Orig.). 1995. pap. 5.95 (0-88270-097-9) Bridge Pub.
***Robertson, Patricia.** Cure for Heartache. large type ed. 1994. 17.95 (0-263-13988-3, Pub. by Mills & Boon Ltd UK) Chivers N Amer.
— Daily Meditations (with Scripture) for Busy Moms. (Illus.). 368p. (Orig.). 1993. pap. 8.95 (0-87946-085-7) ACTA Pubns.
— Doctor to the Rescue. large type ed. (Medical Romance Ser.). 1992. 16.95 (0-263-13144-0, Pub. by Mills & Boon Ltd UK) Chivers N Amer.
— Heart in Jeopardy. large type ed. (Medical Romance Ser.). 1993. 17.95 (0-263-13523-3, Pub. by Mills & Boon Ltd UK) Chivers N Amer.
Robertson, Patrick. Guinness Book of Movie Facts & Feats. (Illus.). 240p. 1991. 19.95 (1-55859-236-9) Abbeville Pr.
— Guinness Book of Movie Facts & Feats. 5th ed. 1993. pap. 19.95 (1-55859-697-6) Abbeville Pr.
Robertson, Patrick, ed. Reshaping Europe in the Twenty-First Century. LC 91-24191. 288p. 1992. text ed. 65.00 (0-312-06889-1) St Martin.
Robertson, Paul, jt. auth. see Langlois, Richard N.
Robertson, Paul, jt. auth. see Pollard, Sidney.
Robertson, Paul B. & Musser, Guy G. A New Species of Peromyscus (Rodentia: Cricetidae), & a New Specimen of P. Simulatus from Southern Mexico, with Comments on Their Ecology. (Occasional Papers: No. 47). 8p. 1976. pap. 1.00 (0-317-04909-7) U of KS Mus Nat Hist.
Robertson, Paul R. & Vincent, James. A Vision with Wings: The Story of Missionary Aviation. 1992. pap. 8.99 (0-8024-9174-X) Moody.
Robertson, Pauline D. Borrowed Moccasins: Poems from Other Viewpoints. 64p. 1987. 10.95 (0-942376-12-9) Paramount TX.
— Field Notes: Poems on Late Light. 64p. 1987. 10.95 (0-942376-14-5) Paramount TX.
— Fringe Benefits: Light Verse from Living. 64p. 1987. 9.95 (0-942376-13-7) Paramount TX.
— Poetry Writing Self-Taught. (Illus.). 208p. 1995. 15.95 (0-942376-10-2) Paramount TX.
Robertson, Pauline D. & Robertson, R. L. Cowman's Country: Fifty Frontier Ranches in the Texas Panhandle, 1876-1887. 2nd ed. (Illus.). 192p. 1993. 24.95 (0-942376-04-8) Paramount TX.
— Goodnight: A Pictorial History of the Pioneer Cattleman. (Illus.). 192p. 1995. 19.95 (0-942376-09-9) Paramount TX.
— Mystery Woman of Old Tascosa: The Legend of Frenchy McCormick. (Illus.). 1977. pap. 1.00 (0-942376-02-1) Paramount TX.
— Panhandle Pilgrimage: Illustrated Tales Tracing History in the Texas Panhandle. 5th ed. LC 78-68222. (Illus.). 400p. 1989. 27.95 (0-942376-00-5) Paramount TX.
— Quanah: A Pictorial History of the Last Comanche Chief. (Illus.). 192p. 1994. 24.95 (0-942376-08-0) Paramount TX.
— Tascosa: Historic Site in the Texas Panhandle. (Illus.). 72p. 1977. pap. 3.00 (0-942376-01-3) Paramount TX.
Robertson, Peter. Beyond Southern Skies: Radio Astronomy & the Parkes Telescope. (Illus.). 336p. (C). 1992. 75.00 (0-521-41408-3) Cambridge U Pr.
Robertson, Priscilla. Revolutions of 1848: A Social History. 1952. pap. 17.95x (0-691-00756-X) Princeton U Pr.
Robertson, R. L., jt. auth. see Robertson, Pauline D.
Robertson, Ralston S., jt. auth. see Holzman, Eric L.
Robertson, Raymond. B-Trees for BASIC: Create Your Own Lightning-Fast Database. 256p. (C). 1992. pap. disk, pap. text ed. 32.50 (0-89496-008-3, Baldar) Ross Bks.
Robertson, Richard G., ed. Robertson's Practical English-Thai Dictionary. LC 79-87787. 320p. (ENG & THA.). 1969. pap. 12.95 (0-8048-0706-X) C E Tuttle.
Robertson, Richard J. & Powers, William T., eds. Introduction to Modern Psychology: The Control-Theory View. (Illus.). 220p. (Orig.). (C). 1990. pap. text ed. write for info. (0-9624154-1-3) Control Systs Group.
Robertson, Ritchie & Timms, Edward, eds. The Austrian Enlightenment & Its Aftermath. 256p. 1991. text ed. 35. 00 (0-7486-0231-3, Pub. by Edinburgh U Pr UK); pap. text ed. 19.50 (0-7486-0236-4, Pub. by Edinburgh U Pr UK) Col U Pr.
— The Habsburg Legacy: National Identity in Historical Perspective. (Austrian Studies: No. 5). (Illus.). 256p. 1994. 50.00 (0-7486-0487-1, Pub. by Edinburgh U Pr UK) Col U Pr.
Robertson, Ritchie, tr. see Bitterli, Urs.
Robertson, Ritchie, tr. see Heine, Heinrich.
Robertson, Ritchie, ed. see Hoffmann, E. T.
Robertson, Ritchie, jt. ed. see Timms, Edward.
Robertson, Robert. Confessions of an Abusive Husband. 1993. pap. 10.95 (0-9631739-0-1) Heritage Pk Pub.
Robertson, Robin. After the End of Time: Revelation & the Growth of Consciousness. 250p. (Orig.). 1990. pap. 12. 95 (0-917483-26-X) InnerVision.
— Beginner's Guide to Jungian Psychology. LC 91-47189. (Illus.). 240p. (Orig.). 1992. reprint ed. pap. 12.95 (0-89254-022-2) Nicolas-Hays.
— Beginner's Guide to Revelation: A Jungian Interpretation. rev. ed. (Illus.). 288p. 1994. reprint ed. pap. 12.95 (0-89254-030-3) Nicolas-Hays.
— Jungian Archetypes: Jung, Godel & the History of the Archetypes. 256p. 1995. pap. 14.95 (0-89254-029-X) Nicolas-Hays.
***Robertson, Robin & Combs, Allan, eds.** Chaos Theory in Psychology & the Life Sciences. 424p. 1995. text ed. 79. 95 (0-8058-1736-0) L Erlbaum Assocs.
— Chaos Theory in Psychology & the Life Sciences. 424p. 1995. pap. text ed. 39.95 (0-8058-1737-9) L Erlbaum Assocs.
Robertson, Robin A., jt. ed. see Freidel, David A.
Robertson, Roin, jt. auth. see Robertson, Vincent.
Robertson, Roland. Globalization: Social Theory & Global Culture. (Theory, Culture & Society Ser.). 240p. (C). 1992. 62.00 (0-8039-8186-4); pap. 22.95 (0-8039-8187-2) Sage.
Robertson, Roland & Garrett, William P., eds. Religion & Global Order. LC 90-44569. 1990. 29.95 (0-89226-090-4, New Era Bks); pap. 14.95 (0-89226-091-2, New Era Bks) Paragon Hse.
Robertson, Roland, jt. ed. see Robbins, Thomas.
Robertson, S., jt. ed. see Suci, G. J.

R

An Asterisk (*) at the beginning of an entry indicates that the title is appearing in BIP for the first time.

***Robertson, S. A., ed.** Contemporary Ergonomics 1995. 512p. 1995. pap. 95.00 (0-7484-0328-0, Pub. by Tay Francis Ltd UK) Taylor & Francis.

Robertson, Sandra. Lorca, Alberti, & the Theater of Popular Poetry. LC 91-17755. (American University Studies: Romance Languages & Literature: Ser. II, Vol. 170). 267p. 1992. 44.95 (0-8204-1565-0) P Lang Pubs.

Robertson, Sandy. The Aleister Crowley Scrapbook. (Illus.). 128p. 1988. pap. 19.95 (0-87728-689-2) Weiser.

— Bryan Adams: The Illustrated Biography. (Illus.). 64p. 1992. pap. 10.95 (0-7119-3101-1, OP47086) Omnibus NY.

Robertson, Sarah A., ed. see Underwood, Paula.

***Robertson, Scot.** The Development of RAF Strategic Bombing Doctrine, 1919-1939. LC 94-22654. (Studies in Diplomacy & Strategic Thought). 224p. 1995. text ed. 55.00 (0-275-94997-4, Praeger Pubs) Greenwood.

Robertson, Scott. Model Ships from Scratch. (Illus.). 190p. 1994. 31.95 (1-55750-589-6) Naval Inst Pr.

Robertson, Scott, ed. see Pattak, Evan M. & Wilson, Andrew G.

Robertson-Scott, John W. Story of the Pall Mall Gazette. LC 73-141266. (Illus.). ix, 470p. 1971. reprint ed. text ed. 79.50 (0-8371-5826-5, ROPM, Greenwood Pr) Greenwood.

Robertson, Scott P., et al. Cognition, Computing & Cooperation. LC 89-14895. (Cognition & Computing Ser.: Vol. 2). 440p. (C). 1990. text ed. 59.50 (0-89391-536-X); pap. text ed. 29.50 (0-89391-615-3) Ablex Pub.

Robertson, Seonaid M. Rosegarden & Labyrinth: A Study in Art Education. LC 89-21822. xxix, 216p. 1963. reprint ed. pap. 14.50 (0-88214-319-0) Spring Pubns.

Robertson, Shirley. Lou Who? The Odyssey of a French Poodle in England & America. LC 93-84751. (Illus.). 216p. (Orig.). 1993. pap. text ed. 13.95 (1-880222-16-7) Red-Apple Pub.

Robertson, Stephen. Blood Tells. (Decoy Ser.: No. 3). 1990. pap. 3.95 (1-55817-325-0, Pinnacle NY) Windsor NY.

— Blood Ties. (Decoy Ser.: No. 2). 1989. pap. 3.95 (1-55817-279-3, Pinnacle NY) Windsor NY.

— Decoy. 1989. pap. 3.95 (1-55817-239-4, Pinnacle NY) Windsor NY.

— Handyman. 1990. pap. 3.95 (1-55817-377-3, Pinnacle NY) Windsor NY.

Robertson, Struan. The Cold Choice: Pictures of a South African Reality. 1991. 24.95 (0-86543-217-1) Africa World.

— The Cold Choice: Pictures of a South African Reality. 128p. reprint ed. pap. 36.50 (0-7837-6567-3, 2046132) Bks Demand.

Robertson, Stuart, tr. see Alfeyeva, Valeria.

Robertson, Sue & Punkus, Sue. Let's All Draw Cars, Trucks & Other Vehicles. (Illus.). 144p. (J). (gr. 3-7). 1991. pap. 9.95 (0-8230-2704-X, Watsn-Guptill) Watsn-Guptill.

Robertson, Susanne M. Programme: Lowell Musicale & Musical Portrait of the Spindle City. (Illus.). 131p. (Orig.). 1986. pap. 8.95 (0-9616315-0-3) Euterpe Pr.

Robertson, Suzanne, jt. auth. see Robertson, James.

Robertson, T. W., ed. see Ward, Artemus, pseud.

Robertson, Theodosia S., tr. see Fiut, Aleksander.

Robertson, Thomas. Human Ecology, 2 Vols. 560p. 1973. 500.00 (0-87968-340-6) Gordon Pr.

Robertson, Thomas, jt. auth. see Tucker, Benjamin R.

Robertson, Thomas S., jt. auth. see Kassarjian, Harold H.

Robertson, Thomas S., et al. Consumer Behavior. (C). 1984. text ed. 54.00 (0-673-15841-1) HarpCollege.

— Televised Medicine Advertising & Children. LC 79-4280. 192p. 1979. text ed. 49.95 (0-275-90413-X, C0413, Praeger Pubs) Greenwood.

Robertson, Tim, et al. Order Restricted Statistical Inference. LC 87-27896. (Probability & Mathematical Statistics Ser.). 521p. 1988. text ed. 145.00 (0-471-91787-7) Wiley.

Robertson, Tom G., jt. auth. see Great American Opportunities Staff.

Robertson, Tomas. Baja California & Its Missions. (Illus.). 1990. pap. 4.50 (0-910856-66-4) La Siesta.

Robertson, Victoria. Breeding Rottweilers. (Illus.). 128p. 1993. 11.95 (0-86622-816-0, KW229) TFH Pubns.

Robertson, Vincent & Robertson, Roin. Alternate Energy-Solar Energy. 1977. pap. 3.95 (0-685-59747-4) Alternate Energy.

Robertson, Virginia. Osage County Quilt Factory. Weiland, Barbara, ed. LC 92-13119. (Quilt Shop Ser.). (Illus.). 80p. 1992. pap. 19.95 (1-56477-013-3, B144) That Patchwork.

Robertson, W. Francisco de Miranda & the Revolutionizing of South America. 1976. lib. bdg. 59.95 (0-8490-1862-5) Gordon Pr.

— On Christian Doctrine: Augustine. 192p. (C). 1958. pap. write for info. (0-02-402150-4) Macmillan.

— Pocahontas: Alias Matoaka, & Her Descendants Through Her Marriage at Jamestown, Virginia, with John Rolfe, Gentleman. 84p. 1993. reprint ed. lib. bdg. 20.00 (0-8328-3384-3); reprint ed. pap. 10.00 (0-8328-3385-1) Higginson Bk Co.

Robertson, W. & Siddle, W. Technical Writing & Presentation. LC 66-25317. 1966. 49.00 (0-08-011559-4, Pub. by Pergamon Repr UK) Franklin.

Robertson, W., jt. auth. see Hill, C.

Robertson, W. H. An Illustrated History of Contraception: A Concise Account of the Quest for Fertility Control. (History of Medicine Ser.). (Illus.). 150p. 1989. 48.00 (1-85070-108-3) Prthnon Pub.

Robertson, W. P., jt. auth. see Robertson, John P.

Robertson, Wallace J. Black Street. 1972. 1.00 (0-685-67932-2) Windless Orchard.

Robertson, William. K. D. Lang: Carrying the Torch. (Illus.). 112p. (Orig.). 1993. pap. 9.95 (1-55022-158-2, Pub. by ECW Pr CN) InBook.

— Soldiers & Statesmen, 2 vols., Set. (Modern Revivals in Military History Ser.). 685p. 1992. 87.50 (0-7512-0035-2, Pub. by Gregg Revivals UK) Ashgate Pub Co.

— Tin: Its Production & Marketing. LC 82-9269. (Contributions in Economics & Economic History Ser.: No. 51). (Illus.). 212p. 1982. text ed. 55.00 (0-313-23637-2, RTN/, Greenwood Pr) Greenwood.

Robertson, William B., Jr. Everglades - The Park Story. rev. ed. LC 89-80983. (Illus.). 64p. (C). 1989. pap. 8.95 (0-945142-01-3) FL Natl Parks.

Robertson, William B., ed. The Cardiovascular System: General Considerations & Congenital Malformations. 3rd ed. LC 92-20957. (Systemic Pathology Ser.: Vol. 10, Pt. A). 1993. pap. text ed. 139.00 (0-443-03096-0) Churchill.

Robertson, William E. The Woodstock & Sycamore Traction Company. LC 85-4886. (Illus.). 56p. 1985. pap. 10.00 (0-933449-00-3) Transport Trails.

Robertson, William G. Back Door to Richmond: The Bermuda Hundred Campaign, April-June 1864. LC 85-41048. (Illus.). 284p. 1991. pap. 9.95 (0-8071-1672-6) La State U Pr.

— Back Door to Richmond: The Bermuda Hundred Campaign, April-June 1864. LC 85-41048. (Illus.). 288p. 1987. 42.50 (0-87413-303-3) U Delaware Pr.

— The Battle of Chickamauga. (Civil War Ser.). (Illus.). 52p. (Orig.). 1995. pap. 3.95 (0-915992-77-9) Eastern Acorn.

— Counterattack on the Naktong 1950. LC 86-2637. (Leavenworth Papers: No. 13). (Illus.). 149p. (Orig.). 1985. pap. 7.00 (0-16-001643-6, S/N 008-020-01079-1) USGPO.

— The Petersburg Campaign the Battle of Old Men & Young Boys June 9, 1864. (Virginia Civil War Battles & Leaders Ser.). (Illus.). 143p. 1989. 19.95 (0-930919-70-X) H E Howard.

Robertson, William J. A Century of French Verse: Brief Biographical & Critical Notices of Thirty-Three French Poets of the Nineteenth Century. LC 77-11481. (Symbolists Ser.). 392p. reprint ed. 52.50 (0-404-16342-4) AMS Pr.

Robertson, William O. Medical Malpractice: A Preventive Approach. LC 84-40322. 212p. 1985. text ed. 20.00 (0-295-96162-7) U of Wash Pr.

Robertson, William O., jt. auth. see Dreisbach, Robert H.

Robertson, William S. Rise of the Spanish American Republics As Told in the Lives of Their Liberators. 1976. lib. bdg. 59.95 (0-8490-2527-3) Gordon Pr.

Robertson, William S., ed. see De Miranda, Francisco.

***Robertson, Willie.** Calum's Way of It. 144p. (C). 1994. pap. 32.00x (1-874640-75-0, Pub. by Argyll Pubng UK) St Mut.

Robertson, Wilmot. The Dispossessed Majority. rev. ed. LC 71-167649. 364p. 1981. 25.00 (0-914576-15-1); pap. 10.00 (0-914576-16-X); Condensed popular edition. pap. 3.95 (0-914576-18-6) Howard Allen.

— The Ethnostate. 233p. (Orig.). 1993. pap. 12.00 (0-914576-22-4) Howard Allen.

— Ventilations. rev. ed. LC 74-20120. 115p. 1982. pap. 4.95 (0-914576-06-2) Howard Allen.

Robertson, Wilmot, ed. Best of Instauration 1976. 117p. 1980. pap. 10.00 (0-914576-11-9) Howard Allen.

— Best of Instauration 1977. 127p. 1982. pap. 10.00 (0-914576-19-4) Howard Allen.

— Best of Instauration 1978. 119p. 1986. pap. 12.00 (0-914576-20-8) Howard Allen.

Robertson, Wyndam. Pocahontas, Alias Matoaka & Her Descendants: Through Her Marriage at Jamestown, Virginia, in April, 1614, with John Rolfe, Gentleman. 84p. 1993. reprint ed. 10.00 (0-8063-0299-2, 4980) Genealog Pub.

Robertus, Polly. The Dog Who Had Kittens. LC 90-39174. (Illus.). 32p. (J). (ps-3). 1991. lib. bdg. 15.95 (0-8234-0860-4); pap. 5.95 (0-8234-0974-0) Holiday.

***Robertus, Polly M.** The Dog Who Had Kittens. (Illus.). (J). (gr. k-3). 1992. audio, pap. 14.95 (0-87499-284-2) Live Oak Media.

— The Dog Who Had Kittens. (Illus.). (J). (gr. k-3). 1992. audio 22.95 (0-87499-285-0) Live Oak Media.

— The Dog Who Had Kittens, 4 bks., Set. (Illus.). (J). (gr. k-3). 1992. audio, pap. 33.95 (0-614-06493-7) Live Oak Media.

***Roberty, Marc.** Complete Guide to the Music of Eric Clapton. (Illus.). 150p. (Orig.). 1995. pap. 7.95 (0-7119-4305-2, OP 47739, Pub. by Omnibus Press UK) Omnibus NY.

— Eric Clapton. (CD Bks.). (Illus.). 120p. 1994. pap. 7.99 (1-886894-12-4, MBS Paperbk) Mus Bk Servs.

— Eric Clapton: The Complete Recording Sessions, 1963-1992. (Illus.). 192p. 1993. 29.95 (0-312-09798-0) St Martin.

— Eric Clapton: The New Visual Documentary. (Illus.). 112p. 1990. pap. 24.95 (0-7119-2223-3, OP43579) Omnibus NY.

— Eric Clapton in His Own Words. Date not set. pap. 15.95 (0-7119-3215-8) Omnibus NY.

— Eric Clapton Scrapbook. (Illus.). 160p. 1993. pap. 16.95 (0-8065-1454-X, Citadel Pr) Carol Pub Group.

— Slowhand: The Life & Music of Eric Clapton. 1993. 19.00 (0-517-88118-7, Crown) Crown Pub Group.

Roberty, Mark. The Eric Clapton Album: Thirty Years of Music & Memorabilia. 192p. 1994. 29.95 (0-670-85364-X) Studio Bks.

— Slowhand: The Life & Music of Eric Clapton. 1991. 30.00 (0-517-58351-8, Harmony) Crown Pub Group.

Robeson, Eslanda. African Journey. LC 73-164468. (Illus.). 154p. 1972. reprint ed. text ed. 35.00 (0-8371-6222-X, ROAJ, Greenwood Pr) Greenwood.

Robeson, James F. & House, Robert G., eds. The Distribution Handbook. LC 83-49340. 978p. (C). 1984. 95.00 (0-02-922700-3) Free Pr.

Robeson, James F., jt. ed. see Copacino, William C.

Robeson, Kenneth. The Forgotten Realm. 1993. mass mkt. 4.99 (0-553-29555-1, Spectra) Bantam.

Robeson, Paul. Here I Stand. LC 87-47882. 144p. 1988. pap. 11.00 (0-8070-6445-9) Beacon Pr.

Robeson, Paul, Jr. Paul Robeson Jr. Speaks to America. LC 92-36164. 225p. (C). 1993. 17.95 (0-8135-1985-3) Rutgers U Pr.

Robeson, Susan. The Whole World in His Hands: A Pictoral Biography of Paul Robeson. (Illus.). 256p. 1981. 17.95 (0-8065-0754-3, Citadel Pr) Carol Pub Group.

— The Whole World in His Hands: A Pictorial Biography of Paul Robeson. (Illus.). 256p. 1985. reprint ed. pap. 14.95 (0-8065-0977-5, Citadel Pr) Carol Pub Group.

Robey, Cora, et al. The New Handbook of Basic Writing Skills. 3rd ed. 470p. (C). 1992. pap. text ed. 16.00 (0-15-565730-5); 13.50 (0-15-565731-3) HB Coll Pubs.

Robey, Cora L., et al. New Workbook of Basic Writings Skills. 2nd ed. 320p. (C). 1984. write for info. (0-318-57829-8) HB Coll Pubs.

***Robey, Daniel.** Designing Organizations. (C). 1981. 62.95 (0-256-02513-4) Irwin.

— Designing Organizations. 3rd ed. 608p. (C). 1990. text ed. 60.95 (0-256-06999-9, 08-1397-03) Irwin.

— Designing Organizations: A Macro Perspective. 3rd ed. (C). 1990. 46.50 (0-685-38299-0) Irwin.

Robey, David & Sales, Carol A. Designing Organizations. 4th ed. LC 93-3727. 560p. (C). 1994. text ed. 65.95 (0-256-11699-7) Irwin.

Robey, David H. Two for Missions: Courageous Stories Come to Life Through Readers Theater. 1987. 8.50 (0-8341-9175-X, MP-640) Lillenas.

Robey, Jim. Ohio Fishing Guide. (Illus.). 164p. (Orig.). 1991. pap. 5.50 (0-9616347-1-5) Dayton Newspapers.

Robey, John S., ed. The Analysis of Public Policy: A Bibliography of Dissertations, 1977-1982. LC 83-22556. x, 225p. 1984. text ed. 47.95 (0-313-23957-6, RPU/, Greenwood Pr) Greenwood.

Robey, Melvin J. African Violets: Gifts from Nature. LC 84-45563. (Illus.). 320p. 1988. 45.00 (0-8453-4766-7, Cornwall Bks) Assoc Univ Prs.

Robey, Randall R. & Schultz, Martin C. Optimizing Theory & Experiments. LC 92-25260. (Illus.). (Orig.). (C). 1993. pap. text ed. 32.50x (1-56593-078-9) Singular Publishing.

Robey, Richard C., ed. Research Library of Colonial Americana, 54 bks. 1972. 2,012.00 (0-405-03270-6) Ayer.

Robey, Tom. Gringo's Guide to Mexican Whitewater. 1992. pap. 9.95 (0-910467-10-2) Heritage Assocs.

***Robey, William Grafton, Jr.** Robey, Roby, Robie; The Family History from Early England to America. 1078p. (Orig.). 1994. pap. text ed. 80.00 (0-7884-0032-0) Heritage Bk.

Robi, James M., jt. ed. see Monastersky, Glenn M.

Robichau. Vegetation of New Jersey. 1985. pap. 15.00 (0-8135-1020-1) Rutgers U Pr.

***Robichaud, Beryl & Buell, Murray F.** Vegetation of New Jersey: A Study of Landscape Diversity. LC 72-4205. (Illus.). 352p. Date not set. reprint ed. pap. 100.40 (0-7837-9210-7, 2049960) Bks Demand.

Robichaud, Beryl, et al. Data Processing Work Kit. 2nd ed. 96p. (gr. 9-12). 1983. text ed. 13.56 (0-07-053207-9) McGraw.

— Introduction to Data Processing. 3rd ed. Orig. Title: Understanding Modern Business Data Processing. 368p. (gr. 9-12). 1983. text ed. 21.12 (0-07-053194-3) McGraw.

***Robichaud, Heidi.** Alaska over the Rainbow: A Colorable Journey Thru the North, Saddlestitch. (Illus.). 40p. 1994. 7.95 (0-9644019-0-8) Goode River.

Robichaud, Raymond, tr. see Hubbard, R. H.

***Robichaux, Harry D.** Mirrored Images. 325p. 1996. pap. 9.95 (0-7610-0524-2) NW Pub.

Robichaux, John W., ed. see Hensche, Henry.

Robicheaux, Jack & Jons, John A. Basic Narcotic Detection Dog Training. (Illus.). 52p. (Orig.). 1990. pap. text ed. write for info. (0-9623099-1-5) J Jons LA.

Robichek, A. Alexander, ed. Financial Research & Management Decisions. LC 67-22552. 248p. reprint ed. pap. 70.70 (0-8357-9890-9, 2014846) Bks Demand.

Robichez, ed. see Verlaine, Paul.

Robicsek, Francis. Extracranial Cerebrovascular Disease: Diagnosis & Management. 1988. text ed. 105.00 (0-07-105306-9) McGraw.

***Robideau, Henri.** Flapjacks & Photographs: A History of Mattie Gunterman, Camp Cook & Photographer. (Illus.). 224p. (Orig.). 1995. pap. 19.95 (1-896095-03-8) Orca Bk Pubs.

Robie, David. Blood on Their Banner: Nationalist Struggles in the South Pacific. LC 89-28954. (Illus.). 304p. (C). 1989. text ed. 49.95 (0-86232-864-0, Pub. by Zed Books UK); pap. 17.50 (0-86232-865-9, Pub. by Zed Books UK) Humanities.

Robie, Diane C. Searching in Florida: A Reference Guide to Public & Private Records. (ISC State Search Bks.: No. 2). (Orig.). 1982. 10.95 (0-942916-01-8) ISC Pubns.

Robie, Joan H. Devotion in Motion. 160p. 1981. pap. 5.95 (0-914984-00-4) Starburst.

— Reverse the Curse in Your Life. 176p. 1991. pap. 7.95 (0-914984-24-1) Starburst.

— Teenage Mutant Ninja Turtles Exposed. 80p. (J). 1991. pap. 5.95 (0-914984-31-4) Starburst.

— The Truth about Dungeons & Dragons. 1992. audio 7.95 (0-914984-25-X) Starburst.

— The Truth about Dungeons & Dragons. 80p. 1992. pap. 5.95 (0-914984-37-3) Starburst.

— Turmoil in the Toy Box II. 1989. audio 7.95 (0-914984-26-8) Starburst.

— Turmoil in the Toy Box II. 224p. 1989. pap. 9.95 (0-914984-20-9) Starburst.

Robie, William. For the Greatest Achievement: A History of the Aero Club of America & the National Aeronautic Association. LC 92-31823. (Illus.). 416p. 1993. 35.00 (1-56098-187-3) Smithsonian.

Robiette, A. G. Electric Smelting Processes. (Illus.). 276p. 1973. text ed. 50.00 (0-85264-096-X, Pub. by H & S UK) Lubrecht & Cramer.

Robilio, Victor. Redneck Guide to Wine Snobbery. 1993. pap. 8.95 (1-55793-015-5) Guild Bindery Pr.

Robillard, Albert B., ed. Social Change in the Pacific Islands. 320p. (C). 1990. text ed. 74.00 (0-7103-0400-5, A5632, Pub. by Kegan Paul Intl UK) Routledge Chapman & Hall.

Robillard, Albert B. & Marsella, Anthony J., eds. Contemporary Issues in Mental Health Research in the Pacific. 300p. 1987. pap. text ed. 12.50 (0-8248-1105-4) UH Pr.

Robillard, David A. Public Space Design in Museums. (Publications in Architecture & Urban Planning: No. R84-7). (Illus.). iv, 73p. 1984. 12.50 (0-938744-36-4) U of Wis Ctr Arch-Urban.

Robillard, Doug, ed. see Cooper, James Fennimore.

Robillard, Douglas, ed. see London, Jack & Strunski, Anna.

Robillard, Douglas, ed. see Melville, Herman.

Robillard, Edmond. Reincarnation: Illusion or Reality. Whitehead, K. D., tr. LC 82-1638. 190p. (Orig.). 1982. pap. 9.95 (0-8189-0432-1) Alba.

Robillard, Jane A., jt. ed. see Rice, Patricia O.

Robillard, Jean & Caulfield, H. John, eds. Industrial Applications of Holography. (Illus.). 224p. 1990. 45.00 (0-19-505855-0) OUP.

Robillard, Mark J. Microprocessor Based Robotics. 220p. (Orig.). 1983. pap. 18.95 (0-317-39379-0) Robot Inst Am.

***Robillard, Walter G. & Bouman, Lane J.** Clark on Surveying & Boundaries. suppl. ed. 1148p. 1993. 80.00 (1-55834-022-X) Michie Butterworth.

— Clark on Surveying & Boundaries. 5th suppl. ed. 966p. 1991. Incl. 1991 cummulative supplement. 65.00 (0-87473-296-4) Michie Butterworth.

Robillard, Walter G. & Hemansen, Knud E. Handbook of Annotated Forms for the Surveying Practice. 150p. 1993. reprint ed. ring bd. 84.95 (0-471-55311-5) Wiley.

Robiller, Franz. Birds Throughout the World. 262p. 1980. 60.00 (0-905418-39-5, Pub. by Gresham Bks UK) St Mut.

Robilliard, David & Zalopany, Michele. Baby Lies Truthfully. Igliori, Paola, ed. (Illus.). 150p. 1990. pap. 15.00 (0-9625119-5-1) Inanout Pr.

Robilotta, Peter, jt. auth. see Bird, Stewart.

Robilotta, Peter T., jt. auth. see Bird, Stewart.

Robin. Farewell to Innocence. 470p. 1989. 49.00 (0-935016-73-2, Assoc Sci Pubs) Excelsior Music Pub Co.

— Illustrated Handbook of Drug Abuse Recognition & Diagnosis. (Illus.). 208p. 1988. pap. 33.95 (0-8151-5871-8, Yr Bk Med Pubs) Mosby Yr Bk.

— Lasers in Ophthalmology. 1991. 75.00 (0-8151-7311-3, Yr Bk Med Pubs) Mosby Yr Bk.

Robin, ed. Aetiology - Idiopathic Scoliosis. 1990. 78.95 (0-8493-6722-0, R) CRC Pr.

Robin, jt. auth. see Simes.

***Robin, et al.** Disorders of Motor Speech: Recent Advances in Assessment, Treatment, & Clinical Characterization. 448p. 1995. boxed 45.00 (1-55766-223-1) P H Brookes.

Robin, Abbe. New Travels Through North America. Decker, Peter, ed. Freneau, Philip, tr. LC 73-77110. (Eyewitness Accounts of the American Revolution Ser., No. 1). 1969. reprint ed. 16.95 (0-405-01176-8) Ayer.

Robin, Anand, ed. see Osho.

Robin, Anand, ed. see Rajneesh, Osho.

Robin, Arthur L. & Foster, Sharon L. Negotiating Parent-Adolescent Conflict: A Behavioral-Family Systems Approach. LC 87-31502. (Guilford Family Therapy Ser.). 338p. 1989. lib. bdg. 37.95 (0-89862-072-4) Guilford Pr.

Robin, C. C. Voyage to Louisiana: 1803-1805. 1966. reprint ed. 27.95 (0-911116-20-6) Pelican.

Robin, Christopher. How to Build Your Own Stereo Speakers: Construction, Applications, Circuits & Characteristics. (Illus.). 1978. 28.95 (0-87909-374-9, Reston) P-H.

Robin, Diana. Filelfo in Milan: Writings 1451-1477. (Illus.). 397p. 1991. text ed. 45.00 (0-691-03185-1) Princeton U Pr.

Robin, Donald P., jt. auth. see Reidenbach, R. Eric.

Robin, Doris, et al. In a Faraway Galaxy: A Literary Approach to a Film Saga. (Illus.). 149p. (Orig.). 1984. pap. 6.95 (0-935892-07-9) Exequer.

Robin, Eddie. Position Play in Three Cushion Billiards. (Three Cushion Billiards Ser.: Vol. III). (Illus.). 431p. 1983. 36.00 (0-686-43838-8) Billiard Wld.

— Position Play in Three-Cushion Billiards. Arreola, Danielle et al, trs. (Three-Cushion Billiards Ser.). (Illus.). 341p. 1980. text ed. 36.00 (0-936362-00-6) Billiard Wld.

— Position Play in Three Cushion Billiards, Vol. III. rev. ed. Haake, James W. & Fels, George, eds. (Three Cushion Billiards Ser.). (Illus.). 352p. (DUT, ENG, FRE & GER.). 1994. 36.00 (0-936362-01-4); text ed. 36.00 (0-936362-02-2) Billiard Wld.

Robin, Eddie, illus. & pref. Winning Nine Ball: As Taught by the Game's Greatest Players. (Pocket Billiards Ser.). 318p. Date not set. text ed. 36.00 (0-936362-06-5) Billiard Wld.

Robin, Eddie, illus. & intro. Winning Straight Pool: As Taught by the Game's Greatest Players. (Pocket Billiards Ser.). 318p. 1994. text ed. 36.00 (0-936362-07-3) Billiard Wld.

R

Robin, Eddie, pref. One-Pocket Shots, Moves & Strategies: As Taught by the Game's Greatest Players. (Pocket Billiards Ser.). (Illus.). 318p. 1993. text ed. 36.00 (0-936362-04-9) Billiard Wld.

Robin, Eddie, et al. Winning One-Pocket: As Taught by the Game's Greatest Players. Haake, James W. & Fels, George, eds. (Illus.). 318p. 1993. lib. bdg. 36.00 (0-936362-03-0) Billiard Wld.

Robin, Eugene D., ed. Claude Bernard & the Internal Environment: A Memorial Symposium. LC 79-23206. (Illus.). 319p. reprint ed. pap. 91.00 (0-8357-6056-1, 2034563) Bks Demand.

— Extrapulmonary Manifestations of Respiratory Disease. LC 78-1279. (Lung Biology in Health & Disease Ser.: No. 8). (Illus.). 536p. reprint ed. pap. 152.80 (0-7837-0733-9, 2041057) Bks Demand.

Robin, G. C. Scoliosis & Neurological Disease. 200p. 1975. text ed. 48.00 (0-7065-1522-6, Pub. by Keter Pub IS) Coronet Bks.

Robin, Gerald D. Violent Crime & Gun Control. LC 91-70555. (ACJS-Anderson Monograph Ser.). 98p. (C). 1991. pap. text ed. 12.95 (0-87084-747-3) Anderson Pub Co.

— Waging the Battle Against Drunk Driving: Issues, Countermeasures, & Effectiveness. LC 91-8235. (Contributions in Criminology & Penology Ser.: No. 32). 160p. 1991. text ed. 49.95 (0-313-27856-3, RWB, Greenwood Pr); pap. text ed. 14.95 (0-275-94040-3, B4040, Praeger Pubs) Greenwood.

Robin, Gerald D. & Anson, Richard H. Introduction to the Criminal Justice System. 4th ed. 656p. (C). 1990. text ed. 60.00 (0-06-045516-0) HarpCollege.

Robin, Gordon C., ed. see Muscular Dystrophy Symposium Staff.

Robin, Hardy. Call of the Wendigo. (YA). 1994. pap. 3.50 (0-553-29828-3) Bantam.

***Robin, Harry.** I, Morgain: A Novella. Caso, Adolfo, ed. LC 94-42544. 192p. 1995. 17.95 (0-8283-2004-7) Branden Pub Co.

— Scientific Image: From Cave to Computer. LC 93-48053. 1995. pap. text ed. write for info. (0-7167-2504-5) W H Freeman.

Robin, J. B., jt. ed. see Schanzlin, D. J.

Robin, Jean. Elmdon: Continuity & Change in a North-West Essex Village, 1861-1964. LC 79-12964. 294p. reprint ed. pap. 83.80 (0-318-34664-8, 2031720) Bks Demand.

Robin, Jeff. The Second Good News - Bad News Joke Book. 176p. (Orig.). 1994. pap. 3.99 (0-451-17986-2, Sig) NAL-Dutton.

Robin, Jeffrey. Mental Health Care & Substance Abuse: A Review of Evidence on Insurance Coverage & Utilization. (Illus.). 69p. (Orig.). (C). 1992. pap. text ed. 34.95 (1-56806-131-5) Diane Pub.

Robin, Jennifer. Clothe Your Spirit: Dressing for Self-Expression. LC 87-23494. (Illus.). 176p. (Orig.). 1988. pap. 15.95 (0-944296-03-3) Spirit Pr.

Robin, Joanna, tr. see Glad, John, ed.

Robin, Lee, jt. auth. see Styne, Jule.

Robin, Leon. Aristotle. Mayer, J. P., ed. LC 78-67380. (European Political Thought Ser.). (FRE.). 1980. reprint ed. lib. bdg. 25.95 (0-405-11730-2) Ayer.

— La Theorie Platonicienne Des Idees et Des Nombres d'Apres Aristote. xvii, 702p. 1984. reprint ed. write for info. (3-487-00344-9, Pub. by Georg Olms GW) Lubrecht & Cramer.

Robin, M. Canadian Provincial Politics. 2nd ed. 1978. pap. write for info. (0-13-113233-4) P-H.

Robin, Marc, jt. auth. see Barrie, James M.

***Robin, Marc R.** Handbook of Sexually Transmitted Diseases: A Clinical Approach. LC 94-78412. (Illus.). 240p. 1995. pap. text ed. 34.95 (0-929894-15-4) K-W Pubns.

Robin, Marc R. & Dessery, Bradford L. The Medical Guide for Third World Travelers: A Comprehensive Self-Care Handbook. (Illus.). 360p. (Orig.). 1990. pap. 16.95 (0-929894-05-7) K-W Pubns.

— The Medical Guide for Third World Travelers: A Comprehensive Self-Care Handbook. 2nd ed. LC 92-73362. (Illus.). 340p. (Orig.). 1992. pap. 14.95 (0-929894-06-5) K-W Pubns.

Robin, Marcy, jt. auth. see Resch, Kathleen.

Robin, Martin. Shades of Right: Nativist & Fascist Politics in Canada, 1920-1940. (Illus.). 384p. (Orig.). 1992. 60.00 (0-8020-5962-7); pap. 16.95 (0-8020-6892-8) U of Toronto Pr.

Robin, Michael, ed. Assessing Child Maltreatment Reports: The Problem of False Allegations. LC 91-20799. (Child & Youth Services Ser.). (Illus.). 297p. 1991. lib. bdg. 39.95 (0-86656-931-6); pap. text ed. 19.95 (1-56024-161-6) Haworth Pr.

Robin, Mickey, ed. see Zidonis, Nancy A. & Sooerberg, Marie K.

***Robin, Mitchell W. & Balter, Rochelle.** Performance Anxiety. 1994. pap. 12.00 (1-55850-441-9) Adams Pubng.

***Robin, Peggy.** Bottle Feeding Without Guilt: A Reassuring Guide for Loving Parents. LC 95-885. 1995. write for info. (0-7615-0001-4) Prima Pub.

— How to Be a Successful Fertility Patient: Your Guide to Getting the Best Possible Medical Help to Have a Baby. LC 92-41043. 1993. 15.00 (0-688-11732-5, Quill) Morrow.

— Saving the Neighborhood: You Can Fight Developers & Win! (Illus.). 428p. (Orig.). 1993. pap. 16.95 (0-89133-205-7) Preservation Pr.

Robin, Peggy, jt. auth. see Adler, Bill, Jr.

Robin, Regine. Socialist Realism: An Impossible Aesthetic. Porter, Catherine, tr. 376p. 1992. 45.00 (0-8047-1655-2) Stanford U Pr.

Robin, Richard. Russian Listening Comprehension I, Pt. A: News & Public Affairs. (Illus.). 315p. (RUS.). 1991. Incl. audiotape. teacher ed, audio 19.00 (0-87415-175-9, 71) OSU Foreign Lang.

— Russian Listening Comprehension II, Part A, Units 45-49 Scripts. (OSU Foreign Language Publications: No. 73D). 86p. (Orig.). (RUS.). (C). 1994. pap. text ed. 5.00 (0-87415-275-5) OSU Foreign Lang.

Robin, Richard & Lekic, Maria. Russian Listening Comprehension I & II: Sample Packet, No. 89. (Illus.). 54p. (Orig.). (RUS.). (C). 1993. audio 17.00 (0-87415-174-0) OSU Foreign Lang.

Robin, Richard M., tr. see Glad, John, ed.

Robin, Richard M., et al. Golosa: A Beginning Russian Course, Books 1 & 2. LC 93-22993. (ENG & RUS.). 1993. text ed. write for info. (0-13-257429-2) P-H.

Robin, Richard S., jt. ed. see Moore, Edward C.

Robin, Robert. Above the Law. 1992. 20.00 (0-671-74425-9) PB.

— Above the Law. Rosenman, Jane, ed. 384p. 1993. reprint ed. mass mkt. 5.50 (0-671-74424-0, Pocket Star Bks) PB.

Robin, Ron. Enclaves of America: The Rhetoric of American Political Architecture Abroad, 1900-1965. LC 92-8520. (Illus.). 201p. 1992. text ed. 29.95 (0-691-04805-3) Princeton U Pr.

— Signs of Change: Urban Iconographies in San Francisco, 1880-1915. LC 90-3506. (European Immigrants & American Society Ser.). 184p. 1990. reprint ed. 15.00 (0-8240-0317-9) Garland.

Robin, Stanley & Wagenfeld, Morton, eds. Paraprofessionals in the Human Services. LC 80-18011. (Community Psychology Ser.: Vol. VI). 368p. 1981. 45.95 (0-87705-490-8) Human Sci Pr.

Robin, Stanley S., jt. ed. see Bosco, James J.

Robin, Swami A., ed. see Osho.

Robin, Thomas J., ed. see Bennett, A. E. & Siy, Louis J.

Robin, Vicki, jt. auth. see Dominguez, Joe.

Robine, J., et al, eds. Health Expectancy Studies on Medical & Population Subjects, No. 54. 187p. 1992. pap. 35.00 (0-11-691436-X, HM1436X, Pub. by HMSO UK) UNIPUB.

Robine, Maurice, tr. see Flato, Moshe.

Robineault, Manfred J. Communicable Diseases: Medical Subject Analysis & Research Bibliography. LC 84-45644. 150p. 1985. 44.50 (0-88164-194-4); pap. 39.50 (0-88164-195-2) ABBE Pubs Assn.

— Psychology & Health: Index of Modern Information with Bibliography. LC 89-78054. 150p. 1990. 44.50 (1-55914-228-6); pap. 39.50 (1-55914-229-4) ABBE Pubs Assn.

Robinet, Andre, jt. auth. see Descartes, Rene.

Robinet, Andre, ed. see Rousseau, Jean-Jacques.

Robinet, B., ed. International Symposium on Programming. (Lecture Notes in Computer Science Ser.: Vol. 83). 341p. 1980. pap. 27.00 (0-387-09981-6) Spr-Verlag.

Robinet, B. & Wilhelm, R., eds. ESOP '86. (Lecture Notes in Computer Science Ser.: Vol. 213). vi, 374p. 1986. pap. 42.00 (0-387-16442-1) Spr-Verlag.

Robinet, B., jt. ed. see Paul, M.

Robinet, Harriette G. Children of the Fire. LC 91-9484. 144p. (J). (gr. 3-7). 1991. text ed. 13.95 (0-689-31655-0, Atheneum Bks Young) S&S Childrens.

— If You Please, President Lincoln! (J). (gr. 3-7). 1995. 15.00 (0-689-31969-X, Atheneum Bks Young) S&S Childrens.

— Mississippi Chariot. LC 94-11092. (J). (gr. 4 up). 1994. text ed. 14.95 (0-689-31960-6, Atheneum S&S) S&S Trade.

Robinet, Isabelle. Taoist Meditation: The Mao-shan Tradition of Great Purity. Pas, Julian F. & Girardot, Norman J., trs. LC 92-23086. (SUNY Series in Chinese Philosophy & Culture). (Illus.). 285p. (C). 1993. 59.50 (0-7914-1359-4); pap. 19.95 (0-7914-1360-8) State U NY Pr.

Robinet, J. F., et al. Dictionnaire Historique et Biographique de la Revolution et de l'Empire: 1789-1815, 2 vols. 1899. 220.00 (0-318-23476-9) Periodicals Srv.

Robinet, Jean F. Le Mouvement Religieux a Paris Pendant la Revolution: 1789-1801, 2 vols. reprint ed. write for info. (0-318-50670-X) AMS Pr.

— Le Mouvement Religieux a Paris Pendant la Revolution: 1789-1801, 2 vols., 1. LC 70-174331. (Collection de documents relatifs a l'histoire de Paris pendant la Revolution francaise). reprint ed. 96.50 (0-404-52568-7) AMS Pr.

— Le Mouvement Religieux a Paris Pendant la Revolution: 1789-1801, 2 vols., 2. LC 70-174331. (Collection de documents relatifs a l'histoire de Paris pendant la Revolution francaise). reprint ed. 96.50 (0-404-52569-5) AMS Pr.

— Le Mouvement Religieux a Paris Pendant la Revolution: 1789-1801, 2 vols., Set. LC 70-174331. (Collection de documents relatifs a l'histoire de Paris pendant la Revolution francaise). reprint ed. 193.00 (0-404-52567-9) AMS Pr.

Robinett, Betty W. Teaching English to Speakers of Other Languages: Substance & Technique. LC 78-11448. 335p. reprint ed. pap. 95.50 (0-8357-3334-3, 2039559) Bks Demand.

Robinett, Betty W. & Schachter, Jacqueline. Second Language Learning: Contrastive Analysis, Error Analysis & Related Aspects. 432p. 1983. pap. text ed. 18.95 (0-472-08033-4) U of Mich Pr.

Robinett, Betty W., jt. auth. see Prator, Clifford H., Jr.

Robinett, Jane. This Rough Magic Vol. 13: Technology in Latin American Fiction. LC 92-17509. (Worcester Polytechnic Institute Studies in Science, Technology & Culture: Vol. 13). 284p. (C). 1994. text ed. 53.95 (0-8204-1889-7) P Lang Pubs.

Robinett, Jane & Barquin, Ramon, eds. Computers & Ethics: A Sourcebook for Discussions. 46p. (Orig.). (C). 1989. pap. text ed. write for info. (0-918902-25-8) Polytechnic Pr.

Robinett, Joseph & Chauls, Robert. Trail of Goldilocks - Musical. 40p. (Orig.). 1991. pap. 4.95 (0-87129-030-8, T08) Dramatic Pub.

Robinett, Stephen. Final Option. 256p. 1990. pap. 3.50 (0-380-75848-2) Avon.

— Unfinished Business. 1990. pap. 3.50 (0-380-75849-0) Avon.

Robinette, Danny R. & Scrivner, Louise M. Guide to Oral Interpretation: Solo & Group Performance. 2nd ed. 1980. pap. write for info. (0-318-51113-4) Macmillan.

Robinette, Diane, jt. auth. see Taraschi, Rosaria.

Robinette, Gary O. Local Landscape Ordinances. (Community Landscape Development Ser.). 348p. 1992. pap. text ed. 24.95 (1-882240-00-6) Agora Comms.

— Parking Lot Landscape Development. 2nd ed. (Community Landscape Development Ser.). (Illus.). 200p. 1994. pap. text ed. 29.95 (1-882240-01-4) Agora Comms.

Robinette, Gary O., ed. see Lofgren, David E.

Robinette, Hillary M. Burnout in Blue: Managing the Police Marginal Performer. LC 87-14581. 173p. 1987. text ed. 55.00 (0-275-92687-7, C2687, Praeger Pubs); pap. text ed. 22.95 (0-275-92688-5, B2688, Praeger Pubs) Greenwood.

Robinette, Joseph. ABC (America Before Columbus) 40p. (J). (gr. k-8). 1984. pap. 4.00 (0-88680-212-1) I E Clark.

— Ashes, Ashes, All Fall Down. 1982. 4.95 (0-87129-251-3, A29) Dramatic Pub.

— Beanstalk! (Illus.). 44p. (Orig.). (J). (gr. 2 up). 1985. pap. 4.00 (0-88680-236-9); 10.00 (0-88680-237-7) I E Clark.

— Dorothy Meets Alice: Wizard of Wonderland. 1991. pap. 4.25 (0-87129-079-0, D51) Dramatic Pub.

— The Fabulous Fable Factory: Musical. 1975. 4.95 (0-87129-348-X, F01) Dramatic Pub.

— Get Bill Shakespeare Off the Stage! 1981. 4.95 (0-87129-309-9, G36) Dramatic Pub.

— Once upon a Shoe - Str. 1979. write for info. (0-87129-491-5, O29) Dramatic Pub.

— Once upon a Shoe or The Rhymes & Mimes of Mother Goose & Her Traveling Troubadours: The Musical. 1988. 3.45 (0-87129-322-6, O04) Dramatic Pub.

— Phantom of the Opera: Musical. (Orig.). 1992. pap. 5.45 (0-87129-173-8, P08) Dramatic Pub.

— Stuart Little. 52p. 1991. pap. 4.95 (0-87129-155-X, S99) Dramatic Pub.

— Trail of Goldilocks - Straight. 34p. (Orig.). 1991. pap. 4.95 (0-87129-003-0, T81) Dramatic Pub.

— The Trumpet of the Swan: Musical. 1992. pap. 4.95 (0-87129-206-8, T85) Dramatic Pub.

***Robinette, Joseph, adapt.** The Adventures of Beatrix Potter & Her Friends - Musical. Date not set. 5.50 (0-87129-523-7, A56) Dramatic Pub.

Robinette, Joseph & Shaw, James R. Penny & the Magic Medallion. (Illus.). 44p. (Orig.). (J). (gr. k up). 1987. pap. 4.00 (0-88680-283-0); 12.50 (0-88680-284-9) I E Clark.

Robinette, Joseph, ed. see Lewis, C. S.

Robinette, Joseph, jt. auth. see Osborn, John J., Jr.

Robinette, Joseph, jt. auth. see White, E. B.

Robinette, Richard & Pasqua, Thomas M. Historical Perspectives in Popular Music: A Historical Outline. 3rd ed. 544p. (Orig.). 1992. per. 35.95 (0-8403-6436-9) Kendall-Hunt.

Robinowitz, C., jt. ed. see Spurlock, J.

Robinowitz, Carolyn B., jt. ed. see Nadelson, Carol C.

Robinowitz, Carolyn B., jt. auth. see Talbott, John A.

Robinowitz, Carolyn B., et al, eds. Directory of Psychiatry Residency Training Programs. 3rd ed. 647p. reprint ed. pap. 180.00 (0-8357-3038-7, 2039287) Bks Demand.

Robins, Adrienne. The Analytical Writer: A College Rhetoric. 600p. (C). 1989. pap. text ed. 30.75 (0-939693-09-7) Collegiate Pr.

Robins, Adrienne, jt. auth. see Robins, Steven.

Robins, Arthur J. Alcohol Detoxification Manual: A Guide to Administering Comprehensive Services. 120p. 1988. 29.95 (0-89885-402-4) Human Sci Pr.

Robins, Ashley H. Biological Perspectives on Human Pigmentation. (Studies in Biological Anthropology: No. 7). (Illus.). 250p. (C). 1991. 79.95 (0-521-36514-7) Cambridge U Pr.

Robins, C. R., et al. Common & Scientific Names of Fishes from the United States & Canada. 5th ed. LC 90-86052. (Special Publication Ser.: No. 20). 183p. 1991. 32.50 (0-913235-70-9); pap. 24.50 (0-913235-69-5) Am Fisheries Soc.

— World Fishes Important to North Americans Exclusive of Species from the Continental Waters of the United States & Canada. (Special Publication Ser.: No. 21). 243p. 1991. text ed. 38.50 (0-913235-54-7); pap. 30.50 (0-913235-53-9) Am Fisheries Soc.

Robins, C. Richard, jt. auth. see Ray, G. Carleton.

Robins, Corinne. Art in the Seventh Power. (Illus.). 72p. (Orig.). 1984. pap. 5.00 (0-930557-00-X) Pratt Press.

Robins, David. Tarnished Vision: Crime & Community Action in the Inner City. LC 92-22144. 160p. 1993. 35.00 (0-19-825751-1); pap. 12.95 (0-19-825816-X) OUP.

Robins, Denise. Dear Loyalty. 192p. 1993. lib. bdg. 18.00 (0-7278-4488-1) Severn Hse.

— Set Me Free. large type ed. 1993. 17.95 (0-7505-0479-X, Pub. by Magna Print Bks) Ulverscroft.

***Robins, Deri.** Christmas Fun. LC 95-2454. (Illus.). (J). 1995. pap. write for info. (1-85697-567-3) Kingfisher.

— The Great Pirate Activity Book. LC 94-43140. (Illus.). 1995. 5.95 (1-85697-578-9, Kingfisher LKC) LKC.

— The Kids' Around the World Cookbook. LC 93-42504. (Illus.). 40p. (J). (gr. 3-7). 1994. pap. 5.95 (1-85697-997-0, Kingfisher LKC) LKC.

— The Kids' Around the World Cookbook. (Illus.). 40p. (J). (gr. 3-7). 1994. lib. bdg. 12.90 (1-85697-627-0, Kingfisher LKC) LKC.

— Making Prints. LC 92-40216. (Step-by-Step Ser.). 40p. (J). (gr. 3-7). 1993. 10.95 (1-85697-925-3, Kingfisher LKC); pap. 5.95 (1-85697-924-5, Kingfisher LKC) LKC.

— Papier Mache. LC 92-41102. (Step-by-Step Ser.). (Illus.). 40p. (J). (gr. 3-7). 1993. 10.95 (1-85697-927-X, Kingfisher LKC); pap. 5.95 (1-85697-926-1, Kingfisher LKC) LKC.

Robins, Deri & Buchanan, George. Santa's Sackful of Best Christmas Ideas. LC 92-41103. 32p. (J). (gr. 2-6). 1993. pap. 5.95 (1-85697-919-9, Kingfisher LKC) LKC.

Robins, Deri & Stowell, Charlotte. Making Books. LC 93-48560. (J). 1994. lib. bdg. 10.95 (1-85697-517-7, Kingfisher LKC); pap. 5.95 (1-85697-518-5, Kingfisher LKC) LKC.

Robins, Deri, et al. The Kids Can Do It Book: Fun Things to Make and Do. LC 92-43345. (Illus.). 80p. (J). (gr. k-4). 1993. pap. 9.95 (1-85697-860-5, Kingfisher LKC) LKC.

Robins, Dorothy. Katie's Birthday Wish. LC 88-81467. (Illus.). 32p. (Orig.). (J). (ps-2). 1988. pap. 8.95 (0-937124-18-4) Kimbo Educ.

Robins, E. Ibsen & the Actress. LC 73-10253. (Studies in Drama: No. 39). 1973. reprint ed. lib. bdg. 75.00 (0-8383-1718-9) M S G Haskell Hse.

Robins, Eleanor. Meg Parker, 5 in each set, Sets 1 & 2. (Illus.). (J). (gr. 2-7). 1984. Set. pap. 15.00 (0-685-61074-8); Set 1. write for info. (0-87879-439-5); Set 2. write for info. (0-87879-472-7) High Noon Bks.

Robins, Elizabeth. Ancilla's Share: An Indictment of Sex Antagonism. LC 75-21815. (Pioneers of the Woman's Movement an International Perspective Ser.). 1976. reprint ed. 23.65 (0-88355-272-8) Hyperion Conn.

— The Convert. 320p. 1980. pap. 11.95 (0-912670-83-5) Feminist Pr.

— The Magnetic North. LC 72-96893. reprint ed. lib. bdg. 19.50 (0-8398-1760-6) Irvington.

Robins, Fred C. Overseas Diary: India & Burma, World War Two. LC 90-62686. (Illus.). 244p. 1990. 17.95 (0-9627280-0-4) Rumaro Pr.

Robins, Gay. Egyptian Painting & Relief. (Shire Egyptology Ser.). (Illus.). 62p. 1990. pap. 12.00 (0-85263-789-6, Pub. by Shire Pubns UK) Lubrecht & Cramer.

— Proportion & Style in Ancient Egyptian Art. LC 93-65. (Illus.). 296p. (Orig.). 1994. text ed. 40.00 (0-292-77060-X); pap. 19.95 (0-292-77064-2) U of Tex Pr.

— Reflections of Women in the New Kingdom: Ancient Egyptian Art from the British Museum. (EUMILOP Ser.: No. 7). 24p. 1995. pap. 10.00 (0-9638169-6-9) M C Carlos Mus.

— Rhind Mathematical Papyrus: An Ancient Egyptian Text. 1990. pap. 8.95 (0-486-26407-6) Dover.

— Women in Ancient Egypt. 205p. 1993. pap. text ed. 18.95 (0-674-95469-6) HUP.

— Women in Ancient Egypt. LC 92-38221. 205p. 1993. reprint ed. pap. 18.95 (0-674-95468-8) HUP.

***Robins, Gay, ed.** Beyond the Pyramids: Egyptian Regional Art from the Museo Egizio, Turin. (EUMILOP Ser.: No. 4). (Illus.). 95p. 1995. pap. text ed. 24.95 (0-9638169-2-6) M C Carlos Mus.

Robins, Gina. Always & Forever. 448p. 1992. mass mkt. 4.99 (1-55817-647-0, Pinnacle NY) Windsor NY.

— Captive Enchantress. 448p. 1989. pap. 3.95 (0-8217-2678-1) Zebra.

— Deception's Sweet Kiss. 1990. mass mkt. 4.50 (0-8217-2960-8) Zebra.

— Diamond Fire. 496p. 1986. pap. 3.95 (0-8217-1943-2) Zebra.

— Love's Reckless Rebel. 512p. 1988. pap. 3.95 (0-8217-2450-9) Zebra.

— Love's Sweetest Secret. 448p. 1991. mass mkt. 4.50 (0-8217-3335-4) Zebra.

— Mississippi Mistress. 1990. mass mkt. 4.50 (0-8217-3118-1) Zebra.

— Secret Splendor. 512p. 1988. pap. 3.95 (0-8217-2254-9) Zebra.

— Texas Temptation. 1989. pap. 3.95 (0-8217-2782-6) Zebra.

— Whispers of Love. 1991. mass mkt. 4.95 (1-55817-553-9, Pinnacle NY) Windsor NY.

— Wyoming Ecstasy. 1993. mass mkt. 4.50 (1-55817-740-X, Pinnacle NY) Windsor NY.

Robins, Jan. Honey for the Devil. large type ed. (Linford Romance Library). 288p. 1994. pap. 14.95 (0-7089-7547-X, Linford) Ulverscroft.

Robins, Joan. Addie Meets Max. LC 84-48329. (Early I Can Read Bk.). (Illus.). 32p. (J). (ps-3). 1985. lib. bdg. 14.89 (0-06-025064-X) HarpC Child Bks.

— Addie Runs Away. LC 88-24350. (Trophy Early I Can Read Bk.). (Illus.). 32p. (J). (ps-2). 1991. pap. 3.50 (0-06-444147-4, Trophy) HarpC Child Bks.

— Addie's Bad Day. LC 92-13101. (I Can Read Bk.). (Illus.). 32p. (J). (ps-2). 1993. 14.00 (0-06-021297-7); lib. bdg. 14.89 (0-06-021298-5) HarpC Child Bks.

— Addie's Bad Day. LC 92-13101. (Trophy I Can Read Book). (Illus.). (J). (ps-3). 1994. pap. 3.50 (0-06-444183-0, Trophy) HarpC Child Bks.

Robins, Joyce. Natural Wonders of the World. 1992. 16.98 (1-55521-760-5) Bk Sales Inc.

— World's Greatest Disasters. 1990. 14.98 (1-55521-566-1) Bk Sales Inc.

***Robins, Kevin, ed.** Understanding Information: Business, Technology & Geography. LC 09-140511. 1994. text ed. 59.95 (0-471-94763-6) Wiley.

R

An Asterisk (*) at the beginning of an entry indicates that the title is appearing in BIP for the first time.

Robins, Kevin & Webster, Frank. Information Technology: Post-Industrial Society or Capitalist Control? Voigt, Melvin J., ed. LC 85-46065. (Communication & Information Science Ser.). 400p. 1986. text ed. 65.00 (*0-89391-343-X*) Ablex Pub.
— The Technical Fix: Education, Computers & Industry. LC 89-4189. (Illus.). 320p. 1989. text ed. 45.00 (*0-312-03111-4*) St Martin.
Robins, Kevin, jt. auth. see Morley, David.
Robins, Lee N. & Barrett, James E. The Validity of Psychiatric Diagnosis. (American Psychopathological Association Ser.). 349p. 1989. 114.50 (*0-88167-499-0*, 1965) Raven.
Robins, Lee N. & Regier, Darrel A., eds. Psychiatric Disorders in America. 400p. 1990. text ed. 55.00 (*0-02-926571-1*) Free Pr.
Robins, Lee N. & Rutter, Michael, eds. Straight & Devious Pathways from Childhood to Adulthood. (Illus.). 416p. (C). 1990. 79.95 (*0-521-36408-6*) Cambridge U Pr.
— Straight & Devious Pathways from Childhood to Adulthood. (Illus.). 389p. (C). 1992. pap. 24.95 (*0-521-42739-8*) Cambridge U Pr.
Robins, Leonard S., jt. auth. see Litman, Theodor J.
Robins, Lewis, jt. auth. see Sackheim, George I.
Robins, Lynton, jt. ed. see Pyper, Robert.
Robins, Lynton, jt. ed. see Savage, Stephen P.
Robins, Lynton, et al, eds. Britain's Changing Party System. LC 94-13743. 1994. pap. 19.00 (*0-7185-1505-6*, Pub. by Leicester Univ Pr) St Martin.
— Britain's Changing Party System. LC 94-13743. 1994. 49.00 (*0-7185-1494-7*, Pub. by Leicester Univ Pr) St Martin.
Robins, M. O., jt. auth. see Massey, H.
Robins, Madeleine. Heiress Companion. 1989. pap. 2.95 (*0-449-21700-0*) Fawcett.
— The Heiress Companion, No. 155. 224p. 1981. pap. 1.50 (*0-449-50228-7*, Coventry) Fawcett.
— My Dear Jenny. 224p. 1980. pap. 1.75 (*0-449-50041-1*, Coventry) Fawcett.
Robins, Marc. Speech Recognition Reference Manual & Buyer's Guide. 225p. (Orig.). 1991. pap. 85.00 (*0-9624360-5-4*) Robins Pr.
— The Voice Mail Reference Manual & Buyer's Guide. 304p. (Orig.). (C). 1989. pap. 75.00 (*0-9624360-0-3*) Robins Pr.
— A Voice Processing Primer. 200p. (Orig.). 1990. pap. 24.95 (*0-9624360-2-X*) Robins Pr.
— The Voice Response Reference Manual & Buyer's Guide. (Illus.). 292p. (Orig.). (C). 1991. pap. 85.00 (*0-9624360-1-1*) Robins Pr.
Robins, Melinda, ed. see Rhodes, Naomi.
Robins, Michael H. Promising, Intending, & Moral Autonomy. (Studies in Philosophy). 160p. 1984. 64.95 (*0-521-26076-0*) Cambridge U Pr.
Robins, Monty. The Manuscript of Jow Smithwitz. 323p. (C). 1989. text ed. 50.00 (*1-872795-58-7*, Pub. by Pentland Pr UK) St Mut.
Robins-Mowry, Dorothy. What's Wrong with Japan, Anyway? 112p. (Orig.). 1993. pap. text ed. 9.95 (*1-883223-00-8*) Pacific NY.
Robins-Mowry, Dorothy, ed. Canada-U. S. Relations: Perceptions & Misperceptions. 64p. (Orig.). (C). 1988. pap. text ed. 9.00 (*0-8191-6873-4*, Aspen Inst for Humanistic Studies) U Pr of Amer.
— What's Wrong with the U. S. A., Anyway? LC 93-47930. 1994. 9.50 (*1-883223-03-2*) Pacific NY.
Robins, Natalie. Alien Ink: The FBI's War on Freedom of Expression. LC 92-36943. (Illus.). 495p. (C). 1993. reprint ed. pap. 14.95 (*0-8135-1954-3*) Rutgers U Pr.
Robins, Natalie & Aronson, M. L. Savage Grace. 1986. mass mkt. 5.99 (*0-440-17576-3*) Dell.
Robins, Owen H. With Love & Better Health: Onward Christian Soldiers. LC 91-90518. 160p. 1993. 16.95 (*0-9630319-0-2*) Larksdale.
Robins, Patricia. Forbidden. 160p. 1992. reprint ed. 17.95 (*0-7278-4325-7*) Severn Hse.
— Forever. 1991. reprint ed. 18.95 (*0-7278-4243-9*) Severn Hse.
— Forsaken. large type ed. 1994. 22.95 (*0-7089-3192-8*) Ulverscroft.
— Fulfillment. 224p. 1993. lib. bdg. 18.00 (*0-7278-4389-3*) Severn Hse.
— No Stone Unturned. large type ed. 280p. 1989. pap. 12.95 (*0-8161-4438-9*, Large Print Bks) Hall.
— Return to Love. large type ed. 271p. 1994. pap. 16.95 (*1-85389-460-5*, Medcom-Trainex) Ulverscroft.
— Topaz Island. large type ed. (Dales Large Print Ser.). 1994. pap. 16.95 (*1-85389-462-1*, Pub. by Magna Print Bks) Ulverscroft.
Robins, Perry. Play It Safe in the Sun. (Illus.). 40p. (J). 1994. pap. 9.95 (*0-9627688-1-2*) Skin Cancer Fndtn.

—Sun Sense: A Complete Guide to the Prevention, Early Detection, & Treatment of Skin Cancer. (Illus.). 272p. 1990. 19.95 (*0-685-54251-3*); pap. 14.95 (*0-9627688-0-4*) Skin Cancer Fndtn.
SUN SENSE is for everyone who is concerned about skin health, sun protection, & skin cancer prevention. In a highly readable style, Dr. Robins reveals the devastating effects of the sun on the skin, including premature aging & of course, skin cancer. This complete guide includes color photographs & descriptions to aid in early detection of tumors & precancerous growths, & detailed information on such subjects as the most common types of skin cancer, skin cancer causes & risk factors, sunscreens & sun susceptibility, protecting children & teenagers, selecting sunglasses, the perils of tanning parlors, ozone depletion & what it means for the future, self-examination of the skin, options for treatment, reconstructive surgery, skin cancer patients' own stories, techniques for treating sun-damaged & aging skin, & promising research in malignant melanoma, the most deadly form of skin cancer. Chockful of information & simple, practical suggestions, this is a valuable resource for health-conscious readers, patients, parents, & health educators. To order contact: The Skin Cancer Foundation, 245 Fifth Ave., Suite 2402, N.Y, N.Y. 10016 or call (212) 725-5176. ***Publisher Provided Annotation.***

Robins, Perry, ed. Surgical Gems in Dermatology, Vol. 2. LC 88-31982. (Illus.). 144p. 1991. 49.50 (*0-89640-206-1*) Igaku-Shoin.
Robins, Philip. Future of the Gulf: Politics & Oil in the 1990s. (Joint Energy Programme Ser.). 157p. 1989. text ed. 52.95 (*1-85521-011-8*, Pub. by Dartmth Pub UK) Ashgate Pub Co.
Robins, Philip, jt. auth. see Royal Institute of International Affairs Staff.
Robins, R. Diseases of Goats. (Library of Veterinary Practice). 250p. 1994. pap. 39.95 (*0-632-03362-2*, Pub. by Blckwell Sci Pubns UK) Blackwell Sci.
Robins, R. H. General Linguistics. 4th ed. 445p. (C). 1989. pap. text ed. 21.95 (*0-582-29144-5*, 78022) Longman.
— A Short History of Linguistics. 3rd ed. (Linguistics Library). 288p. (C). 1990. pap. text ed. 21.95 (*0-582-29145-3*, 78586) Longman.
Robins, R. H. & Uhlenbeck, E. M., eds. Endangered Languages. 291p. 1992. 45.00 (*0-85496-313-8*) Berg Pubs.
Robins, R. J. & Rhodes, M. J., eds. Manipulating Secondary Metabolism in Culture. (Illus.). 328p. (C). 1989. 64.95 (*0-521-36254-7*) Cambridge U Pr.
Robins, R. S., et al. Psychopathology & Political Leadership, Vol. 16. LC 77-85747. 1977. pap. text ed. 11.00 (*0-930598-16-4*) Tulane Stud Pol.
Robins, Richard C. Texas Civil Appeals Forms. 420p. 1991. ring bd. 115.00 (*0-409-25502-5*) Michie Butterworth.
— Texas Discovery Forms, 1991-1992. 360p. 1994. ring bd. 115.00 (*0-409-25534-3*) Michie Butterworth.
— Texas Discovery Forms, 1991-1992. suppl. ed. 400p. 1993. 32.50 (*1-56257-974-6*) Butterworth Legal Pubs.
— Texas Special Issues Forms, 1988-1993. LC 88-2589. 640p. 1994. ring bd. 115.00 (*0-409-25339-1*) Michie Butterworth.
— Texas Special Issues Forms, 1988-1993. suppl. ed. LC 88-2589. 640p. 1993. 55.00 (*0-685-44084-2*) Butterworth Legal Pubs.
Robins, Robert H. The Byzantine Grammarians: Their Place in History. LC 92-47496. (Trends in Linguistics, Studies & Monographs: Vol. 70). xi, 278p. (C). 1993. lib. bdg. 129.25 (*3-11-013574-4*) Mouton.
Robins, Robert S., jt. auth. see Post, Jerrold M.
***Robins, Ron.** The Barbed-Wire College: Educating German POWs in the United States During World War II. LC 94-21161. 1995. 29.95 (*0-691-03700-0*) Princeton U Pr.
***Robins, Sam.** Unleashed. 384p. (Orig.). 1995. pap. 18.95 (*0-86534-035-8*) Sunstone Pr.
Robins, Sam, jt. auth. see Crandall, Richard L.
Robins, Steven & Robins, Adrienne. Readings for Composition: A Writer's Anthology. LC 91-67516. 432p. (Orig.). (C). 1992. pap. text ed. 8.00 (*0-312-04005-9*) St Martin.
— Readings for Composition: A Writer's Anthology. LC 91-67516. 432p. (Orig.). (C). 1992. pap. text ed. 0.38 (*0-312-04007-5*) St Martin.
Robins, Suki, jt. ed. see Hennessy, James E.
Robins, W. P. Phase Noise in Signal Sources (Theory & Applications) rev. ed. Flood, J. E. & Hughes, C. J., eds. 336p. 1984. 69.00 (*0-86341-026-X*, TE009) Inst Elect Eng.
Robinsion, Bonnie. Through the Mists of Darkness. Date not set. pap. 9.98 (*1-55503-704-6*, 01111728) Covenant Comms.
Robinson. Atomic Spectroscopy. 448p. 1990. 125.00 (*0-8247-8311-5*) Dekker.
— Best Christmas Pageant. (J). 1990. mass mkt. 3.95 (*0-06-107017-3*, Harp PBks) HarpC.
— Concepts & Themes in the Regional Geography of Canada. (NFS Canada Ser.). 1993. pap. 17.95 (*0-88922-264-9*, Pub. by Talonbooks CN) InBook.
— Federal Income Taxation of Real Estate: Forms & Analysis. 1989. ring bd. 98.00 (*0-7913-0297-0*); Supplemented annually; write for info. write for info. (*0-318-67194-8*) Warren Gorham & Lamont.
— The Ghost of Whispering Rock. 1994. pap. write for info. (*0-671-86952-3*) PB.
— The Golden Age. Kahan, ed. (Illus.). 200p. 1995. pap. 19.95 (*1-56389-203-0*) DC Comics.
— Green Mars. 1995. mass mkt. (*0-553-57239-3*) Bantam.
— Happiness & Self Esteem. (Illus.). Date not set. pap. text ed. 8.95 (*1-884780-11-3*) Phoenix Pubng.
— Kinesiology One. 600p. 1990. 28.95 (*0-8016-4144-6*) Mosby Yr Bk.
— Least Squares Regression Analysis in Terms of Linear Algebra. 508p. 1988. text ed. 41.00 (*0-13-528233-0*) P-H.
— Lord Meren Mystery. 3rd ed. Date not set. pap. write for info. (*0-345-39532-8*) Ballantine.
— Lord Meren Mystery. 4th ed. Date not set. pap. write for info. (*0-345-39533-6*) Ballantine.
— Lovely in Her Bones. 1993. per. 12.95 (*0-88978-260-1*, Pub. by Arsenal Pulp CN) InBook.
— Medical Emergencies. 5th ed. 366p. 1987. pap. text ed. 34.95 (*0-433-28107-3*) Buttrwrth-Heinemann.
— Migration of Geophysical Data. 214p. 1988. text ed. 55.00 (*0-13-582263-7*) P-H.
— Mom, You're Fired! (Orig.). (J). 1992. pap. 3.50 (*0-590-44903-6*, Apple Paperbacks) Scholastic Inc.
— Motorcycle Tuning: Four-Stroke. 1988. 27.95 (*0-7506-0266-X*); 24.95 (*0-685-63314-4*) Buttrwrth-Heinemann.
— Murder at God's Gate. Date not set. pap. write for info. (*0-345-39531-X*) Ballantine.
— The Odyssey (Homer) (Book Notes Ser.). (C). 1984. pap. 2.95 (*0-8120-3429-5*) Barron.
— Power Paragraphs: Building Blocks for Eloquent Essays. 72p. (Orig.). (C). 1987. student ed 12.95 (*0-88725-081-5*) Hunter Textbks.
— Seagulls Day, Finest Day. 1987. pap. 6.95 (*0-930096-88-6*) G Gannett.
— Seismic Velocity & the Convolutional Model. 290p. 1988. text ed. 55.00 (*0-13-799826-0*) P-H.
— Skin Cancer: Biology, Diagnosis, Treatment, & Prevention. 95.00 (*0-8016-5032-1*) Mosby Yr Bk.
— Sugar Ray. 29.95 (*0-8488-1537-8*) Amereon Ltd.
— Time Series Analysis & Applications. 621p. 1988. text ed. 59.00 (*0-13-921677-4*) P-H.
— When Your Parents Need You. pap. 9.95 (*0-685-73090-5*) Newcastle Pub.
Robinson, ed. Selections from Greek & Roman Historians. 341p. (C). 1957. pap. text ed. 21.00 (*0-03-009425-9*) HB Coll Pubs.
Robinson & Hewison. Southeast Asia in 1980's. 1989. pap. text ed. 14.95 (*0-04-176012-3*, Pub. by Allen Unwin AT) Paul & Co Pubs.
Robinson & Lee. Controlled Drug Delivery: Fundamentals & Applications. 2nd ed. (Drugs & the Pharmaceutical Sciences Ser.: Vol. 29). 744p. 1988. 250.00 (*0-8247-7588-0*) Dekker.
Robinson & Miller. Automated Inspection & Quality Assurance. (Quality & Reliability Ser.: Vol. 16). 272p. 1989. 59.75 (*0-8247-8002-7*) Dekker.
— Colby, Kerr, & Robinson's Color Atlas of Oral Pathology. 5th ed. (Illus.). 198p. 1989. text ed. 57.50 (*0-397-51043-8*) Lippincott.
Robinson & Wickwire, eds. Write It on Your Heart: The Epic World of an Okanagan Story Teller. (NFS Canada Ser.). Date not set. pap. 16.95 (*0-88922-273-8*, Pub. by Talonbooks CN) InBook.
Robinson, jt. auth. see Hall.
Robinson, jt. auth. see Ryan.
Robinson, jt. auth. see Strong.
Robinson, et al. Audio-Visual Guide to Sources of the African Past. 1980. 280.00 (*0-8419-0537-1*, Africana) Holmes & Meier.
Robinson & Cole Land Use, Staff, jt. auth. see Marine Law Institute, Staff.
Robinson, A. Complete Theories. 2nd rev. ed. (Studies in Logic & the Foundations of Mathematics: Vol. 46). 130p. 1977. 56.50 (*0-7204-0690-0*, North Holland) Elsevier.
— The Repair of Vehicle Bodies. 2nd ed. 1989. pap. 27.95 (*0-434-91739-7*) Buttrwrth-Heinemann.
Robinson, A. D., jt. ed. see Czernichow, P.
Robinson, A. G., jt. ed. see Amico, J. A.
Robinson, A. G., jt. ed. see Horbury, A. D.
Robinson, A. L., jt. auth. see Robinson, Antony M.
Robinson, A. R. Theodor Fontane: An Introduction to the Man & His Work. LC 76-383573. 219p. (ENG & GER.). reprint ed. pap. 62.50 (*0-7837-5190-7*, 2044924) Bks Demand.
Robinson, A. R., ed. The Counting House: Thomas Thompson of Hull & His Family, 1751-1828. (C). 45.00 (*1-85072-102-5*, Pub. by W Sessions UK) St Mut.
Robinson, A. S. & Hooper, G., eds. Fruit Flies, Vols. A & B: Their Biology, Natural Enemies & Control, Vol. A. (World Crop Pests Ser.: Vols. 3A & 3B). 384p. 1990. 169.25 (*0-444-42763-5*) Elsevier.
— Fruit Flies, Vols. A & B: Their Biology, Natural Enemies & Control, Vol. B. (World Crop Pests Ser.: Vols. 3A & 3B). 464p. 1990. 171.25 (*0-444-42750-3*) Elsevier.
Robinson, A. T., jt. auth. see Marks, R.
Robinson, Aaron S. Through Faith There's Hope. 1994. 7.95 (*0-8062-4895-5*) Carlton.
Robinson, Abraham. Numbers & Ideals. LC 65-16747. (Illus.). 1965. 16.00 (*0-8162-7234-4*) Holden-Day.
Robinson, Abraham & Laurmann, J. A. Wing Theory. LC 57-601. (Cambridge Aeronautical Ser.: No. 2). 579p. reprint ed. pap. 165.10 (*0-317-10805-0*, 2051692) Bks Demand.
Robinson, Adam. The Princeton Review: Cracking the SAT & PSAT, 1994. 1993. pap. 15.00 (*0-679-74676-5*, Villard Bks) Random.
— The Princeton Review: Cracking the System: The GRE. 1,992th ed. 1991. 15.00 (*0-679-73487-2*, Villard Bks) Random.
— Princeton Review: GRE. 1988. pap. 10.95 (*0-394-75684-3*) Random.
— Princeton Review: The GRE System, 1993. 1992. pap. 16.00 (*0-679-74104-6*, Villard Bks) Random.
— Princeton Review: The LSAT System, 1993. 1992. pap. 16.00 (*0-679-74103-8*, Villard Bks) Random.
— The Princeton Review: The Student Access Guide to College Admissions. 1993. pap. 12.00 (*0-679-74590-4*, Villard Bks) Random.
— The Princeton Review: Word Smart. 1993. pap. 10.00 (*0-679-74589-0*, Villard Bks) Random.
— Princeton Review Cracking SAT & PSAT with Diagnostic Tests on Disk 1995. 1994. pap. 29.95 (*0-679-75348-6*, Villard Bks); pap. 29.95 (*0-679-75368-0*, Villard Bks) Random.
— Princeton Review Cracking the GRE with Diagnostic Tests on Disk 1995. 1994. pap. 29.95 (*0-679-75350-8*, Villard Bks); pap. 29.95 (*0-679-75370-2*, Villard Bks) Random.
— Princeton Review Cracking the LSAT with Diagnostic Test on Disk. 1994. pap. 29.95 (*0-679-75349-4*, Villard Bks) Random.
— Princeton Review Cracking the LSAT with Diagnostic Tests on Disk. 1994. pap. 29.95 (*0-679-75369-9*, Villard Bks) Random.
— Princeton Review Cracking the LSAT 1995 Edition. 1994. pap. 17.00 (*0-679-75339-7*, Villard Bks) Random.
— Princeton Review Cracking the SAT & PSAT 1995 Edition. 1994. pap. 17.00 (*0-679-75338-9*, Villard Bks) Random.
— The Princeton Review-Cracking the System: The GMAT, 1992 Edition. 1991. pap. 15.00 (*0-679-73367-1*, Villard Bks) Random.
— The Princeton Review-Cracking the System: The Last LSAT. 1,992th ed. 1991. 13.00 (*0-679-73488-0*, Villard Bks) Random.
— The Princeton Review-Cracking the System: The SAT & PSAT. 1,992th ed. 1991. pap. 14.00 (*0-679-73486-4*, Villard Bks) Random.
— Princeton Review, SAT & PSAT, 1993. 1992. pap. 15.00 (*0-679-73907-6*, Villard Bks) Random.
— Princeton Review SAT & PSAT-89. 1988. pap. 9.95 (*0-679-72135-5*) McKay.
— Princeton Review SAT Math Workbook. 1995. pap. 12.00 (*0-679-75363-X*, Villard Bks) Random.
— Princeton Review Word Smart 2: Seven Hundred More Words to Help Build an Educated Vocabulary. 1992. pap. 10.00 (*0-679-73863-0*, Villard Bks) Random.
— SAT Verbal Workbook. 1995. pap. 15.00 (*0-679-75362-1*, Villard Bks) Random.
— What Smart Students Know: Maximum Grades Optimum Learning, Minimum Time. LC 93-20437. 1993. 16.00 (*0-517-88085-7*, Crown) Crown Pub Group.
***Robinson, Adam & Katzman, John.** Cracking the GRE 1996. 1995. pap. 17.00 (*0-679-76136-5*, Villard Bks) Random.
— Cracking the GRE '96: With Sample Tests on Computer Disk (MAC) (Princeton Review Ser.). 1995. disk, pap. 29.95 (*0-679-76141-1*, Villard Bks) Random.
— Cracking the GRE '96: With Sample Tests on Computer Disk (WIN) (Princeton Review Ser.). 1995. disk, pap. 29.95 (*0-679-76140-3*, Villard Bks) Random.
— Cracking the SAT & PSAT '96. (Princeton Review Ser.). 1995. pap. 17.00 (*0-679-76132-2*, Villard Bks) Random.
— Cracking the SAT & PSAT '96: With Sample Tests on Computer Disk (MAC) (Princeton Review Ser.). 1995. disk, mac ld 29.95 (*0-679-76134-9*, Villard Bks) Random.
— Cracking the SAT & PSAT '96: With Sample Tests on Computer Disk (WIN) (Princeton Review Ser.). 1995. disk, pap. 29.95 (*0-679-76133-0*, Villard Bks) Random.
— The Princeton Review - Cracking the System: The SAT & PSAT - 1990. LC 89-5631. 304p. 1989. pap. 10.95 (*0-679-72633-0*, Villard Bks) Random.
— The Princeton Review - Word Smart: Building an Educated Vocabulary. LC 87-40580. (Illus.). 256p. 1988. 10.00 (*0-394-75686-X*, Villard Bks) Random.
— The Princeton Review-Cracking the System: The GRE, 1991 Edition. 1990. pap. 11.95 (*0-679-73142-3*, Villard Bks) Random.
***Robinson, Adam & Princeton Review Staff.** Cracking the LSAT '96. (Princeton Review Ser.). 1995. pap. 17.00 (*0-679-76139-X*, Villard Bks) Random.
— Cracking the LSAT '96: With Sample Tests on Computer Disk (MAC) (Princeton Review Ser.). 1995. disk, pap. 29.95 (*0-679-76143-8*, Villard Bks) Random.
— Cracking the LSAT '96: With Sample Tests on Computer Disk (WIN) (Princeton Review Ser.). 1995. disk, pap. 29.95 (*0-679-76142-X*, Villard Bks) Random.
Robinson, Adam, jt. auth. see Katzman, John.
Robinson, Adam, jt. auth. see Princeton Review Editors.
Robinson, Adele J., ed. Portland Symphony Cookbook. 5th ed. LC 74-84052. 336p. 1974. 9.95 (*0-9601266-1-9*) Portland Symphony Cookbook.
***Robinson, Alan.** Clouds of Glory. 94p. 1992. pap. text ed. 24.95x (*0-85439-480-X*, Pub. by St Paul Pubns UK) St Mut.
— The Repair of Vehicle Bodies. 3rd ed. (Illus.). 488p. 1993. pap. write for info. (*0-7506-0955-9*) Buttrwrth-Heinemann.
— The Six Chaplet Rosary. 80p. 1992. pap. 24.95 (*0-85439-473-7*, Pub. by St Paul Pubns UK) St Mut.
— Tongues of Angeles. 190p. 1992. pap. 24.95 (*0-85439-471-0*, Pub. by St Paul Pubns UK) St Mut.
— The Treasures of Jesus. 144p. 1993. pap. 35.00 (*0-85439-466-4*, Pub. by St Paul Pubns UK) St Mut.
— The Treasures of St. Paul: Selected Themes from Paul's Theology & Ethics. 220p. 1994. pap. 39.00 (*0-85439-500-8*, Pub. by St Paul Pubns UK) St Mut.
Robinson, Alan, ed. Continuous Improvement in Operations: A Systematic Approach to Waste Reduction. LC 90-21651. (Illus.). 406p. 1991. 35.00x (*0-915299-51-8*); pap. text ed. 22.95 (*0-915299-86-0*) Prod Press.
— Modern Approaches to Manufacturing Improvement: The Shingo System. LC 89-43673. 420p. 1990. pap. 23.00 (*0-915299-64-X*) Prod Press.

R

An Asterisk (*) at the beginning of an entry indicates that the title is appearing in BIP for the first time.

Robinson, Alan H. Virgin Islands National Park: The Story Behind the Scenery. LC 74-81560. (Illus.). 48p. 1974. pap. 6.95 (*0-916122-14-X*) KC Pubns.
Robinson, Alan S., jt. auth. see Block, Julian.
Robinson, Albert G. Cuba & the Intervention. 1976. lib. bdg. 59.95 (*0-8490-1690-8*) Gordon Pr.
Robinson, Alfred. Life in California Before the Conquest. LC 68-30553. (American Scene Ser.). (Illus.). 1969. reprint ed. lib. bdg. 39.50 (*0-306-71142-7*) Da Capo.
— Life in California Before the Conquest. 1992. reprint ed. lib. bdg. 75.00 (*0-7812-5081-1*) Rprt Serv.
Robinson, Alfred S. Hartford Numismatist. 28p. reprint ed. 3.00 (*0-940748-55-X*) Conn Hist Soc.
Robinson, Alice M. Betty Comden & Adolph Green: A Bio-Bibliography. LC 93-21050. (Bio-Bibliographies in the Performing Arts Ser.: No. 45). 384p. 1993. text ed. 59.95 (*0-313-27659-5*, Greenwood Pr) Greenwood.
Robinson, Alice M., et al, eds. Notable Women in the American Theatre: A Biographical Dictionary. LC 89-17065. 1008p. 1989. text ed. 115.00 (*0-313-27217-4*, RNW/, Greenwood Pr) Greenwood.
Robinson, Allan R. & Lee, Ping. Oceanography & Acoustics: Prediction & Propagation Models. (AIP Series on Modern Acoustics & Signal Processing). (Illus.). 300p. 1994. text ed. 65.00 (*1-56396-203-9*, AIP Pr) Am Inst Physics.
Robinson, Allan R., jt. ed. see Malanotte-Rizzoli, Paola.
Robinson, Amelia B. A Bridge over Jordan. 2nd rev. ed. Huth, Christina & Wertz, Marianna, eds. LC 90-62730. (Illus.). 415p. (YA). (gr. 12 up). 1991. reprint ed. pap. 10.00 (*0-9621095-4-1*) Schiller Inst.
Robinson, Aminah B. The Teachings: Drawn from African-American Spirituals. LC 92-18614. 1992. 26.95 (*0-15-188126-X*); pap. 12.95 (*0-15-688247-7*) HarBrace.
Robinson, Andrew. The Art of Rabindranath Tagore. (Illus.). 224p. 1989. 110.00 (*0-233-98359-7*, Pub. by A Deutsch UK) Trafalgar.
— Challenges for Champions. Bell, Rob, ed. (Champions Ser.). (Illus.). 64p. (Orig.). (C). 1989. pap. 9.00 (*1-55806-046-4*, 404) Hero Games.
— Earthshock. LC 93-60201. (Illus.). 304p. 1993. pap. 19.95 (*0-500-27738-9*) Thames Hudson.
— Satyajit Ray: The Inner Eye. 430p. 1990. 40.00 (*0-520-06905-6*) U CA Pr.
— Satyajit Ray: The Inner Eye. 430p. 1992. pap. 18.00 (*0-520-06946-3*) U CA Pr.
— The Story of Writing: Alphabets, Hieroglyphs, & Pictographs. LC 95-60276. (Illus.). 224p. 1995. 29.95 (*0-500-01665-8*) Thames Hudson.
— Wrath of the Seven Horsemen. MacDonald, George & Charlton, S. Coleman, eds. 32p. (Orig.). (YA). (gr. 10-12). 1987. pap. 6.00 (*0-915795-86-8*, 31) Iron Crown Ent Inc.
Robinson, Andrew & Terlevich, Roberto J., eds. The Nature of Compact Objects in Active Galactic Nuclei. (Illus.). 435p. (C). 1994. 59.95 (*0-521-46480-3*) Cambridge U Pr.
Robinson, Andrew, jt. auth. see Emery, Dominic.
Robinson, Andrew, tr. see Montalban, Manuel V.
Robinson, Andrew J., jt. auth. see Snyder-Mackler, Lynn.
Robinson, Andrew M. The Gadgets! 48p. (J). (gr. 10-12). 1986. pap. 8.00 (*0-915795-64-7*, 23) Iron Crown Ent Inc.
Robinson, Ann. Cappy Claus. (Illus.). 16p. (J). (ps-6). 1992. pap. 4.95 (*0-9633373-0-0*) Chameleon FL.
— Parliament & Public Spending. LC 79-307097. 1978. text ed. 52.95 (*0-435-83750-8*) Ashgate Pub Co.
Robinson, Ann, et al. Tax Policy-Making in the United Kingdom. xi, 256p. 1983. text ed. 54.95 (*0-435-84784-8*) Ashgate Pub Co.
Robinson, Anne, jt. auth. see Hall, Nigel.
Robinson, Anthony. In the Cockpit. 1991. 19.98 (*1-55521-743-5*) Bk Sales Inc.
— The Member-Guest. 1991. 19.95 (*1-55611-268-8*) D I Fine.
— The Whole Truth. 1990. 19.95 (*1-55611-202-5*) D I Fine.
— The Whole Truth. 480p. 1992. mass mkt. 5.99 (*0-8217-3792-9*) Zebra.
Robinson, Antony M. & Robinson, A. L. Systematic Bibliography: A Practical Guide to the Work of Compilation. 4th rev. ed. LC 79-40542. 135p. reprint ed. pap. 38.50 (*0-7837-5325-X*, 2045064) Bks Demand.
Robinson, Armstead L. & Sullivan, Patricia, eds. New Directions in Civil Rights Studies. (Carter G. Woodson Institute Series in Black Studies). 240p. 1991. text ed. 27.50 (*0-8139-1319-5*) U Pr of Va.
Robinson, Arthur. Clinical Genetics Handbook. 2nd ed. 1993. 39.95 (*0-86542-194-3*, 93-010567) Blackwell Sci.
Robinson, Arthur & North, Gary. Fighting Chance: Ten Feet to Survival. LC 86-71490. (Illus.). 289p. (Orig.). 1986. pap. 5.95 (*0-930462-10-6*) Oregon Inst Sci Med.
Robinson, Arthur, et al, eds. Sex Chromosome Aneuploidy: Prospective Studies on Children. LC 78-13921. (Alan R. Liss Ser.: Vol. 15, No. 1). 1979. 38.00 (*0-685-03298-1*) March of Dimes.
Robinson, Arthur E. The Professional Education of Elementary Teachers in the Field of Arithmetic. LC 78-177196. (Columbia University. Teachers College. Contributions to Education Ser.: No. 672). reprint ed. 37.50 (*0-404-55672-8*) AMS Pr.
Robinson, Arthur H. Early Thematic Mapping in the History of Cartography. LC 81-11516. (Illus.). 1982. 39.95 (*0-226-72285-6*) U Ch Pr.
— Elements of Cartography. 6th ed. 560p. 1995. Net. text ed. write for info. (*0-471-55579-7*) Wiley.
— Look of Maps: An Examination of Cartographic Design. 128p. 1986. reprint ed. 20.00 (*0-299-00950-5*) U of Wis Pr.
Robinson, Arthur H., jt. auth. see Hsu, Mei-Ling.
Robinson, Arthur H., et al. Atlas of Wisconsin. LC 73-15262. 126p. 1974. 22.50 (*0-299-06530-8*); pap. 15.00 (*0-299-06534-0*) U of Wis Pr.
— Elements of Cartography. 5th ed. LC 84-11860. 544p. (C). 1984. Net. text ed. write for info. (*0-471-09877-9*) Wiley.
Robinson, B. V., et al. PVP: A Critical Review of the Kinetics & Toxicology of Polyvinylpyrrolidone (Povidone) (Illus.). 200p. 1990. 134.00 (*0-87371-288-9*, RM660) Lewis Pubs.
Robinson, B. W. Fifteenth-Century Persian Painting: Problems & Issues. (Hagop Kevorkian Series on Near Eastern Art & Civilization). (Illus.). 120p. 1991. text ed. 55.00x (*0-8147-7417-2*) NYU Pr.
— Japanese Sword-Fittings: And Associated Metalwork. (Baur Collection). 448p. 1994. 255.00 (*0-7103-0398-X*, Pub. by Kegan Paul Intl UK) Routledge Chapman & Hall.
— Japanese Sword-Fittings & Associated Metalwork. (Baur Collection Geneva: Vol. 7). (Illus.). 448p. 1981. 265.00 (*2-88031-003-2*, Pub. by Baur Foundation SZ) Routledge Chapman & Hall.
Robinson, B. W., jt. auth. see Khalili, Nasser D.
Robinson, B. W., et al. Islamic Art in the Keir Collection. (Keir Collection Ser.). (Illus.). 416p. 1988. 150.00 (*0-571-13753-9*) Faber & Faber.
Robinson, Barbara. The Best Christmas Pageant Ever. LC 72-76501. (Illus.). 96p. (J). (gr. 3 up). 1972. 14.95 (*0-06-025043-7*); lib. bdg. 14.89 (*0-06-025044-5*) HarpC Child Bks.
— The Best Christmas Pageant Ever. LC 72-76501. (Trophy Bk.). (Illus.). 96p. (J). (gr. 3 up). 1988. pap. 31.60 (*0-06-440278-9*, Trophy); pap. 3.95 (*0-06-447044-X*, Trophy) HarpC Child Bks.
— Best Christmas Pageant Ever. (J). 1988. mass mkt. 3.95 (*0-06-440275-4*, Junior Bks) HarpC.
— The Best School Year Ever. LC 93-50891. 128p. (J). (gr. 3 up). 1994. 12.95 (*0-06-023039-8*) HarpC Child Bks.
— The Best School Year Ever. LC 93-50891. 128p. (J). (gr. 3 up). 1994. lib. bdg. 12.89 (*0-06-023043-6*) HarpC Child Bks.
— My Brother Louis Measures Worms: And Other Louis Stories. LC 87-45302. (Charlotte Zolotow Bk.). 160p. (J). (gr. 3-7). 1988. lib. bdg. 14.89 (*0-06-025083-6*) HarpC Child Bks.
— My Brother Louis Measures Worms: and Other Louis Stories. LC 87-45302. (Charlotte Zolotow Bk.). 160p. (J). (gr. 5 up). 1990. pap. 3.95 (*0-06-440362-9*, Trophy) HarpC Child Bks.
— A White Clearing. 192p. (Orig.). 1989. pap. 6.95 (*0-925591-00-9*) Covenant Hse Bks.
— A White Clearing: A Life in the Smokies. 160p. (Orig.). 1989. pap. 9.95 (*0-685-31982-2*) Covenant Hse Bks.
Robinson, Barbara & Wolfson, Evelyn. Environmental Education: A Manual for Elementary Educators. LC 82-741. (Illus.). 233p. reprint ed. pap. 66.50 (*0-7837-1198-0*, 2041728) Bks Demand.
Robinson, Barbara A. And Still, I Cry. LC 90-86221. 220p. (Orig.). 1992. 17.95 (*1-878647-06-7*); pap. 13.95 (*1-878647-01-6*) Duncan & Duncan.
Robinson, Barbara B. This Fragile Eden. (Illus.). 1978. pap. 6.95 (*0-916630-11-0*) Pr Pacifica.
— Words for Carla. (Illus.). 72p. (Orig.). 1986. pap. 4.95 (*0-916630-48-X*) Pr Pacifica.
Robinson, Barbara C., et al, eds. Proceedings of the Ninth International Congress of Arachnology. LC 86-60475. (Illus.). 304p. (Orig.). 1986. pap. 29.95 (*0-87474-401-6*, EBPNP) Smithsonian.
Robinson, Barbara J., ed. Artistic Representation of Latin American Diversity: Sources & Collections. (Illus.). xviii, 518p. (Orig.). 1993. pap. 52.50 (*0-917617-32-0*) SALALM.
Robinson, Barbara J. & Robinson, J. Cordell. The Mexican American: A Critical Guide to Research Aids. Stueart, Robert D., ed. LC 76-5643. (Foundations in Library & Information Science: Vol. 1). 287p. 1980. lib. bdg. 73.25 (*0-89232-006-0*) Jai Pr.
Robinson, Barrie W., jt. auth. see Nelson, Adie.
Robinson, Bart. Columbia Icefield - a Solitude of Ice. (Illus.). 112p. 1981. 29.95 (*0-89886-035-0*) Mountaineers.
***Robinson, Bernadette.** Achieving Quality in Open & Flexible Learning. Lockwood, Fred, ed. 160p. 1995. pap. 32.95 (*0-7494-1372-7*) Nichols Pub.
Robinson, Bert. The Basket Weavers of Arizona. LC 91-22832. (Illus.). 180p. 1991. reprint ed. pap. 29.95 (*0-8263-1263-2*) U of NM Pr.
Robinson, Betty. A Guide to Arkansas Horse Trails. (Illus.). 82p. (Orig.). (YA). (gr. 8 up). 1991. pap. 8.95 (*0-929183-03-7*) Equestrian Unlimited.
— A Guide to Arkansas Horse Trails. 2nd ed. (Illus.). 100p. (Orig.). (YA). (gr. 8 up). 1995. pap. 10.95 (*0-929183-04-5*) Equestrian Unlimited.
Robinson, Bettye W., jt. auth. see Calhoun, Calfrey C.
Robinson, Beverly J. Aunt (Ant) Phyllis. 42p. (Orig.). 1989. pap. 10.95 (*0-916147-10-X*) Regent Pr.
Robinson, Bill. Best Sailing Spots Worldwide. (Illus.). 256p. 1991. 23.00 (*0-688-10214-X*, Hearst Marine Bks) Morrow.
— Destruction at Noonday. 224p. 1992. 22.95 (*0-924486-21-X*) Sheridan.
— Getting Beyond the Small Talk. 1990. pap. 5.95 (*0-89066-191-X*) World Wide Pubs.
— Novice in the North. (Illus.). 176p. (Orig.). 1984. pap. 9.95 (*0-88839-977-4*) Hancock House.
— The Sailing Mystique: The Challenges & Rewards of a Life under Sail. (Illus.). 250p. 1994. pap. 14.95 (*0-924486-63-5*) Sheridan.
— Where to Cruise. (Illus.). 320p. 1991. pap. 14.95 (*0-393-30796-4*) Norton.
— A Winter in the Sun. (Illus.). 180p. 1995. pap. text ed. 17.95 (*0-924486-69-4*) Sheridan.
Robinson, Blackwell P. Five Royal Governors of North Carolina, 1729-1775. (Illus.). 1968. reprint ed. pap. 3.00 (*0-86526-076-1*) NC Archives.
Robinson, Bonnie D., jt. auth. see Ellul, Joseph A., Jr.
Robinson, Bradford, tr. see Dahlhaus, Carl.
Robinson, Brent. Microcomputers & the Language Arts. LC 85-11581. (English, Language & Education Ser.). 160p. 1985. pap. 27.00 (*0-335-15075-6*, Open Univ Pr) Taylor & Francis.
Robinson, Brian. Dialysis, Transplantation, Nephrology: Proceedings, European Dialysis & Transplant Association. (Illus.). 1978. 65.00 (*0-8464-0329-3*) Beekman Pubs.
— The Fischer-Indole Synthesis. LC 81-14749. 923p. 1983. text ed. 395.00 (*0-471-10009-9*, Wiley-Interscience) Wiley.
— The Fischer Indole Synthesis. LC 81-14749. (Illus.). 939p. reprint ed. pap. 180.00 (*0-8357-8643-9*, 2035067) Bks Demand.
Robinson, Brian, ed. Dialysis, Transplantation, Nephrology: Proceedings European Dialysis & Transplant Assoc. Volume 13. (Illus.). 1977. 65.00 (*0-8464-0328-5*) Beekman Pubs.
— Dialysis, Transplantation, Nephrology: Proceedings, European Dialysis & Transplant Association, Vol. 15. (Illus.). 662p. 1979. 65.00 (*0-8464-1087-7*) Beekman Pubs.
Robinson, Brian S. The Nelson Island & Seabrook Marsh Sites Part 1: Late Archaic, Marine Oriented People on the Central New England Coast. (Ocassional Publications in Northeastern Anthropology: No. 9). (Illus.). xii, 107p. 15.00 (*0-318-32508-X*) F Pierce College.
Robinson, Brian S., et al. Early Holocene Occupation in Northern New England. (Occasional Publications in Maine Archaeology). 200p. (C). 1992. pap. text ed. 15.00 (*0-935447-10-5*) ME Hist Preserv.
Robinson, Bruce, ed. see Hamilton, Barbara S.
Robinson, Bruce, jt. auth. see White, Anthony.
***Robinson, Bruce R. & Peterson, Walter.** Strategic Acquisitions: A Guide to Growing & Enhancing the Value of Your Business. LC 94-21386. 264p. 1994. text ed. 65.00 (*1-55623-853-3*) Irwin Prof Pubng.
Robinson, Bryan. Soothing Moments: Daily Meditations for Fast-Track Living. 380p. 1990. pap. 6.95 (*1-55874-075-9*, 0759) Health Comm.
Robinson, Bryan & McCullers, Jamey. How to Conquer Your Fears. (Healograms Ser.). 72p. 1993. pap. 1.95 (*1-55874-285-9*) Health Comm.
— How to Find Peace of Mind. (Healograms Ser.). 72p. 1993. pap. 1.95 (*1-55874-286-7*) Health Comm.
— How to Overcome Self-Doubt. (Healograms Ser.). 72p. 1993. pap. 1.95 (*1-55874-283-2*) Health Comm.
— How to Take Charge of Your Life. (Healograms Ser.). 72p. 1993. pap. 1.95 (*1-55874-284-0*) Health Comm.
Robinson, Bryan & McCullers, Jamie. Six Hundred Eleven Ways to Boost Your Self Esteem. 160p. (Orig.). 1994. pap. 8.95 (*1-55874-297-2*, 2972) Health Comm.
Robinson, Bryan E. Heal Your Self Esteem: Recovery from Addictive Thinking. 1991. pap. 9.95 (*1-55874-119-4*) Health Comm.
— Home Alone Kids: Working Parents Guide to Providing the Best Care for Your Child. 1990. pap. 10.95 (*0-669-19506-5*) Free Pr.
— Overdoing It: How to Slow down & Take Care of Yourself. 275p. 1993. pap. 11.95 (*1-55874-288-3*) Health Comm.
— Stressed Out: A Workbook for Balance & Serenity. 1991. pap. 4.95 (*1-55874-142-9*) Health Comm.
— Teenage Fathers. LC 86-45896. 192p. (C). 1987. pap. 12.95 (*0-669-14587-4*) Free Pr.
— Work Addiction: Hidden Legacies of Adult Children. 1989. pap. 8.95 (*1-55874-023-6*) Health Comm.
— Working with Children of Alcoholics: The Practitioner's Handbook. LC 87-45558. 288p. 1988. text ed. 34.95 (*0-669-16638-3*) Free Pr.
Robinson, Bryan E. & Barret, Robert L. The Developing Father: Emerging Roles in Contemporary Society. LC 86-4637. 224p. 1986. pap. text ed. 18.95 (*0-89862-905-5*) Guilford Pr.
Robinson, Bryan E., jt. auth. see Barrett, Robert L.
Robinson, Bryan E., et al. Latchkey Kids: Unlocking Doors for the Children & Their Families. LC 85-45521. 240p. 1987. text ed. 27.95 (*0-669-11929-6*) Free Pr.
Robinson, Bryan V. MCQs in Pharmacology. 286p. 1980. reprint ed. pap. text ed. 26.00 (*0-443-03873-2*) Churchill.
Robinson, Bud. Honey in the Rock. 1988. pap. 11.99 (*0-88019-235-6*) Schmul Pub Co.
Robinson, Buddy, jt. auth. see Hanna, Mark G.
Robinson, Buffy S. Creative Differences. LC 89-77189. 275p. 1990. 18.95 (*0-939149-32-X*) Soho Press.
Robinson, Byron F., jt. auth. see Bakeman, Roger.
Robinson, C., jt. ed. see Church, M. K.
Robinson, C. Clough. A Glossary of Words Pertaining to the Dialect of Mid-Yorkshire: With Others Peculiar to Lower Nidderdale. (English Dialect Society Publications Ser.: No. 14). 1969. reprint ed. pap. 20.00 (*0-8115-0446-8*) Periodicals Srv.
Robinson, C. W., jt. ed. see Moo-Young, M.
Robinson, Calvin, et al. The Journey of the Songhai People. 227p. 1988. pap. text ed. 13.95 (*1-880205-25-4*) Songhai.
— The Journey of the Songhai People. 2nd ed. (Illus.). 460p. (C). reprint ed. text ed. 29.95 (*1-880205-28-9*); reprint ed. pap. text ed. 14.95 (*1-880205-29-7*) Songhai.
Robinson, Carl. Australia: The Island Continent. 2nd ed. 1993. pap. 16.95 (*0-8442-9887-5*, Passport Bks) NTC Pub Grp.
Robinson, Carlan M. Breaking up? Moving On . . . LC 89-92013. (Illus.). 54p. 1989. pap. 14.95 (*0-9623896-0-9*) Cable Pub.
Robinson, Carol. My Life with Thomas Aquinas. (Illus.). 307p. (Orig.). 1992. pap. text ed. 12.50 (*0-935952-83-7*) Angelus Pr.
***Robinson, Carol, et al.** Raising Children. Angelus Press Staff, ed. (Integrity Magazine Anthology Ser.: No. I). 75p. 1995. pap. 3.95 (*0-935952-27-6*) Angelus Pr.
Robinson, Caroline H. Seventy Birth Control Clinics: A Survey & Analysis Including the General Effects of Control on Size & Quality of Population. LC 71-169398. (Family in America Ser.). 380p. 1972. reprint ed. 18.95 (*0-405-03875-5*) Ayer.
Robinson, Carolyn & Robinson, Ed. The Have-More Plan: A Little Land-A Lot of Living. LC 90-50353. (Illus.). 72p. 1973. pap. 7.95 (*0-88266-024-1*, Garden Way Pub) Storey Comm Inc.
***Robinson, Catherine.** Leaving Mrs. Ellis. (Illus.). 32p. (J). (ps-2). 1995. 19.95 (*0-370-31856-0*, Pub. by Bodley Head UK) Trafalgar.
***Robinson, Catherine & Ker, Phil.** Understanding Accounting Principles. 338p. 1993. pap. 65.00 (*0-409-79000-1*, NZ) Butterworth Legal Pubs.
Robinson, Catherine & Rowekamp, Jenise. Speaking up at Work. (Illus.). 180p. 1985. pap. 9.95 (*0-19-434196-8*) OUP.
— Speaking up at Work. (Illus.). 180p. 1985. teacher ed 5.95 (*0-19-434197-6*) OUP.
Robinson, Cecil. Mexico & the Hispanic Southwest in American Literature. LC 76-24082. 391p. 1977. pap. 17.95 (*0-8165-0593-4*) U of Ariz Pr.
— No Short Journeys: The Interplay of Cultures in the History & Literature of the Borderlands. LC 91-28170. 148p. 1992. 32.50 (*0-8165-1270-1*) U of Ariz Pr.
Robinson, Cecil, ed. & tr. The View from Chapultepec: Mexican Writers on the Mexican-American War. LC 88-36260. 223p. 1989. 35.00 (*0-8165-1083-0*) U of Ariz Pr.
Robinson, Cedric J. Black Marxism: The Making of the Black Radical Tradition. (Third World Studies). 500p. (C). 1983. text ed. 60.00 (*0-86232-126-3*, Pub. by Zed Books UK); pap. 19.95 (*0-86232-127-1*, Pub. by Zed Books UK) Humanities.
Robinson, Celeste. Best Book of Paradox, No. 3. 1990. pap. 27.95 (*0-672-22704-5*, Bobbs) Macmillan.
— Paradox X.0 for Windows Handbook. 1994. pap. 28.00 (*0-679-75409-1*) Random.
— Paradox 4.0 Handbook. 1992. pap. 29.95 (*0-679-79101-9*) Random.
Robinson, Cervin. Cervin Robinson - Cleveland, Ohio. LC 89-22050. (Published in Association with the Cleveland Museum of Art Ser.). 124p. 1989. 44.95 (*0-910386-98-6*); pap. 21.95 (*0-910386-99-4*) Cleveland Mus Art.
Robinson, Cervin & Herschmann, Joel. Architecture Transformed: A History of the Photography of Buildings from 1839 to the Present. (Illus.). 224p. 1990. reprint ed. pap. 32.50x (*0-262-68064-5*) MIT Pr.
Robinson, Charles, III. The Frontier World of Fort Griffin: The Life & Death of a Western Town. LC 91-73890. (Western Lands & Waters Ser.: No. XVII). (Illus.). 236p. 1992. 27.50 (*0-87062-212-9*) A H Clark.
Robinson, Charles. A Stomachful of Laughs: First Premise & Other Stories. 1992. pap. 13.95 (*0-533-10359-2*) Vantage.
Robinson, Charles A., Jr. Alexander the Great: The Meeting of East & West in World Government & Brotherhood. LC 84-10951. 252p. 1984. reprint ed. text ed. 52.50 (*0-313-24572-X*, ROGR, Greenwood Pr) Greenwood.
— Athens in the Age of Pericles. (Centers of Civilization Ser.: Vol. 1). (Illus.). 180p. 1971. pap. 9.95 (*0-8061-0935-1*) U of Okla Pr.
Robinson, Charles A., Jr., ed. see Gibbon, Edward.
Robinson, Charles B. Auditing a Quality System for the Defense Industry. (Auditing Ser.). (Illus.). 156p. (Orig.). 1990. pap. 29.95 (*0-87389-078-7*) ASQC Qual Pr.
— How to Make the Most of Every Audit: An Etiquette Handbook for Auditing. 126p. 1992. 21.95 (*0-87389-158-9*) ASQC Qual Pr.
Robinson, Charles E. Shelley & Byron: The Snake & Eagle Wreathed in Fight. LC 75-36927. 304p. 1976. 38.00 (*0-8018-1707-2*) Johns Hopkins.
Robinson, Charles E., ed. Lord Byron & His Contemporaries: Essays from the Sixth International Byron Seminar. LC 80-66848. (Illus.). 256p. 1982. 35.00 (*0-87413-180-4*) U Delaware Pr.
— Mary Shelley: Collected Tales & Stories. (Illus.). 399p. 1990. reprint ed. pap. text ed. 16.95 (*0-8018-4062-7*) Johns Hopkins.
— Mary Shelley's Plays & Her Translation of the Cenci Story: Bodleian MSS Shelley Adds, Nos. d.2 & e.13. LC 92-23188. (Bodleian Shelley Manuscripts: Vol. 10). 282p. 1992. 125.00 (*0-8240-6986-2*) Garland.
Robinson, Charles E., ed. see Shelley, Mary Wollstonecraft.
***Robinson, Charles J. & Ginder, Andrew P.** Implementing TPM: The North American Experience. (Illus.). 250p. 1995. text ed. 45.00 (*1-56327-087-0*) Prod Press.
Robinson, Charles K., jt. auth. see Nicholson, Kenyon.
Robinson, Charles M. Bad Hand: A Biography of General Ranald S. Mackenzie. (Illus.). 392p. 1993. 29.95 (*1-880510-00-6*); pap. 17.95 (*1-880510-02-2*) State House Pr.
— Bad Hand: A Biography of General Ranald S. Mackenzie. limited ed. (Illus.). 392p. 1993. 60.00 (*1-880510-01-4*) State House Pr.
***Robinson, Charles M., III.** The Buffalo Hunters. LC 95-7590. 1995. write for info. (*1-880510-18-9*); pap. write for info. (*1-880510-19-7*) State House Pr.
— The Buffalo Hunters. deluxe ed. LC 95-7590. 1995. lib. bdg. write for info. (*1-880510-20-0*) State House Pr.
— The Court Martial of Lieutenant Henry Flipper. LC 93-60328. (Southwestern Studies: No. 100). (Illus.). 120p. (Orig.). 1994. pap. 12.50 (*0-87404-196-1*) Tex Western.

R

An Asterisk (*) at the beginning of an entry indicates that the title is appearing in BIP for the first time.

— Frontier Forts of Texas. LC 86-10436. (Illus.). 86p. (Orig.). 1986. pap. 9.95 (*0-88415-597-8*) Gulf Pub.

— A Good Year to Die: The Story of the Great Sioux War. LC 95-7820. 1995. 27.50 (*0-679-43025-3*) Random.

Robinson, Charles M. The Kansas Conflict. LC 70-37599. (Black Heritage Library Collection). reprint ed. 29.95 (*0-8369-8975-9*) Ayer.

— Modern Civic Art: Or, the City Made Beautiful. 4th ed. LC 79-112570. (Rise of Urban America Ser.). (Illus.). 1978. reprint ed. 29.95 (*0-405-02473-8*) Ayer.

Robinson, Charles M., III. Shark of the Confederacy: The Story of the CSS Alabama. LC 94-13816. (Illus.). 230p. 1994. 25.00 (*1-55750-728-7*) Naval Inst Pr.

Robinson, Charles N. British Tar in Fact & Fiction. (Illus.). 1968. reprint ed. 43.00 (*1-55888-938-8*) Omnigraphics Inc.

***Robinson, Charles T.** The New England Ghost Files. LC 95-126. (Illus.). 1995. pap. write for info. (*0-924771-48-8*) Covered Bridge.

***Robinson, Chris.** Collegiate Reader. 1995. pap. text ed. write for info. (*1-56226-228-9*) CT Pub.

— Plotting Directions: An Activist's Guide. LC 82-80105. (Illus.). 68p. 1982. pap. 4.00 (*0-685-04290-1*) Recon Pubns.

— Say It with Style. rev. ed. (Plus Ser.). 1991. pap. 39.40 (*1-56226-088-X*) CT Pub.

Robinson, Christine. Collegiate Reader. rev. ed. 252p. (C). 1990. pap. text ed. 18.15 (*1-56226-021-9*) CT Pub.

— Good Grief Grammar. rev. ed. 92p. (C). 1990. pap. text ed. 12.55 (*1-56226-022-7*) CT Pub.

— Proper Grammarian. rev. ed. (C). 1990. pap. text ed. 12.55 (*1-56226-023-5*) CT Pub.

Robinson, Christine, et al, eds. Transitions: Exeter Remembered. 195p. 1990. 15.95 (*0-939618-06-0*); pap. 9.95 (*0-939618-07-9*) Phillips Exeter.

Robinson, Christopher. C. P. Cavafy. (Studies in Modern Greek: No. 1). xiv, 112p. (Orig.) (C). 1988. 25.00 (*0-89241-469-3*); pap. text ed. 16.00 (*0-89241-470-7*) Caratzas.

— Lucian & His Influence in Europe. LC 79-16580. (Illus.). 258p. reprint ed. pap. 73.60 (*0-7837-3758-0*, 2043575) Bks Demand.

— Scandal in the Ink. Date not set. 60.00 (*0-304-32703-4*) InBook.

— Scandal in the Ink. 1995. pap. 17.95 (*0-304-32705-0*) InBook.

***Robinson, Chuck & Robinson, Debbie.** The Art of Shelling: A Complete Guide to Finding Shells & Other Beach Collectibles at Shelling Locations from Florida to Maine. LC 95-69822. (Illus.). 152p. (Orig.). 1995. pap. 14.95 (*0-9647267-6-9*) Old Squan Vill Pub.

Robinson, Clara L. Psychology & Preparation of the Teacher for the Elementary School. LC 71-177197. (Columbia University. Teachers College. Contributions to Education Ser.: No. 418). reprint ed. 37.50 (*0-404-55418-0*) AMS Pr.

Robinson, Clarie. Penguin. LC 91-44727. (Life Story Ser.). (Illus.). 32p. (J). (gr. 4-6). 1993. teacher ed 3.95 (*0-8167-2772-4*); text ed. 11.59 (*0-8167-2771-6*) Troll Assocs.

***Robinson, Clark.** Dynamical Systems: Stability, Symbolic Dynamics, & Chaos. LC 94-24456. (Studies in Advanced Mathematics). 400p. 1994. 59.95 (*0-8493-8493-1*, 8493) CRC Pr.

Robinson, Claude E. Straw Votes, a Study of Political Prediction. LC 75-41231. reprint ed. 19.50 (*0-685-70797-0*) AMS Pr.

— Straw Votes, a Study of Political Prediction. LC 75-41231. reprint ed. 19.50 (*0-404-14677-5*) AMS Pr.

Robinson, Clay, jt. auth. see Gibson, L. Tucker.

Robinson, Clement. Handful of Pleasant Delights. Rollins, Hyder E., ed. 1965. pap. 4.95 (*0-486-21382-X*) Dover.

Robinson, Clinton D. Language Choice in Rural Development. LC 92-60918. x, 52p. 1992. pap. 5.00 (*0-88312-180-8*); fiche 8.00 (*0-88312-858-6*) Summer Instit Ling.

Robinson, Clive. Lipid Mediators in Allergic Diseases of the Respiratory Tract. 1994. 195.00 (*0-8493-5416-1*, RC859) CRC Pr.

Robinson, Colin, jt. auth. see Marshall, Eileen.

***Robinson, Colin, et al, eds.** Dental Enamel: Formation to Destruction. LC 95-1383. 336p. 1995. 195.00 (*0-8493-4589-8*, 4589) CRC Pr.

Robinson, Conway. The Wild White Shepherd. (Orig.). (J). (gr. 6-9). 1994. lib. bdg. 15.00 (*0-88092-092-0*); pap. 5.00 (*0-88092-091-2*) Royal Fireworks.

Robinson, Conway, ed. see Virginia Company of London, 1619-1624 Staff.

Robinson, Corinne H. Normal & Therapeutic Nutrition. 17th rev. ed. 784p. (C). 1990. write for info. (*0-02-402605-0*) Macmillan.

Robinson, Corinne H., et al. Basic Nutrition & Diet Therapy. 7th ed. 544p. (C). 1993. pap. write for info. (*0-02-402502-X*) Macmillan.

Robinson, Craig. Ted Hughes As Shepherd of Being. 240p. 1989. text ed. 39.95 (*0-312-03202-1*) St Martin.

Robinson-Cutler, Marjory L., jt. auth. see Cutler, Maxwell.

***Robinson, Cynny.** Much Love, Cynny-san. 300p. 1994. 22.95 (*1-878208-49-7*) Guild Pr IN.

Robinson, Cyril. Isms of the Lives & Times of the Modern Painters. (Illus.). 84p. 1993. pap. 10.95 (*0-8059-3384-0*) Dorrance.

***Robinson, Cyril D.** Legal Rights, Duties, & Liabilities of Criminal Justice Personnel: History & Analysis. 2nd ed. 516p. 1992. pap. 39.95 (*0-398-06405-9*) C C Thomas.

— Legal Rights, Duties, & Liabilities of Criminal Justice Personnel: History & Analysis. 2nd ed. 516p. (C). 1992. text ed. 75.95x (*0-398-05779-6*) C C Thomas.

Robinson, Cyril D. & Scaglion, Richard. Police in Contradiction: The Evolution of the Police Function in Society. LC 93-25071. (Contributions in Criminology & Penology Ser.: No. 44). 216p. 1993. text ed. 55.00 (*0-313-28891-7*, GM8891, Greenwood Pr) Greenwood.

Robinson, Cyril E. Everyday Life in Ancient Greece. LC 75-41232. reprint ed. 22.50 (*0-404-14592-2*) AMS Pr.

— Everyday Life in Ancient Greece. LC 77-27627. 159p. 1978. reprint ed. text ed. 49.75 (*0-8371-9078-9*, ROEL, Greenwood Pr) Greenwood.

— A History of Greece. 9th ed. (Illus.). 1957. pap. 16.50 (*0-423-71290-X*, NO. 2411) Routledge Chapman & Hall.

— A History of Rome from Seven Hundred Fifty-Three B.C. to A.D. Four Hundred Ten. (Illus.). 1950. pap. 17.95 (*0-423-87420-9*, NO. 2412) Routledge Chapman & Hall.

Robinson, D., jt. ed. see Paukert, F.

Robinson, D. A. & Williams, R. B., eds. Rock Weathering & Landform Evolution. LC 94-4636. (British Geomorphological Research Group Symposia Ser.). 1994. text ed. 89.95 (*0-471-95119-6*) Wiley.

Robinson, D. F. & Foulds, L. R. Digraphs: Theory & Techniques. 272p. 1980. text ed. 149.00 (*0-677-05470-X*) Gordon & Breach.

Robinson, D. G., Jr. Gerbils. (Illus.). 80p. 1984. pap. 5.95 (*0-86622-715-6*, PB-110) TFH Pubns.

Robinson, D. G., et al, eds. Methods of Preparation for Electron Microscopy: An Introduction for the Biomedical Sciences. (Illus.). 200p. 1987. pap. 55.00 (*0-387-17592-X*) Spr-Verlag.

Robinson, D. J. Course in Linear Algebra with Applications: Solutions to the Exercises. 208p. 1992. pap. text ed. 21.00 (*981-02-1048-5*) World Scientific Pub.

— A Course in the Theory of Groups. (Graduate Texts in Mathematics Ser.: Vol. 80). 480p. 1982. 59.00 (*0-387-90600-2*) Spr-Verlag.

— A Course in the Theory of Groups. 2nd ed. (Graduate Texts in Mathematics Ser.: Vol. 80). (Illus.). 500p. 1993. pap. text ed. write for info. (*3-540-94092-8*) Spr-Verlag.

— A Course in the Theory of Groups. Ewing, J. H. et al, eds. (Graduate Texts in Mathematics Ser.: Vol. 80). (Illus.). 502p. 1994. reprint ed. pap. 42.50 (*0-387-94092-8*) Spr-Verlag.

— Finiteness Conditions & Generalized Soluble Groups, Pt. 1. (Ergebnisse der Mathematik und Ihrer Grenzgebiete Ser.: Vol. 62). (Illus.). 240p. 1972. 45.00 (*0-387-05620-3*) Spr-Verlag.

Robinson, D. Keith. Introductory Physics Laboratory. 64p. 1993. spiral bd. 15.95 (*0-8403-8852-7*) Kendall-Hunt.

Robinson, D. Keith, jt. auth. see Bevington, Philip.

Robinson, D. R., jt. auth. see Bowman, A. W.

Robinson, D. W. & Mollan, R. C., eds. Energy Management & Agriculture: Proceedings of the First International Summer School in Agriculture Held in Cooperation with W. K. Kellogg Foundation 1982. 442p. 1985. reprint ed. 100.00 (*0-444-99577-3*, Pub. by Elsevier Applied Sci UK) Elsevier.

Robinson, D. W. & Reid, G. T., eds. Interferogram Analysis: Digital Fringe Pattern Measurement Techniques. (Illus.). 302p. 1993. 118.00 (*0-7503-0197-X*) IOP Pub.

Robinson, D. W., jt. auth. see Bratteli, O.

Robinson, D. W., jt. ed. see Cavalloro, R.

***Robinson, Dale & Fernandes, Dale.** The Definitive Andy Griffith Show Reference: Episode-by-Episode, with Cast & Production Biographies & a Guide to Collectibles. 344p. 1995. lib. bdg. 39.95 (*0-7864-0136-2*) McFarland & Co.

Robinson, Dan & McKean, S., eds. Shifting Cultivation & Alternatives: An Annotated Bibliography, 1974-1989. 280p. (Orig.). 1992. pap. text ed. 47.50 (*0-85198-680-3*) CAB Intl.

***Robinson, Dana G. & Robinson, James C.** Performance Consulting: Moving Beyond Training. LC 94-47066. (Illus.). 240p. 1995. 32.95x (*1-881052-30-3*) Berrett-Koehler.

— Training for Impact: How to Link Training to Business Needs & Measure the Results. LC 88-46088. (Management Ser.). 336p. 1989. 32.95x (*1-55542-153-9*) Jossey-Bass.

Robinson, Daniel. Capital Maintenance for Colleges & Universities. Weizenbach, Lanora, ed. 35p. 1986. write for info. (*0-915164-34-5*) NACUBO.

— An Intellectual History of Psychology. LC 86-15916. 496p. (C). 1986. reprint ed. pap. text ed. 17.50 (*0-299-10984-4*) U of Wis Pr.

Robinson, Daniel & Logan, Leanne. France: A Travel Survival Kit. (Illus.). 1088p. (Orig.). 1994. pap. 21.95 (*0-86442-192-3*) Lonely Planet.

Robinson, Daniel & Storey, Robert. Vietnam: A Travel Survival Kit. 2nd ed. (Illus.). 454p. 1993. pap. 15.95 (*0-86442-197-4*) Lonely Planet.

— Vietnam: Travel Survival Kit. 3rd ed. (Illus.). 512p. 1995. pap. 15.95 (*0-86442-316-0*) Lonely Planet.

Robinson, Daniel & Wheeler, Tony. Cambodia: A Travel Survival Kit. (Illus.). 132p. (Orig.). 1992. pap. 12.95 (*0-86442-174-5*) Lonely Planet.

Robinson, Daniel J., jt. ed. see Taylor, William J.

Robinson, Daniel N. Aristotle's Psychology. 160p. 1989. text ed. 31.50 (*0-231-07002-0*) Col U Pr.

— Enlightened Machine: An Analytical Introduction to Neuropsychology. rev. ed. LC 79-29756. (Illus.). 158p. 1980. text ed. 39.00 (*0-231-04954-4*); pap. text ed. 15.00 (*0-231-04955-2*) Col U Pr.

— An Intellectual History of Psychology. 3rd ed. LC 95-5697. 1995. write for info. (*0-299-14840-8*); pap. write for info. (*0-299-14844-0*) U of Wis Pr.

— Mind Unfolded: Essays on Psychology's Historic Texts. LC 78-53510. 539p. 1978. text ed. 75.00 (*0-313-27076-7*, U7076); pap. text ed. 19.95 (*0-313-27077-5*, P7077) Greenwood.

— Philosophy of Psychology. 176p. 1989. text ed. 32.50 (*0-231-05922-1*); pap. text ed. 14.50 (*0-231-05923-X*) Col U Pr.

— Toward a Science of Human Nature: Aspirations of Nineteenth Century Psychology. LC 81-38458. 256p. 1982. text ed. 50.00 (*0-231-05174-3*); pap. text ed. 21.00 (*0-231-05175-1*) Col U Pr.

Robinson, Daniel N., ed. Social Discourse & Moral Judgment. (Illus.). 260p. 1992. text ed. 39.95 (*0-12-590155-0*) Acad Pr.

Robinson, Daniel N. & Mos, Leendert P., eds. Annals of Theoretical Psychology, Vol. 6. LC 84-644088. (Illus.). 254p. 1990. 85.00 (*0-306-43588-8*, Plenum Pr) Plenum.

Robinson, Daniel N., ed. see Kohlberg, Lawrence, et al.

Robinson, Daniel S., ed. The Story of Scottish Philosophy: A Compendium of Selections from the Writings of Nine Pre-Eminent Scottish Philosophers, with Biobibliographical Essays. LC 78-12114. (Illus.). 290p. 1979. reprint ed. text ed. 38.50 (*0-313-21082-9*, ROST) Greenwood.

Robinson, Daniel S., ed. see Hoernle, Reinhold F.

Robinson, Darrell W. Total Church Life. LC 85-7900. 1985. 8.99 (*0-8054-6250-3*) Broadman.

Robinson, David. Chaplin: His Life & Art. (Illus.). 896p. 1994. reprint ed. pap. 21.95 (*0-306-80600-2*) Da Capo.

— Chaplin: The Mirror of Opinion. LC 82-48615. (Illus.). 220p. 1984. pap. 12.95 (*0-253-21160-3*) Ind U Pr.

— Encyclopedia of Pet Rabbits. (Illus.). 320p. 1979. 17.95 (*0-87666-911-9*, H-984) TFH Pubns.

— From Drinking to Alcoholism: A Sociological Commentary. LC 75-26597. 223p. reprint ed. pap. 63.60 (*0-317-27737-5*, 2052094) Bks Demand.

— Laricollaguas: Ecology, Economy & Demography in a Seventeenth-Century Peruvian Village, Vol. 29. 400p. (C). 1929. text ed. 45.00 (*0-8133-8022-7*) Westview.

— Saving Graces. (Illus.). 128p. 1995. 25.00 (*0-393-03794-0*, Norton Paperbks) Norton.

— Saving Graces. (Illus.). 128p. 1995. pap. 14.95 (*0-393-31333-6*, Norton Paperbks) Norton.

— The Unitarians & the Universalists. LC 84-9031. (Denominations in America Ser.: No. 1). xiii, 368p. 1985. text ed. 45.00 (*0-313-20946-4*, RUN/) Greenwood.

— The Unitarians & the Universalists. LC 84-9031. (Denominations in America Ser.: No. 1). xiii, 368p. 1985. pap. text ed. 29.95 (*0-313-24893-1*, RUNPB) Greenwood.

Robinson, David, ed. Alcohol Problems: Reviews, Research & Recommendations. LC 79-13367. 254p. 1980. 36.50 (*0-8419-0524-X*) Holmes & Meier.

— Experimentation & Reconstruction in Environmental Archaeology. (Oxbow Monographs in Archaeology). (Illus.). 278p. 1992. pap. 50.00 (*0-946897-23-9*) David Brown.

— William Ellery Channing: Selected Writings. LC 84-62567. (Sources of American Spirituality Ser.: Vol. 2). 320p. 1985. 12.95 (*0-8091-0359-1*) Paulist Pr.

***Robinson, David & Dunkley, John, eds.** Public Interest Perspectives in Environmental Law. 1995. pap. text ed. 45.00 (*0-471-95173-0*) Wiley.

Robinson, David & Smith, Douglas. Sources of the African Past. LC 79-5399. 203p. 1979. 44.50 (*0-8419-0337-9*, Africana) Holmes & Meier.

Robinson, David & Staffordshire Record Society Staff, eds. Visitations of the Archdeaconry of Stafford, 1829-1841. (Joint Publications Ser.: No. 25). 182p. 1980. 19.00 (*0-11-440066-0*, Pub. by HMSO UK) UNIPUB.

Robinson, David, ed. see Aranda, Francisco.

Robinson, David, jt. ed. see Godfrey, Christine.

Robinson, David, ed. see Hanson, Haldore.

Robinson, David, jt. ed. see Hanson, John.

Robinson, David, et al. Thailand: Adjusting to Success: Current Policy Issues. (Occasional Paper Ser.: No. 85). viii, 50p. (Orig.). 1991. pap. 10.00 (*1-55775-221-4*) Intl Monetary.

Robinson, David, et al, eds. Controlling Legal Addictions: Proceedings of the Twenty-Fifth Annual Symposium of the Eugenics Society, London, 1988. LC 89-34300. 230p. 1989. text ed. 49.95 (*0-312-03253-6*) St Martin.

Robinson, David B., ed. see Johnson, Adelaide M.

Robinson, David F. All about Internet FTP: Learning & Teaching to Transfer Files on the Internet. (Internet Workshop Ser.: Vol. 2). 1994. spiral bd. 30.00 (*1-882208-04-8*) Library Solns.

Robinson, David F., ed. Living on the Earth. 320p. 1988. 29.95 (*0-87044-734-3*); 41.95 (*0-87044-735-1*); lib. bdg. 31.95 (*0-87044-736-X*) Natl Geog.

Robinson, David G. Plant Membranes: Endo- & Plasma Membranes. LC 84-7539. (Cell Biology: A Series of Monographs: Vol. 3). 352p. 1985. 83.95 (*0-471-86210-X*) Krieger.

Robinson, David J., ed. Migration in Colonial Spanish America. (Studies in Historical Geography: No. 16). (Illus.). 416p. (C). 1990. 64.95 (*0-521-36281-4*) Cambridge U Pr.

— Social Fabric & Spatial Structure in Colonial Latin America. LC 79-15744. (Dellplain Latin American Studies: No. 1). 496p. reprint ed. pap. 141.40 (*0-317-28161-5*, 2022589) Bks Demand.

— Studying Latin America: Essays in Honor of Preston E. James. LC 80-12413. (Dellplain Latin American Studies: No. 4). 289p. reprint ed. pap. 82.40 (*0-317-28159-3*, 2022591) Bks Demand.

Robinson, David M. Emerson's Pragmatic Turn. LC 93-156. (Studies in American Literature & Culture: Vol. 70). 240p. (C). 1993. 47.95 (*0-521-44497-7*) Cambridge U Pr.

Robinson, David M. & Fluck, Edward J. A Study of the Greek Love Names. Vlastos, Gregory, ed. LC 78-19375. (Morals & Law in Ancient Greece Ser.). 1979. reprint ed. lib. bdg. 23.95 (*0-405-11569-5*) Ayer.

Robinson, Dean. Seaforth. (Illus.). 84p. (Orig.). pap. 10.95 (*0-919783-53-8*, Pub. by Boston Mills Pr CN) Genl Dist Srvs.

Robinson, Deanna, et al. Music at the Margins: Popular Music & Cultural Diversity. (Communication & Human Values Ser.: Vol. 8). (Illus.). 320p. 1991. 49.95 (*0-8039-3192-1*); pap. 24.00 (*0-8039-3193-X*) Sage.

Robinson, Debbie, jt. auth. see Robinson, Chuck.

Robinson, Debby. Medieval Needlepoint: Twenty-Four Easy-to-Make Projects for the Home. (Illus.). 128p. 1994. pap. 19.95 (*0-8069-8821-5*) Sterling.

— The Odd-Ball Knitting Book. (Illus.). 96p. (Orig.). 1989. pap. 12.95 (*0-312-02452-5*) St Martin.

Robinson, Debby, jt. auth. see Coss, Melinda.

Robinson, Dennis W., jt. ed. see Lam, Alven H. S.

Robinson, Derek. Artillery of Lies. large type ed. 1993. 39.95 (*0-7066-1018-0*, Pub. by Remploy Pr CN) St Mut.

— Civil Service Pay in Africa. xi, 220p. (Orig.). 1990. lib. bdg. 22.00 (*92-2-106459-X*) Intl Labour Office.

— A Good Clean Fight. 453p. (Orig.). 1994. pap. 15.00 (*0-00-271338-1*, IntlDept) HarpC.

— Piece of Cake. 1994. reprint ed. lib. bdg. 45.95 (*1-56849-323-1*) Buccaneer Bks.

***Robinson, Derek J.** A Course in the Theory of Groups. 2nd ed. LC 95-4025. (Graduate Texts in Mathematics: Vol. 80). 1995. write for info. (*0-387-94461-3*) Spr-Verlag.

Robinson, Derek J., ed. A Course in Linear Algebra with Applications. 436p. (C). 1991. text ed. 78.00 (*981-02-0567-8*); pap. text ed. 44.00 (*981-02-0568-6*) World Scientific Pub.

Robinson, Derek W. Elliptic Operators & Lie Groups. (Oxford Mathematical Monographs). 578p. 1991. 89.00 (*0-19-853591-0*) OUP.

Robinson, Diana G. Revenge So Sweet. 384p. 1991. mass mkt. 4.25 (*0-8217-3329-X*) Zebra.

Robinson, Diana M. To Stretch a Plank: A Survey of Psychokinesis. LC 80-12335. 282p. 1981. 26.95 (*0-88229-404-0*) Nelson-Hall.

Robinson, Diane. Ashes & Mead. Zarucchi, Roy & Page, Carolyn, eds. (Chapbook Ser.). (Illus.). 28p. (Orig.). 1991. pap. 5.00 (*1-879205-12-2*) Nightshade Pr.

Robinson, Diane G. Delta Desire. 1991. mass mkt. 4.25 (*0-8217-3489-X*) Zebra.

— The Eagle & the Rose. 448p. 1993. mass mkt. 4.50 (*0-8217-4092-X*) Zebra.

— The Falcon & the Swan. 1992. mass mkt. 4.50 (*0-8217-3692-2*) Zebra.

— The Rogue & the Lily. 448p. 1993. mass mkt. 4.50 (*0-8217-4364-3*) Zebra.

Robinson, Dianne P., jt. auth. see Poole, Lisa I.

***Robinson, Dindy.** World Cultures Through Art Activities. 200p. 1996. pap. text ed. 23.00 (*1-56308-271-3*) Teacher Ideas Pr.

Robinson, Donald S., jt. ed. see Prien, Robert F.

Robinson, Doris, ed. Fine Arts Periodicals: An International Directory of the Visual Arts. 570p. (Orig.). 1992. pap. 89.00 (*1-879796-03-1*) Peri Press.

— Music & Dance Periodicals: An International Directory & Guidebook. (Orig.). 1989. pap. 65.00 (*0-9617844-4-X*) Peri Press.

— Stamps, Coins, Postcards & Related Materials: A Directory of Periodicals. 150p. (Orig.). 1991. pap. text ed. 29.00 (*0-9617844-7-4*) Peri Press.

Robinson, Doris & Mopsik, Wendy. Mainstreaming - Inclusion: A Program Designed for Students with a Variety of Handicapping Conditions. (Special Student Series Book). 30p. 1993. 7.95 (*1-884063-07-1*) Mar Co Prods.

Robinson, Dorothy. The Legend of Africania. LC 74-4781. (Ebony Jr. Bks.). (Illus.). 32p. (J). (gr. k-5). 1974. 10.95 (*0-87485-037-1*) Johnson Chi.

Robinson, Dorothy R. The Bells Rings at Four: A Black Teacher's Chronicle of Change. LC 78-61472. (Illus.). 1979. 15.50 (*0-89052-024-0*) Madrona Pr.

Robinson, Dorothy W. Martin Luther King & the Civil Rights Movement. 26p. (Orig.). 1986. pap. text ed. 4.95 (*0-9616227-0-9*) Jehara Pr.

Robinson, Doug, jt. auth. see Benson, Lee.

Robinson, Douglas. American Apocalypses: The Image of the End of the World in American Literature. LC 84-28865. 304p. reprint ed. pap. 86.70 (*0-7837-4402-1*, 2044142) Bks Demand.

— No Less a Man: Masculist Transformations in Post-Feminist Popular Culture. LC 93-72885. 323p. (C). 1994. text ed. 45.95 (*0-87972-637-7*); pap. text ed. 18.95 (*0-87972-638-5*) Bowling Green Univ.

— The Translator's Turn. LC 90-4629. (Parallax: Re-Visions of Culture & Society Ser.). 368p. 1991. text ed. 48.50x (*0-8018-4046-5*); pap. text ed. 15.95x (*0-8018-4047-3*) Johns Hopkins.

— The Zeppelin in Combat: A History of the German Naval Airship Division, 1912-1918. (Illus.). 400p. 1994. 49.95 (*0-88740-510-X*) Schiffer.

Robinson, Douglas, tr. Aleksis Kivi's Heath Cobblers (Nummisuutarit) & Kullervo. LC 93-20724. 1993. 14.95 (*0-87839-081-2*) North Star.

Robinson, Douglas, ed. see Starr, Walter A., Jr.

Robinson, Douglas H. The Dangerous Sky: A History of Aviation Medicine. LC 68-11049. (Illus.). 316p. 1974. 25.00 (*0-295-95304-7*) U of Wash Pr.

— Ring Lardner & the Other. (Illus.). 336p. 1992. 49.95 (*0-19-507600-1*) OUP.

Robinson, Douglas H., jt. auth. see Dick, Harold G.

Robinson, Douglas H., tr. see Eckener, Hugo.

Robinson, Douglas J. & James, Stephen E., eds. Anodes for Electrowinning: Proceedings of the Sessions. LC 84-60151. (Illus.). 119p. reprint ed. pap. 34.00 (*0-8357-5619-X*, 2032592) Bks Demand.

Robinson, Duane, jt. auth. see Sagerson, Mary.

Robinson, Duncan. Stanley Spencer. (Illus.). 128p. (C). 1993. reprint ed. pap. 22.95 (*0-7148-2810-6*, Pub. by Phaidon Press UK) Chronicle Bks.

— William Morris, Edward Burne-Jones, & The Kelmscott Chaucer. (Illus.). 116p. 1987. 45.00 (*0-918825-17-2*) Moyer Bell.

Robinson, Duncan, et al. Acquisitions: The First Decade. LC 86-51189. (Illus.). 40p. (Orig.). 1986. pap. 5.95 (*0-930606-54-X*) Yale Ctr Brit Art.

Robinson, Dwight R., et al. Clinical Therapeutics; Rheumatoid Arthritis; Metabolic Bone Disease. (Current Opinion in Rheumatology Ser.). (Illus.). 115p. (Orig.). 1994. pap. text ed. 39.95 (*1-85922-644-2*) Current Science.

Robinson, E., jt. ed. see Musson, A. E.

Robinson, E. A. Tilbury Score: Centennial Edition. 1987. reprint ed. pap. 5.00 (*0-912156-05-8*) Masterwork Pr.

Robinson, E. A., jt. ed. see Kaser, Michael C.

Robinson, E. A., jt. auth. see Silvia, M. T.

Robinson, E. E. The Roosevelt Leadership Nineteen Thirty-three to Nineteen Fourty-Five. LC 75-146154. (American Scene Ser.). 1972. reprint ed. lib. bdg. 49.50 (*0-306-70202-9*) Da Capo.

Robinson, E. L., jt. ed. see Dancy, T. E.

Robinson, E. R., ed. Time Dependent Chemical Processes. (Illus.). 370p. 1975. 63.00 (*0-85334-608-9*, Pub. by Elsevier Applied Sci UK) Elsevier.

Robinson, E. S. Basic Physical Geology. 3rd ed. (Illus.). 689p. (C). 1991. text ed. 29.00 (*1-878907-21-2*) TechBooks.

Robinson, E. S., jt. auth. see Mattingly, H.

Robinson, Earl. The Bible Fact or Fiction? 1992. pap. 4.99 (*0-88019-296-8*) Schmul Pub Co.

— Marks of a Christian. pap. 2.99 (*0-88019-179-1*) Schmul Pub Co.

Robinson, Ed. Not Ashamed. 32p. 1992. pap. 1.95 (*0-8341-1438-0*) Beacon Hill.

— Walking Worthy. 32p. 1989. pap. 1.95 (*0-8341-1273-6*) Beacon Hill.

Robinson, Ed & Mowry, Kathryn L. Preteen Ministry: Between a Rock & a Hard Place. 95p. (Orig.). 1993. pap. 6.95 (*0-8341-1409-7*) Beacon Hill.

Robinson, Ed, jt. auth. see Robinson, Carolyn.

Robinson, Edgar E. & Bornet, Vaughn D. Herbert Hoover: President of the United States. 1975. 14.95 (*0-8179-1491-9*) Hoover Inst Pr.

Robinson, Edgar E., ed. see Wilbur, Ray L.

Robinson, Edna M. Tennyson's Use of the Bible. 119p. (C). 1968. reprint ed. 40.00 (*0-87752-093-3*) Gordian.

Robinson, Edward. Biblical Researches in Palestine: Mount Sinai & Arabia Petraea: A Journal of Travels in the Year 1838, 3 vols, 1. Davis, Moshe, ed. LC 77-70738. (America & the Holy Land Ser.). 1977. reprint ed. lib. bdg. 58.95 (*0-405-10282-8*) Ayer.

— Biblical Researches in Palestine: Mount Sinai & Arabia Petraea: A Journal of Travels in the Year 1838, 3 vols, 2. Davis, Moshe, ed. LC 77-70738. (America & the Holy Land Ser.). 1977. reprint ed. lib. bdg. 58.95 (*0-405-10283-6*) Ayer.

— Biblical Researches in Palestine: Mount Sinai & Arabia Petraea: A Journal of Travels in the Year 1838, 3 vols, 3. Davis, Moshe, ed. LC 77-70738. (America & the Holy Land Ser.). 1977. reprint ed. lib. bdg. 58.95 (*0-405-10284-4*) Ayer.

— Biblical Researches in Palestine: Mount Sinai & Arabia Petraea: A Journal of Travels in the Year 1838, 3 vols, Set. Davis, Moshe, ed. LC 77-70738. (America & the Holy Land Ser.). 1977. reprint ed. lib. bdg. 173.95 (*0-405-10281-X*) Ayer.

— Icons of the Present. 160p. (Orig.). (C). 1993. pap. 19.00 (*0-334-02548-6*, SCM Pr) TPI PA.

— The Language of Mystery. LC 89-5021. 1990. pap. 8.95 (*0-334-02138-3*) TPI PA.

— Later Biblical Researches in Palestine & in Adjacent Regions: Journal of Travels in the Year 1852. Davis, Moshe, ed. LC 77-70739. (America & the Holy Land Ser.). 1977. reprint ed. lib. bdg. 58.95 (*0-405-10285-2*) Ayer.

Robinson, Edward, tr. see Gesenius, William.

Robinson, Edward A. Selected Poems of E. A. Robinson. Zabel, Morton D., ed. 288p. 1966. pap. 12.95 (*0-02-070530-1*, Collier S&S) S&S Trade.

Robinson, Edward E., jt. auth. see Ash, Peter F.

Robinson, Edward S., tr. see Jaeger, Werner W.

***Robinson, Edwin.** Untriangulated Stars. (American Autobiography Ser.). 348p. 1995. reprint ed. lib. bdg. 89.00 (*0-7812-8626-3*) Rprt Serv.

Robinson, Edwin A. The Children of the Night. 1974. 200.00 (*0-87968-186-1*) Gordon Pr.

— Edwin Arlington Robinson's Letters to Edith Brower. Cary, Richard, ed. LC 68-17623. (Illus.). 242p. 1968. text ed. 29.00 (*0-674-24035-9*) Belknap Pr.

— The Essential Robinson. LC 93-14493. (Essential Poets Ser.: Vol. 19). 1993. pap. 8.00 (*0-88001-336-2*) Ecco Pr.

— Miniver Cheevy & Other Poems. LC 95-8708. (Thrift Editions Ser.). 1995. pap. 1.00 (*0-486-28756-4*) Dover.

— Van Zorn: A Comedy in Three Acts. LC 72-97890. reprint ed. 29.50 (*0-404-05363-7*) AMS Pr.

Robinson, Edwin A. & Torrence, Ridgely. Selected Letters of Edwin Arlington Robinson. LC 79-15514. (Illus.). 191p. 1980. reprint ed. text ed. 39.75 (*0-313-21266-X*, ROSL, Greenwood Pr) Greenwood.

Robinson, Edwin A., ed. see Perry, Thomas S.

Robinson, Edwin S. & Coruh, Cahit. Basic Expoloration Geophysics. 562p. 1988. Net. text ed. write for info. (*0-471-87941-X*) Wiley.

Robinson, Edythe. A Long Lonely Time: A Woman's Search for Justice. (Illus.). 160p. (Orig.). 1990. pap. 8.95 (*0-936101-11-3*) RBH.

Robinson, Edythe F. My Little Ole Cookbook: A Down-Home-Pretty-Good-Stuff Yankee - Southern Cook Book. (Illus.). 86p. (Orig.). 1992. pap. 3.50 (*0-9631983-0-0*) RBH.

Robinson, Eleanor. The Freak. 224p. 1985. reprint ed. pap. 2.50 (*0-8439-2281-8*) Dorchester Pub Co.

Robinson, Eleanor M. Concise Guide for Writing Research Papers, 1984 MLA System. LC 84-90682. 54p. 1984. pap. 5.00 (*0-932587-00-3*) E M Robinson.

Robinson, Elizabeth. Bed of Lists. Rosenwasser, Rena & Dienstfrey, Patricia, eds. LC 90-39994. 48p. (Orig.). (C). 1990. pap. text ed. 8.00 (*0-932716-25-3*) Kelsey St Pr.

— Eight Etudes. (Orig.). 1988. pap. 3.50 (*0-945926-00-6*) Paradigm RI.

— In the Sequence of Falling Things. 96p. 1990. 10.00 (*0-945926-20-0*) Paradigm RI.

— In the Sequence of Falling Things. deluxe ed. 96p. 1990. 25.00 (*0-945926-21-9*) Paradigm RI.

— My Name Happens Also. deluxe ed. (Poetry Chapbooks). 32p. (Orig.). 1987. pap. 10.00 (*0-930901-44-4*) Burning Deck.

Robinson, Enders. The Devil Discovered. (Illus.). 390p. 1992. reprint ed. pap. 12.95 (*0-7818-0104-4*) Hippocrene Bks.

Robinson, Enders A. The Devil Discovered: Salem Witchcraft, 1692. (Illus.). 381p. 1991. 19.95 (*0-87052-009-1*) Hippocrene Bks.

— Einstein's Relativity in Metaphor & Mathematics. 1990. 29.95 (*0-13-246497-7*) P-H.

— Least Squares Regression Analysis in Terms of Linear Algebra. 508p. 1981. text ed. 35.00 (*0-934634-58-0*) Intl Human Res.

— Migration of Geophysical Data. LC 82-82537. (Illus.). 214p. 1983. text ed. 39.00 (*0-934634-14-9*) Intl Human Res.

— Probability Theory & Applications. LC 84-29678. (Illus.). 420p. 1985. 39.00 (*0-934634-90-4*) Intl Human Res.

— Salem Witchcraft & Hawthorne's "House of the Seven Gables" (Illus.). 388p. (Orig.). 1992. pap. 29.50 (*1-55613-515-7*) Heritage Bk.

— Seismic Velocity Analysis & the Convolutional Model. LC 83-12631. (Illus.). 290p. 1983. 46.00 (*0-934634-63-7*) Intl Human Res.

— Time Series Analysis & Applications. 612p. 1981. text ed. 35.00 (*0-934634-57-2*) Intl Human Res.

Robinson, Enders A. & Silvia, Manual T. Digital Foundations of Time Series Analysis: Wave-Equation Space-Time Processing. 464p. 1981. Vol. I, 464. 1979. 49.95 (*0-8162-7270-0*); Vol. II, 450. 1981. text ed. 49.95 (*0-8162-7271-9*) Holden-Day.

Robinson, Enders A. & Silvia, Manuel T. Digital Signal Processing & Time Series Analysis. 1978. 49.95 (*0-8162-7264-6*) Holden-Day.

Robinson, Eric. One Dark Mile: A Widower's Story. LC 89-32046. 200p. 1990. 27.50x (*0-87023-684-9*) U of Mass Pr.

Robinson, Eric, jt. ed. see Bate, Raymond H.

Robinson, Eric, ed. see Clare, John.

Robinson, Everett T. Why Aren't You More Like Me? 1994. pap. 12.95 (*0-87425-970-3*) Human Res Dev Pr.

Robinson, F. A. The Vitamin Co-Factors of Enzyme Systems. 1966. 364.00 (*0-08-011319-2*, Pub. by Pergamon Repr UK) Franklin.

Robinson, F. K. A Glossary of Words Used in the Neighbourhood of Whitby. (English Dialect Society Publications Ser.: Nos. 9, 13). 1969. reprint ed. pap. 25.00 (*0-8115-0442-5*) Periodicals Srv.

Robinson, Famous, illus. Brandon's First Baseball Game. LC 90-63290. (I Promise to Do My Best Ser.). 37p. (Orig.). (J). (ps-6). 1990. pap. text ed. 5.00 (*0-9627951-0-0*) JRBB Pubs.

Robinson, Fay. A Frog Inside My Hat. LC 93-22200. (Illus.). 64p. (J). (ps-3). 1993. lib. bdg. 16.95 (*0-8167-3129-2*); pap. 4.95 (*0-8167-3130-6*) BrdgeWater.

— A Ghost in the Toy Box. LC 92-10758. (Bear & Alligator Tales Ser.). (Illus.). 32p. (J). (ps-2). 1993. lib. bdg. 11.70 (*0-516-02371-3*); pap. 3.95 (*0-516-42371-1*) Childrens.

— Great Snakes! LC 95-10531. (Hello Reader! Ser.: Level 2). (Illus.). (J). 1995. write for info. (*0-590-26243-2*) Scholastic Inc.

— Might Spiders! LC 95-10530. (Hello Reader! Ser.: Level 2). (Illus.). (J). 1996. write for info. (*0-590-26262-9*) Scholastic Inc.

— Old MacDonald Had a Farm. LC 92-10757. (Bear & Alligator Tales Ser.). (Illus.). 32p. (J). (ps-2). 1993. lib. bdg. 11.70 (*0-516-02372-1*); pap. 3.95 (*0-516-42372-X*) Childrens.

— Pizza Soup. LC 92-10756. (Bear & Alligator Tales Ser.). (Illus.). 32p. (J). (ps-2). 1993. lib. bdg. 11.70 (*0-516-02373-X*); pap. 3.95 (*0-516-42373-8*) Childrens.

— Real Bears & Alligators. LC 92-10755. (Bear & Alligator Tales Ser.). (Illus.). 32p. (J). (ps-2). 1992. lib. bdg. 11.70 (*0-516-02374-8*) Childrens.

— Real Bears & Alligators. LC 92-10755. (Bear & Alligator Tales Ser.). (Illus.). 32p. (J). (ps-2). 1993. pap. 3.95 (*0-516-42374-6*) Childrens.

— Recycle That! LC 94-35626. (Rookie Read-About Science Ser.). 32p. (J). (ps-2). 1995. lib. bdg. 10.80 (*0-516-06033-8*) Childrens.

— Rhymes We Like. LC 92-10754. (Bear & Alligator Tales Ser.). (Illus.). 32p. (J). (ps-2). 1993. lib. bdg. 11.70 (*0-516-02375-6*); pap. 3.95 (*0-516-42375-4*) Childrens.

— Solid, Liquid or Gas? LC 95-5563. (Rookie Read-About Science Ser.). (J). 1995. write for info. (*0-516-06041-4*) Childrens.

— Sound All Around. LC 93-38592. (Rookie Read-about Science Ser.). (Illus.). 32p. (J). (ps-2). 1994. lib. bdg. 10.80 (*0-516-06024-9*) Childrens.

— Sound All Around. (J). (ps-2). 1994. pap. 3.95 (*0-516-46024-2*) Childrens.

— Space Probes to the Planets. Grant, Christy, ed. LC 92-10792. (Illus.). 32p. (J). (gr. k-3). 1993. 14.95 (*0-8075-7548-8*) A Whitman.

— Too Much Trash! LC 95-5560. (Rookie Read-About Ser.). (J). 1995. write for info. (*0-516-06042-2*) Childrens.

— The Upside-Down Sloth. LC 93-18981. (Rookie Read-about Science Ser.). (Illus.). 32p. (J). (ps-2). 1993. lib. bdg. 11.93 (*0-516-06018-X*); pap. 3.95 (*0-516-46018-8*) Childrens.

— Vegetables, Vegetables. LC 94-14075. (Cornerstones of Freedom Ser.). (Illus.). 32p. (J). (ps-2). 1994. lib. bdg. 10.80 (*0-516-06030-9*); pap. 3.95 (*0-516-46030-7*) Childrens.

— We Love Fruit! LC 92-13312. (Rookie Read-about Science Ser.). (Illus.). 32p. (J). (ps-2). 1992. lib. bdg. 10.80 (*0-516-06006-6*); 22.95 (*0-516-49633-6*) Childrens.

— We Love Fruit. LC 92-13312. (Rookie Read-about Science Ser.). (Illus.). 32p. (J). (ps-2). 1993. pap. 3.95 (*0-516-46006-4*) Childrens.

— When Nicki Went Away. LC 92-13835. (Bear & Alligator Tales Ser.). (Illus.). 32p. (J). (ps-2). 1992. lib. bdg. 11.70 (*0-516-02376-4*) Childrens.

— When Nicki Went Away. LC 92-13835. (Bear & Alligator Tales Ser.). (Illus.). 32p. (J). (ps-2). 1993. pap. 3.95 (*0-516-42376-2*) Childrens.

— Where Did All the Dragons Go? LC 95-3620. (Illus.). 32p. (J). (gr. k-3). 1996. lib. bdg. 13.95 (*0-8167-3808-4*) BrdgeWater.

Robinson, Fay, jt. auth. see Mathews, Judith.

Robinson, Fay, jt. auth. see Matthews, Judith.

Robinson, Fayette & Street, Franklin. The Gold Mines of California: Two Guidebooks. LC 72-9445. (Far Western Frontier Ser.). 230p. 1973. reprint ed. 18.95 (*0-405-05002-X*) Ayer.

Robinson, Forbes & Kilpack, Gilbert. An Inward Legacy. (C). 1956. pap. 7.00 (*0-87574-092-8*) Pendle Hill.

Robinson, Forrest. After the Fire. 45p. (Orig.). 1988. pap. 7.00 (*0-935153-10-1*) Stormline Pr.

Robinson, Forrest, jt. ed. see Gillman, Susan.

Robinson, Forrest G. Having It Both Ways: Self-Subversion in Western Popular Classics. LC 92-39359. 167p. 1993. 29.95x (*0-8263-1453-8*) U of NM Pr.

— In Bad Faith. LC 86-4668. 272p. 1986. 32.00 (*0-674-44527-9*) HUP.

— In Bad Faith: The Dynamics of Deception in Mark Twain's America. 272p. (C). 1992. pap. 15.95 (*0-674-44528-7*) HUP.

— Love's Story Told: A Life of Henry A. Murray. LC 92-8705. 459p. (Orig.). 1992. 29.95 (*0-674-53928-1*) HUP.

— Love's Story Told: A Life of Henry A. Murray. (Illus.). 496p. (Orig.). (C). 1995. pap. 18.95 (*0-674-53929-X*) HUP.

Robinson, Forrest G., ed. An Apology for Poetry: Sidney. 128p. (C). 1970. pap. write for info. (*0-02-402560-7*) Macmillan.

— The Cambridge Companion to Mark Twain. LC 94-24658. (Cambridge Companions to Literature Ser.). 288p. (C). 1995. 59.95 (*0-521-44036-X*); pap. 16.95 (*0-521-44593-0*) Cambridge U Pr.

Robinson, Frances, jt. auth. see Brass, Paul.

***Robinson, Frances M.** Visitors Who Never Left: The Origin of the People of Damelahamid. 171p. 1974. pap. 13.95 (*0-7748-0034-8*) U of Wash Pr.

***Robinson, Frances R.** Antonio & His Enchanted Watering Can. 48p. (J). (gr. 3-4). 1994. pap. text ed. 6.95 (*1-886114-01-3*) Arrow Pubns.

Robinson, Francis. Atlas of the Islamic World since 1500. (Cultural Atlas Ser.). (Illus.). 240p. 1982. 45.00 (*0-87196-629-8*) Facts on File.

— Separatism among Indian Muslims: The Politics of the United Provinces' Muslims. 496p. 1993. reprint ed. pap. 15.95 (*0-19-563126-9*) OUP.

— Separatism among Indian Muslims: The Politics of the United Provinces' Muslims, 1860-1923. LC 73-93393. (Cambridge South Asian Studies: No. 16). 487p. reprint ed. pap. 138.80 (*0-317-26379-X*, 2024521) Bks Demand.

Robinson, Francis, ed. The Cambridge Encyclopedia of India, Pakistan, Bangladesh, Sri Lanka, Nepal, Bhutan & the Maldives. (Illus.). (C). 1989. 64.95 (*0-521-33451-9*) Cambridge U Pr.

Robinson, Francis, jt. auth. see Harcourt, Freda.

Robinson, Francis T. & Dennis, Roger D. Preventing Pain & Injury from Your Computer. LC 93-93633. (Illus.). 50p. (Orig.). 1993. pap. write for info. (*0-9638697-0-1*) R&D Pubng.

Robinson, Frank K., comp. Edgar Lee Masters: An Exhibition in Commemoration of the Centenary of His Birth. LC 71-31042. (Illus.). 1970. pap. 8.00 (*0-87959-015-7*) U of Tex H Ransom Ctr.

Robinson, Frank K., ed. The Harmony of Deeper Music: Posthumous Poems of Edgar Lee Masters. LC 79-108963. (Tower Poetry Ser.: No. 10). 1976. 15.00 (*0-87959-091-2*) U of Tex H Ransom Ctr.

— The Harmony of Deeper Music: Posthumous Poems of Edgar Lee Masters. aniversary ed. LC 79-108963. (Tower Poetry Ser.: No. 10). 1976. 25.00 (*0-87959-021-1*) U of Tex H Ransom Ctr.

Robinson, Frank M. The Dark Beyond the Stars. 1992. mass mkt. 4.99 (*0-8125-1383-5*) Tor Bks.

***Robinson, Frank M. & Smith, Joe.** Death of a Marionette. 1995. 22.95 (*0-614-03855-3*) Forge NYC.

Robinson, Frank M., jt. auth. see Scortia, Thomas N.

***Robinson, Frank M., et al.** Coping: Dimensions of Disability. LC 94-22650. 280p. 1995. text ed. 55.00 (*0-275-94544-8*, Praeger Pubs) Greenwood.

Robinson, Frank S. Machine Politics: A Study of Albany's O'Connells. LC 76-3785. Orig. Title: Albany's O'Connell Machine. (Illus.). 262p. 1977. reprint ed. 32.95 (*0-87855-147-6*) Transaction Pubs.

Robinson, Franklin, ed. Illustrated Bartsch, Vol. 5: Netherlandish Artists. LC 79-50679. 1979. 140.00 (*0-89835-005-0*) Abaris Bks.

Robinson, Franklin, jt. auth. see Shapiro, Robert.

Robinson, Franklin E., jt. auth. see Plochmann, George K.

Robinson, Franklin W. Gabriel Metsu, the Letter. (Focus Exhibition Catalogues Ser.). (Illus.). 16p. (Orig.). 1985. pap. text ed. 1.50 (*0-9610866-3-7*) Putnam Found.

Robinson, Franklin W. & Nichols, Stephen G., Jr., eds. The Meaning of Mannerism. LC 71-189512. (Illus.). 142p. reprint ed. pap. 40.50 (*0-317-10530-2*, 2022327) Bks Demand.

Robinson, Fred C. Beowulf & the Appositive Style. LC 84-11889. (Hodges Lectures Ser.). 120p. (C). 1985. text ed. 20.00 (*0-87049-444-9*); pap. 10.00 (*0-87049-531-3*) U of Tenn Pr.

— The Editing of Old English. LC 93-30396. (Illus.). 320p. (C). 1994. 59.95 (*1-55786-438-1*) Blackwell Pubs.

— Old English Literature: A Select Bibliography. LC 76-464039. (Toronto Medieval Bibliographies Ser.: No. 2). 86p. reprint ed. pap. 25.00 (*0-685-15278-2*, 2026470) Bks Demand.

— The Tomb of Beowulf & Other Essays. LC 92-27331. 1993. 49.95 (*0-631-17328-5*) Blackwell Pubs.

Robinson, Fred C., jt. auth. see Greenfield, Stanley B.

Robinson, Fred C., jt. auth. see Mitchell, Bruce.

Robinson, Fred M. The Comedy of Language: Studies in Modern Comic Literature. LC 80-125. 200p. 1980. lib. bdg. 27.50x (*0-87023-297-5*) U of Mass Pr.

— Comic Moments. LC 91-43694. (Illus.). 208p. 1992. 27.50 (*0-8203-1424-2*) U of Ga Pr.

— The Man in the Bowler Hat: His History & Iconography. LC 92-37188. (Illus.). xvi, 199p. (C). 1993. 24.95 (*0-8078-2073-3*) U of NC Pr.

Robinson, Fred M., jt. ed. see Heath, Mary.

***Robinson, Freddie.** The Book of Daniel Unsealed. 1995. pap. 12.95 (*0-9640487-3-6*) Transfig Prod.

— A Voice Crying Out. 1994. pap. 8.95 (*0-9640487-0-1*) Transfig Prod.

Robinson, G. & Elliott, G. Children Politics & Medicare: Experiences in a Canadian Province. 335p. (Orig.). 1993. pap. text ed. 24.95 (*1-895176-31-X*, Pub. by Univ Calgary CN) Paul & Co Pubs.

Robinson, G. W., tr. see Wang-Wei.

Robinson, Gabrielle. A Private Mythology: The Manuscripts & Plays of John Whiting. LC 87-47983. (Illus.). 160p. 1989. 29.50 (*0-8387-5140-7*) Bucknell U Pr.

Robinson, Gaden S. & Nielsen, Ebbe S. Tineid Genera of Australia. (Monographs on Australian Lepidoptera: Vol. 2). (C). 1993. 80.00 (*0-643-05025-6*, Pub. by CSIRO AT) Intl Spec Bk.

Robinson, Gary C., jt. ed. see Linebaugh, Donald W.

Robinson, Geoffrey. Marriage, Divorce & Nullity: A Guide to the Annulment Process in the Catholic Church. 96p. 1987. pap. 6.95 (*0-8146-1570-8*) Liturgical Pr.

— Yorkshire Smiles. (C). 1989. text ed. 40.00 (*0-948929-26-X*) St Mut.

***Robinson, Geoffrey B.** The Dark Side of Paradise: Political Violence in Bali. (Asia East by South Ser.). (Illus.). 376p. 1995. 35.00x (*0-8014-2965-X*) Cornell U Pr.

Robinson, George. Yellowstone: Cycle of the Seasons. Leach, Nicky, ed. (Wish You Were Here Ser.). 96p. (Orig.). 1994. 24.95 (*0-939365-32-4*); pap. 14.95 (*0-939365-31-6*) Sierra Pr CA.

Robinson, George, photos. Vermont: A Harvest of Color. LC 90-60429. (Illus.). 32p. 1990. pap. 8.95 (*0-933050-81-X*) New Eng Pr VT.

— Vermont Scenes & Seasons. LC 89-63661. (Illus.). 80p. 1989. pap. 12.95 (*0-933050-65-8*) New Eng Pr VT.

Robinson, George & Robinson, Sandra. In Pictures Yellowstone: The Continuing Story. LC 90-60040. (Illus.). 48p. 1990. pap. 6.95 (*0-88714-047-5*) KC Pubns.

Robinson, George, jt. auth. see Moulton, Janice.

Robinson, George C., jt. auth. see Cowdery, Ray.

Robinson, George F. History of Greene County, Ohio. 927p. 1993. reprint ed. lib. bdg. 92.50 (*0-8328-3123-9*) Higginson Bk Co.

Robinson, George L. Twelve Minor Prophets. LC 54-13359. 1978. pap. 8.99 (*0-8010-7669-2*) Baker Bk.

Robinson, George W. Minerals. LC 94-6344. 1994. 40.00 (*0-671-88002-0*) S&S Trade.

Robinson, George W., ed. Bert Combs the Politician: An Oral History. LC 90-19970. (Kentucky Remembered: An Oral History Ser.). 240p. 1991. text ed. 30.00 (*0-8131-1740-2*) U Pr of Ky.

Robinson, George W., ed. see Combs, Bert T.

Robinson, Gerald, jt. auth. see Pagnoni, Mario.

Robinson, Gerald A., jt. auth. see Turner Publishing Co. Staff.

Robinson, Gerald J. Federal Income Taxation of Real Estate: Forms & Checklists. 1989. ring bd. 105.00 (*0-685-69562-X*, FREF) Warren Gorham & Lamont.

Robinson, Gerald S. Federal Income Taxation of Real Estate, No. 1. suppl. ed. 1992. Supplement, 1992-1. 63.00 (*0-7913-0567-8*) Warren Gorham & Lamont.

— Federal Income Taxation of Real Estate, No. 2. suppl. ed. 1992. Supplement, 1992-2. 65.00 (*0-685-28239-2*) Warren Gorham & Lamont.

— Federal Income Taxation of Real Estate, No. 3. suppl. ed. 1992. Supplement, 1992-3. 66.00 (*0-7913-0957-6*) Warren Gorham & Lamont.

— Federal Income Taxation of Real Estate, Set. 1,988th ed. 1992. ring bd. 110.00 (*0-88712-990-0*, FIRE) Warren Gorham & Lamont.

Robinson, Geroid T. Rural Russia under the Old Regime: A History of the Landlord-Peasant World & a Prologue to the Peasant Revolution of 1917. (C). 1967. pap. 14.00 (*0-520-01075-2*) U CA Pr.

An Asterisk (*) at the beginning of an entry indicates that the title is appearing in BIP for the first time.

Robinson, Gertrude. David Urquhart: Some Chapters in the Life of a Victorian Knight Errant of Justice & Liberty. LC 78-110120. 1970. reprint ed. 39.50 (*0-678-00609-1*) Kelley.

Robinson, Gertrude J., ed. see Lukic, Sveta.

Robinson, Gilbert. Representation Theory of the Symmetric Group. LC 63-424. (Mathematical Expositions Ser.: No. 12). 214p. reprint ed. pap. 61.00 (*0-317-09069-0*, 2014385) Bks Demand.

Robinson, Gilbert de Beauregard. The Foundations of Geometry. 4th ed. LC 48-3776. (Mathematical Expositions Ser.: No. 1). 184p. reprint ed. pap. 52.50 (*0-317-08573-5*, 2020515) Bks Demand.

***Robinson, Gillian.** The Slow Reign of Calamity Jane. 1995. pap. 10.95 (*1-55082-117-2*) InBook.

Robinson, Gillian & Rundell, John, eds. Rethinking Imagination: Culture & Creativity. LC 93-17209. 1993. write for info. (*0-415-09192-6*); pap. write for info. (*0-415-09193-4*) Routledge.

Robinson, Gillian & Stringer, Peter. Social Attitudes in Northern Ireland. (Illus.). 240p. (Orig.). 1992. pap. 24.00 (*0-85640-483-7*, Pub. by Blackstaff Pr IE) Dufour.

Robinson, Gillian, jt. ed. see Stringer, Peter.

***Robinson, Glen.** The Case of the Secret Code. LC 94-23914. (Shoebox Kids Ser.: Vol. 2). (J). 1995. 5.95 (*0-8163-1249-4*) Pacific Pr Pub Assn.

— Fifty-Two Things to Do on Sabbath. Wheeler, Gerald, ed. (Orig.). (J). 1983. pap. 2.95 (*0-8280-0199-5*) Review & Herald.

Robinson, Glen, ed. Communications for Tomorrow. 8.95 (*0-686-26005-8*) Aspen Inst Human.

Robinson, Glen E. & Protheroe, Nancy J. Cost of Education: An Investment in America's Future. 102p. 1987. 26.00 (*0-318-37608-3*) Ed Research.

Robinson, Glen O. American Bureaucracy: Public Choice & Public Law. 276p. (C). 1991. text ed. 42.50 (*0-472-10243-5*) U of Mich Pr.

— The Forest Service: A Study in Public Land Management. LC 75-11352. (Resources for the Future Ser.). (Illus.). 358p. 1975. 28.50 (*0-8018-1723-4*) Johns Hopkins.

Robinson, Glen O. & Gellhorn, Ernest. The Administrative Process. 4th ed. Bruff, Harold H., ed. (American Casebook Ser.). 800p. 1993. text ed. 45.50 (*0-314-02377-1*) West Pub.

***Robinson, Glen O., et al.** Administrative Process, 1995 Supplement to The. (American Casebook Ser.). 53p. (C). 1995. pap. text ed. 7.00 (*0-314-06720-5*) West Pub.

***Robinson, Glenn.** The Mysterious Treasure Map. LC 94-46118. (Shoebox Kids Ser.: Vol. 1). (J). 1995. pap. 5.95 (*0-8163-1256-7*) Pacific Pr Pub Assn.

Robinson, Gloria, ed. Preludes to Genetics. 17.50 (*0-87291-127-6*) Coronado Pr.

Robinson, Gnana. Let Us Be Like the Nations: First & Second Samuel. (New International Commentary on the Old Testament Ser.). 320p. (Orig.). 1993. pap. 19.99 (*0-8028-0608-2*) Eerdmans.

Robinson, Gordon. The Forest & The Trees: Guide to Excellent Forestry. LC 88-9011. (Illus.). 252p. (C). 1988. 34.95 (*0-933280-41-6*); pap. 22.00 (*0-933280-40-8*) Island Pr.

Robinson, Gordon R. Arab Gulf States: A Travel Survival Kit. (Illus.). 352p. (Orig.). 1993. pap. 15.95 (*0-86442-120-6*) Lonely Planet.

Robinson, Graham, jt. auth. see Lee, Stan.

Robinson, Gregory H., ed. Coordination Chemistry of Aluminum. LC 93-12703. 1993. write for info. (*1-56081-059-9*); pap. write for info. (*1-56081-656-2*) VCH Pubs.

Robinson, H. Prostaglandin Synthetase Inhibitors. Vane, J. E., ed. 1974. 37.50 (*0-7204-7529-5*, North Holland) Elsevier.

Robinson, H. & Smith, Nila B. Reading Instruction for Today's Children. 2nd ed. 1980. write for info. (*0-13-755157-6*) P-H.

Robinson, H. Alan & Thomas, Ellen L., eds. Fusing Reading Skills & Content. LC 70-21420. 233p. reprint ed. pap. 66.50 (*0-685-23548-3*, 2027944) Bks Demand.

Robinson, H. Alan, jt. ed. see Berger, Allen.

Robinson, H. Alan, et al. Reading Comprehension Instruction, 1783-1987: A Review of Trends & Research. 212p. 1990. pap. 9.00 (*0-87207-745-4*) Intl Reading.

Robinson, H. B., et al. Early Child Care in the United States of America. (International Monographs on Early Child Care). 236p. 1974. text ed. 86.00 (*0-677-05080-1*) Gordon & Breach.

Robinson, H. Basil. Diefenbaker's World: A Populist in Foreign Affairs. (Illus.). 352p. 1991. pap. 19.95 (*0-8020-6922-3*) U of Toronto Pr.

— Diefenbaker's World: A Populist in World Affairs. 1989. 35.00 (*0-8020-2678-8*) U of Toronto Pr.

Robinson, H. C., jt. auth. see Annandale, Nelson.

Robinson, H. E. Grant: American Ancestry of U. S. Grant. 17p. 1993. reprint ed. pap. 7.50 (*0-8328-3326-6*) Higginson Bk Co.

Robinson, H. P. Redemption, Conceived & Revealed. 3.95 (*0-911866-59-0*); pap. 2.95 (*0-911866-89-2*) LifeSprings Res.

Robinson, H. Russell, ed. see Hakuseki, Arai.

Robinson, H. Wheeler. The Life & Faith of the Baptists. 158p. 1985. reprint ed. pap. 6.95 (*0-913029-09-2*) Stevens Bk Pr.

Robinson, H. Wheeler & Payne, Ernest A. British Baptists: An Original Anthology. Gaustad, Edwin S., ed. LC 79-52583. (Baptist Tradition Ser.). 1980. lib. bdg. 33.95 (*0-405-12450-3*) Ayer.

Robinson, Haddon. Biblical Preaching: The Development & Delivery of Expository Messages. LC 80-66776. 1980. 14.99 (*0-8010-7700-1*) Baker Bk.

— Decision Making by the Book. 168p. 1991. 14.99 (*0-89693-913-8*) SP Pubns.

— The Good Shepherd: Reflections on Psalm 23. 1987. pap. 3.50 (*0-8024-6688-5*) Moody.

— What Jesus Said about Successful Living. 1991. 10.99 (*0-929239-43-1*) Discovery Hse Pubs.

Robinson, Haddon W., ed. Biblical Sermons: How Twelve Preachers Apply the Principles of Biblical Preaching. LC 89-428. 224p. 1989. 16.99 (*0-8010-7751-6*) Baker Bk.

Robinson-Hammerstein, Helga, ed. The Transmission of Ideas in the Lutheran Reformation. 240p. 1988. 39.50 (*0-7165-2376-0*, Pub. by Irish Acad Pr IE) Intl Spec Bk.

***Robinson, Harlow.** The Last Impresario: The Life, Times, & Legacy of Sol Hurok. (Illus.). 560p. 1995. 14.95 (*0-14-011620-6*, Penguin Bks) Viking Penguin.

— The Last Impressario: The Life, Times, & Legacy of Sol Hurok. LC 93-22138. (Illus.). 521p. 1994. 26.95 (*0-670-82529-8*, Viking) Viking Penguin.

Robinson, Harold. A Generic Review of the Tribe Liabeae (Asteraceae) LC 82-10807. (Smithsonian Contributions to Botany Ser.: No. 54). 73p. reprint ed. pap. 25.00 (*0-317-28805-9*, 2020337) Bks Demand.

Robinson, Harold, jt. auth. see Mohamed, Haji.

Robinson, Harold E. A Palynological Study of the Liabeae (Asteraceae) LC 86-600032. (Smithsonian Contributions to Botany Ser.: No. 64). 54p. reprint ed. pap. 25.00 (*0-317-55528-6*, 2029552) Bks Demand.

Robinson, Harriet H. Loom & Spindle. 144p. (C). 1976. write for info. (*0-318-55344-9*); pap. 7.95 (*0-916630-02-1*) Pr Pacifica.

***Robinson-Harris, Tracey & Sowin-Williams, Ritch C.** Beyond Pink & Blue: Exploring Our Stereotypes of Sexuality & Gender. 80p. 1994. 19.00 (*1-55896-322-7*) Unitarian Univ.

Robinson, Harry. Men Born Equal. LC 74-22806. 384p. 1983. reprint ed. 45.00 (*0-404-58462-4*) AMS Pr.

— Nature Power: Stories from an Okanagan Elder. Wickwire, Wendy, ed. LC 92-32934. 272p. 1992. pap. 17.95 (*0-295-97223-8*) U of Wash Pr.

Robinson, Heather. The Simply Wonderful Cookbook. (Illus.). 48p. (J). (gr. 4-8). 1992. text ed. 12.95 (*0-7459-2204-X*) Lion USA.

Robinson, Helene. Basic Piano for Adults for Class & Individual Instruction. 108p. (C). 1964. pap. 18.95 (*0-534-00065-7*) Intl Thomson.

***Robinson, Helja A.** The Ethnography of Empowerment: The Transformative Power of Classroom Interaction. LC 94-24726. 150p. 1994. 65.00x (*0-7507-0367-9*, Falmer Pr); pap. 24.95x (*0-7507-0368-7*, Falmer Pr) Taylor & Francis.

***Robinson, Henry.** The Little Pearls of Wisdom Book: For the Successful Dental Team. LC 95-1025. 1995. write for info. (*0-87814-442-0*) PennWell Bks.

Robinson, Henry C. Blake, Coleridge, Wordsworth, Lamb, Etc., Being Selections from the Remains of Henry Crabb Robinson. Morley, Edith J., ed. LC 23-6630. reprint ed. 24.50 (*0-404-05364-5*) AMS Pr.

— Diary, Reminiscences, & Correspondence, 3 vols., Set. (BCL1-PR English Literature Ser.). 1992. reprint ed. lib. bdg. 225.00 (*0-7812-7622-5*) Rprt Serv.

— Diary, Reminiscences, & Correspondence of Henry Crabb Robinson, 2 Vols. Sadler, Thomas, ed. reprint ed. write for info. (*0-318-50557-6*) AMS Pr.

— Diary, Reminiscences, & Correspondence of Henry Crabb Robinson, 2 Vols, 1. Sadler, Thomas, ed. LC 28-15241. reprint ed. write for info. (*0-404-05366-1*) AMS Pr.

— Diary, Reminiscences, & Correspondence of Henry Crabb Robinson, 2 Vols, 2. Sadler, Thomas, ed. LC 28-15241. reprint ed. write for info. (*0-404-05367-X*) AMS Pr.

— Diary, Reminiscences, & Correspondence of Henry Crabb Robinson, 2 Vols, Set. Sadler, Thomas, ed. LC 28-15241. reprint ed. 115.00 (*0-404-05365-3*) AMS Pr.

— Henry Crabb Robinson on Books & Their Writers, 3 Vols. Morley, Edith J., ed. reprint ed. write for info. (*0-318-50599-1*) AMS Pr.

— Henry Crabb Robinson on Books & Their Writers, 3 Vols, 1. Morley, Edith J., ed. LC 75-182705. reprint ed. write for info. (*0-404-05411-0*) AMS Pr.

— Henry Crabb Robinson on Books & Their Writers, 3 Vols, 2. Morley, Edith J., ed. LC 75-182705. reprint ed. write for info. (*0-404-05412-9*) AMS Pr.

— Henry Crabb Robinson on Books & Their Writers, 3 Vols, 3. Morley, Edith J., ed. LC 75-182705. reprint ed. write for info. (*0-404-05413-7*) AMS Pr.

— Henry Crabb Robinson on Books & Their Writers, 3 vols., Set. Morley, Edith J., ed. 1136p. 1938. 69.50x (*0-614-01807-2*) Elliots Bks.

— Henry Crabb Robinson on Books & Their Writers, 3 Vols, Set. Morley, Edith J., ed. LC 75-182705. reprint ed. 155.00 (*0-404-05410-2*) AMS Pr.

Robinson, Henry H. Negotiability in the Federal Sector. LC 80-28672. 232p. 1981. pap. 14.95 (*0-87546-081-X*) ILR Pr.

Robinson, Henry M. Fantastic Interim. LC 77-148895. (Select Bibliographies Reprint Ser.). 1977. 25.95 (*0-8369-5658-3*) Ayer.

Robinson, Henry M., jt. auth. see Campbell, Joseph.

Robinson, Henry P. The Elements of a Pictorial Photograph. LC 72-9228. (Literature of Photography Ser.). 1978. reprint ed. 12.95 (*0-405-04934-X*) Ayer.

— Letters on Landscape Photography. LC 72-9229. (Literature of Photography Ser.). 1973. reprint ed. 17.95 (*0-405-04935-8*) Ayer.

— Picture-Making by Photography. 5th ed. LC 72-9230. (Literature of Photography Ser.). 1973. reprint ed. 18.95 (*0-405-04936-6*) Ayer.

— The Studio: And What to Do in It. LC 72-9231. (Literature of Photography Ser.). 1973. reprint ed. 18.95 (*0-405-04937-4*) Ayer.

Robinson, Henry P. & Abney, W. D. The Art & Practice of Silver Printing. LC 72-9227. (Literature of Photography Ser.). 1973. reprint ed. 18.95 (*0-405-04933-1*) Ayer.

Robinson, Henry W. Corporate Personality in Ancient Israel. rev. ed. LC 79-8887. 64p. reprint ed. pap. 25.00 (*0-317-55504-9*, 2029603) Bks Demand.

— Inspiration & Revelation in the Old Testament. LC 78-9891. 298p. 1979. reprint ed. text ed. 59.75 (*0-313-21068-3*, ROIR, Greenwood Pr) Greenwood.

Robinson, Henry W., ed. The Bible in Its Ancient & English Version. LC 76-109832. 337p. 1970. text ed. 59.75 (*0-8371-4323-3*, ROBI, Greenwood Pr) Greenwood.

— Record & Revelation. LC 76-29395. reprint ed. 35.50 (*0-404-15354-2*) AMS Pr.

Robinson, Herbert S. & Wilson, Knox. Myths & Legends of All Nations. (Quality Paperback Ser.: No. 319). 244p. 1978. reprint ed. pap. 11.95 (*0-8226-0319-5*) Littlefield.

Robinson, Herbert S., et al. The Dictionary of Biography. (Quality Paperback Ser.: No. 281). 530p. 1975. reprint ed. pap. 7.25 (*0-8226-0281-4*) Littlefield.

Robinson, Herbert W. The Challenge to Government: Management of a Capitalist Economy. (Illus.). 300p. 1991. 39.95 (*0-9628558-1-2*) IMS Press.

Robinson, Hilary. Somerville & Ross: A Critical Appreciation. 220p. 1980. text ed. 29.95 (*0-312-74426-9*) St Martin.

***Robinson, Hoke, ed.** Proceedings of the Eighth International Kant Congress Vol. II, Pt. 1, Sec. 1-9. LC 94-80267. 1995. 25.00 (*0-87462-477-0*) Marquette.

— Proceedings of the Eighth International Kant Congress Vol. II, Pt. 2, Sec. 10-18. LC 94-80267. 1995. 25.00 (*0-87462-478-9*) Marquette.

Robinson, Hoke, tr. see Kamlah, Wilhelm & Lorenzen, Paul.

Robinson, Horace. Architecture for the Educational Theatre. LC 79-88930. (Illus.). 1970. 7.50 (*0-87114-052-7*) U of Oreg Bks.

Robinson-Horley, E. W. Last Post: An Indian Army Memoir. (Illus.). 192p. 1987. 35.95 (*0-436-42058-9*, Pub. by Seck & Warburg UK) Trafalgar.

Robinson, Howard. British Post Office: A History. LC 76-88930. 467p. 1970. reprint ed. text ed. 75.00 (*0-8371-3142-1*, ROPO, Greenwood Pr) Greenwood.

— Perception. LC 93-49381. (Problems of Philosophy: Their Past & Present Ser.). 280p. 1994. 55.00 (*0-415-03364-0*, B4651, Routledge NY) Routledge.

Robinson, Howard, ed. Objections to Physicalism. LC 92-28443. (Illus.). 336p. 1993. 47.00 (*0-19-824256-5*, Clarendon Pr) OUP.

Robinson, Howard, jt. ed. see Blumenthal, Henry.

Robinson, I. K., jt. ed. see Zabel, H.

Robinson, I. S. The Papacy, 1073-1198: Continuity & Innovation. (Cambridge Medieval Textbooks Ser.). 560p. (C). 1990. 79.95 (*0-521-26498-7*); pap. 22.95 (*0-521-31922-6*) Cambridge U Pr.

Robinson, Ian. Chaucer & the English Tradition. (C). 1986. 125.00 (*0-907839-29-0*, Pub. by Brynmill Pr Ltd UK) St Mut.

— Chaucer & the English Tradition. LC 79-163179. 308p. reprint ed. pap. 87.80 (*0-317-26392-7*, 2024530) Bks Demand.

Robinson, Ian, ed. Life & Death under High Technology Medicine. LC 94-17574. (Fulbright Papers: Vol. 14). 1995. text ed. 79.95 (*0-7190-3590-2*, Pub. by Manchester Univ Pr UK) St Martin.

Robinson, Ian & Mencher, Elaine, eds. The Market Bell. 322p. (C). 1989. 95.00 (*0-907839-42-8*, Pub. by Brynmill Pr Ltd UK) St Mut.

Robinson, Ian & Sims, David, eds. The Decline & Fall of Mr. Heath: Essays in Criticism of Recent British Politics. 78p. (C). 1989. 40.00 (*0-9502723-4-5*, Pub. by Brynmill Pr Ltd UK) St Mut.

Robinson, Ian, jt. ed. see Knight, Roger.

Robinson, Ira. Moses Cordovero's Introduction to Kabbalah: An Annotated Translation of His Or Neerav. LC 93-45501. 1993. write for info. (*0-88125-439-8*, Yeshiva Univ Pr) Ktav.

Robinson, Ira, ed. Cyrus Adler - Selected Letters. 1985. 50.00 (*0-317-64460-2*) Jewish Sem.

Robinson, Ira, jt. ed. see Rabkin, Yakov.

Robinson, Ira, et al, eds. The Thought of Moses Maimonides: Philosophical & Legal Studies. (Studies in the History of Philosophy: Vol. 17). 424p. (ENG & FRE.). 1991. lib. bdg. 109.95 (*0-88946-286-0*) E Mellen.

Robinson, J. Architecture Through the Looking Glass. 1992. pap. write for info. (*0-442-01003-6*) Van Nos Reinhold.

Robinson, J., ed. The First Book of Kings. LC 72-80592. (Cambridge Bible Commentary on the New English Bible, New Testament Ser.). (Illus.). 228p. 1972. pap. 24.95 (*0-521-09734-7*) Cambridge U Pr.

— The Second Book of Kings. LC 75-39371. (Cambridge Bible Commentary on the New English Bible, New Testament Ser.). (Illus.). 1976. pap. 24.95 (*0-521-09774-6*) Cambridge U Pr.

Robinson, J., ed. see Valery, Paul.

Robinson, J. A. Euthaliana, Studies of Euthalius: Codex H of the Pauline Epistles & the Armenian Version. (Texts & Studies Ser.: No. 1, Vol. 3, Pt. 3). 1972. reprint ed. pap. 15.00 (*0-8115-1690-3*) Periodicals Srv.

Robinson, J. A., ed. The Passion of S. Perpetua. (Texts & Studies Ser.: No. 1, Vol. 1,Pt. 2). 1974. reprint ed. pap. 15.00 (*0-8115-1680-6*) Periodicals Srv.

Robinson, J. B., ed. Diagnosis of Mineral Disorders in Plants. 1984. Vol. 1, Principles. 66.50 (*0-8206-0311-2*); Vol. 2, Vegetables. 82.50 (*0-8206-0312-0*) Chem Pub.

— Diagnosis of Mineral Disorders in Plants: Vegetables, Vol. II. 100p. 1982. 110.00 (*0-11-240804-4*, Pub. by HMSO UK) UNIPUB.

Robinson, J. B., jt. ed. see Reuter, D. J.

Robinson, J. Bradford, tr. see Dahlhaus, Carl.

Robinson, J. Bradford, tr. see Knepler, Georg.

Robinson, J. Bradford, tr. see Luz, Ulrich.

Robinson, J. Cordell, jt. auth. see Robinson, Barbara J.

Robinson, J. E., ed. Abnormal Load on Power Systems: Report on the Symposium on Transient, Fluctuating & Distorting Loads & Their Effects on Power Systems & Communications, 25th & 26th February. LC 65-63212. (Institution of Electrical Engineers Conference Report Ser.: No. 8). 192p. reprint ed. pap. 54.80 (*0-8357-5011-6*, 2050830) Bks Demand.

Robinson, J. F. & Lowe, Stephen. Videotape Recording. 4th ed. 1987. write for info. (*0-240-51298-7*, Focal) Buttrwrth-Heinemann.

Robinson, J. Gregg, jt. auth. see McIlwee, Judith S.

Robinson, J. H. & Robinson, R. D. Involving Children in One Hundred Four Sunday School Openings. 72p. (J). 1983. pap. 5.99 (*0-570-03912-6*, 12HH2851) Concordia.

Robinson, J. H., et al, eds. Dialysis, Transplantation, Nephrology: Proceedings, European Dialysis & Transplant Association, Vol. 16. (Illus.). 785p. 1979. 65.00 (*0-8464-1067-2*) Beekman Pubs.

Robinson, J. Hedley, ed. God & the Universe. 70p. (C). 1989. pap. 40.00 (*0-7223-2220-8*, Pub. by A H S Ltd UK) St Mut.

Robinson, J. Lewis, ed. British Columbia. LC 72-197301. (Studies in Canadian Geography Ser.). 149p. reprint ed. pap. 42.50 (*0-8357-7420-1*, 2026536) Bks Demand.

Robinson, J. O. Medical Milestones: A Record of Men, Discoveries & Progress at St. Bartholomew's Hospital. (History of Medicine Ser.). (Illus.). 150p. 1994. 48.00 (*1-85070-408-2*) Prthnon Pub.

Robinson, J. Paul, et al, eds. Handbook of Flow Cytometry Methods. LC 92-47082. 260p. 1993. pap. text ed. 49.95 (*0-471-59634-5*, Wiley-Liss) Wiley.

***Robinson, J. Russell.** Radical Systems Development: An Introduction to Rapid Application Development. 152p. 1995. pap. 34.95 (*1-57087-105-1*) Prof Pr NC.

Robinson, J. S., ed. Extrusion of Plastics. LC 82-62311. 270p. (Orig.). 1982. pap. 45.00 (*0-942378-01-6*) Polymers & Plastics Tech Pub Hse.

— Hazardous Chemical Spill Cleanup. LC 79-16362. (Pollution Technology Review Ser.: No. 59). (Illus.). 406p. 1980. 48.00 (*0-8155-0767-4*) Noyes.

— Plastics Molding: Equipment, Processes, & Materials. LC 81-90745. x, 299p. 1981. pap. 42.00 (*0-942378-00-8*) Polymers & Plastics Tech Pub Hse.

Robinson, J. T., jt. auth. see Broom, Robert.

Robinson, J. W. Handbook of Spectroscopy, Vol. 3. 560p. 1981. 146.00 (*0-8493-0333-8*, QD95) CRC Pr.

— Studies in Fifteenth-Century Stagecraft. (Early Drama, Art & Music Monograph: No. 14). 1990. pap. 16.95 (*0-918720-39-7*); boxed 26.95 (*0-918720-38-9*) Medieval Inst.

Robinson, Jack. Finishing Touches, Vol. I. Baum, Samuel J., ed. (Illus.). 56p. 1991. pap. 7.95 (*0-89778-045-0*, 10-6600) Greenberg Bks.

Robinson, Jack F. History of the Illinois Conference, United Church of Christ. LC 90-81374. 57p. 1990. pap. text ed. 5.50 (*0-913552-43-7*) Exploration Pr.

Robinson, Jack H. John Calvin & the Jews. LC 91-34889. (American University Studies: Theology & Religion: Ser. VII, Vol. 123). 152p. (C). 1993. text ed. 35.95 (*0-8204-1752-1*) P Lang Pubs.

Robinson, Jack W., Jr., et al. Pritchard on the Law of Wills & Administration of Estates, 3 vols., Set. 5th suppl. ed. 1995. 225.00 (*0-87215-605-2*) Michie Butterworth.

Robinson, Jack W., jt. auth. see Phillips, Harry.

***Robinson, Jack W., Jr., et al.** Tennessee Forms, 3 vols., Set. 1991. 300.00 (*0-87473-714-1*) Michie Butterworth.

Robinson, Jackie. Animas Quilts. Reikes, Ursula, ed. LC 93-25007. (Quilt Shop Ser.). (Illus.). 88p. (Orig.). 1993. pap. 19.95 (*1-56477-037-0*, B160) That Patchwork.

— Dining Dazzle. 68p. 1993. pap. text ed. 16.00 (*1-885156-04-9*) Animas Quilts.

— I Never Had It Made: An Autobiography. LC 94-45279. 1995. 24.00 (*0-88001-419-9*) Ecco Pr.

— Quadcentrics. 18p. 1991. pap. text ed. 7.00 (*1-885156-02-2*) Animas Quilts.

— Tessellations. 46p. 1992. pap. text ed. 12.00 (*1-885156-03-0*) Animas Quilts.

— Weaver Fever. 14p. 1991. pap. text ed. 6.50 (*1-885156-01-4*) Animas Quilts.

Robinson, Jackie & Duckett, Alfred. Breakthrough to the Big League: The Story of Jackie Robinson. LC 90-48588. (American Cavalcade Ser.). (Illus.). 160p. (J). (gr. 6-10). 1991. lib. bdg. 9.95 (*1-55905-094-2*) Marshall Cavendish.

Robinson, Jacky. Saltwater Adventure in the Florida Keys: An Introduction to Fishing for Kids. LC 94-60394. (Illus.). 104p. (J). (gr. 3-7). 1994. lib. bdg. 19.95 (*0-9641228-0-4*) White Heron.

Robinson, Jacob. Guide to Jewish History Under Nazi Impact. 1974. 45.00 (*0-87068-231-8*) Ktav.

— Palestine & the United Nations: Prelude to Solution. LC 71-147221. 269p. 1971. reprint ed. text ed. 59.75 (*0-8371-5986-5*, ROPU, Greenwood Pr) Greenwood.

Robinson, Jacob, ed. The Holocaust & After: Sources & Literature in English. 353p. 1973. boxed 34.95 (*0-87855-186-7*) Transaction Pubs.

Robinson, Jacob S. A Journal of the Santa Fe Expedition under Colonel Doniphan. LC 75-87634. (American Scene Ser.). (Illus.). 96p. 1972. reprint ed. lib. bdg. 15.00 (*0-306-71798-0*) Da Capo.

Robinson, Jacqueline, et al. High School Entrance Exams. LC 94-4836. (J). 1994. write for info. (*0-671-89196-0*) P-H.

— High School Entrance Exams. 4th ed. 512p. 1991. pap. 12.00 (*0-13-388612-3*, Arco Test) P-H Gen Ref & Trav.

Robinson, Jacqueline S. I'm Ready for Reading. (J). (ps-00). 1990. 19.95 (*0-9624827-0-6*) A Plus Lrn.

— More Ready for Reading. (J). (gr. k-2). 1990. 19.95 (*0-9624827-1-4*) A Plus Lrn.

Robinson, James. The Art of Curing, Pickling & Smoking Meat & Fish. 1973. 250.00 (*0-87968-053-9*) Gordon Pr.

An Asterisk (*) at the beginning of an entry indicates that the title is appearing in BIP for the first time.

— Better Speeches in Ten Simple Steps. 2nd rev. ed. LC 94-39592. 1995. 9.95 (*1-55958-691-5*) Prima Pub.

— A Cup Running Over. (Orig.). 1987. pap. 6.55 (*0-89536-873-0*, 7859) CSS OH.

— Grendel Tales Bk. 1: Four Devils, One Hell. (Illus.). 168p. 1994. pap. 17.95 (*1-56971-027-9*) Dark Horse Comics.

— Illegal Alien. (Illus.). 80p. (YA). 1994. pap. 9.95 (*0-87816-297-6*) Kitchen Sink.

— The Terminator: One Shot. Schutz, Diana, ed. (Illus.). 52p. (Orig.). 1992. pap. 5.95 (*1-878574-22-1*) Dark Horse Comics.

— The Terminator: Secondary Objectives Collection. Schutz, Diana & Prosser, Jerry, eds. (Illus.). 112p. 1992. pap. 13.95 (*1-878574-31-0*) Dark Horse Comics.

Robinson, James & Mino, Yutaka. A Collector's Choices: Asian Art from the Collection of Dr. Walter A. Compton. LC 82-84073. (Illus.). 72p. (Orig.). 1983. pap. text ed. 9.00 (*0-936260-08-4*) Ind Mus Art.

Robinson, James & Nielson, Nancy. Natural Healing & Prevention Secrets. Date not set. pap. 19.95 (*0-9638596-1-7*) Amer Pubng.

Robinson, James, tr. see Abhayadatta.

Robinson, James, jt. auth. see Mino, Yutaka.

Robinson, James, ed. see Spear, Robert K. & Moak, D. Michael.

Robinson, James A. Congress & Foreign Policy-Making: A Study in Legislative Influence & Initiative. LC 80-20372. x, 262p. (C). 1980. reprint ed. text ed. 59.75 (*0-313-22706-3*, ROCF, Greenwood Pr) Greenwood.

— The House Rules Committee. LC 83-18495. xiv, 142p. 1983. reprint ed. text ed. 49.75 (*0-313-24300-X*, ROHO, Greenwood Pr) Greenwood.

— Political Science Annual: An International Review, Vol. 3. LC 66-29710. 1972. 17.95 (*0-672-51743-4*, Bobbs) Macmillan.

Robinson, James C. Peter Taylor. (Study of the Short Fiction Ser.: No. 3). 192p. 1988. text ed. 22.95 (*0-8057-8303-2*, Twayne) Macmillan.

— Toil & Toxics: Workplace Struggles & Political Strategies for Occupational Health. LC 90-20986. 253p. 1991. 35.00 (*0-520-07164-6*); pap. 13.00 (*0-520-08448-9*) U CA Pr.

Robinson, James C., jt. auth. see Robinson, Dana G.

Robinson, James D. How to Use The Bible. 1982. pap. 4.50 (*0-570-03853-7*, 12-2808) Concordia.

Robinson, James H. Essays in Intellectual History, Dedicated to James Harvey Robinson by His Former Seminar Students. LC 68-14903. (Essay Index Reprint Ser.). 1977. 23.95 (*0-8369-0425-7*) Ayer.

— Humanizing of Knowledge. LC 72-165742. (American Education Ser, No. 2). 1972. reprint ed. 11.95 (*0-405-03613-2*) Ayer.

— One Legged Lion. Van Treese, James B., ed. 366p. 1994. pap. 12.95 (*1-56901-092-7*) NW Pub.

— Petrarch. LC 75-127999. (World History Ser.: No. 48). 1970. reprint ed. lib. bdg. 59.95 (*0-8383-1148-2*) M S G Haskell Hse.

Robinson, James H. & Darline, R. One Hundred Bible Quiz Activities for Church School Classes. 1981. pap. 4.95 (*0-570-03829-4*, 12-2794) Concordia.

Robinson, James H. & Robinson, Rowena D. Bulletin Board Ideas. LC 72-94108. 80p. 1981. pap. 5.95 (*0-570-03141-9*, 12-2525) Concordia.

Robinson, James K. & Collins, Lynn M., eds. Introducing Evidence: A Practical Guide for Michigan Lawyers. suppl. ed. LC 88-81316. 260p. 1991. ring bd. 80.00 (*0-685-22722-7*, 88-010) U MI Law CLE.

— Introducing Evidence 1990: A Practical Guide for Michigan Lawyers. suppl. ed. LC 88-81316. 260p. 1988. 35.00 (*0-685-44339-6*) U MI Law CLE.

— Introducing Evidence 1991: A Practical Guide for Michigan Lawyers. suppl. ed. LC 88-81316. 260p. 1988. 35.00 (*0-685-22723-5*, 90-024) U MI Law CLE.

Robinson, James K. & Rideout, Walter B. A College Book of Modern Verse. 1977. 24.95 (*0-8369-6406-3*, 7470) Ayer.

Robinson, James K., ed. see Hardy, Thomas.

***Robinson, James L.** Racism or Attitude? The Ongoing Struggle for Black Liberation & Self-Esteem. 269p. 1995. 24.95 (*0-306-44945-5*) Da Capo.

Robinson, James M. West from Fort Pierre: The World of Scotty Philip. (Great West & Indian Ser.: Vol. 43). (Illus.). 1974. 19.95 (*0-87026-032-4*) Westernlore.

Robinson, James M., ed. A Facsimile Edition of the Dead Sea Scrolls, 1. LC 91-58627. (Illus.). 1785p. (ARC, GRE & HEB.). 1992. reprint ed. write for info. (*1-880317-01-X*) Biblical Arch Soc.

— A Facsimile Edition of the Dead Sea Scrolls, 2. LC 91-58627. (Illus.). 1785p. (ARC, GRE & HEB.). 1992. reprint ed. write for info. (*1-880317-02-8*) Biblical Arch Soc.

— A Facsimile Edition of the Dead Sea Scrolls, Vols. 1-2. LC 91-58627. (Illus.). 1785p. (ARC, GRE & HEB.). 1992. reprint ed. text ed. 195.00 (*1-880317-00-1*, 7H21) Biblical Arch Soc.

— The Nag Hammadi Library in English. rev. ed. LC 88-45154. 576p. 1990. reprint ed. pap. 18.00 (*0-06-066935-7*) Harper SF.

Robinson, James M. & Cobb, John B., Jr., eds. The Later Heidegger & Theology. LC 78-23619. 212p. 1979. reprint ed. text ed. 38.50 (*0-313-20783-6*, ROLH, Greenwood Pr) Greenwood.

Robinson, James O. Frederick Amasa Coller, MD: Biography. Jones, Claudella, ed. LC 86-50838. (Illus.). 278p. 1987. 66.00 (*0-917478-39-8*) Natl Inst Burn.

Robinson, James O., ed. Clio Chirurgical: Biliary Tract. rev. ed. (Surgery Ser.). (Illus.). 227p. 1988. 65.00 (*0-941432-14-9*); pap. 35.00 (*0-941432-15-7*) R G Landes.

Robinson, James R. Four Voices - One Gospel: The Synergistic Gospel of the New Testament - King James Edition. 608p. 1992. pap. 29.95 (*1-881426-00-9*) Quest Pub AZ.

Robinson, James W. Atomic Absorption Spectroscopy. 2nd rev. ed. LC 75-328457. (Illus.). 197p. reprint ed. pap. 56.20 (*0-7837-0896-3*, 2041201) Bks Demand.

— The Beauty of Being Prepared. 1982. 4.45 (*0-89536-548-0*, 0213) CSS OH.

— Better Speeches in Ten Simple Steps. 1989. pap. 7.95 (*0-914629-86-7*) Prima Pub.

— Doing Business in Vietnam. LC 94-13044. 1994. write for info. (*1-55958-591-9*) Prima Pub.

Robinson, James W., et al. The Grievance Procedure & Arbitration: Text & Cases. LC 77-18573. 1978. pap. text ed. 27.00 (*0-8191-0411-6*) U Pr of Amer.

Robinson, James W. Practical Handbook Spectroscopy. (Illus.). 880p. 1991. 83.95 (*0-8493-3708-9*, QD95) CRC Pr.

— Undergraduate Instrumental Analysis. 5th expanded rev. ed. LC 94-21455. 872p. 1994. 65.00 (*0-8247-9215-7*) Dekker.

— Winning Them Over: Get Your Message Across by Dealing Successfully with the Media & Giving Powerful Speeches. Mikesell, Suzanne, ed. 200p. 1986. 17.95 (*0-685-13477-6*, St Martin) Prima Pub.

***Robinson, James W. & Colliau, Russ.** After the Revolution: A Citizen's Guide to the First Republican Congress in Forty Years. LC 94-47409. 1995. pap. 9.95 (*0-7615-0072-3*) Prima Pub.

Robinson, James W. & Walker, Roger W. Introduction to Labor. 2nd ed. (Illus.). 176p. (C). 1985. pap. text ed. write for info. (*0-13-485509-4*) P-H.

Robinson, Jan. Sea to Shore. 288p. 1989. pap. 14.95 (*0-9612686-3-8*) Ship-Shore.

— Ship to Shore, Vol. II. (Illus.). 288p. 1986. pap. 14.95 (*0-9612686-1-1*) Ship-Shore.

— Sip to Shore. 128p. 1986. pap. 10.95 (*0-9612686-2-X*) Ship-Shore.

— Slim to Shore: Recipes for a Healthy Lifestyle. Martin, Jan, ed. (Illus.). 288p. 1994. pap. 14.95 (*0-9612686-5-4*) Ship-Shore.

— Sweet to Shore. 288p. 1990. pap. 14.95 (*0-9612686-4-6*) Ship-Shore.

Robinson, Jan, comp. Ship to Shore: Caribbean Charter Yacht Recipes. (Illus.). 448p. (Orig.). 1987. reprint ed. pap. 15.95 (*0-13-808932-9*) P-H.

Robinson, Jan & Fowler, Cheryl A., eds. Ship to Shore, Vol. I. (Illus.). 336p. 1983. pap. 14.95 (*0-9612686-0-3*) Ship-Shore.

Robinson, Jancis, ed. The Oxford Companion to Wine. (Illus.). 1040p. 1994. 49.95 (*0-19-866159-2*) OUP.

Robinson, Jane. Wayward Women: A Guide to Women Travellers. (Illus.). 368p. 1990. 39.95 (*0-19-212261-4*) OUP.

— Wayward Women: A Guide to Women Travellers. (Illus.). 368p. 1994. reprint ed. pap. 14.95 (*0-19-282822-3*) OUP.

— The Whale in Lowell's Cove. LC 91-77670. (Illus.). 48p. (J). (gr. 1-4). 1992. 14.95 (*0-89272-308-4*) Down East.

***Robinson, Jane, sel.** Unsuitable for Ladies: An Anthology of Women Travelers. (Illus.). 496p. 1995. pap. 14.95 (*0-19-282489-9*) OUP.

— Unsuitable for Ladies: An Anthology of Women Travellers. LC 93-34644. (Illus.). 496p. 1994. 30.00 (*0-19-211681-9*) OUP.

Robinson, Jane, et al, eds. Policy Issues in Nursing. 192p. 1991. 90.00 (*0-335-09467-8*, Open Univ Pr); pap. 34.00 (*0-335-09466-X*, Open Univ Pr) Taylor & Francis.

Robinson, Jane E. The Amazon Chronicles: An Historical Novel. 401p. (Orig.). 1994. pap. 15.95 (*1-878533-12-6*) Clothespin Fever Pr.

Robinson, Jane W. A Birder's Guide to Japan. (Illus.). 358p. 1988. reprint ed. 15.95 (*0-934797-02-1*) Cornell U Pr.

Robinson, Janet E. Underground Storage Tank Management: Closure & Financial Assurance. 1993. 59.95 (*0-87371-402-4*, TD1050) Lewis Pubs.

Robinson, Jay L., ed. Conversations on the Written Word: Essays on Language & Literacy. (Illus.). 335p. (Orig.). 1990. pap. text ed. 21.00 (*0-86709-252-1*) Boynton Cook Pubs.

Robinson, Jayme, ed. see Rice, Jayne.

Robinson, Jean & McVan, Barbara. Medications & IVs. LC 86-30096. (Clinical Pocket Manual Ser.). 187p. 1987. spiral bd., pap. 15.95 (*0-87434-013-6*) Springhouse Pub.

— Neurologic Care. LC 85-27706. (Clinical Pocket Manual Ser.). (Illus.). 187p. 1986. spiral bd., pap. 15.95 (*0-87434-011-X*) Springhouse Pub.

— OB-GYN Care. LC 86-31386. (Clinical Pocket Manual Ser.). 187p. 1987. spiral bd. 15.95 (*0-87434-014-4*) Springhouse Pub.

— Pediatric Care. LC 86-31385. (Clinical Pocket Manual Ser.). 187p. 1987. spiral bd. 15.95 (*0-87434-015-2*) Springhouse Pub.

— Surgical Care. LC 85-27702. (Clinical Pocket Manual Ser.). 187p. 1986. spiral bd. 15.95 (*0-87434-012-8*) Springhouse Pub.

Robinson, Jeanne, jt. auth. see Robinson, Spider.

Robinson, Jeffrey. Europe at Low Cost. 359p. 1978. 5.95 (*0-686-63830-1*) Allsport Pub.

— The Ginger Jar. large type ed. (Mystery Ser.). 560p. 1988. 15.95 (*0-7089-1905-7*) Ulverscroft.

— Rainier & Grace. 1990. mass mkt. 4.95 (*0-380-71310-1*) Avon.

Robinson, Jeffrey & McCann, Brian, eds. High on Hope: Gwyn Thomas. 120p. (C). 1989. 40.00 (*0-905928-40-7*, Pub. by D Brown & Sons Ltd UK) St Mut.

Robinson, Jeffrey C. The Current of Romantic Passion. LC 91-6580. 214p. (Orig.). (C). 1991. lib. bdg. 40.75 (*0-299-12960-8*); pap. 16.95 (*0-299-12964-0*) U of Wis Pr.

— Radical Literary Education: A Classroom Experiment with Wordsworth's "Ode" LC 86-23366. 224p. 1986. pap. text ed. 14.95 (*0-299-11064-8*) U of Wis Pr.

— Radical Literary Education: A Classroom Experiment with Wordsworth's "Ode" LC 86-23366. 224p. (C). 1987. text ed. 30.00 (*0-299-11060-5*) U of Wis Pr.

— The Walk: Notes on a Romantic Image. LC 88-37876. (Illus.). 160p. 1989. 22.95 (*0-8061-2181-5*) U of Okla Pr.

Robinson, Jeffrey C., ed. see Van Ghent, Dorothy.

Robinson, Jeremy. Gloryland: Passionate Poetry Three. 72p. (C). 1989. pap. text ed. 29.00 (*1-871846-25-0*, Pub. by Crescent Moon UK) St Mut.

— Love into Magic. (C). 1990. pap. text ed. 29.00 (*1-871846-95-1*, Pub. by Crescent Moon UK) St Mut.

— The Madona Glorified: The Paintings of Karen Arthurs & Exhibition Hours of the Virgin. 60p. (C). 1991. text ed. 39.00 (*1-871846-06-4*, Pub. by Crescent Moon UK) St Mut.

— Sacred. (C). 1989. pap. text ed. 29.00 (*0-685-63519-8*, Pub. by Crescent Moon UK) St Mut.

Robinson, Jerome. The Complete Plays of Gilbert & Sullivan. 711p. 1991. reprint ed. text ed. 119.00 (*0-7812-9326-X*) Rprt Serv.

Robinson, Jerome B. Training the Hunting Retriever. 232p. 1993. 18.95 (*1-55821-263-9*) Lyons & Burford.

Robinson, Jerry. Something's Out There: A Newspaperman's Columns from Days Gone By. 248p. 1992. pap. 16.95 (*0-9635444-9-7*) Robinson Comm.

— Syner Abs II. (Illus.). 46p. 1990. pap. 14.95 (*0-944831-27-3*) Health Life.

— The Weightless Workout. (Illus.). 158p. (Orig.). 1990. pap. 19.95 (*0-944831-26-5*) Health Life.

Robinson, Jerry & Carrino, Frank. MAXO2. LC 93-73083. (Illus.). 222p. 1993. pap. 19.95 (*0-944831-30-3*) Health Life.

Robinson, Jerry & Horrigan, Joseph. The Seven-Minute Rotator Cuff Solution. (Illus.). 64p. (Orig.). 1990. pap. 16.95 (*0-944831-25-7*) Health Life.

Robinson, Jerry & Miller, Robert. The Transfigure System Two. (Illus.). 132p. (Orig.). 1990. pap. 19.95 (*0-944831-24-9*) Health Life.

Robinson, Jerry W., jt. ed. see Christenson, James A.

Robinson, Jerry W., Jr.

Robinson, Jerry W., et al. Applied Keyboarding. 3rd ed. LC 93-7454. (YA). 1994. text ed. 19.95 (*0-538-62297-0*) S-W Pub.

— Applied Keyboarding. 3rd ed. LC 93-7454. (YA). 1994. text ed. 23.95 (*0-538-62298-9*) S-W Pub.

— Basic Information Keyboarding Skills: A Collegiate Course. 2nd ed. (C). 1988. text ed. 26.95 (*0-538-26160-9*, Z16) S-W Pub.

— Keyboarding & Computer Applications: Includes Commands & Directions for WordPerfect 5.1 MS-DOS, Microsoft Works 2.0 & 3.0 MS-DOS, Microsoft Works 2.0 Macintosh, Lotus 1-2-3. LC 93-32416. 1995. text ed. 29.95 (*0-538-62193-1*) S-W Pub.

Robinson, Jesse S. The Amalgamated Association of Iron, Steel & Tin Workers. LC 74-22757. reprint ed. 24.50 (*0-404-58510-8*) AMS Pr.

Robinson, Jessie B., jt. auth. see Eisenberg, Azriel.

Robinson, Jill. Bed-Time-Story. 272p. 1979. pap. 1.95 (*0-449-24064-9*, Crest) Fawcett.

Robinson, Jill & Fox, A. Dale. Scuba Diving with Disabilities. LC 86-18532. (Illus.). 144p. (Orig.). 1987. pap. 20.00 (*0-88011-280-8*, PROB0280) Human Kinetics.

Robinson, Jim. Roggy Lived on Planet Sun. 288p. 1992. 22.00 (*0-9634367-0-8*) Swallows In-Hse.

Robinson, Jim, photos. Morehouse College - Then & Now. (First Edition Ser.). (Illus.). 112p. 1992. 39.95 (*0-916509-86-9*) Harmony Hse Pub LO.

Robinson, Jo & Staeheli, Jean. Unplug the Christmas Machine: How to Really Participate in the Joys of Christmas. LC 82-13154. 1982. pap. 8.95 (*0-688-01461-5*, Quill) Morrow.

Robinson, Jo & Staeheli, Jean C. The Leader's Guide to the Unplug the Christmas Machine Workshop. 128p. 1991. spiral bd. 20.00 (*0-688-11103-3*, Quill) Morrow.

— Unplug the Christmas Machine: A Complete Guide to Putting Love & Joy Back into the Season. rev. ed. 256p. 1991. pap. 9.00 (*0-688-10961-6*, Quill) Morrow.

Robinson, Jo, jt. auth. see Allen, Marvin.

Robinson, Jo, jt. auth. see Love, Patricia.

Robinson, Jo A. The Montgomery Bus Boycott & the Women Who Started It. Garrow, David J., ed. LC 86-14684. (Illus.). 208p. 1987. pap. 14.95 (*0-87049-527-5*) U of Tenn Pr.

Robinson, Jo Ann. A. J. Muste: Pacifist & Prophet. Mather, Eleanore P., ed. LC 81-80219. 31p. 1981. pap. 3.00 (*0-87574-235-1*) Pendle Hill.

Robinson, Joan. The Accumulation of Capital. 3rd ed. LC 85-12465. xvi, 440p. 1986. reprint ed. lib. bdg. 45.00 (*0-87991-266-9*); reprint ed. pap. 22.95 (*0-87991-260-X*) Porcupine Pr.

— Collected Economic Papers of Joan Robinson, 5 vols. 1980. Index. 20.00 (*0-262-18098-7*) MIT Pr.

— Collected Economic Papers of Joan Robinson, 5 vols., 1. 1980. 37.50 (*0-262-18093-6*) MIT Pr.

— Collected Economic Papers of Joan Robinson, 5 vols., 2. 1980. 37.50 (*0-262-18094-4*) MIT Pr.

— Collected Economic Papers of Joan Robinson, 5 vols., 5. 1980. 37.50 (*0-262-18097-9*) MIT Pr.

— An Essay on Marxian Economics. 2nd ed. xxiv, 104p. 1991. reprint ed. pap. 12.95 (*0-87991-270-7*, Orion Editions) Porcupine Pr.

— Essays in the Theory of Employment. LC 78-14138. (Illus.). 1985. reprint ed. 21.00 (*0-88355-812-2*) Hyperion Conn.

— Notes from China. LC 64-23734. 46p. reprint ed. pap. 25.00 (*0-317-08499-2*, 2001707) Bks Demand.

— The Rate of Interest & Other Essays. LC 79-51867. 1986. reprint ed. 19.00 (*0-88355-959-5*) Hyperion Conn.

— What Are the Questions? Other Essays. LC 80-28062. 244p. 1981. pap. 24.95 (*0-87332-200-2*) M E Sharpe.

— WordBuilding. (Roots of Language Ser.). (J). (gr. 4-8). 1989. pap. 9.99 (*0-8224-7450-6*) Fearon Teach Aids.

— WordStrength. (Roots of Language Ser.). (J). (gr. 4-8). 1989. pap. 9.99 (*0-8224-7451-4*) Fearon Teach Aids.

— WordWise. (Roots of Language Ser.). (J). (gr. 4-8). 1989. pap. 9.99 (*0-8224-7452-2*) Fearon Teach Aids.

Robinson, JoAnn G. The Montgomery Bus Boycott & the Women Who Started It. Garrow, David J., ed. LC 86-14684. (Illus.). 208p. 1987. text ed. 36.00x (*0-87049-524-0*) U of Tenn Pr.

Robinson, John. How Americans Use Time: A Social-Psychological Analysis of Everyday Behavior. LC 76-58838. (Special Studies). 224p. 1977. text ed. 40.95 (*0-275-90273-0*, C0273, Praeger Pubs) Greenwood.

— A Justification of Separation from the Church of England. LC 77-7427. (English Experience Ser.: No. 888). 1977. reprint ed. lib. bdg. 65.00 (*90-221-0888-0*) Walter J Johnson.

— Legends of the Lost. 160p. (Orig.). 1989. pap. 12.95 (*1-882021-07-X*) Salt River Pr.

— Motor Cycle Tuning (Four-stroke) 1988. pap. 24.95 (*0-434-91743-5*) Buttrwrth-Heinemann.

— Motor Cycle Tuning (Two-stroke) 1988. pap. 27.95 (*0-7506-0682-7*) Buttrwrth-Heinemann.

— Motorcycle Service & Set-Up Data. 2nd ed. 256p. 1991. 32.95 (*0-7506-0082-9*) Buttrwrth-Heinemann.

— Motorcycle Tuning: Chassis. (Illus.). 272p. 1994. pap. 24.95 (*0-7506-1840-X*) Buttrwrth-Heinemann.

— Motorcycle Tuning: Four-Stroke. 2nd ed. 178p. 1994. pap. 24.95 (*0-7506-1805-1*) Buttrwrth-Heinemann.

— Motorcycle Tuning: Two-Stroke. 2nd ed. 169p. 1994. pap. 24.95 (*0-7506-1806-X*) Buttrwrth-Heinemann.

— Motorcycle Tuning (Chassis) (Illus.). 176p. 1990. pap. 27.95 (*0-7506-0798-X*) Buttrwrth-Heinemann.

— My Own Story. (American Autobiography Ser.). 172p. 1995. reprint ed. lib. bdg. 69.00 (*0-7812-8627-1*) Rprt Serv.

— The Rock & Roll Connoisseur's Guide to Song Trivia: Footnotes to Some of Rock & Roll's Greatest Hits. 130p. 1988. pap. 9.95 (*0-685-44319-1*) Baruba Bros Inc.

Robinson, John A. The Body: A Study in Pauline Theology. LC 88-40316. 95p. (C). 1988. pap. text ed. 14.95 (*1-55605-050-X*) Wyndhall Pr.

— Exploration into God. LC 67-26529. x, 166p. 1967. 10.95 (*0-8047-0322-1*) Stanford U Pr.

— Honest to God. LC 63-13819. 144p. 1963. pap. 9.99 (*0-664-24465-3*, Westminster) Westminster John Knox.

Robinson, John B. Economics of Liberty. 1972. 59.95 (*0-8490-0084-X*) Gordon Pr.

— Pictures of Slavery & Anti-Slavery. LC 70-83875. (Black Heritage Library Collection). 1977. 20.95 (*0-8369-8646-6*) Ayer.

— Rebuilding the World. 1972. 59.95 (*0-8490-0934-0*) Gordon Pr.

Robinson, John B., ed. see Proudhon, Pierre-Joseph.

Robinson, John C. An Annotated Checklist of the Birds of Tennessee. LC 89-77251. 288p. 1990. 29.95 (*0-87049-642-5*) U of Tenn Pr.

— Death of a Hero, Birth of the Soul: Answering the Call of Midlife. 352p. 1995. pap. 16.95 (*0-929999-09-6*) Tzedakah Pubns.

Robinson, John G. & Redford, Kent H., eds. Neotropical Wildlife Use & Conservation: With Forty-Seven Contributors. LC 90-44430. (Illus.). 512p. 1991. lib. bdg. 62.00 (*0-226-72258-9*); pap. 29.95 (*0-226-72259-7*) U Ch Pr.

Robinson, John H. A Reason to Live. (American Heroes Ser.). (Illus.). 446p. 1989. 19.95 (*0-916693-12-0*) Castle Bks.

Robinson, John J. Born in Blood. LC 89-23703. 396p. 1990. 18.95 (*0-87131-602-1*) M Evans.

— Dungeon, Fire & Sword: The Knights Templar in the Crusades. LC 91-27495. 494p. 1992. 24.95 (*0-87131-657-9*) M Evans.

— A Pilgrim's Path: One Man's Road to the Masonic Temple. LC 93-9178. 192p. 1993. 17.95 (*0-87131-732-X*); pap. 11.95 (*0-87131-722-2*) M Evans.

Robinson, John L., jt. ed. see Levy, Maurice.

Robinson, John M. Cardinal Consalvi, Seventeen Fifty-Seven to Eighteen Twenty-Four. LC 87-17220. 218p. 1987. text ed. 29.95 (*0-312-01297-7*) St Martin.

— The Country House at War. (Illus.). 184p. 1990. 29.95 (*0-370-31306-2*, Pub. by Jonathan Cape UK) Trafalgar.

— Introduction to Early Greek Philosophy. LC 68-1065. (C). 1972. pap. 41.56 (*0-395-05316-1*) HM.

— Pagan Christs. 1967. 5.95 (*0-8216-0136-9*, Univ Bks) Carol Pub Group.

— Shugborough. (Illus.). 96p. 1989. pap. 9.95 (*0-7078-0101-X*, Pub. by Natl Trust UK) Trafalgar.

— Treasures of the English Churches. (Illus.). 288p. 1995. 45.00 (*1-85619-286-5*, Sinclair-Stevenson) Trafalgar.

Robinson, John M., jt. auth. see Erdos, Paul.

Robinson, John M., jt. auth. see Woodcock, Thomas.

Robinson, John P., ed. Social Science & the Arts Nineteen Eighty-Four: A State-of-the-Arts Review from the Tenth Annual Conference on Social Theory, Politics & the Arts University of Maryland, College Park, October 12-14, 1984. (Illus.). 190p. (Orig.). 1986. lib. bdg. 46.00 (*0-8191-4925-X*); pap. text ed. 20.00 (*0-8191-4926-8*) U Pr of Amer.

Robinson, John P. & Levy, Mark R. The Main Source: Learning from Television News. LC 85-22195. (People & Communication Ser.: No. 17). (Illus.). 272p. (Orig.). reprint ed. pap. 77.60 (*0-7837-4559-1*, 2044087) Bks Demand.

R

An Asterisk (*) at the beginning of an entry indicates that the title is appearing in BIP for the first time.

Robinson, John P. & Shaver, Philip R. Measures of Social Psychological Attitudes. rev. ed. LC 79-627967. 750p. 1973. pap. 40.00 (*0-87944-130-5*) Inst Soc Res.

Robinson, John P., et al, eds. Measures of Personality & Social Psychological Attitudes, Vol. 1. (Measure of Social Psychological Changes Ser.). 753p. 1990. pap. text ed. 54.95 (*0-12-590244-1*); boxed 127.00 (*0-12-590241-7*) Acad Pr.

Robinson, John R. The Last Earls of Barrymore, 1769-1824. LC 72-80506. 1972. reprint ed. 24.95 (*0-405-08895-7*, Pub. by Blom Pubns UK) Ayer.

— The Octopus: A History of the Construction, Conspiracies, Extortions, Robberies & Villainous Acts of Subsidized Railroads. Bruchey, Stuart, ed. LC 80-1340. (Railroads Ser.). 1981. reprint ed. lib. bdg. 15.95 (*0-405-13812-1*) Ayer.

Robinson, John S., jt. auth. see Chatham, Russell.

Robinson, John W. Mines of the San Bernardinos. (California Mines Ser.). (Illus.). (Orig.). 1990. pap. text ed. 3.95 (*0-910856-64-8*) La Siesta.

— Mines of the San Gabriels. (Illus.). 1990. 3.95 (*0-910856-52-4*) La Siesta.

— Mount Wilson Story. (Illus.). 1991. 2.50 (*0-910856-53-2*) La Siesta.

— San Bernardino Mountain Trails. 4th ed. LC 85-41027. (Illus.). 272p. (Orig.). 1986. pap. 12.95 (*0-89997-063-X*) Wilderness Pr.

— Trails of the Angeles. 6th ed. LC 83-51479. (Illus.). 248p. (Orig.). 1990. pap. 12.95 (*0-89997-110-5*) Wilderness Pr.

Robinson, John W. & Selters, Andy. High Sierra Hiking Guide to Mt. Goddard. LC 86-40025. (High Sierra Hiking Guide Ser.). (Illus.). 96p. (Orig.). 1986. pap. 11.95 (*0-89997-074-5*) Wilderness Pr.

Robinson, John W., ed. see American Society of Mechanical Engineers Staff.

Robinson, Jon. Property Valuation & Investment Analysis: A Cash Flow Approach. vii, 161p. 1989. pap. 36.50 (*0-455-20830-1*, Pub. by Law Bk Co) W W Gaunt.

Robinson, Jonathan. Bridges to Heaven: How Well-Known Seekers Define & Deepen Their Connection with God. LC 94-67620. 256p. (Orig.). 1994. pap. 14.95 (*0-913299-98-7*) Stillpoint.

— Duty & Hypocrisy in Hegel's Phenomenology of Mind: An Essay in the Real & Ideal. LC 78-300950. 164p. reprint ed. pap. 46.80 (*0-8357-6402-8*, 2035760) Bks Demand.

— The Little Book of Big Questions: 200 Ways to Explore Your Spiritual Nature. (Illus.). 150p. (Orig.). 1995. pap. 8.95 (*1-57324-014-1*) Conari Press.

Robinson, Jonathan, ed. Faith & Reform: A Reinterpretation of Aggiornamento. LC 70-75039. 182p. reprint ed. pap. 51.90 (*0-7837-0469-0*, 2040792) Bks Demand.

Robinson, Jontyle, jt. auth. see Greehouse, Wendy.

Robinson, Jontyle T. & Powell, Richard. The Art of Ronald Burns. (Illus.). 25p. 1994. write for info. (*0-9621349-1-0*) Spelman Coll Art.

Robinson, Joseph A. Gilbert Crispin, Abbot of Westminster: A Study of the Abby under Norman Rule. LC 80-2211. reprint ed. 37.50 (*0-404-18785-4*) AMS Pr.

Robinson, Josephine D. The Circus Lady. Baxter, Annette K., ed. LC 79-8808. (Signal Lives Ser.). (Illus.). 1980. reprint ed. lib. bdg. 35.95 (*0-405-12854-1*) Ayer.

Robinson, Joy M. Antoine de Saint-Exupery. (World Authors Ser.: No. 705). 200p. 1984. text ed. 22.95 (*0-8057-6552-2*, Twayne) Macmillan.

Robinson, Judith. The Hearsts: An American Dynasty. LC 89-40768. (Illus.). 1991. 55.00 (*0-87413-383-1*) U Delaware Pr.

— The Hearsts: An American Dynasty. 432p. 1992. reprint ed. pap. 15.00 (*0-380-71947-9*) Avon.

— You're in Your Mother's Arms: The Life & Legacy of Congressman Phil Burton. LC 94-92365. (Illus.). 700p. (Orig.). 1994. pap. 35.00x (*0-9643382-0-3*) M J Robinson.

Robinson, Judith, ed. see Valery, Paul.

Robinson, Judith S. Tapping the Government Grapevine: The User Friendly Guide to U. S. Government Information Sources. 2nd ed. (Illus.). 240p. 1993. pap. 34.50 (*0-89774-712-7*) Oryx Pr.

Robinson, Julian. Body Packaging. LC 88-6888. (Illus.). 192p. (C). 1988. 32.95 (*1-55599-027-4*) Elysium.

Robinson, Julian, jt. auth. see Langner, Lawrence.

Robinson, Julian P. Chemical & Biological Warfare Developments, 1986-87. (SIPRI Chemical & Biological Warfare Studies: No. 11). 160p. Date not set. pap. 29.95 (*0-19-829140-X*) OUP.

Robinson, Julian P., ed. Chemical & Biological Warfare Development, 1985. (SIPRI Chemical & Biological Warfare Studies). 1986. pap. 29.95 (*0-19-829110-8*) OUP.

Robinson, Julian P., ed. see Stockholm International Peace Research Institute Staff.

Robinson, June K. Fundamentals of Skin Biopsy. (Illus.). 124p. 1986. 34.95 (*0-8151-7312-1*, WKJ-1, Yr Bk Med Pubs) Mosby Yr Bk.

***Robinson, June K., et al.** Atlas of Cutaneous Surgery. LC 94-25752. (Illus.). 432p. 1995. text ed. 150.00 (*0-7216-5404-5*) Saunders.

Robinson, K., jt. auth. see Greenough, C.

Robinson, K. S. The Novels of Philip K. Dick. Scholes, Robert, ed. LC 84-2621. (Studies in Speculative Fiction: No. 9). 162p. reprint ed. pap. 46.20 (*0-8357-1589-2*, 2070623) Bks Demand.

Robinson, Kara L., jt. auth. see Haas, Leslie.

***Robinson, Kate & Shakespeare, Pam.** Open Learning in Nursing, Health & Welfare Education. LC 94-43323. 160p. 1995. 85.00 (*0-335-19075-8*, Open Univ Pr); pap. 29.00 (*0-335-19074-X*, Open Univ Pr) Taylor & Francis.

Robinson, Kate, jt. auth. see Vaughan, Barbara.

Robinson, Katherine. The Clothing Care Handbook. 1985. pap. 7.95 (*0-449-90150-5*, Columbine) Fawcett.

Robinson, Kathleen. Heaven's Only Daughter. 368p. 1993. 21.95 (*0-312-09304-7*) St Martin.

— Heaven's Only Daughter. large type ed. LC 94-2966. 476p. 1994. reprint ed. lib. bdg. 21.95 (*0-8161-5961-0*) Hall.

Robinson, Kathleen & Luckett, Pete. Pete Luckett's Cookbook & Guide to Fresh Fruits & Vegetables. LC 90-25227. (Illus.). 272p. 1990. pap. 12.95 (*1-55561-041-2*) Fisher Bks.

Robinson, Kathleen M., jt. auth. see DeGrandpre, Charles A.

Robinson, Kathryn. The Other Puerto Rico. (Illus.). 164p. (Orig.). 1984. pap. 11.95 (*0-915393-19-0*) Perm Pr.

Robinson, Kathryn, jt. ed. see Irving, Stephanie.

Robinson, Kathryn M. The Stepchildren of Progress: The Political Economy of Development in an Indonesian Mining Town. LC 86-5847. (Anthropology of Work Ser.). 315p. (Orig.). (C). 1986. 64.50 (*0-88706-119-2*); pap. 24.95 (*0-88706-120-6*) State U NY Pr.

Robinson, Kathy, ed. see Houston, Yvonnia M.

Robinson, Kay. Model Plan for Implementation of Title I of the Americans with Disabilities Act: The Human Resource Perspective. (ADA Practice Ser.). 24p. 1994. pap. 9.00 (*0-934753-90-3*) LRP Pubns.

Robinson, Keith & Lehman, Fred. South Fork of the American River: From Chili Bar Dam to Salmon Falls Road. (Whitewater Ser.). (Illus.). 1982. pap. 3.95 (*0-941838-00-5*) Lore Unlim.

— Stanislaus River: From Camp Nine to Parrots Ferry. (Whitewater Ser.). (Illus.). 1982. pap. 3.95 (*0-941838-01-3*) Lore Unlim.

— Tuolumne River: From Lumsden Bridge to Ward's Ferry. (Whitewater Ser.). (Illus.). 1982. pap. 3.95 (*0-941838-02-1*) Lore Unlim.

Robinson, Keith, jt. auth. see Berrisford, Graham.

Robinson, Ken, ed. The Arts & Higher Education: SRHE Leverhulme V. 220p. 1982. pap. 21.00 (*0-900868-89-9*, Open Univ Pr) Taylor & Francis.

Robinson, Ken, jt. ed. see Cain, Tom.

Robinson, Ken, ed. see Oldham, John.

Robinson, Kenneth. Critical Study of Chu Tsai-yu's Contribution to the Theory of Equal Temperament in Chinese Music. 146p. (Orig.). 1980. pap. text ed. 42.50 (*3-515-02732-7*) Coronet Bks.

Robinson, Kenneth & Madden, Frederick, eds. Essays in Imperial Government: Presented to Margery Perham by Kenneth Robinson & Frederick Madden. LC 84-12970. viii, 293p. 1984. reprint ed. text ed. 89.50 (*0-313-24226-7*, REIG, Greenwood Pr) Greenwood.

Robinson, Kenneth A. Thoreau & the Wild Appetite. LC 80-2682. (Thoreau Ser.). (Illus.). reprint ed. 18.50 (*0-404-19079-0*) AMS Pr.

Robinson, Kenneth D., jt. auth. see Little, Gregory L.

Robinson, Kenneth D., ed. see Little, Gregory L.

Robinson, Kenneth D., jt. auth. see Little, Gregory L.

Robinson, Kenneth D., ed. see Little, Gregory L.

Robinson, Kenneth L., jt. auth. see Tomek, William G.

Robinson, Kerry. Foundation Guide for Religious Grant Seekers. 4th ed. (Handbook Ser.). 287p. (C). 1992. pap. 19.95 (*1-55540-677-7*, 001506) Scholars Pr GA.

***Robinson, Kerry A., ed.** Foundation Guide for Religious Grant Seekers. LC 94-48790. (Handbook Ser.: Vol. 9). 1995. pap. write for info. (*0-7885-0090-2*) Scholars Pr GA.

Robinson, Kevin. Mall Rats: A Stick Foster Mystery. 202p. 1992. 19.95 (*0-8027-3215-1*) Walker & Co.

— A Matter of Perspective. LC 93-15674. (Stick Foster Mystery Ser.). 1993. 19.95 (*0-8027-3242-9*) Walker & Co.

— Split Seconds. 208p. 1991. 18.95 (*0-8027-5785-5*) Walker & Co.

Robinson, Kim S. The Blind Geometer. deluxe limited ed. (Illus.). 96p. (Orig.). 1986. boxed 95.00 (*0-941826-13-9*) Cheap St.

— Escape from Kathmandu. 320p. 1994. pap. 10.95 (*0-312-89006-0*) Orb NYC.

— The Gold Coast. 1988. 18.95 (*0-685-20156-2*) St Martin.

— The Gold Coast. 416p. 1988. pap. 3.95 (*0-8125-5239-3*) Tor Bks.

— The Gold Coast. 400p. 1995. pap. 13.95 (*0-312-89037-0*) Orb NYC.

— Pacific Edge. 336p. 1995. pap. 13.95 (*0-312-89038-9*) Orb NYC.

— The Planet on the Table. 256p. 1987. reprint ed. pap. 3.50 (*0-8125-5237-7*) Tor Bks.

— Red Mars. LC 92-21607. 1993. pap. 11.95 (*0-553-37134-7*) Bantam.

— Red Mars, No. 1. 1993. mass mkt. 5.99 (*0-553-56073-5*, Spectra) Bantam.

— Remaking History & Other Stories. 528p. 1994. pap. 10.95 (*0-312-89012-5*) Orb NYC.

— A Short Sharp Shock. 160p. 1990. 18.00 (*0-929480-18-X*) Mark Ziesing.

— A Short Sharp Shock. limited ed. 160p. 1990. 45.00 (*0-929480-19-8*) Mark Ziesing.

— The Wild Shore. 384p. 1995. pap. 13.95 (*0-312-89036-2*) Orb NYC.

Robinson, Kim S., ed. Future Primitive: The New Ecotopias. 384p. 1994. 23.95 (*0-312-85474-9*) Tor Bks.

Robinson, Kim S. & Vance, Jack. Short, Sharp Shock & The Dragon Masters. 1990. pap. 3.50 (*0-8125-0895-5*) Tor Bks.

Robinson, Kimberly. Bubbles: A Thematic Unit. (Thematic Units Ser.). (Illus.). 80p. (gr. 1-3). 1991. student ed 8.95 (*1-55734-275-X*) Tchr Create Mat.

***Robinson-Kimyon, Barbara.** Focus: Interactive Grammar for Students of ESL. 352p. 1995. pap. text ed. 22.61 (*0-312-09229-6*) St Martin.

— Focus: Interactive Grammar for Students of ESL. 170p. (C). 1995. student ed, pap. text ed. 17.29 (*0-312-09230-X*) St Martin.

***Robinson, Kit.** Balance Sheet. LC 93-85180. 111p. (Orig.). 1993. pap. 9.95 (*0-937804-52-5*) Segue NYC.

— The Champagne of Concrete. 104p. (Orig.). 1990. pap. 9.00 (*0-937013-32-3*) Potes Poets.

— Counter Meditation. 42p. 1991. pap. 7.00 (*84-87467-09-1*) SPD-Small Pr Dist.

— Covers. 1988. 4.00 (*0-935724-37-0*) Figures.

— Down & Back. 1978. pap. 7.50 (*0-685-99355-8*); per. 10.00 (*0-935724-58-3*) Figures.

— Ice Cubes. LC 87-63136. 90p. 1988. pap. 6.00 (*0-937804-27-4*) Segue NYC.

Robinson, Kit, tr. see Kutik, Ilya.

Robinson-Kurpius, Sharon E., jt. auth. see Weiner, Neil.

Robinson, L. Strata Title Units in New South Wales. 4th ed. 230p. 1989. Australia. pap. 44.00 (*0-409-30248-1*) Butterworth Legal Pubs.

Robinson, L., jt. auth. see Marks, T.

***Robinson, L. D.** I Broke the Ten Commandments. 122p. (Orig.). 1994. pap. write for info. (*1-885591-08-X*) Morris Pubng.

Robinson, L. H. Mud Cleaners & Combination Separators. (Mud Equipment Manual Ser.: No. 7). 24p. (Orig.). 1982. pap. 19.00 (*0-87201-619-6*) Gulf Pub.

Robinson, L. Louis. Poetic Ventures, Vol. 1: Introspection of a Poet. LC 90-92023. 138p. (Orig.). 1991. pap. text ed. 12.95 (*0-9628034-0-5*) L L Robinson.

Robinson, L. R., jt. auth. see McGann, Daniel M.

Robinson, Lady S. Dreamer's Dictionary. 1994. mass mkt. 5.99 (*0-446-77879-6*) Warner Bks.

Robinson, Lady S. & Corbett, Tom. The Dreamer's Dictionary. 384p. 1986. mass mkt. 5.99 (*0-446-34296-3*) Warner Bks.

Robinson, Lafayette. Penmanship from A to Z. (Illus.). 72p. (J). (gr. 3-4). 1988. student ed 7.95 (*0-9621081-1-1*) Educ Graphics.

— Rite Easy from A to Z. Gonzalez, Inez, tr. (Illus.). 48p. (ENG & SPA.). (J). (gr. 1-3). 1993. lib. bdg. write for info. (*0-9621081-0-3*) Educ Graphics.

Robinson, Lamar. Maine Guide to Fish. 1984. pap. 1.95 (*0-930096-40-1*) G Gannett.

Robinson, Lana. The Best of Little Spouse on the Prairie. 1993. pap. 9.95 (*0-9636248-0-6*) Bedford Hse.

Robinson, Larry. The Art of Inlay: Contemporary Design & Technique. LC 94-12076. (Illus.). 112p. 1994. text ed. 24.95 (*0-87930-332-8*) Miller Freeman.

Robinson, Larry M. & Adler, Roy D., eds. Marketing Megaworks: The Top 150 Books & Articles. LC 86-25248. 224p. 1987. text ed. 55.00 (*0-275-92318-5*, C2318, Praeger Pubs) Greenwood.

Robinson, Larry M., jt. auth. see Cooper, Philip D.

Robinson, Lawrence W. Quantitative Concepts for Management: Decision-Making Without Algorithms. 2nd ed. (Illus.). 384p. (C). 1985. pap. text ed. write for info. (*0-13-746652-8*) P-H.

Robinson, Lee A., jt. auth. see Hill, Steven C.

Robinson, Leif J. Outdoor Optics. (Illus.). 160p. 1990. pap. 13.95 (*1-55821-065-2*) Lyons & Burford.

Robinson, Leif J., ed. see Harrington, Philip S.

***Robinson, Leigh.** Eviction Book for California: A Handy Manual for Scrupulous Landlords & Landladies. 1995. pap. 21.95 (*0-932956-19-X*) ExPress.

— The Eviction Book for California: A Handy Manual for Scrupulous Landlords & Landladies Who Do Their Own Evictions. 6th ed. 238p. 1991. pap. 19.95 (*0-932956-15-7*) ExPress.

— Landlording: A Handy Manual for Scrupulous Landlords & Landladies Who Do It Themselves. 1994. pap. 23.95 (*0-932956-18-1*) ExPress.

— Landlording: A Handy Manual for Scrupulous Landlords & Landladies Who Do It Themselves. 6th ed. 414p. 1992. pap. 21.95 (*0-932956-16-5*) ExPress.

Robinson, Leigh, ed. see Gadow, Sandy.

Robinson, Leland R. Foreign Credit Facilities in the United Kingdom. LC 68-57579. (Columbia University. Studies in the Social Sciences: No. 244). reprint ed. 20.00 (*0-404-51244-5*) AMS Pr.

***Robinson, Lena.** Psychology for Social Workers: Black Perspectives. LC 95-8131. 1996. write for info. (*0-415-10107-7*); pap. write for info. (*0-415-10108-5*) Routledge.

Robinson, Lennox. Irish Theatre. LC 79-92980. (Studies in Drama: No. 39). 1969. reprint ed. lib. bdg. 75.00 (*0-8383-1201-2*) M S G Haskell Hse.

— Selected Plays. Murray, Christopher, ed. LC 82-71455. (Irish Drama Selections Ser.: No. 1). (Illus.). 288p. (C). 1982. 27.95 (*0-8132-0574-3*); pap. 14.95 (*0-8132-0575-1*) Cath U Pr.

— Towards an Appreciation of the Theatre. LC 74-6447. (Studies in Drama: No. 39). (C). 1974. lib. bdg. 49.95 (*0-8383-1915-7*) M S G Haskell Hse.

Robinson, Lennox, jt. auth. see Ohaodha, M.

Robinson, Leonard A., et al. Accounting Information Systems: A Cycle Approach. 2nd ed. 656p. (C). 1986. text ed. 37.95 (*0-06-045515-2*) HarpCollege.

Robinson, Leonard W. In the Whale. LC 83-70061. 80p. 1983. pap. 6.95 (*0-935306-21-8*) Barnwood Pr.

***Robinson, Les.** Field Guide to the Native Plants of Sydney. 2nd ed. (Illus.). 448p. 1995. pap. 19.95 (*0-86417-639-2*) Seven Hills Bk.

Robinson, Lesley, jt. auth. see Cousins, Jill.

Robinson, Lila W. & Armagost, James. Comanche Dictionary & Grammar. (Publications in Linguistics: No. 93). 1990. pap. 26.00 (*0-88312-715-6*) Summer Instit Ling.

— Comanche Dictionary & Grammar, 6 fiche, Set. (Publications in Linguistics: No. 93). 1990. fiche 24.00 (*0-88312-554-4*) Summer Instit Ling.

Robinson, Lillian. Sex, Class & Culture. 388p. 1986. pap. text ed. 13.95 (*0-416-01241-8*, 9874) Routledge Chapman & Hall.

Robinson, Lillian H., ed. Psychiatry & Religion: Overlapping Concerns. LC 85-28728. (Clinical Insights Ser.). 190p. reprint ed. pap. 54.20 (*0-8357-7841-X*, 2036216) Bks Demand.

Robinson, Lillian S. Sex, Class, & Culture. LC 77-15762. 373p. reprint ed. pap. 106.40 (*0-317-27848-7*, 2056052) Bks Demand.

***Robinson, Lillian S., ed. & comp.** Modern Women Writers. LC 94-43197. (Library of Literary Criticism). 2100p. 1995. 300.00 (*0-8264-0823-0*) Continuum.

— Modern Women Writers, 3 vols., Vol. 1. LC 94-43197. (Library of Literary Criticism). 700p. 1995. 100.00 (*0-8264-0813-3*) Continuum.

— Modern Women Writers, 3 vols., Vol. 2. LC 94-43197. (Library of Literary Criticism). 700p. 1995. 100.00 (*0-8264-0814-1*) Continuum.

— Modern Women Writers, 3 vols., Vol. 3. LC 94-43197. (Library of Literary Criticism). 700p. 1995. 100.00 (*0-8264-0815-X*) Continuum.

Robinson, Lillie & Fitch, Stanley. Insights into Child Development II. 1992. pap. 30.00 (*1-56226-127-4*) CT Pub.

— Insights into Infant Development I. 1992. pap. 35.00 (*1-56226-126-6*) CT Pub.

Robinson, Lillie M. Starting & Operating A Child Care Center: A Guide. 1994. 29.95 (*0-9637908-6-2*) Readers Press.

Robinson, Linda. Intervention or Neglect: The United States & Central America Beyond the 1980s. 342p. 1991. pap. 14.95 (*0-87609-097-8*) Coun Foreign.

Robinson, Linda, ed. see Rubin, Alvin B. & LeVan, Gerald.

Robinson, Linda, jt. auth. see Steinberg, Ruth.

Robinson, Linton H. Mexican Slang: A Guide. 160p. (Orig.). (YA). 1994. reprint ed. pap. 6.95 (*0-9627080-7-0*) In One EAR.

Robinson, Lisa. Psychiatric Nursing As a Human Experience. 3rd ed. (Illus.). 1983. text ed. 48.95 (*0-7216-7622-7*) Saunders.

— Psychological Aspects of the Care of Hospitalized Patients. 4th ed. LC 83-20972. 152p. (C). 1984. pap. text ed. 9.95 (*0-8036-7473-2*) Davis Co.

— Substitute Teachers Step by Step Survival Handbook: Elementary Level. (Illus.). 24p. (Orig.). 1994. teacher ed, pap. 6.00 (*1-878276-34-4*) Educ Systs Assocs Inc.

Robinson, Lisa S., jt. auth. see McLaughlin, Kenneth, Jr.

Robinson, Logan. Evil Star. 256p. 1987. pap. 2.95 (*0-8217-1992-0*) Zebra.

Robinson, Lorraine, jt. auth. see Luthert, Joanna M.

Robinson, Lou. Extremes of High & Low Regard. 32p. 1988. pap. 3.00 (*0-917061-27-6*) Top Stories.

— Napoleon's Mare. 177p. 1991. 18.95 (*0-932511-47-3*); pap. 8.95 (*0-932511-48-1*) Fiction Coll.

Robinson, Lou & Norton, Camille, eds. Resurgent: New Writing by Women. 264p. 1992. 39.95 (*0-252-01835-4*); pap. 13.95 (*0-252-06203-5*) U of Ill Pr.

Robinson, Lou, ed. see Kelly, Mary B.

Robinson, Louis N. History & Organization of Criminal Statistics in the United States. LC 69-16246. (Criminology, Law Enforcement, & Social Problems Ser.: No. 83). 1969. reprint ed. 18.00 (*0-87585-083-9*) Patterson Smith.

Robinson, Ludmilla. Handbook for Legal Interpreters. 1994. pap. write for info. (*0-455-21225-2*, Pub. by Law Bk Co) W W Gaunt.

***Robinson, Lynda S.** Murder at the Feast of Rejoicing: A Lord Meren Mystery. 1996. write for info. (*0-8027-3274-7*) Walker & Co.

— Murder at the God's Gate: A Lord Meren Mystery. LC 94-28806. 248p. 1995. 19.95 (*0-8027-3198-8*) Walker & Co.

— Murder in the Place of Anubis. 1995. mass mkt. 4.99 (*0-345-38922-0*) Ballantine.

— Murder in the Place of Anubis. 203p. 1994. 18.95 (*0-8027-3249-6*) Walker & Co.

***Robinson, Lynn.** Coming Out of Your Psychic Closet: How to Unlock Your Naturally Intuitive Self. 176p. (Orig.). 1994. 20.95 (*0-9626531-7-9*) Factor Pr.

***Robinson, Lynn B.** Coming Out of Your Psychic Closet: How to Unlock Your Naturally Intuitive Self. 176p. (Orig.). 1994. pap. 11.95 (*0-9626531-6-0*) Factor Pr.

***Robinson, Lynne & Lowther, Richard.** Stencilling: Projects, Techniques, Pull-Out Stencils. (Illus.). 96p. 1995. pap. 22.95 (*1-57076-028-4*, Trafalgar Sq Pub) Trafalgar.

Robinson, Lytle W. Edgar Cayce's Story of the Origin & Destiny of Man. 1985. mass mkt. 5.99 (*0-425-09320-4*) Berkley Pub.

Robinson, M., ed. The Concise Scots Dictionary: A Comprehensive One-Volume Dictionary of the Scots Language from the 12th Century to the Present Day. 928p. 1987. 22.75 (*0-685-11462-7*, Pub. by Aberdeen U Pr); lib. bdg. 85.00 (*0-08-032447-9*, Pub. by Aberdeen U Pr); pap. 20.50 (*0-08-028492-2*, Pub. by Aberdeen U Pr) Macmillan.

Robinson, M. B., jt. auth. see Porter, B. E.

Robinson, M. E., jt. auth. see Jeremy, Michael.

Robinson, M. J., ed. Practical Paediatrics. 2nd ed. (Illus.). 668p. (Orig.). 1990. pap. text ed. 52.00 (*0-443-04053-2*) Churchill.

Robinson, M. S. The Paintings of the Willem van de Veldes. (Illus.). 1136p. 1990. 395.00 (*0-85667-389-7*, Pub. by P Wilson Pubs) Sothebys Pubns.

Robinson, Marc. Cock-a-Doodle Doo! What Does It Sound Like to You? LC 92-30961. (Illus.). 32p. (J). 1993. 12.95 (*1-55670-267-1*) Stewart Tabori & Chang.

— The Other American Drama. LC 93-43793. (Cambridge Studies in American Theatre & Drama: No. 2). 150p. (C). 1994. 49.95 (*0-521-45437-9*) Cambridge U Pr.

Robinson, Marc, ed. Altogether Elsewhere: Writers in Exile. LC 93-46457. 360p. 1994. 26.95 (*0-571-19829-5*) Faber & Faber.

R

An Asterisk (*) at the beginning of an entry indicates that the title is appearing in BIP for the first time.

Robinson, Marcel. Fingerpicking Cat Stevens. (Illus.). 32p. 1988. pap. 9.95 (*0-8256-2549-1*, AM71358) Music Sales.

— Fingerpicking Dylan. (Illus.). 56p. 1990. pap. 9.95 (*0-8256-1281-0*, AM79740) Music Sales.

— Fingerpicking Leonard Cohen. (Illus.). 56p. 1989. pap. 9.95 (*0-8256-2586-6*, AM76621) Music Sales.

— Fingerpicking Paul Simon. (Illus.). 40p. 1988. pap. 9.95 (*0-8256-1184-9*, PS10909) Music Sales.

— Fingerpicking Paul Simon, No. 2. (Illus.). 64p. 1993. pap. 9.95 (*0-8256-3312-5*) Music Sales.

Robinson, Marcel, sel. Paul Simon: Themes & Variations Clarinet. (Illus.). 48p. 1988. pap. 9.95 (*0-685-65790-6*, PS10917) Music Sales.

— Paul Simon: Themes & Variations, Flute. (Illus.). 48p. 1988. pap. 9.95 (*0-8256-2554-8*, PS10925) Music Sales.

— Paul Simon: Themes & Variations, Trumpet. (Illus.). 48p. 1988. pap. 9.95 (*0-8256-2555-6*, PS10933) Music Sales.

***Robinson, Marcus S.** One Song Hero: The Inward Journey of an Urban Shaman. Lyons, Charles et al, eds. (Illus.). (Orig.). 1994. pap. 12.95 (*0-9639703-5-6*) Magna Publications.

— Quest of the One Song Hero: The Inward Journey of an Urban Shaman. (Illus.). 184p. 1994. pap. 12.95 (*0-9963970-3-5*) Magna Publications.

Robinson, Marcus S. & Kammer, Murray P. The Quest for Excellence. 158p. (Orig.). 1993. student ed 8.95 (*0-9639703-1-3*); pap. 12.95 (*0-9639703-0-5*); audio 8.95 (*0-9639703-2-1*) Magna Publications.

Robinson, Margaret. Family Transformation During Divorce & Remarriage: A Systematic Approach. 368p. 1993. pap. 22.50 (*0-415-05228-9*, B0223) Routledge.

— Family Transformation During Divorce & Remarriage: A Systemic Approach. 320p. (C). 1991. text ed. 72.50 (*0-415-05227-0*, A5135) Routledge.

Robinson, Margaret A. A Woman of Her Tribe. (YA). 1991. mass mkt. 3.99 (*0-449-70405-X*, Juniper) Fawcett.

— A Woman of Her Tribe. LC 90-31534. 144p. (YA). (gr. 7 up). 1990. text ed. 13.95 (*0-684-19223-3*, C Scribner Sons Young) S&S Childrens.

Robinson, Margot. Egos & Eggshells: Managing for Success in Today's Workplace. 209p. 1993. 20.00 (*0-9630151-1-7*) Stanton & Harper.

— Egos & Eggshells: The Complete Guide for Today's Supervisor. 202p. 1991. 20.00 (*0-9630151-0-9*) Stanton & Harper.

Robinson, Marguerite S. Local Politics: The Law of the Fishes: Development Through Political Change in Medak District, Andhra Pradesh (South India) 364p. 1989. 17.95 (*0-19-561992-7*) OUP.

Robinson, Marian D. Meaningful Counseling: A Guide for Students, Counselors, & Clergy. 204p. 1988. 32.95 (*0-89885-385-0*) Human Sci Pr.

Robinson, Marilyn. Holiday Windows: Pillows with Zippered Vinyl Pockets. Holmes, Sharon, ed. (Illus.). 28p. 1992. pap. 8.95 (*1-880972-00-X*) Pssblts Denver.

— Window Zips: Zippered Vinyl Pockets in Memory Pillows. Holmes, Sharon, ed. (Illus.). 28p. 1992. pap. 8.95 (*0-9622477-9-0*) Pssblts Denver.

Robinson, Marilyn & Bisignano, Judith. Creating Your Future: Level 2. (Illus.). 72p. 1982. 6.95 (*0-9607366-8-9*, KP108) Kino Pubns.

Robinson, Marilyn, jt. ed. see Coldwell, Lynn.

Robinson, Marilyn, jt. auth. see Haller, Dolores.

Robinson, Marilyn, tr. see Smith, Nancy J. & Milligan, Lynda S.

Robinson, Marilynne. Housekeeping. 224p. 1984. mass mkt. 5.99 (*0-553-27872-X*, Bantam Classics) Bantam.

— Mother Country. 1989. 18.95 (*0-374-21361-5*) FS&G.

Robinson, Marion & Thurston, Rozetta L. Poetry for Men to Speak Chorally. 148p. 3.00 (*0-686-15465-7*) Expression.

***Robinson, Mark & Riddell, Roger.** Working for the Poor: NGO's & Rural Poverty Alleviation. (Illus.). 380p. 1995. 59.00 (*0-19-823330-2*) OUP.

Robinson, Mark A. Rough Water Power Boating. 268p. (C). 1990. 90.00 (*0-7316-4701-7*, Pub. by Pascoe Pub AT) St Mut.

Robinson, Marlene. What Good Is a Tail? (J). (gr. 4-7). 1994. pap. 7.95 (*1-56171-086-5*) Sure Sellers.

— Who Knows This Nose? (J). (gr. 4-7). 1995. pap. 7.95 (*1-56171-085-7*) Sure Sellers.

Robinson, Marlene M. The Crystal Kit. rev. ed. (Discovery Kit Ser.). (Illus.). 96p. (Orig.). 1993. pap. 17.95 (*1-56138-239-6*) Running Pr.

Robinson, Marlyn & Simoni, Christopher, eds. The Flag & the Law: A Documentary History of the Treatment of the American Flag by the Supreme Court & Congress, 3 vols., Set. LC 93-12055. 7410p. 1993. ring bd. 395.00 (*0-89941-834-1*, 306430) W S Hein.

Robinson, Marsha, jt. auth. see Jarest, Jackie.

Robinson, Martha. The Zoo at Night. LC 94-12773. (Illus.). (J). 1995. text ed. 15.95 (*0-689-50608-2*, McElderry) S&S Childrens.

Robinson, Martha H. Helen Erskine. LC 74-164574. (American Fiction Reprint Ser.). 1977. reprint ed. 24.95 (*0-8369-7051-9*) Ayer.

***Robinson, Martha H., ed.** Culinary Secrets from the Virginia Chefs Association. 272p. 1995. 18.95 (*1-55853-335-4*) Rutledge Hill Pr.

Robinson, Martin. Old Letter Boxes. 1989. pap. 25.00 (*0-85263-846-9*, Pub. by Shire UK) St Mut.

Robinson, Mary. The Amazing Valvano & the Mystery of the Hooded Rat. 160p. (J). (gr. 5). 1990. pap. 2.75 (*0-380-70713-6*, Camelot) Avon.

— The Amazing Valvano & the Mystery of the Hooded Rat. LC 87-26179. 168p. (J). (gr. 3-7). 1988. 13.95 (*0-395-44314-8*) HM.

— Beloved Notes. 1993. pap. 4.50 (*0-8220-0227-2*) Cliffs.

— Give It up, Mom. 144p. (J). (gr. 4). 1992. pap. 2.99 (*0-380-71126-5*, Camelot) Avon.

— I Know Why the Caged Bird Sings Notes. (Illus.). 69p. (Orig.). 1993. pap. text ed. 4.95 (*0-8220-0641-3*) Cliffs.

— Sappho & Phaon: In a Series of Legitimate Sonnets (1796) fac. ed. LC 95-14726. (Scholars' Facsimiles & Reprints Ser.: Vol. 494). 1995. write for info. (*0-8201-1494-4*) Schol Facsimiles.

— A Voice for Somalia. 96p. 1993. pap. 13.95 (*0-86278-329-1*, Pub. by OBrien Pr IE) Dufour.

Robinson, Mary & Ryan, Sandy. You Are a Success! 61 Proven Strategies for Developing Success. LC 90-85787. 195p. (Orig.). 1991. pap. 14.95 (*0-9628496-4-2*) Heart Pub Prodns.

Robinson, Mary A. Alpines: Step by Step to Growing Success. (Crowood Gardening Guides Ser.). (Illus.). 128p. 1992. pap. 16.95 (*1-85223-669-8*, Pub. by Crowood Pr UK) Trafalgar.

— Primulas: The Complete Guide. (Illus.). 272p. 1994. pap. 19.95 (*1-85223-811-9*, Pub. by Crowood Pr UK) Trafalgar.

***Robinson, Mary A. & Shotkin, Andrea, eds.** Listing of Materials Submitted to the Curriculum & Resources Review Fair. (Annual Conference Ser.: Vol. 23). 26p. (Orig.). Date not set. pap. write for info. (*1-884008-16-X*) NAAEE.

Robinson, Mary A., et al. Simple Scrumptious Microwaving. 224p. (Orig.). 1986. pap. 9.95 (*0-449-90174-2*, Columbine) Fawcett.

Robinson, Mary E. Newell D. Goff: The Life of a Young Entrepreneur at the Turn of the Twentieth Century. LC 92-27885. (Illus.). 1992. 9.95 (*0-914659-57-X*) Phoenix Pub.

Robinson, Matt. Gordon of Sesame Street Storybook. (Illus.). (J). (gr. 7-9). 1972. lib. bdg. 5.99 (*0-394-92406-1*) Random Bks Yng Read.

Robinson, Maureen K. Developing the Nonprofit Board. 24p. (Orig.). (C). 1994. pap. text ed. 12.00 (*0-925299-33-2*) Natl Ctr Nonprofit.

Robinson, Mei L. Farewell to Manzanar Notes. 76p. (Orig.). 1994. pap. 4.25 (*0-8220-0463-1*) Cliffs.

Robinson, Michael. Groups. LC 83-10352. 352p. 1984. text ed. 67.95 (*0-471-90009-5*, Wiley-Interscience) Wiley.

— Strindberg & Autobiography. LC 87-62756. 192p. (Orig.). 1986. pap. 22.00 (*1-870041-00-3*, Pub. by Norvik Pr UK) Dufour.

Robinson, Michael, ed. Strindberg & Genre. (Norvik Press Series A: No. 9). 1991. 45.00 (*1-870041-18-6*, Pub. by Norvik Pr UK) Dufour.

Robinson, Michael & Hofmann, Ulrike. Giovanni Paisiello (1741-1816) A Thematic Catalogue of His Music Vol. I: The Dramatic Works. LC 90-7273. (Thematic Catalogues Ser.: No. 15). (Illus.). 400p. 1990. lib. bdg. 120.00 (*0-918728-75-4*) Pendragon NY.

Robinson, Michael, ed. see Strindberg, August.

Robinson, Michael C., ed. see Stewart, J. David & Buehler, Dan Y.

***Robinson, Michael D.** Eternity & Freedom: A Critical Analysis of Divine Timelessness As a Solution to the Foreknowledge - Free Will Debate. LC 95-3456. 266p. (C). 1995. lib. bdg. 42.00 (*0-8191-9895-1*) U Pr of Amer.

Robinson, Michael E. Cultural Nationalism in Colonial Korea, 1920-1925. LC 88-18804. 240p. 1989. 30.00 (*0-295-96600-9*) U of Wash Pr.

Robinson, Michael F. Naples & Neapolitian Opera. LC 83-18918. (Music Reprint Ser.). 281p. 1984. reprint ed. lib. bdg. 35.00 (*0-306-76226-9*) Da Capo.

***Robinson, Michael H. & Challinor, David.** Zoo Animals: A Smithsonian Guide. LC 94-48288. (J). 1995. 24.95 (*0-02-860406-7*); pap. 18.00 (*0-02-860407-5*) Macmillan.

Robinson, Michael H. & Tiger, Lionel, eds. Man & Beast Revisited. LC 90-9953. (Illus.). 416p. (Orig.). (C). 1991. pap. 16.95 (*0-87474-775-9*) Smithsonian.

Robinson, Michael J., et al. Over the Wire & on TV: CBS & UPI in Campaign '80. LC 81-66977. 350p. 1983. 17.50 (*0-87154-722-8*) Russell Sage.

Robinson, Mike. The Greening of British Party Politics. O'Riordan, Timothy & Weale, Albert, eds. (Issues in Environmental Politics Ser.). 208p. 1992. text ed. 19.95 (*0-7190-3199-0*, Pub. by Manchester Univ Pr UK) St Martin.

Robinson, Mirian H. The Mystery of the Blanket. 1995. 7.95 (*0-8062-4988-9*) Carlton.

Robinson-Mitzel, Edith. Mother's Recipes Seasoned with Memories. (Seasoned with Memories Ser.: Vol. 1). (Illus.). 120p. 1991. 12.50 (*0-9628852-0-7*) Twinberry.

Robinson, Mona. Who's Your Hoosier Ancestor? Genealogy for Beginners. LC 91-39969. (Illus.). 240p. 1992. 27.95 (*0-253-34996-6*); pap. 12.95 (*0-253-20731-2*, MB-731) Ind U Pr.

Robinson, Morgan P. Virginia Counties: Those Resulting from Virginia Legislation. (Illus.). 283p. 1992. 25.00 (*0-8063-1335-8*, 4985) Genealog Pub.

Robinson, N., jt. auth. see Hayes, G. M.

Robinson, N. E., jt. ed. see Gillespie, J. R.

Robinson, N. Edward. Current Therapy in Equine Medicine Two. 2nd ed. (Illus.). 784p. 1987. text ed. 115.00 (*0-7216-1491-4*) Saunders.

Robinson, N. F. Monasticism in the Orthodox Church. LC 72-131506. reprint ed. 27.50 (*0-404-05375-0*) AMS Pr.

Robinson, Nancy K. Angela & the Broken Heart. (J). 1991. 12.95 (*0-590-43212-5*, Scholastic Hardcover) Scholastic Inc.

— Countess Veronica. 176p. (J). (gr. 3-7). 1994. 13.95 (*0-590-44485-9*, Scholastic Hardcover) Scholastic Inc.

— The Ghost of Whispering Rock. LC 92-52856. (Illus.). 64p. (J). (gr. 2-6). 1992. 13.95 (*0-8234-0944-9*) Holiday.

— Just Plain Cat. (Orig.). (YA). 1992. pap. 2.95 (*0-590-45850-7*, Apple Paperbacks) Scholastic Inc.

— Just Plain Cat. LC 82-18258. 128p. (Orig.). (J). (gr. 3-6). 1984. text ed. 13.95 (*0-02-777350-7*, Four Winds Pr) S&S Childrens.

— Oh Honestly, Angela! (Illus.). 128p. (J). 1991. pap. 2.95 (*0-590-44902-8*, Apple Paperbacks) Scholastic Inc.

— Veronica Knows Best. 128p. (J). (gr. 4-6). 1987. pap. 10.95 (*0-590-40509-8*) Scholastic Inc.

— Veronica Knows Best. 160p. (J). 1992. pap. 2.95 (*0-590-44900-1*, Apple Paperbacks) Scholastic Inc.

— Veronica Meets Her Match. 128p. (J). 1992. pap. 2.95 (*0-590-45766-7*, Apple Paperbacks) Scholastic Inc.

— Veronica the Show-Off. LC 85-4483. 128p. (J). (gr. 3-6). 1984. text ed. 13.95 (*0-02-777360-4*, Four Winds Pr) S&S Childrens.

— Wendy & the Bullies. (J). (gr. 4-7). 1991. pap. 2.95 (*0-590-44899-4*) Scholastic Inc.

— Wendy on the Warpath. LC 93-32739. (J). (gr. 3 up). 1994. 13.95 (*0-590-45571-0*) Scholastic Inc.

Robinson, Nancy M., ed. Guidelines for Freelancers. 160p. (Orig.). 1989. pap. 14.00 (*0-9623563-0-1*) J R Matthews.

Robinson, Natalie M., jt. auth. see Hardy, Edward.

Robinson, Neal. Christ in Islam & Christianity. LC 90-36383. 248p. 1991. 64.50 (*0-7914-0558-3*); pap. 21.95 (*0-7914-0559-1*) State U NY Pr.

***Robinson, Neil.** Ideology & the Collapse of the Soviet System: A Critical History of Soviet Ideological Discourse. LC 94-48418. (Studies of Communism in Transition). 1995. 61.95 (*1-85898-167-0*, Pub. by E Elgar Pub UK) Ashgate Pub Co.

Robinson, Nicholas A. Environmental Law Lexicon. 300p. 1992. ring bd. 75.00 (*0-317-05396-5*, 00618) NY Law Pub.

— Environmental Regulation of Real Property. 1200p. 1986. reprint ed. 98.00 (*0-318-21431-8*, 00575) NY Law Pub.

Robinson, Nicholas A., ed. New York Environmental Law. LC 92-53528. 1000p. 1992. 110.00 (*0-942954-48-3*) NYS Bar.

Robinson, Nicholas A., jt. ed. see Burhenne, Wolfgang E.

Robinson, Nicholas A., jt. ed. see Commission on Environmental Law of IUCN, World Conservation Union Staff.

Robinson, Nicholas A., ed. see New York State Bar Association Staff.

Robinson, Nicholas A., et al, eds. Agenda Twenty-One & the UNCED Proceedings, 6 vols., Set. LC 92-61109. (International Protection of the Environment, 3rd Ser.). 1993. lib. bdg. 450.00 (*0-379-10350-8*) Oceana.

Robinson, Nick. Paper Airplanes. 1991. 12.98 (*1-55521-724-9*) Bk Sales Inc.

— The Planting Design Handbook. 1992. 99.95 (*0-566-09008-2*, Pub. by Gower UK) Ashgate Pub Co.

Robinson, Nigel. Doctor Who: Edge of Destruction. 1988. pap. 3.95 (*0-426-20327-5*) Carol Pub Group.

— Doctor Who: The Third Quiz Book. pap. 2.95 (*0-426-20212-0*) Carol Pub Group.

Robinson, Nina H. Aunt Dice: The Story of a Faithful Slave. LC 72-2036. (Black Heritage Library Collection). 1977. reprint ed. 17.95 (*0-8369-9058-7*) Ayer.

Robinson, Norborne T., III. The Vietnam Victory Option. LC 93-73398. 248p. 1993. 35.00 (*0-9638286-0-6*) Gram Pr.

Robinson, O. Lesser Antilles: Barbados & Grenada to Virgin Islands. (Illus.). 1991. 69.95 (*0-85288-153-3*, Pub. by Imray Laurie Norie & Wilson UK) Bluewater Bks.

Robinson, O. A. & Bien, Joseph, eds. Ethics & Politics. (Orig.). (C). 1992. pap. write for info. (*0-934135-02-9*) Klare Ltd.

— Leviathan. (Orig.). 1986. pap. write for info. (*0-934135-00-2*) Klare Ltd.

Robinson, O. F. Ancient Rome: City Planning & Administration. 224p. 1992. 35.00 (*0-415-02234-7*, A6063) Routledge.

— Ancient Rome: City Planning & Administration. (Illus.). 272p. 1994. pap. 17.95 (*0-415-10618-4*, B3813) Routledge.

***Robinson, O. F., ed.** The Register of Walter Bronescombe, 1258-1280 No. I. (Canterbury & York Society Ser.: Vol. 82). 224p. (C). 1995. text ed. 45.00 (*0-907239-51-X*, Canterbury & York Soc) Boydell & Brewer.

Robinson, O. F., jt. intro. see Gaius, Gordon W.

***Robinson, O. F., et al.** European Legal History. 2nd ed. 264p. 1994. pap. text ed. 58.00 (*0-406-02976-8*, UK) Butterworth Legal Pubs.

Robinson, Orrin W. Old English & Its Closest Relatives: A Survey of the Earliest Germanic Languages. 304p. (C). 1993. pap. 16.95 (*0-8047-2221-8*) Stanford U Pr.

— Old English & Its Closest Relatives: Survey of the Earliest Germanic Languages. (Illus.). 304p. (C). 1992. 45.00 (*0-8047-1454-1*) Stanford U Pr.

Robinson, Osborne. Vocabulary Development for Science & Technology. 112p. 1989. spiral bd. 12.95 (*0-8403-5292-1*) Kendall-Hunt.

Robinson, Oz & Sadler, Mike. Atlantic Spain & Portugal. (Illus.). 196p. (C). 1990. 64.95 (*0-85288-150-9*, Pub. by Imray Laurie Norie & Wilson UK) Bluewater Bks.

Robinson, Oz, jt. auth. see Sheffield, Barry.

Robinson, P. Anchor Proteins & T Cell Activation. (Molecular Biology Intelligence Unit Ser.). write for info. (*1-57059-118-0*) R G Landes.

Robinson, P. & Rawnsley, J. The Metaplectic Representation, MPC Structures & Geometric Quantization. LC 89-15191. (MEMO Ser.: Vol. 81/410). 93p. 1989. pap. 18.00 (*0-8218-2473-2*, MEMO 81/410) Am Math.

Robinson, P. C. Declan's Night. 224p. (Orig.). 1992. pap. 12.95 (*1-881333-01-9*) White Mount Pubns.

Robinson, P. J., jt. auth. see Henderson-Sellers, A.

Robinson, P. K. Organizational Strategies for Older Workers. (Work in America Institute Studies in Productivity: No. 31). (Illus.). 36p. pap. 39.00 (*0-317-66850-1*, Pergamon Pr) Elsevier.

Robinson, P. R. Catalogue of Dated & Datable Manuscripts c. 737-1600 in Cambridge Libraries, 2 vols., Set. (Illus.). 144p. 1988. text ed. 390.00 (*0-85991-249-3*) Boydell & Brewer.

Robinson, Paschal, tr. see Frances D'Assisi.

Robinson, Patricia. A Trick of the Light. 240p. 1994. 19.95 (*0-312-10564-9*) St Martin.

Robinson, Patricia, tr. see Mori, Takeo & Milenkovic, Dragen.

Robinson, Patricia A. Fundamentals of Technical Writing. LC 84-81802. 320p. (C). 1985. pap. 39.96 (*0-395-35035-2*) HM.

— Fundamentals of Technical Writing. LC 84-81802. 320p. (C). 1985. teacher ed, pap. 2.36 (*0-395-35036-0*) HM.

Robinson, Patricia A., jt. auth. see Schoff, Gretchen H.

***Robinson, Patrick.** Billionaire Wars: The Struggle for Power in America's Wealthiest Oil Family. 1995. 24.95 (*1-56530-170-6*) Summit TX.

Robinson, Paul. The Freudian Left: Wilhelm Reich, Geza Roheim, Herbert Marcuse. LC 89-28749. 280p. 1990. pap. 13.95 (*0-8014-9716-7*) Cornell U Pr.

— Instant Print Estimator: Offset Prices That Reflect Your Costs. rev. ed. (Illus.). 550p. 1981. ring bd. 69.95 (*0-9607084-0-5*) Cushman Pubs.

— The Modernization of Sex: Havelock Ellis, Alfred Kinsey, William Masters & Virginia Johnson. LC 88-47784. 224p. 1988. reprint ed. pap. 14.95 (*0-8014-9539-3*) Cornell U Pr.

— Operas & Ideas: From Mozart to Strauss. LC 86-47637. 288p. 1986. pap. 14.95x (*0-8014-9428-1*) Cornell U Pr.

Robinson, Paul, jt. auth. see Plymen, Roger.

***Robinson, Paul E.** Hope Beneath the Surface. 1995. pap. write for info. (*0-7880-0436-0*) CSS OH.

Robinson, Paul H. Criminal Law Defenses, Vol. 1 & 2. 784p. 1984. Vol. 2, 784 pgs. write for info. (*0-318-57626-0*); Vol. 1, 585 pgs. text ed. 115.00 (*0-314-81513-9*) West Pub.

***Robinson, Paul H. & Darley, John M.** Justice, Liability & Blame: Community Views & the Criminal Law. LC 94-29250. (New Directions in Social Psycholog Ser.). 1995. text ed. 56.50 (*0-8133-2450-5*) Westview.

Robinson, Paul W. Freud & His Critics. LC 92-12935. (C). 1993. 30.00 (*0-520-08029-7*) U CA Pr.

Robinson, Paul W. & Hall, Leo D. Answers: A Parent's Guidebook for Solving Problems. LC 83-17538. (Illus.). 224p. 1984. 16.95 (*0-914107-01-1*); pap. 12.95 (*0-914107-00-3*) Lion House Pr.

Robinson, Pauline K. ESP Today: A Practitioner's Guide. 224p. (C). 1991. pap. text ed. 13.00 (*0-13-284084-7*, 640305) P-H.

— Organizational Strategies for Older Workers. (Studies in Productivity: Vol. 31). 88p. 1983. pap. 55.00 (*0-08-030954-2*) Work in Amer.

Robinson, Pearl T. & Skinner, Elliott P., eds. Transformation & Resiliency in Africa. LC 82-23211. 336p. 1982. 19.50 (*0-88258-054-X*) Howard U Pr.

Robinson, Percy. Handel & His Orbit. LC 79-13828. (Music Reprint Ser.). 1979. reprint ed. lib. bdg. 35.00 (*0-306-79522-1*) Da Capo.

Robinson, Percy J., tr. see Du Creux, Francois.

Robinson, Peter. Caedmon's Song. large type ed. 419p. 1993. 21.95 (*0-7505-0347-5*, Pub. by Magna Print Bks) Ulverscroft.

— A Dedicated Man. 272p. 1992. mass mkt. 4.99 (*0-380-71645-3*) Avon.

— A Dedicated Man. 272p. 1991. text ed. 18.95 (*0-684-19265-9*, Scribners) S&S Trade.

— Final Account: An Inspector Banks Mystery. LC 95-1381. 320p. (Orig.). 1995. text ed. 21.95 (*0-425-14935-8*, Prime Crime) Berkley Pub.

— Full Employment in Britain in the Nineteen Nineties: Lessons from Other Industrial Nations. (Campaign for Work Ser.). 235p. 1991. text ed. 68.95 (*1-85628-124-8*, Pub. by Avebury Pub UK) Ashgate Pub Co.

— Gallows View. 272p. 1991. mass mkt. 3.99 (*0-380-71400-0*) Avon.

— The Hanging Valley. (Chief Inspector Banks Ser.: No. 4). 288p. 1992. text ed. 20.00 (*0-684-19393-0*, Scribners) S&S Trade.

— Hanging Valley. 1994. mass mkt. 4.99 (*0-425-14196-9*) Berkley Pub.

— The Hanging Valley. large type ed. (Magna Mystery Ser.). 406p. 1992. 21.95 (*0-7505-0345-9*) Ulverscroft.

— In the Circumstances: About Poems & Poets. 272p. 1992. 69.00 (*0-19-811248-3*) OUP.

— A Necessary End. 336p. 1993. mass mkt. 4.99 (*0-380-71946-0*) Avon.

— A Necessary End. large type ed. 466p. 1992. 21.95 (*0-7505-0343-2*, Pub. by Magna Print Bks) Ulverscroft.

— A Necessary End: An Inspector Banks Mystery. 320p. 1992. text ed. 19.95 (*0-684-19385-X*, Scribners) S&S Trade.

— Past Reason Hated. (Inspector Banks Mystery Ser.). 320p. 1994. pap. 4.99 (*0-425-14489-5*, Prime Crime) Berkley Pub.

— Past Reason Hated: An Inspector Banks Mystery. 352p. 1993. text ed. 20.00 (*0-684-19529-1*, Scribners) S&S Trade.

— School Days: An Essay on the Hoover Institution Conference "Choice & Vouchers - The Future of American Education?" LC 93-35680. (Essays in Public Policy Ser.: No. 45). 1993. 5.00 (*0-8179-5502-X*) Hoover Inst Pr.

— Snapshots from Hell: The Making of an MBA. (Illus.). 304p. 1994. 22.95 (*0-446-51786-0*) Warner Bks.

— Snapshots from Hell: The Making of an MBA. 304p. 1995. pap. 11.99 (*0-446-67117-7*) Warner Bks.

— Unemployment & Local Labour Markets. (Campaign for Work Ser.). 125p. 1991. text ed. 68.95 (*1-85628-125-6*, Pub. by Avebury Pub UK) Ashgate Pub Co.

R

An Asterisk (*) at the beginning of an entry indicates that the title is appearing in BIP for the first time.

— The Water Garden: A Practical Guide to Planning & Planting. LC 94-31830. (Wayside Gardens Collection). (Illus.). 128p. 1995. pap. 19.95 (*0-8069-0845-9*) Sterling.
— Wednesday's Child. 320p. 1993. pap. text ed. 4.99 (*0-425-14834-3*, Prime Crime) Berkley Pub.
— Wednesday's Child: An Inspector Banks Mystery. 352p. 1994. text ed. 20.00 (*0-684-19644-1*, Scribners) S&S Trade.
— Wednesday's Child: An Inspector Banks Mystery. large type ed. LC 94-19361. 1994. 18.95 (*0-7862-0276-9*) Thorndike Pr.
***Robinson, Peter, ed.** Can Congress Be Fixed (& Is It Broken)? Five Essays on Congressional Reform. LC 95-5853. (Publication Ser.: Vol. 428). 1995. write for info. (*0-8179-9362-2*) Hoover Inst Pr.
— Geoffrey Hill: Essays on His Work. 224p. 1984. 90.00 (*0-335-10588-2*, Open Univ Pr); pap. 32.00 (*0-335-10587-4*, Open Univ Pr) Taylor & Francis.
Robinson, Peter, jt. auth. see Dillon, Helen.
Robinson, Peter, jt. auth. see Hesp, Paul.
Robinson, Peter B. & Tambunlertchai, Somsak. Africa & Asia: Can High Rates of Economic Growth be Replicated? LC 93-10021. (Occasional Papers - International Center for Economic Growth: No. 40). 1993. pap. 6.95 (*1-55815-261-X*) ICS Pr.
***Robinson, Peter G.** Marine Engineer's Guide to Fluid Flow. LC 75-25933. (Illus.). reprint ed. pap. 25.10 (*0-7837-9066-X*, 2049815) Bks Demand.
Robinson, Peter J. HOOD: Hierarchical Object Oriented Design. LC 92-16817. 320p. 1992. pap. text ed. 47.00 (*0-13-390816-X*) P-H.
Robinson, Peter M. Practical Fungal Physiology. LC 78-4243. 131p. reprint ed. pap. 37.40 (*0-685-20684-X*, 2030473) Bks Demand.
Robinson, Phil. Apple IIe: Step-by-Step Programming Guides, 2 Vols., I. 64p. 1984. 19.95 (*0-685-08723-9*) P-H.
Robinson, Philip. Perspectives on the Sociology of Education. 250p. (C). 1981. write for info. (*0-318-55559-X*); pap. 15.95 (*0-7100-0787-6*) Routledge Chapman & Hall.
Robinson, Philip J., jt. auth. see Harding, L. K.
Robinson, Phillip. Joy of Cybersex: An Underground Tour of Digital Erotica. 1993. pap. 24.95 (*1-56686-107-1*) Brady Compu Bks.
— Personal Finance on Your Computer: A Starter Kit. 352p. 1995. cd-rom, pap. text ed. 29.95 (*1-55828-420-6*) MIS Press.
— Using QEMM. 1994. pap. 26.95 (*1-55851-349-3*) M&T Bks.
— Using QEMM. 2nd ed. 482p. 1994. pap. 26.95 (*1-55828-349-8*) MIS Press.
— Welcome to Memory Management. LC 94-17282. 1994. pap. 19.95 (*1-55828-343-9*) H Holt & Co.
— Welcome to Personal Finance on Your Computer: A Guide to Saving, Spending, Taxing & Investing with Your Computer. 1994. pap. 19.95 (*1-55828-372-2*) MIS Press.
Robinson, Quay H. The Palmer & Hendrick Family. LC 94-70396. 432p. 1994. 75.00 (*1-55618-141-8*) Brunswick Pub.
Robinson, R. The Achievement Planner: Executive Edition for Winners. 102p. 1993. student ed 39.95 (*1-884780-06-7*) Phoenix Pubng.
— Gene Mapping in Laboratory Animals. Incl. Pt. A. 160p. 1972. 32.50 (*0-306-37551-6*); 1972. write for info. (*0-318-55320-1*, Plenum Pr) Plenum.
— Genetics for Cat Breeders. 3rd ed. (Illus.). 220p. 1991. text ed. 47.00 (*0-08-037506-5*, Pergamon Pr) Elsevier.
— Genetics of the Norway Rat. LC 64-19588. (International Series Mono on Pure & Applied Mathematics: Vol. 24). 1965. 334.00 (*0-08-010664-1*, Pub. by Pergamon Repr UK) Franklin.
Robinson, R., ed. People in Organizations. (C). 1989. 100.00 (*0-09-173152-6*, Pub. by S Thornes Pubs UK) St Mut.
Robinson, R. & Stott, R. Medical Emergencies. 6th ed. 320p. 1993. pap. 35.00 (*0-7506-0897-8*) Buttrwrth-Heinemann.
Robinson, R. & Wiggin, W. Animal Types One: Invertebrates. (C). 1970. text ed. 54.00 (*0-09-118931-4*, Pub. by S Thornes Pubs UK) St Mut.
— Animal Types Two: Vertebrates. (C). 1971. text ed. 55.00 (*0-09-108781-3*, Pub. by S Thornes Pubs UK) St Mut.
Robinson, R., jt. auth. see Astbury, R.
Robinson, R., jt. auth. see Bennett, A.
Robinson, R., jt. auth. see Bentley, K.
Robinson, R., jt. auth. see Berry, R.
Robinson, R., jt. auth. see Davies, J.
Robinson, R., jt. auth. see Dodsworth, T. L.
Robinson, R., jt. auth. see Evans, V.
Robinson, R., jt. auth. see Fox, P.
Robinson, R., jt. auth. see Harned, H.
Robinson, R., jt. auth. see Helsdon, R.
Robinson, R., jt. auth. see Illing, R.
Robinson, R., jt. auth. see King, E.
Robinson, R., jt. auth. see Kureishi, R.
Robinson, R., jt. auth. see Manning, J.
Robinson, R., jt. auth. see Schwartz, B.
Robinson, R., jt. auth. see Smith, C.
Robinson, R., jt. auth. see Sporn, Philip.
Robinson, R., jt. auth. see Ulbricht, T.
Robinson, R., tr. see Van Meteren, Emanuel.
Robinson, R. D., jt. auth. see Robinson, J. H.
Robinson, R. K. Therapeutic Properties of Fermented Milks. 192p. 1991. 92.00 (*1-85166-552-8*) Elsevier.
Robinson, R. K., ed. Developments in Food Microbiology, No. 2. 200p. 1986. 66.75 (*0-85334-432-9*, Pub. by Elsevier Applied Sci UK) Elsevier.
— Developments in Food Microbiology, Vol. 4. 250p. 1988. 84.75 (*1-85166-169-7*) Elsevier.
— Microbiology of Frozen Foods. 304p. 1985. 79.25 (*0-85334-335-7*, Pub. by Elsevier Applied Sci UK) Elsevier.
— Modern Dairy Technology. 2nd ed. LC 92-40279. 1993. write for info. (*1-85166-924-8*) Elsevier.
— Modern Dairy Technology, Vol. 1: Advances in Milk Processing. 400p. 1986. 99.00 (*0-85334-391-8*, Pub. by Elsevier Applied Sci UK) Elsevier.
— Modern Dairy Technology, Vol. 2: Advances in Milk Products. 400p. 1986. 99.00 (*0-85334-394-2*, Pub. by Elsevier Applied Sci UK) Elsevier.
Robinson, R. L., et al, eds. Reactions Between Complex Nuclei: Proceedings, 2 vols., 1. LC 74-81324. 680p. 1975. 28.25 (*0-444-10664-2*) Elsevier.
— Reactions Between Complex Nuclei: Proceedings, 2 vols., 2. LC 74-81324. 680p. 1975. 82.00 (*0-444-10746-0*) Elsevier.
— Reactions Between Complex Nuclei: Proceedings, 2 vols., Set. LC 74-81324. 680p. 1975. 92.75 (*0-685-57108-4*) Elsevier.
Robinson, R. R., ed. Nephrology. (Illus.). lv, 1756p. 1984. 266.00 (*0-387-96072-4*) Spr-Verlag.
Robinson, R. W., jt. auth. see Likar, I. V.
Robinson, R. W., et al, eds. Glycosaminoglycans & Arterial Diseases. (Monographs on Atherosclerosis: Vol. 5). (Illus.). viii, 134p. 1975. 55.25 (*3-8055-2089-1*) S Karger.
Robinson, Rachel. Sources for the History of Greek Athletics. 289p. 1980. pap. 20.00 (*0-89005-297-2*) Ares.
Robinson, Rachel S. The Size of the Slave Population of Athens. LC 73-10760. 136p. 1974. reprint ed. text ed. 55.00 (*0-8371-7034-6*, ROSP, Greenwood Pr) Greenwood.
Robinson, Ralph. Christ All & in All. 640p. 1992. reprint ed. 29.95 (*1-877611-49-2*) Soli Deo Gloria.
***Robinson, Ramsey.** Deadly Encounters. LC 94-90165. 128p. (Orig.). 1995. pap. 9.00 (*1-56002-450-X*, Univ Edtns) Aegina Pr.
Robinson, Randall N. Chemical Engineering Practice Exam Set. 2nd ed. (Engineering Reference Manual Ser.). 136p. (C). 1989. pap. text ed. 18.95 (*0-932276-93-8*) Prof Pubns CA.
— Chemical Engineering Reference Manual. 4th ed. (Engineering Reference Manual Ser.). 408p. 1988. 49.95 (*0-932276-75-X*) Prof Pubns CA.
— Solutions Manual for the Chemical Engineering Reference Manual. 4th ed. (Engineering Reference Manual Ser.). 64p. 1990. pap. text ed. 17.95 (*0-912045-26-4*) Prof Pubns CA.
Robinson, Ras. Free Indeed! (Illus.). 26p. 1983. pap. 1.50 (*0-937778-08-7*) Fulness Hse.
— How to Receive God's Anointing. (Illus.). 73p. 1985. pap. text ed. 4.00 (*0-937778-10-9*) Fulness Hse.
Robinson, Ras, ed. The Finest of Fulness. 187p. 1979. pap. 4.00 (*0-937778-00-1*) Fulness Hse.
— Spiritual Warfare. (Illus.). 59p. 1982. reprint ed. pap. 3.00 (*0-937778-05-2*) Fulness Hse.
Robinson, Ray. The Hero: The Life & Career of Christy Mathewson. LC 92-40974. (C). 1993. 23.00 (*0-19-507629-X*) OUP.
— Iron Horse: Lou Gehrig in His Time. LC 90-56212. 288p. 1991. pap. 12.00 (*0-06-097408-7*, PL) HarpC.
— Iron Horse: Lou Gehrig in His Time. 1990. 22.50 (*0-393-02857-7*) Norton.
— Iron Horse: Lou Gehrig in His Time. large type ed. 478p. 1991. reprint ed. bds. 22.95 (*1-56054-133-4*) Thorndike Pr.
— Matty, an American Hero: Christy Mathewson of the New York Giants. (Illus.). 272p. 1994. reprint ed. pap. 12.95 (*0-19-509263-5*) OUP.
Robinson, Ray, ed. Choral Music: Norton Historical Anthology. (C). 1978. pap. text ed. 42.95 (*0-393-09062-0*) Norton.
***Robinson, Ray & Le Grand, Julia.** Evaluating the National Health Service Reforms. (Reshaping the Public Sector Ser.: Vol. 8). 275p. (C). 1994. 34.95 (*1-56000-194-1*); pap. 21.95 (*1-56000-796-6*) Transaction Pubs.
Robinson, Ray & Winold, Allen. The Choral Experience: Literature, Materials, & Methods. (Illus.). 510p. (C). 1992. reprint ed. text ed. 33.95 (*0-88133-650-5*) Waveland Pr.
Robinson, Ray, jt. ed. see Le Grand, Julian.
Robinson, Ray, jt. auth. see LeGrand, Julian.
Robinson, Ray, et al. Up Front! Becoming the Complete Choral Conductor. (Illus.). 304p. (Orig.). (C). 1994. pap. 27.95 (*0-911318-19-4*) E C Schirmer.
Robinson, Raymond H. The Growing of America, 1789-1848. 2nd ed. (American History Ser.). (Illus.). 256p. (C). 1991. pap. text ed. write for info. (*0-88273-171-8*) Forum Pr IL.
Robinson, Raymond S., jt. auth. see Kaufman, Harold R.
Robinson, Rebecca Y. & Petrek, Jeanne A. A Step by Step Guide to Dealing with Your Breast Cancer. LC 94-18102. 1994. 18.95 (*1-55972-257-6*, Birch Ln Pr) Carol Pub Group.
Robinson, Red & Hodgins, Peggy. Rockbound. 232p. 1983. 19.95 (*0-88839-162-5*) Hancock House.
***Robinson, Reuel.** History of Camden & Rockport, Maine. (Illus.). 644p. 1995. reprint ed. lib. bdg. 65.00 (*0-8328-4669-4*) Higginson Bk Co.
Robinson, Richard & Weiss, Arthur. Tax Planning for S Corporations. 1988. write for info. (*0-8205-1496-9*) Bender.
Robinson, Richard, tr. see Aristotle.
Robinson, Richard, tr. see Bataille, Georges.
Robinson, Richard, tr. see Jaeger, Werner W.
Robinson, Richard, jt. auth. see Pearce, John A., II.
Robinson, Richard, jt. auth. see Pearce, John.
Robinson, Richard B., Jr. Business History of the World: A Chronology. LC 93-25476. 576p. 1993. text ed. 79.50 (*0-313-26094-X*, Greenwood Pr) Greenwood.
— United States Business History, 1602-1988: A Chronology. LC 90-34102. 672p. 1990. text ed. 69.50 (*0-313-26095-8*, RUB/, Greenwood Pr) Greenwood.
Robinson, Richard B., Jr., jt. auth. see Pearce, John A., II.
Robinson, Richard B., Jr., jt. auth. see Perce, John A., II.
Robinson, Richard D. Cases on International Technology Transfer. 369p. (Orig.). (C). 1989. teacher ed 15.00 (*0-317-93733-2*); pap. text ed. 27.50 (*0-317-93732-4*) Hamlin Pubns.
— Direct Foreign Investment: Costs & Benefits. LC 87-17750. 244p. 1987. text ed. 65.00 (*0-275-92717-2*, C2717, Praeger Pubs) Greenwood.
— The First Turkish Republic: A Case Study in National Development. LC 63-17210. (Harvard Middle Eastern Studies: No. 9). 379p. reprint ed. pap. 108.10 (*0-7837-2321-0*, 2057409) Bks Demand.
— High-Level Manpower in Economic Development: The Turkish Case. LC 67-25400. (Middle Eastern Monographs: No. 17). 147p. 1967. 8.95 (*0-674-39050-4*) HUP.
— International Business Policy. LC 82-970. (Modern Management Ser.). xvi, 252p. 1982. text ed. 59.75 (*0-313-23356-X*, ROINT, Greenwood Pr) Greenwood.
— The Japan Syndrome -- Is There One? Cases to the Point. (Research Monograph: No. 97). 225p. 1985. spiral bd. 30.00 (*0-88406-182-5*) GA St U Busn Pr.
— Performance Requirements for Multinational Corporations: U. S. Management Response. LC 82-22469. 224p. 1983. text ed. 55.00 (*0-275-91066-0*, C1066, Praeger Pubs) Greenwood.
— Teacher Effectiveness & Reading Instruction. LC 91-31023. (Illus.). 100p. (Orig.). (C). 1991. pap. text ed. 14.95 (*0-927516-25-X*) ERIC-REC.
— Teaching Notes for Cases on International Technology Transfer. (Illus.). 107p. (Orig.). (C). 1988. pap. text ed. 15.00 (*0-317-93295-0*) Hamlin Pubns.
Robinson, Richard D., ed. Foreign Capital & Technology in China. LC 87-2450. 224p. 1987. text ed. 59.95 (*0-275-92716-4*, C2716, Praeger Pubs) Greenwood.
— The International Communication of Technology. (International Business & Trade Ser.: Vol. 1). 288p. 1991. 58.00 (*0-8448-1655-8*, Pub. by Tay Francis Ltd UK) Taylor & Francis.
Robinson, Richard D., jt. auth. see McKenna, Michael C.
Robinson, Richard E. Don't Buy a Used Car! Until You Read This! (Illus.). 44p. 1986. pap. 2.95 (*0-9618898-0-2*, 73291) RER Servs.
Robinson, Richard H. & Johnson, Willard L. The Buddhist Religion: A Historical Introduction. 3rd ed. 290p. (C). 1982. pap. 19.95 (*0-534-01027-X*) Intl Thomson.
Robinson, Richard H., tr. see Cranmer-Byng, J. L., ed.
Robinson, Richard R., Jr., jt. auth. see Pearce, John A., II.
Robinson, Rick E., jt. auth. see Csikszentmihalyi, Mihaly.
Robinson, Rita. Center of the World: Native American Spirituality. 1992. pap. 12.95 (*0-87877-172-7*) Newcastle Pub.
— Color Your World: Using the Power of Color & Light in Your Life. Misiroglu, Gina, ed. 192p. (Orig.). 1994. pap. 10.95 (*0-87877-189-1*) Newcastle Pub.
— Friendship Book: The Art of Making & Keeping Friends. 1992. pap. 12.95 (*0-87877-173-5*) Newcastle Pub.
— Health in Your Hands: A New Look at Modern Palmistry & Your Health. Gross, Gina R., ed. (Illus.). 176p. (Orig.). 1993. pap. 12.95 (*0-87877-181-6*) Newcastle Pub.
— The Palm: A Guide to Your Hidden Potential. 128p. 1988. pap. 10.95 (*0-87877-133-6*) Newcastle Pub.
— Survivors of Suicide. (Orig.). 1992. pap. 9.95 (*0-87877-174-3*) Newcastle Pub.
— When Women Choose to Be Single. (Orig.). 1992. pap. 9.95 (*0-87877-170-0*) Newcastle Pub.
Robinson, Rita, ed. see Neumann, Jeff & Ruth, Romy.
Robinson, Robbie. F-100 Super Sabre in Color. (Fighting Colors Ser.). (Illus.). 32p. 1992. pap. 9.95 (*0-89747-284-5*, 6565) Squad Sig Pubns.
— USAFE in Color, Vol. 2. (Fighting Colors Ser.). (Illus.). 32p. 1990. pap. 9.95 (*0-89747-250-0*, 6563) Squad Sig Pubns.
Robinson, Robby, jt. auth. see Lie, Arne B.
Robinson, Robert. Ecclesiastical Researches. 1984. reprint ed. 37.00 (*0-317-11349-6*) Church History.
— Research in Social Stratification & Mobility, Vol. 3. 244p. 1984. 73.25 (*0-89232-331-0*) Jai Pr.
Robinson, Robert, jt. ed. see Chao, K. C.
Robinson, Robert, ed. see Kirsch, Sylvia J.
Robinson, Robert, tr. see Montaner, Carlos.
Robinson, Robert A. ECA Benefit Communications. (ECA Employee Benefit Communications Ser.). (Illus.). 140p. 1990. ring bd. 679.00 (*1-884780-00-8*) Phoenix Pubng.
— ELA Prospecting Kit. (ECA Benefit Communications Ser.). 19p. 1992. student ed 24.95 (*1-884780-01-6*) Phoenix Pubng.
— ELA Salesmaker Kit. abr. ed. (ECA Benefit Communications Ser.). 82p. 1991. student ed 89.95 (*1-884780-10-5*) Phoenix Pubng.
— Employee Enrollment Presentation. (ECA Employee Benefit Communications Ser.). Date not set. audio, pap. text ed. 12.95 (*1-884780-09-1*) Phoenix Pubng.
— Happiness & Self Esteem. Wallace, D., ed. 72p. (Orig.). Date not set. pap. text ed. 8.95 (*1-884780-17-2*) Phoenix Pubng.
— The Hidden Paycheck. (ECA Employee Benefit Communications Ser.). Date not set. audio, pap. text ed. 12.95 (*1-884780-08-3*) Phoenix Pubng.
— Magic Magnifying Mind. Date not set. pap. text ed. 8.95 (*1-884780-02-4*) Phoenix Pubng.
— Positive Power Thinking. (Magic Magnifying Mind Ser.). Date not set. pap. text ed. 8.95 (*1-884780-03-2*) Phoenix Pubng.
Robinson, Robert B. Roman Catholic Exegesis since Divino Afflante Spiritu. LC 88-11432. (Society of Biblical Literature Ser.). 192p. 1988. 18.95 (*1-55540-240-2*, 06 21 11); pap. 12.95 (*1-55540-241-0*, 06 21 11) Scholars Pr GA.
Robinson, Robert B., jt. ed. see Culley, Robert C.
Robinson, Robert E., jt. auth. see Prichard, Robert W.
Robinson, Robert G. Aging & Clinical Practice: Depression & Coexisting Disease. LC 88-28444. 248p. 1989. 52.00 (*0-89640-152-9*) Igaku-Shoin.
Robinson, Robert G., jt. ed. see Starkstein, Sergio E.
Robinson, Robert H. Clambake Sans Sand in Pots & Woks. 1983. pap. 2.95 (*0-911145-04-4*) Sussex Prints.
— Craft of Dismantling a Crab. (Illus.). 120p. (Orig.). 1977. pap. 5.95 (*0-685-07066-2*) Chapter & Cask.
— The Craft of Dismantling Crabs & Other Shellfish. 96p. (Orig.). 1982. pap. 4.95 (*0-685-08789-1*) Sussex Prints.
— The Essential Book of Shellfish. LC 82-184274. (Illus.). 160p. 1983. pap. 6.95 (*0-89709-040-3*) Liberty Pub.
Robinson, Robert H., ed. see Walthers, Lynette L.
Robinson, Robert L. Blinded Veterans of the Vietnam Era. LC 74-191191. 39p. reprint ed. pap. 25.00 (*0-8357-7321-3*, 2027342) Bks Demand.
— Complete Course in Professional Locksmithing. LC 73-174584. (Illus.). 414p. 1973. 63.95 (*0-911012-15-X*) Nelson-Hall.
Robinson, Robert L., jt. ed. see Chao, K. C.
Robinson, Robert V. Research in Social Stratification & Mobility, Vol. 6. 1987. 73.25 (*0-89232-717-0*) Jai Pr.
Robinson, Robert V., ed. Research in Social Stratification & Mobility, Vol. 2. 1983. 73.25 (*0-89232-302-7*) Jai Pr.
— Research in Social Stratification & Mobility, Vol. 4. 1985. 73.25 (*0-89232-563-1*) Jai Pr.
— Research in Social Stratification & Mobility, Vol. 5. 1986. 73.25 (*0-89232-660-3*) Jai Pr.
***Robinson-Roberts, Laura N. & Kirschbaum, Mark A.** Paleogeography of the Upper Cretaceous of the Western Interior of Middle North America: Coal Distribution & Sediment Accumulation. (U.S. Geological Survey Professional Paper: No. 1561). 1996. write for info. (*0-615-00320-6*) US Geol Survey.
Robinson, Rodney P., jt. auth. see Tacitus.
Robinson, Roger. Ace Science-Fiction Double Books. 16p. (C). 1990. reprint ed. lib. bdg. 15.00x (*0-8095-4604-3*) Borgo Pr.
— DAW Science-Fiction Books. 20p. (C). 1990. reprint ed. lib. bdg. 17.00x (*0-8095-4606-X*) Borgo Pr.
— Hale & Gresham Hardback Science Fiction. 16p. (C). 1990. reprint ed. lib. bdg. 17.00x (*0-8095-4605-1*) Borgo Pr.
— Science Fiction & Fantasy Magazines, 1923-1980. 28p. (C). 1990. reprint ed. lib. bdg. 17.00x (*0-8095-4603-5*) Borgo Pr.
— Who's Hugh? An SF Reader's Guide to Pseudonyms. 176p. (C). 1989. reprint ed. lib. bdg. 29.00x (*0-8095-4600-0*) Borgo Pr.
— The Writings of Henry Kenneth Bulmer. rev. ed. 52p. (C). 1989. reprint ed. lib. bdg. 20.00x (*0-8095-4602-7*) Borgo Pr.
Robinson, Roger, ed. Katherine Mansfield: In from the Margin. LC 93-25541. 224p. (C). 1994. text ed. 27.50 (*0-8071-1865-6*) La State U Pr.
Robinson, Roland I. Postwar Market for State & Local Government Securities. (Studies in Capital Formation & Financing: No. 5). 251p. 1960. reprint ed. 65.30 (*0-87014-103-1*) Natl Bur Econ Res.
Robinson, Roland I. & Wrightman, Dwayne. Financial Markets: The Accumulation & Allocation of Wealth. 2nd ed. (Illus.). 1980. text ed. write for info. (*0-07-053274-5*) McGraw.
***Robinson, Ron.** Kitchen Dance: A Pas de Deux in Two Acts. Date not set. 9.95 (*0-929925-10-6*) Ex Machina.
Robinson, Ronald. Tumours That Secrete Catecholamines: Their Detection & Clinical Chemistry. LC 79-41731. 144p. reprint ed. pap. 41.10 (*0-317-29342-7*, 2024034) Bks Demand.
Robinson, Ronald, ed. see Egan, C. John, Jr.
Robinson, Ronald, ed. see Holzach, Michael.
Robinson, Ronald, ed. see Woster, Jim, et al.
Robinson, Ronald D., jt. auth. see Hubbard, Elaine.
Robinson, Ronald L., ed. see Fryxell, David A.
Robinson, Ronald W. Stanley, the Talking Parrot. LC 89-60801. (Illus.). 22p. (Orig.). (J). (gr. 3-4). 1989. Incl. cassette & filmstrip pkg. audio, flmstrp 12.95 (*0-9622692-2-0*); Incl. cassette pkg. audio 8.95 (*0-9622692-1-2*); pap. 4.95 (*0-9622692-0-4*) R W Robinson.
Robinson, Ronn & Vando, David, eds. The New York City Model Agency Directory. 64p. 1987. pap. 9.95 (*0-87314-024-9*) Peter Glenn.
Robinson, Ronn, jt. ed. see Vando, David.
Robinson, Rony. The Beano. 176p. 1988. 16.95 (*0-15-111229-0*) HarBrace.
Robinson, Rosalind, jt. auth. see Lavrack, Kevin R.
Robinson, Rowena D., jt. auth. see Robinson, James H.
***Robinson, Rowland E.** Danvis Tales: Selected Stories. Budbill, David, ed. LC 95-13841. (Hardscrabble Bks.). (Illus.). 320p. (C). 1995. 24.95 (*0-87451-718-4*) U Pr of New Eng.
— Sam Lovel's Boy, with Forest & Stream Fables. Perkins, Llewellyn R., ed. LC 70-160949. (Short Story Index Reprint Ser.). 1977. reprint ed. 20.95 (*0-8369-3928-X*) Ayer.
— Sam Lovel's Camps: & Other Stories, Including 'In the Green Wood' Perkins, Llewellyn R., ed. LC 77-37558. (Short Story Index Reprint Ser.). 1977. reprint ed. 21.95 (*0-8369-4117-9*) Ayer.
— Uncle Lisha's Shop: Life in A Corner of Yankeeland. LC 79-96892. 187p. reprint ed. lib. bdg. 19.00 (*0-8398-1761-4*) Irvington.

R

— Uncle Lisha's Shop: Life in a Corner of Yankeeland. 187p. (C). 1986. reprint ed. pap. text ed. 6.95 (0-8290-2045-4) Irvington.
— Vermont: A Study of Independence. LC 72-3751. (American Commonwealths Ser.: No. 14). reprint ed. 39.50 (0-404-57214-6) AMS Pr.
Robinson, Roxana. Georgia O'Keeffe. LC 89-45061. (Illus.). 656p. 1990. reprint ed. pap. 14.00 (0-06-092000-9, PL) HarpC.
— Georgia O'Keeffe: A Life. LC 89-45061. (Illus.). 496p. 1989. pap. 12.95 (0-685-25760-6, E Burlingame Bks) HarpC.
— Summer Light. (Hardscrabble Bks.). 208p. (C). 1995. pap. 12.95 (0-87451-738-9) U Pr of New Eng.
Robinson, Roy. Genetics for Cat Breeders. 2nd ed. LC 77-120591. 1977. text ed. 36.00 (0-08-021209-3, Pergamon Pr) Elsevier.
— Genetics for Dog Breeders. LC 81-15891. (Illus.). 272p. 1982. text ed. 32.00 (0-08-025917-0, H235, Pergamon Pr) Elsevier.
— Lepidoptera Genetics. (C). 1971. 284.00 (0-08-006659-3, Pub. by Pergamon Repr UK) Franklin.
Robinson, Russell & Gammond, Peter. Bluff Your Way in Music. (Bluffers Ser.). 77p. (Orig.). 1993. pap. 3.95 (1-57143-006-7) RDR Bks.
***Robinson, Russell D.** An Introduction to Dynamics of Group Leadership & Organizational Change. 5th rev. ed. 250p. 1995. pap. text ed. 21.95 (1-877837-02-4) Bible Study Pr.
— An Introduction to Helping Adults Learn & Change. rev. ed. 180p. (C). 1994. pap. text ed. 19.75 (1-877837-28-8) Bible Study Pr.
— Jerusalem Journey & Other Poems. 68p. 1985. reprint ed. pap. 7.95 (1-877837-18-0) Bible Study Pr.
— Teaching the Scriptures: A Study Guide for Bible Students & Teachers. 6th rev. ed. (Illus.). 220p. 1993. pap. text ed. 19.95 (1-877837-11-3) Bible Study Pr.
***Robinson, Russell M., II.** Robinson on North Carolina Corporation Law. 850p. 1990. 95.00 (0-87473-657-9) Michie Butterworth.
***Robinson, Russell S.** A Man for All Ages. 1994. 19.95 (0-533-10971-X) Vantage.
Robinson, Ruth & Farudi, Daryush. Buy Books Where - Sell Books Where, 1988-1989: A Directory of Out of Print Booksellers & Their Author-Subject Specialties. 6th rev. ed. 270p. (Orig.). 1988. pap. 29.75 (0-317-67852-3) Robinson Bks.
Robinson, Ruth E. Buy Books Where - Sell Books Where, 1992-1993: A Directory of Out of Print Booksellers & Collectors & Their Author-Subject Specialties. 8th rev. ed. 308p. (Orig.). 1992. pap. 29.75 (0-9603556-9-3) Robinson Bks.
— Buy Books Where - Sell Books Where, 1994-1995: A Directory of Out of Print Booksellers & Collectors & Their Author-Subject Specialties. 9th rev. ed. 329p. (Orig.). 1994. pap. 34.95 (0-930284-53-4) Robinson Bks.
Robinson, Ruth E. & Farudi, Daryush. Buy Books Where-Sell Books Where. 6th ed. 1988. 29.75 (0-9603556-7-7) Robinson Bks.
Robinson, S. Drafting - Its Application to Conveyancing & Commercial Documents. 1980. U.K. 115.00 (0-406-35890-7) Butterworth Legal Pubs.
— Transfer of Land in Victoria. lxv, 517p. 1979. 123.00 (0-455-19746-6, Pub. by Law Bk Co) W W Gaunt.
Robinson, S. & Marks, T. Woven Cloth Construction. 178p. 1973. 70.00 (0-686-63810-7) St Mut.
***Robinson, S. & Thomson, A. M., eds.** Midwives, Research & Childbirth No. 3. 1994. 45.00 (1-56593-043-6, 0291) Singular Publishing.
— Midwives, Research & Childbirth Vol. 4. 224p. 1995. 44.75 (1-56593-289-7, 0613) Singular Publishing.
Robinson, S. J., jt. auth. see Urwin, J.
Robinson, S. P., jt. auth. see Bacon, D. R.
Robinson, S. Scott. The Law of Game, Salmon & Freshwater Fishing in Scotland. 1990. 124.00 (0-406-11201-0, U.K.) Butterworth Legal Pubs.
— The Law of Interdict. 1987. U.K. pap. 48.00 (0-406-10445-X) Butterworth Legal Pubs.
Robinson, Sallie. Buddie & I. 54p. 1987. reprint ed. pap. 2.95 (0-8341-1216-7) Beacon Hill.
Robinson, Sally. Engendering the Subject: Gender & Self Representation in Contemporary Women's Fiction. LC 90-10249. (SUNY Series in Feminist Criticism & Theory). 240p. (C). 1991. 59.50 (0-7914-0727-6); pap. 19.95 (0-7914-0728-4) State U NY Pr.
— Seasons of a Marriage. LC 93-24559. 190p. (Orig.). 1993. pap. 8.95 (1-882185-12-9) Crnrstone Pub.
Robinson, Sam. Winning Against the Odds. LC 92-29120. (Illus.). 256p. 1993. 17.50 (0-912526-58-0) Lib Res.
Robinson, Sandra, jt. auth. see Robinson, George.
Robinson, Sandra C. The Everywhere Bear. (Wonder Ser.). (Illus.). 64p. (J). (gr. 4-6). 1992. pap. 7.95 (1-879373-07-6) R Rinehart.
— Last Bit Bear: A Fable. 1991. pap. 4.95 (0-911797-09-2) R Rinehart.
— Mountain Lion: Puma, Panther, Painter, Cougar. (Wonder Ser.). (Illus.). 64p. (J). (gr. 4-6). 1991. pap. 7.95 (1-879373-00-9) R Rinehart.
— Sea Otters, River Otters: A Story & Activity Book. LC 92-62078. (Wonder Ser.). (Illus.). 64p. (Orig.). (J). (gr. 1-6). 1993. pap. 7.95 (1-879373-41-6) R Rinehart.
— The Wonder of Wolves: A Story & Activity Book. (Illus.). (J). (gr. 1-6). 1989. pap. 7.95 (0-911797-65-3) R Rinehart.
***Robinson, Sandra C. & Grosshauser, Peter.** The Rainstick: A Fable. LC 94-21587. (Illus.). 40p. (Orig.). (J). (gr. 2 up). 1994. pap. text ed. 9.95 (1-56044-284-0) Falcon Pr MT.
Robinson, Sandra C., et al. Water, a Gift of Nature: The Story Behind the Scenery. LC 93-77028. (Illus.). 48p. 1993. pap. 6.95 (0-88714-077-7) KC Pubns.
Robinson, Sandra R. & McAuliffe, Lindsay. Origins. (Illus.). 336p. (Orig.). 1989. Vol. 1: Bringing Words to Life. write for info. (0-318-64647-1); Vol. 2: The Word Families. write for info. (0-318-64648-X) Tchrs & Writers Coll.
— Origins, Set. (Illus.). 336p. (Orig.). 1989. pap. 25.95 (0-915924-90-0) Tchrs & Writers Coll.
Robinson, Sara T. Kansas: Its Interior & Exterior Life. LC 77-160991. (Select Bibliographies Reprint Ser.). 1977. reprint ed. 25.95 (0-8369-5859-4) Ayer.
Robinson, Sarah & Thomson, Ann, eds. Midwives, Research & Childbirth, Vol. 2. 256p. 1990. pap. 25.50 (0-412-31650-1, A4455) Chapman & Hall.
Robinson, Scott. Indy Cars. LC 87-30509. (Super-Charged Ser.). (Illus.). 48p. (J). (gr. 5-6). 1988. lib. bdg. 11.95 (0-89686-356-5, Crstwood Hse) Silver Burdett Pr.
Robinson, Scott R., jt. ed. see Smotherman, William P.
Robinson, Serjeant. Bench & Bar: Reminiscences of One of the Last of an Ancient Race. (Illus.). xi, 327p. 1988. reprint ed. lib. bdg. 32.50 (0-8377-2537-2) Rothman.
***Robinson, Sheila C.** Along the Lewis & Clark Trail in North Dakota. 142p. 1993. pap. 8.50 (0-9643057-0-4) Dakota Trails.
Robinson, Sheila K. How to Open a Family Child Care Home in Rhode Island: A Practical Guide on How to Become a Family Child Care Provider & How to Start a Family Child Care Home in Rhode Island. 175p. 1994. pap. 9.95 (0-9637673-1-3) Napa Sonoma.
— Stanford House Staff Auxiliary Guidebook to the Bay Area: A Guide for Finding Your Way Around the Bay from Napa to Monterey. LC 93-86355. (Illus.). 170p. (Orig.). 1994. pap. 9.95 (0-9637673-3-X) Napa Sonoma.
Robinson, Shepard, ed. Manufactured Housing: What It Is, Where It Is, How It Operates. 1988. pap. 60.00 (0-9603502-1-7) Ingleside.
Robinson, Shepard D. How to Turn-Around a Troubled Company. (Illus.). 100p. (Orig.). 1979. pap. 15.00 (0-9603502-0-9) Ingleside.
Robinson, Sherman, jt. auth. see Adelman, Irma.
Robinson, Sherry. El Malpais, Mt. Taylor, & the Zuni Mountains: A Hiking Guide & History. LC 94-18694. (Coyote Book Ser.). (Illus.). 293p. 1994. pap. 19.95 (0-8263-1527-5) U of NM Pr.
Robinson, Sidney K. The Architecture of Alden B. Dow. LC 82-247370. (Illus.). 168p. 1983. pap. 19.95 (0-8143-1721-9) Wayne St U Pr.
— The Continuous Present of Organic Architecture. (Illus.). 80p. (Orig.). 1991. pap. 25.00 (0-917562-56-9) Contemp Arts.
— Inquiry into the Picturesque. LC 90-20338. 112p. 1991. 19.95 (0-226-72251-1) U Ch Pr.
Robinson, Sidney K., jt. ed. see Wilson, Richard G.
Robinson, Simon. Whitesnake. (Illus.). 96p. Date not set. pap. 17.95 (0-685-69180-2) Omnibus NY.
Robinson, Sinclair & Smith, Donald, eds. NTC's Dictionary of Canadian French. 300p. 1991. pap. 14.95 (0-8442-1486-8, Natl Textbk) NTC Pub Grp.
Robinson, Skip. Charitable Employee Benefit Design. 270p. 1985. ring bd. 16.00 (0-936434-17-1) SF Study Ctr.
Robinson, Solon. Solon Robinson, Pioneer & Agriculturist. Kellar, Herbert A., ed. LC 74-145268. (Illus.). 1971. reprint ed. 59.00 (0-403-01183-3) Scholarly.
Robinson, Spider. The Callahan Touch. LC 92-21155. (Orig.). 1993. 18.95 (0-441-09075-3) Ace Bks.
— The Callahan Touch. 240p. (Orig.). 1995. pap. text ed. 5.50 (0-441-00133-5) Ace Bks.
— Callahan's Crosstime Saloon. 192p. 1989. pap. 4.50 (0-441-09043-5) Ace Bks.
— Callahan's Lady. 1990. mass mkt. 4.99 (0-441-09072-9) Ace Bks.
— Kill the Editor. 1991. 35.00 (1-56146-114-8, Axolotl Press) Pulphouse Pub.
— Lady Slings the Booze. 272p. 1993. mass mkt. 4.99 (0-441-46929-9) Ace Bks.
— Off the Wall at Callahan's. 160p. 1994. pap. 9.95 (0-312-85661-X) Tor Bks.
Robinson, Spider & Robinson, Jeanne. Stardance. 1991. reprint ed. mass mkt. 3.99 (0-671-72097-X) Baen Bks.
— Starmind. LC 94-33374. 304p. (Orig.). 1995. text ed. 21.95 (0-441-00209-9) Ace Bks.
— Starseed. 256p. 1992. mass mkt. 4.99 (0-441-78360-0) Ace Bks.
Robinson, Stanley. The Property Law Act Victoria. 616p. 1992. 157.50 (0-455-21050-0, Pub. by Law Bk Co) W W Gaunt.
Robinson, Stanley L. Harnessing Technology: The Management of Technology for the Nontechnologist. 120p. 1991. pap. 24.95 (0-442-00753-1) Van Nos Reinhold.
— How to Avoid Old Age. LC 90-91721. (Illus.). 152p. 1990. write for info. (0-9626830-0-0) Remington NJ.
Robinson, Stephen E. Are Mormons Christians? 1991. 8.95 (0-88494-784-X) Bookcraft Inc.
— Believing Christ: The Parable of the Bicycle & Other Good News. LC 92-20924. 131p. 1992. 11.95 (0-87579-634-6) Deseret Bk.
— The Testament of Adam: An Examination of the Syriac & Greek Traditions. LC 80-12209. (Society of Biblical Literature. Dissertation Ser.: No. 52). 208p. reprint ed. pap. 59.30 (0-7837-5440-X, 2045205) Bks Demand.
Robinson, Stephen H. & Reich, Paul R., eds. Hematology: Pathophysiologic Basis for Clinical Diagnosis. 3rd rev. ed. LC 92-48886. 480p. 1993. 39.95 (0-316-73864-6) Little.
Robinson, Stephen M., jt. ed. see Day, Richard H.
Robinson, Stephen T., jt. auth. see Gray, Rhonda.
Robinson, Steve. A Handbook of Financial Management. (Financial Times Management Ser.). 256p. 1994. 75.00x (0-273-60338-8, Pub. by Pitman Pubng UK) St Mut.
Robinson, Steve & Hogan, Stephen. Starting Your Own Successful Indian Business. 160p. 1991. pap. 45.00 (0-945253-08-7) Thornsbury Bailey Brown.
Robinson, Stewart. Successful Simulation: A Practical Approach to Simulation Projects. LC 94-12966. 1994. write for info. (0-07-707622-2) McGraw.
Robinson, Sue. Amendment. 1990. 17.95 (1-55972-018-2, Birch Ln Pr) Carol Pub Group.
— The Amendment. 256p. 1991. pap. 4.50 (0-8216-2501-2, Carol Paperbacks) Carol Pub Group.
Robinson, Sue & Tobin-Singer, Joan F. First Steps: A Divorce Information Guidebook, Arizona Edition. 86p. (Orig.). 1986. pap. text ed. 9.95 (0-9617332-0-9) Sue Robinson.
Robinson, Sugar Ray & Anderson, Dave. Sugar Ray. (Illus.). 400p. 1994. reprint ed. pap. 14.95 (0-306-80574-X) Da Capo.
Robinson, Suzanne. Lady Dangerous. 1994. mass mkt. 5.50 (0-553-29576-4, Fanfare) Bantam.
— Lady Defiant. 1993. mass mkt. 4.99 (0-553-29574-8) Bantam.
— Lady Gallant. 1992. pap. 4.50 (0-553-29430-X) Bantam.
— Lady Hellfire. 1992. 4.99 (0-553-29678-7) Bantam.
— Lady Valiant. 1993. 5.50 (0-553-29575-6) Bantam.
— Lord of Enchantment. 1995. mass mkt. 5.50 (0-553-56344-0) Bantam.
***Robinson, Suzanne S.** Remflash. 470p. Date not set. pap. 12.95 (0-7610-0226-X) NW Pub.
Robinson, Sylvia. HomeWork Coach Student Workbook. (HomeWork Coach Ser.). 1988. 17.95 (0-88671-353-6, 4972) Am Guidance.
— HomeWork Coach Teachers Guide. (HomeWork Coach Ser.). 1988. 16.95 (0-88671-352-8, 4971) Am Guidance.
Robinson, T. The Life & Death of Mary Magdalene. Sommer, H. O., ed. (EETS, ES Ser.: Vol. 78). 1969. reprint ed. 20.00 (0-8115-3401-4) Periodicals Srv.
Robinson, T. F. & Kinnel, R. K., eds. Cardiac Myocyte - Connective Tissue Interactions in Health & Disease. (Issues in Biomedicine Ser.: Vol. 13). (Illus.). x, 150p. 1990. 118.50 (3-8055-5028-6) S Karger.
Robinson, T. H. Decline & Fall of the Hebrew Kingdoms. LC 74-137284. reprint ed. 39.50 (0-404-05376-9) AMS Pr.
Robinson, T. H., et al. Palestine in General History. (British Academy, London, Schweich Lectures on Biblical Archaeology Series, 1930). 1974. reprint ed. pap. 20.00 (0-8115-1268-1) Periodicals Srv.
***Robinson, T. M.** Plato's Psychology. 2nd rev. ed. (Phoenix Supplementary Volumes Ser.). 264p. 1995. 60.00 (0-8020-0635-3); pap. 22.95 (0-8020-7590-8) U of Toronto Pr.
— Plato's Psychology. LC 76-465044. 215p. reprint ed. pap. 61.30 (0-317-08828-9, 2051216) Bks Demand.
Robinson, T. M., ed. Heraclitus: Fragments: A Text & Translation with a Commentary. (Phoenix Supplementary Volumes Ser.: No. XXII: Pre-Socratics II). 228p. 1991. pap. 19.95 (0-8020-6913-4) U of Toronto Pr.
Robinson, T. W., ed. Debt Management & Collection. 1986. pap. write for info. (0-406-35880-X) Butterworth Legal Pubs.
Robinson, Tara. How to Catch Really Big Fish. (Illus.). 64p. (Orig.). 1983. pap. 6.95 (0-88839-967-7) Hancock House.
Robinson, Ted, jt. auth. see Kelly, Tom.
Robinson, Ted, jt. auth. see Woodley, Jeremy D.
Robinson, Terrance, jt. auth. see Pollock, Herman W.
Robinson, Terry. Purchasing Oil & Gas. 99p. (C). 1989. 210.00 (0-685-36124-1, Inst Pur & Supply) St Mut.
Robinson, Terry, ed. see Axiom Information Resources Staff.
Robinson, Terry E. Behavioral Approaches to Brain Research. (Illus.). 1983. 32.50 (0-19-503258-6) OUP.
Robinson, Tery. Star Guide 1990-1991: Where to Reach Movie Stars, TV Stars, Rock Stars, Sports Stars, & Other Famous Celebrities. 191p. 1989. pap. 9.95 (0-317-93093-1) Axiom Info Res.
Robinson, Thelma S. Creatures of Habit. 28p. (Orig.). 1989. pap. text ed. 5.00 (0-685-28348-8) In Tradition Pub.
Robinson, Thomas. The Schoole of Musicke, Wherein Is Taught the Perfect Method of True Fingering of the Lute, Pandora, Orpharion & Viol da Gamba. LC 73-6122. (English Experience Ser.: No. 589). 1973. reprint ed. 25.00 (90-221-0589-X) Walter J Johnson.
Robinson, Thomas & Shambaugh, David, eds. Chinese Foreign Policy: Theory & Practice. (Studies on Contemporary China). 640p. 1994. 65.00 (0-19-828389-X) OUP.
Robinson, Thomas A. The Bauer Thesis Examined: The Geography of Heresy in the Early Christian Church. LC 87-28288. (Studies in the Bible & Early Christianity: Vol. 11). 240p. 1988. lib. bdg. 89.95 (0-88946-611-4) E Mellen.
— Mastering Greek Vocabulary. 2nd rev. ed. 192p. (Orig.). 1990. pap. 7.95 (0-943575-85-0) Hendrickson MA.
Robinson, Thomas A. & St. David's University Press Staff. Greek Verb Endings. LC 86-31268. 96p. 1986. pap. text ed. 39.95 (0-88946-206-2) E Mellen.
Robinson, Thomas A., jt. ed. see Greenshields, Malcolm R.
Robinson, Thomas A., et al. The Early Church: An Annotated Bibliography of Literature in English. LC 93-34350. (American Theological Library Association Monograph: No. 33). 522p. 1993. 57.50 (0-8108-2763-8) Scarecrow.
Robinson, Thomas M. Contrasting Arguments. Connor, W. R., ed. LC 78-18598. (Greek Texts & Commentaries Ser.). (Illus.). (ENG & GRE.). 1979. lib. bdg. 28.95 (0-405-11439-7) Ayer.
Robinson, Thomas P. Radio Networks & the Federal Government. Sterling, Christopher H., ed. LC 78-21735. (Dissertations in Broadcasting Ser.). 1980. reprint ed. lib. bdg. 23.95 (0-405-11772-8) Ayer.
***Robinson, Thomas W. & Shambaugh, David, eds.** Chinese Foreign Policy: Theory & Practice. (Studies on Contemporary China). (Illus.). 664p. 1995. reprint ed. pap. 29.95 (0-19-829016-0) OUP.
Robinson, Thomas W., jt. ed. see Lin, Zhiling.
Robinson, Tim. Economic Theories of Exhaustible Resources. 288p. 1988. lib. bdg. 59.95 (0-415-00988-X) Routledge.
***Robinson, Timothy A.** The Philosophy of Aristotle. LC 94-46137. 128p. (C). 1995. lib. bdg. 24.95x (0-87220-315-8); pap. text ed. 5.95x (0-87220-314-X) Hackett Pub.
Robinson, Tom. The Longcase Clock. (Illus.). 472p. 1981. 79.50 (0-907462-07-3) Antique Collect.
Robinson, Tom, jt. ed. see Hawkin, David J.
Robinson, Tom H. Arkansas Merchant Tokens. Schenkman, David E., ed. LC 85-51498. (Illus.). 259p. 1985. 32.50 (0-918492-07-6) TAMS.
Robinson, Tracy, jt. auth. see Monday, Lori.
Robinson-Treiman, Robert, ed. Research in Social Stratification & Mobility: An Annual Compilation of Research, Vol. 1. 1980. lib. bdg. 73.25 (0-89232-067-2) Jai Pr.
Robinson, Trevor. The Amateur Wind Instrument Maker. rev. ed. LC 80-5381. (Illus.). 128p. 1981. pap. 10.95 (0-87023-312-2) U of Mass Pr.
— The Organic Constituents of Higher Plants. 6th ed. (Illus.). iv, 346p. 1991. 18.50 (0-935118-03-9) Cordus Pr.
Robinson-Valery, Judith, ed. see Valery, Paul.
Robinson, Vaughan. Transients, Settlers, & Refugees. (Illus.). 264p. 1986. 49.95 (0-19-878009-5) OUP.
Robinson, Vaughan, jt. auth. see Black, Richard.
Robinson, Vaughan, jt. ed. see Black, Richard.
Robinson, Velma G. Variety. 1993. 9.95 (0-8062-4666-9) Carlton.
Robinson, Vera M. Humor & the Health Professions: The Therapeutic Use of Humor in Health Care. 2nd ed. 256p. 1990. pap. 25.00 (1-55642-141-9) SLACK Inc.
Robinson, Vicki, jt. ed. see Richardson, Diane.
Robinson, Victor. William Godwin & Mary Wollstonecraft. 1972. 250.00 (0-8490-1304-6) Gordon Pr.
Robinson, Victoria, ed. see Riley, Jan.
***Robinson, Vincent B. & Tom, Henry, eds.** Towards SQL Database Language Extensions for Geographic Information Systems. LC 94-24762. 1994. write for info. (0-929306-19-8) Silicon Pr.

***Robinson, Vincent W. Engine & Drivetrain Performance: Mathematics & Theory. LC 94-92239. (Illus.). 106p. (Orig.). 1995. pap. 16.95 (0-9643024-0-3) Robinson.**
ENGINE & DRIVETRAIN PERFORMANCE: MATHEMATICS & THEORY is a book written to enhance the knowledge of the beginner & the more experienced performance enthusiast. This book provides a mathematical approach to solving these problems. You do not have to know algebra or trigonometry to solve the problems in this book. Just follow the examples shown & substitute any practical data into the desired equation(s). All you need is a simple arithmetic calculator, or a scientific calculator for some equations &/or trigonometry functions to make it much simpler to perform some calculations. This book also includes many features such as: * THEORY - Principles used to analyze &/or explain the function of each subject * EQUATIONS - Given in order to calculate the various parameters * EXAMPLE PROBLEMS - To explain & familiarize the user with the use of each equation * DATA - Made available to make solving related problems easier for the user * GRAPHS - Given in order to show the relationship between two or more pieces of data * CHARTS - To show the relationship between related data * ABBREVIATIONS - To reduce word length & to make them more easily recognizable * MATHEMATICAL CONVERSIONS - To convert from one unit to another * GLOSSARY - A definition of the terms used in this book. The information in this book is applicable to all street, racetrack (such as the drag strip & oval track), & other mechanical related applications. Order from Robinson Publishing., 135 East Newcomen St., Alcoa, TN 37701; 615-681-2584 (phone or FAX). ***Publisher Provided Annotation.***

R

An Asterisk (*) at the beginning of an entry indicates that the title is appearing in BIP for the first time.

Robinson, Vinnie. Devil in Disguise. 145p. 1982. 9.95 (*0-9610404-0-8*) Mogul Bk.
— Ex-- the Unknown. 92p. 1987. pap. 3.95 (*0-9610404-2-4*) Mogul Bk.
— Too. 64p. 1985. 5.95 (*0-9610404-1-6*) Mogul Bk.

Robinson, Virginia P. The Development of a Professional Self: Teaching & Learning in Professional Helping Processes, Selected Writings, 1930-1968. LC 77-78322. (Studies in Modern Society: Political & Social Issues: No. 12). 42.50 (*0-404-16015-8*) AMS Pr.

Robinson, Viviane. Problem Based Methodology: Research for the Improvement of Practice. LC 92-36833. 1993. text ed. 67.00 (*0-08-041925-9*, Pergamon Pr) Elsevier.

Robinson, W., jt. auth. see Luria, Aleksandr R.

***Robinson, W. Douglas.** Southern Illinois Birds: An Annotated List & Sight Guide. LC 95-14767. (Illus.). 480p. (C). 1996. 39.95x (*0-8093-2032-0*) S Ill U Pr.

Robinson, W. Heath. Adventures of Uncle Lubin. (J). (ps-3). 1992. 15.95 (*0-87923-884-4*) Godine.

Robinson, W. I. The Relationship of the Tetracoralla to the Hexacoralla. (Connecticut Academy of Arts & Sciences Ser., Trans.: Vol. 21). 1917. pap. 49.50 (*0-685-22842-8*) Elliots Bks.

Robinson, W. Stitt. Mother Earth: Land Grants in Virginia, 1607-1699. (Illus.). 77p. 1993. reprint ed. pap. 9.00 (*0-685-65681-0*, 9410) Clearfield Co.

Robinson, W. Stitt, Jr. Mother Earth: Land Grants in Virginia, 1607-1699. (Illus.). 77p. 1957. pap. 5.95 (*0-8139-0136-7*) U Pr of Va.

Robinson, W. W. Los Angeles from the Days of the Pueblo. 2nd ed. Nunis, Doyce B., Jr., ed. (Illus.). 128p. 1981. pap. 7.95 (*0-910312-45-1*) Calif Hist.

Robinson, W. Wright. Incredible Facts about the Ocean: The Land Below, the Life Within, Vol. 2. LC 85-25430. (Ocean World Library). (Illus.). 120p. (J). (gr. 4 up). 1987. text ed. 13.95 (*0-87518-358-1*, Dillon Silver Burdett) Silver Burdett Pr.
— Incredible Facts about the Ocean, Vol. 3: How We Use It, How We Abuse It, Vol. 3. (Ocean World Library). (Illus.). 128p. (J). (gr. 4 up). 1990. text ed. 13.95 (*0-87518-435-9*, Dillon Silver Burdett) Silver Burdett Pr.

***Robinson, Walter.** Instant Art History: From Cave Art to Pop Art. (Illus.). 256p. (Orig.). 1995. pap. 10.00 (*0-449-90698-1*) Fawcett.

Robinson, Wayne. How'd They Design & Print That? (Illus.). 144p. 1992. 26.95 (*0-89134-403-9*, 30372) North Light Bks.
— Yo He Hablado en Lenguas: I Once Spoke in Tongues. (SPA.). 4.25 (*84-7228-184-1*, 220980, Pub. by Edit Clie SP) TSELF.

Robinson, Wayne B., ed. Journeys Toward Narrative Preaching. LC 89-36683. 144p. (C). 1990. pap. 10.95 (*0-8298-0832-9*) Pilgrim OH.

Robinson, Wayne F. & Huxtable, Clive R., eds. Clinicopathologic Principles for Veterinary Medicine. (Illus.). 452p. 1988. 69.95 (*0-521-30883-6*) Cambridge U Pr.

Robinson, Willard B. American Forts: Architectural Form & Function. LC 76-25130. (Illus.). 244p. reprint ed. 69.60 (*0-8357-9662-0*, 2011138) Bks Demand.
— Gone from Texas: Our Lost Architectural Heritage. LC 80-5518. (Centennial Series of the Association of Former Students: No. 9). (Illus.). 320p. 1981. 29.95 (*0-89096-106-9*) Tex A&M Univ Pr.
— The People's Architecture: Texas Courthouses, Jails & Municipal Buildings. 1983. 35.00 (*0-87611-060-X*) Tex St Hist Assn.
— Reflections of Faith: Houses of Worship in the Lone Star State. LC 94-20796. (Illus.). 268p. (Orig.). 1994. 45.00 (*0-918954-57-6*) Baylor Univ Pr.

Robinson, Willard B. & Webb, Todd. Texas Public Buildings of the Nineteenth Century. LC 74-578. (Illus.). 304p. 1974. 29.95 (*0-292-78006-0*) U of Tex Pr.

***Robinson, William.** The English Flower Garden. rev. ed. LC 95-3742. (Illus.). 800p. 1995. 35.00 (*0-89831-031-8*) Sagapr.
— The English Flower Garden. LC 84-8325. (Illus.). 800p. 1984. reprint ed. 35.00 (*0-943276-08-X*) Sagapr.
— An Exhibition of Drawings & Watercolors by John Groth. (Illus.). 12p. 1970. pap. 5.00 (*0-87959-116-1*) U of Tex H Ransom Ctr.
— Gravetye Manor. 1984. 125.00 (*0-88192-133-5*) Timber.
— Gravetye Manor or Twenty Years' Work Round an Old Manor House. limited ed. Thomas, Graham S. & Ingwersen, Will, eds. LC 84-22168. (Illus.). 159p. 1984. 125.00 (*0-89831-001-6*) Sagapr.
— The Wild Garden. LC 93-44917. 356p. 1994. 24.95 (*0-88192-284-6*) Timber.

***Robinson, William & Hauri, Christine.** Promotional Marketing. 2nd ed. Knudsen, Anne, ed. (Orig.). 1995. pap. 23.95 (*0-614-03290-3*, NTC Busn Bks) NTC Pub Grp.

Robinson, William & Wellborn, Clay. Knowledge, Power & the Congress. 200p. 1991. 41.95 (*0-87187-632-9*); pap. 24.95 (*0-87187-631-0*) Congr Quarterly.

Robinson, William, jt. auth. see Brezen, Tamara.

Robinson, William, jt. ed. see Cikovsky, Nicolai.

Robinson, William A. Best Sales Promotions. 6th ed. 384p. 1987. 29.95 (*0-8442-3122-3*, NTC Busn Bks) NTC Pub Grp.
— Jeffersonian Democracy in New England. LC 16-22344. (Illus.). 190p. 1969. reprint ed. text ed. 49.75 (*0-8371-0639-7*, ROJE, Greenwood Pr) Greenwood.
— Thomas B. Reed, Parliamentarian. (History - United States Ser.). 423p. 1992. reprint ed. lib. bdg. 99.00 (*0-7812-6200-3*) Rprt Serv.

Robinson, William A. & Hauri, Christine. Promotional Marketing: Ideas & Techniques for Success in Sales Promotion. Orig. Title: Strategic Sales Promotion. (Illus.). 192p. 1991. 39.95 (*0-8442-3150-9*, NTC Busn Bks) NTC Pub Grp.

Robinson, William A. & Schultz, Don E. Sales Promotion Management. LC 82-70974. 512p. (C). 1982. 33.95 (*0-8442-3072-3*, Crain Bks) NTC Pub Grp.

Robinson, William A., jt. auth. see Schultz, Don E.

Robinson, William A., jt. auth. see Schultz, Don.

Robinson, William B., jt. auth. see Fritze, Ronald H.

Robinson, William B., jt. auth. see Skvarcius, Romualdas.

Robinson, William C. Elements of American Jurisprudence. lviii, 401p. 1985. reprint ed. lib. bdg. 37.50 (*0-8377-1041-3*) Rothman.
— Forensic Oratory: A Manual for Advocates. xxix, 357p. 1993. reprint ed. 45.00 (*0-8377-2548-8*) Rothman.
— The Law of Patents for Useful Inventions, 3 vols., Set. LC 12-38173. 1972. reprint ed. lib. bdg. 125.00 (*0-89941-350-1*, 500480) W S Hein.

Robinson, William D., ed. The Solid Waste Handbook: A Practical Guide. LC 85-12454. 848p. 1986. text ed. 135.00 (*0-471-87711-5*) Wiley.

***Robinson, William H.** The Adventures of Uncle Lubin. (Pocket Paragon Ser.). (Illus.). 128p. 1995. pap. 10.95 (*1-56792-059-4*) Godine.
— Black New England Letters: The Uses of Writing in Black New England. 1978. 3.00 (*0-89073-051-2*) Boston Public Lib.

Robinson, William I. A Faustian Bargain: U.S. Intervention in the Nicaraguan Elections & American Foreign Policy in the Post-Cold War Era. 310p. (C). 1992. text ed. 67.00 (*0-8133-8233-5*); pap. text ed. 21.50 (*0-8133-8234-3*) Westview.

Robinson, William L. Fool Hen: The Spruce Grouse on the Yellow Dog Plains. LC 79-3962. (Illus.). 242p. 1980. 21.50 (*0-299-07960-0*) U of Wis Pr.

Robinson, William L. & Bolen, Eric G. Wildlife Ecology & Management. 2nd ed. 592p. (C). 1988. write for info. (*0-02-402251-9*) Macmillan.

Robinson, William L., jt. auth. see Bolen, Eric G.

Robinson, William M. Confederate Privateers. 1994. pap. 15.95 (*1-57003-005-7*) U of SC Pr.

Robinson, William M., Jr. Justice in Grey. LC 91-55437. 734p. 1991. reprint ed. lib. bdg. 105.00 (*0-912004-94-0*) W W Gaunt.

Robinson, William R., ed. Man & the Movies. LC 67-24549. (Illus.). 387p. reprint ed. 110.30 (*0-8357-9389-3*, 2051660) Bks Demand.

Robinson, William R., jt. auth. see Holtzclaw, Henry F., Jr.

Robinson, William R., et al. Chemistry: Concepts & Models. 753p. (C). 1992. text ed. write for info. (*0-669-32800-6*); Study guide. student ed write for info. (*0-669-28948-5*); Instr.'s guide. teacher ed write for info. (*0-669-28949-3*); Transparencies. trans. write for info. (*0-318-70089-1*); Solutions guide. write for info. (*0-669-28950-7*) Heath.

Robinson, William S. Brains & People: An Essay on Mentality & Its Causal Conditions. LC 87-32174. 248p. (C). 1988. 37.95 (*0-87722-548-6*) Temple U Pr.
— Computers, Minds & Robots. 350p. (C). 1992. 44.95 (*0-87722-915-5*) Temple U Pr.
— Computers, Minds, & Robots. 230p. 1993. pap. 19.95 (*1-56639-082-6*) Temple U Pr.

Robinson, William S. & Tucker, Stephanie. Texts & Contexts: A Contemporary Approach to College Writing. 412p. (C). 1991. pap. 24.95 (*0-534-13044-5*) Intl Thomson.
— Texts & Contexts: A Contemporary Approach to College Writing. 2nd ed. 526p. 1994. pap. 28.95 (*0-534-21474-6*) Intl Thomson.

Robinson, William W. Land in California. Bruchey, Stuart, ed. LC 78-56665. (Management of Public Lands in the U. S. Ser.). (Illus.). 1979. reprint ed. lib. bdg. 23.95 (*0-405-11352-8*) Ayer.
— Land in California: The Story of Mission Lands, Ranchos, Squatters, Mining Claims, Railroad Grants, Land Scrip, Homesteads. (Illus.). 1979. pap. 14.00 (*0-520-03875-4*) U CA Pr.
— Seventeenth-Century Dutch Drawings: A Selection from the Maida & George Abrams Collection. (Illus.). 234p. 1991. pap. 39.95 (*0-685-63136-2*) Pierpont Morgan.
— Seventeenth-Century Dutch Drawings: From the Maida & George Abrams Collection. (Illus.). 236p. 1992. 65.00 (*0-8109-3829-4*) Abrams.

Robinson, William W. & Schatborn, Peter. Seventeenth-Century Dutch Drawings: A Selection from the Maida & George Abrams Collection. (Pierpont Morgan Library Ser.). (Illus.). 236p. 1994. pap. 39.95 (*0-87598-107-0*) Pierpont Morgan.

Robinson, William W., jt. ed. see Oberhuber, Konrad.

***Robinson, Zan D.** Ferdie the Fay Meets Flutterey the Butterfly: A Forest Fable. (Ferdie the Fay Adventure Ser.: No. 1). (Illus.). 52p. (Orig.). (J). (ps-4). Date not set. write for info. (*0-9635587-4-9*) E W Connors.
— A Semiotic & Psychoanalytic Interpretation of Herman Melville's Fiction. LC 91-30813. 220p. 1991. lib. bdg. 89.95 (*0-7734-9957-1*) E Mellen.
— The Workplace. 209p. (Orig.). 1992. pap. text ed. 15.00 (*0-9603888-7-7*) Labor Arts.

Robinsunne. Nannee. (Illus.). 36p. (J). (ps). 1993. 15.95 (*0-9636986-0-5*) Robinsunne Pstcrd.

Robiquet, Paul. Le Personnel Municipal de Paris Pendant la Revolution. LC 73-174332. (Collection de documents relatifs a l'histoire de Paris pendant la Revolution francaise). reprint ed. 96.50 (*0-404-52557-1*) AMS Pr.

Robisheaux, Thomas. Rural Society & the Search for Order in Early Modern Germany. (Illus.). 352p. (C). 1989. 64.95 (*0-521-35626-1*) Cambridge U Pr.

Robison, Andrew. Piranesi: Early Architectural Fantasies - A Catalogue Raisonne of the Etchings. (Illus.). x, 206p. 1987. pap. text ed. 39.95 (*0-226-72320-8*, 72319-4) U Ch Pr.
— Piranesi: Early Architectural Fantasies: A Catalogue Raisonne of the Etchings. LC 78-3540. (Illus.). 1985. pap. 8.49 (*0-89468-081-1*) Natl Gallery Art.

Robison, Andrew, ed. The Glory of Venice: Art in the Eighteenth Century. (Illus.). 432p. 1995. 55.00 (*0-300-06185-4*) Yale U Pr.

Robison, Andrew, et al. Durer to Diebenkorn: Recent Acquisitions of Art on Paper. LC 92-12706. (Illus.). 100p. (Orig.). 1992. pap. 24.00 (*0-89468-182-6*) Natl Gallery Art.

Robison, B. C. & Tveten, John L. Birds of Houston. LC 90-53175. (Illus.). 144p. 1990. 22.50 (*0-89263-303-4*); pap. 12.95 (*0-89263-304-2*) Rice Univ.

Robison, Cathy A. Archaeological Excavations at the Fitzgibbons Site, Gallatin County, Illinois. LC 86-72024. (Center for Archaeological Investigations Research Paper Ser.: No. 53). (Illus.). xxi, 294p. 1986. pap. 18.50 (*0-88104-061-4*) Center Archaeo.

Robison, Clarence F., et al. Modern Techniques of Track & Field. LC 74-850. (Health Education, Physical Education, & Recreation Ser.). 357p. reprint ed. pap. 101.80 (*0-317-26702-7*, 2056007) Bks Demand.

Robison, Dale W. Wisconsin & the Mentally Ill. Grob, Gerald N., ed. LC 78-22588. (Historical Issues in Mental Health Ser.). 1980. lib. bdg. 28.95 (*0-405-11939-9*) Ayer.

Robison, David. Alternative Work Patterns: Changing Approaches to Work Scheduling. LC 76-42369. 40p. 1976. pap. text ed. 5.00 (*0-89361-001-1*) Work in Amer.

Robison, David F. All about Internet FTP Plus: Learning & Teaching to Transfer Files on the Internet. (Internet Workshop Ser.: Vol. 2). 1994. disk, spiral bd. 45.00 (*1-882208-06-4*) Library Solns.

Robison, Debra. The Storm Within. 1994. pap. 4.95 (*1-55673-934-6*) CSS OH.

Robison, Diane L., jt. auth. see Stern, Leonard B.

Robison, Esther, jt. auth. see Stern, Raphael.

Robison, G. A., jt. auth. see Cehovic, G.

Robison, G. Alan, jt. auth. see Greengard, Paul.

Robison, G. Alan, jt. ed. see Greengard, Paul.

Robison, Henry W. Fresh Water Fish. (American Nature Guide Ser.). (Illus.). 192p. 1992. spiral bd. 9.98 (*0-8317-6968-8*) Smithmark.

***Robison, Henry W. & Allen, Robert T.** Only in Arkansas: A Study of the Endemic Plants & Animals of the State. 1995. write for info. (*1-55728-326-5*) U of Ark Pr.

Robison, Henry W. & Buchanan, Thomas M. Fishes of Arkansas. LC 87-10757. 544p. (Orig.). 1988. 50.00 (*1-55728-000-2*); pap. 30.00 (*1-55728-001-0*) U of Ark Pr.

Robison, James. Sexo y Amor No Son Lo Mismo: Sex Is Not Love. (SPA.). 3.25 (*84-7228-770-X*, 222430, Pub. by Edit Clie SP) TSELF.

Robison, Jarene. Avenues of Involvement. Howard, Gina, ed. 48p. (Orig.). 1993. pap. text ed. 3.95 (*1-56309-084-8*, New Hope) Womans Mission Union.

Robison, Jarene, et al. Ideas for Exciting Mission Study. 64p. (Orig.). 1989. pap. text ed. 3.95 (*0-936625-59-7*) Womans Mission Union.

***Robison, Jim & Andrews, Mark.** Flashbooks: The Story of Central Florida's Past. LC 94-48818. 1995. write for info. (*1-56943-051-9*) Contemp Bks.

Robison, John. Proofs of a Conspiracy. 1979. lib. bdg. 59.95 (*0-8490-2987-2*) Gordon Pr.

Robison, Joleen. Advertising Dolls. 1980. pap. 9.95 (*0-89145-134-X*) Collector Bks.

Robison, Lindon. Becoming a Zion People. Ingram, tr. 1992. pap. 6.95 (*1-880416-22-0*) NW Pub.

Robison, Lindon J. & Barry, Peter J. The Competitive Firm's Response to Risk. 1987. 43.00 (*0-07-053342-3*) McGraw.

Robison, Margaret. The Naked Bear. LC 77-83730. 70p. 1977. pap. 6.00 (*0-89924-011-9*) Lynx Hse.
— Red Creek: A Requiem. (Illus.). (Orig.). 1992. pap. 10.00 (*0-941895-08-4*) Amherst Wri Art.

Robison, Mary. Amateur's Guide to the Night. LC 89-1904. 1989. reprint ed. pap. 9.95 (*0-87923-802-X*) Godine.
— Oh! A Novel. LC 86-46251. 224p. 1987. pap. 9.95 (*0-87923-675-2*) Godine.

Robison, Nancy. Buffalo Bill. LC 90-47221. (First Bks.). (Illus.). 64p. (J). (gr. 3-5). 1991. lib. bdg. 13.93 (*0-531-20007-8*) Watts.
— Dear Son, about Your Wedding: A Guide for the Groom-to-Be. 1989. pap. 5.95 (*0-671-67329-7*, Fireside) S&S Trade.

Robison, Olin, et al, eds. The Arts in the World Economy: Public Policy & Private Philanthropy for a Global Cultural Community. LC 94-21200. 192p. 1994. 22.00 (*0-87451-698-6*) U Pr of New Eng.

Robison, Pamela L. LIMHI, Son of Noah. 1989. pap. 7.00 (*0-8309-0558-8*) Herald Hse.
— Living with Chronic Illness. 1988. pap. 6.50 (*0-8309-0507-3*) Herald Hse.

Robison, Phyllis, jt. auth. see Smith, Mary.

Robison, R. A., ed. Treatise on Invertebrate Paleontology, Part G: Bryoza, Vol. 1. rev. ed. 641p. 1983. 52.00 (*0-8137-3107-0*) Geol Soc.
— Treatise on Invertebrate Paleontology, Pt. W, Suppl. 2: Conodonta. LC 53-12913. (Illus.). 230p. 1982. 22.00 (*0-8137-3028-7*) Geol Soc.

Robison, R. Warren. Louisiana Church Architecture. LC 84-70619. (U. S. L. Architecture Ser.: No. 2). 90p. 1984. 25.00 (*0-940984-20-2*) U of SW LA Ctr LA Studies.

Robison, Richard. Indonesia: The Rise of Capital. 440p. (C). 1987. pap. 24.95 (*0-04-909024-0*, Pub. by Allen Unwin AT) Paul & Co Pubs.

Robison, Richard, et al, eds. Southeast Asia in the 1990s: Authoritarianism, Democracy & Capitalism. 240p. 1993. pap. 22.95 (*1-86373-230-6*, Pub. by Allen Unwin AT) Paul & Co Pubs.

Robison, Richard A. & Tiechert, Curt, eds. Treatise on Invertebrate Paleontology, Pt. A: Introduction: Fossilization (Taphonomy), Biogeography, & Biostratigraphy. LC 53-12913. 1979. 47.50 (*0-8137-3001-5*) Geol Soc.

Robison, Samuel S. A History of Naval Tactics from 1530-1930: The Evolution of Tactical Maxims. LC 75-41234. reprint ed. 52.50 (*0-404-14698-8*) AMS Pr.

Robison, Sophia. Can Delinquency Be Measured? LC 75-129307. (Criminology, Law Enforcement, & Social Problems Ser.: No. 129). (Illus.). 312p. 1972. reprint ed. 24.00 (*0-87585-129-0*) Patterson Smith.

Robison, Susan, ed. see Children & Youth Program Staff.

Robison, Wade L. Decisions in Doubt: The Environment & Public Policy. LC 94-20549. (Nelson A. Rockefeller Series in Social Science & Public Policy). 288p. 1994. 39.95 (*0-87451-695-1*) U Pr of New Eng.

Robison, Wade L. & Pritchard, Michael S., eds. Medical Responsibility: Paternalism, Informed Consent, & Euthanasia. LC 79-87656. (Contemporary Issues in Biomedicine, Ethics, & Society Ser.). 224p. 1979. 39.50 (*0-89603-007-5*) Humana.

Robison, Wade L., et al, eds. Profits & Professions: Essays in Business & Professional Ethics. LC 82-23399. (Contemporary Issues in Biomedicine, Ethics, & Society Ser.). 336p. 1983. 44.50 (*0-89603-039-3*) Humana.

Robison, William B. Biographic Dictionary of Tyrants, Despots, & Dictators. 1995. lib. bdg. 65.00 (*0-87436-747-6*) ABC-CLIO.

Robitaille, Julie. Jinx. LC 91-73540. (Brown Bag Mystery Line Ser.). 358p. 1992. 14.95 (*0-933031-58-0*) Coun Oak Bks.

Robl, Ernest H., ed. Picture Sources Four. LC 83-625. 200p. 1983. pap. text ed. 43.75 (*0-87111-274-4*) SLA.

Robledo, Juan. The Elusive Knowledge. 187p. 1987. pap. 9.95 (*0-9633822-1-7*) J Robledo.
— Fox: An Ancient Tale. 49p. 1986. pap. 7.95 (*0-9633822-0-9*) J Robledo.

Roblee, Charles L., et al. The Investigation of Fires. 2nd ed. (Illus.). 240p. 1988. text ed. 41.00 (*0-89303-642-0*) P-H.

Roblee, Richard D. Interdisciplinary Dentofacial Therapy: A Comprehensive Approach to Optimal Patient Care. LC 94-20093. 1995. text ed. 128.00 (*0-86715-188-9*) Quint Pub Co.

Robles, Albert G., jt. auth. see Levy, Sidney J.

Robles, Alfredo C., Jr. French Theories of Regulation & Concepts of the International Division of Labour. 1994. text ed. 59.95 (*0-312-10744-7*) St Martin.

Robles de Medina, E. D., ed. New Coding System for Electrocardiography. 1972. pap. 20.00 (*90-219-2073-5*, Excerpta Medica) Elsevier.

***Robles, Edward.** Ted & George: Two Boys Alone. 1995. 9.95 (*0-8062-5308-8*) Carlton.

Robles, Emmanuel. Three Plays by Emmanuel Robles: Plaidoyer Pour un Rebelle (Case for a Rebel), L'Horloge (the Clock), & Porfirio. Kilker, James A., tr. LC 77-24662. (Illus.). 223p. 1977. 17.50 (*0-8093-0822-3*) S Ill U Pr.

Robles, Felix R. De los Gallos De Pelea y De Otros Temas. (Illus.). 402p. (Orig.). 1991. pap. 20.00 (*0-685-51538-9*) Saeta.

***Robles-Garcia, Nelly M.** Las Canteras de Mitla, Oaxaca Tecnologia para la Arquitectura Monumental. (Vanderbilt University Publications in Anthropology: No. 47). (Illus.). 66p. (Orig.). (SPA.). 1994. pap. 12.00 (*0-935462-38-4*) Vanderbilt Pubns.

Robles, Harold. Albert Schweitzer: An Adventurer for Humanity. (Illus.). 64p. (J). (gr. 4-6). 1994. lib. bdg. 15.40 (*1-56294-352-9*) Millbrook Pr.

Robles, Harold, ed. see Schweitzer, Albert.

Robles, Jose. Cartilla Espanola. (Illus.). (Orig.). (SPA.). 1935. pap. text ed. 9.95 (*0-89197-064-9*) Irvington.

Robles, Laureano, ed. see Unamuno, Miguel de.

Robles, Mariana, tr. La Gata a la Que le Gustaba el Rojo. (Illus.). 8p. (J). (gr. 1). 1994. pap. 3.50 (*1-880612-26-7*) Seedling Pubns.

Robles, Mariana, tr. see Bordelon, Carolyn, ed.

Robles, Mariana, tr. see Gorman, Kate.

Robles, Mariana, tr. see Salem, Lynn & Stewart, Josie.

Robles, Mariana, tr. see Stewart, Josie & Salem, Lynn.

Robles, Mariana, tr. see Worthington, Denise.

Robles, Mireya. Profecia y Luz en la Poesia de Maya Islas. Cardenas, Juan, ed. 40p. (Orig.). (SPA.). 1987. pap. 4.00 (*0-913983-05-5*) M & A Edns.

***Robles, Rob.** The Claim. 1994. pap. 8.95 (*1-55503-743-7*) Covenant Comms.

***Robles, Teresa.** Concert for Four Brain Hemispheres in Psychotherapy. 1995. 16.95 (*0-533-11183-8*) Vantage.

Robleto, Adolfo. Amor, Fe y Esperanza, No. 1. 96p. 1987. reprint ed. pap. 3.25 (*0-311-08755-8*) Casa Bautista.
— Amor, Fe y Esperanza, No. 2. (No. 2). 96p. 1990. reprint ed. pap. 3.25 (*0-311-08757-4*) Casa Bautista.
— Catecismo Biblico y Doctrinal Para el Nuevo Creyente. 164p. 1987. reprint ed. pap. 2.25 (*0-311-09088-5*) Casa Bautista.
— Conozca Quienes Son. 112p. (SPA.). 1986. pap. 3.75 (*0-311-05764-0*) Casa Bautista.
— Dramas y Poemas para Dias Especiales, No. 1. 94p. (SPA.). 1985. reprint ed. pap. 4.50 (*0-311-07004-3*, Edit Mundo) Casa Bautista.
— Dramas y Poemas para Dias Especiales, No. 2. 96p. 1986. reprint ed. 3.75 (*0-311-07008-6*, Edit Mundo) Casa Bautista.
— Dramas y Poemas para Dias Especiales, No. 3 - Dramas & Poems for Special Days, Vol. 3. 96p. (Orig.). (SPA.). 1992. pap. 3.45 (*0-311-07012-4*) Casa Bautista.
— Manual de Mayordomia Cristiana. 148p. 1991. 4.95 (*0-89922-245-5*) Edit Caribe.
— Que Hacer En Tiempos de Cri. (SPA.). Date not set. pap. 6.99 (*0-89922-150-5*) Edit Caribe.

— Sermones para Dias Especiales, Tomo I. 112p. (SPA.). 1989. reprint ed. 3.95 (0-311-07009-4) Casa Bautista.
— Sermones para Dias Especiales, Tomo II. 96p. 1991. reprint ed. 3.75 (0-311-07011-6) Casa Bautista.
— Un Vistazo a la Doctrina Romana. 128p. 1984. reprint ed. pap. 4.25 (0-311-05319-X) Casa Bautista.
Robleto, Adolfo, comp. Quinientas una Ilustraciones Nuevas. 320p. 1990. reprint ed. pap. 7.50 (0-311-42062-1) Casa Bautista.
Robleto, Adolfo, tr. see Conner, T.
Robleto, Adolfo, tr. see Cowman, Mrs. Charles E.
Robleto, Adolfo, tr. see Dana, H. E. & Mantey, J. R.
Robleto, Adolfo, tr. see Dana, H. E.
Robleto, Adolfo, tr. see Elmore, Vernon O.
Robleto, Adolfo, tr. see Keller, W. P.
Robleto, Adolfo, tr. see Lester, Andrew D.
Robleto, Adolfo, tr. see McClanahan, John H.
Robley, G. & Robley, R. The Spirit Led Family. 160p. pap. 2.99 (0-88368-033-5) Whitaker Hse.
Robley, R., jt. auth. see Robley, G.
Robley, T. F. History of Bourbon County, Kansas: To the Close of 1865. 1976. reprint ed. pap. 11.00 (0-9601568-4-4) Historic Pres Bourbon.
Roblin, Ann. Easy Russian Phrasebook & Dictionary. 1994. pap. 12.95 (0-8442-4279-9) NTC Pub Grp.
Roblin, Ronald. The Bettor's Guide to Harness Racing: A New Guide to Successful Handicapping. 1979. 9.95 (0-8065-0645-8, Citadel Pr) Carol Pub Group.
Roblin, Ronald, ed. The Aesthetics of the Critical Theorists: Studies on Benjamin, Adorno, Marcuse, & Habermas. LC 90-30955. (Problems in Contemporary Philosophy Ser.: Vol. 23). 532p. 1990. lib. bdg. 119.95 (0-88946-368-9) E Mellen.
Roblin, Ronald, ed. see Dickie, George & Sclafani, Richard J.
Roblot, R. French Business Taxation. (European Commercial Law Library: No. 2). 1974. pap. text ed. 24.00 (0-8464-0429-X) Beekman Pubs.
Roblyer, M. D., et al. Assessing the Impact of Computer-Based Instruction: A Review of Recent Research. LC 88-24377. (Computers in the Schools Ser.: Vol. 5, Nos. 3-4). (Illus.). 149p. 1988. text ed. 39.95 (0-86656-893-X) Haworth Pr.
***Robock, Stefan & Simmonds, Kenneth.** International Business & Multinational Enterprises. 4th ed. 800p. (C). 1988. text ed. 35.50 (0-256-07346-5) Irwin.
Robock, Stefan H. Brazil's Developing Northeast: A Study of Regional Planning & Foreign Aid. LC 79-26655. (Illus.). xv, 213p. 1980. reprint ed. text ed. 55.00 (0-313-22295-9, ROBD, Greenwood Pr) Greenwood.
Robock, Stefan H. & Simmonds. International Business & Multinational Enterprises. 4th ed. 800p. (C). 1988. text ed. 65.95 (0-256-03634-9) Irwin.
***Robotham.** Varga. 1995. (0-7858-0217-7) Bk Sales Inc.
Robotham, John & Shields, Gerald. Freedom of Access to Library Materials. LC 82-14309. 221p. 1982. 35.00 (0-918212-31-6) Neal-Schuman.
Robotham, Tom. Ghost Towns. LC 92-54930. (Illus.). 128p. 1993. 12.98 (1-56138-269-8) Courage Bks.
Robotham, Tom, comp. Native Americans in Early Photographs. LC 94-12504. 1994. 14.98 (1-57145-008-4) Thunder Bay CA.
Robotic Industries Association, Robot Safety Subcommittee. ANSI-RIA Robot Safety Standard. 2nd rev. ed. 12p. (Orig.). 1986. pap. 8.00 (0-317-39388-X) Robot Inst Am.
Robots 12 & Vision '88 Conference (1988: Detroit, MI) Staff. Robots 12 & Vision '88: Conference Proceedings, June 5-9, 1988, Detroit, MI, Vol. 2. LC 88-61194. (Illus.). 806p. reprint ed. pap. 180.00 (0-8357-6501-6, 2035872) Bks Demand.
Robotti, Frances D. Indexing Books & Periodicals: Guidelines for Authors & Indexers. write for info. (0-935497-01-3) Fountainhead.
— Tracing Your Family Roots: The Ancestor Hunt. write for info. (0-935497-03-X) Fountainhead.
— Whaling & Old Salem: A Chronicle of the Sea. (Illus.). 292p. 1983. reprint ed. 17.95 (0-685-41738-7) Fountainhead.
Robottom, Ian. Science Education: Exploring the Tension. 70p. (C). 1988. 41.00 (0-7300-0562-3, Pub. by Deakin Univ AT) St Mut.
***Robottom, Ian & Hart, Paul.** Research in Environmental Education: Engaging the Debate. 81p. 1993. pap. 50.00 (0-7300-1673-0, ESC822, Pub. by Deakin Univ AT) St Mut.
Robottom, Ian M. Environmental Education: Practice & Possibility. 122p. (C). 1987. pap. 47.00x (0-7300-0543-7, ECT317, Pub. by Deakin Univ AT) St Mut.
Robottom, John. Castles & Cathedrals. (Longman Origin Ser.). 1991. pap. text ed. 10.64 (0-582-08250-1) Longman.
Robottom, John, jt. auth. see Claypole, William.
Roboz. Mass Spectrometry in Cancer Research. 1995. write for info. (0-8493-0167-X) CRC Pr.
Roboz, Helga, tr. see Marion-Wild, E. C.
Roboz, Steven, ed. Christian Rosenkreutz: From the Works of Rudolf Steiner. 20p. 1982. pap. 3.25 (0-919924-16-6, Pub. by Steiner Book Centre CN) Anthroposophic.
— The Holy Grail: From the Works of Rudolf Steiner. 2nd ed. 1984. pap. 4.75 (0-919924-24-7, Pub. by Steiner Book Centre CN) Anthroposophic.
Roboz, Steven, tr. see Marion-Wild, E. C.
Robrock, David P., ed. Missouri Forty-Niners: The Journal of William Hunter on the Southern Gold Trail. LC 91-40563. (Historical Society of New Mexico Publications Ser.). 328p. 1992. 35.00x (0-8263-1337-X) U of NM Pr.
Robrock, K. H. Mechanical Relaxation of Interstitials in Irradiated Metals. (Tracts in Modern Physics Ser.: Vol. 118). (Illus.). 112p. 1990. 64.00 (0-387-51090-7) Spr-Verlag.
***Robroek, L. M.** The Development of Rubber Forming As a Rapid Thermoforming Technique for Continuous Fibre Reinforced Thermoplastic Composites. 268p. (Orig.). 1994. pap. 57.50x (90-6275-988-2, Pub. by Delft U Pr NE) Coronet Bks.
Robsky, Paul, jt. auth. see Fraley, Oscar.
Robson. Eternal Truths of Life. 1952. 3.95 (0-8356-7030-9) Theos Pub Hse.
— Mishkat al-Masabih, 2 vols. 59.00 (1-56744-141-6) Kazi Pubns.
— Ride the Wind. 1985. mass mkt. (0-345-32522-2) Ballantine.
Robson, A. D., ed. Soil Acidity & Plant Growth. 306p. 1989. text ed. 85.00 (0-12-590655-2) Acad Pr.
— Zinc in Soils & Plants: Proceedings of the International Symposium Held at the University of Western Australia, Perth, Western Australia, 27-28 September, 1993. LC 93-40339. (Developments in Plants & Soil Sciences Ser.: Vol. 55). 220p. (C). 1994. lib. bdg. 80.00 (0-7923-2631-8) Kluwer Ac.
Robson, A. D. & Abbott, L. K., eds. Management of Mycorrhizas in Agriculture, Horticulture & Forestry: Proceedings of an International Symposium, Held in Perth, Western Australia, September 28-October 2, 1992. LC 94-685. (Developments in Plant & Soil Sciences Ser.). 248p. (C). 1994. lib. bdg. 93.00 (0-7923-2700-4) Kluwer Ac.
***Robson, A. Diedre.** Prestige, Profit & Pleasure: The Market for Modern Art in New York in the 1940s & 1950s. LC 94-40929. (Garland Publications in the Fine Arts). (Illus.). 375p. 1995. 75.00 (0-8153-1364-0) Garland.
***Robson, Andrew J.** Designing & Building Business Models Using Microsoft Excel. LC 95-6597. 1995. pap. write for info. (0-07-709058-6) McGraw.
Robson, Ann P. & Robson, John M., eds. Newspaper Writings: The Collected Works of John Stuart Mill, 4-vol. set, Set, Vols. XXII-XXV. (Illus.). Set. 195.00 (0-8020-2602-8) U of Toronto Pr.
— Sexual Equality: Writings by John Stuart Mill, Harriet Taylor Mill, & Helen Taylor. 409p. 1994. 60.00 (0-8020-0513-6) U of Toronto Pr.
— Sexual Equality: Writings by John Stuart Mill, Harriet Taylor Mill, & Helen Taylor. 352p. 1994. pap. 19.95 (0-8020-6949-5) U of Toronto Pr.
Robson, B. Pre-School Provision for Children with Special Needs. Mittler, Peter, ed. (Special Needs in Ordinary Schools Ser.). 208p. 1989. pap. text ed. 22.50 (0-304-31559-1) Cassell.
Robson, B. & Garnier, J., eds. Introduction to Proteins & Protein Engineering. 699p. 1988. pap. 77.00 (0-444-81047-1) Elsevier.
***Robson, Brian.** Fuzzy Wuzzy: The Campaigns in the Eastern Sudan, 1884-85. (Illus.). 264p. 1994. 24.95 (1-885119-05-4) Sarpedon.
— Those Inner Cities: Reconciling the Social & Economic Aims of Urban Policy. (Illus.). 264p. 1989. 59.00 (0-19-874148-0) OUP.
Robson, Brian, ed. Roberts in India: The Military Papers of Field Marshall Lord Roberts, 1876-1893. LC 93-26403. (Publications of the Army Records Society: Vol. 9). 1993. 80.00 (0-7509-0401-1) A Sutton Pub.
Robson, Brian, jt. auth. see Kershaw, Ronald.
Robson, Brian T., ed. Managing the City: The Aims & Impacts of Urban Policy. LC 87-1827. 240p. 1987. 57.00 (0-389-20731-4, N8289) B&N Imports.
Robson, Bryan. Bryan Robson's Soccer Skills. (Illus.). 128p. (Orig.). 1987. pap. 14.95 (0-8069-6654-8) Sterling.
Robson, Cliff, jt. auth. see Sterling, Chris M.
Robson, Clive, jt. auth. see Cossali, Paul.
Robson, Colin. Real World Research: A Resource for Social Scientists & Practitioner-Researchers. LC 92-21782. 512p. 1993. pap. 24.95 (0-631-17689-6) Blackwell Pubs.
Robson, Colin, et al. In-Service Training & Special Educational Needs: Running Short, School-Focused Courses. (Impact Ser.). 208p. 1988. text ed. 55.00 (0-7190-2547-8, Pub. by Manchester Univ Pr UK) St Martin.
— In-Service Training & Special Educational Needs: Running Short, School-Focused Courses. LC 87-28808. 227p. 1989. reprint ed. text ed. 22.95 (0-7190-2790-X, Pub. by Manchester Univ Pr UK) St Martin.
Robson, David, jt. auth. see Goldberg, Adele.
Robson, David, jt. auth. see Rees, Mike.
Robson, David W. Educating Republicans: The College in the Era of the American Revolution, 1750-1800. LC 84-22436. (Contributions to the Study of Education Ser.: No. 15). (Illus.). xvi, 272p. 1985. text ed. 59.95 (0-313-24606-8, RER/) Greenwood.
Robson, Deb, ed. & intro. Socks: A Spin-off Special Publication for Knitters & Spinners. 56p. Date not set. pap. 7.00 (0-934026-94-7) Interweave.
Robson, Denny. Animal Homes. (Animal Concept Ser.). (J). (ps). 1991. 5.95 (0-8120-6242-6) Barron.
Robson, Douglas S., jt. auth. see Skalski, John R.
Robson, E. & Wendt, L. Shadows of the Voice. 1982. pap. 14.00 (0-934982-09-0) Primary Pr.
— Shadows of the Voice. deluxe limited ed. 1982. 35.00 (0-934982-08-2) Primary Pr.
Robson, E. & Wimp, J., eds. Against Infinity: An Anthology of Contemporary Mathematical Poetry. LC 79-90106. 1979. 17.00 (0-934982-00-7); pap. 8.95 (0-934982-01-5) Primary Pr.
Robson, E. W. & Robson, M. M. Film Answers Back: An Historical Appreciation of the Cinema. LC 73-169350. (Arno Press Cinema Program Ser.). (Illus.). 402p. 1972. reprint ed. 24.95 (0-405-03923-9) Ayer.
Robson, Eric. The American Revolution. LC 74-171392. (Era of the American Revolution Ser.). 254p. 1971. reprint ed. lib. bdg. 29.50 (0-306-70417-X) Da Capo.
Robson, Ernest. Freedom, Cannibalism, Creative Love & the Values of Cosmic Nonsense: A Philosophical Manifesto. LC 86-62122. (Illus.). 1986. 14.00 (0-934982-11-2) Primary Pr.
— Thomas Onetwo. (Illus.). 1971. 6.95 (0-87110-074-6) Primary Pr.
— Transcualisticas: Bilingual Edition. Lopez De Thorogood, Lucy, tr. LC 78-65323. (Illus.). (ENG & SPA.). 1978. pap. 8.95 (0-934982-04-X) Primary Pr.
— Transcualisticas: Bilingual Edition. deluxe ed. Lopez De Thorogood, Lucy, tr. LC 78-65323. (Illus.). (ENG & SPA.). 1978. 25.00 (0-934982-03-1) Primary Pr.
— Transwhichics. LC 74-121306. 1970. 17.00 (0-8023-1249-7); pap. 8.95 (0-8023-1250-0) Primary Pr.
Robson, Ernest & Wendt, Larry. Phonetic Music with Electronic Music. LC 81-90189. 1981. 19.45 (0-934982-02-3); audio 23.45 (0-686-31759-9); audio 12.00 (0-686-34446-4) Primary Pr.
Robson, Ernest M. Thomas Onetwo. (Illus.). 1971. 20.00 (0-89366-258-5) Ultramarine Pub.
***Robson, Frank.** The Basics of Gravure Printing. (Illus.). (Orig.). 1995. write for info. (1-880290-01-4) Gravure Assn.
Robson, George D. Continuous Process Improvement: Simplifying Work Flow Systems. 352p. 1991. text ed. 35.00 (0-02-926645-9) Free Pr.
Robson, Graham. A-Z of Cars of the 1970s. (Illus.). 216p. 1993. pap. 19.95 (1-870979-40-0) Motorbooks Intl.
— A-Z of Works Rally Cars. (Illus.). 176p. 1994. 32.95 (1-870979-42-7, Pub. by Bay View Bks UK) Motorbooks Intl.
— Austin-Healey 100 & 3000 Series. (Illus.). 200p. 1994. 35.95 (1-85223-787-2, Pub. by Crowood UK) Motorbooks Intl.
— The Big Healey's: Collector's Guide. (Collector's Guide Ser.). (Illus.). 1982. 27.95 (0-900549-55-6, Pub. by Motor Racing UK) Motorbooks Intl.
— The Big Jaguars 3 1/2 Litre-420G. 192p. 1995. 34.95 (1-85223-922-0, Pub. by Crowood UK) Motorbooks Intl.
— Cars of the Roots Group: Hillman, Humber, Singer, Sunbeam & Sunbeam Talbot. (Illus.). 240p. 1990. 49.95 (0-947981-35-7, Pub. by Motor Racing UK) Motorbooks Intl.
— Cosworth: The Search for Power. 3rd ed. (Illus.). 328p. 1995. 44.95 (1-85260-503-0, Pub. by J H Haynes & Co UK) Motorbooks Intl.
— Desert Airliners. LC 93-49485. (Illus.). 112p. 1994. pap. 19.95 (0-87938-904-4) Motorbooks Intl.
— The Lotus (Album 294) (C). 1989. pap. text ed. 25.00x (0-7478-0217-3, Pub. by Shire UK) St Mut.
— Lotus since the 70's, Vol. 1: Elite, Eclat, Excel, Elan Collector's Guide. (Collector's Guide Ser.). (Illus.). 128p. 1993. 27.95 (0-947981-70-5, Pub. by Motor Racing UK) Motorbooks Intl.
— Lotus since the 70's, Vol. 2: Esprit, Etna & V8 Engines Collector's Guide. (Collector's Guide Ser.). (Illus.). 128p. 1993. 27.95 (0-947981-69-1, Pub. by Motor Racing UK) Motorbooks Intl.
— Rallying - the 4 Wheel Drive Revolution. LC 86-82147. (Foulis Motoring Bk.). (Illus.). 192p. 34.95 (0-85429-547-X, F723, Pub. by G T Foulis Ltd) Haynes Pubns.
— RR & Bentley Collector Guide, Vol. 1. (Collector's Guide Ser.). (Illus.). 144p. 1984. 27.95 (0-900549-86-6, Pub. by Motor Racing UK) Motorbooks Intl.
— Sporting Fords: Cortinas. (Collector's Guide Ser.). (Illus.). 130p. 1990. 27.95 (0-947981-39-X, Pub. by Motor Racing UK) Motorbooks Intl.
— The Sporting Fords: Escorts. (Collector's Guide Ser.). (Illus.). 130p. 1983. 27.95 (0-900549-71-8, 65-06422, Pub. by Motor Racing UK) Motorbooks Intl.
— Sporting Fords, Vol. 4: Sierras Collector Guide. (Illus.). 128p. 1991. 27.95 (0-947981-55-1, Pub. by Motor Racing UK) Motorbooks Intl.
— The T Series MG: A Collector's Guide. (Collector's Guide Ser.). (Illus.). 128p. 1981. 27.95 (0-900549-51-3, Pub. by Motor Racing UK) Motorbooks Intl.
— Triumph Spitfire GT-6. (Illus.). 128p. 1991. 27.95 (0-947981-60-8, Pub. by Motor Racing UK) Motorbooks Intl.
— Triumph Sports Cars. 1989. pap. 25.00 (0-85263-926-0, Pub. by Shire UK) St Mut.
— Triumph TR's: The Complete Story. (Illus.). 208p. 1991. 35.95 (1-85223-451-2, Pub. by Crowood UK) Motorbooks Intl.
— Triumph 2000 & 2.5 P. I. The Complete Story. (Illus.). 192p. 1995. 34.95 (1-85223-854-2, Pub. by Crowood UK) Motorbooks Intl.
— TVRs, Vol. 1: Grantura to Taimar Collector's Guide. (Collector's Guide Ser.). (Illus.). 128p. 1994. 27.95 (0-947981-80-2, Pub. by Motor Racing UK) Motorbooks Intl.
— TVR's, Vol. 2: Tasmin to Chimaera Collector's Guide. (Collector's Guide Ser.). (Illus.). 128p. 1994. 27.95 (0-947981-81-0, Pub. by Motor Racing UK) Motorbooks Intl.
— Works Triumphs: The Complete Story of Triumph Cars in Motorsport. (Haynes-U. K. Ser.). (Illus.). 296p. 1993. 39.95 (0-85429-926-2) Motorbooks Intl.
— The World's Most Powerful Cars. 1990. 12.98 (1-55521-563-7) Bk Sales Inc.
Robson, Harry, jt. ed. see Occelli, Mario.
Robson, Harry E., jt. ed. see Occelli, Mario L.
Robson, Ian. Active Galactic Nucleii. 350p. 1994. text ed. 110.95 (0-13-005463-1) P-H.
Robson, J., et al. After Abuse: Papers on Caring & Planning for a Child Who Has Been Sexually Abused. (C). 1989. 400.00 (0-903534-82-7, Pub. by Brit Ag for Adopt & Fost UK) St Mut.
Robson, J. C., jt. auth. see Gordon, Robert.
Robson, J. C., jt. auth. see McConnell, J. C.
Robson, J. K. R., ed. Food, Ecology & Culture: Readings in the Anthropology of Dietary Practices. 154p. 1980. text ed. 104.00 (0-677-16090-9) Gordon & Breach.
Robson, J. M., ed. see Mill, John Stuart.
Robson, J. R. Famine: Its Causes, Effects & Management. (Food & Nutrition in History & Anthropology Ser.). 180p. 1981. text ed. 86.00 (0-677-16180-8) Gordon & Breach.
Robson, J. S. How a One-Legged Rebel Lives. 19.95 (0-8488-1141-0) Amereon Ltd.
Robson, J. T., ed. see Meares, L. G. & Hymowitz, C. E.
Robson, Jenny. Winner's Magic. (Junior African Writers Ser.). (Illus.). (J). (gr. 3-4). 1992. pap. 2.95 (0-7910-2906-9) Chelsea Hse.
Robson, John. The Pilgrim Goes Forth. 276p. (Orig.). 1986. pap. 8.75 (0-685-17666-5) Lake Crest Hse.
Robson, John, ed. A Guide to Growing Up. (Illus.). 45p. (Orig.). (gr. 4-6). 1982. pap. 2.50 (0-936098-32-5) Intl Marriage.
— Me & You. (Illus.). 48p. (Orig.). (J). (gr. 6-9). 1982. pap. 2.50 (0-936098-33-3) Intl Marriage.
— Origin & Evolution of the Universe: Evidence for Design? 328p. 1987. pap. 24.95 (0-7735-0618-7, Pub. by McGill CN) U of Toronto Pr.
— Parents, Children & Sex. (Illus.). (Orig.). 1981. pap. 2.50 (0-936098-31-7) Intl Marriage.
— Parents, Teenagers & Sex. (Illus.). 40p. (Orig.). 1982. pap. 2.50 (0-936098-34-1) Intl Marriage.
— Three Early English Metrical Romances. (Camden Society, London. Publications, First Ser.: No. 18). reprint ed. 42.50 (0-404-50118-4) AMS Pr.
— You & Your Family. (Illus.). 30p. (Orig.). (J). (gr. 2-4). 1981. pap. 2.50 (0-936098-30-9) Intl Marriage.
Robson, John A. Wyclif & the Oxford Schools: The Relation of the "Summa de Ente" to Scholastic Debates at Oxford in the Later Fourteenth Century. LC 61-16171. (Cambridge Studies in Medieval Life & Thought: Vol. 8). 282p. reprint ed. pap. 80.40 (0-317-08005-9, 2051448) Bks Demand.
Robson, John H., ed. see Mill, John Stuart.
Robson, John M. The Improvement of Mankind: The Social & Political Thought of John Stuart Mill. LC 68-140051. (University of Toronto, Department of English Studies & Texts: No. 15). 306p. reprint ed. pap. 87.30 (0-317-26963-1, 2023671) Bks Demand.
— James & John Stuart Mill: Papers of the Centenary Conference. Laine, Michael, ed. LC 76-16177. 172p. reprint ed. pap. 49.10 (0-8357-8190-9, 2034058) Bks Demand.
— Marriage or Celibacy? The Daily Telegraph on a Victorian Dilemma. 320p. 1995. 60.00 (0-8020-0473-3) U of Toronto Pr.
Robson, John M., ed. Editing Nineteenth-Century Texts: Papers Given at the Editorial Conference, University of Toronto, November, 1966. (Conference on Editorial Problems Ser.: No. 2). 1987. 37.50 (0-404-63652-7) AMS Pr.
— Journals & Debating Speeches. (Collected Works of John Stuart Mill: Nos. XXVI-XXVII). 900p. 1988. 135.00 (0-8020-2674-5) U of Toronto Pr.
Robson, John M., ed. see Editorial Conference (2nd: 1966: University of Toronto) Staff.
Robson, John M., jt. ed. see Filipiuk, Michael L.
Robson, John M., ed. see Mill, John Stuart.
Robson, John M., jt. ed. see Robson, Ann P.
Robson, John R., jt. auth. see Elias, Joel.
Robson, John R., et al. Malnutrition, Its Causation & Control, Set. 632p. 1972. text ed. 173.00 (0-677-03140-8) Gordon & Breach.
***Robson, Julien.** David Levinthal: Die Nibelungen. 1994. pap. 15.00 (1-881616-41-X) Dist Art Pubs.
***Robson, Ken.** Riley's Annotated Bills of Exchange Act & Cheques & Payment Orders Act. 4th ed. 320p. 1994. pap. 65.00 (0-455-21294-5, Pub. by Law Bk Co) W W Gaunt.
Robson, Kenneth S., ed. Manual of Clinical Child & Adolescent Psychiatry. 2nd rev. ed. LC 93-28362. Orig. Title: Manual of Clinical Child Psychiatry. 432p. 1993. text ed. 36.50 (0-88048-528-0) Am Psychiatric.
Robson, L. L., jt. auth. see Dawes, J. N.
Robson, Larry J. & Bouwman, Dorothy W. Carotid Artery Disease. Bouwman, Dorothy W. & Grin, Oliver D., eds. (Patient Education Ser.). (Illus.). 26p. (Orig.). 1990. pap. text ed. 3.00 (0-929689-39-9) Ludann Co.
Robson, Lloyd. The Convict Settlers of Australia. (Illus.). 257p. 1994. 29.95 (0-522-84585-1) Intl Spec Bk.
— The First AIF: A Study of its Recruitment 1914 - 1918. (Illus.). 240p. 1982. pap. 19.95 (0-522-84237-2) Intl Spec Bk.
Robson, Lucia S. Light a Distant Fire. 1991. mass mkt. 5.99 (0-345-37561-0) Ballantine.
Robson, M. & Heggers. Surgical Infections: Biology & Management. 1988. write for info. (0-8151-7309-1, Yr Bk Med Pubs) Mosby Yr Bk.
Robson, M., jt. auth. see France, R.
Robson, M. M., jt. auth. see Robson, E. W.
Robson, Mark, jt. auth. see OECD Staff.
Robson, Martin C., jt. auth. see Heggers, John P.
Robson, Michael. Rona the Distant Island. 179p. (C). 1992. text ed. 75.00 (0-86152-867-0, Pub. by Acair Ltd UK); pap. text ed. 39.00 (0-86152-823-9, Pub. by Acair Ltd UK) St Mut.
Robson, Michel. Opium: The Poisoned Poppy. (Illus.). 88p. 1994. 40.00 (962-7283-08-8) Weatherhill.
***Robson, Michelle & Clarke, Tim.** LPC Case Study: Civil Litigation. 239p. 1994. pap. 24.00 (1-85431-388-6, Pub. by Blackstone Pr UK) W W Gaunt.
Robson, Mike. Facilitating. 200p. 1995. 49.95 (0-566-07449-4, Pub. by Gower UK) Ashgate Pub Co.

— Problem Solving in Groups. 2nd ed. 160p. 1993. 42.95 (0-566-07414-1, Pub. by Gower UK); pap. 18.95 (0-566-07415-X, Pub. by Gower UK) Ashgate Pub Co.
— Quality Circles: A Practical Guide. 2nd ed. 256p. 1988. text ed. 54.95 (0-566-02748-8, Pub. by Gower UK) Ashgate Pub Co.
— Quality Circles in Action. LC 84-4095. 176p. 1984. text ed. 54.95 (0-566-02433-0) Ashgate Pub Co.
Robson, N. K., ed. see Sivarajan, V. V.
***Robson, N. K., et al.** Flora of Tropical East Africa: Celastraceae. 78p. 1994. 19.50 (90-6191-365-9) Balkema RSA.
Robson, P. D., jt. auth. see Harris, D. J.
Robson, P. N. & Kendall, P. C., eds. Rib Waveguide Theory by the Spectral Index Method. 200p. 1990. text ed. 125.00 (0-471-92923-9) Wiley.
Robson, Pam, jt. auth. see Chapman, Gillian.
Robson, Pat, illus. Oil. (Butterfly Bks.). 32p. (J). (gr. 3-5). 1985. 7.95 (0-86685-449-5) Intl Bk Ctr.
— Rain. (Butterfly Bks.). 32p. (J). (gr. 3-5). 1985. 7.95 (0-86685-451-7) Intl Bk Ctr.
Robson, Patrick. Structural Appraisal of Traditional Buildings. 200p. 1990. text ed. 69.95 (0-566-09081-3, Pub. by Gower UK) Ashgate Pub Co.
Robson, Peter. Economic Integration in Africa. LC 68-25582. 320p. reprint ed. 91.20 (0-8357-9455-5, 2014775) Bks Demand.
— The Economics of International Integration. 3rd rev. ed. LC 93-16558. 1993. reprint ed. pap. write for info. (0-415-09880-7) Routledge.
— Integration, Development & Equity: Economic Integration in West Africa. (Illus.). 192p. (C). 1983. text ed. 39.95 (0-04-338109-X) Routledge Chapman & Hall.
Robson, Peter, ed. Transnational Corporations & Regional Economic Integration. LC 93-18758. (United Nations Library on Transnational Corporations: Vol. 9). 1993. write for info. (0-415-08542-X, Routledge NY) Routledge.
— Welfare Law. (International Library of Essays in Law & Legal Theory). 550p. 1992. text ed. 150.00 (0-8147-7426-1) NYU Pr.
***Robson, Peter & Poustie, Mark.** Homeless People & the Law. 3rd ed. 344p. 1994. pap. text ed. 50.00 (0-406-02772-2, UK) Butterworth Legal Pubs.
Robson, Peter & Watchman, Paul, eds. Justice, Lord Denning & the Constitution. 272p. 1981. text ed. 59.95 (0-566-00399-6) Ashgate Pub Co.
Robson, Peter, jt. ed. see Dunning, John.
***Robson, Philip.** Forbidden Drugs. (Illus.). 248p. 1995. pap. 17.95 (0-19-262429-6) OUP.
Robson, R. Thayne, ed. Employment & Training R&D: Lessons Learned & Future Directions. LC 84-7584. 133p. 1984. pap. text ed. 12.00 (0-88099-018-X) W E Upjohn.
***Robson Rhodes Financial Services Ltd., Personal Financial Planning Department Staff.** Robson Rhodes: Personal Financial Planning Manual 1994-95. 10th ed. 1994. pap. 29.95 (0-406-03597-0) Butterworth Legal Pubs.
Robson Rhodes Staff. Getting Started: How to Set up Your Own Business. 3rd ed. pap. text ed. write for info. (0-7494-0874-X, Pub. by Kogan Page Educ UK) Taylor & Francis.
Robson, Robert. The Attorney in Eighteenth-Century England. LC 85-48164. (Cambridge Studies in English Legal History). 194p. 1986. reprint ed. 47.00 (0-912004-34-7) W W Gaunt.
Robson, Ruthann. Cecile. LC 91-29775. 168p. (Orig.). 1991. lib. bdg. 18.95 (1-56341-002-8); pap. 8.95 (1-56341-001-X) Firebrand Bks.
— Eye of a Hurricane. LC 89-23603. 130p. (Orig.). 1989. lib. bdg. 18.95 (0-932379-65-6); pap. 8.95 (0-932379-64-8) Firebrand Bks.
— Gays & Lesbians & the Law. Duberman, Martin, ed. (Issues in Gay & Lesbian Life Ser.). (Illus.). 196p. (YA). (gr. 9 up). 1995. lib. bdg. 24.95 (0-7910-2612-4); pap. 12.95 (0-7910-2963-8) Chelsea Hse.
— Lesbian (Out) Law: Surviving under the Rule of Law. LC 92-8333. 188p. (Orig.). 1992. lib. bdg. 20.95 (1-56341-013-3); pap. 9.95 (1-56341-012-5) Firebrand Bks.
Robson, S. O., jt. ed. see Ras, J. J.
Robson, T., et al. Major Weeds of the Near East. (Plant Production & Protection Papers: No. 104). 244p. 1991. pap. 30.00 (92-5-103003-0, F0013) UNIPUB.
Robson, Tom. Musical Wisdom: Songs & Drawings for the Child in Us All. (Illus.). 88p. (Orig.). (J). (gr. k-6). 1992. pap. 16.95 (0-9633332-0-8) Laughing Cat.
Robson, Vivian E. A Beginner's Guide to Practical Astrology. 184p. 1991. pap. 17.00 (0-89540-123-1, SB-123, Sun Bks) Sun Pub.
— Fixed Stars & Constellations in Astrology. 264p. 1995. pap. 22.00 (0-89540-281-5, Sun Bks) Sun Pub.
— A Students' Text-Book of Astrology. 243p. 1981. pap. 20.00 (0-89540-117-7, SB-117, Sun Bks) Sun Pub.
Robson, Vivian E., jt. auth. see Leo, Alan.
Robson, W., tr. see Michaud, Joseph F.
Robson, W. W. Critical Essays. 240p. 1993. text ed. 39.95 (0-312-09612-7) St Martin.
Robson, W. W., ed. see Doyle, Arthur Conan.
Robson, Walter. An English View of American Quakerism: The Journal of Walter Robson 1842-1929 Written During the Fall of 1877, While Traveling among American Friends. Bronner, Edwin B., ed. LC 71-107345. (American Philosophical Society, Memoirs Ser.: Vol. 79). 175p. reprint ed. pap. 49.90 (0-317-27898-3, 2025135) Bks Demand.
Robson, Wendy. Strategic Management & Information Systems: An Integrated Approach. 368p. (Orig.). 1993. pap. 44.50 (0-273-60042-7, Pub. by Pitman Pub Ltd UK) Trans-Atl Phila.
Robson, William. James Chalmers: Pioneer Missionary to Papua New Guinea, Vol. 9. 1988. pap. 6.99 (0-88019-236-4) Schmul Pub Co.
Robson, William A. Civilization & the Growth of Law: Study of Relations Between Men's Ideas About the Universe & the Institutions of Law & Government. LC 74-25779. (European Sociology Ser.). 374p. 1975. reprint ed. 31.95 (0-405-06532-9) Ayer.
— Governors & the Governed. LC 64-15876. (Edward Douglass White Lectures). 68p. reprint ed. pap. 25.00 (0-8357-9385-0, 2013639) Bks Demand.
— Justice & Administrative Law: A Study of the British Constitution. 3rd ed. LC 72-98792. xxxiii, 674p. 1970. reprint ed. text ed. 38.50 (0-8371-3143-X, ROJU, Greenwood Pr) Greenwood.
Robson, William A., ed. The Civil Service in Britain & France. LC 75-26777. 191p. 1975. reprint ed. text ed. 35.00 (0-8371-8347-2, ROCSB, Greenwood Pr) Greenwood.
Robson, William A. & Crick, Bernard, eds. China in Transition. LC 75-11135. (Sage Contemporary Social Science Issues Ser.: No. 17). 120p. reprint ed. pap. 34.20 (0-317-11057-8, 2021945) Bks Demand.
Robson, William B., jt. ed. see Lemco, Jonathan.
***Robuchon, Joel & Rabaudy, Nicholas.** Joel Robuchon Cooking Through the Seasons: Cooking Through the Seasons. LC 95-7377. (Illus.). 184p. 1995. 40.00 (0-8478-1899-3) Rizzoli Intl.
Robuchon, Joel, jt. auth. see Wells, Patricia.
Robuck, J. E. My Own Personal Experience & Observation As a Soldier in the Confederate Army During the Civil War, 1861-1865, Also During the Period of Reconstruction. (Illus.). 136p. 1977. reprint ed. 14.00 (0-937130-03-6) Burke's Bk Store.
Robutti, Andreina, jt. auth. see Nissim-Momigliano, Luciana.
Robutti, G. Boggio & De Nicola, Pietro. Plastic Surgery in the Aged. 142p. 1987. pap. text ed. 65.95 (0-471-56572-5) Wiley.
Roby, Cynthia. Feeling Different, Feeling Fine: Kids Talk about Their Learning Problems. LC 93-6532. (J). 1993. write for info. (0-8075-2334-8) A Whitman.
— When Learning Is Tough: Kids Talk about Learning Disabilities. (J). (ps-3). 1993. 12.95 (0-8075-8892-X) A Whitman.
Roby, H. J. Roby: Pedigree of Roby of Castle Donington, County Leicester. 69p. 1993. reprint ed. lib. bdg. 24.00 (0-8328-3740-7); reprint ed. pap. 14.00 (0-8328-3741-5) Higginson Bk Co.
Roby, Henry J. Roman Private Law in the Times of Cicero & of the Antonines, 2 vols. 1977. lib. bdg. 195.00 (0-8490-2533-8) Gordon Pr.
Roby, Mary L. This Land Turns Evil Slowly. Bd. with Dig a Narrow Grave. 1982. Set pap. 2.50 (0-451-11696-8, AE1696, Sig) NAL-Dutton.
Roby, Norman S. & Olken, Charles E. The New Connoisseur's Handbook of California Wines. 2nd ed. LC 93-9393. 1993. 25.00 (0-679-42689-2) Knopf.
Roby, Pamela. Women in the Workplace. 138p. 1981. 18.95 (0-87073-172-6); pap. 11.95 (0-87073-173-4) Schenkman Bks Inc.
Roby, Paul, jt. auth. see Huang, Samuel.
Robyn, Dorothy L. Braking the Special Interests: Trucking Deregulation & the Politics of Policy Reform. LC 86-16015. (Illus.). xii, 296p. (C). 1987. 24.95 (0-226-72328-3) U Ch Pr.
Robyns, Gwen. The Mystery of Agatha Christie. LC 77-76259. (Illus.). 247p. 1978. 18.95 (0-385-12623-9) Boulevard.
Robyt, John F. & White, Bernard J. Biochemical Techniques: Theory & Practice. LC 86-26874. (Illus.). 407p. (C). 1990. reprint ed. text ed. 32.95x (0-88133-556-8) Waveland Pr.
Roc, John. Fire! A Play. LC 69-15511. 181p. 1969. 12.95 (0-910278-46-6) Boulevard.
Roc, Margaret. Little Koala. (Illus.). 32p. (J). (ps-1). 1993. 7.00 (0-207-17039-8) HarperColl Wrld.
Roca, Alexander. Crusader: The Story of the Shelton Flying Wing. LC 89-91607. (Illus.). 184p. (C). 1989. text ed. 59.50 (0-9622886-0-8) Rare Birds Pub.
Roca, Ana & Lipski, John M., eds. Spanish in the United States: Linguistic Contact & Diversity. LC 93-14956. (Studies in Anthropological Linguistics: No. 6). viii, 212p. (C). 1993. lib. bdg. 106.15 (3-11-013204-4) Mouton.
Roca, Castells A., et al. Enciclopedia de la Salud. 6th ed. 1043p. (SPA.). 1974. 70.00 (0-7859-0868-4, S-13678) Fr & Eur.
Roca, Iggy. Generative Phonology. LC 93-4066. (Linguistic Theory Guides Ser.). 1993. write for info. (0-415-04140-6); pap. write for info. (0-415-04141-4) Routledge.
Roca, Iggy M., ed. Logical Issues in Language Acquisition. (Linguistic Models Ser.: No. 15). xxiii, 298p. (Orig.). (C). 1990. pap. text ed. 92.35 (3-11-013373-3) Mouton.
Roca, Miguel A. & Toyu, Maggie. Miguel Angel Roca. (Architectural Monographs: No. 39). (Illus.). 144p. 1994. 50.00 (1-85490-275-X, Academy Edits) St Martin.
— Miguel Angel Roca. (Architectural Monographs: No. 39). (Illus.). 144p. 1994. pap. 38.00 (1-85490-276-8, Academy Edits) St Martin.
Roca Muntanola, Julio. Dictionary of Parapsychology: Diccionario de Parapsicologia. 272p. (SPA.). 1979. 29.95 (0-8288-4761-4, S50093) Fr & Eur.
***Roca, Nuria & Serrano, Marta.** The Respiratory System: The Breath of Life. LC 95-9821. (Invisible World Ser.). (Illus.). 32p. (J). 1996. pap. write for info. (0-7910-3158-6) Chelsea Hse.
— The Respiratory System: The Breath of Life. LC 95-9821. (Invisible World Ser.). (Illus.). 32p. (J). (gr. 4 up). 1996. lib. bdg. 14.95 (0-7910-3153-5) Chelsea Hse.
Roca, Octavio & Korsmo, M. Owen, eds. Shorts: An Anthology. 115p. (Orig.). 1987. pap. 7.95 (0-9618239-0-9) Thane Pr.
Roca, Philippe, jt. auth. see Davis, Wayne H.
Roca, Roberto L. Oil Birds of Venezuela: Ecology & Conservation. (Publications Ser.: No. 24). (Illus.). 83p. 1994. 11.00 (1-877973-35-1) Nuttall Ornith.
Roca, Ruben A., intro. Market Research for Shopping Centers. LC 79-92292. 210p. (Orig.). 1988. pap. 39.95 (0-913598-11-9, 504); pap. 28.95 (0-685-68040-1) Intl Coun Shop.
Rocabado & Iglarsh. Musculoskeletal Approach to Maxillofacial Pain. (Illus.). 500p. 1991. text ed. 59.95 (0-397-54850-8) Lippincott.
Rocard, Ann. Cool Calvin. (Illus.). (J). (ps-4). 1991. 9.95 (1-56182-030-X) Atomium Bks.
— Hobee Scrogneenee. (Illus.). 28p. (J). (ps-4). 1991. 9.95 (1-56182-000-8) Atomium Bks.
— Hobee Scrogneenee at Joey's School. (Illus.). 28p. (J). (ps-4). 1991. 9.95 (1-56182-001-6) Atomium Bks.
— Kouk & the Ice Bear. (Illus.). 38p. (J). (ps-1). 1991. 9.95 (1-56182-029-6) Atomium Bks.
Rocard, Marcienne. The Children of the Sun: Mexican-Americans in the Literature of the United States. Brown, Edward G., Jr., tr. LC 88-39772. 393p. 1989. 45.00 (0-8165-0992-1) U of Ariz Pr.
Rocard, Michael. Europe & the United States. (Critical Issues Ser.: No. 2). 38p. 1992. pap. 4.95 (0-87609-128-1) Coun Foreign.
Rocawich, Linda. Our Food, Our Common Ground. (Southern Exposure Ser.). (Illus.). 112p. (Orig.). 1983. write for info. (0-943810-16-7) Inst Southern Studies.
Rocca, Al M. The Shasta Dam Boomtowns: Community Building in the New Deal Era. LC 93-84961. (Illus.). 180p. (Orig.). 1993. pap. 12.95 (1-884055-00-1) Redding Mus.
***Rocca, Al M. & Capener, J. Paul.** America's Shasta Dam: A History of Construction, 1936-1945. (Illus.). 165p. (Orig.). 1994. pap. 15.95 (0-9643378-0-0) Renown Pubng.
Rocca, F. & Persoglia, S. Seismic Wave Propagation Anomalies Due to Shallow & Deep Causes, No. EUR 13164. 303p. 1991. pap. 35.00 (92-826-2236-3, CD-NA-13164-EN-C, Pub. by Europ Com) UNIPUB.
Rocca, Frank C., II. American Bull Terriers: A Legacy in Gameness. (Orig.). 1992. pap. write for info. (0-941223-01-9) Rocca Ent.
Roccapriore, Maria. Anointing the Sick. LC 80-65722. (Illus.). 144p. (Orig.). 1980. pap. 2.95 (0-8189-1160-3, 160, Pub. by Alba Bks AT) Alba.
Roccasalvo, Joan L. The Eastern Catholic Church: An Introduction to Their Worship & Spirituality. (American Essays in Liturgy Ser.). 80p. (Orig.). 1992. pap. text ed. 4.95 (0-8146-2047-7) Liturgical Pr.
— The Ignatian Influence on the Spirituality of the Sisters of St. Joseph. (Illus.). 111p. (Orig.). 1993. pap. write for info. (0-9638407-0-3) Congreg St Joseph.
— The Plainchant Tradition of Southwestern Rus. 200p. 1986. text ed. 38.50 (0-88033-096-1) East Eur Quarterly.
***Roccasalvo, Joseph.** Portrait of a Woman: A Novel. 263p. (Orig.). Date not set. pap. 12.95 (0-89870-545-2) Ignatius Pr.
Roccatagliata, Giuseppe. A History of Ancient Psychiatry. LC 84-15721. (Contributions in Medical Studies: No. 16). 305p. 1986. text ed. 69.50 (0-313-24419-7, RHI/, Greenwood Pr) Greenwood.
Rocchi, Marc, ed. High-Speed Digital IC Technologies. (Artech House Microwave Library). 320p. 1990. text ed. 88.00 (0-89006-326-5) Artech Hse.
Rocchini, jt. auth. see Rosenthal.
Rocco, Ellen, ed. European Accountancy Yearbook, 1992. 1992. pap. text ed. 235.00 (1-85333-610-6, Pub. by Graham & Trotman UK) Kluwer Ac.
***Rocco, Nola.** The Hollywood Facelift: Facelifting, Cosmetic Surgery & the New You. 1995. pap. 19.95 (0-935016-32-5, Barclay House) Excelsior Music Pub Co.
Rocco, S. Ancient Sex Worship & the Masculine Cross. 1991. lib. bdg. 75.00 (0-87700-971-6) Revisionist Pr.
Rocco, Sha. The Masculine Cross & Ancient Sex Worship. 65p. 1993. pap. 6.00 (0-89540-210-6, SB-210) Sun Pub.
— The Musculine Cross & Ancient Sex Worship. 65p. 1994. reprint ed. spiral bd. 4.95 (0-7873-1117-0) Mokelumne.
— Sex Mythology. (Illus.). 55p. (C). 1982. reprint ed. 4.00 (0-911826-34-3, 5440) Am Atheist.
Rocco, Thomas M. & Murphy, Lawrence R., eds. Institutional & Staff Structures for Nontraditional Programs. LC 84-23655. (Alliance Manual Ser.: No. 2). 128p. 1985. 12.50 (0-8108-1772-1) Scarecrow.
***Rocek, Thomas R.** Navajo Multi-Household Social Units: Archaeology on Black Mesa, Arizona. LC 94-33277. 240p. 1995. 50.00x (0-8165-1472-0) U of Ariz Pr.
Rocek, Thomas R. & Speth, John D. The Henderson Site Burials: Glimpses of a Late Prehistoric Population in the Pecos Valley. (Technical Reports: No. 18). (Illus.). xx, 348p. (Orig.). 1986. pap. 13.00 (0-915703-08-4) U Mich Mus Anthro.
Roceric, Alexandra. Memento. 1982. 5.00 (0-917944-06-2) Am Inst Writing Res.
— Romanian Textbook. LC 89-85238. 356p. 1990. 44.00 (0-931745-57-8) Dunwoody Pr.
Roceric, Alexandra, jt. auth. see Juilland, Alphonse.
Roces, Alfredo & Roces, Grace. Culture Shock! Philippines. (Illus.). 248p. 1992. 10.95 (1-55868-089-6) Gr Arts Ctr Pub.
Roces, Grace, jt. auth. see Roces, Alfredo.
Roch, Edward. Eating Out in Provence & the Cote D'Azur: A Personal Guide to Over 220 Restaurants. LC 92-4803. (Illus.). 192p. 1992. pap. 12.95 (0-940793-93-8) Interlink Pub.
Roch, John, jt. tr. see Yannella, Donald.
Roch, Patrick A. Minority Access to Higher Education: An Analysis of a Pipeline Approach Through Neighborhood Learning Centers - the Minnestoa Experiment. LC 94-4719. 156p. (Orig.). (C). Date not set. lib. bdg. 44.50 (0-8191-9496-4) U Pr of Amer.
Rocha, A., jt. ed. see Catto, S.
***Rocha, Adriana & Jorde-Rocha, Kristi.** Convocation. LC 94-26633. 1995. 23.00 (0-345-38945-X) Ballantine.
Rocha E Silva, M. Mode of Action of Anti-Parasitic Drugs: Proceedings of the 3rd International Pharmacological Meeting, Sao Paulo, July 1966, Vol. 1. LC 67-19416. 1968. 60.00 (0-08-012367-8, Pub. by Pergamon Repr UK) Franklin.
Rocha E Silva, M. & Leme, J. Garcia. Chemical Mediators in the Acute Inflammatory Reaction. 374p. 1972. 118.00 (0-08-017040-4, Pub. by Pergamon Repr UK) Franklin.
Rocha E Silva, M., jt. auth. see Ariens, E.
Rocha E Silva, M., jt. auth. see Raskova, H.
Rocha, Glauber, et al. Reviewing Histories: Selections from New Latin American Cinema. Fusco, Coco, ed. Davis, Jon et al, trs. (Illus.). 224p. (Orig.). 1987. pap. 8.00 (0-936739-06-1) Hallwalls Inc.
Rocha, Guy L., jt. auth. see Kintop, Jeffrey M.
Rocha, Guy L., jt. auth. see Zanjani, Sally.
Rochard, Henri. For the Love of Kate. 1963. reprint ed. 12.00 (0-686-21177-4, 41132) Maple Mont.
— I Was a Male War Bride. (Illus.). 1977. reprint ed. lib. bdg. 5.00 (0-686-21179-0) Maple Mont.
— Pensees. (Illus.). 1977. reprint ed. pap. 5.00 (0-686-21180-4) Maple Mont.
Rochberg-Halton, Eugene. Meaning & Modernity: Social Theory in Pragmatic Attitude. LC 86-7060. (Illus.). 320p. (C). 1987. pap. text ed. 14.95 (0-226-72331-3) U Ch Pr.
Rochberg-Halton, Eugene, jt. auth. see Csikszentmihalyi, Mihaly.
Rochberg-Halton, Francesca, ed. Language, Literature, & History: Philological & Historical Studies Presented to Erica Reiner. (American Oriental Ser.). (Illus.). 439p. (C). 1987. 35.00 (0-940490-67-6, #PJ3189: L35) Am Orient Soc.
Roche, jt. auth. see Estrin.
Roche, jt. auth. see Muller.
Roche, A. F., ed. Predicting Adult Stature for Individuals. (Monographs in Pediatrics: Vol. 3). 1975. 39.25 (3-8055-1843-9) S Karger.
Roche, A. F., et al. Serial Changes in Subcutaneous Fat Thicknesses of Children & Adults. (Monographs in Pediatrics: Vol. 17). (Illus.). x, 110p. 1982. pap. 63.25 (3-8055-3496-5) S Karger.
Roche, Alex F. Growth, Maturation, & Body Composition: The Fels Longitudinal Study, 1929-1991. (Studies in Biological Anthropology: No. 9). (Illus.). 300p. (C). 1992. 69.95 (0-521-37449-9) Cambridge U Pr.
Roche, Alex F. & Malina, Robert M., eds. Manual of Physical Status & Performance in Childhood, Vol. 1: Physical Status, Set with Vol. 2. LC 82-16515. 1456p. 1983. Set with vol. 2: 275.00. 275.00 (0-306-41136-9, Plenum Pr) Plenum.
— Manual of Physical Status & Performance in Childhood, Vol. 2: Physical Performance. LC 82-16515. 814p. 1983. 145.00 (0-306-41137-7, Plenum Pr) Plenum.
— Manual of Physical Status & Performance in Childhood, Vol. 2: Physical Performance, Set with Vol. 1. LC 82-16515. 814p. 1983. 295.00 (0-685-06442-5, Plenum Pr) Plenum.
Roche, Alex F., et al. Assessing the Skeletal Maturity of the Hand-Wrist: FELS Method. (Illus.). 348p. (C). 1988. text ed. 78.95x (0-398-05452-5) C C Thomas.
Roche, Alphonse. Alphonse Daudet. LC 75-25549. (Twayne's World Authors Ser.). (C). 1976. lib. bdg. 17.95 (0-317-38183-0) Irvington.
Roche, Alphonse V. Provencal Regionalism. LC 74-128942. (Northwestern University. Humanities Ser.: No. 30). reprint ed. 37.50 (0-404-50730-1) AMS Pr.
Roche, Anne, jt. auth. see Peguy, Charles.
***Roche, Anthony.** Contemporary Irish Drama: From Beckett to McGuinness. LC 94-22566. (C). 1995. write for info. (0-312-12325-6); pap. write for info. (0-312-12326-4) St Martin.
Roche, Billy. Tumbling Down. 160p. 1986. 17.95 (0-86327-052-2, Pub. by Wolfhound Pr IE) Dufour.
***Roche, Brien A.** Virginia Domestic Relations Case Finder. 2nd ed. 273p. 1991. 75.00 (0-87473-765-6) Michie Butterworth.
— Virginia Domestic Relations Case Finder with 1992 Supplement. 2nd ed. 273p. 1991. 70.00 (0-685-59626-5) Michie Butterworth.
— Virginia Domestic Relations Case Finder with 1992 Supplement. 2nd suppl. ed. 273p. 1992. 25.00 (0-87473-978-0) Michie Butterworth.
— Virginia Torts Case Finder. 3rd ed. 863p. 1994. 90.00 (1-55834-161-7) Michie Butterworth.
— Virginia Torts Case Finder: With 1992 Cumulative Supplement. 2nd ed. 792p. 1990. 80.00 (0-87473-652-8) Michie Butterworth.
— Virginia Torts Case Finder: With 1992 Cumulative Supplement. 2nd suppl. ed. 792p. 1992. 27.50 (0-87473-979-9) Michie Butterworth.
Roche, Charles. Football's Stunting Defenses. LC 82-6321. 181p. 1982. 16.95 (0-13-324020-7, Parker Publishing Co) P-H.
Roche, Chris. A Boy, a Ball, a Dream. LC 92-72559. (Illus.). 1993. 21.95 (0-8158-0488-1) Chris Mass.
Roche, Christine, jt. auth. see Gilbert, Harriet.
Roche, Daniel. The Culture of Clothing: Dress & Fashion in the Ancien Regime. (Past & Present Publications). (Illus.). 528p. (C). 1994. 74.95 (0-521-41119-X) Cambridge U Pr.

R

— The People of Paris. LC 86-24506. (Studies on the History of Society & Culture: No. 2). 300p. 1987. pap. 16.00 (0-520-06031-8) U CA Pr.

Roche, Daniel, jt. ed. see Darnton, Robert.

Roche, Daniel, ed. see Menetra, Louis.

Roche de Coppens, Peter. Apocalypse Now: The Challenges of Our Times. LC 87-45742. (Spiritual Sciences Ser.). 288p. (Orig.). 1988. pap. 9.95 (0-87542-677-8) Llewellyn Pubns.

— Divine Light & Fire: Experiencing Esoteric Christianity. 192p. 1994. reprint ed. pap. text ed. 12.95 (0-8264-0765-X) Continuum.

— Divine Light & Love: Practicing Esoteric Christianity. 192p. 1994. reprint ed. pap. text ed. 14.95 (0-8264-0766-8) Continuum.

— The Invisible Temple. LC 87-45111. (Spiritual Sciences Ser.). (Illus.). 304p. (Orig.). 1987. pap. 9.95 (0-87542-676-X) Llewellyn Pubns.

— The Nature & Use of Ritual for Spiritual Attainment. LC 85-10270. (Spiritual Perspectives Ser.). (Illus.). 256p. (Orig.). (C). 1985. pap. 9.95 (0-87542-675-1) Llewellyn Pubns.

Roche De Coppens, Peter. The Sociological Adventure: A Holistic Perspective. 2nd ed. 304p. (C). 1992. pap. text ed. 21.95 (0-8403-7552-2) Kendall-Hunt.

Roche, Don, Jr. Easy 123 Macros. 1992. pap. 19.95 (1-56529-105-0) Que.

— Excel Four for Windows Quick Reference. (Quick Reference Ser.). (Illus.). 160p. (Orig.). 1992. pap. 9.95 (0-88022-958-6) Que.

— Quattro Pro Four Quickstart. 1992. pap. 21.95 (0-88022-938-1) Que.

Roche, Edward. Business Telecommunications. 512p. (C). 1991. text ed. 51.00 (0-03-032914-0) Dryden Pr.

Roche, Edward J., Jr. & Vogel, Mark A. Individual Taxation. LC 92-19537. (Tax & Estate Planning Ser.). 1200p. 1992. text ed. 130.00 (0-07-172104-5) Shepards-McGraw.

Roche, Edward M. Managing Information Technology in Multinational Corporations. (Illus.). 464p. (C). 1992. text ed. write for info. (0-02-402690-5) Macmillan.

Roche, Elizabeth, jt. auth. see Roche, Jerome.

Roche, Evan. The De Primo Principio of John Duns Scotus: A Revised Text & Translation. (Philosophy Ser.). 1949. 8.00 (0-686-11535-X) Franciscan Inst.

Roche, Francis. The Roche Collection of Traditional Irish Music. 1983. pap. 17.95 (0-8256-0292-0, Oak) Music Sales.

Roche, Francis X. Pension & Profit Sharing Plans for Small & Medium Size Businesses. LC 79-92397. 1984. 150.00 (0-916592-48-0) Panel Pubs.

Roche, George, III. America by the Throat: The Stranglehold of American Bureaucracy. 1982. 14.95 (0-686-81784-2) Devin.

— America by the Throat: The Stranglehold of Federal Bureaucracy. LC 82-12793. 200p. 1983. 14.95 (0-8159-6844-2) Devin.

Roche, George. The Fall of the Ivory Tower: Government Funding, Corruption, & the Bankrupting of Higher Education. LC 93-47561. 320p. 1994. 24.00 (0-89526-487-0) Regnery Pub.

— Free Markets, Free Men: Frederic Bastiat, 1801-1850. 178p. 1993. pap. 14.95 (0-916308-73-1) Hillsdale Coll Pr.

— A Reason for Living. LC 89-36663. 156p. 1990. 17.95 (0-89526-545-1) Regnery Pub.

— A World Without Heroes: The Modern Tragedy. LC 87-80235. 368p. 1987. pap. 12.95 (0-916308-89-8) Hillsdale Coll Pr.

Roche, George C. Going Home. LC 86-3559. (Illus.). 192p. 1987. 14.95 (0-915463-34-2) Green Hill.

Roche, Henri-Pierre. Jules et Jim. (FRE.). 1979. pap. 10.95 (0-7859-4115-0) Fr & Eur.

— Jules et Jim. (Folio Ser.: No. 1096). 242p. (FRE.). 1953. pap. 8.95 (2-07-037096-8) Schoenhof.

— Jules et Jim. Evans, Patrick, tr. LC 92-19043. 256p. 1993. reprint ed. pap. 13.95 (0-7145-2958-3) M Boyars Pubs.

Roche, J., ed. Physicists Look Back: Studies in the History of Physics. (Illus.). 404p. 1990. 114.00 (0-85274-001-8) IOP Pub.

Roche, J., jt. auth. see Van Thoai, N.

Roche, J. F. & O'Callaghan, D., eds. Follicular Growth & Ovulation Rate in Farm Animals. (Current Topics in Veterinary Medicine & Animal Science Ser.). 1987. lib. bdg. 117.00 (0-89838-855-4) Kluwer Ac.

— Manipulation of Growth in Farm Animals. (Current Topics in Veterinary Medicine & Animal Science Ser.). 316p. 1984. text ed. 46.50 (0-685-08511-2) Kluwer Ac.

Roche, J. G. Product Liability. (Illus.). xxviii, 200p. 1990. 57.00 (0-387-51819-3) Spr-Verlag.

Roche, Jerome & Roche, Elizabeth. A Dictionary of Early Music. (Illus.). 1981. 30.00 (0-19-520255-4) OUP.

***Roche, Jim.** Unsigned, Unsung . . . Whereabouts Unknown: Make-Do Art of the American Outlands. (Illus.). 80p. 1994. pap. 19.95 (0-295-97343-9) U of Wash Pr.

Roche, John F. Joseph Reed: A Moderate in the American Revolution. LC 68-59259. (Columbia University. Studies in the Social Sciences: No. 595). reprint ed. 37.50 (0-404-51595-9) AMS Pr.

Roche, John P. The History & Impact of Marxist-Leninist Organizational Theory. LC 84-4582. (Foreign Policy Reports). 73p. 1984. 11.95 (0-89549-059-5) Inst Foreign Policy Anal.

Roche, Jorg & Webber, Mark. Fur- und Wider- Spruche: Ein integriertes Text-Buch fur Colleges und Universitaten. (Illus.). 512p. (C). 1995. text ed. 35.00 (0-300-05769-5) Yale U Pr.

Roche, Judith. Ghosts. 80p. 1989. pap. 6.00 (0-912887-08-7) Empty Bowl.

— Myrrh. 100p. (Orig.). 1993. pap. 11.00 (0-930773-30-6) Black Heron Pr.

Roche, Judith, ed. Ergo! The Bumbershoot Literary Magazine, Vol. 3, No. 1. (Illus.). 100p. (Orig.). 1988. pap. 5.00 (0-929696-00-X) Bumbershoot.

— Ergo! The Bumbershoot Literary Magazine, Vol. 4, No. 1. (Illus.). 100p. (Orig.). 1989. pap. 5.00 (0-929696-01-8) Bumbershoot.

— Ergo! Vol. IX: The Bumbershoot 1994 Literary Magazine. (Illus.). 112p. Date not set. pap. 8.00 (0-929696-06-9) Bumbershoot.

***Roche, Julian.** Forecasting Commodity Markets: Using Technical, Fundamental & Econometric Analysis. 450p. 1995. 42.50 (1-55738-899-7) Probus Pub Co.

— Property Equities: Evaluation & Trading. 192p. 1992. 150.00 (1-85573-107-X, Pub. by Woodhead Pubng UK) St Mut.

Roche, Julian, ed. The International Cotton Trade. 192p. 1993. 150.00 (1-85573-104-5, Pub. by Woodhead Pubng UK) St Mut.

Roche, Liam P. The Chemical Elements: Chemistry, Physical Properties & Uses in Science & Industry. 256p. 1992. pap. text ed. write for info. (0-13-126558-X) P-H.

***Roche, Lissa, ed.** A Christian Treasury of Stories & Songs, Prayers & Poems & Much More for Young & Old. 560p. 1995. 25.00 (0-89107-857-6) Crossway Bks.

Roche, Luane. The Proud Tree. 64p. (J). (gr. 2-6). 1981. pap. 3.95 (0-89243-146-6) Liguori Pubns.

— Proud Tree. (Illus.). 48p. 1995. 14.95 (0-89243-768-5) Liguori Pubns.

— Proud Tree. rev. ed. (Illus.). 64p. 1995. pap. 3.95 (0-89243-769-3) Liguori Pubns.

***Roche, Lyn.** Meditations & Reflections to Uplift the Caregiver. 1995. 10.95 (0-943873-29-0) Elder Bks.

Roche, M. ARL - RLG Interlibrary Loan Cost Study. 64p. 1993. 10.00 (0-918006-70-8) ARL.

Roche, M. F. Dictionary of Surface Water Hydrology. 288p. (ENG, FRE, GER & SPA.). 1986. pap. 65.00 (2-225-80739-6, Masson) IBD Ltd.

Roche-Mahdi, Sarah, ed. & tr. Silence: A Thirteenth-Century French Romance. (Medieval Texts & Studies: No. 10). 367p. 1992. 42.00 (0-937191-31-0); pap. text ed. 15.95 (0-937191-32-9) Colleagues Pr Inc.

Roche, Marcel F. French, English, Spanish & German Dictionary of Surface Hydrology. 288p. (ENG, FRE, GER & SPA.). 1986. pap. 69.95 (0-8288-0962-3, F46020) Fr & Eur.

Roche, Mark W. Gottfried Benn's Static Poetry: Aesthetic & Intellectual-Historical Interpretations. LC 90-40007. (Germanic Languages & Literatures Ser.: No. 112). xi, 123p. (C). 1991. 22.50 (0-8078-8112-0) U of NC Pr.

Roche, Maurice. Compact. Polizzatti, Mark, tr. & intro. by. LC 88-14194. 160p. 1988. 19.95 (0-916583-29-5) Dalkey Arch.

— Rethinking Citizenship: Welfare, Ideology, & Change in Modern Society. LC 92-20497. 280p. 1992. 39.95 (0-7456-0306-8); pap. 19.95 (0-7456-0307-6) Blackwell Pubs.

Roche, Nan. The New Clay: Techniques & Approaches to Jewelry Making. 2nd ed. Bress, Seymour, ed. (Illus.). 160p. 1992. pap. 22.95 (0-9620543-4-8) Flower Valley Pr.

Roche, Orion. Anarclaw. 92p. 1972. pap. 5.95 (0-912282-04-5) Pulse-Finger.

Roche, P. K. Webster & Arnold Go Camping. (Illus.). 32p. (J). (ps-3). 1991. pap. 3.95 (0-14-050806-6, Puffin) Puffin Bks.

Roche, P. K., illus. & sel. At Christmas Be Merry. 32p. (J). (ps-1). 1989. pap. 3.95 (0-14-050680-2, Puffin) Puffin Bks.

Roche, Patrick. Fishermen of the Coromandel: The Social Study of the Paravas of the Coromandel. 1985. 18.50 (0-8364-1345-8, Pub. by Manohar II) S Asia.

Roche, Patrick A. Minority Access to Higher Education: An Analysis of a Pipeline Approach Through Neighborhood Learning Centers - the Minnestoa Experiment. LC 94-4719. 156p. (Orig.). (C). Date not set. pap. text ed. 24.50 (0-8191-9497-2) U Pr of Amer.

Roche, Patrick J. & Barton, Brian. The Northern Ireland: Myth & Reality. 225p. 1991. text ed. 59.95 (1-85628-147-7, Pub. by Avebury Pub UK) Ashgate Pub Co.

Roche, Paul. Aeschylus: Prometheus Bound. (Illus.). 148p. 1990. reprint ed. 12.00 (0-86516-238-7) Bolchazy-Carducci.

— Bible's Greatest Stories. 1990. pap. 5.99 (0-451-62779-2) NAL-Dutton.

— Love Songs of Sappho. 1991. pap. 4.95 (0-451-52535-3, Sig Classics) NAL-Dutton.

— Orestes: The Plays of Aeschylus. 1963. pap. 4.99 (0-451-62819-5) NAL-Dutton.

— Three Plays by Plautus. 1984. pap. 7.00x (0-86516-035-X) Bolchazy-Carducci.

— With Duncan Grant in Southern Turkey. 144p. (C). 1990. 49.00 (0-907855-00-8, Pub. by Honeyglen Pub Ltd UK) St Mut.

Roche, Paul, tr. The Oedipus Plays of Sophocles. 224p. 1958. pap. 3.99 (0-451-62847-0, Sig Classics) NAL-Dutton.

— Orestes: Plays of Aeschylus. pap. 3.95 (0-451-62321-5, ME2321, Ment) NAL-Dutton.

Roche, Philip. The Criminal Mind: A Study of Communication Between the Criminal Law & Psychiatry. LC 76-28524. 299p. 1976. reprint ed. text ed. 38.50 (0-8371-9056-8, ROCM, Greenwood Pr) Greenwood.

Roche, R. L., ed. Design Codes & Structural Mechanics: Based on Papers Presented at the Second International Seminar Held at the Ecole Polytehnique de Lausanne, Switzerland, 24-25 Aug., 1987. 314p. 1989. 108.00 (1-85166-297-9) Elsevier.

Roche, Regina M. Nocturnal Visit: A Tale, 2 vols. Varma, Devendra P., ed. LC 77-2045. (Gothic Novels III Ser.). 1977. reprint ed. lib. bdg. 91.95 (0-405-10143-0) Ayer.

Roche, Richard. The Call of the Wood Pigeon: A Day in the Life of a Monk in Pre-Viking Ireland. 1989. pap. 30.00 (0-685-65152-5, Pub. by Veritas IE) St Mut.

— The Call of the Wood Pigeon - Glaoch an Choluir Choille: A Day in the Life of a Monk in Pre-Viking Ireland. (Illus.). (Orig.). (J). (gr. 1-8). 1990. pap. 9.95 (1-85390-047-8, Pub. by Veritas Pubns IE) Irish Bks Media.

— The Norman Invasion of Ireland. 134p. 1994. pap. 15.95 (0-947962-81-6, Pub. by Anvil Bks Ltd IE) Irish Bks Media.

Roche, Richard & Merne, Oscar. Saltees: Birds & Legends. 160p. 1987. pap. 19.95 (0-86278-147-7, Pub. by OBrien Pr IE) Dufour.

Roche, Ruth L. The Child & Science: Wondering, Exploring, Growing. LC 76-55313. (Illus.). 48p. reprint ed. pap. 25.00 (0-7837-0547-6, 2040877) Bks Demand.

Roche, Thomas P., Jr. Petrarch & the English Sonnet Tradition. LC 85-48062. (Studies in the Renaissance: No. 18). 1990. 57.50 (0-404-62288-7) AMS Pr.

Roche, Thomas P., Jr., jt. ed. see Cullen, Patrick.

Roche, Thomas P., Jr., ed. see Spenser, Edmund.

Roche, Thomas P.

Rochecouste, Gabrielle M. The Role of Parallel Catamorphic Systems in the Structure of Zola's "Rougon-Maquart" (Romanistische Texte und Studien: Vol. 2). (Illus.). 276p. 1988. 35.10 (3-487-07964-X, Pub. by Georg Olms GW) Lubrecht & Cramer.

Rochedieu, C. Comentario Practico - Epistolas, Vol. III: Practical Comment. III - Epist. (SPA.). 6.95 (84-7228-567-7, 220127, Pub. by Edit Clie SP) TSELF.

— Comentario Practico - Hebreos, Vol. IV: Practical Comment. IV - Heb. - Rev. (SPA.). 5.50 (84-7228-568-5, 220128, Pub. by Edit Clie SP) TSELF.

— Comentario Practico - Juan, Vol. II: Practical Comment.I - John. (SPA.). 5.50 (84-7228-570-7, 220126, Pub. by Edit Clie SP) TSELF.

— Comentario Practico - Sinopticos, Vol. I: Practical Comment. I - Synoptics. (SPA.). 5.95 (84-7228-569-3, 220125, Pub. by Edit Clie SP) TSELF.

Rochefort, Christiane. Archaos du le Jardin Etincelant. 448p. (FRE.). 1984. pap. 11.95 (0-7859-1465-X, 2253001074) Fr & Eur.

— C'est Bizarre l'Ecriture. 160p. (FRE.). 1970. pap. 27.95 (0-7859-5436-8) Fr & Eur.

— Encore Heureux Qu'On Va Vers l'Ete. 218p. (FRE.). 1977. pap. 10.95 (0-7859-1469-2, 2253015741); pap. 26.95 (0-686-55222-9) Fr & Eur.

— L' Enfants d'Abord. 192p. (FRE.). 1976. pap. 28.95 (0-7859-5437-6) Fr & Eur.

— Les Petits Enfants du Siecle. 159p. 1969. 14.95 (0-686-55224-5); pap. 24.95 (0-686-55225-3) Fr & Eur.

— La Porte du Fond. (FRE.). 1990. pap. 12.95 (0-7859-3154-6, 2253052779) Fr & Eur.

— Printemps Au Parking. 192p. (FRE.). 1971. pap. 9.95 (0-7859-5564-X); pap. 3.95 (0-686-55227-X) Fr & Eur.

— Quand Tu Vas Chez les Femmes. (FRE.). 1983. pap. 4.95 (0-7859-3112-0) Fr & Eur.

— Le Repos du Guerrier. (Idees Ser.). 280p. 1958. 12.50 (0-686-55228-8) Fr & Eur.

— Une Rose Pour Morrison. 1966. 18.95 (0-686-55230-X) Fr & Eur.

— Les Stances a Sophie. 250p. (FRE.). 1978. 8.95 (0-686-55231-8, 2246005892); pap. 24.95 (0-7859-1452-8) Fr & Eur.

Rochefort, David A. From Poor Houses to Homelessness: Policy Analysis & Mental Health Care. LC 93-18522. 320p. 1993. text ed. 59.95 (0-86569-216-5, T216, Auburn Hse) Greenwood.

— From Poorhouses to Homelessness: Policy Analysis & Mental Health Care. LC 93-18522. 320p. 1993. pap. text ed. 22.95 (0-86569-237-8, Auburn Hse) Greenwood.

Rochefort, David A., ed. Handbook of Mental Health Policy in the United States. LC 88-32052. 563p. 1989. text ed. 99.50 (0-313-25009-X, RHM, Greenwood Pr) Greenwood.

Rochefort, David A. & Cobb, Roger W., eds. The Politics of Problem Definition: Shaping the Policy Agenda. LC 94-11031. (Studies in Government & Public Policy). 240p. 1994. 29.95 (0-7006-0646-7); pap. 14.95 (0-7006-0647-5) U Pr of KS.

Rocheleau, Dianne, jt. auth. see Thomas-Slayter, Barbara.

Rocheleau, Paul. Radio on Wheels: Eastern Edition. 1991. pap. 8.95 (0-425-12860-1, Berkley Trade) Berkley Pub.

— Radio on Wheels: Western Edition. 1991. pap. 8.95 (0-425-12861-X, Berkley Trade) Berkley Pub.

Rocheleau, Paul & Sprigg, June. Shaker Built: The Form & Function of Shaker Architecture. Larkin, David, ed. LC 94-76580. (Illus.). 272p. 1994. 50.00 (1-885254-03-2) Monacelli Pr.

Rochell, Carlton & Spellman, Christina. Dreams Betrayed: Working in the Technological Age. 160p. 1987. text ed. 18.95 (0-669-11105-8) Free Pr.

Rochell, Carlton C., ed. In Praise of Libraries & Librarians. (Illus.). 104p. 1989. 40.00 (0-8147-7409-1) NYU Pr.

Rochelle, Belinda. When Jo Louis Won the Title. LC 93-34317. (Illus.). (J). (gr. 4 up). 1994. 14.95 (0-395-66614-7) HM.

— Witnesses to Freedom: Young People Who Fought for Civil Rights. LC 93-16165. (Illus.). 112p. (J). (gr. 3-7). 1993. 15.99 (0-525-67377-6, Lodestar Bks) Dutton Child Bks.

Rochelle, D. P. The Real World of Alternate ID Acquisition. 28p. 1987. pap. 8.00 (0-87364-440-9) Paladin Pr.

Rochelle, Gary T., jt. ed. see Hudson, John L.

Rochelle, Gerald. The Life & Philosophy of J. McT. E. McTaggart, 1866-1925. LC 91-27674. (Studies in the History of Philosophy: Vol. 22). (Illus.). 268p. 1991. lib. bdg. 89.95 (0-7734-9692-0) E Mellen.

Rochelle, Gerald, ed. see Keeling, Stanley V.

Rochelle, Jay. An Attender of the Altar. LC 88-62023. (Orig.). 1988. pap. 3.00 (0-87574-280-7) Pendle Hill.

Rochelle, Jay C., tr. see Bonhoeffer, Dietrich.

Rochelle, Jeffrey La, jt. auth. see Laforest, Thomas J.

Rochelle, Mercedes. Historical Art Index, A. D. 400-1650: People, Places, & Events Depicted. LC 89-42749. 223p. 1989. lib. bdg. 49.95x (0-89950-449-3) McFarland & Co.

— Mythological & Classical World Art Index: A Locator of Paintings, Sculptures, Frescoes, Manuscript Illuminations, Sketches, Woodcuts & Engravings Executed 1200 B.C. to A.D. 1900, with a Directory of the Institutions Holding Them. LC 91-52503. 287p. 1991. lib. bdg. 62.50x (0-89950-566-X) McFarland & Co.

— Post-Biblical Saints Art Index: A Locator of Paintings, Sculptures, Mosaics, Icons, Frescoes, Manuscripts, Illuminations, Sketches, Woodcuts & Engravings Created from the 4th Century to 1950, with a Directory of the Institutions Holding Them. 367p. 1994. lib. bdg. 65.00 (0-89950-942-8) McFarland & Co.

Rochelson, Meri-Jane, jt. ed. see Manos, Nikki L.

Rochemont, Michael S. & Culicover, Peter W. English Focus Constructions & the Theory of Grammar. (Cambridge Studies in Linguistics: No. 52). (Illus.). 240p. (C). 1990. 64.95 (0-521-36412-4) Cambridge U Pr.

Rocher, A., ed. see Sixth International Conference on Intergranular & Interphase Boundaries in Materials Staff.

Rocher, D., jt. auth. see Clediere, J.

Rocher, Daniel, jt. auth. see Clediere, Jean.

Rocher, Francois & Smith, Miriam, eds. New Trends in Canadian Federalism. 1995. pap. 24.95 (1-55111-019-9) Broadview Pr.

Rocher, Ludo, intro. Ezourvedam: A French Veda of the Eighteenth Century. LC 84-6308. (University of Pennsylvania Studies on South Asia: No. 1). viii, 214p. 1984. 55.00 (0-915027-05-4); pap. 24.00 (0-915027-06-2) Benjamins North Am.

Rocher, Marie-Paule. The French Connection. LC 88-17247. (Illus.). 90p. (Orig.). (C). 1988. pap. text ed. 15.00 (0-8191-7075-5) U Pr of Amer.

Rocher, Rosane. Alexander Hamilton (1762-1824) A Chapter in the Early History of Sanskrit Philology. (American Oriental Ser.: Vol. 51). 1968. pap. 8.00 (0-940490-51-X) Am Orient Soc.

— Orientalism, Poetry & Millenium. 1983. 44.00 (0-8364-0870-5) S Asia.

Rocher, Rosane, ed. see Brown, W. Norman.

Rochester, Anne. Why Farmers Are Poor: The Agricultural Crisis in the United States. McCurry, Dan C. & Rubenstein, Richard E., eds. LC 74-30649. (American Farmers & the Rise of Agribusiness Ser.). 1975. reprint ed. 31.95 (0-405-06821-2) Ayer.

Rochester Civic Music Guild Staff. Recipes of Note. (Illus.). 215p. (Orig.). 1988. write for info. (0-318-63718-9) Rochester Civic Mus Guild.

— Recipes of Note for Entertaining. 346p. (Orig.). 1994. 18.00 (0-9621066-1-5) Rochester Civic Mus Guild.

Rochester, Colin H., jt. ed. see Parfitt, Geoffrey D.

Rochester, David, Jr. Contractor's Information "Sourcebook" The Building Code Simplified. Rene, Wendy, ed. (Illus.). 170p. (Orig.). (C). 1988. text ed. 45.00 (0-685-19927-4); pap. 35.00 (0-685-19928-2) CIS Pub.

Rochester, Dudley F. Hypercapnic Respiratory Failure. 300p. 1990. text ed. 42.00 (0-9626521-5-6, Andover Med Pubs) Buttrwrth-Heinemann.

***Rochester Elementary School Third-Graders.** The Chocolate Dinosaurs. (Wee Write Bks.: No. 1). (Illus.). 16p. (J). (ps-3). 1994. 32.95 (1-884987-00-1) WeWrite.

— The Chocolate Dinosaurs. (Wee Write Bks.: No. 1). (Illus.). 16p. (J). (ps-3). 1994. pap. text ed. 7.95 (1-884987-02-8) WeWrite.

— The Nightmare Dragon. rev. ed. (Wee Write Bks.: No. 2). (Illus.). 16p. (J). (ps-3). 1994. 17.95 (1-884987-01-X) WeWrite.

— The Nightmare Dragon. rev. ed. (Wee Write Bks.: No. 2). (Illus.). 16p. (J). (ps-3). 1994. pap. 7.95 (1-884987-03-6) WeWrite.

— The Nightmare Dragon, Big Bk. rev. ed. (Wee Write Bks.: No. 2). (Illus.). 16p. (J). (ps-3). 1994. 32.95 (1-884987-09-5) WeWrite.

Rochester Folk Art Guild Staff. Little Shooter of Birds & the Great Sun. (J). (ps-7). 1981. 9.50 (0-686-33125-7) Rochester Folk Art.

— More Simple Dishes. 1977. 4.50 (0-686-21777-2) Rochester Folk Art.

— Sunlight in the Morning: Songs from the Farm. (Illus.). 40p. (J). (gr. k-6). 1983. 13.00 (0-686-40298-7); audio 6.00 (0-317-00393-3) Rochester Folk Art.

Rochester General Hospital Laser Group Staff. Color Atlas of CO2 Laser Surgical Techniques. Lanzafame, Raymond, ed. (Illus.). 300p. 1988. 145.00 (0-912791-34-9) Ishiyaku Euro.

***Rochester, Illinois, Elementary School Third-Graders Staff.** The Chocolate Dinosaurs, Big Bk. (Wee Write Bks.: No. 1). (Illus.). 16p. (J). (ps-3). 1994. 32.95 (1-884987-08-7) WeWrite.

***Rochester (Illinois) School Class.** Fantasy Fun. (Wee Write Bks.: No. 20). (Illus.). 40p. (J). (ps-3). 1995. 32.95 (1-884987-69-9); lib. bdg. 18.95 (1-884987-64-8); pap. 8.95 (1-884987-65-6) WeWrite.

Rochester, J. Martin. Waiting for the Millennium: The United Nations & the Future of World Order. LC 92-45145. (Studies in International Relations). 361p. (C). 1993. text ed. 39.95 (0-87249-882-4) U of SC Pr.

Rochester, J. Martin, jt. auth. see Coplin, William D.

An Asterisk (*) at the beginning of an entry indicates that the title is appearing in BIP for the first time.

Rochester, J. Martin, jt. auth. see Pearson, Frederic S.

***Rochester, Jack & Rochester, Jon.** Computers for People: Basic Programming. 88p. (C). 1991. text ed. 11.00 (*0-256-10214-7*) Irwin.

***Rochester, Jack, et al.** Computers for People & Using Microsoft Works Package. (C). 1991. text ed. 43.95 (*0-256-10735-1*) Irwin.

Rochester, Jack B. Computers: Tools for Knowledge Workers. LC 92-16801. 640p. (C). 1993. pap. text ed. 39.95 (*0-256-11015-8*) Irwin.

Rochester, Jack B. & Rochester, Jon. Computers for People. 2nd ed. LC 93-3703. 280p. (C). 1993. pap. text ed. 26.95 (*0-256-10777-7*) Irwin.

— Computers for People: Concepts & Applications. (Illus.). 512p. (C). 1991. pap. text ed. 23.95 (*0-256-06680-9*, 14-2710-01) Irwin.

Rochester, John W. Collected Works. (BCL1-PR English Literature Ser.). 407p. 1992. reprint ed. lib. bdg. 99.00 (*0-7812-7398-6*) Rprt Serv.

— The Complete Poems of John Wilmot, Earl of Rochester. LC 68-27768. 325p. reprint ed. pap. 92.70 (*0-8357-8077-5*, 2033910) Bks Demand.

Rochester, Jon, jt. auth. see Rochester, Jack B.

Rochester, Jon, jt. auth. see Rochester, Jack.

Rochester, Junius. Little St. Simons Island on the Coast of Georgia. LC 93-44483. 1994. 30.00 (*0-913720-90-9*) Beil.

Rochester, Junius, jt. auth. see Buerge, David M.

Rochester, Larry. Publicity for Non-Profits: How to Get It, Be Effective & Make the Best Use of It (Radio, Television & the Press) (Publicity Ser.: Bk. No. 2). 230p. (C). 1993. pap. 19.95 (*1-881447-02-2*) Sunset Hill.

Rochester, Larry J. Book Publicity for Authors & Publishers; Radio, Television. (Publicity Ser.). 168p. 1992. pap. 16.95 (*1-881447-00-6*) Sunset Hill.

Rochester, Lois & Mandell, Judy. The One Hour College Applicant. rev. ed. LC 90-52815. (Illus.). 112p. (Orig.). (YA). (gr. 10-12). 1990. pap. 8.95 (*0-914457-38-1*) Mustang Pub.

Rochester, Maxine K. Foreign Students in American Library Education: Impact on Home Countries. LC 85-12675. (Contributions in Librarianship & Information Science Ser.: No. 55). (Illus.). 218p. 1986. text ed. 55.00 (*0-313-24201-1*, ROF/) Greenwood.

Rochester, Myrna B. Rene Crevel: Le Pays des Miroirs Absolus. (Stanford French & Italian Studies: No. 12). x, 174p. 1979. pap. 46.50 (*0-915838-25-7*) Anma Libri.

Rochester, Myrna B. & Convert-Chalmers, Claudine. Entree en Scene: Cours Premier de Langue et de Culture. (C). 1985. text ed. write for info. (*0-07-554525-X*) McGraw.

— Entree en Scene: Cours Premier de Langue et de Culture. (C). 1985. student ed, pap. text ed. 13.96 (*0-07-554526-8*); student ed, pap. text ed. 13.96 (*0-07-554527-6*); student ed, audio 200.00 (*0-685-08397-7*) McGraw.

Rochester, Myrna B., et al. Bonjour, Ca Va? An Introductory Course. 439p. (C). 1987. student ed 12.95 (*0-685-06847-1*); student ed 12.95 (*0-685-06848-X*); student ed, audio 264.95 (*0-685-06849-8*) McGraw.

— Bonjour, Ca Va? An Introductory Course. 1991. Listening Comprehension Instr's. manual. teacher ed, pap. text ed. write for info. (*0-07-053403-9*) McGraw.

— Bonjour, Ca Va? An Introductory Course. 3rd ed. 1991. pap. text ed. 11.84 (*0-07-557445-4*) McGraw.

— Bonjour, Ca Va? An Introductory Course. 3rd ed. 1991. text ed. write for info. (*0-07-557441-1*); Cahier D'Exercices. pap. text ed. write for info. (*0-07-557443-8*); audio 100.00 (*0-07-557459-4*) McGraw.

— Bonjour, Ca Va? An Introductory Course. 3rd ed. 1991. write for info. (*0-07-053401-2*); write for info. (*0-07-053402-0*) McGraw.

Rochette, Edward. Southwest Traveler: Lost Mines: Buried Treasure: a Guide to Sites & Legends of the Southwest. (American Traveler Ser.). (Illus.). 48p. (Orig.). 1992. pap. 4.95 (*1-55838-130-9*) R H Pub.

Rochette, Edward C. The Romance of Coin Collecting. (Illus.). 184p. (Orig.). 1991. pap. text ed. 12.95 (*0-943161-28-2*) Bowers & Merena.

Rochford, E. Burke. Hare Krishna in America. (Illus.). 300p. (C). 1985. 40.00 (*0-8135-1113-5*); pap. 15.00 (*0-8135-1114-3*) Rutgers U Pr.

***Rochford, Joni.** Is This House Safe? 105p. (Orig.). Date not set. pap. 4.95 (*1-886618-00-3*) Rochford.

Rochkind-Dubinsky. Microbiological Decomposition of Chlorinated Aromatic Compounds. (Microbiology Ser.: Vol. 18). 336p. 1987. 135.00 (*0-8247-7527-9*) Dekker.

Rochkind, Marc J. Advanced C Programming for Displays: Character Displays, Windows, & Keyboards for Unix & MS-DOS. (Illus.). 272p. 1987. 35.95 (*0-13-010240-7*) P-H.

— Advanced UNIX Programming. 265p. 1985. pap. 35.95 (*0-13-011800-1*) P-H.

Rochlin, Gene I. Plutonium, Power, & Politics: International Arrangements for the Disposition of Spent Nuclear Fuel. LC 78-68833. (Studies in International Political Economy: Vol. 3). 1979. 50.00 (*0-520-03887-8*) U CA Pr.

Rochlin, Gene I. & Demchak, Chris C. Lessons of the Gulf War: Ascendant Technology & Declining Capability. LC 91-77818. (Policy Papers in International Affairs Ser.: No. 39). 42p. (Orig.). (C). 1991. pap. text ed. 5.50 (*0-87725-539-3*) U of Cal IAS.

Rochlitz, Steven. Allergies & Candida: With the Physicist's Rapid Solution. 2nd ed. (Towards a Science of Healing Ser.: Vol. I). (Illus.). 272p. (Orig.). (C). 1989. pap. 19.95 (*0-945262-26-4*) HEBS Inc.

— Allergies & Candida: With the Physicist's Rapid Solution. 3rd ed. LC 91-3199. (Towards a Science of Healing Ser.: Vol. I). (Illus.). 272p. (Orig.). 1991. text ed. 23.95 (*0-945262-20-5*); pap. text ed. 19.95 (*0-945262-21-3*) HEBS Inc.

— Allergies & Candida: With the 21st Century Solution. LC 87-83364. (Towards a Science of Healing Ser.: Vol. I). (Illus.). 176p. (Orig.). 1988. audio 22.00 (*0-945262-35-3*) HEBS Inc.

— Towards a Science of Healing, Vol. II: Advanced Human Ecology & Energy Balancing Sciences. deluxe ed. (Illus.). 100p. (C). 1991. spiral bd. 59.95 (*0-945262-40-X*) HEBS Inc.

Rochliz, Steven. Why Do Music Conductors Live into their 90s? The Simple, Revolutionary Discovery that Can Make You Live Longer, Increase Your Stamina & Stretch & Normalize Your Blood Pressure in Minutes. LC 93-33432. (Illus.). 140p. (Orig.). 1994. pap. 12.95 (*0-945262-42-6*) HEBS Inc.

Rochman, H. Clinical Pathology in the Elderly: A Textbook of Laboratory Interpretations. (Illus.). xiv, 222p. 1988. 71.25 (*3-8055-4694-7*) S Karger.

— Voices in the Dark. (J). Date not set. 14.00 (*0-06-025024-0*); lib. bdg. 13.89 (*0-06-025025-9*) HarpC Child Bks.

Rochman, Hazel. Against Borders: Promoting Books for a Multicultural World. LC 93-17840. 288p. (Orig.). (YA). (gr. 5-12). 1993. pap. text ed. 18.95 (*0-8389-0601-X*) ALA.

— Tales of Love & Terror: Booktalking the Classics, Old & New. LC 86-32285. 128p. 1987. pap. text ed. 22.00 (*0-8389-0463-7*) ALA.

— Who Do You Think You Are? Stories of Friends & Enemies. (YA). 1993. 15.95 (*0-316-75355-6*) Little.

Rochman, Hazel, ed. Somehow Tenderness Survives: Stories of Southern Africa. LC 88-916. (Charlotte Zolotow Bk.). 160p. (YA). (gr. 7 up). 1988. lib. bdg. 14.89 (*0-06-025023-2*) HarpC Child Bks.

— Somehow Tenderness Survives: Stories of Southern Africa. LC 88-916. (Charlotte Zolotow Bk.). 208p. (YA). (gr. 7 up). 1990. pap. 3.95 (*0-06-447063-6*, Trophy) HarpC Child Bks.

***Rochman, Hazel & McCampbell, Darlene Z., sels.** Bearing Witness: Stories of the Holocaust. LC 95-13352. 144p. (YA). (gr. 7 up). 1995. 15.95 (*0-531-09488-X*); lib. bdg. 15.99 (*0-531-08788-3*) Orchard Bks Watts.

Rochmis, Jon, ed. see Bernstein, Gary.

Rochmis, Jon, ed. see Dobbins, Dick & Twichell, Jon.

Rochmis, Jon, jt. ed. see Hyman, Laurence J.

Rochmis, Jon, ed. see Jansen, Joyce.

Rochmis, Jon, ed. see Lott, Ronnie.

Rochmis, Jon, ed. see Morgan, Joe.

Rochon, Richard & Linton, Harold. Color in Architectural Illustration. LC 88-3649. (Illus.). 200p. 1991. pap. 39.95 (*0-442-00635-7*) Van Nos Reinhold.

Rochon, Thomas R. Mobilizing for Peace: The Antinuclear Movements in Western Europe. (Illus.). 264p. 1988. 37.50 (*0-691-05671-4*) Princeton U Pr.

Rochow, E. G. Silicon & Silicones. (Illus.). 190p. 1987. pap. 18.50 (*0-387-17565-2*) Spr-Verlag.

Rochow, Theodore G. Light-Microscopical Resinography, Vol. 47. LC 83-61635. (Illus.). 1983. 30.00 (*0-904962-10-5*) Microscope Pubns.

Rochow, Theodore G. & Tucker, Paul A. Introduction to Microscopy by Means of Light, Electrons, X-Rays, or Acoustics. (Illus.). 455p. (C). 1994. 49.50 (*0-306-44684-7*, Plenum Pr) Plenum.

Rochowanski, L. W., ed. Der Formwille der Zeit in der Angewandten Kunst. (Bauhaus Ser.). 1990. reprint ed. 40.00 (*3-601-00288-4*); reprint ed. pap. 30.00 (*0-685-27118-8*) Periodicals Srv.

Rochut, Joannes, ed. Melodious Etudes for Trombone, Bk. 1. (Illus.). 88p. 1928. pap. 9.95 (*0-8258-0149-4*, 0-1594) Fischer Inc NY.

***Rochvarg, Arnold.** Watergate Victory: Mardian's Appeal. LC 95-5695. 1995. write for info. (*0-8191-9916-8*) U Pr of Amer.

Rochwarger, Arnold, jt. auth. see Miskovitz, Paul.

Rocine, V. G. Building a New Stomach. (Nutrition Ser.). 1991. lib. bdg. 75.00 (*0-8490-4260-7*) Gordon Pr.

— Building a New Stomach. reprint ed. spiral bd. 4.95 (*0-7873-0732-7*) Mokelumne.

— Eating for Beauty. reprint ed. spiral bd. 7.70 (*0-7873-0731-9*) Mokelumne.

— Secrets of Eternal Youth. (Orig.). reprint ed. spiral bd. 8.80 (*0-7873-0733-5*) Mokelumne.

— Secrets of Eternal Youth: Why Diet Should Be Based upon Bio-Chemical Food Analysis for Health & Long Life. (Longevity Ser.). 1991. lib. bdg. 79.95 (*0-8490-4103-1*) Gordon Pr.

Rocine, Victor G. Mind-Training. 225p. 1976. reprint ed. 11.00 (*0-7873-1146-4*) Mokelumne.

— Mind Training: A Practical System for Developing Self Confidence, Memory, Mental Concentration & Character. reprint ed. spiral bd. 11.00 (*0-7873-0734-3*) Mokelumne.

Rocissano, Lorraine. Helping Baby Talk: A Pressure-Free Approach to Your Child's First Words from Birth to 3 Years. 1994. pap. 5.50 (*1-56171-327-9*) Sure Sellers.

Rocissano, Lorraine & Fitzpatrick, Jean G. Helping Baby Talk: A Pressure-Free Approach to Your Child's First Words from Birth to 3 Years. 224p. 1990. mass mkt. 4.95 (*0-380-75681-1*) Avon.

Rock. Diagnostic Picture Test in Pediatric Dentistry. 1988. 19.95 (*0-8151-7381-4*, Yr Bk Med Pubs) Mosby Yr Bk.

— Diagnostic Picture Tests in Pediatric Dentistry. 1988. 14.95 (*0-7234-0984-6*, Wolfe Pub) Mosby Yr Bk.

Rock & Kennedy. Power, Performance & Ethics. 1991. 54.95 (*0-7506-0104-3*) Buttrwrth-Heinemann.

Rock, jt. ed. see Horricks.

Rock, jt. auth. see Palmer, Scott.

Rock, jt. auth. see Rosenshein.

***Rock & Learn, Inc., Staff.** Colors, Shapes & Counting. (J). 1994. audio, pap. 9.95 (*1-878489-32-1*) Rock & Learn Educ Prod.

Rock, Andrea, ed. see Smith, Jack A.

Rock, Calvin. Seeing Christ: Windows on His Saving Grace. LC 93-40955. 1994. write for info. (*0-8280-0794-2*) Review & Herald.

Rock, Calvin B. Church Leadership, Call to Virtue. (Anchor Ser.). 96p. 1989. pap. 2.99 (*0-8163-0859-4*) Pacific Pr Pub Assn.

Rock, Cheryl L., ed. Are You Really Serious about Losing Weight? 17th rev. ed. 65p. 1992. pap. 7.95 (*0-9608846-9-6*) PM Inc.

Rock Creek Research Staff. China Statistical Handbook, 1987. Keidel, Albert, ed. 25p. (Orig.). (C). 1987. pap. text ed. 4.50 (*0-943085-02-0*) Rock Creek Res.

Rock, David. Authoritarian Argentina: The Nationalistic Movement, Its History & Its Impact. 334p. (C). 1993. 35.00 (*0-520-07920-5*) U CA Pr.

— Authoritarian Argentina: The Nationalistic Movement, Its History & Its Impact. (C). 1995. pap. 14.95 (*0-520-20352-6*) U CA Pr.

Rock, David, ed. Latin America in the Nineteen Forties: War & Postwar Transitions. LC 93-29798. 285p. 1994. 42.00 (*0-520-08416-0*); pap. 16.00 (*0-520-08417-9*) U CA Pr.

Rock, David, intro. Five Stories. LC 93-27930. (German Texts Ser.). 1993. text ed. 16.95 (*0-7190-3586-4*, Pub. by Manchester Univ Pr UK) St Martin.

Rock, David, jt. ed. see Horrocks, David.

Rock-Evans, Rosemary. Analysis Within the Systems Development Life-Cycle: Activity Analysis - the Deliverables. (RRES Ser.: No. 3). (Illus.). 600p. 1987. pap. 59.95 (*0-08-034107-1*, Pergamon Pr) Elsevier.

— Analysis Within the Systems Development Life-Cycle: Data Analysis - the Methods. (RRES Ser.: No. 2). (Illus.). 360p. 1987. pap. 59.95 (*0-08-034106-3*, Pergamon Pr) Elsevier.

— Data Modelling & Process Modelling: Using the Most Popular Methods. 383p. 1992. pap. 64.95 (*0-7506-0739-4*) Buttrwrth-Heinemann.

— An Introduction to Data & Activity Analysis. LC 89-10661. 264p. 1989. pap. text ed. 39.95 (*0-89435-309-8*) Wiley.

Rock-Evans, Rosemary, ed. Analysis Within the Systems Development Life-Cycle: Data Analysis - the Deliverables, Bk. 1. (RRES Ser.: No. 1). (Illus.). 300p. 1987. pap. 59.95 (*0-08-034105-5*, Pergamon Pr) Elsevier.

Rock, Fern. Slaying the English Jargon. 42p. 1983. pap. text ed. 8.00 (*0-914548-43-3*) Soc Tech Comm.

Rock, G., jt. ed. see Decary, F.

Rock, Gail. The House Without a Christmas Tree. LC 74-162. (Illus.). 96p. (J). (gr. 2 up). 1974. lib. bdg. 9.99 (*0-394-92833-4*) Knopf Bks Yng Read.

Rock, Gail A., jt. ed. see Decary, Francine.

Rock, Harry. The Basic Essentials of Canoe Poling. LC 90-26423. (Basic Essentials Ser.). (Illus.). 72p. (Orig.). 1992. pap. 5.99 (*0-934802-36-X*) ICS Bks.

Rock, Howard B. New York City Artisan, 1789-1825: A Documentary History. LC 88-32412. (SUNY Series in American Labor History). 273p. 1989. 74.50 (*0-7914-0096-4*); pap. 24.95 (*0-7914-0097-2*) State U NY Pr.

Rock, Howard B., jt. auth. see Gilje, Paul A.

***Rock, Howard B., et al, eds.** American Artisans: Crafting Social Identity, 1750-1850. LC 95-1296. (Illus.). 272p. 1995. text ed. 45.00x (*0-8018-5029-0*); pap. text ed. 16.95x (*0-8018-5030-4*) Johns Hopkins.

Rock, Ian, tr. see Chevalier, Jean-Marie.

***Rock, Irvin.** Perception. (Illus.). 243p. 1995. pap. text ed. 19.95 (*0-7167-6011-8*) W H Freeman.

— The Perceptual World: Readings from Scientific American. (Illus.). 224p. (C). 1995. text ed. 15.95 (*0-7167-2068-X*) W H Freeman.

Rock, Irvin, ed. The Legacy of Solomon Asch: Essays in Cognition & Social Psychology. 320p. 1990. text ed. 59.95 (*0-8058-0440-4*) L Erlbaum Assocs.

Rock, J. F. A Monographic Study of the Hawaiian Species of the Tribe Lobelioideae, Family Campanulaceae. (BMB Ser.). (Orig.). 1919. 128.00 (*0-527-01651-9*) Periodicals Srv.

Rock, J. W., jt. auth. see Duncan, Barry L.

Rock, James, et al, eds. Debt & the Twin Deficits Debate. LC 90-46310. 279p. (C). 1991. pap. text ed. 23.95 (*1-55934-040-1*) Mayfield Pub.

Rock, Joe, jt. auth. see Patterson, David.

Rock, John A. & Schlaff, William D., eds. Decision-Making in Reproductive Endocrinology. LC 92-21892. (Illus.). 672p. 1993. 135.00 (*0-86542-214-1*) Blackwell Sci.

Rock, John A., jt. auth. see Carpenter, Sue E.

Rock, John A., jt. auth. see Thompson, John D.

Rock, John A., et al. Female Reproductive Surgery. (Illus.). 404p. 1992. 90.00 (*0-683-07317-6*) Williams & Wilkins.

Rock, Judith. Theology in the Shape of Dance: Using Dance in Worship & Theological Process. 1977. 3.00 (*0-941500-16-0*) Sharing Co.

Rock, Judith, jt. auth. see Adams, Doug.

Rock, Judith, jt. auth. see Mealy, Norman.

Rock, Leo. Making Friends with Yourself: Christian Growth & Acceptance. 1990. pap. 7.95 (*0-8091-3155-2*) Paulist Pr.

Rock, Leo P. Making Friends with Yourself: Christian Growth & Self Acceptance. 144p. (C). 1990. text ed. 39.00 (*0-85439-333-1*, Pub. by St Paul Pubns UK) St Mut.

Rock, Leon. Preparation & Pursuance of Civil Litigation. LC 76-24398. (Illus.). ix, 753p. 1983. 37.50 (*0-317-00679-7*) Natl Ctr PT.

***Rock, Lois.** Christmas Deck the Tree: Decorations, Gifts, & Food to Put Joy into Your Christmas. (Illus.). 48p. (J). (gr. 3-5). 1995. pap. 8.99 (*0-7459-3041-7*) Lion USA.

— The Lord's Prayer for Children. (Illus.). 32p. (J). (gr. k-2). 1993. 8.99 (*0-7459-2542-1*) Lion USA.

— Simply Wonderful Craftbook. (Illus.). 48p. (J). (gr. 3-6). 1993. 13.95 (*0-7459-2503-0*) Lion USA.

— Ten Commandments for Children. (J). (ps-3). 1995. 8.99 (*0-7459-3055-7*) Lion USA.

Rock, Louise, ed. see Allen, Robert A.

Rock, Marcia, jt. auth. see Sanders, Marlene.

Rock, Maxine. The Automobile & The Environment. (Earth at Risk Ser.). (Illus.). (YA). (gr. 5 up). 1992. lib. bdg. 19.95 (*0-7910-1592-0*) Chelsea Hse.

Rock Mechanics Symposium Staff. Applications of Rock Mechanics: Proceedings - 15th Symposium on Rock Mechanics Held at the State Game Lodge, Custer State Park, South Dakota, Sept. 17-19, 1973. LC 78-307544. (Symposium on Rock Mechanics Proceedings Ser.: Vol. 15). (Illus.). 670p. reprint ed. pap. 180.00 (*0-8357-5672-6*, 2019534) Bks Demand.

— Design Methods in Rock Mechanics: Proceedings - 16th Symposium on Rock Mechanics, University of Minnesota, Sept. 22-24, 1975. Fairhurst, Charles & Crouch, Steven L., eds. (Illus.). 427p. reprint ed. pap. 121.70 (*0-317-08309-0*, 2019540) Bks Demand.

— Rock Mechanics - Theory & Practice: Proceedings of the Symposium, 11th, University of California, Berkeley, 1969. Somerton, Wilbur H., ed. LC 73-103203. (Illus.). 772p. reprint ed. pap. 180.00 (*0-317-10996-0*, 2004326) Bks Demand.

— Rock Mechanics Symposium: Presented at the Winter Annual Meeting of the American Society of Mechanical Engineers, Detroit, Michigan, November 11-15, 1973. Sikarskie, D. L., ed. LC 73-87731. (AMD Ser.: Vol. 3). (Illus.). 134p. reprint ed. pap. 38.20 (*0-8357-2880-3*, 2039117) Bks Demand.

— Stability of Rock Slopes: Proceedings of the Symposium on Rock Mechanics, 13th, University of Illinois, Urbana, August 30-September 1, 1971. Cording, Edward J., ed. LC 76-380975. (Illus.). 922p. reprint ed. pap. 180.00 (*0-317-08305-8*, 2019553) Bks Demand.

Rock, Milton L. Mergers & Acquisitions Handbook. 2nd ed. 1993. text ed. 84.95 (*0-07-053353-9*) McGraw.

— The Mergers & Acquistions Handbook. 544p. 1987. text ed. 75.50 (*0-07-053350-4*) McGraw.

Rock, Milton L. & Berger, Lance A. The Compensation Handbook: A State-of-the-Art Guide to Compensation Strategy & Design. 3rd ed. 592p. 1991. text ed. 89.50 (*0-07-053352-0*) McGraw.

Rock, Milton L. & Rock, Robert H. Corporate Restructuring: A Guide to Creating the Premium-Valued Company. 304p. 1990. text ed. 32.95 (*0-07-053351-2*) McGraw.

Rock, N. M. Lamprophyres. 288p. 1991. text ed. 139.95 (*0-442-30396-3*) Chapman & Hall.

Rock, Nicholas L., jt. auth. see Easson, William M.

Rock-Ola Manufacturing Corporation Staff. Rock-Ola Model 1452 of 1955-56-57 Installation & Operation Manual, Service, Parts Manual & Schematic. Adams, Frank, ed. 40p. 1984. reprint ed. spiral bd. 32.50 (*0-913599-39-5*, R-279) AMR Pub Co.

— Rock-Ola Model 1455-D & 1455-S of 1957: Installation, Operation, Service Manual & 3 Schematics. 40p. 1983. reprint ed. spiral bd. 32.50 (*0-913599-28-X*, R-241) AMR Pub Co.

— Rock-Ola Model 1493 "Princess" of 1962 Service Manual, Parts List & Schematic: Service Manual, Parts List & Schematic for the 100 Selection Model "Princess" Jukebox of 1962. 80p. 1984. reprint ed. spiral bd. 35.00 (*0-913599-29-8*, R-269) AMR Pub Co.

— Rock-Ola Model 1544 & 1546 120 Selection Wall Box Models Service Manual, Installation Instructions & Parts List. 10p. 1984. reprint ed. spiral bd. 19.50 (*0-913599-32-8*, R-272) AMR Pub Co.

— Rock-Ola Model 426 "Grand Prix 2" of 1965-66: Service, Parts Manual & Shematic. Adams, Frank, ed. 94p. 1984. reprint ed. spiral bd. 35.00 (*0-913599-30-1*, R282) AMR Pub Co.

— Rock-Ola Model 429 "Starlet" of 1965-66 Service Manual: Service Manuals of 1965-1966 (100 Selections) Adams, Frank, ed. 52p. 1984. reprint ed. spiral bd. 29.50 (*0-913599-38-7*, R-283) AMR Pub Co.

— Rock-Ola, Models 1488 & 1495 "Regis" of 1961 Service, Parts Manual, Installation & Operation Manual & Fold-Out Schematics. 80p. 1984. reprint ed. spiral bd. 35.00 (*0-913599-05-0*, R-248) AMR Pub Co.

Rock, Pam. Love's Changing Moon. 400p. (Orig.). 1994. mass mkt., pap. text ed. 4.99 (*0-505-51965-8*) Dorchester Pub Co.

— Moon of Desire. 400p. (Orig.). 1993. pap. 4.99 (*0-505-51913-5*, Love Spell) Dorchester Pub Co.

— A World Away. 400p. (Orig.). 1995. mass mkt. 4.99 (*0-505-52043-5*) Dorchester Pub Co.

Rock, Pamela A. Going off on Her Own. Warren, Shirley, ed. 24p. (Orig.). 1989. pap. 4.95 (*1-877801-01-1*) Still Waters.

Rock, Paul, ed. Drugs & Politics. LC 76-1766. (Society Bks.). 333p. 1977. 34.95 (*0-87855-076-3*); pap. text ed. 21.95 (*0-87855-572-2*) Transaction Pubs.

— History of Criminology. 666p. 1994. 139.95 (*1-85521-331-1*, Pub. by Dartmth Pub UK) Ashgate Pub Co.

— Victimology: International Library of Criminology & Criminal Justice. 324p. 1994. 89.95 (*1-85521-405-9*, Pub. by Dartmth Pub UK) Ashgate Pub Co.

Rock, Paul, jt. auth. see Downes, David.

Rock, Paul E. Helping Victims of Crime: The Home Office & the Rise of Victim Support in England & Wales. (Oxford Socio-Legal Studies). 464p. 1991. 95.00 (*0-19-825422-9*) OUP.

R

— The Social World of an English Crown Court: Witness & Professionals in the Crown Court Centre at Wood Green. LC 93-16309. (Oxford Socio-Legal Studies). (Illus.). 400p. 1993. 62.00 (*0-19-825843-7*, Old Oregon Bk Store) OUP.
Rock, Paul E., ed. see Davis, John.
Rock, Paul E., jt. auth. see Downes, David.
Rock, Peter A. Chemical Thermodynamics. McQuarrie, Donald A., ed. LC 82-51233. (Physical Chemistry Ser.). (Illus.). 553p. (C). 1983. 54.00 (*0-935702-12-1*) Univ Sci Bks.
Rock, Robert C., jt. auth. see Noe, Dennis A.
Rock, Robert H., jt. auth. see Rock, Milton L.
Rock, Robert T. The Influence upon Learning of the Quantitative Variation of After-Effects. LC 79-177199. (Columbia University. Teachers College. Contributions to Education Ser.: No. 650). reprint ed. 37.50 (*0-404-55650-7*) AMS Pr.
Rock, Roger O., comp. The Native American in American Literature: A Selectively Annotated Bibliography. LC 84-27972. (Bibliographies & Indexes in American Literature Ser.: No. 3). xvi, 211p. 1985. text ed. 55.00 (*0-313-24550-9*, RKN/, Greenwood Pr) Greenwood.
***Rock, Sherry L.** Caged Innocence. LC 94-60632. 192p. 1994. text ed. 14.95 (*1-884570-07-0*) Research Triangle.
— Skippy: An Adventure in Stewardship. (Orig.). 1993. pap. 6.95 (*1-55673-581-2*) CSS OH.
Rock, Stephen R. Why Peace Breaks Out: Great Power Rapprochement in Historical Perspective. LC 88-33824. xii, 220p. (C). 1989. 34.95 (*0-8078-1857-7*) U of NC Pr.
Rock, Tim. Diving & Snorkeling Guide to Guam & Yap. LC 93-30820. Date not set. write for info. (*1-55992-076-9*, Pisces Bks) Gulf Pub.
— Diving & Snorkeling Guide to Truk Lagoon. LC 93-30789. 96p. 1994. 11.95 (*1-55992-069-6*, Pisces Bks) Gulf Pub.
Rock, Tim & Toribiong, Francis. Diving & Snorkeling Guide to Palau. LC 93-27894. (Illus.). 96p. 1994. 11.95 (*1-55992-068-8*, Pisces Bks) Gulf Pub.
Rock, Victoria, ed. see King, Celia.
Rock, Vincent P., ed. Policymakers & Model Builders Cases & Concepts. 672p. 1969. text ed. 237.00 (*0-677-13170-4*) Gordon & Breach.
***Rock, W. J.** The Mass Confusion of "Values Clarification" A Retrospective Look. LC 95-60993. 367p. 1996. 16.95 (*1-55523-749-5*) Winston-Derek.
Rock, W. P., jt. auth. see Andlaw, R. J.
Rockafellar, R. T. Monotone Processes of Convex & Concave Type. LC 52-42839. (Memoirs Ser.: No. 1/77). 74p. 1967. pap. 16.00 (*0-8218-1277-7*, MEMO 1/77) Am Math.
Rockafellar, R. T., tr. see Gol'Stein, E. G.
Rockafellar, R. Tyrell. Network Flows & Monotropic Optimization. LC 83-23478. (Pure & Applied Mathematics: A Wiley Interscience Series of Texts, Monographs & Tracts: No. 1-237). 616p. 1984. text ed. 138.00 (*0-471-88078-7*, Wiley-Interscience) Wiley.
Rockafellar, R. Tyrrell. Conjugate Duality & Optimization. (CBMS-NSF Regional Conference Ser.: No. 16). vi, 74p. (Orig.). 1974. pap. text ed. 16.50 (*0-89871-013-8*) Soc Indus-Appl Math.
— Convex Analysis. LC 68-56318. (Mathematical Ser.: No. 28). 1969. 69.50 (*0-691-08069-0*) Princeton U Pr.
Rockart, John F. & Bullen, Christine V. The Rise of Managerial Computing: The Best of the Center for Information Systems Research. 350p. 1986. text ed. 45.00 (*0-87094-757-5*) Irwin Prof Pubng.
Rockart, John F. & DeLong, David W. Executive Support Systems: The Emergence of Top Management Computer Use. 288p. 1988. text ed. 52.00 (*0-87094-955-1*) Irwin Prof Pubng.
Rockas, Lee. Style in Writing: A Prose Reader. 431p. (C). 1992. pap. text ed. write for info. (*0-669-20878-7*); Instr.'s ed. teacher ed write for info. (*0-669-28172-7*) Heath.
Rockas, Leo. A Creative Copybook. LC 88-81496. 282p. (C). 1988. pap. text ed. 15.00 (*0-669-14073-2*); Instr.'s guide. teacher ed write for info. (*0-669-14074-0*) Heath.
— Ways In: Analyzing & Responding to Literature. 196p. 1984. pap. text ed. 14.50 (*0-86709-075-8*) Boynton Cook Pubs.
Rockaway, Robert A. But - He Was Good to His Mother: The Lives & Crimes of Jewish Gangsters. (Illus.). 272p. 1993. 24.95 (*0-317-05837-1*, Pub. by Gefen Pub Hse IS) Gefen Bks.
— But - He Was Good to His Mother: The Lives & Times of Jewish Gangsters. (Illus.). 272p. (Orig.). 1994. pap. 8.95 (*965-229-092-0*) Gefen Bks.
— The Jews of Detroit: From the Beginning, 1762-1914. LC 86-15866. (Illus.). 175p. 1986. 24.95 (*0-8143-1808-8*) Wayne St U Pr.
Rockcastle, Garth, ed. Type & the (Im) Possibilities of Convention. (Midgard: the University of Minnesota Architectural Review Ser.: Vol. 2). (Illus.). 176p. (Orig.). 1991. pap. 14.95 (*1-878271-30-X*) Princeton Arch.
Rockcastle, Mary, ed. Remembering the Dance: Writing by Older Minnesotans. (Illus.). 224p. (Orig.). 1989. pap. 7.00 (*0-927663-00-7*) COMPAS.
Rockcastle, Mary F. Rainy Lake. 256p. 1994. 22.50 (*1-55597-218-7*) Graywolf.
Rockdale Temple Sisterhood Staff. Beginning Again: More Hors D'oeuvres for Cooks Who Love in the Beginning. (Illus.). 200p. (Orig.). 1981. pap. 10.95 (*0-9602338-1-4*) Rockdale Ridge.
— Beginning Again: More Hors D'oeuvres for Cooks Who Love in the Beginning. braille ed. (Illus.). 200p. (Orig.). 1981. Braille ed. pap. write for info. (*0-318-55537-9*) Rockdale Ridge.
— In the Beginning: A Collection of Hors d'Oeuvres. braille rev. ed. 1982. Braille ed. pap. write for info. (*0-318-56779-2*) Rockdale Ridge.
— In the Beginning: A Collection of Hors d'Oeuvres. rev. ed. 1982. pap. 21.90 (*0-9602338-2-2*); pap. 8.95 (*0-9602338-3-0*) Rockdale Ridge.
— In the Beginning: A Collection of Hors d'Oeuvres, Set. rev. ed. 1982. boxed 17.90 (*0-685-06087-X*) Rockdale Ridge.
Rocke, Alan J. Chemical Atomism in the Nineteenth Century: From Dalton to Cannizzaro. LC 83-25082. 404p. 1984. 57.50 (*0-8142-0360-4*) Ohio St U Pr.
— The Quiet Revolution: Hermann Kolbe & the Science of Organic Chemistry. LC 92-28190. (California Studies in the History of Science: No. 11). 1993. 50.00 (*0-520-08110-2*) U CA Pr.
Rocke, David M., jt. auth. see Downs, George W.
Rocke, Herman H. Check Your Panoply. 240p. 1977. pap. text ed. 6.00 (*0-910424-71-3*) Concordant.
Rockefeller, Edwin S. Antitrust Questions & Answers. LC 73-93042. 703p. reprint ed. pap. 180.00 (*0-8357-5643-2*, 2024302) Bks Demand.
Rockefeller, H. O., ed. Rockefeller, Vol. II: Transactions of the Rockefeller Family Assoc. (Illus.). 338p. 1992. reprint ed. lib. bdg. 56.50 (*0-8328-2203-5*); reprint ed. pap. 46.50 (*0-8328-2204-3*) Higginson Bk Co.
Rockefeller, John D. Random Reminiscences of Men & Events. (Illus.). 124p. 1984. 12.95 (*0-912882-58-1*) Sleepy Hollow.
— Random Reminiscences of Men and Events. 188p. Date not set. 24.95 (*0-9931133-1-1*, Busn Class) Pac Pub Grp.
— Random Reminiscences of Men & Events. LC 73-2533. (Big Business; Economic Power in a Free Society Ser.). 1979. reprint ed. 22.95 (*0-405-05111-5*) Ayer.
— Random Reminiscences of Men & Events. 195p. reprint ed. 25.00 (*0-931133-11-4*, Busn Class) Pac Pub Grp.
Rockefeller, John D., Jr. & Albright, Horace M. Worthwhile Places: The Correspondence of John D. Rockefeller Jr. & Horace M. Albright. Ernst, Joseph W., ed. LC 91-70235. 354p. 1991. pap. 19.95 (*0-8232-1330-7*) Fordham.
Rockefeller, R. D. Nobel Prize Winning Investment Strategies. 1992. pap. 12.95 (*0-9632572-1-8*) MDMI Int Pubns.
Rockefeller, R. D. & Chen, Gerald H. World Famous Investors Advice for 1993-2000: The Greatest Investors of All Time & Their Favorite Stocks, Bonds, Mutual Funds, Income & New Strategies for 1993-2000. Folder, M. Michael, ed. LC 93-77404. 96p. (YA). (gr. 9 up). 1993. pap. 12.95 (*0-9632572-2-6*) MDMI Int Pubns.
Rockefeller, Ruth, ed. see Murdock, Dick.
Rockefeller, Stephen C., jt. ed. see Lopez, Donald S., Jr.
Rockefeller, Steven C. John Dewey: Religious Faith & Democratic Humanism. 584p. 1991. text ed. 50.00 (*0-231-07348-8*) Col U Pr.
Rockefeller, Steven C. & Elder, John C. Spirit & Nature: Visions of Interdependence. (Illus.). 94p. (Orig.). 1990. pap. 15.00 (*0-9625262-1-5*) Middlebury Coll Mus.
Rockefeller, Steven C. & Elder, John C., eds. Spirit & Nature: Why the Environment Is a Religious Issue - an Interfaith Dialogue. LC 91-37116. (Illus.). 240p. 1992. pap. 16.00 (*0-8070-7709-7*) Beacon Pr.
Rocker, I. & Laurence, K. M., eds. Fetoscopy. 336p. 1981. 123.75 (*0-444-80337-8*) Elsevier.
Rocker, Rudolf. Anarchism & Anarcho-Syndicalism. rev. ed. (Anarchist Classics Ser.). 48p. 1988. reprint ed. pap. 3.50 (*0-900384-45-X*) Left Bank.
— Anarcho-Syndicalism. 1972. 250.00 (*0-87968-038-5*) Gordon Pr.
— Anarcho-Syndicalism. 93p. (Orig.). (C). 1993. pap. 5.95 (*0-948984-05-8*, Pub. by Phoenix Pr UK) AK Pr Dist.
— Bolshevism & Anarchism. 1976. lib. bdg. 250.00 (*0-8490-1522-7*) Gordon Pr.
— Nationalism & Culture. Chase, Ray E., tr. LC 78-5960. 1978. 20.00 (*0-9602574-1-1*) M E Coughlin.
— Nationalism & Culture. 1973. 79.95 (*0-87700-076-X*) Revisionist Pr.
— Pioneers of American Freedom. 1971. 250.00 (*0-87700-077-8*) Revisionist Pr.
— The Six. 1972. 69.95 (*0-87700-079-4*) Revisionist Pr.
— Socialism & State. 1972. 250.00 (*0-8490-1069-1*) Gordon Pr.
— Spain: Tragedy & Truth. 1972. 250.00 (*0-8490-1098-5*) Gordon Pr.
Rocker, Rudolph. Anarcho-Syndicalism. 166p. (C). 1989. pap. text ed. 19.00 (*0-85305-077-5*, Pub. by Pluto Pr UK); pap. text ed. 16.95 (*0-685-68138-6*, Pub. by Pluto Pr UK) Westview.
Rocker, Willard. Marriages & Obituaries from the Macon Messenger, 1818-1865. 588p. 1988. 47.50 (*0-89308-340-2*, GA 65) Southern Hist Pr.
Rockers, Dolore & Pierre, Kenneth J. Shared Ministry: An Integrated Approach to Leadership & Service. (Illus.). 120p. (Orig.). 1984. ring bd. 18.95 (*0-88489-158-5*) St Marys.
Rockett, A. M. & Szusz, P. Continued Fractions. 200p. 1992. text ed. 55.00 (*981-02-1047-7*); pap. text ed. 25.00 (*981-02-1052-3*) World Scientific Pub.
***Rockett, James M. & Ungles, Keith D.** Bank Sales of Nondeposit Investment Products: A Compliance Guide. 600p. (Orig.). 1994. pap. 130.00 (*0-8366-0028-2*) Clark Boardman Callaghan.
Rockett, Kevin, et al. Cinema & Ireland. (Irish Studies). (Illus.). 288p. (C). 1988. text ed. 39.95x (*0-8156-2424-7*) Syracuse U Pr.
— Cinema & Ireland. LC 87-7121. (Irish Studies). (Illus.). 288p. 1989. reprint ed. pap. text ed. 15.95 (*0-8156-2459-X*) Syracuse U Pr.
Rockett, Rocky L. Ethnic Nationalities in the Soviet Union: Sociological Perspectives on an Historical Problem. LC 81-304. 190p. 1981. text ed. 45.00 (*0-275-90711-2*, C0711, Praeger Pubs) Greenwood.
Rockett, Will H. Devouring Whirlwind: Terror & Transcendence in the Cinema of Cruelty. LC 88-10254. (Contributions to the Study of Popular Culture Ser.: No. 21). 221p. 1988. text ed. 49.95 (*0-313-25998-4*, RCY/, Greenwood Pr) Greenwood.
***Rockey, Clancy O.** Abused. Jacob, Karen L., ed. 240p. 1995. per., pap. text ed. 14.95 (*0-936417-50-1*) Axelrod Pub.
Rockey, Edward H. Communicating in Organizations. (Illus.). 168p. 1984. reprint ed. pap. text ed. 32.50 (*0-8191-3751-0*) U Pr of Amer.
Rockey, J. L. & Bancroft, R. J. History of Clermont County, Ohio. (Illus.). 557p. 1993. reprint ed. lib. bdg. 57.00 (*0-8328-3614-1*) Higginson Bk Co.
Rockey, K. C. & Hill, H. V., eds. Thin Walled Steel Structures: Their Design & Use in Buildings. 608p. 1969. text ed. 406.00 (*0-677-61270-2*) Gordon & Breach.
***Rockey, Linda D. & Kitzinger, Beth.** Creative Caring: Support & Encouragement Ideas to Help Others Through Life's Challenges. LC 95-68237. 160p. 1995. pap. 6.95 (*0-9646115-0-3*) Support Pubns.
Rockfeller, Steven C. John Dewey: Religious Faith & Democratic Humanism. LC 90-28619. 683p. 1994. pap. 19.50 (*0-231-07349-6*) Col U Pr.
Rockford, Doris E. Drug Effects on the Fetus: Medical Research Subject Analysis with Bibliography. LC 84-45735. 150p. 1987. 39.50 (*0-88164-248-7*); pap. 34.50 (*0-88164-249-5*) ABBE Pubs Assn.
— Hospitalization: Index of Modern Information. LC 88-47569. 150p. 1988. 39.50 (*0-88164-786-1*); pap. 34.50 (*0-88164-787-X*) ABBE Pubs Assn.
— Human Pregnancy Complications: Medical Scientific Subject Analysis & Research Index with Bibliography. LC 83-71671. 150p. 1985. 37.50 (*0-88164-054-9*); pap. 34.50 (*0-88164-055-7*) ABBE Pubs Assn.
— Intra-Uterine Devices: Medical Subject Index with Research Bibliography. 150p. 1987. 37.50 (*0-88164-502-8*); pap. 34.50 (*0-88164-503-6*) ABBE Pubs Assn.
Rockford, T. Jay & Parr, Daniel. T. Jay's Log: The Last Voyage of the Frisco Felucca. 1994. 12.95 (*0-8062-4971-4*) Carlton.
Rockhill, Kathleen. Academic Excellence Versus Public Service: The Development of Adult Higher Education in California. 320p. 1983. 34.95 (*0-87855-491-2*) Transaction Pubs.
Rockhill, William W. The Land of the Lamas: Notes of a Journey Through China, Mongolia & Tibet. (C). 1988. reprint ed. 32.00 (*81-206-0354-0*, Pub. by Asian Educ Servs II) S Asia.
Rockhill, William W., ed. The Journey of William of Rubruck to the Eastern Parts of the World, 1253-55: With Two Accounts of the Earlier Journey of John of Pian de Carpine. (Hakluyt Society Works Ser.: No. 2, Vol. 4). 1969. reprint ed. 48.00 (*0-8115-0327-5*) Periodicals Srv.
Rockin, Donna, jt. auth. see Rockin, Jan.
Rockin, Jan & Rockin, Donna. The Determined Dieter's Diary. (Illus.). 78p. (Orig.). 1985. pap. 3.25 (*0-9616081-0-2*) Rockin Enter.
Rockis, G. Residential Wiring. (Illus.). 260p. 1994. 20.96 (*0-8269-1652-X*) Am Technical.
— Solid State Fundamentals for Electricians. 2nd ed. LC 93-5537. (Illus.). 232p. 1993. 28.96 (*0-8269-1631-7*) Am Technical.
Rockis, G. & Mazur, G. A. Electrical Motor Controls: Automated Industrial Systems. 3rd ed. LC 92-41113. 526p. 1992. 36.96 (*0-8269-1666-X*) Am Technical.
Rockland & Beuchat. Water Activity: Theory & Applications to Food. (IFT Basic Symposium Ser.: Vol. 2). 424p. 1987. 99.75 (*0-8247-7759-X*) Dekker.
Rockland, K. S., jt. ed. see Peters, A.
Rockland, Lawrence H. Supportive Therapy: A Psychodynamic Approach. LC 89-42801. 320p. (C). 1989. text ed. 32.00 (*0-465-08337-4*) Basic.
Rockland, Lawrence H., et al. Supportive Therapy for Borderline Patients: A Psychodynamic Approach. LC 92-1538. (Diagnosis & Treatment of Mental Illness Ser.). 308p. 1992. lib. bdg. 34.95 (*0-89862-182-8*) Guilford Pr.
Rockland, Louis B. & Stewart, George F., eds. Water Activity: Influences on Food Quality: Proceedings of Second International Symposium on Properties of Water Affecting Food Quality. LC 79-26632. 1981. text ed. 158.00 (*0-12-591350-8*) Acad Pr.
Rockland, Michael. Snowshoeing: Adventures in New York City, New Jersey, & Philadelphia. LC 94-10145. 165p. (C). 1994. 21.95 (*0-8135-2115-7*) Rutgers U Pr.
Rockland, Michael A. A Bliss Case. LC 89-36392. 176p. (Orig.). (C). 1989. pap. 9.95 (*0-918273-55-2*) Coffee Hse.
Rockland, Michael A., jt. auth. see Gillespie, Angus K.
Rockland, Michael A., tr. see Sarmiento, Domingo F.
Rockler, Julia, jt. auth. see Fletcher, Tana.
Rockliff, B. J. Crackerjack. large type ed. (General Fiction Ser.). 432p. 1992. 21.95 (*0-7089-2701-7*) Ulverscroft.
Rockliff, V. Saturday Bloody Saturday. 1987. 39.00 (*0-7223-2097-3*, Pub. by A H S Ltd UK) St Mut.
Rockliffe, N. J., jt. ed. see Castro, I. P.
Rocklin. Grandmaman the Hockey Fan. (J). 1996. 15.95 (*0-8050-2322-4*) H Holt & Co.
— Histamine & H2 Antagonists in Inflammation & Immunodeficiency. (Allergic Disease & Therapy Ser.: Vol. 1). 376p. 1990. 135.00 (*0-8247-8280-1*) Dekker.
Rocklin, jt. auth. see Walton.
***Rocklin, J.** Discovering Martha. 1994. pap. 2.99 (*0-517-13319-9*) Random.
***Rocklin, Joanne.** How Much Is That Guinea Pig in the Window? LC 95-13231. (Hello Math Reader Ser.: Level 4). (Illus.). (J). 1995. write for info. (*0-590-22716-5*, Cartwheel) Scholastic Inc.
— Jace the Ace. LC 90-34095. (Illus.). 112p. (J). (gr. 2-6). 1990. text ed. 13.95 (*0-02-777445-7*, Mac Bks Young Read) S&S Childrens.
— Sonia Begonia. 112p. (J). (gr. 3-7). 1987. pap. 2.50 (*0-380-70307-6*, Camelot) Avon.
— Three Smart Pals. (Hello Reader! Ser.). (Illus.). 48p. (J). (ps-4). 1994. pap. 3.50 (*0-590-47431-6*, Cartwheel) Scholastic Inc.
Rocklin, Joanne, jt. auth. see Levinson, Nancy S.
Rockmaker, Gordon & Adams, Susan B. Beepers: Twenty-One Electronics Projects for the Timex-Sinclair 1000 & 1500. 112p. 1984. pap. text ed. 8.95 (*0-685-09096-5*) McGraw.
Rockmaker, Gordon, jt. auth. see Adams, J.
Rockmaker, Gordon, jt. auth. see Adams, Susan B.
Rockman, Bert A., jt. ed. see Linden, Ronald H.
Rockman, Bert A., jt. ed. see Weaver, R. Kent.
Rockman, Richard G., Jr. Rainbow Man. Ouellette, Dean C., ed. (Illus.). 200p. (Orig.). 1991. pap. 9.95 (*0-9630916-0-3*) R G Rockman.
— Rainbow Man. rev. ed. Ouellette, Dean C., ed. (Illus.). 201p. (Orig.). 1992. pap. 9.95 (*0-9630916-1-1*) R G Rockman.
Rockman, Robert. Monarch Notes on Shaw's Plays. pap. 4.25 (*0-671-00646-0*, Arco Test) P-H Gen Ref & Trav.
Rockmore, Tom. Before & after Hegel: A Historical Introduction to Hegel's Thought. LC 93-9719. 1993. 38.00 (*0-520-08205-2*); pap. 14.00 (*0-520-08206-0*) U CA Pr.
— Habermas on Historical Materialism. LC 88-45449. (Studies in Phenomenology & Existential Philosophy). 216p. 1989. 35.00 (*0-253-32709-1*); pap. 14.95 (*0-253-20504-2*, MB-504) Ind U Pr.
— Hegel's Circular Epistemology. LC 85-45037. (Studies in Phenomenology & Existential Philosophy). 220p. (C). 1986. 25.00 (*0-253-32713-X*) Ind U Pr.
— Heidegger & French Philosophy: Humanism, Antihumanism, & Being. LC 93-47961. 304p. 1994. 59.95x (*0-415-11180-3*, B4728, Routledge NY); pap. 18.95 (*0-415-11181-1*, B4732, Routledge NY) Routledge.
— Irrationalism: Lukacs & the Marxist View of Reason. (C). 1991. 44.95 (*0-87722-867-1*) Temple U Pr.
— On Hegel's Epistemology & Contemporary Philosophy. 320p. (C). 1996. text ed. 60.00 (*0-391-03918-0*) Humanities.
— On Heidegger's Nazism & Philosophy. LC 91-22072. (C). 1992. 45.00 (*0-520-07711-3*) U CA Pr.
Rockmore, Tom, ed. Lukacs Today. (C). 1988. lib. bdg. 100.50 (*90-277-2661-2*) Kluwer Ac.
Rockmore, Tom & Margolis, Joseph, eds. The Heidegger Case: On Philosophy & Ethics. 500p. (C). 1992. 49.95 (*0-87722-907-4*); pap. 29.95 (*0-87722-908-2*) Temple U Pr.
Rockmore, Tom & Singer, Beth J., eds. Antifoundationalism Old & New. (C). 1991. 44.95 (*0-87722-881-7*) Temple U Pr.
Rockmore, Tom, jt. ed. see Breazeale, Daniel.
Rockmore, Tom, ed. see Farias, Victor.
Rockmuller, Seth. School Law in New York State: A Manual for Parents. LC 93-77622. 152p. (Orig.). 1993. pap. 12.95 (*0-9636096-4-5*) Longview NY.
Rockne, Jon, tr. see Alefeld, Gotz & Herzberger, Jurgen.
Rockne, Knute. The Four Winners. 1946. 15.00 (*0-8159-5509-X*) Devin.
Rockne, Knute, jt. auth. see Meanwell, Ernest.
Rockner, M. A Dirichlet Problem for Distributions & Specifications for Random Fields. LC 84-29009. (Memoirs of the AMS Ser.: No. 54/324). 76p. 1988. reprint ed. pap. text ed. 18.00 (*0-8218-2325-6*, MEMO 54/324) Am Math.
Rockner, Michael & Ma, Zhi-Ming. Introduction to the Theory of (Non-Symmetric) Dirichlet Forms. LC 92-28120. (Universitext Ser.). 1992. 39.00 (*0-387-55848-9*) Spr-Verlag.
Rockness, Howard D., jt. auth. see Zmud, Robert W.
Rockoff, Hugh. Drastic Measures: A History of Wage & Price Controls in the United States. LC 83-21019. (Studies in Economic History & Policy: The United States in the Twentieth Century). 1984. 49.95 (*0-521-24496-X*) Cambridge U Pr.
— The Free Banking Era: A Re-Examination. LC 75-2593. (Dissertations in American Economic History Ser.). (Illus.). 1979. 21.95 (*0-405-07215-5*) Ayer.
— Price Controls. 400p. 1992. 112.95 (*1-85278-431-8*, Pub. by E Elgar Pub UK) Ashgate Pub Co.
— The Sinews of War: Essays on the Economic History of World War II. Mills, Geoffrey T., ed. LC 92-26832. (Illus.). 320p. 1993. text ed. 42.95 (*0-8138-1312-3*) Iowa St U Pr.
Rockoff, Hugh, jt. ed. see Goldin, Claudia D.
Rockoff, Hugh, jt. auth. see Walton, Gary M.
Rockowitz, et al. Barron's Pass Key to the GED. (Barron's Pass Key Ser.). 1992. pap. 6.95 (*0-8120-1381-6*) Barron.
***Rockowitz, Murray, et al.** How to Prepare for the GED High School Equivalency Examination. 9th ed. LC 94-35332. 1995. write for info. (*0-8120-9196-5*) Barron.
— How to Prepare for the High School Equivalency Examination: GED. 8th ed. 900p. 1990. pap. 11.95 (*0-8120-4397-9*) Barron.
Rockport - Allworth Editions Staff. Computer Graphics: The Best of Computer Art & Design. (Illus.). 160p. 1992. pap. 29.99 (*1-56496-015-3*, 30395) Rockport Pubs.
— Graphic Design America: The Top U. S. & Canadian Design Firms. (Illus.). 248p. 1993. 49.99 (*1-56496-030-7*, 30543) Rockport Pubs.
— Signs & Spaces: International Survey of the Leading Environmental Design Firms. (Illus.). 200p. 1993. 49.99 (*1-56496-031-5*, 30509) Rockport Pubs.
Rockport Book Staff. Best of Business Card Design. 160p. 1994. 34.99 (*1-56496-045-5*, 30583) Rockport Pubs.

R

An Asterisk (*) at the beginning of an entry indicates that the title is appearing in BIP for the first time.

— Guild 9: The Architect's Source of Artists & Artisans. (Illus.). 320p. 1994. 34.99 (*1-56496-094-3*, 30604) Rockport Pubs.
— International Brand Packaging Awards 2 No. 2. 1995. 39. 99 (*1-56496-154-0*) Rockport Pubs.
— Label Design 4: The Best New U. S. & International Design. (Illus.). 240p. 1994. 49.99 (*1-56496-069-2*, 30600) Rockport Pubs.
— 3-Dimensional Illustration Awars Annual IV. (Illus.). 256p. 1993. 59.99 (*1-56496-058-7*, 30556) Rockport Pubs.
Rockport Press Staff. Best of Colored Pencil. (Illus.). 160p. 1993. 24.99 (*1-56496-049-8*, 30503) Rockport Pubs.
***Rockport Publishers Staff.** Best Magazine Publication Design No. 29. 1995. 49.99 (*1-56496-152-4*) Rockport Pubs.
— Complete Process Color Finder. 1995. 24.99 (*1-56496-134-6*) Rockport Pubs.
— Three-Dimensional Illustrator's Awards Annual, Vol. 3. (Illus.). 256p. 1993. 59.99 (*1-56496-024-2*, 30456) Rockport Pubs.
Rockport Publishing. Sourcebook of Craft Artists. 80p. 1994. pap. 19.99 (*1-56496-131-1*) Rockport Pubs.
Rockport Publsihers Editors. The Best of Brochure Design. (Illus.). 256p. 1992. 49.99 (*1-56496-004-8*, 30455) Rockport Pubs.
Rocks, David T. W. C. Fields - an Annotated Guide: Chronology, Bibliographies, Discography, Filmographies, Press Books, Cigarette Cards, Film Clips & Impersonators. LC 92-56688. (Illus.). 143p. 1993. lib. bdg. 27.50 (*0-89950-794-8*) McFarland & Co.
Rockstein, Morris, ed. Biochemistry of Insects. LC 77-1121. 1978. text ed. 118.00 (*0-12-591640-X*) Acad Pr.
Rockstein, Morris & Sussman, Marvin. Biology of Aging. 203p. (C). 1979. pap. 18.95 (*0-534-00687-6*) Intl Thomson.
Rockswold, E. Palmer. Per-Immigrant & Pioneer. 1982. 13. 95 (*0-934860-19-X*); pap. 6.95 (*0-934860-22-X*) Adventure Pubns.
***Rockwell.** El Toro Pinto: And Other Songs in Spanish. (J). 1995. pap. 5.95 (*0-689-71880-2*, Aladdin Paperbacks) S&S Childrens.
Rockwell & Hurlburt. Educating the Horse. (Illus.). 227p. 1984. pap. 15.00 (*0-87556-355-4*) Saifer.
Rockwell, A. D., ed. see Beard, George M.
Rockwell, Anne. Apples & Pumpkins. LC 88-22628. (Illus.). 24p. (J). (ps-1). 1989. text ed. 13.95 (*0-02-777270-5*, Mac Bks Young Read) S&S Childrens.
— Apples & Pumpkins. LC 94-629. (Illus.). 24p. (J). (ps-1). 1994. pap. 3.95 (*0-689-71861-6*, Aladdin Paperbacks) S&S Childrens.
— At the Beach. LC 86-2943. (Illus.). 24p. (J). (ps-1). 1987. text ed. 13.95 (*0-02-777940-8*, Mac Bks Young Read) S&S Childrens.
— At the Beach. LC 90-45620. (Illus.). 24p. (J). (ps-1). 1991. reprint ed. pap. 3.95 (*0-689-71494-7*, Aladdin Paperbacks) S&S Childrens.
— Bear Child's Book of Special Days. LC 89-1633. (Illus.). 32p. (J). (ps-1). 1989. 12.95 (*0-525-44508-0*, DCB) Dutton Child Bks.
— Bikes. LC 86-19923. (Illus.). 24p. (J). (ps-1). 1991. pap. 3.95 (*0-525-44736-9*, Puffin) Puffin Bks.
— Boats. (Illus.). 24p. (J). 1993. pap. 4.99 (*0-14-054988-9*, Puff Unicorn) Puffin Bks.
— Cars. LC 83-14080. (Illus.). 24p. (J). (ps-1). 1984. 13.99 (*0-525-44079-8*, DCB) Dutton Child Bks.
— Cars. LC 83-14080. (Unicorn Paperbacks Ser.). (Illus.). 24p. (J). (ps-1). 1986. pap. 3.95 (*0-525-44241-3*, DCB) Dutton Child Bks.
— Cars. (J). 1992. pap. 4.99 (*0-14-054741-X*, Puff Unicorn) Puffin Bks.
— Ducklings & Polliwogs. LC 93-16600. (Illus.). 32p. (J). (ps-2). 1994. text ed. 14.95 (*0-02-777452-X*, Mac Bks Young Read) S&S Childrens.
— The Emergency Room. LC 84-20161. (Illus.). 24p. (J). (ps-2). 1985. lib. bdg. 13.95 (*0-02-777300-0*, Mac Bks Young Read) S&S Childrens.
— Fire Engines. LC 86-4464. 24p. (J). (ps-1). 1986. 13.99 (*0-525-44259-6*, DCB) Dutton Child Bks.
— Fire Engines. (Illus.). 24p. (J). (ps-1). 1993. pap. 4.99 (*0-14-055250-2*, Puff Unicorn) Puffin Bks.
— First Comes Spring. LC 84-45331. (Illus.). 32p. (J). (ps-1). 1991. pap. 4.95 (*0-06-107412-8*) HarpC Child Bks.
— Hugo at the Park. LC 89-2417. (Illus.). 32p. (J). (ps-k). 1990. text ed. 13.95 (*0-02-777301-9*, Mac Bks Young Read) S&S Childrens.
— Mr. Panda's Painting. LC 92-9220. (Illus.). 32p. (J). (ps-1). 1993. text ed. 14.95 (*0-02-777451-1*, Mac Bks Young Read) S&S Childrens.
— My Spring Robin. LC 88-13333. (Illus.). 24p. (J). (ps-1). 1989. text ed. 13.95 (*0-02-777611-5*, Mac Bks Young Read) S&S Childrens.
— No! No! No! (Illus.). (J). (ps-1). 1995. 14.00 (*0-02-777782-0*, Mac Bks Young Read) S&S Childrens.
— On Our Vacation. LC 88-29996. (Illus.). 32p. (J). (ps-1). 1989. 12.95 (*0-525-44487-4*, DCB) Dutton Child Bks.
— On Our Vacation. (Illus.). 32p. (J). (ps-1). 1994. pap. 4.50 (*0-14-055287-1*, Puff Unicorn) Puffin Bks.
— The One-Eyed Giant & Other Monsters from the Greek Myths. (Illus.). 32p. (J). 1996. write for info. (*0-688-13809-8*); lib. bdg. write for info. (*0-688-13810-1*) Greenwillow.
— Our Garage Sale. LC 80-16704. (Illus.). 24p. (J). (ps-1). 1984. 10.25 (*0-688-80278-8*); lib. bdg. 10.88 (*0-688-84278-X*) Greenwillow.
— Our Yard Is Full of Birds. LC 90-30436. (Illus.). 32p. (J). (ps-2). 1992. text ed. 13.95 (*0-02-777273-X*, Mac Bks Young Read) S&S Childrens.
— Planes. LC 84-13732. (Illus.). 24p. (J). (ps-1). 1985. 13.99 (*0-525-44159-X*, DCB) Dutton Child Bks.
— Planes. (J). 1993. pap. 4.99 (*0-14-054782-7*, Puff Unicorn) Puffin Bks.
— Pots & Pans. LC 91-4976. (Illus.). 32p. (J). (ps-1). 1993. text ed. 13.95 (*0-02-777631-X*, Mac Bks Young Read) S&S Childrens.
— The Robber Baby: Stories from the Greek Myths. LC 90-39560. (Illus.). 80p. (J). (gr. k up). 1994. 18.00 (*0-688-09740-5*); lib. bdg. 17.93 (*0-688-09741-3*) Greenwillow.
— Root-a-Toot-Toot. LC 90-46747. (Illus.). 24p. (J). (ps-1). 1991. text ed. 12.95 (*0-02-777272-1*, Mac Bks Young Read) S&S Childrens.
— The Storm. LC 93-40976. (Illus.). 32p. (J). (ps-3). 1994. 15.95 (*0-7868-0017-8*); lib. bdg. 15.89 (*0-7868-2013-6*) Hyprn Child.
— Sweet Potato Pie. LC 94-34990. (Early Step into Reading Ser.). (J). 1995. 3.99 (*0-679-86440-7*) Random.
— Sweet Potato Pie. LC 94-34990. (Step into Reading Ser.: No. 2). (J). 1995. lib. bdg. 9.99 (*0-679-96440-1*) Random.
— Things That Go. LC 86-6199. (Unicorn Paperback Ser.). (Illus.). 24p. (J). (ps-1). 1991. pap. 3.95 (*0-525-44703-2*, Puffin) Puffin Bks.
— Things to Play With. (Illus.). 24p. (J). (ps-1). 1994. pap. 3.99 (*0-14-050308-0*, Puff Unicorn) Puffin Bks.
— Toolbox. LC 89-34818. (Illus.). 24p. (J). (ps-1). 1990. pap. 3.95 (*0-689-71382-7*, Aladdin Paperbacks) S&S Childrens.
— Trains. LC 87-22180. (Illus.). 24p. (J). (ps-1). 1988. 13.99 (*0-525-44377-0*, 01063-320, DCB) Dutton Child Bks.
— Trains. (J). 1993. pap. 4.99 (*0-14-054979-X*, Puff Unicorn) Puffin Bks.
— Trucks. LC 84-1556. (Unicorn Paperbacks Ser.). (Illus.). 24p. (J). (ps-1). 1988. pap. 3.95 (*0-525-44432-7*, DCB) Dutton Child Bks.
— Trucks. (J). (ps-3). 1992. pap. 4.99 (*0-14-054790-8*) Viking Child Bks.
— The Way to Captain Yankee's. LC 92-44644. (Illus.). 32p. (J). (ps-2). 1994. text ed. 13.95 (*0-02-777271-3*, Mac Bks Young Read) S&S Childrens.
— What We Like. LC 91-4990. (Illus.). 24p. (J). (ps-1). 1992. text ed. 13.95 (*0-02-777274-8*, Mac Bks Young Read) S&S Childrens.
— When Hugo Went to School. LC 89-13211. (Illus.). 32p. (J). (ps-1). 1991. text ed. 13.95 (*0-02-777305-1*, Mac Bks Young Read) S&S Childrens.
— Willy Can Count. (Illus.). 32p. (J). (ps). 1989. 13.95 (*1-55970-013-0*) Arcade Pub Inc.
Rockwell, Anne, illus. & teller. Puss in Boots & Other Stories. LC 87-14976. 96p. (J). (gr. k-4). 1988. text ed. 16.95 (*0-02-777781-2*, Mac Bks Young Read) S&S Childrens.
Rockwell, Anne & Brion, David. Space Vehicles. LC 93-43594. (Illus.). 24p. (J). (ps-1). 1994. 13.99 (*0-525-45270-2*, DCB) Dutton Child Bks.
Rockwell, Anne & Rockwell, Harlow. The First Snowfall. LC 86-23712. (Illus.). 24p. (J). (ps-1). 1987. text ed. 13. 95 (*0-02-777770-7*, Mac Bks Young Read) S&S Childrens.
— The First Snowfall. LC 91-41247. (Illus.). 24p. (J). (ps-1). 1992. reprint ed. pap. 3.95 (*0-689-71614-1*, Aladdin Paperbacks) S&S Childrens.
— Happy Birthday to Me. LC 81-3738. (My World Ser.). (Illus.). 24p. (J). (ps-k). 1981. text ed. 10.95 (*0-02-777680-8*, Mac Bks Young Read) S&S Childrens.
— How My Garden Grew. LC 81-17145. (My World Ser.). (Illus.). 24p. (J). (ps-k). 1982. text ed. 10.95 (*0-02-777660-3*, Mac Bks Young Read) S&S Childrens.
— I Play in My Room. LC 81-2634. (My World Ser.). (Illus.). 24p. (J). (ps-k). 1981. text ed. 10.95 (*0-02-777670-0*, Mac Bks Young Read) S&S Childrens.
— Machines. LC 72-185149. (Illus.). 24p. (J). (ps-2). 1972. text ed. 13.95 (*0-02-777520-8*, Mac Bks Young Read) S&S Childrens.
— My Baby-Sitter. LC 85-5000. (My World Ser.). (Illus.). 24p. (J). (ps-k). 1985. text ed. 9.95 (*0-02-777780-4*, Mac Bks Young Read) S&S Childrens.
— Sick in Bed. LC 81-15637. (My World Ser.). (Illus.). 24p. (J). (ps-k). 1982. text ed. 10.95 (*0-02-777730-8*, Mac Bks Young Read) S&S Childrens.
— Toolbox. LC 72-119836. (Illus.). 24p. (J). (ps-2). 1971. lib. bdg. 13.95 (*0-02-777540-2*, Mac Bks Young Read) S&S Childrens.
***Rockwell, Anne F.** I Fly. LC 94-29278. (Illus.). (J). 1996. write for info. (*0-517-59683-0*) Crown Bks Yng Read.
***Rockwell, Anne F., ed.** The Acorn Tree & Other Folktales. LC 94-29277. (Illus.). 40p. (J). (gr. 4 up). 1995. 16.00 (*0-688-10746-X*); lib. bdg. 15.93 (*0-688-13723-7*) Greenwillow.
Rockwell, Bart. The World's Strangest Baseball Stories. LC 92-10120. (Illus.). 96p. (J). (gr. 3-7). 1992. lib. bdg. 9.89 (*0-8167-2933-6*); pap. text ed. 2.95 (*0-8167-2850-X*) Troll Assocs.
— World's Strangest Basketball Stories. LC 92-25676. (J). 1992. lib. bdg. 9.89 (*0-8167-2935-2*); pap. 2.95 (*0-8167-2852-6*) Troll Assocs.
— The World's Strangest Football Stories. LC 92-10121. (Illus.). 96p. (J). (gr. 3-7). 1992. lib. bdg. 9.89 (*0-8167-2934-4*); pap. text ed. 2.95 (*0-8167-2851-8*) Troll Assocs.
— World's Strangest Hockey Stories. LC 92-25992. (Illus.). 96p. (J). (gr. 3-7). 1992. lib. bdg. 9.89 (*0-8167-2936-0*); pap. text ed. 2.95 (*0-8167-2853-4*) Troll Assocs.
Rockwell, Charles. The Catskill Mountains & the Region Around. 1973. reprint ed. 15.95 (*0-910746-15-X*, TCM01) Hope Farm.
— Catskill Mountains & the Region Around. 351p. 1993. reprint ed. lib. bdg. 89.00 (*0-7812-5134-6*) Rprt Serv.
Rockwell, Colleen. I Wuz Absent Because. 1993. pap. 7.95 (*0-533-10675-3*) Vantage.
Rockwell, Coralie. Kagok: A Traditional Korean Vocal Form. LC 72-87568. (D (Monographs): No. 3). (Illus.). 302p. (Orig.). (C). 1972. pap. text ed. 9.50 (*0-913360-05-8*) Asian Music Pub.
Rockwell, David. Financing Residential Real Estate. 10th ed. (Illus.). 392p. 1994. pap. 32.95 (*0-915799-95-2*) Rockwell WA.
— Giving Voice to Bear. Date not set. pap. 9.99 (*0-517-10801-1*) Random Hse Value.
— Giving Voice to Bear: Native American Indian Myths, Images, & Rituals of the Bear. LC 92-61908. (Illus.). 224p. 1993. pap. 14.95 (*1-879373-48-3*) R Rinehart.
— Giving Voice to Bear: North American Myths, Rituals, & Images of the Bear. (Illus.). 242p. 1991. 25.00 (*0-911797-97-1*) R Rinehart.
— Glacier National Park: A Natural History Guide. LC 95-6058. (National Parks Natural History Ser.). (Illus.). 240p. 1995. pap. 16.95 (*0-395-69981-9*) HM.
***Rockwell, David L., et al.** Oregon Real Estate Law. 4th ed. (Illus.). 245p. (Orig.). 1995. pap. 32.95 (*0-915799-96-0*) Rockwell WA.
— Oregon Real Estate Practices. 4th ed. (Illus.). 296p. (Orig.). 1995. pap. 32.95 (*0-915799-97-9*) Rockwell WA.
— Washington Real Estate Fundamentals. 7th ed. (Illus.). 530p. 1993. pap. 32.95 (*0-915799-92-8*) Rockwell WA.
Rockwell, Gray. A Century of Enterprise: St. Louis, 1894-1994. O'Connor, Candace & Schreiner, Lee A., eds. (Illus.). 135p. (Orig.). 1993. pap. 14.95 (*1-883982-02-2*) MO Hist Soc.
Rockwell, Harlow. I Did It. LC 86-22146. (Ready-to-Read Ser.). (Illus.). 64p. (J). (gr. 1-3). 1987. reprint ed. pap. 3.95 (*0-689-71126-3*, Aladdin Paperbacks) S&S Childrens.
— Look at This. LC 87-1033. (Ready-to-Read Ser.). (Illus.). 64p. (J). (gr. 1-4). 1987. reprint ed. pap. 3.95 (*0-689-71165-4*, Aladdin Paperbacks) S&S Childrens.
— My Dentist. LC 75-6974. (Illus.). 32p. (J). (ps-3). 1975. 16.00 (*0-688-80011-4*); lib. bdg. 15.93 (*0-688-84004-3*) Greenwillow.
— My Dentist. LC 75-6974. (Illus.). 32p. (J). (ps up). 1987. pap. 4.95 (*0-688-07040-X*, Mulberry) Morrow.
— My Doctor. LC 72-92442. (Illus.). 24p. (J). (ps-1). 1973. text ed. 13.95 (*0-02-777480-5*, Mac Bks Young Read) S&S Childrens.
— My Doctor. LC 91-27163. (Illus.). 24p. (J). (ps-2). 1992. reprint ed. pap. 3.95 (*0-689-71606-0*, Aladdin Paperbacks) S&S Childrens.
— My Kitchen. LC 79-15929. (Illus.). 24p. (J). (ps-2). 1980. 13.95 (*0-688-80236-2*); lib. bdg. 15.88 (*0-688-84236-4*) Greenwillow.
— My Nursery School. LC 75-25871. (Illus.). 32p. (J). (ps up). 1990. reprint ed. pap. 3.95 (*0-688-09351-5*, Mulberry) Morrow.
Rockwell, Harlow, jt. auth. see Rockwell, Anne.
Rockwell, James R., Jr., jt. auth. see Goldman, Leon.
Rockwell, Jane. All about Ponds. LC 83-4835. (Question & Answer Bks.). (Illus.). 32p. (J). (gr. 3-6). 1984. lib. bdg. 10.59 (*0-89375-971-6*); pap. text ed. 2.95 (*0-89375-972-4*) Troll Assocs.
Rockwell, Jeanne & Noonan, Thomas E., eds. Good Company: Poets at Michigan. LC 77-91403. 1978. 9.00 (*0-9602934-0-X*) Noon Rock.
Rockwell, Jeanne, ed. see Noonan, Thomas E.
Rockwell, Jerry. The American Dulcimer. LC 85-754651. (Illus.). 52p. (Orig.). 1985. pap. text ed. 5.95 (*0-9614939-2-5*) Backyard Music.
Rockwell, Llewellyn H., Jr., ed. Man, Economy, & Liberty: Essays in Honor of Murray N. Rothbard. 423p. (Orig.). 1988. pap. text ed. 20.00 (*0-945466-02-1*) Ludwig von Mises.
Rockwell, Llewellyn H., Jr., intro. The Economics of Liberty. 392p. (Orig.). 1990. pap. text ed. 12.00 (*0-945466-08-0*) Ludwig von Mises.
— The Gold Standard: Perspectives in the Austrian School. 148p. (Orig.). 1992. reprint ed. pap. text ed. 10.00 (*0-945466-11-0*) Ludwig von Mises.
Rockwell Manufacturing Company Staff. Getting the Most out of Your Shaper. (Illus.). 108p. 1984. reprint ed. pap. 7.95 (*0-941936-01-5*) Linden Pub Fresno.
***Rockwell, Margaret.** Davy's Lake. (Orig.). 1995. pap. text ed. 10.95 (*0-9608496-1-0*) Caribou Pr.
Rockwell, Mark, ed. see McDaniel, Nello & Thorn, George.
Rockwell, Molly, ed. Norman Rockwell's Christmas Book. LC 93-9925. 1993. pap. 12.98 (*0-8109-8121-1*, Abradale Pr) Abrams.
Rockwell Museum Staff. Great Paintings of the Old West. 1987. pap. 3.95 (*0-486-25360-0*) Dover.
Rockwell, Norm. Badger Digs. 104p. (Orig.). 1980. pap. 3.95 (*0-9612002-0-0*) Moonlight Press.
— Murder in Menomonie. 120p. (Orig.). 1984. pap. 3.95 (*0-9612002-3-5*) Moonlight Press.
— Twin City Slickers. rev. ed. 104p. (Orig.). 1983. pap. 3.95 (*0-9612002-1-9*) Moonlight Press.
Rockwell, Norman. American Fisherman. (Norman Rockwell's America Ser.). 1990. 10.99 (*0-517-67899-3*) Random Hse Value.
— American Sportsman. (Norman Rockwell's America Ser.). 1990. 10.99 (*0-517-67900-0*) Random Hse Value.
— My School Days: A Keepsake Album. 1994. 16.95 (*0-8109-4450-2*) Abrams.
— Norman Rockwell. (American Art Ser.). (Illus.). 112p. 1989. 16.99 (*0-517-67599-4*) Random Hse Value.
— Norman Rockwell: My Adventures As an Illustrator. (Illus.). 432p. 1995. pap. 19.95 (*0-8109-2596-6*) Abrams.
— Norman Rockwell's American Children. 128p. 1990. 10. 99 (*0-517-03172-8*) Random Hse Value.
— Norman Rockwell's American Christmas Postcard Book. (Postcard Book Ser.). (Illus.). 64p. (Orig.). 1990. pap. 7.95 (*0-89471-894-0*) Running Pr.
— Portrait of American: Norman Rockwell's America. (Illus.). 1989. 2.00 (*0-517-67897-7*) Random Hse Value.
— Saturday Evening Post, Vol. 1. (Illus.). 120p. 1995. pap. 55.00 (*4-8457-0955-4*, Pub. by Treville JA) Bks Nippan.
— Saturday Evening Post, Vol. 2. (Illus.). 120p. 1995. pap. 55.00 (*4-8457-0961-9*, Pub. by Treville JA) Bks Nippan.
— Willie Was Different. LC 94-8785. (J). 1994. 16.95 (*0-936399-61-9*) Berkshire Hse.
Rockwell, Norman, illus. An American Family Album. 40p. 1993. 6.95 (*0-8362-4711-6*) Andrews & McMeel.
— American Memories. 40p. 1993. 6.95 (*0-8362-4710-8*) Andrews & McMeel.
— Home for Christmas: An Advent Book. (J). 1993. 13.99 (*0-525-44894-2*, DCB) Dutton Child Bks.
— Norman Rockwell Postcard Book. (Postcard Book Ser.). 64p. (Orig.). 1987. pap. 7.95 (*0-89471-554-2*) Running Pr.
— Romance: Norman Rockwell. 40p. 1993. 6.95 (*0-8362-4709-4*) Andrews & McMeel.
— Saturday Evening Post Norman Rockwell Book. 1987. 14. 99 (*0-517-62607-1*) Random Hse Value.
— Wit & Humor of Norman Rockwell. 40p. 1993. 6.95 (*0-8362-4708-6*) Andrews & McMeel.
Rockwell, Norman, jt. auth. see Montgomery, Elizabeth M.
***Rockwell, Paul V.** Rewriting Resemblance in Medieval French Romance: Ceci n'est Pas un Graal. LC 95-13705. (Garland Studies in Medieval Literature Ser.: Vol. 13). 1995. write for info. (*0-8153-2035-3*) Garland.
Rockwell Publishing Staff, ed. How to Pass the California Real Estate Exam. 4th ed. (Illus.). 347p. (C). 1990. pap. 32.95 (*0-915799-69-3*) Rockwell WA.
— How to Pass the New York Real Estate Exam. 242p. (C). 1989. pap. 21.95 (*0-915799-54-5*) Rockwell WA.
— How to Pass the Washington Real Estate Exam. 4th ed. (Illus.). 313p. (C). 1990. pap. 27.95 (*0-915799-75-8*) Rockwell WA.
Rockwell, Robert E. Everybody Has a Body: Science from Head to Toe. 1992. pap. 14.95 (*0-87659-158-6*) Gryphon Hse.
Rockwell, Robert E., jt. auth. see Endres, Jeanette.
Rockwell, Robert E., et al. Hug a Tree & Other Things to Do Outdoors with Young Children. 112p. (ps-1). 1983. pap. 9.95 (*0-87659-105-5*) Gryphon Hse.
***Rockwell, Robin A.** Handprints. 136p. 1994. pap. 7.95 (*1-56901-535-X*) NW Pub.
Rockwell, Sylvia. Tough to Reach, Tough to Teach: Students with Behavior Problems. LC 92-43363. 1993. 22.00 (*0-86586-235-4*, P387) Coun Exc Child.
Rockwell, Theodore. The Rickover Effect: How One Man Made a Difference. LC 92-3909. (Illus.). 411p. 1992. 32. 95 (*1-55750-702-3*) Naval Inst Pr.
Rockwell, Theodore, 3rd, ed. see AEC Technical Information Center Staff.
Rockwell, Thomas. How to Eat Fried Worms. 128p. (J). 1953. mass mkt. 3.99 (*0-440-44545-0*, YB) Dell.
— How to Eat Fried Worms. (J). (gr. 4 up). 1994. pap. 1.99 (*0-440-21940-X*) Dell.
— How to Eat Fried Worms. LC 73-4262. (Illus.). (J). (gr. 4-6). 1973. lib. bdg. 14.77 (*0-531-02631-0*) Watts.
— How to Fight a Girl. 144p. (J). (gr. k-6). 1988. pap. 3.50 (*0-440-40111-9*, YB) Dell.
— How to Get Fabulously Rich. (J). (gr. 4-7). 1991. pap. 3.50 (*0-440-40546-7*, YB) Dell.
— How to Get Fabulously Rich. (Illus.). 128p. (J). (gr. 5-8). 1990. lib. bdg. 14.77 (*0-531-10877-5*) Watts.
Rockwell, W. J., jt. ed. see Talley, Joseph E.
Rockwood, C. H. Atlas of Cheshire County, New Hampshire, 1877. 1,982th ed. LC 82-62166. (Illus.). 53p. 1982. reprint ed. pap. 15.95 (*0-911653-01-5*) Old Maps.
Rockwood, Charles A., Jr. The Shoulder, 2 vol. (Illus.). 1184p. 1990. text ed. 235.00 (*0-7216-2828-1*) Saunders.
Rockwood, Charles A., Jr., et al. Fractures, Vol. 3: Fractures in Children. 3rd ed. (Illus.). 1530p. 1991. text ed. 195.00 (*0-397-51152-3*) Lippincott.
— Fractures, Vols. 1 & 2: Rockwood & Green's Fractures in Adu, 2 vols., Set. 3rd ed. (Illus.). 2384p. 1991. text ed. 350.00 (*0-397-51151-5*) Lippincott.
Rockwood, Charles A., Jr., et al, eds. Fractures in Children, 3 vols., Set. 3rd ed. (Illus.). 3914p. 1991. 475.00 (*0-397-50975-8*) Lippincott.
Rockwood, D. Stephen, jt. ed. see Miller, William.
Rockwood, Jerome. The Craftsmen of Dionysus: An Approach to Acting. LC 92-25206. (Acting Ser.). 1992. pap. 18.95 (*1-55783-155-6*) Applause Theatre Bk Pubs.
Rockwood, John P., jt. auth. see Coler, Robert A.
Rockwood, Joyce. Groundhog's Horse. LC 77-22676. (Illus.). 128p. (J). (gr. 2-4). 1978. 12.95 (*0-8050-1173-0*, Bks Young Read) H Holt & Co.
— To Spoil the Sun. (YA). (gr. 7 up). 1994. pap. 7.95 (*0-8050-3465-X*, Bks Young Read) H Holt & Co.
Rockwood, Roy. The Jungle Boy. 208p. 1991. reprint ed. lib. bdg. 18.95 (*0-89966-825-9*) Buccaneer Bks.
Rocky Mountain Institute Staff. Homemade Money: How to Save Energy & Dollars in Your Home. 258p. 1994. pap. 14.95 (*1-883178-07-X*) Brick Hse Pub.
Rocky Mountain Institute Staff & Sardinsky, Robert. The Efficient House Sourcebook: Reviews of Selected Books & Directory of Organizations Devoted to Resource Efficient Housing. rev. ed. 180p. 1992. pap. 15.00 (*1-881071-00-6*) Rocky Mtn Inst.
Rocky Mountain Institute Water Program Staff. Water Efficiency: A Resource for Utility Managers, Community Planners, & Other Decisionmakers. 114p. (Orig.). 1991. pap. text ed. 15.00 (*1-881071-02-2*, W91-27) Rocky Mtn Inst.
Rocky Mountain Mineral Law Foundation Staff. Public Land & Resources Law Digest, 1984-1988, Cumulative Index. 1989. pap. text ed. 35.00 (*0-929047-08-7*) Rocky Mtn Mineral Law Found.
Rocky Mountain Mineral Law Staff & Reid, Joan A. Law of Federal Oil & Gas Leases, 2 vols. 1964. Updates. ring bd. write for info. (*0-8205-1515-9*) Bender.

R

Rocky Mountain News Staff. Pope John Paul II: The North American Journey of His Holiness. (Illus.). 112p. (Orig.). 1993. pap. 12.95 (0-8362-8042-3) Andrews & McMeel.

Rocky Mountain Region Japan Project Model District Teams Staff. A Look at Japanese Culture Through the Family. Parisi, Lynn, ed. (Illus.). 96p. (Orig.). 1989. pap. 10.95 (0-89994-349-7) Soc Sci Ed.

Rocky Mountain Translators Staff, tr. see Buttner-Janz, Karin.

Roco, M. C., ed. Particulate Two-Phase Flow. 1993. 95.00 (0-7506-9275-8) Buttrwrth-Heinemann.

***Roco, M. C., et al, eds.** Liquid-Solid Flows 1994. LC 93-75377. (Fluid Engineering Division Conference Ser.: Vol. 189). 257p. 1994. pap. 45.00 (0-7918-1372-X) ASME.

Rocole, Terri, ed. see Fantus, James E.

Rocq, Margaret M., ed. California Local History: A Bibliography & Union List of Library Holdings. 2nd ed. LC 70-97912. xvi, 611p. 1970. 57.50 (0-8047-0716-2) Stanford U Pr.

— California Local History, a Bibliography & Union List of Library Holdings: Supplement to the Second Edition Covering Works Published 1961 Through 1970. x, 114p. 1976. 22.50 (0-8047-0908-4) Stanford U Pr.

Rocques, Margaret, tr. see Cassis, Youssef.

Rocquet, Claude-Henri. Bruegel, or the Workshop of Dreams. Scott, Nora, tr. (Illus.). 224p. 1991. 24.95 (0-226-72342-9) U Ch Pr.

Rod Grantham Printing Staff, tr. see Diede, Pauline N.

Roda, E., et al. Workshops in Bile Acid Research: Serum Bile Acids in Health & Disease-Pathophysiology of the Enterohepatic Circulation. 144p. 1983. lib. bdg. 73.00 (0-85200-749-3) Kluwer Ac.

Roda, Giovanni. Troposcatter Radio Links. (Telecommunications Engineering Library). 250p. 1988. text ed. 72.00 (0-89006-293-5) Artech Hse.

Rodabaugh, Barbara J., et al. Developing Consultation & Education Services for Sexual Assault. 1978. pap. 3.00 (0-89785-565-5) Am Inst Res.

Rodabaugh, E. C., jt. ed. see Schneider, R. W.

Rodabaugh, Stephen E., ed. Applications of Category Theory to Fuzzy Subsets. (Theory & Decision Library Series B). 412p. (C). 1991. lib. bdg. 115.50 (0-7923-1511-1) Kluwer Ac.

Rodack, Jaine. As Cool As a Cucumber. Rolfes, Ellen, ed. (Something to Talk about Ser.). 96p. (J). (gr. k-6). 1993. spiral bd. 5.95 (1-879958-19-8) Tradery Hse.

Rodack, Jane. Forgotten Recipes. 190p. 1980. spiral bd. 12.95 (0-918544-60-2) Tradery Hse.

Rodack, Madeleine T., tr. see Bandelier, Adolph F.

Rodahl, Kaare. Stress Monitoring for Improved Worker Performance. 1993. 59.95 (0-87371-655-8, RC963) Lewis Pubs.

Rodahl, Kaare, ed. The Physiology of Work. 250p. 1989. 99.00 (0-85066-478-0); pap. 45.00 (0-85066-483-7) Taylor & Francis.

Rodahl, Kaare, jt. auth. see Astrand, Per-Olof.

Rodak, Bernadette F. Diagnostic Hematology. LC 94-11097. (Illus.). 608p. 1995. text ed. 57.00 (0-7216-4727-8) Saunders.

Rodak, Frederick. Homeowners Guide to Wildfires: In the Urban Interface. 84p. 1991. pap. 6.95 (0-9630493-0-5) Wildfire Tech.

***Rodale.** Save Three Lives. 1994. 3.99 (0-517-13565-5) Random Hse Value.

Rodale, Ardath. Climbing Toward the Light: A Journey of Growth, Understanding & Love. LC 89-32896. (Illus.). 240p. 1989. 17.95 (0-87857-834-X, 05-406-0) Rodale Pr Inc.

Rodale Books Editors, sel. The Weekend Woodworker, Quick-&-Easy Projects: Furniture & Accents, Plywood Projects, Toys, Kitchen Projects, Shelving & Storage. LC 91-33573. (Illus.). 256p. (Orig.). 1992. 22.95 (0-87596-128-2, 14-047-2); pap. 12.95 (0-87857-997-4, 14-047-1) Rodale Pr Inc.

Rodale Center for Women's Health Staff. The Healthy Woman. Feinstein, Alice, ed. LC 93-32831. (Illus.). 304p. (Orig.). 1994. pap. 14.95 (0-87596-197-5) Rodale Pr Inc.

Rodale Craft Books Editors. Special Occasions in Cross-Stitch: Warm & Welcoming Designs for Holidays & Celebrations. (Illus.). 256p. 1992. 26.95 (0-87596-146-0, 11-409-0) Rodale Pr Inc.

Rodale Food Center Staff, jt. auth. see Claessens, Sharon.

***Rodale Garden Books Editors.** Rodale's Guide to Low-Maintenance Gardening Techniques: Shortcuts & Time-Saving Hints for Your Greatest Garden Ever. (Illus.). 384p. 1995. 26.95 (0-87596-641-1) Rodale Pr Inc.

Rodale, J. I. Synonym Finder. rev. ed. LC 78-11440. 1368p. 1978. 21.95 (0-87857-236-8, 10-342-2) Rodale Pr Inc.

Rodale Press Editors. Cut Your Bills in Half. (Illus.). 400p. 1993. 7.98 (0-8317-1892-7) Smithmark.

— Cut Your Spending in Half, Without Settling for Less! How to Pay the Lowest Price for Everything. (Illus.). 480p. 1994. 27.95 (0-87596-188-6) Rodale Pr Inc.

— Prevention's Guide to High-Speed Healing. 1995. reprint ed. 9.98 (1-56731-072-9, MJF Bks) Fine Comms.

Rodale Press Editors & Halpin, Anne M. Foolproof Planting: How to Successfully Start & Propagate More Than 250 Vegetables, Flowers, Trees, & Shrubs. LC 89-10991. (Illus.). 320p. 1992. pap. 14.95 (0-87857-994-X, 01-953-1) Rodale Pr Inc.

Rodale Press Garden Books Editors, jt. auth. see Cox, Jeff.

Rodale Press Staff. Rodale's Illustrated Encyclopedia of Gardening & Landscaping Techniques. LC 90-31521. 432p. 1990. 26.95 (0-87857-898-6, 01-027-0) Rodale Pr Inc.

— Shape up Your Business Workbook. Hill, Chris, ed. LC 94-31012. 1994. write for info. (0-87596-246-7) Rodale Pr Inc.

Rodale Press Staff, et al, eds. Rodale's Illustrated Encyclopedia of Herbs. (Illus.). 552p. 1987. 24.95 (0-87857-699-1, 01-316-0) Rodale Pr Inc.

Rodale Press Staff & Claessens, Sharon. The Lose Weight Naturally Cookbook. Tkac, Debra, ed. LC 85-1687. (Illus.). 400p. 1985. 24.95 (0-87857-539-1, 07-401-0) Rodale Pr Inc.

Rodale Press Staff & Hupping, Carol. Stocking Up III: The All-New Edition of America's Classic Preserving Guide. LC 86-10225. (Illus.). 400p. 1986. 24.95 (0-87857-613-4, 09-091-0) Rodale Pr Inc.

Rodale Press Woodworking Editors. Shop Tips: Expert Advice on Making the Most of Your Shop Time & Tools. LC 93-6356. (Illus.). 312p. 1994. 27.95 (0-87596-591-1) Rodale Pr Inc.

Rodale, Robert. Save Three Lives: A Plan for Famine Prevention. LC 91-15224. 256p. 1991. 20.00 (0-87156-621-4) Sierra.

Rodale, Robert, ed. The Basic Book of Organic Gardening. 384p. 1987. mass mkt. 4.95 (0-345-34522-3) Ballantine.

Rodale's Home Improvement Books Staff & Burton, Ken. Adding On: How to Design & Built the Perfect Addition for Your Home. (Illus.). 384p. 1994. 27.95 (0-87596-605-5) Rodale Pr Inc.

Rodan, Garry, ed. Singapore Changes Guard. LC 93-16580. 272p. 1993. text ed. 49.95 (0-312-09687-9) St Martin.

Rodanas, Kristina. Dance of the Sacred Circle. LC 93-19626. (J). 1994. 14.95 (0-316-75358-0) Little.

— Dragonfly's Tale. LC 90-28758. (J). (ps-3). 1995. pap. 5.95 (0-395-72076-1, Clarion Bks) HM.

— The Story of Wali Dad. LC 86-34423. (Illus.). 32p. (J). (gr. k-3). 1988. 13.95 (0-688-07262-3); lib. bdg. 13.88 (0-688-07263-1) Lothrop.

Rodanas, Kristina, adapt. The Eagle's Song: A Tale from the Pacific Northwest. LC 94-6596. (J). 1995. 15.95 (0-316-75375-0) Little.

***Rodanas, Kristina, illus. & ret.** The Birds of Summer: An Ojibwa Tale. LC 95-7103. (J). 1996. write for info. (0-316-75333-5) Little.

Rodanas, Kristina, ret. Dragonfly's Tale. (Illus.). 32p. (J). (gr. k-3). 1992. 14.95 (0-395-57003-4, Clarion Bks) HM.

Rodano, Philip J. Me-ow: A Book of Pur-rific Cat Cartoons. LC 90-90370. (Illus.). 144p. (Orig.). 1990. pap. text ed. 8.95 (0-9627648-1-7) Top Cat.

Rodari, Florian. A Weekend with Matisse. Knight, Joan, tr. LC 93-41671. 64p. (J). 1994. 19.95 (0-8478-1792-X) Rizzoli Intl.

— A Weekend with Picasso. LC 91-12427. (Weekend with... Ser.). (Illus.). 64p. 1991. 19.95 (0-8478-1437-8) Rizzoli Intl.

Rodarmor, William, tr. see Belloc, Denis.

Rodarmor, William, tr. see Collard, Cyril.

Rodarmor, William, tr. see Modiano, Patrick.

Rodarmor, William, tr. see Moitessier, Bernard.

Rodas-Carroll, Edith B., tr. see Fankhauser, Jerry.

Rodaway, Paul. Sensuous Geographies: Body, Sense, & Place. LC 93-40331. 224p. 1994. 59.95x (0-415-08829-1, B0835) Routledge.

***Rodbell, Donald T.** Subdivision, Subsurface Stratigraphy, & Estimated Age Offluvial-Terrace Deposits in Northwestern Tennessee. LC 95-9815. (U. S. Geological Survey Bulletin: vol. 2128). Date not set. write for info. (0-615-00641-8) US Geol Survey.

Rodbell, K., et al, eds. Materials Reliability in Microelectronics III. (Symposium Proceedings Ser.: Vol. 309). 1993. text ed. 72.00 (1-55899-205-7) Materials Res.

Rodbell, Philip D., ed. Make Our Cities Safe for Trees: Proceedings of the Fourth Urban Forestry Conference. (Illus.). 255p. (Orig.). 1990. pap. 27.95 (0-685-46349-4) Am Forests.

Rodbertus, J. Karl. Over Production & Crises. Franklin, Julia, tr. LC 69-18027. (Reprints of Economic Classics Ser.). 1969. reprint ed. 27.50 (0-678-00497-8) Kelley.

Rodbraugh, Don. Roaring Roadsters: Track Roadsters from 1930-1960. (Illus.). 200p. 1994. pap. 19.95 (1-884089-06-2) CarTech.

Rodby, John, contrib. Solos for Jazz Piano. (All That Jazz Ser.). 64p. (Orig.). 1988. pap. 9.95 (0-8258-0398-5, ATJ305) Fischer Inc NY.

Rodby, Judith. Appropriating Literacy: Writing & Reading in English As a Second Language. LC 92-18835. 151p. 1992. pap. text ed. 18.50 (0-86709-308-0) Boynton Cook Pubs.

— Writing by Choice: Intermediate Composition for Students of ESL. (Illus.). 144p. (C). 1987. pap. text ed. 12.00 (0-13-970328-4) P-H.

Rodchue, Soawalak, jt. auth. see Moore, John.

Rodd, jt. auth. see Motion.

Rodd, Cyril. The Book of Job. LC 90-33941. (Narrative Commentaries Ser.). 160p. (Orig.). (C). 1990. pap. 12.95 (0-334-02473-0) TPI PA.

Rodd, Cyril S., ed. The Pastor's Opportunities. 256p. (Orig.). 1989. pap. 24.95 (0-567-29167-7, Pub. by T & T Clark UK) Bks Intl VA.

— The Pastor's Problems. 240p. pap. 24.95 (0-567-29117-0, Pub. by T & T Clark UK) Bks Intl VA.

Rodd, Jillian. Leadership in Early Childhood: The Pathway to Professionalism. LC 93-39282. (Early Childhood Education Ser.). 200p. 1994. pap. text ed. 18.95 (0-8077-3353-9) Tchrs Coll.

***Rodd, John.** Repairing & Restoring Antique Furniture. (Illus.). 224p. 1995. 27.95 (0-7153-0304-X, Pub. by D & C Pub UK) Sterling.

***Rodd, Judith S.** A Guide to Coopers Rock State Forest. (Illus.). 80p. (Orig.). 1994. pap. 7.95 (0-9630920-2-2) South Wind.

Rodd, Judy. Coopers Rocks State Forest: A Complete Guide. (Illus.). 100p. 1993. pap. write for info. (0-318-69745-9) South Wind.

— West Virginia State Parks, National Forests & Wilderness Areas. (Pocket Guide Ser.). (Illus.). 160p. (Orig.). 1993. pap. 6.95 (0-9630920-6-5) South Wind.

Rodd, Laurel R. Nichiren: A Biography. (Occasional Paper Ser.: No. 11). 86p. 1978. pap. text ed. 8.00 (0-939252-07-4) ASU Ctr Asian.

— Nichiren: Selected Writings. LC 79-17054. (Asian Studies at Hawaii: No. 26). 201p. reprint ed. pap. 57.30 (0-317-28681-1, 2020444) Bks Demand.

Rodd, M. G., ed. see IFAC Workshop on Distributed Computer Control Systems Staff.

Rodd, M. G., jt. ed. see Verbruggen, H. B.

Rodd, Michael G., jt. auth. see Motus, Leo.

Rodd, Mike G. & Lalive D'Epinay, Th., eds. Distributed Computer Control Systems 1988: Proceedings of the 8th IFAC Workshop, Vitznau, Switzerland, 13-15 September, 1988. (IFAC Publication Ser.: No. 84). (Illus.). 145p. 1989. 89.00 (0-08-036938-3, Pergamon Pr) Elsevier.

Rodd, Mike G., jt. auth. see IFAC Symposium Staff.

Rodd, Mike G., jt. ed. see Knuth, Elod.

Rodd, Mike G., jt. auth. see Motus, Leo.

Rodd, R. Frederick, Crown Prince & Emperor. 208p. reprint ed. pap. 8.95 (0-935005-72-2) Lincoln-Rembrandt.

Rodd, Rosemary. Biology, Ethics, & Animals. 280p. 1992. reprint ed. pap. 18.95 (0-19-824052-X) OUP.

Rodda, Annabel. Women & the Environment. (Women & World Development Ser.). (Illus.). 192p. (C). 1991. text ed. 49.95 (0-86232-984-1, Pub. by Zed Books UK) Humanities.

— Women & the Environment. 2nd ed. (Women & World Development Ser.). (Illus.). 192p. (C). 1991. pap. 15.95 (0-86232-985-X, Pub. by Zed Books UK) Humanities.

Rodda, Dorothy. Church & Synagogue Library Resources. 5th ed. LC 75-1178. 24p. 1992. pap. 6.00 (0-915324-33-4) CSLA.

Rodda, Emily. The Best-Kept Secret. 112p. (J). (gr. 5). 1991. reprint ed. pap. 2.95 (0-380-75870-9, Camelot) Avon.

— Finders Keepers. LC 90-47850. (Illus.). (J). (gr. 5 up). 1991. 13.95 (0-688-10516-5) Greenwillow.

— Finders Keepers. LC 92-43776. (Illus.). 192p. (J). (gr. 5 up). 1993. pap. 3.95 (0-688-11846-1, Pub. by Beech Tree Bks) Morrow.

— The Pigs Are Flying! Orig. Title: Pigs Might Fly. (Illus.). 144p. (J). (gr. 2 up). 1989. reprint ed. pap. 2.95 (0-380-70555-9, Camelot) Avon.

— The Pigs Are Flying! LC 88-2449. Orig. Title: Pigs Might Fly. (Illus.). 160p. (J). (gr. 4-6). 1988. reprint ed. 13.95 (0-688-08130-4) Greenwillow.

— Power & Glory. LC 95-1842. (Illus.). 32p. (J). 1996. write for info. (0-688-14214-1); lib. bdg. write for info. (0-688-14215-X) Greenwillow.

— The Timekeeper. LC 92-31512. (Illus.). 160p. (J). (gr. 5 up). 1993. 14.00 (0-688-12448-8) Greenwillow.

Rodda, Gordon H. The Mating Behavior of Iguana. LC 92-2499. (Smithsonian Contributions to Zoology Ser.: No. 534). (Illus.). 44p. reprint ed. pap. 25.00 (0-7837-3877-3, 2043719) Bks Demand.

***Rodda, Jeanette & Smith, Nancy.** Experience Jerome. rev. ed. Caillou, Aliza, ed. (Illus.). 68p. 1995. pap. text ed. 5.95 (0-9628329-7-9) Thorne Enterprises.

Rodda, John C., ed. Facets of Hydrology. LC 75-26568. 384p. reprint ed. pap. 109.50 (0-317-09887-X, 2019670) Bks Demand.

— Facets of Hydrology, Vol. 2. LC 75-26568. 447p. 1985. text ed. 234.95 (0-471-90338-8, Wiley-Interscience) Wiley.

Rodda, Michael & Grove, Carl. Language, Cognition & Deafness. (Zillman-Bryant: Communication Ser.). 456p. 1987. text ed. 79.95 (0-89859-877-X) L Erlbaum Assocs.

Roddan, Brooks. The Light of the Light. 10p. 1987. pap. 12.00 (0-944034-00-4) Blue Earth.

Rodden, C. J., ed. see AEC Technical Information Center Staff.

Rodden, Clement J., ed. see AEC Technical Information Center Staff.

Rodden, John. Critical Essays on Lionel Trilling. (Critical Thoughts Ser.: Vol. 6). 400p. 1994. 35.00 (0-85967-890-3, Pub. by Scolar Pr UK) Ashgate Pub Co.

— The Politics of Literary Reputation: The Making & Claiming of "St. George" Orwell. (Illus.). 496p. 1991. reprint ed. pap. 12.95 (0-19-506711-8) OUP.

Rodden, Lois. Astro Data, No. IV. pap. 35.00 (0-86690-355-0, 3045-014) Am Fed Astrologers.

— Astro Data Two. rev. ed. 1993. pap. 29.00 (0-917086-23-6) Am Fed Astrologers.

— Mercury Method of Chart Comparison. 228p. 1973. 16.00 (0-86690-150-7, R1413-014) Am Fed Astrologers.

— Modern Transits. LC 78-56415. 200p. 1978. 14.00 (0-86690-151-5, R1414-014) Am Fed Astrologers.

Rodden, Lois M. Astro-Data V: Profiles in Crime. 238p. 1992. pap. text ed. 36.00 (0-9633716-0-6) Data News Pr.

— Money, How to Find It with Astrology. Rodden, Lynn, ed. 275p. 1994. pap. text ed. 20.00 (0-9633716-1-4) Data News Pr.

Rodden, Lynn, ed. see Rodden, Lois M.

Roddenberry, Gene. Star Trek-the Motion Picture. 1980. 9.95 (0-686-60888-7) S&S Trade.

Roddenberry, Gene & Friedman, Michael J. The God Thing. Stern, Dave, ed. (Star Trek: The Next Generation Ser.). 1992. 20.00 (0-671-78070-0) PB.

Roddenberry, Gene & Sackett, Susan. Star Trek: The First Twenty-Five Years. 256p. 1991. 45.00 (0-671-73233-1) PB.

Roddenberry, Gene, jt. auth. see Whitfield, Stephen E.

Roddenberry, Seaborn A. I Swear by Apollo: A Black Surgeon in the Deep South. 186p. Date not set. 20.00 (0-9640075-0-9) Grandy Pr.

Roddey, G. J. & Gemayel, A. H. Wolves Come Down on the Fold: A War Story from the Lebanon. 428p. (Orig.). 1993. pap. write for info. (1-881272-04-4) Whitehurst-Wynn.

Roddick, Anita. Body & Soul: Profits with Principles-The Amazing Success Story of Anita Roddick. 1994. 14.00 (0-517-88134-9, Crown) Crown Pub Group.

— Body & Soul: Profits with Principles-The Amazing Success Story of Anita Roddick & the Body Shop. 256p. 1991. 22.00 (0-517-58542-1, Crown) Crown Pub Group.

Roddick, B. The Thirteenth Juror at the Lawrencia Bembenek Murder Trial. 1982. pap. 4.95 (0-937816-23-X) Tech Data.

Roddick, Bill & Korotko, Robin. Bembenek: After the Verdict. 240p. (Orig.). 1991. pap. 9.95 (0-9629136-0-X) Composition Hse.

Roddick, Ellen. Writing That Means Business: How to Get Your Message Across Quickly & Effectively. 198p. 1986. pap. 11.00 (0-02-015380-5, Pub. by Gebrueder Borntraeger GW) Macmillan.

Roddick, J. A., ed. Circum-Pacific Plutonic Terranes. LC 83-1557. (Geological Society of America, Memoir Ser.: No. 159). (Illus.). 322p. reprint ed. pap. 91.80 (0-8357-3830-2, 2036554) Bks Demand.

Roddick, Jackie. Dance of the Millions: Latin America & the Debt Crisis. (Latin America Bureau Ser.). 258p. (C). 1988. pap. text ed. 11.00 (0-906156-30-0) Monthly Rev.

Roddick, Nick. A New Deal in Entertainment: Warner Brothers in the 1930s. LC 83-152420. (Illus.). 332p. 1983. 37.50 (0-85170-125-6, Pub. by British Film Inst UK); pap. 16.95 (0-85170-126-4, Pub. by British Film Inst UK) Ind U Pr.

Roddick, Nick, jt. ed. see Auty, Martyn.

Roddie, Shen. Animal Stew. (Illus.). 32p. (J). (ps). 1992. 13.95 (0-395-57582-6) HM.

— Chicken Pox. LC 92-53851. (Illus.). (J). 1993. 14.95 (0-316-75347-5, Joy St Bks) Little.

— Hatch, Egg, Hatch: Touch & Feel Action Flap Book. (J). (ps). 1991. 14.95 (0-316-75345-9) Little.

— Help, Mama, Help! A Top-&-Feel Pull-Tab Pop-up Book. (Illus.). (J). (ps). 1995. 14.95 (0-316-75357-2) Little.

— The Terrible Itch. (Illus.). 24p. (J). (ps-1). 1993. boxed 13.00 (0-671-79169-9, S&S Bks Young Read) S&S Childrens.

Roddier, F., ed. Active Telescope Systems. 568p. 1989. 77.00 (0-8194-0150-1, VOL. 1114) SPIE.

Roddis, Ingrid. Sudan. (Let's Visit Places & Peoples of the World Ser.). (Illus.). 96p. (J). (gr. 5 up). 1988. 14.95 (0-222-00964-0) Chelsea Hse.

Roddis, Louis H. A Short History of Nautical Medicine. LC 75-23757. reprint ed. 30.50 (0-404-13363-0) AMS Pr.

Roddis, W. M., jt. ed. see Easterling, W. Samuel.

Roddon, Guy. Pastel Painting Techniques. (Illus.). 144p. 1991. pap. 21.95 (0-89134-396-2, 30306) North Light Bks.

Roddy, Dennis. Introduction to Microelectronics. 2nd ed. 1978. text ed. 99.00 (0-08-022687-6, Pub. by Pergamon Repr UK) Franklin.

— Microwave Technology. (C). 1986. teacher ed write for info. (0-8359-4391-7, Reston) P-H.

Roddy, Dennis & Coolen, John. Electronic Communications. 4th ed. LC 94-14041. 1995. text ed. 72.00 (0-13-312083-X) P-H.

— Electronics: Theory, Devices & Circuits. (C). 1982. teacher ed write for info. (0-8359-1644-8, Reston) P-H.

Roddy, Edward G. Mills, Mansions & Mergers: The Life of William M. Wood. LC 82-81081. (Illus.). 1982. 15.00 (0-937474-04-5) Mus Am Textile Hist.

Roddy, Kevin P. RICO in Business & Commercial Litigation. 1840p. 1991. ring bd. 160.00 (0-07-017989-1) Shepards-McGraw.

— UNIX NROFF-TROFF: A User's Guide. LC 85-27223. 362p. (C). 1986. pap. text ed. 29.00 (0-03-000167-6) HB Coll Pubs.

***Roddy, Lee.** The Bear Cub's Adventure. 132p. (J). 1996. pap. 4.99 (1-56476-503-2, 6-3503) SP Pubns.

— Case of the Dangerous Cruise. (Ladd Family Adventure Ser.: No. 11). 1995. pap. text ed. 4.99 (1-56179-349-3) Focus Family.

— The City Bear's Adventures. (D. J. Dillon Ser.: No. 2). 144p. (J). (gr. 3-7). 1985. pap. 4.99 (0-88207-496-2, Victor Books) SP Pubns.

— Danger on Thunder Mountain. (American Adventure Ser.). 176p. (Orig.). (J). (gr. 3 up). 1989. pap. 5.99 (1-55661-028-9) Bethany Hse.

— The Dangerous Canoe Race. (Ladd Family Adventure Ser.: No. 4). (Orig.). (J). (gr. 3-6). 1990. pap. 4.99 (0-929608-62-3) Focus Family.

— Dooger, the Grasshopper. 132p. (J). 1996. pap. 4.99 (1-56476-504-0, 6-3504) SP Pubns.

— Dooger, the Grasshopper Hound. (D. J. Dillon Ser.: No. 3). 144p. (J). (gr. 3-7). 1985. pap. 4.99 (0-88207-497-0, Victor Books) SP Pubns.

— Escape down the Raging Rapids: Escape down the Raging Rapids, Bk. 10. 132p. 1989. pap. 4.99 (0-89693-477-2, Victor Books) SP Pubns.

— Eye of the Hurricane. (Ladd Family Adventure Ser.: No. 9). 170p. 1994. pap. 4.99 (1-56179-220-9) Focus Family.

— The Flaming Trap. (American Adventure Ser.). 176p. (Orig.). (YA). (gr. 4-8). 1990. pap. 5.99 (1-55661-095-5) Bethany Hse.

— The Ghost Dog of Stoney Ridge. (D. J. Dillon Ser.: No. 4). 144p. (J). (gr. 3-7). 1985. pap. 4.99 (0-88207-498-9, Victor Books) SP Pubns.

— Ghost Dog of Stoney Ridge. 132p. (J). 1996. pap. 4.99 (1-56476-505-9, 6-3505) SP Pubns.

— Ghost of the Moaning Mansion. 132p. (J). (gr. 3-7). 1987. pap. 4.99 (0-89693-349-0, Victor Books) SP Pubns.

— Giants on the Hill. LC 94-21915. 1994. 10.99 (0-8499-3492-3) Word Inc.

An Asterisk (*) at the beginning of an entry indicates that the title is appearing in BIP for the first time.

— The Gold Train Bandits. (American Adventure Ser.). 176p. (Orig.). (J). (gr. 3-8). 1992. pap. 5.99 (1-55661-211-7) Bethany Hse.

— The Hair-Pulling Bear Dog. (D. J. Dillon Ser.: No. 1). 144p. (J). (gr. 3-7). 1985. pap. 4.99 (0-88207-499-7, Victor Books) SP Pubns.

— The Hair-Pulling Bear Dog. 132p. (J). 1996. pap. 4.99 (1-56476-502-4, 6-3502) SP Pubns.

— High Country Ambush. (American Adventure Ser.). 176p. (Orig.). (J). (gr. 3-8). 1992. pap. 5.99 (1-55661-287-7) Bethany Hse.

— The Legend of Fire. (Ladd Family Adventure Ser.: No. 2). 148p. (J). (gr. 3-6). 1989. reprint ed. pap. 4.99 (0-929608-17-8) Focus Family.

— The Legend of the White Raccoon. 144p. (J). (gr. 3-7). 1986. pap. 4.99 (0-89693-500-0, Victor Books) SP Pubns.

— Legend of White Raccoon. 132p. (J). 1996. pap. 4.99 (1-56476-507-5, 6-3507) SP Pubns.

— The Mad Dog of Lobo Mountain. 132p. (YA). (gr. 8-12). 1986. pap. 4.99 (0-89693-482-9, Victor Books) SP Pubns.

— Mad Dog of Lobo Mountain. 132p. (J). 1996. pap. 4.99 (1-56476-506-7, 6-3506) SP Pubns.

— Mystery of the Island Jungle. (Ladd Family Adventure Ser.: No. 3). 160p. (Orig.). (J). (gr. 3-7). 1989. pap. 4.99 (0-929608-19-4) Focus Family.

— Mystery of the Phantom Gold. (American Adventure Ser.: Bk. 7). 176p. (Orig.). (J). (gr. 3-8). 1991. pap. 5.99 (1-55661-210-9) Bethany Hse.

— Mystery of the Wild Surfer. (Ladd Family Adventure Ser.: No. 6). 160p. (Orig.). (J). (gr. 3-7). 1990. pap. 4.99 (0-929608-64-X) Focus Family.

— Night of the Vanishing Lights. (Ladd Family Adventure Ser.: No. 10). (J). 1994. pap. 4.99 (1-56179-256-X) Focus Family.

— The Overland Escape. LC 88-63471. (American Adventure Ser.). 160p. (J). (gr. 2-6). 1989. pap. text ed. 5.99 (1-55661-026-2) Bethany Hse.

— Robert E. Lee: Gallant Christian Soldier. (Sower Ser.). (Illus.). (J). (gr. 3-6). 1977. pap. 6.95 (0-915134-40-3) Mott Media.

— The Secret of the Howling Cave. (American Adventure Ser.). 192p. (Orig.). (J). (gr. 4-10). 1990. pap. 5.99 (1-55661-094-7) Bethany Hse.

— Secret of the Shark Pit. (Ladd Family Adventure Ser.: No. 1). 136p. (Orig.). (J). (gr. 3-6). 1989. pap. 4.99 (0-929608-14-3) Focus Family.

— Secret of the Sunken Sub. (Ladd Family Adventure Ser.: No. 5). 160p. (Orig.). (J). (gr. 3-6). 1990. pap. 4.99 (0-929608-63-1) Focus Family.

— Terror at Forbidden Falls. LC 93-3379. (Ladd Family Adventure Ser.: Vol. 8). (J). 1993. write for info. (1-56179-137-7) Focus Family.

— Terror in the Sky. (American Adventure Ser.). 176p. (Orig.). (J). (ps-8). 1991. pap. 5.99 (1-55661-096-3) Bethany Hse.

Roddy, Michael. Beginning English Day by Day. 224p. 1991. pap. text ed. 16.00 (0-87879-907-9) Acad Therapy.

— English Day by Day. Kratoville, Betty L., ed. LC 88-27428. (Illus.). 304p. (Orig.). 1989. pap. text ed. 18.00 (0-87879-668-1) Acad Therapy.

Roddy, Moya. The Long Way Home. 256p. (Orig.). (C). 1992. pap. 11.99x (1-85594-039-6, Pub. by Attic IE) InBook.

Roddy, Patricia. Api & the Boy Stranger: A Village Creation Tale. LC 93-8359. (Illus.). (J). 1994. 14.99 (0-8037-1221-9); lib. bdg. 14.89 (0-8037-1222-7) Dial Bks Young.

Roddy, Ray. Stonekiller. 1992. 13.95 (0-533-10115-8) Vantage.

Roddy, Ruth M. Kids' Stuff. 64p. (Orig.). (J). (gr. 1-7). 1993. pap. 7.95 (0-940669-23-4, D30) Dramaline Pubns.

— Monologues for Kids. 64p. (Orig.). (J). (gr. 1-3). 1987. pap. 6.95 (0-940669-02-1) Dramaline Pubns.

— More Monologues for Kids. 64p. (Orig.). (J). (gr. 6-9). 1992. pap. 7.95 (0-940669-18-8) Dramaline Pubns.

— Scenes for Kids. 64p. (Orig.). (J). (gr. 2-6). 1990. pap. 7.95 (0-940669-14-5) Dramaline Pubns.

Roddy, Vernon. The Lost Town of Bledsoesborough, Tennessee: Its Beginning, Its End: Two Essays in the Record of Tennessee's Upper Cumberland of Old. 1984. pap. 8.45 (0-318-03885-4) Upper Country.

— Whatever Happened to Epperson Springs? 1974. pap. 5.50 (0-686-40797-0) Upper Country.

Rode, A., jt. ed. see Shephard, R. J.

Rode, A. A. Podzol-Forming Process. 392p. 1970. text ed. 100.00 (0-7065-1011-9, Pub. by Keter Pub IS) Coronet Bks.

— The Soil-Forming Process & Soil Evolution. 104p. 1961. 36.00 (0-7065-0149-7, Pub. by Keter Pub IS) Coronet Bks.

Rode, Pierre. Twenty-Four Caprices in the Form of Etudes for Violin. Saenger, Gustave, ed. (Carl Fischer Music Library: No.583). 52p. 1910. pap. 9.00 (0-8258-0076-5, L583) Fischer Inc NY.

Rode, Reinhard, ed. GATT & Conflict Management: A Transatlantic Strategy for a Stronger Regime. 126p. (C). 1990. pap. text ed. 45.00 (0-8133-7967-9) Westview.

Rodean, Howard C. Nuclear-Explosion Seismology. LC 73-170333. (AEC Critical Review Ser.). 168p. 1971. pap. 12.00 (0-87079-288-1, TID-25572); fiche 9.00 (0-87079-289-X, TID-25572) DOE.

Rodecap, Vera E. The Country Schoolteacher: A Kansas Legacy. 141p. (Orig.). 1993. pap. text ed. 12.00 (0-9639944-0-9) V E Rodecap.

Rodecap, Vera E., jt. auth. see Hamm, W. Howard.

Rodechko, James P. Patrick Ford & His Search for America: A Case Study of Irish-American Journalism, 1870-1913. LC 76-6362. (Irish Americans Ser.). 1976. 29.95 (0-405-09354-3) Ayer.

Roded, Ruth. Women in Islamic Biographical Collections: From Ibn Sad to Who's Who. LC 93-28276. 158p. 1993. lib. bdg. 34.00 (1-55587-442-8) Lynne Rienner.

Rodee, Marian. Weaving of the Southwest. LC 86-63764. (Illus.). 248p. 1987. 39.95 (0-88740-095-7); pap. 24.95 (0-88740-091-4) Schiffer.

Rodee, Marian & Ostler, James. Zuni Pottery. LC 87-60505. (Illus.). 92p. 1987. pap. 9.95 (0-88740-100-7) Schiffer.

Rodee, Marian & Ostler, Jim. Zuni Contemporary Pottery. LC 87-655. (Illus.). 92p. 1987. pap. 9.95 (0-317-60740-5) Max Mus.

Rodee, Marian E. One Hundred Years of Navajo Rugs. LC 94-3211. Orig. Title: Old Navajo Rugs. 200p. 1995. pap. 29.95 (0-8263-1576-3) U of NM Pr.

Rodefer, Stephen. Four Lectures. 1982. pap. 10.00 (0-935724-13-3) Figures.

— Passing Duration. (Burning Deck Poetry Ser.). 80p. (Orig.). 1991. pap. 8.00 (0-930901-76-2) Burning Deck.

— Passing Duration. deluxe ed. (Burning Deck Poetry Ser.). 80p. (Orig.). 1991. Signed. pap. 15.00 (0-930901-77-0) Burning Deck.

Rodegast, Pat & Stanton, Judith. Emmanuel's Book. (New Age Ser.). 1987. pap. 11.95 (0-553-34387-4) Bantam.

— Emmanuel's Book II: The Choice for Love. 1989. pap. 11.95 (0-553-34750-0) Bantam.

***Rodegast, Pat & Stanton, Judith, eds.** What Is an Angel Doing Here? LC 94-16006. (Emmanuel's Bks.: 3). 1994. pap. 11.95 (0-553-37412-5) Bantam.

Rodegast, Roland, jt. auth. see Reardon, Ruth.

Rodeghier, Mark. UFO Reports Involving Vehicle Interference: A Catalogue & Data Analysis. 156p. (C). 1981. pap. 8.00 (0-929343-55-7) J A Hynek Ctr UFO.

Rodehaver, Myles W., et al. The Sociology of the School. LC 80-26021. x, 262p. (C). 1981. reprint ed. text ed. 59.75 (0-313-22897-3, ROSSC, Greenwood Pr) Greenwood.

Rodeheaver, Homer A. Hymnal Handbook for Standard Hymns & Gospel Songs. LC 72-1686. reprint ed. 31.50 (0-404-09913-0) AMS Pr.

— Singing Black. LC 72-1681. reprint ed. 31.50 (0-404-08330-7) AMS Pr.

Rodeike, Peter, jt. auth. see Prien, Jochen.

Rodeiro, Joseph, illus. The Immanentist Anthology: Art of the Superconscious. LC 72-96447. 120p. 1973. pap. 6.00 (0-912292-30-X) The Smith.

Rodell, Fred. Nine Men: A Political History of the Supreme Court from 1790-1955. xii, 338p. 1988. reprint ed. lib. bdg. 35.00 (0-8377-2541-0) Rothman.

Rodell, Fred & Frank, Jerome. Woe unto You, Lawyers! 2nd ed. 184p. 1987. reprint ed. lib. bdg. 22.50 (0-8377-2536-4) Rothman.

Rodell, M. J. & Skinner, R. J., eds. People, Poverty & Shelter: Problems of Self-Help Housing in the Third World. LC 83-7967. (Illus.). 195p. 1983. pap. 15.95 (0-416-30960-7, NO. 3953) Routledge Chapman & Hall.

Rodell, Susanna. Dear Fred. LC 94-19926. (Illus.). (J). 1995. 13.95 (0-395-71544-X) Ticknor & Flds Bks Yng Read.

Roden, Bob, ed. see Health for Life Staff.

Roden, Christopher, ed. see Doyle, Arthur Conan.

Roden, Claudia. A Book of Middle Eastern Food. (Illus.). 1974. pap. 16.00 (0-394-71948-4) Knopf.

— Coffee. (Handbook Ser.). 144p. (Orig.). 1981. mass mkt. 8.00 (0-14-046489-1, Penguin Bks) Viking Penguin.

— Coffee: A Connoisseur's Companion. rev. ed. LC 94-18119. (Illus.). 1994. 15.00 (0-679-43739-8) Random.

— Everything Tastes Better Outdoors. LC 94-39695. (Illus.). 1995. reprint ed. write for info. (0-517-12234-0) Wings Bks.

— Good Food of Italy. 1990. 30.00 (0-394-58250-0) Knopf.

— Mediterranean Cookery. 1992. pap. 19.00 (0-679-72835-X) McKay.

Roden, Donald. Schooldays in Imperial Japan: A Study in the Culture of a Student Elite. LC 79-64477. (Illus.). 314p. reprint ed. pap. 89.50 (0-7837-4842-6, 2044489) Bks Demand.

Roden, Martin S. Analog & Digital Communication Systems. 3rd ed. 1990. text ed. 76.00 (0-13-033325-5) P-H.

— Analog & Digital Communication Systems. 4th ed. LC 95-11659. 1995. text ed. 75.00 (0-13-372046-2) P-H.

— Micro-Cap II: Student Manual & Software. (C). 1989. pap. text ed. 24.95 (0-685-18622-9); 5.25 hd 37.45 (0-201-50542-8) Benjamin-Cummings.

— The Student Edition of MICRO-CAP IV. LC 92-41039. 1993. pap. text ed. 47.50 (0-8053-1714-7); pap. text ed. 47.50 (0-8053-1715-5) Benjamin-Cummings.

***Roden, Robert B.** Journey to Wholeness: How to Create Lasting Change & Discover True Happiness. 288p. 1995. 24.95 (0-9646217-3-8) WillowBrk Pub.

Rodenas, Paula. The Random House Book of Horses & Horsemanship. LC 86-42934. (Illus.). 192p. (J). (gr. 3-7). 1991. 17.95 (0-394-88705-0) Random Bks Yng Read.

Rodenbach, Georges. Bruges-La-Morte. Mosley, Philip, tr. LC 86-51023. 78p. (FRE.). 1986. pap. 12.95 (0-905075-23-4, Pub. by Wilfion Bks UK) Dufour.

Rodenbeck, Adolph J. The Anatomy of the Law: A Logical Presentation of the Parts of the Body of the Law. xi, 292p. 1992. reprint ed. 37.50 (0-8377-2546-1) Rothman.

Rodenbeck, John, ed. see Mahfouz, Naguib.

***Rodenberger, Lou H.** Jane Gilmore Rushing. LC 95-75725. (Western Writers Ser.: No. 118). (Illus.). 49p. (C). 1995. pap. 3.95x (0-88430-117-6) Boise St U W Writ Ser.

Rodenborg, L. Epilithische Vegetation in Einem Alten Waldgebiet auf Mittel-Oeland, Schweden. (Bibliotheca Lichenologica Ser.: No. 8). (Illus.). 1977. pap. text ed. 20.00 (3-7682-1151-7) Lubrecht & Cramer.

Rodenborn, Billie J. Double Image. 1994. 11.95 (0-8062-4883-1) Carlton.

Rodenbough, T. F., et al. The Photographic History of the Civil War, 3 vols. in 1. (Illus.). 1024p. 1990. 19.99 (0-517-69266-X) Random Hse Value.

Rodenbough, Theo F. Photographic History of the Civil War, Vol. II. (Illus.). 1987. 14.98 (1-55521-199-2) Bk Sales Inc.

— Photographic History of the Civil War, Vol. IV. (Illus.). 1987. 14.98 (1-55521-201-8) Bk Sales Inc.

— Photographic History of the Civil War, Vol. III: Forts & Artillery - The Navies. 1987. 14.98 (1-55521-200-X) Bk Sales Inc.

— Photographic History of the Civil War, Vol. V: The Armies & Leaders - Poetry & Eloquence. 1987. 14.98 (1-55521-202-6) Bk Sales Inc.

Rodenbough, Theo R. Photographic History of the Civil War, Vol. I: The Opening Battles - Two Years of Grim War. (Illus.). 1987. 14.98 (1-55521-174-7) Bk Sales Inc.

Rodenburg, J., jt. auth. see Hengeveld, R.

Rodenburg, Patsy. The Need for Words. LC 93-7959. 45.00 (0-685-65135-5) Routledge Chapman & Hall.

— Need for Words: Voice & Text. 1993. pap. 16.95 (0-87830-051-1, Theatre Arts Bks) Routledge Chapman & Hall.

— The Right to Speak: Working with the Voice. LC 93-17448. 1993. 45.00 (0-87830-054-6); pap. write for info. (0-87830-055-4) Routledge Chapman & Hall.

Rodengen, Jeffery. Iron Fist: The Lives of Carl Kiekhaefer. 640p. 1992. 24.95 (0-945903-04-9) Write Stuff Syndicate.

Rodengen, Jeffrey L. Evinrude, Johnson & the Legend of OMC. 144p. 1992. 39.95 (0-945903-10-3) Write Stuff Syndicate.

— The Legend of Chris-Craft. (Illus.). 304p. 1988. 49.95 (0-945903-02-2) Write Stuff Syndicate.

— The Legend of Chris-Craft. 2nd ed. (Illus.). 272p. 1993. 49.95 (0-945903-20-0) Write Stuff Syndicate.

— The Legend of Honeywell. Nitkin, Karen, ed. (Illus.). 240p. 1995. 39.95 (0-945903-25-1) Write Stuff Syndicate.

— Serving the Silent Service: The Legend of Electric Boat. (Illus.). 144p. Date not set. 39.95 (0-945903-24-3) Write Stuff Syndicate.

Rodengen, Jeffrey L., ed. see Aronow, Michael.

Rodenhauser, Paul, ed. see Reichard, Birge D. & Siewers, Christiane M.

***Rodenhouse, Mary P. & Torregrosa, Constance H., eds.** HEP Higher Education Directory, 1995. annuals 640p. 1994. pap. 47.00 (0-614-04755-2) Higher Ed Pubns.

Rodenstein, Judith. Dietetic Career Recruitment Study. 32p. 1990. spiral bd. 16.50 (0-88091-075-5, 0405) Am Dietetic Assn.

— Microcomputers in Vocational Education: Programs & Practices. (Illus.). 224p. 1986. pap. text ed. 25.00 (0-13-580507-4) P-H.

***Rodent.** Explaining the Inexplicable: The Rodent's Guide to Lawyers. 224p. 1995. 16.00 (0-671-52294-9) PB.

Rodenwalt, Gerhart. The Acropolis. 2nd ed. LC 58-6859. (Illus.). 167p. reprint ed. pap. 47.60 (0-8357-5082-5, 2016258) Bks Demand.

Roder, Michael M. Guide for Evaluating the Performance of Chemical Protective Clothing. (Illus.). 93p. 1990. pap. 4.75 (0-16-024958-9, S/N 017-033-00446-3) USGPO.

Roder-Thiede, Maike. Chinchillas: A Complete Pet Owner's Manual. LC 92-32050. (Complete Pet Owner's Manuals Ser.). 80p. 1993. pap. 5.95 (0-8120-1471-5) Barron.

Roder, Wolf. Human Adjustment to Kainji Reservoir in Nigeria: An Assessment of the Economic & Environmental Consequences of a Major Man-Made Lake in Africa. 206p. (Orig.). (C). 1994. lib. bdg. 42.50 (0-8191-9333-X); pap. text ed. 29.50 (0-8191-9334-8) U Pr of Amer.

Rodereda, Merce. The Time of the Doves. Rosenthal, David H., tr. LC 85-80976. 201p. 1986. reprint ed. pap. 12.00 (0-915308-75-4) Graywolf.

***Roderer, Phyllis.** Human Resource Management in Associations. Sabo, Sandy, ed. LC 94-21905. 1994. 45.00 (0-88034-083-5) Am Soc Assn Execs.

Roderick, Don, ed. see Lawson, L. & Hardy, H.

Roderick, G. W., jt. auth. see Stephens, M. D.

Roderick, Gary, jt. auth. see Sims, Charles.

Roderick, Gordon W., jt. ed. see Stephens, Michael D.

Roderick, Hilliard. Acid Rain & Friendly Neighbors: The Policy Dispute Between Canada & the United States. rev. ed. Schmandt, Jurgen, ed. LC 88-25605. (Duke Press Policy Studies). (Illus.). 340p. (C). 1989. lib. bdg. 48.00 (0-8223-0870-3) Duke.

Roderick, Hilliard & Magnusson, Ulla, eds. Avoiding Inadvertent War: Crisis Management. (Tom Slick World Peace Ser.). 175p. 1983. 5.00 (0-89940-005-1) LBJ Sch Pub Aff.

Roderick, John. Covering China: The Story of an American Reporter from Revolutionary Days to the Deng Era. (Illus.). 230p. 1993. 39.95 (1-879176-18-1); pap. 19.95 (1-879176-17-3) Imprint Pubns.

Roderick, Kyle. Married in the Movies. LC 93-34291. 80p. 1994. 14.95 (0-00-255368-6) Collins SF.

Roderick, Lee. Leading the Charge: Orrin Hatch & 20 Years of America. LC 94-2048. 447p. 1994. 22.95 (1-882723-09-0) Gold Leaf Pr.

***Roderick, Libby.** When I Hear Music. (Illus.). 118p. (Orig.). 1994. pap. write for info. (0-9641114-1-1) Turtle Islnd.

Roderick, Melissa. The Path to Dropping Out: Evidence for Intervention. LC 92-42905. 240p. 1993. text ed. 49.95 (0-86569-206-8, T206, Auburn Hse) Greenwood.

Roderick, Timothy. The Once Unknown Familiar: Shamanic Paths to Unleash Your Animal Powers. LC 94-5748. 1994. pap. 10.00 (0-87542-439-2) Llewellyn Pubns.

Roderick, Wanda W. Legal Studies to Wit: Basic Legal Terminology & Transcription. 2nd ed. 1984. write for info. (0-538-11360-X, K36) S-W Pub.

***Rodero, Cristina G.** Espana Oculta: Public Celebrations in Spain, 1974-1989. (Illus.). 140p. 1995. pap. 39.95 (1-56098-530-5) Smithsonian.

Rodero, Cristina G., photos. Spain: Festivals & Rituals. LC 93-23289. (Illus.). 1994. 49.50 (0-8109-3839-1) Abrams.

Roders, Mary M., jt. auth. see Hoff, Mary.

Roderus, Frank. Charlie & the Sir. large type ed. LC 93-6616. (Nightingale Ser.). 1993. 14.95 (0-8161-5774-X) G K Hall.

— Duster. LC 85-14759. (Chaparral Bks.). (Illus.). 266p. (J). (gr. 4 up). 1987. reprint ed. 14.95 (0-87565-055-4); reprint ed. pap. 10.95 (0-87565-095-3) Tex Christian.

— Hell Creek Cabin. 1994. 14.95 (0-7451-4597-3, Gunsmoke) Chivers N Amer.

— J. A. Whitford & the Great California Gold Hunt. large type ed. (Nightingale Series Large Print Bks.). 276p. 1991. pap. 14.95 (0-8161-5173-3, Nightingale) Hall.

Rodes, Barbara, jt. auth. see Irwin, Frances.

Rodes, Barbara K. & Odell, Rice. A Dictionary of Environmental Quotations. 288p. 1992. 35.00 (0-13-210576-4) S&S Trade.

Rodes, David S., ed. see Shadwell, Thomas.

Rodes, David S., ed. see Southerne, Thomas.

Rodes, Robert. Lay Authority & Reformation in the English Church. LC 82-7038. 319p. 1982. 30.00 (0-268-01265-2) U of Notre Dame Pr.

Rodes, Robert E. Law & Liberation. LC 85-41011. 240p. 1986. text ed. 29.95 (0-268-01279-2) U of Notre Dame Pr.

Rodes, Robert E., Jr. Law & Modernization in the Church of England: Charles II to the Welfare State. LC 91-50567. (Study of the Legal History of Establishment in England Ser.: Vol. 3). (C). 1991. text ed. 34.95 (0-268-01293-8) U of Notre Dame Pr.

Rodewald, Fred A., ed. see Hays, John Q.

Rodewald, G., jt. ed. see Willner, A. E.

Rodewald, Janet D. Reviewing German Grammar: A Self-Instructional Reference Book for Elementary German Grammar. LC 84-21884. 364p. (Orig.). 1985. pap. text ed. 38.00 (0-8191-4366-9) U Pr of Amer.

***Rodewalt, Vance.** Rodewalt: With Weapons Drawn. (Illus.). 128p. (Orig.). 1994. pap. 16.95 (1-55059-092-8) Temeron Bks.

Rodey, Dickason, Sloan, Akin & Robb Staff. New Mexico Environmental Law Handbook. 2nd ed. (State Environmental Law Ser.). 404p. 1991. pap. text ed. 74.00 (0-86587-268-6) Gov Insts.

Rodey, Glenn. HLA Beyond Tears. 190p. 1991. pap. text ed. 24.95 (0-9631020-0-1) De Novo GA.

***Rodger, Alison & Rodger, P. Mark.** Molecular Geometry. (Illus.). 208p. (C). 1995. pap. text ed. 32.95 (0-7506-2295-4, Focal) Buttrwrth-Heinemann.

***Rodger, David & Hazlett, Deborah.** Creative Production Source Book: 1995 Edition. 526p. (Orig.). (C). 1995. pap. 35.00 (0-911747-28-1) Broadway Pr.

Rodger, Eleanor J. Commitment to Renewal: Baltimore County Public Library Long Range Plan, 1989-1993. (Illus.). 55p. 1988. pap. 20.00 (0-937076-04-X) Baltimore Co Pub Lib.

— Repositioning for the Future: Baltimore County Public Library Long Range Plan 1994-1999. (Illus.). 32p. 1994. 20.00 (0-937076-05-8) Baltimore Co Pub Lib.

Rodger, Elizabeth. Boo to You, Too. LC 92-40023. (J). 1993. write for info. (0-671-86765-2, S&S Bks Young Read); pap. 2.95 (0-671-86766-0, S&S Bks Young Read) S&S Childrens.

— Christmas Without a Tree. LC 94-44399. (J). 1995. pap. write for info. (0-689-80157-2, Aladdin Paperbacks) S&S Childrens.

— Ollie Solves a Messy Mystery. (Read with Me Paperback Ser.). (Illus.). 32p. (J). (ps-2). 1993. pap. 2.50 (0-590-44885-4) Scholastic Inc.

Rodger, Frederick C., ed. Onchocerciasis in Zaire. LC 76-39949. 1977. 90.00 (0-08-020619-0, Pub. by Pergamon Repr UK) Franklin.

Rodger, Jude. Dragon Book. (J). 1993. pap. 15.95 (1-85756-042-6, Pub. by Janus Pub UK) Intl Spec Bk.

Rodger, N. A. The Admiralty. 216p. (C). 1988. 120.00 (0-900963-94-8, Pub. by T Dalton UK) St Mut.

— The Armada in the Public Records. LC 88-179916. (Illus.). 75p. 1988. 5.95 (0-11-440215-9, HM1919, Pub. by HMSO UK) UNIPUB.

— Articles of War: The Statutes Which Governed Our Fighting Navies 1661-1749 & 1866. 62p. 1987. 40.00 (0-85937-275-8, Pub. by K Mason Pubns Ltd UK) St Mut.

— The Insatiable Earl. 480p. 1994. 30.00 (0-393-03587-5) Norton.

Rodger, P. Mark, jt. auth. see Rodger, Alison.

Rodger, R. Fish Facts. 1990. pap. 38.95 (0-442-00543-1) Chapman & Hall.

Rodger, Richard. Research in Urban History: A Classified Survey of Doctoral & Masters' Theses. 281p. 1994. 78.95 (1-85928-082-X, Pub. by Scolar Pr UK) Ashgate Pub Co.

— Urban History Yearbook, 1989. 280p. 1989. 42.00 (0-7185-6089-2, Pub. by Pinter Pubs UK) St Martin.

Rodger, Richard, ed. European Urban History: Prospect & Retrospect. 224p. 1993. text ed. 54.00 (0-7185-1432-7, Pub. by Pinter Pubs UK) St Martin.

— Scottish Housing in the Twentieth Century. 264p. 1993. pap. 20.00 (0-7185-1493-9, Pub. by Pinter Pubs UK) St Martin.

— Urban History Yearbook, 1988. 280p. 1989. 39.00 (0-7185-6088-4, Pub. by Pinter Pubs UK) St Martin.

— Urban History Yearbook, 1990. (Illus.). 300p. 1990. 39.00 (0-7185-6090-6, Pub. by Pinter Pubs UK) St Martin.

— Urban History Yearbook, 1991. (Illus.). 300p. 1992. text ed. 65.00 (0-7185-6091-4, Pub. by Pinter Pubs UK) St Martin.

Rodger, Richard, jt. auth. see Aldcroft, Derek H.

Rodger, Richard, jt. ed. see Morris, R. J.

Rodger, Rosemary, jt. auth. see Abbott, Lesley.

***Rodgers.** Comic Fun. 1995. pap. (0-590-47027-2) Scholastic Inc.

Rodgers & Hammerstein. Carousel: Vocal Selections from the Show. rev. ed. (Illus.). 56p. 1989. pap. 8.95 (0-88188-636-X, 01121008) H Leonard.

— Cinderella - Vocal Selections: Vocal Selections from the Show. rev. ed. (Illus.). 1989. pap. 8.95 (0-88188-069-8, HL 00312091) H Leonard.

— Sound of Music. 1960. 12.95 (0-394-40724-5) Random.

Rodgers, A. Mary. A Billion for Boris. LC 74-3586. 192p. (J). (gr. 5 up). 1974. lib. bdg. 14.89 (0-06-025054-2) HarpC Child Bks.

***Rodgers, Alan.** Bone Music. LC 95-15526. 1995. write for info. (0-681-10086-9) Longmeadow Pr.

— Pandora. 1995. mass mkt. 5.50 (0-553-56305-X) Bantam.

Rodgers, Alan, jt. auth. see Diaz, Gisele.

Rodgers, Allan, ed. Soviet Far East: Geographical Perspectives on Development. (Illus.). 336p. 1990. 52.50 (0-415-02406-4, A4721) Routledge.

Rodgers, Andrew D., III. Bernhard Eduard Fernow: A Story of North American Forestry. 640p. 1991. reprint ed. text ed. 21.95 (0-89030-047-X) Duke.

Rodgers, Audrey T. Denise Levertov: The Poetry of Engagement. LC 92-53065. (Illus.). 240p. (C). 1993. 37. 50 (0-8386-3494-X) Fairleigh Dickinson.

Rodgers, Barbara S., jt. auth. see Nixon, C. E.

Rodgers, Bernard F., Jr. Philip Roth: A Bibliography. 2nd ed. LC 84-5452. (Author Bibliographies Ser.: No. 19). 399p. 1984. 32.50 (0-8108-1699-7) Scarecrow.

Rodgers, Beth L. & Knafl, Kathleen A. Concept Development in Nursing: Foundations, Techniques, & Applications. (Illus.). 256p. 1993. pap. text ed. 36.95 (0-7216-3674-8) Saunders.

Rodgers, Bill, et al. Bill Rodgers & Priscilla Welch on Masters Running & Racing. LC 91-11263. (Illus.). 192p. 1991. 16.95 (0-87857-972-9, 12-751-0) Rodale Pr Inc.

Rodgers, C. Leland, jt. auth. see Snyder, John A.

Rodgers, C. Leland, jt. auth. see Snyder, John.

***Rodgers, Carrie.** My Husband Jimmie Rodgers. 2nd ed. LC 95-68521. (Illus.). 224p. 1995. reprint ed. pap. 14.95 (0-915608-16-2) Country Music Found.

***Rodgers, Christopher P.** Private Sector Housing Law. 344p. 1994. pap. text ed. 65.00 (0-406-12909-6, UK) Butterworth Legal Pubs.

Rodgers, Christopher P. & Margrave-Jones, Clive V. Agricultural Law. 1991. U.K. pap. 99.00 (0-406-11269-X) Butterworth Legal Pubs.

Rodgers, Cook & Rutherford, Clarice. Kids & Pets: A Family Guide to Living & Growing Together. (Illus.). (Orig.). Date not set. pap. write for info. (0-931866-61-8) Alpine Pubns.

Rodgers, Daniel T. The Work Ethic in Industrial America: 1850-1920. LC 77-81737. 1979. pap. text ed. 11.95 (0-226-72352-6) U Ch Pr.

Rodgers, David L. Killer Sleep. (Illus.). 201p. (Orig.). 1988. pap. 6.95 (0-9621251-0-5) D L Rodgers.

Rodgers, Dirk. John a Lasco in England Vol. 168. LC 93-41633. (American University Studies: No. VII). 205p. (C). 1994. text ed. 42.95 (0-8204-2340-8) P Lang Pubs.

***Rodgers, Drew.** Communication: International Case Studies in English. 176p. (C). 1995. pap. text ed. 19.95 (0-312-11171-1) St Martin.

Rodgers, Edith C. Discussion of Holidays in the Latter Middle Ages. LC 41-3851. (Columbia University. Studies in the Social Sciences: No. 474). reprint ed. 20. 00 (0-404-51474-X) AMS Pr.

Rodgers, Elizabeth. Ollie Goes to School. (Illus.). 32p. (J). (ps-2). 1992. pap. 2.50 (0-590-44785-8, Cartwheel) Scholastic Inc.

Rodgers, Eugene. Beyond the Barrier: The Story of Byrd's First Expedition to Antarctica. LC 89-28450. 320p. 1990. 25.95 (0-87021-022-X) Naval Inst Pr.

Rodgers, Frank. I Can't Get to Sleep. LC 90-19607. (Illus.). 32p. (J). (ps-1). 1993. pap. 7.95 (0-671-79848-0, S&S Bks Young Read) S&S Childrens.

— Who's Afraid of the Ghost Train? (Illus.). 23p. (J). (ps-1). 1989. 12.95 (0-15-200642-7, Gulliver Bks) HarBrace.

Rodgers, G. Kryptic: The Little Space Guy. (Illus.). 32p. (J). (gr. 2-6). 1989. 10.95 (0-88625-246-6) Durkin Hayes Pub.

Rodgers, Gerry, ed. Urban Poverty & the Labour Market: Access to Jobs & Incomes in Asian & Latin American Cities. vi, 257p. (Orig.). 1989. pap. 28.00 (92-2-106500-6); pap. 38.00 (92-2-106499-9) Intl Labour Office.

Rodgers, Gerry & Rodgers, Janine, eds. Precarious Jobs in Labour Market Regulation: The Growth of Atypical Employment in Western Europe. x, 301p. (Orig.). 1989. pap. 20.00 (92-9014-453-X); pap. 28.00 (92-9014-452-1) Intl Labour Office.

Rodgers, Gerry & Standing, Guy, eds. Child Work, Poverty & Underdevelopment: Issues for Research in Low-Income Countries. (WEP Study Ser.). xii, 310p. (Orig.). 1981. 28.00 (92-2-102812-7); pap. 20.00 (92-2-102813-5) Intl Labour Office.

Rodgers, Gerry, jt. ed. see Deshpande, L. K.

Rodgers, Glen E. Introduction to Coordination, Solid State, & Descriptive Inorganic Chemistry. LC 93-15952. 1993. text ed. write for info. (0-07-053384-9) McGraw.

Rodgers, Glendon J., jt. auth. see Boyd, William H.

Rodgers, H. J. Twenty-Three Years Under a Skylight; or, Life & Experiences of a Photographer. LC 72-9233. (Literature of Photography Ser.). (Illus.). 1973. reprint ed. 21.95 (0-405-04938-2) Ayer.

Rodgers, Harold R., et al, eds. Arlington Dictionary of Electronics. (Illus.). 1971. text ed. 25.00 (0-8464-0146-0) Beekman Pubs.

Rodgers, Harrell & Weiher, Gregory, eds. Rural vs. Urban Poverty. (Orig.). 1988. pap. 12.00 (0-944285-05-8) Pol Studies.

Rodgers, Harrell R., Jr. Cost of Human Neglect: America's Welfare Failure. LC 82-10390. 236p. 1982. pap. text ed. 22.95 (0-87332-238-X) M E Sharpe.

— Poor Women, Poor Families: The Economic Plight of America's Female-Headed Households. rev. ed. LC 89-24372. 208p. (C). 1990. 46.95 (0-87332-594-X); pap. text ed. 20.95 (0-87332-595-8) M E Sharpe.

— Poverty Amid Plenty: A Political & Economic Analysis. (Political Science Ser.). (Illus.). 240p. (C). 1979. text ed. 9.75 (0-394-34937-7) Random.

Rodgers, Harrell R., Jr., ed. Beyond Welfare: New Approaches to the Problem of Poverty in America. LC 87-28876. 184p. 1988. pap. text ed. 25.95 (0-87332-461-7) M E Sharpe.

Rodgers, Harrell R., Jr. & Weiher, Gregory, eds. Rural Poverty: Special Causes & Policy Reforms. LC 88-35817. (Studies in Social Welfare Policies & Programs: No. 12). 190p. 1989. text ed. 47.95 (0-313-26630-1, RRR/, Greenwood Pr) Greenwood.

Rodgers, Harrell R., jt. auth. see Leichter, H. M., Jr.

Rodgers, J. An Archaeological Investigation of Buckeye Hills East, Maricopa County, Arizona. (Anthropological Research Papers: No. 10). (Illus.). vii, 116p. 1976. 10.00 (0-685-19295-4) AZ Univ ARP.

— Archaeological Investigations along the Granite Reef Aqueduct, Cave Creek Archaeological District, Arizona. (Anthropological Research Papers: No. 12). (Illus.). ix, 185p. 1977. 15.00 (0-685-19296-2) AZ Univ ARP.

Rodgers, Jack. Navigator's Log (Of a Tour in Bomber Command) (C). 1989. 35.00 (0-86303-254-0) St Mut.

— Selected Options for Expanding Health Insurance Coverage. (Illus.). 79p. (Orig.). (C). 1994. pap. text ed. 50.00 (0-7881-0418-7) Diane Pub.

Rodgers, James B., jt. auth. see Henderson, T. Kathleen.

Rodgers, James T., jt. auth. see Rodgers-Rose, La Francis.

Rodgers, James W. A Winnie-the-Pooh Christmas Tail: Christmas Musical. 1994. 4.25 (0-87129-225-4, W03) Dramatic Pub.

***Rodgers, James W. & Rodgers, Wanda C.** Play Director's Survival Kit: A Complete Step-by-Step Guide to Producing Theater in Any School or Community Setting. LC 94-43944. (Illus.). 1995. spiral bd. 29.95 (0-87628-862-X) Ctr Appl Res.

Rodgers, Janine, jt. ed. see Rodgers, Gerry.

Rodgers, Jimmie. Jimmie Rodgers Memorial Folios, 2 vols., 1. pap. 9.95 (0-686-09063-2, Peer-Southern) CPP Belwin.

— Jimmie Rodgers Memorial Folios, 2 vols., 2. pap. 9.95 (0-686-09064-0, Peer-Southern) CPP Belwin.

Rodgers, Joann. Cancer. (Medical Disorders & Their Treatment Ser.). (Illus.). 112p. (YA). (gr. 6 up). 1990. 18.95 (0-7910-0059-1) Chelsea Hse.

— Drugs & Pain. (Encyclopedia of Psychoactive Drugs Ser.: No. 2). (Illus.). 144p. 1987. lib. bdg. 19.95 (1-55546-212-X) Chelsea Hse.

— Drugs & Sexual Behavior. (Encyclopedia of Psychoactive Drugs Ser.: No. 2). (Illus.). 96p. (YA). (gr. 5 up). 1988. lib. bdg. 19.95 (1-55546-215-4) Chelsea Hse.

Rodgers, Joann & Adams, William C. Media Resource Guide. 2nd ed. Ferring, Mike, ed. (Illus.). 87p. 1994. pap. 10.00 (0-910755-02-7) Foun Am Comm.

Rodgers, John. Liturgy & Communication. (C). 1988. 39.00 (0-85439-113-4, Pub. by St Paul Pubns UK) St Mut.

Rodgers, John, jt. auth. see Schaer, Jean-Paul.

Rodgers, Joseph J., Jr., tr. see Gounard, Jean-Francois.

Rodgers, Judith. Winston Churchill. (World Leaders - Past & Present Ser.). (Illus.). 112p. (YA). (gr. 5 up). 1986. lib. bdg. 17.95 (0-87754-563-4) Chelsea Hse.

Rodgers, Kathleen E., jt. auth. see DiZerega, Gere S.

Rodgers, M. A., jt. auth. see Farhataziz.

Rodgers, M. J. The Adventuress. (American Romance Ser.). 1994. mass mkt. 3.50 (0-373-16520-X, 1-16520-8) Harlequin Bks.

— Baby vs. the Bar. 1995. mass mkt. 3.50 (0-373-22342-0, 1-22342-9) Harlequin Bks.

— Beauty vs. the Beast. (Intrigue Ser.). 1995. mass mkt. 3.50 (0-373-22335-8, 1-22335-3) Harlequin Bks.

— Bones of Contention. (Intrigue Ser.: No. 176). 1991. pap. 2.79 (0-373-22176-2, 1-22176-1) Harlequin Bks.

— Fire Magic. (American Romance Ser.). 1993. mass mkt. 3.50 (0-373-16492-0, 1-16492-0) Harlequin Bks.

— The Gift-Wrapped Groom. (American Romance Ser.). 1994. mass mkt. 3.50 (0-373-16563-3, 1-16563-8) Harlequin Bks.

— Heart vs. Humbug. 1995. pap. 3.50 (0-373-22350-1, 1-22350-2) Harlequin Bks.

— Santa Claus Is Coming. (Intrigue Ser.). 1993. mass mkt. 2.99 (0-373-22254-8, 1-22254-6) Harlequin Bks.

— To Die For. (Intrigue Ser.). 1993. pap. 2.89 (0-373-22214-9, 1-22214-0) Harlequin Bks.

— Who Is Jane Williams? (Intrigue Ser.). 1994. mass mkt. 2.99 (0-373-22290-4, 1-22290-0) Harlequin Bks.

Rodgers, Marion E. Mencken & Sara: A Life in Letters: The Correspondence of H. L. Mencken & Sara Hardt. 1992. pap. 15.00 (0-385-41980-5) Doubleday.

Rodgers, Marion E., ed. Impossible H. L. Mencken: A Selection of His Best Newspaper Stories. 707p. 1991. pap. 15.00 (0-385-26208-6) Doubleday.

Rodgers, Mary. A Billion for Boris. LC 74-3586. (Trophy Bk.). 192p. (J). (gr. 5 up). 1976. reprint ed. pap. 3.95 (0-06-440075-1, Trophy) HarpC Child Bks.

— Freaky Friday. LC 74-183158. 156p. (J). (gr. 5-8). 1972. 14.95 (0-06-025048-8); lib. bdg. 14.89 (0-06-025049-6) HarpC Child Bks.

— Freaky Friday. LC 74-183158. (Trophy Bk.). 156p. (J). (gr. 5 up). 1973. reprint ed. pap. 3.95 (0-06-440046-8, Trophy) HarpC Child Bks.

— Freaky Friday - Viernes Embrujado. McShane, Barbara & Alfaya, Javier, trs. 118p. (SPA.). (J). (gr. 5-8). 1987. pap. 5.95 (84-204-3640-2) Santillana.

— Summer Switch. LC 79-2690. (Charlotte Zolotow Bk.). 192p. (J). (gr. 5 up). 1982. 14.95 (0-06-025058-5); lib. bdg. 12.89 (0-06-025059-3) HarpC Child Bks.

— Summer Switch. LC 79-2690. (Trophy Bk.). 192p. (J). (gr. 5 up). 1984. pap. 3.50 (0-06-440140-5, Trophy) HarpC Child Bks.

Rodgers, Mary C. Access List to the Open University Literary Trust. 50p. (Orig.). 1993. pap. 7.00 (0-89848-273-9) Open Univ Am.

— Catholic Marriage Poems 1962-1979. LC 94-15579. (Illus.). 72p. 1994. pap. 14.95 (0-7734-0013-3) E Mellen.

— Catholic Widow with Children Poems 1979-1993: Poems, 1979-1993. LC 94-48866. 84p. 1995. pap. 14.95 (0-7734-2756-2, Mellen Poetry Pr) E Mellen.

— Convent Poems, 1943-1961. LC 92-32473. 76p. 1992. pap. 12.95 (0-7734-0037-0) E Mellen.

Rodgers, Mary M. & Hoff, Mary. Our Endangered Planet: Oceans. (Illus.). 72p. (J). (gr. 4 up). 1991. lib. bdg. 21.50 (0-8225-2505-4, Lerner Publctns) Lerner Group.

Rodgers, Mary M., jt. auth. see Hoff, Mary K.

Rodgers, Mary M., jt. auth. see Hoff, Mary.

Rodgers, Mary M., jt. auth. see Mutel, Cornelia F.

Rodgers, Mary M., jt. auth. see Winckler, Suzanne.

Rodgers, Mary M., jt. auth. see Yount, Lisa.

Rodgers, Patricia H. A Symphony of Color: Stained Glass at First Church. (Illus.). 63p. (Orig.). 1990. pap. write for info. (0-9626196-0-4) United Ch Cambridge.

Rodgers, Peter. Knowing Jesus. rev. ed. 44p. (Orig.). 1990. pap. 1.95 (0-88028-110-3, 1076) Forward Movement.

Rodgers, R. E. The Incarnation of the Antithesis. 105p. (C). 1989. pap. text ed. 40.00 (1-872795-91-9, Pub. by Pentland Pr UK) St Mut.

Rodgers, R. J. & Cooper, S. J., eds. Endorphins, Opiates & Behavioural Processes. LC 87-18890. 361p. 1988. text ed. 199.95 (0-471-91675-7) Wiley.

— Five-Ht 1A Agonists, 5-Ht 3 Antagonists & Benzodiazepines: Their Comparative Behavioral Pharmacology. 387p. 1991. text ed. 159.95 (0-471-92793-7, Wiley-Liss) Wiley.

Rodgers, Raboo. Magnum Fault. 192p. (J). (gr. 5 up). 1984. 11.95 (0-685-07882-5, 5-95260) HM.

Rodgers, Raymond S., ed. Free Speech Yearbook, Vol. 28, 1990. 312p. (C). 1991. 34.95x (0-8093-1700-1); pap. 14. 95 (0-8093-1701-X) S Ill U Pr.

***Rodgers, Rich.** The Perfect Party: Birthday Celebrations. (Illus.). 64p. 1996. write for info. (0-446-91096-1) Warner Bks.

***Rodgers, Richard.** Do Re Mi: Sing-a-Song Storybooks. (J). (ps-3). 1994. 9.95 (0-7935-3196-9) H Leonard.

Rodgers, Richard, et al. Do Re Mi. (Sing-a-Song Storybook Ser.). (Illus.). 24p. (J). 1994. 9.95 (0-685-74740-9) H Leonard.

Rodgers, Richard. Letters to Dorothy (1926-1937) Appleton, William W., ed. (Illus.). 253p. 1988. 50.00 (0-87104-405-6) NY Pub Lib.

— Musical Stages: An Autobiography. (Illus.). 379p. 1995. reprint ed. pap. 14.95 (0-306-80634-7) Da Capo.

Rodgers, Richard & Hart, Lorenz. Rodgers & Hart: A Musical Anthology. (Illus.). 144p. 1984. pap. 19.95 (0-88188-337-9, 00307940) H Leonard.

Rodgers, Richard, jt. auth. see Hammerstein, Oscar, II.

Rodgers, Richard K. Marketing Legal Services: ...Developing & Growing Client Relationships for the 1990s. 212p. 1993. student ed, spiral bd. write for info. (0-9641994-0-8) K Rodgers Grp.

Rodgers, Rick. Mister Pasta's Health Pasta Cookbook: More Than 150 Delicious, Low-Fat Pastas, Pasta Sauces... 1994. 15.95 (0-688-13077-1) Morrow.

— The Perfect Party: Bridal & Baby Showers. (Illus.). 1996. write for info. (0-446-91097-X) Warner Bks.

— The Perfect Party: Picnics, Tailgate Parties. (Illus.). 64p. 1996. write for info. (0-446-91094-5) Warner Bks.

— The Perfect Party: Romantic Dinners. (Illus.). 64p. 1996. write for info. (0-446-91095-3) Warner Bks.

— Three Hundred Sixty-Five Ways to Cook Hamburger: And Other Meats. 1994. mass mkt. 5.99 (0-06-109331-9) HarpC.

— Three Hundred Sixty-Five Ways to Cook Hamburger & Other Ground Meats. LC 91-50445. (Three Hundred Sixty-Five Ways Ser.). 256p. 1992. 17.95 (0-06-016535-9, HarpT) HarpC.

Rodgers, Rick, ed. Ready & Waiting: One Hundred Sixty All-New Recipes for the Slow Cooker. LC 92-9862. 1992. 20.00 (0-688-11023-1) Hearst Bks.

Rodgers, Rick & Delta Queen Steamboat Company Staff. Mississippi Memories. LC 94-4163. 1994. 18.00 (0-688-12799-1) Hearst Bks.

Rodgers-Rose, La Frances, ed. The Black Woman. LC 79-28712. (Focus Editions Ser.: Vol. 21). (Illus.). 316p. 1980. pap. 24.95 (0-8039-1312-5) Sage.

Rodgers-Rose, La Francis & Rodgers, James T. Resolving Conflict in Black Male-Female Relationships. 70p. (Orig.). 1985. pap. 8.95 (0-934185-00-X) Traces Inst.

Rodgers-Rose, LaFrancis, jt. ed. see Aldridge, Delores.

Rodgers, Roy H., jt. auth. see Ahrons, Constance R.

Rodgers, Slats, jt. auth. see Stilwell, Hart.

Rodgers, Susan, ed. Power & Gold: Jewelry from Indonesia, Malaysia & the Philippines from the Collection of the Barkier-Mueller Museum. (Illus.). 369p. 1988. 80.00 (3-7913-0859-9, Pub. by Prestel) TeNeues.

— Telling Lives, Telling Histories: Autobiography & Historical Imagination in Modern Indonesia. LC 94-30282. 1995. 20.00 (0-520-08547-7); pap. text ed. 55.00 (0-520-08546-9) U CA Pr.

Rodgers, Susan, jt. ed. see Kipp, Rita S.

Rodgers, Terry C., jt. ed. see Volkan, Vamik D.

Rodgers, Theodore S., jt. auth. see Richards, Jack C.

Rodgers, Thomas H. Beginners Handbook of Christian Service. LC 92-90930. 70p. (Orig.). 1991. pap. write for info. (0-9633656-1-4) T H Rodgers.

— Joseph's Christmas Story. (Illus.). 12p. (Orig.). 1990. pap. write for info. (0-9633656-0-6) T H Rodgers.

— New Life Handbook: A Study Guide for Christian Growth. Somsak, Lin, ed. & illus. by. 60p. (YA). 1995. write for info. (0-9633656-2-2) T H Rodgers.

Rodgers, Ulka. Oracle: A Database Developer's Guide. (Illus.). 320p. 1991. pap. 32.95 (0-13-488925-8) P-H.

— UNIX Database Management Systems. 352p. 1989. pap. 29.95 (0-13-945593-0) P-H.

Rodgers, Vimala. Change Your Handwriting, Change Your Life. LC 93-6843. (Orig.). 1993. pap. 11.95 (0-89087-693-2) Celestial Arts.

Rodgers, W. A., jt. auth. see Holmwood, K. M.

Rodgers, Wanda C., jt. auth. see Rodgers, James W.

Rodgers, Willard L. & Bachman, Jerald G. The Subjective Well-Being of Young Adults: Trends & Relationships. LC 88-9455. (ISR Research Report Ser.). 256p. (Orig.). 1988. pap. text ed. 20.00 (0-87944-323-5) Inst Soc Res.

Rodgers, William H., Jr. Environmental Law. 2nd ed. LC 94-11577. (Hornbook Ser.). 1994. text ed. 41.00 (0-314-03576-1) West Pub.

— Environmental Law. (Hornbook Ser.). 956p. 1991. reprint ed. text ed. 34.50 (0-314-33231-6) West Pub.

— Environmental Law: Air & Water, 2 vols. LC 86-5578. 1222p. 1987. reprint ed. text ed. write for info. (0-314-98410-0) West Pub.

— Environmental Law: Hazardous Waste & Substance, Vol. 4. 702p. (C). 1991. pap. text ed. write for info. (0-314-90896-X) West Pub.

— Environmental Law: 1984 Pocket Part. (Hornbook Ser.). 223p. 1988. reprint ed. 9.50 (0-314-84121-0) West Pub.

— Environmental Law, Vol. 3: Pesticides & Toxic Substances. 662p. 1989. reprint ed. text ed. write for info. (0-314-43778-9) West Pub.

Rodgers, William L. Greek & Roman Naval Warfare. LC 79-121795. (Illus.). 555p. 1964. reprint ed. 29.95 (0-87021-226-5) Naval Inst Pr.

Rodgerson, Thomas E. Spirituality, Stress & You. LC 94-31705. (Illumination Bks.). 80p. 1994. pap. 3.95 (0-8091-3514-0) Paulist Pr.

Rodgon, Maris M. Single-Word Usage, Cognitive Development, & the Beginnings of Combinatorial Speech: A Study of Ten English-Speaking Children. LC 75-7211. 173p. reprint ed. pap. 49.40 (0-317-26378-1, 2024520) Bks Demand.

Rodhe, Henning & Herrera, R., eds. Acidification in Tropical Countries: (SCOPE 36) LC 88-5667. 405p. 1988. text ed. 350.00 (0-471-91870-9) Wiley.

Rodhe, W., et al, eds. Lake Metabolism & Management: Papers Emanating from the Limnological Symposium of Uppsala University 1977. (Limnology Report: No. 13). (Illus.). 354p. (Orig.). 1979. pap. text ed. 97.50 (3-510-47011-7, Pub. by E Schweizerbartsche GW) Lubrecht & Cramer.

Rodi, Robert. Closet Case: A Novel. LC 93-47343. 336p. 1994. pap. 10.95 (0-452-27211-4, Plume) NAL-Dutton.

— Drag Queen. 224p. 1995. 21.95 (0-525-93925-3, Dutton) NAL-Dutton.

— Fag Hag. LC 91-20293. 304p. 1993. pap. 10.95 (0-452-26940-7, Plume) NAL-Dutton.

— What They Did to Princess Paragon. LC 93-40187. 1994. 19.95 (0-525-93772-2) Dutton Child Bks.

— What They Did to Princess Paragon. 1995. pap. 10.95 (0-452-27163-0, Plume) NAL-Dutton.

Rodi, W., ed. Turbulent Buoyant Jets & Plumes, Vol. 6. (HMT Ser.). 192p. 1982. text ed. 86.00 (0-08-026492-1, Pub. by Pergamon Repr UK) Franklin.

Rodi, W. & Martelli, F., eds. Engineering Turbulence Modelling & Experiments - 2: Proceedings of the 2nd International Symposium, Florence, Italy, 31 May-2 June, 1993. LC 93-7748. xviii, 994p. 1993. 371.50 (0-444-89802-6) Elsevier.

Rodi, Wolfgang. Turbulence Models & Their Application in Hydraulics: A State of the Art Review. 116p. (C). 1984. text ed. 35.00 (90-212-7002-1, Pub. by A A Balkema NE) Ashgate Pub Co.

— Turbulence Models & Their Application in Hydraulics: A-State-of-the-Art Review. rev. ed. (IAHR Monograph Ser.). (Illus.). 120p. (C). Date not set. pap. 35.00 (90-5410-150-4, Pub. by A A Balkema NE) Ashgate Pub Co.

Rodichok, Lawrence D., jt. ed. see Russell, Garfield B.

Rodick, A., tr. see Fedoryuk, M. V.

Rodick, Burleigh C. Appomattox: The Last Campaign. 220p. 1988. reprint ed. 25.00 (0-942211-58-8) Olde Soldier Bks.

Rodieck, Jorma. The Little Bitty Snake. Confreras, Moyra, tr. LC 82-60393. (Illus.). 24p. (J). (ps up). 1983. English-Spanish. pap. 4.95 (0-940880-03-2) Open Hand.

— The Little Bitty Snake. Burnett, Yumiko M., tr. LC 82-60393. (Illus.). 24p. (J). (ps up). 1983. English-Japanese. pap. 4.95 (0-940880-07-5) Open Hand.

— The Little Bitty Snake. Burnett, Yumiko M. et al, trs. LC 82-60393. (Illus.). 24p. (J). (ps up). 1983. English-French. pap. 4.95 (0-940880-05-9) Open Hand.

Rodiek, Jon E. & Bolen, Eric G. Wildlife & Habitats in Managed Landscapes. LC 90-41593. (Illus.). 217p. 1991. 45.00 (1-55963-053-1); pap. 24.95 (1-55963-052-3) Island Pr.

Rodier, David F., jt. ed. see Durfee, Harold A.

Rodier, G., tr. see Aristotle.

Rodig, Oscar R., et al. Organic Chemistry Laboratory: Standard & Microscale Experiments. 533p. (C). 1990. pap. text ed. 36.75 (0-03-012644-4) SCP.

Rodiger, Georgiana. The Miracle of Therapy. 177p. 1989. 12.99 (0-8499-0628-8) Word Inc.

R

An Asterisk (*) at the beginning of an entry indicates that the title is appearing in BIP for the first time.

Rodimtseva, I. Moscow Kremlin: A Guide. 126p. (C). 1987. 60.00 (0-685-22597-6, Pub. by Collets UK) Pro-Am Music.
Rodimzeva, C. The Kremlin & Its Treasures. (C). 1990. 575.00 (0-685-34389-8, Pub. by Collets) St Mut.
Rodin. Rodin on Art & Artists: With Sixty Illustrations of His Work. 2nd ed. (Fine Art Ser.). (Illus.). 160p. 1983. reprint ed. pap. 7.95 (0-486-24487-3) Dover.
Rodin, A. E. & Dey, Jack. Medicine, Literature & Eponyms: Encyclopedia of Medical Eponyms Derived from Literary Characters. LC 88-542. 370p. (C). 1989. lib. bdg. 44.50 (0-89464-277-4) Krieger.
Rodin, A. E. & Key, Jack D. Medical Casebook of Doctor Arthur Conan Doyle: From Practitioner to Sherlock Holmes & Beyond. LC 83-16232. 506p. 1984. 46.50 (0-89874-592-6) Krieger.
Rodin, Alvin E., intro. Oslerian Pathology: An Assessment & Annotated Atlas of Museum Specimens. (Illus.). 250p. (C). 1981. 25.00 (0-87291-144-6) Coronado Pr.
Rodin, Auguste. Cathedrals of France. rev. ed. Geissbuhler, Elisabeth C., tr. (Art of the Middle Ages Ser.). (Illus.). 278p. 1981. 30.00 (0-933806-07-8) Black Swan CT.
— Drawings of Rodin. Longstreet, Stephen, ed. (Master Draughtsman Ser.). (Illus.). (Orig.). 1965. 10.95 (0-87505-031-X); pap. 4.95 (0-87505-184-7) Borden.
***Rodin, Cuia & Rodin, Tibor S.** King Solomon's Feast: Culinary Delights from the Cuisine of Biblical Israel. Lee, Linda, ed. 175p. (Orig.). 1994. pap. 14.95 (0-9644036-0-9) C & T Rodin.
Rodin, E. A., jt. ed. see Degen, R.
Rodin, Ervin Y. Computers & Mathematics with Applications: A Memorial Dedicated to Cornelius Lanczos. 1976. pap. 100.00 (0-08-020521-6, Pergamon Pr) Elsevier.
Rodin, Ervin Y. & Avula, Xavier J. Mathematical Modelling in Science & Technology: Proceedings of 6th International Conference, St Louis, MO, August 1987. (Mathematical Modeling Ser.). 1300p. 1989. pap. 315.00 (0-08-036380-6, Pergamon Pr) Elsevier.
Rodin, Gary, et al. Depression in the Medically Ill: An Integrated Approach. LC 90-26064. 384p. 1991. 44.95 (0-87630-596-6) Brunner-Mazel.
Rodin, Gary M., ed. see Craven, John.
Rodin, J. & Collins, A., eds. Women & New Reproductive Technologies: Medical, Psychosocial, Legal & Ethical Dilemmas. 176p. (C). 1991. text ed. 36.00 (0-8058-0919-8) L Erlbaum Assocs.
Rodin, Judith. Body Traps: Breaking the Binds That Keep You from Feeling Good about Your Body. 1993. pap. 12.00 (0-688-12836-X, Quill) Morrow.
— Body Traps: How to Unlock the Cage of Body Obsessions. 1992. 22.00 (0-688-08843-0) Morrow.
Rodin, Judith, jt. auth. see Brownell, Kelly D.
Rodin, Judith, et al, eds. Self-Directedness: Causes & Effects Throughout the Life Course. 280p. 1990. 59.95 (0-8058-0562-1) L Erlbaum Assocs.
Rodin, S. N. Graphs & Genes. Mirkin, B. G. & Beus, H. L., trs. (Biomathematics Ser.: Vol. II). 197p. 1984. 54.00 (0-387-12657-0) Spr-Verlag.
Rodin, Tibor S., jt. auth. see Rodin, Cuia.
Rodin, Y. L. Generalized Analytic Functions on Riemann Surfaces. (Lecture Notes in Mathematics Ser.: Vol. 1288). v, 128p. 1987. pap. 28.90 (0-387-18572-0) Spr-Verlag.
— The Riemann Boundary Problem on Riemann Surfaces. (C). 1988. lib. bdg. 93.00 (90-277-2653-1) Kluwer Ac.
Rodine, Floyd H. Yalta-Responsibility & Response: January-March 1945. 156p. 1974. pap. 7.50 (0-87291-049-0) Coronado Pr.
Rodine, Sharon, jt. auth. see Lindsay, Jeanne W.
Rodini, Robert J. Antonfrancesco Grazzini, Poet, Dramatist, & Novelliere, 1503-1584. LC 71-106041. (Illus.). 262p. reprint ed. pap. 74.70 (0-8357-6780-9, 2035457) Bks Demand.
— Le Opere Di Dio. LC 75-39907. (ITA.). (C). 1976. pap. 27.96 (0-395-13399-8) HM.
Rodini, Robert J. & Di Maria, Salvatore. Ludovico Ariosto: An Annotated Bibliography of Criticism, 1956-1980. LC 84-2196. 288p. 1985. 32.00 (0-8262-0445-7) U of Mo Pr.
Rodino, L. Linear Partial Differential Operators in Gevrey Spaces. 250p. 1993. text ed. 61.00 (981-02-0845-6) World Scientific Pub.
Rodino, L., jt. ed. see Cattabriga, L.
Rodino, Simonetta P. Three Centuries of Roman Drawings from the Villa Farnesina, Rome. LC 93-490. 1993. write for info. (0-88397-106-2) Art Srvc Intl.
Rodinson, M. Cult, Ghetto & State: The Persistance of the Jewish Question. 240p. 1993. pap. 11.95 (0-86356-020-2, Pub. by Saqi Books UK) Interlink Pub.
Rodinson, Maxime. The Arabs. Goldhammer, Arthur, tr. LC 80-25916. (Illus.). 208p. (C). 1981. pap. text ed. 10.95 (0-226-72356-9) U Ch Pr.
— Cult, Ghetto, & State: The Persistence of the Jewish Question. Rothschild, Jon, tr. 239p. (Orig.). 1984. pap. 10.95 (0-685-08870-7) Evergreen Dist.
— Europe & the Mystique of Islam. Veinus, Roger, tr. LC 86-30761. (Illus.). 170p. 1987. pap. 12.95 (0-295-96485-5) U of Wash Pr.
— Israel: A Colonial-Settler State? LC 73-78187. 96p. (Orig.). 1988. reprint ed. pap. 11.95 (0-913460-23-0) Pathfinder NY.
— Marxism & the Muslim World. Matthews, Jean, tr. LC 81-81695. 349p. reprint ed. pap. 99.50 (0-7837-3910-9, 2043758) Bks Demand.
Rodionov, Sergei N. Global & Regional Climate Interaction: The Caspian Sea Experience. (Water Science & Technology Library). 256p. (C). 1994. lib. bdg. 86.00 (0-7923-2784-5) Kluwer Ac.
Rodionova. Russian-English Dictionary of Socio-Economic Terms. (ENG & RUS.). 1987. 75.00 (0-8288-3974-3, F39311) Fr & Eur.
Roditi, Edouard. Aphorisms: (Or Life with God the Father) 16p. 1991. 5.00 (0-88031-068-5) Invisible-Red Hill.
— Choose Your Own World. LC 91-73681. (Illus.). 112p. (Orig.). 1992. 20.00 (1-878580-40-X); pap. 7.95 (1-878580-39-6) Asylum Arts.
— The Delights of Turkey: Twenty Tales. LC 77-9588. 192p. 1977. 6.95 (0-8112-0669-6) New Directions.
— Dialogues on Art. LC 79-91612. 250p. 1980. pap. 11.95 (0-915520-21-4) R-E CA.
— More Dialogues on Art. (Illus.). 250p. (Orig.). 1983. pap. 11.95 (0-915520-57-5) R-E CA.
— Oscar Wilde. enl. rev. ed. LC 86-8578. 224p. 1986. 4.50 (0-8112-0504-5); pap. 10.95 (0-8112-0995-4, NDP633) New Directions.
— Thrice Chosen. LC 81-9946. 135p. (Orig.). (C). 1981. pap. 5.00 (0-87685-350-5) Black Sparrow.
Roditi, Edouard, tr. see Bosquet, Alain.
Roditi, Edouard, tr. see Emre, Yunus.
Roditi, Edouard, tr. see Kemal, Yashar.
***Rodkey.** Newtisms: Newt Gingrich on the Issues -- from A to Z. 1995. pap. 5.00 (0-671-53533-1) PB.
Rodkin, Henry H. The Ultimate Overseas Business Guide for Growing Companies. 300p. 1990. pap. 50.00 (1-55623-300-0) Irwin Prof Pubng.
Rodkinson, Michael L. History of Amulets, Charms & Talismans. 1977. lib. bdg. 59.95 (0-8490-1966-4) Gordon Pr.
Rodley, Chris, ed. Cronenberg on Cronenberg. (Directors on Directors Ser.). (Illus.). 256p. 1994. pap. 10.95 (0-571-16993-7) Faber & Faber.
Rodley, Chris, ed. see Cronenberg, David.
Rodley, Lyn. Byzantine Art & Architecture: An Introduction. LC 92-33797. (Illus.). 320p. (C). 1992. pap. write for info. (0-521-35724-1) Cambridge U Pr.
— Byzantine Art & Architecture: An Introduction. LC 92-33797. (Illus.). 320p. (C). 1994. 79.95 (0-521-35440-4) Cambridge U Pr.
Rodley, Nigel S. The Treatment of Prisoners under International Law. LC 86-16433. 1987. pap. 39.00 (0-19-825563-2) OUP.
Rodley, Nigel S., ed. To Loose the Bands of Wickedness: International Intervention in Defense of Human Rights. 287p. 1992. 40.00 (1-85753-047-0, Pub. by Brasseys UK) Brasseys Inc.
Rodli, Agnes. Alone in My Kayak. 280p. (Orig.). 1993. pap. 8.95 (1-56043-768-5) Destiny Image.
Rodman, Barbara. Love Stories for All Centuries. 96p. 1984. 8.95 (0-89697-143-0) Intl Univ Pr.
Rodman, Blake H., jt. ed. see Wolk, Ronald A.
Rodman, Dennis, et al. Rebound: The Enduring Friendhsip of Dennis Rodman & Byrne Rich. LC 93-14373. 1994. 22.00 (0-517-59294-0, Crown) Crown Pub Group.
***Rodman, Edmon J.** Let's Dig a Dinosaur. (Illus.). 10p. (J). 1995. 9.95 (0-8362-4243-2) Andrews & McMeel.
— Let's Dig a Treasure. (Illus.). 10p. (J). 1995. 9.95 (0-8362-4244-0) Andrews & McMeel.
Rodman, F. Robert. Not Dying: A Memoir. 1988. pap. 7.95 (0-393-30534-1) Norton.
Rodman, F. Robert, ed. The Spontaneous Gesture: Selected Letters of D. W. Winnicott. LC 86-18483. (Illus.). 256p. 1987. pap. 32.00 (0-674-83336-8) HUP.
Rodman, George. Public Speaking. 3rd ed. 336p. (C). 1986. pap. text ed. 26.75 (0-03-002498-6) HB Coll Pubs.
Rodman, George, jt. auth. see Adler, Ron.
Rodman, George, jt. auth. see Adler, Ronald B.
Rodman, George R. Mass Media Issues. 4th ed. 528p. (C). 1992. per. 26.95 (0-8403-6757-0) Kendall-Hunt.
Rodman, Hyman, et al. The Sexual Rights of Adolescents: Competence, Vulnerability, & Parental Control. LC 83-14440. 183p. 1988. text ed. 40.50 (0-231-04916-1); pap. text ed. 14.50 (0-231-04917-X) Col U Pr.
Rodman, Hyman & Trost, Jan, eds. The Adolescent Dilemma: International Perspectives on Family Planning - Rights of Minors. LC 86-608. 272p. 1986. text ed. 49.95 (0-275-92080-1, C2080, Praeger Pubs) Greenwood.
Rodman, Hyman, et al. The Abortion Question. 250p. 1990. pap. text ed. 15.50 (0-231-05333-9) Col U Pr.
Rodman, Jane, jt. auth. see Hoover, Dwight W.
Rodman, Kenneth. Sanctity vs. Sovereignty: The United States & the Nationalization of Natural Resource Investments. 448p. 1988. text ed. 54.00 (0-231-06448-9) Col U Pr.
Rodman, L., jt. auth. see Lancaster, P.
Rodman, Leiba. An Introduction to Operator Polynomials. (Operator Theory Ser.: No. 38). 394p. 1989. 127.50 (0-8176-2324-8) Birkhauser.
Rodman, Margaret & Cooper, Matthew, eds. The Pacification of Melanesia. LC 83-14551. (ASAO Monograph: No. 7). 246p. (C). 1983. reprint ed. lib. bdg. 52.00 (0-8191-3404-X) U Pr of Amer.
Rodman, Margaret C., jt. auth. see Cooper, Matthew.
Rodman, Paul, ed. see Foote, Mary H.
Rodman, Peter. More Precious Than Peace. 1994. text ed. 29.95 (0-684-19427-9, Scribners) S&S Trade.
Rodman, Peter S., ed. Adaptations for Foraging in Nonhuman Primates: Contributions to an Organismal Biology of Prosimians, Monkeys, & Apes. 1984. text ed. 56.00 (0-231-05226-X, King's Crown Paperbacks); pap. text ed. 22.50 (0-231-05227-8, King's Crown Paperbacks) Col U Pr.
Rodman, Robert, jt. auth. see Fromkin, Victoria.
Rodman, Robert M. Commercial Arbitration with Forms. LC 84-15345. (Handbook Ser.). 767p. 1988. reprint ed. text ed. 80.00 (0-314-86732-5) West Pub.
— Commercial Arbitration with Forms: 1992 Pocket Parts. 180p. 1992. pap. text ed. write for info. (0-318-68976-6) West Pub.
— Commercial Arbitration with Forms: 1995 Pocket Part. Fever, William, ed. (West's Handbook Ser.). 240p. 1994. write for info. (0-314-05582-X) West Pub.
Rodman, Selden. The Brazil Traveler. LC 75-13350. (Illus.). 104p. 1975. pap. 9.95 (0-8159-5113-2) Devin.
— Eye of Man. (Illus.). 1955. 15.00 (0-8159-5403-4) Devin.
— Genius in the Backlands: The Popular Artists of Brazil. 10.00 (0-8159-5616-9) Devin.
— Geniuses & Other Eccentrics. (Illus.). 280p. Date not set. 29.50 (1-883740-16-9) Pebble Bch Pr Ltd.
— Tongues of Fallen Angels. LC 73-89485. (Illus.). 288p. 1974. 12.00 (0-8112-0528-2); pap. 3.75 (0-8112-0529-0, NDP373) New Directions.
— Where Art Is Joy: Haitian Art--The First Forty Years. 1988. 60.00 (0-938291-01-7) R deLatour.
Rodman, Selden, ed. Poetry of Flight. LC 75-76939. (Granger Index Reprint Ser.). 1977. 19.95 (0-8369-6041-6) Ayer.
Rodman, Selden & Cleaver, Carole. Spirits of the Night: The Vaudun Gods of Haiti. (Illus.). 144p. (Orig.). 1992. pap. 16.00 (0-88214-354-9) Spring Pubns.
Rodman, Selden & Kearns, James. The Heart of Beethoven. LC 76-51291. (Illus.). 157p. 1977. reprint ed. text ed. 49.75 (0-8371-9441-5, ROHE, Greenwood Pr) Greenwood.
Rodman, Selden, jt. ed. see Bingham, Alfred M.
Rodman, Selden, jt. ed. see Eberhart, Richard.
Rodman, William L. & Counts, Dorothy A., eds. Middlemen & Brokers in Oceania. (ASAO Monograph: No. 9). 318p. (C). 1983. reprint ed. pap. text ed. 23.00 (0-8191-3468-6) U Pr of Amer.
***Rodmann, Dorothy, et al, eds.** Career Transitions for Chemists: Making It Happen. LC 94-38410. 178p. 1994. 29.95 (0-8412-3052-8); pap. 14.95 (0-8412-3038-2) Am Chemical.
Rodmell, Graham. French Drama of the Revolutionary Years. 288p. 1990. 59.95 (0-415-00808-5, A4165) Routledge.
Rodney, Janet. Orphydice. 56p. (Orig.). 1986. 17.50 (0-938535-76-5); pap. 7.00 (0-938535-75-7) Salt-Works Pr.
***Rodney, Janet, illus.** Incloser: An Essay by Susan Howe. 54p. 1992. 175.00 (1-878460-01-3) Weaselsleeves Pr.
Rodney, Janet, ed. see Prechtel, Martin.
Rodney, Richards S. & Konkle, Burton A. Early Relations of Delaware & Pennsylvania. Incl. Delaware: A Grant Yet Not a Grant. LC 79-164622. (0-318-50814-1); LC 79-164622. (Select Bibliographies Reprint Ser.). 1977. reprint ed. 15.95 (0-8369-5905-1) Ayer.
Rodney, Robert M. Mark Twain Overseas. (Time - Place Ser.: No. 5). 1993. pap. 18.00 (0-89410-721-6) Three Continents.
Rodney, Robert M., ed. Mark Twain International: A Bibliography & Interpretation of His Worldwide Popularity. LC 81-13441. lxix, 275p. 1982. text ed. 65.00 (0-313-23135-4, RMT/, Greenwood Pr) Greenwood.
Rodney, Thomas. Diary of Captain Thomas Rodney. (American Biography Ser.). 53p. 1991. reprint ed. lib. bdg. 59.00 (0-7812-8325-6) Rprt Serv.
— Diary of Captain Thomas Rodney 1776-1777: Papers of the Historical Society of Delaware No. 8. LC 74-8011. (American Constitutional & Legal History Ser.). 53p. 1974. reprint ed. lib. bdg. 17.50 (0-306-70621-0) Da Capo.
Rodney, Walter. A History of the Guyanese Working People, 1881-1905. 312p. 1981. 42.00 (0-8018-2428-1); pap. 14.95 (0-8018-2447-8) Johns Hopkins.
— A History of the Upper Guinea Coast, 1545-1800. LC 79-48070. 1980. reprint ed. pap. 10.00 (0-85345-546-5) Monthly Rev.
— How Europe Underdeveloped Africa. rev. ed. LC 81-6240. 312p. 1982. pap. 9.95 (0-88258-096-5) Howard U Pr.
Rodney, William S., jt. auth. see Rolfs, Claus E.
Rodnick, David. The Fort Belknap Assiniboine of Montana: A Study in Culture Change. LC 76-43811. reprint ed. 37.50 (0-404-15666-5) AMS Pr.
Rodnight, Richard, jt. ed. see Marks, Neville.
Rodning, C. B., et al. Papering Dreams: Haiku & Sumie Ink Drawings. deluxe limited ed. (Illus.). 1994. 95.00 (1-879009-13-7) S P-Persephone Pr.
Rodning, Charles B. Love Knot. (Illus.). 64p. (Orig.). 1994. pap. write for info. (1-56167-143-6) Am Literary Pr.
Rodning, Charles B. & Rodning, Christopher B. Ponderings on Mobile Bay: Haiku. (Scots Plaid Press Poetry Ser.: No. 3). (Illus.). 64p. (Orig.). 1990. pap. 12.00 (1-879009-02-1) S P-Persephone Pr.
Rodning, Charles B. & Rodning, Mary E. Elan Vital: A Chapbook of Oriental Poetry & Sumi-e Painting. LC 88-50166. (Illus.). 78p. 1988. 15.95 (0-8048-1539-9) C E Tuttle.
Rodning, Charles B., et al. Papering Dreams: Haiku & Sumie Ink Paintings. limited ed. Campbell, MaryBelle, ed. (Scots Plaid Press Poetry Ser.: No. 5). (Illus.). 96p. 1994. 95.00 (1-879009-15-3) S P-Persephone Pr.
— Snowbound Below the Firn Line: Haiku. (Scots Plaid Press Poetry Ser.: No. 4). (Illus.). 64p. (Orig.). 1991. pap. 14.00 (1-879009-08-0) S P-Persephone Pr.
Rodning, Christopher B., jt. auth. see Rodning, Charles B.
Rodning, Mary E., jt. auth. see Rodning, Charles B.
***Rodnitzky, Donna.** 101 Great Lowfat Desserts: No Butter, No Cream, No Kidding! LC 94-33548. 1995. write for info. (1-55958-666-4) Prima Pub.
Rodnitzky, Jerome L. Minstrels of the Dawn: The Folk-Protest Singer As a Cultural Hero. LC 76-4520. 214p. 1976. 28.95 (0-88229-284-6); pap. 18.95 (0-88229-427-X) Nelson-Hall.
Rodo, Jose E. Ariel. Peden, Margaret S., tr. 156p. 1988. 16.95 (0-292-70395-3); pap. 8.95 (0-292-70396-1) U of Tex Pr.
— Ariel: Estudio Critico de Leopaldo Alas (Clarin) (Nueva Austral Ser.: Vol. 216). (SPA.). 1991. pap. text ed. 24.95x (84-239-7216-X) Elliots Bks.
— The Motives of Proteus. 1973. lib. bdg. 250.00 (0-87968-384-8) Gordon Pr.
Rodolff, Rebecca, ed. see Cutburth, Ronald W.
Rodolfo, Kelvin S., ed. see Lisitzin, Alexander P.
Rodolph, Stormy. Quest for Courage. (Indian Culture Ser.). (Illus.). 102p. (Orig.). (J). (gr. 5-12). 1984. pap. 8.95 (0-89992-092-6) Coun India Ed.
— Quest for Courage. (Council for Indian Education Ser.). (Illus.). 112p. (Orig.). (J). (gr. 4-6). 1993. pap. 8.95 (1-879373-57-2) R Rinehart.
Rodolphe de la Chavanne Dareste. La Science Du Droit En Grece: Platon, Aristote, Theophraste. LC 75-13259. (History of Ideas in Ancient Greece Ser.). (FRE.). 1976. reprint ed. 23.95 (0-405-07301-1) Ayer.
Rodon, Francesc, jt. auth. see Vila-Grau, Joan.
Rodono, Marcello, jt. ed. see Byrne, Patrick B.
Rodoreda, Merce. Camellia Street: A Novel. Rosenthal, David H., tr. & intro. by. LC 93-12588. 208p. 1993. 20.00 (1-55597-192-X) Graywolf.
— My Christina & Other Stories. Rosenthal, David H., tr. LC 84-81626. (Short Fiction Ser.). 135p. 1984. pap. 11.00 (0-915308-65-7) Graywolf.
Rodorf, E. Hugh, jt. ed. see Hodges, Richard E.
***Rodor's Travel Staff.** Fodor's Golf Digest. 2nd ed. Date not set. pap. write for info. (0-679-03025-5) Fodors Travel.
***Rodowick, D. N.** Crisis of Political Modernism: Criticism & Ideology in Contemporary Film Criticism. LC 94-25112. 1994. pap. 15.00 (0-520-08771-2) U CA Pr.
— The Crisis of Political Modernism: Criticism & Ideology in Contemporary Film Theory. 320p. 1988. 29.95 (0-252-01533-9) U of Ill Pr.
Rodowick, David. The Difficulty of Difference: Psychoanalysis, Sexual Difference & Film Theory. (Illus.). 200p. 1991. 37.50 (0-415-90331-9, A4616, Routledge NY); pap. 13.95 (0-415-90332-7, A4620, Routledge NY) Routledge.
Rodowksy, Colby. Lucy Peale. large type ed. 216p. 1993. reprint ed. bds. 15.95 (1-56054-611-5) Thorndike Pr.
***Rodowsky.** Jenny & Great Old Aunts. 1994. pap. 2.99 (0-517-13346-6) Random.
Rodowsky, Colby. Dog Days. (Illus.). 96p. (J). (gr. 2-6). 1990. 14.00 (0-374-36342-0) FS&G.
— Dog Days. (J). (gr. 4-7). 1993. pap. 4.50 (0-374-41818-7, Sunburst Bks) FS&G.
— Fitchett's Folly. LC 86-31859. 160p. (J). (gr. 4 up). 1987. 15.00 (0-374-32342-9) FS&G.
— The Gathering Room. LC 81-5360. 186p. (J). (gr. 5 up). 1981. 11.95 (0-374-32520-0) FS&G.
— H, My Name Is Henley. LC 82-12164. 184p. (J). (gr. 5 up). 1982. 14.00 (0-374-32831-5) FS&G.
— Hannah in Between. (YA). (gr. 7 up). 1994. 15.00 (0-374-32837-4) FS&G.
— Julie's Daughter. LC 85-47589. 231p. (J). (gr. 7 up). 1985. 15.00 (0-374-33963-5) FS&G.
— Julie's Daughter. (YA). (gr. 7 up). 1992. reprint ed. pap. 3.95 (0-374-43973-7) FS&G.
— Keeping Time. LC 83-14122. 137p. (J). (gr. 5 up). 1983. 14.00 (0-374-34061-7) FS&G.
— Lucy Peale. 208p. (YA). 1992. 15.00 (0-374-36381-1) FS&G.
— Lucy Peale. (Aerial Fiction Ser.). 176p. (YA). (gr. 7 up). 1994. pap. text ed. 3.95 (0-374-44659-8, Sunburst Bks) FS&G.
— P. S. Write Soon. (Sunburst Ser.). 158p. (J). (gr. 5 up). 1987. reprint ed. pap. 3.50 (0-374-46032-9) FS&G.
— Sydney, Herself. 176p. (YA). (gr. 7 up). 1989. 12.95 (0-374-30649-4) FS&G.
— Sydney, Herself. (YA). 1993. pap. 4.50 (0-374-47390-0) FS&G.
— Sydney, Invincible. LC 94-22440. 160p. 1995. 15.00 (0-374-37365-5) FS&G.
— What about Me? 144p. (J). (gr. 3 up). 1989. pap. 3.50 (0-374-48316-7, Sunburst Bks) FS&G.
Rodrick. Advances in Seafood Technology. 1995. write for info. (0-8493-4526-X) CRC Pr.
Rodrick, Gary E., jt. auth. see Otwell, Steven.
Rodricks, Dan. Mencken Doesn't Live Here Anymore. (Orig.). 1989. 18.95 (0-913123-27-7) Galileo.
Rodricks, Joseph. Calculated Risks: The Toxicity & Human Health Hazards of Chemicals in Our Environment. (Illus.). 288p. (C). 1994. pap. 13.95 (0-521-42331-7) Cambridge U Pr.
Rodricks, Joseph V., ed. Mycotoxins & Other Fungal Related Food Problems. LC 76-4547. (Advances in Chemistry Ser.: No. 149). 1976. 49.95 (0-8412-0222-2) Am Chemical.
Rodricks, Joseph V. & Tardiff, Robert C., eds. Assessment & Management of Chemical Risks. LC 83-25851. (ACS Symposium Ser.: No. 239). 184p. 1984. lib. bdg. 44.95 (0-8412-0821-2) Am Chemical.
Rodricks, Joseph V., jt. ed. see Tardiff, Robert G.
***Rodrigo, contrib.** Guitar Music of Spain No. 3. 1994. 14.95 (0-7119-3305-7, AM90242) Omnibus NY.
Rodrigo Garcia, Ignacio, ed. see Pauchet, V. & Dupret, S.
Rodrigo, Juan J. Orthopaedic Surgery: Basic Science & Clinical Science. 770p. 1985. 80.00 (0-316-75369-6, Little Med Div) Little.
Rodrigo, R. G., jt. ed. see Manske, R. H.
Rodrigo, R. G., jt. ed. see Manske, R.
Rodrigo, R. G., et al, eds. Progress in Atmospheric Physics. (C). 1988. lib. bdg. 107.50 (90-277-2753-8) Kluwer Ac.
Rodrigue, Aron. French Jews, Turkish Jews: The Alliance Israelite Universelle & the Politics of Jewish Schooling in Turkey, 1860-1925. LC 89-46327. (Illus.). 250p. 1990. 27.95 (0-253-35021-2) Ind U Pr.

R

— Images of Sephardi & Eastern Jewries in Transition: The Teachers of the Alliance Israelite Universelle, 1860-1939. LC 93-15121. 320p. (C). 1993. 40.00 (*0-295-97281-5*) U of Wash Pr.

Rodrigue, Aron, jt. auth. see Benbassa, Esther.

Rodrigue, Barry H. Tom Plant: The Making of a Franco-American Entrepreneur, 1859-1941. LC 93-42755. (Studies in Entrepreneurship). 304p. 1994. 59.00 (*0-8153-0988-0*) Garland.

Rodrigue, Garry. Parallel Computations, Vol. 1. (Computational Techniques Ser.). 1982. text ed. 126.00 (*0-12-592101-2*) Acad Pr.

Rodrigue, George & Freundlich, Lawrence S. Blue Dog. LC 93-39794. (Illus.). 96p. 1994. 39.95 (*0-670-85538-3*, Viking Studio) Studio Bks.

— Blue Dog. limited ed. (Illus.). 96p. 1995. 50.00 (*0-670-86621-0*, Viking Studio) Studio Bks.

Rodrigue, Yves. Nat-Pwe: Burma's Supernatural Subculture. (Illus.). 128p. (C). 1995. pap. 25.00 (*1-870838-11-4*, Pub. by Kiscadale UK) Weatherhill.

Rodrigues, A. E., ed. Ion Exchange: Science & Technology. (NATO Advanced Science Institutes Series C: Mathematical & Physical Sciences). 1986. lib. bdg. 193.50 (*90-247-3281-6*) Kluwer Ac.

Rodrigues, A. E., et al. Multiphase Chemical Reactors: Design Methods, Vol. II. 1981. lib. bdg. 121.50 (*90-286-2821-5*) Kluwer Ac.

Rodrigues, A. Guimaraes, ed. Operations Research & Management in Fishing. (NATO Advanced Study Institutes Series E, Applied Sciences). (C). 1990. lib. bdg. 133.00 (*0-7923-1051-9*) Kluwer Ac.

Rodrigues-Bachiller, Agustin. Town Planning Education. 240p. 1988. text ed. 68.95 (*0-566-05500-7*, Pub. by Avebury Pub UK) Ashgate Pub Co.

Rodrigues, Clarissa. The Social & Political Thought of Dr. S. Radhakrishnan. 1993. text ed. 30.00 (*81-207-0389-8*, Pub. by Sterling Pubs II) Apt Bks.

Rodrigues, Dawn, jt. auth. see Gebhardt, Richard C.

Rodrigues, Dawn, jt. auth. see Zimmerman, Donald E.

Rodrigues, Eusebio L. Quest for the Human: An Exploration of Saul Bellow's Fiction. LC 80-66707. 380p. 1982. 38.50 (*0-8387-2368-3*) Bucknell U Pr.

Rodrigues, Hillary. Insight & Religious Mind: An Analysis of Krishnamurti's Teachings. LC 90-36352. (American University Studies: Theology & Religion: Ser. VII, Vol. 64). 228p. (C). 1990. text ed. 39.95 (*0-8204-0993-6*) P Lang Pubs.

Rodrigues, J. F. Mathematical Models for Phase Change Problems. (International Series of Numerical Mathematics: No. 88). 408p. 1989. 116.00 (*0-8176-2309-4*) Birkhauser.

— Obstacle Problems in Mathematical Physics. (North-Holland Mathematics Studies: No. 134). 352p. 1987. 87.25 (*0-444-70187-7*, North Holland) Elsevier.

Rodrigues, J. F. & Sequeira, A., eds. Mathematical Topics in Fluid Mechanics: Proceedings of the Summer Course Held in Lisbon, Portugal, September 9-13, 1991. (Pitman Research Notes in Mathematics Ser.). 261p. (Orig.). 1993. pap. text ed. 72.95 (*0-470-22069-4*) Halsted Pr.

Rodrigues, Jose H., jt. auth. see Hilton, Stanley E.

Rodrigues, Larry. It's All in Your Hands: Hand Analysis Guidebook to Self-Understanding. (Illus.). 278p. (Orig.). 1994. pap. 19.95 (*0-9640866-5-4*) EastWest Inst.

— It's All in Your Hands: Hand Analysis Guidebook to Self-Understanding. 2nd rev. ed. Howell, Joan, ed. (Illus.). 300p. (Orig.). 1995. pap. 23.95 (*0-9640866-7-0*) EastWest Inst.

Rodrigues, Louis J. Anglo-Saxon Verse Charms, Maxims & Heroic Legends. 176p. (Orig.). 1993. pap. text ed. 14.95 (*0-317-05875-4*, Pub. by Anglo-Saxon Bks UK) Paul & Co Pubs.

— Harrap's Glossary of English & Spanish Commercial & Industrial Terms. 288p. (ENG & SPA.). 1990. 35.00 (*0-8288-7966-4*, 133833992) Fr & Eur.

Rodrigues, Louis J. & Bernet De Rodrigues, Josefina. Harrap's Spanish Idioms. 896p. 1991. 25.00 (*0-13-377649-2*, Harraps) P-H Gen Ref & Trav.

Rodrigues, Louis J. & Bernet de Rodrigues, Josefina. Harrap's Spanish Synonyms & Antonyms. 800p. 1991. 25.00 (*0-13-384983-X*, Harraps) P-H Gen Ref & Trav.

Rodrigues, M. R., jt. auth. see Abbott, Peter.

Rodrigues, Otilio, jt. tr. see Kavanaugh, Kieran.

Rodrigues, P. R., jt. auth. see De Leon, Manuel.

Rodrigues, P. R., jt. ed. see De Leon, Manuel.

Rodrigues, Santan. I Exist. (Writers Workshop Redbird Ser.). 41p. 1976. 8.00 (*0-86578-267-9*); 4.00 (*0-86578-268-7*) Ind-US Inc.

Rodrigues, W. A. & Letelier, P. S., Jr. Gravitation: The Spacetime Structure - Proceedings of the VIII Latin American Symposium on Relativity & Gravitation. 604p. 1994. text ed. 135.00 (*981-02-1601-7*) World Scientific Pub.

Rodriguez, ed. Directory of Simulation Software, 1993. 56p. 1992. pap. 30.00 (*1-56555-015-3*, DSS-93) Soc Computer Sim.

Rodriguez, A. R., jt. ed. see Stricker, George.

Rodriguez, Abraham, Jr. Boy Without a Flag: Tales of the South Bronx. LC 91-45672. (Illus.). 120p. (Orig.). 1992. pap. 11.00 (*0-915943-74-3*) Milkweed Ed.

— Spidertown. 336p. 1994. reprint ed. pap. 9.95 (*0-14-023838-7*, Penguin Bks) Viking Penguin.

— Spidertown: A Novel. LC 92-34088. 336p. 1993. 19.95 (*1-56282-845-2*) Hyperion.

Rodriguez Adrados, Francisco. Diccionario Griego-Espanol. 2nd ed. 320p. (GRE & SPA.). 1989. pap. 85.00 (*0-7859-5682-4*, 8400046528) Fr & Eur.

Rodriguez, Agatha A. Catability. (Illus.). 20p. (Orig.). (J). 1990. pap. text ed. 7.95 (*0-933196-04-0*) Bilingue Pubns.

— Paracaidas, Paracaidas. (Children's Storybook Ser.). (Illus.). 20p. (Orig.). (SPA.). (J). 1992. pap. 5.00 (*0-933196-05-9*) Bilingue Pubns.

R

***Rodriguez, Albert F. Touche: Programming Tools for Shaping Solutions. 50p. (Orig.). (C). 1994. pap. text ed. 12.50 (*0-9642829-4-1*) AFR Software.**

Throughout all of its three sections, this book accomplishes its purpose & goal of providing tenets & principles to programmers so that they can use them to be more productive, less inefficient & better organized to deal with the task of writing computer programs. Section number one (1) uses a specific program for the purpose of deriving & creating a paradigm that truly optimizes the task of composing any kind of software. Section number two (2) builds on the preceding section by determining what is the most correct programming method used to design, define, & describe computer programs. Section number three (3) suggests that all information covered in the preceding sections can be used in combination with subject matter, specifically taught, in an introductory college-level course dealing with "programming methodology." The main thrust of the material is to help programmers reduce the software cost-line on a graph, improve on its quality & maintain its reliability through economically cost-effective methods of programming. Finally, all of the above information is applicable, regardless of the machine or programming language used to write computer programs. For orders & information, contact: A.F.R. Software (R), 1605 Pennsylvania Ave., #204, Miami Beach, FL 33139; TELEPHONE: 305-531-6464; FAX: 305-538-2483. S&H U.S. $1.74 Domestic; U.S. $3.48 Foreign, per unit.

Publisher Provided Annotation.

***Rodriguez, Alberto.** La Conversacion En el Quijote: Subdialogo, Memoria y Asimetria. LC 94-67394. 180p. (SPA.). (C). 1995. 30.00x (*0-938972-26-X*) Spanish Lit Pubns.

Rodriguez, Aleida, ed. see Labbe, Armand J.

Rodriguez, Alejo. I'm Tired of Being Quiet. LC 93-60258. 140p. 1994. pap. 7.95 (*1-55523-609-X*) Winston-Derek.

— It's Tough Being a Kid These Days. LC 93-85309. 65p. (J). (gr. 6-12). 1994. pap. 5.95 (*1-55523-638-3*) Winston-Derek.

— Simple Poems for Children: Hey What Kind of World Is This? LC 90-71368. 126p. (J). (gr. 3-9). 1991. pap. 5.95 (*1-55523-393-7*) Winston-Derek.

— Simple Poems for Life Experiences. LC 87-51040. 65p. 1988. 6.95 (*1-55523-121-7*) Winston-Derek.

— Simple Poems Looking at Life Through a Broken Glass. LC 89-50713. 82p. 1990. pap. 5.95 (*1-55523-239-6*) Winston-Derek.

Rodriguez, Alfonso. La Estructura Mitica del Popol Vuh. LC 84-81886. (Coleccion Polymita Ser.). 108p. (Orig.). (SPA.). 1985. pap. 10.00 (*0-89729-360-6*) Ediciones.

Rodriguez, Alfonso R., et al. Soil Mechanics in Highway Engineering. (Series on Rock & Soil Mechanics: Vol. 16). 900p. 1987. text ed. 118.00 (*0-87849-072-8*, Pub. by Trans Tech GW) LPS Dist Ctr.

Rodriguez, Alfred, tr. see Perez de Villagra, Gaspar.

Rodriguez, Alfred, ed. see Rojas Zorrilla, Francisco D.

Rodriguez, Alfredo. Biografia De Spurgeon: C. H. Spurgeon's Biography. (SPA.). 7.95 (*84-7645-226-8*, 223317, Pub. by Edit Clie SP) TSELF.

— Estas Tierras. 104p. (SPA.). 1987. pap. 12.00 (*0-9615403-1-1*) Dos Pasos Ed.

Rodriguez, Alison W., jt. auth. see Rivers, William L.

***Rodriguez, Ana & Garvin, Glenn.** Diary of a Survivor: 19 Years in Castro's Prisons. 336p. 1995. 22.95 (*0-312-13050-3*) St Martin.

Rodriguez, Andres. The Book of the Heart: The Poetics, Letters, & Life of John Keats. 256p. (Orig.). 1993. pap. 16.95 (*0-940262-57-6*) Lindisfarne Pr.

***Rodriguez, Angel & Black, Carla.** The Tandem Book. (Illus.). 154p. (Orig.). 1994. pap. 14.95 (*0-924272-03-1*) Info Net Pub.

Rodriguez, Angel, jt. auth. see Black, Carla.

Rodriguez, Anita. Aunt Martha & the Golden Coin. LC 92-7316. (Illus.). 32p. (J). (ps-2). 1993. 14.00 (*0-517-59337-8*, Clarkson Potter); lib. bdg. 14.99 (*0-517-59338-6*, Clarkson Potter) Crown Bks Yng Read.

— Jamal & the Angel. LC 91-11636. (Illus.). 32p. (J). (ps-2). 1992. 14.00 (*0-517-58601-0*); lib. bdg. 15.99 (*0-517-59115-4*) Crown Bks Yng Read.

Rodriguez, Armando R. The Gypsy Wagon. (Creative Ser.: No. 2). 90p. 1974. pap. 5.95 (*0-89551-005-7*) UCLA Chicano Studies.

Rodriguez-Artalejo, M., jt. ed. see Levi, G.

Rodriguez-Bachiller, A. A Small, Robust & Updated Computer Program for Lowry Type Models. (C). 1979. 29.00 (*0-685-30301-2*, Pub. by Oxford Polytechnic UK) St Mut.

Rodriguez-Bachiller, A., ed. Streamlining Local Government? (C). 1984. 35.00 (*0-685-30265-2*, Pub. by Oxford Polytechnic UK) St Mut.

Rodriguez-Badendyck, C., tr. Lope de Vega: The Duchess of Amalfi's Steward. 133p. 1985. pap. 8.00 (*0-919473-53-9*, DH48, Pub. by Dovehouse CN) MRTS.

Rodriguez, Barbara, ed. see Hylton, Hilary.

Rodriguez, Bertha D., et al. Amigo. (ENG & SPA.). 1989. 93.25 (*0-8442-7674-X*, Passport Bks) NTC Pub Grp.

Rodriguez Bravo, Juan L., jt. ed. see Del Mar Martinez Rodriquez, Maria.

***Rodriguez, C.** Cesar Chavez: Mexican-American Labor Leader. Cardona, Rodolfo & Cockcroft, James, eds. (Hispanics of Achievement Ser.). (Illus.). 128p. (YA). (gr. 5 up). 1995. pap. 7.95 (*0-7910-1259-X*) Chelsea Hse.

Rodriguez, Camille, ed. see Bonilla, Frank & Campos, Ricardo.

***Rodriguez, Camilo.** Patrones de Asentamiento de los Agricultores Prehispanicos en "El Limon," Municipio de Chaparral (Tolima) (Illus.). 108p. (SPA.). 1991. pap. 8.50 (*1-877812-29-3*) UPLAAP.

Rodriguez Castro, Maria E., jt. ed. see Alvaraz-Curbelo, Silvia.

***Rodriguez, Cheryl R.** Women, Microenterprise, & the Politics of Self-Help. rev. ed. LC 94-49558. (Garland Studies in Entrepreneurship). 160p. 1995. 41.00 (*0-8153-1969-X*) Garland.

Rodriguez, Chi C. & Andrisani, John. One Hundred One Supershots: Every Golfer's Guide to Lower Scores. LC 89-45709. (Illus.). 208p. 1991. reprint ed. pap. 12.00 (*0-06-092070-X*, PL) HarpC.

Rodriguez, Clara E. Puerto Rican: Born in the USA. 256p. 1989. 44.95 (*0-04-497041-2*); pap. 14.95 (*0-04-497042-0*) Routledge Chapman & Hall.

— Puerto Ricans: Born in the U. S. A. 218p. 1990. pap. 14.95 (*0-685-32963-1*) Routledge Chapman & Hall.

— Puerto Ricans: Born in the U. S. A. 218p. (C). 1989. text ed. 63.00 (*0-8133-1267-1*); pap. text ed. 17.95 (*0-8133-1268-X*) Westview.

***Rodriguez, Claudio.** El Poeta y Su Obra. (Autores Modernos Ser.). 146p. 1994. 10.00 (*84-599-3368-7*) Hispanic Inst.

Rodriguez-Clemente, R. & Paorici, C., eds. Crystalline Materials: Growth & Characterization. 250p. 1992. text ed. 82.00 (*0-87849-543-6*, Pub. by Trans Tech SZ) LPS Dist Ctr.

Rodriguez, Conchita. The Cash-Credit Connection: The Way to Solve All Your Credit & Financial Problems Plus Make a Fortune. 200p. (Orig.). 1990. 19.95 (*1-879497-02-6*) Natl Crdt Ctr.

Rodriguez-Consuegra, F. A. The Mathematical Philosophy of Bertrand Russell: Origins & Development. xiv, 236p. 1991. 84.50 (*0-8176-2656-5*) Birkhauser.

Rodriguez, Consuelo. Cesar Chavez. (Hispanics of Achievement Ser.). (Illus.). 112p. (YA). (gr. 5 up). 1991. lib. bdg. 17.95 (*0-7910-1232-8*) Chelsea Hse.

Rodriguez, Cookie. Please Make Me Cry! 224p. 1974. pap. 4.99 (*0-88368-042-4*) Whitaker Hse.

Rodriguez Cuadros, Evangelina, ed. see Calderon De La Barca, Pedro.

***Rodriguez, Dave & Rodriguez, Judy.** Times Tables the Fun Way Book for Kids: A Picture Method of Learning the Multiplication Facts, Posters. (Illus.). 15p. (J). (gr. 2-8). 1994. 39.95 (*1-883841-31-3*) Key Pubs UT.

Rodriguez, Dave, jt. auth. see Rodriguez, Judy.

Rodriguez, David & Rodriguez, Judy. Times Tables the Fun Way Book for Kids: A Picture Method of Learning the Multiplication Facts. enl. rev. ed. LC 93-79769. (Illus.). 86p. (J). (gr. 2-8). 1994. 4.95 (*1-883841-29-1*) Key Pubs UT.

— Times Tables the Fun Way Book for Kids: A Picture Method of Learning the Multiplication Facts. 2nd enl. rev. ed. LC 93-79769. (Illus.). 86p. (J). (gr. 2-8). 1994. 19.95 (*1-883841-26-7*) Key Pubs UT.

— Times Tables the Fun Way Posters: To Be Used with Time Tables the Fun Way Book for Kids. 2nd rev. ed. (Illus.). 15p. (J). (gr. 2-6). 1995. teacher ed 39.95 (*1-883841-32-1*) Key Pubs UT.

Rodriguez De Castro, Jose. Biblioteca Espanola, 2 vols., Set. (Textos y Estudios Clasicos De las Literaturas Hispanicas Ser.). 1417p. 1977. reprint ed. write for info. (*3-487-06272-0*, Pub. by Georg Olms GW) Lubrecht & Cramer.

Rodriguez de la Fuen, Felix. Enciclopedia Salvat de la Fauna, Vol. 1. 162p. 1986. 24.95 (*0-7859-6127-5*, 8471378507) Fr & Eur.

— Enciclopedia Salvat de la Fauna, Vol. 2. 162p. 1986. 24.95 (*0-7859-6128-3*, 8471378515) Fr & Eur.

— Enciclopedia Salvat de la Fauna, Vol. 3. 162p. 1986. 24.95 (*0-7859-6129-1*, 8471378523) Fr & Eur.

— Enciclopedia Salvat de la Fauna, Vol. 4. 162p. 1986. 24.95 (*0-7859-6130-5*, 8471378531) Fr & Eur.

— Enciclopedia Salvat de la Fauna, Vol. 5. 162p. 1986. 24.95 (*0-7859-6482-7*) Fr & Eur.

— Enciclopedia Salvat de la Fauna, Vol. 6. 162p. 1986. 24.95 (*0-7859-6131-3*, 8471378558) Fr & Eur.

— Enciclopedia Salvat de la Fauna, Vol. 7. 162p. 1986. 24.95 (*0-7859-6132-1*, 8471378566) Fr & Eur.

— Enciclopedia Salvat de la Fauna, Vol. 9. 162p. 1986. 24.95 (*0-7859-6134-8*, 8471378582) Fr & Eur.

— Enciclopedia Salvat de la Fauna, Vol. 10. 162p. 1986. 24.95 (*0-7859-6135-6*, 8471378590) Fr & Eur.

— Enciclopedia Salvat de la Fauna, Vol. 11. 162p. 1986. 24.95 (*0-7859-6136-4*, 8471378604) Fr & Eur.

— Enciclopedia Salvat de la Fauna, Vol. 12. 162p. 1986. 24.95 (*0-7859-6137-2*, 8471378612) Fr & Eur.

— Enciclopedia Salvat de la Fauna, Vol. 13. 162p. 1986. 24.95 (*0-7859-6138-0*, 8471378620) Fr & Eur.

— Enciclopedia Salvat de la Fauna, Vol. 14. 162p. 1986. 24.95 (*0-7859-6139-9*, 8471378639) Fr & Eur.

— Enciclopedia Salvat de la Fauna, Vol. 15. 162p. 1986. 24.95 (*0-7859-6140-2*, 8471378647) Fr & Eur.

— Enciclopedia Salvat de la Fauna, Vol. 16. 162p. 1986. 24.95 (*0-7859-6141-0*, 8471378655) Fr & Eur.

— Enciclopedia Salvat de la Fauna, Vol. 18. 162p. 1986. 24.95 (*0-7859-6142-9*, 8471378663); 24.95 (*0-7859-6143-7*, 8471378671) Fr & Eur.

— Enciclopedia Salvat de la Fauna Iberica y Europea, Vol. 1. 308p. 1984. 69.95 (*0-7859-5944-0*, 8434536463) Fr & Eur.

— Enciclopedia Salvat de la Fauna Iberica y Europea, Vol. 2. 308p. 1984. 69.95 (*0-7859-5945-9*, 8434536471) Fr & Eur.

— Enciclopedia Salvat de la Fauna Iberica y Europea, Vol. 3. 308p. 1984. 69.95 (*0-7859-6467-3*) Fr & Eur.

— Enciclopedia Salvat de la Fauna Iberica y Europea, Vol. 4. 308p. 1984. 69.95 (*0-7859-5946-7*, 8434536498) Fr & Eur.

— Enciclopedia Salvat de la Fauna Iberica y Europea, Vol. 5. 308p. 1984. 69.95 (*0-7859-5947-5*, 8434536501) Fr & Eur.

— Enciclopedia Salvat de la Fauna Iberica y Europea, Vol. 7. 308p. 1984. 69.95 (*0-7859-5948-3*, 8434536528) Fr & Eur.

— Enciclopedia Salvat de la Fauna Iberica y Europea, Vol. 8. 308p. 1984. 69.95 (*0-7859-5949-1*, 8434536536) Fr & Eur.

Rodriguez de la Fuente, Felix. Enciclopedia Salvat de la Fauna, 16 vols. 2916p. (SPA.). 1986. 450.00 (*0-7859-5121-0*) Fr & Eur.

— Enciclopedia Salvat de la Fauna Iberica y Europea, 8 vols., Set. 2464p. (SPA.). 1975. 395.00 (*0-8288-5873-X*, S50539) Fr & Eur.

Rodriguez, Debbie R. Journey to the Crystal City. LC 93-79271. (Illus.). 45p. (Orig.). 1993. pap. 14.95 (*0-9637772-3-8*) Crystal Dimensns.

Rodriguez del Pino, Salvador. La Novela Chicana Escrita en Espanol: Cinco Autores Comprometidos. LC 81-71730. iv, 159p. (SPA.). 1982. pap. 16.00 (*0-916950-28-X*) Biling Rev-Pr.

***Rodriguez, Douglas.** Nuevo Latino. 176p. 1995. 27.95 (*0-89815-752-8*) Ten Speed Pr.

Rodriguez, E. M. & Van Wimersma Greidanus, T. B., eds. The Cerebrospinal Fluid (CSF) & Peptide Hormones. (Frontiers of Hormone Research Ser.: Vol. 9). (Illus.). viii, 220p. 1982. 105.75 (*3-8055-2823-X*) S Karger.

***Rodriguez, Edgar E.** Fauna Precolombina de Narino. (Illus.). 122p. (SPA.). 1992. pap. 10.00 (*1-877812-23-4*) UPLAAP.

Rodriguez, Elizabeth, ed. Engineering Test Principles for Operational Suitability. 181p. 1992. 37.00 (*0-937194-23-9*) A Deepak Pub.

Rodriguez, Estevan A., et al. Agua Fresca. (Illus.). 59p. 1980. pap. 3.50 (*0-918358-10-8*) Pajarito Pubns.

Rodriguez, Esther & Kirvatis, Joanna. Selected Experiments in General Chemistry & Qualitative Analysis. 1994. spiral bd. 15.50 (*0-88252-163-2*) Paladin Hse.

Rodriguez, Eugene, Jr. Henry B. Gonzalez: A Political Profile. Cortes, Carlos E., ed. LC 76-1568. (Chicano Heritage Ser.). 1977. 15.95 (*0-405-09522-8*) Ayer.

Rodriguez, Evangelina & Tordera, Antonio. Calderon Y la Obra Corta Dramatica del Siglo XVII. (Serie A: Monagrafias, XCI). 228p. (Orig.). (SPA.). (C). 1983. pap. 27.00 (*0-7293-0159-1*, Pub. by Tamesis Bks Ltd UK) Boydell & Brewer.

Rodriguez, F. & Marchetti, N. Italian Commercial Correspondence: Corrispondenza Comerciale Italiana. 272p. (ITA.). 1980. pap. 39.95 (*0-8288-1559-3*, M14183) Fr & Eur.

Rodriguez, Ferdinand. Principles of Polymer Systems. 3rd ed. (Illus.). 612p. 1989. 59.50 (*0-89116-176-7*); Instr's. manual. teacher ed write for info. (*1-56032-015-X*) Hemisp Pub.

Rodriguez Forteza, Adela. Manual De Investigacion Intelectual. (UPREX, Manuales: No. 7). 114p. (C). 1972. pap. 1.50 (*0-8477-0007-0*) U of PR Pr.

Rodriguez-Fraticelli, Carlos. Education & Imperialism: The Puerto Rican Experience in Higher Education, 1898-1986. 51p. 1986. lib. bdg. 5.00 (*1-878483-07-2*) Hunter Coll CEP.

Rodriguez, Fred. Equity Education: Issues & Strategies. 320p. (C). 1990. per. 26.95 (*0-8403-5665-X*) Kendall-Hunt.

Rodriguez, G. & Venkataraman, S., eds. Intelligent Control & Adaptive Systems. 310p. 1990. 62.00 (*0-8194-0235-4*, VOL. 1196) SPIE.

Rodriguez Garcia. Juan Bunyan: John Bunyan - A Biography. (SPA.). 8.95 (*84-7645-152-0*, 223198, Pub. by Edit Clie SP) TSELF.

Rodriguez-Garcia, Rosalia, et al. The Health-Development Link. 164p. 1993. pap. text ed. write for info. (*0-9636369-0-1*) GWU Ctr Int Hlth.

Rodriguez, Gina M. Green Corn Tamales - Tamales de Elote. (Illus.). 40p. (ENG & SPA.). (J). 1994. 14.95 (*0-938243-00-4*) Hispanic Bk Dist.

Rodriguez, Gloria F., ed. see Kemvichanuvat, Cherdchai.

Rodriguez, Gloria F., ed. see Rausiri, Supa.

***Rodriguez, Graciela, et al.** Sueno en el Yunque. (Illus.). 36p. (J). 1993. 12.95 (*0-8477-0204-9*) U of PR Pr.

Rodriguez, Helen. Helen of Burma. large type ed. 320p. 1984. 15.95 (*0-7089-1189-7*) Ulverscroft.

Rodriguez-Hunter, Suzanne. Found Meals of the Lost Generation: Recipes & Anecdotes from 1920s Paris. 252p. 1994. 21.95 (*0-571-19855-4*) Faber & Faber.

Rodriguez, Ileana. House - Garden - Nation: Space, Gender, & Ethnicity in Post-Colonial Latin American Literatures by Women. Carr, Robert, tr. LC 93-42502. (Post-Contemporary Interventions Ser.). 272p. 1994. lib. bdg. 49.95 (*0-8223-1450-9*); pap. text ed. 16.95 (*0-8223-1465-7*) Duke.

An Asterisk (*) at the beginning of an entry indicates that the title is appearing in BIP for the first time.

Rodriguez, Isabel. Sin Tiempo ni Distancia. LC 90-81212. (Coleccion Cuba y Sus Jueces Ser.). (Illus.). 94p. (Orig.). (SPA.). 1990. pap. 9.95 (*0-89729-566-8*) Ediciones.

Rodriguez, Israel. La Estatua de Sal. LC 88-80053. (Coleccion Espejo de Paciencia Ser.). (Illus.). 63p. (Orig.). (SPA.). 1989. pap. 9.95 (*0-89729-474-2*) Ediciones.

— El Hombre y las Metaforas de Dios en la Literatura Hispanoamericana. LC 90-8496. 144p. (Orig.). (SPA.). 1991. pap. 19.95 (*0-89729-585-4*) Ediciones.

— Poemas de Israel. LC 80-51403. 91p. 1980. pap. 12.00 (*0-89295-016-1*) Society Sp & Sp-Am.

Rodriguez-Iturbe, Ignacio, jt. auth. see Bras, Rafael L.

Rodriguez, Ivan, tr. see Wycoff, Cynthia.

Rodriguez, J. Costas, ed. Frontinus - Frontini Index. (Alpha-Omega, Reihe A Ser.: Bd. LI). iii, 804p. 1985. write for info. (*3-487-07708-6*, Pub. by Georg Olms GW) Lubrecht & Cramer.

Rodriguez, J. F. Angel de la Bondad: Angel of Kindness. (SPA.). 2.95 (*84-7228-017-9*, 220035, Pub. by Edit Clie SP) TSELF.

— Paginas Luminosas para Micro: Effective Radio Sermons. (SPA.). 3.25 (*84-7228-281-3*, 220108, Pub. by Edit Clie SP) TSELF.

Rodriguez, J. G., jt. ed. see Nault, L. R.

Rodriguez, J. G., jt. ed. see Slansky, Frank.

Rodriguez, Jaime E. Down from Colonialism: Mexico's Nineteenth Century Crisis. LC 83-14331. (Popular Ser.: No. 3). 84p. (Orig.). 1983. pap. 5.50 (*0-89551-064-2*, S161) UCLA Chicano Studies.

— The Evolution of the Mexican Political System. LC 92-29839. (Latin American Silhouettes Ser.). 322p. (ENG & SPA.). 1993. 45.00 (*0-8420-2448-4*, SR Bks) Scholarly Res Inc.

Rodriguez, Jaime E., ed. The Independence of Mexico & the Creation of the New Nation. LC 89-2665. 374p. 1989. 32.50 (*0-87903-070-4*) UCLA Lat Am Ctr.

— The Mexican & Mexican American Experience in the 19th Century. LC 88-64099. 136p. 1989. 20.00 (*0-916950-93-X*); pap. 12.00 (*0-916950-94-8*) Biling Rev-Pr.

— Patterns of Contention in Mexican History. LC 91-38845. (Latin American Silhouettes Ser.). 368p. (ENG & SPA.). 1992. lib. bdg. 45.00 (*0-8420-2399-2*) Scholarly Res Inc.

— The Revolutionary Process in Mexico. (Latin American Studies: Vol. 72). 374p. 1990. 34.50 (*0-87903-073-9*) UCLA Lat Am Ctr.

Rodriguez, Jaime E., jt. auth. see MacLachlan, Colin M.

***Rodriguez, Janel.** Gloria Estefan. LC 95-16152. (Contemporary Hispanic Americans Ser.). (J). 1995. write for info. (*0-8172-3982-0*) Raintree Steck-V.

Rodriguez, Jeanette. Our Lady of Guadalupe: Faith & Empowerment among Mexican-American Women. LC 93-31267. (Illus.). 248p. (Orig.). (C). 1994. text ed. 35.00 (*0-292-77061-8*); pap. 13.95 (*0-292-77062-6*) U of Tex Pr.

Rodriguez, Joaquin P. Reflexiones De un Agricultor. 1978. pap. 10.00 (*0-89729-203-0*) Ediciones.

Rodriguez, Joe. The Oddsplayer. LC 88-10484. 224p. (Orig.). 1989. pap. 9.50 (*0-934770-88-3*) Arte Publico.

Rodriguez, Joe, ed. see Bernar, Noel.

Rodriguez, Jorge. Politica Militar y Dominacion. LC 88-80499. 270p. 1988. pap. 8.95 (*0-940238-59-4*) Ediciones Huracan.

Rodriguez, Jorge A., tr. see Westberg, Granger.

Rodriguez, Jose. Bankruptcy. 28p. pap. 2.75 (*0-685-23159-3*, 41,575B) NCLS Inc.

Rodriguez, Jose M., tr. see Campbell, Doak S.

***Rodriguez, Joseph.** Spanish Harlem. LC 94-35015. (American Scene Ser.: Vol. 3). (Illus.). 1994. pap. 27.50 (*1-881616-24-X*) Dist Art Pubs.

Rodriguez, Jovita, jt. auth. see Torres, Vivian.

Rodriguez, Juan, ed. see Ulica, Jorge, pseud.

Rodriguez, Juan L., et al, eds. Text & Concordance of Biblioteca Nacional Manuscript 9218 Historia del gran Tamerlan. (Spanish Ser.: No. 20). 1986. 10.00 (*0-942260-62-7*) Hispanic Seminary.

Rodriguez, Judith. New & Selected Poems: The House by Water. (Illus.). 180p. (Orig.). 1989. pap. text ed. 16.95 (*0-7022-2138-4*, Pub. by Univ Queensland Pr AT) Intl Spec Bk.

Rodriguez, Judith, ed. Jennifer Rankin: Collected Poems. 256p. 1990. pap. 17.95 (*0-7022-2288-7*, Pub. by Univ Queensland Pr AT) Intl Spec Bk.

Rodriguez, Judith, jt. auth. see Pardo-Maurer, R.

Rodriguez, Judy. Times Tables the Fun Way Book for Kids: A Picture Method of Learning the Multiplication Facts. LC 93-79769. (Illus.). 47p. (J). (gr. 2-8). 1994. student ed 7.95 (*1-883841-27-5*); teacher ed 24.95 (*1-883841-28-3*) Key Pubs UT.

— Times Tables the Fun Way Teacher's Manual. 2nd rev. ed. (Illus.). 145p. 1995. teacher ed 24.95 (*0-614-04517-7*) Key Pubs UT.

***Rodriguez, Judy & Rodriguez, Dave.** Times Tables the Fun Way Book for Kids: A Picture Method of Learning the Multiplication Facts, Flash Cards. 2nd rev. ed. (Illus.). 47p. (J). (gr. 2-8). 1995. 5.95 (*1-883841-30-5*) Key Pubs UT.

Rodriguez, Judy, jt. auth. see Rodriguez, Dave.

Rodriguez, Judy, jt. auth. see Rodriguez, David.

Rodriguez-Julia, Edgardo. El Entierro de Cortijo. LC 83-80312. (Nave y el Puerto Ser.). (Illus.). 96p. (SPA.). 1983. pap. 5.95 (*0-940238-21-7*) Ediciones Huracan.

— Puertorriquenos: Album de la Sagrada Familia Puertorriguena a Partir de 1898. (Biblioteca de Autores de Puerto Rico Ser.). (Illus.). 176p. (Orig.). (SPA.). 1992. reprint ed. pap. 6.00 (*1-56328-025-6*) Edit Plaza Mayor.

Rodriguez, June N. Texas: Off the Beaten Path: A Guide to Unique Places. LC 94-12357. (Off the Beaten Path Ser.). (Illus.). 160p. 1994. pap. 10.95 (*1-56440-483-8*) Globe Pequot.

Rodriguez, Kathryn, jt. auth. see Vredevelt, Pamela.

Rodriguez, Laura, jt. auth. see Taylor, Jill M.

Rodriguez Lee, Maria L. Juegos Sicologicos en la Narrativa de Mario Vargas Llosa. LC 80-70772. (Coleccion Polymita Ser.). 189p. (Orig.). (SPA.). 1984. pap. 14.95 (*0-89729-279-0*) Ediciones.

Rodriguez-Lee, Maria L., tr. see Ponce, Manuel.

Rodriguez, Levine. Maestros Hispanicos del Siglo Viente. 194p. (SPA.). (C). 1979. pap. text ed. write for info. (*0-318-69171-X*) HB Coll Pubs.

***Rodriguez, Lily O. & Duellman, William E.** Guide to the Frogs of the Equitos Region, Amazonian Peru. Trueb, Linda, ed. (Peruvian Field Guides Ser.: No. SP 22). 80p. (Orig.). (C). 1994. pap. text ed. 19.95 (*0-89338-047-4*) U of KS Mus Nat Hist.

Rodriguez, Linda. Skin Hunger. (Petites Major Ser.). 42p. 1993. pap. 4.00 (*1-884754-07-4*) Potpourri Pubns.

Rodriguez, Linda A., ed. Rank & Privilege: The Military & Society in Latin America. LC 94-14393. (Jaguar Books on Latin America: No. 8). 239p. 1994. 40.00 (*0-8420-2432-8*); pap. 14.95 (*0-8420-2433-6*) Scholarly Res Inc.

Rodriguez-Lopez, M., et al. Blue-Green Algae: Current Research, 4 vols., Vol. 1. 213p. 1974. text ed. 26.50 (*0-8422-7187-2*) Irvington.

Rodriguez, Louis C., Jr. So You Want to Be a Federal Agent. 84p. 1992. Career Book. 8.95 (*0-9634286-0-8*) Ancur Comms.

***Rodriguez, Louis J.** Midwestern State University in Photographs. (Illus.). 1995. 34.95 (*0-915323-07-9*) Midwestern St U Pr.

Rodriguez, Luis F. Test Bank to Accompany Allison, Prentice, "The Legal Environment of Business," 4th ed. 270p. (C). 1993. pap. text ed. 8.00 (*0-03-098056-9*) Dryden Pr.

Rodriguez, Luis J. Always Running: Gang Days in L. A. LC 92-39002. (Orig.). (J). (gr. 9 up). 1993. 19.95 (*1-880684-06-3*) Curbstone.

— Always Running: La Vida Loca: Gang Days in L.A. 1994. pap. 10.00 (*0-671-88231-7*, Touchstone Bks) S&S Trade.

— The Concrete River. LC 90-56217. 128p. (Orig.). 1991. pap. 9.95 (*0-915306-42-5*) Curbstone.

— Poems Across the Pavement. (Illus.). 48p. (Orig.). (C). 1991. pap. 5.00 (*0-9624287-0-1*) Tia Chucha Pr.

— La Vida Loca: El Testimonio de una Pandilla Callejera en Los Angeles. 1995. pap. 10.00 (*0-684-81551-6*, Scribners) S&S Trade.

Rodriguez-Luis, Julio. The Contemporary Praxis of the Fantastic: Borges & Cortazar. LC 91-23877. (Latin American Studies: Vol. 1). 220p. 1991. 19.00 (*0-8153-0101-4*, 1435) Garland.

Rodriguez, Luz I. Entonces. (Biblioteca de Autores de Puerto Rico Ser.). 64p. (Orig.). (SPA.). 1991. pap. text ed. 5.00 (*1-56328-003-5*) Edit Plaza Mayor.

Rodriguez, M. A., jt. ed. see Ibort, L. A.

Rodriguez, M. A., jt. ed. see Pesquera, L.

Rodriguez, M. B. Cuentos Alegres. 3rd ed. LC 78-153486. (C). 1972. pap. text ed. 22.75 (*0-03-080276-8*) HB Coll Pubs.

Rodriguez, M. R., tr. see Malgorn, G.

Rodriguez, Maria, tr. see McBride, Jere J.

Rodriguez, Mario. William Burke & Francisco de Miranda: The Word & Deed in Spanish America's Emancipation. LC 94-4182. 600p. (C). 1994. lib. bdg. 64.50 (*0-8191-9485-9*) U Pr of Amer.

Rodriguez, Mario B., et al. Cuentos de Ambos Mundos. Eoff, Sherman H., ed. (Graded Spanish Readers Ser.: Bk. 2). (C). 1972. pap. 15.56 (*0-395-04125-2*) HM.

Rodriguez, Mary, jt. auth. see Knox, Maxine.

Rodriguez-Matos, Carlos, et al. Hispanic Immigrant Writers & the Family: La Escritura de Los Inmigrantes Hispanos y la Familia. Torres-Saillant, Silvio, ed. & intro. by. (Literature - Conversation Ser.: Vol. 2). 100p. (Orig.). (SPA.). (C). 1989. pap. 7.00 (*0-685-30056-0*) Ollantay Pr.

Rodriguez-Matos, Carlos A. Llama de Amor Vivita Jarchas. LC 88-80881. (Arte y Poesia Ser.). (Illus.). 50p. (Orig.). (SPA.). 1988. pap. 6.00 (*0-685-20049-3*) Ichali.

Rodriguez Matos, Carlos A., jt. auth. see Villanueva-Collado, Alfredo.

Rodriguez Monino, Antonio. Diccionario Bibliografico De Liegos Sueltos Poeticos, Siglo XVI. 740p. (SPA.). 1970. 53.95 (*0-8288-6494-2*, S-7006) Fr & Eur.

Rodriguez-Monino, Antonio. Diccionario de Pliegos Sueltos Poeticos: Poetry Manuscripts, 16th Century. 735p. (SPA.). 1970. 49.95 (*0-8288-8564-8*) Fr & Eur.

Rodriguez-Monino, Antonio & Marino, Maria B., eds. Catalogo de los Manuscritos Poeticos Castellanos de la Sociedad Hispana de America, 3 vols. (Illus.). 1966. 50.00 (*0-87535-103-4*); lib. bdg. 60.00 (*0-87535-129-8*) Hispanic Soc.

Rodriguez Monino, Antonio, ed. see Melendez Valdes, Juan.

Rodriguez-Montiel, Zitha & Stevens, Wendelle C. UFO Contact from Andromeda: Extraterrestrial Prophecy. (Factbooks Ser.). (Illus.). 300p. 1989. lib. bdg. 16.95 (*0-934269-12-2*) UFO Photo.

Rodriguez, Narcisco, jt. auth. see Kuhtas, Candace.

Rodriguez-Nieto, Alcides, ed. see Salinas-Norman, Bobbi.

Rodriguez-Nieto, Catherine, tr. Fireflight: Three Latin American Poets. 1976. pap. 2.50 (*0-685-73658-X*) Oyez.

Rodriguez-Nieto, Catherine, tr. see Corpi, Lucha.

Rodriguez-Nieto, Catherine, ed. see Salinas-Norman, Bobbi.

Rodriguez-Nogues, Lourdes, jt. ed. see Rasi, Richard A.

Rodriguez O, Jaime E. Mexico in the Age of Democratic Revolutions, 1750-1850. LC 93-33325. 330p. 1994. lib. bdg. 38.00 (*1-55587-476-2*) Lynne Rienner.

Rodriguez, Olga, ed. The Politics of Chicano Liberation. 1977. lib. bdg. 40.00 (*0-87348-513-0*); pap. 13.95 (*0-87348-514-9*) Pathfinder NY.

Rodriguez, Oscar. The Credit Improvement & Protection Hbk. LC 93-70051. (Illus.). 132p. (Orig.). 1993. pap. 19.95 (*0-918751-32-2*) J O Flores.

Rodriguez, Oscar E., tr. see Rusbuldt, Richard E., et al.

Rodriguez, Otilio, jt. tr. see Kavanaugh, Kieran.

Rodriguez, P. Pedro. Matrimono y Familia Cristiana. 116p. 1984. pap. 4.25 (*0-915388-20-0*, 171, Buckley Pubns) ACTA Pubns.

Rodriguez, Pablo. Al Borde del Abismo. LC 91-77144. 221p. (Orig.). (C). 1992. pap. text ed. 8.00 (*0-9622522-9-8*) Editorial Academica.

Rodriguez, Patricia, ed. see Riley, Gay.

Rodriguez, Paul. Breast Cancer: What Every Woman Should Know. (Illus.). 138p. (Orig.). 1988. pap. text ed. 11.45 (*0-9622118-0-X*) Aurora KS.

Rodriguez Perez, Luis. Diccionario de Dificultades Matematicas Resueltas. 440p. (SPA.). 1984. pap. 55.00 (*0-8288-1900-9*, S60045) Fr & Eur.

Rodriguez, R., et al, eds. Plant Aging: Basic & Applied Approaches. LC 90-6996. (NATO ASI Series A, Life Sciences: Vol. 186). (Illus.). 448p. 1990. 115.00 (*0-306-43518-7*, Plenum Pr) Plenum.

Rodriguez, R. L. & Tait, R. C. Recombinant DNA Experiments: An Introduction. 1983. pap. text ed. 29.25 (*0-201-10870-4*) Benjamin-Cummings.

Rodriguez, Rafael, jt. ed. see Zavala, Iris M.

Rodriguez, Rafael A. Homiletica Simplificada: Homiletics Simplified. (SPA.). 4.25 (*84-7645-305-1*, 223448, Pub. by Edit Clie SP) TSELF.

Rodriguez-Ramos, Walter E. Interactive Engineering Graphics Preliminary. 680p. 1987. pap. 24.95 (*0-07-053395-4*) McGraw.

Rodriguez, Raymond & Denhardt, David T. Vectors: A Survey of Molecular Cloning Vectors & Their Uses. (Biotechnology Ser.). (Illus.). 578p. 1987. text ed. 32.00 (*0-409-90042-7*) Buttrwrth-Heinemann.

Rodriguez, Raymond, jt. auth. see Balderrama, Francisco E.

Rodriguez-Reinoso, F., et al, eds. Characterization of Porous Solids, No. Two: Proceedings of the IUPAC Symposium (COPS II), Alicante, Spain, May 6-9, 1990. (Studies in Surface Science & Catalysis: No. 62). 782p. 1991. 243.00 (*0-444-88569-2*) Elsevier.

Rodriguez, Reymundo & Coleman, Marion T., eds. Mental Health Issues of the Mexican Origin Population in Texas: Proceedings of the Fifth Robert L. Sutherland Seminar. 240p. (Orig.). 1987. pap. 9.45x (*0-943463-00-9*) Hogg Found.

Rodriguez, Ricardo J., jt. auth. see Kolb, Robert W.

Rodriguez, Richard. Days of Obligation: An Argument with My Mexican Father. 256p. 1993. reprint ed. pap. 11.00 (*0-14-009622-1*, Penguin Bks) Viking Penguin.

— Hunger of Memory: The Education of Richard Rodriguez. 208p. 1983. mass mkt. 5.99 (*0-553-27293-4*, Bantam Classics) Bantam.

Rodriguez, Rita M., ed. The Export-Import Bank at Fifty: The International Environment & the Institution's Role. 224p. 1986. text ed. 40.00 (*0-669-14828-8*) Free Pr.

Rodriguez, Rita M., jt. auth. see Riehl, Heinz.

Rodriguez, Robert. Rebel Without a Crew: or How a 23-Year Old Filmmaker with 7,000 Dollars Became a Hollywood Player. (Illus.). 256p. 1995. 21.95 (*0-525-93794-3*) NAL-Dutton.

Rodriguez-Roque, Oswaldo. American Furniture at Chipstone. LC 83-40270. (Illus.). 480p. 1984. 50.00 (*0-299-09760-9*) U of Wis Pr.

Rodriguez-Salgado, M. J., jt. ed. see Adams, Simon.

Rodriguez Santidrian, Pedro. Diccionario de las Religiones. 472p. (SPA.). 1989. pap. 18.95 (*0-7859-5718-9*, 8420603732) Fr & Eur.

Rodriguez-Saona, Roberto. Colloquial Spanish of Latin America. (Colloquial Ser.). 1994. write for info. (*0-415-08952-2*); Incl. casette. audio write for info. (*0-415-08954-9*) Routledge.

Rodriguez-Seda de Laguna, Asela. Shaw en el Mundo Hispanico. LC 79-22415. (Coleccion Mente y Palabra). 142p. (SPA.). 1981. 9.60 (*0-8477-0564-1*); pap. 8.00 (*0-8477-0565-X*) U of PR Pr.

Rodriguez, Spain. She: Anthology of Big Bitch. 1993. pap. 14.95 (*0-86719-398-0*) Last Gasp.

Rodriguez, Stephanie. Time to Stop Pretending: A Mother's Story of Domestic Violence, Homelessness & Escape. LC 93-8299. 192p. 1994. 19.95 (*0-8397-8060-5*) Eriksson.

Rodriguez, Susan. Art Smart: Ready-to-Use Slides & Activities for Teaching Art History & Appreciation. 288p. 1988. pap. text ed. 69.95 (*0-13-047754-0*, Busn) P-H.

— Art Smart: Supplementary Slide Portfolio II: Manet - Impressionism to African Magical Sculpture. 1989. text ed. 29.95 (*0-13-047648-X*) P-H.

— Special Artist's Handbook: Art Activities & Adaptive Aids for Handicapped Children. LC 84-4704. (Illus.). 288p. (Orig.). 1984. pap. 17.95 (*0-13-826355-8*) P-H.

Rodriguez, Teresa B. Modalidades Del Caso y Del Proceso Juridico En el Drama Hispanoamericano. LC 89-83954. (Coleccion Polymita Ser.). 141p. (Orig.). (SPA.). 1991. pap. 19.00 (*0-89729-534-X*) Ediciones.

Rodriguez-Valera, Fransisco, ed. Halophilic Bacteria, 2 vols., Set. (Bacteriologists Ser.). 1988. 187.00 (*0-8493-4366-6*, QR97, CRC Reprint) Franklin.

Rodriguez, Victor. Eldorado in East Harlem. LC 92-14985. 156p. 1992. 9.50 (*1-55885-054-6*) Arte Publico.

***Rodriguez, Victoria & Ward, Peter.** Policymaking, Politics, & Urban Governance in Chihuahua: The Experience of Recent Panista Governments. (Policy Report Ser.: No. 3). 152p. 1992. 15.00 (*0-89940-317-4*) LBJ Sch Pub Aff.

***Rodriguez, Victoria E. & Ward, Peter M.** Political Change in Baja California: Democracy in the Making? (Monograph Ser.). 140p. 1994. pap. 14.95 (*1-878367-25-0*, MN-40) UCSD Ctr US-Mex.

***Rodriguez, Victoria E. & Ward, Peter M., eds.** Opposition Government in Mexico. LC 94-36197. 270p. 1995. 45.00x (*0-8263-1577-1*) U of NM Pr.

— Opposition Government in Mexico. LC 94-36197. 270p. 1995. pap. 22.50 (*0-8263-1578-X*) U of NM Pr.

Rodriguez, Victorino R. The Theology of Peace. LC 88-70763. (Illus.). 62p. (Orig.). (C). 1988. pap. 4.00 (*1-877905-04-6*) Am Soc Defense TFP.

Rodriguez, Victorio, jt. ed. see Bodey, Gerald P.

Rodriguez, W. R. The Shoe Shine Parlor Poems Et Al. 48p. 1984. pap. 6.50 (*0-941160-08-4*) Ghost Pony Pr.

Rodriguez, Walter. The Modeling of Design Ideas: Graphics & Visualization Techniques for Engineers. 1992. pap. text ed. write for info. (*0-07-053394-6*) McGraw.

Rodriguez, Walter E. Modeling of Design Ideas. 1992. text ed. write for info. (*0-07-079744-7*) McGraw.

Rodriguez, Zobeida. Mensajes en Poesia: Messages in Poetry. (SPA.). 5.00 (*84-7645-479-1*, 223663, Pub. by Edit Clie SP) TSELF.

Rodrik, Dani, jt. ed. see Aricanli, Tosun.

Rodrik, Dani, jt. auth. see Collins, Susan M.

Rodrik, Dani, jt. auth. see Diwan, Ishac.

Rodrique, Daniel R. Heading Home. Keith, Randy, ed. 252p. (Orig.). 1992. pap. 3.95 (*0-9633988-0-6*) Minuteman Pub Hse.

Rodrique, Gary, ed. Parallel Processing for Scientific Computing. (Proceedings in Applied Mathematics Ser.: No. 35). xxix, 428p. 1988. pap. 50.50 (*0-89871-228-9*) Soc Indus-Appl Math.

Rodriques, A. & Tondeur, D., eds. Percolation Processes: Theory & Applications. (NATO Advanced Study Institute Ser.: Applied Science, No. 33). 594p. 1981. lib. bdg. 121.50 (*90-286-0579-7*) Kluwer Ac.

Rodriquez, Andres. Night Song. 84p. (Orig.). 1994. pap. 7.95 (*1-882688-05-8*) Tia Chucha Pr.

Rodriquez-Barrientos. Diccionario Maritimo: Ingles - Espanol, Espanol - Ingoles. (ENG & SPA.). 1987. write for info. (*0-7859-3684-X*, 8428315140) Fr & Eur.

Rodriquez-Barrueco, C., jt. auth. see Subbarao, N. S.

Rodriquez, Birgitte. Glimpses of the Divine: Working with the Teachings of Sai Baba. 272p. (Orig.). 1993. pap. 12.95 (*0-87728-766-X*) Weiser.

Rodriquez-Castellano, Juan. En Busca de Oro Negro. (Illus.). (SPA.). (C). 1945. 18.95 (*0-8290-2396-8*) Irvington.

Rodriquez de Lecea, Teresa, ed. see Giner de los Rios, Francisco.

Rodriquez de Montalvo, Garci. Amadis de Gaula, I. Avalle-Arce, Juan B., ed. (Nueva Austral Ser.: Vol. 119). (SPA.). 1991. pap. text ed. 42.95x (*84-239-1919-6*) Elliots Bks.

— Amadis de Gaula, II. Avalle-Arce, Juan B., ed. (Nueva Austral Ser.: Vol. 120). (SPA.). 1991. pap. text ed. 42.95x (*84-239-1920-X*) Elliots Bks.

Rodriquez, Doris. Diego Wants to Be - Diego Quiere Ser. (Illus.). 32p. (J). (ps-2). 1994. lib. bdg. 15.00 (*0-917846-35-4*, 95611) Highsmith Pr.

Rodriquez, Fred. Affirming Equity: A Framework for Teachers & Schools. 336p. (C). 1993. per. 24.76 (*0-8403-9024-6*) Kendall-Hunt.

***Rodriquez, George L.** Civil Engineering: Problem Solving Flowcharts. (Illus.). 110p. (Orig.). 1995. pap. 25.50 (*0-910554-07-2*, 072) Engineering.

Rodriquez, Judy, tr. see Brinkley, Ginny & Sampson, Sherry.

Rodriquez, M. J. & Adams, Simon. England, Spain & the Grand Armada 1585-1604. 324p. (C). 1991. text ed. 78.00 (*0-389-20955-4*) B&N Imports.

Rodriquez, Mario. The Cadiz Experiment in Central America, 1808 to 1826. LC 76-50256. 328p. reprint ed. pap. 93.50 (*0-7837-4844-2*, 2044491) Bks Demand.

Rodriquez O., Jaime E., tr. see Flores Caballero, Romeo.

Rodriquez, Orlando, jt. ed. see Malgady, Robert G.

Rodriquez, Otillo, tr. see Kavanaugh, Kieran.

Rodriquez, Pedro, tr. see Lewinski, Ron.

Rodriquez-Peralta, Phyllis W. Jose Santos Chocano. LC 71-99529. (Twayne's World Authors Ser.). 1970. lib. bdg. 17.95 (*0-685-02668-X*) Irvington.

***Rodriquez, R. & Costas, M.** Lectures on Thermodynamics & Statistical Mechanics: Proceedings of the XXIII Winter Meeting on Statistical Physics. 240p. 1994. text ed. 71.00 (*981-02-1915-6*) World Scientific Pub.

Rodriquez, Susan. Art Smart! Supplementary Slide Portfolio I. (Illus.). 1989. sl. 29.95 (*0-13-047622-6*) P-H.

Rodson, Johan. Alone in the Dark: Official Strategy Guide. 1994. pap. 19.95 (*1-55958-604-4*) Prima Pub.

Rodstein, Harvey E. Pick for Professionals: Advanced Methods & Techniques. 1990. text ed. 34.95 (*0-07-156991-X*) McGraw.

— Pick for Professionals: Advanced Methods & Techniques. (Pick Library). (Illus.). 256p. 1989. 34.95 (*0-8306-0125-2*) TAB Bks.

***Rodu, Brad.** For Smokers Only: How Smokeless Tobacco Can Save Your Life. (Illus.). (Orig.). 1995. pap. text ed. 11.99 (*0-945819-77-3*) Sulzburger & Graham Pub.

Roduit, M. A., tr. see Cusson, Gilles.

Roduit, Mary A., tr. see Cusson, Gilles.

Rodway, Allan E., ed. Godwin & the Age of Transition. LC 76-52953. (English Literature Ser.: No. 33). 1977. lib. bdg. 75.00 (*0-8383-2146-1*) M S G Haskell Hse.

Rodway, Allan E., jt. auth. see De Sola Pinto, Vivian.

Rodway, Howard. Old Path Tarot. 48p. 1990. 17.00 (*0-88079-490-9*) US Games Syst.

— Old Path Tarot Set: Includes Tarot of the Old Path. 160p. 1990. 32.00 (*0-88079-492-5*) US Games Syst.

R

Rodway, James. In the Guiana Forest: Studies of Nature in Relations to the Struggle for Life. LC 69-18997. (Illus.). 242p. 1970. reprint ed. 45.00 (0-8371-1027-0, ROG&, Greenwood Pr) Greenwood.

Rodway, Juliet. Little Book of Renoir. 1994. 4.98 (1-55521-985-3) Bk Sales Inc.

— Little Book of Van Gogh. 1994. 4.98 (1-55521-986-1) Bk Sales Inc.

Rodway, Margaret. Counseling Diverse Client Groups: An International Perspective on Human Social Functioning. LC 89-9297. (Studies in Health & Human Services). 376p. 1989. lib. bdg. 99.95 (0-88946-139-2) E Mellen.

Rodway, Margaret & Wright, Marianne, eds. Sociopsychological Aspects of Sexually Transmitted Diseases. LC 88-638. (Journal of Social Work & Human Sexuality: Vol. 6, No. 2). (Illus.). 162p. 1988. text ed. 32.95 (0-86656-737-2) Haworth Pr.

Rodway, Margaret R. & Trute, Barry, eds. The Ecological Perspective in Family-Centered Therapy. LC 93-29860. (Studies in Health & Human Services: Vol. 19). 364p. 1993. text ed. 99.95 (0-7734-9362-X) E Mellen.

Rodway, Margaret R. & Wingrove, Brian L. Healthy Homosexual. LC 84-90340. 1984. 9.95 (0-87212-180-1) Libra.

Rodway, Stella, tr. see Wiesel, Elie.

Rodwell. Antibody Mediated Delivery Systems: Formulation Solvency & Physical Properties. (Targeted Diagnosis & Therapy Ser.: Vol. 1). 400p. 1988. 140.00 (0-8247-7960-6) Dekker.

Rodwell, jt. auth. see Quash.

Rodwell, Dorothy, jt. auth. see American Production.

Rodwell, J. S., ed. British Plant Communities Vol. 1: Woodlands & Scrub. (Illus.). 395p. (C). 1991. 160.00 (0-521-23558-8) Cambridge U Pr.

— British Plant Communities Vol. 2: Mires & Heaths. (Illus.). 700p. (C). 1992. 195.00 (0-521-39165-2) Cambridge U Pr.

— British Plant Communities Vol. 3: Grasslands & Montane Communities. (Illus.). 750p. (C). 1993. 195.00 (0-521-39166-0) Cambridge U Pr.

— British Plant Communities Vol. 4: Aquatic Communities, Swamps & Tall-Herb Fens. (Illus.). 350p. (C). 1995. 99.95 (0-521-39168-7) Cambridge U Pr.

Rodwell, Jenny. Beginner's Guides: Painting Flowers. (Illus.). 96p. 1993. pap. 17.95 (0-289-80081-1, Pub. by Studio Vista Bks UK) Sterling.

— Beginner's Guides: Painting in Pastels. (Illus.). 96p. (YA). (gr. 10-12). 1993. pap. 17.95 (0-289-80073-0, Pub. by Cassell UK) Sterling.

— Beginner's Guides: Painting in Watercolour. (Illus.). 96p. (YA). (gr. 10-12). 1992. pap. 17.95 (0-289-80056-0, Pub. by Studio Vista Bks UK) Sterling.

— Beginner's Guides: Painting Still Life in Oils. (Illus.). 96p. 1994. pap. 17.95 (0-289-80083-8) Sterling.

— Coloured Pencil Drawing. (Illus.). 96p. 1995. 17.95 (0-289-80119-2, Pub. by Studio Vista Bks UK) Sterling.

— Make Your Own Picture Frames. (Illus.). 144p. 1988. pap. 12.95 (0-89134-248-6, 30065) North Light Bks.

— Painting with Acrylics. (Illus.). 176p. 1990. 19.95 (0-89134-354-7, 30264) North Light Bks.

— Portraits in Oil. (Illus.). 96p. 1995. 17.95 (0-289-80120-6, Pub. by Studio Vista Bks UK) Sterling.

— Step by Step Art School: Drawing. 1987. 12.98 (0-671-08906-4) S&S Trade.

Rodwell, John. Participative Training Skills. Taylor, Billie, ed. LC 94-1072. 1994. 63.95 (0-566-07444-3, Pub. by Gower UK) Ashgate Pub Co.

***Rodwell, John & Patterson, Gordon.** Creating New Native Woodlands. (Forestry Commission Bulletin Ser.: No. 112). 85p. 1994. pap. 17.00 (0-11-710320-9, HM03209, Pub. by HMSO UK) UNIPUB.

Rodwell, Lee. Ward Lock Family Health Guide: Arthritis & Rheumatism. (Illus.). 80p. 1994. pap. 9.95 (0-7063-7257-3, Pub. by Ward Lock UK) Sterling.

Rodwell, Warwick. The Archaeology of Religious Places: Churches & Cemeteries in Britain. rev. ed. LC 89-24964. (Illus.). 208p. (C). 1990. text ed. 37.95x (0-8122-8244-2) U of Pa Pr.

— The Fishermen's Chapel, St. Brelade, Jersey: Its Archaeology, Architecture, Wall-Paintings & Conservation. (Illus.). 190p. 1993. text ed. 63.00 (0-901897-19-1) A Sutton Pub.

Rodwin, Lloyd. Cities & City Planning. LC 81-13956. (Environment, Development, & Public Policy: Public Policy & Social Services Ser.). 318p. (C). 1981. 49.50 (0-306-40666-7, Plenum Pr) Plenum.

Rodwin, Lloyd, ed. Shelter, Settlement & Development. LC 87-1038. 448p. (C). 1987. text ed. 39.95 (0-04-711023-6) Routledge Chapman & Hall.

Rodwin, Lloyd & Hollister, Robert M., eds. Cities of the Mind: Images & Themes of the City in the Social Sciences. LC 84-1991. (Environment, Development, & Public Policy: Public Policy & Social Services Ser.). 370p. 1984. 54.50 (0-306-41426-0, Plenum Pr) Plenum.

Rodwin, Lloyd & Sazanami, Hidehiko. European Deindustrialization & Regional Economic Transformation. 256p. (C). 1990. text ed. 65.00 (0-04-445882-7); pap. text ed. 24.95 (0-04-445883-5) Routledge Chapman & Hall.

Rodwin, Lloyd & Sazanami, Hidehiko, eds. Deindustrialization & Regional Economic Transformation: The Experience of the United States. (Illus.). 288p. 1989. 65.00 (0-04-445538-0); pap. 27.95 (0-04-445539-9) Routledge Chapman & Hall.

Rodwin, Lloyd & Schon, Donald A., eds. Rethinking the Development Experience: Essays Provoked by the Work of Albert O. Hirschman. LC 94-12644. 320p. (C). 1994. 38.95x (0-8157-7552-0); pap. 16.95x (0-8157-7551-2) Brookings.

Rodwin, Marc A. Medicine, Money & Morals: Physicians' Conflicts of Interest. LC 92-49488. (Illus.). 432p. (C). 1993. 25.00 (0-19-508096-3) OUP.

— Medicine, Money, & Morals: Physician's Conflicts of Interest. (Illus.). 432p. 1995. pap. 13.95 (0-19-509647-9) OUP.

Rodwin, Victor G., et al, eds. Public Hospital Systems in New York & Paris. 320p. 1992. text ed. 40.00 (0-8147-7422-9) NYU Pr.

Rody, Lee. The Desperate Search. LC 88-63476. (American Adventure Ser.). 160p. (J). (gr. 2-6). 1989. pap. 5.99 (1-55661-027-0) Bethany Hse.

Rody, Martyn. The Breakup of Yugoslavia. (Conflicts Ser.). (Illus.). 48p. (J). (gr. 6 up). 1994. text ed. 13.95 (0-02-792529-3, New Dscvry Bks) Silver Burdett Pr.

Rodymans, C. & Rabenau, A., eds. Crystal Structure & Chemical Bonding in Inorganic Chemistry. 1975. 51.50 (0-444-10961-7) Elsevier.

Rodzianko, M. The Truth about the Russian Church Abroad. Hilko, Michael P., tr. LC 74-29321. (Illus.). 48p. (Orig.). 1975. pap. 1.50 (0-88465-004-9) Holy Trinity.

Rodzianko, M. V. Krushenie Imperii. rev. ed. LC 85-52365. (Illus.). 384p. 1986. pap. 16.00 (0-9616413-0-4) Multilingual.

Rodzinski, Witold. History of China, Vol. 1. 1983. text ed. 200.00 (0-08-021806-7, Pub. by Pergamon Repr UK) Franklin.

— The People's Republic of China: A Concise Political History. 304p. 1988. 32.95 (0-02-926871-0); pap. 14.95 (0-02-926872-9) Free Pr.

— The Walled Kingdom: A History of China from Antiquity to the Present. 1984. text ed. 29.95 (0-02-926870-2) Free Pr.

***Roe.** From Mechanism to Organism. Date not set. 24.95 (0-8057-9518-9, Twayne); pap. 14.95 (0-8057-9519-7, Twayne) Macmillan.

Roe & Campbell. Drugs & Nutrients: The Interactive Effects. (Drugs & the Pharmaceutical Sciences Ser.: Vol. 21). 624p. 1984. 210.00 (0-8247-7054-4) Dekker.

Roe, Alan. Financial Sector Reform in Transitional Socialist Economies. LC 92-16768. (EDI Policy Seminar Report Ser.: No. 29). 56p. 1992. 6.95 (0-8213-2145-5, 12145) World Bank.

***Roe, Alan & Roy, Jayanta.** Trade Reform & External Adjustment: The Experiences of Hungary, Poland, Portugal, Turkey & Yugoslavia. (EDI Policy Seminar Report Ser.: No. 16). 32p. 1989. 6.95 (0-614-02873-6, 11178) World Bank.

Roe, Alan, jt. auth. see Pyatt, F. Graham.

Roe, Alan, et al. International Finance Strategies for Developing Countries. LC 92-35776. (EDI Policy Seminar Report Ser.: No. 31). 50p. 1992. 6.95 (0-8213-2283-4, 12283) World Bank.

Roe, Alan R. Instruments of Economic Policy in Africa. 238p. (C). 1992. text ed. 50.00 (0-685-62996-1, 08074) Heinemann.

***Roe, Alfred S.** Civil War Infantry, the 10th Regiment, Mass. Volunteer Infantry, 1861-1864, a Western Massachusetts Regiment. (Illus.). 535p. 1995. reprint ed. lib. bdg. 57.50 (0-614-03921-5) Higginson Bk Co.

— Civil War Infantry, 5th Regiment, Mass. Volunteers Infantry, in Its Three Tours of Duty, 1861, 1862-3, 1864. (Illus.). 510p. 1995. reprint ed. lib. bdg. 56.00 (0-8328-4639-2) Higginson Bk Co.

***Roe, Alfred S. & Nutt, Chas.** Civil War Artillery, 1st Regiment of Heavy Artillery, Mass. Volunteers, (Formerly the 14th Regiment of Infantry), 1861-1865. 507p. 1995. reprint ed. lib. bdg. 55.00 (0-8328-4640-6) Higginson Bk Co.

Roe, Anne. The Making of a Scientist. LC 73-15059. 244p. 1974. reprint ed. text ed. 59.75 (0-8371-7151-2, ROMS, Greenwood Pr) Greenwood.

— The Psychology of Occupations. Stein, Leon, ed. LC 77-70529. (Work Ser.). (Illus.). 1977. reprint ed. lib. bdg. 35.95 (0-405-10197-X) Ayer.

Roe, Anne & Simpson, George G. Behavior & Evolution. LC 58-11260. 567p. reprint ed. pap. 161.60 (0-8357-7105-9, 2003070) Bks Demand.

Roe, Anne K., et al. Nursing Communication Skills: Workbook. LC 75-8753. (Wiley Biomedical-Health Publication Ser.). (Illus.). 90p. reprint ed. pap. 25.70 (0-317-09230-8, 2012584) Bks Demand.

Roe, Barbara. Donald Barthelme: A Study of the Short Fiction. (Twayne's Studies in Short Fiction). 200p. (C). 1992. text ed. 22.95 (0-8057-8338-5, Pub. by Royal Botanic Garden UK) Macmillan.

Roe, Betty D. & Ross, Elinor P. Developing Power in Reading. 5th ed. 432p. 1993. per. 26.95 (0-8403-7919-6) Kendall-Hunt.

— Student Teaching & Field Experience Handbook. 3rd ed. (Illus.). 321p. (C). 1994. pap. write for info. (0-02-402661-1, Merrill Pub Co) Macmillan.

Roe, Betty D., jt. auth. see Burns, Paul C.

Roe, Betty D., et al. Secondary School Reading Instruction: The Content Areas. 4th ed. (C). 1991. write for info. (0-395-43233-2) HM Soft Schl Col Div.

Roe, Bonnie C., jt. auth. see Anderson, Peter.

Roe, Byron P. Probability & Statistics in Experimental Physics. LC 92-12653. (Illus.). 224p. 1992. write for info. (3-540-97849-6) Spr-Verlag.

— Probability & Statistics in Experimental Physics. LC 92-12653. (Illus.). 224p. 1994. 39.00 (0-387-97849-6) Spr-Verlag.

Roe, C. F. A Bonny Case of Murder: Dr. Jean Montrose Mystery. 256p. (Orig.). 1994. pap. 3.99 (0-451-18067-4) NAL-Dutton.

— A Classy Touch of Murder. (Dr. Jean Montrose Mystery Ser.: No. 3). 256p. (Orig.). 1993. pap. 3.99 (0-451-17713-4, Sig) NAL-Dutton.

— A Fiery Hint of Murder. (Dr. Jean Montrose Mystery Ser.: No. 2). 272p. 1993. reprint ed. pap. 3.99 (0-451-17606-5, Sig) NAL-Dutton.

— A Nasty Bit of Murder. 272p. 1992. pap. 3.99 (0-451-17468-2, Sig) NAL-Dutton.

— A Relative Act of Murder. 256p. (Orig.). 1995. mass mkt. 4.99 (0-451-18183-2, Sig) NAL-Dutton.

— A Torrid Piece of Murder: A Dr. Jean Montrose Mystery. 256p. (Orig.). 1994. pap. 3.99 (0-451-18182-4, Sig) NAL-Dutton.

Roe, Charles. North Carolina Wildlife Viewing Guide. Cauble, Chris, ed. (Watchable Wildlife Ser.). (Illus.). 96p. (Orig.). 1992. pap. 5.95 (1-56044-055-4) Falcon Pr MT.

Roe, Cheryl. Tym, the Turtle Boy. LC 89-51373. (Illus.). 40p. (Orig.). (J). (gr. 2-5). 1990. pap. 9.95 (0-9624183-1-5) Timeless Sales.

Roe, Cheryl A. Tym, the Turtle Boy. (Illus.). 52p. (Orig.). (J). (ps-3). 1989. pap. write for info. (0-9624183-0-7) Timeless Sales.

Roe, Clifford A., Jr. The Ohio Corporation: Legal Aspects of Organization & Operation. (Corporate Practice Ser.: No. 55). 1989. 95.00 (1-55871-102-3) BNA.

Roe, Daphne A. Clinical Nutrition for the Health Scientist. 144p. 1980. 81.95 (0-8493-5417-X, QP141, CRC Reprint) Franklin.

— Diet & Drug Interactions. (Illus.). 288p. 1989. text ed. 52.95 (0-442-20487-6) Van Nos Reinhold.

— Handbook on Drug & Nutrient Interactions: A Problem-Oriented Reference Guide. 4th ed. LC 89-17781. 150p. 1989. spiral bd. 21.95 (0-88091-046-1, 0102) Am Dietetic Assn.

— Handbook on Drug & Nutrient Interactions: A Reference & Study Guide. 5th ed. LC 94-35993. (Illus.). 1994. spiral bd. 29.95 (0-88091-135-2) Am Dietetic Assn.

— A Plague of Corn: The Social History of Pellagra. LC 72-12408. (Illus.). 217p. 1973. 32.50 (0-8014-0773-7) Cornell U Pr.

Roe, David. Gustave Flaubert. LC 88-24029. (Modern Novelists Ser.). 133p. 1989. text ed. 29.95 (0-312-02446-0) St Martin.

Roe, David B. & Wilpon, Jay G. Voice Communication Between Humans & Machines. 560p. (C). 1994. text ed. 79.95 (0-309-04988-1) Natl Acad Pr.

Roe, Derek A. Prehistory: An Introduction. LC 70-81799. (Illus.). 288p. reprint ed. pap. 82.10 (0-685-23982-9, 2031546) Bks Demand.

Roe, Doug. Rochester Carburetors. rev. ed. LC 86-81204. 176p. 1986. 14.95 (0-89586-301-4) Price Stern.

Roe, Earl, comp. Dream Big: The Henrietta Mears Story. LC 90-33489. (Illus.). 368p. 1990. 16.99 (0-8307-1254-2, 5111768) Regal.

Roe, Earl, ed. see Aldrich, Sandra P.

Roe, Earl, ed. see Greig, Doris W.

Roe, Earl, ed. see Haystead, Wes.

Roe, Earl, ed. see Murren, Doug.

Roe, Earl, ed. see Slater, Michael.

Roe, Earl, ed. see Sproul, R. C.

Roe, Earl O., ed. see Aldrich, Sandra P.

Roe, Earl O., ed. see Meador, Prentice A. & Chisholm, Bob G.

Roe, Earl O., ed. see Reid, John C.

Roe, Earl O., ed. see Stowell, Gordon.

Roe, Edward P. Barriers Burned Away. LC 70-129370. reprint ed. 24.50 (0-404-05378-5) AMS Pr.

— Barriers Burned Away. LC 71-104552. (Illus.). 480p. (C). 1988. reprint ed. lib. bdg. 8.00 (0-8398-1762-2); reprint ed. pap. text ed. 4.95 (0-317-66470-0) Irvington.

— Barriers Burned Away. (BCL1-PS American Literature Ser.). 472p. 1992. reprint ed. lib. bdg. 99.00 (0-7812-6845-1) Rprt Serv.

— Barriers Burned Away. (Illus.). 1971. reprint ed. 9.00 (0-403-01185-X) Scholarly.

Roe, Eileen. All I Am. LC 88-30510. (Illus.). 32p. (J). (ps-1). 1990. text ed. 13.95 (0-02-777372-8, Bradbury S&S) S&S Childrens.

— Con Mi Hermano with My Brother. LC 90-33983. (Illus.). 32p. (J). (ps-3). 1991. text ed. 14.00 (0-02-777373-6, Bradbury S&S) S&S Childrens.

— Mi Hermano with My Brother. (J). (ps-3). 1994. pap. 4.95 (0-689-71855-1, Aladdin Paperbacks) S&S Childrens.

Roe, Elizabeth A. Recollections of Frontier Life. Baxter, Annette K., ed. LC 79-8809. (Signal Lives Ser.). (Illus.). 1980. reprint ed. lib. bdg. 34.95 (0-405-12855-X) Ayer.

Roe, Emery. Development of Livestock, Agriculture & Water Supplies in Botswana Before Independence: A Short History & Policy Analysis. (Occasional Paper Ser.: No. 10). 56p. 1980. 6.45 (0-86731-023-5) Cornell CIS RDC.

Roe, Emery & Fortmann, Louise. Season & Strategy: The Changing Organization of the Rural Water Sector in Botswana. (Special Series on Resource Management: No. 1). 257p. (Orig.). (C). 1982. pap. text ed. 10.00 (0-86731-082-0) Cornell CIS RDC.

Roe, Emery M. Narrative Policy Analysis: Theory & Practice. LC 94-7248. (Illus.). 240p. 1994. lib. bdg. 39.95 (0-8223-1502-5); pap. text ed. 15.95 (0-8223-1513-0) Duke.

Roe, Ernest, jt. auth. see Moses, Ingrid.

Roe, Frances M. Army Letters from an Officer's Wife, 1871-1888. LC 81-7571. (Illus.). xxii, 387p. 1981. pap. 11.95 (0-8032-8905-7) U of Nebr Pr.

— Army Letters from an Officer's Wife, 1871-1888. Kohn, Richard H., ed. LC 78-22395. (American Military Experience Ser.). (Illus.). 1980. reprint ed. lib. bdg. 30.95 (0-405-11871-6) Ayer.

Roe, Francis. Dangerous Practices. 416p. 1993. pap. 5.99 (0-451-17790-8, Sig) NAL-Dutton.

— Doctors & Doctors' Wives. 424p. 1991. pap. 5.99 (0-451-16910-7, Sig) NAL-Dutton.

— Intensive Care. 416p. 1992. pap. 5.99 (0-451-17282-5, Sig) NAL-Dutton.

— The Surgeon. 416p. (Orig.). 1994. pap. 5.99 (0-451-18024-0, Sig) NAL-Dutton.

Roe, Frank G. The North American Buffalo: Critical Study of the Species in Its Wild State. 2nd ed. LC 79-18945. 1010p. reprint ed. pap. 180.00 (0-317-26999-2, 2023663) Bks Demand.

Roe, Frederick W. Social Philosophy of Carlyle & Ruskin. LC 76-116555. 342p. (C). 1970. reprint ed. 60.00 (0-87752-095-X) Gordian.

— The Social Philosophy of Carlyle & Ruskin. (BCL1-PR English Literature Ser.). 335p. 1992. reprint ed. lib. bdg. 89.00 (0-7812-7493-1) Rprt Serv.

— Victorian Prose. LC 47-12149. 773p. reprint ed. pap. 180.00 (0-317-28653-6, 2055090) Bks Demand.

Roe, Frederick W., ed. English Prose: A Series of Related Essays for the Discussion & Practice of the Art of Writing. LC 77-37838. (Essay Index Reprint Ser). 1977. reprint ed. 27.95 (0-8369-2621-8) Ayer.

— Nineteenth Century English Prose: Early Essayists. LC 73-152209. (Essay Index Reprint Ser.). 1977. reprint ed. 31.95 (0-8369-2331-6) Ayer.

Roe, Frederick W., ed. see Ruskin, John.

Roe, George, jt. auth. see Afterman, Allan B.

Roe, George M., ed. Our Police: A History of the Cincinnati Police Force, from the Earliest Period Until the Present Day. LC 77-156024. reprint ed. 37.50 (0-404-09125-3) AMS Pr.

Roe, Gerald, jt. auth. see Anthony, Rebecca J.

Roe, Gerald, jt. auth. see Anthony, Rebecca.

Roe, H. S. Progress in Oceanography, Vol. 13, Nos. 3-4. (Illus.). 276p. 1984. pap. 83.00 (0-08-031735-9, Pergamon Pr) Elsevier.

Roe-Hafer, Ann. Medical & Health Sciences Word Book. 3rd ed. 448p. 1992. 9.95 (0-395-60664-0) HM.

Roe, Ian F. Franz Grillparzer: A Century of Criticism. (Literary Criticism in Perspective Ser.). 180p. 1995. 54.95 (1-57113-008-X) Camden Hse.

— An Introduction to the Major Works of Franz Grillparzer, 1791-1872, Austrian Dramatist & Poet. LC 91-20515. (Studies in German Language & Literature: Vol. 7). 320p. 1991. lib. bdg. 99.95 (0-7734-9725-0) E Mellen.

Roe, Ivan. Shelley: The Last Phase. LC 72-97078. (Illus.). 256p. 1973. reprint ed. lib. bdg. 35.00 (0-8154-0464-6) Cooper Sq.

Roe, JoAnn. Alaska Cat, 3 bks. (Illus.). 64p. (J). (gr. k-5). Alaska Cat. lib. bdg. 11.95 (0-931551-05-6); Alaska Cat. pap. 6.95 (0-931551-04-8) Montevista Pr.

— Castaway Cat, 3 bks. (Illus.). 56p. (Orig.). (J). (gr. k-5). Castaway Cat. pap. 6.95 (0-931551-03-X) Montevista Pr.

— Castaway Cat, 3 bks. (Illus.). 56p. (Orig.). (J). (gr. k-5). 1988. Fisherman Cat, 1988. pap. 6.95 (0-931551-01-3) Montevista Pr.

— The Columbia River: A Historical Travel Guide. LC 91-58486. (Illus.). 240p. (Orig.). 1992. pap. 15.95 (1-55591-102-1) Fulcrum Pub.

— Fisherman Cat, 3 bks. (Illus.). 64p. (J). (gr. k-5). 1988. Fisherman Cat, 1988. lib. bdg. 11.95 (0-931551-02-1) Montevista Pr.

— Fisherman Cat. rev. ed. (Marco the Manx Ser.). (Illus.). 60p. (J). (gr. k-5). 1994. pap. 6.95 (0-931551-09-9) Montevista Pr.

— Fisherman Cat. 2nd rev. ed. (Marco the Manx Ser.). (Illus.). 60p. (J). (gr. k-5). 1994. lib. bdg. 11.95 (0-685-75288-7) Montevista Pr.

— Ghost Camps & Boom Towns. (Illus.). 288p. (Orig.). 1995. pap. write for info. (0-931551-19-6) Montevista Pr.

— The North Cascadians. LC 80-21620. (Illus.). 214p. 1980. 14.95 (0-914842-49-8) Montevista Pr.

— Samurai Cat: Marco the Manx Ser. Bk. 4. (Illus.). 64p. (J). (gr. k-5). 1993. lib. bdg. 11.95 (0-931551-08-0) Montevista Pr.

— Samurai Cat: Marco the Manx Ser., Bk. 4. (Illus.). 64p. (J). (gr. k-5). 1993. pap. 6.95 (0-931551-07-2) Montevista Pr.

— Stevens Pass: The Story of Railroading & Recreation in the North Cascades. (Illus.). 200p. 1995. pap. 14.95 (0-89886-371-6) Mountaineers.

Roe, John. Coarse Cohomology & Index Theory on Complete Riemannian Manifolds. LC 93-17166. (Memoirs of the American Mathematical Society Ser.: No. 497). 90p. 1993. pap. 29.00 (0-8218-2559-3) Am Math.

— Elementary Geometry. LC 92-41660. (Illus.). 320p. 1993. pap. 28.00 (0-19-853456-6) OUP.

Roe, John, ed. see Shakespeare, William.

Roe, Kathleen M., jt. auth. see Minkler, Meredith.

Roe, Keith E. & Frederick, Richard G. Dictionary of Theoretical Concepts in Biology. LC 80-19889. 380p. 1981. 32.50 (0-8108-1353-X) Scarecrow.

Roe, Kenn S. Coyote Cry. 1993. mass mkt. 3.99 (0-449-14864-5, GM) Fawcett.

Roe, M. F. Unacceptable Essays. 112p. 1987. 35.00 (0-946095-19-1, Pub. by Gresham Bks UK) St Mut.

Roe, Mark J. Strong Managers, Weak Owners: The Political Roots of American Corporate Finance. LC 94-12179. 1994. 24.95 (0-691-03683-7) Princeton U Pr.

Roe, Mary A. Total Quality Education - Teaching Techniques for Technical Educators. 32p. (C). 1991. pap. text ed. 4.95 (0-940017-16-4) Info Tec OH.

***Roe, Mary A., et al.** Teaching Factories: A Strategy for World Class Manufacturing Application & Education Networks. 208p. 1993. pap. 16.95 (1-887406-01-8) ICTwo Inst.

Roe, Melvin W., ed. Readings in the History of the American Indian. 1971. pap. 6.95 (0-8422-0134-3) Irvington.

An Asterisk (*) at the beginning of an entry indicates that the title is appearing in BIP for the first time.

***Roe, Michael.** Australia, Britain & Migration: A Study of Desperate Hopes, 1915-1940. (Studies in Australian History). (Illus.). 328p. (C). 1995. 59.95 (*0-521-46507-9*) Cambridge U Pr.

— East European International Road Haulage. 174p. 1992. 68.95 (*1-85628-310-0*, Pub. by Avebury Pub UK) Ashgate Pub Co.

— Evaluation Methodologies for Transport Investment. 307p. 1988. text ed. 75.00 (*0-566-05421-3*, Pub. by Avebury Pub UK) Ashgate Pub Co.

Roe, Michael, ed. The Journal & Letters of Captain Charles Bishop on the North-West Coast of America, in the Pacific & in New South Wales, 1794-1799. (Hakluyt Society Works Ser.: No. 2, Vol. 131). (Illus.). 1969. reprint ed. 42.00 (*0-8115-0411-5*) Periodicals Srv.

Roe, Nancy, ed. The New Quilt: Quilt National, 1989. LC 88-63933. (Illus.). 96p. 1989. pap. 14.95 (*0-88740-157-0*) Schiffer.

Roe, Nicholas. The Politics of Nature: Wordsworth & Some Contemporaries. LC 91-24827. 200p. 1992. text ed. 49.95 (*0-312-06823-9*) St Martin.

***Roe, Nicholas, ed.** Keats & History. (Illus.). 360p. (C). 1995. 59.95 (*0-521-44245-1*) Cambridge U Pr.

Roe, Nicholas, intro. William Wordsworth: Selected Poetry. 336p. 1993. pap. 8.00 (*0-14-058661-X*, Penguin Bks) Viking Penguin.

Roe, Nicholas, ed. see Keats, John.

Roe, Patrick R., tr. see Rossi, Mario.

***Roe, Paul F.** Choral Music Education. 2nd ed. (Illus.). 355p. (C). 1994. pap. text ed. 27.95x (*0-88133-807-9*) Waveland Pr.

Roe, Peter. A Further Exploration of the Rowe Chavin Seriation & Its Implications for North Central Coast Chronology. LC 74-16852. (Studies in Pre-Columbian Art & Archaeology: No. 13). (Illus.). 80p. 1974. pap. 7.00 (*0-88402-056-8*) Dumbarton Oaks.

Roe, Peter, jt. auth. see Braun, Barbara.

Roe, Peter G. The Cosmic Zygote: Cosmology in the Amazon Basin. (Illus.). 451p. 1982. 50.00 (*0-8135-0896-7*) Rutgers U Pr.

Roe, R. A., jt. ed. see Koopman-Iwema, A. M.

Roe, R. J. Computer Simulation of Polymers. 416p. 1990. text ed. 94.00 (*0-13-161480-0*) P-H.

Roe, R. J., et al, eds. Structure Relaxation & Physical Aging of Glassy Polymers: Materials Research Society Symposium Proceedings, Vol. 215. 228p. 1991. text ed. 58.00 (*1-55899-107-7*) Materials Res.

Roe, Richard. Baby Animals. LC 85-2223. (Knee-High Bks.). (Illus.). 24p. (J). (ps-1). 1985. 3.95 (*0-394-86956-7*) Random Bks Yng Read.

— Bringer of Songs. 54p. (Orig.). 1994. pap. 6.00 (*1-878660-13-6*) Fireweed WI.

— Burnt Toast. LC 79-87687. (Orig.). pap. 7.95 (*0-9602100-2-4*) St Wrks Cooperative.

Roe, Richard L., jt. auth. see Arbetman, Lee P.

Roe, Shirley A. Matter, Life & Generation: Eighteenth Century Embryology & the Haller-Wolff Debate. LC 80-19611. (Illus.). 216p. 1981. 54.95 (*0-521-23540-5*) Cambridge U Pr.

Roe, Shirley A. & Cohen, I. Bernard, eds. The Natural Philosophy of Albrecht Von Haller. LC 80-2109. (Development of Science Ser.). (Illus.). 1981. lib. bdg. 44.95 (*0-405-13874-1*) Ayer.

Roe, Sue. Women Reading Women's Writing. LC 87-9494. 304p. 1988. text ed. 39.95 (*0-312-00952-6*) St Martin.

— Writing & Gender: Virginia Woolf's Writing Practice. LC 90-19424. 214p. 1990. text ed. 45.00 (*0-312-05766-0*) St Martin.

Roe, William H., jt. auth. see Drake, Thelbert L.

Roeber, A. G. Faithful Magistrates & Republican Lawyers: Creators of Virginia Legal Culture, 1680-1810. LC 80-19524. (Studies in Legal History). xix, 292p. 1981. 37.50 (*0-8078-1461-X*) U of NC Pr.

— Palatines, Liberty, & Property: German Lutherans in Colonial British America. LC 92-25647. (Early America: History, Context, Culture Ser.). 448p. 1993. text ed. 49.95 (*0-8018-4459-2*) Johns Hopkins.

Roeberg, ed. see DeMatteis.

Roebke, John, jt. auth. see Melchert, Paul A.

Roebling, Karl. The Age of Individuality: America's Kinship with the Brooklyn Bridge. 190p. 1983. 10.95 (*0-942910-05-2*) Dynapress.

— Christian Science-Kingdom or Cult? 190p. 1984. 12.95 (*0-942910-09-5*) Dynapress.

— Great Myths of World War II. LC 85-60763. (Illus.). 288p. 1985. 14.95 (*0-942910-11-7*) Dynapress.

— Me, Me the People. (Illus.). 128p. 1991. pap. 9.95 (*0-942910-15-X*) Dynapress.

— Not His Death-His Overcoming of Death. 30p. 1983. pap. 5.00 (*0-942910-10-9*) Dynapress.

— Pentecostal Origins & Trends: Early & Modern. 3rd rev. ed. LC 85-63631. 112p. 1985. 10.00 (*0-942910-12-5*) Dynapress.

— Prophecy from Here to Two Thousand. 144p. 1983. pap. 4.95 (*0-942910-06-0*) Dynapress.

— Sea Nation. (Illus.). 245p. 1987. 14.95 (*0-942910-14-1*) Dynapress.

Roebuck. Circle of Stars. 1992. pap. 15.95 (*1-85230-303-4*) Element MA.

Roebuck, Carl. Economy & Society In the Early Greek World: Collected Essays. Thomas, Carol G., ed. 172p. 1984. 25.00 (*0-89005-261-1*) Ares.

— Ionian Trade & Colonization. 154p. 1985. reprint ed. 25.00 (*0-89005-528-9*, ROEO2) Ares.

— The World of Ancient Times. (Illus.). 758p. (C). 1974. pap. write for info. (*0-02-402700-6*, Scribners) S&S Trade.

— World of Ancient Times. 1984. 18.95 (*0-684-13726-7*, Scribners) S&S Trade.

Roebuck, Deborah M. Improving Business Communication Skills: Writing, Speaking, & Interacting. 256p. (C). 1992. pap. text ed. 39.95 (*0-8403-8044-5*) Kendall-Hunt.

Roebuck, Derek. Cheques. 120p. (C). 1991. pap. text ed. 22.00 (*962-209-288-8*, Pub. by Hong Kong U Pr HK) St Mut.

Roebuck, Derek, ed. Law Relating to Banking in Hong Kong. 340p. (Orig.). 1993. pap. 52.50x (*960-209-319-6*, Pub. by Hong Kong Univ Pr HK) Coronet Bks.

Roebuck, Derek, jt. auth. see Chui, Carole.

Roebuck, E. J. & Blam. Clinical Breast Radiology. 1990. text ed. 95.00 (*0-433-00066-X*) Buttrwrth-Heinemann.

Roebuck, John A., Jr. Anthropometric Methods: Designing to Fit the Human Body. LC 93-16975. 200p. 1995. pap. 20.00 (*0-945289-01-4*) Human Factors.

Roebuck, John A. & Kroemer, K. H. Engineering Anthropometry Methods. LC 74-34272. (Wiley Series in Human Factors). 477p. reprint ed. pap. 136.00 (*0-7837-0006-7*, 2015849) Bks Demand.

Roebuck, Johnnie J. Celebrate the Temporary. LC 91-67362. (Illus.). xii, 124p. (Orig.). 1992. pap. 9.95 (*0-934955-23-9*) Watercress Pr.

Roebuck, Julian B. & Hickson, Mark L., III. The Southern Redneck: A Phenomenological Class Study. LC 82-9831. 222p. 1982. text ed. 38.50 (*0-275-90886-0*, C0886, Praeger Pubs) Greenwood.

Roebuck, Julian B. & Murty, Komanduri S. Historically Black Colleges & Universities: Their Place in American Higher Education. LC 93-2858. 223p. 1993. text ed. 49.95 (*0-275-94267-8*, C4267, Praeger Pubs) Greenwood.

Roebuck, Kenneth C. Gun-Dog Training Pointing Dogs. LC 83-4948. 192p. 1983. 16.95 (*0-8117-0714-8*) Stackpole.

— Gun-Dog Training Spaniels & Retrievers. LC 82-5667. (Illus.). 192p. 1982. 16.95 (*0-8117-0778-4*) Stackpole.

Roebuck, M. T. From Me to You: Wartime Memories. 72p. 1994. pap. 12.00 (*0-8059-3591-6*) Dorrance.

Roebuck, Nigel & Townsend, John. Grand Prix World Formula One Championship, 1987-88. (Illus.). 160p. 1988. 24.95 (*0-908081-27-8*) Motorbooks Intl.

Roebuck, R. Cornelius Nepos: Three Lives, Alcibiades-Dion-Atticus. (Illus.). 138p. (ENG & LAT.). 1987. reprint ed. pap. 11.00 (*0-86516-207-7*) Bolchazy-Carducci.

Roebuck, Scott, ed. see Marshall, John A.

Roebuck, Susan H. Alaska Wildlife: A Coloring Book. Holen, Anne M., ed. Heshiki, Kazumi, tr. (Illus.). 48p. (Orig.). (JPN.). (J). (gr. 3-8). 1990. pap. 5.95 (*0-922127-01-8*) Paisley Pub.

***Roecker, W. A.** Fresh One! Standup Fishing: Saltwater Methods, Tackle & Techniques. (Standup Ser.). (Illus.). 264p. (Orig.). 1990. pap. 14.95 (*0-9645319-0-9*) Oceanic Prod.

Roecklein, John C. & Leung, PingSun, eds. A Profile of Economic Plants. 608p. 1987. 89.95 (*0-88738-167-7*) Transaction Pubs.

Roed, Tom, ed. Bradley's Top Movie Tunes: Twenty-Three of the Best Movie Hits! 96p. (Orig.). (YA). 1994. pap. text ed. 11.95 (*0-89898-770-9*) CPP Belwin.

— Dave's Diary: A Collection of Dave Brubeck Piano Solos. 56p. (Orig.). (YA). 1995. pap. text ed. 12.95 (*0-89724-613-6*) Warner Brothers.

— Floyd Cramer: Just Me & My Piano. 60p. 1990. pap. text ed. 13.95 (*0-89898-631-1*) CPP Belwin.

Roed, Tom, ed. see Garson, Mike.

Roed, Tom, ed. see Petty, Tom.

Roeda, Daniel. Amigos y Enemigos de Jesucristo-bL-Alumno. (SPA.). 1993. 0.20 (*1-55955-154-2*) CITE MI.

— Amigos y Enemigos de Jesucristo-C-Alumno. (SPA.). 1993. 0.20 (*1-55955-150-X*) CITE MI.

— Amigos y Enemigos de Jesucristo-Db-Alumno. (SPA.). 1993. 0.20 (*1-55955-152-6*) CITE MI.

— Nacimiento de Jesucristo: Promesas y Profecias bL-Alumno. (SPA.). 1991. 0.50 (*1-55955-134-8*) CITE MI.

— Nacimiento de Jesucristo: Promesas y Profecias C-Alumno. (SPA.). 1991. 0.50 (*1-55955-130-5*) CITE MI.

— Nacimiento de Jesucristo: Promesas y Profecias Db-Alumno. (SPA.). 1991. 0.50 (*1-55955-132-1*) CITE MI.

Roeda, Jack. Decisions. 2nd ed. (Illus.). 80p. (YA). (gr. 9-12). 1992. teacher ed 8.50 (*1-56212-000-X*, 1240-4940); pap. text ed. 6.50 (*0-930265-96-3*, 1240-4920); 4.95 (*0-685-60757-7*, 1240-4910) CRC Pubns.

Roedder, E. Fluid Inclusions. (Reviews in Mineralogy Ser.: Vol. 12). 644p. 1984. per. 22.00 (*0-939950-16-2*) Mineralogical Soc.

***Roede, Ann.** The Ghost of Brannock Hall. Reccenda, Ann B., ed. 268p. (Orig.). (J). (gr. 5-9). 1994. pap. 4.95 (*0-9638237-0-1*) Playgrnd Bks.

Roedel, Phil M. & Ripley, William E. Common Marine Fishes & California Sharks & Rays. LC 87-51660. (Illus.). 248p. reprint ed. write for info. (*0-9610602-6-3*) Teaparty Bks.

Roedell, Wendy C., et al. Gifted Young Children. Tannenbaum, Abraham J., ed. LC 80-10707. (Perspectives on Gifted & Talented Education Ser.). (Orig.). 1980. pap. text ed. 8.95 (*0-8077-2587-0*) Tchrs Coll.

***Roeder.** Censored War: American Visual Experience During World War II. 1995. pap. text ed. 16.00 (*0-300-06291-5*) Yale U Pr.

Roeder, Beatrice A. Chicano Folk Medicine from Los Angeles, California. (UC Publications in Folklore & Mythology Studies: Vol. 34). 1988. pap. 45.00 (*0-520-09723-8*) U CA Pr.

Roeder, Charles W., ed. Composite & Mixed Construction: Proceedings of a U. S.-Japan Joint Seminar. 352p. 1985. 31.00 (*0-87262-476-5*) Am Soc Civil Eng.

Roeder, Dietrich H. Rocky Mountains: Der Geologische Aufbau des Kanadischen Felsengebirges. (Illus.). 1967. 99.50 (*3-443-11005-3*) Lubrecht & Cramer.

***Roeder, Dorothy.** Crystal Co-Creators. 288p. 1994. pap. 14.95 (*0-929385-40-3*) Light Tech Comns Servs.

— The Next Dimension is Love. 148p. (Orig.). 1993. pap. 11.95 (*0-929385-50-0*) Light Tech Comns Servs.

— Reach for Us. 168p. (Orig.). 1995. pap. 13.00 (*0-929385-69-1*) Light Tech Comns Servs.

Roeder, Edward, ed. PACs Americana: The Directory of Political Action Committees & Their Interests. 2nd ed. 1986. 250.00 (*0-942236-01-7*) Sunshine Serv.

Roeder, George H., Jr. The Censored War: American Visual Experience During World War II. LC 92-31859. (C). 1993. 32.50x (*0-300-05723-7*) Yale U Pr.

Roeder, Kenneth D. Nerve Cells & Insect Behavior. rev. ed. LC 67-27092. (Books in Biology: No. 4). 91p. 1967. 15.95 (*0-674-60800-3*) HUP.

Roeder, Michael T. A History of the Concerto. LC 92-41967. (Illus.). 480p. 1994. 39.95 (*0-931340-61-6*, Amadeus Pr) Timber.

Roeder, Philip G. Red Sunset: The Failure of Soviet Politics. LC 93-4047. (Illus.). 344p. (C). 1993. text ed. 49.50 (*0-691-03306-4*); pap. text ed. 16.95 (*0-691-01942-8*) Princeton U Pr.

Roeder, Phillip W. Public Opinion & Policy Leadership in the American States. LC 93-12870. (Institute for Social Science Research Monograph Ser.: No. 5). 256p. (Orig.). 1994. pap. 26.95 (*0-8173-0677-3*) U of Ala Pr.

Roeder, Ralph. Man of the Renaissance: Four Law Givers - Savonarola, Machiavelli, Castiglione, Aretino. LC 78-122059. (Illus.). 1977. reprint ed. 49.50 (*0-678-03171-1*) Kelley.

Roeder, Ralph, tr. see Goncourt, Edmond L.

Roeder, Rick. A Quizzical Look at the Rock Era. McLean, Diane, ed. (Illus.). 136p. (Orig.). pap. 9.95 (*0-9619648-0-4*) Big Bop Bks.

Roederer, J. G. Introduction to the Physics & Psychophysics of Music. 2nd ed. (Heidelberg Science Library). (Illus.). 202p. 1975. reprint ed. pap. 21.00 (*3-540-90116-7*) Spr-Verlag.

— Physics & Psychophysics of Music. 1994. pap. 29.50 (*0-387-94366-8*) Spr-Verlag.

— Progress in Solar-Terrestrial Physics. 1983. lib. bdg. 196.00 (*90-277-1559-9*) Kluwer Ac.

Roederer, Juan G. Introduction to the Physics & Psychophysics of Music. LC 94-16447. 1994. write for info. (*0-387-94298-X*) Spr-Verlag.

Roederer, Pierre L. The Spirit of the Revolution of 1789: And Other Writings on the Revolutionary Epoch. Forsyth, Murray, ed. 152p. 1989. text ed. 47.95 (*0-85967-813-X*, Pub. by Scolar Pr UK) Ashgate Pub Co.

Roederer, Scott, jt. auth. see Hafele, Rick.

Roediger, Dave, ed. & intro. Fellow Worker: The Life of Fred Thompson. 94p. (Orig.). 1993. pap. 10.00 (*0-88286-220-0*) C H Kerr.

Roediger, Dave & Rosemont, Franklin, eds. Haymarket Scrapbook: A Centennial Anthology. LC 86-80843. (Illus.). 256p. 1986. 35.00 (*0-88286-147-6*); pap. 18.95 (*0-88286-122-0*) C H Kerr.

Roediger, Dave, ed. see Abrams, Irving.

Roediger, David, intro. Dreams & Dynamite: Selected Poems. (Poets of Revolt Ser.: No. 1). 56p. 1985. pap. 10.00 (*0-88286-111-5*) C H Kerr.

Roediger, David & Fitz, Don, eds. Within the Shell of the Old: Essays in Workers' Self Organization. A Tribute to George Rawick. 112p. (Orig.). (C). 1990. pap. 15.00 (*0-88286-170-0*) C H Kerr.

Roediger, David R. Towards the Abolition of Whiteness: Essays on Race, Politics, & Working Class History. LC 93-49387. (Haymarket Ser.). 1994. 39.95 (*0-86091-438-0*, Pub. by Verso UK); pap. 17.95 (*0-86091-658-8*, Pub. by Verso UK) Routledge Chapman & Hall.

— The Wages of Whiteness: Race & the Making of the American Working Class. (Haymarket Ser.). 192p. 1991. 54.95 (*0-86091-334-1*, A6413, Pub. by Verso UK); pap. 16.95 (*0-86091-550-6*, A6417, Pub. by Verso UK) Routledge Chapman & Hall.

Roediger, David R. & Foner, Philip S. Our Own Time: A History of American Labor & the Working Day. LC 87-29543. (Contributions in Labor Studies: No. 23). 392p. 1989. text ed. 59.95 (*0-313-26062-1*, ROO/, Greenwood Pr) Greenwood.

— Our Own Time: A History of American Labor & the Working Day. 425p. 1989. pap. 19.95 (*0-86091-963-3*, A3752, Pub. by Verso UK) Routledge Chapman & Hall.

Roediger, Fiona J. Smocking Ideas. (Illus.). 80p. (Orig.). 1993. pap. 12.95 (*0-86417-508-6*, Pub. by Kangaroo Pr AT) Seven Hills Bk.

Roediger, H. L., III & Craik, F. I., eds. Varieties of Memory & Consciousness: Essays in Honour of Endel Tulving. 464p. 1989. 89.95 (*0-89859-935-0*); pap. 34.50 (*0-8058-0546-X*) L Erlbaum Assocs.

Roediger, Henry L., III. Discover & Psychology. 3rd ed. (C). 1991. text ed. 44.50 (*0-673-52188-5*) HarpCollege.

Roediger, Henry L., III, et al. Psychology: Study Guide. 3rd ed. (C). 1991. 16.50 (*0-673-39698-3*) HarpCollege.

Roediger, Virginia M. Ceremonial Costumes of the Pueblo Indians: Their Evolution, Fabrication, & Significance in the Prayer Drama. (Illus.). 268p. 1991. 50.00 (*0-520-07630-3*); pap. 25.00 (*0-520-07631-1*) U CA Pr.

Roegdke, Soren & Busse, Kay. Crockett: The True Story of a Cowboy. 300p. (Orig.). 1993. pap. 20.00 (*0-9629242-1-0*) WKB Enterp.

— Quien Es? The True Story of Billy the Kid. 403p. (Orig.). 1991. pap. write for info. (*0-9629242-0-2*) WKB Enterp.

— Sadie: The True Story of a Western Lady. (True Story Ser.). 268p. (Orig.). 1994. pap. 20.00 (*0-9629242-2-9*) WKB Enterp.

— Silk: An Expose of Commercial Fishing. 364p. (Orig.). (C). 1995. pap. 20.00 (*0-9629242-3-7*) WKB Enterp.

Roeges, Noel P. G. A Guide to the Complete Interpretation of Infrared Spectra of Organic Structures. LC 94-2445. 1994. text ed. 69.95 (*0-471-93998-6*) Wiley.

Roegiers, Jean-Claude, ed. Rock Mechanics As a Multidisciplinary Science: Proceedings of the 32nd U. S. Symposium on Rock Mechanics, Norman, Oklahoma, 10-12 July 1991. (Illus.). 1236p. (C). 1991. text ed. 135.00 (*90-6191-194-X*, Pub. by A A Balkema NE) Ashgate Pub Co.

Roegner, Grace. Princeton Review Cracking the SAT II: History 1995 Edition. 1994. pap. 16.00 (*0-679-75352-4*, Villard Bks) Random.

Roeher, H. D., jt. ed. see Clark, O.

Roehl, Bernie. Playing God: Building Virtual Worlds with Rend 386. LC 94-5041. 370p. 1994. disk, pap. 26.95 (*1-878739-62-X*) Waite Group Pr.

Roehl, Carl, jt. auth. see Spielman, Patrick.

Roehl, Evelyn. Whole Food Facts. (Illus.). 192p. 1988. pap. 12.95 (*0-89281-231-1*, Heal Arts VT) Inner Tradit.

Roehl, H., ed. Inscriptiones Graecae Antiquissimae: Praeter Atticas in Attica Repertas. (Illus.). 193p. 1977. reprint ed. 30.00 (*0-89005-221-2*) Ares.

Roehl, Harvey, ed. see Leverett, Willard M.

Roehl, Harvey N. A Carousel of Limericks. LC 85-22538. (Illus.). 60p. (Orig.). (J). (gr. 4-8). 1986. pap. 7.95 (*0-911572-47-3*) Vestal.

— Cornell & Ithaca in Postcards. LC 86-18937. (Illus.). 112p. (Orig.). 1986. pap. 11.95 (*0-911572-59-7*) Vestal.

— Player Piano Scrapbook. (Orig.). 1958. pap. 3.00 (*0-87282-090-4*, 18) Am Life Foun.

Roehl, Harvey N., jt. auth. see Palmer, Richard F.

Roehl, P. O. & Choquette, P. W. Carbonate Petroleum Reservoir. (Casebooks in Earth Sciences Ser.). (Illus.). 480p. 1985. 119.00 (*0-387-96012-0*) Spr-Verlag.

Roehl, Thomas W., jt. ed. see Hanson, Kermit.

Roehler, Laura R., jt. auth. see Duffy, Gerald G.

***Roehlkepartain, Eugene C.** Getting the Word Out: An Idea Book for Users of Profiles of Student Life. 40p. 1993. pap. 10.00 (*1-57482-315-9*) Search Inst.

— The Teaching Church: Moving Christian Education to Center Stage. LC 92-41987. 208p. (Orig.). 1993. pap. 12.95 (*0-687-41083-5*) Abingdon.

— Youth Development in Congregations: An Exploration of the Potential & Barriers. 1995. pap. 14.95 (*1-57482-121-0*) Search Inst.

Roehlkepartain, Eugene C. & Benson, Peter L. Beyond Leaf Raking: Service: Learning & Youth Ministry. LC 93-28845. (Essentials for Christian Youth Ser.). 122p. (Orig.). 1993. pap. 11.95 (*0-687-21328-2*) Abingdon.

Roehlkepartain, Eugene C., jt. auth. see Benson, Peter L.

Roehlkepartain, Eugene C., jt. auth. see Blyth, Dale A.

Roehlkepartain, Eugene C., jt. auth. see Draayer, Donald.

Roehlkepartain, Eugene C., jt. auth. see Feldmeyer, Dean.

Roehlkepartain, Eugene C., jt. auth. see Geraghty, Laura L.

Roehlkepartain, Eugene C., jt. auth. see Melton, Hope.

Roehlkepartain, Eugene C., jt. auth. see Seefeldt, Glenn A.

Roehlkepartain, Eugene C., jt. auth. see Williams, Dorothy L.

***Roehlkepartain, Jolene.** Building Assets Together: One-Hundred-One Group Activities for Helping Youth Succeed. 1995. pap. 18.95 (*1-57482-333-7*) Search Inst.

— Wiggle Tamers. Parolini, Stephen, ed. 96p. 1995. pap. 11.99 (*1-55945-615-9*) Group Pub.

Roehlkepartain, Jolene L. Fidget Busters: One Hundred One Quick Attention-Getters for Children's Ministry. (Illus.). 96p. 1992. pap. 11.99 (*1-55945-058-4*) Group Pub.

— 101 Creative Worship Ideas for Children's Church. Yount, Christine & Wolf, Beth, eds. LC 95-13912. (Illus.). 120p. 1995. pap. 12.99 (*1-55945-601-9*) Group Pub.

Roehlkepartain, Jolene L., ed. Children's Ministry That Works! (Illus.). 228p. (Orig.). 1991. pap. 15.99 (*0-931529-69-7*, Group Bks) Group Pub.

Roehm, Klaus-Jurgen. Polyphonie und Improvisation: Zur Offenen Form in Gunter Grass' Die Rattin. LC 91-31480. (Studies in Modern German Literature: Vol. 47). 200p. (GER.). (C). 1993. text ed. 36.95 (*0-8204-1693-2*) P Lang Pubs.

Roehm, Marjorie C. The Letters of George Catlin & His Family: A Chronicle of the American West. LC 66-13090. (Illus.). 485p. reprint ed. pap. 138.30 (*0-685-23581-5*, 2029061) Bks Demand.

Roehm, Michelle, ed. see Acker, Loren E., et al.

Roehm, Michelle, ed. see Burke-Weiner, Kimberly.

Roehm, Michelle, ed. see Lewis, Paul O.

Roehm, Michelle, ed. see White Deer of Autumn Staff.

Roehmann, Franz L., ed. Music & Child Development. (Illus.). 442p. (Orig.). 1990. pap. 25.00 (*0-918812-58-5*, ST011) MMB Music.

***Roehner, Bertrand M.** Theory of Markets: Trade & Space-Time Patterns of Price Fluctuations: A Study in Analytical Economics. LC 95-5873. (Advances in Spatial & Network Economics Ser.). 1995. 125.00 (*3-540-58815-9*) Spr-Verlag.

Roehr, Mary A. Altering Men's Ready-to-Wear. (Illus.). 150p. (Orig.). 1987. pap. 14.95 (*0-685-71938-3*) M Roehr Cust Tailor.

— Altering Men's Ready-to-Wear. (Illus.). 150p. (Orig.). (C). 1987. pap. text ed. 17.95 (*0-9619229-1-5*) M Roehr Cust Tailor.

— Altering Women's Ready-to-Wear. (Illus.). 190p. (Orig.). (C). 1987. pap. 19.95 (*0-9619229-0-7*) M Roehr Cust Tailor.

— Sew Hilarious. (Illus.). 64p. (Orig.). 1995. pap. 9.95 (*0-9619229-4-X*) M Roehr Cust Tailor.

— Sewing As a Home Business. (Illus.). 130p. (Orig.). 1992. pap. 11.95 (*0-685-71937-5*) M Roehr Cust Tailor.

— Sewing As a Home Business. (Illus.). 135p. (Orig.). (C). 1987. reprint ed. pap. 12.95 (*0-9619229-2-3*) M Roehr Cust Tailor.

— Speed Tailoring. (Illus.). 45p. (C). 1992. reprint ed. pap. 14.95 (*0-9619229-3-1*) M Roehr Cust Tailor.

R

An Asterisk (*) at the beginning of an entry indicates that the title is appearing in BIP for the first time.

Roehr, Robert J. Electronic Advancement: Fund Raising, Set 2. 202p. 1990. vhs 123.00 (*0-89964-278-0*) Coun Adv & Supp Ed.

— Electronic Advancement: Student Recruitment, Set 3. 334p. 1991. vhs 183.00 (*0-89964-280-2*) Coun Adv & Supp Ed.

***Roehr, Sabine.** A Primer on German Enlightenment: With a Translation of Karl Leonhard Reinhold's "The Fundamental Concepts & Principles of Ethics" 304p. 1995. 39.95 (*0-8262-0997-1*) U of Mo Pr.

Roehrborn, Claus G., tr. see Schild, Hans H., et al, eds.

Roehrick, Kaye L., ed. Brevet's North Dakota Historical Markers & Sites. LC 74-79978. (Historical Markers-Sites Ser.). (Illus.). 176p. 1975. 12.95 (*0-88498-024-3*) Brevet Pr.

Roehrig, Catherine. Fun with Hieroglyphs: From the Metropolitan Museum of Art. (J). 1990. 19.95 (*0-670-83576-5*) Viking Child Bks.

— Mummies & Magic: Introduction to Egyptian Funerary Beliefs. Purvis, Cynthia, ed. (Illus.). 32p. (Orig.). 1988. pap. 7.50 (*0-87846-304-6*) Mus Fine Arts Boston.

Roehrig, Michael F. Foreign Joint Ventures in Contemporary China. LC 94-11018. 1994. text ed. 49.95 (*0-312-12131-8*) St Martin.

Roehrkasse, Lucille, jt. auth. see Kramin, Norma.

Roehrman, Hendrik. The Way of Life. LC 70-144677. Orig. Title: Marlow & Shakespeare. reprint ed. 21.50 (*0-404-05386-6*) AMS Pr.

Roehrs & Franzmann. Concordia Self-Study Commentary. LC 15-2721. 1979. 28.99 (*0-570-03277-6*) Concordia.

Roehrs, Mark D., jt. auth. see Renzi, William A.

Roehrs, Walter R. Survey of Covenant History. 208p. 1989. 14.95 (*0-570-04244-5*, 15-2197) Concordia.

Roekard, Karen. The Santa Cruz Haggadah: A Passover Haggadah, Coloring Book & Journal for the Evolving Consciousness. 1992. Participants Version. student ed 5.95 (*0-9628913-8-X*) Hineni Concisus.

— The Santa Cruz Haggadah: A Passover Haggadah, Coloring Book & Journal for the Evolving Consciousness, Leaders Version. 1992. 21.95 (*0-9628913-9-8*) Hineni Concisus.

— The Santa Cruz Haggadah Kids Passover Fun Book. (Illus.). 56p. (Orig.). (J). (ps-10). 1994. pap. 4.95 (*0-9628913-0-4*) Hineni Concisus.

— The Santa Cruz Haggadah Leader's Edition: A Passover Haggadah, Coloring Book & Journal for the Evolving Consciousness. 1992. Leaders Version. 13.95 (*0-9628913-4-7*) Hineni Concisus.

Roelandt, J. R., et al, eds. Cardiac Ultrasound. (Illus.). 800p. 1993. text ed. 275.00 (*0-443-04692-1*) Churchill.

Roelandt, Jos. Practical Echocardiology. LC 77-1619. (Ultrasound in Biomedicine Ser.: No. 1). (Illus.). 330p. reprint ed. pap. 94.10 (*0-8357-4554-6*, 2037453) Bks Demand.

Roelandt, Jos R. The Practice of M-Mode & Two-Dimensional Echocardiagraphy. 1983. lib. bdg. 126.50 (*90-247-2745-6*) Kluwer Ac.

Roelandt, Jos R., ed. Color Doppler Flow Imaging. (Developments in Cardiovascular Medicine Ser.). 1986. lib. bdg. 147.00 (*0-89838-806-6*) Kluwer Ac.

— Digital Techniques in Echocardiography. (Developments in Cardiovascular Medicine Ser.). 1987. lib. bdg. 121.50 (*0-89838-861-9*) Kluwer Ac.

Roelandt, Jos R. & Hugenholtz, P. G. Long-Term Ambulatory Electrocardiography. 1982. lib. bdg. 84.00 (*90-247-2664-6*) Kluwer Ac.

Roelandt, Jos R., jt. ed. see Bom, N.

Roelandt, Jos R., jt. auth. see Meltzer, R. S.

Roelandt, Jos R., et al, eds. Intravascular Ultrasound. LC 93-1382. (Developments in Cardiovascular Medicine Ser.). 184p. (C). 1993. lib. bdg. 59.50 (*0-7923-2301-7*) Kluwer Ac.

Roelants, G. E., jt. ed. see Loor, F.

***Roelcke, Thorsten.** Dramatische Kommunikation: Modell und Reflexion bei Duerrenmatt, Handke, Weiss. (Quellen & Forschungen Zur Sprach- & Kulturgeschichte der Germanischen Voelker Ser.: No. 231). xii, 313p. (GER.). (C). 1994. lib. bdg. 113.85 (*3-11-014646-0*, 98-94) De Gruyter.

Roelfe, Alan P. & Bushnell, William R., eds. The Cereal Rusts: Vol. 2, Diseases, Distribution, Epidemiology, & Control. 1985. text ed. 157.00 (*0-12-148402-5*) Acad Pr.

Roelfs, Alan P., jt. auth. see Bushnell, William R.

Roeliff Jansen Historical Society Staff. The Mill on the Roeliff Jansen Kill: Two Hundred Fifty Years of American Industrial History. Faber, Harold, ed. (Illus.). 110p. (Orig.). 1993. pap. 15.00 (*0-9628523-9-2*) Blk Dome Pr.

Roelker, Nancy L. Queen of Navarre, Jeanne D'Albret, 1528-1572. LC 68-54024. (Illus.). 515p. 1968. 42.50 (*0-674-74150-1*) Belknap Pr.

Roell, Craig H. The Piano in America, 1890-1940. LC 88-14326. (Illus.). xx, 396p. 1991. reprint ed. 45.00x (*0-8078-1802-X*); reprint ed. pap. 16.95 (*0-8078-4322-9*) U of NC Pr.

— Remember Goliad! A History of La Bahia. LC 94-25973. (Fred Rider Cotten Popular History Ser.: No. 9). (Illus.). 108p. (Orig.). 1994. pap. 5.95 (*0-87611-141-X*) Tex St Hist Assn.

Roell, Craig H., ed. Lyndon B. Johnson: A Bibliography, Vol. 2. 378p. 1988. 30.00 (*0-292-74648-2*) U of Tex Pr.

Roell, Craig H., jt. auth. see Gould, Lewis L.

Roelli, H. J. Das Behinderte Kind. Anderhalden, A., ed. (Paediatrische Fortbildungskurse fuer die Praxis Ser.: Vol. 56). (Illus.). vi, 110p. 1982. pap. 42.50 (*3-8055-3493-0*) S Karger.

***Roelofs, Faith.** Adventures Around Kilauea: Kilauea Volcano. (Exploring the Islands: Island of Hawai'i Ser.). 1994. pap. write for info. (*1-882163-30-3*) Moanalua Grdns Fnd.

— Aiea Loop Trail & Keaiwa Heiau Field Site Guide for Teachers. (Exploring the Islands Ser.). 1992. teacher ed write for info. (*1-882163-38-9*) Moanalua Grdns Fnd.

— Central & East Molokai Field Site Guide for Teachers. (Exploring the Islands Ser.). 1994. teacher ed write for info. (*1-882163-27-3*) Moanalua Grdns Fnd.

— Exploring Molokai: Field Site Guides for Teachers, 2 vols., Set. (Exploring the Islands Ser.). 1994. teacher ed write for info. (*1-882163-24-9*) Moanalua Grdns Fnd.

— Exploring the Islands: Island of Hawai'i, 4 vols., Set. 1994. pap. write for info. (*1-882163-44-3*) Moanalua Grdns Fnd.

— Exploring the Islands: Island of Kaua'i, 3 vols., Set. 1994. pap. write for info. (*1-882163-42-7*) Moanalua Grdns Fnd.

— Exploring the Islands: Island of O'ahu, 4 vols., Set. 1994. pap. write for info. (*1-882163-41-9*) Moanalua Grdns Fnd.

— Exploring the Islands: Islands of Maui & Moloka'i, 4 vols., Set. 1994. pap. write for info. (*1-882163-43-5*) Moanalua Grdns Fnd.

— Hamakua to Waipio Field Site Guide for Teachers. (Exploring the Islands Ser.). 1994. teacher ed write for info. (*1-882163-35-4*) Moanalua Grdns Fnd.

— Hauula Loop Trail Field Site Guide for Teachers. (Exploring the Islands Ser.). 1992. teacher ed write for info. (*1-882163-39-7*) Moanalua Grdns Fnd.

— High & Wild: Waikamoi & Halemau'u Trail. (Exploring the Islands: Islands of Maui & Moloka'i Ser.). 24p. 1993. pap. write for info. (*1-882163-15-X*) Moanalua Grdns Fnd.

— Investigating the South Caost: Punalu'u to Manuka. (Exploring the Islands: Island of Hawai'i Ser.). 1994. pap. write for info. (*1-882163-32-X*) Moanalua Grdns Fnd.

— Kilauea Volcano Field Site Guide for Teachers. (Exploring the Islands Ser.). 1994. teacher ed write for info. (*1-882163-34-6*) Moanalua Grdns Fnd.

— Koolaupoko Field Site Guide for Teachers. (Exploring the Islands Ser.). 1992. teacher ed write for info. (*1-882163-37-0*) Moanalua Grdns Fnd.

— Makewehi Dunes & Sinkhole Field Site Guide for Teachers. (Exploring the Islands Ser.). 1993. teacher ed write for info. (*1-882163-22-2*) Moanalua Grdns Fnd.

— On the Wild Side: West Moloka'i. (Exploring the Islands: Islands of Maui & Moloka'i Ser.). 28p. 1994. pap. write for info. (*1-882163-26-5*) Moanalua Grdns Fnd.

— Place of Power: Central & East Moloka'i. (Exploring the Islands: Islands of Maui & Moloka'i Ser.). 36p. 1994. pap. write for info. (*1-882163-25-7*) Moanalua Grdns Fnd.

— Punaluu to Manuka Field Site Guide for Teachers. (Exploring the Islands Ser.). 1994. teacher ed write for info. (*1-882163-36-2*) Moanalua Grdns Fnd.

— Saddle Road Field Site Guide for Teachers. (Exploring the Islands Ser.). 1994. teacher ed write for info. (*1-882163-33-8*) Moanalua Grdns Fnd.

— Saddle Sojourn: Saddle Road, Big Island. (Exploring the Islands: Island of Hawai'i Ser.). 1994. pap. write for info. (*1-882163-29-X*) Moanalua Grdns Fnd.

— Up the Coast & into the Past: Hamakua to Waipio. (Exploring the Islands: Island of Hawai'i Ser.). 1994. pap. write for info. (*1-882163-31-1*) Moanalua Grdns Fnd.

— Waianae Coast & Kuaokala Trail Field Site Guide for Teachers. (Exploring the Islands Ser.). 1992. teacher ed write for info. (*1-882163-40-0*) Moanalua Grdns Fnd.

— Waihe'e Trail & Haleki'i Field: Site Guide for Teachers. (Exploring the Islands Ser.). 36p. 1993. pap. write for info. (*1-882163-16-8*) Moanalua Grdns Fnd.

— Waihee Trail & Halekii Field Site Guide for Teachers. 1993. teacher ed write for info. (*0-614-00211-7*) Moanalua Grdns Fnd.

— Waikamoi & Halemauu Trail: Field Site Guide for Teachers. (Exploring the Islands Ser.). 1993. teacher ed write for info. (*1-882163-17-6*) Moanalua Grdns Fnd.

— Wailua Basin & Heiau Complex Field Site Guide for Teachers. (Exploring the Islands Ser.). 1994. teacher ed write for info. (*1-882163-21-4*) Moanalua Grdns Fnd.

— Waimea Canyon & Kaluapuhi Trail Field Site Guide for Teachers. (Exploring the Islands Ser.). 1994. teacher ed write for info. (*1-882163-23-0*) Moanalua Grdns Fnd.

— West Molokai Field Site Guide for Teachers. (Exploring the Islands Ser.). 1994. teacher ed write for info. (*1-882163-28-1*) Moanalua Grdns Fnd.

Roelofs, Faith M. Aiea Loop Trail & Keaiwa Heiau. (Exploring Oahu: Field Site Guides for Teachers Ser.). 24p. 1992. pap. write for info. (*1-882163-02-8*) Moanalua Grdns Fnd.

— Exploring Hawaii: Field Site Guides for Teachers, Set. 1993. teacher ed write for info. (*1-882163-07-9*) Moanalua Grdns Fnd.

— Exploring Kauai: Field Site Guides for Teachers, 3 vols., Set. 1993. teacher ed write for info. (*1-882163-05-2*) Moanalua Grdns Fnd.

— Exploring Maui: Field Site Guides for Teachers, Set. 1993. teacher ed write for info. (*0-318-69543-X*) Moanalua Grdns Fnd.

— Hauula Loop Trail. (Exploring Oahu: Field Site Guides for Teachers Ser.). 20p. 1992. pap. write for info. (*1-882163-03-6*) Moanalua Grdns Fnd.

— Makawehi Dunes & Sinkhole. (Exploring Kauai: Field Site Guides for Teachers Ser.). 1993. pap. write for info. (*1-882163-11-7*) Moanalua Grdns Fnd.

— Waianae Coast & Kuaokala Ridge Trail. (Exploring Oahu: Field Site Guides for Teachers Ser.). 24p. 1992. pap. write for info. (*1-882163-04-4*) Moanalua Grdns Fnd.

— Wailua Basin & Heiau Complex. (Exploring Kauai: Field Site Guides for Teachers Ser.). 1993. pap. write for info. (*1-882163-10-9*) Moanalua Grdns Fnd.

— Waimea Canyon & the Kaluapuhi Trail. (Exploring Kauai: Field Site Guides for Teachers Ser.). 1993. pap. write for info. (*1-882163-12-5*) Moanalua Grdns Fnd.

Roelofs, Faith M. & Gill, Lorin T. Exploring Oahu: Field Site Guides for Teachers, 4 vols., Set. 1992. teacher ed write for info. (*1-882163-00-1*) Moanalua Grdns Fnd.

— Koolaupoko. (Exploring Oahu: Field Site Guides for Teachers Ser.). 24p. 1992. pap. write for info. (*1-882163-01-X*) Moanalua Grdns Fnd.

Roelofs, Gerrit H., jt. ed. see Coffin, Charles M.

Roelofs, H. Mark. The Poverty of American Politics: A Theoretical Interpretation. (C). 1991. 44.95 (*0-87722-877-9*); pap. 22.95 (*0-87722-878-7*) Temple U Pr.

Roelofse, J., jt. auth. see Foster, P. A.

Roels, Edwin D. Alguien Se Preocupa. Cosby, John, tr. (Friendship Ser.). (Illus.). 48p. (SPA.). 1992. pap. write for info. (*1-882536-27-4*, A110-0016) Bible League.

— Dios Comprende. Cosby, John, tr. (Friendship Ser.). (Illus.). 48p. (SPA.). 1992. pap. write for info. (*1-882536-26-6*, A110-0012) Bible League.

— God Understands. (Friendship Ser.). (Illus.). 48p. (Orig.). 1993. pap. write for info. (*1-882536-02-9*, A100-0019) Bible League.

— El Milagro de Vida. Compeau, Jane, tr. (Friendship Ser.). (Illus.). 48p. (SPA.). 1992. pap. write for info. (*1-882536-28-2*, A110-0015) Bible League.

— A Miracle of Love: The Gift of Life. (Friendship Ser.). (Illus.). 48p. (Orig.). 1993. reprint ed. pap. write for info. (*1-882536-06-1*, A100-0022) Bible League.

— Someone Cares: Scripture Truths for Those Who Are Ill. large type ed. (Friendship Ser.). (Illus.). 48p. (Orig.). 1993. reprint ed. pap. 0.55 (*1-882536-04-5*, A100-0050) Bible League.

— Someone Cares: Scripture Truths for Those Who Are Ill. (Friendship Ser.). (Illus.). 48p. (Orig.). 1993. reprint ed. pap. write for info. (*1-882536-03-7*, A100-0018) Bible League.

— Who Cares When I Hurt? Help from the Bible for Those Who Are Hurting. (Friendship Ser.). (Illus.). 48p. (Orig.). 1993. pap. write for info. (*1-882536-05-3*, A100-0020) Bible League.

Roels, Edwin D., comp. Answers to Live By: Answers You Can Trust to Some of Life's Most Important Questions. 64p. (Orig.). 1993. pap. write for info. (*1-882536-00-2*, A100-0001); Pocket size. pap. write for info. (*1-882536-01-0*, A100-0002) Bible League.

Roels, Frank. Peroximones: A Personal Account. (Illus.). 151p. 1994. pap. 23.00 (*90-70289-94-6*) Paul & Co Pubs.

Roels, J. A. Energetics & Kinetics in Biotechnology. 340p. 1983. 150.50 (*0-444-80442-0*) Elsevier.

Roels, Oswald A., ed. Hudson River Colloquium, Vol. 250. (Annals Ser.). 185p. 1974. 29.00 (*0-89072-764-3*) NY Acad Sci.

Roemer. Flushing Battery. 27.95 (*0-8488-1560-2*) Amereon Ltd.

— Health Care Systems & Comparative Manpower Policies. (Health Policy Ser.: Vol. 1). 472p. 1981. 110.00 (*0-8247-1389-3*) Dekker.

Roemer, Ferdinand. Texas: With Particular Reference to German Immigration & the Physical Appearance of the Country. 1993. reprint ed. lib. bdg. 75.00 (*0-7812-5973-8*) Rprt Serv.

Roemer, John E. Analytical Foundations of Marxian Economic Theory. LC 80-22646. (Illus.). 224p. 1989. pap. 17.95 (*0-521-34775-0*) Cambridge U Pr.

— Egalitarian Perspectives: Essays in Philosophical Economics. 384p. (C). 1994. 59.95 (*0-521-45066-7*) Cambridge U Pr.

— Free to Lose: An Introduction to Marxist Economic Philosophy. LC 87-12121. 216p. (Orig.). 1988. 32.00 (*0-674-31875-7*); pap. 13.95 (*0-674-31876-5*) HUP.

— A Future for Socialism. LC 93-23208. 188p. 1994. 29.95 (*0-674-33945-2*) HUP.

— Future for Socialism. 188p. 1994. pap. 16.95 (*0-674-33946-0*) HUP.

— A General Theory of Exploitation & Class. LC 81-13329. (Illus.). 419p. 1982. 40.00 (*0-674-34440-5*) HUP.

— U. S.-Japanese Competition in International Markets: A Study of the Trade - Investment Cycle in Modern Capitalism. LC 75-620086. (Research Ser.: No. 22). (Illus.). 225p. 1975. pap. 3.95 (*0-87725-122-3*) U of Cal IAS.

— Value, Exploitation & Class. (Fundamentals of Pure & Applied Economics Ser.: Vol. 4). 88p. 1986. pap. text ed. 33.00 (*3-7186-0278-4*) Gordon & Breach.

Roemer, John E., ed. Analytical Marxism. (Studies in Marxism & Social Theory). 280p. 1986. pap. 21.95 (*0-521-31731-2*) Cambridge U Pr.

— Foundations of Analytical Marxism. (International Library of Critical Writings in Business History: Vol. 36). 840p. 1994. 224.95 (*1-85278-784-8*, Pub. by E Elgar Pub UK) Ashgate Pub Co.

Roemer, John E., jt. auth. see Bardhan, Pranab K.

Roemer, John E., jt. ed. see Elster, Jon.

Roemer, Judith. The Group Meeting As a Contemplative Experience. 12p. (Orig.). 1983. pap. 1.00 (*0-943316-02-2*) Typrofile Pr.

Roemer, Kenneth M. The Obsolete Necessity: America in Utopian Writings, 1888-1900. LC 75-17279. 254p. reprint ed. pap. 72.40 (*0-318-34937-X*, 2030729) Bks Demand.

Roemer, Kenneth M., ed. Approaches to Teaching Momaday's The Way to Rainy Mountain. LC 88-8959. (Approaches to Teaching World Literature Ser.: No. 17). xiv, 172p. 1988. 37.50 (*0-87352-509-4*, AP17C); pap. 18.00x (*0-87352-510-8*, AP17P) Modern Lang.

Roemer, Linda, jt. auth. see Lorentzen, Karen M.

Roemer, M. I. Evaluation of Community Health Centres. (Public Health Papers: No. 48). 1972. pap. 2.00 (*92-4-130048-5*) World Health.

Roemer, M. I., jt. auth. see Bridgman, R. F.

Roemer, M. I., jt. auth. see Flahault, D. M.

Roemer, M. I., jt. auth. see Fulop, T.

Roemer, Michael. Fishing for Growth: Export-led Development in Peru, 1950-1967. LC 72-135189. 224p. 1970. 30.00 (*0-674-30480-2*) HUP.

— Telling Stories: Postmodernism, Free Will, & the Invalidation of Narrative. 386p. (C). 1995. lib. bdg. 58.50 (*0-8476-8041-X*); pap. text ed. 22.95 (*0-8476-8042-8*) Rowman.

Roemer, Michael & Jones, Christine. Markets in Developing Countries: Parallel, Fragmented & Black. 267p. 1991. pap. 12.95 (*1-55815-082-X*); 2.00 (*1-55815-142-7*) ICS Pr.

Roemer, Michael, jt. auth. see Kim, Kwang S.

Roemer, Michael, jt. auth. see Lindauer, David L.

Roemer, Michael, jt. ed. see Perkins, Dwight H.

Roemer, Milton I. Comparative National Policies on Health Care. (Political Science & Public Administration Ser.: Vol. 2). 264p. 1977. 65.00 (*0-8247-7730-1*) Dekker.

— National Health Systems of the World, Vols. I & II. (Illus.). 1056p. 1993. 140.00 (*0-19-508623-6*) OUP.

— National Health Systems of the World Vol. 2: The Issues. 368p. 1993. 55.00 (*0-19-507845-4*) OUP.

— National Health Systems of the World, Vol. 1: Countries. (Illus.). 688p. 1991. 85.00 (*0-19-505320-6*) OUP.

— National Strategies for Health Care Organization: A World Overview. LC 84-12878. (Illus.). 428p. 1985. text ed. 38.00 (*0-914904-99-X*, 0657) Health Admin Pr.

Roemer, Milton R. An Introduction to the U. S. Health Care System. 2nd ed. 176p. 1986. pap. 18.95 (*0-8261-3983-3*) Springer Pub.

Roemer, R. B., ed. Advances in Bioheat & Mass Transfer 1993. LC 93-73599. (HTD Ser.: Vol. 268). 145p. Date not set. pap. 47.50 (*0-7918-1047-X*) ASME.

Roemer, Ruth & McKray, George, eds. Legal Aspects of Health Policy: Issues & Trends. LC 79-8583. (Illus.). x, 473p. 1980. text ed. 59.95 (*0-313-21430-1*, RIH/, Greenwood Pr) Greenwood.

Roemer, Theodore. The Ludwig-Missionsverein & the Church in the United States (1838-1918) LC 73-3571. (Catholic University of America. Studies in Romance Languages & Literatures: No. 16). reprint ed. 32.50 (*0-404-57766-0*) AMS Pr.

***Roemer, William.** Mob Power Plays: The Mob Attempts Control of Congress, Casinos & Baseball. 1994. pap. 5.50 (*1-56171-370-8*, S P I Bks) Sure Sellers.

***Roemer, William F., Jr.** Accardo: The Genuine Godfather. (Illus.). 368p. 1995. 23.95 (*1-55611-467-2*) D I Fine.

Roemer, William F. The Enforcer: Spilotro - the Chicago Mob's Man over Law Vegas. LC 93-74484. (Illus.). 384p. 1994. 23.95 (*1-55611-399-4*) D I Fine.

***Roemer, William F., Jr.** The Enforcer. 1995. mass mkt. 5.99 (*0-8041-1310-6*) Ivy Books.

— Mob Power Plays: The Mob Attempts Control of Congress, Casinos & Baseball. 360p. 1993. 18.95 (*1-56171-168-3*, S P I Bks) Sure Sellers.

— Roemer: Man Against the Mob. (Illus.). 1989. 19.95 (*1-55611-146-0*) D I Fine.

— Roemer: Man Against the Mob. 416p. 1991. mass mkt. 4.95 (*0-8041-0718-1*) Ivy Books.

— War of the Godfathers: The Bloody Confrontation Between the Chicago & New York Families for Control of Las Vegas. (Illus.). 1990. 19.95 (*1-55611-193-2*) D I Fine.

Roemer, William R. War of the Godfathers. 1991. mass mkt. 5.99 (*0-8041-0831-5*) Ivy Books.

Roemheld, Diethard. Wege der Weisheit: Die Legren Amenemopes und Proverbein 22, 17-24, 22. (Beiheft zur Zeitschrift fuer die Alttestamentliche Wissenschaft Ser.: No. 184). x, 233p. (GER.). (C). 1989. lib. bdg. 69.25x (*3-11-011958-7*) De Gruyter.

Roemig, Sue, ed. Scandinavian Christmas Recipes & Traditions. (Illus.). 40p. 1985. pap. 4.95 (*0-941016-28-5*) Penfield.

Roemisch, Jerry. The Ten Most Wanted List: Ten Things You Must Do to Get the Job You Really Want. 33p. (Orig.). 1993. pap. 4.95 (*1-883439-00-0*) Jericho Pr.

Roen, Duane H., jt. auth. see Johnson, Donna M.

Roen, Duane H., jt. ed. see Kirsch, Gesa.

Roen, Fran. Classic Quilts in a Day. LC 94-26051. (Illus.). 128p. 1994. pap. 14.95 (*0-8069-0758-4*) Sterling.

— Country Quilts in a Day: Using Strip Quilting & Other Speed Techniques. LC 91-2937. (Illus.). 128p. 1991. pap. 14.95 (*0-8069-8288-8*) Sterling.

— Forty-Eight-Hour Country Quilts. LC 93-5088. (Illus.). 128p. 1993. pap. 14.95 (*0-8069-0386-4*) Sterling.

— Seven-Day Country Quilts. LC 92-17516. (Illus.). 128p. 1992. pap. 14.95 (*0-8069-8685-9*) Sterling.

Roen, Gary. Look at Me World. LC 76-2745. (Illus.). 1976. pap. 2.50 (*0-88435-006-1*) Chateau Pub.

Roen, J. B. & Kepferle, R. C., eds. Petroleum Geology of the Devonian & Mississippian Black Shale of North America. (Illus.). 358p. (Orig.). (C). 1994. pap. text ed. 95.00 (*0-7881-0354-7*) Diane Pub.

Roen, Leona. Using MicroFocus Workbench for COBOL. LC 94-25416. 1994. write for info. (*0-87709-813-1*) Boyd & Fraser.

Roen, Olive. Nurses in Texas: Nurse Aides to Advanced Nurse Practitioners, 1971-1991. (Working Paper Ser.: No. 62). 84p. 1992. 5.00 (*0-685-66567-4*) LBJ Sch Pub Aff.

Roen, Paul. High Camp: A Gay Guide to Camp & Cult Films. (Illus.). 224p. (Orig.). 1993. lib. bdg. 25.00 (*0-943595-45-2*); pap. 15.95 (*0-943595-42-8*) Leyland Pubns.

Roen, Samuel. Murder of a Little Girl. LC 73-82981. 343p. 1974. 8.95 (*0-88435-000-2*) Chateau Pub.

R

 An Asterisk (*) at the beginning of an entry indicates that the title is appearing in BIP for the first time.

Roen, William H. The Inward Ear: A Sermon Evaluation Method for Preachers & Hearers of the Word. LC 89-85375. 91p. (Orig.). 1989. pap. 7.95 (*1-56699-076-9*, OD80) Alban Inst.

Roenback, Patricia. Golden Temptress. 368p. (Orig.). 1991. pap. 3.95 (*0-8439-3111-6*) Dorchester Pub Co.

Roenbeck, Patricia. Golden Conquest. 368p. (Orig.). 1992. pap. 4.50 (*0-8439-3325-9*) Dorchester Pub Co.

Roencranz, Herman, jt. auth. see Pollack, Benny.

Roenicke, Judy, ed. see Dean, Jean, et al.

Roenigk. Dermatologic Surgery: Principles & Practice. 1472p. 1989. 210.00 (*0-8247-7926-6*) Dekker.

Roenigk, Henry H. Surgical Dermatology: Advances in Current. 1993. 125.00 (*0-8151-7414-4*, Yr Bk Med Pubs) Mosby Yr Bk.

Roenigk, Henry H. & Maibach, H., eds. Psoriasis. 2nd ed. 992p. 1991. 250.00 (*0-8247-8223-2*) Dekker.

Roenisch, Rowan, jt. auth. see Conway, Hazel.

Roennfeldt, Ray C. Clark H. Pinnock on Biblical Authority: An Evolving Position. (Andrews University Seminary Doctoral Dissertation Ser.: Vol. 16). 452p. 1993. pap. 19.99 (*0-943872-70-7*) Andrews Univ Pr.

Roensch, Eleanor S. Life Within Limits. (Illus.). 66p. (Orig.). 1993. pap. 9.00 (*0-941232-14-X*) Los Alamos Hist Soc.

Roeper. Educating Children for Life. 1990. pap. 9.99 (*0-89824-198-7*) Trillium Pr.

***Roeper, Annemarie.** Annemarie Roeper: Selected Writings & Speeches. Medeiros, Richard & Silverman, Linda, eds. 136p. (Orig.). 1995. pap. 15.95 (*0-915793-93-8*) Free Spirit Pub.

Roeper, Tom & Williams, Edwin B., eds. Parameter Setting. (C). 1986. pap. text ed. 42.50 (*90-277-2316-8*) Kluwer Ac.

— Parameter Setting. (C). 1987. lib. bdg. 103.00 (*90-277-2315-X*) Kluwer Ac.

Roepke, Fritz. Glossary of Financial & Economic Terms: Glossarium Finanzieller & Wirtschaftlicher Fachausdruecke. 2nd ed. 540p. (FRE & GER.). 1983. 125.00 (*0-8288-0813-9*, M15103) Fr & Eur.

Roepke, Fritz, et al. Glossarium Finanzieller & Wirtschaftlicher Fachausdruecke. 6th ed. 480p. (FRE & GER.). 1982. 125.00 (*0-8288-0814-7*, M15104) Fr & Eur.

Roepke, Howard G. Movements of the British Iron & Steel Industry, 1720 to 1951. LC 80-23128. (Illinois Studies in the Social Sciences: Vol. 36). (Illus.). vii, 198p. 1981. reprint ed. text ed. 52.50 (*0-8371-9096-7*, ROMB, Greenwood Pr) Greenwood.

Roepke, Howard G., ed. Readings in Economic Geography. LC 67-19451. 678p. reprint ed. pap. 180.00 (*0-317-10035-1*, 2012580) Bks Demand.

Roepke, Wilhelm. The Social Crisis of Our Time. 290p. (C). 1991. pap. text ed. 24.95 (*1-56000-580-7*) Transaction Pubs.

Roepstorff, Gert. Path Integral Approach to Quantum Physics: An Introduction. LC 93-43689. (Texts & Monographs in Physics). 1994. 59.00 (*0-387-55213-8*) Spr-Verlag.

***Roer, Kathleen M.** Minnesota Legal Forms: Residential Real Estate. 150p. 1994. disk, ring bd. 69.95 (*0-614-05906-2*) Michie Butterworth.

— Minnesota Legal Forms, 1981-1993: Residential Real Estate. 200p. disk, ring bd. 69.95 (*0-917126-86-6*) Butterworth Legal Pubs.

— Minnesota Legal Forms, 1981-1993: Residential Real Estate. suppl. ed. 200p. 1994. ring bd. 39.00 (*0-685-52223-7*) Butterworth Legal Pubs.

Roerden, Chris. Open Gate: Teaching in a Foreign Country--a Personal Account. LC 90-82649. (Illus.). 288p. (Orig.). (C). 1990. pap. 11.95 (*0-9626859-3-3*) Edit It Pubns.

Roerden, Chris, ed. see Harrell, Earl & Harrell, Cassandra.

Roerden, Chris, ed. see Nelson, Danette L. & Waters, Cynthia V.

Roerden, Chris, ed. see Retzlaff, Nancy.

Roerich, George N. The Blue Annals. (C). 1988. reprint ed. 43.00 (*81-208-0471-6*, Pub. by Motilal Banarsidass II) S Asia.

— Tibetan Paintings. (Illus.). 176p. 1986. 49.95 (*0-318-36347-X*) Asia Bk Corp.

Roerich, Helena. Foundations of Buddhism. 1971. reprint ed. 8.00 (*0-686-79661-6*) Agni Yoga Soc.

Roerich, Nicholas. Heart of Asia: Memoirs from the Himalayas. 192p. 1990. pap. 10.95 (*0-89281-302-4*) Inner Tradit.

— Shambhala. 16.00 (*0-685-00147-4*); pap. 12.00 (*0-686-79666-7*) Agni Yoga Soc.

— Shambhala: In Search of the New Era. 328p. 1990. pap. 10.95 (*0-89281-305-9*) Inner Tradit.

Roerich, Nicholas, Museum Staff. Nicholas Roerich: A Short Biography. 1.50 (*0-686-79662-4*) Agni Yoga Soc.

— Roerich Pact & Banner of Peace. 2.00 (*0-686-79664-0*) Agni Yoga Soc.

Roerich, Y. N. Tibetan-Russian-English Dictionary. Parionovich, Y. & Dylykova, V., eds. 432p. 1985. 39.00 (*0-317-42710-5*, Pub. by Collets UK) Pro-Am Music.

— Tibetan-Russian-English Dictionary with Sanskrit Parallels, Vol. 5. 312p. (ENG, RUS & TIB.). 1985. 45.00 (*0-317-59449-4*, Pub. by Collets UK) Pro-Am Music.

Roerick, Kaye L., jt. ed. see Plucker, Lina S.

Roerig, Fred. Collectors Encyclopedia of Cookie Jars. 1991. 24.95 (*0-89145-438-1*) Collector Bks.

— Collector's Encyclopedia of Cookie Jars, Vol. 2. 1993. 24.95 (*0-89145-563-9*) Collector Bks.

Roers, Louis, ed. see Al-Jerrahi, Muzaffer O.

***Roersch, C.** Plantas Medicinales en el Sur Andino del Peru, 2 vols., Set. (Illus.). 1188p. (SPA.). 1994. 177.00 (*1-878762-67-2*) Koeltz Sci Bks.

Roes, Mimi. The Do Nothing Way to Health & Beauty. (Illus.). 128p. 1979. pap. 4.95 (*0-89780-000-1*) NAR Pubns.

— Poems for Young Children. (Illus.). (J). (ps-6). 1979. pap. 1.95 (*0-89780-003-6*) NAR Pubns.

Roes, Mon. Inherited Memories: Biogenetic Evolution of Intellect. rev. ed. 148p. (C). 1992. 18.00 (*0-9618960-6-X*) M M Fain.

— El Mejor: And Other Stories. 151p. (Orig.). (C). 1988. pap. 1.95 (*0-9618960-1-9*) M M Fain.

— The Orgy Room: And Other Stories. 118p. (C). 1988. pap. 1.95 (*0-9618960-2-7*) M M Fain.

— Sex Preferences. 2nd rev. ed. 190p. (C). 1990. 14.00 (*0-9618960-5-1*) M M Fain.

— Sex Preferences: Origins & Influences. 126p. (Orig.). (C). 1988. pap. 8.95 (*0-9618960-0-0*) M M Fain.

— Sitting on a Wall: Selected Writings of Mon Roes. 194p. 1993. 18.00 (*0-685-67895-4*) M M Fain.

Roes, Nicholas A. America's Lowest Cost Colleges. 256p. (Orig.). 1985. 12.95 (*0-88191-026-0*) Freundlich.

— America's Lowest Cost Colleges. 6th rev. ed. 128p. (Orig.). 1989. pap. 8.95 (*0-89780-010-9*) NAR Pubns.

— America's Lowest Cost Colleges. 9th rev. ed. 156p. (Orig.). 1995. pap. 9.95 (*0-89780-041-9*) NAR Pubns.

— America's Lowest Cost Colleges: A Comprehensive Directory of More Than 1,000 Fully Accredited Colleges & Universities with Low or No Tuition. rev. ed. 144p. 1991. pap. 9.95 (*0-89780-012-5*) NAR Pubns.

— America's Lowest Cost Colleges: A Comprehensive Directory of More Than 1,000 Fully Accredited Colleges & Universities with Low or No Tuition. 8th rev. ed. 1993. pap. 9.95 (*0-89780-014-1*) NAR Pubns.

— Helping Children Watch TV. (Illus.). 52p. 1977. text ed. 6.95 (*0-89780-031-1*); pap. text ed. 4.95 (*0-89780-030-3*) NAR Pubns.

— Helping Children Watch TV: A Practical Handbook with More Than 100 TV-Related Learning Activities. rev. ed. 108p. 1992. pap. 8.95 (*0-89780-013-3*) NAR Pubns.

Roes, Nicholas A. & DuBacher, Monique E. Pick-Your-Own Farms: A Comprehensive Guide to Over 3,000 Farms Where You Can "Pick-Your-Own" Fruits & Vegetables. 242p. (Orig.). 1990. pap. 24.95 (*0-89780-011-7*) NAR Pubns.

Roes, Nick. Gambling for Fun. 100p. 1988. pap. 9.95 (*0-89780-009-5*) NAR Pubns.

Roes, Ruth, ed. see Johnson, Connie.

Roesch, E. P. Ashana. 1991. mass mkt. 5.99 (*0-345-37298-0*) Ballantine.

— Ashana. 1990. 19.95 (*0-394-56963-6*) Random.

Roesch, J., jt. auth. see Lanzer, P.

Roesch, Joseph E., tr. see Chapuis, Alfred.

Roesch, Roberta. The Encyclopedia of Depression. 270p. (C). 1990. 45.00 (*0-8160-1936-3*) Facts on File.

— Smart Talk: The Art of Savvy Business Conversation. LC 89-45455. 256p. 1989. pap. 14.95 (*0-8144-7713-5*) AMACOM.

— The Working Woman's Guide to Managing Time. 1995. text ed. 24.95 (*0-13-097437-4*); pap. text ed. 14.95 (*0-13-097429-3*) P-H.

— You Can Make It Without a College Degree. 1986. 8.95 (*0-13-976812-2*) S&S Trade.

Roesch, Roberta, jt. auth. see Schlenger, Sunny.

Roesdahl, Else. The Vikings. (Illus.). 368p. 1991. 24.95 (*0-7139-9048-1*, A Lane) Viking Penguin.

— The Vikings. (Illus.). 368p. 1992. reprint ed. pap. 12.95 (*0-14-012561-2*, Penguin Bks) Viking Penguin.

***Roese, Neal J. & Olson, James M., eds.** What Might Have Been: The Social Psychology of Counterfactual Thinking. 408p. 1995. text ed. 80.00 (*0-8058-1613-5*) L Erlbaum Assocs.

— What Might Have Been: The Social Psychology of Counterfactual Thinking. 408p. 1995. pap. text ed. 40.00 (*0-8058-1614-3*) L Erlbaum Assocs.

Roesel, Catherine E. Immunology: A Self-Instructional Approach. 1978. pap. text ed. 26.95 (*0-07-053411-X*) McGraw.

Roesel, Martin. Uebersetzung Als Vollendung der Auslegung: Studien Zur Genesis-Septuaginta. (Beiheft zur Zeitschrift fuer die Alttestamentliche Wissenschaft Ser.: Bd. 223). viii, 290p. (GER.). (C). 1994. lib. bdg. 106.15 (*3-11-014234-1*, 8-94) De Gruyter.

***Roeseler, Karl.** The Adventures of Gesso Martin. 111p. (Orig.). 1994. pap. 8.95 (*0-9639192-1-0*) Trip St Pr.

Roeser, M. Karyologische, Systematische und Chorologische Untersuchungen an der Gattung Helictotrichon Besser Ex Schultes & Schultes (Poaceae), Im Westlichen Mittelmeergebiet. (Dissertationes Boranicae Ser.: Vol. 145). (Illus.). 252p. (GER.). 1989. pap. text ed. 63.00 (*3-443-64056-7*, Pub. by Gebruder Borntraeger GW) Lubrecht & Cramer.

***Roeser, Ross J. & Downs, Marion P., eds.** Auditory Disorders in School Children: Identification & Remediation. 3rd ed. (Illus.). 400p. 1995. text ed. 39.00 (*0-86577-550-8*) Thieme Med Pubs.

Roeske, Nancy A. Examination of the Personality. LC 72-8914. 176p. reprint ed. pap. 50.20 (*0-317-08140-3*, 2055441) Bks Demand.

Roeske, Paulette. Breathing under Water. 64p. 1988. pap. 7.95 (*0-935153-08-X*) Stormline Pr.

— Divine Attention: Poems. LC 94-38208. 80p. (C). 1995. text ed. 17.95 (*0-8071-1950-4*); pap. 9.95 (*0-8071-1951-2*) La State U Pr.

Roesky, H. W., ed. Rings, Clusters & Polymers of Main Group & Transition Elements. 560p. 1989. 179.50 (*0-444-88172-7*) Elsevier.

Roesler, H., ed. see Medical Cyclotron Users Conference Staff.

Roesler, Theodore W., jt. auth. see Lamphear, F. Charles.

Roesliep, Raymond. Rabbit in the Moon: Haiku. LC 83-6445. (Illus.). 128p. 1983. 12.00 (*0-934184-15-1*); pap. 6.00 (*0-934184-16-X*) Alembic Pr.

Roesner, Edward H., jt. ed. see Wolf, Eugene K.

Roesner, Larry A., jt. ed. see Urbonas, Ben.

Roesner, Larry A., et al, eds. Design of Urban Runoff Quality Controls. 502p. 1989. 43.00 (*0-87262-695-4*) Am Soc Civil Eng.

Roess, Anne C. Public Utilities: An Annotated Guide to Information Sources. LC 91-22954. 406p. 1991. 45.00 (*0-8108-2443-4*) Scarecrow.

Roess, Christine, jt. auth. see Black, Joanne.

Roess, Roger P., jt. auth. see McShane, William R.

Roessel, David, jt. ed. see Rampersad, Arnold.

Roessel, Monty. Kinaalda: A Navajo Girl Grows Up. (J). (gr. 3-6). 1993. pap. 6.95 (*0-8225-9641-5*, Lerner Publctns) Lerner Group.

— Songs from the Loom: A Navajo Girl Learns to Weave. LC 94-48765. (We Are Still Here Ser.). (J). 1995. text ed. 19.95 (*0-8225-2657-3*, Lerner Publctns); pap. 6.95 (*0-8225-9711-X*, Lerner Publctns) Lerner Group.

Roessel, Monty, photos & text. Kinaalda: A Navajo Girl Grows Up. LC 92-35204. (We are Still Here Ser.). (Illus.). 48p. (J). (gr. 3-6). 1993. 19.95 (*0-8225-2655-7*, Lerner Publctns) Lerner Group.

Roessel, Robert, Jr. Coyote Stories of the Navajo People. 141p. pap. 10.00 (*0-89019-039-9*) Rough Rock Pr.

Roessel, Robert A. Dinetah: Navajo History, Vol. II. 180p. 1983. 24.00 (*0-936008-09-1*) Rough Rock Pr.

Roessel, Robert A., Jr. Navajo Arts & Crafts. 176p. 1983. 24.00 (*0-936008-02-4*) Rough Rock Pr.

— Navajo Education in Action: The Rough Rock Demonstration School. 149p. 1977. 24.00 (*0-317-01681-4*) Rough Rock Pr.

Roessel, Robert A. Navajo Education 1948-78, Its Progress & Its Problems. 340p. 1979. 24.00 (*0-912586-38-9*) Rough Rock Pr.

Roessel, Robert A., Jr. Pictorial History from 1860-1910. (Illus.). 204p. pap. 20.00 (*0-936008-00-8*) Rough Rock Pr.

Roessel, Ruth. Navajo Stories of the Long Walk Period. LC 73-78328. 272p. 1973. pap. 15.00 (*0-912586-16-8*) Navajo Coll Pr.

— Women in Navajo Society. LC 81-1293. (Illus.). 184p. 1981. 24.00 (*0-936008-01-6*) Rough Rock Pr.

Roesset, Jose, jt. auth. see Leet, Kenneth M.

Roesset, Jose M., ed. Dynamics of Structures. 892p. 1987. 77.00 (*0-87262-615-6*) Am Soc Civil Eng.

Roessing, H. Two Thousand Two Hundred Eighty-Six Traditional Stencil Designs. (Illus.). 128p. reprint ed. pap. 6.95 (*0-486-26845-4*) Dover.

Roessing-Hager, Monika, ed. Wortindex zu Georg Buechner, Dichtungen und Uebersetzungen. (Deutsche Wortindices Ser.: No. 1). (C). 1970. 132.30 (*3-11-006448-0*) De Gruyter.

Roessing-Hager, Monika & Soerensen, Niels, eds. Wortindex zu Gottfried Keller, Die Leute von Seldwyla, 2 Pts. (Deutsche Wortindices Ser.: No. 2). (C). 1971. 280.75 (*3-11-006441-3*) De Gruyter.

Roessler, A. C. A. C. Roessler's Standard Historical Souvenir Airmail Catalog. Mellone, Michael, ed. (Illus.). 1978. pap. 4.50 (*0-89794-007-5*) FDC Pub.

Roessler, Carl. Coral Kingdoms. (Illus.). 244p. 1990. 39.95 (*0-8109-0774-7*); pap. 19.98 (*0-8109-8095-9*) Abrams.

— Diving & Snorkeling Guide to Australia: Coral Sea & Great Barrier Reef. 96p. 1991. 11.95 (*1-55992-044-0*, Pisces Bks) Gulf Pub.

— Diving & Snorkeling Guide to the Cayman Islands. 2nd ed. 96p. 1993. 11.95 (*1-55992-042-4*, Pisces Bks) Gulf Pub.

— Great Reefs of the World. (Illus.). 128p. 1992. pap. 19.95 (*1-55992-058-0*, 2058, Pisces Bks) Gulf Pub.

— The Undersea Predators. (Illus.). 192p. 28.95 (*1-55992-014-9*); 45.00 (*1-55992-028-9*) Gulf Pub.

Roessler, Dietrich. Grundriss der Praktischen Theologie. 2nd enl. ed. xvii, 660p. (GER.). 1993. lib. bdg. 60.00 (*3-11-013534-5*) De Gruyter.

Roessler, Eberhard, jt. auth. see Koehl, Fritz.

Roessler, Mark. The Last Magician in Blue Haven. LC 94-75954. (Illus.). 52p. (Orig.). (J). (gr. 4-8). 1994. pap. 12.95 (*0-9638293-0-0*) Hundelrut Studio. THE LAST MAGICIAN is an imaginative tale for children & adults, filled with numerous delicate pen drawings by Donald Hundgen. A sophisticated city doctor comes to Blue Haven to serve the rural community but ends up becoming a thorn in their side. The simple villagers love magic. The doctor, Fortunamus Gengeloof, drives off all the magicians by revealing their secrets, until one comes along who is a match for the doctor. For prepublication order & general information: write Hundelrut Studio, 10 Hawthorne Street, Plymouth, NH 03264. USA. Phone: 603-536-4396. ***Publisher Provided Annotation.***

***Roessler, Martin.** Schleiermachers Programm der Philosophischen Theologie. (Schleiermacher-Archiv Ser.: Bd. 14). 247p. (GER.). (C). 1994. lib. bdg. 121.55 (*3-11-014171-X*) De Gruyter.

Roessler, Richard & Rubin, Stanford E. Case Management & Rehabilitation Counseling: Procedures & Techniques. 2nd ed. LC 91-26385. 227p. 1992. pap. text ed. 26.00 (*0-89079-519-3*, 3657) PRO-ED.

Roessler, Richard T. & Brolin, Donn E. Life Centered Career Education: Competency Units for Occupational Guidance & Preparation. LC 92-18255. 1992. ring bd. 300.00 (*0-86586-226-5*, P369) Coun Exc Child.

Roessler, Richard T., jt. auth. see Marr, John N.

Roessler, Richard T., jt. auth. see Rubin, Stanford E.

Roessler, Robert & Decker, Norman. Emotional Disorders in Physically Ill Patients. LC 85-15120. (Illus.). 269p. 1986. 35.95 (*0-89885-254-4*) Human Sci Pr.

Roessler, Robert & Greenfield, Norman S., eds. Physiological Correlates of Psychological Disorder: Proceedings of an Interdisciplinary Research Conference Sponsored by the Wisconsin Psychiatric Institute & the Dept. of Psychiatry of the University of Wisconsin Medical Center, August 29-31, 1961. LC 62-15990. 294p. reprint ed. pap. 83.80 (*0-317-30077-6*, 2021145) Bks Demand.

Roessler, Rudolf. Woerterbuch des Steuerrechts. (GER.). 1971. 75.00 (*0-8288-6491-8*, M-6934) Fr & Eur.

Roesslin, Eucharius. On Minerals & Mineral Products. (Ars Medica Ser.: Section 1V, Vol. 1). (C). 1978. 300.00 (*3-11-006907-5*) De Gruyter.

Roessner, A., jt. ed. see Vollmer, E.

Roessner, David, ed. Innovation Policy. (Orig.). 1984. pap. 12.00 (*0-918592-66-6*) Pol Studies.

Roessner, J. David, ed. Government Innovation Policy: Design, Implementation, Evaluation. LC 86-21958. (Policy Studies Organization). 256p. 1988. text ed. 39.95 (*0-312-34134-2*) St Martin.

Roessner, J. David, et al. The Impact of Office Automation on Clerical Employment, 1985-2000: Forcasting Techniques & Plausible Futures in Banking & Insurance. LC 85-6523. (Illus.). xii, 297p. 1985. text ed. 69.50 (*0-89930-119-3*, ROU/, Quorum Bks) Greenwood.

***Roessner, Michaela.** The Stars Dispose. (De Medici Fantasy Bks.: No. 1). 1996. 22.95 (*0-312-85754-3*) Tor Bks.

— Vanishing Point. 384p. 1993. 21.95 (*0-312-85213-4*) Tor Bks.

— Vanishing Point. 1994. pap. 4.99 (*0-8125-1672-9*) Tor Bks.

Roest, Aryan I. A Key-Guide to Mammal Skulls & Lower Jaws. 39p. (C). 1986. pap. 5.95 (*0-916422-71-2*) Mad River.

Roest, Jaijer M. Catalog der Reichhalltigen Sammlungen Hebraischer und Judischer Bucher und Handschriften, Kupferstiche, Portraits Etc. viii, 429p. 1990. reprint ed. write for info. (*3-487-09292-1*, Pub. by Georg Olms GW) Lubrecht & Cramer.

Roest, Mark, jt. auth. see Flynn, Rebecca.

Roeta, Perry J. The Person in the Social Order. 390p. reprint ed. pap. 111.20 (*0-317-08068-7*, 2021162) Bks Demand.

Roetger, Doris. Weather Watch. (J). (gr. k-3). 1991. pap. 8.99 (*0-86653-969-7*) Fearon Teach Aids.

Roethel, David A., ed. Professional Directory Nineteen Eighty-Seven. rev. ed. 225p. 1987. pap. 50.00 (*0-939293-01-3*) Amer Inst Chem.

Roethel, Hans K. & Benjamin, Jean K. Kandinsky. LC 79-12966. (Illus.). 172p. 1979. 65.00 (*0-933920-00-8*) Hudson Hills.

— Kandinsky: Catalogue Raisonne of the Oil Paintings: Vol. II, 1916-1944. LC 81-69483. (Illus.). 560p. 1984. 275.00 (*0-8014-1636-1*) Cornell U Pr.

— Kandinsky: Catalogue Raisonne of the Oil Paintings, Vol. I: 1900-1915. LC 81-69483. (Illus.). 480p. 1982. 275.00 (*0-8014-1478-4*) Cornell U Pr.

Roethel, Louis F., et al. Logic, Sets & Numbers. 3rd ed. 415p. (C). 1983. text ed. 57.95 (*0-534-02687-7*) PWS Pubs.

Roether, Barbara, ed. see Codrescu, Andrei.

***Roether, Darlene.** Hair Wrapping Techniques: Step by Step Creative Jewelry for the Hair. (Illus.). 96p. 1995. pap. 9.95 (*0-9644178-0-4*) Roaring Forties.

Roethke, Theodore. Collected Poems. LC 65-23785. 288p. 1975. reprint ed. 12.95 (*0-385-08601-6*, Anchor NY) Doubleday.

Roethlisberger-Bianco, Marcel. Cavalier Pietro Tempesta & His Time. LC 78-101052. (Illus.). 313p. 75.00 (*0-87413-105-7*) U Delaware Pr.

Roethlisberger, Fritz J. The Elusive Phenomena: An Autobiographical Account of My Work in the Field of Organizational Behavior at the Harvard Business School. 1978. text ed. 24.95 (*0-07-103283-5*) McGraw.

— Man-In-Organization: Essays of F. J. Roethlisberger. LC 68-28695. (Illus.). 322p. 1968. 39.95 (*0-674-54500-1*) Belknap Pr.

— Management & Morale. LC 41-4302. 317p. reprint ed. pap. 90.40 (*0-317-09739-3*, 2001587) Bks Demand.

Roethlisberger, Fritz J. & Dickson, William J. Management & the Worker: An Account of a Research Program Conducted by the Western Electric Co, Hawthorne Works, Chicago. 639p. 1939. 44.50 (*0-674-54676-8*) HUP.

Roethlisberger, Marcel. Bartholomeus Breenbergh: The Paintings. (Illus.). 332p. 1980. 246.15 (*3-11-001837-3*) De Gruyter.

— Claude Lorrain: The Drawings, 2 vols., boxed. Incl. Vol. 1. Catalogue. LC 66-24050. 1901. 155.00 (*0-520-01458-8*); Vol. 2. Plates. LC 66-24050. 1901. 155.00 (*0-520-01805-2*); LC 66-24050. (California Studies in the History of Art: No. VIII). (Illus.). 1969. write for info. (*0-318-56005-4*) U CA Pr.

Roethlisberger, Marcel, ed. see Gelee, Glaude Lorrain.

Roets, Lois. Basic Skills Reading Workbook: Grade 1. (Basic Skills Workbooks). 32p. (gr. 1). 1982. teacher ed 1.98 (*0-8209-0363-9*, RW-B) ESP.

— Famous People. 48p. (J). (gr. 3 up). 1988. teacher ed 8.00 (*0-911943-15-3*) Leadership Pub.

— In-Service Manual for Gifted & Talented. 64p. 1995. teacher ed, pap. 26.00 (*0-911943-44-7*) Leadership Pub.

R

— Incomplete Plays. 1990. teacher ed, pap. 8.00 (*0-911943-23-4*) Leadership Pub.

— Leadership: A Skills Training Program. 128p. 1992. 16.00 (*0-911943-26-9*) Leadership Pub.

— Philosophy & Philosophers. 52p. (J). (gr. 5-12). 1994. teacher ed, pap. 8.00 (*0-911943-37-4*) Leadership Pub.

— Public Speaking, Grades 2-12. 40p. 1989. teacher ed 8.00 (*0-911943-17-X*) Leadership Pub.

— Readers' Theater Vol. 3: Entrepreneurs. 104p. (Orig.). (YA). (gr. 5-12). 1995. pap. 15.00 (*0-911943-43-9*) Leadership Pub.

— Readers' Theater, Vol. 1: General Interest. 106p. (Orig.). (YA). (gr. 5-12). 1992. pap. text ed. 15.00 (*0-911943-29-3*) Leadership Pub.

— Readers' Theater, Vol. 2: Famous People. 108p. (Orig.). (YA). (gr. 5-12). 1992. pap. text ed. 15.00 (*0-911943-30-7*) Leadership Pub.

— Student Projects: Ideas & Plans. 272p. (YA). (gr. 3 up). 1994. pap. text ed. 30.00 (*0-911943-39-0*) Leadership Pub.

Roets, Lois F. Christopher Columbus Revisited. 32p. 1992. pap. 8.00 (*0-911943-25-0*) Leadership Pub.

— How to Survive & Thrive As Educator of Talented & Gifted. 72p. 1990. 8.00 (*0-911943-18-8*) Leadership Pub.

— Jumbo Reading Yearbook: Grade 1. (Jumbo Reading Ser.). 96p. (gr. 1). 1979. 18.00 (*0-8209-0012-5*, JRY 1) ESP.

— Modifying Standard Curriculum for High-Ability Learners. 4th ed. 80p. 1993. 14.00 (*0-911943-35-8*) Leadership Pub.

— Outline Wizard. (Study Skills Ser.). 48p. (J). (gr. 4-6). 1980. 5.95 (*0-88160-034-2*, LW 219) Learning Wks.

— Survey & Public Opinion Research: Grades Five to Twelve. 2nd ed. 120p. (J). (gr. 3 up). 1988. 14.00 (*0-911943-14-5*) Leadership Pub.

Roets, Lois S. Understanding Success & Failure. 36p. (J). (gr. 5 up). 1985. 8.00 (*0-911943-07-2*) Leadership Pub.

— Writing Fiction: Grades Three & Above. 60p. 1989. reprint ed. teacher ed 8.00 (*0-911943-16-1*) Leadership Pub.

Roets, Perry J. The Economic Ideas of Bernard W. Dempsey, S.J. LC 90-63708. 1991. 15.00 (*0-87462-995-0*) Marquette.

Roets, Philip G. Books of the Bible. 155p. (Orig.). (C). 1992. pap. text ed. 19.95 (*0-911943-34-X*) Leadership Pub.

Roett, Riordan. Brazil: Politics in a Patrimonial Society. 1978. 16.95 (*0-275-90312-5*, C0312, Praeger Pubs); pap. 16.95 (*0-275-91475-5*, B1475, Praeger Pubs) Greenwood.

— Brazil: Politics in a Patrimonial Society. 4th ed. LC 92-13657. 256p. 1992. text ed. 59.95 (*0-275-94121-3*, C4121, Praeger Pubs); pap. text ed. 19.95 (*0-275-94122-1*, B4122, Praeger Pubs) Greenwood.

— Brazil in the Seventies. LC 76-54880. (AEI Studies: No. 132). 126p. reprint ed. pap. 36.00 (*0-8357-4437-X*, 2037271) Bks Demand.

— The Challenge of Institutional Reform in Mexico. LC 95-3465. 216p. 1995. lib. bdg. 36.50 (*1-55587-545-9*) Lynne Rienner.

— Politics of Foreign Aid in the Brazilian Northeast. LC 72-166403. (Illus.). 1972. 17.50 (*0-8265-1177-5*) Vanderbilt U Pr.

Roett, Riordan, ed. Mexico's External Relations in the 1990s. LC 90-29996. 282p. 1991. lib. bdg. 36.50 (*1-55587-238-7*) Lynne Rienner.

— Political & Economic Liberalization in Mexico: At a Critical Juncture? LC 92-38414. 184p. 1993. 32.00 (*1-55587-382-0*) Lynne Rienner.

Roett, Riordan & Sacks, Richard S. Paraguay: The Personalist Legacy. 188p. 1990. text ed. 49.50 (*0-86531-272-9*) Westview.

Roett, Riordan & Smyth, Frank. Dialogue & Armed Conflict: Negotiating the Civil War in El Salvador. (FPI Case Studies: No. 12). 56p. (Orig.). (C). 1989. lib. bdg. 26.75 (*0-941700-36-4*); pap. text ed. 10.00 (*0-941700-37-2*) JH FPI SAIS.

Roettgen, Steffi. Anton Raphael Mengs: And His British Patrons. 1993. 50.00 (*0-302-00623-0*, Pub. by Zwemmer Bks UK) Sothebys Pubns.

Roettger, Doris. Bugs & Other Insects. 1991. 8.99 (*0-86653-992-1*) Fearon Teach Aids.

— The Environment. (J). (gr. 4-6). 1993. pap. 8.99 (*0-86653-939-5*) Fearon Teach Aids.

— Growing up Healthy. (J). (gr. k-3). 1991. pap. 8.99 (*0-86653-970-0*) Fearon Teach Aids.

— Our Ecosystem. (J). (gr. 4-6). 1993. pap. 8.99 (*0-86653-936-0*) Fearon Teach Aids.

— Pollution, Recycling, Trash, & Litter. 1991. 8.99 (*0-86653-981-6*) Fearon Teach Aids.

— Seeds & Plants. 1991. 8.99 (*0-86653-982-4*) Fearon Teach Aids.

Roettger, Dorye. Rivals of Rockwell. 1992. 14.99 (*0-517-06688-2*) Random Hse Value.

Roettger, Gregory, tr. see Gruen, Anselm.

Roettger, Gregory J., tr. see Colombas, Garcia M.

Roettger, Gregory J., tr. see Gruen, Anselm, et al.

Roettger, Gregory J., tr. see Gruen, Anselm.

Roettger, Gregory J., tr. see Gruen, Anselm & Dufner, Meinrad.

Roettger, Gregory J., tr. see Ruppert, Fidelis & Gruen, Anselm.

Roettgers, Kurt. Kritik und Praxis: Zur Geschichte des Kritikbegriffs Von Kant bis Marx. LC 73-93165. (Quellen und Studien zur Philosophie Ser.: Vol. 8). x, 302p. (C). 1974. 115.40 (*3-11-004604-0*) De Gruyter.

Roettges, Heinz. Nietzsche und die Dialektik der Aufklaerung. (Monographien und Texte zur Nietzscge-Forschung Ser.: Vol. 2). (C). 1972. 130.80 (*3-11-004018-2*) De Gruyter.

Roetz, Heiner. Confucian Ethics of the Axial Age: A Reconstruction under the Aspect of the Breakthrough Toward Postconventional Thinking. (Chinese Philosophy & Culture Ser.). 373p. (C). 1993. 59.50 (*0-7914-1649-6*); pap. 19.95 (*0-7914-1650-X*) State U NY Pr.

Roetzel, Calvin J. The Letters of Paul: Conversations in Context. 3rd ed. 240p. 1991. pap. 14.99 (*0-664-25201-X*) Westminster John Knox.

— The World That Shaped the New Testament. LC 85-12492. 180p. 1985. pap. 14.99 (*0-8042-0455-1*, John Knox) Westminster John Knox.

Roetzel, W., et al, eds. Design & Operation of Heat Exchangers: Proceedings of the EUROTHERM Seminar No. 18 Hamburg, February 27 - March 1, 1991. (EUROTHERM Seminar Ser.: No. 18). (Illus.). 432p. 1992. 110.00 (*0-387-53771-6*) Spr-Verlag.

Roetzheim, William. PC Magazine Programming Windows with Borland C++ (Programming Ser.). (Illus.). 464p. (Orig.). 1992. disk 39.95 (*1-56276-040-8*) Ziff-Davis.

— Programming Windows with Borland C++ 4.0. (Illus.). (Orig.). 1994. disk, pap. 39.95 (*1-56276-269-9*) Ziff-Davis.

Roetzheim, William H. The C Programmer's Guide to the IBM Token Ring. 288p. 1990. pap. text ed. 52.00 (*0-13-723768-5*) P-H.

— Developing Software to Government Standards. 1990. text ed. 60.00 (*0-13-829755-X*) P-H.

— Structured Design Using HIPO II. 240p. 1990. text ed. 36.00 (*0-13-853599-X*) P-H.

— Uncharted Windows Programming. 1993. pap. 34.95 (*0-672-30299-3*) Sams.

Roever, Joan M. Snake Secrets. LC 78-4318. (Illus.). (J). (gr. 5 up). 1979. lib. bdg. 11.85 (*0-8027-6333-2*) Walker & Co.

Rof Carballo, Juan. Entre el Silencio y la Palabra. (Nueva Austral Ser.: Vol. 147). (SPA.). 1991. pap. text ed. 24.95x (*84-239-1947-1*) Elliots Bks.

— Violencia y Ternura. (Nueva Austral Ser.: Vol. 19). (SPA.). 1991. pap. text ed. 24.95x (*84-239-1819-X*) Elliots Bks.

Rofe, A. The Prophetical Stories: The Narratives about the Prophets in the Hebrew Bible, Their Literary Types & History. 218p. 1988. text ed. 20.00 (*0-685-72504-9*, Pub. by Magnes Press IS) Eisenbrauns.

Rofe, Alexander. The Book of Balaam (Numbers 22: 2 - 24: 25) A Study in Methods of Criticism & the History of Biblical Literature & Religion. (Jerusalem Biblical Studies: Vol. 1). 77p. (HEB.). 1979. pap. text ed. 6.50 (*0-685-49416-0*, Pub. by Simor Ltd IS) Eisenbrauns.

Rofe, Husein. The Path of Subud. 1972. 250.00 (*0-8490-0805-0*) Gordon Pr.

— The Path of Subud. 2nd ed. 162p. 1988. reprint ed. pap. text ed. 8.95 (*0-945126-03-4*) Undiscovd Worlds Pr.

Rofe, Yacov. Repression & Fear: New Approaches to Resolve the Crisis in Psychopathology. 500p. 1989. 67.00 (*0-89116-056-6*) Hemisp Pub.

Rofes, Eric E. I Thought People Like That Killed Themselves: Lesbians, Gay Men & Suicide. LC 82-9301. 176p. 1983. 12.00 (*0-912516-70-4*); pap. 7.95 (*0-912516-69-0*) Grey Fox.

Rofes, Eric E., ed. The Kids' Book of Divorce: By, for & about Kids. LC 82-4004. (Illus.). 144p. (J). (gr. 2 up). 1982. pap. 9.00 (*0-394-71018-5*, Vin) Random.

Rofes, Eric E., ed. see Fayerweather Street School Staff.

Roff, Derek A. The Evolution of Life Histories: Theory & Analysis. LC 92-13507. 528p. 1992. 79.00 (*0-412-02381-4*, A3979, Chapman & Hall); pap. 35.00 (*0-412-02391-1*, A3983, Chapman & Hall) Chapman & Hall.

Roff, Lucinda & Atherton, Charles. Promoting Successful Aging. 283p. 1989. text ed. 19.95 (*0-8304-1167-4*) Nelson-Hall.

Roff, Renee, comp. Directory of American Book Workers. LC 80-52837. 1981. 19.95 (*0-935164-05-7*) Prairie Bk Ctr.

***Roff, Sue R.** Hotspots: The Legacy of Hiroshima & Nagasaki. LC 95-15514. 1995. pap. write for info. (*0-304-33438-3*) Cassell.

— Hotspots: The Legacy of Hiroshima & Nagasaki. LC 95-15514. (Global Issues Ser.). 288p. 1995. 70.00 (*0-304-33437-5*); 70.00 (*0-614-07396-0*) Cassell.

— Overreaching in Paradise: United States Policy in Palau since 1945. LC 90-3608. (Illus.). xii, 244p. (Orig.). (C). 1991. pap. 27.50 (*0-938737-22-8*) Denali Press.

— Timor's Anschluss: Indonesian & Australian Policy in East Timor, 1974-76. (Illus.). 142p. 1992. lib. bdg. 69.95 (*0-7734-9500-2*) E Mellen.

Roff, Sue R., ed. see Eleanor Roosevelt Institute Staff.

Roff, William R. The Origins of Malay Nationalism. (Illus.). 352p. 1995. pap. 24.95 (*967-65-3059-X*) OUP.

Roffel, Brian & Chin, Patrick. Computer Control in the Process Industries. (Illus.). 257p. (C). 1987. text ed. 95.00 (*0-87371-122-X*, TS156, CRC Reprint) Franklin.

***Roffey.** Bathtime. Date not set. pap. 2.99 (*0-517-13360-1*) Random.

— Mealtime. Date not set. pap. 2.99 (*0-517-13361-X*) Random.

— Partytime. (J). write for info. (*0-679-87624-3*) Random.

— Playtime. (J). write for info. (*0-679-87623-5*) Random.

Roffey, C. G. Photopolymerization of Surface Coatings. LC 81-12916. (Wiley-Interscience Publication Ser.). 371p. reprint ed. pap. 105.80 (*0-7837-1880-2*, 2042081) Bks Demand.

Roffey, Maureen. Bathtime. LC 89-18413. (Illus.). 32p. (J). (ps). 1990. reprint ed. pap. 4.95 (*0-689-70808-4*, Aladdin Paperbacks) S&S Childrens.

— I Spy at the Zoo. LC 88-19360. (Illus.). 32p. (J). (ps-2). 1989. reprint ed. pap. 3.95 (*0-689-71227-8*, Aladdin Paperbacks) S&S Childrens.

— Mealtime. LC 89-48006. (Illus.). 32p. (J). (ps). 1990. reprint ed. pap. 4.95 (*0-689-70809-2*, Aladdin Paperbacks) S&S Childrens.

— Quick, Catch Dan! (Illus.). 24p. (J). (ps). 1991. 6.95 (*0-395-57583-4*, Sandpiper) HM.

***Roffey, Maureen, illus.** Clown's Vacation. (Duplo Playbks.). 14p. (J). (ps up). 1995. bds. 7.50 (*0-316-72383-5*) Little.

— Cock-a-Doodle-Doo! (Duplo Playbks.). 14p. (J). (ps up). 1995. bds. 7.50 (*0-316-72384-3*) Little.

— Goldilocks & the Three Bears. (Duplo Fold-Out Playbks.). 10p. (J). (ps up). 1995. 11.95 (*0-316-72385-1*) Little.

— The Grand Old Duke of York. rev. ed. LC 92-21339. 32p. (J). (ps-3). 1993. 13.95 (*1-879085-79-8*) Whsprng Coyote Pr.

— Humpty Dumpty & Other Rhymes. (Slip-Slide Nursery Rhymes Ser.). 6p. (J). (ps). 1994. 5.99 (*0-679-86707-4*) Random Bks Yng Read.

— If I Were Bigger. (Duplo Playbks.). 14p. (J). (ps up). 1995. bds. 7.50 (*0-316-72387-8*) Little.

— Jack & the Beanstalk. (Duplo Fold-Out Playbks.). 10p. (J). (ps up). 1995. 11.95 (*0-316-72388-6*) Little.

— Lucy's Birthday. (Duplo Tab Index Playbks.). 8p. (J). (ps up). 1995. 11.95 (*0-316-72389-4*) Little.

— Miss Muffet & Other Rhymes. (Slip-Slide Nursery Rhymes Ser.). 6p. (J). (ps). 1994. 5.99 (*0-679-86708-2*) Random Bks Yng Read.

— Play with Dan. (Duplo Tab Index Playbks.). 8p. (J). (ps up). 1995. 11.95 (*0-316-72390-8*) Little.

— Play with Me! (Duplo Playbks.). 14p. (J). (ps up). 1995. bds. 7.50 (*0-316-72391-6*) Little.

Roffman, Howard. Understanding the Cold War. LC 75-5251. 198p. (C). 1976. 29.50 (*0-8386-1740-9*) Fairleigh Dickinson.

Roffman, Marvin B. & Schwager, Michael J. Fire Your Broker: Straight Talk on Managing Your Money from the Financial Analyst Who Defied Donald Trump. (Illus.). 224p. 1993. 18.95 (*1-55972-207-X*, Birch Ln Pr) Carol Pub Group.

Roffman, Peter & Purdy, Jim. The Hollywood Social Problem Film: Madness, Despair, & Politics from the Depression to the Fifties. LC 80-8100. 384p. reprint ed. pap. 109.50 (*0-8357-3961-9*, 2056053) Bks Demand.

***Roffman, Randolph S.** Historic Georgetown: A Guide to Walking, Shopping & Dining in Old Georgetown. 70p. 1994. 2.50 (*1-886183-00-7*) HistoriCity.

Roffman, Rosaly, jt. ed. see Walker, Sue B.

Roffmann, Harold. Maintenance Management. 187p. 1988. 39.95 (*0-929442-05-9*) Publicare Pr.

Roffmann, Harold, jt. auth. see Stipanuk, David M.

Rog, Debra J., jt. ed. see Bickman, Leonard.

Rog, James A., jt. ed. see Baker, William J.

Rogacheva. Theory of Piezoelectric Plates & Shells. 1993. write for info. (*0-8493-4459-X*) CRC Pr.

Rogahn, Cinda B. Achievement Through Attitude. 65p. 1988. student ed 15.00 (*0-9616898-1-1*) Phoenix Pr FL.

Rogahn, Kenneth W. Begin with Prayer: Prayers & Devotional Outlines for Church Meetings. 112p. 1985. 7.95 (*0-570-03962-2*, 15-2178) Concordia.

Rogak, Lisa. Cat on My Shoulder. LC 92-31333. 192p. 1993. 17.95 (*0-681-41458-8*) Longmeadow Pr.

— Moving to the Country Once & for All. (Illus.). 180p. (Orig.). 1995. pap. 9.95 (*1-56626-142-2*) Country Rds.

— New England Farm Vacations. LC 93-37245. (Illus.). 120p. (Orig.). 1994. pap. 9.95 (*1-56626-044-2*) Country Rds.

— The Quotable Cat. 144p. 1992. 8.95 (*0-8092-3941-8*) Contemp Bks.

— Steroids: Dangerous Game. (Coping with Modern Issues Ser.). 64p. (J). (gr. 4 up). 1992. lib. bdg. 17.50 (*0-8225-0048-5*, Lerner Publctns) Lerner Group.

— Vermont: Off the Beaten Path. (Illus.). 160p. (Orig.). 1992. pap. 9.95 (*1-56440-055-7*) Globe Pequot.

Rogak, Lisa A. UPS Guide to Owning & Managing a B & B. 250p. 1994. pap. 15.95 (*0-936894-65-2*, 610059-01, Upstart) Dearborn Finan.

— UPS Guide to Owning & Managing an Antiques Business. 250p. 1994. pap. 15.95 (*0-936894-66-0*, 610061-01, Upstart) Dearborn Finan.

***Rogak, Lisa A., ed.** The Cat on My Shoulder. 192p. 1994. pap. 10.00 (*0-380-72337-9*) Avon.

Rogak, Lisa A. & Bangs, David H., Jr. One Hundred Best Retirement Businesses. 304p. (Orig.). 1994. pap. 15.95 (*0-936894-54-7*) Upstart Pub.

Rogak, Lisa A. & Blackert, Virginia R. Latin for Pigs: An Illustrated History from Oedipork Rex to Hog & Das. (Illus.). 96p. 1994. 10.95 (*0-525-93820-6*) NAL-Dutton.

***Rogal, Owen.** Headache Rx: A Doctor's Proven Guide to Lasting Headache Relief. 1995. pap. 9.95 (*0-13-156944-9*) P-H.

Rogal, Samuel J. Calendar of Literary Facts. 2nd ed. 1995. 59.00 (*0-8103-8402-7*) Gale.

— A Chronological Outline of American Literature. LC 86-33472. (Bibliographies & Indexes in American Literature Ser.: No. 8). 460p. 1987. text ed. 69.95 (*0-313-25471-0*, RCE/, Greenwood Pr) Greenwood.

— A Chronological Outline of British Literature. LC 79-8577. 341p. 1980. text ed. 42.95 (*0-313-21477-8*, ROB/, Greenwood Pr) Greenwood.

— The Educational & Evangelical Missions of Mary Emilie Holmes (1850-1906) "Not to Seem, but to Be" LC 94-12361. (Studies in Women & Religion: Vol. 33). (Illus.). 113p. 1994. text ed. 59.95 (*0-7734-9095-7*) E Mellen.

— A General Introduction to Hymnody & Congregational Song. LC 91-16693. (American Theological Library Association Monograph). 336p. 1991. 42.50 (*0-8108-2416-7*) Scarecrow.

— An Index to the Biblical References, Parallels, & Allusions in the Poetry & Prose of John Milton. LC 93-48814. 356p. 1994. 99.95 (*0-7734-2390-7*, Mellen Biblical Pr) E Mellen.

— John Wesley in Ireland, 1747-1789, 2 pts., Pt. 1. LC 92-47035. (Studies in the History of Missions: Vol. 9). (Illus.). 418p. 1993. text ed. 109.95 (*0-7734-9243-7*) E Mellen.

— John Wesley in Ireland, 1747-1789, 2 pts., Pt. 2. LC 92-47035. (Studies in the History of Missions: Vol. 9). (Illus.). 420p. 1993. text ed. 109.95 (*0-7734-9245-3*) E Mellen.

— John Wesley in Wales, 1739-1790: Lions & Lambs. LC 93-30969. (Studies in the History of Missions: Vol. 11). 452p. 1993. text ed. 109.95 (*0-7734-9397-2*) E Mellen.

— John Wesley's London: A Guidebook. LC 87-22038. (Texts & Studies in Religion: Vol. 34). (Illus.). 480p. 1988. lib. bdg. 109.95 (*0-88946-823-0*) E Mellen.

— John Wesley's Mission to Scotland. LC 87-31371. (Studies in the History of Missions: Vol. 2). (Illus.). 1988. lib. bdg. 109.95 (*0-88946-070-1*) E Mellen.

Rogal, Samuel J., comp. The Children's Jubilee: A Bibliographical Survey of Hymnals for Infants, Youth & Sunday Schools Published in Britain & America, 1655-1900. LC 83-1661. (Illus.). xliv, 91p. 1983. text ed. 42.95 (*0-313-23880-4*, RCJ/) Greenwood.

— The Education of the British Literati: A Guide to Their Schools, Colleges, & Universities. LC 92-21163. 432p. 1993. text ed. 109.95 (*0-7734-9232-1*) E Mellen.

— Guide to the Hymns & Tunes of American Methodism. LC 85-27114. (Music Reference Collection Ser.: No. 7). 337p. 1986. text ed. 55.00 (*0-313-25123-1*, RGH/, Greenwood Pr) Greenwood.

— Medicine in Great Britain from the Restoration to the Nineteenth Century, 1660-1800: An Annotated Bibliography. LC 91-39004. (Bibliographies & Indexes in Medical Studies: No. 8). 272p. 1992. text ed. 69.50 (*0-313-28115-7*, RMH, Greenwood Pr) Greenwood.

Rogal, Samuel J., ed. Agriculture in Britain & America, 1660-1820: An Annotated Bibliography of the Eighteenth-Century Literature. LC 94-12323. (Bibliographies & Indexes in World History Ser.: No. 33). 280p. 1994. text ed. 75.00 (*0-313-29352-X*, Greenwood Pr) Greenwood.

— A Calendar of Literary Facts: A Daily Guide to Noteworthy Events in World Literature from 1450 Through 1988. 500p. 1990. 59.00 (*0-8103-2943-3*) Gale.

Rogalin, Elizabeth, ed. see Bacchus, Noel C.

***Rogalla & Harremoes.** Biofilm Reactors. (Water Science & Technology). 548p. 1994. pap. 270.00 (*0-08-042544-5*, Pergamon Pr) Elsevier.

Rogalla, Hanna & Rogalla, Willy. German for Academic Purposes: A Reading Course. 110p. (GER.). 17.50 (*3-468-49880-2*) Langenscheidt.

— Grammar Handbook for Reading German Texts. 208p. pap. 21.95 (*3-468-49881-0*) Langenscheidt.

Rogalla, Willy, jt. auth. see Rogalla, Hanna.

Rogalski, Antoni. New Ternary Alloy Systems for Infrared Detectors. LC 94-10019. 1994. write for info. (*0-8194-1583-9*); pap. write for info. (*0-8194-1582-0*) SPIE.

Rogalski, Antoni, ed. Selected Papers on Semiconductor Infrared Detectors. LC 92-31686. (Milestone Ser.: Vol. 66). 1993. 109.00 (*0-8194-1063-2*); pap. 124.00 (*0-8194-1064-0*) SPIE.

***Rogalski, Antoni, et al.** Infrared Photodetectors. LC 94-48051. 1995. write for info. (*0-8194-1798-X*) SPIE.

Rogalski, Richard J., jt. auth. see Logue, Dennis E.

Rogalski, Ron & Moore, Rich. Bow Down. 1991. 5.25 (*0-685-72879-X*, MB-630); audio 10.98 (*0-685-72880-3*, TA-9132C); audio 60.00 (*0-685-72882-X*, MU-9132C); audio 45.00 (*0-685-72884-6*, MU-9132R); cd-rom 60.00 (*0-685-72883-8*, MU-9132T); 6.00 (*0-685-72881-1*, L-9132C); 8.00 (*0-685-72885-4*, MU-926); 36.00 (*0-685-72886-2*, OR-9132); 5.00 (*0-685-72887-0*, MB-630A) Lillenas.

Rogalski, Ron, jt. auth. see Moore, Rich.

Rogalsky, Yakov, jt. auth. see Clorfene, Chaim.

***Rogan.** Morrissey & Marr. 1991. pap. (*0-7119-3000-7*) Omnibus NY.

Rogan, jt. auth. see Murphy.

Rogan, Arthur. The Street Smart Salesman: Making Opportunities Happen. LC 91-19025. 224p. (Orig.). 1991. pap. 9.95 (*0-89529-487-7*) Avery Pub.

Rogan, Barbara. A Heartbeat Away. LC 92-32023. 1993. 20.00 (*0-688-11582-9*) Morrow.

— A Heartbeat Away. large type ed. LC 93-49832. 1994. 25.95 (*0-7927-1981-6*, Contemp Lrg Print); pap. 24.95 (*0-7927-1980-8*, Contemp Lrg Print) Chivers N Amer.

***Rogan, Eugene.** Village, Steppe & State Vol. 1: The Social Origins of Modern Jordan. 1995. text ed. 59.50 (*1-85043-829-3*, Pub. by I B Tauris UK) St Martin.

Rogan, Johnny. Morrissey & Marr: The Severed Alliance - The Definitive Story of the Smiths. (Illus.). 376p. 1992. pap. 22.95 (*0-7119-1838-4*, OP45525) Omnibus NY.

— Timeless Flight: The Definitive Biography of the Byrds. 3rd rev. ed. (Illus.). 278p. (Orig.). 1991. pap. 19.95 (*1-872747-00-0*, Pub. by Sq One Bks UK) Hallenbook.

Rogan, Tom, et al. Beyond the Wall: Adventures in the North of Arthur's Britain. Shirley, Sam, ed. (Pendragon Roleplaying Ser.). (Illus.). 128p. (Orig.). 1995. pap. 12.95 (*1-56882-026-7*, 2717) Chaosium.

Rogasa, M., et al. Coding Microbiological Data for Computers. (Microbiology Ser.). (Illus.). 310p. 1986. 68.00 (*0-387-96417-7*) Spr-Verlag.

Rogasky, Barbara. The Golem: A Version. LC 94-13040. (Illus.). (J). Date not set. write for info. (*0-8234-0964-3*) Holiday.

— Smoke & Ashes: The Story of the Holocaust. LC 87-28617. (Illus.). 192p. (YA). (gr. 5 up). 1988. 19.95 (*0-8234-0697-0*); pap. 9.95 (*0-8234-0878-7*) Holiday.

R

An Asterisk (*) at the beginning of an entry indicates that the title is appearing in BIP for the first time.

Rogawski, Jonathan D. Automorphic Representations of Unitary Groups in Three Variables. (Annals of Mathematics Studies: No. 123). 288p. 1990. text ed. 60.00 (*0-691-08586-2*); pap. text ed. 24.95x (*0-691-08587-0*) Princeton U Pr.

Rogawski, Jonathan D., ed. see Lubotzky, Alexander.

Rogawski, Michael A. & Barker, Jeffrey L., eds. Neurotransmitter Actions in the Vertebrate Nervous System. 536p. 1985. 110.00 (*0-306-41991-2*, Plenum Pr) Plenum.

Rogel, Anne M. Songs of Nature. (Illus.). 109p. (Orig.). 1995. pap. 10.00 (*0-9645205-0-8*) Dandelion Drms. SONGS OF NATURE is a philosophical journal written by a poet with a doctorate in nutritional science. Presented with clarity of style, the 88 poems are filled with vivid & powerful images. They speak of friendship & love, dreams & spirituality, maturation & discovery. They convey an earthy wisdom that looks to nature for answers about the human condition. The book is illustrated with simple line drawings by the author & a cover photograph taken on Heron Island in the Great Barrier Reef. It is a work of art which can be appreciated by young & old - by poetry lovers & by people who never thought they liked poetry. Bob Hollibaugh, a former marine & a retired steel worker, writes, "You did something that no other poet has ever done. You brought back my interest in nature. You reminded me of things that I had forgotten & awoke something in my inner self that I forgot was there." To order, write or call Anne M. Rogel, Dandelion Dreams, P.O. Box 55811, Hayward, CA 94545- 0811. (510) 888-1499.** ***Publisher Provided Annotation.

Rogelberg, David, ed. see Becker, Wayne M. & Deamer, David W.

Roger. Life from Within: Prayers by Brother Roger of Taize. 32p. (Orig.). 1990. pap. 5.99 (*0-664-25162-5*) Westminster John Knox.

Roger, A., jt. auth. see Haatley, J. S.

Roger, Alan. Blue Tortoise. LC 90-9833. (Little Giants Ser.). (Illus.). 16p. (J). (ps-1). 1990. lib. bdg. 14.60 (*0-8368-0404-X*) Gareth Stevens Inc.

— Bonsai. rev. ed. (Wisley Handbooks Ser.). (Illus.). 64p. (Orig.). 1990. pap. 5.95 (*0-304-32001-3*, Pub. by Cassell UK) Sterling.

— Teaching Adults. 224p. 1986. pap. 24.00 (*0-335-15234-1*, Open Univ Pr) Taylor & Francis.

Roger, Cynthia A. Why Aren't There Any Dinosaurs Here at the Zoo? (J). 1993. 7.95 (*0-533-10582-X*) Vantage.

Roger, Derek, jt. ed. see Bull, Peter.

Roger, E. H., jt. auth. see Lambert, P. M.

Roger, Emma, jt. auth. see Roger, Paul.

Roger, F. H., et al, eds. Medical Informatics Europe, 1984: Proceedings. (Lecture Notes in Medical Informatics Ser.: Vol. 24). xxvii, 778p. 1984. pap. 74.00 (*0-387-13374-7*) Spr-Verlag.

Roger-France, F. & Santucci, G., eds. Perspectives of Information Processing in Medical Application: Strategic Issues, Requirements & Options for the European Community. (Health Systems Research Ser.). 320p. 1991. 58.00 (*0-387-53856-9*) Spr-Verlag.

***Roger-France, F., et al.** Case-Based Telematic Systems: Towards Equity in Health Care. LC 94-77522. (Studies in Health Technology & Informatics: Vol. 14). 207p. 1994. 93.00 (*90-5199-182-7*) IOS Press.

Roger, Gertrude M. Lady Rancher. (Illus.). 182p. pap. 12.95 (*0-88839-099-8*) Hancock House.

Roger, J. Identity in Adolescence: The Balance Between Self & Other. (Adolescence & Society Ser.). 200p. 1989. 47.50 (*0-415-01087-X*, A3362); pap. 15.95 (*0-415-01088-8*, A3366) Routledge.

Roger, John. Blessings of Light. 1981. pap. 5.00 (*0-914829-02-5*, 949-1) Mandeville LA.

— Loving Each Day. 1989. 10.00 (*0-914829-26-2*) Mandeville LA.

— The Spiritual Promise. rev. ed. 60p. 1989. lib. bdg. 7.00 (*0-914829-22-X*) Mandeville LA.

***Roger-Marx, C.** Vuillard: Interiors. (Rhythm & Color Two Ser.). 76p. (FRE.). 1948. pap. write for info. (*0-7859-5250-0*) Fr & Eur.

Roger-Marx, Claude. Vuillard, His Life & Work. LC 75-41229. reprint ed. 25.00 (*0-404-14718-6*) AMS Pr.

— Vuillard's Graphic Work: A Catalogue Raisonne. (Illus.). 192p. 1990. 150.00 (*1-55660-123-9*) A Wofsy Fine Arts.

Roger, Maurice. L' Enseignement des Lettres Classiques d'Ausone a Alcuin. xvi, 459p. 1968. reprint ed. write for info. (*0-318-71277-6*, Pub. by Georg Olms GW) Lubrecht & Cramer.

— L' Enseignement Des Lettres Classiques d'Ausone A Alcuin. xvi, 459p. 1968. reprint ed. write for info. (*0-318-71404-3*, Pub. by Georg Olms GW) Lubrecht & Cramer.

Roger of Taize, jt. auth. see Mother Teresa of Calcutta.

Roger of Wendover. Flowers of History, 2 Vols, Set. Giles, J. A., tr. LC 68-55556. (Bohn's Antiquarian Library). reprint ed. 95.00 (*0-404-50070-6*) AMS Pr.

***Roger, Paul & Roger, Emma.** Quacky Duck. (Illus.). (J). (ps-2). 1995. 14.95 (*0-316-37647-7*) Little.

Roger, Pierre A., jt. auth. see Pingali, Prabhu L.

Roger, R. S. & Dewdney, P. E., eds. Regions of Recent Star Formation. 1982. lib. bdg. 131.50 (*90-277-1383-9*) Kluwer Ac.

Roger, R. S. & Landecker, T. L., eds. The Interaction of Supernova Remnants with the Interstellar Medium: Colloquium One Hundred One of the International Astronomical Union. 560p. 1988. 79.95 (*0-521-35062-X*) Cambridge U Pr.

***Roger, Sherry A.** You Are What You Ate. 303p. 1995. pap. text ed. 17.95 (*0-9618821-8-2*) Prestige NY.

Rogers. The Anesthesia Handbook. 1993. 27.95 (*0-8016-7997-4*) Mosby Yr Bk.

— Current Practice in Anesthesiology. 2nd ed. 536p. (C). 1991. 82.00 (*1-55664-269-5*) Mosby Yr Bk.

— Essentials of Optoelectronics. 1995. pap. (*0-412-40890-2*) Chapman & Hall.

— Fission Product & Transport Processes in Reactor Accidents. 1990. 172.00 (*0-89116-876-1*) Hemisp Pub.

— Geriatric Nursing Care Plans. 336p. 1990. 26.95 (*0-8016-5210-3*) Mosby Yr Bk.

— Grammar for Biblical Hebrew Handbook. 1995. pap. (*0-687-01155-8*) Abingdon.

— Happy Trails: Our Life Story. 1995. pap. 12.00 (*0-684-80436-0*, Fireside) S&S Trade.

— Hidden Hearts. 1989. mass mkt. 5.50 (*0-671-65880-8*) PB.

— Making Wreaths. 1994. pap. 9.95 (*1-56799-026-6*, Friedman-Fairfax) M Friedman Pub Grp Inc.

— Nurses At Risk. (Illus.). 186p. 1988. pap. text ed. 29.95 (*0-433-00040-6*) Buttrwrth-Heinemann.

— Poverty Chastity & Change. Date not set. 27.95 (*0-8057-9136-1*, Twayne) Macmillan.

— Presbyterian Creeds Supplement. 1991. pap. 1.99 (*0-664-25311-3*) Westminster John Knox.

— Site Guides: Costa Rica: A Guide to the Best Birding Locations. (Illus.). 96p. 1994. pap. 14.50 (*0-9637765-2-5*) Cinclus Pubns.

— Site Guides: la Ruta Maya: A Guide to the Best Birding Locations in the Yucatan, Belize, Guatemala, Honduras & El Salvador. (Illus.). 60p. 1994. pap. 8.95 (*0-9637765-3-3*) Cinclus Pubns.

— Year Book of Critical Care Medicine, 1991. 356p. 1991. 54.95 (*0-8151-7252-4*, Yr Bk Med Pubs) Mosby Yr Bk.

— Year Book of Critical Care Medicine, 1993. 400p. 1993. 63.95 (*0-8151-7254-0*, Yr Bk Med Pubs) Mosby Yr Bk.

— Year Book of Critical Care Medicine, 1994. 348p. 1994. 63.95 (*0-8151-7255-9*, Yr Bk Med Pubs) Mosby Yr Bk.

— Year Book of Critical Care Medicine, 1995. 348p. 1995. 63.95 (*0-8151-7256-7*, Yr Bk Med Pubs) Mosby Yr Bk.

— Year Book of Critical Care Medicine, 1996. 348p. 1996. 63.95 (*0-8151-7257-5*, Yr Bk Med Pubs) Mosby Yr Bk.

— Year Book of Medicine, 1991. 858p. 1991. 57.95 (*0-8151-7264-8*, Yr Bk Med Pubs) Mosby Yr Bk.

— Year Book of Medicine, 1993. 805p. 1993. 59.95 (*0-8151-7266-4*, Yr Bk Med Pubs) Mosby Yr Bk.

— Year Book of Medicine, 1994. 805p. 1994. 59.95 (*0-8151-7267-2*, Yr Bk Med Pubs) Mosby Yr Bk.

— Year Book of Medicine, 1995. 805p. 1995. 59.95 (*0-8151-7268-0*, Yr Bk Med Pubs) Mosby Yr Bk.

— Year Book of Medicine, 1996. 805p. 1996. 59.95 (*0-8151-7269-9*, Yr Bk Med Pubs) Mosby Yr Bk.

— Yearbook of Critical Care Medicine, 1990. 360p. 1990. 54.95 (*0-8151-7251-6*, Yr Bk Med Pubs) Mosby Yr Bk.

— Yearbook of Critical Care Medicine, 1992. 400p. 1992. 59.95 (*0-8151-7253-2*) Mosby Yr Bk.

— Yearbook of Medicine, 1992. 804p. 1992. 59.95 (*0-8151-7265-6*) Mosby Yr Bk.

Rogers & McMillin. Reducing Depression. (Runs In Your Family Ser.: No. 7). 1993. mass mkt. 4.99 (*0-553-56382-3*) Bantam.

Rogers & Salem. Student's Guide to Mediation & the Law. 1987. write for info. (*0-8205-0401-7*, 675); teacher ed write for info. (*0-8205-0402-5*) Bender.

Rogers & Wat. German Through Conversational Patterns. 3rd ed. 1981. student ed, pap. 29.95 (*0-8384-3602-1*) Heinle & Heinle.

— German Through Conversational Patterns. 3rd ed. 1981. text ed. 37.95 (*0-8384-3598-X*) Heinle & Heinle.

Rogers, jt. auth. see Andersen.

Rogers, jt. auth. see Coleman.

Rogers, jt. auth. see Palmanteer.

Rogers, jt. auth. see Thurman.

***Rogers & Chuvala Staff.** Killer Dbase for Windows. 1994. disk, pap. 49.99 (*1-56529-923-X*) Que.

Rogers & Manson Staff. One Hundred Turn-of-the-Century Brick Bungalows with Floor Plans. LC 94-6540. (Illus.). 128p. 1994. reprint ed. pap. 8.95 (*0-486-28119-1*) Dover.

Rogers, A. Southwell Minster after the Civil Wars. (C). 1974. text ed. 40.00 (*0-685-22172-5*, Pub. by Univ Nottingham UK) St Mut.

— The Spirit & the Form. 159p. (C). 1976. text ed. 60.00 (*0-685-22165-2*, Pub. by Univ Nottingham UK) St Mut.

— The Spirit & the Form Essays in Adult Education in Honour of Professor Harold Wiltshire. (C). 1976. 39.00 (*0-902031-38-4*, Pub. by Univ Nottingham UK) St Mut.

Rogers, A. & Howe, P. Supermanifolds: Theory & Applications. 300p. 1995. text ed. 53.00 (*981-02-1228-3*) World Scientific Pub.

Rogers, A., tr. see Beveridge, Henry.

Rogers, A., et al, eds. Innovation in Process Energy Utilization. (European Federation of Chemical Engineering Ser.). 412p. 1988. 136.00 (*0-89116-844-3*) Hemisp Pub.

Rogers, A. C., jt. auth. see Cohen, Leon J.

Rogers, A. G., jt. ed. see Eden, Frederick M.

Rogers, A. J., ed. see Zhilin, V. G.

Rogers, A. K. English & American Philosophy Since 1800, a Critical Survey. 1922. 29.00 (*0-527-76200-8*) Periodicals Srv.

Rogers, A. M., et al. Earthquake Hazards in the Pacific Northwest: An Overview. (Illus.). 74p. (Orig.). (C). 1994. pap. text ed. 60.00 (*0-7881-0437-3*) Diane Pub.

Rogers, A. P., jt. auth. see Biggs, A. K.

Rogers, A. R. & McChesney, Kathryn. The Library in Society. LC 85-15440. (Library Science Text Ser.). 1984. lib. bdg. 32.00 (*0-87287-379-X*); pap. text ed. 23.50 (*0-87287-398-6*) Libs Unl.

Rogers, A. W. Textbook of Anatomy. (Illus.). 779p. (Orig.). 1992. pap. text ed. 45.95 (*0-443-02672-6*) Churchill.

Rogers, Adam. The Earth Summit: A Planetary Reckoning: An Analysis of Events at the 1992 United Nations Conference on Environment & Development. (Illus.). 352p. (Orig.). (C). 1993. write for info. (*1-881294-93-5*) Global View.

— The Intrepid Traveler: Getting the Ultimate Experience for Your Travel Dollars. 192p. 1992. pap. 14.95 (*1-881294-07-2*) Global View.

— The Intrepid Traveler: Getting the Ultimate Experience for Your Travel Dollars. 2nd rev. ed. (Illus.). 224p. 1993. pap. 14.95 (*1-881294-15-3*) Global View.

***Rogers, Adrian.** The Power of His Presence. LC 94-24968. 192p. 1995. 14.99 (*0-89107-841-X*) Crossway Bks.

Rogers, Alan. Adults Learning for Development. 256p. 1992. text ed. 60.00 (*0-304-32523-6*); pap. text ed. 19.95 (*0-304-32420-5*) Cassell.

— Approaches to Local History. 2nd ed. LC 76-54265. 283p. reprint ed. pap. 80.70 (*0-8357-5695-5*, 2025253) Bks Demand.

— Green Bear. LC 90-9831. (Little Giants Ser.). (Illus.). (J). (ps). 1990. lib. bdg. 14.60 (*0-8368-0406-6*) Gareth Stevens Inc.

— Little Giants, 4 vols., Set. (Illus.). 64p. (J). (ps-1). 1990. lib. bdg. 58.40 (*0-8368-0434-1*) Gareth Stevens Inc.

— Red Rhino. LC 90-9830. (Little Giants Ser.). (Illus.). 16p. (J). (ps-1). 1990. lib. bdg. 14.60 (*0-8368-0403-1*) Gareth Stevens Inc.

— Yellow Hippo. LC 90-9834. (Little Giants Ser.). (Illus.). 16p. (J). (ps-1). 1990. lib. bdg. 14.60 (*0-8368-0405-8*) Gareth Stevens Inc.

Rogers, Alan, jt. auth. see Rogers, Joyce.

Rogers, Alexis. Cost of Love. 160p. (Orig.). 1990. pap. 8.95 (*0-938743-10-4*) Lavender CT.

Rogers, Alisdair, ed. Peoples & Cultures. (Illustrated Encyclopedia of World Geography Ser.: Vol. 7). (Illus.). 256p. 1992. 45.00 (*0-19-520928-1*) OUP.

Rogers, Alisdair, jt. ed. see Keith, Michael.

***Rogers, Alisdair, et al, eds.** The Urban Context: Ethnicity, Social Networks, & Situational Analysis. LC 94-25313. (Explorations in Anthropology Ser.). (Illus.). 320p. 1995. 45.95 (*0-85496-317-0*); pap. 19.95 (*1-85973-072-8*) Berg Pubs.

Rogers, Alison. Luke Has Asthma, Too. LC 87-40053. (Illus.). 32p. (Orig.). (J). (ps-2). 1987. pap. 6.95 (*0-914525-06-9*) Waterfront Bks.

***Rogers, Allan, et al.** Peonies. LC 94-48535. (Illus.). 220p. 1995. write for info. (*0-88192-317-6*) Timber.

Rogers, Alvin L., jt. auth. see Beneke, Everette S.

***Rogers, Amy.** Red Pepper Fudge & Blue Ribbon Biscuits: Favorite Recipes & Cooking Stories from North Carolina State Fair Winners. (Illus.). 160p. (Orig.). 1995. pap. 13.95 (*1-878086-43-X*) Down Home NC.

***Rogers, Andrei, ed.** Elderly Migration & Population Redistribution: A Comparative Study. 1993. text ed. 74.95 (*0-471-94766-0*) Wiley.

Rogers, Andrei & Willekens, Frans. Molecular Astrophysics: Migration & Settlement. 1985. lib. bdg. 129.50 (*90-277-2119-X*) Kluwer Ac.

Rogers, Andrei, jt. ed. see Land, Kenneth C.

Rogers, Andrei, et al. Elderly Migration & Population Redistribution: A Comparative Perspective. Frey, William H., ed. LC 92-24769. 204p. 1992. text ed. 64.95 (*0-470-21934-3*) Halsted Pr.

Rogers, Andy W., ed. Cells & Tissues. 1983. pap. text ed. 43.00 (*0-12-593120-4*) Acad Pr.

Rogers, Ann, jt. auth. see Rogers, Minor.

Rogers, Anne, jt. auth. see Pilgrim, David.

Rogers, Annie, jt. ed. see Shibles, Loana.

***Rogers, Annie G.** The Jerusalem Calender 1996. 1995. 14.95 (*0-670-86362-9*, Penguin Bks) Viking Penguin.

— A Shining Affliction. LC 94-45171. 1995. 23.95 (*0-670-85727-0*, Viking) Viking Penguin.

Rogers, Annie G., et al, eds. Women, Girls, & Psychotherapy: Reframing Resistance. LC 91-20845. (Women & Therapy Ser.). 243p. 1991. lib. bdg. 39.95 (*1-56024-196-9*) Haworth Pr.

— Women, Girls & Psychotherapy: Reframing Resistance. LC 91-20845. (Women & Therapy Ser.). 243p. 1991. lib. bdg. 14.95 (*1-56023-012-6*) Haworth Pr.

***Rogers, Anthony, et al.** Flashpoint! At the Front Line of Today's Wars. (Illus.). 160p. 1995. 24.95 (*1-85409-247-2*) Sterling.

***Rogers, April R.** My Teen Years. (YA). (gr. 6-12). 1993. spiral bd. 12.95 (*0-9643763-1-8*) Spec Moments.

— My Teen Years Memory Journal. (YA). (gr. 6-12). 1995. spiral bd. 12.95 (*0-9643763-2-6*) Spec Moments.

Rogers, Arthur K. Morals in Review. LC 72-126697. reprint ed. 31.50 (*0-404-05379-3*) AMS Pr.

Rogers, Arvey I., jt. ed. see Barkin, Jamie S.

Rogers, Austin F. & Staples, Lloyd. Introduction to the Study of Minerals. 3rd ed. LC 75-41235. reprint ed. 47.50 (*0-404-14699-6*) AMS Pr.

Rogers, B. Nature of Metals. 1964. 142.00 (*0-08-011856-9*, Pub. by Pergamon Repr UK) Franklin.

Rogers, B. G., jt. auth. see Jong, I. C.

Rogers, Barbara. Domestication of Women: Discrimination in Developing Societies. 1981. pap. 15.95 (*0-422-77630-0*, NO.6529, Pub. by Tavistock UK) Routledge Chapman & Hall.

— Drying Flowers. 1994. pap. 9.95 (*1-56799-025-8*, Friedman-Fairfax) M Friedman Pub Grp Inc.

— Giant Pandas. 1994. pap. 11.95 (*1-56799-070-3*, Friedman-Fairfax) M Friedman Pub Grp Inc.

— God Rescues His People Activity Book. 72p. (Orig.). (J). (ps-1). 1983. pap. 3.00 (*0-8361-3338-2*) Herald Pr.

— God's Chosen King Activity Book. 88p. (Orig.). (J). (ps-1). 1984. pap. 3.00 (*0-8361-3370-6*) Herald Pr.

— White Wealth & Black Poverty: American Investments in Southern Africa. LC 75-35353. (Studies in Human Rights: No. 2). 288p. 1976. text ed. 55.00 (*0-8371-8277-8*, RWW/, Greenwood Pr) Greenwood.

***Rogers, Barbara & Rogers, Stillman.** Natural Wonders of Vermont: A Guide to Parks, Preserves & Wild Places. (Natural Wonders Ser.). (Illus.). 200p. (Orig.). 1995. pap. 12.95 (*1-56626-145-7*) Country Rds.

Rogers, Barbara, jt. tr. see Scholz, Bernard W.

Rogers, Barbara R. Safari. 1991. 17.99 (*0-517-69341-0*) Random Hse Value.

— South Africa. LC 89-43188. (Children of the World Ser.). (Illus.). 64p. (J). (gr. 5-6). 1991. lib. bdg. 21.26 (*0-8368-0247-0*) Gareth Stevens Inc.

— Zambia. LC 89-43178. (Children of the World Ser.). (Illus.). 64p. (J). (gr. 5-6). 1991. lib. bdg. 21.26 (*0-8368-0257-8*) Gareth Stevens Inc.

Rogers, Barbara R. & Rogers, Stillman. Exploring Europe by Boat: A Practical Guide to Water Travel in Europe. LC 93-14061. (Voyager Book Ser.). (Illus.). 320p. (Orig.). 1994. pap. 12.95 (*1-56440-252-5*) Globe Pequot.

— New Hampshire: Off the Beaten Path: A Guide to Unique Places. 2nd ed. LC 94-37251. (Off the Beaten Path Ser.). 160p. (Orig.). 1995. pap. 9.95 (*1-56440-627-X*) Globe Pequot.

Rogers, Bernard. Art of Orchestration: Principles of Tone Color in Modern Scoring. LC 73-97353. 198p. 1970. reprint ed. text ed. 49.75 (*0-8371-2969-9*, ROAO, Greenwood Pr) Greenwood.

Rogers, Bertha. Sleeper, You Wake: Poems. Schultz, Patricia, ed. LC 91-29832. (Poetry Ser.: Vol. 17). (Illus.). 84p. 1991. pap. 12.95 (*0-7734-9669-6*) E Mellen.

***Rogers, Bertha, ed.** Speaking the Words Anthology. 48p. 1994. pap. 5.00 (*0-9646844-0-3*) Bright Hill.

— The Word Thursdays Anthology of Poetry & Fiction. 198p. 1995. pap. 12.95 (*0-9646844-1-1*) Bright Hill.

Rogers, Betty. Will Rogers. (Illus.). 312p. (YA). (gr. 8 up). 1982. pap. 13.95 (*0-8061-1600-5*) U of Okla Pr.

Rogers, Betty P., et al. In the Company of Their Peers: A Geriatric Peer Counselor Training Manual. (Illus.). 415p. (Orig.). 1993. 19.95 (*0-9632698-2-8*) Veda Vangarde.

Rogers, Bettye. Prairie Dog Town. LC 93-13357. (Smithsonian Wild Heritage Collection). (Illus.). 32p. (J). (gr. k-3). 1993. 11.95 (*1-56899-005-7*); digital audio 16.95 (*1-56899-004-9*); digital audio 39.95 (*1-56899-002-2*); digital audio 25.95 (*1-56899-003-0*); digital audio write for info. (*1-56899-006-5*) Soundprints.

— Prairie Dog Town. (Smithsonian Wild Heritage Collection). (Illus.). 32p. (J). (gr. k-3). 1995. pap. 4.95 (*1-56899-201-7*) Soundprints.

— Prairie Dog Town. (Smithsonian Wild Heritage Collection). (Illus.). 32p. (J). (gr. k-3). 1995. pap. 14.95 (*1-56899-207-6*) Soundprints.

Rogers, Bill. You Know the Fair Rule. (C). 1990. 75.00 (*0-86431-068-4*, Pub. by Aust Council Educ Res AT) St Mut.

Rogers, Billi M., jt. ed. see Sewell, Ernestine.

Rogers, Bob & Dunn, Ralph. Non-Fiction Poems & by the Blood: A Chapbook Duet. (Illus.). 40p. 1985. pap. 5.00 (*0-929170-07-5*) Paper Plant.

Rogers, Bonnie. Occupational Health Nursing: Concepts & Practice. LC 93-48841. 1994. text ed. 51.50 (*0-7216-7588-3*) Saunders.

Rogers, Bruce. Centaur Types. (Illus.). 90p. 1948. 50.00 (*1-55753-052-1*) Purdue U Pr.

— Complete Guide to TOEFL. 1993. cd-rom 22.00 (*0-8384-5093-8*) Heinle & Heinle.

— Complete Guide to TOEFL. 1993. cd-rom, text ed. 23.95 (*0-8384-4225-0*); audio, text ed. 22.95 (*0-8384-4226-9*); pap. 20.95 (*0-8384-3415-0*); teacher ed, pap. 5.95 (*0-8384-4134-3*); audio 21.00 (*0-8384-4133-5*) Heinle & Heinle.

— Complete Guide to TOEFL: Intermediate to Advanced. 1993. pap. 28.95 (*0-8384-4227-7*) Heinle & Heinle.

— Complete Guide to TOEFL: Practice Tests. (College ESL Ser.). 1994. pap. 15.95 (*0-8384-4279-X*) Heinle & Heinle.

— Paragraphs on Printing. LC 79-50699. (Illus.). 1980. reprint ed. pap. 6.95 (*0-486-23817-2*) Dover.

— PI: A Hodge-Podge of the Letters, Papers, & Addresses Written During the Last Sixty Years. LC 79-167407. (Essay Index Reprint Ser.). 1977. reprint ed. 20.95 (*0-8369-2669-2*) Ayer.

Rogers, Bruce H. Tales & Declarations. (Dog River Review Poetry Ser.: No. 9). 32p. (Orig.). (YA). (gr. 10 up). 1991. pap. 4.00 (*0-916155-13-7*) Trout Creek.

Rogers, C., jt. auth. see Gibson, J.

Rogers, C. A. & Ames, William F., eds. Nonlinear Boundary Value Problems in Science & Engineering. (Mathematics in Science & Engineering Ser.: Vol. 183). 417p. 1989. text ed. 104.00 (*0-12-593110-7*) Acad Pr.

Rogers, C. A. & Moodie, T. B. Wave Phenomena: Modern Theory & Applications. (Mathematical Studies: Vol. 97). 1984. 102.75 (*0-444-87586-7*, North Holland) Elsevier.

Rogers, C. A. & Rogers, R. C. Recent Advances in Adaptive & Sensory Materials & Their Applications. LC 92-80289. 850p. 1992. text ed. 145.00 (*0-87762-947-1*) Technomic.

R

An Asterisk (*) at the beginning of an entry indicates that the title is appearing in BIP for the first time.

Rogers, C. A. & Shadwick, William F. Backlund Transformations & Their Applications. LC 81-22783. (Mathematics in Science & Engineering Ser.). 1982. text ed. 106.00 (*0-12-592850-5*) Acad Pr.

Rogers, C. A., et al, eds. Analytic Sets. LC 80-40647. (London Mathematical Society Symposia Ser.). 1981. text ed. 154.00 (*0-12-593150-6*) Acad Pr.

Rogers, C. Clark. The Guest Log. (Illus.). 98p. (Orig.). 1988. pap. 13.25 (*1-878797-07-7*) C Plath North Amer.

Rogers, C. E., ed. see American Chemical Society Symposium on Permselective Membranes Staff.

Rogers, C. M. Linaceae. LC 84-14891. (North American Flora Ser.: No. 2, Pt. 12). (Illus.). 58p. 1984. 10.75 (*0-89327-260-4*) NY Botanical.

Rogers, C. Paul, III, jt. auth. see Andersen, William R.

Rogers, C. Stewart & McCue, Jack D., eds. Managing Chronic Disease. 456p. 1987. pap. 38.95 (*0-87489-391-7*) Med Economics.

Rogers, Carl & Skinner, B. F. A Dialogue on the Control of Human Behavior. Gladstein, Gerald, ed. 30p. 1976. audio 49.50 (*0-88432-028-6*, S29244) Audio-Forum.

Rogers, Carl R. Client Centered Therapy. LC 51-9139. (C). 1951. pap. 33.96 (*0-395-05322-6*) HM.

— Measuring Personality Adjustment in Children Nine to Thirteen Years of Age. LC 76-177202. (Columbia University. Teachers College. Contributions to Education Ser.: No. 458). reprint ed. 37.50 (*0-404-55458-X*) AMS Pr.

— On Becoming a Person. 1972. pap. 10.95 (*0-395-08409-1*) HM.

— The Therapeutic Relationship & Its Impact. LC 76-14790. 625p. 1976. reprint ed. text ed. 62.50 (*0-8371-8358-8*, ROTR, Greenwood Pr) Greenwood.

— Therapist's View of Personal Goals. LC 60-11607. (Orig.). 1960. pap. 3.00 (*0-87574-108-8*) Pendle Hill.

— A Way of Being. LC 80-82291. 288p. 1980. pap. 10.95 (*0-395-30067-3*) HM.

Rogers, Carl R. & Freiberg, H. Jerome. Freedom to Learn. 3rd rev. ed. LC 93-34791. (Illus.). 352p. (C). 1994. pap. write for info. (*0-02-403121-6*, Merrill Pub Co) Macmillan.

***Rogers, Carleton.** I Remember: Memories from My Ministry. LC 94-79190. (Illus.). 134p. 1994. 12.95 (*0-916445-41-0*) Crossroads Comm.

Rogers, Carol & Ulsafer-Von Lanen, Jane, eds. Nursing Interventions in Depression. 272p. 1985. text ed. 62.95 (*0-8089-1710-2*, 793574, Grune) Saunders.

Rogers, Carol, et al, comps. Directory of European Anthropologists in North America. 1987. 6.00 (*0-913167-20-7*) Am Anthro Assn.

Rogers, Carol A. Just Picture This: My Own Photo Album. (Illus.). 10p. (J). 1993. vinyl bd. 24.95 (*0-9635899-0-3*) New Vision VA.

Rogers, Carol L., jt. ed. see Friedman, Sharon M.

Rogers, Carole, ed. see Westport Young Woman's League Staff.

***Rogers, Cathy, ed.** Malibu's Cooking Again. (Illus.). 126p. (Orig.). 1995. pap. 19.95 (*0-9644695-0-2*) Image Maker Pub.

Rogers, Charles. Book of Robert Burns, 3 Vols, Set. LC 78-144470. reprint ed. 155.00 (*0-404-08530-X*) AMS Pr.

— Colt: Genealogical Memoirs of the Families of Colt & Coutts. 59p. 1992. reprint ed. pap. 12.00 (*0-8328-2647-2*) Higginson Bk Co.

— Knox: Genealogical Memoirs of John Knox, & of the Family of Knox. (Illus.). 184p. 1994. reprint ed. lib. bdg. 38.00 (*0-8328-4027-0*); reprint ed. pap. 28.00 (*0-8328-4028-9*) Higginson Bk Co.

Rogers, Charles B. Art Observations. (Illus.). 64p. 1980. pap. 5.95 (*0-686-64396-8*) Rogers Hse Mus.

— Country Neighbor. (Illus.). (Orig.). 1977. pap. 1.49 (*0-685-77026-5*) Rogers Hse Mus.

Rogers, Charles E. & Irvine, Jerry. Model Rocket Computer Programs: Malewicki Closed-Form Altitude, Coefficient of Drag & Center of Pressure. 1983. 39.95 (*0-912468-12-2*) CA Rocketry.

— Near-Orbital Rocket: Multi-Stage Capable Altitude Prediction, Drag, Center of Pressure, Plotting Ogive Nose Cones, Trajectory, Reentry. 60p. 1983. 99.95 (*0-912468-14-9*) CA Rocketry.

— Sub & Supersonic Experimental Rocket Computer Programs: Fourth Order Range-Kutta, Altitude Prediction, Drag , Center of Pressure. 50p. 1983. 49.95 (*0-912468-13-0*) CA Rocketry.

Rogers, Chester B., jt. auth. see Renstrom, Peter G.

Rogers, Chris. Haynes Honda G L-1100 Goldwing Owners Workshop Manual, No. 669: 1979 Thru 1981. 180p. 1982. pap. 16.95 (*0-85696-669-X*) Haynes Pubns.

— Haynes Honda XL-XR 80, 100, 125, 185 & 200 Owners' Workshop Manual, No. M566: 1978-1987. 16.95 (*1-85010-347-X*) Haynes Pubns.

— Haynes Yamaha XV750, 920 & TR1 V-Twins Owners Workshop Manual, No. M802: '81-'85. pap. 16.95 (*1-85010-697-5*) Haynes Pubns.

Rogers, Chris & Shoemark, Pete. Haynes Suzuki GS-GSX 250, 400 & 450 Twins Owners Workshop Manual, M736: '79-'85. pap. 16.95 (*1-85010-253-8*) Haynes Pubns.

Rogers, Chris, jt. auth. see Clew, Jeff.

Rogers, Chris, jt. auth. see Darlington, Mansur.

Rogers, Chris, jt. auth. see Miller, Bert.

Rogers, Chuck, jt. auth. see Irvine, Jerry.

***Rogers, Cindy.** A Family for Casey. Stortz, Diane, ed. LC 94-67877. (Really Reading! Bks.). (Illus.). 48p. (Orig.). (J). (gr. k-2). 1995. pap. 4.49 (*0-614-00533-7*, 24-03977) Standard Pub.

Rogers, Cleon L. Topical Josephus. 1992. 18.99 (*0-310-57440-4*) Zondervan.

Rogers, Cleon L., jt. auth. see Rienecker, Fritz.

***Rogers, Clifford J., ed.** Military Revolution Debate. (History & Warfare Ser.). 1995. text ed. 65.00 (*0-8133-2053-4*) Westview.

— Military Revolution Debate. (History & Warfare Ser.). (C). 1995. pap. text ed. 24.95 (*0-8133-2054-2*) Westview.

Rogers, Colin D. Money, Interest & Capital: A Study in the Foundations of Monetary Theory. (Modern Cambridge Economics Ser.). (Illus.). 320p. (C). 1989. pap. 21.95 (*0-521-35956-2*) Cambridge U Pr.

— The Surname Detective: Investigating Surname Distribution in England, 1086-Present Day. LC 94-24441. 1995. text ed. write for info. (*0-7190-4047-7*, Pub. by Manchester Univ Pr UK); text ed. write for info. (*0-7190-4048-5*, Pub. by Manchester Univ Pr UK) St Martin.

— Tracing Your English Ancestors: A Manual for Analysing & Solving Genealogical Problems in England & Wales, 1538 to the Present Day. 196p. 1989. text ed. 22.95 (*0-7190-3172-9*, Pub. by Manchester Univ Pr UK) St Martin.

Rogers, Colin D. & Kutnick, Peter, eds. The Social Psychology of the Primary School. 267p. 1991. 55.00 (*0-415-02400-5*, A4352) Routledge.

Rogers, Colin D. & Smith, John. Local Family History in England, 1538-1914. LC 91-17939. (Illus.). 200p. 1992. text ed. 16.95 (*0-7190-3201-6*, Pub. by Manchester Univ Pr UK) St Martin.

Rogers, Colin D., jt. ed. see Ames, William F.

Rogers, Constance, jt. auth. see Rogers, David J.

Rogers-Cordon, Sue, jt. auth. see MacDonald, Marion.

Rogers, Cornish R., jt. ed. see Jeter, Joseph R., Jr.

Rogers, Cosby S. & Sawyers, Janet K. Play in the Lives of Children. LC 87-62314. 135p. 1988. pap. 6.00 (*0-935989-09-9*, NAEYC #301) Natl Assn Child Ed.

Rogers, Cosby S., jt. auth. see Sawyers, Janet K.

Rogers, Craig A. Smart Materials, Structures & Mathematical Issues: Selected Papers from the U. S. Army Research Office Workshop, Smart Materials, Structures & Mathematical Issues, September 1988. LC 89-85344. 244p. 1989. pap. 49.00 (*0-87762-682-0*) Technomic.

Rogers, Craig A. & Crawley, Edward F. Intelligent Materials Systems & Structures (Seminar Notes) March 29-30, 1990. 434p. 1991. 225.00 (*0-87762-845-9*) Technomic.

***Rogers, Craig A. & Wallace, Gordon G., eds.** Proceedings of the Second International Conference on Intelligent Materials. (Illus.). 1409p. 1994. 285.00 (*1-56676-171-9*) Technomic.

Rogers, Cynthia Shade. Chocolate Companion. LC 93-74032. (Traditional Country Life Recipe Ser.). (Illus.). 96p. (Orig.). 1994. pap. 9.95 (*1-883283-02-7*) Brick Tower.

Rogers, D., ed. Gabriel Tellez: El Condenado por Desconfiado. LC 73-7964. 172p. (C). 1974. 26.00 (*0-08-017247-4*, Pergamon Pr); pap. 15.50 (*0-08-017248-2*, Pergamon Pr) Elsevier.

Rogers, D. F., ed. Computer Applications in the Automation of Shipyard Operation & Ship Design, Vol. IV. (Computer Applications in Shipping & Shipbuilding Ser.: Vol. IX). 356p. 1982. 72.00 (*0-444-86408-3*, I-300-82, North Holland) Elsevier.

— Computer Graphics in Engineering Education. 136p. 1982. 54.00 (*0-08-028949-5*, Pub. by Pergamon Repr UK) Franklin.

Rogers, D. F. & Earnshaw, P. A., eds. State of the Art in Computer Graphics: Visualization & Modeling. (Illus.). 368p. 1991. 89.00 (*0-387-97560-8*) Spr-Verlag.

Rogers, D. F. & Earnshaw, R. A., eds. Computer Graphics Techniques: Theory & Practice. (Illus.). v, 542p. 1990. 89.00 (*0-387-97237-4*) Spr-Verlag.

— Techniques for Computer Graphics. (Illus.). 590p. 1987. 81.00 (*0-387-96492-4*) Spr-Verlag.

Rogers, D. Laurence. Paul Bunyan: How a Terrible Timber Feller Became a Legend. LC 90-84346. (Illus.). 208p. 1993. 19.95 (*0-9635369-0-7*) Hist Pr MI.

Rogers, D. M., jt. auth. see Allison, A. F.

Rogers, Dale E. Angel Unaware. 64p. (Orig.). 1991. reprint ed. lib. bdg. 10.95 (*0-89966-811-9*) Buccaneer Bks.

— God in the Hard Times. large type ed. (Large Print Inspirational Ser.). 1985. pap. 8.95 (*0-8027-2516-3*) Walker & Co.

Rogers, Dale Evans & Thatcher, Floyd W. Say Yes to Tomorrow. LC 93-29464. 160p. 1993. 9.99 (*0-8007-1696-5*) Revell.

Rogers, Daniel. Motor Disorder in Psychiatry: Towards a Neurological Approach. 200p. 1993. text ed. 74.95 (*0-471-93616-2*) Wiley.

— The Thames. LC 92-44702. (Rivers of the World Ser.). (Illus.). 48p. (J). (gr. 5-6). 1993. lib. bdg. 22.80 (*0-8114-3104-5*) Raintree Steck-V.

***Rogers, Daniel B.** How to Talk Country. 40p. 1995. pap. 7.95 (*0-614-03592-9*) NW Pub.

***Rogers, Daniel E.** Politics after Hitler: The Western Allies & the German Party System. 1995. 40.00 (*0-8147-7461-X*) NYU Pr.

Rogers, Dave. Comp Avengers. 1989. pap. 13.95 (*0-312-03187-4*) St Martin.

— The ITV Encyclopedia of Adventure. 800p. 1988. 60.00 (*1-85283-205-3*, Pub. by Boxtree Ltd UK); pap. 40.00 (*0-317-89942-2*, Pub. by Boxtree Ltd UK) St Mut.

— The ITV Encyclopedia of Adventure. 593p. (C). 1990. 125.00 (*1-85283-217-7*, Pub. by Boxtree Ltd UK) St Mut.

Rogers, Dave, jt. auth. see Peel, John.

***Rogers, David.** The Bodleian Library & Its Treasures, 1320-1700. (Illus.). 176p. 1995. 50.00 (*0-85628-128-X*, 128-X) A Schwartz & Co.

— The Complete Book of Hors-d'Oeuvres. 288p. (Orig.). 1992. pap. 29.95 (*0-273-03779-X*, Pub. by Pitman Pub Ltd UK) Trans-Atl Phila.

— Flowers for Algernon - One Act. 1969. 2.75 (*0-87129-387-0*, F28) Dramatic Pub.

— Foundations of Psychology: Some Personal Views. LC 84-13374. 292p. 1984. text ed. 55.00 (*0-275-91253-1*, C1253, Praeger Pubs) Greenwood.

— Future of American Banking. 1992. text ed. 24.95 (*0-07-053538-8*) McGraw.

— Here & Now. 1973. 5.00 (*0-87129-538-5*, H16) Dramatic Pub.

— The In-Laws. (Orig.). 1979. pap. 1.95 (*0-449-14252-3*, GM) Fawcett.

— Monarch Notes on O'Neill's Plays. (Orig.). (C). pap. 3.95 (*0-671-00627-4*, Arco Test) P-H Gen Ref & Trav.

— Never Mind What Happened, How Did It End? 104p. 1976. pap. 4.95 (*0-87129-103-7*, N11) Dramatic Pub.

— Soft Soap. 1982. 5.00 (*0-87129-529-6*, S65) Dramatic Pub.

— Stories by an Atheist. 267p. (Orig.). 1991. pap. 5.95 (*0-9618064-1-9*) D Rogers NY.

— Sunday Morning. LC 86-90807. 95p. (Orig.). 1986. pap. 6.95 (*0-9618064-0-0*) D Rogers NY.

Rogers, David, adapt. The Sting. 1985. 4.95 (*0-87129-280-7*, S69) Dramatic Pub.

Rogers, David & Chung, Norman H. One Hundred Ten Livingston Street Revisited: Decentralization in Action. LC 83-3937. 264p. 1983. 50.00x (*0-8147-7387-7*) NYU Pr.

Rogers, David, jt. auth. see Keyes, Daniel.

Rogers, David, jt. ed. see Whiting, Larry.

Rogers, David B. Prehistoric Man of the Santa Barbara Coast. LC 76-43812. reprint ed. 74.50 (*0-404-15667-3*) AMS Pr.

Rogers, David E. & Ginzberg, Eli, eds. Improving the Life Chances of Children at Risk. 184p. (C). 1990. text ed. 54.50 (*0-8133-8036-7*) Westview.

— Medical Care & the Health of the Poor. LC 92-49555. 144p. (C). 1993. text ed. 54.50 (*0-8133-1720-7*) Westview.

— Metropolitan Academic Medical Center. 1995. text ed. 55.00 (*0-8133-2574-9*) Westview.

Rogers, David E., ed. see Ryan, Will G.

Rogers, David E., et al, eds. Year Book of Medicine, 1989. (Illus.). 848p. 1989. 57.95 (*0-8151-7262-1*, Yr Bk Med Pubs) Mosby Yr Bk.

Rogers, David F. Laminar Flow Analysis. (Illus.). 422p. (C). 1992. 120.00 (*0-521-41152-1*) Cambridge U Pr.

— Procedural Elements for Computer Graphics. 1985. text ed. write for info. (*0-07-053534-5*) McGraw.

Rogers, David F. & Adams, J. Alan. Mathematical Elements for Computer Graphics. 2nd ed. 1989. pap. text ed. write for info. (*0-07-053530-2*) McGraw.

— Mathematical Elements for Computer Graphics. 2nd ed. 512p. (C). 1989. text ed. write for info. (*0-07-053529-9*) McGraw.

Rogers, David F. & Earnshaw, Rae A., eds. State-of-the-Art in Computer Graphics: Aspects of Visualization. LC 93-33016. 1993. 149.00 (*0-387-94164-9*) Spr-Verlag.

Rogers, David F., ed. see Bechtolsheim, Stephen V.

Rogers, David J. Waging Business Warfare. 448p. 1988. mass mkt. 4.95 (*0-8217-2510-6*) Zebra.

Rogers, David J. & Appun, S. G. Manihot (Manihotoides: Euphorbiaceae) LC 72-88251. (Flora Neotropica Monograph Ser.: No. 13). (Illus.). 272p. (Orig.). 1973. pap. 23.95 (*0-89327-295-7*) NY Botanical.

Rogers, David J. & Rogers, Constance. Woody Ornamentals for Deep South Gardens. (Illus.). 325p. 1991. lib. bdg. 32.95 (*0-8130-1011-X*); pap. 16.95 (*0-8130-1021-7*) U Press Fla.

Rogers, David S., jt. ed. see Davies, R. L.

Rogers, Dawn, jt. ed. see McFadden, E.

Rogers, Debbie, ed. see Punches, Laurie.

***Rogers, Deborah, ed.** Two Gothic Classics by Women: The Italian by Ann Radcliffe & Northanger Abbey by Jane Austen. 688p. 1995. pap. 6.95 (*0-451-52607-4*, Sig Classics) NAL-Dutton.

Rogers, Deborah D. Bookseller As Rogue: John Almon & the Politics of Eighteenth-Century Publishing. (American University Studies: English Language & Literature: Ser. IV, Vol. 28). 153p. 1986. text ed. 28.50 (*0-8204-0221-4*) P Lang Pubs.

Rogers, Deborah D., ed. The Critical Response to Ann Radcliffe. LC 93-28048. (Critical Responses in Arts & Letters Ser.: No. 7). 320p. 1993. text ed. 59.95 (*0-313-28031-2*, Greenwood Pr) Greenwood.

Rogers, Deborah W. & Rogers, Ivor A. J. R. R. Tolkien. (English Authors Ser.: No. 304). 168p. 1980. text ed. 21.95 (*0-8057-6796-7*, Pub. by Royal Botanic Garden UK) Macmillan.

Rogers, Deborah W., tr. see De Troyes, Chretien.

Rogers, Del M. Close to Ground. LC 90-61426. (Poets Ser.: No. 8). 68p. (Orig.). 1991. pap. 6.95 (*0-931722-85-3*) Corona Pub.

Rogers, Delores J. The American Empirical Movement in Theology. LC 89-77291. (American University Studies: Theology & Religion: Ser. VII, Vol. 70). 254p. (C). 1990. text ed. 47.50 (*0-8204-1218-X*) P Lang Pubs.

Rogers, Denis. Home Grown. Campbell, Cole, ed. 198p. (Orig.). 1979. 12.95 (*0-935400-02-8*); pap. 7.95 (*0-935400-03-6*) News & Observer.

— Second Harvest. Davis, Owen, ed. LC 81-84333. 196p. (Orig.). 1981. 12.95 (*0-935400-07-9*); pap. 7.95 (*0-935400-08-7*) News & Observer.

Rogers, Denise, comp. Selected Bibliography of Books & Articles on Censorship (1950-1983) LC 83-204879. (Washington University Law Library Bibliography Ser.: No. 4). vi, 22p. (Orig.). 1983. pap. text ed. 8.00 (*0-317-00753-X*) Wash U Law Lib.

Rogers, Dennis. Crossroads. 1989. 12.95 (*0-935400-10-9*); 7.95 (*0-685-27877-8*) News & Observer.

— It's Bad News When the Bartender Cries. Munger, Guy, ed. (Illus.). 208p. 1988. 12.95 (*0-935400-14-1*) News & Observer.

— Site Guides Venezuela: A Guide to the Best Birding Spots. 54p. 1993. spiral bd. 14.50 (*0-9637765-0-9*) Cinclus Pubns.

***Rogers, Derek J.** To Hell with Morpheus. 300p. 1995. pap. 8.95 (*1-56901-866-9*) NW Pub.

Rogers, Diane L., jt. auth. see Fullerton, Don.

Rogers, Dick, jt. auth. see Gallagher, Lyn.

Rogers, Dilwyn J., ed. A Bibliography of African Ecology: A Geographically & Topically Classified List of Books & Articles. LC 78-19935. (Special Bibliographic Ser.: No. 6). 499p. 1979. text ed. 105.00 (*0-313-20552-3*, RAE/, Greenwood Pr) Greenwood.

Rogers, Don & Sloboda, John A., eds. The Acquisition of Symbolic Skills. LC 83-9464. (NATO Conference Series III, Human Factors: Vol. 22). 636p. 1983. 115.00 (*0-306-41368-X*, Plenum Pr) Plenum.

Rogers, Don, jt. ed. see Branthwaite, Alan.

Rogers, Don, jt. auth. see Sloboda, John A.

Rogers, Donald B., ed. Urban Church Education. LC 89-4024. 213p. 1989. 16.95 (*0-89135-070-5*) Religious Educ.

Rogers, Donald J. Banned! Censorship in the Schools. LC 87-7736. 128p. (YA). (gr. 5 up). 1987. lib. bdg. 12.98 (*0-671-63708-8*, Julian Messner) Silver Burdett Pr.

Rogers, Donald W. BASIC Microcomputing & Biostatistics. LC 81-85465. (Contemporary Instrumentation & Analysis Ser.). 304p. 1983. 59.50 (*0-89603-015-6*) Humana.

— Computational Chemistry Using the PC. LC 90-12309. 224p. 1990. lib. bdg. 59.50 (*0-89573-770-1*) VCH Pubs.

Rogers, Donald W., ed. Voting & the Spirit of American Democracy: Essays on the History of Voting & Voting Rights in America. 136p. 1992. 17.50 (*0-252-01918-0*); pap. 7.95 (*0-252-06247-7*) U of Ill Pr.

***Rogers, Donna C. & Mayer, Susan B.** Kuba: People of Central Africa. (Illus.). 16p. 1978. pap. 4.95 (*0-614-02732-2*) A M Huntington Art.

Rogers, Dorothy. The Adult Years: An Introduction to Aging. 3rd ed. (Illus.). 416p. 1986. text ed. write for info. (*0-13-008939-7*) P-H.

— Classroom Discipline: An Idea Handbook for Elementary School Teachers. 2nd ed. 288p. 1987. text ed. 24.95 (*0-87628-011-4*) P-H.

— How to Market Your College Degree. 1992. pap. 12.95 (*0-8442-4163-6*, VGM Career Bks) NTC Pub Grp.

Rogers, Dorothy & Gamans, Lynda. Fashion: A Marketing Approach. 334p. (C). 1983. text ed. 36.00 (*0-03-053231-0*) HB Coll Pubs.

Rogers, Dorothy S., et al. Retailing: New Perspectives. 2nd ed. 570p. (C). 1992. text ed. 55.25 (*0-03-054172-7*) Dryden Pr.

Rogers, Douglas G., ed. Many Marriages by Sherwood Anderson. LC 78-2353. 316p. 1978. 22.50 (*0-8108-1122-7*) Scarecrow.

***Rogers, Douglas G., et al, eds.** A Book of Meditations: Readings from Phillips Exeter Academy, 1983-1994. (Orig.). 1995. pap. write for info. (*0-939618-09-5*) Phillips Exeter.

Rogers, E. Looking at Vertebrates: A Practical Guide to Vertebrate Adaptations. 195p. 1986. text ed. 47.95 (*0-470-20660-8*) Halsted Pr.

Rogers, E. & Shoemaker, F. Communication of Innovations. 2nd ed. LC 78-122276. 1971. text ed. 19.95 (*0-02-926680-7*) Free Pr.

Rogers, E. T. & Owens, D. H. Stability Analysis for Linear Repetitive Processes. (Lecture Notes in Control & Information Sciences Ser.: Vol. 175). (Illus.). 201p. 1992. pap. 50.00 (*0-387-55264-2*) Spr-Verlag.

Rogers, Earl M. & Rogers, Susan H. The American Farm Crisis: An Annotated Bibliography. LC 89-31667. 162p. 1989. 26.00 (*0-8240-7243-X*) Garland.

Rogers, Edgar. A Handy Guide to Jewish Coins. LC 77-77252. (Illus.). 1990. reprint ed. pap. 16.00 (*0-915262-14-2*) S J Durst.

Rogers, Edith R. The Perilous Hunt: Symbols in Hispanic & European Balladry. LC 79-4010. (Studies in Romance Languages: No. 22). 187p. reprint ed. pap. 53.30 (*0-7837-5787-5*, 2045453) Bks Demand.

Rogers, Edward. Essay on Some General Principles of Political Economy. LC 74-11496. (Reprints of Economic Classics Ser.). 1974. reprint ed. 19.50 (*0-678-01247-4*) Kelley.

Rogers, Elizabeth. The Children's Book of Talking Numbers. (Illus.). 16p. (J). (gr. 1-3). 1994. 6.95 (*0-8059-3470-7*) Dorrance.

Rogers, Elizabeth & Stoval, Iris. Beginning Chemistry: A Workbook to Use in the Laboratory. 6th ed. 1994. pap. 9.80 (*0-87563-499-0*) Stipes.

Rogers, Elizabeth A., jt. ed. see Hopp, Joyce W.

Rogers, Elizabeth B., et al. Rebuilding Central Park: A Management & Restoration Plan. Berendt, John, ed. (Illus.). 176p. 1987. 37.50 (*0-262-18127-4*) MIT Pr.

Rogers, Elizabeth F. Peter Lombard & the Sacramental System. 250p. 1976. reprint ed. lib. bdg. 19.50 (*0-915172-22-4*) Richwood Pub.

Rogers, Elizabeth F., ed. The Archives of British History & Culture, Vols. I-II: Letters of Sir John Hackett, 1526-1534. LC 70-105970. 419p. 1974. 25.00 (*0-87012-089-1*) West Va U Pr.

— Letters of Sir John Hackett. LC 70-105570. (Archives of British History & Culture Ser). 419p. 1971. 15.00 (*0-937058-05-X*) West Va U Pr.

Rogers, Elizabeth F., ed. see More, Thomas.

Rogers, Elizabeth J. Create Your Own Joy: A Guide for Transforming Your Life. LC 94-2565. 240p. 1994. pap. 10.00 (*1-56718-354-9*) Llewellyn Pubns.

An Asterisk (*) at the beginning of an entry indicates that the title is appearing in BIP for the first time.

Rogers, Elizabeth S. & Rogers, Timothy J. In Retrospect: Essays on Latin American Literature (In Memory of Willis Knapp Jones) LC 86-61056. 195p. 1987. 20.00 (*0-938972-10-3*) Spanish Lit Pubns.

Rogers, Ellen. The Lone Wolf. (Stolen Moments Ser.). 1993. pap. 1.99 (*0-373-83287-7*, 1-83287-2) Harlequin Bks.

Rogers, Ellen S., ed. Genealogical Periodical Annual Index, 1963, Vol. 2. 133p. 1983. reprint ed. pap. 15.00 (*0-917890-31-0*) Heritage Bk.

— Genealogical Periodical Annual Index, 1964, Vol. 3. 151p. 1983. reprint ed. pap. 15.00 (*0-917890-32-9*) Heritage Bk.

— Genealogical Periodical Annual Index, 1965, Vol. 4. 151p. 1983. reprint ed. pap. 15.00 (*0-917890-33-7*) Heritage Bk.

Rogers, Elliot C., jt. auth. see Copeland, Melvin T.

***Rogers, Emma, ed.** Life & Letters of William Barton Rogers, 2 vols., Set. (Illus.). 874p. 1995. reprint ed. lib. bdg. 97.50 (*0-8328-4502-7*) Higginson Bk Co.

Rogers, Emma, jt. auth. see Rogers, Paul.

Rogers, Eric & Li, Yun, eds. Parallel Processing in a Control Systems Environment. LC 92-36364. (International Systems & Control Engineering Ser.). 300p. 1993. text ed. 54.00 (*0-13-651530-4*) P-H.

Rogers, Eric M. Astronomy for the Inquiring Mind: The Growth & Use of Theory in Science. LC 81-47286. (Illus.). 173p. reprint ed. pap. 49.40 (*0-8357-2921-4*, 2039161) Bks Demand.

Rogers, Ethel T. Piano Duets for All Seasons. 1985. 8.95 (*0-8341-9082-6*, MB-548) Lillenas.

— Thanks, God! (J). 1985. 7.95 (*0-8341-9281-0*, MB-551) Lillenas.

Rogers, Ethel T., comp. Christmas Joy, Level One. 1984. 6.50 (*0-685-68308-7*, BCMC-260) Lillenas.

Rogers, Ethel T., contrib. Christmas Joy, Level Two. 1984. 6.50 (*0-685-68309-5*, BCMC-261) Lillenas.

— Duets Plus. 1990. 9.95 (*0-685-68327-3*, MB-617) Lillenas.

— Holiday Joy. 1985. 7.95 (*0-685-71353-9*, MB-556) Lillenas.

— Preludes for Organ. 1988. 8.95 (*0-8341-9238-1*, MB-585) Lillenas.

***Rogers, Eugene F., Jr.** Thomas Aquinas & Karl Barth: Sacred Doctrine & the Natural Knowledge of God. LC 94-42830. (Revisions: A Series of Books on Ethics: Vol. 13). (C). 1995. text ed. 34.95x (*0-268-01889-8*) U of Notre Dame Pr.

Rogers, Evan. A Funny Old Quist: Memories of a Gamekeeper. 288p. 1986. pap. 14.95 (*0-907871-61-5*) Hippocrene Bks.

Rogers, Evelyn. Desert Fire. 448p. 1992. mass mkt. 4.50 (*0-8217-3988-3*) Zebra.

— Desert Heat. 448p. 1993. mass mkt. 4.50 (*0-8217-4216-7*) Zebra.

— Flame. 448p. 1994. mass mkt. 4.50 (*0-8217-4491-7*) Zebra.

— Love So Wild. 448p. 1991. mass mkt. 4.50 (*0-8217-3267-6*) Zebra.

— Midnight Sins. 1989. pap. 3.75 (*0-8217-2694-3*) Zebra.

— Raven. 384p. 1995. mass mkt. 4.99 (*0-8217-4800-9*) Zebra.

— Surrender to the Night. 448p. 1991. mass mkt. 4.50 (*0-8217-3444-X*) Zebra.

— Sweet Texas Magic. 1992. mass mkt. 4.50 (*0-8217-3716-3*) Zebra.

— Texas Kiss. 1989. mass mkt. 4.25 (*0-8217-2828-8*) Zebra.

— Wanton Slave. 1990. mass mkt. 4.50 (*0-8217-3039-8*) Zebra.

Rogers, Everett, et al, eds. The Media Revolution in America & in Western Europe. LC 84-21680. (Communication & Information Science Ser.). 352p. 1985. text ed. 59.50 (*0-89391-258-1*) Ablex Pub.

Rogers, Everett M. Communication Technology. (Communication Technology & Society Ser.: Vol. 1). 288p. 1986. 29.95 (*0-02-927110-X*); pap. 16.95 (*0-02-927120-7*) Free Pr.

— Diffusion of Innovations. 3rd ed. (Illus.). 512p. 1982. text ed. 29.95 (*0-02-926650-5*) Free Pr.

— Diffusion of Innovations. 4th ed. LC 94-24947. 1995. pap. 29.95 (*0-02-926671-8*) Free Pr.

— The High Technology of Silicon Valley. (Urban Studies Monograph Ser.: No. 4). (Illus.). 35p. (Orig.). 1985. pap. 5.00 (*0-685-10291-2*) U MD Urban Stud.

— A History of Communication: A Bibliographic Approach. 550p. 1994. text ed. 35.00 (*0-02-926735-8*) Free Pr.

Rogers, Everett M. & Agarwala-Rogers, Rekha. Communication in Organizations. LC 75-32368. (Illus.). 1976. pap. 18.95 (*0-02-926710-2*) Free Pr.

Rogers, Everett M. & Kincaid, D. Lawrence. Communication Networks: Towards a New Paradigm for Research. LC 80-65202. (Illus.). 1981. text ed. 29.95 (*0-02-926740-4*) Free Pr.

Rogers, Everett M., jt. ed. see Backer, Thomas E.

Rogers, Everett M., jt. auth. see Gibson, David V.

Rogers, Everett M., jt. auth. see Singhal, Arvind.

Rogers, Everett M., et al. Social Change in Rural Societies: An Introduction to Rural Sociology. 3rd ed. (Illus.). 480p. (C). 1988. text ed. write for info. (*0-13-815481-3*) P-H.

Rogers, Floyd. Hangman's Gulch. large type ed. (Linford Western Library). 1991. pap. 13.95 (*0-7089-7124-5*) Ulverscroft.

***Rogers, Ford.** Olives. 128p. (Orig.). 1995. pap. 15.95 (*0-89815-679-3*) Ten Speed Pr.

Rogers, Ford B. Citrus: A Cookbook. (Illus.). 120p. (Orig.). 1993. pap. 18.00 (*0-671-74534-4*, Fireside) S&S Trade.

— Nuts, a Cookbook. LC 92-27046. (Illus.). 1993. pap. 18.00 (*0-671-79326-8*, Fireside) S&S Trade.

Rogers, Forrest J. & Dewitt, Hugh E., eds. Strongly Coupled Plasma Physics. (NATO ASI Series B, Physics: Vol. 154). (Illus.). 610p. 1987. 115.00 (*0-306-42581-5*, Plenum Pr) Plenum.

Rogers, Francis. Some Famous Singers of the 19th Century. Farkas, Andrew, ed. LC 76-29963. (Opera Biographies Ser.). (Illus.). 1977. reprint ed. lib. bdg. 18.95 (*0-405-09703-4*) Ayer.

Rogers, Francis M. Atlantic Islanders of the Azores & Madeiras. LC 78-72837. (Illus.). 1979. 17.50 (*0-8158-0373-7*) Chris Mass.

— The Quest for Eastern Christians: Travels & Rumor in the Age of Discovery. LC 62-18138. 233p. reprint ed. pap. 66.50 (*0-317-41750-9*, 2055901) Bks Demand.

Rogers, Francis M. & Haberly, David T. Brazil, Portugal, & Other Portuguese-Speaking Lands: A List of Books Primarily in English. LC 68-7564. (Texts from the Romance Languages Ser.: No. 4). 75p. (C). 1968. pap. 1.95 (*0-674-08050-5*) HUP.

***Rogers, Frank & VanVoorhis, Steven.** Roosevelt & the Magic Box. (Illus.). 24p. (J). 1994. 10.95 (*0-9642564-9-5*) Bookbuddy.

Rogers, Frank C. The Great Saltmine & Hifwip Direct Phonics Reading Program. 50p. 1987. ring bd. 10.00 (*0-9616691-0-1*) Parents as Tchrs.

Rogers, Franklin R. Occidental Ideographs: Image, Sequence, & Literary History. LC 89-45972. 288p. 1991. 39.50 (*0-8387-5179-2*) Bucknell U Pr.

— Painting & Poetry: Forms, Mataphor & the Language of Literature. LC 83-46175. (Illus.). 248p. 1986. 42.50 (*0-8387-5077-X*) Bucknell U Pr.

Rogers, Franklin R., ed. see Twain, Mark.

Rogers, Fred. Going to the Dentist. (Mr. Rogers' First Experience Bks.). (Illus.). 32p. (Orig.). (J). (ps-2). 1989. pap. 5.95 (*0-399-21634-0*, Putnam) Putnam Pub Group.

— Going to the Hospital. (First Experience Bks.). (Illus.). 32p. (J). (ps-4). 1988. pap. 5.95 (*0-399-21530-1*, Putnam) Putnam Pub Group.

— Going to the Potty. (Mister Rogers' First Experience Bks.). (Illus.). 32p. (J). (ps-2). 1986. pap. 5.95 (*0-399-21297-3*, Putnam) Putnam Pub Group.

— Let's Talk about It. LC 94-2312. (J). Date not set. write for info. (*0-399-22449-1*); pap. write for info. (*0-399-22800-4*) Putnam Pub Group.

— Let's Talk about It: Adoption. (Illus.). (J). 1995. pap. 6.95 (*0-399-22525-0*, Putnam) Putnam Pub Group.

— Making Friends. (First Experience Bks.). (Illus.). (J). (ps-1). 1987. 12.95 (*0-399-21382-1*, Putnam); pap. 5.95 (*0-399-21385-6*, Putnam) Putnam Pub Group.

— You Are Special: Words of Wisdom for All Ages from a Beloved Neighbor. 192p. 1995. 8.95 (*0-14-023514-0*, Penguin Bks) Viking Penguin.

— You Are Special: Words of Wisdom from America's Most Beloved Neighbor. LC 94-335. 176p. 1994. 18.95 (*0-670-85412-3*, Viking) Viking Penguin.

Rogers, Fred & Head, Barry. Mister Rogers Talks with Parents. 320p. 1993. pap. 7.95 (*0-7935-2642-6*, 00815004) H Leonard.

Rogers, Fred B. Montgomery & the Portsmouth. LC 90-20215. (Portsmouth Marine Society Ser.: Vol. 17). (Illus.). 176p. 1990. reprint ed. 25.00 (*0-915819-16-3*, 17) Portsmouth Marine Soc.

Rogers, Frederick R. Physical Capacity Tests in the Administration of Physical Education. LC 70-177203. (Columbia University. Teachers College. Contributions to Education Ser.: No. 173). reprint ed. 37.50 (*0-404-55173-4*) AMS Pr.

Rogers, Fritzie. Falling Through the Cracks. LC 91-43724. 192p. (Orig.). 1992. pap. 8.95 (*0-934678-29-4*) New Victoria Pubs.

Rogers, G. A., ed. Locke's Philosophy: Content & Context. 280p. 1994. 49.95 (*0-19-824076-7*) OUP.

Rogers, G. A. & Ryan, Alan, eds. Perspectives on Thomas Hobbes. (Mind Association Occasional Ser.). 224p. 1991. pap. 19.95 (*0-19-823914-9*) OUP.

Rogers, G. A., ed. see Locke, John.

Rogers, G. E., et al, eds. The Biology of Wool & Hair. (Illus.). 500p. 1988. text ed. 105.00 (*0-412-32120-3*) Chapman & Hall.

***Rogers, G. F. & Mayhew, Y.** Thermodynamic & Transport Properties of Fluids: SI Units. 5th ed. 30p. 1995. pap. 11.95 (*0-631-19703-6*) Blackwell Pubs.

Rogers, G. G. Colloquial Nepali. (C). 1991. reprint ed. 16.00 (*81-206-0634-5*, Pub. by Asian Educ Servs II) S Asia.

Rogers, G. K. Gleasonia, Henriquezia & Platycarpum. LC 84-19080. (Flora Neotropica Monograph Ser.: No. 39). (Illus.). 135p. 1984. 26.00 (*0-89327-257-4*) NY Botanical.

Rogers, G. S., jt. auth. see Nguyen, H. T.

Rogers-Gallagher, Kim. Astrology for the Light Side of the Brain: A User-Friendly Guide. 300p. (Orig.). 1995. pap. 12.95 (*0-935127-35-6*) ACS Pubns.

Rogers-Gardner, Barbara. Jung & Shakespeare: Hamlet, Othello, & the Tempest. (Chiron Monograph Ser.: Vol. VII). 128p. (Orig.). 1992. pap. 12.95 (*0-933029-55-1*) Chiron Pubns.

Rogers-Gardner, Barbara & Sabbath, Linda, frwds. Jesus & the Single Mother. LC 90-37193. 145p. (Orig.). 1990. spiral bd. 7.95 (*0-8294-0695-6*) Loyola Univ Pr.

Rogers-Gardner, Barbara J., jt. auth. see Maloney, G.

Rogers, Garry F. Then & Now: A Photographic History of Vegetation Change in the Central Great Basin Desert. LC 82-4825. (Illus.). 164p. (Orig.). reprint ed. pap. 46.80 (*0-7837-6865-6*, 2046695) Bks Demand.

Rogers, Garry F., et al. Bibliography of Repeat Photography for Evaluating Landscape Change. LC 84-23437. (Illus.). 215p. reprint ed. pap. 61.30 (*0-7837-6867-2*, 2046697) Bks Demand.

Rogers, Gary R. The COBOL Programmer's Design Book. 304p. (C). 1986. reprint ed. pap. text ed. 34.95 (*0-471-82666-9*) Wiley.

Rogers, Gay A. American Silver Thimbles. LC 88-82066. (Illus.). 224p. 1989. 47.95 (*1-869812-03-4*) Needlewrk Unltd.

— An Illustrated History of Needlework Tools. (Illus.). 243p. 1989. reprint ed. 45.00 (*0-9622310-0-2*) Needlewrk Unltd.

Rogers, Gayla, jt. auth. see Schneck, Dean.

Rogers, Gayle T., jt. auth. see Alsalam, Nabeel.

Rogers, George, ed. Change in Alaska. LC 75-11734. 213p. 1970. 7.95 (*0-912006-40-4*) U of Alaska Pr.

Rogers, George A. & Saunders, R. Frank. Swamp Water & Wiregrass: Historical Sketches of Coastal Georgia. LC 84-701. x, 254p. 1984. 19.95 (*0-86554-099-3*, MUP/H91) Mercer Univ Pr.

Rogers, George C., Jr. Charleston in the Age of the Pinckneys. (Illus.). xvi, 202p. 1984. pap. 10.95 (*0-87249-297-4*) U of SC Pr.

— Generations of Lawyers: A History of the South Carolina Bar (1690-1990) (Illus.). 367p. 1992. write for info. (*0-945036-01-9*) SC Bar Found.

— The History of Georgetown County, South Carolina. (Illus.). xviii, 566p. 1990. reprint ed. 37.50 (*0-87152-443-0*) Reprint.

— A Social Portrait of the South at the Turn of the Eighteenth Century. 14p. 1988. reprint ed. pap. 4.00 (*0-944026-03-6*) Am Antiquarian.

Rogers, George C., Jr. & Taylor, C. James. A South Carolina Chronology, 1497-1992. 2nd ed. LC 93-27306. 144p. (C). 1993. 12.95 (*0-87249-971-5*) U of SC Pr.

Rogers, George C., ed. see Laurens, Henry.

Rogers, George C., Jr.

Rogers, George C.

Rogers, George C., Jr.

Rogers, George L. Mac & Zach from Hackensack. (Illus.). 32p. (J). (gr. k-6). 1992. lib. bdg. 12.95 (*0-938399-07-1*); pap. 4.95 (*0-938399-06-3*) Acorn Pub MN.

Rogers, George L., ed. see Franklin, Benjamin.

Rogers, George W. Alaska in Transition: The Southeast Region. LC 59-14895. 398p. reprint ed. pap. 113.50 (*0-8357-5293-3*, 2052110) Bks Demand.

Rogers, Gerald S. Matrix Derivatives. LC 80-24248. (Lecture Notes in Statistics Ser.). 221p. reprint ed. pap. 63.00 (*0-7837-3548-0*, 2043385) Bks Demand.

Rogers, Gerhild B. Das Romanwerk von Ingeborg Drewitz. (Studies in Modern German Literature: Vol. 26). 246p. (C). 1989. text ed. 37.00 (*0-8204-0715-1*) P Lang Pubs.

Rogers, Ginger. Ginger: My Story. large type ed. LC 92-15294. (General Ser.). 608p. 1992. text ed. 22.95 (*0-8161-5436-8*, Large Print Bks); pap. 16.95 (*0-8161-5437-6*, Large Print Bks) Hall.

— Ginger My Story. 1992. mass mkt. 5.99 (*0-06-109114-6*, Harp PBks) HarpC.

Rogers, Glenn. Serving & Saving. LC 88-63244. 150p. (Orig.). 1989. pap. 6.99 (*0-89900-326-5*) College Pr Pub.

Rogers, Glenn C., jt. auth. see Rogers, Judy R.

Rogers, Glenn T. English-Spanish, Spanish-English Medical Dictionary: (Diccionario Medico) 220p. 1992. pap. text ed. 19.95 (*0-07-053537-X*) Hlth Prof Div.

Rogers, Gloree. Love, Or a Reasonable Facsimile. 2nd ed. 160p. (Orig.). 1989. pap. 10.00 (*0-932112-27-7*) Carolina Wren.

Rogers, Glyn & Badham, Linda. Evaluation in Schools. 128p. 1992. pap. 33.50 (*0-415-08077-0*, A7627) Routledge.

Rogers, Glynn B., Sr. The Packet Radio Operator's Manual. (Illus.). 176p. (Orig.). 1993. pap. 15.95 (*0-943016-04-5*) CQ Commns Inc.

Rogers, Glynn E., Sr. The Packet User's Notebook. (Illus.). 160p. (Orig.). 1988. pap. write for info. (*0-318-64319-7*) CQ Commns Inc.

Rogers, Godfrey, tr. see Lepetit, Bernard.

Rogers, Godfrey, tr. see Rioux, Jean-Pierre.

Rogers, Gregg & Swanson, Kathryn, eds. CPT Coder's Choice 1994. deluxe rev. ed. 850p. 1993. 49.95 (*1-878487-97-3*) Practice Mgmt Info.

— CPT Coder's Choice 1994. rev. ed. 850p. 1993. 42.95 (*1-878487-93-0*); spiral bd., pap. 39.95 (*1-878487-95-7*); Timesaver ver. ring bd. 49.95 (*1-878487-96-5*) Practice Mgmt Info.

— CPT 1995 Coder's Choice. 850p. 1994. spiral bd., pap. 44.95 (*1-57066-016-6*) Practice Mgmt Info.

— CPT 1995 Deluxe. 850p. 1994. 49.95 (*1-57066-019-0*) Practice Mgmt Info.

— CPT 1995 Plain? 850p. 1994. spiral bd., pap. 41.95 (*1-57066-017-4*) Practice Mgmt Info.

— CPT 1995 Timesaver. 850p. 1994. ring bd. 49.95 (*1-57066-018-2*) Practice Mgmt Info.

— HCPCS Coder's Choice 1994. rev. ed. 300p. 1993. ring bd. 44.95 (*1-878487-99-X*); spiral bd. 34.95 (*1-878487-98-1*) Practice Mgmt Info.

— Health Insurance Carrier Directory, 1994. rev. ed. 330p. 1994. pap. text ed. 49.95 (*1-57066-001-8*); ring bd. write for info. (*1-57066-000-X*) Practice Mgmt Info.

— Health Insurance Carrier Directory 1995: Coder's Choice. 325p. 1995. spiral bd. 44.95 (*1-57066-021-2*) Practice Mgmt Info.

— Health Insurance Carrier Directory 1995: Time-Saver. rev. ed. 325p. 1995. ring bd. 49.95 (*1-57066-022-0*) Practice Mgmt Info.

— ICD-9-CM Coder's Choice, 1995, Vols. 1, 2 & 3. rev. ed. 1700p. (C). 1994. pap. text ed. 49.95 (*1-57066-011-5*) Practice Mgmt Info.

— ICD-9-CM Coder's Choice, 1995, Vos. 1 & 2. rev. ed. 1400p. (C). 1994. pap. text ed. 44.95 (*1-57066-010-7*) Practice Mgmt Info.

— ICD-9-CM Deluxe, 1995. rev. ed. 1400p. (C). 1994. text ed. 54.95 (*1-57066-012-3*) Practice Mgmt Info.

— ICD-9-CM Timesaver, 1995. 1700p. (C). 1994. student ed 59.95 (*1-57066-009-3*) Practice Mgmt Info.

— ICD-9-CM, 1994, Vols. 1-2: Diagnosis Codes Required by Medicare & Most Insurance Companies. rev. ed. 1400p. 1993. pap. 44.95 (*1-878487-90-6*) Practice Mgmt Info.

— ICD-9-CM, 1994, Vols. 1-2: Diagnosis Codes Required by Medicare & Most Insurance Companies, Set. rev. ed. 1400p. 1993. 54.95 (*1-878487-92-2*) Practice Mgmt Info.

— ICD-9-CM, 1994, Vols. 1-3: Diagnosis Codes Required by Medicare & Most Insurance Companies, 1994. rev. ed. 1700p. 1993. pap. 49.95 (*1-878487-91-4*) Practice Mgmt Info.

— ICD-9-CM, 1994, Vols. 1-3: Diagnosis Codes Required by Medicare & Most Insurance Companies, 1994, Set. rev. ed. 1700p. 1993. text ed. 59.95 (*1-878487-94-9*) Practice Mgmt Info.

— Physician Fees, 1994. rev. ed. 400p. 1994. 99.95 (*1-878487-22-1*) Practice Mgmt Info.

Rogers, Gregg, ed. see Alpiar, Hal.

Rogers, Gregg, ed. see Costain, Lynne R. & Moawad, Karen.

Rogers, Gregg, ed. see Davis, James B. & Farber, Lawrence.

Rogers, Gregg, ed. see Davis, James B.

Rogers, Gregg, ed. see Fish, Raymond M., et al.

Rogers, Gregg, ed. see Goyette, Richert E.

Rogers, Gregg, ed. see Isler, Charlotte.

Rogers, Gregg, ed. see Knaus, Denise L. & Davis, James B.

Rogers, Gregg, ed. see Lorenzini, Jean A. & Lorenzini-Ley, Laura.

Rogers, Gregg, ed. see Perez-Sabido, Jesus.

Rogers, Gregg, ed. see Prather, Stephen, et al.

Rogers, Gregory A. Impact. abr. ed. 380p. 1995. pap. 9.95 (*1-56901-317-9*) NW Pub.

Rogers, Guy, jt. auth. see Rogers, Nell.

Rogers, Guy M. The Sacred Identity of Ephesos: Foundation Myths of a Roman City. 192p. (C). 1991. text ed. 49.95 (*0-415-05530-X*, A5619) Routledge.

Rogers, Guy M., jt. ed. see Lefkowitz, Mary R.

Rogers, H., ed. see Howe, John.

Rogers, H. C. A History of Artillery. 1977. pap. 4.95 (*0-8065-0597-4*, Citadel Pr) Carol Pub Group.

Rogers, H. Kendall. Before the Revisionist Controversy: Kautsky, Bernstein, & the Meaning of Marxism, 1895-1898. LC 92-29718. (Modern European History Ser.). (Illus.). 496p. 1992. 112.00 (*0-8153-0674-1*) Garland.

Rogers, Hal. Generals. LC 92-9478. (Football Heroes Ser.). (YA). 1992. 12.95 (*0-685-59323-1*); lib. bdg. 17.26 (*0-86593-154-2*) Rourke Corp.

— Skiing. LC 93-23410. (Pro-Am Sports Ser.). (J). 1993. write for info. (*0-86593-348-0*) Rourke Corp.

Rogers, Hal, jt. auth. see Reinhardt, Ed.

Rogers, Harrell. Public Policy Studies: A Multi-Volume Treatise. (Public Policy & Social Institutions Ser.: Vol. 1). 1984. 73.25 (*0-89232-377-9*) Jai Pr.

Rogers, Hartley. Problems Book: Engineering Drawing & Graphic Technology. 13th ed. (Illus.). 256p. 1986. pap. text ed. write for info. (*0-07-053491-8*) McGraw.

Rogers, Hartley, Jr. Theory of Recursive Functions & Effective Computability. 504p. (Orig.). 1987. pap. 23.50 (*0-262-68052-1*) MIT Pr.

Rogers, Heather, jt. auth. see Nicol, Andrew.

***Rogers, Helen, ed.** Adult Exercise & Instruction Sheets: More Home Exercises for Rehabilitation. 222p. 1993. pap. text ed., ring bd. 59.00 (*0-88450-685-1*, 4294) Commun Skill.

Rogers, Helen P. The American Deficit-Fulfillment of a Prophecy? "America Will Spend Herself Out of Existence" (Lenin 1917) LC 85-52235. 244p. 1988. 17.95 (*0-915915-07-3*) Wellington Pubns.

— The Deficit: Twelve Steps to Ease the Crisis. LC 87-51350. 465p. 1988. 17.95 (*0-915915-06-5*) Wellington Pubns.

— The Election Process: A Grass Roots Call for Reform. LC 87-51351. 280p. 1988. 12.95 (*0-915915-05-7*) Wellington Pubns.

— Everyone's Guide to Financial Planning. LC 83-51159. (Winn-When If Not Now Ser.). (Illus.). 325p. 1984. 12.95 (*0-915915-00-6*) Wellington Pubns.

— Social Security: An Idea Whose Time Has Passed. 2nd ed. LC 85-51900. (Illus.). 150p. 1986. pap. 6.95 (*0-915915-04-9*) Wellington Pubns.

— Taking a Stand on Banking. 64p. (Orig.). 1991. pap. 6.95 (*0-915915-18-9*) Wellington Pubns.

— Taking a Stand on Civil Rights. LC 91-66842. 80p. (Orig.). 1991. pap. 6.95 (*0-915915-19-7*) Wellington Pubns.

— Taking a Stand on Education. LC 91-67469. 80p. (Orig.). 1991. pap. text ed. 6.95 (*0-915915-11-1*) Wellington Pubns.

— Taking a Stand on Health Care. LC 91-75100. 64p. (Orig.). 1991. pap. 6.95 (*0-915915-08-1*) Wellington Pubns.

— Taking a Stand on Housing. LC 91-75106. 64p. (Orig.). 1991. pap. 6.95 (*0-915915-15-4*) Wellington Pubns.

— Taking a Stand on Our National Debt. LC 91-66841. 128p. (Orig.). 1991. pap. 6.95 (*0-915915-10-3*) Wellington Pubns.

— Taking a Stand on Poverty. LC 91-67468. 96p. (Orig.). 1991. pap. 6.95 (*0-915915-17-0*) Wellington Pubns.

— Taking a Stand on Regulation. LC 91-75101. 96p. (Orig.). 1991. pap. 6.95 (*0-915915-13-8*) Wellington Pubns.

— Taking a Stand on Taxes. 90p. (Orig.). 1991. pap. 6.95 (*0-915915-16-2*) Wellington Pubns.

— Taking a Stand on the Environment. LC 91-67467. 90p. (Orig.). 1991. pap. 6.95 (*0-915915-12-X*) Wellington Pubns.

— Taking a Stand on U. S. Competitiveness. LC 91-67462. 128p. (Orig.). 1991. pap. 6.95 (*0-915915-14-6*) Wellington Pubns.

***Rogers, Henry C.** History of the Town of Paris: And the Valley of the Sauquoit. 432p. 1994. 20.00 (*0-614-03845-6*) North Country.

— Rogers' Rules for Success: Tips That Will Take You to the Top by One of America's Foremost Public Relations Experts. 304p. 1986. pap. 8.95 (*0-312-68830-X*) St Martin.

R

An Asterisk (*) at the beginning of an entry indicates that the title is appearing in BIP for the first time.

Rogers, Henry W. The Law of Expert Testimony. 2nd ed. xlvii, 542p. 1991. reprint ed. lib. bdg. 47.50 (0-8377-2544-5) Rothman.

Rogers, Hiram. Exploring the Black Hills & Badlands: A Guide for Hikers, Cross-Country Skiers & Mountain Bikers. LC 93-24675. 192p. (Orig.). 1993. pap. 14.95 (1-55566-111-4) Johnson Bks.

Rogers, Homer. Uncommon Sense: An Introduction to Christian Belief. 416p. 1993. pap. 16.00 (0-00-599323-7, Pub. by HarperCollins UK) Harper SF.

Rogers, Horatio. Hadden's Journal & Orderly Books. LC 72-8761. (American Revolutionary Ser.). (Illus.). 704p. 1979. reprint ed. lib. bdg. 94.50 (0-8398-1772-X) Irvington.

Rogers, Howard & Lee, Sherman E. Masterworks of Ming & Qing Painting from the Forbidden City: A Color Catalogue of Paintings from the Palace Museum in Bejing, China. (Illus.). 224p. (Orig.). 1989. 60.00 (0-9621061-2-7); pap. 50.00 (0-9621061-1-9) Intl Arts Coun.

Rogers, Howard E. Yes Means No. 1950. pap. 4.75 (0-8222-1286-2) Dramatists Play.

Rogers, Howard J., ed. Congress of Arts & Science. LC 73-14177. (Perspectives in Social Inquiry Ser.). 342p. 1974. reprint ed. 24.95 (0-405-05520-X) Ayer.

Rogers, Hugh F. Workbook in Graphics. 1991. pap. text ed. write for info. (0-07-053536-1) McGraw.

Rogers, Ian T., jt. ed. see Oliver, J. David.

***Rogers, Ingrid.** Glimpses of China. fac. ed. LC 88-39447. (Illus.). 159p. (Orig.). 1994. pap. 45.40 (0-7837-7349-8, 2047302) Bks Demand.

Rogers, Ivor A., jt. auth. see Rogers, Deborah W.

Rogers, J. Presbyterian Creeds & Supplement. 1991. pap. 10.99 (0-664-25496-9) Westminster John Knox.

Rogers, J. A. Africa's Gift to America. rev. ed. (Illus.). 272p. 1961. 17.95 (0-9602294-6-9) H M Rogers.

— As Nature Leads. LC 89-61275. 1987. reprint ed. pap. text ed. 11.95 (0-933121-15-6) Black Classic.

— Five Negro Presidents. 19p. 1965. 1.95 (0-9602294-8-5) H M Rogers.

— From Superman to Man. 20.95 (0-8488-1462-2) Amereon Ltd.

— From "Superman to Man" rev. ed. 132p. 1968. reprint ed. 11.95 (0-9602294-4-2) H M Rogers.

— Ku Klux Spirit. 36p. 1980. reprint ed. pap. 3.00 (0-933121-06-7) Black Classic.

— Nature Knows No Color Line. 242p. 1980. reprint ed. 12.95 (0-9602294-5-0) H M Rogers.

— One Hundred Amazing Facts about the Negro. rev. ed. (Illus.). (Orig.). 1980. reprint ed. pap. 3.95 (0-9602294-7-7) H M Rogers.

— The Real Facts about Ethiopia. (Illus.). 34p. 1982. reprint ed. pap. 3.00 (0-933121-07-5) Black Classic.

— Sex & Race, 3 vols. (Illus.). 1074p. 41.85 (0-9602294-3-4) H M Rogers.

— Sex & Race, Vol. I: The Old World. (Illus.). 411p. 1970. reprint ed. 13.95 (0-9602294-0-X) H M Rogers.

— Sex & Race, Vol. II: The New World. (Illus.). 304p. 1967. reprint ed. 13.95 (0-9602294-1-8) H M Rogers.

— Sex & Race, Vol. III: Why White & Black Do Mate. (Illus.). 359p. 1972. reprint ed. 13.95 (0-9602294-2-6) H M Rogers.

— World's Great Men of Color, Vol. 1. 448p. 1972. pap. 13.95 (0-02-081300-7, Pub. by Gebrueder Borntraeger GW) Macmillan.

— World's Great Men of Color, Vol. 2. 592p. 1972. pap. 14.00 (0-02-081310-4) Macmillan.

— Your History. LC 89-61277. (Illus.). 100p. 1983. reprint ed. pap. 8.95 (0-933121-04-0, BC-10) Black Classic.

Rogers, J. Arthur. Sailaway Advisor Report. 2nd ed. LC 93-93640. 1993. spiral bd. 14.95 (0-9633412-0-0) Sailaway.

Rogers, J. D. & Wilson, S. M., eds. Ethnohistory & Archaeology: Approaches to Postcontract Change in the Americas. (Interdisciplinary Contributions to Archaeology Ser.). (Illus.). 245p. (C). 1993. 35.00 (0-306-44176-4, Plenum Pr) Plenum.

Rogers, J. Daniel. Objects of Change: The Archaeology & History of Arikara Contact with Europeans. LC 89-600382. (Archaeological Inquiry Ser.). (Illus.). 336p. 1990. 32.50 (0-87474-840-2) Smithsonian.

***Rogers, J. Daniel & Smith, Bruce D., eds.** Mississippian Communities & Households. LC 94-44049. 320p. 1995. pap. 29.95 (0-8173-0768-0) U of Ala Pr.

Rogers, J. M. Mughal Miniatures. LC 93-60225. (Eastern Art Ser.). (Illus.). 128p. 1993. pap. 15.95 (0-500-27732-X) Thames Hudson.

— Uses of Anachrohism on Cultural Methodological Diversity in Islamic Art. (C). 1994. 8.50 (0-7286-0225-3, Pub. by Sch Orient & African Stud UK) S Asia.

Rogers, J. Philip. Through a Glass Darkly: The Impact of Cognitive Psychological Factors on Crisis Decision-Making. (Ridgeway International Security Studies). 320p. (C). 1995. text ed. 55.00 (0-8133-8592-X) Westview.

Rogers, J. Philips, ed. The Future of European Security. LC 92-10695. 1993. text ed. 55.00 (0-312-04782-7) St Martin.

Rogers, J. S. James Rogers of New London, Connecticut, & His Descendants. (Illus.). 514p. 1989. reprint ed. lib. bdg. 85.00 (0-8328-1026-6); reprint ed. pap. 77.00 (0-8328-1027-4) Higginson Bk Co.

Rogers, J. W. & Millan, W. H. Coil Slitting. LC 73-7903. 127p. 1967. reprint ed. pap. 55.00 (0-08-017696-8, Pub. by Pergamon Repr UK) Franklin.

Rogers, Jack B. & Baird, Forrest. Introduction to Philosophy: A Case Study Approach. LC 80-8344. (Case Study Ser.). 240p. (Orig.). 1981. pap. text ed. 14.95 (0-06-066997-7, RD 346) Harper SF.

Rogers, Jacqueline. Best Friends Sleep Over. LC 92-56895. (J). 1993. 14.95 (0-590-44793-9) Scholastic Inc.

— The Christmas Pageant. (Sandcastle Ser.). (Illus.). 32p. (J). (ps-3). 1992. pap. 5.95 (0-448-40256-4, G&D) Putnam Pub Group.

— You Can Stop Smoking. 288p. 1990. mass mkt. 5.50 (0-671-70295-5) PB.

Rogers, Jacqueline, tr. see Dumas, Alexandre.

Rogers, Jacqueline M. Aspects of the Female Novel. LC 91-6859. 200p. (C). 1991. text ed. 30.00 (0-89341-663-0); pap. text ed. 17.50 (0-89341-664-9) Hollowbrook.

***Rogers, Jacquelyn.** You Can Stop Smoking. Rubenstein, Julie, ed. 1995. mass mkt. 5.99 (0-671-52303-1) PB.

Rogers, James. The Dictionary of Cliches. 1986. mass mkt. 5.99 (0-345-33814-6) Ballantine.

— The Dictionary of Cliches. 320p. 1992. reprint ed. pap. 8.99 (0-517-06020-5, Pub. by Wings Bks) Random.

Rogers, James A., jt. auth. see Dorland, Wayne E.

Rogers, James E. The Story of Holland. 1977. lib. bdg. 59.95 (0-8490-2680-6) Gordon Pr.

Rogers, James H. Capitalism in Crisis. 1938. 59.50 (0-686-83499-2) Elliots Bks.

Rogers, James M. The Impact of Policy Analysis. LC 87-17181. (Series in Policy & Institutional Studies). 210p. (C). 1988. 49.95 (0-8229-3571-6) U of Pittsburgh Pr.

Rogers, James N., ed. see Shumacker, Harris B.

***Rogers, James R.** A Uniform Approach to Rate & Ratio Problems. (Hi Map Ser.: No. 15). (Illus.). 60p. Date not set. pap. text ed. 11.99 (0-614-05311-0, HM 5615) COMAP Inc.

***Rogers, James S.** The Early History of the Law of Bills & Notes: A Study of the Origins of Anglo-American Commerical Law. (Cambridge Studies in English Legal History). 296p. (C). 1995. 59.95 (0-521-44212-5) Cambridge U Pr.

Rogers, James S., ed. Anatomy of a Personal Injury Lawsuit. 3rd ed. (Illus.). 556p. 1991. boxed 80.00 (0-941916-61-8) ATLA Pr.

Rogers, James T. The Antislavery Movement. LC 93-40960. (Social Reform Movements Ser.). (J). 1994. write for info. (0-8160-2907-5) Facts on File.

— The Secret War: Espionage in World War II. (World Espionage Ser.). (Illus.). 128p. (YA). (gr. 7-10). 1991. lib. bdg. 16.95 (0-8160-2395-6) Facts on File.

Rogers, Janice, jt. auth. see Cunningham, Loren.

Rogers, Janice L., ed. see Dittman, Richard & Schmieg, Glenn.

Rogers, Jean. Dinosaurs Are 568. LC 88-5501. (Illus.). 96p. (J). (gr. 3 up). 1988. 10.95 (0-688-07931-8) Greenwillow.

— Goodbye, My Island. LC 82-15816. (Illus.). 96p. (J). (gr. 5-7). 1983. 12.95 (0-688-01964-1); lib. bdg. 12.88 (0-688-01965-X) Greenwillow.

— King Island Christmas. LC 84-25865. (Illus.). 32p. (J). (gr. k-3). 1985. 13.00 (0-688-04236-8); lib. bdg. 12.93 (0-688-04237-6) Greenwillow.

— Prevention's Quick & Healthy Low-Fat Cooking, 1993: From Entertaining to the Everyday. 1993. 25.95 (0-87596-174-6); pap. 15.95 (0-87596-175-4) Rodale Pr Inc.

— Raymond's Best Summer. LC 89-34772. (Illus.). 80p. (J). (gr. 1 up). 1990. 12.95 (0-688-09391-4) Greenwillow.

— Runaway Mittens. LC 87-12024. (Illus.). 24p. (J). (ps-3). 1988. 15.00 (0-688-07053-1); lib. bdg. 14.93 (0-688-07054-X) Greenwillow.

— The Secret Moose. LC 84-12897. (Illus.). 64p. (J). (gr. 3-5). 1985. 15.00 (0-688-04248-1); lib. bdg. 14.93 (0-688-04249-X) Greenwillow.

Rogers, Jean, ed. Prevention's Cooking for Good Health: Easy Recipes for Low-Fat Living. (Illus.). 384p. 1994. 27.95 (0-87596-210-6) Rodale Pr Inc.

— Prevention's Quick & Healthy Low-Fat Cooking: Featuring All-American Food. LC 94-39507. (Illus.). 320p. 1995. pap. 15.95 (0-87596-237-8) Rodale Pr Inc.

— Prevention's Quick & Healthy Low-Fat Cooking: Featuring Healthy Cuisines from the Mediterranean. LC 93-35544. (Illus.). 272p. 1994. 25.95 (0-87596-192-4); pap. 15.95 (0-87596-193-2) Rodale Pr Inc.

***Rogers, Jean & Prevention Magazine Health Books Staff, eds.** Prevention's Quick & Healthy Low-Fat Cooking: Featuring All-American Food. LC 94-39507. (Prevention Magazine's Quick & Healthy Low-Fat Cooking Ser.). (Illus.). 320p. 1995. 25.95 (0-87596-235-1) Rodale Pr Inc.

Rogers, Jean B. A Prolog Primer. LC 85-22846. 214p. (C). 1986. pap. text ed. 23.75 (0-201-06467-7) Addison-Wesley.

— A Turbo Prolog Primer. LC 86-28707. (Illus.). 240p. (C). 1987. pap. text ed. 23.75 (0-201-12198-0) Addison-Wesley.

Rogers, Jeff. Business Planning for Healthcare Organizations: The Experts' Guide to Creating & Maintaining a Competitive Advantage. (Illus.). 102p. (C). 1988. student ed 87.00 (0-923680-00-4) Amer ComVision Inc.

Rogers, Jeffrey S., jt. auth. see Hamilton, Jeffries M.

Rogers, Jennifer. Adults Learning. 256p. 1977. pap. 16.00 (0-335-00044-4, Open Univ Pr) Taylor & Francis.

— Jigsaws. 87p. (Orig.). 1990. pap. 4.95 (0-87129-016-2, J19) Dramatic Pub.

— Pride & Pregnancy: The Guide to Being a Mother-to-Be. (Illus.). 208p. (Orig.). 1993. pap. 12.00 (0-671-75867-5, Fireside) S&S Trade.

Rogers, Jenny. Adults Learning. 3rd ed. 256p. 1989. pap. 22.00 (0-335-09215-2, Open Univ Pr) Taylor & Francis.

— Caring for People. 192p. 1990. 75.00 (0-335-09430-9, Open Univ Pr); pap. 22.00 (0-335-09429-5, Open Univ Pr) Taylor & Francis.

Rogers, Jerry. The Art of Knitting. (Illus.). 240p. 1991. pap. 29.95 (0-207-17026-6, Pub. by Angus & Robertson AT) HarpC.

Rogers, Jerry, ed. Global Risk Assessments: Issues, Concepts & Applications, Bk. 1. (Illus.). 176p. 1983. pap. 29.95 (0-914325-00-0) Global Risk.

— Global Risk Assessments: Issues, Concepts & Applications, Bk. 2. (Illus.). 240p. 1986. pap. 32.50 (0-914325-01-9) Global Risk.

— Global Risk Assessments: Issues, Concepts & Applications, Bk. 3. 239p. 1988. pap. 32.50 (0-914325-02-7) Global Risk.

Rogers, Jerry, ed. see Suzman, Cedric L. & Srivastava, Mahendra.

***Rogers, Jerry S. & Bullock, William P., Jr., eds.** Revenue Enhancement for Water & Wastewater Systems: Proceedings of the Session. LC 94-34443. 1994. write for info. (0-7844-0030-X) Am Soc Civil Eng.

Rogers, Jim. In Care of the Conductor. 270p. 1994. pap. 5.95 (0-929292-77-4) Hannibal Bks.

Rogers, Jimmie N. The Country Music Message: Revisited. LC 88-17176. 288p. (Orig.). 1988. 20.00 (1-55728-051-7); pap. 11.00 (1-55728-052-5) U of Ark Pr.

Rogers, Joann V. Nonprint Cataloging for Multimedia Collections. 2nd ed. LC 87-22589. (Library Science Text Ser.). 200p. 1987. lib. bdg. 29.50 (0-87287-523-7) Libs Unl.

***Rogers, Joel & Streeck, Wolfgang, eds.** Work Councils: Consultation, Representation, & Cooperation in Industrial Relations. LC 95-13423. (NBER Comparative Labor Markets Ser.). 1995. 55.00 (0-226-72376-3) U Ch Pr.

Rogers, Joel, jt. auth. see Cohen, Joshua.

Rogers, Joel, jt. ed. see Ferguson, Thomas.

Rogers, Joel A. Selected Writings of Joel Augustus Rogers. Kiongozi, Kinya, ed. 100p. (Orig.). 1989. write for info. (0-939841-04-5); pap. write for info. (0-939841-03-7) Pyramid MD.

Rogers, Joel Townsley. The Red Right Hand. 198p. 1983. reprint ed. pap. 3.50 (0-88184-008-4) Carroll & Graf.

Rogers, Joel W. The Hidden Coast: Kayak Explorations from Alaska to Mexico. LC 90-45968. (Illus.). 168p. (Orig.). 1991. pap. 19.95 (0-88240-403-2) Alaska Northwest.

Rogers, John. Crime, Justice & Society in Colonial Sri Lanka. (University of London, School of Oriental & African Studies, Centre of South Asian Studies, London Studies on South Asia Ser.: No. 5). 271p. (C). 1987. 42.00 (0-913215-24-4) Riverdale Co.

— John Rogers & the Rogers Groups, (1829-1904) LC 88-50731. (Illus.). (Orig.). (C). 1990. pap. text ed. write for info. (0-939958-03-1) New Canaan.

— Terminal Option. 168p. (Orig.). 1992. pap. 8.99 (1-56043-656-5) Destiny Image.

Rogers, John, ed. Medical Ethics, Human Choices: A Christian Perspective. LC 87-29747. 176p. (Orig.). 1988. pap. 10.95 (0-8361-3460-5) Herald Pr.

Rogers, John & Crawford, Warren. Maryland Supplement for Modern Real Estate Practice. 7th rev. ed. LC 93-4091. 136p. 1993. pap. 12.95 (0-7931-0629-X, 1510-08, Real Estate Ed) Dearborn Finan.

Rogers, John A. The Elephant on the Tracks & Other Stories. 72p. 1992. pap. 8.00 (1-882265-01-7) Muse Pr ME.

Rogers, John B., Jr. In Him Is Life: How Christ Meets Our Deepest Needs. LC 93-24245. 1994. 9.99 (0-8066-2652-6, 9-2652, Augsburg) Augsburg Fortress.

Rogers, John C., III, ed. see Conference of the Academy of Marketing Science.

Rogers, John E. & Whitman, William B., eds. Microbial Production & Consumption of Greenhouse Gases: Methane, Nitrogen Oxides, & Halomethanes. (Illus.). 308p. 1991. text ed. 64.00 (1-55581-035-7) Am Soc Microbio.

Rogers, John E., et al. Fundamentals of Business Mathematics. LC 92-33170. 624p. 1993. pap. 54.95 (0-534-92476-X) PWS Pubs.

— Fundamentals of Business Mathematics. LC 92-33170. 624p. 1993. student ed, pap. 17.95 (0-534-93292-4) PWS Pubs.

Rogers, John G. Origins of Sea Terms. (American Maritime Library: Vol. 11). xv, 220p. 1984. 15.00 (0-913372-31-5) Mystic Seaport.

***Rogers, John H.** The Giant Planet Jupiter. (Practical Astronomy Handbooks Ser.: 6). (Illus.). 586p. (C). 1995. write for info. (0-521-41008-8) Cambridge U Pr.

Rogers, John J. A History of the Earth. (Illus.). 417p. (C). 1993. 89.95 (0-521-39480-5); pap. 39.95 (0-521-39782-0) Cambridge U Pr.

Rogers, John N. PC Write for Students. 2nd ed. LC 90-42093. 64p. (Orig.). 1991. pap. 5.00 (0-914061-19-4) Orchises Pr.

Rogers, John R. Free Land, Inalienable Rights of Man. LC 00-5557. 52p. (C). 1987. reprint ed. pap. 5.00 (0-942153-17-0) Entropy Conserv.

***Rogers, Joseph P.** Realm of Haden: A Space-Age Fantasy. 183p. 1995. pap. 8.95 (0-9642331-0-X) Rogers Pubng.

Rogers, Joseph P. & Zucker, Howard. ABCs of Housing Bonds. 4th ed. 300p. 1989. pap. 30.00 (0-936093-22-6) Packard Pr Fin.

Rogers, Joseph P., Jr. & Zucker, Howard. ABCs of Housing Bonds. 5th ed. 329p. 30.00 (0-685-71081-5) Packard Pr Fin.

Rogers, Joseph W. U. S. National Bibliography & the Copyright Law: An Historical Study. LC 60-15545. 119p. reprint ed. pap. 34.00 (0-317-10597-3, 2050963) Bks Demand.

Rogers, Joy J. Third Party Billing for Special Education: Panacea or Mirage? LC 92-44211. 1993. pap. text ed. 27.95 (0-914797-83-2) Brookline Bks.

Rogers, Joyce. The Second Best Bed: Shakespeare's Will in a New Light. LC 92-33763. (Contributions to the Study of World Literature Ser.: No. 48). 160p. 1993. text ed. 47.95 (0-313-28831-3, GM8831, Greenwood Pr) Greenwood.

Rogers, Joyce & Rogers, Alan. Let's Eat Out: In Montgomery County. 3rd ed. 256p. 1993. pap. text ed. 9.95 (1-883720-00-1) A Siegel Assocs.

Rogers, Judith & Matsumura, Molleen. Mother-To-Be: A Guide to Pregnancy & Birth for Women with Disabilities. 457p. 1991. 39.95 (0-939957-30-2); pap. 24.95 (0-939957-29-9) Demos Vermande.

Rogers, Judy R. & Rogers, Glenn C. Patterns & Themes: A Basic English Reader. 3rd ed. 240p. (C). 1993. pap. 21.95 (0-534-17988-6) Intl Thomson.

— Variations: A Rhetoric & Reader for College Writing. 298p. (C). 1991. pap. 25.95 (0-534-14658-9) Intl Thomson.

Rogers, Judy S., ed. see Liebhardt, Paul W.

Rogers, Julie. Understanding People or, How to Be Your Very Own Shrink. LC 78-31175. 232p. 1979. 25.95 (0-88229-273-0) Nelson-Hall.

***Rogers, Juliet & Waldron, Tony.** A Field Guide to Joint Disease in Archaeology. LC 94-45111. 1995. pap. text ed. 48.00 (0-471-95506-X) Wiley.

Rogers, June W. Heidi. (J). 1969. pap. 3.75 (0-87129-200-9, H14) Dramatic Pub.

— A Little Princess. 1978. pap. 3.75 (0-87129-197-5, L40) Dramatic Pub.

— The Magic Flute. 1976. pap. 3.75 (0-87129-078-2, M10) Dramatic Pub.

— The Nutcracker. 1975. write for info. (0-87129-543-1, N22) Dramatic Pub.

— The Truth about Cinderella. 1974. 4.95 (0-87129-235-1, T03) Dramatic Pub.

***Rogers, June W., adapt.** Snow White & the 7 Dwarfs of the Black Forest. 1969. write for info. (0-87129-440-0, S42) Dramatic Pub.

***Rogers, June W., et al.** Twelve Dancing Princesses - Musical. 1976. 5.00 (0-87129-516-4, T04) Dramatic Pub.

Rogers, Justus H. Colusa County (California) (Illus.). 473p. 1993. reprint ed. lib. bdg. 49.50 (0-8328-3524-2) Higginson Bk Co.

Rogers, K. & Coup, A. J. Surgical Pathology of the Breast. 348p. 1990. text ed. 95.00 (0-7236-0965-9, Pub. by John Wright UK) Buttrwrth-Heinemann.

***Rogers, Kalen.** Green Day. (Illus.). 48p. (Orig.). 1995. pap. 11.95 (0-8256-1504-6, OP 47781, Pub. by Omnibus Press UK) Omnibus NY.

— Tori Amos: All These Years. (Illus.). 96p. (Orig.). (C). 1994. pap. 19.95 (0-8256-1448-1, OP47756) Omnibus NY.

Rogers, Katharine M. Feminism in Eighteenth-Century England. LC 81-16236. 302p. 1982. 29.95 (0-252-00900-2) U of Ill Pr.

Rogers, Katharine M., ed. The Meridian Anthology of Restoration & Eighteenth-Century Plays by Women. 592p. (Orig.). 1994. pap. 14.95 (0-452-01110-8, Mer) NAL-Dutton.

Rogers, Katherine. The Sternberg Fossil Hunters: A Dinosaur Dynasty. (Illus.). 301p. 1991. pap. 12.00 (0-87842-300-1) Mountain Pr.

Rogers, Katherine M. & McCarthy, William, eds. The Meridian Anthology of Early Women Writers. 1987. pap. 14.95 (0-452-00848-4, Mer) NAL-Dutton.

Rogers, Kathleen A. Writing to Explain. (J). (gr. 3-6). 1987. pap. 8.99 (0-8224-7537-5) Fearon Teach Aids.

— Writing to Inform. (J). (gr. 3-6). 1987. pap. 8.99 (0-8224-7536-7) Fearon Teach Aids.

— Writing to Persuade. (J). (gr. 3-6). 1987. pap. 8.99 (0-8224-7538-3) Fearon Teach Aids.

Rogers, Kathryn S. U. S. Coal Goes Abroad: A Social Action Perspective in Interorganizational Networks. LC 85-12467. 272p. 1985. text ed. 55.00 (0-275-90036-3, C0036, Praeger Pubs) Greenwood.

Rogers, Kathy. Animals: An Integrated Unit. (Primary Thematic Units Ser.). (Illus.). 96p. (Orig.). 1993. pap. 12.95 (0-944459-75-7) ECS Lrn Systs.

— Bears Everywhere: An Integrated Unit. (Primary Thematic Units Ser.). (Illus.). 96p. (Orig.). 1993. pap. 12.95 (0-944459-78-1) ECS Lrn Systs.

— Dinosaurs: An Integrated Unit. (Primary Thematic Units Ser.). (Illus.). 96p. (Orig.). 1993. pap. 12.95 (0-944459-79-X) ECS Lrn Systs.

— Fairy Tales: An Integrated Unit. (Primary Thematic Units Ser.). (Illus.). 96p. (Orig.). 1994. pap. 12.95 (0-944459-80-3) ECS Lrn Systs.

— Fall Harvest: An Integrated Unit. (Primary Thematic Units Ser.). (Illus.). 80p. (Orig.). 1993. pap. 12.95 (0-944459-73-0) ECS Lrn Systs.

— Folktales: An Integrated Unit. (Primary Thematic Units Ser.). (Illus.). 96p. (Orig.). 1994. pap. 12.95 (0-944459-81-1) ECS Lrn Systs.

— Love & Friendship: An Integrated Unit. (Primary Thematic Units Ser.). (Illus.). 96p. (Orig.). 1994. pap. 12.95 (0-944459-88-9) ECS Lrn Systs.

— Maps & Globes: An Integrated Unit. (Primary Thematic Units Ser.). (Illus.). 96p. (Orig.). 1993. pap. 12.95 (0-944459-76-5) ECS Lrn Systs.

— Native Americans: An Integrated Unit. (Primary Thematic Units Ser.). (Illus.). 80p. (Orig.). 1993. pap. 12.95 (0-944459-74-9) ECS Lrn Systs.

— Oceans & Sea Life: An Integrated Unit. (Primary Thematic Units Ser.). (Illus.). 96p. (Orig.). 1993. pap. 12.95 (0-944459-82-X) ECS Lrn Systs.

— Plants: An Integrated Unit. (Primary Thematic Units Ser.). (Illus.). 96p. (Orig.). 1994. pap. 12.95 (0-944459-83-8) ECS Lrn Systs.

— Sports: An Integrated Unit. (Primary Thematic Units Ser.). (Illus.). 96p. (Orig.). 1993. pap. 12.95 (0-944459-84-6) ECS Lrn Systs.

An Asterisk (*) at the beginning of an entry indicates that the title is appearing in BIP for the first time.

— Stars & Planets: An Integrated Unit. (Primary Thematic Units Ser.). (Illus.). 96p. (Orig.). 1993. pap. 12.95 (0-944459-85-4) ECS Lrn Systs.

— Toys: An Integrated Unit. (Primary Thematic Units Ser.). (Illus.). 96p. (Orig.). 1993. pap. 12.95 (0-944459-86-2) ECS Lrn Systs.

— Ugh! Bugs! An Integrated Unit. (Primary Thematic Units Ser.). (Illus.). 96p. (Orig.). 1994. pap. 12.95 (0-944459-87-0) ECS Lrn Systs.

— Weather: An Integrated Unit. (Primary Thematic Units Ser.). (Illus.). 96p. (Orig.). 1993. pap. 12.95 (0-944459-77-3) ECS Lrn Systs.

Rogers, Katrina S. Hermeneutics, Political Science, & Theory. LC 94-10288. (San Francisco State University Series in Philosophy: Vol. 3). 1994. write for info. (0-8204-2486-2) P Lang Pubs.

Rogers, Kay, ed. Vikings & Surnames. (C). 1989. pap. 35.00 (1-85072-086-X, Pub. by W Sessions UK) St Mut.

Rogers, Ken. Everton Greats. 176p. (C). 1989. pap. text ed. 21.00 (0-85976-274-2, Pub. by J Donald) St Mut.

Rogers, Kim L. Righteous Lives: Narratives of the New Orleans Civil Rights Movement. (Illus.). 254p. (C). 1993. text ed. 45.00 (0-8147-7431-8); pap. text ed. 16.95 (0-8147-7456-3) NYU Pr.

Rogers, Kim L., jt. ed. see McMahan, Eva M.

Rogers, Krista F., ed. see Fritz, E. Mae.

Rogers, L. E., ed. Methods in Plant Biochemistry, Vol. 5: Amino Acids, Proteins & Nucleic Acids. 341p. 1991. text ed. 99.00 (0-12-461015-3) Acad Pr.

***Rogers, L. J.** The Development of Brain & Behaviour in the Chicken. 280p. 1995. 77.50x (0-85198-924-1) CAB Intl.

Rogers, L. W. Dreams & Premonitions. 144p. 1993. pap. 12.00 (0-89540-225-4, SB-225) Sun Pub.

— The Ghosts in Shakespeare. LC 72-3658. (Studies in Shakespeare: No. 24). 1972. reprint ed. lib. bdg. 75.00 (0-8383-1567-4) M S G Haskell Hse.

— The Occultism in the Shakespeare Plays. 1993. reprint ed. pap. 6.00 (1-56459-401-7) Kessinger Pub.

Rogers-Lafferty, Sarah. Encore: Celebrating Fifty Years: The Contemporary Arts Center's Fiftieth Anniversary. Krause, Carolyn, ed. (Illus.). 72p. 1989. pap. 25.00 (0-917562-54-2) Contemp Arts.

Rogers-Lafferty, Sarah, jt. auth. see Grundberg, Andy.

Rogers, Larry. Boatowner's Legal & Financial Advisor. (Illus.). 256p. 1993. pap. text ed. 17.95 (0-87742-341-5, 60270) Intl Marine.

— Boatowner's Legal & Financial Advisor. 1994. pap. text ed. 17.95 (0-07-158007-7) McGraw.

Rogers, Laura. A Collection of Fashion Drawings, 1901. (Illus.). 165p. 1983. pap. text ed. 19.95 (0-914921-00-2) Graphic Ent.

Rogers, Laurine, jt. auth. see Rogers, Richard A.

Rogers, Lawrence, tr. see Agawa, Hiroyuki.

***Rogers, L.C.G. & Williams, D.** Diffusion, Markov Processes & Martingales. 2nd ed. (Probability & Mathematic Ser.: 1). 1995. text ed. 79.95 (0-471-95061-0) Wiley.

Rogers, Leah L., jt. auth. see Dowla, Farid U.

Rogers, Lee. All These Splendid Sins. (Orig.). 1979. pap. 2.50 (0-89083-480-6) Zebra.

Rogers, Lee F. Radiology of Skeletal Trauma, 2 vols., Set. 2nd ed. LC 92-9204. (Illus.). 1619p. 1992. text ed. 375.00 (0-443-08550-1) Churchill.

— Radiology of Skeletal Trauma, Vol. 1. LC 82-4181. (Illus.). 467p. reprint ed. pap. 121.50 (0-8357-6563-6, 2035936) Bks Demand.

— Radiology of Skeletal Trauma, Vol. 2. LC 82-4181. (Illus.). 519p. reprint ed. pap. 148.00 (0-8357-6564-4) Bks Demand.

Rogers, Len. The Barclays Guide to Marketing for the Small Business. (Barclays Small Business Ser.). (Illus.). 180p. 1990. pap. text ed. 24.95 (0-631-17247-5) Blackwell Pubs.

— Pricing for Profit. 380p. (C). 1991. text ed. 49.95 (0-631-16994-6) Blackwell Pubs.

Rogers, Leon. Basic Construction Management. 3rd ed. Lamberton, Sharon, ed. 80p. 1994. 23.00 (0-685-74771-9) Home Builder.

— Basic Construction Management: The Superintendent's Job. 3rd rev. ed. LC 95-12274. (Illus.). 96p. 1995. pap. 27.50 (0-86718-406-X) Home Builder.

Rogers, Leon & Householder, Jerry. Basic Construction Management: The Superintendent's Job. 2nd ed. (Illus.). 63p. 1990. pap. 21.00 (0-86718-342-X) Home Builder.

Rogers, Leon & Weidman, Brent. Your Business Plan: How to Create It, How to Use It. Lamberton, Sharon, ed. LC 93-37571. (Illus.). 128p. (Orig.). 1993. pap. 22.00 (0-86718-390-X) Home Builder.

Rogers, Lesley, jt. auth. see Bradshaw, John.

Rogers, Lewis M., et al. Toward Understanding the New Testament. LC 88-22730. 462p. 1990. 19.95 (0-941214-76-1) Signature Bks.

Rogers, Lilian, tr. see Spykman, Gordon, et al.

Rogers, Lilja. More Laughter Than Tears. 1984. 6.50 (0-8233-0381-0) Golden Quill.

***Rogers, Linda.** Fifth-Five County Doughcraft Designs. (Illus.). 128p. 1995. 24.95 (0-7153-0168-3, Pub. by D & C Pub UK) Sterling.

Rogers, Linda, jt. auth. see Rogers, Neal.

Rogers, Linda T. How to Start a Leadership Class. Rough, Jackie, ed. 64p. (Orig.). 1990. pap. 8.00 (0-88210-245-1) Natl Assn Student.

Rogers, Lindsay. The Postal Powers of Congress: A Study in Constitutional Expansion. LC 78-63956. (Johns Hopkins University. Studies in the Social Sciences. Thirtieth Ser. 1912: 2). reprint ed. 19.00 (0-404-61204-0) AMS Pr.

Rogers, Liz, jt. auth. see Hill, Harold.

Rogers, Lloyd. Zane Grey First Editions: An Analytic Compendium of Determination Points. 1985. 24.00 (0-916620-77-8) Portals Pr.

***Rogers, Lori & Thornock, Chriscilla M.** Too Busy to Cook. (Illus.). 108p. 1994. pap. text ed. 9.95 (0-9629060-7-7) Thornock Intl.

Rogers, Louis, ed. see Al-Jerrahi, Muzaffer O.

Rogers, Louisa. Book of Forms for Everyday Living. 2nd ed. 1990. pap. 8.95 (0-8442-5327-8, Natl Textbk) NTC Pub Grp.

Rogers, Lynn. Great American Bear. (Illus.). 1990. 39.00 (1-55971-079-9, 0164) NorthWord.

Rogers, Lynn, photos. The Wonder of Black Bears. LC 92-16944. (Animal Wonders Ser.). (Illus.). (J). 1992. lib. bdg. 18.60 (0-8368-0855-X) Gareth Stevens Inc.

***Rogers, M.** Clip! Clop! (Sound Board Bks.). 16p. (J). Date not set. bds. 4.98 (0-86112-954-7) Brimax Bks.

— Count with Teddy One Two Three. (Learn with Teddy Ser.). 32p. (J). 1995. 3.98 (1-85854-149-2) Brimax Bks.

— Dear God. (My First Prayers Ser.). 12p. (J). (ps). 1994. bds. 2.98 (0-86112-218-6) Brimax Bks.

— God Bless. (My First Prayers Ser.). 12p. (J). (ps). 1994. bds. 2.98 (0-86112-195-3) Brimax Bks.

— God Made. (My First Prayers Ser.). 12p. (J). (ps). 1994. bds. 2.98 (0-86112-219-4) Brimax Bks.

— How to Overcome Nervousness. 1973. lib. bdg. 250.00 (0-87968-552-2) Krishna Pr.

— Learn with Teddy ABC. (Learn with Teddy Ser.). 32p. (J). 1995. 3.98 (1-85854-150-6) Brimax Bks.

— The Little Red Train. (Sound Board Bks.). 16p. (J). Date not set. bds. 5.98 (0-86112-992-X) Brimax Bks.

— Moo! Moo! (Sound Board Bks.). 16p. (J). Date not set. bds. 4.98 (0-86112-953-9) Brimax Bks.

— Teddy & the Duckling. (Read to Me Ser.). 10p. (J). 1995. bds. 3.98 (1-85854-244-8) Brimax Bks.

— Teddy & the Frog. (Read to Me Ser.). 10p. (J). 1995. bds. 3.98 (1-85854-247-2) Brimax Bks.

— Teddy & the Mice. (Read to Me Ser.). 10p. (J). 1995. bds. 3.98 (1-85854-246-4) Brimax Bks.

— Teddy & the Puppy. (Read to Me Ser.). 10p. (J). 1995. bds. 3.98 (1-85854-245-6) Brimax Bks.

— Thank You God. (My First Prayers Ser.). 12p. (J). (ps). 1994. bds. 2.98 (0-86112-196-1) Brimax Bks.

Rogers, M. H., jt. auth. see Abramson, Harvey.

Rogers, Malcolm. Elizabeth II: Portraits of Sixty Years. (Illus.). 112p. 1986. pap. 11.95 (0-904017-74-5, Pub. by Natl Port Gall UK) Antique Collect.

— From Elizabeth I to Elizabeth II: Master Drawings from the National Portrait Gallery, London. LC 93-23993. 1993. write for info. (0-88397-112-7) Art Srvc Intl.

— Master Drawings: From the National Portrait Gallery. (Illus.). 224p. 1993. 49.50 (1-85514-134-5) Antique Collect.

— Museums & Galleries of London. 3rd rev. ed. (Blue Guides Ser.). (Illus.). 408p. 1991. pap. 22.95 (0-393-30774-3) Norton.

— William Dobson, 1611-1646. Date not set. 14.95 (0-904017-52-4) Antique Collect.

Rogers, Malcolm, ed. see Piper, David.

Rogers, Mara. Decorating Easter Eggs. (J). (ps-3). 1994. 14.95 (0-316-75414-5) Little.

Rogers, Mara R. Contemporary One-Dish Meals. LC 90-62524. (New Country Fare Ser.). (Illus.). 200p. 1991. 21.95 (0-9627403-0-6) Lake Isle Pr.

— Creative Garnishing: Beautiful Ways to Enhance Meals. LC 94-7777. 1994. pap. write for info. (1-56799-100-9, Friedman-Fairfax) M Friedman Pub Grp Inc.

— Instant Ethnic Cook: An Herb & Spice Blend Cookbook. LC 93-78928. 1993. 19.95 (0-9627403-4-9) Lake Isle Pr.

— Onions: A Celebration of the Onion Through Recipes, Lore, & History. 1995. 15.38 (0-201-62680-2) Addison-Wesley.

Rogers, Marc. Saving Seeds: The Gardner's Guide to Growing & Storing Vegetable & Flower Seeds. Watson, Ben, ed. LC 90-50353. 176p. 1990. pap. 9.95 (0-88266-634-7) Storey Comm Inc.

Rogers, Margaret. Fifty Spiritually Powerful Meditations. 132p. pap. 9.98 (0-87554-560-2, B934) Valley Sun.

Rogers, Margaret & Rogers, Robin. Off the Beaten Track: Scandinavia. LC 93-10709. (Illus.). 317p. (Orig.). 1993. pap. 14.95 (1-56440-303-3) Globe Pequot.

Rogers, Margaret, jt. auth. see Makiya, Hind.

***Rogers, Maria M., comp.** In Other Words: Oral Histories of the Colorado Frontier. (Illus.). 204p. 1995. 24.95 (1-55591-218-4) Fulcrum Pub.

Rogers, Marianne. Dolphins Swim Free. (Illus.). 48p. (Orig.). 1994. pap. 10.95 (0-86417-573-6, Pub. by Kangaroo Pr AT) Seven Hills Bk.

Rogers, Marion. Caribbean ABC. (Illus.). 26p. (Orig.). (J). (ps-1). 1992. reprint ed. pap. 3.50 (0-935357-02-5) CRIC Prod.

Rogers, Mark, jt. auth. see Jackson, R. Eugene.

Rogers, Mark C. Handbook of Pediatric Intensive Care. (Illus.). 464p. 1989. pap. 45.00 (0-683-07321-4) Williams & Wilkins.

— Textbook of Pediatric Intensive Care. 2nd ed. (Illus.). 1792p. 1992. text ed. 195.00 (0-683-07319-2) Williams & Wilkins.

Rogers, Mark C. & Helfaer, Mark A. Handbook of Pediatric Intensive Care. 2nd ed. (Illus.). 873p. 1994. 59.00 (0-683-07326-5) Williams & Wilkins.

Rogers, Mark C. & Helfaer, Mark A., eds. Case Studies in Pediatric Intensive Care. LC 93-12263. (Illus.). 392p. 1993. 45.00 (0-683-07323-0) Williams & Wilkins.

Rogers, Mark C., et al, eds. Principles & Practice of Anesthesiology, Set. LC 92-49205. 2880p. 1992. 179.00 (0-8016-5818-7) Mosby Yr Bk.

Rogers, Mark E. Samurai Cat Goes to the Movies. 288p. 1994. pap. 10.95 (0-312-85744-6) Tor Bks.

— Samurai Cat in the Real World. (Illus.). 128p. (Orig.). 1989. pap. 12.95 (0-312-93198-0) St Martin.

— Sword of Samurai Cat. 1991. pap. 7.95 (0-312-85156-1) St Martin.

Rogers, Marlin N. & Tjia, Benny O. Gerbera Production. Armitage, Allan M., ed. LC 89-20598. (Growers Handbook Ser.: Vol. 4). (Illus.). 120p. 1990. pap. 12.95 (0-88192-172-6) Timber.

Rogers, Marliss, ed. Weekly Prayer Services for Parish Meetings, Cycle C. LC 94-60153. 120p. (Orig.). 1994. pap. 12.95 (0-89622-599-2) Twenty-Third.

— Weekly Prayer Services for Parish Meetings, Year A. LC 94-62052. 120p. (Orig.). 1995. pap. 12.95 (0-89622-646-8) Twenty-Third.

Rogers, Marliss, jt. auth. see Rademacher, William.

Rogers, Marshall, jt. auth. see Englehart, Steve.

Rogers, Martha E. An Introduction to the Theoretical Basis of Nursing. 144p. 1970. pap. 14.95 (0-8036-7490-2) Davis Co.

Rogers, Martin. Opting Out: Choice & the Future of Schools. 200p. (C). 1992. pap. 18.50 (0-85315-769-3, Pub. by Lawrence & Wishart UK) Humanities.

Rogers, Marvin L. Local Politics in Rural Malaysia: Patterns of Change in Sungai Raya. 150p. (C). 1992. pap. text ed. 37.00 (0-8133-8353-6) Westview.

Rogers, Mary. Baby Birds. (Cityscapes Ser.). 33p. (J). (ps-00). 1992. pap. text ed. 23.00 (1-56843-003-5); pap. text ed. 4.50 (1-56843-053-1) BGR Pub.

— Big Brother. (Cityscapes Ser.). 19p. (J). (gr. k). 1992. pap. text ed. 23.00 (1-56843-010-8); pap. text ed. 4.50 (1-56843-060-4) BGR Pub.

— Daniel's First Bus Ride. (Cityscapes Ser.). 30p. (J). (gr. k). 1992. pap. text ed. 23.00 (1-56843-008-6); pap. text ed. 4.50 (1-56843-058-2) BGR Pub.

— The Ducks. (Cityscapes Ser.). 28p. (J). (ps-00). 1992. pap. text ed. 23.00 (1-56843-000-0); pap. text ed. 4.50 (1-56843-050-7) BGR Pub.

— Funny Names. (Cityscapes Ser.). 35p. (J). (gr. 1). 1992. pap. text ed. 23.00 (1-56843-016-7); pap. text ed. 4.50 (1-56843-066-3) BGR Pub.

— I Want to Play. (Cityscapes Ser.). 26p. (J). (gr. 1). 1992. pap. text ed. 23.00 (1-56843-020-5); pap. text ed. 4.50 (1-56843-070-1) BGR Pub.

— Mary Rogers on Pottery & Porcelain: A Handbuilder's Approach. LC 86-70687. (Illus.). 152p. 1986. 19.95 (0-8019-7731-2) Chilton.

— Moving. (Cityscapes Ser.). 32p. (J). (ps-00). 1992. pap. text ed. 23.00 (1-56843-001-9); pap. text ed. 4.50 (1-56843-051-5) BGR Pub.

— New Puppy. (Cityscapes Ser.). 35p. (J). (gr. k). 1992. pap. text ed. 23.00 (1-56843-012-4); pap. text ed. 4.50 (1-56843-062-0) BGR Pub.

— Too Little. (Cityscapes Ser.). 30p. (J). (ps-00). 1992. pap. text ed. 23.00 (1-56843-002-7); pap. text ed. 4.50 (1-56843-052-3) BGR Pub.

— The Torn Jacket. (Cityscapes Ser.). 30p. (J). (gr. 1). 1992. pap. text ed. 23.00 (1-56843-018-3); pap. text ed. 4.50 (1-56843-068-X) BGR Pub.

— The Twins' First Bike. (Cityscapes Ser.). 34p. (J). (gr. 1). 1992. pap. text ed. 23.00 (1-56843-019-1); pap. text ed. 4.50 (1-56843-069-8) BGR Pub.

Rogers, Mary & Rosario, Bernada D. New Glasses. (Cityscapes Ser.). 28p. (J). (gr. 1). 1992. pap. text ed. 23.00 (1-56843-021-3); pap. text ed. 4.50 (1-56843-071-X) BGR Pub.

Rogers, Mary A. Country Roads of Kentucky. LC 92-81832. (Country Roads Ser.). (Illus.). 120p. (Orig.). 1993. pap. 9.95 (1-56626-008-6) Country Rds.

Rogers, Mary A., ed. see Laborde, Errol.

Rogers, Mary B. Cold Anger: A Story of Faith & Power Politics. LC 90-35619. 320p. (Orig.). 1990. pap. 14.95 (0-929398-13-0) UNTX Pr.

Rogers, Mary B., et al. We Can Fly: Stories of Katherine Stinson & Other Gutsy Texas Women. LC 82-80441. (Illus.). 184p. (Orig.). (J). (gr. 7-p). 1983. 14.95 (0-936650-02-8) E C Temple.

Rogers, Mary E. Domestic Life in Palestine. 390p. 1988. pap. 19.95 (0-7103-0290-8) Routledge Chapman & Hall.

Rogers, Mary F. Novels, Novelists, & Readers: Toward a Phenomenological Sociology of Literature. LC 90-9890. (SUNY Series in the Sociology of Culture). 332p. (C). 1991. 64.50 (0-7914-0602-4); pap. 21.95 (0-7914-0603-2) State U NY Pr.

Rogers, Mary R. The International Spud: Fun & Feast with the World's Favorite Tuber. (Illus.). 160p. 1992. pap. 17.95 (0-316-75412-9) Little.

Rogers, Marylyle. Chanting the Dawn. Marrow, Linda, ed. 288p. (Orig.). 1991. mass mkt. 4.95 (0-671-70951-8, Pocket Star Bks) PB.

— Chanting the Storm. Tolley, Carolyn, ed. 320p. (Orig.). 1994. mass mkt. 5.50 (0-671-87185-4) PB.

— Dark Whispers. Tolley, Carolyn, ed. 368p. (Orig.). 1992. mass mkt. 4.99 (0-671-70952-6) PB.

— The Eagle's Song. Tolley, Carolyn, ed. 368p. (Orig.). 1992. mass mkt. 4.99 (0-671-74561-1, Pocket Star Bks) PB.

— The Keepsake. Tolley, Carolyn, ed. 336p. (Orig.). 1993. mass mkt. 5.50 (0-671-74562-X, Pocket Star Bks) PB.

— Proud Hearts. Tolley, Carolyn, ed. 352p. (Orig.). 1990. mass mkt. 5.50 (0-671-70235-1) PB.

— Twilight Secrets. Tolley, Caroline, ed. 336p. (Orig.). 1994. mass mkt. 5.50 (0-671-87186-2, Pocket Star Bks) PB.

Rogers, Maureen, ed. see Monahan, Jean.

Rogers, May. The Waverley Dictionary. 1972. 75.00 (0-8490-1279-1) Gordon Pr.

Rogers, Meyric R. American Interior Design: The Traditions & Development of Domestic Design from Colonial Times to the Present. LC 75-22838. (America in Two Centuries Ser.). (Illus.). 1976. reprint ed. 34.95 (0-405-07709-2) Ayer.

Rogers, Meyric R., et al. Four American Painters: George Caleb Bingham, Winslow Homer, Thomas Eakins, Albert P. Ryder. LC 72-86438. (Museum of Modern Art Publications in Reprint). (Illus.). 1969. reprint ed. 20.95 (0-405-01547-X) Ayer.

Rogers, Michael C., et al. College Korean. 380p. 1991. pap. 25.00 (0-520-06994-3) U CA Pr.

***Rogers, Michael D., ed.** Business & the Environment. LC 94-48399. 1995. write for info. (0-312-12573-9) St Martin.

Rogers, Michael J. From Sherborne to a See: The Life of Bishop David Coutts. 205p. (C). 1989. 100.00 (0-7223-2364-6, Pub. by A H S Ltd UK) St Mut.

Rogers, Michael R. Teaching Approaches in Music Theory: An Overview of Pedagogical Philosophies. LC 83-10167. 236p. 1984. 29.95 (0-8093-1147-X) S Ill U Pr.

Rogers, Michael S. The A to Z Guide to Alternative Medicine. 130p. 1994. pap. 12.95 (0-9641646-0-4) Rogers Bks.

Rogers, Millard B., jt. auth. see Moseley, Spencer.

Rogers, Millard F. Sketches & Bozzetti by American Sculptors, 1800-1950. Schoellkopf, Carol, ed. (Illus.). 243p. (C). 1989. text ed. 65.00 (0-931537-08-8) Cincinnati Mus.

Rogers, Minor & Rogers, Ann. Rennyo: The Second Founder of Shin Buddhism. LC 91-43551. (Nanzan Studies in Asian Religions: Vol. 3). (Illus.). 456p. (C). 1992. text ed. 75.00 (0-89581-929-5, Asian Human Pr); pap. text ed. 30.00 (0-89581-930-9, Asian Human Pr) Jain Pub Co.

Rogers, Miriam, jt. auth. see Yardley, Maili.

Rogers, Mondel. Old Ranches of the Texas Plains. LC 76-17980. (Joe & Betty Moore Texas Art Ser.: No. 1). (Illus.). 126p. 1976. 29.95 (0-89096-019-4) Tex A&M Univ Pr.

Rogers, Murphy P. A State's Supervision of Its Elementary Schools. LC 73-177204. (Columbia University. Teachers College. Contributions to Education Ser.: No. 679). reprint ed. 37.50 (0-404-55679-5) AMS Pr.

Rogers, N. Bruce, tr. see Swedenborg, Emanuel.

***Rogers, Nancy H. & McEwen, Craig A.** Mediation: Law, Policy & Practice. 2nd ed. LC 94-39341. 1994. 120.00 (0-615-00494-6) Clark Boardman Callaghan.

Rogers, Naomi. Dirt & Disease: Polio Before FDR. LC 91-32642. (Health & Medicine in American Society Ser.). (Illus.). 276p. (C). 1992. text ed. 45.00 (0-8135-1785-0); pap. text ed. 15.00 (0-8135-1786-9) Rutgers U Pr.

Rogers, Natalie. The Creative Connection. LC 93-83958. 1993. 29.95 (0-8314-0080-3) Sci & Behavior.

— Emerging Woman: A Decade of Midlife Transitions. LC 79-92627. 1980. 9.95 (0-9605634-0-7) Personal Press.

— Farewell Fatigue. 144p. (Orig.). 1977. pap. 6.95 (0-88976-022-5) Gordon Soules Bk.

Rogers, Neal & Rogers, Linda. Powder Paradise: Helicopter Skiing in the Cariboo & Monashee Mountains of British Columbia. (Illus.). 128p. 1992. 39.95 (1-56037-009-2) Am Wrld Geog.

— Saltwater Fly-Fishing Magic. (Illus.). 144p. 1993. 45.00 (1-55821-253-1) Lyons & Burford.

Rogers, Nell & Rogers, Guy. The Medical Mischief, You Say! (Degerminating the Germ Theory) reprint ed. spiral bd. 5.50 (0-7873-0735-1) Mokelumne.

Rogers, Neville. Keats, Shelley & Rome. LC 75-22076. (English Literature Ser.: No. 33). 1975. lib. bdg. 75.00 (0-8383-2080-5) M S G Haskell Hse.

Rogers, Nicholas. Whigs & Cities: Popular Politics in the Age of Walpole & Pitt. 456p. 1990. 79.00 (0-19-821785-4) OUP.

Rogers, Nicholas, jt. ed. see Lovejoy, Paul E.

Rogers, Nicholas, jt. ed. see Lovejoy, Paul.

***Rogers, Noel, ed. & comp.** Christmas Joy: Favorite Holiday Stories. (Die-Cuts Ser.). (Illus.). 80p. (Orig.). 1995. pap. 6.99 (0-88088-951-9) Peter Pauper.

Rogers, P. L. & Fleet, G. H., eds. Biotechnology & the Food Industry. 320p. 1989. text ed. 56.00 (2-88124-354-1) Gordon & Breach.

Rogers, P. M., jt. ed. see Cairns, W. J.

Rogers, P. P. & Lapuente, F. A. Diccionario de Seudonimos Literarios Espanoles, Con Algunas Iniciales. 610p. (SPA.). 1977. 75.00 (0-8288-5322-3, S50152); pap. 49.95 (0-8288-5325-8, S31444) Fr & Eur.

— Diccionario de Seudonimos Literarios Espanoles, Con Algunas Iniciales. 610p. (SPA.). 1993. 69.50x (84-249-1352-3) Elliots Bks.

***Rogers, P. Thomas.** The Medical Student's Guide to Top Board Scores. (Illus.). 236p. (Orig.). (C). 1994. pap. text ed. 24.95 (0-9632231-0-0) Innovat Pub & Graph.

Rogers, Pat. The Economy of the Arts in the 18th Century. 224p. 1989. 39.00 (0-7185-1281-2, Pub. by Pinter Pubs UK) St Martin.

— Essays on Pope. LC 92-29785. 264p. (C). 1993. 54.95 (0-521-41869-0) Cambridge U Pr.

— Johnson. (Past Masters Ser.). 128p. (C). Date not set. 7.95 (0-19-287593-0) OUP.

— The Transit of Caledonia: Johnson, Boswell, & Scotland. (Illus.). 290p. 1995. 49.95 (0-19-818259-7) OUP.

Rogers, Pat, ed. The Eighteenth Century. LC 78-15568. (Context of English Literature Ser.). 246p. (C). 1978. pap. 18.50 (0-8419-0422-7) Holmes & Meier.

— An Outline of English Literature. 512p. 1992. pap. 13.95 (0-19-282938-6) OUP.

— The Oxford Illustrated History of English Literature. (Illus.). 450p. 1987. 45.00 (0-19-812816-9) OUP.

— The Oxford Illustrated History of English Literature. (Illus.). 544p. 1990. reprint ed. pap. 22.95 (0-19-282728-6) OUP.

***Rogers, Pat & Kaiser, Gabriele, eds.** Equity in Mathematics Education: Influences of Feminism & Culture. LC 94-43477. 1995. write for info. (0-7507-0400-4, Falmer Pr); pap. write for info. (0-7507-0401-2, Falmer Pr) Taylor & Francis.

Rogers, Pat, ed. see Defoe, Daniel.

Rogers, Pat, ed. see Johnson, Samuel & Boswell, James.

Rogers, Pat, ed. see Pope, Alexander.

Rogers, Pat, jt. ed. see Rousseau, G. S.

Rogers, Pat, ed. see Swift, Jonathan.

An Asterisk (*) at the beginning of an entry indicates that the title is appearing in BIP for the first time.

Rogers, Patricia N., ed. JTEC Program Summary. (Program Summaries Ser.). xvi, 99p. 1991. pap. write for info. (*1-883712-18-1*, JTEC) Intl Tech Res.

Rogers, Patricia S., jt. auth. see Rogers, Steve.

Rogers, Patrick, tr. see Martini, Carlo C.

Rogers, Patrick F. Target Zone. (Omega Ser.). 1993. mass mkt. 3.50 (*0-373-63209-6*, 1-63209-0) Harlequin Bks.

— War God. 1990. mass mkt. 4.50 (*1-55817-436-2*, Pinnacle NY) Windsor NY.

— War Machine. (Omega Ser.). 1993. mass mkt. 3.50 (*0-373-63207-X*, 1-63207-4) Harlequin Bks.

— Zero Hour. (Omega Ser.). 1993. mass mkt. 3.50 (*0-373-63208-8*, 1-63208-2) Harlequin Bks.

Rogers, Patrick J. Continuo Realization in Handel's Vocal Music. Buelow, George J., ed. LC 88-37937. (Studies in Musicology: No. 104). 286p. 1991. 64.95 (*0-8357-1875-1*) Univ Rochester Pr.

Rogers, Patrick V. Colossians. LC 80-83063. (New Testament Message Ser.: Vol. 15). 98p. 1981. 10.95 (*0-8146-5203-4*); pap. 5.95 (*0-8146-5138-0*) Liturgical Pr.

Rogers, Pattiann. Firekeeper: New & Selected Poems. LC 94-10655. 168p. (Orig.). 1994. pap. 12.95 (*1-57131-400-8*) Milkweed Ed.

— Legendary Performance. 96p. (Orig.). 1987. pap. text ed. 9.95 (*0-938507-07-9*) Ion Books.

— Splitting & Binding. LC 88-28065. (Wesleyan Poetry Ser.). 61p. 1989. 22.50 (*0-8195-2172-8*, Wesleyan Univ Pr); pap. 10.95 (*0-8195-1173-0*, Wesleyan Univ Pr) U Pr of New Eng.

Rogers, Paul. Funimals. (Illus.). 32p. (J). (ps-1). 1991. 12.95 (*0-8120-6216-7*) Barron.

— Letter to Grandma. (J). 1994. 14.95 (*0-689-31947-9*, Atheneum Bks Young) S&S Childrens.

— The Shapes Game. LC 89-19957. (Illus.). 32p. (J). (ps-2). 1990. 12.95 (*0-8050-1280-X*, Bks Young Read) H Holt & Co.

— What Will the Weather Be Like Today? LC 88-32736. (Illus.). (J). (ps up). 1990. 13.95 (*0-688-08950-X*); lib. bdg. 13.88 (*0-688-08951-8*) Greenwillow.

***Rogers, Paul, text.** Subject of Painting: A Selection by Paul Rogers of 9 Contemporary Painters Working in France. (Illus.). 1982. pap. 20.00 (*0-905836-32-4*, Pub. by Museum Modern Art UK) St Mut.

Rogers, Paul & Rogers, Emma. Bat Boy. (Illus.). 96p. (J). (gr. 5-8). 1993. pap. 6.95 (*0-460-88153-1*, J M Dent & Sons) Trafalgar.

— Our House. LC 92-53015. (Illus.). 40p. (J). (ps up). 1993. 14.95 (*1-56402-134-3*) Candlewick Pr.

Rogers, Paul, jt. auth. see Dando, Malcolm.

Rogers, Paul, jt. auth. see Landais-Stamp, Paul.

Rogers, Paul, jt. auth. see Randle, Michael.

Rogers, Paul, jt. auth. see Williams, David J.

Rogers, Paul P. The Bitter Years: MacArthur & Sutherland. LC 90-36984. 376p. 1990. text ed. 69.50 (*0-275-92919-1*, C2919, Praeger Pubs) Greenwood.

Rogers, Paul P., et al. Insurance in Socialist East Europe. LC 87-29248. 192p. 1988. text ed. 59.95 (*0-275-92903-5*, C2903, Praeger Pubs) Greenwood.

Rogers, Paul P. Insurance in the Soviet Union. LC 86-9437. 222p. 1986. text ed. 65.00 (*0-275-92255-3*, C2255, Praeger Pubs) Greenwood.

— MacArthur & Sutherland: The Good Years. LC 89-27560. 408p. 1990. text ed. 69.50 (*0-275-92918-3*, C2918, Praeger Pubs) Greenwood.

Rogers, Paul P., comp. The Spanish Civil War: An Exhibit. (Illus.). 1978. pap. 8.00 (*0-87959-083-1*) U of Tex H Ransom Ctr.

Rogers, Paul T. Forget-Me-Not. (Picture Puffins Ser.). (Illus.). 32p. (J). (ps-00). 1986. pap. 3.50 (*0-685-43615-2*, Puffin) Puffin Bks.

— Saul's Book. 1983. 15.95 (*0-916366-16-2*) Pushcart Pr.

Rogers, Penelope R., jt. auth. see Essa, Eva.

Rogers, Perry M. Aspects of Western Civilization: Problems & Sources in History, Vol. 1. 2nd ed. 480p. (C). 1991. pap. text ed. write for info. (*0-13-050758-X*) P-H.

— Aspects of Western Civilization: Problems & Sources in History, Vol. 2. 2nd ed. 528p. (C). 1992. pap. text ed. write for info. (*0-13-051897-2*) P-H.

Rogers, Peter. Painter's Quest: Art As a Way of Revelation. 1994. pap. 17.95 (*1-879041-22-7*) Sigo Pr.

— Red Letter Days. (Illus.). 240p. 1995. 39.95 (*1-85223-783-X*, Pub. by Crowood Pr UK) Trafalgar.

***Rogers, Peter & Lydon, Peter, eds.** Water in the Arab World: Perspectives & Prognoses. LC 94-37287. 1994. write for info. (*0-674-94789-4*) HUP.

— Water in the Arab World: Perspectives & Prognoses. (Illus.). 389p. 1995. pap. text ed. 25.00 (*0-674-94780-0*, ROGWAT) HUP.

Rogers, Peter P. America's Water: Federal Roles & Responsibilities. LC 93-1740. (Illus.). 285p. 1993. 29.95x (*0-262-18156-8*) MIT Pr.

Rogers, Peter S. Proust: Speculative Scripture: The Reader of His Own Self. Olds, Marshall C., ed. (STCL Monographs: No. 2). 200p. (Orig.). 1992. pap. 4.40 (*0-9624892-1-2*) Studies Twentieth.

Rogers, Phil. Ash Glazes. 144p. 1991. text ed. 29.95 (*0-8019-8243-X*) Chilton.

Rogers, Phillip A., jt. auth. see Craig, John R.

Rogers, Quint. The Guardian Coloring Book, Safety Tips for Children. (Illus.). 20p. (J). (gr. k-4). 1995. pap. 1.50 (*0-9637930-0-4*) Creat Wrld.

Rogers, R. Colossians. 1989. pap. 22.00 (*0-86217-032-X*, Pub. by Veritas IE) St Mut.

— How to Make Money from Ideas & Inventions. pap. text ed. write for info. (*0-7494-0862-6*, Pub. by Kogan Page Educ UK) Taylor & Francis.

— The Language of Discipline. 1990. pap. 33.00 (*0-7463-0651-2*, Pub. by Northcote UK) St Mut.

Rogers, R. C., jt. auth. see Rogers, C. A.

Rogers, R. H., jt. auth. see Owen, J. M.

Rogers, R. Mark. Handbook of Key Economic Indicators. 288p. 1994. text ed. 45.00 (*0-7863-0193-7*) Irwin Prof Pubng.

Rogers, R. R. & Yau, M. K. Short Course in Cloud Physics. (International Series in Natural Philosophy). (Illus.). 350p. 1989. pap. 33.00 (*0-08-034863-7*, Pergamon Pr) Elsevier.

— Short Course in Cloud Physics. 3rd ed. (International Series in Natural Philosophy). (Illus.). 350p. 1989. 65.00 (*0-08-034864-5*, Pergamon Pr) Elsevier.

Rogers, R. Vashon, Jr. Drinks, Drinkers & Drinking or the Law & History of Intoxicating Liquors. iv, 241p. 1985. reprint ed. lib. bdg. 24.00 (*0-8377-1043-X*) Rothman.

— The Law & Medical Men. xiii, 214p. 1981. reprint ed. lib. bdg. 22.00 (*0-8377-1032-4*) Rothman.

***Rogers, Raleigh.** Alison. LC 93-94366. 208p. (Orig.). 1995. pap. 12.00 (*1-56002-433-X*, Univ Edtns) Aegina Pr.

Rogers, Ralph B. Splendid Torch. LC 93-39006. (Illus.). 1993. 25.00 (*0-914659-66-9*) Phoenix Pub.

Rogers, Randall. Latin Siege Warfare in the Twelfth Century. LC 92-8978. (Oxford Historical Monographs). (Illus.). 310p. 1993. 65.00 (*0-19-820277-6*, Clarendon Pr) OUP.

Rogers, Randy. Collier Farm Bankruptcy Guide. 1989. Updates. ring bd. write for info. (*0-8205-1233-8*) Bender.

Rogers, Raymond A. How to Report Research & Development Findings to Management. rev. ed. LC 72-78965. 32p. 1986. pap. 3.95 (*0-87576-040-6*) Pilot Bks.

Rogers, Raymond F. My Childhood's Eden. 96p. 1992. 12. 95 (*1-56167-080-4*) Noble Hse MD.

Rogers, Rex & Rogers, Wendy. Stories of Childhood: Shifting Agendas of Child Concern. 228p. 1992. 65.00 (*0-8020-2974-4*) U of Toronto Pr.

Rogers, Rex S. Stories of Childhood: Shifting Agendas of Child Concern. LC 93-136336. 228p. 1994. pap. 19.95 (*0-8020-6944-4*) U of Toronto Pr.

Rogers, Rex S., ed. Sex Education, Rationale & Reaction. LC 73-89764. 295p. reprint ed. pap. 84.10 (*0-317-26377-3*, 2024519) Bks Demand.

***Rogers, Rex S., et al.** Social Psychology: A Critical Agenda. (Illus.). 300p. (C). 1995. text ed. 54.95 (*0-7456-1182-6*, Pub. by Polity Pr UK); pap. text ed. 21. 95 (*0-7456-1183-4*, Pub. by Polity Pr UK) Blackwell Pubs.

***Rogers, Ricard.** Diagnostic & Structured Interviewing: A Handbook for Psychologists. LC 94-42415. 411p. 1995. 59.00 (*0-911907-20-3*) Psych Assess.

Rogers, Richard. Architecture: A Modern View. LC 90-71314. (Walter Neurath Memorial Lecture Ser.). (Illus.). 64p. 1991. 14.95 (*0-500-55022-0*) Thames Hudson.

— Architecture: A Modern View. LC 90-71314. (Walter Neurath Memorial Lecture Ser.). (Illus.). 64p. 1992. pap. 9.95 (*0-500-27651-X*) Thames Hudson.

— Judges. 1983. 65.95 (*0-85151-377-8*) Banner of Truth.

Rogers, Richard, ed. Clinical Assessment of Malingering & Deception. LC 88-11212. 370p. 1988. lib. bdg. 39.50 (*0-89862-721-4*) Guilford Pr.

Rogers, Richard & Ward, Samuel. Two Elizabethan Puritan Diaries. Knappen, Marshall M., ed. 1933. 11.75 (*0-8446-1387-8*) Peter Smith.

Rogers, Richard, jt. contrib. see Cook, Peter.

Rogers, Richard A. & Rogers, Laurine. The Outrageous Atlas: A Guide to North America's Strangest Places. (Illus.). 160p. 1993. pap. 9.95 (*0-8065-1445-0*, Citadel Pr) Carol Pub Group.

Rogers, Rick. Earth Tales & Bird Song. (Illus.). 125p. (Orig.). (J). (gr. k-9). 1991. pap. 7.50 (*0-9631017-0-6*) Timberdoodle.

— Education & Social Class. 206p. 1985. 60.00 (*1-85000-094-8*, Falmer Pr); pap. 33.00 (*1-85000-095-6*, Falmer Pr) Taylor & Francis.

— Teaching Information Skills: A Review of the Research & Its Impact on Education. LC 93-33414. (British Library Research Ser.). 240p. 1994. 50.00 (*1-85739-054-7*) Bowker-Saur.

Rogers, Rita S., jt. auth. see Mack, John E.

Rogers, Robert. Rogers' Reminiscences of the French War & Memoir of General Stark. LC 88-80441. (Illus.). 343p. (Orig.). 1988. pap. 20.00 (*0-9620261-3-1*) Freedom Historical.

— Self & Other: Object Relations in Psychoanalysis & Literature. (Psychoanalytic Crosscurrents Ser.). 228p. 1991. text ed. 45.00x (*0-8147-7418-0*); pap. text ed. 17. 50 (*0-8147-7443-1*) NYU Pr.

Rogers, Robert C. Old Dorset. LC 76-140338. (Short Story Index Reprint Ser.). 1977. 17.95 (*0-8369-3730-9*) Ayer.

Rogers, Robert C., jt. auth. see Renardy, Michael.

Rogers, Robert D., jt. auth. see Vemuri, V. Rao.

Rogers, Robert F. Destiny's Downfall: A History of the Island of Guam. LC 94-25845. (Illus.). 416p. (C). 1995. text ed. 45.00x (*0-8248-1616-1*); pap. text ed. 24.95 (*0-8248-1678-1*) UH Pr.

Rogers, Robert J. & White, David. Payroll Deduction Life Insurance. 27p. (Orig.). (C). 1989. pap. text ed. 10.00 (*1-878204-08-4*) APIS Inc.

Rogers, Robert S. Studies in the Reign of Tiberius. LC 77-152601. 181p. 1972. reprint ed. text ed. 52.50 (*0-8371-6036-7*, RORT, Greenwood Pr) Greenwood.

Rogers, Robert S. & Chamberlain, V. B., eds. National Account Marketing Handbook. LC 80-25435. 299p. reprint ed. pap. 85.30 (*0-317-42070-4*, 2056089) Bks Demand.

Rogers, Robert T. Love Will Live & Other Selected Poems. Ware, Claude, ed. & frwd. by. (Illus.). 80p. 1995. pap. 8.00 (*0-9640995-1-9*) Mitram Bks. LOVE WILL LIVE is a collection of poems in chronological order by the two periods in the author's life: BEGINNING, ages 14-24 & FLOWERING, ages 50-73. They arouse a sense of beauty for nature - the sea, magnificent floral arrangements, wild violets in a dense forest, verbenas stretched across dunes & columbines planted on a star. R.T.R., born & raised in So. Carolina & migrating to California at 18, writes in both free verse & stanzaic form; some poems patterned after Millay & Robinson Jeffers (his mentors) have also the spirit & fight of Rimbaud. Rogers' first lines are stimulating, calming, seductive & will stir the reader's imagination; some are an explosive launching of both a smooth & raucous ride the short distance down the page; they accent life, sacred beliefs in NATURE & a dislike for stereotyping humanity. These poems exemplify his love for beauty in all weeds & flowers, which attributed to his success as a florist. R.T.R.'s remission from lung cancer for 12 yrs. & recovery from alcoholism for 19 yrs. was his strength, & poetry his therapy. The people he touched daily & through his writings know his formula for conquering adversities ..."all you have to have is just a thimble full of willingness to be willing." Rogers died from complications of a stroke in 1994. MITRAM BOOKS, P.O. Box 236, Monterey, CA 91754. Voice & FAX 213-664-8146.** ***Publisher Provided Annotation.

Rogers, Robert W. A History of Ancient Persia. LC 70-168502. (Select Bibliographies Reprint Ser.). 1977. reprint ed. 42.95 (*0-8369-5942-6*) Ayer.

— A History of Babylonia & Assyria, 2 vols, Set. LC 76-165806. (Select Bibliographies Reprint Ser.). 1977. reprint ed. 60.95 (*0-8369-5961-2*) Ayer.

Rogers, Robert W., ed. Cuneiform Parallels to the Old Testament. 1977. lib. bdg. 250.00 (*0-8490-1695-9*) Gordon Pr.

Rogers, Robin, jt. auth. see Rogers, Margaret.

***Rogers, Robin D. & Eiteman, Mark A., eds.** Aqueous Biphasic Separations: Biomolecules to Metal Ions. 200p. 1995. 79.50 (*0-306-45019-4*) Plenum.

Rogers, Ronald C., jt. auth. see Doeleman, David.

Rogers, Ronald L. Freeing Someone You Love from Alcohol & Other Drugs. 1992. pap. 14.00 (*0-399-51727-8*, Body Pr-Perigree) Berkley Pub.

Rogers, Ronald L. & McMillan, C. Scott. The Healing Bond: Treating Addictions in Groups. (C). 1989. 19.95 (*0-393-70083-6*); pap. 11.95 (*0-393-70088-7*) Norton.

Rogers, Ronald L. & McMillin, Chandler S. Under Your Own Power: A Guide to Recovery for Nonbelievers--& the Ones Who Love Them. LC 93-4803. 1993. pap. 10. 95 (*0-399-51849-5*, Perigree Bks) Berkley Pub.

— Under Your Own Power: A Guide to Recovery for Nonbelievers, & the Ones Who Love Them. 224p. 1992. 19.95 (*0-399-13775-0*, Putnam) Putnam Pub Group.

Rogers, Rosemary. Bound by Desire. 416p. 1988. mass mkt. 4.95 (*0-380-75451-7*) Avon.

— The Crowd Pleasers. 528p. 1980. mass mkt. 4.95 (*0-380-75622-6*) Avon.

— Dark Fires. (Steve & Ginny Ser.: Bk. 1). 1976. mass mkt. 5.99 (*0-380-00425-9*) Avon.

— The Insiders. 1979. mass mkt. 5.50 (*0-380-40576-8*) Avon.

— Lost Love, Last Love. (Steve & Ginny Ser.: Bk. 3). 1980. mass mkt. 5.99 (*0-380-75515-7*) Avon.

— Love Play. 1982. mass mkt. 4.95 (*0-380-81190-1*) Avon.

— Surrender to Love. 624p. 1982. mass mkt. 4.95 (*0-380-80630-4*) Avon.

— Sweet Savage Love. (Steve & Ginny Ser.: Bk. 1). 640p. 1976. mass mkt. 5.99 (*0-380-00815-7*) Avon.

— The Tea Planter's Bride. 416p. (Orig.). 1995. mass mkt. 6.50 (*0-380-76477-6*) Avon.

— The Wanton. 336p. 1985. mass mkt. 4.95 (*0-380-86165-8*) Avon.

— Wicked Loving Lies. 672p. 1983. mass mkt. 5.99 (*0-380-00776-2*) Avon.

— The Wildest Heart. 608p. 1976. mass mkt. 5.99 (*0-380-00137-3*) Avon.

Rogers, Rosemary, jt. auth. see Kelly, Sean.

Rogers, Roxanne S. The Successful Job Search: A Step-by-Step Guide for a Successful Job Search in the 1990's. 320p. 1993. 29.95 (*1-884274-00-5*) Rogers Res.

Rogers, Roy. Happy Trails. 1994. 23.50 (*0-671-89714-4*) S&S Trade.

***Rogers, Roy, et al.** Happy Trails: Our Life Story. large type ed. LC 95-13694. 390p. 1995. 24.95 (*0-7862-0478-8*) Thorndike Pr.

Rogers, Roy A. Jackson's Mountain. LC 89-26717. 176p. (Orig.). 1990. pap. 9.95 (*1-877674-05-2*) Hampshire Bks.

Rogers, Rudy E. Coalbed Methane Technology. 368p. 1994. text ed. 89.00 (*0-13-016353-8*) P-H.

Rogers, S., ed. Applications of Artificial Neural Networks. 1990. 86.00 (*0-8194-0345-8*, VOL. 1294) SPIE.

Rogers, S. K. Applications of Artificial Neural Networks, Vol. 1469. 1991. 109.00 (*0-8194-0578-7*) SPIE.

Rogers, Sally. Breathless Surge of Words. Spurr, Anna M., ed. LC 91-90407. (Illus.). 80p. (Orig.). 1991. pap. 12.95 (*0-9629738-0-7*) Sentimntl Sal.

Rogers, Sally J., et al, eds. Hospitals & the Uninsured Poor: Measuring & Paying for Uncompensated Care. 192p. 1985. 30.00 (*0-934459-00-2*) United Hosp Fund.

Rogers, Samuel. The Pleasures of Memory. LC 90-118393. 86p. 1989. reprint ed. 48.00 (*1-85477-003-9*, Pub. by Woodstock Bks UK) Cassell.

***Rogers, Sandra.** Lessons from the Light: Insights from a Journey to the Other Side. 128p. (Orig.). 1995. mass mkt. 4.99 (*0-446-60277-9*) Warner Bks.

Rogers, Sandra B. Anatomy Charts for Reflexology. Issel, Christine, ed. (Illus.). 21p. 1994. student ed write for info. (*0-9638862-0-7*) B J Scott.

— Anatomy Charts for Reflexology: Student Edition. Issel, Christine, ed. (Illus.). 55p. 1994. write for info. (*0-9638862-1-5*) B J Scott.

— Anatomy Charts for Reflexology: Teacher's Edition. Issel, Christine, ed. (Illus.). 56p. 1994. write for info. (*0-9638862-2-3*) B J Scott.

***Rogers, Sandra H.** Lessons from the Light: A Spiritual Light. 1994. 10.95 (*0-89176-990-0*) R Bemis Pub.

***Rogers, Sarah.** Maya Lin: Public/Private. 1994. pap. 12.95 (*1-881390-05-5*) OSU Wexner Ctr.

Rogers, Sarah B. Ezra Hardman, M. A. of Wayback College. LC 78-163046. (Short Story Index Reprint Ser.). 1977. reprint ed. 19.95 (*0-8369-3960-3*) Ayer.

Rogers-Seidl. Geriatric Nursing Care Plans. 2nd ed. 340p. 1995. spiral bd. 25.95 (*0-8016-7697-5*) Mosby Yr Bk.

Rogers, Sharon & Person, Ruth. Recruiting Academic Library Director: A Companion to the Search Committee Handbook. 1991. 18.95 (*0-8389-7484-8*); 15. 95 (*0-685-59004-6*) Assn Coll & Res Libs.

Rogers, Sheena J., jt. ed. see Epstein, William.

***Rogers, Sherbrooke.** Grandfather Webster's Strange Will. (Illus.). 90p. (Orig.). (J). (gr. 6-7). 1995. lib. bdg. 15.00 (*0-88092-067-X*); pap. 5.00 (*0-88092-066-1*) Royal Fireworks.

Rogers, Sheridan. Seasonal Entertaining. (Illus.). 144p. 1993. 30.00 (*0-207-17716-3*, Pub. by Angus & Robertson AT) HarpC.

Rogers, Sherry. Chemical Sensitivity. Bensen, Don R., ed. 1995. 3.95 (*0-87983-634-2*) Keats.

Rogers, Sherry A. The Cure Is in the Kitchen. 368p. 1991. 14.95 (*0-9618821-3-1*) Prestige NY.

— The E. I. Syndrome: Environmental Illness. rev. ed. 1995. pap. text ed. 17.95 (*0-9618821-7-4*) Prestige NY.

— The E.I. Syndrome: Are You Allergic to the Twenty-First Century? (Illus.). 667p. (Orig.). (C). 1988. pap. text ed. 14.95 (*0-9618821-0-7*) Prestige NY.

— Tired or Toxic. 438p. 1990. 17.95 (*0-9618821-2-3*) Prestige NY.

— You Are What You Ate. 225p. (Orig.). (C). 1988. pap. text ed. 9.95 (*0-9618821-1-5*) Prestige NY.

Rogers, Sherry A. & Gallinger, Shirley. Macro Mellow. (Orig.). 1992. pap. 12.95 (*0-9618821-4-X*) Prestige NY.

Rogers, Shirle, jt. auth. see Russ, Diane.

Rogers, Sid, jt. auth. see Courtright, John.

Rogers, Spencer L. The Aging Skeleton: Aspects of Human Bone Involution. (Illus.). 120p. (C). 1982. 24.95 (*0-398-04710-3*) C C Thomas.

— The Colors of Mankind: The Range & Role of Human Pigmentation. (Illus.). 68p. (C). 1990. text ed. 21.95x (*0-398-05643-9*) C C Thomas.

— The Human Skull: Its Mechanics, Measurements & Variations. (Illus.). 118p. (C). 1984. 25.95 (*0-398-04955-6*) C C Thomas.

— Personal Identification from Human Remains. (Illus.). 94p. 1987. 33.95x (*0-398-05307-3*) C C Thomas.

— The Shaman: His Symbols & His Healing Power. (Illus.). 224p. 1982. pap. 19.95 (*0-614-02370-X*) C C Thomas.

— The Shaman: His Symbols & His Healing Power. (Illus.). 224p. (C). 1982. 38.95 (*0-398-04594-1*) C C Thomas.

— The Testimony of Teeth: Forensic Aspects of Human Dentition. (Illus.). 126p. (C). 1988. text ed. 35.95x (*0-398-05450-9*) C C Thomas.

Rogers, Steve. Model Boat Building Made Simple. LC 91-67007. (Illus.). 64p. 1992. pap. 12.95 (*0-88740-388-3*) Schiffer.

Rogers, Steve & Rogers, Patricia S. Model Boat Building: The Lobster Boat. LC 94-66369. (Illus.). 64p. (Orig.). 1994. pap. 12.95 (*0-88740-642-4*) Schiffer.

Rogers, Steve & Rosa, Tina. The Shopper's Guide to Mexico. (Illus.). 224p. (Orig.). 1989. pap. 9.95 (*0-912528-90-7*) John Muir.

— Twenty-Two Days in Mexico: The Itinerary Planner. 2nd ed. (Illus.). 128p. 1989. pap. 7.95 (*0-945465-41-6*) John Muir.

Rogers, Steve & Staby-Rogers, Patricia. Model Boat Building: The Spritsail Skiff. (Illus.). 64p. 1993. pap. 12. 95 (*0-88740-534-7*) Schiffer.

Rogers, Steve, jt. auth. see Franz, Carl.

Rogers, Steven K. & Kabrisky, Matthew. An Introduction to Biological & Artificial Neural Networks for Pattern Recognition. 220p. 1991. 42.00 (*0-8194-0534-5*, VOL. TT04) SPIE.

Rogers, Stillman, photos. South Africa Is My Home. LC 92-17722. (My Home Country Ser.). (Illus.). (J). 1992. lib. bdg. 18.60 (*0-8368-0851-7*) Gareth Stevens Inc.

Rogers, Stillman, jt. auth. see Rogers, Barbara R.

Rogers, Stillman, jt. auth. see Rogers, Barbara.

Rogers, Stuart & Thompson, Richard, Jr. The Medical Marketing Plan. 450p. 1992. ring bd. 150.00 (*1-55623-770-7*) Irwin Prof Pubng.

Rogers, Stuart C. & Lubbers, Ronald J. How to Market Your Accounting Services Vol. 1: Developing Your Plan. 400p. 1994. pap. 75.00 (*1-55623-991-2*) Irwin Prof Pubng.

— How to Market Your Accounting Services Vol. 2: Implementing Your Plan. 304p. 1994. pap. 75.00 (*1-55623-994-7*) Irwin Prof Pubng.

Rogers, Stuart C. & Thompson, Richard H., Jr. The Medical Marketing Plan: A Comprehensive Course & Programmed Guide to Writing a Successful Marketing Plan for Your Practice. LC 90-61646. 498p. 1990. 180.00 (*0-9626911-0-0*) Prof Prac Mktg.

Rogers, Sue, jt. ed. see Ruthven, Beverly.

Rogers, Susan. The Worth of a Woman Through God's Eyes. 1988. 4.95 (*0-89274-485-5*) Harrison Hse.

Rogers, Susan, jt. auth. see Abadi, Mauricio.

Rogers, Susan C. Shaping Modern Times in Rural France: The Transformation & Reproduction of an Aveygronnais Community. (Illus.). 235p. 1991. text ed. 47.50 (*0-691-09458-6*); pap. text ed. 16.95 (*0-691-02858-3*) Princeton U Pr.

Rogers, Susan F. Sportsdykes: Stories from On & Off the Field. 224p. 1994. 18.95 (*0-312-11072-3*) St Martin.

Rogers, Susan F., ed. Another Wilderness: New Outdoor Writing by Women. 288p. (Orig.). 1994. pap. 14.95 (*1-878067-54-0*) Seal Pr Feminist.

— Sportsdykes: Stories from on & off the Field. LC 95-5497. 1995. pap. 8.95 (*0-312-13187-9*) St Martin.

Rogers, Susan H., tr. see Rascovsky, Arnaldo.

Rogers, Susan H., jt. auth. see Rogers, Earl M.

***Rogers, Suzanne.** Amazing Alligators - Story Hour Friends. (Illus.). 193p. (J). (ps-1). 1990. teacher ed, pap. 8.95 (*1-878279-11-4*, MM 193) Monday Morning Bks.

Rogers, T. Georgian Poetry, Nineteen Eleven to Nineteen Twenty-Two: The Critical Heritage. (Critical Heritage Ser.). 1977. 69.50 (*0-7100-8278-9*, RKP) Routledge.

Rogers, T., tr. see Buddhaghosa.

Rogers, T. D., jt. auth. see Clapinson, Mary.

Rogers, T. K. Forchess: The Ultimate Social Game. 64p. 1992. pap. 4.95 (*0-9632959-0-X*) Smallbook Assocs.

Rogers, T. N. Too Far from Home & Other Stories. LC 87-25514. 128p. (Orig.). 1988. pap. 10.95 (*0-8262-0671-9*) U of Mo Pr.

***Rogers, Ted.** Fit & Fast Foods. 164p. 1994. pap. 12.00 (*0-9647006-0-3*) Fit Forty Plus.

Rogers, Terence A. Elementary Human Physiology. LC 61-11245. (Illus.). 429p. reprint ed. 122.30 (*0-8357-9880-1*, 2016101) Bks Demand.

Rogers, Teresa. George Washington Carver: Nature's Trailblazer. (Earth Keepers Ser.). (Illus.). 72p. (J). (gr. 4-7). 1992. lib. bdg. 14.98 (*0-8050-2115-9*) TFC Bks NY.

Rogers, Teresa, jt. auth. see Shulman, Jeffrey.

Rogers, Theresa F., jt. auth. see Friedman, Natalie.

Rogers, Theresa F., jt. auth. see Friedman, Nathalie.

Rogers, Thomas. Confessions of a Child of the Century by Samuel Heather. LC 72-189740. 1972. 25.00 (*0-671-21266-4*) Ultramarine Pub.

— Leicester's Ghost. Williams, Franklin B., Jr., ed. (Renaissance English Text Society Ser.: Vol. 4). 94p. 1972. 7.50 (*0-911028-16-1*) Newberry.

Rogers, Thomas E., jt. auth. see Reid, Robert L.

***Rogers, Thomas F.** A Good Man Is Hard to Find. 11p. (Orig.). 1993. pap. 3.00 (*1-57514-114-0*, 3019) Encore Perform Pub.

— Myth & Symbol in Soviet Fiction: Images of the Savior Hero, Great Mother, "Anima," & Child in Selected Novels & Films. LC 91-46783. (Illus.). 348p. 1992. lib. bdg. 99.95 (*0-7734-9849-4*) E Mellen.

— Superfluous Men & the Post-Stalin Thaw: The Alienated Hero in Soviet Prose During the Decade 1953-1963. 1972. text ed. 76.00 (*90-279-2118-0*) Mouton.

Rogers, Thomas G. Stepping Inside the Story: Sermons for Pentecost, Last Third - First Lesson. LC 94-1001. (Orig.). 1994. pap. write for info. (*0-7880-0045-4*) CSS OH.

Rogers, Thomas J., jt. auth. see Gilman, Steven C.

Rogers, Tim B. The Psychological Testing Enterprise: An Introduction. (Psychology Ser.). 1995. text ed. 59.95 (*0-534-21648-X*) Brooks-Cole.

Rogers, Timothy J., ed. Autobiography at the Trigger by Etelvina Astrada. LC 82-60922. 128p. 1984. 13.00 (*0-938972-04-9*) Spanish Lit Pubns.

Rogers, Timothy J., intro. Death on the Run. LC 86-62497. 99p. 1987. 13.00 (*0-938972-11-1*) Spanish Lit Pubns.

Rogers, Timothy J., jt. auth. see Rogers, Elizabeth S.

Rogers, Timothy L. The Power of Goalsetting. 96p. (Orig.). 1991. pap. 5.95 (*0-9630182-0-5*) T L Rogers.

Rogers, Tom. The Soviet Withdrawal from Afghanistan: Analysis & Chronology. LC 92-24260. 256p. 1992. text ed. 59.95 (*0-313-27907-1*, RSE, Greenwood Pr) Greenwood.

— Understanding PCM. 2nd ed. (ABC Pocket Guide for the Field Ser.). (Illus.). 56p. (C). 1986. pap. text ed. 6.95 (*1-56016-028-4*) ABC TeleTraining.

***Rogers, Truett.** West Virginia Baptist History: The Convention Years, 1865-1965. 1994. 21.95 (*0-929915-12-7*) Headline Bks.

— West Virginia Baptist History: The Early Years: 1770-1865. (Illus.). 185p. 1990. 12.95 (*0-929915-04-6*) Headline Bks.

***Rogers, Trumbull.** Editorial Freelancing: A Practical Guide. 200p. (Orig.). 1995. pap. 14.95 (*0-614-01360-7*) Aletheia.

— Editorial Freelancing: A Practical Guide. 1995. pap. write for info. (*0-9639260-1-2*) Aletheia.

***Rogers, Vicki & Stewart, Sharon.** The Tale of a Silly Goose & Other Stories. (Illus.). 44p. (Orig.). (J). 1993. pap. 12.95 (*0-88865-082-5*, Pub. by Pacific Educ Pr CN) Orca Bk Pubs.

Rogers, Vickie L. Ambulataory Care Coding. 1993. 49.00 (*0-317-05420-1*) Am Hlth Info.

— ICD-9-CM: Focus on Pediatrics. 1993. 42.00 (*0-317-05431-7*) Am Hlth Info.

— Intermediate ICD-9-CM for Hospitals. 349p. 1993. 42.00 (*0-317-05432-5*) Am Hlth Info.

— Total Data Quality for the Coding Manager. 1993. 42.00 (*0-317-05443-0*) Am Hlth Info.

Rogers, Virgil M., jt. auth. see Marks, John H.

Rogers, W. G. Wise Men Fish Here: The Story of Frances Steloff & the Gotham Book Mart. 288p. 1994. reprint ed. pap. 14.95 (*1-879923-08-4*) Booksellers Pub.

***Rogers, W. Lane.** Crimes & Misdeeds: Headlines from Arizona's Past. Murphy, Erin, ed. (Illus.). 176p. (Orig.). 1995. pap. 9.95 (*0-87358-631-X*) Northland AZ.

Rogers, Walter T. A Manual of Bibliography. 1977. lib. bdg. 75.00 (*0-8490-2204-5*) Gordon Pr.

Rogers, Warren. When I Think of Bobby: A Personal Memoir of the Kennedy Years. (Illus.). 208p. 1994. reprint ed. pap. 11.00 (*0-06-092533-7*, PL) HarpC.

Rogers, Warren S. My Own Los Angeles, Eighteen Ninety-Four to Nineteen Eighty-Two. (Los Angeles Miscellany Ser.: No. 13). (Illus.). 53p. 1982. 15.00 (*0-87093-313-2*) Dawsons.

Rogers, Wendy. The Return. abr. ed. 210p. 1995. pap. 8.95 (*1-56901-334-9*) NW Pub.

Rogers, Wendy, jt. auth. see Rogers, Rex.

Rogers, Will. Autobiography of Will Rogers. Day, Donald, ed. LC 76-6592. reprint ed. 39.50 (*0-404-15293-7*) AMS Pr.

— Convention Articles of Will Rogers, Ser. II, Vol. I. Stout, Joseph A., Jr. & Rollins, Peter C., eds. LC 76-5609. (Writings of Will Rogers Ser.: Vol. 2). 174p. 1976. 10.50 (*0-914956-08-6*) Okla State Univ Pr.

— The Cowboy Philosopher on Prohibition. Stout, Joseph A., Jr. & Rollins, Peter C., eds. LC 75-21295. (Writings of Will Rogers Ser.: Ser. I, Vol. 5). (Illus.). 52p. 1975. 6.95 (*0-914956-06-X*) Okla State Univ Pr.

— The Cowboy Philosopher on the Peace Conference. Stout, Joseph A., Jr. & Rollins, Peter C., eds. LC 75-8471. (Writings of Will Rogers Ser.: Ser. I, Vol. 4). (Illus.). 47p. 1975. 6.95 (*0-914956-05-1*) Okla State Univ Pr.

— Ether & Me or "Just Relax" Stout, Joseph A., Jr., ed. LC 73-79456. (Writings of Will Rogers Ser.: Ser. I, Vol. 1). (Illus.). 64p. 1973. 8.95 (*0-914956-01-9*) Okla State Univ Pr.

— How to Be Funny & Other Writings of Will Rogers, 3. Gragert, Steven K., ed. LC 82-80505. (Writings of Will Rogers Ser.: Ser. V, Vol. 3). (Illus.). 187p. 1983. 10.95 (*0-914956-23-X*) Okla State Univ Pr.

— The Illiterate Digest. Stout, Joseph A., Jr., ed. LC 74-82796. (Writings of Will Rogers Ser.: Ser. I, Vol. 3). (Illus.). 230p. 1974. 10.50 (*0-914956-04-3*) Okla State Univ Pr.

— Letters of a Self-Made Diplomat to His President. Stout, Joseph A., Jr. et al, eds. LC 76-47737. (Writings of Will Rogers Ser.: Ser. I, Vol. 6). (Illus.). 149p. 1977. 10.50 (*0-914956-09-4*) Okla State Univ Pr.

— More Letters of a Self-Made Diplomat. Gragert, Steven K., ed. LC 82-80504. (Writings of Will Rogers Ser.: Ser. V, Vol. 2). (Illus.). 203p. 1982. 10.95 (*0-914956-22-1*) Okla State Univ Pr.

— Radio Broadcasts of Will Rogers. Gragert, Steven K., ed. LC 82-61001. (Writings of Will Rogers Ser.: Ser. VI, Vol. I). (Illus.). 211p. 1983. 10.95 (*0-914956-24-8*) Okla State Univ Pr.

— There's Not a Bathing Suit in Russia & Other Bare Facts. Stout, Joseph A., Jr., ed. LC 73-89307. (Writings of Will Rogers Ser.: Ser. I, Vol. 2). (Illus.). 95p. 1973. 9.25 (*0-914956-03-5*) Okla State Univ Pr.

— Will Rogers' Daily Telegrams: The Coolidge Years, 1926-1929, Vol. 1. Smallwood, James M. & Gragert, Steven K., eds. LC 77-91791. (Writings of Will Rogers Ser.: Ser. III, Vol. 1). (Illus.). 453p. 1978. 19.95 (*0-914956-10-8*) Okla State Univ Pr.

— Will Rogers' Daily Telegrams: The Hoover Years, 1929-1931, Vol. 2. Smallwood, James M. & Gragert, Steven K., eds. LC 78-70066. (Writings of Will Rogers Ser.: Ser. III, Vol. 2). (Illus.). 390p. 1978. 19.95 (*0-914956-11-6*) Okla State Univ Pr.

— Will Rogers' Daily Telegrams: The Hoover Years, 1931-1933, Vol. 3. Smallwood, James M. & Gragert, Steven K., eds. LC 78-78290. (Writings of Will Rogers Ser.: Ser. III, Vol. 3). (Illus.). 389p. 1979. 19.95 (*0-914956-12-4*) Okla State Univ Pr.

— Will Rogers' Daily Telegrams: The Roosevelt Years, 1933-1935, Vol. 4. Smallwood, James M. & Gragert, Steven K., eds. LC 77-91791. (Writings of Will Rogers Ser.: Ser. III, Vol. 4). (Illus.). 457p. 1979. 19.95 (*0-914956-13-2*) Okla State Univ Pr.

— Will Rogers Treasury: Reflections & Observations. 1987. 7.99 (*0-517-62544-X*) Random Hse Value.

— Will Rogers' Weekly Articles: The Coolidge Years, 1925-1927, Vol. 2. Smallwood, James M. & Gragert, Steven K., eds. LC 79-57650. (Writings of Will Rogers Ser.: Ser. IV, Vol. 2). (Illus.). 368p. 1980. 19.95 (*0-914956-16-7*) Okla State Univ Pr.

— Will Rogers' Weekly Articles: The Coolidge Years, 1927-1929, Vol. 3. Smallwood, James M. & Gragert, Steven K., eds. LC 79-57650. (Writings of Will Rogers Ser.: Ser. IV, Vol. 3). (Illus.). 304p. 1981. 19.95 (*0-914956-17-5*) Okla State Univ Pr.

— Will Rogers' Weekly Articles: The Harding-Coolidge Years, 1922-1925, Vol. 1. Smallwood, James M. & Gragert, Steven K., eds. LC 79-57650. (Writings of Will Rogers Ser.: Ser. IV, Vol. 1). (Illus.). 431p. 1980. 19.95 (*0-914956-15-9*) Okla State Univ Pr.

— Will Rogers' Weekly Articles: The Hoover Years: 1929-1931, Vol. 4. Gragert, Steven K., ed. LC 79-57650. (Writings of Will Rogers Ser.: Ser. IV, Vol. 4). (Illus.). 278p. 1981. 17.95 (*0-914956-18-3*) Okla State Univ Pr.

— Will Roger's Weekly Articles: The Hoover Years 1931-1933, Vol. 5. Gragert, Steven K., ed. LC 79-57650. (Writings of Will Rogers Ser.: Ser. IV, Vol. 5). (Illus.). 280p. 1982. 17.95 (*0-914956-19-1*) Okla State Univ Pr.

— Will Rogers' Weekly Articles: The Roosevelt Years: 1933-1935, Vol. 6. Gragert, Steven K., ed. LC 79-57650. (Writings of Will Rogers Ser.: Ser. IV, Vol. 6). (Illus.). 309p. 1982. 17.95 (*0-914956-21-3*) Okla State Univ Pr.

Rogers, Will, et al. Storm Center: The USS Vincennes & Iran Air Flight 655. LC 92-9202. (Illus.). 264p. 1992. 23.95 (*1-55750-727-9*) Naval Inst Pr.

***Rogers, William.** Recovered Memory & Other Assaults Upon the Mysteries of Consciousness: Hypnosis, Psychotherapy, Fraud & the Mass Media. 176p. 1995. lib. bdg. 26.50 (*0-7864-0109-5*) McFarland & Co.

Rogers, William A. The Shepherd & His Sheep. 1983. pap. 6.99 (*1-56632-011-9*) Revival Lit.

***Rogers, William B.** We Are All Together Now: Fredrick Douglass, William Lloyd Garrison, & the Prophetic Tradition. LC 94-24749. (Studies in African American History & Culture). 182p. 1994. 41.00 (*0-8153-1868-5*) Garland.

Rogers, William E. How to Cut Workers' Comp Costs: 115 Proven Ways. 276p. 1991. ring bd. 125.00 (*0-9635070-0-1*) Cntry Rd Pubns.

— Interpreting Interpretation: Textual Hermeneutics as an Ascetic Discipline. 256p. 1993. 35.00 (*0-271-01059-2*); pap. text ed. 16.95 (*0-685-63308-X*) Pa St U Pr.

— The Three Genres & the Interpretation of Lyric. LC 82-12293. 288p. reprint ed. pap. 82.10 (*0-7837-1936-1*, 2042151) Bks Demand.

Rogers, William Elford. The Three Genres & the Interpertation of Lyric. LC 82-12293. 280p. 1983. pap. 42.50x (*0-691-06554-3*) Princeton U Pr.

Rogers, William F., Jr. Dorothy Maynor & the Harlem School of the Arts: The Diva & the Dream. LC 93-32243. (Illus.). 308p. 1993. 99.95 (*0-7734-9377-8*) E Mellen.

Rogers, William J. Ischemic Heart Disease. (Current Opinion in Cardiology 1993 Ser.). (Illus.). 164p. (Orig.). 1993. pap. 39.95 (*1-870485-88-2*) Current Science.

— Ischemic Heart Disease. (Current Opinion in Cardiology Ser.). (Illus.). 502p. (Orig.). 1994. pap. text ed. 39.95 (*1-85922-603-5*) Current Science.

Rogers, William P. & Kirkham, Robert M. Contributions to Colorado Siesmicity & Tectonics: A 1986 Update. (Special Publication Ser.: No. 28). (Illus.). 301p. (Orig.). 1986. pap. 15.00 (*1-884216-43-9*) Colo Geol Survey.

Rogers, William P., jt. auth. see Kirkham, Robert M.

Rogers, William P., et al. Guidelines & Criteria for Identification & Land-Use Controls of Geologic Hazard & Mineral Resource Areas. (Special Publication Ser.: No. 6). (Illus.). 146p. (Orig.). 1974. pap. 6.00 (*1-884216-35-8*) Colo Geol Survey.

Rogers, William W., Jr. Black Belt Scalawag: Charles Hays & Southern Republicans in the Era of Reconstruction. LC 92-25885. (Illus.). 216p. 1993. 32.50 (*0-8203-1513-3*) U of Ga Pr.

Rogers, William W. Favored Land: A History of Tallahassee & Leon County. 1988. 29.95 (*0-89865-642-7*) Donning Co.

— Outposts on the Gulf: Saint George Island & Apalachicola from Early Exploration to World War II. LC 85-17802. (Illus.). 312p. 1987. text ed. 34.95 (*0-8130-0832-8*) U Press Fla.

Rogers, William W., jt. ed. see Ward, Robert D.

Rogers, William W., et al. Alabama: The History of a Deep South State. LC 93-27240. (Illus.). 768p. 1994. 49.95 (*0-8173-0712-5*); pap. 29.95 (*0-8173-0714-1*) U of Ala Pr.

Rogers, Woodes. Cruising Voyage Around the World. (Illus.). 10.50 (*0-8446-0881-5*) Peter Smith.

Rogers, Yvonne, et al, eds. Models in the Mind: Perspective, Theory & Application. (Computers & People Ser.). (Illus.). 330p. 1992. text ed. 65.00 (*0-12-592970-6*) Acad Pr.

Rogerson, Barnaby. Cyprus. LC 93-5568. (Cadogan Guides Ser.). (Illus.). 220p. (Orig.). 1993. pap. 14.95 (*1-56440-177-4*) Globe Pequot.

— Morocco. 2nd ed. LC 93-5573. (Cadogan Guides Ser.). (Illus.). 480p. 1993. pap. 17.95 (*1-56440-005-0*) Globe Pequot.

Rogerson, Barnaby & Baring, Rose. Tunisia. LC 91-8895. (Cadogan Guides Ser.). (Illus.). 384p. (Orig.). 1992. pap. 17.95 (*0-87106-323-9*) Globe Pequot.

***Rogerson, C. M.** Managing Urban Growth in the Developing World. Date not set. text ed. 59.95 (*0-471-94974-4*) Wiley.

— Managing Urban Growth in the Development World. Date not set. pap. text ed. 24.95 (*0-470-22137-2*) Wiley.

***Rogerson, C.M.** Managing Urban Growth in the Developing World. Date not set. text ed. 59.95 (*0-470-22111-9*) Wiley.

— Managing Urban Growth in the Developing World. Date not set. pap. text ed. 24.95 (*0-470-22112-7*) Wiley.

Rogerson, Dr. Clark T., ed. This Issue Commemorating the 70th Birthday of Dr. Josiah L. Lowe. LC 66-6394. (Memoirs Ser.: Vol. 28, No. 1). 231p. 1976. pap. 20.00 (*0-89327-004-0*) NY Botanical.

Rogerson, Fred. Weird Is the Night. 50p. 1973. pap. 2.50 (*0-87129-114-2*, W14) Dramatic Pub.

Rogerson, J. H. Quality Assurance in Process Plant Manufacture. 168p. 1986. 57.75 (*1-85166-003-8*, Pub. by Elsevier Applied Sci UK) Elsevier.

Rogerson, J. W. Myth in Old Testament Interpretation. LC 73-78234. (Beiheft zur Zeitschrift fuer die Alttestamentliche Wissenschaft Ser.). (C). 1974. 76.95 (*3-11-004220-7*) De Gruyter.

Rogerson, John. The Atlas of the Bible. (Cultural Atlas Ser.). (Illus.). 240p. 1984. 45.00 (*0-8160-1207-5*) Facts on File.

— The Bible. Evans, Gillian, ed. (Cultural Atlases for Young People Ser.). (Illus.). 96p. (YA). (gr. 6-9). 1993. 17.95 (*0-8160-2908-3*) Facts on File.

— The History of Christian Theology: The Study & Use of the Bible, Vol. 2. fac. ed. Avis, Paul, ed. LC 87-47429. 427p. 1988. reprint ed. pap. 121.70 (*0-7837-7943-7*, 2047699) Bks Demand.

Rogerson, John W. W.M.L. de Welte, Founder of Modern Biblical Criticism: An Intellectual Biography. (JSOT Supplement Ser.: No. 126). 296p. (C). 1991. 30.00 (*1-85075-330-X*, Pub. by Sheffield Acad UK) CUP Services.

Rogerson, Kenneth F. Introduction to Ethical Theory. 416p. (C). 1991. pap. text ed. 29.50 (*0-03-023094-2*) HB Coll Pubs.

Rogerson, Margaret, jt. ed. see Johnston, Alexandra F.

Rogerson, Peter, jt. ed. see Fotheringham, A. Stewart.

Rogerson, Peter A., jt. auth. see Plane, David A.

Rogerson, Sidney. Propaganda in the Next War. LC 72-4678. (International Propaganda & Communications Ser.). 188p. 1972. reprint ed. 17.95 (*0-405-04762-2*) Ayer.

— Twelve Days. 172p. 1988. 65.00 (*0-947893-10-5*, Pub. by Gliddon Bks UK) St Mut.

Roget, Gwendoline L. Elans under a Wynnewood Sky. LC 93-44181. 64p. 1994. pap. 12.95 (*0-7734-2716-3*) E Mellen.

Roget, John L., ed. see Roget, Peter M.

Roget, P. Roget's II: The New Thesaurus. rev. ed. 1989. mass mkt. 4.99 (*0-425-11769-3*) Berkley Pub.

Roget, Paul. New Roget's Thesaurus in Dictionary Form: Student Edition. 1990. mass mkt. 4.99 (*0-425-12361-8*) Berkley Pub.

Roget, Peter M. Roget's International Thesaurus. 1994. mass mkt. 4.99 (*0-06-100709-9*, Harp PBks) HarpC.

— Roget's Thesaurus of English Words & Phrases. 832p. 1992. 8.99 (*0-517-03552-9*) Random Hse Value.

— Thesaurus of English Words & Phrases. rev. ed. Roget, John L. & Roget, Samuel R., eds. 42.50 (*0-87559-049-7*); 47.50 (*0-87559-050-0*) Shalom.

Roget, Peter M. & Day, A. Colin. Roget's International Thesaurus of the Bible Index. LC 92-53896. 944p. 1992. 28.00 (*0-06-061773-X*); 30.00 (*0-06-061772-1*) Harper SF.

Roget, Samuel R., ed. see Roget, Peter M.

Rogg, Bernd, jt. ed. see Peters, Norbert.

Rogg, Carla S. & Rogg, Oskar H. Atlanta Eldercare Sourcebook: A Resource Guide for Older Adults, Caregivers & Eldercare Professionals. 2nd ed. 1993. pap. 19.95 (*0-9631939-2-9*) Care Solutions.

— Georgia Mental Health Sourcebook: A Resource Guide for Consumers & Professionals. 177p. (Orig.). 1994. pap. 19.95 (*0-9631939-6-1*); spiral bd. 24.95 (*0-9631939-8-8*) Care Solutions.

— Georgia Senior Resource Guide: A Guide for Older Adults, Caregivers & Eldercare Professionals. 258p. (Orig.). 1995. pap. 19.95 (*0-9631939-9-6*) Care Solutions.

— Health Insurance Options: A Guide to Health Insurance & Health Care Benefits for Consumers with Disabilities & Ongoing Health Care Needs. (Orig.). 1995. pap. 19.95 (*1-887203-00-1*) Care Solutions.

— Houston Eldercare Directory: A Resource Guide for Older Adults, Caregivers, & Eldercare Professionals. (Orig.). 1992. pap. 24.95 (*0-9631939-1-0*) Care Solutions.

— North Carolina Eldercare Sourcebook: A Resource Guide for Older Adults & Caregivers. (Orig.). 1995. spiral bd. 24.95 (*0-9631939-4-5*) Care Solutions.

— North Carolina Senior Resource Guide: A Resource Guide for Older Adults, Caregivers & Eldercare Professional. 277p. (Orig.). 1995. pap. 19.95 (*0-9631939-7-X*) Care Solutions.

— North Texas Eldercare Sourcebook: A Resource Guide for Older Adults, Caregivers & Eldercare Professionals. 186p. (Orig.). 1995. pap. 14.95 (*0-9631939-3-7*) Care Solutions.

Rogg, Carla S., jt. auth. see Rogg, Oskar H.

Rogg, Fay F. & Borsi, Emilia. El Arte de Escribir. 1994. pap. text ed. write for info. (*0-07-053543-4*) McGraw.

Rogg, Oskar. The Atlanta Area School Directory: Your Complete Guide to Greater Atlanta Area Public & Private Education. 3rd ed. 240p. 1994. pap. text ed. 9.95 (*0-9631939-5-3*) Care Solutions.

Rogg, Oskar H. & Rogg, Carla S. The Metropolitan Atlanta Eldercare Directory: A Resource Guide for Older Adults, Caregivers & Eldercare Professionals. 250p. 1992. pap. 24.95 (*0-9631939-0-2*) Care Solutions.

Rogg, Oskar H., jt. auth. see Rogg, Carla S.

Roggan, Andre, jt. ed. see Muller, Gerhard J.

Rogge, jt. ed. see Haggarty.

Rogge, A. E., jt. auth. see Brown, Patricia E.

***Rogge, A. E., et al.** Raising Arizona's Dams: Daily Life, Danger, & Discrimination in the Dam Construction Camps of Central Arizona, 1890s-1940s. LC 94-21368. (Illus.). 215p. 1995. lib. bdg. 45.00x (*0-8165-1491-7*) U of Ariz Pr.

Rogge, Benjamin A. Can Capitalism Survive? LC 78-17378. 1979. 12.00 (*0-913966-46-0*) Liberty Fund.

Rogge, John. Refugees: A Third World Dilemma. LC 87-9605. 384p. (C). 1987. text ed. 61.00 (*0-8476-7557-2*, R7557) Rowman.

Rogge, John R. Too Many, Too Long: Sudan's Twenty-Year Refugee Dilemma. LC 85-2058. (Illus.). 214p. (C). 1985. 56.50 (*0-8476-7412-6*, R7412) Rowman.

***Rogge, Michelle.** Ceaseless Explorer: Conversations with Joseph Spies. LC 95-10734. 1995. write for info. (*0-929925-29-7*) Univ SD Pr.

Rogge, O. John. First & the Fifth. LC 71-140377. (Civil Liberties in American History Ser.). 1971. reprint ed. lib. bdg. 39.50 (*0-306-70087-5*) Da Capo.

— Why Men Confess. LC 74-22067. (Quality Paperbacks Ser.). iv, 298p. 1975. reprint ed. pap. 5.95 (*0-306-80006-3*) Da Capo.

Roggeman, Willem M. Vanishing Emptiness. LC 88-8259. 108p. 1989. pap. 16.95 (0-948259-51-5) Dufour.

Roggemans, Paul, ed. Handbook for Visual Meteor Observations. 2nd ed. (Illus.). 192p. 1989. student ed 18.95 (0-933346-57-3) Sky Pub.

Roggendorf, H., et al. Investigation of the Long Term Behaviour of HLW Glass under Conditions Relevant, EUR 13609. 85p. 1992. pap. 11.00 (92-826-3732-8, CD-NA-13609-EN-C, Pub. by Europ Com) UNIPUB.

Roggenkamp, Klaus W. & Taylor, Martin J. Group Rings & Class Groups. LC 92-10083. (DMV Seminar Ser.: Bd. 18). 216p. 1992. pap. 56.50 (0-8176-2734-0, Pub. by Birkhauser Vlg SZ) Birkhauser.

Roggenkamp, Klaus W., jt. ed. see Reiner, I.

***Roggenthen, Eileen S.** Teenage Violence: A Deadly Trend. 111p. 1992. pap. write for info. (1-57515-015-8) PPI Pubng.

Rogger, Hans. Russia in the Age of Modernization & Revolution, 1881-1917. LC 83-714. (History of Russia Ser.). 323p. (Orig.). (C). 1983. pap. text ed. 24.95 (0-582-48912-1, 73395) Longman.

Rogger, Hans J. National Consciousness in Eighteenth-Century Russia. LC 60-8450. (Russian Research Center Studies: No. 38). 327p. 1960. 29.95 (0-674-60150-5) HUP.

***Roggero, Alex.** Greyhound: Every Mile a Magnificent Mile. (Osprey Color Library). (Illus.). 128p. 1995. pap. 15.95 (1-85532-525-X, Pub. by Osprey UK) Motorbooks Intl.

***Roggli, Linda S. & McLain, Kay.** Durham: An American Enterprise Book. Harris, Bonnie & Turner, James E., eds. (Illus.). 192p. 1995. 39.00 (1-885352-19-0) Community Comm.

Roggli, Victor L., et al. Pathology of Asbestos-Associated Diseases. LC 92-13417. 1992. 155.00 (0-316-75423-4) Little.

Roggo, Constance, ed. see Achad, Frater.

Roggow, Linda M., jt. auth. see Owens, Carolyn.

Roggow, Paul A., et al. The Home Rehabilitation Program Guide. rev. ed. LC 89-43335. (Illus.). 184p. 1993. pap. text ed. 27.00 (1-55642-231-8) SLACK Inc.

Roghair, Gene H., jt. tr. see Rao, Velcheru N.

Rogich, Daniel. Sebian Patericon, Vol. 1: Saints of the Serbian Orthodox Church. Herman, Abbot, ed. LC 94-64911. (Illus.). 330p. (Orig.). 1994. pap. 15.00 (0-938635-75-1) St Herman AK.

***Rogich, Daniel M.** St. Gregory Palamas: Treatise on the Spiritual Life. 105p. (Orig.). 1994. pap. 8.95 (1-880971-05-4) Light&Life Pub Co MN.

Rogier, June & Wolfe, MaryLou, prefs. Nursery & Seed Catalogs: A Directory of Collections. 87p. (Orig.). 1989. pap. write for info. (0-9621791-2-4) CBHL Inc.

Rogiers, Vera, et al, eds. Human Cells in In-Vitro Pharmaco-Toxicology: Present Status Within Europe. (Illus.). 328p. 1994. 55.00 (90-5487-041-9) Paul & Co Pubs.

***Rogilds, Flemming.** In the Land of the Elephant Bird: Voices of South Africa. 165p. 1994. 65.95 (1-85628-892-7, Pub. by Avebury Pub UK) Ashgate Pub Co.

Rogin, Leo. Meaning & Validity of Economic Theory. LC 78-134129. (Essay Index Reprint Ser.). 1977. 42.95 (0-8369-2126-7) Ayer.

Rogin, Michael P. Fathers & Children: Andrew Jackson & the Subjugation of the American Indian. 383p. (C). 1991. pap. 19.95 (0-88738-886-8) Transaction Pubs.

— Ronald Reagan the Movie, & Other Episodes in Political Demonology. 480p. (C). 1987. pap. 14.00 (0-520-06469-0) U CA Pr.

— Subversive Genealogy: The Politics & Art of Herman Melville. 370p. 1985. pap. 14.00 (0-520-05178-5) U CA Pr.

Rogin, Michael P. & Shover, John L. Political Change in California: Critical Elections & Social Movements, 1890-1966. LC 72-95506. (Contributions in American History Ser.: No. 5). 231p. 1970. text ed. 55.00 (0-8371-2346-1, ROP/, Greenwood Pr) Greenwood.

Rogin, Neal, ed. see Emery, Stewart.

Roginets, I. I., jt. auth. see Plotikov, N. I.

Roginets, I. I., jt. auth. see Plotnikov, N. I.

Roginski, Jim. Behind the Covers: Interviews with Authors & Illustrators of Books for Children & Young Adults. 261p. 1989. lib. bdg. 27.50 (0-87287-627-6) Libs Unl.

— Behind the Covers: Interviews with Authors & Illustrators of Books for Children & Young Adults, Vol. 1. LC 85-18129. 249p. 1985. lib. bdg. 23.50 (0-87287-506-7) Libs Unl.

Roginski, Jim, ed. see Brown, Muriel & Foudray, Rita S.

Roginski, Jim, ed. see Cooper, Kay.

Roginski, Jim, ed. see Sharkey, Paulette B.

Roginskii, S. Z. & Shnol', S. E. Isotopes in Biochemistry. 320p. 1965. text ed. 79.50 (0-7065-0555-7, Pub. by Keter Pub IS) Coronet Bks.

Roginsky, Rachel J., jt. auth. see Fisher, Justin S.

Roginsky, Rachel J., jt. ed. see Raleigh, Lori E.

***Rogister, John.** Louis the XV & the "Parlement" of Paris, 1737-1755. (Illus.). 320p. (C). 1995. 64.95 (0-521-40395-2) Cambridge U Pr.

Rogland, Robert. Romans: A Study Manual. 1988. pap. 6.99 (0-87552-403-6) Presby & Reformed.

Rogler, Ingrid. Small Folk Quilters. Watts, Pamela M., ed. (Illus.). 66p. (Orig.). (J). (gr. 3-10). 1989. pap. 9.95 (0-9622565-0-1) Chariot Pub PA.

Rogler, Lloyd H. Hispanics & Mental Health: A Framework for Research. LC 88-37203. 174p. (Orig.). (C). 1989. lib. bdg. 21.50 (0-89464-248-0) Krieger.

Rogler, Lloyd H., jt. auth. see Farber, Anne.

Rogliatti, Gianni. Ferrari Ecurie Garage Francorchamps. (Illus.). 244p. 60.00 (88-7911-083-7, Pub. by Giorgio Nada Editore IT) Howell Pr VA.

Rogliatti, Gianni, et al. Ferrari - Design of a Legend: The Official History & Catalog. (Illus.). 264p. 1991. 65.00 (1-55859-026-9) Abbeville Pr.

Rogne, Carol. Control & Power in Relationships. 68p. 1991. pap. text ed. 4.95 (1-881565-01-7) Discov Counsel.

— Dealing with Anger. 51p. 1991. pap. text ed. 4.95 (1-881565-02-5) Discov Counsel.

— Understanding & Enhancing Self-Esteem. 527p. 1991. pap. text ed. 8.95 (1-881565-00-9) Discov Counsel.

Rognebakke, Myrtle, jt. auth. see Driessle, Hannelore.

Rogner, E. A. Living in Arcadia: Ocean Pines, Maryland. (Illus.). 80p. (Orig.). 1990. pap. text ed. 9.95 (0-935045-07-4) D-OR Pr.

— The Pentagon: "A National Institution": Its History, Its Functions, Its People. rev. ed. LC 85-72559. (Illus.). 1986. pap. text ed. 3.50 (0-935045-05-8) D-OR Pr.

— The Pentagon: "A National Showplace"; What to See & Where to See It. (Illus.). 48p. (Orig.). pap. text ed. 4.95 (0-935045-06-6) D-OR Pr.

— The Pentagon: Facts about the Building (Monograph) rev. ed. 1986. pap. text ed. 0.95 (0-935045-04-X) D-OR Pr.

— The Pentagon: Flags Displayed in the Building. LC 85-72558. (Illus.). 36p. (Orig.). 1985. pap. 3.50 (0-935045-03-1) D-OR Pr.

— The Pentagon: Flags Displayed in the Flag Corridor (Monograph) (Orig.). pap. 0.95 (0-935045-02-3) D-OR Pr.

Rognes, Knut. Blowflies (Diptera, Calliphoridae) of Fennoscandia & Denmark. LC 90-40545. (Fauna Entomologica Scandinavica Ser.: No. 24). (Illus.). 272p. 1990. 80.00 (90-04-09304-4) E J Brill.

Rogness, Alvin N. My Personal Prayer Book. LC 88-28625. (Illus.). 64p. (Orig.). 1988. kivar 4.99 (0-8066-2358-6, 10-4599, Augsburg) Augsburg Fortress.

— Remember the Promise. LC 76-27082. 64p. 1977. 10.99 (0-8066-1619-9, 10-5481, Augsburg); kivar 4.99 (0-8066-1567-2, 10-5480, Augsburg) Augsburg Fortress.

— Today & Tomorrow. LC 77-84095. 96p. 1978. pap. 9.99 (0-8066-1621-0, 10-6660, Augsburg) Augsburg Fortress.

— The Word for Every Day: Three Hundred & Sixty-Five Devotional Reading. LC 81-65650. 376p. 1981. kivar 16.99 (0-8066-1886-8, 10-7284, Augsburg) Augsburg Fortress.

***Rogness, Andrew.** Crossing Boundary Waters: A Spiritual Journey in Canoe Country. 1994. pap. 9.99 (0-8066-2730-1, Augsburg) Augsburg Fortress.

Rogness, Michael. Preaching to a TV Generation: Preaching for an Electronic Age. LC 93-47208. 1994. pap. write for info. (1-55673-838-2) CSS OH.

Rognli, O. A., et al, eds. Breeding Fodder Crops for Marginal Conditions: Proceedings of the 18th Eucarpia Fodder Crops Section Meeting, Loen, Norway, 25-28 August 1993. LC 94-21242. (Developments in Plant Breeding Ser.: Vol. 2). 300p. (C). 1994. lib. bdg. 130.00 (0-7923-2948-1) Kluwer Ac.

Rogo, D. Scott. Beyond Reality: The Role Unseen Dimensions Play in Our Lives. 1990. pap. 12.95 (0-85030-886-0) Thorsons SF.

— Man Does Survive Death. 1977. pap. 3.95 (0-8065-0582-6, Citadel Pr) Carol Pub Group.

— Methods & Models for Education in Parapsychology. LC 73-75209. (Parapsychological Monograph Ser.: No. 14). 1973. pap. 5.00 (0-912328-22-3) Parapsych Foun.

— Nad: A Study of Some Unusual Other World Experiences, Vol. I. 1970. 5.95 (0-8216-0125-3, Univ Bks) Carol Pub Group.

— Nad: Psychic Study of the Music of the Spheres, Vol. 2. 1972. 6.95 (0-8216-0140-7, Univ Bks) Carol Pub Group.

— New Techniques of Inner Healing. 248p. (Orig.). 1994. pap. 12.95 (1-56924-930-X) Marlowe & Co.

— On the Track of the Poltergeist. 1985. 16.95 (0-13-634445-3) P-H.

Rogoff, Barbara. Apprenticeship in Thinking: Cognitive Development in Social Context. (Illus.). 272p. (C). 1991. reprint ed. pap. text ed. 18.95 (0-19-507003-8) OUP.

Rogoff, Barbara & Lave, Jean, eds. Everyday Cognition: Its Development in Social Context. (Illus.). 320p. 1984. 38.00 (0-674-27030-4) HUP.

Rogoff, Barbara, et al. Guided Participation in Cultural Activity by Toddlers & Caregivers. (Monographs of the Society for Research on Child Development). 180p. 1993. pap. text ed. 14.00 (0-226-72391-7) U Ch Pr.

Rogoff, Herbert, ed. see Van Wyk, Helen.

Rogoff, Irit, ed. The Divided Heritage: Themes & Problems in German Modernism. (Illus.). 424p. (C). 1991. 74.95 (0-521-34553-7) Cambridge U Pr.

Rogoff, Irit, jt. ed. see Sherman, Daniel J.

***Rogoff, Jay.** The Cutoff. 72p. (Orig.). 1995. pap. 10.00 (0-915380-31-5) Word Works.

Rogoff, Leonard. Office Guide to Business Letters. 2nd ed. pap. 6.00 (0-671-89664-4) P-H.

Rogoff, Marc J. & Williams, John F. Approaches to Implementing Solid Waste Recycling Facilities. LC 94-3865. (Illus.). 216p. 1994. 48.00 (0-8155-1352-6) Noyes.

***Rogoff, Marianne.** Silvie's Life. Logsdon, Wendy, ed. LC 95-60133. 135p. (Orig.). 1995. pap. 9.95 (1-57143-045-8, Zenobia Pr) RDR Bks.

Rogoff, Marianne, ed. see Petterle, Elmo A.

Rogoff, Mark J. How to Implement Waste-to-Energy Projects. LC 87-12211. (Illus.). 202p. 1988. 45.00 (0-8155-1132-9) Noyes.

Rogoff, Mike. Israel. LC 90-10027. (World in View Ser.). (Illus.). 96p. (YA). (gr. 6-12). 1990. lib. bdg. 24.26 (0-8114-2432-4) Raintree Steck-V.

Rogoff, Natalie. Recent Trends in Occupational Mobility. Coser, Lewis A. & Powell, Walter W., eds. LC 79-7016. (Perennial Works in Sociology Ser.). (Illus.). 1979. reprint ed. lib. bdg. 18.95 (0-405-12115-6) Ayer.

Rogols-Siegel, Linda, tr. see Lewald, Fanny.

Rogolsky, Janet, ed. see Thompson, Alan.

***Rogondino, M.** Computer Type. Date not set. pap. 12.99 (0-517-13021-1) Random.

Rogondino, Michael. Computer Color, Ten Thousand Computer-generated Process Colors. 1990. pap. 24.95 (0-87701-739-5) Chronicle Bks.

Rogosheske, Walter, jt. auth. see Houts, Marshall.

***Rogosin, Donn.** Invisible Men: Life in Baseball's Negro Leagues. Turner, Philip, ed. (Kodansha Globe Trade Paperback Ser.). (Illus.). 320p. 1995. pap. 14.00 (1-56836-085-1, Kodansha Globe) Kodansha.

— Invisible Men: Life in Baseball's Negro Leagues. LC 82-73026. (Illus.). 320p. 1985. pap. 11.95 (0-689-70687-1, 327, Pub. by Ctrl Bur voor Schimmel NE) Macmillan.

Rogosta, Ray. From the Varieties of Religious Experience, Bk. II. 24p. 4.00 (0-945926-31-6) Paradigm RI.

Rogove, Susan T. & Steinhauer, Marcia B. Pyrex by Corning: A Collector's Guide. (Illus.). 134p. (Orig.). 1993. 32.95 (0-915410-95-8); pap. 24.95 (0-915410-94-X) Antique Pubns.

Rogovin, Anne. Let Me Do It! rev. ed. LC 90-30226. 160p. 1990. pap. 10.95 (0-687-21376-2) Abingdon.

— One Thousand One Wonderful Wonders: Activities for All Children. 208p. (Orig.). 1992. pap. 12.95 (0-687-29193-3) Abingdon.

— Turn off the TV & 224p. (Orig.). 1995. pap. 14.95 (0-687-00233-8) Abingdon.

Rogovin, Janice. A Sense of Place - Tu Barrio: Jamaica Plain People & Where They Live - La Gente de Jamaica Plain y Donde Ellos Viven. Rivas, Yolanda, tr. (Illus.). 48p. (Orig.). (ENG & SPA.). 1981. pap. text ed. 10.00 (0-9621783-1-4) Stonybrook Pr.

Rogovin, Milton, photos. Triptychs: Buffalo's Lower West Side Revisited. 160p. 1994. 40.00 (0-393-03588-5) Norton.

Rogovin, Milton & Frisch, Michael, photos. Portraits in Steel. LC 92-56776. (Illus.). 288p. 1993. 49.95 (0-8014-2253-1); pap. 28.95 (0-8014-8102-3) Cornell U Pr.

Rogovin, Sarah, jt. ed. see Grady, John.

Rogow, Arnold A., ed. Politics, Personality & Social Science in the Twentieth Century: Essays in Honor of Harold D. Lasswell. LC 76-75812. 1969. lib. bdg. 27.50 (0-226-72399-2) U Ch Pr.

Rogow, Arnold A. & Shore, Peter. The Labour Government & British Industry, 1945-1951. LC 73-22508. 196p. (C). 1974. reprint ed. text ed. 79.50 (0-8371-6374-9, ROLG, Greenwood Pr) Greenwood.

Rogow, Arnold A., jt. auth. see Burks, Ardath W.

Rogow, Faith. Gone to Another Meeting: The National Council of Jewish Women, 1893-1993. LC 92-24721. (Judaic Studies). 320p. (C). 1993. pap. 24.95 (0-8173-0671-4) U of Ala Pr.

Rogow, Sally M. Helping the Visually Impaired Child with Developmental Problems: Effective Practice in Home, School & Community. (Special Education Ser.). 216p. (C). 1988. text ed. 29.95 (0-8077-2903-5); pap. text ed. 16.95 (0-8077-2902-7) Tchrs Coll.

Rogow, Sally M. & Hass, Julia L. Shared Moments: Learning Games for Disabled Children. 64p. 1993. pap. 8.95 (0-936389-33-8) Tudor Pubs.

Rogow, Zack. Preview of the Dream. 64p. (Orig.). 1985. pap. 6.00 (0-940584-10-7) Gull Bks.

Rogow, Zack, tr. see Breton, Andre.

Rogow, Zack, tr. see Sand, George.

Rogowitz, B., jt. ed. see Allebach, J. P.

Rogowitz, B. E., ed. Human Vision, Visual Processing, & Digital Display III. 1992. 77.00 (0-8194-0820-4, 1666) SPIE.

— Human Visions, Visual Processing, & Digital Display. 401p. 1989. 70.00 (0-8194-0112-9, VOL. 1077) SPIE.

Rogowski, Christian. Distinguished Outsider: Robert Musil & His Critics. (Literary Criticism in Perspective Ser.). 230p. 1994. 55.95 (1-879751-52-6) Camden Hse.

— Implied Dramaturgy: Robert Musil & the Crisis of Modern Drama. (Studies in Austrian Literature, Culture, & Thought). 313p. 1993. 37.50 (0-929497-59-7) Ariadne CA.

Rogowski, Jeannette A. Private vs Public Sector Insurance Coverage for Drug Abuse. LC 93-12592. 1993. write for info. (0-8330-1345-9, MR-166-OPRC) Rand Corp.

Rogowski, Jeannette A., jt. auth. see Carter, Grace M.

***Rogowski, Ralf.** Drafting & Negotiating Commerical Leases. 4th ed. 347p. 1994. pap. text ed. 143.00 (0-406-01026-9, UK) Butterworth Legal Pubs.

— German Law. Date not set. pap. text ed. write for info. (0-406-02291-7, UK) Butterworth Legal Pubs.

***Rogowski, Ralf, ed.** Civil Law. LC 95-8007. (International Library of Essays in Law & Legal Theory: No. 10). 500p. 1995. 150.00x (0-8147-7465-2) NYU Pr.

Rogowski, Ronald. Commerce & Coalitions: How Trade Affects Domestic Political Alignments. (Illus.). 224p. (C). 1990. text ed. 35.00 (0-691-07812-2); pap. text ed. 13.95 (0-691-02330-1) Princeton U Pr.

— Rational Legitimacy: A Theory of Political Support. LC 74-2975. 256p. 1974. 49.50x (0-691-07563-8) Princeton U Pr.

— Rational Legitimacy: A Theory of Political Support. LC 74-2975. (Illus.). Date not set. reprint ed. pap. 92.40 (0-7837-9434-7, 2060176) Bks Demand.

***Rogowski, Ronald, ed.** Comparative Politics & the International Political Economy. LC 94-22995. (Library of International Political Economy: Vol. 8). 560p. 1995. 287.95 (1-85278-654-X, Pub. by E Elgar Pub UK) Ashgate Pub Co.

Rogowski, Ronald, jt. ed. see Tiryakian, Edward A.

Rogozhin, Nikolai, jt. auth. see Jansson, Maija.

Rogozhnikova, R., ed. Dictionary of Combinations Equivalent to a Word. 144p. (C). 1983. 75.00 (0-685-46807-0, Pub. by Collets) St Mut.

***Rogozinski, J.** Smokeless Tobacco in the Western World. 194p. 1990. 25.00 (0-8159-6856-6) Devin.

Rogozinski, Jan. A Brief History of the Caribbean: From the Arawak & the Carib to the Present. (Illus.). 256p. 1992. lib. bdg. 29.95 (0-8160-2451-0) Facts on File.

— A Brief History of the Caribbean: From the Arawak & the Carib to the Present. (Illus.). 336p. 1994. pap. 13.95 (0-452-01134-5, Mer) NAL-Dutton.

— Pirates! Brigands, Buccaneers, & Privateers in Fact, Fiction & Legend. LC 94-12717. 1995. 45.00 (0-8160-2761-7) Facts on File.

— Pirates! Brigands, Buccaneers, & Privateers in Fact, Fiction & Legend. 1996. pap. 19.95 (0-8160-2773-0) Facts on File.

— Power, Caste & Law: Social Conflict in Fourteenth-Century Montpellier. LC 78-70247. (Medieval Academy Bks.: No. 91). 1982. 30.00 (0-910956-72-3) Medieval Acad.

— Smokeless Tobacco in the Western World, 1550-1950. LC 90-6899. 208p. 1990. text ed. 49.95 (0-275-93600-7, C3600, Praeger Pubs) Greenwood.

Rogozkin, Victor A. Metabolism of Anabolic-Androgenic Steroids. (Illus.). 168p. 1991. 190.00 (0-8493-6415-9, QP) CRC Pr.

***Rogriquez, K. S.** The Dolphins of Coral Cove. LC 94-70052. (Little Mermaid Novels Ser.: No. 11). (Illus.). 80p. (J). (gr. 1-4). 1994. pap. text ed. 3.50 (0-7868-4001-3) Disney Pr.

Roguet, A. M. Homilies for the Celebration of Baptism. Du Charme, Jerome, tr. LC 76-53546. 1977. pap. 2.95 (0-8199-0655-7, Frncscn Herld) Franciscan Pr.

— Homilies for the Celebration of Marriage. Du Charme, Jerome, tr. LC 76-53538. 1977. pap. 5.95 (0-8199-0656-5, Frncscn Herld) Franciscan Pr.

— The New Mass. 2.95 (0-89942-130-X, 130/05) Catholic Bk Pub.

Rogulic-Newsome, Lisa. Theme for a Day. 128p. (J). (gr. 1-6). 1990. 11.95 (0-86653-545-4, GA1154) Good Apple.

— Theme of the Week. 208p. 1991. 14.95 (0-86653-602-7, GA1321) Good Apple.

Rogus, Joseph & Yeager, Robert J. The Development Director, Making Each Moment Count. 1987. 7.30 (0-317-60168-7) Natl Cath Educ.

Rogus, Joseph F., jt. auth. see Ristau, Karen M.

Roguski & Palmberg. Academic Mini-Lectures. 1990. pap. 22.95 (0-8384-3381-2); teacher ed, pap. 7.95 (0-8384-3382-0); audio 20.00 (0-8384-3383-9) Heinle & Heinle.

Roh, Franz & Tschichold, Jan, eds. Foto-Auge, Oeil et Photo, Photo-Eye. LC 72-9234. (Literature of Photography Ser.). 1977. reprint ed. 18.95 (0-405-04939-0) Ayer.

Rohan, Michael S. The Anvil of Ice Vol. I. (The Winter of the World). 368p. 1989. mass mkt. 4.99 (0-380-70547-8, AvoNova) Avon.

— Chase the Morning. 352p. 1992. mass mkt. 4.99 (0-380-70871-X, AvoNova) Avon.

— Cloud Castles. 1994. pap. 22.00 (0-688-13419-X) Morrow.

— Cloud Castles. (Spiral Ser.). 336p. 1995. reprint ed. mass mkt. 5.50 (0-380-77554-9, AvoNova) Avon.

— The Forge in the Forest Vol. II. (The Winter of the World). 416p. 1989. mass mkt. 4.99 (0-380-70548-6, AvoNova) Avon.

— The Gates of Noon. 320p. 1994. mass mkt. 4.99 (0-380-71718-2, AvoNova) Avon.

— The Gates of Noon. 1993. 22.00 (0-688-12507-7) Morrow.

— The Hammer of the Sun. 512p. 1990. mass mkt. 4.99 (0-380-70549-4) Avon.

— The Hammer of the Sun. 512p. 1995. pap. 4.99 (0-380-30549-6, AvoNova) Avon.

Rohan, P. Surveillance Radar Performance Prediction. Wait, J. R. et al, eds. (Electromagnetic Waves Ser.). 336p. 1983. boxed 119.00 (0-906048-98-2, EW017) Inst Elect Eng.

Rohan, Patrick J. Home Owner Associations & Planned Unit Developments: Law & Forms, 3 vols. (Real Estate Transactions Ser.). 1977. Updates available. ring bd. write for info. (0-8205-1327-X) Bender.

— New York Civil Practice: EPTL, 7 vols. 1969. Updates. ring bd. write for info. (0-8205-1806-9) Bender.

— Real Estate Brokerage: Law & Practice, 1 vol. (Real Estate Transactions Ser.). 1985. Looseleaf updates avail. write for info. (0-8205-1486-1) Bender.

— Real Estate Financing: Text, Forms, Tax Analysis, 7 vols. (Real Estate Transactions Ser.). 1973. Updates. ring bd. write for info. (0-8205-1592-2) Bender.

— Real Estate Tax Appeals: Law, Practice & Forms, 3 vols. (Real Estate Transactions Ser.). 1984. write for info. (0-8205-1575-2) Bender.

— Zoning & Land Use Controls, 10 vols., Set. 1977. ring bd. write for info. (0-8205-1845-X) Bender.

Rohan, Patrick J. & Donovan, Caroline. Current Leasing Law & Techniques: Forms, 4 vols., Updates available. (Real Estate Transactions Ser.). 1982. ring bd. write for info. (0-8205-1401-2) Bender.

Rohan, Patrick J. & Frankel, B. Harrison. Real Estate Syndications: Law, Practice & Forms, 2 vols. 1985. Looseleaf updates avail. write for info. (0-8205-1587-6) Bender.

Rohan, Patrick J. & Reskin, Melvin A. Condemnation Procedures & Techniques-Forms, 6 vols. (Real Estate Transactions Ser.). 1968. ring bd. write for info. (0-8205-1243-5) Bender.

— Condominium Law & Practice-Forms, 8 vols. (Real Estate Transactions Ser.). 1965. Updates. ring bd. write for info. (0-8205-1235-4) Bender.

— Cooperative Housing: Law & Practice-Forms, 4 vols. (Real Estate Transactions Ser.). 1967. Updates. ring bd. write for info. (0-8205-1239-7) Bender.

Rohan, Patrick J., jt. auth. see Powell, Richard R.

Rohan, Patrick J., jt. auth. see Sackman, Julius.

Rohan, Paul. Introduction to Electromagnetic Wave Propagation. (Sensing Library). 358p. 1991. text ed. 79.00 (*0-89006-545-4*) Artech Hse.

Rohan, Rebecca. Got a Minute? 101 Marketing Tips for Writers. 136p. (Orig.). 1990. pap. 8.95 (*0-942980-12-3*) CNW.

Rohan, Zina. The Book of Wishes & Complaints. 214p. 1992. 23.95 (*0-09-174778-3*, Pub. by Hutchinson UK) Trafalgar.

Rohani, M. Contemplating Life's Great Questions. 96p. (Orig.). 1991. pap. 7.95 (*1-85168-024-1*) Onewrld Pubns.

Rohani, M. K. The Accents of God: A Treasury of the World's Sacred Scriptures. (Illus.). 96p. 1992. 12.95 (*1-85168-023-3*) Onewrld Pubns.

Rohatgi, P., ed. Friction Lubrication & Wear Technology for Advanced Composite Materials: Proceedings from ASM Materials Week '93. 310p. 1993. 97.00 (*0-87170-490-0*, 6322U) ASM.

— Solidification of Metal Matrix Composites. (Illus.). 370p. 1989. 104.00 (*0-87339-155-1*, 389) Minerals Metals.

Rohatgi, P. K., ed. Principles of Solidification of Cast Composites. 163p. 1993. 48.00 (*0-87339-214-0*, 471) Minerals Metals.

***Rohatgi, U. S. & Ogut, A., eds.** Fluid Machinery 1994. LC 90-55406. (Fluid Engineering Division Conference Ser.: Vol. 195). 1994. pap. 22.50 (*0-7918-1379-7*) ASME.

Rohatgi, U. S., jt. ed. see Sharma, M. P.

Rohatgi, U. S., jt. ed. see Zakem, S. B.

Rohatgi, U. S., et al, eds. Gas-Liquid Flows 1993. LC 93-71646. (FED Ser.: Vol. 165). 223p. 1993. pap. 45.00 (*0-7918-0973-0*, H00805) ASME.

Rohatgi, Vijay K. An Introduction to Probability Theory & Mathematical Statistics. LC 75-14378. (Series in Probability & Mathematical Statistics). 684p. 1976. text ed. 119.00 (*0-471-73135-8*, Wiley-Interscience) Wiley.

Rohatyn, Dennis. The Reluctant Naturalist: A Study of G.E. Moore's Principia Ethica. 150p. (Orig.). (C). 1987. lib. bdg. 40.50 (*0-8191-5767-8*) U Pr of Amer.

Rohatyn, Dennis A. Naturalism & Deontology. LC 73-92240. (Studies in Philosophy: No. 27). 128p. (Orig.). 1975. pap. text ed. 25.35 (*90-279-3233-6*) Mouton.

— Two Dogmas of Philosophy & Other Essays in the Philosophy of Philosophy. LC 75-63. 199p. (C). 1976. 29.50 (*0-8386-1673-9*) Fairleigh Dickinson.

Rohatyn, Dennis A., jt. auth. see Nolt, John E.

Rohde, Barbara. In the Simple Morning Light: A Meditation Manual. LC 93-40866. 1994. 7.00 (*1-55896-275-1*, Skinner Hse Bks) Unitarian Univ.

Rohde, Betty. So Fat, Low Fat, No Fat. 94p. 1993. 9.00 (*0-9637239-0-1*) Be Ro Pub.

Rohde, David W. Parties & Leaders in the PostReform House. LC 90-22984. (American Politics & Political Economy Ser.). (Illus.). 224p. 1991. pap. text ed. 14.95 (*0-226-72407-7*) U Ch Pr.

— Parties & Leaders in the PostReform House. LC 90-22984. (American Politics & Political Economy Ser.). (Illus.). 224p. 1991. lib. bdg. 39.95 (*0-226-72406-9*) U Ch Pr.

Rohde, David W., jt. ed. see Fiorina, Morris P.

Rohde, Deborah J., et al. Planning & Managing Major Construction Projects: A Guide for Hospitals. LC 84-28997. 112p. (C). 1985. pap. text ed. 25.00 (*0-910701-01-6*, 0651) Health Admin Pr.

Rohde, Edith C. Letters from Alaska: Hazards & Humor of Life in Subrrrbia. LC 79-66091. (Illus.). 1979. 10.95 (*0-918270-04-9*) That New Pub.

Rohde, Eleanor S. Shakespeare's Wild Flowers. LC 76-153350. reprint ed. 8.50 (*0-404-05385-8*) AMS Pr.

Rohde, Eleanour S. Culinary & Salad Herbs. (Illus.). 128p. 1972. pap. 3.50 (*0-486-22865-7*) Dover.

— Garden-Craft in the Bible, & Other Essays. LC 67-26775. (Essay Index Reprint Ser.). 1977. 23.95 (*0-8369-0829-5*) Ayer.

— Garden of Herbs. LC 75-81736. 1969. reprint ed. pap. 7.95 (*0-486-22308-6*) Dover.

— Old English Herbals. 1989. pap. 7.95 (*0-486-26193-X*) Dover.

— Rose Recipes from Olden Times. (Illus.). 95p. 1973. reprint ed. pap. 2.95 (*0-486-22957-2*) Dover.

— Scented Garden. 1974. reprint ed. 46.00 (*1-55888-222-7*) Omnigraphics Inc.

Rohde, Elliot S. Producing Corrugated Packaging Profitably. 228p. 1995. 65.00 (*0-9616302-7-2*) Jelmar Pub.

Rohde, Erwin. Der Griechische Roman und Seine Vorlaufer. xxxi, 636p. (GER.). 1964. reprint ed. write for info. (*0-318-70495-1*, Pub. by Georg Olms GW) Lubrecht & Cramer.

— Der Griechische Roman und Seine Vorlaufer. xxxi, 636p. 1974. reprint ed. write for info. (*3-487-05401-9*, Pub. by Georg Olms GW) Lubrecht & Cramer.

— Kleine Schriften, 2 vols. xxxi, 917p. (GER.). 1969. reprint ed. write for info. (*0-318-70496-X*, Pub. by Georg Olms GW); reprint ed. Bd. I: Beitrage zur Chronologie, Quellenkunde und Geschichte der Griechischen Literatur. write for info. (*0-318-70497-8*, Pub. by Georg Olms GW); reprint ed. Bd. II: Beitrage zur Geschichte des Romans und der Novelle zur Sagen-, Marchen- und Alterthumskunde. write for info. (*0-318-70498-6*, Pub. by Georg Olms GW); reprint ed. Bd. I: Beitrage zur Chronologie, Quellenkunde und Geschichte der Griechischen Literatur. write for info. (*0-318-71009-9*, Pub. by Georg Olms GW); reprint ed. Bd. II: Beitrage zur Geschichte des Romans und der Novelle zur Sagen-, Marchen- und Alterthumskunde. write for info. (*0-318-71010-2*, Pub. by Georg Olms GW) Lubrecht & Cramer.

— Kleine Schriften, 2 vols., Set. xxxi, 917p. 1969. reprint ed. write for info. (*0-318-71008-0*, Pub. by Georg Olms GW) Lubrecht & Cramer.

— Psyche: The Cult of Souls & Belief in Immortality Among the Greeks. LC 75-37911. (Select Bibliographies Reprint Ser.). 1980. reprint ed. 57.95 (*0-8369-6749-6*) Ayer.

— Psyche, the Cult of Souls & Belief in Immortality among Ancient Greeks. xvi, 626p. 1987. reprint ed. pap. 35.00 (*0-89005-477-0*) Ares.

Rohde, Fred C., et al. Freshwater Fishes of the Carolinas, Virginia, Maryland, & Delaware. LC 93-32535. (Illus.). 340p. (C). 1994. 24.95 (*0-8078-2130-6*) U of NC Pr.

Rohde, Gisela, jt. auth. see Rohde, Jerry.

Rohde, Jerry & Rohde, Gisela. Humboldt Redwoods State Park: A Complete Guide. LC 92-60250. (Illus.). 301p. (Orig.). 1992. pap. 15.95 (*0-936810-25-4*) R&E Miles.

— Redwood National & State Parks: Tales, Trails, & Auto Tours. LC 94-75098. 288p. 1994. pap. 15.95 (*0-9640261-0-4*) MtnHome Bks.

Rohde, Jon E., et al, eds. Reaching Health for All. (Illus.). 500p. 1993. 12.95 (*0-19-563236-2*) OUP.

Rohde, Klaus. Ecology of Marine Parasites. LC 81-12934. (Australian Ecology Ser.). (Illus.). 245p. (C). 1982. pap. text ed. 24.95 (*0-7022-1670-4*) Intl Spec Bk.

— Ecology of Marine Parasites. 2nd ed. 300p. 1993. pap. text ed. 38.00 (*0-85198-845-8*) CAB Intl.

Rohde, Peter P., ed. see Kierkegaard, Soren.

Rohde, Richard A., jt. ed. see Zuckerman, Bert M.

Rohde, S. M., ed. see American Society of Mechanical Engineers Staff.

Rohde, S. M., ed. see Design Engineering Conference (1979: Chicago, IL).

Rohde, S. M., ed. see Fluid Film Bearing Committee of the Lubrication Division.

Rohden, Peter R., jt. auth. see Bayle, Francis.

Rohdie, Sam. Antonioni. (Illus.). 224p. 1990. 49.95 (*0-85170-273-2*, Pub. by British Film Inst UK); pap. 19.95 (*0-85170-274-0*, Pub. by British Film Inst UK) Ind U Pr.

— Rocco & His Brothers. (BFI Film Classics Ser.). (Illus.). 1993. pap. 9.95 (*0-85170-340-2*, Pub. by British Film Inst UK) Ind U Pr.

Rohds, Richard, jt. auth. see Mackie, Thomas T.

Rohe, Deborah, jt. auth. see Breighner, Kathryn.

Rohe, M. Untersuchungen zur Phylogenense Linearer Element: Extrachromosomale DNA des Ascomyceten Morchella Conica. (Bibliotheca Mycologica Ser.: Vol. 146). (Illus.). 118p. (GER.). 1992. pap. text ed. 42.00 (*3-443-59047-0*, Pub. by Cramer-Borntraeger GW) Lubrecht & Cramer.

Rohe, Terry & Cohen, Sally. Good Old-Fashioned Maine Cookery: From Red Flannel Hash to Maine Lobster Stew - Here Is a Collection of 125 Traditional Down East Recipes. LC 93-33001. 1994. spiral bd. 14.95 (*1-55958-430-0*) Prima Pub.

Rohe, William M. & Gates, Lauren B. Planning with Neighborhoods. LC 84-17221. (Urban & Regional Policy & Development Studies). xi, 238p. (C). 1985. pap. 16.95 (*0-8078-4133-1*) U of NC Pr.

Roheim, Geza. Eternal Ones of the Dream: Myth & Ritual, Dreams & Fantasies-Their Role in the Lives of Primitive Man. 1970. reprint ed. pap. text ed. 24.95 (*0-8236-8044-4*, 021760) Intl Univs Pr.

— The Eternal Ones of the Dream, a Psychoanalytic Interpretation of Australian Myth & Ritual. 290p. reprint ed. pap. 82.70 (*0-317-10577-9*, 2010425) Bks Demand.

— Fire in the Dragon & Other Psychoanalytic Essays on Folklore. 1992. 39.50 (*0-691-09471-3*); pap. 12.95 (*0-691-02868-0*) Princeton U Pr.

— Gates of the Dream. 1969. reprint ed. pap. text ed. 24.95 (*0-8236-8060-6*, 22110) Intl Univs Pr.

— The Gates of the Dream. LC 53-10679. 564p. reprint ed. pap. 160.80 (*0-317-10573-6*, 2010428) Bks Demand.

— Hungarian & Vogul Mythology. LC 84-45522. (American Ethnological Society Monographs: No. 23). 1988. reprint ed. 20.00 (*0-404-62922-9*) AMS Pr.

— Psychoanalysis & Anthropology. 496p. 1968. reprint ed. pap. text ed. 24.95 (*0-8236-8234-X*, 25120) Intl Univs Pr.

— War, Crime & the Covenant. Branham, V. C., ed. LC 46-5116. (Journal of Clinical Psychopathology. Monograph Ser.: No. 1). 166p. reprint ed. pap. 47.40 (*0-317-08250-7*, 2010705) Bks Demand.

Rohen. Photographic Color Atlas of Head & Neck Anatomy. (Illus.). 1990. 60.00 (*1-55664-276-8*) Mosby Yr Bk.

Rohen, Harold. The Tennessee Locator. 387p. (Orig.). 1992. pap. 19.95 (*0-9634555-0-9*) Budro.

Rohen, Johannes, jt. auth. see Yokochi, Chihiro.

Rohen, Johannes W., jt. ed. see Muller, Werner E.

Rohen, Johannes W., et al. Color Atlas of Anatomy: A Photographic Study of the Human Body. LC 92-49387. (Illus.). 494p. 1993. 59.00 (*0-89640-228-2*) Igaku-Shoin.

Roher, H. D., jt. ed. see Goretzki, P. E.

Roherty, James M. State Security in South Africa: Civil-Military Relations under P W Botha. LC 91-14446. 240p. 1992. 51.95 (*0-87332-877-9*) M E Sharpe.

Roherty, James M., ed. & intro. Defense Policy Formation: Towards Comparative Analysis. LC 79-54443. 315p. 1980. lib. bdg. 29.75 (*0-89089-152-4*) Carolina Acad Pr.

Rohfritsch, Odette, jt. ed. see Shorthouse, Joseph D.

***Rohl, Ernst.** Deutsch-Deutsch: Ein Satirisches Woerterbuch. 103p. (GER.). 1991. 29.95 (*0-7859-8322-8*, 3359004957) Fr & Eur.

Rohl, John & Sombart, Nicolaus, eds. Kaiser Wilhelm II - New Interpretations: The Corfu Papers. LC 81-7706. 352p. 1982. 69.95 (*0-521-23898-6*) Cambridge U Pr.

Rohl, John C. From Bismarck to Hitler: The Problem of Continuity in German History. LC 72-181319. (Problems & Perspectives in History Ser.). 207p. reprint ed. pap. 59.00 (*0-8357-2532-4*, 2057145) Bks Demand.

— The Kaiser & His Court: Wilhelm the Second & the Government of Germany. Cole, Terence F., tr. 304p. (C). 1995. 49.95 (*0-521-40223-9*) Cambridge U Pr.

Rohleder, J. W. & Munn, R. W. Magnetism & Optics of Molecular Crystals. 137p. 1992. text ed. 79.95 (*0-471-93171-3*) Wiley.

***Rohleiser, Ronald.** The Shatted Lantern: Rediscovering the Felt Presence of God. 172p. (Orig.). 1995. pap. 12.95 (*0-8245-1497-1*) Crossroad NY.

Rohlen, Thomas P. For Harmony & Strength: Japanese White-Collar Organization in Anthropological Perspective. LC 73-91668. (Center for Japanese Studies, UC Berkeley: No. 9). 1974. pap. 14.00 (*0-520-03849-5*) U CA Pr.

— Japan's High Schools. (Center for Japanese Studies, UC Berkeley: No. 21). (Illus.). 360p. 1983. pap. 15.00 (*0-520-04863-6*) U CA Pr.

***Rohlen, Thomas P. & LeTendre, Gerald K., eds.** Teaching & Learning in Japan. (Illus.). 350p. (C). 1995. write for info. (*0-521-49587-3*) Cambridge U Pr.

Rohlen, Thomas P., jt. ed. see Okimoto, Daniel I.

***Rohler, Lloyd.** Ralph Waldo Emerson: Preacher & Lecturer. LC 95-2105. (Great American Orators: Vol. 21). 216p. 1995. text ed. 59.95 (*0-313-26328-0*, Greenwood Pr) Greenwood.

Rohler, Lloyd & Cook, Roger. Great Speeches for Criticism & Analysis. 2nd ed. 358p. (C). 1992. pap. text ed. 17.95 (*0-9616489-4-5*) Alistair Pr.

Rohlf, Daniel. The Endangered Species Act: Protection & Implementation. 207p. (Orig.). (C). 1989. pap. 12.00 (*0-942007-33-6*) Stanford Enviro.

Rohlf, F. James. BIOM-pc: A Package of Statistical Programs. 70p. (C). 1981. pap. 60.00 (*0-925031-01-1*) Exeter NY.

— NTSYS-pc: Numerical Taxonomy & Multivariate Analysis System. (Illus.). 180p. (C). 1988. teacher ed 440.00 (*0-317-93052-4*) Exeter NY.

— NTSYS-pc: Numerical Taxonomy & Multivariate Analysis System. rev. ed. (Illus.). 180p. (C). 1988. 110.00 (*0-925031-00-3*) Exeter NY.

Rohlf, F. James, jt. auth. see Sokal, Robert.

Rohlf, James W. Modern Physics from A to Z. LC 93-48737. 646p. 1994. text ed. 70.95 (*0-471-57270-5*) Wiley.

Rohlf, William D., Jr. Introduction to Economic Reasoning. (Illus.). 510p. (C). 1989. text ed. 41.95 (*0-201-15743-8*) Addison-Wesley.

— Introduction to Economic Reasoning. 2nd ed. (Illus.). 540p. (C). 1993. pap. text ed. 41.95 (*0-201-57261-3*) Addison-Wesley.

— Introduction to Economic Reasoning. 3rd ed. 592p. (C). 1996. pap. text ed. write for info. (*0-201-60994-0*) Addison-Wesley.

— Introduction to Economic Reasoning: Test Bank & Transparency. 3rd ed. 375p. 1995. trans. write for info. (*0-201-47600-2*) Addison-Wesley.

Rohlfing, Christian F. Greenberg's Guide to Lionel Trains, 1901-1942, Vol. II. (Illus.). 152p. 1988. text ed. 29.95 (*0-89778-101-5*, 10-7080) Greenberg Bks.

Rohlfing, R., tr. see Peseschkian, N.

Rohlfs, Anna K. The Forsaken Inn: A Novel. LC 78-164575. (American Fiction Reprint Ser.). 1977. reprint ed. 29.95 (*0-8369-7052-7*) Ayer.

Rohlfs, Gerhard. From Vulgar Latin to Old French: An Introduction to the Study of the Old French Language. Almazan, Vincent & McCarthy, Lillian, trs. LC 71-98131. 291p. reprint ed. pap. 83.00 (*0-7837-3685-1*, 2043559) Bks Demand.

Rohlfs, Gerhard, jt. ed. see Rohlfs, Heinrich.

Rohlfs, Heinrich & Rohlfs, Gerhard, eds. Deutsches Archiv: Fur Geschichte der Medicin und Medicinische Geographie. xxvii, 3896p. 1971. reprint ed. write for info. (*3-487-04127-8*, Pub. by Georg Olms GW) Lubrecht & Cramer.

Rohlfs, K. Tools of Radio Astronomy. (Astronomy & Astrophysics Library). (Illus.). xii, 319p. 1986. 79.00 (*0-387-16188-0*) Spr-Verlag.

— Tools of Radio Astronomy: Study Edition. 2nd ed. Harwit, Martin D. et al, eds. (Astronomy & Astrophysics Library). (Illus.). xv, 319p. 1990. reprint ed. pap. 45.00 (*0-387-52744-3*) Spr-Verlag.

Rohlich, Gerard A. & Howe, Richard S. Environmental Regulation & the Chemical Industry. LC 82-83536. 122p. 1982. 8.00 (*0-89940-806-0*) LBJ Sch Pub Aff.

Rohlich, P. & Bacsy, E., eds. Tissue Culture & Reticuloendothelial System. 569p. 1984. lib. bdg. 193.00 (*0-317-65951-0*, Pub. by VSP NE) Coronet Bks.

Rohlich, Thomas H., tr. A Tale of Eleventh-Century Japan: Hamamatsu Chunagon Monogatari. LC 82-61380. (Library of Asian Translations). 256p. 1983. 47.50x (*0-691-05377-4*) Princeton U Pr.

Rohling, Augustus. Louise Lateau: Her Stigmas & Ecstasy. 55p. 1994. reprint ed. spiral bd. 11.00 (*0-7873-1288-6*) Mokelumne.

Rohlman, Jeff, jt. auth. see Beecham, John J.

Rohlmeier, Charles. Drafting: Metric. LC 79-55761. 320p. reprint ed. pap. 91.20 (*0-317-19778-9*, 2023202) Bks Demand.

***Rohlsen, Beatrix.** The Art of Taste: A Gourmet Guide to Vegeterian Cooking. (Illus.). 141p. 1994. pap. 19.95 (*0-9643302-0-2*) Gourmet Creat.

Rohm & Haas Company Staff, et al, eds. Artificial Intelligence Applications in Chemistry. LC 86-3315. (ACS Symposium Ser.: No. 306). (Illus.). 394p. 1986. 65.95 (*0-8412-0966-9*) Am Chemical.

Rohm, Ernst. Why S. A.? 1982. lib. bdg. 59.95 (*0-87700-368-8*) Revisionist Pr.

Rohm, Robert & Shaw, John W. Real World Measurement. LC 79-730249. (Illus.). 1979. student ed, audio 165.00 (*0-89290-097-0*, A513-SATC) Soc for Visual.

Rohm, Robert A. Positive Personality Profiles: Discover Personality Insights to Understand Yourself & Others. Carey, Chris & Enis, Nancy, eds. (Illus.). 200p. 1994. reprint ed. pap. 10.00 (*0-9641080-0-3*) Prsnality Insights.

Rohman, Dale L. A Time for Flowers. LC 82-14362. (Illus.). 140p. 1983. 50.00 (*0-935284-26-5*) Patrice Pr.

***Rohman, Jane M.** The Dogs' Guide to New York City with Jack, the City Dog: With over 200 Wonderful Walks, Outings, Activities, Getaways & Places You Never Thought You Could Take Your Pooch. (Illus.). 200p. (Orig.). 1994. pap. 14.95 (*0-9641824-0-8*) Richmond Pr.

Rohmann, Eric. Time Flies. LC 93-28200. (Illus.). 32p. (J). (ps-4). 1994. 15.00 (*0-517-59598-2*); lib. bdg. 15.99 (*0-517-59599-0*) Crown Bks Yng Read.

Rohmann, Steven O. & Lilienthal, Nancy. Tracing a River's Toxic Pollution: A Case Study of the Hudson, 2 vols. LC 85-60234. Phase I, 1985, 162p. write for info. (*0-918780-30-6*); Phase II, 1987, 218p. write for info. (*0-318-68255-9*) INFORM NY.

— Tracing a River's Toxic Pollution: A Case Study of the Hudson, 2 vols., Set. LC 85-60234. pap. 20.00 (*0-918780-40-3*) INFORM NY.

Rohmer, Eric. The Taste for Beauty. Volk, Carol, tr. (Cambridge Studies in Film). (Illus.). 207p. (C). 1990. pap. 17.95 (*0-521-38592-X*) Cambridge U Pr.

Rohmer, Harriet, ed. Mr. Sugar Came to Town Read-Along. LC 88-38781. (ENG & SPA.). (J). (ps-7). 1990. audio 22.95 (*0-89239-062-X*) Childrens Book Pr.

Rohmer, Harriet & Anchondo, Mary. How We Came to the Fifth World (Como Vinimos al Quinto Mundo) LC 76-7240. (Illus.). 24p. (ENG & SPA.). (J). (gr. 2-6). 1988. 13.95 (*0-89239-024-7*) Childrens Book Pr.

Rohmer, Harriet & Guerrero Rea, Jesus. Atariba & Niguayona. LC 76-17495. (Illus.). 24p. (ENG & SPA.). (J). (gr. 2-6). 1988. 13.95 (*0-89239-026-3*) Childrens Book Pr.

Rohmer, Harriet & Wilson, Dorminster. Mother Scorpion Country: La tierra de la madre escorpion. LC 86-32649. (Illus.). (ENG & SPA.). (J). (gr. 2-7). 1987. 13.95 (*0-89239-032-8*) Childrens Book Pr.

Rohmer, Sax. Bimbashi Baruk of Egypt. 1970. 8.50 (*0-685-26777-6*) Bookfinger.

— The Bride of Fu Manchu. 1976. reprint ed. lib. bdg. 19.95 (*0-89190-801-3*, Rivercity Pr) Amereon Ltd.

— The Day the World Ended. 1976. reprint ed. lib. bdg. 22.95 (*0-89190-804-8*, Rivercity Pr) Amereon Ltd.

— The Devil Doctor. 256p. 1994. 16.95 (*0-7451-8647-5*, Black Dagger) Chivers N Amer.

— Dream Detective. 16.95 (*0-89190-810-2*, Am Repr) Amereon Ltd.

— Drums of Fu Manchu. 18.95 (*0-8488-0619-0*) Amereon Ltd.

— The Emperor of America. 1976. reprint ed. lib. bdg. 22.95 (*0-89190-805-6*) Amereon Ltd.

— Exploits of Captain O'Hagan. 1968. 6.00 (*0-685-22715-4*) Bookfinger.

— Fu Manchu. (Sax Rohmer Reader Ser.). 434p. 1984. pap. 6.95 (*0-8065-0899-X*, Citadel Pr) Carol Pub Group.

— The Golden Scorpion. 1976. reprint ed. lib. bdg. 22.95 (*0-89190-806-4*, Rivercity Pr) Amereon Ltd.

— The Hand of Fu Manchu. 1976. reprint ed. lib. bdg. 22.95 (*0-89190-802-1*, Rivercity Pr) Amereon Ltd.

— Hangover House. 20.95 (*0-89190-807-2*, Am Repr) Amereon Ltd.

— The Insidious Dr. Fu Manchu. 1976. lib. bdg. 13.95 (*0-89968-143-3*, Lghtyr Pr) Buccaneer Bks.

— The Island of Fu Manchu. 320p. 1986. pap. 3.50 (*0-8217-1912-2*) Zebra.

— The Mask of Fu Manchu. 1976. reprint ed. lib. bdg. 19.95 (*0-89190-803-X*, Rivercity Pr) Amereon Ltd.

— The Moon Is Red. 1976. 12.50 (*0-685-80029-6*) Bookfinger.

— The Mystery of Dr. Fu-Manchu. large type ed. 1994. 18.95 (*0-7451-6454-4*, Scarlet Dagger Lrg Print) Chivers N Amer.

— Orchard of Tears. 1969. 8.50 (*0-685-22716-2*) Bookfinger.

— Return of Dr. Fu Manchu. 18.95 (*0-89190-828-5*) Amereon Ltd.

— Return of Dr. Fu Manchu. 1976. lib. bdg. 13.95 (*0-89968-141-7*, Lghtyr Pr) Buccaneer Bks.

— The Romance of Sorcery. 1976. reprint ed. lib. bdg. 22.95 (*0-89190-808-0*, Rivercity Pr) Amereon Ltd.

— Salute to Bazarada & Other Stories. 311p. 1972. 12.50 (*0-685-26828-4*) Bookfinger.

— Sand & Satin. 1978. 8.50 (*0-685-90566-7*) Bookfinger.

— Sax Rohmer: Two Complete Fu Manchu Adventures. Mason, Tom, ed. (Illus.). 112p. 1990. pap. 12.95 (*0-944735-24-X*) Malibu Graphics.

— Seven Sins. 1972. 8.50 (*0-685-33437-6*) Bookfinger.

— Shadow of Fu Manchu. 272p. 1986. pap. 3.50 (*0-8217-1870-3*) Zebra.

— Sinister Madonna. (Sumuru Ser.). 1977. reprint ed. 8.50 (*0-685-88226-8*) Bookfinger.

— Sins of Severac Bablon. 1967. 10.00 (*0-685-22714-6*) Bookfinger.

— Sins of Sumuru. 1977. reprint ed. 8.50 (*0-685-88227-6*) Bookfinger.

— Slaves of Sumuru. (Sumuru Ser.). 1979. 8.50 (*0-686-65266-5*) Bookfinger.

Rohmer, Sax, pseud. Tales of Chinatown. LC 75-178459. (Short Story Index Reprint Ser.). 1977. reprint ed. 22.95 (*0-8369-4060-1*) Ayer.

Rohmer, Sax. Tales of East & West. 1976. 8.50 (*0-685-79490-3*) Bookfinger.

— Tales of Secret Egypt. 1976. reprint ed. lib. bdg. 22.95 (*0-89190-809-9*) Amereon Ltd.

— Trail of Fu Manchu. 23.95 (*0-8488-0317-5*) Amereon Ltd.

— Virgin in Flames. 1978. 8.50 (*0-685-90567-5*) Bookfinger.

— Wulfheim. 1972. 12.50 (*0-685-33438-4*) Bookfinger.

— The Yellow Claw. 1976. lib. bdg. 13.95 (*0-89968-142-5*, Lghtyr Pr) Buccaneer Bks.

— Yellow Claw. 12.95 (*0-8488-1463-0*) Amereon Ltd.

R

Rohmert, Walter & Landau, Kurt. A New Technique for Job Analysis. LC 83-8425. 100p. 1983. pap. 46.00 (*0-8002-3089-2*) Taylor & Francis.

Rohmert, Walter, jt. ed. see Landau, Kurt.

Rohn. Seven Strategies for Wealth. 1989. pap. 9.95 (*0-914629-73-5*) Prima Pub.

Rohn, Arthur H., jt. auth. see Ferguson, William M.

Rohn, Arthur H., et al. Rock Art of Bandelier National Monument. LC 88-4736. (Illus.). 170p. 1989. pap. 32.50 (*0-8263-1052-4*) U of NM Pr.

***Rohn, Charles L.** Analytical Polymer Rheology: Structure - Processing - Property Relationships. 320p. (C). 1995. text ed. write for info. (*1-56990-149-X*) Hanser-Gardner.

Rohn, E. James. Seven Strategies for Wealth & Happiness: Power Ideas from America's Foremost Business Philosopher. Dominitz, Nancy D., ed. 160p. (Orig.). 1986. 13.95 (*0-685-10528-8*, St Martin); pap. 9.95 (*0-685-10529-6*, St Martin) Prima Pub.

Rohn, E. James & Reynolds, Ronald L. The Seasons of Life. LC 81-66145. (Illus.). 117p. 1981. text ed. 9.95 (*0-939490-00-5*) Total Impact.

Rohn, Jim. The Holo Brothers, Bk. 1. (Illus.). 92p. (Orig.). 1988. pap. 8.95 (*0-930193-36-9*) Fantagraph Bks.

Rohn, Jim & Reynolds, Ron. The Five Major Pieces to the Life Puzzle. Chinell, Kathryn, ed. 135p. 1991. 30.00 (*0-939490-02-1*) Total Impact.

Rohn, Matthew. Visual Dynamics in Jackson Pollock's Abstractions. LC 86-30746. (Studies in the Fine Arts - Art Theory: No. 14). 190p. reprint ed. pap. 54.20 (*0-8357-1790-9*, 2070662) Bks Demand.

Rohn, Peter H. World Treaty Index, 5 vols., 1. 2nd ed. LC 83-3872. 4271p. 1984. lib. bdg. 210.00 (*0-87436-159-1*) ABC-CLIO.

— World Treaty Index, 5 vols., 2. 2nd ed. LC 83-3872. 4271p. 1984. lib. bdg. 210.00 (*0-87436-160-5*) ABC-CLIO.

— World Treaty Index, 5 vols., 3. 2nd ed. LC 83-3872. 4271p. 1984. lib. bdg. 210.00 (*0-87436-161-3*) ABC-CLIO.

— World Treaty Index, 5 vols., 4. 2nd ed. LC 83-3872. 4271p. 1984. lib. bdg. 210.00 (*0-87436-162-1*) ABC-CLIO.

— World Treaty Index, 5 vols., 5. 2nd ed. LC 83-3872. 4271p. 1984. lib. bdg. 210.00 (*0-87436-163-X*) ABC-CLIO.

— World Treaty Index, 5 vols., Set. 2nd ed. LC 83-3872. 4271p. 1984. lib. bdg. 999.00 (*0-87436-141-9*) ABC-CLIO.

Rohne. Total Auto Body Repair. 2nd ed. 1985. 34.64 (*0-02-682110-9*) Macmillan.

Rohner, Eric. My Night at Maud's. LC 92-32891. (Films in Print Ser.: Vol. 19). (Illus.). 220p. (C). 1993. text ed. 40.00 (*0-8135-1939-X*); pap. text ed. 16.00 (*0-8135-1940-3*) Rutgers U Pr.

Rohner, Linda K., ed. A Dictionary for Lupus Patients. 60p. 1993. pap. text ed. 9.95 (*0-9638245-0-3*) Mtn Gem Pubng.

Rohner, Peter. Industrial Hydraulic Control. 184p. (C). 1988. 170.00 (*0-86787-080-X*, Pub. by S Thornes Pubs UK) St Mut.

Rohner, Peter & Smith, Gordon. Pneumatic Control for Industrial Automation. 272p. (C). 1988. 110.00 (*0-86787-075-3*, Pub. by S Thornes Pubs UK) St Mut.

— Pneumatic Control for Industrial Automation. 272p. (C). 1988. 60.00x (*0-471-33449-9*, Pub. by S Thornes Pubs UK) St Mut.

Rohner, Ronald P. & Bettauer, Evelyn C. The Kwakiutl: Indians of British Columbia. (Illus.). 111p. (C). 1986. reprint ed. pap. text ed. 8.50 (*0-88133-225-9*) Waveland Pr.

Rohner, Ronald P. & Chaki-Sircar, Manjusri. Women & Children in a Bengali Village. LC 87-25463. (Illus.). 231p. 1988. text ed. 35.00 (*0-87451-431-2*) U Pr of New Eng.

Rohner, Ronald P. & Cournoyer, David E. Handbook for the Study of Parental Acceptance & Rejection. rev. ed. 181p. 1990. pap. text ed. 15.00 (*1-881628-00-0*); disk 25.00 (*1-881628-01-9*) U CT Parent Accept & Reject.

***Rohnke & Butler.** Quicksilver. 192p. 1994. per., pap. text ed. 23.50 (*0-7872-0032-8*) Kendall-Hunt.

Rohnke, Karl. The Bottomless Bag. 384p. 1991. pap. 29.00 (*0-8403-6633-7*) Kendall-Hunt.

— Bottomless Baggie. 144p. 1991. pap. text ed. 16.50 (*0-8403-6813-5*) Kendall-Hunt.

— Forget Me Knots. 80p. (C). 1991. spiral bd. 8.50 (*0-8403-7138-1*) Kendall-Hunt.

— Forget Me Knots: All the Knots You Need to Know to Run a Ropes Course. (Illus.). 75p. (Orig.). 1991. pap. 8.50 (*0-934387-10-9*) Project Advent.

— Slightly Skewed Vignettes: Confessions of an Incorrigible Kid. 144p. 1992. pap. text ed. 10.95 (*0-8403-7852-1*) Kendall-Hunt.

Rohnke, Karl E. Cranking Out Adventure: A Bike Leader's Guide to Trial & Error Touring. 46p. 1977. pap. 4.50 (*0-934387-04-4*) Project Advent.

— High Profile: A How to Book for Building, Belaying, & Use of Indoor Climbing Walls & Selected Ropes Course Elements. (Illus.). 55p. 1981. pap. 7.00 (*0-934387-02-8*) Project Advent.

Rohonyi, K. & Marot, M. Walking Around Budapest: Budapest Corvina, 1988. (Illus.). 156p. (C). 1988. pap. 65.00 (*0-569-08215-3*, Pub. by Collets) St Mut.

Rohr, Charles J. The Governor of Maryland, a Constitutional Study. LC 78-64147. (Johns Hopkins University. Studies in the Social Sciences. Thirtieth Ser. 1912: No. 3). reprint ed. 21.00 (*0-404-61258-X*) AMS Pr.

Rohr-Dietschi, Ursula. Zur Genese des Selbstbewusstseins: Eine Studie ueber den Beitrag des phaenomenologischen Denkens zur Frage der Entwicklung des Selbstbewusstseins. LC 72-81567. (Phaenomenologisch-Psychologische Forschungen Ser.: Vol. 14). 197p. (C). 1975. 79.25 (*3-11-004048-4*) De Gruyter.

Rohr, Donald G., jt. auth. see Ergang, Robert.

Rohr, Erwin K. Meditations. (Illus.). 260p. 1989. 13.95 (*0-931660-07-6*) R Oman Pub.

Rohr, J. A. Ethics for Bureaucrats: An Essay on Law & Values. 2nd expanded rev. ed. (Public Administration & Public Policy Ser.: Vol. 36). 352p. 1989. 59.75 (*0-8247-8032-9*) Dekker.

Rohr, Janelle. Science & Religion: Opposing Viewpoints. LC 87-38066. (Opposing Viewpoints Ser.). (Illus.). (YA). (gr. 10 up). 1988. pap. text ed. 11.55 (*0-89908-406-0*) Greenhaven.

Rohr, Janelle, ed. Animal Rights: Opposing Viewpoints. LC 89-2227. (Opposing Viewpoints Ser.). (Illus.). 235p. (YA). (gr. 10 up). 1989. lib. bdg. 19.95 (*0-89908-440-0*); pap. 11.55 (*0-89908-415-X*) Greenhaven.

— Eastern Europe: Opposing Viewpoints. LC 90-44330. (Opposing Viewpoints Ser.). (Illus.). 240p. (YA). (gr. 10 up). 1990. lib. bdg. 19.95 (*0-89908-480-X*); pap. text ed. 11.55 (*0-89908-455-9*) Greenhaven.

— Violence in America: Opposing Viewpoints. LC 89-25943. (Opposing Viewpoints Ser.). (Illus.). 288p. (YA). (gr. 10 up). 1990. lib. bdg. 19.95 (*0-89908-449-4*); pap. text ed. 11.55 (*0-89908-424-9*) Greenhaven.

***Rohr, John A.** Founding Republics in France & America: A Study in Constitutional Governance. (Studies in Government & Public Policy). 400p. (C). 1995. 45.00x (*0-7006-0733-1*); pap. 19.95x (*0-7006-0734-X*) U Pr of KS.

— The President & the Public Administration. Belz, Herman, ed. (Bicentennial Essays on the Constitution Ser.). 78p. 1989. 7.00 (*0-87229-045-X*) Am Hist Assn.

— To Run a Constitution: The Legitimacy of the Administrative State. LC 85-28867. xvi, 272p. 1986. 35.00 (*0-7006-0291-7*); pap. 12.95 (*0-7006-0301-8*) U Pr of KS.

***Rohr, Richard.** Enneagram II: Advancing Spiritual Discernment. LC 94-41710. 160p. 1995. 17.95 (*0-8245-1451-3*) Crossroad NY.

— Near Occasions of Grace. LC 92-33193. 125p. (Orig.). 1993. pap. 9.95 (*0-88344-852-1*) Orbis Bks.

— Quest for the Grail: Soul Work & the Sacred Journey. 160p. 1994. 17.95 (*0-8245-1411-4*) Crossroad NY.

— Radical Grace: Daily Meditations. Feister, John B., ed. 410p. 1993. 22.95 (*0-86716-151-5*) St Anthony Mess Pr.

— Simplicity: The Art of Living. 180p. 1992. pap. 19.95 (*0-8245-1251-0*) Crossroad NY.

Rohr, Richard & Ebert, Andreas. Discovering the Enneagram: An Ancient Tool a New Spiritual Journey. 256p. 1992. pap. 12.95 (*0-8245-1185-9*) Crossroad NY.

Rohr, Richard & Martos, Joseph. The Great Themes of Scripture: New Testament. (Great Themes of Scripture Ser.). 192p. (Orig.). 1988. pap. 6.95 (*0-86716-098-5*) St Anthony Mess Pr.

— The Great Themes of Scripture: Old Testament. (Great Themes of Scripture Ser.). 144p. (Orig.). 1987. pap. 5.95 (*0-86716-085-3*) St Anthony Mess Pr.

— Why Be Catholic? Understanding Our Experience & Tradition. 146p. (Orig.). 1990. pap. 6.95 (*0-86716-101-9*) St Anthony Mess Pr.

— The Wild Man's Journey: Reflections on Male Spirituality. 225p. 1992. 17.95 (*0-86716-128-0*) St Anthony Mess Pr.

Rohr, Richard, et al. Experiencing the Enneagram. 288p. (Orig.). 1992. pap. 13.95 (*0-8245-1201-4*) Crossroad NY.

— Grace in Action. 160p. (Orig.). 1994. pap. 12.95 (*0-8245-1379-7*) Crossroad NY.

Rohr-Rouendal, Petra, illus. Talking AIDS, A Guide for Community Work. 110p. (Orig.). 1989. pap. 9.95 (*0-333-49781-3*, Pub. by Macmill Press UK) Scholium Intl.

Rohrbach, David H. & Timpl, Rupert, eds. Molecular & Cellular Aspects of Basement Membranes. (Cell Biology Ser.). (Illus.). 448p. 1993. text ed. 115.00 (*0-12-593165-4*) Acad Pr.

Rohrbach, Jim. Business Success Skills. 100p. (Orig.). 1994. pap. 19.95 (*0-9627754-1-X*) J M Rohrbach.

— The Social Skills Playbook: Why Be Shy? LC 90-91986. 96p. (Orig.). 1990. pap. 11.95 (*0-9627754-0-1*) J M Rohrbach.

Rohrbach, Lewis B. Hoffelbauer Genealogy, 1660-1989. LC 93-85401. 640p. 1993. 69.50 (*0-929539-12-5*) Picton Pr.

— Rohrbach Genealogy, Vol. III: The Rorabaugh, Rohrbough, Rohrbaugh, Rohrabough, Rohrabaugh, Rorabough & Rhorabaugh Families of America Who Are Descendants of Johann Reinhart Rohrbach Who Emigrated from Germany to America in 1749. LC 71-118879. 376p. 1982. 45.00 (*0-929539-00-1*) Picton Pr.

Rohrbach, Lewis B., ed. The Records of the Church of Christ in Buxton, Maine, 1763-1817. rev. ed. LC 88-63778. 104p. 1989. reprint ed. 20.00 (*0-929539-02-8*) Picton Pr.

Rohrbach, Lewis B., intro. Boston Taxpayers in Eighteen Twenty-One. rev. ed. LC 88-90540. 256p. 1988. reprint ed. 25.00 (*0-929539-01-X*) Picton Pr.

***Rohrbach, Mike & Rydberg, Denny.** Run to Win: Devotions & Chapel Talks for Athletes, Coaches & Sports Fans. 142p. (Orig.). (YA). (gr. 6 up). 1993. pap. 8.95 (*1-887002-05-7*) Cross Trng.

Rohrbach, Peter T. Conversation with Christ. LC 82-50586. 171p. 1982. reprint ed. pap. 8.00 (*0-89555-180-2*) TAN Bks Pubs.

— The Largest Event: A Library of Congress Resource Guide for the Study of World War II. LC 93-16487. 1993. write for info. (*0-8444-0782-8*) Lib Congress.

Rohrbach, Peter T. & Newman, Lowell S. American Issue: The U. S. Postage Stamp, 1842-1869. LC 83-27146. (Illus.). 232p. 1984. text ed. 32.50 (*0-87474-816-X*, ROAI) Smithsonian.

Rohrbach, Peter-Thomas, tr. see St. Therese.

Rohrbach, Roger P., jt. auth. see Christianson, Leslie L.

Rohrbacher, jt. auth. see Burfeindt-Moral, H.

Rohrbacher, Charles. Icon: Image of the Invisible Workbook. 1995. write for info. (*1-879038-11-0*) Oakwood Pubns.

Rohrbacher, Richard W., jt. auth. see Westwood, Phoebe L.

Rohrbacher, T. J., et al. Coal Resource Recoverability: A Methodology. 1993. write for info. (*0-318-70285-1*) US Interior.

Rohrbacher, Timothy J., et al. Coal Reserves of the Boltsfork Quadrangle, Kentucky: A Coal Recoverability Study. 1993. write for info. (*0-318-72293-3*) US Interior.

Rohrback. Introduction of Chemometrics. 1993. write for info. (*0-8493-7323-9*) CRC Pr.

Rohrbaugh, John W., et al, eds. Event-Related Brain Potentials: Basic Issues & Applications. (Illus.). 402p. 1990. 75.00 (*0-19-504891-1*) OUP.

Rohrbaugh, Richard L., jt. auth. see Malina, Bruce J.

Rohrborn, Claus, tr. see Sokeland, Jurgen.

Rohrbough, Edward, jt. auth. see Jardine, John.

Rohrbough, F. W. Rohrbaugh Family. (Illus.). 130p. 1993. reprint ed. lib. bdg. 36.00 (*0-8328-3742-3*); reprint ed. pap. 26.00 (*0-8328-3743-1*) Higginson Bk Co.

Rohrbough, Linda. Mailing List Services on Your Home-Based PC. 1993. pap. text ed. 14.95 (*0-07-041397-5*) McGraw.

— Mailing List Services on Your Home-Based PC. 1994. text ed. 24.95 (*0-07-041396-7*) McGraw.

— Mailing List Services on Your Home-Based PC. 1993. 14.95 (*0-8306-4473-3*, Windcrest); pap. 14.60 (*0-8306-4474-1*, Windcrest) TAB Bks.

— Small Business Computing Made Easy: Everything You Need to Know to Get Started with a Computer. Rohrbough, Mark, ed. (Illus.). 240p. 1989. disk 24.95 (*1-877855-00-6*) SoftServe Pr.

— Start Your Own Computer Repair Business. 1995. disk, pap. text ed. 32.95 (*0-07-911901-8*) McGraw.

Rohrbough, Malcolm J. Aspen: The History of a Silver-Mining Town, 1879-1893. (Illus.). 288p. 1988. pap. 10.95 (*0-19-505428-8*) OUP.

— The Trans-Appalachian Frontier: People, Societies, & Institutions, 1775-1850. 403p. (C). 1990. pap. 22.95 (*0-534-12336-8*) Intl Thomson.

Rohrbough, Mark, ed. see Rohrbough, Linda.

Rohreke, H. G., ed. see Pineus, K.

Rohrer, Alyce. The True Believers. LC 85-18521. 1987. 22.95 (*0-87949-253-8*) Ashley Bks.

Rohrer, Ann & Flamholtz, Cathy J. The Tibetan Mastiff: Legendary Guardian of the Himalayas. (Illus.). 160p. (Orig.). 1989. 16.95 (*0-940269-02-3*) OTR Pubns.

Rohrer, C., jt. ed. see Guenthner, Franz.

Rohrer, C., jt. ed. see Reyle, U.

Rohrer, Doug. More Thought Provokers. (YA). (gr. 9-12). 1994. 9.95 (*1-55953-070-7*) Key Curr Pr.

— Thought Provokers. 57p. (YA). (gr. 9-12). 1993. pap. 9.95 (*1-55953-065-0*) Key Curr Pr.

Rohrer, James E. Quality Assurance in Long-Term Care: Managing the Process. (Learning the Continuum: AUPHA Modules for Management Education Ser.). (Illus.). 48p. (Orig.). (C). 1989. pap. text ed. 45.00 (*0-910591-21-0*) AUPHA Pr.

***Rohrer, James R.** Keepers of the Covenant: Frontier Missions & the Decline of Congregationalism, 1774-1818. (Religion in America Ser.). 240p. 1995. text ed. 35.00 (*0-19-509166-3*) OUP.

Rohrer, John N. & Sherif, Muzafer, eds. Social Psychology at the Crossroads: Conference on Social Psychology, University of Oklahoma, 1950. LC 73-111822. (Essay Index Reprint Ser.). 1977. 28.95 (*0-8369-1600-X*) Ayer.

Rohrer, Josef, ed. see Hildebrand, Sigrid S. & Hildebrand, Eckart.

Rohrer, Josef, tr. see Winitz, Harris.

Rohrer, Josef, ed. see Winitz, Harris.

***Rohrer, Matthew.** A Hummock in the Malookas: Poems. 96p. 1995. 17.95 (*0-393-03798-3*) Norton.

Rohrer, Norman. Indomitable Mr. O. 150p. 1970. pap. 5.99 (*1-55976-124-5*) CEF Press.

Rohrer, Norman B., jt. auth. see Engstrom, Ted W.

Rohrer, P. Project Management Software & Systems. 1988. text ed. write for info. (*0-442-27707-5*) Van Nos Reinhold.

Rohrer, R. System Theory. Date not set. write for info. (*0-318-51860-0*) Entropy Ltd.

Rohrer, Richard L., jt. auth. see Greenwood, L. Larry.

Rohrer, Wayne & Douglas, Louis H. Agrarian Transition in America: Dualism & Change. LC 68-15586. 1969. 29.50 (*0-672-60806-5*) Irvington.

Rohrich, Lutz. Folktales & Reality. Tokofsky, Peter, tr. LC 90-26381. (Folklore Studies in Translation). 324p. 1991. 39.95 (*0-253-35028-X*) Ind U Pr.

***Rohrich, Rod, et al.** Secondary Rhinoplasty & Nasal Reconstruction. 1995. 95.00 (*0-942219-80-5*) Quality Med Pub.

Rohricht, Jo Anne, jt. auth. see Nelson, James B.

Rohrig, Carl-W. Rohrig Tarot. 72p. 1995. 19.50 (*1-885394-08-X*) Bluestar Commun.

Rohrl, Vivian J. Change for Continuity: The People of a Thousand Lakes. LC 80-6077. 269p. 1981. pap. text ed. 24.00 (*0-8191-1539-8*) U Pr of Amer.

Rohrlich, Beulah F. A Handbook for Visitors to the U. S. A. (Illus.). 114p. (Orig.). 1986. pap. 6.50 (*971-10-0214-0*, Pub. by New Day Pub PH) Cellar.

Rohrlich, Chester. Law & Practice in Corporate Control. LC 34-1197. (Business Enterprises Reprint Ser.). vii, 268p. 1982. reprint ed. lib. bdg. 65.00 (*0-89941-184-3*, 302360) W S Hein.

Rohrlich, Chester & Bender's Editorial Staff. Organizing Corporate & Other Business Enterprises. 5th ed. 1975. Looseleaf updates avail. write for info. (*0-8205-1595-7*) Bender.

Rohrlich, Fritz. From Paradox to Reality: Basic Concepts of the Physical World. (Illus.). 240p. (C). 1989. pap. 24.95 (*0-521-37605-X*) Cambridge U Pr.

Rohrlich, Fritz, jt. auth. see Jauch, J. M.

Rohrlich-Leavitt, Ruby, ed. Women Cross-Culturally: Change & Challenge. (World Anthropology Ser.). (Illus.). xiv, 670p. 1975. 50.70 (*90-279-7649-X*) Mouton.

Rohrman, Larry G. Fit to Be Tied: How to Be Married & Happy. (Illus.). (Orig.). 1990. pap. 6.00 (*0-9628956-0-1*) Carousel AL.

Rohrs, Charles E. Linear Control Systems. 2nd ed. 1993. text ed. write for info. (*0-07-041525-0*) McGraw.

Rohrs, Richard C., jt. auth. see Darcy, R.

Rohrs, Walter F., jt. auth. see Colton, Raymond R.

Rohse, Mitch. Land Use Planning in Oregon: A No-Nonsense Handbook in Plain English. LC 86-12457. (Illus.). 296p. 1987. text ed. 29.95x (*0-87071-349-3*) Oreg St U Pr.

Rohsenow, John S. A Chinese-English Dictionary of Enigmatic Folk Similes (Xiehouyu) LC 90-25213. 325p. 1991. 50.00 (*0-8165-1031-8*) U of Ariz Pr.

***Roht-Arriaza, Naomi.** Impunity & Human Rights in International Law & Practice. 384p. 1995. 55.00 (*0-19-508136-6*) OUP.

Rohter, Ira. A Green Hawaii: Sourcebook for Development Alternatives. LC 92-82826. (Illus.). 480p. (Orig.). 1992. 25.95 (*1-878751-12-3*); pap. 16.95 (*1-878751-13-1*) Na Kane O Ka Malo.

Rohwedder, W. J., ed. Computer-Aided Environmental Education. (Monograph Ser.: Vol. 8). (Illus.). 250p. (Orig.). 1990. pap. 17.00 (*1-884008-02-X*) NAAEE.

***Rohwedder, W. J. & Alm, Andy.** Using Computers in Environmental Education: Interactive Multimedia & On-Line Learning. 72p. 1994. teacher ed 8.00 (*1-884782-11-6*) Natl Consort EET.

Rohwer, C., jt. ed. see Campbell, D.

Rohwer, Claude D., jt. auth. see Schaber, Gordon D.

Rohwer, Gotz, jt. auth. see Blossfeld, Hans-Peter.

Rohwer, Jens G. Lauraceae: Nectandra. (Flora Neotropica Monograph Ser.: No. 60). (Illus.). 1993. pap. text ed. 43.50 (*0-89327-373-2*) NY Botanical.

Rohwer, Jurgen & Hummelchen, Gerhard. Chronology of the War at Sea, 1939-1945: The Naval History of World War Two. 416p. 1992. 55.00 (*1-55750-105-X*) Naval Inst Pr.

Rohwer, Lee O. What Is God Like? (Illus.). 64p. (Orig.). (J). (gr. k-4). 1986. pap. 5.95 (*0-9617788-0-6*) Damon Pub.

— What Is God Like? 2nd rev. ed. (Illus.). 68p. (Orig.). (YA). (gr. 8 up). 1989. reprint ed. pap. 7.95 (*0-9617788-1-4*) Damon Pub.

Rohwer, Sievert. Specific Distinctness & Adaptive Differences in Southwestern Meadowlarks. (Occasional Papers: No. 44). 14p. 1976. pap. 1.00 (*0-317-04634-9*) U of KS Mus Nat Hist.

Rohwer, William D., et al. Educational Psychology: Teaching for Student Diversity. LC 79-24238. 340p. (C). 1980. pap. text ed. 25.50 (*0-03-019531-4*) HB Coll Pubs.

Ro'i, Yaacov. From Encroachment to Involvement: A Documented Study of Soviet Policy in the Middle East 1945-1973. 616p. 1974. boxed 49.95 (*0-87855-158-1*) Transaction Pubs.

— Soviet Decision Making in Practice: The U. S. S. R. & Israel, 1947-1954. LC 79-64857. 540p. 1980. 44.95 (*0-87855-267-7*) Transaction Pubs.

— The Struggle for Soviet Jewish Emigration, 1948-1967. (Cambridge Russian, Soviet & Post-Soviet Studies: No. 75). (Illus.). 512p. (C). 1991. 69.95 (*0-521-39084-2*) Cambridge U Pr.

***Ro'i, Yaacov, ed.** Jews & Jewish Life in Russia & the Soviet Union. LC 94-33683. (Cummings Center Ser.). 1995. 35.00 (*0-7146-4619-9*, Pub. by F Cass Pubs UK); pap. 18.00 (*0-7146-4149-9*, Pub. by F Cass Pubs UK) Intl Spec Bk.

Ro'i, Yaacov & Beker, Avi. Jewish Culture & Identity in the Contemporary Soviet Union. 420p. 1989. 45.00 (*0-8147-7408-3*) NYU Pr.

Ro'i, Yaacov & Beker, Avi, eds. Jewish Culture & Identity in the Soviet Union. 480p. (C). 1992. pap. text ed. 20.00 (*0-8147-7432-6*) NYU Pr.

Roicek, M., jt. ed. see Hawking, S. W.

Roid, Gale & Haladyna, Tom. A Technology for Test-Item Writing. (Educational Technology Ser.). 1981. text ed. 51.00 (*0-12-593250-2*) Acad Pr.

Roider, Karl A. Austria's Eastern Question, Seventeen Hundred to Seventeen Ninety. LC 81-48141. 271p. reprint ed. pap. 77.30 (*0-8357-4195-8*, 2036973) Bks Demand.

Roider, Karl A., Jr. Baron Thugut & Austria's Response to the French Revolution. LC 87-2240. (Illus.). 448p. 1987. text ed. 67.50 (*0-691-05135-6*) Princeton U Pr.

***Roider, Karl A.** The Reluctant Ally: Austria's Policy in the Austro-Turkish War, 1737-1739. LC 72-79336. 206p. 1972. pap. 58.80 (*0-7837-8521-6*, 2049330) Bks Demand.

Roidon Co. Staff. Yo-Leven. (United States Ser.). (Illus.). 108p. (Orig.). 1990. pap. 7.00 (*1-879374-00-5*) Roidon.

Roig de Lluis, Luis, tr. see Platon.

Roig, Jose G., tr. see Oberlander, June R.

Roig, Pedro. La Guerra de Marti. LC 84-81165. (Coleccion Cuba y Sus Jueces Ser.). (Illus.). 257p. (Orig.). (SPA.). 1984. pap. 9.95 (*0-89729-353-3*) Ediciones.

Roillaexxur. Macabre Affectatious. (Illus.). 40p. (Orig.). 1992. pap. text ed. 6.95 (*1-56315-057-3*) Sterling Hse.

Roinard, P. M., et al. La Poesie Symboliste. LC 77-11482. reprint ed. 40.00 (*0-404-16343-2*) AMS Pr.

Roiphe, Anne. If You Knew Me. 224p. 1995. pap. 11.99 (*0-446-67071-5*) Warner Bks.

R

An Asterisk (*) at the beginning of an entry indicates that the title is appearing in BIP for the first time.

— If You Knew Me: A Novel. LC 92-38200. 1993. 19.95 (*0-316-75430-7*) Little.
— Lovingkindness. 256p. 1989. mass mkt. 4.99 (*0-446-35274-8*) Warner Bks.
— The Pursuit of Happiness. 1991. 22.95 (*0-685-48600-1*) Summit Bks.
— The Pursuit of Happiness. 579p. 1992. mass mkt. 5.99 (*0-446-36334-0*) Warner Bks.
Roiphe, Anne, jt. auth. see Roiphe, Herman.
Roiphe, Anne R. If You Knew Me. large type ed. LC 93-34586. 1994. bds. 20.95 (*0-7862-0077-4*) Thorndike Pr.
Roiphe, Herman & Galenson, Eleanor. Infantile Origins of Sexual Identity. LC 81-14290. 301p. 1981. 42.50 (*0-8236-2368-8*) Intl Univs Pr.
Roiphe, Herman & Roiphe, Anne. Your Child's Mind: The Complete Guide to Infant & Child Emotional Well-Being. 448p. 1986. pap. 10.95 (*0-312-89784-7*) St Martin.
Roiphe, Katherine. The Morning After: Fear, Sex, & Feminism on College Campuses. LC 93-18783. 1993. 19.95 (*0-316-75431-5*) Little.
***Roiphe, Katie.** Morning After: Sex, Fear, & Feminism, Vol. 1. 1994. pap. 8.95 (*0-316-75432-3*) Little.
***Roisman, Joseph.** Alexander the Great. (Problems in European Civilization Ser.). 250p. (C). 1995. pap. text ed. write for info. (*0-669-34501-6*) Heath.
— The General Demosthenes & His Use of Military Surprise. 84p. (Orig.). 1993. pap. 39.50 (*3-515-06277-7*) Coronet Bks.
Roitberg, Bernard D. & Isman, Murray B., eds. Insect Chemical Ecology. LC 92-12249. 1992. 69.95 (*0-412-01871-3*); pap. 35.00 (*0-412-01881-0*) Chapman & Hall.
Roitblat, H. L., et al, eds. Animal Cognition. (Comparative Cognition & Neuroscience Ser.). 696p. 1984. pap. text ed. 99.95 (*0-89859-334-4*) L Erlbaum Assocs.
***Roitblat, Herbert L. & Meyer, Jean-Arcady, eds.** Comparative Approaches to Cognitive Science. (Illus.). 550p. 1995. 50.00 (*0-262-18166-5*) MIT Pr.
Roitblat, Herbert L., et al, eds. Language & Communication: Comparative Perspectives. (Comparative Cognition & Neuroscience Ser.). 520p. 1992. text ed. 110.00 (*0-8058-0946-5*); pap. 39.95 (*0-8058-0947-3*) L Erlbaum Assocs.
Roiter, Howard, jt. auth. see Kohn, Nahum.
Roith, Estelle. The Riddle of Freud: Jewish Influences on His Theory of Female Sexuality. 250p. (C). 1987. lib. bdg. 55.00 (*0-422-61380-0*, Pub. by Tavistock UK); pap. 16.95 (*0-422-61760-1*, Pub. by Tavistock UK) Routledge Chapman & Hall.
Roitman, Judith. Introduction to Modern Set Theory. 156p. 1990. text ed. 69.95 (*0-471-63519-7*) Wiley.
Roitt, I. M. Slide Atlas of Essential Immunology. 236p. 1992. sl. 995.00 (*0-632-03273-1*) Blackwell Sci.
Roitt, Ivan M., ed. Immune Intervention Vol. 1: New Trends in Vaccines. 1984. text ed. 55.00 (*0-12-593301-0*) Acad Pr.
Roitt, Ivan M. & Delves, Peter J., eds. Encyclopedia of Immunology, 3 vols., 1. (Illus.). 1800p. 1992. text ed. 175.00 (*0-12-226761-3*) Acad Pr.
— Encyclopedia of Immunology, 3 vols., 2. (Illus.). 1800p. 1992. text ed. 175.00 (*0-12-226762-1*) Acad Pr.
— Encyclopedia of Immunology, 3 vols., 3. (Illus.). 1800p. 1992. text ed. 175.00 (*0-12-226763-X*) Acad Pr.
— Encyclopedia of Immunology, 3 vols., Set. (Illus.). 1800p. 1992. text ed. 475.00 (*0-12-226760-5*) Acad Pr.
Roitt, Ivan M., et al. Case Studies in Immunology. 77p. 1994. pap. 14.95 (*0-7234-2052-1*) Mosby Yr Bk.
Roizen, Judith & Jepson, Mark. Degrees for Jobs: Employer Expectations of Higher Education. 225p. 1985. pap. write for info. (*0-335-15617-7*, Open Univ Pr) Taylor & Francis.
— Degrees for Jobs: Employer Expectations of Higher Education. LC 85-15343. 224p. 1985. pap. 38.00 (*1-85059-005-2*, Open Univ Pr) Taylor & Francis.
Roizen, Michael F. Anesthesia for Vascular Surgery. (Illus.). 518p. 1990. text ed. 93.00 (*0-443-08567-6*) Churchill.
Roizin, Leon, jt. auth. see Kolb, Lawrence C.
Roizin, Leon, et al, eds. Neurotoxicology, Vol. 1. LC 77-4632. 686p. 1977. 174.50 (*0-89004-148-2*) Raven.
Roizman, Bernard, ed. The Herpesviruses, Vol. 1. LC 82-15034. (Viruses Ser.). 460p. 1982. 89.50 (*0-306-40922-4*, Plenum Pr) Plenum.
— The Herpesviruses, Vol. 2. LC 82-15034. (Viruses Ser.). 458p. 1983. 89.50 (*0-306-41083-4*, Plenum Pr) Plenum.
— The Herpesviruses, Vol. 3. LC 82-15034. (Viruses Ser.). 432p. 1985. 89.50 (*0-306-41778-2*, Plenum Pr) Plenum.
Roizman, Bernard & Lopez, Carlos, eds. The Herpesviruses, Vol. 4: Immunobiology & Prophylaxis of Human Herpesvirus Infections. LC 82-15034. (Viruses Ser.). 458p. 1985. 89.50 (*0-306-41793-6*, Plenum Pr) Plenum.
Roizman, Bernard, jt. ed. see Lopez, Carlos.
Roizman, Bernard, ed. see New York Academy of Sciences Staff.
Roizman, Bernard, et al, eds. The Human Herpesviruses: Biology, Pathogenesis, & Treatment. LC 93-21719. 448p. 1993. 94.50 (*0-7817-0024-8*) Raven.
Roja, Harry, jt. auth. see Blackwell, Kenneth.
Rojahn, Jurgen, jt. ed. see Van der Linden, Marcel.
Rojankovsky, Feodor. Award Puzzles: Frog Went a-Courting. (Caldecott Collection). (J). 1991. 6.95 (*0-938971-69-7*) JTG Nashville.
— Tall Book of Mother Goose. (Harper Tall Bk.). (Illus.). 120p. (J). (ps up). 1942. 9.95 (*0-06-025055-0*) HarpC Child Bks.
— Tall Book of Nursery Tales. LC 44-3881. (Tall Bks.). (Illus.). 120p. (J). (ps-3). 1944. 9.95 (*0-06-025065-8*) HarpC Child Bks.
Rojankovsky, Feodor, jt. auth. see Langstaff, John.
Rojansky, Vladimir. Electromagnetic Fields & Waves. LC 79-52648. 1980. pap. text ed. 8.95 (*0-486-63834-0*) Dover.
***Rojany, Lisa.** Casper. LC 94-25837. (J). 1995. 3.95 (*0-8431-3854-8*) Price Stern.
— Dena Dinosaur. LC 94-66568. (Fuzzy Friends Ser.). (Illus.). 10p. (J). (ps up). 1995. bds. 3.95 (*0-8431-3786-X*) Price Stern.
— Hands-On Book of Big Machines. (J). (ps-3). 1992. 11.95 (*0-316-41904-4*) Little.
— Hippo & Pals. LC 94-61415. (Giant Animal Fold-Outs Ser.). (Illus.). 20p. (J). (ps up). 1995. bds., spiral bd. 14.95 (*0-8431-3910-2*) Price Stern.
— Jake & Jenny on the Town. 18p. (J). (ps-2). 1993. 7.95 (*0-8431-3584-0*) Price Stern.
— Kangaroo & Company. LC 94-61416. (Giant Animal Fold-Outs Ser.). (Illus.). 20p. (J). (ps up). 1995. bds., spiral bd. 14.95 (*0-8431-3909-9*) Price Stern.
— Melvin Martian. LC 94-66567. (Fuzzy Friends Ser.). (Illus.). 10p. (J). (ps up). 1995. bds. 3.95 (*0-8431-3787-8*) Price Stern.
— Morty Monster. LC 94-66565. (Fuzzy Friends Ser.). (Illus.). 10p. (J). (ps up). 1995. bds. 3.95 (*0-8431-3788-6*) Price Stern.
— Santa's New Suit! (Surprise Bks.). (Illus.). 24p. (J). (ps-2). 1993. 7.95 (*0-8431-3587-5*) Price Stern.
— The Story of Hanukkah: A Lift-the-Flap Rebus Book. (Illus.). 16p. (J). (ps-3). 1993. 12.95 (*1-56282-420-1*) Hyprn Child.
— Wanda Witch. LC 94-66566. (Fuzzy Friends Ser.). (Illus.). 10p. (J). (ps up). 1995. bds. 3.95 (*0-8431-3789-4*) Price Stern.
***Rojany, Lisa, adapt.** Gold Diggers: The Novelization. 144p. (J). (gr. 5 up). 1995. pap. 3.95 (*0-8431-3917-X*) Price Stern.
***Rojany, Lisa, ed.** The Magic Feather: A Jamaican Legend. LC 95-9982. (Legends of the World Ser.). (Illus.). 32p. (J). (gr. 1-4). 1995. lib. bdg. 11.89 (*0-8167-3751-7*); pap. text ed. 3.95 (*0-8167-3752-5*) Troll Assocs.
Rojany, Lisa & Strong, Stacie. Exploring the Human Body. LC 92-7514. (Illus.). (J). (gr. 4-7). 1992. 13.95 (*0-8120-6298-1*) Barron.
Rojany, Lisa, jt. auth. see Walker, Craig.
Rojas, Alfonso V., jt. auth. see Redfield, Robert.
Rojas, Carlos. Salvador Dali, or the Art of Spitting on Your Mother's Portrait. Amell, Alma, tr. 208p. (C). 1993. 29.95 (*0-271-00842-3*) Pa St U Pr.
Rojas, Carmen. Draw Me: Prayers for Every Occasion in a Woman's Life. 200p. (Orig.). 1990. pap. 7.99 (*0-89283-660-1*) Servant.
— How to Read the Bible Everyday: A Guide for Catholics. 48p. (Orig.). 1988. pap. 2.99 (*0-89283-399-8*) Servant.
Rojas, Carmen, ed. The Catholic Book of Bible Promises. 176p. (Orig.). 1988. pap. 4.99 (*0-89283-659-8*) Servant.
Rojas, Delores. Treasury of Mexican Cuisine. 1994. 9.98 (*0-8317-5167-3*) Smithmark.
Rojas, Don, ed. One People, One Destiny: The Caribbean & Central America Today. LC 88-62937. (Orig.). 1988. lib. bdg. 35.00 (*0-87348-536-X*); pap. 11.95 (*0-87348-535-1*) Pathfinder NY.
Rojas, Emilio. Little Friend. (Illus.). 125p. 1992. 14.95 (*1-85230-281-X*) Element MA.
Rojas, Enrique. El Laberinto de la Afectividad. (Nueva Austral Ser.: Vol. 11). (SPA.). 1991. pap. text ed. 24.95 (*84-239-1811-4*) Elliots Bks.
Rojas, Gonzalo. Schizotext & Other Poems: Esquizotexto y Otros Poemas. Quackenbush, Howard & Cluff, Russel, eds. 135p. (ENG & SPA.). (C). 1988. text ed. 34.00 (*0-8204-0561-2*) P Lang Pubs.
Rojas, Hector. Origami Animals. LC 92-18266. (Illus.). 160p. (J). (gr. 3-9). 1992. 24.95 (*0-8069-8648-4*) Sterling.
— Origami Animals. LC 91-18266. (Illus.). 160p. (J). (gr. 7 up). 1993. pap. 14.95 (*0-8069-8649-2*) Sterling.
Rojas, John, Jr., intro. Chula Vista: The Early Years. 80p. (Orig.). 1992. pap. 7.95 (*0-938711-14-8*) Tecolote Pubns.
Rojas, John, Jr., et al. Chula Vista: The Early Years, Vol. 3. (Illus.). 72p. (Orig.). Date not set. pap. 7.95 (*0-938711-24-5*) Tecolote Pubns.
Rojas, Juan. Dic. Popular De la Biblia (Popular Bible Dictionary) (Illus.). (SPA.). 1992. 8.99 (*1-56063-191-0*, 497693); pap. 5.99 (*0-685-74928-2*, 497692) Editorial Unilit.
Rojas, Juan, tr. see Graham, Billy.
Rojas-Lombardi, Felipe. The Art of South American Cooking. LC 90-56395. 416p. 1991. 30.00 (*0-06-016425-5*, HarpT) HarpC.
— Game Cookery. LC 72-12215. (Illus.). 1973. spiral bd. 3.95 (*0-915180-16-2*) Harrowood Bks.
— Soup, Beautiful Soup. 224p. 1992. pap. 14.95 (*0-8050-1939-1*, Owl) H Holt & Co.
Rojas, Maria P., jt. auth. see Pascal, Nanette R.
Rojas, Mary H. Lady in Waiting: Poems in English & Spanish. Lombeida, Ernesto, tr. LC 93-87093. (Illus.). 88p. (Orig.). 1994. pap. 8.95 (*0-9634090-1-8*) Spillway Pubns.
Rojas, Miriam M., tr. see Bartel, Nettie R., et al.
Rojas, Nelson. Redaccion Comercial Estructurada. 2nd ed. 200p. 1982. text ed. 15.36 (*0-07-053566-3*) McGraw.
Rojas, Nelson & Curry, Richard. Gramatica para la Comunicacion: Repaso y Conversacion. (C). 1987. pap. 29.96 (*0-395-36411-6*) HM.
Rojas, Sonia R. & Rehbein, Edna A. Critical Approaches to Isabel Allende's Novels. LC 91-11499. (American University Studies: Latin American Literature: Ser. XXII, Vol. 14). 201p. (C). 1991. text ed. 35.95 (*0-8204-1495-6*) P Lang Pubs.
Rojas-Suarez, Liliana, jt. auth. see Mathieson, Donald J.
Rojas, Tony H. TDR vs Gravimetric: A Comparison of Soil Moisture Determination Methods. (University of Michigan Report Ser.: No. 030613-1-T). 15p. reprint ed. pap. 25.00 (*0-7837-6780-3*, 2046610) Bks Demand.
***Rojas Zorrilla, Francisco D.** Progne y Filomena de Francisco de Rojas Zorrilla: Edicion, Introduccion y Notas de Dr. Alfred Rodriguez y Saul Roll-Velez. Rodriguez, Alfred & Roll-Velez, Saul, eds. LC 93-2531. (Iberica Ser.: No. 8). 147p. (C). 1994. text ed. 38.95 (*0-8204-2080-8*) P Lang Pubs.
Rojcewicz, Richard, tr. see Heidegger, Martin.
Rojcewicz, Richard, tr. see Husserl, Edmund.
Rojczyk, Ursula, jt. auth. see Roos, Werner.
***Rojeck, Chris.** Decentring Leisure. (Theory, Culture & Society Ser.). 240p. 1995. text ed. 65.00 (*0-8039-8812-5*); pap. text ed. 21.95 (*0-8039-8813-3*) Sage.
Rojek, Chris. Capitalism & Leisure Theory. LC 85-2869. 224p. (Orig.). 1985. 45.00 (*0-422-79060-5*, 9558, Pub. by Tavistock UK); pap. 14.95 (*0-422-79070-2*, 9559, Pub. by Tavistock UK) Routledge Chapman & Hall.
— Ways of Escape: Modern Transformation in Leisure & Travel. LC 93-33328. (Postmodern Social Futures Ser.). 250p. (C). 1994. lib. bdg. 45.00 (*0-8476-7898-9*) Rowman.
Rojek, Chris, ed. Leisure for Leisure: Critical Essays. 256p. 1989. text ed. 32.50 (*0-415-90065-4*, Routledge NY) Routledge.
Rojek, Chris & Turner, Bryan S., eds. Forget Baudrillard? LC 93-14835. 1993. write for info. (*0-415-05988-7*); pap. write for info. (*0-415-05989-5*) Routledge.
Rojek, Chris, jt. ed. see Dunning, Eric.
Rojek, Dean, jt. auth. see Jensen, Gary.
***Rojek, Dean G. & Jensen, Gary F., eds.** Exploring Delinquency: Causes & Control (An Anthology) 350p. (Orig.). (C). 1995. pap. text ed. write for info. (*0-935732-71-3*) Roxbury Pub Co.
Rojek, Dean G., jt. auth. see Jensen, Gary F.
Rojer, Olga E. Exile in Argentina, 1933-1945: A Historical & Literary Introduction. (American University Studies: Ser. XXII, Vol. 3). 250p. (C). 1989. text ed. 55.80 (*0-8204-0785-2*) P Lang Pubs.
Rojiani, Kamal B. Programming in Basic for Engineers. (C). 1988. pap. 57.95 (*0-534-91899-9*) PWS Pubs.
— Programming in C for Engineers. 500p. 1992. pap. text ed. 32.00 (*0-13-726498-4*) P-H.
Rojkind, Marcos, ed. Connective Tissue in Health & Disease. 224p. 1989. 144.00 (*0-8493-4161-2*, RC924) CRC Pr.
Rojkind, Marcos, jt. ed. see Perez-Tamayo, Ruy.
Rojo, A. Diccionario Enciclopedico de Anatomia de Peces: Ingles-Espanol. (ENG & SPA.). write for info. (*0-318-56672-9*, S-36994) Fr & Eur.
Rojo, Alfonso L. Diccionario Enciclopedico de Anatomia de Peces, Ingles-Espanol. 564p. 1988. write for info. (*0-7859-6226-3*) Fr & Eur.
— Dictionary of Evolutionary Fish Osteology. (Illus.). 280p. 1991. 49.95 (*0-8493-4214-7*, QL639) CRC Pr.
Rojo, Grinor & Hassett, John J. Chile: Dictatorship & the Struggle for Democracy. LC 88-82164. 112p. 1988. 12.00 (*0-935318-14-3*) Edins Hispamerica.
Rojo, Grinor & Steele, Cynthia. Ritos de Iniciacion: Tres Nouvelas Cortas de Hispanoamerica. LC 85-80939. 224p. (SPA.). (C). 1985. text ed. 23.96 (*0-395-38125-8*) HM.
Rojo, J. P. Pterocarpus (Leguminosae-Papilionaceae) Revised for the World. 1971. 36.00 (*3-7682-0726-9*) Lubrecht & Cramer.
Rojot, J., jt. auth. see Despax, M.
Roka, Alex. Wishes at the Bottom of the Well. LC 90-84625. 216p. 1991. 24.00 (*0-9627936-0-4*) Bk Elan.
Rokach, A., jt. auth. see Weitz, R.
Rokach, Abraham J. Schaum's Outline of Structural Steel Design. (Schaum Outline Ser.). 1991. pap. text ed. 13.95 (*0-07-053563-9*) McGraw.
Rokach, Allen, ed. & photos. Focus on Travel: Creating Memorable Photographs of Journeys to New Places. LC 92-27282. 228p. 1993. 45.00 (*1-55859-371-3*) Abbeville Pr.
***Rokach, Allen & Millman, Anne.** The Field Guide to Photographing Flowers. LC 94-36839. (Center for Nature Photography Ser.). (Illus.). 128p. 1995. pap. 16.95 (*0-8174-3870-X*, Amphoto) Watsn-Guptill.
— The Field Guide to Photographing Landscapes. LC 94-36840. (Center for Nature Photography Ser.). 16.95p. 1995. 16.95 (*0-8174-3871-8*, Amphoto) Watsn-Guptill.
— The Field Guide to Photographing Trees. LC 95-12035. (Center for Nature Photography Ser.). (Illus.). 1995. write for info. (*0-8174-3872-6*, Amphoto) Watsn-Guptill.
— Focus on Flowers: Discovering & Photographing Beauty in Gardens & Wild Places. (Illus.). 228p. 1990. 39.95 (*1-55859-066-8*) Abbeville Pr.
Rokach, J., ed. Leukotrienes & Lipoxygenases. (Bioactive Molecules Ser.: No. 11). 518p. 1989. 184.75 (*0-444-87464-X*) Elsevier.
Rokach, Livia. The Catholic Church & the Question of Palestine. 228p. 1990. 39.95 (*0-86356-128-4*, Pub. by Saqi Bks UK) Interlink Pub.
— Israel's Sacred Terrorism: A Study Based on Moshe Sharett's "Personal Diary" & Other Documents. 3rd rev. ed. LC 85-19946. (Information Papers: No. 23). 90p. 1985. pap. 5.95 (*0-937694-70-3*) Assn Arab-Amer U Grads.
Rokeach, Milton. Beliefs, Attitudes, & Values: A Theory of Organization & Change. LC 68-21322. (Social & Behavioral Science Ser.). 230p. 1968. 30.95x (*0-87589-013-X*) Jossey-Bass.
— Understanding Human Values: Individual & Societal. LC 78-24753. (Illus.). 1979. text ed. 29.95 (*0-02-926760-9*) Free Pr.
Rokeah, D. Jews, Pagans & Christians in Conflict. 232p. (C). 1982. text ed. 25.00 (*90-04-06560-1*, Pub. by Magnes Press IS) Eisenbrauns.
Rokem, Freddie. Theatrical Space in Ibsen, Chekhov & Strindberg: Public Forms of Privacy. Brockett, Oscar, ed. LC 85-16415. (Theater & Dramatic Studies: No. 32). (Illus.). 106p. reprint ed. 34.00 (*0-8357-1707-0*, 2070441) Bks Demand.
Rokem, J. Stefan, jt. auth. see Goldberg, Israel.
Rokes, Willis P. Human Relations in Handling Insurance Claims. 2nd rev. ed. (C). 1981. text ed. 53.95 (*0-256-02504-5*) Irwin.
Rokey, Roxann, jt. ed. see Rolak, Loren A.
Rokhlin, L. L., et al, eds. Problems of Psychopharmacology. 336p. 1964. text ed. 77.75x (*0-7065-0532-8*, Pub. by Keter Pub IS) Coronet Bks.
Rokhlin, V. A., jt. auth. see Fuks, D. B.
Rokicki, Thomas, jt. auth. see Borde, Arvind.
Rokkan, Elizabeth, tr. see Borgen, Johan.
Rokkan, Elizabeth, tr. see Sandel, Cora, pseud.
Rokkan, Elizabeth, tr. see Vesaas, Tarjei.
Rokkan, Elizabeth, tr. see Vesass, Terjei.
***Rokkan, Stein.** State Formation, Nation-Building, & Mass Politics in Europe. Kuhnle, Stein et al, eds. (Comparative European Politics Ser.). (Illus.). 360p. 1995. 59.00 (*0-19-828032-7*) OUP.
Rokkan, Stein, ed. Comparative Research Across Cultures & Nations. 1968. text ed. 50.00 (*3-10-800123-X*) Mouton.
Rokkan, Stein & Meyriat, Jean, eds. International Guide to Electoral Statistics: National Elections in Western Europe, Vol. 1. 1969. text ed. 46.00 (*0-686-22601-1*) Mouton.
Rokkan, Stein, jt. ed. see Eisenstadt, Shmuel N.
Rokkan, Stein, et al. Comparative Survey Analysis. (Confluence Ser: Vol. 12). 1969. text ed. 28.00 (*90-279-6246-4*) Mouton.
Rokne, J., tr. see Robert, F.
Rokop, Frank J., jt. auth. see Brandon, Jeffrey L.
Rokosz, Francis M. Procedures for Structuring & Scheduling Sports Tournaments: Elimination, Consolation, Placement, & Round Robin Design. 2nd ed. (Illus.). 300p. (C). 1993. spiral bd. 51.95x (*0-398-05829-6*) C C Thomas.
Rokosz, Francis M. & Taylor, Howard H. Administrative Procedures for Conducting Recreational Sports Tournaments, from Archery to Wrestling. 2nd ed. LC 93-33148. (Illus.). 418p. (C). 1994. spiral bd. 71.95 (*0-398-05895-4*) C C Thomas.
Rokumoto, Kahei, ed. Sociological Theories of Law. LC 93-27760. (International Library of Essays in Law & Legal Theory: Vol. 12). 1993. 150.00 (*0-8147-7425-3*) NYU Pr.
Rokwaho. Covers. (Illus.). 50p. (Orig.). 1981. pap. 4.00 (*0-936574-05-4*) Strawberry Pr NY.
Rola, Fatima & Buster, Dave, eds. Formwork for Contractor's Exams: Sample Questions & Solutions Based on Tables in ACI's Formwork for Concrete (Hurd) 66p. 1985. pap. 7.50 (*0-935715-09-6*, 1586) Construct Bkstore.
Rola-Pleszczynski, M., jt. ed. see Sirois, R.
Rola-Pleszczynski, Marek, ed. Immunopharmacology of Lymphocytes. (Handbook of Immunopharmacology Ser.). (Illus.). 304p. 1994. text ed. 67.50 (*0-12-593390-8*) Acad Pr.
Rolak, Loren A., ed. Neurology Secrets. (Secrets Ser.). 480p. (Orig.). 1993. pap. text ed. 35.95 (*1-56053-056-1*) Hanley & Belfus.
Rolak, Loren A. & Rokey, Roxann, eds. Coronary & Cerebral Vascular Disease: A Practical Guide. (Illus.). 400p. 1990. 52.00 (*0-87993-353-4*) Futura Pub.
Roland. Chanson de Roland. Calin, William C., ed. LC 67-29335. (Medieval French Literature Ser.). (FRE.). (C). 1968. pap. text ed. 9.95 (*0-89197-071-1*) Irvington.
— Ten Hungry Mice. (J). 1995. 6.99 (*0-679-86865-8*) Random.
Roland & Michaud, Sabrina. Caravans To Tartary. LC 84-51676. (Illus.). 104p. 1990. pap. 17.95 (*0-500-27359-6*) Thames Hudson.
Roland, Alan. In Search of Self in India & Japan: Toward a Cross-Cultural Psychology. 418p. 1991. text ed. 55.00 (*0-691-08617-6*); pap. text ed. 17.95 (*0-691-02458-8*) Princeton U Pr.
Roland, Alan, ed. Psychoanalysis: Creativity & Literature, a French-American Inquiry. LC 77-26613. 368p. 1978. text ed. 48.00 (*0-231-04324-4*) Col U Pr.
Roland, Alan & Harris, Barbara, eds. Career & Motherhood: Struggles for a New Identity. LC 78-8026. 212p. 1979. 35.95 (*0-87705-372-3*) Human Sci Pr.
Roland, Alex. Underwater Warfare in the Age of Soil. LC 77-74436. (Illus.). 254p. reprint ed. pap. 72.40 (*0-8357-6698-5*, 2056878) Bks Demand.
Roland, Berta, jt. ed. see Waide, Linda.
Roland, C., comp. Secondary Sources in the History of Canadian Medicine: A Bibliography. 190p. (C). 1984. text ed. 29.95 (*0-88920-182-X*, Pub. by Wilfrid Laurier CN) Humanities.
Roland, Charles G. Courage under Siege: Starvation, Disease, & Death in the Warsaw Ghetto. (Studies in Jewish History). (Illus.). 352p. 1992. 30.00 (*0-19-506285-X*) OUP.
Roland, Charles G., jt. ed. see Barondess, Jeremiah A.
Roland, Charles G., jt. auth. see Golden, Richard L.
Roland, Charles P. Albert Sidney Johnston: Soldier of Three Republics. (Illus.). 408p. (Orig.). 1987. reprint ed. pap. 18.95 (*0-292-70399-6*) U of Tex Pr.
— An American Iliad: The Story of the Civil War. 1991. pap. text ed. write for info. (*0-07-053594-9*) McGraw.
— An American Iliad: The Story of the Civil War. LC 90-38392. (Illus.). 304p. 1991. text ed. 32.00 (*0-8131-1737-2*) U Pr of Ky.

R

— Confederacy. LC 60-12573. (Chicago History of American Civilization Ser.). (Illus.). 1962. pap. text ed. 11.95 (0-226-72451-4, CHAC18) U Ch Pr.
— The Improbable Era: The South Since World War II. rev. ed. LC 76-46033. (Illus.). 240p. 1976. pap. 10.00 (0-8131-0139-5) U Pr of Ky.
— Reflections on Lee: A Historian's Assessment. (Illus.). 128p. 1995. 16.95 (0-8117-0719-9) Stackpole.
Roland, Christopher, jt. auth. see Smith, Thomas.
***Roland, Christopher, et al.** Corporate Experiential Learning. 256p. 1994. boxed, per. 50.00 (0-7872-0308-4) Kendall-Hunt.
Roland, Claude, jt. auth. see Grosjean, Didier.
Roland de la Platiere, Jeanne M. Appeal to Impartial Posterity. LC 90-36680. 364p. 1990. reprint ed. 55.00 (1-85477-054-3, Pub. by Woodstock Bks UK) Cassell.
Roland de la Platiere, Marie. The Private Memoirs of Madame Roland. 2nd ed. LC 78-37719. (Women of Letters Ser.). (Illus.). reprint ed. 47.50 (0-404-56829-7) AMS Pr.
Roland de la Platiere, Marie J. An Appeal to Impartial Posterity, 2 vols., Set. LC 74-37718. reprint ed. 125.00 (0-404-56826-2) AMS Pr.
Roland, Donna. Grandfather's Stories. (Illus.). (Orig.). (J). (gr. k-3). 1993. Flannelboard set. 12.00 (0-685-73481-1); Video cass. vhs 32.00 (0-685-73482-X) Open My World.
— Grandfather's Stories. (Illus.). (Orig.). (J). (gr. k-3). 1995. pap. 5.95 (0-941996-00-X); Audio cass., per culture. audio 5.95 (0-685-73483-8) Open My World.
— Grandfather's Stories from Cambodia. (J). (gr. k-3). 1984. pap. 5.95x (0-941996-05-0) Open My World.
— Grandfather's Stories from Germany. (J). (gr. k). 1984. teacher ed 6.50 (0-941996-15-8) Open My World.
— Grandfather's Stories from Germany. (J). (gr. k-3). 1984. pap. 5.95x (0-941996-03-4) Open My World.
— Grandfather's Stories from Mexico. (J). (gr. k-3). 1986. teacher ed 6.50 (0-941996-16-6); pap. 5.95 (0-941996-09-3) Open My World.
— More of Grandfather's Stories. (Grandfather's Stories Ser.). (Illus.). 25p. (Orig.). (J). (gr. k-3). 1995. teacher ed 6.50 (0-941996-13-1); pap. 5.95 (0-941996-02-6) Open My World.
— More of Grandfather's Stories from Cambodia. (J). (gr. k-3). 1984. teacher ed 6.50 (0-941996-14-X); pap. 5.95 (0-941996-06-9) Open My World.
— More of Grandfather's Stories from Germany. (J). (gr. k-3). 1984. pap. 5.95x (0-941996-04-2) Open My World.
— More of Grandfather's Stories from Mexico. (J). (gr. k-3). 1986. pap. 5.95 (0-941996-10-7) Open My World.
— More of Grandfather's Stories from the Philippines. (J). (gr. k-3). 1985. teacher ed 6.50 (0-941996-17-4); pap. 5.95x (0-941996-08-5) Open My World.
— More of Grandfather's Stories from Vietnam. (J). (gr. k-3). 1985. pap. 5.95x (0-941996-12-3) Open My World.
Roland, Erling & Munthe, Elaine, eds. Bullying: An International Perspective. 144p. (Orig.). 1990. pap. 34.95 (0-8464-1481-3) Beekman Pubs.
Roland, Harold E. & Moriarity, Brian. System Safety Engineering Management. 2nd ed. 367p. 1990. text ed. 79.95 (0-471-61816-0) Wiley.
Roland, Harold E. & Moriarty, Brian. System Safety Engineering & Management. (Wiley Interscience Ser.). 368p. 1983. 34.95 (0-317-01156-1, 1-09695-4) DeLeuw-Cather Co.
***Roland, Henri.** Dictionnaire des Expressions Juridiques. 440p. (FRE.). 1983. pap. 36.95 (0-7859-8116-0, 2859341102) Fr & Eur.
Roland, J. L. European Cooperation in the Field of Scientific & Technical Research, EUR 13914. 105p. 1992. pap. 25.00 (92-826-4371-9, CG-NA-13914-EN-C, Pub. by Europ Com) UNIPUB.
Roland, Jacques, et al, eds. Extragalactic Radio Sources: From Beams to Jets. (Illus.). 380p. (C). 1992. 69.95 (0-521-41602-7) Cambridge U Pr.
***Roland, Jeffrey.** A Mister in Kindergarten. 210p. 1995. pap. 7.95 (1-56901-664-X) NW Pub.
Roland, Joan G. Jews in British India: Identity in a Colonial Era. LC 88-40113. (Tauber Institute Ser.: No. 9). (Illus.). 371p. 1989. text ed. 45.00 (0-87451-457-6) U Pr of New Eng.
Roland, John. Human Biology Activities Kit: Ready-to-Use Lessons & Worksheets for General Science & Health. 320p. 1993. spiral bd. 27.95 (0-87628-121-8) Ctr Appl Res.
Roland, L., jt. auth. see Blum, W.
Roland, Lillian D. Women in Robbe-Grillet: A Study in Thematics & Diegetics. LC 91-43247. (American University Studies: Romance Languages & Literature: Ser. II, Vol. 177). 302p. (C). 1993. text ed. 59.95 (0-8204-1643-6) P Lang Pubs.
Roland, M. O. & Jenner, J. R., eds. Back Pain: New Approaches to Rehabilitation & Education. LC 89-2491. 320p. 1989. text ed. 95.00 (0-7190-2789-6, Pub. by Manchester Univ Pr UK) St Martin.
Roland-Manuel. Histoire de la Musique, 2 vols. 2260p. (FRE.). 1973. 145.00 (0-7859-4542-3) Fr & Eur.
— Histoire de la Musique, 2 vols., 1. (Historique Ser.). 69.95 (0-686-56457-X) Fr & Eur.
— Histoire de la Musique, 2 vols., 2. (Historique Ser.). 65.50 (0-686-56458-8) Fr & Eur.
— Histoire de la Musique, Vol. 2. (Historique Ser.). 1894p. 65.50 (0-686-56459-6) Fr & Eur.
Roland-Manuel, Claude. Histoire de la Musique, Vol. 2: Du XVIIIe Siecle a Nos Jours. 1896p. (FRE.). 1975. lib. bdg. 145.00 (0-7859-3773-0, 2070104044) Fr & Eur.
Roland, Marie-Jeanne. Memoirs of Madame Roland: A Heroine of French Revolution. Shuckburgh, Evelyn, tr. 264p. 1992. pap. 9.95 (1-55921-015-X) Moyer Bell.
Roland, Marie-Jeanne P. Memoirs of Madame Roland. Shuckburgh, Evelyn, tr. 1990. 19.95 (1-55921-014-1) Moyer Bell.
Roland, Martin & Coulter, Angela, eds. Hospital Referrals. LC 92-19067. (Oxford General Practice Ser.: No. 22). (Illus.). 240p. 1993. pap. 32.50 (0-19-262174-2) OUP.
Roland, N. L., et al. Key Topics in Otolaryngology. 368p. (Orig.). 1995. pap. 57.50x (1-872748-68-6, Pub. by Bios Scientific UK) Coronet Bks.
Roland, Nelson, jt. auth. see D'Hondt, Jacques.
Roland, P. E. Brain Activation. LC 92-49741. (Series in Neuroscience). 600p. 1993. text ed. 94.95 (0-471-50867-5, Wiley-Liss) Wiley.
***Roland, Paul.** Revelations: Wisdom of the Ages. (Illus.). 160p. (Orig.). 1995. 17.95 (1-56975-047-5) Ulysses Pr.
Roland, Paula. Faro's Lady. 1990. pap. 3.95 (0-8217-2932-2) Zebra.
— The Rogue's Bride. 304p. 1990. pap. 3.95 (0-8217-2880-6) Zebra.
Roland, Regina & Sandberg, Jane L. A Hat for All Seasons: Fall & Winter. (ECS Activity Book for Language Arts Ser.). (Illus.). 128p. (Orig.). 1994. pap. 15.95 (0-944459-96-X) ECS Lrn Systs.
***Roland, Regina E. & Sandberg, Jane L.** Hats on the Go. (ECS Activity Book Ser.). (Illus.). 144p. (Orig.). (J). (ps-2). 1995. teacher ed. pap. write for info. (1-57022-058-1) ECS Lrn Systs.
***Roland, Richard G.** Pilgrim in Rome. LC 94-92066. (Illus.). 80p. 1994. per. 18.75 (0-9640694-0-7) R G Roland.
Roland, Timothy. Detective Dan & the Flying Frog Mystery. (Detective Dan Ser.). 48p. (J). (gr. 2-5). 1993. pap. 4.99 (0-310-38121-5) Zondervan.
— Detective Dan & the Gooey Gumdrop Mystery. (Detective Dan Ser.). 48p. (J). (gr. 2-5). 1993. pap. 4.99 (0-310-38111-8) Zondervan.
— Detective Dan & the Missing Marble Mystery. 2nd abr. rev. ed. (Detective Dan Ser.). 48p. (J). (gr. 2-5). 1993. pap. 4.99 (0-310-38091-X) Zondervan.
— Detective Dan & the Puzzling Pizza Mystery. (Detective Dan Ser.). 48p. (J). (gr. 2-5). 1993. pap. 4.99 (0-310-38101-0) Zondervan.
Roland, Tom. The Billboard Book of Number One Country Hits. (Illus.). 592p. 1991. pap. 19.95 (0-8230-7553-2, Billboard Bks) Watsn-Guptill.
Rolander-Chilo, Brita, ed. Nutritional Research: An International Approach. (Illus.). 1979. 58.00 (0-08-024399-1, Pub. by Pergamon Repr UK) Franklin.
Rolandi, L., jt. auth. see Blum, W.
Rolater. Japanese Americans. (American Voices Ser.). (J). 1991. 13.95 (0-86593-138-0); 18.60 (0-685-59186-7) Rourke Corp.
***Rolbein, Seth.** The Enemy Within: The Struggle to Clean up Cape Cod's Military SuperFund Site. 177p. (Orig.). 1995. pap. 12.00 (0-9645260-0-X) APCC.
Rolcik, Karen A. & Haman, Edward A. How to File for Divorce in Texas. LC 94-66932. 146p. (Orig.). 1994. pap. 19.95 (0-913825-91-3) Sphinx Pub FL.
***Rolcik, Karen A. & Warda, Mark.** How to Form a Simple Corporation in Texas. 135p. (Orig.). 1995. pap. 19.95 (1-57248-009-2) Sphinx Pub FL.
— How to Make a Texas Will. LC 94-66930. 96p. (Orig.). 1994. pap. 9.95 (0-913825-89-1) Sphinx Pub FL.
Rold, Jim. First Degree Love: A Novel of Euthanasia. 208p. (Orig.). 1992. pap. 9.95 (0-89407-106-8) Strawberry Hill.
Roldan, Arturo A., jt. ed. see Vermeulen, Han.
Roldan, Aurora H., ed. Gifted & Talented Children, Youth, & Adults: Their Social Perspectives & Culture. 563p. 1985. pap. 15.00 (0-89824-047-6) Trillium Pr.
***Roldan, Marggi, ed.** College Facts Chart. 39th rev. ed. 92p. 1994. pap. 5.00 (0-9614726-6-9) Natl Beta Club.

—College Facts Chart. 40th rev. ed. 92p. 1995. pap. 5.00 (0-9614726-7-7) Natl Beta Club.
The new edition of the COLLEGE FACTS CHART published by the National Beta Club is now available to college-bound students & their parents. This 92-page book in chart format provides information on 14 aspects of each of 3500 U.S. college & universities. Listed in the charts are the name of the institution, address, telephone, president, date founded, affiliation &/or support, level of school, type (coed/men/women), session plan, degrees offered, enrollment, number of teachers, estimated tuition, estimated room & board & estimated total cost. Institutions are listed by state with an alphabetical index by college name. A list of toll-free admission office telephone numbers & a key to abbreviations for degrees are in the back of the book. The book can be purchased for $5.00 (check or money order) from College Facts Chart, 40th edition, National Beta Club, 151 W. Lee Street, P.O. Box 730, Spartanburg, SC 29304; 803-583-4555. *Publisher Provided Annotation.*

Roldan, Martha, jt. auth. see Beneria, Lourdes.
Rolde, Neil. Maine: A Narrative History. (Illus.). 368p. (Orig.). (YA). 1990. pap. 19.95 (0-88448-069-0) Tilbury Hse.
— So You Think You Know Maine. LC 84-47758. (Illus.). 216p. (Orig.). (J). (gr. 6-12). 1984. pap. 13.95 (0-88448-025-9) Tilbury Hse.
Role of Karl Marx in the Development of Contemporary Symposium Staff. Marx & Contemporary Scientific Thought: Proceedings. (Publications of the International Social Science Council: No. 13). 1970. 69.25 (90-279-6276-6) Mouton.
Rolef, Susan Hattis. Political Dictionary of the State of Israel. 2nd ed. LC 93-20521. 420p. 1993. text ed. 65.00 (0-02-897193-0, Collier S&S) S&S Trade.
Roles, Patricia. Facing Teenage Pregnancy: A Handbook for the Pregnant Teen. 1990. pap. 12.95 (0-87868-210-4) Child Welfare.
— Saying Goodbye to a Baby, Vol. 2: A Counselor's Guide to Birthparent Grief & Loss. 34p. 1990. pap. 10.95 (0-87868-393-3) Child Welfare.
Rolett, Karin. Organizing Community Resources in Sexuality Counseling & Family Planning for the Retarded: a Community Workers' Manual. 1976. pap. 3.00 (0-89055-118-9) Carolina Pop Ctr.
Rolewicz, Stefan. Metric Linear Spaces. 1985. lib. bdg. 178.00 (90-277-1480-0) Kluwer Ac.
Roley, Paul, ed. see Egger, Bruce E. & Otts, Lee M.
Rolf. Inventory of World Topographic Mapping: Eastern Europe, Asia, Oceania & Antartica, Vol. 3. LC 89-7760. 1993. 305.00 (1-85861-034-6) Elsevier.
Rolf, Asal, jt. auth. see Hanks, Joyce M.
Rolf, Eckard. Die Funktionen der Gebrauchstextsorten. (Grundlagen der Kommunikation & Kognition (Foundations of Communication & Cognition) Ser.). xii, 339p. (GER.). (C). 1993. lib. bdg. 120.00 (3-11-012551-X) De Gruyter.
Rolf, F. James & Sokal, Robert R. Statistical Tables. 3rd ed. LC 94-11121. (C). 1995. pap. text ed. write for info. (0-7167-2412-X) W H Freeman.
Rolf, Gustavsen & Streeck, Renate. Training Therapy: Prophylaxis & Rehabilitation. 2nd rev. ed. Gilliar, Wolfgang G., tr. & adapt. by. LC 92-48359. (Flexibook Ser.). (Illus.). 240p. 1993. pap. text ed. 27.00 (0-86577-483-8) Thieme Med Pubs.
Rolf, Howard L. & Williams, Gareth. Finite Mathematics. 2nd ed. 720p. (C). 1991. boxed write for info. (0-697-08577-5) Wm C Brown Pubs.
— Finite Mathematics. 3rd ed. 672p. (C). 1993. text ed. 59.95 (0-697-16171-4) Wm C Brown Pubs.
— Finite Mathematics. 3rd ed. 672p. (C). 1993. Solutions manual. teacher ed write for info. (0-697-16173-0) Wm C Brown Pubs.
Rolf, Howard L., et al. Mathematics for Management, Social & Life Sciences. 1200p. (C). 1991. student ed write for info. (0-697-09873-7) Wm C Brown Pubs.
— Mathematics for Management, Social & Life Sciences. 1200p. (C). 1991. text ed. write for info. (0-697-08579-1) Wm C Brown Pubs.
Rolf, Ida. Rolfing & Physical Reality. 224p. 1990. pap. 12.95 (0-89281-380-6) Inner Tradit.
Rolf, Ida P. Rolfing. (Illus.). 304p. 1989. pap. 19.95 (0-89281-335-0, Heal Arts VT) Inner Tradit.
— Rolfing: The Integration of Human Structures. LC 76-52192. (Illus.). 1977. 27.50 (0-930422-10-4) Dennis-Landman.
— What in the World is Rolfing? 1975. pap. 4.00 (0-930422-05-8) Dennis-Landman.
Rolf, Jon, et al, eds. Risk & Protective Factors in the Development of Psychopathology. (Illus.). 560p. (C). 1990. 74.95 (0-521-35099-9) Cambridge U Pr.
— Risk & Protective Factors in the Development of Psychopathology. (Illus.). 576p. (C). 1993. pap. 24.95 (0-521-43972-8) Cambridge U Pr.
Rolf, Robert T. & Gillespie, John K., eds. Alternative Japanese Drama: Ten Plays. LC 92-5185. (Illus.). 520p. 1992. text ed. 38.00 (0-8248-1347-2); pap. 14.95 (0-8248-1379-0) UH Pr.
***Rolfe.** Spiral of Life. 1995. pap. 12.50 (0-85435-432-8) Atrium Pubs.
Rolfe, Bari. Behind the Mask. LC 77-76975. (Illus.). 66p. 1977. pap. 6.50 (0-932456-01-4) Personabks.
— Commedia Dell'Arte: A Scene Study Book. LC 77-73190. (Illus.). 100p. (gr. 9-12). 1977. pap. 7.50 (0-932456-00-6) Personabks.
— Farces, Italian Style. LC 78-60783. (Illus.). 86p. (gr. 9-12). 1978. pap. 7.50 (0-932456-02-2) Personabks.
— Movement for Period Plays. LC 85-73125. (Illus.). 160p. 1985. pap. 15.00 (0-932456-04-9) Personabks.
— Movement for Period Plays, Appendix B. LC 85-73125. (Illus.). 160p. 1985. vhs 70.00 (0-932456-05-7) Personabks.
Rolfe, Bari, ed. Mimes on Miming: An Anthology of Writings on the Art of Mime. (Illus.). 256p. (C). 1980. 15.95 (0-915572-32-X); pap. 8.95 (0-915572-31-1) Panjandrum.
Rolfe, Christopher, jt. ed. see Parrinder, Patrick.
Rolfe, E. J., jt. ed. see Hawthorne, J.
Rolfe, Edwin. Collected Poems. Nelson, Cary & Hendricks, Jefferson, eds. LC 92-42324. (American Poetry Recovery Ser.). 352p. 1993. 34.95 (0-252-02026-X) U of Ill Pr.
— Lincoln Battalion. LC 74-651. (World History Ser.: No. 48). 1974. lib. bdg. 75.00 (0-8383-1762-6) M S G Haskell Hse.
— Trees Became Torches: Selected Poems. Nelson, Cary & Hendricks, Jefferson, eds. LC 94-6722. (American Poetry Recovery Ser.). Date not set. write for info. (0-252-02131-2); pap. write for info. (0-252-06417-8) U of Ill Pr.
Rolfe, Eugene. Encounter with Jung. 1989. 32.50 (0-938434-26-8); pap. 15.95 (0-938434-27-6) Sigo Pr.
— Intelligent Agnostics Introduction to Christianity. 2nd ed. 1991. 29.95 (0-938434-90-X); pap. 14.95 (0-938434-89-6) Sigo Pr.
Rolfe, Eugene, tr. see Meier, C. A.
Rolfe, Eugene, tr. see Neumann, Erich.
Rolfe, F. W., jt. auth. see Rolfe, R. T.
Rolfe, Frederick, see Baron Corvo, pseud..
Rolfe, Frederick C. The Desire & Pursuit of the Whole: A Romance of Modern Venice. LC 77-10836. 299p. 1977. reprint ed. text ed. 35.00 (0-8371-9808-9, RODP, Greenwood Pr) Greenwood.
Rolfe, Frederick W. The Desire & Pursuit of the Whole: A Romance of Modern Venice. LC 78-21374. (Gay Experience Ser.). reprint ed. 25.50 (0-404-61536-8) AMS Pr.
— In His Own Image. LC 70-157795. (Short Story Index Reprint Ser.). 1977. reprint ed. 26.95 (0-8369-3907-7) Ayer.
Rolfe, Frederick W., et al. Hubert's Arthur: Being Certain Curious Documents Found Among the Literary Remains of Mr. N. C., Here Produced by Prospero & Caliban. Reginald, R. & Melville, Douglas, eds. LC 77-92409. (Lost Race & Adult Fantasy Ser.). 1978. reprint ed. lib. bdg. 40.95 (0-405-11005-7) Ayer.
Rolfe, J. C., tr. see Cornelius Nepos.
Rolfe, J. M. & Staples, K. J., eds. Flight Simulation. (Cambridge Aerospace Ser.). 250p. 1988. pap. 39.95 (0-521-35751-9) Cambridge U Pr.
Rolfe, John. Bo Jackson. (Sports Illustrated for Kids Ser.). (Illus.). 124p. (J). (gr. 3-6). 1991. lib. bdg. 19.95 (0-8225-3109-7, Lerner Publctns) Lerner Group.
— Curveballs Strikes Again: More Wacky Facts to Bat Around. (Illus.). 32p. (J). (gr. 3-7). 1992. mass mkt. 4.95 (0-316-75460-9, Spts Illus Kids) Little.
— David Robinson. (Illus.). (J). (gr. 3-7). 1991. mass mkt. 4.95 (0-316-75461-7, Spts Illus Kids) Little.
— Jerry Rice. (J). 1993. mass mkt. 3.99 (0-553-48157-6) Bantam.
— Jim Abbott. (Sports Illustrated for Kids Ser.). 144p. (J). (gr. 3-6). 1991. lib. bdg. 19.95 (0-8225-3108-9, Lerner Publctns) Lerner Group.
— Ken Griffey, Jr. (J). (gr. 4-7). 1995. 3.99 (0-553-48291-2) Bantam.
— Nolan Ryan. (Illus.). 144p. (J). (gr. 3-7). 1992. mass mkt. 4.95 (0-316-75462-5, Spts Illus Kids) Little.
Rolfe, John C., ed. see Horace.
Rolfe, Lionel. In Search of Literary L. A. (Illus.). 208p. (Orig.). 1991. pap. 11.95 (1-879395-00-2) CA Classics Bks.
— Last Train North. 1987. pap. 6.95 (0-915572-95-8) Panjandrum.
Rolfe, Lionel & Lennon, Nigey. The Heal Yourself Home Handbook of Unusual Remedies. LC 82-14274. 205p. 1982. pap. 4.95 (0-13-384677-6, Parker Publishing Co) P-H.
Rolfe, Lionel M. The Menuhins: A Family Odyssey. LC 78-13051. 256p. 1978. 15.95 (0-915572-22-2) Panjandrum.
Rolfe, Margaret. Go Wild with Quilts: Fourteen North American Birds & Animals. Reikes, Ursula & Weiland, Barbara, eds. LC 93-9765. (Illus.). 80p. (Orig.). 1993. pap. text ed. 19.95 (1-56477-019-2, B155) That Patchwork.
— Patchwork Quilts to Make for Children. LC 91-21702. (Illus.). 160p. (Orig.). 1991. pap. 14.95 (0-8069-8498-8) Sterling.
***Rolfe, Margaret & Hodges, Beryl.** Australian Houses in Patchwork. (Lothian Australian Craft Ser.). (Illus.). 64p. (Orig.). 1995. pap. 14.95 (0-85091-452-3, Pub. by Lothian Pub AT) Seven Hills Bk.
Rolfe, Margaret, et al. Metric Quiltmaking. (Illus.). 136p. 1994. pap. 14.95 (1-86351-116-4, Pub. by S Milner AT) Sterling.
Rolfe, Mona. Initiation by the Nile. 140p. (Orig.). Date not set. 20.95 (0-8464-4241-8) Beekman Pubs.
— Radiation of the Light. 144p. (Orig.). Date not set. pap. 8.95 (0-8464-4280-9) Beekman Pubs.
— The Sacred Vessel. 140p. Date not set. 12.95 (0-8464-4286-8) Beekman Pubs.
— The Spiral of Life. 176p. (Orig.). Date not set. pap. 18.95 (0-8464-4291-4) Beekman Pubs.
Rolfe, Peter. Noninvasive Physiological Measurements, Vol. 2. (Medical Physics Ser.). 1984. text ed. 137.00 (0-12-593402-5) Acad Pr.
Rolfe, Peter, ed. Fetal Physiological Measurements. 440p. 1987. text ed. 145.00 (0-407-00450-5) Buttrwrth-Heinemann.
Rolfe, R. A. Orchidaceae in Flora of Tropical Africa. 595p. (C). 1984. 50.00 (0-685-22343-4, Scientific) St Mut.
Rolfe, R. A. & Hurst, C. C. The Orchid Stud Book: Enumeration of Hybrid Orchids of Artificial Origin: With Historical Introduction. (Illus.). 327p. 1986. reprint ed. text ed. 32.50 (81-211-0003-8) Lubrecht & Cramer.
Rolfe, R. T. & Rolfe, F. W. The Romance of the Fungus World: An Account of Fungus Life in Its Numerous Guises, Both Real & Legendary. LC 74-81401. (Illus.). 352p. 1974. reprint ed. pap. 6.95 (0-486-23105-4) Dover.
Rolfe, Randall C. You Can Postpone Anything but Love: Expanding Our Potential As Parents. 1990. pap. 9.95 (0-446-39058-5) Warner Bks.
Rolfe, Randy C. Adult Children Raising Children: Sparing Your Child from Co-dependency Without Being Perfect Yourself. 160p. 1989. 8.95 (1-55874-055-4) Health Comm.
Rolfe, Rial D. & Finegold, Sydney M., eds. Clostridium Difficile. (Its Role in Intestinal Disease Ser.). 384p. 1988. text ed. 136.00 (0-12-593410-6) Acad Pr.
Rolfe, Robert. The Alpine House: Its Plants & Purposes. (Illus.). 144p. 1991. 27.50 (0-88192-185-8) Timber.
Rolfe, Sidney E. & Burtle, James. The Great Wheel: The World Monetary System - a Reinterpretation. LC 73-79929. 1974. write for info. (0-8129-0378-1, Times Bks) Random.
Rolfe, Stanley T., jt. auth. see Barsom, John M.
Rolfe, William J. Life of William Shakespeare. LC 70-174961. reprint ed. 57.50 (0-404-05387-4) AMS Pr.
— Shakespeare the Boy. 251p. 1982. reprint ed. 22.50 (0-87928-111-1) Corner Hse.

An Asterisk (*) at the beginning of an entry indicates that the title is appearing in BIP for the first time.

— Shakespeare the Boy. LC 78-128411. (Studies in Shakespeare: No. 24). 1970. reprint ed. lib. bdg. 49.95 (*0-8383-1103-2*) M S G Haskell Hse.

Rolfes, Ellen, ed. Why Didn't I Think of That? 96p. 1979. spiral bd. 5.95 (*1-882232-15-1*) Kitchen Collect.

Rolfes, Ellen, ed. see National Alliance to End Homelessness Staff.

Rolfes, Ellen, ed. see Neill, Robert H.

Rolfes, Ellen, ed. see Ransom, Judith.

Rolfes, Ellen, ed. see Rodack, Jaine.

Rolfes, Ellen, ed. see Sharp, Emily.

Rolfes, Ellen, ed. see Southeast Out Press Writers Assoc. Staff.

Rolfes, Ellen, ed. see Williams, Thelma.

Rolfes, Harold L., jt. auth. see Basu, Sam N.

Rolfes, Sharon R., jt. auth. see Whitney, Eleanor N.

Rolfes, Sharon R., et al. Lifespan Nutrition: Conception Through Aging. Marshall, ed. 528p. (C). 1990. text ed. 49.75 (*0-314-66811-X*) West Pub.

Rolfo, Luigi. James Alberione: Apostle for Our Times. LC 87-1102. 442p. 1987. pap. 19.95 (*0-8189-0518-2*) Alba.

Rolfs, A., et al, eds. PCR: Clinical Diagnostics & Research. (Laboratory Ser.). (Illus.). 280p. 1992. 59.00 (*0-387-55440-8*) Spr-Verlag.

***Rolfs, Arndt, et al, eds.** Methods in DNA Amplification: Proceedings of the Second International PCR Symposium on Usage of PCR & Alternative Amplification Methods in Infectious & Genetic Diseases Held in Berlin, Germany, February 26-27, 1993. LC 94-43082. 251p. 1995. 85.00 (*0-306-44908-0*, Plenum Pr) Plenum.

Rolfs, Claus E. & Rodney, William S. Cauldrons in the Cosmos: Nuclear Astrophysics. (Theoretical Astrophysics Ser.). (Illus.). xviii, 562p. 1988. pap. text ed. 34.95 (*0-226-72457-3*) U Ch Pr.

Rolfs, Donald, jt. auth. see Foreman, Dale M.

Rolfsen, D., ed. Knot Theory & Manifolds. (Lecture Notes in Mathematics Ser.: Vol. 1144). v, 163p. 1985. pap. 31.10 (*0-387-15680-1*) Spr-Verlag.

Rolfsen, Dale. Knots & Links. LC 76-15514. (Mathematics Lecture Ser.: No. 7). (Illus.). 439p. 1976. pap. text ed. 40.00 (*0-914098-16-0*) Publish or Perish.

Rolfson, H., tr. see Van Ruusbroec, Jan.

Rolheiser, Ronald. Forgotten among the Lilies: Learning to Live Beyond Our Own Obsessions. 284p. 1991. pap. 15.95 (*0-340-53624-1*, Pub. by Hodder & Stoughton Ltd UK) Lubrecht & Cramer.

Rolheiser, Ronald, et al. A Fresh Approach to St. John of the Cross: Growth Through Pain & Sexuality. 160p. 1993. 29.00 (*0-85439-450-8*, Pub. by St Paul Pubns UK) St Mut.

Rolin, Dominique, jt. auth. see Gage, Jennifer C.

Roling, B. V., jt. ed. see Cassese, Antonio.

Rolinson, G. N. & Watson, A. Augmentin: Clavulanate Potentiated Amoxycillin. (International Congress Ser.: Vol. 544). 310p. 1981. 84.75 (*0-444-90188-4*, Excerpta Medica) Elsevier.

Rolka, Gail M. One Hundred Women Who Shaped World History. (One Hundred Ser.). (Illus.). 112p. (Orig.). 1994. pap. 7.95 (*0-912517-06-9*) Bluewood Bks.

Rolke, Karl-Hermann. Die Bildhaften Vergleiche in Den Fragmenten der Stoiker von Zenon Bis Panaitios. (Spudasmata Ser.: Bd. 32). vii, 531p. (GER.). 1975. write for info. (*3-487-05595-3*, Pub. by Georg Olms GW) Lubrecht & Cramer.

Roll, jt. auth. see Elliman.

***Roll, Bob.** Bobke: A Ride on the Wild Side of Cycling. 175p. 1995. pap. 19.95 (*1-884737-12-9*) VeloPress.

***Roll, Charles.** Colonel Dick Thompson, the Persistent Whig. 315p. 1948. 2.50 (*1-885323-11-5*) IN Hist Bureau.

Roll, Eric. The Combined Food Board: A Study in Wartime International Planning. xiii, 385p. 1956. 47.50 (*0-8047-0472-4*) Stanford U Pr.

— A History of Economic Thought. 5th ed. 656p. (Orig.). 1992. pap. 24.95 (*0-571-16553-2*) Faber & Faber.

Roll, Eric L. Early Experiment in Industrial Organization: Being a History of the Firm of Boulton & Watt 1775-1804. LC 68-56059. (Reprints of Economic Classics Ser.). (Illus.). 1968. reprint ed. 39.50 (*0-678-05193-5*) Kelley.

Roll, F., jt. auth. see Rapatz, F.

Roll, Hans U., tr. see Dietrich, Gunter.

Roll-Hansen, Nils, jt. auth. see Broberg, Gunnar.

Roll, Susanne, tr. see Dietrich, Gunter.

Roll-Velez, Saul, ed. see Rojas Zorrilla, Francisco D.

Roll, William G. Theory & Experiment in Psychical Research. LC 75-7398. (Perspectives in Psychical Research Ser.). (Illus.). 1975. 42.95 (*0-405-07047-0*) Ayer.

Roll, William G., ed. see Parapsychological Association Staff.

Rolla, G., jt. auth. see Embery, G.

Rolla, Gregory M. Your Inner Music: Creative Analysis & Music Memory. 144p. (Orig.). 1993. pap. 16.95 (*0-933029-74-8*) Chiron Pubns.

Rolland. Life of Vivekananda: Universal Gospel. pap. 4.95 (*0-87481-210-0*) Vedanta Pr.

— Pharmaceutical Particulate Carriers: Therapeutic Applications. (Drugs & the Pharmaceutical Sciences Ser.: Vol. 61). 448p. 1993. 170.00 (*0-8247-9016-2*) Dekker.

Rolland, C., et al, eds. Advanced Information Systems Engineering: Proceedings of the 5th International Conference, CAISE '93, Paris, France, June 8-11, 1993. (Lecture Notes in Computer Science Ser.: Vol. 685). v, 648p. 1993. pap. 92.00 (*0-387-56777-1*) Spr-Verlag.

— Temporal Aspects in Information Systems: Proceedings of the IFIP TC8 WG8.1 Working Conference, Sophia-Antipolis, France, 13-15 May, 1987. 265p. 1988. 64.00 (*0-444-70373-X*, North Holland) Elsevier.

Rolland, Eugene. Faune Populaire de la France: Noms Vulgaires, Dictons, Proverbes, Legendes, Etc., 7 tomes, Set. 72p. (FRE.). 1967. 795.00 (*0-7859-5314-0*) Fr & Eur.

— Flore Populaire de la France: Historie Naturelle des Plantes dans leurs Rapports avec la Linguistique, 5 tomes, Set. 2948p. (FRE.). 1968. 695.00 (*0-7859-5315-9*) Fr & Eur.

Rolland, Fred. Relational Database Management with Oracle. 2nd ed. (C). 1992. pap. text ed. 39.75 (*0-201-56520-X*) Addison-Wesley.

Rolland, Jim, ed. Sing Out Your Praise, Vol. 1. 128p. 1989. ring bd., pap. 6.95 (*0-937779-21-0*) Greenlawn Pr.

— Sing Out Your Praise, Vol. 2. 160p. 1993. ring bd., pap. 8.95 (*0-937779-26-1*) Greenlawn Pr.

Rolland, John. Seven Sages, in Scotish Metre. Laing, David, ed. LC 74-144429. (Bannatyne Club, Edinburgh. Publications: No. 57). reprint ed. 57.50 (*0-404-52767-1*) AMS Pr.

Rolland, John S. Families, Illness, & Disability: An Integrative Treatment Model. LC 94-206. 304p. 1994. text ed. 35.00 (*0-465-02915-9*) Basic.

Rolland, Paul, ed. see Szigeti, J.

Rolland, R., ed. Gamete Quality & Fertility Regulation: Proceedings of the Renier de Graaf Symposium, 5th, Nijmegen, The Netherlands, 13-15 August, 1984. (International Congress Ser.: No. 658). 368p. 1985. 122.75 (*0-444-80660-1*, Excerpta Medica) Elsevier.

Rolland, R., et al, eds. Neuroendocrinology of Reproduction: Proceedings of the VIth Reinier de Graaf Symposium, Nijmegen, the Netherlands 27-29 August, 1987. (International Congress Ser.: No. 751). 322p. 1988. 102.75 (*0-444-80953-8*, Excerpta Medica) Elsevier.

Rolland, Romain. Un Beau Visage a Tous Sens: Avec: Choix de Lettres de R. Rolland (1886-1944) 400p. (FRE.). 1967. pap. 15.95 (*0-7859-5439-2*) Fr & Eur.

— Beethoven. LC 76-95077. (Select Bibliographies Reprint Ser.). 1977. 29.95 (*0-8369-5077-1*) Ayer.

— Beethoven. Hull, A. Eaglefield, ed. Hull, B. Constanace, tr. 244p. 1990. reprint ed. lib. bdg. 69.00 (*0-7812-9046-5*) Rprt Serv.

— Beethoven: Les Grandes Epoques Creatices. 1520p. (FRE.). 1992. reprint ed. 115.00 (*0-7859-5440-6*) Fr & Eur.

— Choix de Lettres a Malwida Von Meysenburg. 336p. (FRE.). 1948. pap. 9.95 (*0-7859-5443-0*) Fr & Eur.

— Le Cloitre de la Rue D'Ulm: Avec: Journal de Romain Rolland a l'Ecole Normal (1886-1899) 416p. (FRE.). 1952. pap. 9.95 (*0-7859-5444-9*) Fr & Eur.

— Colas Breugnon. 280p. (FRE.). 1988. 28.95 (*0-686-55241-5*); pap. 10.95 (*0-7859-5445-7*) Fr & Eur.

— De la Decadence de la Peinture Italienne au 16e Siecle. (Illus.). 169p. (FRE.). 1957. pap. 9.95 (*0-7859-5446-5*) Fr & Eur.

— D'une Rive a l'Autre: Herman Hess et Romain Rolland, Correspondance et Fragments du Journal. (Illus.). 192p. (FRE.). 1972. pap. 9.95 (*0-7859-5448-1*) Fr & Eur.

— Empedocle d'Agrigente. (Illus.). 136p. (FRE.). 1931. pap. 19.95 (*0-7859-5449-X*) Fr & Eur.

— Fraulein Elsa. Wolff, Elsa, ed. 328p. (FRE.). 1964. pap. 9.95 (*0-7859-5450-3*) Fr & Eur.

— Goethe & Beethoven. LC 67-13338. (Illus.). 1972. reprint ed. 24.95 (*0-405-08896-5*, Pub. by Blom Pubns UK) Ayer.

— Haendel. (Illus.). 320p. (FRE.). 1975. pap. 18.95 (*0-7859-1449-8*, 2226001255) Fr & Eur.

— Handel. LC 75-151597. (Illus.). reprint ed. 34.50 (*0-404-05388-2*) AMS Pr.

— Handel. 210p. 1990. reprint ed. lib. bdg. 69.00 (*0-7812-9066-X*) Rprt Serv.

— I Will Not Rest. 1977. text ed. 18.95 (*0-8369-8190-1*, 8328) Ayer.

— Inde Journal Nineteen Fifteen to Nineteen Forty-Three. 628p. (FRE.). 1960. pap. 36.95 (*0-7859-5451-1*) Fr & Eur.

— Je Commence a Devenir Dangereux. (FRE.). 1973. pap. 14.95 (*0-7859-5452-X*) Fr & Eur.

— Jean-Christophe, 3 vols. 1962. 4.50 (*0-685-73292-4*) Fr & Eur.

— Jean-Christophe. 1656p. (FRE.). 1978. 115.00 (*0-7859-5283-7*) Fr & Eur.

— Le Jeu de l'Amour et de la Mort. 192p. (FRE.). 1955. pap. 9.95 (*0-7859-5453-8*) Fr & Eur.

— Les Leonides. 252p. (FRE.). 1928. pap. 8.95 (*0-7859-5565-8*) Fr & Eur.

— Life of Ramakrishna. 1928. 4.95 (*0-87481-080-9*, Pub. by Advaita Ashrama II) Vedanta Pr.

— Life of Vivekananda. 1987. 4.95 (*0-87481-090-6*, Pub. by Advaita Ashrama II) Vedanta Pr.

— Liluli. 218p. (FRE.). 1926. pap. 10.95 (*0-7859-5454-6*) Fr & Eur.

— Mahatma Gandhi. Groth, Catherine, tr. 132p. (C). 1994. 10.00 (*0-934676-81-X*) Greenlf Bks.

— Memoires, Souvenires de Jeunesse, Complements, Fragments du Journal. 336p. (FRE.). 1956. pap. 18.95 (*0-686-55260-1*) Fr & Eur.

— Musical Tour Through the Land of the Past. Miall, Bernard, tr. LC 67-30229. (Essay Index Reprint Ser.). 1977. 19.95 (*0-8369-0830-9*) Ayer.

— Musicians of To-Day. Blaiklock, M., tr. LC 72-86777. (Essay Index Reprint Ser.). 1977. 21.95 (*0-8369-1188-1*) Ayer.

— Les Origines du Theatre Lyrique Moderne. 332p. 1971. 85.00 (*0-7859-5566-6*) Fr & Eur.

— Peguy, 2 vols. 696p. (FRE.). 1973. pap. 16.95 (*0-7859-5456-2*) Fr & Eur.

— Pierre et Luce. 160p. (FRE.). 1959. pap. 15.95 (*0-7859-5457-0*) Fr & Eur.

— Printemps Romain: Avec: Choix de Lettres de Romain Rolland a sa Mere (1889-1890) 360p. (FRE.). 1954. pap. 8.95 (*0-7859-5459-7*) Fr & Eur.

— Recueil de Chansons Populaires, 6 tomes, Set. 85.00 (*0-685-36691-X*) Fr & Eur.

— Retour au Palais Farnese: Avec: Choix de Lettres de Romain Rolland a sa Mere (1890-1891) (Illus.). 368p. (FRE.). 1956. pap. 8.95 (*0-7859-5461-9*) Fr & Eur.

— Robespierre. 318p. (FRE.). 1939. pap. 15.95 (*0-7859-5463-5*) Fr & Eur.

— Romain Rolland et le Mouvement Florentin de la Voce. (Illus.). 400p. (FRE.). 1966. pap. 14.95 (*0-7859-5464-3*) Fr & Eur.

— Salut et Fraternite: Avec: Alain et R. Rolland. 184p. (FRE.). 1969. pap. 8.95 (*0-7859-5465-1*) Fr & Eur.

— Selected Letters of Romain Rolland. Dore, Francis & Prevost, Marie-Laure, eds. (Illus.). 168p. 1990. 12.95 (*0-19-562551-X*) OUP.

— Some Musicians of Former Days. LC 76-177517. 1972. 26.95 (*0-405-08897-3*, Pub. by Blom Pubns UK) Ayer.

— Some Musicians of Former Days. LC 68-8490. (Essay Index Reprint Ser.). 1977. 23.95 (*0-8369-0831-7*) Ayer.

— Textes Politiques, Sociaux & Philosophiques Choisis. Albertini, Jean, ed. (FRE.). 1973. pap. 13.95 (*0-7859-5466-X*) Fr & Eur.

— Les Tragedies de la Foi. 296p. (FRE.). 1970. pap. 11.95 (*0-7859-5467-8*) Fr & Eur.

— Le Triomphe de la Raison. 88p. (FRE.). 1971. pap. 8.95 (*0-7859-5468-6*) Fr & Eur.

— La Vie de Ramakrishna. 320p. (FRE.). 1978. pap. 36.95 (*0-7859-5469-4*) Fr & Eur.

— La Vie de Vivekananda. 352p. (FRE.). 1978. pap. 36.95 (*0-7859-5470-8*) Fr & Eur.

— Voyage Musical Aux Pays du Passe. (Illus.). 271p. (FRE.). 1976. pap. 49.95 (*0-7859-5471-6*) Fr & Eur.

Rolland, Romain & Bertolini Guerrieri-Gonzaga. Chere Sofia: Choix de Lettres de Romain Rolland a Sofia Bertolini Guerrieri-Gonzaga (1901-1908), 2 vols. (Illus.). 387p. 1959. 6.95 (*0-685-73254-1*) Fr & Eur.

Rolland, Romain & Bloch, Jean-Richard. Deux Hommes Se Rencontrent. 384p. (FRE.). 1964. pap. 10.95 (*0-7859-5447-3*) Fr & Eur.

Rolland, Romain & Peguy, Charles. Une Amitie Francaise: Avec: Correspondance entre Charles Peguy et Romain Rolland. 360p. (FRE.). 1955. pap. 8.95 (*0-7859-5438-4*) Fr & Eur.

— Pour l'Honneur de l'Esprit: Correspondance, 1898-1914. (Illus.). 352p. (FRE.). 1973. pap. 12.95 (*0-7859-5458-9*) Fr & Eur.

Rolland, Romain & Seche, Alphonse. Ces Jours Lointains: Avec: Alphonse Sechee et Romain Rolland, Lettres et autres Ecrits. 176p. (FRE.). 1962. pap. 8.95 (*0-7859-5441-4*) Fr & Eur.

Rolland, Romain & Strauss, Richard. Richard Strauss et Romain Rolland. (Illus.). 248p. (FRE.). 1951. pap. 8.95 (*0-7859-5462-7*) Fr & Eur.

Rolland, Romain & Suares, Andre. Cette Ame Ardente: Avec: Choix de Lettres d'Andre Suares a Romain Rolland (1887-1891) 408p. (FRE.). 1954. pap. 8.95 (*0-7859-5442-2*) Fr & Eur.

Rolland, Romain & Tagore, Rabindranath. Rabindranath Tagore et Romain Rolland: Lettres et Autres Ecrits. (Illus.). 208p. (FRE.). 1961. pap. 8.95 (*0-7859-5460-0*) Fr & Eur.

Rolland, Romain, et al. French Thought in the Eighteenth Century. LC 70-152172. (Essay Index Reprint Ser.). 1977. reprint ed. 29.95 (*0-8369-2316-2*) Ayer.

Rolland, Solange C., jt. auth. see Graham, Gwethalyn.

Rolland, Thomas, jt. auth. see McLean, Mick.

Rollason, David. Saints & Relics in Anglo-Saxon England. (Illus.). 256p. 1989. text ed. 49.95 (*0-631-16506-1*) Blackwell Pubs.

Rollason, David, et al, eds. Anglo-Norman Durham, 1093-1193. LC 94-18926. (Illus.). 448p. (C). 1994. text ed. 117.00 (*0-85115-390-9*, Boydell Pr) Boydell & Brewer.

Rollason, Jane, jt. auth. see Owen, Peter.

Rollband, James. Basic Cantonese Cooking. (Illus.). 224p. 1993. reprint ed. pap. 10.95 (*1-880188-45-7*) Bess Pr.

Rolle, Andrew. California: A History. 4th ed. LC 86-4790. (Illus.). 600p. (C). 1987. text ed. write for info. (*0-88295-839-9*) Harlan Davidson.

— Henry Mayo Newhall & His Times: A California Legacy. (Illus.). 184p. 1991. 29.95 (*0-87328-136-5*) Huntington Lib.

— The Italian Americans: Troubled Roots. LC 84-40282. 240p. 1984. reprint ed. pap. 12.95 (*0-8061-1907-1*) U of Okla Pr.

— John Charles Fremont: Character As Destiny. LC 91-50305. (Illus.). 432p. 1991. 29.95 (*0-8061-2380-X*) U of Okla Pr.

— Los Angeles. 2nd ed. Hundley, Norris, Jr. & Schutz, John A., eds. (Golden State Ser.). (Illus.). 192p. 1995. pap. 10.00 (*0-929651-01-4*) MTL.

— The Lost Cause: The Confederate Exodus to Mexico. LC 65-11228. (Illus.). 272p. 1992. pap. 14.95 (*0-8061-1961-6*) U of Okla Pr.

Rolle, Andrew & Gaines, John S. The Golden State: California History & Government. 3rd ed. (Illus.). 310p. (C). 1989. text ed. write for info. (*0-88295-866-6*); pap. text ed. write for info. (*0-88295-868-2*) Harlan Davidson.

Rolle, Andrew F. An American in California: The Biography of William Heath Davis 1822-1909. LC 56-10064. (Illus.). 155p. 1981. reprint ed. pap. 9.95 (*0-87328-120-9*) Huntington Lib.

— Immigrant Upraised: Italian Adventurers & Colonists in an Expanding America. LC 68-10302. (Illus.). 1970. 32.95 (*0-8061-0810-X*) U of Okla Pr.

***Rolle, Claude H.** Denise & Other Stories. LC 94-90533. 64p. (Orig.). 1995. pap. 8.95 (*1-56002-504-2*, Univ Edtns) Aegina Pr.

***Rolle, Gunter.** Lexikon Computerwissen Von A-Z: German-English, English-German. 124p. 1990. 19.95 (*0-7859-8441-0*, 3572033500) Fr & Eur.

Rolle, Kurt C. Thermodynamics & Heat Power. 4th ed. (Illus.). 864p. (C). 1993. teacher ed, disk write for info. (*0-318-69909-5*) Macmillan.

— Thermodynamics & Heat Power. 4th ed. (Illus.). 864p. (C). 1994. text ed. write for info. (*0-02-403201-8*) Macmillan.

Rolle, Renate. Totenkult der Skythen. (Vorgeschichtliche Forschungen Ser.). (Illus.). (C). 1979. 307.70 (*3-11-006620-3*) De Gruyter.

— The World of the Scythians. 1990. 40.00 (*0-520-06864-5*) U CA Pr.

Rolle, Richard. The Contra Amatores Mundi of Richard Rolle of Hampole. Theiner, Paul F., ed. LC 68-64641. 196p. 1983. reprint ed. lib. bdg. 33.00x (*0-89370-791-0*) Borgo Pr.

— English Prose Treatises. Perry, G. G., ed. (EETS, OS Ser.: No. 20). 1972. reprint ed. 20.00 (*0-527-00021-3*) Periodicals Srv.

— English Writings. 180p. 1931. reprint ed. 49.00 (*0-403-04052-3*) Somerset Pub.

— English Writings of Richard Rolle: Hermit of Hampole. LC 74-161958. 180p. 1931. reprint ed. 29.00 (*0-403-01328-3*) Scholarly.

— The Fire of Love. Wolters, Clifton, tr. (Classics Ser.). 192p. 1972. mass mkt. 9.95 (*0-14-044256-1*, Penguin Classics) Viking Penguin.

— Selected Works of Richard Rolle, Hermit. LC 78-20488. 1980. reprint ed. 25.85 (*0-88355-865-3*) Hyperion Conn.

— Some Minor Works of Richard Rolle, with the Privity of the Passion by S. Bonaventura. (BCL1-PR English Literature Ser.). 225p. 1992. reprint ed. lib. bdg. 79.00 (*0-7812-7191-6*) Rprt Serv.

Rolle, Richard, ed. see Harvey, Ralph & Misyn, R.

Rolle Richard of Hampole. The Pricke of Conscience (Stimulus Conscientiae) A Northumbrian Poem. LC 74-178551. reprint ed. 52.50 (*0-404-56666-9*) AMS Pr.

Rolle-Whatley, R., ed. see Jones, Richard O.

Rolle-Whatley, R., ed. see Parham, Vanessa R.

Rolle-Whatley, R., ed. see Wunder, Matthew R.

Rolle-Whatley, Renee M. Baby Products Basics: The Busy Person's Guide to Baby Products on a Budget. LC 90-92125. (Illus.). 128p. (Orig.). 1991. pap. 8.95 (*0-9627756-0-6*) Sandcastle Pub.

Rollenhagen, Gabriel. Nucleus Emblematum Selectissimorum. 45p. (GER.). 1985. reprint ed. write for info. (*3-487-07505-9*, Pub. by Georg Olms GW) Lubrecht & Cramer.

Roller, jt. ed. see Thomas, J. R.

Roller, Bill, ed. see Roller, Twila J.

Roller, Cathy M., jt. auth. see Jackson, Nancy E.

Roller, Dave. How to Make Big Money in Multi-Level Marketing. 216p. 1989. 19.95 (*0-13-417858-0*, Busn) P-H.

— How to Make Big Money in Multi-Level Marketing. 216p. 1989. pap. text ed. 14.00 (*0-13-417866-1*, Busn) P-H.

Roller, Dick. Indiana Glass Factories Notes. (Illus.). 140p. (Orig.). 1994. pap. 40.00 (*0-915627-00-0*) Acorn Pr IL.

Roller, Duane. Early Travellers in Eastern Boiotia. (McGill University Monographs in Classical Archaeology & History: Vol. 8). 211p. 1989. 49.00 (*90-5063-006-5*, Pub. by Gieben NE) Benjamins North Am.

— Fundamental Physics: Mechanics, Waves & Thermodynamics, Vol. 1. (Illus.). 818p. 1981. text ed. 40.00 (*0-8162-7284-0*) Holden-Day.

— Tanagran Studies, No. I: Sources & Documents on Tanagra in Boiotia. (McGill University Monographs in Classical Archaeology & History: Vol. 9.1). xii, 173p. 1989. 44.00 (*90-5063-030-8*, Pub. by Gieben NE) Benjamins North Am.

— Tanagran Studies, No. II: The Prosopography of Tanagra in Boiotia. (McGill University Monographs in Classical Archaeology & History: Vol. 9.2). 122p. 1989. 41.00 (*90-5063-031-6*, Pub. by Gieben NE) Benjamins North Am.

Roller, Duane & Blum, Ronald. Fundamental Physics, 2 vols. Incl. Vol. 2. Electricity, Magnetism & Light. LC 81-81011. (Illus.). 790p. 1981. (*0-318-53449-5*); Vol. 2. Electricity, Magnetism & Light. LC 81-81011. (Illus.). 790p. 1981. 40.00 (*0-8162-7285-9*); LC 81-81011. (Illus.). 1981. write for info. (*0-318-53448-7*) Holden-Day.

Roller, Duane E. The Early Development of the Concepts of Temperature & Heat: The Rise & Decline of the Caloric Theory. LC 50-8653. (Harvard Case Histories in Experimental Science Ser.: Case 3). 110p. reprint ed. pap. 31.40 (*0-317-09176-X*, 2011607) Bks Demand.

Roller, Gerhard, jt. auth. see Von Wilmowsky, Peter.

Roller, Judi M. The Politics of the Feminist Novel. LC 85-12718. (Contributions in Women's Studies: No. 63). 206p. 1986. text ed. 49.95 (*0-313-24663-7*, RPN); pap. 12.95 (*0-313-25445-1*, RPNPB) Greenwood.

Roller, Karen L., ed. Women Pray. LC 86-15117. 96p. (Orig.). 1986. pap. 5.95 (*0-8298-0737-3*) Pilgrim OH.

Roller, Leonard H. The Profits of Persuasion: Speaking Effectively for Your Company. (Illus.). 224p. 1988. 18.95 (*0-914598-24-4*) Intl Resources.

Roller, Lynn E. Gordon Special Studies I: The Nonverbal Graffiti, Dipinti, & Stamps. Kohler, Ellen L., ed. (University Museum Monographs: No. 63). (Illus.). xxii, 100p. 1987. text ed. 45.00 (*0-934718-70-9*) U PA Mus Pubns.

Roller, Lynn E., tr. see Schleiner, Louise.

Roller, Martin, jt. ed. see Niblo, Graham.

Roller, Twila J. Methodism in Their Madness. Roller, Bill, ed. (Illus.). 152p. (Orig.). (C). 1993. pap. text ed. 6.95 (*1-880047-04-7*) Creative Des.

R

Roller, William & Nelson, Vivian. The Art of Co-Therapy: How Therapists Work Together. LC 90-44744. 256p. 1991. lib. bdg. 33.50 (0-89862-557-2) Guilford Pr.
Roller, William L., jt. auth. see Shashkan, Donald A.
Rollerson, Michael, tr. see Helakisa, Kaarina.
Rolleston, F. S., jt. auth. see Halperin, M. L.
Rolleston, Humphrey D. Internal Medicine. LC 75-23653. (Clio Medica Ser.: No. 4). reprint ed. 20.00 (0-404-58904-9) AMS Pr.
Rolleston, James. Narratives of Ecstasy: Romantic Temporality in Modern German Poetry. LC 87-2020. 244p. 1987. 34.95 (0-8143-1841-X) Wayne St U Pr.
— Rilke in Transition: An Exploration of His Earliest Poetry. LC 73-99839. (Yale Germanic Studies: 4). 256p. reprint ed. pap. 73.00 (0-317-29716-3, 2022035) Bks Demand.
Rolleston, James, tr. see Witte, Bernd.
Rolleston, T. W. Celtic Myths & Legends. 1990. pap. 9.95 (0-486-26507-2) Dover.
Rollet, B., et al. Stratification of Tropical Forests as Seen in Leaf Structure, Pt. 2. (Tasks for Vegetation Science Ser.). (C). 1990. lib. bdg. 188.50 (0-7923-0397-0) Kluwer Ac.
Rollet, Jean. Les Maitres De la Lumiere. (Illus.). 301p. (FRE.). 1980. lib. bdg. 75.00 (2-04-010496-8) Hacker.
Rollett, A., jt. ed. see Anderson, M. P.
Rollett, A. D., ed. see Minerals, Metals & Materials Society Staff.
Rollett, J. Computing Methods in Crystallography. LC 64-17189. 1965. 115.00 (0-08-010590-4, Pub. by Pergamon Repr UK) Franklin.
Rollett, R., et al. Fertilizers & Soil Amendments. 1981. text ed. 54.20 (0-13-314336-8) P-H.
Rolley, Claude. Greek Bronzes. LC 85-51623. (Illus.). 300p. 1986. lib. bdg. 95.00 (0-85667-300-5, Pub. by P Wilson Pubs) Sothebys Pubns.
Rolley, Katrina & Aish, Caroline. Fashions in Photographs, 1900-1920. 144p. (C). 1992. text ed. 82.50 (0-7134-6119-5) B&N Imports.
Rollfinke, Dieter & Rollfinke, Jacqueline. The Call of Human Nature: The Role of Scatology in Modern German Literature. LC 86-1490. (Illus.). 256p. 1986. lib. bdg. 30.00 (0-87023-536-2) U of Mass Pr.
Rollfinke, Jacqueline, jt. auth. see Rollfinke, Dieter.
Rolliet, D. G. Your Name & Colors: Blueprints to Your Chemistry--The Rolliet Letter-Color Theory. (Illus.). (Orig.). 1988. pap. text ed. write for info. (0-318-64366-9) Spectra Pubns Hse.
— Your Name & Colors: Secret Keys to Your Beauty, Personality & Success, the Rolliett Letter-Color Theory. Reanult, Michael & Wolf, Jeannie, eds. LC 89-91991. (Illus.). 192p. (Orig.). (YA). 1990. pap. 12.95 (0-9621693-0-7) Spectra Pubns Hse.
Rollig, Aaron E. Jurisprudence & Medical Mistakes: Index & Bibliography. LC 88-47579. 150p. 1988. 44.50 (0-88164-718-7); pap. 39.50 (0-88164-719-5) ABBE Pubs Assn.
Rollin. The Experimental Animal in Biomedical Research, I. 1990. 240.00 (0-8493-4981-8, HV4915) CRC Pr.
— The Experimental Animal in Biomedical Research, Vol. II. 1993. write for info. (0-8493-4982-6) CRC Pr.
Rollin, A., ed. see Bille-de Mot, Eleonore.
Rollin, A. L. & Rigo, J. M., eds. Geomembranes: Identification & Performance Testing. 352p. 1991. 88.95 (0-442-31272-5) Chapman & Hall.
Rollin, B. E. The Teaching of Responsibility. 1983. 20.00 (0-317-43863-8) St Mut.
Rollin, Bernard E. Animal Rights & Human Morality. rev. ed. 248p. (C). 1992. pap. 17.95 (0-87975-789-2) Prometheus Bks.
— The Frankenstein Syndrome. (Cambridge Studies in Philosophy & Public Policy). (Illus.). 272p. (C). 1995. 49.95 (0-521-47230-X); pap. 18.95 (0-521-47807-3) Cambridge U Pr.
— The Unheeded Cry: Animal Consciousness, Animal Pain & Science. (Studies in Bioethics). (Illus.). 336p. 1990. reprint ed. pap. 14.95 (0-19-286104-2) OUP.
Rollin, Betty. First, You Cry. 1993. mass mkt. 5.50 (0-06-104235-8, Harp PBks) HarpC.
— Last Wish. 240p. 1986. pap. 8.95 (0-446-37032-0) Warner Bks.
Rollin, Frank A. Life & Public Services of Martin R. Delany, Sub-Assistant Commissioner, Bureau Relief of Refugees, Freedmen & of Abandoned Lands, & Late Major 104th U. S. Colored Troops. LC 77-92236. (American Negro: His History & Literature, Ser. No. 3). 1970. reprint ed. 19.95 (0-405-01934-3) Ayer.
Rollin, Jack. World Cup, 1930-1990. (Illus.). 208p. 1990. 24.95 (0-8160-2523-1, Pub. by Guinness Pub UK) Facts on File.
***Rollin, Libby.** Age Plus Wisdom: The ARt of Thriving in a Retirement Community. 276p. 1995. 23.00 (1-885420-07-2) Peradam Pr.
Rollin, Lucy. Cradle & All: A Cultural & Psychoanalytic Study of Nursery Rhymes. LC 91-38995. (Studies in Popular Culture Ser.). 176p. 1992. 28.50 (0-87805-556-8) U Pr of Miss.
Rollin, Lucy, ed. The Antic Art: Enhancing Children's Literary Experiences Through Film & Video. (Illus.). 243p. 1994. pap. text ed. 29.00 (0-917846-27-3, 95552) Highsmith Pr.
Rollin, Roger, ed. The Americanization of the Global Village: Essays in Comparative Popular Culture. LC 89-83393. (Illus.). 154p. (C). 1990. lib. bdg. 26.95 (0-87972-469-2); pap. 13.95 (0-87972-470-6) Bowling Green Univ.
Rollin, Roger B. Robert Herrick. (Twayne's English Authors Ser.: No. 34). 180p. 1992. text ed. 22.95 (0-8057-7012-7, Twayne) Macmillan.
Rollin, Roger B., ed. see Robert Herrick Memorial Conference, University of Michigan Staff.
Rolling, L., jt. auth. see Goetschalckx, J.
Rolling Stone Editors. Neil Young: The Rolling Stone Files: The Ultimate Compendium of Interviews, Articles, Facts, & Opinions from the Files of "Rolling Stone" LC 94-11012. 320p. 1994. pap. 12.95 (0-7868-8043-0) Hyperion.
— REM: The "Rolling Stone" Files: The Ultimate Compendium of Interviews, Articles, Facts & Opinions from the Files of "Rolling Stone" 208p. 1995. pap. 12.95 (0-7868-8054-6) Hyperion.
— U2: The Rolling Stone Files: The Ultimate Compendium of Interviews, Articles, Facts & Opinions from the Files of "Rolling Stone" 256p. 1994. pap. 12.95 (0-7868-8001-5) Hyperion.
Rolling Stone Magazine Editors. Rolling Stone Journalism Awards. 160p. 1992. pap. 7.95 (0-8065-1314-4, Citadel Pr) Carol Pub Group.
Rolling Stone Magazine Staff, ed. The Rolling Stone Environmental Reader. LC 92-5175. 268p. (Orig.). 1992. 25.00 (1-55963-167-8); pap. 15.00 (1-55963-166-X) Island Pr.
Rolling Stone Press Staff. The Rolling Stone Encyclopedia of Rock & Roll. Pareles, Jon & Romanowski, Patty, eds. LC 83-4791. (Illus.). 704p. (Orig.). 1983. 16.00 (0-671-44071-3) Summit Bks.
— The Rolling Stone Illustrated History of Rock & Roll, 1950-1980. rev. ed. Miller, Jim, ed. (Illus.). 1980. 25.00 (0-394-51322-3); pap. 19.95 (0-394-73938-8) Random.
— Rolling Stone Interviews 1967-1980. 1989. pap. 15.95 (0-312-03486-5) St Martin.
— Rolling Stone Rock Almanac. 1987. pap. 19.95 (0-02-604490-0) Macmillan.
***Rolling Stones Editors.** Cobain. 1994. 24.95 (0-316-88034-5) Little.
Rollings, Alane. In Your Own Sweet Time. LC 88-5746. (Wesleyan Poetry Ser.). 72p. 1989. 22.50 (0-8195-2156-6, Wesleyan Univ Pr); pap. 10.95 (0-8195-1157-9, Wesleyan Univ Pr) U Pr of New Eng.
— Struggle to Adore. 106p. 1993. pap. 12.95 (0-934257-97-3) Story Line.
Rollings, Charles. Stalag Luft III: The Full Story. 1000p. (C). 1992. 125.00 (0-946771-58-8, Pub. by Spellmount UK) St Mut.
Rollings, Laurie M. Mother Goose Rhymes-Versos Infantiles-Vers D'Enfance. 64p. 1988. Including 2 cassettes. audio 19.95 (0-945206-00-3) Matterplay.
***Rollings, Marian P.** Geotechnical Materials in Construction. 1995. text ed. 56.00 (0-07-053665-1) McGraw.
Rollings, Willard H. The Comanche. (Indians of North America Ser.). (Illus.). 112p. (YA). (gr. 5 up). 1989. 17.95 (1-55546-702-4); pap. 9.95 (0-7910-0359-0) Chelsea Hse.
— The Osage: An Ethnohistorical Study of Hegemony on the Prairie-Plains. (Illus.). 336p. 1995. pap. 17.95 (0-8262-1006-6) U of Mo Pr.
Rollini, Art. When Will Summer Come? LC 90-70904. (Illus.). 21p. (J). (ps-6). 1991. pap. 5.95 (1-55523-354-6) Winston-Derek.
Rollini, Arthur. Thirty Years with the Big Bands. (Illus.). 144p. 1987. 19.95 (0-252-01454-5) U of Ill Pr.
Rollins. Art to Choke Hearts - Pissing in the Gene Pool. 254p. (Orig.). 1992. reprint ed. pap. 15.00 (1-880985-10-1) Two Thirteen Sixty-one.
— Bang! (Illus.). 144p. (Orig.). 1992. reprint ed. pap. 11.00 (1-880985-03-9) Two Thirteen Sixty-one.
— Black Coffee Blues. 142p. (Orig.). 1992. reprint ed. pap. 11.00 (1-880985-05-5) Two Thirteen Sixty-one.
— High Adventure in the Great Outdoors. 2nd ed. 140p. (Orig.). 1992. reprint ed. pap. 11.00 (1-880985-02-0) Two Thirteen Sixty-one.
— Now Watch Him Die. 188p. (Orig.). 1993. pap. 11.00 (1-880985-14-4) Two Thirteen Sixty-one.
— One from None. (Illus.). 144p. (Orig.). 1992. reprint ed. pap. 11.00 (1-880985-04-7) Two Thirteen Sixty-one.
— See a Grown Man Cry. 190p. (Orig.). 1992. pap. 11.00 (1-880985-12-8) Two Thirteen Sixty-one.
Rollins & Baker. The Renaissance in England: Nondramatic Prose & Verse of the Sixteenth Century. 1014p. (C). 1954. text ed. 34.00 (0-669-21352-7) Heath.
Rollins, ed. see Bajema, Don.
Rollins, ed. see Cole, Joe.
Rollins, Alden. Rome in the Fourth Century A.D. An Annotated Bibliography with Historical Overview. LC 91-52762. 358p. 1991. lib. bdg. 55.00x (0-89950-624-0) McFarland & Co.
Rollins, Arline M., jt. auth. see Gouke, Mary N.
Rollins, Boyd C., jt. ed. see Barber, Brian K.
Rollins, Catherine. Building Self-Esteem & Confidence in Yourself & Your Child. 1994. 7.98 (0-88365-857-7) Galahad Bks.
Rollins, Charlemae H., ed. Christmas Gif' An Anthology of Christmas Poems, Songs, & Stories, Written by & about Black People. LC 92-18976. (Illus.). 128p. (J). 1993. 14.00 (0-688-11667-1) Morrow Jr Bks.
Rollins, Dan. IBM-PC: 8088 Macro Assembler Programming. 368p. (C). 1984. pap. write for info. (0-02-403210-7) Macmillan.
Rollins, Doug. John Metcalf & His Works. (Canadian Author Studies). 57p. (C). 1985. pap. text ed. 9.95 (0-920802-73-7, Pub. by ECW Press CN) Genl Dist Srvs.
Rollins, George W. The Struggle of the Cattleman, Sheepman & Settler for Control of Lands in Wyoming, 1867-1910. Bruchey, Stuart, ed. LC 78-56671. (Management of Public Lands in the U. S. Ser.). (Illus.). 1979. lib. bdg. 35.95 (0-405-11353-6) Ayer.
Rollins, Harold. Geology Lecture Notes. 72p. 1993. spiral bd. 8.50 (0-8403-8884-5) Kendall-Hunt.
***Rollins, Henry.** Get in the Van: On the Road with Black Flag. (Illus.). 256p. 1994. 25.00 (1-880985-23-3) Two Thirteen Sixty-one.
— Get in the Van: On the Road with Black Flag. (Illus.). 1995. pap. write for info. (1-880985-24-1) Two Thirteen Sixty-one.
Rollins, Hyder. Contribution to the History of English Commonwealth Drama. (Studies in Drama: No. 39). (C). 1970. reprint ed. pap. 39.95 (0-8383-0065-0) M S G Haskell Hse.
— Troilus-Cressida Story from Chaucer to Shakespeare. LC 76-100782. (English Literature Ser.: No. 33). (C). 1970. reprint ed. lib. bdg. 49.95 (0-8383-0338-2) M S G Haskell Hse.
Rollins, Hyder & Baker, Herschel, eds. The Renaissance in England: Non-Dramatic Prose & Verse of the Sixteenth Century. 1014p. (C). 1992. reprint ed. pap. text ed. 37.95 (0-88133-673-4) Waveland Pr.
Rollins, Hyder E. The Keats Circle: Letters & Papers, & More Letters & Poems of the Keats Circle, 2 vols., 1. 2nd ed. LC 65-13632. (Illus.). 492p. 1965. reprint ed. pap. 140.30 (0-7837-4890-6, 2059058) Bks Demand.
— The Keats Circle: Letters & Papers, & More Letters & Poems of the Keats Circle, 2 vols., 2. LC 65-13632. (Illus.). 661p. 1965. reprint ed. pap. 180.00 (0-7837-4891-4) Bks Demand.
Rollins, Hyder E., ed. Pack of Autolycus or Strange & Terrible News of Ghosts: Broadside Ballads of the Years 1624-1693. LC 27-4308. (Illus.). 287p. 1969. 17.50 (0-674-65125-1) HUP.
— Phoenix Nest, Fifteen Ninety-Three. LC 31-4893. (Illus.). 285p. 1959. 16.50 (0-674-66610-0) HUP.
Rollins, Hyder E., ed. see Keats, John.
Rollins, Hyder E., ed. see Pepys, Samuel.
Rollins, Hyder E., ed. see Robinson, Clement.
Rollins, Hyder E., ed. see Shakespeare, William.
Rollins, Hyder E., ed. see Tottel, R.
Rollins, Jack, jt. auth. see Nelson, Steve.
***Rollins, Jennifer.** Embroidery. 1994. 5.99 (0-517-10252-8) Random Hse Value.
— Quilting: Country Crafts. 1993. 5.99 (0-517-08799-5) Random Hse Value.
Rollins, John P., ed. Compressed Air & Gas. 5th ed. 384p. 1988. reprint ed. text ed. 130.00 (0-13-162611-6) P-H.
***Rollins, Judith.** All Is Never Said: The Narrative of Odette Harper Hines. (Illus.). 320p. (Orig.). (C). 1995. lib. bdg. 39.95 (1-56639-307-8); pap. text ed. 16.95 (1-56639-308-6) Temple U Pr.
— Between Women: Domestics & Their Employers. LC 85-8022. (Labor & Social Change Ser.). 256p. 1985. pap. 17.95 (0-87722-491-9) Temple U Pr.
Rollins, Judy H., ed. see Wong, Donna L. & Whaley, Lucille F.
Rollins, Kay D. & Patrick, Freda. Invitation to a Discussion: With Blacks Around the Table. 114p. 1992. pap. 8.95 (0-9635390-0-0) Rohill Pubns.
***Rollins, Kyle M., ed.** In-Situ Deep Soil Improvement: Proceedings of Sessions Sponsored by the Geotechnical Engineering Division of the American Society of Civil Engineers in Conjunction with the ASCE National Convention in Atlanta, Georgia, October 9-13, 1994. LC 94-34442. (Geotechnical Special Pubns.: Vol. 45). 1994. write for info. (0-7844-0058-X) Am Soc Civil Eng.
Rollins, L. A. Lucifer's Lexicon. 144p. (Orig.). 1987. pap. text ed. 6.95 (0-915179-43-1) Loompanics.
— The Myth of Natural Rights. 50p. (Orig.). 1983. pap. 5.95 (1-55950-007-7) Loompanics.
Rollins, Leighton & Corrigan, Daniel. Disasters of War. LC 80-69430. (Illus.). 48p. 1981. pap. 4.00 (0-932274-15-3) Cadmus Eds.
— Disasters of War. deluxe limited ed. LC 80-69430. (Illus.). 48p. 1981. 15.00 (0-932274-16-1) Cadmus Eds.
Rollins, Leslie E., ed. see Assoc. of Theatrical Artists & Craftspeople Staff.
Rollins, Marilyn. Lifestyle Changes! LC 91-24619. 128p. (Orig.). 1991. pap. 7.95 (0-934125-23-6) Hazelden.
Rollins, Marion J. The God of the Old Testament in Relation to War. LC 72-176551. (Columbia University. Teachers College. Contributions to Education Ser.: No. 263). reprint ed. 37.50 (0-404-55263-3) AMS Pr.
Rollins, Mark. Mental Imagery: On the Limits of Cognitive Science. 187p. (C). 1992. reprint ed. pap. text ed. 13.00 (0-300-05472-6) Yale U Pr.
Rollins, Mark, ed. Danto & His Critics. LC 93-6590. (Philosophers & Their Critics Ser.: No. 4). 256p. 1993. 49.95 (0-631-18337-X); pap. 19.95 (0-631-18338-8) Blackwell Pubs.
Rollins, Mark, jt. ed. see Campbell, Mary B.
Rollins, Mary R. Patients, Pain & Politics: Nursing Home Inspector's Shocking True Story & Expert Advice for You & Your Family. Davis, Barbara, ed. 248p. (Orig.). 1994. pap. 11.95 (1-884348-20-3) N Century Pubng.
Rollins, Nancy. Child Psychiatry in the Soviet Union: Preliminary Observations. LC 72-76560. (Illus.). 315p. 1972. 36.00 (0-674-11475-2) HUP.
Rollins, Patrick J., ed. U. S. S. R. Legislative Documents Series, 2 vols. in 1, Ea. 1993. 170.00 (0-87569-166-8) Academic Intl.
Rollins, Peter, jt. ed. see Rollins, Susan.
Rollins, Peter C. Will Rogers: A Bio-Bibliography. LC 83-10696. (Popular Culture Bio-Bibliographies Ser.). xiii, 282p. 1984. text ed. 42.95 (0-313-22633-4, RWR/, Greenwood Pr) Greenwood.
Rollins, Peter C., ed. Hollywood As Historian: American Film in a Cultural Context. LC 82-49118. (Illus.). 288p. 1983. pap. 12.00 (0-8131-0154-9) U Pr of Ky.
Rollins, Peter C., ed. see Rogers, Will.
***Rollins, Philip A., ed.** The Discovery of the Oregon Trail: Robert Stuart's Narratives of His Overland Trip Eastward from Astoria in 1812-13. LC 95-2134. (Illus.). 535p. (J). 1995. pap. 18.95 (0-8032-9234-1, Bison Books) U of Nebr Pr.
Rollins, R., jt. auth. see Cooke, G.
Rollins, R., jt. auth. see Schultes, Richard E.
Rollins, R., jt. auth. see Szafer, W.
Rollins, R., jt. auth. see Turrill, W.
Rollins, Reed C. The Cruciferae of Continental North America: Systematics of the Mustard Family from the Arctic to Panama. LC 92-35018. (Illus.). 1000p. (C). 1993. 125.00 (0-8047-2064-9) Stanford U Pr.
Rollins, Reed C. & Shaw, Elizabeth A. Genus Lesquerella (Cruciferae) in North America. LC 72-87777. (Illus.). 300p. 1973. 34.50 (0-674-34775-7) HUP.
***Rollins, Richard, ed.** The Damned Reg Flags of the Rebellion: The Confederate Battle Flag at Gettysburg. 1995. write for info. (0-9638993-3-3) Rank & File.
— A Day with Mr. Lincoln: Essays in Honor of the Lincoln Exhibit at the Huntington Library. 1994. write for info. (0-9638993-2-5) Rank & File.
— Double Canister at Ten Yards: The Federal Artillery at Gettysburg. 1995. pap. write for info. (0-9638993-5-X) Rank & File.
— Pickett's Charge: Eyewitness Accounts. 1994. 35.00 (0-9638993-1-7); pap. 18.00 (0-9638993-0-9) Rank & File.
— The Returned Battle Flags. 1995. pap. write for info. (0-9638993-4-1) Rank & File.
Rollins, Richard M., intro. The Autobiographies of Noah Webster: From the Letters & Essays, Memoir & Diary. 394p. 1989. lib. bdg. 39.95 (0-87249-574-4) U of SC Pr.
***Rollins, Ronald G.** Sean O'Casey's Drama: Verisimilitude & Vision. LC 77-14462. (Illus.). 150p. 1979. pap. 42.80 (0-7837-8401-5, 2059212) Bks Demand.
***Rollins, Scott.** Borderlines. (Essential Poets Ser.: No. 66). 160p. 1995. 15.00 (1-55071-009-5) Guernica Editions.
Rollins, Scott, tr. see Barkan, Stanley H., ed.
Rollins, Scott, tr. see Bernlef, J.
Rollins, Scott, tr. see De Winter, Leon.
Rollins Staff, ed. see Shields, Bill.
***Rollins, Susan & Rollins, Peter, eds.** Gender in Popular Culture: Images of Men & Women in Literature, Visual Media, Material Culture. (Illus.). 234p. (Orig.). (C). 1995. pap. 16.50 (0-9641755-0-9) Ridgemont Pr.
Rollins, Wayne G. Jung & the Bible. LC 82-48091. 156p. (C). 1980. pap. 12.99 (0-8042-1117-5, John Knox) Westminster John Knox.
Rollins, William, Jr. The Shadow Before. LC 74-22808. reprint ed. 45.00 (0-404-58464-0) AMS Pr.
Rollins, Wilma E., jt. auth. see Ranucci, Ernest R.
Rollins, Yuriko U., jt. auth. see Young, John.
Rollinson, David & Anderson, R. M. Ecology & Genetics of Host-Parasite Interactions. (Linnean Society Symposium Ser.: No. 11). 1985. text ed. 124.00 (0-12-593690-7) Acad Pr.
Rollinson, David & Simpson, Andrew J., eds. The Biology of Schistosomes: From Genes to Latrines. 472p. 1988. text ed. 117.00 (0-12-593692-3) Acad Pr.
Rollinson, David, ed. see Oxford, Geoffrey S.
Rollinson, Hugh R. Using Geochemical Data: Evaluation, Presentation, Interpretation. LC 93-3887. (Geochemistry Ser.). 1993. pap. text ed. 67.95 (0-470-22154-2) Halsted Pr.
Rollinson, John K. Pony Trails in Wyoming: Hoofprints of a Cowboy & U. S. Ranger. LC 88-14313. (Illus.). 465p. 1988. pap. 11.95 (0-8032-8932-4) U of Nebr Pr.
Rollinson, Mark. Popular Legal Delusions. viii, 169p. 1992. 22.95 (0-9614303-6-2) Summertown.
Rollinson, Mark, jt. auth. see Harvey, Carolyn.
Rollinson, Philip. Classical Theories of Allegory & Christian Culture. LC 81-4891. (Duquesne Studies: Language & Literature Ser.: Vol. 3). 196p. (C). 1981. text ed. 20.00 (0-391-01712-8) Duquesne.
Rollinson, Philip & Ross, Mark E. The Children's Catechism: A New, Modern Version. 26p. (Orig.). 1988. pap. text ed. 1.75 (0-9614303-2-X) Summertown.
Rollinson, Philip, jt. ed. see Ball, John H., III.
Rollinson, Philip, jt. auth. see Kelly, Douglas.
Rollinson, Philip, tr. see Viperano, Giovanni A.
Rollison, David. The Local Origins of Modern Society: Gloucestershire 1500-1800. LC 91-41500. 256p. 1992. 49.95 (0-415-07000-7, A7877) Routledge.
Rollison, Jeffrey, jt. auth. see Tatem, Jill M.
Rollnick, Stephen, jt. auth. see Miller, William R.
Rollnik, H. & Pfeil, W. E., eds. Electron & Photon Interactions at High Energies. 1974. 107.75 (0-444-10626-X) Elsevier.
Rollo, Duncan J., jt. auth. see Gehle, Quentin L.
Rollo, E. M., ed. see Flemming, John.
Rollo, J. M. The New Eastern Europe: Western Responses. LC 90-34197. (Chatham House Papers). 148p. 1990. pap. 14.95 (0-87609-085-4) Coun Foreign.
Rollo, May. Discovery of Being. 192p. 1994. pap. 11.00 (0-393-31240-2) Norton.
Rollo, Naomi J. Goldy Lark: A Novel. LC 91-48138. 224p. (Orig.). 1992. pap. 10.95 (1-56474-018-8) Fithian Pr.
Rollo, Ned. Man, I Need a Job! Finding Employment with a Criminal History. 2nd ed. (Information Ser.). 76p. (Orig.). 1993. pap. 5.95 (1-878436-15-5) OPEN TX.
— Necesito Empleo! La Busqueda do Emleo con Historial Penal. (Information Ser.). 75p. (Orig.). (SPA.). 1993. pap. 5.95 (1-878436-13-9) OPEN TX.
— Ninety-Nine Days & a Get Up: A Pre- & Post-Release Survival Manual for Inmates & Their Loved Ones. 2nd ed. (Information Ser.). 29p. (Orig.). 1988. pap. 3.95 (1-878436-04-X) OPEN TX.

R

An Asterisk (*) at the beginning of an entry indicates that the title is appearing in BIP for the first time.

Rollo, Ned & Adams, Louis W. A Map Through the Maze: A Guide to Surviving the Criminal Justice System with Advice for Families of Offenders. (Illus.). 119p. (Orig.). 1993. pap. 8.95 (*1-878436-14-7*) OPEN TX.
Rollo, Ned & Greene, Katherine S. Tears, Fears & a Lonely Highway: Secrets to Successful Prison Visits in Texas. (Information Ser.). 33p. (Orig.). 1989. pap. 3.95 (*1-878436-05-8*) OPEN TX.
Rollo, Ned, jt. auth. see Udashen, Robert N.
***Rollo, Terry.** Right to Remain Silent. 700p. 1995. pap. 14.95 (*1-56901-703-4*) NW Pub.
***Rollo, Vera.** Aviation Programs in the Postsecondary Schools of the United States: 1950 & 1985. 240p. 1990. 50.00 (*0-614-01410-7*); pap. 40.00 (*0-614-01411-5*) MD Hist Pr.
Rollo, Vera F. The American Flag. LC 89-42930. (Illus.). 78p. 1989. pap. 5.95 (*0-917882-31-8*); boxed 12.95 (*0-917882-28-8*) MD Hist Pr.
— Aviation Insurance. LC 86-62107. 438p. 1987. lib. bdg. 14.50 (*0-917882-22-9*) MD Hist Pr.
— Aviation Insurance: Instructor's Manual. 97p. 1987. pap. 14.00 (*0-614-01409-3*) MD Hist Pr.
— Aviation Law: An Introduction. 3rd ed. LC 79-64803. 514p. 1994. lib. bdg. 24.50 (*0-917882-40-7*) MD Hist Pr.
— Burt Rutan: Reinventing the Airplane. LC 91-52844. (Illus.). 300p. 1991. 24.50 (*0-917882-33-4*) MD Hist Pr.
— Maryland Today: A Geography. 1994. teacher ed, pap. 10.00 (*0-614-06587-9*) MD Hist Pr.
— Maryland Today: A Geography. (Illus.). 188p. (J). (gr. 4). 1994. 19.50 (*0-917882-37-7*); teacher ed, pap. 10.00 (*0-685-71072-6*) MD Hist Pr.
— Maryland's Government. LC 85-61164. (Illus.). 300p. 1985. teacher ed, pap. 10.00 (*0-685-14546-8*) MD Hist Pr.
— Maryland's Government. LC 85-61164. (Illus.). 300p. 1985. 16.75 (*0-917882-18-0*) MD Hist Pr.
— The Presidents & Their Pets. 120p. 1993. pap. 14.25 (*0-917882-36-9*); boxed 19.50 (*0-917882-29-6*) MD Hist Pr.
— The Proprietorship of Maryland: A Documented Account. LC 87-43200. 550p. 1988. 49.75 (*0-917882-26-1*) MD Hist Pr.
— Your Maryland: A History. 414p. 1993. ring bd. 22.50 (*0-917882-35-0*) MD Hist Pr.
Rollock, Barbara. Black Authors & Illustrators of Children's Books: A Biographical Dictionary. 2nd ed. LC 91-37402. (Illus.). 252p. 1992. 35.00 (*0-8240-7078-X*, H01316) Garland.
Rollock, Barbara T. Public Library Services for Children. LC 88-12863. xv, 228p. (C). 1988. 35.00 (*0-208-02016-0*, Lib Prof Pubns) Shoe String.
Rollot, Jean-Claude. English-French, French-English Lexicon of Management Terms: Lexique Anglais-Francais-Anglais des Termes de Gestion. (ENG & FRE.). 1987. 15.95 (*0-8288-0085-5*, F127520) Fr & Eur.
Rolls, jt. auth. see Williston.
Rolls, Charles J. His Glorious Name. LC 85-6926. (Names & Titles of Jesus Christ Beginning with T-Z: No. 5). 267p. 1986. reprint ed. pap. 7.99 (*0-87213-735-X*) Loizeaux.
— The Indescribable Christ. rev. ed. LC 83-19890. (Names & Titles of Jesus Christ Beginning with T-Z). 1984. pap. 7.99 (*0-87213-731-7*) Loizeaux.
— Name above Every Name: The Names & Titles of Jesus Christ Beginning with P-S. rev. ed. LC 85-6927. 1985. pap. 7.99 (*0-87213-734-1*) Loizeaux.
— The Names & Titles of Jesus Christ, 5 vols., Set. 1985. 39.95 (*0-87213-736-8*) Loizeaux.
— Time's Noblest Name: The Names & Titles of Jesus Christ, L-O. rev. ed. 1985. pap. 7.99 (*0-87213-733-3*) Loizeaux.
— The World's Greatest Name, Names & Titles of Jesus Christ Beginning with H-K. rev. ed. 183p. 1985. pap. 7.99 (*0-87213-732-5*) Loizeaux.
Rolls, Eric. From Forest to Sea: Australia's Changing Environment. 176p. Date not set. pap. 14.95 (*0-7022-2576-2*, Pub. by Univ Queensland Pr AT) Intl Spec Bk.
— Sojourners: The Epic Story of China's Centuries-Old Relationship with Australia. (Orig.). 1992. 49.95 (*0-7022-2478-2*, Pub. by Univ Queensland Pr AT) Intl Spec Bk.
Rolls, Mark G., jt. ed. see McInnes, Colin.
Rolls Royce, Ltd. Staff. Rolls Royce Catalog: 1910-1911. (Illus.). 70p. 1973. reprint ed. 37.95 (*0-8464-1129-6*) Beekman Pubs.
Rollwagen, J. R. Anthropological Filmmaking: Anthropological Perspectives on the Production of Film & Video for General Public Audiences. 416p. 1988. pap. text ed. 42.00 (*3-7186-0478-7*) Gordon & Breach.
Rollwagen, Jack R., intro. Anthropological Film & Video in the Nineteen Nineties. LC 93-79690. (Case Studies in Documentary Filmmaking). (Illus.). 450p. (Orig.). (C). 1993. pap. text ed. 30.00 (*0-9635206-1-X*) Institute NY.
Rolly, Kent, jt. auth. see Valencia, Heather.
Rollyson, Carl. The Arts - Pablo Picasso. LC 92-44757. (Biographies Ser.). (J). 1992. 19.93 (*0-86625-488-9*); 14.95 (*0-685-67772-9*) Rourke Pubns.
— Biography. (Magill Bibliographies Ser.). 215p. 1992. 40.00 (*0-8108-2803-0*) Scarecrow.
Rollyson, Carl E. Marilyn Monroe: A Life of the Actress. LC 86-11322. (Studies in Cinema: No. 39). (Illus.). 269p. reprint ed. pap. 76.70 (*0-8357-1771-2*, 2070520) Bks Demand.
Rollyson, Carl E., Jr. Marilyn Monroe: A Life of the Actress. (Illus.). 269p. 1993. reprint ed. pap. 14.95 (*0-306-80542-1*) Da Capo.
Rollyson, Carl E. Uses of the Past in the Novels of William Faulkner. LC 84-2745. (Studies in Modern Literature: No. 37). 234p. reprint ed. pap. 66.70 (*0-8357-1554-X*, 2070598) Bks Demand.
Rolnick, Philip A. Analogical Possibilities: How Words Refer to God. LC 92-46630. (American Academy of Religion Academy Ser.: No. 81). 328p. 1993. 29.95 (*1-55540-824-9*, 010181); pap. 19.95 (*1-55540-825-7*, 010181) Scholars Pr GA.
Rolnick, William B. The Fundamental Particles & Their Interactions. (Illus.). 544p. (C). 1994. text ed. 60.25 (*0-201-57838-7*) Addison-Wesley.
Rolnick, William B., ed. see American Institute of Physics.
Rol'nik, V. V. Bird Embryology. 386p. 1970. text ed. 102.50 (*0-7065-1014-3*, Pub. by Keter Pub IS) Coronet Bks.
Rolo, Charles J., ed. Psychiatry in American Life. LC 76-156711. (Essay Index Reprint Ser.). 1977. reprint ed. 20.95 (*0-8369-2424-X*) Ayer.
Rolo, Charles J. & Klein, Robert J. Gaining on the Market: Your Complete Guide to Investment Strategy. rev. ed. LC 87-29758. 1988. 18.95 (*0-316-75456-0*) Little.
Rolodex Staff. Rolodex Toll-Free Directory. 1990. 4.95 (*0-87833-719-9*) Taylor Pub.
***Rolof, Marcia C.** Tie the Moon to Your Car: My Cancer, My Way. 1994. 10.95 (*0-533-10890-X*) Vantage.
Roloff, Hans G., ed. see Brant, Sebastian.
Roloff, Hans-Gert, ed. Georg Wickram - Samtliche Werke: Band XIII: Ovids Metamorphosen, 2 vols., Vol. 1. (Ausgaben Deutscher Literatur des XV bis XVIII Jahrhunderts Ser.). iv, 490p. (C). 1990. lib. bdg. 298.50 (*3-11-012121-2*) De Gruyter.
— Georg Wickram - Samtliche Werke: Band XIII: Ovids Metamorphosen, 2 vols., Vol. 2. (Ausgaben Deutscher Literatur des XV bis XVIII Jahrhunderts Ser.). iv, 405p. (C). 1990. lib. bdg. 247.70 (*3-11-012644-3*) De Gruyter.
— Thomas, Naogeorg, Werke, Vol. 1: Tragoedia Nova Pammachius, Mit der Deutschen Uebersetzung des Johann Tyrolff. (Ausgaben Deutscher Literatur des XV bis XVIII Jahrhunderts Ser.). (C). 1974. 426.95 (*3-11-004074-3*) De Gruyter.
Roloff, Hans-Gert, ed. see Czepko, Daniel.
Roloff, Louis. Retinal Nerve Fiber Layer Photography. LC 89-43408. 174p. 1990. 100.00 (*1-55642-161-3*) SLACK Inc.
Roloff, M. Val, ed. Human Risk Assessment: The Roles of Animal Selection & Extrapolation, Proceedings of the Symposium, St. Louis, Missouri, 1985. 280p. 1987. 120.00 (*0-85066-368-7*) Taylor & Francis.
Roloff, Michael, tr. see Handke, Peter.
Roloff, Michael, tr. see Hesse, Hermann.
Roloff, Michael, tr. see Schindel, Robert.
Roloff, Michael, tr. see Skwara, Erich W.
Roloff, Michael, tr. see Zauner, Friedrich C.
Roloff, Michael E. Interpersonal Communication: The Social Exchange Approach. LC 81-4451. (CommText Ser.: Vol. 6). (Illus.). 149p. (C). 1981. 37.00 (*0-8039-1604-3*); pap. 16.95 (*0-8039-1605-1*) Sage.
— Interpersonal Communication: The Social Exchange Approach. LC 81-4451. (Sage Commtext Ser.: No. 6). 151p. reprint ed. pap. 43.10 (*0-7837-1130-1*, 2041660) Bks Demand.
Roloff, Michael E. & Berger, Charles R., eds. Social Cognition & Communication. LC 82-10715. 328p. reprint ed. pap. 93.50 (*0-8357-4850-2*, 2037781) Bks Demand.
Roloff, Michael E. & Miller, Gerald R., eds. Interpersonal Processes: New Directions in Communication Research. (Annual Reviews of Communication Research Ser.: Vol. 14). 304p. 1987. text ed. 52.00 (*0-8039-2654-5*); pap. text ed. 24.00 (*0-8039-2655-3*) Sage.
Roloff, Michael E., jt. auth. see Putnam, Linda L.
Roloff, Nan. Patterns of the Past: A Collection of Current Quilt Designs. Green, Elaine M., ed. LC 92-75415. (Illus.). 60p. (Orig.). 1993. pap. 16.20 (*0-944943-19-5*, CODE 18143-0) Current Inc.
Roloff, Nan & Flynn, Amy. The Bunnies' Easter Bonnet. LC 94-6728. (Illus.). (J). 1994. 2.25 (*0-448-40739-6*, G&D) Putnam Pub Group.
Rolofson, Kristine. Baby Blues. 1994. mass mkt. 2.99 (*0-373-25594-2*, 1-25594-2) Harlequin Bks.
— I'll Be Seeing You: Lovers & Legends. (Temptation Ser.). 1993. mass mkt. 2.99 (*0-373-25569-1*, 1-25569-4) Harlequin Bks.
— Jessie's Lawman. (Temptation Ser.). 1995. mass mkt. 3.25 (*0-373-25648-5*, 1-25648-6) Harlequin Bks.
— Madeleine's Cowboy. (Temptation Ser.). 1994. mass mkt. 2.99 (*0-373-25578-0*, 1-25578-5) Harlequin Bks.
— Make-Believe Honeymoon. 1995. mass mkt. 3.25 (*0-373-25660-4*, 1-25660-1) Harlequin Bks.
Rolofson, Mark, jt. auth. see Hubbel, Peter.
Rolph, Daniel N. To Shoot, Burn & Hang: Folk History from a Kentucky Mountain Family & Community. LC 93-48781. (Illus.). 192p. (C). 1994. text ed. 25.00 (*0-87049-844-4*) U of Tenn Pr.
Rolph, Earl R. The Theory of Fiscal Economics. LC 54-10435. (Publications of the Bureau of Business & Economic Research, University of California, California Library Reprint Ser.). (Illus.). 324p. reprint ed. pap. 92.40 (*0-685-44495-3*, 2031511) Bks Demand.
***Rolph, Elizabeth & Moller, Erik.** Evaluating Agency Alternative Dispute Resolution Programs: A User's Guide to Data Collection & Use. LC 95-3897. (MR-534-ACUS-ICJ Ser.). 104p. 1995. pap. text ed. 13.00 (*0-8330-1630-X*) Rand Corp.
***Rolph, Elizabeth, et al.** Escaping the Courthouse: Private Alternative Dispute Resolution in Los Angeles. LC 94-24074. 1995. write for info. (*0-8330-1611-3*) Rand Corp.
Rolphe, Anne. Generation Without Memory: A Jewish Journey in Christian America. 1989. pap. 8.95 (*0-671-69001-9*) Summit Bks.
Rolshoven, Jurgen & Tietz, Manfred, eds. Pedro Calderon de la Barca: Konkordanz Zu Calderon, Pt. II. Date not set. write for info. (*0-318-71994-0*, Pub. by Georg Olms GW) Lubrecht & Cramer.
Rolski, T. Stationary Random Processes Associated with Point Processses. (Lecture Notes in Statistics Ser.: Vol. 5). 152p. 1981. pap. 34.00 (*0-387-90575-8*) Spr-Verlag.
Rolstad, B., jt. ed. see Fossum, S.
Rolstad, Bent. Natural Immunity to Normal Hemopoietic Cells. 1993. 159.95 (*0-8493-4837-4*, QR185) CRC Pr.
Rolstadaas, A., ed. Computer-Aided Production Management. (IFIP State-of-the-Art Reports). (Illus.). 415p. 1988. 113.00 (*0-387-18748-0*) Spr-Verlag.
***Rolstadas.** Benchmarking. 1995. (*0-412-62680-2*) Chapman & Hall.
— Performance Management. 1995. (*0-412-60560-0*) Chapman & Hall.
Rolstadas, A., jt. ed. see Falster, P.
Rolstadas, A., jt. ed. see Kimura, F.
Rolston, Adam, jt. auth. see Crimp, Douglas.
Rolston, Bill. Politics & Painting: Murals & Conflict in Northern Ireland. LC 89-45981. (Illus.). 1991. 60.00 (*0-8386-3386-2*) Fairleigh Dickinson.
Rolston, Bill & Eggert, Anna, eds. Abortion in the New Europe: A Comparative Handbook. LC 93-44510. 344p. 1994. text ed. 75.00 (*0-313-28723-6*, Greenwood Pr) Greenwood.
Rolston, Bill, jt. auth. see Munck, Ronnie.
Rolston, David L., ed. How to Read the Chinese Novel. (Library of Asian Translations). 464p. (C). 1989. text ed. 67.50 (*0-691-06753-8*) Princeton U Pr.
Rolston, David W. Principles of Artificial Intelligence & Expert Systems Development. (Computing That Works Ser.). 1988. 53.00 (*0-07-053614-7*) McGraw.
Rolston, Dennis E., et al, eds. Agricultural Ecosystem Effects on Trace Gases & Global Climate Change: Proceedings of a Symposium. LC 92-45593. (ASA Special Publication: No. 55). 1993. write for info. (*0-89118-113-X*) Am Soc Agron.
Rolston, Holmes, III. Biology Ethics & the Origin of Life. (Philosophy Ser.). 300p. (C). 1994. pap. text ed. 26.25 (*0-86720-875-9*) Jones & Bartlett.
Rolston, Holmes. Conserving Natural Value. 1994. 45.00 (*0-231-07901-X*); write for info. (*0-231-07900-1*) Col U Pr.
Rolston, Holmes, III. Environmental Ethics: Duties to & Values in the Natural World. (Ethics & Action Ser.). 408p. 1989. 44.95 (*0-87722-501-X*); pap. 19.95 (*0-87722-628-8*) Temple U Pr.
— Philosophy Gone Wild: Environmental Ethics. 2nd ed. 269p. (C). 1989. pap. 18.95 (*0-87975-556-3*) Prometheus Bks.
Rolston, Matthew. Big Pictures. (Illus.). 144p. 1991. 60.00 (*0-8212-1832-8*) Bulfinch Pr.
Rolt, C. E. Dionysius the Areopagite. 225p. 1992. reprint ed. pap. 19.95 (*0-922802-97-1*) Kessinger Pub.
Rolt, Francis. On the Brink in Bengal. (Illus.). 192p. 1992. 39.95 (*0-7195-4907-8*, Pub. by John Murray UK) Trafalgar.
Rolt, L. T. High Horse Riderless. 180p. (Orig.). 1991. pap. 9.95 (*1-870098-14-5*, Pub. by Green Bks UK) Seven Hills Bk.
— Landscape with Canals: The Second Part of His Autobiography. (Illus.). 192p. 1994. pap. 18.00 (*0-86299-141-2*) A Sutton Pub.
— Landscape with Figures: The Final Part of His Autobiography. (Illus.). 256p. 1994. pap. 18.00 (*0-7509-0593-X*) A Sutton Pub.
— Landscape with Machines: The First Part of His Autobiography. (Illus.). 240p. 1994. pap. 18.00 (*0-86299-140-4*) A Sutton Pub.
— The Making of a Railway. (Illus.). 160p. 1990. 28.00 (*0-86299-582-5*) A Sutton Pub.
— Railway Adventure. (Illus.). 192p. 1992. 30.00 (*0-86299-367-9*) A Sutton Pub.
Rolt, Lionel T. George & Robert Stephenson: The Railway Revolution. LC 77-22800. (Illus.). 356p. 1977. reprint ed. text ed. 38.50 (*0-8371-9747-3*, RORR, Greenwood Pr) Greenwood.
Rolt, Sonia, jt. auth. see Rolt, Tom.
Rolt, Tom & Rolt, Sonia. Hold on a Minute. 188p. (C). 1989. 65.00 (*0-947712-14-3*, Pub. by S A Baldwin UK) St Mut.
Rolt-Wheeler, F. Mystic Gleams from the Holy Grail. 1972. 59.95 (*0-8490-0694-5*) Gordon Pr.
Rolte, J., tr. Palatinate-a Full Declaration of the Faith & Ceremonies Professed in the Dominions of Prince Fredericke, 5. Prince Elector Palatine. LC 79-84129. (English Experience Ser.: No. 947). 208p. 1979. reprint ed. lib. bdg. 20.00 (*90-221-0947-X*) Walter J Johnson.
Roltgen, Ingrid, jt. auth. see Muller-Lux, William.
Roluti, Michael J., ed. Waterpower '85, 3 vols., Set. (Conference Proceedings Ser.). 2280p. 1986. 140.00 (*0-87262-536-2*) Am Soc Civil Eng.
Rolvaag, O. E. The Boat of Longing. Solum, Nora O., tr. LC 84-29466. 304p. (C). 1985. reprint ed. pap. 9.95 (*0-87351-184-0*, Borealis Book) Minn Hist.
— Peder Victorious: A Tale of the Pioneers Twenty Years Later. Solum, Nora O., tr. LC 81-16402. xxii, 325p. 1982. reprint ed. pap. 10.95 (*0-8032-8906-5*, Bison Books) U of Nebr Pr.
— Their Fathers' God. Ager, Trygve M., tr. LC 82-17636. x, 338p. 1983. reprint ed. pap. 10.95 (*0-8032-8911-1*, Bison Books) U of Nebr Pr.
Rolvaag, Ole E. The Boat of Longing, a Novel. Solum, Nora O., tr. LC 73-11844. 304p. 1974. reprint ed. text ed. 59.75 (*0-8371-7069-9*, ROBL, Greenwood Pr) Greenwood.
— Giants in the Earth: A Saga of the Prairie. 1965. pap. 7.00 (*0-06-083047-6*, PL) HarpC.
— Peder Victorious. Solum, Nora O., tr. LC 73-11845. 350p. 1973. reprint ed. text ed. 65.00 (*0-8371-7067-2*, ROPV, Greenwood Pr) Greenwood.
— Pure Gold. Erdahl, Sivert, tr. LC 73-11846. 346p. 1973. reprint ed. text ed. 65.00 (*0-8371-7070-2*, ROPG, Greenwood Pr) Greenwood.
Rolwing, Richard J. Israel's Original Sin: A Catholic Confession. 500p. 1994. 74.95 (*1-883255-62-7*); pap. 54.95 (*1-883255-61-9*) Intl Scholars.
Rolzinski, Catherine A., jt. ed. see Charner, Ivan.
Rom, Christine S. Creepy Castles. LC 89-28986. (Incredible Histories Ser.). (Illus.). 48p. (J). (gr. 5-6). 1990. text ed. 11.95 (*0-89686-505-3*, Crstwood Hse) Silver Burdett Pr.
— Everglades. LC 88-18644. (National Parks Ser.). (Illus.). 48p. (J). (gr. 4-5). 1988. text ed. 13.95 (*0-89686-404-9*, Crstwood Hse) Silver Burdett Pr.
Rom, Elena, jt. auth. see Koester, Soia.
Rom, Mark C., jt. auth. see Peterson, Paul E.
Rom, R. & Sidi, M. Multiple Access Protocols: Performance & Analysis. Gerla, M. et al, eds. (Telecommunications Networks & Computer Systems Ser.). (Illus.). viii, 177p. 1990. 43.00 (*0-387-97253-6*) Spr-Verlag.
Rom, Roy C. & Carlson, Robert F., eds. Rootstocks for Fruit Crops. LC 86-15730. 494p. 1987. text ed. 99.95 (*0-471-80551-3*) Wiley.
Rom, Rudolf. Salvador Dali: The Surrealist Angel. rev. ed. LC 85-71012. (Illus.). 181p. 1985. 125.00 (*0-933709-00-5*) deLorenzo diSalvo.
Romack, Janice R. The Glass Jar. LC 93-85311. (Illus.). 40p. (J). (gr. k-3). 1994. 6.95 (*1-55523-643-X*) Winston-Derek.
Romadanov, Alexander. Ozhivi Pokoinika (To Wake the Dead) Roman (A Novel) LC 90-86134. (Illus.). 240p. (Orig.). (RUS.). 1991. pap. text ed. 15.00 (*0-911971-63-7*) Effect Pub.
Romagnano, Lew. Wrestling with Change: The Dilemmas of Teaching Real Mathematics. LC 93-38257. (Illus.). 192p. (J). 1994. pap. text ed. 18.00 (*0-435-08342-2*, 08342) Heinemann.
Romagnesi, H. Les Fondements de la Taxonomie des Rhodophylles et Leur Classification. (Nova Hedwigia Beiheft Ser.: No. 59). (Illus.). 1979. pap. text ed. 15.00 (*3-7682-1191-6*) Lubrecht & Cramer.
— Petit Atlas Des Champignons, 2 vols., Vols. 1 & 2. (Illus.). 1964. 25.00 (*0-934454-91-4*) Lubrecht & Cramer.
Romagnesi, H. & Gilles, G. Les Rhodophylles des Forets Cotieres du Gabon et de la Cote d'Ivoire. (Nova Hedwigia Beiheft Ser.: No. 59). (Illus.). 1979. lib. bdg. 150.00 (*3-7682-5459-3*) Lubrecht & Cramer.
Romagnesi, H., jt. auth. see Kuhner, R.
Romagnesi, Henri. Les Russules d'Europe et d'Afrique du Nord: With English Translation of the Keys by R. W. G. Dennis. (Illus.). 1030p. 1985. reprint ed. lib. bdg. 150.00 (*3-7682-1316-1*) Lubrecht & Cramer.
Romagnoli, G. Franco, jt. auth. see Romagnoli, Margaret O'Neill.
Romagnoli, G. Franco, jt. auth. see Romagnoli, Margaret.
Romagnoli, Margaret. Romagnolis' Italian Fish Cookbook. 1995. pap. 15.95 (*0-8050-2538-3*) H Holt & Co.
Romagnoli, Margaret & Romagnoli, G. Franco. The New Romagnolis' Table: Classic & Contemporary Italian Family Recipes Designed for Today's Faster Pace & Lighter Palate. (Illus.). 320p. 1988. pap. 15.95 (*0-87113-214-1*) Grove-Atltic.
Romagnoli, Margaret O'Neill & Romagnoli, G. Franco. Romagnolis' Italian Fish Cookery: A Large Embrace & A Light Touch. LC 93-21633. 1994. 25.00 (*0-8050-2526-X*) H Holt & Co.
***Romagnoli, Maureen S.** Manchester Children's Directory. rev. ed. 75p. 1995. pap. 5.95 (*0-9645068-0-7*) Romagnoli.
***Romain, A.** German-English Dictionary of Legal & Commercial Terms. 3rd ed. 939p. (ENG & GER.). 1994. write for info. (*0-7859-8762-2*) Fr & Eur.
— German-English Dictionary of Legal & Commercial Terms. 3rd rev. ed. 939p. (ENG & GER.). 1994. 125.00x (*3-406-35836-5*, Pub. by BCH Verlag GW) IBD Ltd.
Romain, Alfred. Dictionary of German & English Legal & Economic Terminology: Woerterbuch der Rechtssprache und Wirtschaftssprache, Vol. 1. 4th ed. 854p. (ENG & GER.). 1989. 225.00 (*0-8288-0393-5*, M 7101) Fr & Eur.
— Dictionary of German & English Legal & Economic Terminology: Woerterbuch der Rechtssprache und Wirtschaftssprache, Vol. 2. 2nd ed. 882p. (ENG & GER.). 1985. 225.00 (*0-8288-0394-3*, M7100) Fr & Eur.
Romain, E. & Colby, F. Let's Go Dancing: Introduction to Social Dancing. 1984. lib. bdg. 79.95 (*0-87700-513-3*) Revisionist Pr.
Romain, Effie, jt. auth. see Brown, Kathleen.
Romain, Elizabeth, ed. Popular Variations in Latin-American Dancing. 1984. lib. bdg. 79.95 (*0-87700-514-1*) Revisionist Pr.
Romain, Joseph. Hockey Superstars. 1991. 9.98 (*0-8317-4508-8*) Smithmark.
— Pictorial History Hockey. (Illus.). 176p. 1994. 19.98 (*0-8317-6805-3*) Smithmark.
— Two Minutes for Roughing. (J). (gr. 3-8). 1995. pap. 8.95 (*1-55028-458-4*); bds. 16.95 (*1-55028-459-2*) Formac Dist Ltd.
Romain, Michael, ed. A Profile of Jonathan Miller. (Illus.). 272p. (C). 1991. 64.95 (*0-521-40137-2*); pap. 19.95 (*0-521-40953-5*) Cambridge U Pr.
***Romain, Simon.** How to Live Safely in a Dangerous World: The Essential, Practical Guide. (Illus.). 121p. 1995. pap. 8.95 (*0-86051-723-3*, Robson-Parkwest) Parkwest Pubns.
Romain, Trevor. The Big Cheese. (Illus.). 32p. (Orig.). (J). (ps-3). 1992. pap. 5.25 (*1-880092-00-X*) Bright Bks TX.
— The Boy Who Swallowed a Rainbow. (Illus.). 32p. (J). (ps-5). 1993. 13.95 (*1-880092-05-0*) Bright Bks TX.
— How to Go to Bed with an Elephant in Your Head. (Illus.). 32p. (J). (ps-5). 1996. 13.95 (*1-880092-10-7*) Bright Bks TX.
— The Keeper of the Dreams. (Illus.). 32p. (J). (ps-5). 1992. 13.50 (*1-880092-03-4*) Bright Bks TX.

— The Little People's Guide to the Big World Vol. 1. (Illus.). 48p. (J). (ps-5). 1993. 13.95 (1-880092-04-2) Bright Bks TX.
— The Little People's Guide to the Big World Vol. 1, Vol. 2. (Illus.). 32p. (J). (ps-5). 1994. 13.95 (1-880092-16-6) Bright Bks TX.
— The Little People's Guide to the Big World Vol. 3. (Illus.). 32p. (J). (gr. 5). 1995. 13.95 (1-880092-24-7) Bright Bks TX.
— The Other Side of the Invisible Fence. Willerman, Benne, ed. 96p. (J). (gr. 3-11). 1994. pap. 7.95 (1-880092-17-4) Bright Bks TX.
— The Silent Voice. 32p. (J). (gr. k-5). 1995. 13.95 (1-880092-23-9) Bright Bks TX.
— There's a Lady in the Attic & I Don't Like Her Face. (Illus.). 32p. (J). (ps-5). 1996. 13.95 (1-880092-07-7) Bright Bks TX.
— Under the Big Sky. (Illus.). 64p. (YA). (gr. 5-12). 1994. 13.95 (1-880092-13-1) Bright Bks TX.
— Where the Moonbeams Waltz. (Illus.). 32p. (J). (gr. k-5). 1996. 13.95 (1-880092-09-3) Bright Bks TX.
Romaine. Pidgin & Creole Languages. (Linguistics Library). (Illus.). 376p. (C). 1988. text ed. 39.95 (0-582-01474-3, 71828); pap. text ed. 20.95 (0-582-29647-1, 71828) Longman.
Romaine-Davis, Ada. John Gibbon & His Heart-Lung Machine. LC 91-40290. (Illus.). 278p. (C). 1992. text ed. 39.95 (0-8122-3073-6) U of Pa Pr.
Romaine-Davis, Ada, et al. Encyclopedia of Home Care for the Elderly. LC 94-17989. 456p. 1995. text ed. 85.00 (0-313-28532-2, Greenwood Pr) Greenwood.
Romaine, Lawrence B. Guide to American Trade Catalogs, 1744-1900. 1990. pap. 12.95 (0-486-26475-0) Dover.
— A Guide to American Trade Catalogs, 1744-1900. LC 75-22839. (America in Two Centuries Ser.). 1976. reprint ed. 37.95 (0-405-07710-6) Ayer.
Romaine, Mary L., ed. see Waymer, Bob.
Romaine, Suzanne. Bilingualism. (Language in Society Ser.). (Illus.). 384p. 1989. pap. text ed. 19.95 (0-631-15226-1) Blackwell Pubs.
— Bilingualism. 2nd ed. LC 94-9462. (Language in Society Ser.: Vol. 13). 416p. 1994. pap. 24.95 (0-631-19539-4) Blackwell Pubs.
— Language, Education, & Development: Urban & Rural Tok Pisin in Papua New Guinea. (Oxford Studies in Language Contact). (Illus.). 416p. 1992. 89.00 (0-19-823966-1) OUP.
— Language in Society: An Introduction to Sociolinguistics. (Illus.). 256p. 1994. pap. 9.95 (0-19-875134-6) OUP.
Romaine, Suzanne, ed. Language in Australia. (Illus.). 384p. (C). 1991. 89.95 (0-521-32786-5) Cambridge U Pr.
Romains, Jules. Amities et Rencontres. 231p. (FRE.). 1970. pap. 17.95 (0-7859-1412-9, 2080604899) Fr & Eur.
— Le Besoin de Voir Clair. 256p. (FRE.). 1958. pap. 10.95 (0-7859-1394-7, 2080505890) Fr & Eur.
— Body's Rapture. (Black & Gold Library). 1937. 7.95 (0-87140-855-4) Liveright.
— Boen Ou la Possession des Biens. 160p. (FRE.). 1959. pap. 10.95 (0-7859-1311-4, 2070255247) Fr & Eur.
— Choix de Poemes. 286p. (FRE.). 1948. pap. 10.95 (0-7859-1309-2, 2070255220) Fr & Eur.
— Les Copains. (FRE.). 1982. pap. 10.95 (0-7859-3987-3) Fr & Eur.
— Les Copains. (Folio Ser.: No. 182). 160p. (FRE.). 1972. pap. 6.95 (2-07-036182-9) Schoenhof.
— Le Couple France-Allemagne. 140p. (FRE.). 1965. pap. 10.95 (0-7859-1597-4, 208050794X) Fr & Eur.
— Cromedeyre le Vieil. 172p. (FRE.). 1926. pap. 11.95 (0-7859-1392-0, 2080255093) Fr & Eur.
— Le Dieu des Corps. 244p. (FRE.). 1928. pap. 10.95 (0-7859-1306-8, 2070255123) Fr & Eur.
— Donogoo Tonga: Avec: Le Bourg Regenere. 246p. (FRE.). 1920. pap. 18.95 (0-7859-1308-4, 2070255190) Fr & Eur.
— Examen de Conscience des Francais. 168p. (FRE.). 1954. pap. 10.95 (0-7859-1395-5, 2080505904) Fr & Eur.
— Eyeless Sight. 1978. pap. 4.95 (0-8065-0632-6, Citadel Pr) Carol Pub Group.
— Le Fils de Jerphanion. 320p. (FRE.). 1956. pap. 10.95 (0-7859-1396-3, 2080505912) Fr & Eur.
— Un Grand Honnete Homme. 268p. 4.95 (0-686-55309-8) Fr & Eur.
— Les Hauts et les Bas de la Liberte. 272p. (FRE.). 1960. pap. 10.95 (0-7859-1397-1, 2080505920) Fr & Eur.
— L' Homme Blanc. 144p. (FRE.). 1953. pap. 10.95 (0-7859-1398-X, 2080505939) Fr & Eur.
— Hommes, Medecins, Machines. 256p. (FRE.). 1959. pap. 10.95 (0-7859-1399-8, 2080505947) Fr & Eur.
— Jean le Maufranc. 176p. (FRE.). 1959. pap. 10.95 (0-7859-1310-6, 2070255239) Fr & Eur.
— Knock. (Folio Ser.: No. 60). 1972. pap. 6.95 (2-07-036060-1) Schoenhof.
— Knock ou le Triomphe de la Medecine. (FRE.). 1972. pap. 10.95 (0-7859-2857-X, 2070360601) Fr & Eur.
— Lettre Ouverte Contre une Vaste Conspiration. 176p. (FRE.). 1965. pap. 10.95 (0-7859-5472-4) Fr & Eur.
— Lettres a un Ami, 1. 238p. (FRE.). 1964. pap. 4.95 (0-686-55316-0, 2080506137) Fr & Eur.
— Lettres a un Ami, 2. 238p. (FRE.). 1964. pap. 10.95 (0-7859-1400-5) Fr & Eur.
— Lucienne. (Folio Ser.: No. 1671). 280p. (FRE.). 1922. 14.95 (2-07-037671-0) Schoenhof.
— Lucienne - le Dieu des Corps Quand le Navire: Psyche I, II, III. (FRE.). 1985. pap. 18.95 (0-7859-4228-9) Fr & Eur.
— Marc Aurele. 252p. (FRE.). 1968. pap. 16.95 (0-7859-1411-0, 2080603620) Fr & Eur.
— Le Mariage de M. le Trouhadec. 160p. (FRE.). 1959. pap. 10.95 (0-7859-1313-0, 2070255271) Fr & Eur.
— Memoires de Madame Chauverel, 2 vols. 304p. (FRE.). 1959. pap. 10.95 (0-7859-1640-7, 2080505955) Fr & Eur.
— Memoires de Madame Chauverel, 2 vols., Set. 304p. (FRE.). 1959. pap. 10.95 (0-7859-1642-3, 2080505963) Fr & Eur.
— Mission a Rome. (Illus.). 356p. (FRE.). 1958. pap. 14.95 (0-7859-1402-1, 2080506161) Fr & Eur.
— Monsieur le Trouhadec Saisi Par la Debauche. 160p. (FRE.). 1975. pap. 10.95 (0-7859-1371-8, 2070366510) Fr & Eur.
— Mort de Quelqu'un. (Folio Ser.: No. 1882). 160p. (FRE.). 1970. pap. 6.95 (2-07-037882-9) Schoenhof.
— Le Moulin et l'Hospice. 240p. (FRE.). 1950. pap. 10.95 (0-7859-1596-6, 208050617X) Fr & Eur.
— Musse ou l'Ecole de l'Hypocrisie. 144p. (FRE.). 1959. pap. 10.95 (0-7859-1312-2, 2070255255) Fr & Eur.
— Odes et Prieres. 176p. (FRE.). 1923. pap. 10.95 (0-7859-1304-1, 2070255026) Fr & Eur.
— Paul Landowski, la Main et L'Esprit: Le Main et l'Esprit. 308p. 39.50 (0-686-55328-4) Fr & Eur.
— Pieces en un Acte: Avec: La Scintillante, Amedes et les Messieurs en rang. 176p. (FRE.). 1930. pap. 10.95 (0-7859-1307-6, 2070255166) Fr & Eur.
— Portraits d'Inconnue. 240p. (FRE.). 1962. pap. 10.95 (0-7859-1620-2, 208050620X) Fr & Eur.
— Pour Raison Garder, 3 vols., 1. 272p. (FRE.). 1967. pap. 10.95 (0-7859-1408-0, 2080507486) Fr & Eur.
— Pour Raison Garder, 3 vols., 2. 272p. (FRE.). 1967. pap. 13.95 (0-7859-1409-9, 2080602098) Fr & Eur.
— Pour Raison Garder, 3 vols., 3. 272p. (FRE.). 1967. pap. 13.95 (0-7859-1410-2, 2080602101) Fr & Eur.
— Recherche d'une Eglise. 192p. (FRE.). 1962. pap. 10.95 (0-7859-1403-X, 2080506226) Fr & Eur.
— Saints de Notre Calendrier. 256p. (FRE.). 1952. pap. 10.95 (0-7859-1404-8, 2080506234) Fr & Eur.
— Seven Mysteries of Europe. Bree, Germaine, tr. LC 78-152210. (Essay Index Reprint Ser.). 1977. reprint ed. 20.95 (0-8369-2294-8) Ayer.
— Situation de la Terre. 244p. (FRE.). 1958. pap. 10.95 (0-7859-1405-6, 2080506242) Fr & Eur.
— Verdun. 376p. (FRE.). 1964. pap. 17.95 (0-7859-1598-2, 208060211X) Fr & Eur.
— Le Vin Blanc de la Villette. 224p. (FRE.). 1923. pap. 10.95 (0-7859-1305-X, 2070255034) Fr & Eur.
— Violations de Frontieres. 288p. (FRE.). 1951. pap. 10.95 (0-7859-1406-4, 2080506277) Fr & Eur.
Romaji Kai, Hyojun. All-Romanized English-Japanese Dictionary. 9th ed. 732p. (ENG & JPN.). 1980. pap. 14.95 (0-8288-1611-5, M9548) Fr & Eur.
Romalov, Nancy T., jt. ed. see Dyer, Carolyn S.
Roman, Agnes, jt. auth. see Lasker, Bruno.
Roman, Alfred. The Military Operations of General Beauregard: In the War Between the States, 1861 to 1865, 2 Vols., I. (Illus.). 1994. reprint ed. write for info. (0-306-80546-4) Da Capo.
— The Military Operations of General Beauregard: In the War Between the States, 1861 to 1865, 2 Vols., II. (Illus.). 1994. reprint ed. write for info. (0-306-80547-2) Da Capo.
— The Military Operations of General Beauregard: In the War Between the States, 1861 to 1865, 2 Vols., Set. (Illus.). 1994. reprint ed. pap. 17.95 (0-306-80551-0) Da Capo.
Roman, Beverly. The Graduate's Handbook: Surviving Successfully & Happily on Your Own after College. Brisco, Paula J., ed. LC 92-97493. (Illus.). 64p. 1992. pap. 10.00 (0-9627470-4-1) BR Anchor.
***Roman, Beverly D.** Let's Make a Move! A Creative Visualization Activity Book for Children. Lawson, Cathleen, ed. (Illus.). 32p. (J). (gr. 1-8). 1995. pap. 4.95 (0-9627470-7-6) BR Anchor.
— Let's Make a Move with American Red Ball World Wide Movers: A Creative Visualization Activity Book for Children. Lawson, Cathie, ed. (Illus.). 32p. (Orig.). (J). (gr. 1-8). 1995. pap. write for info. (0-9627470-6-8) BR Anchor.
— Moving Minus Mishaps: A Practical Guide for Successful Family Relocation Including Foreign & Domestic Moves. rev. ed. Brisco, Paula J., ed. LC 92-90346. (Illus.). 152p. (Orig.). 1992. pap. 12.95 (0-9627470-3-3) BR Anchor.
— When in Rome... Living & Working in a Foreign Country. Lawson, Cathleen, ed. LC 93-90795. (Personal & Professional Management Ser.). (Illus.). 96p. (Orig.). 1993. pap. text ed. 12.95 (0-9627470-5-X) BR Anchor.
Roman, Bruce W., jt. auth. see Monet, Gabriel.
Roman, Camille, et al, eds. The Women & Language Debate: A Sourcebook. LC 93-7642. 500p. (C). 1993. text ed. 48.00 (0-8135-2011-8); pap. text ed. 18.00 (0-8135-2012-6) Rutgers U Pr.
Roman, Camille P., jt. auth. see Brandler, Sondra.
Roman, Carlos, ed. Almanaque Mundial, 1988. LC 55-22432. (Illus.). (Orig.). (SPA.). 1986. pap. text ed. 6.00 (0-944499-07-4) Editorial Amer.
— Almanaque Mundial, 1990. (Illus.). 592p. (Orig.). (SPA.). 1989. pap. 6.00 (0-944499-61-9) Editorial Amer.
— Almanaque Mundial, 1991. (Illus.). 608p. (Orig.). (SPA.). 1990. pap. write for info. (0-944499-85-6) Editorial Amer.
— Almanaque Mundial, 1994. (Illus.). 592p. (SPA.). 1993. pap. 6.00 (1-56259-026-X) Editorial Amer.
— Almanaque Universal 1990. (Illus.). 608p. (Orig.). (SPA.). 1989. pap. 6.00 (0-944499-65-1) Editorial Amer.
— Almanaque Universal 1991. (Illus.). 608p. (Orig.). (SPA.). 1990. pap. write for info. (0-944499-86-4) Editorial Amer.
— Quince Mil Nuevas Minibiografias. (Illus.). 608p. (Orig.). (SPA.). 1989. pap. 5.95 (0-944499-26-0) Editorial Amer.
Roman, Carlos, ed. see Editorial America, S. A. Staff.
Roman, Carlos, ed. see Lebelson, Harry & Rush, Bette.
Roman, Charles V. American Civilization & the Negro. LC 74-37316. (Black Heritage Library Collection). 1977. reprint ed. 39.95 (0-8369-8953-8) Ayer.
— Meharry Medical College. LC 71-38019. (Black Heritage Library Collection). 1977. reprint ed. 26.95 (0-8369-8986-4) Ayer.
Roman Corporation Staff, ed. see Roman, Dan.
Roman, D. Project Management. 240p. 1985. 42.25 (0-444-00966-3) P-H.
Roman, D. D. & Puett, J. F. International Business & Technological Innovation. 498p. 1982. 53.50 (0-444-00715-6, North Holland) Elsevier.
Roman-D'Amat, Jean-Claude, jt. auth. see Prevost, Michel.
Roman-D'Amat, Jean-Claude, jt. auth. see Prevot, Floriane.
Roman, Dan. D A N: A Man Without Youth. LC 87-50276. 416p. 1987. write for info. (0-9618449-0-6) Teneco Corp.
— The Satanic Conspiracy, Pts. 1 & 2: A Man Without Youth & A Dead Man Alive. Roman Corporation Staff, ed. LC 90-91755. 612p. 1990. write for info. (0-9627447-0-0) Roman Corp.
***Roman, Daniel.** Asi Era Cuba. LC 94-61122. (Coleccion Caniqui). 160p. (Orig.). (SPA.). 1994. pap. 16.00 (0-89729-760-1) Ediciones.
— Managing Projects: A System Approach. pap. text ed. 39.00 (0-13-116238-1) P-H.
— Los Seis Grandes Errores de Marti. LC 93-70879. (Coleccion Cuba y Sus Jueces Ser.). 181p. (Orig.). (SPA.). 1993. pap. 18.00 (0-89729-679-6) Ediciones.
Roman de Bera, P. Diccionario Castellano-Vasco. 4th ed. 524p. (BAQ & SPA.). 1975. 39.95 (0-8288-5804-7, S50440) Fr & Eur.
Roman, Ernan. Integrated Direct Marketing: Techniques & Strategies for Success. 2nd ed. Knudsen, Anne, ed. LC 94-17508. (International Business Culture Ser.). 1995. 45.00 (0-8442-3349-8, NTC Busn Bks) NTC Pub Grp.
Roman, Eva. Art of Dictation. (Illus.). 135p. 1971. pap. 11.95 (0-8464-1077-X) Beekman Pubs.
— Skills of Dictation. (Illus.). 128p. 1990. pap. text ed. 11.95 (0-566-02908-1, Pub. by Gower UK) Ashgate Pub Co.
Roman, Frank. El Apocalipsis Al Descubierto: Revelation Unveiled. (SPA.). 4.95 (84-7645-424-4, 223548, Pub. by Edit Clie SP) TSELF.
Roman, G. Martin. How to Maximize Your Job Security: By Knowing Your Employment Rights. 165p. 1992. pap. text ed. 19.95 (0-9635073-0-3) Employ Rights.
Roman, Gail H. & Marquardt, Virginia H., eds. The Avant-Garde Frontier: Russia Meets the West, 1910-1930. LC 92-11323. (Illus.). 320p. 1992. lib. bdg. 49.95 (0-8130-1157-4) U Press Fla.
Roman, Harry T. Building Internal Team-Partnerships: Engineers Guide to Business Series. LC 93-2702. 1993. 19.95 (0-7803-0365-2, HL0465-5) Inst Electrical.
Roman, Herschel L., et al, eds. Annual Review of Genetics, Vol. 1. LC 67-29891. (Illus.). 1967. 40.00 (0-8243-1201-5) Annual Reviews.
— Annual Review of Genetics, Vol. 2. LC 67-29891. (Illus.). 1968. 40.00 (0-8243-1202-3) Annual Reviews.
— Annual Review of Genetics, Vol. 3. LC 67-29891. (Illus.). 1969. 40.00 (0-8243-1203-1) Annual Reviews.
— Annual Review of Genetics, Vol. 4. LC 67-29891. (Illus.). 1970. 40.00 (0-8243-1204-X) Annual Reviews.
— Annual Review of Genetics, Vol. 5. LC 67-29891. (Illus.). 1971. 40.00 (0-8243-1205-8) Annual Reviews.
— Annual Review of Genetics, Vol. 6. LC 67-29891. (Illus.). 1972. text ed. 40.00 (0-8243-1206-6) Annual Reviews.
— Annual Review of Genetics, Vol. 7. LC 67-29891. (Illus.). 1973. text ed. 40.00 (0-8243-1207-4) Annual Reviews.
— Annual Review of Genetics, Vol. 8. LC 67-29891. (Illus.). 1974. text ed. 40.00 (0-8243-1208-2) Annual Reviews.
— Annual Review of Genetics, Vol. 9. LC 67-29891. (Illus.). 1975. text ed. 40.00 (0-8243-1209-0) Annual Reviews.
— Annual Review of Genetics, Vol. 10. LC 67-29891. (Illus.). 1976. text ed. 40.00 (0-8243-1210-4) Annual Reviews.
— Annual Review of Genetics, Vol. 11. LC 67-29891. (Illus.). 1977. text ed. 40.00 (0-8243-1211-2) Annual Reviews.
— Annual Review of Genetics, Vol. 12. LC 67-29891. (Illus.). 1978. text ed. 40.00 (0-8243-1212-0) Annual Reviews.
— Annual Review of Genetics, Vol. 14. LC 67-29891. (Illus.). 1980. text ed. 40.00 (0-8243-1214-7) Annual Reviews.
— Annual Review of Genetics, Vol. 15. LC 67-29891. (Illus.). 1981. text ed. 40.00 (0-8243-1215-5) Annual Reviews.
— Annual Review of Genetics, Vol. 16. LC 67-29891. (Illus.). 1982. text ed. 40.00 (0-8243-1216-3) Annual Reviews.
— Annual Review of Genetics, Vol. 17. LC 67-29891. (Illus.). 1983. text ed. 40.00 (0-8243-1217-1) Annual Reviews.
— Annual Review of Genetics, Vol. 18. LC 67-29891. (Illus.). 1984. text ed. 40.00 (0-8243-1218-X) Annual Reviews.
Roman, I., jt. auth. see Baum, H.
Roman, Jose M. Enciclopedia de la Cocina: Encyclopedia of Cooking, 3 vols. 6th ed. 824p. (SPA.). 1986. pap. 325.00 (0-7859-5074-5) Fr & Eur.
Roman, Joseph. King Philip. (North American Indians of Achievement Ser.). (Illus.). 112p. (YA). (gr. 5 up). 1992. lib. bdg. 17.95 (0-7910-1704-4) Chelsea Hse.
— Octavio Paz: Mexican Poet & Critic. LC 92-47051. (Hispanics of Achievement Ser.). (Illus.). (J). 1994. lib. bdg. 18.95 (0-7910-1249-2, Am Art Analog); pap. write for info. (0-7910-1276-X, Am Art Analog) Chelsea Hse.
— Pablo Neruda. (Hispanics of Achievement Ser.). (Illus.). (YA). (gr. 5 up). 1992. lib. bdg. 17.95 (0-7910-1248-4) Chelsea Hse.
Roman, Judith A. Annie Adams Fields: The Spirit of Charles Street. LC 89-46328. (Illus.). 204p. 1991. 27.95 (0-253-35022-0) Ind U Pr.
Roman, Kenneth. How to Advertise: Expanded, Updated, & Completely Revised for the 90's. 1992. 21.95 (0-312-07789-0, Pub. by Thomas Dunne Bks) St Martin.
— Writing That Works. 1994. pap. 4.99 (0-06-109381-5, Harp PBks) HarpC.
Roman, Kenneth & Maas, Jane. The New How to Advertise. pap. text ed. write for info. (0-7494-0843-X, Pub. by Kogan Page Educ UK) Taylor & Francis.
— The New How to Advertise. 2nd ed. LC 92-61005. (Illus.). 193p. (C). 1992. pap. text ed. 14.00 (0-312-08352-1) St Martin.
— The New How to Advertise: Expanded, Updated, & Completely Revised for the '90s. (Illus.). 192p. 1992. 22.95 (0-685-52426-4, Pub. by Thomas Dunne Bks) St Martin.
Roman, Kenneth & Raphaelson, Joel. Writing That Works. enl. rev. ed. LC 91-58285. 144p. 1992. pap. 10.00 (0-06-273144-0, HarpT) HarpC.
Roman-Lagunas, Jorge. The Chilean Novel: A Critical Study of Its Secondary Sources & a Bibliography. LC 94-4566. 1994. write for info. (0-8108-2868-5) Scarecrow.
Roman-Lagunas, Jorge, ed. La Literatura Centroamericana: Visiones y Revisiones. LC 94-5647. 364p. (SPA.). 1994. text ed. 99.95 (0-7734-9082-5) E Mellen.
Roman-Lagunas, Jorge, jt. ed. see Promis, Jose.
Roman, Lawrence. Under the Yum Yum Tree. 1961. pap. 4.75 (0-8222-1195-5) Dramatists Play.
Roman, Leslie G., jt. ed. see Dworkin, Dennis L.
Roman, Leslie G., et al, eds. Becoming Feminine: The Politics of Popular Culture. 230p. 1988. 65.00 (1-85000-328-9, Falmer Pr); pap. 29.00 (1-85000-329-7, Falmer Pr) Taylor & Francis.
Roman, Lewis. Principate. 1973. 20.00 (0-88866-574-1) Edgar Kent.
Roman, Margaret. Sarah Orne Jewett: Reconstructing Gender. LC 90-20598. 264p. 1992. 28.95 (0-8173-0533-5) U of Ala Pr.
***Roman, Michael.** Black September. 350p. 1995. pap. 9.95 (1-56901-547-3) NW Pub.
Roman, Michael & Weingrod, Alex. Living Together Separately: Arabs & Jews in Contemporary Jerusalem. (Near East Studies). 270p. 1991. text ed. 24.95 (0-691-09455-1) Princeton U Pr.
Roman, Michael, ed. see Splaver, Bernard.
Roman, Murray. Telephone Marketing Techniques. LC 78-32000. (AMA Management Briefing Ser.). 34p. reprint ed. pap. 25.00 (0-317-09567-6, 2051565) Bks Demand.
Roman, Nat. Why Can't We Say Goodbye? 516p. 1981. pap. 16.95 (0-686-32931-7) Roman Enter.
Roman, O. V., jt. ed. see Arunachalam, V. S.
Roman, Paul M. Alcohol: The Development of Sociological Perspectives on Use & Abuse. 401p. 1991. 27.95 (0-911290-23-0) Rutgers Ctr Alcohol.
— Some Modern Mathematics for Physicists & Other Outsiders, Vol. 2: Introduction to Algebra, Topology, & Functional Analysis. LC 75-101. 1975. 140.00 (0-08-018134-1, Pub. by Pergamon Repr UK) Franklin.
Roman, Paul M., ed. Alcohol Problem Intervention in the Workplace: Employee Assistance Programs & Strategic Alternatives. LC 89-27239. 448p. 1990. text ed. 89.50 (0-89930-459-1, RAD/, Quorum Bks) Greenwood.
Roman, Paul M., jt. ed. see Macdonald, Scott.
Roman, Paul M., jt. auth. see Trice, Harrison M.
***Roman, Peter J.** Eisenhower & the Missile Gap. (Studies in Security Affairs). (Illus.). 280p. 1996. 35.00 (0-8014-2797-5) Cornell U Pr.
Roman, Robert. Survival 21: Futurology for the 21st Century. 17.50 (0-912314-00-1) Academy Santa Clara.
Roman, Sanaya. Living with Joy: Keys to Personal Power & Spiritual Transformation. Ratner, Elaine, ed. LC 86-80207. (Earth Life Ser.: Bk. I). 216p. (Orig.). 1986. pap. 10.95 (0-915811-03-0) H J Kramer Inc.
— Personal Power Through Awareness: A Guidebook for Sensitive People. Ratner, Elaine, ed. (Earth Life Ser.: Bk. II). 216p. 1986. pap. 10.95 (0-915811-04-9) H J Kramer Inc.
— Spiritual Growth: Being Your Higher Self. Ratner, Elaine, ed. LC 88-81721. (Earth Life Ser.: Bk. III). 252p. 1989. pap. 10.95 (0-915811-12-X) H J Kramer Inc.
Roman, Sanaya & Packer, Duane. Creating Money: Keys to Abundance. Ratner, Elaine, ed. (Life Mastery Ser.). 288p. 1988. pap. 12.95 (0-915811-09-X) H J Kramer Inc.
— Opening to Channel: How to Connect with Your Guide. Armstrong, Gregory, ed. (Birth into Light Ser.). 252p. (Orig.). 1987. pap. 12.95 (0-915811-05-7) H J Kramer Inc.
Roman, Santa I. Quien Era Ella? (Romance Real Ser.). 192p. (SPA.). 1981. pap. 1.50 (0-88025-005-4) Roca Pub.
Roman, Stephan. The Development of Islamic Library Collections in Western Europe & North America. 272p. 1990. text ed. 100.00 (0-7201-2065-9, Mansell Pub) Cassell.
Roman, Steven. Advanced Linear Algebra. LC 92-11860. (Graduate Texts in Mathematics Ser.: Vol. 135). (Illus.). xii, 363p. 1992. 49.90 (0-387-97837-2) Spr-Verlag.
— College Algebra. 526p. (C). 1987. student ed. pap. text ed. 17.00 (0-15-507892-5) SCP.
— College Algebra. 526p. (C). 1988. text ed. 43.00 (0-15-507890-9); pap. text ed. 8.25 (0-15-507891-7) SCP.
— College Algebra & Trigonometry. 702p. (C). 1987. teacher ed write for info. (0-15-507914-X); text ed. 41.25 (0-15-507911-5); student ed. pap. text ed. 17.00 (0-15-507913-1) SCP.

R

An Asterisk (*) at the beginning of an entry indicates that the title is appearing in BIP for the first time.

— Field Theory. LC 94-36400. (Graduate Texts in Mathematics Ser: Vol. 158). 1994. 59.00 (*0-387-94407-9*); pap. 29.00 (*0-387-94408-7*) Spr-Verlag.

— An Introduction to Discrete Mathematics. 2nd ed. 469p. (C). 1989. text ed. 51.00 (*0-15-541730-4*); pap. text ed. 28.50 (*0-15-541732-0*) SCP.

— An Introduction to Discrete Mathematics. 2nd suppl. ed. 469p. (C). 1989. write for info. (*0-318-64380-4*) SCP.

— An Introduction to Linear Algebra with Applications. 2nd ed. 504p. (C). 1988. teacher ed write for info. (*0-15-542737-7*); text ed. 48.00 (*0-15-542736-9*) SCP.

— Precalculus. 672p. (C). 1987. text ed. 47.00 (*0-15-571052-4*); Instr's. manual with tests. teacher ed write for info. (*0-15-571055-9*) SCP.

— Precalculus. 672p. (C). 1987. Student solution manual. student ed, text ed. 17.00 (*0-15-571054-0*) SCP.

— Supplement to Accompany Discrete Mathematics. 2nd ed. (C). 1989. text ed. 65.25 (*0-15-541733-9*) SCP.

— The Umbral Calculus. LC 83-11940. (Pure & Applied Mathematics Ser.). 1983. text ed. 75.00 (*0-12-594380-6*) Acad Pr.

Roman, Steven, et al. Coding & Information Theory. Ewing, J. H. et al, eds. (Graduate Texts in Mathematics Ser.: Vol. 134). (Illus.). 496p. 1992. 49.95 (*0-387-97812-7*) Spr-Verlag.

Roman, Susan, ed. see Association for Library Service to Children Staff.

Roman, Trish F. Voices under One Sky: Contemporary Native Literature. LC 94-12477. 224p. 1994. pap. 12.95 (*0-89594-720-X*) Crossing Pr.

Roman, Z. Industrial Development & Industrial Policy. 426p. 1979. 100.00 (*0-317-53877-2*, Pub. by Collets UK) Pro-Am Music.

Roman, Zoltan. Gustav Mahler & Hungary, No. 5. (Studies in Central & Eastern European Music: No. 5). 255p. 1991. 126.00 (*963-05-5609-X*, Pub. by Akad Kiado HU) St Mut.

— Gustav Mahler's American Years 1907-1911. LC 88-18639. (Illus.). 530p. 1989. lib. bdg. 62.00 (*0-918728-73-8*) Pendragon NY.

— Productivity & Economic Growth. 276p. 1982. 47.50 (*0-685-17058-6*, Pub. by Collets UK) Pro-Am Music.

Romana, M., ed. Rock Mechanics & Power Plants: Proceedings of the ISRM Symposium, 12-16 September, 1988, 2 vols., Set. 900p. (C). 1988. text ed. 195.00 (*90-6191-827-8*, Pub. by A A Balkema NE) Ashgate Pub Co.

Romanach, Julio, Jr. Dictionary of Legal Terms - Spanish-English - English-Spanish: Diccionario de Terminos Juridicos - Espanol-Ingles - Ingles-Espanol. 216p. 1992. pap. text ed. 34.50 (*0-9633610-0-7*) Lawrence LA.

***Romanach, Julio, Jr., tr.** Civil Code of Spain. 521p. 1994. pap. text ed. 65.00 (*0-9633610-1-5*) Lawrence LA.

***Romanack, Mark.** Advanced Walleye Strategies. LC 92-62042. (Complete Angler's Library). 250p. 1993. write for info. (*0-914697-52-8*) N Amer Outdoor Grp.

Romance, Trisha. The World of Trisha Romance. (Illus.). 160p. 1992. 40.00 (*0-670-84201-X*, Viking Studio) Studio Bks.

Romanch, Pedro, tr. see Shepard, Martin.

Romanchik, Brenda. A Birthmother's Book of Memories. 60p. 1994. 15.95 (*0-9641035-2-4*) R-Squared Pr.

Romanczyk. Clinical Utilization of Microcomputer. (C). 1986. pap. 19.95 (*0-205-14468-3*, H4468) Allyn.

Romanczyk, Raymond G. & Lockshin, Stephanie. How to Create a Curriculum for Autistic & Other Handicapped Children. (Teaching the Autistic Ser.). 46p. 1981. pap. 8.00 (*0-89079-057-4*, 1038) PRO-ED.

Romand, Didier & Schurr, Gerald. Le Dictionnaire du Marche de l'Art: Dictionary of the Art market. 416p. (FRE.). 1978. pap. 95.00 (*0-8288-5193-X*, M6490) Fr & Eur.

Romand, J., jt. auth. see Vodar, Boris.

Romane, F., et al, eds. Quercus Ilex L. Ecosystems: Function, Dynamics, & Management. LC 92-13699. (Advances in Vegetation Science Ser.: Vol. 13). 384p. (C). 1992. lib. bdg. 281.50 (*0-7923-1764-5*) Kluwer Ac.

Romanec, Carolyn, jt. auth. see Romanec, Jaroslav.

***Romanec, Jaroslav & Romanec, Carolyn.** Get Bigger & Stronger with Your Own "Personal Training Journal" (Illus.). 194p. 1995. 9.95 (*0-9645091-0-5*) Pulsar Publ.

Romanek, Betty. GED Preparation for the High School Equivalency Examination Literature & the Arts: New GED Test. 1987. pap. 9.93 (*0-8092-5040-3*) Contemp Bks.

Romanek, Elizabeth. Foundations: Social Studies. LC 92-36112. 1993. pap. 10.33 (*0-8092-3831-4*) Contemp Bks.

— GED Literature & the Arts. LC 93-43846. 1994. pap. 10.60 (*0-8092-3779-2*) Contemp Bks.

Romanell, Patrick. Croce Versus Gentile: A Dialogue on Contemporary Italian Philosophy. LC 78-63709. (Studies in Fascism: Ideology & Practice). (Illus.). 80p. reprint ed. 20.00 (*0-404-16979-1*) AMS Pr.

— John Locke & Medicine. LC 84-42846. 225p. 1984. 35.95x (*0-87975-250-5*) Prometheus Bks.

— A Letter Concerning Toleration: Locke. 64p. (C). 1955. pap. write for info. (*0-02-403400-2*) Macmillan.

— Making of the Mexican Mind: A Study in Recent Mexican Thought. LC 76-86778. (Essay Index Reprint Ser.). 1977. 18.95 (*0-8369-1189-X*) Ayer.

Romanell, Patrick, tr. see Croce, Benedetto.

Romanelli, Charles S. How to Make Money in One Day at the Track: Everything the Occasional Racegoer Needs to Know to Come Home from the Track a Winner. 1989. pap. 12.00 (*0-671-66652-5*, Fireside) S&S Trade.

Romanelli, Dorothy H., ed. see Romanelli, Nicholas.

Romanelli, Nicholas. Una Vita: A Grandfather's Story. Romanelli, Dorothy H., ed. (Illus.). 185p. (Orig.). 1981. pap. 6.50 (*0-9606104-0-5*) Port Pr.

Romanelli, Samuel. Travail in an Arab Land. Stillman, Yedida K. & Stillman, Norman A., trs. LC 88-3931. (Judaic Studies). 240p. 1989. 29.50 (*0-8173-0409-6*) U of Ala Pr.

Romanes, David. Let Ego Go. 1993. 12.95 (*0-533-10423-8*) Vantage.

Romanes, G. J., ed. see Cunningham.

Romanes, George J. An Examination of Weismannism. reprint ed. 30.00 (*0-404-19358-7*) AMS Pr.

— Mental Evolution in Animals: With a Posthumous Essay on Instinct by Charles Darwin. LC 71-96472. reprint ed. 37.50 (*0-404-05389-0*) AMS Pr.

— Mental Evolution in Man: Origin of Human Faculty. LC 74-21426. (Classics in Child Development Ser.). 466p. 1975. reprint ed. lib. bdg. 38.95 (*0-405-06475-6*) Ayer.

Romani, Cinzia. Tainted Goddesses: Female Film Stars of the Third Reich. Teal, D., ed. Connolly, Bob, tr. (Illus.). 192p. 1992. pap. 19.95 (*0-9627613-1-1*) Sarpedon.

Romanides, John S. Franks, Romans, Feudalism, & Doctrine: An Interplay Between Theology & Society. (Patriarch Athenagoras Memorial Lectures). 98p. (Orig.). (C). 1982. pap. text ed. 4.95 (*0-916586-54-5*) Holy Cross Orthodox.

Romanilos, Jose L. Antonio Torres - Guitar Maker: His Life & His Work. rev. ed. (Illus.). 1995. 62.50 (*0-933224-26-5*) Bold Strummer Ltd.

Romanini, C., et al, eds. Experimental Models in Obstetrics & Gynecology. (Advances in Gynecological & Obstetric Research Ser.). (Illus.). 466p. (C). 1991. 98.00 (*1-85070-280-2*) Prthnon Pub.

Romaniouk, Mikhass. Belorussian National Dress: Belaruskae Narodnae Adzenne. (BEL, ENG, FRE, GER, RUS & SPA.). 1981. 143.00 (*0-317-57297-0*, Pub. by Collets UK) St Mut.

Romanish, Bruce. Empowering Teachers: Restructuring Schools for the 21st Century. 162p. (C). 1992. lib. bdg. 38.00 (*0-8191-8422-5*); pap. text ed. 18.00 (*0-8191-8423-3*) U Pr of Amer.

Romaniuk, jt. ed. see Deangelis.

Romaniuk, jt. ed. see Wolinski.

***Romaniuk, Bohdan, ed.** Who's Wealthy in America 1995: A Prospect List & Directory of Nearly 100,000 Affluent Americans, 2 vols. 5th ed. 2300p. 1994. pap. 415.00 (*0-930807-54-5*) Taft Group.

***Romaniuk, Bohdan & DeAngelis, James, eds.** Corporate & Foundation Grants 1995: A Comprehensive Listening of Nearly 95,000 Recent Grants to Nonprofit Organizations in the U. S., 2 Vol., Vol. 2. 3916p. 1994. pap. 195.00 (*0-930807-67-7*) Taft Group.

Romaniuk, Bohdan R. America's New Foundation 1997. Date not set. 150.00 (*1-56995-001-6*) Taft Group.

— America's New Foundations 1996, Vol. 1. 1995. 170.00 (*1-56995-000-8*) Taft Group.

— Corporate & Foundation Grants 1997, 2 vol., 1. 1996. write for info. (*1-56995-029-6*) Taft Group.

— Corporate & Foundation Grants 1997, 2 vol., 2. 1996. write for info. (*1-56995-030-X*) Taft Group.

— Corporate & Foundation Grants 1997, 2 vol., Set. 1996. 195.00 (*1-56995-028-8*) Taft Group.

— Corporate Giving Directory 1995. 1994. 365.00 (*1-56995-002-4*) Taft Group.

— Corporate Giving Directory 1996. 1995. 375.00 (*1-56995-003-2*) Taft Group.

— Corporate Giving Directory 1997. Date not set. 350.00 (*1-56995-004-0*) Taft Group.

— Corporate Giving Yellow Page 1995, Vol. 1. 1994. 88.00 (*1-56995-005-9*) Taft Group.

— Corporate Giving Yellow Pages 1996. 1995. 90.00 (*1-56995-006-7*) Taft Group.

— Corporate Giving Yellow Pages 1997. Date not set. 82.00 (*1-56995-007-5*) Taft Group.

— Foundation Reporter 1996. 1995. 375.00 (*1-56995-055-5*) Taft Group.

— Foundation Reporter 1997. 1996. 375.00 (*1-56995-056-3*) Taft Group.

— FR Guide to Human Service 1995. 1994. 120.00 (*1-56995-017-2*) Taft Group.

— Fundraiser's Guide to Human Resources 1996. 1995. 125.00 (*1-56995-018-0*) Taft Group.

— Fundraiser's Guide to Human Services 1997. 1996. 105.00 (*1-56995-019-9*) Taft Group.

Romaniuk, R. S. & Szustakowski, M. Optical Fibres & Their Applications Five, Vol. 1085: SPIE Proceedings, Feb. 1989, Warsaw, Poland. 638p. 1990. 92.00 (*0-8194-0120-X*, 1085) SPIE.

Romankiewicz, J., jt. auth. see Krinov, E.

***Romankiw, L. T. & Herman, D. A., Jr., eds.** Proceedings of the International Symposium on Magnetic Materials, Processe & Devices, 3rd. LC 93-72865. (Proceedings Ser.: Vol. 94-06). 312p. 1994. 48.00 (*1-56677-036-X*) Electrochem Soc.

— Second International Symposium on Magnetic Materials, Processes, & Devices. LC 92-71336. (Proceedings Ser.: Vol. 92-10). 600p. 1992. 60.00 (*1-56677-010-6*) Electrochem Soc.

***Romankiw, L. T., et al, eds.** Proceedings of the International Symposium on Electrochemical Technology Applications in Electronics, 2nd. LC 93-70065. (Proceedings Ser.: Vol. 93-20). 560p. 1993. 54.00 (*1-56677-062-9*) Electrochem Soc.

***Romano.** Pocket Guide to Digital Prepress. 1996. pap. text ed. (*0-8273-7198-5*) Delmar.

Romano, jt. auth. see CCFA Staff.

Romano, A. Thermomechanics of Phase Transition in Classical Field Theory. (Advances in Mathematics for Applied Sciences Ser.). 272p. 1993. text ed. 48.00 (*981-02-1398-0*) World Scientific Pub.

Romano, Alba C. Irony in Juvenal. (Altertumswissenschaftliche Texte und Studien Ser.: Bd. 7). viii, 366p. 1979. write for info. (*3-487-06892-3*, Pub. by Georg Olms GW) Lubrecht & Cramer.

Romano, Angelo. U. S. Navy Fighters. (Illus.). 128p. 1992. 15.95 (*1-85532-222-6*, Pub. by Osprey Pubng Ltd UK) Motorbooks Intl.

Romano, Anne T. Taking Charge: Crisis Intervention in Criminal Justice. LC 89-37995. (Contributions in Criminology & Penology Ser.: No. 25). 208p. 1990. text ed. 49.95 (*0-313-26890-8*, RTA/, Greenwood Pr) Greenwood.

Romano, Anne T., jt. auth. see Martin, John M.

Romano, Antonio. The Charism of the Founder. 160p. 1993. 29.00 (*0-85439-453-2*, Pub. by St Paul Pubns UK) St Mut.

***Romano, Bernardo.** Lexikon der Italienische Wirtschaftsfachbegriffe: German-Italian. 312p. (GER & ITA.). 1991. 29.95 (*0-7859-7053-3*) Fr & Eur.

Romano, Branko E. Chicken Toons. LC 82-83844. 1982. pap. 2.00 (*0-89229-010-2*) TQS Pubns.

Romano, Carl. Philosophers American Style. Date not set. 22.95 (*0-06-016578-2*, HarpT) HarpC.

Romano, Clare & Ross, John. The Complete Collagraph: The Art & Technique of Printmaking from Collage Plates. (Illus.). 1980. 35.00 (*0-02-926770-6*) Macmillan.

Romano, Clare, jt. auth. see Ross, John.

Romano, David G. Athletics & Mathematics in Archaic Corinth: An Early Design of the Greek Stadion. LC 92-75705. (Memoirs Ser.: Vol. 206). (Illus.). 117p. (C). 1993. 25.00 (*0-87169-206-6*, M206-ROD) Am Philos.

Romano, Deane L. The Rainbows of Moon. LC 92-82544. 240p. 1993. pap. 12.00 (*1-56002-204-3*, Univ Edtns) Aegina Pr.

Romano, Dennis. Patricians & Popolani: The Social Foundations of the Venetian Renaissance State. LC 87-2826. 220p. 1988. text ed. 36.00x (*0-8018-3513-5*) Johns Hopkins.

Romano, Dugan. Intercultural Marriage: Promises & Pitfalls. LC 88-81393. 166p. 1988. pap. 15.95 (*0-933662-71-8*) Intercult Pr.

Romano, Elizabeth, ed. see Alimonti, Joan M.

Romano, Emily. Pear Blossoms Drift. 20p. 1981. pap. 2.00 (*0-913719-51-X*) High-Coo Pr.

Romano, Eugene L. The Way of Desert Spirituality: The Rule of Life of the Hermits of Bethlehem of the Heart of Jesus. LC 92-37733. 1993. pap. 6.95 (*0-8189-0661-8*) Alba.

Romano, Frank. The TypEncyclopedia: A User's Guide to Better Typography. 224p. 1984. pap. 34.95 (*0-8352-1925-9*) Bowker.

***Romano, Frank & Knaflewska, Magda, eds.** QUI's QuarkXPress Slick Tricks. 1995. 19.99 (*0-941845-13-3*) Micro Pub Pr.

***Romano, Frank, et al.** Biology Laboratory: An Inquiry. 256p. (C). 1994. pap. text ed., ring bd. 41.95 (*0-8403-8456-4*) Kendall-Hunt.

Romano, Frank J. Desktop Typography with QuarkXPress. 1992. pap. 19.95 (*0-07-053558-2*) McGraw.

— Desktop Typography with QuarkXPress. 2nd ed. 1992. 29.95 (*0-07-053559-0*) McGraw.

— Desktop Typography with QuarkXPress(R) 2nd ed. 256p. 1992. 29.95 (*0-8306-3058-9*, 3968, Windcrest); pap. 19.95 (*0-8306-3057-0*, 3968, Windcrest) TAB Bks.

— Machine Writing & Typesetting. (Illus.). 146p. 1986. lib. bdg. 24.95 (*0-938853-00-7*) GAMA Comns.

***Romano, Giuseppe.** Opus Dei: Who, How, Why. Lane, Edmund C., tr. (Orig.). 1995. pap. write for info. (*0-8189-0739-8*) Alba.

Romano, Jaime, ed. see De Romano, Dora R.

Romano, James F. Daily Life of the Ancient Egyptians. LC 89-85823. (Illus.). 56p. (Orig.). 1990. pap. text ed. 7.95 (*0-911239-18-9*) Carnegie Mus.

— Death, Burial & Afterlife in Ancient Egypt. LC 89-85822. (Illus.). 48p. (Orig.). (C). 1990. pap. text ed. 7.95 (*0-911239-19-7*) Carnegie Mus.

Romano, James V., ed. Poetica de la Poblacion Marginal: Sensibilidades Determinantes. (Literature & Human Rights Ser.: No. 2). 488p. (Orig.). (SPA.). 1988. pap. 14.95 (*0-910235-20-1*) Prisma Bks.

***Romano, Joe.** It All Comes Together Right Here. 28p. 1993. 12.95 (*0-614-00506-X*) Non-Toxic Music.

Romano, John F. & McHale, Michael J. Strategic Use of Circumstantial Evidence. 2nd ed. 773p. 1991. 80.00 (*0-87473-774-5*) Michie Butterworth.

Romano, Joseph P. & Siegel, Andrew F. Counterexamples in Probability & Statistics. LC 85-19024. (Statistics Ser.). 303p. (C). 1986. boxed 46.50 (*0-534-05568-0*) Chapman & Hall.

Romano-Lax, Andromeda. Sea Kayaking in Baja. LC 93-27790. 144p. 1993. pap. 13.95 (*0-89997-157-1*) Wilderness Pr.

Romano, Locus G., jt. auth. see Georgrady, Nicholas P.

Romano, Locus G., ed. see Georgrady, Nicholas P. & Romano, Locus G.

Romano, Louis & Georgiady, Nicholas P. Building an Effective Middle School. 318p. (C). 1994. pap. text ed. write for info. (*0-697-15179-4*) Brown & Benchmark.

Romano, Louis A. Manual & Industrial Education at Girard College 1831-1965: An Era in American Educational Experimentation. Cordasco, Francesco, ed. LC 80-1075. (American Ethnic Groups Ser.). 1981. lib. bdg. 47.95 (*0-405-13450-9*) Ayer.

Romano, Louis G., ed. Focus on a Middle School Belief System. (Illus.). 1979. pap. text ed. 3.00 (*0-918449-01-4*) MI Middle Educ.

Romano, Louis G., ed. see Bouth, Anita J.

Romano, Louis G., ed. see Costar, James W.

Romano, Louis G., jt. auth. see Georgiady, Nicholas P.

Romano, Louis G., jt. auth. see Georgisky, Nicholas P.

Romano, Louis G., ed. see Gilliland, Katherine.

Romano, Louis G., jt. auth. see Hamachek, Alice L.

Romano, Louis G., ed. see Kaminski, Lorraine B. & Dornbos, Karen L.

Romano, Louis G., ed. see Maksimowicz, Michelle.

Romano, Louis G., ed. see Marlow, Jean, et al.

Romano, Louis G., ed. see McEwin, C. Kenneth.

Romano, Louis G., ed. see Mowen, Carol & Mowen, Gregg.

Romano, Louis G., ed. see Muldrew, Jessie.

Romano, Louis G., ed. see Powell, William.

Romano, Louis G., ed. see Scullen, Thomas.

Romano, Louis G., et al, eds. Focus on Successful Characteristics of a Middle School. rev. ed. 12p. 1985. pap. text ed. 2.50 (*0-918449-04-9*) MI Middle Educ.

— The Middle School: Selected Readings on an Emerging School Program. LC 72-97847. 509p. 1973. 35.95 (*0-911012-82-6*) Nelson-Hall.

Romano, M. E., tr. see Zoja, Luigi.

Romano, Marc, tr. Men of Dishonor: Inside the Sicilian Mafia. LC 93-15397. 1993. 23.00 (*0-688-04574-X*) Morrow.

Romano, Marc, tr. see Messadie, Gerald.

Romano, Marc, tr. see Yermakov, Oleg.

Romano, Nicholas. Chemistry. 2nd ed. Garnsey, Wayne, ed. (Science Ser.). (Illus.). 320p. 1992. pap. text ed. 4.13 (*0-935487-41-7*) N & N Pub Co.

Romano, Nicholas, jt. auth. see Moreau, Nancy.

Romano, Octavio I. Geriatric Fu. LC 89-20500. 256p. 1990. pap. 12.00 (*0-89229-018-8*) TQS Pubns.

Romano, Octavio I., ed. The Grito del Sol Collection: Anthology, Annual, Winter 1984. LC 81-649163. 255p. 1985. 10.00 (*0-89229-016-1*) TQS Pubns.

Romano, Osservatore, tr. see O'Byrne, Seamus, ed.

***Romano, Patrick L. & Barth, Claire, eds.** Activity-Based Management in Action. (Illus.). 160p. 1994. pap. 35.00 (*0-86641-227-1*, 94289) Inst Mgmt Account.

Romano, Paul & Stone, Ria. The American Worker. ix, 70p. 1972. reprint ed. pap. 3.00 (*0-935590-01-3*) Bewick Edns.

Romano, Roberta. The Genius of American Corporate Law. LC 93-18917. 164p. (Orig.). 1993. 24.75 (*0-8447-3837-9*); pap. 9.75 (*0-8447-3836-0*) Am Enterprise.

Romano, Roberta, ed. Foundations of Corporate Law. LC 92-34550. (Interdisciplinary Readers in Law Ser.). (Illus.). 352p. (C). 1993. 47.00 (*0-19-507412-2*); pap. text ed. 19.95 (*0-19-507413-0*) OUP.

Romano, Rose. Vendetta. 48p. (Orig.). 1990. pap. 3.00 (*1-883112-01-X*) Malafemmina.

Romano, Rose, ed. La Bella Figura: A Choice. 192p. (Orig.). 1993. pap. 8.95 (*1-883112-00-1*) Malafemmina.

Romano, Tom. Clearing the Way: Working with Teenage Writers. LC 86-29558. 191p. 1987. pap. text ed. 19.00 (*0-435-08439-9*) Heinemann.

— Writing with Passion: Life Stories, Multiple Genres. LC 95-8647. 1995. write for info. (*0-86709-362-5*) Boynton Cook Pubs.

Romano, V., ed. Advances in Phenylketonuria Research. (Journal: Developmental Brain Dysfunction: Vol. 6, Nos. 1-3, 1993). (Illus.). 192p. 1993. pap. 78.50 (*3-8055-5759-0*) S Karger.

***Romanoff, Alan, ed.** Birthdays of the Rich & Famous: How Old 10,000 Celebrities Really Are! 128p. 1995. pap. 14.95 (*1-887320-00-8*) Darco Pr OH.

Romanoff, Alexis L. The Avian Embryo: Structural & Functional Development. LC 59-7975. 1323p. reprint ed. pap. 180.00 (*0-8357-5932-6*, 2051970) Bks Demand.

Romanoff, Lena. Your People, My People: Finding Acceptance & Fulfillment As a Jew by Choice. 280p. 1990. 22.95 (*0-8276-0360-6*) JPS Phila.

Romanoff, Marjorie. Language & Study Skills for Learners of English. 144p. (C). 1991. pap. text ed. 14.00 (*0-13-847229-7*, 640306) P-H.

Romanoff, Steve. The Steve Romanoff Songbook: Songs Written for Schooner Fare. 160p. 1993. spiral bd. 24.95 (*0-9638602-0-8*) Outer Green Recs.

Romanofsky, Peter, ed. Social Service Organizations, 2 vols. LC 77-84754. (Encyclopedia of American Institutions Ser.: No. 2). 1978. text ed. 150.00 (*0-8371-9829-1*, RSS/) Greenwood.

— Social Service Organizations, 2 vols., 1. LC 77-84754. (Encyclopedia of American Institutions Ser.: No. 2). 1978. text ed. 95.00 (*0-8371-9902-6*, RSS/1) Greenwood.

— Social Service Organizations, 2 vols., Vol. 2. LC 77-84754. (Encyclopedia of American Institutions Ser.: No. 2). 1978. text ed. 95.00 (*0-8371-9903-4*, RSS/2) Greenwood.

Romanofsky, Peter, jt. ed. see Fisher, Robert M.

Romanos, Christos S. Poetics of a Fictional Historian: A Synchronic-Diachronic Approach with a Focus on Alexandros Kotzias in the Context of European Fiction. LC 73-49255. (American University Studies: Comparative Literature: Ser. III, Vol. 7). 267p. (C). 1984. text ed. 28.00 (*0-8204-0088-2*) P Lang Pubs.

Romanov, et al. Azure Cities. LC 72-3284. (Short Story Index Reprint Ser.). 1977. reprint ed. 23.95 (*0-8369-4143-8*) Ayer.

Romanov, A. & Rado, Rudolf, eds. Modified Polymers, Their Preparation & Properties: Modified Polymers, Their Preparation & Properties - Proceedings. 1977. 40.00 (*0-08-020953-X*, Pub. by Pergamon Repr UK) Franklin.

Romanov, A. C. & Wedel, E. Romanov's Russian - English, English - Russian Dictionary. 3rd ed. 509p. (ENG & RUS.). 1992. 29.95 (*0-7859-1083-2*, 5850540113) Fr & Eur.

Romanov, A. S. Russian-English Dictionary. 1990. mass mkt. 5.99 (*0-671-70924-0*) PB.

Romanov, Jane F., jt. ed. see Anderson, Owen.

Romanov, Panteleimon S. On the Volga & Other Stories. Gretton, Ann, tr. LC 75-39013. (Soviet Literature in English Translation Ser.). 286p. 1978. reprint ed. 21.45 (*0-88355-415-1*) Hyperion Conn.

R

An Asterisk (*) at the beginning of an entry indicates that the title is appearing in BIP for the first time.

— Three Pairs of Silk Stockings. Graham, Stephen, ed. Zarine, Leonide, tr. LC 72-90308. (Soviet Literature in English Translation Ser.). 344p. 1973. reprint ed. 22.50 (*0-88355-019-9*) Hyperion Conn.
— Without Cherry Blossom. Graham, Stephen, ed. Zarine, L., tr. LC 78-142275. (Short Story Index Reprint Ser.). 1977. 17.95 (*0-8369-3759-7*) Ayer.
— Without Cherry Blossom. Graham, Stephen, ed. Zarine, L., tr. LC 72-90310. (Soviet Literature in English Translation Ser.). 287p. 1973. reprint ed. 21.25 (*0-88355-020-2*) Hyperion Conn.
Romanov, V. G. Inverse Problems of Mathematical Physics. Yuzina, L. Ya., tr. 248p. 1986. lib. bdg. 182.00 (*90-6764-056-5*, Pub. by VSP NE) Coronet Bks.
***Romanov, V. G. & Kabanikhin, S. I.** Inverse Problems for Maxwell's Equations. (Inverse & Ill-Posed Problems Ser.). 257p. 1994. 177.50 (*90-6764-172-3*, Pub. by VSP NE) Coronet Bks.
Romanov, V. V. Hydrophysics of Bogs. 312p. 1968. text ed. 79.50 (*0-7065-0512-3*, Pub. by Keter Pub IS) Coronet Bks.
Romanova, Natalia. Once There Was a Tree. (J). 1985. 14. 99 (*0-8037-0235-3*) Dial Bks Young.
— Once There Was a Tree. LC 85-6730. (Pied Piper Bks.). (Illus.). (J). (ps up). 1989. pap. 4.99 (*0-8037-0705-3*) Dial Bks Young.
Romanovsky, M. Y., jt. auth. see Korobkin, V. V.
Romanowich, Barbara, jt. auth. see Kemnitz, Thomas M.
Romanowicz, Zofia. Passage Through the Red Sea. 151p. 1962. 4.00 (*0-686-30917-0*) Polish Inst Art & Sci.
Romanowski, Jerome. Mackmen. (Illus.). 160p. (Orig.). 1980. 8.95 (*0-940056-08-9*) Chapter & Cask.
— Sages of Sport. (Illus.). 44p. 1984. pap. 4.95 (*0-940056-10-0*) Chapter & Cask.
***Romanowski, Nick.** Farming in Ponds & Dams. (Illus.). 224p. (Orig.). 1995. pap. 22.95 (*0-85091-630-5*, Pub. by Lothian Pub AT) Seven Hills Bk.
— Grasses, Bamboos & Related Plants in Australia. (Illus.). 168p. (Orig.). 1995. pap. 24.95 (*0-85091-554-6*, Pub. by Lothian Pub AT) Seven Hills Bk.
— Water & Wetland Plants for Southern Australia: For Southern Australia. (Illus.). 168p. (Orig.). 1995. pap. 19. 95 (*0-85091-487-6*, Pub. by Lothian Pub AT) Seven Hills Bk.
***Romanowski, Patricia & George-Warren, Holly, eds.** The New Rolling Stone Encyclopedia of Rock & Roll: Completely Revised & Updated. rev. ed. 1995. pap. 22. 50 (*0-684-81044-1*, Fireside) S&S Trade.
Romanowski, Patricia, jt. auth. see Funicello, Annette.
Romanowski, Patricia, jt. auth. see Martin, Joel.
Romanowski, Patricia, jt. auth. see Wilson, Mary.
Romanowski, Patty, ed. see Rolling Stone Press Staff.
***Romanowski, Sylvie & Bilezikian, Monique, eds.** Homage to Paul Benichou. LC 94-67074. 340p. 1994. lib. bdg. 44. 95 (*0-917786-98-X*) Summa Pubns.
Romans, John R., et al. Meat We Eat. 13th ed. (Illus.). 1216p. 1994. 86.60 (*0-8134-2881-5*); text ed. 64.95 (*0-685-64926-1*) Interstate.
Romans, Joseph C. In the Company of Angels. Theune, Claire, ed. LC 88-80676. 256p. 1988. 9.95 (*0-945586-03-5*) Editech Pr.
***Romans, Lois E.** Introduction to Computed Tomography. LC 94-43673. 1995. write for info. (*0-683-07353-2*) Williams & Wilkins.
Romanski, Kate D., jt. ed. see McKinney, Beth C.
Romanski, Kate D., jt. auth. see McKinney, Beth.
Romantic Hotel & Restaurant Association Staff, ed. Romantik Hotels & Restaurants 1989: Charming Historic Hotels in Europe & America. (Illus.). 294p. 1989. pap. 6.95 (*1-55832-012-1*) Harvard Common Pr.
Romantowski, Jane, jt. auth. see Lipson, Greta.
Romanucci-Ross, Lola. Mead's Other Manus: Phenomenology of the Encounter. (Illus.). 256p. 1985. text ed. 34.95 (*0-89789-064-7*, H064, Bergin & Garvey) Greenwood.
— One Hundred Towers: An Italian Odyssey of Cultural Survival. LC 90-1123. 240p. 1991. text ed. 55.00 (*0-89789-250-X*, H250, Bergin & Garvey) Greenwood.
Romanucci-Ross, Lola, et al, eds. The Anthropology of Medicine: From Culture to Method. (Illus.). 416p. (C). 1985. text ed. 44.95 (*0-03-062192-5*, Bergin & Garvey) Greenwood.
— The Anthropology of Medicine: From Culture to Method. LC 91-21999. 464p. 1991. pap. text ed. 22.95 (*0-89789-263-1*, G263, Bergin & Garvey) Greenwood.
— The Anthropology of Medicine: From Culture to Method. 2nd ed. LC 91-21999. 464p. 1991. text ed. 75.00 (*0-89789-262-3*, H262, Bergin & Garvey) Greenwood.
Romanus, Peter, ed. Lyonel Feininger: Die Halle-Bilder. (Illus.). 120p. (GER.). 1991. 64.00 (*3-7913-1155-7*, Pub. by Prestel) TeNeues.
Romany, Celina, jt. auth. see Fernandez, Demetrio.
Romanyshyn, Robert. Technology As Symptom & Dream. (Illus.). 320p. 1989. 45.00 (*0-415-00786-0*, A3877); pap. 16.95 (*0-415-00787-9*, A3881) Routledge.
***Romao, Jorge C. & Freire, Filipe, eds.** Electroweak Physics & the Early Universe: Proceedings of a NATO ARW Held in Sintra, Portugal, Lisbon, March 23-25, 1994. (NATO ASI Series B: Vol. 338). 415p. 1995. 125.00 (*0-306-44909-9*) Plenum.
Romas, Nicholas A. & Cohen, Herman, eds. Prostatic Acid Phosphatase Measurement: Detection & Management of Prostatic Cancer. (Annals Ser.: Vol. 390). 145p. 1982. lib. bdg. 30.00 (*0-89766-170-2*); pap. 30.00 (*0-89766-171-0*) NY Acad Sci.
Romas, Nicholas A. & Vaughan, E. Darracott, eds. Alternate Methods in the Treatment of Benign Prostatic Hyperlasia. LC 92-48354. 1993. write for info. (*3-540-56389-X*); 109.00 (*0-387-56389-X*) Spr-Verlag.
Romashkevitch, P. A., ed. Polnij Russkij Orthografficheskij Slovar' 264p. reprint ed. pap. 10.00 (*0-317-29290-0*) Holy Trinity.
Romashko, Sandra. The Complete Collector's Guide to Shells & Shelling. 2nd ed. LC 81-51067. (Illus.). 112p. (Orig.). 1994. pap. 9.95 (*0-89317-032-1*) Windward Pub.
— Handbook of Saltwater Fishes. LC 91-65377. (Illus.). 64p. (Orig.). 1992. pap. 3.95 (*0-89317-040-2*) Windward Pub.
Romashko, Sandra, ed. see Ashton, Ray E., Jr. & Ashton, Patricia S.
Romashko, Sandra, ed. see Erwin, Wilma C.
Romashko, Sandra, ed. see Stachowicz, Jim.
Romashko, Sandra D. Birds of Water, Sea & Shore. LC 77-81169. (Illus.). 64p. 1990. pap. 4.95 (*0-89317-016-X*) Windward Pub.
— The Shark: Lord of the Sea. 6th ed. LC 76-150452. (Illus.). 64p. 1991. pap. 4.95 (*0-89317-001-1*) Windward Pub.
— The Shell Book: A Complete Guide to Collecting & Identifying. 6th ed. LC 76-360976. (Illus.). 64p. 1992. pap. 5.95 (*0-89317-000-3*) Windward Pub.
— Wild Ducks & Geese of North America. LC 77-81167. (Illus.). 1978. pap. 3.95 (*0-89317-018-6*) Windward Pub.
Romatowski, Jane, jt. auth. see Lipson, Greta.
Romb, Anselm. Kolbe Reader. (Orig.). 1987. pap. 10.95 (*0-913382-35-3*, 101-35) Prow Bks-Franciscan.
— Man of Peace: Casimir Michael Cypher: His Meaning in Life Was Found in Death. (Illus.). 67p. (Orig.). 1985. pap. 3.75 (*0-913382-17-5*, 105-42) Prow Bks-Franciscan.
— Total Consecration to Mary, Spouse of the Holy Spirit. 64p. 1982. pap. 2.00 (*0-913382-13-2*, 105-37) Prow Bks-Franciscan.
Romb, Anselm W. Maximilian Kolbe: Authentic Franciscan. (Illus.). 192p. (Orig.). 1990. pap. 7.95 (*0-913382-56-6*, 101-37) Prow Bks-Franciscan.
— Walk with the Lord: Sharing the Cross, Sharing the Glory. LC 89-49678. 328p. (Orig.). 1990. pap. 8.95 (*0-8198-8240-2*) Pauline Bks.
— Walk with the Lord: Sharing the Silence, Sharing the Life. LC 90-44397. 182p. (Orig.). 1990. pap. 6.95 (*0-8198-8245-3*) Pauline Bks.
Romb, Anselm W., ed. see McHugh, Joan C.
Romba, John J. Controlling Your Dog Away from You. LC 84-71305. (Illus.). 112p. 1984. pap. 9.95 (*0-915359-00-6*) Abmor Pub.
***Rombach-de Kievid, J. E. & Sorenson, Veronica.** Technique of Bruges Flower Lace. (Illus.). 144p. 1995. 34.95 (*0-7134-7329-0*, Pub. by Batsford UK) Trafalgar.
Rombach, H. D., et al, eds. Experimental Software Engineering Issues - Critical Assessment & Future Directions: Proceedings of an International Workshop, Dagstuhl Castle, Germany, September 14-18, 1992. (Lecture Notes in Computer Science Ser.: Vol. 706). xviii, 261p. 1993. pap. write for info. (*3-540-57092-6*) Spr-Verlag.
— Experimental Software Engineering Issues - Critical Assessment & Future Directions: Proceedings of the International Workshop Held at Dagstuhl Castle, Germany, September 14-18, 1992. (Lecture Notes in Computer Science Ser.: Vol. 706). xviii, 261p. 1993. pap. 44.00 (*0-387-57092-6*) Spr-Verlag.
Rombauer, Irma S. Joy of Cooking, 2 vols., Set. 1991. boxed 9.98 (*0-451-92511-4*, Sig) NAL-Dutton.
Rombauer, Irma S. & Becker, Marion R. Joy of Cooking. 930p. 1985. text ed. 23.00 (*0-02-604570-2*) Macmillan.
— Joy of Cooking. LC 61-7902. (Illus.). 864p. 1973. pap. 11. 95 (*0-452-26333-6*, Plume) NAL-Dutton.
— Joy of Cooking. LC 61-7902. (Illus.). 864p. 1985. spiral bd. 13.95 (*0-452-26332-8*, Plume) NAL-Dutton.
— Joy of Cooking. rev. ed. LC 75-10772. (Illus.). 930p. 1975. write for info. (*0-672-51831-7*); write for info. (*0-672-52385-X*) Macmillan.
— The Joy of Cooking, Vol. II. 1989. pap. 4.50 (*0-451-15666-8*) NAL-Dutton.
Rombauer, Irma S., jt. auth. see Becker, Marion R.
Rombauer, Marjorie D. Legal Problem Solving: Analysis, Research & Writing. 5th ed. (American Casebook Ser.). 524p. 1991. pap. text ed. 34.50 (*0-314-84243-8*) West Pub.
— Legal Problem Solving: Analysis, Research & Writing, Teacher's Manual & 1991-92 Problem Supplement. 5th ed. (American Casebook Ser.). 69p. (C). 1992. reprint ed. pap. text ed. write for info. (*0-314-00076-3*) West Pub.
Rombauer, Marjorie D., jt. auth. see Squires, Lynn B.
Rombaut, C., et al. Power Electronic Converters: AC-DC Conversion. 340p. 1987. text ed. 50.00 (*0-07-053630-9*) McGraw.
Rombaut, Marc. Paul Delvaux. LC 89-43581. (Twentieth Century Artists Ser.). (Illus.). 128p. 1990. 24.95 (*0-8478-1201-4*) Rizzoli Intl.
Rombeau, John L. Atlas of Nutritional Support Techniques. 1989. 51.00 (*0-316-75575-3*) Little.
Rombeau, John L. & Caldwell. Clinical Nutrition: Enteral & Tube Feeding. 2nd ed. (Illus.). 688p. 1990. text ed. 125. 00 (*0-7216-2814-1*) Saunders.
Rombeau, John L. & Caldwell, Michael D. Clinical Nutrition: Parenteral Nutrition. 2nd ed. (Illus.). 912p. 1993. text ed. 115.00 (*0-7216-3600-4*) Saunders.
Romberg, Alan. The United States, the Soviet Union & Korea: Beyond Confrontation. 25p. 1989. pap. 4.95 (*0-87609-058-7*) Coun Foreign.
Romberg, Alan & Yamamoto, Tadashi, eds. Same Bed, Different Dreams: America & Japan - Societies in Transition. LC 90-1523. (Illus.). 160p. 1990. pap. 14.95 (*0-87609-082-X*) Coun Foreign.
Romberg, Alan, et al. The United States & Japan: Changing Societies in a Changing Relationship - A Conference Report. 56p. 1987. pap. 4.95 (*0-87609-022-6*) Coun Foreign.
Romberg, Alan D. U. S.-Japan Relations: A Partnership in Search of Definition. (Critical Issues 1988 Ser.: No. 1). 32p. 1988. pap. 3.95 (*0-87609-031-5*) Coun Foreign.
Romberg, Jenean. Let's Discover Crayon. (Arts & Crafts Discovery Units Ser.). (Illus.). 1973. pap. 9.95 (*0-87628-523-X*) Ctr Appl Res.
— Let's Discover Mobiles. (Arts & Crafts Discovery Units Ser.). (Illus.). 1974. pap. 9.95 (*0-87628-524-8*) Ctr Appl Res.
— Let's Discover Paper. (Arts & Crafts Discovery Units Ser.). (Illus.). 1974. pap. 9.95 (*0-87628-525-6*) Ctr Appl Res.
— Let's Discover Printing. (Arts & Crafts Discovery Units Ser.). (Illus.). 1974. pap. 9.95 (*0-87628-527-2*) Ctr Appl Res.
— Let's Discover Puppets. (Arts & Crafts Discovery Units Ser.). (Illus.). 1974. pap. 9.95 (*0-87628-528-0*) Ctr Appl Res.
— Let's Discover Tempera. (Arts & Crafts Discovery Units Ser.). (Illus.). 1974. pap. 9.95 (*0-87628-529-9*) Ctr Appl Res.
— Let's Discover Tissue. (Arts & Crafts Discovery Units Ser.). (Illus.). 1974. pap. 9.95 (*0-87628-530-2*) Ctr Appl Res.
— Let's Discover Watercolor. (Arts & Crafts Discovery Units Ser.). (Illus.). 1974. pap. 9.95 (*0-87628-531-0*) Ctr Appl Res.
— Let's Discover Weaving. (Arts & Crafts Discovery Units Ser.). (Illus.). 1974. pap. 9.95 (*0-685-01335-9*) Ctr Appl Res.
Romberg, Nina. Shadow Walkers. 304p. 1993. mass mkt. 4.50 (*1-55817-696-9*, Pinnacle NY) Windsor NY.
— Spirit Stalker. 1989. pap. 3.95 (*1-55817-271-8*, Pinnacle NY) Windsor NY.
Romberg, Thomas, jt. auth. see Webb, Norman.
Romberg, Thomas A. Toward Effective Schooling: The IGE Experience. LC 85-3156. (Illus.). 246p. (Orig.). 1985. lib. bdg. 48.00 (*0-8191-4580-7*); pap. text ed. 22.50 (*0-8191-4581-5*) U Pr of Amer.
Romberg, Thomas A., ed. Mathematics Assessment & Evaluation: Imperatives for Mathematics Educators. LC 91-11157. (SUNY Series, Reform in Mathematics Education). 369p. (C). 1992. 64.50 (*0-7914-0899-X*); pap. 21.95 (*0-7914-0900-7*) State U NY Pr.
— Reform in School Mathematics & Authentic Assessment. (SUNY Series, Reform in Mathematics Education). 320p. 1995. pap. text ed. 19.95 (*0-7914-2162-7*) State U NY Pr.
— Reform in School Mathematics & Authentic Assessment. (SUNY Series, Reform in Mathematics Education). 320p. 1995. text ed. 59.50 (*0-7914-2161-9*) State U NY Pr.
Romberg, Thomas A., et al, eds. Integrating Research on the Graphical Representation of Functions. (Studies in Mathematical Thinking & Learning). 368p. 1994. text ed. 79.95 (*0-8058-1134-6*) L Erlbaum Assocs.
Romberger, J. A. Plant Structure: Function & Development - A Treatise on Anatomy & Vegetative Development, With Special Reference to Woody Plants. LC 93-20242. 1993. Acid-free paper. 219.00 (*0-387-56305-9*) Spr-Verlag.
Romberger, John A. Virology in Agriculture. LC 76-42139. (Beltsville Symposia in Agricultural Research Ser.: No. 1). 320p. 1977. text ed. 41.00 (*0-916672-14-X*) Rowman.
Rombke, Jorg, jt. ed. see Moltmann, Johann F.
Rombouts, A. Pecten Shells: Guide Book. Coomans, H. E. et al, eds. (Illus.). 184p. 1992. 40.00 (*90-73348-07-2*) Am Malacologists.
Rome, David, jt. auth. see Langlais, Jacques.
Rome, Donald L., et al. Business Workouts Manual. 2nd ed. (Bankruptcy Law Ser.). 736p. 1992. 130.00 (*0-7913-1014-0*) Warren Gorham & Lamont.
— Business Workouts Manual. 2nd suppl. ed. (Bankruptcy Law Ser.). 736p. 1992. Supplemented annually, write for info. 50.00 (*0-685-56392-8*) Warren Gorham & Lamont.
Rome, Dorothy, ed. see Parr, Judith D.
Rome, Edwin P. & Roberts, William H. Corporate & Commercial Free Speech: First Amendment Protection of Expression in Business. LC 84-26496. xii, 320p. 1985. text ed. 59.95 (*0-89930-041-3*, RCR/, Quorum Bks) Greenwood.
Rome, Marcus. Abreactions. 144p. (Orig.). 1989. pap. 15.00 (*0-913559-13-X*) Birch Brook Pr.
— Abreactions. deluxe limited ed. 144p. (Orig.). 1989. 35.00 (*0-913559-12-1*) Birch Brook Pr.
Rome, Margaret. Chateau of Flowers. large type ed. 1990. 21.95 (*0-7089-2340-2*) Ulverscroft.
— The Girl at Eagle's Mount. large type ed. 288p. 1992. 21. 95 (*0-7089-2595-2*) Ulverscroft.
— The Wild Man. large type ed. (Linford Romance Library). 288p. 1985. pap. 11.95 (*0-7089-6156-8*) Ulverscroft.
***Romei, Francesca.** Leonardo Da Vinci: Artist, Inventor & Scientist of the Renaissance. (Masters of Art Ser.). (Illus.). 64p. 1994. lib. bdg. 19.95 (*0-87226-313-4*) P Bedrick Bks.
— The Story of Sculpture: From Prehistory to the Present. LC 95-7006. (Masters of Art Ser.). (Illus.). 64p. 1995. 19.95 (*0-87226-316-9*) P Bedrick Bks.
Romeijn, H. E. Global Optimization by Random Walk Sampling Methods. (Tinbergen Institute Research Ser.). 144p. 1992. pap. 25.00 (*90-5170-157-8*, Pub. by Thesis Pubs NE) IBD Ltd.
Romeis, James C. & Coe, Rodney, eds. Quality & Cost-Containment in Care of the Elderly: Health Services Research Perspectives. LC 90-10439. 248p. 1991. 42.95 (*0-8261-7170-2*) Springer Pub.
Romeis, Robert S. The Encouraging Word. 2nd ed. 1989. write for info. (*0-318-66812-2*) Hibiscus Pr.
— The Encouraging Word: A Limited Edition. 1989. write for info. (*0-943787-01-7*) Hibiscus Pr.
Romeiser, John B. Andre Malraux: A Reference Guide, 1940-1990. LC 93-46322. (Reference Publications in Literature). 384p. 1994. text ed. 45.00 (*0-8161-9071-2*) G K Hall.
— Critical Reception of Andre Malraux's l'Espoir in the French Press: December 1937-June 1940. LC 79-19837. (Romance Monographs: No. 37). 176p. 1980. 24.00 (*84-499-3368-4*) Romance.
Romen, A. S. Self-Suggestion & Its Influence on the Human Organism. Lewis, A. J. & Forsky, Valentina, trs. LC 80-28703. Orig. Title: Samovnushenie I Ego Vliianie Na Organizm Cheloveka. (Illus.). 235p. reprint ed. pap. 67. 00 (*0-685-23745-1*, 2032786) Bks Demand.
Romenesko, James. Death Log. LC 82-90083. (Orig.). 1982. pap. 7.95 (*0-942724-00-3*) Police Beat Pr.
***Romeny, Bart M., ed.** Geometry-Driven Diffusion in Computer Vision. (Computational Imaging & Vision Ser.). 472p. (C). 1994. lib. bdg. 152.00 (*0-7923-3087-0*) Kluwer Ac.
Romeo, Catherine, jt. auth. see Panuthos, Claudia.
Romeo, Felicia F. Understanding Anorexia Nervosa. 116p. (C). 1986. 28.95 (*0-398-05191-7*) C C Thomas.
Romeo, Jean B., jt. auth. see Wolf, Jack S.
Romeo, Leticia B., ed. see American Institute of Certified Public Accountants Staff.
Romeo, Luigi. Ecce Homo! A Lexicon of Man. xv, 163p. 1979. 46.00x (*90-272-2006-9*) Benjamins North Am.
Romeo-Mark, Althea. Palaver: West Indian Poems. 1978. pap. 1.50 (*0-917402-10-3*) Downtown Poets.
Romeo, Sharon L., tr. see Lesourne, Jacques.
Romeo, Thomas J. Marfan Syndrome: Physcial Activity Guideline for Physical Educators, Coaches & Physicians. 77p. pap. 15.00 (*0-918335-08-6*) Natl Marfan Foun.
— The Marfan Syndrome: Physical Activity Guidelines for Physical Educators, Coaches & Physicians. 78p. 1992. pap. 15.00 (*0-918335-06-X*) Natl Marfan Foun.
Romer, jt. auth. see Haring, Norris G.
Romer, Alfred S. Notes & Comments on Vertebrate Paleontology. LC 66-13886. 1968. 17.50 (*0-226-72486-7*) U Ch Pr.
Romer, Alfred S. & Parsons, Thomas S. The Vertebrate Body. 6th ed. (Illus.). 656p. (C). 1986. text ed. 57.00 (*0-03-058446-9*) SCP.
Romer, Alfred S. & Price, Llewellyn I. Review of the Pelycosauria: Geological Society of American Special Papers, No. 28. Gould, Stephen J., ed. LC 79-8346. (History of Paleontology Ser.). (Illus.). 1980. reprint ed. lib. bdg. 55.95 (*0-405-12740-5*) Ayer.
Romer, Alfred S., et al. Bibliography of Fossil Vertebrates, Exclusive of North America, 1509-1927. LC 63-1118. (Geological Society of America, Memoir Ser.: No. 87, Vol. 2). 779p. reprint ed. pap. 180.00 (*0-8357-7183-0*, 2031792) Bks Demand.
Romer, David, jt. ed. see Mankiw, N. Gregory.
Romer, Elizabeth. The Tuscan Year: Life & Food in an Italian Valley. LC 88-37226. 192p. 1989. pap. 9.95 (*0-86547-387-0*, North Pt Pr) FS&G.
— Tuscan Year: Life & Food in an Italian Valley. 1994. 20. 00 (*0-86547-478-8*, North Pt Pr) FS&G.
Romer, Elizabeth, jt. auth. see Romer, John.
Romer, Hartmann, jt. auth. see Honerkamp, Josef.
Romer, Joe. Hydroponic Crop Production. (Illus.). 170p. 1993. 24.95 (*0-86417-527-2*, Pub. by Kangaroo Pr AT) Seven Hills Bk.
Romer, John. Ancient Lives: Daily Life in Egypt of the Pharaohs. LC 84-12908. (Owl Bks.). (Illus.). 256p. 1990. pap. 18.95 (*0-8050-1244-3*) H Holt & Co.
— Testament: The Bible & History. (Illus.). 368p. 1989. 29. 95 (*0-8050-0939-6*) H Holt & Co.
— Testament: The Bible & History. (Illus.). 368p. 1993. pap. 18.95 (*0-8050-2692-4*) H Holt & Co.
— Valley of the Kings. (Illus.). 288p. 1994. pap. 19.95 (*0-8050-3027-1*) H Holt & Co.
Romer, John & Romer, Elizabeth. The Rape of Tutankhamun. (Illus.). 160p. 1993. 44.50 (*1-85479-169-9*, Pub. by M OMara Books UK) Trans-Atl Phila.
Romer, Ken. Dorothy & the Wooden Soldiers. (Illus.). 52p. (J). (gr. 3-7). 1987. Colorina book with story. pap. 3.95 (*0-932458-35-1*) Star Rover.
Romer, R. Legislative Action to Combat the World Tobacco Epidemic. 2nd ed. xiii, 297p. 1993. pap. text ed. 53.10 (*92-4-156157-2*) World Health.
Romer, Robert H. Energy Facts & Figures. LC 84-16278. 72p. (Orig.). 1985. pap. 8.95 (*0-931691-17-6*) Spring St Pr.
Romer, Stephen. Idols. 64p. 1987. pap. 7.95 (*0-19-281984-4*) OUP.
— Plato's Ladder. 80p. 1993. pap. 11.95 (*0-19-282986-6*) OUP.
Romer, Theodore. Fight to Live - Live to Fight. 180p. (Orig.). 1989. pap. text ed. 4.95 (*0-9616898-3-8*, TX 2-779-127) Phoenix Pr FL.
Romer, Therese, tr. see Dion, Leon.
Romeralo, Antonio S., ed. see Jimenez, Juan R.
Romero. Essentials of Neuroanatomy. 1990. 34.00 (*1-55664-121-4*) Mosby Yr Bk.
Romero, Adrian, jt. auth. see Browne, Louis.
Romero, Arthur, jt. auth. see Romero, Cynthia.
Romero, Bernice, jt. ed. see Tulchin, Joseph S.
Romero, C. & Rehman, T. Multiple Criteria Analysis for Agricultural Designs. (Developments in Agricultural Economics Ser.: No. 5). 257p. 1989. 92.50 (*0-444-87408-9*) Elsevier.
Romero, Carlos. Handbook of Critical Issues in Goal Programming. 160p. 1991. text ed. 83.00 (*0-08-040661-0*, Pergamon Pr) Elsevier.
***Romero, Christie.** Warman's Jewelry. 304p. 1995. pap. 18. 95 (*0-87069-696-3*) Chilton.

R

An Asterisk (*) at the beginning of an entry indicates that the title is appearing in BIP for the first time.

Romero, Cynthia & Romero, Arthur. Albuquerque Trivia: A Treasury of Niceties. (Illus.). 101p. (Orig.). 1993. pap. text ed. 7.95 (1-880047-06-3) Creative Des.

***Romero, Edna.** A Bug C. (Illus.). 48p. (J). (ps-3). 1993. pap. 10.95 (1-880812-07-X) S Ink WA.

Romero, Emilio. Las Ratas Suben a la Ciudad. Verde Doncella O el Marido para Despues. (Nueva Austral Ser.: Vol. 76). (SPA.). 1991. pap. text ed. 24.95x (84-239-1876-9) Elliots Bks.

Romero, Enrique, jt. auth. see Avenell, Donne.

Romero, Enrique M, jt. ed. see Cassaro, Michael A.

Romero, Federico. The United States & the European Trade Union Movement, 1944-1951. Fergusson, Harvey, II, tr. LC 92-27645. xvi, 292p. (C). 1993. 39.95 (0-8078-2065-2) U of NC Pr.

Romero Garcia, Luz V. El Aldeanismo en la Poesia de Luis Pales Matos. (UPREX, Estudios Literarios Ser.: No. 42). 119p. (C). 1976. pap. 1.50 (0-8477-0042-9) U of PR Pr.

Romero, George, jt. auth. see Skulan, Tom.

Romero, Gilbert C. Hispanic Devotional Piety: Tracing the Biblical Roots. LC 91-18620. (Faith & Cultures Ser.). 175p. (Orig.). 1991. pap. 16.95 (0-88344-767-3) Orbis Bks.

Romero Gualda, Maria V. Vocabulario de Cine y Television en Espana. 400p. (SPA.). 1976. pap. 29.95 (0-8288-5763-6, S50002) Fr & Eur.

Romero, Hector H. Nuevas Perspectivas Sobre La Generacion Del 27: Ensayos Literaries. LC 81-69021. (Coleccion Polymita Ser.). 169p. (Orig.). (SPA.). 1983. pap. 14.95 (0-89729-299-5) Ediciones.

Romero, Hector R. La Evolucion Literaria De Juan Goytisolo. LC 78-74702. (Coleccion Polymita Ser.). 162p. (SPA.). 1979. pap. 10.00 (0-89729-222-7) Ediciones.

Romero, Javier. Instante e Intensidad. (UPREX, Poesia Ser.: No. 56). 64p. (SPA.). 1978. pap. text ed. 1.50 (0-8477-0056-9) U of PR Pr.

Romero, Joan A., ed. see Plaskow, Judith.

***Romero, John.** How to Beat Stress. 1992. pap. 9.95 (0-9630158-4-2) Baker-Hill.

***Romero, John S.** Casino Marketing. Quiroga, Robin M., ed. LC 94-78077. 288p. 1994. 49.95 (0-9642414-0-4) J R Direct Mktg.

Romero, Jose L. A History of Argentine Political Thought. McGann, Thomas F., tr. xvii, 270p. 1963. 35.00 (0-8047-0108-3) Stanford U Pr.

— A History of Argentine Political Thought. 294p. reprint ed. pap. 83.80 (0-7837-3948-6, 2043777) Bks Demand.

Romero, Jose R. Notes of a Villager: A Mexican Poet's Youth & Revolution. Mitchell, John & de Aguilar, Ruth M., trs. LC 88-4042. 224p. 1995. 15.95 (0-917635-04-3); pap. 9.95 (0-917635-05-1) Plover Pr.

Romero, Juan. Inspirational Pathways: Senderos De Inspiracion. (SPA.). 2.50 (84-7228-738-6, 220809, Pub. by Edit Clie SP) TSELF.

Romero, Leo. Agua Negra. 4th ed. Boyer, Dale, ed. LC 81-68459. (Ahsahta Press Modern & Contemporary Poets of the West Ser.). 55p. 1981. pap. 6.95 (0-916272-17-6) Ahsahta Pr.

— Celso. LC 84-72302. 80p. (Orig.). (C). 1984. pap. 7.00 (0-934770-36-0) Arte Publico.

— Going Home Away Indian. Boyer, Dale K., ed. LC 89-80859. (Ahsahta Press Modern & Contemporary Poets of the West Ser.). 110p. (Orig.). 1990. pap. 6.95 (0-916272-41-9) Ahsahta Pr.

— Rita & Los Angeles. 144p. (Orig.). 1995. pap. 12.00 (0-927534-44-4) Biling Rev-Pr.

Romero, Leo M. An Administrative Model of Juvenile Justice. 55p. 1975. 4.00 (0-318-15762-4, JLD) Natl Juv & Family Ct Judges.

Romero, Luis. Cuerda Tensa. LC 79-66063. 62p. 1979. pap. 12.00 (0-89295-012-9) Society Sp & Sp-Am.

Romero, Luis A. Latin America: Its Cities & Ideas. (C). 1929. text ed. 45.00 (0-8133-1320-1) Westview.

Romero, Mary. Maid in the U.S.A. (Perspectives on Gender Ser.). 256p. 1992. 49.95 (0-415-90611-3, A7362, Routledge NY); pap. 15.95 (0-415-90612-1, A7366, Routledge NY) Routledge.

***Romero-Oak, Judy.** The Secret Place. 97p. 1994. pap. 14.95 (0-9644174-0-5) Writing Designs.

Romero, Orlando. Nambe-Year One. LC 76-13385. 1976. pap. 6.00 (0-89229-003-X) TQS Pubns.

Romero, Orlando & Larkin, David. Adobe: Building & Living with Earth. LC 94-11692. (Illus.). 1994. 50.00 (0-395-56693-2) HM.

Romero, Oscar. Voice of the Voiceless: The Four Pastoral Letters & Other Statements. Walsh, Michael J., tr. LC 84-14722. 208p. (Orig.). 1985. pap. 14.95 (0-88344-525-5) Orbis Bks.

Romero, Patricia, ed. Life Histories of African Women. LC 87-1441. (C). 1987. pap. 15.95 (0-948660-05-8, Pub. by Ashfield Pr UK) Humanities.

Romero, Patricia, ed. see Balewa, Alhaji S.

Romero, Patricia W. E. Sylvia Pankhurst. LC 86-7796. 325p. 1987. 40.00 (0-300-03691-4) Yale U Pr.

— E. Sylvia Pankhurst: Portrait of a Radical. 352p. (C). 1990. reprint ed. 22.00 (0-300-04482-8) Yale U Pr.

Romero, Patricia W., intro. Women's Voices on Africa. LC 91-36228. (Topics in World History Ser.). (Illus.). 324p. (C). 1992. text ed. 39.95 (1-55876-047-4); pap. text ed. 14.95 (1-55876-048-2) Wiener Pubs Inc.

Romero, Patricia W., ed. see Taylor, Susie K.

Romero, Roberto, et al. Prenatal Diagnosis of Congenital Anomalies. (Illus.). 466p. 1987. boxed 105.00 (0-8385-7921-3, A7921-8) Appleton & Lange.

Romero-Sierra, C. Neuroanatomy: A Conceptual Approach. LC 85-28060. (Illus.). 463p. (Orig.). reprint ed. pap. 132.00 (0-7837-1609-5, 2041901) Bks Demand.

Romero, Vicki L. & Henry, Judith B. CFO's Expectations for Patient Financial Services. 50p. 1992. 20.00 (0-930228-87-1) Hlthcare Fin Mgmt.

Romerstein, Herbert. The World Peace Council & Soviet Active Measures. 1983. pap. 5.00 (0-935067-01-9) Nathan Hale Inst.

Romerstein, Herbert & Levchenko, Stanislav. The KGB Against the "Main Enemy" 384p. 1989. text ed. 22.95 (0-669-11228-3) Free Pr.

***Romesburg, Don A., ed.** Young, Gay, & Proud! 4th ed. (Illus.). 120p. (YA). (gr. 7-12). 1995. pap. 5.95 (1-55583-279-2) Alyson Pubns.

Romesburg, H. Charles. Cluster Analysis for Researchers. LC 89-24453. 350p. (C). 1990. reprint ed. lib. bdg. 46.50 (0-89464-426-2) Krieger.

Romeu, Jose A. Panorama del Periodismo Puertorriqueno. (UPREX, Communicacion Ser.: No. 67). 225p. 1985. pap. 6.00 (0-8477-0067-4) U of PR Pr.

Romeu, Xavier. Breu Diccionari Ideologic Catala. 270p. (CAT.). 1977. pap. 19.95 (0-8288-5291-X, S50236) Fr & Eur.

Romey, William D. & Hibert, Mary L. Teaching the Gifted & Talented in the Science Classroom. 2nd ed. 64p. 1987. 8.95 (0-8106-0748-4) NEA.

***Romeyn, Mary.** Nutrition & HIV: A New Model for Treatment. LC 95-10538. (Social & Behavioral Studies). 1995. 25.00 (0-7879-0107-5) Jossey-Bass.

Romfo, Chey, jt. auth. see Cobb, Stephen.

Romhild, Jurgen, ed. see Richter, Hans.

Romicki, R., jt. auth. see Meshcherskii, I.

Romig, et al. Juvenile Delinquency: Visionary Approaches. 160p. (C). 1989. pap. write for info. (0-675-21013-5, Merrill Pub Co) Macmillan.

Romig, A. D., Jr., ed. see Metallurgical Society of AIME Staff.

Romig, A. D., et al, eds. Structure-Property Relationships for Metal-Metal Interfaces: Materials Research Society Symposium Proceedings, Vol. 229. 1991. text ed. 74.00 (1-55899-123-9) Materials Res.

Romig, Anne L., jt. auth. see Romig, Ronald E.

Romig, Candace L., ed. see NCSL Children, Families & Social Services Committee Staff.

***Romig, Emily.** Pioneer Woman in Alaska. (American Autobiography Ser.). 140p. 1995. reprint ed. lib. bdg. 69.00 (0-7812-8628-X) Rprt Serv.

Romig, Harry G., jt. auth. see Dodge, Harold F.

Romig, Jack, jt. auth. see Bennett, Carolyn.

***Romig, Nancy B.** Scrips & Scraps: Scrapbook Abstracts Venango County & Surrounding Counties. 318p. 1995. pap. 24.95 (1-55856-191-9) Closson Pr.

Romig, Ralph. Sacred Refuge. LC 80-14984. 1987. pap. 13.95 (0-87949-189-2) Ashley Bks.

Romig, Robert E. Reasonable Religion: A CommonSense Approach. LC 84-42823. 183p. 1984. 27.95 (0-87975-252-1) Prometheus Bks.

Romig, Ronald E. & Romig, Anne L. Stewardship Concepts & Practices. LC 92-24180. (Studies in Restoration History). 35p. 1992. pap. 4.50 (0-8309-0622-3) Herald Hse.

Romig, Walter. Michigan Place Names. LC 86-15858. (Great Lakes Bks.). 675p. 1986. reprint ed. 55.00 (0-8143-1837-1); reprint ed. pap. 19.95 (0-8143-1838-X) Wayne St U Pr.

Romig, Walter, ed. Book of Catholic Authors, Fourth Series: Informal Self-Portraits of Famous Modern Catholic Writers. LC 70-179740. (Biography Index Reprint Ser.). 1977. reprint ed. 30.95 (0-8369-8108-1) Ayer.

Romijn, J. C., et al, eds. Mechanisms of Progression to Hormone-Independent Growth of Breast & Prostatic Cancer. (Illus.). (C). 1991. 35.00 (1-85070-356-6) Prthnon Pub.

Romijn & Seely. Live Action English. 68p. 1979. pap. text ed. 6.25 (0-88084-025-0); Set of 2 cassettes. audio 19.00 (0-88084-221-0) Alemany Pr.

Romijn, Elizabeth, jt. auth. see Seely, Contee.

Romilly, Hugh H. From My Verandah in New Guinea: Sketches & Traditions. 1977. text ed. 18.95 (0-8369-9233-4, 9087) Ayer.

Romine, A. Russell, jt. auth. see Evans, Lynn D.

Romine, A. Russell, jt. auth. see Smith, Kelly L.

Romine, A. Russell, jt. auth. see Wilson, Thomas P.

Romine, Charles, ed. see Winter, Gerald A.

Romine, Jack S. Vocabulary for Adults. LC 75-17660. (Self-Teaching Guides Ser.). 221p. (C). 1975. pap. text ed. 12.95 (0-471-73285-0) Wiley.

Romine, Jack S., et al. College Business English. 3rd ed. (Illus.). 400p. 1981. pap. text ed. write for info. (0-13-141960-9) P-H.

— College Business English. 4th ed. (Illus.). 352p. 1988. pap. text ed. write for info. (0-13-141888-2) P-H.

Romine, James, jt. auth. see Shah, Rawn.

Romines, Ann. The Home Plot: Women, Writing, & Domestic Ritual. LC 91-34053. 336p. (C). 1992. pap. text ed. 16.95 (0-87023-794-2) U of Mass Pr.

Rominger, James M., jt. auth. see Mayes, Vernon O.

Rominski, F. Zarod. Seven Windows, Stories of Women. LC 85-22394. 151p. (Orig.). 1985. pap. 7.95 (0-9615216-1-9) Crones Own Pr.

Romiszowski, A. J. Designing Instructional Systems: Decision-Making in Course Planning & Curriculum Design. 418p. 1984. 34.95 (0-89397-181-2) Nichols Pub.

— Developing Auto-Instructional Materials. 460p. (Orig.). 1987. pap. 35.95 (0-89397-269-X) Nichols Pub.

— New Technologies in Education & Training: Efficient Tools or Seeds of Change? 300p. (C). 1994. text ed. 54.95 (0-89397-417-X) Nichols Pub.

— Producing Instructional Systems. 286p. 1986. pap. 33.95 (0-89397-244-4) Nichols Pub.

— The Selection & Use of Instructional Media. 2nd rev. ed. 400p. 43.95 (0-89397-376-9) Nichols Pub.

Romiszowski, Alexander, et al. Case Studies in Instructional Design & Development. 300p. 1994. text ed. 74.95 (0-8464-1423-6) Beekman Pubs.

Romiszowski, Alexander J. Computer Mediated Communication: A Selected Bibliography. LC 91-43966. 55p. (Orig.). 1992. pap. 19.95 (0-87778-243-1) Educ Tech Pubns.

***Romiszowski, Alexander J. & Gratch, Bonnie.** Telecommunications & Teleconferencing in Education & Training: A Selected Bibliography. LC 95-6110. (Educational Technology Selected Bibliography Ser.: Vol. 13). 63p. 1995. 19.95 (0-87778-281-4) Educ Tech Pubns.

Romita, A. C., et al, eds. Accelerated Processing of Meat: Proceedings of a Workshop on Accelerated Processing in the Slaughter House, Istituto Sperimentale per la Zootecnia, Monterotondo, Rome, Itlay, 29-31 October, 1985. 292p. 1987. 63.00 (1-85166-156-5, Pub. by Elsevier Applied Sci UK) Elsevier.

***Romke, Adam & Novak, Derry, eds.** The Communist States in the Era of Detente. 360p. 1995. lib. bdg. 33.00 (0-8095-4934-4) Borgo Pr.

Romkey, Michael. I, Vampire. 368p. (Orig.). 1990. mass mkt. 4.95 (0-449-14638-3, GM) Fawcett.

Romkowska, S. English-Polish Dictionary of Abbreviations in Electronics. 150p. (C). 1988. 59.00 (0-685-54135-5, Pub. by Collets) St Mut.

Romm. The Changing Face of Beauty. 346p. 1991. 99.00 (0-8016-5505-6) Mosby Yr Bk.

Romm, J. Leonard. The Swastika on the Synagogue Door. 2nd ed. LC 94-46454. (Lazarus Family Mystery Ser.). (Illus.). 168p. (Orig.). (J). (gr. 6-9). 1994. reprint ed. pap. 5.95 (1-881283-05-4) Alef Design.

Romm, James S. The Edges of the Earth in Ancient Thought: Geography, Exploration, & Fiction. 256p. 1992. text ed. 35.00 (0-691-06933-6) Princeton U Pr.

— Edges of the Earth in Ancient Thought: Geography, Exploration, & Fiction. 1994. pap. 14.95 (0-691-03788-4) Princeton U Pr.

Romm, Joseph J. Defining National Security. (Pew Project Ser.). 96p. 1993. pap. 10.95 (0-87609-135-4) Coun Foreign.

— Lean & Clean Management: How to Boost Profits & Productivity by Reducing Pollution. 224p. 1994. 23.00 (1-56836-037-1) Kodansha.

— The Once & Future Superpower: How to Restore America's Economic, Energy, & Environmental Security. 320p. 1992. 23.00 (0-688-11868-2) Morrow.

Romm, Sharon. The Unwelcome Intruder: Freud's Struggle with Cancer. LC 83-13649. (Illus.). 188p. 1983. text ed. 55.00 (0-275-91409-7, C1409, Praeger Pubs) Greenwood.

Romme, Jac, jt. ed. see Hoekstra, Sjoerd.

Rommel, Bart. Dirty Tricks Cops Use: (And Why They Do Them) LC 93-77151. 160p. (Orig.). 1993. pap. 14.95 (1-55950-101-4, 58084) Loompanics.

— Execution: Tools & Techniques. LC 90-63309. 400p. (Orig.). 1990. pap. 12.95 (1-55950-051-4, 34056) Loompanics.

Rommel, Carol A. Integrating Beginning Math & Literature. (Illus.). 80p. (Orig.). 1991. pap. text ed. 8.95 (0-86530-215-4, IP 192-9) Incentive Pubns.

Rommel, Erwin. Attacks. rev. ed. Allen, Lee, ed. Driscoll, J. R., tr. LC 79-52022. (Illus.). (GER.). 1979. pap. 15.45 (0-9602736-0-3) Athena Pr.

— Infantry Attacks. (Illus.). 288p. 1995. pap. 17.95 (1-85367-199-1, Pub. by Greenhill Bks UK) Stackpole.

***Rommel, Gunter, et al.** Simplicity Wins: How Germany's Mid-Sized Industrial Companies Succeed. LC 94-34599. 1995. 27.95 (0-87584-504-5) Harvard Busn.

Rommel, J., jt. auth. see Leonard, P.

Rommel, John G. Connecticut's Yankee Patriot: Roger Sherman. LC 79-57127. (Connecticut Bicentennial Ser.: Vol. XXXIV). 1980. write for info. (0-918676-20-7) Conn Hist Com.

Rommell, Otto, ed. see Nestroy, Johann N.

Rommen, Edward, jt. auth. see Hesselgrave, David J.

Rommen, Heinrich A. The Natural Law. Mayer, J. P., ed. LC 78-67382. (European Political Thought Ser.). 1980. reprint ed. lib. bdg. 23.95 (0-405-11732-9) Ayer.

— Die Staatslehre des Franz Suarez, S. J. Mayer, J. P., ed. LC 78-67381. (European Political Thought Ser.). (GER.). 1980. reprint ed. lib. bdg. 30.95 (0-405-11731-0) Ayer.

— State in Catholic Thought: A Treatise in Political Philosophy. LC 74-91770. 747p. 1970. reprint ed. text ed. 38.50 (0-8371-2437-9, ROCT, Greenwood Pr) Greenwood.

Rommetveit, R. & Blaker, R. M., eds. Studies of Language, Thought & Verbal Communication. 1979. text ed. 186.00 (0-12-594660-0) Acad Pr.

Rommetveit, Ragnar. On Message Structure: A Framework for the Study of Language & Communication. LC 74-174. reprint ed. pap. 37.80 (0-317-29388-5, 2024284) Bks Demand.

— On Message Structure: A Framework for the Study of Language & Communication. LC 74-174. 151p. reprint ed. pap. 43.10 (0-317-39678-1, 2024284) Bks Demand.

Rommey, Marshall B., jt. auth. see Cushing, Barry E.

Romney, A. Kimball, jt. auth. see Weller, Susan C.

Romney, Brad, jt. auth. see Romney, Keith B.

***Romney, David M., ed.** Improving the Quality of Life: Recommendations for People with & Without Disabilities. 1995. write for info. (0-7923-3234-2) Kluwer Ac.

Romney, David M. & Bynner, John M. The Structure of Personal Characteristics. LC 92-18845. 160p. 1992. text ed. 47.95 (0-275-93995-2, C3995, Praeger Pubs) Greenwood.

***Romney, Ed.** Fixing up Nice Old Radios. 186p. 1990. pap. text ed. 25.00 (0-614-04287-9) Hillcrst Pub.

— Romney Dealer Text: How to Make Money Buying & Selling Old Cameras. 84p. 1977. pap. text ed. 24.00 (1-886996-59-8) Hillcrst Pub.

Romney, Ed, jt. auth. see Tannehill, James.

***Romney, Edward H.** Basic Training in Camera Repair Tape Learning Program. 122p. 1993. audio 99.00 (1-886996-55-5) Hillcrst Pub.

— Contax Camera Repair. 44p. 1992. pap. text ed. 18.00 (1-886996-65-2) Hillcrst Pub.

— Ed Romney & His Cameras. 52p. 1995. pap. write for info. (1-886996-57-1) Hillcrst Pub.

— Ed Romney's Graphic Repair for Graphic Cameras. 35p. 1989. pap. text ed. 19.00 (1-886996-58-X) Hillcrst Pub.

— Ed Romney's Rolleiflex Rollei Cord Camera Repair: Repair & User's Guide. 36p. 1978. pap. 25.00 (1-886996-61-X) Hillcrst Pub.

— Home Repair & Restoration of Antique Cameras. 33p. 1976. pap. text ed. 12.00 (1-886996-62-8) Hillcrst Pub.

— Leica Camera Repair. 64p. 1985. pap. text ed. 25.00 (1-886996-56-3) Hillcrst Pub.

— Living Well on Practically Nothing. (Illus.). 160p. 1992. pap. 19.95 (0-87364-694-0) Paladin Pr.

— Original Search for Human Theory. 252p. 1994. pap. 29.00 (1-886996-53-9) Hillcrst Pub.

— Restoring Traditional Values: The Search for Human Theory. 110p. 1995. 25.00 (1-886996-51-2); pap. 19.95 (1-886996-50-4) Hillcrst Pub.

— Revised Basic Training in Camera Repair. 132p. 1993. pap. text ed. 29.00 (1-886996-52-0) Hillcrst Pub.

— Stereo Realist Camera Repair Manual: Repair & User's Manual. 26p. 1992. pap. text ed. 18.00 (1-886996-64-4) Hillcrst Pub.

Romney, Eldon C. World's Stupidest I. Q. Test. (Illus.). 64p. (Orig.). (C). 1992. pap. 4.95 (0-9632451-0-4) Creat Diversions.

Romney, George. Drawings of Romney. Longstreet, Stephen, ed. (Master Draughtsman Ser.). 1970. 10.95 (0-87505-032-8); pap. 4.95 (0-87505-185-5) Borden.

Romney, Keith B. & Romney, Brad. Condominium Development Guide. 2nd ed. 1000p. 1990. boxed 98.00 (0-88262-908-5) Warren Gorham & Lamont.

— Condominium Development Guide, No. 1. 2nd suppl. ed. 1000p. 1990. 59.50 (0-7913-0699-2) Warren Gorham & Lamont.

Romney, Kimball & Romney, Romaine. The Mixtecans of Juxtlahuaca, Mexico. LC 66-17616. 186p. 1974. reprint ed. pap. text ed. 9.50 (0-88275-136-0) Krieger.

Romney, Marshall B. & Hansen, James V. Data Communications: Concepts & Controls. Campbell, Lee A., ed. (IIA Monograph). 66p. 1987. pap. text ed. 15.00 (0-89413-162-1) Inst Inter Aud.

— An Introduction to Microcomputers & Their Controls. Holman, Richard, ed. (Illus.). 1985. pap. text ed. 33.00 (0-89413-131-1) Inst Inter Aud.

Romney, Marshall B., jt. auth. see Cushing, Barry E.

Romney, Marshall D., jt. auth. see Cushing, Barry E.

Romney, Mary. The Devil Take You, Sweetest. large type ed. 336p. 1987. 16.95 (0-7089-1669-4) Ulverscroft.

— The Long Vacation. large type ed. 304p. 1987. 16.95 (0-7089-1715-1) Ulverscroft.

— Love Lies Waiting. large type ed. (General Ser.). 432p. 1993. 21.95 (0-7089-2867-6) Ulverscroft.

Romney, Paul. Mr. Attorney: The Attorney General for Ontario in Court, Cabinet & Legislature, 1791-1899. 456p. 1986. 47.50 (0-8020-3431-4) U of Toronto Pr.

Romney, Rodney R. Love Without Conditions. (Orig.). 1986. pap. write for info. (0-936415-01-0) Riverrun Piermont.

Romney, Romaine, jt. auth. see Romney, Kimball.

Romo, Alberto. Sombrero De Tres Picos. (Classics in Spanish Literature Ser.). 1987. pap. text ed. 11.25 (0-13-273814-7) Prentice ESL.

Romo, Alberto, tr. see Marzollo, Jean.

Romo, Alberto, tr. see San Souci, Robert.

Romo De Mease, Ana M. & Biksler Mease, Larry. Encuentros: A Communicative Work Text for Spanish. 216p. (C). 1994. per. 19.95 (0-8403-9338-5) Kendall-Hunt.

Romo, Harriet D., ed. Latinos & Blacks in the Cities: Policies for the 1990's. (Symposia Ser.). 236p. 1990. 10.00 (0-89940-423-5) LBJ Sch Pub Aff.

Romo, Jesus, jt. auth. see Sanchez, Guadalupe L.

Romo, Miguel P., jt. ed. see Resendiz, Daniel.

Romo, Oscar. American Mosaic: Church Planting in Ethnic America. (Orig.). 1993. pap. 8.95 (0-8054-6070-5) Broadman.

Romo, Ricardo. East Los Angeles: History of a Barrio. LC 82-10891. 232p. 1983. pap. 10.95 (0-292-72041-6) U of Tex Pr.

Romo, Ricardo & Paredes, Raymund, eds. New Directions in Chicano Scholarship. rev. ed. (Monographs in Chicano Studies). 279p. (C). 1977. reprint ed. pap. 18.95 (0-930929-00-4) U CA Ctr Chicano Stud.

Romo, Rora. Jesus Is Here for His World Again: Repent & Pray. 1992. 16.95 (0-533-10022-4) Vantage.

Romond, Edwin. Home Fire. 72p. 1992. pap. 8.00 (1-879462-01-X) Belle Mead Pr.

Romond, Janis. Children Facing Grief. LC 88-83363. 40p. (Orig.). 1989. pap. 2.95 (0-87029-221-8, 20211-9) Abbey.

Romond, Marguerite P., ed. see Pfeiffer, Philip A.

Romonovski, P. & Slater, M. Mathematical Methods for Engineers & Technologists. LC 60-14989. 1961. 113.00 (0-08-009430-9, Pub. by Pergamon Repr UK) Franklin.

***Romos, Alcida R.** Sanuma Memories: Yanomani Ethnography in Times of Crisis. LC 94-39614. (New Directions in Anthropological Writing Ser.). (Illus.). 320p. 1995. lib. bdg. 50.00 (0-299-14650-2); pap. text ed. 19.95 (0-299-14654-5) U of Wis Pr.

Romoser, George K., jt. ed. see Wallach, H. G.

Romoser, William & Stoffolano, John G., Jr. The Science of Entomology. 3rd ed. 552p. (C). 1993. text ed. 63.00 (0-697-03349-X) Wm C Brown Pubs.

Rompelman, O., jt. ed. see Kitney, R. I.

R

Rompf, Kraft. Five Fingers. (Orig.). 1981. pap. 4.00 (*0-939162-00-8*) Numen Chapbks.
Rompf, Kraft, jt. auth. see Diyanni, Robert.
Rompf, Kraft, jt. auth. see DiYanni, Robert.
Rompf, Shirley J., jt. auth. see Mackie, Benita.
Rompkey, Ronald. Grenfell of Labrador: A Biography. 448p. 1991. 35.00 (*0-8020-5919-8*) U of Toronto Pr.
Rompkey, Ronald, ed. Expeditions of Honour: The Journal of John Salusbury in Halifax, Nova Scotia, 1749-1753. LC 79-13797. (Illus.). 224p. 1982. 32.50 (*0-87413-169-3*) U Delaware Pr.
Romportle, Milan. Studies in Phonetics. (Janua Linguarum, Ser. Major: No. 61). 217p. (C). 1973. text ed. 46.15 (*90-279-2667-0*) Mouton.
Rompp, Georg. Husserls Phanomenologie der Intersubjektivitat: Und Ihre Bdedutung Fur eine Theorie Intersubjektiver Objektivitat und die Konzeption Einer Phanomenologischen Philosophie. 248p. (C). 1992. lib. bdg. 115.50 (*0-7923-1361-5*) Kluwer Ac.
Romrell, Lynn J., et al. Sectional Anatomy of the Head & Neck with Correlative Radiology. LC 92-49088. (Illus.). 230p. 1994. text ed. 125.00 (*0-8121-1673-9*) Williams & Wilkins.
Romsics, Ignac, ed. Wartime America Plans for a New Hungary: Developments from the U. S. Department of State, 1942-44. (Atlantic Studies on Society & Change: No. 77). 316p. (C). 1993. text ed. 45.00 (*0-88033-251-4*) Col U Pr.
Romstedt. Building Academic Fluency. 1992. pap. 18.95 (*0-8384-3412-6*) Heinle & Heinle.
— Building Academic Fluency. 1992. teacher ed, pap. 7.95 (*0-8384-3988-8*) Heinle & Heinle.
Romtvedt, David. Crossing Wyoming. 1992. pap. 12.00 (*1-877727-23-7*) White Pine.
— A Flower Whose Name I Do Not Know. (National Poetry Ser.). 80p. (Orig.). 1992. pap. 10.00 (*1-55659-046-6*) Copper Canyon.
— Moon. LC 82-22812. (Illus.). 1984. 112.50 (*0-931460-14-X*); pap. 6.95 (*0-931460-16-6*) Bieler.
Romtvedt, David, jt. ed. see Iberlin, Dollie.
Romulo, Beth D. Forty Years: A Third World Soldier at the UN. LC 85-30200. (Studies in Freedom: No. 3). (Illus.). 240p. 1986. text ed. 55.00 (*0-313-25358-7*, RFY/, Greenwood Pr) Greenwood.
— Forty Years: A Third World Soldier at the UN. LC 87-2370. (Studies in Freedom: No. 3). (Illus.). 240p. 1987. pap. text ed. 14.95 (*0-275-92729-6*, B2729, Praeger Pubs) Greenwood.
Romulo, Beth D., jt. auth. see Romulo, Carlos P.
Romulo, Carlos P. Crusade in Asia: Philippine Victory. LC 73-5206. 309p. 1973. reprint ed. text ed. 35.00 (*0-8371-6865-1*, ROCA, Greenwood Pr) Greenwood.
— I See the Philippines Rise. LC 79-163491. reprint ed. 27.50 (*0-404-09038-9*) AMS Pr.
Romulo, Carlos P. & Romulo, Beth D. The Philippine Presidents: Memoirs. (Illus.). (Orig.). (C). 1989. pap. 12.50 (*971-10-0384-8*, Pub. by New Day Pub PH) Cellar.
Romvary, F., jt. auth. see Hars, E.
Romweber, Marilyn. Favorites from the Little Mushroom: Elegant & Easy Recipes from Marilyn Romweber. LC 87-21049. 376p. 1987. pap. 13.95 (*0-87833-594-3*) Taylor Pub.
Romzek, Barbara S., jt. auth. see Ingraham, Patricia W.
Ron, Aviva, et al. Health Insurance in Developing Countries: The Social Security Approach. x, 231p. (Orig.). 1993. pap. 24.00 (*92-2-106475-1*) Intl Labour Office.
Ron B, comp. My Mind Is Out to Get Me: Humor & Wisdom in Recovery. LC 93-42421. 1994. write for info. (*0-15-683010-8*, Hazelden SF) Harper SF.
Ron, E. Z. & Rottem, S., eds. Microbial Surface Components & Toxins in Relation to Pathogenesis. (FEMS Symposium Ser.: No. 51). (Illus.). 210p. 1991. 75.00 (*0-306-43908-5*, Plenum Pr) Plenum.
Ron, Yacov, jt. ed. see Sigal, Leonard H.
Rona, D. C. Guide to Professional Records. (Illus.). 50p. (Orig.). 1982. pap. 8.50 (*0-911127-00-3*) CRS Pr.
Rona, Donna C. Environmental Permits: A Time-Saving Guide. (Illus.). 320p. 1988. text ed. 52.95 (*0-442-27838-1*) Chapman & Hall.
Rona, G., ed. see Schibsbye, K. & Kossmann, H.
Rona, Jeff. MIDI - The In's, Out's & Thru's. 96p. (Orig.). 1987. pap. 12.95 (*0-88188-560-6*, 00183495) H Leonard.
— The MIDI Companion. (Illus.). 96p. 1994. pap. 14.95 (*0-7935-3077-6*, HL00183500) H Leonard.
— Synchronization: From Reel to Reel - A Complete Guide for the Synchronization of Audio, Film & Video. (Illus.). 80p. (Orig.). 1988. pap. 16.95 (*0-88188-905-9*, 00239235) H Leonard.
Rona, Peter A., ed. Mid-Atlantic Ridge. LC 76-47736. (Microform Publication: No. 5). (Illus.). 1976. mic. film 1.25 (*0-8137-6005-4*) Geol Soc.
Rona, Peter A., et al, eds. Hydrothermal Processes at Seafloor Spreading Centers. LC 83-17747. (NATO Conference Series IV, Marine Sciences: Vol. 12). 810p. 1983. 145.00 (*0-306-41482-1*, Plenum Pr) Plenum.
Rona-Tas, A. An Introduction to Turkology. (Studio Uralo-Altaica (SUA) Ser.: No. 33). 170p. 1993. pap. 76.00 (*0-685-68160-2*) Benjamins North Am.
Rona-Tas, A., ed. Studies in Chuvash Etymology I. (Studia Oralo-Altaica Ser.: No. 17). 240p. 1982. 48.00 (*0-686-36268-3*) Benjamins North Am.
Rona-Tas, Andras. Language & History: Contributions to Comparative Altaistics. (Studia Uralo-Altaica Ser.: No. 25). iv, 270p. (C). 1986. pap. 78.00 (*0-317-60113-X*) Benjamins North Am.
Rona, Thomas P. . Our Changing Geopolitical Premises. LC 81-16192. (Illus.). 360p. 1982. pap. text ed. 9.95 (*0-87855-897-7*) Transaction Pubs.
Rona, Thomas P. Our Changing Geopolitical Premises. LC 81-16192. 364p. reprint ed. pap. 103.80 (*0-317-27257-8*, 2024159) Bks Demand.
Rona, Zoltan P. The Joy of Health: A Doctor's Guide to Nutrition & Alternative Medicine. LC 92-34054. 272p. 1992. pap. 12.95 (*0-87542-684-0*) Llewellyn Pubns.
***Rona, Zoltan P. & Martin, Jeanne M.** Return to the Joy of Health: Natural Medicine & Alternative Treatments for All Your Health Complaints. LC 95-910586. 408p. (Orig.). 1995. pap. 19.95 (*0-920470-62-9*) Alive Bks.
Ronai, Andras Z., jt. ed. see Szekeley, Jozsef I.
Ronai, Andras Z., jt. ed. see Szekely, Jozsef I.
***Ronald, Ann.** Earthtones: A Nevada Album. LC 94-45450. (Illus.). 136p. 1995. 39.95 (*0-87417-270-5*) U of Nev Pr.
— Functions of Setting in the Novel: From Mrs. Radcliffe to Charles Dickens. Varma, Devendra P., ed. LC 79-8475. (Gothic Studies & Dissertations). 1980. lib. bdg. 31.95 (*0-405-12659-X*) Ayer.
— Zane Grey. LC 75-7010. (Western Writers Ser.: No. 17). (Illus.). 46p. (Orig.). 1975. pap. 3.95 (*0-88430-016-1*) Boise St U W Writ Ser.
Ronald, Ann, ed. Words for the Wild: The Sierra Club Trailside Reader. LC 86-22097. (Totebook Ser.). 384p. (Orig.). 1987. pap. 12.00 (*0-87156-709-1*) Sierra.
***Ronald, Barnett.** The Limits of Competence: Knowledge, Higher Education & Society. LC 94-22170. 160p. 1994. 79.00x (*0-335-19070-7*, Open Univ Pr); pap. 29.00x (*0-335-19341-2*, Open Univ Pr) Taylor & Francis.
Ronald, Belluomini. Thirteenth Labor. LC 85-70532. (Living Poets' Library Ser.). 1985. pap. 5.00 (*0-934218-32-3*) Dragons Teeth.
Ronald, Judith & Skiba, Diane. Guidelines for Basic Computer Education in Nursing. 78p. (Orig.). 1987. pap. 18.95 (*0-88737-361-5*, 41-2177) Natl League Nurse.
Ronald, K., ed. see International Conference on the Mediterranean Monk Seal Staff.
Ronald, Kate & Roskelly, Hephzibah, eds. Farther Along: Transforming Dichotomiesin Rhetoric & Composition. 208p. 1990. pap. text ed. 18.50 (*0-86709-249-1*, 0249) Boynton Cook Pubs.
Ronald McDonald House Staff, ed. see Mott Hospital Staff.
Ronald, Story, jt. auth. see Boller, Paul F., Jr.
Ronall, Ruth, ed. Beyond the Hot Seat: Gestalt Approaches to Group. 272p. 1994. reprint ed. pap. 20.00 (*0-939266-13-X*) Gestalt Journal.
Ronan. Deep Space. 1982. 24.95 (*0-02-604510-9*) Macmillan.
— Practical Astronomer. 1981. 20.00 (*0-02-604500-1*) Macmillan.
Ronan, Charles E. Francisco Javier Clavigero, S. J., Figure of the Mexican Enlightment: His Life & Work. 1978. pap. 26.00 (*88-7041-340-3*) Jesuit Hist.
— Francisco Javier Clavigero, S. J. (1731-1787) Figure of the Mexican Enlightenment. 1978. pap. 26.00 (*0-685-03108-X*) Loyola Univ Pr.
Ronan, Charles E., ed. see Spence, Jonathan D., et al.
Ronan, Christine, jt. auth. see Bartok, Mira.
Ronan, Clifford. Antike Roman: Power Symbology & the Roman Play in Early Modern England, 1585-1635. LC 94-7604. 240p. 1995. 50.00 (*0-8203-1672-5*) U of Ga Pr.
Ronan, Colin A. Science: Its History & Development among the World's Cultures. LC 82-12176. 543p. reprint ed. pap. 154.80 (*0-7837-2675-9*, 2043046) Bks Demand.
— Shorter Science & Civilisation in China, Vol. 1. LC 77-82513. (Illus.). 337p. 1980. pap. 27.95 (*0-521-29286-7*) Cambridge U Pr.
— Shorter Science & Civilisation in China, Vol. 2. LC 77-82513. (Illus.). 250p. 1985. pap. 29.95 (*0-521-31536-0*) Cambridge U Pr.
— Shorter Science & Civilisation in China, Vol. 3. 280p. 1986. 59.95 (*0-521-25272-5*); pap. 24.95 (*0-521-31560-3*) Cambridge U Pr.
— The Shorter Science & Civilisation in China Vol. 4: An Abridgement of Joseph Needham's Original Text of Volume IV. 1994. 69.95 (*0-521-32995-7*); pap. 34.95 (*0-521-33873-5*) Cambridge U Pr.
— The Shorter Science & Civilisation in China Vol. 5. (Illus.). 360p. (C). 1995. write for info. (*0-521-46214-2*); pap. write for info. (*0-521-46773-X*) Cambridge U Pr.
— Skywatchers Handbook. 1989. pap. 15.00 (*0-517-57326-1*, Crown) Crown Pub Group.
Ronan, Colin A., ed. Science Explained: The World of Science in Everyday Life. LC 93-15439. (Reference Book Ser.). (Illus.). 240p. 1993. 45.00 (*0-8050-2551-0*, Bks Young Read) H Holt & Co.
— The Universe Explained: The Earth-Dweller's Guide to the Mysteries of Space. LC 94-16294. 1994. 35.00 (*0-8050-3488-9*) H Holt & Co.
Ronan, David T., jt. auth. see PCDI Staff.
Ronan, Johanna, jt. auth. see O'Kelly, Sile P.
Ronan, Mark. Lectures on Buildings. (Perspectives in Mathematics Ser.). 175p. 1989. text ed. 42.00 (*0-12-594750-X*) Acad Pr.
Ronan, Peter. Historical Sketch of the Flathead Nation. 1965. reprint ed. 15.00 (*0-87018-054-1*) Ross.
Ronan, Richard. Narratives from America. LC 81-67639. 139p. 1982. 12.00 (*0-937872-04-0*); pap. 6.00 (*0-937872-05-9*) Dragon Gate.
— A Radiance Like Wind or Water. LC 83-72376. 73p. 1984. 14.00 (*0-937872-14-8*); pap. 6.00 (*0-937872-15-6*) Dragon Gate.
Ronan, S. Orphic Fragments. 150p. (C). 1988. text ed. 95.00 (*0-948366-22-2*, Pub. by Chthonios Bks UK) St Mut.
Ronart, Nandy. Lexikon der Arabischen Welt. (GER.). 295.00 (*3-7608-0138-2*, M-7277); 295.00 (*0-8288-7969-9*, M7277) Fr & Eur.
Ronay, Bill & Ronay, Camille, eds. The Ronay Guide: Arts & Crafts Shown in the Carolinas, 1994. 1994. 7.95 (*1-56736-019-X*) A Step Ahead.
— The Ronay Guide: Arts & Crafts Shown in Virginia, 1994. 1994. 7.95 (*1-56736-020-3*) A Step Ahead.
— The Ronay Guide: Arts & Crafts Shows in Alabama, 1994. 1994. 7.95 (*1-56736-017-3*) A Step Ahead.
— The Ronay Guide: Arts & Crafts Shows in Florida, 1994. 1994. 7.95 (*1-56736-016-5*) A Step Ahead.
— The Ronay Guide: Arts & Crafts Shows in Georgia, 1994. 1994. 7.95 (*1-56736-015-7*) A Step Ahead.
— The Ronay Guide: Arts & Crafts Shows in Tennessee, 1994. 1994. 7.95 (*1-56736-018-1*) A Step Ahead.
Ronay, Camille, jt. ed. see Ronay, Bill.
Ronay, Egon. Egon Ronay's Guide, 1994: And Baby Comes, Too. 1994. pap. 15.95 (*0-312-10606-8*) St Martin.
— Egon Ronay's Guide, 1994: Just a Bite. 1994. pap. 15.95 (*0-312-10613-0*) St Martin.
— Egon Ronay's Guide, 1994: Pubs & Inns. 1993. pap. 17.95 (*0-312-10604-1*) St Martin.
— Egon Ronay's Guide 1995: Europe. LC 95-2603. 1995. pap. 19.95 (*0-312-13061-9*) St Martin.
— Egon Ronay's Guide 1995: Ireland. LC 95-2711. 1995. pap. 22.95 (*0-312-13060-0*) St Martin.
— Egon Ronay's Guide 1995: Paris. LC 95-2132. 1995. pap. 17.95 (*0-312-13059-7*) St Martin.
Ronay, Gabriel. The Lost King of England: The East European Adventures of Edward the Exile. (Illus.). 224p. (C). 1990. 39.95 (*0-85115-541-3*) Boydell & Brewer.
Ronayne. Freemasonry Handbook. 16.95 (*0-685-21949-6*) Wehman.
— Masters Carpet. 15.95 (*0-685-41897-9*) Wehman.
Ronayne, Edmond. Blue Lodge. 18.95 (*0-685-38430-6*) Wehman.
— Blue Lodge & Chapter. 1947. 17.00 (*0-685-19465-5*) Powner.
— Chapter Degrees. 13.00 (*0-685-19469-8*) Powner.
— Handbook of Freemasonry. 13.00 (*0-685-19476-0*) Powner.
— Mah Hah Bone. 17.00 (*0-685-19485-X*) Powner.
— Master's Carpet. 13.00 (*0-685-19490-6*) Powner.
— Ranayne's Handbook of Freemasonry. enl. rev. ed. reprint ed. spiral bd. 22.00 (*0-7873-0736-X*) Mokelumne.
Ronayne, John. Introduction to Digital Communications Switching. 216p. (C). 1986. pap. text ed. 130.00 (*0-273-02178-8*, Pub. by Pitman Pubng UK) St Mut.
Ronayne, John, ed. Integrated Services Digital Networks: From Concept to Application. 240p. (C). 1987. pap. text ed. 200.00 (*0-273-02677-1*, Pub. by Pitman Pubng UK) St Mut.
Ronayne, John, jt. auth. see Langley, Graham.
Ronberg, Gary. The Illustrated Hockey Encyclopedia. LC 84-11169. (Illus.). 399p. 1984. 24.95 (*0-917439-03-1*) Balsam Pr.
Ronberg, Gert. A Way with Words: The Language of English Renaissance Literature. 192p. 1992. pap. 14.95 (*0-340-49307-0*, A6109, Pub. by E Arnold UK) Routledge Chapman & Hall.
Roncaglia, Alessandro. Sraffa & the Theory of Prices. Kregel, J. A., tr. LC 77-7241. 196p. reprint ed. pap. 55.90 (*0-685-23761-3*, 2032835) Bks Demand.
Roncarelli, R. Computer Animation Dictionary. 1989. pap. 28.00 (*0-387-97022-3*, 2937) Spr-Verlag.
***Roncarolo, Maria-Garzia, et al, eds.** Human Hematopoiesis in SCID Mice. LC 95-6539. (Medical Intelligence Unit Ser.). 165p. 1995. 79.00 (*1-57059-202-0*) R G Landes.
Ronce, David. California Hazardous Waste Directory, 1991-1992. 482p. 1991. pap. text ed. 199.00 (*1-880720-00-0*) In Media Res.
Ronch, Judah L. Alzheimer's Disease: A Practical Guide for Those Who Help Others. 144p. 1991. 17.95 (*0-8245-1283-9*); pap. 12.95 (*0-8245-1284-7*) Crossroad NY.
Ronch, Judah L., et al, eds. The Counseling Sourcebook: A Practical Reference on Contemporary Issues. 536p. (Orig.). 1994. pap. 21.95 (*0-8245-1241-3*) Crossroad NY.
Ronchetti, Elvezio, jt. auth. see Field, Christopher A.
Ronchi, C. & Turrini, F. Thermochemical Data for Reactor Materials, No. EUR 12819. 186p. 1990. pap. 18.00 (*92-826-1558-8*, CD-NA-12819-EN) UNIPUB.
Ronchi, C., ed. see European Institute for Transuranium Elements Staff.
Ronchi, C., et al. X - Points in the Spectral Emissivity of Solid & Liquid Refactory Transmission, EUR 14220. 54p. 1993. pap. 12.00 (*92-826-5699-3*, CD-NA-14220-EN-C, Pub. by Europ Com) UNIPUB.
Ronchi, Susanna, illus. Where in the World Is Geo? A Child's First Atlas. 12p. (J). (ps-4). 1991. bds. 15.95 (*0-8120-6251-5*) Barron.
Ronchi, Vasco. Optics: The Science of Vision. (Illus.). ix, 360p. reprint ed. pap. 9.95 (*0-486-66846-0*) Dover.
Ronck, Ron, jt. auth. see Buffet, Guy.
Ronck, Ronn, ed. Kauai: A Many Splendored Island. (Illus.). 155p. 1985. 24.95 (*0-935180-18-4*) Mutual Pub HI.
Ronck, Ronn & Rankin, Jack. Panorama California: Scenic Views of the Golden State. (Illus.). 144p. 1988. 24.95 (*0-935180-57-5*) Mutual Pub HI.
Ronck, Ronn, ed. see Baker, Ray J.
Ronco, C., jt. ed. see Bellomo, R.
Ronco, W. & Peattie, L. Making Work: Self-Created Jobs in Participatory Organizations. LC 83-9527. (Environment, Development, & Public Policy: Public Policy & Social Services Ser.). (Illus.). 224p. 1983. 49.50 (*0-306-41230-6*, Plenum Pr) Plenum.
Roncucci, Romeo R., ed. see International Symposium on Quantitative Mass Spectrometry in Life Science Staff.
Ronda, James P. Astoria & Empire. LC 89-38464. (Illus.). xiv, 400p. 1990. 27.50 (*0-8032-3896-7*); pap. 12.95 (*0-8032-8942-1*) U of Nebr Pr.
— The Exploration of North America. Phillips, Carla R. & Weber, David J., eds. (Essays on the Columbian Encounter Ser.). 72p. (Orig.). (C). 1992. 8.00 (*0-87229-067-0*) Am Hist Assn.
— Lewis & Clark among the Indians. LC 84-3544. (Illus.). xviii, 310p. 1984. pap. 12.00 (*0-8032-8929-4*) U of Nebr Pr.
Ronda, James P., ed. see Eliot, John.
Rondal, Jean A. Adult-Child Interaction & the Promise of Language Acquisition. 240p. 1985. text ed. 55.00 (*0-275-90157-2*, C0157, Praeger Pubs) Greenwood.
— Exceptional Language Development in Down Syndrome: Implications for the Cognition-Language Relationship. (Cambridge Monographs & Texts in Applied Psycholinguistics). (Illus.). 350p. (C). 1995. 59.95 (*0-521-36167-2*); pap. 24.95 (*0-521-36966-5*) Cambridge U Pr.
Rondanelli, E. G. Amphizoic Amoebae: Human Pathology. (Infectious Diseases Color Atlas Monographs: No. 1). 276p. 1988. text ed. 32.00 (*1-57235-028-8*) Piccin NY.
— Blood Transfusions & Infectious Diseases. (Infectious Diseases Color Atlas Monographs: No. 2). 322p. 1989. text ed. 45.00 (*1-57235-029-6*) Piccin NY.
Rondanelli, E. G., et al. Human Pathogenic Protozoa: Atlas of Electron-Microscopy. 356p. 1987. text ed. 64.00 (*1-57235-027-X*) Piccin NY.
— Pathology of Erythroblastic Mitosis in Occupational Benzenic Erythropathy & Erythremia. (Bibliotheca Haematologica Ser.: No. 35). (Illus.). 1970. pap. 61.00 (*3-8055-0139-0*) S Karger.
Rondanelli, R. Clinical Pharmacology of Drug Interactions. 864p. 1988. text ed. 50.00 (*1-57235-032-6*) Piccin NY.
Ronde, S. M., ed. Fluid Film Lubrication: A Century of Progress. 217p. 1983. pap. text ed. 44.00 (*0-317-03526-6*, 100162) ASME.
***Rondeau, Edmond P. & Lapides, Paul D.** Facility Management. (Real Estate Practice Library). Date not set. text ed. 69.95 (*0-471-03806-7*) Wiley.
Rondeau, Rene. The Watch of the Future: The Story of the Hamilton Electric Watch. 2nd rev. ed. (Illus.). 168p. (Orig.). 1992. 29.95 (*0-9622219-1-0*) R Rondeau.
***Rondebush.** Cassatt. (Art Library). 1995. pap. 12.00 (*0-517-88371-6*, Crown) Crown Pub Group.
Rondebush, Jay. Mary Cassatt. (CAL Art Ser.). (Illus.). 1988. 14.95 (*0-517-53740-0*, Crown) Crown Pub Group.
Rondel, R. K., et al, eds. Clinical Data Management. 300p. 1994. text ed. 59.95 (*0-471-94092-5*) Wiley.
Rondia, D., et al, eds. Mobile Source Emissions Included Polycyclic Organic Species. 1983. lib. bdg. 121.50 (*90-277-1633-1*) Kluwer Ac.
***Rondina, Marisa.** Vocabulary of Family Violence. (Terminology Bulletin Ser.: No. 222). 209p. (Orig.). 1994. pap. 25.95x (*0-660-59106-5*, Pub. by Canada Commun Grp CN) Accents Pubns.
Rondinelli, Dennis A. Development Projects As Policy Experiments: An Adaptive Approach to Development Administration. LC 83-8117. (Development & Underdevelopment Ser.). 180p. 1983. pap. 10.95 (*0-416-73640-8*, NO. 3914) Routledge Chapman & Hall.
— Development Projects As Policy Experiments: An Adaptive Approach to Development Administration. 2nd ed. LC 92-17773. (Development & Underdevelopment Ser.). (Illus.). 192p. 1993. 59.95 (*0-415-06622-0*, A9845, Routledge NY); pap. 16.95 (*0-415-06623-9*, A9849, Routledge NY) Routledge.
— Secondary Cities in Developing Countries: Policies for Diffusing Urbanization. LC 82-23165. (Sage Library of Social Research: No. 145). 288p. reprint ed. pap. 82.10 (*0-8357-4851-0*, 2037782) Bks Demand.
Rondinelli, Dennis A., ed. Expanding Sino-American Business & Trade: China's Economic Transition. LC 94-8543. 288p. 1994. text ed. 55.00 (*0-89930-932-1*, Quorum Bks) Greenwood.
— Privatization & Economic Reform in Central Europe: The Changing Business Climate. LC 93-27714. 304p. 1994. text ed. 59.95 (*0-89930-851-1*, Quorum Bks) Greenwood.
Rondinelli, Dennis A., et al. Planning Education Reforms in Developing Countries: The Contingency Approach. LC 89-36234. 225p. (C). 1990. lib. bdg. 39.50 (*0-8223-0966-1*); pap. text ed. 19.95 (*0-8223-0974-2*) Duke.
Rondinone, et al. The Advancing Writer, Bk. I. (C). 1994. text ed. 32.50 (*0-06-500301-2*) HarpCollege.
Rondon, Javier. The Absent-Minded Toad. Corbett, Kathryn, tr. LC 94-14407. (Illus.). 32p. (J). (ps-1). 1994. 9.95 (*0-916291-53-7*) Kane-Miller Bk.
Rondot, Jean. La Compagnie Francaise Des Petroles: Du Franc-or Au Petrole-Franc. Wilkins, Mira, ed. LC 76-29773. (European Business Ser.). (FRE.). 1977. reprint ed. lib. bdg. 19.95 (*0-405-09785-9*) Ayer.
Rondthaler, Ed. Artron Area Copyfitting. LC 84-72106. 48p. 1984. pap. 8.95 (*0-88108-016-0*) Art Dir.
Rondthaler, Katharine B. Tell Me a Story. (Illus.). 64p. (J). (ps-5). 1992. reprint ed. pap. 4.00 (*1-878422-06-5*) Moravian Ch in Amer.
***Rondurham, et al.** Higley: Sunday School Commentary, 1995-1996, Vol. 63. Reagan, Wesley C., ed. (Illus.). 1995. text ed. 14.99 (*1-886763-01-1*) Higley.
— Higley: Sunday School Commentary, 1995-1996, Vol. 63. large type ed. Reagan, Wesley C., ed. (Illus.). 1995. 10.99 (*1-886763-02-X*) Higley.
Rone, Christine, tr. see Richer, Jean.
Rone, Jemera & Meier, Aryeh. Settling into Routine: Human Rights Abuses in Duarte's Second Year. LC 86-202472. 162p. 1986. 10.00 (*0-938579-19-3*, Fund Free Exp) Hum Rts Watch.
Ronell, Avital. Crack Wars: Literature Addiction Mania. LC 91-18917. (Texts & Contexts Ser.). xii, 175p. 1992. 25.00 (*0-8032-3903-3*); pap. 9.95 (*0-8032-8944-8*) U of Nebr Pr.
— Dictations: On Haunted Writing. LC 93-8475. xxix, 205p. 1993. pap. 12.00 (*0-8032-8945-6*, Bison Books) U of Nebr Pr.
— Finitude's Score: Essays for the End of the Millennium. LC 93-11942. xvi, 370p. 1994. 35.00 (*0-8032-3911-4*) U of Nebr Pr.

An Asterisk (*) at the beginning of an entry indicates that the title is appearing in BIP for the first time.

— The Telephone Book: Technology - Schizophrenia - Electric Speech. LC 88-27960. (Illus.). xviii, 466p. 1989. 50.00 (*0-8032-3876-2*); pap. 25.00 (*0-8032-8938-3*) U of Nebr Pr.

Ronen, ed. High Converting Water Reactors. 1989. 180.00 (*0-8493-6081-1*, TK9203) CRC Pr.

Ronen, Avraham. Stones & Bones! How Archaeologists Trace Human Origins. LC 93-2480. (Buried Worlds Ser.). (YA). (gr. 6 up). 1993. lib. bdg. 22.95 (*0-8225-3207-7*, Lerner Publctns) Lerner Group.

Ronen, Dov. Dahomey: Between Tradition & Modernity. LC 74-25375. (Africa in the Modern World Ser). (Illus.). 320p. 1975. 36.50 (*0-8014-0927-6*) Cornell U Pr.

Ronen, Ela & Baefour, Bernice. Migraine Headache: Prevention & Treatment by Phytotherapy, Herbal Medicine. 68p. (Orig.). 1993. pap. 15.95 (*0-9638677-0-9*) E M D Ent.

Ronen, Joshua, ed. Accounting & Financial Globalization. LC 90-26406. 184p. 1991. text ed. 55.00 (*0-89930-618-7*, RAF/, Quorum Bks) Greenwood.

Ronen, Joshua & Sorter, George H. Relevant Financial Statements: Original Anthology. Brief, Richard P., ed. LC 77-87318. (Development of Contemporary Accounting Thought Ser.). 1978. lib. bdg. 30.95 (*0-405-10930-X*) Ayer.

Ronen, Joshua, et al, eds. Off-Balance Sheet Activities. LC 90-8909. 192p. 1990. text ed. 49.95 (*0-89930-613-6*, ROD/, Quorum Bks) Greenwood.

Ronen, Ruth. Possible Worlds in Literary Theory. (Literature, Culture, Theory Ser.: No. 7). 249p. (C). 1994. 59.95 (*0-521-45017-9*); pap. 17.95 (*0-521-45648-7*) Cambridge U Pr.

Ronen, Simcha. Comparative & Multinational Management. LC 85-17971. (International Business Ser.). 636p. (C). 1986. Net. text ed. write for info. (*0-471-86875-2*) Wiley.

Ronen, Yigal. Uncertainty Analysis. 272p. 1988. 166.00 (*0-8493-6714-X*, Q375, CRC Reprint) Franklin.

Ronen, Yigal, ed. Handbook of Nuclear Reactors Calculations, 3 vols., Set. 1986. 885.00 (*0-8493-2924-8*, TK9153) CRC Pr.

— Handbook of Nuclear Reactors Calculations, Vol. I. 448p. 1986. 321.95 (*0-8493-2925-6*, TK9153, CRC Reprint) Franklin.

— Handbook of Nuclear Reactors Calculations, Vol. I: Introduction. 448p. 1986. write for info. (*0-318-60779-4*) CRC Pr.

— Handbook of Nuclear Reactors Calculations, Vol. II. 1986. write for info. (*0-318-60777-8*) CRC Pr.

— Handbook of Nuclear Reactors Calculations, Vol. III: Ctrl Rods & Burnable Absorber Calculatns. 492p. 1986. Vol. III: Control Rods & Burnable Absorber Calculations, 492pp. write for info. (*0-318-60778-6*) CRC Pr.

Ronenau, J. N., jt. ed. see Knorr, Klaus.

Ronet, Jorge & Carriles, Lazaro G. Diptico Cubano: La Mueca de la Paloma Negra Desertores del Paraiso. (Biblioteca Cubana Contemporanea Ser.). 126p. (Orig.). (SPA.). 1988. pap. 12.00 (*84-359-0539-X*, Pub. by Editorial Playor SP) Ediciones.

Ronet, Jorge & Hernandez-Alende, Andres. Guaguasi-Los Simbolos del Delirio. (Biblioteca Cubana Contemporanea Ser.). (Illus.). 325p. (Orig.). (SPA.). 1986. pap. 9.95 (*84-359-0452-0*, Pub. by Editorial Playor SP) Ediciones.

Roney, Bob, et al. Guide to Yosemite High Sierra Trails. (Illus.). 1981. 2.50 (*0-939666-34-0*) Yosemite Assn.

Roney, Deborah W., jt. auth. see Krzyzanowski, Jerzy R.

Roney-Dougal, Serena. Where Science & Magic Meet: The Psychology of Occultism. 1990. pap. 18.95 (*1-85230-162-7*) Element MA.

— Where Science Magic Meet: Quantum Physics & Parapsychology: the Reunion of Intellect Intuition. rev. ed. 272p. 1993. pap. 19.95 (*1-85230-446-4*) Element MA.

Roney, Frank. Frank Roney: Irish Rebel & California Labor Leader. LC 74-22758. (Labor Movement in Fiction & Non-Fiction Ser.). reprint ed. 45.00 (*0-404-58511-6*) AMS Pr.

— Frank Roney: Irish Rebel & California Labor Leader: An Autobiography. (American Biography Ser.). 573p. 1991. reprint ed. lib. bdg. 99.00 (*0-7812-8326-4*) Rprt Serv.

— Irish Rebel & California Labor Leader: An Autobiography. Cross, Ira B., ed. LC 76-6363. (Irish Americans Ser.). (Illus.). 1976. reprint ed. 54.95 (*0-405-09355-1*) Ayer.

Roney, Lois. Chaucer's Knight's Tale & Theories of Scholastic Psychology. 376p. (C). 1990. lib. bdg. 39.95 (*0-8130-1006-3*); pap. text ed. 18.95 (*0-8130-1027-6*) U Press Fla.

Roney, Lois, jt. ed. see Wasserman, Julian N.

Roney, Lonzell. A Whale of a Tale. (J). 1994. 7.95 (*0-8062-4807-6*) Carlton.

Roney, Raymond G., jt. auth. see Casciero, Albert J.

Ronfeldt, David. Atencingo: The Politics of Agrarian Struggle in a Mexican Ejido. LC 74-190528. xii, 284p. 1973. 37.50 (*0-8047-0820-7*) Stanford U Pr.

Ronfeldt, David, jt. auth. see Gonzalez, Edward.

Ronfeldt, David F., ed. The Modern Mexican Military: A Reassessment. (Monograph Ser.: No. 15). (Illus.). 218p. (Orig.). (C). 1984. ring bd. 12.95 (*0-935391-52-5*, MN-15) UCSD Ctr US-Mex.

Ronfor, Philip A. Rio Grande Southern Album. Lankenau, Walter C., ed. (Illus.). 36p. (Orig.). 1989. pap. 18.00 (*0-685-29056-5*) E Crist.

Rong, Du, et al. Speaking Chinese about China, No. 1. (Chinese Language Library). (Illus.). 490p. (Orig.). (C). 1985. pap. 18.95 (*0-8351-1583-6*) China Bks.

Rong, Du, et al, eds. Speaking Chinese about China, No. 2. (Chinese Language Library). (Illus.). 602p. (Orig.). (C). 1987. pap. 18.95 (*0-8351-1905-X*) China Bks.

Rong Yang. P-Prolog: a Parallel Logic Programming Language. (Series in Computer Science: Vol. 9). 152p. (C). 1988. text ed. 49.00 (*9971-5-0508-8*) World Scientific Pub.

***Rongsheng, Chen.** Dictionnaire Chinois-Francais de Termes et Expressions Moder. 1989. 75.00 (*0-7859-8706-1*, 7800280144) Fr & Eur.

Rongstad, James. How to Respond to the Lodge. (Response Ser.). 1977. 2.79 (*0-570-07677-3*, 12-2660) Concordia.

Roniger, Luis. Hierarchy & Trust in Modern Mexico & Brazil. LC 90-37775. 256p. 1990. text ed. 59.95 (*0-275-93628-7*, C3628, Praeger Pubs) Greenwood.

Roniger, Luis, jt. auth. see Eisenstadt, S. N.

Roniger, Luis, ed. see Gunes-Ayata, Ayse.

Roningen, Vernon O. Managing Free Trade for Agriculture. LC 93-87573. 200p. 1993. pap. 25.00 (*0-9640007-0-9*) Natl Ctr Food.

Roninson, I. B., ed. Molecular & Cellular Biology of Multidrug Resistance in Tumor Cells. (Illus.). 400p. 1990. 95.00 (*0-306-43547-0*, Plenum Pr) Plenum.

Ronish, Martha J., jt. auth. see Burrows, Donald.

Ronk, A. T. History of Brethren Missionary Movements. LC 70-184490. 1971. pap. 1.50 (*0-934970-02-5*) Brethren Church.

— History of the Brethren Church. LC 68-23554. 1968. 5.00 (*0-934970-03-3*) Brethren Church.

— A Search for Truth. LC 73-82191. 1973. pap. 0.75 (*0-934970-04-1*) Brethren Church.

Ronk, Martha. Desert Geometries. (Littoral Bks.). 1993. pap. 9.95 (*1-55713-151-1*) Sun & Moon CA.

Ronk, Martha C. Desire in L. A. LC 89-34552. (Contemporary Poetry Ser.). 96p. 1990. 15.00 (*0-8203-1175-8*); pap. 7.95 (*0-8203-1176-6*) U of Ga Pr.

Ronkainen, Ilkka A., jt. auth. see Czinkota, Michael R.

Ronkin, Bruce, ed. see Londeix, Jean-Marie.

Ronkin, L. I. Introduction to the Theory of Entire Functions of Several Variables. Israel Program for Scientific Translations Staff, tr. LC 74-12068. (Translations of Mathematical Monographs: Vol. 44). 273p. 1974. 80.00 (*0-8218-1594-6*, MMONO-44) Am Math.

Ronn, Ehud I. & Bliss, Robert R., Jr. A New Method for Valuing Treasury Bond Futures Options. 1992. pap. text ed. 20.00 (*0-943205-15-8*) ICFARF.

Ronnenberg, Herman W. Beer & Brewing in the Inland Northwest, 1850 to 1950. Allebery, Louie W., ed. LC 92-16284. (Northwest Folklife Ser.). (Illus.). 240p. 1993. pap. 26.95 (*0-89301-162-2*) U of Idaho Pr.

Ronner, Amy D. W. H. Hudson: The Man, the Novelist, the Naturalist. LC 85-48068. (Studies in Modern Literature: No. 16). 1986. 34.50 (*0-404-61586-4*) AMS Pr.

Ronner, Heinz, et al, eds. Louis I. Kahn: Complete Works 1935-74. 2nd enl. rev. ed. (Illus.). 500p. 1990. 139.50 (*0-8176-1347-1*) Birkhauser.

***Ronner, John.** Angels of Cokeville: And Other True Stories of Heavenly Intervention. 192p. (Orig.). 1995. pap. 10. 95 (*0-932945-43-0*) Mamre Pr.

Ronner, John E. Do You Have a Guardian Angel? & Other Questions Answered about Angels. LC 84-62980. (Illus.). (Orig.). 1985. pap. 10.95 (*0-932945-37-6*) Mamre Pr.

— Know Your Angels: The Angel Almanac with Biographies of 100 Prominent Angels in Legend & Folklore - & Much More. (Illus.). 192p. (Orig.). 1993. pap. 10.95 (*0-932945-40-6*) Mamre Pr.

— Seeing Your Future: A Modern Look at Prophecy & Prediction. (Illus.). 190p. (Orig.). 1990. pap. 10.95 (*0-932945-38-4*) Mamre Pr.

Ronnestad, M. H., jt. auth. see Skovholt, T. M.

Ronnestad, Michael H., jt. auth. see Skovholt, Thomas M.

Ronnett, Alexander . Romanian Nationalism: The Legionary Movement. Barsan, Uasile C., tr. LC 74-3350. 93p. reprint ed. pap. 26.60 (*0-8357-9431-8*, 2015062) Bks Demand.

Ronnholm, Paul, ed. see Ronnholm, Ursula O.

Ronnholm, Paul F., ed. see Ronnholm, Ursula O.

Ronnholm, Paul F., jt. auth. see Ronnholm, Ursula O.

Ronnholm, Ursala O. Aprende a Leer a Traves de Musica, Juegos y Ritmos. Deliz, Osdila O., ed. (Illus.). 42p. (SPA.). (J). (gr. k up). 1986. audio, text ed. 20.00 (*0-941911-01-2*) Two Way Bilingual.

Ronnholm, Ursula O. Aprende a Leer a Traves de Musica, Juegos y Ritmos. rev. ed. Rabell, Edda, ed. & tr. by. (Illus.). 42p. (SPA.). (J). (gr. k-2). 1989. audio, pap. text ed. 20.00 (*0-941911-07-1*) Two Way Bilingual.

— Learning to Read Through Music, Games & Reading. Ronnholm, Paul F., ed. Montero, Miguel, tr. (Illus.). 60p. (Orig.). (J). (gr. k up). 1985. pap. text ed. 20.00 (*0-941911-00-4*); audio (*0-318-61899-0*) Two Way Bilingual.

— Mi Libro de Escritura. (Illus.). 74p. (SPA.). (J). (gr. k-3). 1986. 4.00 (*0-941911-05-5*) Two Way Bilingual.

— Mi Libro de Palabras: Oraciones y Cuentos. rev. ed. Rabell, Edda, ed. & tr. by. Montero, Miguel, tr. & illus. by. 100p. (SPA.). (J). (gr. k-6). 1989. reprint ed. pap. 7.00 (*0-941911-08-X*) Two Way Bilingual.

— Mi Libro de Palabras, Oraciones y Cuentos. Deliz, Osdila O., ed. (Illus.). 100p. (J). (gr. k-6). pap. text ed. 7.00 (*0-941911-02-0*) Two Way Bilingual.

— Two Way Bilingual Songs for Elementary School. 41p. (J). (gr. k-12). 1987. Incl. cass. audio 8.00 (*0-941911-06-3*) Two Way Bilingual.

— Writing Through Music. rev. ed. Ronnholm, Paul, ed. Montero, Miguel, tr. (Illus.). 74p. (J). (gr. k-3). 1989. pap. text ed. 4.00 (*0-941911-09-8*) Two Way Bilingual.

Ronnholm, Ursula O. & Ronnholm, Paul F. My Book of Words, Songs & Sentences. (Illus.). 91p. (J). (gr. k-3). 1986. pap. text ed. 7.00 (*0-941911-03-9*) Two Way Bilingual.

***Ronnie, Art.** Counterfeit Hero: Fritz Duquesne, Adventurer & Spy. LC 95-12401. (Illus.). 360p. 1995. 29.95 (*1-55750-733-3*) Naval Inst Pr.

Ronning, C. Neale. Jose Marti & the Emigre Colony in Key West: Leadership & State Formation. LC 89-38802. 175p. 1990. text ed. 39.95 (*0-275-93368-7*, C3368, Greenwood Pr) Greenwood.

Ronning, C. Neale & Vannucci, Albert P., eds. Ambassadors in Foreign Policy: The Influence of Individuals on U. S. - Latin American Policy. LC 87-2833. 166p. 1987. text ed. 55.00 (*0-275-92393-2*, C2393, Praeger Pubs) Greenwood.

Ronning, Philip L., et al. Successful Management Strategies in Cardiovascular Services. LC 91-47042. 316p. (Orig.). 1992. 49.95 (*1-55648-083-0*, 067300) AHPI.

Ronning, Royce R., jt. ed. see Glover, John A.

Ronningen, Micheline, jt. auth. see McNeilan, Ray A.

Ronningen, Thor. Butler's Battlin Blue Bastards: The Story of Men of the 3rd Battalion-395th Infantry in WW II under the Leadership of Lt. Col. McClernand Butler. LC 93-9515. (Illus.). 236p. 1993. pap. 19.95 (*1-55618-132-9*) Brunswick Pub.

Ronnow, Robert. Janie Huzzie Bows. LC 83-70121. 64p. (Orig.). 1983. pap. 6.95 (*0-935306-18-8*) Barnwood Pr.

— White Waits. LC 83-71219. 64p. (Orig.). 1984. pap. 6.95 (*0-935306-27-7*) Barnwood Pr.

Ronsard, Nicole. Beyond Cellulite: Nicole Ronsard's Ultimate Strategy to Slim, Firm & Reshape Your Lower Body. 1992. 12.00 (*0-679-73936-X*, Villard Bks) Random.

Ronsard, Pierre D. Poems of Pierre De Ronsard. Kilmer, Nicholas, ed. LC 75-17287. (Illus.). 1979. 38.00 (*0-520-03078-8*) U CA Pr.

— Poesies Choisies. Joukovsky, Francois, ed. (Illus.). 539p. (FRE.). 1989. 45.00 (*0-7859-1271-1*, 2040173234) Fr & Eur.

— Le Second Livre des Amours. 227p. (FRE.). 1951. pap. 14.95 (*0-7859-5473-2*) Fr & Eur.

— Sonnets pour Helene. (Illus.). 228p. (FRE.). 1970. pap. 29.95 (*0-7859-5474-0*) Fr & Eur.

Ronsard, Pierre D. & Baillou, Jean. Discours des Miseres de Ce Temps. 290p. (FRE.). 1949. pap. 18.95 (*0-7859-1460-9*, 2251360913) Fr & Eur.

Ronsard, Pierre de. Oeuvres Completes, Vol. 1. Cerard, Jean, ed. 1184p. (FRE.). 1993. lib. bdg. 110.00 (*0-7859-3787-0*, 2070104850) Fr & Eur.

Ronsch, Hermann. Itala und Vulgata. xvi, 526p. 1979. reprint ed. write for info. (*3-487-06728-5*, Pub. by Georg Olms GW) Lubrecht & Cramer.

Ronse, Christian & Devijver, Pierre A. Connected Components in Binary Images: The Detection Problem. LC 84-3312. (Pattern Recognition & Image Processing Research Studies). 165p. 1984. text ed. 107.95 (*0-471-90456-2*) Wiley.

Ronsivalli, Louis J. & Vierra, Ernest. Elementary Food Science. 3rd rev. ed. (Illus.). 432p. 1991. pap. 45.00 (*0-442-00532-6*) Chapman & Hall.

Ronsley, Joseph. Yeats's Autobiography: Life As Symbolic Pattern. LC 68-15642. 180p. reprint ed. pap. 51.30 (*0-7837-6088-4*, 2059134) Bks Demand.

Ronsley, Joseph, frwd. The Dramatic Works of Denis Johnston, Vol. 3: The Radio & Television Plays. 516p. 1992. 70.00 (*0-86140-080-1*, Pub. by Colin Smythe Ltd UK) Dufour.

Ronsley, Joseph, ed. see Johnston, Denis.

***Ronson, Jon.** Clubbed Class. (Illus.). 224p. 1995. 22.95 (*1-85793-320-6*, Pub. by Pavilion UK) Trafalgar.

Ronson, Stephen J., jt. auth. see Thaw, Barbara L.

Ronstadt, Edward F., ed. Borderman: Memoirs of Federico Jose Maria Ronstadt. LC 93-3853. (Illus.). 181p. 1993. 19.95 (*0-8263-1462-7*) U of NM Pr.

Ronstadt, Robert. Art of Case Analysis: A Guide to the Diagnosis of Business Situations. 3rd ed. 1994. pap. 9.95 (*0-685-69348-1*) Lord Pub.

— Entrepreneurial Finance. Date not set. 39.95 (*0-685-69355-4*); pap. 17.95 (*0-685-69356-2*) Lord Pub.

— Entrepreneurship: Text, Cases & Notes. 800p. (C). 1985. text ed. 39.95 (*0-930204-11-5*) Lord Pub.

Ronstadt, Robert & Shuman. Venture Feasibility Planning Guide. 150p. 1988. pap. 19.95 (*0-930204-21-2*) Lord Pub.

Ronstadt, Robert, et al. Ronstadt's Financials. 250p. 1988. 99.00 (*0-930204-24-7*) Lord Pub.

Ronstadt, Robert, et al, eds. Frontiers of Entrepreneurship Research, 1986. 730p. (Orig.). 1986. pap. text ed. 50.00 (*0-910897-07-7*) Babson College.

Ronstadt, Robert C. Entrepreneurial Finance: Taking Control of Your Financial Decision Making. 250p. 1988. 32.95 (*0-930204-23-9*); pap. 19.95 (*0-930204-22-0*) Lord Pub.

— Venture Feasibility Plan. 1988. 19.95 (*0-930204-25-5*) Lord Pub.

Ronstadt, Robert C., ed. Entrepreneurship: Bibliography 1985. 1985. pap. 20.95 (*0-930204-10-7*) Lord Pub.

Ronsvalle, John & Ronsvalle, Sylvia. Hidden Billions: The Potential of the Church in the U. S. 175p. (Orig.). 1984. pap. 8.00 (*0-914527-18-5*) C-Four Res.

— The Poor Have Faces: Loving Your Neighbor in the Twenty-First Century. LC 92-916. 156p. 1992. pap. 8.99 (*0-8010-7764-8*) Baker Bk.

***Ronsvalle, John L. & Ronsvalle, Sylvia.** The State of Church Giving Through 1991. 75p. 1993. pap. 18.00 (*0-9639962-2-3*) Empty Tomb.

— The State of Church Giving Through 1992. 74p. 1994. pap. 15.00 (*0-9639962-3-1*) Empty Tomb.

Ronsvalle, Sylvia, jt. auth. see Ronsvalle, John L.

Ronsvalle, Sylvia, jt. auth. see Ronsvalle, John.

Rontgen, Robert. The Book of Meissen. LC 84-51186. (Illus.). 333p. 1984. 95.00 (*0-88740-014-0*) Schiffer.

Rontgen, Robert E. Marks on German, Bohemian & Austrian Porcelain, 1710 to the Present. LC 80-85431. (Illus.). 640p. 1981. 75.00 (*0-916838-38-2*) Schiffer.

***Ronto, G. & Tarjan, I., eds.** An Introduction to Biophysics with Medical Orientation: With Medical Orientation. 441p. 1994. 190.00 (*963-05-6757-1*, Pub. by Akad Kiado HU) St Mut.

***Rony, A. Kohar, comp.** Philippine Holdings in the Library of Congress, 1960-1987: A Bibliography. LC 92-3438. 702p. 1993. 46.00 (*0-8444-0744-5*) Lib Congress.

— Vietnamese Holdings in the Library of Congress: A Bibliography. LC 81-2847. 236p. 1982. Incls. Supplement, 1979-1985, 1987, 167p. 13.00 (*0-8444-0564-7*, 030-000-00196-6) Lib Congress.

Rony, Fatimah T., jt. auth. see Griffin, Farah J.

***Rony, Peter R.** Fundamentals of Z-80 Microcomputer Programming Interfacing with Experiments. (Foxware Ser.: Module 11). 300p. 1988. ring bd. write for info. (*0-89704-042-2*) E&L Instru.

Ronyoung, Kim. Clay Walls. LC 86-60589. 304p. 1986. 22. 00 (*0-932966-66-7*) Permanent Pr.

Ronzheimer, Philip. Trust Me! Trust Me! 1992. 1.19 (*0-87509-498-8*) Chr Pubns.

Ronzio, Camille & Wilkinson, Trina. Microwave Delights. 4th rev. ed. LC 80-65640. (Illus.). 206p. 1980. pap. 7.95 (*0-686-85760-7*) Cam-Tri Prods.

Ronzio, Robert A. & Pillepich, John A. Metabolic Mastery. (Illus.). 116p. 1991. 39.95 (*0-9630057-0-7*); pap. text ed. 19.95 (*0-9630057-1-5*) RJ Innov.

Ronzitti, Natalino, ed. The Law of Naval Warfare. (C). 1988. lib. bdg. 283.50 (*90-247-3652-8*) Kluwer Ac.

— Maritime Terrorism & International Law. (C). 1990. lib. bdg. 85.50 (*0-7923-0734-8*) Kluwer Ac.

Ronzitti, Natalino, jt. ed. see De Guttry, Andrea.

Roobeek, A. J. Beyond the Technology Race: An Analysis of Technology Policy in Seven Industrial Countries. 268p. 1990. 92.50 (*0-444-88637-0*) Elsevier.

Roobeek, Annemieke & Verolme, Cornelis. Strategic Management from Below: The Business Benefits. (Financial Times Management Ser.). 256p. 1995. 83.50 (*0-273-60159-8*, Pub. by Pitman Pub Ltd UK) Trans-Atl Phila.

Roobel, Norman R. Industrial Painting: Principles & Practices. 297p. (C). 1993. text ed. 35.00 (*1-56990-123-6*) Hanser-Gardner.

Roobol. Tsereteli: A Democrat in the Russian Revolution. (Studies in Social History: No. 1). 1977. lib. bdg. 99.00 (*90-247-1915-1*) Kluwer Ac.

Roobol, M. J., jt. auth. see Smith, A. L.

Roobol, Norman R. Painting Practices Handbook. 290p. 1988. 34.95 (*0-933931-10-7*) Hitchcock Pub.

— Painting Problems: Solved Questions & Answers. 250p. (Orig.). 1987. pap. 22.95 (*0-933931-01-8*) Hitchcock Pub.

Roochnik, David. The Tragedy of Reason: Towards a Platonic Conception of Logos. 256p. 1990. 39.95 (*0-415-90315-7*, A4592, Routledge NY); pap. 14.95 (*0-415-90316-5*, A4596, Routledge NY) Routledge.

Roochvarg, Alida, ed. The Alida Roochvarg Collection of Books About Books. (Illus.). 300p. 1981. 45.00 (*0-938768-00-X*) Oak Knoll.

***Roocroft, Alan & Zoll, Donald A.** Managing Elephants: An Introduction to Their Training & Management. 198p. (Orig.). 1994. pap. text ed. 20.00 (*0-9640073-0-4*) Fever Tree.

Roocroft, Alan, jt. auth. see Tibbitts, Alison.

Rood, Arnold, ed. Edward Gordon Craig, Artist of the Theatre, 1872-1966: A Memorial Exhibition in the Amsterdam Gallery. LC 73-137703. (New York Public Library Publications in Reprint). (Illus.). 1971. reprint ed. 11.95 (*0-405-18768-8*) Ayer.

Rood, Beverly, jt. auth. see Pisano, Ronald G.

Rood, E. P., ed. Holographic Particle Image Velocimetry. LC 93-71635. (FED Ser.: Vol. 148). 67p. 1993. pap. 25. 00 (*0-7918-0956-0*, H00788) ASME.

***Rood, E. P. & Katz, J., eds.** Free-Surface Turbulence. LC 94-71261. (Fluid Engineering Division Conference Ser.: Vol. 181). 169p. 1994. pap. 37.50 (*0-7918-1364-9*) ASME.

Rood, Harold J. Logic & Structured Design for Computer Programmers. 2nd ed. 304p. 1992. pap. 39.95 (*0-534-92966-4*) PWS Pubs.

Rood, Jean. Country Harvest. (Illus.). (Orig.). 1984. pap. 6.50 (*0-941284-23-9*) J Shaw Studio.

Rood, John. Sculpture in Wood. LC 50-9725. 191p. reprint ed. pap. 54.50 (*0-317-39699-4*, 2055902) Bks Demand.

— Sculpture with a Torch. LC 63-13883. (Illus.). 117p. reprint ed. pap. 33.40 (*0-318-39691-2*, 2033286) Bks Demand.

Rood, Karen, ed. American Literary Almanac: From 1608 to the Present. (Illus.). 448p. 1989. pap. 19.95 (*0-8160-1575-9*) Facts on File.

Rood, Karen L., ed. American Writers in Paris, Nineteen Twenty to Nineteen Thirty-Nine, Vol. 4. LC 79-26101. (Dictionary of Literary Biography Ser.: Vol. 4). (Illus.). 448p. 1980. 128.00 (*0-8103-0916-5*) Gale.

Rood, Karen L., et al, eds. Dictionary of Literary Biography Yearbook, 1980. LC 81-4188. 344p. 1981. 128.00 (*0-8103-1600-5*) Gale.

Rood, Lois S. Beyond Severe Disability: Models & Strategies for Change. 43p. (Orig.). 1983. pap. 3.15 (*1-55719-006-2*) U NE CPAR.

— Beyond Severe Disability: Nebraska Services Guide. 38p. (Orig.). 1985. pap. 3.15 (*1-55719-013-5*) U NE CPAR.

Rood, Lois S. & Davis, Carole M. Beyond Severe Disability: The Challenge of Private Enterprise. 38p. (Orig.). 1985. pap. 3.15 (*1-55719-015-1*) U NE CPAR.

Rood, Lois S. & Faison, Karen. Beyond Severe Disability: A Functional Bibliography. 32p. (Orig.). 1985. pap. 2.50 (*1-55719-014-3*) U NE CPAR.

Rood, Ron. Beachcombers All: Exploring the New England Seashore. LC 90-5817. (Illus.). 128p. (Orig.). 1990. pap. 9.95 (*0-933050-80-1*) New Eng Pr VT.

R

Rood, Ronald. Animals Nobody Loves. LC 87-62516. (Illus.). 215p. 1987. pap. text ed. 8.95 (*0-933050-54-2*) New Eng Pr VT.
— How Do You Spank a Porcupine? LC 83-62565. (Illus.). 160p. (J). (gr. 7 up). 1983. reprint ed. pap. 9.95 (*0-933050-19-4*) New Eng Pr VT.
— A Land Alive: The World of Nature at One Family's Door. LC 92-61232. (Illus.). 160p. (Orig.). 1992. pap. 9.95 (*0-933050-89-5*) New Eng Pr VT.
— Loon in My Bathtub. LC 85-61031. (Illus.). 192p. (Orig.). 1985. reprint ed. pap. 9.95 (*0-933050-28-3*) New Eng Pr VT.
— Ron Rood's Vermont: A Nature Guide. LC 88-9856. (Illus.). 224p. (Orig.). 1988. pap. 10.95 (*0-933050-56-9*) New Eng Pr VT.
— Tide Pools. LC 92-2581. (Nature Study Ser.: Trophy Nonfiction Bk.). (Illus.). 48p. (J). (gr. 2-5). 1993. pap. 7.95 (*0-06-446151-3*, Trophy) HarpC Child Bks.
— Wetlands. LC 92-47140. (Nature Study Book Ser.). (Illus.). 48p. (J). (gr. 2-5). 1994. 15.00 (*0-06-023010-X*); lib. bdg. 14.89 (*0-06-023011-8*) HarpC Child Bks.
Rood, Royal D. On Drawing up a Will. 10p. 1969. reprint ed. spiral bd. 5.00 (*0-7873-1287-8*) Mokelumne.
Rood, Stewart R., jt. auth. see Johns, Michael E.
Rood, W. A. Dominican Republic Investors Handbook: A Guide for Investing in Santo Domingo. 1978. lib. bdg. 69.95 (*0-8490-1389-5*) Gordon Pr.
Roodenburg, Herman, ed. see Bremmer, Jan.
Roodman, David, jt. auth. see Lenssen, Nicholas.
Roodyn, D. B. Automated Enzyme Assays, Vol. 2, Pt. 1. (Laboratory Techniques in Biochemistry & Molecular Biology Ser.). 1970. pap. 22.00 (*0-444-10056-3*, North Holland) Elsevier.
Roodyn, Donald B., ed. Subcellular Biochemistry, Vol. 9. LC 73-643479. 442p. 1983. 85.00 (*0-306-41091-5*, Plenum Pr) Plenum.
— Subcellular Biochemistry, Vol. 10. LC 73-643479. 568p. 1984. 110.00 (*0-306-41528-3*, Plenum Pr) Plenum.
— Subcellular Biochemistry, Vol. 11. LC 73-643479. 308p. 1985. 75.00 (*0-306-41959-9*, Plenum Pr) Plenum.
***Roodyn, Paltiel, tr.** Pathways in Medicine: A Journal of Topics in Medicine in the Spirit of Halacha & Jewish Thought. 167p. 1995. 16.95 (*1-56871-060-7*) Targum Pr.
Roof, Anita W. Sherard Families of South Carolina & Beyond. (Illus.). 100p. 1993. 35.00 (*0-9623070-1-7*) A W Roof.
Roof, Anita W., ed. see Thompson, James L.
Roof, Christopher, ed. see Montague, Bill.
Roof, Jonathan. Pathways to God: A Study Guide to the Teachings of Sathya Sai Baba. LC 91-61787. 224p. 1991. pap. 12.00 (*0-9629835-0-0*) Leela Pr.
Roof, Judith. A Lure of Knowledge: Lesbian Sexuality & Theory. Faderman, Lillian & Gross, Larry, eds. (Gay & Lesbian Ser.). 285p. (C). 1993. text ed. 40.00 (*0-231-07486-7*); pap. 14.50 (*0-231-07487-5*) Col U Pr.
***Roof, Judith & Wiegman, Robyn.** Who Can Speak? Authority & Critical Identity. LC 95-4115. 1995. pap. write for info. (*0-252-06487-9*) U of Ill Pr.
***Roof, Judith & Wiegman, Robyn, eds.** Who Can Speak? Authority & Critical Identity. LC 95-4115. 1995. write for info. (*0-252-02191-6*) U of Ill Pr.
Roof, Judith, jt. ed. see Feldstein, Richard.
Roof, Wade C. A Generation of Seekers: The Spiritual Journeys of the Baby Boom Generation. LC 92-53920. 304p. 1993. pap. 12.00 (*0-06-066964-0*) Harper SF.
— World Order & Religion. LC 90-45447. (SUNY Series in Religion, Culture, & Society). 328p. (C). 1991. 59.50 (*0-7914-0739-X*); pap. 19.95 (*0-7914-0740-3*) State U NY Pr.
Roof, Wade C. & McKinney, William. America Mainline Religion: Its Changing Shape of the Religious Establishment. 272p. 1987. text ed. 40.00 (*0-8135-1215-8*); pap. text ed. 15.00 (*0-8135-1216-6*) Rutgers U Pr.
Roof, Wade C., jt. ed. see Ammerman, Nancy T.
Roof, Wade C., jt. ed. see Carroll, Jackson W.
Roohan, James E. American Catholics & the Social Question, 1865-1900. LC 76-6364. (Irish Americans Ser.). 1976. 41.95 (*0-405-09356-X*) Ayer.
Roohizadegan, Olya. Olya's Story: A Survivor's Personal & Dramatic Account of the Persecution of Baha In. 1993. pap. 12.95 (*1-85168-073-X*) Onewrld Pubns.
Rook. Federal Income Taxation of Banks & Financial Institutions, No. 1317. rev. ed. 640p. 1989. Supplemented quarterly; write for info. write for info. (*0-318-67193-X*) Warren Gorham & Lamont.
Rook, A. & Dawber, R. Diseases of the Hair & Scalp. 2nd ed. 1990. 165.00 (*0-632-02719-3*) Blackwell Sci.
Rook, Arthur, et al. History of Addenbrooke's Hospital, Cambridge. (Illus.). 464p. (C). 1992. 69.95 (*0-521-40529-7*) Cambridge U Pr.
Rook, E. C. & Rook, Lizzie J., comps. Child's Own Speaker. LC 71-116413. (Granger Index Reprint Ser.). 1977. 16.95 (*0-8369-6154-4*) Ayer.
Rook, E. C. & Rook, Lizzie J., eds. Drills & Marches. LC 75-116414. (Granger Index Reprint Ser.). 1977. 16.95 (*0-8369-6155-2*) Ayer.
— Young Folks' Entertainments: Comprising Many New & Novel Motion Songs, Charades, Pantomimes, Tableaux, Concert Recitations, Drills, etc., for Home - School Entertainment. LC 72-168787. (Granger Index Reprint Ser.). 1977. reprint ed. 17.95 (*0-8369-6307-5*) Ayer.
— Young People's Speaker: Designed for Young People of Twelve Years. LC 70-37019. (Granger Index Reprint Ser.). (YA). (gr. 7 up). 1977. reprint ed. 17.95 (*0-8369-6318-0*) Ayer.
Rook, Lance W. Federal Income Taxation of Banks & Financial Institutions. 6th ed. 1990. ring bd. 205.00 (*0-685-69566-2*, FITB) Warren Gorham & Lamont.
— Tax Planning for the Alternative Minimum Tax. 1989. Updates available. ring bd. write for info. (*0-8205-1694-5*) Bender.
Rook, Lizzie J. & Goodfellow, E. J. Tiny Tot's Speaker. LC 73-160907. (Granger Index Reprint Ser.). (YA). (gr. 7 up). 1977. reprint ed. 17.95 (*0-8369-6271-0*) Ayer.
Rook, Lizzie J., jt. comp. see Rook, E. C.
Rook, Lizzie J., jt. ed. see Rook, E. C.
Rook, P., ed. Software Reliability Handbook. 548p. 1990. 135.00 (*1-85166-400-9*) Elsevier.
Rook, P. F. & Carter, P. B. Offences Against the Person. (Criminal Law Library). 400p. 1991. 100.00 (*0-08-039202-4*, K130, Waterlow) Macmillan.
Rook, P. F. & Ward, R. Sexual Offences. (Waterlow Criminal Law Library). 320p. 1990. 72.01 (*0-685-33555-0*, Waterlow) Macmillan.
Rook, Pearl N. Where Still the Source Endures. 64p. 1987. 7.50 (*0-8233-0426-4*) Golden Quill.
Rook, Tony. Roman Baths in Britain. 1989. pap. 25.00 (*0-7478-0157-6*, Pub. by Shire UK) St Mut.
Rooke, jt. auth. see Aliabadi, M. H.
Rooke, D. P. Compounding Stress Intensity Factors. (Research Reports in Materials Science Ser.: Vol. 1). (Illus.). 214p. 1986. 75.00 (*1-85070-110-5*) Prthnon Pub.
Rooke, D. P., jt. auth. see Aliabadi, M. H.
Rooke, Daphne. Mittee. (Twentieth-Century Classics Ser.). 224p. 1991. 9.95 (*0-14-018431-7*, Penguin Classics) Viking Penguin.
Rooke, John. Inquiry into the Principles of National Wealth. LC 68-56573. (Reprints of Economic Classics Ser.). 1969. reprint ed. 49.50 (*0-678-00566-4*) Kelley.
Rooke, Leon. A Bolt of White Cloth. 176p. 1985. pap. 8.50 (*0-88001-078-9*) Ecco Pr.
— The Broad Back of the Angel. LC 77-70901. 1977. 15.95 (*0-914590-42-1*); pap. 6.95 (*0-914590-43-X*) Fiction Coll.
— Fat Woman. 179p. 1986. reprint ed. pap. 8.50 (*0-88001-107-6*) Ecco Pr.
— A Good Baby. LC 91-50043. (Vintage Contemporaries Ser.). 320p. 1991. pap. 10.00 (*0-679-72939-9*, Vin) Random.
— Shakespeare's Dog. 176p. 1986. reprint ed. pap. 8.50 (*0-88001-093-2*) Ecco Pr.
— Sing Me No Love Songs, I'll Say You No Prayers. 1984. 15.50 (*0-88001-036-3*, Norton) Ecco Pr.
— Sing Me No Love Songs, I'll Say You No Prayers. 270p. 1986. pap. 9.50 (*0-88001-047-9*) Ecco Pr.
Rooke, Patricia T. & Schnell, R. L. Discarding the Asylum: From Child Rescue to the Welfare State in English-Canada (1800-1950) LC 83-10569. (Illus.). 510p. (Orig.). (C). 1983. pap. text ed. 36.00 (*0-8191-3305-1*) U Pr of Amer.
Rooke, Richard. Crossing the Border. (Illus.). 48p. 1992. 25.00 (*0-930126-37-8*) Typographeum.
Rooker, Margaret, ed. see Davis, Carolyn O.
Rooker, O. E., ed. see Barnes, Oliver.
***Rooker, Oliver E.** Riding the Travel Bureau: Ghost Riders Network on Route 66 During the Great Depression. Speer, Bonnie, ed. LC 93-80883. (Illus.). 80p. (YA). 1995. pap. write for info. (*0-9621622-2-1*) Nat Trning.
Rookledge, Gordon. Rookledge's International Handbook of Type Designers. (Illus.). 224p. 1993. 19.95 (*1-55921-092-3*) Moyer Bell.
Rookledge, Gordon, jt. auth. see Perfect, Christopher.
Rooklin, Anthony R. & Masline, Shelagh R. Living with Asthma. LC 94-18487. (Illus.). 1995. 9.95 (*0-452-27250-5*, Plume) NAL-Dutton.
***Rookmaaker, H. R.** Modern Art & the Death of a Culture. Chang, Robert, tr. 229p. (CHI.). 1985. pap. 6.50 (*1-56582-051-7*) Christ Renew Min.
— Modern Art & the Death of a Culture. LC 94-16587. 256p. 1994. reprint ed. pap. 14.99 (*0-89107-799-5*) Crossway Bks.
Rookmaaker, H. R., Jr. Towards a Romantic Conception of Nature: Coleridge's Poetry up to 1803. LC 84-24633. (Utrecht Publications in Literature: 20). ix, 214p. 1984. 71.00x (*90-272-2205-3*); pap. 37.00x (*90-272-2215-0*) Benjamins North Am.
Rookmaaker, L. C. The Zoological Exploration of Southern Africa 1650-1790. (Illus.). 392p. (C). 1989. text ed. 130.00 (*90-6191-867-7*, Pub. by A A Balkema NE) Ashgate Pub Co.
Rooks, B., ed. Robot Vision & Sensory Controls III: Proceedings of the 3rd International Conference, Cambridge, MA, Nov. 6-10, 1983. 700p. 1984. 151.50 (*0-444-86872-0*) Elsevier.
Rooks, B., ed. see European Automated Manufacturing Conference Staff.
Rooks, B., jt. ed. see Mortimer, J.
Rooks, Belvie, jt. ed. see Bomani, Asake.
Rooks, Charles S. The Hopeful Spirit. LC 87-7277. 184p. (Orig.). 1987. pap. 9.95 (*0-8298-0760-8*) Pilgrim OH.
— Revolution in Zion: Reshaping African American Ministry, 1960-1974. LC 90-39633. 248p. (Orig.). 1990. pap. 14.95 (*0-8298-0873-6*) Pilgrim OH.
Rooks, George. Can't Stop Talking. 2nd ed. 128p. 1990. pap. 17.95 (*0-8384-2914-9*, Newbury) Heinle & Heinle.
— Non-Stop Discussion Workbook: Problems for Intermediate & Advanced Students of English. 2nd ed. 162p. (C). 1988. pap. 17.95 (*0-8384-2938-6*, Newbury) Heinle & Heinle.
Rooks, George, et al. Conversar Sin Parar. 144p. (C). 1982. pap. 25.95 (*0-8384-3474-6*, Newbury) Heinle & Heinle.
Rooks, George M. Let's Start Talking: Conversation for High Beginning & Low Intermediate Students of English. LC 93-41508. 1994. pap. 17.95 (*0-8384-4825-9*) Heinle & Heinle.
— Paragraph Power. 128p. (C). 1989. pap. write for info. (*0-13-648668-1*) P-H.
— Paragraph Power: Communicating Ideas Through Paragraphs. (Illus.). 176p. 1988. pap. text ed. 18.95 (*0-13-648585-5*) P-H.
— Share Your Paragraph: The Process Approach to Writing. (Illus.). 144p. 1987. pap. text ed. 15.25 (*0-13-808271-5*) P-H.
Rooks, James E., jt. auth. see Turley, Windle.
Rooks, John. Love's Courtly Ethic in "The Faerie Queene" From Garden to Wilderness. LC 91-37408. (University of Kansas Humanistic Studies: Vol. 58). 244p. (C). 1992. text ed. 38.95 (*0-8204-1708-4*) P Lang Pubs.
Rooks, Sharon E., tr. see Asper, Kathrin.
Rooksby, Rikky & Shrimpton, Nicholas, eds. The Whole Music of Passion: New Essays on Swinburne. 300p. 1993. 67.95 (*0-85967-925-X*, Pub. by Scolar Pr UK) Ashgate Pub Co.
Rooley, Anthony. Performance: Revealing the Orpheus Within. 1990. pap. 13.95 (*1-85230-160-0*) Element MA.
Room, Adrian. African Placenames: Origins & Meanings of the Names for over 2000 Natural Features, Towns, Cities, Provinces & Countries. LC 93-40261. 245p. 1994. lib. bdg. 49.95 (*0-89950-943-6*) McFarland & Co.
— Cassell Dictionary of First Names. 336p. 1995. 19.95 (*0-304-34398-6*, Pub. by Cassell UK) Sterling.
— Cassell Dictionary of Proper Names. 640p. 1994. 22.95 (*0-304-34447-8*, Pub. by Cassell UK) Sterling.
— Corporate Eponymy: A Biographical Dictionary of the Persons Behind the Names of Major American, British, European & Asian Businesses. LC 92-53502. 302p. 1992. lib. bdg. 38.50x (*0-89950-679-8*) McFarland & Co.
— Dictionary of Astronomical Names. 1988. 27.50 (*0-415-01298-8*) Routledge.
— Dictionary of Contrasting Pairs. 492p. (C). 1988. text ed. 35.00 (*0-415-00217-6*) Routledge.
— A Dictionary of Irish Place Names. 2nd ed. 144p. 1994. reprint ed. pap. 12.95 (*0-86281-460-X*, Pub. by Appletree Pr IE) Irish Bks Media.
— A Dictionary of Pseudonyms & Their Origins, with Stories of Name Changes. LC 89-42750. 350p. 1989. lib. bdg. 38.50x (*0-89950-450-7*) McFarland & Co.
— Dictionary of Trade Name Origins. 1990. 39.95 (*0-7102-0174-5*, RKP) Routledge.
— Dictionary of Trade Name Origins. rev. ed. 1991. 39.95 (*0-8442-3190-8*, Natl Textbk) NTC Pub Grp.
— Dictionary of Translated Names & Titles. 336p. 1986. 57.50 (*0-7100-9953-3*, RKP) Routledge.
— Dictionary of World Place-Names Derived from English Names. (Illus.). 272p. 1989. 35.00 (*0-415-02811-6*) Routledge.
— The Guinness Book of Numbers. (Illus.). 158p. 1991. pap. 12.95 (*0-8160-2562-2*, Pub. by Guinness Pub UK) Facts on File.
— Literally Entitled: A Dictionary of the Origins of the Titles of over 1,300 Major Literary Works of the Nineteenth & Twentieth Century. 320p. 1995. lib. bdg. 48.50 (*0-7864-0110-9*) McFarland & Co.
— The Naming of Animals: An Appelative Reference to Domestic, Work & Show Animals Real & Fictional. LC 92-56689. 244p. 1993. lib. bdg. 35.00 (*0-89950-795-6*) McFarland & Co.
— NTC Dictionary of Word Origins. 1994. pap. 12.95 (*0-8442-5179-8*) NTC Pub Grp.
— NTC's Dictionary of Changes in Meanings. 304p. 1991. 29.95 (*0-8442-5136-4*, Natl Textbk) NTC Pub Grp.
— NTC's Dictionary of World Origins. 208p. 1991. 16.95 (*0-8442-5137-2*, Natl Textbk) NTC Pub Grp.
Room, Adrian, comp. Place-Name Changes Since Nineteen Hundred: A World Gazetteer. LC 79-4300. 224p. 1979. 25.00 (*0-8108-1210-X*) Scarecrow.
— Place-Name Changes, 1900-1991. LC 93-5159. 322p. 1993. 39.50 (*0-8108-2600-3*) Scarecrow.
Room, Graham. Cross-National Innovation in Social Policy: European Perspectives on the Evaluation of Action-Research. LC 85-18302. 189p. 1986. text ed. 29.95 (*0-312-17676-7*) St Martin.
Room, M. B. Wanted Your Daily Life. 1979. pap. 3.50 (*0-87508-011-1*) Chr Lit.
Room, Robin, jt. ed. see Barrows, Susanna.
Room, Robin, jt. auth. see Cahalan, Don.
Roomans, G. M. & Forslind, Bo, eds. Cell Structure & Cell Function: A Symposium in Honor of Bjorn Afzelius on His Sixtieth Birthday Stockholm, Dec. 1985. (Illus.). vi, 138p. 1988. pap. text ed. 23.00 (*0-931288-38-X*) Scanning Microscopy.
Roomans, Godfried M., ed. see Murphy, Judith A.
Roome, D. Faith, Hope & Cyanide. 1973. pap. 2.50 (*0-87129-085-5*, F10) Dramatic Pub.
Roome, Diana R., jt. auth. see Gluckman, Perry.
***Roome, Nigel.** Taking Responsibility: Management & Business. LC 94-33847. (Environmental Agenda Ser.). (C). 1995. pap. text ed. write for info. (*0-7453-0925-9*, Pub. by Pluto Pr UK) Westview.
Roome, William D., jt. auth. see Gehani, Narain.
Roomkin, Myron J., ed. Managers As Employees: An International Comparison of the Changing Character of Managerial Employment. 304p. 1989. 39.95 (*0-19-504322-7*) OUP.
— Profit Sharing & Gain Sharing. LC 90-8777. (Institute of Management & Labor Relations Ser.: No. 2). (Illus.). 190p. 1990. 29.50 (*0-8108-2335-7*) Scarecrow.
Roon, Robert J., jt. auth. see Van Pilsum, John F.
Rooney, Andrew. Sweet & Sour. 320p. 1994. reprint ed. mass mkt. 5.99 (*0-425-14232-9*) Berkley Pub.
Rooney, Andrew A. And More by Andy Rooney. 256p. 1991. reprint ed. pap. 9.95 (*0-02-010202-X*, Collier S&S) S&S Trade.
— A Few Minutes with Andy Rooney. (Illus.). 272p. 1991. reprint ed. pap. 9.95 (*0-02-010201-1*, Pub. by Gebrueder Borntraeger GW) Macmillan.
— Not That You Asked... 1989. 15.95 (*0-394-57837-6*) Random.
— Not That You Asked . . . 288p. 1990. pap. 7.95 (*0-14-013172-8*, Penguin Bks) Viking Penguin.
— Not That You Asked... large type ed. (General Ser.). 482p. 1990. lib. bdg. 20.95 (*0-8161-4943-7*); pap. 14.95 (*0-8161-4944-5*) G K Hall.
— Pieces of My Mind. 1985. mass mkt. 4.95 (*0-380-69885-4*) Avon.
— Sweet & Sour. 256p. 1992. 18.95 (*0-399-13774-2*, Putnam) Putnam Pub Group.
— Sweet & Sour. large type ed. LC 92-40343. (Basic Ser.). 350p. 1994. reprint ed. lib. bdg. 20.95 (*1-56054-628-X*); reprint ed. pap. 13.95 (*1-56054-887-8*) Thorndike Pr.
— Word for Word. 1987. pap. 4.95 (*0-425-10526-1*) Berkley Pub.
Rooney, Andy. Most of Andy Rooney. 1990. 12.98 (*0-88365-765-1*) Galahad Bks.
— My War. LC 94-41322. 1995. 25.00 (*0-8129-2532-7*, Times Bks) Random.
— My War. large type ed. 1995. pap. 24.00 (*0-679-76282-5*) Knopf.
Rooney, Anne. Hunting in Middle English Literature. 160p. (C). 1993. text ed. 59.00 (*0-85991-379-1*) Boydell & Brewer.
Rooney, Charles J., Jr. Dreams & Visions: A Study of American Utopias, 1865-1917. LC 84-8932. (Contributions in American Studies: No. 77). (Illus.). xi, 209p. 1985. text ed. 49.95 (*0-313-23727-1*, RUL/, Greenwood Pr) Greenwood.
Rooney, Christine M. Football in Twenty Minutes. 32p. 1992. pap. write for info. (*1-884144-01-2*) Fill Ins.
— Table Manners in Twenty Minutes. 44p. 1991. pap. write for info. (*1-884144-00-4*) Fill Ins.
Rooney, D. E., ed. Human Cytogenetics, Vol. 1. (Practical Approach Ser. 96). 269p. 1992. 79.00 (*0-19-963288-X*, IRL Pr) OUP.
***Rooney, D. E. & B., Czepulkowski, eds.** Human Cytogenetics: Essential Data. LC 94-20736. (Essential Data Ser.). 1995. pap. text ed. 19.95 (*0-471-95076-9*) Wiley.
Rooney, D. E. & Czepulkowski, B. H., eds. Human Cytogenetics: A Practical Approach, 2 vols. Vols. I-II. (Illus.). 1992. 60.00 (*0-318-69015-2*); pap. 40.00 (*0-318-69016-0*) OUP.
— Human Cytogenetics: A Practical Approach, 2 vols., I. (Practical Approach Ser.: Vols. I-II). (Illus.). 1992. 44.00 (*0-19-963287-1*) OUP.
— Human Cytogenetics: A Practical Approach, 2 vols., II. (Practical Approach Ser.: Vols. I-II). (Illus.). 1992. 79.00 (*0-19-963290-1*); pap. 44.00 (*0-19-963289-8*) OUP.
— Human Cytogenetics: A Practical Approach, 2 vols., Set. (Practical Approach Ser.: Vols. I-II). (Illus.). 1992. pap. 79.00 (*0-19-963313-4*) OUP.
— Human Cytogenetics: A Practical Approach, 2 vols., Set. (Practical Approach Ser.: Vols. I-II). (Illus.). 1992. 131.00 (*0-19-963314-2*) OUP.
Rooney, Dawn. Angkor: Temples of Cambodia's Kings. 1993. pap. 15.95 (*0-8442-9888-3*, Passport Bks) NTC Pub Grp.
Rooney, Dawn F. The Betel Chewing Traditions in South-East Asia. LC 93-400. (Images of Asia Ser.). (Illus.). 104p. 1994. 16.95 (*0-19-588620-8*) OUP.
Rooney, Dawn F., ed. see Khoo, Joo E.
Rooney, Diane, ed. The Hidden Link: Energy & Economic Development. 86p. (Orig.). 1987. pap. 15.00 (*1-55657-003-1*) Pub Tech Inc.
Rooney, E. Gene. Amphorae: Metaphoric Techniques for Understanding, Enhancing, & Improving Your Self-Image. 244p. (Orig.). 1993. student ed 19.95 (*1-881596-03-6*) L E A D Cnslts.
— Listening with the Mind's Inner Ear: The Value of Metaphors in Forming & Developing Belief Systems & Attitudes. 165p. (Orig.). 1993. student ed 19.95 (*1-881596-02-8*) L E A D Cnslts.
— Metaphors for Metamorphosis: The Power of Metaphors & Personal Story. 93p. 1992. student ed 19.95 (*1-881596-00-1*) L E A D Cnslts.
— Metaphors for Metamorphosis: The Power of Metaphors & Personal Story. 2nd ed. 94p. reprint ed. student ed 19.95 (*1-881596-04-4*) L E A D Cnslts.
— The Simon Syndrome: A Wholistic Metaphoric Approach to 20th Century Problems of Leaders, Leading & Leadership. 507p. (Orig.). 1995. write for info. (*1-881596-06-0*) L E A D Cnslts.
— Speaking Heart to Heart: Metaphors & Parables As a Communication Form. 102p. (Orig.). 1993. student ed 19.50 (*1-881596-01-X*) L E A D Cnslts.
— When the Bough Breaks: Metaphors & Meanings about Institutional Problems & Dysfunctional Organizations. (Illus.). 384p. (Orig.). 1995. student ed 35.00 (*1-881596-05-2*) L E A D Cnslts.
***Rooney, Edward.** The Reign of Error. 24p. 1995. pap. 8.95 (*0-8059-3679-3*) Dorrance.
Rooney, Ellen. Seductive Reasoning: Pluralism as the Problematic of Contemporary Literary Theory. LC 88-47917. 288p. 1989. 34.95 (*0-8014-2192-6*) Cornell U Pr.
Rooney, Frances. Our Lives: Lesbian Personal Writings. (Orig.). Date not set. pap. 14.95 (*0-929005-21-X*, Pub. by Second Story Pr CN) InBook.
Rooney, James. Bossmen: Bill Monroe & Muddy Waters. (Quality Paperbacks Ser.). (Illus.). 163p. 1991. reprint ed. pap. 11.95 (*0-306-80427-1*) Da Capo.
— The Demon Cat. (Short Play Ser.). 1974. pap. 1.00 (*0-912262-34-6*) Proscenium.
— The Lame Horse. (Illus.). 237p. 1984. reprint ed. text ed. 19.95 (*0-914327-04-6*) Breakthrgh NY.
Rooney, James F., jt. auth. see Frederickson, Jon.
Rooney, James R. Lame Horse - Causes, Symptoms & Treatment. 1975. pap. 10.00 (*0-87980-308-8*) Wilshire.
— Mechanics of the Horse. LC 78-8774. 104p. 1981. lib. bdg. 21.50 (*0-88275-693-1*) Krieger.

R

An Asterisk (*) at the beginning of an entry indicates that the title is appearing in BIP for the first time.

Rooney, Jim. Organizing the South Bronx. LC 93-49671. (SUNY Series, the New Inequalities). 295p. (C). 1994. 49.50x (*0-7914-2209-7*); pap. 16.95x (*0-7914-2210-0*) State U NY Pr.

Rooney, Jim, jt. auth. see Von Schmidt, Eric.

Rooney, Joe & Steadman, Philip, eds. Principles of Computer-Aided Design: An Open University Set Book. 356p. (C). 1987. pap. text ed. 160.00 (*0-273-02672-0*, Pub. by Pitman Pubng UK) St Mut.

Rooney, John. Struggling to Be Prophets: The Mill Hill Missionaries in North America, 1871-1985. 188p. 1991. pap. 10.00 (*0-317-04686-1*) Mill Hill Fthrs.

Rooney, John, tr. see Thomas a Kempis.

Rooney, John F. The Recruiting Game: Toward a New System of Intercollegiate Sports. 2nd rev. ed. LC 86-19152. 254p. reprint ed. pap. 72.40 (*0-7837-6177-5*, 2045899) Bks Demand.

Rooney, John F., Jr. & Pillsbury, Richard. Atlas of American Sport. 198p. 1993. text ed. 95.00 (*0-02-897351-8*) Macmillan.

Rooney, John W., Jr. Revolt in the Netherlands: Brussels-Eighteen Thirty. 250p. (C). 1982. pap. text ed. 15.00 (*0-87291-156-X*) Coronado Pr.

Rooney, Liam & Christini, Ed. Wreck Diving: The Diver's Field Guide to Wreck Exploration Procedures. 31p. 1986. pap. text ed. 5.50 (*0-943717-29-9*) Concept Sys.

Rooney, Liam & Hardy, Jon. Boat Diving: The Diver's Field Guide to Planning & Procedures for Diving from Boats. 27p. 1986. pap. text ed. 5.50 (*0-943717-30-2*) Concept Sys.

Rooney, Lisa, jt. auth. see Bell, Alison.

***Rooney, Lucy & Faricy, Robert.** Lord Jesus, Teach Me to Pray: A Seven Week Course in Personal Prayer. 2nd ed. LC 95-68113. 111p. 1994. pap. 5.95 (*1-882972-55-4*) Queenship Pub.

— Mary, Queen of Peace: Is the Mother of God Appearing in Medjugorje? 98p. (Orig.). 1985. pap. 4.95 (*0-8189-0475-5*) Alba.

— Medjugorje Journal: Mary Speaks to the World. (Illus.). 205p. (Orig.). 1988. reprint ed. pap. 9.50 (*0-8199-0916-5*, Frncscn Herld) Franciscan Pr.

— Medjugorje Up-Close: Mary Speaks to the World. 1986. pap. 5.95 (*0-8199-0902-5*, Frncscn Herld) Franciscan Pr.

Rooney, Lucy, jt. auth. see Faricy, Robert.

Rooney, Margaret, jt. auth. see Harms, Richard.

Rooney, Mickey. Life Is Too Short. 1992. mass mkt. 5.99 (*0-345-37643-9*) Ballantine.

— Life Is Too Short. 1991. 22.00 (*0-679-40195-4*, Villard Bks) Random.

— Life Is Too Short. large type ed. (Illus.). 544p. 1991. 24.50 (*0-679-40287-X*) Random.

— The Search for Sonny Skies: A Novel. large type ed. LC 95-2631. 1995. 21.95 (*0-7838-1254-X*) Hall.

— The Search for Sunny Skies: A Novel. LC 93-44187. 1994. 19.95 (*1-55972-231-2*, Birch Ln Pr) Carol Pub Group.

Rooney, Miriam T. Lawlessness, Law, & Sanction: A Dissertation. (Catholic University of America Philosophical Studies: Vol. XXXIV). 176p. 1982. reprint ed. lib. bdg. 24.00 (*0-8377-1036-7*) Rothman.

Rooney, Pat, jt. auth. see Doty, Betty.

Rooney, Patty, jt. auth. see Rooney, Theodore.

Rooney, Philip. Captain Boycott. 190p. 1966. reprint ed. 13.95 (*0-900068-90-6*, Pub. by Anvil Bks Ltd IE); reprint ed. pap. 4.95 (*0-900068-27-2*) Irish Bks Media.

Rooney, Robert & Lipuma, Anthony. Learn to Be the Master Student: How to Develop Self-Confidence & Effective Study Skills. LC 92-80281. (Illus.). 248p. (Orig.). (YA). (gr. 9-12). 1992. pap. 14.95 (*0-9632530-8-5*) Maydale Pub.

Rooney, Robert C., ed. Equal Opportunity in the United States: A Symposium on Civil Rights. 185p. 1973. pap. 3.00 (*0-89940-400-6*) LBJ Sch Pub Aff.

Rooney, Ronald H. Strategies for Work with Involuntary Clients. (Illus.). 392p. 1992. text ed. 60.00 (*0-231-06768-2*); pap. text ed. 22.50 (*0-231-06769-0*) Col U Pr.

Rooney, Theodore & Rooney, Patty. The Arthritis Handbook. 1986. mass mkt. 5.99 (*0-345-33561-9*) Ballantine.

Rooney, Thomas. Fine Arts: Humanities. 56p. 1989. 8.95 (*0-8106-0302-0*) NEA.

***Rooney, Tim.** Brain Lord: Official Players Guide. (Illus.). 96p. (Orig.). 1994. pap. 9.95 (*1-57280-016-X*) IFTW Bks.

Rooney, Tim, jt. auth. see Sandler, Corey.

Rooney, Victor M., jt. auth. see Ismail, Amin R.

Rooney, William J. The Problem of "Poetry & Belief" in Contemporary Criticism. 175p. LC 50-2632. 175p. reprint ed. pap. 49.90 (*0-685-17807-2*, 2029494) Bks Demand.

Rooney, William R. Chapter & Verse: The Life of Christ in Poetry. 1993. 11.95 (*0-533-10319-3*) Vantage.

Roonwal, G. S. The Indian Ocean: Exploitable Mineral & Petroleum Resources. (Illus.). 235p. 1986. 91.00 (*0-387-16881-8*) Spr-Verlag.

Roonwal, M. L. Termite Life & Termite Control in Tropical South Asia. 117p. (C). 1979. 80.00 (*81-85046-02-6*, Scientific) St Mut.

Roonwal, Mithan L. & Mohnot, S. M. Primates of South Asia: Ecology, Sociobiology, & Behavior. LC 76-28309. (Illus.). 439p. reprint ed. pap. 125.20 (*0-7837-4184-7*, 2059034) Bks Demand.

Roop, Connie, ed. see Columbus, Christopher.

Roop, Connie, jt. auth. see Roop, Peter.

Roop, Connie, jt. ed. see Roop, Peter.

Roop, D. Haigh. An Introduction to the Burmese Writing System. LC 70-179476. (Linguistic Ser.). 136p. (C). 1972. pap. text ed. 15.00 (*0-300-01528-3*) Yale U Pr.

Roop, D. Haigh, jt. auth. see Cornyn, William S.

Roop, Edward. Best Deals for New Wheels. 144p. (Orig.). 1992. pap. 3.99 (*0-425-13473-3*) Berkley Pub.

***Roop, Eugene.** Heard in Our Land. 112p. 1991. pap. 7.95 (*0-87178-351-7*) Brethren.

Roop, Eugene F. Genesis. LC 87-10969. (Believers Church Bible Commentary Ser.: No. 2). 352p. (Orig.). 1987. pap. 17.95 (*0-8361-3443-5*) Herald Pr.

— Let the Rivers Run: Stewardship & the Biblical Story. fac. ed. LC 91-26338. (Library of Christian Stewardship). 120p. (Orig.). 1991. reprint ed. pap. 34.20 (*0-7837-7972-0*, 2047728) Bks Demand.

Roop, Peter. Go Hog Wild! (J). (gr. 1-4). 1990. pap. 2.95 (*0-8225-9555-9*, Lerner Publctns) Lerner Group.

— Little Blaze & the Buffalo Jump. (Indian Culture Ser.). (Illus.). 28p. (Orig.). (J). (gr. 3-8). 1984. pap. 4.95 (*0-89992-089-6*) Coun India Ed.

— Natosi: Strong Medicine. 32p. (J). (gr. 3-8). 1984. pap. 4.95 (*0-89992-090-X*) Coun India Ed.

— Sik-Ki-Mi. (Indian Culture Ser.). 32p. (J). (gr. 3-6). 1984. pap. 3.95 (*0-89992-091-8*) Coun India Ed.

Roop, Peter & Roop, Connie. Ahyoka & the Talking Leaves. LC 91-3036. (Illus.). 48p. (J). (gr. 1 up). 1992. text ed. 14.00 (*0-688-10697-8*) Lothrop.

— Ahyoka & the Talking Leaves. Cohn, Amy, ed. LC 91-30366. (Illus.). 64p. (J). (gr. 3 up). 1994. reprint ed. pap. 3.95 (*0-688-13082-8*, Pub. by Beech Tree Bks) Morrow.

— Buttons for General Washington. LC 86-6120. (Carolrhoda On My Own Bks.). (Illus.). 48p. (J). (gr. k-3). 1986. lib. bdg. 15.95 (*0-87614-294-3*, Carolrhoda); pap. 5.95 (*0-87614-476-8*, Carolrhoda) Lerner Group.

— Buttons for General Washington. (Illus.). 48p. (J). (gr. k-4). 1987. reprint ed. pap. 5.95 (*0-685-18657-1*, Lerner Publctns) Lerner Group.

— Going Buggy! Jokes about Insects. (Make Me Laugh! Joke Bks.). (Illus.). 32p. (J). (gr. 1-4). 1986. lib. bdg. 11.96 (*0-8225-0988-1*, Lerner Publctns); pap. 2.95 (*0-8225-9530-3*, Lerner Publctns) Lerner Group.

— Keep the Lights Burning, Abbie. LC 84-27446. (Carolrhoda On My Own Bks.). (Illus.). 40p. (J). (gr. k-3). 1985. lib. bdg. 15.95 (*0-87614-275-7*, Carolrhoda); pap. 5.95 (*0-87614-454-7*, Carolrhoda) Lerner Group.

— Keep the Lights Burning, Abbie. (Illus.). (J). (gr. 2-4). 1989. audio 19.95 (*0-87499-135-8*); audio 12.95 (*0-87499-134-X*) Live Oak Media.

— Keep the Lights Burning, Abbie, 4 bks., Set. (Illus.). (J). (gr. 2-4). 1989. audio 27.95 (*0-87499-136-6*) Live Oak Media.

— Let's Celebrate! Jokes about Holidays. (Make Me Laugh! Joke Bks.). (Illus.). 32p. (J). (gr. 1-4). 1986. lib. bdg. 11.96 (*0-8225-0989-X*, Lerner Publctns); pap. 2.95 (*0-8225-9529-X*, Lerner Publctns) Lerner Group.

— Off the Map: The Journals of Lewis & Clark. LC 92-18340. (Illus.). 48p. (J). (gr. 3-7). 1993. 14.95 (*0-8027-8207-8*); lib. bdg. 15.85 (*0-8027-8208-6*) Walker & Co.

— One Earth, a Multitude of Creatures. LC 92-14057. 32p. (J). 1992. 14.95 (*0-8027-8192-6*); lib. bdg. 15.85 (*0-8027-8193-4*) Walker & Co.

— Out to Lunch: Jokes about Food. LC 84-4416. (Make Me Laugh! Joke Bks.). (Illus.). 32p. (J). (gr. 1-4). 1984. lib. bdg. 11.95 (*0-8225-0983-0*, Lerner Publctns); pap. 2.95 (*0-8225-9552-4*, Lerner Publctns) Lerner Group.

— Pilgrim Voices: Our First Year in the New World. LC 95-10114. (Illus.). 48p. (J). (gr. 2-6). 1995. 16.95 (*0-8027-8314-7*); lib. bdg. 17.85 (*0-8027-8315-5*) Walker & Co.

— Seasons of the Cranes. (Illus.). 32p. (J). (gr. 4-7). 1989. 14.95 (*0-8027-6859-8*); lib. bdg. 15.85 (*0-8027-6860-1*) Walker & Co.

— Stick Out Your Tongue! Jokes about Doctors & Patients. (Make Me Laugh! Joke Bks.). (Illus.). 32p. (J). (gr. 1-4). 1986. lib. bdg. 11.96 (*0-8225-0990-3*, Lerner Publctns); pap. 2.95 (*0-8225-9546-X*, Lerner Publctns) Lerner Group.

— Stonehenge: Opposing Viewpoints. LC 89-37441. (Great Mysteries Ser.). (Illus.). 112p. (J). (gr. 5-8). 1989. lib. bdg. 16.95 (*0-89908-066-9*) Greenhaven.

Roop, Peter & Roop, Connie, eds. Capturing Nature: The Writings & Art of John James Audubon. LC 92-15662. (Illus.). 48p. (J). (gr. 5 up). 1993. 16.95 (*0-8027-8204-3*); lib. bdg. 17.85 (*0-8027-8205-1*) Walker & Co.

— I, Columbus: My Journal - 1492. (Illus.). 57p. (J). (gr. 4-7). 1990. 13.95 (*0-8027-6977-2*); lib. bdg. 14.85 (*0-8027-6978-0*) Walker & Co.

Roop, Peter, ed. see Columbus, Christopher.

Roop, Peter, et al. Go Hog Wild: Jokes from down on the Farm. LC 84-5662. (Make Me Laugh! Joke Bks.). (Illus.). 32p. (J). (gr. 1-4). 1984. lib. bdg. 11.96 (*0-8225-0982-2*, Lerner Publctns) Lerner Group.

— Space Out: Jokes about Outer Space. LC 84-5650. (Make Me Laugh! Joke Bks.). (Illus.). 32p. (J). (gr. 1-4). 1984. lib. bdg. 11.96 (*0-8225-0984-9*, Lerner Publctns) Lerner Group.

Roop, Peter G., jt. auth. see McCown, Rick R.

Roopnarine, J. L. & Johnson, J. E., eds. Approaches to Early Childhood Education. 2nd ed. LC 92-14849. 416p. (C). 1992. pap. write for info. (*0-02-403545-9*, Merrill Pub Co) Macmillan.

Roopnarine, Jaipaul L. & Carter, D. Bruce. Parent-Child Socialization in Diverse Cultures. Sigel, Irving E., ed. (Advances in Applied Developmental Psychology Ser.). 336p. (C). 1992. text ed. 49.50 (*0-89391-849-0*) Ablex Pub.

Roopnarine, Jaipaul L., et al, eds. Children's Play in Diverse Cultures. LC 93-12177. (SUNY Series, Children's Play in Society). 234p. (C). 1994. 59.50 (*0-7914-1753-0*); pap. 19.95 (*0-7914-1754-9*) State U NY Pr.

Roorbach, O. A. Bibliotheca Americana: Eighteen Fifty-Two to Eighteen Sixty-One, 3 vols. in 1, Vols. 2, 3 & 4. 30.00 (*0-8446-1389-4*) Peter Smith.

***Roorda, Berend.** Global Total Least Squares: A Method for the Construction of Open Approximate Models from Vector Time Series. (Tinbergen Institute Research Ser.: No. 88). 168p. 1995. pap. 25.00 (*90-5170-323-6*) IBD Ltd.

Roorda, Randall, ed. see Rossini, Frank.

Roos, Aarand, ed. Estonia: A Nation Unconquered. (Illus.). 96p. (Orig.). 1985. pap. 5.00 (*0-932595-00-6*) Estonian Wrld.

Roos, B. O., jt. ed. see European Summer School in Quantum Chemistry Staff.

Roos, B. O., ed. see Third European Summer School in Quantum Chemistry Staff.

Roos, C. F. NRA Economic Planning. LC 72-171693. (FDR & the Era of the New Deal Ser.). 596p. 1971. reprint ed. lib. bdg. 59.50 (*0-306-70396-3*) Da Capo.

Roos-Collins, Margit. Flavors of Home: A Guide to Wild Edible Plants of the San Francisco Bay Area. (Illus.). 224p. (Orig.). 1990. pap. 11.95 (*0-930588-46-0*) Heyday Bks.

— The Flavors of Home: A Guide to Wild Edible Plants of the San Francisco Bay Area. (Illus.). 224p. 1991. reprint ed. lib. bdg. 31.00x (*0-8095-4966-2*) Borgo Pr.

***Roos, Daniel.** Agile-Lean: A Common Strategy for Success. (Perspectives on Agility Ser.). 10p. (Orig.). 1995. pap. 10.00 (*1-885166-01-X*) Agile Manufact.

Roos, Diane F. Yazoo County, Mississippi, Eighteen Fifty Census & Marriages. 140p. (Orig.). 1990. pap. 20.00 (*1-55613-343-X*) Heritage Bk.

Roos, Frank J., Jr. Bibliography of Early American Architecture: Writings on Architecture Constructed Before 1860 in Eastern & Central U. S. LC 68-24624. (Illus.). 399p. reprint ed. pap. 113.80 (*0-8357-9665-5*, 2014984) Bks Demand.

Roos, George H. Collie Concept. rev. ed. (Illus.). 232p. 1988. 26.95 (*0-931866-36-7*) Alpine Pubns.

Roos, J. E., ed. Algebra, Algebraic Topology & Their Interactions. (Lecture Notes in Mathematics Ser.: Vol. 1183). xi, 396p. 1986. pap. 53.40 (*0-387-16453-7*) Spr-Verlag.

Roos, J. L., ed. Economics & Artificial Intelligence. (IFAC Proceedings Ser.). (Illus.). 245p. 1987. 90.00 (*0-08-034350-3*) Franklin.

Roos, J. P. & Sicinski, Andrzej. Ways of Life in Finland & Poland: Comparative Studies on Urban Population. 200p. 1987. text ed. 63.95 (*0-566-05342-X*, Pub. by Avebury Pub UK) Ashgate Pub Co.

Roos, J. W., jt. ed. see Hjortso, Martin A.

Roos, Johan. European Casebook on Cooperative Strategies. LC 94-17228. (European Casebook Series in Management). 1994. write for info. (*0-13-097155-3*) P-H.

***Roos, Kelley.** Ghost of a Chance. 200p. 1994. 16.95 (*0-7451-8648-3*, Black Dagger) Chivers N Amer.

Roos, Leslie L., Jr., jt. ed. see Caporaso, James A.

Roos, Matts. Introduction to Cosmology. LC 93-32956. 1994. pap. text ed. 42.95 (*0-471-94298-7*) Wiley.

Roos, Murphre. Sonnets & Other Dead Forms. 1980. pap. 3.50 (*0-916696-15-4*) Cross Country.

Roos, Norbert & Morgan, A. John. Cryopreparation of Thin Biological Specimens for Electron Microscopy: Methods & Applications. (Royal Microscopical Society Microscopy Handbooks Ser.: No. 21). (Illus.). 120p. 1990. pap. 19.95 (*0-19-856424-4*) OUP.

Roos, Paavo. Survey of Rock-Cut Chamber-Tombs in Caria, Pt. I: Southeastern Caria & the Lyco-Carian Borderland. (Studies in Mediterranean Archaeology). (Illus.). 132p. (Orig.). 1985. pap. text ed. 156.00x (*0-685-16885-9*, Pub. by Almqv & Wiksell SW) Coronet Bks.

Roos, Patricia A., jt. auth. see Reskin, Barbara F.

Roos, Raymond P., ed. Molecular Neurovirology: Pathogenesis of Viral CNS Infections. LC 91-20851. (Illus.). 1992. 125.00 (*0-89603-222-1*) Humana.

Roos, Robert A., jt. auth. see McKenzie, Evan.

Roos, Rosalie. Travels in America, 1851-1855. Anderson, Carl L., ed. LC 81-187. 170p. 1982. 19.95 (*0-8093-1018-X*) S Ill U Pr.

Roos, Stephen. And the Winner Is . . . LC 88-27519. (Illus.). 128p. (J). (gr. 3-7). 1989. text ed. 13.95 (*0-689-31300-4*, Atheneum Bks Young) S&S Childrens.

— Cottontail Caper: The Pet Lovers Club. (J). (gr. 4-7). 1994. pap. 3.50 (*0-440-40925-X*) Dell.

— Dear Santa, Make Me a Star. (Maple Street Kids Ser.). (Illus.). 96p. (J). (gr. 2-6). 1991. per., pap. 1.95 (*0-89486-764-4*, 5174A) Hazelden.

— The Fair-Weather Friends. LC 86-17246. (Plymouth Island Chronicles Ser.: Bk. 1). (Illus.). 144p. (J). (gr. 3-6). 1987. text ed. 13.95 (*0-689-31297-0*, Atheneum Bks Young) S&S Childrens.

— Fair-Weather Friends. 128p. (J). (gr. 2-9). 1988. reprint ed. pap. 2.95 (*0-8167-1306-5*) Troll Assocs.

— Leave It to Augie. (Maple Street Kids Ser.). (Illus.). 96p. (J). (gr. 2-6). 1991. per. 1.50 (*0-89486-774-1*, T5172) Hazelden.

— My Blue Tongue. (Maple Street Kids Ser.). (Illus.). 96p. (J). (gr. 2-6). 1991. per., pap. 1.50 (*0-89486-784-9*, T5173) Hazelden.

— My Favorite Ghost. LC 87-15186. 128p. (J). (gr. 3-7). 1988. text ed. 13.95 (*0-689-31301-2*, Atheneum Bks Young) S&S Childrens.

— Never Trust a Sister over Twelve. LC 92-34406. (Illus.). (J). 1993. 13.95 (*0-385-31048-X*) Delacorte.

— Silver Secrets: Maple Street Kids Ser. (Illus.). 96p. (J). (gr. 2-6). 1991. per. 1.50 (*0-89486-777-6*, T5171) Hazelden.

— Thirteenth Summer. 112p. (J). (gr. 4-7). 1992. pap. 2.95 (*0-8167-1840-7*) Troll Assocs.

— A Young Person's Guide to the Twelve Steps. LC 92-21818. 128p. (YA). (gr. 7 up). 1992. 6.00 (*0-89486-851-9*, 5432A) Hazelden.

Roos, Werner & Rojczyk, Ursula. Construction of Simple Kiln Systems. 34p. 1984. pap. 7.00 (*3-528-02012-1*, Pub. by Vieweg & Sohn GW) Ballen Bkslr.

***Roos, Wilma.** Shaping Brazil's Petrochemical Industry: The Importance of Foreign Firm Origin in Tripartite Joint Ventures. 272p. 1991. pap. 28.50 (*90-70280-53-1*, Pub. by Thesis Pubs NE) IBD Ltd.

***Roos, Yrjo.** Phase Transitions in Food. LC 95-5987. (Food Science & Technology International Ser.). (Illus.). 384p. 1995. boxed write for info. (*0-12-595340-2*) Acad Pr.

Roosa, Bertha. The HoBERT Bears' Big Surprise!! (Illus.). 88p. 1994. 28.00 (*0-9639391-0-6*) Hobert Ent.

Roosa, Dean M., jt. auth. see Eilers, Lawrence J.

Roosa, Dean M., jt. auth. see Runkel, Sylvan T.

Roosa, Robert V. The United States & Japan in the International Monetary System: 1946-1985. (Occasional Paper Ser.: No. 21). 75p. 1986. pap. write for info. (*1-56708-020-0*) Grp of Thirty.

Roosa, Vernon, jt. auth. see Bronzino, Joseph D.

Roose, Dirk, jt. ed. see Mittlemann, Hans D.

Roose, Dirk, et al, eds. Continuation & Bifurcations: Numerical Techniques & Applications. (C). 1990. lib. bdg. 150.00 (*0-7923-0855-7*) Kluwer Ac.

Roose-Evans, James. The Inner Stage: Finding a Center in Prayer & Ritual. LC 89-29269. 216p. 1990. pap. 9.95 (*1-56101-001-4*) Cowley Pubns.

— Passages of the Soul. 1995. pap. 11.95 (*1-85230-708-0*) Element MA.

— Passages of the Soul: Rituals for Today. 1994. 19.95 (*1-85230-474-X*) Element MA.

Roose, Steven P. & Glassman, Alexander H., eds. Treatment Strategies for Refractory Depression. LC 90-10. (Progress in Psychiatry Ser.: No. 25). 160p. 1990. text ed. 31.00 (*0-88048-184-6*, 8184) Am Psychiatric.

***Roose, Steven P. & Glick, Robert A., eds.** Anxiety: Symptom & Signal. 200p. 1995. text ed. write for info. (*0-88163-118-3*) Analytic Pr.

Roose, Steven T., jt. ed. see Glick, Robert A.

Roosen, G., ed. Nonlinear Optical Materials, Vol. 1017. 1989. 51.00 (*0-8194-0052-1*) SPIE.

***Roosen, G., et al, eds.** Photorefractive Materials. (European Materials Research Society Symposia Proceedings Ser.: Vol. 48). 300p. 1995. 173.50 (*0-444-82167-8*, North Holland) Elsevier.

Roosen-Runge, Edward C. The Process of Spermatogenesis in Animals. LC 76-9169. (Developmental & Cell Biology Ser.: 5). 222p. reprint ed. pap. 63.30 (*0-685-16061-0*, 2027239) Bks Demand.

Roosen, William. Daniel Defoe & Diplomacy. LC 85-40508. (Illus.). 144p. 1986. 32.50 (*0-941664-12-0*) Susquehanna U Pr.

Roosen, William J. The Age of Louis the Fourteenth: The Rise of Modern Diplomacy. 208p. 1976. pap. text ed. 32.95 (*0-87073-581-0*) Transaction Pubs.

Roosens, Eugeen E. Creating Ethnicity: The Process of Ethnogenesis. (Frontiers of Anthropology Ser.). 200p. (C). 1989. text ed. 49.95 (*0-8039-3422-X*); pap. text ed. 24.00 (*0-8039-3423-8*) Sage.

Roosens, Laurent & Salu, Luc. History of Photography: A Bibliography of Books, Vol. 2. 192p. 1994. 100.00 (*0-7201-2152-3*, Mansell Pub) Cassell.

Roosens, Laurent P. & Salu, Luc. History of Photography: A Bibliography of Books. 456p. 1989. text ed. 100.00 (*0-7201-2008-X*, Mansell Pub) Cassell.

Rooses, Max. Art in Flanders. LC 75-100819. (Illus.). reprint ed. 22.50 (*0-404-05397-1*) AMS Pr.

***Roosevelt.** Letters Vol. 5-6. Date not set. 25.00 (*0-674-52802-6*) HUP.

— Murder in the East Room. 1995. mass mkt. 4.99 (*0-312-95410-7*) St Martin.

Roosevelt, Anna, ed. Amazonian Indians from Prehistory to the Present: Anthropological Perspectives. 400p. 1994. 60.00x (*0-8165-1436-4*) U of Ariz Pr.

Roosevelt, Anna C. Moundbuilders of the Amazon: Geophysical Archaeology on Marajo Island, Brazil. 495p. 1991. text ed. 105.00 (*0-12-595348-8*) Acad Pr.

Roosevelt, Anna C. & Smith, James G., eds. The Ancestors: Native Artisans of the Americas. LC 79-89536. (Illus.). 230p. 1986. pap. 17.50 (*0-295-95780-8*) U of Wash Pr.

Roosevelt, Archibald, ed. see Roosevelt, Theodore.

Roosevelt, Constance, ed. see Lewis, Mina B.

Roosevelt, Corinne A. & Roosevelt, Kermit, III. Exploring Nature on Nantucket. LC 93-78238. (Illus.). 112p. (Orig.). 1993. pap. 9.00 (*0-9640372-0-3*) Kerriemuir Pr.

Roosevelt, Eleanor. The Autobiography of Eleanor Roosevelt. (Illus.). 498p. 1992. reprint ed. pap. 15.95 (*0-306-80476-X*) Da Capo.

— This I Remember. LC 74-11884. (Illus.). 387p. 1975. reprint ed. text ed. 85.00 (*0-8371-7702-2*, ROTI, Greenwood Pr) Greenwood.

— You Learn by Living. LC 83-6838. 224p. 1983. reprint ed. pap. 10.99 (*0-664-24494-7*, Westminster) Westminster John Knox.

Roosevelt, Elliott. A First Class Murder. large type ed. (General Ser.). 339p. 1992. text ed. 20.95 (*0-8161-5317-5*); pap. 16.95 (*0-8161-5318-3*) G K Hall.

— A First Class Murder. 224p. 1993. reprint ed. mass mkt. 4.99 (*0-380-71238-5*) Avon.

— The Hyde Park Murder. 240p. 1986. mass mkt. 4.50 (*0-380-70058-1*) Avon.

— Murder & the First Lady. 240p. 1985. mass mkt. 4.99 (*0-380-69937-0*) Avon.

— Murder at Hobcaw Barony. 224p. 1987. mass mkt. 4.50 (*0-380-70021-2*) Avon.

— Murder at the Palace. 272p. 1989. mass mkt. 4.99 (*0-380-70405-6*) Avon.

— Murder at the Palace. large type unabridged ed. (General Ser.). 315p. 1989. lib. bdg. 17.95 (*0-8161-4663-2*) G K Hall.

— Murder in the Blue Room. 240p. 1992. mass mkt. 4.99 (*0-380-71237-7*) Avon.

R

An Asterisk (*) at the beginning of an entry indicates that the title is appearing in BIP for the first time.

— Murder in the Blue Room. large type ed. (General Ser.). 377p. 1991. pap. 13.95 (0-8161-5112-1) G K Hall.

— Murder in the Blue Room. large type ed. (General Ser.). 377p. 1991. text ed. 20.95 (0-8161-5100-8, Large Print Bks) Hall.

— Murder in the East Room: An Eleanor Roosevelt Mystery. 208p. 1993. 18.95 (0-312-09878-2, Pub. by Thomas Dunne Bks) St Martin.

— Murder in the Executive Mansion: An Eleanor Roosevelt Mystery. 208p. 1995. 19.95 (0-312-13128-3, Pub. by Thomas Dunne Bks) St Martin.

— Murder in the Oval Office. 1990. mass mkt. 4.99 (0-380-70528-1) Avon.

— Murder in the Red Room. 256p. 1994. mass mkt. 4.99 (0-380-72143-0) Avon.

— Murder in the Red Room: An Eleanor Roosevelt Mystery. 256p. 1992. 18.95 (0-312-07637-1, Pub. by Thomas Dunne Bks) St Martin.

— Murder in the Rose Garden. 256p. 1991. reprint ed. mass mkt. 4.95 (0-380-70529-X) Avon.

— Murder in the Rose Garden: An Eleanor Roosevelt Mystery. large type ed. (General Ser.). 384p. 1990. reprint ed. 19.95 (0-8161-4998-4, Large Print Bks); reprint ed. pap. 11.95 (0-8161-5000-1, Large Print Bks) G K Hall.

— Murder in the West Wing. 1993. mass mkt. 4.99 (0-312-95144-2) St Martin.

— Murder in the West Wing: An Eleanor Roosevelt Mystery. 256p. 1992. 18.95 (0-312-08144-8, Pub. by Thomas Dunne Bks) St Martin.

— New Deal for Death. (Blackjack Endicott Novel Ser.). 256p. 1993. 18.95 (0-312-09267-9, Pub. by Thomas Dunne Bks) St Martin.

— New Deal for Death. (Blackjack Endicott Ser.: No. 2). 288p. 1994. mass mkt. 4.99 (0-312-95238-4) St Martin.

— President's Man. 1992. mass mkt. 4.99 (0-312-92828-9) St Martin.

— The President's Man: A "Blackjack" Endicott Novel. large type ed. LC 92-17879. (General Ser.). 354p. 1992. pap. 16.95 (0-8161-5397-3) G K Hall.

— A Royal Murder. large type ed. LC 94-40019. 1995. 22.95 (1-56895-171-X) Wheeler Pub.

— A Royal Murder: An Eleanor Roosevelt Mystery. 240p. 1994. 19.95 (0-312-10970-9, Pub. by Thomas Dunne Bks) St Martin.

— The White House Pantry Murder. 224p. 1988. mass mkt. 4.50 (0-380-70404-8) Avon.

Roosevelt, F. D. On Our Way. LC 72-2383. (FDR & the Era of the New Deal Ser.). 216p. 1973. reprint ed. lib. bdg. 39.50 (0-306-70476-5) Da Capo.

Roosevelt, Frank & Belkin, David. Why Market Socialism? Voices from Dissent. 392p. 1994. text ed. 52.00 (1-56324-465-9); pap. text ed. 21.95 (1-56324-466-7) M E Sharpe.

***Roosevelt, Franklin.** Wartime Correspondence Between President Roosevelt & Pope Pius XII. (American Autobiography Ser.). 127p. 1995. reprint ed. lib. bdg. 69.00 (0-7812-8629-8) Rprt Serv.

Roosevelt, Franklin D. The Complete Presidential Press Conferences of Franklin Delano Roosevelt (1933-1945), 12 annual vols., Set. LC 78-155953. (FDR & the Era of the New Deal Ser.). 7000p. 1973. 495.00 (0-306-77500-X) Da Capo.

— The Essential Franklin Delano Roosevelt. Hunt, John G., ed. LC 94-40318. (Library of Freedom). 1994. write for info. (0-517-12289-8) Random.

— Franklin D. Roosevelt & Foreign Affairs, 3 vols. Nixon, Edgar B., ed. Incl. Vol. 1. January 1933 - Feburary 1934. LC 68-25617. 1969. (0-674-31816-1); Vol. 2. March 1934 - August 1935. LC 68-25617. 1969. (0-674-31818-8); Vol. 3. September 1935 - January 1937. LC 68-25617. 1969. (0-674-31819-6); LC 68-25617. 1969. 100.00 (0-674-31815-3) HUP.

— Looking Forward. LC 72-2382. (FDR & the Era of the New Deal Ser.). 284p. 1973. reprint ed. lib. bdg. 35.00 (0-306-70477-3) Da Capo.

Roosevelt, Franklin D., Jr. Nothing to Fear. LC 76-128302. (Essay Index Reprint Ser.). 1977. 30.95 (0-8369-1845-2) Ayer.

Roosevelt, Grace G. Reading Rousseau in the Nuclear Age. 288p. 1990. 44.95 (0-87722-679-2) Temple U Pr.

Roosevelt, Hilborne L. Hilborne L. Roosevelt Organs. (Illus.). 1978. reprint ed. 30.00 (0-913746-12-6) Organ Lit.

Roosevelt, James, ed. Liberal Papers. LC 79-111861. (Essay Index Reprint Ser.). 1977. 26.95 (0-8369-1716-2) Ayer.

Roosevelt, Kermit, III, jt. auth. see Roosevelt, Corinne A.

Roosevelt, Kermit, jt. auth. see Roosevelt, Theodore.

Roosevelt, Nicholas. Philippines: A Treasure & a Problem. LC 71-100510. reprint ed. 24.00 (0-404-00618-3) AMS Pr.

***Roosevelt, Priscilla.** Life on the Russian Country Estate: A Social & Cultural History. LC 94-42337. 1995. write for info. (0-300-05595-1) Yale U Pr.

Roosevelt, R. B., ed. see Halpine, Charles G.

Roosevelt, Rita K., jt. auth. see Laird, Nick L.

Roosevelt, Robert B. Superior Fishing: The Striped Bass, Trout, & Black Bass of the Northern States. LC 84-29451. xxiii, 310p. 1985. reprint ed. 19.95 (0-87351-187-5, Borealis Book); reprint ed. pap. 8.95 (0-87351-176-X, Borealis Book) Minn Hist.

Roosevelt, Ruth & Lofas, Jeannette. Living in Step. (Paperbacks Ser.). 1977. reprint ed. pap. text ed. 8.95 (0-07-053596-5) McGraw.

Roosevelt, T. & Grinnell, G., eds. Hunting in Many Lands. (Illus.). 447p. 1986. reprint ed. pap. 19.95 (0-940864-10-X) Boone & Crockett.

Roosevelt, Theodore, Jr. African Game Trails. (Peter Capstick Library). (Illus.). 620p. 1988. 19.95 (0-312-02151-8) St Martin.

Roosevelt, Theodore. American Bears: Selections from the Writings of Theodore Roosevelt. LC 82-71701. (Illus.). 206p. reprint ed. pap. 58.80 (0-7837-5167-2, 2044896) Bks Demand.

— American Ideals & Other Essays, Social & Political. LC 70-106519. reprint ed. 34.50 (0-404-05398-X) AMS Pr.

— American Ideals & Other Essays, Social & Political. 1971. reprint ed. 15.00 (0-403-00195-1) Scholarly.

— Autobiography of Theodore Roosevelt. (Quality Paperbacks Ser.). 628p. 1985. reprint ed. pap. 15.95 (0-306-80232-5) Da Capo.

— A Bully Father: Theodore Roosevelt's Letters to His Children. LC 95-8585. 1995. 25.00 (0-679-43948-X) Random.

Roosevelt, Theodore, Jr. Colonial Policies of the United States. LC 71-111705. (American Imperialism: Viewpoints of United States Foreign Policy, 1898-1941 Ser.). 1977. reprint ed. 19.95 (0-405-02048-1) Ayer.

***Roosevelt, Theodore.** The Essential Theodore Roosevelt. 1994. 8.99 (0-517-11848-3) Random Hse Value.

— Frontier Types in Cowboy Land. (Illus.). 28p. 1988. pap. 3.00 (0-86541-024-0) Filter.

— Gouverneur Morris. Morse, John T., Jr., ed. LC 76-128972. (American Statesmen Ser.: No. 8). reprint ed. 45.00 (0-404-50858-8) AMS Pr.

— Gouverneur Morris. LC 68-24996. (American Biography Ser.: No. 32). 1969. reprint ed. lib. bdg. 62.95 (0-8383-0274-2) M S G Haskell Hse.

— Gouverneur Morris. (BCL1 - U. S. History Ser.). 341p. 1992. reprint ed. lib. bdg. 89.00 (0-7812-6128-7) Rprt Serv.

— Gouverneur Morris. LC 70-108532. 1971. reprint ed. 20.00 (0-403-00313-X) Scholarly.

— Maxims. LC 79-104554. reprint ed. lib. bdg. 17.00 (0-8398-1764-9) Irvington.

— Naval War of Eighteen Twelve. LC 68-24994. (American History & Americana Ser.: No. 47). 1969. reprint ed. lib. bdg. 75.00 (0-8383-0235-1) M S G Haskell Hse.

— Naval War of Eighteen Twelve or the History of the United States Navy During the Last War. 1988. reprint ed. lib. bdg. 59.00 (0-7812-0174-8) Rprt Serv.

— Naval War of Eighteen Twelve or the History of the United States Navy During the Last War with Great Britain to Which Is Appended an Account of the Battle of New Orleans. LC 74-108533. (Illus.). 1971. reprint ed. 49.00 (0-403-00312-1) Scholarly.

— The Naval War of 1812. Sweetman, Jack, ed. LC 87-7747. (Classics of Naval Literature Ser.). 1987. reprint ed. 32.95 (0-87021-445-4) Naval Inst Pr.

— New Nationalism. 11.25 (0-8446-0237-X) Peter Smith.

— Outdoor Pastimes of an American Hunter. LC 90-9884. (Classics of American Sport Ser.). (Illus.). 480p. 1990. reprint ed. pap. 16.95 (0-8117-3033-6) Stackpole.

Roosevelt, Theodore, Jr. Outdoor Pastimes of an American Hunter. LC 70-25762. (American Environmental Studies). 1971. reprint ed. 31.95 (0-405-02687-0) Ayer.

Roosevelt, Theodore. Ranch Life & the Hunting-Trail. LC 82-20091. (Illus.). x, 210p. 1983. reprint ed. pap. 10.95 (0-8032-8913-8, Bison Books) U of Nebr Pr.

Roosevelt, Theodore, Jr. Ranch Life & the Hunting Trail. LC 76-125761. (American Environmental Studies). 1971. reprint ed. 18.95 (0-405-02688-9) Ayer.

Roosevelt, Theodore. Ranch Life in the Far West. (Illus.). 1978. reprint ed. pap. 8.95 (0-89646-034-7) Vistabooks.

Roosevelt, Theodore, Jr. Realizable Ideals. LC 77-90676. (Essay Index Reprint Ser.). 1977. 19.95 (0-8369-1233-0) Ayer.

Roosevelt, Theodore. Rough Riders. (Illus.). 384p. 1971. reprint ed. 25.00 (0-87928-018-2) Corner Hse.

— The Rough Riders. (Quality Paperbacks Ser.). (Illus.). 296p. 1990. reprint ed. pap. 12.95 (0-306-80405-0) Da Capo.

— Selections from the Correspondence of Theodore Roosevelt & Henry Cabot Lodge, 1884-1918. (American Biography Ser.). 72p. 1991. reprint ed. lib. bdg. 59.00 (0-7812-8327-2) Rprt Serv.

— Selections from the Correspondence of Theodore Roosevelt & Henry Cabot Lodge, 1884-1918, 2 vols., Set. (History - United States Ser.). 1992. reprint ed. lib. bdg. 150.00 (0-7812-6221-6) Rprt Serv.

Roosevelt, Theodore, Jr. Social Justice & Popular Rule: Essays, Addresses, & Public Statements of the Progressive Movement, 1910-1916. LC 73-19173. (Politics & People Ser.). (Illus.). 604p. 1974. reprint ed. 44.95 (0-405-05909-4) Ayer.

Roosevelt, Theodore. The Strenuous Life. 1991. 8.95 (1-55709-142-0) Applewood.

— Strenuous Life: Essays & Addresses. 1902. 39.00 (0-403-00311-3) Scholarly.

— Theodore Roosevelt on Race, Riots, Reds, & Crime. 2nd ed. Roosevelt, Archibald, ed. 101p. 1983. pap. 5.00 (0-89562-174-6) Sons Lib.

— Theodore Roosevelt's America: American Naturalists Ser. Wiley, Farida, ed. (Selections from the Writings of the Oyster Bay Naturalist). (Illus.). 1955. 14.95 (0-8159-6714-4) Devin.

— Thomas H. Benton. Morse, John T., Jr., ed. LC 79-128972. (American Statesmen Ser.: No. 23). reprint ed. 45.00 (0-404-50873-1) AMS Pr.

— Thomas Hart Benton. LC 68-24995. (American Biography Ser.: No. 32). 1969. reprint ed. lib. bdg. 52.95 (0-8383-0275-0) M S G Haskell Hse.

— Through the Brazilian Wilderness. (Classics of American Sport Ser.). (Illus.). 448p. 1994. pap. 16.95 (0-8117-2569-3) Stackpole.

— The Wilderness Hunter: An Account of the Big Game of the United States & its Chase with Horse Hound & Rifle. 279p. reprint ed. write for info. (0-8290-1955-3) Irvington.

— Winning of the West. Wish, Harvey, ed. & intro. by. 12.00 (0-8446-2827-1) Peter Smith.

— The Winning of the West, 4 vols. 1900. reprint ed. 295.00 (0-403-04339-5) Somerset Pub.

— The Winning of the West Vol. 1: From the Alleghanies to the Mississippi, 1769-1776. (Illus.). 384p. 1995. pap. 15.00 (0-8032-8954-5, Bison Books) U of Nebr Pr.

— The Winning of the West Vol. 2: From the Alleghanies to the Mississippi, 1777-1783. (Illus.). 448p. 1995. pap. 15.00 (0-8032-8955-3, Bison Books) U of Nebr Pr.

— The Winning of the West Vol. 3: The Founding of the Trans-Alleghany Commonwealths, 1784-1790. LC 94-46645. (Illus.). 360p. 1995. pap. 15.00 (0-8032-8956-1, Bison Books) U of Nebr Pr.

— The Winning of the West Vol. 4: Louisiana & the Northwest, 1791-1807. (Illus.). 384p. 1995. pap. text ed. 15.00 (0-8032-8957-X, Bison Books) U of Nebr Pr.

— The Writings of Theodore Roosevelt. Harbaugh, William H., ed. LC 66-14828. 407p. 1967. 39.50 (0-8290-0221-9) Irvington.

Roosevelt, Theodore, ed. Desk Drawer Anthology. LC 72-99032. (Granger Index Reprint Ser.). 1977. 24.95 (0-8369-6107-2) Ayer.

Roosevelt, Theodore & Roosevelt, Kermit. East of the Sun & West of the Moon. 1988. 25.00 (0-935632-70-0) Wolfe Pub Co.

Roosevelt, Theodore, et al. Elk Hunting Tales: An Anthology of Historic Outdoor Adventures from the Pages of BUGLE Magazine. Schelvan, Lance, ed. LC 90-62302. (Rocky Mountain Elk Foundation Conservation Library: Vol. 1). (Illus.). 210p. (C). 1990. 14.95 (0-9627248-1-5); write for info. (0-9627248-2-3); Series. write for info. (0-9627248-0-7) Rocky Mntn Elk.

Root. Contrary Bear. (J). 1996. 15.00 (0-06-025085-2); lib. bdg. 14.89 (0-06-025086-0) HarpC Child Bks.

— No Place for a Pig. 1995. pap. text ed. (0-8114-8405-X) Raintree Steck-V.

— Wordsmithery: A Guide to Working at Writing. 147p. (C). 1994. pap. write for info. (0-02-403541-6) Macmillan.

Root, A. I. Eighteen Ninety ABC of Bee Culture. (Illus.). 403p. 1981. reprint ed. 17.95 (0-931308-08-9); reprint ed. pap. 11.50 (0-931308-09-7) Molly Yes.

Root, Ann, jt. auth. see Gladden, Linda.

Root, Ann R., ed. Survey of Marketing Research, 1988. LC 79-641017. (Illus.). 89p. 1989. text ed. 50.00 (0-685-33269-1) Am Mktg.

Root, Barrett, illus. April, Bubbles, Chocolate. LC 92-17100. (J). 1994. pap. 14.00 (0-671-75911-6, S&S Bks Young Read) S&S Childrens.

Root, Barry, ed. see Ray, M. L.

Root-Bernstein, Michele. Boulevard Theater & Revolution in Eighteenth- Century Paris. LC 84-2545. (Theater & Dramatic Studies: No. 22). (Illus.). 340p. reprint ed. pap. 96.90 (0-8357-1551-5, 2070573) Bks Demand.

Root-Bernstein, Robert S. Discovering. LC 88-35768. (Illus.). 520p. 1989. text ed. 39.95 (0-674-21175-8) HUP.

— Discovering: Inventing & Solving Problems at the Frontiers of Scientific Knowledge. 520p. (C). 1991. pap. text ed. 15.95 (0-674-21176-6) HUP.

— Rethinking AIDS: The Tragic Cost of Premature Consensus. LC 92-26843. 1993. text ed. 29.95 (0-02-926905-9) Free Pr.

Root, Betty. Dictionary. LC 91-26178. (Picture Pockets Ser.). (Illus.). 96p. (J). (gr. 1-5). 1992. pap. 13.00 (0-671-76002-5, S&S Bks Young Read); pap. 8.00 (0-671-76003-3, S&S Bks Young Read) S&S Childrens.

— Help Your Child Learn to Read. (Parents' Guides Ser.). 1989. lib. bdg. 13.96 (0-88110-366-7) EDC.

— Help Your Child Learn to Read. (Parents' Guides Ser.). 1989. pap. 6.95 (0-7460-0224-6, Usborne) EDC.

— My First Dictionary. LC 93-20145. (Illus.). 96p. (J). (gr. k-4). 1993. 16.95 (1-56458-277-9) Dorling Kindersley.

— Three Hundred First Words. 156p. (J). (ps). 9.95 (0-8120-6356-2) Barron.

— Three Hundred First Words - Palabras Primeras. 156p. (ENG & SPA.). (J). (ps). 9.95 (0-8120-6358-9) Barron.

— Three Hundred First Words - Premiers Mots. 156p. (ENG & FRE.). (J). (ps). 1993. 9.95 (0-8120-6357-0) Barron.

Root, Christine B., jt. auth. see Blanchard, Karen L.

Root, Claudia, jt. auth. see Root, Jerry.

Root, Darrell K., jt. auth. see Basarab, David J., Sr.

Root, Deane L. American Popular Stage Music, 1860-1880. LC 81-1512. (Studies in Musicology: No. 44). (Illus.). 294p. reprint ed. pap. 83.80 (0-8357-1509-4, 2070293) Bks Demand.

Root, Deane L., jt. auth. see Saunders, Steven.

Root, Edward. Philip Hooker. 242p. 1993. reprint ed. lib. bdg. 79.00 (0-7812-5305-5) Rprt Serv.

Root, Eileen. Hawaiian Names - English Names. 163p. (Orig.). 1988. pap. 9.95 (0-916630-62-5) Pr Pacifica.

Root, Elihu. Addresses on Government & Citizenship. LC 70-86779. (Essay Index Reprint Ser.). 1977. 29.95 (0-8369-1190-3) Ayer.

— Addresses on International Subjects. LC 74-86780. (Essay Index Reprint Ser.). 1977. 26.95 (0-8369-1191-1) Ayer.

— The Citizen's Part in Government & Experiments in Government & the Essentials of the Constitution, 2 vols. in 1. LC 73-19174. (Politics & People Ser.). 220p. 1974. reprint ed. 19.95 (0-405-05895-0) Ayer.

— Men & Policies: Addresses. Bacon, Robert & Scott, J. B., eds. LC 68-22942. (Essay Index Reprint Ser.). 1977. reprint ed. 23.95 (0-8369-0832-5) Ayer.

— Military & Colonial Policy of the United States. LC 70-121030. reprint ed. 47.50 (0-404-05399-8) AMS Pr.

— North Atlantic Coast Fisheries Arbitration at the Hague: Argument on Behalf of the United States. Bacon, Robert & Scott, James, eds. (Illus.). cix, 445p. 1982. reprint ed. lib. bdg. 38.50 (0-8377-1035-9) Rothman.

Root, Elizabeth. Hawaiian Quilting. 1989. pap. 3.95 (0-486-25948-X) Dover.

Root, Esther S. Over Periscope Pond: Letters from Two American Girls in Paris, October 1916-January 1918. (American Biography Ser.). 295p. 1991. reprint ed. lib. bdg. 69.00 (0-7812-8328-0) Rprt Serv.

Root, Frank A. & Connelly, William E. The Overland Stage to California: Personal Reminiscences & Authentic History of the Great Overland Stage Line & Pony Express. (Illus.). xvii, 630p. 1989. reprint ed. lib. bdg. 64.00 (0-8328-1428-8) Higginson Bk Co.

Root, Franklin R. Entry Strategies for International Markets. 288p. 1986. text ed. 40.00 (0-669-13701-4); pap. 24.95 (0-669-13702-2) Free Pr.

— Entry Strategies for International Markets. 2nd rev. ed. 310p. 1994. text ed. 35.00 (0-02-926903-2) Free Pr.

— International Strategic Management: Challenges & Opportunities. (International Business & Trade Ser.). 240p. 1992. 59.50 (0-8448-1665-5); pap. 29.00 (0-8448-1666-3) Taylor & Francis.

— International Trade & Investment. 7th ed. LC 93-20445. (C). 1994. text ed. 58.95 (0-538-82286-4, HV61GA) S-W Pub.

Root, G. A., jt. auth. see Cone, W. W.

Root, George F. Story of a Musical Life. LC 71-174964. reprint ed. 20.00 (0-404-07205-4) AMS Pr.

— The Story of a Musical Life: An Autobiography. LC 70-126072. (Music Ser.). 1970. reprint ed. lib. bdg. 35.00 (0-306-70031-X) Da Capo.

— The Story of a Musical Life: An Autobiography. (American Biography Ser.). 256p. 1991. reprint ed. lib. bdg. 69.00 (0-7812-8329-9) Rprt Serv.

***Root, Gineke.** Innovative Beaded Jewelry Techniques. 56p. 1994. pap. 14.00 (0-916896-60-9) Lacis Pubns.

Root, H. E., ed. see Hume, David.

Root, Hal & Koenig, Steve. The Small Business Start-up Guide: Make or Break Factors to Successfully Launch Your Own Business. LC 93-31432. (Small Business Sourcebooks Ser.). 144p. 1993. 17.95 (0-942061-70-5); pap. 8.95 (0-942061-67-5) Sourcebks.

Root, Hilton L. The Fountain of Privilege: Political Foundations of Economic Markets in Old Regime France & England. LC 93-5066. (California Series on Social Choice & Political Economy: Vol. 26). 1994. 45.00 (0-520-08415-2) U CA Pr.

— Has China Lost Its Way? Getting Stuck in Transition. LC 95-12510. (Essays in Public Policy: No. 62). 1995. write for info. (0-8179-5672-7) Hoover Inst Pr.

— Peasants & King in Burgundy: Agrarian Foundations of French Absolutism. (California Series on Social Choice & Political Economy: Vol. 9). (C). 1992. pap. 14.00 (0-520-08097-1) U CA Pr.

Root, J. P. Root Genealogical Records, 1600-1870, Comprising the History of the Root & Roots Family in America. 533p. 1989. reprint ed. lib. bdg. 88.00 (0-8328-1030-4); reprint ed. pap. 80.00 (0-8328-1031-2) Higginson Bk Co.

***Root, Jack B., Sr. & Mortensen, Douglas L.** The Seven Secrets of Financial Success: Applying the Time-Tested Principles of Creating, Managing & Building Personal Wealth. 275p. 1995. text ed. 25.00 (0-7863-0459-6) Irwin Prof Pubng.

Root, Jacqueline C. Canine Therapy Groups: Organization & Management. LC 90-31708. (Other Dog Bks.). (Illus.). 1990. 12.95 (0-87714-143-6) Denlingers.

Root, Jane, jt. auth. see Colvin, Ruth J.

Root, Jane H., jt. ed. see Colvin, Ruth J.

Root, Janet. Open the Box: About Television. (Comedia Bks.). 128p. 1988. pap. text ed. 13.95 (0-906890-78-0, Pub. by Comedia NY) Routledge Chapman & Hall.

Root, Jerry & Root, Claudia. Friendship Evangelism. (NetWork Discussion Guides Ser.). 48p. (Orig.). 1990. 4.99 (0-87788-273-8) Shaw Pubs.

Root, Jerry, jt. auth. see Martindale, Wayne.

Root, John W. & Krohn, Kenneth A., eds. Short-Lived Radionuclides in Chemistry & Biology. LC 81-19148. (Advances in Chemistry Ser.: No. 197). 1982. 80.95 (0-8412-0603-1) Am Chemical.

Root, Judith. Weaving the Sheets. 1988. pap. 9.95 (0-88748-070-5) Carnegie-Mellon.

Root, Kathleen B. & Byers, Edward E. Medical Secretary: Terminology & Transcription. 3rd ed. 1967. text ed. 38.95 (0-07-053586-8) McGraw.

— Medical Typing Practice. 2nd ed. 1967. text ed. 18.25 (0-07-053585-X) McGraw.

Root, Kimberly B., illus. Billy Beg & His Bull: An Irish Tale. LC 93-7730. 32p. (J). (ps-3). 1994. lib. bdg. 15.95 (0-8234-1100-1) Holiday.

— Boots & His Brothers: A Tale from Norway. LC 90-23659. 32p. (J). (ps-3). 1992. lib. bdg. 14.95 (0-8234-0886-8) Holiday.

— Gulliver in Lilliput. LC 94-15037. (J). (ps-3). 1995. lib. bdg. 15.95 (0-8234-1147-8) Holiday.

Root, Kimberly B., jt. auth. see Wolff, Patricia R.

Root, Leon. No More Aching Back: Dr. Root's New, Fifteen-Minute-a-Day Program for a Healthy Back. 240p. 1991. pap. 5.99 (0-451-17091-1, Sig) NAL-Dutton.

— No More Aching Back: Dr. Root's New 15-Minute-a-Day Program for a Healthy Back. (Illus.). 256p. 1990. 17.95 (0-394-58794-4, Villard Bks) Random.

Root, Loren F. Radio Frequency: Microwave Robust Design Techniques Applied to a Transistor Amplifier Test Fixture. LC 92-26383. (Six Sigma Research Institute Ser.). 1992. pap. write for info. (0-201-63428-7) Addison-Wesley.

Root, Loretta P. Outflowing Love: Auntie-Bai, Effie Southworth's Life. Benson, Mary C., ed. (Illus.). 124p. (Orig.). (J). 1989. pap. 5.95 (0-89367-142-8) Light & Life.

Root, Maria P. Racially Mixed People in America: Within, Between & Beyond Race. (Illus.). 400p. 1992. 55.00 (0-8039-4101-3); pap. 23.95 (0-8039-4102-1) Sage.

R

An Asterisk (*) at the beginning of an entry indicates that the title is appearing in BIP for the first time.

Root, Maria P., jt. ed. see Brown, Laura S.
Root, Maria P., et al. Bulimia: A Systems Approach to Treatment. (Professional Bks.). (Illus.). 1986. 34.95 (*0-393-70024-0*) Norton.
Root, Martha L. Tahirih the Pure. rev. ed. LC 80-39945. (Illus.). 1981. reprint ed. boxed 12.95 (*0-933770-14-6*) Kalimat.
Root, Michael. Philosophy of Social Science: The Methods, Ideals & Politics of Social Inquiry. 272p. 1994. 49.95 (*0-631-19041-4*); pap. 19.95 (*0-631-19042-2*) Blackwell Pubs.
Root, Mike. REV. LC 88-50590. 162p. (Orig.). 1989. pap. 8.00 (*0-916383-65-2*, Univ Edtns) Aegina Pr.
— Spilt Grape Juice: Re-Thinking the Worship Tradition. (Orig.). 1992. pap. 9.99 (*0-89900-421-0*) College Pr Pub.
Root, Monica, jt. auth. see NCSL Legislative Management Staff.
Root, Orrin. Training for Service: A Survey of the Bible. 128p. 1983. teacher ed 6.99 (*0-87239-703-3*, 3211); pap. 3.99 (*0-87239-704-1*, 3212) Standard Pub.
Root, Phyllis. Coyote & the Magic Words. LC 92-3893. (J). (gr. 4-7). 1993. 14.00 (*0-688-10308-1*) Lothrop.
— Coyote & the Magic Words. LC 92-3893. (J). (ps-3). 1993. 13.93 (*0-688-10309-X*) Lothrop.
— Glacier. LC 88-18945. (National Parks Ser.). (Illus.). 48p. (J). (gr. 4-5). 1988. text ed. 13.95 (*0-89686-408-1*, Crstwood Hse) Silver Burdett Pr.
— The Listening Silence. LC 90-37425. (Illus.). 128p. (J). (gr. 3-7). 1992. lib. bdg. 13.89 (*0-06-025093-3*) HarpC Child Bks.
— Moon Tiger. LC 85-7572. (Illus.). 32p. (J). (ps-2). 1985. 14.95 (*0-8050-0896-9*, Bks Young Read) H Holt & Co.
— Moon Tiger. LC 85-7572. (Illus.). 32p. (J). (ps-2). 1988. pap. 4.95 (*0-8050-0803-9*, Bks Young Read) H Holt & Co.
— The Old Red Rocking Chair. 32p. (J). (ps-3). 1992. 14.95 (*1-55970-063-7*) Arcade Pub Inc.
— Sam Who was Swallowed by a Shark. LC 93-2884. (Illus.). 32p. (J). (ps up). 1994. 12.95 (*1-56402-198-X*) Candlewick Pr.
Root, Phyllis & McCormick, Maxine. Galapagos. LC 89-7918. (National Parks Ser.). (Illus.). 48p. (J). (gr. 4-5). 1989. text ed. 13.95 (*0-89686-434-0*, Crstwood Hse) Silver Burdett Pr.
— Great Basin. LC 88-18645. (National Parks Ser.). (Illus.). 48p. (J). (gr. 4-5). 1988. text ed. 13.95 (*0-89686-410-3*, Crstwood Hse) Silver Burdett Pr.
Root, Richard K. & Sande, Merle A. Viral Infections. (Contemporary Issues in Infectious Diseases Ser.: Vol. 10). (Illus.). 218p. 1993. text ed. 69.00 (*0-443-08859-4*) Churchill.
Root, Richard K. & Sande, Merle A., eds. New Dimensions in Antimicrobial Therapy. (Contemporary Issues in Infectious Diseases Ser.: Vol. 1). (Illus.). 350p. 1984. text ed. 58.00 (*0-443-08290-1*) Churchill.
— New Dimensions in Antimicrobial Therapy. fac. ed. LC 83-23135. (Contemporary Issues in Infectious Diseases Ser.: No. 1). (Illus.). 360p. 1984. reprint ed. pap. 102.60 (*0-7837-7872-4*, 2047629) Bks Demand.
— Septic Shock. (Contemporary Issues in Infectious Diseases Ser.: Vol. 4). (Illus.). 281p. 1985. text ed. 52.00 (*0-443-08397-5*) Churchill.
Root, Richard K., jt. ed. see Sande, Merle A.
Root, Richard K., et al, eds. Immunization. (Contemporary Issues in Infectious Diseases Ser.: Vol. 8). (Illus.). 272p. 1989. text ed. 74.00 (*0-443-08611-7*) Churchill.
— New Surgical & Medical Approaches in Infectious Diseases. (Contemporary Issues in Infectious Diseases Ser.: Vol. 6). (Illus.). 295p. 1987. text ed. 63.00 (*0-443-08540-4*) Churchill.
Root, Robert. Critical Essays on E. B. White. (Critical Essays on American Literature Ser.). 224p. 1994. text ed. 45.00 (*0-8161-7321-4*, Twayne) Macmillan.
Root, Robert K. Classical Mythology in Shakespeare. LC 65-24996. 134p. 1965. reprint ed. 40.00 (*0-87752-096-8*) Gordian.
— Classical Mythology in Shakespeare. (BCL1-PR English Literature Ser.). 134p. 1992. reprint ed. lib. bdg. 69.00 (*0-7812-7306-4*) Rprt Serv.
— The Poetical Career of Alexander Pope. 12.00 (*0-8446-1392-4*) Peter Smith.
— The Poetry of Chaucer. 1972. 59.95 (*0-8490-0860-3*) Gordon Pr.
— The Poetry of Chaucer: A Guide to Its Study & Appreciation. rev. ed. 11.25 (*0-8446-1391-6*) Peter Smith.
Root, Robert L., Jr. The Rhetorics of Popular Culture: Advertising, Advocacy & Entertainment. LC 86-14974. (Contributions to the Study of Popular Culture Ser.: No. 16). 192p. 1987. text ed. 45.00 (*0-313-24403-0*, Greenwood Pr) Greenwood.
— Working at Writing: Columnists & Critics Composing. LC 90-38873. 264p. (C). 1991. 24.95 (*0-8093-1686-2*) S Ill U Pr.
Root, Ross, des. With Heart & Hands: Hymns for the Worshiping Organist. 1994. 7.95 (*0-8341-9115-6*, MB-688) Lillenas.
Root, Steven J., jt. auth. see Willson, James D.
Root, Susan, jt. ed. see Wellish, Pam.
Root, Terry. Atlas of Wintering North American Birds: An Analysis of Christmas Bird Count Data. LC 88-8591. (Illus.). 336p. 1989. lib. bdg. 60.00 (*0-226-72539-1*); pap. text ed. 35.00 (*0-226-72540-5*) U Ch Pr.
***Root, W. & Pavlicek, R.** Modern Bridge Conventions. 1995. 15.00 (*0-517-88429-1*) Random.
Root, W. H. German Criticism of Zola, Eighteen Seventy-Five to Eighteen Ninety-Three. 1972. 59.95 (*0-8490-0226-5*) Gordon Pr.
Root, Waverley & De Rochemont, Richard. Eating in America. LC 76-16145. 488p. 1981. reprint ed. pap. 17.00 (*0-912946-88-1*) Ecco Pr.
Root, Waverly. The Food of France. 1977. pap. 10.95 (*0-394-72428-3*, Vin) Random.
— Food of France. 1992. pap. 13.00 (*0-679-73897-5*, Vin) Random.
— Food of Italy. 1992. pap. 15.00 (*0-679-73896-7*, Vin) Random.
***Root, Waverly & De Rochemont, Richard.** Eating in America: A History. 488p. 1994. pap. 18.00 (*0-88001-399-0*) Ecco Pr.
Root, Wayne A. & Cross, Wilbur. Betting to Win on Sports. 1989. pap. 8.95 (*0-685-28265-1*) Bantam.
Root, Wells. Writing the Script: A Practical Guide for Films & Television. LC 79-1927. 228p. 1980. pap. 11.95 (*0-8050-0237-5*, Owl) H Holt & Co.
Root, William A. & Liebman, John R. United States Export Controls. 3rd ed. 914p. 1991. ring bd. 116.00 (*0-13-109281-2*) Aspen Law.
Root, William L., jt. auth. see Davenport, Wilbur B.
Root, William P. In the World's Common Grasses. LC 81-81272. 72p. (Orig.). 1981. lib. bdg. 35.00 (*0-939952-02-5*) Moving Parts.
— Invisible Guests. LC 83-73490. 1984. pap. 4.00 (*0-917652-28-2*) Confluence Pr.
— Trace Elements from a Recurring Kingdom. 1994. 25.00 (*1-881090-12-4*); pap. 15.00 (*1-881090-11-6*) Confluence Pr.
Root, William P., et al. The Tribute of His Peers: Elegies for Robinson Jeffers. 85p. (Orig.). 1989. pap. write for info. (*0-318-65051-7*) Tor Hse Pr.
Root, William S. Common Sense Bidding. 1986. pap. 14.00 (*0-517-56129-8*, Crown) Crown Pub Group.
— Common Sense Bidding. 1995. 15.00 (*0-517-88430-5*) Random.
— How to Defend a Bridge. 1995. 16.00 (*0-517-88393-7*) Random.
— How to Defend a Bridge Hand. Alder, Phillip, ed. LC 93-39169. 1994. 25.00 (*0-517-59160-X*, Crown) Crown Pub Group.
— How to Play a Bridge Hand. 1990. 21.95 (*0-517-57457-8*, Crown) Crown Pub Group.
Root, William S. & Pavlicek, Richard. Modern Bridge Conventions. 256p. 1981. 19.95 (*0-517-54573-X*, Crown) Crown Pub Group.
— Modern Bridge Conventions. 264p. 1992. 15.00 (*0-517-58727-0*, Crown) Crown Pub Group.
Root, Winfred T. Relations of Pennsylvania with the British Government, 1696-1765. LC 71-99249. reprint ed. 28.50 (*0-404-00608-6*) AMS Pr.
— The Relations of Pennsylvania with the British Government, 1696-1765. (BCL1 - United States Local History Ser.). 422p. 1991. reprint ed. lib. bdg. 99.00 (*0-7812-6278-X*) Rprt Serv.
Rootes, Chris & Davis, Howard, eds. Social Change & Political Transformation: A New Europe? 224p. 1994. 75.00 (*1-85728-147-0*, Pub. by UCL Pr UK); pap. 27.50 (*1-85728-148-9*, Pub. by UCL Pr UK) Taylor & Francis.
Rootes, Chris, jt. ed. see Richardson, Dick.
***Rootes, David.** Exploration of the Polar Regions. LC 94-26498. (Illus.). (J). (gr. 4 up). 1995. 15.95 (*0-02-718083-2*, New Dscvry Bks) Silver Burdett Pr.
Rootes, Nina, tr. see Apollinaire, Guillaume.
Rootes, Nina, tr. see Cendrars, Blaise.
Rootes, Nina, tr. see Lacarriere, Jacques.
Rooth, Anna Birgitta. The Cinderella Cycle. Dorson, Richard M., ed. LC 80-748. (Folklore of the World Ser.). 1981. reprint ed. lib. bdg. 29.95 (*0-405-13322-7*) Ayer.
Rooth, G., jt. auth. see Huch, R.
Rooth, Marianne. Sarah Vaughn: Jazz Singer. (Black American Ser.). (Illus.). 208p. (Orig.). (YA). 1994. pap. 3.95 (*0-87067-592-3*, Melrose Sq) Holloway.
Rooth, Tim. British Protectionism & the International Economy: Overseas Commercial Policy in the 1930s. (Illus.). 340p. (C). 1993. 64.95 (*0-521-41608-6*) Cambridge U Pr.
Rootham, Helen, tr. see Rimbaud, Jean N.
Rootman, Jack. Diseases of the Orbit. LC 65-8162. (Illus.). 704p. 1988. text ed. 130.00 (*0-397-50651-1*, Lippincott Medical) Lippincott.
***Rootman, Jack, et al.** Orbital Surgery: A Conceptual Approach. 1995. write for info. (*0-7817-0254-2*) Raven.
Roots & Rhythm Mail Order Staff, et al. The Roots & Rhythm Guide to Rock: Over 3,000 Annotated Entries on LPs, Cassettes, & CDs. LC 93-8143. (Illus.). 400p. 1993. pap. 16.95 (*1-55652-154-5*) A cappella Bks.
Roots, B., jt. auth. see Johnston, P.
Roots, Betty, jt. ed. see Vernadakis, Antonia.
Roots, Guy, et al. Ryde on Rating & the Community Charge, 2 vols. 14th ed. 1990. U.K. ring bd. 562.00 (*0-406-36319-6*) Butterworth Legal Pubs.
Roots, Ivan, ed. Conflicts in Tudor & Stuart England. LC 68-97374. (Selections from History Today Ser.: No. 5). (Illus.). 1969. pap. 8.95 (*0-05-001536-2*) Dufour.
Rooum, Donald. What Is Anarchism? An Introduction. 74p. (Orig.). 1992. pap. 5.00 (*0-900384-66-2*) Left Bank.
— Wildcat: ABC of Bosses. (Illus.). 48p. (Orig.). 1991. pap. 5.00 (*0-900384-60-3*) Left Bank.
— Wildcat: Anarchist Comics. rev. ed. (Illus.). 47p. 1987. pap. 4.00 (*0-900384-30-1*) Left Bank.
— Wildcat Strikes Again. (Illus.). 48p. (Orig.). 1989. pap. 5.00 (*0-900384-47-6*) Left Bank.
Rooy, Cristina. En El Pais del Sol. 41p. (SPA.). 1990. pap. 1.00 (*0-939125-56-0*) Evangelical Lit.
Rooy, E. L., ed. Light Metals, 1991. (Illus.). 1150p. 1991. 170.00 (*0-87339-161-6*, 394) Minerals Metals.
***Rooyackers, Paul.** One Hundred & One Dance Games for Children: Fun & Creativity with Movement. 1994. pap. 9.95 (*0-89793-171-8*) Hunter Hse.
— One Hundred & One Dance Games for Children: Fun & Creativity with Movement. 1994. pap. 12.95 (*0-89793-172-6*) Hunter Hse.
Roozen, David, jt. auth. see Hadaway, C. Kirk.
Roozen, David A., jt. auth. see Hadaway, C. Kirk.
Roozen, David A., et al. Varieties of Religious Presence: Mission in Public Life. LC 84-19045. 288p. (Orig.). 1984. pap. 14.95 (*0-8298-0724-1*) Pilgrim OH.
***Roozenburg, N. F. & Eekels, J.** Product Design: Fundamentals & Methods. LC 94-26737. 1994. text ed. 105.00 (*0-471-94351-7*) Wiley.
Ropars, C., et al, eds. Red Blood Cells As Carriers for Drugs: Potential Therapeutic Applications. (Illus.). 272p. 1987. 120.00 (*0-08-036137-4*, Pergamon Pr) Elsevier.
Roparz. Dictionnaire Historique du Breton: Geriadur Istorel ar Brezhoneg. (FRE.). 1975. reprint ed. 695.00 (*0-8288-9534-1*) Fr & Eur.
Roparz, Hemon. Dictionanaire Francais-Breton. 42p. (BRE & FRE.). 1984. pap. 14.95 (*0-7859-4890-2*) Fr & Eur.
Rope, Frederick T. Opinion Conflict & School Support. LC 70-177206. (Columbia University. Teachers College. Contributions to Education Ser.: No. 838). reprint ed. 37.50 (*0-404-55838-0*) AMS Pr.
Ropeberson, Elizabeth W. In Care of Yellow River. abr. ed. 142p. 1995. pap. write for info. (*1-878853-53-8*) Venture Pr FL.
Roper, ed. Active Infrared Systems & Technology. 138p. 1987. 36.00 (*0-89252-841-9*, 806) SPIE.
Roper, A. Woman to Woman. (C). 1990. 36.00 (*0-946211-23-X*, Pub. by Attic Pr IE) St Mut.
Roper, Alan. Arnold's Poetic Landscapes. LC 70-86097. 280p. reprint ed. pap. 79.80 (*0-8357-5751-X*, 2020749) Bks Demand.
Roper, Allen G. Ancient Eugenics. 1982. reprint ed. 15.00 (*0-941694-05-4*) Cliveden Pr.
***Roper, Beryl C.** Trementina Revisited. 82p. 1994. 24.95 (*1-885812-00-0*) Aquamarine.
Roper, Brent D. Computers & the Law: Concepts & Applications. Hannan, ed. 481p. (C). 1992. pap. text ed. 50.75 (*0-314-93374-3*) West Pub.
— Practical Law Office Management for Legal Assistants. LC 94-19945. 400p. 1994. text ed. 37.00 (*0-314-04305-5*) West Pub.
Roper, Brent S., jt. comp. see Chalfant, H. Paul.
Roper, Brian & Rudd, Chris, eds. State & Economy in New Zealand. (Oxford Readings in New Zealand Politics Ser.: No. 2). (Illus.). 292p. 1993. pap. 35.00 (*0-19-558273-X*) OUP.
Roper, C. How to Open Handcuffs Without Keys. (Criminology Ser.). 1986. lib. bdg. 79.95 (*0-8490-3659-3*) Gordon Pr.
Roper, C. A. & Phillips, Bill. The Complete Book of Locks & Locksmithing. 3rd ed. 1991. pap. 19.95 (*0-07-155241-3*) McGraw.
— The Complete Book of Locks & Locksmithing. 3rd ed. (Illus.). 360p. 1991. 26.95 (*0-8306-7522-1*, 3522); pap. 19.95 (*0-8306-3522-X*) TAB Bks.
***Roper Center for Public Opinion Research Staff & Ladd, Everett C.** America at the Polls, 1994. (Occasional Papers & Monographs Ser.: No. 12). (Illus.). 170p. (Orig.). (C). 1995. pap. text ed. 19.95 (*1-887415-01-7*) RCPOR.
***Roper, Daniel.** Fifty Years of Public Life. (American Autobiography Ser.). 422p. 1995. reprint ed. lib. bdg. 99.00 (*0-7812-8630-1*) Rprt Serv.
Roper, Daniel C. Fifty Years of Public Life. (History - United States Ser.). 422p. 1993. reprint ed. lib. bdg. 99.00 (*0-7812-4923-6*) Rprt Serv.
***Roper, David.** Bart. (Illus.). 200p. 1995. 34.95 (*1-85793-330-3*, Pub. by Pavilion UK) Trafalgar.
— A Burden Shared. 1991. 9.99 (*0-929239-40-7*) Discovery Hse Pubs.
— Precious Memories. 1987. pap. 2.50 (*0-89137-443-4*) Quality Pubns.
— Psalm Twenty-Three: The Song of the Passionate Heart - Hope & Rest from the Shepherd. 1994. pap. 7.99 (*0-929239-86-5*) Discovery Hse Pubs.
— Seeing Through: Clinging to God's Active Presence in an Age Gone Mad. 1995. pap. 10.99 (*0-88070-735-6*) Questar Pubs.
— The Strength of a Man: Encouragement for Today. 1989. 7.99 (*0-929239-07-5*) Discovery Hse Pubs.
Roper, David H. Getting the Job You Want...Now! Fifty Winning Moves for Spotting Hot Companies, Identifying Hiring Patterns, & Landing a Great Job. LC 93-3339. 192p. (Orig.). 1994. pap. 11.99 (*0-446-39451-3*) Warner Bks.
Roper, David L. Getting Serious about Love. 219p. 1992. pap. write for info. (*0-945441-11-8*) Res Pubns AR.
Roper, Derek. Reviewing Before the Edinburgh, 1788-1802. LC 77-2446. (Illus.). 1978. 40.00 (*0-87413-128-6*) U Delaware Pr.
Roper, Derek & Chitham, Edward, eds. The Poems of Emily Bronte. (English Texts Ser.). 420p. 1995. 70.00 (*0-19-812641-7*) OUP.
Roper, Derek, ed. see Ford, John.
Roper, Donna C. Airport Site: A Multicomponent Site in the Sangamon River Drainage. (Research Series: Papers in Anthropology: No. 4). (Illus.). 32p. 1978. pap. 2.00 (*0-89792-074-0*) Ill St Museum.
— Archeological Survey & Settlement Pattern Models in Central Illinois. (Scientific Papers: Vol. XVI). (Illus.). 156p. 1979. pap. 4.50 (*0-89792-081-3*) Ill St Museum.
— The Distribution of Middle Woodland Sites Within the Environment of the Lower Sangamon River, Illinois. (Reports of Investigations Ser.: No. 30). (Illus.). 22p. 1974. pap. 1.00 (*0-89792-054-6*) Ill St Museum.
Roper, E. The Ropers of Sterling & Rutland. (Illus.). 473p. 1989. reprint ed. lib. bdg. 71.00 (*0-8328-1032-0*); reprint ed. pap. 71.00 (*0-8328-1033-9*) Higginson Bk Co.
Roper, Ed M. Guidelines for Health & Safety in Metal Finishing. 80p. 1991. 75.00 (*0-904477-06-1*, Pub. by FMJ Intl UK) St Mut.
Roper, Eric, jt. auth. see Shaw, Malcolm.
Roper-Evans, Emma, tr. see Hankiss, Agnes.
Roper, Gail. Seventh Grade Soccer Star. LC 88-9496. 132p. (J). (gr. 3-7). 1988. pap. 4.99 (*1-55513-507-2*, Chariot Bks) Chariot Family.
Roper, Gayle. The Case of the Missing Melody. LC 92-39317. (East Edge Mysteries Ser.: No. 4). (Illus.). (J). 1993. pap. 4.99 (*1-55513-702-4*, Chariot Bks) Chariot Family.
— Cat Burglars? (Adventures of Scooter & Jake Ser.). (Illus.). 48p. (Orig.). (J). (gr. 1-3). 1995. pap. 2.99 (*0-7814-0077-5*, Chariot Bks) Chariot Family.
— Here, Boy! (Adventures of Scooter & Jake Ser.). (Illus.). 48p. (Orig.). (J). (gr. 1-3). 1995. pap. 2.99 (*0-7814-0078-3*, Chariot Bks) Chariot Family.
— Mystery at Harmony Hill. LC 92-27105. 1993. pap. 4.99 (*1-55513-701-6*, Chariot Bks) Chariot Family.
— The Puzzle of the Poison Pen. LC 94-6755. (J). 1994. write for info. (*0-7814-1507-1*, Chariot Bks) Chariot Family.
— A Race to the Finish. LC 90-21160. (Sports Stories for Boys Ser.). 128p. (J). (gr. 3-7). 1991. pap. 4.99 (*1-55513-816-0*, 38166, Chariot Bks) Chariot Family.
Roper, Gayle G. Balancing Your Emotions: For Women Who Want Consistency under Stress. LC 92-30983. 144p. 1992. pap. 7.99 (*0-87788-075-1*) Shaw Pubs.
— Who Cares? Cultivating the Fine Art of Loving One Another. 112p. (Orig.). 1992. pap. 6.99 (*0-87788-948-1*) Shaw Pubs.
Roper, Geoffrey. World Survey of Islamic Manuscripts, Vol. 2: Iraq-Russian Federation. 724p. 1993. 143.00 (*1-873992-02-5*, Pub. by Al-Furqan Islamic UK) E J Brill.
Roper, Geoffrey, ed. World Survey of Islamic Manuscripts, Vol. 1. xvi, 569p. 1992. 143.00 (*1-873992-01-7*) E J Brill.
Roper, Gordon, ed. see Hawthorne, Nathaniel.
Roper-Hall, M. J. Stallard's Eye Surgery. 7th ed. 1989. 225.00 (*0-7236-0714-1*, Pub. by John Wright UK) Buttrwrth-Heinemann.
Roper-Hall, M. J., ed. Microsurgery of the Anterior & Posterior Segments for the Eye. (Developments in Ophthalmology Ser.: Vol. 5). (Illus.). vi, 134p. 1982. pap. 72.00 (*3-8055-2711-X*) S Karger.
Roper-Hall, M. J., et al, eds. Advances in Ophthalmology, Vol. 26. 1972. 107.25 (*3-8055-1354-2*) S Karger.
— Advances in Ophthalmology, Vol. 35. (Illus.). (GER.). 1978. 105.75 (*3-8055-2657-1*) S Karger.
— Advances in Ophthalmology, Vol. 39. (Illus.). 1979. 150.50 (*3-8055-3030-7*) S Karger.
— Advances in Ophthalmology, Vol. 40. (Illus.). 1979. 125.75 (*3-8055-3031-5*) S Karger.
— Commemorative Volume in Honour of Prof. Streiff. (Advances in Ophthalmology Ser.: Vol. 36). (Illus.). (FRE & GER.). 1978. 150.50 (*3-8055-2828-0*) S Karger.
Roper, Harlin J. In the Beginning God: Genesis - Exodus 18. (Through the Bible Study Ser.: No. 1Y). 64p. (YA). (gr. 7-12). 1988. student ed 4.98 (*0-86606-362-5*, 1Y) Roper Pr.
— In the Beginning God: Genesis - Exodus 18. (Through the Bible Study Ser.: No. 1J). (Illus.). 64p. (J). (gr. 4-6). 1989. student ed 4.98 (*0-86606-374-9*, 1J) Roper Pr.
— In the Beginning God: Genesis - Exodus 18. (Through the Bible Study Ser.: No. 1). 64p. (J). 1989. student ed 4.98 (*0-86606-350-1*, 1) Roper Pr.
Roper, Harold, jt. auth. see Campbell-Allen, Denison.
Roper, Hazel A., jt. auth. see Burt, Steven E.
Roper, James E. The Founding of Memphis, 1818-1820. (Illus.). 100p. 1970. 10.00 (*0-937130-07-9*) Burke's Bk Store.
Roper, John, ed. The Future of the British Defense Policy. (Joint Studies in Public Policy). 200p. 1985. text ed. 53.95 (*0-566-00922-6*) Ashgate Pub Co.
Roper, John, et al. Keeping the Peace in the Post-Cold War Era: Strengthening Multilateral Peacekeeping. LC 93-30079. (Triangle Papers: Vol. 43). 101p. (C). 1993. pap. 9.00 (*0-930503-70-8*) Trilateral Comm.
Roper, John H. C. Vann Woodward, Southerner. LC 86-25020. 398p. 1987. 30.00 (*0-8203-0933-8*) U of Ga Pr.
— U. B. Phillips: A Southern Mind. LC 84-682. vi, 204p. 1984. 16.95 (*0-86554-112-4*, MUP/H103) Mercer Univ Pr.
Roper, John H., ed. see Green, Paul.
Roper, Jon, jt. auth. see Melling, Phil.
Roper, K. N., jt. auth. see Gatehouse, Anthony L.
Roper, Katherine. German Encounters with Modernity: Novels of Imperial Berlin. LC 90-38585. (Studies in German Histories). 280p. (C). 1991. text ed. 49.95 (*0-391-03695-5*) Humanities.
Roper, Lyndal. The Holy Household: Women & Morals in Reformation Augsburg. (Oxford Studies in Social History). (Illus.). 310p. 1991. reprint ed. pap. 24.00 (*0-19-820280-6*) OUP.
— Oedipus & the Devil: Witchcraft, Sexuality, & Religion in Early Modern Europe. LC 93-5903. 1994. write for info. (*0-415-08894-1*); pap. write for info. (*0-415-10581-1*) Routledge.
Roper, Marc. Software Testing. 1994. text ed. 40.00 (*0-07-707466-1*) McGraw.
Roper, Michael. Masculinity & the British Organisation Man, 1945 to the Present. 272p. 1994. 37.00 (*0-19-825693-0*) OUP.
Roper, Michael & Tosh, John, eds. Manful Assertions: Masculinities in Britain since 1800. (Illus.). 240p. 1991. 59.95 (*0-415-05322-6*, A6030); pap. 15.95 (*0-415-05323-4*, A6034) Routledge.
Roper, Nancy. The Elements of Nursing. 3rd ed. (Illus.). 376p. 1990. pap. text ed. 45.00 (*0-443-03950-X*) Churchill.
— New American Pocket Medical Dictionary. 2nd ed. 392p. 1988. pap. 17.00 (*0-684-19031-1*, Scribners) S&S Trade.

R

An Asterisk (*) at the beginning of an entry indicates that the title is appearing in BIP for the first time.

— Principles of Nursing in Process Context. 4th ed. (Illus.). 336p. (Orig.). 1988. text ed. 30.00 (*0-443-03576-8*) Churchill.

Roper, Nancy, ed. New American Pocket Medical Dictionary. 2nd ed. (Illus.). 368p. 1988. pap. text ed. 10.95 (*0-443-08581-1*) Churchill.

***Roper, Peter.** Badminton: The Skills of the Game. (Illus.). 128p. 1995. pap. 17.95 (*1-85223-887-9*, Pub. by Crowood Pr UK) Trafalgar.

— Jedediah Hotchkiss: Rebel Mapmaker. LC 92-9456. (Illus.). 300p. (C). 1992. 29.95 (*0-942597-26-5*) White Mane Pub.

Roper, R. Wordsworth & Coleridge: Lyrical Ballads 1805. 1990. pap. 27.00 (*0-7463-0382-3*, Pub. by Northcote UK) St Mut.

Roper, R. G., ed. Interim Results of the Middle Atmosphere Program: A Selection of Invited Papers from the Symposium Jointly Sponsored by the IAGA & IAMAP at the XVIII General Assembly of the IUGG, Hamburg, Federal Republic of Germany, August 1985. 112p. 1985. pap. 36.00 (*0-08-032594-7*, Pergamon Pr) Elsevier.

Roper, Robert. Cuervo Tales. LC 93-145. 256p. 1993. 19.95 (*0-89919-988-7*) Ticknor & Fields.

— State Court Caseload Statistics: Annual Report, 1984. 276p. (Orig.). 1986. pap. text ed. write for info. (*0-318-69221-X*, R098) Natl Ctr St Courts.

Roper, Sally E. Medieval English Benedictine Liturgy: Studies in the Formation, Structure, & Content of the Monastic Votive Office, c. 950-1540. Caldwell, John, ed. LC 93-15812. (Outstanding Dissertations in Music from British Universities Ser.). 424p. 1993. 88.00 (*0-8153-0953-8*) Garland.

Roper, Stephen D., jt. ed. see Simon, Sidney A.

Roper, Steve. Camp Four: Recollections of a Yosemite Rock Climber. (Illus.). 240p. 1994. 24.95 (*0-89886-381-3*) Mountaineers.

— Climber's Guide to the High Sierra. rev. ed. LC 75-45108. (Totebook Ser.). (Illus.). 384p. 1976. pap. 12.00 (*0-87156-147-6*) Sierra.

— Climbers Guide to Yosemite Valley. LC 71-157530. (Totebook Ser.). (Illus.). 320p. 1971. pap. 10.95 (*0-87156-048-8*) Sierra.

— Timberline Country: The Sierra High Route. LC 82-714. (Totebook Ser.). (Illus.). 320p. (Orig.). 1982. pap. 9.95 (*0-87156-298-7*) Sierra.

Roper, Steve & Steck, Allen, eds. The Best of Ascent: Twenty-Five Years of the Mountaineering Experience. LC 92-24722. (Illus.). 416p. 1993. 25.00 (*0-87156-517-X*) Sierra.

Roper, Steve, jt. ed. see Steck, Allen.

Roper, Tony. The Steamie. (C). 1989. 75.00 (*0-685-52511-2*, Pub. by Jordanhill College UK) St Mut.

Roper, Trey. Japanese-English Idioms. 500p. (C). 1994. pap. text ed. 30.00 (*0-9640744-3-5*) US-Asia Res.

Roper, Walter F., jt. auth. see McHenry, Roy C.

Roper, William. Sequoia & His Miracle. (J). (gr. 5-12). 1972. 4.95 (*0-89992-056-X*) Coun India Ed.

Ropers, R. H. Persistent Poverty: The American Dream Turned Nightmare. LC 91-14. (Illus.). 238p. 1991. 23.95 (*0-306-43764-3*, Plenum Insight) Plenum.

Ropers, Richard H. The Invisible Homeless: A New Urban Ecology. (Illus.). 224p. (C). 1988. 32.95 (*0-89885-406-7*) Human Sci Pr.

— Toward a Kinder & Gentler America: Ending Poverty & Homelessness & Fulfilling the American Dream. (Distinguished Faculty Lecture Ser.). 29p. Date not set. pap. text ed. write for info. (*0-935615-08-3*) S Utah St Coll.

***Ropers, Richard H. & Pence, Daniel J.** American Prejudice: With Liberty & Justice for Some. 290p. 1995. 27.95 (*0-306-44946-3*) Da Capo.

Ropes, Hannah A. Six Months in Kansas, by a Lady. LC 76-38020. (Black Heritage Library Collection). 1977. reprint ed. 23.95 (*0-8369-8987-2*) Ayer.

Ropes, James H. Singular Problem of the Epistle to the Galatians. (Harvard Theological Studies: Vol. 14). 1929. pap. 15.00 (*0-527-01014-6*) Periodicals Srv.

— St. James: Critical & Exegetical Commentary. LC 16-6543. (International Critical Commentary Ser.). 336p. 1916. 36.95 (*0-567-05035-1*, Pub. by T & T Clark UK) Bks Intl VA.

Ropes, Linda B. Health Care Crisis in America. (Contemporary World Issues Ser.). 1991. lib. bdg. 39.50 (*0-87436-616-X*) ABC-CLIO.

— Health Care Crisis in America. (Contemporary World Issues Ser.). 200p. 1992. lib. bdg. 45.00 (*0-87436-642-9*) ABC-CLIO.

Ropes, Marian W. Systemic Lupus Erythematosus. LC 75-31988. 179p. reprint ed. pap. 51.10 (*0-7837-6089-2*, 2059135) Bks Demand.

Ropka, Gerald W. The Evolving Residential Patterns of the Mexican, Puerto Rican, & Cuban Population in the City of Chicago. Cortes, Carlos E., ed. LC 79-6222. (Hispanics in the United States Ser.). (Illus.). 1981. lib. bdg. 23.95 (*0-405-13169-0*) Ayer.

Ropke, Wilhelm. A Humane Economy: The Social Framework of the Free Market. 320p. 1983. reprint ed. pap. text ed. 18.50 (*0-8191-3314-0*) U Pr of Amer.

— International Economic Disintegration. LC 78-11239. (Studies in International Economics: No. 4). xii, 283p. 1979. reprint ed. lib. bdg. 39.50 (*0-87991-853-5*) Porcupine Pr.

Ropp, Kathy, jt. auth. see Frantz, Angel.

Ropp, Paul S., ed. The Heritage of China: Contemporary Perspectives on Chinese Civilization. 1990. 65.00 (*0-520-06440-2*); pap. 18.00 (*0-520-06441-0*) U CA Pr.

Ropp, R. C. The Chemistry of Artificial Lighting Devices: Lamps, Phosphors, & Cathode Ray Tubes. LC 93-33113. (Studies in Inorganic Chemistry: No. 17). 1993. write for info. (*0-444-81709-3*) Elsevier.

— Inorganic Polymeric Glasses. LC 92-14445. (Studies in Inorganic Chemistry: Vol. 15). 1992. write for info. (*0-444-89500-0*) Elsevier.

— Luminescence & the Solid State. (Studies in Inorganic Chemistry: No. 12). 450p. 1991. 185.50 (*0-444-88940-X*) Elsevier.

Ropp, Robert S. Man Against Aging. Kastenbaum, Robert, ed. LC 78-22216. (Aging & Old Age Ser.). 1979. reprint ed. lib. bdg. 28.95 (*0-405-11829-5*) Ayer.

Ropp, Steve. One on One: Making the Most of Your Mentoring Relationship. Janzen, Susan E., ed. LC 93-71182. 90p. (Orig.). 1993. spiral bd., pap. 15.95 (*0-87303-206-3*) Faith & Life.

Ropp, Steve C. Panamanian Politics: From Guarded Nation to National Guard. LC 81-17831. (Politics in Latin America, A Hoover Institution Ser.). 174p. 1982. text ed. 33.95 (*0-275-91817-3*, C1817, Praeger Pubs) Greenwood.

Ropp, Theodore. The Development of a Modern Navy: French Naval Policy 1871-1904. Roberts, Stephen S., ed. (Illus.). 439p. 1987. 36.95 (*0-87021-141-2*) Naval Inst Pr.

— War in Modern World. 416p. 1985. pap. 11.00 (*0-02-036390-7*, Pub. by Gebrueder Borntraeger GW) Macmillan.

— War in the Modern World. LC 60-5274. 416p. reprint ed. pap. 118.60 (*0-317-08033-4*, 2010250) Bks Demand.

— War in the Modern World. LC 81-6448. xv, 400p. 1981. reprint ed. text ed. 89.50 (*0-313-22844-2*, ROWM, Greenwood Pr) Greenwood.

Roppel, Patricia. Alaska's Salmon Hatcheries, Eighteen-Ninety-One to Nineteen-Fifty-Nine. LC 82-600591. (Alaska Historical Commission Studies in History: No. 20). (Illus.). 299p. 1982. 20.00 (*0-943712-09-2*) Alaska Hist.

— Fortunes from the Earth: An History of the Base & Industrial Minerals of Southeast Alaska. (Illus.). 152p. (Orig.). 1991. pap. 18.95 (*0-89745-136-8*) Sunflower U Pr.

Roppelt, Donna & Mowl, Mary. Tomorrow, We're Taking a Test, Set. 1982. 1.95 (*0-932666-16-7*) T J Pubs.

Ropper, Allan H., ed. Neurological & Neurosurgical Intensive Care. 3rd ed. LC 92-49216. 528p. 1994. 104.00 (*0-88167-981-X*) Raven.

Ropper, Allan H., et al. Guillain-Barre Syndrome. LC 90-15721. (Contemporary Neurology Ser.: No. 34). (Illus.). 369p. (C). 1991. 70.00 (*0-8036-7572-0*) Davis Co.

Rops, Daniel. Jesus & His Times. 478p. 1990. reprint ed. lib. bdg. 35.95 (*0-89966-747-3*) Buccaneer Bks.

Roque, Ana. Luz y Sombra. 200p. 1991. pap. 8.50 (*0-8477-3648-2*) U of PR Pr.

Roque Dalton Cultural Brigade, tr. see Fernandez, Magaly & Volpendesta, David, eds.

Roque, Marichelle, jt. auth. see Arienda, Roger.

Roque, Oswaldo R. Directions in American Painting 1875-1925: Works from the Collection of Dr. & Mrs. John J. McDonough. LC 82-6473. (Illus.). 112p. (Orig.). 1982. pap. text ed. 12.95 (*0-88039-003-4*) Mus Art Carnegie.

Roque, Oswaldo R., jt. auth. see Caldwell, John.

Roque, Raquel R. Las Mejozes Recetas de la Cocina Cubana. 176p. (SPA.). 1987. pap. 4.95 (*0-941010-02-3*) Downtown Bk.

Roque, Waldir L., ed. see MacCallum, Malcolm A., et al.

***Roquebert, Anne.** Degas. (Grandes Monografias). (Illus.). 200p. (SPA.). 1993. 200.00 (*84-343-0538-0*) Elliots Bks.

Roquefeuil, Camille de. Voyage Around the World, Eighteen Sixteen to Eighteen Nineteen. 143p. 1983. 14.95 (*0-87770-258-6*) Ye Galleon.

Roquelaure, A. N. Beauty's Punishment. 1984. pap. 10.95 (*0-452-26662-9*, Plume) NAL-Dutton.

— Beauty's Release. 1985. pap. 10.95 (*0-452-26663-7*, Plume) NAL-Dutton.

— Claiming of Sleeping Beauty. 1983. pap. 10.95 (*0-452-26656-4*, Plume) NAL-Dutton.

Roquelaure, A. N., pseud. The Sleeping Beauty Novels: The Claiming of Sleeping Beauty; Beauty's Punishment; Beauty's Release, Set. 1991. Boxed set. pap. 32.85 (*0-452-15298-4*, Plume) NAL-Dutton.

Roquemore, Cliff, ed. see Roquemore, Erma.

Roquemore, Erma. How to Develop a Goal Mind: Using Left & Right Brain Functions to Achieve Your Goals. Roquemore, Cliff, ed. (Illus.). 119p. 1995. pap. 11.95 (*1-882518-70-5*) Roquemore Sem.

Roques, Henri. The "Confessions" of Kurt Gerstein. Percival, Ronald, tr. 297p. (Orig.). 1989. pap. 11.00 (*0-939484-27-7*) Inst Hist Rev.

Roques, Marlo, ed. Le Roman de Renart, 6 tomes, Set. 75.00 (*0-685-34018-X*) Fr & Eur.

Roques, Marlo, jt. auth. see Chretien de Troyes.

Roques, Marlo, jt. ed. see Mujumdar, Arun S.

Roquette, P., jt. auth. see Prestel, A.

Roquette, Peter, ed. see Hasse, Helmut.

Rorabacher, David B. & Endicott, John F., eds. Mechanistic Aspects of Inorgnic Reactions. LC 82-13817. (ACS Symposium Ser.: No. 198). 480p. 1982. 60.95 (*0-8412-0734-8*) Am Chemical.

***Rorabaugh, Britt.** Mechanical Devices for the Electronics Experimenter. LC 94-36306. 1995. text ed. 29.95 (*0-07-053546-9*); pap. text ed. 18.95 (*0-07-053547-7*) TAB Bks.

— Signal Processing Design Techniques. (Illus.). 304p. 1986. 32.50 (*0-8306-0457-X*, NO. 2657, TAB/TPR) TAB Bks.

Rorabaugh, C. Britton. Circuit Design & Analysis: Featuring C Routines. 1992. pap. 34.95 (*0-07-053659-7*) McGraw.

— Circuit Design & Analysis: Featuring C Routines. 256p. 1992. pap. 34.95 (*0-8306-4275-7*, 4308) TAB Bks.

— Circuit Design & Anaylsis: Featuring C Routine. 240p. 1992. text ed. 50.00 (*0-07-053653-8*) McGraw.

— Communications Formulas & Algorithms: For Systems Analysis & Design. 1990. text ed. 40.00 (*0-07-053644-9*) McGraw.

— Digital Filter Designer's Handbook: Featuring C Routines. 1993. text ed., disk 49.50 (*0-07-911166-1*) McGraw.

— Digital Filter Designer's Handbook: Featuring C Routines. 1993. pap. text ed. 34.95 (*0-07-053661-9*) McGraw.

— Digital Filter Designer's Handbook: Featuring C Routines. 1993. pap. 34.95 (*0-8306-4431-8*) TAB Bks.

— Error Coding Cookbook: Practical C Routines & Recipes for Error Detection & Correction. 1995. text ed. 50.00 (*0-07-911720-1*) McGraw.

Rorabaugh, W. J. The Alcoholic Republic: An American Tradition. (Illus.). 1981. pap. 11.95 (*0-19-502990-9*) OUP.

— Berkeley at War: The Nineteen Sixties. 336p. 1990. pap. 11.95 (*0-19-506667-7*) OUP.

— The Craft Apprentice: From Franklin to the Machine Age in America. (Illus.). 288p. 1988. pap. 16.95 (*0-19-505189-0*) OUP.

Rorabaugh, William J. & Critchlow, Donald T. America! A Concise History. 626p. 1994. pap. 28.95 (*0-534-13614-1*) Intl Thomson.

Rorden, Judith W. Discharge Planning Handbook. (Illus.). 384p. 1990. pap. text ed. 32.95 (*0-7216-2845-1*) Saunders.

— Nurses As Health Teachers: A Practical Guide. (Illus.). 320p. 1987. pap. text ed. 27.95 (*0-7216-1804-9*) Saunders.

***Rorem.** Knowing When to Stop. 1995. pap. 16.00 (*0-684-80440-9*) S&S Trade.

Rorem, C. Rufus. Accounting Method. LC 82-48382. (Accountancy in Transition Ser.). 613p. 1982. lib. bdg. 20.00 (*0-8240-5327-3*) Garland.

Rorem, Ned. Knowing When to Stop. 1994. 30.00 (*0-671-72872-5*) S&S Trade.

— The Paris & New York Diaries of Ned Rorem. LC 82-73718. (First in A Ser.). 432p. 1982. reprint ed. pap. 15.00 (*0-86547-109-6*, North Pt Pr) FS&G.

— Settling the Score: Essays on Music. 352p. 1988. 27.95 (*0-15-180895-3*) HarBrace.

Rorem, Paul. Pseudo-Dionysius: A Commentary on the Texts & an Introduction to Their Influence. LC 92-15353. 288p. (C). 1993. 45.00 (*0-19-507664-8*) OUP.

Rorem, Paul, ed. see Fredriksen, Paula, et al.

Rorer, David. American Inter-State Law. Mayer, Levy, ed. lvii, 400p. 1983. reprint ed. lib. bdg. 35.00 (*0-8377-1038-3*) Rothman.

Rorick, William G. Your Brain & the Mind of Christ. LC 84-50081. 140p. 1984. 12.95 (*0-938232-43-6*) Winston-Derek.

Rorie, David, jt. ed. see Simpkins, John E.

Rorig, Fritz. The Medieval Town. Matthew, D. J., tr. 1967. reprint ed. pap. 14.00 (*0-520-01579-7*) U CA Pr.

***Rorimer, Anne, intro.** Graham, Dan: Buildings & Signs. (Illus.). 1981. pap. 20.00 (*0-941548-00-7*, Pub. by Museum Modern Art UK) St Mut.

Rorimer, Anne, jt. ed. see Goldstein, Ann.

Rorison, I. H. & Hunt, Roderick, eds. Amenity Grassland: An Ecological Perspective. LC 79-40823. (Illus.). 275p. reprint ed. pap. 78.40 (*0-8357-5345-X*, 2030384) Bks Demand.

Rorison, I. H., et al, eds. Frontiers of Comparative Plant Ecology. 317p. (Orig.). 1987. pap. text ed. 52.00 (*0-12-595960-5*) Acad Pr.

Rorke, Lucy B. Pathology of Perinatal Brain Injury. (Illus.). 160p. 1982. text ed. 40.50 (*0-89004-688-3*) Raven.

Rorlich, Azade-Ayse. The Volga Tatars: A Profile in National Resilience. (Publication Series: Studies of Nationalities in the U. S. S. R.). 288p. (C). 1986. text ed. 31.95 (*0-8179-8391-0*); pap. 15.95 (*0-8179-8392-9*) Hoover Inst Pr.

Rorres, Chris, jt. auth. see Anton, Howard.

Rorrison, Hugh. Erwin Piscator: Political Theatre in the Weimar Republic. (Theatre in Focus Ser.). 120p. 1987. pap. 105.00 (*0-85964-166-X*) Chadwyck-Healey.

Rorro, Thomas A. Assessing Risk on Wall Street. LC 83-51720. 224p. 1984. 19.95 (*0-89709-134-5*) Liberty Pub.

Rorschach, H. Psychodiagnostics: A Diagnostic Test Based on Perception. 9th ed. 228p. 1981. 29.00 (*3-456-30279-7*) Hogrefe & Huber Pubs.

Rorschach, Kimerly. Blake to Beardsley: The Artist As Illustrator. (Illus.). 55p. 1988. pap. 12.50 (*0-939084-24-4*) R Mus & Lib.

— Drawings by Jean-Baptiste Le Prince for the Voyage en Siberie. (Illus.). 36p. 1986. pap. 14.95 (*0-939084-20-1*) R Mus & Lib.

— Eighteenth-Century French Book Illustration: Drawings by Fragonard & Gravelot from the Rosenbach Museum & Library. (Illus.). 40p. 1985. pap. 14.95 (*0-939084-17-1*, U Pr of Va) R Mus & Lib.

Rorty, Amelia O., jt. ed. see McLaughlin, Brian P.

Rorty, Amelie O. Essays on Aristotle's Ethics. LC 78-62858. (Major Thinkers Ser.: No. 2). 446p. reprint ed. pap. 127.20 (*0-685-23528-9*, 2029062) Bks Demand.

— Essays on Descartes' Meditations. Oksenberg, ed. (Major Thinkers Ser.: No. 4). 1986. pap. 17.00 (*0-520-05509-8*) U CA Pr.

— Mind in Action: Essays in the Philosophy of Mind. LC 87-47876. 378p. 1991. pap. 19.00x (*0-8070-1405-2*) Beacon Pr.

Rorty, Amelie O., ed. Essays on Aristotle's Ethics. LC 78-62858. (Major Thinkers Ser.: No. 2). 1980. pap. 16.00 (*0-520-04041-4*) U CA Pr.

— Essays on Aristotle's Poetics. 480p. 1992. pap. text ed. 75.00 (*0-691-06872-0*); pap. text ed. 19.95 (*0-691-01498-1*) Princeton U Pr.

— Essays on Aristotle's Rhetoric. LC 95-14304. (Philosophical Traditions Ser.: Vol. 6). Date not set. write for info. (*0-520-20227-9*); pap. write for info. (*0-520-20228-7*) U CA Pr.

— Explaining Emotions. LC 78-62859. (Topics in Philosophy Ser.: Vol. V). 1980. pap. 15.00 (*0-520-03921-1*) U CA Pr.

— The Identities of Persons. LC 75-13156. (Topics in Philosophy Ser.: Vol. III). 1976. pap. 16.00 (*0-520-03309-4*) U CA Pr.

Rorty, Amelie O., jt. ed. see Flanagan, Owen.

Rorty, Amelie O., jt. ed. see Nussbaum, Martha C.

Rorty, James. McCarthy & the Communists. LC 78-138179. 163p. 1972. reprint ed. text ed. 65.00 (*0-8371-5636-X*, ROCO, Greenwood Pr) Greenwood.

— Our Master's Voice: Advertising. LC 75-39272. (Getting & Spending: the Consumer's Dilemma Ser.). 1976. reprint ed. 33.95 (*0-405-08044-1*) Ayer.

Rorty, James & Norman, N. Philip. Tomorrow's Food. enl. rev. ed. LC 56-8132. 309p. reprint ed. pap. 88.10 (*0-317-28232-8*, 2022712) Bks Demand.

Rorty, James & Norman, Philip. Tomorrow's Food. 9.95 (*0-8159-6906-6*) Devin.

Rorty, Mary V., tr. see Albert, Hans.

Rorty, Richard. The Barber of Kasbeam: Nabokov on Cruelty. (Chapbooks in Literature Ser.). 32p. 1988. pap. text ed. 5.00 (*0-9614940-6-9*) Bennington Coll.

— Consequences of Pragmatism: Essays 1972-1980. LC 82-2597. 239p. (C). 1992. pap. text ed. 14.95x (*0-8166-1064-9*) U of Minn Pr.

— Contingency, Irony, & Solidarity. 208p. (C). 1989. 54.95 (*0-521-35381-5*); pap. 15.95 (*0-521-36781-6*) Cambridge U Pr.

— Philosophical Papers, Set, Vols. 1 & 2. (C). 1991. Set. 84.95 (*0-521-40476-2*); Set. pap. 27.95 (*0-521-40915-2*) Cambridge U Pr.

— Philosophical Papers, Vol. 1: Objectivity, Relativism, & Truth. (Illus.). 280p. (C). 1990. 49.95 (*0-521-35369-6*); pap. 16.95 (*0-521-35877-9*) Cambridge U Pr.

— Philosophical Papers, Vol. 2: Essays on Heidegger & Others. 250p. (C). 1991. 49.95 (*0-521-35370-X*); pap. 16.95 (*0-521-35878-7*) Cambridge U Pr.

— Philosophy & the Mirror of Nature. LC 79-84013. 401p. 1979. pap. 16.95 (*0-691-02016-7*) Princeton U Pr.

Rorty, Richard, et al, eds. Philosophy in History: Essays in the Historiography of Philosophy. (Ideas in Context Ser.). 380p. 1984. pap. 19.95 (*0-521-27330-7*) Cambridge U Pr.

Rorty, Richard M., ed. The Linguistic Turn: Essays in Philosophic Method. 416p. 1992. pap. text ed. 17.95 (*0-226-72569-3*) U Ch Pr.

— The Linguistic Turn: Recent Essays in Philosophic Method. viii, 394p. 1988. pap. text ed. 19.95 (*0-226-72568-5*, Midway Reprint) U Ch Pr.

Rorvick, David, jt. auth. see Shettles, Landrum B.

Ros. Abdominal Magnetic Resonance Imaging. 576p. 1992. 99.00 (*0-8016-6310-5*) Mosby Yr Bk.

Ros, Amanda M. Thine in Storm & Calm: An Amanda McKittrick Ros Reader. LC 88-7510. 166p. 1989. pap. 12.95 (*0-85640-408-X*, Pub. by Blackstaff Pr IE) Dufour.

***Ros, Enrique.** Giron la Verdadera Historia. LC 94-71749. (Coleccion Cuba y sus Jueces). (Illus.). 314p. (Orig.). (SPA.). 1994. pap. 25.00 (*0-89729-738-5*) Ediciones.

Ros, Frank. The Lost Secrets of Ayurvedic Acupuncture: An Ayurvedic Guide to Acupuncture. LC 93-80314. 215p. (Orig.). 1994. pap. 15.95 (*0-914955-12-8*) Lotus Pr WI.

Ros, Fred, et al. Dreaming of Paradise: Islamic Art from the Collection of the Museum of Ethnology Rotterdam. (Illus.). 224p. 1994. 75.00 (*90-5349-101-5*) U of Wash Pr.

Ros, Jaime, jt. ed. see Bouzas, Roberto.

Ros, Martin. Night of Fire: The Black Napoleon & the Battle for Haiti. Ford, Karen, tr. (Illus.). 256p. 1994. 27.50 (*0-9627613-8-9*); pap. 14.95 (*0-9627613-7-0*) Sarpedon.

Ros, Milenko. Respirometry of Activated Sludge. LC 93-60579. 155p. 1993. text ed. 65.00 (*1-56676-029-1*) Technomic.

Ros, Saphan, jt. auth. see Ho, Minfong.

Rosa, Albert J., jt. auth. see Thomas, Roland E.

***Rosa, Alfred & Eschholz, Paul.** Models for Writers: Short Essays for Composition. 5th ed. 480p. 1994. pap. text ed. 16.50 (*0-312-10120-1*) St Martin.

— Outlooks & Insights: A Reader for College Writers. 4th ed. 736p. (C). 1994. pap. text ed. 18.50 (*0-312-10110-4*) St Martin.

Rosa, Alfred, jt. auth. see Eschholz, Paul.

Rosa, Alfred F. Salem, Transcendentalism, & Hawthorne. LC 77-89784. 108p. 1978. 28.50 (*0-8386-2159-7*) Fairleigh Dickinson.

Rosa, Alfred F., ed. The Old Century & the New. LC 76-2853. 287p. 1978. 38.50 (*0-8386-1954-1*) Fairleigh Dickinson.

Rosa, Alfred F. & Eschholz, Paul A. The Writer's Brief Handbook. 375p. (C). 1994. pap. write for info. (*0-02-403591-2*) Macmillan.

Rosa, Alfred F., jt. ed. see Eschholz, Paul A.

Rosa, Alfred F., et al. Controversies: Contemporary Arguments for College Writers. 656p. (C). 1991. pap. write for info. (*0-02-403611-0*) Macmillan.

***Rosa, David.** A Soul to Weep for Others to Keep. 1995. 10.95 (*0-8062-5186-7*) Carlton.

Rosa, Don, jt. auth. see Barks, Carl.

Rosa, Don, jt. illus. see Barks, Carl.

Rosa, Elva, ed. see Stamper, Melvin.

Rosa, Frank. Legionnaires' Disease: Prevention & Control. LC 92-45807. 1993. 49.95 (*0-912524-79-0*) Busn News.

— Water Treatment Specification Manual. LC 92-45808. 1993. 47.95 (*0-912524-80-4*) Busn News.

Rosa, Jean J., ed. World Crisis in Social Security. 245p. (Orig.). 1982. pap. text ed. 9.95 (*0-917616-44-8*) Transaction Pubs.

Rosa, Jean-Jacques. France: 1950-1985. 24p. 1987. pap. 5.00 (*0-917616-97-9*) ICS Pr.

R

An Asterisk (*) at the beginning of an entry indicates that the title is appearing in BIP for the first time.

Rosa, Jose & Altman, Nathaniel. Power Spots. 96p. 1988. pap. 8.95 (*0-85030-474-1*, Pub. by Aquarian Pr UK) Thorsons SF.

Rosa, Joseph. Albert Frey, Architect. LC 89-43557. (Illus.). 160p. 1990. pap. 29.95 (*0-8478-1183-2*) Rizzoli Intl.

— A Constructed View: The Architectural Photography of Julius Shulman. LC 93-39735. (Illus.). 224p. 1994. 50.00 (*0-8478-1777-6*) Rizzoli Intl.

Rosa, Joseph G. Age of the Gunfighter: Men & Weapons of the Frontier 1840-1900. (Illus.). 192p. 1995. 24.98 (*0-8317-0381-4*) Smithmark.

— Age of the Gunfighter: Men & Weapons on the Frontier, 1840-1900. LC 95-4992. 1995. write for info. (*0-8061-2761-9*) U of Okla Pr.

— Gunfighter: Man or Myth? LC 68-31378. (Illus.). 1979. reprint ed. pap. 14.95 (*0-8061-1561-0*) U of Okla Pr.

— Guns of the American West. 1988. 12.98 (*0-671-10036-X*) S&S Trade.

— They Called Him Wild Bill. 2nd ed. (Illus.). 1979. pap. 19.95 (*0-8061-1538-6*) U of Okla Pr.

— The West of Wild Bill Hickok. LC 81-21945. (Illus.). 202p. 1994. pap. 15.95 (*0-8061-2680-9*) U of Okla Pr.

Rosa, Joseph G. & May, Robin. Buffalo Bill & His Wild West: A Pictorial Biography. LC 88-34426. (Illus.). xii, 244p. 1989. pap. 14.95 (*0-7006-0399-9*) U Pr of KS.

Rosa, Joseph G., jt. auth. see Davis, William C.

Rosa, L. Guerra, jt. ed. see Branco, C. Moura.

Rosa-Nieves. Voz Folklorica de Puerto Rico. 1967. 16.95 (*0-87751-009-1*) E Torres & Sons.

Rosa-Nieves & Melon. Biografias Puertorriquenas. 1970. 18. 95 (*0-685-73206-1*) E Torres & Sons.

Rosa Nieves, Cesareo. Plumas Estelares de Puerto Rico, Bk. 2: Siglo XX. 518p. (C). 1971. 5.00 (*0-8477-3148-0*) U of PR Pr.

Rosa-Nieves, Cesario. Romanticism in Puerto Rican Literature. (Puerto Rico Ser.). 1979. lib. bdg. 59.95 (*0-8490-3003-X*) Gordon Pr.

***Rosa, Paul.** Idiot Letters: One Man's Relentless Assault on Corporate America. LC 94-38428. 1995. 7.95 (*0-385-47508-X*) Doubleday.

Rosa, Paul M. How Electrons Whirl Our Wheels: Nikola Tesla. 1995. pap. 20.00 (*1-885522-03-7*) Telecommunity Pr.

Rosa, Peter, ed. The Role & Contribution of Small Business Research: Proceedings of the Ninth National Small Firms Policy & Research Conference, 1986. (Illus.). 256p. 1989. text ed. 68.95 (*0-566-07103-7*, Pub. by Avebury Pub UK) Ashgate Pub Co.

Rosa, Portada de Rafael, jt. auth. see Agramonte, Roberto D.

Rosa, Richard J. Magnetohydrodynamic Energy Conversion. rev. ed. LC 66-56029. 234p. 1987. 68.00 (*0-89116-690-4*) Hemisp Pub.

Rosa, Rodrigo R. El Agua Quieta. 108p. (Orig.). (SPA.). (C). 1991. pap. 6.95 (*0-9626221-2-5*) Vista Pubns FL.

— El Cuchillo del Mendigo. 80p. (Orig.). (SPA.). (C). 1987. pap. 5.95 (*0-9626221-0-9*) Vista Pubns FL.

— El Salvador De Buques. 98p. (Orig.). (SPA.). (C). 1993. pap. 5.95 (*0-9626221-3-3*) Vista Pubns FL.

Rosa, Rosa, jt. auth. see Jaffe, Hilda.

Rosa, Tina, jt. auth. see Rogers, Steve.

Rosa, Vincent, jt. auth. see Horan, George J.

Rosa, Vincent, jt. auth. see Horan, George.

Rosaaen, Robin. All the King's Things: The Ultimate Elvis Memorabilia Book. (Illus.). 40p. 1993. text ed. 12.95 (*0-912517-04-2*) Bluewood Bks.

Rosadi, Giovanni. The Trial of Jesus. 1977. lib. bdg. 59.95 (*0-8490-2767-5*) Gordon Pr.

Rosado, Anibal C. Filosofia de la Tecnica. 162p. 1992. pap. 8.50 (*0-8477-2832-3*) U of PR Pr.

Rosado, Caleb. Broken Walls. 160p. 1989. pap. 0.99 (*0-8163-0862-4*) Pacific Pr Pub Assn.

— What Is God Like? Coffen, Richard W., ed. 96p. (Orig.). 1988. pap. 6.95 (*0-8280-0414-5*) Review & Herald.

Rosado, Olga. Donde Termina la Noche. LC 78-74598. (Coleccion Caniqui Ser.). (Illus.). 1979. pap. 6.00 (*0-89729-217-0*) Ediciones.

— Dos Decadas (Versos) LC 86-83334. (Coleccion Espejo de Paciencia Ser.). 41p. (Orig.). (SPA.). 1987. pap. 5.00 (*0-89729-424-6*) Ediciones.

— Guajiro. LC 89-83448. (Coleccion Espejo de Paciencia Ser.). 69p. (Orig.). (SPA.). 1990. pap. 9.00 (*0-89729-526-9*) Ediciones.

— Pecadora (Seleccion de Poesias) LC 80-68759. 66p. (Orig.). (SPA.). 1984. pap. 5.00 (*0-89729-268-5*) Ediciones.

— Tengo Prisa. (Coleccion Espejo de Paciencia Ser.). 1978. pap. 5.00 (*0-89729-197-2*) Ediciones.

Rosage, David. Praying the Scriptural Rosary. 140p. 1989. 6.99 (*0-89283-630-X*) Servant.

— Rejoice in Me: A Pocket Guide to Daily Scriptural Prayer. 256p. 1986. 5.99 (*0-89283-298-3*) Servant.

Rosage, David E. Abide in Me: A Pocket Guide to Daily Scriptural Prayer. 229p. (Orig.). 1985. pap. text ed. 5.99 (*0-89283-243-6*, Vine Bks) Servant.

— Beginning Spiritual Direction. 170p. (Orig.). 1994. pap. 7.99 (*0-89283-759-4*, Charis) Servant.

— Comfort for the Losses in Life. 280p. 1995. 9.99 (*0-89283-887-6*, Charis) Servant.

— Discovering Pathways to Prayer. 160p. (Orig.). 1975. pap. 6.95 (*0-914544-08-X*) Living Flame Pr.

— Encountering the Lord in Daily Life. 160p. (Orig.). 1983. pap. 5.95 (*0-914544-45-4*) Living Flame Pr.

— Follow Me. (Inspirational Library Ser.). 256p. 1992. 4.98 (*0-8317-4977-6*) Smithmark.

— Follow Me: A Pocket Guide to Daily Scriptural Prayer. 240p. 1982. pap. 5.99 (*0-89283-168-5*) Servant.

— Habla Senor, Tu Siervo Te Escucha (Speak, Lord, Your Servant Is Listening) Una Guia Diaria para Orar con las Sagradas Escrituras (A Daily Guide to Scriptural Prayer) 160p. (SPA.). 1991. pap. 4.99 (*0-89283-723-3*) Servant.

— Know Me: A Pocket Guide to Daily Scriptural Prayer. 278p. 1991. pap. 5.99 (*0-89283-693-8*) Servant.

— Linger with Me: Moments Aside with Jesus. 212p. (Orig.). 1979. pap. 6.95 (*0-914544-29-2*) Living Flame Pr.

— Living Here & Hereafter. (Christian Dying, Death & Resurection Ser.). 128p. (Orig.). 1982. pap. 5.95 (*0-914544-44-6*) Living Flame Pr.

— Praying with Mary. 122p. (Orig.). 1980. pap. 6.95 (*0-914544-31-4*) Living Flame Pr.

— Reconciliation: The Sacramental Path to Peace. 144p. (Orig.). 1984. pap. 6.95 (*0-914544-56-X*) Living Flame Pr.

— Speak Lord, Your Servant Is Listening. large type ed. (Large Print Inspirational Ser.). 1987. pap. 9.95 (*0-8027-2568-6*) Walker & Co.

— Speak, Lord, Your Servant Is Listening. rev. ed. 112p. 1987. pap. 4.99 (*0-89283-371-8*) Servant.

Rosai. Ackerman's Surgical Pathology. 7th ed. (Illus.). 2112p. 1988. text ed. 230.00 (*0-8016-4176-4*) Mosby Yr Bk.

Rosai, Juan. Ackerman's Surgical Pathology. 8th ed. 2300p. 1994. 259.00 (*0-8016-7004-7*) Mosby Yr Bk.

— Manual of Surgical Pathology Gross Room Procedures. (Illus.). 132p. (C). 1981. spiral bd. 29.95 (*0-8166-1027-4*) U of Minn Pr.

Rosai, Juan & Levine, Gerald D. Atlas of Tumor Pathology: Tumors of the Thymus. (Second Ser.: Fascicle 13). (Illus.). 240p. 1990. reprint ed. per., pap. 8.50 (*0-16-001843-9*, S/N 008-023-000) USGPO.

***Rosair, David.** The Facts on File Photographic Guide to the Shorebirds of the World. LC 95-2502. (Illus.). 1995. write for info. (*0-8160-3309-9*) Facts on File.

Rosak, Theodore. Why Astrology Endures. (Broadside Editions Ser.). 20p. (C). 1986. pap. 1.95 (*0-9609850-9-3*) Rob Briggs.

Rosakis, A. J., jt. ed. see Knauss, W. G.

Rosal, Lorenca. Eternal Vigilance: The Story of the N.H. Constitution. (Illus.). 425p. 1987. 16.95 (*0-685-19457-4*) Equity Pubng NH.

— The Liberty Key: The Story of the N.H. Constitution. (Illus.). 300p. (J). 1987. 12.95 (*0-685-19456-6*) Equity Pubng NH.

Rosaldo, Michael Z. Knowledge & Passion. LC 79-12632. (Cambridge Studies in Cultural Systems). (Illus.). 1980. pap. 19.95 (*0-521-29562-9*) Cambridge U Pr.

Rosaldo, Michelle Z. & Lamphere, Louise, eds. Woman, Culture, & Society. LC 73-89861. 360p. 1974. 45.00 (*0-8047-0850-9*); pap. 13.95 (*0-8047-0851-7*) Stanford U Pr.

Rosaldo, Renato. Culture & Truth: The Remaking of Social Analysis. LC 93-18158. 288p. 1993. pap. 14.00 (*0-8070-4623-X*) Beacon Pr.

— Ilongot Headhunting, 1883-1974: A Study in Society & History. LC 79-64218. (Illus.). xii, 313p. 1980. 42.50 (*0-8047-1046-5*); pap. 13.95 (*0-8047-1284-0*) Stanford U Pr.

Rosalee. The Music of Women. (Illus.). 40p. (Orig.). 1992. pap. text ed. 6.95 (*1-56315-071-9*) Sterling Hse.

Rosaler, R. C. & Rice, James O. Industrial Maintenance Reference Guide. (Reference Guide Ser.). 232p. 1987. text ed. 53.00 (*0-07-052162-X*) McGraw.

Rosaler, Robert C. Standard Handbook of Plant Engineering. 2nd ed. 1994. text ed. 104.50 (*0-07-052164-6*) McGraw.

Rosales-Dordelly, Carmen L. & Short, Edmund C. Curriculum Professors' Specialized Knowledge. (Illus.). 124p. (Orig.). 1985. pap. text ed. 13.50 (*0-8191-4639-0*) U Pr of Amer.

Rosales, F. Arturo & Foster, David W. Hispanics & the Humanities in the Southwest: A Directory of Resources. 256p. (C). 1983. pap. 2.00 (*0-87918-055-2*) ASU Lat Am St.

Rosales, Gaudencio & Arevalo, Catalino, eds. For All the Peoples of Asia: Federation of Asian Bishops' Conferences Documents from 1970 to 1991. LC 92-5033. 342p. 1992. 39.95 (*0-88344-837-8*) Orbis Bks.

***Rosales, Guillermo.** El Juego de la Viola. LC 93-73441. (Coleccion Caniqui). 96p. 1994. pap. 9.95 (*0-89729-707-5*) Ediciones.

Rosales, Melodye. Double Dutch & the Voodoo Shoes: An Urban Folktale. LC 91-13153. (Adventures in Storytelling Ser.). (Illus.). 32p. (J). (ps-3). 1991. lib. bdg. 13.85 (*0-516-05133-4*); pap. 5.95 (*0-516-45133-2*) Childrens.

Rosalind, ed. see Laurence Urdang Associates, Ltd. Staff.

Rosamond, Peggy. Bear Record Book. 48p. 1983. 16.95 (*0-87588-195-5*, 2402) Hobby Hse.

Rosamond, Peggy J. American Colonial Brides Paper Dolls. 32p. 1981. pap. 4.95 (*0-87588-239-0*, 49) Hobby Hse.

— Antique French Doll Paper Dolls: An Armenian-American Memoir. 8p. (J). (gr. 8-12). 1976. pap. 4.00 (*0-914510-07-X*) Evergreen.

— Black Doll Paper Dolls. (Illus.). 32p. (Orig.). 1991. pap. 4.95 (*0-87588-382-6*) Hobby Hse.

— Paper Doll Diary. (Illus.). 32p. (C). spiral bd. 4.95 (*0-87588-334-6*, 3723) Hobby Hse.

— Paper Doll Masquerade. (Illus.). 16p. 1987. pap. 4.95 (*0-87588-296-X*, 3573) Hobby Hse.

— The Teddy Bear & Friends Paper Doll Fantasy. (Illus.). 32p. (Orig.). 1984. pap. 4.95 (*0-87588-224-2*, 2860) Hobby Hse.

Rosamond, Peggy-Jo. Paper Doll Greeting Cards - Act B. 32p. 1984. spiral bd. 5.95 (*0-87588-327-3*) Hobby Hse.

Rosamond, Peggy Jo. Paper Doll Portrait: Antique German Bisque Dolls. 16p. 1985. pap. 5.95 (*0-87588-246-3*, 2916) Hobby Hse.

— Teddy Bear & Friends Paper Dolls Go Hollywood. (Illus.). 32p. 1986. spiral bd. 4.95 (*0-87588-287-0*, 3407) Hobby Hse.

Rosamonds. Doll Record Book. 48p. 1984. 16.95 (*0-87588-197-1*, 641) Hobby Hse.

— Doll Record Book Refill Set. 24p. 1984. ring bd. 3.95 (*0-87588-198-X*, 642) Hobby Hse.

Rosamonds, Peggy. Bear Record Book Refill Set. 24p. 1984. ring bd. 3.95 (*0-87588-196-3*, 2403) Hobby Hse.

Rosan, Burton, jt. ed. see Mergenhagen, Stephan E.

Rosand, David. The Meaning of the Mark: Leonardo & Titian. (Franklin D. Murphy Lectures: No. 8). 1988. 12. 00 (*0-913689-01-7*) Spencer Muse Art.

Rosand, David, jt. auth. see Hanning, Robert W.

Rosand, Ellen. Opera in Seventeenth-Century Venice: The Creation of a Genre. (Illus.). 710p. 1990. 125.00 (*0-520-06808-4*) U CA Pr.

Rosander. Applications of Quality Control to the Service Industry. (Quality & Reliability Ser.: Vol. 5). 432p. 1985. 69.75 (*0-8247-7466-3*) Dekker.

Rosander, A. C. Deming's Fourteen Points Applied to Services. (Quality & Reliability Ser.: Vol. 25). 168p. 1991. 55.00 (*0-8247-8517-7*) Dekker.

— The Quest for Quality in Services. (Illus.). 579p. 1989. text ed. 37.50 (*0-527-91644-7*, 916447) Qual Resc.

— Washington Story: Behind the Scenes in the Federal Government - An Official under Civil Service Describes His Experiences. LC 85-227965. xiii, 546p. 1985. 7.95 (*0-9615168-0-1*) Natl Directions.

Rosander, Arlyn C. Case Studies in Sample Design. LC 76-12283. (Statistics, Textbooks & Monographs: 21). 438p. reprint ed. pap. 124.90 (*0-685-17120-5*, 2027836) Bks Demand.

Rosander, Eva E. Women in a Borderland: Managing Muslim Identity Where Morocco Meets Spain. (Stockholm Studies in Social Anthropology: No. 26). 313p. (Orig.). 1991. pap. 58.50x (*91-7146-918-4*, Pub. by Almqv & Wiksell SW) Coronet Bks.

Rosanes-Berrett, Marilyn. Do You Really Need Eyeglasses? enl. ed. (Illus.). 140p. 1990. 20.95 (*0-88268-107-9*); pap. 10.95 (*0-88268-104-4*) Station Hill Pr.

Rosanik, Ralph. Hawk Safari: The Search for a Rare Bird. 200p. 1993. pap. 12.95 (*0-9637153-0-5*) C & D Mktg.

Rosano. Microemulsion Systems. (Surfactant Science Ser.: Vol. 24). 440p. 1987. 199.00 (*0-8247-7439-6*) Dekker.

Rosano, Aureleo. The Rosano Sculptures. LC 83-90393. (Illus.). 120p. 1984. 38.00 (*0-914817-00-0*) Rose Pubns AZ.

Rosanoff, Nancy. Intuition Workout: A Practical Guide to Discovering & Developing Your Inner Knowing. LC 88-19437. (Illus.). 168p. (Orig.). 1988. pap. 9.95 (*0-944031-13-7*) Aslan Pub.

— Intuition Workout: A Practical Guide to Discovering & Developing Your Inner Knowing. rev. ed. LC 91-76. (Illus.). 176p. (Orig.). 1991. reprint ed. pap. 10.95 (*0-944031-14-5*) Aslan Pub.

Rosanore of Redthorn. Rose & Nefr Dance Manual. (Illus.). 136p. (C). 1989. teacher ed 26.00 (*0-685-27241-9*); pap. text ed. 20.00 (*1-877934-03-8*) Rose & Nefr Pr.

Rosanova, A. M. Ballroom Dancing Made Easy. (Ballroom Dance Ser.). 1986. lib. bdg. 79.95 (*0-8490-3358-6*) Gordon Pr.

— Ballroom Dancing Made Easy. (Ballroom Dance Ser.). 1985. lib. bdg. 250.00 (*0-87700-685-7*) Revisionist Pr.

Rosansky, Lynne M., jt. auth. see Giovannini, Maureen J.

Rosario. El Espanol de America. 1970. 12.95 (*0-685-73205-3*) E Torres & Sons.

Rosario, Benjamin, jt. auth. see Martinez, Felix J.

Rosario, Bernada D., jt. auth. see Rogers, Mary.

Rosario-Braid, Florangel. Communication Strategies for Productivity Improvement. rev. ed. 300p. 1983. text ed. 24.75 (*92-833-1053-5*, Pub. by APO JA) Qual Resc.

Rosario, Idalia. Idalia's Project ABC-Proyecto ABC: An Urban Alphabet Book in English & Spanish. LC 80-21013. (Illus.). (J). (ps-2). 1988. pap. 5.95 (*0-8050-0296-0*, Bks Young Read) H Holt & Co.

Rosario, Jose C. The Development of the Puerto Rican Jibaro & His Present Attitude Towards Society. LC 74-14248. (Puerto Rican Experience Ser.). (Illus.). 124p. 1975. reprint ed. 11.95 (*0-405-06234-6*) Ayer.

***Rosario, Nahum.** Atrevete a Cambiar. 45p. (Orig.). (SPA.). 1995. pap. 5.00 (*0-9634761-6-5*) Pub Maranatha.

— Confrontando a Satana's. (Orig.). (SPA.). 1993. pap. text ed. write for info. (*0-9634761-3-0*) Pub Maranatha.

— La Escalera del Exito. 64p. 1992. pap. 5.50 (*0-9634761-0-6*) Pub Maranatha.

— Las Riquezas de Su Gracia. 151p. (Orig.). (SPA.). 1994. pap. 8.00 (*0-9634761-4-9*) Pub Maranatha.

— Los Secretos de la Uncion. 120p. (Orig.). 1993. pap. 7.00 (*0-9634761-1-4*) Pub Maranatha.

— The Secrets of the Anointing. Toledo, Efren, tr. 112p. (Orig.). 1994. pap. 7.00 (*0-9634761-5-7*) Pub Maranatha.

Rosario, Ruben D. Diccionario de Terminos Aerauticos. (ENG & SPA.). 125.00 (*0-685-42438-3*, S-37343) Fr & Eur.

— Vocabulario Puertorriqueno. 92p. (SPA.). 1980. 24.95 (*0-8288-2058-9*, S5253) Fr & Eur.

***Rosario-Sievert, Heather.** Honor My Father. LC 94-24145. 1995. write for info. (*0-7734-2736-8*) Irwin.

Rosario, Vernon, 2nd, jt. ed. see Bennett, Paula.

Rosas, Allan, ed. International Human Rights Norms in Domestic Law: Finnish & Polish Perspectives. 300p. (Orig.). 1990. pap. 118.00x (*951-640-509-6*, Pub. by Almqv & Wiksell SW) Coronet Bks.

***Rosas, Allan & Antola, Esko, eds.** A Citizens' Europe: In Search of a New Order. 272p. (C). 1995. 69.95 (*0-8039-7560-0*); pap. 21.95 (*0-8039-7561-9*) Sage.

Rosas, Allan & Helgesen, Jan, eds. The Strength of Diversity: Human Rights & Pluralist Democracy. LC 92-32721. (International Studies in Human Rights: Vol. 25). 1992. lib. bdg. 95.50 (*0-7923-1987-7*) Kluwer Ac.

***Rosas, Carlos.** Misa de Tepeyac. (SPA.). Date not set. write for info. (*0-614-04900-8*) Mex Am Cult.

Rosas, Debbie, et al. Non-Impact Aerobics. 192p. 1988. pap. 9.95 (*0-380-70522-2*) Avon.

Rosas, Joseph, III. Scripture in the Thought of Soren Kierkegaard. LC 93-15865. 1994. 24.99 (*0-8054-1624-2*) Broadman.

***Rosas, Juan C. & Young, Roberto.** El Cultivo de la Soya. 60p. (C). 1993. pap. text ed. 3.50 (*1-885995-10-5*) Escuela Agricola.

— Principios y Practicas de Mejoramiento de Plantas. 119p. (C). 1992. pap. text ed. 4.75 (*1-885995-06-7*) Escuela Agricola.

Rosas, Yolanda. Villasandino y su Hablante Lirico. (American University Studies: Romance Languages & Literature: Ser. II, Vol. 53). 186p. (C). 1987. text ed. 32. 90 (*0-8204-0342-3*) P Lang Pubs.

Rosasco, Gregory J., ed. Workshop on Federal Programs Involving Supercritical Water Oxidation: Proceedings. 303p. (Orig.). (C). 1993. pap. text ed. 65.00 (*0-7881-0042-4*) Diane Pub.

Rosasco-Soule, Adelia. Panhandle Memories. Cannon, Ron, ed. & intro. by. (Illus.). 143p. 1987. text ed. 12.95 (*0-944206-00-X*) W FL Lit Fed.

Rosati, Jeral A. The Politics of United States Foreign Policy. 560p. (C). 1993. pap. text ed. write for info. (*0-03-047024-2*) HB Coll Pubs.

Rosati, Jerel, jt. ed. see Coate, Roger A.

Rosati, Jerel A. The Carter Administration's Quest for Global Community: Beliefs & Their Impact on Behavior. 268p. 1987. text ed. 39.95 (*0-87249-508-6*) U of SC Pr.

— The Carter Administration's Quest for Global Community: Beliefs & Their Impact on Behavior. LC 87-6006. (Illus.). 268p. 1991. reprint ed. pap. text ed. 21.95 (*0-87249-787-9*) U of SC Pr.

Rosati, L. A., ed. Buildings & the Geometry of Diagrams. (Lecture Notes in Mathematics Ser.: Vol. 1181). vii, 277p. 1986. pap. 34.80 (*0-387-16466-9*) Spr-Verlag.

Rosati, S., jt. ed. see Fantoni, S.

Rosato, Amelia, jt. auth. see O'Neal, Debbie T.

Rosato, Angelo A. Encyclopedia of the Modern Elongated: Encyclopedia on Elongated Coins. LC 90-83073. (Illus.). 1760p. 1990. 129.95 (*0-9626996-2-4*) Angros Pubs.

— Rerolls - Restrikes: Supplement. (Encyclopedia of the Modern Elongated Ser.). (Illus.). 40p. 1992. pap. text ed. 25.00 (*0-9626996-3-2*) Angros Pubs.

Rosato, D. Plastics Processing Data Handbook. 256p. 1989. 42.00 (*0-685-27060-2*) T-C Pubns CA.

Rosato, D. V. & Grove, C. S., Jr. Filament Winding: Its Development, Manufacture, Applications, & Design. LC 64-14998. (Polymer Engineering & Technology Ser.). 371p. reprint ed. pap. 105.80 (*0-317-28942-X*, 2055989) Bks Demand.

Rosato, Dominick V. Rosato's Plastics Encyclopedia & Dictionary. 2nd ed. 884p. (C). 1992. text ed. 148.00 (*1-56990-088-4*) Hanser-Gardner.

***Rosato, Dominick V. & Rosato, Donald V., eds.** Injection Molding Handbook. 2nd ed. LC 94-29399. 1995. 139.95 (*0-412-99381-3*) Chapman & Hall.

Rosato, Dominick V., jt. auth. see Rosato, Donald V.

Rosato, Donald V. Plastics Processing Data Handbook. 1989. text ed. 52.95 (*0-442-31869-3*) Chapman & Hall.

Rosato, Donald V. & Rosato, Dominick V. Blow Molding Handbook. 1010p. (C). 1989. text ed. 184.50 (*1-56990-089-2*) Hanser-Gardner.

Rosato, Donald V., jt. ed. see Rosato, Dominick V.

Rosato, Donald V., et al. Designing with Plastics & Composites: A Handbook. LC 90-46378. (Illus.). 928p. 1991. text ed. 105.00 (*0-442-00133-9*) Chapman & Hall.

Rosato, Francis R., jt. auth. see Strombeck, Jan Olaf.

***Rosato, Frank.** Jogging & Walking. (Illus.). 160p. (C). 1995. pap. text ed. 14.95x (*0-89582-295-4*) Morton Pub.

Rosato, Frank D. Fitness for Wellness: The Physical Connection. 3rd ed. Westby, ed. LC 93-6048. 350p. (C). 1994. pap. text ed. 34.25 (*0-314-02814-5*) West Pub.

Rosato, Philip. The Spirit As Lord. 240p. 1981. 37.95 (*0-567-09305-0*, Pub. by T & T Clark UK) Bks Intl VA.

***Rosaw, Jerome M. & Lotto, Jill C.** People, Partnership, & Profits Pt. 2: The New Labor-Management Agenda. (Strategic Partners for High Performance Ser.). 138p. 1994. per., pap. text ed. 95.00 (*0-89361-051-8*) Work in Amer.

Rosazza, John P., ed. Microbial Transformations of Bioactive Compounds, Vol. II. 200p. 1982. 144.00 (*0-8493-6066-8*, QR88, CRC Reprint) Franklin.

***Rosbach-Chandler, Ruth.** Attention Training & Healing: What Other Books Didn't Tell You. 64p. Date not set. pap. text ed. 9.95 (*0-9645303-0-9*) Olympic Press.

Rosberg, Carl G. & Callaghy, Thomas M., eds. Socialism in Sub-Saharan Africa: A New Assessment. LC 79-84635. (Research Ser.: No. 38). (Illus.). 1979. pap. 12.95 (*0-87725-138-X*) U of Cal IAS.

Rosberg, Carl G., jt. auth. see Apter, David E.

Rosberg, Carl G., Jr., jt. ed. see Friedland, William H.

Rosberg, Carl G., jt. auth. see Jackson, Robert H., Jr.

Rosberg, Carl G., jt. ed. see Price, Robert M.

Rosberg, Gary. Choosing to Love Again. 1992. 14.99 (*1-56179-095-8*) Focus Family.

— Choosing to Love Again. 1995. pap. 9.99 (*1-56179-257-8*) Focus Family.

— Guard Your Heart. 1994. 16.99 (*0-88070-655-4*, Multnomah Bks) Questar Pubs.

Rosberg, Rose. Breathe in, Breathe Out. 56p. (Orig.). 1992. pap. 7.50 (*1-880286-09-2*) Singular Speech Pr.

— The Country of Connections. LC 92-91130. 112p. (Orig.). 1994. pap. 5.95 (*1-56002-251-5*, Univ Edtns) Aegina Pr.

Rosberger, Paul. The Theory of Total Consonance. LC 71-92560. (Illus.). 108p. 1975. 16.50 (*0-8386-7570-0*) Fairleigh Dickinson.

Rosbert, C. Joseph. Flying Tiger Joe's Adventure Story Cookbook. 343p. 1985. 18.95 (*0-9616536-0-4*) Giant Poplar Pr.

An Asterisk (*) at the beginning of an entry indicates that the title is appearing in BIP for the first time.

— The Pictorial History of Civil Air Transport. 290p. (C). 1990. 30.00 (*0-932298-82-6*) Giant Poplar Pr.

Rosborough, Brian A., ed. United States Map Book: Environmental Atlas. (Illus.). 188p. 1991. 15.95 (*1-879856-01-8*) Interarts.

Rosborough, E. H. Tying & Fishing the Fuzzy Nymphs. 4th rev. ed. LC 88-2190. (Illus.). 192p. 1988. 21.95 (*0-8117-1818-2*) Stackpole.

Rosbotham, Lyle. Extinction Event: A Workbook. (Illus.). 96p. (Orig.). 1988. pap. 12.00 (*0-917796-04-7*) Press Four Fifty One.

— High School Students. (Illus.). 120p. 1983. 12.00 (*0-917796-03-9*) Press Four Fifty One.

Rosbottom, Betty. Betty Rosbottom's Cooking School Cookbook. LC 87-42746. 416p. 1987. 19.95 (*0-89480-526-6*, 1526); pap. 10.95 (*0-89480-525-8*, 1525) Workman Pub.

Rosbrow-Reich, Susan, jt. auth. see Raymond, Laurie.

Rosch, Eleanor & Lloyd, Barbara B., eds. Cognition & Categorization. LC 78-6570. 336p. reprint ed. pap. 95.80 (*0-8357-3404-8*, 2039661) Bks Demand.

Rosch, J. Thomas. Manual of Federal Trade Commission Practice. 2nd ed. (Corporate Practice Series Portfolio: No. 21). 1989. ring bd. 92.00 (*1-55871-144-9*) BNA.

Rosch, T. & Classen, M. Gastroenterologic Endosonography. (Illus.). 120p. 1992. text ed. 119.00 (*0-86577-454-4*) Thieme Med Pubs.

Rosch, Winn. Winn L. Rosch Hardware Bible. 3rd ed. 1248p. (Orig.). 1994. 35.00 (*1-56686-127-6*) Sams.

Rosch, Winn L. This Old PC. 1993. pap. 24.95 (*1-56686-104-7*) Brady Compu Bks.

— Winn L. Rosch Hardware Bible. 2nd ed. (Illus.). (Orig.). 1992. pap. 29.95 (*0-13-932260-4*) Brady Compu Bks.

— The Winn L. Rosch PC Upgrade Bible. 1991. 26.95 (*0-13-932252-3*) Brady Compu Bks.

Rosch, Winn L., jt. auth. see Heath, Chet.

Roschar, Frans M., jt. auth. see Mokken, Robert J.

Rosche, Larry, ed. A Field Book of Birds of the Cleveland Region. 2nd ed. (Illus.). 44p. 1988. pap. 3.50 (*1-878600-05-2*) Cleve Mus Nat Hist.

Roscher, Marina & Fishman, Charles, eds. Catlives: Sarah Kirsch's Katzenleben. Fishman, Charles, tr. 177p. 1990. 24.95 (*0-89672-232-5*); pap. 12.95 (*0-89672-231-7*) Tex Tech Univ Pr.

Roscher, Wilhelm H. Ausfuhrliches Lexikon der Griechischen und Romischen Mythologie, 10 vols. (GER.). 1992. reprint ed. write for info. (*3-487-00915-3*, Pub. by Georg Olms GW) Lubrecht & Cramer.

Roscher, William. Principles of Political Economy. LC 72-38255. (Evolution of Capitalism Ser.). 964p. 1972. reprint ed. 65.95 (*0-405-04136-5*) Ayer.

Roschlau & Kadar. Pharmacology Study Aid. 167p. 1991. pap. 21.95 (*1-55664-303-9*) Mosby Yr Bk.

***Roschwalb, Susanne A. & Stack, Richard A.** Litigation Public Relations: Courting Public Opinion. LC 95-6541. 1995. write for info. (*0-8377-1048-0*) Rothman.

***Rosciglione, Salvatore.** Possible e l'Improbabile: Italian Novel. 167p. (ITA.). 1988. pap. 10.00 (*0-89304-657-4*) Cross-Cultrl NY.

Rosciszewski, Jan. Ionizing Fronts in Plasma Propulsion & Power Generation Systems. LC 70-131402. 191p. 1969. 19.00 (*0-403-04532-0*) Scholarly.

Rosco, Jerry, ed. see Wescott, Glenway.

Roscoe, A. W. & Reed, G. M. Domains Denotational Semantics. 300p. 1994. text ed. 34.00 (*0-13-219023-0*) P-H.

Roscoe, Adrian & Msika, Hangson. Quiet Chameleon: Modern Poetry from Central Africa. (New Perspectives on African Literature Ser.: No. 2). 216p. 1992. lib. bdg. 85.00 (*0-905450-52-3*, Pub. by H Zell Pubs UK) Bowker-Saur.

Roscoe, David, tr. see Meier, Carl A.

Roscoe, Edward S. The Growth of English Law. Being Studies in the Evolution of Law & Procedure in England. viii, 260p. 1980. reprint ed. lib. bdg. 26.00 (*0-8377-1029-4*) Rothman.

Roscoe, Fred. From Humboldt to Kodiak, 1886-1895: Recollections of a Frontier Childhood & the Founding of the First American School & the Baptist Mission of Kodiak, Alaska. Roscoe, Stanley N., ed. (Alaska History Ser.: 40). (Illus.). 232p. (Orig.). 1992. pap. 14.95 (*0-919642-40-3*) Limestone Pr.

Roscoe, George B. Here's the Dirt. LC 84-50310. (Illus.). 140p. 1984. 13.95 (*0-932673-01-5*) Sense Pubns.

***Roscoe, Gerald & Larkin, David.** Westward: The Epic Crossing of the American Landscape. (Illus.). 256p. 1995. 60.00 (*1-885254-09-1*) Monacelli Pr.

— Westward: The Epic Crossing of the American Landscape, 4 vols., Set. (Illus.). 256p. 1995. 240.00 (*1-885254-19-9*) Monacelli Pr.

Roscoe, Henry. Lives of Eminent British Lawyers. 428p. 1982. reprint ed. lib. bdg. 35.00 (*0-8377-1037-5*) Rothman.

Roscoe, J. T. Fundamental Research Statistics for the Behavioral Sciences. 2nd ed. LC 74-14795. (International Series in Decision Processes). (C). 1975. text ed. 46.00 (*0-03-091934-7*) HB Coll Pubs.

Roscoe, John. Logica Post-Moderna. LC 93-37303. (Revisioning Philosophy Ser.: Vol. 16). 1994. write for info. (*0-8204-2352-1*) P Lang Pubs.

— Northern Bantu. (Illus.). 305p. 1966. reprint ed. 35.00 (*0-7146-1713-X*, BHA-01713, Pub. by F Cass Pubs UK) Intl Spec Bk.

Roscoe, Lorraine, jt. auth. see Denenberg, Dennis.

Roscoe Moss Company Staff. Handbook of Ground Water Development. 493p. 1990. text ed. 115.00 (*0-471-85611-8*) Wiley.

Roscoe, Patrick. Beneath the Western Slopes. 190p. (Orig.). 1987. pap. 14.95 (*0-88784-502-9*, Pub. by Hse of Anansi Pr CN) Genl Dist Srvs.

— The Lost Oasis. (Orig.). 1995. pap. 14.95 (*0-7710-7579-0*, Pub. by McClelland & Stewart CN) Firefly Bks Ltd.

Roscoe, Paul B., jt. ed. see Lutkehaus, Nancy C.

Roscoe, Paul B., jt. ed. see Lutkehaus, Nancy.

Roscoe Pound-American Trial Lawyers Association Staff & Colley, Michael F. Product Safety in America. LC 85-60392. (Annual Chief Justice Earl Warren Conference on Advocacy in the U.S. Ser.). 127p. (Orig.). 1985. pap. 25.00 (*0-933067-00-3*) Roscoe Pound Found.

Roscoe Pound-American Trial Lawyers Foundation Staff. Church, State & Politics: Final Report of the 1981 Chief Justice Earl Warren Conference on Advocacy in the United States. LC 81-85556. (Annual Chief Earl Warren Conference on Advocacy in the U. S. Ser.). 147p. 1982. pap. 25.00 (*0-933067-03-8*) Roscoe Pound Found.

— The Courts: The Pendulum of Federalism: Final Report of the 1979 Chief Justice Earl Warren Conference on Advocacy in the United States. 166p. 1979. pap. 25.00 (*0-317-57758-1*) Roscoe Pound Found.

— Dispute Resolution Devices in a Democratic Society: Final report of the 1985 Chief Justice Earl Warren Conference on Advocacy in the United States. 152p. 1985. pap. 25.00 (*0-941916-41-3*) Roscoe Pound Found.

Roscoe, S. & Brimmell, R. A. James Lumsden & Son of Glasgow. 134p. 1981. 28.00 (*0-900002-04-2*, Pub. by Priv Lib Assn UK) Oak Knoll.

Roscoe, Stanley, jt. auth. see O'Hare, David.

Roscoe, Stanley N. Aviation Psychology. LC 79-27539. (Illus.). 318p. 1990. reprint ed. pap. text ed. 18.95 (*0-8138-1927-X*) Iowa St U Pr.

Roscoe, Stanley N., ed. see Roscoe, Fred.

Roscoe, Theodora & Were, Mary W., eds. Poems by Contemporary Women. LC 79-51967. (Granger Poetry Library). 1980. reprint ed. 15.00 (*0-89609-195-3*) Roth Pub Inc.

Roscoe, Theodore. United States Destroyer Operations in World War II. LC 53-4273. (Illus.). 581p. 1953. 42.95x (*0-87021-726-7*) Naval Inst Pr.

— United States Submarine Operations in World War II. LC 50-5198. (Illus.). 577p. 1949. 42.95x (*0-87021-731-3*) Naval Inst Pr.

— The Wonderful Lips of Thibong Linh. (Illus.). 1981. 15.00 (*0-937986-36-4*) D M Grant.

Roscoe, Thomas, ed. see Roscoe, William.

Roscoe, Will. The Zuni Man-Woman. LC 90-21397. (Illus.). 328p. 1992. pap. 14.95 (*0-8263-1370-1*) U of NM Pr.

Roscoe, Will, ed. Living the Spirit: A Gay American Indian Anthology. (Stonewall Inn Editions Ser.). (Illus.). 240p. 1989. pap. 10.95 (*0-312-03475-X*) St Martin.

— Queer Spirits: A Gay Men's Myth Book. LC 94-30970. 336p. 1995. 24.00 (*0-8070-7938-3*) Beacon Pr.

Roscoe, William. A Classical Mind: Essays in Honour of Car Hoare. 472p. 1994. text ed. 70.00 (*0-13-294844-3*) P-H.

— Life & Pontificate of Pope Leo the Tenth, 2 vols. 6th rev. ed. Roscoe, Thomas, ed. LC 75-174965. reprint ed. 125. 00 (*0-404-05430-7*) AMS Pr.

***Roscoe, William E.** History of Schoharie County, N. Y. 1713-1882 with Illustrations & Biographical Sketches of Some of Its Prominent Men & Pioneers. (Illus.). 502p. (Orig.). 1994. pap. text ed. 54.00 (*0-7884-0060-6*) Heritage Bk.

— History of Schoharie County, New York. (Illus.). 470p. 1994. reprint ed. lib. bdg. 49.50 (*0-8328-4353-9*) Higginson Bk Co.

Roscoe, Wilma J., ed. Accreditation of Historically & Predominantly Black Colleges & Universities. LC 88-39408. (Illus.). 68p. (Orig.). (C). 1989. lib. bdg. 25.00 (*0-8191-7288-X*, NAEOHE) U Pr of Amer.

Roscow, Gregory, ed. see Bliss, Arthur.

Roscow, Judith, jt. auth. see Klein, Barbara.

Rosdahl, Caroline. Student Workbook for Textbook of Basic Nursing. 5th ed. (Illus.). 384p. 1990. text ed. 15.95 (*0-397-54771-4*) Lippincott.

— Textbook of Basic Nursing. 5th ed. (Illus.). 1168p. 1990. text ed. 43.95 (*0-397-54772-2*) Lippincott.

***Rosdahl, Caroline B.** Textbook of Basic Nursing. 6th ed. LC 94-30640. 1995. write for info. (*0-397-55109-6*) Lippincott.

Rosdahl, Kurt, tr. see Jackins, Harvey.

Rosden, George E. & Rosden, Peter E. Law of Advertising, 4 vols. 1973. Updates available. ring bd. write for info. (*0-8205-1357-1*) Bender.

Rosden, Peter E., jt. auth. see Rosden, George E.

Rosdolsky, Roman. The Making of Marx's "Capital", 2 vols., I. 320p. (C). 1977. pap. text ed. 19.50 (*0-86104-915-2*, Pub. by Pluto Pr UK) Westview.

— Making of Marx's "Capital" Vol. 2, Vol. 2. (C). 1977. pap. text ed. 20.50 (*0-86104-305-7*, Pub. by Pluto Pr UK) Westview.

***Rose.** Concrete Evidence. 1995. mass mkt. 3.50 (*0-590-20358-4*) Scholastic Inc.

— Heathcliff in Outer Space. 1987. pap. 1.95 (*0-8167-1264-6*) Troll Assocs.

— Like Mother, Like Daughter. pap. write for info. (*0-345-37572-6*) Ballantine.

— Year of Flowers. 1995. 12.98 (*1-56138-576-X*) Courage Bks.

Rose, ed. Wheels of Progress? Motor Transport, Pollution & the Environment. 170p. 1973. text ed. 78.00 (*0-677-15425-9*) Gordon & Breach.

Rose & Kaye. Internal Medicine for Dentistry. 2nd ed. (Illus.). 1240p. 1989. 76.95 (*0-8016-4301-5*) Mosby Yr Bk.

Rose & Myers, eds. Clinical Decision Making. 95p. 1989. 10.00 (*0-912452-71-4*, P-68) Am Phys Therapy Assn.

Rose, jt. auth. see Drier.

Rose, A. G. The Pathology of Heart Valve Replacement. 1987. lib. bdg. 129.50 (*0-85200-984-4*) Kluwer Ac.

***Rose, A. H.** Insects of Eastern Spruces, Fir, & Hemlock. 2nd rev. ed. (Illus.). 159p. (Orig.). 1994. pap. 51.95x (*0-317-06258-1*, Pub. by Canada Commun Grp CN) Accents Pubns.

Rose, A. H., ed. Advances in Microbial Physiology, Vol. 33. (Illus.). 424p. 1992. text ed. 115.00 (*0-12-027733-6*) Acad Pr.

— Advances in Microbial Physiology, Vol. 34. (Illus.). 356p. 1993. text ed. 110.00 (*0-12-027734-4*) Acad Pr.

— Advances in Microbial Physiology, Vol. 35. (Illus.). 352p. 1993. text ed. 99.00 (*0-12-027735-2*) Acad Pr.

— Advances in Microbial Physiology, Vols. 11-13. Incl. Vol. 13. 1976. 65.00 (*0-12-027713-1*); (Serial Publication Ser.). write for info. (*0-318-50201-1*) Acad Pr.

— Economic Microbiology Vol. 7. (Economic Microbiology Ser.). 1982. text ed. 141.00 (*0-12-596557-5*) Acad Pr.

— Economic Microbiology, Vol. 6: Microbial Biodeterioration. 516p. 1981. text ed. 184.00 (*0-12-596556-7*) Acad Pr.

— Products of Metabolism. 1978. text ed. 184.00 (*0-12-596552-4*) Acad Pr.

Rose, A. H. & Harrison, J. S. The Yeasts: Edited Treatise, Vol. 1. 2nd ed. 391p. 1987. text ed. 118.00 (*0-12-596411-0*) Acad Pr.

Rose, A. H. & Harrison, J. S., eds. The Yeasts, Vol. 2. 2nd ed. 282p. 1987. text ed. 116.00 (*0-12-596412-9*) Acad Pr.

— The Yeasts, Vol. 5. 2nd ed. (Illus.). 660p. 1993. text ed. 120.00 (*0-12-596415-3*) Acad Pr.

— The Yeasts, Vol. 3: Metabolism & Physiology of Yeasts. 2nd ed. 635p. 1989. text ed. 143.00 (*0-12-596413-7*) Acad Pr.

— The Yeasts, Vol. 4: Yeast Organelles. 2nd ed. (Serial Publication Ser.). 765p. 1991. text ed. 175.00 (*0-12-596414-5*) Acad Pr.

Rose, A. H. & Morris, Gareth, eds. Advances in Microbial Physiology, Vol. 21. LC 67-19850. (Serial Publication Ser.). 1981. text ed. 187.00 (*0-12-027721-2*) Acad Pr.

Rose, A. H. & Morris, J. G., eds. Advances in Microbial Physiology, Vol. 22. (Serial Publication Ser.). 1981. text ed. 187.00 (*0-12-027722-0*) Acad Pr.

Rose, A. H. & Morris, J. Gareth, eds. Advances in Microbial Physiology, Vol. 23. (Serial Publication Ser.). 268p. 1982. text ed. 154.00 (*0-12-027723-9*) Acad Pr.

Rose, A. H. & Tempest, David W., eds. Advances in Microbial Physiology. (Serial Publication Ser.: Vol. 30). 276p. 1990. text ed. 120.00 (*0-12-027730-1*) Acad Pr.

— Advances in Microbial Physiology, Vol. 27. (Serial Publication Ser.). 368p. 1986. text ed. 154.00 (*0-12-027727-1*) Acad Pr.

— Advances in Microbial Physiology, Vol. 28. (Serial Publication Ser.). 268p. 1987. text ed. 136.00 (*0-12-027728-X*) Acad Pr.

— Advances in Microbial Physiology, Vol. 29. (Serial Publication Ser.). 365p. 1988. text ed. 129.00 (*0-12-027729-8*) Acad Pr.

— Advances in Microbial Physiology, Vol. 31. 311p. 1990. text ed. 116.00 (*0-12-027731-X*) Acad Pr.

— Advances in Microbial Physiology, Vol. 32. (Illus.). 257p. 1991. text ed. 110.00 (*0-12-027732-8*) Acad Pr.

Rose, A. H., et al, eds. Advances in Microbial Physiology, Vol. 24. (Serial Publication Ser.). 1983. text ed. 154.00 (*0-12-027724-7*) Acad Pr.

— Advances in Microbial Physiology, Vol. 25. (Serial Publication Ser.). 1985. text ed. 154.00 (*0-12-027725-5*) Acad Pr.

Rose, A. James. Inquiring Children & Their Teachers. (Catherine Molony Memorial Lecture 1987 Ser.). 1987. pap. text ed. 5.00 (*0-918374-26-X*) City Coll Wk.

Rose, A. W. & Gundlach, H., eds. Geochemical Exploration Nineteen Eighty: Proceedings of the 1980 International Symposium in Hanover. (Developments in Economic Geology Ser.: Vol. 15). 698p. 1981. 210.25 (*0-444-42012-6*) Elsevier.

***Rose-Ackerman, Susan.** Controlling Environmental Policy: The Limits of Public Law in Germany & the United States. 1995. write for info. (*0-300-06065-3*) Yale U Pr.

— Corruption: A Study in Political Economy. 1978. text ed. 51.00 (*0-12-596350-5*) Acad Pr.

— Rethinking the Progressive Agenda: The Reform of the American Regulatory State. 224p. 1992. text ed. 27.95 (*0-02-926915-6*) Free Pr.

Rose-Ackerman, Susan, jt. auth. see James, Estelle.

Rose, Adam & Kolk, David, eds. Forecasting Natural Gas Demand in a Changing World. (Contemporary Studies in Economic & Financial Analysis: Vol. 60). 1987. 73.25 (*0-89232-838-X*) Jai Pr.

Rose, Adam, jt. auth. see Edmunds, Stahrl.

Rose, Adam, et al. Natural Resource Policy & Income Distribution. LC 87-2788. 176p. 1988. text ed. 31.00 (*0-8018-3523-2*) Johns Hopkins.

Rose, Adam Z. & Stevens, Benjamin H. Transboundary Income & Expenditure Flows in Regional Input-output Models. (Discussion Paper Ser.: No. 133). 32p. (C). 1989. pap. 10.00 (*1-55869-138-3*) Regional Sci Res Inst.

Rose, Adam Z., jt. auth. see Polenske, Karen R.

Rose, Adrian, ed. see Dolmetsch, Rudolph.

Rose, Agatha. Hide-&-Seek in the Yellow House. (Illus.). 32p. (J). (ps-1). 1992. lib. bdg. 14.00 (*0-670-84383-0*) Viking Child Bks.

— Hide & Seek in the Yellow House. (Illus.). 32p. (J). 1995. pap. 4.99 (*0-14-054482-8*) Puffin Bks.

Rose, Aidan, jt. auth. see Lawton, Alan.

Rose, Al. Born in New Orleans: Notables of Two Centuries. (Illus.). 1983. 17.50 (*0-916620-68-9*) Portals Pr.

— I Remember Jazz. LC 86-15307. (Illus.). xii, 257p. 1987. 24.95 (*0-8071-1315-8*) La State U Pr.

— Storyville New Orleans: Being an Authentic, Illustrated Account of the Notorious Red Light District. 1974. pap. 16.50 (*0-8173-4403-9*) U of Ala Pr.

Rose, Al & Souchon, Edmond. New Orleans Jazz: A Family Album. enl. rev. ed. LC 84-5721. (Illus.). vii, 362p. 1984. pap. 19.95 (*0-8071-1173-2*) La State U Pr.

Rose, Alan. Build Your Own Empire State Building. LC 94-2619. 1994. pap. 14.38 (*0-201-62705-1*) Addison-Wesley.

— Surrealism & Communism: The Early Years. LC 91-2231. (American University Studies: History: Ser. IX, Vols. 96). 343p. (C). 1991. text ed. 49.95 (*0-8204-1384-4*) P Lang Pubs.

Rose, Alan, jt. auth. see Boyles, Denis.

Rose, Albert. Electron Phonon Interactions: A Novel Semiclassical Approach. 192p. 1989. text ed. 46.00 (*9971-5-0635-1*) World Scientific Pub.

— Governing Metropolitan Toronto: A Social & Political Analysis. LC 72-157821. 201p. 1972. 19.95 (*0-87772-353-2*) UCB IGS.

— Governing Metropolitan Toronto: A Social & Political Analysis, 1953-1971. LC 72-157821. (Lane Studies in Regional Government). 227p. reprint ed. pap. 64.70 (*0-685-23958-6*, 2031512) Bks Demand.

Rose, Alexander G., III & Savoye, Jeffrey A. Such Friends As These. 1986. pap. 5.00 (*0-910556-24-5*) Enoch Pratt.

Rose, Alice, jt. auth. see Rose, Kent.

Rose, Allen J., jt. auth. see Gilman, Leonard.

Rose, Amber. Bee in Balance: A Guide to Healing the Whole Person with Honeybees, Oriental Medicine & Common Sense. Dumoff, Alan, ed. (Illus.). 320p. 1994. pap. 34.95 (*0-9641810-0-2*) Starpoint Ent.

Rose, Andrea. Pre-Raphaelites. (Color Library). (Illus.). 128p. (C). 1994. pap. 14.95 (*0-7148-2907-2*, Pub. by Phaidon Press UK) Chronicle Bks.

— Pre-Raphaelites. (Color Library). (Illus.). 128p. (C). 1994. reprint ed. 19.95 (*0-7148-3240-5*, Pub. by Phaidon Press UK) Chronicle Bks.

Rose, Andrea, pref. The Germ: Literary Magazine of the Pre-Raphaelites. (Illus.). 194p. 1995. 19.95 (*1-85444-023-3*, 0233, Pub. by Ashmolean Mus UK); pap. 15.95 (*1-85444-024-1*, 0241, Pub. by Ashmolean Mus UK) A Schwartz & Co.

Rose, Andy, ed. Twice Blessed: On Being Lesbian or Gay & Jewish. LC 89-42598. 320p. 1991. pap. 16.00 (*0-8070-7909-X*) Beacon Pr.

***Rose, Angie & Weiss, Lynn.** Self Esteem: Giving Children from Birth to Six the Freedom to Grow. LC 83-81434. (Illus.). 192p. (Orig.). 1995. lib. bdg. 26.95 (*0-614-07068-6*, 2246X09) Humanics Ltd.

— Self Esteem: Giving Children from Birth to Six the Freedom to Grow. rev. ed. LC 83-81434. 170p. (Orig.). (C). 1984. pap. 16.95 (*0-89334-046-4*) Humanics Ltd.

Rose, Anne C. Victorian America & the Civil War. (Illus.). 272p. (C). 1992. 49.95 (*0-521-41081-9*) Cambridge U Pr.

— Victorian America & the Civil War. (Illus.). 320p. (C). 1994. pap. 15.95 (*0-521-47883-9*) Cambridge U Pr.

— Voices of the Marketplace: American Thought & Culture, 1830-1860. (American Thought & Culture Ser.). (Illus.). 272p. 1994. text ed. 27.95x (*0-8057-9065-9*, Twayne); pap. 15.95 (*0-8057-9075-6*, Twayne) Macmillan.

Rose, Anthony H. Chemical Microbiology. 2nd ed. LC 68-28664. 324p. reprint ed. pap. 92.40 (*0-685-15664-8*, 2026288) Bks Demand.

Rose, Arnold M. Assuring Freedom to the Free: A Century of Emancipation in the U. S. A. LC 63-14634. 311p. reprint ed. pap. 88.70 (*0-7837-3789-0*, 2043609) Bks Demand.

— The Institutions of Advanced Societies. LC 57-11006. 703p. reprint ed. pap. 180.00 (*0-317-41639-1*, 2055903) Bks Demand.

— Libel & Academic Freedom: A Lawsuit Against Political Extremists. LC 68-19743. 299p. reprint ed. pap. 85.30 (*0-317-29499-7*, 2055905) Bks Demand.

— Migrants in Europe: Problems of Acceptance & Adjustment. LC 76-76162. 206p. reprint ed. pap. 58.80 (*0-318-39692-0*, 2033287) Bks Demand.

Rose, Arnold M., ed. Aging in Minnesota: A Report of the Minnesota Planning Committee for the White House Conference on Aging, Governor's Citizens Council on Aging. LC 63-13884. 334p. reprint ed. pap. 95.20 (*0-8357-5260-7*, 2055904) Bks Demand.

Rose, Arthur, et al. Geochemistry in Mineral Exploration. 2nd ed. 1980. pap. text ed. 61.00 (*0-12-596252-5*) Acad Pr.

Rose, Augustus F. How to Work Copper for Fun & Profit. (Illus.). 125p. 1993. reprint ed. 23.00 (*1-877767-89-1*) Univ Publng Hse.

Rose, Augustus F. & Cirino, Antonio. Jewelry Making & Design. (Illus.). 1949. pap. 7.95 (*0-486-21750-7*) Dover.

Rose, Barbara. American Painting: The Twentieth Century, Vol. II. LC 85-43548. (Illus.). 180p. 1986. pap. 25.00 (*0-8478-0716-9*) Rizzoli Intl.

— Ellsworth Kelly: Curves - Rectangles. Bell, Suzanne, ed. 32p. 1989. pap. 20.00 (*0-924008-04-0*) Blum Helman.

— Magdalena Abakanowicz. LC 93-26843. 1994. 49.50 (*0-8109-1947-8*) Abrams.

— Ronald Davis: Dodecagons, 1968-69. (Illus.). 32p. (Orig.). 1989. pap. 15.00 (*0-924008-03-2*) Blum Helman.

— Tsuda Umeko & Women's Education in Japan. (Illus.). 224p. 1992. text ed. 27.00 (*0-300-05177-8*) Yale U Pr.

Rose, Barbara, ed. Art As Art: The Selected Writings of Ad Reinhardt. (Illus.). 253p. 1991. reprint ed. pap. 13.00 (*0-520-07670-2*) U CA Pr.

Rose, Barbara, ed. see Namuth, Hans.

Rose, Barbara, jt. auth. see Spender, Matthew.

Rose, Barbara A., jt. auth. see Baron, Howard C.

Rose, Barry. The Family Guide to Homeopathy. LC 93-3586. 1993. 32.95 (*0-89087-695-9*) Celestial Arts.

***Rose, Ben L.** The History of Hebron Presbyterian Church: Manakin-Sabot, Virginia. (Illus.). 128p. 1993. 19.95 (*1-881576-12-4*) Providence Hse.

R

— T. U. L. I. P. Sermons on the Five Points of Calvinism. 64p. (Orig.). 1992. pap. 5.95 (1-881576-01-9) Providence Hse.

— T. U. L. I. P. Study Guide. 8p. 1994. pap. 2.50 (1-881576-07-8) Providence Hse.

Rose, Bernice. Allegories of Modernism: Contemporary Drawing. 1992. pap. 19.95 (0-8109-6103-2) Abrams.

— Allegories of Modernism: Contemporary Drawing. (Illus.). 128p. 1992. pap. 19.95 (0-87070-325-0, 0-8109-6103-2) Mus of Modern Art.

— Henry Moore: A Sculptor's Drawings. 70p. (Orig.). 1993. pap. write for info. (1-878283-39-1) PaceWildenstein.

— New Work on Paper Three. (Illus.). 100p. (Orig.). 1985. pap. 12.50 (0-87070-508-3) Mus of Modern Art.

***Rose, Bernice, contrib.** Picasso & Drawing. (Illus.). 120p. (Orig.). 1995. pap. write for info. (1-878283-50-2) PaceWildenstein.

Rose, Bernice & Temkin, Ann. Thinking Is Form: The Drawings of Joseph Beuys. LC 92-81535. (Illus.). 224p. 1993. 50.00 (0-500-01547-3) Thames Hudson.

Rose, Bernice, jt. auth. see Temkin, Ann.

***Rose, Billy.** Wine, Women & Words. (American Autobiography Ser.). 295p. 1995. reprint ed. lib. bdg. 79.00 (0-7812-8631-X) Rprt Serv.

Rose, Brian, jt. auth. see Matsuoka, Mikihiro.

Rose, Brian G. An Examination of Narrative Structure in Four Films of Frank Capra. Jowett, Garth S., ed. LC 79-6683. (Dissertations on Film, 1980 Ser.). 1980. lib. bdg. 18.95 (0-405-12915-7) Ayer.

— Televising the Performing Arts: Interviews with Merrill Brockway, Kirk Browning, & Roger Englander. LC 92-10677. (Contributions to the Study of Music & Dance Ser.: No. 29). 216p. 1992. text ed. 47.95 (0-313-28617-5, RTR/, Greenwood Pr) Greenwood.

— Television & the Performing Arts: A Handbook & Reference Guide to American Cultural Programming. LC 85-14655. 291p. 1986. text ed. 49.95 (0-313-24159-7, RTV/, Greenwood Pr) Greenwood.

Rose, Brian G., ed. Modern Trends in Education. LC 79-174706. 1972. text ed. 29.95 (0-312-54250-X) St Martin.

Rose, Brian G. & Alley, Robert S., eds. TV Genres: A Handbook & Reference Guide. LC 84-22460. ix, 453p. 1985. text ed. 65.00 (0-313-23724-7, RHG/, Greenwood Pr) Greenwood.

Rose, Burton D. Clinical Physiology of Acid-Base & Electrolyte Disorders. 4th ed. (Illus.). 915p. 1994. pap. text ed. 37.00 (0-07-053663-5) Hlth Prof Div.

— Manual of Complete Neph ISE. 1988. 15.95 (0-316-75635-0) Little.

Rose, Burton D., ed. Pathophysiology of Renal Disease. 2nd ed. (Illus.). 623p. 1987. pap. text ed. 35.00 (0-07-053629-5) Hlth Prof Div.

Rose, Burton D. & Black, Robert. Manual of Clinical Problems in Nephrology. 375p. 1988. 29.95 (0-316-75637-7, Little Med Div) Little.

Rose, Burton D. & Rennke, Helmut G. Renal Pathophysiology. LC 93-13959. (Illus.). 352p. 1994. 26.00 (0-683-07354-0) Williams & Wilkins.

Rose, C. L. & De Torres, A. R. Storage of Natural History Collections: Ideas & Practical Solutions. 360p. (C). 1992. spiral bd. 30.00 (0-9635476-0-7) Soc Preser NHC.

Rose, Calvin W., jt. ed. see Ghadiri, Hossein.

***Rose, Candi & Thomas, Dirk.** Net.Sex: A Discreet Guide to the Adult Side of the Internet. (Illus.). 250p. (Orig.). 1995. pap. text ed. 19.99 (0-672-30702-2) Sams.

Rose, Carla. It's a Mad, Mad, Mad, Mad Mac. LC 93-33691. 1994. pap. text ed. 27.95 (0-07-053662-7, Windcrest) TAB Bks.

— It's Mad, Mad, Mad Mac. 1994. disk 27.95 (0-8306-4535-7, Windcrest) TAB Bks.

— Mac Online: Making the Connection. (Illus.). 448p. 1992. pap. 24.95 (0-8306-4254-4, 4296, Windcrest) TAB Bks.

— Mac Online! Making the Connection. 1993. pap. 24.95 (0-07-053656-2) McGraw.

— Turbocharge Your MAC! Make Any Mac Faster & Smarter. 1993. pap. text ed. 32.95 (0-8306-4443-1, Windcrest) TAB Bks.

— Turbocharge Your Mac! Make Any Mac Faster & Smarter. 1993. pap. text ed. 32.95 (0-07-053660-0) TAB Bks.

Rose, Carla & Lewis, R. The Essential Pagemaker 5.0. (Illus.). 400p. (Orig.). 1993. pap. 24.95 (1-56761-249-0) Alpha Bks IN.

Rose, Carla & Rose, Jay. First Book of the Mac. 2nd ed. (First Bks.). (Illus.). 375p. 1992. pap. 18.95 (0-672-27418-3) Alpha Bks IN.

Rose, Carol, ed. see Evans, K., et al.

Rose, Carol J. The Full Four. 135p. (C). 1990. 39.00 (1-878490-60-5); lib. bdg. 49.00 (1-878490-61-3) Rosehips Ink.

— Step Mother: An Epistolary Novel. LC 89-92530. 300p. (C). 1990. 49.00 (1-878490-58-3); lib. bdg. 59.00 (1-878490-59-1) Rosehips Ink.

— The Tarot Gypsy Tales. LC 89-92413. (Illus.). 300p. (C). 1990. 59.00 (1-878490-50-8); lib. bdg. 69.00 (1-878490-51-6) Rosehips Ink.

— The Tarot Gypsy Trips. 1995. 49.00 (1-878490-64-8); lib. bdg. 59.00 (1-878490-65-6) Rosehips Ink.

Rose, Carol M. Property & Persuasion: Essays on the History, Theory, & Rhetoric of Ownership. LC 94-10741. (New Perspectives on Law, Culture, & Society Ser.). 1994. text ed. 65.00 (0-8133-8554-7) Westview.

— Property & Persuasion: Essays on the History, Theory, & Rhetoric of Ownership. LC 94-10741. (New Perspectives on Law, Culture, & Society Ser.). (C). 1994. pap. text ed. 22.95 (0-8133-8555-5) Westview.

Rose, Cecy, illus. Profound Writings, East & West. 242p. 1988. 14.00 (1-878683-05-5) TAT Found.

Rose, Charles G. Netware Power Tools for Window. 1993. pap. 54.95 (0-679-79099-3) Random.

— Netware Power Tools for Windows. 1993. disk, pap. 54.95 (0-553-37039-1) Bantam.

***Rose, Charlotte.** A Dangerous Day. (Orig.). 1995. pap. text ed. 5.95 (1-56333-293-0) Masquerade.

— The Doctor Is In. (Orig.). 1994. pap. 4.95 (1-56333-195-0) Masquerade.

— Women at Work. (Orig.). 1993. pap. 4.95 (1-56333-088-1) Masquerade.

Rose, Christiana. Healing Wonders. 80p. (Orig.). 1984. pap. 5.95 (0-87961-145-6) Naturegraph.

Rose, Christine. Ancestors & Descendants of Robert Rose of Wethersfield & Branford, Connecticut, Who Came on the Ship "Francis" in 1634 from Ipswich, England. LC 83-62117. (Illus.). xvi, 512p. 1983. write for info. (0-929626-02-8) Rose Family Assn.

— Ancestors & Descendants of the Brothers Rev. Robert Rose & Rev. Charles Rose of Colonial Virginia & Wester Alves, Morayshire, Scotland: With Information on Their Brothers Patrick, James, Hugh, George & Alexander. LC 84-62409. (Illus.). xvi, 318p. 1985. write for info. (0-929626-01-X) Rose Family Assn.

— Nicknames: Past & Present. 29p. 1991. pap. 4.50 (0-929626-04-4) Rose Family Assn.

— Rose War Files, Vol. I: Abstracts of Rose Land Bounty Records. 210p. 1987. pap. 13.50 (0-929626-00-1) Rose Family Assn.

— Santa Clara County, California Declarations of Intention, Bk. A, B, & C. iv, 76p. 1990. Book A (1850-1857), Book B (1862-1867), Book C (1848-1870). per. 9.75 (0-929626-03-6) Rose Family Assn.

Rose, Clare. Children's Clothes. (Illus.). 160p. 1990. pap. 24.95 (0-89676-111-8) Drama Bk.

Rose, Clare & Nyre, G. F., eds. Agents of Academic Change: The Pandora's Box. (Journal: Vol. 6, No. 1, 1980). 1980. pap. 15.25 (3-8055-0554-X) S Karger.

Rose, Clifford F., ed. Methodological Problems of Clinical Trials in Dementia. (Journal: Neuroepidemiology: Vol. 9, No. 4, 1990). (Illus.). 60p. 1990. pap. 36.00 (3-8055-5239-4) S Karger.

— Modern Approaches to the Dementias, Part I: Etiology & Pathophysiology. (Interdisciplinary Topics in Gerontology Ser.: Vol. 19). (Illus.). x, 230p. 1985. 142.50 (3-8055-3980-0) S Karger.

Rose, Clifford F. & Capildeo, Rudy E. Stroke: The Facts. (Facts Ser.). (Illus.). 1981. text ed. 19.95 (0-19-261170-4) OUP.

Rose, Clifford F. & Fields, W S., eds. Neuro Oncology. (Progress in Experimental Tumor Research Ser.: Vol. 29). (Illus.). xiv, 274p. 1985. 184.00 (3-8055-4054-X) S Karger.

Rose, Clive. Campaigns Against Western Defense: NATO's Adversaries & Critics. LC 84-18067. 320p. 1985. text ed. 32.50 (0-312-11469-9) St Martin.

Rose, Clive & Blaker, Peter. Perception & Reality: An Opion Poll on Defence & Disarmament Commentaries. (C). 1990. 45.00 (0-907967-72-8, Pub. by Inst Euro Def & Strat UK) St Mut.

Rose, Colin. Accelerated Learning. (Orig.). 1987. pap. 11.95 (0-440-50044-3, Dell Trade Pbks) Dell.

Rose, Colin & Rose, Diana. Accelerated Learning. (Illus.). 240p. (Orig.). (C). 1985. pap. text ed. 9.95 (0-905553-12-8, Pub. by Accel Lrn Sys UK) Acclrtd Learn.

Rose, Colliston R. Fundamental Approaches in Mastering the Sciences: A Practical Guide for Science Students. LC 89-81166. (Illus.). 350p. (Orig.). (C). 1988. pap. text ed. 24.95 (0-935132-10-4) C H Fairfax.

Rose, Constance H. Alonso Nunez de Reinoso. LC 77-99324. 309p. 1975. 35.00 (0-8386-7612-X) Fairleigh Dickinson.

Rose, Cordelia. Courierspeak: A Phrase Book for Couriers of Museum Objects. LC 92-33621. (Illus.). 160p. (Orig.). 1993. pap. text ed. 14.95 (1-56098-195-4) Smithsonian.

Rose, Cornelia B., Jr. National Policy for Radio Broadcasting. LC 71-161172. (History of Broadcasting: Radio to Television Ser.). 1977. reprint ed. 26.95 (0-405-03580-2) Ayer.

Rose, Courtice G., jt. ed. see Rittenhouse, Jonathan.

Rose, Cynthia. Design after Dark. LC 92-62131. (Illus.). 160p. 1993. pap. 22.50 (0-500-27648-X) Thames Hudson.

— Living in America: The Soul Saga of James Brown. 1991. pap. 10.95 (1-85242-209-2) Serpents Tail.

— Lottie Deno: Gambling Queen of Hearts. LC 93-5335. (Illus.). 120p. 1993. 22.95 (0-940666-33-2); pap. 12.95 (0-940666-38-3) Clear Light.

Rose, D. J., ed. Nuclear-Electric Power in the Asia-Pacific Region: Proceedings of the Workshop Held in Honolulu, Hawaii, 23-28 January 1983. 265p. 1985. pap. 61.00 (0-08-031654-9, Pergamon Pr) Elsevier.

Rose, Dan. Black American Street Life: South Philadelphia, 1969-1971. LC 87-17830. (Conduct & Communication Ser.). (Illus.). 288p. (C). 1987. text ed. 46.95 (0-8122-8071-7); pap. text ed. 17.95x (0-8122-1245-2) U of Pa Pr.

— Living the Ethnographic Life. (Qualitative Research Methods Ser.: Vol. 23). 64p. (C). 1990. text ed. 21.50 (0-8039-3998-1); pap. text ed. 9.50 (0-8039-3999-X) Sage.

— Patterns of American Culture: Ethnography & Estrangement. LC 89-33964. (Contemporary Ethnography Ser.). (Illus.). 138p. (C). 1989. pap. text ed. 14.95x (0-8122-1285-1) U of Pa Pr.

Rose, Daniel E. A Symbolic & Connectionist Approach to Legal Information Retrieval. 328p. 1994. text ed. 59.95 (0-8058-1388-8) L Erlbaum Assocs.

Rose, Danis, jt. auth. see McCarthy, Jack.

Rose, Daphne A. Geriatric Nutrition. 3rd ed. 288p. 1991. text ed. 62.00 (0-13-353046-9) P-H.

Rose, Darlene D. Evidence Not Seen: A Woman's Miraculous Faith in the Jungles of World War II. LC 86-43018. 192p. 1990. reprint ed. pap. 11.00 (0-06-067020-7) Harper SF.

Rose, Darrell D. Digital Circuit Logic & Design Through Experimentation. (Illus.). 256p. (C). 1982. pap. text ed. 12.50 (0-911908-13-7) Tech Ed Pr.

Rose, Dave. DOS: For Real Life. 6th ed. 1993. 10.95 (1-56901-211-3) NW Pub.

Rose, David. Home, School & Faith: Towards an Understanding of Religious Diversity. 128p. 1992. pap. 23.00 (1-85346-179-2, Pub. by D Fulton UK) Taylor & Francis.

***Rose, David & Dobson, Vernon G., eds.** Models of the Visual Cortex. LC 84-29143. (Illus.). 608p. 1985. reprint ed. pap. 173.30 (0-7837-8873-8, 2049584) Bks Demand.

Rose, David & Gregson, Richard. Beneath the Mountains. large type ed. 416p. 1988. 15.95 (0-7089-1886-7) Ulverscroft.

Rose, David & Sullivan, Oriel. Introducing Data Analysis for Social Scientists. LC 92-31162. 1993. pap. 39.00 (0-335-09708-1, Open Univ Pr) Taylor & Francis.

Rose, David, jt. auth. see Radford, John.

Rose, David, jt. ed. see Radford, John.

Rose, David J. Learning about Energy. LC 85-28218. (Modern Perspectives in Energy Ser.). 528p. 1986. 85.00 (0-306-42124-0, Plenum Pr) Plenum.

Rose, David P. Endocrinology of Cancer, 3 vols., Vol. 1. 160p. 1982. 67.95 (0-8493-5337-8, RC271, CRC Reprint) Franklin.

— Endocrinology of Cancer, 3 vols., Vol. 2. 160p. 1982. 67.95 (0-8493-5338-6, CRC Reprint) Franklin.

— Endocrinology of Cancer, 3 vols., Vol. 3. 208p. 1982. Vol. III, 208p. 75.00 (0-8493-5339-4, RC271, CRC Reprint) Franklin.

Rose, David S. Lord, Make Everything All Right. (Illus.). 158p. (Orig.). 1982. pap. 5.95 (0-918769-31-0) Univ South Pr.

— Loving God: Journey to a More Mature Faith. (Illus.). 70p. (Orig.). 1990. pap. text ed. 9.50 (0-9627687-0-7) Proctors Hall Pr.

— Loving God: Journey to a More Mature Faith. 70p. (Orig.). 1990. pap. 9.50 (0-918769-32-9) Univ South Pr.

— Maynard's Dreams. LC 92-43146. (Illus.). 32p. (J). (ps-3). 1993. text ed. 14.95 (0-689-31847-2, Atheneum Bks Young) S&S Childrens.

Rose, Deborah B. Dingo Makes Us Human. 250p. (C). 1992. 54.95 (0-521-39269-1) Cambridge U Pr.

Rose, Deborah F., jt. auth. see Smith, Barbara J.

Rose, Deborah L. Meredith's Mother Takes the Train. Levine, Abby, ed. LC 90-12756. (Illus.). 24p. (J). (ps-00). 1991. 11.95 (0-8075-5061-2) A Whitman.

— The People Who Hugged the Trees. LC 90-62832. (Illus.). 32p. (J). (gr. 4-8). 1994. pap. 6.95 (1-879373-50-5) R Rinehart.

— The People Who Hugged the Trees: An Environmental Folk Tale. (Illus.). 32p. 1990. lib. bdg. 12.95 (0-911797-80-7) R Rinehart.

— The Rose Horse. LC 94-19629. (Illus.). 1996. write for info. (0-15-200068-2) HarBrace.

Rose, Dennis. Lewis: Australian Bankruptcy Law. 9th ed. xxiv, 301p. 1990. pap. 39.00 (0-455-20968-5, Pub. by Law Bk Co) W W Gaunt.

— Lewis: Australian Bankruptcy Law. 10th ed. 1994. write for info. (0-455-21236-8, Pub. by Law Bk Co); pap. write for info. (0-455-21237-6, Pub. by Law Bk Co) W W Gaunt.

Rose, Diana, ed. see Bate, Michele & Miller, Arthur.

Rose, Diana, ed. see Gateva, Evelyna.

Rose, Diana, ed. see Gatti-Doyle, Gigi & Doyle, Terry.

Rose, Diana, ed. see Kattan-Ibarra, Juan & Stockton, Dennis.

Rose, Diana, ed. see Labiosa-Cassone, Libyan.

Rose, Diana, ed. see Margulies, Nancy.

Rose, Diana, jt. auth. see Rose, Colin.

Rose, Diana, ed. see Schlotmann, Lisa, et al.

Rose, Dilys. Red Tides. 176p. 1994. pap. 17.95 (0-436-42581-5, Pub. by Seck & Warburg UK) Trafalgar.

***Rose, Donald.** Internet Chat Quick Tour: Carrying on Real-Time Conversations & Communication Online. (Illus.). 200p. 1995. 14.00 (1-56604-223-2) Ventana Pr.

— Minding Your CyberManners on the Internet. (Illus.). 208p. (Orig.). 1994. pap. 12.99 (1-56761-521-X) Alpha Bks IN.

Rose, Donald K. The Vacation-Condo Game. LC 84-60563. (Illus.). 126p. 1984. pap. 11.95 (0-88100-042-6) Natl Writ Pr.

Rose, Donna, ed. see Krigger, John T.

Rose, Donna L., ed. see Magnin, John D.

Rose, Dorothy. Baby Games: Follow Me. (J). (ps). 1994. pap. 3.50 (0-671-88361-5, Litl Simon S&S) S&S Childrens.

— Baby Games: Peek A Boo. (J). (ps). 1994. pap. 3.50 (0-671-88358-5, Litl Simon S&S) S&S Childrens.

— Baby Games: What Do Lambs Say? (J). (ps). 1994. pap. 3.50 (0-671-88359-3, Litl Simon S&S) S&S Childrens.

— Baby Games: Where's Your Nose. (J). (ps). 1994. pap. 3.50 (0-671-88360-7, Litl Simon S&S) S&S Childrens.

— Haunted House. 1985. pap. 2.25 (0-671-52539-5) S&S Trade.

Rose, Dorothy, ed. see Harvey, William J., III.

Rose, Dorothy J., ed. see Harvey, William J., III.

Rose, Douglas, ed. The Emergence of David Duke & the Politics of Race. LC 92-5331. (Tulane Studies in Political Science). (Illus.). xxvi, 270p. (C). 1992. pap. 13.95 (0-8078-4381-4) U of NC Pr.

Rose, Earlene. Rose's for You: Inspirational. 1982. 4.95 (0-916620-66-2) Portals Pr.

Rose, Edgar. New Roles for Old Cities: Adapting to Economic Social Change. 240p. 1986. text ed. 56.50 (0-566-05182-6, Pub. by Avebury Pub UK) Ashgate Pub Co.

Rose, Edward J. Henry George. (Twayne's United States Authors Ser.). 1968. lib. bdg. 17.95 (0-8290-1700-3) Irvington.

— Henry George. (Twayne's United States Authors Ser.). 1968. pap. 13.95 (0-8084-0003-7, T128) NCUP.

Rose, Elaine O., jt. auth. see Irvin, Judith L.

Rose, Elisabeth. Body Sharers: A Novel. LC 92-28944. (Fiction Ser.). 205p. (C). 1993. 17.95 (0-8135-1934-9) Rutgers U Pr.

Rose, Elizabeth. Lady of Gray, Healing Candida: Nightmare Chemical Epidemic. 2nd ed. LC 85-70122. (Illus.). 178p. 1986. reprint ed. pap. 10.95 (0-9614637-1-6) Butterfly NY.

— Sainthood & Single Motherhood: Laugh Yourself Back to Sanity. 1990. 10.45 (0-9614637-7-5) Butterfly NY.

Rose, Ellen C. The Novels of Margaret Drabble: Equivocal Figures. (Illus.). 141p. 1980. 44.00 (0-389-20006-9, N6783) B&N Imports.

Rose, Ellen C., jt. auth. see Kaplan, Carey.

Rose, Ellen C., jt. ed. see Kaplan, Carey.

Rose, Elliot. Cases of Conscience: Alternatives Open to Recusants & Puritans under Elizabeth I & James I. LC 74-76947. 274p. reprint ed. pap. 78.10 (0-685-16075-0, 2027243) Bks Demand.

— A Razor for a Goat: A Discussion of Certain Problems in the History of Witchcraft & Diabolism. 265p. 1989. pap. 15.95 (0-8020-6768-9) U of Toronto Pr.

***Rose, Emerald.** You're the Reason Our Kids Are Ugly. 1995. pap. 7.50 (0-06-273363-X, Harper Ref) HarpC.

Rose, Emma, tr. see Morazzoni, Marta.

Rose, Enid. Gordon Craig & the Theatre. LC 72-6840. (Studies in Drama: No. 39). (Illus.). 260p. 1972. reprint ed. lib. bdg. 59.95 (0-8383-1641-7) M S G Haskell Hse.

***Rose, Eugene.** Nihilism: The Root of the Revolution of the Modern Age. 1994. pap. 5.95 (0-938635-15-8) St Herman AK.

Rose, Evelyn. Jewish Cooking. 1991. 10.99 (0-517-06146-5) Random Hse Value.

— The New Complete International Jewish Cookbook. rev. ed. LC 92-44700. 736p. 1993. 29.95 (0-88184-927-8) Carroll & Graf.

Rose, F., ed. Contract & Tort Statutes. (C). 1991. 75.00 (1-85431-181-6, Pub. by Blackstone Pr UK) W W Gaunt.

Rose, F. Clifford. Amyotrophic Lateral Sclerosis. (Illus.). 275p. 1990. 69.95 (0-939957-23-X) Demos Vermande.

— James Parkinson: His Life & Times by A. D. Morris. 308p. 1989. 76.50 (0-8176-3401-0) Birkhauser.

Rose, F. Clifford, ed. Advances in Migraine Research & Therapy. 248p. 1982. text ed. 94.50 (0-89004-848-7) Raven.

— Advances in Stroke Therapy. 348p. 1982. text ed. 134.00 (0-89004-847-9) Raven.

— Clinical Trials in Multiple Sclerosis. (Journal: Neuroepidemiology: Vol. 6, No. 1-2, 1987). (Illus.). 92p. 1987. pap. 54.50 (3-8055-4577-0) S Karger.

— The Control of the Hypothalamo-Pituitary-Andrenocortical Axis. 470p. 1989. 65.00 (0-8236-1070-5) Intl Univs Pr.

— Interdisciplinary Topics in Gerontology, Set, Vols. 19 & 20. (Illus.). xx, 432p. 1985. Set. 269.00 (3-8055-3982-7) S Karger.

— The Management of Headache. 192p. 1988. text ed. 28.00 (0-88167-246-7) Raven.

— Modern Approaches to the Dementias, Pt. II: Clinical & Therapeutic Aspects. (Interdisciplinary Topics in Gerontology Ser.: Vol. 20). (Illus.). x, 202p. 1985. 126.50 (3-8055-3981-9) S Karger.

— Progress in Aphasiology. fac. ed. LC 84-15979. (Advances in Neurology Ser.: No. 42). (Illus.). 382p. Date not set. pap. 108.90 (0-7837-7269-6, 2047036) Bks Demand.

***Rose, F. D.** Blackstone's Statutes on Contract, Tort & Restitution: 1994-95. 5th ed. 309p. 1994. pap. 22.00 (1-85431-385-1, Pub. by Blackstone Pr UK) W W Gaunt.

— New Foundations for Insurance Law: Current Legal Problems. (C). 1987. 210.00 (0-685-32709-4, Pub. by Witherby & Co UK) St Mut.

Rose, F. D. & Johnson, D. A., eds. Recovery from Brain Damage: Reflections & Directions. (Advances in Experimental Medicine & Biology Ser.: Vol. 325). (Illus.). 200p. (C). 1993. 69.50 (0-306-44344-9, Plenum Pr) Plenum.

Rose, Ferrel. The Guises of Modesty: Marie von Ebner-Eschenbach's Female Artists. 250p. 1994. 49.95 (1-879751-69-0) Camden Hse.

Rose, Frances L. Wildflowers of the Llano Estacado. 1990. 12.95 (0-9617102-0-9) Rose-Strandtmann.

Rose, Francis. Blackstone's Statutes on Commercial Law. 2nd ed. 1992. pap. 34.00 (1-85431-247-2, Pub. by Blackstone Pr UK) W W Gaunt.

— International Commercial & Maritime Arbitration. (C). 1988. 150.00 (0-685-32767-1, Pub. by Witherby & Co UK) St Mut.

***Rose, Frank.** The Agency: The William Morris Agency & the Hidden History of Show Business. 1995. 30.00 (0-88730-749-3) Harper Busn.

— Employment Law. (C). 1987. 125.00 (0-901812-45-5); pap. 89.00 (0-901812-46-3) St Mut.

— West of Eden: The End of Innocence at Apple Computer. LC 88-40302. 288p. 1990. 19.95 (0-685-23144-5); pap. 8.95 (0-685-23145-3) Viking Penguin.

Rose, G., jt. auth. see Barker, D. J.

R

Rose, G. A. & Blackburn, H. Cardiovascular Survey Methods. (Monograph Ser.: No. 56). 188p. (ENG, FRE, RUS & SPA.). 1968. 11.20 (92-4-140056-0) World Health.

Rose, Gary L. Connecticut Politics at the Crossroads. LC 92-16636. 122p. (Orig.). (C). 1992. lib. bdg. 38.50 (0-8191-8755-0) U Pr of Amer.

— Connecticut Politics at the Crossroads. LC 92-16636. 122p. (Orig.). (C). 1992. pap. text ed. 14.50 (0-8191-8756-9) U Pr of Amer.

Rose, Gary L., ed. Controversial Issues in Presidential Selection. LC 90-46019. (SUNY Series on the Presidency). 343p. 1991. 57.50 (0-7914-0747-0); pap. 18.95 (0-7914-0748-9) State U NY Pr.

— Controversial Issues in Presidential Selection. 2nd ed. LC 93-5713. (SUNY Series on the Presidency: Contemporary Issues). 358p. 1994. 49.50 (0-7914-1935-5); pap. 16.95 (0-7914-1936-3) State U NY Pr.

***Rose, Gene.** Reflections of Shaver Lake. (Illus.). 128p. Date not set. pap. 14.95 (1-884995-04-7) Word Dancer.

Rose, Geoffrey. The Strategy of Preventive Medicine. (Illus.). 160p. 1994. reprint ed. pap. 16.95 (0-19-262486-5) OUP.

Rose, Geoffrey, ed. see Coggin, D.

Rose, Gerald. Grumps. (Illus.). 32p. (J). (gr. k-2). 1993. 17.95 (0-370-31575-8, Pub. by Bodley Head UK) Trafalgar.

— Trouble in the Ark. LC 89-37270. (J). (ps-1). 1989. 12.95 (0-8192-1511-2) Morehouse Pub.

— Trouble in the Ark. (Illus.). 32p. (J). 1995. pap. 8.95 (0-8192-1651-8) Morehouse Pub.

Rose, Gerald L. Management Decision Making. (C). 1987. text ed. 22.00 (0-316-75638-5) Little.

***Rose, Gilbert J.** Necessary Illusion: Art As "Witness" Resonance & Attunement to Forms & Feelings. 120p. 1995. text ed. 25.00 (0-8236-3510-4) Intl Univs Pr.

— The Power of Form: A Psychoanalytic Approach to Aesthetic Form. 2nd ed. 288p. (C). 1992. reprint ed. pap. text ed. 24.95 (0-8236-8188-2) Intl Univs Pr.

Rose, Gilbert J. & Farge, Andrew. The Power of Form. LC 79-53592. (Psychological Issues Monograph: No. 49, Vol. 13, No. 1). (Illus.). 252p. 1980. text ed. 32.50 (0-8236-4171-6) Intl Univs Pr.

Rose, Gilbert P. Plato: Crito. 2nd ed. 1983. pap. text ed. 6.00 (0-929524-24-1) Bryn Mawr Commentaries.

— Plato Apology. (Greek Commentaries Ser.). 104p. (Orig.). (C). 1989. pap. text ed. 7.00 (0-929524-56-X) Bryn Mawr Commentaries.

— Plato's Republic, Bk. 1. (Greek Commentaries Ser.). 91p. (Orig.). (C). 1983. pap. text ed. 6.00 (0-929524-31-4) Bryn Mawr Commentaries.

— Plato's Symposium. 2nd ed. (Greek Commentaries Ser.). 158p. (C). 1985. pap. text ed. 8.00 (0-929524-32-2) Bryn Mawr Commentaries.

— Sophocles Oedipus at Colonus. (Greek Commentaries Ser.). 132p. (Orig.). (C). 1988. pap. text ed. 7.00 (0-929524-34-9) Bryn Mawr Commentaries.

Rose, Gillian. The Broken Middle: Out of Our Ancient History. 336p. 1992. text ed. 54.95 (0-631-16359-X); pap. text ed. 22.95 (0-631-18221-7) Blackwell Pubs.

— Feminism & Geography: The Limits of Geographical Knowledge. LC 93-10411. 206p. 1993. text ed. 44.95 (0-8166-2417-8); pap. 17.95 (0-8166-2418-6) U of Minn Pr.

— Hegel: Contra Sociology. 260p. (C). 1995. pap. 25.00 (0-485-12036-4, Pub. by Athlone Pr UK) Humanities.

— Judaism & Modernity: Philosophical Essays. 256p. 1993. 49.95 (0-631-16436-7); pap. 19.95 (0-631-18971-8) Blackwell Pubs.

— Melancholy Science: An Introduction to the Thought of Theodor W. Adorno. 212p. 1979. text ed. 46.50 (0-231-04584-0) Col U Pr.

Rose, Gillian, jt. ed. see Blunt, Alison.

Rose, Gloria. The Color Purple Notes. 74p. (Orig.). (C). 1986. pap. text ed. 3.75 (0-8220-0308-2) Cliffs.

— Cooking for Good Health: Creative Recipes Without Added Fat, Sugar, or Salt. LC 93-617. 384p. 1993. pap. 13.95 (0-89529-577-6) Avery Pub.

— Enjoying Good Health. 320p. (Orig.). 1987. 12.50 (0-944785-00-X) Herm Barr Pub.

Rose, Gordon & Marshall, Tony F. Counselling & School Social Work: An Experimental Study. LC 74-2449. 355p. reprint ed. pap. 101.20 (0-317-09856-X, 2016524) Bks Demand.

Rose, Graham. The Low Maintenance Garden. New York Botanical Garden Institute of Urban Horticulture, ed. LC 83-3498. (Home Gardening Book Shelf Ser.). (Illus.). 168p. 1983. pap. 12.95 (0-670-44349-2) Viking Penguin.

— The Low-Maintenance Garden. 1987. pap. 19.95 (0-14-046807-2) Viking Penguin.

— The Romantic Garden: A Practical Guide to Creating a Beautiful Garden That Appeals to the Emotions As Well As the Senses. (Illus.). 168p. 1988. pap. 16.95 (0-14-046828-5, Penguin Bks) Viking Penguin.

***Rose, Graham & King, Peter, eds.** Good Gardens Guide 1995: Over 1,000 of the Best Gardens in the British Isles & Europe. (Illus.). 592p. 1995. pap. 22.95 (0-09-178365-8, Vermillion) Trafalgar.

***Rose, H. E.** A Course in Number Theory. 2nd ed. 416p. (C). 1995. text ed. 46.95 (0-19-853479-5) OUP.

— Subrecursion: Functions & Hierarchies. (Oxford Logic Guides Ser.). 1984. 39.95 (0-19-853189-3) OUP.

Rose, H. J. A Handbook of Latin Literature. 550p. reprint ed. 25.00 (0-8196-0356-2) Biblo.

Rose, H. J., tr. see Plutarchus.

Rose-Hancock, Marga, jt. ed. see McCrone, Carole N.

***Rose, Harold.** The Changing World of Finance & Its Problems. 57p. (Orig.). 1993. pap. text ed. 9.00 (0-89068-116-3, NPA 264) Natl Planning.

— The Question of Saving. 53p. (Orig.). 1991. pap. text ed. 8.00 (0-89068-106-6, BNAC 38(NPA249)) Natl Planning.

Rose, Harold M., ed. Geography of the Ghetto: Perceptions, Problems, & Alternatives. LC 72-1388. (Perspectives in Geography Ser.: Vol. 2). (Illus.). 273p. 1972. 22.00 (0-87580-031-9) N Ill U Pr.

Rose, Harold M. & McClain, Paula D. Race, Place, & Risk: Black Homicide in Urban America. LC 89-48538. (Series in Afro-American Studies). 297p. 1990. 64.50 (0-7914-0393-9); pap. 21.95 (0-7914-0394-7) State U NY Pr.

Rose, Harriet W. Something's Wrong with My Child! A Straightforward Presentation to Help Professionals & Parents to Better Understand Themselves in Dealing with the Emotionally-Charged Subject of Disabled Children. 210p. 1987. 37.95x (0-398-05325-1) C C Thomas.

— Something's Wrong with My Child! A Straightforward Presentation to Help Professionals & Parents to Better Understand Themselves in Dealing with the Emotionally-Charged Subject of Disabled Children. 210p. 1987. pap. 22.95 (0-398-06407-5) C C Thomas.

Rose, Harvey, jt. ed. see Campbell, David R.

Rose, Helen. Just Make Them Beautiful. LC 76-4764. (Illus.). 1982. 17.50 (0-930422-09-0) Dennis-Landman.

Rose, Helen W. Quilting with Strips & Strings: Full with Complete Instructions for Making 12 Patchwork Quiltblocks. (Quilting Ser.). (Illus.). 48p. (Orig.). 1983. pap. 3.95 (0-486-24357-5) Dover.

Rose, Helen Whitson. Quick & Easy Strip Quilting. 1989. pap. 4.95 (0-486-26018-6) Dover.

Rose, Henry. Henrik Ibsen: Poet, Mystic & Moralist. LC 72-1323. (Studies in Scandinavian Life & Literature: No. 18). 1972. reprint ed. lib. bdg. 75.00 (0-8383-1428-7) M S G Haskell Hse.

— Nonmodular Lattice Varieties. LC 83-22449. (Memoirs Ser.: No. 47/292). 76p. 1984. 16.00 (0-8218-2292-6, MEMO 47/292) Am Math.

— On Maeterlinck. LC 73-21891. (Studies in French Literature: No. 45). 1974. lib. bdg. 49.95 (0-8383-1829-0) M S G Haskell Hse.

Rose, Henry, jt. auth. see Jipsen, Peter.

Rose, Herbert J. Primitive Culture in Italy. LC 73-168503. (Select Bibliographies Reprint Ser.). 1977. reprint ed. 27.95 (0-8369-5948-5) Ayer.

Rose, Herbert J., ed. see Plutarch.

Rose, Herbert N., jt. ed. see Menendez-Botet, Celia.

Rose, Hieromonk S., tr. see Saint Theophan the Recluse.

Rose, Hilary. Love, Power, & Knowledge: Towards a Feminist Transformation of the Sciences. LC 94-1883. 1994. 45.00 (0-253-35046-8) Ind U Pr.

— Love, Power & Knowledge: Towards a Feminist Transformation of the Sciences. LC 94-1883. 1994. pap. 18.95 (0-253-20907-2) Ind U Pr.

Rose, Hilary, jt. ed. see Nowotny, Helga.

Rose, Horace A., ed. see Brown, John P.

Rose, Howard. The Marrano. LC 92-60817. 256p. 1992. 20.00 (1-878352-08-3); pap. 10.00 (1-878352-09-1) R Saroff Pub.

— Oak Street Beach. 120p. 1990. 16.00 (1-878352-06-7); pap. 9.00 (1-878352-07-5) R Saroff Pub.

— The Pooles of Pismo Bay. 430p. 1990. 20.00 (1-878352-04-0); pap. 10.00 (1-878352-05-9) R Saroff Pub.

— Twelve Ravens. 405p. 1990. reprint ed. 20.00 (1-878352-02-4); reprint ed. pap. 10.00 (1-878352-03-2) R Saroff Pub.

— Unexpected Eloquence: The Art in American Folk Art. (Illus.). 160p. 1990. 25.00 (1-878352-00-8); pap. 15.00 (1-878352-01-6) R Saroff Pub.

Rose, Howard A. No Bull Diet: A Lifetime Beyond Dieting. 1992. pap. 10.00 (0-9631828-0-3) Hart Mktg.

Rose, Hugh. Macroeconomic Dynamics: A Marshallian Synthesis. 200p. (C). 1990. text ed. 47.95 (1-55786-037-8) Blackwell Pubs.

Rose-Hulman, jt. auth. see Grimaldi, Ralph P.

Rose, I. Nelson. Gambling & the Law. (Illus.). 308p. 1985. 19.95 (0-89746-066-9) Gambling Times.

Rose-Innes, A. Vocabulary of Common Japanese Words. (JPN.). 1945. 4.95 (0-88710-123-2) Yale Far Eastern Pubns.

Rose-Innes, A. C. & Rhoderick, E. H. Introduction to Superconductivity. 1978. pap. 48.00 (0-08-021652-8, Pergamon Pr) Elsevier.

— Introduction to Superconductivity. 2nd ed. 1978. text ed. 92.00 (0-08-021651-X, Pergamon Pr) Elsevier.

Rose-Innes, Arthur. Beginners' Dictionary of Chinese-Japanese Characters & Compounds. (CHI & JPN.). 1977. reprint ed. pap. 11.95 (0-486-23467-3) Dover.

Rose, Irene B., jt. auth. see Conger, Flora S.

Rose, J. Progress of Cybernetics, Vol. 1. xiv, 522p. 1970. text ed. 308.00 (0-677-14310-9) Gordon & Breach.

— Progress of Cybernetics, Vol. 2. xvi, 438p. 1970. 206.00 (0-685-47155-1) Gordon & Breach.

— Progress of Cybernetics, 3 vols., Vol. 3. 1420p. 1970. Set. text ed. 812.00 (0-677-14190-4); text ed. 275.00 (0-677-14330-3) Gordon & Breach.

Rose, J., ed. Acid Rain: Current Situation & Remedies. LC 94-1936. (Environmental Topics Ser.: Vol. 4, No. 1945-5294). 1993. text ed. 95.00 (2-88124-850-0) Gordon & Breach.

— Advances in Cybernetics & Systems, 3 vols., Set. 1790p. 1975. text ed. 826.00 (0-677-15650-2) Gordon & Breach.

— Human Stress & the Environment: Health Aspects. LC 94-2603. (Environmental Topics Ser.: Vol. 5). 1994. text ed. 147.00 (2-88124-851-9) Gordon & Breach.

— Survey of Cybernetics. 394p. 1969. text ed. 220.00 (0-677-60560-9) Gordon & Breach.

— Technological Injury: The Effect of Technological Advances on Environment Life & Society. 244p. 1969. pap. 63.00 (0-677-13645-5) Gordon & Breach.

— Trace Elements in Health: A Review of Current Issues. 320p. 1983. text ed. 95.00 (0-407-00255-3) Buttrwrth-Heinemann.

***Rose, J. & Smith, M.** Basic Hockey & Skating Skills: The Backyard Rink Approach. (Illus.). 160p. (Orig.). (J). (gr. 4-8). 1993. pap. 14.95 (0-919591-84-1, Pub. by Polestar Bk Pubs CN) Orca Bk Pubs.

Rose, J., jt. ed. see Menzies, J.

Rose, J. C., jt. auth. see Woollard, G. P.

Rose, J. L. Durative & Aoristic Tenses in Thucydides. (LD Ser.: No. 35). 1942. pap. 16.00 (0-527-00781-1) Periodicals Srv.

Rose, J. N., jt. auth. see Britton, Nathaniel L.

Rose, J. R., ed. see Gattefosse, Rene M.

Rose, Jack & Phil, M. Square Feet: The Autobiography of Jack Rose. 160p. 1993. pap. 59.00 (0-85406-565-2, Pub. by R-I-C-S Bks UK) St Mut.

Rose, Jack H. Christianity & Education: A Manifesto. LC 86-90551. 302p. (Orig.). 1986. pap. 34.95 (0-9617430-0-X) J H Rose.

Rose, Jacqueline. The Case of Peter Pan: or The Impossibility of Children's Fiction. rev. ed. LC 92-30533. (New Cultural Studies). 208p. (C). 1993. reprint ed. pap. text ed. 13.95 (0-8122-1435-8) U of Pa Pr.

— The Haunting of Sylvia Plath. (Convergences Ser.). 288p. (C). 1992. text ed. 24.95 (0-674-38225-0) HUP.

— Haunting of Sylvia Plath. 288p. 1993. pap. text ed. 14.95 (0-674-38226-9) HUP.

— Why War? Psychoanalysis, Politics & the Return to Melanie Klein. Schweizer, Harold, ed. (Bucknell Lectures in Literary Theory). 144p. 1993. 27.95 (0-631-18923-8); pap. 14.95 (0-631-18924-6) Blackwell Pubs.

Rose, Jacqueline, jt. ed. see Mitchell, Juliet.

Rose, James B. A Guide to American Christian Education for the Home & School: The Principle Approach. LC 85-82560. (Illus.). 550p. 1987. lib. bdg. 35.00 (0-9616201-1-0) Am Christ Hist.

Rose, James C. Gardens Make Me Laugh: A New Edition. LC 89-36437. (Illus.). 136p. 1990. text ed. 24.95 (0-8018-3861-4) Johns Hopkins.

Rose, James M. New York Vehicle & Traffic Law. LC 84-80365. 1984. 105.00 (0-318-01917-5) Lawyers Cooperative.

— New York Vehicle & Traffic Law. suppl. ed. LC 84-80365. 1993. Suppl. 1993. 45.00 (0-317-03245-3) Lawyers Cooperative.

Rose, James M. & Brown, Barbara W. Tapestry. (Illus.). 163p. (Orig.). 1979. pap. 4.95 (0-9607744-2-4) New London County.

Rose, Jane, ed. see Bouciault, Dion.

Rose, Jane, ed. see Davis, Rebecca H.

Rose, Jane A. Rebecca Harding Davis. (Twayne's United States Authors Ser.). 216p. 1993. text ed. 22.95 (0-8057-3958-0, Twayne) Macmillan.

Rose, Jay, jt. auth. see Rose, Carla.

Rose, Jeanne. Aroma-Color-Plant-Sound Correlations for Healing: A Practical Reference Table. (Illus.). 1990. student ed 9.95 (0-9620838-7-9, J R Herb Pubns) Herb Studies.

— The Aromatherapy Book: Applications & Inhalations. (Jeanne Rose Herbal Library). (Illus.). 395p. (Orig.). 1992. pap. 18.95 (1-55643-073-6) North Atlantic.

— Ask Jeanne Rose about Herbs. Passwater, Richard A. & Mindell, Earl, eds. (Good Health Guide Ser.). 32p. (Orig.). 1984. pap. text ed. 2.25 (0-87983-315-7) Keats.

— Guide to Essential Oils: Over Two Hundred Twenty-Five EO Listed. (Illus.). 90p. (Orig.). (C). 1994. spiral bd. 25.00 (1-879687-02-X) Herb Studies.

— Heart of Dreams. (Shadows Ser.). 1995. mass mkt. 3.50 (0-373-27055-0, 1-27055-2) Silhouette.

— The Herbal Body Book Pt. II: Herbs & Aromatherapy for Healthy Skin & Hair. Earle, Susan, ed. & intro. by. (Jeanne Rose Earth Medicine Ser.). (Illus.). 55p. (Orig.). 1994. per., pap. 4.95 (1-879687-04-6) Herb Studies.

— Herbs & Things: Jeanne Rose's Herbal. (Illus.). 1972. 12.00 (0-399-50944-5, Perigree Bks) Berkley Pub.

— Herbs for the Reproductive System. LC 94-19980. 128p. (Orig.). (C). 1994. pap. 7.95 (1-883319-17-X) Frog CA.

— Herbs for the Reproductive System, with Charts: Herbs for Men & Women, for Health, for Reproduction, Menstrual Regularity & Abortives. (Illus.). 1988. student ed 10.95 (0-9620838-9-5, J R Herb Pubns) Herb Studies.

— A History of Herbs & Herbalism: A Chronology from 10,000 BC to the Present. (Illus.). 52p. 1988. student ed 10.95 (0-9620838-6-0, J R Herb Pubns) Herb Studies.

— Jeanne Rose's Herbal Body Book. (Illus.). 400p. 1976. pap. 12.00 (0-399-50790-6, Perigree Bks) Berkley Pub.

— Jeanne Rose's Herbal Guide to Food: Eating Healthy the Herbal Way. 250p. (Orig.). 1989. 25.00 (1-55643-063-9); pap. 14.95 (1-55643-056-6) North Atlantic.

— Jeanne Rose's Herbal Studies Course: A Complete Home Study Herb Course, 3 vols. (Herbal Studies). (Illus.). 1200p. 1988. 125.00 (0-685-74261-X, J R Herb Pubns); Pt. II: The Medicinal Herbal, 400p. write for info. (0-9620838-3-6, J R Herb Pubns); Pt. III: The Reference Herbal, 450p. write for info. (0-9620838-4-4, J R Herb Pubns) Herb Studies.

— Jeanne Rose's Herbal Studies Course: A Complete Home Study Herb Course, 3 vols., Pt. I: The Seasonal Herbal. (Herbal Studies). (Illus.). 350p. 1988. 125.00 (0-9620838-2-8, J R Herb Pubns) Herb Studies.

— Jeanne Rose's Herbal Studies Course: A Complete Home Study Herb Course, 3 vols., Set. (Herbal Studies). (Illus.). 1200p. 1988. ring bd. 375.00 (0-9620838-1-X, J R Herb Pubns) Herb Studies.

— Jeanne Rose's Kitchen Cosmetics: Using Herbs, Fruit & Flowers for Natural Bodycare. 3rd ed. 1991. pap. 11.95 (1-55643-101-5) North Atlantic.

— Jeanne Rose's Modern Herbal. (Illus.). 224p. 1987. pap. 9.95 (0-399-51394-9, Perigree Bks) Berkley Pub.

— Kitchen Cosmetics: Using Plants & Herbs in Cosmetics. LC 77-17077. 128p. 1978. 12.95 (0-915572-25-7); pap. 6.95 (0-915572-24-9) Panjandrum.

— Love on the Run. (Silhouette Romance Ser.). 1994. pap. 2.75 (0-373-19027-1, 1-19027-1) Harlequin Bks.

***Rose, Jeanne & Earle, Susan, eds.** Women of Aromatherapy: Complete Aromatherapy by the People Who Made It So. (Illus.). 310p. (Orig.). 1996. pap. 12.95 (1-879687-06-2) Herb Studies.

Rose, Jed, jt. auth. see Shipley, Robert H.

Rose, Jennifer, ed. see Fleming, Red.

Rose, Jerome G. Landlords & Tenants. LC 72-82194. 288p. 1976. text ed. 34.95 (0-87855-042-9); pap. text ed. 18.95 (0-87855-538-2) Transaction Pubs.

Rose, Jerome G., ed. The Transfer of Development Rights: A New Technique of Land Use Regulation. 356p. 1975. boxed 29.95x (0-87855-119-0) Transaction Pubs.

Rose, Jerry & Shelkin, Lisa. Fresh Flower Arranging: A Year of Flowers. LC 93-85512. (Illus.). 128p. 1994. 21.95 (1-56138-401-1) Running Pr.

Rose, Jerry D. Outbreaks. 256p. (C). 1982. pap. 16.95 (0-02-926790-0) Free Pr.

Rose, Jessica & Gamble, James G., eds. Human Walking. 2nd ed. LC 93-13823. (Illus.). 256p. 1994. 50.00 (0-683-07360-5) Williams & Wilkins.

Rose, Joel. Kill the Poor. (Atlantic Monthly Press Fiction Ser.). 312p. (Orig.). 1988. pap. 8.95 (0-87113-260-5) Grove-Atltic.

Rose, Joel & Texier, Catherine, eds. Love Is Strange: Stories of Postmodern Romance. LC 92-15411. 288p. 1993. pap. 12.95 (0-393-30965-7) Norton.

Rose, John, ed. Nutrition & Killer Diseases: The Effects of Dietary Factors on Fatal Chronic Diseases. LC 82-3401. (Illus.). 185p. 1982. 25.00 (0-8155-0902-2) Noyes.

Rose, John & Hankin, Linda. Running Your Own Photographic Business. 2nd ed. 145p. (Orig.). 1992. pap. 20.95 (0-8464-1378-7) Beekman Pubs.

Rose, John & Pillider, Sarah. Breeding the Competition Horse. 2nd ed. LC 93-27092. 1993. 24.00 (0-632-03727-X) Blackwell Sci.

Rose, John, jt. auth. see Steinhorst, Lori.

Rose, John H. Mediterranean in the Ancient World. 1970. reprint ed. text ed. 55.00 (0-8371-1933-2, ROME, Greenwood Pr) Greenwood.

— Nationality in Modern History. 1977. 13.95 (0-8369-6989-8, 7866) Ayer.

— William Pitt & the Great War. LC 71-110862. (Illus.). xiv, 596p. 1971. reprint ed. text ed. 65.00 (0-8371-4533-3, ROWP, Greenwood Pr) Greenwood.

Rose, John H., et al. Germany in the Nineteenth Century: Five Lectures. LC 67-30189. (Manchester University Publications Historical Series No. 13, Essay Index Reprint Ser.). 1977. 18.95 (0-8369-0471-0) Ayer.

Rose, John R. Beyond Reason. 432p. 1993. pap. 19.95 (1-881170-03-9) Rose Pub OR.

— The Donkey Hide. 261p. (Orig.). (J). 1993. pap. 10.00 (1-881170-04-7) Rose Pub OR.

— Keys to Success. 128p. (YA). 1992. pap. write for info. (1-881170-00-4) Rose Pub OR.

— Manual for Legal Investigators. rev. ed. 319p. (C). 1995. 50.00 (1-881170-05-5) Rose Pub OR.
The most comprehensive book ever written for the apprentice investigator. This is the ONLY TEXTBOOK on the market today written for the purpose of teaching Private Investigations & has been used every day in the classroom by the Academy of Legal Investigators for the last seven years. The author covers nearly every aspect of the BUSINESS OF INVESTIGATION from notes to billing. You can use this book as a guideline for starting a new agency or to enhance the margin of profit in any agency. The techniques of investigative reporting taught will guarantee repeat business for those in need of a professional reporting procedure. This book is not limited to the P.I.; it will enhance the job performance of anyone in the realm of investigations, research, security, collections, sales & merchandising. There is something in this book for everyone because the author even shows you how to beat a traffic ticket & that alone is worth the price of the book! Volume discounts available from publisher - Rose Publishing, 3303 Ward Dr. NE, Salem OR 97305, Phone: 800-842-7421. ***Publisher Provided Annotation.***

— The Old Roper. 224p. 1992. pap. write for info. (1-881170-01-2) Rose Pub OR.

— Ten Thousand Dollars Per Month as a Private Investigator. 264p. (Orig.). 1992. pap. 29.95 (1-881170-02-0) Rose Pub OR.

Rose, John S. A Course of Group Theory. LC 76-22984. 320p. reprint ed. pap. 91.20 (*0-318-34665-6*, 2031721) Bks Demand.
— A Course on Group Theory. unabridged ed. LC 94-20435. 310p. 1994. reprint ed. pap. text ed. 8.95 (*0-486-68194-7*) Dover.
Rose, Jon. Classic U. S. Imperforate Stamps. (Illus.). 100p. (Orig.). 1990. pap. 14.95 (*0-940403-29-3*) Linns Stamp News.
Rose, Jonathan. Otto von Bismarck. (World Leaders - Past & Present Ser.). (Illus.). 112p. (YA). (gr. 5 up). 1987. lib. bdg. 17.95 (*0-87754-510-3*) Chelsea Hse.
***Rose, Joshua.** The Pattern Maker's Assistant: Embracing Lathe Work, Branch Work, Core Work, Sweep Work & Practical Gear Construction, & Preparation & Use of Tools. 6th ed. (Illus.). 249p. 1995. reprint ed. pap. 19.95 (*1-879335-59-X*) Astragal Pr.
Rose, Judith A., ed. Timberline Lodge: A Love Story. LC 86-82136. (Illus.). 128p. 1986. 29.50 (*0-932575-24-2*) Gr Arts Ctr Pub.
Rose, Julie, tr. see Virilio, Paul.
Rose, June. Marie Stopes & the Sexual Revolution. (Illus.). 256p. 1992. 22.95 (*0-571-16260-6*) Faber & Faber.
— Marie Stopes & the Sexual Revolution. (Illus.). 256p. 1993. pap. 10.95 (*0-571-16970-8*) Faber & Faber.
Rose, K. D., jt. ed. see Bown, T. M.
Rose, Kalima. Where Women Are Leaders: The SEWA Movement in India. (Illus.). 272p. (C). 1993. text ed. 55.00 (*1-85649-083-1*, Pub. by Zed Books UK); pap. 19.95 (*1-85649-084-X*, Pub. by Zed Books UK) Humanities.
Rose, Karel. Teaching Language Arts to Children. 510p. (C). 1982. text ed. 40.00 (*0-15-588808-0*) HB Coll Pubs.
Rose, Karen. That First Bite: Journal of a Compulsive Overeater. 1990. 8.95 (*0-88282-070-2*) New Horizon NJ.
Rose, Karen, jt. auth. see Person, Ron.
Rose, Karol. Work & Family: Program Models & Policies. (Employee Benefits - Human Resource Library). 928p. 1993. ring bd. 128.00 (*0-471-58135-6*) Wiley.
Rose, Karol, jt. auth. see Adolf, Barbara.
Rose, Kathleen M. Review of Pharmacology. (Board Review Ser.). 288p. (Orig.). 1989. pap. text ed. 19.95 (*0-683-07363-X*) Williams & Wilkins.
***Rose, Kenneth.** Knowing the Real: John Hick on the Cognitivity of Religions & Religious Pluralism. LC 94-23673. (Toronto Studies in Religion: Vol. 19). 1995. write for info. (*0-8204-2636-9*) P Lang Pubs.
***Rose, Kenneth D.** American Women & the Repeal of Prohibition. (American Social Experience Ser.). (Illus.). 230p. 1996. 40.00 (*0-8147-7464-4*) NYU Pr.
Rose, Kenneth D., et al. Sport Medicine: Physiology. LC 73-11032. (Sport Medicine Ser.: Vol. 4). 202p. 1974. text ed. 29.00 (*0-8422-7139-2*) Irvington.
Rose, Kenneth J. Classification of the Animal Kingdom. (YA). (gr. 7 up). 1980. 8.95 (*0-679-20508-X*) McKay.
— Lawful Hiring: A Primer for California Employers. rev. ed. 186p. (C). 1995. reprint ed. pap. text ed. 29.95 (*0-9645377-0-2*) R & J Legal.
— Quick Scientific Terminology: A Self-Teaching Guide. LC 88-725. 267p. 1988. pap. text ed. 16.95 (*0-471-85763-7*) Wiley.
Rose, Kenneth W., et al. Survey of Sources at the Rockefeller Archive Center for the Study of African-American History & Race Relations. Sherman, Lois, ed. 120p. (Orig.). (C). Date not set. pap. write for info. (*1-884354-01-7*) IN Univ Ctr.
Rose, Kent & Rose, Alice. Cemetery Quilt. LC 94-17617. (Illus.). (J). 1995. 14.95 (*0-395-70948-2*) HM.
Rose, Kurt. The Islands of the Sulu Sea. LC 93-61096. (Illus.). (Orig.). 1993. pap. 15.95 (*0-9637586-1-6*) Glencannon Pr.
***Rose, L. J., Jr.** L. J. Rose of Sunnyslope. (Illus.). 236p. 1994. 19.95 (*0-87328-144-6*) Huntington Lib.
Rose, L. M. Application of Mathematical Modelling to Process Development & Design. (Illus.). 364p. 1974. 93.75 (*0-85334-584-8*, Pub. by Elsevier Applied Sci UK) Elsevier.
— Distillation Design in Practice. (Computer Aided Chemical Engineering Ser.: No. 1). 308p. 1985. 89.75 (*0-444-42477-6*); pap. 37.50 (*0-444-42481-4*) Elsevier.
— Engineering Investment Decisions. 478p. 1976. 77.00 (*0-444-41522-X*) Elsevier.
Rose, L. M., ed. Chemical Reactor Design in Practice. (Chemical Engineering Monographs: Vol. 13). 378p. 1981. 102.75 (*0-444-42018-5*); pap. 29.75 (*0-444-42476-8*) Elsevier.
Rose, L. M., jt. auth. see Wells, G. L.
***Rose, Lance.** Netlaw: Your Rights in the Online World. 1995. pap. text ed. 19.95 (*0-07-882077-4*) McGraw.
Rose, Lance & Wallace, Jonathan. SysLaw. 2nd ed. 336p. 1992. pap. 34.95 (*1-879705-01-X*) PC Info Grp.
***Rose, Larry.** Show Me the Way to Go Home. LC 94-61038. 150p. (Orig.). 1995. pap. 10.95 (*0-943873-08-8*) Elder Bks.
Rose, Laura. Life Isn't Weighed on the Bathroom Scales. 192p. 1994. 18.95 (*1-56796-037-5*) WRS Group.
— Picture This: Teaching Reading Through Visualization. 176p. (Orig.). (J). (gr. 4-8). 1989. pap. text ed. 17.95 (*0-913705-32-2*) Zephyr Pr AZ.
— Picture This for Beginning Readers: Teaching Reading Through Visualization. 136p. (J). (gr. k-3). 1991. pap. text ed. 17.95 (*0-913705-63-2*) Zephyr Pr AZ.
— Teaching Thinking Through Literature: A Practical Model & Ten Theme-Based Units for Growing Minds. LC 95-15696. 1995. write for info. (*1-56976-029-2*) Zephyr Pr AZ.
— Write to Read & Spell: Teaching the Basics Through a Whole-Language Journal Program. LC 92-36612. 176p. (J). (gr. k-2). 1993. 21.95 (*0-913705-83-7*) Zephyr Pr AZ.
Rose, Laurel L. The Politics of Harmony: Land Dispute Strategies in Swaziland. (African Studies: No. 69). (Illus.). 256p. (C). 1992. 64.95 (*0-521-39296-9*) Cambridge U Pr.
Rose, Laurence M. Fitzgerald vs. Nita & Western R. R. 210p. 1988. 17.95 (*1-55681-114-4*, FBA0114) Natl Inst Trial Ad.
Rose, Leo, jt. auth. see Sisson, Richard.
Rose, Leo E., ed. Nepal: Perspectives on Development Issues. LC 87-72277. (Occasional Paper Ser.: No. 12). 121p. (Orig.). (C). 1987. pap. 7.00 (*0-318-23776-8*) UC Berkeley Ctrs SE Asia.
Rose, Leo E. & Gonsalves, Eric, eds. Toward a New World Order: Adjusting India-U. S. Relations. LC 92-70529. (Research Papers & Policy Studies: No. 38). 1992. pap. 15.00 (*1-55729-032-6*) IEAS.
Rose, Leo E. & Husain, Noor A., eds. U. S.-Pakistan Relations. LC 85-80563. (Research Papers & Policy Studies: No. 13). 245p. 1985. pap. 8.50 (*0-912966-78-5*) IEAS.
Rose, Leo E. & Matinuddin, Kamal, eds. Beyond Afghanistan: The Emerging U. S. - Pakistan Relations. LC 89-81688. (Research Papers & Policy Studies). 336p. (Orig.). (C). 1990. pap. text ed. 20.00 (*1-55729-017-2*) IEAS.
Rose, Leo E., jt. ed. see Husain, Noor A.
Rose, Linda. Hands: The Total Guide to Beauty, Health, Language & Lore. LC 84-22665. (Illus.). 188p. 1985. pap. 9.95 (*0-87951-991-6*) Overlook Pr.
***Rose, Linda M.** Mortgaging a Home Vol. 1: Simple Guide to Financing a Home in Basic Terms - What to Do... What Not to Do...& Why. Di Ianni, Marisa, ed. 200p. (Orig.). 1994. pap. 14.95 (*1-885878-00-1*) Essent Finan.
Rose, Lionel. The Erosion of Childhood: Childhood in Britain, 1860-1918. 288p. 1991. 69.95 (*0-415-00165-X*, A6236) Routledge.
— Massacre of the Innocents: Infanticide in Britain 1800-1939. (Illus.). 215p. (C). 1986. 45.00 (*0-7102-0339-X*, RKP) Routledge.
— Rogues & Vagabonds: The Vagrant Underworld in Britain 1815-1985. 272p. (C). 1988. lib. bdg. 65.00 (*0-415-00275-3*) Routledge.
Rose, Lisle. Survey of American Economic Fiction. (BCL1-PS American Literature Ser.). 22p. 1993. reprint ed. lib. bdg. 59.00 (*0-7812-6593-2*) Rprt Serv.
Rose, Lisle A. The Roots of Tragedy: The United States & the Struggle for Asia, 1945-1953. LC 75-35354. (Contributions in American History Ser.: No. 48). 352p. 1976. text ed. 55.00 (*0-8371-8592-0*, RRT/, Greenwood Pr) Greenwood.
— The Ship That Held the Line: The U. S. S. Hornet & the First Year of the Pacific War. LC 95-8683. (Illus.). 320p. 1995. 34.95 (*1-55750-729-5*) Naval Inst Pr.
***Rose, Loretta.** Daycare: What Can a Mother Do. 16p. 1994. per., pap. 6.00 (*0-8059-3653-X*) Dorrance.
Rose, Louis F., ed. Year Book of Dentistry, 1989. (Illus.). 496p. 1989. 54.95 (*0-8151-1896-1*, Yr Bk Med Pubs) Mosby Yr Bk.
Rose, Louis J. How to Investigate Your Friends & Enemies. rev. ed. Byrne, Robert & Fiquette, Lawrence, eds. LC 81-68851. (Illus.). 137p. 1983. pap. 7.95 (*0-9606846-1-1*) Albion Pr.
Rose, Lyn. Mom's Diary: 30 Days to Being a Better Mom. 180p. 1994. 10.95 (*1-878990-30-6*) Howard Pub LA.
Rose, Lynn E., ed. see Velikovsky, et al.
Rose, M. The Highest Form of Killing. (J). 1992. 16.95 (*0-15-234270-2*, HB Juv Bks) HarBrace.
Rose, M., ed. Heidelberg Congress on Taxing Consumption: Proceedings of the International Congress on Taxing Consumption, Heidelberg, June 28-30, 1989. (Illus.). xvii, 541p. 1990. 120.00 (*0-387-52728-1*) Spr-Verlag.
***Rose, M. E.** Elementary Theory of Angular Momentum. LC 94-41223. (Illus.). 256p. 1995. pap. text ed. 7.95 (*0-486-68480-6*) Dover.
Rose, M. E., ed. Nuclear Orientation. (International Science Review Ser.). (Illus.). 336p. 1963. text ed. 255.00 (*0-677-00730-2*) Gordon & Breach.
— Proceedings of the Eastern Theoretical Physics Conference. 472p. 1963. text ed. 169.00 (*0-677-12710-3*) Gordon & Breach.
Rose, M. Gaddis, tr. see Villiers de l'Isle-Adam, Philippe A.
Rose, Malcolm. Formula for Murder. (YA). 1994. pap. 3.50 (*0-590-48320-X*) Scholastic Inc.
— The Highest Form of Killing. LC 91-31889. 304p. (YA). (gr. 9 up). 1995. pap. 5.00 (*0-15-200373-8*) HarBrace.
Rose, Marcia. Hospital. LC 91-58981. 384p. 1993. mass mkt. 5.99 (*0-345-36829-0*) Ballantine.
— A House of Her Own. (Orig.). 1990. mass mkt. 5.95 (*0-345-35723-X*) Ballantine.
— Like Mother, Like Daughter. 448p. 1994. 21.95 (*0-345-38769-4*) Ballantine.
— Summer Times. 320p. (Orig.). 1985. pap. 3.95 (*0-345-31854-4*) Ballantine.
Rose, Margaret. Parody: Ancient, Modern, & Post-Modern. LC 92-39133. (Literature, Culture, Theory Ser.: No. 5). 300p. (C). 1993. 59.95 (*0-521-41860-7*); pap. 18.95 (*0-521-42924-2*) Cambridge U Pr.
Rose, Margaret A. Marx's Lost Aesthetic: Karl Marx & the Visual Arts. (Illus.). 228p. 1988. pap. 22.95 (*0-521-36979-7*) Cambridge U Pr.
— The Post-Modern & the Post-Industrial: A Critical Analysis. (Illus.). 296p. (C). 1991. pap. 22.95 (*0-521-40952-7*) Cambridge U Pr.
Rose, Marilyn G. Katharine Tynan. LC 71-126276. (Irish Writers Ser.). 97p. 1975. 8.50 (*0-8387-7770-8*); pap. 1.95 (*0-8387-7771-6*) Bucknell U Pr.
— Translation Spectrum: Essays in Theory & Practice. LC 80-20302. 172p. 1980. pap. 12.95 (*0-87395-437-8*) State U NY Pr.
Rose, Marilyn G., tr. see De L'Isle-Adam, Villers.
Rose, Marilyn G., tr. see Sainte-Beuve, Charles-Augustin.
Rose, Marilyn P. On the Move: A Study of Migration & Ethnic Persistence among Mennonites from East Freeman, South Dakota. LC 87-45793. (Immigrant Communities & Ethnic Minorities in the U. S. & Canada Ser.: No. 28). 1988. 45.00 (*0-404-19438-9*, F659) AMS Pr.
Rose, Marilyn S. My First Horse. 53p. (Orig.). (J). (gr. 3-4). 1991. pap. 9.95 (*0-9632117-0-6*) AMI & Arabian Mktg.
Rose, Marilynn J., tr. see Hamburger, Kate.
Rose, Marion H., et al. The Preschool Behavior Inventory: Mental Health Screening for Children Ages Eighteen Months Through Five Years. 66p. (Orig.). 1985. pap. text ed. 15.00 (*0-933373-06-6*) Early Learn Assoc.
Rose, Mark. Alien Encounters: Anatomy of Science Fiction. LC 81-683. 220p. 1982. pap. text ed. 11.95 (*0-674-01566-5*) HUP.
— Authors & Owners: The Invention of Copyright. LC 92-43010. 190p. (Orig.). 1993. text ed. 29.00 (*0-674-05308-7*) HUP.
— Authors & Owners: The Invention of Copyright. 192p. (Orig.). (C). 1995. pap. text ed. 14.95 (*0-674-05309-5*) HUP.
— Heroic Love: Studies in Sidney & Spenser. LC 68-29182. 163p. reprint ed. pap. 47.90 (*0-7837-2322-9*, 2057410) Bks Demand.
— Shakespearean Design. LC 72-88129. (Illus.). 201p. reprint ed. pap. 57.30 (*0-7837-4185-5*, 2059035) Bks Demand.
— Spenser's Art: A Companion to Book One of "The Faerie Queene" LC 74-21229. 160p. (C). 1975. 19.00 (*0-674-83193-4*) HUP.
Rose, Mark, ed. Shakespeare's Early Tragedies: A Collection of Critical Essays. LC 94-11740. (New Century Views Ser.). 264p. 1994. write for info. (*0-13-035544-5*) P-H.
Rose, Mark D., et al. Methods in Yeast Genetics: A Laboratory Course Manual. (Illus.). 200p. (C). 1990. text ed. 20.00 (*0-87969-354-1*) Cold Spring Harbor.
Rose, Mark H. Cities of Light & Heat: Domesticating Gas & Electricity in Urban America. LC 94-16202. (Illus.). 240p. 1995. 34.50 (*0-271-01349-4*) Pa St U Pr.
— Interstate: Express Highway Politics, 1939-1989. LC 90-12343. 208p. 1990. reprint ed. pap. text ed. 18.95x (*0-87049-671-9*) U of Tenn Pr.
— Interstate: Express Highway Politics, 1941-1956. LC 78-14940. 1979. 25.00 (*0-7006-0186-4*) U Pr of KS.
Rose, Mark H., jt. ed. see Daniels, George H.
Rose, Mark V. The Actor & His Double: Mime & Movement for the Theatre of Cruelty. LC 85-73269. 80p. 1986. pap. 8.95 (*0-9616087-0-6*) Actor Train Res.
Rose, Marsha, jt. auth. see Malloy, Merrit.
Rose, Marshall T. The Internet Message: Closing the Book with Electronic Mail. 384p. 1993. text ed. 56.00 (*0-13-092941-7*) P-H.
— The Little Black Book: Mail Bonding with OSI Directory Services. 416p. 1991. text ed. 58.00 (*0-13-683210-5*) P-H.
— Open Book: Practical Perspective on ASI. 1989. text ed. 71.00 (*0-13-643016-3*) P-H.
— The Simple Book. 2nd ed. 1993. text ed. 58.00 (*0-13-177254-6*) P-H.
— Simple Book: Management of TCP-IP Based Internets. 384p. 1990. text ed. 54.00 (*0-13-812611-9*) P-H.
***Rose, Marshall T. & McCloghrie, Keith.** How to Manage Your Network Using SNMP: The Networking Management Practicum. LC 94-5350. 576p. 1994. pap. text ed. 48.00 (*0-13-141517-4*) P-H.
Rose, Marshall T., jt. auth. see Lynch, Daniel C.
Rose, Martin R., jt. auth. see Altschul, Jeffrey H.
Rose, Martin R., et al. The Past Climate of Arroyo Hondo, New Mexico, Reconstructed from Tree Rings. LC 80-21834. (Arroyo Hondo Archaeological Ser.: Vol. 4). (Illus.). 138p. (Orig.). 1981. pap. 10.00 (*0-933452-05-5*) Schol Am Res.
Rose, Mary, jt. ed. see Brown, Jonathan.
Rose, Mary, jt. ed. see Jones, Geoffrey.
Rose, Mary, jt. auth. see Wood, Erskine.
Rose, Mary B. The Expense of Spirit: Love & Sexuality in English Renaissance Drama. LC 88-47742. 272p. 1991. reprint ed. pap. 12.95 (*0-8014-9695-0*) Cornell U Pr.
— The Gregs of Quarry Bank Mill: The Rise & Decline of a Family Firm, 1750-1914. (Illus.). 170p. 1986. 54.95 (*0-521-32382-7*) Cambridge U Pr.
— Women in the Middle Ages & the Renaissance: Literary & Historical Perspectives. LC 85-22153. 272p. (Orig.). 1986. pap. 15.95 (*0-8156-2352-6*) Syracuse U Pr.
***Rose, Mary B., ed.** Family Business. LC 95-11877. (International Library of Critical Writings in Business History: Vol. 13). 1995. write for info. (*1-85898-049-6*, Pub. by E Elgar Pub UK) Ashgate Pub Co.
— International Competition & Strategic Response in Textile Industries since 1870. 165p. 1991. text ed. 32.00 (*0-7146-3412-3*, Pub. by F Cass Pubs UK) Intl Spec Bk.
— Renaissance Drama: Disorder & Drama. (New Ser.: No. XXI). 260p. 1991. 49.95 (*0-8101-0684-1*) Northwestern U Pr.
— Renaissance Drama: Dramatic Intertextuality & Theatrical Conditions. (New Ser.: No. XXII). (Illus.). 275p. 1993. 49.95 (*0-8101-0685-X*) Northwestern U Pr.
— Renaissance Drama: New Series, No. XXIV. 270p. 1995. 49.95 (*0-8101-1195-0*) Northwestern U Pr.
— Renaissance Drama New Series, No. XX: Essays on Renaissance Dramatic Traditions. 238p. 1990. 49.95 (*0-8101-0681-7*) Northwestern U Pr.
— Renaissance Drama New Series XIX: Essays on Texts of Renaissance Plays. 270p. 1989. 49.95 (*0-8101-0680-9*) Northwestern U Pr.
— Renaissance Drama, Vol. XXIII: Renaissance Drama in an Age of Colonization. 210p. 1994. 49.95 (*0-8101-0686-8*) Northwestern U Pr.
Rose, Mary B., jt. ed. see Kirby, Maurice W.
Rose, Mary C. Clara Barton: Soldier of Mercy. (Discovery Biographies Ser.). (Illus.). 80p. (J). (gr. 2-6). 1991. reprint ed. lib. bdg. 12.95 (*0-7910-1403-7*) Chelsea Hse.
Rose, Mary E., ed. see Tyrrell, Albert E.
Rose, Mary K. The Children's Tarot: The Road Is a River. (Illus.). 52p. (Orig.). (J). (gr. k-6). 1993. pap. 18.95 (*0-9636234-0-0*) Wild Rose CO.
Rose, Mavis. Indonesia Free: A Political Biography of Mohammad Hatta. (Monograph Ser.: No. 67). 244p. (Orig.). 1987. pap. 10.50 (*0-87763-033-X*) Cornell Mod Indo.
Rose, Melvyn. Healing Hurt Minds: The Peper Harow Experience. 234p. 1990. 25.00 (*0-415-04943-1*, A4161) Routledge.
Rose, Michael, jt. auth. see Amis, John.
Rose, Michael, jt. auth. see Koben, Shelly.
Rose, Michael D. The Law of Federal Income Taxation, 1994: Pocket Part. 3rd ed. (Hornbook Ser.). 150p. 1994. pap. text ed. 9.50 (*0-314-04332-2*) West Pub.
— Selected Federal Taxation, Statutes & Regulations: 1996 Edition. 1664p. (C). 1995. pap. text ed. 25.00 (*0-314-06723-X*) West Pub.
Rose, Michael D. & Chommie, June R. Federal Income Taxation. 3rd ed. (Hornbook Ser.). 923p. (C). 1993. reprint ed. text ed. 38.00 (*0-314-64224-2*) West Pub.
Rose, Michael E., ed. The Poor & the City: The English Poor Law in its Urban Context 1834-1914. LC 85-2139. (Themes in Urban History Ser.). (Illus.). 192p. 1985. text ed. 35.00 (*0-312-56897-5*) St Martin.
Rose, Michael R. Evolutionary Biology of Aging. (Illus.). 240p. 1994. reprint ed. pap. 19.95 (*0-19-509530-8*) OUP.
— Quantitative Ecological Theory: An Introduction to Basic Models. LC 86-46274. 200p. 1987. text ed. 32.50x (*0-8018-3509-7*) Johns Hopkins.
Rose, Michael R. & Finch, Caleb E., eds. Genetics & Evolution of Aging. LC 94-16569. (Contemporary Issues in Genetics & Evolution Ser.: Vol. 3). 312p. (C). 1994. lib. bdg. 150.00 (*0-7923-2902-3*) Kluwer Ac.
Rose, Michael T. A Prayer for Relief: The Constitutional Infirmities of the Military Academies' Conduct, Honor, & Ethics Systems. vii, 194p. (Orig.). 1973. pap. text ed. 7.50 (*0-8377-1025-1*) Rothman.
Rose, Mike. Lives on the Boundary: A Moving Account of the Struggles & Achievements of America's Educational Underclass. 256p. 1990. pap. 11.95 (*0-14-012403-9*, Penguin Bks) Viking Penguin.
— Lives on the Boundary: The Struggles & Achievements of America's Underprepared. 288p. 1989. text ed. 29.95 (*0-02-926821-4*) Free Pr.
— Selected Federal Taxation, Statutes & Regulations, Supplement to 1994 Edition Revenue Reconciliation Act of 1993, Selected Sections of the Conference Report on H. R. 2264, Omnibus Reconciliation Act of 1993. 231p. 1993. pap. text ed. 5.00 (*0-314-02995-8*) West Pub.
Rose, Mike, jt. auth. see Kiniry, Malcolm.
Rose, Mike, et al. How to Save Your Child or Baby: When Every Second Counts. (C). 1987. 19.95 (*0-685-28882-X*) Pacific Stat.
Rose, Minnie B., jt. ed. see Cahill, Matthew.
Rose, Minnie B., jt. ed. see Hamilton, Helen.
Rose, Minnie B., jt. ed. see Potter, Diana O.
***Rose, Miriam.** Baker's Dozen No. 12: The Baker Family Circus. 172p. (J). (gr. 6-8). Date not set. pap. 9.95 (*1-56871-062-3*) Targum Pr.
Rose, Mitchell, jt. illus. see Young, Ruth.
Rose, N. A. Gentile Zionists: Study in Anglo-Zionist Diplomacy, 1929-1939. 246p. 1973. 32.50 (*0-7146-2940-5*, Pub. by F Cass Pubs UK) Intl Spec Bk.
Rose, N. R., ed. see International Convocation on Immunology Staff.
Rose, Nancy E. Put to Work: Relief Programs in the Great Depression. LC 93-26617. (J). (ps-12). 1993. 10.00 (*0-85345-871-5*) Monthly Rev.
— Workfare or Fair Work: Women, Welfare & Government Work Programs. LC 95-8589. 320p. (C). 1995. text ed. 52.00 (*0-8135-2232-3*); pap. text ed. 19.95 (*0-8135-2233-1*) Rutgers U Pr.
Rose, Nicholas D., ed. Essential Psychiatry. 2nd ed. LC 93-34958. 336p. 1994. pap. write for info. (*0-632-03737-7*, Pub. by Blckwell Sci Pubns UK) Blackwell Sci.
Rose, Nicholas J., jt. auth. see Ritger, Paul D.
Rose, Nikolas. Governing the Soul: Technologies of Human Subjectivity. 1990. 25.00 (*0-415-02856-6*, A4031) Routledge.
— Governing the Soul: The Shaping of the Private Self. LC 90-138198. 320p. 1993. pap. 17.95 (*0-415-06477-5*, A7773) Routledge.
Rose, Noel R. & Mackay, Ian R., eds. The Autoimmune Disease. 1985. text ed. 154.00 (*0-12-596920-1*) Acad Pr.
— The Autoimmune Diseases Two. (Illus.). 444p. 1992. text ed. 99.95 (*0-12-596922-8*) Acad Pr.
Rose, Noel R. & Siegel, Benjamin V., eds. The Reticuloendothelial System: A Comprehensive Treatise, Vol. 4: Immunopathology. LC 79-25933. 464p. 1983. 105.00 (*0-306-40979-8*, Plenum Pr) Plenum.
Rose, Noel R., ed. see American Society for Microbiology Staff, et al.
Rose, Noel R., jt. ed. see Schwartz, Robert S.
Rose, Noel R., et al, eds. Immune Mediated Heart Disease. LC 92-49773. 1992. write for info. (*0-387-55614-1*) Spr-Verlag.
— International Convocation on Immunology. 1969. 96.00 (*3-8055-0888-3*) S Karger.
— Manual of Clinical Laboratory Immunology. 4th ed. (Illus.). 1016p. 1992. 79.00 (*1-55581-044-6*); text ed. 89.00 (*1-55581-043-8*) Am Soc Microbio.
***Rose, Norman.** Churchill: An Unruly Life. LC 95-4125. 450p. 1995. 25.00 (*0-02-874009-2*) Free Pr.
— Favorite Foods: No Fat Cooking. (Illus.). 360p. 1994. 21.95 (*1-56796-039-1*) WRS Group.

R

An Asterisk (*) at the beginning of an entry indicates that the title is appearing in BIP for the first time.

— Favorite Foods No Fat Cooking. 2nd ed. (Illus.). 288p. 1995. ring bd. 21.95 (1-56796-100-2) WRS Group.

— Just No Fat: No Fat Cooking with over 400 Recipes of Regular Food for Regular People from Chili Dogs to Cheesecake. 354p. 1992. spiral bd. write for info. (0-9631847-1-7) N Rose Co.

— No Fat Fudge: Forever Changing the Way America Makes Fudge. 100p. (Orig.). 1994. 19.95 (0-9631847-5-X); pap. 15.95 (0-9631847-4-1) N Rose Co.

— No Fat Greatness: The Ten Master Tips to Guaranteed No Fat Cooking Success. 100p. 1993. 10.95 (0-9631847-2-5) N Rose Co.

— No Fat Please: Feast Without Fat & Lose Weight. 169p. 1992. spiral bd., pap. write for info. (0-9631847-0-9) N Rose Co.

Rose, Norman, ed. From Palmerston to Balfour: Collected Essays of Mayir Verete. 248p. 1992. text ed. 42.00 (0-7146-3441-7, Pub. by F Cass Pubs UK) Intl Spec Bk.

Rose, P. R. & Lidz, B. Diagnostic Foraminiferal Assemblages of Shallow-Water Modern Environments: South Florida & the Bahamas, No. VI. (Sedimenta Ser.: Vol. VI). 55p. 1977. 9.00 (0-932981-05-4) Univ Miami CSL.

Rose-Paradise, Helen. Timothy O'Toole: Irish Stories for Little Folk. LC 93-94368. (Illus.). 136p. (J). 1994. 14.95 (1-56002-431-3, Univ Edtns) Aegina Pr.

Rose, Pat R. The Solar Boat Book. rev. ed. LC 83-70115. (Illus.). 266p. 1983. pap. 8.95 (0-89815-086-8) Ten Speed Pr.

Rose, Patti E. In Search of Serenity: A Black Family's Struggle with the Threat of AIDS. LC 92-60058. 200p. (Orig.). 1993. pap. 10.95 (0-88378-069-0) Third World.

Rose, Paul A., jt. auth. see Dreier, William A.

Rose, Paul L. German Question-Jewish Question: Revolutionary Antisemitism in Germany from Kant to Wagner. 411p. (C). 1992. text ed. 49.50 (0-691-03144-4); pap. text ed. 16.95 (0-691-00890-6) Princeton U Pr.

— Wagner: Race & Revolution. 288p. (C). 1992. text ed. 27.00 (0-300-05182-4) Yale U Pr.

Rose, Paul L. & Druks, Herbert, eds. The Hecht Archive, University of Haifa. LC 89-16915. (Archives of the Holocaust Ser.: Vol. 12). 520p. 1990. reprint ed. 130.00 (0-8240-5494-6) Garland.

Rose, Pauline, tr. see Grekov, Boris.

Rose, Peter, ed. Working with Refugees. LC 85-47916. (CMS Migration & Ethnicity Ser.). 175p. (C). 1986. pap. 12.95 (0-913256-97-8) Ctr Migration.

Rose, Peter G. Foods of the Hudson: A Seasonal Sampling of the Region's Bounty. LC 92-35040. 272p. 1993. 22.95 (0-87951-489-2) Overlook Pr.

— The Sensible Cook: Dutch Foodways in the Old & the New World. LC 89-33457. (Illus.). 160p. 1989. 24.95 (0-8156-0241-3) Syracuse U Pr.

Rose, Peter I. Group Status in America. (Task Force on the Eighties Ser.). 30p. 1981. pap. 2.50 (0-87495-039-2) Am Jewish Comm.

— Mainstream & Margins: Jews, Blacks, & Other Americans. LC 83-4693. 241p. 1983. 28.95 (0-87855-473-4) Transaction Pubs.

— Strangers in Their Midst: Small-Town Jews & Their Neighbors. 1977. lib. bdg. 12.95 (0-915172-32-1) Richwood Pub.

— They & We: Racial & Ethnic Relations in the United States. 3rd ed. 252p. (C). 1980. pap. text ed. write for info. (0-07-554317-6) McGraw.

— They & We: Racial & Ethnic Relations in the United States. 4th ed. 1990. pap. text ed. write for info. (0-07-053640-6) McGraw.

Rose, Peter I., ed. Socialization & the Life Cycle. LC 78-65243. 1979. pap. text ed. 17.00 (0-312-73800-5) St Martin.

— The Study of Society: An Integrated Anthology. 4th ed. 1977. pap. text ed. 14.50 (0-394-31229-5) Random.

Rose, Peter I. & Kahn, Roger. Pete Rose: My Story. 288p. 1989. text ed. 18.95 (0-02-560611-5) Macmillan.

Rose, Peter I., et al. Sociology: Understanding Society. (gr. 11-12). 1978. text ed. 24.88 (0-13-821322-4) P-H.

Rose, Peter J. They & We. 190p. reprint ed. pap. 7.95 (0-686-95008-9) ADL.

***Rose, Peter R., ed.** Guiding Your Career As a Professional Geologist. iv, 78p. 1994. pap. 5.00 (0-89181-818-9) AAPG.

Rose, Peter S. The Changing Structure of American Banking: Competition, Concentration, & Performance. LC 86-18843. (Columbia Studies in Business, Government & Society). 392p. 1987. text ed. 64.00 (0-231-05980-9) Col U Pr.

— Commercial Bank Management. 2nd ed. 800p. (C). 1992. pap. text ed. 66.95 (0-256-11557-5) Irwin.

— The Interstate Banking Revolution: Benefits, Risks, & Tradeoffs for Bankers & Consumers. LC 89-10476. 244p. 1989. text ed. 55.00 (0-89930-438-9, REC/, Greenwood Pr) Greenwood.

— Japanese Banking & Investment in the United States: An Assessment of Their Impact upon U. S. Markets & Institutions. LC 91-2275. 224p. 1991. text ed. 55.00 (0-89930-622-5, RJB, Quorum Bks) Greenwood.

— Money & Capital Market. 5th ed. LC 93-30804. (Series in Finance). 864p. (C). 1993. text ed. 65.95 (0-256-12199-0) Irwin.

— Money & Capital Markets: The Financial System in an Increasingly Global Economy. 4th ed. 380p. (C). 1991. text ed. 65.95 (0-256-08300-2) Irwin.

Rose, Peter S., ed. Readings on Financial Institutions & Markets. 5th ed. LC 92-32270. 448p. (C). 1992. pap. text ed. 21.95 (0-256-09454-3) Irwin.

— Readings on Financial Institutions & Markets. 7th ed. LC 94-30043. (Finance Ser.). 456p. (C). 1994. 21.95 (0-256-14526-1) Irwin.

Rose, Peter S. & Kolari, James. Financial Institutions: Understanding & Managing Financial Services. 5th ed. LC 94-14030. (Finance Ser.). 766p. (C). 1994. text ed. 66.95 (0-256-13569-X) Irwin.

Rose, Peter S., jt. auth. see Fraser, Donald R.

Rose, Peter S., et al. Financial Institutions: Understanding & Managing Financial Services. 4th ed. LC 92-30862. 800p. (C). 1993. text ed. 66.95 (0-256-09233-8) Irwin.

Rose, Peter W. Sons of the Gods, Children of Earth: Ideology & Literary Form in Ancient Greece. LC 91-31562. 432p. 1992. 48.95 (0-8014-2425-9); pap. 16.95 (0-8014-9983-6) Cornell U Pr.

Rose, Philip M. The Italians in America. LC 74-17946. (Italian American Experience Ser.). (Illus.). 168p. 1975. reprint ed. 15.95 (0-405-06416-0) Ayer.

Rose, Phyllis. Jazz Cleopatra. LC 90-50267. 352p. 1990. 14.00 (0-679-73133-4, Vin) Random.

— The Norton Book of Womens' Lives. 832p. 1995. pap. 17.95 (0-393-31290-9, Norton Paperbks) Norton.

— Parallel Lives: Five Victorian Marriages. LC 84-40026. 336p. 1984. pap. 11.00 (0-394-72580-8, Vin) Random.

— Woman of Letters: A Life of Virginia Woolf. (Illus.). 1987. pap. 8.95 (0-15-698190-4, Harvest Bks) HarBrace.

— Writing of Women: Essays in a Renaissance. rev. ed. LC 84-23446. 187p. 1986. pap. 12.95 (0-8195-6173-8, Wesleyan Univ Pr) U Pr of New Eng.

Rose, Phyllis, ed. The Norton Book of Women's Lives. LC 92-40015. 1993. 30.00 (0-393-03532-8) Norton.

Rose, R., jt. auth. see Bryan, W. S.

Rose, R., et al. The Banks & Their Competitors. (C). 1989. 40.00 (0-85297-057-9, Pub. by Inst Bankers UK) St Mut.

Rose, R. B. Gracchus Babeuf: The First Revolutionary Communist. LC 76-54099. xii, 434p. 1978. 47.50 (0-8047-0949-1) Stanford U Pr.

Rose, Reginald. Dear Friends. 1968. pap. 4.75 (0-8222-0287-5) Dramatists Play.

— Thunder on Sycamore Street. 1986. 4.95 (0-87129-325-0, T27) Dramatic Pub.

— Twelve Angry Men: A Screen Adaptation, Directed by Sidney Lumet. Garrett, George P. et al, eds. LC 71-135273. (Film Scripts Ser.). 1989. reprint ed. pap. text ed. 19.95 (0-89197-970-0) Irvington.

— Twelve Angry Men (or Twelve Angry Women. rev. ed. 1983. 4.95 (0-87129-327-7); Men. 4.95 (0-685-74683-6, T42) Dramatic Pub.

— Twelve Angry Women. rev. ed. 1983. Women. 5.95 (0-87129-401-X, T43) Dramatic Pub.

Rose, Reuben J. & Hodgson, David R. Manual of Equine Practice. LC 92-21745. (Illus.). 544p. 1992. pap. text ed. 61.00 (0-7216-3739-6) Saunders.

Rose, Reuben J., jt. auth. see Hodgson, David R.

Rose, Rich. Drafting Scenery for Theater, Film, & Television. LC 94-7095. (Illus.). 176p. 1994. pap. 18.99 (1-55870-348-9) Betterway Bks.

Rose, Richard. The Albigen Papers. rev. ed. 240p. 1978. reprint ed. pap. 9.00 (1-878683-00-4) TAT Found.

— The Albigen Papers. 3rd rev. ed. 240p. 1978. reprint ed. 12.00 (1-878683-07-1) TAT Found.

— AppleWorks User's Handbook. 288p. 1986. pap. 15.95 (0-938862-78-2) Weber Systems.

— Carillon: Poems, Essays & Philosophy of Richard Rose. (Illus.). 147p. (Orig.). 1982. pap. 8.00 (1-878683-03-9) TAT Found.

— The Direct-Mind Experience. (Illus.). 316p. (Orig.). 1985. 14.00 (1-878683-08-X); pap. 10.00 (1-878683-01-2) TAT Found.

— Do Parties Make a Difference? 2nd ed. LC 84-9560. (Chatham House Series on Change in American Politics). 238p. reprint ed. pap. 67.90 (0-8357-3452-8, 2039713) Bks Demand.

— Energy Transmutation, Between-Ness & Transmission. 2nd rev. ed. 68p. 1985. reprint ed. pap. 8.00 (1-878683-02-0) TAT Found.

— Lesson-Drawing in Public Policy: A Guide to Learning Across Time & Space. LC 92-36205. 192p. (Orig.). (C). 1993. pap. text ed. 19.95x (0-934540-32-2) Chatham Hse Pubs.

— Managing Presidential Objectives. LC 76-4424. 1976. 24.95 (0-02-926840-0) Free Pr.

— Ministers & Ministries: A Functional Analysis. LC 86-23739. 298p. 1987. 59.00 (0-19-827486-6) OUP.

— Northern Ireland: Time of Choice. LC 76-10080. (Foreign Affairs Study Ser.: No. 33). (Illus.). 185p. reprint ed. pap. 52.80 (0-8357-4515-5, 2037373) Bks Demand.

— Northern Ireland Loyalty Study, 1968. LC 75-32210. 1975. write for info. (0-89138-116-3) ICPSR.

— Ordinary People in Public Policy: A Behavioural Analysis. 208p. (C). 1989. text ed. 45.00 (0-8039-8135-X); pap. text ed. 17.95 (0-8039-8136-8) Sage.

— Politics in England: Change & Persistence. 5th ed. (C). 1989. pap. text ed. 28.50 (0-673-39892-7) HarpCollege.

— The Postmodern President. 2nd ed. LC 91-12614. 408p. (C). 1991. pap. text ed. 24.95x (0-934540-94-2) Chatham Hse Pubs.

— Psychology of the Observer. (Illus.). 92p. 1979. pap. 15.00 (1-878683-06-3) TAT Found.

— The Territorial Dimension in Government: Understanding the United Kingdom. LC 82-9680. 240p. reprint ed. pap. 68.40 (0-8357-4827-8, 2037764) Bks Demand.

— Understanding Big Government: The Programme Approach. LC 83-51198. iii, 261p. 1984. 39.95 (0-8039-9778-7); pap. 16.95 (0-8039-9779-5) Sage.

— The Wolf. 1982. pap. 2.50 (0-89083-961-1) Zebra.

Rose, Richard & Davies, Phillip L. Inheritance in Public Policy: Change Without Choice in Britain. LC 93-49088. 256p. 1994. 27.50 (0-300-05877-2) Yale U Pr.

Rose, Richard & McAllister, Ian. The Loyalties of Voters: A Lifetime Learning Model. 256p. (C). 1990. text ed. 45.00 (0-8039-8274-7); pap. text ed. 19.95 (0-8039-8275-5) Sage.

— Voters Begin to Choose: From Closed-Class to Open Elections in Britain. 192p. (Orig.). 1986. text ed. 45.00 (0-8039-9743-4); pap. text ed. 17.50 (0-8039-9744-2) Sage.

Rose, Richard, jt. auth. see Mackie, Thomas T.

Rose, Richard C. & Garrett, Echo M. How to Make a Buck & Still Be a Decent Human Being: A Week with Rick Rose at Dataflex. LC 92-352611. (Illus.). 272p. 1993. reprint ed. pap. 10.00 (0-88730-654-3) Harper Busn.

Rose, Robert. Creating Your Giant Self. LC 89-81557. 224p. (Orig.). 1990. pap. 12.95 (0-941404-61-7) New Falcon Pubns.

Rose, Robert & Tilton, Buck. Sex in the Outdoors: A Humerous Approach to Recreation. LC 93-27919. (Illus.). 96p. (Orig.). 1993. pap. 6.99 (0-934802-86-6) ICS Bks.

Rose, Robert, jt. auth. see Bryan, William S.

Rose, Robert, jt. ed. see Geahigan, Priscilla C.

Rose, Robert C. The Lonely Eagles. (Illus.). 1976. 20.00 (0-917612-00-0) Aviation.

Rose, Robert G. Practical Issues in Employment Testing. LC 93-27798. 156p. 1993. pap. 19.95 (0-911907-09-2) Psych Assess.

— Psychological Consultation to Business. LC 94-8302. 195p. 1994. pap. 19.95 (0-911907-15-7) Psych Assess.

Rose, Robert M. & Barrett, James E., eds. Alcoholism: Origins & Outcome. (American Psychopathological Association Ser.). (Illus.). 314p. 1988. text ed. 104.00 (0-88167-333-1) Raven.

Rose, Robert M., jt. ed. see Barrett, James E.

Rose, Robert M., jt. auth. see Chernyak, Yuri B.

Rose, Roger G. Reconciling the Past: Two Basketry Ka'ai & the Legendary Liloa & Lonoikamakahiki. (Bishop Museum Bulletin in Anthropology Ser.: No. 5). 1992. pap. 12.95 (0-930897-76-5) Bishop Mus.

Rose, Roger G., jt. ed. see Dark, Philip J.

Rose, Ron. Dad's Diary: 30 Days to Being a Better Dad. 180p. 1994. 10.95 (1-878990-29-2) Howard Pub LA.

— Seven Things Kids Never Forget: And How to Make the Most of Them. 175p. 1993. pap. 8.99 (0-945564-79-1, Multnomah Bks) Questar Pubs.

Rose, Ron, jt. auth. see Allen, Roger.

Rose, Ronald E. English Dial Clocks. 2nd ed. (Illus.). 256p. 1988. 69.50 (1-85149-062-0) Antique Collect.

Rose, Ruth P., jt. auth. see Netherton, Nan.

Rose, Saul. Britain & South-East Asia. LC 62-18415. (Britain in the World Today Ser.: No. 2). 208p. reprint ed. pap. 59.30 (0-8357-7407-4, 2005249) Bks Demand.

Rose, Seraphim. The Future of Russia & the End of the World. 12p. (Orig.). 1985. pap. 1.00 (0-912927-16-X, X016) St John Kronstadt.

— God's Revelation to the Human Heart. (Illus.). 40p. (Orig.). 1988. pap. 4.00 (0-938635-03-4) St Herman AK.

— Heavenly Realm. LC 84-51410. (Illus.). 116p. 1984. pap. 5.00 (0-938635-05-0) St Herman AK.

— Orthodoxy & the Religion of the Future. LC 75-16940. 246p. 1989. pap. 5.00 (0-938635-22-0) St Herman AK.

— The Place of Blessed Augustine in the Orthodox Church. (Illus.). 50p. 1983. pap. 3.00 (0-938635-12-3) St Herman AK.

— The Soul after Death: Contemporary "After-Death" Experiences in the Light of the Orthodox Teaching on the Afterlife. 3rd ed. LC 93-25175. 296p. 1993. pap. 8.95 (0-938635-14-X) St Herman AK.

Rose, Seraphim, tr. see Andrew of New Diveyevo.

Rose, Seraphim, ed. see Archbishop Averky.

Rose, Seraphim, tr. see Maximovitch, John.

Rose, Seraphim, tr. see Pomazansky, Michael.

Rose, Seraphim, tr. see Schema-monk Plato n.

Rose, Seraphim, ed. see St. Gregory of Tours.

Rose, Seraphim, tr. see St. Symeon the New Theologian.

***Rose, Sharon, ed.** CD's, Super Glue, & Salsa: How Everyday Products Are Made, 2. Incl. Vol. 1. Automobile to Lawn Mower, 2. LC 94-35243. (J). 1994. (0-8103-9792-7, UXL); Vol. 2. Light Bulb to Zipper, 2. (J). 1994. (0-8103-9793-5, UXL); LC 94-35243. write for info. (0-8103-9791-9, UXL) Gale.

***Rose, Sharon & Stevens, Cris, eds.** Bisexual Horizons: Politics, Histories & Lives. 288p. (C). 1995. pap. 19.95 (0-85315-831-2, Pub. by Lawrence & Wishart UK) Humanities.

Rose, Sharon, ed. see Chapelle.

Rose, Sharon, ed. see Edwards, Lynne.

Rose, Sharon, ed. see Rice, Lynn.

Rose, Sheldon D. A Casebook in Group Therapy: A Behavioral-Cognitive Approach. (Social Work Practice Ser.). (Illus.). 1979. text ed. write for info. (0-13-117408-8) P-H.

— Treating Children in Groups: A Behavioral Approach. LC 78-189609. (Jossey-Bass Behavioral Science Ser.). 239p. reprint ed. pap. 68.20 (0-8357-6890-2, 2037942) Bks Demand.

— Working with Adults in Groups: Integrating Cognitive-Behavioral & Small Group Strategies. LC 89-45589. (Social & Behavioral Science Ser.). 382p. 1989. 34.95x (1-55542-166-0) Jossey-Bass.

Rose, Sheldon D. & Edleson, Jeffrey L. Working with Children & Adolescents in Groups: A Multimethod Approach. LC 86-20181. (Social & Behavioral Science Ser.). 404p. 1987. 34.95x (1-55542-009-5) Jossey-Bass.

Rose, Sheldon D. & Feldman, Ronald A., eds. Research in Social Group Work. LC 86-25176. (Social Work with Groups Ser.: Vol. 9, No. 3). 124p. 1987. text ed. 29.95 (0-86656-645-7) Haworth Pr.

Rose, Sheldon D., jt. ed. see Brower, Aaron M.

***Rose, Shirley.** Let's Discover the Bible, 2 vols., Set. (Illus.). 64p. (J). (gr. k-2). Date not set. pap. 3.95 (0-87441-538-1) Behrman.

***Rose, Silver.** Women Who Joke Too Much. LC 95-8210. 192p. (Orig.). 1995. pap. 9.00 (0-399-52154-2, Perigree Bks) Berkley Pub.

Rose, Sonia O. Limited Livelihoods: Gender & Class in Nineteenth-Century England. (Studies on the History of Society & Culture: No. 13). (Illus.). 320p. 1991. 40.00 (0-520-07478-5); pap. 14.00 (0-520-07479-3) U CA Pr.

Rose, Stanley M. Real Estate Buying-Selling Guide for Ontario. 9th ed. (Legal Ser.). 224p. Canadian Edition. 9.95 (0-88908-392-4) Self-Counsel Pr.

Rose, Stephen & Fasenfest, David. Family Incomes in the Nineteen Eighty's. (Working Paper Ser.: No. 103). 1988. 10.00 (0-944826-28-8) Economic Policy Inst.

Rose, Stephen C., et al. Design Engineering Aspects of Waterflooding. 108p. 1989. 45.00 (1-55563-016-2, 30411) Soc Petrol Engineers.

Rose, Stephen J. Social Stratification in the United States: The American Profile Poster. LC 92-18940. 48p. 1992. pap. 14.95 (1-56584-021-6) New Press NY.

Rose, Stephen J., jt. auth. see Joss, Vanda.

Rose, Stephen M. The Betrayal of the Poor: The Transformation of Community Action. LC 76-178829. 199p. 1972. pap. text ed. 15.95 (0-87073-285-4) Schenkman Bks Inc.

Rose, Stephen M., ed. Case Management & Social Work Practice. 320p. (Orig.). (C). 1992. pap. text ed. 27.50 (0-8013-0332-X, 78104) Longman.

Rose, Stephen M. & Black, Bruce. Advocacy & Empowerment: Mental Health Care in Community. LC 85-1802. 256p. 1985. 27.50 (0-7100-9963-0, RKP) Routledge.

Rose, Steven. Molecules & Minds: Biology & the Social Order. 160p. 1991. text ed. 99.95 (0-471-93260-4, Wiley-Liss); pap. text ed. 42.95 (0-471-93259-0, Wiley-Liss) Wiley.

— Molecules & Minds: Essays on Biology & the Social Order. 176p. 1987. 75.00 (0-335-15814-5); pap. 28.00 (0-335-15813-7) Wiley.

Rose, Steven R., jt. auth. see Fatout, Marian.

Rose, Stewart. Ignatius Loyola & the Early Jesuits. LC 83-45596. reprint ed. 52.00 (0-404-19889-9) AMS Pr.

Rose, Stuart R. International Travel Health Guide, 1995. 6th ed. (Illus.). 454p. 1995. pap. 17.95 (0-923947-05-1) Travel Med.

***Rose, Stuart W.** Mandeville: A Guide for the Marketing of Professional Services. 379p. 1995. 89.00 (1-887133-00-3) Prof Dev Res.

Rose, Susan D. Keeping Them Out of the Hands of Satan: Evangelical Schooling in America. (Critical Social Thought Ser.). 224p. 1990. text ed. 35.00 (0-415-90004-2, Routledge NY); pap. 13.95 (0-415-90299-1, Routledge NY) Routledge.

***Rose, Susan E., pseud.** Celestial Inspirations: Channeled Affirmations & Prayers by the "Nameless Ones", St. Therese, Archangel Michael, St. Germain, & Thalius. 48p. 1995. pap. write for info. (0-9644840-0-5) Celestial Insp.

Rose, Susan L. Clinical Laboratory Safety. (Illus.). 304p. 1984. pap. 34.95 (0-397-50615-5, 65-07800) Van Nos Reinhold.

Rose, Suzanna. Career Guide for Women Scholars. 224p. 1986. pap. 27.95 (0-8261-5411-5) Springer Pub.

Rose, Suzanna & Larwood, Laurie, eds. Women's Careers: Pathways & Pitfalls. LC 88-2344. 234p. 1988. text ed. 55.00 (0-275-92724-5, C2724, Praeger Pubs) Greenwood.

Rose, T. K. & Newman, W. A. C. The Metallurgy of Gold. write for info. (0-931913-05-5) Met-Chem Rsch.

***Rose, T. L., et al, eds.** Proceedings of the Symposium on Water Purification by Photocatalytic, Photoelectrochemical, & Electrochemical Processes. LC 94-70851. (Proceedings Ser.: Vol. 94-19). 384p. 1994. 48.00 (1-56677-076-9) Electrochem Soc.

***Rose, Tania.** Aspects of Political Censorship, 1914-1918. 104p. 1995. pap. 17.95 (0-85958-632-4, Pub. by Hull Univ Pr UK) Paul & Co Pubs.

***Rose, Ted.** Discovering Drawing. LC 93-74645. (Illus.). 1995. teacher ed 34.50 (0-87192-282-7) Davis Mass.

Rose, Tessa. Coronation Ceremony & the Crown Jewels. 134p. 1992. 19.95 (0-11-701361-7, HM2676, Pub. by HMSO UK) UNIPUB.

Rose, Thomas, jt. auth. see Ansello, Edward F.

Rose, Thomasine. Verbivocovisual. (Illus.). 72p. (C). 1982. 9.85 (0-9606540-3-8) Classic Nonfic.

Rose, Tom. Economics: Principles & Policy from a Christian Perspective. 2nd ed. LC 85-72235. (Illus.). 380p. 1985. teacher ed 7.50 (0-9612198-6-6); text ed. 21.95 (0-9612198-5-8) A E P.

— Economics: The American Economy from a Christian Perspective. LC 83-72165. (Illus.). 388p. 1985. 21.95 (0-9612198-0-7); teacher ed 7.50 (0-9612198-1-5) A E P.

— Free Enterprise Economics. 2nd ed. LC 88-70057. 20p. 1988. pap. 1.75 (0-9612198-7-4) A E P.

— Freeing the Whales: How the Media Created the World's Greatest Non-Event. Black, Hillel, ed. (Illus.). 252p. 1989. 16.95 (1-55972-011-5, Birch Ln Pr) Carol Pub Group.

— How to Succeed in Business. LC 74-33827. (Illus.). 88p. 1975. 4.95 (0-9612198-2-3); pap. 1.95 (0-9612198-3-1) A E P.

Rose Township Historical Society. Rose Township Eighteen Thirty-Seven - Nineteen Eighty-Seven. Trimmer, Betty, ed. LC 86-63912. (Illus.). 141p. 1987. 15.00 (0-9617648-0-5) Rose Twsp Hist Soc.

Rose, Tricia. Black Noise: Rap Music & Black Culture in Contemporary America. LC 93-41386. (Music - Culture Ser.). (Illus.). 257p. (C). 1994. text ed. 35.00x (0-8195-5271-2, Wesleyan Univ Pr); pap. 14.95 (0-8195-6275-0, Wesleyan Univ Pr) U Pr of New Eng.

Rose, Tricia, jt. ed. see Ross, Andrew.

Rose-Troup, Frances. Massachusetts Bay Company & Its Predecessors. LC 73-15804. 1973. reprint ed. 29.50 (0-678-00871-X) Kelley.

R

An Asterisk (*) at the beginning of an entry indicates that the title is appearing in BIP for the first time.

Rose, Tui. How to Make a Snail Sneeze: 301 Greenthumbs-up Gardening Successes. Roberts, Jackie et al, eds. (Illus.). 100p. (Orig.). 1995. per. write for info. (*1-885735-05-7*) Crown Jewel.

— Money Is Honey: 501 Dollar-Wise Ways to Save Thousands and Prevent Big Losses. Roberts, Jackie & Love, Karen, eds. (Crown Jewel of Home Help Ser.). (Illus.). 263p. 1995. pap. 9.95 (*1-885735-13-8*) Crown Jewel.

— My Very Own Kitchen Maid: 1500 Smart & Trouble Saving Hints for Cooking Success, Kitchen Efficiency & Ease. Allison, Valerie et al, eds. (Illus.). 200p. 1995. pap. write for info. (*1-885735-07-3*) Crown Jewel.

— My Very Own Nurse: One Thousand One Body, Mind, & Beauty Briefs. Roberts, Jackie & Love, Karen, eds. (Illus.). 350p. 1995. per. write for info. (*1-885735-08-1*) Crown Jewel.

— The Right Royal Clean-Up: Five Hundred One Quick N' Easy Hints for Cleaning, Laundry & Those Jack-of-All-Trades Jobs. Allison, Valerie et al, eds. (Illus.). 150p. 1995. pap. write for info. (*1-885735-04-9*) Crown Jewel.

Rose-Turner, Clarinda. Ruminations: Poetry, Images & Memories. (Illus.). 30p. (Orig.). 1989. pap. 4.00 (*0-924120-02-9*) Intl Oil Work.

Rose, V. M. The Anti-Representational Response: Gertrude Stein's Lucy Church Amiably. 232p. (Orig.). 1985. pap. text ed. 33.00x (*91-554-1751-5*) Coronet Bks.

Rose, Valentin. Aristoteles Pseudepigraphus. 728p. 1971. reprint ed. write for info. (*0-318-71011-0*, Pub. by Georg Olms GW) Lubrecht & Cramer.

Rose, Valentin & Schillmann, Fritz. Verzeichnis der Lateinischen Handschriften der Koniglichen Bibliothek Zu Berlin, 5 vols. in 3, Set. 1, 2035p. 1976. reprint ed. write for info. (*3-487-06038-8*, Pub. by Georg Olms GW) Lubrecht & Cramer.

Rose, Vattel T., ed. Aesthetic & Philosophical Issues in Afro-American Art. (Papers on Afro-American, African, & Caribbean Studies). (Illus.). 150p. 1985. pap. 6.00 (*0-911393-04-8*) Ctr Afro Stud Ohio.

Rose, Vernon E., jt. ed. see Perkins, Jimmy L.

Rose, W. K., ed. see Lewis, Wyndham.

Rose, Walter. Good Neighbours. 160p. (Orig.). 1991. pap. 9.95 (*1-870098-16-1*, Pub. by Green Bks UK) Seven Hills Bk.

— The Village Carpenter. LC 88-3. (Illus.). 146p. (YA). (gr. 10 up). 1988. reprint ed. pap. 9.95 (*0-941533-18-2*) New Amsterdam Bks.

Rose, Wendy. Bone Dance: New & Selected Poems, 1965-1993. LC 93-21117. (Sun Tracks Ser.: Vol. 27). 120p. (Orig.). (C). 1994. lib. bdg. 19.95 (*0-8165-1412-7*); pap. 10.95 (*0-8165-1428-3*) U of Ariz Pr.

— Going to War with All My Relations: New & Selected Poems. LC 92-46217. 96p. (Orig.). 1993. pap. 9.95 (*0-87358-556-9*, Entrada Bks) Northland AZ.

— The Halfbreed Chronicles & Other Poems. (Illus.). 72p. (Orig.). (C). 1985. pap. 8.95 (*0-931122-39-2*) West End.

— Lost Copper. LC 80-81849. 1992. pap. 10.00 (*0-939046-35-0*) Malki Mus Pr.

— Now Poof She Is Gone. 80p. (Orig.). 1994. lib. bdg. 18.95 (*1-56341-049-4*); pap. 8.95 (*1-56341-048-6*) Firebrand Bks.

— What Happened When the Hopi Hit New York. (Chapbook Ser.). (Illus.). 56p. (Orig.). (C). 1982. pap. 3.50 (*0-936556-08-0*) Contact Two.

Rose, Will. The Vanishing Village. 350p. 1970. 5.50 (*0-9600350-0-1*) Catskill Art.

Rose, Willi, jt. auth. see McMahan, Dean.

Rose, William. From Goethe to Byron: The Development of Weltschmerz in German Literature. 1972. 59.95 (*0-8490-0203-6*) Gordon Pr.

— U. S. Unilateral Arms Control Initiatives: When Do They Work? LC 88-17774. (Contributions in Military Studies: No. 82). 209p. 1988. text ed. 55.00 (*0-313-25787-6*, RUR/, Greenwood Pr) Greenwood.

Rose, William & Isaacs, Jacob, eds. Contemporary Movements in European Literature. (Essay Index Reprint Ser.). 1977. 20.95 (*0-8369-0833-3*) Ayer.

Rose, William, tr. see Bejar-Rivera, Hector.

Rose, William, jt. auth. see Lindemann, Mark.

Rose, William, ed. see Rilke, Rainer Maria.

Rose, William, et al. R. M. Rilke: Aspects of His Mind & Poetry. Houston, G. C., ed. LC 72-6484. (Studies in German Literature: No. 13). (Illus.). 190p. 1972. reprint ed. lib. bdg. 39.95 (*0-8383-1617-4*) M S G Haskell Hse.

Rose, William G. Cleveland: The Making of a City (1950) 1, 950th ed. LC 90-4853. (Black Squirrel Bks.: No. 1). (Illus.). 1286p. 1990. 75.00 (*0-87338-428-8*) Kent St U Pr.

Rose, William J. The English Memoirs of William John Rose. Stone, Daniel, ed. LC 74-79986. reprint ed. pap. 28.50 (*0-317-26961-5*, 2023673) Bks Demand.

— The Polish Memoirs of William John Rose. Stone, Daniel, ed. LC 74-79986. 274p. reprint ed. pap. 78.10 (*0-317-41778-9*, 2023673) Bks Demand.

Rose, William M. Pleading Without Tears: A Guide to Legal Drafting. 2nd ed. 316p. (C). 1992. pap. 32.00 (*1-85431-216-2*, Pub. by Blackstone Pr UK) W W Gaunt.

— Pleadings Without Tears: A Guide to Legal Drafting, Vol. 1. 3rd ed. 340p. 1994. pap. text ed. 32.00 (*1-85431-405-X*, Blckstone AT) W W Gaunt.

Rose, Willie L. Rehearsal for Reconstruction: The Port Royal Experiment. 1976. reprint ed. pap. 14.95 (*0-19-519882-4*) OUP.

Rose, Xenia. Widow's Journey: A Return to the Loving Self. 224p. 1991. pap. 9.95 (*0-8050-1837-9*, Owl) H Holt & Co.

Roseau, M. Asymptotic Wave Theory. LC 74-26167. (Applied Mathematics & Mechanics Ser.: Vol. 20). 349p. 1976. 97.50 (*0-444-10798-3*, North Holland) Elsevier.

— Vibrations in Mechanical Systems. (Illus.). 530p. 1987. 74.00 (*0-387-17950-X*) Spr-Verlag.

Rosebault, Charles J. When Dana Was the Sun. LC 77-103657. (Select Bibliographies Reprint Ser.). 1977. 30.95 (*0-8369-5157-3*) Ayer.

— When Dana Was the Sun: A Story of Personal Journalism. 1970. reprint ed. text ed. 69.50 (*0-8371-4009-9*, RODS, Greenwood Pr) Greenwood.

Rosebaum, Robert A., ed. see Neumann, Inge S.

Rosebberg, Janet, ed. see Landis, Carney & Bolles, M. Marjorie.

Roseberry, C. R. Flashback: A Fresh Look at Albany's Past. Dumbleton, Susanne, ed. (Illus.). 208p. (Orig.). 1986. 22.95 (*0-9605460-5-7*); pap. 14.95 (*0-9605460-4-9*) Wash Park.

— Glenn Curtiss: Pioneer of Flight. (Illus.). 526p. (Orig.). 1991. reprint ed. pap. 17.95 (*0-8156-0264-2*) Syracuse U Pr.

Roseberry, Eric. Shostakovich. (Illustrated Lives of the Great Composers Ser.). (Illus.). 192p. 1987. pap. 14.95 (*0-7119-0258-5*, OP42449) Omnibus NY.

— W. A. Mozart. LC 60-3144. (Great Masters Ser.). 1960. pap. 4.00 (*0-913932-20-5*) Boosey & Hawkes.

Roseberry, J. Royal, III. Imperial Rule in Punjab: The Conquest & Administration of Multan, 1818-1881. LC 86-63596. 272p. 1987. 34.00 (*0-913215-23-6*) Riverdale Co.

***Roseberry, John.** Self-Development Through Self-Defense: A Course in Personal Security. (Illus.). 58p. (Orig.). 1994. student ed, pap. 19.95 (*0-9639936-0-7*) J Samuel Pubng.

Roseberry, John L. & Klimstra, Willard D. Population Ecology of the Bobwhite. LC 83-2481. (Illus.). 282p. 1983. 29.95 (*0-8093-1116-X*) S Ill U Pr.

Roseberry, Robert & Weinstock, Rachel. Reading Etc. An Integrated Skills Text. 304p. (C). 1991. pap. text ed. 20.50 (*0-13-763467-6*, 640806) P-H.

Roseberry, Sherry. Love Only Once. 336p. (Orig.). 1993. mass mkt. 4.99 (*1-55773-924-2*) Diamond.

Roseberry, William. Anthropologies & Histories: Essays in Culture, History, & Political Economy. LC 89-30378. 256p. (C). 1989. text ed. 38.00 (*0-8135-1445-2*); pap. text ed. 16.00 (*0-8135-1446-0*) Rutgers U Pr.

Roseberry, William, jt. ed. see O'Brien, Jay.

Roseberry, William, et al, eds. Coffee, Society, & Power in Latin America. LC 94-14193. (Johns Hopkins Studies in Atlantic History & Culture Ser.). 304p. 1995. text ed. 48.50 (*0-8018-4884-9*); pap. text ed. 15.95 (*0-8018-4887-3*) Johns Hopkins.

Rosebery, Archibald. Pitt. LC 68-25264. (English Biography Ser.: No. 31). 1969. reprint ed. lib. bdg. 59.95 (*0-8383-0236-X*) M S G Haskell Hse.

Rosebery, Archibald P. Miscellanies: Literary & Historical, 2 vols. LC 71-152211. (Essay Index Reprint Ser.). 1977. reprint ed. 47.95 (*0-8369-2253-0*) Ayer.

— Pitt. LC 78-106521. reprint ed. 34.00 (*0-404-05405-6*) AMS Pr.

Roseblade, James E., jt. ed. see Gruenberg, Karl W.

Roseblade, James E., ed. see Hall, Philip.

Roseblum, Richard. Stars & Stripes & Soldiers. (J). (ps-3). 1993. pap. 3.95 (*0-590-45222-3*) Scholastic Inc.

Roseboom. History of Presidential Elections. 1985. 17.95 (*0-02-604890-6*) Macmillan.

Roseboom & Weisenburger Staff. A History of Ohio. pap. 12.95 (*0-318-42416-9*) Ohio Hist Soc.

Roseboom, Eugene H. History of Ohio. 1993. reprint ed. lib. bdg. 89.00 (*0-7812-5398-5*) Rprt Serv.

Roseboom, Johannes, jt. ed. see Pardey, Philip G.

Roseboro, Viola. Players & Vagabonds. LC 70-101291. (Short Story Index Reprint Ser.). 1977. 21.95 (*0-8369-3228-5*) Ayer.

Roseborough, Margaret M. Outline of Middle English Grammar. LC 70-109833. 112p. 1970. reprint ed. text ed. 35.00 (*0-8371-4324-1*, ROMI, Greenwood Pr) Greenwood.

Rosebrock, Ellen F. Counting-House Days in South Street: New York's Early Brick Seaport Buildings. (Illus.). (Orig.). 1975. pap. 2.50 (*0-913344-18-4*) South St Sea Mus.

— Farewell to Old England, New York in Revolution. LC 75-3941. (Illus.). 64p. (Orig.). 1976. pap. 1.95 (*0-913344-21-4*) South St Sea Mus.

— South Street: A Photographic Guide to New York City's Historic Seaport. 1977. pap. 5.95 (*0-486-23396-0*) Dover.

— Walking Around in South Street: Discoveries in New York's Old Shipping District. (Illus.). (Orig.). 1974. pap. 3.95 (*0-913344-17-6*) South St Sea Mus.

Rosebrough, jt. auth. see Grossman.

Rosebrough, Robert F. The San Juan Mountains: A Climbing & Hiking Guide. LC 86-4530. (Illus.). 274p. 1986. 12.95 (*0-917895-07-X*) Cordillera CO.

Rosebury, Brian. Art & Desire: A Study in the Aesthetics of Fiction. LC 88-6566. 272p. 1988. text ed. 39.95 (*0-312-02062-7*) St Martin.

— Tolkein: A Critical Assessment. LC 91-33345. 176p. 1992. text ed. 49.95 (*0-312-07583-9*) St Martin.

Rosebury, Fred. Handbook of Electron Tube & Vacuum Techniques. LC 92-46418. (AVS Classics of Vacuum Science & Technology Ser.). 1993. write for info. (*1-56396-121-0*) Am Inst Physics.

— Symbols: Myth, Magic, Fact, & Fancy. LC 74-22888. (Illus.). 411p. reprint ed. pap. 117.20 (*0-685-23681-1*, AU00358) Bks Demand.

Rosebush, James S. First Lady, Public Wife: A Behind-the-Scenes History of the Evolving Role of First Ladies in American Political Life. LC 87-24051. (Illus.). 128p. 1987. 24.95 (*0-8191-6497-6*) U Pr of Amer.

Rosebush, Judson. Computer-Generated Animation. 1991. text ed. write for info. (*0-442-20526-0*) Van Nos Reinhold.

Rosebush, Judson, jt. auth. see Kerlow, Isaac V.

Rosebush, Waldo E. American Firearms & the Changing Frontier. 1962. pap. 4.50 (*0-910524-01-7*) Eastern Wash.

Rosecan, Jeffrey S., jt. ed. see Spitz, Henry I.

Rosecrance, Barbara. Forster's Narrative Vision. LC 23-71598. 248p. 1982. 34.95 (*0-8014-1502-0*) Cornell U Pr.

Rosecrance, John. The Degenerates of Lake Tahoe: A Study of Persistence in the Social World of Horse Race Gambling. (American University Studies: Anthropology & Science: Ser. XI, Vol. 8). 169p. (C). 1985. text ed. 32.00 (*0-8204-0187-0*) P Lang Pubs.

— Gambling Without Guilt: The Legitimation of an American Pastime. 174p. 1988. pap. 16.00 (*0-534-08954-2*) Intl Thomson.

Rosecrance, Richard. Cooperation in a World Without Enemies: Solving the Public Goods Problem in International Relations. (CISA Working Paper Ser.: No. 2). 54p. Date not set. 10.00 (*0-86682-092-2*) Ctr Intl Relations.

Rosecrance, Richard, ed. America As an Ordinary Country: U. S. Foreign Policy & the Future. LC 75-38427. 288p. 1976. 34.00 (*0-8014-1010-X*) Cornell U Pr.

Rosecrance, Richard & Stein, Arthur A., eds. The Domestic Bases of Grand Strategy. LC 93-15396. (Cornell Studies in Security Affairs). 256p. 1993. 36.50 (*0-8014-2880-7*); pap. 13.95 (*0-8014-8116-3*) Cornell U Pr.

Rosecrance, Richard N. Action & Reaction in World Politics: International Systems in Perspective. LC 77-2329. 314p. 1977. reprint ed. text ed. 35.00 (*0-8371-9548-9*, ROAR, Greenwood Pr) Greenwood.

— The Rise of the Trading State: Commerce & Conquest in the Modern World. LC 85-47558. 288p. 1987. pap. text ed. 17.00 (*0-465-07037-X*) Basic.

Rosedahl, Else, ed. From Viking to Crusader: The Scandinavians & Europe, 800-1200. (Illus.). 432p. 1992. 65.00 (*0-8478-1625-7*) Rizzoli Intl.

***Roseen, Sven, et al.** The Dansbury Diaries: Moravian Travel Diaries of Reverend Sven Roseen & Others 1748-1755 in the Area of Dansbury, Now Stroudsburg, PA. Schwarze, William N. & Hillman, Ralf R., trs. LC 94-667111. (Illus.). 288p. 1994. 29.95x (*0-89725-176-8*, 522) Picton Pr.

Rosefeld, Stuart. Vocational Education & Economic Growth: Connections & Conundrums. 22p. 1986. 3.00 (*0-318-22232-9*, OC 112) Ctr Educ Trng Employ.

***Rosefeldt, Paul.** The Absent Father in Modern Drama. 54. LC 94-28595. (American University Studies: Series III, Vol. 54). 176p. (C). 1995. text ed. 38.95 (*0-8204-2629-6*) P Lang Pubs.

Rosefielde, Steven. False Science: Underestimating the Soviet Arms Buildup. 2nd rev. ed. 452p. 1987. 42.95 (*0-88738-088-3*) Transaction Pubs.

Rosefielde, Steven, ed. World Communism at the Crossroads: Military Ascendancy, Political Economy & Human Welfare. 1980. lib. bdg. 49.50 (*0-89838-041-3*) Kluwer Ac.

Rosefsky, Bob. Financial Wisdom: Lessons from Life. LC 94-16686. 1995. text ed. 24.95 (*0-471-58729-X*) Wiley.

Rosefsky, Robert S. Personal Finance. 5th ed. LC 92-34971. 719p. 1993. Net. text ed. write for info. (*0-471-54978-9*) Wiley.

— Personal Finance. 6th ed. LC 95-17418. 1996. text ed. write for info. (*0-471-11620-3*) Wiley.

— Personal Finance Newsletter, Set. 3rd ed. 1994. text ed. write for info. (*0-471-11713-7*) Wiley.

Rosegg. Natural Childbirth: The Bradley Way. 1985. pap. 15.00 (*0-452-26724-2*, Plume) NAL-Dutton.

Rosegger, Gerhard. The Economics of Production & Innovation: An Industrial Perspective. (Illus.). 1980. text ed. 35.60 (*0-08-024047-X*, Pergamon Pr); pap. text ed. 17.00 (*0-08-024046-1*, Pergamon Pr) Elsevier.

— The Economics of Production & Innovation: An Industrial Perspective. 2nd ed. (OMEGA Management Science Ser.). (Illus.). 260p. 1986. text ed. 110.00 (*0-08-033958-1*, Pergamon Pr); pap. text ed. 59.00 (*0-08-033959-X*, Pergamon Pr) Elsevier.

Rosegrant, Mark W., jt. auth. see Mendoza, Meyra S.

Rosegrant, Susan & Lampe, David. Route One Twenty-Eight: Lessons from Boston's High-Tech Community. LC 91-58600. 256p. 1993. pap. 14.00 (*0-465-07147-3*) Basic.

Rosegrant, Teresa, jt. ed. see Bredekamp, Sue.

Rosei, Peter. From Here to There. Thorpe, Kathleen, tr. & aft. by. (Studies in Austrian Literature, Culture, & Thought. Translation Ser.). 94p. 1991. pap. 10.50 (*0-929497-43-0*) Ariadne CA.

— Try Your Luck. Thorpe, Kathleen E., tr. & aft. by. LC 93-25580. (Studies in Austrian Literature, Culture, & Thought. Translation Ser.). (GER.). 1994. pap. 10.50 (*0-929497-76-7*) Ariadne CA.

Rosei, R., jt. ed. see Campagna, M.

Roseinnes, A., jt. auth. see Hilsum, C.

Roseire, Gabrielle. Fortune Telling & Character Reading. reprint ed. spiral bd. 6.60 (*0-7873-0737-8*) Mokelumne.

Rosekrans, Spreck, jt. auth. see Rasmussen, Steven.

Rosekraus, Spreck, jt. auth. see Rasmussen, Steven.

Roseler, Robert O., ed. see Von le Fort, Gertrud.

Roseliep, Raymond. Love Makes the Air Light. (Orig.). 1965. pap. 1.95 (*0-393-04243-X*) Norton.

— The Still Point. 1979. pap. 2.50 (*0-930600-12-6*) Uzzano Pr.

Roselius, Ted & Benton, Douglas. Black Market Operations. LC 89-45800. (Illus.). 1979. pap. 7.95 (*1-55950-017-4*) Loompanics.

Rosell, Garth, jt. auth. see Dupuis, Richard.

Rosell, Rosendo. Mas Cuentos Picantes de Rosendo Rosell. LC 79-5001. (Coleccion Caniqui Ser.). (Illus.). 138p. 1980. pap. 6.00 (*0-89729-219-7*) Ediciones.

— Vida y Milagros de la Farandula de Cuba. 2nd ed. LC 91-72527. (Coleccion Arte Ser.). (Illus.). 427p. (SPA.). 1992. reprint ed. pap. 19.00 (*0-89729-608-7*) Ediciones.

— Vida y Milagros de la Farandula de Cuba, Vol. III. LC 91-72527. (Coleccion Cuba y Sus Jueces Ser.). (Illus.). 468p. (SPA.). 1994. pap. 20.00 (*0-89729-754-7*) Ediciones.

— Vida y Milagros de la Farandula de Cuba 2. LC 91-72527. 494p. (Orig.). (SPA.). 1992. pap. 20.00 (*0-89729-668-0*) Ediciones.

Rosell, Steven A., et al. Governing in an Information Society. 167p. 1992. pap. text ed. 14.95 (*0-88645-147-7*, Pub. by Inst Res Pub CN) Ashgate Pub Co.

Roselle, Daniel. A Parent's Guide to the Social Studies. 16p. 1974. pap. 1.25 (*0-87986-053-7*, 491-15274) Nat Coun Soc Studies.

Roselle, Daniel, ed. Voices of Social Education, Nineteen Thirty-Seven to Nineteen Eighty-Seven. 528p. (C). 1987. text ed. 34.95 (*0-02-922380-6*) Macmillan.

Roselle, Laurie P. Litigation Techniques for Legal Assistants: Becoming a More Effective Member of the Litigation Team. 476p. 1991. 70.00 (*0-685-69462-3*); vhs 195.00 (*0-685-69463-1*) PLI.

Roselle, Leone R. Secrets of Word Power: The Anatomy of Words. 320p. 1994. pap. 18.95 (*0-8059-3423-5*) Dorrance.

Roselle, William C., jt. auth. see Gabriel, Michael R.

Rosellini, Gayle. Stinking Thinking. 24p. (Orig.). 1985. pap. 1.55 (*0-89486-326-6*, 5451B) Hazelden.

Rosellini, Gayle & Worden, Mark. Barriers to Intimacy: For People Torn by Addiction & Compulsive Behavior. 176p. 1990. reprint ed. mass mkt. 4.99 (*0-345-36735-9*) Ballantine.

— Here Comes the Sun: Dealing with Depression. 190p. (Orig.). 1987. pap. 10.00 (*0-89486-466-1*, 5026A) Hazelden.

— Of Course You Are Angry. (Hazelden Bks.). (Orig.). 1986. pap. 10.00 (*0-06-255442-5*, Hazelden SF) Harper SF.

— Of Course You're Angry. 92p. (Orig.). 1985. pap. 9.00 (*0-89486-333-9*, 1169A) Hazelden.

— Of Course You're Anxious: By the Authors of "Of Course You're Angry" 170p. (Orig.). 1990. pap. 10.00 (*0-89486-619-2*, 5075A) Hazelden.

Roseman & Mansdorf. Controlled Released Delivery Systems. 424p. 1983. 140.00 (*0-8247-1728-7*) Dekker.

Roseman, Christina H. Pytheas of Massalia: On the Ocean. (Illus.). 190p. (Orig.). 1994. pap. 15.00 (*0-89005-545-9*) Ares.

Roseman, Curtis C. Changing Migration Patterns Within the United States. Natoli, Salvatore J., ed. LC 76-57033. (Resource Papers for College Geography). (Illus.). 1977. pap. text ed. 10.00 (*0-89291-123-9*) Assn Am Geographers.

***Roseman, Curtis C., et al, eds.** EthniCity: Geographic Perspectives on Ethnic Change in Modern Cities. 245p. (C). 1995. text ed. 58.50 (*0-8476-8032-0*) Rowman.

— EthniCity: Geographic Perspectives on Ethnic Change in Modern Cities. 245p. (C). 1995. pap. text ed. 22.95 (*0-8476-8033-9*) Rowman.

Roseman, Dennis M. Elementary Topology. 192p. 1998. text ed. write for info. (*0-697-14964-1*) Wm C Brown Pubs.

***Roseman, Donald P., ed.** The MarAd Systematic Series of Full-Form Ship Models. 421p. 1987. 60.00 (*0-614-06722-7*) Soc Naval Arch.

Roseman, Edward. Managing Employee Turnover: A Positive Approach. LC 80-69690. 272p. reprint ed. pap. 77.60 (*0-317-42072-0*, 2056088) Bks Demand.

Roseman, Herbert C., ed. see Tucker, Benjamin.

***Roseman, Janet L.** The Way of the Woman Writer. LC 94-22764. 156p. (Orig.). 1994. lib. bdg. 29.95 (*1-56024-905-6*) Haworth Pr.

— The Way of the Woman Writer. LC 94-22764. (Illus.). 120p. (Orig.). 1994. pap. 12.95 (*1-56023-860-7*) Haworth Pr.

Roseman, Kenneth. All in My Jewish Family. (Illus.). 32p. (J). (gr. k-3). 1984. student ed, pap. 5.00 (*0-8074-0266-4*, 103800) UAHC.

— The Cardinal's Snuffbox. (Illus.). 128p. (J). (gr. 4-6). 1982. pap. text ed. 7.95 (*0-8074-0059-9*, 140060) UAHC.

— Escape from the Holocaust. 192p. (Orig.). (J). (gr. 4-6). 1985. pap. 7.95 (*0-8074-0307-5*, 140070) UAHC.

— The Melting Pot. (Do-It-Yourself Jewish Adventure Ser.). (Illus.). 144p. (Orig.). (J). (gr. 4-6). 1984. pap. 7.95 (*0-8074-0269-9*, 146065) UAHC.

Roseman, Kenneth D. The Other Side of the Hudson. (Orig.). (J). (gr. 4-6). 1993. pap. 7.95 (*0-8074-0506-X*, 140061) UAHC.

— The Tenth of Av. (Do-It-Yourself Jewish Adventure Ser.). 96p. (Orig.). (J). (gr. 4-6). 1988. pap. text ed. 7.95 (*0-8074-0359-8*, 123928) UAHC.

Roseman, Kenneth D., et al. Gates of Prayer for Young People: Youth & Family Services. (Illus.). 228p. 1995. Hebrew. 12.95 (*0-88123-045-6*) Central Conf.

Roseman, Marina. Healing Sounds from the Malaysian Rainforest: Temiar Music & Medicine. LC 90-11253. (Comparative Studies of Health Systems & Medical Care: Vol. 28). (Illus.). 278p. 1991. 40.00 (*0-520-06682-0*); pap. 14.00 (*0-520-08281-8*) U CA Pr.

Roseman, Mark. Recasting the Ruhr, 1945-1958: Manpower, Economic Recovery & Labour Relations. (Illus.). 370p. 1992. 75.00 (*0-85496-606-4*) Berg Pubs.

***Roseman, Mark, ed.** Generations in Conflict: Youth Revolt & Generation Formation in Germany 1770-1968. 360p. (C). 1995. 59.95 (*0-521-44183-8*) Cambridge U Pr.

Roseman, Mill. Detectionary. Fenzler, Otto et al, eds. LC 75-27326. (Illus.). 320p. 1977. pap. 12.95 (*0-87951-114-1*) Overlook Pr.

— Detectionary. Fenzler, Otto et al, eds. LC 75-27326. (Illus.). 320p. 1980. 22.95 (*0-87951-041-2*) Overlook Pr.

Roseman, Mindy, jt. auth. see Gesensway, Deborah.

Roseman, Pearl, ed. California Kosher. 286p. 1991. spiral bd. 19.95 (*0-9630953-0-7*) WLOAAE.

R

An Asterisk (*) at the beginning of an entry indicates that the title is appearing in BIP for the first time.

Roseman, V. S. Model Railroading's Guide to the Railway Express. 100p. 1992. pap. 12.95 (*0-9612692-5-1*) Rocky Mntn Pub Co.

Rosemary. One Day at a Time in Phobics Victorious. LC 94-71004. Date not set. pap. 14.95 (*0-8158-0500-4*) Chris Mass.

Rosemary, Kristine. The War Against Gravity. 192p. 1993. 19.95 (*0-930773-20-9*); pap. 10.95 (*0-930773-24-1*) Black Heron Pr.

Rosemergy, Jim. A Daily Guide to Spiritual Living. LC 90-71582. 505p. 1991. 12.95 (*0-87159-027-1*) Unity Bks.

Rosemeyer, Nita. The Bamboo & the Heather. (Orig.). 1980. pap. 2.75 (*0-345-28740-1*) Ballantine.

Rosemire, Adeline. The Other Mid-Life Crisis: Everything You Need to Know about Wills, Hospitals, Life-&-Death Decisions, & Final Matters (but Were Never Taught) 98p. (Orig.). 1994. pap. 14.95 (*0-9640044-0-2*) Meridian Calif.

— The 2-Ingredient Cookbook. 120p. 1995. pap. 9.95 (*0-614-04902-4*) Meridian Calif.

Rosemond, Irene, ed. Reflections: An Oral History of Detroit. LC 92-90956. 106p. (YA). (gr. 12 up). 1992. 10.00 (*0-940713-08-X*) Broadside Pr.

Rosemond, John. Ending the Homework Hassle: Understanding, Preventing, & Solving School Performance Problems. 204p. (Orig.). 1990. pap. 8.95 (*0-8362-2807-3*) Andrews & McMeel.

— A Family of Value. 1995. pap. 8.95 (*0-8362-0505-7*) Andrews & McMeel.

— John Rosemond's Daily Guide to Parenting. (Orig.). 1994. spiral bd. 8.50 (*1-882835-44-1*) STA-Kris.

— Making the "Terrible" Twos Terrific! 160p. 1993. pap. 8.95 (*0-8362-2811-1*) Andrews & McMeel.

— Parent Power! A Common-Sense Approach to Parenting in the '90s & Beyond. 288p. (Orig.). 1991. pap. 9.95 (*0-8362-2808-1*) Andrews & McMeel.

Rosemond, John K. John Rosemond's Six-Point Plan for Raising Happy Healthy Children. 196p. (Orig.). 1989. pap. 8.95 (*0-8362-2806-5*) Andrews & McMeel.

— To Spank or Not to Spank: A Parent's Handbook. LC 94-30050. (Illus.). 1994. pap. 8.95 (*0-8362-2813-8*) Andrews & McMeel.

Rosemont, Franklin. The Apple of the Automatic Zebra's Eye. 2nd ed. (Surrealist Research & Development Monographs). (Illus.). 1971. pap. 9.00 (*0-941194-03-5*) Black Swan Pr.

— Arsenal, No. 4: Surrealist Subversion. (Illus.). 224p. (Orig.). 1989. lib. bdg. 27.50 (*0-941194-28-0*); pap. 17.00 (*0-941194-27-2*) Black Swan Pr.

— Lamps Hurled at the Stunning Algebra of Ants. (Illus.). 72p. (Orig.). 1990. pap. 12.00 (*0-941194-22-1*) Black Swan Pr.

— The Morning of a Machine Gun: Including Surrealist Documents 1966-68. (Illus.). 1968. pap. 12.00 (*0-941194-00-0*) Black Swan Pr.

— The One Hundredth Anniversary of Hysteria: Catalog of 1978 International Surrealist Exhibition. (Illus.). 24p. pap. 8.00 (*0-941194-11-6*) Black Swan Pr.

Rosemont, Franklin, ed. Apparitions of Things to Come: Edward Bellamy's Tales of Mystery & Imagination. 160p. 1990. 25.95 (*0-88286-164-6*); pap. 9.95 (*0-88286-165-4*) C H Kerr.

— Juice Is Stranger Than Friction: Selected Writings of T-Bone Slim. (Illus.). 160p. 1992. lib. bdg. 25.00 (*0-88286-069-0*); pap. 9.95 (*0-88286-070-4*) C H Kerr.

— Marvelous Freedom: Vigilance of Desire. (Catalog of the 1976 World Surrealist Exhibition Ser.). (Illus.). 1976. pap. 15.00 (*0-941194-09-4*) Black Swan Pr.

Rosemont, Franklin, intro. Mister Block: IWW Comics. (Illus.). 36p. (J). reprint ed. pap. 7.00 (*0-88286-062-3*) C H Kerr.

— Written in Red: Selected Poems. (Poets of Revolt Ser.: No. 2). 56p. 1991. lib. bdg. 20.00 (*0-88286-146-8*); pap. 5.00 (*0-88286-121-2*) C H Kerr.

— You Have No Country! Workers' Struggle Against War. 80p. pap. 4.95 (*0-88286-058-5*) C H Kerr.

Rosemont, Franklin & Garon, Paul. The Forecast Is Hot: Collective Statements of the Surrealist Movement in the U. S. 380p. 1993. pap. text ed. 14.95 (*0-941194-67-1*) Black Swan Pr.

Rosemont, Franklin, ed. see Breton, Andre.

Rosemont, Franklin, ed. see Duncan, Isadora.

Rosemont, Franklin, jt. ed. see Roediger, Dave.

Rosemont, Henry, Jr. A Chinese Mirror: Moral Reflections on Political Economy & Society. LC 91-29013. 140p. (C). 1991. 27.95 (*0-8126-9161-X*); pap. 9.95 (*0-8126-9162-8*) Open Court.

— Chinese Texts & Philosophical Contexts: Essays Dedicated to Angus C. Graham. LC 90-41104. 352p. (C). 1991. 54.95 (*0-8126-9121-0*); pap. 24.95 (*0-8126-9122-9*) Open Court.

— Explorations in Early Chinese Cosmology. (Thematic Studies). 1984. 30.95 (*0-89130-656-0*, 01 25 02) Scholars Pr GA.

Rosemont, Henry, ed. see Leibniz, Gottfried W.

Rosemont, Henry, Jr., ed. see Workshop on Classical Chinese Thought Staff.

Rosemont, Henry P. Benjamin Franklin & the Philadelphia Typographical Strikers of 1786. (UPHS Monographs: No. 1). 32p. 5.00 (*0-686-37775-3*) Union Printers Hist Soc.

Rosemont, Penelope & Baj, Enrico. Beware of the Ice. (Illus.). 64p. 1992. pap. 12.00 (*0-941194-29-9*) Black Swan Pr.

Rosemoor, Patricia. Crimson Nightmare. (Intrigue Ser.). 1994. mass mkt. 2.99 (*0-373-22291-2*, 1-22291-8) Harlequin Bks.

— Dead Heat. (Intrigue Ser.). 1993. mass mkt. 2.99 (*0-373-22243-2*, 1-22243-9) Harlequin Bks.

— The Desperado (Timeless Love) 1995. mass mkt. 3.50 (*0-373-22346-3*) Harlequin Bks.

— Drop Dead Gorgeous: (Dangerous Man) (Intrigue Ser.). 1995. mass mkt. 3.50 (*0-373-22317-X*, 1-22317-1) Harlequin Bks.

— Haunted. (Intrigue Ser.). 1993. mass mkt. 2.99 (*0-373-22250-5*, 1-22250-4) Harlequin Bks.

— No Holds Barred. (Intrigue Ser.: No. 165). 1991. pap. 2.75 (*0-373-22165-7*) Harlequin Bks.

— Pushed to the Limit. (Intrigue Ser.: No. 161). 1991. pap. 2.75 (*0-373-22161-4*) Harlequin Bks.

— Squaring Accounts. (Intrigue Ser.: No. 163). 1991. pap. 2.75 (*0-373-22163-0*) Harlequin Bks.

— Torch Job. (Intrigue Ser.). 1993. pap. 2.89 (*0-373-22219-X*, 1-22219-9) Harlequin Bks.

Rosen. Bruno Bauer & Karl Marx. (Studies in Social History: No. 2). 1977. lib. bdg. 99.00 (*90-247-1948-8*) Kluwer Ac.

— Georgian Republic. 1995. pap. text ed. 15.95 (*0-8442-9679-1*) NTC Pub Grp.

— Lobster Boy. 1995. mass mkt. (*0-7860-0133-X*, Pinnacle NY) Windsor NY.

— Marketing Your Accounting Practice the Big 6 Way: Tricks of the Trade Made Easy for the Small Accounting Firm. 1995. text ed. 55.00 (*0-471-11169-4*) Wiley.

— Maybe He's Just a Jerk. 1995. mass mkt. 4.99 (*0-312-95457-3*) St Martin.

— Species of Aphytis of the World (Hymenoptera: Aphelinidae) (Entomologica Ser.: No. 17). 1979. lib. bdg. 281.50 (*90-6193-127-4*) Kluwer Ac.

— Surfactants in Emerging Technology. (Surfactant Science Ser.: Vol. 26). 216p. 1987. 125.00 (*0-8247-7801-4*) Dekker.

***Rosen & Fechner.** Pathology Annual 1995, Pt. 1. (C). 1995. text ed. 75.00 (*0-8385-7699-0*) Appleton & Lange.

— Pathology Annual, 1995 Pt. 2. (Illus.). 208p. (C). 1995. pap. text ed. 80.00 (*0-8385-8109-9*) Appleton & Lange.

***Rosen & Helman.** Phacoemulsification: A Practical Handbook. 224p. 1995. 49.95 (*0-7506-1887-6*, Focal) Buttrwrth-Heinemann.

Rosen, jt. auth. see Barkin.

Rosen, jt. auth. see Reiser.

Rosen, et al. The Articling Handbook. 192p. 1988. pap. 42.00 (*0-409-80480-0*) Butterworth Legal Pubs.

— Diagnostic Radiology in Emergency Medicine. (Illus.). 704p. 1991. 120.00 (*0-8016-6267-2*) Mosby Yr Bk.

— Diagnostic Radiology in Emergency Medicine. (SPA.). 1993. 109.65 (*84-8086-047-2*) Mosby Yr Bk.

— Essentials of Emergency Medicine. (Illus.). 706p. 1990. pap. 43.95 (*0-8016-5315-0*) Mosby Yr Bk.

Rosen, et al, eds. Biology of Lung Cancer: Diagnosis & Treatment. (Lung Biology in Health & Disease Ser.: Vol. 37). 384p. 1988. 140.00 (*0-8247-7642-9*) Dekker.

Rosen, A. & Wilbur, V. Long-Term Care: Needs, Costs, & Financing. 203p. 1992. pap. text ed. write for info. (*1-879143-14-3*) Health Ins Assn Am.

Rosen, Aaron. Taps for Space. LC 80-52194. 79p. (Orig.). 1980. pap. 7.95 (*0-935296-16-6*) Sheep Meadow.

— Traces. LC 91-13792. 77p. 1991. pap. 10.95 (*1-878818-10-4*) Sheep Meadow.

Rosen, Al. Business Rescue: How to Fix a Company That's Losing Money. 1989. pap. 11.95 (*0-9620675-0-4*) Busn Univ Pr.

— Mint Card Price Guide. 1994. pap. 14.95 (*0-87341-327-X*) Krause Pubns.

Rosen, Alan. Mr. Mint's Insider's Guide to Investing in Baseball Cards & Collectibles. 1991. pap. 8.99 (*0-446-39252-9*) Warner Bks.

***Rosen, Albert P.** Health Hints for Hikers. LC 94-31690. 1994. write for info. (*1-880775-02-6*) NY-NJ Trail Confer.

Rosen, Alexander. How to Find, Hire, Train & Manage Salespeople. (Illus.). 83p. (Orig.). 1990. student ed. pap. 19.95 (*0-9620675-1-2*) Busn Univ Pr.

Rosen, Allen D. Kant's Theory of Justice. 240p. 1993. 28.50 (*0-8014-2757-6*) Cornell U Pr.

Rosen, Andrew. Rise Up, Women! The Militant Campaign of the Women's Social & Political Union, 1903-1914. (Modern Revivals in History Ser.). 340p. 1993. 61.95 (*0-7512-0173-1*, Pub. by Gregg Revivals UK) Ashgate Pub Co.

***Rosen, Ann.** Achieving Sexual Ecstasy: Using Your Body & Mind to Experience Total Satisfaction. 1995. pap. 16.95 (*0-935016-31-7*, Barclay House) Excelsior Music Pub Co.

— Better Shape Up. (Illus.). 32p. 1984. pap. 6.00 (*0-318-35556-6*) Visual Studies.

Rosen, Anne, et al. Family Passover. LC 79-89298. 64p. (J). (gr. 2 up). 1980. 9.95 (*0-8276-0169-7*) JPS Phila.

Rosen, Arlene M. Cities of Clay: The Geoarcheology of Tells. LC 85-11215. (Prehistoric Archeology & Ecology Ser.). (Illus.). 208p. 1987. pap. text ed. 9.00 (*0-226-72627-4*) U Ch Pr.

Rosen, Arnold. Desktop Publishing: Applications & Exercises. 202p. (C). 1988. spiral bd. 21.50 (*0-15-517373-1*) Dryden Pr.

— Office Automation & Information Systems. 363p. (C). 1987. pap. write for info. (*0-675-20557-3*, Merrill Pub Co) Macmillan.

— Quick Reference Guide to PageMaker 4.0: IBM Version. 80p. (C). 1992. spiral bd. write for info. (*0-697-14661-8*) Bus & Educ Tech.

— Telecommunications. 304p. (C). 1987. text ed. 39.00 (*0-15-589815-9*) Dryden Pr.

— The WordPerfect Book. 282p. (C). 1988. spiral bd. 20.00 (*0-15-596580-8*) HB Coll Pubs.

Rosen, Arnold & Dolan, James. Quick Reference Guide to Lotus 1-2-3, Version 2.3. 128p. 1994. spiral bd. write for info. (*0-697-20028-0*) Bus & Educ Tech.

— Quick Reference Guide to PageMaker 5.0, Windows Version. 112p. 1993. spiral bd. write for info. (*0-697-22531-3*) Bus & Educ Tech.

— Quick Reference Guide to Windows. 96p. 1994. spiral bd. write for info. (*0-697-22284-5*) Bus & Educ Tech.

— Quick Reference Guide to Wordperfect 6.0. 128p. (C). 1994. spiral bd. write for info. (*0-697-24278-1*) Bus & Educ Tech.

Rosen, Arnold & Hubbard, William H. Information Processing: Keyboarding Applications & Exercises. 2nd ed. LC 84-27056. 352p. 1985. pap. text ed. 35.50 (*0-471-80855-5*) P-H.

— Text Editing: Keyboarding, Applications & Exercises. LC 84-27090. 231p. 1985. pap. text ed. 30.95 (*0-471-81068-1*) P-H.

***Rosen, Arye & Rosen, Harel D., eds.** New Frontiers in Medical Device Technology. LC 94-26892. (Series in Microwave & Optical Engineering). 1995. text ed. 74.95 (*0-471-59189-0*) Wiley.

Rosen, Arye & Zutavern, Fred J., eds. High-Power Optically Activated Solid-State Switches. (Optoelectronics Ser.). 368p. 1993. text ed. 88.00 (*0-89006-507-1*) Artech Hse.

Rosen, Barbara. Arriaga, the Forgotten Genius: The Short Life of a Basque Composer. LC 88-19219. (Basque Studies Program Occasional Papers Ser.: No. 3). (Illus.). 78p. 1989. 12.00 (*1-877802-01-8*) UNV Reno Basque.

Rosen, Barbara, ed. Witchcraft in England, 1558-1618. LC 91-18279. (Illus.). 424p. 1991. reprint ed. pap. 18.95 (*0-87023-753-5*) U of Mass Pr.

***Rosen, Barry.** The Dog That Did Give Up. (Illus.). 32p. (J). (gr. 1-7). Date not set. pap. 6.95 (*0-614-07270-0*) B R Pub Co TN.

— I'm Not Stupid, I'm Dyslexic. Date not set. pap. write for info. (*0-9625593-3-4*) B R Pub Co TN.

— Marriage 101: Back to the Basics. (Marriage & Family Romance Selfhelp Ser.). 98p. 1993. pap. 4.25 (*0-9625593-1-8*) B R Pub Co TN.

— 250 Ways to Be Romantic: The King of Romance. 189p. 1990. pap. 9.95 (*0-9625593-0-X*) B R Pub Co TN.

Rosen, Barry A., ed. Iran since the Revolution: Internal Dynamics, Regional Conflict, & the Superpowers. (Brooklyn College Studies in Society in Change: No. 47). 200p. 1985. 20.00 (*0-88033-075-9*) Brooklyn Coll Pr.

Rosen, Barry P., ed. Bacterial Transport. LC 78-16191. (Microbiology Ser.: No. 4). 700p. reprint ed. pap. 180.00 (*0-7837-3383-6*, 2043341) Bks Demand.

Rosen, Ben. Digital Type Specimens: The Designer's Computer Type Book. 1991. pap. 44.95 (*0-442-23501-1*) Van Nos Reinhold.

— Digital Type Specimens; Type & Typography, 2 vols., Set. (Illus.). 968p. 1991. pap. 59.95 (*0-442-00761-2*) Van Nos Reinhold.

Rosen, Bernard. Ethical Theory: Strategies & Concepts. LC 92-15891. 306p. (C). 1993. pap. text ed. 30.95 (*1-55934-088-6*) Mayfield Pub.

— Ethics Companion. 144p. (C). 1989. pap. text ed. write for info. (*0-13-291691-6*) P-H.

— Holding Government Bureaucracies Accountable. 2nd ed. LC 88-35731. 224p. 1989. text ed. 55.00 (*0-275-92981-7*, C2981, Praeger Pubs); pap. text ed. 18.95 (*0-275-92982-5*, B2982, Praeger Pubs) Greenwood.

Rosen, Bernard & Caplan, Arthur L. Ethics in the Undergraduate Curriculum. LC 80-12351. (Teaching of Ethics Ser.). 67p. 1980. pap. 4.00 (*0-916558-13-4*) Hastings Ctr.

Rosen, Bernard C. Women, Work & Achievement: The Endless Revolution. LC 88-7802. 256p. 1992. pap. text ed. 18.95 (*0-333-48869-5*) St Martin.

Rosen, Bernard C., et al, eds. Achievement in American Society. 640p. (C). 1969. text ed. 18.50 (*0-87073-000-2*) Schenkman Bks Inc.

Rosen, Betty. And None of It Was Nonsense: The Power of Storytelling in School. LC 87-35272. 176p. 1988. pap. text ed. 16.00 (*0-435-08464-X*) Heinemann.

— How to Set & Achieve Goals. 1981. pap. 5.95 (*0-917386-47-7*) Exec Ent Pubns.

Rosen, Bill, jt. auth. see Drooyan, Irving.

Rosen, Brenda, jt. ed. see Nicholson, Shirley.

Rosen, Bruce K. & Law, Margaret H. Guide to Data Administration. LC 89-600766. (Computer Systems Technology Ser.: Pub. No. 500-173). (Illus.). 81p. (Orig.). 1989. pap. 4.25 (*0-16-000292-3*, S/N 003-003-02967-0) USGPO.

Rosen, C. Party Fun. (Simple Activities Ser.). (Illus.). 14p. (J). (gr. 2-6). 1986. pap. 4.50 (*0-7460-0124-X*) EDC.

Rosen, C., jt. auth. see Wilkes, A.

Rosen, C., et al, eds. Piezoelectricy. LC 90-24044. (Illus.). 552p. (C). 1992. 125.00 (*0-88318-647-0*) Am Inst Physics.

Rosen, Carol. Plays of Impasse: Contemporary Drama Set in Confining Institutions. LC 82-61381. (Illus.). 304p. 1983. 47.50 (*0-691-06565-9*) Princeton U Pr.

— Sam Shepard. (Modern Dramatists Ser.). (Illus.). 160p. 1991. write for info. (*0-312-06051-3*) St Martin.

Rosen, Carole. The Goossens: A Musical Century. 546p. 1994. text ed. 40.00 (*1-55553-210-1*) NE U Pr.

Rosen, Ceil & Rosen, Moishe. Christ in the Passover. LC 77-10689. (C). 1978. pap. 5.99 (*0-8024-1392-7*) Moody.

Rosen, Charles. The Cockroach Basketball League. LC 92-53074. 288p. 1992. 21.00 (*1-55611-329-3*) D I Fine.

— The Frontiers of Meaning: Three Informal Lectures on Music. LC 93-39614. 1994. 21.00 (*0-8090-7254-8*) Hill & Wang.

— The Romantic Generation. LC 94-46239. (Illus.). 736p. 1995. 39.95 (*0-674-77933-9*, ROSROM) HUP.

— Sonata Forms. rev. ed. (Illus.). 352p. 1988. reprint ed. 19.95 (*0-685-08784-0*); reprint ed. pap. 16.95 (*0-393-30219-9*) Norton.

Rosen, Charles, ed. see Cherubini, Maria L.

Rosen, Cheryl B., ed. see Rudrananda, Swami.

Rosen, Christine. The Limits of Power: Great Fires & the Process of City Growth in America. 416p. 1986. 74.95 (*0-521-30319-2*) Cambridge U Pr.

Rosen, Corey & Young, Karen M., eds. Understanding Employee Ownership. 248p. (Orig.). 1991. 32.00 (*0-87546-171-9*); pap. 16.95 (*0-87546-172-7*) ILR Pr.

Rosen, Corey, jt. auth. see Kumin, Matthew.

Rosen, Corey, et al. The Employee Ownership Buyout Handbook. rev. ed. Young, Karen M., ed. 70p. (C). 1991. pap. 25.00 (*0-926902-06-7*) NCEO.

— Employee Ownership in America: The Equity Solution. LC 85-40000. (Issues in Organization & Management Ser.). 240p. 1985. text ed. 27.95 (*0-669-10307-1*) Free Pr.

— The Employee Ownership Reader. rev. ed. Young, Karen M., ed. 79p. (C). 1989. pap. 25.00 (*0-926902-00-8*) NCEO.

— International Developments in Employee Ownership. rev. ed. 132p. (C). 1991. pap. text ed. 25.00 (*0-926902-11-3*) NCEO.

Rosen, D. Armored Scale Insects, Vols. A & B: Their Biology, Natural Enemies & Control, 2 vols., Vol. A. (World Crop Pests Ser.: Vol. 4). 386p. 1991. 159.00 (*0-444-42854-2*) Elsevier.

— Armored Scale Insects, Vols. A & B: Their Biology, Natural Enemies & Control, 2 vols., Vol. B. (World Crop Pests Ser.: Vol. 4). 616p. 1991. 200.00 (*0-444-42902-6*) Elsevier.

Rosen, David. The Changing Fictions of Masculinity. LC 92-35300. (Illus.). 216p. 1993. 29.95 (*0-252-02004-9*); pap. 14.95 (*0-252-06309-0*) U of Ill Pr.

— Henry's Tower. LC 84-61581. (Illus.). 36p. (J). (gr. k-5). 1984. 10.95 (*0-930905-01-6*); pap. 4.95 (*0-930905-00-8*) Platypus Bks.

— Making Money with Multimedia. 1994. pap. 16.95 (*0-201-82283-0*) Addison-Wesley.

— The Role of Hyperparasitism in Biological Control: A Symposium. LC 81-65779. (Illus.). 52p. 1981. pap. 3.00 (*0-931876-47-8*, 4103) ANR Pubns CA.

— Verdi: Requiem. (Cambridge Music Handbooks Ser.). 125p. (C). 1995. write for info. (*0-521-39448-1*); pap. write for info. (*0-521-39767-7*) Cambridge U Pr.

Rosen, David & Hamilton, Peter. Off-Hollywood: The Making & Marketing of Independent Films. 288p. 1989. pap. 13.95 (*0-8021-3187-5*) Grove-Atltic.

Rosen, David, jt. auth. see DeBach, Paul.

Rosen, David, ed. see Reagle, Merl.

Rosen, David, jt. auth. see Rosen, Harry.

Rosen, David, ed. see Verdi, Giuseppe.

Rosen, David H. Transforming Depression: A Jungian Approach Using the Creative Arts. LC 92-45220. (Illus.). 304p. 1993. 24.95 (*0-87477-675-9*, J P T-Putnam) Putnam Pub Group.

Rosen, David H., ed. see Beebe, John.

Rosen, David P. Public Capital: Revitalizing America's Communities. 150p. 1987. 14.95 (*0-89788-102-8*) CPA Washington.

Rosen, David S., jt. auth. see Helen Keller International Vitamin A Technical Assistance Program Staff.

Rosen, Dennis. Mathematics Recovered: For the Natural & Medical Sciences. (Illus.). 224p. (C). 1991. pap. text ed. 35.00 (*0-412-41040-0*, A6503) Chapman & Hall.

***Rosen, Donald, et al.** Dictionary of Educational Opportunities. LC 94-24738. 166p. 1994. pap. 18.00 (*0-911907-19-X*) Psych Assess.

Rosen, Donn E., jt. ed. see Nelson, Gareth.

Rosen, Dorothy, jt. auth. see Rosen, Sidney.

Rosen, Dorothy S. A Fire in Her Bones: The Story of Mary Lyon. LC 94-1978. 96p. (J). (gr. 3-7). 1994. lib. bdg. 17.50 (*0-87614-840-2*, Carolrhoda) Lerner Group.

Rosen, Edward. Copernicus & the Scientific Revolution. LC 83-9380. (Anvil Ser.). 220p. (Orig.). 1984. pap. text ed. 11.50 (*0-89874-573-X*) Krieger.

— Three Imperial Mathematicians. 367p. 1986. 20.00 (*0-89835-242-8*) Abaris Bks.

Rosen, Edward, tr. see Copernicus, Nicholas.

Rosen, Edward, tr. see Kepler, Johann.

Rosen, Efrem, jt. auth. see Weinstein, Estelle.

Rosen, Ellen D. Improving Public Productivity: Concepts & Practice. (Illus.). 288p. 1993. 49.00 (*0-8039-4572-8*); pap. 21.95 (*0-8039-4573-6*) Sage.

Rosen, Ellen F., jt. auth. see Harcum, E. Rae.

Rosen, Ellen I. Bitter Choices: Blue Collar Women In & Out of Work. LC 87-5867. (Women in Culture & Society Ser.). (Illus.). 232p. (C). 1987. 25.95 (*0-226-72644-4*) U Ch Pr.

— Bitter Choices: Blue Collar Women In & Out of Work. LC 87-5867. (Women in Culture & Society Ser.). (Illus.). 232p. (C). 1990. pap. text ed. 12.95 (*0-226-72645-2*) U Ch Pr.

Rosen, Elliott J. Families Facing Death. 208p. 1990. text ed. 27.95 (*0-669-21685-2*) Free Pr.

Rosen, Esther K. A Comparison of the Intellectual & Educational Status of Neurotic & Normal Children in Public Schools. LC 78-177208. (Columbia University. Teachers College. Contributions to Education Ser.: No. 188). reprint ed. 37.50 (*0-404-55188-2*) AMS Pr.

Rosen, F., ed. see Bentham, Jeremy.

Rosen, Fechner. Pathology Annual 1994 Pt. 2. (C). 1994. text ed. 80.00 (*0-8385-7700-8*) Appleton & Lange.

Rosen, Fred. Doctors from Hell. (Illus.). 320p. 1993. mass mkt. 4.99 (*1-55817-764-7*, Pinnacle NY) Windsor NY.

— Lobster Boy. 352p. 1995. pap. 4.99 (*0-8217-0133-9*) Zebra.

***Rosen, Fred & McFadyen, Deidre, eds.** Free Trade & Economic Restructuring in Latin America: A NACLA Reader. 288p. 1995. 30.00 (*0-85345-952-5*, CL9525) Monthly Rev.

— Free Trade & Economic Restructuring in Latin America: A NACLA Reader. 288p. 1995. pap. 15.00 (*0-85345-953-3*, PB9533) Monthly Rev.

Rosen, Fred, jt. auth. see Proctor, Dorothy.

Rosen, Fred S. & Seligmann, Maxime, eds. Immunodeficiencies. LC 92-48452. 1993. text ed. 250.00 (*3-7186-5343-5*); pap. text ed. 98.00 (*3-7186-5344-3*) Gordon & Breach.

Rosen, Frederic, ed. see Muhammad Ibn Musa, Al K.

Rosen, Frederick S. Bentham, Byron, & Greece: Constitutionalism, Nationalism, & Early Liberal Political Thought. 344p. 1992. 76.00 (*0-19-820078-1*) OUP.

— Jeremy Bentham & Representative Democracy: A Study of the Constitutional Code. 1983. 59.00 (*0-19-822656-X*) OUP.

Rosen, Frederick S., jt. ed. see Eibl, M. M.

Rosen, Frederick S., ed. see Gentham, Jeremy.

Rosen, Frederick S., et al, eds. Dictionary of Immunology. 233p. 1990. pap. 28.00 (*0-444-01478-0*) Elsevier.

— Dictionary of Immunology. 200p. 1988. 60.00 (*0-935859-58-6*, Stockton Pr) Groves Dictionaries.

Rosen, George. Contrasting Styles of Industrial Reform: China & India in the 1980s. LC 91-31762. 184p. 1992. 25.95 (*0-226-72646-0*) U Ch Pr.

— A History of Public Health. LC 93-9821. 535p. 1993. reprint ed. pap. text ed. 19.95 (*0-8018-4645-5*) Johns Hopkins.

— Industrial Change in India, 1970-2000: Present State of Indian Manufactures & Outlook of the Same. LC 86-62578. 123p. 1988. 29.00 (*0-913215-20-1*) Riverdale Co.

— Madness in Society: Chapters in the Historical Sociology of Mental Illness. LC 68-13112. 352p. 1980. pap. text ed. 14.95 (*0-226-72642-8*, P913) U Ch Pr.

— Preventive Medicine in the United States, 1900-1975, Trends & Interpretations. LC 75-35978. (Illus.). 128p. 1976. lib. bdg. 15.00 (*0-88202-103-6*, Sci Hist); pap. text ed. 6.95 (*0-685-63141-9*, Sci Hist) Watson Pub Intl.

— The Specialization of Medicine with Particular Reference to Ophthalmology. LC 79-180586. (Medicine & Society in America Ser.). 106p. 1972. reprint ed. 13.95 (*0-405-03966-2*) Ayer.

— Western Economists & Eastern Societies: Agents of Change in South Asia, 1950-1970. LC 84-4370. (Studies in Development). 296p. 1985. text ed. 43.00x (*0-8018-3187-3*) Johns Hopkins.

Rosen, George, jt. auth. see Bullough, Bonnie.

Rosen, Gerald. Growing up Bronx. LC 84-1193. 190p. 1984. 18.95 (*0-938190-37-7*); pap. 7.95 (*0-938190-36-9*) North Atlantic.

Rosen, Gladys. Jewish Life in America: Historical Perspectives. 17.50 (*0-87068-346-2*); pap. 9.95 (*0-686-52683-X*) Ktav.

Rosen, Gladys, jt. auth. see Reisman, Bernard.

Rosen, Gladys L., ed. Jewish Life in America: Historical Perspectives. LC 78-16560. 198p. 1978. pap. 6.95 (*0-686-74514-0*) Am Jewish Comm.

Rosen, H., jt. ed. see Keating, D.

Rosen, Haiim B. A Textbook of Israeli Hebrew: With an Introduction to the Classical Language. 2nd ed. LC 62-9116. 1976. pap. text ed. 25.00 (*0-226-72603-7*, P689) U Ch Pr.

Rosen, Harel D., jt. ed. see Rosen, Arye.

Rosen, Harold. Old High German Preposition Compounds in Relation to Their Latin Originals. (LD Ser.: No. 16). 1934. pap. 16.00 (*0-527-00762-5*) Periodicals Srv.

— Religious Education & Our Ultimate Commitment: An Application of Henry Nelson Wieman's Philosophy of Creative Interchange. LC 84-19651. 196p. (Orig.). 1985. pap. text ed. 19.50 (*0-8191-4342-1*, Unitarian Univ) U Pr of Amer.

Rosen, Harold J. & Heineman, Tom. Construction Specifications Writing: Principles & Procedures. 3rd ed. 286p. 1990. text ed. 64.95 (*0-471-61892-6*) Wiley.

Rosen, Harry & Rosen, David. But Not Next Door. 1962. 12.95 (*0-8392-1007-8*) Astor-Honor.

Rosen, Harry R. The Complete Guide for Building Your New Jewish Community Center. Wundohl, Frank F., ed. LC 83-80776. (Illus.). 217p. 1983. text ed. 225.00 (*0-914820-11-7*) JWB.

Rosen, Harvet S., jt. auth. see Katz, Michael L.

Rosen, Harvey. Public Finance. 4th ed. 1994. write for info. (*0-318-72960-1*) Irwin.

— Public Finance. 4th ed. 623p. (C). 1994. text ed. 63.95 (*0-256-16019-8*) Irwin.

— Public Finance, International. 3rd ed. (C). 1991. student ed, text ed. 32.50 (*0-256-11393-9*) Irwin.

Rosen, Harvey S. Fiscal Federalism: Quantitative Studies. (National Bureau of Economic Research Project Report Ser.). (Illus.). x, 262p. 1988. lib. bdg. 39.95 (*0-226-72619-3*) U Ch Pr.

— Public Finance. 3rd ed. 640p. (C). 1991. text ed. 63.95 (*0-256-08376-2*) Irwin.

Rosen, Harvey S., ed. Studies in State & Local Public Finance. (National Bureau of Economic Research Project Report Ser.). x, 236p. 1986. lib. bdg. 33.00 (*0-226-72621-5*) U Ch Pr.

Rosen, Harvey S., jt. auth. see Katz, Michael L.

Rosen, Harvey S., jt. auth. see Quandt, Richard E.

Rosen, Helen. Unspoken Grief: Coping with Childhood Sibling Loss. LC 85-40389. 144p. 1985. text ed. 24.95 (*0-669-11024-8*); text ed. 12.95 (*0-669-11022-1*) Free Pr.

Rosen, Howard & Greenwood, John, prefs. The Flood Control Challenge: Past, Present, & Future Proceedings of a National Symposium in Commemoration of the 50th Anniversaray of the 1936 Flood Control Act, September 1986, New Orleans. (Illus.). 160p. (C). 1988. text ed. 20.00 (*1-882102-00-2*, TC423, F58) Pub Works Hist Soc.

Rosen, Howard & Keating, Ann D., eds. Water & the City: The Next Century. (Illus.). 300p. (C). 1990. 25.00 (*1-882102-01-0*) Pub Works Hist Soc.

Rosen, Howard & Mendes, Joel, eds. One Hundred Years of Public Works Equipment: An Illustrated History. (Illus.). 96p. 1986. pap. text ed. 10.00 (*1-882102-03-7*) Pub Works Hist Soc.

Rosen, Howard, jt. auth. see Armstrong, Ellis L.

Rosen, Hugh. The Development of Sociomoral Knowledge: A Cognitive Structural Approach. LC 80-20. 208p. 1980. text ed. 50.00 (*0-231-04998-6*); pap. text ed. 19.50 (*0-231-04999-4*) Col U Pr.

— Piagetian Dimensions of Clinical Relevance. LC 85-2608. 320p. 1985. text ed. 49.00 (*0-231-06076-9*) Col U Pr.

Rosen, Hugh, jt. auth. see Kuehlwein, Kevin T.

Rosen, Hugo. Clincal Psychopharmacology for the Busy Practitioner. 2nd rev. ed. Wills, Susan E., ed. LC 93-76875. (Illus.). 362p. 1993. lib. bdg. 88.00 (*1-883122-01-5*) Pearce Pub.

Rosen, J. C. & McReynolds, P., eds. Advances in Psychological Assessment, Vol. 8. (Illus.). 260p. (C). 1992. 55.00 (*0-306-44251-5*, Plenum Pr) Plenum.

Rosen, Jamie H., et al. Sip of San Diego: Urban Espresso Guide. (Illus.). 85p. (Orig.). 1993. pap. 9.95 (*0-9639169-0-4*) Ethno Trek.

Rosen, Jay & Taylor, Paul, eds. The New News vs. the Old News: Press & Politics in the 1990s. LC 92-32299. (Perspectives on the News Ser.). 1992. 9.95 (*0-87078-344-0*) TCFP-PPP.

Rosen, Jay, jt. ed. see Harris, Joseph.

Rosen Jervis, Alice De, tr. see Landucci, Luca.

Rosen, Joan M. Guessing: Reading As Prediction. (Illus.). 198p. (YA). 1986. pap. text ed. 11.95 (*0-9616224-0-7*); 11.95 (*0-685-13952-2*) Innovative Lrn.

— TPR Student Kit Stories. (Illus.). 80p. 1992. pap. 10.95 (*1-56018-420-5*) Sky Oaks Prodns.

Rosen, Joe. The Capricious Cosmos: Universe Beyond Law. 192p. 1992. text ed. 19.95 (*0-02-604931-7*) Macmillan.

Rosen, Joe, ed. Symmetry & Group Theory in Physics. 160p. 1982. 18.00 (*0-318-41556-9*, RB34) Am Assn Physics.

***Rosen, Joseph.** Symmetry in Science: An Introduction to the General Theory. LC 94-30622. 1995. 49.00 (*0-387-94375-7*) Spr-Verlag.

Rosen, Joseph, jt. auth. see Essinger, James.

Rosen, Joseph D., et al, eds. Sulfur in Pesticide Action & Metabolism. LC 81-7916. (ACS Symposium Ser.: No. 158). 1981. 38.95 (*0-8412-0635-X*) Am Chemical.

Rosen, Judith. Bacewicz, Her Life & Works. Wilk, Wanda & Lutoslawski, Witold, eds. LC 84-80101. (Polish Music History Ser.: No. 2). (Illus.). 70p. (Orig.). 1984. pap. 10.00 (*0-916545-02-4*, ML 410 B05 R7) Friends of Pol Mus.

Rosen, Karen. Twenty-Five Years of the Peachtree Road Race. LC 93-81144. (Illus.). 144p. 1994. 20.00 (*1-56352-127-X*) Longstreet Pr Inc.

Rosen, Karen, jt. auth. see Rosen, Mel.

Rosen, Kay. XY Equals Z. (Illus.). 40p. 1992. pap. text ed. 20.00 (*1-881138-02-X*) Tallgrass Pr.

Rosen, Kenneth. Longfellow Square. Burke, Elizabeth, ed. (Illus.). 64p. (Orig.). 1992. pap. 11.95 (*1-878112-00-7*) Ascensius Pr.

Rosen, Kenneth H. The Best Unix Tips Ever. 1994. pap. text ed. 29.95 (*0-07-881924-5*) Osborne-McGraw.

— Discrete Mathematics. 600p. (C). 1988. text ed. 38.95 (*0-685-13440-7*) McGraw.

— Discrete Mathematics & Its Applications. 2nd ed. 1991. text ed. write for info. (*0-07-053744-5*) McGraw.

— Discrete Mathematics & Its Applications. 2nd ed. 1991. pap. text ed. write for info. (*0-07-053746-1*) McGraw.

— Discrete Mathematics & Its Applications. 3rd ed. LC 95-942. 1995. text ed. write for info. (*0-07-053965-0*) McGraw.

— Elementary Number Theory & Its Applications. 1984. write for info. (*0-201-06561-4*) Addison-Wesley.

— Elementary Number Theory & Its Applications. 2nd ed. 480p. (C). 1988. text ed. write for info. (*0-201-11959-5*, Adv Bk Prog) Addison-Wesley.

— Elementary Number Theory & Its Applications. 3rd ed. (Mathematics Ser.). (Illus.). 496p. (C). 1993. text ed. 61.25 (*0-201-57889-1*) Addison-Wesley.

— Unix System V Release 4: Introduction. 1990. pap. text ed. 34.95 (*0-07-881552-5*) Osborne-McGraw.

Rosen, Kenneth H., ed. Hemingway Repossessed. LC 93-16260. 208p. 1994. Alk. paper. text ed. 49.95 (*0-275-94546-4*, C4546, Praeger Pubs) Greenwood.

— Voices of the Rainbow: Contemporary Poetry by Native Americans. 256p. 1993. pap. 11.95 (*1-55970-224-9*) Arcade Pub Inc.

Rosen, Kenneth H., intro. The Man to Send Rain Clouds: Contemporary Stories by American Indians. 192p. 1992. reprint ed. pap. 9.95 (*0-14-017317-X*, Penguin Bks) Viking Penguin.

Rosen, Kenneth H., jt. auth. see Michaels, John G.

Rosen, L., jt. auth. see Feldman, J.

***Rosen, Larry S., et al.** Values-Based Teaching Skills: Introduction & Implementation. rev. ed. 180p. 1995. pap. 25.95 (*1-885435-02-9*) Twin Lights.

Rosen, Laura. Profiles: Who's Who in American Crafts. LC 92-29778. (Illus.). 368p. (Orig.). 1993. lib. bdg. 24.95 (*1-881930-00-9*) Rosen Pub.

Rosen, Lawrence. American Indians & the Law. LC 77-80868. 230p. 1978. reprint ed. 39.95x (*0-87855-266-9*) Transaction Pubs.

— The Anthropology of Justice: Law As Culture in Islamic Society. (Lewis Henry Morgan Lectures). (Illus.). 134p. (C). 1989. pap. 16.95 (*0-521-36740-9*) Cambridge U Pr.

— Bargaining for Reality: The Construction of Social Relations in a Muslim Community. LC 84-2501. (Illus.). 264p. 1984. pap. 13.95 (*0-226-72611-8*) U Ch Pr.

***Rosen, Lawrence & Harris, Jennifer.** Other Intentions: Cultural Contexts & the Attribution of Inner States. Ziegfeld, Richard, ed. LC 94-27115. (Advanced Seminar Ser.). 230p. 1995. text ed. 35.00x (*0-933452-88-8*) Schol Am Res.

Rosen, Lawrence, ed. see Harris, Jennifer.

Rosen, Lawrence R. McGraw-Hill Handbook of Interest, Yields, & Returns. 1995. text ed. 59.50 (*0-07-053766-6*) McGraw.

***Rosen, Leonard J.** Discovery & Commitment: A Guide for College Writers. LC 94-39162. 1994. text ed. write for info. (*0-205-14249-4*) Allyn.

— Discovery & Commitment: A Guide for College Writers. LC 94-39163. 1994. pap. text ed. write for info. (*0-205-17126-5*) Allyn.

— Elementary Number Theory. 480p. 1988. teacher ed 40.95 (*0-318-35471-3*) Addison-Wesley.

Rosen, Leonard J. & Behrens, Laurence. The Allyn & Bacon Handbook. 864p. (C). 1992. text ed. 23.00 (*0-205-13347-9*) Allyn.

— The Allyn & Bacon Handbook. 2nd ed. LC 93-39768. 1994. text ed. 25.00 (*0-205-15327-5*) Allyn.

— Writing Papers in College. (C). 1987. pap. text ed. 13.00 (*0-673-39235-X*) HarpCollege.

Rosen, Leonard J., jt. auth. see Behrens, Laurence.

Rosen, Louis. School Discipline Practices. LC 92-64180. (Illus.). 131p. 1992. pap. 14.95 (*0-9633825-4-3*) Schl Justice Inst.

Rosen, Louis & Glasser, Robert, eds. Climate Change & Energy Policy. 564p. 1992. pap. 55.00 (*1-56396-017-6*) Am Inst Physics.

Rosen, Marc. Let's Talk! 425p. (Orig.). 1992. pap. 14.95 (*0-9629821-0-5*) Baron Pied.

Rosen, Marcia. How the Animals Got Their Colors: Animal Myths from Around the World. (J). 1992. 14.95 (*0-15-236783-7*, HB Juv Bks) HarBrace.

— Journey Back to Me. Date not set. pap. write for info. (*0-345-36798-7*) Ballantine.

— Management of Labor: Physician Judgement & Patient Care. 300p. 1990. 55.00 (*0-444-01528-0*) Elsevier.

Rosen, Marcia & Hunt, Gerry. The Cheers Bartending Guide. 192p. 1986. pap. 3.95 (*0-380-70189-8*) Avon.

Rosen, Marcia & Lisk, Eunice A. Test Your Fitness I. Q. (Illus.). 96p. 1986. pap. 6.95 (*0-13-906868-6*) P-H.

Rosen, Marcia, jt. auth. see Ireland, K.

Rosen, Marcia, jt. auth. see Latto, L. P.

Rosen, Marion. Don't Speak to Strangers. 1993. mass mkt. 4.99 (*0-312-95000-4*) St Martin.

Rosen, Marion & Brenner, Susan. Rosen Method of Movement. 97p. (Orig.). 1991. pap. 12.95 (*1-55643-117-1*) North Atlantic.

Rosen, Marjorie, ed. see Groteke, Kristi.

Rosen, Marvin J. & DeVries, David L. Introduction to Photography. 4th ed. 494p. (C). 1993. pap. 35.95 (*0-534-17850-2*) Intl Thomson.

Rosen, Mel. Mailbox Crosswords: A Postcard Book. (Postcard Book Ser.). 64p. (Orig.). 1992. pap. 7.95 (*1-56138-161-6*) Running Pr.

— Sports Illustrated Tracking - Running. 1988. pap. 9.95 (*1-56800-040-5*, Pub. by Sports Illus Bks) Natl Bk Netwk.

Rosen, Mel, ed. Crosswords, No. 16. 96p. (Orig.). 1990. pap. 5.95 (*0-89471-865-7*) Running Pr.

— Crosswords, No. 17. 96p. (Orig.). 1991. pap. 5.95 (*0-89471-987-4*) Running Pr.

— Crosswords, No. 19. 96p. (Orig.). 1992. pap. 6.95 (*1-56138-084-9*) Running Pr.

— Crosswords, No. 20. 96p. (Orig.). 1992. pap. 6.95 (*1-56138-136-5*) Running Pr.

— Crosswords, No. 21. 96p. (Orig.). 1993. spiral bd. 6.95 (*1-56138-203-5*) Running Pr.

— Crosswords, No. 22. (Illus.). 96p. (Orig.). 1993. spiral bd., pap. 6.95 (*1-56138-283-3*) Running Pr.

— Crosswords, No. 23. 96p. (Orig.). 1994. spiral bd. 6.95 (*1-56138-397-X*) Running Pr.

— Crosswords, No. 24. 96p. (Orig.). 1994. 6.95 (*1-56138-424-0*) Running Pr.

— Crosswords, No. 11. 96p. (Orig.). 1988. spiral bd. 5.95 (*0-89471-594-1*) Running Pr.

— Crosswords No. 4. 96p. (Orig.). 1984. spiral bd., pap. 5.95 (*0-89471-277-2*) Running Pr.

— Crosswords No. 8. 96p. 1986. spiral bd., pap. 5.95 (*0-89471-451-1*) Running Pr.

— Crosswords No. 9. 96p. (Orig.). 1987. spiral bd., pap. 5.95 (*0-89471-497-X*) Running Pr.

— Large Print Crosswords. large type ed. (Large Print Omnibus Ser.: No. 9). 240p. 1994. spiral bd. 12.95 (*1-56138-399-6*) Running Pr.

— Large Print Crosswords Omnibus, No. 5. large type ed. 240p. (Orig.). 1992. pap. 9.95 (*1-56138-086-5*) Running Pr.

— Large Print Crosswords Omnibus, No. 8. (Illus.). 240p. (Orig.). 1993. spiral bd. 9.95 (*1-56138-285-X*) Running Pr.

— Large Print Crosswords Omnibus, No. 10. 240p. (Orig.). 1994. 12.95 (*1-56138-426-7*) Running Pr.

— Large Print Omnibus Crosswords. (Orig.). 1989. pap. 8.95 (*0-89471-770-7*) Running Pr.

— Large Print Omnibus Crosswords, No. 3. large type ed. (Large Print Omnibus Ser.). 240p. (Orig.). 1991. pap. 8.95 (*0-89471-989-0*) Running Pr.

— Large-Type Omnibus Crosswords, No. 2. large type ed. 96p. (Orig.). 1990. pap. 8.95 (*0-89471-867-3*) Running Pr.

— Pen & Pencil Club Crosswords, No. 13. 90p. (Orig.). 1990. pap. 5.95 (*0-89471-866-5*) Running Pr.

— Pen & Pencil Club Crosswords, No. 14. 80p. (Orig.). 1991. pap. 5.95 (*0-89471-988-2*) Running Pr.

— The Pen & Pencil Club Crosswords, No. 15. 80p. (Orig.). 1991. spiral bd. 6.95 (*1-56138-048-2*) Running Pr.

— Pen & Pencil Club Crosswords, No. 16. 80p. (Orig.). 1992. pap. 6.95 (*1-56138-085-7*) Running Pr.

— Pen & Pencil Club Crosswords, No. 17. 96p. (Orig.). 1992. pap. 6.95 (*1-56138-137-3*) Running Pr.

— Pen & Pencil Club Crosswords, No. 18. (Pen & Pencil Club Ser.). 96p. (Orig.). 1993. spiral bd. 6.95 (*1-56138-204-3*) Running Pr.

— The Pen & Pencil Club Crosswords, No. 19. (Illus.). 80p. (Orig.). 1993. spiral bd. 6.95 (*1-56138-284-1*) Running Pr.

— Pen & Pencil Club Crosswords, No. 20. 80p. (Orig.). 1994. spiral bd. 6.95 (*1-56138-398-8*) Running Pr.

Rosen, Mel & Rosen, Karen. Sports Illustrated Track: Championship Running. LC 93-28169. (Illus.). 1993. pap. 12.95 (*1-56800-008-1*, Pub. by Sports Illus Bks) Natl Bk Netwk.

Rosen, Mel, jt. auth. see Kurzban, Stan.

Rosen, Mel, et al. Practical Coaching Techniques for Sprints & Relays, 10 bks., Set. 1980. 34.95 (*0-932741-95-9*) Championship Bks & Vid Prodns.

Rosen, Menahem. Problems of the Hegelian Dialectic: Dialectic Reconstructed as a Logic of Human Reality. 1992. lib. bdg. 104.00 (*0-7923-2047-6*) Kluwer Ac.

Rosen, Meyer R. A Novel Synergy of AuriculoTherapy, Kinesiology & Temporomandibular Dysfunction (TMD) Treatment Protocols for the Quantitative Characterization & Treatment Of: Hyperacusis - a Pain-Causing Ultra-Sensitivity to Normal Sounds. LC 94-77159. 112p. 1994. pap. text ed. 60.00 (*0-9641617-0-2*) Interact Cnslting.
Will be of high interest to western & eastern health practitioners & researchers involved with TMJ & Orofacial Pain (Diagnostic Classification #11, International Headache Society). A research inquiry into the two most difficult to treat ear disorders: Hyperacusis & Tinnitus. Provides a new treatment approach for otolaryngologists, dentists, chiropractors & acupuncturists. Takes the reader through the developmental thinking associated with formulation of new clinical methodology. The author draws from an eclectic background of 30 years of research & development experience in science & engineering, applied kinesiology, body acupuncture & Auriculotherapy. Makes a convincing case for a causal relationship between Temporomandibular Dysfunction & Hyperacusis. Includes experimental data documenting effectiveness of the proposed clinical protocol for diagnosis & treatment. A must for libraries, & medical/acupuncture schools at the cutting edge of new technology. "...a remarkable example to all of us...that when we have real, difficult problems, we should call forth all the creative energies & technology that we have & put them all together to solve our problems..." - Ralph Alan Dale, Ed.D., Ph.D., C.A., Dipl. Ac. To order, contact: Interactive Consulting Inc., P.O. Box 66, E. Norwich, NY 11732, Phone: 516-922-4010; FAX 516-922-3830. $60.00 plus $5.00 S & H. ***Publisher Provided Annotation.***

— Quantitative Auriculotherapy. 52p. 1994. pap. text ed. 35.00 (*0-9641617-1-0*) Interact Cnslting.

***Rosen, Michael.** The Best of Michael Rosen: Poetry for Kids. (Illus.). 150p. (Orig.). (J). (gr. 1-5). 1995. pap. 15.95 (*0-614-03292-X*, Wetlands Pr) RDR Bks.

— A Drink at the Mirage. LC 84-15016. (Contemporary Poets Ser.). 80p. 1985. text ed. 21.95 (*0-691-06627-2*); pap. 9.95 (*0-691-01417-5*) Princeton U Pr.

— Itsy-Bitsy Beasties: Poems from Around the World. (J). (ps-3). 1992. 19.95 (*0-87614-747-3*, Carolrhoda) Lerner Group.

— Mind Your Own Business. LC 74-9969. (Illus.). 96p. (J). (gr. 3 up). 1974. 22.95 (*0-87599-209-9*) S G Phillips.

— Off the Wall: A Very Silly Story Book. LC 93-28643. (Illus.). 64p. (Orig.). (J). (gr. 1-4). 1994. pap. 2.95 (*1-85697-949-0*, Kingfisher LKC) LKC.

— South & North, East & West: The Oxfam Book of Children's Stories. LC 91-58749. (Illus.). 96p. (J). (ps-3). 1994. pap. 12.99 (*1-56402-396-6*) Candlewick Pr.

— Walking the Bridge of Your Nose. LC 95-3007. (Illus.). (J). 1995. 12.95 (*1-85697-596-7*, Kingfisher LKC) LKC.

— We're Going on a Bear Hunt. LC 88-13338. (Illus.). 40p. (J). (ps-4). 1989. text ed. 15.95 (*0-689-50476-4*, McElderry) S&S Childrens.

— We're Going on a Bear Hunt. LC 92-8836. (Illus.). 40p. (J). (ps-1). 1992. bds. 5.95 (*0-689-71653-2*, Aladdin Paperbacks) S&S Childrens.

***Rosen, Michael, ed. & ret.** Crow & Hawk: A Traditional Pueblo Indian Story. LC 94-15176. (Illus.). (J). 1995. 15.00 (*0-15-200257-X*) HarBrace.

Rosen, Michael, ed. Poems for the Very Young. LC 92-45574. (Illus.). 80p. (J). (gr. k-3). 1993. 15.95 (*1-85697-908-3*, Kingfisher LKC) LKC.

— South & North, East & West: The Oxfam Book of Children's Stories. LC 91-58749. (Illus.). 96p. (J). (ps up). 1992. 19.95 (*1-56402-117-3*) Candlewick Pr.

R

An Asterisk (*) at the beginning of an entry indicates that the title is appearing in BIP for the first time.

Rosen, Michael, sel. The Kingfisher Book of Children's Poetry. LC 92-26444. (Illus.). 256p. (J). (gr. 3-9). 1993. 16.95 (*1-85697-910-5*, Kingfisher LKC); pap. 10.95 (*1-85697-909-1*, Kingfisher LKC) LKC.

***Rosen, Michael A.** Sexual Art: Photographs That Test the Limits. (Illus.). 64p. (Orig.). 1994. pap. 30.00 (*0-936705-03-5*) Shaynew Pr.

— Sexual Magic: The S-M Photographs. (Illus.). 72p. (Orig.). 1986. pap. 25.00 (*0-936705-69-8*) Shaynew Pr.

— Sexual Portraits: Photographs of Radical Sexuality. (Illus.). 64p. (Orig.). 1990. pap. 30.00 (*0-936705-88-4*) Shaynew Pr.

Rosen, Michael J. All Eyes on the Pond. LC 93-11743. (Illus.). 32p. (J). (ps-2). 1994. 14.95 (*1-56282-475-9*); lib. bdg. 14.89 (*1-56282-476-7*) Hyprn Child.

— All Eyes on the Pond. LC 93-11743. (Illus.). 32p. (J). (ps-2). 1995. pap. 4.95 (*0-7868-1078-5*) Hyprn Ppbks.

— Bonesy & Isabel. LC 93-7892. (Illus.). (J). 1995. 15.00 (*0-15-209813-5*) HarBrace.

— Down at the Doctor's: The Sick Book. (Illus.). 24p. (J). (gr. k-4). 1988. 10.95 (*0-13-218942-9*, Litl Simon S&S) S&S Childrens.

— Elijah's Angel. (Illus.). (J). 1992. 13.95 (*0-15-225394-7*, HB Juv Bks) HarBrace.

— Goodnight Hands: A Bedtime Adventure. LC 91-67933. (Illus.). 32p. (J). (ps-3). 1992. pap. 14.95 (*1-880444-01-1*) Times to Treas.

— The Greatest Table: A Banquet to Fight Against Hunger. LC 94-1611. 1994. 18.95 (*0-15-200028-3*) HarBrace.

— Hegel's Dialectic & Its Criticism. LC 81-24211. 210p. 1982. 44.95 (*0-521-24484-6*) Cambridge U Pr.

— I Love My Dog Best Dog Book & Neighborhood Field Guide. (J). (gr. 4-7). 1993. pap. 12.95 (*1-56305-317-9*, 3317) Workman Pub.

— The Kids' Book of Fishing. LC 90-50949. (Illus.). 96p. (Orig.). (J). (gr. 2-6). 1991. pap. 12.95 (*0-89480-866-4*, 1866) Workman Pub.

— Little Rabbit Foo Foo. LC 90-9598. (Illus.). 32p. (J). (ps-1). 1990. pap. 14.00 (*0-671-70968-2*, S&S Bks Young Read) S&S Childrens.

— Little Rabbit Foo Foo. LC 90-9598. (Illus.). 32p. (J). (ps-1). 1993. pap. 4.95 (*0-671-79604-6*, Litl Simon S&S) S&S Childrens.

— The Lullaby & Goodnight Sleepkit: The Gift of Sweet Dreams & Family Memories. (Illus.). 32p. (J). (ps-3). 1992. Mini ed. 14.95 (*1-880444-02-X*) Times to Treas.

— The Lullaby & Goodnight Sleepkit: The Gift of Sweet Dreams & Family Memories, Set. (Illus.). 32p. (J). (ps-3). 1992. Boxed gift set incl. cass. & parents' guide. teacher ed, audio 29.95 (*1-880444-00-3*) Times to Treas.

— Moving. (Illus.). 32p. (J). (ps-1). 1993. 12.99 (*0-670-84865-4*) Viking Child Bks.

— A School for Pompey Walker. LC 94-6240. (J). 1995. write for info. (*0-15-200114-X*, HB Juv Bks) HarBrace.

Rosen, Michael J., ed. Home: A Collaboration of Thirty Authors & Illustrators of Children's Books to Aid the Homeless. LC 91-29125. (Illus.). 32p. (J). (ps-3). 1992. 16.00 (*0-06-021788-X*); lib. bdg. 15.89 (*0-06-021789-8*) HarpC Child Bks.

— Purr-- Children's Book Illustrators Brag About Their Cats. LC 95-17622. (Illus.). (J). 1996. write for info. (*0-15-200837-3*) HarBrace.

— Speak! Children's Book Illustrators Brag about Their Favorite Dogs. LC 92-30325. (J). 1993. 16.95 (*0-15-277848-9*) HarBrace.

Rosen, Michael J., jt. auth. see Ireland, K.

Rosen, Michael J., tr. see Kant, Immanuel.

Rosen, Michael J., ed. see Thurber, James.

Rosen, Michael R., ed. Paleoclimate & Basin Evolution of Playa Systems. LC 93-50091. (Special Paper Ser.: No. 289). 1994. pap. 45.00 (*0-8137-2289-6*) Geol Soc.

Rosen, Michael R. & Hoffman, Brian F., eds. Cardiac Therapy. 1983. lib. bdg. 125.00 (*0-89838-564-4*) Kluwer Ac.

Rosen, Michael R. & Palti, Yoram, eds. Lethal Arrhythmias Resulting from Myocardial Ischemia & Infarction: Proceedings of Second Rappaport Symposium Haifa, Israel, March 13-16, 1988. (Developments in Cardiovascular Medicine Ser.). (C). 1988. lib. bdg. 113.50 (*0-89838-401-X*) Kluwer Ac.

Rosen, Michael R., et al, eds. Cardiac Electrophysiology: A Textbook: In Honor of Brian F. Hoffman, MD. 1215p. 1990. 160.00 (*0-87993-391-7*) Futura Pub.

Rosen, Milt, ed. see Berle, Milton.

Rosen, Milton. Surfactants & Interfacial Phenomena. 2nd ed. LC 88-5404. 431p. 1989. text ed. 79.95 (*0-471-83651-6*) Wiley.

Rosen, Milton J. Structure-Performance Relationships in Surfactants. LC 84-6384. (ACS Symposium Ser.: No. 253). 356p. 1984. lib. bdg. 60.95 (*0-8412-0839-5*) Am Chemical.

Rosen, Milton J. & Goldsmith, Henry A. Systematic Analysis of Surface-Active Agents. 2nd ed. LC 78-173678. (Chemical Analysis Ser.: Vol. 12). 617p. reprint ed. pap. 175.90 (*0-317-28059-7*, 2055772) Bks Demand.

Rosen, Moishe. Demystifying Personal Evangelism. (Illus.). 48p. (Orig.). 1992. pap. 1.99 (*1-881022-01-3*) Purple Pomegranate.

— The Universe is Broken: Who on Earth Can Fix It? LC 91-67710. (Illus.). 52p. (Orig.). 1991. pap. write for info. (*0-9616148-8-9*) Purple Pomegranate.

— Y'shua. 128p. (Orig.). 1983. pap. 4.50 (*0-8024-9842-6*) Moody.

Rosen, Moishe, jt. auth. see Rosen, Ceil.

Rosen, Nancy, jt. auth. see Drucker, Mindy.

Rosen, Ned. Teamwork & the Bottom Line: Groups Make a Difference. (Series in Applied Psychology). 240p. 1989. pap. text ed. 24.50 (*0-8058-0461-7*) L Erlbaum Assocs.

— Teamwork & the Bottom Line: Groups Make a Difference. 240p. 1989. 49.95 (*0-8058-0459-5*) L Erlbaum Assocs.

Rosen, Nina G. Javier: A Young Man Arrives in the U. S. 224p. 1994. pap. text ed. 11.25 (*0-13-512120-5*) P-H.

Rosen, Norma. Accidents of Influence: Writing As a Woman & a Jew in America. LC 91-29320. (Modern Jewish Literature & Culture Ser.). 210p. (C). 1992. 57.50 (*0-7914-1091-9*); pap. 18.95 (*0-7914-1092-7*) State U NY Pr.

— Touching Evil. LC 89-38145. 277p. (C). 1990. reprint ed. 32.50 (*0-8143-2298-0*); reprint ed. pap. 11.95 (*0-8143-2299-9*) Wayne St U Pr.

Rosen, Ora M. & Krebs, Edwin G., eds. Protein Phosphorylation, 2 bks. LC 81-10184. (Cold Spring Harbor Conferences on Cell Proliferation Ser.: Vol. 8). 1421p. (C). 1981. 177.00 (*0-87969-140-9*) Cold Spring Harbor.

Rosen, Paul & Brother, Marvin. Accounting Applications for Spreadsheets. 104p. 1988. 15.50 (*0-936862-37-8*, AC/SP); teacher ed 10.00 (*0-936862-44-0*, AS-TM); trans. 175.00 (*0-936862-42-4*, AS-TOR); disk 65.00 (*0-936862-71-8*, SAD-1, SAD-3) DDC Pub.

Rosen, Paul, jt. auth. see Brother, Marvin.

Rosen, Paul M., jt. auth. see Walsh, Barent W.

Rosen, Paul P. Pathology Annual 1993 Pt. 2. Fechner, Robert E., ed. 272p. 1993. 80.00 (*0-8385-7722-9*, A7722-0) Appleton & Lange.

Rosen, Paul P. & Fechner, Robert E. Pathology Annual 1990 Vol. 25, Pt. 1. (Illus.). 416p. 1989. text ed. 80.00 (*0-8385-7714-8*, A7714-7) Appleton & Lange.

— Pathology Annual 1990 Vol. 25, Pt. 1. (Illus.). 400p. 1990. text ed. 80.00 (*0-8385-7814-4*, A7814-5) Appleton & Lange.

— Pathology Annual 1994 Pt. 1. (Illus.). 320p. 1994. text ed. 80.00 (*0-8385-7723-7*, A7723-8) Appleton & Lange.

Rosen, Paul P. & Fechner, Robert E., eds. Pathology Annual 1988 Vol. 23, Pt. 1. (Illus.). 352p. 1988. boxed 80.00 (*0-8385-7781-4*, A7781-6) Appleton & Lange.

— Pathology Annual 1988 Vol. 23, Pt. 2. (Illus.). 416p. 1988. boxed 80.00 (*0-8385-7789-X*, A7789-9) Appleton & Lange.

— Pathology Annual 1989, Vol. 24, Pt. 1. 400p. 1989. boxed 75.00 (*0-8385-7733-4*, A7733-7) Appleton & Lange.

— Pathology Annual 1989 Vol. 24, Pt. 2. 352p. 1989. boxed 80.00 (*0-8385-7713-X*, A7713-9) Appleton & Lange.

— Pathology Annual 1991 Vol. 26, Pt. 1. (Illus.). 323p. (C). 1991. boxed 80.00 (*0-8385-7716-4*, A7716-2) Appleton & Lange.

— Pathology Annual 1992 Vol. 27, Pt. 1. (Illus.). 320p. (C). 1992. text ed. 80.00 (*0-8385-7720-2*, A7720-4) Appleton & Lange.

Rosen, Paul P. & Fechner, Robert F. Pathology Annual 1993 Vol. 28, Pt. 1. (Illus.). 304p. (C). 1992. text ed. 80.00 (*0-8385-7721-0*, A7721-0) Appleton & Lange.

***Rosen, Penni.** CC: Mail Release X Plain & Simple. 1995. write for info. (*0-7821-1797-X*) Sybex.

Rosen, Peter. The Luminous Life: How to Shine Like the Sun. Iozzi, Carol, ed. 420p. (Orig.). Date not set. pap. 20.00 (*1-878682-01-6*) Roaring Lion Pub.

Rosen, Peter, jt. ed. see Barkin, Roger M.

Rosen, Peter, et al, eds. Emergency Medicine: Concepts & Clinical Practice. 3rd ed. 3240p. 1992. 230.00 (*0-8016-4303-1*) Mosby Yr Bk.

Rosen, Peter S., jt. ed. see FitzGerald, Duncan M.

Rosen, Philip. Narrative, Apparatus, Ideology: A Film Theory Reader. LC 86-2619. 560p. 1986. pap. text ed. 19.50 (*0-231-05881-0*) Col U Pr.

Rosen, Philip T. The Modern Stentors: Radio Broadcasters & the Federal Government, 1920-1934. LC 79-8952. (Contributions in Economics & Economic History Ser.: No. 31). (Illus.). 267p. 1980. text ed. 59.95 (*0-313-21231-7*, RMS/, Greenwood Pr) Greenwood.

Rosen, Philip T., ed. International Handbook of Broadcasting Systems. LC 87-29986. 336p. 1988. text ed. 79.50 (*0-313-24348-4*, ROH/, Greenwood Pr) Greenwood.

Rosen, Philip T., jt. ed. see Mellencamp, Patricia.

Rosen, R., ed. see Cole, Barbara S.

Rosen, R., ed. see Cooney, Judith.

Rosen, R., ed. see Kurland, Morton L.

Rosen, R., ed. see Lee, Mary P. & Lee, Richard.

Rosen, R., ed. see Schauer, Donald D.

Rosen, Ralph. Old Comedy & the Iambographic Tradition. LC 88-33324. (American Philological Association, American Classical Studies). 110p. 1989. 15.95 (*1-55540-304-2*, 40 04 19); pap. 12.95 (*1-55540-305-0*, 40 04 19) Scholars Pr GA.

Rosen, Ralph M. & Farrell, Joseph, eds. Nomodeiktes: Greek Studies in Honor of Martin Ostwald. (Illus.). 750p. (C). 1992. text ed. 59.50 (*0-472-10297-4*) U of Mich Pr.

Rosen, Randy, et al. Making Their Mark: Women Artists Move into the Mainstream, 1970-85. Brawer, Catherine, ed. (Illus.). 300p. 1991. 59.95 (*0-89659-958-2*); pap. 29.95 (*1-55859-161-3*) Abbeville Pr.

Rosen, Raymond C. & Beck, J. Gayle. Patterns of Sexual Arousal: Psychophysiological Processes & Clinical Applications. LC 87-19726. 404p. 1988. lib. bdg. 47.50 (*0-89862-712-5*) Guilford Pr.

***Rosen, Raymond C. & Leiblum, Sandra R.** Case Studies in Sex Therapy. 1995. lib. bdg. 40.00 (*0-89862-848-2*, C2848) Guilford Pr.

Rosen, Raymond C. & Leiblum, Sandra R., eds. Erectile Disorders: Assessment & Treatment. LC 91-38062. 378p. 1992. lib. bdg. 37.95 (*0-89862-792-3*) Guilford Pr.

Rosen, Raymond C., jt. ed. see Leiblum, Sandra R.

Rosen, Richard. World of Hurt. LC 94-11253. 1994. 20.95 (*0-8027-3251-8*) Walker & Co.

Rosen, Richard D. Strike Three, You're Dead. 1986. pap. 2.95 (*0-451-14233-0*, Sig) NAL-Dutton.

Rosen, Robert. Life Itself. (Illus.). 320p. 1991. text ed. 45.00 (*0-231-07564-2*) Col U Pr.

Rosen, Robert, ed. Foundations of Mathematical Biology, 3 vols. Incl. Vol. 1. Subcellular Systems. 1972. 57.50 (*0-12-597201-6*); Vol. 2. Cellular Systems. 1972. 65.00 (*0-12-597202-4*); Vol. 3. 1973. 74.50 (*0-12-597203-2*); Vol. 1. Subcellular Systems. 1972. 57.50 (*0-12-597201-6*); Vol. 2. Cellular Systems. 1972. 65.00 (*0-12-597202-4*); Set. 198.50 (*0-685-00055-9*) Acad Pr.

— Theoretical Biology & Complexity. 1985. text ed. 103.00 (*0-12-597280-6*) Acad Pr.

Rosen, Robert C. John Dos Passos: Politics & the Writer. LC 81-1928. 207p. reprint ed. pap. 59.00 (*0-7837-6178-3*, 2045900) Bks Demand.

Rosen, Robert C. & Simon, Wayne, eds. International Securities Regulation: Stock Exchanges of the World: Selected Rules & Regulations. 1992. Approx. 2 releases per yr. ring bd. 150.00 (*0-379-20827-X*) Oceana.

Rosen, Robert C., jt. auth. see Annas, Pamela J.

Rosen, Robert C., et al, eds. International Securities Regulation, 4 vols. of 5 projected bds. 1986. Approx. 2 releases per yr. write for info. (*0-318-59392-0*) Oceana.

— International Securities Regulation, 5 vols., Set. LC 86-12602. 1986. ring bd. 650.00 (*0-379-20825-3*) Oceana.

Rosen, Robert H. & Berger, Lisa. The Healthy Company: Eight Strategies to Develop People, Productivity & Profits. LC 92-29602. 304p. 1992. pap. 14.95 (*0-87477-708-9*) J P Tarcher.

Rosen, Robert J. & Nosher, John. Angiography & Interventional Radiology. (Illus.). 184p. 1991. Extracted from Atlas of Radiologic Imaging. 65.00 (*1-56375-003-1*, GM0193) Mosby Yr Bk.

Rosen, Robert L., jt. ed. see Bone, Roger C.

Rosen, Robert N. Confederate Charleston: An Illustrated History of the City & the People During the Civil War. LC 94-13751. 1994. write for info. (*0-87249-991-X*) U of SC Pr.

— A Short History of Charleston. rev. ed. Howe, M. Rita & Cole, Tom, eds. (Illus.). 176p. (Orig.). 1992. 25.00 (*0-9635154-1-1*); pap. 13.95 (*0-9635154-0-3*) Peninsula SC.

Rosen, Rochelle S. College in California, the Inside Track: The Comprehensive & Practical Guide for Students, Parents, & Educators. LC 92-96890. (Illus.). 576p. (Orig.). 1992. pap. 24.95 (*1-880403-11-0*) Baywood.

— College in California, the Inside Track, 1994 Edition: The Comprehensive & Practical Guide for Students, Parents, & Educators. LC 93-72476. (Illus.). 592p. (YA). (gr. 8 up). 1993. pap. 24.95 (*1-880403-12-9*) Baywood.

— College in California: The Inside Track 1995: Comprehensive Guide for Students, Parents, & Educators. 3rd ed. 592p. (YA). (gr. 9-12). 1994. per., pap. 24.95 (*1-880403-13-7*) Baywood.

Rosen, Roger. The Georgian Republic. (Soviet Guides Ser.). (Illus.). 320p. 1991. pap. 15.95 (*0-8442-9677-5*, Passport Bks) NTC Pub Grp.

***Rosen, Roger, ed.** A Guide to African American Genealogy. (Oryx American Family Tree Ser.: Vol. 1). (Illus.). 192p. 1995. 22.50 (*0-89774-972-3*, 2372) Oryx Pr.

— A Guide to Italian American Genealogy. (Oryx American Family Tree Ser.: Vol. 2). (Illus.). 192p. 1995. 22.50 (*0-89774-973-1*, 2373) Oryx Pr.

— A Guide to Native American Genealogy. (Oryx American Family Tree Ser.: Vol. 4). (Illus.). 192p. 1996. 22.50 (*0-89774-975-8*, 2375) Oryx Pr.

— A Guide to Polish American Genealogy. (Onyx American Family Tree Ser.: Vol. 3). (Illus.). 192p. 1996. 22.50 (*0-89774-974-X*, 2374) Oryx Pr.

Rosen, Roger & Sevastiades, Patra, eds. Celebration: Visions & Voices of the African Diaspora. LC 93-47413. (Icarus World Issues Ser.). 1994. 16.95 (*0-8239-1808-4*); pap. 8.95 (*0-8239-1809-2*) Rosen Group.

***Rosen, Roger & Sevstiades, Patra M., eds.** End of Empire: Fifteen New Works from the Fifteen Republics of the Former Soviet Union. LC 94-29833. (Icarus World Issues Ser.). 1994. write for info. (*0-8239-1802-5*) Rosen Group.

Rosen, Roger, ed. see Allman, Paul.

Rosen, Roger, ed. see Beit-Hallahmi, Benjamin.

Rosen, Roger, ed. see Bleich, Alan R.

Rosen, Roger, ed. see Buckalew, Walker.

Rosen, Roger, ed. see Dumond, Michael.

Rosen, Roger, ed. see Edwards, Gabrielle I.

Rosen, Roger, ed. see Epstein, Lawrence.

Rosen, Roger, ed. see Hughes, Tracy.

Rosen, Roger, ed. see Macdonald, Robert.

Rosen, Roger, ed. see Mahoney, Ellen V.

Rosen, Roger, ed. see McClaskey, Marilyn H.

Rosen, Roger, jt. ed. see McSharry, Patra.

Rosen, Roger, ed. see Parrot, Andrea.

Rosen, Roger, ed. see Rue, Nancy N.

Rosen, Roger, ed. see Rue, Nancy.

Rosen, Roger, ed. see Southworth, Scott.

Rosen, Roger, ed. see Webb, Margot.

Rosen, Rosanne. The Living Together Trap: Everything Women & Men Should Know. LC 92-63124. 176p. 1993. pap. 12.95 (*0-88282-075-3*) New Horizon NJ.

Rosen, Roseanne. Marriage Secrets: How to Have a Lifetime Love Affair. LC 93-9442. 1993. 17.95 (*1-55972-166-9*, Birch Ln Pr) Carol Pub Group.

Rosen, Ruth. The Lost Sisterhood: Prostitution in America, 1900-1918. LC 81-23678. 272p. (C). 1982. 32.50 (*0-8018-2664-0*) Johns Hopkins.

— The Lost Sisterhood: Prostitution in America, 1900-1918. LC 81-23678. 272p. (C). 1984. pap. 14.95x (*0-8018-2665-9*) Johns Hopkins.

Rosen, Ruth, ed. Jesus for Jews. LC 87-20343. (Illus.). 336p. (Orig.). (YA). (gr. 12). 1987. 13.95 (*0-9616148-3-8*); pap. 7.95 (*0-9616148-4-6*); mass mkt. 4.95 (*0-9616148-2-X*) Purple Pomegranate.

— Testimonies of Jews Who Believe in Jesus: If Jesus Is the Messiah at All, Then He Is the Messiah for All. rev. ed. LC 92-3656. Orig. Title: Jesus for Jews. 349p. 1992. pap. 5.95 (*1-881022-00-5*) Purple Pomegranate.

Rosen, Ruth & Davidson, Sue, eds. The Maimie Papers. LC 84-42837. (Illus.). 496p. 1985. reprint ed. pap. 10.95 (*0-253-23600-2*) Ind U Pr.

Rosen, Ruth, ed. see Allman, Paul.

Rosen, Ruth, ed. see Ayer, Eleanor.

Rosen, Ruth, ed. see Beyer, Kay.

Rosen, Ruth, ed. see Black, Beryl.

Rosen, Ruth, ed. see Bowen-Woodward, Kathy.

Rosen, Ruth, ed. see Brown, Margaret F.

Rosen, Ruth, ed. see Buckalew, M. Walker.

Rosen, Ruth, ed. see Carlson, Linda.

Rosen, Ruth, ed. see Carter, Sharon.

Rosen, Ruth, ed. see Carter, Sharon & Monnig, Judith.

Rosen, Ruth, ed. see Clayton, Lawrence.

Rosen, Ruth, ed. see Clayton, Lawrence & Carter, Sharon.

Rosen, Ruth, ed. see Clayton, Lawrence & Morrison, Jaydene.

Rosen, Ruth, ed. see Clayton, Lawrence.

Rosen, Ruth, ed. see Cohen, Payl & Cohen, Shari.

Rosen, Ruth, ed. see Cohen, Shari.

Rosen, Ruth, ed. see Collins, Robert F.

Rosen, Ruth, ed. see Cristall, Barbara.

Rosen, Ruth, ed. see Diskavich, Laura & Woods, Samuel, Jr.

Rosen, Ruth, ed. see Edwards, E. W.

Rosen, Ruth, ed. see Feller, Robyn M.

Rosen, Ruth, ed. see Field, Shelly.

Rosen, Ruth, ed. see Gartner, Bob.

Rosen, Ruth, ed. see Gooden, Kimberly W.

Rosen, Ruth, ed. see Grant, Edgar.

Rosen, Ruth, ed. see Greenwald, Dorothy.

Rosen, Ruth, ed. see Grosshandler, Janet.

Rosen, Ruth, ed. see Haddock, Patricia.

Rosen, Ruth, ed. see Heron, Jackie.

Rosen, Ruth, ed. see Hill, Margaret.

Rosen, Ruth, ed. see Hopkins, Del & Hopkins, Margaret.

Rosen, Ruth, ed. see Hurwitz, Ann R. & Hurwitz, Sue.

Rosen, Ruth, ed. see Hurwitz, Sue & Hurwitz, Jane.

Rosen, Ruth, ed. see Johnson, Barbara L.

Rosen, Ruth, ed. see Kane, June K.

Rosen, Ruth, ed. see Keyishian, Elizabeth.

Rosen, Ruth, ed. see Lee, Mary P. & Lee, Richard S.

Rosen, Ruth, ed. see Lee, Mary P.

Rosen, Ruth, ed. see Lee, Richard S. & Lee, Mary P.

Rosen, Ruth, ed. see Lobus, Catherine O.

Rosen, Ruth, ed. see Lytle, Elizabeth S.

Rosen, Ruth, ed. see Macdonald, Robert W.

Rosen, Ruth, ed. see Mahoney, Ellen V.

Rosen, Ruth, ed. see McFarland, Rhoda.

Rosen, Ruth, ed. see McGlothin, Bruce.

Rosen, Ruth, ed. see Milios, Rita.

Rosen, Ruth, ed. see Miller, Deborah.

Rosen, Ruth, ed. see Miller, Maryann.

Rosen, Ruth, ed. see Moe, Barbara.

Rosen, Ruth, ed. see Nelson, Cordner.

Rosen, Ruth, ed. see Neufeld, Rose.

Rosen, Ruth, ed. see Ottens, Allen & Myer, Rick.

Rosen, Ruth, ed. see Parker, Julie F.

Rosen, Ruth, ed. see Peck, Lee.

Rosen, Ruth, ed. see Peck, Rodney.

Rosen, Ruth, ed. see Raab, Robert A.

Rosen, Ruth, ed. see Ratto, Linda L.

Rosen, Ruth, ed. see Rawls, Bea O. & Johnson, Gwen.

Rosen, Ruth, ed. see Reynolds, Moira.

Rosen, Ruth, ed. see Santamaria, Peggy.

Rosen, Ruth, ed. see Schleifer, Jay.

Rosen, Ruth, ed. see Shapiro, Stanley J.

Rosen, Ruth, ed. see Shniderman, Nancy & Hurwitz, Sue.

Rosen, Ruth, ed. see Shuker-Haines, Frances.

Rosen, Ruth, ed. see Simpson, Carolyn.

Rosen, Ruth, ed. see Simpson, Carolyn & Simpson, Dwain.

Rosen, Ruth, ed. see Smith, Judie.

Rosen, Ruth, ed. see Smith, Sandra L.

Rosen, Ruth, ed. see Spencer, Jean.

Rosen, Ruth, ed. see Spies, Karen B.

Rosen, Ruth, ed. see St. Pierre, Stephanie.

Rosen, Ruth, ed. see Strauss, Linda.

Rosen, Ruth, ed. see Taylor, Barbara.

Rosen, Ruth, ed. see Vandenburg, Mary L.

Rosen, Ruth, ed. see Wagonseller, Bill, et al.

Rosen, Ruth, ed. see Webb, Margot.

Rosen, Ruth, ed. see White, Carl P.

Rosen, Ruth, ed. see Wilkinson, Beth.

Rosen, Ruth, ed. see Zeldis, Yona.

Rosen, Samuel R. A Judge Judges Mushrooms. (Illus.). 92p. 1988. pap. 8.00 (*0-913617-01-6*) Lubrecht & Cramer.

Rosen, Sara. My Lost World: A Survivor's Tale. (Library of Holocaust Testimonies Ser.). 320p. 1993. pap. text ed. 19.50 (*0-85303-254-8*, Pub. by Vallentine Mitchell UK) Intl Spec Bk.

Rosen, Saul. Lectures on the Measurement & Evaluation of the Performance of Computing Systems. (CBMS-NSF Regional Conference Ser.: No. 23). vii, 138p. (Orig.). 1976. reprint ed. pap. text ed. 20.50 (*0-89871-020-0*) Soc Indus-Appl Math.

Rosen-Sawyer, Fran. I Wish I Had Known. (Orig.). 1990. pap. 13.00 (*0-944909-02-7*) Fivefold Path.

Rosen, Selma. Children's Clothing: Designing, Selecting Fabrics, Patternmaking, Sewing. LC 82-83319. (Illus.). 168p. 1983. text ed. 18.50 (*0-87005-430-9*) Fairchild.

— Master Patterns for Children's Clothing. 1984. pap. 18.50 (*0-87005-433-3*) Fairchild.

Rosen, Sherwin, ed. Implicit Contract Theory. LC 93-39146. (International Library of Critical Writings in Business History: No. 35). 1994. 134.95 (*1-85278-748-1*, Pub. by E Elgar Pub UK) Ashgate Pub Co.

R

An Asterisk (*) at the beginning of an entry indicates that the title is appearing in BIP for the first time.

— Studies in Labor Markets. LC 81-7488. (National Bureau of Economic Research Ser.: Universities-Nat'l Conference Series No. 31). (Illus.). 400p. (C). 1981. lib. bdg. 47.00 (*0-226-72628-2*) U Ch Pr.

Rosen, Sherwin, jt. auth. see Nadiri, M. Ishaq.

Rosen, Shirley. Truman of St. Helens: The Man & His Mountain. 3rd rev. ed. LC 81-4304. (Illus.). 192p. 1989. reprint ed. pap. 9.95 (*0-685-44698-0*) Rosebud Pub.

— Truman of St. Helens: The Man & His Mountain. 4th ed. (Illus.). 163p. reprint ed. pap. 9.95 (*0-9623297-1-1*) Rosebud Pub.

Rosen, Sidney. Can You Find a Planet? (Question of Science Book Ser.). 40p. (J). (gr. k-3). 1991. lib. bdg. 19.95 (*0-87614-683-3*, Carolrhoda) Lerner Group.

— Can You Hitch a Ride on a Comet? LC 92-16808. (Question of Science Book Ser.). (Illus.). (J). (gr. k-3). 1993. 19.95 (*0-87614-719-8*, Carolrhoda) Lerner Group.

— How Far Is a Star? (Question of Science Book Ser.). (Illus.). 40p. (J). (gr. k-3). 1992. 19.95 (*0-87614-684-1*, Carolrhoda) Lerner Group.

— My Voice Will Go with You. 1991. pap. 9.95 (*0-393-30135-4*) Norton.

— Where Does the Moon Go? (Question of Science Book Ser.). (Illus.). 40p. (J). (gr. k-3). 1992. lib. bdg. 19.95 (*0-87614-685-X*, Carolrhoda) Lerner Group.

— Which Way to the Milky Way? (J). (gr. k-3). 1992. 19.95 (*0-87614-709-0*, Carolrhoda) Lerner Group.

Rosen, Sidney & Rosen, Dorothy. The Baghdad Mission. LC 93-36965. (J). (gr. 4-7). 1994. 19.95 (*0-87614-828-3*, Carolrhoda) Lerner Group.

— The Magician's Apprentice. LC 93-10781. (J). (gr. 4-7). 1993. 19.95 (*0-87614-809-7*, Carolrhoda) Lerner Group.

Rosen, Stanley. The Ancients & the Moderns: Rethinking Modernity. 246p. (C). 1991. reprint ed. pap. text ed. 14.00 (*0-300-05030-5*) Yale U Pr.

— Hermeneutics As Politics. (Odeon Ser.). 224p. 1990. reprint ed. pap. 16.95 (*0-19-506161-6*) OUP.

— The Mask of Enlightenment: Nietzsche's Zarathustra. (Modern European Philosophy Ser.). 272p. (C). 1995. write for info. (*0-521-49546-6*); pap. write for info. (*0-521-49889-9*) Cambridge U Pr.

— Nihilism: A Philosophical Essay. LC 70-81428. 261p. reprint ed. pap. 74.40 (*0-8357-8250-6*, 2033877) Bks Demand.

— Plato's Sophist: The Drama of Original & Image. LC 83-3512. 341p. 1986. text ed. 18.00 (*0-300-03761-9*) Yale U Pr.

— Plato's Statesman: The Web of Politics. LC 94-44016. 1995. write for info. (*0-300-06264-8*) Yale U Pr.

— Plato's Symposium. LC 86-23342. 432p. 1987. 18.00 (*0-300-03762-7*, Y-632) Yale U Pr.

— The Quarrel Between Philosophy & Poetry: Studies in Ancient Thought. 256p. 1988. text ed. 29.95 (*0-415-00184-6*) Routledge.

— The Quarrel Between Philosophy & Poetry: Studies in Ancient Thought. 223p. 1993. pap. 16.95 (*0-415-90745-4*, B0257, Routledge NY) Routledge.

— The Question of Being: A Reversal of Heidegger. LC 92-34934. 368p. (C). 1993. text ed. 40.00 (*0-300-05356-8*) Yale U Pr.

— Rethinking Modernity: The Ancients & the Moderns. LC 88-26155. 272p. (C). 1989. 32.00 (*0-300-04331-7*) Yale U Pr.

Rosen, Stanley, jt. ed. see Burns, John P.

Rosen, Stanley L. D. C. Circuits. LC 80-12328. (Avionics Technician Training Course Ser.). 158p. (Orig.). 1980. pap. text ed. 10.95 (*0-89100-121-2*, EA-DCC) IAP.

— Electricity & Electronics for the Microcomputer Age. LC 86-15912. 588p. 1987. student ed 22.95 (*0-471-88003-5*); text ed. 43.95 (*0-471-88195-3*) P-H.

Rosen, Stephen L. Fundamental Principles of Polymeric Materials. (SPE Monograph). 346p. 1982. 42.00 (*0-686-48122-4*, 0814) T-C Pubns CA.

— Fundamental Principles of Polymeric Materials. 2nd ed. LC 92-10973. (SPE Monographs). 448p. 1993. text ed. 64.00 (*0-471-57525-9*, Wiley-Interscience) Wiley.

Rosen, Stephen P. Winning the Next War: Innovation & the Modern Military. LC 91-55235. (Cornell Studies in Security Affairs). 288p. 1991. 37.50 (*0-8014-2556-5*) Cornell U Pr.

— Winning the Next War: Innovation & the Modern Military. (Cornell Studies in Security Affairs). 288p. 1994. pap. 14.95 (*0-8014-8196-1*) Cornell U Pr.

Rosen, Steve. Alpha Hand Dictionary. (Alpha Hand Ser.). 63p. 1980. 4.00 (*0-936862-08-4*, AHD) DDC Pub.

Rosen, Steve & Palmer, Rose. Alpha Hand ABC Shorthand: Notetaking & Secretarial. (Alpha Hand Ser.). 172p. 1989. 14.00 (*0-936862-02-5*, AH-1); teacher ed 10.00 (*0-936862-49-1*, AHM); student ed 6.00 (*0-936862-09-2*, AHWB); audio 7.50 (*0-936862-33-5*, 98) DDC Pub.

Rosen, Steven. Food for the Spirit: Vegetarianism & the World Religions. Greene, Joshua M., ed. (Illus.). 144p. (Orig.). 1987. pap. 6.95 (*0-89647-021-0*) Bala Bks.

— India's Spiritual Renaissance: The Life & Times of Lord Chaitanya. (Illus.). 250p. (Orig.). 1988. pap. 12.95 (*0-9619763-0-6*) Folk Bks.

— Passage from India: The Life & Times of His Divine Grace A. C. Bhaktivedanti Swami Prabhupada. A Summary Study of Satsvarupa Dasa Goswami's Srila Prabhupada Lilamrta. (C). 1992. 14.00 (*81-215-0558-5*, Pub. by Munshiram Manoharial II) S Asia.

Rosen, Steven, et al, eds. Innovations in Urologic Oncology. LC 91-67426. 144p. 1992. 39.95 (*0-944496-25-3*) Precept Pr.

Rosen, Steven J. The Proliferation of Land-Based Technologies: Implications for Local Military Balances. (CISA Working Paper Ser.: No. 12). 35p. (Orig.). Date not set. pap. 10.00 (*0-86682-011-6*) Ctr Intl Relations.

— Samuel Beckett & the Pessimistic Tradition. LC 76-2506. 262p. 1976. reprint ed. pap. 74.70 (*0-7837-5662-3*, 2059088) Bks Demand.

— What a Fifth Arab-Israeli War Might Look Like: An Exercise in Crisis Forecasting. (CISA Working Paper Ser.: No. 8). 46p. (Orig.). Date not set. pap. 10.00 (*0-86682-007-8*) Ctr Intl Relations.

Rosen, Steven J., ed. Vaisnavism: Contemporary Scholars Discuss the Gaudiya Tradition. LC 92-71546. 1992. pap. write for info. (*0-9619763-6-5*) Folk Bks.

Rosen, Steven M. Science, Paradox, & the Moebius Principle: The Evolution of a "Transcultural" Approach to Wholeness. LC 93-3091. (SUNY Series in Science, Technology, & Society). 317p. (C). 1994. 59.50 (*0-7914-1769-7*); pap. 19.95 (*0-7914-1770-0*) State U NY Pr.

Rosen, Steven T. & Kuzel, Timothy M., eds. Immunoconjugate Therapy of Hematologic Malignancies. LC 93-15382. (Cancer Treatment & Research Ser.: Vol. 68). 224p. (C). 1993. lib. bdg. 127.50 (*0-7923-2270-3*) Kluwer Ac.

Rosen, Steven W., intro. A Catalog of the Ceramics Collection of the Nora Eccles Harrison Museum of Art. (Illus.). 72p. (Orig.). 1993. pap. write for info. (*1-882710-00-2*) USU N E H Mus.

Rosen, Steven W. & Fergus-Jean, John. Columbus Collects American Painting, Sculpture, Photography. Roberts, Norma J. & Parsons, Merribell, eds. (Illus.). (Orig.). 1988. pap. 3.95 (*0-918881-22-6*) Columbus Mus Art.

Rosen, Steven W., et al. Henry Moore: The Reclining Figure. LC 84-71383. (Illus.). 148p. (Orig.). 1984. pap. 17.50 (*0-918881-12-9*) Columbus Mus Art.

Rosen, Stuart & Howell, Peter. Signals & Systems for Speech & Hearing. 332p. (C). 1991. text ed. 99.00 (*0-12-597230-X*); pap. text ed. 49.95 (*0-12-597231-8*) Acad Pr.

Rosen, Sumner M. Building a Program for Full Employment in New York. LC 84-167076. 66p. 1983. pap. 6.00 (*0-88156-010-3*) Comm Serv Soc NY.

— Economic Power Failure: The Current American Crisis. 1975. 8.95 (*0-07-053657-0*) McGraw.

Rosen, Teresa. The OTA Children's Coloring Book. (Illus.). 24p. (J). (ps-8). 1989. pap. 3.95 (*0-685-27024-6*) Prac Psych Pr.

— The OTA Children's Coloring Book: Time for College. 2nd ed. LC 91-50640. (Illus.). 24p. (J). (ps-8). 1989. pap. 3.95 (*0-944227-03-1*) Prac Psych Pr.

Rosen, Theodore, et al. Nurse's Atlas of Dermatology. 203p. 1983. 25.50 (*0-316-75705-5*) Little.

Rosen, Theodore A., jt. auth. see Daniels, Aubrey C.

Rosen, Valentina S. German Indologists: Biographies of Scholars in Indian Studies Writing German - with a Summary of Indology German Speaking Countries. 1990. 22.50 (*0-685-34759-1*, Pub. by Manohar II) S Asia.

***Rosen, Vicki.** The Cellular & Molecular Basis of Bone Formation & Repair. Thies, R. Scott, ed. (Molecular Biology Intelligence Unit Ser.). 161p. 1995. write for info. (*1-57059-289-6*) R G Landes.

Rosen, Walter, jt. auth. see Tellalian, Chuck.

Rosen, Wendy. Crating As a Business. 160p. 1994. pap. 19.95 (*0-8019-8632-X*) Chilton.

Rosen, William. Shakespeare & the Craft of Tragedy. LC 60-8002. 245p. 1960. reprint ed. pap. 69.00 (*0-7837-4127-8*, 2057950) Bks Demand.

Rosen, William, jt. auth. see Drooyan, Irving.

Rosen, Wilma G., jt. ed. see Mayeux, Richard.

Rosen, Winifred, jt. auth. see Weil, Andrew.

Rosenak, Chuck & Rosenak, Jan. Museum of American Folk Art Encyclopedia of Twentieth-Century American Folk Art & Artists. (Illus.). 416p. 1991. 75.00 (*1-55859-041-2*) Abbeville Pr.

— The People Speak: Navajo Folk Art. LC 93-40024. (Illus.). 173p. 1994. 40.00 (*0-87358-565-8*) Northland AZ.

Rosenak, Jan, jt. auth. see Rosenak, Chuck.

Rosenak, Michael. Commandments & Concerns. 320p. 1987. 37.50 (*0-8276-0279-0*) JPS Phila.

— The Road to the Palace Jewish Texts & Teaching. (Faith & Culture in Contemporary Education Ser.). 288p. (C). 1995. text ed. 39.95 (*1-57181-058-7*) Berghahn Bks.

Rosenast, Eleanor S. Soup Alive! LC 93-6656. (Illus.). 196p. (Orig.). 1993. pap. 9.95 (*0-88007-198-2*) Woodbridge Pr.

Rosenau, Hartmut. Allversoehnung: Ein Transzendentaltheologischer Grundlegungsversuch. (Theologische Bibliothek Toepelmann Ser.: No. 57). x, 544p. (GER.). 1993. lib. bdg. 163.10 (*3-11-013738-0*) De Gruyter.

Rosenau, Helen. The Ideal City: & Its Architectural Evolution in Europe. 3rd ed. (Illus.). 210p. 1983. 49.50 (*0-416-32850-4*, NO.3768) Routledge Chapman & Hall.

Rosenau, James N. International Politics & Foreign Policy. 2nd ed. LC 61-14106. 1969. text ed. 37.95 (*0-02-926980-6*) Free Pr.

— National Leadership & Foreign Policy: A Case Study in the Mobilization of Public Support. LC 63-7160. 427p. reprint ed. pap. 121.70 (*0-685-23412-6*, 2032637) Bks Demand.

— Turbulence in World Politics: A Theory of Change & Continuity. (Illus.). 459p. (Orig.). 1990. text ed. 65.00 (*0-691-07820-3*); pap. text ed. 16.95 (*0-691-02308-5*) Princeton U Pr.

— The United Nations in a Turbulent World. LC 91-45522. (International Peace Academy Occasional Paper Ser.). 88p. 1992. pap. text ed. 8.95 (*1-55587-330-8*) Lynne Rienner.

Rosenau, James N., ed. Global Voices: Dialogues in International Relations. 155p. (C). 1993. pap. text ed. 16.95 (*0-8133-1405-4*) Westview.

— Global Voices: Dialogues in International Relations. 155p. (C). 1993. text ed. 45.00 (*0-8133-1404-6*) Westview.

Rosenau, James N. & Czempiel, Ernst-Otto, eds. Governance Without Government: Order & Change in World Politics. (Studies in International Relations: No. 20). (Illus.). 288p. (C). 1992. 64.95 (*0-521-40531-9*); pap. 19.95 (*0-521-40578-5*) Cambridge U Pr.

***Rosenau, James N. & Durfee, Mary.** Thinking Theory Thoroughly: Coherent Approaches to an Incoherent World. LC 95-1095. (C). 1995. pap. text ed. 14.95 (*0-8133-2595-1*) Westview.

— Thinking Theory Thoroughly: Coherent Approaches to an Incoherent World. LC 95-1095. (C). 1995. text ed. 45.00 (*0-8133-2594-3*) Westview.

Rosenau, James N., jt. ed. see Czempiel, Ernst-Otto.

Rosenau, James N., jt. ed. see Kruzel, Joseph J.

Rosenau, Milton, Jr. Faster New Product Development: Time-Tested Techniques for Developing Products Faster to Gain the Competitive Edge. LC 89-81027. 432p. 1990. 55.00 (*0-8144-5942-0*) AMACOM.

Rosenau, Milton D., Jr. Project Management for Engineers. (Illus.). 328p. 1984. text ed. 54.95 (*0-534-03383-0*) Van Nos Reinhold.

— Successful Project Management. 2nd enl. ed. (Project Management Ser.). (Illus.). 320p. 1992. text ed. 59.95 (*0-442-00655-1*) Van Nos Reinhold.

Rosenau, Milton D., Jr. & Moran, John J. Managing the Development of New Products: Achieving Speed & Quality Simultaneously Through Multifunctional Teamwork. LC 93-14968. 1993. text ed. 49.95 (*0-442-01395-7*) Van Nos Reinhold.

Rosenau, Milton D., Jr., jt. auth. see Lewin, Marsha D.

Rosenau, Pauline M. Post-Modernism & the Social Sciences: Insights, Inroads, & Intrusions. 220p. 1992. text ed. 39.50 (*0-691-08619-2*); pap. text ed. 13.95 (*0-691-02347-6*) Princeton U Pr.

Rosenau, Pauline V., ed. Health Care Reform in the Nineties. LC 94-6009. 268p. (C). 1994. text ed. 48.00 (*0-8039-5729-7*); pap. text ed. 23.95 (*0-8039-5730-0*) Sage.

Rosenau, William. Jewish Ceremonial Institutions & Customs. 3rd rev. ed. LC 89-71334. 190p. 1992. reprint ed. lib. bdg. 45.00 (*1-55888-912-4*) Omnigraphics Inc.

Rosenauer, Johnnie L., jt. auth. see Lyon, Robert L.

Rosenauer, Libby. The Aware Person Series. Date not set. pap. write for info. (*1-881762-05-X*) Aware Pr.

— One Hundred Fifty-One Ways to Raise Your Self-Esteem: A Book of Activities That Will Enhance Your Life. (Aware Person Ser.). (Illus.). 96p. (Orig.). 1993. pap. 9.95 (*1-881762-00-9*) Aware Pr.

— You Are More Prosperous Than You Think: A Book of Activities That Will Enhance Your Life. (Aware Person Ser.). 96p. 1993. pap. 9.95 (*1-881762-01-7*) Aware Pr.

Rosenaur, Johnnie. Effective Real Estate Sales & Marketing. 2nd ed. (Illus.). 258p. 1987. pap. 23.95 (*0-88462-599-0*, 1562-02, Real Estate Ed) Dearborn Finan.

Rosenbach, Abraham S. An American Jewish Bibliography: Being a List of Books & Pamphlets by Jews, or Relating to Them, Printed in the United States from the Establishment of the Press in the Colonies until 1850. (American Jewish Historical Society Publications: No. 30). (Illus.). 509p. reprint ed. pap. 145.10 (*0-8357-5376-X*, 2017816) Bks Demand.

— Book Hunter's Holiday: Adventures with Books & Manuscripts. LC 68-29242. (Essay Index Reprint Ser.). 1977. reprint ed. 23.95 (*0-8369-0834-1*) Ayer.

— The Unpublished Memoirs. (American Biography Ser.). 151p. 1991. reprint ed. lib. bdg. 59.00 (*0-7812-8330-2*) Rprt Serv.

Rosenbach, Detlev. Alexej Von Jawlensky's Life & Graphic Work. (Illus.). 176p. (GER.). 1985. 120.00 (*0-915346-96-6*) A Wofsy Fine Arts.

— Bargheer's Graphic Work. (Illus.). 200p. 1974. 120.00 (*0-915346-97-4*) A Wofsy Fine Arts.

— Bremer's Graphic Work. (Illus.). 230p. 1974. 120.00 (*0-915346-98-2*) A Wofsy Fine Arts.

— Heinrich Zille's Graphic Work. (Illus.). 228p. 1984. 165.00 (*0-915346-95-8*) A Wofsy Fine Arts.

Rosenbach, Joseph B. College Algebra with Trigonometry. LC 73-79572. 512p. reprint ed. pap. 146.00 (*0-317-09359-2*, 2055103) Bks Demand.

Rosenbach, Kevin P. Pharmacology: MedCharts, Tables & Summaries for Review. LC 92-49118. 1993. pap. 14.95 (*1-882531-00-0*) ILOC.

Rosenbach, Margo L. The Use of Physicians' Services by Low-Income Children. LC 92-48901. (Children of Poverty Ser.). 200p. 1993. 53.00 (*0-8153-1113-3*) Garland.

Rosenbach, William E. & Taylor, Robert L. Leadership: Challenges for Today's Manager. 220p. 1989. 29.95 (*0-89397-317-3*) Nichols Pub.

Rosenbach, William E. & Taylor, Robert L., eds. Contemporary Issues in Leadership. 3rd ed. LC 93-1255. 233p. (C). 1993. text ed. 52.50 (*0-8133-1754-1*); pap. text ed. 19.95 (*0-8133-1755-X*) Westview.

Rosenbach, William E., jt. ed. see Taylor, Robert L.

Rosenband, Leonard N., jt. ed. see Safley, Thomas M.

Rosenbauer, Tom. The Orvis Fly-Fishing Guide. (Illus.). 260p. 1988. 26.95 (*0-941130-91-6*); pap. 17.95 (*0-941130-92-4*) Lyons & Burford.

— Prospecting for Trout: Flyfishing Secrets from a Streamside Observer. LC 92-29642. 1993. pap. 14.95 (*0-385-30816-7*, Delta) Dell.

— Reading Trout Streams: An Orvis Guide. (Illus.). 160p. 1988. pap. 16.95 (*0-941130-78-9*) Lyons & Burford.

Rosenbauer, Tom, text. Casting Illusions: The World of Fly-Fishing. LC 88-4053. (Illus.). 144p. 1989. 19.98 (*0-934738-50-5*) Thomasson-Grant.

Rosenbaum. Edwardian Bloomsbury: The Early Literary History of the Bloomsbury Group, Vol. 2. 1994. text ed. 35.00 (*0-312-23909-2*) St Martin.

Rosenbaum, jt. auth. see Jabs.

Rosenbaum, Alan S. Coercion & Autonomy: Philosophical Foundations, Issues & Practices. LC 86-7578. (Contributions in Philosophy Ser.: No. 31). 208p. 1986. text ed. 49.95 (*0-313-22819-1*, RHA/, Greenwood Pr) Greenwood.

— Prosecuting Nazi War Criminals. LC 92-46912. 144p. 1993. text ed. 39.00 (*0-8133-8357-9*) Westview.

Rosenbaum, Alan S., ed. Constitutionalism: The Philosophical Dimension. LC 88-5634. (Contributions in Legal Studies: No. 46). 288p. 1988. text ed. 59.95 (*0-313-25671-3*, RCU/, Greenwood Pr) Greenwood.

— The Philosophy of Human Rights: International Perspectives. LC 79-6191. (Contributions in Philosophy Ser.: No. 15). xv, 272p. 1980. text ed. 49.95 (*0-313-20985-5*, RHR/, Greenwood Pr) Greenwood.

Rosenbaum, Allan, ed. Employment Training Policy. 204p. (Orig.). 1987. pap. 12.00 (*0-918592-92-5*) Pol Studies.

***Rosenbaum, Alvin.** The Complete Home Office: Planning Your Work Space for Maximum Efficiency. LC 94-45190. 1995. write for info. (*0-670-85293-7*, Viking Studio) Studio Bks.

— Usonia: Frank Lloyd Wright's Design for America. LC 93-7612. (Illus.). 216p. 1993. 29.95 (*0-89133-201-4*) Preservation Pr.

— Works in Progress. LC 94-7912. (Illus.). 208p. 1994. 39.95 (*0-87654-069-8*) Pomegranate Calif.

Rosenbaum, Art. Art of the Mountain Banjo. 84p. (Orig.). 1988. reprint ed. pap. text ed. 9.95 (*0-931759-24-2*) Centerstream Pub.

— Old Time Mountain Banjo. (Illus.). 88p. 1968. pap. 11.95 (*0-8256-0116-9*, OK62034, Oak) Music Sales.

Rosenbaum, Art & Rosenbaum, Margo. Folk Visions & Voices: Traditional Music & Song in North Georgia. LC 83-6473. (Illus.). 256p. 1983. 29.95 (*0-8203-0682-7*) U of Ga Pr.

Rosenbaum, Arthur L., ed. State & Society in China: The Consequences of Reform. 240p. (C). 1992. text ed. 52.50 (*0-8133-1175-6*); pap. text ed. 19.95 (*0-8133-1176-4*) Westview.

Rosenbaum, B. Index of English Literary Manuscripts, 1800-1900, Vol. IV, Pt. 2: Hardy-Lamb. (Illus.). 768p. 1990. text ed. 500.00 (*0-7201-1660-0*, Mansell Pub) Cassell.

Rosenbaum, B. & White, P. Index of English Literary Manuscripts, 1800-1900, Vol. IV, Pt. 1, A-G. (Illus.). 864p. 1982. text ed. 360.00 (*0-7201-1587-6*, Mansell Pub) Cassell.

Rosenbaum, Barbara & Pearson, Richard. Index of English Literary Manuscripts, 1800-1900, Vol. IV, Pt. 3: Landor-Patmore. (Index of English Literary Manuscripts Ser.). (Illus.). 860p. 1994. 500.00 (*0-7201-2153-1*, Mansell Pub) Cassell.

Rosenbaum, Brenda. How to Avoid the Evil Eye: Five Thousand Years of Jewish Superstition. (Illus.). 96p. 1985. pap. 5.95 (*0-312-39584-1*) St Martin.

— With Our Heads Bowed: The Dynamics of Gender in a Maya Community. LC 92-76220. (IMS Studies on Culture & Society: No. 5). (Illus.). 239p. (Orig.). (C). 1993. pap. 18.00 (*0-942041-14-3*) SUNYA Inst Mesoam.

Rosenbaum, C. Peter. Italian for Educated Guessers: Shortcuts to the Language. (Illus.). 254p. (Orig.). 1984. pap. 12.00 (*0-9614045-1-5*) Forza Pr.

Rosenbaum, Cindy, et al. For the Love of Animals: Six Delightful Songs & a Story about How the Children Save the Animals. (Illus.). 24p. (Orig.). (J). (ps-4). 1992. audio, pap. text ed. 12.95 (*1-881567-00-1*) Happy Kids Prods.

Rosenbaum, Claire M. A Gem of a College: History of Westhampton College, 1914-1989. Lancaster, Ann & Beville, Don, eds. (Illus.). 156p. 1989. text ed. 19.95 (*0-685-29350-5*) Westhampton College.

Rosenbaum, David. Sasha's Trick. 400p. 1995. 21.95 (*0-89296-591-6*) Mysterious Pr.

— Sasha's Trick. 1996. mass mkt. write for info. (*0-446-40441-1*, Mysterious Paperbk) Warner Bks.

— Zaddik. LC 92-50695. 448p. 1993. 19.95 (*0-89296-540-1*) Mysterious Pr.

— Zaddik. 464p. 1994. mass mkt. 5.99 (*0-446-40322-9*, Mysterious Paperbk) Warner Bks.

Rosenbaum, David A. Human Motor Control. 411p. (C). 1990. text ed. 45.00 (*0-12-597300-4*) Acad Pr.

Rosenbaum, David G. Patents, Trademarks & Copyrights. 2nd ed. (Layman's Law Guides Ser.). 128p. 1994. pap. 8.95 (*1-56414-085-7*) Career Pr Inc.

— Patents, Trademarks & Copyrights: Practical Strategies for Protecting Your Ideas & Inventions. 1993. pap. 9.95 (*0-9630356-6-5*) Makai.

Rosenbaum, Dennis P., ed. see Bayley, David H., et al.

***Rosenbaum, Dennis P., et al.** Community Responses to Drug Abuse: A Program Evaluation. (Illus.). 52p. (Orig.). (C). 1994. pap. text ed. 25.00x (*0-7881-1435-2*) Diane Pub.

Rosenbaum, Dora, jt. auth. see McGreevy, Mary.

Rosenbaum, Eduard & Sherman, A. J. M. M. Warburg & Co., 1798-1938: Merchant Bankers of Hamburg. LC 79-511. (Illus.). 190p. 1979. 37.95 (*0-8419-0477-4*) Holmes & Meier.

Rosenbaum, Edward E. Doctor. 1991. mass mkt. 4.99 (*0-8041-0873-0*) Ivy Books.

— A Taste of My Own Medicine: When the Doctor Is the Patient. LC 87-43218. 192p. 1988. 16.95 (*0-394-56282-8*) Random.

— A Taste of My Own Medicine: When the Doctor Is the Patient. braille ed. 320p. 1991. vinyl bd. 25.60 (*1-56956-319-5*, BR7660) W A T Braille.

Rosenbaum, Eli & Hoffer, William. Betrayal: The Untold Story of the Kurt Waldheim Investigation & Cover-Up. (Illus.). 576p. 1993. 25.95 (*0-312-08219-3*, Pub. by Thomas Dunne Bks) St Martin.

Rosenbaum, Elisabeth, ed. see Erasmus.

R

Rosenbaum, Eliza. Friends Afloat. LC 92-39029. (Publish-a-Book Contest Ser.). (Illus.). 24p. (J). (gr. 2-3). 1992. lib. bdg. 19.97 (0-8114-3584-9) Raintree Steck-V.

— Friends Afloat. (J). (ps-3). 1994. pap. 4.95 (0-8114-7776-2) Raintree Steck-V.

Rosenbaum, Elizabeth. A Catalogue of Cyrenaican Portrait Sculpture. 160p. 1979. 26.00 (0-686-26936-5) St Mut.

Rosenbaum, Ernest H. You Can Prevent Cancer. Mahoney, Sheila & Wiltsek, Nancy, eds. (Illus.). 29p. 1984. pap. 2.50 (0-933161-00-X) Better H Prog.

Rosenbaum, Ernest H., jt. auth. see Ramstack, Janet.

Rosenbaum, Ernest H., jt. auth. see Wheat, Mary E.

Rosenbaum, Ernest H., et al. Lifestyle & Cancer Prevention. Mahoney, Sheila & Wiltsek, Nancy, eds. (Illus.). 49p. 1985. pap. 2.50 (0-933161-05-0) Better H Prog.

— Tobacco, Alcohol & Cancer Prevention. Mahoney, Sheila & Wiltsek, Nancy, eds. (Illus.). 29p. 1984. pap. 2.50 (0-933161-02-6) Better H Prog.

Rosenbaum, Fred. Architects of Reform: Congregation & Community Leadership, Emanu-El of San Francisco, 1849-1980. LC 80-54032. 241p. 1980. 19.95 (0-943376-14-9); pap. 9.95 (0-943376-13-0) Magnes Mus.

Rosenbaum, H. Jon & Tyler, William G., eds. Contemporary Brazil: Issues in Economic & Political Development. LC 73-180851. (Special Studies in International Economics & Development). 1972. 64.50 (0-275-28289-9) Irvington.

Rosenbaum, Harold D. Pearls in Diagnostic Radiology. LC 80-19014. 296p. reprint ed. pap. 84.40 (0-7837-3148-5, 2042837) Bks Demand.

Rosenbaum, Herbert D. & Bartelme, Elizabeth, eds. Franklin D. Roosevelt: The Man, the Myth, the Era, 1882-1945. LC 87-8456. (Contributions in Political Science Ser.: No. 189). 400p. 1987. text ed. 75.00 (0-313-25949-6, RRS/, Greenwood Pr) Greenwood.

Rosenbaum, Herbert D. & Ugrinsky, Alexej, eds. Jimmy Carter: Foreign Policy & Post-Presidential Years. LC 93-9320. (Contributions in Political Science Ser.: No. 328). 528p. 1993. text ed. 75.00 (0-313-28844-5, GM8844, Greenwood Pr) Greenwood.

— The Presidency & Domestic Policies of Jimmy Carter. LC 93-9321. (Contributions in Political Science Ser.: No. 327). 876p. 1993. text ed. 95.00 (0-313-28845-3, GM8845, Greenwood Pr) Greenwood.

Rosenbaum, I. Holocaust & Halakhah. (Library of Jewish Law & Ethics: No. 2). 12.95 (0-87068-296-2); pap. 9.95 (0-685-02915-8) Ktav.

Rosenbaum, J. F., jt. ed. see Fava, M.

Rosenbaum, J. F., jt. ed. see Jonsson, B.

Rosenbaum, James E. Careers in a Corporate Hierarchy: Structural Timetables & Historical Effects (Monograph) LC 83-22406. 1984. text ed. 55.00 (0-12-597080-3) Acad Pr.

Rosenbaum, Jean & Prine, Mary. Opportunites in Fitness Careers. (Illus.). 160p. 1987. 13.95 (0-8442-6151-3, VGM Career Bks); pap. 10.95 (0-8442-6152-1, VGM Career Bks) NTC Pub Grp.

— Opportunities in Fitness Careers. LC 90-50731. (Opportunities in...Ser.). 160p. (YA). (gr. 7 up). 1991. 13.95 (0-8442-8185-9, VGM Career Bks); pap. 10.95 (0-8442-8186-7, VGM Career Bks) NTC Pub Grp.

Rosenbaum, Jean & Rosenbaum, Veryl. Living with Teenagers. LC 79-3711. 192p. (C). 1982. pap. 7.95 (0-8128-6144-2, Scrbrough Hse) Madison Bks UPA.

Rosenbaum, Jean, jt. auth. see Rosenbaum, Veryl.

Rosenbaum, Joel. Bulk Acoustic Wave Theory & Devices. (Acoustics Library). 400p. 1988. text ed. 49.00 (0-89006-265-X) Artech Hse.

Rosenbaum, Joel & Gallo, Tom. The Broadway Limited. LC 88-32103. (Illus.). 96p. (C). 1988. pap. 18.00 (0-9621541-0-5) Railpace Co.

Rosenbaum, Jonathan. Film: The Front Line 1983. (Illus.). 238p. (Orig.). 1983. pap. 10.95 (0-912869-03-8) Arden Pr.

— Greed. (Illus.). 64p. (C). 1993. pap. 9.95 (0-85170-358-5, Pub. by British Film Inst UK) Ind U Pr.

— Moving Places: A Life at the Movies. LC 94-28364. (Orig.). 1995. reprint ed. pap. text ed. 16.00 (0-520-08907-3) U CA Pr.

— Placing Movies: The Practice of Film Criticism. LC 93-42954. 1995. 45.00 (0-520-08632-5); pap. 16.00 (0-520-08633-3) U CA Pr.

Rosenbaum, Jonathan, tr. see Bazin, Andre.

Rosenbaum, Jonathan, jt. auth. see Hoberman, J.

Rosenbaum, Jonathan, ed. see Welles, Orson & Bogdanovich, Peter.

Rosenbaum, Judith, jt. auth. see Lubet, Steven.

Rosenbaum, Kurt. Community of Fate: German-Soviet Diplomatic Relations, 1922-1928. LC 65-18573. 1965. 34.95x (0-8156-2079-9) Syracuse U Pr.

***Rosenbaum, Larry.** Quick Reference Guide for Lotus Notes 3 for Windows. 1994. pap. 8.95 (1-56243-205-2) DDC Pub.

— You Shall Be My Witnesses: How to Reach Your City for Christ. LC 86-90426. 144p. (Orig.). 1986. pap. 5.00 (0-938573-00-4) SOS Minist Pr.

Rosenbaum, Lilian. Biofeedback Frontiers: Self-Regulation of Stress Reactivity. LC 86-82030. (Stress in Modern Society Ser.: No. 15). 1988. 32.50 (0-404-63266-1) AMS Pr.

Rosenbaum, M. & Elizari, M., eds. Frontiers of Cardiac Electrophysiology. 1983. lib. bdg. 314.00 (90-247-2663-8) Kluwer Ac.

Rosenbaum, M., jt. auth. see Silbermann, A. M.

Rosenbaum, Margo, jt. auth. see Rosenbaum, Art.

Rosenbaum, Marsha. Women on Heroin. (Crime, Law & Deviance Ser.). 205p. (Orig.). (C). 1981. pap. 15.00 (0-8135-0946-7) Rutgers U Pr.

Rosenbaum, Marsha, jt. auth. see Beck, Jerome.

Rosenbaum, Martin. Children & the Environment. 90p. 1994. pap. 22.00 (1-874579-01-6, Pub. by Natl Childrens Bur UK) Paul & Co Pubs.

Rosenbaum, Mary H. & Rosenbaum, Stanley N. Celebrating Our Differences: Living Two Faiths in One Marriage. LC 94-8447. 240p. (C). 1994. 19.95 (0-942597-69-9, Ragged Edge) White Mane Pub.

Rosenbaum, Maurice, tr. see Mehnert, Klaus.

Rosenbaum, Maury, jt. ed. see Neumann, Karl.

Rosenbaum, Max, ed. Complaint Behavior: Beyond Obedience to Authority. 254p. 1983. 35.95 (0-89885-115-7) Human Sci Pr.

— Drug Abuse & Drug Addiction. 102p. (Orig.). 1973. text ed. 79.00 (0-677-15710-X) Gordon & Breach.

— Group Psychotherapy from the Southwest. 130p. 1974. text ed. 59.00 (0-677-15790-8) Gordon & Breach.

Rosenbaum, Max & Muroff, Melvin, eds. Anna O. Fourteen Contemporary Reinterpretations. LC 83-48147. (C). 1984. text ed. 32.95 (0-02-926940-7) Free Pr.

Rosenbaum, Max, jt. ed. see Rabin, H. M.

Rosenbaum, Michael. Street Fighting Tactics From Karate-Do. 96p. (Orig.). 1985. pap. 5.95 (0-89826-015-9) Natl Paperback.

Rosenbaum, Michael, ed. Learned Resourcefulness: On Coping Skills, Self-Control & Adaptive Behavior. LC 90-9637. (Behavior Therapy & Behavioral Medicine Ser.: Vol. 24). 288p. 1990. 38.95 (0-8261-4860-3) Springer Pub.

Rosenbaum, Michael, jt. auth. see Lee, William H.

Rosenbaum, Michael, jt. auth. see Susser, Murray.

Rosenbaum, Michael E. & Bosco, Dominick. Super Fitness Beyond Vitamins. 1989. pap. 4.95 (0-318-40124-X, Sig) NAL-Dutton.

— Super Supplements: Your Guide to Today's Newest Amino Acids & Glandulars. 288p. 1989. pap. 4.99 (0-451-15809-1, Sig) NAL-Dutton.

Rosenbaum, Myron G. Understanding Arthritis. LC 73-9498. (Illus.). 112p. 1975. 8.50x (0-87527-121-9) Green.

Rosenbaum, Nelson M. Citizen Involvement in Land Use Governance: Issues & Methods. (Illus.). 82p. (Orig.). 1976. pap. text ed. 11.00 (0-87766-140-5) Urban Inst.

***Rosenbaum, Paul R.** Observational Studies. LC 95-2178. (Springer Series in Statistics). 1995. write for info. (0-387-94482-6) Spr-Verlag.

Rosenbaum, Peter A., jt. auth. see Volpe, E. Peter.

Rosenbaum, Philip. The Promise. LC 93-44778. 1994. 16.99 (0-8054-6141-8) Broadman.

Rosenbaum, R. A. & Johnson, G. P. Calculus: Basic Concepts & Applications. LC 83-14257. 422p. 1984. 47.95 (0-521-25012-9) Cambridge U Pr.

***Rosenbaum, Ray.** Condors: A Novel. LC 94-32681. 1995. 21.95 (0-89141-478-9, Lyford Bks) Presidio Pr.

— Falcons: A Novel. LC 92-29016. 362p. 1993. 21.95 (0-89141-476-2, Lyford Bks) Presidio Pr.

— Falcons: Wings of War. 416p. 1995. pap. 9.95 (0-89141-559-9) Presidio Pr.

— Hawks: A Novel. LC 93-34197. 314p. 1994. 21.95 (0-89141-477-0) Presidio Pr.

Rosenbaum, Richard B. & Ochoa, Jose L. Carpal Tunnel Syndrome & Other Disorders of the Median Nerve. 1992. text ed. 95.00 (0-7506-9229-4) Buttrwrth-Heinemann.

Rosenbaum, Robert. Aviators. (American Profiles Ser.). (Illus.). 128p. (YA). (gr. 6-12). 1992. lib. bdg. 16.95 (0-8160-2539-8) Facts on File.

Rosenbaum, Robert A. The Public Issues Handbook: A Guide for the Concerned Citizen. LC 82-15812. (Illus.). vii, 409p. 1983. text ed. 69.50 (0-313-23504-X, RPI/, Greenwood Pr) Greenwood.

Rosenbaum, Robert D. & Parker, L. Stevenson. State Takeover Statutes & Poison Pills, 2 Vols., Set. 2006p. 1989. ring bd. 185.00 (0-13-808882-9) Aspen Law.

Rosenbaum, Robert J. History of Mexican Americans in Texas. (Texas History Ser.). (Illus.). 38p. 1981. pap. text ed. 3.95x (0-89641-042-0) American Pr.

Rosenbaum, Robert J. Mexicano Resistance in the Southwest: "The Sacred Right of Self-Preservation" (Illus.). 253p. 1986. reprint ed. 25.00 (0-292-77562-8); reprint ed. pap. 13.95 (0-292-75097-8) U of Tex Pr.

Rosenbaum, Robert J., ed. People in Texas. (Illus.). 192p. (C). 1982. pap. text ed. 7.95x (0-89641-102-8) American Pr.

— Readings in Texas History. (Illus.). 216p. (C). 1982. pap. text ed. 7.95x (0-89641-136-2) American Pr.

Rosenbaum, Roberta, jt. auth. see Highland, Esther H.

Rosenbaum, S. E. A Voyage to America Ninety Years Ago: The Diary of a Bohemian Jew on His Voyage from Hamburg to New York in 1847. Kravetz, Nathan, tr. LC 93-2898. (Studies in Judaica & the Holocaust: No. 3). 144p. Date not set. reprint ed. write for info. (0-89370-371-0); reprint ed. pap. write for info. (0-89370-471-7) Borgo Pr.

Rosenbaum, S. P. Victorian Bloomsbury: The Early Literary History of the Bloomsbury Group, Vol. 1. 298p. 1987. text ed. 29.95 (0-312-84051-9) St Martin.

***Rosenbaum, S. P., ed.** The Bloomsbury Group: A Collection of Memoirs & Commentary. (C). 1995. pap. 22.95 (0-8020-7640-8) U of Toronto Pr.

— The Bloomsbury Group: A Collection of Memoirs & Commentary. rev. ed. 500p. (C). 1995. 60.00 (0-8020-0690-6) U of Toronto Pr.

— The Bloomsbury Group: A Collection of Memoirs, Commentary & Criticism. 1975. pap. 21.95 (0-8020-6268-7) U of Toronto Pr.

— A Bloomsbury Group Reader. LC 92-44808. 1993. 54.95 (0-631-17318-8); pap. 21.95 (0-631-19059-7) Blackwell Pubs.

Rosenbaum, S. P., ed. see James, Henry.

Rosenbaum, S. P., ed. see Woolf, Virginia.

Rosenbaum, Sindy. Stepping into Yourself, Grades Three to Six. (Illus.). 42p. (Orig.). 1988. pap. 7.95 (0-673-38244-3) GdYrBks.

Rosenbaum, Stanford P., ed. see Dickinson, Emily.

Rosenbaum, Stanley N. Amos of Israel: A New Interpretation. LC 89-39065. xii, 129p. (C). 1990. 25.00 (0-86554-355-0, MUP/H296) Mercer Univ Pr.

Rosenbaum, Stanley N., jt. auth. see Rosenbaum, Mary H.

Rosenbaum, Stuart, jt. ed. see Baird, Robert.

Rosenbaum, Stuart E., jt. auth. see Baird, Robert M.

Rosenbaum, Stuart E., jt. ed. see Baird, Robert M.

Rosenbaum, Veryl & Rosenbaum, Jean. Stepparenting. LC 77-22070. 160p. 1977. 12.95 (0-88316-530-9) Chandler & Sharp.

Rosenbaum, Veryl, jt. auth. see Rosenbaum, Jean.

Rosenbaum, Virginia. Corporate Takeover Defenses, 1993. 1530p. 1993. 495.00 (1-879775-09-3) IRRC Inc DC.

Rosenbaum, Virginia K. Corporate Takeover Defenses. 2nd ed. 1551p. 1990. 495.00 (0-685-48385-1) IRRC Inc DC.

— Corporate Takeover Defenses 1990. 1551p. 1990. text ed. 495.00 (0-685-48000-3) IRRC Inc DC.

Rosenbaum, Walter A. Environmental Politics & Policy. 2nd ed. 336p. 1990. 22.95 (0-87187-546-2) Congr Quarterly.

Rosenbek, John C., et al. Aphasia: A Clinical Approach. LC 90-52763. 311p. (C). 1989. pap. text ed. 36.00 (0-89079-270-4, 1781) PRO-ED.

Rosenberg. Harper's Grammar of French. 1983. text ed. 37.95 (0-8384-3746-X) Heinle & Heinle.

— In Our Times: America since World War II. 5th ed. (Illus.). 336p. (C). 1994. pap. text ed. write for info. (0-13-106477-0) P-H.

— Occupational & Environmental Neurology. 1995. write for info. (0-7506-9515-3, Focal) Buttrwrth-Heinemann.

Rosenberg, et al. Nineteen Ninety-Three Case Supplement to Civil Procedure. 5th ed. 1993. pap. text ed. 6.50 (1-56662-081-3) Foundation Pr.

Rosenberg, A. Nicolas Gueudeville & His Work Sixteen Fifty-Two to Seventeen Twenty-Five. 1982. lib. bdg. 107.50 (90-247-2533-X) Kluwer Ac.

Rosenberg, A. J., ed. Chronicles I & II: Hebrew Text, English Translation & Commentary Digest. 2nd rev. ed. LC 93-8763. 1995. 14.95 (1-871055-85-7) Soncino Pr.

— Ezekiel, Vol. 2. 1991. 17.95 (0-685-49569-8) Judaica Pr.

— Ezekiel: Hebrew Text, English Translation & Commentary Digest. LC 93-5029. 1995. 14.95 (1-871055-95-4) Soncino Pr.

Rosenberg, A. J., tr. Book of Isaiah, Vol. 1. 261p. (HEB.). 1982. 17.95 (0-910818-50-9) Judaica Pr.

— Book of Isaiah, Vol. 2. 292p. (HEB.). 1983. 17.95 (0-910818-52-5) Judaica Pr.

— Book of Jeremiah, Vol. 1. (Books of the Prophet Ser.). 474p. (HEB.). 1985. 17.95 (0-910818-59-2) Judaica Pr.

— Book of Jeremiah, Vol. II. (Books of the Prophet Ser.). 464p. (HEB.). 1985. 17.95 (0-910818-60-6) Judaica Pr.

— Book of Job - Hebrew Text & Commentary with English Translation: Hebrew Text, English Translation & Commentary Digest. (Books of Prophets & Holy Writings Ser.). 249p. (HEB.). 1989. 17.95 (0-910818-80-0) Judaica Pr.

— Book of Joshua - Hebrew Text & Commentary with English Translation: Hebrew Text, English Translation & Commentary Digest. 357p. (HEB.). 1984. 17.95 (0-910818-08-8) Judaica Pr.

— Book of Judges: Hebrew Text, English Translation & Commentary Digest. 400p. (HEB.). 1979. 17.95 (0-910818-17-7) Judaica Pr.

— Book of Kings, Vol. 1. 521p. (HEB.). 1980. 17.95 (0-910818-30-4) Judaica Pr.

— Book of Kings, Vol. 2. 447p. (HEB.). 1980. 17.95 (0-910818-31-2) Judaica Pr.

— Book of Samuel, Vol. 1. 512p. (HEB.). 1981. 17.95 (0-910818-07-X) Judaica Pr.

— Book of Samuel, Vol. 2. 450p. (HEB.). 1982. 17.95 (0-910818-11-8) Judaica Pr.

— Book of Twelve Prophets, Vol. 1. 268p. (HEB.). 1986. 17.95 (0-910818-70-3) Judaica Pr.

— Book of Twelve Prophets, Vol. II. 213p. (HEB.). 1988. 17.95 (0-910818-78-9) Judaica Pr.

— Chronicles I: Hebrew Text, English Translation & Commentary Digest. 1992. 17.95 (0-910818-97-5) Judaica Pr.

— Chronicles II: Hebrew Text, English Translation & Commentary Digest. 1992. 17.95 (0-910818-98-3) Judaica Pr.

— Daniel, Ezra, & Nehemiah - Hebrew Text & Commentary with English Translation: Hebrew Text, English Translation & Commentary Digest. 1992. 17.95 (0-910818-94-0) Judaica Pr.

— Ezekiel Vol. 2, Chaps. 26-48. 275p. 1991. 17.95 (0-910818-88-6) Judaica Pr.

— Ezekiel - Hebrew Text & Commentary with English Translation Vol. 1, Chaps. 1-25. 1991. 17.95 (0-910818-87-8) Judaica Pr.

— The Five Megilloth: Hebrew Text, English Translation & Commentary Digest. LC 92-13500. (Judaica Bks. of the Hagiographa - the Holy Writings). (ENG & HEB.). 1992. 39.90 (1-880582-01-5) Judaica Pr.

— Five Megilloth Vol. 2: A New English Translation. LC 92-13500. (Judaica Bks. of the Hagiographa - the Holy Writings). (HEB.). 1992. 39.90 (1-880582-02-3) Judaica Pr.

— Genesis: A New Translation with Hebrew Text & Commentary Digest. 1995. write for info. (1-880582-09-0) Judaica Pr.

— Genesis: A New Translation, with Hebrew Text & Hebrew Commentary, Vol. III. LC 93-4128. 534p. 1994. 22.50 (1-880582-10-4) Judaica Pr.

— Genesis: Hebrew Text, English Translation & Commentary Digest, Vol. I. LC 93-1547. 1993. 22.50 (1-880582-08-2) Judaica Pr.

***Rosenberg, A J., tr.** Genesis Vol. 2: A New Translation, with Hebrew Text & Commentary Digest. Date not set. 22.50 (0-614-04072-8) Judaica Pr.

Rosenberg, A. J., tr. Megillath Esther: Hebrew Text, English Translation & Commentary Digest. 86p. 1984. pap. 6.95 (0-900689-97-8) Soncino Pr.

— Psalms, Vol. I (Chaps. 1-41) 250p. 1990. 17.95 (0-910818-84-3) Judaica Pr.

— Psalms, Vol. II (Chaps. 42-89) 250p. 1990. 17.95 (0-910818-85-1) Judaica Pr.

— Psalms, Vol. III (Chaps. 90-150) 250p. 1990. 17.95 (0-910818-86-X) Judaica Pr.

Rosenberg, A. Y. Mishnah-Moed: Shabbos. Danziger, Y. & Gold, A., eds. (ArtScroll Mishnah Ser.). (Illus.). 396p. 1982. 22.95 (0-89906-250-4) Mesorah Pubns.

Rosenberg, A. Y. Mishnah-Nashim: Kesubos. Arem, T. Z., ed. (ArtScroll Mishnah Ser.). (Illus.). 258p. 1984. 22.95 (0-89906-277-6) Mesorah Pubns.

Rosenberg, A. Y. Mishnah-Nezikin. Finkel, G., ed. (ArtScroll Mishnah Ser.). (Illus.). 310p. 1987. 22.95 (0-89906-297-0) Mesorah Pubns.

— Mishnah-Nezikin: Bava Kamma. Arem, T. Z., ed. (ArtScroll Mishnah Ser.). 240p. 1986. 22.95 (0-89906-289-X) Mesorah Pubns.

— Mishnah-Nezikin: Bava Metzia. Arem, T. Z., ed. (ArtScroll Mishnah Ser.). (Illus.). 264p. 22.95 (0-89906-291-1) Mesorah Pubns.

***Rosenberg, Abraham, ed.** Biology of the Sialic Acids. 375p. 1995. 95.00 (0-306-44974-9) Plenum.

Rosenberg, Alan & Myers, Gerald, eds. Echoes from the Holocaust: Philosophical Reflections on a Dark Time. 472p. 1990. pap. 22.95 (0-87722-686-5) Temple U Pr.

Rosenberg, Alan & Myers, Gerald E., eds. Echoes from the Holocaust: Philosophical Reflections on a Dark Time. LC 87-18109. 453p. (C). 1988. 39.95 (0-87722-539-7) Temple U Pr.

Rosenberg, Alan, jt. ed. see Marcus, Paul.

Rosenberg, Alan, jt. ed. see Milchman, Alan.

Rosenberg, Alex, ed. see Packel, Edward W.

Rosenberg, Alexander. Economics: Mathematical Politics or Science of Diminishing Returns? (Science & Its Conceptual Foundations Ser.). xvii, 266p. 1994. pap. text ed. 13.95 (0-226-72724-6) U Ch Pr.

— Economics - Mathematical Politics or Science of Diminishing Returns? (Science & Its Conceptual Foundations Ser.). (Illus.). 288p. 1992. lib. bdg. 32.50 (0-226-72723-8) U Ch Pr.

— Instrumental Biology, or the Disunity of Science. (Science & Its Conceptual Foundations Ser.). 184p. 1994. pap. text ed. 15.95 (0-226-72726-2) U Ch Pr.

— Instrumental Biology, or the Disunity of Science. (Science & Its Conceptual Foundations Ser.). 184p. 1994. lib. bdg. 38.00 (0-226-72725-4) U Ch Pr.

— Philosophy of Social Science. (Dimensions of Philosophy Ser.). 218p. (C). 1988. pap. text ed. 21.50 (0-8133-0617-5) Westview.

— Sociobiology & the Preemption of Social Science. LC 80-8091. 240p. 1981. text ed. 35.00x (0-8018-2423-0) Johns Hopkins.

— The Structure of Biological Science. (Illus.). 352p. 1985. 69.95 (0-521-25566-X); pap. 21.95 (0-521-27561-X) Cambridge U Pr.

***Rosenberg, Alexander L.** Noncommutative Algebraic Geometry & Representations of Quantized Algebras. (Mathematics & Its Applications Ser.). 328p. (C). 1995. lib. bdg. 155.00 (0-7923-3575-9) Kluwer Ac.

Rosenberg, Alfred. Kampf Um die Macht: Aufsatze Von 1921-1932, Herausgegeben Von Thilo Von Trotha. LC 77-180426. reprint ed. 54.00 (0-404-56160-8) AMS Pr.

— The Myth of the Twentieth Century. Orig. Title: Der Mythos des 20. Jahrhunderts. 1984. lib. bdg. 250.00 (0-87700-605-9) Revisionist Pr.

— Der Mythus des 20 Jahrhunderts. LC 78-63710. (Studies in Fascism: Ideology & Practice). reprint ed. 64.50 (0-404-16983-X) AMS Pr.

— Nietzsche. 1975. lib. bdg. 250.00 (0-8490-0732-1) Gordon Pr.

Rosenberg, Allison A., et al, eds. American Psychologist Special Issue, Vol. 46, No. 11: Homelessness. 156p. 1991. pap. 16.00 (1-55798-161-2) Am Psychol.

Rosenberg, Amy, jt. auth. see Slesin, Louis.

Rosenberg, Amye. Good Job, Jelly Bean! (Sticker Bks.). (Illus.). 24p. (J). (ps-1). 1992. pap. 2.95 (0-671-75512-9, Litl Simon S&S) S&S Childrens.

— Is It Christmas Yet? (J). (ps). 1990. write for info. (0-307-12168-2) Western Pub.

— Jewels for Josephine. (Illus.). 28p. (J). (ps-2). 1993. 12.95 (0-448-40457-5, G&D) Putnam Pub Group.

— A Magic Merry Christmas! (Illus.). 24p. (J). (ps-2). 1994. 12.95 (0-448-40579-2, G&D) Putnam Pub Group.

— Melly's Menorah. (Illus.). 24p. (J). (ps-1). 1991. pap. 2.95 (0-671-74495-X, Litl Simon S&S) S&S Childrens.

— Mitzvot. (Illus.). 30p. (J). (gr. 1-5). pap. text ed. 4.50 (0-87441-387-7) Behrman.

— My Calendar. 66p. (J). (gr. 1-2). 1984. pap. text ed. 4.50 (0-87441-385-0) Behrman.

— Sam the Detective's Reading Readiness Book. (Illus.). 63p. (J). (ps). 1982. pap. text ed. 4.95x (0-87441-361-3) Behrman.

— Ten Treats for Ginger. (Sticker Bks.). (Illus.). 24p. (J). (ps-1). 1992. pap. 2.95 (0-671-75511-0, Litl Simon S&S) S&S Childrens.

— Tzedakah. (Jewish Awareness Ser.). (Illus.). (J). (gr. k-1). 1979. pap. text ed. 4.25 (0-87441-279-X) Behrman.

Rosenberg, Amye, illus. Nursery Rhymes. (Happytime Ser.). 24p. (J). (ps-1). 1987. pap. 1.25 (0-7214-9550-8, S871-6) Ladybird Bks.

— The Pudgy Peek-a-Boo Book. (Pudgy Board Bks.). 16p. (J). (ps). 1983. pap. 2.95 (0-448-10205-6, G&D) Putnam Pub Group.

R

An Asterisk (*) at the beginning of an entry indicates that the title is appearing in BIP for the first time.

Rosenberg, Amye & Mason, Patrice G. Sam the Detective & the Alef Bet Mystery. Rossel, Seymour, ed. (Illus.). 64p. (Orig.). (J). (gr. 1-3). 1980. pap. text ed. 4.95 (*0-87441-328-1*) Behrman.

Rosenberg, Amye & Newman, Shirley. A Child's Introduction to the Early Prophets, No. 1. LC 75-14052. (Illus.). 128p. (J). (gr. 3-4). 1975. student ed, pap. 2.95 (*0-87441-268-4*) Behrman.

Rosenberg, Andrew D., jt. auth. see Bernstein, Ralph L.

***Rosenberg, Andrew E.** Case Records of the Massachusetts General Hospital. 1995. vdisk 700.00 (*1-56815-028-8*) Image Premast.

Rosenberg, Arnold J., jt. ed. see Utterback, Ann S.

Rosenberg, Arthur. Untersuchungen Zur Romischen Zenturienverfassung. LC 75-7337. (Roman History Ser.). (GER.). 1975. reprint ed. 13.95 (*0-405-07058-6*) Ayer.

Rosenberg, Arthur & Hizer, David. Resume Handbook. 2nd ed. 1990. pap. 5.95 (*1-55850-933-X*) Adams Pubng.

***Rosenberg, Arthur D.** Manipulative Memos. 1994. pap. 9.95 (*0-89815-659-9*) Ten Speed Pr.

— Manipulative Memos: The Art of Control Through the Medium of the Memo. 1994. 18.95 (*0-89815-614-9*) Ten Speed Pr.

***Rosenberg, Aura & Tillman, Lynne, photos.** Head Shots. (Illus.). 96p. Date not set. pap. 24.95 (*1-881616-56-8*) Dist Art Pubs.

Rosenberg, Avrohom Y. Mishnah-Kodashim, Vol. 2A: Chullin. Danzigger, H., ed. (ArtScroll Mishnah Ser.). (Illus.). 286p. 1989. 22.95 (*0-89906-305-5*) Mesorah Pubns.

— The Mishnah-Seder Moed, Vol. 4: Tranis-Megillah-Moed Katan-Chaggigah. (ArtScroll Mishnah Ser.). 352p. 1979. 22.95 (*0-89906-258-X*) Mesorah Pubns.

Rosenberg, Barbara S., et al. How to Succeed with Chicken Without Even Frying. LC 84-90615. (Illus.). (Orig.). 1984. pap. 8.95 (*0-9613733-7-7*) Marlance Bks.

Rosenberg, Barry. Kornshell Programming Tutorial. (Illus.). 348p. 1991. pap. text ed. write for info. (*0-318-68379-2*) Addison-Wesley.

— Kornshell Script Programming. 1991. pap. 35.95 (*0-201-56324-X*) Addison-Wesley.

Rosenberg, Barry A. Assembled. 1990. per. 12.00 (*0-932706-17-7*) WSU Art Gallrs.

Rosenberg, Barry A. & Nathanson, Carol. Words & Numbers: An Exhibition Organized by the Museum of Contemporary Art at Wright State University Curated by Barry A. Rosenberg with Assistance by Teresa Schalnat. Wukeson, Ron, ed. 72p. (Orig.). 1991. pap. 15.00 (*0-932706-18-5*) WSU Art Gallrs.

Rosenberg, Barry A., ed. see University Art Galleries, Wright State University.

Rosenberg, Bernard & Fliegel, Norris. The Vanguard Artist. 366p. (C). 1990. reprint ed. pap. 14.95 (*0-941533-97-2*) New Amsterdam Bks.

— The Vanguard Artist: Portrait & Self-Portrait. Coser, Lewis A. & Powell, Walter W., eds. LC 79-7017. (Perennial Works in Sociology Ser.). 1980. reprint ed. lib. bdg. 24.95 (*0-405-12116-4*) Ayer.

Rosenberg, Bernard & Goldstein, Ernest. Creators & Disturbers: Reminiscences by Jewish Intellectuals of New York. LC 82-4281. 432p. 1982. text ed. 37.00 (*0-231-04712-6*) Col U Pr.

Rosenberg, Bernard & Harburg, Ernest. The Broadway Musical: A Collaboration in Hits & Flops. (Illus.). 350p. 1993. 39.95 (*0-8147-7433-4*) NYU Pr.

Rosenberg, Bernard & Rosenberg, Deena. The Music Makers. LC 78-15564. 1979. text ed. 49.50 (*0-231-03953-0*) Col U Pr.

Rosenberg, Bernard, jt. ed. see Coser, Lewis A.

Rosenberg, Bernhard H. & Heuman, Fred S., eds. Theological & Halakhic Reflections on the Holocaust. write for info. (*0-88125-375-8*) Ktav.

***Rosenberg, Beth C.** Virginia Woolf & Samuel Johnson: Common Readers. LC 94-27520. 1995. text ed. 39.95 (*0-312-10741-2*) St Martin.

Rosenberg, Betsy, tr. see Grossman, David.

Rosenberg, Betsy, tr. see Kenaz, Yehoshua.

Rosenberg, Betty & Herald, Diana T. Genreflecting: A Guide to Reading Interests in Genre Fiction. 3rd ed. 300p. 1991. lib. bdg. 40.00 (*0-87287-930-5*) Libs Unl.

Rosenberg, Bianca, jt. intro. see Sterret, Frances.

Rosenberg, Blanca. To Tell at Last: Survival under False Identity, 1941-45. LC 92-32695. (Illus.). 192p. (C). 1993. 22.50 (*0-252-01998-9*) U of Ill Pr.

Rosenberg, Brian. Mary Lee Settle's Beulah Quintet: The Price of Freedom. LC 85-23683. (Southern Literary Studies). 203p. 1991. 27.50 (*0-8071-1674-2*) La State U Pr.

Rosenberg, Bruce. Can These Bones Live? The Art of the American Folk Preacher. rev. ed. LC 87-5895. 328p. 1988. 39.95 (*0-252-01415-4*); pap. 14.95 (*0-252-01416-2*) U of Ill Pr.

— Folklore & Literature: Rival Siblings. LC 90-40630. 296p. 1991. text ed. 34.95 (*0-87049-681-6*) U of Tenn Pr.

Rosenberg, Bruce A. The Code of the West. LC 81-47014. (Illus.). 213p. reprint ed. pap. 60.80 (*0-7837-1760-1*, 2057297) Bks Demand.

— Folksongs of Virginia: A Checklist of the WPA Holdings at Alderman Library, University of Virginia. LC 75-88185. 167p. reprint ed. pap. 47.60 (*0-685-07765-9*, 2017209) Bks Demand.

— The Neutral Ground: The Andre Affair & the Background of Cooper's The Spy. LC 94-16127. (Contributions to the Study of Popular Culture Ser.: No. 42). 168p. 1994. text ed. 45.00 (*0-313-29319-8*, Greenwood Pr) Greenwood.

Rosenberg, Bruce A. & Stewart, Ann H. Ian Fleming. (English Authors Ser.). 168p. 1989. text ed. 21.95 (*0-8057-6977-3*, TEAS 466, Pub. by Royal Botanic Garden UK) Macmillan.

Rosenberg, Bruce A., jt. auth. see Cawelti, John G.

Rosenberg, Carl. As God Is My Witness. Lewis, Sol, ed. LC 90-55237. (Illus.). 146p. 1991. 20.95 (*0-89604-142-5*); pap. 10.95 (*0-89604-143-3*) Holocaust Pubns.

***Rosenberg, Carol F.** Versed Edit: A Potpourri of Poems & Parodies. 264p. 1994. pap. 12.00 (*0-8059-3641-6*) Dorrance.

Rosenberg, Carroll-Smith, jt. auth. see Rosenberg, Charles E.

Rosenberg, Carroll-Smith, jt. ed. see Rosenberg, Charles E.

***Rosenberg, Charles B.** The Trial of O. J. How to Watch the Trial & Understand What's Really Going On. 100p. 1994. pap. text ed. write for info. (*0-9643415-0-6*) Pubng Partners.

***Rosenberg, Charles E.** The Care of Strangers: The Rise of America's Hospital System. LC 94-36036. (Illus.). 448p. 1994. pap. text ed. 16.95x (*0-8018-5082-7*) Johns Hopkins.

— The Cholera Years: The United States in 1832, 1849, & 1866. LC 62-18121. (Illus.). x, 266p. (C). 1987. pap. text ed. 11.95 (*0-226-72677-0*) U Ch Pr.

— Explaining Epidemics: And Other Studies in the History of Medicine. 384p. (C). 1992. 49.95 (*0-521-39340-X*); pap. 16.95 (*0-521-39569-0*) Cambridge U Pr.

— No Other Gods: On Science & American Social Thought. LC 75-36942. 288p. reprint ed. pap. 82.10 (*0-8357-7882-7*, 2036300) Bks Demand.

— Trial of the Assassin Guiteau: Psychiatry & the Law in the Gilded Age. LC 68-16713. 1976. pap. text ed. 10.00x (*0-226-72717-3*, P682) U Ch Pr.

— The Trial of the Assassin Guiteau: Psychiatry & the Law in the Gilded Age. xviii, 290p. 1989. pap. text ed. 17.50 (*0-226-72718-1*, Midway Reprint) U Ch Pr.

Rosenberg, Charles E., ed. Caring for the Working Man: The Rise & Fall of the Dispensary. (Medical Care in the United States Ser.). 304p. 1989. reprint ed. lib. bdg. 20.00 (*0-8240-8341-5*) Garland.

— The Community Hospitals of Kansas City, Missouri, 1870-1915. (Medical Care in the United States Ser.). 232p. 1989. lib. bdg. 15.00 (*0-8240-8337-7*) Garland.

— An Emerging Profession: Philadelphia Doctors, 1860-1900. (Medical Care in the United States Ser.). 270p. 1989. lib. bdg. 25.00 (*0-8240-8339-3*) Garland.

— Healing & History: Essays for George Rosen. 1979. lib. bdg. 27.00 (*0-88202-180-X*) Watson Pub Intl.

— Medical Care in the United States: The Debate before 1940, 14 vol. 433.00 (*0-8153-0321-1*) Garland.

— Medicine & Society in America, 47 bks., Set. 1972. 1,073.00 (*0-405-03930-1*) Ayer.

— On the Administrative Frontier of Medicine: The First Ten Years of the American Hospital Association, 1899-1908. (Medical Care in the United States Ser.). 440p. 1989. lib. bdg. 25.00 (*0-8240-8330-X*) Garland.

— The Origins of Specialization in American Medicine. (Medical Care in the United States Ser.). 200p. 1989. reprint ed. lib. bdg. 15.00 (*0-8240-8342-3*) Garland.

Rosenberg, Charles E. & Golden, Janet, eds. Framing Disease: Studies in Cultural History. LC 91-19164. (Health & Medicine in American Society Ser.). 450p. (C). 1992. text ed. 48.00 (*0-8135-1756-7*); pap. text ed. 16.00 (*0-8135-1757-5*) Rutgers U Pr.

Rosenberg, Charles E. & Rosenberg, Carroll-Smith. Fertility Controlled: The British Argument for Family Limitation. LC 73-20644. (Sex, Marriage & Society Ser.). 137p. 1974. reprint ed. 17.95 (*0-405-05799-7*) Ayer.

— The Male-Midwife & the Female Doctor. LC 73-20642. (Sex, Marriage & Society Ser.). (Illus.). 224p. 1979. reprint ed. 28.95 (*0-405-05810-1*) Ayer.

Rosenberg, Charles E. & Rosenberg, Carroll-Smith, eds. Sexual Indulgence & Denial. LC 73-20650. (Sex, Marriage & Society Ser.). 188p. 1974. reprint ed. 19.95 (*0-405-05818-7*) Ayer.

Rosenberg, Charles E. & Smith-Rosenberg, Carroll, eds. Sex, Marriage & Society, 35 bks. 1974. 832.00 (*0-405-05790-3*) Ayer.

Rosenberg, Charles E., jt. auth. see Golden, Janet.

Rosenberg, Charles M., ed. Art & Politics in Late Medieval & Early Renaissance Italy, 1250-1500. LC 89-40744. (Conferences in Medieval Studies: Vol. 2). (C). 1992. pap. text ed. 22.95 (*0-268-00628-8*) U of Notre Dame Pr.

Rosenberg, Claude. Wealthy and Wise: How you and America can get the most of your giving. 1994. 23.95 (*0-316-75741-1*) Little.

Rosenberg, Claude N., Jr. Investing with the Best: What to Look for, What to Look for in Your Search for a Superior Investment Manager. 2nd ed. 256p. 1993. text ed. 29.95 (*0-471-55827-3*) Wiley.

Rosenberg, Claude N. Stock Market Primer. rev. ed. 1991. pap. 13.99 (*0-446-38718-5*) Warner Bks.

Rosenberg, D. J., jt. auth. see Cushman, W. H.

Rosenberg, D. N. Oaten Reeds & Trumpets: Pastoral & Epic in Virgil, Spenser, & Milton. LC 80-17974. 288p. 1981. 38.50 (*0-8387-5002-8*) Bucknell U Pr.

***Rosenberg, Dale.** Reflections for Living. 1995. pap. text ed. write for info. (*1-56226-223-8*) CT Pub.

— Reflections for Living: A Monograph. 60p. (C). 1990. pap. text ed. 14.99 (*0-929655-88-5*) CT Pub.

Rosenberg, Dan, ed. see Carlock, Marty.

Rosenberg, Dan, ed. see Jamison, Bill & Jamison, Cheryl.

Rosenberg, Dan, ed. see Jamison, Cheryl A. & Jamison, Bill.

Rosenberg, Dan, ed. see Jarratt, Claudia J.

Rosenberg, Dan, ed. see Kelleher, James B.

Rosenberg, Dan, ed. see Lieberman, Adrienne B.

Rosenberg, Dan, ed. see Naylor, Honey.

Rosenberg, Dan, ed. see Sinai, Lee.

Rosenberg, Dan, ed. see Ziedrich, Linda.

Rosenberg, Daniel. New Orleans Dockworkers: Race, Labor, & Unionism 1892-1923. LC 87-10156. (SUNY Series in American Labor History). 233p. 1988. 64.50 (*0-88706-649-6*); pap. 21.95 (*0-88706-650-X*) State U NY Pr.

Rosenberg, Daniel, jt. ed. see Foner, Phillip S.

Rosenberg, David. Blues of the Sky: Interpreted from the Original Hebrew Book of Psalms. LC 76-991. 53p. 1976. 15.00 (*0-89366-241-0*) Ultramarine Pub.

— Congregation: Contemporary Writers Read the Jewish Bible. braille ed. 1178p. 1990. vinyl bd. 94.24 (*1-56956-216-4*, BR8094) W A T Braille.

— The Hidden Holmes: His Theory of Torts in History. 288p. (C). 1995. text ed. 45.00 (*0-674-39002-4*) HUP.

— Job Speaks. 101p. 1980. reprint ed. 9.95 (*0-934450-09-9*) Unmuzzled Ox.

— Lightworks: Interpreted from the Original Hebrew Book of Isaiah. LC 78-3356. 78p. 1978. 15.00 (*0-89366-249-6*) Ultramarine Pub.

— The Lost Book of Paradise: Adam & Eve in the Garden of Eden. 192p. 1995. pap. 12.95 (*0-7868-8073-2*) Hyperion.

Rosenberg, David, ed. Congregation: Contemporary Writers Read the Jewish Bible. 1987. 29.95 (*0-15-146350-6*) HarBrace.

— Testimony: Contemporary Writers Make the Holocaust Personal. LC 89-40185. 1989. 24.95 (*0-8129-1817-7*, Times Bks) Random.

Rosenberg, David, tr. see Bloom, Harold.

Rosenberg, David, et al, eds. Textbook of Pharmacotherapy for Child & Adolescent Psychiatric Disorders. LC 94-6401. 576p. 1994. 65.00 (*0-87630-740-3*) Brunner-Mazel.

Rosenberg, David A. & Rosenberg, Jean G. Landless Peasants & Rural Poverty in Selected Asian Countries. (Special Series on Landlessness & Near-Landlessness: No. 2). 108p. (Orig.). (C). 1978. pap. text ed. 7.95 (*0-86731-069-3*) Cornell CIS RDC.

Rosenberg, David A., jt. auth. see Rosenberg, Jean G.

Rosenberg, David A., jt. ed. see Ross, Steven T.

Rosenberg, David M. & Resh, Vincent H., eds. Freshwater Biomonitoring & Benthic Macroinvertebrates. LC 92-13702. (Illus.). 512p. 1992. 65.00 (*0-412-02251-6*, A3729, Chapman & Hall) Chapman & Hall.

Rosenberg, David M., jt. ed. see Resh, Vincent H.

Rosenberg, Deena, jt. auth. see Rosenberg, Bernard.

Rosenberg, Donna. World Literature. 896p. 1992. pap. 24.95 (*0-8442-5482-7*, Natl Textbk) NTC Pub Grp.

— World Mythology. 552p. pap. 23.95 (*0-8442-5548-3*, Natl Textbk) NTC Pub Grp.

— World Mythology. 2nd ed. 1994. pap. 19.95 (*0-8442-5767-2*, Natl Textbk) NTC Pub Grp.

Rosenberg, Donna & Baker, Sorelle. Mythology & You. 304p. pap. 18.95 (*0-8442-5594-7*, Passport Bks) NTC Pub Grp.

Rosenberg, Dorothy, jt. ed. see Lukens, Nancy.

Rosenberg, Dorothy B., jt. auth. see Camurati, Mireya.

Rosenberg, Duska & Hutchinson, Chris. Design Issues in CSCW. LC 94-13514. (Computer Supported Cooperative Work Ser.). 1994. 59.00 (*0-387-19810-5*) Spr-Verlag.

Rosenberg, E. Meat & Dairy. 1991. 17.95 (*0-89906-898-7*); pap. 14.95 (*0-89906-899-5*) Mesorah Pubns.

Rosenberg, Edgar. From Shylock to Svengali: Jewish Stereotypes in English Fiction. (Illus.). viii, 388p. 1960. 47.50 (*0-8047-0586-0*) Stanford U Pr.

Rosenberg, Eileen P. Principles of Law Office Management: Concepts & Applications. Hannan, ed. LC 93-9794. 510p. (C). 1994. Acid-free paper. text ed. 41.00 (*0-314-01359-8*) West Pub.

Rosenberg, Elinor B. The Adoption Life Cycle: The Children & Their Families Through the Years. LC 92-9031. 250p. 1992. text ed. 24.95 (*0-02-927055-3*) Free Pr.

Rosenberg, Ellen. College Life. 416p. (Orig.). 1992. pap. 12.00 (*0-14-014484-6*, Penguin Bks) Viking Penguin.

— Growing up Feeling Good. LC 95-5617. (J). 1995. pap. 12.99 (*0-14-037718-2*) Puffin Bks.

— Growing up Feeling Good: A Growing up Handbook Especially for Kids. (J). 1989. pap. 11.99 (*0-14-034264-8*, Puffin) Puffin Bks.

Rosenberg, Ellen M. The Southern Baptists: A Subculture in Transition. LC 88-31610. 256p. 1989. 28.00x (*0-87049-598-4*) U of Tenn Pr.

Rosenberg, Emily. Spreading the American Dream: American Economic & Cultural Expansion 1890-1945. (American Century Ser.). 269p. 1982. pap. 9.95 (*0-8090-0146-2*) Hill & Wang.

***Rosenberg, Emily A.** California Biotechnology Corporate Directory: Instant Access to 200 Plus Companies. (Orig.). 1995. spiral bd. 95.00 (*0-9623687-0-9*) Venture Info.

— The Job Hunter's Guide to Biotechnology in California. rev. ed. 1995. spiral bd. 45.00 (*0-9623687-6-8*) Venture Info.

Rosenberg, Emily A., ed. Biotechnology in the Bay Area: The Job Hunters Guide to 100 Plus Leading Companies. rev. ed. 90p. (Orig.). 1990. pap. 65.00 (*0-9624687-4-6*) Venture Info.

Rosenberg, Eugene, ed. Microorganisms to Combat Pollution. LC 93-3223. 288p. (C). 1993. lib. bdg. 151.50 (*0-7923-2226-6*) Kluwer Ac.

— Myxobacteria: Development & Cell Interactions. (Molecular Biology Ser.). (Illus.). 325p. 1984. 108.00 (*0-387-90962-1*) Spr-Verlag.

Rosenberg, Eugene & Cohen, Irun. Microbial Biology. 433p. (C). 1983. text ed. 51.00 (*0-03-085658-2*) SCP.

Rosenberg, Eugene, jt. ed. see Cohen, Yehuda.

Rosenberg, Fred. The Violin - the Technic of Relaxation & Power. 1987. 4.75 (*0-89917-504-X*) Am String Tchrs.

Rosenberg, G. D. & Runcorn, S. K., eds. Growth Rhythms & the History of the Earth's Rotation. LC 74-18096. 575p. reprint ed. pap. 163.90 (*0-317-29706-6*, 2024008) Bks Demand.

Rosenberg, Gail S., jt. auth. see McCarthy, Maureen E.

Rosenberg, Gary & Clarke, Sylvia S., eds. Social Workers in Health Care Management: The Move to Leadership. LC 87-15026. (Social Work in Health Care Ser.: Vol. 12, No. 3). 159p. 1987. 39.95 (*0-86656-672-4*); pap. text ed. 14.95 (*0-86656-815-8*) Haworth Pr.

Rosenberg, Gary & Rehr, Helen, eds. Advancing Social Work Practice in the Health Care Field: Emerging Issues & New Perspectives. LC 82-9249. (Social Work in Health Care Ser.: Vol. 8, No. 3). 162p. 1983. text ed. 39.95 (*0-917724-91-7*); pap. text ed. 19.95 (*0-86656-232-X*, B232) Haworth Pr.

***Rosenberg, Gary & Weissman, Andrew, eds.** Social Work in Ambulatory Care: New Implications for Health & Social Services. (Social Work in Health Care Ser.). (Illus.). 108p. 1994. lib. bdg. 19.95 (*1-56024-697-9*) Haworth Pr.

Rosenberg, Gary, jt. ed. see Lurie, Abraham.

Rosenberg, Gary A. Brain Fluids & Metabolism. (Illus.). 224p. 1990. 39.95 (*0-19-505324-9*) OUP.

Rosenberg, Gary B., jt. auth. see Gardner, Sandra.

Rosenberg, George, jt. auth. see Broadbent, Bill.

Rosenberg, George S. The Worker Grows Old. LC 78-110628. (Jossey-Bass Behavioral Science Ser.). 222p. reprint ed. pap. 63.30 (*0-317-08640-5*, 2013919) Bks Demand.

Rosenberg, Gerald N. The Hollow Hope: Can Courts Bring about Social Change? LC 90-22391. (Illus.). 424p. 1991. 29.95 (*0-226-72702-5*) U Ch Pr.

— The Hollow Hope: Can Courts Bring about Social Change? LC 90-22391. (American Politics & Political Economy Ser.). (Illus.). xii, 425p. (C). 1993. pap. text ed. 16.95 (*0-226-72703-3*) U Ch Pr.

Rosenberg, Graciella, tr. see Dragon, Osvaldo.

Rosenberg, H. M. The Solid State: An Introduction to the Physics of Crystals for Students of Physics, Materials Science, & Engineering. 3rd ed. (Oxford Physics Ser.: No. 9). (Illus.). 326p. (C). 1988. pap. text ed. 19.95 (*0-19-851870-6*) OUP.

Rosenberg, H. S., ed. Transplantation & Developmental Biology of the Liver. (Perspectives in Pediatric Pathology Ser.: Vol. 14). xii, 220p. 1991. 221.00 (*3-8055-5156-8*) S Karger.

Rosenberg, H. S. & Bernstein, J., eds. Cardiovascular Diseases. (Perspectives in Pediatric Pathology Ser.: Vol. 12). (Illus.). x, 162p. 1988. 158.50 (*3-8055-4716-1*) S Karger.

— Central Nervous System Diseases. (Perspectives in Pediatric Pathology Ser.: Vol. 10). viii, 264p. 1987. 211.25 (*3-8055-4403-0*) S Karger.

— Neoplasia in Infancy & Childhood. (Perspectives in Pediatric Pathology Ser.: Vol. 9). viii, 248p. 1986. 176.00 (*3-8055-4373-5*) S Karger.

— Respiratory & Alimentary Tract Disease. (Perspectives in Pediatric Pathology Ser.: Vol. 11). (Illus.). x, 218p. 1987. 176.00 (*3-8055-4435-9*) S Karger.

Rosenberg, H. S., et al, eds. Pediatric Molecular Pathology: Quantitation & Applications. (Perspectives in Pediatric Pathology Ser.: Vol. 16). (Illus.). xii, 170p. 1992. 168.00 (*3-8055-5496-6*) S Karger.

Rosenberg, Harold. Abstract Expressionism - A Tribute to Harold Rosenberg: Paintings & Drawings from Chicago Collections. LC 79-67698. (Illus.). 48p. (Orig.). 1979. pap. 4.00 (*0-935573-06-2*) D & A Smart Museum.

— The Anxious Object. 272p. (C). 1982. pap. 17.95 (*0-226-72682-7*) U Ch Pr.

— Arshile Gorky: The Man, the Times, the Idea. LC 62-11237. (Illus.). 144p. 1981. reprint ed. pap. 7.95 (*0-935296-20-4*) Sheep Meadow.

— Art on the Edge: Creators & Situations. LC 82-24807. (Illus.). xiv, 304p. (C). 1983. pap. 17.95 (*0-226-72674-6*) U Ch Pr.

— Barnett Newman. (Contemporary Artists Ser.). 1994. 75.00 (*0-8109-1360-7*) Abrams.

— The Case of the Baffled Radical. LC 84-27996. viii, 294p. 1985. 25.00 (*0-226-72692-4*) U Ch Pr.

— The De-Definition of Art. LC 83-1101. (Illus.). 256p. (C). 1983. pap. 17.95 (*0-226-72673-8*) U Ch Pr.

— Discovering the Present: Three Decades in Art, Culture & Politics. LC 72-92852. xii, 336p. 1985. pap. 10.95 (*0-226-72681-9*) U Ch Pr.

— Tradition of the New. LC 72-134130. (Essay Index Reprint Ser.). 1977. 21.95 (*0-8369-2127-5*) Ayer.

— The Tradition of the New. 286p. 1994. reprint ed. pap. 14.95 (*0-306-80596-0*) Da Capo.

Rosenberg, Harold S. Nutrition & Stress. Passwater, Richard A. & Mindell, Earl, eds. (Good Health Guide Ser.). 32p. (Orig.). 1983. pap. 2.50 (*0-87983-298-3*) Keats.

Rosenberg, Harriet G. Negotiated World: Three Centuries of Change in a French Alpine Community. (Illus.). 256p. 1988. 35.00 (*0-8020-2640-0*) U of Toronto Pr.

Rosenberg, Harvey. Joey's Cabbage Patch. 32p. (J). (gr. k-3). 1991. write for info. (*0-9629587-0-0*) Go Jolly Pubns.

Rosenberg, Harvey S. & Bolande, Robert P., eds. Perspectives in Pediatric Pathology, Vol. 3. LC 72-88828. 377p. reprint ed. pap. 107.50 (*0-317-10977-4*, 2022730) Bks Demand.

— Perspectives in Pediatric Pathology, Vol. 4. LC 72-88828. 533p. pap. 152.00 (*0-317-58151-1*, 2029740) Bks Demand.

Rosenberg, Helane S. Creative Drama & Imagination: Transforming Ideas into Action. 350p. (C). 1987. text ed. 29.50 (*0-03-064051-2*) HB Coll Pubs.

Rosenberg, Helane S. & Epstein, Yakov M. Getting Pregnant When You Thought You Couldn't. 400p. (Orig.). 1993. pap. 13.99 (*0-446-39388-6*) Warner Bks.

R

Rosenberg, Helane S. & Prendergast, Christine. Theatre for Young People: A Sense of Occasion. 366p. (C). 1983. pap. text ed. 33.25 (*0-03-039911-4*) HB Coll Pubs.

Rosenberg, Helen, ed. see Kalb, Ira S.

Rosenberg, Hilary. The Vulture Investors: The Winners & Losers of the Great American Bankruptcy Feeding Frenzy. LC 91-58511. 416p. 1993. pap. 12.00 (*0-88730-648-9*) Harper Busn.

Rosenberg, Howard G. How to Succeed Without a Career: Jobs for People with No Corporate Ladder. 1994. pap. 13.95 (*1-57023-003-X*) Impact VA.

Rosenberg, Howard R. & Egan, Daniel L. Labor Management Laws in California Agriculture. LC 90-85383. viii, 128p. 1990. reprint ed. pap. 10.00 (*0-931876-75-3*, 21404) ANR Pubns CA.

Rosenberg, I. Protein Analysis & Purification: Benchtop Techniques. 450p. 1993. pap. 45.00 (*0-8176-3665-X*) Birkhauser.

Rosenberg, I. G., jt. ed. see Deza, M. M.

Rosenberg, I. J. Comeback! The Inside Story, in Words & Pictures of the 1991 Atlanta Braves' Race for Baseball Glory. 192p. 1991. 29.95 (*0-9631594-0-2*) AJ & the AC.

— Encore! Inside Story of the Atlanta Braves' Second Consecutive National League Championship. LC 92-84003. (Illus.). 1992. 29.95 (*1-56352-062-1*) Longstreet Pr Inc.

— Miracle Season: The Inside Story, in Words & Pictures, of the 1991 Atlanta Braves' Race for Glory. (Illus.). 192p. 1991. pap. 19.95 (*1-878685-21-X*); write for info. (*1-878685-22-8*) Turner Pub GA.

Rosenberg, Irene, jt. auth. see Wellness International, Ltd Staff.

***Rosenberg, Irwin H., ed.** Nutritional Assessment of Elderly Populations: Measure & Function: Proceedings of the 13th Annual Briston-Myers Squibb/Mead Johnson Symposium on Nutrition Research, Held in boston on Oct. 11-13, 1993. LC 94-26017. (Bristol-Meyers Squibb-Mead Johnson Nutrition Symposia Ser.: Vol. 13). 336p. 1995. 65.00 (*0-7817-0232-1*) Raven.

Rosenberg, Ivo G., ed. Algebras & Orders: Proceedings of the NATO Advanced Study Institute & Seminaire De Mathematiques Superieures, Montreal, Canada, July 29-August 9, 1991. (NATO Advanced Science Institutes Series C: Mathematical & Physical Sciences). 572p. (C). 1993. lib. bdg. 220.00 (*0-7923-2143-X*) Kluwer Ac.

Rosenberg, J. & Schochet, C. The Kunneth Theorem & the Universal Coefficient Theorem for Equivariant K-Theory & KK-Theory. LC 86-10959. (Memoirs of the AMS Ser.: Vol. 62/348). 95p. 1986. pap. text ed. 18.00 (*0-8218-2349-3*, MEMO 62/348) Am Math.

Rosenberg, J., et al. Multi-Media Document Translation: ODA & the EXPRES Project. (Illus.). 824p. 1990. 65.00 (*0-387-97397-4*) Spr-Verlag.

Rosenberg, J., et al, eds. Persistent Object Systems: Third International Workshop, 10-13 January 1989, Newcastle, Australia. (Workshops in Computing Ser.). xvii, 408p. 1990. pap. 59.00 (*0-387-19626-9*) Spr-Verlag.

Rosenberg, J. F. Linguistic Representation. LC 74-26886. (Philosophical Studies: No. 1). 166p. 1974. lib. bdg. 56.50 (*90-277-0533-X*) Kluwer Ac.

— Linguistic Representation. LC 74-26886. (Philosophical Studies: No. 1). 166p. 1978. pap. text ed. 26.50 (*90-277-0946-7*) Kluwer Ac.

Rosenberg, Jack, et al. Body Self & Soul: Sustaining Integration. LC 85-2293. (Illus.). 352p. 1985. lib. bdg. 28.95 (*0-89334-196-7*, 196-7) Humanics Ltd.

Rosenberg, Jack L., et al. Body, Self & Soul: Sustaining Integration. 2nd ed. LC 85-2293. 352p. (Orig.). 1985. pap. 18.95 (*0-89334-082-0*) Humanics Ltd.

Rosenberg, Jack M. & Rosenberg, Marilyn S. Prescriber's Guide to Drug Interactions. 2nd ed. 424p. 1984. 33.95 (*0-87489-340-2*) Med Economics.

Rosenberg, Jakob. Great Draughtsmen from Pisanello to Picasso. LC 59-7661. 296p. reprint ed. pap. 124.30 (*0-7837-2323-7*, 2057411) Bks Demand.

— Rembrandt: Life & Work. rev. ed. (Landmarks in Art History Ser.). (Illus.). 398p. 1980. pap. 19.95 (*0-8014-9198-3*) Cornell U Pr.

***Rosenberg, Jakob & Slive, Seymour.** Dutch Painting 1600-1800. rev. ed. LC 95-14215. (Pelican History of Art Ser.). (Illus.). 1995. write for info. (*0-300-06418-7*) Yale U Pr.

Rosenberg, Jakob, et al. Dutch Art & Architecture: 1600-1800. 3rd ed. (Pelican History of Art Ser.). (Illus.). 502p. (C). 1987. reprint ed. pap. text ed. 26.50 (*0-300-05312-6*) Yale U Pr.

Rosenberg, James L. The Death & Life of Sneaky Fitch: A Farcical Tragedy in Three Acts. 47p. 1987. reprint ed. pap. 4.75 (*0-8222-0289-1*) Dramatists Play.

— Mel Says to Give You His Best. 1975. pap. 2.75 (*0-8222-0746-X*) Dramatists Play.

Rosenberg, Jan. Women's Reflections: The Feminist Film Movement. Kirkpatrick, Diane, ed. LC 83-1271. (Studies in Cinema: No. 22). 154p. reprint ed. 43.70 (*0-8357-1400-4*, 2070759) Bks Demand.

Rosenberg, Jane. Dance Me a Story. LC 84-51701. (Illus.). 128p. 1993. pap. 15.95 (*0-500-27739-7*) Thames Hudson.

— Play Me a Story. LC 93-33490. (J). (gr. 3 up). 1994. 25.00 (*0-679-84391-4*) Knopf Bks Yng Read.

— Play Me a Story. Date not set. write for info. (*0-679-86214-5*) Random.

— Sing Me a Story: The Metropolitan Opera's Book of Opera Stories for Children. LC 88-51929. (Illus.). 160p. 1989. 24.95 (*0-500-01467-1*) Thames Hudson.

Rosenberg, Jane A. Nation's Great Library: Herbert Putnam & the Library of Congress. LC 92-37287. 248p. (C). 1993. 39.95 (*0-252-02001-4*) U of Ill Pr.

Rosenberg, Janet, ed. see Anderson, Roy N.

Rosenberg, Janet, ed. see Axford, Wendy A. & McMurtrie, Douglas C.

Rosenberg, Janet, ed. see Barton, George E.

Rosenberg, Janet, ed. see Berkowitz, Edward D.

Rosenberg, Janet, ed. see Carling, Finn & Haecker, Theodor.

Rosenberg, Janet, ed. see Charity Organisation Society Staff.

Rosenberg, Janet, ed. see Giralestone, Gathrone R.

Rosenberg, Janet, ed. see Graham, Earl C. & Mullen, Marjorie.

Rosenberg, Janet, ed. see Hathaway, Katharine B.

Rosenberg, Janet, ed. see Hinshaw, David.

Rosenberg, Janet, ed. see Hoyer, Louis & Hay, Charles K.

Rosenberg, Janet, ed. see Hunt, Agnes.

Rosenberg, Janet, ed. see Kenny, Elizabeth.

Rosenberg, Janet, ed. see Kessler, Henry H.

Rosenberg, Janet, ed. see Leavitt, Moses A.

Rosenberg, Janet, ed. see Macdonald, Mary E.

Rosenberg, Janet, ed. see Mallinson, Vernon.

Rosenberg, Janet, ed. see Mawson, Thomas.

Rosenberg, Janet, ed. see McMurtrie, Douglas C.

Rosenberg, Janet, ed. see Obermann, C. Esco.

Rosenberg, Janet, ed. see Orr, H. Winnett.

Rosenberg, Janet, jt. ed. see Phillips, William R.

Rosenberg, Janet, ed. see Pitner, Rudolf, et al.

Rosenberg, Janet, ed. see Sullivan, Oscar M. & Snortum, Kenneth O.

Rosenberg, Janet, ed. see Tracy, Susan R.

Rosenberg, Janet, ed. see Watson, Frederick.

Rosenberg, Janet, ed. see Wright, Beatrice A.

Rosenberg, Janet, ed. see Wright, Henry C.

Rosenberg, Janet, ed. see Wurtz, Hans.

Rosenberg, Janet, ed. see Ziegler, Carlos R.

Rosenberg, Jay F. Beyond Formalism: Naming & Necessity for Human Beings. LC 93-12691. 256p. 1994. 44.95 (*1-56639-118-0*) Temple U Pr.

— The Practice of Philosophy: A Handbook for Beginners. 2nd ed. 128p. (C). 1983. pap. text ed. write for info. (*0-13-687467-3*) P-H.

Rosenberg, Jean G. & Rosenberg, David A. Landless Peasants & Rural Poverty in Indonesia & the Philippines. (Special Series on Landlessness & Near-Landlessness: No. 3). 133p. (Orig.). (C). 1980. pap. text ed. 8.65 (*0-86731-070-7*) Cornell CIS RDC.

Rosenberg, Jean G., jt. auth. see Rosenberg, David A.

Rosenberg, Jeanette L. Secrets to Running a Successful Business: How to Have Fun Getting More Business. 120p. 1993. student ed 19.95 (*0-9639304-0-0*) JLR Pub.

Rosenberg, Jerome H. Margaret Atwood. (World Authors Ser.: No. 740). 220p. 1984. lib. bdg. 22.95 (*0-8057-6586-7*, Twayne) Macmillan.

Rosenberg, Jerome L. & Epstein, L. Schaum's Outline of College Chemistry. 7th ed. (Schaum's Outline Ser.). 1990. pap. text ed. 12.95 (*0-07-053707-0*) McGraw.

Rosenberg, Jerry M. Business Dictionary of Computers. 3rd ed. (Business Dictionaries Ser.). 416p. 1993. text ed. 45.00 (*0-471-58575-0*); pap. text ed. 14.95 (*0-471-58574-2*) Wiley.

— Diccionario de Administracio y Finanzas - Dictionary of Administration & Finance. 2nd ed. 652p. 1991. 195.00 (*0-7859-5222-5*) Fr & Eur.

— The Dictionary of Banking. (Business Dictionaries Ser.). 384p. 1992. text ed. 49.95 (*0-471-57435-X*); pap. text ed. 14.95 (*0-471-57436-8*) Wiley.

— Dictionary of Business & Management. 2nd ed. 684p. 1985. 49.95 (*0-8288-4408-9*, M7802) Fr & Eur.

— Dictionary of Business & Management. 3rd ed. (Business Dictionaries Ser.). 384p. 1992. text ed. 45.00 (*0-471-57812-6*); pap. text ed. 14.95 (*0-471-54536-8*) Wiley.

— Dictionary of International Trade. (Business Dictionaries Ser.). 336p. 1993. text ed. 45.00 (*0-471-59732-5*); pap. text ed. 14.95 (*0-471-59731-7*) Wiley.

— Dictionary of Investing. (Business Dictionaries Ser.). 384p. 1992. text ed. 49.95 (*0-471-57433-3*); pap. text ed. 14.95 (*0-471-57434-1*) Wiley.

— Dictionary of Marketing & Advertising. LC 94-25576. 1995. text ed. 39.95 (*0-471-02503-8*); pap. text ed. 17.95 (*0-471-02502-X*) Wiley.

— Dictionary of Retailing & Merchandising. (Wiley Small Business Editions). Date not set. text ed. 27.95 (*0-471-11023-X*) Wiley.

— Encyclopedia of the North American Free Trade Agreement, the New American Community, & Latin-American Trade. LC 94-16984. 576p. 1994. text ed. 79.50 (*0-313-29069-5*, Greenwood Pr) Greenwood.

— The Investor's Dictionary. 508p. 1986. pap. text ed. 16.95 (*0-471-84567-1*) Wiley.

— McGraw-Hill Dictionary of Information Technology & Computer Acronyms, Initials & Abbreviations. 240p. 1992. text ed. 24.95 (*0-07-053936-7*); pap. text ed. 12.95 (*0-07-053735-6*) McGraw.

— McGraw-Hill Dictionary of Wall Street Acronyms, Initials, & Abbreviations. 240p. 1992. text ed. 24.95 (*0-07-053934-0*); pap. text ed. 12.95 (*0-07-053736-4*) McGraw.

— The New American Community: A Response to the European & Asian Economic Challenge. LC 91-35038. 200p. 1992. text ed. 42.95 (*0-275-94206-6*, C4206, Praeger Pubs) Greenwood.

Rosenberg, Jerry M., ed. McGraw-Hill Dictionary of Business Acronyms, Initials & Abbreviations. 336p. 1992. text ed. 29.95 (*0-07-053734-8*); pap. text ed. 14.95 (*0-07-053935-9*) McGraw.

***Rosenberg, Joe, ed.** Aplauso! Hispanic Childrens Theatre. (J). 1995. 12.95 (*1-55885-136-4*, Pinata Bks) Arte Publico.

— Aplauso! Hispanic Children's Theater. LC 94-36005. 120p. (YA). (gr. 7 up). 1995. 12.95 (*1-55885-127-5*) Arte Publico.

— Aplauso! Hispanic Children's Theater. 120p. (YA). 1995. pap. 7.95 (*0-614-03967-3*) Arte Publico.

Rosenberg, Joe, tr. see Dragon, Osvaldo.

Rosenberg, Joe, jt. auth. see Vallejo, Teresita G.

Rosenberg, Joel. D'shai. 1991. pap. 4.95 (*0-441-15751-3*) Ace Bks.

— The Fire Duke. LC 94-42586. (Keepers of the Hidden Ways Ser.). 1995. write for info. (*0-688-14153-6*) Morrow.

— Guardians of the Flame: The Heroes, 2 vols. in 1. (Illus.). 448p. 1989. 10.98 (*1-56865-050-7*, GuildAmerica) Dblday Bk Music.

— Guardians of the Flame: The Warriors, 3 vols. in 1. 736p. 1985. 12.98 (*1-56865-061-2*, GuildAmerica) Dblday Bk Music.

— Heir Apparent. (Guardians of the Flame Ser.: No. 4). 256p. 1987. pap. 3.50 (*0-451-14820-7*, Sig) NAL-Dutton.

— The Heir Apparent. (Guardians of the Flame Ser.: No. 4). 320p. 1987. pap. 3.95 (*0-451-16212-9*, ROC) NAL-Dutton.

— Hour of the Octopus. 272p. (Orig.). 1994. pap. text ed. 4.99 (*0-441-16975-9*) Ace Bks.

— King & Kin: Political Allegory in the Hebrew Bible. LC 85-45160. (Indiana Studies in Biblical Literature). (Illus.). 270p. 1986. 29.95 (*0-253-14624-0*); pap. 10.95 (*0-253-20396-1*, MB-396) Ind U Pr.

— The Road Home. LC 94-27301. 272p. 1995. 21.95 (*0-451-45433-2*, ROC) NAL-Dutton.

— The Road Home. 320p. 1995. mass mkt. 5.99 (*0-451-45450-2*, ROC) NAL-Dutton.

— The Road to Ehvenor. (Guardians of the Flame Ser.). 320p. (Orig.). 1992. pap. 5.50 (*0-451-45191-0*, ROC) NAL-Dutton.

— Road to Ehvenor: Guardians of the Flame Novel. 384p. 1991. 19.95 (*0-451-45140-6*, ROC) NAL-Dutton.

— The Sleeping Dragon. (Guardians of the Flame Ser.: Bk. 1). 256p. 1986. pap. 3.50 (*0-451-14833-9*, Sig) NAL-Dutton.

— The Sleeping Dragon. (Guardians of the Flame Ser.: No. 1). 256p. 1986. pap. 3.95 (*0-451-16213-7*, ROC) NAL-Dutton.

— Sleeping Dragon. (Guardians of the Flame Ser.). 256p. 1993. pap. 4.99 (*0-451-45350-6*, ROC) NAL-Dutton.

— The Sword & the Chain. (Guardians of the Flame Ser.: Bk. 2). 256p. 1987. pap. 3.95 (*0-451-15982-9*, ROC) NAL-Dutton.

— The Sword & The Chain. (Guardians of the Flame Ser.). 256p. 1993. pap. 4.99 (*0-451-45351-4*, ROC) NAL-Dutton.

— The Warrior Lives. (Guardians of the Flame Ser.: No. 5). 272p. 1990. pap. 4.99 (*0-451-45001-9*, ROC) NAL-Dutton.

Rosenberg, Joel, tr. see Green, Arthur, ed.

Rosenberg, John, jt. auth. see Glossbrenner, Alfred.

Rosenberg, John D. Carlyle & the Burden of History. LC 85-8407. (Illus.). 1986. 32.00 (*0-674-09754-8*) HUP.

— The Darkening Glass. LC 86-17148. 274p. 1986. pap. text ed. 18.00 (*0-231-06387-3*) Col U Pr.

— The Fall of Camelot: A Study of Tennyson's Idylls of the King. LC 73-77992. 144p. (C). 1973. 16.95 (*0-674-29175-1*) HUP.

Rosenberg, John R. The Circular Pilgrimage: An Anatomy of Confessional Autobiography in Spain. LC 92-17656. (University of Kansas Humanistic Studies: Vol. 59). 204p. (C). 1994. text ed. 41.95 (*0-8204-1952-4*) P Lang Pubs.

Rosenberg, John S., jt. auth. see Healy, Robert G.

Rosenberg, Jonathan. Algebraic K-Theory & Its Applications. LC 94-8077. (Graduate Texts in Mathematics Ser.: Vol. 147). (Illus.). 408p. 1994. 49.95 (*0-387-94248-3*) Spr-Verlag.

Rosenberg, Joseph. German: How to Speak & Write It. (Illus.). 1962. pap. 5.95 (*0-486-20271-2*) Dover.

Rosenberg, Joshua D., ed. see Lind, Stephen A. & Schwarz, Stephen.

***Rosenberg, Judith P.** A Question of Balance: Artists & Writers on Motherhood. (Illus.). 288p. 1995. 25.00 (*0-918949-54-8*); pap. 14.00 (*0-918949-53-X*) Papier-Mache Press.

Rosenberg, Judy. Rosie's Bakery All Butter, Fresh Cream, Sugar- Packed, No-Holds-Barred Baking Book. LC 91-50380. (Illus.). 256p. (Orig.). 1991. 22.95 (*1-56305-126-5*, 3126); pap. 12.95 (*0-89480-723-4*, 1723) Workman Pub.

Rosenberg, Justin. The Empire of Civil Society: The Critique of the Realist Theory of International Relations. LC 93-47997. 1994. 64.95 (*0-86091-442-9*, Pub. by Verso UK); pap. 18.95 (*0-86091-607-3*, Pub. by Verso UK) Routledge Chapman & Hall.

Rosenberg, Ken & Daly, Helen. Foundations of Psychological Research: A Basic Question. LC 92-70921. (Illus.). 420p. (C). 1993. text ed. 22.00 (*0-03-055558-2*) HB Coll Pubs.

Rosenberg, Kenneth A. Wilderness Preservation: A Reference Handbook. (Contemporary World Issues Ser.). 250p. 1994. lib. bdg. 39.50 (*0-87436-731-X*) ABC-CLIO.

Rosenberg, Kenneth M. Statistics for the Behavioral Sciences. 496p. (C). 1990. student ed write for info. (*0-697-11257-8*); boxed write for info. (*0-697-09740-4*); write for info. (*0-318-66913-7*) Brown & Benchmark.

Rosenberg, Kenneth V., et al. Birds of the Lower Colorado River Valley. LC 90-11120. (Illus.). 416p. 1990. 45.00 (*0-8165-1174-8*) U of Ariz Pr.

Rosenberg, Kenyon C. A Basic Classical & Operatic Recordings Collection for Libraries. LC 87-12747. 269p. 1987. 29.50 (*0-8108-2041-2*) Scarecrow.

— A Basic Classical & Operatic Recordings Collection on Compact Discs for Libraries: A Buying Guide. LC 90-8317. 395p. 1990. 39.50 (*0-8108-2322-5*) Scarecrow.

— Dictionary of Library & Educational Technology. 3rd enl. ed. 196p. 1989. lib. bdg. 32.50 (*0-87287-623-3*) Libs Unl.

Rosenberg, Kris. Talk to Me: A Therapist's Guide to Breaking Through Male Silence. LC 93-10362. 240p. 1994. 19.95 (*0-87477-749-6*, J P T-Putnam) Putnam Pub Group.

Rosenberg, L. M., ed. see Kessler, Milton.

Rosenberg, Larry J. & Assael, Henry, eds. The Roots of Marketing Strategy: An Original Anthology. LC 78-289. (Century of Marketing Ser.). 1979. lib. bdg. 47.95 (*0-405-11189-4*) Ayer.

Rosenberg, Lawrence. Muffins & Cupcakes. Levine, Marian, ed. (Collector's Ser.: Vol. 18). 64p. (Orig.). 1986. pap. 3.49 (*0-942320-13-1*) Am Cooking.

***Rosenberg, Lawrence M. & Gamon, David.** Cake Decorating Simplified. (Illus.). 168p. 1995. 24.95 (*0-8317-1187-6*) A D Bragdon.

Rosenberg, Lee. Retirement Ready or Not. 250p. (Orig.). 1993. pap. 14.95 (*1-56414-052-0*) Career Pr Inc.

Rosenberg, Lee & Rosenberg, Saralee. Fifty Fabulous Places to Raise Your Family. 320p. (Orig.). 1992. pap. 17.95 (*1-56414-034-2*) Career Pr Inc.

— Fifty Fabulous Places to Retire in America. 256p. 1991. pap. 14.95 (*0-934829-29-2*) Career Pr Inc.

Rosenberg, Leon E., jt. auth. see Bondy, Philip K.

Rosenberg, Leon J. Dillard's, the First Fifty Years. LC 87-25499. 162p. (Orig.). 1988. 15.95 (*1-55728-021-5*) U of Ark Pr.

Rosenberg, Liz. The Carousel. LC 94-7332. (J). 1995. 15.95 (*0-399-22704-0*, Philomel Bks) Putnam Pub Group.

— The Carousel. LC 94-47323. (Illus.). (J). 1995. 14.00 (*0-15-200853-5*) HarBrace.

— Children of Paradise. LC 92-62426. (Poetry Ser.). 80p. (C). 1993. text ed. 19.95 (*0-8229-3750-6*); pap. text ed. 10.95 (*0-8229-5502-4*) U of Pittsburgh Pr.

— The Fire Music. LC 85-40856. (Poetry Ser.). 58p. 1986. pap. 10.95 (*0-8229-5381-1*) U of Pittsburgh Pr.

— Grandmother & the Runaway Shadow. LC 92-42349. (Illus.). (J). 1994. write for info. (*0-399-22545-5*, Philomel Bks) Putnam Pub Group.

— Monster Mama. (Illus.). 32p. (J). (ps-3). 1993. lib. bdg. 14.95 (*0-399-21989-7*, Philomel Bks) Putnam Pub Group.

— My Grandmother & Her Runaway Shadow. LC 95-7603. (Illus.). (J). 1996. write for info. (*0-15-200948-5*) HarBrace.

Rosenberg, Lory D. The Fair Hearings Pleadings Manual: Administrative & Federal Actions at Your Fingertips. 396p. 1992. pap. text ed. 45.00 (*1-878677-39-X*) Amer Immi Law Assn.

Rosenberg, Louis. Canada's Jews: A Social & Economic Study of Jews in Canada in the 1930s. (McGill-Queen's Studies in Ethnic History). (Illus.). 464p. 1993. 49.95 (*0-7735-0997-6*, Pub. by McGill CN); pap. 24.95 (*0-7735-1109-1*, Pub. by McGill CN) U of Toronto Pr.

Rosenberg, M. B. English-Russian Dictionary of Refrigerating & Cryogenic Engineering. 467p. (ENG & RUS.). 1978. 75.00 (*0-8288-5237-5*, M9063) Fr & Eur.

Rosenberg, M. E., tr. see Kovalevsky, A. L.

Rosenberg, M. J. The Cybernetics of Art: Reason & the Rainbow. (Studies in Cybernetics: Vol. 4). (Illus.). 236p. 1983. text ed. 76.00 (*0-677-05970-1*) Gordon & Breach.

Rosenberg, Madge. The Best Bread Machine Cookbook Ever. LC 92-52548. 224p. 1992. spiral bd. 16.95 (*0-06-016927-3*, HarpT) HarpC.

— The Best Bread Machine Cookbook Ever: International Breads. 224p. 1994. 16.95 (*0-06-017093-X*, HarpT) HarpC.

— The Best Low-Fat, No-Sugar Bread Machine Cookbook Ever. 1995. 16.95 (*0-06-017174-X*) HarpC.

Rosenberg, Magda & Rossman, Isadore. Sixty-Plus & Fit Again: Exercises for Older Men & Women. LC 76-49130. (Illus.). 156p. 1977. 12.95 (*0-87131-224-7*) M Evans.

Rosenberg, Marc. Dingo. 1993. pap. 12.95 (*0-86819-317-8*, Pub. by Currency Pr AT) St Mut.

Rosenberg, Marc L., ed. Violence in America: A Public Health Approach. (Illus.). 216p. 1991. 35.00 (*0-19-506437-2*) OUP.

***Rosenberg, Marc L. & Nadolny, Paul R.** CPA Firm Administration Handbook. 1995. text ed. 95.00 (*0-471-58548-3*) Wiley.

Rosenberg, Marie B. & Bergstrom, Len V., eds. Women & Society: A Critical Review of the Literature with a Selected Annotated Bibliography. LC 73-77874. 360p. reprint ed. pap. 102.60 (*0-317-10619-8*, 2021948) Bks Demand.

Rosenberg, Marilyn R. Circumambience Can Be. 18p. 1985. pap. 100.00 (*0-913615-09-9*) M Rosenberg.

— Coming Around. 14p. 1985. pap. 100.00 (*0-913615-10-2*) M Rosenberg.

— One Way. 4p. 1977. pap. 8.00 (*0-317-14975-X*) M Rosenberg.

— Philip One. 55p. 1980. pap. 8.00 (*0-913615-01-3*) M Rosenberg.

— Philip Two. 70p. 1980. pap. 8.00 (*0-913615-02-1*) M Rosenberg.

— Unit of Measure. 18p. 1977. pap. 8.00 (*0-913615-04-8*) M Rosenberg.

— Wheelwork. 14p. 1986. pap. 100.00 (*0-913615-11-0*) M Rosenberg.

Rosenberg, Marilyn S., jt. auth. see Rosenberg, Jack M.

Rosenberg, Mark B., ed. The Changing Hemispheric Trade Environment: Opportunities & Obstacles. LC 91-32431. (Orig.). (C). 1991. pap. text ed. 11.95 (*1-879862-01-8*) FL Intl U Latin.

Rosenberg, Mark B. & Hiskey, Jonathan. Florida-Mexico: Strategies & Recommendations for an Expanding Market. 91p. 1992. 35.00 (*1-879862-02-6*) FL Intl U Latin.

Rosenberg, Mark B., et al, eds. Americas: An Anthology. (Illus.). 416p. (C). 1992. pap. 17.95 (*0-19-507792-X*) OUP.

An Asterisk (*) at the beginning of an entry indicates that the title is appearing in BIP for the first time.

Rosenberg, Mark L. & Baer, Katie, eds. Report of the Secretary's Task Force on Youth Suicide, Vol. 4: Strategies for the Prevention of Youth Suicide. 207p. 1989. per. 11.00 (*0-16-002509-5*, S/N 017-024-01375-7) USGPO.

Rosenberg, Marshall. A Model for Nonviolent Communication. 36p. 1983. pap. 3.95 (*0-86571-029-5*) New Soc Pubs.

Rosenberg, Martin. Opportunities in Accounting Careers. (Illus.). 160p. 1991. 13.95 (*0-8442-8577-3*, VGM Career Bks); pap. 10.95 (*0-8442-8578-1*, VGM Career Bks) NTC Pub Grp.

— Raphael & France: The Artist As Paradigm & Symbol. (Illus.). 265p. (C). 1995. 49.50 (*0-271-01300-1*) Pa St U Pr.

Rosenberg, Martin & Moore, Gordon P., eds. The Pharmacology of Monoclonal Antibodies. LC 93-44948. (Handbook of Experimental Pharmacology Ser.: Vol. 113). (Illus.). 460p. 1994. 291.00 (*0-387-57123-X*) Spr-Verlag.

Rosenberg, Marvin. The Masks of Hamlet. LC 92-22566. 992p. (C). 1993. 69.50 (*0-87413-480-3*) U Delaware Pr.

— The Masks of King Lear. LC 74-115492. 440p. 1993. reprint ed. 30.00 (*0-87413-482-X*); reprint ed. pap. 15.00 (*0-87413-485-4*) U Delaware Pr.

— The Masks of Macbeth. LC 76-14295. 816p. 1993. reprint ed. 30.00 (*0-87413-483-8*); reprint ed. pap. 15.00 (*0-87413-486-2*) U Delaware Pr.

— The Masks of Othello: The Search for the Identity of Othello, Iago, & Desdemona by Three Centuries of Actors & Critics. LC 61-7521. 328p. 1993. reprint ed. 30.00 (*0-87413-481-1*); reprint ed. pap. 15.00 (*0-87413-484-6*) U Delaware Pr.

Rosenberg, Marvin M., et al. Periodontal & Prosthetic Management for Advanced Cases. (Illus.). 415p. 1988. text ed. 178.00 (*0-86715-162-5*, 1625) Quint Pub Co.

Rosenberg, Maurice & Hay, Peter. Conflict of Laws, 1994: Cases & Materials. 9th ed. (University Casebook Ser.). 47p. 1994. pap. text ed. 4.95 (*1-56662-171-2*) Foundation Pr.

Rosenberg, Maurice, et al. Elements of Civil Procedure: Cases & Materials On. 5th ed. (University Casebook Ser.). 1155p. 1990. text ed. 43.75 (*0-88277-797-1*) Foundation Pr.

— Elements of Civil Procedure: Cases & Materials, 1994 Supplement. 5th ed. (University Casebook Ser.). 110p. 1994. pap. text ed. 6.95 (*1-56662-186-0*) Foundation Pr.

— Elements of Civil Procedure, Cases & Materials, Teachers Manual For. 5th ed. (University Casebook Ser.). 137p. 1990. pap. text ed. write for info. (*0-88277-842-0*) Foundation Pr.

Rosenberg, Max. The Building of Perry's Fleet on Lake Erie: 1812-1813. LC 50-9593. 72p. (Orig.). 1988. pap. 7.95 (*0-911124-49-7*) Pa Hist & Mus.

Rosenberg, Maxine B. Being a Twin, Having a Twin. LC 84-17159. (Illus.). 48p. (J). (gr. 1-4). 1985. lib. bdg. 11.88 (*0-688-04329-1*) Lothrop.

— Being Adopted. LC 83-17522. (Illus.). 48p. (J). (gr. 1-4). 1984. 16.00 (*0-688-02672-9*); lib. bdg. 15.93 (*0-688-02673-7*) Lothrop.

— Brothers & Sisters. (Illus.). 32p. (J). (gr. k-3). 1991. 14.95 (*0-395-51121-6*, Clarion Bks) HM.

— Finding a Way: Living with Exceptional Brothers & Sisters. LC 88-6776. 48p. (J). (gr. 1-4). 1988. 12.95 (*0-688-06873-1*); lib. bdg. 12.88 (*0-688-06874-X*) Lothrop.

— Growing up Adopted. LC 89-9899. 128p. (J). (gr. 4 up). 1989. text ed. 14.95 (*0-02-777912-2*, Bradbury S&S) S&S Childrens.

— Hiding to Survive: Fourteen Jewish Children & the Gentiles Who Rescued Them from the Holocaust. LC 93-28328. (J). (gr. 4 up). 1994. 15.95 (*0-395-65014-3*, Clarion Bks) HM.

— Living in Two Worlds. LC 85-23990. 48p. (J). (ps-3). 1986. lib. bdg. 11.88 (*0-688-06279-2*) Lothrop.

— Living with a Single Parent. LC 92-3883. (Illus.). 128p. (J). (gr. 4 up). 1992. text ed. 14.95 (*0-02-777915-7*, Bradbury S&S) S&S Childrens.

— Making a New Home in America. LC 85-11642. (Illus.). 48p. (J). (gr. 1-4). 1986. 11.95 (*0-688-05824-8*); lib. bdg. 11.88 (*0-688-05825-6*) Lothrop.

— My Friend Leslie: The Story of a Handicapped Child. LC 82-12734. (Illus.). (J). (gr. 1-3). 1983. 13.95 (*0-688-01690-1*); lib. bdg. 13.88 (*0-688-01691-X*) Lothrop.

— Not My Family: Sharing the Truth about Alcoholism. LC 88-10468. 112p. (J). (gr. 4-7). 1988. text ed. 14.95 (*0-02-777911-4*, Bradbury S&S) S&S Childrens.

— On the Mend: Getting Away from Drugs. LC 91-11202. (Illus.). 128p. (J). (gr. 4 up). 1991. text ed. 14.95 (*0-02-777914-9*, Bradbury S&S) S&S Childrens.

— Talking about Stepfamilies. LC 90-33540. (Illus.). 160p. (J). (gr. 4-7). 1990. lib. bdg. 14.95 (*0-02-777913-0*, Bradbury S&S) S&S Childrens.

Rosenberg, Mel, jt. ed. see Doyle, Ronald J.

Rosenberg, Michael & Edmond-Rosenberg, Irene. The Special Education Sourcebook. LC 94-21554. 325p. (Orig.). 1994. pap. 21.95 (*0-933149-52-2*) Woodbine House.

Rosenberg, Michael J. Smoking & Reproductive Health. 352p. 1987. 49.00 (*0-88416-549-3*, Yr Bk Med Pubs) Mosby Yr Bk.

Rosenberg, Michael S., et al. Educating Students with Behavior Disorders. 352p. (C). 1991. text ed. 47.00 (*0-205-13136-0*) Allyn.

— Student Teacher to Master Teacher: A Handbook for Preservice & Beginning Teachers of Students with Mild & Moderate Handicaps. 352p. (C). 1991. pap. write for info. (*0-02-403650-1*) Macmillan.

Rosenberg, Milton J., ed. Beyond Conflict & Containment: Critical Studies of Military & Foreign Policy. LC 79-189565. 250p. 1972. 32.95 (*0-87855-038-0*); pap. text ed. 17.95x (*0-87855-534-X*) Transaction Pubs.

Rosenberg, Milton J., et al. Attitude Organization & Change: An Analysis of Consistency among Attitude Components. LC 80-14704. (Yale Studies in Attitude & Communication: Vol. 3). (Illus.). x, 239p. 1980. reprint ed. text ed. 59.75 (*0-313-22435-8*, ROAT) Greenwood.

Rosenberg, Mona. Stick-tivity. (J). (gr. k-1). 1991. write for info. (*1-880056-07-0*) Play-Media.

— Stick-tivity, Bk. 1: The Talking Drum & Trumpet. 16p. (J). (gr. k-1). 1991. write for info. (*1-880056-08-9*) Play-Media.

— Stick-tivity, Bk. 2: Bob's Zoo. 16p. (J). (gr. k-1). 1991. write for info. (*1-880056-09-7*) Play-Media.

— Stick-tivity, Bk. 3: On a Wet Day in Botswana. 16p. (J). (gr. k-1). 1991. write for info. (*1-880056-10-0*) Play-Media.

— Stick-tivity, Bk. 4: Magical Thoughts on a Hot Day. 16p. (J). (gr. k-1). 1991. write for info. (*1-880056-11-9*) Play-Media.

— Stick-tivity, Bk. 5: Planning to See the Whole World. 16p. (J). (gr. k-1). 1991. write for info. (*1-880056-12-7*) Play-Media.

— Stick-tivity, Bk. 6: Mainly Math. 16p. (J). (gr. k-1). 1991. write for info. (*1-880056-13-5*) Play-Media.

Rosenberg, Morris. Conceiving the Self. LC 86-7431. 336p. 1986. reprint ed. text ed. 36.50 (*0-89874-961-1*) Krieger.

— Occupations & Values. Zuckerman, Harriet & Merton, Robert K., eds. LC 79-9020. (Dissertations on Sociology Ser.). 1980. reprint ed. lib. bdg. 18.95 (*0-405-12989-0*) Ayer.

— Society & the Adolescent Self-Image. rev. ed. LC 89-14706. 380p. 1989. pap. 22.00 (*0-8195-6228-9*, Wesleyan Univ Pr) U Pr of New Eng.

Rosenberg, Morris, ed. Children & Mental Health: Group Rejection & Self-Rejection. (Research in Community & Mental Health Ser.: Vol. 1). 1979. lib. bdg. 73.25 (*0-89232-063-X*) Jai Pr.

Rosenberg, Morris & Kaplan, Howard B., eds. Social Psychology of the Self-Concept. (Illus.). 576p. (C). 1982. text ed. write for info. (*0-88295-214-5*); pap. text ed. write for info. (*0-88295-215-3*) Harlan Davidson.

Rosenberg, Morris & Turner, Ralph H., eds. Social Psychology: Sociological Perspectives. 798p. (C). 1990. pap. 24.95 (*0-88738-854-X*) Transaction Pubs.

***Rosenberg, Nancy T.** California Angel. LC 94-22686. (J). 1995. 17.95 (*0-525-93945-8*, DCB) Dutton Child Bks.

— California Angel. large type ed. LC 95-15713. (Large Print Bks.). 1995. 25.95 (*1-56895-214-7*) Wheeler Pub.

— First Offense. 320p. 1994. 22.95 (*0-525-93853-2*) NAL-Dutton.

— First Offense. 448p. 1995. mass mkt. 6.99 (*0-451-18432-7*, Sig) NAL-Dutton.

— First Offense. large type ed. LC 94-19115. Date not set. 26.95 (*1-56895-108-6*) Wheeler Pub.

— First Offense. large type ed. LC 94-35474. 1994. 25.00 (*1-56895-155-8*) Wheeler Pub.

— Interest of Justice. 448p. 1994. pap. 5.99 (*0-451-18021-6*, Sig) NAL-Dutton.

— Interest of Justice. LC 93-40896. 1993. 25.95 (*1-56895-047-0*) Wheeler Pub.

— Mitigating Circumstances. 448p. 1993. pap. 5.99 (*0-451-17672-3*, Sig) NAL-Dutton.

Rosenberg, Nancy Taylor. Mitigating Circumstances. large type ed. LC 93-2164. 1994. 21.95 (*0-7927-1753-8*, Paragon Lrg Print); pap. 21.95 (*0-7927-1752-X*, Paragon Lrg Print) Chivers N Amer.

Rosenberg, Nathan. Exploring the Black Box: Technology, Economics & History. (Illus.). 325p. (C). 1994. 54.95 (*0-521-45270-8*); pap. 17.95 (*0-521-45955-9*) Cambridge U Pr.

— Inside the Black Box: Technology & Economics. LC 82-4563. 304p. 1983. pap. 21.95 (*0-521-27367-6*) Cambridge U Pr.

— Technology & American Economic Growth. LC 76-52621. 214p. (C). 1976. reprint ed. pap. 20.95 (*0-87332-104-9*) M E Sharpe.

Rosenberg, Nathan, ed. The Emergence of Economic Ideas: Essays in the History of Economics. LC 94-21289. (Economists of the Twentieth Century Ser.). 1994. 59.95 (*1-85898-047-X*, Pub. by E Elgar Pub UK) Ashgate Pub Co.

Rosenberg, Nathan & Birdzell, L. E., Jr. How the West Grew Rich: The Economic Transformation of the Industrial World. LC 85-47551. 368p. 1987. pap. text ed. 16.00 (*0-465-03109-9*) Basic.

Rosenberg, Nathan, jt. auth. see Mowery, David C.

Rosenberg, Nathan, ed. see National Research Council, Committee on Vision Staff.

Rosenberg, Nathan, et al, eds. Technology & the Wealth of Nations. 464p. (C). 1992. 49.50 (*0-8047-2082-7*); pap. 16.95 (*0-8047-2083-5*) Stanford U Pr.

Rosenberg, Neil V. Bluegrass: A History. LC 84-15747. (Music in American Life Ser.). (Illus.). 464p. 1985. 29.95 (*0-252-00265-2*) U of Ill Pr.

— Bluegrass: A History. LC 93-3590. 464p. (C). 1993. pap. 18.95 (*0-252-06304-X*) U of Ill Pr.

Rosenberg, Neil V., ed. Transforming Tradition: Folk Music Revivals Examined. LC 92-26727. (Music in American Life, Folklore & Society Ser.). 336p. (C). 1993. 37.50 (*0-252-01982-2*) U of Ill Pr.

Rosenberg, Norman. Handbook of Carotid Artery Surgery: Facts & Figures. 328p. 1989. 155.95 (*0-8493-2957-4*, RD598) CRC Pr.

— Handbook of Carotid Artery Surgery: Facts & Figures. 2nd ed. LC 93-29684. 1994. reprint ed. 139.95 (*0-8493-3252-4*, RD598) CRC Pr.

Rosenberg, Norman J., et al. Microclimate: The Biological Environment. 2nd ed. LC 83-7031. 495p. 1983. text ed. 79.95 (*0-471-06066-6*, Wiley-Interscience) Wiley.

Rosenberg, Norman J., ed. Drought in the Great Plains: Research on Impacts & Strategies. LC 80-51532. 1980. 25.00 (*0-918334-34-9*) WRP.

— Towards an Integrated Impact Assessment of Climate Change: The Mink Study. LC 93-26849. 172p. (C). 1993. lib. bdg. 69.00 (*0-7923-2448-X*) Kluwer Ac.

Rosenberg, Norman J., jt. ed. see Frederick, Kenneth D.

Rosenberg, Norman J., et al. Greenhouse Warming: Abatement & Adaptation. LC 89-8483. 182p. 1989. pap. 18.95 (*0-915707-50-0*) Resources Future.

Rosenberg, Norman L. Protecting the Best Men: An Interpretive History of the Law of Libel. LC 85-1174. (Studies in Legal History). xi, 369p. (C). 1990. reprint ed. 39.95 (*0-8078-1665-5*); reprint ed. pap. 16.95 (*0-8078-4290-7*) U of NC Pr.

Rosenberg, P., ed. Topical French. 10p. 1979. pap. 14.95 (*0-8288-4838-6*, M9205) Fr & Eur.

Rosenberg, Paul. The Alternative Energy Handbook. LC 92-30937. 1992. write for info. (*0-88173-140-4*) Fairmont Pr.

— Electrical Estimating: Work for a Profit. 208p. 1989. boxed 42.00 (*0-13-247586-3*) P-H.

— High-Tech Electrical Installation Techniques. 160p. 1992. text ed. 40.00 (*0-13-388349-3*) P-H.

— How to Be a Successful Computer Consultant. 320p. 1993. text ed. write for info. (*0-13-396771-9*) P-H.

— Installation Requirements of the National Electrical Code, 1993. 263p. 1993. pap. 22.00 (*0-02-077760-4*) Macmillan.

— Installation Requirements of the 1990 National Electrical Code. 256p. 1991. text ed. 24.95 (*0-02-604941-4*, Audel) Macmillan.

— Installation Requirements of the 1993 National Electrical Code. LC 92-33276. 1993. write for info. (*0-02-604963-5*) Macmillan.

— Introduction to the National Electrical Code. LC 93-19186. 228p. 1993. pap. text ed. 26.95 (*0-8273-5305-7*) Delmar.

— Introduction to the National Electrical Code - Instructor's Guide. 39p. 1993. 12.00 (*0-8273-5306-5*) Delmar.

— Introduction to the NEC. 228p. 1993. pap. text ed. 25.95 (*0-685-67799-0*) Delmar.

— Questions & Answers for Electrician's Examinations: Includes NEC Rulings, 1993. 272p. 1993. pap. 20.00 (*0-02-077762-0*) Macmillan.

— Questions & Answers for Electricians Ten. 1990. text ed. 22.95 (*0-02-604955-4*) Macmillan.

— Vest Pocket Guide to Electrical Estimating. 1989. pap. 14.95 (*0-13-942930-1*) P-H.

Rosenberg, Paul, rev. Guide to the 1993 National Electrical Code. LC 92-36482. 1993. write for info. (*0-02-604964-3*, Audel) Macmillan.

— Questions & Answers for Electricians' Examinations. 11th ed. LC 92-33277. 1993. write for info. (*0-02-604962-7*) Macmillan.

Rosenberg, Paul & Fairmont, Press. The Illustrated Energy Dictionary. 1994. text ed. 43.50 (*0-13-100348-8*) P-H.

Rosenberg, Paul, jt. auth. see Fairmont Press Staff.

Rosenberg, Paul, jt. auth. see Traister, John E.

Rosenberg, Peter D. Patent Law Basics. LC 92-15593. (IP Ser.). 1992. ring bd. 125.00 (*0-87632-897-4*) Clark Boardman Callaghan.

— Patent Law Fundamentals, 3 vols., Set. 2nd ed. LC 80-10710. (IP Ser.). (C). 1980. ring bd. 425.00 (*0-87632-098-1*) Clark Boardman Callaghan.

Rosenberg, Philip. Cost Finding for Public Libraries: A Manager's Handbook. LC 85-20091. 112p. 1986. pap. 5.00 (*0-8389-0442-4*) ALA.

— Tygers of Wrath. 1992. mass mkt. 5.99 (*0-312-92705-3*) St Martin.

Rosenberg, Philip, ed. Toxins: Animal, Plant & Microbial. LC 77-30440. 1978. 466.00 (*0-08-022640-X*, Pub. by Pergamon Repr UK) Franklin.

Rosenberg, Philip, jt. auth. see Tanenbaum, Robert K.

Rosenberg, Phillip. The Seventh Hero: Thomas Carlyle & the Theory of Radical Activism. LC 73-87659. 288p. 1974. 25.95 (*0-674-80260-8*) HUP.

Rosenberg, Pierre. Chardin. LC 90-50883. (Illus.). 1991. pap. 25.00 (*0-8478-1350-9*) Rizzoli Intl.

Rosenberg, Pierre & Stewart, Marion C. French Paintings, Fifteen Hundred to Eighteen Twenty-Five. 376p. 1988. pap. 39.95 (*0-295-96660-2*) U of Wash Pr.

— French Paintings 1500-1825: The Fine Museums of San Francisco. (Illus.). 376p. 1987. pap. 39.95 (*0-88401-055-4*, ND544.F56) Fine Arts Mus.

Rosenberg, Pierre, et al. French Paintings from Dutch Collections, 1600-1800. (Illus.). 184p. 1993. pap. 49.00 (*90-6918-098-7*) U of Wash Pr.

Rosenberg, R., et al, eds. In-Situ Patterning: Selective Area Deposition & Etching: Material Research Society Symposium Proceedings, Vol. 158. 1990. text ed. 45.00 (*1-55899-046-1*) Materials Res.

Rosenberg, R. C. Software Toolkit: Apple II Plus Version. 1986. write for info. (*0-07-053912-X*) McGraw.

Rosenberg, R. N. & Harding, A. E. Molecular Biology of Neurological Disease. (International Medical Reviews Neurology Ser.: Vol. 9). 263p. 1988. text ed. 65.00 (*0-407-02400-X*) Buttrwrth-Heinemann.

Rosenberg, R. Robert. Business Mathematics, Exercises, Problems, & Tests. 7th rev. ed. 1970. text ed. 16.12 (*0-07-053772-0*) McGraw.

— Mathematicas Para Contabilidad y Administracion. 1972. text ed. 18.25 (*0-07-053722-4*) McGraw.

Rosenberg, R. Robert, et al. Understanding Business & Consumer Law. 6th ed. (Illus.). (YA). (gr. 11-12). 1978. text ed. 25.12 (*0-07-053631-7*) McGraw.

Rosenberg, R. Robert & Bonnice, Joseph G. Business Law-Thirty. 2nd ed. (C). 1976. 7.72 (*0-07-053670-8*) McGraw.

Rosenberg, R. Robert & Karnopp, D. C. Introduction to Physical Systems Dynamics. 512p. 1983. text ed. write for info. (*0-07-053905-7*) McGraw.

Rosenberg, R. Robert & Sexton, J. E. Business Math on the Job: Practice Set. 1969. text ed. 12.96 (*0-07-053770-4*) McGraw.

Rosenberg, R. Robert, jt. auth. see Alvey, G. C.

Rosenberg, R. Robert, jt. auth. see Bonnice, Joseph G.

Rosenberg, R. Robert, jt. auth. see Brown, Gordon W.

Rosenberg, R. Robert, et al. Business Law: UCC Applications. 6th ed. LC 82-13001. 640p. 1983. text ed. 33.50 (*0-07-053901-4*) McGraw.

— Business Mathematics. 9th rev. ed. LC 80-18533. 576p. (gr. 9-12). 1982. text ed. 24.88 (*0-07-053726-7*) McGraw.

— Consumer Math & You: Activity Guide. (Illus.). 1978. text ed. 24.56 (*0-07-053641-4*) McGraw.

Rosenberg, Ralph G., jt. auth. see Millet, Gary W.

Rosenberg, Richard. Competence in Mathematics, Bk. I. (Mathematics Ser.). 96p. 1981. student ed 4.95 (*0-9602800-4-9*) Comp Pr.

— Competence in Mathematics, Bk. II. (Mathematics Ser.). 90p. 1981. student ed 4.95 (*0-9602800-5-7*) Comp Pr.

Rosenberg, Richard S. The Social Impact of Computers. (Illus.). 375p. 1992. pap. text ed. 42.50 (*0-12-597130-3*) Acad Pr.

Rosenberg, Richard S., ed. see Herman, Herbert.

***Rosenberg, Rita.** Mushrooms: Over 100 Tantalizing International Recipes. 1995. 12.95 (*1-55561-071-4*) Fisher Bks.

Rosenberg, Rob. Shareware Compendium: The ASP Shareware Catalog, 1993. 1993. pap. 25.00 (*1-55623-914-9*) Irwin Prof Pubng.

Rosenberg, Robert. Bill Cosby: The Changing Black Image. (YA). 1992. pap. 5.92 (*0-395-63615-9*) HM.

— Bill Cosby: The Changing Black Image. (New Directions Ser.). (Illus.). 96p. (YA). (gr. 7 up). 1991. lib. bdg. 15.40 (*1-878841-17-3*); pap. 5.95 (*1-56294-828-8*) Millbrook Pr.

— The Cutting Room: A Detective Avram Cohen Mystery. 320p. 1993. reprint ed. mass mkt. 5.95 (*0-14-023112-9*, Penguin Bks) Viking Penguin.

— The Cutting Room: An Avram Cohen Mystery. 320p. 1993. 20.00 (*0-671-74344-9*) S&S Trade.

Rosenberg, Robert & Hand, August. Electric Motor Repair. 3rd ed. 752p. (C). 1987. text ed. 60.00 (*0-03-059584-3*) SCP.

***Rosenberg, Robert A., et al, eds.** The Papers of Thomas A. Edison Vol. 3: Menlo Park: the Early Years April 1876-December 1877. (Illus.). 752p. 1994. 65.00x (*0-8018-3102-4*) Johns Hopkins.

— The Papers of Thomas A. Edison, Vol. 2: From Workshop to Laboratory, June 1873-March 1876. LC 88-9017. (Illus.). 776p. 1991. text ed. 75.00 (*0-8018-3101-6*) Johns Hopkins.

Rosenberg, Robert G. Wyoming's Last Frontier: Sublette County, Wyoming. LC 89-24701. (Illus.). 284p. (Orig.). 1990. pap. 11.95 (*0-931271-12-6*) Hi Plains Pr.

Rosenberg, Robert J. Bankruptcy Developments for Workout Officers & Lenders Counsel. 758p. 1990. pap. text ed. 17.50 (*0-685-49896-4*, A4-4348) PLI.

— Doing Business with Troubled Companies, 1991. 732p. 1991. pap. text ed. 17.50 (*0-685-49892-1*, A4-4340) PLI.

Rosenberg, Robert J., et al. Collier Lending Institutions & the Bankruptcy Code. 1986. write for info. (*0-8205-1119-6*) Bender.

Rosenberg, Robert M., jt. auth. see Klotz, Irving M.

Rosenberg, Robin, jt. ed. see Munoz, Heraldo.

Rosenberg, Robin L. Spain & Central America: Democracy & Foreign Policy. LC 91-824. (Contributions in Political Science Ser.: No. 288). 280p. 1992. text ed. 55.00 (*0-313-27885-7*, RSJ, Greenwood Pr) Greenwood.

Rosenberg, Roger N. Comprehensive Neurology. 944p. 1991. 243.50 (*0-88167-717-5*) Raven.

— Neurogenetics: Principles & Practice. (Illus.). 336p. 1986. text ed. 95.50 (*0-88167-151-7*) Raven.

Rosenberg, Roger N., et al, eds. The Molecular & Genetic Basis of Neurological Disease. 1248p. 1992. 225.00 (*0-7506-9069-0*) Buttrwrth-Heinemann.

Rosenberg, Ronald H., jt. auth. see Schoenbaum, Thomas J.

Rosenberg, Rosalind. Beyond Separate Spheres: Intellectual Roots of Modern Feminism. LC 81-15967. (Illus.). 1983. pap. 15.00 (*0-300-03092-4*, Y-464) Yale U Pr.

— Divided Lives: American Women in the Twentieth Century. Foner, Eric, ed. (American Century Ser.). 288p. 1992. pap. 10.95 (*0-374-52347-9*) Hill & Wang.

Rosenberg, Roy A. The Concise Guide to Judaism: History, Practice, Faith. 160p. 1994. pap. 10.95 (*0-452-01136-1*, Mer) NAL-Dutton.

— The Veneration of Divine Justice: The Dead Sea Scrolls & Christianity. LC 95-5266. (Contributions to the Study of Religion Ser.: Vol. 40). 160p. 1995. text ed. 45.00 (*0-313-29655-3*, Greenwood Pr) Greenwood.

Rosenberg, Roy A., et al. Happily Intermarried: Authoritative Advice for a Joyous Jewish-Christian Marriage. 1989. pap. 7.95 (*0-02-036430-X*, Collier S&S) S&S Trade.

Rosenberg, Rutger, jt. ed. see Barrett, Gary W.

Rosenberg, Ruthan, jt. auth. see Jukes, Jill.

Rosenberg, S., ed. The State & Labor Market. LC 89-33437. (Studies & Work & Industry). (Illus.). 276p. 1989. 42.50 (*0-306-43170-X*, Plenum Pr) Plenum.

Rosenberg, Samuel. Naked Is the Best Disguise: The Death & Revolution of Sherlock Holmes. 20.95 (*0-89190-169-8*, Am Repr) Amereon Ltd.

R

Rosenberg, Samuel N. Modern French CE: The Neuter Pronoun in Adjectival Predication. (Janua Linguarum, Ser. Practica: No. 116). 1970. pap. text ed. 90.80 (*90-279-0747-1*) Mouton.

Rosenberg, Samuel N. & Tischler, Hans. The Monophonic Songs in the ROMAN de FAUVEL. LC 90-751897. (Illus.). x, 171p. 1991. 50.00 (*0-8032-3898-3*) U of Nebr Pr.

Rosenberg, Samuel N. & Tischler, Hans, eds. Chanter M'estuet: Songs of the Trouveres. LC 80-8383. (Illus.). 608p. (C). 1981. 34.95 (*0-253-14942-8*) Ind U Pr.

Rosenberg, Saralee, jt. auth. see Rosenberg, Lee.

Rosenberg, Seth, jt. auth. see Silverstein, Herbert.

Rosenberg, Seymour & Goldstein, Richard S., eds. The AILA Consular Post Handbook. 3rd ed. 125p. 1990. pap. text ed. 18.00 (*1-878677-14-4*) Amer Immi Law Assn.

Rosenberg, Shawn, et al. Political Reasoning & Cognition: A Piagetian View. LC 88-16225. 192p. (C). 1988. lib. bdg. 36.95 (*0-8223-0856-8*) Duke.

Rosenberg, Shawn W. Reason, Ideology, & Politics. 250p. 1988. 42.50 (*0-691-07785-1*) Princeton U Pr.

Rosenberg, Sheldon, ed. Advances in Applied Psycholinguistics, Vols. 1. (Cambridge Monographs & Texts in Applied Psycholinguistics). (Illus.). 380p. 1987. Vol. 1: Disorders of First Language, 380 pgs. pap. 29.95 (*0-521-31732-0*) Cambridge U Pr.

— Advances in Applied Psycholinguistics, Vols. 1 & 2. (Cambridge Monographs & Texts in Applied Psycholinguistics). (Illus.). 1987. Single Vol. ed. 94.95 (*0-521-30027-4*) Cambridge U Pr.

— Advances in Applied Psycholinguistics, Vols. 2. (Cambridge Monographs & Texts in Applied Psycholinguistics). (Illus.). 380p. 1987. Vol. 2: Reading, Writing & Language Learning, 380 pgs. pap. 32.95 (*0-521-31733-9*) Cambridge U Pr.

— Handbook of Applied Psycholinguistics: Major Thrusts of Research & Theory. LC 81-9891. (Illus.). 608p. 1982. text ed. 120.00 (*0-89859-173-2*) L Erlbaum Assocs.

Rosenberg, Sheldon & Abbeduto, Leonard. Language & Communication in Mental Retardation: Development, Processes, & Intervention. (Topics in Applied Psycholinguistics Ser.). 272p. 1993. text ed. 59.95 (*0-8058-0302-5*); pap. 27.50 (*0-8058-0303-3*) L Erlbaum Assocs.

Rosenberg, Sidney. Any Dog Named Papageno Rosenberg Must Be a Little Bit of All Right! LC 77-79785. (Illus.). 1977. 5.95 (*0-88435-008-8*) Chateau Pub.

Rosenberg, Sondra, jt. auth. see Silverman, Stuart J.

Rosenberg, Stanley, jt. auth. see Farrell, Michael P.

Rosenberg, Stanley D. & Bergen, Bernard J. The Cold Fire: Alienation & the Myth of Culture. LC 76-3918. 224p. reprint ed. pap. 63.90 (*0-317-41766-5*, 2025637) Bks Demand.

Rosenberg, Stephen M. Keep Uncle Sam (& Cousin George) from Devouring Your Estate. LC 91-75531. 330p. (Orig.). 1992. pap. text ed. 19.95 (*1-880380-11-0*) Capital Pub GA.

— Keep Uncle Sam (& Cousin George) from Devouring Your Estate - Physician's Edition. LC 91-75532. (Orig.). 1991. pap. 19.95 (*1-880380-10-2*) Capital Pub GA.

— Keep Uncle Sam from Devouring Your Life Savings. 250p. (Orig.). 1994. pap. 14.95 (*1-56414-120-9*) Career Pr Inc.

Rosenberg, Stephen M. & Peterson, Ann Z. Every Woman's Guide to Financial Security. 382p. 1994. pap. 16.95 (*1-880380-14-5*) Capital Pub GA.

Rosenberg, Steve. Diving & Snorkeling Guide to Northern California & the Monterey Peninsula. 2nd ed. 96p. 1992. pap. 11.95 (*1-55992-052-1*, Pisces Bks) Gulf Pub.

— Diving Cozumel. (Illus.). 114p. (Orig.). 1992. pap. 18.95 (*0-9623389-7-4*) Aqua Quest.

— Diving Hawaii. LC 90-82635. (Illus.). 128p. (Orig.). 1990. pap. 18.95 (*0-9623389-1-5*) Aqua Quest.

Rosenberg, Steve & Ratterree, John. Pisces Guide to Shooting Underwater Video. 256p. 1991. 18.95 (*1-55992-041-6*, Pisces Bks) Gulf Pub.

Rosenberg, Steven & Barry, John M. The Transformed Cell: Unlocking the Mysteries of Cancer. viii, 376p. 1993. reprint ed. pap. 12.50 (*0-380-72115-5*) Avon.

Rosenberg, Steven A. Radiographic Measurements. (Illus.). 112p. 1989. text ed. 16.50 (*0-397-50987-1*) Lippincott.

Rosenberg, Steven A. & Barry, John M. The Transformed Cell: Unlocking the Mysteries of Cancer. (Illus.). 352p. 1992. 24.95 (*0-399-13749-1*, Putnam) Putnam Pub Group.

Rosenberg, Steven A., jt. ed. see Whipple, Terry L.

Rosenberg, Stuart E. Judaism. 159p. pap. 2.45 (*0-686-95139-5*) ADL.

— Secrets of the Jews. 220p. 1995. 45.00 (*0-8095-4901-8*) Borgo Pr.

Rosenberg, Stuart G., jt. ed. see Duke, James C.

Rosenberg, Sue E., intro. West Wind Review. 216p. (C). 1994. write for info. (*0-9630694-3-8*) So Oregon.

***Rosenberg, Terry J.** Poverty in New York City: An Update. 75p. 1994. 10.00 (*0-88156-162-2*) Comm Serv Soc NY.

— Residence, Employment, & Mobility of Puerto Ricans in New York City. LC 73-87828. (Research Papers Ser.: No. 151). (Illus.). 230p. 1974. pap. 12.00 (*0-89065-058-6*) U Chicago Comm Geo.

Rosenberg, Tina. Children of Cain: Violence & the Violent in Latin America. 400p. 1992. reprint ed. pap. 12.95 (*0-14-017254-8*, Penguin Bks) Viking Penguin.

— The Haunted Land: Facing Europe's Ghosts after Communism. LC 94-24750. 437p. 1995. 25.00 (*0-679-42215-3*) Random.

Rosenberg, Victor & Whitney, Gretchen, eds. The Transfer of Scholarly Scientific & Technical Information Between North & South America: Proceedings of a Conference. LC 86-15625. (Illus.). 739p. 1986. 59.50 (*0-8108-1935-X*) Scarecrow.

Rosenberg, Vivian. Reading, Writing, & Thinking: Critical Connections. 208p. (C). 1989. pap. text ed. 14.95 (*0-394-37057-0*) Random.

Rosenberg, Vivian G. Turn of the Century American Journalist, Ray Stannard Baker. (Illus.). 1977. 10.00 (*0-686-15375-8*); pap. 8.00 (*0-686-15376-6*) V G Rosenberg.

Rosenberg, Warren, et al. American Voices: A Thematic-Rhetorical Reader. 493p. (C). 1989. pap. text ed. 26.50 (*0-06-045763-5*) HarpCollege.

Rosenberg, William, ed. Social & Cultural History of the Soviet Union: The Lenin & Stalin Years. LC 91-44186. (Articles on Russian & Soviet History, 1500-1991 Ser.: Vol. 6). 536p. 1992. 79.00 (*0-8153-0563-X*) Garland.

Rosenberg, William G., ed. Bolshevik Visions: First Phase of the Cultural Revolution in Soviet Russia, Pt. 1: The Culture of a New Society: Ethics, Gender & the Family, Law & Problems of Tradition. 2nd rev. ed. LC 90-10958. 250p. 1990. text ed. 44.50 (*0-472-09424-6*); pap. text ed. 16.95 (*0-472-06424-X*) U of Mich Pr.

— Bolshevik Visions: First Phase of the Cultural Revolution in Soviet Russia, Pt. 2: Creating Soviet Cultural Forms: Art, Architecture, Music, Film & the New Tasks of Education. 2nd rev. ed. LC 90-10958. 250p. 1990. text ed. 44.50 (*0-472-09425-4*); pap. text ed. 16.95 (*0-472-06425-8*) U of Mich Pr.

Rosenberg, William G. & Siegelbaum, Lewis H., eds. Social Dimensions of Soviet Industrialization. LC 92-19627. (Indiana-Michigan Series in Russian & East European Studies). 320p. 1993. 39.95 (*0-253-34993-1*); pap. 14.95 (*0-253-20772-X*) Ind U Pr.

Rosenberg, William G. & Young, Marilyn B. Transforming Russia & China: Revolutionary Struggle in the Twentieth Century. 1982. pap. text ed. 16.95 (*0-19-502966-6*) OUP.

Rosenberg, William G., jt. auth. see Koenker, Diane P.

Rosenberg, Yvette, jt. ed. see Kodera, Tsukasa.

Rosenberger, Alfred L., jt. ed. see Fleagle, John G.

Rosenberger, F. Fundamentals of Crystal Growth I: Macroscopic Equilibrium & Transport Concepts. 2nd ed. (Solid-State Sciences Ser.: Vol. 5). (Illus.). 530p. 1981. 75.00 (*0-387-09023-1*) Spr-Verlag.

Rosenberger, Francis C. One Season Here: Poems, 1943-1946. LC 76-150451. 87p. reprint ed. pap. 25.00 (*0-7837-4345-9*, 2044055) Bks Demand.

Rosenberger, Francis C., ed. Washington & the Poet. LC 77-81771. 87p. reprint ed. pap. 25.00 (*0-317-55499-9*, 2029601) Bks Demand.

Rosenberger, Homer T. Adventures & Philosophy of a Pennsylvania Dutchman: An Autobiography in a Broad Setting. LC 79-165295. (Illus.). 665p. 1971. lib. bdg. 15.00 (*0-917264-03-7*) Rose Hill.

— The Enigma: How Shall History Be Written? LC 78-68731. (Illus.). 453p. 1980. lib. bdg. 12.00 (*0-917264-02-9*) Rose Hill.

— Grassroots Philosophy for the Modern Mind. LC 75-32703. (Horizons of the Humanities Ser.: Vol. 2). 255p. 1976. lib. bdg. 9.00 (*0-917264-00-2*) Rose Hill.

— Letters from Africa. LC 65-16638. 209p. 1965. pap. 3.50 (*0-917264-04-5*) Rose Hill.

— Man & Modern Society: Philosophical Essays. LC 72-85861. (Horizons of the Humanities Ser.: Vol. 1). 272p. 1972. lib. bdg. 8.00 (*0-917264-05-3*) Rose Hill.

— The Philadelphia & Erie Railroad: Its Place in American Economic History. LC 74-75110. (Illus.). 748p. 1975. lib. bdg. 22.50 (*0-685-04372-X*) Rose Hill.

— Vignettes of Philosophy: Thirty-Five Vital Subjects. LC 77-71070. (Horizons of the Humanities Ser.: Vol. 3). 258p. 1977. lib. bdg. 9.00 (*0-917264-01-0*) Rose Hill.

Rosenberger, Jesse L. Pennsylvania Germans. 1993. reprint ed. lib. bdg. 89.00 (*0-7812-5825-1*) Rprt Serv.

Rosenberger, Lisa. Integrated Programs of Incentives & Controls for Farmland Preservation in Three Metropolitan Areas. (Discussion Paper Ser.: No. 121). 1980. pap. 10.00 (*1-55869-059-X*) Regional Sci Res Inst.

Rosenberger, Lisa & Coughlin, Robert E. Planning for Vegetation in Urbanizing Areas. (Discussion Paper Ser.: No. 115). 1979. pap. 10.00 (*1-55869-096-4*) Regional Sci Res Inst.

Rosenberger, Margaret, comp. Issues in Focus. LC 89-31025. 233p. 1989. pap. 6.99 (*0-8307-1332-8*, S501112) Regal.

Rosenberger, Margaret, ed. see Fickett, Harold L.

Rosenberger, Margaret, ed. see Stedman, Ray C.

Rosenberger, Mary S. Abundant Living: Wellness from a Biblical Perspective. (Covenant Bible Study Ser.). 48p. 1991. pap. 3.95 (*0-87178-006-2*) Brethren.

— The Lord's Prayer. (Covenant Bible Study Ser.). 48p. 1989. pap. 3.95 (*0-87178-541-2*) Brethren.

Rosenberger, Nancy R., ed. Japanese Sense of Self. (Publications of the Society for Psychological Anthropology). (Illus.). 192p. (C). 1994. pap. 14.95 (*0-521-46637-7*) Cambridge U Pr.

Rosenberger, Noah B. The Place of the Elementary Calculus in the Senior High School Mathematics. LC 71-177209. (Columbia University. Teachers College. Contributions to Education Ser.: No. 117). reprint ed. 37.50 (*0-404-55117-3*) AMS Pr.

Rosenberger, Richard F. & Kaufmann, Charles. The Longrifles of Western Pennsylvania: Allegheny & Westmoreland Counties. LC 92-12625. (Illus.). 192p. (C). 1993. text ed. 60.00 (*0-8229-3727-1*) U of Pittsburgh Pr.

Rosenberry, C. R. The Challenging Skies: The Colorful Story of Aviation's Most Exciting Years, 1919-1939. Gilbert, James B., ed. LC 79-7294. (Flight: Its First Seventy-Five Years Ser.). (Illus.). 1980. reprint ed. lib. bdg. 80.95 (*0-405-12201-2*) Ayer.

Rosenberry, Katharine, jt. auth. see Treese, Clifford.

Rosenberry, Katharine N., jt. auth. see Sproul, Curtis C.

Rosenberry, Sara & Hartman, Chester, eds. Housing Issues of the Nineties. LC 88-15560. 416p. 1989. text ed. 65.00 (*0-275-92362-2*, C2362, Praeger Pubs) Greenwood.

Rosenberry, Ward & Teague, Jim. Distributing Applications Across DCE & Windows NT. 302p. 1993. pap. 24.95 (*1-56592-047-3*) OReilly & Assocs.

Rosenberry, Ward, et al. Understanding DCE. (Nutshell Handbook Ser.). (Illus.). 266p. (Orig.). 1992. pap. text ed. 24.95 (*1-56592-005-8*) OReilly & Assocs.

***Rosenblat, Rebecca.** An Eastern Seduction. 200p. 1995. pap. 7.95 (*0-614-03589-9*) NW Pub.

Rosenblatt. King Lear (Shakespeare) (Book Notes Ser.). (C). 1984. pap. 2.50 (*0-8120-3425-2*) Barron.

Rosenblatt, Aaron. Virginia Woolf for Beginners. (Writers & Readers Documentary Comic Bks.). (Illus.). (Orig.). (YA). (gr. 11 up). 1987. pap. 7.95 (*0-86316-133-2*) Writers & Readers.

Rosenblatt, Aaron & Waldfogel, Diana, eds. Handbook of Clinical Social Work. LC 82-49042. (Jossey-Bass Social & Behavioral Science Ser.). 1211p. reprint ed. pap. 180.00 (*0-8357-4920-7*, 2037850) Bks Demand.

Rosenblatt, Allan & Thickstun, James. Modern Psychoanalytic Concepts in a General Psychology: Including General Concepts & Principles(Part 1); & Motivation(Part 2), 2 pts. Incl. Pt. 1. General Concepts & Principles. LC 77-14712. 1978. text ed. (*0-318-53693-5*); Pt. 2. Motivation Psychological Issues. LC 77-14712. 1978. text ed. (*0-318-53694-3*); LC 77-14712. (Psychological Issues Monograph: Nos. 42 & 43; Vol. 11, Nos. 2 & 3). 348p. 1978. Set text ed. 45.00 (*0-8236-3430-2*) Intl Univs Pr.

Rosenblatt, Arthur, jt. auth. see Benjamin, Ruth.

Rosenblatt, Arthur S. Please Hang Up. 18p. 1984. pap. 2.50 (*0-87129-107-X*, P58) Dramatic Pub.

***Rosenblatt, Barry, et al.** Advances in Organization Development Vol. 3. 200p. 1995. write for info. (*1-56750-102-8*) Ablex Pub.

Rosenblatt, Bernard A. Two Generations of Zionism. LC 67-18134. 1967. 12.95 (*0-88400-017-6*) Shengold.

Rosenblatt, Bill. Learning the Korn Shell. Loukides, Mike, ed. (Nutshell Handbook Ser.). (Illus.). 363p. (Orig.). 1993. pap. 27.95 (*1-56592-054-6*) OReilly & Assocs.

Rosenblatt, Bill, jt. auth. see Cameron, Debra.

***Rosenblatt, Daniel.** The Gestalt Therapy Primer. 153p. (C). 1944. pap. 10.00 (*0-9647037-1-8*) Yurisha Pr.

— Opening Doors: What Happens in Gestalt Therapy. rev. ed. 220p. 1989. 20.00 (*0-939266-07-5*) Gestalt Journal.

Rosenblatt, David J. An Inventory to the Kingsley a Taft Collection. 103p. 1973. 1.50 (*0-318-03222-8*) Ohio Hist Soc.

Rosenblatt, Donald & Rosenblatt, Jackie. The Curie Conundrum. 328p. (Orig.). 1992. pap. 12.95 (*1-56672-001-X*) Seabar Pub.

***Rosenblatt, Emil & Rosenblatt, Ruth, eds.** Hard Marching Every Day: The Civil War Letters of Private Wilbur Fisk, 1861-1865. LC 91-46739. (Modern War Studies). 416p. 1994. pap. 15.95 (*0-7006-0681-5*) U Pr of KS.

— Hard Marching Every Day: The Civil War Letters of Private Wilbur Fisk, 1861-1865. LC 91-46739. (Modern War Studies). 416p. 1992. reprint ed. 25.00 (*0-7006-0529-0*) U Pr of KS.

Rosenblatt, F. F. The Chartist Movement in Its Social & Economic Aspects, 2 vols., Set. LC 74-120203. (Columbia University. Studies in the Social Sciences: No. 171-172). reprint ed. 74.50 (*0-404-51696-3*) AMS Pr.

Rosenblatt, Frank F. Chartist Movement in Its Social & Economic Aspects. 248p. 1967. reprint ed. 32.50 (*0-7146-1103-4*, BHA-01103, Pub. by F Cass Pubs UK) Intl Spec Bk.

Rosenblatt, G. M., ed. Progress in Solid State Chemistry, Vol. 12. (Illus.). 332p. 1980. 147.00 (*0-08-022846-1*, Pub. by Pergamon Repr UK) Franklin.

Rosenblatt, G. M. & Worrell, W. L., eds. Progress in Solid State Chemistry, Vol. 13. (Illus.). 376p. 1982. 140.00 (*0-08-029712-9*, Pergamon Pr) Elsevier.

— Progress in Solid State Chemistry, Vol. 14. (Illus.). 302p. 1983. 130.00 (*0-08-030998-4*, Pergamon Pr) Elsevier.

— Progress in Solid State Chemistry, Vol. 15. (Illus.). 374p. 1985. 145.00 (*0-08-033664-7*, E115, E125, C140, Pub. by PPL UK) Elsevier.

***Rosenblatt, George L., ed.** A Marmac Guide to Houston & Galveston. 3rd ed. (Illus.). 304p. Date not set. pap. 10.95 (*1-56554-100-6*) Pelican.

Rosenblatt, J., tr. see Sirjaev, A. N.

Rosenblatt, Jack & Friedman, M. Harold. Direct & Alternating Current Machinery. 2nd ed. 568p. (C). 1984. write for info. (*0-675-20160-8*, Merrill Pub Co) Macmillan.

Rosenblatt, Jackie, jt. auth. see Rosenblatt, Donald.

Rosenblatt, Jason P. Torah & Law in Paradise Lost. LC 93-37043. 1994. 39.50 (*0-691-03340-4*) Princeton U Pr.

Rosenblatt, Jason P. & Sitterson, Joseph C., Jr., eds. Not in Heaven: Coherence & Complexity in Biblical Narrative. LC 91-6317. (Indiana Studies in Biblical Literature). (Illus.). 272p. 1991. 39.95 (*0-253-35036-0*); pap. 14.95 (*0-253-20678-2*, MB-678) Ind U Pr.

Rosenblatt, Jay S. Advances in the Study of Behavior, Vol. 16. (Serial Publication Ser.). 368p. 1986. text ed. 106.00 (*0-12-004516-8*) Acad Pr.

Rosenblatt, Jay S., ed. Advances in the Study of Behavior, Vol. 18. (Serial Publication Ser.). 199p. 1988. text ed. 70.00 (*0-12-004518-4*) Acad Pr.

Rosenblatt, Jeanette, jt. auth. see Schoenfield, Mark.

Rosenblatt, Judith, ed. see Ebbott, Elizabeth.

Rosenblatt, Judith, ed. see Moses, John G. & Nassar, Eugene P.

Rosenblatt, Judith, jt. ed. see Radovich, Milan.

Rosenblatt, Jules. Key Punch. 1969. student ed write for info. (*0-672-96027-3*); student ed write for info. (*0-672-96029-X*) Macmillan.

Rosenblatt, Julia C. & Sonnenschmidt, Fredric H. Dining with Sherlock Holmes: A Baker Street Cookbook. 2nd ed. LC 76-11610. (Illus.). 287p. 1990. pap. 18.95 (*0-8232-1271-8*) Fordham.

Rosenblatt, Julius, et al. The Common Agricultural Policy of the European Community: Principles & Consequences. (Occasional Paper Ser.: No. 62). 70p. 1988. pap. 7.50 (*1-55775-036-X*) Intl Monetary.

Rosenblatt, L., tr. see Sirjaev, A. N.

Rosenblatt, L., tr. see Walter, Wolfgang.

Rosenblatt, Lily. Fire Diary. Grant, Christy, ed. LC 93-45917. (Illus.). 32p. (J). (gr. 2-5). 1994. lib. bdg. 13.95 (*0-8075-2439-5*) A Whitman.

Rosenblatt, Louise M. L' Idee de l'Art pour l'Art dans la Litterature Anglaise Pendant la Periode Victorienne. LC 75-148289. reprint ed. 45.00 (*0-404-08896-1*) AMS Pr.

— Literature As Exploration. 4th ed. xiv, 304p. 1983. pap. 9.00 (*0-87352-103-X*, T3010) Modern Lang.

—Literature as Exploration. 5th ed. 300p. 1996. lib. bdg. 28.00 (*0-87352-567-1*, T301C); pap. 12.50 (*0-87352-568-X*, T301P) Modern Lang.
First published in 1938, LITERATURE AS EXPLORATION is widely recognized as the first exposition of reader-response criticism. Rosenblatt discusses the psychological, social & aesthetic aspects of the reading experience & argues that teachers must consider what students bring to literature. The fifth edition includes a new foreword by the distinguished literary critic Wayne Booth & an updated list of suggestions for further reading. ***Publisher Provided Annotation.***

— The Reader, the Text, the Poem: The Transactional Theory of the Literary Work. LC 78-16335. 214p. 1978. 22.50 (*0-8093-0883-5*) S Ill U Pr.

— The Reader, the Text, the Poem: The Transactional Theory of the Literary Work. LC 94-1302. 232p. (C). 1994. pap. 14.95x (*0-8093-1805-9*) S Ill U Pr.

Rosenblatt, M., ed. Errett Bishop: Reflections on Him & His Research. LC 85-152. (Contemporary Mathematics Ser.: Vol. 39). 91p. 1985. pap. text ed. 24.00 (*0-8218-5040-7*, CONM-39) Am Math.

Rosenblatt, Marie-Eloise. Paul the Accused: His Portrait in the Acts of the Apostles. LC 94-16103. (Zacchaeus Studies, New Testament). 128p. (Orig.). 1995. pap. text ed. 8.95 (*0-8146-5750-8*, M Glazier) Liturgical Pr.

Rosenblatt, Murray. Markov Processes: Structure & Asymptotic Behavior. LC 70-161441. (Grundlehren der Mathematischen Wissenschaften Ser.: Vol. 184). 1971. 75.00 (*0-387-05480-4*) Spr-Verlag.

— Random Processes. LC 74-10956. (Graduate Texts in Mathematics Ser.: Vol. 17). (Illus.). 225p. 1974. 49.00 (*0-387-90085-3*) Spr-Verlag.

— Stationary Sequences & Random Fields. 288p. 1985. 42.50 (*0-8176-3264-6*) Birkhauser.

Rosenblatt, Murray, ed. Studies in Probability Theory. LC 78-71935. (MAA Studies in Mathematics: Vol. 18). 268p. 1978. 12.00 (*0-88385-118-0*) Math Assn.

Rosenblatt, Murray, jt. auth. see Grenander, Ulf.

Rosenblatt, Naomi. Rainforest for Beginners. (Illus.). 96p. (Orig.). 1992. pap. 7.95 (*0-86316-005-0*) Writers & Readers.

***Rosenblatt, Naomi H. & Horwitz, Joshua.** Wrestling with Angels: What the First Family of Genesis Teaches Us about Our Spiritual Identity, Sexuality & Personal Relationships. LC 95-2563. 1995. write for info. (*0-385-31330-6*) Delacorte.

Rosenblatt, Nate. Encyclopedia of Money Making Sales Letters. 372p. 1992. pap. 19.95 (*0-929543-08-4*) Round Lake Pub.

Rosenblatt, Nate & Fritsch, Edward L. The Art & Skill of Conversation. 64p. 1989. student ed, audio 49.95 (*0-13-048760-0*) P-H.

Rosenblatt, Nate, jt. auth. see Barton, Judi.

Rosenblatt, Nate, ed. see York, David & York, Phyllis.

Rosenblatt, Paul. A Constant Lover. 175p. 1990. 17.50 (*0-922820-11-2*) Watermark Pr.

— John Woolman. (Great American Thinkers Ser.). 1969. lib. bdg. 17.95 (*0-89197-813-5*) Irvington.

— The Sun in Capricorn. 185p. 1989. 18.50 (*0-922820-00-7*) Watermark Pr.

Rosenblatt, Paul & Koppel, Gene. Isaac Bashevis Singer on Literature & Life: An Interview. LC 79-116461. 40p. reprint ed. pap. 25.00 (*0-7837-7015-4*, 2046829) Bks Demand.

***Rosenblatt, Paul, et al.** Multiracial Couples. (Understanding Families Ser.: Vol. 1). 304p. (C). 1995. 44.00 (*0-8039-7258-X*); pap. 21.95 (*0-8039-7259-8*) Sage.

Rosenblatt, Paul C. Bitter, Bitter Tears: Nineteenth-Century Diarists & Twentieth-Century Brief Theories. LC 83-3485. 214p. reprint ed. pap. 61.00 (*0-7837-2924-3*, 2057530) Bks Demand.

— Farming Is in Our Blood: Farm Families in Economic Crisis. LC 89-26967. 198p. 1990. text ed. 24.95 (*0-8138-0238-5*) Iowa St U Pr.

— Metaphors of Family Systems Theory: Toward New Constructions. LC 93-19476. (Perspectives on Marriage & the Family Ser.). 230p. 1993. lib. bdg. 26.95 (*0-89862-321-9*) Guilford Pr.

Rosenblatt, Paul C., et al. The Family in Business: Understanding & Dealing with the Challenges Entrepreneurial Families Face. LC 84-43033. (Management Ser.). 343p. 1985. 36.95 (*0-87589-640-5*) Jossey-Bass.

— Grief & Mourning in Cross-Cultural Perspective. LC 76-29270. (Comparative Studies). 242p. 1976. pap. 12.00 (*0-87536-334-2*) HRAFP.

Rosenblatt, Richard, jt. auth. see Kellner, Jenny.

Rosenblatt, Richard H., jt. auth. see Matsui, Tetsuo.

Rosenblatt, Roger. Black Fiction. LC 74-81387. 272p. 1974. 29.00 (*0-674-07620-6*) HUP.

— Black Fiction. LC 74-81387. 272p. 1976. pap. 11.50 (*0-674-07622-2*) HUP.

— Life Itself: Abortion in the American Mind. LC 91-52686. 224p. 1992. 19.50 (*0-394-58244-6*) Random.

— Life Itself: Abortion in the American Mind. LC 92-56377. 1992. pap. 10.00 (*0-679-74373-1*, Vin) Random.

— The Man in the Water: Essays & Stories. LC 93-5006. 1994. 25.00 (*0-679-42693-0*) Random.

Rosenblatt, Ruth, jt. ed. see Rosenblatt, Emil.

Rosenblatt, Ruth Y., jt. auth. see Beebe, Brooke M.

Rosenblatt, Samuel, tr. Saadia Gaon: Book of Beliefs & Opinions. 1989. pap. 20.00 (*0-300-04490-9*) Yale U Pr.

— Saadia Gaon Book of Beliefs & Opinions. (Judaica Ser.: No. 1). 1948. 60.00 (*0-300-00865-1*) Yale U Pr.

Rosenblatt, Samuel, tr. see Abraham Ben Moses Ben Maimon.

Rosenblatt, Stanley M. Murder of Mercy: Euthanasia on Trial. (Illus.). 352p. (C). 1992. 25.95 (*0-87975-772-8*) Prometheus Bks.

— Trial Lawyer. LC 84-73. 416p. 1984. 19.95 (*0-8184-0360-8*); pap. 9.95 (*0-8184-0361-6*) Carol Pub Group.

Rosenblatt, Suzanne. Shorelines. (Open Meeting Bks.). (Illus.). 64p. 1991. pap. 15.00 (*0-87924-072-5*) Membrane Pr.

Rosenblith, Judy F. In the Beginning: Development from Conception to Age Two. 2nd ed. (Illus.). 600p. (C). 1992. 55.00 (*0-8039-4690-2*) Sage.

Rosenbloom & Schwartz, eds. Handbook of Regulation & Administrative Law. (Public Administration & Public Policy Ser.: Vol. 54). 592p. 1994. 175.00 (*0-8247-9167-3*) Dekker.

Rosenbloom, jt. auth. see Bureau in the U. S. Staff.

Rosenbloom, Alfred J. & Morgan, Meredith W. Vision & Aging. 2nd ed. 463p. 1993. 69.95 (*0-7506-9311-8*) Buttrwrth-Heinemann.

Rosenbloom, Arlan, jt. ed. see Shiverick, Kathleen T.

Rosenbloom, Arlan L. & Tonnessen, Diana. Living with Diabetes. 192p. (Orig.). 1993. pap. 10.95 (*0-452-27093-6*, Plume) NAL-Dutton.

Rosenbloom, Bert. Marketing Channels: A Management View. 4th ed. 707p. (C). 1991. text ed. 57.25 (*0-03-032762-8*) Dryden Pr.

Rosenbloom, Bert, intro. Direct Selling Channels. LC 92-40395. (Journal of Marketing Channels: Vol. 2, No. 2). (Illus.). 124p. 1993. lib. bdg. 29.95 (*1-56024-445-3*); pap. text ed. 14.95 (*1-56024-446-1*) Haworth Pr.

— Wholesale Distribution Channels: New Insights & Perspectives. LC 93-44293. (Journal of Marketing Channels). (Illus.). 167p. 1994. lib. bdg. 29.95 (*1-56024-617-0*); pap. text ed. 14.95 (*1-56024-618-9*) Haworth Pr.

Rosenbloom, D. L., ed. see Twentieth Century Fund, Task Force on Financing Congressional Campaigns Staff.

Rosenbloom, David, ed. Public Personnel Policy in a Political Environment: A Symposium. (Orig.). 1982. pap. 12.00 (*0-918592-59-3*) Pol Studies.

Rosenbloom, David & Morgan. Principles & Practice of Pediatric Optometry. (Illus.). 496p. 1990. text ed. 69.50 (*0-397-50917-0*) Lippincott.

Rosenbloom, David, jt. ed. see Ingraham, Patricia W.

Rosenbloom, David, jt. ed. see Ingraham, Patricia.

Rosenbloom, David, et al. Clinical Trials in the Rheumatic Diseases: A Selected Critical Review. LC 84-9911. 400p. 1985. text ed. 85.00 (*0-275-91323-6*, C1323, Praeger Pubs) Greenwood.

Rosenbloom, David H. & Carroll, James D. Toward Constitutional Competence: A Casebook for Public Administrators. 176p. (C). 1989. pap. text ed. write for info. (*0-13-926122-2*) P-H.

Rosenbloom, David H. & Goldman, Deborah D. Public Administration: Understanding Management, Politics, & Law in Public Sector. 3rd ed. LC 92-11250. 1992. text ed. write for info. (*0-07-053937-5*) McGraw.

— Public Administration: Understanding Management, Politics, & Law in the Public Sector. 2nd ed. (Illus.). 576p. (C). 1989. text ed. write for info. (*0-318-62942-9*) Random.

Rosenbloom, David H. & Shafritz, Jay M. Essentials of Labor Relations. (C). 1985. teacher ed write for info. (*0-8359-1766-5*, Reston) P-H.

Rosenbloom, David H., jt. ed. see Ingraham, Patricia W.

Rosenbloom, David H., jt. auth. see Nachmias, David.

Rosenbloom, David H., jt. ed. see Nivola, Pietro S.

Rosenbloom, David H., et al, eds. Centenary Issues of the Pendleton Act of 1883: The Problematic Legacy of Civil Service Reform. LC 82-10041. (Annals of Public Administration Ser.: No. 3). 149p. reprint ed. pap. 42.50 (*0-7837-3357-7*, 2043315) Bks Demand.

— Contemporary Public Administration. LC 93-47904. 1994. write for info. (*0-07-053939-1*) P-H Gen Ref & Trav.

Rosenbloom, Gerry & Hallman, Victor G. Employee Benefit Planning. 3rd ed. 496p. 1990. text ed. 73.00 (*0-13-275496-7*) P-H.

***Rosenbloom, Jerry.** Automobile Liability Claims: Insurance Company Philosophies & Practices. (C). 1968. 9.50 (*0-256-00677-6*) Irwin.

Rosenbloom, Jerry S. The Handbook of Employee Benefits: Design, Funding & Administration. 2nd ed. 1200p. 1988. pap. 52.00 (*1-55623-175-X*) Irwin Prof Pubng.

— The Handbook of Employee Benefits: Design, Funding & Administration. 2nd ed. 1988. 85.00 (*1-55623-068-0*) Irwin Prof Pubng.

— Handbook of Employee Benefits Vol. 1: Designing, Funding & Administration. 3rd ed. 1040p. 1992. text ed. 75.00 (*1-55623-483-X*) Irwin Prof Pubng.

— Handbook of Employee Benefits Vol. 2: Designing, Funding & Administration. 3rd ed. 640p. 1992. text ed. 55.00 (*1-55623-884-3*) Irwin Prof Pubng.

— Handbook of Employee Benefits Vol. 2: Designing, Funding & Administration. 3rd ed. 1992. text ed. 117.95 (*1-55623-944-0*) Irwin Prof Pubng.

Rosenbloom, Jerry S., jt. auth. see Hallman, G. Victor.

Rosenbloom, Joseph. Biggest Riddle Book in the World. LC 76-1165. (Illus.). (YA). (gr. 5 up). 1979. pap. 6.95 (*0-8069-8884-3*) Sterling.

— Deputy Dan & the Bank Robbers. LC 84-159969. (Step into Reading Bks.). (Illus.). 48p. (J). (gr. 2-3). 1985. 3.50 (*0-394-87045-X*); lib. bdg. 7.99 (*0-394-97045-4*) Random Bks Yng Read.

— Deputy Dan Gets His Man. (Step into Reading Bks.: Step 3). 48p. (J). (gr. 2-3). 1985. pap. 3.50 (*0-394-87250-9*) Random Bks Yng Read.

— Doctor Knock-Knock's Official Knock-Knock Dictionary. LC 76-19796. (Illus.). 128p. (J). (gr. 3 up). 1980. pap. 3.95 (*0-8069-8936-X*) Sterling.

— Funny Insults & Snappy Put-Downs. LC 82-50547. (Illus.). 128p. (J). (gr. 4 up). 1982. pap. 3.95 (*0-8069-7644-6*) Sterling.

— Gigantic Joke Book. LC 77-93310. (Illus.). 256p. (J). (gr. 4-6). 1981. pap. 6.95 (*0-8069-7514-8*) Sterling.

— Giggles, Gags & Groaners. LC 86-30052. (Illus.). 128p. (J). (gr. 2-8). 1988. pap. 3.95 (*0-8069-6536-3*) Sterling.

— Looniest Limerick Book in the World. (J). 1991. 3.99 (*0-517-07355-2*) Random Hse Value.

— Monster Madness. (J). 1991. 3.99 (*0-517-07354-4*) Random Hse Value.

— Nutty Knock Knocks! LC 85-27626. (Illus.). 128p. (Orig.). (J). (gr. 2 up). 1986. pap. 3.95 (*0-8069-6304-2*) Sterling.

— Perfect Put-Downs & Instant Insults. LC 88-11710. (Illus.). 128p. (J). (gr. 2-8). 1989. pap. 3.95 (*0-8069-6940-7*) Sterling.

— School's Out! Vacation Riddles & Jokes. LC 88-31868. (Illus.). 128p. (J). (gr. 2-8). 1990. pap. 3.95 (*0-8069-5760-3*) Sterling.

— Six Hundred Ninety-Six Silly School Jokes & Riddles. (Illus.). 128p. (J). (gr. 2 up). 1987. pap. 3.95 (*0-8069-6392-1*) Sterling.

— Spooky Riddles & Jokes. LC 87-17972. (Illus.). 128p. (J). (gr. 4 up). 1988. pap. 3.95 (*0-8069-6736-6*) Sterling.

— World's Toughest Tongue Twisters. LC 86-5983. (Illus.). 128p. (J). (gr. 2-8). 1987. pap. 3.95 (*0-8069-6596-7*) Sterling.

— The Zaniest Riddle Book in the World. LC 83-18102. (Illus.). 128p. (J). (gr. 3 up). 1985. pap. 3.95 (*0-8069-6252-6*) Sterling.

Rosenbloom, Joseph R. Conversion to Judaism: From the Biblical Period to the Present. LC 78-9409. 192p. reprint ed. pap. 54.80 (*0-7837-2999-5*, 2042942) Bks Demand.

Rosenbloom, P., jt. auth. see Evyatar, A.

Rosenbloom, Paul S. The Soar Papers: Research on Integrated Intelligence, 2 vols. (Artificial Intelligence Ser.). (Illus.). 1300p. (C). 1993. 95.00 (*0-262-18152-5*); pap. 65.00 (*0-262-68071-8*) MIT Pr.

Rosenbloom, Richard S., ed. Research on Technological Innovation, Management & Policy, Vol. 1. 1983. 73.25 (*0-89232-273-X*) Jai Pr.

— Research on Technological Innovation, Management & Policy, Vol. 2. 1985. 73.25 (*0-89232-426-0*) Jai Pr.

— Research on Technological Innovation, Management & Policy, Vol. 3. 1986. 73.25 (*0-89232-688-3*) Jai Pr.

— Research on Technological Innovation, Management & Policy, Vol. 4. 1988. 73.25 (*0-89232-798-7*) Jai Pr.

Rosenbloom, Richard S. & Marris, Robin, eds. Social Innovation in the City: New Enterprises for Community Development, A Collection of Working Papers. LC 69-72560. (Studies in Technology & Society). 212p. 1969. pap. 4.00 (*0-674-81350-2*) HUP.

Rosenbloom, Richard S. & Wolek, Francis W. Technology & Information Transfer: A Survey of Practice in Industrial Organizations. LC 70-119550. 190p. reprint ed. pap. 54.20 (*0-317-10820-4*, 2002225) Bks Demand.

Rosenbluh, Edward. Crisis Counseling. 416p. 1986. per. 26.95 (*0-8403-3903-8*) Kendall-Hunt.

***Rosenblum.** Who Stole the News? Why We Can't Keep up with What Happens in the World & What We Can Do about It. 1995. pap. text ed. 14.95 (*0-471-12032-4*) Wiley.

Rosenblum, jt. auth. see Bracey, Hyler.

Rosenblum, A., ed. Relativity, Supersymmetry, & Strings. LC 87-21294. (Illus.). 136p. 1990. 59.50 (*0-306-42680-3*, Plenum Pr) Plenum.

Rosenblum, Andrew, jt. ed. see Magura, Stephen.

Rosenblum, Art. The Natural Birth Control Book. 6th rev. ed. (Illus.). 168p. 1984. reprint ed. pap. 6.00 (*0-916726-03-7*, 84-70295) Aquarian Res.

Rosenblum, Barbara. Photographers at Work: A Sociology of Photographic Styles. LC 78-8986. 144p. 1978. 35.00 (*0-8419-0402-2*) Holmes & Meier.

Rosenblum, Barbara, jt. auth. see Butler, Sandra.

Rosenblum-Cale, Karen. Thinking Skills: Teaching Social Studies. 48p. 1987. 7.95 (*0-8106-0205-9*) NEA.

Rosenblum-Cale, Karen, jt. ed. see Gruenwald, Oskar.

Rosenblum, Daniel. A Time to Hear, a Time to Help: Listening to People with Cancer. 250p. 1993. text ed. 24.95 (*0-02-927105-3*) Free Pr.

Rosenblum, Dolores. Christina Rossetti: The Poetry of Endurance. LC 85-30739. (Ad Feminam: Women & Literature). 264p. 1987. text ed. 26.95 (*0-8093-1269-7*) S Ill U Pr.

Rosenblum, I. Y. & Heyner, Susan, eds. Growth Factors in Mammalian Development. 240p. 1989. 179.00 (*0-8493-4540-5*, QP552) CRC Pr.

***Rosenblum, Ira.** The Music Lover's Guide to New York. 1995. 15.00 (*1-885492-21-9*) City & Co.

Rosenblum, J. Reb Yaakov. 1993. 19.95 (*0-89906-413-2*); pap. 16.95 (*0-89906-415-9*) Mesorah Pubns.

Rosenblum, James B. The Defense Lawyer's Trial Handbook: Successful Courtroom Strategies for Defending Personal Injury & Malpractice Cases. LC 84-481. 1984. 99.50 (*0-13-197807-1*) Exec Reports.

Rosenblum, James B., ed. Podiatric Liability. 1990. ring bd. 125.00 (*0-9626905-0-3*) Med Litigation.

***Rosenblum, Jonathan D.** Copper Crucible: How the Arizona Miners' Strike of 1983 Recast Labor-Management Relations in America. LC 94-27852. 264p. 1994. 38.00 (*0-87546-331-2*) ILR Pr.

— Copper Crucible: How the Arizona Miners' Strike of 1983 Recast Labor-Management Relations in America. LC 94-27852. 264p. 1994. pap. 16.95 (*0-87546-332-0*) ILR Pr.

***Rosenblum, Joseph.** A Bibliographic History of the Book: An Annotated Guide to the Literature. annot. ed. LC 95-5327. (History of the Book Ser.: No. 3). 439p. 1995. 55.00 (*0-8108-3009-4*) Scarecrow.

— Fun Two: Daffy Definitions. (J). 1992. 3.99 (*0-517-07776-0*) Random Hse Value.

— Land Banking. Linger, Juyne, ed. 8p. (Orig.). 1978. pap. 8.00 (*0-317-04908-9*) Natl Coun Econ Dev.

— Shakespeare. (Magill Bibliographies Ser.). 307p. 1992. 40.00 (*0-8108-2802-2*) Scarecrow.

— Urban Industrial Parks. Bell, Stephanie, ed. 8p. (Orig.). 1978. pap. 8.00 (*0-317-05496-1*) Natl Coun Econ Dev.

***Rosenblum, L., et al, eds.** Scientific Visualization: Advances & Challenges. (Illus.). 532p. 1994. boxed 49.95 (*0-12-227742-2*) Acad Pr.

Rosenblum, Leonard A. & Coe, Christopher L. Handbook of Squirrel Monkey Research. LC 84-24859. 524p. 1985. 110.00 (*0-306-41754-5*, Plenum Pr) Plenum.

Rosenblum, Leonard A., jt. ed. see Lewis, Michael.

Rosenblum, Leonard A., ed. see Moltz, Howard.

Rosenblum, M. L. & Wilson, C. B., eds. Brain Tumor Biology. (Progress in Experimental Tumor Research Ser.: Vol. 27). (Illus.). xvi, 260p. 1984. 125.75 (*3-8055-3698-4*) S Karger.

— Brain Tumor Therapy. (Progress in Experimental Tumor Research Ser.: Vol. 28). (Illus.). xvi, 288p. 1984. 125.75 (*3-8055-3699-2*) S Karger.

Rosenblum, M. L., jt. auth. see Ocko, Judy Y.

Rosenblum, M. L., jt. auth. see Rosenblum, Ocko.

Rosenblum, Mark L., et al, eds. AIDS & the Nervous System. (Illus.). 424p. 1988. text ed. 87.50 (*0-88167-259-9*) Raven.

Rosenblum, Martin J. Divisions-One. 4.00 (*0-686-15300-6*) Great Raven Pr.

— The Holy Ranger: Harley-Davidson Poems. LC 89-83936. 75p. (Orig.). 1989. pap. 14.95 (*0-89018-053-9*) Lion Pub-Roar Rec.

— The Holy Ranger: Harley-Davidson Poems. deluxe limited ed. LC 89-83936. 75p. (Orig.). 1989. pap. 29.95 (*0-89018-054-7*) Lion Pub-Roar Rec.

— Home. LC 74-171995. (Orig.). 1971. pap. 5.00 (*0-87924-015-6*) Membrane Pr.

— Home. 2nd deluxe limited ed. LC 74-171995. 50p. (Orig.). (C). 1989. reprint ed. pap. 10.00 (*0-89018-056-3*) Lion Pub-Roar Rec.

— Home. 2nd ed. LC 74-171995. 50p. (Orig.). (C). 1989. reprint ed. pap. 5.00 (*0-89018-055-5*) Lion Pub-Roar Rec.

— Protractive Verse. 1976. pap. 0.50 (*0-89018-001-6*) Cats Pajamas.

— The Werewolf Sequence (a Poem in 100 Sequences) 150p. (Orig.). 1974. pap. 50.00 (*0-87924-029-6*) Membrane Pr.

Rosenblum, Martin J., ed. & frwd. Brewing: Twenty Milwaukee Poets. LC 72-89435. 1972. 6.95 (*0-89018-008-3*); pap. 6.00 (*0-89018-007-5*) Pentagram.

***Rosenblum, Marvin & Rovnyak, James.** Topics in Hardy Classes & Univalent Functions. LC 94-23454. (Baser Lehrb Ucher). 1994. write for info. (*3-7643-5111-X*) Birkhauser.

— Topics in Hardy Classes & Univalent Functions. LC 94-23454. (Baser Lehrb Ucher). xii, 250p. 1994. 49.50 (*0-8176-5111-X*) Birkhauser.

Rosenblum, Mary. Chimera. 1993. mass mkt. 4.99 (*0-345-38528-4*) Ballantine.

— Selkies. Date not set. pap. write for info. (*0-345-39525-5*) Ballantine.

— The Stone Garden. (Orig.). 1995. pap. 4.99 (*0-345-38958-1*, Del Rey Discovery) Ballantine.

***Rosenblum, Mendel.** The Design & Implementation of a Log-Structured File System. (International Series in Engineering & Computer Science). 144p. (C). 1994. lib. bdg. 76.00 (*0-7923-9541-7*) Kluwer Ac.

Rosenblum, Morris, jt. auth. see Nurnberg, Maxwell.

Rosenblum, Mort. The Secret Life of the Seine. LC 93-42107. 1994. 20.19 (*0-201-62461-3*) Addison-Wesley.

— Who Stole the News? Why We Can't Keep up with What's Happening in the World & What We Can Do about It. 304p. 1993. text ed. 24.95 (*0-471-58522-X*) Wiley.

Rosenblum, Nancy L. Another Liberalism: Romanticism & the Reconstruction of Liberal Thought. LC 87-365. 240p. 1987. 37.00 (*0-674-03765-0*) HUP.

— Bentham's Theory of the Modern State. LC 77-17034. (Harvard Political Studies). 184p. reprint ed. pap. 53.60 (*0-7837-2324-5*, 2057412) Bks Demand.

Rosenblum, Nancy L., ed. Liberalism & the Moral Life. LC 89-30983. 336p. 1989. 40.00 (*0-674-53020-9*) HUP.

— Liberalism & the Moral Life. 336p. (C). 1991. pap. 16.95 (*0-674-53021-7*) HUP.

Rosenblum, Naomi. A History of Women Photographers: All You Need Is Courage. LC 94-6713. 1994. write for info. (*1-55859-761-1*) Abbeville Pr.

— A World History of Photography. rev. ed. (Illus.). (Orig.). (C). Date not set. pap. text ed. 35.00x (*1-55859-055-2*) Abbeville Pr.

— A World History of Photography. rev. ed. (Illus.). 673p. (Orig.). 1989. 60.00 (*1-55859-054-4*) Abbeville Pr.

Rosenblum, Naomi & Heinemann, Larry, eds. Changing Chicago: A Photodocumentary. LC 88-38929. (Visions of Illinois Ser.). (Illus.). 208p. 1989. pap. 29.95 (*0-252-06083-0*) U of Ill Pr.

Rosenblum, Ocko & Rosenblum, M. L. The Specialty Store & Its Advertising. 12.00 (*0-87102-056-4*, 60-6657); teacher ed 4.00 (*0-685-03543-3*) Natl Ret Merch.

Rosenblum, R. Transformation in Late Eighteenth Century Art. 1967. 65.00x (*0-691-03846-5*); pap. 19.95x (*0-691-00302-5*) Princeton U Pr.

Rosenblum, Ralph & Karen, Robert. When the Shooting Stops... The Cutting Begins: A Film Editor's Story. (Illus.). 304p. 1986. pap. 11.95 (*0-306-80272-4*) Da Capo.

Rosenblum, Richard. Brooklyn Dodger Days. LC 90-36691. (Illus.). 32p. (J). (gr. 1-5). 1991. text ed. 13.95 (*0-689-31512-0*, Atheneum Bks Young) S&S Childrens.

— Journey to the Golden Land. LC 91-44941. (Illus.). 32p. (J). (gr. k-4). 1992. 14.95 (*0-8276-0405-X*) JPS Phila.

— The Old Synagogue. 32p. (J). (gr. k-3). 1989. 12.95 (*0-8276-0322-3*) JPS Phila.

Rosenblum, Robert. Cubism & Twentieth Century Art. 1976. 20.95 (*0-685-03819-X*) P-H.

— Ingres. (Masters of Art Ser.). (Illus.). 128p. 1990. 22.95 (*0-8109-3451-5*) Abrams.

— The Jeff Koons Handbook. LC 92-33348. (Illus.). 176p. 1993. 19.95 (*0-8478-1696-6*) Rizzoli Intl.

— Modern Painting & the Northern Romantic Tradition: Friedrich to Rothko. LC 74-6579. (Icon Editions Ser.). (Illus.). 240p. 1977. pap. text ed. 18.00i (*0-06-430057-9*, IN-057, Icon Edns) HarpC.

— Paintings in the Musee D'Orsay. LC 89-11338. (Illus.). 686p. 1995. 59.95 (*1-55670-099-7*) Stewart Tabori & Chang.

— The Romantic Child: From Runge to Sendak. (Walter Neurath Memorial Lecture). (Illus.). 1989. 12.95 (*0-500-55020-4*) Thames Hudson.

Rosenblum, Robert & Bantens, Robert J. Eugene Carriere: The Symbol of Creation. Wasilik, Jeanne M., ed. (Illus.). 132p. 1990. 40.00 (*1-878607-08-1*) Kent Gallery.

Rosenblum, Robert & Ingres, Jean A. Ingres. (Library of Great Painters). (Illus.). 176p. 1967. 49.50 (*0-8109-0195-1*) Abrams.

Rosenblum, Robert & Janson, H. W. Nineteenth-Century Art. LC 83-3882. (Illus.). 528p. 1984. 60.00 (*0-8109-1362-3*) Abrams.

— Nineteenth Century Art (Abrams Book) (Illus.). 528p. 1983. text ed. 60.95 (*0-13-622621-3*) P-H.

Rosenblum, Robert, jt. auth. see Ballatore, Sandy.

Rosenblum, Robert, jt. auth. see Geldzahler, Henry.

Rosenblum, Robert, jt. auth. see Ratcliff, Carter.

Rosenblum, Robert, et al. The Landscape in Twentieth-Century American Art: Selections from the Metropolitan Museum of Art. (Illus.). 174p. 1991. pap. 25.00 (*0-917418-93-X*) Am Fed Arts.

— The Romantic Spirit in German Art: 1790-1990. LC 94-60293. (Illus.). 400p. 1994. 75.00 (*0-500-23693-3*) Thames Hudson.

Rosenblum, S. & Louis, K. S. Stability & Change: Innovation In an Educational Context. LC 80-28291. (Environment, Development, Public Policy & Social Services Ser.). 370p. 1981. 55.00 (*0-306-40665-9*, Plenum Pr) Plenum.

Rosenblum, Sandra P. Performance Practices in Classic Piano Music: Their Principles & Applications. LC 87-45437. (Music: Scholarship & Applications Ser.). 544p. 1988. 49.50 (*0-253-34314-3*, MB-680); pap. 22.50 (*0-253-20680-4*) Ind U Pr.

Rosenblum, Sheila, ed. Leadership Skills for Jewish Educators: A Casebook. LC 93-37122. 1994. 35.00 (*0-87441-555-1*) Behrman.

Rosenblum, Simon, jt. ed. see Joseph, Paul.

Rosenblum, Victor G. & Castberg, A. Didvick, eds. Cases on Constitutional Law: Political Roles of the Supreme Court. LC 72-86627. (Dorsey Series in Political Science). 676p. reprint ed. pap. 180.00 (*0-317-09076-3*, 2021662) Bks Demand.

Rosenblum, Walter. Walter Rosenblum. (Illus.). 224p. 1991. 49.95 (*0-89381-472-5*) Aperture.

Rosenblum, William, jt. auth. see Blaker, J. Warren.

Rosenblum, William M. & Benjamin, William J., eds. Selected Papers on Optometry. LC 92-29543. (Milestone Ser.: Vol. MS 62). 1992. 100.00 (*0-8194-1051-9*); pap. 115.00 (*0-8194-1050-0*) SPIE.

Rosenblum, Y., jt. auth. see Birnbaum, M.

***Rosenbluth.** Rolf & Edgar. (J). Date not set. 11.95 (*0-671-75272-3*, S&S Bks Young Read) S&S Childrens.

Rosenbluth, Frances M. Financial Politics in Contemporary Japan. LC 89-30074. (Studies of the East Asian Institute-Columbia University). 248p. 1989. 29.95 (*0-8014-2274-4*) Cornell U Pr.

Rosenbluth, Frances M., jt. auth. see Ramseyer, J. Mark.

Rosenbluth, Gideon. Concentration in Canadian Manufacturing Industries. (General Ser.: No. 61). 168p. 1957. reprint ed. 43.70 (*0-87014-060-4*); reprint ed. mic. film 21.90 (*0-685-61309-7*) Natl Bur Econ Res.

R

An Asterisk (*) at the beginning of an entry indicates that the title is appearing in BIP for the first time.

Rosenbluth, Gideon & Thorburn, H. G. Canadian Anti-Combines Administration, 1952-1960. LC 64-982. 114p. reprint ed. pap. 32.50 (*0-8357-7992-0*, 2026535) Bks Demand.

Rosenbluth, Hal. Customer Comes Second: And Other Secrets. 1992. 20.00 (*0-688-11466-0*) Morrow.

Rosenbluth, Hal F. Customer Comes Second: And Other Secrets of Exceptional Service. 1994. pap. 12.00 (*0-688-13246-4*, Quill) Morrow.

Rosenbluth, James M., jt. auth. see Bertsch, Gary K.

Rosenbluth, Marshall N. New Ideas in Tokamak Confinement. (Research Trends in Physics Ser.). (Illus.). 496p. 1994. boxed 85.00 (*1-56396-131-8*) Am Inst Physics.

Rosenbluth, Michael, jt. ed. see Silver, Daniel.

Rosenbluth, Rosalyn. The Brave Little Mouse. (Storytime Bks.). (Illus.). 24p. (J). (ps-2). 1993. pap. text ed. 0.99 (*1-56293-346-9*) McClanahan Bk.

— The Land of Peek-A-Boo. (Storytime Bks.). (Illus.). 24p. (J). (ps-2). 1993. pap. text ed. 0.99 (*1-56293-344-2*) McClanahan Bk.

— Scaredy-Cat Kitten. (Storytime Bks.). (Illus.). 24p. (J). (ps-2). 1993. pap. text ed. 0.99 (*1-56293-352-3*) McClanahan Bk.

Rosenbluth, Vera. Keeping Family Stories Alive: A Creative Guide to Taping Your Family Life & Lore. LC 90-47912. 184p. 1990. pap. 11.95 (*0-88179-026-5*) Hartley & Marks.

Rosenboltz, Heidi K., jt. auth. see Howkins, Nan L.

Rosenboom, David. Extended Musical Interface with the Human Nervous System: Assessment & Prospectus. (Illus.). 64p. (Orig.). 1990. pap. 25.00 (*0-9625355-0-8*) Intl Soc Arts Sci & Tech.

Rosenbrock, Howard. Machines with a Purpose. (Illus.). 240p. 1990. 49.95 (*0-19-856346-9*) OUP.

Rosenbrock, Howard, ed. Designing Human-Centered Technology. (Artificial Intelligence & Society Ser.). (Illus.). 225p. 1990. pap. 69.00 (*0-387-19567-X*, 3414) Spr-Verlag.

Rosenbrock, J. & Storey, C. Computational Techniques for Chemical Engineers. LC 65-14227. (International Series Mono in Chemical Engineering: Vol. 7). 1966. 144.00 (*0-08-010889-X*, Pub. by Pergamon Repr UK) Franklin.

Rosenburg, Joel. The Silver Crown. (Book of Guardians of the Flame Ser.: No. 3). 304p. 1985. pap. 4.99 (*0-451-15983-7*, ROC) NAL-Dutton.

Rosenburg, Louis, jt. auth. see Grigsby, William G.

Rosenburg, Maurice & Hay, Peter. Conflict of Laws, 1993: Cases & Materials. 9th suppl. ed. (University Casebook Ser.). 35p. 1993. pap. text ed. 4.95 (*1-56662-082-1*) Foundation Pr.

Rosenburg, Nathan & Frischtak, Claudio, eds. International Technology Transfer: Concepts, Measures, & Comparisons. LC 85-6276. 364p. 1985. text ed. 69.50 (*0-275-90221-8*, C0221, Praeger Pubs) Greenwood.

Rosenburg, Pierre. Chardin: New Thoughts. LC 83-50337. (Franklin D. Murphy Lectures: No. 1). (Illus.). 1983. 12.00 (*0-913689-11-4*) Spencer Muse Art.

Rosenburg, R. B. Living Monuments: Confederate Soldiers' Homes in the New South. LC 93-12465. (Illus.). xvi, 240p. (C). 1993. 34.95 (*0-8078-2109-8*) U of NC Pr.

Rosenburg, R. B., ed. For the Sake of My Country: The Diary of Col. W. W. Ward, 9th Tennessee Cavalry, Morgan's Brigade, C. S. A. LC 92-28143. (Confederate Nation Ser.). 1992. 15.00 (*0-9631963-3-2*); pap. 10.99 (*0-9631963-2-4*) So Herit Pr.

Rosenburg, Seymour, ed. Consular Posts Handbook. 5th ed. 150p. (Orig.). Date not set. pap. text ed. 24.00 (*1-878677-49-7*) Amer Immi Law Assn.

Rosenburgh, Bob. Snake Driver! Cobras in Vietnam. 1993. mass mkt. 5.99 (*0-8041-0538-3*) Ivy Books.

Rosenburgh, V. A. Malayan Fern Allies: Handbook to the Determination of the Fern Allies of the Malayan Islands. 261p. (C). 1985. reprint ed. 175.00 (*81-7089-033-0*, Pub. by Intl Bk Distr II) St Mut.

— Malayan Fern Allies. Handbook to the Determination of the Fern Allies of the Malayan Island. 261p. (C). 1985. text ed. 175.00 (*0-89771-649-3*, Pub. by Intl Bk Distr II) St Mut.

Rosenbusch, Gerd, jt. auth. see Reeders, Jacques W.

Rosenbusch, Marcia, intro. Colloquium on Foreign Languages in the Elementary Schools: Proceedings. (Illus.). 110p. (C). 1992. pap. text ed. 15.00 (*0-942017-10-2*) Amer Assn Teach German.

Rosencher, Emmanuel, jt. ed. see Nissim, Yves I.

Rosencher, Emmanuel, et al, eds. Intersubband Transitions in Quantum Wells. LC 92-10016. (NATO ASI Series B, Physics: Vol. 288). (Illus.). 340p. (C). 1992. 95.00 (*0-306-44204-3*, Plenum Pr) Plenum.

Rosencrans, Glen. Music Notation Primer. (Illus.). 64p. 1993. pap. 5.95 (*0-8256-9149-4*) Music Sales.

Rosencrantz, Barbara G., ed. From Consumption to Tuberculosis: A Documentary History. LC 93-23171. (Reference Library of Social Science, Vol. 903, Library of Sociology: Vol. 1). 648p. 1994. 95.00 (*0-8153-0608-3*, SS808) Garland.

Rosencrantz, Peter. Sco Security Handbook. 1994. pap. text ed. 26.25 (*0-13-123423-4*) P-H.

Rosencwaig. Photoacoustics & Photoacoustic Spectroscopy. 320p. 1990. 69.50 (*0-89464-450-5*) Krieger.

Rosendahl, Carl O. Trees & Shrubs of the Upper Midwest. LC 55-8489. (Illus.). 419p. reprint ed. pap. 119.50 (*0-318-39693-9*, 2033288) Bks Demand.

Rosendahl, Mona. Conflict & Compliance: Class Consciousness among Swedish Workers. 214p. (Orig.). 1985. pap. text ed. 54.00x (*91-85284-24-6*) Coronet Bks.

Rosendahl, Pearl P., ed. see Bullock, Barbara L., et al.

Rosendahl, Pearl P., jt. auth. see Bullock, Barbara L.

Rosendahl, Peter J. More han Ola og han Per. Haugen, Einar & Buckley, Joan N., eds. LC 87-30208. (Bur Oak Bk.). (Illus.). 195p. (Orig.). 1988. pap. 25.95 (*0-87745-192-3*) U of Iowa Pr.

Rosendall, Heidi J. A Phonological Study of the Gwari Lects. LC 92-81460. (Language Data, African Ser.: No. 24). x, 128p. 1992. pap. 10.00 (*0-88312-186-7*); fiche 12.00 (*0-88312-861-6*) Summer Instit Ling.

Rosendorfer, Herbert. The Architect of Ruins. Mitchell, Mike, tr. (Dedalus European Fiction Classics Ser.). 384p. 1992. pap. 14.95 (*0-7818-0001-3*, Pub. by Dedalus Bks UK) Hippocrene Bks.

Rosendorff, Clive. Clinical Cardiovascular & Pulmonary Physiology. (Illus.). 382p. 1983. pap. 39.50 (*0-89004-919-X*) Raven.

Rosene, Candace, jt. auth. see Olson, Melfried.

Rosene, Marcella. Pasta & Co. by Request: Coveted Recipes from Seattle's Leading Take-Out Foodshop. 262p. (Orig.). 1991. 13.95 (*0-912365-49-8*) Sasquatch Bks.

Rosene, Marcella, ed. see Pasta & Co. Staff.

***Roseneil, Sasha.** Disarming Patriarchy: Feminism & Political Action at Greenham. LC 94-40164. 1995. write for info. (*0-335-19058-8*, Open Univ Pr) Taylor & Francis.

— Disarming Patriarchy: Feminism & Political Action at Greenham. LC 94-40164. 1995. pap. write for info. (*0-335-19057-X*, Open Univ Pr) Taylor & Francis.

***Rosener, Judy B.** America's Competitive Secret: Women Managers. (Illus.). 288p. 1995. 25.00 (*0-19-508079-3*) OUP.

Rosener, Judy B., jt. auth. see Loden, Marilyn.

Rosener, Werner. The Peasantry of Europe. Barker, Thomas M., tr. (Making of Europe Ser.). (Illus.). 256p. 1994. 24.95 (*0-631-17503-2*) Blackwell Pubs.

— Peasants in the Middle Ages. Stutzer, Alexander, tr. & frwd. by. (Illus.). 352p. (Orig.). (C). 1993. pap. 21.95 (*0-252-06289-2*) U of Ill Pr.

Rosenfeld & Berko, Roy M. Communicating with Competency Plus TIME Package. (C). 1990. pap. text ed. 24.25 (*0-673-46250-1*) HarpCollege.

Rosenfeld, jt. auth. see Merdinger.

Rosenfeld, et al. Turner Syndrome. 647p. 1990. 199.00 (*0-8247-8108-2*) Dekker.

Rosenfeld, A. A., jt. auth. see Shapiro, E. G.

Rosenfeld, A. H., ed. see American Institute of Physics.

Rosenfeld, Abraham, tr. Selichot for the Whole Year. 832p. (ENG & HEB.). 1956. 17.95 (*0-910818-10-X*) Judaica Pr.

Rosenfeld, Alvin & Wasserman, Saul. Healing the Heart: A Therapeutic Approach to Disturbed Children in Group Care. 96p. 1990. pap. 13.95 (*0-87868-391-7*) Child Welfare.

Rosenfeld, Alvin A., jt. auth. see Bettelheim, Bruno.

Rosenfeld, Alvin H. A Double Dying: Reflections on Holocaust Literature. LC 79-3006. 222p. 1980. 29.95 (*0-253-13337-8*); pap. 9.95 (*0-253-20492-5*, MB-492) Ind U Pr.

— Imagining Hitler. LC 84-48456. 144p. 1985. 15.00 (*0-253-13960-0*) Ind U Pr.

Rosenfeld, Alvin H. & Greenberg, Irving, eds. Confronting the Holocaust: The Impact of Elie Wiesel. LC 78-15821. 255p. reprint ed. pap. 72.70 (*0-317-27853-3*, 2056054) Bks Demand.

Rosenfeld, Alvin H., ed. see Wheelwright, John.

Rosenfeld, Andree, jt. ed. see Bahn, Paul.

Rosenfeld, Arthur. Dark Money. 256p. (Orig.). 1992. mass mkt. 4.99 (*0-380-76486-5*) Avon.

— Dark Tracks. 224p. (Orig.). 1992. mass mkt. 4.99 (*0-380-76487-3*) Avon.

Rosenfeld, Arthur H., jt. ed. see De Almeida, Anibal T.

Rosenfeld, Azriel. Human & Machine Vision II. (Perspectives in Computing Ser.). 376p. 1986. text ed. 69.00 (*0-12-597345-4*) Acad Pr.

Rosenfeld, Azriel, ed. Image Modeling. LC 81-3562. 1981. text ed. 84.00 (*0-12-597320-9*) Acad Pr.

— Multiresolution Image Processing & Analysis. (Information Sciences Ser.: Vol. 12). (Illus.). 400p. 1984. 66.00 (*0-387-13006-3*) Spr-Verlag.

— Techniques for Three D Machine Perception: Machine Intelligence & Pattern Recognition, Vol. 3. 320p. 1986. 59.50 (*0-444-87901-3*, North Holland) Elsevier.

Rosenfeld, Azriel & Kak, Avinash C. Digital Picture Processing, 1. 2nd ed. LC 81-17611. (Computer Science & Applied Mathematics Ser.). 1982. text ed. 72.00 (*0-12-597301-2*) Acad Pr.

— Digital Picture Processing, 2. 2nd ed. LC 81-17611. (Computer Science & Applied Mathematics Ser.). 1982. text ed. 72.00 (*0-12-597302-0*) Acad Pr.

Rosenfeld, Azriel, jt. ed. see Kanal, L. N.

Rosenfeld, Azriel, jt. ed. see Simon, J. C.

Rosenfeld, B. A. The History of Non-Euclidean Geometry. (Studies in the History of Mathematics & Physical Sciences: Vol. 12). (Illus.). 488p. 1988. 89.00 (*0-387-96458-4*) Spr-Verlag.

Rosenfeld, B. A., jt. auth. see Akivis, M. A.

Rosenfeld, C., jt. auth. see Serrou, B.

Rosenfeld, C., jt. ed. see Serrou, B.

Rosenfeld, Charles, ed. The Uterine Circulation. LC 89-16219. (Reproductive & Perinatal Medicine Ser.: No. X). 1989. 102.50 (*0-916859-30-4*) Perinatology.

Rosenfeld, D., ed. see Pertzig, F.

Rosenfeld, D., ed. see Sandman, Rochel.

Rosenfeld, Daniel, ed. European Painting & Sculpture in the Museum of Art, Rhode Island School of Design, Circa 1770-1937. LC 91-61492. (Illus.). 286p. (Orig.). 1992. pap. text ed. 30.00 (*0-911517-55-3*, U of Pa Pr) Mus of Art RI.

Rosenfeld, David. Psychoanalysis & Groups: History & Dialectics. 216p. 1988. reprint ed. pap. 32.95 (*0-946439-48-6*, Pub. by Karnac Bks UK) Brunner-Mazel.

— The Psychotic: Aspects of the Personality. 336p. 1992. pap. 40.95 (*0-946439-96-6*, Pub. by Karnac Bks UK) Brunner-Mazel.

Rosenfeld, Dina. All about Us. (Illus.). 32p. (J). (ps-1). 1989. 8.95 (*0-922613-02-8*); pap. 6.95 (*0-922613-03-6*) Hachai Pubns.

— A Chanukah Story for Night Number Three. Pape, David S., ed. (Illus.). 32p. (J). (ps-1). 1989. 9.95 (*0-922613-16-8*); pap. 7.95 (*0-922613-17-6*) Hachai Pubns.

— David the Little Shepherd. (Little Greats Ser.). (Illus.). 32p. (J). (ps-1). 1995. 8.95 (*0-922613-67-2*) Hachai Pubns.

— Kind Little Rivka. (Little Greats Ser.). (Illus.). 32p. (J). (ps-1). 1991. 8.95 (*0-922613-44-3*); pap. 6.95 (*0-922613-45-1*) Hachai Pubns.

— Kind Little Rivka. Englin, A., tr. (Little Greats Ser.). (Illus.). 32p. (RUS.). (J). (ps-1). 1993. 8.95 (*0-922613-29-X*) Hachai Pubns.

— Labels for Laibel. (Illus.). 32p. (J). (ps-1). 1990. 8.95 (*0-922613-35-4*); pap. 6.95 (*0-922613-36-2*) Hachai Pubns.

— A Little Boy Named Avram. (Little Greats Ser.). (Illus.). 32p. (J). (ps-1). 1989. 8.95 (*0-922613-08-7*); pap. 6.95 (*0-922613-09-5*) Hachai Pubns.

— Peanut Butter & Jelly for Shabbos. (Illus.). 32p. (J). (ps-1). 1995. 8.95 (*0-922613-69-9*); pap. 6.95 (*0-922613-70-2*) Hachai Pubns.

— Why the Moon Only Glows. (Illus.). 32p. (J). (ps-1). 1992. 8.95 (*0-922613-00-1*); pap. 6.95 (*0-922613-01-X*) Hachai Pubns.

— Yossi & Laibel Hot on the Trail. (Illus.). 32p. (J). (ps-1). 1991. 8.95 (*0-922613-47-8*); pap. 6.95 (*0-922613-48-6*) Hachai Pubns.

Rosenfeld, Dina, ed. see Jacobs, Chana R.

Rosenfeld, Dina, ed. see Sharfstein, Chana.

Rosenfeld, Edward, jt. ed. see Anderson, James A.

Rosenfeld, Edward, jt. auth. see Wysong, Joe.

Rosenfeld, Erwin & Geller, Harriet. Global Studies, Vol. I. 2nd ed. 656p. 1993. 25.95 (*0-8120-6197-7*); pap. 19.95 (*0-8120-4771-0*) Barron.

Rosenfeld, Eugene, jt. auth. see Prouty, Chris.

Rosenfeld, F. H. & Bojnicic, J. Adel von Galizien, Lodomerien U. der Bukowina. 275p. (GER & POL.). 1990. reprint ed. 195.00 (*0-317-03845-1*) Szwede Slavic.

Rosenfeld, Gary C., et al. Pharmacology. 2nd ed. LC 93-18750. (Board Review Ser.). (Illus.). 275p. 1993. pap. 19.95 (*0-683-07361-3*) Williams & Wilkins.

Rosenfeld, Georglyn, jt. auth. see Johnson, Laurene.

Rosenfeld, Gerry. Shut Those Thick Lips! A Study of Slum School Failure. 120p. (C). 1983. reprint ed. pap. text ed. 8.50 (*0-88133-022-1*) Waveland Pr.

Rosenfeld, Harvey. The Great Chase: The Dodgers-Giants Pennant Race of 1951. LC 91-51208. 287p. 1992. pap. 28.50x (*0-89950-713-1*) McFarland & Co.

— Raoul Wallenberg. rev. ed. 290p. 1994. pap. 20.00 (*0-8419-1359-5*) Holmes & Meier.

— Roger Maris: A Title to Fame. (Illus.). 288p. 1991. 19.95 (*0-911007-12-1*) Prairie Hse.

Rosenfeld, Harvey & Huttenbach, Henry, eds. A Legacy Recorded: An Anthology of Martyrdom & Resistance. (Illus.). 320p. 1989. write for info. (*0-9619503-0-7*) Martyrdom & Resist Found.

Rosenfeld, Herbert. Impasse & Interpretation: Therapeutic & Anti-therapeutic Factors in the Psyco-analytic Treatment of Psychotic, Boderline, & Neutrotic Patients. Tuckett, David, ed. (New Library of Psychoanalysis). 250p. 1987. lib. bdg. 37.50 (*0-422-61010-0*, Pub. by Tavistock UK) Routledge Chapman & Hall.

***Rosenfeld, Hy.** Money Isn't Everything--It's Nothing. LC 93-7299. 149p. (Orig.). 1994. pap. 9.95 (*0-9638145-3-2*) Carillon Hse.

Rosenfeld, Isaac. Passage from Home. LC 87-40105. (Masterworks of Modern Jewish Writing Ser.). 300p. 1988. reprint ed. pap. 9.95 (*0-910129-75-4*) Wiener Pubs Inc.

Rosenfeld, Isadore. Am I Sick? Is It Serious? What Your Symptoms Really Mean. 1989. 18.95 (*0-318-41500-3*) S&S Trade.

— Best Treatment. 1992. mass mkt. 5.99 (*0-553-29879-8*) Bantam.

— The Best Treatment. large type ed. LC 92-32815. (General Ser.). 1993. 22.95 (*0-8161-5657-3*) G K Hall.

— But Doctor, What Should I Eat? LC 94-8942. 1994. 25.00 (*0-679-42818-6*) Random.

— Distress Signals. 1989. 18.95 (*0-318-37668-7*) S&S Trade.

— Modern Prevention: The New Medicine. 1991. pap. 5.99 (*0-553-27301-9*) Bantam.

— Second Opinion. 1991. mass mkt. 5.99 (*0-553-20562-5*) Bantam.

— Symptoms. 1990. pap. 13.95 (*0-553-34902-3*) Bantam.

— Symptoms. 1994. pap. 5.99 (*0-553-56813-2*) Bantam.

Rosenfeld, J. L., ed. Information Processing Seventy-Four. LC 74-76063. 1107p. 1975. 128.25 (*0-444-10689-8*, North Holland) Elsevier.

Rosenfeld, J. L. & Morton, J. Long-Term Energy Storage in Solar Systems. (C). 1984. 140.00 (*0-685-33080-X*, Pub. by Interntl Solar Energy Soc UK) St Mut.

— Long-Term Energy Storage in Solars Systems (C35) 77p. (C). 1984. 140.00 (*0-685-30221-0*, Pub. by Interntl Solar Energy Soc UK) St Mut.

Rosenfeld, Jeffrey P. The Legacy of Aging: Inheritance & Disinheritance in Social Perspective. LC 78-24209. (Modern Sociology Ser.). (Illus.). 152p. 1979. 35.00 (*0-89391-011-2*) Ablex Pub.

— Relationships: Marriage & Family Reader. LC 81-8941. (C). 1982. pap. text ed. write for info. (*0-394-33293-8*) Random.

Rosenfeld, Joan. Flute Music. 52p. 1987. pap. 4.95 (*0-912159-00-6*) Center Pr CA.

Rosenfeld, Joseph G., jt. auth. see Blanco, Ralph F.

Rosenfeld, Lawrence B., jt. auth. see Berko, Roy M.

***Rosenfeld, Lois G.** The Garden Tourist, 1995: A Guide to Garden Tours, Garden Days, Shows & Special Events. 4th ed. (Illus.). 172p. 1994. pap. write for info. (*0-9639082-1-9*) Garden Tourist.

— The Garden Tourist, '94: A Guide to Garden Tours, Garden Days, Shows & Special Events. 160p. 1993. pap. write for info. (*0-9639082-0-0*) Garden Tourist.

Rosenfeld, Louis. Thomas Hodgkin: Morbid Anatomist & Social Activist. LC 92-28528. (Illus.). 356p. 1992. 24.95 (*0-8191-8633-3*) Madison Bks UPA.

***Rosenfeld, Louis, et al, eds.** Internet Compendium: Subject Guides to Humanities Resources. LC 95-11521. 1995. write for info. (*1-55570-218-X*) Neal-Schuman.

***Rosenfeld, Louis B., et al.** The Internet Compendium: Guides to Resources by Subject. LC 94-36685. 1994. write for info. (*1-55570-188-4*) Neal-Schuman.

Rosenfeld, Lucy D., jt. auth. see Harrison, Marina.

Rosenfeld, Lulla A. The Yiddish Theatre & Jacob P. Adler. rev. ed. LC 86-29677. (Illus.). 408p. 1988. 11.95 (*0-933503-26-1*) Sure Sellers.

Rosenfeld, Lynn R. Your Child & Health Care: A "Dollars & Sense" Guide for Families with Special Needs. 608p. 1994. pap. 29.00 (*1-55766-154-5*, 1545) P H Brookes.

Rosenfeld, M. & Zaks, J., eds. Convexity & Graph Theory. (Mathematics Studies: No. 87). 340p. 1985. pap. 95.00 (*0-444-86571-3*, I-501-83, North Holland) Elsevier.

Rosenfeld, Mark S. Wellness & Lifestyle Renewal: A Manual for Personal Change. (Orig.). 1993. pap. text ed. 28.00 (*0-910317-92-5*) Am Occup Therapy.

Rosenfeld, Max, ed. see Albert, Nachum.

Rosenfeld, Max, ed. see Alpert, Nachum.

Rosenfeld, Max, tr. see Blinkin, Meir.

Rosenfeld, Max, tr. see Smolar, Hersh.

Rosenfeld, Michel. Affirmative Action & Justice: A Philosophical & Constitutional Inquiry. 384p. (C). 1991. text ed. 40.00 (*0-300-04781-9*) Yale U Pr.

— Affirmative Action & Justice: A Philosophical & Constitutional Inquiry. 384p. (C). 1993. reprint ed. pap. text ed. 19.00 (*0-300-05508-0*) Yale U Pr.

Rosenfeld, Michel, ed. Constitutionalism, Identity, Difference & Legitimacy: Theoretical Perspectives. LC 94-15777. 448p. 1994. lib. bdg. 49.95 (*0-8223-1505-X*); pap. text ed. 19.95 (*0-8223-1516-5*) Duke.

Rosenfeld, Mordecai. A Backhanded View of the Law: Irreverent Essays on Justice. LC 91-27013. 1992. 24.95 (*0-918024-90-0*) Ox Bow.

— The Lament of the Single Practitioner: Essays on the Law. LC 88-17515. 256p. 1988. 22.95 (*0-8203-1066-2*) U of Ga Pr.

Rosenfeld, Morris. Collected Works, 3 vols. 1972. 300.00 (*0-87968-897-1*) Gordon Pr.

— Songs from the Ghetto. LC 76-104556. 123p. reprint ed. lib. bdg. 19.00 (*0-8398-1766-5*) Irvington.

Rosenfeld, Morris & Rosenfeld, Stanley, photos. A Century under Sail. (Illus.). 288p. 1988. pap. 29.95 (*0-201-07963-1*) Mystic Seaport.

Rosenfeld, Nancy. Unfinished Journey: Two People, Two Worlds - from Tyranny to Freedom. LC 93-17961. 294p. (Orig.). (C). 1993. lib. bdg. 47.50 (*0-8191-9195-7*); pap. text ed. 18.95 (*0-8191-9196-5*) U Pr of Amer.

Rosenfeld, Paul. By Way of Art: Criticisms of Music, Literature, Painting, Sculpture & the Dance. LC 67-30230. (Essay Index Reprint Ser.). 1977. 20.95 (*0-8369-0835-X*) Ayer.

— Men Seen: Twenty Four Modern Authors. LC 67-26776. (Essay Index Reprint Ser.). 1977. 24.95 (*0-8369-0836-8*) Ayer.

— Musical Chronicle, 1917-1923. LC 77-175877. 17.00 (*0-685-26463-7*) Ayer.

— Musical Portraits: Interpretations of Twenty Modern Composers. LC 68-29243. (Essay Index Reprint Ser.). 1977. 20.95 (*0-8369-0837-6*) Ayer.

Rosenfeld, Paul, jt. ed. see Giacalone, R. A.

Rosenfeld, Paul, jt. ed. see Giacalone, Robert A.

Rosenfeld, Paul, tr. see Schumann, Robert.

Rosenfeld, Paul, et al, eds. Improving Organizational Surveys: New Directions, Methods, & Applications. (Focus Editions Ser.: Vol. 158). (Illus.). 280p. (C). 1993. text ed. 49.95 (*0-8039-5193-0*); pap. text ed. 24.95 (*0-8039-5194-9*) Sage.

Rosenfeld, Peri. Profiles of the Newly Licensed Nurse. 152p. 1989. 99.00 (*0-88737-432-8*) Natl League Nurse.

Rosenfeld, Rachel A. Farm Women: Work, Farm, & Family in the United States. (Institute for Research in Social Science Ser.). xiii, 354p. 1986. 32.50 (*0-8078-1674-4*) U of NC Pr.

— Farm Women: Work, Farm & Family in the United States. LC 85-13945. (Institute for Research in Social Science Ser.). xiii, 354p. (C). 1987. reprint ed. pap. 12.95x (*0-8078-4193-5*) U of NC Pr.

Rosenfeld, Richard, jt. auth. see Messner, Steven F.

Rosenfeld, Robert. Learning about Business Statistics: The McGraw-Hill 36-Hour Business Statistics Course. 248p. 1992. text ed. 35.00 (*0-07-053837-9*) McGraw.

— McGraw Hill Thirty-Six-Hour Business Statistics Course. 1992. pap. text ed. 19.95 (*0-07-053836-0*) McGraw.

Rosenfeld, Robert, jt. auth. see Christy, Dennis T.

Rosenfeld, Robert, jt. auth. see Everly, George S., Jr.

Rosenfeld, Robert, jt. auth. see Zirkel, Gene.

Rosenfeld, Ron G., jt. ed. see Hintz, Raymond L.

Rosenfeld, Sheila D. & White, Susan A. Nuclear Medicine Technology Review. LC 76-57458. (Illus.). 264p. reprint ed. pap. 75.30 (*0-8357-7601-8*, 2056923) Bks Demand.

Rosenfeld, Sidney, ed. see Amery, Jean.

Rosenfeld, Sidney, tr. see Richarz, Monika, ed.

Rosenfeld, Stanley, jt. photos see Rosenfeld, Morris.

Rosenfeld, Stella, tr. see Amery, Jean.

Rosenfeld, Stella P., tr. see Amery, Jean.

Rosenfeld, Stella P., tr. see Richarz, Monika, ed.

Rosenfeld, Stephanie, jt. auth. see Bello, Walden.

R

An Asterisk (*) at the beginning of an entry indicates that the title is appearing in BIP for the first time.

Rosenfeld, Steven. Making History in Vermont: The Election of a Socialist to Congress. LC 91-34055. 500p. (C). 1992. text ed. 35.00 (*0-89341-698-3*); pap. text ed. 17.50 (*0-89341-699-1*) Hollowbrook.

***Rosenfeld, Stuart A.** Advancing Opportunity in Advanced Manufacturing. 145p. 1995. 15.00 (*0-9636927-1-2*) Reg Tech Strat.

— Competitive Manufacturing: New Strategies for Regional Development. LC 91-39699. 418p. (C). 1992. 39.95 (*0-88285-137-3*) Ctr Urban Pol Res.

— New Technologies & New Skills: Two Year Colleges at the Vanguard of Modernization. 159p. (Orig.). (C). 1995. 15.00 (*0-9636927-2-0*) Reg Tech Strat.

Rosenfeld, Tzvi A., ed. see Nachman of Breslov.

Rosenfeld, U., jt. ed. see Miller, H.

Rosenfeld, V. Kleines Fachwoerterbuch Geologie. 197p. (GER.). 1966. 39.95 (*0-8288-6724-0*, M-7500) Fr & Eur.

Rosenfeld, W. The Practical Specifier: A Manual of Construction Documentation for Architects. 194p. 1985. text ed. 39.00 (*0-07-053779-8*) McGraw.

Rosenfeld, Zvi A., ed. see Nachman of Breslov.

Rosenfelder, Lewis. Advanced IBM BASIC Faster & Better, Vol. I. (IBM Information Ser.). (Illus.). 396p. (Orig.). 1985. pap. 19.95 (*0-932679-01-3*); disk 29.95 (*0-685-43124-X*) Blue Cat.

— BASIC Disk I-O Faster & Better & Other Mysteries. 432p. 1984. 29.95 (*0-936200-09-X*) Blue Cat.

— BASIC Faster & Better & Other Mysteries. (TRS-80 Information Ser.: Vol. 4). (Illus.). 290p. (Orig.). 1981. pap. text ed. 29.95 (*0-936200-03-0*) Blue Cat.

— IBM BASIC Faster & Better. Evans, Carl M. & Trapp, Charles, eds. (IBM PC Information Ser.: Vol. 1). (Illus.). 392p. 1984. pap. text ed. 19.95 (*0-936200-52-9*) Blue Cat.

Rosenfelder, Ruth, jt. auth. see Setoguchi, Yoshio.

Rosenfels, Paul. Freud & the Scientific Method. LC 80-118217. (Ninth Street Center Monographs). (Orig.). 1980. pap. 3.95 (*0-932961-06-1*) Ninth St Ctr.

— Homosexuality: The Psychology of the Creative Process. LC 86-23698. 1989. reprint ed. pap. 9.95 (*0-932961-08-8*) Ninth St Ctr.

— Letters to Dean. LC 87-402040. (Ninth Street Center Monographs). (Orig.). 1981. pap. 3.95 (*0-932961-07-X*) Ninth St Ctr.

— Love & Power: The Psychology of Interpersonal Creativity. LC 66-25081. 1966. 12.95 (*0-87212-009-0*) Libra.

— The Nature of Civilization: A Psychological Analysis. LC 86-143005. (Ninth Street Center Monographs). (Orig.). 1977. pap. 3.95 (*0-932961-03-7*) Ninth St Ctr.

— The Nature of Psychological Maturity. LC 86-143042. (Ninth Street Center Monographs). (Orig.). 1978. pap. 3.95 (*0-932961-04-5*) Ninth St Ctr.

— Psychic Exhaustion & the Growth Process (An Appendix to Homosexuality: The Psychology of the Creative Process) LC 86-142957. (Ninth Street Center Monographs). (Orig.). 1976. pap. 3.95 (*0-932961-02-9*) Ninth St Ctr.

— Psychoanalysis & Civilization. LC 62-18668. 1963. 10.95 (*0-87212-016-3*) Libra.

— The Relationship of Adaptation & Fun & Pleasure to Psychological Growth (An Appendix to Homosexuality: The Psychology of the Creative Process) LC 86-142926. (Ninth Street Center Monographs). (Orig.). 1975. pap. 3.95 (*0-932961-01-0*) Ninth St Ctr.

— A Renegade Psychiatrist's Story: An Introduction to the Science of Human Nature. LC 86-142970. (Ninth Street Center Monographs). (Orig.). 1979. pap. 3.95 (*0-932961-05-3*) Ninth St Ctr.

— Subjectivity & Objectivity: Further Aspects of Psychological Growth (An Appendix to Homosexuality: The Psychology of the Creative Process) LC 86-143018. (Ninth Street Center Monographs). (Orig.). 1974. pap. 3.95 (*0-932961-00-2*) Ninth St Ctr.

Rosenfelt, D., jt. ed. see Newton, Judith L.

Rosenfelt, Deborah, jt. ed. see Hoffman, Leonore.

Rosenfelt, Deborah S., ed. see Olson, Tillie.

Rosenfield, A. & Fathalla, M. F., eds. The F. I. G. O. Manual of Human Reproduction, 3 vols., Set, Vols. 1-3. (Illus.). 1990. Set. text ed. 90.00 (*1-85070-190-3*) Prthnon Pub.

Rosenfield, A., et al, eds. Family Planning. (F. I. G. O. Manual of Human Reproduction Ser.: Vol. 2). (Illus.). 244p. 1990. text ed. 35.00 (*1-85070-193-8*) Prthnon Pub.

— Reproductive Health: Global Issues. (F. I. G. O. Manual of Human Reproduction Ser.: Vol. 3). (Illus.). 224p. 1990. text ed. 35.00 (*1-85070-194-6*) Prthnon Pub.

— Reproductive Physiology. (F. I. G. O. Manual of Human Reproduction Ser.: Vol. 1). (Illus.). 120p. 1990. text ed. 35.00 (*1-85070-192-X*) Prthnon Pub.

Rosenfield, A. R., et al, eds. What Does the Charpy Test Really Tell Us? Proceedings of a Symposium Held at the Annual Meeting of the American Institute of Mining, Metallurgical & Petroleum Engineers, 1978. LC 78-10109. 240p. reprint ed. pap. 68.40 (*0-317-26236-X*, 2052145) Bks Demand.

Rosenfield, Aaron & Mann, Roger, eds. Dispersal of Living Organisms into Aquatic Ecosystems. 1992. 35.00 (*0-943676-56-8*) MD Sea Grant Col.

Rosenfield, Geraldine. The Heroes of Masada. (Illus.). 38p. (J). (gr. 6-10). pap. 1.50 (*0-8381-0733-8*, 10-732) United Syn Bk.

Rosenfield, Geraldine, jt. ed. see Ettenberg, Sylvia C.

Rosenfield, Israel. La Conscience: Une Biologie du Moi. exp. ed. 1991. write for info. (*0-318-68136-6*) Knopf.

— A Critique of Artificial Intelligence: The Enchanted Loom. 400p. 1990. 60.00 (*0-685-47601-4*) OUP.

— The Strange, Familiar, & Forgotten: An Anatomy of Consciousness. LC 92-50651. 1993. pap. 10.00 (*0-679-74305-7*, Vin) Random.

Rosenfield, Israel, et al. DNA for Beginners. 1983. 14.95 (*0-86316-022-0*); pap. 9.95 (*0-86316-023-9*) Writers & Readers.

***Rosenfield, James R.** Bank Marketer's Self-Assessment Guide: A Financial Services Marketing Guide to Help You Improve Your Customer Service, Marketing & Profitability. 200p. 1995. 50.00 (*1-55738-779-6*) Probus Pub Co.

— Financial Services Direct Marketing: Tactics, Techniques & Strategies. LC 90-49288. 240p. 1991. boxed 55.00 (*0-942061-13-6*, Financial Sourcebks) Sourcebks.

***Rosenfield, John.** Extraordinary Persons: Japanese Artists (1560-1860) in the Kimiko & John Powers Collection. (Illus.). 31p. 1995. boxed 25.00 (*0-614-06905-X*) A Schwartz & Co.

Rosenfield, John, ed. see Kageyama, Haruki.

Rosenfield, John, ed. see Miki, Fujio.

Rosenfield, John, tr. see Noma, Seiroku.

Rosenfield, John, ed. see Okudaira, Hideo.

***Rosenfield, John, et al, eds.** Courtly Tradition in Japanese Art & Literature; Selected from the Hofer & Hyde Collections. LC 73-85473. (Illus.). 316p. 1973. 12.00 (*0-614-02674-1*) Japan Soc.

***Rosenfield, John M.** Dynastic Arts of the Kushans. (C). 1993. 110.00x (*81-215-0579-8*, Pub. by Munshiram Manoharial II) S Asia.

Rosenfield, John M. & Ten Grotenhuis, Elizabeth. Journey of the Three Jewels: Japanese Buddhist Paintings from Western Collections. LC 79-15072. (Illus.). 1979. 19.95 (*0-87848-054-4*) Asia Soc.

Rosenfield, John M., jt. auth. see Coolidge, John.

Rosenfield, John M., jt. auth. see Shimizu, Yoshiaki.

Rosenfield, Judith F., jt. auth. see Mulpeter, Virginia A.

Rosenfield, Lawrence W. Aristotle & Information Theory: A Comparison of the Influence of Causal Assumptions on Two Theories of Communication. (Janua Linguarum, Ser. Major: No. 35). 1971. text ed. 81.55 (*90-279-1849-X*) Mouton.

Rosenfield, Leonara C., tr. see Koyre, Alexandre.

***Rosenfield, Louis, ed.** The Internet Compendium: Subject Guides to Social Sciences, Business and Law Resources. LC 95-2183. 424p. 1995. 75.00 (*1-55570-220-1*) Neal-Schuman.

Rosenfield, Nancy S. The Radiology of Childhood Leukemia & Its Therapy. (Illus.). 126p. (C). 1981. pap. text ed. 22.50 (*0-87527-173-1*) Green.

Rosenfield, Patricia L. The Management of Schistosomiasis. (Resources for the Future Ser.). 148p. 1979. pap. text ed. 10.00 (*0-8018-2328-5*) Johns Hopkins.

Rosenfield, Paul. Accounting & Auditing for Employee Benefit Plans, No. 2254. 2nd ed. 624p. 1987. boxed 142.00 (*0-88712-793-2*) Warren Gorham & Lamont.

— Accounting & Auditing for Employee Benefit Plans, No. 2254. 2nd suppl. ed. 624p. 1991. Supplemented annually, write for info. 68.00 (*0-7913-1038-8*) Warren Gorham & Lamont.

— The Club Rules: Power, Money, Sex, & Fear - How It Works in Hollywood. 480p. 1993. mass mkt. 5.99 (*0-446-36423-1*) Warner Bks.

Rosenfield, S. A. Instructional Consultation. 304p. 1987. 36.00 (*0-8058-0014-X*) L Erlbaum Assocs.

Rosenfield, Sybil. The Richmond Theatre, Yorkshire: A History of the Georgian Theatre, One of Only Four Remaining 18th Century English Playhouses. (C). 1989. 34.00 (*0-900657-91-X*, Pub. by W Sessions UK); 71.00 (*0-685-37107-7*, Pub. by W Sessions UK) St Mut.

***Rosengard, Jay K.** Building on a Land Mine: Property Tax Reform in Developing Countries. LC 94-41955. (ICEG Sector Studies: Vol. 13). 1995. 12.95 (*1-55815-312-8*) ICS Pr.

Rosengard, Jay K., jt. auth. see Patten, Richard H.

Rosengard, Peter, jt. auth. see Wilmut, Roger.

Rosengart, Axel, jt. ed. see Kessler, Christof M.

Rosengart, Linda E., jt. auth. see Williams, Robert P.

***Rosengart, Terry.** Folk Tales from Around the World. 40p. (J). (gr. 3-6). 1994. 5.95 (*0-88160-245-0*, LW340) Learning Wks.

Rosengarten, Dale. Row upon Row: Sea Grass Baskets of the South Carolina Lowcountry. (Illus.). 64p. (Orig.). 1986. pap. 10.00 (*0-938983-02-4*) McKissick.

Rosengarten, Frank, ed. see Gramsci, Antonio.

Rosengarten, Frederic, Jr. Wilson Popenoe: Agricultural Explorer, Educator, & Friend of Latin America. 92p. 1994. 22.95 (*0-935868-53-4*) Allen Pr.

Rosengarten, Herbert & Goldrick-Jones, Amanda, eds. The Broadview Anthology of Poetry. 1993. pap. 17.95 (*1-55111-006-7*) Broadview Pr.

Rosengarten, Herbert, ed. see Bronte, Anne.

Rosengarten, Herbert, ed. see Bronte, Charlotte.

Rosengarten, Ian B. How to Market Your Business. LC 92-41062. (Small Business Sourcebooks Ser.). 17.95 (*0-942061-48-9*); pap. 8.95 (*0-942061-45-4*) Sourcebks.

— How to Market Your Business: An Introduction to Tools and Tactics for Marketing Your Business. (Small Business Sourcebooks Ser.). 160p. 1995. pap. 8.95 (*1-57071-032-5*) Sourcebks.

Rosengarten, J. G. French Colonists & Exiles in the United States. 234p. 1989. reprint ed. pap. 16.50 (*1-55613-247-6*) Heritage Bk.

Rosengarten, Sudy. Worlds Apart. 214p. 1992. 14.95 (*0-944070-81-7*); pap. 11.95 (*0-944070-82-5*) Targum Pr.

Rosengarten, Theodore. All God's Dangers: The Life of Nate Shaw. 1984. pap. 12.95 (*0-394-72245-0*) Random.

— All God's Dangers: The Life of Nate Shaw. LC 83-19828. 608p. 1989. pap. 14.00 (*0-679-72761-2*, Vin) Random.

— Tombee: Portrait of a Cotton Planter. 1992. pap. 15.00 (*0-688-11609-4*, Quill) Morrow.

Rosengarten, Theodore, jt. auth. see Jacob, Mary J.

Rosengaus, Joseph. Soviet Steam Generator Technology (Fossil Fuel & Nuclear Power Plants) Tamberg, Andreas, ed. (Illus.). (Orig.). 1987. pap. text ed. 75.00 (*1-55831-042-8*) Delphic Associates.

Rosengrant, Sandra & Lifschitz, Elena. Focus on Russian: An Interactive Approach to Writing & Reading. 314p. 1991. Net. pap. text ed. write for info. (*0-471-50659-1*) Wiley.

***Rosengren, Frank H., et al.** Internationalizing Your School: A Resource Guide for Teachers, Administrators, Parents, & School Board Members. 63p. 1983. 5.00 (*0-614-03007-2*) Amer Forum.

Rosengren, Karl E., ed. Media Effects & Beyond: Culture, Socialization & Lifestyles. LC 94-385. (Communication & Society Ser.). 1994. write for info. (*0-415-09141-1*) Routledge.

Rosengren, Karl E. & Windahl, Sven. Media Matter: TV Use in Childhood & Adolescence. Dervin, Brenda, ed. LC 88-38458. (Communication & Information Science Ser.). 304p. (C). 1989. text ed. 52.50 (*0-89391-499-1*); pap. text ed. 29.50 (*0-89391-570-X*) Ablex Pub.

Rosengren, N. J., ed. see Isachenko, A. G.

Rosenhan, David L. & Seligman, Martin E. Abnormal Psychology. (C). 1989. Casebook & study guide. student ed, pap. text ed. 17.95 (*0-393-95698-9*); Test item file. pap. text ed. write for info. (*0-393-95702-0*) Norton.

— Abnormal Psychology. 2nd ed. (C). 1989. Instr's. manual. teacher ed, pap. text ed. write for info. (*0-393-95700-4*); disk write for info. (*0-318-63776-6*) Norton.

— Abnormal Psychology. 3rd ed. LC 94-27953. (C). 1995. text ed. 61.95 (*0-393-96644-5*) Norton.

— Abnormal Psychology. 3rd ed. LC 94-27953. (C). Date not set. teacher ed, pap. text ed. write for info. (*0-393-96659-3*) Norton.

***Rosenhan, David L., et al.** Abnormal Psychology. 3rd ed. LC 94-41703. (C). 1995. student ed, pap. text ed. 17.95x (*0-393-96658-5*) Norton.

Rosenhaum, Stephanie, jt. auth. see Lees, John.

Rosenhead, Jonathan, ed. Rational Analysis for a Problematic World: Problems Structuring Methods for Complexity, Uncertainty & Conflict. 370p. 1989. text ed. 60.50 (*0-471-92285-4*) Wiley.

Rosenhead, L., ed. Laminar Boundary Layers: An Account of the Development, Structure & Stability of Laminar Boundary Layers in Incompressible Fluids, Together with a Description of the Associated Experimental Techniques. (Illus.). 708p. 1988. reprint ed. pap. 15.95 (*0-486-65646-2*) Dover.

Rosenhead, L., tr. see Prandtl, Ludwig & Tietjens, O. G.

Rosenheim, James M. The Townshends of Raynham: Nobility in Transition in Restoration & Early Hanoverian England. LC 89-31140. (Illus.). 288p. 1989. text ed. 40.00 (*0-8195-5217-8*, Wesleyan Univ Pr) U Pr of New Eng.

Rosenheim, Jeff L. Walker Evans & Jane Ninas in New Orleans, 1935-1936. LC 90-86149. (Illus.). 24p. 1991. pap. 10.00 (*0-917860-31-4*) Historic New Orleans.

Rosenheim, Margaret K. & Testa, Mark T., eds. Early Parenthood & Coming of Age in the 1990s. LC 91-40325. 280p. (C). 1992. text ed. 40.00 (*0-8135-1815-6*); pap. text ed. 15.00 (*0-8135-1816-4*) Rutgers U Pr.

***Rosenheim, Shawn & Rachman, Stephen, eds.** The American Face of Edgar Allen Poe. LC 95-10302. 408p. 1995. text ed. 55.00x (*0-8018-5024-X*); pap. text ed. 19.95x (*0-8018-5025-8*) Johns Hopkins.

Rosenhein, Neil B., jt. ed. see Rader, Janet S.

Rosenholtz, Stephen. Monkey Moves. LC 93-93549. (J). (ps-3). 1993. audio, pap. 14.95 (*0-9630979-2-X*) Rosewd Pubns.

— Move Like the Animals. LC 91-66970. (Illus.). 32p. (J). (ps-3). 1992. audio 19.95 (*0-9630979-1-1*); audio, pap. 14.95 (*0-9630979-0-3*) Rosewd Pubns.

Rosenholtz, Susan. Teachers' Workplace: The Organizational Context of Schooling. (Research on Teaching Ser.). 256p. (C). 1991. pap. text ed. 19.95 (*0-8077-3149-8*) Tchrs Coll.

***Rosenhouse, G.** Active Noise Suppression: Fundamentals & Technologies. 200p. 1995. 85.00 (*1-56252-297-3*) Computational Mech MA.

Rosenhouse, Sandra. Identifying the Poor: Is "Headship" a Useful Concept? (Living Standards Measurement Study Working Paper Ser.: No. 58). 60p. 1989. 6.95 (*0-8213-1263-4*, 11263) World Bank.

Rosenkoetter, Sharon, et al. Bridging Early Services for Children with Special Needs & Their Families: A Practical Guide for Transition Planning. 300p. (C). 1993. pap. text ed. 22.00 (*1-55766-160-X*, 160X) P H Brookes.

Rosenkrans, A. Rosenkrans: Family in Europe & America. (Illus.). 333p. 1990. reprint ed. lib. bdg. 60.50 (*0-8328-1620-5*); reprint ed. pap. 52.50 (*0-8328-1621-3*) Higginson Bk Co.

Rosenkrantz & Gutmann, Barbara, eds. Philanthropic Foundations & Resources for Health: An Anthology of Sources. (Medical Care in the United States Ser.). 200p. 1990. lib. bdg. 15.00 (*0-8240-8343-1*) Garland.

Rosenkrantz, Barbara G. Public Health & the State: Changing Views in Massachusetts, 1842-1936. LC 70-172321. (Illus.). 271p. 1972. 29.95 (*0-674-72235-3*) HUP.

— Public Health & the State: Changing Views in Massachusetts, 1842-1936. LC 70-172321. (Illus.). 271p. 1980. pap. 15.95 (*0-674-72236-1*) HUP.

Rosenkrantz, Barbara G., ed. Animalcular & Cryptogamic Theories on the Origins of Fevers: An Original Anthology. LC 76-40658. (Public Health in America Ser.). 1977. reprint ed. 23.95 (*0-405-09839-1*) Ayer.

— Carrier State: An Original Anthology. LC 76-40660. (Public Health in America Ser.). (Illus.). 1977. reprint ed. 18.95 (*0-405-09870-7*) Ayer.

— Clean Water & the Health of the Cities: An Original Anthology. LC 76-40661. (Public Health in America Ser.). (Illus.). 1977. reprint ed. lib. bdg. 23.95 (*0-405-09871-5*) Ayer.

— First American Medical Association Reports on Public Hygiene in American Cities: An Original Anthology. LC 76-40663. (Public Health in America Ser.). 1977. reprint ed. lib. bdg. 21.95 (*0-405-09872-3*) Ayer.

— Health in the Southern United States: An Original Anthology. LC 76-40667. (Public Health in America Ser.). (Illus.). 1977. reprint ed. lib. bdg. 29.95 (*0-405-09875-8*) Ayer.

— Health in the Twentieth Century: An Original Anthology. LC 76-40666. (Public Health in America Ser.). 1977. reprint ed. lib. bdg. 39.95 (*0-405-09874-X*) Ayer.

— Public Health in America, 46 bks. (Public Health in America Ser.). 1977. reprint ed. lib. bdg. 1,242.50 (*0-405-09804-9*) Ayer.

— Selections from Public Health in Reports and Papers: American Public Health Association (1873-1883) LC 76-4065. (Public Health in America Ser.). 1977. reprint ed. lib. bdg. 34.95 (*0-405-09838-3*) Ayer.

— Selections from Public Health Reports & Papers Presented at the Meetings of the American Public Health Association (1884-1907) An Original Anthology. LC 76-40657. (Public Health in America Ser.). 1977. reprint ed. lib. bdg. 21.95 (*0-405-09883-9*) Ayer.

— Selections from the Health-Education Series: An Original Anthology. LC 76-40664. (Public Health in America Ser.). 1977. reprint ed. lib. bdg. 17.95 (*0-405-09873-1*) Ayer.

— Selections from the Journal of the Massachusetts Association of Boards of Health, 1891-1904: An Original Anthology. LC 76-40669. (Public Health in America Ser.). 1977. lib. bdg. 41.95 (*0-405-09878-2*) Ayer.

— Sewering the Cities: An Original Anthology. LC 76-40352. (Public Health in America Ser.). (Illus.). 1977. reprint ed. lib. bdg. 23.95 (*0-405-09879-0*) Ayer.

— Smallpox in Colonial America: An Original Anthology. LC 76-40353. (Public Health in America Ser.). (Illus.). 1977. reprint ed. lib. bdg. 23.95 (*0-405-09880-4*) Ayer.

— Yellow Fever Studies: An Original Anthology. LC 76-40355. (Public Health in America Ser.). 1977. reprint ed. lib. bdg. 26.95 (*0-405-09882-0*) Ayer.

Rosenkrantz, Barbara G., ed. see Ackerknecht, Erwin H.

Rosenkrantz, Barbara G., ed. see Boston Medical Commission.

Rosenkrantz, Barbara G., ed. see Bowditch, Henry I.

Rosenkrantz, Barbara G., ed. see Buck, Albert H.

Rosenkrantz, Barbara G., ed. see Budd, William.

Rosenkrantz, Barbara G., ed. see Chapin, Charles V.

Rosenkrantz, Barbara G., ed. see Davis, Michael M., Jr. & Warner, Andrew R.

Rosenkrantz, Barbara G., ed. see Dublin, Louis I. & Lotka, Alfred J.

Rosenkrantz, Barbara G., ed. see Dunglison, Robley.

Rosenkrantz, Barbara G., ed. see Emerson, Haven & Luginbuhl, Martha.

Rosenkrantz, Barbara G., ed. see Emerson, Haven.

Rosenkrantz, Barbara G., ed. see Fish, Hamilton.

Rosenkrantz, Barbara G., ed. see Frost, Wade H.

Rosenkrantz, Barbara G., ed. see Gardner, Mary S.

Rosenkrantz, Barbara G., ed. see Greenwood, Major.

Rosenkrantz, Barbara G., ed. see Hartley, Robert M.

Rosenkrantz, Barbara G., ed. see Hill, Hibbert W.

Rosenkrantz, Barbara G., ed. see Knopf, S. Adolphus.

Rosenkrantz, Barbara G., ed. see MacNutt, J. Scott.

Rosenkrantz, Barbara G., ed. see National Quarantine & Sanitary Convention Staff.

Rosenkrantz, Barbara G., ed. see Richards, Ellen H.

Rosenkrantz, Barbara G., ed. see Richardson, Joseph G.

Rosenkrantz, Barbara G., ed. see Royal College of Physicians of London Staff & Greenwood, Major.

Rosenkrantz, Barbara G., ed. see Rumsey, Henry W.

Rosenkrantz, Barbara G., ed. see Shryock, Richard H.

Rosenkrantz, Barbara G., ed. see Simon, John.

Rosenkrantz, Barbara G., ed. see Sternberg, George M.

Rosenkrantz, Barbara G., ed. see Straus, Lina G.

Rosenkrantz, Barbara G., ed. see Wanklyn, J. Alfred & Chapman, Ernest T.

Rosenkrantz, Barbara G., ed. see Whipple, George C.

Rosenkrantz, Gary S. Haecceity: An Ontological Essay. LC 93-27789. (Philosophical Studies in Philosophy Ser.). 266p. (C). 1993. lib. bdg. 104.50 (*0-7923-2438-2*) Kluwer Ac.

Rosenkrantz, Gary S., jt. auth. see Hoffman, Joshua.

Rosenkrantz, Joel, jt. auth. see Conner, Janis.

***Rosenkrantz, Linda.** Beyond Jennifer & Jason Vol. 1. 1995. mass mkt. 4.99 (*0-312-95444-1*) St Martin.

— Last Word on First Names: The Definite Guide to the Best & Worst in Baby Names. 1995. pap. 9.95 (*0-312-11748-5*) St Martin.

Rosenkrantz, Linda & Satran, Pamela R. Beyond Charles & Diana: An Anglophile's Guide to Baby Naming. 128p. (Orig.). 1992. pap. 8.95 (*0-312-06902-2*) St Martin.

— Beyond Jennifer & Jason. 2nd rev. ed. 320p. (Orig.). 1994. pap. 10.95 (*0-312-10426-X*) St Martin.

— Beyond Sarah & Sam: An Enlightened Guide to Jewish Baby Naming. 128p. (Orig.). 1992. pap. 8.95 (*0-312-06904-9*) St Martin.

— Beyond Shannon & Sean: An Enlightened Guide to Irish Baby Naming. 128p. 1992. pap. 8.95 (*0-312-06905-7*) St Martin.

— The Last Word on First Names: The Definitive Guide to the Best & Worst in Baby Names by America's Leading Experts. LC 94-42081. 1995. 21.95 (*0-312-11747-7*) St Martin.

Rosenkrantz, Roger D. E. T. Jaynes: Papers on Probability, Statistics & Statistical Physics. 1983. lib. bdg. 106.50 (*90-277-1448-7*) Kluwer Ac.

R

An Asterisk (*) at the beginning of an entry indicates that the title is appearing in BIP for the first time.

— Foundations & Applications of Inductive Probability. xiv, 326p. (Orig.). (C). 1981. lib. bdg. 36.00 (*0-917930-23-1*); pap. text ed. 20.00 (*0-917930-03-7*) Ridgeview.

— Inference, Method & Decision. (Synthese Library: No. 115). 1977. lib. bdg. 70.00 (*90-277-0817-7*); pap. text ed. 36.50 (*90-277-0818-5*) Kluwer Ac.

Rosenkrantz, Timme, jt. auth. see Smith, Stuff.

Rosenkranz, Bernhard. Vergleichende Untersuchungen der Altanatolischen Sprachen. (Trends in Linguistics, State-of-the-Art Reports: No. 8). 1978. pap. 66.15 (*90-279-7696-1*) Mouton.

Rosenkranz, Friedrich. An Introduction to Corporate Modeling. LC 79-63071. (Illus.). xiv, 498p. 1979. 41.95 (*0-8223-0426-0*) Duke.

Rosenkranz, George. Bid Your Way to the Top. Hirsch, Tannah, ed. 1978. 5.95 (*0-87643-026-4*) Barclay Bridge.

— Eywtka Trump Leads. 1988. pap. 7.95 (*0-910791-49-X*) Devyn Pr.

Rosenkranz, Margie & Chappell, Jon, eds. The Minstrel Boy - (Guitar - Vocal) (Illus.). 134p. (Orig.). 1990. pap. text ed. 19.95 (*0-89524-437-3*) Cherry Lane.

Rosenkranz, Shirley A., ed. Beyond the Doors. LC 88-72070. (Illus.). 240p. (YA). (gr. 5-12). 1988. pap. 5.95 (*0-9620953-3-8*) A Class Act.

Rosenlicht, Maxwell. Introduction to Analysis. 254p. 1986. reprint ed. pap. text ed. 7.95 (*0-486-65038-3*) Dover.

Rosenlund, Sigurd J. The Chemical Laboratory - It's Design & Operation: A Practical Guide for Planners of Industrial, Medical, or Educational Facilities. LC 86-31183. (Illus.). 158p. 1987. 36.00 (*0-8155-1110-8*) Noyes.

Rosenman, Ellen B. The Invisible Presence: Virginia Woolf & the Mother-Daughter Relationship. LC 85-23683. (Illus.). xiii, 181p. 1986. text ed. 27.50 (*0-8071-1290-9*) La State U Pr.

— A Room of One's Own: Women Writers & the Politics of Creativity. (Twayne's Masterwork Studies Ser.: No. 151). 124p. 1994. text ed. 22.95x (*0-8057-8374-1*, Twayne) Macmillan.

— A Room of One's Own: Women Writers & the Politics of Creativity. (Twayne's Masterwork Studies Ser.: No. 151). 124p. 1994. pap. 12.95 (*0-8057-8594-9*, Twayne) Macmillan.

Rosenman, Helen, ed. see Dumont d'Urville, Jules S.

Rosenman, Helen, tr. see Dumont d'Urville, Jules S.

Rosenman, Jane, ed. American Voices: Best Short Fiction by Contemporary Authors. LC 92-30087. 400p. 1993. pap. 12.00 (*0-671-78315-7*, WSP) PB.

Rosenman, Jane, ed. see Barrett, Andrea.

Rosenman, Jane, ed. see Bennett, James G.

Rosenman, Jane, ed. see Berkey, Brian F.

Rosenman, Jane, ed. see Burgess, Anthony.

Rosenman, Jane, ed. see Carkeet, David.

Rosenman, Jane, ed. see Castaneda, Carlos.

Rosenman, Jane, ed. see Davidson, Cathy N.

Rosenman, Jane, ed. see DeFerrari, Gabriella.

Rosenman, Jane, ed. see Dixon, Melvin.

Rosenman, Jane, ed. see Fried, Stephen.

Rosenman, Jane, ed. see Goddard, Robert.

Rosenman, Jane, ed. see Gold, Ivan.

Rosenman, Jane, ed. see Goodman, Eric.

Rosenman, Jane, ed. see Gotfryd, Bernard.

Rosenman, Jane, ed. see Graham, Martha.

Rosenman, Jane, ed. see Griffith, Patricia.

Rosenman, Jane, ed. see Haines, John A.

Rosenman, Jane, ed. see Harrison, Jim.

Rosenman, Jane, ed. see Helprin, Mark.

Rosenman, Jane, ed. see Houston, Pam.

Rosenman, Jane, ed. see Hynes, James.

Rosenman, Jane, ed. see Johnson, Fenton.

Rosenman, Jane, ed. see Johnson, Joyce.

Rosenman, Jane, ed. see Johnson, Thomas.

Rosenman, Jane, ed. see Kay, Terry.

Rosenman, Jane, ed. see Klavan, Andrew.

Rosenman, Jane, ed. see Lederer, Richard.

Rosenman, Jane, ed. see Lipman, Elinor.

Rosenman, Jane, ed. see Lombreglia, Ralph.

Rosenman, Jane, ed. see Lott, Bret.

Rosenman, Jane, ed. see Malone, Michael.

Rosenman, Jane, ed. see McCauley, Stephen.

Rosenman, Jane, ed. see McMillan, Terry.

Rosenman, Jane, ed. see Meriwether, Louise.

Rosenman, Jane, ed. see Minot, Susan.

Rosenman, Jane, ed. see Narayan, Kirin.

Rosenman, Jane, jt. ed. see O'Brien, Peggy.

Rosenman, Jane, ed. see Pelletier, Cathie.

Rosenman, Jane, ed. see Phillips, Jayne A.

Rosenman, Jane, ed. see Ransmayr, Christoph.

Rosenman, Jane, ed. see Robin, Robert.

Rosenman, Jane, ed. see Stark, Stephen.

Rosenman, Jane, ed. see Steinke, Darcey.

Rosenman, Jane, ed. see Strempek-Shea, Suzanne.

Rosenman, Jane, ed. see Upman, Elinor.

Rosenman, Jane, ed. see Walker, Walter.

Rosenman, Jane, ed. see Ward, Robert.

Rosenman, Jane, ed. see Watson, Larry.

Rosenman, Jane, ed. see Wickersham, Joan.

Rosenman, Jane, ed. see Wilson, Wayne.

Rosenman, Jane, ed. see Yoshimoto, Banana.

Rosenman, John B. The Best Laugh Last. LC 81-12990. 218p. 1983. reprint ed. pap. 6.95 (*0-914232-62-2*) McPherson & Co.

Rosenman, Martin E. Loving Styles. 192p. 1988. reprint ed. pap. 6.95 (*0-913660-22-1*) Magic Cir Pr CT.

Rosenman, Ray H., jt. ed. see Byrne, D. G.

Rosenman, Ray H., jt. auth. see Friedman, Meyer.

Rosenman, Samuel I. Working with Roosevelt. LC 75-168391. (FDR & the Era of the New Deal Ser.). (Illus.). 1972. reprint ed. lib. bdg. 55.00 (*0-306-70328-9*) Da Capo.

Rosenmann, E., jt. ed. see Cohen, A. M.

Rosenmeier, Rosamond. Anne Bradstreet Revisited. (Twayne's United States Authors Ser.: No. 580). 200p. (C). 1991. text ed. 22.95 (*0-8057-7625-7*, Twayne) Macmillan.

— Lines Out. LC 89-14855. 72p. 1989. pap. 9.95 (*0-914086-88-X*) Alicejamesbooks.

Rosenmeyer, Patricia A. The Poetics of Imitation: Anacreon & the Anacreontic Tradition. (Illus.). 288p. (C). 1992. 69.95 (*0-521-41044-4*) Cambridge U Pr.

Rosenmeyer, Thomas G. The Art of Aeschylus. LC 81-1289. (Illus.). 393p. (C). 1982. pap. 14.00 (*0-520-04608-0*) U CA Pr.

— Deina Ta Polla: A Classicist's Checklist of Twenty Literary-Critical Positions. (Arethusa Monographs: No. 12). vii, 74p. (C). 1988. pap. 10.00 (*0-930881-09-5*) Dept Classics.

— The Green Cabinet: Theocritus & the European Pastoral Lyric. LC 78-82376. (C). 1969. pap. 13.00 (*0-520-02362-5*) U CA Pr.

— Masks of Tragedy, Essays on Six Greek Dramas. LC 78-150417. 261p. (C). 1971. reprint ed. 50.00 (*0-87752-140-9*) Gordian.

— Senecan Drama & Stoic Cosmology. 1989. 42.00 (*0-520-06445-3*) U CA Pr.

Rosenmeyer, Thomas G., ed. see Johnson, W. R.

Rosenmeyer, Thomas G., et al. Meters of Greek & Latin Poetry. LC 62-21264. (C). 1973. reprint ed. pap. text ed. 9.95 (*0-8290-1666-X*) Irvington.

Rosenn, Keith S. Foreign Investment in Brazil. 405p. (C). 1991. pap. text ed. 61.00 (*0-8133-8128-2*) Westview.

— Law & Inflation. LC 81-51139. 491p. reprint ed. pap. 140.00 (*0-7837-3004-7*, 2042937) Bks Demand.

Rosenn, Keith S., jt. ed. see Dolinger, Jacob.

Rosenne, Shabtai. Breach of Treaty. 154p. (C). 1985. 50.00 (*0-906496-36-5*, Pub. by Grotius Pubns UK) St Mut.

— Developments in the Law of Treaties. (Cambridge Studies in International & Comparative Law). 566p. (C). 1989. 94.95 (*0-521-33318-0*) Cambridge U Pr.

— An International Law Miscellany. LC 92-34736. 1993. lib. bdg. 308.00 (*0-7923-1742-4*) Kluwer Ac.

— Intervention in the International Court of Justice. LC 92-42957. (Nova et Vetera Iuris Gentium Series, Modern International Law: No. 16). 228p. (C). 1993. lib. bdg. 107.00 (*0-7923-2109-X*) Kluwer Ac.

— The Law & Practice of the International Court. LC 85-2997. 1985. lib. bdg. 283.50 (*90-247-2986-6*) Kluwer Ac.

— Practice & Methods of International Law. LC 83-43170. 169p. 1984. lib. bdg. 30.00 (*0-379-20140-2*) Oceana.

— Procedure in International Court: A Commentary on the 1978 Rules of the International Court of Justice. 1983. lib. bdg. 130.00 (*90-247-3045-7*) Kluwer Ac.

— Reflections on International Arbitration & Litigation in the International Court of Justice. (Forum Internationale Ser.: No. 9). 1987. 24.00 (*90-6544-351-7*) Kluwer Law Tax Pubs.

— The World Court: What It Is & How It Works. 5th rev. ed. LC 94-15816. (Legal Aspects of International Organizations Ser.: Vol. 16). 1995. lib. bdg. 127.00 (*0-7923-2861-2*) Kluwer Ac.

Rosenne, Shabtai, ed. Documents on the International Court of Justice - Documents Relatifs a la Cour International de Justice: First Bilingual Edition - Premiere Edition Bilinque. (C). 1991. lib. bdg. 310.00 (*0-7923-0912-X*) Kluwer Ac.

— The International Law Commission's Draft Article on State Responsibility, Pt. 1 Articles 1-35. 392p. (C). 1991. lib. bdg. 142.50 (*0-685-48750-4*) Kluwer Ac.

— The International Law Commission's Draft Articles on State Responsibility, Pt. 1, Articles 1-35. 392p. 1991. lib. bdg. 161.50 (*0-7923-1179-5*) Kluwer Ac.

— League of Nations Committee of Experts for the Progressive Codification of International Law (1925-1928), 2 Vols., Set. LC 77-165998. 1972. lib. bdg. 150.00 (*0-379-00147-0*) Oceana.

— League of Nations Conference for the Codification of International Law (1930), 4 vols, Set. LC 74-23544. 1975. lib. bdg. 200.00 (*0-379-10100-9*) Oceana.

Rosenne, Shabtai & Sohn, Louis B., eds. United Nations Convention on the Law of the Sea. 2nd ed. (C). 1989. lib. bdg. 207.50 (*90-247-3719-2*) Kluwer Ac.

Rosennow, Diane, illus. Meeker County Minnesota Cemeteries, Vol. 1: Cedar Mills, Collinwood, Cosmos, Danielson, Ellsworth, Greenleaf & Litchfield Townships. LC 93-31365. 132p. (Orig.). 1993. pap. 15.00 (*0-915709-10-4*) Pk Geneal Bk.

Rosenoer, V. & Rothschild, M. A., eds. Controversies in Clinical Care. LC 80-21593. (Illus.). 312p. 1981. text ed. 40.00 (*0-88331-125-9*) Luce.

Rosenoer, Victor, et al, eds. Albumin: Structure, Function & Uses. 1977. 173.00 (*0-08-019603-9*, Pub. by Pergamon Repr UK) Franklin.

Rosenof, Howard & Ghosh, Asish. Batch Process Automation: Theory & Practice. (Illus.). 1987. text ed. 67.95 (*0-442-27708-3*) Chapman & Hall.

Rosenow, Diane, illus. & comp. Meeker County Cemeteries, Vol. 2: Acton, Darwin, Dassel, Forest City, Forest Prairie, Kingston, Manannah, North Kingston, Swede Grove & Union Grove Townships. LC 93-31365. 140p. (Orig.). 1993. pap. 15.00 (*0-915709-11-2*) Pk Geneal Bk.

Rosenow, Edward C., Jr. History of the American College of Physicians: Executive Perspectives 1959-1977. 451p. 1978. 26.00 (*0-943126-01-0*, EXP84) Amer Coll Phys.

Rosenow, Frank. Seagoing Knots. 1990. 19.95 (*0-393-03338-4*) Norton.

Rosenquist, Glenn C. & Bergsma, Daniel, eds. Morphogenesis & Malinformation of the Cardiovascular System. LC 78-14527. (Alan R. Liss Ser.: Vol. 14, No. 7). 1978. 64.00 (*0-685-03292-2*) March of Dimes.

Rosenquist, John, ed. see Anderson, Jim.

Rosenquist, Valerie. The Iron Ore Eaters: A Portrait of the Mining Community of Moriah, New York. LC 90-3588. (European Immigrants & American Society Ser.). 260p. 1990. reprint ed. 20.00 (*0-8240-7430-0*) Garland.

Rosenqvist, I. & Graff-Petersen, P. International Clay Conference, 1963: Proceedings of Conference, Stockholm, August 1963, 2 vols., Set. LC 63-18137. (International Series Mono on Earth Sciences: Vols. 1-2). 1965. 178.00 (*0-08-011016-9*, Pub. by Pergamon Repr UK) Franklin.

Rosenqvist, Jan O., jt. ed. see Ryden, Lennart.

Rosenqvist, Terkel. Principles of Extractive Metallurgy. (Illus.). 576p. (C). reprint ed. text ed. 50.00 (*1-878907-13-1*) TechBooks.

Rosensaft, Menachem Z. The Legal Status of Soviet Jewry: De Jure Equality & De Facto Discrimination. 30p. 1.00 (*0-686-74962-6*) ADL.

— Moshe Sharett. LC 66-25854. (Illus.). 1966. 12.95 (*0-88400-019-2*) Shengold.

Rosenschein, Jeffrey S. & Zlotkin, Gilad. Rules of Encounter: Designing Convention for Automated Negotiation among Computers. (Artificial Intelligence Ser.). (Illus.). 225p. 1994. pap. 35.00 (*0-262-18159-2*) MIT Pr.

Rosensfiel, Leonie, ed. see Rosenstiel, Leonie, et al.

***Rosensfit.** Beowulf. (Max Notes Ser.). 128p. 1995. pap. text ed. 3.95 (*0-87891-998-8*) Res & Educ.

Rosenshein & Rock. Surgery in the Retroperitoneal Space. 1989. 125.00 (*0-397-50949-9*) Lippincott.

Rosenshein, Joseph & Bennett, Gordon D., eds. Groundwater Hydraulics. (Water Resources Monograph Ser.: Vol. 9). (Illus.). 407p. (Orig.). 1983. 18.00 (*0-87590-310-X*) Am Geophysical.

Rosenshein, Neil B., jt. auth. see Hernandez, Enrique.

Rosensohn, William L. The Phenomenology of Charles S. Pierce: From the Doctrine of Categories to Phaneroscopy. 109p. (Orig.). 1974. pap. 17.00x (*90-6032-024-7*, Pub. by Gruner NE) Benjamins North Am.

***Rosenstand, Nina.** Instructor's Manual for the Moral of the Story: An Introduction to Questions of Ethics & Human Nature. (C). 1993. teacher ed, pap. text ed. write for info. (*1-55934-028-2*) Mayfield Pub.

— The Moral of the Story: An Introduction to Questions of Ethics & Human Nature. LC 93-25790. 524p. (C). 1993. pap. 35.95 (*1-55934-027-4*) Mayfield Pub.

— The Moral of the Story: An Introduction to Questions of Ethics & Human Nature, Testbank. (C). 1993. disk write for info. (*0-614-02718-7*) Mayfield Pub.

Rosenstark, Sol. Transmission Lines in Computer Engineering. LC 93-41585. 1994. text ed. 50.00 (*0-07-053953-7*) McGraw.

Rosenstein. Pediatric Pearls. 384p. 1989. pap. 24.95 (*0-8151-7396-2*, Yr Bk Med Pubs) Mosby Yr Bk.

— Pediatric Pearls. (SPA.). 1992. 22.10 (*0-8016-6721-6*) Mosby Yr Bk.

Rosenstein, Alan H. Stress. Chesney, Margaret & Wiltsek, Nancy, eds. (Illus.). 23p. 1986. pap. 2.50 (*0-933161-06-9*) Better H Prog.

Rosenstein, Beryl J. & Forsarelli, Patricia D. Pediatric Pearls: The Handbook of Practical Pediatrics. 2nd ed. LC 93-4445. 410p. 1993. pap. 21.95 (*0-8016-7171-X*) Mosby Yr Bk.

Rosenstein, Carolyn, jt. auth. see Light, Ivan.

Rosenstein, Eliezer, jt. ed. see Lafferty, William M.

Rosenstein, Emilio S. Diccionario de Especialidades Odontolgicas. 360p. (SPA.). 1989. 85.00 (*0-7859-3446-4*) Fr & Eur.

— Specialized Pharmaceuticals Dictionary: Diccionario de Especialidades Farmaceuticas. 28th ed. 1350p. (SPA.). 1982. 49.95 (*0-8288-1877-0*, S39848) Fr & Eur.

***Rosenstein, Emilio S., ed.** Diccionario de Especialidades Farmaceuticas. 40th ed. (SPA.). 1994. pap. 72.00 (*1-56363-112-1*) Drug Intell Pubns.

— Diccionario de Especialidades Farmaceuticas. 40th ed. 1994. pap. 72.00 (*968-460-094-1*) Drug Intell Pubns.

Rosenstein, G. Z., ed. Income & Choice in Biological Control Systems: A Framework for Understanding the Function & Dysfunction of the Brain. 176p. (C). 1991. text ed. 49.95 (*0-8058-0072-7*) L Erlbaum Assocs.

Rosenstein, Ira. Left on the Field to Die, Part 1: Timothy Richardson. LC 84-242659. 27p. (Orig.). 1980. pap. 3.00 (*0-9605438-0-5*) Starlight Pr.

— Left on the Field to Die, Part 2: Yehudi Weismann. LC 84-242659. 42p. (Orig.). 1982. pap. 4.00 (*0-9605438-1-3*) Starlight Pr.

— Left on the Field to Die, Part 3: Peter Koslov. LC 84-242659. 30p. (Orig.). 1984. pap. 3.00 (*0-9605438-2-1*) Starlight Pr.

— Twenty-Two Sonnets. LC 87-102639. 44p. (Orig.). 1986. pap. 4.00 (*0-9605438-3-X*) Starlight Pr.

Rosenstein, Ira, ed. Starlight Poets One. 32p. (Orig.). 1990. pap. 4.00 (*0-9605438-4-8*) Starlight Pr.

— Starlight Poets Two: Sonnets. 40p. (Orig.). 1992. pap. 5.00 (*0-9605438-5-6*) Starlight Pr.

Rosenstein, Joseph G. Linear Orderings. LC 80-2341. (Pure & Applied Mathematics Ser.). 1982. text ed. 121.00 (*0-12-597680-1*) Acad Pr.

Rosenstein, Marvin, jt. ed. see Kereiakes, James G.

Rosenstein, Milton. Data Structures for Programmers. LC 88-262. 224p. 1992. text ed. 39.95 (*0-471-63520-0*) Krieger.

Rosenstein, Milton & Morris, Paul. Modern Electronic Devices: Circuit Design & Application. 1985. write for info. (*0-8359-4549-9*, Reston) P-H.

Rosenstein, Nathan S. Imperatores Victi: Military Defeat & Aristocratic Competition in the Middle & Late Republic. LC 89-20653. 208p. 1990. 35.00 (*0-520-06939-0*) U CA Pr.

Rosenstein, Neil. The Unbroken Chain. (C). 1990. 69.95 (*1-56062-023-4*) CIS Comm.

Rosenstein, Neil & Bernstein, Charles B. From King David to Baron David: The Genealogical Connections Between Baron Guy de Rothschild & Baroness Alix de Rothschild. LC 89-81367. (Illus.). 78p. (Orig.). 1990. write for info. (*0-9610578-3-1*); pap. 7.00 (*0-685-33278-0*) Computer Ctr Jewish Geog.

Rosenstein, Sheldon, jt. auth. see Kernahan, Desmond A.

Rosenstein, Sophie, et al. Modern Acting: A Manual. 1936. 5.00 (*0-573-69017-0*) French.

Rosenstengel, Janet. Spirals. 20p. (Orig.). 1991. pap. 2.29 (*0-685-48292-8*) Dayspring Pr.

Rosenstiehl, Agnes. Livre de la Langue Francaise. (Gallimard - Decouverte Cadet Ser.: No. 24). (Illus.). 93p. (FRE.). (J). (gr. 4-9). 1985. 16.95 (*2-07-039524-3*) Schoenhof.

Rosenstiel, et al. Contemporary Fixed Prosthodontics. (Illus.). 544p. 1988. text ed. 54.95 (*0-8016-4172-1*) Mosby Yr Bk.

Rosenstiel, Leonie. The Life & Works of Lili Boulanger. LC 75-18244. 408p. (C). 1978. 42.50 (*0-8386-1796-4*) Fairleigh Dickinson.

— Nadia Boulanger: A Life in Music. (Illus.). 449p. 1982. 35.00 (*0-393-01495-9*) Norton.

Rosenstiel, Leonie, jt. auth. see Orrmont, Arthur.

Rosenstiel, Leonie, jt. ed. see Orrmont, Arthur.

Rosenstiel, Leonie, et al. Schirmer History of Music. Rosensfiel, Leonie, ed. 992p. (C). 1982. text ed. 25.00 (*0-02-872190-X*) Schirmer Bks.

Rosenstiel, Stephen F., et al. Contemporary Fixed Prosthodontics. 2nd ed. LC 93-40196. (Illus.). 530p. 1994. 55.00 (*0-8016-6528-0*) Mosby Yr Bk.

Rosenstiel, Tom. The Beat Goes On: President Clinton's First Year with the Media. LC 94-25761. 1994. 9.95 (*0-87078-369-6*) TCFP-PPP.

— Strange Bedfellows: How Television & the Presidential Candidates Changed American Politics, 1992. (Illus.). 384p. 1994. pap. 14.95 (*0-7868-8022-8*) Hyperion.

Rosenstock. Felix & Blackie. (Road to Avonlea Ser.). 1994. mass mkt. 3.99 (*0-553-48121-5*) Bantam.

Rosenstock, Adele. Etruria. (Illus.). 64p. (Orig.). 1994. pap. write for info. (*0-9641829-0-4*) A Rosenstock.

***Rosenstock Arts Staff.** American Art in Colorado Collections. (Documents of Colorado Art Ser.). (Illus.). 30p. (Orig.). 1983. pap. 19.95 (*0-938075-47-0*) Ocean View Bks.

Rosenstock, D. Misfits & Miracles. (YA). 1994. pap. 3.99 (*0-553-48046-4*) Bantam.

Rosenstock, Gabriel. Portrait of the Artist As an Abominable Snowman. LC 89-82064. 112p. (ENG & IRI.). 1990. pap. 18.95 (*0-948259-56-6*, Pub. by Forest Bks UK) Dufour.

Rosenstock, Gabriel, tr. The Wasp in the Mug: Unforgettable Irish Proverbs. (Illus.). 111p. 1993. pap. 13.95 (*1-85635-043-6*, Pub. by Mercier Pr IE) Dufour.

Rosenstock, Gabriel, tr. see Conaola, Dara O.

Rosenstock, Harvey A., jt. auth. see Rosenstock, Judith D.

Rosenstock, Harvey A., et al. Journey Through Divorce: Five Stages Toward Recovery. 128p. 1988. 28.95 (*0-89885-403-2*) Human Sci Pr.

***Rosenstock-Huessy, Eugen.** American Social History - 1959, Vol. 19. (Eugen Rosenstock-Huessy Lectures). 622p. Date not set. audio, pap. 275.00 (*0-614-05384-6*); pap. 135.00 (*0-912148-38-1*); audio 205.00 (*0-614-05383-8*) Argo Bks.

— Applied Science of the Soul. 40p. 1984. pap. text ed. 3.95 (*0-910727-04-X*) Golden Phoenix.

— Christian Future. 248p. pap. 9.50 (*0-912148-10-1*) Argo Bks.

— Circulation of Thought - 1949, Vol. 1. (Eugen Rosenstock-Huessy Lectures). 114p. Date not set. audio, pap. 45.00 (*0-614-05347-1*); pap. 25.00 (*0-912148-20-9*); audio 30.00 (*0-614-05346-3*) Argo Bks.

— Circulation of Thought - 1954, Vol. 9. (Eugen Rosenstock-Huessy Lectures). 570p. Date not set. audio, pap. 215.00 (*0-614-05363-3*); pap. 125.00 (*0-912148-28-4*); audio 125.00 (*0-614-05362-5*) Argo Bks.

— Circulation of Thought - 1956, Vol. 15. (Eugen Rosenstock-Huessy Lectures). 21p. Date not set. audio, pap. 10.00 (*0-614-05376-5*); pap. 7.50 (*0-912148-34-9*); audio 5.00 (*0-614-05375-7*) Argo Bks.

— Comparative Religion - 1954, Vol. 8. (Eugen Rosenstock-Huessy Lectures). 638p. Date not set. audio, pap. 200.00 (*0-614-05361-7*); pap. 125.00 (*0-912148-27-6*); audio 125.00 (*0-614-05360-9*) Argo Bks.

— Cross of Reality - 1953, Vol. 5. (Eugen Rosenstock-Huessy Lectures). 520p. Date not set. audio, pap. 195.00 (*0-614-05355-2*); pap. 125.00 (*0-912148-24-1*); audio 120.00 (*0-614-05354-4*) Argo Bks.

— Cross of Reality - 1965, Vol. 28. (Eugen Rosenstock-Huessy Lectures). 10p. Date not set. audio, pap. 10.00 (*0-614-05402-8*); pap. 7.50 (*0-912148-47-0*); audio 5.00 (*0-614-05401-X*) Argo Bks.

— Cruciform Character - 1967, Vol. 31. (Eugen Rosenstock-Huessy Lectures). 65p. Date not set. audio, pap. 35.00 (*0-614-05408-7*); pap. 15.00 (*0-912148-50-0*); audio 25.00 (*0-614-05407-9*) Argo Bks.

— Economy of Times - 1965, Vol. 26. (Eugen Rosenstock-Huessy Lectures). 79p. Date not set. audio, pap. 40.00 (*0-614-05398-6*); pap. 20.00 (*0-912148-45-4*); audio 25.00 (*0-614-05397-8*) Argo Bks.

— Fashions of Atheism - 1968, Vol. 33. (Eugen Rosenstock-Huessy Lectures). 20p. Date not set. audio, pap. 10.00 (*0-614-05412-5*); pap. 7.50 (*0-912148-52-7*); audio 5.00 (*0-614-05411-7*) Argo Bks.

— Four Disangelists - 1954, Vol. 10. (Eugen Rosenstock-Huessy Lectures). 23p. Date not set. pap. 7.50 (*0-912148-29-2*); audio, pap. 22.50 (*0-614-05366-8*); audio 15.00 (*0-614-05365-X*) Argo Bks.

R

An Asterisk (*) at the beginning of an entry indicates that the title is appearing in BIP for the first time.

— Grammatical Method - 1962, Vol. 24. (Eugen Rosenstock-Huessy Lectures). 51p. Date not set. audio, pap. 25.00 (0-614-05394-3); pap. 15.00 (0-912148-43-8); audio 15.00 (0-614-05393-5) Argo Bks.
— Greek Philosophy - 1956, Vol. 16. (Eugen Rosenstock-Huessy Lectures). 664p. Date not set. audio, pap. 220.00 (0-614-05378-1); pap. 125.00 (0-912148-35-7); audio 150.00 (0-614-05377-3) Argo Bks.
— Hinge of Generations - 1953, Vol. 6. (Eugen Rosenstock-Huessy Lectures). 201p. Date not set. audio, pap. 90.00 (0-614-05357-9); pap. 45.00 (0-912148-25-X); audio 70.00 (0-614-05356-0) Argo Bks.
— Historiography - 1959, Vol. 20. (Eugen Rosenstock-Huessy Lectures). 581p. Date not set. audio, pap. 210.00 (0-614-05386-2); pap. 125.00 (0-912148-39-X); audio 135.00 (0-614-05385-4) Argo Bks.
— History Must Be Told - 1954, Vol. 11. (Eugen Rosenstock-Huessy Lectures). 14p. Date not set. audio, pap. 15.00 (0-614-05368-4); pap. 7.50 (0-912148-30-6); audio 7.00 (0-614-05367-6) Argo Bks.
— History Must Be Told - 1955, Vol. 13. (Eugen Rosenstock-Huessy Lectures). 14p. Date not set. audio, pap. 10.00 (0-614-05372-2); pap. 7.50 (0-912148-32-2); audio 5.00 (0-614-05371-4) Argo Bks.
— I Am an Impure Thinker. LC 77-103630. 206p. 1970. 9.50 (0-912148-03-9) Argo Bks.
— Liberal Arts College - 1960, Vol. 22. (Eugen Rosenstock-Huessy Lectures). 26p. Date not set. audio, pap. 20.00 (0-614-05390-0); pap. 10.00 (0-912148-41-1); audio 10.00 (0-614-05389-7) Argo Bks.
— Life Lines: Quotations from the Work of Eugen Rosenstock-Huessy. Gardner, Clinton C., ed. LC 88-19392. 1988. pap. 5.95 (0-912148-16-0) Argo Bks.
— Lingo of Linguistics - 1966, Vol. 29. (Eugen Rosenstock-Huessy Lectures). 63p. Date not set. audio, pap. 25.00 (0-614-05404-4); pap. 15.00 (0-912148-48-9); audio 15.00 (0-614-05403-6) Argo Bks.
— Make Bold to Be Ashamed, Vol. 7. (Eugen Rosenstock-Huessy Lectures). 37p. Date not set. audio, pap. 20.00 (0-614-05359-5); pap. 10.00 (0-912148-26-8); audio 14.00 (0-614-05358-7) Argo Bks.
— Man Must Teach - 1959, Vol. 21. (Eugen Rosenstock-Huessy Lectures). 20p. Date not set. audio, pap. 10.00 (0-614-05388-9); pap. 7.50 (0-912148-40-3); audio 5.00 (0-614-05387-0) Argo Bks.
— Multiformity of Man. 1973. pap. 5.00 (0-912148-06-3) Argo Bks.
— Origin of Speech. LC 81-20527. 1981. pap. 9.50 (0-912148-13-6) Argo Bks.
— Out of Revolution: Autobiography of Western Man. LC 93-24321. 820p. 1993. 79.95 (0-85496-400-2); pap. 34.95 (0-85496-390-1) Berg Pubs.
— Peace Corps - 1966, Vol. 30. (Eugen Rosenstock-Huessy Lectures). 40p. Date not set. audio, pap. 22.50 (0-614-05406-0); pap. 12.50 (0-912148-49-7); audio 15.00 (0-614-05405-2) Argo Bks.
— Planetary Service. Huessy, Mark & Von Moltke, Freya, trs. LC 78-68422. 1978. pap. 8.00 (0-912148-09-8) Argo Bks.
— Potential Teachers - 1952, Vol. 4. (Eugen Rosenstock-Huessy Lectures). 34p. Date not set. audio, pap. 20.00 (0-614-05353-6); pap. 10.00 (0-912148-23-3); audio 10.00 (0-614-05352-8) Argo Bks.
— Practical Knowledge of the Soul. Gardner, Clinton C., ed. Huessy, Mark & Von Moltke, Freya, trs. 66p. 1988. pap. 5.00 (0-912148-00-4) Argo Bks.
— Rosenstock-Huessy Papers, Vol. 1. 1981. pap. 25.00 (0-912148-15-2) Argo Bks.
— St. Augustine - 1962, Vol. 25. (Eugen Rosenstock-Huessy Lectures). 149p. Date not set. audio, pap. 60.00 (0-614-05396-X); pap. 30.00 (0-912148-44-6); audio 45.00 (0-614-05395-1) Argo Bks.
— Speech & Reality. LC 72-103629. 1970. 9.50 (0-912148-01-2); pap. 15.00 (0-912148-02-0) Argo Bks.
— Talk with Franciscans - 1965, Vol. 27. (Eugen Rosenstock-Huessy Lectures). 36p. Date not set. audio, pap. 20.00 (0-614-05400-1); pap. 10.00 (0-912148-46-2); audio 10.00 (0-614-05399-4) Argo Bks.
— Universal History - 1949, Vol. 2. (Eugen Rosenstock-Huessy Lectures). 141p. Date not set. audio, pap. 60.00 (0-614-05349-8); pap. 35.00 (0-912148-21-7); audio 35.00 (0-614-05348-X) Argo Bks.
— Universal History - 1951, Vol. 3. (Eugen Rosenstock-Huessy Lectures). 22p. Date not set. audio, pap. 10.00 (0-614-05351-X); pap. 7.50 (0-912148-22-5); audio 5.00 (0-614-05350-1) Argo Bks.
— Universal History - 1954, Vol. 12. (Eugen Rosenstock-Huessy Lectures). 540p. Date not set. audio, pap. 200.00 (0-614-05370-6); pap. 125.00 (0-912148-31-4); audio 130.00 (0-614-05369-2) Argo Bks.
— Universal History - 1955, Vol. 14. (Eugen Rosenstock-Huessy Lectures). 91p. Date not set. audio, pap. 35.00 (0-614-05374-9); pap. 20.00 (0-912148-33-0); audio 20.00 (0-614-05373-0) Argo Bks.
— Universal History - 1956, Vol. 17. (Eugen Rosenstock-Huessy Lectures). 218p. Date not set. audio, pap. 80.00 (0-614-05380-3); pap. 45.00 (0-912148-36-5); audio 55.00 (0-614-05379-X) Argo Bks.
— Universal History - 1957, Vol. 18. (Eugen Rosenstock-Huessy Lectures). 595p. Date not set. audio, pap. 220.00 (0-614-05382-X); pap. 130.00 (0-912148-37-3); audio 145.00 (0-614-05381-1) Argo Bks.
— Universal History - 1967, Vol. 32. (Eugen Rosenstock-Huessy Lectures). 396p. Date not set. audio, pap. 155.00 (0-614-05410-9); pap. 90.00 (0-912148-51-9); audio 100.00 (0-614-05409-5) Argo Bks.
— The University - 1968, Vol. 34. (Eugen Rosenstock-Huessy Lectures). 8p. Date not set. audio, pap. 10.00 (0-614-05414-1); pap. 7.50 (0-912148-53-5); audio 5.00 (0-614-05413-3) Argo Bks.
— What Future Professions - 1960, Vol. 23. (Eugen Rosenstock-Huessy Lectures). 93p. Date not set. audio, pap. 40.00 (0-614-05392-7); pap. 20.00 (0-912148-42-X); audio 25.00 (0-614-05391-9) Argo Bks.

Rosenstock-Huessy, Eugen, ed. Judaism Despite Christianity. 81p. 1969. pap. 9.00 (0-8052-0315-X) Argo Bks.
Rosenstock-Huessy, Eugen & Battles, Ford L. Magna Carta Latina: The Privilege of Singing, Articulating & Reading a Language & Keeping It Alive. 2nd ed. LC 75-23378. (Pittsburgh Reprint Ser.: No. 1). 296p. reprint ed. pap. text ed. 10.00 (0-915138-07-7) Argo Bks.
Rosenstock, Janet, jt. auth. see Adair, Dennis.
Rosenstock, Judith D. & Rosenstock, Harvey A. Your Hospital Stay...It'll Be Okay. 36p. (Orig.). (J). (gr. 1-5). 1988. pap. 4.95 (0-9622172-0-4) D Miller Fndtn.
Rosenstock, Laura. Christopher Wilmarth. (Illus.). 48p. (Orig.). 1989. pap. 9.95 (0-87070-644-6, 0-8109-6084-2) Mus of Modern Art.
Rosenstock, Laura, ed. see Krauss, Rosalind E., et al.
Rosenstock, Linda & Cullen, Mark R. Textbook of Clinical Occupational & Environmental Medicine. LC 93-8640. (Illus.). 944p. 1994. text ed. 127.00 (0-7216-3482-6) Saunders.
Rosenstock, Morton. Louis Marshall: Defender of Jewish Rights. LC 65-19608. 335p. reprint ed. pap. 95.50 (0-7837-3680-0, 2043554) Bks Demand.
Rosenstock, Norman. Tales of an Ancient Modeler. (Illus.). 181p. 1990. pap. 14.95 (0-934575-10-X) Vip Pubs.
Rosenstone, Robert A. Mirror in the Shrine: American Encounters with Meiji Japan. LC 87-31053. (Illus.). 336p. 1988. text ed. 34.50 (0-674-57641-1) HUP.
— Mirror in the Shrine: American Encounters with Meiji Japan. 336p. 1991. pap. 15.95 (0-674-57642-X, ROSMIX) HUP.
— Revisioning History: Film & the Construction of the Past. 1994. pap. 14.95 (0-691-02534-7) Princeton U Pr.
— Romantic Revolutionary: A Biography of John Reed. 464p. 1990. pap. text ed. 12.95 (0-674-77938-X) HUP.
— Visions of the Past: The Challenge of Film to Our Idea of History. LC 95-6720. 288p. (C). 1995. text ed. 35.00 (0-674-94097-0); pap. text ed. 16.95 (0-674-94098-9) HUP.
Rosenstone, Robert A., ed. Revisioning History: Film & the Construction of the Past. LC 94-19563. (Studies in Culture - Power - History). 1994. pap. text ed. 49.50 (0-691-08629-X) Princeton U Pr.
Rosenstone, Steven J. & Hansen, John M. Mobilization, Participation, & Democracy in America. LC 92-34552. (New Topics in Politics Ser.). (Illus.). 352p. (Orig.). (C). 1993. pap. write for info. (0-02-403660-9) Macmillan.
Rosenstone, Steven J., jt. auth. see Wolfinger, Raymond E.
Rosenstone, Steven J., et al. Third Parties in America. LC 83-43091. 266p. 1984. pap. 15.95 (0-691-02225-9) Princeton U Pr.
Rosensweig, Jim, et al. Frank & Earnest Manager. Crisp, Michael G., ed. LC 90-83480. (Illus.). 125p. (Orig.). 1991. pap. 10.95 (1-56052-077-9) Crisp Pubns.
Rosensweig, Linda & Prevention Magazine Editors. New Vegetarian Cuisine: Two Hundred & Fifty Satisfying Recipes for Superior Health. LC 93-17792. 1993. 26.95 (0-87596-168-1) Rodale Pr Inc.
Rosensweig, Roy. Park & the People. 1994. pap. 19.95 (0-8050-3242-8) H Holt & Co.
Rosentahl, A., et al. Deutsch-Finnisches Schulworterbuch. 673p. (FIN & GER.). 1976. 39.95 (0-8288-5577-3, M9637) Fr & Eur.
Rosental, I. L., jt. auth. see Nikitin, Yu. P.
Rosenteur, P. I., jt. auth. see Haddad, H. M.
Rosenthal. How Cooking Works. 1981. 19.95 (0-02-605090-0) Macmillan.
Rosenthal & Rocchini. Clinical Pediatric Cardiology. 576p. 1994. 80.00 (0-8016-7678-9) Mosby Yr Bk.
Rosenthal, jt. auth. see Shaw.
Rosenthal, A. M., jt. ed. see Gelb, Arthur.
Rosenthal, Abby. Ardor's Hut. 64p. (Orig.). 1990. 15.00 (0-934184-22-4); pap. 7.00 (0-934184-21-6) Alembic Pr.
Rosenthal, Abigail L. Conversions: A Philosophical Memoir. LC 93-44719. 240p. (C). 1994. text ed. 44.95 (1-56639-219-5) Temple U Pr.
— Conversions: A Philosophical Memoir. LC 93-44719. 240p. (C). 1994. pap. 19.95 (1-56639-220-9) Temple U Pr.
Rosenthal, Alan. The Documentary Conscience: A Casebook in Film-Making. LC 79-64487. (Illus.). 1980. pap. 14.00 (0-520-04022-8) U CA Pr.
— Governors & Legislatures: Contending Powers. 223p. 1990. 22.95 (0-87187-545-4) Congr Quarterly.
— Impurely Academic. LC 79-65226. 88p. 1979. pap. text ed. 15.95 (0-87855-745-8) Transaction Pubs.
— Legislative Performance in the States: Explorations of Committee Behavior. LC 73-10576. 1974. text ed. 14.95 (0-02-927300-5) Free Pr.
— The Third House: Lobbyists & Lobbying in the States. LC 92-28705. 1992. 33.95 (0-87187-671-X); pap. 19.95 (0-87187-672-8) Congr Quarterly.
— Writing, Directing, & Producing Documentary Films. 416p. (C). 1990. 39.95 (0-8093-1636-6); pap. 24.95 (0-8093-1637-4) S Ill U Pr.
— Writing Docudrama: Dramatizing Reality for Film & TV. 224p. 1994. pap. 24.95 (0-240-80195-4, Focal) Buttrwrth-Heinemann.
Rosenthal, Alan, ed. New Challenges to Documentary. 1987. 58.00 (0-520-05725-2); pap. 22.50 (0-520-05724-4) U CA Pr.
Rosenthal, Alan & Fuhrman, Susan. Legislative Education Leadership in the States. 118p. 1981. lib. bdg. 14.00 (0-318-03013-6); pap. 8.00 (0-318-03014-4) Inst Educ Lead.
Rosenthal, Alan & Katz, Illana. Show Me Where It Hurts! Chiropractic Care. (J). (ps-3). 1993. pap. 9.95 (1-882388-10-0) Real Life Strybks.
Rosenthal, Alan, jt. ed. see Fuhrman, Susan.
Rosenthal, Alan, jt. ed. see Huwa, Randy.
Rosenthal, Alan, et al. Objectif France: Introduction to French & the Francophone World. LC 92-33450. (ENG & FRE.). 1993. text ed. 48.95 (0-8384-3736-2) Heinle & Heinle.
Rosenthal, Alan D., jt. auth. see Katz, Illana.
Rosenthal, Albert H. The Social Programs in Sweden: A Search for Security in a Free Society. LC 67-27098. 213p. reprint ed. pap. 60.80 (0-317-29497-0, 2055906) Bks Demand.
Rosenthal, Albi, ed. & intro. Mozart's "Thematic Catalogue" 2nd ed. (Illus.). 160p. 1990. 44.95 (0-8014-2545-X) Cornell U Pr.
Rosenthal, Allen M. Your Mind the Magician. LC 90-82481. (Illus.). 143p. (Orig.). 1991. pap. 10.95 (0-87516-619-9) DeVorss.
Rosenthal, Barbara. Clues to Myself. (Illus.). 48p. 1981. pap. 15.00 (0-89822-015-7) Visual Studies.
— Homo Futurus. (Artist's Bks.). (Illus.). 88p. (Orig.). 1986. pap. 8.95 (0-89822-046-7) Visual Studies.
— Sensations. (Illus.). 48p. 1984. pap. 8.95 (0-89822-022-X) Visual Studies.
Rosenthal, Ben J. To Life! To Life! abr. ed. 250p. 1995. pap. 8.95 (1-56901-203-2) NW Pub.
Rosenthal, Bernard. City of Nature: Journeys to Nature in the Age of American Romanticism. LC 78-68879. 280p. 1980. 38.50 (0-87413-147-2) U Delaware Pr.
— Salem Story: Reading the Witch Trials of 1692. (Studies in American Literature & Culture: No. 73). 297p. (C). 1993. 49.95 (0-521-44061-0) Cambridge U Pr.
— Salem Story: Reading the Witch Trials of 1692. (Studies In American Literature & Culture: No. 73). 288p. (C). 1995. pap. write for info. (0-521-55820-4) Cambridge U Pr.
Rosenthal, Bernard & Szarmach, Paul E., eds. Medievalism in American Culture. (Medieval & Renaissance Texts & Studies: Vol. 55). (Illus.). 320p. 1989. 21.00 (0-86698-039-3) MRTS.
Rosenthal, Bernice G., ed. Nietzsche & Soviet Culture: Ally & Adversary. LC 93-29255. (Cambridge Studies in Russian Literature). (Illus.). 417p. (C). 1994. 59.95 (0-521-45281-3) Cambridge U Pr.
— Nietzsche in Russia. (Illus.). 440p. 1986. text ed. 70.00 (0-691-06695-7); pap. text ed. 25.00 (0-691-10209-0) Princeton U Pr.
Rosenthal, Bernice G. & Bohachevsky-Chomiak, Martha, eds. A Revolution of the Spirit: Crisis of Value in Russia, 1890-1924. 2nd ed. LC 90-81779. 350p. 1990. reprint ed. 35.00 (0-8232-1285-8); reprint ed. pap. 19.95 (0-8232-1286-6) Fordham.
Rosenthal, Bert. Basketball. LC 82-19745. (New True Bks.). (Illus.). 48p. (J). (gr. k-4). 1983. lib. bdg. 12.90 (0-516-01674-1); pap. 4.95 (0-516-41674-X) Childrens.
— Basketball. (New True Bks.). 48p. (J). (gr. k-4). 1995. lib. bdg. 18.00 (0-516-01080-8) Childrens.
— Dwight Gooden: King of the Ks. LC 85-11687. (Sports Stars Ser.). (Illus.). 48p. (J). (gr. 2-8). 1985. pap. 3.95 (0-516-44348-8) Childrens.
— Soccer. LC 82-19753. (New True Bks.). (Illus.). 48p. (J). (gr. k-4). 1983. lib. bdg. 12.90 (0-516-01658-X); pap. 4.95 (0-516-41658-8) Childrens.
— Soccer. rev. ed. (New True Bks.). 48p. (J). (gr. k-4). 1995. lib. bdg. 18.00 (0-516-01084-0) Childrens.
***Rosenthal, Beth E.** Meltdown! Diet & Cookbook: Burn Fat 24 Hours a Day, Even While You Sleep. Bradley, Margaret, ed. (Illus.). 134p. (Orig.). 1994. pap. text ed. 9.95 (1-885676-01-8) Meltdown Intl.
Rosenthal, Beth E., jt. auth. see Naxon, Jan L.
***Rosenthal, Bianca, ed.** Pathways to Paul Celan: A History of Critical Responses as a Chorus of Discordant Voices. LC 94-23691. (Studies in Modern German Literature: Vol. 73). 1995. write for info. (0-8204-2695-4) P Lang Pubs.
Rosenthal, Bob. Rude Awakenings. LC 81-21943. 1981. pap. 3.50 (0-916328-16-3) Yellow Pr.
Rosenthal, Burt. Track & Field. LC 93-23281. (How to Play the All-Star Way Ser.). (J). 1993. lib. bdg. 22.13 (0-8114-5778-8) Raintree Steck-V.
Rosenthal, C. J. & Rotman, M., eds. Clinical Applications of Continuous Infusion Chemotherapy & Concomitant Radiation Therapy. LC 86-4890. 262p. 1986. 75.00 (0-306-42260-3, Plenum Pr) Plenum.
Rosenthal, C. Julian, ed. Neoplastic Diseases. LC 91-62100. 675p. 1991. 129.00 (0-944496-24-5) Precept Pr.
Rosenthal, Carolyn J. & Hendricks, Jon, eds. The Remainder of Their Days: Domestic Policy & Older Families in the United States & Canada. LC 92-44317. 248p. 1993. 36.00 (0-8153-0483-8, SS795) Garland.
Rosenthal, Charles L. The Art World at Your Fingertips: For Artists, Students, Art Dealers & Their Patrons & Essential for Those Interested in the Visual Arts. (Illus.). 100p. 1991. text ed. 17.50 (0-9629041-1-2); pap. 8.95 (0-9629041-0-4); spiral bd., pap. 8.95 (0-9629041-2-0) J-C Ranch Pr.
Rosenthal, Curt, tr. see Simmel, Georg.
Rosenthal, D. & Kety, Seymour S. Transmission of Schizophrenia: Proceedings 2nd Research Conference in Psychiatry 7-67. LC 69-14242. 1968. 180.00 (0-08-013018-6, Pub. by Pergamon Repr UK) Franklin.
Rosenthal, D., jt. auth. see Davenport, W.
Rosenthal, Daniel. How Gold Dealers Legally Defraud You - While the Industry Tries to Cover It Up. 52p. 1988. pap. text ed. 29.00 (0-938689-06-1) Inst Preserv Wealth.
— Insider's Guide to Buying Silver & Gold: How Gold Dealers Lie, Cheat, & Rip You Off - All Within the Letter of the Law. 229p. 1988. pap. text ed. 78.00 (0-938689-08-8) Inst Preserv Wealth.
— Resistance & Deformation of Solid Media. LC 72-10583. 372p. 1974. 152.00 (0-08-017100-1, Pub. by Pergamon Repr UK) Franklin.
Rosenthal, Daniel & Young, Ellen. The New Case for Silver. rev. ed. 157p. 1986. pap. text ed. 82.00 (0-9615814-1-7) Rosenthal Assocs.
— Which Three Silver & Gold Dealers Give You the Worst Prices (& Which Give You the Best!) 58p. (Orig.). 1986. pap. text ed. 59.95 (0-9615814-3-3) Rosenthal Assocs.
Rosenthal, Daniel, et al. Radiological-Pathological Conferences of the Massachusetts General Hospital. (C). 1991. disk 500.00 (1-56815-008-3) Image Premast.
Rosenthal, Daniel I., ed. see Chew, Felix S. M., et al.
Rosenthal, David, tr. see Abuli, Sanchez.
Rosenthal, David, tr. see Catala, Victor, pseud.
Rosenthal, David, tr. see Nazario.
Rosenthal, David, tr. see Segura, Antonio.
Rosenthal, David, tr. see Torres, Daniel.
Rosenthal, David, tr. see Trillo, Carlos.
Rosenthal, David A. An Inquiry Driven Vision System Based on Visual & Conceptual Hierarchies. LC 81-7616. (Computer Science: Artificial Intelligence Ser.: No. 7). (Illus.). 210p. reprint ed. pap. 59.90 (0-685-20833-8, 2070049) Bks Demand.
Rosenthal, David H. Hard Bop: Jazz & Black Music, 1955-1965. 224p. 1992. 23.00 (0-19-505869-0) OUP.
— Hard Bop: Jazz & Black Music 1955-1965. 224p. 1993. reprint ed. pap. 9.95 (0-19-508556-6) OUP.
— The Journey: Poems. LC 92-20333. 1992. 9.95 (0-89255-181-X) Persea Bks.
— Loves of the Poets: Poems. 86p. 1989. 17.95 (0-89255-139-9); pap. 9.95 (0-89255-132-1) Persea Bks.
— Postwar Catalan Poetry. LC 89-43048. (Illus.). 128p. 1991. 29.50 (0-8387-5178-4) Bucknell U Pr.
Rosenthal, David H., ed. Modern Catalan Poetry. 1979. pap. 6.00 (0-89823-000-4) New Rivers Pr.
Rosenthal, David H., tr. Four Postwar Catalan Poets. LC 78-67773. (Cross Cultural Review Ser.: No. 1). (Illus.). (CAT & ENG.). 1978. 15.00 (0-89304-600-0, CCC14); pap. 5.00 (0-89304-601-9) Cross-Cultrl NY.
Rosenthal, David H., tr. & intro. When I Sleep, Then I See Clearly: Selected Poems of J. V. Foix. (Illus.). 1988. pap. 12.95 (0-89255-130-5) Persea Bks.
Rosenthal, David H., tr. see Abuli, Sanchez.
Rosenthal, David H., tr. see Estelles, Vicent A.
Rosenthal, David H., tr. see Rodereda, Merce.
Rosenthal, David H., tr. see Rodoreda, Merce.
Rosenthal, David K. The Complete Guide to Racetrack Betting. 160p. (Orig.). 1986. pap. 9.95 (0-89709-144-2) Liberty Pub.
Rosenthal, David M., ed. & intro. Materialism & the Mind-Body Problem. LC 87-23794. 249p. (C). 1987. reprint ed. lib. bdg. 29.95 (0-87220-024-8); reprint ed. pap. text ed. 8.95 (0-87220-023-X) Hackett Pub.
Rosenthal, David M., ed. The Nature of Mind. 656p. (C). 1991. 55.00 (0-19-504670-6); pap. text ed. 22.00 (0-19-504671-4) OUP.
Rosenthal, David M. & Shehadi, Fadlou, eds. Applied Ethics & Ethical Theory. LC 88-14304. (Ethics in a Changing World Ser.: Vol. 1). 320p. 1988. 30.00 (0-87480-289-X) U of Utah Pr.
Rosenthal, David W. Introduction to Marketing. 1990. pap. text ed. 8.95 (0-07-053884-0) McGraw.
Rosenthal, Debra. At the Heart of the Bomb. 1991. pap. 9.57 (0-201-56752-0) Addison-Wesley.
***Rosenthal, Dennis.** Guide to Consumer Credit & Hire Law. 304p. 1994. pap. text ed. 64.00 (0-406-01310-1, UK) Butterworth Legal Pubs.
Rosenthal, Donald. British Watercolors from the West Foundation. Morris, Kelly & Woods, Amanda, eds. (Illus.). 56p. 1988. pap. 10.00 (0-939802-47-3) High Mus Art.
Rosenthal, Donald, et al. Selected Works in the High Museum. LC 87-80790. (Illus.). 86p. (Orig.). 1987. 25.00 (0-685-18200-2); pap. 15.00 (0-939802-43-0) High Mus Art.
Rosenthal, Donald A. La Grande Maniere: Religious & Historical Painting in France, 1700-1800. (Illus.). 200p. 1987. pap. 24.95 (0-295-96475-8) U of Wash Pr.
Rosenthal, Donald B. Urban Housing & Neighborhood Revitalization: Turning a Federal Program into Local Projects. LC 87-32259. (Contributions in Political Science Ser.: No. 208). 238p. 1988. text ed. 59.95 (0-313-26148-2, RND/, Greenwood Pr) Greenwood.
Rosenthal, Donna M., jt. auth. see Epstein, Charles J.
Rosenthal, Donne, jt. ed. see Nadel, Lynn.
Rosenthal, Doreen A., jt. auth. see Moore, Susan M.
Rosenthal, Dorothy L. Cytology of the Central Nervous System. (Monographs in Clinical Cytology: Vol. 8). (Illus.). x, 206p. 1984. 78.50 (3-8055-3808-1) S Karger.
— Cytopathology of Pulmonary Disease. (Monographs in Clinical Cytology: Vol. 11). (Illus.). x, 238p. 1988. 107.25 (3-8055-4740-4) S Karger.
Rosenthal, Douglas E. Lawyer & Client: Who's in Charge. LC 73-83891. 230p. 1974. 29.95 (0-87154-725-2) Russell Sage.
Rosenthal, Earl. The Palace of Charles V in Granada. LC 85-3366. (Illus.). 508p. 1985. text ed. 99.50 (0-691-04034-6) Princeton U Pr.
Rosenthal, Ed. Closet Cultivator. 1991. pap. 16.95 (0-86719-359-X) Last Gasp.
— Marijuana Growers Handbook: Indoor - Greenhouse Edition. (Illus.). 250p. (Orig.). 1989. reprint ed. pap. 19.95 (0-932551-00-9); reprint ed. Spiral bdg. spiral bd. 23.95 (0-932551-02-5) Quick Am Pub.
— Marijuana Growing Tips. (Illus.). 140p. reprint ed. pap. 12.95 (0-932551-05-X) Quick Am Pub.
— Marijuana Question? Ask Ed. (Illus.). 300p. (Orig.). reprint ed. 19.95 (0-932551-01-7) Quick Am Pub.

R

— Marijuana, the Law & You: A Guide to Minimizing Consequences. 1995. pap. 17.95 (0-932551-18-1) Quick Am Pub.

Rosenthal, Ed, ed. Hemp Today. (Illus.). (Orig.). 1994. pap. 19.95 (0-932551-14-9) Quick Am Pub.

Rosenthal, Ed, jt. auth. see Frank, Mel.

Rosenthal, Ed, ed. see Gold, D. & Green, Bud.

Rosenthal, Ed, ed. see Gold, Dave.

Rosenthal, Edwin I., ed. Averroe's Commentary on Plato's Republic. (University of Cambridge Oriental Publications: No. 1). 1966. 74.95 (0-521-06130-X) Cambridge U Pr.

Rosenthal, Ellie. What Can I Do? Asked the Kangaroo. (J). 1993. 7.95 (0-533-10358-4) Vantage.

— Why, Oh, Why Do You Laugh At Me? (J). 1994. 7.95 (0-533-10765-2) Vantage.

Rosenthal, Eric. Civilians at Risk: Military & Police Abuses in the Mexican Countryside. (North America Project Special Report Ser.). 37p. 1993. 5.00 (0-911646-58-2) World Policy.

Rosenthal, Erik. The Calculus of Murder. large type ed. 416p. 1988. 15.95 (0-7089-1887-5) Ulverscroft.

Rosenthal, Erwin I. Political Thought in Medieval Islam: An Introductory Outline. LC 85-21909. ix, 345p. 1985. reprint ed. text ed. 55.50 (0-313-25094-4, ROPTH, Greenwood Pr) Greenwood.

— Studia Semitica, 2 vols. Incl. Vol. 1. Jewish Themes. 1971. 64.95 (0-521-07958-6); Vol. 2. Islamic Themes. 1971. 54.95 (0-521-07959-4); (University of Cambridge Oriental Publications: Nos. 16 & 17). 1971. write for info. (0-318-51296-3) Cambridge U Pr.

Rosenthal, Erwin I. & Katz, Steven, eds. Saadya Studies: In Commemoration of the One Thousandth Anniversary of the Death of R. Saadya Gaon. LC 79-7170. (Jewish Philosophy, Mysticism & History of Ideas Ser.). 1980. reprint ed. lib. bdg. 28.95 (0-405-12284-5) Ayer.

Rosenthal, Evelyn. Woman Aging & Ageism. 1990. pap. 12. 95 (0-918393-73-6) Harrington Pk.

— Women, Aging & Ageism. LC 90-4644. (Journal of Women & Aging: Vol. 2, No. 2). 161p. 1990. text ed. 29.95 (0-86656-984-7) Haworth Pr.

Rosenthal, F., jt. auth. see Brann, M.

Rosenthal, Franz. Ahmad B. at-Tayyib as-Sarahsi. (American Oriental Ser.: Vol. 26). 1943. pap. 5.00 (0-940490-26-9) Am Orient Soc.

— Greek Philosophy in the Arab World: A Collection of Essays. 300p. 1990. text ed. 82.50 (0-86078-271-9, Pub. by Variorum UK) Ashgate Pub Co.

— Muslim Intellectual & Social History: A Collection of Essays. (Collected Studies: No. CS309). 336p. 1990. text ed. 89.95 (0-86078-257-3, Pub. by Variorum UK) Ashgate Pub Co.

— Science & Medicine in Islam: A Collection of Essays. (Collected Studies: No. 330). 250p. 1991. text ed. 79.95 (0-86078-282-4, Pub. by Variorum UK) Ashgate Pub Co.

Rosenthal, Franz, ed. & tr. The History of al-Tabari, Vol. 38: The Return of the Caliphate to Baghdad: The Caliphate of al-Muctadid al-Muktafi & al-Mugtzdir, A.D. 892-915 - A.H. 279-302. LC 83-18115. (SUNY Series in Near Eastern Studies). 239p. 1985. 44.50 (0-87395-876-4); pap. 16.95 (0-7914-0626-1) State U NY Pr.

Rosenthal, Franz, tr. The History of al-Tabari, Vol. 1: General Introduction & from the Creation to the Flood. LC 87-33532. (SUNY Series in Near Eastern Studies). 413p. 1989. 64.50 (0-88706-562-7); pap. 24.95 (0-88706-563-5) State U NY Pr.

Rosenthal, Franz, tr. see Khaldun, Ibn.

Rosenthal, Gary. Soccer: The Game & How to Play It. rev. ed. LC 72-129116. (Illus.). 256p. (J). (gr. 3-9). 1978. lib. bdg. 14.95 (0-87460-258-0) Lion Bks.

— Soccer Skills & Drills. (Illus.). 224p. (gr. 7 up). 1984. pap. 14.00 (0-684-18217-3, Scribners) S&S Trade.

— Soccer Skills & Drills. rev. ed. LC 93-32462. 288p. 1994. pap. 14.00 (0-02-036435-0, Collier S&S) S&S Trade.

— Volleyball: The Game & How to Play It. (Illus.). 256p. 1983. pap. 11.00 (0-684-17908-3, Scribners) S&S Trade.

Rosenthal, Gerald A. & Berenbaum, May R., eds. Herbivores: Their Interactions with Secondary Plant Metabolites Vol. 1: The Chemical Participants. 2nd ed. (Illus.). 468p. 1991. text ed. 120.00 (0-12-597183-4) Acad Pr.

— Herbivores: Their Interactions with Secondary Plant Metabolites Vol. 2: Ecological & Evolutionary Processes. 2nd ed. (Illus.). 493p. 1992. text ed. 99.00 (0-12-597184-2) Acad Pr.

Rosenthal, Gert. Erhaltung & Regeneration von Feuchtwiesen: Vegetationsoekologische Untersuchungen auf Dauerflaechen, 1992. (Dissertationes Botanicae Ser.: Vol. 182). (Illus.). 284p. (GER.). 1992. pap. 84.00 (3-443-64094-X, Pub. by Cramer-Borntraeger GW) Lubrecht & Cramer.

Rosenthal, Gertrude. From El Greco to Pollock: Early & Late Works by European & American Artists. LC 68-58201. (Illus.). 1968. pap. 12.00 (0-912298-05-7) Baltimore Mus.

Rosenthal, Gertrude, ed. Italian Paintings, XIV-XVIIIth Centuries from the Collection of the Baltimore Museum of Art. LC 80-66714. 1981. pap. 19.98 (0-912298-51-0) Baltimore Mus.

Rosenthal, Gilbert S. Contemporary Judaism: Patterns of Survival. 2nd ed. 423p. 1986. 43.95 (0-89885-260-9); pap. 22.95 (0-89885-277-3) Human Sci Pr.

— The Many Faces of Judaism: Orthodox, Conservative, Reconstructionist, & Reform. Rossel, Seymour, ed. LC 78-25898. (YA). (gr. 9-10). 1979. pap. 6.95 (0-87441-311-7) Behrman.

Rosenthal, Gilbert S., ed. Maimonides: His Wisdom for Our Time. large type ed. (Large Print Jewish Classics Ser.). 1991. pap. 9.95 (0-8027-2646-1) Walker & Co.

Rosenthal, Gilbert S., jt. auth. see Ben-Aharon, Moshe.

Rosenthal, Gilbert S., jt. auth. see Singer, Ellen.

Rosenthal, Glenda & Zupnick, Elliot, eds. Contemporary Western Europe: Problems & Responses. LC 84-6835. 512p. 1984. text ed. 55.00 (0-275-91255-8, C1255, Praeger Pubs) Greenwood.

Rosenthal, Glenda G., jt. ed. see Cafruny, Alan W.

Rosenthal, Gloria, jt. auth. see Salamon, Michael J.

Rosenthal, Gottfried E. Literatur der Technologie. (Documenta Technica Ser.: No. 11). 420p. 1972. reprint ed. write for info. (3-487-04206-1, Pub. by Georg Olms GW) Lubrecht & Cramer.

Rosenthal, H. D. Their Day in Court: A History of the Indian Claims Commission. LC 90-3688. (Distinguished Studies in American Legal & Constitutional History: Vol. 21). 310p. 1990. reprint ed. 70.00 (0-8240-0028-5) Garland.

Rosenthal, H. P. Projections onto Translation-Invariant Subspaces of Lp(G) (Memoirs Ser.: No. 1/63). 84p. 1966. pap. 16.00 (0-8218-1263-7, MEMO 1/63) Am Math.

Rosenthal, H. P., jt. ed. see Odell, E.

***Rosenthal, Harald & Wilson, J. Scott.** Bibliography on Ozone, Its Biological Effects & Technical Applications. 249p. (Orig.). (C). 1993. pap. text ed. 95.00x (0-7881-0110-2) Diane Pub.

Rosenthal, Harold D. Great Singers of Today. Farkas, Andrew, ed. LC 76-29964. (Opera Biographies Ser.). (Illus.). 1977. reprint ed. lib. bdg. 21.95 (0-405-09704-2) Ayer.

Rosenthal, Harold D., ed. Opera, 5 vols., Set. (Music Reprint Ser.). (Illus.). 1980. reprint ed. lib. bdg. 350.00 (0-306-79583-3) Da Capo.

Rosenthal, Harold D. & Warrack, John. Dictionnaire de l'Opera. 420p. (FRE.). 1974. pap. 59.95 (0-8288-6014-9, M416) Fr & Eur.

Rosenthal, Harold D. & Warrack, John, eds. The Concise Oxford Dictionary of Opera. 2nd ed. (OPR Ser.). 573p. 1986. pap. 15.95 (0-19-311321-X) OUP.

Rosenthal, Harry. German & Pole National Conflict & Modern Myth. LC 76-2402. 185p. reprint ed. pap. 52.80 (0-317-27758-8, 2015529) Bks Demand.

Rosenthal, Henry M. The Consolations of Philosophy: Hobbes's Secret; Spinoza's Way. LC 88-24927. 248p. (C). 1989. 29.95 (0-87722-610-5) Temple U Pr.

Rosenthal, Henry M. & Berson, S. Cathy, eds. Canadian Jewish Outlook Anthology. 325p. (C). 1988. pap. 5.00 (0-685-30699-2) Left Bank.

Rosenthal, Howard. Encyclopedia of Counseling Master Review & Tutorial. LC 93-2805. 520p. (Orig.). 1993. pap. text ed. 35.95 (1-55959-041-6) Accel Devel.

— Not with My Life I Don't: Preventing Your Suicide & That of Others. LC 88-70011. vi, 266p. (YA). (gr. 9 up). 1988. pap. text ed. 18.95 (0-915202-77-8) Accel Devel.

— Test Anxiety Prevention. 1994. audio 8.95x (1-55959-067-X) Accel Devel.

Rosenthal, Howard & Hollis, Joseph W. Help Yourself to Positive Mental Health. LC 94-19050. (Conduct of Life Ser.). 112p. 1994. pap. 12.95 (1-55959-069-6) Accel Devel.

Rosenthal, Howard, jt. auth. see Alesina, Alberto.

Rosenthal, I. Electromagnetic Radiations in Food Science. Yaron, B. et al, eds. LC 92-19937. (Advanced Series in Agricultural Sciences: Vol. 19). (Illus.). 184p. 1992. 100. 00 (0-387-54833-5) Spr-Verlag.

Rosenthal, Ionel. Milk & Dairy Products: Properties & Processing. (Illus.). 217p. 1991. text ed. 89.50 (0-89573-938-0) VCH Pubs.

Rosenthal, Ionel, jt. ed. see Ben-Hur, Ehud.

Rosenthal, J., ed. Arterial Hypertension: Pathogenisis, Diagnosis, & Therapy. Telger, Terry C., tr. (Illus.). 576p. 1982. 168.00 (0-387-90611-8) Spr-Verlag.

— Calcium Antagonists & Hypertension: Current Status. (Current Clinical Practice Ser.: No. 39). 254p. 1987. 103.00 (0-444-90455-7) Elsevier.

— Focus on Angiotensin-Converting Enzyme Inhibition. (Journal: Clinical Physiology & Biochemistry: Vol. 8, Suppl. 1, 1990). (Illus.). iv, 52p. 1990. pap. 16.00 (3-8055-5258-0) S Karger.

— Focus on Beta-Adrenergic Blockade: Journal: Clinical Physiology & Biochemistry, Supplement 2, 1990, Vol. 8. (Illus.). iv, 56p. 1991. pap. 17.00 (3-8055-5329-3) S Karger.

Rosenthal, J. & Franz, H. E., eds. Medical & Surgical Aspects of Renovascular Hypertension. (Contributions to Nephrology Ser.: Vol. 3). (Illus.). 200p. 1976. 51.25 (3-8055-2341-6) S Karger.

Rosenthal, J. & Stumpe, K. O., eds. Angiotensin-Converting-Enzym-Hemmer Bei Hypertonie, Teil 1 - Angiotensin Converting Inhibitors in Treatment of Hypertension, Pt. I: Schwerpunkt auf Cilazapril - Emphasis on Cilazapril. (Journal: Cardiology: Vol. 82, Suppl. 1, 1993). (Illus.). iv, 80p. 1993. pap. 32. 00 (3-8055-5764-7) S Karger.

— Angiotensin-Konversionsenzyme-Hemmer Bei Hypertonie, Teil 2 (Angiotensin Converting Inhibitors in Treatment of Hypertension, Pt. 2) Schwerpunkt auf Cilazapril (Emphasis on Cilazapril) (Journal: Cardiology: Vol. 82, Suppl. 2, 1993). (Illus.). iv, 84p. 1993. pap. 32. 00 (3-8055-5772-8) S Karger.

Rosenthal, J. & Van Zwieten, Pieter A., eds. Serotonin & Serotonin Antagonists: Journal: Clinical Physiology & Biochemistry, Vol. 8, Suppl. 3. (Illus.). iv, 128p. 1991. pap. 37.00 (3-8055-5456-7) S Karger.

Rosenthal, J., et al, eds. The Biochemistry of Hypertension. (Journal: Clinical Physiology & Biochemistry: Vol. 6, No. 3-4, 1988). (Illus.). 124p. 1988. pap. 53.75 (3-8055-4849-4) S Karger.

Rosenthal, James & Ocampo, Juan. Securitization of Credit: Inside the New Technology of Finance. 266p. 1988. text ed. 79.95 (0-471-61368-1) Wiley.

Rosenthal, James A. & Groze, Victor K. Special-Needs Adoption: A Study of Intact Families. LC 91-30278. 264p. 1992. text ed. 49.95 (0-275-93790-9, C3790, Praeger Pubs) Greenwood.

Rosenthal, Jean-Laurent. The Fruits of Revolution: Property Rights, Litigation & French Agriculture, 1700-1860. (Political Economy of Institutions & Decisions Ser.). (Illus.). 224p. (C). 1992. 59.95 (0-521-39220-9) Cambridge U Pr.

***Rosenthal, Jesse & Soroka, Mort.** Managed Vision Benefits. Brzezinski, Mary J., ed. LC 94-74488. 189p. (Orig.). 1995. pap. 35.00 (0-89154-487-9) Intl Found Employ.

Rosenthal, Jim, jt. auth. see Gwynn, Tony.

Rosenthal, Jim, jt. auth. see Haney, Lee.

Rosenthal, Jim, jt. auth. see Tom, Kiana.

Rosenthal, Joe, et al, eds. The Trainee's Companion to General Practice. LC 93-3406. 320p. 1993. text ed. 44. 95 (0-443-04703-0) Churchill.

***Rosenthal, Joel, ed.** Ethics & International Affairs: A Reader. LC 94-32277. 224p. 1995. pap. text ed. 18.95 (0-87840-578-X) Georgetown U Pr.

— Moral Education. 82p. 1992. pap. (0-87641-119-7) Carnegie Ethics & Intl Affairs.

— Moral Education, Vol. 2. 88p. 1992. pap. (0-87641-120-0) Carnegie Ethics & Intl Affairs.

— Moral Education, Vol. 3. 121p. 1993. pap. (0-318-72241-0) Carnegie Ethics & Intl Affairs.

Rosenthal, Joel & Richmond, Colin, eds. People, Politics & Community in the Later Middle Ages. 192p. 1988. text ed. 39.95 (0-312-01220-9) St Martin.

Rosenthal, Joel H. Righteous Realists: Political Realism, Responsible Power, & American Culture in the Nuclear Age. LC 90-48592. (Political Traditions in Foreign Policy Ser.). 184p. 1991. text ed. 27.50x (0-8071-1649-1) La State U Pr.

Rosenthal, Joel H., jt. ed. see Myers, Robert J.

Rosenthal, Joel T. Anglo-Saxon History: An Annotated Bibliography: 450-1066. LC 84-45279. (Studies in the Middle Ages: No. 7). vii, 178p. 1985. 39.50 (0-404-61437-X) AMS Pr.

— Late Medieval England (1377-1485) A Bibliography of Historical Scholarship, 1975-1989. LC 94-6595. 1994. boxed 45.00 (1-879288-16-8) Medieval Inst.

— Patriarchy & Families of Privilege in Fifteenth-Century England. LC 91-17228. (Middle Ages Ser.). (Illus.). 304p. (C). 1991. text ed. 38.95 (0-8122-3072-8) U of Pa Pr.

Rosenthal, Joel T., ed. Medieval Women & the Sources of Medieval History. LC 89-20296. (Illus.). 456p. 1990. 45. 00 (0-8203-1214-2); pap. 20.00 (0-8203-1226-6) U of Ga Pr.

Rosenthal, Jon K. Antique Map Price Record & Handbook for 1993, Vol. 11. (Illus.). viii, 344p. 1993. lib. bdg. 36. 00 (0-9638100-0-6) Kimmel Pubns.

— Antique Map Price Record & Handbook for 1994 Vol. 12. 360p. 1994. lib. bdg. 36.00 (0-9638100-1-4) Kimmel Pubns.

Rosenthal, Joyce, jt. auth. see Beyea, Jan.

Rosenthal, Judah, intro. Meyer Waxman Jubilee Volume. 427p. (ENG & HEB.). (C). 1967. 30.00 (0-935982-07-8, JMR-01) Spertus Coll.

Rosenthal, Judah M., intro. Perspectives in Jewish Learning, Vol. III. LC 65-27991. 56p. (Orig.). (C). 1967. pap. 3.95 (0-935982-36-1, PJL-03) Spertus Coll.

***Rosenthal, Judith W.** Teaching Science to Language Minority Students: Theory & Practice. LC 95-6554. (Bilingual Education & Bilingualism Ser.: Vol. 3). 1995. 69.00 (1-85359-273-0, Pub. by Multilingual Matters UK); pap. 24.00 (1-85359-272-2, Pub. by Multilingual Matters UK) Taylor & Francis.

Rosenthal, Karl T. Interview with Mrs. Karl (Trudie) Rosenthal: Concentration Camp Survivor Given 1976 to Rabbi Martin M. Wietz Transcribed by A. D. Warshauer, M. D. September 1979. 45p. (Orig.). 1993. pap. 15.00 (0-9630383-2-X) Pambrit.

Rosenthal, Lawrence. Exploring Careers in Accounting. rev. ed. (Careers in Depth Ser.). (Illus.). 148p. (YA). (gr. 7-12). 1993. lib. bdg. 14.95 (0-8239-1501-8); pap. 9.95 (0-8239-1721-5) Rosen Group.

Rosenthal, Leslie. Resolving Resistance in Group Psychotherapy. LC 85-19940. 230p. 1994. reprint ed. pap. 27.50 (1-56821-193-7) Aronson.

Rosenthal, Liliana H., tr. see Biller, Geraldine P.

Rosenthal, Lisa & Rowland, Susan. Academic Reading & Study Skills for International Students. (Illus.). 300p. (C). 1985. pap. text ed. 19.25 (0-13-000563-0) P-H.

Rosenthal, Lucy, ed. Great American Love Stories. 1988. 24.95 (0-316-75734-9) Little.

— The World Treasury of Love Stories. 768p. 1995. 30.00 (0-19-509361-5) OUP.

Rosenthal, Ludwig. The Final Solution to the Jewish Question: Mass-Murder or Hoax? (Illus.). 145p. (Orig.). 1984. pap. 9.95 (0-318-04673-3) Magnes Mus.

— How Was It Possible? 83p. 1971. 6.00 (0-943376-02-5) Magnes Mus.

Rosenthal, M., et al, eds. Rehabilitation of the Adult & Child with Traumatic Brain Injury. 2nd ed. LC 89-7929. 652p. (C). 1990. text ed. 82.00 (0-8036-7626-3) Davis Co.

Rosenthal, M . L. She. (American Poets Continuum Ser.: No. 2). 40p. 1977. pap. 7.00 (0-918526-06-X) BOA Edns.

Rosenthal, M. L. Our Life in Poetry: Selected Essays & Reviews. 550p. 1990. 47.50 (0-89255-149-6) Persea Bks.

— Poetry & the Common Life. 148p. 1987. reprint ed. pap. 8.95 (0-89255-118-6) Persea Bks.

Rosenthal, M. L., ed. see Williams, William Carlos.

Rosenthal, M. M., ed. The Political Dynamics of Physician Manpower Policy. (Health Policy Monographs). 216p. 1991. 113.75 (0-444-81397-7) Elsevier.

***Rosenthal, M. Sara.** The Fertility Sourcebook. 192p. 1995. 25.00 (1-56565-213-4) Lowell Hse.

— The Gynecological Sourcebook: Everything You Need to Know. 300p. 1994. 25.00 (1-56565-123-5) Lowell Hse.

— The Pregnancy Sourcebook: Everything You Need to Know. 288p. 1994. 25.00 (1-56565-156-1) Lowell Hse.

— The Thyroid Sourcebook. 228p. 1995. pap. 14.95 (1-56565-215-0) Lowell Hse.

— The Thyroid Sourcebook: Everything You Need to Know. LC 93-10425. 228p. 1993. 23.95 (1-56565-087-5, Legcy) Lowell Hse.

Rosenthal, Macha L. As for Love: Poems & Translations. 64p. 1987. pap. 11.95 (0-19-505268-4) OUP.

— The Poet's Art. 1989. pap. 7.95 (0-393-30584-8) Norton.

— Running to Paradise: Yeats's Poetic Art. LC 93-20178. 1994. 30.00 (0-19-505200-5) OUP.

Rosenthal, Macha L., ed. Poetry in English: An Anthology. (Illus.). 1234p. 1987. pap. text ed. 24.95 (0-19-520539-1) OUP.

Rosenthal, Macha L. & Gall, Sally M. The Modern Poetic Sequence: The Genius of Modern Poetry. 528p. 1983. 39.95 (0-19-503170-9) OUP.

Rosenthal, Macha L., ed. see Yeats, William Butler.

Rosenthal, Manuel & Thomson, Virgil. Satie, Ravel, Poulenc. 86p. (Orig.). 1987. pap. 5.95 (0-937815-09-8) Hanuman Bks.

Rosenthal, Margaret F. The Honest Courtesan: Veronica Franco, Citizen & Writer in Sixteenth-Century Venice. LC 92-14540. (Women in Culture & Society Ser.). 350p. (C). 1992. lib. bdg. 50.00 (0-226-72811-0); pap. text ed. 18.95 (0-226-72812-9) U Ch Pr.

Rosenthal, Marilyn, ed. see Graham, Carolyn.

Rosenthal, Marilyn S. The Magic Boxes: Children & Black English. (CAL-ERIC - CLL Series on Languages & Linguistics: No. 43). 79p. reprint ed. pap. 25.00 (0-8357-3360-2, 2039598) Bks Demand.

Rosenthal, Marilyn S. & Freeman, Daniel B. Longman English-Chinese Photo Dictionary. 103p. (CHI & ENG.). 1989. pap. 12.95 (0-8013-0810-0, 78471) Longman.

— Longman English-Chinese Photo Dictionary: Hanyu Pinyin Edition. (Illus.). 1989. pap. text ed. 13.98 (0-8013-0931-X, 79196) Longman.

— Longman English-Japanese Photo Dictionary. (Illus.). 113p. 1991. pap. text ed. 12.95 (0-582-07245-X, 78929) Longman.

— Longman Photo Dictionary. 91p. (C). 1986. pap. text ed. 12.95 (0-8013-0004-5, 75670) Longman.

— Longman Photo Dictionary. 91p. (C). 1987. text ed. 18.95 (0-8013-0244-7, 75900) Longman.

— Longman Photo Dictionary: Edicion Bilingue en Espanol. (Photo Dictionary Ser.). (Illus.). 93p. (SPA.). (C). 1990. pap. text ed. 12.95 (0-582-08011-8, 78774) Longman.

— Longman Photo Dictionary: Wall Charts - Sets 1 & 2, Set 1. (Illus.). 1989. text ed. 64.95 (0-8013-0146-7, 75899) Longman.

— Longman Photo Dictionary: Wall Charts - Sets 1 & 2, Set 2. (Illus.). 1989. text ed. 74.69 (0-8013-0243-9) Longman.

Rosenthal, Marilyn S. & Ioudine, P. Petit Dictionnaire Philosophique. 638p. (FRE.). 1977. pap. 29.95 (0-8288-5507-2, M6446) Fr & Eur.

Rosenthal, Marilyn S., et al. Longman Photo Dictionary: Intermediate. (Illus.). 1989. text ed. 28.69 (0-8013-0145-9, 75808); student ed, pap. text ed. 10.45 (0-8013-0056-8, 75720) Longman.

***Rosenthal, Marilynn.** The Incompetent Doctor: Behind Closed Doors. (State of Health Ser.). 160p. 1994. 79.00x (0-335-19110-X, Open Univ Pr); pap. 24.95x (0-335-19109-6, Open Univ Pr) Taylor & Francis.

Rosenthal, Marilynn M. Dealing with Medical Malpractice: The British & Swedish Experience. LC 87-27245. xviii, 270p. (C). 1988. lib. bdg. 48.00 (0-8223-0830-4) Duke.

Rosenthal, Marilynn M. & Frenkel, Marcel, eds. Health Care Systems & Their Patients: An International Perspective. 345p. (C). 1992. pap. text ed. 49.00 (0-8133-8078-2) Westview.

Rosenthal, Mark. Anselm Kiefer. LC 87-29007. (Illus.). 216p. (Orig.). 1987. pap. 35.00 (0-87633-071-5) Phila Mus Art.

— Anselm Kiefer. (Illus.). 216p. (Orig.). 1988. pap. 55.00 (3-7913-0847-5, Pub. by Prestel) TeNeues.

— Artists at Gemini G.E.L. Celebrating the 25th Year. LC 92-43357. 1993. 60.00 (0-8109-1933-8) Abrams.

— Bears. LC 82-17910. (New True Bks.). (Illus.). 48p. (J). (gr. k-4). 1983. lib. bdg. 12.90 (0-516-01675-X); pap. 4.95 (0-516-41675-8) Childrens.

— Critiques of Pure Abstraction. 72p. 1995. pap. 20.00 (0-916365-43-3) Ind Curators.

— Jasper Johns: Work since Nineteen Seventy-Four. LC 88-50233. (Illus.). 112p. 1990. pap. 19.95 (0-500-27600-5) Thames Hudson.

— Jasper Johns: Work Since 1974. LC 88-50233. (Illus.). 112p. (Orig.). 1988. pap. 15.95 (0-87633-074-X) Phila Mus Art.

— Juan Gris. LC 83-6060. (Illus.). 192p. 1983. 59.95 (0-89659-400-9) Abbeville Pr.

— Philadelphia Collects: Art Since Nineteen Forty. (Illus.). 128p. 1986. 59.95 (0-8122-7955-7, PA Mus Art) U of Pa Pr.

Rosenthal, Mark, ed. Franz Marc. (Illus.). 160p. 1989. 55.00 (3-7913-1024-0, Pub. by Prestel) TeNeues.

Rosenthal, Mark, told to. Richard Serra: Drawings & Prints from Iceland. (Illus.). 90p. 1992. text ed. 20.00 (1-880146-03-7) M Marks Inc.

Rosenthal, Mark & Marshall, Richard. Jonathan Borofsky. (Illus.). 202p. 1984. pap. 19.95 (0-87633-059-6) Phila Mus Art.

Rosenthal, Mark, jt. contrib. see Baptista, Lynne H.

Rosenthal, Martin R. CPCS Training Manual. LC 89-64082. 200p. 1989. pap. 50.00 (0-944490-19-0) Mass CLE.

Rosenthal, Marvin J. The Prewrath Rapture of the Church. (Illus.). 320p. 1989. 17.95 (*0-685-28847-1*) Zions Hope.

Rosenthal, Maureen R. Cookin' on Special: Recipe Reminder System. 97p. (Orig.). 1993. pap. text ed. 6.95 (*0-9634217-1-9*) MorFor Pubns.

Rosenthal, Mel. In the South Bronx of America. 2nd ed. (Illus.). 1994. 39.95 (*0-915306-96-4*) Curbstone.

Rosenthal, Michael. British Landscape Painting. (Illus.). 192p. 1982. 45.00 (*0-8014-1489-X*) Cornell U Pr.

— Centennial. 1986. pap. 9.95 (*0-918223-86-5*) Pindar Pr.

— Constable. LC 86-50221. (World of Art Ser.). (Illus.). 168p. 1987. pap. 11.95 (*0-500-20211-7*) Thames Hudson.

— Constable: The Painter & His Landscape. LC 82-48908. (Illus.). 264p. 1983. 50.00x (*0-300-03014-2*) Yale U Pr.

— Constable: The Painter & His Landscape. LC 82-48908. (Illus.). 264p. 1986. text ed. 30.00 (*0-300-03753-8*) Yale U Pr.

— Official CBS Viewers Guide to the 1992 Winter Olympics. 1991. pap. 3.95 (*0-918223-90-3*) Pindar Pr.

— Official NBC Viewers Guide to the 1992 Summer Olympics. 1992. pap. 14.95 (*0-918223-92-X*) Pindar Pr.

— Virginia Woolf. 270p. 1987. pap. text ed. 16.00 (*0-231-04849-1*, King's Crown Paperbacks) Col U Pr.

Rosenthal, Miriam & Reeves, Marjorie. The French Revolution. (Then & There Ser.). (Illus.). 106p. (Orig.). (gr. 7-12). 1965. pap. text ed. 8.76 (*0-582-20403-8*, 70739) Longman.

Rosenthal, Miriam B. & Smith, D. H., eds. Psychosomatic Obstetrics & Gynecology. (Advances in Psychosomatic Medicine Ser.: Vol. 12). (Illus.). vi, 190p. 1985. 65.75 (*3-8055-3967-3*) S Karger.

Rosenthal, Miriam K. An Ecological Approach to the Study of Child Care: Family Day Care in Israel. 184p. 1994. text ed. 36.00 (*0-8058-1163-X*) L Erlbaum Assocs.

Rosenthal, Miriam P. Radiology Syllabus. (Illus.). 64p. (Orig.). (C). 1987. pap. text ed. 12.95 (*0-942801-02-4*) Apogee Pr.

Rosenthal, Monroe. Wars of the Jews: A Military History from Biblical to Modern Times. 1995. pap. 12.95 (*1-56171-054-7*) Sure Sellers.

Rosenthal, Myron R. Numerical Methods in Computer Programming. LC 06-24614. (Irwin Series in Quantitative Analysis for Business). 576p. reprint ed. pap. 164.20 (*0-317-08771-1*, 2001049) Bks Demand.

***Rosenthal, Nadine, comp.** Speaking of Reading. LC 95-5102. 240p. 1995. 23.95 (*0-435-08119-5*) Heinemann.

Rosenthal, Nan. Tucson Adventures for Tots Through Teens: Everything for Kids to See & Do in Tucson. rev. ed. 96p. 1992. pap. 5.95 (*0-918080-62-2*) Treas Chest Bks.

Rosenthal, Nan, intro. Hans Haacke: Four Recent Works of Art. (Illus.). 30p. (Orig.). 1977. pap. 10.00 (*0-939982-01-3*) Sesnon Art Gall.

Rosenthal, Nan & Fine, Ruth E. The Drawings of Jasper Johns. LC 90-70396. (Illus.). 294p. 1990. 60.00 (*0-500-23606-2*) Thames Hudson.

Rosenthal, Nan, jt. auth. see Hartt, Frederick N.

Rosenthal, Neal H. & Pilot, Michael. National Occupational Projections for Voc Ed Planning. 26p. 1983. 3.25 (*0-318-22159-4*, IN252) Ctr Educ Trng Employ.

Rosenthal, Norman E. Winter Blues: Seasonal Affective Disorder: What It Is & How to Overcome It. LC 93-30354. 325p. (Orig.). 1993. pap. 14.95 (*0-89862-149-6*) Guilford Pr.

Rosenthal, Norman E. & Blehar, Mary C., eds. Seasonal Affective Disorders & Phototherapy. LC 88-24402. 386p. 1989. lib. bdg. 50.00 (*0-89862-741-9*) Guilford Pr.

Rosenthal, Odeda. Never Said I Was a Lady. (Illus.). 48p. 1983. pap. 5.00 (*0-910425-03-5*) Starchand Pr.

— Not Strictly Kosher: Pioneer Jews of New Zealand (1831-1901) (Illus.). 208p. (Orig.). 1988. 26.95 (*0-910425-07-8*) Starchand Pr.

Rosenthal, P., jt. auth. see Radjavi, H.

Rosenthal, Paul. Where on Earth: A Geografunny Guide to the Globe. LC 92-1227. (Illus.). 112p. (Orig.). (J). (gr. 3-7). 1992. lib. bdg. 15.99 (*0-679-90833-1*); pap. 11.00 (*0-679-80833-7*) Knopf Bks Yng Read.

Rosenthal, Phil, jt. auth. see Groneman, Bill.

Rosenthal, Ray. Astanga Yoga, an Aerobic Yoga System, Taught by K. Paltabhi Jois. 1988. vhs 39.95 (*0-685-23252-2*) Hart Prodns.

Rosenthal, Ray, jt. auth. see Jois, Paltabhi.

Rosenthal, Raymond, tr. Gabriele D'Annunzio: Nocturne & Five Tales of Love & Death. LC 88-60729. 1988. 20.95 (*0-910395-40-3*); pap. 13.00 (*0-910395-41-1*) Marlboro Pr.

— The Vatican Frescoes of Michelangelo, 2 vols. limited ed. LC 80-66646. (Illus.). 528p. 1980. 8,500.00 (*0-89659-158-1*) Abbeville Pr.

Rosenthal, Raymond, tr. see Alvera, Pierluigi & Spada, Marco, eds.

Rosenthal, Raymond, tr. see Aretino, Pietro.

Rosenthal, Raymond, tr. see Brelich, Mario.

Rosenthal, Raymond, tr. see Crotti, Renato.

Rosenthal, Raymond, tr. see Giorello, Giulio.

Rosenthal, Raymond, tr. see Gramsci, Antonio.

Rosenthal, Raymond, tr. see Levi, Primo & Regge, Tullio.

Rosenthal, Raymond, tr. see Levi, Primo.

Rosenthal, Raymond, tr. see Redondi, Pietro.

Rosenthal, Raymond, tr. see Verga, Giovanni.

Rosenthal, Raymond F. & Gordon, James S. The Healing Partnership. 92p. (Orig.). 1984. pap. text ed. 4.95 (*0-931211-01-8*) Aurora Assocs.

— New Directions in Medicine: A Directory of Learning Opportunities. 1984. pap. 15.95 (*0-931211-00-X*) Aurora Assocs.

Rosenthal, Richard. Sky Cops. Tobias, Eric, ed. 384p. (Orig.). 1994. mass mkt. 5.50 (*0-671-79516-3*) PB.

Rosenthal, Rick J. Reef Animals of the Pacific Northwest. 192p. (C). 1990. pap. 125.00 (*0-907151-54-X*, Pub. by IMMEL Pubng UK) St Mut.

Rosenthal, Rob. Homeless in Paradise: A Map of the Terrain. LC 93-17275. 352p. 1994. 44.95 (*1-56639-129-6*); pap. 18.95 (*1-56639-130-X*) Temple U Pr.

Rosenthal, Robert. Judgement Studies: Design, Analysis & Meta-Analysis. (Illus.). 235p. 1987. 59.95 (*0-521-33191-9*) Cambridge U Pr.

— Meta-Analytic Procedures for Social Research. rev. ed. (Applied Social Research Methods Ser.: Vol. 6). (Illus.). 148p. 1991. text ed. 37.00 (*0-8039-4245-1*); pap. text ed. 16.95 (*0-8039-4246-X*) Sage.

Rosenthal, Robert & Jacobson, Lenore. Pygmalion in the Classroom: Teacher Expectation & Pupils' Intellectual Development. enl. ed. 265p. 1989. text ed. 39.50 (*0-8290-1768-2*); pap. text ed. 14.95 (*0-8290-1265-6*) Irvington.

Rosenthal, Robert & Rosnow, Ralph L. Essentials of Behavioral Research: Methods & Data Analysis. 2nd ed. (Psychology Ser.). 1991. text ed. write for info. (*0-07-053929-4*) McGraw.

Rosenthal, Robert, jt. auth. see Rosnow, Ralph L.

Rosenthal, Robert, jt. ed. see Sebeok, Thomas A.

Rosenthal, Robert, et al. PONS (Profile of Nonverbal Sensitivity) Test Manual. (Illus.). 1979. pap. text ed. 12.95 (*0-89197-647-7*); audio 11.00 (*0-8290-0753-9*) Irvington.

— Sensitivity to Nonverbal Communication: The PONS Test. LC 78-17322. (Illus.). 432p. 1979. reprint ed. pap. 123.20 (*0-7837-1618-4*, 2041911) Bks Demand.

Rosenthal, Rose. Not All Soldiers Wore Pants: Witty World War II WAC Tells All. 239p. 1994. pap. write for info. (*0-9636931-0-7*) Ryzell Bks.

Rosenthal, S. The Pragmatic a Priori. LC 75-41707. 104p. 1975. 8.50 (*0-87527-142-1*) Green.

Rosenthal, S., et al, eds. Gene Function: Proceedings of the 12th FEBS Meeting, Dresden, 1978. (Federation of European Biochemical Societies Ser.: Vol. 51). (Illus.). 1979. 234.00 (*0-08-023175-6*, Pub. by Pergamon Repr UK) Franklin.

Rosenthal, Sandra. Speculative Pragmatism. 213p. 1990. pap. 17.95 (*0-8126-9109-1*) Open Court.

Rosenthal, Sandra B. Charles Peirce's Pragmatic Pluralism. LC 93-46977. (SUNY Series in Philosophy). 177p. (C). 1994. text ed. 51.50x (*0-7914-2157-0*); pap. text ed. 18.95x (*0-7914-2158-9*) State U NY Pr.

— Speculative Pragmatism. LC 85-31813. 248p. 1986. lib. bdg. 27.50 (*0-87023-526-5*) U of Mass Pr.

Rosenthal, Sandra B. & Bourgeois, Patrick L. Mead & Merleau-Ponty: Toward a Common Vision. LC 90-20226. 231p. (C). 1991. 59.50 (*0-7914-0789-6*); pap. 19.95 (*0-7914-0790-X*) State U NY Pr.

— Pragmatism & Phenomenology: A Philosophic Encounter. viii, 199p. (Orig.). 1980. pap. 30.00 (*90-6032-179-0*, Pub. by Gruner NE) Benjamins North Am.

Rosenthal, Sandra B., jt. auth. see Bourgeois, Patrick L.

Rosenthal, Saul. A Sociology of Chiropractic. LC 86-8532. (Studies in Health & Human Services: Vol. 6). 1986. lib. bdg. 89.95 (*0-88946-130-9*) E Mellen.

Rosenthal, Saul H. Sex over Forty. 288p. 1989. pap. 9.95 (*0-87477-495-0*) J P Tarcher.

Rosenthal-Schneider, Ilse. Reality & Scientific Truth: Discussions with Einstein, von Laue, & Planck. LC 80-13950. (Illus.). 149p. reprint ed. pap. 42.50 (*0-318-39785-4*, 2033187) Bks Demand.

Rosenthal, Sherri Z., jt. auth. see Adams, Gordan.

***Rosenthal, Sol R.** Challenge: The Joy of Life. (Illus.). 1995. write for info. (*0-9635392-1-3*) Sci-Tech Commun.

Rosenthal, Stephany & Ebone, Jane. Confessions of a Clever Cook. (Illus.). 234p. (Orig.). 1993. spiral bd. 14.95 (*0-9638405-0-9*) Clever Cooks.

Rosenthal, Stephen & Russ, Peter. The Politics of Power: Inside Australia's Electric Utilities. 1988. 24.95 (*0-522-84264-X*) Intl Spec Bk.

Rosenthal, Stephen R. Effective Produce Design & Development: How to Cut Lead Time & Increase Customer Satisfaction. (APICS Ser.). 270p. 1992. 45.00 (*1-55623-603-4*) Irwin Prof Pubng.

Rosenthal, Stephen R., jt. auth. see Salzman, Harold.

Rosenthal, Steve, jt. auth. see Crosbie, Michael J.

Rosenthal, Steven. Rosenthal's Computer Glossary. 350p. 1985. 17.95 (*0-13-783192-7*) P-H.

— Rosenthal's Dictionary of the Automated Office. 350p. 1985. 19.95 (*0-13-783218-4*); pap. 12.95 (*0-13-783200-1*) P-H.

Rosenthal, Steven T. The Politics of Dependency: Urban Reform in Istanbul. LC 79-7588. (Contributions in Comparative Colonial Studies: No. 3). (Illus.). 220p. 1980. text ed. 69.50 (*0-313-20927-8*, RPO/, Greenwood Pr) Greenwood.

***Rosenthal, Susan, ed.** Myoscint: Indium-Labeled Antimyosin Monoclonal Antibody. LC 91-61674. (Illus.). 78p. 1992. 32.95 (*0-924428-06-6*) Phys Sci Pub.

Rosenthal, Susan, et al. Medical Care of the Cancer Patient. 2nd ed. (Illus.). 349p. 1992. pap. text ed. 44.00 (*0-7216-3959-3*) Saunders.

***Rosenthal, Susan R., et al, eds.** Dysphagia & the Child with Developmental Disabilities: Medical, Clinical & Family Interventions. (Illus.). 432p. (Orig.). (C). 1994. pap. text ed. 65.00 (*1-56593-089-4*, 0394) Singular Publishing.

Rosenthal, Sylvia, jt. auth. see Hovis, Gene.

Rosenthal, T. & Silverberg, D., eds. Hypertension in the Community. (Bibliotheca Cardiologica Ser.: No. 42). (Illus.). x, 178p. 1987. 136.00 (*3-8055-4521-5*) S Karger.

Rosenthal, T. G. The Art of Jack B. Yeats. (Illus.). 305p. 1994. 65.00 (*0-233-98849-1*, Pub. by A Deutsch UK) Trafalgar.

Rosenthal, Ted. How Could I Not Be Among You? LC 73-80922. (Illus.). 80p. 1987. reprint ed. pap. 8.95 (*0-89255-117-8*) Persea Bks.

Rosenthal, Uriel, ed. Crisis Management & Decision Making: Simulation Oriented Scenarios. 168p. (C). 1991. lib. bdg. 69.00 (*0-7923-1177-9*) Kluwer Ac.

Rosenthal, Uriel, et al, eds. Coping with Crises: The Management of Disasters, Riots & Terrorism. (Illus.). 498p. (C). 1989. text ed. 86.95x (*0-398-05597-1*) C C Thomas.

— Coping with Crises: The Management of Disasters, Riots & Terrorism. (Illus.). 198p. 1989. pap. 45.95 (*0-398-06408-3*) C C Thomas.

Rosenthal, Yaffa. Mitzvos We Can Do. (ArtScroll Youth Ser.). (Illus.). 32p. (J). (gr. 1-8). 1982. 11.95 (*0-89906-775-1*); pap. 8.95 (*0-89906-776-X*) Mesorah Pubns.

— Thank You Hashem. (ArtScroll Youth Ser.). (Illus.). 32p. (J). (gr. 1-8). 1983. 11.95 (*0-89906-777-8*); pap. 8.95 (*0-89906-778-6*) Mesorah Pubns.

Rosenthale, M. E., ed. Suprofen. (Journal: Pharmacology: Vol. 27, Suppl. 1). (Illus.). viii, 96p. 1983. pap. 30.50 (*3-8055-3789-1*) S Karger.

Rosenthall, Gary. Soccer - the Game & How to Play It. 1981. pap. 7.00 (*0-87980-310-X*) Wilshire.

Rosenthall, Leonard. The Application of Radioiodinated Rose Bengal & Colloidal Radiogold in the Detection of Hepatobiliary Disease. LC 68-59353. (Illus.). 98p. 1969. 8.00 (*0-87527-068-9*) Green.

Rosentheil, Agnes. Mimi Makes a Splash. Stryker, Sandra & Paine, Penelope, eds. Paine, Penelope, tr. LC 91-11286. (Mimi Ser.). (Illus.). 48p. (Orig.). (J). (ps-4). 1991. pap. 6.95 (*0-911655-51-4*) Advocacy Pr.

— Mimi Takes Charge. Stryker, Sandra & Paine, Penelope, eds. Paine, Penelope, tr. LC 91-11285. (Mimi Ser.). (Illus.). 48p. (Orig.). (J). (ps-4). 1991. pap. 6.95 (*0-911655-50-6*) Advocacy Pr.

Rosenthine, Barak, jt. ed. see Berliner, David C.

Rosentraub, Mark & Warren, Robert, eds. Urban Policy Problems. (Orig.). 1984. pap. 12.00 (*0-918592-67-4*) Pol Studies.

Rosentraub, Mark S., ed. Urban Policy Problems: Federal Policy & Institutional Change. LC 86-596. 270p. 1986. text ed. 49.95 (*0-275-92120-4*, C2120, Praeger Pubs) Greenwood.

Rosentreter, Roger, jt. auth. see Leonard, Benjamin F.

Rosentsweig, Gerry. Los Angeles Graphic Design. 1993. 49.95 (*0-942604-33-4*) Madison Square.

— New Logo from California. 1993. 37.50 (*0-942604-28-8*) Madison Square.

Rosentswieg, Gerry. The Advertising Art of Coca-Cola. 192p. 1994. (*0-942604-46-6*) Madison Square.

— The Advertising Art of Coca-Cola. 256p. 1996. 59.95 (*0-942604-52-0*) Madison Square.

— Graphic Design: San Francisco. 1993. 49.95 (*0-942604-29-6*) Madison Square.

— The New Typeographic Logo. (Illus.). 211p. 1996. 37.50 (*0-942604-55-5*) Madison Square.

Rosentswieg, Gerry, ed. The Best New America Logo. (Illus.). 211p. 1994. 37.50 (*0-942604-34-2*) Madison Square.

— Type Faces. (Illus.). 211p. 1996. 37.50 (*0-614-07060-0*) Madison Square.

Rosentswieg, Gerry & Hunt, Wayne. Designing & Planning Environmental Graphics. (Illus.). 256p. 1995. 55.00 (*0-942604-35-0*) Madison Square.

Rosentswieg, Gerry, jt. ed. see Hunt, Wayne.

Rosenus, Alan. Devil Stories: Modern Man in Search of a Resort. LC 78-64543. (Illus.). 1979. 18.95 (*0-913522-07-4*); pap. 10.95 (*0-913522-08-2*) Urion Pr CA.

— Devil Stories: Modern Man in Search of a Resort. limited ed. LC 78-64543. (Illus.). 1979. 40.00 (*0-913522-09-0*) Urion Pr CA.

— General M. G. Vallejo & the Advent of the Americans: A Biography. LC 94-18678. (Illus.). 304p. 1995. pap. 22.50 (*0-8263-1611-5*) U of NM Pr.

Rosenus, Alan, ed. see Miller, Joaquin.

Rosenvall, E. Alan. The Twelve Tribes of Israel Through History. Van Treese, James B., ed. Ingram, tr. 420p. 1992. text ed. write for info. (*1-880416-98-0*) NW Pub.

Rosenvall, Vernice G., et al. The Classic Wheat for Man Cookbook: 300 Ways with Stone Ground Wheat. LC 75-17276. (Illus.). 224p. (Orig.). 1975. pap. 5.95 (*0-912800-16-X*) Woodbridge Pr.

Rosenvold, Lloyd. Can a Gluten-Free Diet Help You...How? 224p. (Orig.). 1990. pap. 9.95 (*0-87983-538-9*) Keats.

Rosenwaike, Ira. Population History of New York City. LC 75-39829. (New York State Bks.). (Illus.). 274p. 1972. 29.95x (*0-8156-2155-8*) Syracuse U Pr.

Rosenwaike, Ira, ed. Mortality of Hispanic Populations: Mexicans, Puerto Ricans, & Cubans in the United States & in the Home Country. LC 91-2. (Studies in Population & Urban Demography: No. 6). 240p. 1991. text ed. 55.00 (*0-313-27500-9*, RMY, Greenwood Pr) Greenwood.

Rosenwaike, Ira & Logue, Barbara. The Extreme Aged in America: A Portrait of an Expanding Population. LC 85-8014. (Contributions to the Study of Aging Ser.: No. 3). (Illus.). xx, 253p. 1985. text ed. 55.00 (*0-313-24857-5*, REA/, Greenwood Pr) Greenwood.

Rosenwaks, S., ed. Gas Flow & Chemical Lasers: Proceedings of the International Symposium, Jerusalem, 6th, September 8-12, 1986. (Physics Ser.: Vol. 15). (Illus.). 545p. 1987. 85.00 (*0-387-17481-8*) Spr-Verlag.

Rosenwaks, Zev. Gynecology: Principles & Practice. 668p. 1987. text ed. 99.00 (*0-07-105307-7*) Hlth Prof Div.

Rosenwaks, Zev, et al. Gynecology: Principles & Practices. 2nd ed. 1992. text ed. 110.00 (*0-07-105423-5*) McGraw.

Rosenwald, Carol, jt. auth. see Beker, Gisela.

Rosenwald, George C. & Ochberg, Richard L., eds. Storied Lives: The Cultural Politics of Self-Understanding. 336p. (C). 1992. text ed. 37.00 (*0-300-05455-6*) Yale U Pr.

Rosenwald, Lawrence. Emerson & the Art of the Diary. 176p. 1988. 35.00 (*0-19-505333-8*) OUP.

Rosenwald, Lawrence, tr. see Buber, Martin & Rosenzweig, Franz.

Rosenwald, Lawrence, tr. see Connaud, Maurice.

Rosenwasser, et al, eds. Hair-Raising. 1976. 3.75 (*0-932716-05-9*) Kelsey St Pr.

Rosenwasser, Edward. Directory of College Alumni Groups: Networking - Local & International Business Sales, Grants & Information for Students. Komer, Barbara, ed. 304p. (Orig.). 1993. pap. 19.95 (*0-932495-06-0*) Student Coll.

— How to Obtain Maximum College Financial Aid: Helps Students Maximize Their Financial Aid Awards. 3rd ed. 250p. 1993. pap. 17.95 (*0-932495-07-9*) Student Coll.

— How to Obtain Maximum College Financial Aid: Little Known Grants for College Students. 4th ed. 214p. (YA). (gr. 11-12). 1994. pap. 12.95 (*0-932495-08-7*) Student Coll.

Rosenwasser, Edward H. How & Where to Get Good Paying, Career Oriented, College Jobs. 48p. (Orig.). 1985. pap. 7.50 (*0-932495-01-X*) Student Coll.

— How to Obtain Maximum College Financial Aid. 38p. (Orig.). 1984. pap. 8.00 (*0-932495-00-1*) Student Coll.

— How to Obtain Maximum College Financial Aid. 2nd ed. 144p. (Orig.). 1991. pap. 16.95 (*0-932495-04-4*) Student Coll.

Rosenwasser, Harvey M. Malpractice & Contact Lenses: A Guide to Limiting Liability in Contact Lens Practice. 96p. (Orig.). (C). 1988. pap. 15.00 (*0-9620349-0-8*) Gillman-Marcuse.

— Malpractice & Contact Lenses: An Updated Edition. 2nd ed. 136p. 1991. pap. text ed. 25.00 (*0-7506-9192-1*) Buttrwrth-Heinemann.

Rosenwasser, Lanny J. Year Book of Allergy & Clinical Immunology, 1994. 320p. 1994. 59.95 (*0-8151-7275-3*, Yr Bk Med Pubs) Mosby Yr Bk.

— Year Book of Allergy & Clinical Immunology, 1995. 320p. Date not set. write for info. (*0-8151-7276-1*, Yr Bk Med Pubs) Mosby Yr Bk.

— Year Book of Allergy & Clinical Immunology, 1996. 320p. 1996. 59.95 (*0-8151-7277-X*, Yr Bk Med Pubs) Mosby Yr Bk.

— Year Book of Allergy & Clinical Immunology, 1996. 320p. 1997. 59.95 (*0-8151-7278-8*, Yr Bk Med Pubs) Mosby Yr Bk.

— Year Book of Allergy & Clinical Immunology, 1998. 320p. 1998. 59.95 (*0-8151-7279-6*, Yr Bk Med Pubs) Mosby Yr Bk.

Rosenwasser, Penny. Voices from a Promised Land: Palestinian & Israeli Peace Activists Speak Their Hearts. LC 91-55411. (Illus.). 288p. (Orig.). 1992. pap. 12.95 (*0-915306-57-3*) Curbstone.

Rosenwasser, Penny, ed. Visionary Voices: Women on Power: Conversations with Shaman, Activists, Teachers, Artists & Healers. LC 92-5113. 204p. (Orig.). 1992. pap. 9.95 (*1-879960-20-6*) Aunt Lute Bks.

Rosenwasser, Rena. Desert Flats. (Illus.). 1979. 5.75 (*0-932716-06-7*) Kelsey St Pr.

— Elephants & Angels. LC 84-14413. (Illus.). 48p. 1985. 8.00 (*0-932716-19-9*) Kelsey St Pr.

— Isle. LC 91-43512. (Illus.). 56p. (C). 1992. pap. text ed. 12.95 (*0-932716-28-8*) Kelsey St Pr.

— Isle. limited ed. Dienstfrey, Pat, ed. (Illus.). 56p. 1992. 40.00 (*0-932716-29-6*) Kelsey St Pr.

Rosenwasser, Rena & Delos, Kate. Simulacra. LC 86-18836. (Illus.). 48p. (Orig.). 1986. pap. text ed. 23.00 (*0-932716-21-0*) Kelsey St Pr.

— Simulacra. deluxe limited ed. LC 86-18836. (Illus.). 48p. (Orig.). 1986. 75.00 (*0-685-16475-6*) Kelsey St Pr.

Rosenwasser, Rena, ed. see Berssenbrugge, Mei-Mei & Tuttle, Richard.

Rosenwasser, Rena, ed. see Einzig, Barbara.

Rosenwasser, Rena, ed. see Fraser, Kathleen.

Rosenwasser, Rena, ed. see Kitrilakis, Thalia.

Rosenwasser, Rena, ed. see Myung Mi Kim.

Rosenwasser, Rena, ed. see Robinson, Elizabeth.

Rosenwasser, Rena, ed. see Waldrop, Rosmarie & MacDonald, Jennifer.

Rosenwasser, Robert H., et al, eds. Cerebral Ischemia: Clinical Implications & Therapeutics. (Illus.). 179p. (C). 1994. lib. bdg. 62.00 (*1-56072-137-5*) Nova Sci Pubs.

***Rosenweig, David J.** Spend Less, Sell More: Thirteen Simple Steps You Can Take Right Now to Grow Your Business. 1994. pap. 21.95 (*1-55738-819-9*) Probus Pub Co.

Rosenweig, Mark R., jt. auth. see Pitt, Mark M.

Rosenwein, Barbara. To Be the Neighbor of Saint Peter: The Social Meaning of Cluny's Property, 909-1049. LC 88-47912. 264p. 1989. 36.50 (*0-8014-2206-X*) Cornell U Pr.

Rosenwein, Robert, jt. auth. see Barner-Barry, Carol.

Rosenzweig, Anne. The Arcadia Seasonal Mural & Cookbook. (Illus.). 28p. 1986. 14.95 (*0-8109-1843-9*) Abrams.

***Rosenzweig, Bill.** Republic of Tea: The Story of the Creation of a Business As Told Through the Personal Letters. 1994. pap. 15.00 (*0-385-42057-9*) Doubleday.

***Rosenzweig, Cynthia, et al, eds.** Climate Change & Agriculture: Analysis of Potential International Impacts: Proceedings of a Symposium. LC 95-14069. (Special Publication Ser.: Vol. 59). 1995. write for info. (*0-89118-126-1*) Am Soc Agron.

Rosenzweig, Daphne L. Contemporary Japanese Ceramics. 1988. pap. 5.00 (*0-9619219-1-9*) Polk Mus Art.

Rosenzweig, Franz. The Star of Redemption. Hallo, William W., tr. LC 84-40833. 464p. (C). 1985. reprint ed. pap. text ed. 16.95 (*0-268-01718-2*) U of Notre Dame Pr.

R

Rosenzweig, Franz & Rosenzweig, Rafael. Sprachdenken. 1984. lib. bdg. 114.50 (90-247-2695-6) Kluwer Ac.
Rosenzweig, Franz, jt. auth. see Buber, Martin.
Rosenzweig, Ilene. The I Hate Madonna Handbook. LC 93-44463. 1994. 83.70 (0-312-10480-4); pap. 12.95 (0-312-10481-2, Pub. by Thomas Dunne Bks) St Martin.
Rosenzweig, James, jt. auth. see Kast, Fremont.
Rosenzweig, Jim. Frank & Earnest Manager. 1991. pap. 10.95 (1-56020-779-5) Three G Home.
Rosenzweig, Linda W. The Anchor of My Life: Middle-Class American Mothers & Daughters, 1880-1920. LC 92-44560. (History of Emotion Ser.). 293p. 1993. 45.00 (0-8147-7438-5); pap. 18.50 (0-8147-7455-5) NYU Pr.
Rosenzweig, Lionel. The Anatomy of the Nectarus: Text & Dissection Guide. 112p. (C). 1988. spiral bd. write for info. (0-697-03025-3) Wm C Brown Pubs.
— Anatomy of the Shark: Text & Dissection Guide. 128p. (C). 1988. Wire Coil. write for info. (0-697-01542-4) Wm C Brown Pubs.
Rosenzweig, Louis E., jt. auth. see Cleverdon, Dorthy.
Rosenzweig, Luc & Cohen, Bernard. Waldheim. Bacon, Josephine, tr. (Illus.). 224p. 1987. 17.95 (1-55774-010-0) Modan-Adama Bks.
Rosenzweig, M. L., jt. ed. see Patil, G. P.
Rosenzweig, Mark, tr. see Kott, Jan.
Rosenzweig, Mark R., ed. International Psychological Science: Progress, Problems, & Prospects. 318p. 1992. pap. text ed. 30.00 (1-55798-168-X) Am Psychol.
Rosenzweig, Mark R. & Leiman, Arnold L. Physiological Psychology. 640p. (C). 1989. student ed 10.50 (0-394-37617-X) Random.
— Physiological Psychology. abr. ed. 640p. (C). 1989. text ed. 32.95 (0-394-37237-9) Random.
Rosenzweig, Mark R. & Porter, Lyman W., eds. Annual Review of Psychology, Vol. 26. LC 50-13143. (Illus.). 1975. text ed. 40.00 (0-8243-0226-5) Annual Reviews.
— Annual Review of Psychology, Vol. 27. LC 50-13143. (Illus.). 1976. text ed. 40.00 (0-8243-0227-3) Annual Reviews.
— Annual Review of Psychology, Vol. 28. LC 50-13143. (Illus.). 1977. text ed. 40.00 (0-8243-0228-1) Annual Reviews.
— Annual Review of Psychology, Vol. 29. LC 50-13143. (Illus.). 1978. text ed. 40.00 (0-8243-0229-X) Annual Reviews.
— Annual Review of Psychology, Vol. 30. LC 50-13143. (Illus.). 1979. text ed. 40.00 (0-8243-0230-3) Annual Reviews.
— Annual Review of Psychology, Vol. 33. LC 50-13143. (Illus.). 1982. text ed. 40.00 (0-8243-0233-8) Annual Reviews.
— Annual Review of Psychology, Vol. 34. LC 50-13143. (Illus.). 1983. text ed. 40.00 (0-8243-0234-6) Annual Reviews.
— Annual Review of Psychology, Vol. 36. LC 50-13143. (Illus.). 1985. text ed. 40.00 (0-8243-0236-2) Annual Reviews.
— Annual Review of Psychology, Vol. 37. LC 50-13143. (Illus.). 1986. text ed. 40.00 (0-8243-0237-0) Annual Reviews.
— Annual Review of Psychology, Vol. 39. (Illus.). 1988. text ed. 40.00 (0-8243-0239-7) Annual Reviews.
— Annual Review of Psychology, Vol. 40. (Illus.). 1989. text ed. 40.00 (0-8243-0240-0) Annual Reviews.
— Annual Review of Psychology, Vol. 41. 1990. text ed. 40.00 (0-8243-0241-9) Annual Reviews.
— Annual Review of Psychology, Vol. 42. 1991. text ed. 40.00 (0-8243-0242-7) Annual Reviews.
— Annual Review of Psychology, Vol. 43. 1992. text ed. 43.00 (0-8243-0243-5) Annual Reviews.
Rosenzweig, Mark R., jt. ed. see Binswanger, Hans P.
Rosenzweig, Mark R., jt. auth. see Jasso, Guillermina.
Rosenzweig, Mark R., jt. ed. see Mussen, Paul H.
Rosenzweig, Mark R., jt. ed. see Mussen, Paul.
Rosenzweig, Mark R., jt. ed. see Porter, Lyman W.
Rosenzweig, Mark R., jt. auth. see Renner, M. J.
Rosenzweig, Mark R., jt. ed. see Sinz, R.
Rosenzweig, Mark R., et al, eds. Annual Review of Psychology, Vol. 35. LC 50-13143. (Illus.). 1984. text ed. 40.00 (0-8243-0235-4) Annual Reviews.
***Rosenzweig, Michael L.** Species Diversity in Space & Time. (Illus.). 458p. (C). 1995. 74.95 (0-521-49618-7); pap. 27.95 (0-521-49952-6) Cambridge U Pr.
Rosenzweig, N., jt. ed. see Narkis, M.
Rosenzweig, Norman. Community Mental Health Programs in England: An American View. LC 74-13365. 282p. reprint ed. pap. 80.40 (0-685-15717-2, 2027664) Bks Demand.
Rosenzweig, Norman & Griscon, Hilda, eds. Psychopharmacology & Psychotherapy: Synthesis or Antithesis? LC 78-4088. 256p. 1978. 35.95 (0-87705-354-5) Human Sci Pr.
Rosenzweig, P. M. Married & Alone: The Way Back. (Illus.). 265p. 1992. 24.50 (0-306-44125-X, Plenum Insight) Plenum.
Rosenzweig, Philip M., jt. auth. see Riccomini, Donald R.
Rosenzweig, Rafael, jt. auth. see Rosenzweig, Franz.
Rosenzweig, Rafael N. The Economic Consequences of Zionism. LC 89-17405. xiii, 260p. (Orig.). 1989. pap. text ed. 57.25 (90-04-09147-5) E J Brill.
Rosenzweig, Robert M. & Turlington, Barbara. The Research Universities & Their Patrons. LC 81-19685. 200p. 1982. pap. 11.00 (0-520-04735-4) U CA Pr.
***Rosenzweig, Rosie, ed.** The Jewish Guide to Boston & New England. 260p. 1995. 19.95 (0-9645367-0-6) Jewish Adv.
Rosenzweig, Roy. Eight Hours for What We Will: Workers & Leisure in an Industrial City, 1870-1920. (Interdisciplinary Perspectives on Modern History Ser.). (Illus.). 320p. 1985. pap. 15.95 (0-521-31397-X) Cambridge U Pr.
Rosenzweig, Roy & Blackmar, Elizabeth. The Park & the People: A History of Central Park. LC 92-7062. (Illus.). 600p. 1992. 39.95x (0-8014-2516-6) Cornell U Pr.
Rosenzweig, Roy, jt. ed. see Leon, Warren.
Rosenzweig, Roy, et al, eds. Government & the Arts in Thirties America: A Guide to Oral Histories & Other Research Materials. (Illus.). 344p. (Orig.). 1986. 64.50 (0-913969-18-4, G Mason Univ Pr); 57.00 (0-8026-0002-6, G Mason Univ Pr); pap. 39.00 (0-8026-0003-4, G Mason Univ Pr) Univ Pub Assocs.
Rosenzweig, Saul. Freud & Experimental Psychology: The Emergence of Idiodynamics. LC 85-19142. 1985. 18.50 (0-930172-04-3) Rana Hse.
— Freud, Jung & Hall the Kingmaker: The Historic Expedition to America (1909) with G. Stanley Hall As Host & William James As Guest. Including the Complete Correspondence of Sigmund Freud & G. Stanley Hall & a New Translation of Freud's Lectures at Clark University on the Origin & Development of Psychoanalysis. 1994. 27.50 (0-930172-07-8) Rana Hse.
— Freud, Jung & Hall the Kingmaker - The Historic Expedition to America (1909) with G. Stanley Hall As Host & William James As Guest: Including the Complete Correspondence of Sigmund Freud & G. Stanley Hall & a New Translation of Freud's Lectures at Clark University on the Origin & Development of Psychoanalysis. (Illus.). 480p. 1992. 29.50 (0-88937-110-5) Hogrefe & Huber Pubs.
— The Historic Expedition to America (1909) Freud, Jung & Hall the Kingmaker with G. Stanley Hall As Host & William James As Guest, Including the Complete Correspondence of Sigmund Freud & G. Stanley Hall & a New Translation of Freud's Lectures at Clark University on the Origin & Development of Psychoanalysis. 2nd rev. ed. Orig. Title: Freud, Jung & Hall the King-Maker. (Illus.). 490p. 1994. pap. 14.95 (0-930172-05-1) Rana Hse.
— The Rosenzweig Picture-Frustration (P-F) Study--Basic Manual. LC 77-95428. 1978. 9.00 (0-930172-02-7) Rana Hse.
Roser, Bill, et al, eds. The Tale of the Frog Prince. (J). 1979. pap. 3.75 (0-87129-199-1, T48) Dramatic Pub.
Roser, H. N. Sales Engineering. (Instructional Resource Package Ser.). 132p. 1983. Student text, 132 p. student ed, pap. text ed. 30.00 (0-87664-665-8, 1665-8) Instru Soc.
Roser, Hermann-Josef & Meisenheimer, Klaus. Jets in Extragalactic Radio Sources: Proceedings of a Workshop Held at Ringberg Castle, Tegernsee, FRG, September 22-28, 1991. LC 93-29538. (Lecture Notes in Physics Ser.: Vol. 421). 1993. 62.00 (0-387-57164-7) Spr-Verlag.
Roser, Hermann-Josef, jt. ed. see Meisenheimer, Klaus.
Roser, Nancy & Frith, Margaret, eds. Children's Choices: Teaching with Books Children Like. LC 83-10697. 128p. reprint ed. pap. 36.50 (0-7837-1235-9, 2041372) Bks Demand.
Roser, Nancy, jt. auth. see Farr, Roger.
Roser, Nancy L. Helping Your Child Become a Reader. 20p. 1989. pap. 1.75 (0-87207-161-8) Intl Reading.
***Roser, Nancy L. & Martinez, Miriam, eds.** Book Talk & Beyond: Children & Teachers Respond to Literature. 320p. 1995. pap. 19.00 (0-87207-129-4) Intl Reading.
Roser, Nancy L., jt. ed. see Jensen, Julie M.
Roser, Susan E. Mayflower Births & Deaths: From the Files of George Ernest Bowman, at the Massachusetts Society of Mayflower Descendants, 2 vols., Set. 1075p. 1992. 75.00 (0-8063-1340-4, 4999) Genealog Pub.
— Mayflower Deeds & Probates: From the Files of George Ernest Bowman, at the Massachusetts Society of Mayflower Descendants. 660p. 1994. pap. 44.95 (0-614-03825-1, 4994) Genealog Pub.
— Mayflower Increasings. 2nd ed. 159p. 1995. 20.00 (0-685-58998-6, 4995) Genealog Pub.
— Mayflower Marriages: From the Files of George Ernest Bowman, at the Massachusetts Society of Mayflower Descendants. 415p. 1994. 29.95 (0-685-48610-9, 4996) Genealog Pub.
Roses, Daniel F., et al. Diagnosis & Management of Cutaneous Malignant Melanoma. (Major Problems in Clinical Surgery Ser.: Vol. 27). (Illus.). 336p. 1983. text ed. 121.00 (0-7216-7706-1) Saunders.
Roses De Irizarry, Estelle. English the Laboratory Way. 97p. 1965. pap. 1.00 (0-8477-3316-5) U of PR Pr.
Roses, Lorraine E. Voices of the Storyteller: Cuba's Lino Novas Calvo. LC 85-27148. (Contributions to the Study of World Literature Ser.: No. 14). 170p. 1986. text ed. 49.95 (0-313-25077-4, RVS, Greenwood Pr) Greenwood.
Roses, Lorraine E. & Randolph, Ruth E. Harlem Renaissance & Beyond: Literary Biographies of One Hundred Black Women Writers, 1900-1945. (Illus.). 536p. 1989. text ed. 45.00 (0-8161-8926-9, Hall Reference) Macmillan.
Roseta, Steve, jt. auth. see Dobler, Joe.
Rosetree, Laura. I Can Read Your Face: A Systemic Introduction to Wholistic Face Reading. 2nd ed. (Illus.). 368p. (Orig.). 1991. reprint ed. pap. 8.95 (0-440-50309-4) Dell.
Rosett, Arthur. Contract Law & Its Application. 4th ed. (University Casebook Ser.). 1049p. 1991. reprint ed. text ed. 37.75 (0-88277-633-9) Foundation Pr.
— Contract Law & Its Application. 5th ed. LC 94-9882. (University Casebook Ser.). 1071p. 1994. text ed. 46.00 (1-56662-151-8) Foundation Pr.
— Contract Law & Its Application: Teacher's Manual. 4th ed. (University Casebook Ser.). 191p. 1990. pap. text ed. write for info. (0-88277-847-1) Foundation Pr.
Rosett, Henry L. & Weiner, Lyn. Alcohol & the Fetus: A Clinical Perspective. LC 84-919. (Illus.). 1984. text ed. 37.50 (0-19-503458-9) OUP.
Rosett, Richard N., ed. The Role of Health Insurance in the Health Services Sector: A Conference of the Universities-National Bureau Committee for Economic Research. LC 76-8856. (Universities-National Bureau Conference Ser.: 27). 562p. reprint ed. pap. 160.20 (0-317-42091-7, 2052158) Bks Demand.
Rosett, Richard N., jt. auth. see Universities-National Bureau Staff.
Rosetta, M. T. Compositional Translation. LC 94-20091. (International Series in Engineering & Computer Science, VLSI, Computer Architecture, & Digital Screen Processing: Vol. 273). 496p. (C). 1994. lib. bdg. 88.00 (0-7923-9462-3) Kluwer Ac.
Rosette, Jack. Improving Tamper-Evident Packaging: Problems, Tests, & Solutions. LC 91-67903. 135p. 1992. text ed. 65.00 (0-87762-906-4) Technomic.
Rosetti, A. Etudes Linguistiques. (Janua Linguarum, Series Major: No. 95). 1973. 110.75 (90-279-2596-8) Mouton.
Rosetti, Rosalie. Report Writing Lesson Plan. Scott, Katherine, ed. 91p. 1991. 209.99 (0-929310-65-9, 142) Am Correctional.
Rosetti, Rosalie & Geiman, Diane, eds. Correctional Food Service Correspondence Course, 2 Vols., Set. (Illus.). (Orig.). 1985. pap. 54.00 (0-942974-67-0, 166) Am Correctional.
Rosetti, Rosalie, ed. see American Correctional Association Staff.
Rosetti, Rosalie, ed. see Cornelius, Gary F.
Rosetti, Rosalie, jt. auth. see Geiman, Diane.
Rosetti, William M., ed. see Blake, William.
Rosevear, Bernie & Rosevear, Stephen. Canadians with Custer in Eighteen Seventy-Six. (Illus.). 24p. (Orig.). 1992. pap. 8.95 (0-940696-32-0) Monroe County Lib.
Rosevear, Francis & McMartin, Barbara. Colvin in the Adirondacks. 150p. 1992. 22.00 (0-932052-98-3) North Country.
Rosevear, John. Pot: A Handbook of Marijuana. 2.25 (0-8065-0204-5, Citadel Pr) Carol Pub Group.
Rosevear, Stephen, jt. auth. see Rosevear, Bernie.
Roseveare, Henry. Markets & Merchants of the Late Seventeenth Century: The Marescoe-David Letters, 1668-1680. (Records of Social & Economic History, New Series British Academy: No. XII). (Illus.). 690p. 1992. reprint ed. pap. 69.00 (0-19-726106-X) OUP.
— The Treasury: The Evolution of a British Institution. 1970. text ed. 50.00 (0-231-03405-9) Col U Pr.
Roseveare, N. T. Mercury's Perihelion from Le Verrier to Einstein. (Illus.). 1982. 47.50 (0-19-858174-2) OUP.
Rosevold, Doreen, ed. see Bjerke, Luther.
Rosewater, Frank. Ninety-Six: A Romance of Utopia. LC 72-154460. (Utopian Literature Ser.). 1976. reprint ed. 23.95 (0-405-03542-X) Ayer.
Rosewater, Lynne B. New Roles - New Rules: A Guide to Transforming Relationships Between Women & Men. LC 92-61899. 175p. (Orig.). 1993. pap. 12.95 (0-9623879-3-2) Trilogy Bks.
Rosewater, Lynne B. & Walker, Lenore E. A Handbook of Feminist Therapy: Women's Issues in Psychotherapy. 384p. 1985. 44.95 (0-8261-4970-7) Springer Pub.
Rosewater, Victor. Special Assessments: A Study in Municipal Finance. LC 68-56686. (Columbia University. Studies in the Social Sciences: No. 7). reprint ed. 29.50 (0-404-51007-8) AMS Pr.
Rosewell, Pamela. The Five Silent Years of Corrie Ten Boom. Hazzard, David, ed. 192p. 1986. pap. 8.99 (0-310-61121-0, 13228P) Zondervan.
— The Five Silent Years of Corrie Ten Boom. large type ed. (Large Print Inspirational Ser.). 1987. pap. 12.95 (0-8027-2577-5) Walker & Co.
Roshal, A., jt. auth. see Karpov, Anatoly.
Roshberg, Robert. Game of Thieves. 1980. 19.95 (0-405-13687-0) Ayer.
Roshchin, Mikhail. First Love. 140p. 1991. 19.95 (0-7145-2932-X) M Boyars Pubs.
Roshchina, Valentina D., jt. auth. see Roshchina, Victoria V.
Roshchina, Victoria V. & Roshchina, Valentina D. The Excretory Function of Higher Plants. LC 93-4993. 1993. 198.00 (0-387-56544-2) Spr-Verlag.
Roshco, Bernard. Newsmaking. LC 75-5076. x, 160p. 1975. lib. bdg. 12.00 (0-226-72814-5) U Ch Pr.
***Roshefsky, Eve F. & Hessel, Carolyn S.** How to Promote a Jewish Book. rev. ed. 15p. 1994. pap. text ed. 10.00 (1-885838-01-8) Jwsh Bk Council.
Rosheim, David L. Galaxy Magazine: The Dark & the Light Years. 1986. 17.00 (0-911682-28-7) Advent.
— Old Iowegian Legends. (Illus.). 196p. (Orig.). 1991. pap. 12.95 (0-9602996-2-9) Andromeda.
— Old Iowegian Sagas. (Illus.). 181p. (Orig.). 1989. pap. 12.95 (0-9602996-1-0) Andromeda.
— The Other Minneapolis. (Illus.). (Orig.). pap. 6.50 (0-9602996-0-2) Andromeda.
Rosheim, Mark E. Robot Evolution: The Development of Anthrobotics. LC 94-13687. 423p. 1994. text ed. 44.95 (0-471-02622-0) Wiley.
— Robot Wrist Actuators. LC 88-22762. 271p. 1989. text ed. 84.95 (0-471-61595-1) Wiley.
***Roshelle, Ariel.** The Voices of Angels, Vol. I. (Illus.). 32p. (Orig.). 1995. pap. write for info. (0-9644530-1-0) AR-L Pubns.
Roshelle, Ariel, ed. see Roshelle, Danille.
***Roshelle, Danille.** The Shepherd & His Shepherdess Are Leading Their Sheep to the Ark Vol. I. Roshelle, Ariel, ed. 340p. (Orig.). 1995. pap. 21.00 (0-9644530-0-2) AR-L Pubns.
Roshi, Shodo H. Morning Dewdrops of the Mind: Teachings of a Contemporary Zen Master. Storandt, Daichi-Priscilla, tr. LC 93-8465. 90p. (Orig.). 1993. pap. 9.95 (1-883319-10-2) Frog CA.
Roshier, Bob. Controlling Crime: The Classical Perspective in Criminology. LC 89-8022. 153p. (C). 1989. 38.95 (0-925065-24-2); pap. text ed. 19.95 (0-925065-19-6) Lyceum IL.
Roshko, A., jt. auth. see Liepmann, Hans W.
Rosholt, Malcolm. Days of the Ching Pao. rev. ed. LC 78-52589. (Illus.). 192p. 1986. 30.00 (0-910417-07-5) Rosholt Hse.
— Flight in the China Air Space. LC 84-61079. (Illus.). 238p. 1984. 30.00 (0-910417-04-0) Rosholt Hse.
— The Press Corps of Old Shanghai. (Illus.). 36p. (Orig.). 1994. pap. write for info. (0-910417-10-5) Rosholt Hse.
— Trains of Wisconsin. 176p. 1992. text ed. 29.95 (0-9635065-0-1) Nat Railrd Mus.
— Trains of Wisconsin. LC 85-90436. (Illus.). 176p. 1985. 29.95 (0-910417-06-7) Rosholt Hse.
Rosholt, Malcolm & Rosholt, Margaret. The Child of Two Mothers. LC 83-63177. (Illus.). 108p. (J). (gr. 4 up). 1983. lib. bdg. 9.95 (0-910417-03-2) Rosholt Hse.
— The Story of Old Abe Wisconsin's Civil War Hero. (Illus.). 110p. (J). (gr. 4-12). 1987. 14.95 (0-910417-09-1) Rosholt Hse.
Rosholt, Malcolm, tr. see Nelson, Clifford, ed.
Rosholt, Malcom. Indian Lands. (Illus.). 352p. pap. text ed. 17.50 (0-87341-084-X) Krause Pubns.
Rosholt, Margaret, jt. auth. see Rosholt, Malcolm.
Roshton, M. Legal Secretary's Concise Dictionary. 1974. 8.00 (0-87511-099-1) Claitors.
Roshwald, Aviel. Estranged Bedfellows: Britain & France in the Middle East During World War II. (Studies in Middle Eastern History). (Illus.). 328p. 1990. 49.95 (0-19-506266-3) OUP.
***Roshwald, Miriam.** Ghetto, Shtetl, or Polis? The Jewish Community in the Writings of Karl Emil Franzos, Sholom Aleichem, & Shemuel Yosef Agnon. LC 95-924. (I. O. Evans Studies in the Philosophy & Criticism of Literature: No. 30). 1995. lib. bdg. write for info. (0-89370-145-9) Borgo Pr.
— Ghetto, Shtetl, or Polis? The Jewish Community in the Writings of Karl Emil Franzos, Sholom Aleichem, & Shemuel Yosef Agnon. LC 95-924. (I. O. Evans Studies in the Philosophy & Criticism of Literature: Nol 30). 1995. pap. write for info. (0-89370-245-5) Borgo Pr.
Roshwald, Mordecai. Level Seven. LC 89-25157. 192p. 1989. reprint ed. pap. 8.95 (1-55652-065-4) L Hill Bks.
— Modern Technology: The Promise & the Menace. LC 95-3868. (Great Issues of the Day Ser.: No. 8). 1995. lib. bdg. write for info. (0-8095-0600-9); pap. write for info. (0-8095-1600-4) Borgo Pr.
Rosic, George S., jt. auth. see Klein, Carl R.
Rosicky, J., jt. auth. see Adamek, Jiri.
Rosicruciae. Evolution of Immortality. reprint ed. spiral bd. 6.60 (0-7873-0738-6) Mokelumne.
Rosicrucian Fellowship Staff. Astrology: The Mystery of the Ductless Glands. 2nd rev. ed. (Illus.). 87p. (C). 1983. reprint ed. pap. text ed. 4.50 (0-911274-68-5) Rosicrucian.
— Children, Aquarian Age Stories For..., 7 vols., Set, Vols. 1-7. 2nd ed. (Illus.). (J). 1989. Set. pap. text ed. 15.00 (0-911274-94-4) Rosicrucian.
— Children, Sunday School Lessons For..., 6 vols., Set, Vols. 1-6. (J). 1985. Set. pap. text ed. 11.25 (0-911274-63-4) Rosicrucian.
— Ephemerides Two Thousand to Two Thousand One Hundred (Noon) - 2000-2100. 1992. pap. 35.95 (0-911274-24-3) Rosicrucian.
— Ephemeris, Any Year - 1857 Through 1999: Single Year (Noon) 1991. pap. text ed. 1.50 (0-685-50472-7) Rosicrucian.
— Ephemeris, 1880-1889: Ten Year (Noon) 1918. pap. text ed. 9.50 (0-911274-40-5) Rosicrucian.
— Ephemeris, 1890-1899: Ten Year (Noon) 1918. pap. text ed. 9.50 (0-911274-41-3) Rosicrucian.
— Ephemeris, 1900-1909: Ten Year (Noon) 1918. pap. text ed. 9.50 (0-911274-42-1) Rosicrucian.
— Ephemeris, 1910-1919: Ten Year (Noon) 1918. pap. text ed. 9.50 (0-911274-43-X) Rosicrucian.
— Ephemeris, 1920-1929: Ten Year (Noon) 1918. pap. text ed. 9.50 (0-911274-44-8) Rosicrucian.
— Ephemeris, 1930-1939: Ten Year (Noon) 1918. pap. text ed. 9.50 (0-911274-45-6) Rosicrucian.
— Ephemeris, 1950-1959: Ten Year (Noon) 1949. reprint ed. pap. text ed. 9.50 (0-911274-47-2) Rosicrucian.
— Ephemeris, 1960-1969: Ten Year (Noon) 1959. reprint ed. pap. text ed. 9.50 (0-911274-48-0) Rosicrucian.
— Ephemeris, 1970-1979: Ten Year (Noon) 1969. reprint ed. pap. text ed. 9.50 (0-911274-49-9) Rosicrucian.
— Ephemeris, 1980-1989: Ten Year (Noon) 1979. reprint ed. pap. text ed. 9.50 (0-911274-75-8) Rosicrucian.
— Ephemeris, 1990-1999: Ten Year (Noon) 1989. reprint ed. pap. text ed. 9.50 (0-911274-46-4) Rosicrucian.
— Ephemeris, 1990-1999: Ten Year (Noon) 1989. reprint ed. pap. text ed. 9.50 (0-911274-76-6) Rosicrucian.
— Ephmeris, 1950-2000 (Midnight) (Illus.). 1993. pap. text ed. 17.95 (0-88112-029-4) Rosicrucian.
— Index: Complete of the Books by Max Heindel. 278p. 1950. text ed. 7.95 (0-911274-07-3) Rosicrucian.
Rosicrucian Fellowship Staff, ed. Shakespeare: The Deeper Truths Of. 2nd ed. (Illus.). 143p. (C). 1990. reprint ed. pap. text ed. 5.00 (0-911274-91-X) Rosicrucian.
— Vision, Etheric: And What It Reveals. 2nd ed. 110p. (C). 1989. reprint ed. pap. text ed. 3.95 (0-911274-59-6) Rosicrucian.
Rosicrucian Fellowship Staff, ed. see Heindel, Max & Heindel, Augusta F.
Rosicrucian Fellowship Staff, ed. see Heindel, Max.
Rosicrucian Fellowship Staff, jt. auth. see Heindel, Max.
Rosicrucian Fellowship Staff, ed. see Heindel, Max, et al.
Rosicrucian Fellowship Staff, ed. see Swainson, Esme.
Rosicrucian Fellowship Staff, ed. see Tucker, Prentiss.

R

Rosicrucian Foundation Staff. The Brotherhood of the Rosy Cross. 76p. 1935. 5.95 (*0-932785-06-9*) Philos Pub.
Rosie, A. M. Information & Communication Theory. 188p. 1968. text ed. 81.00 (*0-677-70380-5*) Gordon & Breach.
Rosiek, Jan. Figures of Failure: Paul de Man's Criticism 1953-1970. 247p. (Orig.). 1992. pap. 33.50 (*87-7288-403-7*, Pub. by Aarhus Univ Pr DK) Coronet Bks.
Rosiello, Luigi, jt. ed. see Dogliotti, Miro.
Rosier, Annemarie. Microwave Cookbook. 1986. 4.98 (*0-671-07750-3*) S&S Trade.
***Rosier, David, ed.** Snow Faculty Studies: The Journal of the Faculty of Snow College, Vol. 5. 101p. (C). 1995. text ed. 14.95 (*1-886632-05-7*) Snow Coll Eng.
Rosier, David & Rosier, Vernette. Equally Yoked. 112p. (Orig.). 1993. pap. 7.99 (*1-56043-763-4*) Destiny Image.
Rosier, James, tr. see Rosier, James L. & Lapidge, M., eds.
Rosier, James L. & Lapidge, M., eds. Aldhelm: The Poetic Works. Lapidge, Michael & Rosier, James, trs. LC 84-29781. 274p. 1985. 63.00 (*0-85991-146-2*) Boydell & Brewer.
Rosier, James L., ed. see Aldhelm.
Rosier, James L., tr. see Aldhelm.
Rosier, Malcoln & Banks, Diana. The Scientific Literacy of Australian Students. (C). 1992. 75.00 (*0-86431-069-2*, Pub. by Aust Council Educ Res AT) St Mut.
Rosier, Malcoln & Long, Michael. The Science Achievement of Year 12 Students in Australia. (C). 1992. 75.00 (*0-86431-089-7*, Pub. by Aust Council Educ Res AT) St Mut.
Rosier, Pat, jt. auth. see Singh, Jasbindar.
Rosier, Patricia & Weiss, Jessica L. The Leftover Gourmet. (Illus.). 160p. 1991. spiral bd. 9.95 (*0-915765-80-2*) Natl Pr Bks.
Rosier, Vernette, jt. auth. see Rosier, David.
Rosies, Toos. Mas Preciosa Que el Oro: More Precious Than Gold. (SPA.). 3.95 (*84-7645-371-X*, 223509, Pub. by Edit Clie SP) TSELF.
— Virtuosa, Pero No Perfecta: Virtuous but Not Perfect. (SPA.). 4.25 (*84-7645-385-X*, 223510, Pub. by Edit Clie SP) TSELF.
Rosignoli. Army Badges & Insignia, Bk. 2: World War 1. 10.95 (*0-02-605080-3*) Macmillan.
— Army Badges Insignia World War 2. 1974. pap. (*0-7137-0697-X*, Pub. by Blandford Pr UK) Sterling.
Rosik, Christopher H. & Malony, H. Newton, eds. The Nineteen Eighty-Three Travis Papers in the Integration of Psychology & Theology. 1986. pap. 10.00 (*0-9609928-5-5*) Integ Pr.
Rosin, Arielle. Eclairs & Brown Bears. LC 93-24971. (Young Gourmet Ser.). (Illus.). 60p. (J). (gr. 3 up). 1994. 12.95 (*0-395-68380-7*) Ticknor & Flds Bks Yng Read.
— Pizzas & Punk Potatoes. LC 93-24970. (Young Gourmet Ser.). (Illus.). 60p. (J). (gr. 3 up). 1994. 12.95 (*0-395-68381-5*) Ticknor & Flds Bks Yng Read.
Rosin, Carol, jt. auth. see Sheffield, Charles.
***Rosin, David.** Minimal Access General Surgery. 1994. 95.00 (*1-870905-72-5*) Scovill Paterson.
— Minimal Access Medicine & Surgery. 1993. 89.95 (*1-870905-67-9*) Scovill Paterson.
Rosin, David, jt. ed. see Greene, Frederick.
Rosin, Gary & Closen, Michael. Agency & Partnership Law: Cases & Materials. LC 92-71956. 1992. 45.00 (*0-89089-515-5*); write for info. (*0-318-69288-0*) Carolina Acad Pr.
— Agency & Partnership Law: Cases & Materials. suppl. ed. 1993. write for info. (*0-318-69289-9*) Carolina Acad Pr.
Rosin, Laurie, ed. see Scott, Carlton T.
Rosin, Mark B., jt. auth. see Burkan, Tolly.
Rosin, R. Thomas. Land Reform & Agrarian Change: Study of a Marwar Village from Raj to Swaraj. 260p. 1987. 36.00 (*81-7033-033-5*, Pub. by Rawat II) S Asia.
Rosin, Robert, ed. Worship in the Lutheran Congregation: The '90s & Beyond. (Monograph Series - Symposium Papers: No. I). (Orig.). 1992. pap. 5.00 (*0-911770-58-5*) Concordia Seminary.
Rosin, W., jt. ed. see Preus, R.
Rosina. What to Do with Those Green Chiles. 1992. write for info. (*1-881935-02-7*) Vaya con Dios.
Rosine, Lawrence L., ed. Advances in Electronic Circuit Packaging: Proceedings of the 5th International Electronic Circuit Packaging Symposium Held at Boulder, Colorado, August 19-21, 1964, Vol. 5. LC 72-187718. 303p. reprint ed. pap. 86.40 (*0-8357-5160-0*, 2020719) Bks Demand.
Rosing, Jens. The Sky Hangs Low. Groves, Naomi J., tr. 60p. 1986. 14.95 (*0-920806-86-4*, Pub. by Penumbra Pr CN) U of Toronto Pr.
Rosing, Ruth. Val Rosing: Musical Genius. (Illus.). 238p. 1993. pap. 20.95 (*0-89745-167-8*) Sunflower U Pr.
Rosing, Wayne C. Laboratory Experiences in Botany. 144p. (C). 1992. spiral bd. 15.95 (*0-8403-7906-4*) Kendall-Hunt.
— Laboratory Experiences in Botany. 144p. (C). 1994. spiral bd. 17.25 (*0-8403-9230-3*) Kendall-Hunt.
Rosinger, Elemer E., jt. auth. see Oberguggenberger, Michael B.
Rosinger, F. E. Non-Linear Partial Differential Equations: An Algebraic View of Generalized Solutions. (North-Holland Mathematics Studies: No. 164). 380p. 1991. 120.00 (*0-444-88700-8*, North Holland) Elsevier.
Rosinger, F. E., ed. Generalized Solutions of Nonlinear Partial Differential Equations. 410p. 1987. 95.00 (*0-444-70310-1*) Elsevier.
Rosinger, Lawrence K., et al. State of Asia. LC 76-134131. (Essay Index Reprint Ser.). 1977. 30.95 (*0-8369-2069-4*) Ayer.
Rosini, Neil J. The Practical Guide to Libel Law. LC 91-9566. 256p. 1991. text ed. 39.95 (*0-275-93782-8*, C3782, Praeger Pubs) Greenwood.
Rosinsky, Therese D. Suzanne Valadon. (Women Artists Ser.). 1994. 14.95 (*0-87663-777-2*) Universe.
Rosio, Bob. Hitler & the New Age. LC 91-78345. 208p. 1992. 9.99 (*1-56384-009-X*) Huntington Hse.
— The Satanization of America. 208p. 1994. pap. 9.99 (*0-933451-04-0*) Prescott Pr.
***Rosium, David R.** The Mechanice of Winding. LC 94-26503. 1994. 81.00 (*0-89852-281-1*, 0101R236) TAPPI.
Rosivach, Vincent J. The System of Public Sacrifice in Fourth-Century Athens. LC 93-47180. (American Philological Association, American Classical Studies: No. 34). 171p. 1994. 29.95 (*1-55540-942-3*, 400434); pap. 19.95 (*1-55540-943-1*) Scholars Pr GA.
Roska & Vandewalle. Cellular Neural Networks. LC 93-1593. 224p. 1994. text ed. 198.00 (*0-471-93836-X*) Wiley.
Roskam, E. E., ed. Mathematical Psychology in Progress. (Recent Research in Psychology Ser.). viii, 385p. 1989. pap. 66.00 (*0-387-51686-7*) Spr-Verlag.
Roskam, E. E. & Suck, R., eds. Progress in Mathematical Psychology, Pt. 1. 538p. 1987. 120.50 (*0-444-70257-1*, North Holland) Elsevier.
Roskam, J. C., ed. see Mamaev, B. M. & Krivosheina, N. P.
Roskam, K. S. Feeling the Sound. (Illus.). 1992. pap. 15.00 (*0-911302-69-7*) San Francisco Pr.
Roskamm, H., ed. Myocardial Infarction at Young Age: Proceedings. (Illus.). 228p. 1982. 35.50 (*0-387-11090-9*) Spr-Verlag.
— Nitroglycerin 6: Unstable Angina Pectoris & Extracardial Indications. (Illus.). 165p. (C). 1990. pap. 60.00 (*0-89925-580-9*) De Gruyter.
— Nitroglycerin 6: Unstable Angina Pectoris & Extracardial Indications. (Illus.). 165p. (C). 1990. pap. 60.00 (*3-11-012061-5*) De Gruyter.
— Prognosis of Coronary Heart Disease-Progression of Coronary Arteriosclerosis. (Illus.). 248p. 1983. 44.00 (*0-387-12367-9*) Spr-Verlag.
Roskamm, H., ed. see Oberrheinisches Kardiologen Symposium Staff.
Roskamm, Helmut & Csapo, Georg, eds. Disorders of Cardiac Function. LC 82-2406. (Basic & Clinical Cardiology Ser.: No. 2). (Illus.). 376p. reprint ed. pap. 107.20 (*0-7837-0933-1*, 2041238) Bks Demand.
Roskamp, Karl W. Capital Formation in West Germany. LC 64-22331. (Wayne State University, Center for Economic Studies, Monograph: No. 3). 288p. reprint ed. pap. 82.10 (*0-7837-3683-5*, 2043557) Bks Demand.
Roskamp, Karl W., ed. The International Institute of Public Finance Semicentennial, 1937-1987. LC 87-10724. 106p. (C). 1987. 19.95 (*0-8143-1984-X*) Wayne St U Pr.
Roskamp, Karl W., jt. ed. see Neumann, Manfred.
Roskams, Julian, ed. The Lawyer's Remembrancer 1992. 250p. 1991. 37.00 (*0-406-26934-3*) Butterworth Legal Pubs.
— The Lawyer's Remembrancer 1993. 250p. 1993. 35.00 (*0-406-01591-0*) Butterworth Legal Pubs.
Roske, Mildred D. Housing in Transition. 371p. (C). 1983. text ed. 37.25 (*0-03-051256-5*) HB Coll Pubs.
Roske, Ralph J. His Own Counsel: The Life & Times of Lyman Trumbull. LC 79-19409. (Wilbur S. Shepperson Series in History & Humanities: No. 14). 240p. 1980. pap. 14.95 (*0-87417-055-9*) U of Nev Pr.
***Roske, Ralph J. & Van Doren, Charles.** Lincoln's Commando: The Biography of Cdr. W. B. Cushing, USN. (Illus.). 320p. 1995. pap. 13.95 (*1-55750-737-6*) Naval Inst Pr.
— Lincoln's Commando: The Biography of Commander W. B. Cushing, U.S.N. LC 73-7311. (Illus.). 310p. 1973. reprint ed. text ed. 38.50 (*0-8371-6923-2*, ROLC, Greenwood Pr) Greenwood.
Roskell, J. S. Parliament & Politics in Late Medieval England, 3 Vols., Vol. 1. 225p. (C). 1985. text ed. 55.00 (*0-685-73659-8*) Hambledon Press.
— Parliament & Politics in Late Medieval England, 3 Vols., Vol. 2. 360p. (C). 1985. text ed. 60.00 (*0-9506882-9-0*) Hambledon Press.
— Parliament & Politics in Late Medieval England, 3 Vols., Vol. 3. 424p. (C). 1985. text ed. 65.00 (*0-907628-30-3*) Hambledon Press.
Roskelley, Fenton, ed. Flies of the Northwest. (Illus.). 132p. 1986. spiral bd. 14.95 (*0-936608-48-X*) F Amato Pubns.
Roskelley, John. Last Days: A World-Famous Climber Challenges the Himalayas' Tawoche & Menlungtse. LC 91-12872. (Illus.). 272p. 1991. 24.95 (*0-8117-0889-6*) Stackpole.
— Nanda Devi: The Tragic Expedition. 224p. 1988. mass mkt. 4.50 (*0-380-70568-0*) Avon.
— Nanda Devi: The Tragic Expedition. LC 87-9949. (Illus.). 208p. 1987. 16.95 (*0-8117-1647-3*) Stackpole.
— Stories off the Wall. LC 93-22667. (Illus.). 224p. 1993. 22.95 (*0-89886-349-X*) Mountaineers.
Roskelley, R. W., et al. The Farmer Scholar Program, 3 vols., I. 1296p. 1975. write for info. (*0-942717-07-4*) Intl Inst Rural.
— The Farmer Scholar Program, 3 vols., II. 1296p. 1975. write for info. (*0-942717-08-2*) Intl Inst Rural.
— The Farmer Scholar Program, 3 vols., III. 1296p. 1975. write for info. (*0-942717-09-0*) Intl Inst Rural.
— The Farmer Scholar Program, 3 vols., Set. 1296p. 1975. 70.50 (*0-318-14578-2*) Intl Inst Rural.
Roskelly, Hephzibah, jt. auth. see Kutz, Eleanor.
Roskelly, Hephzibah, jt. ed. see Ronald, Kate.
Roskey, William. Fifth Gospel: The Odyssey of a Time Traveler in First Century Palestine. LC 83-81189. 240p. 1984. 12.95 (*0-9612112-0-2*) Elghund Pub.
Roski, Steve. Data Structures on the IBM PC. write for info. (*0-318-59629-6*) S&S Trade.
Roskies, D. M. Imperial Perceptions: Examples of Colonial Fiction from the Netherlands East Indies. (Occasional Papers: No. 9). 54p. (Orig.). (C). 1988. pap. 12.50 (*0-318-32899-2*, Pub. by CSEAS UK) Cellar.
Roskies, D. M., ed. Text - Politics in Island Southeast Asia: Essays in Interpretation. (Monographs in International Studies, Southeast Asia Ser.: No. 91). x, 360p. (C). 1993. pap. text ed. 25.00 (*0-89680-175-6*, Ohio U Ctr Intl) Ohio U Pr.
Roskies, David G. Against the Apocalypse: Responses to Catastrophe in Modern Jewish Culture. (Illus.). 352p. 1984. 32.00 (*0-674-00915-0*) HUP.
— Against the Apocalypse: Responses to Catastrophe in Modern Jewish Culture. LC 83-18663. (Illus.). 352p. 1986. pap. text ed. 12.50 (*0-674-00916-9*) HUP.
— A Bridge of Longing: The Lost Art of Yiddish Storytelling. (Illus.). 400p. 1995. text ed. 37.50 (*0-674-08139-0*, ROSBRI) HUP.
— The Literature of Destruction: Jewish Responses to Catastrophe. 650p. 1992. 47.50 (*0-8276-0314-2*); pap. 24.95 (*0-8276-0414-9*) JPS Phila.
Roskies, David G., jt. auth. see Roskies, Diane K.
Roskies, David G
Roskies, Diane K. & Roskies, David G. The Shtetl Book. 327p. pap. 5.95 (*0-686-95146-8*) ADL.
Roskies, Diane K. & Roskies, David G. The Shtetl Book. rev. ed. pap. 12.95 (*0-87068-455-8*) Ktav.
Roskies, Ethel. Abnormality & Normality: The Mothering of Thalidomide Children. LC 70-37757. (Illus.). 365p. 1972. 44.95 (*0-8014-0691-9*) Cornell U Pr.
— Stress Management for the Healthy Type A: A Skills-Training Program. LC 86-31856. 224p. 1987. spiral bd. 19.95 (*0-89862-692-7*) Guilford Pr.
— Stress Management for the Healthy Type A: Theory & Practice. LC 86-31856. 252p. 1987. lib. bdg. 30.95 (*0-89862-689-7*) Guilford Pr.
Roskill, Mark. The Interpretation of Pictures. LC 88-22112. (Illus.). 144p. 1989. pap. 12.95x (*0-87023-661-X*) U of Mass Pr.
— Klee, Kandinsky, & the Thought of Their Time: A Critical Perspective. (Illus.). 304p. 1992. 49.95 (*0-252-01857-5*) U of Ill Pr.
— Klee, Kandinsky, & the Thought of Their Time: A Critical Perspective. (Illus.). 304p. (C). 1995. pap. 19.95 (*0-252-06469-0*) U of Ill Pr.
— What Is Art History? 2nd ed. LC 89-4749. (Illus.). 200p. 1989. pap. 13.95x (*0-87023-675-X*) U of Mass Pr.
Roskill, Mark & Carrier, David. Truth & Falsehood in Visual Images. LC 83-5123. (Illus.). 160p. 1983. lib. bdg. 12.95 (*0-87023-404-8*) U of Mass Pr.
Roskill, Mark, ed. see Van Gogh, Vincent.
***Roskill, S. W.** The War at Sea, 1939-1945, Vol. III, Pt. 2. (Illus.). 632p. 1994. reprint ed. 49.95 (*0-89839-210-1*) Battery Pr.
Roskill, Stephen W. The Strategy of Sea Power: Its Development & Application. LC 80-27028. (Lees-Knowles Lecture Ser., Cambridge, 1961). 287p. 1981. reprint ed. text ed. 52.50 (*0-313-22801-9*, ROSSP, Greenwood Pr) Greenwood.
***Roskin, Gary.** Photo Masters for Diamond Grading. 94p. 1994. 75.00 (*0-9641733-0-1*) Gemwrld Intl.
***Roskin, Michael G.** Countries & Concepts: An Introduction to Comparative Politics. 5th ed. LC 94-32876. 464p. 1994. text ed. 32.00 (*0-13-176025-4*) P-H.
— The Rebirth of East Europe. 2nd ed. LC 93-27337. 1993. pap. text ed. write for info. (*0-13-035957-2*) P-H.
— The Rebirth of Europe. 224p. (C). 1991. pap. text ed. write for info. (*0-13-763442-0*) P-H.
Roskin, Michael G. & Berry, Nicholas O. IR: An Introduction to International Relations. 448p. (C). 1989. pap. text ed. write for info. (*0-13-505603-9*) P-H.
— IR: The New World of International Relations. 2nd ed. LC 92-30054. 480p. 1993. pap. text ed. write for info. (*0-13-505892-9*) P-H.
Roskin, Michael G., et al. Political Science: An Introduction. 4th ed. 432p. (C). 1990. text ed. write for info. (*0-13-682410-2*) P-H.
— Political Science: An Introduction. 5th ed. LC 93-26956. 1993. text ed. write for info. (*0-13-156423-4*) P-H.
Roskin, Rick, jt. auth. see Stuart-Kotze, Robin.
Roskin, Ronald R., jt. auth. see Vitello, Stanley J.
Roskind, Robert. Building Your Own House. LC 83-40029. (Illus.). 448p. 1984. pap. 19.95 (*0-89815-110-4*) Ten Speed Pr.
— Building Your Own House, Bk. II. (Illus.). 288p. 1991. pap. 14.95 (*0-89815-358-1*) Ten Speed Pr.
— In the Spirit of Business: Applying the Principles of a Course in Miracles. 156p. 1993. pap. 9.95 (*0-89087-677-0*) Celestial Arts.
Roskind, Robert & Owner Builder Center Staff. Before You Build. LC 81-51897. 192p. (Orig.). 1981. pap. 12.95 (*0-89815-036-1*) Ten Speed Pr.
Roskis, A. J., jt. auth. see Rossmanith, H. P.
Rosko, Michael D. & Broyles, Robert W. The Economics of Health Care: A Reference Handbook. LC 87-36101. 448p. 1988. text ed. 95.00 (*0-313-25416-8*, REH/, Greenwood Pr) Greenwood.
Rosko, Michael D., jt. auth. see Broyles, Robert W.
Roskos-Ewoldsen, Beverly, et al, eds. Imagery, Creativity, & Discovery: A Cognitive Perspective. LC 93-17150. (Advances in Psychology Ser.: Vol. 98). 1993. write for info. (*0-444-89591-4*, North Holland) Elsevier.
Roskos, Kathleen A., jt. auth. see Neuman, Susan B.
Roskos, Kathy, jt. auth. see Walker, Barbara M.
***Roskoski, Robert, Jr.** Biochemistry. LC 95-1002. (Illus.). 528p. 1995. pap. text ed. write for info. (*0-7216-5174-7*) Saunders.
Roslak, Deborah & Orber, Linda. Dear Jesus, Dear Child: Guided Meditations for Young Children. LC 91-67713. (Illus.). 96p. (Orig.). 1992. pap. 9.95 (*0-89622-508-9*) Twenty-Third.
Roslavets, H. Museum of Western & Oriental Art: Kiev. (Illus.). 192p. (C). 1985. text ed. 70.00 (*0-685-40290-8*, Pub. by Collets) St Mut.
Roslavleva, Natalia. Era of the Russian Ballet. LC 79-11509. (Series in Dance). 1979. reprint ed. 37.50 (*0-306-79536-1*) Da Capo.
Rosler, H. J. & Lange, H. Geochemical Tables. LC 79-132143. 468p. 1973. 118.00 (*0-444-40894-0*) Elsevier.
Rosler, Lee, jt. auth. see Thomson, Andrew.
Rosler, Martha. If You Lived Here... The City in Art, Theory & Social Activism. Wallis, Brian, ed. LC 89-650815. (Discussions in Contemporary Culture Ser.: No. 6). (Illus.). 312p. (Orig.). (C). 1991. pap. 16.95 (*0-941920-18-6*) Bay Pr.
— Service: A Trilogy on Colonization. 36p. 1978. pap. 5.00 (*0-89439-007-4*) Printed Matter.
Rosloniec, Stanislaw. Algorithms for Computer Aided Design of Linear Microwave Circuits. (Microwave Library). 256p. 1990. 49.00 (*0-89006-354-0*); disk 49.00 (*0-685-45614-5*) Artech Hse.
Roslyakov, G. S., ed. Numerical Methods in Gas Dynamics. 176p. 1966. text ed. 47.00 (*0-7065-0397-X*, Pub. by Keter Pub IS) Coronet Bks.
Roslyakov, G. S., jt. auth. see Pirumov, U. G.
Rosman, Abraham & Rubel, Paula. Feasting with Mine Enemy: Rank & Exchange among Northwest Coast Societies. (Illus.). 221p. 1986. reprint ed. pap. text ed. 9.95 (*0-88133-221-6*) Waveland Pr.
Rosman, Abraham & Rubel, Paula G. Tapestry of Culture. 4th ed. 1992. text ed. write for info. (*0-07-053718-6*) McGraw.
— The Tapestry of Culture: An Introduction to Cultural Anthropology. 5th ed. LC 94-9412. 1994. 24.00 (*0-07-053955-3*) McGraw.
Rosman, Bernice L., jt. ed. see Fishman, H. Charles.
Rosman, Doreen. Evangelicals & Culture. (Modern Revivals in History Ser.). 262p. 1992. 56.95 (*0-7512-0056-5*, Pub. by Gregg Revivals UK) Ashgate Pub Co.
Rosman, M. S. The Lords' Jews: Magnate-Jewish Relations in the Polish-Lithuanian Commonwealth During the 18th Century. (Harvard Ukrainian Research Institute Monograph: Vol. 7). (Illus.). 260p. (C). 1990. reprint ed. 27.00 (*0-916458-18-0*) Harvard Ukrainian.
— The Lords' Jews: Magnate-Jewish Relations in the Polish-Lithuanian Commonwealth During the 18th Century. (Harvard Ukrainian Research Institute Monograph: Vol. 7). (Illus.). 260p. (C). 1992. reprint ed. pap. 17.00 (*0-916458-47-4*) Harvard Ukrainian.
Rosman, Steven. Spiritual Parenting: A Sourcebook for Parents & Teachers. (Illus.). 180p. (Orig.). 1994. pap. 12.00 (*0-8356-0703-8*, Quest) Theos Pub Hse.
Rosman, Steven M. The Bird of Paradise & Other Sabbath Stories. (Illus.). (Orig.). 1994. pap. 8.95 (*0-8074-0529-9*, 123725) UAHC.
— Sidrah Stories: A Torah Companion. 120p. (J). (gr. 4-6). 1989. pap. 7.95 (*0-8074-0429-2*, 121723) UAHC.
— The Twenty-Two Gates to the Garden. LC 93-35944. 224p. (J). 1994. pap. 24.95 (*1-56821-124-4*) Aronson.
Rosman, Steven M., jt. auth. see Schram, Peninnah.
Rosman, Steven S. Deena the Damselfly. LC 91-43472. (J). (gr. k-3). 1992. 10.95 (*0-8074-0477-2*, 101069) UAHC.
Rosmarin, Aden. The Power of Genre. LC 85-8630. 205p. 1986. text ed. 29.95 (*0-8166-1395-8*); pap. text ed. 12.95 (*0-8166-1396-6*) U of Minn Pr.
Rosmarin, Ike. South Africa. LC 92-38755. (Cultures of the World Ser.). (J). 1993. 21.95 (*1-85435-575-9*) Marshall Cavendish.
Rosmarin, Leonard. Saint-Evremond: Artiste de l'Euphorie. LC 86-63080. 112p. (FRE.). 1987. 18.95 (*0-917786-52-1*) Summa Pubns.
Rosmarin, Yvonne W. & Edelman, Daniel A. Consumer Class Actions: A Practical Litigation Guide. 2nd ed. LC 90-6335. (Consumer Credit & Sales Legal Practice Ser.). 237p. (Orig.). 1990. pap. 60.00 (*0-943116-79-1*) Nat Consumer Law.
Rosneck, Mark, jt. auth. see Huber, John P.
Rosner, B. S. & Pickering, J. B. Vowel Perception & Production. LC 93-47078. (Psychology Ser.: No. 23). (Illus.). 416p. (C). 1994. 98.00 (*0-19-852138-3*) OUP.
Rosner, Bernard. Fundamentals of Biostatistics. 3rd ed. 655p. (C). 1990. text ed. 58.95 (*0-534-91973-1*) Intl Thomson.
— Fundamentals of Biostatistics. 4th ed. 682p. 1995. text ed. 58.95 (*0-534-20940-8*) Intl Thomson.
Rosner, Brian. Swindle: How a Man Named John Grambling Cheated Banks out of Thirty-Six Million. 350p. 1990. 30.00 (*1-55623-291-8*) Irwin Prof Pubng.
Rosner, Burt, jt. auth. see Rothstein, Michael F.
***Rosner, David.** Deadly Dust: Silicosis & the Politics of Occupational Disease in Twentieth-Century America. 1994. pap. 15.95 (*0-691-03771-X*) Princeton U Pr.
— A Once Charitable Enterprise: Hospitals & Health Care in Brooklyn & New York, 1855-1915. LC 81-21725. (Interdisciplinary Perspectives on Modern History Ser.). 288p. 1982. 54.95 (*0-521-24217-7*) Cambridge U Pr.
— A Once Charitable Enterprise: Hospitals & Health Care in Brooklyn & New York, 1855-1915. LC 81-21725. (Illus.). 248p. 1986. pap. text ed. 14.95x (*0-691-02835-4*) Princeton U Pr.
***Rosner, David, ed.** Hives of Sickness: Public Health & Epidemics in New York City. LC 94-29784. (Illus.). 230p. (C). 1995. text ed. 35.00 (*0-8135-2158-0*) Rutgers U Pr.
Rosner, David & Markowitz, Gerald. Deadly Dust: Silicosis & the Politics of Occupational Disease in Twentieth-Century America. (Illus.). 219p. 1991. text ed. 35.00 (*0-691-04758-8*) Princeton U Pr.
Rosner, David & Markowitz, Gerald, eds. Dying for Work: Workers' Safety & Health in Twentieth Century America. LC 85-46003. (Interdisciplinary Studies in History). (Illus.). 256p. 1986. 35.00 (*0-253-31825-4*); pap. 10.95 (*0-253-20507-7*, MB-507) Ind U Pr.
Rosner, David, jt. ed. see Markowitz, Gerald E.
Rosner, David, jt. ed. see Reverby, Susan.

R

An Asterisk (*) at the beginning of an entry indicates that the title is appearing in BIP for the first time.

Rosner, Erhard. Medizingeschichte Japans. LC 89-30046. (Handbuch der Orientalistik Ser.: Vol. 5/3/5). viii, 135p. (Orig.). (GER.). 1989. pap. text ed. 97.25 (90-04-08815-6) E J Brill.

Rosner, F. Medicine in the Bible & the Talmud: Selections from Classical Jewish Sources. (Library of Jewish Law & Ethics: Vol. 5). 16.95 (0-87068-326-8) Ktav.

Rosner, Fred. Maimonides' Commentary on Mishnah Sanhedrin. LC 81-51800. 224p. 1981. 16.95 (0-87203-099-7) Hermon.

— Medicine in the Bible & the Talmud: Selections from Classical Jewish Sources. LC 94-29687. 1994. 29.50 (0-88125-506-8) Ktav.

— Medicine in the Mishneh Torah of Maimonides. 1983. 29.50 (0-88125-020-1); pap. 16.95 (0-88125-021-X) Ktav.

— Modern Medicine & Jewish Ethics. LC 86-2910. (C). 1986. text ed. 29.50 (0-685-13545-4); pap. text ed. 19.95 (0-88125-102-X) Ktav.

— Sex Ethics in the Writings of Moses Maimonides. LC 94-19613. 144p. 1994. pap. 20.00 (1-56821-323-9) Aronson.

Rosner, Fred, ed. Medicine & Jewish Law, Vol. I. LC 89-49410. 216p. 1993. pap. 20.00 (1-56821-028-0) Aronson.

— Medicine & Jewish Law, Vol. II. LC 89-49410. 184p. 1993. pap. 20.00 (0-87668-574-2) Aronson.

Rosner, Fred, tr. & anno. Maimonides' Introduction to His Commentary on the Mishnah. LC 94-14644. 256p. 1995. 30.00 (1-56821-241-0) Aronson.

Rosner, Fred, tr. Moses Maimonides' Treatise on Resurrection. 15.00 (0-87068-764-6); pap. 8.95 (0-685-05843-3) Ktav.

Rosner, Fred, tr. & anno. Six Treatises Attributed to Maimonides. LC 89-18590. 280p. 1991. 40.00 (0-87668-804-0) Aronson.

Rosner, Fred & Kottek, Samuel S., eds. Moses Maimonides: Physician, Scientist, & Philosopher. LC 92-41882. 304p. 1993. pap. 24.95 (0-87668-470-3) Aronson.

Rosner, Fred & Tendler, Moshe D. Practical Medical Halakhah. 18.95 (0-88125-336-7) Ktav.

Rosner, Fred, ed. see Preuss, Julius.

Rosner, Gerald, et al, eds. Dying & Death: Perspectives on the Role of the Financial & Estate Planner. (Current Thanatology Ser.). 100p. 1988. pap. 14.95 (0-930194-41-1) Ctr Thanatology.

Rosner, Hilda, tr. see Hesse, Hermann.

***Rosner, Jeremy D.** New Era, New Partnership: Congress, the Executive, & National Security after the Cold War. 110p. (C). 1995. pap. 10.95x (0-87003-059-0) Carnegie Endow.

Rosner, Jerome. Helping Children Overcome Learning Difficulties: A Step-by-Step Guide for Parents & Teachers. 2nd rev. ed. (Illus.). 408p. 1993. pap. 18.95 (0-8027-7396-6) Walker & Co.

— Test of Auditory Analysis Skills (TAAS) teacher ed 10.00 (0-87879-630-4) Acad Therapy.

— Test of Visual Analysis Skills (TVAS) teacher ed 15.00 (0-685-53819-2); teacher ed 2.00 (0-87879-678-9) Acad Therapy.

Rosner, Jerome & Rosner, Joy. Vision Therapy in a Primary Care Practice. (Illus.). 256p. 1988. Text & manual. text ed. 49.95 (0-87873-077-X, Prof Pr Bks NYC); Manual only. text ed. 23.95 (0-87873-082-6, Prof Pr Bks NYC) Buttrwrth-Heinemann.

Rosner, Jonathon L., tr. see Novozhilov, Yuri V.

Rosner, Joy, jt. auth. see Rosner, Jerome.

Rosner, Joyce, jt. auth. see Hoffpauir, Stephan.

***Rosner, Kira.** The Power of Being Human. Charles, Rodney, ed. 100p. (Orig.). 1995. pap. 12.95 (0-9638502-6-1) Sunstar Pubng.

Rosner, Lisa. First Look at Quattro Pro for Windows. 1993. text ed. write for info. (0-07-053830-1) McGraw.

— First Look at Quattro Pro 2.0-3.0. 1992. pap. text ed. write for info. (0-07-053811-5) McGraw.

— Quick Success: DOS 6.2. LC 94-23132. 64p. 1995. pap. text ed. 5.95 (0-534-32402-9) Boyd & Fraser.

— Quick Success: Lotus 1-2-3 for Windows, Release 4. 64p. 1995. pap. 6.95 (0-534-32405-3) Intl Thomson.

— Quick Success: Microsoft Excel 5.0 for DOS. 64p. 1995. pap. 6.95 (0-534-32410-X) Intl Thomson.

— Quick Success: Microsoft Word 6.0 for Windows. LC 94-28229. 64p. 1994. pap. text ed. 5.95 (0-534-32401-0) Boyd & Fraser.

— Quick Success: Micrsoft Excel for Windows. 64p. 1995. pap. 6.95 (0-534-32404-5) Intl Thomson.

— Quick Success: Windows 3.1. LC 94-33239. 1994. write for info. (0-534-21403-7) Boyd & Fraser.

— Quick Success: Windows 3.1. LC 94-33239. (Management Information Systems Ser.). 64p. 1995. pap. 6.95 (0-534-32403-7) Intl Thomson.

— Quick Success: WordPerfect 6.0 for Windows. LC 94-28596. 64p. 1994. pap. text ed. 5.95 (0-534-32400-2) Boyd & Fraser.

— Students & Apprentices at Edinburgh University. 1991. text ed. 40.00 (0-7486-0245-3, Pub. by Edinburgh U Pr UK) Col U Pr.

Rosner, Louis J. & Ross, Shelley. Multiple Sclerosis. 256p. 1992. pap. 11.00 (0-671-77809-9, Fireside) S&S Trade.

Rosner, Lydia S. The Soviet Way of Crime: Beating the System in the Soviet Union & the U. S. A. LC 86-6095. 160p. 1986. text ed. 55.00 (0-89789-098-1, Bergin & Garvey) Greenwood.

Rosner, M. E., ed. see Spath, Wilhelm.

Rosner, Martic C. Hormones & Hyacinths. LC 79-82087. 1980. 5.95 (0-87212-126-7) Libra.

Rosner, Martin C. Coracle & Other Poems. LC 75-146469. 1971. 3.95 (0-87212-001-5) Libra.

— Pilgrim at Sunset. Date not set. 11.95 (1-884570-04-6) Research Triangle.

Rosner, Martin M., jt. ed. see Catania, Patrick.

Rosner, Menachem, jt. ed. see Oldenquist, Andrew.

Rosner, Menachem, et al. The Second Generation: Continuity & Change in the Kibbutz. LC 90-3905. (Kibbutz Study Ser.: No. 2). 480p. 1990. text ed. 65.00 (0-313-27287-5, RSG/, Greenwood Pr) Greenwood.

Rosner, Michael & Johnson, Roderick, eds. Computational Linguistics & Formal Semantics. (Studies in Natural Language Processing). 250p. (C). 1992. 79.95 (0-521-41959-X); pap. 27.95 (0-521-42988-9) Cambridge U Pr.

***Rosner, Neal.** On the Road to Freedom: A Pilgrimage in India. 190p. (Orig.). 1987. 6.00 (0-9615875-4-7) M A Ctr.

Rosner, R. Packet Switching. 2nd ed. 1989. text ed. write for info. (0-442-31803-0) Van Nos Reinhold.

Rosner, Raphael, ed. Junior Judaica: Encyclopedia Judaica for Youth, 6 vols. 3rd ed. 1200p. (J). 1994. 167.50 (0-89563-816-9, Pub. by Keter Pub IS) Coronet Bks.

Rosner, Richard, ed. Critical Issues in American Psychiatry & the Law, Vol. 2. LC 81-9059. 324p. 1985. 70.00 (0-306-41954-8, Plenum Pr) Plenum.

Rosner, Richard & Harmon, R. B., eds. Correctional Psychiatry. LC 88-657025. (Critical Issues in American Psychiatry & the Law Ser.: Vol. 6). (Illus.). 320p. 1989. 65.00 (0-306-43070-3, Plenum Pr) Plenum.

— Criminal Court Consultation. (Critical Issues in American Psychiatry & the Law Ser.: Vol. 5). (Illus.). 344p. 1989. 65.00 (0-306-43061-4, Plenum Pr) Plenum.

Rosner, Richard & Schwartz, H. I., eds. Geriatric Psychiatry & the Law. (Critical Issues in American Psychiatry & the Law Ser.: Vol. 3). (Illus.). 386p. 1987. 75.00 (0-306-42522-X, Plenum Pr) Plenum.

— Juvenile Psychiatry & the Law. LC 88-657025. (Critical Issues in American Psychiatry & the Law Ser.: Vol. 4). (Illus.). 452p. 1989. 75.00 (0-306-42958-6, Plenum Pr) Plenum.

Rosner, Richard & Weinstock, R., eds. Ethical Practice in Psychiatry & the Law. LC 88-657025. (Critical Issues in American Psychiatry & the Law Ser.: Vol. 7). (Illus.). 366p. 1990. 85.00 (0-306-43476-8, Plenum Pr) Plenum.

Rosner, Roy D. Packet Switching: Tomorrow's Communications Today. (Illus.). 371p. 1982. text ed. 69.95 (0-534-97965-3) Van Nos Reinhold.

Rosner, Ruth. Arabba, Gah, Zee, Marissa & Me! Fay, Ann, ed. LC 86-15904. (Illus.). 32p. (J). (ps-3). 1987. lib. bdg. 13.95 (0-8075-0442-4) A Whitman.

Rosner, Stanley & Abt, Lawrence E., eds. Essays in Creativity. LC 89-2472. 220p. (C). 1989. reprint ed. lib. bdg. 23.50 (0-89464-384-3) Krieger.

Rosner, Victoria, intro. The Columbia Guide to New York, 1989-1990. (Illus.). 128p. (Orig.). 1989. pap. 9.95 (0-9611970-1-3) Columbia Guide to NY.

Rosness, Russell A. Vitamins & Medicine: Subject, Reference & Research Guide. LC 87-47633. 160p. 1987. 44.50 (0-88164-568-0); pap. 39.50 (0-88164-569-9) ABBE Pubs Assn.

Rosney, C., jt. auth. see Craig, A.

Rosnow, Mimi, jt. auth. see Rosnow, Ralph L.

Rosnow, Ralph L. & Fine, G. A. Rumor & Gossip. 166p. 1976. pap. 24.50 (0-444-99035-6) Elsevier.

Rosnow, Ralph L. & Georgoudi, Marianthi, eds. Contextualism & Understanding in Behavioral Science: Implications for Research & Theory. 392p. 1986. text ed. 69.50 (0-275-92121-2, C2121, Praeger Pubs) Greenwood.

Rosnow, Ralph L. & Rosenthal, Robert. Beginning Behavioral Research: A Conceptual Primer. (Illus.). 528p. (C). 1993. text ed. write for info. (0-02-403781-8) Macmillan.

— Beginning Behavioral Research: A Conceptual Primer. 2nd ed. LC 95-10444. 1995. text ed. write for info. (0-13-436916-5) P-H.

— Understanding Behavioral Science: Research Methods for Research Consumers. 1984. text ed. write for info. (0-07-053809-3) McGraw.

Rosnow, Ralph L. & Rosnow, Mimi. Writing Papers in Psychology: A Student Guide. 2nd ed. 105p. (C). 1991. pap. 13.95 (0-534-16986-4) Brooks-Cole.

— Writing Papers in Psychology: A Student Guide. 3rd ed. LC 94-9163. 1995. pap. 10.95 (0-534-24378-9) Brooks-Cole.

Rosnow, Ralph L., jt. auth. see Rosenthal, Robert.

Rosny, J. H. Quest for Fire. 128p. 1982. pap. 2.50 (0-345-30067-X) Ballantine.

Rosof, Adrienne B. & Felch, William C., eds. Continuing Medical Education: A Primer. 2nd ed. LC 91-24229. 256p. 1992. text ed. 59.95 (0-275-94009-8, C4009, Praeger Pubs); pap. text ed. 15.95 (0-275-94010-1, B4010, Praeger Pubs) Greenwood.

Rosof, Barbara D. Worst Loss. 1994. 25.00 (0-8050-3240-1) H Holt & Co.

— Worst Loss. 1995. pap. 14.95 (0-8050-3241-X) H Holt & Co.

Rosof, Patricia & Zeisel, William, eds. History of Education. LC 84-6626. (Trends in History Ser.: Vol. 3, No. 2). 94p. 1984. text ed. 32.95 (0-86656-137-4) Haworth Pr.

Rosof, Patricia J. & Zeisel, William, eds. Family History. LC 84-22520. (Trends in History Ser.: Vol. 3, Nos. 3-4). 171p. 1985. text ed. 39.95 (0-86656-136-6) Haworth Pr.

Rosof, Patricia J., et al, eds. Black History. LC 83-87. (Trends in History Ser.: Vol. 3, No. 1). 99p. 1983. text ed. 19.95 (0-86656-135-8) Haworth Pr.

— Ethnic & Immigration Groups: The United States, Canada, & England. LC 82-23323. (Trends in History Ser.: Vol. 2, No. 4). 126p. 1983. text ed. 32.95 (0-917724-46-1) Haworth Pr.

— The Middle East & North Africa: Medieval & Modern History. LC 82-11931. (Trends in History Ser.: Vol. 2, No. 3). 134p. 1983. text ed. 39.95 (0-917724-45-3) Haworth Pr.

— The Military & Society: Reviews of Recent Research. LC 81-20073. (Trends in History Ser.: Vol. 2, No. 2). 120p. (C). 1982. text ed. 39.95 (0-917724-44-5) Haworth Pr.

— Urban History: Reviews of Recent Research. LC 80-27903. (Trends in History Ser.: Vol. 2, No. 1). 97p. 1981. text ed. 32.95 (0-917724-26-7) Haworth Pr.

Rosoff, Arnold J. & Bergwall, David F., eds. Teaching Health Law: A Guide on Health Law for Health Services Administration. 1986. pap. text ed. 12.95 (0-910591-01-6) AUPHA Pr.

Rosoff, Barbara, tr. see Cornell, Donald.

Rosoff, Betty & Tobach, Ethel, eds. Challenging Racism & Sexism: Alternatives to Genetic Determinism. (Genes & Gender Ser.: Vol. VII). 350p. (Orig.). (C). 1994. 35.00 (1-55861-089-8); pap. 14.95 (1-55861-090-1) Feminist Pr.

Rosoff, Betty, jt. ed. see Tobach, Ethel.

Rosoff, David. Safed, the Mystical City. 1991. 15.95 (0-87306-566-2) Feldheim.

Rosoff, Iris, ed. see Corwin, Judith H.

Rosoff, Iris, ed. see Greene, Jacqueline D.

Rosoff, Iris, ed. see Landau, Elaine.

Rosoff, Iris, ed. see Markosian, Becky T. & Thayne, Emma L.

Rosoff, Iris, ed. see Newman, Shirlee P.

Rosoff, Iris, ed. see Shepherd, Donna A.

Rosoff, Morton, ed. Controlled Release of Drugs: Polymers & Aggregate Systems. LC 88-19177. 315p. 1989. lib. bdg. 80.00 (0-89573-321-8) VCH Pubs.

Rosolack, Stephen, jt. auth. see Haberlen, John.

Rosolowsky, Diane. West Germany's Foreign Policy: The Impact of the Social Democrats & the Greens. LC 87-12017. (Contributions in Political Science Ser.: No. 192). 168p. 1987. text ed. 45.00 (0-313-25672-1, RWG/, Greenwood Pr) Greenwood.

Rosone, Geraldine A., jt. auth. see DeGaetano, Jean G.

Rosovsky, Henry. University: An Owner's Manual. 1991. pap. 11.95 (0-393-30783-2) Norton.

Rosovsky, Henry, ed. Discord in the Pacific: Challenges to the Japanese-American Alliance. LC 72-93017. 1972. pap. 3.00 (0-910416-16-8) Am Assembly.

Rosovsky, Henry, jt. ed. see Kumon, Shumpei.

Rosovsky, Henry, jt. auth. see Ohkawa, Kazushi.

Rosovsky, Henry, jt. ed. see Patrick, Hugh.

Rosovsky, Henry, et al, eds. Favorites of Fortune: Technology, Growth, & Economic Development since the Industrial Revolution. 558p. (C). 1991. text ed. 50.00 (0-674-29520-X) HUP.

Rosovsky, Henry M., jt. auth. see Middleton, Charles R.

Rosovsky, Nitza. Jerusalemwalks. rev. ed. (Illus.). 272p. 1992. pap. 14.95 (0-8050-1553-1, Owl) H Holt & Co.

***Rosow.** Into Forsaken Hands: The Power of Literacy Theory. LC 94-43727. 1995. 24.95 (0-435-08116-0) Heinemann.

Rosow, C. E., ed. Butorphanol Tartrate: Research Advances in Multiple Clinical Settings. (Journal: Acute Care: Vol. 12, Suppl. 1, 1986). (Illus.). iv, 80p. 1988. pap. 24.00 (3-8055-4752-8) S Karger.

Rosow, Irving. Socialization to Old Age. LC 73-78540. 1975. pap. 11.00 (0-520-03417-1) U CA Pr.

Rosow, Jerome M., ed. The Global Marketplace. LC 88-16279. 237p. reprint ed. pap. 67.60 (0-7837-1580-3, 2041872) Bks Demand.

— Teamwork: Joint Labor-Management Programs in America. 199p. 1986. 27.50 (0-08-032799-0) Work in Amer.

— The Worker & the Job: Coping with Change. LC 74-765. (American Assembly Guides Ser.). 224p. 1974. 6.95 (0-317-00261-9) Am Assembly.

Rosow, Jerome M. & Casner-Lotto, Jill. The Participative Leader: From Autocracy to Empowerment. (New Roles for Managers Ser.: Pt. V). 131p. 1993. 95.00 (0-89361-044-5) Work in Amer.

***Rosow, Jerome M. & Hickey, John V.** The Partnership Paradigm for Competitive Advantage Pt. 1. (Strategic Partners for High Performance Ser.). 115p. 1994. 95.00 (0-89361-050-X) Work in Amer.

Rosow, Jerome M. & Zager, Robert. Employee Involvement & the Supervisor's Job. (New Roles for Managers Ser.: Pt. I). 101p. 1989. pap. 95.00 (0-89361-042-9) Work in Amer.

— The Future of Older Workers in America: New Options for an Extended Working Life. 135p. 1980. pap. 11.00 (0-89361-018-6) Work in Amer.

— Improving Health-Care Management in the Workplace. 162p. 1985. 19.25 (0-08-032797-4) Work in Amer.

— Job Strategies for Urban Youth: Complete Study. 102p. 1979. pap. 8.75 (0-89361-005-4) Work in Amer.

— Job Strategies for Urban Youth: Executive Summary. 18p. 1979. pap. 4.35 (0-89361-004-6) Work in Amer.

— Linking Training Strategy Corporate Strategy. 76p. 1991. pap. 95.00 (0-685-50727-0) Work in Amer.

— Linking Training Strategy to Corporate Strategy. Casner-Lotto, Jill, ed. (Training for New Technology Ser.: Part I). 76p. 1985. 95.00 (0-89361-058-5) Work in Amer.

— Management Involvement for High Commitment. Casner-Lotto, Jill, ed. (New Roles for Managers Ser.: Pt. II). 97p. 1989. pap. 95.00 (0-89361-046-1) Work in Amer.

— The Manager As Trainer, Coach & Leader. (New Roles for Managers Ser.: Pt. III). 94p. 1990. pap. 95.00 (0-89361-045-3) Work in Amer.

— Meeting the Challenge of Change: Basic Skills for a Competitive Workforce. (Job-Linked Literacy: Innovative Strategies at Work Ser.: Pt. II). 99p. 1992. pap. 95.00 (0-89361-048-8) Work in Amer.

— Moving Ahead: Basic Skills for Career Advancement. Casner-Lotto, Jill, ed. (Job-Linked Literacy: Innovative Strategies at Work Ser.: Pt. III). 97p. 1993. 95.00 (0-89361-047-X) Work in Amer.

— New Work Schedules for a Changing Society: Complete Study. 128p. 1981. pap. 12.00 (0-89361-025-9) Work in Amer.

— New Work Schedules for a Changing Society: Executive Summary. 55p. 1981. pap. 5.50 (0-89361-026-7) Work in Amer.

— Productivity Through Work Innovations: Complete Study. 161p. 1982. 18.25 (0-08-029545-2) Work in Amer.

— Productivity Through Work Innovations: Executive Summary. 48p. 1982. pap. 7.75 (0-08-029546-0) Work in Amer.

— Toward a New Social Contract: Employment Security for Managers & Professionals. Casner-Lotto, Jill, ed. (New Roles for Managers Ser.: Pt. IV). 75p. 1991. pap. 95.00 (0-89361-043-7) Work in Amer.

— Vestibule Training: Basic Skills for New Hires, Pt. I. Casner-Lotto, Jill, ed. 97p. 1991. pap. 95.00 (0-89361-049-6) Work in Amer.

Rosow, Jerome M., jt. ed. see Kerr, Clark.

Rosow, Jerome M., et al. Allies in Educational Reform: How Teachers, Unions, & Administrators Can Join Forces for Better Schools. LC 88-46095. (Education-Higher Education Ser.). 353p. 1989. 36.95x (1-55542-158-X) Work in Amer.

— The Continuous Learning Employment Security Connection. (Training for New Technology Ser.: Part IV). 83p. 1987. 95.00 (0-89361-055-0) Work in Amer.

— Cost-Effective Design & Delivery. Casner-Lotto, Jill, ed. (Training for New Technology Ser.: Part III). 118p. 1986. 95.00 (0-89361-056-9) Work in Amer.

— Partners in Learning: Manufacturers & Users. Casner-Lotto, Jill, ed. (Training for New Technology Ser.: Part V). 87p. 1987. 95.00 (0-89361-054-2) Work in Amer.

— Toward Continuous Learning. rev. ed. Casner-Lotto, Jill, ed. (Training for New Technology Ser.: Part II). 87p. 1991. pap. 95.00 (0-89361-057-7) Work in Amer.

— Training--The Competitive Edge: Introducing New Technology into the Workplace. LC 88-42797. (Management Ser.). 243p. 1988. 33.95x (1-55542-109-1) Work in Amer.

Rosow, Michael P., jt. ed. see Zager, Robert.

Rosow, Stephen J., et al, eds. The Global Economy As Political Space. LC 93-33348. (Critical Perspectives on World Politics Ser.). 256p. 1994. lib. bdg. 45.00 (1-55587-462-2) Lynne Rienner.

Rosowski, Susan, ed. see Cather, Willa.

Rosowski, Susan J. Approaches to Teaching Cather's My Antonia. LC 88-31154. (Approaches to Teaching World Literature Ser.: No. 22). xii, 194p. 1989. 37.50 (0-87352-519-1, AP22C); pap. 18.00x (0-87352-520-5, AP22P) Modern Lang.

— The Voyage Perilous: Willa Cather's Romanticism. LC 86-4341. xviii, 284p. 1986. 25.00 (0-8032-3874-6) U of Nebr Pr.

Rosowski, Susan J., ed. Cather Studies, Vol. 1. (Illus.). xii, 189p. 1990. 30.00x (0-8032-3895-9) U of Nebr Pr.

Rosowsky, Andre, ed. Advances in Cancer Chemotherapy, Vol. 1: 1979. LC 79-643464. (Illus.). 309p. reprint ed. pap. 88.10 (0-7837-0796-7, 2041110) Bks Demand.

***Ross.** Birthday Wish. 3.99 (0-517-13577-9) Random Hse Value.

— Craniofacial Anomalies. 1991. 79.50 (1-55664-082-X) Mosby Yr Bk.

— Digital Design & Synthesis with VHDL. (Design Automation Ser.). (Illus.). 300p. (C). 1994. text ed. 59.95 (0-9627488-3-8) Automata Pub.

— Diminished by Death. (Black Dagger Crime Ser.). 16.50 (0-86220-824-6, BD023, Black Dagger) Chivers N Amer.

— Drafting & Negotiating Commercial Leases in Scotland. 2nd ed. 1993. 130.00 (0-406-02006-X, UK) Butterworth Legal Pubs.

— A Family of Strangers. large type ed. 1991. pap. 15.95 (0-7927-0455-X, AS062, Atlantic Lrg Print) Chivers N Amer.

— Gospel of Thomas. 1990. pap. 9.95 (1-85230-302-6, GOTHOP) Element MA.

— Introduction to Oceanography. (C). 1995. text ed. 41.50 (0-673-46938-7) HarpCollege.

— Introduction to Statistics. 2nd ed. 1989. 26.25 (0-536-57704-8) Ginn Pr.

— Italian-English - English-Italian Practical Dictionary. 1995. pap. (0-7818-0354-3) Hippocrene Bks.

— Let's Talk! A Discussion of Group Dynamics. 208p. (C). 1993. pap. text ed. 27.95 (0-8403-8237-5) Kendall-Hunt.

— Making Affirmations & Prayers Work. 52p. 1988. pap. 10.00 (0-87916-026-8) Upstat.

— Scott, Levantate y Anda: Scott Free. (SPA.). 4.25 (0-7228-389-5, 360750, Pub. by Edit Clie SP) TSELF.

Ross & Boyd. Precalculus: Algebra & Trigonometry. LC 90-2668. (C). 1991. text ed. 54.95 (0-534-14550-7) Brooks-Cole.

Ross & Cobb, Stephen. The Family As a Client. Hunter, Debra, ed. 269p. (C). 1990. pap. text ed. 37.75 (0-201-08291-8) Addison-Wesley.

Ross & Sellmeyer. School Publications - The Business Side. 1989. 12.50 (0-317-02685-2) Quill & Scroll.

Ross, jt. auth. see Hill, Bill.

Ross, jt. auth. see MacGibbon.

Ross, jt. auth. see Pollard.

Ross, jt. auth. see Somerville.

Ross, et al. Cardiopulmonary Bypass: Anesthesia & Perioperat. 550p. Date not set. 80.00 (0-8016-4178-0) Mosby Yr Bk.

— Histology: A Text & Atlas. 2nd ed. (Illus.). 815p. 1989. text ed. 52.00 (0-683-07368-0) Williams & Wilkins.

— Love, Lawyers & Lies. 200p. 1991. per. write for info. (0-8187-0147-1) Harlo Press.

Ross, A., jt. auth. see Ball, J. C.

Ross, A. C., tr. see Bachelard, Gaston.

R

Ross, Abraham S. & Grant, Malcolm J. Experimental & Non-Experimental Designs in Social Psychology. 196p. 1994. pap. write for info. (0-697-16603-1) Brown & Benchmark.

Ross, Aileen D. The Hindu Family in Its Urban Setting. LC 62-2801. 339p. reprint ed. pap. 96.70 (0-317-09747-4, 2014388) Bks Demand.

Ross, Al. The Destroyer Campbeltown. LC 90-60099. (Anatomy of the Ship Ser.). (Illus.). 128p. 1990. 36.95 (1-55750-725-2) Naval Inst Pr.

— The Destroyer Escort England. (Anatomy of the Ship Ser.). (Illus.). 96p. 1985. 36.95 (0-87021-140-4) Naval Inst Pr.

— The Destroyer, the Sullivans: Anatomy of the Ship. LC 87-63031. (Anatomy of the Ship Ser.). (Illus.). 120p. 1988. 36.95 (0-87021-617-1) Naval Inst Pr.

— The Escort Carrier Gambier Bay. (Anatomy of the Ship Ser.). (Illus.). 128p. 1993. 36.95 (1-55750-235-8) Naval Inst Pr.

Ross, Al, jt. auth. see Lambert, John.

Ross, Alan. Ehanamani "Walks Among" The Winter Count of a Santee Dakota Educator, Historian And. (Illus.). 1993. pap. 12.00 (0-9621977-2-6) Wiconi Waste.

— Spiritualism & Beyond: A Guide for Life in the World to Come. Jones, Alese, ed. LC 88-70801. (Illus.). 161p. (Orig.). 1988. pap. 6.95 (0-9617038-4-9) Divine Love Pub.

Ross, Alan O. Child Behavior Therapy. LC 87-3517. 444p. (C). 1987. reprint ed. lib. bdg. 44.50 (0-89464-229-4) Krieger.

— Personality: The Scientific Study of Complex Human Behavior. 608p. (C). 1987. text ed. 46.75 (0-03-010959-0) HB Coll Pubs.

— The Sense of Self: Research & Theory. LC 91-868. 208p. (C). 1992. text ed. 32.95 (0-8261-7430-2) Springer Pub.

Ross, Alan S., jt. ed. see Dickins, Bruce.

Ross, Alastair. Dynamic Factory Automation: Creating Flexible Systems for Competitive Manufacturing. (IBM Ser.). 1992. text ed. 47.00i (0-07-707440-8) McGraw.

Ross, Alec & Plant, David. Writing Police Reports: A Practical Guide. LC 76-55879. 1977. pap. 5.95 (0-916070-03-4, MTI Film & Video) Coronet.

Ross, Alexander. Adventures of the First Settlers on the Oregon or Columbia River, 1810-1813. LC 85-24550. 319p. 1986. reprint ed. pap. 7.95 (0-8032-8920-0, Bison Books) U of Nebr Pr.

Ross, Alexander M. The Imprint of the Picturesque on Nineteenth-Century British Fiction. 228p. (C). 1986. text ed. 35.00 (0-88920-191-9, Pub. by Wilfrid Laurier CN) Humanities.

— Recollections & Experiences of an Abolitionist, from 1885-1865. (American Biography Ser.). 224p. 1991. reprint ed. lib. bdg. 69.00 (0-7812-8331-0) Rprt Serv.

— William Henry Bartlett: Artist, Author, & Traveller (Containing a Reprint of Dr. William Beattie's Brief Memoir of the Late William Henry Bartlett. (Illus.). 176p. reprint ed. pap. 50.20 (0-317-10533-7, 2020518) Bks Demand.

Ross, Alice, et al. Whistle Punk. LC 93-14187. (Chaparral Books for Young Readers Ser.). 142p. (J). (gr. 5-8). 1994. pap. 9.95 (0-87565-123-2) Tex Christian.

Ross, Alison, illus. Daytime Baby: Baby Books. 8p. (J). (ps). 1992. bds. 3.50 (0-7214-1515-6, S9212-4) Ladybird Bks.

— Hello Baby: Baby Books. 8p. (J). (ps). 1992. bds. 3.50 (0-7214-1497-4, S9212-3) Ladybird Bks.

— Noisy Baby: Baby Books. 8p. (J). (ps). 1992. bds. 3.50 (0-7214-1496-6, S9212-1) Ladybird Bks.

— Playtime Baby: Baby Books. 8p. (J). (ps). 1992. bds. 3.50 (0-7214-1514-8, S9212-2) Ladybird Bks.

Ross, Alistair, jt. ed. see Ahier, John.

Ross, Allan, Jr. Administrative Manual, Vol. 3. 1990. text ed. 35.00 (0-915355-79-5) Am Assn Blood.

Ross, Allan & Helgesen, Jan, eds. Human Rights in a Changing East-West Perspective. 1991. text ed. 69.00 (0-86187-131-6, Pub. by Pinter Pubs UK) St Martin.

Ross, Allan M., jt. ed. see Wasserman, Alan G.

Ross, Allen. Mitakuye Oyasin: We Are All Related. (Illus.). 215p. (Orig.). 1989. pap. 12.00 (0-9621977-0-X) Wiconi Waste.

Ross, Allen P. Creation & Blessing: A Guide to the Study & Exposition of Genesis. LC 88-6173. 784p. 1988. 29.99 (0-8010-7748-6) Baker Bk.

Ross, Amanda M. Public Virtue, Public Love. 1989. 30.00 (0-86278-123-X, Pub. by OBrien Pr IE) Dufour.

Ross, Amy. Out in Left Field. 112p. 1993. pap. 8.95 (0-8059-3403-0) Dorrance.

Ross, Andrea. All about Turtles. LC 89-92455. 24p. (J). (ps-3). 1990. audio, pap. 5.95 (0-943864-59-3) Davenport.

— Chester's Coloring Book. (Illus.). 70p. (Orig.). (J). (gr. k-2). 1992. 7.00 (1-56002-016-4, Univ Edtns) Aegina Pr.

— Oscar Crab & Rallo Car. LC 86-72872. 64p. (Orig.). (J). (ps-2). 1987. pap. 5.00 (0-916383-18-0) Aegina Pr.

— Poenisha. 43p. 1986. 5.95 (1-55523-016-4) Winston-Derek.

— Seymour. LC 81-71758. 24p. (J). (gr. 2-3). 1992. reprint ed. pap. 3.50 (0-943864-64-X) Davenport.

Ross, Andrea, ed. Selected Figural Works, Vol. 1. (Illus.). 32p. 1989. pap. text ed. write for info. (0-318-66432-1) A Ross Gallery.

Ross, Andrew. The Chicago Gangster Theory of Life: Ecology, Culture & Society. LC 94-18514. 1994. 24.95 (0-86091-429-1, B4529, Pub. by Verso UK) Routledge Chapman & Hall.

— The Failure of Modernism. LC 86-9660. 256p. 1986. text ed. 35.00 (0-231-06330-X) Col U Pr.

— John Philip Seventeen Seventy-Five to Eighteen Fifty-One: Missions, Race & Politics in South Africa. 258p. 1986. text ed. 30.00 (0-08-032457-6, Pub. by Aberdeen U Pr) Macmillan.

— No Respect: Intellectuals & Popular Culture. 288p. 1989. 32.50 (0-415-90036-0, A1574, Routledge NY); pap. 13.95 (0-415-90037-9, A1578, Routledge NY) Routledge.

— Strange Weather: Culture, Science & Technology in the Age of Limits. 240p. 1991. 59.95 (0-86091-354-6, A6397, Pub. by Verso UK); pap. 16.95 (0-86091-567-0, A6401, Pub. by Verso UK) Routledge Chapman & Hall.

Ross, Andrew, ed. Universal Abandon? The Politics of Postmodernism. LC 88-10134. (Cultural Politics Ser.). xviii, 300p. (Orig.). 1989. text ed. 39.95 (0-8166-1679-5); pap. 14.95 (0-8166-1680-9) U of Minn Pr.

Ross, Andrew & Rose, Tricia, eds. Microphone Fiends: Youth Music & Youth Culture. LC 93-44005. 1994. write for info. (0-415-90907-4, Routledge NY); pap. write for info. (0-415-90908-2, Routledge NY) Routledge.

Ross, Andrew, jt. auth. see Penley, Constance.

Ross, Andrew C. A Vision Betrayed: The Jesuits in Japan & China 1542-1742. LC 94-10623. 225p. 1994. 34.95 (0-88344-991-9) Orbis Bks.

Ross, Andrew L., ed. The Political Economy of Defense: Issues & Perspectives. LC 90-25280. (Contributions in Military Studies: No. 112). 240p. 1991. text ed. 55.00 (0-313-26462-7, RPD/, Greenwood Pr) Greenwood.

Ross, Angus, jt. ed. see Heap, Shaun H.

Ross, Angus, ed. see Richardson, Samuel.

Ross, Angus, ed. see Smollett, Tobias G.

Ross, Angus, ed. see Swift, Jonathan.

Ross, Angus, et al, eds. Jonathan Swift. (Oxford Authors Ser.). 1984. pap. text ed. 22.50 (0-19-281337-4) OUP.

Ross, Ann. The Way We Were...the Way We Can Be... - A Vision for the Middle School: Integrated Thematic Instruction. 167p. (Orig.). 1990. pap. 17.95 (1-878631-04-7) S Kovalik.

Ross, Ann & Olsen, Karen. The Way We Were...The Way We Can Be: A Vision for the Middle School. 2nd ed. (Illus.). 211p. 1993. spiral bd. 21.95 (1-878631-05-5); per. write for info. (1-878631-06-3) S Kovalik.

Ross, Ann & Olsen, Karen D. The Way We Were... the Way We Can Be: A Vision for the Middle School. 3rd ed. (Illus.). (C). 1994. pap. write for info. (1-878631-19-5) S Kovalik.

Ross, Ann B. The Murder Stroke. (Orig.). 1981. pap. 1.75 (0-8439-8018-4) Dorchester Pub Co.

Ross, Anna. Be My Friend. LC 89-24389. (Sesame Street Toddler Bks.). (Illus.). 24p. (J). (ps). 1991. 3.95 (0-394-85496-9) Random Bks Yng Read.

— Big Bird's Big Bike. LC 92-60305. (Sesame Street Chunky Shape Bks.). (Illus.). 22p. (J). (ps). 1993. 3.25 (0-679-83271-8) Random Bks Yng Read.

— Elmo's Big Lift-&-Look Book. (Illus.). 12p. (J). (ps-00). 1994. 10.00 (0-679-84468-6) Random Bks Yng Read.

— Elmo's Little Playhouse. LC 91-68111. (Sesame Street Chunky Shape Bks.). (Illus.). 22p. (J). (ps). 1993. 3.25 (0-679-83270-X) Random Bks Yng Read.

— Grover's Ten Terrific Ways to Help Our Wonderful World. LC 91-11095. (Sesame Street R Picturebacks Ser.). (Illus.). 32p. (Orig.). (J). (ps-3). 1992. pap. 2.25 (0-679-81384-5) Random Bks Yng Read.

— I Did It! LC 89-34543. (Sesame Street Toddler Bks.). (Illus.). 24p. (J). (ps). 1990. 3.95 (0-394-86019-5) Random Bks Yng Read.

— I Have to Go. LC 89-34542. (Sesame Street Toddler Bks.). (Illus.). 24p. (J). (ps). 1990. 3.95 (0-394-86051-9) Random Bks Yng Read.

— Knock, Knock, Who's There? A Sesame Street Book. (Chunky Flap Bks.). (Illus.). 22p. (J). (ps-00). 1994. 3.50 (0-679-85304-9) Random Bks Yng Read.

— Little Bert's Book of Numbers. LC 91-4921. (Sesame Street Toddler Bks.). (Illus.). 24p. (J). (ps). 1992. 3.99 (0-679-82239-9) Random Bks Yng Read.

— Little Elmo's Book of Colors. LC 91-23979. (Sesame Street Toddler Bks.). (Illus.). 24p. (J). (ps). 1992. 3.99 (0-679-82238-0) Random Bks Yng Read.

— Little Ernie's ABC's. LC 91-27823. (Sesame Street Toddler Bks.). (Illus.). 24p. (J). (ps). 1992. 3.99 (0-679-82240-2) Random Bks Yng Read.

— Little Grover's Book of Shapes. LC 91-4920. (Sesame Street Toddler Bks.). (Illus.). 24p. (J). (ps). 1992. 3.99 (0-679-82237-2) Random Bks Yng Read.

— Meet the Sesame Street Babies. LC 92-60973. (Board Bks.). 7p. (J). (ps). 1993. bds. 3.95 (0-679-83486-9) Random Bks Yng Read.

— Naptime. LC 89-34545. (Sesame Street Toddler Bks.). (Illus.). 24p. (J). (ps). 1990. 3.95 (0-394-85828-X) Random Bks Yng Read.

— Not the Monster. (Sesame Street Baby Board Bks.). (Illus.). 12p. (J). (ps). 1994. bds. 3.99 (0-679-84739-1) Random Bks Yng Read.

— Open Sesame. LC 91-67671. (Lift-&-Peek-a-Board Bks.). (Illus.). 14p. (J). (ps-00). 1992. bds. 4.50 (0-679-83063-4) Random Bks Yng Read.

— Peekaboo, Puppy! (My Puppy Loves Me Book Ser.). (J). (ps). 1994. 3.50 (0-679-85700-1) Random Bks Yng Read.

— Quiet Time. LC 89-24354. (Sesame Street Toddler Bks.). (Illus.). 24p. (J). (ps). 1991. 3.95 (0-394-85495-0) Random Bks Yng Read.

— Rock-a-Bye Babies. (Sesame Street Baby Board Bks.). (Illus.). 12p. (J). (ps). 1994. bds. 3.99 (0-679-84740-5) Random Bks Yng Read.

— Rubber Duckies Don't Say Quack! (Sesame Street Baby Board Bks.). (Illus.). 12p. (J). (ps). 1994. bds. 3.99 (0-679-84741-3) Random Bks Yng Read.

— Say Bye-Bye. LC 90-52915. (Sesame Street Toddler Bks.). (Illus.). 24p. (J). (ps). 1992. 3.95 (0-394-85485-3) Random Bks Yng Read.

— Say Good Night. LC 90-52914. (Sesame Street Toddler Bks.). (Illus.). 24p. (J). (ps). 1992. 3.95 (0-394-85491-8) Random Bks Yng Read.

— Say the Magic Word, Please. LC 89-34544. (Sesame Street Toddler Bks.). (Illus.). 24p. (J). (ps). 1990. 3.95 (0-394-85857-3) Random Bks Yng Read.

— Sesame Street Busy Little Neighborhood, 4 bks., Set. (Illus.). (J). (ps). 1991. bds. 8.00 (0-679-80252-5) Random Bks Yng Read.

— Sesame Street Whose Knees Are These? (J). (ps). 1994. 3.99 (0-679-84742-1) Random Bks Yng Read.

— Where, Oh, Where? A Sesame Street Book. (Chunky Flap Bks.). (Illus.). 22p. (J). (ps-00). 1994. 3.50 (0-679-85303-0) Random Bks Yng Read.

— Whose Knees Are These? (Illus.). 12p. (J). (ps). 1994. write for info. (0-318-72490-1) Random Bks Yng Read.

Ross, Anne. Druids, Gods & Heroes from Celtic Mythology. LC 93-31615. (World Mythology Ser.). (Illus.). 128p. (YA). 1994. 22.50 (0-87226-918-3); pap. 14.95 (0-87226-919-1) P Bedrick Bks.

— Life & Death Of Druid Prince. 1991. pap. 12.00 (0-671-74122-5, Touchstone Bks) S&S Trade.

Ross, Anne & Cyprien, Michael. Traveller's Guide to Celtic Britain. (Traveller's Guide Ser.). (Illus.). 128p. 1985. 14.95 (0-918678-06-4) Natl Hist Soc.

Ross, Annette L. & Disney, Jean A. The Art of Making Good Cookies. 256p. 1987. reprint ed. pap. 4.95 (0-486-25315-5) Dover.

Ross, Anthony C. Economic Stabilization for Developing Countries. 320p. 1991. text ed. 69.95 (1-85278-314-1, Pub. by E Elgar Pub UK); pap. text ed. 29.95 (1-85278-452-0, Pub. by E Elgar Pub UK) Ashgate Pub Co.

Ross, Arnold, jt. ed. see Newman, William A.

Ross, Austin. Ambulatory Care Management. 2nd ed. 1991. text ed. 41.95 (0-8273-4613-1) Delmar.

— Cornerstones of Leadership for Health Services Executives. LC 91-35345. 220p. 1992. text ed. 42.00 (0-910701-58-X, 0818) Health Admin Pr.

Ross, Austin, et al. Ambulatory Care: Organization & Management. LC 83-16709. (Health Services Ser.: No. 1-456). 453p. 1983. text ed. 41.95 (0-8273-4349-3) Delmar.

Ross, B. Robert. Charts & Tables for Beginning Reading. (Illus.). 48p. 1971. 5.00 (0-87916-003-9) Upstat.

— A Child's Introduction to General Semantics: First Ten Word Games. 60p. pap. 15.00 (0-87916-013-6) Upstat.

— How to Study: To Understand As Well As to Pass Tests, 3 vols., Vols. 1, 2 & 3. 300p. 1989. 50.00 (0-87916-030-6) Upstat.

— How to Study; to Understand As Well As to Pass Tests, Vol. 1: Practical Methods of Study. 120p. 1989. pap. 25.00 (0-87916-012-8); audio write for info. (0-318-60279-2); disk write for info. (0-318-60280-6) Upstat.

— How to Study, To Understand As Well As to Pass Tests, Vol. 2: Theory of Study. 60p. pap. 15.00 (0-87916-028-4) Upstat.

— How to Study, To Understand As Well As to Pass Tests, Vol. 3: Advanced Methods of Study & Thinking. 90p. pap. 25.00 (0-87916-029-2) Upstat.

— Making Affirmations & Prayers Work. 100p. pap. 10.00 (0-87916-027-6) Upstat.

— The Philosophy & Teaching of Reading. 75p. Date not set. 30.00 (0-87916-007-1); pap. 15.00 (0-87916-008-X) Upstat.

Ross, Barbara. The Chef's Table. 208p. 1991. pap. 19.95 (0-04-442221-0, Pub. by Allen Unwin AT) Paul & Co Pubs.

Ross, Barbara T. American Drawings in the Art Museum, Princeton University: 130 Selected Examples. LC 76-27117. (Illus.). 144p. 1977. 45.00x (0-691-03921-6) Princeton U Pr.

Ross, Barry. Hands on Guide to Oscilloscopes. 1994. pap. 21.95 (0-07-053954-5) McGraw.

— Hands on Guide to Oscilloscopes. 1994. pap. text ed. 21.95 (0-07-707818-7) McGraw.

— A Violinist's Guide for Exquisite Intonation. 1988. 9.75 (0-89917-520-1) Am String Tchrs.

Ross, Barry, jt. auth. see Ross, Garry.

Ross, Barry, jt. auth. see Tarr, Bill.

***Ross, Becki.** The House That Jill Built: A Lesbian Nation in Formation. (Illus.). 384p. 1995. 50.00 (0-8020-0460-1); pap. 19.95 (0-8020-7479-0) U of Toronto Pr.

Ross, Bernard D. The Fundamental Pathway to Better Health: A Case for Individualized Replacement Therapy. xvii, 152p. (Orig.). 1984. pap. 8.95 (0-931541-01-8) Mancorp Pub.

— Niacin Can Curb Craving for Alcohol. (Illus.). xiv, 130p. 1990. 16.95 (0-931541-16-6) Mancorp Pub.

Ross, Bernard H., ed. Urban Management: A Guide to Information Sources. LC 78-10310. (Urban Studies Information Guide Ser.: Vol. 8). 304p. 1979. 68.00 (0-8103-1430-4) Gale.

Ross, Bernard H., et al. Urban Politics: Power in Metropolitan America. 4th ed. LC 90-62258. 471p. 1991. pap. 30.00 (0-87581-352-6) Peacock Pubs.

Ross, Bertram. Methods of Summation. ix, 127p. (C). 1987. write for info. (0-936285-08-7, JPY7000, Pub. by Descartes JA); teacher ed write for info. (0-318-64056-2, JPY4000, Pub. by Descartes JA) U New Haven Pr.

Ross, Bertram, jt. auth. see Miller, Kenneth.

Ross, Bette M. Journey of No Return. LC 84-24797. 1987. pap. 7.99 (0-8007-5231-7) Revell.

***Ross, Betty.** Washington D. C. Museum: Museums, Historic Houses, Art Galleries & Other Special Places. 3rd ed. LC 91-39333. (Illus.). 328p. 1992. pap. 14.95 (0-939009-85-4) EPM Pubns.

— Washington, D. C. Museums: A Ross Guide. (Illus.). 325p. (Orig.). 1992. pap. 14.95 (0-9616144-3-9) Americana Pr.

Ross, BevAnne. Freelance: Research for Pay. 187p. (Orig.). 1992. pap. 15.00 (0-9631494-2-3) BAR Pubns.

— A Piece of Parchment. 87p. 1987. pap. 6.00 (0-9631494-0-7) BAR Pubns.

— Presidential Campaigns & the Media: With Special Emphasis Upon the 1988 Campaigns. 732p. (Orig.). (C). 1991. pap. 18.00 (0-9631494-1-5) BAR Pubns.

Ross, Beverlee. Annabelle. (Historical Ser.). 1993. mass mkt. 3.99 (0-373-28778-X, 1-28778-8) Harlequin Bks.

Ross, Beverly B. & Durgin, Jean P. Junior Broadway: How to Produce Musicals with Children 9 to 13. LC 82-23983. (Illus.). 187p. (Orig.). 1983. pap. 21.95x (0-89950-033-1) McFarland & Co.

Ross, Bill, illus. Crazy Christmas Characters. (Orig.). (J). (ps-2). 1991. pap. 3.50 (0-8249-8522-2, Ideals Child) Hambleton-Hill.

— Easter Bunnyheads. 12p. (Orig.). (J). (ps-2). 1992. pap. 2.95 (0-8249-8541-9, Ideals Child) Hambleton-Hill.

— Easter Eggheads. 12p. (Orig.). (J). (ps-2). 1992. pap. 2.95 (0-8249-8540-0, Ideals Child) Hambleton-Hill.

— Funny Bunnyheads. 12p. (J). (ps-2). 1995. pap. 3.50 (1-57102-030-6, Ideals Child) Hambleton-Hill.

— Scrambled Eggheads. 12p. (J). (ps-2). 1995. pap. 3.50 (1-57102-031-4, Ideals Child) Hambleton-Hill.

— Silly Christmas Scenes. (J). (ps-3). 1991. pap. 3.50 (0-8249-8523-0, Ideals Child) Hambleton-Hill.

Ross, Bill, et al. Orange County. (Illus.). 96p. 1988. 19.95 (1-55652-044-1) Chicago Review.

— San Diego. (Illus.). 96p. 1988. 19.95 (1-55652-043-3) Chicago Review.

Ross, Bill D. Iwo Jima: Legacy of Valor. LC 85-40665. (Illus.). 416p. 1986. pap. 12.00 (0-394-74288-5, Vin) Random.

— Peleliu: Tragic Triumph: The Untold Story of the Pacific War's Forgotten Battle. (Illus.). 400p. 1991. 21.50 (0-394-56588-6) Random.

— Special Piece of Hell: The Untold Story of Peleliu - the Pacific War's Forgotten Battle. 1993. mass mkt. 5.99 (0-312-95004-7) St Martin.

Ross, Bob. Campbellites, Cow-Bells, Rosary Beeds, & Snake-Handlers. 1994. 3.95 (1-56186-522-2) Pilgrim Pubns.

— Laugh, Lead & Profit: Building Productive Workplaces with Humor. 125p. (Orig.). (YA). 1989. pap. write for info. (0-318-65545-4) Arrowhead Pub.

Ross, Bob & Kowalski, Annette. The Best of the Joy of Painting. LC 89-62150. (Illus.). 1989. 24.95 (0-688-09246-2) Morrow.

— More Joy of Painting. (Illus.). 256p. 1991. 25.00 (0-688-10046-5) Morrow.

Ross, Bob L. Acts Two: Thirty-Eight. 1976. pap. 2.95 (1-56186-503-6) Pilgrim Pubns.

— Baptism & the Restoration Movement. 1979. pap. 1.95 (1-56186-507-9) Pilgrim Pubns.

— Campbellism: Its History & Heresies. 1962. pap. 3.50 (1-56186-502-8) Pilgrim Pubns.

— History & Heresies of Hardshellism. 1994. pap. 4.95 (1-56186-500-1) Pilgrim Pubns.

— Killing Effects of Calvinism. 1980. pap. 1.95 (1-56186-506-0) Pilgrim Pubns.

— Little Horn of the Book of Daniel. 1983. pap. 2.95 (1-56186-511-7) Pilgrim Pubns.

— Not One Stone. 1993. pap. 5.95 (1-56186-521-4) Pilgrim Pubns.

— Old Landmarkism & the Baptists. 1979. pap. 3.95 (1-56186-504-4) Pilgrim Pubns.

— Pictorial Biography of C. H. Spurgeon. 1974. 8.95 (1-56186-109-X); pap. 5.95 (1-56186-205-3) Pilgrim Pubns.

— The Restoration Movement. 1981. pap. 2.95 (1-56186-509-5) Pilgrim Pubns.

— Salvation by Grace Through Faith in Contrast to the Restorationist Doctrine. 1979. pap. 1.95 (1-56186-508-7) Pilgrim Pubns.

— The Trinity & Eternal Sonship of Christ: A Defense Against "Oneness Pentecostal" Attacks. 1993. pap. 11.95 (1-56186-517-6) Pilgrim Pubns.

Ross, Bonnie, ed. see Vermont Institute of Natural Science Staff.

Ross, Brad. Kidz Sing-Along Poems Car Songbook & Audiocassette. (KIDZ Ser.). (Illus.). 128p. (Orig.). (J). 1994. 9.95 (1-56138-414-3) Running Pr.

Ross, Brian H., jt. auth. see Medin, Douglas L.

Ross, Brion. The Rigger's Locker: Tools & Techniques for Modern & Traditional Rigging. 224p. 1992. 24.95 (0-87742-961-8, 60126) Intl Marine.

Ross, Bruce. Haiku Moment: An Anthology of Contemporary North American Haiku. 368p. 1993. pap. 16.95 (0-8048-1820-7) C E Tuttle.

— The Inheritance of Animal Symbols in Modern Literature & World Culture: Essays, Notes & Lectures. (American University Studies: General Literature: Ser. XIX, Vol. 17). 161p. (C). 1988. text ed. 31.50 (0-8204-0725-9) P Lang Pubs.

Ross, Bruce M. Recovering the Personal Past: The Conceptual Background of Autobiographical Memory. 272p. 1992. 29.95 (0-19-506894-7) OUP.

Ross, C. & Valentine, Ed, eds. Food Industry Environmental Conference Proceedings, 1991. (Illus.). 500p. (C). 1991. 60.00 (0-9624647-5-9) GA Tech Rsch Inst.

Ross, C. Randolph. Common Sense Christianity. LC 88-61552. 266p. 1989. 19.95 (0-929368-00-2) Occam Pubs.

Ross, C. T. Finite Element Programs for Structural Vibrations. (Illus.). x, 187p. 1991. 3.5 hd 129.00 (0-387-19693-5) Spr-Verlag.

— Pressure Vessels under External Pressure: Statics & Dynamics. 250p. 1990. 99.00 (1-85166-433-5) Elsevier.

Ross, C. V. Sheep Production & Management. 512p. 1989. boxed 50.80 (0-13-808510-2) P-H.

Ross, Cal. Counseling the Gifted: Developing the Whole Child. 1990. pap. 6.00 (0-89824-710-1) Trillium Pr.

Ross, Calvert G., et al. War - A Trilogy. 174p. 1993. pap. 6.95 (1-56794-052-8, C-2330) Star Bible.

R

An Asterisk (*) at the beginning of an entry indicates that the title is appearing in BIP for the first time.

Ross, Cameron. Local Government in the Soviet Union: Problems of Implementation & Control. LC 86-29861. 240p. 1987. text ed. 45.00 (*0-312-00545-8*) St Martin.

Ross, Carl, ed. see Appalachian Studies Staff.

Ross, Carl, ed. see Penti, Marsha, et al.

Ross, Carmen F. Personal & Vocational Relationships in Practical Nursing. 5th ed. (Illus.). 290p. 1981. text ed. 19.50 (*0-397-54281-X*, 64-02168, Lippincott Nursing) Lippincott.

Ross, Carol, jt. auth. see Askew, Sue.

Ross, Caroline. Captive of Love. large type ed. (Linford Romance Library). 272p. 1988. pap. 11.95 (*0-7089-6463-X*, Linford) Ulverscroft.

***Ross, Carolyn.** Writing Nature: An Ecological Reader for Writers. 550p. 1995. pap. text ed. 23.28 (*0-312-10391-3*) St Martin.

Ross, Catherine. Cognitive Challenge Cards. 1976. pap. 12.00 (*0-87879-188-4*) Acad Therapy.

Ross, Catherine & Dewdney, Patricia. Communicating Professionally: A How-to-Do-It Manual for Librarians. (How-to-Do-It Ser.). 220p. (Orig.). 1989. pap. text ed. 39.95 (*1-55570-031-4*) Neal-Schuman.

Ross, Catherine E., jt. auth. see Mirowsky, John.

Ross, Catherine H., jt. auth. see Ross, John D.

Ross, Catherine S. Alice Munro: A Double Life. (Illus.). 97p. (Orig.). 1993. pap. 9.95 (*1-55022-153-1*, Pub. by ECW Pr CN) InBook.

— Circles: Fun Ideas for Getting A-Round in Math. LC 92-40159. (Illus.). (J). (gr. 4-7). 1993. pap. 9.57 (*0-201-62268-8*) Addison-Wesley.

Ross, Charles. The Best of Your Personal Finance: Money Management Tips from the Nationally Syndicated Radio Program & Newspaper Column. 164p. (Orig.). 1991. pap. text ed. 12.95 (*0-9629100-0-7*) FMS Pub.

— Computer Systems for Occupational Safety & Health Management. 2nd rev. ed. (Occupational Safety & Health Ser.: Vol. 23). 476p. 1991. 125.00 (*0-8247-8479-0*) Dekker.

— The Inner Sanctuary. 247p. 1992. pap. 7.95 (*0-85151-042-6*) Banner of Truth.

Ross, Charles, ed. Crocodiles & Alligators. 1989. 35.00 (*0-8160-2174-0*) Facts on File.

Ross, Charles A., ed. Paleogeographic Provinces & Provinciality. LC 74-193154. (Society of Economic Paleontologists & Mineralogists, Special Publication Ser.: No. 21). 243p. reprint ed. pap. 69.30 (*0-317-27151-2*, 2024743) Bks Demand.

Ross, Charles C. & Valentine, G. Edd, eds. Food Industry Environmental Conference Proceedings, 1990. (Illus.). 600p. (C). 1990. 60.00 (*0-9624647-3-2*) GA Tech Rsch Inst.

— Food Industry Environmental Conference Proceedings, 1992. (Illus.). 600p. (C). 1992. 60.00 (*0-9624647-6-7*) GA Tech Rsch Inst.

Ross, Charles C., jt. ed. see Valentine, G. Edward.

Ross, Charles L. The Composition of The Rainbow & Women in Love: A History. LC 79-1422. (Illus.). 168p. 1979. 25.00 (*0-8139-0704-7*) U Pr of Va.

— Richard III. LC 81-43381. (English Monarchs Ser.: No. 6). (Illus.). 263p. 1982. pap. 13.00 (*0-520-05075-4*) U CA Pr.

— The Wars of the Roses: A Concise History. LC 85-52289. (Illus.). 190p. 1986. pap. 15.95 (*0-500-27407-X*) Thames Hudson.

— Women in Love: A Novel of Mythic Realism. (Twayne's Masterworks Ser.: No. 65). 152p. 1991. text ed. 21.95 (*0-8057-8057-2*, Pub. by Royal Botanic Garden UK); pap. 12.95 (*0-8057-8106-4*, Pub. by Royal Botanic Garden UK) Macmillan.

***Ross, Charles L. & Jackson, Dennis, eds.** Editing D. H. Lawrence: New Versions of a Modern Author. LC 95-10370. (Editorial Theory & Literary Criticism Ser.). 1995. write for info. (*0-472-10612-0*) U of Mich Pr.

Ross, Charles L., ed. see Lawrence, D. H.

Ross, Christine. Lily & the Present. LC 91-41134. (Illus.). 28p. (J). (ps-3). 1992. 13.95 (*0-395-61127-X*) HM.

— The Whirlys & the West Wind. LC 92-39011. (J). 1993. 13.95 (*0-395-65379-7*) HM.

Ross, Christopher S., ed. see O'Farrell, Valerie & Neville, Peter.

Ross, Cindy. Journey on the Crest: Walking 2,600 Miles from Mexico to Canada. LC 87-28160. (Illus.). 320p. (Orig.). 1987. pap. 11.95 (*0-89886-146-2*) Mountaineers.

— A Woman's Journey. Orig. Title: A Woman's Journey on the Appalachian Trail. (Illus.). 128p. 1991. reprint ed. 9.95 (*0-917953-42-8*) Appalachian Trail.

Ross, Cindy & Gladfelter, Todd. A Hiker's Companion: Twelve Thousand Miles of Trail-Tested Wisdom. LC 92-46568. (Illus.). 224p. (Orig.). 1993. pap. 12.95 (*0-89886-353-8*) Mountaineers.

Ross, Clarissa. Beloved Scoundrel. 1980. pap. 1.95 (*0-8439-0710-X*) Dorchester Pub Co.

— China Shadow. 448p. 1985. reprint ed. pap. 3.75 (*0-8439-2237-0*) Dorchester Pub Co.

— Flame of Love. 1978. pap. 1.95 (*0-8439-0583-2*) Dorchester Pub Co.

— Let Your Heart Answer. large type ed. 1994. 21.95 (*0-7089-3210-X*) Ulverscroft.

— Moscow Mists. 416p. 1985. reprint ed. pap. 3.95 (*0-8439-2280-X*) Dorchester Pub Co.

— A Scandalous Affair. large type ed. 304p. 1995. 23.95 (*0-7089-3248-7*) Ulverscroft.

— So Perilous, My Love. 1979. pap. 2.25 (*0-8439-0606-5*) Dorchester Pub Co.

— The Spectral Mist. large type ed. 1992. pap. 17.95 (*0-7927-1287-0*, Curley Lrg Print) Chivers N Amer.

Ross, Clark G., jt. auth. see Hess, Peter N.

***Ross, Clay C.** Differential Equations: An Introduction with Mathematica. LC 94-36401. (Texts in Mathematical Sciences Ser.: Vol. 1). 1995. 44.95 (*0-387-94301-3*) Spr-Verlag.

— The Relation Between Grade School Record & High School Achievement: A Study of the Diagnostic Value of Individual Record Cards. LC 70-177211. (Columbia University. Teachers College. Contributions to Education Ser.: No. 166). reprint ed. 37.50 (*0-404-55166-1*) AMS Pr.

Ross, Cleon W. Plant Physiology Laboratory Manual. 200p. (C). 1974. pap. 21.95 (*0-534-00351-6*) Intl Thomson.

Ross, Cleon W., jt. auth. see Salisbury, Frank B.

Ross, Clifford, ed. Abstract Expressionism: Creators & Critics. (Illus.). 288p. 1991. 49.50 (*0-8109-1908-7*) Abrams.

Ross, Clifton, tr. see Cardenal, Ernesto.

Ross, Clifton, ed. see Zapatista National Liberation Army Staff.

Ross, Clifton, tr. see Zapatista National Liberation Army Staff.

Ross, Clyde. Valdez Creek Mining District Alaska. 56p. reprint ed. pap. 4.95 (*0-8466-0107-9*, S107) Shorey.

Ross, Colin. Adenocarcinoma & Other Poems. (C). 1989. 60.00 (*0-907839-38-X*, Pub. by Brynmill Pr Ltd UK) St Mut.

Ross, Colin A. Multiple Personality Disorder: Diagnosis, Clinical Features & Treatment. 380p. 1989. text ed. 60.00 (*0-471-61515-3*) Wiley.

— The Osiris Complex: Case Studies in Multiple Personality Disorder. LC 93-95100. 296p. (C). 1994. 50.00 (*0-8020-2858-6*); pap. 17.95 (*0-8020-7358-1*) U of Toronto Pr.

— Satanic Ritual Abuse: Principles of Treatment. 256p. (C). 1995. 45.00 (*0-8020-2857-8*); pap. 16.95 (*0-8020-7357-3*) U of Toronto Pr.

Ross, Connie, illus. Betty Elizabeth Brown: A Keepsake Book. 32p. (J). (ps up). 1992. pap. 2.75 (*1-878893-26-2*) Telcraft Bks.

— Dearie Dot: A Keepsake Book. 32p. (J). (ps up). 1992. pap. 2.75 (*1-878893-25-4*) Telcraft Bks.

Ross, Corinne. To Market to Market. (Illus.). 1980. pap. 4.50 (*0-89182-022-1*) Charles River Bks.

Ross, Courtney. Listen Up. 1990. audio 34.95 (*0-446-39233-2*); cd-rom 39.95 (*0-446-39286-3*) Warner Bks.

Ross-Craig, Stella. Drawings of British Plants, 8 vols., Set. Incl. Vol. 1. 1980. 32.50 (*0-7135-1137-0*); Vol. 2. 1980. 32.50 (*0-7135-1138-9*); Vol. 3. 1980. 32.50 (*0-7135-1139-7*); Vol. 4. 1980. 32.50 (*0-685-73376-9*); Vol. 5. 1980. 32.50 (*0-7135-1141-9*); Vol. 6. 1980. 32.50 (*0-7135-1142-7*); Vol. 7. 1980. 32.50 (*0-7135-1143-5*); Vol. 8. 1980. 32.50 (*0-685-73377-7*); (Illus.). 1980. 256.25 (*0-7135-1110-9*) Lubrecht & Cramer.

Ross, Cynthia. D'Aulaires Book of Greek Myths: A Literature Unit. (Literature Units Ser.). (Illus.). 48p. 1993. student ed 6.95 (*1-55734-423-X*) Tchr Create Mat.

— Medieval Times: A Thematic Unit. (Thematic Units Ser.). (Illus.). 80p. 1992. student ed 8.95 (*1-55734-291-1*) Tchr Create Mat.

Ross, Cynthia M. & Stangl, Karen M. The Music Teacher's Book of Lists. LC 94-2407. 1994. write for info. (*0-13-093832-7*, Parker Publishing Co) P-H.

Ross, D. Mechanics of Underwater Noise. LC 76-18731. 1976. 166.00 (*0-08-021182-8*, Pub. by Pergamon Repr UK) Franklin.

— The U. K. Taxation of Modern Financial Instruments & Transactions. 64p. 1989. text ed. 60.00 (*0-304-31831-0*) Cassell.

Ross, D. A., et al. Woollen Yarn Manufacture, Vol. 15, No. 1/2. 87p. (C). 1986. pap. text ed. 85.00 (*0-900739-86-X*, Pub. by Textile Institue UK) St Mut.

Ross, D. B. & Guder, W. G., eds. Biochemical Aspects of Renal Function: Proceedings of a Symposium Held in Honour of Professor Sir Hans Krebs FRS, at Merton College, Oxford, 16-19 September 1979. (Illus.). 340p. 1980. pap. 67.00 (*0-08-025517-5*, Pergamon Pr) Elsevier.

Ross, D. N., et al. Principles of Cardiac Diagnosis & Treatment: A Surgeon's Guide. 2nd ed. (Illus.). ix, 269p. 1991. 129.00 (*0-387-17494-X*) Spr-Verlag.

Ross, D. S., ed. Machine Control Systems: Proceedings of the International Conference (MACON 1), 1st, Brighton, U. K., 23-25 October, 1984. 260p. 1985. 110.25 (*0-444-87628-6*, North Holland) Elsevier.

Ross, D. W. Introduction to Molecular Medicine. (Illus.). 184p. 1994. pap. 29.50 (*0-387-97724-4*) Spr-Verlag.

— On Drawing & Painting. LC 78-137285. (Illus.). reprint ed. 44.50 (*0-404-05406-4*) AMS Pr.

Ross, Dan. Moscow Maze. 304p. 1983. pap. 3.25 (*0-8439-2055-6*) Dorchester Pub Co.

Ross, Dana F. California Glory. (Holts Ser.: No. 4). 1991. mass mkt. 4.99 (*0-553-28970-5*) Bantam.

— California Glory. large type ed. (General Ser.). 476p. 1992. text ed. 21.95 (*0-8161-5310-8*, Large Print Bks) Hall.

— Carolina Courage. (Holts Ser.: No. 3). 1991. 5.99 (*0-553-28756-7*) Bantam.

— Celebration! large type ed. (General Ser.). 384p. 1991. lib. bdg. 18.95 (*0-8161-4978-X*) G K Hall.

— Expedition! large type ed. LC 92-30415. (General Ser.). 546p. 1993. 22.95 (*0-8161-5514-3*); pap. 16.95 (*0-8161-5515-1*) G K Hall.

— Expedition: Wagons West, the Frontier Trilogy, Bk. 2. 1993. 5.50 (*0-553-29403-2*) Bantam.

— Hawaii Heritage. (Holts, an American Dynasty Ser.: No. 5). 1991. mass mkt. 5.50 (*0-553-29414-8*) Bantam.

— Hawaii Heritage. large type ed. (General Ser.). 464p. 1992. text ed. 20.95 (*0-8161-5421-X*, Large Print Bks) Hall.

— Holts, an American Dynasty, Vol. 6: Sierra Triumph. 1992. mass mkt. 5.50 (*0-553-29750-3*) Bantam.

— Homecoming. large type ed. 1995. 22.95 (*0-7838-1173-X*, Large Print Bks) Hall.

— Homecoming: The Holts, Bk. 9. 1994. mass mkt. 5.99 (*0-553-56150-2*) Bantam.

— Independence! (Wagons West Ser.: No. 1). 1984. 5.50 (*0-553-26822-8*) Bantam.

— New Mexico! large type ed. (General Ser.). 397p. 1990. 20.95 (*0-8161-4771-X*, Large Print Bks) Hall.

— Oklahoma! (Wagons West Ser.: No. 23). 1989. pap. 4.50 (*0-685-25336-8*) Bantam.

— Oklahoma! Wagons West, No. 23. large type ed. (General Ser.). 464p. 1990. 19.95 (*0-8161-4897-X*, Large Print Bks) G K Hall.

— Oklahoma Pride. (Holts, an American Dynasty Ser.: No. 2). 1990. 5.50 (*0-553-28446-0*) Bantam.

— Oklahoma Pride. large type ed. (General Ser.). 416p. 1991. text ed. 20.95 (*0-8161-5101-6*, Large Print Bks) Hall.

— Oregon Legacy. 1989. 5.50 (*0-553-28248-4*) Bantam.

— Oregon Legacy. large type ed. (General Ser.). 482p. 1991. text ed. 20.95 (*0-8161-4989-5*, Large Print Bks) Hall.

— Outpost! large type ed. LC 93-8890. (Wagons West Ser.: Vol. 3). 1993. 22.95 (*0-8161-5516-X*) Hall.

— Outpost! large type ed. LC 93-8890. (Wagons West Ser.: Vol. 3). 1994. pap. 17.95 (*0-8161-5517-8*) Hall.

— Pacific Destiny. 1994. 5.99 (*0-553-56149-9*) Bantam.

— Pacific Destiny. large type ed. LC 94-25460. 507p. 1994. 21.95 (*0-8161-7466-0*) Hall.

— Sierra Triumph Vol. 6: The Holts; An American Dynasty. braille ed. 629p. 1994. text ed. 50.32 (*1-56956-478-7*, BR9322) W A T Braille.

— Wagons West, No. 22: New Mexico. 1988. pap. 4.50 (*0-318-37676-8*) Bantam.

— Westward! large type ed. (General Ser.). 640p. 1992. lib. bdg. 21.95 (*0-8161-5448-1*, Large Print Bks); pap. 16.95 (*0-8161-5449-X*, Large Print Bks) Hall.

— Westward! Wagons West, the Trilogy. 1992. mass mkt. 5.50 (*0-553-29402-4*) Bantam.

— Yankee. large type ed. 1993. 21.95 (*1-56895-044-6*) Wheeler Pub.

— Yankee Rogue. LC 94-8217. 1994. 22.95 (*1-56895-066-7*) Wheeler Pub.

— Yukon Justice. (Holts, an American Dynasty Ser.: No. 7). 1992. 5.50 (*0-553-29763-5*) Bantam.

— Yukon Justice. large type ed. LC 92-15296. (General Ser.). 1992. pap. 16.95 (*0-8161-5488-0*) G K Hall.

— Yukon Justice. large type ed. LC 92-15296. (General Ser.). 464p. 1992. text ed. 21.95 (*0-8161-5487-2*, Large Print Bks) Hall.

— Yukon Justice Vol. 7: The Holts: An American Dynasty. braille ed. 622p. 1994. text ed. 49.76 (*1-56956-485-X*, BR9323) W A T Braille.

Ross, Dana Fuller. Carolina Courage. large type ed. 400p. 1991. text ed. 19.95 (*0-8161-5309-4*, Large Print Bks) Hall.

Ross, Daniel. UFO's & the Complete Evidence from Space: The Truth about Venus, Mars, & the Moon. (Illus.). 242p. (Orig.). (C). 1987. pap. 9.95 (*0-944255-00-0*) Pintado Pub.

Ross, Dave. A Book of Hugs. LC 79-7896. (Illus.). 32p. (J). (gr. k up). 1991. reprint ed. pap. 3.95 (*0-06-107418-7*) HarpC Child Bks.

— How to Prevent Monster Attacks. LC 83-26536. (Illus.). 64p. (J). (gr. 4 up). 1984. 7.00 (*0-688-03790-9*) Morrow Jr Bks.

— Little Mouse's Valentine. LC 85-15357. (Illus.). 32p. (J). (ps-00). 1986. 15.00 (*0-688-06224-5*) Morrow Jr Bks.

Ross, David. Aristotle. 5th ed. 312p. 1964. pap. 17.95 (*0-415-04306-9*, NO.2421) Routledge.

— Aristotle. 6th ed. LC 94-43265. 336p. 1995. pap. 18.95 (*0-415-12068-3*, C0115) Routledge.

— The BiNational: American Art of the Late 80's. (Illus.). 1988. 19.95 (*0-87846-301-1*) ICA Inc.

— Little Book of Scottish Verse. 1993. 7.95 (*0-8118-0515-8*) Chronicle Bks.

— A Little History of Scotland. (Little Irish Book Ser.). (Illus.). 60p. 1995. 7.95 (*0-86281-541-X*, Pub. by Appletree Pr IE) Irish Bks Media.

— Power from the Waves. (Illus.). 224p. 1995. 32.00 (*0-19-856511-9*) OUP.

— Utopia Post Utopia. (Illus.). 1988. 12.95 (*0-685-26094-1*) ICA Inc.

Ross, David & Usher, Peter. From the Roots Up: Economic Development As If Community Mattered. LC 85-27972. 192p. (Orig.). 1986. pap. 13.50 (*0-942850-04-1*) Intermediate Tech.

Ross, David, ed. see Aristotle.

Ross, David, ed. see Joachim, Harold H.

Ross, David, jt. auth. see May, Robin.

Ross, David, et al. Boston Now: Sculpture, Emerging Massachusetts Painters. Institute of Contemporary Art, Inc. Staff & The, Museum of Fine Arts, eds. LC 84-80928. 125p. (Orig.). 1984. pap. 6.00 (*0-910663-41-6*) ICA Inc.

Ross, David A. Introduction to Oceanography. 4th ed. (Illus.). 464p. (C). 1987. text ed. write for info. (*0-13-491408-2*) P-H.

Ross, David A., jt. auth. see Harten, Jurgen.

Ross, David F., et al, eds. Adult Eyewitness Testimony: Current Trends & Developments. LC 93-8004. (Illus.). 384p. (C). 1994. 59.95 (*0-521-43255-3*) Cambridge U Pr.

Ross, David H., jt. ed. see Loh, Horace H.

Ross, David J. A Dynasty Restored: Through the Eyes of Their No. 1 Fan. LC 94-60197. 192p. 1994. pap. text ed. 12.95 (*1-884570-05-4*) Research Triangle.

***Ross, David O.** Virgil's Elements: Physics & Poetry in the Georgics. LC 86-22598. Date not set. reprint ed. pap. 76.40 (*0-7837-9435-5*, 2060177) Bks Demand.

Ross, David O., Jr. Virgil's Elements: Physics & Poetry in the Georgics. 250p. 1987. text ed. 39.50 (*0-691-06699-X*) Princeton U Pr.

Ross, David R., jt. auth. see Scherer, Jeanne C.

Ross, David R., et al. The Emergence of Modern America: 1865-1900. LC 78-101951. (Structure of American History Ser.). 256p. (C). 1970. pap. text ed. write for info. (*0-88295-758-9*) Harlan Davidson.

— Forging the Nation: 1763-1828, Vol. 2. LC 78-101951. (Structure of American History Ser.). 256p. (C). 1970. pap. text ed. write for info. (*0-88295-756-2*) Harlan Davidson.

Ross, David R., et al, eds. Nation in Crisis Eighteen Twenty-Eight to Eighteen Sixty-Five. LC 78-101951. (Structure of American History Ser.: Vol. 3). (C). 1970. pap. text ed. write for info. (*0-88295-757-0*) Harlan Davidson.

— Progress, War & Reaction: 1900-1933. LC 78-101951. (Structure of American History Ser.: Vol. 5). (C). 1970. pap. text ed. write for info. (*0-88295-759-7*) Harlan Davidson.

Ross, David W. Beyond the Stars. 528p. 1991. mass mkt. 5.95 (*0-380-71471-X*) Avon.

— Eye of the Hawk. 512p. 1992. 22.00 (*0-671-75513-7*) S&S Trade.

— Eye of the Hawk. 512p. 1994. mass mkt. 5.99 (*0-380-72232-1*) Avon.

Ross, Deane. The Ross Guide to Rose Growing. (Illus.). 118p. (Orig.). 1995. pap. 22.95 (*0-85091-395-0*, Pub. by Lothian Pub AT) Seven Hills Bk.

Ross, Deborah. The Excellence of Falsehood: Romance, Realism, & Women's Contribution to the Novel. LC 91-22068. 264p. 1992. text ed. 29.00 (*0-8131-1764-X*) U Pr of Ky.

Ross, Deborah & Spencer, Sara. Reading & Writing Task Hierarchy. (Illus.). 350p. (C). 1981. spiral bd. 49.95x (*0-398-04642-5*) C C Thomas.

Ross, Deborah & Spencer, Sara H. Aphasia Rehabilitation: An Auditory & Verbal Task Hierarchy. (Illus.). 272p. 1980. 38.95 (*0-398-04031-1*) C C Thomas.

— Aphasia Rehabilitation: An Auditory & Verbal Task Hierarchy. (Illus.). 272p. 1980. pap. 24.95 (*0-398-06409-1*) C C Thomas.

Ross, Deborah G. Ross Information Processing Assessment: A Cognitive-Linguistic Assessment. 44p. 1986. 69.00 (*0-88120-379-3*, 2102); teacher ed 29.00 (*0-685-17381-X*, 2104); 42.00 (*0-685-17382-8*, 2103) PRO-ED.

Ross, Debra. Federal Equal Opportunity Deskbook, 1994. 1992. pap. 59.50 (*0-934753-70-9*) LRP Pubns.

Ross, Delmer G. Gold Road to La Paz: An Interpretive Guide to the Bradshaw Trail. (Illus.). 304p. 1992. 22.50 (*0-914224-24-7*) Tales Mojave Rd.

Ross, Dennis. The Conservation of Strangeness. LC 80-22044. 1980. pap. 3.95 (*0-914974-18-1*) Holmgangers.

— Incremental or Comprehensive SALT: Is Some SALT Better Than No SALT. (CISA Working Paper Ser.: No. 16). 27p. (Orig.). Date not set. pap. 10.00 (*0-86682-015-9*) Ctr Intl Relations.

— Rethinking Soviet Strategic Policy: Inputs & Implications. (CISA Working Paper Ser.: No. 5). 46p. (Orig.). Date not set. pap. 10.00 (*0-86682-004-3*) Ctr Intl Relations.

Ross, Dennis W. Blood. LC 87-70225. (Carolina Biology Readers Ser.: No. 184). (Illus.). 16p. (Orig.). (YA). (gr. 10 up). 1988. pap. text ed. 2.75 (*0-89278-184-X*, 45-9784) Carolina Biological.

Ross, Derek, et al. International Treasury Management. 1990. 54.95 (*0-317-04754-X*) NY Inst Finance.

Ross, Derek E., jt. auth. see Thorpe, Nicolas M.

Ross, Diana. Secrets of a Sparrow. 1993. 22.00 (*0-679-42874-7*, Villard Bks) Random.

Ross, Don. Metaphor, Meaning, & Cognition. LC 93-6956. (American University Studies: Vol. 149). 210p. 1993. 38.95 (*0-8204-2151-0*) P Lang Pubs.

— Rubber Powered Model Airplanes: The Handbook on Designing-Building-Flying. (Illus.). 144p. 1992. pap. 13.95 (*0-938716-19-0*) Motorbooks Intl.

Ross, Don & Ross, Helen. Zero Seven Fifty-Five: Pearl Harbor Heroes: Heroism of 250 Men & Women 7 December 1941. 200p. 1988. pap. 11.95 (*0-930942-15-9*) Rokalu Pr.

Ross, Donald. Mechanics of Underwater Noise. LC 76-18731. 315p. 1987. reprint ed. 53.95 (*0-932146-16-3*) Peninsula CA.

— A Public Citizen's Action Manual. 238p. pap. 1.95 (*0-686-36537-2*) Ctr Responsive Law.

Ross, Donald, Jr., jt. auth. see Adams, Stephen.

Ross, Donald, jt. auth. see Bila, Dennis.

Ross, Donald K. Newspaper Correspondent's Manual. 40p. reprint ed. pap. 25.00 (*0-317-26680-2*, 2025110) Bks Demand.

***Ross, Donald K. & Ross, Helen L.** More Men of Valor. 2nd rev. ed. 256p. 1994. 20.00 (*0-614-00512-4*) Perry Pub WA.

— Washington State Men of Valor. 2nd rev. ed. LC 94-68497. (Illus.). 259p. 1994. 22.00 (*0-9620552-1-2*) Rokalu Pr.

Ross, Donald M., jt. auth. see Ormiston, Hugh.

Ross, Doran H., ed. Elephant: The Animal & Its Ivory in African Culture. LC 92-73840. (Illus.). 464p. 1992. 69.00 (*0-930741-25-0*); pap. 39.00 (*0-930741-26-9*) UCLA Fowler Mus.

— Visions of Africa: The Jerome L. Joss Collection of African Art at UCLA. (Exhibition Ser.). (Illus.). 164p. 1994. 35.00 (*0-930741-33-1*); pap. 19.00 (*0-930741-34-X*) UCLA Fowler Mus.

Ross, Dorene D., et al. Reflective Teaching for Student Empowerment: Elementary Curriculum & Methods. (Illus.). 496p. (Orig.). (C). 1993. pap. write for info. (*0-02-403960-8*) Macmillan.

Ross, Dorothy. G. Stanley Hall: The Psychologist As Prophet. LC 75-165180. 482p. 1972. lib. bdg. 25.00 (*0-226-72821-8*) U Ch Pr.

An Asterisk (*) at the beginning of an entry indicates that the title is appearing in BIP for the first time.

— The Origins of American Social Science. (Ideas in Context Ser.: No. 19). 528p. (C). 1990. 39.95 (*0-521-35092-1*) Cambridge U Pr.

— The Origins of American Social Science. (Ideas in Context Ser.: No. 19). 544p. (C). 1992. pap. 17.95 (*0-521-42836-X*) Cambridge U Pr.

Ross, Dorothy, ed. Modernist Impulses in the Human Sciences, 1870-1930. LC 93-38354. (C). 1994. 58.00 (*0-8018-4744-3*); pap. 18.95 (*0-8018-4745-1*) Johns Hopkins.

Ross, Dorthy M. Fundraising for Youth. Zapel, Arthur L., ed. LC 84-61477. (Illus.). 256p. (Orig.). 1985. pap. 9.95 (*0-916260-28-3*, B-184) Meriwether Pub.

Ross, Douglas A. In the Interests of Peace: Canada & Vietnam 1954-1973. 496p. 1984. 35.00 (*0-8020-5632-6*) U of Toronto Pr.

— Optoelectronic Devices & Optical Imaging Techniques. (Electrical & Electronic Engineering Ser.). (Illus.). 137p. 1979. pap. text ed. 32.00 (*0-333-25335-3*, Pub. by Macmill Press UK) Scholium Intl.

Ross, Douglas A., jt. ed. see Langdon, Frank C.

Ross, E. The Social Revolution in Mexico. 1976. lib. bdg. 59.95 (*0-8490-2618-0*) Gordon Pr.

Ross, E. C., tr. see Sirhan, Sirhan.

Ross, E. Denison, ed. The Hafez Poems of Gertrude Bell: With the Original Persian on the Facing Page. LC 94-7718. (Classics of Persian Literature Ser.: Vol. 1). (Illus.). 168p. (Orig.). (ENG & PER.). 1994. pap. 14.95 (*0-936347-39-2*) Iran Bks.

Ross, E. Denison, tr. see Lammens, Henri.

Ross, E. Lamar, ed. Interethnic Communication. LC 77-27456. (Southern Anthropological Society Proceedings Ser.: No. 12). 158p. (C). 1978. 10.00x (*0-8203-0441-7*) U of Ga Pr.

Ross, E. M. & Wirtz, K. W. A., eds. Biological Signal Transduction. (NATO ASI Series H: Cell Biology: Vol. 52). xi, 540p. 1991. 198.00 (*0-387-51773-1*) Spr-Verlag.

Ross, E. Wayne, et al, eds. Teacher Personal Theorizing: Connecting Curriculum, Practice, Theory, & Research. LC 91-27209. (SUNY Series, Teacher Preparation & Development). 324p. (C). 1992. 64.50 (*0-7914-1125-7*); pap. 21.95 (*0-7914-1126-5*) State U NY Pr.

Ross, Earle D. Democracy's College: The Land-Grant Movement in the Formative Stage. LC 74-89226. (American Education: Its Men, Institutions & Ideas, Ser. 1). 1973. reprint ed. 15.95 (*0-405-01463-5*) Ayer.

— Liberal Republican Movement. LC 71-137286. reprint ed. 20.00 (*0-404-05407-2*) AMS Pr.

— The Liberal Republican Movement. LC 79-125183. (Americana Library Ser.: No. 20). 292p. 1970. reprint ed. 25.00 (*0-295-95095-1*) U of Wash Pr.

***Ross, Edward.** Murder in Montrose. 191p. 1995. pap. 7.95 (*0-9635448-1-0*) Thornhse Pr.

— The Silver Hammer. LC 92-46184. 192p. (Orig.). 1993. pap. 7.95 (*0-9635448-0-2*) Thornhse Pr.

Ross, Edward A. The Old World in the New: The Significance of Past & Present Immigration to the American People. LC 77-145491. (American Immigration Library). x, 327p. 1971. reprint ed. lib. bdg. 37.95 (*0-89198-024-5*) Ozer.

— Roads to Social Peace. LC 79-117830. (Essay Index Reprint Ser.). 1977. 17.95 (*0-8369-1679-4*) Ayer.

— Seventy Years of It: An Autobiography. Metzger, Walter P., ed. LC 76-55183. (Academic Profession Ser.). (Illus.). 1977. reprint ed. lib. bdg. 29.95 (*0-405-10010-8*) Ayer.

— Social Psychology. LC 73-14178. (Perspectives in Social Inquiry Ser.). 394p. 1974. reprint ed. 25.95 (*0-405-05521-8*) Ayer.

— Social Trend. LC 72-117831. (Essay Index Reprint Ser.). 1977. 20.95 (*0-8369-1680-8*) Ayer.

— Standing Room Only? Grob, Gerald, ed. LC 76-46101. (Anti-Movements in America Ser.). 1977. reprint ed. lib. bdg. 31.95 (*0-405-09972-X*) Ayer.

Ross, Edward D., jt. auth. see Skrine, Francis H.

Ross, Edward S. Ants. LC 92-44257. (J). (gr. 2-6). 1993. lib. bdg. 22.79 (*1-56766-056-8*) Childs World.

— Yellowjackets. LC 92-42934. (Naturebook Ser.). (J). (gr. 2-6). 1993. lib. bdg. 22.79 (*1-56766-017-7*) Childs World.

***Ross, Eileen.** Josh. 93p. (Orig.). (J). (gr. 3-7). 1994. pap. 5.00 (*0-88092-104-8*) Royal Fireworks.

— Josh. 93p. (J). (gr. 3-7). 1994. lib. bdg. 15.00 (*0-88092-105-6*) Royal Fireworks.

— Lucinda the Late. LC 92-14092. (Illus.). 32p. (J). (ps-2). Date not set. 11.95 (*1-56065-164-4*) Capstone Pr.

— Savage Shadows. 272p. (Orig.). 1993. mass mkt. 4.99 (*1-55773-885-8*) Diamond.

Ross, Eileen, et al. Savage Shadows: Eileen Ross's True Story of Blindness, Rape - & Courage. LC 91-66895. 1992. 21.95 (*0-88282-105-9*) New Horizon NJ.

***Ross, Eleanor.** Schooling Exercises for Flatwork & Jumping. (Illus.). 95p. 1992. pap. 20.95 (*1-872082-31-9*) Half Halt Pr.

Ross, Eleanora "Betsy". After Suicide: A Ray of Hope. 2nd rev. ed. 230p. 1990. per. 16.95 (*0-940179-01-6*) Lynn Pubns.

— After Suicide: A Unique Grief Process. 24p. 1987. pap. 4.95 (*0-940179-02-4*) Lynn Pubns.

Ross, Elena & Champlin, Allen R., Sr. Ghost Riders in the Sky. Hartstrom, Noelle, ed. (Orig.). (YA). (gr. 12). Date not set. pap. write for info. (*0-9628802-1-3*) DeChamp CA.

Ross, Elinor P., jt. auth. see Roe, Betty D.

Ross, Elinor P., et al. An Introduction to Teaching the Language Arts. Youngblood, Dawn, ed. LC 89-15243. 432p. (C). 1990. text ed. 42.00 (*0-03-014922-3*) HB Coll Pubs.

Ross, Elizabeth. What for the Future - Famine or Feast? 51p. 1.50 (*0-89567-019-4*) World View Forum.

Ross, Elizabeth, jt. auth. see Patmore, Ruth.

Ross, Elizabeth I. How to Write While You Sleep: And Other Surprising Ways to Increase Your Creativity. LC 92-31266. (Orig.). 1993. pap. 12.95 (*0-89087-688-6*) Celestial Arts.

Ross, Ellen. Love & Toil: Motherhood in Outcast London, 1870-1918. LC 92-40849. (Illus.). 1993. 55.00 (*0-19-503957-2*); pap. 19.95 (*0-19-508321-0*) OUP.

Ross, Elmer L. Factors in Residence Patterns Among Latin Americans in New Orleans, Louisiana. Cortes, Carlos E., ed. LC 79-6223. (Hispanics in the United States Ser.). (Illus.). 1981. lib. bdg. 29.95 (*0-405-13170-4*) Ayer.

Ross, Eric. Full of Hope & Promise: The Canadas in 1841. (Illus.). 1991. 37.95 (*0-7735-0855-4*, Pub. by McGill CN) U of Toronto Pr.

Ross, Eric B., jt. auth. see Harris, Marvin.

Ross, Estelle. Martin Luther. LC 83-45673. (Illus.). reprint ed. 28.00 (*0-404-19862-7*) AMS Pr.

Ross, Euan, ed. Paediatric Perspectives on Epilepsy: A Symposium Held at the Grand Hotel, Eastbourne, December 1984, Vol. 198. LC 85-12009. 163p. 1985. text ed. 84.00 (*0-471-90817-7*, A R Liss) Wiley.

Ross, Euan, et al, eds. Epilepsy in Young People: Symposium Held at the Holiday Inn, Portsmouth, June 1986. 180p. 1987. text ed. 69.95 (*0-471-91469-X*, A R Liss) Wiley.

Ross, Eulalie S. The Spirited Life: Bertha Mahony Miller & Children's Books. LC 73-84132. (Illus.). 274p. 1973. 12.95 (*0-87675-057-9*) Horn Bk.

Ross, Eunice L., jt. auth. see Reed, Thomas J.

Ross, F. Russel & King, Virginia. Multicultural Dance. (Illus.). 174p. (Orig.). 1985. pap. 17.95 (*0-9615280-0-1*); pap. text ed. 14.95 (*0-317-31639-7*) Russel & King.

Ross, Felice, tr. see Durrenmatt, Friedrich & Selz, Peter.

Ross, Floyd H. Shinto, the Way of Japan. LC 83-12970. (Illus.). xvii, 187p. 1983. reprint ed. text ed. 52.50 (*0-313-24240-2*, RSHI, Greenwood Pr) Greenwood.

Ross, Frances. Some Special Times: Selected Poems. (Illus.). 1976. pap. 3.95 (*0-915242-07-9*) Pygmalion Pr.

Ross, Frank, Jr. The Metric System: Measures for All Mankind. LC 74-14503. (Illus.). 128p. (J). (gr. 7-10). 1974. 30.95 (*0-87599-198-X*) S G Phillips.

— Oracles Bones, Stars & the Wheelbarrows: Ancient Chinese Science & Technology. (YA). 1990. pap. 5.95 (*0-395-54967-1*) HM.

Ross, Franz & Kluepfel, Brian, eds. Holography Marketplace. 4th ed. 192p. pap. 19.95 (*0-89496-059-8*) Ross Bks.

Ross, Fred. Conquering Goliath: Cesar Chavez at the Beginning. 145p. 1992. reprint ed. pap. 14.95 (*0-9625298-0-X*) Wayne St U Pr.

Ross, Frederick. Slavery Ordained of God. LC 70-95445. (Studies in Black History & Culture: No. 54). 1970. reprint ed. lib. bdg. 75.00 (*0-8383-1202-0*) M S G Haskell Hse.

Ross, Frederick, et al. A Glossary of Words Used in Holderness in the East Riding of Yorkshire. (English Dialect Society Publications Ser.: No. 16). 1969. reprint ed. pap. 16.00 (*0-8115-0448-4*) Periodicals Srv.

Ross, Frederick A. Slavery Ordained by God. LC 74-83876. (Black Heritage Library Collection). 1977. 17.95 (*0-8369-8647-4*) Ayer.

Ross, Frederick C. Introductory Microbiology. 2nd ed. (C). 1986. text ed. 70.50 (*0-673-18681-4*) HarpCollege.

Ross, G. Computer Programming Examples for Chemical Engineers. (Computer Aided Chemical Engineering Ser.: No. 3). 296p. 1987. 92.50 (*0-444-42836-4*); pap. 51.50 (*0-444-42837-2*); disk 46.25 (*0-444-42843-7*) Elsevier.

Ross, G. J. MLP Manual. 1980. 11.20 (*0-317-52206-X*, Pub. by Rothamsted Stats UK) Numer Algorithms.

— Non-Linear Estimation. Brillinger, David R. et al, eds. (Series in Statistics). (Illus.). viii, 189p. 1990. 39.00 (*0-387-97278-1*) Spr-Verlag.

Ross, G. M., jt. ed. see Dorobek, S. L.

Ross, G. MacLeod. The Business of Tanks, 1933 to 1945. 340p. (C). 1989. 75.00 (*0-685-36176-4*, Pub. by A H S Ltd UK) St Mut.

— The Business of Tanks, 1933-1945. 340p. (C). 1990. 35.00 (*0-685-49137-4*, Pub. by A H S Ltd UK) St Mut.

Ross, G. R., jt. auth. see Descartes, Rene.

Ross, G. W., jt. auth. see Buckingham, W.

Ross, Gaby. Damien the Dragon. 1990. pap. 6.95 (*1-85371-078-4*, Pub. by Poolbeg Pr IE) Dufour.

Ross, Gail E., jt. auth. see Goldfarb, Ronald L.

Ross, Garry & Ross, Barry. Lifelines - Training & Conditioning Program. Wright, Barry, ed. (Illus.). 128p. (Orig.). 1989. pap. text ed. 29.95 (*0-931571-04-9*) Lifetime Pr.

Ross, Gary. At Large: The Fugitive Odyssey of Murray Hill & His Elephants. 1992. 19.50 (*0-679-40937-8*) Random.

— John Ward: Entering Nature. (C). 1993. pap. 12.50 (*0-88920-237-0*, Pub. by Wilfrid Laurier CN) Humanities.

***Ross, Gayle.** Dat-so-la-lee, Artisan. (Illus.). (J). (gr. 1-4). 1995. lib. bdg. 9.95 (*0-8136-5734-2*); pap. 4.95 (*0-8136-5740-7*) Modern Curr.

— How Rabbit Tricked Otter & Other Cherokee Trickster Stories. LC 93-3637. (Illus.). 80p. (J). (gr. 1 up). 1994. 17.00 (*0-06-021285-3*, HarpT) HarpC.

— How Rabbit Tricked Otter & Other Cherokee Trickster Stories. LC 93-3637. (Illus.). 80p. (J). (gr. 1 up). 1994. lib. bdg. 16.89 (*0-06-021286-1*) HarpC.

Ross, Gayle, jt. auth. see Bruchac, Joseph.

***Ross, George.** Jacques Delors & European Integration. (Europe & the International Order Ser.). 320p. (C). 1995. text ed. 35.00 (*0-19-521038-7*); pap. text ed. 14.95 (*0-19-521039-5*) OUP.

Ross, George, jt. ed. see Hollifield, James F.

Ross, George, jt. auth. see Howorth, Jolyon.

Ross, George, jt. ed. see Howorth, Jolyon.

Ross, George, et al. Unions & Economic Crisis: Britain, West Germany & Sweden. 250p. 1984. text ed. 44.95 (*0-04-331094-X*) Routledge Chapman & Hall.

***Ross, George E.** Centralia: A Pictorial History. (Illinois Pictorial History Ser.). (Illus.). 1992. write for info. (*0-943963-31-1*) G Bradley.

Ross, George E. & Novack, Barbara. Vice-Presidents & Their Wives. 1975. pap. 4.95 (*0-89036-052-9*) Hawkes Pub Inc.

Ross, George R. Treating Adolescent Substance Abuse: Understanding the Fundamental Elements. LC 93-11215. 238p. 1993. 34.95 (*0-205-15255-4*, Longwood Div) Allyn.

Ross, George R., tr. see Aristotle.

Ross, Gerald. Toppling the Pyramids: Redefining the Way Companies Are Run. 1994. 25.00 (*0-8129-2341-3*, Times Bks) Random.

Ross, Glen. On Coon Mountain: Scenes from a Childhood in the Oklahoma Hills. LC 91-29392. 192p. (C). 1992. 19.95 (*0-8061-2405-9*) U of Okla Pr.

Ross, Glenn, jt. ed. see Roth, Michael D.

Ross, Gordon. Argentina & Uruguay. 1976. lib. bdg. 59.95 (*0-87968-655-3*) Gordon Pr.

Ross, Gordon D. Immunobiology of the Complement System. 1986. text ed. 84.00 (*0-12-597640-2*) Acad Pr.

Ross-Gordon, Jovita M. Adults with Learning Disabilities: An Overview for the Adult Educator. 1989. 7.00 (*0-317-03009-4*, IN337) Ctr Educ Trng Employ.

Ross-Gordon, Jovita M., et al, eds. Serving Culturally Diverse Populations. LC 85-644750. (New Directions for Adult & Continuing Education Ser.: No. ACE 48). 1990. 16.95 (*1-55542-801-0*) Jossey-Bass.

Ross, Graham. Grand Unified Theories. (Frontiers in Physics Ser.: No. 60). 497p. (C). 1985. pap. 44.95 (*0-8053-6968-6*, 36968, Adv Bk Prog) Addison-Wesley.

— The Great Powers & the Decline of the European States System, 1914-1945. 181p. (C). 1983. pap. text ed. 20.95 (*0-582-49188-6*, 73517) Longman.

Ross, Graham, ed. The Foreign Office & the Kremlin: British Documents on Anglo-Soviet Relations 1941-45. LC 83-18903. 320p. 1984. 69.95 (*0-521-24387-4*) Cambridge U Pr.

Ross, Gwendolyn. A Child's Treasure for a Lifetime. 24p. (J). (gr. 2-6). 1988. pap. 2.95 (*0-88144-134-1*) Christian Pub.

Ross, H. F., jt. ed. see Eggington, S.

Ross, H. John. Integrated Data Processing for Every Office. pap. 2.00 (*0-911056-03-3*) Office Res.

— Technique of Systems & Procedures. (Illus.). 19.50 (*0-911056-01-7*) Office Res.

Ross, H. K. Black American Women, No. 3. (Illus.). 160p. (YA). (gr. 6-12). 1990. lib. bdg. 14.95 (*0-87460-365-X*) Lion Bks.

Ross, H. K., ed. Great Story Poems: Collection. 160p. (YA). (gr. 5-12). 1993. pap. 9.95 (*0-87460-385-4*) Lion Bks.

Ross, H. Laurence. Settled out of Court: The Social Process of Insurance Claims Adjustment. 2nd ed. LC 80-68523. 285p. 1980. lib. bdg. 45.95 (*0-202-30286-5*); pap. text ed. 24.95 (*0-202-30296-2*) Aldine de Gruyter.

Ross, H. W. A Blacksmith Guide to Ruger Flattops & Super Blackhawks. (Illus.). 96p. 1982. reprint ed. pap. 12.50 (*0-941540-08-1*) Blacksmith Corp.

Ross, Harley, et al, eds. Liquid Scintillation Counting & Organic Scintillators. 600p. 1990. 95.00 (*0-87371-246-3*, QC787) Lewis Pubs.

Ross, Harriet, comp. Heroes & Heroines of Many Lands. 160p. (J). (gr. 3-9). 1992. reprint ed. lib. bdg. 14.95 (*0-87460-214-9*) Lion Bks.

Ross, Harriet, ed. Great Horror Stories. (Illus.). 160p. (J). (gr. 3-9). 1992. pap. 11.95 (*0-87460-188-6*) Lion Bks.

— Greek Myths: Tales of the Gods, Heroes & Heroines. 160p. (YA). (gr. 6-12). 1993. lib. bdg. 14.95 (*0-87460-383-8*) Lion Bks.

Ross, Harris. Film As Literature, Literature As Film: An Introduction to & Bibliography of Film's Relationship to Literature. LC 87-132. (Bibliographies & Indexes in World Literature Ser.: No. 10). 355p. 1987. text ed. 49.95 (*0-313-24595-9*, RFL/) Greenwood.

Ross, Harvey M. Fighting Depression. 1992. pap. 9.95 (*0-87983-582-6*) Keats.

Ross, Heather C. Arabian History with Precious Gold in Saudi Arabia. (Illus.). 180p. 1994. 80.00 (*2-88373-003-2*, Pub. by Arabesque Comm SZ) Empire Pub Srvs.

— The Art of Arabian Costume: A Saudi Arabian Profile. (Illus.). 188p. 1990. 65.00 (*0-907513-00-X*, Pub. by Arabesque Comm SZ) Empire Pub Srvs.

— The Art of Arabian Costume: A Saudi Arabian Profile. LC 93-26337. 1993. 65.00 (*0-88734-640-5*) Players Pr.

— The Art of Arabian Costume: A Saudi Arabian Profile. (Illus.). 188p. 1982. 50.00 (*0-7103-0031-X*, Pub. by Kegan Paul Intl UK) Routledge Chapman & Hall.

— The Art of Bedouin Jewellery: A Saudi Arabian Profile. (Illus.). 133p. 1990. 65.00 (*0-907513-01-8*, Pub. by Arabesque Comm SZ) Empire Pub Srvs.

— The Art of Bedouin Jewellery: A Saudi Arabian Profile. LC 93-35828. 1994. 65.00 (*0-88734-641-3*) Players Pr.

— Bedouin Jewellery in Saudi Arabia. (Illus.). 128p. 1990. 50.00 (*2-88373-002-4*, Pub. by Arabesque Comm SZ) Empire Pub Srvs.

Ross, Heather L. & Sawhill, Isabel V. Time of Transition: The Growth of Families Headed by Women. 233p. (Orig.). 1975. pap. text ed. 24.00 (*0-87766-148-0*) Urban Inst.

Ross, Heidi A. China Learns English: Language Teaching & Social Change in the People's Republic. (Illus.). 320p. 1993. 35.00 (*0-300-05562-5*) Yale U Pr.

Ross, Helen, jt. ed. see Alexander, Franz.

Ross, Helen, jt. auth. see Ross, Don.

Ross, Helen L. Touch of Smile. (Illus.). 1978. pap. 5.00 (*0-933992-01-7*) Coffee Break.

Ross, Helen L., jt. auth. see Ross, Donald K.

Ross, Henry D. For Rhyme & Reason: A Potpourri of Light Verse & Prose. LC 88-90586. 136p. (Orig.). 1988. pap. 8.95 (*0-9620231-1-6*) Oleander Pub Hse.

— Free Speech & Talk Radio Hosts & Other Pieces. 75p. (Orig.). 1994. pap. text ed. 9.95 (*0-685-70774-1*) Capricorn Pr.

Ross, Herbert H. Evolution & Classification of the Mountain Caddisflies. LC 56-5681. (Illus.). 221p. reprint ed. 63.00 (*0-8357-9675-2*, 2015025) Bks Demand.

Ross, Herbert H., et al. A Textbook of Entomology. 704p. (C). 1991. reprint ed. lib. bdg. 72.50 (*0-89464-497-1*) Krieger.

Ross, Hildy S., jt. ed. see Rubin, Kenneth H.

Ross, Howard P. Florida Corporations: Florida Practice Systems Library Selection, 2 vols. suppl. ed. LC 79-91141. 1134p. 1992. 135.00 (*0-317-03206-2*) Lawyers Cooperative.

— Florida Corporations: Florida Practice Systems Library Selection, 2 vols., Set. LC 79-91141. 1134p. 1980. ring bd. 220.00 (*0-317-00573-1*) Lawyers Cooperative.

Ross, Hugh. Creation & Time: A Biblical & Scientific Perspective on the Creation-Date Controversy. LC 94-4308. 192p. 1994. pap. 10.00 (*0-89109-776-7*) NavPress.

— Creator & the Cosmos: An Astrophysicist Reconciles Science & Scripture. LC 92-64094. 192p. (Orig.). 1993. pap. 10.00 (*0-89109-700-7*) NavPress.

— The Fingerprint of God. 2nd ed. 248p. 1991. reprint ed. pap. 9.95 (*0-939497-18-2*) Promise Pub.

Ross, Hugh M. The Gospel of Thomas. (C). 1990. 60.00 (*0-685-37372-X*, Pub. by W Sessions UK) St Mut.

— Thirty Essays on the Gospel of Thomas. 1991. pap. 12.95 (*1-85230-183-X*) Element MA.

Ross, Hugh M., ed. George Fox Speaks for Himself. (C). 1989. pap. 21.00 (*1-85072-081-9*, Pub. by W Sessions UK) St Mut.

Ross, Hugh M., notes. The Gospel of Thomas. 115p. (C). 1987. 50.00 (*1-85072-019-3*, Pub. by W Sessions UK) St Mut.

Ross, Iain, ed. The Gude & Godly Ballatis. 70p. 1986. 20.00 (*0-85411-019-4*, Pub. by Saltire Soc) St Mut.

Ross, Ian. How Green Was My Valet. 184p. 1993. 23.95 (*0-434-65275-X*, Pub. by W Heinemann Ltd) Trafalgar.

Ross, Ian C. & Tukey, John W. Tukey Citation Index, Vol. 5: Index to Statistics & Probability: Locations & Authors. LC 72-86075. 1092p. 1973. 115.00 (*0-88274-004-0*) Am Math.

Ross, Ian C., ed. see Sterne, Laurence.

***Ross, Ian S.** The Life of Adam Smith. (Illus.). 448p. 1995. write for info. (*0-19-828821-2*) OUP.

Ross, Irwin. The Loneliest Campaign: The Truman Victory of 1948. LC 75-22761. 304p. 1977. reprint ed. text ed. 35.00 (*0-8371-8353-7*, ROLCT, Greenwood Pr) Greenwood.

— Shady Business: Confronting Corporate Corruption. LC 92-29437. 1992. 19.95 (*0-87078-340-8*); pap. 9.95 (*0-87078-341-6*) TCFP-PPP.

Ross, Isabel. First Lady of the South: The Life of Mrs. Jefferson Davis. LC 73-7381. (Illus.). 475p. 1973. reprint ed. text ed. 35.00 (*0-8371-6927-5*, ROFL, Greenwood Pr) Greenwood.

— Ladies of the Press: The Story of Women in Journalism by an Insider. LC 74-3972. (Women in America Ser.). (Illus.). 642p. 1974. reprint ed. 46.95 (*0-405-06120-X*) Ayer.

— Margaret Fell: Mother of Quakerism. (C). 1989. pap. 36.00 (*0-900657-83-9*, Pub. by W Sessions UK) St Mut.

— Silhouette in Diamonds: The Life of Mrs. Potter Palmer. LC 75-1868. (Leisure Class in America Ser.). (Illus.). 1975. reprint ed. 25.95 (*0-405-06934-0*) Ayer.

Ross, Ishbel. Grace Coolidge & Her Era. LC 62-8017. (Illus.). 370p. (C). 1988. reprint ed. 19.95 (*0-944951-05-8*); reprint ed. pap. 13.95 (*0-944951-04-X*) C Coolidge Memorial.

— Rebel Rose. LC 54-8986. 244p. 1987. pap. 4.95 (*0-89176-026-1*, Mckingbird) R Bemis Pub.

Ross, J., jt. auth. see Heusch, G.

Ross, J., jt. ed. see Myneni, R. B.

Ross, J. A., ed. Illustrated Medieval Alexander-Books in Germany & the Netherlands: A Study of Comparative Inconography. Vol. 3. (Illus.). xx, 202p. 1971. write for info. (*0-318-59945-7*) Modern Humanities Res.

Ross, J. A. & Erichsen, N. The Story of Lucca. (Mediaeval Towns Ser.: Vol. 7). 1974. reprint ed. pap. 40.00 (*0-8115-0849-8*) Periodicals Srv.

— The Story of Pisa. LC 85-47864. (Mediaeval Towns Ser.: Vol. 3). 1974. reprint ed. pap. 50.00 (*0-8115-0845-5*) Periodicals Srv.

Ross, J. A. & Mauldin, W. P., eds. Berelson on Population. (Illus.). 345p. 1988. 44.00 (*0-387-96716-8*) Spr-Verlag.

Ross, J. Elliott. Christian Ethics. 250p. 1951. 12.95 (*0-8159-5202-3*) Devin.

Ross, J. J. Some Facts & More Facts about the Self-Styled "Pastor" C. T. Russell. 48p. 1988. reprint ed. pap. 2.95 (*1-883858-40-2*) Witness CA.

Ross, J. L., jt. ed. see Satz, Paul.

***Ross, J. M.** The Royal New Zealand Air Force. (Official History Ser.: No. 2). (Illus.). 400p. 1993. reprint ed. 49.95 (*0-89839-187-3*) Battery Pr.

***Ross, J. Michael.** Angel Watching. 32p. 1995. 14.95 (*0-9643748-1-1*) Side Door.

— The MotherSong. 32p. 1995. 14.95 (*0-9643748-0-3*) Side Door.

Ross, Jack C. An Assembly of Good Fellows: Voluntary Associations in History. LC 75-35355. 320p. 1976. text ed. 59.95 (*0-8371-8586-6*, RGF/, Greenwood Pr) Greenwood.

Ross, Jack C. & Wheeler, Raymond H. Black Belonging: A Study of the Social Correlates of Work Relations among Negroes. LC 77-105974. (Contributions in Sociology Ser.: No. 7). 292p. 1971. text ed. 59.95 (*0-8371-3298-3*, RBB/, Greenwood Pr) Greenwood.

R

Ross, Jack L., tr. see Meister, Albert.

Ross, Jacob J. The Virtues of the Family. LC 93-42425. 1994. text ed. 27.95 (0-02-927385-4) Free Pr.

Ross, James. They Don't Dance Much. LC 74-23650. (Lost American Fiction Ser.). 308p. 1975. reprint ed. 8.95 (0-8093-0714-6) S Ill U Pr.

Ross, James & Kelson, Michael. Creating Visual C Plus Plus Applications, Incl. disk. (Illus.). 1512p. (Orig.). 1994. pap. 44.99 (1-56529-806-3) Que.

Ross, James, jt. auth. see Kilov, Haim.

Ross, James A. Escape to Shanghai: A Jewish Community in China. 280p. 1993. text ed. 22.95 (0-02-927375-7) Macmillan.

— How to Buy a Car. 3rd ed. 1993. mass mkt. 4.99 (0-312-95151-5) St Martin.

— How to Buy a Car: The Essential Guide for Buying a New Or Used Car, Updated & Revised for the 1990s. 2nd rev. ed. 160p. (Orig.). 1992. pap. 6.95 (0-312-07792-0) St Martin.

Ross, James B. & McLaughlin, Mary M., eds. Portable Medieval Reader. (Portable Library: No. 46). 1977. pap. 12.50 (0-14-015046-3, Penguin Bks) Viking Penguin.

— Portable Renaissance Reader. (Portable Library: No. 61). 1977. pap. 14.95 (0-14-015061-7, Penguin Bks) Viking Penguin.

Ross, James B., ed. see Galbert.

Ross, James D. Cambodia: Justice System & Human Rights Violations. O'Neill, William G. & Posner, Michael J., eds. 74p. (Orig.). 1992. pap. 10.00 (0-934143-53-6) Lawyers Comm Human.

— Malaysia: Assault on the Judiciary. 76p. (Orig.). 1989. 8.00 (0-934143-27-7) Lawyers Comm Human.

Ross, James D., ed. see Gelatt, Timothy.

Ross, James F. Philosophical Theology. 366p. 1982. 49.50 (0-8290-0335-5) Irvington.

— Philosophical Theology. LC 68-17707. (C). 1969. write for info. (0-672-60721-2, Bobbs) Macmillan.

— Portraying Analogy. LC 81-15463. (Cambridge Studies in Philosophy). (Illus.). 280p. 1982. 64.95 (0-521-23805-6) Cambridge U Pr.

Ross, James F., ed. Inquiries into Medieval Philosophy: A Collection in Honor of Francis P. Clarke. LC 74-105984. (Contributions in Philosophy Ser.: No. 4). 329p. 1971. text ed. 49.95 (0-8371-3311-4, RMP/, Greenwood Pr) Greenwood.

Ross, James F., tr. Suarez: Disputation Six, on Formal & Universal Unity. LC 64-7799. (Medieval Philosophical Texts in Translation Ser.: No. 23). 1965. pap. 25.00 (0-87462-215-8) Marquette.

Ross, James R. Caught in a Tornado: A Chinese American Woman Survives the Cultural Revolution. 192p. 1994. text ed. 21.95 (1-55553-192-X) NE U Pr.

Ross, James W. Social Security Disability Benefits: How to Get Them! How to Keep Them! rev. ed. 104p. 1984. 24.95 (0-9615202-6-4); pap. 12.95 (0-9615202-5-6) Ross Pub Co.

Ross, Jane B. The George Medallion. 125p. (J). (gr. 4-7). 1986. 9.95 (0-917949-07-2) Vimach Assocs.

Ross, Janet. The City That She Loved: A Reflection... LC 93-86933. (Illus.). 147p. (Orig.). 1993. pap. 7.95 (0-9624229-6-7) St Thomas Tech.

— Lives of the Early Medici As Told in Their Correspondence. 1977. lib. bdg. 59.95 (0-8490-2175-8) Gordon Pr.

Ross, Janet & Waterfield, Michael. Leaves from Our Tuscan Kitchen. (Illus.). 208p. 1994. 10.95 (0-14-046824-2, Penguin Bks) Viking Penguin.

Ross, Janet, jt. auth. see Doty, Gladys G.

Ross, Janice, jt. auth. see Steinberg, Stephen C.

Ross, Jason. A World Without Homosexuals. LC 94-66316. (Illus.). 104p. (Orig.). 1994. pap. 10.00 (0-9641408-1-0) Road Kill Pr.

Ross, Jean W., ed. Dictionary of Literary Biography Yearbook, 1984. 380p. 1985. 128.00 (0-8103-1628-5) Gale.

Ross, Jeanette. K Ranch. 126p. (Orig.). 1984. 20.00 (0-938190-42-3); pap. 7.95 (0-938190-32-6) North Atlantic.

— Telling Our Tales, Stories & Storytelling for All Ages. 216p. 1994. 20.00 (1-55896-280-8) Unitarian Univ.

***Ross, Jeffrey I., ed.** Controlling State Crime: An Introduction. LC 94-27125. (Current Issues in Criminal Justice Ser.: Vol. 9). 430p. 1995. 67.00 (0-8153-1546-5, SS933) Garland.

***Ross, Jeffrey S.** Magnetic Resonance Angiography of the Head & Neck: A Teaching File. LC 94-31810. (Illus.). 1994. write for info. (0-8151-7409-8) Mosby Yr Bk.

Ross, Jennie-Keith. Old Peoples, New Lives: Community Creation in a Retirement Residence. LC 76-8103. (Illus.). 1977. lib. bdg. 18.00 (0-226-72825-0) U Ch Pr.

— Old Peoples, New Lives: Community Creation in a Retirement Residence. LC 76-8103. (Illus.). 1982. pap. text ed. 8.00 (0-226-42965-2) U Ch Pr.

***Ross, Jeremy.** Acupuncture Point Combinations: The Key to Clinical Success. LC 94-43497. 1995. write for info. (0-443-05006-6) Churchill.

Ross, Jerilyn. Triumph over Fear. 1994. 22.95 (0-553-08132-2) Bantam.

— Triumph over Fear: A Book of Help & Hope for People with Anxiety, Panic Attacks, & Phobias. 1995. pap. 12.95 (0-553-37444-3) Bantam.

Ross, Jim. Saddle up & R-I-I-D-E. (Illus.). 100p. 1990. pap. 6.95 (0-9617932-2-8) J A Ross.

Ross, Jim, jt. auth. see Shearer, Debby.

Ross, Jini K., ed. What Makes You So Strong? Sermons of Joy & Strength from Jeremiah A. Wright, Jr. 176p. 1993. pap. 13.00 (0-8170-1198-6) Judson.

Ross, Jini K., ed. see Wright, Jeremiah A., Jr.

Ross, Joan. Guarded Moments. (Temptation Ser.: No. 296). 1990. pap. 2.65 (0-373-25396-6) Harlequin Bks.

Ross, Joan, jt. auth. see Allen, Layman E.

Ross, Joan C. & Langone, Michael D. Cults: What Parents Should Know. 1989. pap. 5.95 (0-8184-0511-2, L Stuart) Carol Pub Group.

— Cults: What Parents Should Know: A Practical Guide to Help Parents with Children in Destructive Groups. 133p. (Orig.). 1988. pap. text ed. 9.95 (0-931337-00-3) Am Family Foun.

Ross, Joann. Angel of Desire. (Temptation Ser.). 1994. mass mkt. 2.99 (0-373-25582-9, 1-25582-7) Harlequin Bks.

— Dusk Fire. 1995. pap. 4.99 (1-55166-022-9, Mira Bks) Harlequin Bks.

— For Richer or Poorer. (Temptation Ser.). 1995. mass mkt. 3.25 (0-373-25641-8, 1-25641-1) Harlequin Bks.

— In a Class by Himself. (Western Lovers Ser.). 1995. mass mkt. 3.99 (0-373-88520-2, 1-88520-1) Harlequin Bks.

— Legacy of Lies. 1995. pap. 4.99 (1-55166-018-0, Mira Bks) Harlequin Bks.

— Lovestorm. (Temptation Ser.). 1993. mass mkt. 2.99 (0-373-25571-3, 1-25571-0) Harlequin Bks.

— Private Passions (Secret Fantasies) 1995. mass mkt. 3.25 (0-373-25662-0) Harlequin Bks.

— Private Pleasures. 1993. mass mkt. 4.99 (0-312-95026-8) St Martin.

Ross, JoAnn. Private Pleasures. braille ed. 637p. 1993. vinyl bd. 50.96 (1-56956-383-7, BR9151) W A T Braille.

Ross, Joann. The Return of Caine O'Halloran. 1994. 2.99 (0-373-25589-6) Harlequin Bks.

— Secret Sins. 1991. mass mkt. 4.95 (0-312-92461-5) St Martin.

— Star-Crossed Lovers. (Temptation Ser.). 1993. mass mkt. 2.99 (0-373-25532-2, 1-25532-2) Harlequin Bks.

— Stormy Courtship. (Mira Bks.). 1995. mass mkt. 4.99 (1-55166-072-5, 1-66072-9, Mira Bks) Harlequin Bks.

— Tangled Lives. (Temptation Ser.: No. 345). 1991. pap. 2.95 (0-373-25445-8) Harlequin Bks.

— Three Grooms & a Wedding. (Temptation Ser.). 1995. mass mkt. 3.25 (0-373-25645-0, 1-25645-2) Harlequin Bks.

***Ross, Joanne.** Never a Bride: (Bachelor Arms) (Temptation Ser.). 1995. pap. 3.25 (0-373-25637-X, 1-25637-9) Harlequin Bks.

Ross, Joe. An American Voyage. (New American Poetry Ser.: No. 12). 92p. (Orig.). 1993. pap. 9.95 (1-55713-070-1) Sun & Moon CA.

— Guards of the Heart. (Blue Corner Drama: No. 3). 120p. (Orig.). 1991. pap. 10.95 (1-55713-082-5) Sun & Moon CA.

— NESFA Hymnal, Vol. 1. 2nd ed. 220p. 1979. pap. 16.00 (0-915368-69-2) New Eng SF Assoc.

— Productivity, People & Profits. 150p. (C). 1986. 32.95 (0-8359-5626-1, Reston) P-H.

Ross, Joel. Total Quality Management: Text, Cases & Readings. LC 92-61645. 325p. 1993. pap. text ed. 39.95 (0-9634030-0-1) St Lucie Pr.

Ross, Joel, jt. auth. see Omachanu, Vincent.

Ross, Joel E. Managing Productivity. (Illus.). 192p. 1977. text ed. 34.00 (0-87909-459-1, Reston) P-H.

— Mutual Funds: Taking the Worry Out of Investing. 128p. 1988. pap. 16.95 (0-13-608761-2) P-H.

— Total Quality Management: Text, Cases & Readings. 2nd ed. (Illus.). 450p. (C). 1994. pap. text ed. 39.95 (1-884015-08-5) St Lucie Pr.

Ross, Joel E. & Ross, William A. Japanese Quality Circles & Productivity. 1982. 34.95 (0-8359-3325-3, Reston) P-H.

Ross, Joel E., jt. auth. see Murdick, Robert G.

Ross, John. Changing Lives: Motivation Through Perspective. 1991. pap. 10.00 (1-879868-01-6) Mentor Group.

— Comp Printmaker. rev. ed. 1989. text ed. 49.95 (0-02-927371-4) Free Pr.

— Connecting with Windows 95. 1995. 24.99 (0-7821-1713-9) Sybex.

— Dog Talk: Training Your Dog Through a Canine Point of View. 1995. 14.95 (0-312-11778-7) St Martin.

— Internet Power Tools. 1995. pap. 40.00 (0-679-75815-1) Knopf.

— Just the Fax: All about Winfax. LC 93-87026. 376p. 1994. pap. 16.99 (0-7821-1462-8) Sybex.

— Lease-Purchase America! Acquiring Real Estate in the '90s & Beyond. 192p. 1993. pap. 9.95 (0-914984-45-4) Starburst.

— The Manchus, or the Reigning Dynasty of China: Their Rise & Progress. LC 70-38080. (China Classic & Contemporary Works in Reprint Ser.). (Illus.). reprint ed. 89.00 (0-404-56944-7) AMS Pr.

— Narrative of a Second Voyage in Search of a North-West Passage, & of a Residence in the Arctic Regions During the Years 1829, 1830,1831, 1833, 2 vols., 1. LC 68-55217. 1971. reprint ed. text ed. 55.00 (0-8371-1332-6, RONQ) Greenwood.

— Narrative of a Second Voyage in Search of a North-West Passage, & of a Residence in the Arctic Regions During the Years 1829, 1830,1831, 1833, 2 vols., Set. LC 68-55217. 1971. reprint ed. text ed. 75.00 (0-8371-3860-4, RONP) Greenwood.

— Narrative of a Second Voyage in Search of a North-West Passage, & of a Residence in the Arctic Regions During the Years 1829, 1830,1831, 1833, 2 vols., Vol. 2. LC 68-55217. 1971. reprint ed. text ed. 45.00 (0-8371-1333-4, RONR) Greenwood.

— The Papers of Chief John Ross: Volume I, 1807-1839, Volume II, 1840-1866. (Illus.). 1611p. 1985. Vol. II 790p. write for info. (0-318-58377-1) U of Okla Pr.

— The Papers of Chief John Ross: Volume I, 1807-1839, Volume II, 1840-1866, Vol. I. LC 84-21954. (Illus.). 824p. 1985. text ed. 99.50 (0-8061-1865-2) U of Okla Pr.

— Poems on Events of the Day, 1582-1607. LC 91-20371. 1991. 50.00 (0-8201-1456-1) Schol Facsimiles.

— Rags to Riches to Rags to Riches: The John Ross Story. 107p. 1990. pap. 10.00 (1-879868-00-8) Mentor Group.

— Rebellion at the Roots: Indian Uprising in Chiapas. 250p. (Orig.). 1994. lib. bdg. 29.95 (1-56751-043-4); pap. 14.95 (1-56751-042-6) Common Courage.

— The RFC to the RAF India Nineteen Nineteen. 122p. (Orig.). 1987. pap. 35.00 (0-7212-0792-8, Pub. by Regency Press) St Mut.

— The Royal Flying Corps-Boy Service, 1917. 192p. (C). 1990. 39.00 (0-7212-0830-4, Pub. by Regency Press) St Mut.

— Unlock Your Personal Best: From the Inside Out. (Illus.). 264p. (Orig.). 1995. pap. 12.95 (1-879868-02-4) Mentor Group.

Ross, John & McKinney, Barbara. Dog Talk: Training Your Dog Through a Canine Point of View. (Illus.). 288p. 1992. 22.95 (0-312-07726-2) St Martin.

Ross, John & Romano, Clare. The Complete Intaglio Print. LC 74-2697. 1974. pap. text ed. 14.95 (0-02-927400-1) Free Pr.

— The Complete Printmaker. LC 72-77151. (Illus.). 1972. 39.95 (0-02-927370-6) Free Pr.

Ross, John, jt. ed. see Hand, Q. R.

Ross, John, jt. auth. see Lalond, David E.

Ross, John, jt. auth. see Romano, Clare.

Ross, John, et al. The Complete Printmaker: Techniques - Traditions - Innovations. enl. rev. ed. 352p. 1991. pap. 35.00 (0-02-927372-2) Free Pr.

Ross, John A., ed. International Encyclopedia of Population, 2 Vols. LC 82-2326. 1982. text ed. 250.00 (0-02-927430-3) Macmillan.

Ross, John A. & Frankenberg, Elizabeth. Findings from Two Decades of Family Planning Research. LC 93-86577. 108p. 1993. pap. 12.00 (0-87834-080-7) Population Coun.

Ross, John A. & Maynes, Florence J. Teaching Problem-Solving. LC 82-207857. (Informal Ser.: No. 43). (Illus.). 216p. reprint ed. pap. 61.60 (0-7837-0553-0, 2040894) Bks Demand.

Ross, John A., jt. auth. see LaLond, David E.

Ross, John A., jt. auth. see LaLond, David L.

Ross, John A., jt. ed. see Phillips, James F.

Ross, John A., et al. Family Planning & Child Survival Programs: 100 Developing Countries. (Illus.). 258p. (Orig.). 1988. pap. 25.00 (0-685-21889-9) CUCFP&FH.

— Management Strategies for Family Planning Programs. LC 89-6029. (Illus.). 71p. (Orig.). 1989. pap. 10.00 (0-9620952-1-4) CUCFP&FH.

Ross, John A., et al, eds. Family Planning & Population: A Compendium of International Statistics. LC 93-93706. 202p. 1993. pap. 25.00 (0-87834-078-5) Population Coun.

***Ross, John C., ed.** Thomas Shadwell's Bury Fair: A Critical Edition. LC 94-43031. (Renaissance Imagination Ser.). 216p. 1995. 58.00 (0-8153-1740-9) Garland.

Ross, John D. Bonnie Jean, a Collection of Papers & Poems Relating to the Wife of Robert Burns. LC 71-144471. reprint ed. 20.00 (0-404-08526-1) AMS Pr.

— Burns Almanac. LC 72-144474. reprint ed. 27.50 (0-404-08534-2) AMS Pr.

— Burns Handbook. LC 76-144475. reprint ed. 24.50 (0-404-08535-0) AMS Pr.

— Early Critical Reviews on Robert Burns. LC 70-144476. reprint ed. 34.50 (0-404-08536-9) AMS Pr.

— Robert Burns & His Rhyming Friends. LC 77-144478. reprint ed. 14.00 (0-404-08538-5) AMS Pr.

— Round Burns Grave. enl. ed. LC 70-144479. reprint ed. 34.50 (0-404-08539-3) AMS Pr.

— Sixty Years of Life & Adventure in the Far East, 2 vols., Set. (Illus.). 1968. reprint ed. 85.00 (0-7146-2024-6, Pub. by F Cass Pubs UK) Intl Spec Bk.

— Story of the Kilmarnock Burns. LC 76-153519. reprint ed. 32.50 (0-404-08978-X) AMS Pr.

— Who's Who in Burns. LC 75-144480. reprint ed. 34.50 (0-404-08547-4) AMS Pr.

Ross, John D., comp. Scottish Poets in America. LC 72-80502. 1972. reprint ed. lib. bdg. 24.95 (0-405-08899-X, Pub. by Blom Pubns UK) Ayer.

Ross, John D. & Ross, Catherine H. Ross Test of Higher Cognitive Process. 1976. student ed 15.00 (0-87879-151-5); 12.00 (0-685-74188-5); 5.00 (0-685-74189-3); student ed 20.00 (0-87879-152-3); vinyl bd. 55.00 (0-685-74187-7) Acad Therapy.

Ross, John E. Truths to Live by. LC 72-37834. (Essay Index Reprint Ser.). 1977. reprint ed. 21.95 (0-8369-2622-6) Ayer.

Ross, John F. Neutrality & International Sanctions: Sweden, Switzerland & Collective Security. LC 89-32270. 256p. 1989. text ed. 55.00 (0-275-93349-0, C3349, Praeger Pubs) Greenwood.

Ross, John J. Twentieth Annual Institute on Employment Law. (Litigation & Administrative Practice Ser.). 1018p. 1991. 70.00 (0-685-59336-3, H4-5112) PLI.

Ross, John M. How to Use the Major Indexes to U. S. Government Publications. 64p. 1989. pap. text ed. 5.00 (0-8389-0509-9) ALA.

— Trials in Collections: An Index to Famous Trials Throughout the World. LC 82-21635. 218p. 1983. 20.00 (0-8108-1603-2) Scarecrow.

— What Men Want: Mothers, Fathers, & Manhood. LC 93-46057. 252p. 1994. text ed. 29.95 (0-674-95080-1) HUP.

Ross, John M. & Myers, Wayne A. New Concepts in Psychoanalytic Psychotherapy. LC 87-33421. 289p. 1988. 36.50 (0-88048-287-7) Am Psychiatric.

Ross, John M., jt. ed. see Pollock, George.

Ross, John P., ed. Research in Urban Economics, Vol. 5: Causes & Consequences of Urban Change in the World's Developed Countries. 235p. 1985. 73.25 (0-89232-446-5) Jai Pr.

Ross, John R. Salem Electric Against the Odds! (Illus.). 121p. (Orig.). 1991. pap. text ed. 12.95 (0-945490-02-X) Carolina Pacific.

Ross, John R., ed. see Borkin, Ann.

Ross, John W., ed. see Florey, Henry E., Jr.

Ross, Jonathan. Dead Eye. large type ed. 384p. 1985. 15.95 (0-7089-1394-6) Ulverscroft.

— The Deadest Thing You Ever Saw. large type ed. 1992. 18.95 (0-7451-6417-X, Scarlet Dagger Lrg Print) Chivers N Amer.

— The Deadest Thing You Ever Saw. large type ed. 1993. pap. 16.95 (0-7451-6422-6, Scarlet Dagger Lrg Print) Chivers N Amer.

— Fate Accomplished. large type ed. 384p. 1989. 17.95 (0-7089-2046-2) Ulverscroft.

— Murder Be Hanged. LC 92-43890. 1993. 17.95 (0-312-08857-4) St Martin.

Ross, Joseph A., jt. auth. see Pessin, Allan H.

Ross, Joseph E. Krotona of Old Hollywood, 1866-1913, Vol. I. LC 89-50410. (Illus.). 352p. 1989. lib. bdg. 22.95 (0-925943-11-8) El Montecito Oaks.

Ross, Josephine. Princess of Wales. (Profiles Ser.). (Illus.). 64p. (J). (gr. 5-9). 1991. 11.95 (0-237-60023-4, Pub. by Evans Bros Ltd UK) Trafalgar.

— Royalty in Vogue. (Illus.). 208p. 1989. 29.95 (0-318-42768-0) Congdon & Weed.

— Society in Vogue. LC 92-13882. 1992. 45.00 (0-86565-133-7) Vendome.

Ross, Joyce M. Direct Sales: Be Better Than Good - Be Great! LC 91-7387. (Illus.). 208p. 1991. 17.95 (0-88289-782-9) Pelican.

Ross, Judith W., et al. Health Care Ethics Committees: The Next Generation. LC 93-17509. 198p. 1993. 45.00 (1-55648-104-7, 058300) AHPI.

Ross, Judith Wilson, et al. Handbook for Hospital Ethics Committees. LC 86-14130. 176p. (Orig.). 1986. 28.75 (0-939450-96-8, 025101) AHPI.

Ross, Judy, jt. auth. see DeVisser, John.

Ross, Judy, jt. auth. see Visser, John D.

Ross, Juhan. The Radiation Regime & Architecture of Plant Stands. (Tasks for Vegetation Science Ser.: No. 3). 480p. 1981. lib. bdg. 215.00 (90-6193-607-1) Kluwer Ac.

Ross, Julian, jt. auth. see Ross, Noah.

Ross, Julie A. Practical Parenting for the Twenty-First Century: The Manual You Wish Had Come with Your Child. LC 92-55103. 152p. (Orig.). 1993. pap. 10.95 (0-9627226-6-9) Excalibur Pub.

Ross, June R., ed. & intro. Bryozoa: Present & Past. (Illus.). 340p. (Orig.). 1987. pap. 60.00 (0-930216-02-4) West Wash Univ.

Ross, June R., jt. auth. see Dick, Mathew H.

Ross, K. A. Elementary Analysis: The Theory of Calculus. Gehring, F. W. & Halmos, P. R., eds. LC 79-24806. (Undergraduate Texts in Mathematics Ser.). (Illus.). 350p. 1980. 26.40 (3-540-90459-X) Spr-Verlag.

Ross, K. A., jt. auth. see Hewitt, E.

Ross, K. K. Bert's Little Bedtime Story: A Sesame Street Book. LC 89-64283. (Chunky Tales Ser.). (Illus.). 28p. (J). (ps). 1991. bds. 3.25 (0-679-80757-8) Random Bks Yng Read.

— Cozy in the Woods. LC 88-63931. (Chunky Tales Ser.). (Illus.). 28p. (J). (ps). 1990. 2.95 (0-394-85400-4) Random Bks Yng Read.

— The Little Red Car. LC 88-63930. (Chunky Tales Ser.). (Illus.). 28p. (J). (ps). 1990. 2.95 (0-394-85376-8) Random Bks Yng Read.

— Peekaboo, Puppy! A My Puppy Loves Me Book. (Chunky Flap Bks.). (Illus.). 22p. (J). (ps-00). 1994. 3.50 (0-685-71037-8) Random Bks Yng Read.

Ross, Kate. A Broken Vessel. 304p. 1994. 18.95 (0-670-84999-5, Viking) Viking Penguin.

— A Broken Vessel. 304p. 1995. mass mkt. 5.95 (0-14-023453-5, Penguin Bks) Viking Penguin.

— Cut to the Quick. 352p. 1994. mass mkt. 5.95 (0-14-023394-6, Penguin Bks) Viking Penguin.

— Whom the Gods Love. LC 94-43877. 1995. 21.95 (0-670-86207-X, Viking) Viking Penguin.

Ross, Katharine. Bunnies' Ball. LC 92-29930. (Pictureback Ser.). (Illus.). (J). 1994. 2.50 (0-679-83503-2) Random Bks Yng Read.

— Fuzzy Kitten. LC 92-62262. (Fuzzy Chunkies Ser.). (Illus.). 22p. (J). (ps-3). 1993. 3.50 (0-679-84644-1) Random Bks Yng Read.

— Fuzzy Monsters. (J). Date not set. 3.99 (0-679-87274-4) Random.

— Fuzzy Teddy. LC 92-62263. (Fuzzy Chunkies Ser.). (Illus.). 22p. (J). (ps). 1993. 3.50 (0-679-84643-3) Random Bks Yng Read.

— Grover, Grover, Come on Over: A Step 1 Book - Preschool-Grade 1. LC 90-33947. (Sesame Street Step into Reading Bks.). (Illus.). 32p. (Orig.). (J). (ps-1). 1991. lib. bdg. 7.99 (0-679-91117-0); pap. 3.50 (0-679-81117-6) Random Bks Yng Read.

— The Little Ballerina. LC 92-42093. (J). 1994. 2.99 (0-679-84915-7) Random Bks Yng Read.

— The Little City Book. LC 93-84942. (Chunky Bks.). (Illus.). 28p. (J). (ps). 1994. 3.25 (0-679-85290-5) Random Bks Yng Read.

— The Little Noisy Book. LC 88-62100. (Chunky Bks.). (Illus.). 28p. (J). (ps). 1989. bds. 2.95 (0-394-82907-7) Random Bks Yng Read.

— The Little Pumpkin Book. LC 91-67669. (Chunky Shape Bks.). (Illus.). 22p. (J). (ps). 1992. bds. 2.95 (0-679-83384-6) Random Bks Yng Read.

— The Little Quiet Book. LC 88-62101. (Chunky Bks.). (Illus.). 28p. (J). (ps). 1989. bds. 2.95 (0-394-82899-2) Random Bks Yng Read.

— Open the Door, Little Dinosaur. LC 92-80950. (Lift-&-Peek-a-Board Bks.). (Illus.). 14p. (J). (ps-00). 1993. bds. 3.99 (0-679-83689-6) Random Bks Yng Read.

An Asterisk (*) at the beginning of an entry indicates that the title is appearing in BIP for the first time.

— Teeny Tiny Farm. LC 91-50647. (Chunky Shape Bks.). (Illus.). 22p. (J). (ps). 1992. 2.95 (0-679-83388-9) Random Bks Yng Read.

— Twinkle, Twinkle, Little Bug. LC 94-48341. (Step Into Reading, A Step 1 Bk.). (Illus.). 1996. 3.99 (0-679-87666-9); lib. bdg. 9.99 (0-679-97666-3) Random.

— Wooly Bear. (J). Date not set. 3.99 (0-679-87275-2) Random.

Ross, Katharine & Lukas, Noah. Little Dinosaur's Little Sister. (Illus.). 24p. (Orig.). (J). (ps-2). 1994. pap. 2.50 (0-679-86178-5) Random Bks Yng Read.

Ross, Katherine. The Fuzzytail Friends' Great Egg Hunt. LC 87-50812. (Peek-a-Boo Board Bks.). (Illus.). 14p. (J). (ps). 1988. bds. 3.99 (0-394-89475-8) Random Bks Yng Read.

Ross, Kathleen. The Baroque Narrative of Carlos de Siguenza y Gongora: A New World Paradise. (Studies in Latin American & Iberian Literature: No. 8). 240p. (C). 1994. 54.95 (0-521-45113-2) Cambridge U Pr.

Ross, Kathleen, tr. see Campos, Julieta.

Ross, Kathleen, tr. see Dalton, Rogue.

Ross, Kathleen, jt. ed. see Miller, Yvette E.

Ross, Kathleen, tr. see Vallejo, Cesar.

***Ross, Kathryn.** Le Femme Trompee. (Azur Ser.). (FRE.). 1994. pap. 3.50 (0-373-34437-6, 1-34437-3) Harlequin Bks.

— Scent of Betrayal. large type ed. (Traditional Romance Ser.). 1994. 17.95 (0-263-13875-5, Pub. by Mills & Boon Ltd UK) Chivers N Amer.

***Ross, Kathy.** Crafts for Christmas. LC 94-48304. (Holiday Crafts for Kids Ser.). (Illus.). 48p. (J). (gr. k-3). 1995. lib. bdg. 15.40 (1-56294-536-X) Millbrook Pr.

— Crafts for Christmas. LC 94-48304. (Holiday Crafts for Kids Ser.). (Illus.). 48p. (J). (gr. k-3). 1995. pap. 5.95 (1-56294-681-1) Millbrook Pr.

— Crafts for Easter. LC 95-13510. (Holiday Crafts for Kids Ser.). (Illus.). (J). 1995. lib. bdg. write for info. (1-56294-918-7) Millbrook Pr.

— Crafts for Halloween. LC 93-37249. (Holiday Crafts for Kids Ser.). (Illus.). 48p. (J). (gr. k-3). 1994. lib. bdg. 15. 40 (1-56294-411-8); pap. 6.95 (1-56294-741-9) Millbrook Pr.

— Crafts for Kwanzaa. LC 93-36690. (Holiday Crafts for Kids Ser.). (Illus.). 48p. (J). (gr. k-3). 1994. 15.40 (1-56294-412-6); pap. 6.95 (1-56294-740-0) Millbrook Pr.

— Crafts for Thanksgiving. LC 94-48301. (Holiday Crafts for Kids Ser.). (Illus.). 48p. (J). (gr. k-3). 1995. 15.40 (1-56294-535-1) Millbrook Pr.

— Crafts for Thanksgiving. LC 94-48301. (Holiday Crafts for Kids Ser.). (Illus.). 48p. (J). (gr. k-3). 1995. pap. 5.95 (1-56294-682-X) Millbrook Pr.

— Crafts for Valentine's Day. LC 94-9834. (Holiday Crafts for Kids Ser.). (Illus.). 48p. (J). (gr. k-3). 1995. lib. bdg. 15.40 (1-56294-489-4) Millbrook Pr.

— Crafts for Valentine's Day. LC 94-9834. (Holiday Crafts for Kids Ser.). (Illus.). 48p. (J). (gr. k-3). 1995. pap. 5.95 (1-56294-887-3) Millbrook Pr.

— Every Day Is Earth Day. (Holiday Crafts for Kids Ser.). (Illus.). 48p. (J). (gr. k-3). 1995. pap. 5.95 (1-56294-888-1) Millbrook Pr.

— Every Day Is Earth Day: A Craft Book. LC 94-9835. (Holiday Crafts for Kids Ser.). (Illus.). 48p. (J). (gr. k-3). 1995. 15.40 (1-56294-490-8) Millbrook Pr.

***Ross, Kenneth.** Church & Creed in Scotland: The Free Church Case 1900-1904 & Its Origins. 400p. Date not set. 49.50 (0-614-06084-2) Attic Pr.

Ross, Kenneth & Wright, Charles R. Discrete Mathematics. (Illus.). 672p. (C). 1985. pap. text ed. write for info. (0-13-215286-X) P-H.

Ross, Kenneth A. & Wright, Charles R. Discrete Mathematics. 3rd ed. 752p. (C). 1992. text ed. write for info. (0-13-218157-6) P-H.

Ross, Kenneth A., jt. auth. see Lopez, Jorge M.

Ross, Kenneth G. & Matthews, Robert W., eds. The Social Biology of Wasps. LC 90-44178. (Illus.). 688p. 1991. 79. 95 (0-8014-2035-0); pap. 34.95 (0-8014-9906-2) Cornell U Pr.

Ross, Kenneth R. Church & Creed in Scotland: The Free Church Case 1900-1904 & Its Origins. LC 92-5153. (Rutherford Studies in Historical Theology) 424p. 1992. reprint ed. lib. bdg. 109.95 (0-7734-1647-1) E Mellen.

Ross, Kevin. Kingsport. Herber, Keith, ed. (Call of Cthulhu Roleplaying Game System Ser.). (Illus.). 128p. 1991. pap. 18.95 (0-933635-77-X, 2333) Chaosium.

Ross, Kevin, et al. Escape from Innsmouth. Herber, Keith, ed. (Call of Cthulhu System Ser.). (Illus.). 160p. (Orig.). 1992. pap. text ed. 20.95 (0-933635-65-6, 2338) Chaosium.

Ross, Keyo & Krauth, Diane, eds. The National Directory of Certified Public Accountants. LC 82-62277. xvii, 1002p. 1982. 75.00 (0-312-55945-3) St Martin.

Ross, Kimberley M. & Strebeck, Sherry L. Scalies: A Comprehensive Resource for Architects, Designers & Students. (Illus.). 200p. 1988. pap. text ed. 28.50 (0-931541-12-3) Mancorp Pub.

Ross, Kristin. The Emergence of Social Space: Rimbaud & the Paris Commune. LC 88-4205. (Theory & History of Literature Ser.: Vol. 60). xvi, 170p. (Orig.). 1989. text ed. 39.95 (0-8166-1686-8); pap. text ed. 14.95 (0-8166-1687-6) U of Minn Pr.

— Fast Cars, Clean Bodies: Decolonization & the Reordering of French Culture. LC 94-17815. 300p. 1995. 24.95x (0-262-18161-4, October Bk) MIT Pr.

Ross, Kristin, tr. see Ranciere, Jacques.

Ross, Larry, illus. Hardie Gramatky's Little Toot. (All Aboard Bks.). 32p. (J). (ps-2). 1988. pap. 2.25 (0-448-34301-0, Platt & Munk Pubs) Putnam Pub Group.

***Ross-Larson, Bruce.** Edit Yourself: A Manual for Everyone Who Works with Words. 128p. 1995. pap. 9.00 (0-393-31326-3, Norton Paperbks) Norton.

— Edit Yourself: A Manual for Everyone Who Works with Words. 128p. 1985. reprint ed. pap. 7.95 (0-393-30268-7) Norton.

Ross-Larson, Bruce, jt. auth. see Baldwin, Harriet.

Ross, Laura. Hand Puppets: How to Make & Use Them. 1989. pap. 5.95 (0-486-26161-1) Dover.

Ross, Laura, ed. Theatre Profiles Seven: The Illustrated Guide to America's Nonprofit Professional Theatre. 25th ed. (Illus.). 388p. 1986. pap. 18.95 (0-930452-52-6) Theatre Comm.

***Ross, Lawrence S.** Personal Civil War Letters. Morrison, Shelly, ed. Shelton, Perry W., tr. 130p. 1994. 29.50 (0-926158-22-8) W M Morrison.

Ross, Lee & Nisbett, Richard E. The Person & the Situation: Essential Contributions of Social Psychology. 192p. 1991. pap. text ed. write for info. (0-07-053926-X) McGraw.

Ross, Lee, jt. auth. see Nisbett, Richard E.

***Ross, Lena B.** Cast the First Stone: Ethics in Analytical Practice. Guggenbuhl-Craig, Adolf, ed. 168p. (Orig.). 1995. pap. 19.95 (0-933029-89-6) Chiron Pubns.

Ross, Lena B., ed. To Speak or Be Silent: The Paradox of Disobedience in the Lives of Women. LC 92-45106. 288p. (Orig.). 1993. pap. 17.95 (0-933029-68-3) Chiron Pubns.

Ross, Leon T., jt. auth. see Mimms, Kenneth A.

Ross, Leonard Q. Education of Hyman Kaplan. LC 38-6588. 146p. 1968. reprint ed. pap. 6.95 (0-15-627811-1, Harvest Bks) HarBrace.

Ross, Lesli K. Celebrate! The Complete Jewish Holidays Handbook. LC 94-1940. 376p. 1994. pap. 35.00 (1-56821-154-6) Aronson.

Ross, Leslie. Text, Image, Message: Saints in Medieval Manuscript Illustrations. LC 93-35869. (Contributions to the Study of Art & Architecture Ser.: No. 3). 280p. 1994. text ed. 59.95 (0-313-29046-6, Greenwood Pr) Greenwood.

Ross, Lester. Environmental Policy in China. LC 87-45587. 252p. 1988. 35.00 (0-253-31837-8) Ind U Pr.

Ross, Lester & Silk, Mitchell A. Environmental Law & Policy in the People's Republic of China. LC 86-22503. (Illus.). 465p. 1987. text ed. 99.50 (0-89930-204-1, SKV/, Quorum Bks) Greenwood.

Ross, Lillian. Picture. 1993. 10.00 (0-385-46879-2, Anchor NY) Doubleday.

— Picture. LC 82-49210. (Cinema Classics Ser.). 264p. 1985. lib. bdg. 16.00 (0-8240-5775-9) Garland.

Ross, Lillian, jt. auth. see Steig, William.

Ross, Lillian B. Blaze Allen. 281p. 1986. pap. 9.95 (0-88496-241-5) Coast Pub.

— The Stranger in Big Sur. 282p. 1985. pap. 9.95 (0-88496-233-4) Coast Pub.

Ross, Lillian H. Buba Leah & Her Paper Children. (Illus.). 32p. (J). (gr. k-3). 1991. 17.95 (0-8276-0375-4) JPS Phila.

— Sarah, Also Known As Hannah. LC 93-29601. (Illus.). (J). 1994. write for info. (0-8075-7237-3) A Whitman.

Ross, Lissette L. Dark Sun. 1992. pap. 4.75 (0-8222-0274-3) Dramatists Play.

***Ross, Louise, ed.** Jane Austen: Novels, Letters & Memoir. 5918p. 1995. 1,899.00 (0-415-11562-0, C0483) Routledge.

Ross, Ludwig. Inselreisen. xxxvi, 350p. 1985. reprint ed. write for info. (3-487-07668-3, Pub. by Georg Olms GW) Lubrecht & Cramer.

Ross, Lydia. Cycles: In Universe & Man. rev. ed. Small, W. Emmett & Todd, Helen, eds. (Theosophical Manual Ser.: No. 8). 92p. 1975. reprint ed. pap. 3.95 (0-913004-19-7) Point Loma Pub.

Ross, Lydia & Ryan, Charles J. Theosophia: An Introduction. 57p. 1974. pap. 3.00 (0-913004-13-8) Point Loma Pub.

Ross, Lynn. Introduction to Radiologic Technology: A Study Guide Manual. 270p. (C). 1991. text ed. 45.00 (1-880359-02-2) Par Rad.

Ross, Lynn & Parelli, Robert J. Ultrasound - Medical Sonography: Clinical Manual. 124p. (C). 1991. text ed. 42.95 (1-880359-03-0) Par Rad.

Ross, Lynn C. Career Advancement for Women in the Federal Service: An Annotated Bibliography & Resource Book. LC 93-19100. (Public Affairs & Administration Ser.: Vol. 28). 280p. 1993. 40.00 (0-8153-1058-7, SS867) Garland.

Ross, Lynn N., jt. auth. see Jernigan, Anna K.

Ross, Lynne N. Purchasing for Food Service: Self-Instruction. LC 84-81612. (Illus.). 160p. (C). 1985. pap. text ed. 17.95 (0-8138-1461-8) Iowa St U Pr.

— Work Simplification in Food Service: Individualized Instruction. LC 73-171164. 134p. (Orig.). reprint ed. pap. 38.20 (0-317-27203-9, 2023865) Bks Demand.

Ross, M. Aesthetic Impulse. 250p. 1984. 64.00 (0-08-030234-3, 3400-3, 2600-2, Pub. by Pergamon Repr UK) Franklin.

— The Development of Aesthetic Experience. LC 82-3742. (Curriculum Issues in Arts Education Ser.: Vol. 3). 222p. 1982. 92.00 (0-08-028908-8, Pub. by Pergamon Repr UK) Franklin.

Ross, M., ed. The Arts: A Way of Knowing. LC 83-13208. (Curriculum Issues of Education Ser.: Vol. 4). 248p. 1983. 107.00 (0-08-030180-0, Pub. by Pergamon Repr UK) Franklin.

Ross, M. & Temkin, R. J., eds. Space Sensing, Communications, & Networking: 1989 Los Angeles Symposium - OE-LASE '89 (January 1989) (Proceedings Ser.: Vol. 1059). 1989. 62.00 (0-8194-0094-7) SPIE.

Ross, M., jt. auth. see Somerville, E.

Ross, M., et al, eds. Software Quality Management. LC 92-75804. (SQM Ser.: Vol. 1). 960p. 1993. 400.00 (1-56252-149-7) Computational Mech MA.

— Software Quality Management: Proceedings, Southampton, United Kingdom, March 1993. 960p. 1993. 400.00 (1-85166-963-9, Pub. by Elsevier Applied Sci UK) Elsevier.

— Software Quality Management II: Proceedings of the Second International Conference, 2 vols., Set. LC 94-70402. (SQM Ser.). 1592p. 1994. text ed. 435.00 (1-56252-188-8) Computational Mech MA.

— Software Quality Management II Vol. 1: Managing Quality Systems. (SQM Ser.: No. 2). 800p. 1994. 243.00 (1-56252-277-9) Computational Mech MA.

— Software Quality Management II Vol. 2: Building Quality into Software. (SQM Ser.: No. 2). 792p. 1994. 240.00 (1-56252-278-7) Computational Mech MA.

— Software Quality Management III: Proceedings of the Third International Conference, 2 vols., Set. LC 95-67478. (SQM Ser.: Vol. 3). 952p. 1995. 315.00 (1-56252-233-7) Computational Mech MA.

— Software Quality Management III Vol. 1: Quality Management, 2 vols., Set. LC 95-67478. (SQM Ser.: Vol. 3). 494p. 1995. 179.00 (1-56252-337-6) Computational Mech MA.

— Software Quality Management III Vol. 2: Measuring & Maintaining Quality, 2 vols., Set. (SQM Ser.: Vol. 3). 458p. 1995. 168.00 (1-56252-338-4) Computational Mech MA.

***Ross, M. J.** Polar Pioneers: John Ross & James Clark Ross. (Illus.). 456p. 1994. 34.95 (0-7735-1234-9, Pub. by McGill CN) U of Toronto Pr.

Ross, Mabel. Encyclopedia of Handspinning. LC 87-46354. 268p. 1988. 21.95 (0-934026-32-7) Interweave.

— The Essentials of Handspinning. 1988. pap. 8.95 (0-9507292-0-5) Robin & Russ.

— The Essentials of Yarn Design for Handspinners. 1987. pap. 15.95 (0-9507292-1-3) Robin & Russ.

— Handspinner's Workbook: Fancy Yarns. 1989. pap. 20.95 (0-9507292-5-6) Robin & Russ.

Ross, Maggie. The Fire of Your Life: A Solitude Shared. LC 91-55278. 144p. 1992. pap. 10.00 (0-06-067023-1) Harper SF.

— Pillars of Flame: Power, Priesthood, & Spiritual Maturity. LC 87-46227. 160p. 1988. 17.95 (0-06-254840-9) Harper SF.

Ross, Malcolm. The Aesthetic Imperative: Relevance & Responsibility in Arts Education. (Curriculum Issues in Arts Education Ser.: Vol. 2). 187p. 1981. 83.00 (0-08-026766-1, Pub. by Pergamon Repr UK) Franklin.

Ross, Malcolm, ed. The Arts & Personal Growth. LC 80-40260. (Curriculum Issues in Arts Education Ser.: Vol. 1). (Illus.). 136p. 1980. 58.00 (0-08-024714-8, Pub. by Pergamon Repr UK) Franklin.

— Claims of Feeling: Readings in Aesthetic Education. 240p. 1989. 75.00 (1-85000-612-1, Falmer Pr); pap. 38. 00 (1-85000-613-X, Falmer Pr) Taylor & Francis.

Ross, Malcolm, jt. ed. see Durie, Mark.

Ross, Malcolm, et al. Assessing Achievement in the Arts. LC 92-31892. (C). 1993. 90.00 (0-335-19062-6, Open Univ Pr); pap. 32.50 (0-335-19061-8, Open Univ Pr) Taylor & Francis.

Ross, Marc. Quantum Scattering Theory: Selected Papers. LC 63-16622. 313p. reprint ed. pap. 89.30 (0-317-08058-X, 2055227) Bks Demand.

Ross, Marc H. The Culture of Conflict: Interpretations & Interests in Comparative Perspective. LC 92-41994. (Illus.). 164p. (C). 1993. 30.00 (0-300-05273-1) Yale U Pr.

— Grass Roots in an African City: Political Behavior in Nairobi. LC 74-34263. 192p. (C). 1975. 32.50 (0-262-18074-X) MIT Pr.

Ross, Marc Howard. The Management of Conflict: Interpretations & Interests in Comparative Perspective. LC 92-47397. 232p. 1993. 25.00 (0-300-05398-3) Yale U Pr.

Ross, Margery, ed. Robert Ross, Friend of Friends: Letters to Robert Ross, Art Critic & Writer. LC 79-8074. reprint ed. 34.50 (0-404-18384-0) AMS Pr.

Ross, Marie. Child of Icaria. LC 75-343. (Radical Tradition in America Ser.). 147p. 1975. reprint ed. 17.60 (0-88355-246-9) Hyperion Conn.

Ross, Marilyn. The Haiti Circle. large type ed. (Romace Ser.). 272p. 1994. pap. 14.95 (0-7089-7543-7, Trailtree Bookshop) Ulverscroft.

— National Directory of Newspaper Op-Ed Pages. 158p. 1994. 19.95 (0-918880-17-3) Comm Creat.

Ross, Marilyn & Ross, Tom. Big Ideas for Small Service Businesses: How to Successfully Advertise, Publicize, & Maximize Your Business or Professional Practice. 289p. 1994. pap. 15.95 (0-918880-16-5) Comm Creat.

— Country Bound! Trade Your Business Suit Blues for Blue Jean Dreams. 1993. audio 59.95 (0-918880-32-7) Comm Creat.

— Country Bound! Trade Your Business Suit Blues for Blue Jean Dreams. 430p. 1992. pap. 19.95 (0-918880-30-0) Comm Creat.

— How to Make Big Profits Publishing City & Regional Books: A Guide for Entrepreneurs, Writers, & Publishers. 224p. 1987. pap. 14.95 (0-918880-12-2) Comm Creat.

— Marketing Your Books: A Collection of Profit-Making Ideas for Authors & Publishers. (Orig.). 1989. pap. 9.95 (0-918880-21-1) Comm Creat.

Ross, Marilyn, ed. see Alessandra, Tony, et al.

Ross, Marilyn, ed. see Bone, Bob.

Ross, Marilyn, ed. see Fotiades, John M.

Ross, Marilyn, ed. see Glasser, Selma.

Ross, Marilyn, ed. see Ottosen, Joleen.

Ross, Marilyn, jt. auth. see Ross, Tom.

Ross, Marion W. Bibliography of Vietnamese Literature in the Wason Collection at Cornell University. LC 74-173511. (Cornell University, Southeast Asia Program, Data Paper Ser.: No. 90). 196p. reprint ed. pap. 55.90 (0-8357-3679-2, 2036403) Bks Demand.

Ross, Maris & Jeans, David S. Adam & Evolution. 256p. 1974. 25.00 (0-8464-1289-6) Beekman Pubs.

Ross, Marjory, jt. auth. see Schabacker, Jay.

Ross, Mark. Principles of Aural Rehabilitation. LC 78-183116. (Studies in Communicative Disorders). (C). 1972. pap. write for info. (0-672-61283-6, Bobbs) Macmillan.

Ross, Mark, ed. Communication Access for Persons with Hearing Loss: Compliance with the Americans with Disabilities Act. LC 94-2594. (Illus.). 306p. (C). 1994. pap. text ed. 37.50 (0-912752-35-1) York Pr.

— FM Auditory Training Systems: Characteristics, Selection, & Use. LC 92-21604. 234p. 1992. pap. text ed. 24.00 (0-912752-31-9) York Pr.

— Hearing-Impaired Children in the Mainstream. LC 90-71342. (Illus.). 336p. (Orig.). (C). 1990. pap. text ed. 31. 00 (0-912752-22-X) York Pr.

Ross, Mark, jt. auth. see Luterman, David M.

Ross, Mark, jt. auth. see Ross, Raymond S.

Ross, Mark, et al. Assessment & Management of Mainstreamed Hearing-Impaired Children: Principles & Practices. LC 90-27495. 415p. (C). 1991. text ed. 38.00 (0-89079-458-8, 1969) PRO-ED.

Ross, Mark E., jt. auth. see Rollinson, Philip.

Ross, Marlon B. The Contours of Masculine Desire: Romanticism & the Rise of Women's Poetry. 360p. 1990. 49.95 (0-19-505791-0) OUP.

Ross, Martin, jt. auth. see Somerville, Edith O.

Ross, Martin J. Handbook of Everyday Law. 4th ed. 1982. mass mkt. 5.95 (0-449-24515-2) Fawcett.

Ross, Marvin C., jt. auth. see Von Erdberg, Joan P.

***Ross, Mary & Cameron, Ron, eds.** Behind the Scenes: A Canadian Scene Book. 124p. 1990. pap. text ed. 17.00 (0-88924-194-5, Pub. by Simon & Pierre Pub CN) Empire Pub Srvs.

— Behind the Scenes Vol. 2: A Canadian Scene Book. 124p. 1990. pap. text ed. 17.00 (0-88924-196-1, Pub. by Simon & Pierre Pub CN) Empire Pub Srvs.

Ross, Mary, ed. see Mitchell, Brooks.

Ross, Mary Alice. Fitness for the Aging Adult with Visual Impairment: An Exercise & Resource Manual. LC 84-24285. (Illus.). 88p. 1984. pap. 19.95 (0-89128-125-8) Am Foun Blind.

Ross, Meg, ed. see Bergrun, Norman R.

Ross, Mel, jt. auth. see Hall, Betty.

Ross, Melvin H. & Duffy, James P. Sailboat Chartering: The Complete Guide & International Directory. LC 92-36028. 320p. (Orig.). 1993. pap. 13.95 (1-56440-137-5) Globe Pequot.

Ross, Michael. Getting Great Guitar Sounds: A Non-Technical Approach to Developing, Controlling, & Shaping Your Own Personal Sound. (Illus.). 64p. (Orig.). 1989. pap. 10.95 (0-88188-596-7, 00183279) H Leonard.

Ross, Michael, ed. Homosexuality, Masculinity, & Femininity. LC 84-19778. (Journal of Homosexuality Ser.: Vol. 9, No. 1). 107p. 1985. pap. text ed. 9.95 (0-918393-04-3) Harrington Pk.

— Pedigrees of Leading Winners 1960-1980. 198p. 1990. 120.00 (0-85131-372-8, Pub. by J A Allen & Co UK) St Mut.

— Psychopathology & Psychotherapy in Homosexuality. LC 87-29894. (Journal of Homosexuality: Vol. 15, Nos. 1-2). 222p. 1988. text ed. 39.95 (0-86656-499-3) Haworth Pr.

Ross, Michael & DeCecco, John P., eds. The Treatment of Homosexuals with Mental Health Disorders. LC 87-30826. (Journal of Homosexuality Ser.: No. 15, No. 1-2). (Illus.). 222p. 1988. pap. 17.95 (0-918393-47-7) Harrington Pk.

Ross, Michael, jt. auth. see Johnson, Greg.

Ross, Michael, jt. auth. see Pickering, Martin.

Ross, Michael, jt. auth. see Sasso, Mario.

Ross, Michael, ed. see Wilson, Arthur N.

Ross, Michael E. Become a Bird & Fly! LC 91-36562. (Illus.). 32p. (J). (gr. k up). 1992. lib. bdg. 15.90 (1-56294-074-0) Millbrook Pr.

— Cycles, Cycles, Cycles. (Illus.). 88p. (J). (gr. 1-3). 1979. pap. 3.95 (0-939666-01-4) Yosemite Assn.

— Faces in All Kinds of Places: A Worm's Eye View of Flowers. (Illus.). 48p. 1987. 4.95 (0-939666-44-8) Yosemite Assn.

— Rolypolyology. LC 94-22327. (Backyard Buddies Ser.). (Illus.). (J). 1995. 18.95 (0-87614-862-3, Carolrhoda) Lerner Group.

— Sandbox Scientist: Real Science Activities for Little Kids. LC 95-13508. (Illus.). 144p. (J). (ps-3). 1995. pap. 12.95 (1-55652-248-7) Chicago Review.

— What Makes Everything Go? 94p. (J). (gr. k-2). 1979. pap. 4.95 (0-939666-19-7) Yosemite Assn.

— The World of Small: Nature Explorations with a Hand Lens. Medley, Steven P., ed. (Illus.). 64p. (J). (gr. k-6). 1993. spiral bd. 15.95 (0-939666-62-6) Yosemite Assn.

— Yosemite Fun Book. 48p. (J). (gr. 3-8). 1987. pap. 2.95 (0-939666-45-6) Yosemite Assn.

Ross, Michael J. California: Its Government & Politics. 4th ed. LC 91-18891. 272p. (C). 1992. pap. 24.95 (0-534-16434-X) Intl Thomson.

— State & Local Politics & Policy: Change & Reform. (Illus.). 352p. (C). 1987. pap. text ed. write for info. (0-13-843384-4) P-H.

Ross, Michael L. Storied Cities: Literary Imaginings of Florence, Venice, & Rome. LC 93-13011. (Contributions to the Study of World Literature Ser.: No. 51). 328p. 1993. text ed. 55.00 (0-313-28717-1, GM8717, Greenwood Pr) Greenwood.

R

An Asterisk (*) at the beginning of an entry indicates that the title is appearing in BIP for the first time.

Ross, Michael R. Recreational Fisheries of Coastal New England. LC 90-49253. (Illus.). 288p. 1991. lib. bdg. 45.00 (*0-87023-742-X*); pap. 17.95 (*0-87023-743-8*) U of Mass Pr.

Ross, Michael W. The Married Homosexual Man: A Psychological Study. 200p. (Orig.). 1983. pap. 14.95 (*0-7100-9532-5*, RKP) Routledge.

— Psychovenereology: Personality & Lifestyle Factors in Sexually Transmitted Diseases in Homosexual Men, Vol. 3. LC 85-25683. (Series in Sexual Medicine). 258p. 1986. text ed. 55.00 (*0-275-92122-0*, C2122, Praeger Pubs) Greenwood.

Ross, Michael W., ed. Homosexuality & Social Sex Roles. LC 83-12636. (Journal of Homosexuality: Vol. 9, No. 1). 107p. 1983. text ed. 32.95 (*0-86656-235-4*) Haworth Pr.

Ross, Michael W. & Channon-Little, Lorna D., eds. Discussing Sexuality: A Guide for Health Practitioners. 148p. 1991. pap. text ed. 16.95 (*0-8036-9888-7*) Davis Co.

Ross, Mildred. Group Process: Using Therapeutic Activities in Chronic Care. LC 86-63276. 158p. 1987. pap. 22.00 (*1-55642-012-9*) SLACK Inc.

— Integrative Group Therapy: The Structured Five Stage Approach. 2nd ed. LC 88-43457. 182p. 1991. pap. 25.00 (*1-55642-083-8*) SLACK Inc.

Ross, Monica L. Montana Molly & the Peppermint Kid: (Musical) (J). 1989. Playscript. 5.00 (*0-87602-285-9*) Anchorage.

— Wilma's Revenge. (J). 1989. Playscript. 5.00 (*0-87602-288-3*) Anchorage.

Ross, Morton. Sinclair Ross & His Works. (Canadian Author Studies). 42p. (C). 1991. pap. text ed. 9.95 (*1-55022-056-X*, Pub. by ECW Press CN) Genl Dist Srvs.

Ross-Murphy, S. B., ed. Physical Techniques for the Study of Food Biopolymers. LC 93-3412. 1993. write for info. (*1-85861-030-3*, Pub. by Elsevier Applied Sci UK) Elsevier.

Ross-Murphy, S. B., jt. ed. see Burchard, W.

Ross, Murray. Stars & Strikes: Unionization of Hollywood. LC 41-24783. reprint ed. 20.00 (*0-404-05408-0*) AMS Pr.

— The Way Must Be Tried: Memoirs of a University Man. 288p. 1992. 29.95 (*0-7737-2571-7*, Pub. by Stoddart Pubng CN) Genl Dist Srvs.

Ross, Murray G. Canadian Corporate Directors on the Firing Line. LC 80-154129. 146p. 1980. 26.95 (*0-07-092422-8*) McGraw.

Ross, Murray J. Drafting & Negotiating Commercial Leases. 3rd ed. 1989. 100.00 (*0-406-35909-1*, U.K.) Butterworth Legal Pubs.

Ross, Murray J., et al. Drafting & Negotiating Commercial Leases in Scotland. 1985. 90.00 (*0-406-35906-7*, U.K.) Butterworth Legal Pubs.

Ross, Myron H. A Gale of Creative Destruction: The Coming Economic Boom, 1992-2020. LC 89-3556. 184p. 1989. text ed. 45.00 (*0-275-93322-9*, C3322, Praeger Pubs) Greenwood.

Ross, Myron H., ed. The Economics of Aging. LC 85-25470. 138p. (C). 1985. text ed. 19.00 (*0-88099-033-3*); pap. text ed. 9.00 (*0-88099-032-5*) W E Upjohn.

Ross, N., jt. ed. see Price, G.

Ross, N. Phillip, jt. ed. see Cothern, C. Richard.

Ross, Nancy. Cordova's Historic Buildings. LC 83-81337. (Illus.). 20p. 1983. pap. 3.50 (*0-9607358-1-X*) Fathom Pub.

— Westward the Women. LC 76-117832. (Essay Index Reprint Ser.). 1977. 22.95 (*0-8369-1846-0*) Ayer.

***Ross, Nancy P.** Matzo Bunny. (Illus.). 20p. (Orig.). (J). (ps-4). 1995. pap. 8.95 (*0-9645964-0-7*) Powerhse Advert.

Ross, Nancy W. Buddhism: A Way of Life & Thought. LC 81-40081. (Illus.). 224p. 1981. pap. 12.00 (*0-394-74754-2*, Vin) Random.

— Westward the Women. LC 84-62311. 208p. 1985. 10.95 (*0-86547-183-5*, North Pt Pr) FS&G.

Ross, Nancy W., ed. World of Zen. (Illus.). 1964. pap. 15.00 (*0-394-70301-4*, Vin) Random.

Ross, Neil, ed. Marina Research, 1991. (Illus.). 178p. (C). 1991. 75.00 (*0-929803-11-6*) Intl Marina Inst.

Ross, Neil W., ed. Marina Environment, 1990. (Illus.). 322p. (Orig.). (C). 1990. pap. 75.00 (*0-929803-10-8*) Intl Marina Inst.

— Marina Investment & Appraisal Notebook. (Illus.). 282p. 1990. 75.00 (*0-929803-12-4*) Intl Marina Inst.

— Marina Research, 1989. (Illus.). 344p. (Orig.). (C). 1989. pap. 75.00 (*0-929803-04-3*) Intl Marina Inst.

— Marina Research, 1990. (Illus.). 255p. (Orig.). (C). 1990. pap. 75.00 (*0-929803-05-1*) Intl Marina Inst.

Ross, Neil W., intro. Marina Design & Engineering Conference Technical Papers. (Illus.). 305p. (Orig.). (C). 1987. pap. 65.00 (*0-929803-00-0*) Intl Marina Inst.

Ross, Neil W. & Dodson, Paul E., eds. Dockominium: Opportunities & Problems Proceedings of the National Dockominium Conference, 1987. 180p. (Orig.). 1988. pap. 25.00 (*0-929803-02-7*) Intl Marina Inst.

***Ross, Nicholas.** Art in Focus: Florence. (Illus.). 128p. 1995. 12.95 (*0-8212-2157-4*) Bulfinch Pr.

Ross, Nina P. The Norwegian Elkhound. Luther, Luana, ed. LC 93-74007. (Illus.). 320p. 1995. 26.95 (*0-944875-39-4*) Doral Pub.

— Of Gods & Dogs: Norse Mythology. LC 94-6068. (Illus.). 1994. write for info. (*1-881096-14-9*) Towery Pub.

***Ross, Noah & Ross, Julian.** The All-New Allstar Hockey Activity Book. (Illus.). 48p. (Orig.). (J). (gr. 4-8). 1993. pap. 5.95 (*0-919591-89-2*, Pub. by Polestar Bk Pubs CN) Orca Bk Pubs.

— Allstar Hockey Activity Book. (Illus.). 48p. (Orig.). (J). (gr. 4-8). 1990. pap. 5.95 (*0-919591-60-4*, Pub. by Polestar Bk Pubs CN) Orca Bk Pubs.

***Ross, Nola M.** How to Write the Story of Your Family. (Illus.). 67p. 1991. pap. 8.00 (*1-887144-06-4*) N M Ross.

— Jean Laffite Louisiana Buccaneer. (Illus.). 88p. Date not set. pap. 8.00 (*1-887144-05-6*) N M Ross.

— Mardi Gras in Calcasieu Parrish: A Pictorial History. (Illus.). 111p. Date not set. 30.00 (*1-887144-01-3*) N M Ross.

— Pioneers of Calcasieu & Cameron Parish, Vol. III. (Illus.). 102p. 1990. pap. 12.95 (*1-887144-04-8*) N M Ross.

— Pioneers of Calcasieu Parish, Vol. II. (Illus.). 80p. 1988. pap. 12.95 (*1-887144-03-X*) N M Ross.

— Pioneers of Calcasieu Parish: Memories of Early Calcasieu, Vol. I. (Illus.). 72p. 1987. pap. 12.95 (*1-887144-02-1*) N M Ross.

— Southwest Louisiana Veterans Remember: A 50th Anniversary Remembrance of World War II, Vol. I. (Illus.). 157p. 1993. 18.00 (*1-887144-00-5*) N M Ross.

Ross, Norm. Dull Moments, Never. 24p. 1993. pap. 3.00 (*1-884226-02-7*) Dark River.

Ross, Novelene. Lloyd Foltz (1897-1990): A Retrospective: An Exhibition of Prints, Drawings & Paintings by Prairie Print Maker Lloyd Foltz. (Illus.). 6p. (Orig.). 1992. pap. write for info. (*0-939324-45-8*) Wichita Art Mus.

— Passing Seasons: Paintings by Robert Sudlow. (Illus.). 24p. (Orig.). 1993. pap. 12.00 (*0-939324-49-0*) Wichita Art Mus.

Ross, Novelene, ed. Body Adornment. (Illus.). 20p. 1986. pap. 3.50 (*0-939324-27-X*) Wichita Art Mus.

Ross, Novelene, et al. Wan Qingli: The Scholar Artist in Modern China. (Illus.). 12p. 1988. pap. 3.00 (*0-939324-34-2*) Wichita Art Mus.

Ross, Novelene G. East Meets West in Lawrence, Kansas: An Exhibition of Paintings & Photographs by Martin Cheng, Norman Gee, Pok Chi Lau. (Illus.). 12p. (Orig.). 1992. pap. write for info. (*0-939324-48-2*) Wichita Art Mus.

Ross, Novella & Kurth, Paula, eds. Model Entrepreneurship Programs. 283p. 1986. 18.00 (*0-318-23569-2*, SN 53) Ctr Educ Trng Employ.

Ross, Novella, et al. A National Entrepreneurship Education Agenda for Action. 114p. 1984. 9.50 (*0-318-22156-X*, LT66) Ctr Educ Trng Employ.

Ross, Opal. Fields & Pine Trees. 71p. 1977. 9.95 (*0-87770-184-9*); pap. 6.95 (*0-87770-177-6*) Ye Galleon.

Ross, P. J. Fatigue under Superimposed Pressure. (Research Reports in Materials Science Ser.: Vol. 6). (Illus.). 128p. 1986. 75.00 (*1-85070-115-6*) Prthnon Pub.

Ross, P. R. & Lloyd, S. D., eds. Thirteenth-Century England I: Proceedings of the Newcastle-Upon-Tyne Conference 1985. (Thirteenth-Century England Ser.). 1986. 79.00 (*0-85115-452-2*) Boydell & Brewer.

Ross, P. Whitcomb, jt. auth. see Ross, Paul W.

Ross, Pat. Baby Dear: The Sweet Nellie Book of Traditional Advice, Sentiments & Expressions of Endearment from the Past. (Illus.). 64p. 1993. 8.95 (*0-670-84438-1*, Viking Studio) Studio Bks.

— A Christmas Gathering: The Sweet Nellie Book of Entertainment, Diversions, & Traditions of the Holiday Season. LC 91-50164. (Illus.). 64p. 1991. 8.95 (*0-670-83530-7*, Viking Studio) Studio Bks.

— Country Entertaining. LC 95-15983. (Illus.). 1995. 24.99 (*0-517-14695-9*, Pub. by Wings Bks) Random.

— Formal Country. LC 88-40639. (Illus.). 240p. 1989. 35.00 (*0-670-82574-3*, Viking Studio) Studio Bks.

— Formal Country Entertaining: At Home with Family & Friends. (Illus.). 288p. 1992. 35.00 (*0-670-83809-8*, Viking Studio) Studio Bks.

— The Grandest Folks: The Sweet Nellie Book of Traditional Sentiments about Grandmothers & Grandfathers. LC 93-14957. (Illus.). 64p. 1993. 8.95 (*0-670-84731-3*, Viking Studio) Studio Bks.

— Hannah's Fancy Notions: A Story of Industrial New England. LC 92-20286. (Once Upon America Ser.). (Illus.). 64p. (J). (gr. 2-6). 1992. pap. 3.99 (*0-14-032389-9*) Puffin Bks.

— I Thee Wed: The Sweet Nellie Book of Wedding Traditions & Sentiments. LC 90-55263. (Illus.). 64p. 1991. 8.95 (*0-670-83529-3*, Viking Studio) Studio Bks.

— It's Raining Cats & Dogs: An Obsession Book. 72p. 1994. 10.95 (*0-670-85218-X*) Studio Bks.

— M & M & the Bad News Babies. (M & M ser.). (Illus.). 48p. (J). (ps-3). 1985. pap. 3.99 (*0-14-031851-8*, Puffin) Puffin Bks.

— M & M & the Big Bag I Am Reading Book. LC 80-23299. (Illus.). 48p. (J). (gr. 1-4). 1981. 6.95 (*0-394-84340-1*) Pantheon.

— M & M & the Halloween Monster. LC 91-50294. (Illus.). 48p. (J). (gr. 1-2). 1991. text ed. 10.95 (*0-670-83003-8*) Viking Child Bks.

— M & M & the Halloween Monster. LC 93-15183. (Illus.). 64p. (J). (gr. 2-5). 1993. reprint ed. pap. 3.99 (*0-14-034247-8*, Puffin) Puffin Bks.

— M & M & the Haunted House Game. (J). (gr. 4 up). 1990. pap. 4.50 (*0-14-034577-9*, Puffin) Puffin Bks.

— M & M & the Santa Secrets. (Illus.). (J). (gr. 1-4). reprint ed. pap. 2.95 (*0-317-62234-X*, Puffin) Puffin Bks.

— M & M & the Super Child Afternoon. braille ed. 21p. (J). 1992. Braille. vinyl bd. 1.68 (*1-56956-277-6*, BR7953) W A T Braille.

— Meet M & M. (Illus.). 48p. (J). (gr. 1-4). 1988. pap. 3.99 (*0-14-032651-0*, Puffin) Puffin Bks.

— Motherly Devotion: The Sweet Nellie Book of Memories & Expressions of Endearment from the Past. LC 89-40651. (Illus.). 64p. 1990. 8.95 (*0-670-83059-3*, Viking Studio) Studio Bks.

— One Swell Dad: The Sweet Nellie Book of Memories & Expressions of Fatherly Endearment from the Past. (Illus.). 64p. 1992. 8.95 (*0-670-84445-4*, Viking Studio) Studio Bks.

— The Pleasure of Your Company: The Sweet Nellie Book of Traditional Sentiments & Customs of Proper Entertaining. (Illus.). 64p. 1989. 8.95 (*0-670-83038-0*, Viking Studio) Studio Bks.

— Remembering Main Street: An American Album. LC 94-6018. (Illus.). 256p. 1994. 29.95 (*0-670-84784-4*, Viking Studio) Studio Bks.

— Son in a Million: The Sweet Nellie Book of Traditional Sentiments, Endearments, & Appreciations from the Past. (Illus.). 64p. 1994. 8.95 (*0-670-85009-8*, Viking Studio) Studio Bks.

— The Sweet Nellie HomeFile: An Essential Household Record Book & Directory. (Illus.). 144p. 1992. 12.95 (*0-670-83759-8*, Viking Studio) Studio Bks.

— To Have & to Hold: Decorative American Boxes. LC 89-40798. (Illus.). 144p. 1991. 19.95 (*0-670-83061-5*, Viking Studio) Studio Bks.

— With Love & Affection: The Sweet Nellie Book of Traditional Sentiments & Tokens of Romance & Friendship. LC 89-40353. 64p. 1990. pap. 8.95 (*0-670-83058-5*, Viking Studio) Studio Bks.

— With Thanks & Appreciation: The Sweet Nellie Book of Thoughts, Sentiments, Tokens & Traditions of the Past. LC 88-17140. 64p. 1989. pap. 8.95 (*0-670-82521-2*, Viking Studio) Studio Bks.

Ross, Pat, comp. My Delightful Daughter: The Sweet Nellie Book of Traditional Sentiments, Endearments & Affections from the Past. LC 93-47460. 1994. 8.95 (*0-670-85010-1*, Viking) Viking Penguin.

Ross, Pat & Crane, Leisa. A Birthday Wish: The Sweet Nellie Book of Traditional Sentiments & Tokens of Birthtide. LC 92-24798. (Illus.). 1993. 8.95 (*0-670-84437-3*, Viking Studio) Studio Bks.

Ross, Pat & Sedgewood Press Staff. Soft Furnishings. 192p. 1992. 29.95 (*0-696-02378-4*); pap. 19.95 (*0-696-02551-5*) Meredith Bks.

Ross, Pat, ed. see Gray, Arthur.

Ross, Pat, ed. see Hamilton, Gail.

***Ross, Patricia.** Goats: A Guide to Management. (Illus.). 112p. 1995. pap. 19.95 (*1-85223-912-3*, Pub. by Crowood Pr UK) Trafalgar.

Ross, Patricia T., ed. see Hedgecock, Joseph C.

Ross, Paul W. Using ENABLE: An Introduction to Integrated Software. 448p. 1988. pap. 28.50 (*0-87835-295-3*) Boyd & Fraser.

— Using Enable - OA. 416p. 1991. text ed. 28.50 (*0-87835-557-X*, BF557X) Boyd & Fraser.

***Ross, Paul W., ed.** The Handbook of Software for Engineers & Scientists. 2,000p. 1995. 89.95 (*0-8493-2530-7*, 2530) CRC Pr.

Ross, Paul W. & Ross, P. Whitcomb. Using Microsoft Works Effectively: Windows Version. 288p. (C). 1993. spiral bd. write for info. (*0-697-17143-4*) Brown & Benchmark.

— Using Windows 3.0-3.1 Effectively. 272p. (C). 1993. spiral bd. write for info. (*0-697-14535-2*) Bus & Educ Tech.

Ross, Paul W., et al. Understanding Computer Information Systems. Leyh, ed. 204p. (C). 1992. pap. text ed. 15.50 (*0-314-93437-5*) West Pub.

Ross, Paula P., tr. see Chekhov, Anton.

Ross, Penny. Stop Smoking Without Putting on Weight. 176p. 1994. write for info. (*0-318-72608-4*) Thorsons SF.

— Stop Smoking Without Putting on Weight. 1994. pap. 5.99 (*0-7225-3015-3*) Thorsons SF.

Ross, Peter. Advanced Prolog: Techniques & Applications. 250p. (C). 1989. text ed. 37.75 (*0-201-17527-4*) Addison-Wesley.

Ross, Peter R., jt. auth. see Galdy, Nancy K.

Ross, Philip. The Government As a Source of Union Power: The Role of Public Policy in Collective Bargaining. LC 65-10155. 334p. reprint ed. 95.20 (*0-685-15768-7*, 2027521) Bks Demand.

— Talley's Truth. 256p. 1988. pap. 3.50 (*0-8125-8784-7*) Tor Bks.

— True Lies. 256p. 1994. mass mkt. 3.99 (*0-8125-1376-2*) Tor Bks.

***Ross, Philip J.** De-Privatizing Morality. (Philosophy Ser.). 125p. 1994. pap. 54.95 (*1-85628-659-2*, Pub. by Avebury Pub UK) Ashgate Pub Co.

Ross, Philip N., jt. ed. see Lipkowski, Jacek.

Ross, Philip N., jt. ed. see Lipowski, Jacek.

Ross, Phillip J. Taguchi Techniques for Quality Engineering: Loss Function, Orthgonal Experiments, Parameter & Tolerance Design. 304p. 1988. text ed. 57.00 (*0-07-053866-2*) McGraw.

— Taguchi Techniques for Quality Engineering: Loss Function, Orthogonal Experiments, Parameter & Tolerance Design. 2nd ed. LC 95-15415. 1995. write for info. (*0-07-053958-8*) McGraw.

Ross Pipes & Associates Inc., Staff. The Pocket Proposal Style Manual. 2nd deluxe ed. 68p. (Orig.). 1989. Deluxe leatherbound. 49.95 (*0-923768-01-7*) Tekne Pr.

— The Pocket Proposal Style Manual. 2nd ed. 68p. (Orig.). 1989. pap. 12.95 (*0-923768-02-5*) Tekne Pr.

Ross, R. Air Pollution & Industry. 1995. text ed. write for info. (*0-442-00125-8*) Van Nos Reinhold.

Ross, R., ed. Recent & Fossil Diatoms: Proceedings of the Symposia on Taxonomy, Morphology, Ecology & Biology, 6th, Budapest, Sept. 1980. (Illus.). 500p. 1982. text ed. 219.50 (*3-87429-192-8*) Koeltz Sci Bks.

Ross, R., jt. ed. see Baxter, A.

Ross, R. B. Metallic Materials Specification Handbook. 3rd ed. 1980. 120.00 (*0-419-11360-6*, NO. 6339, E & FN Spon) Routledge Chapman & Hall.

Ross, R. T., ed. see Jonesco-Sisesti, N.

Ross, Rachael & Schneider, Robin. From Equality to Diversity: A Business Case for Equal Opportunities. 256p. 1992. 72.50x (*0-273-03370-0*, Pub. by Pitman Pub Ltd UK) Trans-Atl Phila.

Ross, Ralph G., ed. Makers of American Thought: An Introduction to Seven American Writers. LC 74-78993. (Minnesota Library on American Writers). 307p. reprint ed. pap. 87.50 (*0-318-39694-7*, 2033289) Bks Demand.

Ross, Ralph G., ed. see Bosanquet, Bernard.

Ross, Ralph G., ed. see Burke, Edmund.

Ross, Ralph G., et al, eds. Thomas Hobbes in His Time. LC 74-83134. 160p. reprint ed. pap. 45.60 (*0-318-39663-7*, 2033232) Bks Demand.

***Ross, Ramon R.** The Dancing Tree. LC 95-2124. (J). 1995. 15.00 (*0-689-80072-X*, Atheneum S&S) S&S Trade.

— Harper & Moon. 192p. (J). 1995. pap. 3.50 (*0-380-72356-5*, Camelot) Avon.

— Harper & Moon. LC 92-17216. (Illus.). 192p. (J). (gr. 4 up). 1993. text ed. 14.95 (*0-689-31803-0*, Atheneum Bks Young) S&S Childrens.

Ross, Randal. Seven Habits of Winning Relationships. 150p. (Orig.). 1992. pap. text ed. 11.95 (*1-882745-00-0*) YMTN-Stone.

***Ross, Randall R. & Altmaier, Elizabeth M.** Intervention in Occupational Stress: A Handbook of Counselling for Stress at Work. LC 94-65025. 196p. 1994. pap. 17.95 (*0-8039-8673-4*) Sage.

Ross, Randy. Government & the Private Sector: Who Should Do What? LC 88-3803. (Illus.). 140p. (C). 1988. text ed. 29.00 (*0-8448-1554-3*, Crane Russak) Taylor & Francis.

Ross, Randy L., jt. auth. see Kakalik, James S.

Ross, Raymond, jt. ed. see Hendry, Joy.

Ross, Raymond S. Understanding Persuasion. 4th ed. LC 93-9103. 1993. pap. text ed. write for info. (*0-13-501131-0*) P-H.

Ross, Raymond S. & Ross, Mark. Relating & Interacting: An Introduction to Interpersonal Communication. (Illus.). 320p. (C). 1982. pap. text ed. write for info. (*0-13-771923-X*) P-H.

Ross, Rhea B. Bet's on, Lizzie Bingman! (YA). 1992. pap. 4.95 (*0-395-64375-9*) HM.

Ross, Richard. The Bacterial Diseases of Reptiles: Their Epidemiology, Control, Diagnosis & Treatment. (Illus.). 131p. 1984. pap. 22.00 (*0-9631470-1-3*) Inst Herpeto Res.

— Handbook of Stock Brokerage Accounting. 1993. 65.00 (*0-13-374182-6*) P-H.

— Museology. (Illus.). 80p. 1989. 39.95 (*0-89381-376-1*) Aperture.

— One Hundred & One Photographs: Selections from the Arthur & Yolanda Steinman Collection. LC 84-71041. (Illus.). (Orig.). 1984. pap. 3.50 (*0-89951-052-3*) Santa Barb Mus Art.

— Reproductive Husbandry of Pythons & Boas. (Illus.). 270p. 1990. 75.00 (*0-9631470-0-5*) Inst Herpeto Res.

Ross, Richard G., jt. auth. see Ross, Truedie L.

Ross, Robert. Adam Kok's Griquas: A Study in the Development of Stratification in South Africa. LC 75-43368. (African Studies Ser.: 21). 208p. reprint ed. pap. 59.30 (*0-8357-5092-2*, 2024526) Bks Demand.

— American National Government: Institutions, Policy, & Participation. 3rd ed. 544p. 1993. 21.95 (*1-56134-223-8*) Dushkin Pub.

— Beyond the Pale: Essays on the History of Colonial South Africa. LC 92-56910. (Illus.). 284p. 1993. 50.00 (*0-8195-5258-5*, Wesleyan Univ Pr) U Pr of New Eng.

— How to Study, Vol. 1: To Understand As Well As to Pass Tests. 170p. pap. 25.00 (*0-87916-035-7*) Upstat.

Ross, Robert, ed. International Literature in English: Essays on the Major Writers. LC 90-24468. 784p. 1991. 95.00 (*0-8240-3437-6*, H1159) Garland.

Ross, Robert, jt. auth. see MacKichan, Margaret.

Ross, Robert A., et al. Wildflowers of the Western Cascades. LC 87-29648. (Illus.). 204p. (Orig.). 1988. pap. 19.95 (*0-88192-078-9*) Timber.

Ross, Robert B. Handbook of Metal Treatments & Testing. 2nd ed. 550p. 1988. lib. bdg. 69.95 (*0-412-31390-1*) Chapman & Hall.

— Metallic Materials Specification Handbook. 4th enl. ed. 830p. 1992. 211.95x (*0-412-36940-0*, A5567) Chapman & Hall.

Ross, Robert E. Beyond the Rope's End. LC 81-83846. (Illus.). 180p. (Orig.). 1982. pap. 12.95 (*0-9607312-0-2*) Priority Proj.

— Even If You've Never Played Before: You Can Play Hymns & Spirituals Using the New Music Notation System for Keyboards! (Illus.). 190p. 1992. write for info. (*0-9630043-3-6*) Keyboard Mus.

— If You Really Want to Learn Piano: A Quicker & Easier Method for Learning to Play Pianos & Electronic Keyboards. rev. ed. LC 91-77293. Orig. Title: For Beginners Only: An Innovative Method for Learning Piano & Electronic Keyboard Playing. (Illus.). 195p. 1992. write for info. (*0-9630043-1-X*) Keyboard Mus.

— A New Music System Especially for Electronic Keyboards: A Quicker & Easier Method for Learning to Play Keyboard Instruments. LC 92-90282. (Illus.). 195p. 1992. write for info. (*0-9630043-2-8*) Keyboard Mus.

***Ross, Robert E., ed.** The Ross Register of Siberian Industry: A Guide to Factories, Mines & Industrial Establishments Through Siberia. LC 94-28437. 300p. 1995. lib. bdg. 119.00 (*0-88354-125-4*) N Ross.

Ross, Robert H., ed. see Tennyson, Alfred.

Ross, Robert J. The Indochina Tangle: China's Vietnam Policy, 1975-1979. (Studies of the East Asian Institute). 392p. 1988. text ed. 52.50 (*0-231-06564-7*) Col U Pr.

— Infinite Syntax. LC 82-24310. (Language & Being Ser.). 344p. 1986. text ed. 65.00 (*0-89391-042-2*) Ablex Pub.

— Racism & Colonialism. 1982. lib. bdg. 77.50 (*90-247-2634-4*) Kluwer Ac.

Ross, Robert J., ed. Imperialism & Global Capitalism. (Key Concepts in Critical Theory Ser.). (C). Date not set. pap. write for info. (*0-391-03796-X*) Humanities.

Ross, Robert J. & Trachte, Kent C. Global Capitalism: The New Leviathan. LC 89-21858. (SUNY Series in Radical, Social & Political Theory). 1990. 64.50 (*0-7914-0339-4*); pap. 21.95 (*0-7914-0340-8*) State U NY Pr.

Ross, Robert J., tr. see Barbagli, Marzio.

Ross, Robert L. Australian Literary Criticism, 1945-1988: An Annotated Bibliography. 400p. 1989. 58.00 (*0-8240-1510-X*) Garland.

Ross, Robert M. & Allmon, Warren D., eds. Causes of Evolution: A Paleontological Perspective. (Illus.). 368p. 1990. pap. text ed. 24.95 (*0-226-72824-2*) U Ch Pr.

— Causes of Evolution: A Paleontological Perspective. (Illus.). 368p. 1991. lib. bdg. 65.00 (*0-226-72823-4*) U Ch Pr.

Ross, Robert N. Experience the Joy of Painting with Bob Ross, Vol. 2. (Joy of Painting with Bob Ross Ser.). (Illus.). 66p. (Orig.). 1989. reprint ed. pap. 10.50 (*0-924639-06-7*) Bob Ross Inc.

— Experience the Joy of Painting with Bob Ross, Vol. 3. (Joy of Painting with Bob Ross Ser.). (Illus.). 74p. (Orig.). 1989. reprint ed. pap. 10.95 (*0-685-24725-2*) Bob Ross Inc.

— Experience the Joy of Painting with Bob Ross, Vol. 4. (Joy of Painting with Bob Ross Ser.). (Illus.). 78p. (Orig.). 1989. reprint ed. pap. 11.00 (*0-685-24726-0*) Bob Ross Inc.

— The Joy of Painting with Bob Ross, Vol. 6. (Illus.). 76p. (Orig.). 1989. reprint ed. pap. 11.50 (*0-924639-03-2*) Bob Ross Inc.

— The Joy of Painting with Bob Ross, Vol. 8. (Illus.). 80p. (Orig.). 1986. pap. 11.95 (*0-685-24727-9*) Bob Ross Inc.

— The Joy of Painting with Bob Ross, Vol. 9. (Illus.). 84p. (Orig.). 1989. reprint ed. pap. 12.00 (*0-685-24728-7*) Bob Ross Inc.

— The Joy of Painting with Bob Ross, Vol. 10. (Illus.). 76p. (Orig.). 1987. pap. 12.25 (*0-685-24729-5*) Bob Ross Inc.

— The Joy of Painting with Bob Ross, Vol. 11. (Illus.). 76p. (Orig.). 1988. pap. 11.98 (*0-685-24730-9*) Bob Ross Inc.

— The Joy of Painting with Bob Ross, Vol. 12. (Illus.). 76p. (Orig.). 1989. reprint ed. pap. 11.90 (*0-924639-04-0*) Bob Ross Inc.

— The Joy of Painting with Bob Ross, Vol. 13. (Illus.). 80p. (Orig.). 1988. pap. 12.10 (*0-685-24731-7*) Bob Ross Inc.

— The Joy of Painting with Bob Ross, Vol. 14. (Illus.). 76p. (Orig.). 1989. pap. 12.20 (*0-924639-01-6*) Bob Ross Inc.

— The Joy of Painting with Bob Ross, Vol. 16. (Illus.). 76p. (Orig.). 1989. pap. 12.20 (*0-924639-07-5*) Bob Ross Inc.

— Nasalcrom in Clinical Practice. LC 83-81193. (Illus.). 40p. 1983. write for info. (*0-914132-04-0*) Fisons Corp.

— Opticrom Four Percent in Clinical Practice. LC 84-72911. (Illus.). 43p. 1984. write for info. (*0-914132-05-9*) Fisons Corp.

Ross, Robert N., jt. auth. see Cohen, Sanford I.

Ross, Robert N., jt. auth. see Prout, Curtis.

Ross, Robert R. The Non-Existence of God: Linguistic Paradox in Tillich's Thought. LC 78-65486. (Toronto Studies in Theology: Vol. 1). xiv, 216p. 1978. lib. bdg. 89.95 (*0-88946-905-9*) E Mellen.

***Ross, Robert R. & Lightfoot, Lynn O.** Treatment of the Alcohol-Abusing Offender. 164p. 1985. pap. 16.95 (*0-398-06410-5*) C C Thomas.

— Treatment of the Alcohol-Abusing Offender. 164p. (C). 1985. 31.95x (*0-398-05090-2*) C C Thomas.

Ross, Robert R., jt. auth. see Lobanoff, Val S.

***Ross, Robert S.** Negotiating Cooperation: The United States & China, 1969-1989. 1995. 39.50 (*0-8047-2453-9*) Stanford U Pr.

Ross, Robert S., ed. China, the United States & the Soviet Union: Tripolarity & Policymaking in the Cold War. (Studies on Contemporary China). 224p. (C). 1993. text ed. 57.95 (*1-56324-253-2*, East Gate Bk); pap. text ed. 20.95 (*1-56324-254-0*, East Gate Bk) M E Sharpe.

— East Asia in Transition: Toward a New Regional Order. (Illus.). 382p. 1995. 59.95 (*1-56324-560-4*, East Gate Bk) M E Sharpe.

— East Asia in Transition: Toward a New Regional Order. (Illus.). 382p. 1995. pap. 22.50 (*1-56324-561-2*, East Gate Bk) M E Sharpe.

— Perspectives on Local Government. 192p. (C). 1987. pap. 14.95 (*0-89863-119-X*) Star Pub CA.

Ross, Robert T., et al. Lives of the Mentally Retarded: A Forty-Year Follow-up Study. LC 83-42533. 224p. 1985. 42.50 (*0-8047-1189-5*) Stanford U Pr.

Ross, Robert W. So It Was True: The American Protestant Press & the Nazi Persecution of the Jews. 374p. reprint ed. pap. 9.95 (*0-686-95052-6*) ADL.

Ross, Rockford J., jt. auth. see Starkey, J. Denbigh.

Ross-Rodgers, Martha J. Awakenings. LC 93-14401. 180p. 1993. pap. 8.95 (*1-882185-10-2*) Crnrstone Pub.

Ross, Ron. The Tomato Can. LC 93-86844. 192p. 1994. pap. 11.95 (*0-9638230-5-1*) Oyster Bay Bks.

Ross, Ron G., Jr., ed. see Eighth International Cryocoolers Conference.

Ross, Ronald D. Your Family Heritage: A Guide to Preserving Family History. LC 88-60501. 144p. 1988. 19.95 (*0-9620144-0-0*) R D Ross.

Ross, Ronald E. Wild Edible Plants of Mother Nature: A Guide to Eating Hardy on Plants Common to 48 States. (Illus.). 92p. (Orig.). 1991. pap. 7.50 (*0-9632601-0-3*) Plans Plus.

Ross, Ronald G. Entity Modeling: Techniques & Application. (Illus.). 218p. 1987. 39.95 (*0-941049-00-0*) Dbase Res Grp.

Ross, Ronald G. & Michaels, Wanda I. Resource Life Cycle Analysis: A Business Modeling Technique for IS Planning. (Illus.). 90p. 1992. 39.95 (*0-941049-01-9*) Dbase Res Grp.

***Ross, Rosemary.** Creative Living & Health Workbook: A New & Exciting System for Dealing with the Emotional & Physical Stress of Cancer. 44p. (Orig.). 1989. pap. 8.95 (*0-9647382-1-X*) R Ross.

— Creative Living & Health Workbook: A New & Exciting System for Dealing with the Emotional & Physical Stress of Cancer. 36p. 1994. reprint ed. pap. 8.95 (*0-9647382-2-8*) R Ross.

— I'm Glad I Had Cancer, It Changed My Life: A Guide to Starting & Facilitating Cancer Support Groups. 50p. (Orig.). 1994. pap. 14.95 (*0-9647382-3-6*) R Ross.

Ross-Rovertson, David, illus. Speaking As a Writer. 76p. 1979. 7.75 (*0-9602342-1-7*); pap. 5.95 (*0-9602342-0-9*) Westwind Pr.

Ross, Rupert. Dancing with a Ghost: Exploring Indian Reality. 1992. 22.95 (*0-409-90648-4*, Pub. by Buttrwrth Can Acad CN) Buttrwrth-Heinemann.

Ross, Russell, jt. ed. see Sato, Gordon H.

***Ross-Russell, Noel.** Serenade of Fear. 256p. 1995. pap. 12.95 (*1-871871-21-2*) Paul & Co Pubs.

Ross, Russell R. Cambodia: A Country Study. 3rd ed. LC 89-600150. (Area Handbook Ser.). (Illus.). 398p. 1990. Individual mailing box. per. 18.00 (*0-16-020838-6*, S/N 008-020-01203-3) USGPO.

Ross, Russell R. & Savada, Andrea M., eds. Sri Lanka: A Country Study. 2nd ed. LC 89-600470. (Illus.). 360p. 1990. 17.00 (*0-16-024055-7*, 0327-J) USGPO.

Ross, Ruth. Power to Prosper: The Inner Path to Success. 1992. write for info. (*0-9622313-3-9*) Prosper Natural.

— Prospering Woman: A Complete Guide to Achieving the Full, Abundant Life. 2nd ed. LC 94-38598. 224p. 1995. pap. 11.95 (*1-880032-60-0*) New Wrld Lib.

Ross, Ruth, jt. auth. see Iglitzin, Lynne B.

Ross, Ruth, jt. auth. see Weston, David.

Ross, Ruth I. Irish Wildflowers. (Appletree Pocket Guides Ser.). (Illus.). 71p. (Orig.). 1987. pap. 7.95 (*0-86281-192-9*, Pub. by Appletree Pr IE) Irish Bks Media.

Ross, S. Soil Processes: A Systematic Approach. (Illus.). 416p. 1989. text ed. 95.00 (*0-415-00205-2*) Routledge.

Ross, S., ed. see Bertsch, Sharon M. & Bertsch, George.

Ross, S., ed. see Dewdney, A. K.

Ross, S., ed. see Dickson, Paul, Jr. & Clancy, Paul.

Ross, S., jt. ed. see Nash, J.

Ross, S. D., jt. ed. see Considine, Douglas M.

Ross, S. M., ed. Toxic Metals in Soil-Plant Systems. LC 93-46717. 1994. text ed. 125.00 (*0-471-94279-0*) Wiley.

Ross, Sam. Melov's Legacy. Orig. Title: The Sidewalks Are Free. 308p. 1984. reprint ed. 22.00 (*0-933256-56-6*) Second Chance.

— Melov's Legacy. LC 84-50877. Orig. Title: The Sidewalks Are Free. 308p. 1985. reprint ed. pap. 16.00 (*0-933256-57-4*) Second Chance.

Ross, Sandi B., jt. auth. see Nelson, John M.

Ross, Sandra. The Nicelies at Home: A Lil'l Charmers Book. LC 93-70084. (Nicelies Ser.). (Illus.). 76p. (Orig.). (J). (ps-2). 1993. pap. 5.95 (*1-881235-01-7*) Creat Opport.

Ross, Sandra B. The Nicelies Series, 4 vols., Set. (J). (ps-2). 1994. pap. 19.95 (*1-881235-04-1*) Creat Opport.

Ross, Sandra J. The Nicelies Go to School: A Lil'l Charmers Book. LC 93-74878. (Nicelies Ser.). (Illus.). 74p. (J). (ps-2). 1994. pap. 5.95 (*1-881235-02-5*) Creat Opport.

— Traveling with the Nicelies. LC 94-94426. (Nicelies Ser.). (Illus.). 64p. (J). (ps-2). 1994. pap. 5.95 (*1-881235-03-3*) Creat Opport.

— Visiting the Nicelies: A Lil'l Charmers Book. LC 92-70147. (Nicelies Ser.). (Illus.). 60p. (Orig.). (J). (ps-2). 1991. pap. 5.95 (*1-881235-00-9*) Creat Opport.

Ross, Sandy T. Bairnsangs. (C). 1988. pap. 23.00 (*0-907526-11-X*, Alloway Pub) St Mut.

Ross, Sarah, illus. The Ladybird Baby Book. 28p. 1989. 3.95 (*0-7214-5198-5*, S808-1) Ladybird Bks.

Ross, Seamus, et al, eds. Computing for Archaeologists. (Illus.). 216p. 1991. pap. 35.00 (*0-947816-18-6*, Pub. by Univ Comm Archeology UK) David Brown.

***Ross, Seth.** Internet Now! The Consumer's Guide to Internet Access. (Orig.). 1995. pap. 12.95 (*0-9637025-3-X*) Albion Bks.

Ross, Seth & Kehoe, Daniel M. Taking the Next Step: The Buyers' Guide to Nextstep Computing. 148p. 1993. pap. 29.95 (*0-9637025-0-5*) Albion Bks.

Ross, Sharon & Boyd, Linda. Graphing Calculator Exercises & Student Experiments for Precalculus Algebra & Trigonometry. 191p. (C). 1991. pap. 18.95 (*0-534-14558-2*) Brooks-Cole.

***Ross, Sharon M.** Painting & Wallpapering. rev. ed. Beckstrom, Robert J., ed. LC 94-69599. (Illus.). 96p. 1995. pap. 9.95 (*0-89721-259-2*, 05970B) Ortho Info.

Ross, Sheldon. Explorations in Mathematical Thinking. Smart, Margaret, ed. & illus. by. 64p. (Orig.). (J). (gr. 2-8). 1994. pap. 7.95 (*1-882293-03-7*) Activity Resources.

Ross, Sheldon M. Applied Probability Models with Optimization Applications. unabridged ed. LC 92-16013. (Illus.). 198p. 1992. reprint ed. pap. text ed. 6.95 (*0-486-67314-6*) Dover.

— Applied Probability Models with Optimization Applications. LC 73-111376. (Holden-Day Series in Management Science). 208p. reprint ed. pap. 59.30 (*0-8357-5685-8*, 2052131) Bks Demand.

— A Course in Simulation. 326p. (C). 1990. write for info. (*0-02-403891-1*) Macmillan.

— A First Course in Probability. 4th ed. 473p. (C). 1994. write for info. (*0-02-403872-5*) Macmillan.

— Introduction to Probability & Statistics for Engineers & Scientists. LC 87-10406. 492p. 1987. Net. text ed. write for info. (*0-471-81752-X*) Wiley.

— Introduction to Probability Theory. 5th ed. (Illus.). 556p. 1993. text ed. 59.95 (*0-12-598455-3*) Acad Pr.

— Stochastic Processes. LC 82-8619. (Probability & Mathematical Statistics Ser.). 309p. (C). 1982. Net. text ed. write for info. (*0-471-09942-2*); teacher ed 20.00 (*0-471-87236-9*) Wiley.

Ross, Sheldon M., ed. Introduction to Stochastic Dynamic Programming: Probability & Mathematical. LC 82-18163. 1983. text ed. 37.00 (*0-12-598420-0*) Acad Pr.

Ross, Shelley. Fall from Grace: Sex, Scandal & Corruption in American Politics, 1702-1987. 1988. pap. 10.00 (*0-345-35381-1*, Ballantine Trade) Ballantine.

Ross, Shelley, jt. auth. see Rosner, Louis J.

Ross, Shepley L. Differential Equations. 3rd ed. LC 83-21643. 807p. (C). 1984. 24.95 (*0-471-82777-0*) Wiley.

— Differential Equations, Set. 3rd ed. LC 83-21643. 807p. (C). 1984. Net. text ed. write for info. (*0-471-03294-8*) Wiley.

— Introduction to Ordinary Differential Equations. 4th ed. 609p. 1989. Net. text ed. write for info. (*0-471-09881-7*); Net. student ed write for info. (*0-471-63438-7*) Wiley.

***Ross, Sherry.** The Hockey Scouting Report 1995-1996. (Illus.). 480p. 1995. pap. 12.95 (*1-55054-444-6*, Pub. by Doug & McIntyre CN) Sterling.

Ross, Shirley. ABCs Beginning Sounds. (Rainbow Skill Builders Ser.: Level 1). 80p. (Orig.). (J). (ps). 1985. pap. 2.95 (*0-8431-2506-3*) Price Stern.

— Kindergarten Readiness. (Rainbow Skill Builders Ser.: Level 2). 80p. (Orig.). 1986. pap. 2.95 (*0-8431-2513-6*) Price Stern.

— Learning to Print. (Rainbow Skill Builders Ser.: Level 2). 80p. (Orig.). (J). (ps-1). 1984. pap. 2.95 (*0-8431-2507-1*) Price Stern.

— Visual Skills. (Rainbow Skill Builders Ser.: Level 3). 80p. (J). (ps-3). 1986. 2.95 (*0-8431-2516-0*) Price Stern.

Ross, Shirley, jt. auth. see McCord, Cindy.

Ross, Shirley, et al. Alphabet Connections. (Illus.). 352p. 1993. pap. 24.95 (*1-878279-52-1*) Monday Morning Bks.

— Alphabet Connections. (Illus.). 352p. 1993. teacher ed, pap. 24.95 (*0-87827-952-0*, MM 1969) Evan-Moor Corp.

Ross, Sidney S. What Is Sex Education All About? A Guide for Parents. LC 78-64612. 1979. pap. 7.95 (*0-9602028-0-3*) Sidney Scott Ross.

Ross, Sondra. Hines-Fabric Tension. (Illus.). 115p. 1981. 30.00 (*0-940170-00-0*) Open Bk Pubns.

Ross, Stan & Burgess, Phillip. Income Tax: A Critical Analysis. xxii, 236p. 1991. 60.00 (*0-455-21026-8*, Pub. by Law Bk Co); pap. 36.00 (*0-455-21027-6*, Pub. by Law Bk Co) W W Gaunt.

Ross, Stanley R. Francisco I. Madero: Apostle of Mexican Democracy. LC 79-122591. reprint ed. 26.50 (*0-404-05409-9*) AMS Pr.

Ross, Stanley R. & Chaffee, Wilber A., eds. Guide to the Hispanic American Historical Review: 1956-1975. LC 58-8501. vii, 432p. 1980. 41.75 (*0-8223-0429-5*) Duke.

Ross, Stanley R. & McGann, Thomas F., eds. Buenos Aires: Four Hundred Years. 204p. (C). 1982. text ed. 20.00 (*0-292-70738-X*) U of Tex Pr.

Ross, Stanley R., jt. ed. see Erb, Richard D.

Ross, Stanley R., jt. ed. see Glade, William P.

Ross, Stanley R., ed. see Kennedy, Paul P.

Ross, Stanley R., jt. auth. see Nash, Jay R.

Ross, Stanley R., jt. ed. see Nash, Jay R.

Ross, Stanley Ralph, jt. ed. see Nash, Jay Robert.

Ross, Stella. Pain of Betrayal. large type ed. (Linford Romance Library). 272p. 1994. pap. 14.95 (*0-7089-7555-0*) Ulverscroft.

— Shadow of the Past. large type ed. (Linford Romance Library). 1989. pap. 11.95 (*0-7089-6793-0*, Trailtree Bookshop) Ulverscroft.

***Ross, Stephan A., et al.** Corporate Finance, International. 3rd ed. (C). 1992. text ed. 35.50 (*0-256-10827-7*) Irwin.

— Fundamentals of Corporate Finance. 2nd ed. 280p. (C). 1992. student ed, text ed. 22.95 (*0-256-11827-2*) Irwin.

— Fundamentals of Corporate Finance: Canadian. (C). 1993. text ed. write for info. (*0-256-10586-3*) Irwin.

— Fundamentals of Corporate Finance: Ready Notes. 2nd ed. 376p. (C). 1993. text ed. 7.95 (*0-256-11904-X*) Irwin.

Ross, Stephen A., et al. Corporate Finance. 3rd ed. LC 92-25582. (Finance Taking the Lead Ser.). 992p. (C). 1992. text ed. 69.95 (*0-256-09487-X*) Irwin.

— Fundamentals of Corporate Fianance. 3rd ed. LC 94-14328. (Finance Ser.). 816p. (C). 1994. text ed. 66.95 (*0-256-13585-1*); text ed. 61.95 (*0-256-17059-2*) Irwin.

— Fundamentals of Corporate Finance. 512p. (C). 1991. pap. text ed. 22.95 (*0-256-07933-1*, 06-3064-01) Irwin.

— Fundamentals of Corporate Finance. 2nd ed. LC 92-28101. (Series in Finance). 940p. (C). 1992. text ed. 66.95 (*0-256-11113-8*); Pkg. text ed. 63.50 (*0-256-12537-6*) Irwin.

Ross, Stephen D. Art & Its Significance: An Anthology of Aesthetic Theory. 3rd ed. 692p. (C). 1994. pap. 19.95 (*0-7914-1852-9*) State U NY Pr.

— Inexhaustibility & Human Being: An Essay on Locality. LC 88-82222. xvi, 331p. 1989. 40.00 (*0-8232-1227-0*) Fordham.

— Injustice & Restitution: The Ordinance of Time. LC 92-42843. 395p. (C). 1993. 74.50 (*0-7914-1669-0*); pap. 24.95 (*0-7914-1670-4*) State U NY Pr.

— Learning & Discovery. 148p. (C). 1981. text ed. 72.00 (*0-677-05110-7*) Gordon & Breach.

— The Limits of Language. LC 93-17970. 272p. (C). 1994. 35.00 (*0-8232-1518-0*) Fordham.

— Locality & Practical Judgement: Charity & Sacrifice. LC 93-47206. 256p. 1994. 35.00 (*0-8232-1584-9*) Fordham.

— Locality & Practical Judgment: Charity & Sacrifice. LC 93-47206. 256p. 1994. 35.00 (*0-8232-1556-3*) Fordham.

— Metaphysical Aporia & Philosophical Heresy. LC 88-24773. (SUNY Series in Contemporary Continental Philosophy). 411p. 1989. 74.50 (*0-7914-0006-9*); pap. 24.95 (*0-7914-0007-7*) State U NY Pr.

— The Nature of Moral Responsibility. LC 72-3399. 271p. reprint ed. pap. 77.30 (*0-7837-3628-2*, 2043494) Bks Demand.

— Perspective in Whitehead's Metaphysics. LC 82-8332. (SUNY Series in Systematic Philosophy). 295p. 1983. 59.50 (*0-87395-657-5*); pap. 19.95 (*0-87395-658-3*) State U NY Pr.

— Philosophical Mysteries. LC 80-26837. (SUNY Series in Systematic Philosophy). 151p. 1981. 59.50 (*0-87395-524-2*); pap. 19.95 (*0-87395-525-0*) State U NY Pr.

— Plenishment in the Earth: An Ethic of Inclusion. LC 94-9881. 440p. (C). 1995. text ed. 74.50 (*0-7914-2309-3*); pap. text ed. 24.95 (*0-7914-2310-7*) State U NY Pr.

— The Ring of Representation. LC 91-26923. (SUNY Series in Contemporary Continental Philosophy). 262p. (C). 1992. 59.50 (*0-7914-1109-5*); pap. 19.95 (*0-7914-1110-9*) State U NY Pr.

— A Theory of Art: Inexhaustibility by Contrast. LC 81-9027. (SUNY Series in Philosophy). 246p. (C). 1982. 59.50 (*0-87395-554-4*); pap. 19.95 (*0-87395-555-2*) State U NY Pr.

Ross, Stephen D., ed. Art & Its Significance: An Anthology of Aesthetic Theory. LC 83-9683. (SUNY Series in Philosophy). 574p. 1984. 59.50 (*0-87395-764-4*) State U NY Pr.

— Art & Its Significance: An Anthology of Aesthetic Theory. 2nd rev. ed. LC 83-9683. 638p. (C). 1987. pap. 19.95 (*0-88706-600-3*) State U NY Pr.

Ross, Stephen F. Principles of Antitrust Law. (University Textbook Ser.). 542p. 1992. text ed. 34.95 (*1-56662-003-1*) Foundation Pr.

Ross, Stephen M. Fiction's Inexhaustible Voice: Speech & Writing in Faulkner. LC 88-4720. 304p. 1991. pap. 15.00 (*0-8203-1375-0*) U of Ga Pr.

Ross, Steve. Successful Car Buying: How to Come Out a Winner, Whether You Buy New, Buy Used, or Lease. LC 89-35283. (Illus.). 96p. (Orig.). 1990. pap. 9.95 (*0-8117-2246-5*) Stackpole.

Ross, Steve W., et al. Endangered, Threatened, & Rare Fauna of North Carolina, Pt. 2: A Re-evaluation of the Marine & Estuarine Fishes. Potter, Eloise F., ed. (Occasional Papers of the North Carolina Biological Survey). (Illus.). 24p. (Orig.). 1988. pap. text ed. 3.00 (*0-917134-17-6*) NC Natl Sci.

Ross, Steven. The Caregiver's Mission: A Comprehensive Practical Guide on Caring for Your Elderly Parent, Spouse, or Family Member. LC 93-24305. 160p. 1994. pap. 12.95 (*0-942963-41-5*) Distinctive Pub.

— Data Exchange in the PC & MS-DOS Environment. 320p. 1990. pap. text ed. 29.95 (*0-07-053923-5*) McGraw.

— European Diplomatic History Seventeen Eighty-Nine to Eighteen Fifteen: France Against Europe. LC 81-8242. 432p. 1981. reprint ed. lib. bdg. 37.50 (*0-89874-369-9*) Krieger.

— From Flintlock to Rifle: Infantry Tactics, 1740-1866. LC 77-74397. (Illus.). 218p. 1979. 29.50 (*0-8386-2051-5*) Fairleigh Dickinson.

— My Visit to the Nursing Home: A Children's Story of Loving & Sharing Between the Generations. Pabich, Jill, tr. & illus. by. 48p. (J). (ps-2). 1995. pap. 5.95 (*0-942963-59-8*) Distinctive Pub.

— A Parent's Guide: When Young Children Visit the Nursing Home. (Illus.). 64p. 1995. pap. 9.95 (*0-942963-60-1*) Distinctive Pub.

Ross, Steven, ed. How to Maximize Your PC. Van Ollefen, William, tr. (Illus.). 1050p. 1989. ring bd. 49.95 (*0-929321-03-0*) WEKA Pub.

Ross, Steven C. Understanding & Using Application Software, Vol. I. 444p. (C). 1988. pap. text ed. 41.50 (*0-314-34739-9*) West Pub.

— Understanding & Using Data Base III: Including D Base II. (Illus.). 196p. (C). 1986. pap. text ed. 26.75 (*0-314-96211-5*) West Pub.

— Understanding & Using dBASE III Plus. (Microcomputing Ser.). 283p. (C). 1987. pap. text ed. 20.50 (*0-314-34744-5*) West Pub.

— Understanding & Using dBASE III PLUS. 2nd ed. Leyh, ed. 368p. (C). 1991. pap. text ed. 26.75 (*0-314-81984-3*) West Pub.

— Understanding & Using dBASE IV. Leyh, ed. 434p. (C). 1989. pap. text ed. 26.75 (*0-314-47364-5*) West Pub.

— Understanding & Using dBASE IV 2.0. Leyh, ed. LC 94-8269. (Microcomputing Ser.). 450p. (C). 1994. teacher ed, pap. text ed. 26.75 (*0-314-02871-4*) West Pub.

— Understanding & Using dBase 5.0 for Windows. 450p. 1995. pap. write for info. (*0-314-04652-6*) West Pub.

— Understanding & Using Lotus 1-2-3. (Illus.). 196p. (Orig.). (C). 1986. pap. text ed. 26.75 (*0-314-96209-3*) West Pub.

— Understanding & Using Lotus 1-2-3: Release 2. (Microcomputing Ser.). 232p. (C). 1987. pap. text ed. 26.75 (*0-314-34741-0*); teacher ed, pap. text ed. write for info. (*0-314-35880-3*) West Pub.

— Understanding & Using Lotus 1-2-3 Release 2.3 & 2.4. Leyh, ed. LC 92-26257. (Microcomputing Ser.). 416p. (C). 1993. pap. text ed. 26.75 (*0-314-01111-0*) West Pub.

— Understanding & Using Lotus 1-2-3 Release 3. Leyh, ed. 411p. (C). 1991. pap. text ed. 30.50 (*0-314-47365-3*) West Pub.

— Understanding & Using Quattro Pro 5.0 for DOS. LC 94-27988. (Microcomputing Ser.). 1994. pap. write for info. (*0-314-04098-6*) West Pub.

— Understanding & Using WordStar. (Illus.). 237p. (Orig.). (C). 1986. pap. text ed. 26.75 (*0-314-96207-7*) West Pub.

— Understanding Information Systems. Leyh, ed. LC 93-33048. (Microcomputing Ser.). 224p. (C). 1994. pap. text ed. 16.75 (*0-314-02880-3*) West Pub.

Ross, Steven C. & Hutson, Stephen V. Understanding & Using Microsoft Excel 3.0. Leyh, ed. 410p. (C). 1992. spiral bd. 26.75 (*0-314-93406-5*) West Pub.

R

— Understanding & Using Microsoft Excel 4. Leyh, ed. LC 93-28874. (Microcomputing Ser.). 400p. (C). 1994. teacher ed, pap. text ed. 26.75 (*0-314-02588-X*) West Pub.
— Understanding & Using Microsoft Excel 5.0. LC 94-5365. (Microcomputing Ser.). 450p. 1994. pap. text ed. 26.75 (*0-314-04626-7*) West Pub.
— Understanding & Using Quattro Pro 4. Leyh, ed. LC 92-26259. (Microcomputer Ser.). 416p. (C). 1993. pap. text ed. 26.75 (*0-314-01035-1*) West Pub.
Ross, Steven C. & Maestas, Ronald W. Understanding & Using Microsoft Windows 3. Leyh, ed. 309p. (C). 1992. spiral bd. 26.75 (*0-314-93375-1*) West Pub.
— Understanding & Using Microsoft Windows 3.1. Leyh, ed. LC 93-8665. 384p. (C). 1994. pap. text ed. 26.75 (*0-314-02589-8*) West Pub.
— Understanding & Using Microsoft Windows 4. 450p. 1995. pap. write for info. (*0-314-04659-3*) West Pub.
Ross, Steven C. & Reinders, Judy A. Understanding & Using Supercalc 3. (Microcomputing Ser.). 184p. (C). pap. text ed. 26.75 (*0-314-30123-2*) West Pub.
Ross, Steven C., jt. auth. see Pusins, Dolores W.
Ross, Steven C., jt. auth. see Reinders, Judy A.
Ross, Steven C., et al. Developing & Using Decision Support Applications. (Microcomputing Ser.). 266p. (C). 1988. pap. text ed. 28.50 (*0-314-30124-0*) West Pub.
— Essentials of Application Software, Vol. 1. Leyh, ed. 400p. (C). 1991. pap. text ed. 38.75 (*0-314-81734-4*) West Pub.
— Understanding & Using Application Software, Vol. II. 464p. (C). 1988. pap. text ed. 41.50 (*0-314-34740-2*) West Pub.
— Understanding & Using Application Software, Vol. 5. Leyh, ed. 700p. (C). 1991. pap. text ed. 53.75 (*0-314-66779-2*) West Pub.
— Understanding & Using Lotus 1-2-3 for Windows. 450p. (C). 1994. teacher ed, pap. text ed. 27.25 (*0-314-01227-3*) West Pub.
Ross, Steven J. Workers on the Edge: Work, Leisure, & Politics in Industrializing Cincinnati, 1788-1890. (History of Urban Life Ser.). 464p. 1987. text ed. 50.50 (*0-231-05520-X*); pap. text ed. 18.00 (*0-231-05521-8*) Col U Pr.
***Ross, Steven L. & McChrystal, Karen.** How to Get Married after Forty: A Radical Approach to Finding Your Mate. 300p. (Orig.). 1995. pap. 13.95 (*0-9644183-3-9*) Earthly Delights.
Ross, Steven L., ed. see Kierkegaard, Soren.
Ross, Steven M., jt. ed. see Upper, Dennis.
Ross, Steven S. Construction Disasters: Design Failures, Causes & Prevention. 1984. 59.00 (*0-07-053865-4*) McGraw.
— Highway Design Reference Guide. (Engineering Reference Guide Ser.). 1989. text ed. 58.00 (*0-07-053924-3*) McGraw.
— Spreadstat: How to Build Statistics into Your Lotus 1-2-3 Spreadsheet by Busi. 1988. pap. text ed. 29.95 (*0-07-053909-X*) McGraw.
Ross, Steven S., ed. see Council on Economic Priorities Staff, et al.
Ross, Steven T., ed. American War Plans, 1919-1941, 5 vols. rev. ed. LC 92-20669. 1992. Set. 588.00 (*0-8153-0688-1*) Garland.
— Coalition War Plans & Hemispheric Defense Plans, 1940-1941. LC 92-20669. (American War Plans, 1919-1941 Ser.: Vol. 4). 392p. 1992. 127.00 (*0-8153-0692-X*) Garland.
— The French Revolution: Conflict or Continuity? LC 77-21289. (European Problem Studies). 138p. 1978. reprint ed. pap. text ed. 10.50 (*0-88275-633-8*) Krieger.
— Peacetime War Plans, 1919-1935. LC 92-20669. (American War Plans, 1919-1941 Ser.: Vol. 1). 248p. 1992. 89.00 (*0-8153-0689-X*) Garland.
— Plans for Global War: Rainbow-5 & the Victory Program, 1941. LC 92-20669. (American War Plans, 1919-1941 Ser.: Vol. 5). 328p. 1992. 110.00 (*0-8153-0693-8*) Garland.
— Plans for War Against the British Empire & Japan: The Red, Orange, & Red-Orange Plans, 1923-1938. LC 92-20669. (American War Plans, 1919-1941 Ser.: Vol. 2). 440p. 1992. 139.00 (*0-8153-0690-3*) Garland.
Ross, Steven T., intro. Plans to Meet the Axis Threat, 1939-1940, Vol. 3. LC 92-20669. 376p. 1992. 123.00 (*0-8153-0691-1*) Garland.
Ross, Steven T. & Rosenberg, David A., eds. Budgets & Strategy: The Road to Offtackle. (America's Plans for War Against the Soviet Union 1945-1950 Ser.). 432p. 1990. 50.00 (*0-8240-7161-1*) Garland.
— Evaluating the Air Offensive: The WSEG 1 Study. (America's Plans for War Against the Soviet Union 1945-1950 Ser.: Vol. 13). 512p. 1990. 55.00 (*0-8240-7162-X*) Garland.
— The Limits of American Power. (America's Plans for War Against the Soviet Union 1945-1950 Ser.: Vol. 5). 425p. 1990. 55.00 (*0-8240-7154-9*) Garland.
Ross, Stewart. Elizabethan Life. (How It Was Ser.). (Illus.). 72p. (YA). (gr. 7-11). 1991. 19.95 (*0-7134-6356-2*, Pub. by Batsford UK) Trafalgar.
— The Nineteen Eighties. (Living Through History Ser.). (Illus.). 72p. (YA). (gr. 7-11). 1991. 19.95 (*0-7134-6361-9*, Pub. by Batsford UK) Trafalgar.
— Propaganda. LC 93-21730. (World War II Ser.). 48p. (J). (gr. 5-9). 1993. 14.95 (*1-56847-080-0*) Thomson Lrning.
— Shakespeare & Macbeth. (Illus.). 48p. (J). (gr. 5 up). 1994. 16.99 (*0-670-85629-0*) Viking Child Bks.
— Spies & Traitors. LC 95-13147. (Fact or Fiction Ser.). (Illus.). (J). 1995. write for info. (*1-56294-648-X*); pap. write for info. (*1-56294-188-7*) Copper Beech.
— World Leaders. LC 93-20185. (World War II Ser.). (Illus.). 48p. (J). (gr. 5-9). 1993. 14.95 (*1-56847-079-7*) Thomson Lrning.
— World War II. LC 95-7740. (Causes & Consequences Ser.). (J). 1995. write for info. (*0-8172-4050-0*) Raintree Steck-V.
Ross, Stewart H. The Management of Business-to-Business Advertising: A Working Guide for Small to Mid-Size Companies. LC 85-31726. 175p. 1986. text ed. 49.95 (*0-89930-163-0*, RHD/, Quorum Bks) Greenwood.
— Propaganda for War: How the United States Was Conditioned to Fight the Great War of 1914-1918. 304p. 1995. lib. bdg. 42.50 (*0-7864-0111-7*) McFarland & Co.
Ross, Stewart L. Expanding Our Musical Options. 2nd rev. ed. 256p. 1993. per. 20.95 (*0-8403-8996-5*) Kendall-Hunt.
Ross, Stuart. Portugal's Pousada Route: An Insider's Guide. (Illus.). 248p. (Orig.). 1994. pap. 18.95 (*972-804-400-3*, Pub. by Kuperard UK) Seven Hills Bk.
Ross, Susan. Comparative Retirement Benefits for General State Employees & Public Safety Personnel. (State Legislative Reports: Vol. 16, No. 5). 14p. 1991. pap. text ed. 5.00 (*1-55516-304-1*, 7302-1605) Natl Conf State Legis.
— Snowflower for Six Viols. (Contemporary Consort Ser.: No. 10). i, 14p. 1990. 11.00 (*1-56571-005-3*) PRB Prods.
Ross, Susan A., jt. ed. see Tilley, Maureen A.
Ross, Susan D., et al. The Rights of Women: The Basic ACLU Guide to Women's Rights. rev. ed. 336p. (C). 1993. pap. 7.95 (*0-8093-1633-1*) S Ill U Pr.
— The Rights of Women: The Basic ACLU Guide to Women's Rights. 3rd rev. ed. 336p. (C). 1993. 24.95 (*0-8093-1898-9*) S Ill U Pr.
Ross, Suzanne. Nature Activity Book. (Little Activity Bks.). (J). 1994. pap. 1.00 (*0-486-28036-5*) Dover.
— What's in the Rainforest? One Hundred Six Answers from A to Z. LC 91-72682. (Illus.). 48p. (Orig.). (J). (gr. 1-7). 1991. pap. 5.95 (*0-9629895-0-9*) Enchanted Rain Pr.
Ross-Swain, Deborah. The Voice Advantage. (Illus.). 52p. (Orig.). (C). 1991. student ed, pap. text ed. 49.95 (*1-879105-09-8*, 0073) Singular Publishing.
Ross, Sydney. Nineteenth-Century Attitudes: Men of Science. (C). 1991. lib. bdg. 80.50 (*0-7923-1308-9*) Kluwer Ac.
Ross, Sydney & Morris, Ian. Colloidal Systems & Interfaces. LC 87-30529. 422p. 1988. text ed. 110.00 (*0-471-82848-3*) Wiley.
Ross, T. Flash Cards, Bk. 1. 1990. 5.95 (*0-685-32026-X*, P036) Hansen Ed Mus.
— Flash Cards, Bk. 2. 1990. 5.95 (*0-685-32027-8*, P037) Hansen Ed Mus.
Ross, T. J., ed. see Mitchell, Brooks.
Ross, Terry. Cults. (Troubled Society Ser.). (Illus.). 64p. (YA). (gr. 7 up). 1990. lib. bdg. 17.27 (*0-86593-070-8*); lib. bdg. 12.95 (*0-685-36323-6*) Rourke Corp.
Ross, Terry & Wright, Richard D. The Divining Mind. (Illus.). 176p. 1990. pap. 10.95 (*0-89281-263-X*, Destiny Bks) Inner Tradit.
Ross, Thomas E. One Land, Three Peoples: A Geography of Robeson County, North Carolina. LC 94-76044. (Illus.). 130p. (Orig.). 1994. pap. 15.95 (*0-9641628-0-6*) Karo Hollow.
***Ross, Thomas E. & Reiman, Robert E., eds.** World Geography Workbook. 126p. (Orig.). (C). 1994. 11.20 (*0-9641628-1-4*) Karo Hollow.
Ross, Thomas W. & Brooks, Edward, Jr., eds. English Glosses from British Library MS Additional 37075 (A Fifteenth Century Word-List) LC 84-18877. 250p. 1984. 24.95 (*0-937664-66-9*) Pilgrim Bks OK.
Ross, Thomas W., ed. see Chaucer, Geoffrey.
Ross, Thomasina, tr. see Von Humboldt, Alexander.
***Ross, Timothy.** Fuzzy Logic with Engineering Applications. 1994. text ed. 58.00 (*0-07-053917-0*) McGraw.
Ross, Timothy A., jt. ed. see Lau, Joseph S.
Ross, Timothy L., jt. auth. see Graham-Moore, Brian.
Ross, Tom. Eggbert, the Slightly Cracked Egg. (Illus.). 32p. (J). (ps-3). 1994. 14.95 (*0-399-22416-5*) Putnam Pub Group.
— Irma the Flying Bowling Ball. LC 95-3578. (Illus.). (J). 1996. write for info. (*0-399-22641-9*, Putnam) Putnam Pub Group.
Ross, Tom & Ross, Marilyn. The Complete Guide to Self-Publishing: Everything You Need to Know to Write, Publish, Promote, & Sell Your Own Book. 3rd ed. LC 94-16872. 432p. 1994. pap. 18.99 (*0-89879-646-6*) Writers Digest.
— The Force of Us: Living, Loving, & Working Together. 224p. 1995. 19.95 (*0-918880-31-9*) Comm Creat.
Ross, Tom, jt. auth. see Ross, Marilyn.
***Ross, Tony.** Bedtime. LC 94-36611. (Little Princess Board Bks.). (J). 1995. write for info. (*0-15-200317-7*, Red Wagon Bks) HarBrace.
— A Fairy Tale. (Illus.). 32p. (J). (ps-3). 1992. 13.95 (*0-316-75750-0*) Little.
— Hansel & Gretel. LC 93-31047. (Illus.). 32p. (J). (ps-3). 1994. 13.95 (*0-87951-535-X*) Overlook Pr.
— Hansel & Gretel. (Illus.). 32p. (J). (gr. k-3). 1990. 15.95 (*0-86264-210-8*, Pub. by Andersen Pr UK) Trafalgar.
— Happy Blanket. (Illus.). 32p. (J). (ps-2). 1990. 12.95 (*0-374-32843-9*) FS&G.
— I Want a Cat. (Illus.). 26p. (J). (ps up). 1989. 13.00 (*0-374-33621-0*) FS&G.
— I Want a Cat. (Illus.). 26p. (J). (ps up). 1991. pap. 4.95 (*0-374-43544-8*) FS&G.
— I Want My Potty. LC 86-10568. (Illus.). 24p. (J). (ps-00). 1986. 9.95 (*0-916291-08-1*) Kane-Miller Bk.
— I Want My Potty. (Illus.). 24p. (J). (ps-00). 1988. reprint ed. pap. 6.95 (*0-916291-14-6*) Kane-Miller Bk.
— I Want to Be. LC 92-41527. (Illus.). 32p. (J). (ps-1). 1993. 11.95 (*0-916291-46-4*) Kane-Miller Bk.
— I'm Coming to Get You! LC 84-5831. (Pied Piper Bks.). (Illus.). 32p. (J). (ps-2). 1987. pap. 4.95 (*0-8037-0434-8*) Dial Bks Young.
— Mrs. Goat & Her Seven Little Kids. LC 89-17933. (Illus.). 24p. (J). (gr. 1-3). 1990. text ed. 13.95 (*0-689-31624-0*, Atheneum Bks Young) S&S Childrens.
— Pets. (Little Princess Board Bks.). (J). 1995. 4.95 (*0-15-200318-5*, Red Wagon Bks) HarBrace.
— Shapes. (Little Princess Board Bks.). (J). 1995. write for info. (*0-15-200319-3*, Red Wagon Bks) HarBrace.
— Stone Soup. (J). (ps-3). 1990. pap. 3.95 (*0-8037-0890-4*, Puff Pied Piper) Puffin Bks.
— Super Dooper Jezebel. 1990. pap. 3.95 (*0-374-47342-0*) FS&G.
— This Old Man. 12p. (J). (ps-1). 1990. text ed. 10.95 (*0-689-71386-X*, Aladdin Paperbacks) S&S Childrens.
— Towser & the Haunted House. (Illus.). 32p. (J). (ps-1). 1987. 5.95 (*0-86264-079-2*, Pub. by Andersen Pr UK) Trafalgar.
— Towser & the Magic Apple. (Illus.). 32p. (J). (ps-1). 1987. 5.95 (*0-86264-078-4*, Pub. by Andersen Pr UK) Trafalgar.
— Treasure of Cozy Cove. (J). (ps-3). 1990. 14.00 (*0-374-37744-8*) FS&G.
— Weather. (Little Princess Board Bks.). (J). 1995. 4.95 (*0-15-200320-7*, Red Wagon Bks) HarBrace.
***Ross, Tony, illus.** Animals. LC 94-49432. (First Discovery Art Bk.). (ENG & FRE.). (J). 1995. write for info. (*0-590-55202-3*, Cartwheel) Scholastic Inc.
Ross, Tony, illus. & ret. Goldilocks & the Three Bears. 26p. (J). (ps-3). 1992. 13.95 (*0-87951-453-1*) Overlook Pr.
Ross, Truedie L. & Ross, Richard G. Unclaimed Fortunes: How to Discover Your Share. LC 91-78132. 68p. 1992. pap. 9.95 (*0-9631885-0-X*) Kalia Pubns.
Ross, Tweed W., Jr. The Best Way to Destroy a Ship: The Evidence of European Naval Operations in World War II. 219p. (Orig.). 1980. pap. 27.95 (*0-89126-069-2*) MA-AH Pub.
Ross, Tweed W. & Bailey, Gearld D. Technology-Based Learning: A Handbook for Principals & Technology Leaders. LC 94-12518. (Illus.). 192p. 1995. 29.95x (*0-590-49626-3*) Scholastic Inc.
Ross, Veronica, jt. auth. see Anderson, Rob.
Ross, Vicki. Hunger & Discipleship. (Orig.). 1982. pap. 5.00 (*0-8309-0346-1*) Herald Hse.
Ross, Victor J. Bite the Wall! LC 84-10316. 408p. 1986. 19.95 (*0-88280-108-2*) ETC Pubns.
Ross, Victor J. & Marlowe, John. The Forbidden Apple: Sex in the Schools. LC 84-6152. 112p. 1985. 16.95 (*0-88280-107-4*) ETC Pubns.
Ross, W. D. The Right & the Good. LC 88-11019. 184p. (C). 1988. reprint ed. lib. bdg. 27.50 (*0-87220-059-0*); reprint ed. pap. 14.50 (*0-87220-058-2*) Hackett Pub.
Ross, W. D., ed. see Theophrast.
Ross, W. David, ed. see Aristotle.
Ross, W. David, tr. see Aristotle.
Ross, W. David, ed. see Aristotle.
Ross, W. E. One Louisburg Square. (Inflation Fighter Ser.). 192p. 1982. pap. 1.50 (*0-8439-1148-4*) Dorchester Pub Co.
— Only Make-Believe. 1980. pap. 2.50 (*0-8439-0813-0*) Dorchester Pub Co.
— Satan Whispers. 1981. pap. 2.50 (*0-8439-0913-7*) Dorchester Pub Co.
— This Man I Love. large type ed. (Romance Library). 320p. 1995. pap. 14.95 (*0-7089-7665-4*, Linford) Ulverscroft.
Ross, W. E. D. Reunion in Renfrew. large type ed. (Linford Romance Library). 288p. 1992. pap. 14.95 (*0-7089-7190-3*, Trailtree Bookshop) Ulverscroft.
Ross, W. Gillies, ed. see Comer, George.
Ross, W. McGregor. Kenya from Within: A Short Political History. (Illus.). 486p. 1968. 35.00 (*0-7146-1715-6*, Pub. by F Cass Pubs UK) Intl Spec Bk.
Ross, W. O., ed. Middle English Sermons from Manuscript Roy, No. 18 B. (EETS, OS Ser.: Vol. 209). 1974. reprint ed. 58.00 (*0-8115-3385-9*) Periodicals Srv.
Ross, W. Ogden. Marketing in Commercial Banks. LC 68-579749. 1968. 19.95 (*0-912164-07-7*) Masterco Pr.
Ross, W. W., jt. auth. see Gustafson, Ralph.
Ross, Wallace. Sail Power: The Complete Guide to Sails & Sail Handling. rev. ed. (Illus.). 1985. pap. 32.50 (*0-394-72715-0*) Knopf.
Ross, Walter, jt. auth. see Hitchin, David.
Ross, Warner A. My Colored Battalion. 15.95 (*0-8488-1142-9*) Amereon Ltd.
Ross, Webber A. A Guide to Getting Things Done. 1984. pap. 12.95 (*0-317-30515-8*) Free Pr.
Ross, Wilbur L., jt. auth. see Cook, Michael L.
Ross, William A. Sex: There's More to It Than You've Been Told. Carlson, Robert, ed. 96p. (Orig.). 1988. pap. 4.95 (*0-9619246-0-8*) Playful Wisdom.
— The Wonderful Little Sex Book. 288p. (Orig.). 1992. 27.00x (*0-8095-5865-3*) Borgo Pr.
— The Wonderful Little Sex Book. 288p. (Orig.). 1992. pap. 9.95 (*0-943233-34-8*) Conari Press.
Ross, William A., comp. Words from the Masters: A Guide to the God Within. 350p. 1989. pap. 29.95 (*0-9619246-3-2*) Playful Wisdom.
Ross, William A. & Duff, Jon M. Integrated Engineering Drawing & Modeling with VERSACAD. 416p. 1992. pap. text ed. 51.00 (*0-13-278177-8*) P-H.
Ross, William A. & Ford, Judy. Lovers' Quarrels: The Other Side of Romance. Carlson, Robert, ed. 96p. (Orig.). 1988. pap. 4.95 (*0-9619246-1-6*) Playful Wisdom.
Ross, William A., jt. auth. see Ford, Judy.
Ross, William A., jt. auth. see Ross, Joel E.
Ross, William D. Kant's Ethical Theory: A Commentary on the Grundlegung zur Metaphysik der Sitten. LC 78-6730. 96p. 1978. reprint ed. text ed. 38.50 (*0-8371-9059-2*, ROKE, Greenwood Pr) Greenwood.
— Plato's Theory of Ideas. LC 75-36510. 250p. 1976. reprint ed. text ed. 55.00 (*0-8371-8635-8*, ROPTI, Greenwood Pr) Greenwood.
Ross, William G. Forging New Freedoms: Nativism, Education, & the Constitution, 1917-1927. LC 93-44308. (Illus.). (C). 1994. text ed. 40.00x (*0-8032-3900-9*) U of Nebr Pr.
— The Honest Hour: The Ethics of Time-Based Billing by Attorneys. LC 95-68698. (C). 1996. text ed. write for info. (*0-89089-902-9*) Carolina Acad Pr.
— A Muted Fury: Populists, Progressives, & Labor Unions Confront the Courts, 1890-1937. LC 93-13698. 368p. 1993. text ed. 39.50 (*0-691-03264-5*) Princeton U Pr.
Ross, William M. Oil Pollution As an International Problem: A Study of Puget Sound & the Strait of Georgia. LC 73-5610. (Illus.). 296p. 1973. 25.00 (*0-295-95275-X*) U of Wash Pr.
— The Ticket to Harmony. 94p. (Orig.). (J). (gr. 4-9). 1993. pap. 4.95 (*1-883787-00-9*, Baker & Taylor) Trolley Car.
— The Ticket to Harmony, Set. 94p. (Orig.). (J). (gr. 4-9). 1993. pap. 7.95 (*1-883787-01-7*, Baker & Taylor) Trolley Car.
Ross, Williamson H. Sir Walter Raleigh. LC 78-17033. 215p. 1978. reprint ed. text ed. 35.00 (*0-313-20577-9*, ROSI, Greenwood Pr) Greenwood.
Ross-Williamson, Hugh. Poetry of T. S. Eliot. LC 71-156296. (Studies in T. S. Eliot: No. 11). 1971. reprint ed. lib. bdg. 75.00 (*0-8383-1291-8*) M S G Haskell Hse.
Ross, Wilma. X-15 Rocket Plane. LC 93-1844. (Those Daring Machines Ser.). (Illus.). 48p. (J). (gr. 5-6). 1994. text ed. 13.95 (*0-89686-831-1*, Crstwood Hse) Silver Burdett Pr.
Rossa, Jeremiah O. Irish Rebels in English Prisons. rev. ed. 320p. 1991. reprint ed. pap. 15.95 (*0-86322-125-4*, Pub. by Brandon Bk Pubs IE) Irish Bks Media.
Rossabi, Morris. The Jurchens in the Yuan & Ming. (Cornell East Asia Ser.: No. 27). 88p. 1982. 9.00 (*0-939657-27-9*) Cornell East Asia Pgm.
— Khubilai Khan: His Life & Times. LC 86-25031. (Illus.). 344p. 1988. 38.00 (*0-520-05913-1*); pap. 16.00 (*0-520-06740-1*) U CA Pr.
— Voyager from Xanadu: Rabban Sauma & the First Journey from China to the West. (Illus.). 240p. 1992. 22.00 (*4-7700-1650-6*) Kodansha.
Rossabi, Morris, ed. China among Equals: The Middle Kingdom & Its Neighbors, 10th-14th Centuries. LC 81-11486. 400p. (C). 1983. pap. 16.00 (*0-520-04562-9*) U CA Pr.
Rossano, G. S. & Craine, E. R. Near Infrared Photographic Sky Survey: A Field Index. (Astronomy & Astrophysics Ser.: Vol. 8). (Illus.). 208p. 1980. 38.00 (*0-912918-11-X*, 0911) Pachart Pub Hse.
Rossano, Geoffrey L. Creating a Dignified Past: Museums & the Colonial Revival. 144p. (C). 1991. text ed. 35.50 (*0-8476-7690-0*) Rowman.
Rossano, Geoffrey L., ed. The Price of Honor: The World War One Letters of Naval Aviator Kenneth Macleish. LC 90-45844. (Illus.). 320p. 1991. 32.95 (*0-87021-584-1*) Naval Inst Pr.
Rossano, Joan, jt. auth. see Schiller, Pam.
***Rossant, Colette.** My Mother's House & Sido. 1995. 13.50 (*0-679-60157-0*) Random.
Rossant, Colette & Melendez, Marianne. Vegetables: The Art of Growing, Cooking, & Keeping the New American Harvest. LC 91-50153. (Illus.). 288p. 1991. 40.00 (*0-670-82710-X*, Viking Studio) Studio Bks.
Rossant, J. & Pedersen, Roger A., eds. Experimental Approaches to Mammalian Embryonic Development. (Illus.). 558p. 1988. pap. 39.95 (*0-521-36891-X*) Cambridge U Pr.
Rossant, M. J., jt. auth. see Ippolito, Dennis S.
Rossant, M. J., ed. see Twentieth Century Fund, Task Force Report for a National News Council Staff.
Rossbach, August & Westphal, Rudolf. Theorie der Musischen Kunste der Hellenen, 3 vols. in 2. cxii, 1783p. 1966. reprint ed. Bd. I: Griechische Rhythmik. write for info. (*0-318-71013-7*, Pub. by Georg Olms GW); reprint ed. Bd. II: Griechische Harmonik und Melopoesie. write for info. (*0-318-71014-5*, Pub. by Georg Olms GW); reprint ed. Bd. III, 1: Allg. Theorie der Griechischen Metrik. write for info. (*0-318-71015-3*, Pub. by Georg Olms GW); reprint ed. Bd. III, 2: Griechische Metrik mit Besonderer Ruck Sicht auf die Strophengattungen und die Ubrigen M. write for info. (*0-318-71016-1*, Pub. by Georg Olms GW) Lubrecht & Cramer.
— Theorie der Musischen Kunste der Hellenen, 3 vols. in 2, Set. cxii, 1783p. 1966. reprint ed. write for info. (*0-318-71012-9*, Pub. by Georg Olms GW) Lubrecht & Cramer.
Rossbach, Ed. The Nature of Basketry. rev. ed. LC 85-63576. (Illus.). 192p. 1986. reprint ed. pap. 14.95 (*0-88740-059-0*) Schiffer.
Rossbach, Ed & Halper, Vicki. John McQueen: The Language of Containment. (Renwick Contemporary American Craft Ser.). (Illus.). 56p. 1992. pap. 14.95 (*0-295-97153-3*) U of Wash Pr.
Rossbach, J. High Energy Accelerators, '92: Proceedings of the Fifteenth International Conference. 1272p. 1993. text ed. 206.00 (*981-02-1152-X*) World Scientific Pub.
Rossbach, M., et al, eds. Specimen Banking: Environmental Monitoring & Modern Analytical Approaches. LC 92-12244. (Illus.). x, 242p. 1992. 119.00 (*0-387-55001-1*) Spr-Verlag.
Rossbach, Otto. De Senecae Philosophi Librorum Recensione Et Emendatione. Vol. II, 3. xxxii, 184p. 1969. reprint ed. write for info. (*0-318-71218-0*, Pub. by Georg Olms GW) Lubrecht & Cramer.
Rossbach, Sarah. Feng Shui: The Chinese Art of Placement. LC 83-1609. (Illus.). 169p. 1983. pap. 8.95 (*0-525-48061-7*, Dutton) NAL-Dutton.
— Feng Shui: The Chinese Art of Placement. (Illus.). 192p. 1991. pap. 11.95 (*0-14-019353-7*, Arkana) Viking Penguin.

R

An Asterisk (*) at the beginning of an entry indicates that the title is appearing in BIP for the first time.

— Interior Design with Feng Shui. (Illus.). 224p. 1991. pap. 15.00 (*0-14-019352-9*, Arkana) Viking Penguin.

Rossbach, Sarah & Lin Yun. Living Color: Master Lin Yun's Guide to Harmony Through Color. (Illus.). 208p. 1994. pap. 18.00 (*1-56836-014-2*) Kodansha.

Rossbacher, Lisa A. & Buchanan, Rex C. Geomedia: A Guide for Geoscientists Who Meet the Press. 50p. 1988. pap. 5.95 (*0-913312-96-7*) Am Geol.

Rossdale, Peter. The Horse: From Conception to Maturity. (Illus.). 1984. pap. 20.00 (*0-87556-609-X*) Saifer.

— Horse Breeding. (D&C Equestrian Library). (Illus.). 384p. 1992. 34.95 (*0-7153-9975-6*, Pub. by David & Charles UK) Trafalgar.

Rossdale, Peter D. The Horse: From Conception to Maturity. 224p. 1990. write for info. (*0-318-72166-X*, Pub. by J A Allen & Co UK) St Mut.

Rosse, Cornelius, jt. auth. see Hollinshead, W. Henry.

Rosse, Gerard. The Cry of Jesus on the Cross: A Biblical & Theological Study. 1988. pap. 8.95 (*0-8091-2922-1*) Paulist Pr.

Rosse, Richard, et al. Concise Guide to Laboratory & Diagnostic Testing in Psychiatry. LC 89-3. (American Psychiatric Press Concise Guides Ser.). 175p. 1989. pap. text ed. 19.50 (*0-88048-333-4*) Am Psychiatric.

Rosseau, Jean-Jacques. Emile. Jimack, P. D., ed. 512p. 1993. pap. 6.95 (*0-460-87380-6*, Everyman's Classic Lib) C E Tuttle.

Rosseel, Frank R. A Back Number Town: Lewiston, New York. 1984. lib. bdg. 49.95 (*0-88946-025-6*) E Mellen.

Rossein, Merrick T. Employment Discrimination: Law & Litigation, 2 vols. 1990. ring bd. 220.00 (*0-87632-736-6*) Clark Boardman Callaghan.

Rossel Bks Staff. Mitzvah: The Teacher's Guide. 1982. spiral bd. 10.95 (*0-940646-27-7*) Rossel Bks.

Rossel, Muriel. The Lilacs Will Bloom. Zarucchi, Roy & Page, Carolyn, eds. (Chapbook Ser.). (Illus.). 24p. (Orig.). 1990. pap. 5.00 (*0-9623862-1-9*) Nightshade Pr.

Rossel, Seymour. Child's Bible: Lessons from the Writings & Prophets, Vol. 2. (J). (gr. 4-5). 1989. teacher ed, pap. 14. 95 (*0-87441-485-7*); pap. text ed. 8.95 (*0-87441-487-3*) Behrman.

— A Child's Bible: The Torah & Its Lessons. (J). (gr. 3 up). 1988. pap. 8.95 (*0-87441-466-0*); teacher ed, pap. 14.95 (*0-87441-467-9*) Behrman.

— The Holocaust: The World & the Jews, 1933-1945. Altshuler, David, ed. 192p. (YA). (gr. 9-12). 1992. pap. text ed. 7.95 (*0-87441-526-8*) Behrman.

— Introduction to Jewish History. Kozodoy, Neil, ed. (Illus.). 128p. (J). (gr. 4-5). 1981. Malkah L. Avrami. student ed, pap. 4.50 (*0-87441-363-X*); pap. text ed. 6.95 (*0-87441-335-4*) Behrman.

— Israel: Covenant People, Covenant Land. (Illus.). 256p. (C). 1985. teacher ed 5.00 (*0-8074-0329-6*); pap. 8.95 (*0-8074-0303-2*, 208028) UAHC.

— Journey Through Jewish History: The Age of Faith & the Age of Freedom, Vol. II. (Illus.). 128p. (J). (gr. 6). 1983. pap. text ed. 7.95x (*0-87441-366-4*) Behrman.

— Managing the Jewish Classroom: How to Transform Yourself into a Master Teacher. 188p. 1988. pap. 10.95 (*0-933873-20-4*) Torah Aura.

— A Spiritual Journey: The Bar Mitzvah & Bat Mitzvah Handbook. Cutter, William, ed. (Illus.). 64p. Date not set. pap. 3.95 (*0-87441-551-9*) Behrman.

— A Thousand & One Chickens. (Illus.). 1995. pap. 10.00 (*0-8074-0541-8*) UAHC.

— When a Jew Prays. (Illus.). 192p. (J). (gr. 4-5). Date not set. pap. 8.95 (*0-87441-093-2*) Behrman.

— When a Jew Seeks Wisdom: The Sayings of the Fathers. LC 75-14119. (Jewish Values Ser.). (J). (gr. 7). teacher ed 14.95 (*0-685-41999-1*); pap. 8.95 (*0-87441-089-4*); 3.95 (*0-685-00741-3*) Behrman.

Rossel, Seymour, ed. see Ben-Aharon, Moshe & Rosenthal, Gilbert S.

Rossel, Seymour, jt. auth. see Kipper, Lenore C.

Rossel, Seymour, ed. see Kozodoy, Ruth.

Rossel, Seymour, ed. see Newman, Shirley.

Rossel, Seymour, ed. see Rosenberg, Amye & Mason, Patrice G.

Rossel, Seymour, ed. see Rosenthal, Gilbert S.

Rossel, Seymour, ed. see Singer, Ellen & Rosenthal, Gilbert S.

Rossel, Seymour, jt. auth. see Sugarman, Morris J.

Rossel, Sven H. A History of Scandinavian Literature, 1870-1980. Ulmer, Anne C., tr. LC 81-14654. (Nordic Ser.: No. 5). 504p. reprint ed. pap. 143.70 (*0-7837-2923-5*, 2057531) Bks Demand.

Rossel, Sven H., ed. A History of Danish Literature. LC 91-46729. (History of Scandinavian Literature Ser.: Vol. 1). (Illus.). xvi, 709p. 1992. 50.00 (*0-8032-3886-X*) U of Nebr Pr.

— Why Not! A Picture Out of Life. Ingalsbe, Lori A., tr. & intro. by. 120p. (Orig.). (C). 1994. pap. 9.95 (*1-880755-08-4*) Mermaid Pr.

Rossel, Sven H., ed. see Andersen, Hans Christian, et al.

Rossel, Sven H., tr. see Andersen, Hans Christian.

Rossel, Sven H., ed. see Bjornvig, Thorkild.

Rossel, Sven H., tr. see Holberg, Ludvig.

Rossel-Waugh, Carol-Lyn, jt. ed. see Greenberg, Martin H.

Rossel Waugh, Carol-Lynn, ed. see King, Stephen, et al.

Rosselet, Joan, jt. auth. see Daix, Pierre.

Rosseli, Annalisa, jt. auth. see Marcuzzo, Maria C.

Rosselini, G. Vip, Pacap & Related Regulatory Peptides. 648p. 1994. text ed. 137.00 (*981-02-1788-9*) World Scientific Pub.

Rossell, B. A., jt. ed. see Hamilton, R. J.

Rossell, Christine H. The Carrot or the Stick for School Desegregation Policy: Magnet Schools or Forced Busing. (Illus.). 272p. 1990. 49.95 (*0-87722-682-2*) Temple U Pr.

— The Carrot or the Stick for School Desegregation Policy: Magnet Schools or Forced Busing. 1992. pap. 22.95 (*0-87722-924-4*) Temple U Pr.

Rossell, Christine H. & Hawley, Willis D., eds. The Consequences of School Desegregation. LC 83-6755. 221p. 1983. 34.95 (*0-87722-320-3*) Temple U Pr.

Rossell, Denton. Voice: A Dramatic New Concept. Westman, Delorez, ed. (Illus.). 227p. 1984. 28.50 (*0-686-39615-4*) Clark & Westman-Magnolia.

Rosselli, Carlo. Liberal Socialism. Urbinati, Nadia, ed. McCraig, William, tr. LC 93-42365. (C). 1994. 39.50 (*0-691-08650-8*); pap. 12.95 (*0-691-02560-6*) Princeton U Pr.

Rosselli, John. Lord William Bentinck: The Making of a Liberal Imperialist, 1774-1839. LC 72-95302. 386p. reprint ed. pap. 110.10 (*0-685-23983-7*, 2031547) Bks Demand.

— Music & Musicians in Nineteenth Century Italy. (Illus.). 176p. 1991. 29.95 (*0-931340-40-3*, Amadeus Pr) Timber.

— Singers of Italian Opera. 288p. 1995. pap. 17.95 (*0-521-42697-9*) Cambridge U Pr.

— Singers of Italian Opera: The History of a Profession. (Illus.). 275p. (C). 1992. 47.95 (*0-521-41683-3*) Cambridge U Pr.

Rossellini, Roberto. My Method: Writings & Interviews. Cancogni, Annapaola, tr. LC 92-82645. (Illus.). 280p. 1993. 24.00 (*0-941419-64-9*) Marsilio Pubs.

— Roberto Rossellini: The War Trilogy. LC 82-49232. (Cinema Classics Ser.). 487p. 1985. lib. bdg. 16.00 (*0-8240-5776-7*) Garland.

Rosselot, Bernard. Vocabulaire Maritime. 95p. (FRE.). 1980. pap. 19.95 (*0-8288-1581-X*, F136860) Fr & Eur.

Rosselot, Kirsten S., jt. auth. see Allen, David T.

***Rosselson, Leon.** Rosa & Her Grandfather. LC 95-10320. (J). 1996. write for info. (*0-399-22733-4*, Philomel Bks) Putnam Pub Group.

— Where's My Mom? LC 93-32383. (Illus.). 32p. (J). (ps up). 1994. 13.95 (*1-56402-392-3*) Candlewick Pr.

Rossen, Janice. Philip Larkin: His Life's Work. LC 89-51283. 176p. (C). 1990. text ed. 25.95 (*0-87745-271-7*) U of Iowa Pr.

— The World of Barbara Pym. LC 86-24810. 208p. 1987. 29.95 (*0-312-00090-1*) St Martin.

Rossen, Janice, ed. Independent Women: The Function of Gender in the Novels of Barbara Pym. LC 88-699. 160p. 1988. text ed. 39.95 (*0-312-02042-2*) St Martin.

Rossen, Janice, jt. ed. see Wyatt-Brown, Anne M.

Rossen, John, jt. ed. see Rifkin, Jeremy.

Rossen, Susan F., jt. ed. see DelliQuadri, Lyn.

Rossen, Susan F., jt. comment see Mosby, Dewey F.

Rosseneu, Maryvonne, ed. Structure & Function of Apolipoproteins. 437p. 1992. 133.00 (*0-8493-6906-1*, QP99) CRC Pr.

***Rosser.** Esoteric Nature of Music. 1994. 24.95 (*0-8356-4002-7*, Quest) Theos Pub Hse.

— Theosophical Society in America. 1994. 24.95 (*0-8356-4003-5*, Quest) Theos Pub Hse.

Rosser, Aelred. A Workbook for Lectors & Gospel Readers 1995. 176p. (Orig.). 1994. pap. 10.00 (*1-56854-032-9*, WL95) Liturgy Tr Pubns.

— A Workbook for Lectors & Gospel Readers 1996. 176p. (Orig.). 1995. pap. 10.00 (*1-56854-067-1*, WL96) Liturgy Tr Pubns.

***Rosser, Aelred R.** A Word That Will Rouse Them: Reflections on the Ministry of Reader. 80p. (Orig.). 1995. pap. 5.95 (*1-56854-028-0*, ROUSE) Liturgy Tr Pubns.

Rosser, B. R. Gay Catholics down under: The Journeys in Sexuality & Spirituality of Gay Men in Australia & New Zealand. LC 91-47084. 256p. 1992. text ed. 49.95 (*0-275-94229-5*, C4229, Praeger Pubs) Greenwood.

— Male Homosexual Behavior & the Effects of AIDS Education: A Study of Behavior & Safer Sex in New Zealand & South Australia. LC 91-4626. 264p. 1991. text ed. 65.00 (*0-275-93809-3*, C3809, Praeger Pubs) Greenwood.

Rosser, Bill. Up Rode the Troopers: The Black Police in Queensland. 1990. pap. 14.95 (*0-7022-2224-0*, Pub. by Univ Queensland Pr AT) Intl Spec Bk.

Rosser, Caroline S. Planning Activities for Child Care: A Curriculum Guide for Early Childhood Education. LC 92-27485. 504p. 1993. text ed. 31.80 (*0-87006-989-6*) Goodheart.

Rosser, David. A Dragon in the House. 235p. (C). 1987. 21. 00x (*0-86383-357-8*, Pub. by Gomer Pr UK) St Mut.

Rosser, Evelyn C. Too Late for Tears. 52p. 1994. 7.95 (*0-8059-3508-8*) Dorrance.

Rosser, Gervase, jt. ed. see Holt, Richard.

Rosser, J. Allyn. Bright Moves. (Samuel French Morse Poetry Prize Ser.). 88p. 1990. pap. 9.95 (*1-55553-083-4*) NE U Pr.

Rosser, J. Barkley, Jr. From Catastrophe to Chaos: A General Theory of Economic Discontinuities. 416p. (C). 1991. lib. bdg. 93.50 (*0-7923-9157-8*) Kluwer Ac.

Rosser, J. K. Teenage Mutant Ninja Turtles ABC's for a Better Planet. LC 90-52437. (Pictureback Ser.). (Illus.). 32p. (Orig.). (J). (ps-3). 1991. lib. bdg. 5.99 (*0-679-91383-1*) Random Bks Yng Read.

***Rosser, James A.** The Art of Laparoscopic Suturing. 1995. 59.50 (*1-85775-022-5*) Scovill Paterson.

Rosser, Linda K. Christmas in Oklahoma. (Illus.). 122p. 1982. 14.95 (*0-86546-041-8*) Bobwhite Pubns.

— Memory Album of a Territorial Lady. (Illus.). 72p. 1988. 14.95 (*0-929546-00-8*) Bobwhite Pubns.

— Pioneer Cookery Around Oklahoma. (Illus.). 250p. 1978. reprint ed. pap. 9.95 (*0-929546-01-6*) Bobwhite Pubns.

Rosser, M. J., jt. auth. see Mallier, A. T.

Rosser, Mike. Basic Mathematics for Economists. 496p. 1993. 79.95 (*0-415-08424-5*, B0003); pap. 29.95 (*0-415-08425-3*, B0007) Routledge.

Rosser, Phyllis. The SAT Gender Gap: Identifying the Causes. 190p. 1989. pap. 15.00 (*1-877966-00-2*) Ctr Women Policy.

Rosser, R., ed. Mind-Made Disease: A Clinician's Guide to Recent Research. (Journal of Psychosomatic Research: No. 25). (Illus.). 144p. 1982. pap. 30.00 (*0-08-027957-0*, Pergamon Pr) Elsevier.

Rosser, Rosemary A. Cognitive Development: Psychological & Biological Perspectives. 1993. pap. text ed. 33.75 (*0-205-13965-5*) Allyn.

***Rosser, S.** Women's Health. 1994. pap. 14.95 (*0-253-28533-X*) Ind U Pr.

***Rosser, Sue, ed.** Teaching the Majority: Breaking the Gender Barriers in Science, Mathematics, & Engineering. (Athene Ser.). 272p. (C). 1995. pap. text ed. 22.75 (*0-8077-6276-8*) Tchrs Coll.

— Teaching the Majority: Breaking the Gender Barriers in Science, Mathematics, & Engineering. (Athene Ser.). 272p. (C). 1995. text ed. 50.00 (*0-8077-6277-6*) Tchrs Coll.

Rosser, Sue V. Biology & Feminism: A Dynamic Interaction. (Feminist Impact on the Arts & Sciences Ser.). 200p. 1992. pap. 14.95 (*0-8057-9755-6*, Twayne) Macmillan.

— Biology & Feminism: A Dynamic Interaction. (Feminist Impact on the Arts & Sciences Ser.). 200p. 1993. text ed. 26.95 (*0-8057-9770-X*, Twayne) Macmillan.

— Female-Friendly Science: Applying Women's Studies, Methods & Theories to Attract Students. (Athene Ser.). 176p. (C). text ed. 32.50 (*0-8077-6241-5*); pap. text ed. 13.95 (*0-8077-6240-7*) Tchrs Coll.

— Female Friendly Science: Applying Women's Studies Methods & Theories to Attract Students to Science. (Athene Ser.). 160p. 1990. text ed. 32.50 (*0-08-037469-7*, Pub. by PPI UK); pap. text ed. 12.95 (*0-08-037470-0*, Pub. by PPI UK) Elsevier.

— Feminism Within the Science & Health Professions: Overcoming Resistance. (Athene Ser.). 168p. 1988. text ed. 36.50 (*0-08-035558-7*, Pergamon Pr); pap. text ed. 16.95 (*0-08-035557-9*, Pergamon Pr) Elsevier.

— Teaching Health & Science from a Feminist Perspective: A Practical Guide. (Athene Ser.). (Illus.). 200p. 1986. 36.50 (*0-08-033135-1*, Pergamon Pr); pap. 19.95 (*0-08-033997-2*, Pergamon Pr) Elsevier.

— Teaching Science & Health from a Feminist Perspective: A Practical Guide. (Athene Ser.). 256p. (C). pap. text ed. 19.95 (*0-8077-6223-7*) Tchrs Coll.

— Women's Health - Missing from U. S. Medicine. LC 94-9745. (Race, Gender, & Science Ser.). 1994. 29.95 (*0-253-34991-5*) Ind U Pr.

— Women's Health - Missing from U. S. Medicine. 1994. pap. 14.95 (*0-253-20924-2*) Ind U Pr.

Rosser, Sue V., ed. Feminism Within the Science & Health Care Professions: Overcoming Resistance. (Athene Ser.). 178p. (C). text ed. 36.50 (*0-8077-6209-1*); pap. text ed. 16.95 (*0-8077-6208-3*) Tchrs Coll.

Rosser, W. G. Introductory Special Relativity. 260p. 1992. 95.00 (*0-85066-838-7*, Pub. by Tay Francis Ltd UK); pap. 45.00 (*0-85066-839-5*, Pub. by Tay Francis Ltd UK) Taylor & Francis.

Rosset, Barney, ed. Evergreen Review Reader 1957-1966. (Illus.). 368p. 1994. pap. 16.95 (*1-55970-273-7*) Arcade Pub Inc.

Rosset, Barney, et al, eds. Evergreen Review Reader, 1957-1966: The Best from the First Ten Years of America's Most Provocative, Most Controversial, Most Important Literary Magazine. (Illus.). 356p. (Orig.). 1993. pap. 15. 95 (*1-56201-046-8*, North Star Line) Blue Moon Bks.

Rosset, Clement. Joyful Cruelty: Toward a Philosophy of the Real. Bell, David F., tr. (Odeon Ser.). 160p. 1993. 38.00 (*0-19-507741-5*); pap. 16.95 (*0-19-507991-4*) OUP.

Rosset, E. & Dobosz, I. Aging Process of Population. LC 63-19956. 1964. 208.00 (*0-08-010402-9*, Pub. by Pergamon Repr UK) Franklin.

Rosset, Lisa. James Baldwin. (Black Americans of Achievement Ser.). (Illus.). 112p. (Orig.). (J). (gr. 5 up). 1989. 17.95 (*1-55546-572-2*); pap. 9.95 (*0-7910-0230-6*) Chelsea Hse.

— James Baldwin. (Orig.). 1990. pap. 3.95 (*0-685-47668-5*, Melrose Sq) Holloway.

Rosset, M. O. Beziehungen Zwischen Vegetation, Bodenwasser, Mikroklima und Energiehaushalt von Feuchtwiesen Unter Besonderer Beruecksichtigung der Evatranspiration. (Dissertationes Botanicae Ser.: Vol. 159). (Illus.). 244p. (GER.). 1990. pap. text ed. 76.00 (*3-443-64071-0*, Pub. by Cramer-Borntraeger GW) Lubrecht & Cramer.

***Rosset, Peter & Benjamin, Medea, eds.** The Greening of the Revolution: Cuba's Experiment with Organic Farming. 110p. 1995. 11.95 (*1-875284-80-X*, Pub. by Ocean Pr AT) Talman.

Rossett, Allison. Training Needs Assessment. LC 87-9070. (Illus.). 281p. 1987. 37.95 (*0-87778-195-8*) Educ Tech Pubns.

Rossett, Allison & Gautier-Downes, Jeannette. A Handbook of Job Aids. LC 91-9090. (Illus.). 195p. 1991. 39.95 (*0-88390-290-7*) Pfeiffer & Co.

Rossett, Arthur, jt. auth. see Dorff, Elliot N.

Rossetter, Laura. The Mountain Bike Guide to Summit County, Colorado: Backcountry Roads & Trails Around Breckenridge, Keystone-Dillon, Montezuma, Frisco, Copper Mountain, Vail Pass, & the Lower Blue River Valley. 2nd rev. ed. (Illus.). 120p. (Orig.). 1993. reprint ed. pap. write for info. (*0-9621978-1-5*) Sage Creek Pr.

— Mountain Biking Colorado's Historic Mining Districts. LC 90-85222. (Illus.). 150p. (Orig.). 1991. pap. 10.95 (*1-55591-090-4*) Fulcrum Pub.

Rossetti, Ana & Suntree, Susan. Tulips: Ten Poems by Anna Rossetti. Nieman, Nancy D., tr. (Illus.). 24p. (ENG & SPA.). 1990. 7.00 (*1-882623-08-8*) Exiled-Am Pr.

Rossetti, Christina. A Choice of Christina Rossetti's Verse. Jennings, Elizabeth, ed. 96p. 1970. pap. 9.95 (*0-571-09018-4*) Faber & Faber.

— Color. LC 90-25588. (Illus.). 40p. (J). (ps-1). 1994. pap. 4.95 (*0-06-443361-7*, Trophy) HarpC Child Bks.

— Complete Poems of Christina Rossetti: A Variorum Edition, Vol. 1. Crump, R. W., ed. LC 78-5571. 1979. text ed. 37.50 (*0-8071-0358-6*) La State U Pr.

— Complete Poems of Christina Rossetti: A Variorum Edition, Vol. II. Crump, R. W., ed. LC 78-5571. (Illus.). 525p. 1986. text ed. 42.50 (*0-8071-1246-1*) La State U Pr.

— Complete Poems of Christina Rossetti: A Variorum Edition, Vol. III. Crump, R. W., ed. LC 78-5571. 784p. 1990. text ed. 50.00 (*0-8071-1530-4*) La State U Pr.

— Goblin Market. adapted ed. Harmon, Peggy, ed. 1987. spiral bd. 8.95 (*0-8222-0452-5*) Dramatists Play.

— Goblin Market. (Illus.). 64p. 1983. reprint ed. pap. 2.95 (*0-486-24516-0*) Dover.

— Goblin Market & Other Poems. LC 93-40975. (Thrift Editions Ser.). 64p. (Orig.). 1994. pap. 1.00 (*0-486-28055-1*) Dover.

— Love Poems. (Illus.). 88p. 1995. 19.95 (*1-85793-458-X*, Pub. by Pavilion UK) Trafalgar.

— Poems of Christina Rossetti. LC 94-14790. (Illus.). 1994. pap. 8.99 (*0-517-11851-3*, Pub. by Gramercy) Random Hse Value.

Rossetti, Christina & Craik, Dinah M. Maude. Showalter, Elaine, ed. LC 92-38333. (Women's Classics Ser.). 223p. 1993. 55.00 (*0-8147-7442-3*); pap. 17.95 (*0-8147-7451-2*) NYU Pr.

Rossetti, Christina G. Complete Poems. 1992. reprint ed. lib. bdg. 37.95x (*0-89968-293-6*, Lghtyr Pr) Buccaneer Bks.

— The Family Letters of Christina Georgina Rossetti. (BCL1-PR English Literature Ser.). 242p. 1992. reprint ed. lib. bdg. 79.00 (*0-7812-7624-1*) Rprt Serv.

— Family Letters of Christina Georgina Rossetti, with Some Supplementary Letters & Appendices. Rossetti, William M., ed. LC 68-24915. (English Literature Ser.: No. 33). (Illus.). 1969. reprint ed. lib. bdg. 75.00 (*0-8383-0237-8*) M S G Haskell Hse.

— Poems: Rossetti. LC 93-14362. (Pocket Poets Ser.). 1993. 10.95 (*0-679-42908-5*, Everymans Lib) Knopf.

— Poetical Works. (BCL1-PR English Literature Ser.). 507p. 1992. reprint ed. lib. bdg. 99.00 (*0-7812-7623-3*) Rprt Serv.

— Sing Song: A Nursery Rhyme Book. LC 68-55822. (Illus.). x, 130p. (J). (gr. 3-7). 1969. reprint ed. pap. 4.50 (*0-486-22107-5*) Dover.

Rossetti, Concetta M. Rainbows of Love. (Illus.). 72p. (Orig.). 1988. pap. 9.99 (*0-925037-03-6*) Great Lks Poetry.

Rossetti, Dante G. Collected Works, 2 vols., Set. (BCL1-PR English Literature Ser.). 1992. reprint ed. lib. bdg. 150. 00 (*0-7812-7626-8*) Rprt Serv.

— Dante Gabriel Rossetti: His Family Letters, 2 Vols, Set. LC 70-130231. reprint ed. 72.50 (*0-404-05434-X*) AMS Pr.

— Dante Gabriel Rossetti: His Family-Letters, 2 vols., Set. (BCL1-PR English Literature Ser.). 1992. reprint ed. lib. bdg. 150.00 (*0-7812-7629-2*) Rprt Serv.

— The House of Life, a Sonnet-Sequence. (BCL1-PR English Literature Ser.). 242p. 1992. reprint ed. lib. bdg. 79.00 (*0-7812-7628-4*) Rprt Serv.

— Poems & Translations, 1850-1870, Together with the Prose Story "Hand & Soul" (BCL1-PR English Literature Ser.). 492p. 1992. reprint ed. lib. bdg. 99.00 (*0-7812-7627-6*) Rprt Serv.

Rossetti, Dante G., tr. see Dante Alighieri, et al.

Rossetti, Francesca. Psycho-Regression: A New System for Healing & Personal Growth. 240p. (Orig.). 1994. pap. 12.95 (*0-87728-788-0*) Weiser.

Rossetti, G., et al. Double Contrast Radiology of the Aesophagus. 154p. 1985. text ed. 56.00 (*1-57235-035-0*) Piccin NY.

Rossetti, Gabriel C. The Works. (Anglistica & Americana Ser.: No. 135). xxxvii, 684p. 1972. reprint ed. 122.20 (*3-487-04360-2*, Pub. by Georg Olms GW) Lubrecht & Cramer.

Rossetti, Guy, ed. see De la Barca, Pedro C.

Rossetti, Lou. The Rossetti Infant-Toddler Language Scale: A Measure of Communication & Interaction. 80p. (ps). 1990. student ed, spiral bd. 36.00 (*1-55999-121-6*) LinguiSystems.

Rossetti, Louis. Rossetti Assessment & Intervention with High-Risk Infants & Toddlers. 1992. audio 49.95 (*1-55999-215-8*) LinguiSystems.

***Rossetti, Louis M.** Communication Intervention: Birth to Three. 350p. 1995. 34.95 (*1-56593-101-7*, 0404) Singular Publishing.

— High-Risk Infants: Identification, Assessment & Intervention. LC 90-9220. 238p. (C). 1986. pap. text ed. 29.00 (*0-89079-367-0*, 1783) PRO-ED.

— Infant-Toddler Assessment: An Interdisciplinary Approach. LC 90-9185. (Illus.). 294p. (C). 1990. text ed. 29.00 (*0-89079-312-3*, 1782) PRO-ED.

— The Rossetti Infant-Toddler Language Scale Kit: A Measure of Communication & Interaction. 140p. (ps). 1990. student ed 54.95 (*1-55999-143-7*) LinguiSystems.

Rossetti, Louis M., ed. Developmental Problems of Drug-Exposed Infants. (Illus.). 77p. (Orig.). (C). 1992. pap. text ed. 21.50x (*1-56593-064-9*, 0370) Singular Publishing.

Rossetti, Rosemarie, jt. auth. see Powell, Charles.

Rossetti, Stephen. Fire on the Earth: Daily Living in the Kingdom of God. LC 88-51808. 128p. 1989. pap. 7.95 (*0-89622-391-4*) Twenty-Third.

Rossetti, Stephen J. Slayer of the Soul: Child Sexual Abuse & the Catholic Church. LC 90-70990. 224p. (Orig.). 1990. pap. 14.95 (*0-89622-452-X*) Twenty-Third.

Rossetti, William M. American Poems. LC 74-131501. reprint ed. 47.50 (*0-404-05419-6*) AMS Pr.

— Bibliography of the Works of Dante Gabriel Rossetti. LC 71-130242. reprint ed. 24.50 (*0-404-05439-0*) AMS Pr.

R

An Asterisk (*) at the beginning of an entry indicates that the title is appearing in BIP for the first time.

— Dante Gabriel Rossetti As Designer & Writer. LC 73-144678. reprint ed. 36.00 (*0-404-05429-3*) AMS Pr.

— Fine Art, Chiefly Contemporary. LC 73-12670. Orig. Title: Fine Art. reprint ed. 41.50 (*0-404-05417-X*) AMS Pr.

— Letters about Shelley Interchanged by Three Friends-Edward Dowden, Richard Garnett & William Michael Rossetti. LC 77-168058. reprint ed. 24.50 (*0-404-05444-7*) AMS Pr.

— Life of John Keats. LC 75-122695. reprint ed. 29.50 (*0-404-05428-5*) AMS Pr.

— Lives of Famous Poets. LC 77-148292. reprint ed. 42.50 (*0-404-05425-0*) AMS Pr.

— Memoir of Shelley. LC 71-144680. (Shelley Society, Fourth Ser.: No. 2). reprint ed. 34.00 (*0-404-05427-7*) AMS Pr.

— Notes on the Royal Academy Exhibition, 1868. LC 75-144681. reprint ed. 27.50 (*0-404-05418-8*) AMS Pr.

— Rossetti Papers, 1862-1870. LC 76-130238. reprint ed. 32.50 (*0-404-05438-2*) AMS Pr.

— Ruskin: Rossetti: Pre-Raphaelitism, Papers 1854-62. LC 73-127453. reprint ed. 36.00 (*0-404-05437-4*) AMS Pr.

— Some Reminiscences, 2 vols, Set. LC 75-132386. (Illus.). 645p. 1975. reprint ed. 59.50 (*0-404-05440-4*) AMS Pr.

— Swinburne's Poems & Ballads: A Criticism. LC 73-130623. reprint ed. 21.50 (*0-404-05416-1*) AMS Pr.

Rossetti, William M., ed. Humorous Poems. LC 77-139260. reprint ed. 42.50 (*0-404-05426-9*) AMS Pr.

— Preraphaelite Diaries & Letters. LC 70-148293. reprint ed. 34.50 (*0-404-08898-8*) AMS Pr.

Rossetti, William M., ed. see Rossetti, Christina G.

Rossetto, L. Major General Orde Charles Wingate & the Development of Long-Range Penetration. 492p. 1982. 47.95 (*0-89126-107-9*) MA-AH Pub.

Rossfeldt, Klaus. Rolls-Royce & Bentley: A History. (Illus.). 304p. 1991. 150.00 (*0-85429-920-3*) Haynes Pubns.

Rossi, jt. auth. see Cady.

Rossi, A. The Rise of Italian Fascism, 1918-1922. 1975. 300.00 (*0-87968-435-6*) Gordon Pr.

Rossi, A., jt. ed. see Casacchia, M.

Rossi, Agnes. Athletes & Artists. (Creative Writers Ser.). 92p. 1987. 27.50x (*0-8147-7400-8*) NYU Pr.

— Athletes & Artists: Stories. 72p. 1987. pap. 6.95 (*0-89255-115-1*) Persea Bks.

— The Quick: A Novella & Stories. 128p. 1992. 17.95 (*0-393-03086-5*) Norton.

— Split Skirt. LC 93-26887. 1994. 20.00 (*0-679-42543-8*) Random.

Rossi, Albert S. Can I Make a Difference? Christian Family Life Today. LC 89-38001. 128p. (Orig.). 1990. pap. 5.95 (*0-8091-3125-0*) Paulist Pr.

Rossi, Aldo. The Architecture of the City. Ghirardo, Diane, tr. 252p. 1982. pap. 16.95x (*0-262-68043-2*) MIT Pr.

— A Scientific Autobiography. Venuti, Lawrence, tr. (Illus.). 128p. 1981. pap. 13.95 (*0-262-68041-6*) MIT Pr.

***Rossi, Aldo & Gravagnuolo, Benedetto.** Adolf Loos: Theory & Works. (Illus.). 228p. Date not set. pap. 39.95 (*0-948835-16-8*) Dist Art Pubs.

Rossi, Alfred. Astonish Us in the Morning: Tyrone Guthrie Remembered. LC 80-11855. (Illus.). 322p. reprint ed. pap. 91.80 (*0-8357-5820-6*, 2033175) Bks Demand.

Rossi, Alice S. Generational Differences in the Soviet Union. Zuckerman, Harriet & Merton, Robert K., eds. LC 79-9021. (Dissertations on Sociology Ser.). 1980. lib. bdg. 35.95 (*0-405-12990-4*) Ayer.

Rossi, Alice S., ed. The Feminist Papers: From Adams to De Beauvoir. LC 73-8828. 600p. 1973. text ed. 81.00 (*0-231-03795-3*) Col U Pr.

— The Feminist Papers: From Adams to de Beauvoir. 716p. 1988. reprint ed. pap. 16.95 (*1-55553-028-1*) NE U Pr.

— Gender & the Life Course. LC 84-12335. (Illus.). 389p. (C). 1985. pap. text ed. 24.95 (*0-202-30312-8*) Aldine de Gruyter.

— Sexuality Across the Life Course. LC 93-41706. (John D. & Catherine T. MacArthur Foundation Series on Mental Health & Development). 1994. 34.95 (*0-226-72833-1*) U Ch Pr.

Rossi, Alice S. & Rossi, Peter H. Of Human Bonding. (Parent-Child Relations Across the Life Course Ser.). 560p. 1990. pap. 42.95 (*0-202-30361-6*) Aldine de Gruyter.

— Of Human Bonding. (Parent-Child Relations Across the Life Course Ser.). 560p. 1990. 67.95 (*0-202-30360-8*) Aldine de Gruyter.

Rossi, Alice S., ed. see Mill, John Stuart & Mill, Harriet T.

Rossi, Arcangelo, jt. ed. see Garola, Claudio.

Rossi, B. E., ed. Experimental Mechanics: Proceedings, International Congress on Experimental Mechanics - 1st, Vols. 1 & 2. 1963. 175.00 (*0-08-013346-0*, Pub. by Pergamon Repr UK) Franklin.

Rossi, Bobbie L. Reflective Thoughts. (Illus.). 48p. 1994. pap. 7.95 (*0-8059-3512-6*) Dorrance.

Rossi, Bruno. Las Vegas Vengeance. (Sharpshooter Ser.: No. 14). (Orig.). 1975. pap. 1.25 (*0-685-52940-1*, LB261ZK) Dorchester Pub Co.

— Moments in the Life of a Scientist. (Illus.). 200p. (C). 1990. 49.95 (*0-521-36439-6*) Cambridge U Pr.

— Triggerman. (Sharpshooter Ser.: No. 11). 1975. pap. 0.95 (*0-685-51411-0*, LB229NK) Dorchester Pub Co.

Rossi, C. & Tiezzi, Enzo, eds. Ecological Physical Chemistry: Proc. of the Internat. Workshop, Sienna, Italy, Nov. 1990. 652p. 1991. 202.75 (*0-444-87430-5*) Elsevier.

Rossi, Carl L. Ultrasonic Diagnosis: Index of Modern Information. LC 88-47847. 150p. 1988. 44.50 (*0-88164-964-3*); pap. 39.50 (*0-88164-965-1*) ABBE Pubs Assn.

***Rossi, Christina P.** Dostoevsky's Last Night: A Novel. 192p. 1995. 20.00 (*0-312-13054-6*) St Martin.

Rossi, Christopher R. Equity As a Source of International Law? A Legal Realist Approach to the Process of International Decisionmaking. LC 92-46570. (Innovation in International Law Ser.). 280p. (C). 1993. 85.00 (*0-941320-81-2*) Transnatl Pubs.

***Rossi, Cristina P.** Babel Barbara. Decker, tr. (QRL Poetry Book Ser.: Vol. XXXI). 20.00 (*0-614-06448-1*); pap. 10.00 (*0-614-06449-X*) Quarterly Rev.

— Evohe: Poemas Eroticas-Erotic Poems. Decker, Diana P., tr. LC 93-73117. 128p. (Orig.). (C). 1994. pap. 11.95 (*0-9632363-5-0*) Azul Edits.

— A Forbidden Passion. Treacy, Mary J., tr. 184p. (Orig.). (C). 1993. lib. bdg. 24.95 (*0-939416-67-0*); pap. 9.95 (*0-939416-68-9*) Cleis Pr.

— The Ship of Fools. Hughes, Psiche, tr. LC 88-61390. (Readers International Ser.). 225p. (Orig.). 1989. 17.95 (*0-930523-53-9*); pap. 9.95 (*0-930523-54-7*) Readers Intl.

Rossi, D. Romanistische Texte und Studien, Vol. 1: Le 'Egloghe Viscontee' Di Alligretti. write for info. (*0-318-71469-8*, Pub. by Georg Olms GW) Lubrecht & Cramer.

— Romanistische Texte und Studien, Vol. 3: Due Epistole Di Giovanni Conversini Da Ravenna. write for info. (*0-318-71470-1*, Pub. by Georg Olms GW) Lubrecht & Cramer.

Rossi, Diego. Due Epistole Di Giovanni Conversini Da Ravenna. (Romanistische Texte und Studien Ser.: Vol. 3). vi, 64p. 1988. write for info. (*3-487-07965-8*, Pub. by Georg Olms GW) Lubrecht & Cramer.

— Le Egloghe Viscontee Di Lacopo Allegretti. (Romanistische Texte und Studien Ser.: Vol. 1). 55p. 1984. write for info. (*3-487-07566-0*, Pub. by Georg Olms GW) Lubrecht & Cramer.

Rossi, Diego, ed. see Poliziano, Angelo A.

Rossi, Doc. Guitar Styles of Jerry Donahue. (Illus.). 80p. 1993. pap. 14.95 (*0-7119-2948-3*) Music Sales.

Rossi, E., ed. Ernaehrung und Stoffwechsel: Die Adipositas im Kindesalter. (Paediatrische Fortbildungskurse fuer die Praxis Ser.: Band 42). (Illus.). 113p. 1975. 28.00 (*3-8055-2158-8*) S Karger.

— Perinatologie. (Paediatrische Fortbildungskurse fuer die Praxis Ser.: Band 41). 200p. 1975. 63.25 (*3-8055-2115-4*) S Karger.

— Pulmonale Aspekte der Cystischen Fibrose. (Paediatrische Fortbildungskurse fuer die Praxis Ser.: Vol. 48). (Illus.). 1979. pap. 39.25 (*3-8055-2944-9*) S Karger.

— Solide maligne Tumoren im Kindesalter. (Paediatrische Fortbildungskurse fuer die Praxis Ser.: Vol. 39). (Illus.). 100p. 1974. 26.50 (*3-8055-1691-6*) S Karger.

Rossi, E. & Oetliker, O., eds. Nephrologie im Kindesalter III. (Paediatrische Fortbildungskurse fuer die Praxis Ser.: Bd. 45). (Illus.). (GER.). 1978. 42.50 (*3-8055-2825-6*) S Karger.

Rossi, E. & Wyler, F., eds. Neuere Aspekte der Kinderkardiologie, Set. (Paediatrische Fortbildungskurse fuer die Praxis Ser.: Vol. 47). (Illus.). (FRE & GER.). 1978. pap. 29.75 (*3-8055-2865-5*) S Karger.

Rossi, E., ed. see Kinderchirurgisches Symposium Staff.

Rossi, E. Bern, ed. Neue Akquisitionen in der Neonatologie: Nouvelles Acquisitions en Neonatologie. (Paediatrische Fortbildungskurse fuer die Praxis Ser.: Vol. 62). (Illus.). x, 660p. 1988. pap. 31.25 (*3-8055-4742-0*) S Karger.

Rossi, Ennio C., jt. ed. see Wu, Kenneth K.

Rossi, Ennio C., et al. Principles of Transfusion Medicine. (Illus.). 816p. 1991. 115.00 (*0-683-07385-0*) Williams & Wilkins.

***Rossi, Ennio C., et al, eds.** Principles of Transfusion Medicine. 2nd ed. LC 95-11651. 1995. write for info. (*0-683-07386-9*) Williams & Wilkins.

Rossi, Enzo. Malta on the Brink: From Western Democracy to Libyan Satellite. (C). 1986. 35.00 (*0-907967-79-5*, Pub. by Inst Euro Def & Strat UK) St Mut.

Rossi, Ernest. Western Europe: A Political Dictionary. (Dictionary Ser.). 300p. 1994. lib. bdg. 60.00 (*0-87436-754-9*) ABC-CLIO.

Rossi, Ernest E. & McCrea, Barbara. The European Political Dictionary. LC 84-24389. (Clio Dictionaries in Political Science Ser.: No. 7). 408p. 1985. lib. bdg. 55.00 (*0-87436-046-3*); pap. text ed. 20.50 (*0-87436-367-5*) ABC-CLIO.

Rossi, Ernest E. & Plano, Jack C., eds. Latin America: A Political Dictionary. LC 92-28946. (Clio Dictionaries in Political Science Ser.). 1992. lib. bdg. 60.00 (*0-87436-608-9*); pap. text ed. 29.95 (*0-87436-698-4*) ABC-CLIO.

Rossi, Ernest L. Dreams & the Growth of Personality: Expanding Awareness in Psychotherapy. 232p. (C). 1972. 101.00 (*0-08-016787-X*, Pub. by Pergamon Repr UK) Franklin.

— Dreams & the Growth of Personality: Expanding Awareness in Psychotherapy. 2nd ed. LC 85-9693. 264p. 1985. 35.95 (*0-87630-397-1*) Brunner-Mazel.

— The Psychology of Mind-Body Healing: New Concepts of Therapeutic Hypnosis. rev. ed. 304p. (C). 1993. 39.00 (*0-393-70168-9*) Norton.

Rossi, Ernest L. & Cheek, David B. Mind-Body Therapy: Methods of Ideodynamic Healing in Hypnosis. (Professional Bks.). (Illus.). 1988. 36.95 (*0-393-70052-6*) Norton.

— Mind-Body Therapy: Methods of Ideodynamic Healing in Hypnosis. 544p. 1994. pap. 18.95 (*0-393-31247-X*) Norton.

Rossi, Ernest L., ed. see Erickson, Milton H.

Rossi, Ernest L., jt. auth. see Erickson, Milton H.

Rossi, Ernest L., ed. see Erickson, Milton H.

Rossi, Ernest L., jt. auth. see Erickson, Milton H.

Rossi, Ernest L., ed. see Erickson, Milton H.

Rossi, Ernest L., jt. ed. see Lloyd, David.

Rossi, F., jt. auth. see Pleyte, E.

Rossi, Faust. Evidence for the Trial Lawyer. 1994. 35.00 (*1-55917-172-3*, 9322); digital audio 135.00 (*1-55917-171-5*) Natl Prac Inst.

— Evidence for the Trial Lawyer. 1994. vhs 495.00 (*0-614-07112-7*) Natl Prac Inst.

— Experts & Hearsay: What Every Trial Lawyer Must Know. 1994. 35.00 (*0-614-06014-1*, 4129) Natl Prac Inst.

Rossi, Gail. The Dong People of China: A Hidden Civilization. (Illus.). 96p. (Orig.). 1991. pap. 18.95 (*981-00-1551-8*, Pub. by Hagley & Hoyle SI) Seven Hills Bk.

Rossi, Giovanni. Biohydrometallurgy. 620p. 1990. text ed. 90.00 (*0-07-053931-6*) McGraw.

Rossi, Giuseppe, et al, eds. Coping with Floods. LC 94-2615. (NATO Advanced Study Institutes Series E, Applied Sciences: Vol. 257). 1994. lib. bdg. 282.00 (*0-7923-2706-3*) Kluwer Ac.

Rossi, Guido, photos. Italy from the Air. LC 93-12461. 1993. write for info. (*0-86565-140-X*) Vendome.

Rossi, Guido A., photos. Egypt: Gift of the Nile: An Aerial Portrait. (Illus.). 208p. 1992. 49.50 (*0-8109-3254-7*) Abrams.

— Turkey: An Aerial Portrait. LC 93-31352. 1994. 49.50 (*0-8109-3866-9*) Abrams.

***Rossi, H. H.** Microdosimetry & Its Applications. 352p. 1995. 49.00 (*3-540-58541-9*) Spr-Verlag.

Rossi, Harald H. Limitation & Assessment in Radiation Protection. LC 84-11041. (Taylor Lecture Ser.: No. 8). 1984. 20.00 (*0-913392-69-3*) NCRP Pubns.

Rossi, Hugh. Landlord & Tenant Act Nineteen Eighty-Seven. 1987. pap. 110.00 (*0-7219-1070-X*, Scientific) St Mut.

— Shaw's Guide to the Rent (Agriculture) Act, 1976. (C). 1977. 75.00 (*0-7219-0750-4*, Scientific) St Mut.

Rossi, Ino. Community Reconstruction after Earthquake: Dialectical Sociology in Action. LC 93-2856. 208p. 1993. text ed. 59.95 (*0-275-94602-9*, C4602, Praeger Pubs) Greenwood.

— From the Sociology of Symbols to the Sociology of Signs. LC 83-5261. 1983. text ed. 69.00 (*0-231-04844-0*) Col U Pr.

— From the Sociology of Symbols to the Sociology of Signs: Toward a Dialectical Sociology. LC 83-5261. 359p. reprint ed. pap. 102.40 (*0-8357-6123-1*, 2034192) Bks Demand.

Rossi, Ino, ed. The Logic of Culture: Advances in Structural Theory & Method. LC 81-29. 304p. 1982. text ed. 42.95 (*0-89789-015-9*, Bergin & Garvey) Greenwood.

— People in Culture: A Survey of Cultural Anthropology. (Illus.). 640p. 1980. 39.95 (*0-03-028351-5*, Bergin & Garvey); pap. 18.95 (*0-03-051021-X*, Bergin & Garvey) Greenwood.

— Structural Sociology. LC 81-12246. (Illus.). 416p. 1984. text ed. 60.50 (*0-231-04846-7*); pap. text ed. 19.50 (*0-231-04847-5*) Col U Pr.

Rossi, Ino, et al. People in Culture: A Survey of Cultural Anthropology. LC 79-11842. (Praeger Special Studies). 640p. 1979. pap. text ed. 18.95 (*0-275-91481-X*, B1481, Praeger Pubs) Greenwood.

— People in Culture: A Survey of Cultural Anthropology. LC 79-11842. (Praeger Special Studies). 640p. 1980. text ed. 89.50 (*0-275-90542-X*, C0542, Praeger Pubs) Greenwood.

Rossi, Jacques. The Gulag Handbook: An Encyclopedia Dictionary of Soviet Penal Institutions. Burnhans, William, tr. 610p. 1989. 29.95 (*1-55778-024-2*) Prof World Peace.

Rossi, John V. Snakes of the United States & Canada, Vol. One, Eastern Area: Keeping Them Healthy in Captivity. 224p. (Orig.). 1992. lib. bdg. 49.50 (*0-89464-590-0*) Krieger.

Rossi, John V. & Rossi, Roxanne. Snakes of the United States & Canada: Keeping Them Healthy in Captivity, Vol. II: Western Area. 2nd ed. LC 91-2199. 342p. 1994. 74.50 (*0-89464-808-X*) Krieger.

Rossi, Joseph S. American Catholics & the Formation of the United Nations. LC 92-37604. (Melville Studies in Church History: Vol. 4). 1993. 59.50 (*0-8191-8548-5*); pap. 34.00 (*0-8191-8549-3*) U Pr of Amer.

***Rossi, Joyce.** The Gullywasher. Murphy, Erin, ed. (Illus.). 32p. (J). (ps up). 1995. 14.95 (*0-87358-607-7*) Northland AZ.

Rossi, Kevin. Lawn Care & Gardening: A Down-to-Earth Guide to the Business. LC 93-74400. (Illus.). 240p. (Orig.). 1994. pap. 21.95 (*0-9639371-9-7*) Acton Circle.

Rossi-Landi, Ferruccio. Between Sign & Non-Sign. Petrilli, Susan, ed. LC 92-24183. (Critical Theory Ser.: No. 10). xxix, 322p. 1992. 89.00x (*1-55619-177-4*) Benjamins North Am.

— Ideologies of Linguistic Relativity. LC 72-94502. (Approaches to Semiotics Ser.: No. 4). 101p. 1974. pap. text ed. 29.25 (*90-279-2594-1*) Mouton.

— Language As Work & Trade: A Semiotic Homology for Linguistics & Economics. LC 82-4432. 224p. 1983. text ed. 49.95 (*0-89789-022-1*, Bergin & Garvey) Greenwood.

— Linguistics & Economics. (Janua Linguarum, Series Major: No. 81). 240p. 1977. pap. text ed. 30.00 (*90-279-3243-3*) Mouton.

— Marxism & Ideology. Griffin, Roger, tr. (Marxist Introductions Ser.). (Illus.). 384p. 1990. 74.00 (*0-19-876127-9*) OUP.

Rossi, Leandro & Valsecchi, Ambrogio. Diccionario Enciclopedico de Teologia Moral: Encyclopedic Dictionary of Theological Morality. 1488p. (SPA.). 1978. pap. 35.00 (*0-8288-5458-0*, S50078) Fr & Eur.

— Diccionario Enciclopedico de Teologia Moral: Encyclopedic Dictionary of Theological Morality. 3rd ed. 1488p. (SPA.). 1978. 53.95 (*0-8288-5129-8*, S50077) Fr & Eur.

— Diccionario Enciclopedico de Teologia Moral: Suplemento: Encyclopedic Dictionary of Theological Morality, Supplement. 256p. (SPA.). 1978. 49.95 (*0-8288-5130-1*, S50079) Fr & Eur.

Rossi, Lee. Beyond Rescue: New Poems. 72p. (Orig.). 1991. pap. 7.95 (*0-941017-19-2*) Bombshelter Pr.

Rossi, Lee D. The Politics of Fantasy: C. S. Lewis & J. R. R. Tolkien. Scholes, Robert, ed. LC 84-16116. (Studies in Speculative Fiction: No. 10). 154p. reprint ed. 43.70 (*0-8357-1597-3*, 2070437) Bks Demand.

Rossi, Lee D., et al. Computer Notions. (Illus.). 176p. (C). 1985. pap. text ed. 15.50 (*0-13-163932-3*) P-H.

Rossi, Lillian. Process: Vision & Re-Vision. 78p. (C). 1992. pap. text ed. 5.50 (*0-685-67277-8*) Nat Writing Proj.

Rossi, Louis S. Six Years on the West Coast of America, 1856-1862. Wortley, W. Victor, tr. (Illus.). 376p. 1983. 19.95 (*0-87770-293-4*) Ye Galleon.

Rossi, Mario. Acoustics & Electroacoustics. Roe, Patrick R., tr. LC 88-2176. (Illus.). 768p. reprint ed. pap. 180.00 (*0-7837-4620-2*, 2044341) Bks Demand.

— Roosevelt & the French. LC 93-12973. 224p. 1993. text ed. 55.00 (*0-275-94613-4*, C4613, Praeger Pubs) Greenwood.

Rossi, Mary A. Theocritis' "Idyll XVII" A Stylistic Commentary. vii, 249p. 1989. pap. 54.00 (*90-256-0967-8*, Pub. by A M Hakkert NE) Benjamins North Am.

Rossi, Michael, jt. auth. see Goldman, Norma.

Rossi, Miram, jt. auth. see Patterson, Betty K.

Rossi, Mitchell S. Hong Kong Papers. 1989. pap. 3.95 (*1-55817-215-7*, Pinnacle NY) Windsor NY.

Rossi, Nick. Hearing Music: An Introduction. 428p. (Orig.). (C). 1981. pap. text ed. 2.00 (*0-15-535598-8*) HB Coll Pubs.

— Hearing Music: An Introduction, Set of 6. 428p. (Orig.). (C). 1981. lp 28.75 (*0-15-535599-6*) HB Coll Pubs.

— Opera in Italy Today: A Guide. (Illus.). 1995. pap. 24.95 (*0-931340-77-2*, Amadeus Pr) Timber.

Rossi, Norma M., jt. auth. see LoSardo, Mary M.

Rossi, Paolo. The Dark Abyss of Time: The History of the Earth & the History of Nations from Hooke to Vico. Cochrane, Lydia G., tr. LC 84-8481. 352p. 1985. 35.00 (*0-226-72835-8*) U Ch Pr.

— The Dark Abyss of Time: The History of the Earth & the History of Nations from Hooke to Vico. Cochrane, Lydia G., tr. LC 84-8481. 352p. 1987. pap. text ed. 14.95 (*0-226-72832-3*) U Ch Pr.

Rossi, Patrizio. Roberto Rossellini: A Guide to References & Resources. 1988. text ed. 50.00 (*0-8161-7911-5*, Hall Reference) Macmillan.

Rossi, Patrizio & Radcliff-Umstead, Douglas. Italiano Oggi: Italian Review Grammar. LC 71-146362. (ITA.). (C). 1976. reprint ed. pap. text ed. 12.95 (*0-89197-638-8*) Irvington.

Rossi, Paul. Art of the Old West. 1981. 29.98 (*0-88394-045-0*) Promntory Pr.

Rossi, Peter. Without Shelter: Homelessness in the 1980s. (Twentieth Century Fund Paper Ser.). 1989. 18.95 (*0-87078-235-5*); pap. 8.95 (*0-87078-234-7*) TCFP-PPP.

Rossi, Peter & Freeman, Howard E. Evaluation: A Systematic Approach. 5th ed. (Illus.). 512p. (C). 1993. text ed. 42.00 (*0-8039-4458-6*) Sage.

Rossi, Peter, jt. auth. see Senelick, Richard C.

Rossi, Peter H. Down & Out in America: The Origins of Homelessness. LC 89-31598. (Illus.). 264p. 1991. pap. 10.95 (*0-226-72829-3*) U Ch Pr.

— Why Families Move. LC 79-25370. 243p. reprint ed. pap. 69.30 (*0-7837-4558-3*, 2044086) Bks Demand.

Rossi, Peter H., ed. Ghetto Revolts. 2nd ed. LC 72-91469. (Society Bks.). 171p. 1970. reprint ed. 27.95 (*0-87855-067-4*); reprint ed. pap. text ed. 15.95 (*0-87855-564-1*) Transaction Pubs.

Rossi, Peter H. & Biddle, Bruce J., eds. The New Media & Education: Their Impact on Society. LC 66-19580. (Monographs in Social Research: No. 12). 1966. 11.95 (*0-202-09005-1*) NORC.

Rossi, Peter H. & Dentler, Robert A. The Politics of Urban Renewal: The Chicago Findings. LC 81-6327. (Illus.). ix, 308p. 1981. reprint ed. text ed. 65.00 (*0-313-22780-2*, ROPR, Greenwood Pr) Greenwood.

Rossi, Peter H. & Lyall, Katharine C. Reforming Public Welfare: A Critique of the Negative Income Tax Experiment. LC 75-41509. 208p. 1976. 29.95 (*0-87154-754-6*) Russell Sage.

Rossi, Peter H. & Pereira, Joseph A. Who Should Be Supported? New Yorkers' Normative Views of Public Assistance Entitlement. 20p. (Orig.). 1985. pap. 2.25 (*0-88156-040-5*) Comm Serv Soc NY.

Rossi, Peter H., jt. auth. see Berk, Richard A.

Rossi, Peter H., jt. ed. see Chen, Huey-tsyh.

Rossi, Peter H., jt. auth. see Greeley, Andrew M.

Rossi, Peter H., jt. auth. see Rossi, Alice S.

Rossi, Peter H., jt. auth. see Wright, James D.

Rossi, Peter H., jt. ed. see Wright, James D.

Rossi, Peter H., et al. Handbook of Survey Research. (Quantitative Studies in Social Relations). 1985. pap. text ed. 49.95 (*0-12-598227-5*) Acad Pr.

— Victims of the Environment: Loss from Natural Hazards In the United States, 1970-1980. 256p. 1983. 54.50 (*0-306-41413-9*, Plenum Pr) Plenum.

Rossi, Peter M. & White, Wayne E., eds. Articles on the Middle East, 1947-1971: A Cumulation of Bibliographies from the Middle East Journal, 4 vols., Set. LC 79-91337. (Cumulated Bibliography Ser.: No. 7). 1980. 180.00 (*0-87650-030-0*) Pierian.

Rossi, Philip. Together Toward Hope: A Journey to Moral Theology. LC 83-1279. 224p. 1983. 22.95 (*0-268-01844-8*) U of Notre Dame Pr.

Rossi, Philip J. & Soukup, Paul, eds. Mass Media & the Moral Imagination. LC 93-30845. (Orig.). 1994. pap. 24.95 (*1-55612-622-0*) Sheed & Ward MO.

R

Rossi, Philip J. & Wreen, Michael, eds. Kant's Philosophy of Religion Reconsidered. LC 90-27310. (Indiana Series in the Philosophy of Religion). 244p. 1991. 25.00 (*0-253-35027-1*) Ind U Pr.

Rossi, Rita H., jt. ed. see Rossi, Roberto A.

Rossi, Robert J. Schools & Students at Risk: Context & Framework for Positive Change. LC 93-44316. 336p. (C). 1994. text ed. 48.00 (*0-8077-3326-1*); pap. 23.95 (*0-8077-3325-3*) Tchrs Coll.

Rossi, Robert J., jt. ed. see Gilmartin, Kevin J.

Rossi, Robert J., et al. Using the Talent Profiles in Counseling: A Supplement to the Career Data Book. 1975. pap. 5.25 (*0-89785-516-7*) Am Inst Res.

Rossi, Roberto A. & Rossi, Rita H., eds. Aromatic Substitution by the SRN1 Mechanism. LC 82-22829. (ACS Monograph: No. 178). 300p. 1983. lib. bdg. 54.95 (*0-8412-0648-1*) Am Chemical.

Rossi, Roxanne, jt. auth. see Rossi, John V.

Rossi, Sanna B. Anthony T. Rossi. LC 86-27651. 199p. 1986. pap. 9.99 (*0-8308-4999-8*, 4999) InterVarsity.

Rossi, Sara. Collector's Guide to Paperweights. 1990. 12.98 (*1-55521-541-6*) Bk Sales Inc.

Rossi, Steve. Dirty! Dirty! Dirty! You Should Be Ashamed to Buy This Joke Book! 160p. (Orig.). 1989. pap. 2.95 (*0-8439-2869-7*) Dorchester Pub Co.

Rossi, T., jt. auth. see Cittadini, E.

Rossi, Ted. Step by Step: How to Actively Ensure the Best Possible Care for Your Aging Relative. 192p. 1987. pap. 9.95 (*0-446-38427-5*) Warner Bks.

Rossi, Vanessa, jt. auth. see Heri, Erwin W.

Rossi, Vinio. Andre Gide. LC 68-54458. (Columbia Essays on Modern Writers Ser.: No. 35). (Orig.). (C). 1968. pap. text ed. 7.50 (*0-231-02960-8*) Col U Pr.

Rossi, Vinio, tr. see Raboni, Giovanni.

Rossi, William. Profitable Footwear Retailing. 335p. 1988. lib. bdg. 24.00 (*0-87005-630-1*) Fairchild.

Rossi, William, ed. see Thoreau, Henry David.

Rossi, William A. The Complete Footwear Dictionary. LC 91-48230. 171p. 1994. lib. bdg. 34.50 (*0-89464-715-6*) Krieger.

— The Sex Life of the Foot & Shoe. LC 90-24686. 272p. 1993. reprint ed. pap. 26.50 (*0-89464-756-3*) Krieger.

Rossides, Daniel W. American Society: An Introduction to Macrosociology. LC 91-75942. 550p. 1993. lib. bdg. 39.95 (*0-930390-16-4*) Gen Hall.

— American Society: An Introduction to Macrosociology. LC 92-75606. 695p. 1993. text ed. 64.95 (*1-882289-05-6*); pap. text ed. 39.95 (*1-882289-04-8*) Gen Hall.

— Comparative Societies. 592p. (C). 1990. text ed. write for info. (*0-13-155318-6*) P-H.

— Social Stratification. 560p. (C). 1989. Casebound. text ed. write for info. (*0-13-817578-0*) P-H.

Rossides, Eugene T. Foreign Unfair Competition: Practice & Procedure. 3rd rev. ed. (Corporate Practice Ser.: No. 28). 1990. ring bd. 95.00 (*1-55871-107-4*) BNA.

— United States Import Trade Regulation. LC 84-23748. 768p. reprint ed. pap. 180.00 (*0-7837-4597-4*, 2044316) Bks Demand.

Rossides, Eugene T. & Maravel, Alexandra. U. S. Import Trade Law, 2 vols. 1350p. 1992. ring bd. 200.00 (*0-88063-803-6*) Michie Butterworth.

Rossie, John P. Handbook for Aerospace Education. rev. ed. Duca, Victoria, ed. LC 89-83438. 108p. (Orig.). 1989. reprint ed. pap. 6.00 (*0-9620988-0-9*) Aerospace EDP.

Rossie, John P., pref. Handbook Two for Aerospace Education: A Guide to Projects & Applications. LC 91-60903. (Illus.). 398p. (Orig.). 1991. pap. text ed. 19.50 (*0-911168-80-X*) Prakken.

Rossie, Jonathan G. The Politics of Command in the American Revolution. 272p. 1975. 35.00x (*0-8156-0112-3*) Syracuse U Pr.

Rossie, Jonathan G., jt. ed. see Gibson, Frederick W.

***Rossier, Bernard.** Hermeneutical Principles of Pentecostals. 80p. (Orig.). 1994. pap. text ed. 8.95 (*0-930401-72-7*) Artex Pub.

— The New Testament Church. 104p. (Orig.). 1990. pap. 8.00 (*0-930401-31-X*) Artex Pub.

— Prison Epistles: Praise from Prison. 272p. (C). 1987. 14.95 (*0-912981-18-0*) Hse BonGiovanni.

— Professionalism in Pentecostal Education. 96p. 1992. pap. 7.95 (*0-930401-50-6*) Artex Pub.

— Proper Pattern for Pentecostal Postsecondary Education. 96p. 1992. pap. text ed. 7.95 (*0-930401-53-0*) Artex Pub.

Rossier, H. Meditations on Joshua. 7.25 (*0-88172-119-0*) Believers Bkshelf.

— Que Pasa Despues de la Muerte? 2nd ed. Bennett, Gordon H., ed. Bautista, Sara, tr. (Serie Diamante). (Illus.). 36p. (SPA.). 1982. pap. 0.85 (*0-942504-07-0*) Overcomer Pr.

— Second Kings. 11.50 (*0-88172-182-4*) Believers Bkshelf.

Rossier, H. L. Meditations on First Kings. 210p. 8.95 (*0-88172-165-4*) Believers Bkshelf.

Rossignol, J. & Wandsnider, L., eds. Space, Time, & Archeological Landscapes. (Interdisciplinary Contributions to Archaeology Ser.). (Illus.). 275p. 1992. 47.50 (*0-306-44161-6*, Plenum Pr) Plenum.

Rossing, John P. Daring to Hope: Sermons for Pentecost First Lesson, Cycle B. LC 93-2759. 1993. pap. 6.50 (*1-55673-615-0*) CSS OH.

— A Season of Saints. 1991. pap. 8.25 (*1-55673-408-5*, 9221) CSS OH.

Rossing, Karl-Johan. Letters of Henry Handel Richardson to Nettie Palmer. (Essays & Studies on English Language & Literature: Vol. 14). 1953. pap. 15.00 (*0-8115-0212-0*) Periodicals Srv.

***Rossing, T. D. & Fletcher, N. H.** Principles of Vibration & Sound. 250p. 1994. pap. text ed. 34.50 (*0-387-94336-6*) Spr-Verlag.

Rossing, Thomas D. Science of Sound: Musical, Electronic, Environmental. LC 80-12028. (Chemistry Ser.). (Illus.). 512p. 1982. text ed. write for info. (*0-201-06505-3*) Addison-Wesley.

Rossing, Thomas D., ed. Environmental Noise Control. 196p. 1979. 18.00 (*0-318-41411-2*, RB-30) Am Assn Physics.

— Musical Acoustics: Selected Reprints. (Reprint Bks.: No. RB-51). (Illus.). 227p. (Orig.). (C). 1988. pap. text ed. 18.00 (*0-917853-30-X*) Am Assn Physics.

Rossing, Thomas D. & Flechter, N. H. The Physics of Musical Instruments. (Illus.). xvii, 620p. 1991. 69.00 (*0-387-96947-0*) Spr-Verlag.

Rossing, Thomas D. & Fletcher, Neville H. Principles of Vibration & Sound. LC 94-15494. 1994. 49.95 (*0-387-94304-8*) Spr-Verlag.

Rossing, Thomas D., jt. auth. see Fletcher, Neville H.

Rossington, David R., et al, eds. Advances in Materials Characterization. LC 83-4186. (Materials Science Research Ser.: Vol. 15). 692p. 1983. 130.00 (*0-306-41347-7*, Plenum Pr) Plenum.

Rossington, Michael, jt. ed. see Perry, Gill.

Rossini, Francesco P., et al, eds. Recent Progress in Colorectal Cancer: Biology & Management of High Risk Groups, Proceedings of the 5th International Symposium on Colorectal Cancer, Biology & Management of High Risk Groups, Torino, 24-26 September 1991. LC 92-10023. (International Congress Ser.: No. 990). 1992. write for info. (*0-444-89310-5*, Excerpta Medica) Elsevier.

Rossini, Frank. Sparking the Rain. Moody, Rodger & Roorda, Randall, eds. (Illus.). 28p. 1979. pap. 3.00 (*0-9610508-1-0*) Silverfish Rev Pr.

Rossini, Gioachino. Album Francais - Morceaux Reserves: 24 Vocal Pieces (7 Additional Pieces in Appendix) Dalmonte, Rossana, ed. xlii, 404p. 1991. 100.00 (*0-226-72843-9*) U Ch Pr.

— The Barber of Seville & Moses. John, Nicholas, ed. Dent, Edward J. et al, trs. LC 85-52162. (English National Opera Guide Series: Bilingual Libretto, Articles: No. 36). (Illus.). 160p. (Orig.). (C). 1986. pap. 9.95 (*0-7145-4080-3*, LIBRETTO, ARTICLES, NO. 36) Riverrun NY.

— La Cenerentola. John, Nicholas, ed. Jacobs, Arthur, tr. (English National Opera Guide Series: Bilingual Libretto, Articles: No. 1). (Illus.). (Orig.). 1980. pap. 9.95 (*0-7145-3819-1*) Riverrun NY.

— La Donna del Lago: Melo-Dramma in Two Acts, 4 vols. Slim, H. Colin, ed. (Works of Gioachino Rossini Critical Edition Ser.). 1992. 300.00 (*0-226-72844-7*) U Ch Pr.

— Edipo Coloneo. Tozzi, Lorenzo & Weiss, Piero, eds. Cagli, Bruno et al, trs. (Works of Gioachino Rossini Ser.). xxv, 176p. 1986. lib. bdg. 65.00 (*0-226-72837-4*, 728374) U Ch Pr.

— La Gazza Ladra, 3 vols., Set. Zedda, Alberto et al, eds. (Works of Gioachino Rossini Ser.). 220p. 1986. One vol. pap., 220p., set. pap. 260.00 (*0-226-72841-2*) U Ch Pr.

— Guillaume Tell: Melodramma Tragico in Four Acts by Etienne de Jouy & Hippolyte Bis, 4 vols. Bartlet, M. Elizabeth, ed. (Works of Gioachino Rossini Critical Edition Ser.: Section I: Operas). 1993. 400.00 (*0-226-72846-3*) U Ch Pr.

— Le Nozze di Teti, e di Peleo: Azione Coro-Drammatica by Angelo Maria Ricci, Vol. 3. Joerg, Guido J., ed. 390p. 1994. 75.00 (*0-226-72847-1*) U Ch Pr.

— L' Occasione fa il Ladro, Ossia il Cambio della Valigia. Ballola, Giovanni C. et al, eds. 108p. 1995. lib. bdg. 135.00 (*0-226-72849-8*) U Ch Pr.

— Otello, Ossia il Moro di Venezia: Dramma per Musica in Three Acts by Francesco Berio de Salsa, 3 vols. Collins, Michael, ed. (Critical Edition of the Worlds of Gioachino Rossini, Section 1: Operas: Vol. 19). 961p. 1995. 195.00x (*0-226-72850-1*) U Ch Pr.

— Quelques Riens Pour Album, 1 vol. Tartak, Marvin, ed. Cagli, Bruno et al, trs. (Works of Gioachino Rossini Ser.). xxii, 224p. 1986. lib. bdg. 65.00 (*0-226-72839-0*, 728390) U Ch Pr.

— Ricciardo E. Zoraide, 2 vols., Set. LC 76-49184. (Early Romantic Opera Ser.: Vol. 10). 1979. lib. bdg. 30.00 (*0-8240-2909-7*) Garland.

— La Scala Di Seta: Farsa Comica in One Act, 2 vols., Set. Wiklund, Anders, ed. (Works of Gioachino Rossini Critical Edition Ser.). 1992. lib. bdg. 180.00 (*0-226-72845-5*) U Ch Pr.

— Il Signor Bruschino. Fazzanigo, Arrigo, ed. Cagli, Bruno et al, trs. (Works of Gioachino Rossini Ser.). xxxv, 426p. 1987. XXXV, 426 p. plus one vol. pap., 78 p. lib. bdg. 180.00 (*0-226-72836-6*, 728366) U Ch Pr.

— Tancredi, 2 vols. Gossett, Philip, ed. Cagli, Bruno et al, trs. (Works of Gioachino Rossini Ser.). 200p. 1986. One vol. pap., 200 p. pap. 260.00 (*0-226-72838-2*, 718382) U Ch Pr.

— Il Turco in Italia: Dramma Buffo in Two Acts. Bent, Margaret, ed. 1280p. 1988. lib. bdg. 250.00 (*0-226-72842-0*) U Ch Pr.

Rossini, P. M. & Mauguiere, F. New Trends & Advanced Techniques in Clinical Neurophysiology. (Supplement to EEG Ser.: Vol. 41). 1991. 248.25 (*0-444-81352-7*) Elsevier.

Rossini, Stephane. Egyptian Hieroglyphics: How to Read & Write Them. 1989. pap. 4.95 (*0-486-26013-5*) Dover.

Rossino, John. Cobb County . . . a Portrait. 95p. (Orig.). 1988. pap. write for info. (*0-318-64426-6*) CCCC.

Rossinski, K. I., ed. Dynamics & Thermal Regimes of Rivers, Vol. 52. Mishra, R. K., tr. 417p. (C). 1987. text ed. 105.00 (*90-6191-486-8*, Pub. by A A Balkema NE) Ashgate Pub Co.

Rossinskii, K. I. Dynamics & Thermal Regimes of Rivers. 1986. 18.50 (*81-204-0185-9*, Pub. by Oxford IBH II) S Asia.

***Rossipaul.** Woerterbuch Englisch Elektronische Windows Version. (ENG & GER.). 1994. 49.95 (*0-614-00372-5*, 3876865247) Fr & Eur.

— Woerterbuch Englisch Macintosh Version. (ENG & GER.). 1994. 75.00 (*0-614-00377-6*, 3876867622) Fr & Eur.

— Woerterbuch Franzoesich - Windows Version. (FRE & GER.). 1994. 49.95 (*0-614-00373-3*, 3876865255) Fr & Eur.

— Woerterbuch Handelsenglisch - Windows Version. (ENG & GER.). 1994. write for info. (*0-614-00374-1*, 387686528X) Fr & Eur.

— Woerterbuch Italienisch - Windows Version. (GER & ITA.). 1994. 49.95 (*0-614-00375-X*, 3876865263) Fr & Eur.

— Woerterbuch Spanisch - Macintosh Version. (GER & SPA.). 1994. 75.00 (*0-614-00378-4*, 3876867614) Fr & Eur.

— Woerterbuch Spanische - Windows Version. (GER & SPA.). 1994. 49.95 (*0-7859-7230-7*, 3876865271) Fr & Eur.

Rossitch, Eugene, jt. auth. see Black, Peter M.

***Rossiter.** Casper. (J). 1995. pap. text ed. 2.50 (*0-307-12834-2*, Golden Pr) Western Pub.

Rossiter, A. P. Angel with Horns: Fifteen Lectures on Shakespeare. 316p. (Orig.). (C). 1989. pap. text ed. 22.75 (*0-582-01499-9*, 78287) Longman.

***Rossiter, Alan P., ed.** Waste Minimization Through Process Design. LC 94-49707. 1995. text ed. 55.00 (*0-07-053957-X*) McGraw.

Rossiter, B. W., jt. ed. see Weissberger, A.

Rossiter, Bryant W. & Baetzold, Roger C. Physical Methods of Chemistry: Investigations of Surfaces & Interfaces, Vol. 9. 2nd ed. LC 92-24513. 768p. 1993. text ed. 299.00 (*0-471-54405-1*) Wiley.

Rossiter, Bryant W. & Baetzold, Roger C., eds. Determination of Electronic & Optical Properties, Vol. 8. 2nd ed. LC 92-24323. (Physical Methods of Chemistry Ser.: Vol. 8). 544p. 1993. text ed. 165.00 (*0-471-54407-8*) Wiley.

— Investigations of Surfaces & Interfaces, Part A, Vol. 9. 2nd ed. (Physical Methods of Chemistry Ser.: Vol. 9A). 528p. 1992. text ed. 165.00 (*0-471-54406-X*) Wiley.

— Physical Methods of Chemistry, 12, Vol. 12. 2nd ed. 1993. text ed. 2,230.00 (*0-471-02577-1*) Wiley.

Rossiter, Bryant W. & Hamilton, John F. Physical Methods of Chemistry, 3 vols., Vol. 1. 2nd ed. LC 85-6386. (Techniques of Chemistry Ser.). 1986. text ed. 240.00 (*0-471-08034-9*) Wiley.

— Physical Methods of Chemistry, 3 vols., Vol. 2. 2nd ed. LC 85-6386. (Techniques of Chemistry Ser.). 904p. 1986. text ed. 255.00 (*0-471-08027-6*) Wiley.

— Physical Methods of Chemistry, 3 vols., Vol. 3. 2nd ed. LC 85-6386. (Techniques of Chemistry Ser.). 971p. 1989. text ed. 225.00 (*0-471-85051-9*) Wiley.

Rossiter, Bryant W. & Hamilton, John F., eds. Physical Methods of Chemistry: Determination of Thermodynamic Properties, Vol. 6. 2nd ed. 760p. 1992. text ed. 299.00 (*0-471-57087-7*) Wiley.

— Physical Methods of Chemistry: Part A: Determination of Chemical Composition & Molecular Structure, Vol. 3. 2nd ed. 624p. 1987. text ed. 195.00 (*0-471-85041-1*) Wiley.

— Physical Methods of Chemistry Vol. 4: Microscopy, Vol. 4. 2nd ed. 560p. 1991. text ed. 199.00 (*0-471-08026-8*) Wiley.

— Physical Methods of Chemistry Vol. 5: Determination of Structural Features of Crystalline & Amorphous Solids, Vol. 5. 2nd ed. 618p. 1990. text ed. 195.00 (*0-471-52509-X*) Wiley.

Rossiter, Bryant W., et al, eds. Physical Methods of Chemistry Vol. 7: Determination of Elastic & Mechanical Properties, Vol. 7. 2nd ed. 313p. 1991. text ed. 135.00 (*0-471-53438-2*) Wiley.

Rossiter, C. J. Vendor & Purchaser: Commentary & Materials. xxviii, 436p. 1985. pap. 59.00 (*0-455-20607-4*, Pub. by Law Bk Co) W W Gaunt.

Rossiter, Charles, et al. Thirds. LC 85-70935. (Illus.). 64p. (Orig.). 1985. pap. 3.95 (*0-9614525-0-1*) Distant Pr.

Rossiter, Clinton. The American Presidency. LC 87-2824. 304p. (Orig.). 1987. reprint ed. pap. 13.95 (*0-8018-3545-3*) Johns Hopkins.

— Conservatism in America. 320p. 1982. pap. 13.95 (*0-674-16510-1*) HUP.

— The First American Revolution: The American Colonies on the Eve of Independence. rev. ed. LC 56-13741. Orig. Title: Seedtime of the Republic, Pt. 1. 245p. 1956. pap. 9.95 (*0-15-631121-6*, Harvest Bks) HarBrace.

— Parties & Politics in America. 212p. 1960. 34.00 (*0-8014-0364-2*); pap. 12.95 (*0-8014-9021-9*) Cornell U Pr.

— Seventeen Eighty-Seven: The Grand Convention. (Illus.). 464p. 1987. reprint ed. pap. 13.95 (*0-393-30404-3*) Norton.

— The Supreme Court & the Commander in Chief. Longaker, Richard P., ed. LC 76-12815. 280p. 1976. 37.95 (*0-8014-1052-5*); pap. 14.95 (*0-8014-9161-4*) Cornell U Pr.

— Supreme Court & the Commander in Chief. LC 76-98182. 1970. reprint ed. lib. bdg. 22.50 (*0-306-71832-4*) Da Capo.

Rossiter, Clinton & Lare, James, eds. The Essential Lippmann: A Political Philosophy for Liberal Democracy. 576p. 1982. pap. text ed. 15.95 (*0-674-26775-3*) HUP.

Rossiter, Clinton, ed. see Hamilton, Alexander, et al.

Rossiter, Clinton L. Conservatism in America: The Thankless Persuasion. 2nd rev. ed. LC 80-27937. xii, 306p. 1981. reprint ed. text ed. 35.00 (*0-313-22720-9*, ROCN, Greenwood Pr) Greenwood.

Rossiter, Elizabeth. The Lemon Garden. 256p. 1992. 4.50 (*0-88184-888-3*) Carroll & Graf.

— The Lemon Garden. large type ed. LC 91-30943. 455p. 1991. reprint ed. bds. 19.95 (*1-56054-261-6*) Thorndike Pr.

Rossiter, Evelyn, tr. see Boldin, Valery.

Rossiter, Graham, jt. auth. see Crawford, Marisa.

Rossiter, Jane, jt. auth. see Mellett, Peter.

Rossiter, John R. Advertising & Promotion Management. 1987. text ed. write for info. (*0-07-053907-3*) McGraw.

Rossiter, John R., jt. auth. see Percy, Larry.

Rossiter, Louis F., jt. ed. see Scheffler, Richard M.

Rossiter, Luois F., jt. ed. see Scheffler, Richard M.

Rossiter, Margaret, jt. ed. see Kohlstedt, Sally.

Rossiter, Margaret L. Women in the Resistance. LC 85-16746. (Illus.). 256p. 1985. text ed. 59.95 (*0-275-90222-6*, C0222, Praeger Pubs) Greenwood.

***Rossiter, Margaret W.** Women Scientists in America: Before Affirmative Action, 1940-1972. 624p. 1995. 35.95 (*0-8018-4893-8*) Johns Hopkins.

— Women Scientists in America: Struggles & Strategies to 1940. LC 81-20902. 1984. reprint ed. pap. 15.95x (*0-8018-2509-1*) Johns Hopkins.

Rossiter, Margaret W., jt. ed. see Elliott, Clark A.

Rossiter, Paul L. The Electrical Resistivity of Metals & Alloys. (Solid State Science Ser.). (Illus.). 434p. (C). 1991. pap. 44.95 (*0-521-40872-5*) Cambridge U Pr.

Rossiter, Phyllis. The Living History of the Ozarks. LC 92-5309. (Illus.). 192p. 1992. 25.00 (*0-685-59080-1*); pap. 19.95 (*0-88289-801-9*) Pelican.

— Moxie. LC 90-30027. 192p. (J). (gr. 5 up). 1990. text ed. 14.95 (*0-02-777831-2*, Four Winds Pr) S&S Childrens.

— On the Scent of Danger. large type ed. LC 93-30109. 1993. pap. 13.95 (*0-7862-0045-6*) Thorndike Pr.

***Rossiter, Richard.** Best of Boulder Climbs. (Illus.). 180p. (Orig.). 1992. pap. 15.00 (*0-934641-26-9*) Chockstone Pr.

— Boulder Climbs North. 2nd ed. (Illus.). 130p. 1995. pap. write for info. (*0-614-05455-9*) Chockstone Pr.

— Boulder Climbs South. (Illus.). 420p. (Orig.). 1990. pap. 25.00 (*0-934641-15-3*) Chockstone Pr.

— Boulder Sport Climbs. (Illus.). 120p. (Orig.). Date not set. pap. 12.95 (*0-614-05454-0*) Chockstone Pr.

— Climber's Guide to Rocky Mountain National Park: The Crags. (Illus.). 300p. 1995. pap. 20.00 (*0-934641-34-X*) Chockstone Pr.

— Climber's Guide to Rocky Mountain National Park: The High Peaks. (Illus.). 144p. (Orig.). 1995. pap. 15.00 (*0-614-07053-8*) Chockstone Pr.

— Teton Classics: Fifty Selected Climbs in Grand Teton National Park. 2nd ed. (Illus.). 136p. 1994. pap. 15.00 (*0-934641-71-4*) Chockstone Pr.

Rossiter, Rick. The Greedy Man in the Moon. 32p. (J). (gr. k-3). 1994. pap. 4.50 (*0-87406-708-1*) Willowisp Pr.

Rossiter, Sean, jt. auth. see MacLean, Robert M.

Rossiter, Val. Electromagnetism. LC 81-214054. 180p. reprint ed. pap. 51.30 (*0-317-41976-5*, 2025978) Bks Demand.

Rossiter, Walter J., Jr., ed. Roofing Technology Conference, 9th: Proceedings. 98p. 1989. 28.00 (*0-934809-05-4*) Natl Roofing Cont.

Rossiter, Walter J., jt. ed. see Wallace, J.

Rossiter, Walter J., Jr., jt. ed. see Wallace, Thomas J.

Rossitto, Constance C. Daily Lessons for the Visiting Teacher: A Better Way. 1979. text ed. 19.95 (*0-201-06421-9*) Addison-Wesley.

Rossiya, Sovetskaya. Folk Russian Costume. 309p. (C). 1989. 250.00 (*0-89771-819-4*, Pub. by Collets) St Mut.

Rosskam, Edwin, photos. Twelve Million Black Voices. (Classic Reprint Ser.). 160p. 1988. reprint ed. pap. 15.95 (*0-938410-44-X*) Thunders Mouth.

Rosskopf, Myron F. Children's Mathematical Concepts: Six Piagetian Studies in Mathematics Education. LC 75-12872. (Illus.). 224p. reprint ed. pap. 63.90 (*0-317-09439-4*, 2017767) Bks Demand.

Rosskopf, W. J., Jr., jt. auth. see Woerpel, R. W.

***Rossler.** Woerterbuch der Deutschen Geschichte, 3 vols. 2nd rev. ed. (GER.). Date not set. 350.00 (*0-7859-7233-1*, 3907820835) Fr & Eur.

Rossler, jt. auth. see El Naschie.

Rossler, E., jt. auth. see Kothe, H. K.

Rossler, Eberhard. The U-Boat: Evolution & Technical History of German Submarines. LC 81-81198. (Illus.). 384p. 1981. 49.95 (*0-87021-966-9*) Naval Inst Pr.

Rossler, Horst, jt. ed. see Hoerder, Dirk.

Rossler, Otto E. Bifurcation Theory & Applications in Scientific Disciplines, Vol. 316. Gurel, Okan, ed. (Annals Ser.). 708p. (Orig.). 1979. pap. 87.00 (*0-89766-000-5*) NY Acad Sci.

Rossler, Ulrich, ed. Advances in Solid State Physics, 32 - Festkorperprobleme: Plenary Lectures of the Divisions Semiconductor Physics, Thin Films, Dynamics & Statistical Physics of the German Physical Society (DPG), Regensburg, March 16-20, 1992. viii, 372p. 1992. 124.00 (*3-528-08040-X*, Pub. by Vieweg & Sohn GW) Ballen Bkslr.

Rossley, Peter J., jt. auth. see Goudel, Yann.

Rosslin, Eucharius. When Midwifery Became the Male Physician's Province: The Sixteenth Century Handbook "The Rose Garden for Pregnant Women & Midwives," Newly Enlisted. Arons, Wendy, tr. & intro. by. (Illus.). 143p. 1994. lib. bdg. 29.95 (*0-89950-934-7*) McFarland & Co.

Rosslyn, F. Pope's Iliad: A Selection with Commentary. 256p. 1985. 36.95 (*0-86292-049-3*, Pub. by Brstl Class Pr UK) Focus Info Gr.

Rosslyn, Felicity. Alexander Pope: A Literary Life. LC 89-24045. 220p. 1990. text ed. 39.95 (*0-312-04021-0*) St Martin.

R

An Asterisk (*) at the beginning of an entry indicates that the title is appearing in BIP for the first time.

Rossman, A. Y. Mycological Papers, No. 157: The Tubeufiaceae & Similar Loculoascomycetes. 71p. (C). 1987. pap. text ed. 29.00 (*0-85198-580-7*) CAB Intl.

Rossman, A. Y., ed. Mycological Papers, No. 150: The Phragmosporous Species of Nectria & Related Genera. 162p. (C). 1983. pap. text ed. 34.50 (*0-00-000078-7*) CAB Intl.

***Rossman, Allan J.** Workshop Statistics: Discovery with Data. LC 95-16797. (Textbooks in Mathematical Sciences). 1995. pap. write for info. (*0-387-94497-4*) Spr-Verlag.

Rossman, Amy Y., et al. A Literature Guide for the Identification of Plant Pathogenic Fungi. LC 87-70764. 252p. 1987. 26.00 (*0-89054-080-2*) Am Phytopathol Soc.

Rossman, Charles. Enchanted Rock: Views of a Texas Batholith. limited ed. Stark, David, tr. (Illus.). 96p. 1984. 125.00 (*0-9616212-0-6*); ring bd. 300.00 (*0-9616212-1-4*) Duncan & Gladstone.

Rossman, Charles, jt. ed. see Miller, Yvette E.

Rossman, Douglas A. Where Legends Live. (Illus.). 48p. (Orig.). 1988. pap. 4.95 (*0-935741-10-0*) Cherokee Pubns.

Rossman, Gretchen B., jt. auth. see Marshall, Catherine.

Rossman, Gretchen B., jt. auth. see Wilson, Bruce L.

Rossman, Gretchen B., et al. Change & Effectiveness in Schools: A Cultural Perspective. LC 87-33539. (Frontiers in Education Ser.). 173p. 1988. 64.50 (*0-88706-725-5*); pap. 21.95 (*0-88706-726-3*) State U NY Pr.

Rossman, Isadore, ed. Clinical Geriatrics. 3rd ed. LC 65-8386. (Illus.). 742p. 1986. text ed. 79.50 (*0-397-50672-4*, Lippincott Medical) Lippincott.

Rossman, Isadore & Obeck, Victor. Isometrics: The Static Way to Physical Fitness. LC 66-24095. (Illus.). 1966. 7.95 (*0-87396-017-3*); pap. 3.95 (*0-87396-018-1*) Stravon.

Rossman, Isadore, jt. auth. see Rosenberg, Magda.

Rossman, Isadore, jt. auth. see Smith, Jeanne.

Rossman, J. Robert. Recreation Programming: Designing Leisure Experiences. 2nd ed. (Illus.). 465p. 1994. 37.95 (*0-915611-95-3*) Sagamore Pub.

Rossman, Lewis A., jt. ed. see Arciszewski, Tomasz.

Rossman, M. G. The Molecular Replacement Method. (International Science Review Ser.). 276p. 1972. text ed. 239.00 (*0-677-13940-3*) Gordon & Breach.

Rossman, Marcela, tr. see Carmona-Agosto, Vivian, ed.

Rossman, Marcela, tr. see Henderson, Celina, ed.

***Rossman, Mark H.** Negotiating Graduate School: A Guide for Graduate Students. LC 95-3258. 160p. 1995. 36.00 (*0-8039-7114-1*); pap. 17.95 (*0-8039-7115-X*) Sage.

Rossman, Mark H. & Rossman, Maxine E., eds. Applying Adult Development Strategies. LC 85-644750. (New Directions for Adult & Continuing Education Ser.: No. ACE 45). 1990. 16.95 (*1-55542-820-7*) Jossey-Bass.

Rossman, Mark H., et al. Teaching & Learning Basic Skills: A Guide for Adult Basic Education & Developmental Education Programs. LC 83-9118. 188p. reprint ed. pap. 53.60 (*0-7837-3885-4*, 2043733) Bks Demand.

Rossman, Marlene L. The International Businesswoman of the 1990's: A Guide to Success in the Global Marketplace. LC 89-70950. 192p. 1990. text ed. 19.95 (*0-275-93329-6*, C3329, Greenwood Pr) Greenwood.

— Multicultural Marketing: Selling to a Diverse America. LC 93-41996. 192p. 1994. 22.95 (*0-8144-5071-7*) AMACOM.

Rossman, Martin L. Healing Yourself. 1987. 17.95 (*0-8027-0986-9*) Walker & Co.

— Healing Yourself: A Step-by-Step Program for Better Health Through Imagery. Zion, Claire, ed. (Orig.). 1994. pap. 7.95 (*0-671-66769-6*) PB.

Rossman, Maxine E., jt. ed. see Rossman, Mark H.

Rossman, Milton D. & MacGregor, Rob R. Tuberculosis. 352p. 1995. text ed. 60.00 (*0-07-053950-2*) Hlth Prof Div.

Rossman, Neil. Consciousness: Separation & Integration. LC 89-48909. 213p. 1991. 59.50 (*0-7914-0407-2*); pap. 19.95 (*0-7914-0408-0*) State U NY Pr.

Rossman, Parker. The Emerging Worldwide Electronic University: Information Age Global Higher Education. LC 92-3660. (Contributions to the Study of Education Ser.: No. 57). 184p. 1992. text ed. 49.95 (*0-313-27927-6*, REK/, Greenwood Pr) Greenwood.

— The Emerging Worldwide Electronic University: Information Age Global Higher Education. LC 92-3660. (Studies on the 21st Century). 176p. 1993. pap. text ed. 17.95 (*0-275-94776-9*, Praeger Pubs) Greenwood.

Rossman, Parker & Kirby, Richard. Christians & the World of Computers: Professional & Social Excellence in the Computer World. LC 90-41636. 160p. (Orig.). (C). 1990. pap. 12.95 (*0-334-02468-4*) TPI PA.

Rossman, Parker, jt. auth. see Bedell, Kenneth.

Rossman, Thomas D. Rack up a Victory. (Illus.). 182p. (Orig.). 1988. pap. 7.00 (*0-9626414-0-5*) T D Rossman.

Rossman, Toby G., ed. Induced Effects of Genotoxic Agents in Eukaryotic Cells. LC 92-19547. 1992. 59.50 (*1-56032-272-1*) Hemisp Pub.

Rossman, Vladimir. Perspectives of Irony in Medieval French Literature. (De Proprietatibus Litterarum, Series Major: No. 35). 198p. (Orig.). 1975. pap. text ed. 60.80 (*90-279-3291-3*) Mouton.

Rossmanith, H. P., ed. Fracture & Damage of Concrete & Rock: Proceedings of the Second International Conference on Fracture & Damage of Concrete & Rock, Vienna, Austria, 9-13 November 1992. LC 93-12576. 1993. write for info. (*0-419-18470-8*, E & FN Spon) Routledge Chapman & Hall.

— Mechanics of Jointed & Faulted Rock: Proceedings of an International Conference, Vienna, 18-20 April 1990. (Illus.). 1008p. (C). 1991. text ed. 140.00 (*90-6191-155-9*, Pub. by A A Balkema NE) Ashgate Pub Co.

— Rock Fracture Mechanics. (CISM International Centre for Mechanical Sciences Ser.: No. 275). 484p. 1983. pap. 61.00 (*0-387-81747-6*) Spr-Verlag.

— Structural Failure, Product Liability & Technical Insurance: Proceedings of the 4th International Conference on Structural Safety, Product Safety, Product Liability & Technical Insurance, Vienna, Austria, 6-9 July 1992. LC 92-38099. 1992. write for info. (*0-444-89600-7*) Elsevier.

Rossmanith, H. P. & Roskis, A. J. Dynamic Failure of Materials: Theory, Experiments & Numerics. 398p. 1991. 102.00 (*1-85166-665-6*) Elsevier.

Rossmanith, H. P., et al. Structural Failure, Product Liability, & Technical Insurance: Proceedings of the First International Conference Held at the Technical University of Vienna, Austria, September 26-29, 1983. LC 84-1519. 1984. 82.00 (*0-444-86869-0*, I-089-84, North Holland) Elsevier.

Rossmanith, Hans-Peter, ed. Rock Fragmentation by Blasting: Proceedings, 4th International Symposium, Vienna, Austria, July 1993. (Illus.). 532p. 1993. text ed. 115.00 (*90-5410-316-7*, Pub. by A A Balkema NE) Ashgate Pub Co.

Rossmanith, W. G. & Scherbaum, W. A., eds. Neuroendocrinology of Sex Steroids: Basic Knowledge & Clinical Implications. (New Developments in Biosciences Ser.: No. 6). viii, 222p. (Orig.). (C). 1993. pap. text ed. 98.50 (*3-11-013616-3*) De Gruyter.

Rossmoore, H. W., ed. Biodeterioration & Biodegradation 8: Proceedings of the 8th International Symposium 26-31 August 1990, Windsor, Ontario, Canada. 600p. 1991. 229.50 (*1-85166-626-5*) Elsevier.

Rossmoore, Harold W. The Microbes, Our Unseen Friends. LC 76-17795. 238p. reprint ed. pap. 67.90 (*0-7837-3643-6*, 2043512) Bks Demand.

Rossnagel, Stephen M., et al. Handbook of Plasma Processing Technology: Fundamentals, Etching, Deposition, & Surface Interactions. LC 89-22834. (Illus.). 523p. 1990. 86.00 (*0-8155-1220-1*) Noyes.

Rossnagel, W. A. Handbook of Rigging: In Construction & Industrial Operations. 3rd ed. 1964. text ed. 51.50 (*0-07-053940-5*) McGraw.

Rossnagel, W. A., et al. Handbook of Rigging: For Construction & Industrial Operations. 4th ed. 512p. 1988. pap. text ed. 70.50 (*0-07-053941-3*) McGraw.

***Rossner.** Olivia. 1995. mass mkt. 6.99 (*0-8041-1246-0*) Ivy Books.

Rossner, John. In Search of the Primordial Tradition & the Cosmic Christ: Uniting World Religious Experience with a Lost Esoteric Christianity. LC 89-8107. (Spiritual Sciences Ser.). (Illus.). 320p. 1989. pap. 12.95 (*0-87542-685-9*) Llewellyn Pubns.

Rossner, Judith. August. 576p. 1989. mass mkt. 6.99 (*0-446-35224-1*) Warner Bks.

— His Little Women. 1990. 233.40 (*0-671-94344-8*) S&S Trade.

— His Little Women. Rubenstein, Julie, ed. 448p. 1991. reprint ed. mass mkt. 5.95 (*0-671-70124-X*) PB.

— Looking for Mr. Goodbar. 1991. mass mkt. 5.95 (*0-671-73575-6*) PB.

— Olivia, or, the Weight of the Past. LC 93-50211. 1994. 23.00 (*0-517-59720-9*) Crown Pub Group.

— Olivia, or, the Weight of the Past. large type ed. LC 94-42583. (Large Print Book Ser.). 1995. 23.95 (*1-56895-166-3*) Wheeler Pub.

Rossner, M., et al, eds. Constraints, Language & Computation. (Cognitive Science Ser.). 391p. 1994. text ed. 69.95 (*0-12-597930-4*) Acad Pr.

Rossner, Richard. The Whole Story: Short Stories for Pleasure & Language Improvement. (YA). (gr. 9-12). 1988. pap. text ed. 14.95 (*0-582-79109-X*, 78326); audio 22.95 (*0-582-01887-0*, 78325) Longman.

Rosso, G. A. & Watkins, Daniel P., eds. Spirits of Fire: English Romantic Writers & Contemporary Historical Methods. LC 89-45548. (Illus.). 296p. 1990. 45.00 (*0-8386-3376-5*) Fairleigh Dickinson.

Rosso, George A., Jr. Blake's Prophetic Workshop: A Study of the Four Zoas. LC 92-54660. (Illus.). 208p. (C). 1993. 36.50 (*0-8387-5240-3*) Bucknell U Pr.

Rosso, Henry A., et al. Achieving Excellence in Fund Raising: A Comprehensive Guide to Principles, Strategies, & Methods. LC 91-16609. (Nonprofit Sector-Public Administration Ser.). 345p. 1991. 38.95 (*1-55542-387-6*) Jossey-Bass.

Rosso, Julee. Great Good Food. (Illus.). 1993. 29.00 (*0-517-59645-8*, Crown); 20.00 (*0-517-88122-5*, Crown) Crown Pub Group.

— Great Good Food: Luscious, Lower-Fat Cooking. 1993. pap. 19.00 (*0-679-74460-6*) Random.

***Rosso, Julee & Lukens, Sheila.** Silver Palate Desserts: Recipes from the Classic American Cookbooks. (Miniature Editions Ser.). (Illus.). 128p. 1995. 4.95 (*1-56138-498-4*) Running Pr.

Rosso, Julee & Lukins, Sheila. The New Basics Cookbook. LC 88-51581. 864p. 1989. 29.95 (*0-89480-392-1*, 1392); pap. 19.95 (*0-89480-341-7*, 1341) Workman Pub.

— The Silver Palate Cookbook in Large Print. large type ed. LC 93-9108. (Illus.). 650p. 1993. reprint ed. pap. 17.95 (*0-8161-5765-0*) Hall.

— The Silver Palate Cookbook in Large Print. large type ed. LC 93-9108. (Illus.). 650p. 1993. reprint ed. 22.95 (*0-8161-5764-2*) Hall.

Rosso, Julee, et al. The Silver Palate Cookbook. LC 81-43782. (Illus.). 384p. 1982. 22.95 (*0-89480-203-8*, 316); pap. 12.95 (*0-89480-204-6*, 402) Workman Pub.

— The Silver Palate Good Times Cookbook. LC 85-5368. (Illus.). 416p. (Orig.). 1985. 22.95 (*0-89480-832-X*, 832); pap. 12.95 (*0-89480-831-1*, 831) Workman Pub.

Rosso-O'Laughlin, Marta, jt. auth. see Spinelli, Emily.

Rosso-O'Laughlin, Marta, et al. Cuentame: Lecturas Interactivas. Vardy, Katherine L., ed. (Illus.). 288p. (Orig.). (SPA.). (C). 1990. pap. text ed. 22.00 (*0-03-028759-6*) HB Coll Pubs.

Rosso, Pedro. Nutrition Second Metabolism in Pregnancy: Mother & Fetus. (Illus.). 400p. 1990. 59.95 (*0-19-503928-9*) OUP.

***Rosso, R., et al, eds.** Advances in Distributed Hydrology: Selected Papers from International Workshop by ISMES. 1994. 55.00 (*0-918334-81-0*) WRP.

Rosso, Renata. Living Language In-Tense Italian Verb Practice: A Conversational Guide to 75 Essential Verbs. (ENG & ITA.). 1993. 25.00 (*0-517-59602-4*, Living Language) Crown Pub Group.

Rossoff, Irving. Handbook of Veterinary Drugs: A Compendium for Research & Clinical Use. LC 73-88322. 752p. 1975. 63.95 (*0-8261-1530-6*) Springer Pub.

Rossoff, Irving S., ed. see Bailey, J. W.

Rossol, Monona. Artist's Complete Health & Safety Guide. 2nd rev. ed. LC 94-70298. 344p. 1994. pap. 19.95 (*1-880559-18-8*) Allworth Pr.

— Stage Fright: Health & Safety in the Theater. LC 85-28080. (Illus.). 128p. 1986. pap. text ed. 12.95 (*0-918875-02-1*) Ctr Occupational Hazards.

— Stage Fright: Health Hazards in the Theater. LC 90-85553. (Illus.). 144p. (Orig.). 1991. pap. 12.95 (*0-9607118-3-X*) Allworth Pr.

Rossol, Monona & Bartlett, Ben. Danger! Artists at Work: A Guide to Occupational Hazards for Australian Art Workers & Teachers. 200p. 1991. pap. 45.00 (*0-909532-98-2*) D W Thorpe.

Rossol, Monona, jt. auth. see Shaw, Susan D.

Rossomando, Edward F. & Alexander, Stephen, eds. Morphogenesis: An Analysis of the Development of Biological Form: An Analysis of the Development of Biological Form. LC 92-3820. 448p. 1992. 175.00 (*0-8247-8667-X*) Dekker.

Rosson & Bloom. Therapeutic Gastrointestinal Endoscopy. 1991. write for info. (*0-8151-7399-7*, Yr Bk Med Pubs) Mosby Yr Bk.

Rosson, C. Parr, III, et al. North American Free Trade Agreement (NAFTA) Background, Legislative Process, & Provisions for Agricultural Trade. (Illus.). 67p. (Orig.). (C). 1994. pap. text ed. 30.00 (*0-7881-0309-1*) Diane Pub.

Rosson, Philip J. & Reid, Stanley D., eds. Managing Export Entry & Expansion: Concepts & Practice. LC 86-30330. 462p. 1987. text ed. 79.50 (*0-275-92361-4*, C2361, Praeger Pubs) Greenwood.

Rosson, Philip J., jt. auth. see Seringhaus, Rolf.

Rossos, Andrew. Russia & the Balkans: Inter-Balkan Rivalries & Russian Foreign Policy, 1908-1914. LC 81-142342. 327p. reprint ed. pap. 93.20 (*0-685-16003-3*, 2026405) Bks Demand.

Rossotti, Hazel. Fire. LC 92-22005. (Illus.). 336p. 1993. 30.00 (*0-19-855722-1*) OUP.

— The Study of Ionic Equilibria: An Introduction. LC 77-26048. (Illus.). 208p. reprint ed. pap. 59.30 (*0-8357-3555-9*, 2034442) Bks Demand.

***Rossow, Edwin C.** Analysis & Behavior of Structures. (Illus.). 600p. 1995. write for info. (*0-02-403913-6*, Merrill Pub Co) Macmillan.

Rossow, Francis. Preaching the Creative Gospel Creatively. 1983. pap. 9.95 (*0-570-03917-7*, 12-2856) Concordia.

Rossow, Francis & Aho, Gerhard. Lectionary Preaching Resources: Series B. (Illus.). 224p. 1987. pap. 16.95 (*0-570-04468-5*, 12-3085) Concordia.

Rossow, Francis & Aho, Gerhard, eds. Lectionary Preaching Resources Series C. (Orig.). 1988. pap. 16.95 (*0-570-04484-7*, 12-3087) Concordia.

Rossow, Lawrence. The Principalship: Dimensions in Instructional Leadership. 416p. (C). 1989. Casebound. text ed. 65.00 (*0-13-712290-X*) P-H.

Rossow, Lawrence & Parkinson, Jerry. The Law of Teacher Evaluation. 96p. (Orig.). (C). 1991. pap. text ed. 17.95 (*1-56534-031-0*) NOLPE.

Rossow, Lawrence F. The Law of Student Expulsions & Suspensions. 1989. 12.95 (*1-56534-015-9*) NOLPE.

— Search & Seizure in the Public Schools. 1987. 9.95 (*1-56534-010-8*) NOLPE.

Rossow, Lawrence F. & Hininger, Janice A. Students & the Law. LC 91-60202. (Fastback Ser.: No. 317). (Orig.). 1991. pap. 1.25 (*0-87367-317-4*) Phi Delta Kappa.

Rossum, Constance. How to Assess Your Nonprofit Organization with Peter Drucker's Five Most Important Questions: User Guide for Boards, Staff, Volunteers, & Facilitators. LC 93-40200. (Jossey-Bass Nonprofit Sector Ser.). 1993. write for info. (*1-55542-596-8*) Jossey-Bass.

Rossum, Ralph A. The Politics of the Criminal Justice System: An Organizational Analysis. LC 78-18519. (Political Science Ser.: No. 6). (Illus.). 303p. reprint ed. pap. 86.40 (*0-7837-0823-8*, 2041137) Bks Demand.

— Reverse Discrimination: The Constitutional Debate. LC 80-13777. (Political Science Ser.: No. 10). 240p. reprint ed. pap. 68.40 (*0-8357-3517-6*, 2034564) Bks Demand.

***Rossum, Ralph A. & Tarr, G. Alan.** American Constitutional Law. 4th ed. 960p. (C). 1995. pap. text ed. 54.53 (*0-312-10262-3*) St Martin.

— American Constitutional Law, Vol. 1. 4th ed. 416p. (C). 1995. pap. text ed. 33.25 (*0-312-10260-7*) St Martin.

— American Constitutional Law, Vol. 2. 4th ed. 592p. (C). 1995. pap. text ed. 33.25 (*0-312-10261-5*) St Martin.

Rosswall, Thomas, et al. Spatial & Temporal Variability in Biospheric & Geospheric Processes: Scope 35. LC 87-31955. 355p. 1988. text ed. 289.95 (*0-471-91828-8*) Wiley.

Rosswurm, Steve, ed. The CIO's Left-Led Unions. LC 91-19467. 330p. (C). 1992. text ed. 45.00 (*0-8135-1769-9*); pap. text ed. 17.00 (*0-8135-1770-2*) Rutgers U Pr.

Rosswurm, Steven. Arms, Country & Class: The Philadelphia Militia & the "Lower Sort" During the American Revolution. 373p. (C). 1990. pap. text ed. 16.00 (*0-8135-1472-X*) Rutgers U Pr.

Rost, jt. auth. see Heinig.

Rost, Arno & Rost, Jutta. Introduction to Regulation Thermography: Practical Instruction & Therapeutic Consequences. Ware, Barbara & Krag, Juergen, trs. (Illus.). 88p. 1990. pap. text ed. 25.00 (*3-7773-0937-0*, Pub. by Hippokrates Verlag GW) Medicina Bio.

Rost, F. W. Fluorescence Microscopy, Vol. 1. (Illus.). 256p. (C). 1992. 89.95 (*0-521-23641-X*) Cambridge U Pr.

— Fluorescence Microscopy, Vol. 2. (Illus.). 500p. (C). 1995. write for info. (*0-521-41088-6*) Cambridge U Pr.

— Quantitative Fluorescence Microscopy. (Illus.). 300p. (C). 1991. 74.95 (*0-521-39422-8*) Cambridge U Pr.

Rost, H. T. Brilliant Stars. 182p. 1979. pap. 9.95 (*0-85398-083-7*) G Ronald Pub.

— The Golden Rule. 1986. text ed. 16.75 (*0-85398-226-0*); pap. text ed. 9.50 (*0-85398-227-9*) G Ronald Pub.

Rost, J., jt. ed. see Langeheine, R.

Rost, Joseph C. Leadership in the Twenty-First Century. LC 90-40961. 256p. 1991. text ed. 47.95 (*0-275-93670-8*, C3670, Praeger Pubs) Greenwood.

— Leadership in the Twenty-First Century. LC 90-40961. 256p. 1993. pap. text ed. 16.95 (*0-275-94610-X*, B4610, Praeger Pubs) Greenwood.

Rost, Jutta, jt. auth. see Rost, Arno.

***Rost, Leo.** Jake's Revenge. 1995. pap. 10.95 (*0-533-11405-5*) Vantage.

Rost, M. Prime Time English. (YA). 1994. teacher ed 18.95 (*0-582-09224-8*); text ed. 11.44 (*0-582-09222-1*); pap. text ed. 43.64 (*0-582-23082-9*) Longman.

— Real Time English. (YA). 1994. teacher ed 18.95 (*0-582-09223-X*); text ed. 11.44 (*0-582-09221-3*); pap. text ed. 43.64 (*0-582-22927-8*) Longman.

Rost, M. & McGannon, A. Keynote. (Illus.). 1994. teacher ed 14.95 (*0-582-10233-2*); pap. text ed. 12.95 (*0-582-10235-9*); audio 55.00 (*0-582-10225-1*) Longman.

Rost, M., et al. Keynote Plus. (Illus.). (YA). 1994. teacher ed 14.95 (*0-582-10234-0*); pap. text ed. 12.95 (*0-582-10236-7*); audio 55.00 (*0-582-10229-4*) Longman.

Rost, Michael A. Listening in Action. 160p. 1991. pap. 18.25 (*0-13-538778-7*) P-H.

— Listening in Language Learning. (Applied Linguistics & Language Ser.). 278p. (C). 1990. pap. text ed. 25.95 (*0-582-01650-9*) Longman.

— Strategies in Listening: Tasks for Listening Development. 80p. 1986. teacher ed 10.95 (*0-8013-0521-7*, 78367); pap. text ed. 13.50 (*0-8013-0520-9*, 78366); audio 55.00 (*0-8013-0522-5*, 78368) Longman.

Rost, Michael A. & Kumai, Nobuhiro. First Steps in Listening. (Illus.). 52p. 1990. teacher ed 13.95 (*1-85294-001-8*, 78675); pap. text ed. 12.95 (*1-85294-095-6*, 78674) Longman.

— First Steps in Listening, 2 cass., Set. (Illus.). 52p. 1990. audio 55.00 (*1-85294-002-6*, 78676) Longman.

Rost, Michael A. & Stratton, Robert K. Listening in the Real World: Clues to English Conversation. 144p. 1978. pap. text ed. 14.50 (*0-685-03056-3*, 78390); audio 88.00 (*0-685-03057-1*, 78391) Longman.

Rost, Michael A. & Uruno, M. Basics in Listening: Short Tasks for Listening Development. 71p. 1985. 10.95 (*0-8013-0518-7*, 78364); pap. text ed. 13.50 (*0-8013-0517-9*, 78363); audio 55.00 (*0-8013-0519-5*, 78365) Longman.

Rost, Michael A., jt. auth. see Kisslinger, Ellen.

Rost, Michele P. Holiday Hoopla. (Illus.). 144p. 1991. 24.95 (*0-937857-18-1*, 1582) Speech Bin.

Rost, Pat, et al, eds. Celebrate. (Illus.). 1989. 15.00 (*0-9622333-0-7*) Missouri Bankers.

Rost, Paulus, ed. Die Keilschrifttexte Tiglat-Pilessers III, 2 vols. LC 78-72769. (Ancient Mesopotamian Texts & Studies). reprint ed. 45.00 (*0-404-18223-2*) AMS Pr.

Rost, Randi. X & Motif Quick Reference Guide: X Window System 11.4 & Motif 1.1. 2nd ed. (X & Motif Ser.). (Illus.). 301p. (Orig.). 1994. pap. 24.95 (*1-55558-118-8*, EY-P953E-DP, Digital DEC) Buttrwrth-Heinemann.

Rost, Randi J. X & Motif Quick Reference Guide. LC 93-5670. 369p. 1993. pap. 24.95 (*1-55558-061-0*, Digital DEC) Buttrwrth-Heinemann.

Rost, Yuri. Armenian Tragedy: An Eye-Witness Account of Human Conflict & Natural Disaster in Armenia & Azerbaijan. Roberts, Elizabeth, tr. 1990. text ed. 29.95 (*0-312-04611-1*) St Martin.

Rostad, Lee. Fourteen Cents & Seven Green Apples: The Life & Times of Charles Bair. Tobias, Ronald, ed. (Illus.). 128p. (Orig.). 1992. 25.00 (*0-9633909-2-9*); pap. 9.95 (*0-9633909-1-0*) C M R Museum.

Rostagno, Ippolita, tr. see Sereni, Vittorio.

Rostami, S., jt. auth. see Miles, Isabel S.

Rostand, Charles. Liszt. John, Miriam, tr. (Illus.). 192p. 1980. 12.00 (*0-7145-0342-8*) M Boyars Pubs.

Rostand, Claude. French Music Today. LC 73-4333. (Music Reprint Ser.). 146p. 1973. reprint ed. lib. bdg. 25.00 (*0-306-70578-8*) Da Capo.

Rostand, Edmond. Aiglon. (Illus.). 434p. (FRE.). 1986. 15.95 (*0-685-74006-4*, 2070377644) Fr & Eur.

— Aiglon. (Folio Ser.: No. 1764). 434p. 1986. pap. 13.95 (*2-07-037764-4*) Schoenhof.

— Chantecler: A Play in Four Acts. Smith, Kay N., tr. (Illus.). 242p. (Orig.). (C). 1987. pap. text ed. 22.00 (*0-8191-5766-X*) U Pr of Amer.

— Cyrano de Bergerac. (Orig.). 19.95 (*0-8488-0621-2*) Amereon Ltd.

— Cyrano de Bergerac. Hooker, Brian, tr. 208p. (Orig.). 1950. 3.95 (*0-553-21360-1*, Bantam Classics) Bantam.

— Cyrano de Bergerac. Via Luis Marti, Jose O., tr. (Nueva Austral Ser.: Vol. 206). (Orig.). (SPA.). 1991. pap. text ed. 24.95x (*84-239-7206-2*) Elliots Bks.

An Asterisk (*) at the beginning of an entry indicates that the title is appearing in BIP for the first time.

— Cyrano de Bergerac. (Illus.). 216p. (Orig.). (FRE.). 1990. pap. 10.95 (*0-685-74009-9*, 2080705261) Fr & Eur.
— Cyrano de Bergerac. Blair, Lowell, tr. 240p. (Orig.). 1972. pap. 3.95 (*0-451-52548-5*, Sig Classics) NAL-Dutton.
— Cyrano de Bergerac. (Folio Ser.: No. 1487). (Illus.). (Orig.). (FRE.). 1962. pap. 10.95 (*2-07-037487-4*) Schoenhof.
— Cyrano De Bergerac. Burgess, Anthony, tr. 1971. 16.95 (*0-394-47239-X*) Knopf.
— Cyrano De Bergerac. Burgess, Anthony, tr. 1990. 9.95 (*0-679-73413-9*, Vin) Random.
— Cyrano De Bergerac. 1995. pap. 11.95 (*1-880399-68-7*) Smith & Kraus.
— Cyrano de Bergerac. 301p. (Orig.). 1984. reprint ed. lib. bdg. 21.95 (*0-89968-255-3*, Lghtyr Pr) Buccaneer Bks.
— Deux Romanciers de Provence: Honore d'Urfe et Emile Zola. 98p. (FRE.). 1921. pap. 36.95 (*0-318-51977-1*) Fr & Eur.
— The Far Princess. Heard, J., tr. 192p. 1987. reprint ed. lib. bdg. 29.50 (*0-86527-359-6*) Fertig.
— Les Romanesques. 3.95 (*0-686-55337-3*) Fr & Eur.
Rostand, Edmond, et al. Cyrano de Bergerac. (Classics Illustrated Ser.). (Illus.). 52p. (Orig.). (YA). Date not set. pap. 4.95 (*1-57209-019-7*) Classics Int Ent.
Rostankowski, Cynthia, jt. auth. see Velasquez, Manuel G.
***Rostas, Francois, ed.** Spectral Line Shapes: Proceedings, Seventh International Congress Aussois, France, June 11-15, 1984. (Illus.). xx, 769p. 1985. 273.10 (*3-11-010119-X*) De Gruyter.
— Spectral Line Shapes, Vol. 3: Proceedings, Seventh International Congress Aussois, France, June 11-15, 1984. (Illus.). xx, 769p. 1985. 273.10 (*0-89925-013-0*) De Gruyter.
***Rostas, Susanna & Droogers, Andre.** The Popular Use of Popular Religion in Latin America. (CEDLA Latin America Studies (CLAS): No. 70). 240p. 1993. pap. 28. 50 (*90-70280-65-5*, Pub. by Thesis Pubs NE) IBD Ltd.
Rosteck, Thomas. See It Now Confronts McCarthyism: Television Documentary & the Politics of Representation. LC 93-4780. (Studies in Rhetoric & Communication). 264p. (C). 1994. 29.95 (*0-8173-0705-2*) U of Ala Pr.
Rosted, J., jt. ed. see Bjerholt, O.
Rosten, Leo. Hooray for Yiddish. 368p. 1984. pap. 11.00 (*0-671-43026-2*, Touchstone Bks) S&S Trade.
— Joys of Yiddish. 1991. pap. 5.99 (*0-671-72813-X*) S&S Trade.
— The Joys of Yinglish. 610p. 1990. pap. 14.95 (*0-452-26543-6*, Plume) NAL-Dutton.
Rosten, Leo, ed. Leo Rosten's Carnival of Wit: From Aristotle to Groucho Marx. 544p. 1994. 24.95 (*0-525-93716-1*) NAL-Dutton.
— Religions of America. LC 74-11705. 1975. pap. 16.95 (*0-671-21971-5*) S&S Trade.
Rosten, Leo C. Hollywood: The Movie Colony, the Movie Makers. LC 74-124036. (Literature of Cinema, Ser. 1). 1975. reprint ed. 30.95 (*0-405-01636-0*) Ayer.
— The Washington Correspondents. LC 73-19175. (Politics & People Ser.). 456p. 1974. reprint ed. 30.95 (*0-405-05896-9*) Ayer.
Rosten, Norman. Come Slowly, Eden. 1967. pap. 4.75 (*0-8222-0228-X*) Dramatists Play.
— Selected Poems. LC 79-52399. 171p. 1979. 10.00 (*0-8076-0930-7*); pap. 4.95 (*0-8076-0938-2*) Braziller.
— Under the Boardwalk. LC 90-39133. 126p. 1991. pap. 12. 95 (*1-55728-188-2*) U of Ark Pr.
Rosten, Shaw. Marilyn among Friends. 1992. 17.99 (*0-517-06989-X*) Random Hse Value.
Rostenberg, Bill. Design Planning for Freestanding Ambulatory Care Facilities. LC 86-17241. (Illus.). 142p. (Orig.). 1987. 40.00 (*0-939450-95-X*, 043181) AHPI.
Rostenberg, Leona. Bibliately. 61p. 1978. pap. 3.00 (*0-686-24134-7*) Am Philatelic Society.
Rostenberg, Leona, et al. Bookman's Quintet, Five Catalogues about Books, Bibliography, Printing History, Booksellers, Libraries, Presses, Collectors. (Illus.). 283p. 1980. 25.00 (*0-938768-03-4*) Oak Knoll.
Rostenberg, Leona. The Library of Robert Hooke: The Scientific Book Trade of Restoration England. (Illus.). 288p. (Orig.). 1989. pap. 18.00 (*0-929246-01-2*) Modoc Pr.
— Old & Rare: Thirty Years in the Book Business. (American Autobiography Ser.). 234p. 1995. reprint ed. lib. bdg. 79.00 (*0-7812-8632-8*) Rprt Serv.
Rostenberg, Leona & Stern, Madeleine B. Between Boards: New Thoughts on Old Books. 240p. 1989. pap. 18.00 (*0-929246-02-0*) Modoc Pr.
— Connections: Our Selves - Our Books. 238p. (Orig.). 1994. pap. 18.00 (*0-929246-06-3*) Modoc Pr.
— Old & Rare: Forty Years in the Book Business. rev. ed. (Illus.). 272p. 1988. reprint ed. pap. 18.00 (*0-929246-00-4*) Modoc Pr.
— Quest Book - Guest Book: A Biblio-Folly. (Illus.). 124p. (Orig.). 1993. pap. 18.00 (*0-929246-04-7*) Modoc Pr.
Rosters Ltd. Staff & Struthers, S. U. K. Activity Holidays: Over Two Hundred Fifty Ideas Inside. 374p. (C). 1989. pap. text ed. 40.00 (*0-948032-93-6*, Pub. by Rosters Ltd) St Mut.
Rostker, Bernard, et al. The Defense Officer Personnel Management Act of 1980: A Retrospective Assessment. LC 92-42096. 1993. write for info. (*0-8330-1287-8*, R-4246-FMP) Rand Corp.
Rostkowski, Margaret I. After the Dancing Days. LC 85-45810. 240p. (YA). (gr. 6-9). 1986. lib. bdg. 14.89 (*0-06-025078-X*) HarpC Child Bks.
— After the Dancing Days. LC 85-45810. (Trophy Bk.). 224p. (J). (gr. 5-9). 1988. pap. 3.95 (*0-06-440248-7*, Trophy) HarpC Child Bks.
— Moon Dancer. LC 94-39553. 224p. (YA). (gr. 7 up). 1995. 11.00 (*0-15-276638-3*, Browndeer Pr); pap. 5.00 (*0-15-200194-8*, Browndeer Pr) HarBrace.
Rostoker, ed. Microwave & Particle Beam Sources & Propagation. 1988. 59.00 (*0-89252-908-3*, 873) SPIE.
Rostoker-Gruber, Karen. Remote Controls Are Better Than Women Because: or What Men Would Say If They Could. LC 92-84004. (Illus.). 80p. 1993. pap. 5.95 (*1-56352-076-1*) Longstreet Pr Inc.
— The Unofficial College Survival Guide. 78p. (Orig.). 1992. pap. 7.95 (*1-56245-058-1*) Great Quotations.
Rostoker, Michael D. Technology Management: Licensing & Protection for Computers in the World Market. 267p. 1993. 29.95 (*0-9639750-0-5*) Cap Info Assocs.
Rostoker, N., jt. ed. see Reiser, M.
Rostoker, Norman, jt. ed. see Liboff, Richard L.
Rostoker, W. & Domagala, R. A Study Aid for Introductory Materials Science & Engineering. (C). 1974. spiral bd. 7.80 (*0-87563-070-7*) Stipes.
Rostoker, William & Dvorak, Jim. Interpretation of Metallographic Structures. 3rd ed. 282p. 1990. text ed. 69.00 (*0-12-598255-0*) Acad Pr.
Roston, Elspeth, jt. ed. see Jordan, Barbara.
Roston, Jacqueline G. Camus's Recit, La Chute: A Rewriting Through Dante's Commedia. (Studies in the Humanities: Literature-Politics-Society: Vol. 5). 188p. 1985. text ed. 26.75 (*0-8204-0269-9*) P Lang Pubs.
Roston, M., tr. see Rabinovich, Isaiah.
Roston, Murray. Changing Perspectives in Literature & the Visual Arts, 1650-1820. (Illus.). 469p. 1993. text ed. 70. 00 (*0-691-06795-3*); pap. text ed. 26.95 (*0-691-01539-2*) Princeton U Pr.
— Renaissance Perspectives in Literature & the Visual Arts. LC 86-18681. (Illus.). 448p. (Orig.). 1990. text ed. 70.00 (*0-691-06683-3*); pap. text ed. 26.95 (*0-691-01486-8*) Princeton U Pr.
Roston, Ruth. I Live in the Watchmakers Town. LC 81-83880. (Minnesota Voices Project Ser.: No. 4). (Illus.). 76p. 1981. pap. 3.00 (*0-89823-028-4*) New Rivers Pr.
***Roston, Ruth, ed.** Never Like You Plan. (Orig.). 1994. pap. 5.00 (*0-927663-23-6*) COMPAS.
— A Piece of the Moon Is Missing. (Illus.). 192p. (Orig.). 1985. pap. 7.00 (*0-927663-06-6*) COMPAS.
Roston, Ruth, jt. ed. see Buchwald, Emilie.
Rostovsky, Demeter B., jt. auth. see Forter, Norman L.
Rostovtsev, Mikhail I. Caravan Cities. LC 75-137287. reprint ed. 37.50 (*0-404-05445-5*) AMS Pr.
— Dura-Europos & Its Art. LC 75-41237. reprint ed. 34.50 (*0-404-14594-9*) AMS Pr.
Rostovtsev, N. F. Theory & Practice of Livestock Breeding. 216p. 1961. text ed. 55.00 (*0-7065-0355-4*, Pub. by Keter Pub IS) Coronet Bks.
Rostovtzeff, M. A History of the Ancient World, Vol. I: The Orient & Greece. 418p. 1926. 30.00 (*0-8196-2162-5*) Biblo.
— A History of the Ancient World, Vol. II: Rome. 387p. 1927. 30.00 (*0-8196-2163-3*) Biblo.
— The Social & Economic History of the Roman Empire. 695p. 1926. 40.00 (*0-8196-2164-1*) Biblo.
Rostovtzeff, Michael. A Large Estate in Egypt in the Third Century B.C.: A Study in Economic History. Finley, Moses, ed. LC 79-5003. (Ancient Economic History Ser.). 1979. reprint ed. lib. bdg. 27.95 (*0-405-12392-2*) Ayer.
Rostovtzeff, Michael I. Out of the Past of Greece & Rome. LC 63-18047. (Illus.). 1960. 22.00 (*0-8196-0126-8*) Biblo.
Rostovtzeff, Mikhail I. Greece. 2nd ed. Bickerman, Elias J., ed. Duff, J. D., tr. (Illus.). 1963. reprint ed. pap. 16.95 (*0-19-500368-3*) OUP.
— Rome. Bickerman, Elias J., ed. Duff, J. D., tr. 1960. reprint ed. pap. 17.95 (*0-19-500224-5*) OUP.
***Rostow.** Toward Managed Peace: The National Security Interests of the United States, 1759 to the Present. 1995. pap. text ed. 17.00 (*0-300-06316-4*) Yale U Pr.
Rostow, Eugene V. The Democratic Character of Judicial Review. (Reprint Series in Political Science). (C). 1993. reprint ed. pap. text ed. 2.30 (*0-8290-3723-3*, P-247) Irvington.
— The Ideal in Law. LC 77-81733. 1978. 20.00 (*0-226-72818-8*) U Ch Pr.
— Law, Power, & the Pursuit of Peace. LC 67-10669. (Roscoe Pound Lectureship Ser.: 1966). 153p. reprint ed. pap. 43.70 (*0-317-27120-2*, 2024688) Bks Demand.
— The Sovereign Prerogative: The Supreme Court & the Quest for Law. LC 73-17923. 318p. 1974. reprint ed. text ed. 35.00 (*0-8371-7276-4*, RSOP, Greenwood Pr) Greenwood.
— Toward Managed Peace: The National Security Interests of the United States, 1759 to the Present. LC 92-24550. 352p. (C). 1993. text ed. 35.00 (*0-300-05700-8*) Yale U Pr.
Rostow, Eugene V., et al. Power & Policy in Quest of the Law: Essays in Honor of Eugene Victor Rostow. LC 83-26502. 1985. lib. bdg. 190.00 (*90-247-2911-4*) Kluwer Ac.
Rostow, Nicholas. Anglo-French Relations, Nineteen Thirty-Four to Thirty-Six. LC 82-3263. 328p. 1984. text ed. 25. 00 (*0-312-03725-2*) St Martin.
Rostow, Victoria P. & Bulger, Roger J., eds. Medical Professional Liability & the Delivery of Obstetrical Care: An Interdisciplinary Review, Vol. II. 256p. 1989. text ed. 35.00 (*0-309-03986-X*) Natl Acad Pr.
Rostow, W. W. The Barbaric Counter-Revolution: Cause & Cure. 140p. 1983. 13.95 (*0-292-70749-5*) U of Tex Pr.
— The Division of Europe after World War II: 1946. (Ideas & Action Ser.: No. 2). 224p. 1981. text ed. 19.95 (*0-292-70358-9*); pap. 10.95 (*0-292-70359-7*) U of Tex Pr.
— Why the Poor Get Richer & the Rich Slow Down: Essays in the Marshallian Long Period. 394p. 1980. text ed. 25. 00 (*0-292-73012-8*) U of Tex Pr.
Rostow, Walt W. British Economy of the Nineteenth Century: Essays. LC 81-13312. 240p. 1982. reprint ed. text ed. 59.75 (*0-313-23208-3*, ROBR, Greenwood Pr) Greenwood.
— British Trade Fluctuations, 1868-1896: Dissertations in European Economic History II. Bruchey, Stuart, ed. LC 80-2828. (Illus.). 1981. lib. bdg. 49.00 (*0-686-73124-7*) Ayer.
— Stages of Economic Growth: A Non-Communist Manifesto. 3rd ed. 1991. pap. 19.95 (*0-521-40928-4*) Cambridge U Pr.
— Stages of Economic Growth: A Non-Communist Manifesto. 3rd ed. 1991. 59.95 (*0-521-40070-8*) Cambridge U Pr.
— Theorists of Economic Growth from David Hume to the Present: With a Perspective on the Next Century. (Illus.). 736p. 1990. 55.00 (*0-19-505837-2*) OUP.
— Theorists of Economic Growth from David Hume to the Present: With a Perspective on the Next Century. (Illus.). 768p. 1992. pap. 22.00 (*0-19-508043-2*) OUP.
Rostow, Walt W., jt. auth. see Millikan, Max F.
***Rostowski, Jacek, ed.** Banking Reform in Central Europe & the Former Soviet Union. (A Central European University Press Bk.). (Illus.). 256p. 1995. 69.00 (*1-85866-038-6*); pap. 23.00 (*1-85866-039-4*) OUP.
Rostron, Arthur. The Loss of the Titanic. (C). 1991. pap. text ed. 50.00 (*0-9518190-0-3*, Pub. by Cambdge Hse Bks UK) St Mut.
Rostron, S. Nowell. The Christology of St. Paul. 1977. lib. bdg. 59.95 (*0-8490-1620-7*) Gordon Pr.
Rostworowski, Boguslaw, tr. see Karasek, Krzysztof, et al.
Rostworowski, Boguslaw, tr. see Zbigniew, Herbert.
***Rosu, Anca.** The Metaphysics of Sound in Wallace Stevens. LC 94-43107. 1995. write for info. (*0-8173-0797-4*) U of Ala Pr.
— The Metaphysics of Sound in Wallace Stevens. 208p. (FRE, GER & SPA.). (C). 1995. 39.95 (*0-8172-0797-X*) U of Ala Pr.
Rosumek, Peter & Najock, Dietmar, eds. Plinius: Konkordanz Zur Naturalis Historia des C. Plinius Secundus, 3 vols. Vol. LV. Date not set. Set. write for info. (*0-318-71980-0*, Pub. by Georg Olms GW) Lubrecht & Cramer.
Rosumek, Peter, ed. see Plinius Secundus, C.
Rosumek, Peter, ed. see Secundus, C. Plinius.
Rosumek, Peter, ed. see Secundus, Plinius.
Rosvall, J. & Aleby, S., eds. Air Pollution & Conservation: Safeguarding Our Architectural Heritage. 432p. 1989. 143.75 (*0-444-87131-4*) Elsevier.
***Roswell, Galen.** Poles Apart: Parallel Visions of the Arctic & Antarctic. LC 94-42048. (Mountain Light Press Bks.). (Illus.). 184p. 1995. 39.95 (*0-520-20174-4*) U CA Pr.
Roswell, Geoffrey, jt. auth. see Dudley, Martin.
Roswell Symphony Guild, Board of Directors Staff. Savoring the Southwest. LC 83-62041. (Illus.). 332p. 1994. 18.95 (*0-9612466-0-X*) Roswell Symphony Guild.
Roswitha. Plays of Roswitha. St. John, Christopher, tr. LC 65-20048. 1972. reprint ed. 22.95 (*0-405-08900-7*) Ayer.
— Plays of Roswitha. St. John, Christopher, tr. LC 65-20048. 1989. reprint ed. pap. 18.95 (*0-88143-106-0*) Ayer.
Rosy. Basil. (J). (ps-3). 1993. 13.95 (*0-307-17502-2*, Artsts Writrs) Western Pub.
Rosynyaine, J. H. The Xipehuz & the Death of the Earth (les Xipehuz & la Mort De la Terre), 2 vols. in 1. Reginald, R. & Melville, Douglas, eds. LC 77-84283. (Lost Race & Adult Fantasy Ser.). 1978. lib. bdg. 23.95 (*0-405-11020-0*) Ayer.
Roszak, Theodor. Where the Wasteland Ends. LC 88-13860. 1989. pap. 14.95 (*0-89087-561-8*) Celestial Arts.
Roszak, Theodore. The Cult of Information: A Neo-Luddite Treatise on High Tech, Artificial Intelligence, & the True Art of Thinking. LC 93-37189. 1994. pap. 10.00 (*0-520-08584-1*) U CA Pr.
— Fool's Cycle-Full Cycle: Reflections on the Great Trumps of the Tarot. (Broadside Editions Ser.). (Illus.). 36p. (Orig.). (C). 1988. pap. 3.95 (*0-931191-07-6*) Rob Briggs.
— From Satori to Silicon Valley: San Francisco & the American Counter-Culture. 60p. (Orig.). 1986. pap. 3.95 (*0-917583-09-4*, Don't Call Frisco) Lexikos.
— The Making of a Counter Culture: Reflections on the Technocratic Society & Its Youthful Opposition. LC 94-34092. 1995. pap. 12.95 (*0-520-20122-1*) UpClose Pub.
— The Memoirs of Elizabeth Frankenstein. 1995. 22.00 (*0-679-43732-0*) Random.
— The Voice of the Earth. (Illus.). 368p. 1993. pap. 13.00 (*0-671-86753-9*, Touchstone Bks) S&S Trade.
***Roszak, Theodore, et al, eds.** Ecopsychology: Restoring the Earth, Healing the Mind. LC 94-31179. 1995. pap. 15.00 (*0-87156-406-8*) Sierra.
Roszel, Renee. A Bride for Ransom. (Romance Ser.). 1993. pap. 2.89 (*0-373-03251-X*, 1-03251-5) Harlequin Bks.
— A Bride for Ransom. large type ed. 266p. 1993. reprint ed. lib. bdg. 13.95 (*1-56054-686-7*) Thorndike Pr.
— Dare to Kiss a Cowboy. 1994. mass mkt. 2.99 (*0-373-03317-6*, 1-03317-4) Harlequin Bks.
— Ghost Whispers. 1994. mass mkt. 2.99 (*0-373-25612-4*, 1-25612-2) Harlequin Bks.
— Make-Believe Marriage. (Romance Ser.). 1995. mass mkt. 2.99 (*0-373-03370-2*, 1-03370-3) Harlequin Bks.
— No More Mr. Nice. (Temptation Ser.). 1993. mass mkt. 2.99 (*0-373-25568-3*, 1-25568-6) Harlequin Bks.
— Sex, Lies & Leprechauns. (Temptation Ser.). 1994. mass mkt. 2.99 (*0-373-25583-7*, 1-25583-5) Harlequin Bks.
Roszell, Calvert. The Near-Death Experience. LC 91-27842. 96p. (Orig.). 1992. pap. 10.95 (*0-88010-360-4*) Anthroposophic.
Roszia, Sharon K., jt. auth. see Melina, Lois R.
Roszkiewicz, Ron. The Woodturner's Companion. LC 84-8557. (Illus.). 256p. (Orig.). 1985. pap. 17.95 (*0-8069-7940-2*) Sterling.
Roszkowski, Mark. Baseball Crosswords. 2nd rev. ed. LC 94-1718. (Spalding Sports Library). (Illus.). 192p. 1994. pap. 12.95 (*0-940279-83-5*, Spalding Sports) Masters Pr IN.
Roszkowski, Mark E. Business Law: Principles, Cases & Policy. 3rd ed. (C). 1991. text ed. 73.00 (*0-673-52130-3*) HarpCollege.
— Business Law: Principles, Cases & Policy. 3rd ed. (C). 1991. 25.50 (*0-673-52219-9*) HarpCollege.
— Business Law for CPA Candidates. (C). 1992. text ed. 40. 00 (*0-673-52218-0*) HarpCollege.
Roszkowski, Mark E., et al. Business Law: Principles, Cases, & Policy. 2nd ed. (C). 1989. text ed. 43.25 (*0-673-39927-3*) HarpCollege.
Roszkowski, Wojchiech. Landowners in Poland, 1918-1939. 1991. text ed. 35.00 (*0-88033-196-8*) Col U Pr.
Rota, Anthony. Points at Issue: A Bookseller Looks at Bibliography. LC 84-600230. 22p. 1984. Incl. a Lecture Delivered at the Library of Congress on April 24, 1984. 3.95 (*0-8444-0471-3*) Lib Congress.
***Rota, E. Miriandra.** The Story of the People. 209p. (Orig.). 1993. pap. 11.95 (*0-929385-51-9*) Light Tech Comns Servs.
Rota, Gian-Carlo, ed. Probability, Statistical Mechanics, & Number Theory. (Advances in Mathematics Supplementary Studies). 208p. 1986. text ed. 91.00 (*0-12-598543-6*) Acad Pr.
— Studies in Combinatorics. LC 78-60730. (Studies in Mathematics: No. 17). 1978. 30.00 (*0-88385-117-2*) Math Assn.
Rota, Gian-Carlo, jt. auth. see Birkhoff, Garrett.
Rota, Gian-Carlo, jt. ed. see Gessel, I.
Rota, Gian-Carlo, jt. ed. see Metropolis, Nicholas.
Rota, Gian-Carlo, ed. see Polya, George.
Rota, Gian-Carlo, jt. ed. see Reynolds, Mark.
Rota, Maria, tr. see Miravalle, Mark I.
Rotary Club of Chester, South Carolina Staff. Chiefs. Grant, Tommy & Wilson, Sandy, eds. LC 83-73060. 128p. 1983. 16.95 (*0-912081-01-5*) Delmar Co.
Rotatori, Anthony F. & Fox, Robert A. Obesity in Children & Youth: Measurement, Characteristics, Causes & Treatment. (Illus.). 188p. 1989. 49.95 (*0-398-05594-7*) C C Thomas.
Rotatori, Anthony F. & Fox, Robert A., eds. Understanding Individuals with Low Incidence Handicaps: Categorical & Noncategorical Perspectives. (Illus.). 378p. (C). 1989. text ed. 77.95x (*0-398-05538-6*) C C Thomas.
Rotatori, Anthony F., jt. ed. see Burkhardt, Sandra A.
Rotatori, Anthony F., et al. Comprehensive Assessment in Special Education: Approaches, Procedures & Concerns. (Illus.). 578p. (C). 1990. text ed. 99.95x (*0-398-05645-5*) C C Thomas.
Rotatori, Anthony F., et al, eds. Counseling Exceptional Students. 334p. (C). 1986. 45.95 (*0-89885-274-9*); pap. 21.95 (*0-89885-275-7*) Human Sci Pr.
***Rotbart, Harley A., ed.** Human Enterovirus Infections. LC 94-39792. 1994. write for info. (*1-55581-092-6*) Am Soc Microbio.
Rotberg, Iris C., et al, eds. Federal Policy Options for Improving the Education of Low-Income Students, Vol. II: Commentaries. LC 93-36689. 1993. write for info. (*0-8330-1457-9*, MR-210-LE) Rand Corp.
Rotberg, R. I., jt. auth. see Rabb, T.
Rotberg, Robert, jt. auth. see Rabb, Theodore.
Rotberg, Robert I. Africa & Its Explorers: Motives, Methods, & Impact. LC 77-134327. 351p. 1970. pap. 15. 50 (*0-674-00777-8*) HUP.
— Christian Missionaries & the Creation of Northern Rhodesia, 1880-1924. LC 65-12993. (Illus.). 264p. reprint ed. pap. 75.30 (*0-8357-2924-9*, 2039163) Bks Demand.
— The Founder: Cecil Rhodes & the Enigma of Power. (Illus.). 834p. 1988. 45.00 (*0-19-504968-3*) OUP.
— Rise of Nationalism in Central Africa: The Making of Malawi & Zambia, 1873-1964. LC 65-19829. (Center for International Affairs Ser.). (Illus.). 362p. 1965. pap. 13. 95 (*0-674-77191-5*, HP39) HUP.
— Suffer the Future: Policy Choices in Southern Africa. LC 79-25845. 327p. 1980. 32.00 (*0-674-85401-2*) HUP.
Rotberg, Robert I., ed. Africa in the Nineteen Nineties & Beyond: U. S. Policy Opportunities & Choices. LC 88-6724. (Illus.). 300p. (Orig.). 1988. text ed. 24.95 (*0-917256-43-3*); pap. 12.95 (*0-917256-44-1*) Ref Pubns.
Rotberg, Robert I. & Rabb, Theodore K., eds. Art & History: Images Their Meaning. (Studies in Interdisciplinary History). (Illus.). 310p. 1988. pap. 17. 95 (*0-521-33569-8*) Cambridge U Pr.
— Art & History: Images Their Meaning. (Studies in Interdisciplinary History). (Illus.). 310p. 1988. 59.95 (*0-521-34018-7*) Cambridge U Pr.
— Marriage & Fertility: Studies in Interdisciplinary History. LC 80-7816. (Illus.). Date not set. reprint ed. pap. 109. 50 (*0-7837-9428-2*, 2060169) Bks Demand.
— The Origin & Prevention of Major Wars. (Studies in Interdisciplinary History). 350p. (C). 1989. pap. 17.95 (*0-521-37955-5*) Cambridge U Pr.
Rotberg, Robert I. & Robb, Theodore K., eds. Population & Economy: From the Traditional to the Modern World. (Studies in Interdisciplinary History). (Illus.). 220p. 1986. pap. 19.95 (*0-521-31055-5*) Cambridge U Pr.
Rotberg, Robert I., jt. ed. see Chittick, H. Neville.
Rotberg, Robert I., jt. ed. see Kilson, Martin L.
Rotblat, Joseph. Striving for Peace, Security & Development in the World: Annals of Pugwash 1991. 296p. 1993. text ed. 55.00 (*981-02-1249-6*) World Scientific Pub.
Rotblat, Joseph, ed. Scientists, the Arms Race & Disarmament. 320p. 1982. 39.00 (*0-85066-234-6*) Taylor & Francis.

Rotblat, Joseph & Holdren, John P., eds. Building Global Security Through Cooperation: Annals of Pugwash 1989. (Illus.). 320p. 1991. text ed. 83.00 (*0-387-52813-X*) Spr-Verlag.

Rotblat, Joseph & Pascolini, Alessandro, eds. The Arms Race at a Time of Decision: Annals of Pugwash 1983. LC 84-40288. 315p. 1984. text ed. 35.00 (*0-312-04950-1*) St Martin.

Rotblat, Joseph & Valki, Laszlo, eds. Coexistence, Cooperation & Common Security. LC 88-1956. 340p. 1988. text ed. 59.95 (*0-312-01875-4*) St Martin.

Rotblat, Joseph, jt. ed. see Atlmann, J.

Rotblat, Joseph, jt. auth. see Hellman, Sven.

Rotblat, Joseph, jt. ed. see Holdren, John P.

Rotblat, Joseph, et al, eds. A Nuclear-Weapon-Free World: Desirable? Feasible? 228p. (C). 1993. text ed. 55.50 (*0-8133-8718-3*) Westview.

Rotch, William, et al. Cases in Management Accounting & Control Systems. 3rd ed. 1995. pap. text ed. 22.00 (*0-13-103128-7*) P-H.

— The Executive's Guide to Management Accounting & Control Systems. 4th ed. LC 90-84296. 183p. 1991. 39.95 (*0-87393-120-3*) Dame Pubns.

***Rotella.** Critical Essays on James Merrill. 1996. 40.00 (*0-7838-0031-2*) G K Hall.

— Golf Between the Ears. 1995. 21.00 (*0-671-88999-0*) S&S Trade.

Rotella & Coop. Becoming a Winner in the Classroom. 53p. Incl. 3 cass. 34.50 (*0-88432-233-5*, S01830) Audio-Forum.

— Mind Power to Better Golf. 25p. 1985. Incl. 3 cass. audio 34.50 (*0-88432-187-8*, S01820) Audio-Forum.

Rotella, Alexis. Beards & Wings. 40p. 1985. pap. text ed. 6.00x (*0-917951-01-8*) White Peony.

— Camembert Comes from the Sea. (Illus.). 40p. 1984. pap. 6.50 (*0-917951-00-X*) White Peony.

Rotella, Alexis, ed. The Rise & Fall of Sparrows: A Collection of North American Haiku. LC 89-81932. (Orig.). 1990. pap. 8.95 (*0-9623497-2-0*) Los Hombres.

Rotella, Alexis K. Antiphony of Bells. 20p. 1988. 6.00 (*0-917951-02-6*) Jade Mtn.

— The Essence of Flowers: Wisdom for the Aquarian Age. (Illus.). 140p. 1991. per. 10.00 (*0-917951-11-5*) Jade Mtn.

— How Words & Thoughts Affect Your Body: The Book of Affirmations. 94p. 1990. per. 10.00 (*0-917951-10-7*) Jade Mtn.

— The Lace Curtain. 20p. 1988. 6.00 (*0-917951-03-4*) Jade Mtn.

— Moonflowers. 20p. (Orig.). 1987. pap. 7.00 (*0-916133-05-2*) Jade Mtn.

— Musical Chairs: Childhood Haiku. (Illus.). 50p. 1994. per., pap. text ed. 11.00 (*0-917951-26-3*) Jade Mtn.

— Tuning the Lily. 20p. 1983. pap. 2.00 (*0-913719-61-7*) High-Coo Pr.

Rotella, Alexis K., jt. auth. see Miller, Florence.

***Rotella, Bob & Cullen, Bob.** Golf Is Not a Game of Perfect. LC 95-1120. 1995. 20.00 (*0-684-80364-X*) S&S Trade.

Rotella, Elyce J. From Home to Office: U. S. Women At Work, 1870-1930. LC 80-29154. (Studies in American History & Culture: No. 25). 251p. reprint ed. pap. 71.60 (*0-685-44072-9*, 2070112) Bks Demand.

Rotella, Guy. Critical Essays on e. e. cummings. (Critical Essays on American Literature Ser.). 352p. (C). 1984. text ed. 45.00 (*0-8161-8677-4*) G K Hall.

— Reading & Writing Nature: The Poetry of Robert Frost, Wallace Stevens, Marianne Moore, & Elizabeth Bishop. 253p. 1990. text ed. 40.00 (*1-55553-086-9*) NE U Pr.

Rotella, R. J., jt. ed. see Bunker, L. K.

Rotella, Robert. Elements of Successful Trading: Developing Your Comprehensive Strategy Through Psychology. 1992. 29.95 (*0-13-204579-6*) P-H.

Rotella, Robert J. & Bunker, Linda K. Parenting Your Superstar. LC 84-20174. (Illus.). 256p. (Orig.). 1987. pap. 15.95 (*0-88011-262-X*, PROT0262) Human Kinetics.

Rotellar, Carlos. Acute Renal Insufficiency Made Ridiculously Simple. (Illus.). 56p. (Orig.). 1992. pap. text ed. 9.95 (*0-940780-09-7*) MedMaster.

Rotelle, John E. Augustine Day by Day. (Orig.). 1986. pap. 4.50 (*0-89942-170-9*, 170-09) Catholic Bk Pub.

— Lord, Let Me Know You. 72p. (Orig.). 1987. pap. 1.00 (*0-941491-04-8*) Augustinian Pr.

— Woman of Faith. 72p. (Orig.). 1987. pap. 1.00 (*0-941491-03-X*) Augustinian Pr.

Rotelle, John E., ed. Augustine's Heritage: Readings from the Augustinian Tradition, 3 vols., 1. 1986. 1.50 (*0-89942-701-4*, 701-04) Catholic Bk Pub.

— Augustine's Heritage: Readings from the Augustinian Tradition, 3 vols., 2. 1986. write for info. (*0-89942-702-2*, 702-04) Catholic Bk Pub.

— Augustine's Heritage: Readings from the Augustinian Tradition, 3 vols., 3. 1986. write for info. (*0-89942-703-0*, 703-04) Catholic Bk Pub.

— Little Office of the Blessed Virgin Mary. 192p. 1988. 8.95 (*0-89942-450-3*, 450/10) Catholic Bk Pub.

***Rotelle, John E., ed. & pref.** Meditations on the Sunday Gospels: Year A. (Word of God Throughout the Ages Ser.). 168p. (Orig.). 1995. pap. 9.95 (*1-56548-032-5*) New City.

Rotelle, John E., ed. Sermons. Boulding, Maria, tr. LC 93-44267. (Augustinian Ser.: Vol. 20). (ENG & LAT.). 1994. write for info. (*0-941491-60-9*); pap. write for info. (*0-941491-59-5*) Augustinian Pr.

— Take My Advice. rev. ed. 64p. 1987. pap. 1.00 (*0-941491-02-1*) Augustinian Pr.

***Rotelle, John E., ed. & intro.** Tradition Day by Day. 430p. Date not set. pap. 12.95 (*0-941491-74-9*) Augustinian Pr.

Rotelle, John E., ed. We Are Your Servants: Augustine's Homilies on Ministry. Fellowes, Audrey, tr. LC 86-71645. 156p. 1986. pap. 4.50 (*0-941491-10-2*) Augustinian Pr.

— A Word in Season, 4 vols. Barnecut, Edith, tr. (Orig.). 1987. reprint ed. write for info. (*0-318-62742-6*) Augustinian Pr.

— A Word in Season, 4 vols., Vol. I. Barnecut, Edith, tr. 230p. (Orig.). 1987. reprint ed. pap. 12.50 (*0-941491-14-5*) Augustinian Pr.

— A Word in Season, 4 vols., Vol. II. Barnecut, Edith, tr. 230p. (Orig.). 1987. reprint ed. pap. 12.50 (*0-941491-12-9*) Augustinian Pr.

— A Word in Season, 4 vols., Vol. III. Barnecut, Edith, tr. 230p. (Orig.). 1987. reprint ed. pap. 12.50 (*0-941491-13-7*) Augustinian Pr.

— A Word in Season, 4 vols., Vol. IV. Barnecut, Edith, tr. 304p. (Orig.). 1987. reprint ed. 25.00 (*0-941491-45-5*); reprint ed. pap. 15.00 (*0-941491-15-3*) Augustinian Pr.

Rotelle, John E., ed. see Alonso, Carlos.

Rotelle, John E., ed. see Back, Siegfried.

Rotelle, John E., jt. auth. see Bellini, Pietro.

Rotelle, John E., ed. see De Orozco, Alonso.

Rotelle, John E., ed. see Hackett, Benedict.

Rotelle, John E., ed. see Hippo, Augustine of.

Rotelle, John E., ed. see Martin, Francis X.

Rotelle, John E., ed. see Pellegrino, Michele.

Rotelle, John E., ed. see Possidius.

Rotelle, John E., ed. see St. Augustine.

Rotelle, John E., ed. see Trape, Agostino.

Rotem, A., jt. auth. see Lawson, James.

Rotem, J., jt. ed. see Kranz, J.

Rotem, Joseph. The Genus Alternaria: Biology, Epidemiology, & Pathogenicity. LC 93-74153. (Illus.). 326p. 1994. 79.00 (*0-89054-152-3*) Am Phytopathol Soc.

Rotem, Simha. The Past Within Me: Memoirs of a Warsaw Ghetto Fighter. Harshav, Barbara, tr. LC 94-17452. 192p. 1994. 18.50 (*0-300-05797-0*) Yale U Pr.

Rotemberg, Julio, jt. ed. see Bernanke, Ben S.

Rotemberg, Julio J., jt. ed. see Fischer, Stanley.

Rotenberg, Abie. The Place Where I Belong. (Illus.). (J). (ps-1). 1988. 9.95 (*0-935063-43-9*) CIS Comm.

Rotenberg, Alexander. Emissaries. (Illus.). 256p. 1987. 17.95 (*0-8065-1062-5*, Citadel Pr) Carol Pub Group.

Rotenberg, K. J., ed. Children's Interpersonal Trust: Sensitivity to Lying, Deception & Promise Violations. (Illus.). viii, 172p. 1991. 49.00 (*0-387-97511-X*) Spr-Verlag.

***Rotenberg, Ken J., ed.** Disclosure Processes in Children & Adolescents. (Cambridge Studies in Social & Emotional Development). (Illus.). 240p. (C). 1995. 44.95 (*0-521-47098-6*) Cambridge U Pr.

Rotenberg, M., ed. Biomathematics & Cell Kinetics. (Developments in Cell Biology Ser.: Vol. 8). 424p. 1981. 97.50 (*0-444-80371-8*) Elsevier.

Rotenberg, Marc, jt. ed. see Banisar, David.

***Rotenberg, Mark.** I Was a 1950's Pin-up Model. Betrock, Alan, ed. LC 95-69562. (Illus.). 96p. (Orig.). 1995. pap. 12.95 (*0-9626833-7-X*) Shake Bks.

Rotenberg, Mordechai. Dia-Logo Therapy: Psychonarration & the Pardes. LC 90-44250. 192p. 1991. text ed. 55.00 (*0-275-92943-4*, C2943, Praeger Pubs) Greenwood.

— Dialogue with Deviance: The Hasidic Ethic & the Theory of Social Contraction. LC 93-6901. 283p. (C). 1993. reprint ed. pap. 18.95 (*0-8191-8975-8*) U Pr of Amer.

— Re-Biographing & Deviance: Psychotherapeutic Narrativism & the Midrash. LC 87-2451. 256p. 1987. text ed. 52.95 (*0-275-92391-6*, C2391, Praeger Pubs) Greenwood.

Rotenberg, Rena, jt. auth. see Feinberg, Miriam P.

***Rotenberg, Robert.** Landscape & Power in Vienna. (Illus.). 416p. 1994. text ed. 39.95x (*0-8018-4961-6*) Johns Hopkins.

— Time & Order in Metropolitan Vienna: A Seizure of Schedules. LC 91-32894. (Ethnographic Inquiry Ser.). (Illus.). 224p. (C). 1992. text ed. 32.50 (*1-56098-103-2*) Smithsonian.

Rotenberg, Robert & McDonogh, Gary. The Cultural Meaning of Urban Space: Contemporary Urban Studies. LC 92-32179. 248p. 1993. text ed. 55.00 (*0-89789-319-0*, H319, Bergin & Garvey); pap. text ed. 16.95 (*0-89789-320-4*, G320, Bergin & Garvey) Greenwood.

Rotenberg, Shlomo. Am Olam, Vol. 1. 1989. 17.95 (*0-87306-483-6*) Feldheim.

Rotenstreich, Nathan. Jewish Philosophy in Modern Times. rev. ed. 296p. (C). 1995. reprint ed. pap. text ed. 19.95 (*0-8143-2439-8*) Wayne St U Pr.

— Order & Might. LC 87-9980. (SUNY Series in Philosophy). 238p. 1988. 57.50 (*0-88706-628-3*); pap. 18.95 (*0-88706-630-5*) State U NY Pr.

— Philosophy: The Concept & Its Manifestations. LC 72-77878. 255p. 1972. lib. bdg. 84.00 (*90-277-0236-5*); pap. text ed. 41.50 (*90-277-0284-5*) Kluwer Ac.

— Philosophy, History & Politics. (Melbourne International Philosophy Ser.: No. 1). 1976. pap. text ed. 47.00 (*90-247-1743-4*) Kluwer Ac.

— Practice & Realization. 1979. lib. bdg. 62.00 (*90-247-2112-1*) Kluwer Ac.

— Reflection & Action. 1984. lib. bdg. 89.00 (*90-247-2969-6*) Kluwer Ac.

— Reflection & Action. 1988. pap. text ed. 25.00 (*90-247-3128-3*) Kluwer Ac.

— Theory & Practice. (Van Leer Jerusalem Foundation Ser.). 1977. pap. text ed. 65.50 (*90-247-2004-4*) Kluwer Ac.

— Time & Meaning in History. (C). 1987. lib. bdg. 95.00 (*90-277-2467-9*) Kluwer Ac.

Rotenstreich, Nathan, ed. Essays on Zionism & the Contemporary Jewish Condition. 1981. write for info. (*0-318-53299-9*) Herzl Pr.

Rotenstreich, Nathan, jt. ed. see Bauer, Yehuda.

Roter, Debra, jt. ed. see Stewart, Moira.

Roter, Debra L. & Hall, Judith A. Doctors Talking with Patients - Patients Talking with Doctors: Improving Communication in Medical Visits. LC 92-17633. 224p. 1992. text ed. 45.00 (*0-86569-048-0*, T048, Auburn Hse) Greenwood.

— Doctors Talking with Patients - Patients Talking with Doctors: Improving Communication in Medical Visits. 2nd ed. LC 92-17633. 224p. 1993. pap. text ed. 19.95 (*0-86569-234-3*, Auburn Hse) Greenwood.

Roter, Mike, jt. auth. see Wright, Benjamin.

Rotermund, Heinrich W. Das Gelehrte Hannover Oder Lexikon Von Schriftstellern un Schriftstellerinnen, Gelehrten Geschaftsmannern und Kunstlern die Seit der Reformation in und Auberhalb Den Samtlichen Zum Jetzigen Konigreich Hannover Gehorigen Provinzen Gelebt Haben und Noch Leben, 2 vols. 1983. Set incl. microfiches. fiche write for info. (*0-318-71944-4*, Pub. by Georg Olms GW) Lubrecht & Cramer.

Rotert, Richard W., jt. ed. see Butler, Francelia.

Rotert, Ruth, jt. auth. see Taylor, Alf.

Rotfeld, Adam D., ed. A Co-Operative Security Order in & for Europe. 400p. 1995. 65.00 (*0-19-829165-5*) OUP.

— Global Security & the Rule of Law. LC 92-27076. 320p. 1995. 59.00 (*0-19-829163-9*) OUP.

Rotfield, Adam D., ed. From Helsinki to Helsinki & Beyond: Analysis & Documents of the Conference on Security & Co-Operation in Europe, 1973-93. (SIPRI Publication). 608p. 1995. 69.00 (*0-19-829181-7*) OUP.

Roth. Husserls Ethische Untersuchungen Dargestellt Anhand Seiner Vorlesungsmanuskripte. (Phaenomenologica Ser.: No. 7). 1961. lib. bdg. 42.50 (*90-247-0241-0*) Kluwer Ac.

— I'll Cry Tomorrow. 1988. pap. text ed. 9.95 (*0-88391-074-8*, F Fell Pubs) LIFETIME.

— The Radetsky March. pap. write for info. (*0-679-44361-4*) Random.

— Sign Painters Dream. Date not set. pap. 6.99 (*0-517-88541-7*) Random Hse Value.

Roth, jt. auth. see Bergman.

Roth, et al. Thoracic Oncology. 944p. 1989. text ed. 125.00 (*0-7216-1950-9*) Saunders.

Roth, A. Vacuum Sealing Techniques. LC 93-27399. (American Vacuum Society Classics Ser.). (Illus.). 864p. 1994. pap. text ed. 35.00 (*1-56396-259-4*, AIP Pr) Am Inst Physics.

— Vacuum Sealing Techniques. 1966. 346.00 (*0-08-011587-X*, Pub. by Pergamon Repr UK) Franklin.

— Vacuum Technology. 3rd enl. ed. 572p. 1990. write for info. (*0-444-88010-0*, North Holland) Elsevier.

Roth, Al. Great Lights. (Illus.). 77p. 1992. write for info. (*0-9637380-1-1*) Al Roth.

Roth, Alfred C. Small Gas Engines. rev. ed. (Illus.). 352p. (YA). 1992. text ed. 30.00 (*0-87006-919-5*) Goodheart.

Roth, Alvin. Picture Bidding. 317p. 1991. 24.95 (*0-940257-11-4*) Granovetter Bks.

Roth, Alvin E., ed. Game Theoretic Models of Bargaining. (Illus.). 416p. 1985. 79.95 (*0-521-26757-9*) Cambridge U Pr.

— Laboratory Experiments in Economics: Six Points of View. 224p. 1987. 54.95 (*0-521-33392-X*) Cambridge U Pr.

— The Shapley Value: Essays in Honor of Lloyd S. Shapley. (Illus.). 320p. 1988. 74.95 (*0-521-36177-X*) Cambridge U Pr.

Roth, Alvin E. & Sotomayor, Marilda A. Two-Sided Matching: A Study in Game-Theoretic Modeling & Analysis. (Econometric Society Monographs: No. 18). (Illus.). 300p. (C). 1990. 69.95 (*0-521-39015-X*) Cambridge U Pr.

— Two-Sided Matching: A Study in Game-Theoretic Modeling & Analysis. (Econometric Society Monographs: No. 18). (Illus.). 288p. (C). 1992. pap. 19.95 (*0-521-43788-1*) Cambridge U Pr.

Roth, Amy. Season for Change. 24p. 1990. pap. 3.00 (*0-87227-147-1*, RBP5178) Reg Baptist.

Roth, Andrew, jt. auth. see Roth, Jonathan.

Roth, Ann M. Egyptian Phyles in the Old Kingdom: The Evolution of a System of Social Organization. LC 90-63938. (Studies in Ancient Oriental Civilization: No. 48). (Illus.). xxvi, 243p. 1991. pap. 30.00 (*0-918986-68-0*) Orientl Inst Pr IT.

Roth, Ann M., tr. see Zauzich, Karl-Theodor.

Roth, Arlen. Arlen Roth's Complete Acoustic Guitar. (Illus.). 208p. 1985. pap. 18.95 (*0-02-872150-0*) Schirmer Bks.

— Arlen Roth's Heavy Metal Guitar. 186p. (YA). 1990. pap. 16.95 (*0-02-870010-4*) Schirmer Bks.

— Beginning Blues Guitar. LC 75-32888. (Illus.). (Orig.). 1976. pap. 9.95 (*0-8256-2350-2*) Music Sales.

— Nashville Guitar. (Illus.). 144p. pap. 14.95 (*0-8256-0172-X*, OK63321, Oak) Music Sales.

— Traditional, Country & Electric Slide Guitar. (Illus.). 128p. 1975. pap. 14.95 (*0-8256-0162-2*, Oak) Music Sales.

Roth, Arthur. Eiger: Wall of Death. large type ed. 528p. 1988. 15.95 (*0-7089-1806-9*) Ulverscroft.

— Iceberg Hermit. (YA). 1989. pap. 2.95 (*0-590-44112-4*) Scholastic Inc.

Roth, Audrey J. The Research Paper: Process, Form, & Content. 6th ed. 300p. (C). 1989. pap. 15.95 (*0-534-09924-6*) Intl Thomson.

— The Research Paper: Process, Form, & Content. 7th ed. 300p. (C). 1995. pap. 15.95 (*0-534-17454-X*) Intl Thomson.

Roth, Barry. An Annotated Bibliography of Jane Austen Studies, 1973-83. LC 84-20814. 359p. 1985. 35.00 (*0-8139-1054-4*) U Pr of Va.

— Associations: The Memory Book. LC 92-70949. (Illus.). 90p. (Orig.). 1993. pap. 6.95 (*1-881140-01-6*) Benidee Prods.

Roth, Bennett E., et al, eds. Difficult Patient in Group: Group Psychotherapy with Borderline & Narcissistic Disorders. (American Group Psychotherapy Association Monographs: No. 6). 350p. 1990. 40.00 (*0-8236-1286-4*) Intl Univs Pr.

Roth, Bette, jt. auth. see Grad, Eli.

Roth, Bettie G. & Schneider, Harriette, eds. Today's Traditional: Jewish Cooking with a Lighter Touch. LC 93-70841. (Illus.). 208p. (Orig.). 1993. pap. 11.95 (*0-9636626-0-0*) Congreg Beth Shalom.

Roth, Beulah, jt. auth. see Roth, Sanford.

Roth, Bob & Tedesco, Art, eds. The Official Guide to LGB Trains. 192p. 1996. pap. text ed. write for info. (*0-89778-302-6*, 10-7815) Greenberg Bks.

Roth, Byron M. Prescription for Failure: Race Relations in the Age of Social Science. LC 93-42745. (Studies in Social Philosophy & Policy: No. 18). 370p. (C). 1994. 49.95 (*1-56000-161-5*); pap. 21.95 (*1-56000-739-7*) Transaction Pubs.

Roth, Byron M. & Mullen, John D. Decision Making: Its Logic & Practice. 272p. (C). 1990. lib. bdg. 39.95 (*0-8476-7619-6*) Rowman.

Roth, C. H., Jr., jt. auth. see Matney, Roy M., II.

Roth, Carol. Quiet As a Mouse. (Illus.). 32p. (J). (ps-3). 1991. 6.95 (*1-56288-121-3*) Checkerboard.

Roth, Carol Pindar, et al. Medical Record Abstraction Form & Guidelines for Assessing the Quality of Prenatal Care. LC 93-4622. 1993. write for info. (*0-8330-1393-9*, MR-238-HF) Rand Corp.

Roth, Catharine, tr. St. Theodore the Studite on the Holy Icons. LC 81-18319. 115p. (Orig.). 1981. pap. 7.95 (*0-913836-76-1*) St Vladimirs.

Roth, Catharine P., tr. see St. Gregory of Nyssa.

Roth, Catharine P., tr. see St. John Chrysostom.

Roth, Catherine. The Architectural Heritage of Genesee County, New York. (Illus.). 339p. 1989. 40.00 (*0-685-29181-2*); per. 29.50 (*0-685-29182-0*) Lndmrk Soc Genesee.

Roth, Cecil. Dona Gracia of the House of Nasi. LC 77-92984. 232p. 1992. reprint ed. pap. text ed. 13.95 (*0-8276-0411-4*) JPS Phila.

— The Duke of Naxos of the House of Nasi. LC 71-91172. 270p. 1992. reprint ed. pap. text ed. 13.95 (*0-8276-0412-2*) JPS Phila.

— Gleanings: Essays in Jewish History, Letters & Art. 1967. 14.95 (*0-8197-0178-5*) Bloch.

— A History of the Jews: From Earliest Times Through the Six Day War. rev. ed. LC 74-121042. 1970. pap. 16.00 (*0-8052-0009-6*) Schocken.

— A History of the Marranos. LC 74-29516. (Modern Jewish Experience Ser.). (Illus.). 1975. reprint ed. 39.95 (*0-405-06742-9*) Ayer.

— A History of the Marranos. xxiv, 424p. 1992. reprint ed. 24.95 (*0-87203-040-7*); reprint ed. pap. 15.95 (*0-87203-138-1*) Hermon.

— The Jewish Contribution to Civilizaton. 1978. 10.95 (*0-685-42172-4*) Hebrew Pub.

— The Jews in the Renaissance. LC 59-8516. (Illus.). 378p. 1978. reprint ed. pap. 9.95 (*0-8276-0103-4*) JPS Phila.

— A Life of Menasseh Ben Israel: Rabbi, Printer & Diplomat. LC 74-29518. (Modern Jewish Experience Ser.). (Illus.). 1975. reprint ed. 35.95 (*0-405-06743-7*) Ayer.

— The Sassoon Dynasty. Wilkins, Mira, ed. LC 76-29982. (European Business Ser.). (Illus.). 1977. reprint ed. lib. bdg. 25.95 (*0-405-09747-6*) Ayer.

— Short History of the Jewish People. rev. ed. 1969. 14.95 (*0-685-05778-X*); pap. 6.95 (*0-87677-183-5*) Hartmore.

Roth, Cecil & Wigoder, Geoffrey, eds. Encyclopedia Judaica, 18 vols., Set. 1994. reprint ed. 995.00x (*0-685-36253-1*, Pub. by Keter Pub IS) Coronet Bks.

Roth, Cecil, jt. auth. see Wurmbrand, Max.

Roth, Charles. The Amateur Naturalist: Explorations & Investigations. (Amateur Science Ser.). (Illus.). (J). (gr. 5-8). 1994. pap. 6.95 (*0-531-15697-4*) Watts.

— Mind: The Master Power. LC 72-94282. 1984. 7.95 (*0-87159-099-9*) Unity Bks.

— More Power to You! LC 82-50122. 164p. 1982. 7.95 (*0-87159-093-X*) Unity Bks.

— Twelve Power Meditation Exercise. LC 89-50837. 90p. 1989. 6.95 (*0-87159-161-8*) Unity Bks.

Roth, Charles, ed. see Cross, Ruth C.

Roth, Charles B. Fundamentals of Logic Design. 4th ed. Slaughter, Michael, ed. 770p. (C). 1992. text ed. 68.50 (*0-314-92218-0*) West Pub.

— Secrets of Closing Sales. 6th ed. 1993. 18.95 (*0-13-799412-5*) P-H.

Roth, Charles B. & Alexander, Roy. Secrets of Closing Sales. 5th ed. LC 82-12312. 276p. 1986. 18.95 (*0-13-797910-X*, Busn) P-H.

Roth, Charles E. The Amateur Naturalist: Explorations & Investigations. LC 93-13390. (Amateur Science Ser.). (Illus.). 144p. (J). (gr. 6-9). 1993. lib. bdg. 13.93 (*0-531-11002-8*) Watts.

— The Sky Observer's Guidebook. (Phalarope Book Ser.). (Illus.). 256p. 1986. 17.95 (*0-13-812793-X*) P-H.

Roth, Charles E., et al. Beyond the Classroom: Exploration of Schoolground & Backyard. Orig. Title: Schoolground Science. 1991. reprint ed. 9.95 (*0-932691-10-2*) MA Audubon Soc.

***Roth, Cliff.** The Low Budget Video Bible: The Essential Do-It-Yourself Guide to Creating Top-Notch Video on a Shoestring Budget. 2nd ed. (Illus.). 460p. (Orig.). (C). 1995. pap. 27.95 (*0-9635216-1-6*) Desktop Vid.

— The Low Budget Video Bible: The Essential Do-It-Yourself Guide to Making Top-Notch Video on a Shoestring Budget. (Illus.). 300p. (Orig.). 1993. pap. 34.95 (*0-9635216-0-8*) Desktop Video.

R

An Asterisk (*) at the beginning of an entry indicates that the title is appearing in BIP for the first time.

Roth, D. The Girl in the Grass. 1984. pap. 2.25 (*0-449-70092-5*) Fawcett.

Roth, Dana. Complete Book of Bass Chords. (Complete Book Ser.). 1993. 19.95 (*1-56222-548-0*, 94754) Mel Bay.

— Encyclopedia of Scales & Modes for Electric Bass. 1993. 9.95 (*1-56222-290-2*, 94695) Mel Bay.

Roth, Daniel. Why Women Win at Bridge. (Illus.). 192p. (Orig.). 1994. pap. 10.95 (*0-571-16748-9*) Faber & Faber.

Roth, Danny. Awareness - The Way to Improve Your Bridge. (Master Bridge Ser.). 128p. 1991. 24.95 (*0-575-05011-X*, Pub. by V Gollancz UK) Trafalgar.

— Bridge: The Expert Beginner. 256p. (Orig.). 1993. pap. 10.00 (*0-00-258202-3*, Pub. by HarpC UK) HarpC.

— Bridge: The Expert Improver. 256p. (Orig.). 1993. pap. 10.00 (*0-00-258201-5*, Pub. by HarpC UK) HarpC.

— Hand Reading in Bridge: How to Improve Your Card Play. (Illus.). 128p. 1993. 24.95 (*0-575-05434-4*, Pub. by V Gollancz UK) Trafalgar.

— Signal Success in Bridge. (Illus.). 142p. 1993. pap. 15.95 (*0-575-05539-1*, Pub. by V Gollancz UK) Trafalgar.

Roth, Darlene R. Architecture, Archaeology & Landscapes: Resources for Historic Preservation in Unincorporated Cobb County, Georgia. LC 88-62643. (Illus.). 290p. (Orig.). (C). 1988. student ed 25.00 (*0-9621120-2-X*); text ed. 25.00 (*0-9621120-0-3*); pap. text ed. 25.00 (*0-9621120-1-1*) CCHPC.

— Matronage: Patterns in Women's Organizations, Atlanta, Georgia, 1890-1940. LC 94-18184. (Scholarship in Women's History Ser.: Vol. 9). 240p. 1994. 55.00 (*0-926019-70-8*) Carlson Pub.

Roth, David. Sacred Honor: Colin Powell. 1994. mass mkt. 5.99 (*0-06-100849-4*) HarpC.

— Sacred Honor: Colin Powell: The Inside Account of His Life & Triumphs. (Illus.). 272p. 1993. 12.99 (*0-310-61508-9*) Zondervan.

— Sacred Honor: Colin Powell: The Inside Account of His Life & Triumphs. (Illus.). 272p. 1993. 19.99 (*0-310-60480-X*) Zondervan.

Roth, David & Maifair, Linda L. Colin Powell. (Today's Heroes Ser.). 112p. (J). (gr. 3-7). 1993. 4.99 (*0-310-39851-7*) Zondervan.

Roth, David & Warwick, Paul. Study of Comparative Politics. 432p. (C). 1990. text ed. 52.00 (*0-06-045626-4*) HarpCollege.

Roth, David, jt. auth. see North, Oliver.

Roth, David E. Bettmann Archive Illustrated History of the Civil War, 1861-1865. (Illus.). 256p. 1992. 24.98 (*0-8317-0775-5*) Smithmark.

Roth, Deborah. Being Human in the Face of Death. 160p. (C). 1989. reprint ed. lib. bdg. 25.00x (*0-8095-6560-9*) Borgo Pr.

Roth, Deborah, jt. auth. see Center for Help in Times of Loss Staff.

Roth, Dennis M. Rhythm Vision: A Guide to Visual Awareness. LC 90-30610. (Illus.). 128p. (Orig.). 1990. pap. 12.95 (*0-944091-02-4*) Intaglio Pr.

— The Wilderness Movement & the National Forests. 2nd rev. ed. LC 88-9495. (Illus.). 106p. 1995. pap. 12.95 (*0-944091-01-6*) Intaglio Pr.

— The Wilderness Movement & the National Forests. 2nd rev. ed. (Illus.). 106p. (C). 1995. lib. bdg. 22.95 (*0-944091-06-7*); pap. 14.95 (*0-944091-05-9*) Intaglio Pr.

Roth, E., et al. Grundlagen und Technik der Infusionstherapie und Klinischen Ernaehrung. (Handbuch der Infusionstherapie und Klinischen Ernaehrung Ser.: Band 2). x, 278p. 1985. 100.00 (*3-8055-3746-8*) S Karger.

Roth, E. N., ed. see Chien, S. H. & Hammond, L. L.

Roth, E. N., ed. see Cooper, Peter, et al.

Roth, E. N., ed. see Harris, G. T.

Roth, E. N., ed. see Kaddar, T., et al.

Roth, E. N., ed. see Kanwar, J. S. & Mudahar, Mohinder S.

Roth, E. N., ed. see Martinez, Adolfo, et al.

Roth, E. N., ed. see Mudahar, Mohinder S. & Kapusta, Edwin C.

Roth, E. N., ed. see Schultz, James J., et al.

Roth, E. N., ed. see Williams, Lewis B.

Roth, Edward S. Functional Gaging. LC 74-118771. (Society of Manufacturing Engineers Manufacturing Data Ser.). 149p. reprint ed. pap. 42.50 (*0-685-09004-3*, 2004984) Bks Demand.

Roth, Edward S., ed. Gaging: Practical Design & Application. LC 80-53424. 289p. reprint ed. pap. 82.40 (*0-317-27697-2*, 2024170) Bks Demand.

Roth, Edward S. & Runck, Robert F., eds. Functional Inspection Techniques. LC 67-20359. (American Society of Tool & Manufacturing Engineers Manufacturing Data Ser.). 95p. reprint ed. pap. 27.10 (*0-317-10741-0*, 2004985) Bks Demand.

***Roth, Eli & Streicher-Lankin, Sandra L.** Good Cholesterol, Bad Cholesterol. 2nd ed. LC 95-5285. 1995. pap. write for info. (*0-7615-0010-3*) Prima Pub.

Roth, Eli M. & Streicher, Sandra. Good Cholesterol, Bad Cholesterol: What You Need to Know to Reduce Your Risk of Heart Disease. 192p. 1990. reprint ed. 15.95 (*0-914629-85-9*); reprint ed. pap. 8.95 (*1-55958-025-9*) Prima Pub.

Roth, Elizabeth, jt. auth. see Beck, Sydney.

Roth, Ernst & Schuh, Willi. Richard Strauss: Complete Catalog. LC 64-6063. 1964. pap. 5.25 (*0-913932-31-0*) Boosey & Hawkes.

Roth, Etienne & Poty, Bernard, eds. Nuclear Methods of Dating. (C). 1990. lib. bdg. 375.00 (*0-7923-0188-9*) Kluwer Ac.

Roth, Filibert. Forest Regulation. 1925. 10.00 (*0-911586-28-8*) Wahr.

— Forest Valuation. 1926. 10.00 (*0-911586-29-6*) Wahr.

Roth, Francis. Did You Ever Talk to God Above? (Illus.). 1974. 6.99 (*3-901170-23-5*) CEF Press.

Roth, G., ed. see Wake, D. B., et al.

***Roth, Gabriel.** Private Provision of Public Services in Developing Countries. 294p. 1987. 16.95 (*0-614-02835-3*, 60785) World Bank.

Roth, Gabriel & Wynne, George W. Free Enterprise Urban Transportation. (Learning from Abroad Ser.: Vol. 5). 48p. (Orig.). 1982. pap. 10.95 (*0-87855-914-0*) Transaction Pubs.

Roth, Gabriel, jt. auth. see Wynne, George G.

Roth, Gabrielle. Maps to Ecstasy: Teachings of an Urban Shaman. 212p. 1993. reprint ed. pap. 10.95 (*1-882591-08-9*) Nataraj Pub.

Roth, Geneen. Breaking Free from Compulsive Eating. 1986. pap. 4.50 (*0-451-16132-7*, Sig) NAL-Dutton.

— Breaking Free from Compulsive Eating. LC 93-13034. 224p. 1993. reprint ed. pap. 10.95 (*0-452-27084-7*, Plume) NAL-Dutton.

— Feeding the Hungry Heart: The Experience of Compulsive Eating. LC 93-13035. 208p. 1993. reprint ed. pap. 10.95 (*0-452-27083-9*, Plume) NAL-Dutton.

— When Food Is Love: Exploring the Relationship Between Eating & Intimacy. 224p. 1992. pap. 10.00 (*0-452-26818-4*, Plume) NAL-Dutton.

— Why Weight? A Guide to Ending Compulsive Eating. (Illus.). 224p. 1989. pap. 10.95 (*0-452-26254-2*, Plume) NAL-Dutton.

Roth, George. Slaying the Law School Dragon: How to Survive & Thrive in First Year Law School. 2nd ed. 182p. 1991. pap. text ed. 14.95 (*0-471-54298-9*) Wiley.

Roth, George S., jt. auth. see Adelman, Richard C.

Roth, George S., jt. ed. see Adelman, Richard C.

Roth, Gerhard. The Autobiography of Albert Einstein. Green, Malcolm, tr. 120p. (Orig.). 1993. pap. 13.99 (*0-947757-47-3*) Serpents Tail.

— The Calm Ocean. Schreckenberger, Helga & Vansant, Jacqueline, trs. LC 92-45048. (Studies in Austrian Literature, Culture, & Thought. Translation Ser.). 238p. 1993. pap. 20.50 (*0-929497-64-3*) Ariadne CA.

Roth, Glen A., jt. auth. see Schlabach, Sue V.

***Roth, Greg, et al, eds.** Corn Silage Production, Management, & Feeding. LC 95-1562. 1995. write for info. (*0-89118-124-5*) Am Soc Agron.

Roth, Guenther. The Social Democrats in Imperial Germany: A Study in Working-Class Isolation & National Integration. Coser, Lewis A. & Powell, Walter W., eds. LC 79-7018. (Perennial Works in Sociology Ser.). 1980. reprint ed. lib. bdg. 29.95 (*0-405-12117-2*) Ayer.

Roth, Guenther & Schluchter, Wolfgang. Max Weber's Vision of History: Ethics & Methods. 222p. 1979. pap. 13.00 (*0-520-05226-9*) U CA Pr.

Roth, Guenther, jt. auth. see Bendix, Reinhard.

Roth, Guenther, jt. ed. see Lehmann, Hartmut.

Roth, Guenther, tr. see Schluchter, Wolfgang.

Roth, Guenther, ed. see Weber, Max M.

Roth, Gunter D., ed. Compendium of Practical Astronomy, 3 vols. rev. ed. Augensen, Harry J. & Heintz, Wulff D., trs. LC 93-27023. (Illus.). (ENG & GER.). 1993. Vol. 1: Instrumentation & Reduction Techniques, 560p. pap. 59.00 (*0-387-53596-9*); Vol. 2: Earth & Solar System, 384p. pap. 44.50 (*0-387-54885-8*); Vol. 3: Stars & Stellar Systems, 288p. pap. 44.50 (*0-387-54886-6*) Spr-Verlag.

— Compendium of Practical Astronomy, 3 vols., Set. rev. ed. Augensen, Harry J. & Heintz, Wulff D., trs. LC 93-27023. (Illus.). (ENG & GER.). 1994. pap. 125.00 (*0-387-56273-7*) Spr-Verlag.

***Roth, H.** Chasing the Long Rainbow. 1994. 29.95 (*0-393-90794-5*) Norton.

Roth, H. Ling. Oriental Silverwork: Malay & Chinese. (Oxford in Asia Hardback Reprints Ser.). (Illus.). 336p. 1994. 75.00 (*0-19-588605-4*) OUP.

— Studies in Primitive Looms. 1977. reprint ed. pap. 7.95 (*1-56659-020-5*) Robin & Russ.

Roth, Hal. After Fifty Thousand Miles. (Illus.). 1977. 24.95 (*0-393-03202-7*) Norton.

— After Fifty Thousand Miles. 352p. 1993. pap. 16.95 (*0-393-30948-7*) Norton.

— Chasing the Wind: A Book of High Adventure. (Illus.). 280p. (Orig.). 1993. pap. 19.95 (*0-924486-55-4*) Sheridan.

Roth-Hano, Renee. Safe Harbors. LC 93-10782. 224p. (YA). (gr. 12 up). 1993. text ed. 16.95 (*0-02-777795-2*, Four Winds Pr) S&S Childrens.

— Touch Wood: A Girlhood in Occupied France. LC 87-34326. 304p. (J). (gr. 5-9). 1988. lib. bdg. 16.95 (*0-02-777340-X*, Four Winds Pr) S&S Childrens.

— Touch Wood: A Girlhood Occupied In France. (ALA Notable Bk.). 304p. (J). (gr. 5 up). 1989. pap. 5.99 (*0-14-034085-8*, Puffin) Puffin Bks.

Roth, Hans-Dieter. Indian Moneylenders at Work. 1984. 18.50 (*0-8364-1106-4*, Pub. by Manohar II) S Asia.

Roth, Harold. A Day at the Races. LC 83-2345. (Illus.). 64p. (J). (gr. 3-6). 1983. 10.95 (*0-394-85814-X*) Pantheon.

Roth, Harold D. The Textual History of the Huai-nan Tzu. LC 90-85256. (Association for Asian Studies Monograph). (Illus.). 380p. (Orig.). (CHI.). (C). 1991. 36.00 (*0-924304-05-7*); pap. 20.00 (*0-924304-06-5*) Assn Asian Studies.

Roth, Harold P., jt. auth. see Morse, Wayne J.

Roth, Harriet. Deliciously Low: The Gourmet Guide to Low-Sodium, Low-Fat, Low-Cholesterol, Low-Sugar Cooking. 350p. 1984. pap. 11.95 (*0-452-26266-6*, Plume) NAL-Dutton.

— Deliciously Simple. 1988. pap. 8.95 (*0-452-25984-3*, Plume); pap. 11.00 (*0-452-26404-9*, Plume) NAL-Dutton.

— Harriet Roth's Cholesterol Control Cookbook. 1989. 18.95 (*0-317-02813-8*) NAL-Dutton.

— Harriet Roth's Cholesterol-Control Cookbook. (Illus.). 440p. 1991. reprint ed. pap. 11.95 (*0-452-26612-2*, Plume) NAL-Dutton.

— Harriet Roth's Completed Guide to Fats, Calories, & Cholesterol. 224p. 1993. pap. 3.99 (*0-451-17670-7*, Sig) NAL-Dutton.

— Harriet Roth's Deliciously Low-Fat Jewish Cooking: Over 350 Low-Fat, Low-Cholesterol Recipes for Holidays & Every Day. 400p. 1995. 24.95 (*0-525-93931-8*, Dutton) NAL-Dutton.

— Harriet Roth's Fat Counter. 80p. 1995. mass mkt. 2.99 (*0-451-17799-1*, Sig) NAL-Dutton.

— Harriet Roth's Fat Counter. rev. ed. 80p. 1992. pap. 2.50 (*0-451-17264-7*, Sig) NAL-Dutton.

***Roth, Harrison.** The Irwin Yearbook of Listed Stock Options-1995. 320p. 1995. 90.00 (*0-7863-0336-0*) Irwin Prof Pubng.

— LEAPS - Long-Term Equity Anticipation Securities: What They Are & How to Use Them for Profit & Protection. 360p. 1993. 45.00 (*1-55623-819-3*) Irwin Prof Pubng.

Roth, Henry. Call It Sleep. 1976. mass mkt. 4.95 (*0-380-01002-X*, Bard) Avon.

— Call It Sleep. 1992. 30.00 (*0-374-11819-1*); pap. 13.00 (*0-374-52292-8*) FS&G.

— Call It Sleep. limited ed. (Illus.). 482p. 1995. 700.00 (*0-318-72981-4*) Arion Pr.

— A Diving Rock on the Hudson, 2 vols. 418p. Date not set. 23.95 (*0-615-00586-1*) St Martin.

— Diving Rock on the Hudson: Mercy of a Rude Stream, Vol. II. 1995. 23.95 (*0-312-11777-9*) St Martin.

— Mercy of a Rude Stream. LC 93-37270. 304p. 1993. 23.00 (*0-312-10499-5*) St Martin.

— Mercy of a Rude Stream. LC 93-37270. 304p. 1994. 250.00 (*0-312-10501-0*) St Martin.

— Mercy of a Rude Stream: A Star Shines over Mt. Morris Park, Vol. 1. 1994. pap. 13.00 (*0-312-11929-1*) St Martin.

— Mercy of a Rude Stream, Vol. 1: A Star Shines over Mt. Morris Park. 1994. 23.00 (*0-312-16499-8*) St Martin.

— Shifting Landscape. 320p. 1994. pap. 13.95 (*0-312-11139-8*) St Martin.

Roth, Henry H. Boundaries of Love: And Other Stories. 1990. 17.95 (*0-945167-31-8*) British Amer Pub.

— The Cruz Chronicle: A Novel. (Fiction Ser.). 200p. 1988. 18.95 (*0-8135-1404-5*) Rutgers U Pr.

— The Cruz Chronicle: A Novel. (Fiction Ser.). 184p. (C). 1991. reprint ed. pap. 10.95 (*0-8135-1750-8*) Rutgers U Pr.

— In Empty Rooms: Tales of Love. LC 79-50422. (Illus.). 102p. (C). 1980. pap. 12.50 (*0-913204-11-0*) December Pr.

Roth, Henry L. The Natives of Sarawak & British North Borneo, 2 vols., Set. LC 77-87510. reprint ed. 75.00 (*0-404-16780-2*) AMS Pr.

Roth, Herman J., et al. Pharmaceutical Chemistry, Vol. 2: Drug Analysis. 544p. 1991. text ed. write for info. (*0-13-663360-9*) P-H.

Roth, I. Stratification of a Tropical Forest As Seen in Dispersal Types. (Tasks for Vegetation Science Ser.). 1987. lib. bdg. 209.50 (*90-6193-613-6*) Kluwer Ac.

— Stratification of Tropical Forests as seen in Leaf Structure. (Tasks for Vegetation Science Ser.). 1984. lib. bdg. 255.00 (*90-6193-946-1*) Kluwer Ac.

Roth, Ilona, ed. Introduction to Psychology, Vol. 2. 394p. 1990. 49.95 (*0-86377-137-8*); pap. 19.95 (*0-86377-139-4*) L Erlbaum Assocs.

— The Open University's Introduction to Psychology, Vol. 1. 488p. 1990. text ed. 49.95 (*0-86377-136-X*); pap. text ed. 19.95 (*0-86377-138-6*) L Erlbaum Assocs.

***Roth, Ilona & Bruce, Vicki.** Perception & Representation: Current Issues. 2nd ed. LC 94-41284. 1995. write for info. (*0-335-19474-5*, Open Univ Pr) Taylor & Francis.

Roth, Ilona & Frisby, John P. Perception & Representation. LC 85-21649. (Open Guides to Psychology Ser.). 192p. 1986. pap. 29.00 (*0-335-15328-3*, Open Univ Pr) Taylor & Francis.

Roth, Ingrid. Fruits of Angiosperms. (Encyclopedia of Plant Anatomy Ser.: Vol. 10-1). (Illus.). 1978. lib. bdg. 176.00 (*3-443-14010-6*) Lubrecht & Cramer.

— Leaf Structure: Coastal Vegetation & Mangroves of Venezuela. (Encyclopedia of Plant Anatomy Ser.: No. 14/2). (Illus.). 172p. 1992. lib. bdg. 95.00 (*3-443-14020-3*, Pub. by Gebrueder Borntraeger GW) Lubrecht & Cramer.

— Leaf Structure of a Venezuelan Cloud Forest in Relation to the Microclimate. (Encyclopedia of Plant Anatomy Ser.: Vol. 14/1). (Illus.). 248p. 1991. lib. bdg. 93.40 (*3-443-14018-1*, Pub. by Cramer-Borntraeger GW) Lubrecht & Cramer.

— Structural Patterns of Tropical Barks. (Encyclopedia of Plant Anatomy: Special Part Ser.: Vol. 9, Pt. 3). (Illus.). 609p. 1981. 196.00 (*3-443-14012-2*) Lubrecht & Cramer.

Roth, Irene. Cecil Roth, Historian Without Tears: A Memoir. (Illus.). 288p. 1982. 17.50 (*0-87203-103-9*) Hermon.

Roth, J., et al, eds. Polysialic Acid: From Microbes to Men. LC 92-48982. (Advances in Life Sciences Ser.). xxiii, 350p. 1992. 92.50 (*0-8176-2803-7*, Pub. by Birkhauser Vlg SZ) Birkhauser.

Roth, J. D., et al. Propagation of Mammalian Cells in Culture, Vol. I. 1976. text ed. 39.50 (*0-8422-7290-9*) Irvington.

Roth, J. H. Hand & Wrist. (Current Opinion in Orthopedics Ser.). (Illus.). 91p. (Orig.). 1993. pap. text ed. 59.95 (*1-870485-64-5*) Current Science.

***Roth, J. Reece.** Industrial Plasma Engineering. LC 94-42312. 1995. 135.00 (*0-7503-0317-4*); pap. 49.00 (*0-7503-0318-2*) IOP Pub.

— Introduction to Fusion Energy. 600p. (C). 1986. text ed. 43.50 (*0-935005-07-2*) Lincoln-Rembrandt.

Roth, Jack, et al, eds. Lung Cancer. LC 93-2842. 1993. 79.95 (*0-86542-282-6*) Blackwell Sci.

***Roth, Jack, et al.** Thoracic Oncology. 2nd ed. LC 94-26869. (Illus.). 608p. 1995. text ed. write for info. (*0-7216-4769-3*) Saunders.

***Roth, James, ed.** Virulence Mechanisms. 2nd ed. 500p. 1995. write for info. (*1-55581-085-3*) Am Soc Microbio.

Roth, James A., ed. Virulence Mechanisms of Bacterial Pathogens. (Illus.). 390p. 1988. text ed. 83.00 (*0-914826-99-9*) Am Soc Microbio.

Roth, Janice L. Charting: The Systematic Approach to Achieving Control. 38p. 1991. pap. 3.95 (*0-9631701-0-4*) R A Rapaport.

Roth, Jay S. All about AIDS. 320p. (C). 1989. pap. text ed. 30.00 (*3-7186-0488-4*) Gordon & Breach.

— All about Cancer. LC 85-50. (Illus.). 341p. (Orig.). 1985. text ed. 24.95 (*0-397-53068-4*) Lippincott.

Roth, Jeffrey. The Disturbed Subject: Epistemological & Ethical Implication of Reactivity in Videotape Research. (American University Studies: Psychology: Ser. VIII, Vol. 20). 144p. 1990. text ed. 30.50 (*0-8204-1150-7*) P Lang Pubs.

Roth, Jeffrey A., jt. auth. see National Research Council, Panel on the Understanding.

Roth, Jeffrey A., et al, eds. Taxpayer Compliance, 2 vols., Set. LC 88-36250. (Law in Social Context Ser.). 1989. 86.95 (*0-8122-8187-X*) U of Pa Pr.

— Taxpayer Compliance, Vol. 1. LC 88-36250. (Law in Social Context Ser.), 414p. 1989. Vol. I: An Agenda for Research, 414p. text ed. 46.95x (*0-8122-8182-9*) U of Pa Pr.

— Taxpayer Compliance, Vol. 2. LC 88-36250. (Law in Social Context Ser.). 282p. 1989. Vol. II: Social Science Perspectives, 282p. text ed. 44.95 (*0-8122-8150-0*) U of Pa Pr.

Roth, Joachim. Day & Night. (Illus.). 1993. 7.95 (*0-8059-3521-5*) Dorrance.

***Roth, Joan.** Jewish Women: A World of Traditional Changes. Lyons, Harriet, ed. (Illus.). 242p. 1995. 75.00 (*0-942160-12-6*) S Tilatitsky.

— Jewish Women: A World of Traditional Changes. deluxe ed. Lyons, Harriet, ed. 242p. 1995. 75.00 (*0-942160-11-8*) Jolen Pr.

— Shopping Bag Ladies of New York. Walter, Robert, ed. LC 81-85387. (Illus.). 122p. (Orig.). 1982. pap. 10.95 (*0-942160-00-2*) Jolen Pr.

Roth, Joel. The Halakhic Process: A Systemic Analysis. (Moreshet Ser.: No. XIII). 1987. 29.50 (*0-87334-035-3*) Jewish Sem.

Roth, John. Norigami: The Art of Norwegian Paper Folding. 1991. 6.95 (*0-934860-77-7*) Adventure Pubns.

Roth, John, jt. ed. see Magill, Frank N.

***Roth, John E.** American Elves: An Encyclopedia of Little People from the Lore of 340 Ethnic Groups of the Western Hemisphere. 528p. 1995. lib. bdg. 68.50 (*0-89950-944-4*) McFarland & Co.

Roth, John K. American Dreams: Meditations on Life in the United States. LC 76-26877. 194p. 1976. pap. 8.95 (*0-88316-527-9*) Chandler & Sharp.

— Ethics. (Magill Bibliographies Ser.). 169p. 1991. 40.00 (*0-8108-2788-3*) Scarecrow.

***Roth, John K., ed.** American Diversity, American Identity: The Lives & Works of 145 Writers Who Define the American Experience. (Reference Bks.). 736p. 1995. 45.00 (*0-8050-3430-7*) H Holt & Co.

Roth, John K. & Berenbaum, Michael, eds. Holocaust: Religious & Philosophical Implications. 390p. 1989. 29.95 (*1-55778-187-7*); pap. 16.95 (*1-55778-212-1*) Paragon Hse.

Roth, John K. & Rubenstein, Richard L. Approaches to Auschwitz: The Holocaust & Its Legacy. LC 86-27749. 420p. 1987. 20.00 (*0-8042-0778-X*, John Knox); pap. 18.99 (*0-8042-0777-1*, John Knox) Westminster John Knox.

Roth, John K. & Sontag, Frederick. The Questions of Philosophy. 532p. (C). 1988. text ed. 43.95 (*0-534-08064-2*) Intl Thomson.

Roth, John K., jt. ed. see Fossum, Robert H.

Roth, John K., jt. ed. see Peden, Creighton.

Roth, John K., jt. ed. see Rittner, Carol A.

Roth, John K., jt. ed. see Rittner, Carol.

Roth, John K., ed. see Royce, Josiah.

Roth, Jonathan & Roth, Andrew. Devil's Advocates: The Unnatural History of Lawyers. (Illus.). 192p. (Orig.). 1989. pap. 12.95 (*0-87337-101-1*) Nolo Pr.

— Poetic Justice: The Funniest, Meanest Things Ever Said About Lawyers. LC 87-63575. 128p. (Orig.). 1988. pap. 9.95 (*0-87337-072-4*) Nolo Pr.

Roth, Jordan. Black Belt Karate. 380p. 1992. pap. 22.95 (*0-8048-1851-7*) C E Tuttle.

— Black Belt Karate. 22.95 (*0-685-47545-X*) Wehman.

Roth, Jordan & Downey, Robert. Officer Survival: Arrest & Control. (Illus.). 122p. 1976. 7.95 (*1-56325-021-7*, DH005) Davis Pub Law.

Roth, Joseph. Confession of a Murderer. LC 84-20580. 224p. 1987. 22.50 (*0-87951-989-4*); Tusk. pap. 9.95 (*0-87951-287-3*) Overlook Pr.

— The Emperor's Tomb. Hoare, John, tr. LC 84-5663. 157p. 1987. 22.50 (*0-87951-985-1*); Tusk. pap. 9.95 (*0-87951-270-9*) Overlook Pr.

— Flight Without End. LeVay, David, tr. LC 76-47077. 144p. 1987. 22.50 (*0-87951-057-9*); Tusk. pap. 8.95 (*0-87951-279-2*) Overlook Pr.

— Flight Without End. LeVay, David, tr. 144p. 1987. 8.95 (*0-317-60441-4*, Penguin Bks) Viking Penguin.

— Hotel Savoy. Hoare, John, tr. LC 86-125. 192p. 1986. 16.95 (*0-87951-211-3*) Overlook Pr.

— Hotel Savoy. 192p. 1988. Tusk. pap. 8.95 (*0-87951-330-6*) Overlook Pr.

R

An Asterisk (*) at the beginning of an entry indicates that the title is appearing in BIP for the first time.

— Job: The Story of a Simple Man. Thompson, Dorothy, tr. LC 81-18901. 252p. 1985. reprint ed. 22.50 (*0-87951-149-4*); reprint ed. Tusk. pap. 8.95 (*0-87951-202-4*) Overlook Pr.
— The Radetzky March. Tucker, Eva & Dunlop, Geoffrey, trs. LC 72-97581. 324p. 1983. 22.50 (*0-87951-198-2*); Tusk. pap. 12.95 (*0-87951-189-3*) Overlook Pr.
— The Radetzky March. Neugroschel, Joachim, tr. 320p. 1995. 25.00 (*0-87951-548-1*); pap. 13.95 (*0-87951-558-9*) Overlook Pr.
— Right & Left & The Legend of the Holy Drinker. Hofmann, Michael, tr. 320p. 1992. 23.95 (*0-87951-448-5*) Overlook Pr.
— Right & Left & the Legend of the Holy Drinker. Hoffman, Michael, tr. 304p. 1993. pap. 13.95 (*0-87951-456-6*) Overlook Pr.
— The Silent Prophet. Le Vay, David, tr. LC 79-67676. 216p. 1980. 22.50 (*0-87951-110-9*) Overlook Pr.
— The Silent Prophet. Le Vay, David, tr. 224p. 1990. pap. 9.95 (*0-87951-384-5*) Overlook Pr.
— Spider's Web & Zipper & His Father. Hoare, John, tr. 224p. (ENG.). 1990. 18.95 (*0-87951-345-4*) Overlook Pr.
— The Spider's Web & Zipper & His Father. 224p. 1991. reprint ed. pap. 9.95 (*0-87951-361-6*) Overlook Pr.
— Tarabas. Katzin, Winifred, tr. LC 86-31239. 280p. 1987. reprint ed. 18.95 (*0-87951-275-X*) Overlook Pr.
— Tarabas: A Guest on Earth. 280p. 1989. Tusk. pap. 10.95 (*0-87951-299-7*) Overlook Pr.
Roth, Judith P., jt. auth. see Helsel, Sandra K.
Roth, Julee. Get Ready Get Set Go! An Advanced Sailing Manual. (Illus.). 208p. (Orig.). (YA). (gr. 7-12). 1993. pap. text ed. 15.95 (*0-9637423-0-2*) JRC Pubns.
Roth, Julian A., jt. auth. see Douglas, Dorothy J.
Roth, Julius & Douglas, Dorothy. No Appointment Necessary: The Hospital Emergency Department in the Medical Services World. 324p. 1983. pap. text ed. 24.50 (*0-8290-1255-9*) Irvington.
Roth, Julius & Ruzek, Sheryl. Research in the Sociology of Health Care, Vol. 4: The Adoption & Social Consequences of Medical Technologies. 1986. 73.25 (*0-89232-492-9*) Jai Pr.
Roth, Julius A. Health Purifiers & Their Enemies: A Study of the Natural Health Movement in the United States with a Comparison to Its Counterpart in Germany. LC 77-2210. 1977. 15.00 (*0-88202-117-6*); pap. 5.95 (*0-686-67897-4*) Watson Pub Intl.
— International Comparisons of Health Services. (Research in the Sociology of Health Care Ser.: Vol. 5). 1987. 73.25 (*0-89232-597-6*) Jai Pr.
— Timetables: Structuring the Passage of Time in Hospital Treatment & Other Careers. (Orig.). 1963. pap. 4.95 (*0-672-60851-0*, Bobbs) Macmillan.
Roth, Julius A., ed. The Control of Costs & Performance of Medical Services. (Research in the Sociology of Health Care Ser.: Vol. 3). 350p. 1984. 73.25 (*0-89232-310-8*) Jai Pr.
— Research in Sociology of Health Care, Vol. 1. 400p. 1980. lib. bdg. 73.25 (*0-89232-145-8*) Jai Pr.
— Research in the Sociology of Health Care, Vol. 2. 400p. 1981. 73.25 (*0-89232-199-7*) Jai Pr.
Roth, Julius A. & Conrad, Peter, eds. Research in the Sociology of Health Care, Vol. 6. 1987. 73.25 (*0-89232-834-7*) Jai Pr.
Roth, Julius A., ed. see Byrd, Doris Elaine.
Roth, June. How to Cook Like a Jewish Mother. 1993. 5.98 (*1-55521-899-7*) Bk Sales Inc.
Roth, K., jt. auth. see Halberstam, H.
Roth, K., jt. auth. see Jury, W. A.
Roth, K., jt. ed. see Meijer, O. G.
Roth, K., et al, eds. Field-Scale Water & Solute Flux in Soils. (Monte Verita Ser.). 304p. 1991. 72.50 (*0-8176-2510-0*) Spr-Verlag.
***Roth, K. Madsen, ed.** Hollywood Wits. LC 94-47041. 224p. (Orig.). 1995. pap. 7.50 (*0-380-77765-7*) Avon.
***Roth, Kevin.** Kevin Roth Songbook. (Illus.). 36p. (J). (gr. k-6). 1995. audio, pap. text ed. 17.95 (*0-931759-97-8*) Centerstream Pub.
— Lullabies for Little Dreamers. (Kevin Roth Presents Ser.). (Illus.). 24p. (J). (ps-1). 1992. audio 9.95 (*0-679-82382-4*) Random Bks Yng Read.
Roth, Kevin, jt. auth. see Reed, Bella.
***Roth, Klaus & Wolf, Gabriele.** South Slavic Folk Culture: A Bibliography of Literature in English, German, & French. 553p. (ENG, FRE & GER.). 1994. 29.95 (*0-89357-244-6*) Slavica.
Roth, Larry. Living Cheap: The Survival Guide for the 'Nineties. (Illus.). 130p. (Orig.). 1990. pap. 14.95 (*0-9625228-1-3*) Living Cheap.
— Living Cheap News: The First Two Years. 104p. (Orig.). 1994. pap. 11.95 (*0-9625228-2-1*) Living Cheap.
Roth, Larry M., jt. auth. see Rahdent, George K.
Roth, Larry M., jt. auth. see Rahdert, George K.
Roth, Laszlo. A Basic Guide to Plastics for Designers, Technicians, & Crafts People. (Illus.). 192p. 1985. 22.95 (*0-13-062373-3*) P-H.
Roth, Laszlo & Wybenga, George. The Packaging Designer's Book of Patterns. (Illus.). 496p. 1991. pap. 39.95 (*0-442-00524-5*) Van Nos Reinhold.
Roth, Laura M. & Inomata, Akira. Fundamental Questions in Quantum Mechanics: Selected Papers from the Fundamental Questions in Quantum Mechanics Symposium, Albany, NY, April 12-14, 1984. 312p. 1986. text ed. 171.00 (*2-88124-058-5*) Gordon & Breach.
Roth, Laura M., ed. see Karthar, Khenpo.
Roth, Laurie M. A Critical Examination of the Dual Ladder Approach to Career Advancement. 1982. pap. 12.00 (*0-317-11510-3*) CU Ctr Career Res.
— Managing the Technical Workforce: A Study of Computer Professionals. 1984. pap. 17.50 (*0-317-11514-6*) CU Ctr Career Res.
Roth, Lawrence M. & Czernobilsky, Bernard, eds. Tumors & Tumor-Like Conditions of the Ovary. (Contemporary Issues in Surgical Pathology Ser.: Vol. 6). (Illus.). 296p. 1985. text ed. 72.00 (*0-443-08289-8*) Churchill.
Roth, Lawrence M., jt. ed. see Talerman, Aleksander.
Roth, Leland M. America Builds. LC 82-48151. (Illus.). 675p. 1983. pap. text ed. 27.00 (*0-06-430122-2*, IN-122, Icon Edns) HarpC.
— A Concise History of American Architecture. LC 78-2169. (Icon Editions Ser.). (Illus.). 1980. pap. 25.00 (*0-06-430086-2*, IN-86, Icon Edns) HarpC.
— Understanding Architecture: Its Elements, History & Meaning. LC 88-45540. 784p. 1993. 50.00 (*0-06-438493-4*, HarpT) HarpC.
— Understanding Architecture: Its Elements, History, Meaning. LC 88-45540. (Illus.). 576p. 1993. 45.00 (*0-00-001606-3*, PL); pap. text ed. 30.00 (*0-06-430158-3*, PL) HarpC.
Roth, Leo. Jim Kelly: Star Quarterback. LC 93-38637. (Sports Reports Ser.). 104p. (J). (gr. 4-10). 1994. lib. bdg. 17.95 (*0-89490-446-9*) Enslow Pubs.
Roth, Leon. Spinoza. LC 78-14139. 1986. reprint ed. 23.75 (*0-88355-813-0*) Hyperion Conn.
Roth, Lewis, ed. see Prokofiev, Sergei.
Roth, Lewis D., ed. see Symposium on Applications of Artificial Intelligence in Material Science Staff.
Roth, Lillian. I'll Cry Tomorrow. 320p. 1977. pap. 5.95 (*0-8119-0385-0*) LIFETIME.
Roth, Lloyd J., ed. see International Conference on the Uses of Isotopically Labeled Drugs in Experimental Pharmacology Staff.
Roth, Lois, tr. see Sjowall, Maj & Wahloo, Per.
Roth, Loren, jt. auth. see Daley, Dennis.
Roth, Loren H., ed. Clinical Treatment of the Violent Person. LC 86-19543. 270p. 1987. pap. text ed. 23.50 (*0-89862-914-4*) Guilford Pr.
***Roth, Lutz & Rump, Gabriele, eds.** Roth Collection of Natural Products Data: Concise Descriptions & Spectra. 500p. 1995. pap. 190.00 (*3-527-28180-0*) VCH Pubs.
Roth, M., jt. ed. see Hansen, Heine H.
Roth, M., Jr., et al, eds. Biological, Clinical & Cultural Perspectives of Anxiety, Vol. 1. (Handbook of Anxiety Ser.: Vol. 1). 400p. 1988. 201.25 (*0-444-90475-1*) Elsevier.
Roth, Marcia, jt. ed. see Pollock, Mary.
Roth, Mark & Walters, Sally. Twenty Bicycle Tours in the Finger Lakes: Scenic Routes to Central New York's Best Waterfalls, Wineries, Beaches & Parks. 2nd ed. LC 87-1004. (Illus.). 160p. 1987. pap. 11.00 (*0-942440-39-0*, Backcountry) Countryman.
Roth, Martin. The Fiction Writer's Silent Partner. 304p. 1991. 19.95 (*0-89879-482-X*) Writers Digest.
— Making Money in Japanese Stocks. 184p. 1989. pap. 14.95 (*0-8048-1596-8*) C E Tuttle.
— The Writer's Complete Crime Reference Book. rev. ed. 304p. 1993. pap. 19.99 (*0-89879-564-8*) Writers Digest.
Roth, Martin & Cowie, Valerie, eds. Psychiatry, Genetics & Pathography: A Tribute to Eliot Slater. LC 79-20997. 247p. reprint ed. pap. 70.40 (*0-7837-4917-1*, 2044582) Bks Demand.
Roth, Martin & Stevens, John. Zen Guide: Where to Meditate in Japan. (Illus.). 152p. 1985. pap. 7.50 (*0-8348-0202-3*) Weatherhill.
Roth, Marty. Foul & Fair Play: Reading Genre in Classic Detective Fiction. LC 93-30367. 312p. 1995. 45.00 (*0-8203-1622-9*) U of Ga Pr.
Roth, Matthew, jt. auth. see Clouette, Bruce.
Roth, Matthew W. Platt Brothers & Company: Small Business in American Manufacturing. LC 93-11001. (Illus.). 268p. 1994. 40.00 (*0-87451-654-4*) U Pr of New Eng.
Roth, Michael, ed. see Merquior, J. G.
Roth, Michael D. & Galis, Leon, eds. Knowing: Essays in the Analysis of Knowledge. 246p. 1984. reprint ed. pap. text ed. 21.00 (*0-8191-4262-X*) U Pr of Amer.
Roth, Michael D. & Ross, Glenn, eds. Doubting: Contemporary Perspectives on Skepticism. (Philosophical Studies). 225p. (C). 1990. lib. bdg. 77.50 (*0-7923-0576-0*) Kluwer Ac.
Roth, Michael G., et al, eds. Methods in Cell Biology: Protein Expression in Animals Cells, Vol. 43. (Illus.). 379p. 1994. text ed. 90.00 (*0-12-564144-3*) Acad Pr.
***Roth, Michael S.** The Ironist's Cage: Memory, Trauma, & the Construction of History. LC 95-5816. 1995. write for info. (*0-231-10244-5*); pap. write for info. (*0-231-10245-3*) Col U Pr.
— Knowing & History: Appropriations of Hegel in Twentieth-Century France. LC 87-47870. 272p. 1988. 35.00 (*0-8014-2136-5*) Cornell U Pr.
— Psycho-Analysis As History: Negation & Freedom in Freud. LC 86-29192. 208p. 1987. 30.00 (*0-8014-1957-3*) Cornell U Pr.
— Psycho-Analysis As History: Negation & Freedom in Freud. 208p. 1995. pap. 13.95 (*0-8014-8303-4*) Cornell U Pr.
Roth, Michael S., ed. Rediscovering History: Culture, Politics, & the Psyche. LC 93-33732. (Cultural Sitings Ser.). 1994. 75.00 (*0-8047-2309-5*); pap. 22.95 (*0-8047-2313-3*) Stanford U Pr.
Roth, Michael S., jt. ed. see Cohen, Ralph.
Roth, Michael S., jt. ed. see Gourevitch, Victor.
***Roth, Michael-Wolff.** Authentic School Science: Knowing & Learning in Open-Inquiry Science Laboratories. LC 94-30832. (Science & Technology Education Library Ser.: 1). 1995. lib. bdg. 106.00 (*0-7923-3088-9*) Kluwer Ac.
Roth, Milton. Ship Modeling from Stem to Stern. 1988. pap. text ed. 18.95 (*0-07-155060-7*) McGraw.
— Ship Modeling from Stem to Stern. (Illus.). 288p. 1988. pap. 17.95 (*0-8306-2844-4*) TAB Bks.
***Roth, Molly D.** Shadows of the Cross. LC 94-19568. (Illus.). 1994. 21.95 (*0-8294-0810-X*) Loyola Univ Pr.
Roth, Nancy. The Breath of God: An Approach to Prayer. LC 89-29785. 174p. 1990. pap. 9.95 (*0-936384-92-1*) Cowley Pubns.
— A New Christian Yoga. LC 89-22142. 118p. 1989. pap. 10.95 (*0-936384-82-4*) Cowley Pubns.
— Organic Prayer: Cultivating Your Relationship with God. LC 93-12653. (Illus.). 167p. 1993. pap. 10.95 (*1-56101-077-4*) Cowley Pubns.
Roth-Nelson, Stephanie. S. E. E. K. Self-Esteem Enhancement Kit. LC 93-29345. 176p. (Orig.). (YA). (gr. 7-12). 1993. pap. 14.95 (*0-942097-49-1*) BPPbks.
***Roth-Nelson, Stephanie & Jessop, Nancy.** S. E. E. K. Facilitator's Guide: Accompanies the Self-Esteem Enhancement Kit Workbook. 123p. (Orig.). 1994. teacher ed, pap. 29.95 (*0-942097-48-3*) BPPbks.
Roth, Nicki. Integrating the Shattered Self: Psychotherapy with Adult Incest Survivors. LC 92-10687. 200p. 1993. 25.00 (*0-87668-562-9*) Aronson.
Roth, Noble P. Brave Men All. 352p. 1987. pap. 3.50 (*0-8217-1998-X*) Zebra.
***Roth, Norman.** Conversos, Inquisition & the Expulsion of the Jews from Spain. LC 94-23486. 448p. 1995. text ed. 50.00 (*0-299-14230-2*) U of Wis Pr.
— Jews, Visigoths, & Muslims in Medieval Spain: Cooperation & Conflict. LC 94-18401. (Medieval Iberian Peninsula, Texts & Studies: Vol. 10). 1994. 65.75 (*90-04-09971-9*) E J Brill.
Roth, Otavio, ed. Children's Declaration of Human Rights. (Illus.). 45p. 1989. 9.95 (*0-685-50854-4*) Amnesty Intl USA.
Roth, P. Using Powerpoint 4 for the Mac. 1993. pap. 24.95 (*1-56529-442-4*) Que.
***Roth, Pam & Juch, William, eds.** Data Warehousing & Decision Support: The State of the Art. (Enterprise Computing Ser.). (Illus.). 200p. (Orig.). 1995. pap. 44.95 (*1-57109-005-3*) Spiral Communs.
***Roth, Pamela J., ed.** Customer or Employer? Vendor or Employee? A Guide to Knowing Who You Are & Why You Should Care. (Business Management Ser.). 200p. (Orig.). Date not set. pap. 44.95 (*1-57109-004-5*) Spiral Communs.
Roth, Pamela K., jt. ed. see Nicol, Mary M.
Roth, Paul. Seneca Apocolocyntosis. (Latin Commentaries Ser.). 54p. (Orig.). (C). 1988. pap. text ed. 6.00 (*0-929524-51-9*) Bryn Mawr Commentaries.
Roth, Paul A. Meaning & Method in the Social Sciences: A Case for Methodological Pluralism. LC 87-47718. 272p. 1987. 35.95 (*0-8014-1941-7*); pap. 13.95x (*0-8014-9605-5*) Cornell U Pr.
Roth, Paula, ed. Alcohol & Drugs Are Women's Issues, 2 vols., Set. LC 90-49988. (Illus.). 155p. 1991. 50.00 (*0-8108-2437-X*) Scarecrow.
— Alcohol & Drugs Are Women's Issues: The Model Program Guide, Vol. 2. (Illus.). 155p. 1991. 29.50 (*0-8108-2389-6*) Scarecrow.
— Alcohol & Drugs Are Women's Issues, Vol. 1: A Review of the Issues. LC 90-49988. (Copublished with Women's Action Alliance Ser.). (Illus.). 202p. 1991. 32.50 (*0-8108-2360-8*) Scarecrow.
Roth, Philip. The Anatomy Lesson. deluxe limited ed. LC 83-11645. 291p. 1983. boxed 60.00 (*0-374-10492-1*) FS&G.
— The Breast. LC 93-43498. 1994. pap. 9.00 (*0-679-74901-2*, Vin) Random.
— The Conversion of the Jews. (Short Stories Ser.). (J). (gr. 5 up). 1992. lib. bdg. 13.95 (*0-88682-506-7*) Creative Ed.
— The Counterlife. 320p. 1987. 18.95 (*0-374-13026-4*) FS&G.
— The Counterlife. 336p. 1988. mass mkt. 4.95 (*0-14-009769-4*, Penguin Bks) Viking Penguin.
— Deception. Date not set. pap. write for info. (*0-679-75294-3*) Random.
— Deception. 208p. 1991. 18.95 (*0-685-37883-7*, Touchstone Bks) S&S Trade.
— The Facts: A Novelist's Autobiography. 328p. 1988. 17.95 (*0-374-15212-8*) FS&G.
— The Facts: A Novelist's Autobiography. limited ed. 328p. 1988. 75.00 (*0-374-15210-1*) FS&G.
— The Ghost Writer. LC 95-6782. 1995. write for info. (*0-679-74898-9*, Vin) Random.
— Goodbye Columbus. (FRE.). 1980. pap. 11.95 (*0-7859-4130-4*) Fr & Eur.
— Goodbye Columbus. 1995. 13.50 (*0-679-60159-7*) Random.
— Goodbye Columbus. 1994. reprint ed. lib. bdg. 32.95 (*1-56849-325-8*) Buccaneer Bks.
— Goodbye, Columbus: And Five Short Stories. LC 93-1698. 1994. 11.00 (*0-679-74826-1*, Publishers Media) Random.
— Goodbye, Columbus & Other Stories. 19.95 (*0-8488-0622-0*) Amereon Ltd.
— The Great American Novel. 1995. pap. 13.00 (*0-679-74906-3*, Vin) Random.
— His Mistress's Voice. deluxe ed. Wheatcroft, John, ed. (The/Bucknell University Fine Editions). 60p. 1995. boxed 245.00 (*0-916375-21-8*) Press Alley.
— Laisser Courir, Tome 1. 384p. (FRE.). 1983. pap. 15.95 (*0-7859-4186-X*, 2070374777) Fr & Eur.
— Laisser Courir, Tome II. (FRE.). 1983. pap. 17.95 (*0-7859-4187-8*) Fr & Eur.
— Letting Go. 640p. 1984. mass mkt. 4.95 (*0-449-20728-5*, Crest) Fawcett.
— Letting Go. 1962. 12.50 (*0-394-43305-X*) Random.
— Letting Go. 640p. 1991. pap. 10.95 (*0-671-73616-7*, Touchstone Bks) S&S Trade.
— My Life As a Man. LC 93-15504. 1994. pap. 11.00 (*0-679-74827-X*, Vin) Random.
— Operation Shylock. 1994. pap. 12.00 (*0-679-75029-0*, Vin) Random.
— Operation Shylock: A Confession. LC 92-41959. 400p. 1993. 23.00 (*0-671-70376-5*) S&S Trade.
— Patrimony. Date not set. pap. write for info. (*0-679-75293-5*) Random.
— Portnoy et Son Complexe. (FRE.). 1973. pap. 10.95 (*0-7859-4017-0*) Fr & Eur.
— Portnoy's Complaint. LC 83-42950. 288p. 1983. 6.95 (*0-394-60810-0*, Modern Lib) Random.
— Portnoy's Complaint. 1994. pap. 11.00 (*0-679-75645-0*, Vin) Random.
— Portnoy's Complaint. 1994. reprint ed. lib. bdg. 32.95 (*1-56849-324-X*) Buccaneer Bks.
— Professor of Desire. 1994. pap. 10.00 (*0-679-74900-4*, Vin) Random.
— Quand Elle Etait Gentille. (FRE.). 1985. pap. 19.95 (*0-7859-4233-5*) Fr & Eur.
— Sabbath's Theater. LC 95-914. 1995. 24.95 (*0-395-73982-9*) HM.
— Le Sein. (FRE.). 1984. pap. 10.95 (*0-7859-4215-7*) Fr & Eur.
— When She Was Good. LC 94-31360. 1995. pap. 12.00 (*0-679-75925-5*, Vin) Random.
— Zuckerman Bound: A Trilogy & Epilogue. LC 84-23265. 784p. 1985. 22.50 (*0-374-29943-9*) FS&G.
— Zuckerman Unbound. LC 95-6783. 1995. write for info. (*0-679-74899-7*, Vin) Random.
Roth, Philip, ed. see Kundera, Milan.
Roth, Philip, et al. The American West's Acid Rain Test. LC 85-50619. 60p. (Orig.). 1985. pap. text ed. 10.00 (*0-915825-07-4*) World Resources Inst.
Roth Publications, Inc. Staff, ed. Annual Index to Poetry in Periodicals, 1984. 540p. 1985. 39.99 (*0-89609-243-7*) Roth Pub Inc.
Roth Publishing Editorial Board. Core Poetry Collection Index, 3 vols., Set. (Corefiche Ser.). 1127p. (Orig.). (YA). (gr. 9). 1993. pap. text ed. 75.00 (*0-89609-325-5*) Roth Pub Inc.
— Poetry Index Annual 1992. 1993. 54.99 (*0-89609-324-7*) Roth Pub Inc.
— Poetry Index Annual 1993. 1994. 54.99x (*0-89609-329-8*) Roth Pub Inc.
— Roth's Essay Index, Second Cumulative Supplement, Phases VI-X. (Corefiche Ser.). 478p. (Orig.). 1993. pap. text ed. 49.95 (*0-89609-326-3*) Roth Pub Inc.
— Roth's Index to Short Stories. 3rd ed. (Corefiche Ser.). 108p. 1992. pap. text ed. 19.95 (*0-89609-322-0*) Roth Pub Inc.
— The World's Best Poetry, Supplement VIII, Cumulative Index. LC 82-84763. 257p. 1993. 49.95 (*0-89609-327-1*) Roth Pub Inc.
Roth Publishing Editorial Board Staff. Master Index to Poetry. 2nd ed. LC 85-81058. l, 1939p. 1992. 250.00 (*0-89609-309-3*) Roth Pub Inc.
— Poetry Index Annual 1991. 1992. 54.99 (*0-89609-321-2*) Roth Pub Inc.
— Roth's Essay Index, Cumulative Supplement to Phases VI, VII, VIII. 358p. (Orig.). 1992. pap. 29.95 (*0-89609-320-4*) Roth Pub Inc.
Roth Publishing Inc., Editorial Board, ed. American Poetry Index, Vol. 4. 400p. 1988. 52.00 (*0-89609-268-2*) Roth Pub Inc.
Roth Publishing, Inc., Editorial Board Staff. American Poetry Index, 1984, Vol. 3. 570p. 1987. 52.00 (*0-89609-262-3*) Roth Pub Inc.
— Annual Index to Poetry in Periodicals, 1985. 800p. 1987. 39.99 (*0-89609-263-1*) Roth Pub Inc.
— Poetry Index Annual, 1986. 470p. 1987. 54.99 (*0-89609-264-X*) Roth Pub Inc.
— Survey of American Poetry, Vol. IX: World War II & Aftermath (1940-1950) LC 81-83526. 1986. 39.95 (*0-89609-221-6*) Roth Pub Inc.
— Survey of American Poetry, Vol. VII: Poetic Renaissance (1913-1919) LC 81-83526. 380p. 1986. 39.95 (*0-89609-219-4*) Roth Pub Inc.
— Survey of American Poetry, Vol. VIII: Interval Between World Wars (1920-1939) LC 81-83526. 380p. 1986. 39.95 (*0-89609-220-8*) Roth Pub Inc.
— Survey of American Poetry, Vol. X: Midcentury to 1984. LC 81-83526. 370p. 1986. 39.95 (*0-89609-222-4*) Roth Pub Inc.
— World's Best Poetry, Supplement III: Critical Companion, Supplement III. LC 82-84763. 400p. 1986. 49.95 (*0-89609-242-9*) Roth Pub Inc.
Roth Publishing, Inc., Editorial Board Staff, ed. Poetry Index Annual, 1987. 328p. 1988. 54.99 (*0-89609-269-0*) Roth Pub Inc.
Roth Publishing, Inc. Editorial Board Staff. Roth's Index to Great American & English Essays. 87p. 1988. pap. text ed. 29.95 (*0-89609-293-3*) Roth Pub Inc.
Roth Publishing, Inc. Editorial Board Staff, ed. Roth's American Poetry Annual, 1988. 727p. 1989. 60.00 (*0-89609-285-2*) Roth Pub Inc.
— Roth's Essay Index. LC 88-62954. 494p. 1989. 49.95 (*0-89609-286-0*, Poetry Index Pr) Roth Pub Inc.
— World's Best Poetry, Supplement VI: Twentieth Century African & Latin American Verse. LC 82-84763. 238p. 1989. 49.95 (*0-89609-271-2*, Poetry Index Pr) Roth Pub Inc.
Roth Publishing, Inc. Staff. Master Index to Poetry, Supplement, Phase III. 862p. 1990. pap. text ed. 49.95 (*0-89609-298-4*) Roth Pub Inc.
— Roth's Essay Index, Supplement, Phase VI. 177p. 1990. pap. 19.95 (*0-89609-297-6*) Roth Pub Inc.
— Roth's Essay Index, Supplement, Phase Seven. 175p. 1991. pap. 19.95 (*0-89609-310-7*) Roth Pub Inc.
— World's Best Drama Index. 159p. 1989. pap. 24.95 (*0-89609-294-1*) Roth Pub Inc.
Roth Publishing, Inc., Staff, ed. Annual Survey of American Poetry, 1985. LC 86-62135. 300p. 1987. 34.95 (*0-89609-266-6*) Roth Pub Inc.

R

An Asterisk (*) at the beginning of an entry indicates that the title is appearing in BIP for the first time.

Roth Publishing, Inc Staff, ed. Annual Survey of American Poetry, 1986. LC 86-62135. 279p. 1987. 34.95 (0-89609-272-0) Roth Pub Inc.

Roth Publishing, Inc. Staff, ed. Poetry Index Annual, 1988. 320p. 1989. 54.99 (0-89609-283-6, Poetry Index Pr) Roth Pub Inc.

— Poetry Index Annual, 1989. 305p. 1990. 54.99 (0-89609-296-8) Roth Pub Inc.

— Roth's American Poetry Annual, 1989. 700p. 1990. 60.00 (0-89609-295-X) Roth Pub Inc.

— Roth's American Poetry Annual, 1990. 735p. 1991. 60.00 (0-89609-302-6) Roth Pub Inc.

— Survey of British Poetry, Vol. Four: Nineteenth Century. 400p. 1992. 59.95 (0-89609-277-1) Roth Pub Inc.

Roth Publishing Inc Staff, ed. Survey of British Poetry, Vol. I: Old English to Renaissance. 442p. 1988. 59.95 (0-89609-274-7) Roth Pub Inc.

Roth Publishing, Inc. Staff, ed. Survey of British Poetry, Vol. II: Cavalier to Restoration, Vol. 2. 365p. 1989. 59. 95 (0-89609-275-5) Roth Pub Inc.

— Survey of British Poetry, Vol. III: Eighteenth Century. LC 88-60329. 438p. 1991. 59.95 (0-89609-276-3) Roth Pub Inc.

Roth Publishing, Inc., Staff, ed. World's Best Poetry, Supplement IV. LC 82-84763. 370p. 1987. 49.95 (0-89609-265-8) Roth Pub Inc.

Roth Publishing, Inc Staff, ed. World's Best Poetry, Supplement V: Twentieth-Century Women Poets. LC 82-84763. 375p. 1987. 49.95 (0-89609-270-4) Roth Pub Inc.

Roth Publishing, Inc. Staff, ed. World's Best Poetry, Supplement VII: Twentieth-Century Asian Verse. LC 82-84763. 350p. 1990. 49.95 (0-89609-289-5) Roth Pub Inc.

— World's Best Short Stories, 10 vols., Set. LC 89-60440. 35000p. 1994. 499.50 (0-89609-400-6) Roth Pub Inc.

— World's Best Short Stories Vol. 1: Short Story Masters, Vol. I. LC 89-60440. 350p. 1989. 49.95 (0-89609-303-4) Roth Pub Inc.

— World's Best Short Stories Vol. 2: Short Story Masters, Vol. II. LC 89-60440. 378p. 1990. 49.95 (0-89609-304-2) Roth Pub Inc.

— World's Best Short Stories Vol. 3: Famous Stories. LC 89-60440. 376p. 1990. 49.95 (0-89609-305-0) Roth Pub Inc.

— World's Best Short Stories Vol. 4: Fables & Tales. LC 89-60440. 389p. 1991. lib. bdg. 49.95 (0-89609-306-9) Roth Pub Inc.

— World's Best Short Stories Vol. 7: Characters. LC 89-60440. 350p. 1992. 49.95 (0-89609-313-1) Roth Pub Inc.

— World's Best Short Stories Vol. 8: Places. LC 89-60440. 350p. 1993. 49.95 (0-89609-314-X) Roth Pub Inc.

— World's Best Short Stories Vol. 9: Cultures. LC 89-60440. 350p. 1994. 49.95 (0-89609-315-8) Roth Pub Inc.

— World's Best Short Stories Vol. 10: Research & Reference: Criticism & Indexes. LC 89-60440. 350p. 1995. 49.95 (0-89609-316-6) Roth Pub Inc.

Roth Publishing Staff, ed. World's Best Short Stories Vol. 5: Genres, Mystery & Detection. LC 89-60440. 350p. 1991. 49.95 (0-89609-307-7) Roth Pub Inc.

— World's Best Short Stories Vol. 6: Genres, Horror & Science Fiction. LC 89-60440. 350p. 1991. 49.95 (0-89609-312-3) Roth Pub Inc.

Roth, R. S., ed. The Bellman Continuum. 892p. 1987. text ed. 114.00 (9971-5-0090-6) World Scientific Pub.

Roth, R. S., jt. auth. see Bellman, Richard E.

Roth, R. S., et al, eds. Phase Diagrams for Ceramists, Vol. IV, 1981. (Illus.). 330p. 1981. 150.00 (0-916094-40-5, PHASE4) Am Ceramic.

— Phase Diagrams for Ceramists, Vol. V. 404p. 1983. 150. 00 (0-916094-47-2, PHASE5) Am Ceramic.

Roth, Rainer. Lexikon der Arbeits und Soziallere. (GER.). 1976. 65.00 (0-8288-5729-6, M7278) Fr & Eur.

Roth, Randall, ed. Price of Paradise, Vol. II. 320p. 1993. pap. 14.95 (1-56647-042-0) Mutual Pub HI.

— The Price of Paradise: Lucky We Live Hawaii? 268p. 1992. pap. 14.95 (1-56647-016-1) Mutual Pub HI.

***Roth, Randall D.** Prayer Powerpoints. LC 95-1640. 192p. 1995. 11.99 (1-56476-433-8, 6-3433, Victor Books) SP Pubns.

Roth, Randolph A. The Democratic Dilemma: Religion, Reform, & the Social Order in the Connecticut River Valley of Vermont, 1791-1850. 400p. 1987. 49.95 (0-521-30183-1) Cambridge U Pr.

***Roth, Richard & Martin, Douglas C.** Carving Fish & Pond Life. (Illus.). 224p. 1994. text ed. 39.95 (0-88740-589-4) Schiffer.

Roth, Richard J., Jr., jt. auth. see Steinbrugge, Karl V.

Roth, Robert. Transcendental Meditation. 1988. pap. 5.95 (1-55611-085-5, Primus Lib Contemp) D I Fine.

— Transcendental Meditation. rev. ed. LC 94-71116. 160p. 1994. pap. 8.95 (1-55611-403-6, Primus) D I Fine.

Roth, Robert A. Teaching & Teacher Education: Implementing Reform. LC 85-63695. (Fastback Ser.: No. 240). 50p. (Orig.). 1986. pap. 1.25 (0-87367-240-2) Phi Delta Kappa.

Roth, Robert A., jt. auth. see Gold, Yvonne.

Roth, Robert F. International Marketing Communications. LC 81-66513. 1982. 34.95 (0-8442-3058-8, Crain Bks) NTC Pub Grp.

Roth, Robert J. British Empiricism & American Pragmatism: New Directions & Neglected Arguments. LC 93-3064. 205p. 1993. 30.00 (0-8232-1391-9); pap. 19.95 (0-8232-1392-7) Fordham.

Roth, Robert J., ed. Person & Community: A Philosophical Exploration. LC 73-93143. 187p. reprint ed. pap. 53.30 (0-7837-0470-4, 2040793) Bks Demand.

***Roth, Robert S., ed.** Phase Equilibria Diagrams, Phase Diagrams for Ceramists: Oxides. (Phase Equilibria Diagrams Ser.: Vol. XI). (Illus.). 495p. 1995. 150.00 (0-944904-90-4, 3BHP11N) Am Ceramic.

Roth, Robert S., jt. auth. see Bellman, Richard E.

Roth, Robert S., jt. ed. see Davies, Peter K.

Roth, Robert S., jt. ed. see Whitler, John D.

Roth, Robert S., et al, eds. Phase Diagrams for Ceramists, Vol. VI. 550p. 1987. 150.00 (0-916094-90-1, PHASE6) Am Ceramic.

Roth, Robyn E. Coming to Terms. LC 89-4124. (Illus.). 176p. (Orig.). 1989. pap. 9.95 (0-89407-083-5) Strawberry Hill.

Roth, Roger. The Sign Painter's Dream. LC 92-13041. (Illus.). 40p. (J). (ps-3). 1993. 14.00 (0-517-58920-6); lib. bdg. 14.99 (0-517-58921-4) Crown Bks Yng Read.

Roth, Ron. I Want to See Jesus. 187p. pap. 7.95 (0-318-22779-7) Fr Ron Roth Min.

***Roth, Rosemary A., ed.** Perioperative Nursing Core Curriculum: Achieving Competency in Clinical Practice. (Illus.). 448p. 1995. pap. text ed. 35.00 (0-7216-5197-6) Saunders.

Roth, Roswitha & Borkenstein, H. M., eds. Psychosoziale Aspekte in der Betreuung von Kindern und Jugendlichen mit Diabetes. (Illus.). x, 202p. 1991. 32.00 (3-8055-5414-1) S Karger.

Roth, S., jt. ed. see Plocharski, J.

Roth, S., jt. ed. see Przyluski, J.

Roth, Samuel. Jews Must Live. 1980. lib. bdg. 69.95 (0-8490-3204-0) Gordon Pr.

Roth, Sanford & Roth, Beulah. Italy Fifties. LC 89-27617. (Illus.). 144p. 1990. 24.95 (0-916515-72-9) Mercury Hse Inc.

— Paris in the Fifties. LC 88-5360. (Illus.). 136p. 1988. 19. 95 (0-916515-43-5) Mercury Hse Inc.

— Portraits of the Fifties: The Photographs of Sanford Roth. LC 87-12152. (Illus.). xx, 108p. (Orig.). 1987. pap. 19.95 (0-916515-29-X) Mercury Hse Inc.

Roth, Sanford I., jt. auth. see Castleman, Benjamin.

Roth-Scholtz, Friedrich. Bibliotheca Chemica. 238p. 1971. reprint ed. write for info. (3-487-04117-0, Pub. by Georg Olms GW) Lubrecht & Cramer.

— Deutsches Theatrum Chemicum, 3 vols., Set. 1976. reprint ed. write for info. (3-487-05920-7, Pub. by Georg Olms GW) Lubrecht & Cramer.

— Thesaurus Symbolorum Ac Emblematum, I. E. Insignia Bibliopolarum et Typographorum. 184p. reprint ed. write for info. (0-318-71862-6, Pub. by Georg Olms GW) Lubrecht & Cramer.

Roth, Sheldon. Psychotherapy: The Art of Wooing Nature. LC 86-28763. 304p. 1987. 35.00 (0-87668-945-4) Aronson.

Roth, Sheldon H. & Miller, Keith W. Molecular & Cellular Mechanisms of Anesthetics. LC 85-28274. 502p. 1986. 110.00 (0-306-42128-3, Plenum Pr) Plenum.

Roth, Shirley P. & Morse, Joyce S., eds. A Life-Span Approach to Nursing Care for Individuals with Developmental Disabilities. 368p. 1994. 48.00 (1-55766-151-0, 1510) P H Brookes.

Roth, Sid. Time Is Running Short. 238p. (Orig.). 1991. pap. 9.99 (1-56043-030-3) Destiny Image.

Roth, Siegmar, jt. ed. see Przyluski, Jan.

Roth, Sol. Halakhah & Politics: The Jewish Idea of a State. 1988. 19.95 (0-88125-129-1) Ktav.

Roth, Stanley, ed. see Young, Norman S.

Roth, Stephanie, jt. auth. see Weidlein, Marianne.

Roth, Stephen, ed. Molecular Approaches to Supracellular Phenomena. LC 90-12412. (Developmental Biology Ser.). (Illus.). 242p. (C). 1990. reprint ed. text ed. 39.95 (0-8122-8251-5) U of Pa Pr.

Roth, Stephen & Sellers, Don. The Little QuicKeys Book. (Illus.). 288p. (Orig.). 1991. pap. 18.95 (0-938151-59-2) Peachpit Pr.

Roth, Stephen, jt. auth. see Blatner, David.

Roth, Stephen F., ed. Real World PostScript: Techniques from PostScript. 400p. 1988. pap. 22.95 (0-201-06663-7) Addison-Wesley.

Roth, Stephen J., ed. The Impact of the Six-Day War: A Twenty-Year Assessment. LC 88-6737. 304p. 1988. text ed. 45.00 (0-312-02122-4) St Martin.

Roth, Steve. Daws: Some Descendants of Frank Daws of County Sussex, England, with Information on Associate Kiplinger Family. (Illus.). 89p. 1993. reprint ed. lib. bdg. 27.50 (0-8328-3294-4); reprint ed. pap. 17.50 (0-8328-3293-6) Higginson Bk Co.

— Junior Executive. (You Can Do It! Ser.). (Illus.). 68p. (Orig.). (J). (ps up). Date not set. pap. 12.95 (1-56530-070-X) Summit TX.

— Roth: The Family of Nicholas Roth, American Settlers from Germany, with Information on Associate Families of Winters, Darnold & Keppler. (Illus.). 197p. 1993. reprint ed. lib. bdg. 39.50 (0-8328-3396-7); reprint ed. pap. 29.50 (0-8328-3397-5) Higginson Bk Co.

***Roth, Steve & Fleishman, Glenn.** Photos on CD. 1995. cd-rom, pap. 49.95 (1-56609-173-X) Peachpit Pr.

***Roth, Steve & Sellers, Don.** The QuicKeys 3 Book. 2nd ed. LC 94-36390. 1995. pap. 22.95 (0-201-40979-8) Addison-Wesley.

Roth, Sue, jt. auth. see Schaff, Barbara.

***Roth, Susan.** The Biggest Frog in Australia. LC 95-9721. (Illus.). (J). 1996. write for info. (0-671-50134-8, S&S Bks Young Read) S&S Childrens.

— Ishi's Tale of Lizard. (J). (gr. 4-7). 1992. 14.00 (0-374-33643-1) FS&G.

— Moses in the Twentieth Century: A Universal Primer. 1994. 24.95 (0-9638861-0-X) S J R Assocs.

Roth, Susan A. The Four-Season Landscape: Easy-Care Plants & Plans for Year-Round Color. (Illus.). 352p. 1993. 26.95 (0-87596-556-3) Rodale Pr Inc.

— The Weekend Garden Guide: Work-Saving Ways to a Beautiful Backyard. LC 90-9060. 368p. 1991. 23.95 (0-87857-933-8, 01-873-0) Rodale Pr Inc.

Roth, Susan L. Another Christmas. LC 91-33148. (Illus.). 32p. (J). (gr. k). 1992. 15.00 (0-688-09942-4); lib. bdg. 14.93 (0-688-09943-2) Morrow Jr Bks.

— Buddha. LC 93-8240. (J). 1994. 15.95 (0-385-31072-2) Doubleday.

— Fire Came to the Earth People: A Dahomean Folktale. (J). (ps-3). 1994. mass mkt. 4.99 (0-440-40844-X) Dell.

— Gypsy Bird Song. (Illus.). 32p. (J). (gr. 1 up). 1991. 14.95 (0-374-32825-0) FS&G.

— Martha & the Dragon. LC 94-41631. (J). 1996. write for info. (0-8037-1852-7); lib. bdg. write for info. (0-8037-1853-5) Dial Bks Young.

— Princess. LC 92-55042. (Illus.). 32p. (J). (ps-3). 1993. 13. 95 (1-56282-465-1); lib. bdg. 13.89 (1-56282-466-X) Hyprn Child.

— The Story of Light. LC 90-5654. (Illus.). 32p. (J). (ps up). 1990. 12.95 (0-688-08676-4); lib. bdg. 12.88 (0-688-08677-2) Morrow Jr Bks.

— Thump, Creak, Bump! LC 94-14234. (J). (gr. k-3). 1995. text ed. 14.95 (0-02-777916-5, Mac Bks Young Read) S&S Childrens.

— We'll Ride Elephants Through Brooklyn. (J). (ps up). 1989. 13.95 (0-374-38258-1) FS&G.

Roth, Sydell, jt. auth. see Wax, Edith.

Roth, Timothy P. Information, Ideology, & Freedom: The Disenfranchised Electorate. LC 94-1573. 138p. (Orig.). Date not set. lib. bdg. 46.50 (0-8191-9464-6); pap. 21.00 (0-8191-9465-4) U Pr of Amer.

— The Present State of Consumer Theory. 2nd ed. LC 89-34175. 220p. (Orig.). (C). 1989. pap. text ed. 22.50 (0-8191-7506-4) U Pr of Amer.

Roth, Timothy P., jt. ed. see Bartlett, Bruce.

Roth, Viola, tr. see Dauprat, Louis-Francois.

Roth, Walter. Games, Sports & Amusements. LC 75-35076. (Studies in Play & Games). (Illus.). 1976. reprint ed. 17. 95 (0-405-07926-5) Ayer.

Roth, Walter, jt. auth. see Keimel, Klaus.

***Roth, Walter E., ed.** Additional Studies of the Arts, Crafts & Customs of the Guiana Indians, with Special Reference to Those Southern British Guiana. (Bureau of American Ethnology Bulletins Ser.). 110p. 1995. lib. bdg. 79.00 (0-7812-4091-3) Rprt Serv.

Roth, Walton T., ed. Core Concepts in Health. 7th ed. 1994. 15.95 (1-55934-342-7); pap. 39.95 (1-55934-210-2) Mayfield Pub.

Roth, Walton T., jt. auth. see Insel, Paul M.

Roth, Wendy & Tompane, Michael. Easy Access to National Parks: The Sierra Club Guide for People with Disabilities. LC 91-34274. (Illus.). 352p. (Orig.). 1992. pap. 16.00 (0-87156-620-6) Sierra.

Roth, William. The Evolution of Management Theory: Past, Present, Future. LC 93-92548. 150p. (C). 1993. pap. 11. 95 (0-9635680-1-9) Roth & Assocs.

— Personal Computers for Persons with Disabilities: An Analysis, with Directories of Vendors & Organizations. LC 91-50944. 206p. 1992. pap. 32.50x (0-89950-698-4) McFarland & Co.

Roth, William F., Jr. A Systems Approach to Quality Improvement. LC 91-4204. 208p. 1991. text ed. 47.95 (0-275-94107-8, C4107, Praeger Pubs) Greenwood.

— Work & Rewards: Redefining Our Work-Life Reality. LC 88-25572. 206p. 1989. text ed. 52.95 (0-275-93166-8, C3166, Praeger Pubs) Greenwood.

Roth, Wolfgang. Hebrew Gospel: Cracking the Code of Mark. LC 87-62868. 160p. (Orig.). 1988. 34.95 (0-940989-17-4); pap. 16.95 (0-940989-31-X) Meyer Stone Bks.

***Roth-Young, Bette.** Ema Lazarus: In Her World. 1995. 35. 00 (0-8276-0516-1) JPS Phila.

Roth, Zvi S., jt. auth. see Zhuang, Hanqi.

Rotha, Charline T. Weida. 204p. 1993. pap. 11.95 (0-685-69189-6) Prof Pr NC.

Rothacher, Albrecht. Japan's Agro-Food Sector: The Politics & Economics of Excess Protection. LC 88-18640. 256p. 1989. text ed. 59.95 (0-312-01691-3) St Martin.

Rothafel, Samuel L. & Yates, Raymond F. Broadcasting: Its New Day. LC 70-161153. (History of Broadcasting: Radio to Television Ser.). 1977. reprint ed. 31.95 (0-405-03571-3) Ayer.

Rothauge, Kirstie A. Ben O'Wulf: The Canine of a Thousand Faces. LC 93-93771. (Illus.). 72p. (Orig.). 1994. pap. 7.00 (1-56002-306-6, Univ Edtns) Aegina Pr.

Rothaus, Barry, jt. ed. see Scott, Samuel F.

***Rothaus, Don.** Aardvarks. (Nature Bks.). (Illus.). 32p. (J). (gr. 2-6). 1995. lib. bdg. 22.79 (1-56766-181-5) Childs World.

— Eels. (Nature Bks.). (Illus.). 32p. (J). (gr. 2-6). 1995. lib. bdg. 22.79 (1-56766-187-4) Childs World.

— Hyenas. (Nature Bks.). (Illus.). 32p. (J). (gr. 2-6). 1995. lib. bdg. 22.79 (1-56766-183-1) Childs World.

— Monkeys. (Nature Bks.). (Illus.). 24p. (J). (gr. 2-6). 1995. lib. bdg. 22.79 (1-56766-189-0) Childs World.

— Warthogs. (Nature Bks.). (Illus.). 32p. (J). (gr. 2-6). 1995. lib. bdg. 22.79 (1-56766-185-8) Childs World.

Rothaus, James R. Barry Sanders. (Sports Superstars Ser.). 32p. (J). (gr. 2-6). 1991. lib. bdg. 21.36 (0-89565-737-6) Childs World.

— Bo Jackson. (Sports Superstars Ser.). 32p. (J). (gr. 2-6). 1991. lib. bdg. 21.36 (0-89565-731-7) Childs World.

— David Robinson. (Sports Superstars Ser.). 32p. (J). (gr. 2-6). 1991. lib. bdg. 21.36 (0-89565-784-8) Childs World.

— Jennifer Capriati. (Sports Superstars Ser.). 32p. (J). 1991. lib. bdg. 21.36 (0-89565-738-4) Childs World.

— Joe Montana. (Sports Superstars Ser.). 32p. (J). 1991. lib. bdg. 21.36 (0-89565-736-8) Childs World.

— Jose Canseco. (Sports Superstars Ser.). 32p. (J). 1991. lib. bdg. 21.36 (0-89565-735-X) Childs World.

— Ken Griffey, Jr. (Sports Superstars Ser.). 32p. (J). 1991. 21.36 (0-89565-783-X) Childs World.

— Magic Johnson. (Sports Superstars Ser.). 32p. (ENG & SPA.). (J). (gr. 2-6). 1991. lib. bdg. 21.36 (0-89565-732-5) Childs World.

— Michael Jordan. (Sports Superstars Ser.). 32p. (ENG & SPA.). (J). (gr. 2-6). 1991. lib. bdg. 21.36 (0-89565-733-3) Childs World.

— Steffi Graf. (Sports Biographies Ser.). (Illus.). 32p. (ENG & SPA.). (J). (gr. 2-6). 1991. lib. bdg. 21.36 (0-89565-734-1) Childs World.

Rothaus, Jim. Alligators & Crocodiles. (Zoobooks Ser.). 24p. (J). (gr. 3). 1988. lib. bdg. 14.95 (0-88682-220-3) Creative Ed.

— Bears. (Zoobooks Ser.). 24p. (J). (gr. 3). 1991. lib. bdg. 14.95 (0-88682-221-1) Creative Ed.

— Dinosaurs. (Zoobooks Ser.). 24p. (J). (gr. 3). 1988. lib. bdg. 14.95 (0-88682-223-8) Creative Ed.

— The Dream Team. LC 92-37938. (Illus.). 32p. 1992. lib. bdg. 21.36 (1-56766-050-9) Childs World.

— Ducks, Geese, & Swans. (Zoobooks Ser.). 24p. (J). (gr. 3). 1988. lib. bdg. 14.95 (0-88682-224-6) Creative Ed.

— Eagles. (Zoobooks Ser.). 24p. (J). (gr. 3). 1988. lib. bdg. 14.95 (0-88682-225-4) Creative Ed.

— Elephants. (Zoobooks Ser.). 24p. (J). (gr. 3). 1988. lib. bdg. 14.95 (0-88682-226-2) Creative Ed.

— Fairy Tale Jokes. (Funny Side up Ser.). (Illus.). (J). (gr. 1-4). 1992. lib. bdg. 19.93 (0-89565-862-3) Childs World.

— Giant Pandas. (Zoobooks Ser.). 24p. (J). (gr. 3). 1988. lib. bdg. 14.95 (0-88682-228-9) Creative Ed.

— Karl Malone. (Sports Biographies Ser.). (ENG & SPA.). (J). (gr. 2-6). 1992. lib. bdg. 21.36 (0-89565-961-1) Childs World.

— Karl Malone. (Sports Biographies Ser.). (ENG & SPA.). (J). (gr. 2-6). 1992. lib. bdg. 21.36 (1-56766-055-X) Childs World.

— Kirby Puckett. (Sports Biographies Ser.). 32p. (ENG & SPA.). (J). (gr. 2-6). 1992. lib. bdg. 21.36 (0-89565-960-3) Childs World.

— Koalas. (Zoobooks Ser.). 24p. (J). (gr. 3). 1988. lib. bdg. 14.95 (0-88682-227-0) Creative Ed.

— Monster Riddles. (Funny Side up Ser.). (Illus.). 32p. (J). (gr. 1-4). 1992. lib. bdg. 19.93 (0-89565-863-1) Childs World.

— Sharks. (Zoobooks Ser.). 24p. (J). (gr. 3). 1988. lib. bdg. 14.95 (0-88682-229-7) Creative Ed.

Rothaus, Kenneth, jt. auth. see Tyberg, Theodore.

Rothbard, Murray. America's Great Depression. 346p. 1983. 19.95 (0-945999-25-9) Independent Inst.

Rothbard, Murray N. Advance to Revolution, Seventeen Sixty to Seventeen Seventy-Five. LC 76-18978. (Conceived in Liberty Ser.: Vol. III). 373p. (C). 1988. reprint ed. pap. text ed. 13.95 (0-317-90517-1) Independent Inst.

— Classical Economics Vol. II: An Austrian Perspective on the History of Economic Thought. 560p. 1995. 111.95 (1-85278-962-X, Pub. by E Elgar Pub UK) Ashgate Pub Co.

— Conceived in Liberty, 4 vols. 1672p. (C). 1988. reprint ed. pap. text ed. 49.95 (0-685-21085-5) Independent Inst.

— Economic Thought Before Adam Smith Vol. I: An Austrian Perspective on the History of Economic Thought. 608p. 1995. 119.95 (1-85278-961-1, Pub. by E Elgar Pub UK) Ashgate Pub Co.

— For a New Liberty: The Libertarian Manifesto. 3rd ed. 338p. 1985. reprint ed. pap. 12.95 (0-930073-02-9) Fox & Wilkes.

— Man, Economy, & State: A Treatise on Economic Principles. rev. ed. (Illus.). 1001p. (C). 1993. reprint ed. pap. text ed. 25.00 (0-945466-15-3) Ludwig von Mises.

— What Has Government Done to Our Money? 119p. (Orig.). 1990. reprint ed. pap. text ed. 5.00 (0-945466-10-2) Ludwig von Mises.

Rothbard, Murray N., ed. The Review of Austrian Economics, 1990, Vol. 4. (C). 1990. lib. bdg. 57.50 (0-7923-9064-4) Kluwer Ac.

Rothbard, Murray N. & Block, Walter, eds. The Review of Austrian Economics, Vol. II. 304p. 1987. text ed. 49.95 (0-669-16740-1) Free Pr.

— The Review of Austrian Economics, Vol. 3. 288p. 1989. text ed. 49.95 (0-669-20124-3) Free Pr.

Rothbard, Murray N. & Hess, Karl, eds. Libertarian Forum, 1969-1971. LC 77-172217. (Right Wing Individualist Tradition in America Ser.). 1979. reprint ed. 23.95 (0-405-00427-3) Ayer.

Rothbard, Murray N. & Sylvester, Isaiah W. What Is Money: An Original Arno Press Compilation. LC 74-172227. (Right Wing Individualist Tradition in America Ser.). 1972. reprint ed. 13.95 (0-405-00447-8) Ayer.

Rothbard, Murray N. & Tuccille, Jerome, eds. The Right Wing Individualist Tradition in America, 38 bks, Set. 1972. 812.00 (0-405-00410-9) Ayer.

Rothbardt, Don & Harris, Paul N. Love & Attachment: or Falling in Love Is B. S. An Unauthorized Psychological Approach. LC 92-34014. 208p. (Orig.). 1992. pap. 11.95 (0-915180-35-9) Harrowood Bks.

Rothbart, Andrea. The Theory of Remainders. 1994. write for info. (0-939765-82-9, G168) Janson Pubns.

Rothbart, Betty, jt. auth. see Caplan, Ronald M.

***Rothbart, Daniel.** Concise Intro Logic. 150p. (C). 1995. student ed, pap. text ed. 19.95 (0-7872-0958-9) Kendall-Hunt.

Rothbart, Harold A. Cybernetic Creativity. LC 78-175238. 240p. 1972. 10.95 (0-8315-0118-9) Speller.

— Mechanical Systems Reference Guide. 1989. 34.50 (0-07-054025-X) McGraw.

Rothbart, Linda, ed. see American Trucking Association Staff.

Rothbart, Linda S., ed. see American Trucking Association Staff.

Rothbaum, Donald A., jt. ed. see Noble, R. Joe.

***Rothbaum, Leslie.** Rothbaum's Guide to the King County Courthouse. (Illus.). 152p. (Orig.). 1994. pap. 19.95 (0-89716-515-2) P B Pubng.

Rothberg, Abraham, jt. auth. see Simon, Solomon.

R

Rothberg, David L. Insecurity & Success in Organizational Life: Sources of Personal Motivation among Leaders & Managers. LC 81-11881. (Illus.). 238p. 1981. text ed. 55.00 (*0-275-90712-0*, C0712, Praeger Pubs) Greenwood.

Rothberg, Diane & Cook, Barbara. Part-Time Professional: How to Pursue a Career on a Part-Time Basis. LC 85-19964. 160p. 1985. pap. 8.95 (*0-87491-786-7*) Acropolis.

Rothberg, Joel. Poems of the Big Sur. (Illus.). 114p. (Orig.). 1989. pap. 12.95 (*0-9610386-0-8*) Dragons Tail Pr.

Rothberg, Judith. Meet Me in West Africa: The Ivory Coast, Togo & Senegal. 1991. 12.95 (*0-533-09458-5*) Vantage.

— Meet the Rivers of the Commonwealth of Independent States: The Volga & the Dneiper. 1992. 13.95 (*0-533-10317-7*) Vantage.

Rothberg, L., jt. ed. see Alfano, R. R.

Rothberg, Morey & Goggin, Jacqueline, eds. John Franklin Jameson & the Development of Humanistic Scholarship in America: Selected Essays, Vol. 1. LC 92-8221. (Illus.). 432p. 1992. 45.00 (*0-8203-1446-3*) U of Ga Pr.

Rothberg, Robert R., ed. Corporate Strategy & Product Innovation. 2nd ed. LC 80-1857. (Illus.). 1981. text ed. 32.95 (*0-02-927520-2*) Free Pr.

***Rothbert.** Mechanical Design Handbook. 1995. 115.00 (*0-07-054038-1*) McGraw.

Rothblatt, Donald N., ed. Metropolitan Governance: American-Canadian Intergovernmental Perspectives. LC 92-43736. 469p. (C). 1993. pap. 24.95 (*0-87772-334-6*) UCB IGS.

Rothblatt, Donald N. & Garr, Daniel J. Suburbia: An International Assessment. LC 85-22111. 336p. 1986. text ed. 39.95 (*0-312-77487-7*) St Martin.

Rothblatt, Donald N., et al. Suburbia. LC 78-19797. (Praeger Special Studies). 210p. 1979. text ed. 55.00 (*0-275-90414-8*, C0414, Praeger Pubs) Greenwood.

Rothblatt, Henry B. The Art of Cross Examination. 1971. 5.00 (*1-55917-014-X*, 881); audio 50.00 (*1-55917-012-3*); vhs 350.00 (*1-55917-013-1*) Natl Prac Inst.

— Criminal Law of New York, 2 Vols. LC 78-151142. 1386p. 1971. 150.00 (*0-317-00473-5*); Suppl. 1993. 80.00 (*0-317-03181-3*) Lawyers Cooperative.

Rothblatt, Henry B., jt. auth. see Bailey, F. Lee.

Rothblatt, Henry B., et al. How to Stop the Pain of Arthritis. LC 84-61541. 140p. (Orig.). 1985. pap. 4.95 (*0-936320-23-0*) Compact Books.

Rothblatt, J., et al, eds. Guidebook to the Secretory Pathway. (Guidebook Ser. A Sambrook & Tooze Publication at Oxford University Press). (Illus.). 296p. 1995. 75.00 (*0-19-859942-0*); pap. 39.50 (*0-19-859941-2*) OUP.

***Rothblatt, Martine A.** The Apartheid of Sex: A Manifesto on the Freedom of Gender. LC 94-20941. 1995. 21.00 (*0-517-59997-X*) Crown Pub Group.

Rothblatt, Sheldon. The Revolution of the Dons: Cambridge & Society in Victorian England. LC 80-41865. 325p. reprint ed. pap. 92.70 (*0-685-20568-1*, 2030618) Bks Demand.

Rothblatt, Sheldon & Wittrock, Bjorn, eds. The European & American University since 1800: Historical & Sociological Essays. 416p. (C). 1993. 59.95 (*0-521-43165-4*) Cambridge U Pr.

Rothblatt, Sheldon, ed. see May, Henry F.

Rothblum, Esther D., ed. Women & Sex Therapy. LC 88-11068. (Women & Therapy Ser.: Vol. 7, No. 2-3). (Illus.). 300p. 1988. pap. text ed. 17.95 (*0-918393-54-X*) Harrington Pk.

Rothblum, Esther D. & Brehony, Kathleen A., eds. Boston Marriages: Romantic but Asexual Relationships among Contemporary Lesbians. LC 93-4281. 216p. 1993. lib. bdg. 40.00 (*0-87023-875-2*); pap. 15.95 (*0-87023-876-0*) U of Mass Pr.

Rothblum, Esther D. & Brown, Laura S., eds. Fat Oppression & Psychotherapy: A Feminist Perspective. LC 89-19860. (Women & Therapy Ser.: Vol. 8, No. 3). 103p. 1990. text ed. 24.95 (*0-86656-954-5*) Haworth Pr.

Rothblum, Esther D. & Cole, Ellen. Lesbianism: Affirming Nontraditional Roles. LC 88-32028. (Women & Therapy Ser.: Vol. 8, Nos. 1-2). (Illus.). 224p. 1989. text ed. 37.95 (*0-86656-809-3*) Haworth Pr.

— Loving Boldly: Issues Facing Lesbians. LC 88-21415. (Women & Therapy Ser.: Vol. 8, Nos. 1-2). (Illus.). 224p. 1989. pap. text ed. 14.95 (*0-918393-58-2*) Harrington Pk.

— Professional Training for Feminist Therapists: Personal Memoirs. LC 90-26555. (Women & Therapy Ser.). 129p. 1990. text ed. 29.95 (*1-56024-123-3*) Haworth Pr.

Rothblum, Esther D. & Cole, Ellen, eds. Another Silenced Trauma: Twelve Feminist Therapists & Activists Respond to One Woman's Recovery from War. LC 86-9481. 124p. 1986. pap. 9.95 (*0-918393-29-9*) Harrington Pk.

— Treating Women's Fear of Failure. LC 87-25134. (Women & Therapy Ser.: Vol. 6, No. 3). 105p. 1988. text ed. 29.95 (*0-86656-676-7*) Haworth Pr.

— Treating Women's Fear of Failure: From Worry to Enlightenment. LC 87-25132. (Women & Therapy Ser.: Vol. 6, No. 3). 105p. 1988. pap. text ed. 9.95 (*0-918393-41-8*) Harrington Pk.

— Women's Mental Health in Africa. (Women & Therapy Ser.). (Illus.). 98p. 1990. text ed. 24.95 (*1-56024-043-1*); pap. text ed. 9.95 (*0-918393-86-8*) Haworth Pr.

Rothblum, Esther D., jt. ed. see Brown, Laura S.

Rothblum, Esther D., jt. ed. see Cole, Ellen.

Rothblum, Esther D., jt. auth. see Franks, Violet.

Rothbrust, Florian K. Guderian's XIX Panzer Corps & the Battle of France: Breakthrough in the Ardennes, May 1940. LC 89-38182. 224p. 1990. text ed. 49.95 (*0-275-93473-X*, C3473, Greenwood Pr) Greenwood.

Rothchild, B. J., ed. Global Fisheries: Perspectives for the 1980's. (Environmental Management Ser.). (Illus.). 289p. 1983. 84.00 (*0-387-90772-6*) Spr-Verlag.

Rothchild, Donald, ed. Ghana: The Political Economy of Recovery. LC 90-26072. (SAIS African Studies Library). 287p. (C). 1991. lib. bdg. 42.00 (*1-55587-237-9*); pap. text ed. 17.95 (*1-55587-284-0*) Lynne Rienner.

Rothchild, Donald & Chazan, Naomi, eds. The Precarious Balance: State & Society in Africa. 357p. (C). 1989. pap. text ed. 23.50 (*0-8133-0968-9*) Westview.

Rothchild, Donald, jt. ed. see Harbeson, John W.

Rothchild, Donald, jt. ed. see Keller, Edmond J.

Rothchild, John. A Fool & His Money: The Odyssey of an Average Investor. 256p. 1989. pap. 10.95 (*0-14-011989-2*, Penguin Bks) Viking Penguin.

Rothchild, John, jt. auth. see Douglas, Marjory S.

Rothchild, John, jt. auth. see Lynch, Peter.

Rothchild, Seymour, ed. Advances in Tracer Methodology: A Collection of Papers Presented at the Sixth, Seventh & Eighth Symposia on Tracer Methodology & Other Papers Selected by the Editor. LC 62-13475. 329p. reprint ed. pap. 93.80 (*0-8357-5189-9*, 2019408) Bks Demand.

Rothchild, Seymour, ed. see Advances in Tracer Methodology.

Rothchild, Sylvia. Family Stories for Every Generation. LC 89-5561. 229p. (C). 1989. 24.95 (*0-8143-2240-9*) Wayne St U Pr.

Rothe, E. H. Introduction to Various Aspects of Degree Theory in Banach Spaces. LC 86-8038. (Mathematical Surveys & Monographs: Vol. 23). 242p. 1986. text ed. 77.00 (*0-8218-1522-9*, SURV-23) Am Math.

Rothe, F. Global Solutions of Reaction-Diffusion Systems. (Lecture Notes in Mathematics Ser.: Vol. 1072). v, 216p. 1984. pap. 34.10 (*0-387-13365-8*) Spr-Verlag.

***Rothe, Gunter M.** Electrophoresis of Enzymes: Laboratory Methods. LC 94-35142. (Laboratory Ser.). 1994. write for info. (*3-540-58114-6*) Spr-Verlag.

— Electrophoresis of Enzymes: Laboratory Methods. LC 94-35142. (Laboratory Ser.). 1994. 59.00 (*0-387-58114-6*) Spr-Verlag.

Rothe, H. J. Lattice Gauge Theories. 350p. (C). 1992. text ed. 86.00 (*981-02-0606-2*); pap. text ed. 46.00 (*981-02-0607-0*) World Scientific Pub.

Rothe, Hans, ed. Daumier on War. LC 77-9349. (Quality Paperbacks Ser.). (Illus.). 1977. pap. 6.95 (*0-306-80079-9*) Da Capo.

Rothe, J. P., ed. Rethinking Young Drivers. 292p. 1989. pap. 18.95 (*0-88738-785-3*) Transaction Pubs.

Rothe, J. P. & Cooper, P. J., eds. Motorcyclists: Image & Reality. 222p. 1989. pap. 19.95 (*0-88738-784-5*) Transaction Pubs.

Rothe, J. Peter. Beyond Traffic Safety. 366p. (C). 1993. text ed. 39.95 (*1-56000-095-3*) Transaction Pubs.

— The Safety of Elderly Drivers: Yesterday's Young in Today's Traffic. 250p. 1989. pap. 24.95 (*0-88738-728-4*) Transaction Pubs.

— The Trucker's World: Risk, Safety, & Mobility. 240p. (C). 1991. pap. 19.95 (*1-56000-551-3*) Transaction Pubs.

Rothe, J. Peter, ed. Challenging the Old Order: Towards New Directions in Traffic Safety Theory. 250p. 1990. pap. 21.95 (*0-88738-828-0*) Transaction Pubs.

Rothe, J. Peter & Cooper, Peter J. Never Say Always: Perspectives on Seat Belt Use. 192p. 1989. pap. 19.95 (*0-88738-775-6*) Transaction Pubs.

Rothe, Manfred. Introduction to Aroma Research. (C). 1988. lib. bdg. 114.50 (*90-277-2078-9*) Kluwer Ac.

Rothe, P. H., ed. see Basic Mechanisms in Two-phase Flow & Heat Transfer Symposium Staff.

Rothe, Robert. Acadia: The Story Behind the Scenery. LC 78-78121. (Illus.). 48p. 1979. pap. 6.95 (*0-916122-57-3*) KC Pubns.

Rothel, David. An Ambush of Ghosts: A Guide to Great Western Film Locations. LC 90-84532. 306p. 1991. 40.00 (*0-944019-10-2*) Empire NC.

— The Gene Autry Book: A Reference - Trivia - Scrapbook. LC 87-82382. 294p. 1988. 30.00 (*0-944019-02-1*); pap. 25.00 (*0-944019-03-X*) Empire NC.

— The Roy Rogers Book: A Reference-Trivia-Scrapbook. LC 87-8183. 224p. 1987. 25.00 (*0-944019-00-5*); pap. 20.00 (*0-944019-01-3*) Empire NC.

— Those Great Cowboy Sidekicks. LC 84-10513. 338p. 1984. 39.50 (*0-8108-1707-1*) Scarecrow.

— Those Great Cowboy Sidekicks. (Illus.). 325p. 1984. pap. 17.95 (*0-936505-00-1*) World Yesterday.

— Tim Holt. (Illus.). 290p. Date not set. text ed. 30.00 (*0-944019-13-7*) Empire NC.

Rothel, David, jt. auth. see Thornton, Chuck.

Rothenbeck-Neff, Nancy, ed. see Hedge, Christine.

Rothenberg. Advanced Medical Life Support: Adult Medical-Cardiac Emergencies. 224p. 1987. pap. text ed. 29.95 (*0-8016-4284-1*) Mosby Yr Bk.

Rothenberg, et al. Basic Prehospital Care. (Illus.). 688p. 1991. student ed 12.95 (*0-8016-3418-0*); pap. 23.95 (*0-8016-2933-0*) Mosby Yr Bk.

Rothenberg, Albert. The Creative Process of Psychotherapy. (Professional Bks.). 1987. 24.95 (*0-393-70046-1*) Norton.

— Creativity & Madness: New Findings & Old Stereotypes. LC 90-30770. 200p. 1990. 32.50x (*0-8018-4011-2*) Johns Hopkins.

— Creativity & Madness: New Findings & Old Stereotypes. 208p. 1994. reprint ed. pap. text ed. 13.95x (*0-8018-4977-2*) Johns Hopkins.

— The Emerging Goddess: The Creative Process in Art, Science, & Other Fields. LC 78-26486. (Midway Reprint Ser.). (Illus.). xii, 440p. 1989. pap. text ed. 24.95 (*0-226-72950-8*) U Ch Pr.

Rothenberg, Albert & Hausman, Carl R. The Creativity Question. LC 75-30132. xiv, 366p. 1976. 41.95 (*0-8223-0353-1*); pap. 18.95 (*0-8223-0354-X*) Duke.

***Rothenberg, B. Annye.** Understanding & Working with Parents & Children from Rural Mexico: What Professionals Need to Know about Child-Rearing Practices, the School Experience, & Health Care Concerns. LC 94-31386. 285p. 1995. per. 27.50x (*0-9642119-0-4*) CHC Ctr.

Rothenberg, B. Annye, et al. Parentmaking: A Practical Handbook for Teaching Parent Classes about Babies & Toddlers. LC 81-66429. (Illus.). 461p. (Orig.). 1983. pap. 25.95 (*0-9604620-0-7*) Banster Pr.

— Parentmaking: A Practical Handbook for Teaching Parent Classes about Babies & Toddlers. 2nd rev. ed. Whiteley, Carol, ed. LC 95-3150. (Illus.). 495p. (Orig.). 1995. pap. text ed. 35.95x (*0-9604620-2-3*) Banster Pr.

— Parentmaking Educators Training Program: A Comprehensive Skills Development Course to Train Early Childhood Parent Educators (Birth to 5) LC 92-19352. (Illus.). 440p. (Orig.). 1993. pap. text ed., vhs 149.95 (*0-9604620-1-5*, HQ755.7.R665) Banster Pr.

Rothenberg, Benno, ed. Archaeological Haggadah. LC 86-1052. (Illus.). 1986. 24.95 (*0-915361-36-1*) Modan-Adama Bks.

Rothenberg, Bertram. U. S. Postal Service Bicentennial Postmarks, 1972-1984. 42p. 1986. pap. text ed. 5.00 (*0-935991-01-8*) Am Topical Assn.

Rothenberg, Beth & Rothenberg, Oscar. Touch Training for Strength. LC 94-1605. 152p. 1995. pap. 13.95 (*0-87322-437-X*, PROT0437) Human Kinetics.

Rothenberg, David. Hand's End: Technology & the Limits of Nature. LC 92-39341. 1993. 30.00 (*0-685-74493-0*) U CA Pr.

— Hand's End: Technology & the Limits of Nature. LC 92-39341. 1995. pap. 11.95 (*0-520-08055-6*) U CA Pr.

— Is It Painful to Think? Conversations with Arne Naess. (Illus.). 248p. (C). 1992. text ed. 44.95 (*0-8166-2151-9*); pap. 16.95 (*0-8166-2152-7*) U of Minn Pr.

***Rothenberg, David, ed.** Wild Ideas. LC 94-49620. 143p. 1995. text ed. 44.95 (*0-8166-2614-6*); pap. text ed. 18.95 (*0-8166-2615-4*) U of Minn Pr.

Rothenberg, David, tr. see Naess, Arne.

Rothenberg, David, jt. ed. see Reed, Peter.

Rothenberg, Diane, jt. auth. see Rothenberg, Jerome.

Rothenberg, Ed. The Rothenberg Lease-Option Strategy. (Orig.). 1986. pap. 7.95 (*0-9613865-1-7*) E Rothenberg.

Rothenberg, Eric B. & Telego, Dean J., eds. Environmental Risk Management: A Desk Reference. LC 90-63282. 855p. 1991. text ed. 125.00 (*0-9628098-0-2*) RTM Comns.

Rothenberg, Erika, ed. see Cage, John, et al.

Rothenberg, Gunther E. The Art of Warfare in the Age of Napoleon. LC 77-86495. (Illus.). 280p. 1978. 29.95 (*0-253-31076-8*); pap. 10.95 (*0-253-20260-4*, MB-260) Ind U Pr.

— Napoleon's Great Adversary: Archduke Charles & the Austrian Army, 1792-1814. LC 94-77048. (Illus.). 240p. 1995. reprint ed. 29.95 (*1-885119-21-6*) Sarpedon.

Rothenberg, Gunther E., jt. ed. see Kiraly, Bela K.

Rothenberg, Gunther E., et al. East Central European Society & War in Pre-Revolutionary Eighteenth Century. (Brooklyn College Studies on Society in Change). 566p. 1982. text ed. 65.00 (*0-930888-19-7*) East Eur Quarterly.

Rothenberg, Jeff & Narain, Sanjai. The RAND Advanced Simulation Language Project's Declarative Modeling Formalism: DMOD. LC 94-420774. 1994. write for info. (*0-8330-1555-9*, MR376ARPA) Rand Corp.

Rothenberg, Jerome. Abulafia's Circles. 1979. pap. 5.00 (*0-87924-034-2*) Membrane Pr.

— Altar Pieces. (Illus.). 1982. pap. 5.50 (*0-930794-48-6*) Station Hill Pr.

— Economic Evaluation of Urban Renewal: Conceptual Foundation of Benefit-Cost Analysis. LC 67-19190. (Studies of Government Finance). 291p. reprint ed. pap. 83.00 (*0-317-28184-4*, 2022559) Bks Demand.

— Esther K Comes to America. LC 79-134740. 52p. 1973. pap. 7.95 (*0-87775-008-4*) Unicorn Pr.

— Further Sightings & Conversations. 32p. (Orig.). 1989. pap. 4.00 (*0-938631-03-9*) Pennywhistle Pr.

— Gematria. (Sun & Moon Classics Ser.: No. 45). 100p. (Orig.). 1993. pap. 11.95 (*1-55713-097-3*) Sun & Moon CA.

— In a Time of War. deluxe ed. 12p. 1993. 35.00 (*0-9627430-6-2*) diwan.

— In a Time of War. limited ed. 12p. 1993. pap. 10.00 (*0-9627430-5-4*) diwan.

— Khurbn & Other Poems. LC 89-12224. 128p. 1989. 19.95 (*0-8112-1108-8*); pap. 9.95 (*0-8112-1109-6*, NDP679) New Directions.

— The Lorca Variations: One to Thirty-Three. LC 93-794. 128p. (Orig.). 1993. pap. 10.95 (*0-8112-1253-X*, NDP771) New Directions.

— New Selected Poems, Nineteen Seventy to Nineteen Eighty-Five. LC 86-5388. 160p. (Orig.). 1986. 23.50 (*0-8112-0996-2*); pap. 8.95 (*0-8112-0997-0*, NDP625) New Directions.

— The Notebooks. (Illus.). 1977. pap. 5.00 (*0-87924-033-4*) Membrane Pr.

— The Pirke & the Pearl. LC 74-24550. 32p. (Orig.). 1975. pap. 7.50 (*0-686-10821-3*) Tree Bks.

— Poland, Nineteen Thirty-One. LC 74-8646. (Illus.). 160p. 1974. 7.50 (*0-8112-0541-X*); pap. 3.25 (*0-8112-0542-8*, NDP379) New Directions.

— Pre-Faces & Other Writings. LC 80-24031. 224p. 1981. 14.95 (*0-8112-0785-4*); pap. 6.95 (*0-8112-0786-2*, NDP511) New Directions.

— Shaking the Pumpkin: Traditional Poetry of the Indian North Americas. rev. ed. LC 90-39916. 448p. 1991. reprint ed. pap. 17.95 (*0-8263-1246-2*) U of NM Pr.

— That Dada Strain. LC 82-18827. 96p. 1983. pap. 7.25 (*0-8112-0860-5*, NDP550) New Directions.

— Vienna Blood & Other Poems. LC 79-24966. (Orig.). 1980. pap. 4.95 (*0-8112-0759-5*, NDP498) New Directions.

Rothenberg, Jerome, ed. Technicians of the Sacred: A Range of Poetries from Africa, America, Asia, Europe & Oceania. rev. ed. LC 84-16276. 1985. pap. 17.00 (*0-520-04912-8*) U CA Pr.

Rothenberg, Jerome & Joris, Pierre, eds. Poems for the Millennium: The University of California Book of Modern & Postmodern Poetry. LC 93-49839. (Centennial Book Ser.: Vol. 1, From Fin-de-Siecle to Negritude). Date not set. pap. 24.95x (*0-520-07227-8*) U CA Pr.

— Poems for the Millennium: The University of California Book of Modern & Postmodern Poetry. LC 93-49839. (Centennial Book Ser.: Vol. 1,). 1995. 60.00x (*0-520-07225-1*) U CA Pr.

Rothenberg, Jerome & Lenowitz, Harris. Gematria Twenty-Seven. (Illus.). 1977. pap. 10.00 (*0-87924-047-4*) Membrane Pr.

Rothenberg, Jerome & Rothenberg, Diane. Symposium of the Whole: A Range of Discourse Toward an Enthnopoetics. 526p. (C). 1983. pap. 16.00 (*0-520-04531-9*) U CA Pr.

Rothenberg, Jerome, tr. see Andrews, Bruce, et al.

Rothenberg, Jerome, tr. see Garcia Lorca, Federico.

Rothenberg, Jerome, tr. see Gomringer, Eugen.

Rothenberg, Jerome, ed. see Norman, Howard.

Rothenberg, Jerome, ed. see Schwitters, Kurt.

Rothenberg, Jerome, et al. The Maze of Urban Housing Markets: Theory, Evidence, & Policy. LC 90-22756. (Illus.). 480p. 1991. 62.95 (*0-226-72951-6*) U Ch Pr.

***Rothenberg, Joan.** Inside-Out Grandma. LC 94-23677. (Illus.). 32p. (J). (ps-3). 1995. 14.95 (*0-7868-0107-7*); lib. bdg. 14.89 (*0-7868-2092-6*) Hyprn Child.

— Yettele's Feathers. large type ed. LC 94-26623. (Illus.). 40p. (J). (ps-3). 1995. 14.95 (*0-7868-0097-6*); lib. bdg. 14.89 (*0-7868-2081-0*) Hyprn Child.

Rothenberg, Joshua. The Jewish Religion in the Soviet Union. 1971. 25.00 (*0-87068-156-7*) Ktav.

Rothenberg, Karen H. & Thomson, Elizabeth J., eds. Women & Prenatal Testing: Facing the Challlenges of Genetic Technology. (Women & Health Ser.). 256p. 1994. 75.00 (*0-8142-0640-9*); pap. 17.95 (*0-8142-0641-7*) Ohio St U Pr.

Rothenberg, Lawrence S. Linking Citizens to Government: Interest Group Politics at Common Cause. (Illus.). 280p. (C). 1992. 64.95 (*0-521-41560-8*); pap. 19.95 (*0-521-42577-8*) Cambridge U Pr.

— Regulation, Organizations, & Politics: Motor Freight Policy at the Interstate Commerce Commission. 326p. (C). 1993. text ed. 47.50x (*0-472-10443-8*) U of Mich Pr.

Rothenberg, Mace L., ed. Gynecologic Oncology: Controversies & New Developments. LC 93-41309. (Cancer Treatment & Research Ser.). 144p. (C). 1994. lib. bdg. 120.00 (*0-7923-2634-2*) Kluwer Ac.

Rothenberg, Marc. The History of Science & Technology in the United States, Vol. 2: A Critical & Selected Bibliography. LC 81-43355. (Bibliographies on the History of Science & Technology Ser.: Vol. 17). 216p. 1993. 32.00 (*0-8240-8349-0*, H815) Garland.

Rothenberg, Marc, ed. The Papers of Joseph Henry, Vol. 6: The Princeton Years, January 1844 - December 1846. LC 72-2005. (Illus.). 592p. 1992. text ed. 55.00 (*1-56098-112-1*) Smithsonian.

Rothenberg, Marc, jt. ed. see Reingold, Nathan.

Rothenberg, Marie. David. 1986. pap. 4.50 (*0-425-08766-2*) Phoenix Soc.

Rothenberg, Marie & White, Mel. David. (Illus.). 200p. 1984. pap. 3.99 (*0-8007-8589-4*) Revell.

Rothenberg, Melvin, jt. auth. see Dovermann, Karl H.

Rothenberg, Michael. Dahlia. (Illus.). 36p. 1989. 85.00 (*0-685-31054-X*) Big Bridge Pr.

— Favorite Songs. 88p. (Orig.). 1990. pap. 8.95 (*0-685-31055-8*) Big Bridge Pr.

***Rothenberg, Michael, ed.** The Collected Poems of Ann Fields. 281p. (Orig.). Date not set. pap. 12.95 (*1-878471-02-3*) Big Bridge Pr.

Rothenberg, Michael & Kyger, Joanne. Man - Women. (Illus.). 48p. 1988. 65.00 (*0-685-31053-1*) Big Bridge Pr.

Rothenberg, Michael, ed. see Andre, Edouard F.

Rothenberg, Michael, jt. auth. see Spock, Benjamin M.

***Rothenberg, Mikel A.** Anatomy for Trial Lawyers. LC 94-40261. (Personal Injury Library). 1995. text ed. 105.00 (*0-471-09056-5*) Wiley.

— Emergency Medicine Malpractice. 2nd ed. LC 94-11906. (Personal Injury Library). 1994. text ed. 128.00 (*0-471-00083-3*, Pub. by Wiley Law Pubns) Wiley.

Rothenberg, Mikel A. & Chapman, Charles F. Dictionary of Medical Terms for the Nonmedical Person. 3rd ed. LC 93-31122. 628p. 1994. pap. 9.95 (*0-8120-1852-4*) Barron.

Rothenberg, Molly A. Rethinking Blake's Textuality. LC 93-13510. (Illus.). 176p. 1993. text ed. 34.95 (*0-8262-0901-7*) U of Mo Pr.

Rothenberg, Oscar, jt. auth. see Rothenberg, Beth.

***Rothenberg, Paula S.** Race, Class, & Gender in the United States. 3rd ed. 528p. 1994. pap. text ed. 19.00 (*0-312-09652-6*) St Martin.

— Race, Class, & Gender in the United States: An Integrated Study. 2nd ed. 463p. (C). 1992. text ed. 45.00 (*0-312-08578-8*) St Martin.

Rothenberg, Paula S., jt. ed. see Jaggar, Alison M.

Rothenberg, Randall. Where the Suckers Moon: An Advertising Story. LC 94-496. 1994. 25.00 (*0-679-41227-1*) Knopf.

Rothenberg, Rebecca. The Bulrush Murders. 240p. 1991. 18.95 (*0-88184-749-6*) Carroll & Graf.

— The Bulrush Murders. 256p. 1994. mass mkt. 5.50 (*0-446-40404-7*, Mysterious Paperbk) Warner Bks.

R

An Asterisk (*) at the beginning of an entry indicates that the title is appearing in BIP for the first time.

— The Dandelion Murders. 304p. 1994. 18.95 (*0-89296-561-4*) Mysterious Pr.
— The Dandelion Murders. 256p. 1995. mass mkt. 5.50 (*0-446-40378-4*, Mysterious Paperbk) Warner Bks.
— The Shy Tulip Murders. 1996. write for info. (*0-89296-607-6*) Mysterious Pr.
Rothenberg, Robert A., jt. auth. see Hillman, Jimmye S.
Rothenberg, Robert E. New American Medical Dictionary & Health Manual. 5th rev. ed. 1992. pap. 4.95 (*0-451-15152-6*, AE2027, Sig) NAL-Dutton.
— The New American Medical Dictionary & Health Manual. 5th rev. ed. (Illus.). 1988. pap. 9.95 (*0-452-00910-3*, Mer) NAL-Dutton.
— The New American Medical Dictionary & Health Manual. 6th enl. rev. ed. LC 92-80540. (Illus.). 592p. 1992. pap. 14.95 (*0-452-01102-7*, Mer) NAL-Dutton.
— The New American Medical Dictionary & Health Manual. 6th rev. ed. 608p. 1988. pap. 5.99 (*0-451-17277-9*, Sig) NAL-Dutton.
— New Illustrated Medical Encyclopedia. 1990. 19.98 (*0-88365-762-7*) Galahad Bks.
Rothenberg, Ronald J. Probability & Statistics. Thompson, Emily, ed. (College Outline Ser.). (Illus.). 391p. (C). 1992. pap. text ed. 13.50 (*0-15-601676-1*) HB Coll Pubs.
Rothenberg, Stanley. Copyright & Public Performance of Music. xii, 188p. 1987. reprint ed. lib. bdg. 32.50 (*0-8377-2535-6*) Rothman.
— Legal Protection of Literature, Art & Music. xiii, 367p. 1988. reprint ed. lib. bdg. 42.50 (*0-8377-2538-0*) Rothman.
Rothenberg, Stuart. Party Switches: Interviews about Realignment & the Political Parties. LC 85-81687. (Currents in Politics Ser.). v, 61p. 1985. 11.75 (*0-942522-04-4*) Free Congr Res.
Rothenberg, Stuart, ed. Ousting the Ins: Lessons for Congressional Challengers. LC 85-81100. 106p. (Orig.). (C). 1985. pap. text ed. 13.25 (*0-942522-05-2*) Free Congr Res.
Rothenberg, Stuart & Newport, Frank. The Evangelical Voter: Religion & Politics in America. LC 84-82043. 182p. (Orig.). (C). 1984. pap. text ed. 18.25 (*0-942522-07-9*) Free Congr Res.
Rothenberg, Susan. Teach Yourself Excel 4.0 for Windows. 1992. pap. 19.95 (*1-55828-208-4*) MIS Press.
Rothenberg, Susan, jt. auth. see Munoz, Juan.
Rothenberg, Thomas J. Efficient Estimation with a Priori Information. LC 73-77164. (Cowles Foundation for Research in Economics at Yale University. Monograph Ser.: No. 23). 190p. reprint ed. pap. 54.20 (*0-8357-8111-9*, 2033878) Bks Demand.
Rothenberg, Winifred B. From Market-Places to a Market Economy: The Transformation of Rural Massachusetts, 1750-1850. LC 92-13535. (Illus.). 248p. (C). 1992. 37.50 (*0-226-72953-2*) U Ch Pr.
Rothenberger & Ohnsorg. Personal & Community Health: Selected Readings. 272p. (C). 1990. per. 30.95 (*0-8403-6108-4*) Kendall-Hunt.
Rothenberger, A., ed. Brain & Behavior in Child Psychiatry. 496p. 1990. 109.00 (*0-387-52064-3*) Spr-Verlag.
— Event Related Potentials in Children. (Developments in Neurology Ser.: Vol. 6). 488p. 1983. 105.25 (*0-444-80451-X*) Elsevier.
Rothenberger, James H., jt. auth. see Hochhauser, Mark.
***Rothenberger, Otis & Webb, James.** Liberal Arts Chemistry Worktext. 368p. (C). 1994. per., pap. text ed. 26.36 (*0-8403-9736-4*) Kendall-Hunt.
Rothenbuhler, Claire, jt. auth. see Sonntag, Wendy W.
Rothenburg, Michael B., jt. auth. see Spock, Benjamin M.
Rothenburg, Nathan, tr. see Van Nostrand, R., ed.
Rothenhaus, Todd C. & Masterson, Thomas M. The ER Intern Pocket Survival Guide. 78p. (Orig.). (C). 1992. pap. text ed. 6.00 (*0-9634063-2-9*) Intl Med Pub.
Rothenhaus, Todd C., jt. auth. see Masterson, Thomas M.
Rothenstein, John, jt. auth. see John, Augustus E.
Rothenstein, John K. Nineteenth-Century Painting: A Study in Conflict. LC 67-28739. (Essay Index Reprint Ser.). 1977. 18.95 (*0-8369-0838-4*) Ayer.
— Pot of Paint. LC 70-128303. (Essay Index Reprint Ser.). 1977. 20.95 (*0-8369-1847-9*) Ayer.
Rothenstein, Jules. Noah's Aardvark. LC 90-70468. 166p. (Orig.). 1991. pap. text ed. 8.00 (*1-56002-150-0*, Univ Edtns) Aegina Pr.
Rothenstein, Julian, ed. Jose Guadalupe Posada: Mexican Popular Prints. LC 93-9455. (Redstone Editions Ser.). (Illus.). 160p. 1993. 25.00 (*0-87773-942-0*) Shambhala Pubns.
— The Paradox Box. LC 93-5512. (Shambhala Redstone Editions Ser.). (Illus.). 160p. 1993. 25.00 (*0-87773-941-2*) Shambhala Pubns.
Rothenstein, Julian, ed. see Gellner, David N.
Rothenstein, Julian, ed. see Posada, J. G.
Rothenstein, William & Tagore, Rabindranath. Imperfect Encounter: Letters of William Rothenstein & Rabindranath Tagore, 1911-1941. Lago, Mary M., ed. LC 73-182182. (Illus.). 422p. 1972. 37.00 (*0-674-44512-0*) HUP.
Rother, Audrey L. Bastrop County, Texas Cemeteries, Vol. 1. LC 91-75085. 410p. 1991. text ed. 29.98 (*0-9630786-0-7*) A Rother.
— Bastrop County, Texas Cemeteries, Vol. 2. 138p. 1992. text ed. 21.00 (*0-9630786-2-3*) A Rother.
Rother, K. & Rother, U., eds. Hereditary & Acquired Complement Deficiencies in Animals & Man. (Progress in Allergy Ser.: Vol. 39). (Illus.). vi, 406p. 1987. 229.75 (*3-8055-4378-6*) S Karger.
Rother, K. & Till, G. O., eds. The Complement System. (Illus.). 540p. 1988. 121.00 (*0-387-18205-5*) Spr-Verlag.
Rother, K. O., ed. see Collegium Internationale Allergologicum Symposium Staff.
Rother, U., jt. ed. see Rother, K.
Rotheram-Borus, Mary J., et al, eds. Planning to Live: Evaluating & Treating Suicidal Teens in Community Settings. (Illus.). 408p. (C). 1990. 24.95 (*1-878848-00-3*, 119) Natl Res Ctr.
Rotheram, Mary, jt. auth. see Phinney, Jean S.
Rotherham, G. A. It's Really Quite Safe! 304p. (C). 1987. 119.00 (*0-920497-07-1*, Pub. by Picton UK) St Mut.
— It's Really Quite Safe. (Illus.). 304p. 1985. 18.00 (*0-89745-107-4*) Sunflower U Pr.
Rotherham, J. B., et al. The Lord's Supper: Historical Writings on Its Meaning to the Body of Christ. Gresham, Charles & Lawson, Tom, eds. 243p. (C). 1993. 13.99 (*0-89900-603-5*) College Pr Pub.
Rotherham, Joseph B. The Emphasized Bible. LC 59-7560. 1202p. 1994. reprint ed. 44.99 (*0-8254-3601-X*) Kregel.
Rothermel, Dan. Sweet Dreams Robyn. Johnson, Joy, ed. (Illus.). 74p. 1991. pap. 5.50 (*1-56123-026-X*) Centering Corp.
Rothermel, Jerry L. HuMan - a Novel. 207p. (C). 1987. reprint ed. pap. 5.95 (*0-944386-05-9*) SOM Pub.
— Meditation the Answer to Your Prayers. 99p. (C). 1987. reprint ed. pap. 4.95 (*0-944386-01-6*) SOM Pub.
Rothermell, Fred. Fifth Avenue. LC 76-134978. (Short Story Index Reprint Ser.). 1977. 20.95 (*0-8369-3708-2*) Ayer.
Rothermich, John A., ed. see Schanker, Harry H.
Rothermich, Norman O. & Whisler, Ronald L. Rheumatoid Arthritis: Diagnosis & Comprehensive Management. (Manuals of Clinical Medicine Ser.). 288p. 1985. pap. text ed. 37.95 (*0-8089-1716-1*, 793665, Grune) Saunders.
Rothermund, D., et al, eds. Urban Growth & Rural Stagnation: Studies in the Economy of an Indian Coalfield & Its Hinterland. 1980. 36.00 (*0-8364-0662-1*, Pub. by Manohar II) S Asia.
Rothermund, Dietmar. Asian Trade & European Expansion in the Age of Mercantilism. 1981. 17.50 (*0-8364-0812-8*, Pub. by Manohar II) S Asia.
— An Economic History of India. 224p. 1988. text ed. 49.95 (*0-7099-4228-1*) Routledge Chapman & Hall.
— An Economic History of India: From Pre-Colonial Times to 1991. 2nd ed. 224p. 1993. pap. 16.95 (*0-415-08871-2*) Routledge.
— The German Intellectual Quest for India. 73p. 1987. 8.00 (*81-85054-16-9*, Pub. by Manohar II) S Asia.
— Government, Landlord & Peasant in India: Agrarian Relations under British Rule 1865-1935. xii, 211p. (Orig.). 1978. pap. text ed. 28.50 (*3-515-02764-5*) Coronet Bks.
— The Indian Economy Under British Rule. 1983. 17.50 (*0-8364-1021-1*, Pub. by Manohar II) S Asia.
— Mahatma Gandhi: An Essay in Political Biography. (C). 1992. 14.00 (*0-685-59790-3*) S Asia.
Rothermund, Dietmar, jt. auth. see Kulke, Herman.
Rothermund, Dietmar, jt. auth. see Kulke, Hermann.
Rothermund, Dietmar, jt. ed. see Ptak, Roderich.
Rothermund, Dietmar, et al. Regional Desparities in India: Rural & Industrial Dimensions. (C). 1991. 22.00 (*0-8364-2734-3*, Pub. by Manohar II) S Asia.
Rothero, Chris, illus. Strawberry Fair. 96p. (J). (gr. 1-6). 14.95 (*0-7136-2676-3*, Pub. by A&C Black UK) Talman.
Rothero, Christopher. The Armies of Agincourt. (Men-at-Arms Ser.: No. 113). (Illus.). 48p. pap. 11.95 (*0-85045-394-1*, 9046, Pub. by Osprey UK) Stackpole.
— Armies of Crecy & Poitiers. (Men-at-Arms Ser.: No. 111). (Illus.). 48p. pap. 11.95 (*0-85045-393-3*, 9044, Pub. by Osprey UK) Stackpole.
— The Scottish & Welsh Wars 1250-1400. (Men-at-Arms Ser.: No. 151). (Illus.). 48p. pap. 11.95 (*0-85045-542-1*, 9083, Pub. by Osprey UK) Stackpole.
***Rotheroe, Dominic.** London Inn Signs. 1989. pap. 25.00 (*0-7478-0088-X*, Pub. by Shire UK) St Mut.
Rothert, Eugene A. & Daubert, James R. Horticultural Therapy at a Physical Rehabilitation Facility. (Illus.). 130p. (Orig.). (C). 1981. pap. 10.00 (*0-939914-02-6*) Chi Horticult.
— Horticultural Therapy for Nursing Homes, Senior Centers, Retirement Living. (Illus.). 130p. (Orig.). 1981. pap. 10.00 (*0-939914-01-8*) Chi Horticult.
Rothert, Eugene A., Jr., jt. auth. see Daubert, James R.
Rothert, Gene. The Enabling Garden. LC 93-41968. (Illus.). 160p. 1994. pap. 13.95 (*0-87833-847-0*) Taylor Pub.
Rothert, Otto A. Outlaws of Cave-In-Rock. LC 70-140371. (Select Bibliographies Reprint Ser.). 1977. 22.95 (*0-8369-5614-1*) Ayer.
— The Outlaws of Cave-in-Rock. (Shawnee Classics Ser.). (C). 1995. pap. 12.95 (*0-8093-2034-7*) S Ill U Pr.
— The Outlaws of Cave-in-Rock. (Shawnee Classics Ser.). 368p. (C). 1995. reprint ed. 29.95 (*0-8093-2033-9*) S Ill U Pr.
— Story of a Poet: Madison Cawein. LC 76-146871. (Select Bibliographies Reprint Ser.). 1977. reprint ed. 42.95 (*0-8369-5640-0*) Ayer.
Rothery, Agnes E. Joyful Gardener. LC 77-99647. (Essay Index Reprint Ser.). 1977. 21.95 (*0-8369-2128-3*) Ayer.
Rothery, Andrew, ed. see Language & Reading in Mathematics Group Staff.
Rothery, Brian. BS 7750: Implementing the Environment Management Standard. 200p. 1993. 59.95 (*0-566-07392-7*, Pub. by Gower UK) Ashgate Pub Co.
— ISO 9000. 2nd ed. 220p. 1993. 59.95 (*0-566-07402-8*, Pub. by Gower UK) Ashgate Pub Co.
— What Maastricht Meant for Business: Opportunities & Regularities in the EC Internal Market. 200p. 1993. 49.95 (*0-566-07430-3*, Pub. by Gower UK); pap. 21.95 (*0-566-07431-1*, Pub. by Gower UK) Ashgate Pub Co.
***Rothery, Brian & Robertson, Ian.** The Truth about Outsourcing. 200p. 1995. 59.95 (*0-566-07515-6*, Pub. by Gower UK) Ashgate Pub Co.
Rothery, David A. Satellites of the Outer Planets: Worlds in Their Own Right. (Illus.). 208p. 1992. pap. 35.00 (*0-19-854290-9*) OUP.
Rothery, M. & Cameron, G., eds. Child Maltreatment: Expanded Concepts of Helping. 336p. 1990. text ed. 69.95 (*0-8058-0455-2*) L Erlbaum Assocs.
Rothery, P., jt. auth. see Brown, D.
Rothery, P., jt. auth. see Grown, D.
Rothes, John L. Relation of Proceedings Concerning the Affairs of the Kirk of Scotland. LC 79-174966. (Bannatyne Club, Edinburgh. Publications: No. 37). reprint ed. 28.00 (*0-404-52743-4*) AMS Pr.
Rotheva, Brian, jt. auth. see Lawson-Hall, Toni.
Rothfarb, Lee A., ed. see Kurth, Ernst.
Rothfeder, Jeffrey. Heart Rhythms. braille ed. 446p. 1990. Braille. vinyl bd. 35.68 (*1-56956-253-9*, BR7842) W A T Braille.
— Minds over Matter: A New Look at Artificial Intelligence. 226p. 1986. 7.95 (*0-13-583543-7*) P-H.
— Privacy for Sale: How Computerization Has Made Everyone's Private Life an Open Secret. 256p. 1992. 22.00 (*0-671-73492-X*) S&S Trade.
***Rothfeld, Otto.** With Pen & Rifle in Kashmir. (C). 1993. reprint ed. 18.00x (*81-7041-823-2*, Pub. by Anmol II) S Asia.
***Rothfeld, S.** Italian Dreams. Date not set. 25.00 (*0-00-225066-7*, HarpT) HarpC.
Rothfeld, Steven. French Dreams. LC 92-50934. 1993. 19.95 (*1-56305-469-8*, 3469) Workman Pub.
Rothfield, Lawrence. Vital Signs: Medical Realism in Nineteenth-Century Fiction. (Literature in History Ser.). 250p. 1992. text ed. 32.50 (*0-691-06896-8*) Princeton U Pr.
— Vital Signs: Medical Realism in Nineteenth-Century Fiction. (Literature in History Ser.). 250p. 1994. pap. 14.95 (*0-691-02954-7*) Princeton U Pr.
Rothfunchsm, T., et al. Test Disposal of Highly Radioactive Radiation Sources in the Asse Salt Mine. (Nuclear Science & Technology Ser.). 262p. 1993. pap. 40.00 (*92-826-4962-8*, CD-NA-14531-EN-C, Pub. by Europ Com) UNIPUB.
Rothfus, Robert R. Working Concepts of Fluid Flow. (Illus.). 96p. (Orig.). (C). pap. 3.75 (*0-685-23655-2*) Bek Tech.
Rothgarber, Herbert. The Ensemble Recorder, Bk. 2. 1975. 3.00 (*0-913334-23-5*, CM1027) Consort Music.
— Let's Folk Dance. 16p. 1980. pap. 3.25 (*0-918812-10-0*, SE 0440) MMB Music.
— Make a Glad Sound. 1974. 2.75 (*0-913334-17-0*, CM1021) Consort Music.
Rothgarber, Herbert, contrib. The Drunken Sailor. 1975. 4.50 (*0-913334-28-6*, CM1035) Consort Music.
***Rothgeb, Anita B.** Short Stories. LC 95-67130. 1995. 8.95 (*0-8158-0512-8*) Chris Mass.
Rothgeb, Carrie L., ed. Abstracts of the Collected Works of C. G. Jung. 136p. 1993. pap. 19.95 (*1-85575-035-X*, Pub. by Karnac Bks UK) Brunner-Mazel.
— Abstracts of the Standard Edition of the Complete Psychological Works of Sigmund Freud. LC 73-2144. 770p. (C). 1973. text ed. 75.00x (*0-8236-0030-0*) Intl Univs Pr.
— Abstracts of the Standard Edition of the Complete Psychological Works of Sigmund Freud. LC 73-17649. 320p. 1993. pap. 35.00 (*1-56821-140-6*) Aronson.
— Abstracts of the Standard Edition of the Complete Works of Sigmund Freud. 315p. 1987. 35.00 (*0-87668-135-6*) Aronson.
Rothgeb, John, tr. see Jonas, Oswald.
Rothgeb, John, ed. see Schenker, Heinrich.
Rothgeb, John, tr. see Schenker, Heinrich.
Rothgeb, John M., Jr. Defining Power: Influence & Force in the Contemporary International System. LC 92-50035. 1993. text ed. 39.95 (*0-312-08682-2*) St Martin.
— Defining Power: Influence & Force in the Contemporary System. LC 92-50035. (Illus.). 205p. (C). 1992. pap. text ed. 15.00 (*0-312-06105-6*) St Martin.
— Myths & Realities of Foreign Investment in Poor Countries: The Modern Leviathan in the Third World. LC 88-34026. 162p. 1989. text ed. 49.95 (*0-275-93255-9*, C3255, Praeger Pubs) Greenwood.
Rothgeb, Lew, jt. auth. see Mantle, Mickey.
Rothgeb, Wayne P. New Guinea Skies: A Fighter Pilot's View of World War II. LC 92-2916. (Illus.). 278p. 1992. 27.95 (*0-8138-0836-7*) Iowa St U Pr.
Rothhammer, Francisco, jt. ed. see Schull, William J.
Rothholz, Amy. Iced Tigers. 72p. 1987. 10.00 (*0-943959-00-4*) Amagansett Pr.
Rothkegel, Annely. Text Knowledge & Object Knowledge. LC 92-44023. (Communication in Artificial Intelligence Ser.). 220p. 1993. 59.00 (*1-86187-136-8*, Pub. by Pinter Pubs UK) St Martin.
Rothkopf, Michael M. & Askanazi, Jeffrey. Intensive Home Care. (Illus.). 352p. 1992. 70.00 (*0-683-07389-3*) Williams & Wilkins.
Rothkopf, Nancy & Cantor, Gilbert M. Pennsylvania Estates Practice, Vol. 1. LC 79-91161. (Practice Systems Library Manual). ring bd. 120.00 (*0-317-00577-4*) Lawyers Cooperative.
— Pennsylvania Estates Practice, Vol. 1. suppl. ed. LC 79-91161. (Practice Systems Library Manual). 1991. Suppl. 1991. 65.00 (*0-317-03207-0*) Lawyers Cooperative.
Rothkrug, Paul & Olson, Robert, eds. Mending the Earth: A World for Our Grandchildren. 219p. (Orig.). 1990. pap. 9.95 (*1-55643-091-4*) North Atlantic.
Rothlein, Liz & Christman, Terri. Read It Again! A Guide for Teaching Reading Through Literature, K-2, Bk. 1. (Illus.). 116p. (Orig.). 1988. pap. 9.95 (*0-673-38199-4*) GdYrBks.
— Read It Again, Bk 2, Grades 3-5: Grades 3-5. 1990. pap. 9.95 (*0-673-46290-0*) GdYrBks.
— Read It Again, More: Grades 3-5, Bk. 2. 1991. pap. 9.95 (*0-673-36007-5*) GdYrBks.
***Rothlein, Liz & Meinbach, Anita M.** Legacies: Using Children's Literature in the Classroom. LC 94-34987. (C). 1995. 22.50 (*0-673-46985-9*) HarpCollege.
— The Literature Connection: Using Children's Books in the Classroom, K-Grade 8. 1990. pap. 24.95 (*0-673-38450-0*) GdYrBks.
— Take Ten Steps to Successful Research: Grades 5-8. (Illus.). 82p. (Orig.). 1988. pap. 9.95 (*0-673-38087-4*) GdYrBks.
Rothlein, Liz & Wild, Terri C. Read It Again! Multicultural Books for the Intermediate Grades. (Illus.). 144p. (Orig.). (J). (gr. 3-5). 1993. pap. 9.95 (*0-673-36081-4*) GdYrBks.
— Read it Again! Multicultural Books for the Primary Grades, Bk. 1. (Illus.). 144p. (Orig.). (J). 1993. pap. 9.95 (*0-673-36064-4*) GdYrBks.
Rothlein, Liz, jt. auth. see Christman, Terri.
Rothlein, Liz, jt. auth. see Miller, Libby.
Rothlein, Liz, jt. auth. see Vaughn, Sharon.
Rothlein, Valerie, ed. see Hou, Tien.
Rothlisberg, Barbara A., jt. ed. see D'Amato, Rik C.
Rothlisberger, Marcel. Claude Lorrain: The Paintings: Critical Catalogue & Illustrations, 2 vols., Set. LC 79-83839. (Illus.). 1979. reprint ed. lib. bdg. 100.00 (*0-87817-244-0*) Hacker.
Rothluebber, Francis. Nobody Owns Me: A Celibate Woman Discovers Her Sexual Power. Geiger, Lura J., ed. 128p. (Orig.). 1994. pap. 12.95 (*1-880913-13-5*) LuraMedia.
***Rothman.** Health Facility Malpractice Cases: A Management Prevention Guide. 187p. 1995. lib. bdg. write for info. (*1-56072-227-4*) Nova Sci Pubs.
— Saying Goodbye To Daniel: When Death Is a Choice. 150p. 1995. 18.95 (*0-8264-0857-5*) Continuum.
Rothman & Lavin. Fostering Young Learners: Activities for Parents & Teachers in Partnership. 1990. pap. 14.99 (*0-89824-613-X*) Trillium Pr.
Rothman, Barbara K. Encyclopedia of Childbearing: Critical Perspectives. (Illus.). 472p. 1993. 74.50 (*0-89774-648-1*) Oryx Pr.
— In Labor: Women & Power in the Birthplace. 320p. 1991. pap. 10.95 (*0-393-30798-0*) Norton.
— Recreating Motherhood, Ideology & Technology in a Patriarchal Society. 1990. pap. 10.95 (*0-393-30712-3*) Norton.
— The Tentative Pregnancy: How Amniocentesis Changes the Experience of Motherhood. 288p. 1993. pap. 9.95 (*0-393-30998-3*) Norton.
— The Tentative Pregnancy: Prenatal Diagnosis & the Future of Motherhood. 288p. 1987. pap. 9.95 (*0-14-009486-5*, Penguin Bks) Viking Penguin.
Rothman, Barbara K. & King, Donna L., eds. The Encyclopedia of Childbearing. LC 94-20081. (Reference Books Ser.). 480p. 1994. pap. (*0-8050-3390-4*) H Holt & Co.
Rothman, Barbara K., jt. auth. see Simonds, Wendy.
Rothman, Beulah, jt. ed. see Papell, Catherine P.
Rothman, Cynthia. Bread Around the World. (Interactive Photo Big Bks.). 16p. (J). (ps-2). 1994. pap. 14.95 (*1-56784-301-8*) Newbridge Comms.
— Think about the Weather. (Interactive Photo Big Bks.). 16p. (J). (ps-2). 1994. pap. 14.95 (*1-56784-300-X*) Newbridge Comms.
— Under the Sea. (Interactive Photo Big Bks.). 16p. (J). (ps-2). 1994. pap. 14.95 (*1-56784-302-6*) Newbridge Comms.
Rothman, David. IZE Examined: Realize All the Power of IZE to Manage the Resources of the Information Age. 224p. 1988. pap. 25.00 (*1-55623-155-5*) Irwin Prof Pubng.
— NetWorld: What People Are Really Doing on the INTERNET & What It Means To You. LC 95-5287. 1995. 22.95 (*0-7615-0013-8*) Prima Pub.
Rothman, David & Wheeler, Stanton, eds. Social History & Social Policy. LC 80-1772. (Studies in Social Discontinuity). 1981. text ed. 46.00 (*0-12-598680-7*) Acad Pr.
Rothman, David, et al. Humanitarianism or Control? A Symposium on Nineteenth-Century Social Reform in Britain & America. Wiener, Martin, ed. (Rice University Studies: Vol. 67, No. 1). 84p. (Orig.). 1981. pap. 5.50 (*0-89263-248-8*) Rice Univ.
— On Being Homeless. Beard, Rick, ed. (Illus.). 176p. (Orig.). 1987. 29.95 (*0-317-67769-1*) Mus City NY.
Rothman, David H. XYWrite Made Easier: Revised & Expanded to Include Version XYWrite III PLUS. (Illus.). 384p. 1988. pap. 21.95 (*0-318-32704-X*) TAB Bks.
Rothman, David H., jt. auth. see Friedman, Lee A.
Rothman, David J. Conscience & Convenience: The Asylum & Its Alternatives in Progressive America. (C). 1987. pap. text ed. 19.75 (*0-673-39350-X*) HarpCollege.
— Discovery of the Asylum: Social Order & Disorder in the New Republic, Vol. 1. 1990. pap. 15.95 (*0-316-75745-4*) Little.
— Discovery of the Asylum: Social Order & Disorder in the New Republic, Vol. 1. 1994. 42.50 (*0-316-75744-6*) Little.
— Strangers at the Bedside: A History of How Law & Bioethics Transformed Medical Decision-Making. LC 90-55598. 320p. 1992. pap. 16.00 (*0-465-08210-6*) Basic.
Rothman, David J., ed. Poverty U. S. A., the Historical Record, 44 vols. 1971. reprint ed. 1,064.50 (*0-405-03090-8*) Ayer.
Rothman, David J. & Rothman, Sheila M., eds. The Family. LC 88-19594. (Great Contemporary Issues Ser.). 1979. lib. bdg. 27.95 (*0-405-11197-5*) Ayer.
— Family in America, 44 bks., Set. 1972. 973.00 (*0-405-03840-2*) Ayer.

R

Rothman, David J., jt. ed. see Morris, Norval.

***Rothman, David J, et al, eds.** Medicine & Western Civilization. (Illus.). 450p. (C). 1995. text ed. 49.00 (*0-8135-2189-0*) Rutgers U Pr.

— Medicine & Western Civilization. (Illus.). 450p. (C). 1995. pap. text ed. 18.95 (*0-8135-2190-4*) Rutgers U Pr.

Rothman, Ellen K. Hands & Hearts: A History of Courtship in America. LC 86-19575. (Illus.). 384p. 1987. pap. text ed. 9.95 (*0-674-37160-7*) HUP.

Rothman, Esther P. Foundations of Education. (College Review Bk. Ser.). 320p. 1989. pap. text ed. 7.95 (*0-07-054026-8*) McGraw.

Rothman, Eugene, jt. ed. see Polzin, Robert.

Rothman, Frances. My Father, Edward Branstein: His Life & Letters. (Illus.). 109p. 1983. pap. 5.00 (*0-943376-18-1*) Magnes Mus.

Rothman, Frank, jt. auth. see Cotchett, Joseph W.

Rothman, Gerald C. Philanthropists, Therapists & Activists. LC 84-23514. 179p. 1985. 18.95 (*0-87073-521-7*); pap. 11.95 (*0-87073-524-1*) Schenkman Bks Inc.

Rothman, Hal. America's National Monuments: The Politics of Preservation. (Illus.). 280p. 1994. pap. 14.95 (*0-7006-0672-6*) U Pr of KS.

— Preserving Different Pasts: The American National Monuments. (Illus.). 304p. 1989. 29.95 (*0-252-01548-7*) U of Ill Pr.

Rothman, Hal K. On Rims & Ridges: The Los Alamos Area since 1880. LC 91-24418. (Illus.). xvi, 364p. 1992. 45.00 (*0-8032-3901-7*) U of Nebr Pr.

Rothman, Hal K., ed. I'll Never Fight Fire with My Bare Hands Again: Recollections of the First Forest Rangers of the Inland Northwest. (Development of Western Resources Ser.). (Illus.). 260p. 1994. 35.00 (*0-7006-0676-9*); pap. 14.95 (*0-7006-0677-7*) U Pr of KS.

Rothman, Harry, et al. Energy from Alcohol: The Brazilian Experience. LC 82-21956. 200p. 1983. 22.00 (*0-8131-1479-9*) U Pr of Ky.

***Rothman, Howard.** All That Once Was Good: Inside America's National Pastime. LC 95-16199. 1995. write for info. (*0-9644849-0-0*) Pendleton Clay.

— The Employee Handbook for Building a Healthier Lifestyle. Brzezinski, Mary J., ed. LC 91-65846. 97p. (Orig.). 1991. pap. 9.95 (*0-89154-421-6*) Intl Found Employ.

— RX, Inc. The Small Business Handbook for Building a Healthier Workforce. Lyne, Debra J., ed. 84p. (Orig.). 1990. pap. 10.00 (*0-89154-398-8*) Intl Found Employ.

Rothman, Howard, jt. auth. see Scott, Mary.

Rothman, J., et al. Strategies of Community Intervention. 5th ed. LC 94-66869. 550p. 1995. pap. text ed. 36.50 (*0-87581-390-9*) Peacock Pubs.

Rothman, Jack. Guidelines for Case Management: Putting Research to Professional Use. LC 91-76458. 142p. 1992. pap. 18.00 (*0-87581-362-3*) Peacock Pubs.

— Planning & Organizing for Social Change: Action Principles from Social Service Research. LC 74-4434. 1974. pap. text ed. 37.50 (*0-231-08335-1*) Col U Pr.

— Practice with Highly Vulnerable Clients: Case Management & Community-Based Service. LC 93-29021. 1993. text ed. write for info. (*0-13-119058-X*) P-H.

Rothman, Jack & Thomas, Edwin J., eds. Intervention Research: Design & Development for Human Service. LC 92-44915. (Illus.). 488p. 1993. lib. bdg. 59.95 (*1-56024-420-8*); pap. 29.95 (*1-56024-421-6*) Haworth Pr.

Rothman, Jack, et al. Changing Organizations & Community Programs. (Human Services Guides Ser.: Vol. 20). 160p. 1981. 17.95 (*0-8039-1618-3*) Sage.

Rothman, Jay. From Confrontation to Cooperation: Resolving Ethnic & Regional Conflict. (Violence, Cooperation, & Peace Ser.). 304p. (C). 1992. text ed. 52.00 (*0-8039-4693-7*); pap. text ed. 24.00 (*0-8039-4694-5*) Sage.

Rothman, Joel. The Antcyclopedia. (Illus.). (J). 4.95 (*0-685-86236-4*) Pubns Devl Co.

— Around the Drums Compleatly. 1976. 30.00 (*0-913952-05-2*) J R Pubns.

— Compleat Drum Technique. 256p. 1974. 25.00 (*0-913952-02-8*) J R Pubns.

— The Compleat Show Drummer. 370p. 1975. 30.00 (*0-913952-04-4*) J R Pubns.

— A Moment in Time. LC 72-90693. (Illus.). 32p. (J). (ps-2). 1973. 7.95 (*0-87592-034-9*) Scroll Pr.

— Once There Was a Stream. LC 72-90692. (Illus.). 32p. (J). (gr. k-4). 1973. 8.95 (*0-87592-038-1*) Scroll Pr.

— One Thousand Howlers for Kids. 224p. 1990. pap. 3.95 (*0-345-36155-5*) Ballantine.

— Picture Guide to Rock 'n Roll Drums. (Illus.). 32p. 1980. pap. 7.95 (*0-86001-739-7*, AM26337) Music Sales.

— Play Rock 'n Roll Drums. (Illus.). 32p. 1980. pap. 4.95 (*0-685-65791-4*, AM26329) Music Sales.

Rothman, Joel & Whaley, Gar. Compleat Drum Reader. 1976. 30.00 (*0-913952-07-9*) J R Pubns.

Rothman, John. Origin & Development of Dramatic Criticism in the New York Times 1851-1880. LC 78-126346. 1971. 12.95 (*0-405-02560-2*) Ayer.

Rothman, Juliet C. Aristotle's Eudaemonia, Terminal Illness, & the Question of Life Support. LC 92-17507. (American University Studies: Philosophy: Ser. V, Vol. 141). 149p. (C). 1993. text ed. 44.95 (*0-685-71440-3*) P Lang Pubs.

Rothman, Julius. A Glossarial Index to the Biography of the Life of Manuel. (James Branch Cabell Ser.). 1976. lib. bdg. 250.00 (*0-87700-218-5*) Revisionist Pr.

Rothman, Kenneth J. Modern Epidemiology. 358p. 1986. 59.95 (*0-316-75776-4*, Little Med Div) Little.

Rothman, Kenneth J., ed. & intro. Causal Inference. LC 87-22227. 207p. (Orig.). 1988. pap. text ed. 25.00 (*0-917227-03-4*) Epidemiology.

Rothman, L. S., ed. Modeling of the Atmosphere: Critical Reviews. 293p. 1988. 48.00 (*0-89252-963-6*, 928) SPIE.

Rothman, M. F., ed. see American Society for Metals Staff.

Rothman, Marcie. The Five Dollar Chef: How to Save Cash & Cook Fast. 130p. 1992. pap. 5.00 (*0-9630542-0-1*) Five-Spot.

—The Five Dollar Chef: How to Save Cash & Cook Fast. 2nd ed. 130p. 1992. pap. 5.00 (*0-425-13555-1*) Berkley Pub. "America on $5 a meal", says Charles Perry of the LOS ANGELES TIMES "Marcie Rothman has collected more than 100 of her recipes--not quite all-American, not quite ethnic, all tight with a penny-- together with boiled wisdom on strategic shopping, maintaining a cupboard & overcoming the fear of cooking in her book THE $5 CHEF." Ann Byrn of THE ATLANTA JOURNAL/CONSTITUTION says this budget- friendly cookbook offers practical tips & emphasizes ethnic recipes in a well-organized paperback... has comfort foods such as roast chicken & cabbage rolls." Rothman shares her knack for creating flavorful, healthful & delicious food on a tight budget & it's not just spaghetti, rice & beans. College students, newlyweds & just about anyone interested in cooking terrific fresh, seasonal, easy meals will love this book. Seen weekly on Sacramento's KOVR (CBS) TV, as THE $5 CHEF, Marcie shows viewers how to shop & cook fast & easy meals that feed four for just $5. Her recipes appear in THE SACRAMENTO & MODESTO BEE FOODS SECTIONS. ORDERING INSTRUCTIONS: THE BERKLEY PUBLISHING GROUP OR FIVE SPOT PRESS (ISBN 0-9630542-0-1), P.O. BOX 4559, SANTA ROSA, CA 95402-4559. *Publisher Provided Annotation.*

Rothman, Marcy E. The Divided Heart. 224p. (Orig.). 1994. pap. 3.99 (*0-451-17931-5*, Sig) NAL-Dutton.

— The Kinder Heart. (Signet Regency Romance Ser.). 224p. (Orig.). 1994. pap. 3.99 (*0-451-17922-6*, Sig) NAL-Dutton.

Rothman, Mark. The Careful Contributor's Guide to Smart Giving in Oregon & Beyond: Tools for Easy, Efficient Charitable Giving. (Careful Contributor's Guides Ser.). 192p. (Orig.). 1994. pap. 20.00 (*1-884749-00-3*) Careful Contrib.

***Rothman, Mark & Rothman, Patricia, eds.** Staying Human in Seattle & the Puget Sound Area: Sustainable Family Giving When You're Sick of Being Hassled & Too Tired to Save the World. (Staying Human Ser.). (Orig.). 1994. pap. 16.00 (*1-884749-05-4*) Careful Contrib.

Rothman, Michael, jt. auth. see Ryder, Joanne.

Rothman, Milton. Discovering the Natural. 1990. pap. 5.95 (*0-486-26178-6*) Dover.

Rothman, Milton A. A Physicist's Guide to Skepticism. LC 88-4077. (Illus.). 247p. 1988. 26.95 (*0-87975-440-0*) Prometheus Bks.

— The Science Gap: Dispelling the Myths & Understanding the Reality of Science. 254p. 1991. 26.95 (*0-87975-710-8*) Prometheus Bks.

Rothman, Miriam, et al, eds. Industrial Relations Around the World: Labor Relations for Multinational Companies. LC 92-32313. (Studies in Organization: No. 45). xx, 419p. (C). 1992. 74.95 (*3-11-012544-7*); pap. 34.95 (*3-11-012547-1*) De Gruyter.

Rothman, Mitchell S., ed. Chiefdoms & Early States in the Near East: The Organizational Dynamics of Complexity. LC 94-10284. (Monographs in World Archaeology: No. 18). (Illus.). 248p. 1994. pap. 35.00 (*1-881094-07-3*) Prehistory Pr.

Rothman, Patricia, jt. ed. see Rothman, Mark.

Rothman, Paula. Computer Applications, Disk Operating System: Course Code 394-5. Doheny, Cathy, ed. 23p. 1989. reprint ed. pap. text ed. 3.95 (*0-917531-93-0*) CES Compu-Tech.

Rothman, Peter. Intelligent Agents, Artificial Intelligence & Virtual Reality. 1994. pap. 22.95 (*0-672-30379-5*) Sams.

Rothman, Raymond C. Notary Public Practices & Glossary. 4th ed. 1987. 17.95 (*0-933134-50-9*) Natl Notary.

—Programming in Your Words: With Any Database Program, Expert or Novice, Custom-Make Your Programs, Linguistic Technique, Filing & Accounting System. LC 87-81413. 254p. (Orig.). (C). 1989. pap. text ed. 9.95 (*0-9618666-2-4*) DUIMINT. PROGRAMMING IN YOUR WORDS is fun. It's a unique technique for using your own familiar terms (English or any foreign language) to set up a bookkeeping & filing system. It enables the database program user to custom-make virtually any type of application program without using programming language or code. FOR THE NOVICE -- You've already saved yourself thousands of hours of frustration & many dollars if you haven't learned a programming language, hired a programmer or bought package programs. Simply choose the subject & terms vital to your filing &/or bookkeeping needs. Your database program creates the program. Then the newly created program sorts, calculates & prints your terms & information as you want them listed in reports. Explanations with examples show how to set up files, records & fields for programs & order the records sorted by category, totaled & subtotaled for reports on equipment, invoicing & merchandise inventory, real estate, bonds, stocks, loans, accounts receivable & payable, profit, worth, billing for services rendered & much more. Obtain your bank balance anytime. Reconcile your bank statement with income, expense & bank balances listed by category accurate to the penny. Appendix has a glossary of terms, record entry forms for food recipe keeping, job scheduling, & a perpetual calendar table to be used for your daily appointment program described in Chapter 10. To order contact: DUIMINT, 21650 Burbank Blvd., #110, Woodland Hills, CA 91367 USA. Phone: 818-347-5974. FAX: 818-716-0312. *Publisher Provided Annotation.*

Rothman, Richard & Hozack, William. Surgical Technique of Total Hip Arthroplasty. 1995. write for info. (*0-7817-0156-2*) Raven.

Rothman, Richard H. & Hozak. Complications of Total Hip Arthroplasty. 256p. 1988. text ed. 98.50 (*0-7216-2447-2*) Saunders.

***Rothman, Robert.** Measuring Up: Standards, Assessment, & School Reform. (Education Ser.). 240p. 1995. 25.00 (*0-614-05120-7*) Jossey-Bass.

— Tests of Significance. (Education Ser.). 240p. 1995. write for info. (*0-7879-0055-9*) Jossey-Bass.

Rothman, Robert A. Inequality & Stratification: Class, Color & Gender. 2nd ed. 224p. 1992. pap. text ed. write for info. (*0-13-457375-7*) P-H.

Rothman, Robert A., jt. auth. see Inciardi, James A.

Rothman, Rozann. The Great Society at the Grass-Roots Local Adaptation to Federal Initiatives of the 1960's: Champaign Urbana. LC 84-7533. (Illus.). 324p. (Orig.). 1984. lib. bdg. 52.00 (*0-8191-4007-4*); pap. text ed. 27.00 (*0-8191-4008-2*) U Pr of Amer.

Rothman, Sandy, ed. see Aihara, Herman.

Rothman, Sandy, ed. see Ohsawa, George.

Rothman, Seymour. Your Memoirs: Collecting Them for Fun & Posterity. LC 86-43086. 128p. 1987. lib. bdg. 17.95x (*0-89950-267-9*) McFarland & Co.

Rothman, Sheila M. Living in the Shadow of Death: Tuberculosis & the Social Experience of Illness in America. LC 93-9017. (Illus.). 304p. 1994. 25.00 (*0-465-03002-5*) Basic.

— Living in the Shadow of Death: Tuberculosis & the Social Experience of Illness in American History. 352p. 1995. reprint ed. pap. 15.95 (*0-8018-5186-6*) Johns Hopkins.

Rothman, Sheila M., jt. ed. see Rothman, David J.

Rothman, Sherman. Highway Robbery: The Truth about America's Auto Dealers. LC 89-91255. 1989. 18.95 (*0-87212-229-8*) Libra.

— Highway Robbery: The Truth about America's Auto Dealers. LC 89-91255. 1989. pap. 10.95 (*0-87212-245-X*) Libra.

Rothman, Stanley. European Society & Politics. LC 75-92273. (Illus.). 1970. text ed. 15.75 (*0-672-60772-7*, Bobbs) Macmillan.

Rothman, Stanley, ed. The Mass Media in Liberal Democratic Societies. LC 91-4048. 312p. 1992. 34.95 (*0-943852-92-7*); pap. text ed. 17.95 (*0-943852-93-5*) Prof World Peace.

Rothman, Stanley, jt. auth. see Snyderman, Mark.

Rothman, Steven, ed. The Standard Doyle Company: Christopher Morley on Sherlock Holmes. LC 90-82073. (Illus.). 429p. 1990. reprint ed. 19.95 (*0-8232-1292-0*) Fordham.

***Rothman, Tony.** Instant Physics: From Aristotle to Einstein, & Beyond. (Illus.). 256p. (Orig.). 1995. pap. 10.00 (*0-449-90697-3*) Fawcett.

— Long Ago Is Far Away: Figuring Out How the Universe Began. LC 92-29745. (J). 1993. write for info. (*0-7167-9000-9*) W H Freeman.

— A Physicist on Madison Avenue. (Illus.). 200p. 1991. text ed. 25.00 (*0-691-08731-8*) Princeton U Pr.

— Science a la Mode: Physical Factions & Fictions. (Illus.). 224p. 1991. text ed. 35.00 (*0-691-08484-X*); pap. text ed. 12.95 (*0-691-02521-5*) Princeton U Pr.

Rothman, William. Hitchcock: The Murderous Gaze. (Harvard Film Studies). (Illus.). 383p. 1984. pap. 24.95 (*0-674-40411-4*) HUP.

— The I of the Camera: Essays in Film Criticism, History & Aesthetics. (Cambridge Studies in Film). (Illus.). 220p. 1988. 65.00 (*0-521-36048-X*); pap. 17.95 (*0-521-36828-6*) Cambridge U Pr.

Rothman, William A. A Bibliography of Collective Bargaining in Hospitals & Related Facilities, 2 vols. Incl. Vol. 1. 1959-1968. 1970. 6.95 (*0-87736-301-3*); Vol. 2. 1969-1971. 1970. 7.95 (*0-87736-320-X*); 1970. write for info. (*0-318-56089-5*) U of Mich Inst Labor.

— A Bibliography of Collective Bargaining in Hospitals & Related Facilities, 1972-1974. LC 76-21690. (ILR Bibliography Ser.: No. 14). 164p. 1976. pap. 1.00 (*0-87546-287-1*) ILR Pr.

— Interviewing for a Career in Health Care. LC 83-80275. (Illus.). 144p. (C). 1984. pap. 7.95 (*0-938352-51-2*) Hampton Pr MI.

Rothmann, Ralf. Knife Edge. Mitchell, Breon, tr. LC 91-43449. 128p. 1992. 19.95 (*0-8112-1204-1*); pap. 9.95 (*0-8112-1210-6*, NDP744) New Directions.

Rothmann, S. Charles, ed. Constructive Uses of Atomic Energy. LC 73-128304. (Essay Index Reprint Ser.). 1977. 23.95 (*0-8369-2129-1*) Ayer.

Rothmeier, Jeffrey, ed. Proceedings: MUMPS Users' Group Meeting. 1976. 20.00 (*0-918118-03-4*) M Technol.

Rothmiller, Mike. L. A. Secret Police. 1992. mass mkt. 5.99 (*0-671-79657-7*) PB.

Rothmiller, Mike & Goldman, Ivan G. L.A. Secret Police. pap. 5.99 (*0-685-61109-4*) PB.

Rothmund, M. & Wells, S. A., Jr., eds. Parathyroid Surgery. (Progress in Surgery Ser.: Vol. 18). (Illus.). x, 250p. 1986. 141.75 (*3-8055-4217-8*) S Karger.

Rothmyer, Karen. Winning Pulitzers: The Stories Behind Some of the Best News Coverage of Our Time. 256p. 1991. text ed. 29.00 (*0-231-07028-4*) Col U Pr.

Rothney, Murray, jt. auth. see Findley, A. M.

Rothnie, W., jt. auth. see Lahore, J.

***Rothon.** Particulate-Filled Polymer Composites. (Polymer Science & Technology Ser.). Date not set. text ed. 195.00 (*0-470-23509-8*) Wiley.

***Rothra, Elizabeth O.** Florida's Pioneer Naturalist: The Life of Charles Torrey Simpson. (Illus.). 240p. 1995. lib. bdg. 49.95 (*0-8130-1374-7*) U Press Fla.

Rothrock. Perioperative Nursing Care Planning. (Illus.). 592p. 1990. 33.95 (*0-8016-5528-5*) Mosby Yr Bk.

Rothrock, Cynthia, jt. auth. see Chung, George.

Rothrock, George A. The Huguenots: A Biography of a Minority. LC 78-23476. (Illus.). 228p. 1979. 31.95 (*0-88229-277-3*) Nelson-Hall.

Rothrock, George A. & Jones, Tom B. Europe; a Brief History, Vol. I: Prehistory to 1815. 2nd rev. ed. LC 81-43503. (Illus.). 410p. reprint ed. pap. text ed. 23.00 (*0-8191-2070-7*) U Pr of Amer.

Rothrock, George A., jt. auth. see Hebbert, John.

Rothrock, Jane C., ed. The RN First Assistant: An Expanded Perioperative Nursing Role. 2nd ed. LC 92-48997. 1992. 39.95 (*0-397-55014-6*) Lippincott.

Rothrock, Jane C., jt. auth. see Rothrock, Joseph T.

Rothrock, Joseph T. & Rothrock, Jane C. Chesapeake Odysseys: An Nineteen Thousand Eight Hundred Eighty-Three Cruise Revisited. LC 84-40343. (Illus.). 138p. 1984. 15.95 (*0-87033-323-2*, Tidewtr Pubs) Cornell Maritime.

Rothrock, Mary U., ed. The French Broad-Holston Country: A History of Knox County, Tennessee. (Illus.). 573p. 1972. 6.00 (*0-941199-02-9*) ETHS.

Rothrock, Robert W. & D'Amore, Gabriella. The Illustrated Guide to Better Sex for People with Chronic Pain. 19p. 1991. pap. 8.95 (*0-9632602-0-0*) Rothrock & DAmore.

— The Illustrated Guide to Better Sex for People with Chronic Pain. 2nd ed. (Illus.). 50p. 1992. pap. 11.95 (*0-9632602-1-9*) Rothrock & DAmore.

Rothschield, Paul. Holocaust Pawns. (Ben-Gurion Books & Media Production Ser.). 1993. pap. 7.95 (*0-915133-15-6*) Gindi Pr.

Rothschild. Geriatrics for the Internist. (Illus.). 650p. 1990. 49.95 (*0-8016-4302-3*) Mosby Yr Bk.

Rothschild, A. M., ed. Contributions to Autacoid Pharmacology: A Festschrift in Honour of Mauricio Rocha e Silva. LC 92-10713. (Agents & Actions Supplements Ser.: Vol. 36). (Illus.). x, 286p. 1992. 69.00 (*0-8176-2617-4*) Birkhauser.

Rothschild, Brian J. Dynamics of Marine Fish Populations. LC 86-9877. 288p. reprint ed. pap. 83.60 (*0-7837-2325-3*, 2057413) Bks Demand.

Rothschild, Bruce J., ed. Toward a Theory on Biological-Physical Interactions in the World Ocean. (C). 1988. lib. bdg. 212.00 (*90-277-2765-1*) Kluwer Ac.

Rothschild, Bruce M. & Martin, Larry. Paleopathology: Disease in the Fossil Record. 1992. 146.95 (*0-8493-8897-X*, R134) CRC Pr.

***Rothschild, D. Aviva.** Graphic Novels: A Bibliographic Guide to Book-Length Comics. 250p. 1995. lib. bdg. 30.00 (*1-56308-086-9*) Libs Unl.

Rothschild, Deborah M. Picasso's Parade: From Page to Stage. (Illus.). 280p. 1991. 90.00 (*0-85667-392-7*, Pub. by P Wilson Pubs) Sothebys Pubns.

— Yardbird Suite. LC 94-938. (Illus.). 72p. 1995. pap. text ed. 18.95 (*0-913697-19-2*) Williams Art.

Rothschild, Deborah M., ed. James Turrell. LC 91-50616. (Illus.). 48p. (Orig.). 1991. pap. text ed. 12.95 (*0-913697-12-5*, U of Pa Pr) Williams Art.

Rothschild, Deborah M., jt. auth. see Balken, Debra B.

Rothschild, Deborah M., jt. auth. see Mandle, Julia B.

Rothschild, Donald P., et al. Collective Bargaining & Labor Arbitration. 3rd ed. (Contemporary Legal Education Ser.). 1004p. 1980. 7.00 (*0-672-84079-0*) Michie Butterworth.

— Collective Bargaining & Labor Arbitration. 3rd ed. (Contemporary Legal Education Ser.). 1004p. 1988. text ed. 39.00 (*0-87473-381-2*) Michie Butterworth.

Rothschild, Edward F., jt. auth. see Sweeney, James J.

R

An Asterisk (*) at the beginning of an entry indicates that the title is appearing in BIP for the first time.

Rothschild, Frances, ed. see Denner, Richard E.
Rothschild, Fritz. The Lost Tradition in Music: Rhythm & Tempo in J. S. Bach's Time. LC 78-19565. (Encore Music Editions Ser.). (Illus.). 1986. reprint ed. 26.50 (0-88355-760-6) Hyperion Conn.
***Rothschild, Helene.** As I Grow. LC 94-68702. 30p. 1994. pap. 3.95 (1-56875-092-7, 092-7) R & E Pubs.
— Loving Yourself. LC 94-68701. 30p. 1994. pap. 3.95 (1-56875-091-9, 091-9) R & E Pubs.
— A Promise of Love. LC 94-68700. 30p. 1994. pap. 3.95 (1-56875-090-0, 090-0) R & E Pubs.
Rothschild, Helene & Seff, Marsha K. Free to Fly: Dare to Be a Success. LC 85-62441. 150p. (Orig.). (C). 1985. pap. text ed. 9.95 (0-88247-748-X) R & E Pubs.
Rothschild, Henry R., ed. Biocultural Aspects of Disease. LC 81-12714. 1981. text ed. 148.00 (0-12-598720-X) Acad Pr.
Rothschild, Henry R. & Cohen, J. Craig, eds. Virology in Medicine. (Illus.). 1986. pap. text ed. 24.95 (0-19-504017-1) OUP.
Rothschild, Hester. Prayers & Meditations: Imre Lev. 544p. 1928. 6.00 (0-88482-120-X) Hebrew Pub.
Rothschild, Jeffrey, ed. see Nurbakhsh, Javad.
Rothschild, Jeffrey, ed. see Nurbaksh, Javad.
Rothschild, Joan. Teaching Technology from a Feminist Perspective: A Practical Guide. (Athene Ser.). 200p. 1988. 36.50 (0-08-034234-5, Pergamon Pr); pap. 17.95 (0-08-034233-7, Pergamon Pr) Elsevier.
— Teaching Technology from a Feminist Perspective: A Practical Guide. (Athene Ser.). 178p. (C). text ed. 36.50 (0-8077-6263-6); pap. text ed. 17.95 (0-8077-6214-8) Tchrs Coll.
Rothschild, Joan, ed. Machina ex Dea: Feminist Perspectives on Technology. (Athene Ser.). 264p. 1983. text ed. 48.50 (0-08-029404-9, Pergamon Pr); pap. text ed. 19.95 (0-08-029403-0, Pergamon Pr) Elsevier.
— Machina Ex Dea: Feminist Perspectives on Technology. (Athene Ser.). 264p. (C). 1983. reprint ed. pap. text ed. 19.95 (0-8077-6221-0) Tchrs Coll.
— Women, Technology & Innovation. (Journal of Women's Studies International Quarterly 4(Si)). 88p. 1981. 92.00 (0-08-028943-6, Pub. by Pergamon Repr UK) Franklin.
Rothschild, Jon, tr. see Ding, Ya.
Rothschild, Jon, tr. see Kadare, Ismail.
Rothschild, Jon, ed. see Krause, Ulrich.
Rothschild, Jon, tr. see Parboni, Ricardo.
Rothschild, Jon, tr. see Peyrefitte, Alain.
Rothschild, Jon, tr. see Rodinson, Maxime.
Rothschild, Jon, tr. see Spriano, Paulo.
Rothschild, Jon, tr. see Volpe, Galvano D.
Rothschild, Jon, tr. see Wiesel, Elie & De Saint-Cheron, Philippe.
Rothschild, Joseph. Communist Party of Bulgaria. LC 72-174967. reprint ed. 26.00 (0-404-07164-3) AMS Pr.
— East Central Europe Between the Two World Wars. LC 74-8327. (History of East Central Europe Ser.: Vol. 9). (Illus.). 438p. 1990. pap. 25.00 (0-295-95357-8) U of Wash Pr.
— Return to Diversity: A Political History of East Central Europe since World War II. 2nd ed. LC 92-35420. 1993. 39.95 (0-19-507381-9); pap. 14.95 (0-19-507382-7) OUP.
— Return to Diversity: A Political History of East Central Europe since World War II. (Illus.). 272p. (C). 1988. reprint ed. 27.95 (0-19-504574-2) OUP.
Rothschild, Kurt W. Employment, Wages, & Income Distribution: Critical Essays in Economics. LC 92-37260. 352p. 1993. 65.00 (0-415-08579-9, B0139, Routledge NY) Routledge.
— Ethics & Economic Theory. 176p. 1993. 59.95 (1-85278-675-2, Pub. by E Elgar Pub UK) Ashgate Pub Co.
Rothschild, Lincoln. Susan Kahn. LC 79-5388. (Illus.). 164p. 1980. 45.00 (0-87982-031-4) Art Alliance.
— To Keep Art Alive: The Effort of Kenneth Hayes Miller, American Painter (1876-1952) (Illus.). 208p. 1974. 40.00 (0-87982-012-8) Art Alliance.
Rothschild, Lowell E. & Berger, Edward B. Withdrawal, Retirement, & Disputes: What You & Your Firm Need to Know. LC 86-71286. 100p. 1986. 39.95 (0-89707-242-1, 511-0211) Amer Bar Assn.
Rothschild, M. A., jt. ed. see Rosenoer, V.
Rothschild, Mary A. A Case of Black & White: Northern Volunteers & the Southern Freedom Summers, 1964-1965. LC 82-6175. (Contributions in Afro-American & African Studies: No. 69). xiv, 213p. 1982. text ed. 49.95 (0-313-23430-2, RBL/) Greenwood.
Rothschild, Mary L. & Hronek, Pamela C. Doing What the Day Brought: An Oral History of Arizona Women. LC 91-20354. (Illus.). 174p. (Orig.). 1992. 40.00 (0-8165-1032-6); pap. 16.95 (0-8165-1276-0) U of Ariz Pr.
Rothschild, Michael. Advertising: From Fundamentals to Strategies. LC 86-80487. (Illus.). 776p. (C). 1987. text ed. 38.00 (0-669-07213-3); Instr.'s guide with test items. teacher ed 2.00 (0-669-07212-5); Archive testing prog. IBM-PC. 150.00 (0-669-11317-4); Archive testing prog. Apple. 150.00 (0-669-11319-0) Heath.
— Bionomics: Economy As Ecosystem. 448p. 1992. pap. 17.95 (0-8050-1979-0, Owl) H Holt & Co.
— Marketing Communications: From Fundamentals to Strategies. LC 86-80486. (Illus.). 765p. (C). 1987. Instr.'s guide with test items. teacher ed 2.00 (0-669-07209-5); text ed. 37.00 (0-669-07210-9); Archive testing prog. IBM-PC. 150.00 (0-669-11322-0); Archive testing prog. Apple. 150.00 (0-669-11324-7) Heath.
Rothschild, Michael, jt. ed. see Colfelter, Charles T.
Rothschild, Michael, jt. ed. see Diamond, Peter.
Rothschild, Miriam. Animals & Man: The Romane Lecture for 1984-5. 108p. 1987. pap. 13.95 (0-19-854210-0) OUP.
— Butterflies & the Cooing of Doves. 1991. 35.00 (0-385-26376-7) Doubleday.
— Dear Lord Rothschild: Birds, Butterflies & History. (Illus.). 398p. 1983. write for info. (0-86689-019-X) Am Inst Physics.
Rothschild, Miriam, jt. auth. see Hopkins, G. H.
Rothschild, Nan A. New York City Neighborhoods: The Eighteenth Century. 264p. 1990. text ed. 61.00 (0-12-598725-0) Acad Pr.
— Prehistoric Dimensions of Status: Gender & Age in Eastern North America. LC 90-21592. (Evolution of North American Indians Ser.). 248p. 1991. 25.00 (0-8240-2514-8) Garland.
Rothschild, Nan A., jt. ed. see Leacock, Eleanor B.
Rothschild, R. E. & Siegmund, O. H. EUV, X-Ray, & Gamma-Ray Instrumentation for Astronomy Two. 1992. 70.00 (0-8194-0677-5, 1549) SPIE.
Rothschild, Rich, jt. auth. see Brickell, Sean.
Rothschild, Richard C. The Emerging Religion of Science. LC 88-12010. 176p. 1989. text ed. 45.00 (0-275-93097-1, C3097, Praeger Pubs) Greenwood.
Rothschild-Sherwin, Shelley, jt. auth. see Batra, Neelam.
Rothschild, Walter. Dynamics of Molecular Liquids. 432p. (C). 1984. reprint ed. lib. bdg. 64.95 (0-471-73971-5) Krieger.
Rothschild-Whitt, Joyce & Whitt, J. Allen. The Cooperative Workplace: Potentials & Dilemmas of Organizational Democracy & Participation. (American Sociological Assn. Rose Monograph Ser.). (Illus.). 224p. 1986. 49.95 (0-521-32967-1) Cambridge U Pr.
— The Cooperative Workplace: Potentials & Dilemmas of Organizational Democracy & Participation. (American Sociological Assn. Rose Monograph Ser.). (Illus.). 224p. 1989. pap. 18.95 (0-521-37942-3) Cambridge U Pr.
Rothschild-Whitt, Joyce, jt. ed. see Lindenfeld, Frank.
Rothschild, William E. How to Gain & Maintain the Competitive Advantage in Business. (Illus.). 240p. 1989. pap. text ed. 12.95 (0-07-054032-2) McGraw.
— Risktaker, Caretaker, Surgeon, Undertaker: The Four Faces of Strategic Leadership. 314p. 1993. text ed. 29.95 (0-471-53629-6) Wiley.
Rothschuh, Karl E. History of Physiology. Risse, Gunter B., tr. LC 74-158126. Orig. Title: Geschichte der Physiologie. (Illus.). 400p. 1973. 39.50 (0-88275-069-0); pap. 24.50 (0-89874-254-4) Krieger.
***Rothstein.** Emblems of Mind: The Inner Life of Music & Mathematics. 1995. 25.00 (0-8129-2560-2, Times Bks) Random.
— Evidence: Cases, Materials & Problems. 1986. write for info. (0-8205-0236-7, 454) Bender.
Rothstein, jt. auth. see Grant.
Rothstein, Andrew. British Foreign Policy & Its Critics, 1830-1950. 128p. 1969. 19.95 (0-8464-0212-2) Beekman Pubs.
— Peter the Great & Marlborough: Politics & Diplomacy in Converging Wars. LC 85-22125. 224p. 1986. text ed. 32.50 (0-312-60363-0) St Martin.
Rothstein, Arden, et al. Learning Disorders: An Integration of Neuropsychological & Psychoanalytic Considerations. 398p. 1988. text ed. 47.50 (0-8236-2956-2) Intl Univs Pr.
Rothstein, Arnold. Narcissistic Pursuit of Perfection. 2nd rev. ed. LC 84-25159. 327p. 1985. text ed. 42.50 (0-8236-3494-9, 03493) Intl Univs Pr.
— The Structural Hypothesis: An Evolutionary Hypothesis. LC 83-18490. vii, 194p. 1984. text ed. 30.00 (0-8236-6175-X) Intl Univs Pr.
Rothstein, Arnold, ed. How Does Treatment Help? On the Modes of Therapeutic Action of Psychoanalytic Psychotherapy. LC 88-13604. (Workshop Series of the American Psychoanalytic Association: Monograph 4). 242p. 1988. text ed. 32.50 (0-8236-2362-9) Intl Univs Pr.
— The Interpretation of Dreams in Clinical Work. (American Psychoanalytic Association Workshop Ser.: Monograph 3). 1987. text ed. 35.00 (0-8236-2910-4) Intl Univs Pr.
— Models of the Mind: Their Relationship to Clinical Work. LC 85-10844. (Monograph 1 of the American Psychanalytic Association Ser.). x, 160p. 1985. text ed. 25.00 (0-8236-3410-8) Intl Univs Pr.
— The Moscow Lectures on Psychoanalysis. LC 91-30974. 186p. (C). 1991. text ed. 27.50 (0-685-51686-5) Intl Univs Pr.
— The Reconstruction of Trauma: Monograph II. LC 86-10672. (Workshop Series of the American Psychoanalytic Association). 280p. (C). 1986. text ed. 35.00 (0-8236-5786-8) Intl Univs Pr.
Rothstein, Arnold, jt. ed. see Dowling, Scott.
Rothstein, Arnold, jt. ed. see Jacobs, Theodore.
Rothstein, Arnold M. The Jesus Idea. 135p. 1993. 22.95 (0-87975-862-7) Prometheus Bks.
— Re-Thinking Biblical Story & Myth: Selected Lectures at the Theodor Herzl Institute 1986-1995. 104p. (Orig.). Date not set. pap. text ed. write for info. (0-9639999-1-5) Jay St Pubs.
Rothstein, Arthur. Arthur Rothstein's America in Photographs, 1930-1980. LC 84-6147. 96p. 1984. pap. 7.95 (0-486-24735-X) Dover.
— The Depression Years As Photographed by Arthur Rothstein. LC 77-91384. (Illus.). 1978. pap. 10.95 (0-486-23590-4) Dover.
— Photojournalism. 4th ed. (Illus.). 224p. (C). 1983. pap. 14.95 (0-240-51728-8, Focal) Buttrwrth-Heinemann.
— Words & Pictures. (Illus.). 128p. 1983. pap. 12.50 (0-240-51727-X, Focal) Buttrwrth-Heinemann.
***Rothstein, Bo.** The Social Democratic State: Bureaucracy & Social Reforms in Swedish Labor Market & School Policy. LC 95-2869. (Pitt Series in Policy & Institutional Studies). 1995. write for info. (0-8229-3881-2) U of Pittsburgh Pr.
Rothstein, Chaya L. But Then I Remembered. 1991. 10.95 (0-87306-558-1) Feldheim.
— Mentchkins Make Friends. (J). (gr. 4-8). 1988. pap. 4.95 (0-87306-453-4) Feldheim.
— The Mentchkins Make Shabbos. (Sifrei Rimon Ser.). (J). (ps-2). 1986. pap. 2.95 (0-317-42728-8) Feldheim.
Rothstein, Edward. Emblems of Mind: The Inner Life of Music & Mathematics. 1994. 25.00 (0-8129-2298-0, Times Bks) Random.
— Mathematics & Music: The Deeper Links. 1988. write for info. (0-318-61943-1) Knopf.
Rothstein, Elisabeth, jt. auth. see De Lamar, Marie.
Rothstein, Eric. George Farquhar. LC 67-19355. (Twayne's English Authors Ser.). 206p. (C). 1967. lib. bdg. 17.95 (0-8290-1725-9) Irvington.
— Restoration Tragedy: Form & the Process of Change. LC 78-5529. 194p. 1978. reprint ed. text ed. 49.75 (0-313-20472-1, RORET, Greenwood Pr) Greenwood.
Rothstein, Eric, ed. Literary Monographs, Vol. 3. LC 66-25869. 234p. 1970. 25.00 (0-299-05780-1) U of Wis Pr.
— Literary Monographs, Vol. 4. LC 66-25869. 234p. 1971. 25.00 (0-299-05860-3) U of Wis Pr.
Rothstein, Eric & Kavenik, Frances M. The Designs of Carolean Comedy. LC 87-36552. 312p. (C). 1988. text ed. 32.50 (0-8093-1460-6) S Ill U Pr.
Rothstein, Eric & Ringler, Richard N., eds. Literary Monographs, Vol. 2. LC 66-25869. (Illus.). 242p. 1969. 25.00 (0-299-05410-1) U of Wis Pr.
Rothstein, Eric, jt. ed. see Clayton, Jay.
Rothstein, Erica L. The Dell Book of Logic Problems, No. 4. (Orig.). 1989. mass mkt. 10.00 (0-440-50181-4, Dell Trade Pbks) Dell.
Rothstein, Erica L. & Renineke, eds. Dell Book of Logic Problems, No. 3. (Orig.). (J). 1988. pap. 10.99 (0-440-50068-0, Dell Trade Pbks) Dell.
Rothstein, Evelyn. Easy Writer Student Worksheets, 6 levels, Level C. Gess, Diane, ed. (Illus.). (J). (gr. 3-5). 1988. 14.95 (0-9606172-2-1) ERA-CCR.
— Easy Writer Student Worksheets, 6 levels, Level D. Gess, Diane, ed. (Illus.). (J). (gr. 4-6). 1988. 14.95 (0-9606172-3-X) ERA-CCR.
— Easy Writer Student Worksheets, 6 levels, Level A. Gess, Diane, ed. (Illus.). (J). (gr. 1-2). 1988. 14.95 (0-9606172-5-6) ERA-CCR.
— Easy Writer Student Worksheets, 6 levels, Level B. Gess, Diane, ed. (Illus.). (J). (gr. 2-3). 1988. 14.95 (0-9606172-1-3) ERA-CCR.
— Easy Writer Student Worksheets, 6 levels, Level E. Gess, Diane, ed. (Illus.). (J). (gr. 5-7). 1988. 14.95 (0-9606172-4-8) ERA-CCR.
— Easy Writer Student Worksheets, 6 levels, Level F. Gess, Diane, ed. (Illus.). (J). (gr. 6-8). 1988. 14.95 (0-9606172-6-4) ERA-CCR.
— Writer's Book of Synonyms. (Illus.). 52p. (Orig.). (C). (gr. 2-8). 1988. pap. text ed. 5.00 (0-9606172-9-9) ERA-CCR.
Rothstein, Evelyn & Gess, Diane. EarlyWriter. (Illus.). 80p. (J). (gr. k-1). 1989. pap. text ed. 7.95 (0-913935-44-1) ERA-CCR.
— Teaching Writing Manual. rev. ed. (Illus.). 170p. 1987. pap. text ed. 17.95 (0-913935-39-5) ERA-CCR.
Rothstein, Evelyn, ed. see Bierman, Bernard.
Rothstein, Evelyn, et al. Creative Writes, Bk. B. 34p. (J). (gr. 5-12). 1984. pap. 14.95 (0-913935-26-3) ERA-CCR.
— Editing Writes, Blue Edition. (Illus.). (J). (gr. 3-4). 1990. pap. 7.95 (0-913935-46-8) ERA-CCR.
— Editing Writes, Green Edition. (Illus.). (J). (gr. 5-7). 1990. pap. 7.95 (0-913935-47-6) ERA-CCR.
— Editing Writes, Orange Edition. (Illus.). (J). (gr. 2-8). 1990. pap. 7.95 (0-913935-48-4) ERA-CCR.
— Editing Writes, Red Edition. (Illus.). 110p. (J). (gr. 4-6). 1989. pap. 7.95 (0-913935-45-X) ERA-CCR.
— Staying at the Top. Ostacher, Joan, ed. LC 86-80111. (Illus.). 175p. 1986. 9.95 (0-913935-42-5) ERA-CCR.
Rothstein, Frances A. Three Different Worlds: Women, Men, & Children in an Industrializing Community. LC 82-6216. (Contributions in Family Studies: No. 7). (Illus.). xii, 148p. 1982. text ed. 45.00 (0-313-22594-X, RTW/, Greenwood Pr) Greenwood.
Rothstein, Frances A. & Blim, Michael L. Anthropology & the Global Factory. LC 91-18922. (Studies of the New Industrialization in the Late Twentieth Century). 296p. 1991. text ed. 59.95 (0-89789-232-1, H232, Bergin & Garvey); pap. text ed. 19.95 (0-89789-233-X, G233, Bergin & Garvey) Greenwood.
Rothstein, Frances A., jt. ed. see Leons, Madeline B.
Rothstein, Frances R., ed. Commitment to an Aging Workforce: Strategies & Models for Helping Older Workers Achieve Full Potential. 194p. 1988. 15.00 (0-910883-46-7, 352) Natl Coun Aging.
Rothstein, Gustav. Die Dynastie der Lahmiden In Al'Hira. 152p. 1968. reprint ed. write for info. (0-318-71557-0, Pub. by Georg Olms GW) Lubrecht & Cramer.
Rothstein, Horton & Field, Daniel, eds. Quantitative Studies in Agrarian History. LC 93-24729. (Illus.). 280p. 1993. text ed. 39.95 (0-8138-1673-4) Iowa St U Pr.
Rothstein, Joseph. MIDI: A Comprehensive Introduction. LC 91-39701. (Computer Music & Digital Audio Ser.: Vol. 7). (Illus.). 226p. (C). 1992. 27.95 (0-89579-258-3) A-R Eds.
— MIDI: A Comprehensive Introduction. 2nd ed. LC 94-45738. (Computer Music & Digital Audio Ser.: Vol. 7). (Illus.). xvii, 268p. (C). 1995. pap. 28.95 (0-89579-309-1) A-R Eds.
Rothstein, Jules, et al. The Rehabilitation Specialist's Handbook. LC 90-14090. (Illus.). 1022p. 1991. pap. 28.95 (0-8036-7629-8) Davis Co.
Rothstein, Larry, jt. auth. see Paine-Gernee, Karen.
Rothstein, Larry, jt. auth. see Thorne, Julia.
Rothstein, Laura. Special Education Law. 2nd ed. 396p. (Orig.). (C). 1995. pap. text ed. 37.95 (0-8013-1234-5) Longman.
Rothstein, Laura F. Disabilities & the Law. LC 92-34372. (Individual Rights Ser.). 534p. 1992. text ed. 95.00 (0-07-172372-2) Shepards-McGraw.
— Rights of Physically Handicapped Persons. LC 83-20464. 500p. 1984. text ed. 95.00 (0-07-054021-7) Shepards-McGraw.
— Special Education Law. 464p. (Orig.). (C). 1990. pap. text ed. 34.95 (0-8013-0209-9, 75868) Longman.
— Special Education Law. 2nd ed. (Orig.). (C). 1995. teacher ed write for info. (0-8013-1249-3, 79880) Longman.
Rothstein, Lawrence E. Plant Closings: Myths, Power, Politics. LC 85-23025. 250p. 1986. text ed. 49.95 (0-86569-121-5, Auburn Hse) Greenwood.
Rothstein, Marian, tr. Regicide & Revolution: Speeches at the Trial of Louis XVI. LC 92-39235. 240p. (C). 1993. text ed. 35.00 (0-231-08258-4, Mrngside); pap. 16.00 (0-231-08259-2, Mrngside) Col U Pr.
Rothstein, Marian, tr. see Febvre, Lucien.
Rothstein, Mark A. Occupational Safety & Health Law. 3rd ed. (Handbook Ser.). 722p. 1990. text ed. write for info. (0-314-76669-3) West Pub.
***Rothstein, Mark A. & Liebman, Lance.** Employment Law: Cases & Materials. 3rd ed. (University Casebook Ser.). 121p. 1994. teacher ed, pap. text ed. write for info. (1-56662-227-1) Foundation Pr.
— Employment Law: Cases & Materials. 3rd ed. (University Casebook Ser.). 1327p. (C). 1994. pap. text ed. 48.00 (1-56662-158-5) Foundation Pr.
— Supplement to Cases & Materials on Employment Law, 1994 Statutory. (University Casebook Ser.). 271p. 1994. pap. text ed. 12.95 (1-56662-180-1) Foundation Pr.
***Rothstein, Mark A., et al.** Employment Law. Velde, Lea V., ed. (Hornbook Ser.). 693p. 1994. text ed. 38.00 (0-314-03527-3) West Pub.
— Employment Law, Vol. 3. 1994. text ed. write for info. (0-318-72513-4) West Pub.
— Employment Law: Cases & Materials. 2nd ed. (University Casebook Ser.). 111p. 1990. pap. text ed. write for info. (0-88277-876-5) Foundation Pr.
— Employment Law: Cases & Materials On. 2nd ed. (University Casebook Ser.). 1204p. 1990. text ed. 42.50 (0-88277-812-9) Foundation Pr.
— Employment Law, 1993 Supplement to Cases & Materials On. 2nd ed. (University Casebook Ser.). 188p. 1993. pap. text ed. 8.95 (1-56662-110-0) Foundation Pr.
— Human Resources & the Law. LC 94-28869. 500p. 1994. text ed. 95.00 (0-87179-845-X) BNA.
Rothstein, Max, ed. see Propertius, Sextus A.
Rothstein, Michael. ACE the Technical Interview: How to Get Your Next Job in the Computer Industry. LC 93-20953. 420p. 1993. pap. text ed. 19.95 (0-07-054030-6) McGraw.
— Structured Analysis & Design for the Case User. 1993. text ed. 45.00 (0-07-054028-4) McGraw.
Rothstein, Michael F. & Rosner, Burt. Professional's Guide to Database Systems Project Management. 304p. 1990. text ed. 48.95 (0-471-62130-7) Wiley.
Rothstein, Nancy H. & Little, James M. The Handbook of Financial Futures: A Guide for Investors & Professional Financial Managers. 640p. 1984. text ed. 74.95 (0-07-038099-6) McGraw.
Rothstein, Natalie. Four Hundred Years of Fashion. (Illus.). 184p. (Orig.). 1993. pap. 29.95 (1-85177-116-6, Pub. by Victoria & Albert Mus UK) Trafalgar.
Rothstein, Pamela. Educational Psychology. rev. ed. (College Core Bks.). Date not set. pap. text ed. 9.95 (0-07-054029-2) McGraw.
Rothstein, Pamela R. Introduction to Educational Psychology. (College Review Bk. Ser.). 416p. 1990. pap. text ed. 9.95 (0-07-054027-6) McGraw.
Rothstein, Paul. Evidence State & Federal Rules. (Nutshell Ser.). 514p. 1993. reprint ed. pap. text ed. 16.00 (0-8299-2131-1) West Pub.
Rothstein, Paul F. Federal Rules of Evidence. 2nd ed. LC 78-9296. (Federal Court Rules Ser.). (C). 1978. ring bd. 145.00 (0-87632-088-4) Clark Boardman Callaghan.
Rothstein, Richard. Keeping Jobs in Fashion: Alternatives to the Euthanasia of the U. S. Apparel Industry. LC 89-80759. (Illus.). 143p. 1990. 12.00 (0-944826-11-3) Economic Policy Inst.
Rothstein, Robert L. Alliances & Small Powers. LC 68-28401. (Institute of War & Peace Studies). 1968. text ed. 50.00 (0-231-03113-0) Col U Pr.
— The Weak in the World of the Strong: The Developing Countries in the International System. LC 77-7889. 399p. reprint ed. pap. 113.80 (0-8357-7071-0, 2033594) Bks Demand.
— The Weak in the World of the Strong: The Third World in the International System. LC 77-7889. (Institute of War & Peace Studies). 1980. text ed. 53.00 (0-231-04338-4); pap. text ed. 20.50 (0-231-04339-2) Col U Pr.
Rothstein, Robert L., et al, eds. The Evolution of Theory in International Relations. LC 91-12846. (Studies in International Relations). 240p. (Orig.). (C). 1992. pap. text ed. 39.95 (0-87249-862-X) U of SC Pr.
***Rothstein, Rochelle, et al.** MCAT & Medical Admission: The Kaplan All-in-One Guide. LC 94-41581. 1995. 34.95 (0-385-31444-2, Kaplan Source Bks) Doubleday.
***Rothstein, Stanley W.** Class, Culture & Race in American Schools: A Handbook. LC 94-38502. 272p. 1995. text ed. 69.50 (0-313-29102-0, Greenwood Pr) Greenwood.
— Identity & Ideology: Sociocultural Theories of Schooling. LC 91-22987. (Contributions to the Study of Education Ser.: No. 49). 176p. 1991. text ed. 45.00 (0-313-27744-3, RUU, Greenwood Pr) Greenwood.

— The Power to Punish: A Social Inquiry into Coercion & Control in Urban Schools. 188p. (Orig.). (C). 1984. pap. text ed. 23.00 (*0-8191-3732-4*) U Pr of Amer.
— Schooling the Poor: A Social Inquiry into the American Educational Experience. 1994. write for info. (*0-318-72276-3*, Bergin & Garvey) Greenwood.
— Schooling the Poor: A Social Inquiry into the American Educational Experience. LC 93-40161. (Critical Studies in Education & Culture). 189p. 1994. text ed. 49.95 (*0-89789-372-7*, Bergin & Garvey) Greenwood.
— The Voice of the Other: Language As Illusion in the Formation of the Self. LC 92-23059. 192p. 1992. text ed. 45.00 (*0-275-94358-5*, C4358, Praeger Pubs) Greenwood.
Rothstein, Stanley W., ed. Handbook of Schooling in Urban America. LC 93-9323. 440p. 1993. text ed. 75.00 (*0-313-28412-1*, Greenwood Pr) Greenwood.
Rothstein, Susan, jt. ed. see Anderson, Stephen R.
Rothstein, T. From Chartism to Labourism. 265p. (C). 1983. reprint ed. pap. 22.50 (*0-85315-519-4*, Pub. by Lawrence & Wishart UK) Humanities.
Rothstein, Vicki & Goldberg, Rhoda Z. Thinking Through Stories: Predicting, Classifying, Building Vocabulary, Questioning, Storytelling, Discussing. (Language Lessons for the Curriculum Ser.). (gr. k-7). 1993. student ed. spiral bd. 27.95 (*1-55999-253-0*) LinguiSystems.
Rothstein, Vicki, jt. auth. see Goldberg, Rhoda.
Rothstein, William. Phrase Rhythm in Tonal Music. 368p. 1990. text ed. 42.00 (*0-02-872191-8*) Schirmer Bks.
Rothstein, William G. American Physicians in the Nineteenth Century: From Sects to Science. 256p. 1992. reprint ed. pap. text ed. 18.95 (*0-8018-4427-4*) Johns Hopkins.
***Rothstein, William G., ed.** Readings in American Health Care: Current Issues in Socio-Historical Perspective. LC 95-12317. 1995. write for info. (*0-299-14530-1*); pap. write for info. (*0-299-14534-4*) U of Wis Pr.
Rothsteis, Shmuel. Heir to the Throne. LC 90-83945. (Illus.). 224p. (J). (gr. 5-8). 1990. 13.95 (*1-56062-043-9*); pap. 10.95 (*1-56062-044-7*) CIS Comm.
Rothweiler, Paul R. Track of the Assassin. 352p. 1987. pap. 3.95 (*0-380-89898-5*) Avon.
Rothwell, A. B., ed. see American Society for Metals Staff.
Rothwell, Andrew, tr. see Jacques, Francis.
Rothwell, Andrew, ed. see Zola, Emile.
***Rothwell, C. A.** Object Recognition Through Invariant Indexing. (Illus.). 272p. 1995. text ed. 79.00 (*0-19-856512-7*) OUP.
Rothwell, David. Databases: An Introduction. LC 92-28123. 1992. write for info. (*0-07-707703-2*, M-H Bk Intl Group) McGraw.
— Introduction to Ingres. 1992. pap. text ed. 32.95 (*0-07-707482-3*) McGraw.
Rothwell, Donald R., jt. ed. see Crawford, James.
Rothwell, Evelyn. Oboe Technique. 3rd ed. 1983. 26.95 (*0-19-322333-3*) OUP.
Rothwell, F., jt. tr. see Schure, Edouard.
Rothwell, Fred, tr. see David-Neel, Alexandra.
Rothwell, Fred, tr. see Saint-Saens, Camille.
Rothwell, Gar W., jt. auth. see Stewart, Wilson N.
Rothwell, Helen F. & Rothwell, Mel-Thomas. A Catechism on the Christian Religion. 1989. pap. 3.99 (*0-88019-000-0*) Schmul Pub Co.
Rothwell, J. Dan. In Mixed Company: Small Group Communication. LC 91-28038. (Illus.). 350p. (C). 1992. pap. text ed. 27.50 (*0-03-049523-7*) HB Coll Pubs.
— In Mixed Company: Small Group Communication. 2nd ed. (Illus.). 416p. 1994. pap. text ed. write for info. (*0-15-501627-X*) HarBrace.
Rothwell, Kenneth S., Jr. Politics & Persuasion in Aristophanes' Ecclesiazusae. (Mnemosyne Ser.: Supplement 111). xii, 118p. 1990. pap. 31.50 (*90-04-09185-8*) E J Brill.
Rothwell, Kenneth S. & Meltzer, Annabelle H. Shakespeare on Screen: An International Filmography & Videography. 400p. (Orig.). 1990. text ed. 59.95 (*1-55570-049-7*) Neal-Schuman.
Rothwell, Margaret, jt. auth. see Jowett, Paul.
Rothwell, Mel-Thomas, jt. auth. see Rothwell, Helen F.
***Rothwell, N. J.** Immune Responses in the Nervous System. (Molecular & Cellular Neurobiology Ser.). 350p. 1995. 157.50 (*1-872748-79-1*, Pub. by Bios Scientific UK) Coronet Bks.
Rothwell, N. J. & Stock, M. J., eds. Obesity & Cachexia, Vol. 3: Physiological Mechanisms & New Approaches to Pharamcological Control. (Biological Council Symposia on Drug Action Ser.: No. 1937). 304p. 1991. text ed. 195.50 (*0-471-93068-7*, Wiley-Liss) Wiley.
Rothwell, Nancy & Dantzer, Robert, eds. Interleukin-1 in the Brain. LC 92-48945. (Studies in Neuroscience: No. 5). 1992. 150.00 (*0-08-041996-8*, Pergamon Pr) Elsevier.
Rothwell, Nancy J. & Berkenbosch, Frank, eds. Brain Control of Responses to Trauma. (Illus.). 330p. (C). 1994. 79.95 (*0-521-41939-5*) Cambridge U Pr.
Rothwell, Norman V. Understanding Genetics: A Molecular Approach. 672p. 1993. text ed. 56.95 (*0-471-58822-9*, Wiley-Liss) Wiley.
***Rothwell, Robert L.** Henry David Thoreau: An American Journal: Selected Writings from His Journals. (Illus.). 225p. 1995. pap. 12.95 (*1-56924-852-4*) Marlowe & Co.
Rothwell, Roy, jt. ed. see Dodgson, Mark.
Rothwell, Roy G. Minerals & Mineraloids in Marine Sediments: An Optical Identification Guide. 282p. 1990. 84.75 (*1-85166-382-7*) Elsevier.
Rothwell, Roy G. & Bessant, J. Innovation: Apdaptation & Growth, An International Perspective. 320p. 1987. 97.50 (*0-444-42861-5*) Elsevier.
Rothwell, Roy G. & Zegveld, Walter. Industrial Innovation & Public Policy: Preparing for the 1980s & the 1990s. LC 81-493. (Contributions in Economics & Economic History Ser.: No.42). (Illus.). 180p. 1981. text ed. 45.00 (*0-313-22989-9*, RTE/) Greenwood.
— Innovation & the Small & Medium Sized Firm. 1982. lib. bdg. 49.50 (*0-89838-099-5*) Kluwer Ac.
Rothwell, Roy G., jt. ed. see Langdon, Richard.
Rothwell, Roy R. & Zegveld, Walter. Reindustrialization & Technology. LC 85-2064. 288p. 1985. pap. 22.95 (*0-87332-331-9*) M E Sharpe.
Rothwell, Sheila, ed. Strategic Planning for Human Resources. (Best of Long Range Planning Ser.: No. 6). 155p. 1990. text ed. 83.00 (*0-08-037272-4*, Pergamon Pr); pap. text ed. 42.00 (*0-08-037770-X*, Pergamon Pr) Elsevier.
Rothwell, Una. A Long Way to Go. large type ed. 320p. 1987. 16.95 (*0-7089-1617-1*) Ulverscroft.
— The Secret of Sandhills. large type ed. 320p. 1987. 16.95 (*0-7089-1732-1*) Ulverscroft.
— The Welcoming Land. large type ed. 336p. 1987. 16.95 (*0-7089-1661-9*) Ulverscroft.
Rothwell, William. On the Job Training Workshop Coursebook, Set. 1990. 139.95 (*0-87425-127-3*) Human Res Dev Pr.
— On the Job Training Workshop Instructor's Guide, Set. 250p. 1990. 139.95 (*0-87425-128-1*) Human Res Dev Pr.
***Rothwell, William J.** Effective Succession Planning: Ensuring Leadership Continuity & Building Talent from Within. LC 94-27808. 352p. 1994. 59.95 (*0-8144-0206-2*) AMACOM.
— Emerging Issues in HRD Sourcebook. 200p. 1995. pap. 35.00 (*0-87425-266-0*) Human Res Dev Pr.
— The Employee Discipline Workshop, 2 vols., Set. 352p. 1990. ring bd. 99.95 (*0-87425-136-2*) Human Res Dev Pr.
— The Employee Selection Workshop, 2 vols., Set. 286p. 1990. ring bd. 99.95 (*0-87425-134-6*) Human Res Dev Pr.
— The Strategic Planning Workshop. 179p. 1989. ring bd. 139.95 (*0-87425-079-X*) Human Res Dev Pr.
Rothwell, William J. & Kazanas, H. C. The Complete AMA Guide to Management Development. 336p. 1993. 65.00 (*0-8144-5079-2*) AMACOM.
— Human Resource Development: A Strategic Approach. 1993. ring bd. 39.95 (*0-87425-238-5*) Human Res Dev Pr.
— Improving on-the-Job Training: How to Establish & Operate a Comprehensive OJT Program. LC 94-7847. (Management Ser.). 160p. 1994. 27.95 (*1-55542-665-4*) Jossey-Bass.
— Mastering the Instructional Design Process: A Systematic Approach. LC 91-31612. (Management Ser.). 416p. 1992. 49.95 (*1-55542-427-9*) Jossey-Bass.
— Planning & Managing Human Resources. 1993. ring bd. 34.95 (*0-87425-246-6*) Human Res Dev Pr.
Rothwell, William J. & Kazanas, Hercules C. Strategic Human Resources Planning & Management. (Illus.). 416p. (C). 1988. text ed. 72.00 (*0-13-851643-X*) P-H.
Rothwell, William J. & Sredl, Henry J. The ASTD Reference Guide to Professional Human Resource Development Roles & Competencies. 2nd ed. 1000p. 1992. 79.95 (*0-87425-177-X*) Human Res Dev Pr.
***Rothwell, William J., et al.** Practicing OD: A Guide for Consultants. LC 94-69887. 512p. 1995. text ed. 49.95 (*0-88390-379-2*) Pfeiffer & Co.
Rothwell, William S. The Vocabulary of Physics. 188p. (Orig.). 1988. pap. text ed. 13.95 (*0-89420-250-2*, 230500) Natl Book.
Roti, Grant C., tr. see Blaise, Albert.
Rotilio, G. Oxidative Damage & Related Enzymes, Vol. 2. (Life Chemistry Reports Supplement Ser.). 448p. 1984. pap. text ed. 139.00 (*3-7186-0221-0*) Gordon & Breach.
Rotillo, G., ed. Superoxide & Superoxide Dismutase in Chemistry, Biology & Medicine. 688p. 1986. 206.25 (*0-444-80797-7*) Elsevier.
Rotkiewiez, W., ed. Electromagnetic Compatibility in Radio Engineering. (Studies in Electrical & Electronic Engineering: Vol. 6). 314p. 1982. 100.00 (*0-444-99722-9*) Elsevier.
Rotkin, Charles E. Professional Photographer's Survival Guide. rev. ed. 368p. 1992. pap. 16.95 (*0-89879-554-0*, 10327) North Light Bks.
Rotman, A., ed. see Weizman Institute of Science Staff.
Rotman, Brian. Ad Infinitum - the Ghost in Turing's Machine: Taking God Out of Mathematics & Putting the Body Back In: An Essay in Corporeal Semiotics. LC 92-26420. 224p. 1993. 39.50 (*0-8047-2127-0*); pap. 12.95 (*0-8047-2128-9*) Stanford U Pr.
— Signifying Nothing: The Semiotics of Zero. LC 87-15632. 210p. 1988. pap. 12.95 (*0-318-32465-2*) St Martin.
— Signifying Nothing: The Semiotics of Zero. (Illus.). 111p. (C). 1993. reprint ed. pap. 12.95 (*0-8047-2129-7*) Stanford U Pr.
Rotman, Edgardo. Beyond Punishment: A New View on the Rehabilitation of Criminal Offenders. LC 89-37996. (Contributions in Criminology & Penology Ser.: No. 26). 229p. 1990. text ed. 55.00 (*0-313-26493-7*, RCI/, Greenwood Pr) Greenwood.
Rotman, Jayne. If Your Doctor's Busy, Call on God: A Spiritual Journey Through Ecological Illness. 190p. (Orig.). pap. write for info. (*0-931515-05-X*) Triumph Pr.
Rotman, Jeffrey L. Colors of the Deep. LC 91-29. (Illus.). 144p. 1991. 19.98 (*0-934738-87-4*) Thomasson-Grant.
***Rotman, Jeffrey L., illus.** Coral Reef: A City That Never Sleeps. LC 95-6635. (J). 1996. 15.99 (*0-525-65193-4*, Cobblehill Bks) Dutton Child Bks.
Rotman, Joseph. An Introduction to the Theory of Groups. LC 94-6507. (Graduate Texts in Mathematics Ser.). 1994. text ed. 59.00 (*0-387-94285-8*) Spr-Verlag.
Rotman, Joseph J. Galois Theory. xii, 108p. 1994. pap. 29.00 (*0-387-97305-2*) Spr-Verlag.
— An Introduction to Algebraic Topology. (Graduate Texts in Mathematics Ser.: Vol. 119). (Illus.). xiii, 433p. 1994. reprint ed. 49.80 (*0-387-96678-1*) Spr-Verlag.
— An Introduction to Homological Algebra. (Pure & Applied Mathematics Ser.). 1979. text ed. 84.00 (*0-12-599250-5*) Acad Pr.
— An Introduction to the Theory of Groups. 3rd ed. 500p. (C). 1984. pap. write for info. (*0-697-06882-X*) Wm C Brown Pubs.
Rotman, Leslie, jt. auth. see Lampert, Rachel.
Rotman, M., jt. ed. see Rosenthal, C. J.
Rotman, M., et al, eds. Concomitant Continuous Infusion Chemotherapy & Radiation. (Medical Radiology, Diagnostic Imaging & Radiation Oncology Ser.). (Illus.). xiv, 304p. 1991. 149.00 (*0-387-52545-9*) Spr-Verlag.
Rotman, Marcel, tr. see Wake, Harry S.
Rotman, Morris. Opportunities in Public Relations Careers. 1988. pap. 10.95 (*0-8442-6487-3*, VGM Career Bks) NTC Pub Grp.
***Rotman, Morris B.** Opportunities in Public Relations Careers. LC 94-49547. (VGM Opportunities Ser.). 1995. write for info. (*0-8442-4417-1*, VGM Career Bks); pap. write for info. (*0-8442-4419-8*, VGM Career Bks) NTC Pub Grp.
Rotmensz, N. K., et al, eds. Data Management & Clinical Trials: EORTC Study Group on Data Management. 246p. 1989. 77.00 (*0-444-81077-3*) Elsevier.
***Rotner, Shelley.** Action Alphabet. LC 94-32212. 1995. 14.95 (*0-689-80086-X*, Mac Bks Young Read) S&S Childrens.
— Wheels at Work. (Illus.). (J). 1995. 13.95 (*0-395-71815-5*) HM.
***Rotner, Shelley & Kelly, Sheila M.** Lots of Moms. LC 95-7789. (Illus.). (J). 1996. write for info. (*0-8037-1891-8*); lib. bdg. write for info. (*0-8037-1892-6*) Dial Bks Young.
Rotner, Shelley & Kreisler, Ken. Citybook. LC 93-6350. (Illus.). 32p. (J). (ps-1). 1994. 14.95 (*0-531-06837-4*); lib. bdg. 14.99 (*0-531-08687-9*) Orchard Bks Watts.
— Faces. LC 93-46758. 32p. (J). 1994. text ed. 14.95 (*0-02-777887-8*) Macmillan.
— Nature Spy. LC 91-38430. (Illus.). 32p. (J). (ps-1). 1992. text ed. 14.95 (*0-02-777885-1*, Mac Bks Young Read) S&S Childrens.
— Ocean Day. LC 92-6114. (Illus.). 32p. (J). (ps-1). 1993. text ed. 14.95 (*0-02-777886-X*, Mac Bks Young Read) S&S Childrens.
Rotner, Shelley, jt. auth. see Allen, Marjorie N.
Rotola, Al, jt. auth. see United Entrepreneurs Association of America Staff.
Rotola, Albert C., ed. see Gaspar, Stoquerus.
Rotondi, Giovanni. Leges Publicae Populi Romani. (Olms Paperbacks Ser.: Bd. 25). vii, 544p. 1990. reprint ed. pap. write for info. (*3-487-01173-5*, Pub. by Georg Olms GW) Lubrecht & Cramer.
Rotondi, Paul, tr. see Forte, Bruno.
Rotondo, Antonio, ed. Camillo Renato: Opere, Documenti E Testimonianze. LC 72-3454. (Corpus Reformatorum Italicorum & Biblioteca Ser.). (Illus.). 353p. (ITA & LAT.). 1968. 25.00 (*0-87580-034-3*) N Ill U Pr.
Rotondo, Susan, ed. see Schuster, Michael L.
***Rotovision, S. A.** DID 3: Architecture & Design World Review. 264p. 1994. 45.00 (*0-8230-6321-6*) Watsn-Guptill.
— Illustrators 36. 320p. 1994. 57.50 (*0-8230-6365-8*) Watsn-Guptill.
Rotovision, S. A. Staff. Art Directors' Index to Photographers, Set. (Illus.). 1994. boxed 135.00 (*0-8230-6334-8*, Watsn-Guptill) Watsn-Guptill.
— Art Directors' Index to Photographers, 2 vols., Vol. 1: Europe. (Illus.). 400p. 1994. 67.50 (*0-8230-6323-2*, Watsn-Guptill) Watsn-Guptill.
— Art Directors' Index to Photographers, 2 vols., Vol. 2: The Americas, Asia & Australasia. (Illus.). 300p. 1994. 67.50 (*0-8230-6324-0*, Watsn-Guptill) Watsn-Guptill.
Rotovision S. A. Staff. The Best in Digrammatic Graphics. (Illus.). 224p. 1993. 55.00 (*0-8230-6305-4*, Watsn-Guptill) Watsn-Guptill.
— The Best in Industrial Architecture Design. (Illus.). 224p. 1992. 50.00 (*0-8230-6212-0*, Watsn-Guptill) Watsn-Guptill.
Rotovision, S. A. Staff. The Best in Leisure & Public Architecture. (Illus.). 224p. 1994. 55.00 (*0-8230-6360-7*, Watsn-Guptill) Watsn-Guptill.
Rotovision S. A. Staff. The Best in Mixed-Use Development Design. (Illus.). 224p. 1992. 50.00 (*0-8230-6233-3*, Watsn-Guptill) Watsn-Guptill.
RotoVision S. A. Staff. The Best in Point-of-Purchase Design. (Illus.). 224p. 1992. 50.00 (*0-8230-6169-8*, Watsn-Guptill) Watsn-Guptill.
Rotovision S. A. Staff. The Best in Specialist Packaging Design. (Illus.). 224p. 1992. 50.00 (*0-8230-6214-7*, Watsn-Guptill) Watsn-Guptill.
— DID Two: The International Directory of Architecture & Design. (Illus.). 224p. 1992. 65.00 (*0-8230-6207-4*, Watsn-Guptill) Watsn-Guptill.
Rotovision, S. A. Staff. Graphic Designer's Index 8. (Illus.). 275p. 1994. 67.50 (*0-8230-6337-2*, Watsn-Guptill) Watsn-Guptill.
***Rotovision S. A. Staff.** Illustration West 33. (Illus.). 224p. 1995. 39.50 (*0-8230-6435-2*) Watsn-Guptill.
— The Seventy-Second Art Directors Annual. (Illus.). 550p. 1993. 68.00 (*0-8230-6301-1*, Watsn-Guptill) Watsn-Guptill.
***RotoVision Staff.** Art Directors' Index to Illustrators, No. 15. 1995. (*0-8230-6434-4*) Watsn-Guptill.
— Art Directors' Index to Photographers, Vol. 1, No. 20. 1995. (*0-8230-6430-1*) Watsn-Guptill.
— Art Directors' Index to Photographers, Vol. 2, No. 20. 1995. (*0-8230-6429-8*) Watsn-Guptill.
— Best in Catalogue & Brochure Design. 1995. (*0-8230-6441-7*) Watsn-Guptill.
— Best in Cutting Edge Typography. 1995. (*0-8230-6442-5*) Watsn-Guptill.
— Best in Trade & Exhibition Stand Design 2. 1995. (*0-8230-6443-3*) Watsn-Guptill.
— Commercial Spaces: Hotels, Bars & Restaurants. 1995. pap. text ed. (*0-8230-6439-5*) Watsn-Guptill.
— Commercial Spaces: Office Spaces, Furniture & Lighting. 1995. pap. text ed. (*0-8230-6440-9*) Watsn-Guptill.
— Commercial Spaces: Shops, Malls & Boutiques. 1995. pap. text ed. (*0-8230-6438-7*) Watsn-Guptill.
— Europe, Vol. I. 1995. (*0-8230-6428-X*) Watsn-Guptill.
— Graphic Designers' Index Nine. 1995. (*0-8230-6444-1*) Watsn-Guptill.
Rotovision Staff. One Show Fifteen. 1994. 69.00 (*0-8230-6319-4*) Watsn-Guptill.
***RotoVision Staff.** Pro-Lighting: Food Shots. 1995. pap. text ed. (*0-8230-6432-8*) Watsn-Guptill.
— Pro-Lighting: Glamour Shots. 1995. pap. text ed. (*0-8230-6431-X*) Watsn-Guptill.
— Pro-Lighting: Product Shots. 1995. pap. text ed. (*0-8230-6433-6*) Watsn-Guptill.
RotoVision Staff, jt. auth. see European Association of Ad Agencies Staff.
***Rotovison S. A. Staff.** The ADDY Book: The Annual of the American Advertising Federation. (Illus.). 592p. 1995. 65.00 (*0-8230-6436-0*) Watsn-Guptill.
Rotroff, Susan I. Hellenistic Pottery: Athenian & Imported Moldmade Bowls. LC 91-43755. (Athenian Agora Ser.: Vol. 22). (Illus.). xvi, 136p. 1982. 40.00 (*0-87661-222-2*) Am Sch Athens.
Rotroff, Susan I. & Oakley, John W. Debris from a Public Dining Place in the Athenian Agora. (Hesperia Supplement Ser.: No. 25). (Illus.). 116p. 1992. pap. 35.00 (*0-87661-525-6*) Am Sch Athens.
Rotroff, Susan I., jt. auth. see Lamberton, Robert D.
Rotrosen, John, jt. ed. see Stanley, Michael.
Rotschild, Jon, tr. see Franck, Dan.
Rotsfein, Abraham, jt. auth. see Polyani, Karl.
Rotsler, William. Plot-It-Yourself Adventure: Goonies Cavern of Horror. Arico, Diane, ed. 128p. (Orig.). (J). (gr. 3-7). 1985. pap. 3.95 (*0-671-60135-0*) S&S Trade.
— The Star Trek II Gift Set, 3 vols., Set. (J). boxed 9.50 (*0-317-12429-3*) S&S Trade.
***Rotsler, William, ed.** Science Fictionisms. LC 95-13162. 144p. 1995. pap. 5.95 (*0-87905-693-2*) Gibbs Smith Pub.
Rotstein, J., ed. Immunosuppression Systematic Lupus Erythematosus. (Rheumatology Ser.: Vol. 5). (Illus.). 1974. 92.00 (*3-8055-1540-5*) S Karger.
Rotstein, Maurice. The Democratic Myth. 245p. 1983. 15.00 (*0-912598-21-2*); pap. 6.95 (*0-912598-52-2*) Florham.
***Rotstein, Nancy-Gay.** Shattering Glass. 352p. Date not set. 21.00 (*0-374-26223-3*) FS&G.
Rotstein, Ronald D. The Future: Trends & Developments Through the 21st Century. 1989. 19.95 (*0-8184-0505-8*) Carol Pub Group.
Rott, Jean, ed. Correspondance de Martin Bucer Tome II (1524-1526) (Studies in Medieval & Reformation Thought: No. 43). (Illus.). (FRE & LAT.). (C). 1989. text ed. 74.50 (*90-04-08636-6*) E J Brill.
Rott, Joanna R. & Groves, Seli. How on Earth Do We Recycle Glass? LC 91-24241. (Illus.). 64p. (J). (gr. 4-6). 1992. lib. bdg. 13.90 (*1-56294-141-0*) Millbrook Pr.
Rott, R. & Goebel, W. Molecular Basis of Viral & Microbial Pathogenesis. (Colloquium Mosbach Ser.: Vol. 38). (Illus.). 280p. 1988. 69.00 (*0-387-18606-9*) Spr-Verlag.
Rotte, Joanna. Scene Change: A Theatre Diary Prague, Moscow, Leningrad Spring 1991. LC 94-67. (Illus.). 176p. (Orig.). 1994. 25.00 (*0-87910-175-X*); pap. 12.95 (*0-87910-171-7*) Limelight Edns.
Rotte, Joanna & Yamamoto, Koji. Vision: A Holistic Guide to Healing the Eyesight. LC 84-80538. 152p. (Orig.). 1986. pap. 18.00 (*0-87040-622-1*) Japan Pubns USA.
Rotteck, ed. Dictionnaire Allemand-Francais, Francais-Allemand. 980p. (FRE & GER.). 1970. pap. 10.95 (*0-7859-0753-X*, M-6115) Fr & Eur.
***Rotteck, Karl & Kister, G.** Dictionnaire Allemand-Francais et Francais-Allemand. 1978. write for info. (*0-7859-8004-0*, 2-7370-0085-8) Fr & Eur.
Rottem, S. & Kahane, I., eds. Subcellular Biochemistry, Vol. 20: Mycoplasma Cell Membranes. (Illus.). 310p. (C). 1993. 85.00 (*0-306-44394-5*, Plenum Pr) Plenum.
Rottem, S., jt. ed. see Ron, E. Z.
Rottem, S., jt. ed. see Timor-Tritsch, I. E.
Rottenberg, Annette T. Elements of Argument: A Text & Reader. 3rd ed. LC 89-63931. 630p. (C). 1990. pap. text ed. 0.68 (*0-312-04913-7*, Bedford Bks) St Martin.
— Elements of Argument: A Text & Reader. 4th ed. 736p. 1993. pap. text ed. 18.50 (*0-312-08640-7*) St Martin.
— The Structure of Argument. 352p. 1993. pap. text ed. 10.00 (*0-312-09459-0*) St Martin.
Rottenberg, David A. Neurological Complications of Cancer Treatment. (Illus.). 248p. 1990. text ed. 70.00 (*0-409-90143-1*) Buttrwrth-Heinemann.
Rottenberg, P., jt. auth. see Institute of Chemical Engineers Staff.
Rottenberg, Simon. The Cost of Regulated Pricing: A Critical Analysis of Auto Insurance Premium Rate - Setting in Massachusetts. LC 89-22939. (Pioneer Paper Ser.: No. 2). 50p. (Orig.). 1989. pap. 10.00 (*0-929930-02-9*) Pioneer Inst.
Rottenberg, Simon, ed. The Economics of Legal Minimum Wages. LC 80-26563. (AEI Symposia Ser.: No. 81A). (Illus.). 552p. reprint ed. pap. 157.40 (*0-8357-4470-1*, 2037314) Bks Demand.
— The Economics of Medical Malpractice. LC 78-6364. (Illus.). 302p. reprint ed. pap. 86.10 (*0-8357-4471-X*, 2037315) Bks Demand.

R

An Asterisk (*) at the beginning of an entry indicates that the title is appearing in BIP for the first time.

— The Political Economy of Poverty, Equity, & Growth: Costa Rica & Uruguay. (Comparative Study Ser.). 440p. 1993. 39.95 (*0-19-520883-8*, 60883) OUP.

Rottenbucher, Terri, ed. see Metlina, L. S.

Rottensteiner, Franz, ed. see Lem, Stanislaw.

Rotter, Andrew J. The Path to Vietnam: Origins of the American Commitment to Southeast Asia. LC 87-47603. 304p. (C). 1987. pap. 15.95 (*0-8014-9620-9*) Cornell U Pr.

Rotter, Andrew J., ed. Light at the End of the Tunnel: A Vietnam War Anthology. LC 89-63932. 589p. (Orig.). (C). 1990. pap. text ed. 18.50 (*0-312-04529-8*) St Martin.

Rotter, Charles. Monarchs. (Nature Books Ser.). (J). (gr. 2-6). 1992. lib. bdg. 22.79 (*0-89565-840-2*) Childs World.

— Seals & Sea Lions. (Nature Books Ser.). 32p. (J). (gr. 2-6). 1991. lib. bdg. 22.79 (*0-89565-714-7*) Childs World.

— Tornadoes. LC 93-46803. 40p. (J). Date not set. 18.95 (*0-88682-712-4*) Creative Ed.

— Walruses. LC 92-8410. (Nature Books Ser.). (J). (gr. 2-6). 1992. lib. bdg. 22.79 (*0-89565-841-0*) Childs World.

Rotter, Charles M. Fungi. LC 92-44441. (Images Ser.). (J). (gr. 4 up). 1993. 16.95 (*0-88682-593-8*) Creative Ed.

— Hurricanes. LC 92-44442. (Images Ser.). (J). (gr. 6 up). 1994. 16.95 (*0-88682-597-0*) Creative Ed.

— Mountains. LC 92-41340. (Images Ser.). (J). 1994. 16.95 (*0-88682-596-2*) Creative Ed.

— The Prairie. LC 92-44822. (Images Ser.). (J). (gr. 4 up). 1994. 16.95 (*0-88682-598-9*) Creative Ed.

Rotter, Charles M. & Taylor, Nicole. Wetlands. LC 92-41339. (Images Ser.). (J). 1994. 16.95 (*0-88682-594-6*) Creative Ed.

Rotter, George & Rotter, Naomi. Ecstatic 2.01: Selected Procedures, Problems, & Solutions. 340p. 1993. spiral bd. 31.95 (*0-8403-8820-9*) Kendall-Hunt.

Rotter, Joseph C., jt. auth. see Miller, Gary M.

Rotter, Joseph C., et al. Parent-Teacher Conferencing. 2nd ed. 32p. 1987. 3.95 (*0-8106-1075-2*) NEA.

Rotter, Julian B. Clinical Psychology. 2nd ed. LC 74-110493. (Foundations of Modern Psychology Ser.). (Illus.). 1971. pap. 8.95 (*0-685-03791-6*) P-H.

Rotter, Naomi, jt. auth. see Rotter, George.

Rotter, Richard, ed. see Davies, Devi, et al.

Rotterdahn, Lori. Fetal Monitoring & Health Sciences: Medical Analysis Index with Research Bibliography. LC 85-47854. 150p. 1987. 39.50 (*0-88164-382-3*); pap. 34.50 (*0-88164-383-1*) ABBE Pubs Assn.

Rotterdam Conference Staff. Human Gene Mapping: Proceedings of the Rotterdam Conference, 2nd, 1974. Bergsma, Daniel, ed. LC 75-8204. (March of Dimes Ser.: Vol. 11, No. 3). 1976. 20.00 (*0-686-14571-2*) March of Dimes.

— Human Gene Mapping Two: Proceedings of the Rotterdam Conference, 1974 - Journal: Cytogenetics & Cell Genetics, Vol. 14, Nos. 3-6. Bergsma, Daniel, ed. (Illus.). 332p. 1975. pap. 63.25 (*3-8055-2251-7*) S Karger.

Rotterdam, Heidrun, et al. Biopsy Diagnosis of the Digestive Tract, 2 vols., Set. 2nd ed. (Biopsy Interpretation Ser.). 872p. 1993. 168.00 (*0-88167-968-2*) Raven.

***Rotteveel, Jacqueline.** Incest: The Pain & the Healing. 93p. (YA). (gr. 7-12). 1990. pap. write for info. (*1-57515-004-2*) PPI Pubng.

Rottger, H., jt. auth. see Von der Hardt, Peter.

Rottger, Heinz, jt. auth. see Genthon, J. P.

Rottger, Heinz, jt. auth. see Von Der Hardt, Peter.

Rottger, Heinz, jt. ed. see Von der Hardt, Peter.

Rottier, Carol, jt. auth. see Voell, Rick.

Rottier, Jerry & Ogan, Beverly J. Cooperative Learning in Middle-Level Schools. 112p. 1991. 11.95 (*0-8106-3068-0*) NEA.

Rottlevy, Uriel. Adolescent Behavior: Medical Subject Analysis with Research Bibliography. LC 84-45645. 150p. 1987. 39.50 (*0-88164-240-1*); pap. 34.50 (*0-88164-241-X*) ABBE Pubs Assn.

— Behavior & Motivation: Index of Modern Information. LC 90-31679. 150p. 1990. 39.50 (*1-55914-140-9*); pap. 34.50 (*1-55914-141-7*) ABBE Pubs Assn.

Rottlstein, Mark A., et al. Employment Law, 1993 Statutory Supplement to Cases & Materials. 2nd ed. (University Casebook Ser.). 276p. 1993. pap. text ed. 11.95 (*1-56662-118-6*) Foundation Pr.

Rottman, David. State Court Caseload Statistics: Annual Report, 1987. 266p. 1989. pap. text ed. 6.95 (*0-89656-091-0*, R-109) Natl Ctr St Courts.

— State Court Caseload Statistics: Annual Report, 1988. 306p. 1990. pap. text ed. 6.95 (*0-89656-097-X*, R-115) Natl Ctr St Courts.

— State Court Model Statistical Dictionary. 90p. 1989. pap. text ed. 4.50 (*0-89656-093-7*, R-111) Natl Ctr St Courts.

Rottman, Fran. Easy-to-Make Puppets & How to Use Them. Incl. Children & Youth. 96p. 1978. pap. 5.95 (*0-8307-0560-0*, 5202205); Early Childhood. 1978. pap. 6.99 (*0-8307-0559-7*, 5202108); 1978. Set pap. write for info. (*0-318-55489-5*) Regal.

Rottman, G. German Combat Equipments 1939-451. (Men-at-Arms Ser.: No. 234). (Illus.). 48p. pap. 11.95 (*1-85532-952-2*, 9192, Pub. by Osprey UK) Stackpole.

— World Special Forces Insignia. (Elite Ser.: No. 22). (Illus.). 64p. pap. 12.95 (*0-85045-865-X*, 9422, Pub. by Osprey UK) Stackpole.

Rottman, Gordon. Armies of the Gulf War. (Elite Ser.: No. 45). (Illus.). 64p. pap. 12.95 (*1-85532-277-3*, 9460, Pub. by Osprey UK) Stackpole.

— Inside the U. S. Army Today. (Elite Ser.: No. 20). (Illus.). 64p. 1989. pap. 12.95 (*0-85045-855-2*, 9420, Pub. by Osprey Pubng Ltd UK) Stackpole.

— Panama. (Elite Ser.: No. 37). (Illus.). 64p. pap. 12.95 (*1-85532-156-4*, 9452, Pub. by Osprey UK) Stackpole.

— U. S. Army Air Force One. (Elite Ser.: No. 46). (Illus.). 64p. pap. 12.95 (*1-85532-294-3*, 9461, Pub. by Osprey UK) Stackpole.

— U. S. Army Air Force (2) (Elite Ser.). (Illus.). 64p. 1994. pap. 12.95 (*1-85532-339-7*, 9466, Pub. by Osprey UK) Stackpole.

— U. S. Army Airborne 1940-1990: The First Fifty Years. (Elite Ser.: No. 31). (Illus.). 64p. 1990. pap. 12.95 (*0-85045-948-6*, 9431, Pub. by Osprey Pubng Ltd UK) Stackpole.

— U. S. Army Combat Equipments. (Men-at-Arms Ser.: No. 205). (Illus.). 48p. 1989. pap. 11.95 (*0-85045-842-0*, 9138, Pub. by Osprey Pubng Ltd UK) Stackpole.

— U. S. Army Special Forces 1952-84. (Elite Ser.: No. 4). (Illus.). 64p. pap. 12.95 (*0-85045-610-X*, 9403, Pub. by Osprey Pubng Ltd UK) Stackpole.

— Vietnam Airborne. (Elite Ser.: No. 29). (Illus.). 64p. 1990. pap. 12.95 (*0-85045-941-9*, 9429, Pub. by Osprey Pubng Ltd UK) Stackpole.

Rottman, Gordon, et al. The Official Lite History & Cookbook of the Gulf War. (Illus.). 160p. (Orig.). 1991. pap. 6.95 (*0-9623992-1-3*) Electric Strawberry.

Rottman, Gordon L. U. S. Army Rangers & LRRP Units 1942-87. (Elite Ser.: No. 13). (Illus.). 64p. pap. 12.95 (*0-85045-795-5*, 9412, Pub. by Osprey UK) Stackpole.

— Warsaw Pact Ground Forces. (Elite Ser.: No. 10). (Illus.). 64p. pap. 12.95 (*0-85045-730-0*, 9409, Pub. by Osprey Pubng Ltd UK) Stackpole.

***Rottman, Vicki.** The Coffee Break Book: Brief Diversions for Your Busy Day. LC 94-96366. (Illus.). 112p. (Orig.). 1994. pap. 12.95 (*0-9642517-0-1*) VR Prodns.

***Rottmann, Gordon.** U. S. Marine Corps 1941-45. (Elite Ser.). (Illus.). 64p. 1995. pap. 12.95 (*1-85532-497-0*, Pub. by Osprey UK) Stackpole.

Rottmann, Larry. Voices from the Ho Chi Minh Trail. LC 93-71258. (Illus.). 224p. (Orig.). 1993. pap. 19.95 (*1-880391-06-6*) Event Horizon.

Rotton, Peter J. & Ossorio, Nelson A. Soluciones Nuevas Para un Mundo Computarizado. (PC Help Ser.). 120p. (Orig.). (SPA.). 1993. pap. 18.95 (*1-56721-022-8*) Twenty-Fifth Cent Pr.

Rotton, Wendy & Ossorio, Nelson A. Animal Fashions. (Illus.). 48p. (J). (gr. 3-5). 1994. pap. 6.95 (*1-56721-069-4*) Twnty-Fifth Cent Pr.

Rotton, Wendy & Salvadeo, Michele B. The Ill-Tempered Crane. (Illus.). 48p. (J). (gr. 3-5). 1994. pap. 6.95 (*1-56721-060-0*) Twnty-Fifth Cent Pr.

Rotton, Wendy, et al. Cheap Gourmet. 120p. (Orig.). 1994. pap. 6.95 (*1-56721-076-7*) Twnty-Fifth Cent Pr.

— Leftover Magic. 96p. (Orig.). 1994. pap. 15.95 (*1-56721-084-8*) Twnty-Fifth Cent Pr.

Rottschaefer, Henry. The Constitution & Socio-Economic Change. LC 77-173667. (American Constitutional & Legal History Ser). 253p. 1971. reprint ed. lib. bdg. 35.00 (*0-306-70410-2*) Da Capo.

— Constitution & Socio-Economic Change. LC 49-2548. (Michigan Legal Publications). xiii, 253p. 1986. reprint ed. lib. bdg. 42.00 (*0-89941-542-3*, 304710) W S Hein.

Rottschafer, Ronald H. The Search for Satisfaction: Getting More for Yourself & Giving More to Others. LC 91-31387. 320p. 1992. 12.99 (*0-8010-7762-1*) Baker Bk.

Rotunda, D. P. Motif-Index of the Italian Novella in Prose. LC 72-6778. (Studies in Italian Literature: No. 46). 1972. reprint ed. lib. bdg. 75.00 (*0-8383-1653-0*) M S G Haskell Hse.

Rotunda, Ronald D. Constitutional Law. LC 86-26555. 609p. 1987. text ed. 65.25 (*0-314-31127-0*); teacher ed, pap. text ed. write for info. (*0-314-66077-1*) West Pub.

— Modern Constitutional Law: Cases & Notes. 4th ed. LC 93-9233. (American Casebook Ser.). 1126p. 1993. text ed. 47.00 (*0-314-01816-6*) West Pub.

— Modern Constitutional Law: Cases & Notes, 1993 Supplement To. 3rd ed. (American Casebook Ser.). 46p. 1993. pap. text ed. 4.50 (*0-314-02548-0*) West Pub.

— The Politics of Language: Liberalism As Word & Symbol. LC 85-24548. 148p. reprint ed. pap. 42.20 (*0-8357-3406-4*, 2039663) Bks Demand.

— Professional Responsibility. 3rd ed. (Black Letter Ser.). 492p. (C). 1993. reprint ed. pap. text ed. 20.00 (*0-314-92146-X*) West Pub.

— Professional Responsibility. 4th ed. (Black Letter Ser.). 428p. (C). 1995. pap. text ed. write for info. (*0-314-06469-9*) West Pub.

— Six Justices on Civil Rights. LC 82-69327. (David C. Baum Memorial Lectures). 211p. 1983. lib. bdg. 25.00 (*0-379-20044-9*) Oceana.

Rotunda, Ronald D. & Nowak, John E. Constitutional Law. 4th ed. (Hornbook Ser.). 1357p. 1993. reprint ed. text ed. 41.50 (*0-314-84217-9*) West Pub.

Rotunda, Ronald D., jt. auth. see Hay, Peter.

Rotunda, Ronald D., jt. auth. see Morgan, Thomas D.

Rotunda, Ronald D., jt. auth. see Nowak, John E.

Rotundo, E. Anthony. American Manhood. 400p. 1994. reprint ed. pap. 13.00 (*0-465-00169-6*) Basic.

— American Manhood: Transformations in Masculinity from the Revolution to the Modern Era. LC 92-53247. 400p. 1993. 25.00 (*0-465-01409-7*) Basic.

Rotundo, John L., jt. auth. see Ericson, Don.

Rotundo, L. Battle for Stalingrad: The 1943 Soviet General Staff Study. (Illus.). 342p. 1989. 47.00 (*0-08-035974-4*) Brasseys Inc.

Rotundo, Louis. Into the Unknown: The X-1 Story. LC 93-15989. (Illus.). 352p. 1994. Acid-free paper. 29.95 (*1-56098-305-1*) Smithsonian.

Rotundo, R. L., et al. Advances in Gene Technology: Molecular Neurobiology & Neuropharmacology: Molecular Neurobiology & Neuropharmacology, Vol. 9. Ahmad, F. et al, eds. (ICSU Short Series Reports: Vol. 9). (Illus.). 180p. 1989. pap. 50.00 (*1-85221-205-5*, IRL Pr) OUP.

Rotunno, Betsy, jt. auth. see Rotunno, Rocco.

Rotunno, Betsy, jt. auth. see Rotunno, Roccy.

Rotunno, Catalina A., jt. auth. see Cereijido, Marcelino.

Rotunno, Rocco & Rotunno, Betsy. How Snowshoe Saves Christmas. (Stamptime Stories Ser.). (Illus.). 12p. (Orig.). (J). (gr. 2-6). 1993. boxed 7.00 (*1-881980-05-7*) Noteworthy.

— The Incredible Crash Dummies: The Dashboard Sandwich. (Stamptime Stories Ser.). (Illus.). 12p. (Orig.). (J). (gr. 2-6). 1993. boxed 7.00 (*1-881980-06-5*) Noteworthy.

— Little Bear's Best Birthday. (Stamptime Stories Ser.). (Illus.). 12p. (J). (gr. 2-6). 1992. Mixed Media Pkg. incls. stamp pad, stamps & box of 4 crayons. 7.00 (*1-881980-00-6*) Noteworthy.

— The Story of Christmas Tree Lane. (Stamptime Stories Ser.). (Illus.). 12p. (Orig.). (J). (gr. 2-6). 1993. boxed 7.00 (*1-881980-04-9*) Noteworthy.

— Tessa Becomes a Ballerina. (Stamptime Stories Ser.). (Illus.). 12p. (J). (gr. 2-6). 1992. Mixed Media Pkg. incls. stamp pad, stamps, box of 4 crayons. 7.00 (*1-881980-01-4*) Noteworthy.

— A Trick for Magic Bunny. (Stamptime Stories Ser.). (Illus.). 12p. (J). (gr. 2-6). 1992. Mixed Media Pkg. incls. stamp pad, stamps & box of 4 crayons. 7.00 (*1-881980-02-2*) Noteworthy.

Rotunno, Roccy & Rotunno, Betsy. Dennis the Dinosaur Moves to Crystal Pond. (Stamptime Stories Ser.). (Illus.). 12p. (J). (gr. 2-6). 1992. Mixed Media Pkg. incls. stamp pad, stamps & box of 4 crayons. 7.00 (*1-881980-03-0*) Noteworthy.

Rotwein, Eugene, ed. see Hume, David.

Rotwitt, Jeffrey B., jt. auth. see Nasuti, James F.

***Roty, Martine.** Dictionnaire Russe-Francais des Termes en Usage Dans l'Eglise Russe. 2nd ed. 160p. (FRE & RUS.). 1983. pap. 24.95 (*0-7859-7961-1*, 2720401935) Fr & Eur.

Rotz, Anna O. Heritage Hill Farm Cookbook. 96p. 1980. 7.95 (*0-9605108-0-X*) Rotz.

Rotzel, Grace. The School in Rose Valley: A Parent Venture in Education. LC 70-144200. (Illus.). 159p. (C). reprint ed. 45.40 (*0-8357-9284-6*, 2015739) Bks Demand.

Rotzer, Florian. Conversations with French Philosophers. Aylesworth, Gary E., tr. LC 93-30819. 120p. (C). 1995. 39.95 (*0-391-03846-X*); pap. 12.50 (*0-391-03847-8*) Humanities.

Rotzheim, William H. & Gutman, Lew. Guide to Network Management. 375p. 1993. text ed. 32.00 (*0-13-365966-6*) P-H.

Rotzler, Willy. Constructive Concepts: A History of Constructive Art from Cubism to the Present. rev. ed. LC 77-89937. (Illus.). 332p. 1989. reprint ed. 50.00 (*0-8478-1024-0*) Rizzoli Intl.

Rotzoll, Kim, ed. see Gossage, Howard L.

Rotzoll, Kim B. Advertising in Contemporary Society. 2nd ed. (C). 1989. pap. text ed. write for info. (*0-318-65184-X*, SJ70BA) S-W Pub.

Rotzoll, Kim B., ed. Proceedings of the 1989 Conference of the American Academy of Advertising. 1989. pap. 25.00 (*0-931030-12-9*) Am Acad Advert.

Rotzoll, Kim B., jt. auth. see Christians, Clifford G.

Rotzsche, H. Stationary Phases in Gas Chromatography. (Journal of Chromatography Library: Vol. 48). 424p. 1991. 166.50 (*0-444-98733-9*) Elsevier.

Rouan, B. J., jt. auth. see Rouan, C.

Rouan, C. & Rouan, B. J. Basic Biology Questions for GCSE. (C). 1989. text ed. 60.00 (*0-7487-0057-9*, Pub. by S Thornes Pubs UK) St Mut.

Rouanet, Leo. Coleccion De Autos, Farsas y Coloquios Del Siglo, 4 vols., Set, XVI. xxviii, 2124p. 1979. reprint ed. Set. write for info. (*3-487-06804-4*, Pub. by Georg Olms GW) Lubrecht & Cramer.

Rouard, Danielle, jt. auth. see Dibango, Manu.

Rouard, Marguerite, jt. auth. see Simon, Jacques.

Rouard-Snowman, Margo. Museum Graphics. LC 92-80096. (Illus.). 192p. 1992. 40.00 (*0-500-23635-6*) Thames Hudson.

— Romas Cieslewicz. LC 93-60426. (Illus.). 160p. 1993. pap. 34.95 (*0-500-27729-X*) Thames Hudson.

Rouart, Denis. Degas: In Search of His Technique. LC 87-36083. (Illus.). 140p. 1988. pap. 25.00 (*0-8478-0949-8*) Rizzoli Intl.

Rouart, Denis, ed. Berthe Morisot: Correspondence. Hubbard, Betty W., tr. 272p. pap. 9.95 (*0-918825-62-8*) Moyer Bell.

Rouaud, Jean. Fields of Glory. Manheim, Ralph, tr. 160p. 1992. 18.95 (*1-55970-165-X*) Arcade Pub Inc.

— Fields of Glory. Manheim, Ralph, tr. 160p. 1993. reprint ed. pap. 9.95 (*1-55970-216-8*) Arcade Pub Inc.

— Of Illustrious Men. Wright, Barbara, tr. 160p. 1994. 19.95 (*1-55970-265-6*) Arcade Pub Inc.

— Of Illustrious Men. Wright, Barbara, tr. 160p. 1995. pap. 10.95 (*1-55970-319-9*) Arcade Pub Inc.

Rouault, Georges. The Passion. (Illus.). 1983. 15.50 (*0-8446-6006-X*) Peter Smith.

— The Passion. (Fine Art Ser.). (Illus.). 80p. 1983. reprint ed. pap. 8.95 (*0-486-24370-2*) Dover.

Rouault, Isabelle. Rouault's Complete Paintings, 2 vols., Set. (Illus.). (ENG & FRE.). 1988. 1,500.00 (*1-55660-031-3*) A Wofsy Fine Arts.

Rouault, Isabelle, jt. auth. see Chapon, Francois.

Rouault, O. Elements pour un Logiciel Assyriologique. (Computer Aided Research in Near Eastern Studies: Vol. 1, Pt. 2). 82p. 1984. pap. 9.50 (*0-89003-185-1*) Undena Pubns.

Rouault, O., jt. auth. see Buccellati, G.

Rouault, Olivier. Terqa Final Reports, No. 1: L'Archive de Puzurum. LC 81-71741. (Bibliotheca Mesopotamica Ser.: Vol. 16). (Illus.). 130p. (AKK, ENG & FRE.). 1984. pap. 24.25 (*0-89003-102-9*) Undena Pubns.

Roubatis, Yiannis P. Tangled Webs: The U. S. in Greece 1947-1967. LC 87-60390. 228p. (Orig.). 1987. 25.00 (*0-317-64511-0*); pap. 12.00 (*0-918618-34-7*) Pella Pub.

Roubaud, Jacques. Great Fire of London. Di Bernardi, Dominic, tr. LC 91-7722. 330p. 1991. 21.95 (*0-916583-76-7*) Dalkey Arch.

— The Great Fire of London. Di Bernardi, Dominic, tr. (Illus.). 330p. 1992. reprint ed. pap. 12.95 (*0-916583-89-9*) Dalkey Arch.

— Hortense in Exile. Di Bernardi, Dominic, tr. LC 91-29759. 211p. 1992. 19.95 (*1-56478-001-5*) Dalkey Arch.

— Hortense Is Abducted. Di Bernardi, Dominic, tr. LC 88-30390. 230p. 1989. 19.95 (*0-916583-38-4*) Dalkey Arch.

— Plurality of Worlds of Lewis. Waldrop, Rosmarie, tr. 109p. (Orig.). 1995. pap. 9.95 (*1-56478-069-4*) Dalkey Arch.

— The Princess Hoppy: or the Tale of Labrador. Hoepffner, Bernard, tr. (Illus.). 133p. (Orig.). 1993. pap. 9.95 (*1-56478-032-5*) Dalkey Arch.

— Some Thing Black. Waldrop, Rosmarie, tr. LC 89-35216. (Illus.). 160p. 1990. 19.95 (*0-916583-48-1*) Dalkey Arch.

Roubelakis-Angelakis, K. A. & Tran Trahn Van, eds. Morphogenesis in Plants: Molecular Approaches. LC 93-20954. (NATO ASI Series A, Life Sciences: Vol. 256). (Illus.). 284p. 1994. 89.50 (*0-306-44597-2*, Plenum Pr) Plenum.

Roubens, M., ed. Advances in Operations Research: Proceedings of the European Congress on Operation Research, 2nd, Stockholm, Sweden, November 29, 1977. 1977. 97.50 (*0-7204-0718-4*, North Holland) Elsevier.

Roubens, M. & Vincke, P. Preference Modelling. (Lecture Notes in Economics & Mathematical Systems Ser.: Vol. 250). (Illus.). viii, 94p. 1985. pap. 29.50 (*0-387-15685-2*) Spr-Verlag.

Roubens, M., jt. ed. see Kacprzyk, Janusz.

Roubens, Marc, jt. auth. see Fodor, Janos.

Roubicek, Henry L. Doing Business & Professional Speech Communications. 3rd ed. 208p. 1992. per. 16.00 (*0-8403-8204-9*) Kendall-Hunt.

Roubicek, Joseph B. How to Investigate Financial Exploitation of the Elderly: A Training Manual for Police. 64p. (Orig.). (C). 1993. pap. text ed. 11.95 (*1-56806-278-8*) Diane Pub.

Roubiczek, Paul. Existentialism: For & Against. LC 64-21562. 206p. reprint ed. pap. 58.80 (*0-317-08055-5*, 2022466) Bks Demand.

Roubik, David W. Ecology & Natural History of Tropical Bees. (Cambridge Tropical Biology Ser.). (Illus.). 400p. 1989. 79.95 (*0-521-26236-4*) Cambridge U Pr.

— Ecology & Natural History of Tropical Bees. (Cambridge Tropical Biology Ser.). (Illus.). 514p. (C). 1992. pap. 29.95 (*0-521-42909-9*) Cambridge U Pr.

Roubin, Gary S. Coronary Artery Stenting. 400p. 1994. write for info. (*0-86542-283-4*) Blackwell Sci.

Roubin, Gary S., et al, eds. Interventional Cardiovascular Medicine: Principles & Practice. (Illus.). 976p. 1993. 179.95 (*0-443-08834-9*) Churchill.

Roubine, E. & Bolomey, J. C. Antennas Vol. 1: General Principles. LC 66-56953. 218p. 1987. 121.00 (*0-89116-278-X*) Hemisp Pub.

Roubine, E., et al, eds. Mathematics Applied to Physics. (Illus.). 1970. 74.00 (*0-387-04965-7*) Spr-Verlag.

Roucek, Joseph. Tito: Modern Leader of Yugoslavia. Rahmas, D. Steve, ed. LC 73-87625. (Outstanding Personalities Ser.: No. 62). 32p. (Orig.). (YA). (gr. 7-12). 1973. lib. bdg. 4.95 (*0-87157-562-0*) SamHar Pr.

Roucek, Joseph S. Balkan Politics: International Relations in No Man's Land. LC 75-106696. (Illus.). 298p. 1971. reprint ed. text ed. 59.75 (*0-8371-3370-X*, ROBP, Greenwood Pr) Greenwood.

— Capital Punishment. Rahmas, D. Steve, ed. (Topics of Our Times Ser.: No. 15). 32p. (YA). (gr. 7-12). 1975. lib. bdg. 4.95 (*0-87157-816-6*) SamHar Pr.

— Contemporary Roumania & Her Problems: A Study in Modern Nationalism. LC 74-135831. (Eastern Europe Collection Ser.). 1971. reprint ed. 30.95 (*0-405-02773-7*) Ayer.

— Sexual Attack & the Crime of Rape. rev. ed. Rahmas, D. Steve, ed. (Topics of Our Times Ser.: No. 13). 32p. 1980. lib. bdg. 4.95 (*0-87157-814-X*) SamHar Pr.

— Social Control for the Nineteen Eighties: A Handbook for Order in a Democratic Society. LC 77-91112. (Contributions in Sociology Ser.: No. 31). 386p. 1978. text ed. 65.00 (*0-313-20048-3*, RSC/, Greenwood Pr) Greenwood.

Roucek, Joseph S., ed. Challenge of Science Education. LC 77-128305. (Essay Index Reprint Ser.). 1977. 29.95 (*0-8369-2070-8*) Ayer.

— Juvenile Delinquency. LC 70-128306. (Essay Index Reprint Ser.). 1977. 26.95 (*0-8369-1848-7*) Ayer.

Roucek, Joseph S. & Belok, Michael V. The United States & the Persian Gulf: An ANVIL Original. LC 84-19366. (Anvil Ser.). 208p. (C). 1985. reprint ed. pap. text ed. 9.50 (*0-89874-574-8*) Krieger.

Roucek, Joseph S. & Eisenberg, Bernard, eds. America's Ethnic Politics. LC 81-986. (Contributions in Ethnic Studies: No. 5). (Illus.). x, 403p. 1982. text ed. 75.00 (*0-313-22024-7*, ROA/, Greenwood Pr) Greenwood.

Roucek, Joseph S. & Lottich, Kenneth. Behind the Iron Curtain. 631p. 1986. 10.00 (*0-317-52987-0*) Noontide.

Rouch, James. The Zone, No. 2: Blind Fire. 1985. pap. 2.50 (*0-8217-1588-7*) Zebra.

— The Zone, No. 4: Sky Strike. 224p. 1986. pap. 2.50 (*0-8217-1770-7*) Zebra.

— The Zone, No. 6: Plague Bomb. 224p. 1986. pap. 2.50 (*0-8217-1911-4*) Zebra.

— The Zone, No. 7: Killing Ground. 224p. 1988. pap. 2.50 (*0-8217-2494-0*) Zebra.

— Zone No. 8: Civilian Slaughter. 1989. pap. 2.95 (*0-8217-2633-1*) Zebra.

— Zone, No. 9: Body Count. 1990. pap. 2.95 (0-8217-3101-7) Zebra.
Rouchdy, Aleya. Nubians & the Nubian Language in Contemporary Egypt: A Case of Cultural & Linguistic Contact. LC 90-19286. (Studies in Semitic Languages & Linguistics: No. 15). xiv, 83p. 1991. 48.75 (90-04-09197-1) E J Brill.
— Variation on a Theme: Bilingualism, a Case Study. LC 76-47344. (Language Science Monographs: Vol. 17). 1977. pap. text ed. 8.00 (0-87750-209-9) Res Inst Inner Asian Studies.
Rouchdy, Aleya, ed. The Arabic Language in America. LC 91-30156. 345p. 1992. 44.95 (0-8143-2283-2); pap. 19.95 (0-8143-2284-0) Wayne St U Pr.
Roucoules. Terminologie Fondamentale en Odonto-Stomatologie et Lexique: Francais-Anglais, Anglais-Francais. 259p. (ENG & FRE.). 1977. 35.95 (0-8288-5524-2, M6492) Fr & Eur.
***Roucoules, Gil & Perlemuter, Leon.** Dictionnaire Pratique des Soins et du Soutien a Domicile. 1990. write for info. (0-7859-7829-1, 2-225-81308-6) Fr & Eur.
Roucoux, A. & Crommelinck, M. Physiological & Pathological Aspects of Eye Movements. 1982. lib. bdg. 164.50 (90-6193-730-2) Kluwer Ac.
Roud, Paul C. Making Miracles: Exploration Into the Dynamics of Self-Healing. 1990. pap. 9.95 (0-446-39118-2) Warner Bks.
***Roudane.** American Drama Since 1960. Date not set. 24.95 (0-8057-8954-5, Twayne) Macmillan.
Roudane, M. C. Public Issues, Private Tensions: Contemporary American Drama. LC 91-58147. (Georgia State Literary Studies: No. 9). 1993. 45.00 (0-404-63209-2) AMS Pr.
Roudane, Matthew C. Understanding Edward Albee. Bruccoli, Matthew, ed. (Understanding Contemporary American Literature Ser.). 233p. 1987. 34.95 (0-87249-502-7); pap. 14.95 (0-87249-503-5) U of SC Pr.
— Who's Afraid of Virginia Woolf? Necessary Fictions, Terrifying Realities. (Masterwork Studies: No. 34). 142p. 1989. text ed. 21.95 (0-8057-8059-9, MWS-34, Pub. by Royal Botanic Garden UK); pap. 12.95 (0-8057-8105-6, Pub. by Royal Botanic Garden UK) Macmillan.
***Roudane, Matthew C., ed.** Approaches to Teaching Miller's Death of a Salesman. LC 94-32025. (Approaches to Teaching World Literature Ser.: No. 52). 180p. (Orig.). 1995. lib. bdg. 37.50 (0-87352-727-5) Modern Lang.
— Approaches to Teaching Miller's Death of a Salesman. LC 94-32025. (Approaches to Teaching World Literature Ser.: No. 52). 180p. (Orig.). 1995. pap. 18.00 (0-87352-728-3) Modern Lang.
— Conversations with Arthur Miller. LC 87-17931. (Literary Conversations Ser.). 1987. 37.50 (0-87805-322-0); pap. 15.95 (0-87805-323-9) U Pr of Miss.
Roudiez, Leon S. French Fiction Revisited. LC 90-14081. 350p. (Orig.). 1991. pap. 14.95 (0-916583-73-2) Dalkey Arch.
Roudiez, Leon S., tr. see Kristeva, Julia.
Roudiez, Leon S., ed. see Kristeva, Julia.
Roudiez, Leon S., tr. see Kristeva, Julia.
Roudinesco, Elisabeth. Jacques Lacan & Co. A History of Psychoanalysis in France, 1925-1985. LC 89-78164. (Illus.). 816p. 1990. 45.00 (0-226-72997-4) U Ch Pr.
— Revolution & Madness: The Lives & Legends of Theroigne de Mericourt. Thom, Martin, tr. (Illus.). 296p. 1992. pap. 18.95 (0-86091-597-2, A9770, Pub. by Verso UK) Routledge Chapman & Hall.
— Theroigne de Mericourt: Melancholic Woman During the French Revolution. 1991. 34.95 (0-86091-324-4, A5346, Pub. by Verso UK) Routledge Chapman & Hall.
Roueche, Berton. Greener Grass & Some People Who Found It. LC 78-160927. (Biography Index Reprint Ser.). 1977. reprint ed. 19.95 (0-8369-8090-5) Ayer.
— The Medical Detectives. 448p. 1991. pap. 12.95 (0-452-26588-6, Plume-Truman Talley Bks) NAL-Dutton.
— River World. 246p. 11.95 (0-317-27106-7) Yankee Peddler.
— Sea to Shining Sea: People, Travel, Places. 288p. 1987. mass mkt. 4.50 (0-380-70265-7) Avon.
— What's Left. 10.95 (0-911660-21-6) Yankee Peddler.
***Roueche, Breton.** The Man Who Grew Two Breasts: And Other True Tales of Medical Detection. LC 94-42426. 1995. 22.95 (0-525-93934-2, Dutton-Truman Talley) NAL-Dutton.
Roueche, Charlotte, jt. ed. see Beaton, Roderick.
Roueche, John, et al. Underrepresentation & the Question of Diversity: Women & Minorities in Community Colleges. 300p. (C). 1991. text ed. 35.00 (0-87117-225-9) Am Assn Comm Coll.
Roueche, John E. & Baker, George, III. Access & Excellence. 1986. 27.50 (0-87117-162-7) Am Assn Comm Coll.
Roueche, John E. & Baker, George A., III. Profiling Excellence in America's Schools. Dees, Anne, ed. LC 86-70022. 177p. (Orig.). pap. text ed. 16.95 (0-87652-106-5, 021-00157) Am Assn Sch Admin.
Roueche, John E. & Kirk, R. Wade. Catching Up: Remedial Education. LC 73-1851. (Jossey-Bass Higher Education Ser.). 122p. reprint ed. 34.80 (0-8357-9299-4, 2013746) Bks Demand.
Roueche, John E. & Pitman, John C. A Modest Proposal: Students Can Learn. LC 73-184956. (Jossey-Bass Higher Education Ser.). 160p. reprint ed. 45.60 (0-8357-9336-2, 2013864) Bks Demand.
Roueche, John E., et al. Shared Vision: Transformational Leadership in America Community Colleges. 1989. 34.00 (0-87117-190-2, 1100) Am Assn Comm Coll.
Roueche, Nelda W. & Graves, Virginia H. Business Mathematics: A Collegiate Approach. 6th ed. 704p. 1993. text ed. write for info. (0-13-093683-9) P-H.
Rouede, Denise, jt. auth. see Rouede, Pierre.
Rouede, Pierre & Rouede, Denise. Dictionnaire Italien-Francais et Francais-Italien: Italian - French, French - Italian Dictionary. 1256p. (FRE & ITA.). 1970. 55.00 (0-8288-6526-4, M-6493) Fr & Eur.
***Rouet, Jean-Francois, et al, eds.** Hypertext & Cognition. 250p. 1996. text ed. 50.00 (0-8058-2143-0); pap. 25.00 (0-8058-2144-9) L Erlbaum Assocs.
Rouet, Marcel. Dictionnaire de la Culture Physique. 304p. (FRE.). 1975. 39.95 (0-8288-5846-2, M6494) Fr & Eur.
***Rouff, A. L.** Literatures of the American Indian. 1992. pap. 7.95 (0-7910-0370-1) Chelsea Hse.
Rouffet, Denis, jt. auth. see Morgan, Walter L.
Rouge, J. de. Geographie Ancienne de la Basse Egypte. (Illus.). 188p. reprint ed. lib. bdg. 38.50 (0-685-13354-0, Pub. by A M Hakkert SP) Coronet Bks.
***Rouge, Jacques-Marie.** Petit Dictionnaire du Parler de Touraine. 91p. (FRE.). 1991. pap. 32.95 (0-7859-8094-6, 2854432258) Fr & Eur.
Rouge, Janine, jt. auth. see Moureau, Magdeleine.
Rougeau, Darlene H. & Hudak, Deanna M. The Bride's Organizer. 1992. mass mkt. 4.99 (0-345-90224-6) Ballantine.
Rougemont, Claire. The National Dream Book. 188p. 1994. pap. 14.00 (0-89540-247-5, SB-247) Sun Pub.
Rougemont, Denis. The Devil's Share. LC 79-8118. reprint ed. 27.50 (0-404-18431-6) AMS Pr.
Rouger, ed. see Perrault, Charles.
Rouger, P., jt. ed. see Cartron, J. P.
Rouget, Gilbert. Music & Trance: A Theory of the Relations Between Music & Possession. Biebuyck, Brunhilde, tr. LC 85-1107. (Illus.). xx, 398p. 1985. pap. text ed. 19.95 (0-226-73006-9) U Ch Pr.
— Music & Trance: A Theory of the Relations Between Music & Possession. Biebuyck, Brunhilde, tr. LC 85-1107. (Illus.). xx, 398p. 1986. lib. bdg. 60.00 (0-226-73005-0) U Ch Pr.
***Rougeyron, Andre.** Agents for Escape: Inside the French Resistance, 1939-1945. McConnell, Marie-Antoinette, tr. (Illus.). 248p. (C). 1995. 24.95 (0-8071-2019-7) La State U Pr.
Rough, Jackie, ed. Miniversity: Ideas for Student Activities & Projects. 32p. (Orig.). 1989. pap. 7.00 (0-88210-237-0) Natl Assn Student.
Rough, Jackie, ed. see Rogers, Linda T.
Rough Notes Co. Staff. A Brief Outline. 1992. 25.00 (0-942326-05-9, 26199) Rough Notes.
Rough Notes Company Staff. Businessowners Policy Program Guide. 1991. 18.00 (1-56461-051-9, 30153) Rough Notes.
— Earn More-Work Less. 1991. 6.00 (0-942326-48-2, 29412) Rough Notes.
— Forum: Answers to Questions on Ins. Coverage. 1991. 20.00 (0-685-62462-5, 30161) Rough Notes.
— Guide to Liability Insurance. 1992. 29.50 (0-942326-33-4, 30164) Rough Notes.
Rough Notes Staff. The Letter Book. 1991. 27.50 (1-877723-77-0, 29008) Rough Notes.
Roughead, William. Classic Crimes: A Selection from Works of William Roughead. LC 74-10431. (Classics of Crime & Criminology Ser.). 449p. 1975. reprint ed. 18.25 (0-88355-198-5) Hyperion Conn.
Roughead, William, ed. see Galt, John.
***Roughgarden, Jonathan.** Anolis Lizards of the Caribbean: Ecology, Evolution, & Plate Tectonics. (Oxford Series in Ecology & Evolution). (Illus.). 224p. 1995. 59.95 (0-19-506731-2); pap. 29.95 (0-19-509605-3) OUP.
Roughgarden, Jonathan, et al, eds. Perspectives in Ecological Theory. 425p. 1989. text ed. 75.00 (0-691-08507-2); pap. text ed. 27.95 (0-691-08508-0) Princeton U Pr.
Roughgraden, Jonathan, jt. auth. see Erlich, Paul R.
Roughley, Alan. James Joyce & Critical Theory: An Introduction. LC 91-34377. 304p. (C). 1992. text ed. 44.50 (0-472-09489-0); pap. text ed. 16.95 (0-472-06489-4) U of Mich Pr.
Roughsey, Dick. Rainbow Serpent. (J). (ps-3). 1994. pap. 7.00 (0-207-17433-4, Pub. by Angus & Robertson AT) HarpC.
Roughton, Evelyn & Roughton, Tony. Classic Catfish: From the Crown at the Antique Mall. (Illus.). 160p. 1993. write for info. (0-9635571-0-6) Ant Mall & Crown.
***Roughton, James E.** Confined Space Entry: Complying with the Standard. 190p. (Orig.). 1994. per., pap. text ed. 75.00 (0-86587-406-9) Gov Insts.
Roughton, Roger, ed. Contemporary Poetry & Prose. (Illus.). 274p. 1968. 35.00 (0-7146-2106-4, Pub. by F Cass Pubs UK) Intl Spec Bk.
Roughton, Sheila. Breaking & Training Your Horse. (Illus.). 176p. 1994. 24.95 (0-7063-7123-2, Pub. by Ward Lock UK) Sterling.
— Eventing. (Riding School Ser.). (Illus.). 112p. 1993. 14.95 (0-7063-7125-9, Pub. by Ward Lock UK) Sterling.
Roughton, Tony, jt. auth. see Roughton, Evelyn.
***Rougier, Andre, et al, eds.** In Vitro Skin Toxicology Vol. 10: Irritation, Phototoxicity, Sensitization. (Alternative Methods in Toxicology Ser.: No. 10). (Illus.). 448p. 1994. 185.00 (0-913113-65-4) M Liebert.
Rougle, Charles, tr. see Akhundov, Murad D.
Rougle, Charles, tr. see Bogdanov, Alexander.
Rougle, Charles, tr. see Groys, Boris.
Rouhani, Fazullah. Black Tents. (Middle Eastern Ser.: No. 19). Orig. Title: Chadur-ha-ye Siah. (Illus.). 350p. (Orig.). 1986. pap. 17.00 (0-936665-06-8) Jahan Bk Co.
Rouhiainen, Veikko, jt. ed. see Malmn, Y.
Rouhiainen, Veikko, jt. ed. see Suokas, Jouko.
Rouhier, Kathleen M. Lifelong Reading, Bk. 2. (C). 1993. pap. text ed. 6.50 (0-13-016098-9) P-H.
— Lifelong Reading, Bk. 3. (C). 1994. pap. text ed. 6.50 (0-13-016106-3) P-H.
— Lifelong Reading, Bk. 4. 1994. pap. text ed. write for info. (0-13-532292-8) P-H.
— Lifelong Reading, No. 1: A Basic Course. 128p. 1993. pap. text ed. 6.50 (0-13-016080-6) P-H.
***Rouillac, Didier.** Cement Evaluation Logging Handbook. (Illus.). 172p. (C). 1994. pap. text ed. 76.00 (2-7108-0677-0) Technip.
Rouillard, Clarence D. The Turk in French History, Thought & Literature, 1520-1660. LC 71-180375. reprint ed. 67.50 (0-404-56321-X) AMS Pr.
Rouillard, Dom P. Diccionario de los Santos de Cada Dia. 2nd ed. 336p. (SPA.). 1989. pap. write for info. (0-7859-5125-3) Fr & Eur.
Rouillard, Dominique. Building the Slope: Hillside Houses 1920-1960. LC 85-72036. (Illus.). 176p. (Orig.). 1987. pap. 14.95 (0-931228-12-3) Arts & Arch.
Rouillard, Larrie. Goals & Goal Setting. Gerould, W. Philip, ed. (Fifty-Minute Ser.). 100p. (Orig.). 1993. pap. 8.95 (1-56052-183-X) Crisp Pubns.
Rouillard, Philippe. Diccionari dels Sants de Cada Dia. 442p. (SPA.). 1965. pap. 12.95 (0-7859-5852-5, 8428100616) Fr & Eur.
***Rouillard, Wendy W.** Barnaby's Faraway Land. LC 94-70710. (Illus.). 28p. (J). (ps-4). 1993. pap. 9.95 (0-9642836-0-3) Barnaby Books.
— Barnaby's Nantucket Coloring Book. (Illus.). 32p. (J). (ps-4). 1994. pap. 6.95 (0-9642836-1-1) Barnaby Books.
Rouiller, Gregoire, jt. ed. see Bovon, Francois.
Rouillon, F., jt. auth. see Montgomery, S. A.
Rouit, Huguette & Humbert, Jean-Marcel, eds. A la Recherche de la Memoire: Le Patrimoine Culturel Actes du Colloque Organise par la Section des Bibliotheques d'Art de l'IFLA, Paris, 16-19 Aout 1989. (IFLA Publication Ser.: Vol. 62). 330p. 1992. lib. bdg. 65.00 (3-598-21790-0) K G Saur.
Roukes, Nicholas. Acrylics Bold & New. (Illus.). 144p. 1990. pap. 18.95 (0-8230-0059-1, Watsn-Guptill) Watsn-Guptill.
— Art Synectics. (Illus.). 156p. (Orig.). 1982. pap. 18.25 (0-87192-151-0) Davis Mass.
— Design Synectics: Stimulating Creativity in Design. LC 88-70675. (Illus.). 224p. 1988. pap. 24.95 (0-87192-198-7) Davis Mass.
— Sculpture in Paper. LC 92-72329. (Illus.). 160p. 1993. 24.95 (0-87192-246-0) Davis Mass.
Roukis, George S. American Labor & the Conservative Republicans, 1946-1948: A Study in Economic & Political Conflict. LC 88-10266. (Modern American History Ser.). 392p. 1988. 20.00 (0-8240-4338-3) Garland.
Roukis, George S. & Montana, Patrick J., eds. Workforce Management in the Arabian Peninsula: Forces Affecting Development. LC 85-24772. (Contributions in Economics & Economic History Ser.: No. 67). 228p. 1986. text ed. 55.00 (0-313-24209-7) Greenwood.
Roukis, George S., jt. ed. see Montana, Patrick J.
Roukis, George S., et al, eds. Global Corporate Intelligence: Opportunities, Technologies & Threats in the 1990s. LC 89-27240. 352p. 1990. text ed. 75.00 (0-89930-220-3, RMC/, Quorum Bks) Greenwood.
Roulac, John, ed. see Hemptech Staff.
***Rouland, Norbert.** Legal Anthropology. Planel, Philippe G., tr. 364p. 1995. 45.00x (0-8047-1931-4) Stanford U Pr.
Rouland, Steve. Heywood-Wakefield Modern Furniture. 1994. pap. 18.95 (0-89145-624-4) Collector Bks.
Rouleau, Bill. Banker's Blood. 1995. pap. 10.95 (0-9627860-1-2) Lone Oak MN.
Roulet, Jean-Francois. Degradation of Dental Polymers. (Illus.). xiv, 228p. 1986. 158.50 (3-8055-4320-4) S Karger.
Roulet, Jean-Francois & Herder, Stefan. Bonded Ceramic Inlays. (Illus.). 103p. 1991. text ed. 62.00 (0-86715-244-3) Quint Pub Co.
Roulin-Maloney, A. C., ed. Fractography & Failure Mechanisms of Polymers & Composites. 548p. 1989. 153.00 (1-85166-296-0) Elsevier.
Roulston, D. J., jt. ed. see Kapoor, A. K.
Roulston, David J. Bipolar Semiconductor Devices. 1990. text ed. write for info. (0-07-054120-5) McGraw.
Roulston, Helen H., jt. auth. see Roulston, Robert.
Roulston, J. E. & Leonard, R. C. Serological Tumour Markers: An Introduction. LC 92-49368. (Illus.). 192p. 1993. text ed. 71.00 (0-443-04511-9) Churchill.
Roulston, Robert & Roulston, Helen H. The Winding Road to West Egg: The Artistic Development of F. Scott Fitzgerald. LC 94-20157. 1995. 37.50 (0-8387-5280-2) Bucknell U Pr.
Roulstone, Michael, ed. Bibliography of Museum & Art Gallery Publications & Audio Visual Aids in Great Britain & Ireland, 1979-80. 1980. lib. bdg. 100.00 (0-85964-097-3) Chadwyck-Healey.
Roult, Neil J. A Catalog of the Russian War Loan Posters of 1916 & 1917. (Illus.). 36p. (Orig.). 1993. pap. 12.50 (0-9639726-0-X) N J Roult.
Roumain, Jacques. Masters of the Dew. (Caribbean Writers Ser.). 192p. (C). 1978. pap. 10.95 (0-435-98745-3) Heinemann.
— When the Tom-Tom Beats: Selected Poems. Fungaroli, Joann, ed. LC 94-72476. 96p. (Orig.). Date not set. pap. 11.95 (0-9632363-8-5) Azul Edits.
Roumani, Judith, tr. see De Felice, Renzo.
Roumasset, James & Barr, Susan, eds. The Economics of Cooperation: East Asian Development & the Case for Pro-Market Intervention. 207p. (C). 1992. pap. text ed. 39.50 (0-8133-0454-7) Westview.
Roumeliotis, Michael D. A Study of Epistemology in Legal History. LC 94-594. (Series in Philosophy). 1994. write for info. (1-85628-697-5, Pub. by Avebury Pub UK) Ashgate Pub Co.
***Roumenin, Chavdar S., ed.** Solid State Magnetic Sensors. LC 94-26842. 1994. 148.50 (0-444-89401-2) Elsevier.
Rounce, J. F. Science for the Beauty Therapist. (C). 1983. 120.00 (0-85950-331-3, Pub. by S Thornes Pubs UK) St Mut.
Rounce, J. F., jt. auth. see Lowe, T. L.
Round, ed. see De Molina.
Round, ed. see Tirso de Molina.
***Round, David K., ed.** The Australian Trade Practices Act 1974: Proscriptions & Prescriptions for a More Competitive Economy. (Studies in Industrial Organization: Vol. 19). 1995. lib. bdg. 75.00 (0-7923-3228-8) Kluwer Ac.
Round, Dora, tr. see Capek, Karel.
Round, Elizabeth. Dying to Be Thin. (Pocketbooks Ser.). 1990. pap. 2.99 (0-7459-1952-9) Lion USA.
Round, F. E., ed. Algae & the Aquatic Environment: Contributions in Honour of J. W. G. Lund. (Illus.). 460p. 1988. lib. bdg. 106.00 (0-948737-06-9, Pub. by Biopress Ltd UK) Lubrecht & Cramer.
— Proceedings of the Ninth International Diatom Symposium. Bristol, 1986. (Illus.). 480p. 1988. lib. bdg. 219.50 (3-87429-275-4) Koeltz Sci Bks.
Round, F. E. & Chaoman, D. J., eds. Progress in Phycological Research, Vol. 7. (Illus.). 330p. 1990. lib. bdg. 104.00 (0-948737-13-1, Pub. by Biopress Ltd UK) Lubrecht & Cramer.
Round, F. E. & Chapman, D. J. Progress in Phycological Research, Vol 3. (Illus.). 387p. 1984. lib. bdg. 104.00 (0-685-44914-9, Pub. by Biopress Ltd UK) Lubrecht & Cramer.
— Progress in Phycological Research, Vol 5. (Illus.). 299p. 1987. lib. bdg. 104.00 (0-948737-03-4, Pub. by Biopress Ltd UK) Lubrecht & Cramer.
— Progress in Phycological Research, Vol. 6. (Illus.). 286p. 1988. lib. bdg. 104.00 (0-948737-07-7, Pub. by Biopress Ltd UK) Lubrecht & Cramer.
Round, F. E. & Chapman, D. J., eds. Progress. (Progress in Phycological Research Ser.: Vol. 8). (Illus.). 278p. 1992. lib. bdg. 152.50 (0-948737-17-4, Pub. by Biopress Ltd UK) Lubrecht & Cramer.
— Progress in Phycological Research, Vol. 4. (Illus.). 481p. 1986. lib. bdg. 104.00 (0-685-45078-3, Pub. by Biopress Ltd UK) Lubrecht & Cramer.
— Progress in Phycological Research, Vol. 9. (Illus.). 376p. 1993. lib. bdg. 129.95 (0-948737-19-0, Pub. by Biopress Ltd UK) Lubrecht & Cramer.
— Progress in Phycological Research, Vol. 10. (Illus.). 209p. 1994. lib. bdg. 175.00 (0-948737-20-4, Pub. by Biopress Ltd UK) Lubrecht & Cramer.
Round, F. E. & Chapman, David J. Progress in Phycological Research, Vol. 2. 1983. 192.50 (0-444-80502-8, I-355-83) Elsevier.
Round, F. E. & Chapman, David J., eds. Progress in Psychological Research, Vol. 1. 384p. 1982. 180.00 (0-444-80396-3) Elsevier.
Round, F. E., et al. Diatoms. (Illus.). (C). 1990. 285.00 (0-521-36318-7) Cambridge U Pr.
Round, G., jt. auth. see Tyler, J.
Round, G. F., ed. Freight Pipelines: A Selection of Papers Presented at the 7th International Symposium on Freight Pipelines, Wollongong, NSW, Australia, 6-8 July, 1992. LC 93-31563. 1993. write for info. (0-444-89944-8) Elsevier.
Round, George F., ed. Freight Pipelines. 50p. 1990. 110.00 (0-89116-886-9) Hemisp Pub.
Round, Gilbert F., ed. Solid-Liquid Flow Abstracts, 3 Vols, Vol. 1. 448p. 1969. text ed. 284.00 (0-677-40080-2) Gordon & Breach.
— Solid-Liquid Flow Abstracts, 3 Vols, Vol. 2. 460p. 1969. text ed. 275.00 (0-677-40090-X) Gordon & Breach.
— Solid-Liquid Flow Abstracts, 3 Vols, Vol. 3. 1064p. 1969. Set. text ed. 606.00 (0-677-40120-5); text ed. 141.00 (0-677-40100-0) Gordon & Breach.
Round, Graham. God Creates. (J). (ps). 1992. 5.99 (0-8423-0994-2) Tyndale.
— Jesus Saves. (J). (ps). 1992. 5.99 (0-8423-1873-9) Tyndale.
Round, Graham, jt. auth. see Tyler, Jenny.
Round, Graham, jt. auth. see Waters, Gaby.
***Round, J. H.** Feudal England: Historical Studies on the Eleventh & Twelfth Centuries. 587p. (Orig.). 1994. pap. text ed. 35.00 (0-7884-0033-9) Heritage Bk.
Round, J. M., jt. auth. see Jones, Dorothy A.
Round, Jeffery I., jt. ed. see Pyatt, Graham.
Round, Jeffrey I., ed. The European Economy in Perspective. 314p. 1994. 70.00 (0-7083-1240-3, Pub. by Univ Wales Pr UK) Paul & Co Pubs.
Round, Joan M., jt. ed. see Clayton, Barbara E.
Round, John H. Feudal England: Historical Studies on the Eleventh & Twelfth Centuries. LC 78-21143. 444p. 1979. reprint ed. text ed. 35.00 (0-313-21239-2, ROEN, Greenwood Pr) Greenwood.
Round, Nicholas. The Greatest Man Uncrowned: A Study of the Fall of Don Alvaro De Luna. (Series A: Vol. CXI). 267p. 1986. 53.00 (0-7293-0211-3, Pub. by Tamesis Bks Ltd UK) Boydell & Brewer.
Round, Robert H., ed. Advances in Plasmid Molecular Biology, Vol. 1. 1988. 73.25 (0-89232-877-0) Jai Pr.
Round Table Conference on Government Regulation of Accounting & Information (1979: University of Florida). Government Regulation of Accounting & Information. Abdel-Khalik, Rashad, ed. LC 79-26555. (University of Florida Accounting Ser.: No. 11). 328p. reprint ed. pap. 93.50 (0-8357-6712-4, 2035344) Bks Demand.
Roundhill, D. M. Photochemistry & Photophysics of Metal Complexes. (Modern Inorganic Chemistry Ser.). (Illus.). 355p. 1994. 89.50 (0-306-44694-4) Plenum.
Rounds, David. Celebrisi's Journey. 176p. (Orig.). 1976. pap. 4.00 (0-917512-14-6) Buddhist Text.

— Perfecting a Piece of the World: Arthur Imperatore & the Blue-Collar Aristocrats of A-P-A. LC 93-18731. (Illus.). 288p. 1993. 21.11 (*0-201-56794-6*) Addison-Wesley.

Rounds, Glen. The Cowboy Trade. (Illus.). (J). 1994. pap. 6.95 (*0-8234-1083-8*) Holiday.

— The Cowboy Trade. (Illus.). 96p. (J). (gr. 5 up). 1994. reprint ed. 15.95 (*0-8234-1075-7*) Holiday.

— Cowboys. LC 90-46501. (Illus.). 32p. (J). (ps-3). 1991. lib. bdg. 15.95 (*0-8234-0867-1*) Holiday.

— Cowboys. (J). 1993. pap. 5.95 (*0-8234-1061-7*) Holiday.

— Ol' Paul, The Mighty Logger. LC 75-22163. (Illus.). 96p. (J). (gr. 4-6). 1976. 15.95 (*0-8234-0269-X*); pap. 5.95 (*0-8234-0713-6*) Holiday.

— Old MacDonald Had a Farm. LC 88-24640. (Illus.). 32p. (J). (ps-3). 1989. lib. bdg. 15.95 (*0-8234-0739-X*); pap. 5.95 (*0-8234-0846-9*) Holiday.

— The Prairie Schooners. (Illus.). (J). 1994. pap. 6.95 (*0-8234-1087-0*) Holiday.

— The Prairie Schooners. (Illus.). 96p. (J). (gr. 5 up). 1994. reprint ed. 15.95 (*0-8234-1086-2*) Holiday.

— Sod Houses on the Great Plains. LC 94-27390. (J). (ps-3). 1995. lib. bdg. 15.95 (*0-8234-1162-1*) Holiday.

— The Treeless Plains. (Illus.). (J). 1994. pap. 6.95 (*0-8234-1085-4*) Holiday.

— The Treeless Plains. (Illus.). 96p. (J). (gr. 5 up). 1994. reprint ed. 15.95 (*0-8234-1084-6*) Holiday.

— Wild Horses. LC 92-73608. (Illus.). 32p. (J). (ps-3). 1993. lib. bdg. 14.95 (*0-8234-1019-6*) Holiday.

Rounds, Glen, illus. & adapt. The Blind Colt. LC 89-1779. 84p. (J). (gr. 3-6). 1989. reprint ed. 15.95 (*0-8234-0010-7*); reprint ed. pap. 5.95 (*0-8234-0758-6*) Holiday.

Rounds, Glen, illus. I Know an Old Lady Who Swallowed a Fly. LC 89-46244. 32p. (J). (ps-3). 1990. lib. bdg. 15.95 (*0-8234-0814-0*) Holiday.

— I Know an Old Lady Who Swallowed a Fly. LC 89-46244. 32p. (J). (ps-3). 1991. reprint ed. pap. 5.95 (*0-8234-0908-2*) Holiday.

— Soap! Soap! Don't Forget the Soap! An Appalachian Folktale. LC 92-11295. 32p. (ps-3). 1993. lib. bdg. 15.95 (*0-8234-1005-6*) Holiday.

Rounds, Glen, illus. & ret. The Three Billy Goats Gruff. LC 92-23951. 32p. (J). (ps-3). 1993. lib. bdg. 15.95 (*0-8234-1015-3*); pap. 5.95 (*0-8234-1136-2*) Holiday.

— Three Little Pigs & the Big Bad Wolf. LC 91-18173. 32p. (J). (ps-3). 1992. lib. bdg. 14.95 (*0-8234-0923-6*) Holiday.

Rounds, Glen, illus. & teller. Washday on Noah's Ark: A Story of Noah's Ark. LC 91-4507. 32p. (J). (ps-3). 1991. lib. bdg. 14.95 (*0-8234-0555-9*); pap. 5.95 (*0-8234-0880-9*) Holiday.

Rounds, H. L. Abstracts of Bristol County, Massachusetts Probate Records, 1687-1745. 392p. 1993. reprint ed. pap. 30.00 (*0-685-65682-9*, 5020) Clearfield Co.

— Abstracts of Bristol County, Massachusetts Probate Records, 1745-1762. 365p. 1988. 30.00 (*0-8063-1226-2*, 5022) Genealog Pub.

Rounds, Joseph B. The Time Was Right: A History of the Buffalo & Erie County Public Library, 1940-1975. Mahaney, Michael C., ed. (Illus.). x, 172p. 1986. 11.95 (*0-9615896-0-4*) Grosvenor Soc.

***Rounds, Michael F. & Miller, Nancy.** How to Sell Your Ideas & Inventions for Cash. 158p. (Orig.). 1991. pap. text ed. 79.95 (*0-9629944-1-3*) CPM Systems.

— Mechanics of Mail Order. (Orig.). 1992. pap. text ed. 40.00 (*0-9629944-2-1*) CPM Systems.

Rounds, Peter. Vital Records of Swansea, Massachusetts to 1850. 600p. 1992. 40.00 (*0-685-59452-1*) New Eng Hist.

Rounds, R. Stowell. Men & Birds in South America 1492 to 1900. LC 89-43069. (Illus.). 204p. 1989. pap. 14.95 (*0-936609-16-8*) QED Ft Bragg.

Rounds, Richard S. Basic Budgeting Practices for Librarians. 2nd ed. LC 93-47476. 180p. 1994. pap. 25.00 (*0-8389-0630-3*) ALA.

Rounds, Stewart A., jt. auth. see Bonn, Bernadine A.

Rounds, Stowell & O'Connell, Joseph J. How to Save Time & Taxes Preparing Fiduciary Income Tax Returns Federal & State. 2nd ed. (How to Save Time & Taxes Ser.). 1985. Looseleaf updates. ring bd. write for info. (*0-8205-1204-4*) Bender.

Roundtable Assoc. Staff. Managing in the Nineties: or The Truth Eventually Catches On. 96p. 1992. pap. text ed. 12.95 (*0-8403-7762-2*) Kendall-Hunt.

Roundtable Press Editors, ed. see Mead, Judson.

Roundtable Press Editors, ed. see Price, Bernie.

Roundtable Press Staff, ed. see Clapper, James.

Roundtable Press Staff, ed. see Cowan, Tom & Maguire, Jack.

Roundtable Press Staff, ed. see Demske, Dick.

Roundtable Press Staff, ed. see Dorazio, Ralph & Dorazio, Mary.

Roundtable Press Staff, ed. see U Bild Editors & Burch, Monte.

Roundtree, Derek, ed. Teaching Through Self-Instruction: How to Develop Open Learning Materials. rev. ed. 392p. 1990. pap. 33.50 (*0-89397-356-4*) Nichols Pub.

Roundy, Elizabeth, jt. auth. see Tree, Christina.

Roundy, Nancy L. & Mair, David. Strategies for Technical Communication. (C). 1987. text ed. 27.75 (*0-673-39293-7*) HarpCollege.

Rouner, Leroy S. The Long Way Home. LC 89-23363. 122p. 1989. 15.95 (*0-912083-40-9*, Langford Bks) Diamond Communications.

— Within Human Experience: The Philosophy of William Ernest Hocking. LC 71-75433. 395p. 1969. reprint ed. pap. 112.60 (*0-7837-4186-3*, 2059036) Bks Demand.

Rouner, Leroy S., ed. Celebrating Peace. LC 90-36381. (Boston University Studies in Philosophy & Religion: Vol. 11). 256p. (C). 1990. text ed. 31.95 (*0-268-00779-9*) U of Notre Dame Pr.

— The Changing Face of Friendship. LC 94-15462. (Boston University Studies in Philosphy & Religion: Vol. 15). (C). 1994. text ed. 29.95 (*0-268-00804-3*) U of Notre Dame Pr.

— Civil Religion & Political Theology. LC 86-11242. (Boston University Studies in Philosophy & Religion: Vol. 8). 240p. (C). 1986. text ed. 29.95x (*0-268-00757-8*) U of Notre Dame Pr.

— Civil Religion & Political Theology. LC 86-11242. (Boston University Studies in Philosophy & Religion: Vol. 8). (C). 1994. reprint ed. pap. text ed. 10.95 (*0-268-00806-X*) U of Notre Dame Pr.

— The Foundations of Ethics. LC 83-10280. (Boston University Studies in Philosophy & Religion). 232p. 1983. text ed. 29.95 (*0-268-00963-5*) U of Notre Dame Pr.

— Human Rights & the World's Religions. LC 88-17303. (Boston University Studies in Philosophy & Religion: Vol. 9). (C). 1988. text ed. 28.95x (*0-268-01086-2*) U of Notre Dame Pr.

— Human Rights & the World's Religions. LC 88-17303. (Boston University Studies in Philosophy & Religion: Vol. 9). (C). 1994. reprint ed. pap. text ed. 10.95 (*0-268-01107-9*) U of Notre Dame Pr.

— In Pursuit of Happiness. LC 95-16518. (Boston University Studies in Philosophy & Religion: Vol. 16). (C). 1995. text ed. 29.95 (*0-268-01174-5*) U of Notre Dame Pr.

— Meaning, Truth & God. LC 82-7023. (Boston University Studies in Philosophy & Religion: Vol. 3). 240p. (C). 1982. text ed. 29.95x (*0-268-01354-3*) U of Notre Dame Pr.

— Meaning, Truth & God. LC 82-7023. (Boston University Studies in Philosophy & Religion: Vol. 3). (C). 1994. reprint ed. pap. text ed. 10.95 (*0-268-01415-9*) U of Notre Dame Pr.

— On Community. LC 91-50573. (Boston University Studies in Philosophy & Religion: Vol. 12). (C). 1991. text ed. 29.95 (*0-268-01507-4*) U of Notre Dame Pr.

— On Freedom. LC 89-33164. (Boston University Studies in Philosophy & Religion: Vol. 10). (C). 1989. text ed. 29.95 (*0-268-01502-3*) U of Notre Dame Pr.

— On Nature. LC 84-7502. (Boston University Studies in Philosophy & Religion: Vol. 6). 224p. (C). 1984. text ed. 28.95 (*0-268-01499-X*) U of Notre Dame Pr.

— Religious Pluralism. LC 84-7431. (Boston University Studies in Philosophy & Religion: Vol. 5). 256p. (C). 1984. text ed. 31.95 (*0-268-01626-7*) U of Notre Dame Pr.

— Selves, People, & Persons: What Does It Mean to Be a Self? LC 92-53748. (Boston University Studies in Philosophy & Religion: Vol. 13). (C). 1992. text ed. 31.95 (*0-268-01747-6*) U of Notre Dame Pr.

Rouner, Leroy S. & Langford, James R., eds. Philosophy, Religion, & Contemporary Life: Essays on Perennial Problems. (C). 1995. pap. text ed. 10.95 (*0-268-03807-4*) U of Notre Dame Pr.

Rouner, Leroy S., jt. ed. see Dickie, Robert B.

Rouner, Leroy S., jt. ed. see Olson, Alan M.

Rounick, Jack A. Pennsylvania Matrimonial Practice, 4 vols. LC 81-85429. (Pennsylvania Practice Systems Library). 1982. ring bd. 400.00 (*0-317-00357-7*) Lawyers Cooperative.

— Pennsylvania Matrimonial Practice, 4 vols. suppl. ed. LC 81-85429. (Pennsylvania Practice Systems Library). 1993. Suppl. 1993. 175.00 (*0-317-03160-0*) Lawyers Cooperative.

***Rounsefell, Tony.** The Donnington Diaries. 336p. 1995. 19.00 (*0-8059-3596-7*) Dorrance.

***Rounsevell, Mark D. & Loveland, Peter J., eds.** Soil Responses to Climate Change. LC 94-35237. (NATO ASI, Series I, Global Environmental Change: Vol. 23). 1994. write for info. (*0-387-58373-4*) Spr-Verlag.

Rounseville, A. W. The Poetry of the Orient. 1973. 59.95 (*0-8490-0865-4*) Gordon Pr.

Rountree. The Country of Marriage. Date not set. 22.00 (*0-06-250842-3*, HarpT); pap. 11.00 (*0-06-250843-1*, HarpT) HarpC.

Rountree, Cathleen. Coming into Our Fullness: On Women Turning Forty. (Illus.). 200p. (Orig.). 1991. pap. 16.95 (*0-89594-517-7*) Crossing Pr.

— 50 Ways to Meet Your Lover. LC 94-27620. 1994. pap. 9.00 (*0-06-251188-2*) Harper SF.

— On Women Turning Fifty: Celebrating Mid-Life Discoveries. LC 92-54617. 224p. 1994. reprint ed. pap. 14.00 (*0-06-250731-1*) Harper SF.

Rountree, Charlotte. Seoul Sketches: A Visual Sketch of the Yi Dynasty. (Illus.). 84p. 1985. 22.50 (*0-930878-43-4*) Hollym Intl.

Rountree, Charlotte, jt. auth. see Ryan, Joyce.

Rountree, Estelle & Halverstadt, Hugh F., eds. Sometimes They Cry: A Study-Action Book. rev. ed. LC 72-129096. (Illus.). 144p. reprint ed. pap. 41.10 (*0-7837-1957-4*, 2042174) Bks Demand.

Rountree, George. A Govan Childhood. 250p. (C). 1989. pap. text ed. 30.00 (*0-85976-385-4*, Pub. by J Donald) St Mut.

Rountree, Helen C. Pocahontas's People: The Powhatan Indians of Virginia Through Four Centuries. LC 88-27905. (Civilization of the American Indian Ser.: Vol. 196). (Illus.). 416p. 1990. 29.95 (*0-8061-2280-3*) U of Okla Pr.

— The Powhatan Indians of Virginia: Their Traditional Culture. LC 90-33598. (Civilization of the American Indian Ser.: Vol. 193). (Illus.). 232p. 1992. pap. 12.95 (*0-8061-2455-5*) U of Okla Pr.

Rountree, Helen C., ed. Powhatan Foreign Relations, 1500-1722. LC 92-21942. (Illus.). 328p. 1993. 29.95 (*0-8139-1409-4*) U Pr of Va.

Rountree, Melissa. Jasper Johns: Collecting Prints. (Illus.). 32p. (Orig.). 1993. pap. 15.00 (*0-914489-13-5*) Univ Miss-KS Art.

Rountree, Susan H. Christmas Decorations from Williamsburg. LC 91-24638. (Illus.). 144p. 1991. 19.95 (*0-87935-085-7*) Colonial Williamsburg.

— Entertaining Ideas from Williamsburg. LC 93-23178. (Illus.). 164p. 1993. 19.95 (*0-87935-095-4*) Colonial Williamsburg.

Rountree, Thomas J. Emma Notes. 1967. pap. 3.50 (*0-8220-0434-8*) Cliffs.

— Last of the Mohicans Notes. 1965. pap. 3.75 (*0-8220-0717-7*) Cliffs.

— This Mighty Sum of Things: Wordsworth's Theme of Benevolent Necessity. LC 65-12244. reprint ed. 27.00 (*0-8357-9621-3*, 2103214) Bks Demand.

Rountree, Thomas J., ed. Critics on Emerson. LC 73-77552. (Readings in Literary Criticism Ser.: No. 20). 128p. 1973. 10.95 (*0-87024-237-7*) U of Miami Pr.

— Critics on Hawthorne. LC 78-159297. (Readings in Literary Criticism Ser.: No. 16). 1972. 10.95 (*0-87024-209-1*) U of Miami Pr.

— Critics on Melville. LC 74-143456. (Readings in Literary Criticism Ser.: No. 12). 1972. 10.95 (*0-87024-193-1*) U of Miami Pr.

***Roupp, Heidi, ed.** Teaching World History: A Resource Book. (Sources & Studies in World History Ser.). 500p. 1995. 55.00 (*1-56324-419-5*) M E Sharpe.

— Teaching World History: A Resource Book. (Sources & Studies in World History Ser.). 500p. 1995. pap. text ed. 20.00 (*1-56324-420-9*) M E Sharpe.

Rouquerol, J. & Sing, K. S., eds. Adsorption at the Gas-Solid Interface: Proceedings of the International Symposium at Auxen - Provence, Sept. 1981. (Studies in Surface Science & Catalysis: Vol. 10). 512p. 1982. 131.00 (*0-444-42087-8*) Elsevier.

***Rouquerol, J., et al, eds.** Characterization of Porous Solids III: Proceedings of the IUPAC Symposium (COPS III), Marseille, France, May 9-12, 1993. LC 94-27695. 1994. write for info. (*0-444-81491-4*) Elsevier.

Rouquette, Jean. Litterature D'Oc. 125p. (FRE.). 1968. 9.95 (*0-8288-7417-4*) Fr & Eur.

***Rouquette, Max.** Green Paradise. MacGregor, William B., tr. LC 95-1139. 1995. 39.50 (*0-472-09543-9*); pap. 18.95 (*0-472-06543-2*) U of Mich Pr.

Rouquie, Alain. The Military & the State in Latin America. Sigmund, Paul E., tr. 520p. 1987. 55.00 (*0-520-05559-4*); pap. 14.00 (*0-520-06664-2*) U CA Pr.

Rouquier, Magali. Vocabulaire d'Ancien Francais. 127p. (FRE.). 1992. pap. 22.95 (*0-7859-0969-9*, 2091906549) Fr & Eur.

***Roure, F.** Peri-Tethyan Platforms: Proceedings of the IFP/Peritethys Research Conference, Arles, France, 1993. (Illus.). 294p. 1994. pap. text ed. 96.00 (*2-7108-0679-7*) Technip.

Rourk, et al. Guidelines for Occupational Therapy Services in School Systems. 2nd ed. 176p. (C). 1989. ring bd. 50.00 (*0-910317-51-8*) Am Occup Therapy.

Rourke, A. Decorating Your Room. (Looking Good Ser.: Set 2). (Illus.). 32p. (J). (gr. 5 up). 1989. lib. bdg. 15.94 (*0-86625-286-X*) Rourke Corp.

Rourke, Arlene C. Los Manos y los Pies. LC 92-5661. (Buena Presencia Ser.). (ENG & SPA.). (YA). 1992. 15.94 (*0-86625-290-8*); 11.95 (*0-685-59319-3*) Rourke Pubns.

Rourke, Byron P. Nonverbal Learning Disabilities: The Syndrome & the Model. LC 89-1958. 253p. 1989. lib. bdg. 32.00 (*0-89862-378-2*) Guilford Pr.

— Syndrome of Nonverbal Learning Disabilities: Neurodevelopmental Manifestations. LC 95-3981. 1995. lib. bdg. 45.00 (*0-89862-155-0*) Guilford Pr.

Rourke, Byron P., ed. Neuropsychological Validation of Learning Disability Types. LC 90-3912. 398p. 1990. lib. bdg. 42.00 (*0-89862-446-0*) Guilford Pr.

— Neuropsychology of Learning Disabilities: Essentials of Subtype Analysis. LC 84-10860. 351p. 1985. lib. bdg. 40.00 (*0-89862-644-7*) Guilford Pr.

Rourke, Byron P. & Del Dotto, Jerel E. Learning Disabilities: A Neuropsychological Perspective. (Developmental Clinical Psychology & Psychiatry Ser.: Vol. 30). 160p. (C). 1994. text ed. 37.00 (*0-8039-5353-4*); pap. text ed. 16.95 (*0-8039-5354-2*) Sage.

Rourke, Byron P. & Fuerst, Darren R. Learning Disabilities & Psychosocial Functioning: A Neuropsychological Perspective. LC 91-16388. 198p. 1991. lib. bdg. 25.00 (*0-89862-767-2*) Guilford Pr.

Rourke, Byron P., jt. ed. see Adams, Kenneth.

Rourke, Byron P., et al. Child Neuropsychology: An Introduction to Theory, Research, & Clinical Practice. LC 83-1657. 389p. 1983. lib. bdg. 50.00 (*0-89862-620-X*) Guilford Pr.

— Child Neuropsychology: An Introduction to Theory, Research, & Clinical Practice. LC 83-1657. 389p. 1991. reprint ed. pap. text ed. 25.00 (*0-89862-468-1*) Guilford Pr.

— Neuropsychological Assessment of Children: A Treatment-Oriented Approach. LC 86-211316. 285p. 1986. lib. bdg. 35.00 (*0-89862-676-5*) Guilford Pr.

Rourke, Byron P., et al, eds. Methodological & Biostatistical Foundations of Clinical Neuropsychology. 260p. 1992. 100.00 (*90-265-1165-5*, Pub. by Swets Pub Serv NE); pap. 39.95 (*90-265-1245-7*, Pub. by Swets Pub Serv NE) Taylor & Francis.

Rourke, C. P. & Sanderson, B. J. Introduction to Piecewise-Linear Topology. (Springer Study Edition Ser.). (Illus.). 130p. 1982. pap. 35.00 (*0-387-11102-6*) Spr-Verlag.

Rourke, Constance. Aududon. 1993. reprint ed. lib. bdg. 89.00 (*0-7812-5826-X*) Rprt Serv.

— Charles Sheeler: Artist in the American Tradition. LC 70-87603. (Library of American Art Ser.). 1969. reprint ed. lib. bdg. 32.50 (*0-306-71634-8*) Da Capo.

Rourke, Constance & Lhamon, W. T. American Humor: A Study of the National Character. rev. ed. LC 85-26428. 376p. 1986. reprint ed. pap. 15.95 (*0-8130-0837-9*) U Press Fla.

Rourke, Constance M. Troupers of the Gold Coast: or the Rise of Lotta Crabtree. 1992. reprint ed. lib. bdg. 75.00 (*0-7812-5082-X*) Rprt Serv.

Rourke, Dennis J. The American Home Builder & the Housing Industry: A Textbook in Residential Building Management. 2nd ed. (Illus.). 405p. 1994. 70.00 (*0-9641670-0-X*) Mgmt Practice.

Rourke, Francis E. Bureaucracy & Foreign Policy. LC 73-186516. (School of Advanced International Studies: No. 17). 89p. 1972. 12.50 (*0-8018-1394-8*) Johns Hopkins.

— Bureaucracy, Politics & Public Policy. 3rd ed. (C). 1987. pap. text ed. 15.50 (*0-673-39475-1*) HarpCollege.

***Rourke, John.** International Politics on the World Stage. 5th ed. 688p. 1995. 32.95 (*1-56134-382-X*) Dushkin Pub.

Rourke, John T. Making Foreign Policy: U. S., Soviet Union, & China. 336p. (C). 1990. pap. 23.95 (*0-534-12582-4*) Intl Thomson.

Rourke, John T., ed. Taking Sides: Clashing Views on Controversial Issues in World Politics. 6th ed. LC 94-33209. (Illus.). 408p. 1995. pap. text ed. 13.95 (*1-56134-324-2*) Dushkin Pub.

Rourke, John T., et al. Direct Democracy & International Politics: Deciding International Issues Through Referendums. LC 92-8773. 202p. 1992. lib. bdg. 37.00 (*1-55587-263-8*) Lynne Rienner.

— Making American Foreign Policy. LC 93-73227. (Illus.). 512p. (Orig.). (C). 1994. pap. text ed. 34.95 (*1-56134-116-9*) Dushkin Pub.

Rourke, Norman, ed. I Saw the Elephant: The Civil War of George Baily Mclelan. (Illus.). 64p. (C). 1995. pap. text ed. 6.95 (*0-942597-85-0*, Burd St Pr) White Mane Pub.

Rourke, Richard W. Cape Cod: An Artist's Sketchbook. (Illus.). 48p. 1992. pap. 8.50 (*1-884824-01-3*) Tryon Pubng.

— Cape Cod & the Islands: An Artist's Sketchbook. rev. ed. (Illus.). 52p. 1994. pap. 8.50 (*1-884824-08-0*) Tryon Pubng.

Rous, John. Diary of John Rous, Incumbent of Santon Downham, Suffolk, from 1625 to 1642. Green, Mary A., ed. (Camden Society, London. Publications, First Ser.: No. 66). reprint ed. 35.00 (*0-404-50166-4*) AMS Pr.

Rous, S. N. Understanding Urology. (Perspectives in Medicine Ser.: No. 5). (Illus.). 1973. 15.25 (*3-8055-0000-9*) S Karger.

Rous, Stephen. Prostate Book. 288p. 1995. pap. 12.00 (*0-393-30864-2*) Norton.

Rous, Stephen N. The Prostate Book: Sound Advice on Symptoms & Treatment. (Illus.). 256p. 1992. 22.95 (*0-393-03387-2*) Norton.

— Stone Disease: Diagnosis & Management. LC 79-3666. 448p. 1987. text ed. 94.00 (*0-8089-1873-7*, Grune) Saunders.

— Urology Annual, 1987, Vol. 1. (Illus.). 336p. (C). 1987. boxed 80.00 (*0-8385-9318-6*, A9318-5) Appleton & Lange.

— Urology Annual, 1988, Vol. 2. (Illus.). 304p. (C). 1988. boxed 80.00 (*0-8385-9319-4*, A9319-3) Appleton & Lange.

— Urology Annual, 1989, Vol. 3. (Illus.). 356p. 1989. boxed 80.00 (*0-8385-9320-8*, A9320-1) Appleton & Lange.

— Urology Annual, 1990, Vol. 4. (Illus.). 300p. 1989. text ed. 80.00 (*0-8385-9322-4*, A9322-7) Appleton & Lange.

— Urology Annual, 1991, Vol. 5. (Illus.). 288p. (C). 1991. boxed 80.00 (*0-8385-9323-2*, A9323-5) Appleton & Lange.

***Rous, Stephen N., ed.** Urology Annual 1995, Vol. 9. 300p. (C). 1995. 85.00 (*0-393-71022-X*, Norton Medical Bks) Norton.

Rous, Stephen N., jt. auth. see Zobel, Hiller B.

Rous, W. E. & Reid, Brian H., eds. The Science of War: Back to First Principles. LC 92-15504. (Operational Level of War Ser.). 208p. 1993. 59.95 (*0-415-07995-0*, B0307) Routledge.

Rousar, I., et al. Electrochemical Engineering I-II, 2 vols., Set. (Chemical Engineering Monographs: No. 21 A&B). 1986. 140.75 (*0-444-99562-5*) Elsevier.

— Electrochemical Engineering I-II, 2 vols., Vol. 1. (Chemical Engineering Monographs: No. 21 A&B). 350p. 1986. 115.50 (*0-444-99563-3*) Elsevier.

— Electrochemical Engineering I-II, 2 vols., Vol. 2. (Chemical Engineering Monographs: No. 21 A&B). 280p. 1986. 97.50 (*0-444-99548-X*) Elsevier.

Rouse. Human Problem Solving in Failure Situations. write for info. (*0-444-00876-4*) Elsevier.

Rouse & Cardoso, Ersillo. Dictionnaire Portugais. 1820p. (SPA.). (J). (gr. 9-12). 1963. 49.95 (*0-685-57714-7*, M-6495) Fr & Eur.

Rouse, jt. auth. see Scheiman.

Rouse, Anne. Sunset Grill: Poems. 64p. 1993. pap. 12.95 (*1-85224-219-1*, Pub. by Bloodaxe Bks UK) Dufour.

Rouse, Barry T. & Lopez, Carlos, eds. Immunobiology of Herpes Simplex Virus Infection. 176p. 1984. 144.00 (*0-8493-6037-4*, RC147, CRC Reprint) Franklin.

Rouse, Blair. Ellen Glasgow. LC 62-16821. (Twayne's United States Authors Ser.). 1962. lib. bdg. 17.95 (*0-89197-745-7*); pap. text ed. 4.95 (*0-8290-0010-0*) Irvington.

Rouse, C. A., ed. Progress in High Temperature Physics & Chemistry, 5 vols, Vol. 1. 1967. 104.00 (*0-08-012123-3*, Pub. by Pergamon Repr UK) Franklin.

— Progress in High Temperature Physics & Chemistry, 5 vols, Vol. 2. 1973. 83.00 (*0-08-012640-5*, Pub. by Pergamon Repr UK) Franklin.

— Progress in High Temperature Physics & Chemistry, 5 vols, Vol. 3. 1973. 142.00 (*0-08-013959-0*, Pub. by Pergamon Repr UK) Franklin.

— Progress in High Temperature Physics & Chemistry, 5 vols, Vol. 4. 1973. 88.00 (0-08-016439-0, Pub. by Pergamon Repr UK) Franklin.

— Progress in High Temperature Physics & Chemistry, 5 vols, Vol. 5. 1973. 98.00 (0-08-017240-7, Pub. by Pergamon Repr UK) Franklin.

Rouse, Charles E. Philosophy As Method & Process. 104p. (Orig.). 1990. pap. 10.00 (0-9626282-0-4) C E Rouse.

Rouse, E. Clive, ed. Medieval Wall Paintings. 80p. 1989. pap. 25.00 (0-7478-0144-4, Pub. by Shire UK) St Mut.

Rouse, Elizabeth. Understanding Fashion. (Illus.). 256p. (C). 1989. pap. text ed. 24.95 (0-632-01891-7) Blackwell Sci.

Rouse, Geraldine & Birch, Carol. Socialization & Sex Education. (C). 1991. pap. text ed. 99.00 (1-56304-031-X) J Stanfield.

***Rouse, Harvey.** Letters of Endearment & Tranquility from Beyond the Veil. 1995. 9.95 (0-8062-5380-0) Carlton.

Rouse, Hunter. Elementary Mechanics of Fluids. LC 78-57159. (Illus.). 1978. reprint ed. pap. 7.95 (0-486-63699-2) Dover.

Rouse, Irving. Prehistory in Haiti: A Study in Method. LC 64-21834. (Yale University Publications in Anthropology Reprints Ser.: No. 21). 202p. 1964. pap. 20.00x (0-87536-504-3) HRAFP.

— A Survey of Indian River Archeology, Florida. LC 76-43813. (Yale Univ. Publications in Anthropology: No. 45). 376p. reprint ed. 52.50 (0-404-15668-1) AMS Pr.

— The Tainos: Rise & Decline of the People Who Greeted Columbus. (Illus.). 232p. (C). 1992. text ed. 27.50 (0-300-05181-6) Yale U Pr.

— The Tainos: Rise & Decline of the People Who Greeted Columbus. (Illus.). 232p. (C). 1993. pap. 12.00 (0-300-05696-6) Yale U Pr.

Rouse, Irving & Alegria, Ricardo E. Excavations at Maria de la Cruz Cave & Hacienda Grande Village Site, Loiza, Puerto Rico. (Publications in Anthropology: No. 80). (Illus.). viii, 133p. (Orig.). 1990. pap. 13.50 (0-913516-16-3) Yale U Anthro.

Rouse, Jacqueline A. Lugenia Burns Hope: Black Southern Reformer. (Brown Thrasher Bks.). (Illus.). 198p. 1992. reprint ed. pap. 14.95 (0-8203-1464-1) U of Ga Pr.

Rouse, John. Brecht & the West German Theatre: The Practice & Politics of Interpretation. Brockett, Oscar, ed. LC 89-20165. (Theatre & Dramatic Studies: No. 62). 236p. reprint ed. 67.00 (0-8357-2006-3, 2070761) Bks Demand.

— Provocations: The Story of Mrs. M. 103p. (Orig.). 1993. pap. text ed. 11.95 (0-8141-3794-6) NCTE.

Rouse, John, Jr., jt. auth. see Berkley, George E.

Rouse, John D. Garnet. (Gem Bks.). (Illus.). 208p. 1986. text ed. 39.95 (0-408-01534-9) Buttrwrth-Heinemann.

***Rouse, Joseph.** Engaging Science: How to Understand Its Practices Philosophically. 280p. 1996. 39.95x (0-8014-3193-X); pap. 16.95 (0-8014-8289-5) Cornell U Pr.

— Knowledge & Power: Toward a Political Philosophy of Science. LC 87-47604. 304p. (C). 1987. 36.50 (0-8014-1959-X); pap. 13.95 (0-8014-9713-2) Cornell U Pr.

Rouse, Kate. Classic Cameras. 1994. 10.98 (0-7858-0177-4) Bk Sales Inc.

— Classic Cameras. 1994. 10.98 (0-7858-0152-9) Bk Sales Inc.

Rouse, Ken. Putting Money in Its Place. 164p. 1993. per. 14.95 (0-8403-9115-3) Kendall-Hunt.

Rouse, Linda P. You Are Not Alone, 4 bks., Set. 2nd abr. ed. Date not set. 11.95 (0-685-72099-3) Learning Pubns.

— You Are Not Alone: A Guide for Battered Women. abr. ed. LC 83-83182. 136p. 1986. pap. write for info. (0-918452-70-8) Learning Pubns.

— You Are Not Alone: A Guide for Battered Women. 2nd unabridged ed. 136p. Date not set. pap. 12.95 (1-55691-088-6) Learning Pubns.

Rouse, Mary, ed. see Hu Shih.

Rouse, Mary A. & Rouse, Richard H. Authentic Witnesses: Approaches to Medieval Texts & Manuscripts. LC 89-40389. (Mediaeval Studies: Vol. 27). (C). 1993. pap. text ed. 29.95 (0-268-00623-7) U of Notre Dame Pr.

Rouse, Mary A., jt. ed. see Rouse, Richard H.

Rouse, Michael. Coastal Resorts of East Anglia. 192p. (C). 1988. pap. 70.00 (0-86138-010-X, Pub. by T Dalton UK) St Mut.

Rouse, Michael W., jt. auth. see Caloroso, Elizabeth.

Rouse, Michael W., jt. auth. see Scheiman, Mitchell M.

Rouse, Park, Jr. Below the James Lies Dixie. (Illus.). 1968. pap. 7.50 (0-87517-048-X) Dietz.

Rouse, Park. Cows on the Campus. 1987. reprint ed. 8.50 (0-87517-047-1) Dietz.

Rouse, Parke. The Good Old Days in Hampton & Newport News. 1986. pap. 14.95 (0-87517-056-0) Dietz.

***Rouse, Parke, Jr.** The Great Wagon Road. 1992. pap. 13.95 (0-87517-065-X) Dietz.

— A House for a President. 264p. 1983. 14.95 (0-87517-050-1) Dietz.

— The James - Where a Nation Began. 1991. pap. 17.95 (0-87517-062-5) Dietz.

Rouse, Parke. James Blair of Virginia. LC 70-159559. 368p. reprint ed. pap. 104.90 (0-8357-4420-5, 2037240) Bks Demand.

Rouse, Parke, Jr. Living by Design: Leslie Cheek & the Arts. LC 85-73016. (Illus.). 197p. 1985. 29.95 (0-9615670-0-7) Soc Alu Wm.

— Remembering Williamsburg. 1989. pap. 15.95 (0-87517-059-5) Dietz.

Rouse, Parke, Jr., ed. see West, George B.

Rouse, R., ed. Bankers' Lending Techniques. (C). 1989. 125.00 (0-85297-228-8, Pub. by Inst Bankers UK) St Mut.

Rouse, Richard & Rouse, Susan. The Last Week. 1985. 1.00 (0-89536-726-2, 5810) CSS OH.

Rouse, Richard H. & Rouse, Mary A., eds. Authentic Witnesses: Approaches to Medieval Texts & Manuscripts. LC 89-40389. (Mediaeval Studies: No. 27). (C). 1990. text ed. 59.95 (0-268-00622-9) U of Notre Dame Pr.

Rouse, Richard H., ed. see Ferrari, Mirella.

Rouse, Richard H., jt. auth. see Rouse, Mary A.

Rouse, Richard O., jt. auth. see Schwartz, Fred.

Rouse, Roscoe, Jr. A History of the Oklahoma State University Library. (Centennial Histories Ser.). (Illus.). 304p. 1992. 14.95 (0-914956-49-3) Okla State Univ Pr.

Rouse, Susan, jt. auth. see Rouse, Richard.

Rouse, W. D., jt. tr. see Bendall, Cecil.

Rouse, W. H., jt. ed. see Bendall, Cecil.

Rouse, W. H., tr. see Xenophon.

Rouse, William. Best Laid Plans. LC 94-16433. 228p. 1994. write for info. (0-13-300054-0) P-H.

Rouse, William B. Catalysts for Change: Concepts & Principles for Enabling Innovation. (Series in Systems Engineering). 272p. 1993. text ed. 69.95 (0-471-59196-3, Wiley-Interscience) Wiley.

— Design for Success: A Human-Centered Approach to Designing Successful Products & Systems. (Systems Engineering Ser.). 287p. 1991. text ed. 74.95 (0-471-52483-2) Wiley.

— Strategies for Innovation: Creating Successful Products, Systems, & Organizations. (Series in Systems Engineering). 272p. 1992. text ed. 74.95 (0-471-55904-0) Wiley.

— Systems Engineering Models of Human Machine Interactions. (Systems Science & Engineering Ser.: Vol. 6). 152p. 1980. 60.25 (0-444-00366-5) P-H.

Rouse, William B., ed. Advances in Man-Machine Systems Research, Vol. 1. 1984. 73.25 (0-89232-404-X) Jai Pr.

— Advances in Man-Machine Systems Research, Vol. 2. 1985. 73.25 (0-89232-466-X) Jai Pr.

— Advances in Man-Machine Systems Research, Vol. 3. 1987. 73.25 (0-89232-659-X) Jai Pr.

— Advances in Man-Machine Systems Research, Vol. 4. 1988. 73.25 (0-89232-753-7) Jai Pr.

Rouse, William B., jt. ed. see Rasmussen, Jens.

Rouse, William H. Gods, Heroes & Men of Ancient Greece. 192p. (J). (gr. 5). 1957. pap. 4.50 (0-451-62669-9, Ment) NAL-Dutton.

— Gods, Heroes, & Men of Ancient Greece. 1989. pap. 3.95 (0-451-62618-4) NAL-Dutton.

— Greek Votive Offerings: An Essay in the History of Greek Religion. LC 75-10654. (Ancient Religion & Mythology Ser.). (Illus.). 1976. reprint ed. 52.95 (0-405-07262-7) Ayer.

— Greek Votive Offerings: An Essay in the History of Greek Religion. xviii, 463p. 1976. reprint ed. 96.20 (3-487-05828-6, Pub. by Georg Olms GW) Lubrecht & Cramer.

Rouse, William H., tr. Great Dialogues of Plato. 1956. pap. 4.95 (0-451-62522-6, ME2287, Ment) NAL-Dutton.

Rouse, William H., tr. see Homer.

Rouseff, jt. auth. see Ting.

***Rouseff, Russell L. & Leahy, Margaret M., eds.** Fruit Flavors: Biogenesis, Characterization & Authentication. LC 95-8847. (Symposium Ser.: Vol. 596). 1995. write for info. (0-8412-3227-X) Am Chemical.

Rouself, R., ed. Bitterness in Foods & Beverages. (Developments in Food Science Ser.: No. 25). 356p. 1990. 133.50 (0-444-88175-1) Elsevier.

Rousell, Chris. Wilton. (Towns & Villages of England Ser.). (Illus.). (Orig.). 1993. pap. write for info. (0-7509-0464-X) A Sutton Pub.

Rouselle, Melinda M., anno. Sanctuary. LC 89-33872. (William Faulkner Annotations to Novels Ser.). 148p. 1989. 15.00 (0-8240-4232-8) Garland.

Roush, F. W., jt. auth. see Kim, Hang KI.

Roush, George, et al. Cancer Risks & Incidence Trends: The Connecticut Perspective. (Illus.). 435p. 1987. 154.00 (0-89116-412-X) Hemisp Pub.

Roush, Jackson & Matkin, Noel, eds. Infants & Toddlers with Hearing Loss: Family Centered Assessment & Intervention. 360p. 1994. 38.00 (0-912752-28-9) York Pr.

Roush, John H., Jr. Enjoying Fishing Lake Tahoe: The Truckee River & Pyramid Lake. LC 87-70065. (Illus.). 375p. 1987. 21.00 (0-685-19091-9) J H Roush.

— Management Audits of Branch Claims Offices of National Insurance Companies. LC 74-31546. 197p. 1975. 17.00 (0-9600830-1-4); pap. 15.00 (0-685-02680-9) J H Roush.

— Management Audits of Subordinate Claims Offices of National Insurance Companies. LC 74-31546. 197p. 17.00 (0-686-70274-3) J H Roush.

***Roush, John H., Jr., ed. & illus.** World War II Reminiscences. 336p. 1995. pap. write for info. (0-9600830-3-0) J H Roush.

***Roush, Nadine.** Get Moving. 1991. pap. text ed. 11.97 (0-937659-52-5) GCT.

Roush, Patricia B., ed. The Design, Sampling, Handling, & Applications of Infrared Microscopes. LC 87-14345. (Special Technical Publication Ser.: No. 949). (Illus.). viii, 115p. 1987. 24.00 (0-8031-0953-9, 04-949000-39) ASTM.

Roush, Richard T. & Tabashnik, Bruce E., eds. Pesticide Resistance in Arthropods. 352p. 1990. 57.50 (0-412-01971-X, A3545, Chap & Hall NY) Chapman & Hall.

Roush, Ronald C. Bottling Ships & Houses. (Illus.). 224p. (Orig.). 1985. 22.95 (0-8306-0975-X, 1975); pap. 17.95 (0-8306-1975-5, 1975P) TAB Bks.

Roush, Sheryl. Newsletters for the 90s. 1992. write for info. (1-880878-02-X) Creative Comns.

Rousmaniere, John. The Annapolis Book of Seamanship. rev. ed. 1989. 29.95 (0-671-67447-1) S&S Trade.

— A Bridge to Dialogue: The Story of Jewish-Christian Relations. 1991. pap. 8.95 (0-8091-3284-2) Paulist Pr.

— Fastnet. Force Ten. (Illus.). 1980. 19.95 (0-393-03256-6) Norton.

— Fastnet, Force Ten. (Illus.). 288p. 1993. pap. 12.95 (0-393-30865-0) Norton.

— The Low Black Schooner: Yacht America 1851-1945. 80p. (Orig.). (C). 1990. text ed. 59.00 (0-685-65893-7, Pub. by Fernhurst Bks UK) St Mut.

— The Norton Sailor's Log. (Orig.). 1987. pap. 19.95 (0-393-30429-9) Norton.

Rousmaniere, John, ed. see Cruising Club of America Technical Committee, et al.

Rousmaniere, John, et al. A Picture History of the America's Cup. 1989. 39.95 (0-393-02819-4) Norton.

***Rousmaniere, Leah R. & Larom, Peter.** Anchored Within the Vail: A Pictorial History of the Seamen's Church Institute. (Illus.). 135p. (Orig.). 1995. pap. 18.00 (0-9643657-0-7) Seamens Church.

— Anchored Within the Vail: A Pictorial History of the Seamen's Church Institute. deluxe ed. (Illus.). 135p. (Orig.). 1995. 75.00 (0-9643657-1-5) Seamens Church.

Rousmaniere, Peter. The Public Money Managers Handbook. LC 81-67754. (Illus.). 320p. 1982. 39.95 (0-8442-3065-0, Crain Bks) NTC Pub Grp.

***Rouss, Sylvia.** Sammy Spider's First Passover. (Illus.). 32p. (J). (ps-2). 1995. 14.95 (0-929371-81-X); pap. 5.95 (0-929371-82-8) Kar Ben.

Rouss, Sylvia A. Fun with Jewish Holiday Rhymes. LC 91-40931. (J). (ps). 1992. 10.95 (0-8074-0463-2, 101981) UAHC.

— Sammy Spider's First Hanukkah. LC 92-39639. (Illus.). (J). 1993. 13.95 (0-929371-45-3); pap. 5.95 (0-929371-46-1) Kar Ben.

Roussakis, Emmanuel N. Commercial Banking in an Era of Deregulation. 2nd ed. LC 89-3862. (Illus.). 448p. 1989. text ed. 65.00 (0-275-93144-7, C3144, Praeger Pubs) Greenwood.

— Managing Commercial Banks. LC 77-4380. (Special Studies). 202p. 1977. text ed. 35.00 (0-275-90274-9, C0274, Praeger Pubs) Greenwood.

Roussarie, R., jt. ed. see Francoise, J. P.

Roussas, George, ed. Nonparametric Functional Estimation & Related Topics. (C). 1991. lib. bdg. 226.00 (0-7923-1226-0) Kluwer Ac.

Roussaskis, E. N. Cases in Commercial Bank Management. LC 94-75194. 134p. 1994. pap. 20.00 (1-878975-39-0) Kolb Pub.

***rousse Staff.** Larousse Dictionnaire de la Sculpture. 624p. (FRE.). 1992. 195.00 (0-7859-7671-X, 2035113091) Fr & Eur.

Rousseas, S. Capitalism & Catastrophe. LC 78-11996. (Illus.). 1979. 29.95 (0-521-22333-4) Cambridge U Pr.

Rousseas, Stephen. Post Keynesian Monetary Economy. 2nd ed. LC 92-9112. 136p. 1992. 46.95 (1-56324-082-3); pap. 20.95 (1-56324-095-5) M E Sharpe.

Rousseas, Stephen W. The Political Economy of Reaganomics: A Critique. LC 82-10659. 158p. reprint ed. pap. 45.10 (0-8357-2624-X, 2040112) Bks Demand.

Rousseau, Ann Marie & Shulman, Alix K. Shopping Bag Ladies: Homeless Women Speak about Their Lives. LC 81-407. (Illus.). 160p. 1982. pap. 12.95 (0-8298-0603-2) Pilgrim OH.

Rousseau, David, jt. auth. see Le Clair, Kim.

Rousseau, David, et al. Your Home, Your Health & Well Being. LC 87-7080. (Illus.). 320p. 1988. pap. 14.95 (0-89815-223-2) Ten Speed Pr.

Rousseau, Denis L., ed. Optical Techniques. (Physical Techniques in Biology & Medicine Ser.: Vol. 1B). 1984. text ed. 138.00 (0-12-599322-6) Acad Pr.

Rousseau, Denise, jt. ed. see Cooper, Cary L.

***Rousseau, Denise M.** Psychological Contracts in Organizations: Understanding Written & Unwritten Agreements. (Illus.). 264p. 1995. 39.95 (0-8039-7104-4); pap. 19.95 (0-8039-7105-2) Sage.

Rousseau, Francois O. Andree Putman. LC 90-8110. (Illus.). 288p. 1990. 110.00 (0-8478-1210-3) Rizzoli Intl.

Rousseau, Francois-Olivier. L' Enfant d'Edouard. (FRE.). 1984. pap. 11.95 (0-7859-4214-9) Fr & Eur.

Rousseau, G. S. Enlightenment Borders: Pre- & Postmodern Discourses, Vol. 2: Scientific, Medical. LC 90-19452. 384p. 1991. text ed. 90.00 (0-7190-3506-6, Pub. by Manchester Univ Pr UK) St Martin.

— Enlightenment Crossings: Pre- & Postmodern Discourses, Vol. 1: Anthropological. LC 90-19452. 272p. 1991. text ed. 79.95 (0-7190-3072-2, Pub. by Manchester Univ Pr UK) St Martin.

— Goldsmith: The Critical Heritage. (Critical Heritage Ser.). 412p. 1974. 69.50 (0-7100-7720-3, RKP) Routledge.

— Perilous Enlightenment: Pre- & Postmodern Discourses, Vol. 3: Sexual, Historical. LC 90-19452. 320p. 1991. text ed. 90.00 (0-7190-3301-2, Pub. by Manchester Univ Pr UK) St Martin.

— Pre- & Postmodern Discourses on the Enlightenment, 3 vols., Set. LC 90-19452. 976p. 1991. text ed. 200.00 (0-7190-3549-X, Pub. by Manchester Univ Pr UK) St Martin.

Rousseau, G. S., ed. The Languages of Psyche: Mind & Body in Enlightenment Thought. LC 90-34872. (Publications from the Clark Library Professorship, UCLA: No. 12). (Illus.). 494p. 1991. 55.00 (0-520-07044-5); pap. 18.00 (0-520-07119-0) U CA Pr.

— The Letters & Papers of Sir John Hill, 1714-1775. LC 81-68993. (Studies in the Eighteenth Century: No. 6). (Illus.). 264p. 1990. 39.50 (0-404-61472-8) AMS Pr.

Rousseau, G. S. & Porter, R., eds. The Ferment of Knowledge: Studies in the Historiography of Eighteenth-Century Science. LC 80-40001. 550p. 1980. 69.95 (0-521-22599-X) Cambridge U Pr.

Rousseau, G. S. & Porter, Roy, eds. Sexual Underworlds of the Enlightenment. (Illus.). vi, 294p. (C). 1988. 45.00 (0-8078-1782-1) U of NC Pr.

Rousseau, G. S. & Rogers, Pat, eds. The Enduring Legacy: Alexander Pope Tercentenary Essays. (Illus.). 328p. 1988. 74.95 (0-521-30581-0) Cambridge U Pr.

Rousseau, George S. Tobias Smollett. 210p. 1982. 24.95 (0-567-09330-1, Pub. by T & T Clark UK) Bks Intl VA.

Rousseau, J. M., ed. Computer Scheduling of Public Transport, 2. 522p. 1985. 92.50 (0-444-87778-9, North Holland) Elsevier.

Rousseau, J. M., jt. ed. see Goffin, J. L.

Rousseau, Jean J. Contrato Social. De los Rios, Fernando, tr. (Nueva Austral Ser.: Vol. 165). (SPA.). 1991. pap. text ed. 24.95x (84-239-1965-X) Elliots Bks.

— Discourse on the Sciences & Arts (First Discourse) & Polemics. Masters, Roger D. & Kelly, Christopher, eds. Kelly, Christopher et al, trs. LC 91-50820. (Collected Writings of Rousseau: Vol. 2). (Illus.). 259p. 1992. 40.00 (0-87451-580-7) U Pr of New Eng.

— Rousseau on International Relations. Hoffman, Stanley & Fidler, David P., eds. 296p. 1991. 49.95 (0-19-827321-5) OUP.

Rousseau, Jean-Jacques. Basic Political Writings. Cress, Donald A., tr. LC 87-23610. (HPC Classics Ser.). 249p. (C). 1987. lib. bdg. 29.95 (0-87220-048-5); pap. text ed. 5.95 (0-87220-047-7) Hackett Pub.

— A Complete Dictionary of Music. LC 72-1664. reprint ed. 55.00 (0-404-08335-8) AMS Pr.

— Les Confessions. Voisine, ed. (FRE.). 1268. pap. 45.00 (0-7859-1497-8, 2705002529) Fr & Eur.

— Les Confessions, 2 vols. Koenig, Catherine, ed. 384p. (FRE.). 1973. pap. 10.95 (0-7859-1630-X, 2070363767) Fr & Eur.

— Les Confessions. Voisine, ed. (Coll. Prestige). 512p. (FRE.). 1973. pap. 10.95 (0-7859-1631-8, 2070363775) Fr & Eur.

— Confessions. (Orig.). 1992. 20.00 (0-679-41334-0, Everymans Lib) Knopf.

— Confessions. 1094p. (Orig.). 1964. 16.95 (0-8288-7479-4) Fr & Eur.

— Confessions. Cohen, John M., tr. (Classics Ser.). (Orig.). 1953. mass mkt. 7.95 (0-14-044033-X, Penguin Classics) Viking Penguin.

— Confessions, Tome 1. (Folio Ser.: No. 376). (Orig.). (FRE.). pap. 9.95 (2-07-036376-7) Schoenhof.

— Confessions, Tome 2. (Folio Ser.: No. 377). (Orig.). (FRE.). 1990. pap. 9.95 (2-07-036377-5) Schoenhof.

— Deux Lettres a Monsieur le Marechal Duc de Luxembourg. (Illus.). 122p. (FRE.). 1977. pap. 49.95 (0-7859-5567-4) Fr & Eur.

— Discours sur les Sciences et les Arts. Havens, G. R., ed. (MLA Ser.: No. 15). 1946. 26.00 (0-527-77300-X) Periodicals Srv.

— Discours sur les Sciences et les Arts. (Folio Ser.: No. 1874). (FRE.). pap. 12.95 (2-07-037874-8) Schoenhof.

— Discours sur les Sciences et les Arts: Avec: Discours sur l'Origine et l'Inegalite. 510p. (FRE.). 1955. pap. 10.95 (0-7859-1427-7, 2080702432) Fr & Eur.

— Discours sur l'Origine et les Fondements de l'Inegalite Parmi les Hommes. (Folio Essais Ser.: No. 18). 185p. (FRE.). 1985. pap. 11.95 (2-07-032541-5) Schoenhof.

— Discours sur l'Origine et les Fondements de l'Inegalite Parmi les Hommes: Avec: La Reine Fantastique. 192p. (FRE.). 1973. pap. 17.95 (0-7859-5568-2); pap. 4.95 (0-686-55343-8) Fr & Eur.

— A Discourse on Inequality. Cranston, Maurice W., tr. (Classics Ser.). 208p. 1985. mass mkt. 8.95 (0-14-044439-4, Penguin Classics) Viking Penguin.

— Discourse on Political Economy & the Social Contract. Betts, Christopher, tr. & intro. by. LC 93-48985. (World's Classics Ser.). 240p. 1994. pap. 5.95 (0-19-282750-2) OUP.

— Discourse on the Origin of Inequality. Cress, Donald A., tr. LC 92-20421. 112p. (C). 1992. lib. bdg. 27.50 (0-87220-151-1); pap. text ed. 3.95 (0-87220-150-3) Hackett Pub.

— Discourse on the Origin of Inequality. Coleman, Patrick, ed. Philip, Franklin, tr. (World's Classics Ser.). 176p. 1994. pap. 6.95 (0-19-282947-5) OUP.

— Discourse on the Origins of Inequality (Second Discourse), Polemics, & Political Economy. Masters, Roger D. & Kelly, Christopher, eds. Bush, Judith R. et al, trs. LC 92-53866. (Collected Writings of Rousseau: Vol. 3). (Illus.). 242p. 1993. 40.00 (0-87451-603-X) U Pr of New Eng.

— Du Contrat Social. Burgelin, Pierre, ed. 215p. 1971. 3.95 (0-686-55344-6) Fr & Eur.

— Eloisa, 2 vols., Set. LC 90-118291. 1350p. 1989. reprint ed. 105.00 (1-85477-027-6, Pub. by Woodstock Bks UK) Cassell.

— Emile. Bloom, Allan, tr. & intro. by. LC 78-73765. 512p. 1979. pap. text ed. 20.00 (0-465-01931-5) Basic.

— Emile et de l'Education: College Prestige. Richard, ed. 27.95 (0-685-34056-2) Fr & Eur.

— Emile ou de l'Education. Launay, Michel, ed. 636p. 1966. 5.95 (0-686-55346-2) Fr & Eur.

— Emile ou de l'Education. Richard, ed. 189p. (FRE.). 1986. pap. 10.95 (0-7859-1269-X, 2040166300) Fr & Eur.

— Essai sur l'Origine des Langues. (FRE.). 1990. 13.95 (0-686-55347-0, 2070325431); pap. 11.95 (0-7859-1359-9) Fr & Eur.

— Essai sur l'Origine des Langues. (Folio Essais Ser.: No. 135). (FRE.). pap. 11.95 (2-07-032543-1) Schoenhof.

— The Essential Rousseau. 1974. pap. 10.95 (0-452-01031-4, Plume) NAL-Dutton.

— First & Second Discourse, Together with Replies to the Critics, & Essays on the Origin of Languages. Gourevitch, Victor, tr. LC 85-45226. 320p. 1988. pap. text ed. 15.00 (0-06-132083-8, PB2083, Torch) HarpC.

— First & Second Discourses. Masters, Roger D., ed. 1969. pap. text ed. 9.50 (0-312-69440-7) St Martin.

An Asterisk (*) at the beginning of an entry indicates that the title is appearing in BIP for the first time.

— The First & Second Discourses, Together with Replies to Critics, & Essay on the Origin of Languages. Gourevitch, Victor, ed. & tr. by. 400p. 1991. reprint ed. lib. bdg. 37.00x (*0-8095-9091-3*) Borgo Pr.

— The Government of Poland. Kendall, Willmoore, ed. & tr. by. LC 85-5463. (HPC Classics Ser.). 158p. (C). 1985. reprint ed. lib. bdg. 21.50 (*0-915145-96-0*); reprint ed. pap. 6.95 (*0-915145-95-2*) Hackett Pub.

— Jean Jacques Entre Socrate et Caton. 112p. (FRE.). 1972. pap. 12.95 (*0-7859-5476-7*) Fr & Eur.

— Julie: Ou, La Nouvelle Heloise. Launay, Michel, ed. 640p. 1967. 5.95 (*0-686-55351-9*) Fr & Eur.

— Julie: Ou, La Nouvelle Heloise. Pomeau, Rene, ed. 640p. (FRE.). 1967. pap. 14.95 (*0-7859-1383-1*, 2070701487) Fr & Eur.

— Julie ou La Nouvelle Heloise: Ou, La Nouvelle Heloise. Pomeau, Rene, ed. (Coll. Prestige). 35.95 (*0-685-34057-0*) Fr & Eur.

— Lettre a M. d'Alembert sur les Spectacles. 254p. (FRE.). 1967. pap. 10.95 (*0-7859-1420-X*, 2080701606) Fr & Eur.

— Lettres Philosphiques. 232p. (FRE.). 1974. pap. 29.95 (*0-686-55353-5*, 271160666X) Fr & Eur.

— La Nouvelle Heloise, 2 vols., 1. 1993. pap. 19.95 (*0-7859-2932-0*) Fr & Eur.

— La Nouvelle Heloise, 2 vols., 2. 1993. pap. 19.95 (*0-7859-2933-9*) Fr & Eur.

— La Nouvelle Heloise: Julie, or the New Eloise. McDowell, Judith H., tr. LC 67-27114. 428p. 1987. reprint ed. pap. 14.95 (*0-271-00602-1*) Pa St U Pr.

— Oeuvres Completes, Tome III. deluxe ed. 2224p. (FRE.). 1964. 125.00 (*0-7859-1622-9*, 2070104907) Fr & Eur.

— Oeuvres Completes, Tome IV. deluxe ed. 2184p. (FRE.). 1969. write for info. (*0-7859-1623-7*, 2070104915) Fr & Eur.

— Oeuvres Completes, Tome II. Raymont, Andre, ed. (FRE.). 1961. lib. bdg. 130.00 (*0-7859-3954-7*) Fr & Eur.

— On the Social Contract. Masters, Roger D., ed. Masters, Judith R., tr. LC 77-86291. 1978. pap. text ed. 10.50 (*0-312-69446-6*) St Martin.

— On the Social Contract. rev. ed. Cress, Donald A., ed. & tr. by. LC 88-28260. 112p. (C). 1988. lib. bdg. 21.50 (*0-87220-069-8*); pap. 4.95 (*0-87220-068-X*) Hackett Pub.

— Politics & the Arts: Letter to M. D'Alembert on the Theatre. Bloom, Allan, tr. 196p. 1968. reprint ed. pap. 10.95 (*0-8014-9071-5*) Cornell U Pr.

— Profession de Foi du Vicaire Savoyard. Robinet, Andre, ed. (FRE.). 1978. pap. 24.95 (*0-685-73323-8*, 2711606678) Fr & Eur.

— Les Reveries du Promeneur Solitaire. 288p. (FRE.). 1972. pap. 10.95 (*0-7859-3989-X*, 2070361861) Fr & Eur.

— Les Reveries du Promeneur Solitaire. Sacy, S. Sylvestre de, ed. (Folio Ser.: No. 186). 288p. 1972. 6.95 (*2-07-036186-1*) Schoenhof.

— Reveries du Promeneur Solitaire. De Sacy, S. Sylvestre, ed. 288p. 1972. write for info. (*0-318-63590-9*) Fr & Eur.

— Reveries of the Solitary Walker. France, Peter, tr. (Classics Ser.). 1980. pap. 7.95 (*0-14-044363-0*, Penguin Classics) Viking Penguin.

— The Reveries of the Solitary Walker. Butterworth, Charles E., tr. & notes by. LC 92-28212. 288p. (C). 1992. reprint ed. lib. bdg. 29.95 (*0-87220-163-5*); reprint ed. pap. text ed. 7.95 (*0-87220-162-7*) Hackett Pub.

— Rousseau, Judge of Jean-Jacques: Dialogues. Masters, Roger D. et al, eds. Kelly, Christopher et al, trs. LC 89-40234. (Collected Writings of Rousseau: Vol. 1). (Illus.). 309p. 1990. 40.00 (*0-87451-495-9*) U Pr of New Eng.

— Rousseau's Political Writings. Ritter, Alan, ed. Bondanella, Julia C., tr. (Critical Editions Ser.). (C). 1987. pap. text ed. 8.95 (*0-393-95651-2*) Norton.

— Social Contract. 18.95 (*0-8488-0840-1*) Amereon Ltd.

— Social Contract. Frankell, Charles, ed. (Library of Classics: No. 1). 160p. 1970. pap. 11.95 (*0-02-851150-6*) Hafner.

— Social Contract. LC 88-60152. (Great Books in Philosophy). 150p. (C). 1988. pap. 5.95 (*0-87975-444-3*) Prometheus Bks.

— Social Contract. Cranston, Maurice W., tr. (Classics Ser.). 1968. mass mkt. 6.95 (*0-14-044201-4*, Penguin Classics) Viking Penguin.

— The Social Contract. 1969. pap. 9.95 (*0-317-30544-1*) Free Pr.

— Social Contract & Discourse on the Origin of Inequality. Crocker, Lester G., ed. 288p. 1989. mass mkt. 5.99 (*0-671-68956-8*, WSP) PB.

— The Social Contract & Discourses. Brumfitt, J. H., ed. Cole, G. D., tr. 422p. 1993. pap. 6.95 (*0-460-87357-1*, Everyman's Classic Lib) C E Tuttle.

— The Social Contract; &, The Discourses. Cole, G. D., tr. LC 93-22368. 1993. 17.00 (*0-679-42302-8*, Everymans Lib) Knopf.

— Social Contract, Discourse on the Virtue Most Necessary for a Hero, Political Fragments, & Geneva Manuscript. Masters, Roger D. & Kelly, Christopher, eds. Kelly, Christopher et al, trs. (Collected Writings of Rousseau: Vol. 4). (Illus.). 306p. (C). 1994. 45.00x (*0-87451-646-3*) U Pr of New Eng.

Rousseau, Jean-Jacques & Furbank, P. N. Confessions. (Orig.). 1992. 20.00 (*0-679-40998-X*, Everymans Lib) Knopf.

Rousseau, Jean-Jacques & Herder, Johann G. On the Origin of Language. Moran, John H. & Gode, Alexander, trs. LC 85-20945. x, 176p. 1986. pap. text ed. 9.95 (*0-226-73012-3*) U Ch Pr.

***Rousseau, John J.** Jesus & His World: An Archaeological & Cultural Dictionary. 1995. 48.00 (*0-8006-2903-5*, Fortress Pr) Augsburg Fortress.

Rousseau, John J., et al. Jesus & His World: An Archaeological & Cultural Dictionary. LC 94-12733. 1995. pap. 25.00 (*0-8006-2805-5*, 1-2805, Fortress Pr) Augsburg Fortress.

Rousseau, Julie W. Alice Bay Cookbook. LC 85-63063. (Illus.). 256p. (Orig.). 1985. pap. 12.95 (*0-931849-02-0*) Quartzite Bks.

Rousseau, Louis-Jean. English - French Lexicon of the Mining Industry Two: Mineral Processing. 83p. (ENG & FRE.). 1981. pap. 39.95 (*0-8288-9400-0*) Fr & Eur.

Rousseau, Louis-Jean, jt. auth. see Auger, Pierre.

Rousseau, Marie-Andre, tr. see Ogilvie, Lloyd J.

Rousseau, Mark O. & Zariski, Raphael. Regionalism & Regional Devolution in Comparative Perspective. LC 87-47735. 303p. 1987. text ed. 65.00 (*0-275-92546-3*, C2546, Praeger Pubs) Greenwood.

Rousseau, Mary. Community: The Tie That Binds. 188p. (C). 1991. lib. bdg. 43.50 (*0-8191-8209-5*) U Pr of Amer.

Rousseau, Mary & Gallagher, Charles. Sex Is Holy. 150p. (Orig.). 1994. reprint ed. pap. text ed. 11.95 (*0-8264-0776-5*) Continuum.

— Sexual Healing in Marriage. 152p. 1994. reprint ed. pap. text ed. 12.95 (*0-8264-0777-3*) Continuum.

Rousseau, Mary & Gallagher, Chuck. Sex Is Holy. (Wellspring Bks.). 160p. (Orig.). 1986. pap. 9.95 (*0-916349-11-X*) Amity Hse Inc.

Rousseau, Mary F., tr. Liber De Pomo: The Apple or Aristotle's Death. LC 68-28028. (Medieval Philosophical Texts in Translation Ser.: No. 18). 1968. pap. 5.00 (*0-87462-218-2*) Marquette.

Rousseau, May. Everyone Is Dressing Up! (Illus.). 12p. (J). (ps). 1991. bds. 4.95 (*0-916291-38-3*) Kane-Miller Bk.

Rousseau, Philip. Basil of Caesarea. LC 93-3552. (Transformation of the Classical Heritage Ser.: Vol. 20). 1994. Alk. paper. 55.00 (*0-520-08238-9*) U CA Pr.

— Pachomius: The Making of a Community in Fourth-Century Egypt. (Transformation of the Classical Heritage Ser.: Vol. VI). 1985. 45.00 (*0-520-05048-7*) U CA Pr.

Rousseau, R., ed. see Egghe, L.

Rousseau, R., jt. ed. see Egghe, L.

Rousseau, Richard, ed. Christianity & Judaism: The Deepening Dialogue. (Modern Theological Themes: Selections from the Literature Ser.: Vol. 3). (Orig.). 1983. pap. 15.00 (*0-940866-02-1*) U Scranton Pr.

Rousseau, Richard W., ed. Christianity & Islam: The Struggling Dialogue. (Modern Theological Themes: Selections from the Literature Ser.: Vol. 4). 220p. (Orig.). 1985. pap. 17.95 (*0-940866-03-X*) U Scranton Pr.

— Christianity & the Religions of the East: Models for a Dynamic Relationship. (Modern Theological Themes: Selections from the Literature Ser.: Vol. 2). 174p. (Orig.). (C). 1982. pap. 15.00 (*0-940866-01-3*) U Scranton Pr.

Rousseau, Ronald W. Handbook of Separation Process Technology. 1024p. 1987. text ed. 130.00 (*0-471-89558-X*) Wiley.

Rousseau, Ronald W., jt. auth. see Felder, Richard M.

Rousseau, Victor. Messiah of the Cylinder. LC 73-13264. (Classics of Science Fiction Ser.). 334p. 1973. reprint ed. 15.00 (*0-88355-118-7*); reprint ed. pap. 10.00 (*0-88355-147-0*) Hyperion Conn.

— The Sea Demons. LC 75-28861. (Classics of Science Fiction Ser.). 254p. 1976. reprint ed. 15.00 (*0-88355-375-9*); reprint ed. pap. 10.00 (*0-88355-462-3*) Hyperion Conn.

Rousseaux, Colin G., jt. ed. see Haschek, Wanda.

Rousseeuw, Peter J. & Leroy, Annick M. Robust Regression & Outlier Detection. LC 87-8234. (Probability & Mathematical Statistics Ser.). 329p. 1987. text ed. 87.95 (*0-471-85233-3*) Wiley.

Roussel, Fernand. Le Moniteur d'Orientation Rogerienne. fac. ed. LC 72-366473. 249p. (FRE.). reprint ed. pap. 71.00 (*0-7837-6953-9*, 2046782) Bks Demand.

Roussel, Hubert. The Houston Symphony Orchestra, 1913-1971. LC 74-38924. 273p. reprint ed. pap. 77.90 (*0-8357-7760-X*, 2036118) Bks Demand.

Roussel, Mike. Clay. (Craft Projects Ser.). (Illus.). 32p. (J). (gr. 2-6). 1990. lib. bdg. 15.94 (*0-86592-485-6*); lib. bdg. 11.95 (*0-685-36301-5*) Rourke Corp.

— Scrap Materials. (Craft Projects Ser.). (Illus.). 32p. (J). (gr. 2-6). 1990. 11.95 (*0-685-36305-8*); lib. bdg. 15.94 (*0-86592-487-2*) Rourke Corp.

Roussel, Mike, et al. Craft Projects, 6 bks., Set. (Illus.). 192p. (J). (gr. 2-6). 1990. lib. bdg. 95.64 (*0-86592-482-1*); lib. bdg. 71.70 (*0-685-36300-7*) Rourke Corp.

Roussel, Monique. Biographie Legendaire D'Achille. x, 505p. (FRE.). 1991. pap. 79.00 (*90-256-0993-7*, Pub. by A M Hakkert SP) Benjamins North Am.

Roussel, Philip A., et al. Third Generation R & D: Managing the Link to Corporate Strategy. 224p. 1991. 29.95 (*0-87584-252-6*) Harvard Busn.

— Third Generation R&D: Managing the Link to Corporate Strategy. 1991. text ed. 29.95 (*0-07-103284-3*) McGraw.

Roussel, Raymond. How I Wrote Certain of My Books. 1995. pap. 15.95 (*1-878972-14-6*) Exact Change.

— Selections from Certain of His Books. 1991. pap. 13.95 (*0-947757-26-0*) Serpents Tail.

Roussel, Raymond, jt. auth. see Padgett, Ron.

Roussel, Royal. The Metaphysics of Darkness: A Study in the Unity & Development of Conrad's Fiction. LC 74-146458. 208p. reprint ed. 59.30 (*0-8357-9277-3*, 2011004) Bks Demand.

Rousselet-Blanc, Josette, jt. auth. see Rousselet-Blanc, Pierre.

Rousselet-Blanc, Pierre. Dictionary of Animals: Dictionnaire des Animaux. 250p. (FRE.). 1981. 19.95 (*0-8288-4443-7*, M9771) Fr & Eur.

— Larousse Des Animaux Familiers Insolites. (FRE.). 1976. 24.95 (*0-8288-5723-7*, M6334) Fr & Eur.

Rousselet-Blanc, Pierre, ed. Larousse des Poissons d'Aquarium. 120p. (FRE.). 1975. 59.95 (*0-8288-5912-4*, M6336) Fr & Eur.

— Larousse du Chevel. (FRE.). 1976. 85.00 (*0-8288-5726-1*, F12080) Fr & Eur.

Rousselet-Blanc, Pierre & Rousselet-Blanc, Josette. Dictionnaire du Chien. 267p. (FRE.). 1976. 49.95 (*0-8288-5648-6*, M6647) Fr & Eur.

Roussell, Aage. Norse Building Customs in the Scottish Isles. LC 77-87681. reprint ed. 18.00 (*0-404-16477-3*) AMS Pr.

Rousselle, Aline. Porneia: On Desire & the Body in Antiquity. 224p. 1993. pap. 17.95 (*0-631-19208-5*) Blackwell Pubs.

Rousselot, Jean, ed. see Reverdy, Pierre.

Rousselot, John H., jt. ed. see Schulze, Richard.

Rousselot, Pierre. The Eyes of Faith: With Rousselot's "Answer to Two Attacks" Donceel, Joseph & McDermott, John M., trs. LC 90-82352. 117p. 1990. reprint ed. 27.50 (*0-8232-1288-2*) Fordham.

Rousset, David. The Legacy of the Bolshevik Revolution: A Critical History of the U. S. S. R. 1982. text ed. 32.50 (*0-312-47802-X*) St Martin.

— The Other Kingdom. Guthrie, Ramon, tr. LC 81-12572. 173p. 1982. reprint ed. lib. bdg. 35.00 (*0-86527-339-1*) Fertig.

Rousset, Paul. Les Origines et les caracteres de la premiere croisade. LC 76-29837. reprint ed. 37.50 (*0-404-15428-X*) AMS Pr.

Roussin, Andre, jt. auth. see Mitford, Nancy.

Rousso, Harilyn, et al. Disabled, Female, & Proud! Stories of Ten Women with Disabilities. LC 93-26049. (Illus.). 1993. pap. text ed. 12.95 (*0-89789-358-1*, Bergin & Garvey) Greenwood.

Rousso, Henry. Vichy Syndrome: History & Memory in France since 1914. 384p. (C). 1994. pap. text ed. 15.95 (*0-674-93539-X*) HUP.

— The Vichy Syndrome: History & Memory in France since 1944. Goldhammer, Arthur, tr. 384p. (C). 1991. 42.50 (*0-674-93538-1*) HUP.

Rousso, Nira. The Passover Gourmet. (Illus.). 192p. 1987. 22.95 (*0-915361-66-3*) Modan-Adama Bks.

Rousso, Robyn, jt. auth. see Cohen, Robyn.

***Roussos.** The Thorax. 2nd expanded rev. ed. (Lung Biology in Health & Disease Ser.). 1474p. 1995. write for info. (*0-8247-9504-0*) Dekker.

— The Thorax. 2nd expanded rev. ed. (Lung Biology in Health & Disease Ser.). 1080p. 1995. write for info. (*0-8247-9600-4*) Dekker.

— The Thorax. 2nd expanded rev. ed. (Lung Biology in Health & Disease Ser.). 1424p. 1995. write for info. (*0-8247-9601-2*) Dekker.

Roussos, Charis & Macklem, Peter T., eds. The Thorax, Pt. A. LC 85-25254. (Lung Biology in Health & Disease Ser.: No. 29). 655p. reprint ed. Part A, 655p. pap. 176.90 (*0-7837-0322-8*, 2040642) Bks Demand.

— The Thorax, Pt. B. LC 85-25254. (Lung Biology in Health & Disease Ser.: No. 29). 955p. reprint ed. Part B, 955p. pap. 180.00 (*0-7837-0323-6*) Bks Demand.

Roussy De Sales, R. Easy French Reader. (Illus.). 218p. pap. 11.95 (*0-8442-1001-3*, Natl Textbk) NTC Pub Grp.

— French Verb Drills. 152p. 1983. pap. 6.95 (*0-8442-1032-3*, Natl Textbk) NTC Pub Grp.

— Jeux de Grammaire. (Illus.). 64p. (FRE.). (J). (gr. 5 up). 1983. pap. 4.95 (*0-8442-1380-2*, Natl Textbk) NTC Pub Grp.

Roussy de Sales, R. de. Easy French Grammar Puzzles. 64p. pap. 4.95 (*0-8442-1322-5*, Natl Textbk) NTC Pub Grp.

***Roussy, G. & Pearce, J. A.** Foundation & Industrial Applications of Microwaves & Radio Frequency Fields: Physical & Chemical Processes. text ed. write for info. (*0-471-95153-6*) Wiley.

***Roussy, M. G. & Pearce, J. A.** Foundations & Industrial Applications of Microwave & Radio Frequency Fields: Physical & Chemical Processes. LC 94-36676. 1995. text ed. 115.00 (*0-471-93849-1*) Wiley.

Roustan, Marius. The Pioneers of the French Revolution. LC 68-9659. 1970. reprint ed. 45.00 (*0-86527-150-X*) Fertig.

Roustang, Francois. Dire Mastery: Discipleship from Freud to Lacan. Lukacher, Ned, tr. LC 86-20572. 178p. 1986. pap. text ed. 13.00 (*0-88048-259-1*, 48-259-1) Am Psychiatric.

— Dire Mastery: Discipleship from Freud to Lacan. Lukacher, Ned, tr. LC 82-6552. 160p. 1982. text ed. 30.00x (*0-8018-2675-6*) Johns Hopkins.

— The Lacanian Delusion. Sims, Gregg, tr. (Odeon Ser.). 160p. 1990. 32.00 (*0-19-506399-6*) OUP.

— Psychoanalysis Never Lets Go. Lukacher, Ned, tr. LC 82-10042. 176p. (C). 1982. text ed. 38.00x (*0-8018-2674-8*) Johns Hopkins.

— The Quadrille of Gender: Casanova's 'Memoirs' Vila, Anne C., tr. LC 87-27807. 184p. 1988. 27.50 (*0-8047-1456-8*) Stanford U Pr.

Rout, J. K., jt. auth. see Rout, U.

Rout, Kathleen. Eldridge Cleaver. (Twayne's United States Authors Ser.: No. 583). 288p. (C). 1991. text ed. 22.95 (*0-8057-7620-6*, Pub. by Royal Botanic Garden UK) Macmillan.

Rout, Leslie B., Jr. Politics of the Chaco Peace Conference, 1935-1939. (Latin American Monographs: No. 19). (Illus.). 286p. 1970. 12.50 (*0-292-70049-0*) U of Tex Pr.

Rout, Leslie B. & Bratzel, John. The Shadow War: German Espionage & United States Counterespionage in Latin America During World War II. LC 85-295633. (Foreign Intelligence Book Ser.). 540p. 1986. text ed. 55.00 (*0-313-27005-8*, U7005, Greenwood Pr) Greenwood.

Rout, Nancy E., jt. ed. see Buckley, Ellen.

Rout, Pravakar. Environmental Concept Development in Children. (C). 1988. 31.00 (*81-7024-206-1*, Pub. by Ashish II) S Asia.

***Rout, T., ed.** Software Process Assessment & Improvement. (Software Quality Management Ser.: No. 1). 300p. 1995. 93.00 (*1-56252-313-9*) Computational Mech MA.

Rout, U. & Rout, J. K. Stress & General Practitioners. LC 93-18711. 1993. pap. text ed. 25.00 (*0-7923-8815-1*) Kluwer Ac.

Routburg, Marcia. On Becoming a Special Parent: A Mini-Support Group in a Book. (Illus.). 130p. (Orig.). 1987. pap. 7.00 (*0-9619347-0-0*) Parent Prof Pubns.

Route, Anthony. Flies for Alaska: A Guide to Buying & Tying. LC 91-77326. (Illus.). 188p. 1991. 18.95 (*1-55566-087-8*) Johnson Bks.

Route, Anthony J. Flyfishing Alaska. LC 89-83505. 240p. 1989. pap. 12.95 (*1-55566-042-8*) Johnson Bks.

— Kenai River, AK. (River Journal Ser.: Vol. 2, No. 1). (Illus.). 48p. 1994. pap. 14.95 (*1-878175-64-5*) F Amato Pubns.

Routh, C. R., ed. Who's Who in Tudor England. LC 90-63661. (Who's Who in British History Ser.). (Illus.). 494p. 1991. lib. bdg. 45.00 (*1-55862-133-4*) St James Pr.

Routh, D. K., ed. Disruptive Behavior Disorders in Childhood. (Illus.). 219p. (C). 1994. 39.50 (*0-306-44695-2*, Plenum Pr) Plenum.

Routh, David, jt. auth. see Devine, Mike.

Routh, David, jt. auth. see Newhouse, Tom.

Routh, Donald K. Clinical Psychology since 1917: Science, Practice, & Organization. LC 93-50551. (Applied Clinical Psychology Ser.). 281p. 1994. 45.00 (*0-306-44452-6*) Plenum.

Routh, Donald K., ed. Handbook of Pediatric Psychology. LC 87-34754. 612p. 1988. lib. bdg. 65.00 (*0-89862-707-9*) Guilford Pr.

— Handbook of Pediatric Psychology. 2nd ed. LC 95-8536. 1995. lib. bdg. 75.00 (*0-89862-156-9*) Guilford Pr.

— Learning, Speech, & the Complex Effects of Punishment: Essays Honoring George J. Wischner. LC 82-18075. 248p. 1982. 49.50 (*0-306-40960-7*, Plenum Pr) Plenum.

Routh, Donald K., jt. ed. see Wolraich, Mark L.

Routh, H. V. Money, Morals & Manners As Revealed in Modern Literature. 1972. 59.95 (*0-8490-0662-7*) Gordon Pr.

Routh, Harold V. God, Man & Epic Poetry: A Study in Comparative Literature, 2 vols., 1. LC 69-10152. (Illus.). 1968. reprint ed. text ed. 45.00 (*0-8371-0206-5*, ROEA, Greenwood Pr) Greenwood.

— God, Man & Epic Poetry: A Study in Comparative Literature, 2 vols., Set. LC 69-10152. (Illus.). 1968. reprint ed. text ed. 75.00 (*0-8371-9948-4*, ROEP, Greenwood Pr) Greenwood.

— God, Man & Epic Poetry: A Study in Comparative Literature, 2 vols., Vol. 2. LC 69-10152. (Illus.). 1968. reprint ed. text ed. 45.00 (*0-8371-0880-2*, ROEB, Greenwood Pr) Greenwood.

— Towards the Twentieth Century. LC 69-17587. (Essay Index Reprint Ser.). 1977. 21.95 (*0-8369-0091-X*) Ayer.

Routh, Martin J., ed. see Burnet, Gilbert.

Routh, Martinus J. Reliaquiae Sacrae, 5 vols., Set. lv, 2416p. 1974. reprint ed. write for info. (*3-487-05142-7*, Pub. by Georg Olms GW) Lubrecht & Cramer.

Routh, Paul & Kladder, Ronald. Welfare Benefits Guide, 1990-91. 1993. pap. 128.00 (*0-685-31929-6*) Clark Boardman Callaghan.

Routh, Paul J., jt. auth. see Kladder, Ronald A.

Routhier-Graf, Diane, jt. auth. see Schroeder, Betty L.

Routhier, Nicole. Cooking under Wraps: The Art of Wrapping Hors D'Oeuvres, Main Courses, & Desserts. LC 92-26605. 1993. 27.00 (*0-688-10867-9*) Morrow.

— The Foods of Vietnam. LC 89-11320. (Illus.). 240p. 1989. 40.00 (*1-55670-095-4*) Stewart Tabori & Chang.

Routledge. Arabic-English, English-Arabic Computer Dictionary. 350p. (ARA & ENG.). 1986. 125.00 (*0-8288-0227-0*, F62951) Fr & Eur.

— Arabic-English, English-Arabic Dictionary of Civil Engineering. (ARA & ENG.). 1986. 150.00 (*0-7859-0639-8*, F76990) Fr & Eur.

— Colloquial French. 1985. pap. 12.95 (*0-7100-0450-8*, RKP) Routledge.

***Routledge, Gerry.** Using DOS. (Illus.). 450p. (Orig.). 1995. pap. text ed. 19.99 (*0-7897-0095-6*) Que.

Routledge, J. Instructions for Engineers' Slide Rule. (Illus.). 32p. 1990. reprint ed. pap. 4.00 (*1-879335-17-4*) Astragal Pr.

Routledge, K., jt. auth. see Routledge, W. S.

Routledge, Katherine. The Mystery of Easter Island: The Story of an Expedition. LC 77-18690. reprint ed. 84.50 (*0-404-14231-1*) AMS Pr.

Routledge, Marie & Jackson, Marion E. Pudlo: Thirty Years of Drawing. (Illus.). 176p. 1991. pap. 24.95 (*0-88884-603-7*) U Ch Pr.

Routledge, N. W. Anti-Aircraft Artillery, 1914-55: A History of the Royal Regiment of Artillery. (Illus.). 460p. 1994. 66.00 (*1-85753-099-3*, Pub. by Brasseys UK) Brasseys Inc.

Routledge, Paul. Terrains of Resistance: Nonviolent Social Movements & the Contestation of Place in India. 200p. 1993. text ed. 49.95 (*0-275-94517-0*, C4517, Praeger Pubs) Greenwood.

Routledge, Terry, jt. auth. see Walnum, Clayton.

Routledge, W. S. & Routledge, K. With a Prehistoric People: A Kikuyu of British East Africa. (Illus.). 392p. 1968. reprint ed. 37.50 (*0-7146-1716-4*, Pub. by F Cass Pubs UK) Intl Spec Bk.

Routley, Erik. Church Music & the Christian Faith. LC 78-110219. 156p. 1978. pap. 9.95 (*0-916642-10-0*) Agape IL.

— Church Music & the Christian Faith. LC 78-110219. 1979. 9.95 (*0-916642-11-9*) Hope Pub.

R

An Asterisk (*) at the beginning of an entry indicates that the title is appearing in BIP for the first time.

— The English Carol. LC 73-9129. (Illus.). 272p. 1973. reprint ed. text ed. 35.00 (0-8371-6989-5, ROEC, Greenwood Pr) Greenwood.
— The Musical Wesleys. LC 75-36511. (Illus.). 272p. 1976. reprint ed. text ed. 75.00 (0-8371-8644-7, ROMW, Greenwood Pr) Greenwood.
— Our Lives Be Praise. Young, Carlton R., & ed. & intro. by. LC 88-83215. 208p. (Orig.). 1989. pap. 14.95 (0-916642-26-7, CODE NO. 389) Hope Pub.
Routley, Erik & Young, Carlton R. Music Leadership in the Church. 136p. 1985. reprint ed. pap. text ed. 9.95 (0-916642-24-0) Agape IL.
Routley, Erik, ed. see Reformed Church in America Staff.
Routley, Richard. Exploring Meinong's Jungle & Beyond. (Monograph Ser.: No. 3). xxvii, 1035p. (C). 1980. lib. bdg. 49.00 (0-909596-36-0) Ridgeview.
— Relevant Logics & Their Rivals, One. 460p. (C). 1983. pap. text ed. 30.00 (0-917930-66-5) Ridgeview.
— Relevant Logics & Their Rivals, One, Vol. 1. xv, 460p. (C). 1983. lib. bdg. 49.00 (0-917930-80-0) Ridgeview.
Routman, Emily O., ed. St. Louis Zoo Visitor's Guide. (Illus.). 64p. (Orig.). 1990. pap. 5.95 (0-9625506-0-4) St Louis Zoo.
Routman, Regie. Invitations: Changing As Teachers & Learners K-12. LC 91-9304. 644p. 1991. pap. text ed. 27.50 (0-435-08578-6) Heinemann.
— Invitations: Changing as Teachers & Learners, K-12. LC 94-29709. 720p. 1994. pap. text ed. 28.50 (0-435-08836-X) Heinemann.
— Invitations: Changing as Teachers & Learners, K-12. LC 94-29709. 720p. 1994. 38.50 (0-435-08837-8) Heinemann.
— Transitions: From Literature to Literacy. LC 88-4379. 352p. (Orig.). (C). 1988. pap. 20.00 (0-435-08467-4, 08467) Heinemann.
***Routman, Regie, et al.** The Blue Pages: Resources for Teachers: from Invitations. LC 94-31701. 200p. 1994. pap. text ed. 13.50 (0-435-08835-1) Heinemann.
Routtenberg, A., jt. ed. see Gispen, W. H.
Routtenberg, Max J. One in a Minyan & Other Studies. 1979. pap. 6.95 (0-87068-342-X) Ktav.
Rouve, S. & Symons, R. En Directo Desde Espana. (C). 1990. 50.00 (0-7487-0139-7, Pub. by S Thornes Pubs UK) St Mut.
Rouvelas, Marilyn. A Guide to Greek Traditions & Customs in America. Papaioannou, George, ed. (Illus.). 336p. 1993. 25.00 (0-9638051-0-X) Nea Attiki Pr.
Rouverol, Jean. Writing for Daytime Drama. 336p. 1992. pap. 34.95 (0-240-80102-4, Focal) Buttrwrth-Heinemann.
Rouverol, W. S. & Pearce, W. J. The Reduction of Gear Pair Transmission Error by Minimizing Mesh Stiffness Variation. (Fall Technical Meeting Papers 88FTM11). (Illus.). 20p. 1988. pap. text ed. 30.00 (1-55589-516-6) AGMA.
***Rouvez, Alain, et al.** Disconsolate Empires: French, British & Elgian Military Involvement in Post - Colonial Sub - Saharan Africa. 468p. (C). 1994. lib. bdg. 52.50 (0-8191-9643-6) U Pr of Amer.
Rouvray, D. H., ed. Computational Chemical Graph Theory. 329p. (C). 1990. text ed. 115.00 (0-941743-84-5) Nova Sci Pubs.
Rouvray, D. H., jt. auth. see King, R. B.
Rouvray, D. H., et al. Graph Theory & Its Applications to Chemistry: Fundamentals & Specific Chemical Applications, Vol. 1. (Annals of Mathematical Chemistry Ser., Abacus Bks.). (Illus.). 250p. 1991. text ed. 146.00 (0-85626-454-7) Gordon & Breach.
Rouvray, Dennis H., jt. ed. see Bonchev, Danail.
Rouwen, A. J. Corneal Alterations with Contact Lens Wear. (Illus.). 168p. 1992. lib. bdg. 43.00 (90-6299-080-0, Pub. by Kugler NE) Kugler Pubns.
Rouwendal, Jan. Choice & Allocation Models for the Housing Market. (C). 1989. lib. bdg. 120.00 (0-7923-0466-7) Kluwer Ac.
Roux, Albert & Roux, Michel. Cooking for Two. (Illus.). 256p. 1991. 49.50 (0-283-06075-1, Pub. by Sidgwick & Jackson UK) Trans-Atl Phila.
Roux, Barbara & Gordon, Coco. The Opaque Glass. 30p. (Orig.). 1985. 40.00 (0-931956-25-0) Water Mark.
Roux, Bernard, ed. Numerical Simulation of Oscillatory Convection in Low-Pr Fluids: A GAMM-Workshop. (Notes on Numerical Fluid Mechanics Ser.: Vol. 27). vii, 365p. (C). 1990. 84.00 (3-528-07628-3, Pub. by Vieweg & Sohn GW) Ballen Bkslr.
Roux, Claude. Etude Ecologique et Phytosociologique des Peuplements Licheniques Saxicoles-Calcicoles du Sud-Est de la France. (Bibliotheca Lichenologica Ser.: Vol. 15). (Illus.). 558p. (FRE.). 1981. text ed. 90.00 (3-7682-1301-3) Lubrecht & Cramer.
Roux, Edward. Time Longer Than Rope: A History of the Black Man's Struggle for Freedom in South Africa. 2nd ed. 488p. 1967. pap. 12.95 (0-299-03204-3) U of Wis Pr.
Roux, Georges. Ancient Iraq. rev. ed. 480p. 1976. pap. 10.00 (0-14-020828-3, Penguin Bks) Viking Penguin.
— Ancient Iraq. 3rd ed. (Illus.). 576p. 1993. pap. 13.00 (0-14-012523-X, Penguin Bks) Viking Penguin.
Roux, Henry, ed. see Mittelberger, Ernest.
Roux, J. A. & McCay, T. D., eds. Spacecraft Contamination: Sources & Prevention. LC 84-12401. (PAAS Ser.: Vol. 91). 333p. 1984. 74.95 (0-915928-85-X) AIAA.
Roux, J. A., jt. ed. see McCay, T. D.
***Roux, Michel.** Michel Roux's Finest Desserts. LC 95-35427. (Illus.). 192p. 1995. 40.00 (0-8478-1857-8) Rizzoli Intl.
Roux, Michel, jt. auth. see Roux, Albert.
Roux, S., jt. ed. see Hermann, H. J.
Roux, V., ed. The Potters Wheel. (C). 1989. 44.00 (81-204-0436-X) S Asia.
Rouxel, Jean. Crystal Chemistry & Properties of Materials with Quasi-One-Dimensional Structures. 1986. lib. bdg. 136.50 (90-277-2057-6) Kluwer Ac.
Rouzer, Paul F. Writing Another's Dream: The Poetry of Wen Tingyun. LC 92-33907. 276p. (C). 1993. 37.50 (0-8047-2165-3) Stanford U Pr.
Rov, A. B. & Trudinger, P. A. The Biochemistry of Inorganic Compounds of Sulphur. LC 78-79056. 414p. reprint ed. pap. 118.00 (0-8357-7218-7, 2025595) Bks Demand.
Rovan, B., et al, eds. Mathematical Foundations of Computer Science 1990: Banska Bystrica, Czechoslovakia, August 27-31, 1990 Proceedings. (Lecture Notes in Computer Science Ser.: Vol. 452). viii, 544p. 1990. pap. 50.00 (0-387-52953-5) Spr-Verlag.
Roveda, C., ed. see IFAC Symposium Staff.
Rovee-Collier, Carolyn & Lipsitt, Lewis P., eds. Advances in Infancy Research, Vol. 5. 240p. 1988. text ed. 65.00 (0-89391-378-2) Ablex Pub.
— Advances in Infancy Research, Vol. 6. 336p. (C). 1990. text ed. 65.00 (0-89391-512-2) Ablex Pub.
***Rovee-Collier, Carolyn & Lipsitt, Lewis P, eds.** Advances in Infancy Research Vol. 9. (Illus.). 424p. 1995. 74.95 (1-56750-126-5) Ablex Pub.
Rovee-Collier, Carolyn, jt. auth. see Lipsitt, Lewis P.
Rovee-Collier, Carolyn, jt. ed. see Lipsitt, Lewis P.
Rovee, Joanne. Four Walls. Teasley, Jamie, ed. LC 89-51428. 101p. 1989. 6.95 (1-55523-271-X) Winston-Derek.
Roven, Milton D. Non-Disabling Surgical Rehabilitation of the Forefoot. LC 76-176177. (Illus.). 416p. 1976. 27.60 (0-87527-123-5) Green.
Rovenger, Holli & Bosshardt, Alexa. Today's Specials. 328p. 1991. pap. 14.95 (0-9630382-0-6) Nutrit Mktg.
Rover, Michelle. French for Business Studies. (ENG & FRE.). 1980. pap. 14.95 (0-8288-1549-6, M9207) Fr & Eur.
Rover, Red, jt. auth. see Lee, Butch.
Rovere, Richard H. The American Establishment & Other Reports, Opinions, & Speculations. LC 80-22247. x, 308p. 1981. reprint ed. text ed. 59.75 (0-313-22646-6, ROAE, Greenwood Pr) Greenwood.
— Senator Joe McCarthy. 280p. 1991. reprint ed. lib. bdg. 23.00x (0-8095-9078-6) Borgo Pr.
Rovere, Richard H. & Schlesinger, Arthur, Jr. General MacArthur & President Truman: The Struggle for Control of American Foreign Policy. 376p. (C). 1992. pap. 21.95 (1-56000-609-9) Transaction Pubs.
Rovere, Richard H. & Schlesinger, Arthur M., Jr. Final Reports: Personal Reflections on Politics & History in Our Time. LC 86-7735. (Wesleyan Paperback Ser.). 264p. reprint ed. pap. 75.30 (0-7837-0220-5, 2040528) Bks Demand.
Rovere, Vicki. Where to Go: A Guide to Manhattan's Toilets. 52p. 1991. pap. 4.50 (0-9633586-0-X) V Rovere.
— Worn Again, Hallelujah! A Guide to NYC's Thrift Shops & Other Treasure Troves. (Illus.). 140p. (Orig.). 1993. pap. write for info. (0-9633586-1-8) V Rovere.
Roverts, John H. C. H. Graun & Lotti. (Handel Sources Ser.). 1987. 30.00 (0-8240-6479-8) Garland.
Rovet, Ernest & Bernofsky, Stephen. Employee-Employer Rights: A Guide for the Ontario Work Force - Canadian Edition. 9th rev. ed. (Legal Ser.). 128p. (C). 1992. pap. 7.95 (0-88908-391-6) Self-Counsel Pr.
Rovetch, Lissa. Trigwater Did It. LC 88-31791. (Illus.). 32p. (J). (ps up). 1989. lib. bdg. 12.88 (0-688-08058-8) Morrow Jr Bks.
— Trigwater Did It. (Illus.). 32p. (J). (ps-3). 1991. pap. 3.95 (0-14-054238-8, Puffin) Puffin Bks.
Rovetti, Paul, intro. Dwight W. Tryon: A Retrospective Exhibition. 48p. 1971. 3.00 (0-918386-05-5) W Benton Mus.
— Sculpture in the Spring. 36p. 1970. 1.00 (0-918386-03-9) W Benton Mus.
Rovetti, Paul, et al. Nineteenth Century Folk Painting: Our Spirited National Heritage. (Illus.). 210p. 1974. 15.00 (0-918386-08-X); pap. write for info. (0-918386-09-8) W Benton Mus.
Rovetti, Paul F. Connecticut & American Impressionism. 184p. 1980. 19.95 (0-918386-32-2) W Benton Mus.
***Rovin.** GameMaster Complete Video Game Guide 1995. 1995. mass mkt. 5.99 (0-312-95439-5) St Martin.
Rovin, Jeff. Adventure Heroes: Legendary Characters from Odysseus to James Bond. LC 93-46603. 1994. 35.00 (0-8160-2881-8) Facts on File.
— Adventure Heroes: Legendary Characters from Odysseus to James Bond. 1995. pap. 19.95 (0-8160-2886-9) Facts on File.
— Aliens, Robots, & Spaceships. LC 94-24273. 1995. 35.00 (0-8160-3107-X) Facts on File.
— Best of How to Win at Nintendo Games. 1992. mass mkt. 5.99 (0-312-92874-2) St Martin.
— The Book of Dumb Movie Blurbs. 96p. (Orig.). 1995. pap. 8.00 (0-425-14616-2, Berkley Trade) Berkley Pub.
— Classic Science Fiction Films. (Illus.). 256p. 1993. pap. 16.95 (0-8065-1463-9, Citadel Pr) Carol Pub Group.
— Cliffhanger. 1993. pap. 4.50 (0-515-11267-4) Jove Pubns.
— Country Music Babylon. 1993. mass mkt. 4.99 (0-312-95027-6) St Martin.
— Dino-Mite Dinosaur Jokes. Ashby, Ruth, ed. (Illus.). 96p. (J). 1994. pap. 2.99 (0-671-88258-9, Minstrel Bks) PB.
— Encyclopedia of Monsters. (Illus.). 400p. 1989. 35.00 (0-8160-1824-3) Facts on File.
— The Encyclopedia of Monsters. (Illus.). 400p. 1990. pap. 19.95 (0-8160-2303-4) Facts on File.
— The Films of Charlton Heston. 1977. 14.95 (0-8065-0561-3, Citadel Pr); pap. 9.95 (0-8065-0741-1, Citadel Pr) Carol Pub Group.
— The First Good News - Bad News Joke Book. 176p. (Orig.). 1993. pap. 3.50 (0-451-17425-9, Sig) NAL-Dutton.
— Five Hundred Great Doctor Jokes. 176p. (Orig.). 1993. pap. 3.99 (0-451-17596-4, Sig) NAL-Dutton.
— Five Hundred Great Lawyer Jokes. 192p. (Orig.). 1992. pap. 3.99 (0-451-17387-2, Sig) NAL-Dutton.
— Five Hundred Hilarious Jokes for Kids. 144p. (Orig.). (J). 1990. pap. 3.99 (0-451-16549-7, Sig) NAL-Dutton.
— Gamemaster Vol. 1: Conquering Super Nintendo Games. 1994. mass mkt. 4.99 (0-312-95437-9) St Martin.
— Gamemasters Vol. 1: Conquering Sega Genesis Games. 1994. pap. 4.99 (0-312-95438-7) St Martin.
— How to Win at Game Boy Games. 1991. mass mkt. 3.99 (0-312-92632-4) St Martin.
— How to Win at Nintendo. 1988. pap. 2.95 (0-312-91341-9) St Martin.
— How to Win at Nintendo. 1989. pap. 3.95 (0-312-92018-0) St Martin.
— How to Win at Nintendo Games, No. 3. 1990. pap. 3.95 (0-312-92215-9) St Martin.
— How to Win at Nintendo Games, No. 4. 224p. 1991. mass mkt. 3.99 (0-312-92721-5) St Martin.
— How to Win at Nintendo Games, 3 vols., Set. 1991. pap. write for info. (0-312-92696-0); pap. 11.89 (0-312-92697-9) St Martin.
— How to Win At Nintendo, No. 3. 1990. pap. 71.10 (0-312-92251-5) St Martin.
— How to Win At Nintendo Sports Games. 1990. pap. 3.95 (0-312-92371-6) St Martin.
— How to Win at Sega & Genesis Games. 1991. pap. 3.95 (0-312-92364-3) St Martin.
— How to Win at Super Mario Brothers Games. 1991. mass mkt. 4.50 (0-312-92656-1) St Martin.
— How to Win at Super Nintendo Entertainment System Games. 1992. mass mkt. 4.99 (0-312-92871-8) St Martin.
— In Search of Trivia. 1984. pap. 3.95 (0-451-13313-7, Sig); pap. 5.99 (0-451-16250-1) NAL-Dutton.
— The Laserdisc Film Guide: Complete Ratings for the Best & Worst Movies Available on Disc. LC 92-33340. 1992. pap. 15.95 (0-312-08703-9) St Martin.
— Mortal Kombat. (Orig.). 1994. pap. text ed. 4.99 (0-441-00222-6) Ace Bks.
— One Thousand & One Great Jokes. 1989. pap. 4.99 (0-451-15979-9, Sig) NAL-Dutton.
— One Thousand One Great One-Liners. 160p. 1989. pap. 3.99 (0-451-16422-9, 028) NAL-Dutton.
— One Thousand One Great Pet Jokes. 224p. 1992. 3.99 (0-451-17261-2) NAL-Dutton.
— One Thousand One Great Sport Jokes. 1991. pap. 4.99 (0-451-16965-4, Sig) NAL-Dutton.
— A Pictorial History of Science Fiction Films. (Illus.). 1975. 12.00 (0-8065-0475-7, Citadel Pr) Carol Pub Group.
— A Pictorial History of Science Fiction Films. (Illus.). 1976. pap. 9.95 (0-8065-0537-0, Citadel Pr) Carol Pub Group.
— Simpson Fever. 1990. pap. 2.95 (0-312-92502-6) St Martin.
— Starik. 1989. pap. 3.95 (1-55817-270-X, Pinnacle NY) Windsor NY.
— TV Babylon. 304p. 1987. pap. 4.99 (0-451-16633-7, Sig) NAL-Dutton.
— TV Babylon Two. (Illus.). 304p. (Orig.). 1991. pap. 4.99 (0-451-17015-6, Sig) NAL-Dutton.
— Unauthorized Teenage Mutant Ninja Turtles Quiz Book. 1990. pap. 3.50 (0-312-92469-0) St Martin.
— The Unbelievable Truth! 176p. (Orig.). 1994. pap. 3.99 (0-451-17761-4, Sig) NAL-Dutton.
— What's the Difference. 1994. mass mkt. 4.99 (0-345-37827-X) Ballantine.
— World According to Elvis: Quotes from the King. 1992. mass mkt. 5.99 (0-06-100626-2, Harp PBks) HarpC.
Rovin, Jeff, jt. auth. see West, Adam.
Rovin, Sheldon & Ginsberg, Lois, eds. Managing Hospitals: Lessons from the Johnson & Johnson-Wharton Fellows Program in Management for Nurses. LC 91-7087. (Health-Management Ser.). 282p. 1991. 32.95 (1-55542-380-9) Jossey-Bass.
Rovine, Michael J. & Von Eye, Alexander. Applied Computational Statistics Longitudinal Research. 237p. 1991. pap. text ed. 44.00 (0-12-599450-8) Acad Pr.
Rovinski & Zastocki. Home Care: A Technical Manual for the Professional. 1989. pap. text ed. 39.50 (0-7216-2449-9) Saunders.
Rovinski, jt. auth. see Zastocki.
Rovinski, Leonor, tr. see Barzetti, Valerie, ed.
Rovinski, Yanina, tr. see Barzetti, Valerie, ed.
Rovinski, Yanina, jt. ed. see Barzetti, Valerie.
Rovira, Albert. Wax Crayon. (I Draw, I Paint Ser.). (Illus.). 48p. (J). 1991. pap. 7.95 (0-8120-4718-4) Barron.
Rovira, Carmen, ed. & tr. Sears: Lista de Encabezamientos de Materia. LC 84-19619. 753p. (SPA.). 1984. 45.00 (0-8242-0704-1) Wilson.
Rovira, Catherine. Semblanza y Circunstancia de Manuel Gonzalez Prada. LC 93-72951. (Coleccion Polymita Ser.). 142p. (Orig.). (SPA.). 1993. pap. 19.00 (0-89729-704-0) Ediciones.
Rovira, Jose C., ed. see Hernandez, Miguel.
Rovirosa, Dolores. Jorge Manach: Bibliografia. (Bibliography & Reference Ser.: No. 13). 261p. (Orig.). 1985. pap. 18.00 (0-917617-04-5) SALALM.
Rovit, Earl & Brenner, Gerry. Ernest Hemingway. rev. ed. (United States Authors Ser.: No.497). 240p. (C). 1986. text ed. 21.95 (0-8057-7455-6, Pub. by Royal Botanic Garden UK) Macmillan.
Rovit, Earl H. Saul Bellow. LC 67-26665. (University of Minnesota Pamphlets on American Writers Ser.: No. 65). 46p. reprint ed. pap. 25.00 (0-317-29457-1, 2055934) Bks Demand.
Rovit, Richard L., et al. Trigeminal Neuralgia. (Illus.). 218p. 1990. 85.00 (0-683-07393-1) Williams & Wilkins.
Rovner, Arkady. Xod Korolem: (The King's Visit) (Illus.). 164p. (Orig.). (RUS.). 1988. pap. 15.00 (0-922792-00-3) Gnosis Pr.
Rovner, Arkady & Andreyeva, Victoria. Tchaadaev. 76p. (Orig.). (RUS.). 1989. pap. 10.00 (0-922792-05-4) Gnosis Pr.
Rovner, Arkady, et al, eds. Gnosis Anthology of Contemporary American & Russian Literature & Art, 2 vols. 323p. (ENG & RUS.). 1982. Russian, 323p. 22.00 (0-685-70021-6); English, 307p. 22.00 (0-685-70022-4); Russian, 323p. pap. 15.00 (0-685-70023-2); English, 307p. pap. 15.00 (0-685-70024-0) Gnosis Pr.
Rovner, Jerome S., jt. ed. see Witt, Peter N.
Rovner, Mark J. Defense Dollars & Sense: A Common Cause Guide to the Defense Budget Process. (Illus.). 96p. (Orig.). 1983. pap. 4.50 (0-914389-00-9) Common Cause.
Rovner, Uri. Instant Recital Series: Level 1. 1993. 3.95 (1-56222-383-6, 94736) Mel Bay.
— Instant Recital Series: Level 2. 1993. 3.95 (1-56222-384-4, 94755) Mel Bay.
— Instant Recital Series: Level 3. 1993. 3.95 (1-56222-416-6, 94757) Mel Bay.
Rovnyak, James, jt. auth. see Rosenblum, Marvin.
Row, A. Tracy, ed. Frontier Tucson: Hispanic Contributions. (Illus.). 85p. 1987. reprint ed. pap. 9.95 (0-910037-22-1) AZ Hist Soc.
Row, Ann. A Century of Change in Gutemalan Textiles. (Illus.). 150p. 1981. pap. 18.95 (0-89192-328-4, Ctr Inter-Am Rel) Interbk Inc.
Row, Ernest F., tr. see Gide, Charles.
Row, H. J., ed. see Anderson, George B.
Row, John & Row, William. Historie of the Kirk of Scotland, 2 Vols, Set. LC 70-174969. (Maitland Club, Glasgow. Publications: No. 55). reprint ed. 115.00 (0-404-53039-7) AMS Pr.
***Row, Richard.** Anne of Green Gables: Pop-up Dollhouse. (Illus.). (J). (ps-3). 1994. 18.00 (0-679-86391-5) Random Bks Yng Read.
Row, Richard D., ed. Standard Vocal Repertoire, Bk. 2: For High Voice. (Illus.). 80p. 1963. pap. 9.95 (0-8258-0253-9, RB-71) Fischer Inc NY.
Row, Sanjiva. Negotiable Instruments Acts. (C). 1988. 150.00 (0-685-25702-9) St Mut.
Row, Subba T. Esoteric Writings. 1980. 17.95 (0-8356-7544-0) Theos Pub Hse.
Row, T. Subba. Consciousness & Immortality. (Sangam Texts Ser.). 96p. (Orig.). 1983. pap. 8.75 (0-88695-012-0) Concord Grove.
— Notes on the Bhagavad-Gita. LC 77-88628. 182p. 1978. reprint ed. 10.00 (0-911500-81-2); reprint ed. pap. 6.00 (0-911500-82-0) Theos U Pr.
Row, T. Sundara. Geometric Exercises in Paper Folding. (Illus.). pap. 3.95 (0-486-21594-6) Dover.
Row, William, jt. auth. see Row, John.
Rowallan, Lord. Rowallan. (Illus.). 1977. 24.95 (0-8464-0802-3) Beekman Pubs.
***Rowan.** Breakthroughs & Integragation. 1992. 49.95 (1-56593-579-9, 0310) Singular Publishing.
Rowan, jt. ed. see Erwitt, Jennifer.
Rowan, A. James & Gates, John R. Non-Epileptic Seizures. 296p. 1993. 90.00 (0-7506-9415-7) Buttrwrth-Heinemann.
Rowan, Alistair. Robert Adam. (Illus.). 122p. 1990. 55.00 (1-85177-070-4, Pub. by Victoria & Albert Mus UK) Trafalgar.
Rowan, Alistair, jt. ed. see Gow, Ian.
Rowan, Andrew N. Of Mice, Models, & Men: A Critical Evaluation of Animal Research. LC 83-4986. 323p. 1984. 64.50 (0-87395-776-8); pap. 21.95 (0-87395-777-6) State U NY Pr.
Rowan, Andrew N., ed. Animals & People Sharing the World. LC 88-40114. (Illus.). 206p. 1988. text ed. 30.00 (0-87451-449-5); pap. 13.95 (0-87451-465-7) U Pr of New Eng.
Rowan, Barbara A. Handbook on State Laws Regarding Covert Recordings of Conversations. (Private Investigator, 1990 Ser.). 156p. 1991. reprint ed. pap. text ed. 38.00 (0-918487-57-9) Thomas Pubns TX.
Rowan, Bob & Fenn, Melvin. Tradesmen in Business: A Comprehensive Guide & Handbook for the Skilled Tradesman. 226p. (Orig.). 1988. pap. 14.95 (1-55870-103-6) Betterway Bks.
Rowan, Bonnie. Scholars' Guide to Washington D. C. Film & Video Collections. LC 80-607014. (Scholar's Guide to Washington D.C. Ser.: No. 6). 282p. 1980. text ed. 27.50 (0-87474-818-6, Johns Hopkins); pap. text ed. 10.95 (0-87474-819-4, Johns Hopkins) W Wilson Ctr Pr.
Rowan, Bonnie G. & Wood, Cynthia. Scholars' Guide to Washington, D.C., for Media Collections. (Woodrow Wilson Center Press Ser.). 208p. (C). 1994. text ed. 45.00 (0-943875-54-4); pap. text ed. 19.95 (0-943875-55-2) Johns Hopkins.
Rowan, Carl T. Breaking Barriers. 1991. 22.95 (0-316-75977-5) Little.
— Dream Makers, Dream Breakers: The World of Justice Thurgood Marshall. 1993. 24.95 (0-316-75978-3) Little.
— Dream Makes, Dream Breakers: The World of Justice Thurgood Marshall. 1994. pap. 12.95 (0-316-75979-1) Little.
Rowan, David. Jack-up Based Extended Well Test System. (C). 1989. 95.00 (0-89771-725-2, Pub. by Lorne & MacLean Marine) St Mut.
— Jack-up-Based Extended Well Test System. 1989. 125.00 (90-6314-522-5, Pub. by Lorne & MacLean Marine) St Mut.
Rowan, Dennis. My Sheep & I. (Illus.). 160p. (Orig.). 1993. pap. text ed. 5.99 (0-9628579-1-2) Vision WY.
Rowan, Eric. Art in Wales, AD1850-1980: An Illustrated History. 128p. 1985. 65.00 (0-7083-0854-6, Pub. by U of Wales UK) Bks Intl VA.

R

*Rowan, Eric & Wallace, David, comps. The Really Wild Guide to Britain: A Guide to Wildlife Activities for Children over 200 Sites Included. (Illus.). 289p. 1995. pap. 9.95 (0-563-36788-1, Pub. by BBC UK) Parkwest Pubns.

Rowan, Hester. The Linden Tree. large type ed. 320p. 1985. 15.95 (0-7089-1331-8) Ulverscroft.

— Overture in Venice. large type ed. 320p. 1985. 15.95 (0-7089-1353-9) Ulverscroft.

— Snowfall. large type ed. 352p. 1985. 15.95 (0-7089-1395-4) Ulverscroft.

*Rowan, J. O. Physics & the Circulation. fac. ed. LC 81-12790. (Medical Physics Handbooks Ser.: No. 9). (Illus.). 132p. 1981. reprint ed. pap. 37.70 (0-7837-7999-2, 2047755) Bks Demand.

Rowan, James P. Butterflies & Moths. LC 83-7216. (New True Bks.). (Illus.). 48p. (J). (gr. k-4). 1983. lib. bdg. 12.90 (0-516-01692-X); pap. 4.95 (0-516-41692-8) Childrens.

— Prairies & Grasslands. LC 83-7310. (New True Bks.). (Illus.). 48p. (J). (gr. k-4). 1983. lib. bdg. 12.90 (0-516-01706-3); pap. 4.95 (0-516-41706-1) Childrens.

Rowan, Jim. I Can Be a Zoo Keeper. LC 85-11327. (I Can Be Bks.). 32p. (J). (gr. k-3). 1985. pap. 3.95 (0-516-41889-0) Childrens.

Rowan, John. Discovering Your Subpersonalities: Our Inner World & the People in It. LC 93-14812. (Illus.). 160p. 1994. pap. 17.95 (0-415-07366-9, A7634) Routledge.

— Horned God: Feminism & Men As Wounding & Healing. 1987. pap. 13.95 (0-7102-0674-7, RKP) Routledge.

— Ordinary Ecstasy: Humanistic Psychology in Action. rev. ed. 270p. (Orig.). 1988. pap. 15.95 (0-415-00190-0) Routledge.

— Reality Game: A Guide to Humanistic Counselling & Therapy. 1990. pap. 13.95 (0-415-04046-9) Routledge.

— Subpersonalities: The People Inside Us. 1990. pap. 14.95 (0-415-04329-8) Routledge.

— The Transpersonal: Psychotherapy & Counselling. LC 92-15268. (Illus.). 304p. 1992. 49.95 (0-415-05361-7, A7783, Routledge NY); pap. 15.95 (0-415-05362-5, A7787, Routledge NY) Routledge.

Rowan, John & Dryden, Wendy. Innovative Therapy in Britain. (Psychotherapy in Britain Ser.). 320p. 1988. 95.00 (0-335-09837-1, Open Univ Pr); pap. 42.00 (0-335-09827-4, Open Univ Pr) Taylor & Francis.

Rowan, John, jt. ed. see Reason, Peter.

Rowan, Joseph R. Suicide Prevention in Custody Intensive Study Course. Geiman, Diane & Flannery, Denise, eds. 192p. 1991. pap. 35.00 (0-929310-43-8, 173) Am Correctional.

— Suicide Prevention in Custody Intensive Study Course - Final Test. rev. ed. Geiman, Diane & Flannery, Denise, eds. 8p. 1992. pap. 19.00 (1-56991-031-6) Torah Aura.

Rowan, Kingsley S. Photosynthetic Pigments of Algae. (Illus.). (C). 1989. 69.95 (0-521-30176-9) Cambridge U Pr.

Rowan, N. R. Women in the Marines: The Book Camp Challenge. LC 93-9706. (Illus.). (YA). (gr. 5 up). 1993. 22.95 (0-8225-1430-3, Lerner Publctns) Lerner Group.

Rowan, Patricia & Stevenson, Dennis. The Boise Parent Guide. 100p. (Orig.). 1990. pap. write for info. (0-318-66749-5) Boise Parent Guide.

*Rowan, Paul. The Team That Jack Built. (Illus.). 192p. 1995. 29.95 (1-85158-670-9, Pub. by Mnstream UK) Trafalgar.

Rowan, Pete. Some Body! A Life-Size Guide. LC 94-20402. (Illus.). (J). 1995. 20.00 (0-679-87043-1) Knopf.

Rowan, Peter. Bodywise. 64p. 1993. pap. 9.00 (0-11-701707-8, HM17078, Pub. by HMSO UK) UNIPUB.

— Doctor, Doctor. 109p. 1992. pap. 10.00 (0-11-701695-0, HM16950, Pub. by HMSO UK) UNIPUB.

Rowan, Richard L., ed. Collective Bargaining: Survival in the '70's? Proceedings of a Conference. LC 75-189564. (Labor Relations & Public Policy Ser.: No. 5). 499p. reprint ed. pap. 142.30 (0-8357-3150-2, 2039413) Bks Demand.

Rowan, Richard L. & Barr, Robert E. Employee Relations Trends & Practices in the Textile Industry. LC 86-82726. (Employee Relations & Collective Bargaining Ser.). 1987. 30.00 (0-89546-063-7) U PA Wharton Ctr Human Resc.

Rowan, Richard L. & Northrup, Herbert R. Educating the Employed Disadvantaged for Upgrading: A Report on Remedial Education Programs in the Paper Industry. LC 76-184335. (Manpower & Human Resources Studies: No. 2). 184p. reprint ed. pap. 52.50 (0-8357-3157-X, 2039420) Bks Demand.

Rowan, Richard L., jt. auth. see Campbell, Duncan C.

Rowan, Richard L., jt. auth. see Northrup, Herbert R.

Rowan, Richard L., jt. ed. see Northrup, Herbert R.

Rowan, Richard L., jt. auth. see Perry, Charles R.

Rowan, Richard L., et al. Multinational Union Organizations in the Manufacturing Industries. (Multinational Industrial Relations Ser.: No. 7a). 213p. (Orig.). 1982. pap. 15.00 (0-89546-021-1) U PA Wharton Ctr Human Resc.

— Multinational Union Organizations in the White-Collar, Service, & Communications Industries. LC 83-48900. (Multinational Industrial Relations Ser.: No. 7b). 481p. 1983. pap. text ed. 27.50 (0-89546-022-X) U PA Wharton Ctr Human Resc.

Rowan, Robert L. How to Control High Blood Pressure Without Drugs. 320p. 1987. mass mkt. 5.99 (0-8041-0144-2) Ivy Books.

— Men & Their Sex. LC 80-25539. (Illus.). 168p. 1982. pap. 9.95 (0-8290-0446-7) Irvington.

Rowan, Robin & Perry, Clark. Insiders' Guide to Florida's Great Northwest. 1994. pap. 12.95 (0-912367-53-9) Insiders Guide.

*Rowan, Robin H. & Perry, Clark. The Insiders' Guide to Florida's Great Northwest. 2nd ed. 1995. pap. 14.95 (0-912367-70-9) Insiders Guide.

Rowan-Robinson, Jeremy, jt. auth. see Brand, Clive.

Rowan-Robinson, Michael. Our Universe: An Armchair Guide. (Illus.). 180p. (C). 1992. pap. text ed. write for info. (0-7167-2156-2) W H Freeman.

— Our Universe: An Armchair Guide. LC 91-41170. 1995. pap. text ed. 19.95 (0-7167-2359-X) W H Freeman.

— Ripples in the Cosmos: A View Behind the Scenes of the New Cosmology. LC 93-1590. 1995. text ed. write for info. (0-7167-4503-8) W H Freeman.

Rowan-Robinson, Michael, ed. Vistas in Astronomy, Supplement: Far Infrared Astronomy. 352p. 1976. 150.00 (0-08-020513-5, Pub. by Pergamon Repr UK) Franklin.

Rowan, Ronald R. Same Game: Higher Stakes. Van Treese, James B., ed. 336p. 1994. 9.95 (1-56901-181-8) NW Pub.

Rowan, Roy. Connections, Vol. 1. 1989. 18.95 (0-316-75976-7) Little.

— Intuitive Manager. 1991. mass mkt. 4.99 (0-425-13079-7) Berkley Pub.

Rowan, Stephen C. Nicene Creed: Poetic Words for a Prosaic World. LC 90-70989. 80p. (Orig.). 1991. pap. 5.95 (0-89622-451-1) Twenty-Third.

— The Parables of Calvary: Reflections on the Seven Last Words of Jesus. LC 93-61555. 48p. (Orig.). 1994. pap. 4.95 (0-89622-576-3) Twenty-Third.

— Words from the Cross. LC 87-51281. (Illus.). 64p. (Orig.). 1988. pap. 3.95 (0-89622-354-X) Twenty-Third.

Rowan, Steven, ed. see Boernstein, Henry.

Rowan, Steven, ed. see Goetz, Hans-Werner.

Rowan, Steven, tr. see Grundmann, Herbert.

Rowan, Thomas E. & Bourne, Barbara. Thinking Like Mathematicians: Putting the K-4 NCTM Standards into Practice. LC 93-43901. 160p. (YA). 1994. pap. text ed. 16.00 (0-435-08343-0) Heinemann.

Rowan, Thomas E. & Morrow, Lorna J., eds. Implementing the K-Eight Curriculum & Evaluation Standards: Readings from the "Arithmetic Teacher" LC 92-30628. (Illus.). 105p. (Orig.). 1993. pap. 7.50 (0-87353-351-8) NCTM.

Rowan, Walter, jt. auth. see King, L. R.

Rowan, William. The Riddle of Migration. 1977. lib. bdg. 59.95 (0-8490-2523-0) Gordon Pr.

*Rowan, William L., ed. Atomic Processes in Plasmas. (AIP Conference Proceedings Ser.: No. 322). 224p. 1995. text ed. 125.00x (1-56396-411-2) Am Inst Physics.

Rowat. Public Administration in Developed Democracies: A Comparative Study. (Public Administration & Public Policy Ser.: Vol. 32). 528p. 1988. 110.00 (0-8247-7807-3) Dekker.

Rowat, Donald C. The Ombudsman Plan: The Worldwide Spread of an Idea. rev. ed. 208p. (Orig.). (C). 1986. pap. text ed. 22.00 (0-8191-5040-1) U Pr of Amer.

Rowat, Donald C., ed. Administrative Secrecy in Developed Countries. LC 78-16376. (International Institute of Administrative Sciences Ser.). 1979. text ed. 52.00 (0-231-04596-4) Col U Pr.

— The Government of Federal Capitals. LC 72-185733. 394p. reprint ed. pap. 112.30 (0-317-09384-3, 2014390) Bks Demand.

— International Handbook on Local Government Reorganization: Contemporary Developments. LC 79-54063. (Illus.). xv, 626p. 1980. text ed. 95.00 (0-313-21269-4, RHL/, Greenwood Pr) Greenwood.

— The Ombudsman: Citizen's Defender. 401p. reprint ed. pap. 114.30 (0-317-26998-4, 2023664) Bks Demand.

*Rowat, Malcolm, et al, eds. Judicial Reform in Latin America & the Carribbean. LC 95-6392. (Technical Paper Ser.: No. 280). 1995. write for info. (0-8213-3206-6) World Bank.

Rowatt, G. Wade, Jr. Pastoral Care with Adolescents in Crisis. LC 88-28059. 168p. 1989. pap. 13.99 (0-664-25039-4) Westminster John Knox.

Rowberry, John. Lewd Conduct. 1993. pap. text ed. 4.95 (0-685-72890-0) Masquerade.

Rowbotham, Sheila. Friends of Alice Wheeldon. (New Feminist Library). 256p. (C). 1988. 26.00 (0-85345-729-8); pap. 10.00 (0-85345-728-X) Monthly Rev.

— Hidden from History: Three Hundred Years of Women's Oppression & the Fight Against It. 182p. (Orig.). (C). 1989. pap. text ed. 16.95 (0-904383-56-3) Westview.

— The Past Is Before Us: Feminism in Action since the 1960s. LC 90-26157. 376p. 1991. reprint ed. pap. 16.00 (0-8070-6759-8) Beacon Pr.

— Women in Movement: Feminism & Social Action. LC 92-12239. (Revolutionary Thought - Radical Movements Ser.). 320p. 1992. 49.95 (0-415-90651-2, A7615, Routledge NY); pap. 14.95 (0-415-90652-0, A7619, Routledge NY) Routledge.

Rowbotham, Sheila & Mitter, Swasti. Dignity & Daily Bread: New Forms of Economic Organising among Poor Women in the Third World & the First. LC 93-7363. 272p. 1994. 59.95 (0-415-09585-9, B2205, Routledge NY); pap. 16.95 (0-415-09586-7, B2209, Routledge NY) Routledge.

Rowbotham, Sheila, jt. ed. see Swasti, Mitter.

Rowbottom, Derek. Making Georgian Dolls' Houses. (Illus.). 176p. 1993. pap. 14.95 (0-946819-28-9, Pub. by Guild Mstr Craftsman UK) Sterling.

— Making Tudor Dolls' Houses. (Illus.). 128p. 1992. pap. 14.95 (0-946819-21-1, Pub. by Guild Mstr Craftsman UK) Sterling.

Rowbottom, Frederick, jt. auth. see Chapman, Johnathan.

Rowbottom, Margaret & Susskind, Charles. Electricity & Medicine: History of Their Interaction. (Illus.). 1984. 30.00 (0-685-10052-9) San Francisco Pr.

Rowbottom, Ralph. Social Analysis. LC 78-306628. (Heinemann Educational Bks.). 1977. pap. text ed. 34.95 (0-435-82773-1) Ashgate Pub Co.

Rowbottom, Ralph & Billis, David. Organisational Design: The Work Levels Approach. 1987. text ed. 68.95 (0-566-05408-6, Pub. by Avebury Pub UK) Ashgate Pub Co.

Rowcliffe, Irene. And There Was Light. 1993. 15.00 (0-533-10482-3) Vantage.

Rowden, C. Speech Processing. 288p. 1992. text ed. 60.00i (0-07-707324-X) McGraw.

Rowden, Geoffrey, jt. auth. see Lewis, Martin G.

Rowden, Thomas, tr. see Lawson, Myldred.

Rowdon, Maurice. The Spanish Terror: Spanish Imperialism in the Sixteenth Century. LC 74-196578. 343p. reprint ed. pap. 97.80 (0-317-28441-X, 2051265) Bks Demand.

Rowe. Building & Using a Groundwater Database. 85.00 (0-87371-404-0, GB428) Lewis Pubs.

— Critical Care of the Newborn & Infant Surgical Patient. 1991. 75.00 (0-8151-7390-3, Yr Bk Med Pubs) Mosby Yr Bk.

— Giant Dinosaurs. (J). 1989. pap. 19.95 (0-590-73275-7) Scholastic Inc.

Rowe, jt. auth. see Camfield.

Rowe, jt. auth. see Logan.

Rowe, ed. see Plato.

Rowe, et al. Essentials of Pediatric Surgery. 800p. 1994. 95.00 (0-8016-7472-7) Mosby Yr Bk.

Rowe, Alan. Aliens on Earth. (Illus.). 32p. (J). (ps-3). 1994. pap. 2.99 (1-56402-407-5) Candlewick Pr.

— The Topography & History of Beth-shan: With Details of the Egyptian & Other Inscriptions Found on the Site. LC 31-13812. (Publications of the Palestine Section of the Museum of the University of Pennsylvania: Vol. 1). 144p. reprint ed. pap. 41.10 (0-317-28548-3, 2052030) Bks Demand.

Rowe, Alan J. Strategic Management: A Methodological Approach. 4th ed. LC 93-6599. (Illus.). 992p. (C). 1994. pap. text ed. 58.25 (0-201-58638-X) Addison-Wesley.

— Strategic Management & Business Policy: A Methodological Approach. 3rd ed. (C). 1989. pap. text ed. 54.95 (0-201-15736-5) Addison-Wesley.

Rowe, Alan J. & Boulgarides, James D. Managerial Decision Making: A Guide to Successful Business Decisions. (Illus.). 272p. (Orig.). (C). 1992. pap. write for info. (0-02-404111-4) Macmillan.

Rowe, Alan J. & Mason, Richard O. Managing with Style: A Guide to Understanding, Assessing, & Improving Decision Making. LC 87-45570. (Management Ser.). 243p. 1987. 28.95 (1-55542-074-5) Jossey-Bass.

— Strategic Management & Business Policy: A Methodological Approach. 2nd ed. Dickel, Karl E., ed. 700p. 1985. teacher ed write for info. (0-201-06088-4); pap. text ed. write for info. (0-201-06087-6) Addison-Wesley.

Rowe, Alan J., jt. auth. see Willison, M.

Rowe, Alan J., et al. Cases in Strategic Management. (C). 1986. teacher ed write for info. (0-201-06098-1); pap. text ed. write for info. (0-201-16899-5, 85-18612) Addison-Wesley.

— Strategic Management: A Methodological Approach. 2nd ed. 396p. (C). 1986. teacher ed write for info. (0-318-59831-0); pap. text ed. write for info. (0-201-16898-7) Addison-Wesley.

— Strategic Management & Business Planning: A Methodological Approach. 1982. text ed. write for info. (0-201-06387-5) Addison-Wesley.

Rowe, Alan R. Relics, Water & the Kitchen Sink: A Diver's Guide to Underwater Archeology. 2nd ed. 56p. 1988. reprint ed. pap. 6.95 (0-9616399-1-1) Sea Sports Pubns.

Rowe, Allan & Harris, Tim. Practical English 3B. 2nd ed. 178p. (C). 1988. pap. text ed. 7.50 (0-15-570930-5) HB Coll Pubs.

Rowe, Allan, jt. auth. see Harris, Tim.

Rowe, Allen, jt. auth. see Harris, Tim.

Rowe, Ami. AMI Model MM-3 "Music Miracle" & "MM4 "Trimount" Combined Service Manual of 1969-70. rev. ed. Adams, Frank, ed. 164p. 1986. reprint ed. 39.95 (0-939971-12-7, R-370) AMR Pub Co.

— AMI Model MM-3 "Music Miracle" & MM4 "Trimount" Parts Catalog of 1969-70. rev. ed. Adams, Frank, ed. 126p. 1986. reprint ed. 32.95 (0-939971-13-5, R-371) AMR Pub Co.

Rowe Ami. AMI Model MM6 "Super Star" of 1971-72 Service & Parts Manual Supplement. rev. ed. Adams, Frank, ed. 66p. 1986. 25.00 (0-939971-14-3, R-372) AMR Pub Co.

Rowe, Amy & Rowe, Philip. Ernest the Fierce Mouse. rev. ed. (Quality Time Easy Readers Ser.). (Illus.). 32p. (J). (gr. k-2). 1990. reprint ed. lib. bdg. 10.95 (1-878363-08-5) Forest Hse.

Rowe, Anita, jt. auth. see Gardenswartz, Lee.

Rowe, Ann P. Costumes & Featherwork of the Lords of Chimor. LC 84-50103. (Illus.). 192p. 1984. pap. 35.00 (0-87405-023-5) Textile Mus.

Rowe, Ann P., ed. The Junius B. Bird Conference on Andean Textiles. LC 86-51317. (Illus.). 384p. 1986. pap. 35.00 (0-87405-025-1) Textile Mus.

Rowe, Ann P. & Stevens, Rebecca A., eds. Ed Rossbach: Forty Years of Exploration & Innovation in Fiber Art. LC 89-83928. (Illus.). 164p. 1990. pap. 24.95 (0-937274-52-6) Lark Books.

Rowe, Ann P., et al, eds. The Junius B. Bird Pre-Columbian Textile Conference. LC 79-63729. (Illus.). 278p. 1979. 22.50 (0-318-42011-2) Textile Mus.

— Junius B. Bird Pre-Columbian Textile Conference, May 19 & 20,1973. LC 79-63729. (Illus.). 280p. 1979. 30.00 (0-88402-086-X) Dumbarton Oaks.

Rowe, Anne E. The Idea of Florida in the American Literary Imagination. LC 85-18043. (Southern Literary Studies). (Illus.). xiv, 159p. 1986. text ed. 27.50 (0-8071-1262-3) La State U Pr.

— The Idea of Florida in the American Literary Imagination. (Florida Sand Dollar Book Ser.). (Illus.). 176p. 1992. reprint ed. pap. 13.95 (0-8130-1107-8) U Press Fla.

Rowe, B. R., et al, eds. Dissociative Recombination: Theory, Experiment, & Applications. (NATO ASI Series B, Physics: Vol. 313). 286p. (C). 1993. 95.00 (0-306-44568-9, Plenum Pr) Plenum.

Rowe, Barney. Catching More Flounder - Fluke. (Illus.). 36p. (Orig.). 1982. pap. 2.75 (0-940844-74-5) Wellspring.

— Saltwater Fishing. (Illus.). 36p. (Orig.). 1983. pap. 2.75 (0-940844-55-9) Wellspring.

Rowe, Basil. Under My Wings. (Airlines History Project Ser.). reprint ed. 30.00 (0-404-19333-1) AMS Pr.

Rowe, Beverly. Sea Gems. LC 82-60557. (Illus.). 64p. 1982. 24.00 (0-88014-046-1) Mosaic Pr OH.

*Rowe, Bruce M. The College Survival Guide. LC 94-34060. 1994. text ed. 9.50 (0-314-04511-2) West Pub.

— College Survival Guide: Hints & References to Aid College Students. 2nd ed. Perlee, Clyde, ed. 98p. (C). 1992. pap. text ed. 8.25 (0-314-00363-0) West Pub.

Rowe, Bruce M., jt. auth. see Stein, Philip L.

Rowe, C. J., ed. see Plato.

Rowe, Carter R., ed. The Shoulder. (Illus.). 1988p. 1987. 175.00 (0-443-08457-2) Churchill.

Rowe, Clarence J. & Mink, Walter D. An Outline of Psychiatry. 10th ed. 464p. (C). 1993. pap. text ed. write for info. (0-697-10490-7) Brown & Benchmark.

Rowe, Colin. Architecture of Good Intentions. (Illus.). 144p. 1994. pap. 35.00 (1-85490-307-1, Academy Edits) St Martin.

— As I Was Saying: Recollections & Miscellaneous Essays Vol. 1: Texas, Pre-Texas, Cambridge. Caragonne, Alexander, ed. LC 95-15191. (Illus.). 288p. (C). 1995. 30.00 (0-262-18167-3) MIT Pr.

— As I Was Saying: Recollections & Miscellaneous Essays Vol. 2: Cornelliana. (Illus.). 408p. (C). 1995. 35.00 (0-262-18168-1) MIT Pr.

— As I Was Saying: Recollections & Miscellaneous Essays Vol. 3: Urbanistics. (Illus.). 432p. (C). 1995. 35.00 (0-262-18169-X) MIT Pr.

— Mathematics of the Ideal Villa & Other Essays. (Illus.). (C). 1982. pap. 15.95x (0-262-68037-8) MIT Pr.

Rowe, Colin & Koetter, Fred. Collage City. 1978. pap. 19.95x (0-262-68042-4) MIT Pr.

Rowe, Crayton E., Jr. & MacIsaac, David S. Empathic Attunement: The "Technique" of Psychoanalytic Self Psychology. LC 88-8069. 336p. 1993. pap. 35.00x (0-87668-551-3) Aronson.

Rowe, Cyprian, jt. ed. see Bensinger, Gad J.

Rowe, D., jt. auth. see Peavy, H. S.

Rowe, D., jt. auth. see Sisson, H.

Rowe, D. J., ed. Dynamic Structure of Nuclear States: Proceedings of 1971 Mont Tremblant International Summer School. LC 75-186282. 599p. reprint ed. pap. 170.80 (0-317-08960-9, 2014391) Bks Demand.

Rowe, D. M., ed. First European Conference on Thermoelectrics. 424p. 1988. boxed 115.00 (0-86341-134-7, ED007) Inst Elect Eng.

— Handbook of Thermoelectrics. 768p. 1995. 149.95 (0-8493-0146-7, 146) CRC Pr.

Rowe, D. M., jt. auth. see Bhandari, C. M.

Rowe, David. Thunder & Trumpets: The Millerites Dissenting Religion in Upstate New York, 1800-1850. (American Academy of Religion, Studies in Religion: No. 38). 1985. pap. 24.95 (0-89130-769-9, 01 00 38) Scholars Pr GA.

Rowe, David & McCleary, John, eds. The History of Modern Mathematics, Vol. 1. 453p. 1989. text ed. 61.00 (0-12-599661-6) Acad Pr.

— The History of Modern Mathematics, Vol. 2. 325p. 1989. text ed. 59.95 (0-12-599662-4) Acad Pr.

Rowe, David, jt. ed. see Borrowdale, Andrew.

Rowe, David C. Limits of Family Influence: Genes, Experience, & Behavior. LC 93-21876. 232p. 1993. lib. bdg. 30.00 (0-89862-132-1) Guilford Pr.

Rowe, David E., jt. ed. see Knobloch, Eberhard.

Rowe, David E., jt. auth. see Parshall, Karen H.

Rowe, David J. Faith at Work: A Celebration of All We Do. 120p. (Orig.). 1994. pap. 10.95 (1-880837-80-3) Smyth & Helwys.

Rowe, David M., jt. ed. see Nye, Joseph S., Jr.

Rowe, David N. Modern China: A Brief History. 11.25 (0-8446-2841-7) Peter Smith.

*Rowe, Debi M. Introduction to the Siddur: Amidah. Grishaver, Joel L., ed. & illus. by. 143p. (Orig.). (J). (gr. 6-7). 1992. pap. text ed. 6.95 (0-933873-75-1) Torah Aura.

— Introduction to the Siddur: Amidah, Teacher's Guide. Grishaver, Joel L., ed. & illus. by. 150p. (Orig.). (J). (gr. 6-7). Date not set. teacher ed, pap. text ed. 16.95 (0-933873-91-3) Torah Aura.

— Introduction to the Siddur: The Brakhah System. (Illus.). 96p. (J). (gr. 4-5). 1990. student ed 5.50 (0-933873-58-1) Torah Aura.

— Introduction to the Siddur: The Shema & Its Blessings. (Illus.). 164p. (J). (gr. 5-6). 1991. student ed 5.95 (0-933873-60-3) Torah Aura.

Rowe, Deborah. Preschoolers As Authors: Literacy Learning in the Social World of the Classroom. Green, Judith, ed. LC 93-1672. (Language & Social Processes Ser.). 288p. (C). 1993. text ed. 52.50 (1-881303-71-3); pap. text ed. 19.95 (1-881303-72-1) Hampton Pr NJ.

Rowe, Dennis. Considered Responses to Contemporary Terrorism in Democratic Societies. 56p. (C). 3.50 (0-942511-06-9) OICJ.

R

An Asterisk (*) at the beginning of an entry indicates that the title is appearing in BIP for the first time.

Rowe, Dennis, intro. International Drug Trafficking. 168p. (C). 1988. 19.00 (0-942511-16-6); pap. text ed. 14.00 (0-942511-15-8) OICJ.

***Rowe, Donald R. & Mohamed Abdel Magid, Isam.** Handbook of Wastewater Reclamation & Reuse. LC 94-46589. 592p. 1995. 95.00 (0-87371-671-X, L671) Lewis Pubs.

Rowe, Donald W. O Love, O Charite! Contraries Harmonized in Chaucer's "Troilus" LC 76-4816. 211p. 1976. 12.50 (0-8093-0697-2) S Ill U Pr.

— Through Nature to Eternity: Chaucer's "Legend of Good Women" LC 87-5993. x, 218p. 1988. 25.00 (0-8032-3882-7) U of Nebr Pr.

Rowe, Dorothy. Depression: The Way Out of Your Prison. (Illus.). 242p. 1984. pap. 10.95 (0-7100-9586-4, RKP) Routledge.

— The Experience of Depression. LC 77-9609. 292p. reprint ed. pap. 83.30 (0-317-07822-4, 2022406) Bks Demand.

— Living with the Bomb. (Illus.). 256p. 1985. pap. 8.95 (0-7102-0477-9, RKP) Routledge.

Rowe, E., jt. auth. see Yagar, Sam.

Rowe, Ednor, ed. see Kapitza, S. P. & Melekhin, V. N.

***Rowe, Elsebeth.** The Bird of Barjag. 1995. 10.95 (0-8062-5240-5) Carlton.

Rowe, Erna. Los Dinosaurios Gigantes (Giant Dinosaurs) Palacios, Argentina, tr. (Illus.). 32p. (J). (ps-2). pap. 4.95 (0-590-40647-7) Scholastic Inc.

— Giant Dinosaurs. (Illus.). (J). (gr. k-3). 1975. pap. 2.95 (0-590-40262-5) Scholastic Inc.

Rowe, Frank. The Enemy among Us: A Story of Witch-Hunting in the McCarthy Era. LC 79-56759. 160p. 1980. 5.95 (0-917982-18-5) Cougar Bks.

— The Famous Airplanes of Kansas. Lickei, Elizabeth, ed. (Illus.). 64p. (Orig.). (J). 1992. pap. 3.95 (1-880652-12-9) Wichita Eagle.

Rowe, Frank & Miner, Craig. Borne on the South Wind: A Century of Kansas Aviation. Janssen, Bruce, ed. (Illus.). 240p. 1994. 24.95 (1-880652-33-1) Wichita Eagle.

Rowe, Fred. The Career Connection for College Education: A Guide to College Majors & Related Career Opportunities. 272p. (Orig.). 1994. pap. 16.95 (1-56370-142-1, CCCE) JIST Works.

— The Career Connection for Technical Education: A Guide to Technical Education & Related Career Opportunities. 190p. (Orig.). 1994. pap. 14.95 (1-56370-143-X, CCTE) JIST Works.

Rowe, Frederick J. AP Chemistry. 2nd ed. LC 93-18320. 1993. 14.00 (0-671-84778-3, Arco Test) P-H Gen Ref & Trav.

Rowe, Frederick M., et al, eds. Enterprise Law of the Eighties: European & American Perspectives on Competition & Industrial Organization. LC 80-67958. 254p. (Orig.). 1980. 10.50 (0-685-00353-1); pap. text ed. 15.00 (0-89707-018-6, 5030033) Amer Bar Assn.

Rowe, G. S. Embattled Bench: The Pennsylvania Supreme Court & the Forging of a Democratic Society, 1684-1809. LC 93-47888. (C). 1994. write for info. (0-87413-526-5) U Delaware Pr.

Rowe, G. W., et al, eds. Finite Element Plasticity & Metalforming Analysis. (Illus.). 350p. (C). 1991. 110.00 (0-521-38362-5) Cambridge U Pr.

Rowe, Gaelene. Guiding Young Artists: Curriculum Ideas for Teachers. (Illus.). 89p. (Orig.). 1989. pap. text ed. 16.00 (0-435-08499-2) Heinemann.

Rowe, Gail S. Thomas McKean: The Shaping of an American Republicanism. LC 77-94085. (Illus.). 517p. reprint ed. pap. 147.40 (0-8357-5500-2, 2035115) Bks Demand.

Rowe, Gavin, illus. Abraham & Isaac. LC 84-18076. (People of the Bible Ser.). 32p. (J). (gr. k-4). 1985. 14.95 (0-8172-1994-3) Raintree Steck-V.

— The Birth of Jesus. LC 82-9048. (People of the Bible Ser.). 32p. (J). (gr. k-4). 1982. 14.65 (0-8172-1977-3) Raintree Steck-V.

— The Prodigal Son. LC 82-23011. (People of the Bible Ser.). 32p. (J). (gr. k-4). 1983. 14.65 (0-8172-1982-X) Raintree Steck-V.

Rowe, Genevieve B., ed. see Rowe, Josiah P., Jr.

Rowe, George, et al, eds. Building Family Strengths Five: Continuity & Diversity. 505p. 1984. pap. 15.95 (0-89292-090-4) Educ Dev Ctr.

Rowe, George E. Distinguishing Jonson: Imitation, Rivalry, & the Direction of a Dramatic Career. LC 87-13198. xii, 220p. 1988. 25.00 (0-8032-3883-5) U of Nebr Pr.

— Thomas Middleton & the New Comedy Tradition. LC 79-4289. 252p. reprint ed. pap. 71.90 (0-7837-6179-1, 2045901) Bks Demand.

Rowe, George S., ed. see Williams, Thomas & Calvert, James.

Rowe, Gerard P., jt. auth. see Rashkind, Alan B.

Rowe, Gilbert T., ed. Deep-Sea Biology. (Sea Ser.: No. 8). 569p. reprint ed. pap. 162.20 (0-7837-2806-9, 2057666) Bks Demand.

Rowe, Gilbert T. & Pariente, Vita, eds. Deep-Sea Food Chains & the Global Carbon Cycle. (C). 1992. lib. bdg. 137.50 (0-7923-1608-8) Kluwer Ac.

Rowe, Glen W. Theoretical Models In Biology: The Original of Life, the Immune System, & the Brain. LC 93-40873. (Illus.). 440p. 1994. 52.50 (0-19-859688-X); pap. write for info. (0-19-859687-1) OUP.

Rowe, H. A., ed. Intelligence: Reconceptualization & Measurement. 312p. (C). 1991. text ed. 65.00 (0-8058-0942-2) L Erlbaum Assocs.

Rowe, Helga. Learning with Personal Computers. (C). 1992. 75.00 (0-86431-129-X, Pub. by Aust Council Educ Res AT) St Mut.

Rowe, Helga A. Problem Solving & Intelligence. 416p. (C). 1985. text ed. 79.95 (0-89859-347-6) L Erlbaum Assocs.

Rowe, Henry K. Modern Pathfinders of Christianity: The Lives & Deeds of Seven Centuries of Christian Leaders. LC 68-16973. (Essay Index Reprint Ser.). 1977. 19.95 (0-8369-0839-2) Ayer.

Rowe, Hortense M., jt. ed. see Joseph, Gloria I.

Rowe, J. Fostering in the Eighties. (C). 1989. 50.00 (0-903534-48-7, Pub. by Brit Ag for Adopt & Fost UK) St Mut.

Rowe, J. & Lambert, L. Children Who Wait (Extracts) (C). 1989. 50.00 (0-903534-31-2, Pub. by Brit Ag for Adopt & Fost UK) St Mut.

Rowe, J., et al. Child Care Now: A Survey of Placement Patterns. (C). 1989. 50.00 (0-903534-85-1, Pub. by Brit Ag for Adopt & Fost UK) St Mut.

— Long-Term Fostering & the Children Act: A Study of Foster Parents Who Went on to Adopt. (C). 1989. 39.00 (0-903534-49-5, Pub. by Brit Ag for Adopt & Fost UK) St Mut.

Rowe, J. G., ed. Aspects of Late Medieval Government & Society: Essays Presented to J. R. Lander. 278p. 1986. 40.00 (0-8020-5695-4) U of Toronto Pr.

Rowe, J. N. An Investigation of the Effects of Solar Flares & Stratospheric Warmings on the Lower Ionosphere. LC 72-135091. 90p. 1970. 15.00 (0-403-04533-9) Scholarly.

Rowe, J. Phillip, jt. auth. see Gray, John T.

Rowe, J. W., ed. Natural Products of Woody Plants. (Wood Science Ser.). (Illus.). 1280p. 1990. 568.00 (0-387-50300-5) Spr-Verlag.

Rowe, Jack. No-It's Not the Devil: It's You. 80p. (Orig.). 1990. spiral bd. 3.00 (0-9621384-1-X) Rowe Evangelistic Minist.

— The Strait Way, Vol. 1. (Illus.). 128p. (Orig.). 1988. spiral bd. 4.95 (0-9621384-0-1) Rowe Evangelistic Minist.

Rowe, James G., Jr. Love to All, Jim: A Young Man's Letters from Vietnam. Prescott, Gary R., ed. LC 88-35579. (Illus.). 128p. (Orig.). 1989. pap. 9.95 (0-89407-096-7) Strawberry Hill.

Rowe, James N. Five Years to Freedom. 480p. 1984. mass mkt. 5.95 (0-345-31460-3) Ballantine.

Rowe, Jeanine C. Eyes of Desire. Hannan, R., ed. 370p. (YA). 1991. pap. 5.99 (0-9626415-0-2) Intl Info NY.

***Rowe, Jennifer.** Death in Store. 1994. pap. 4.99 (0-553-56875-2) Bantam.

— Makeover Murders. 1994. 4.99 (0-553-29740-6); mass mkt. 5.50 (0-553-29693-0) Bantam.

— Stranglehold. 1995. mass mkt. 4.99 (0-553-56819-1) Bantam.

— Stranglehold. large type ed. LC 94-49410. 1995. pap. 18.95 (0-7838-1247-7) Hall.

***Rowe, Jeremy.** History of Arizona Photography: From Daguerreotypes to World War I. Chapman, Jean, ed. (Illus.). 200p. (Orig.). 1995. pap. text ed. 29.00 (0-9621940-9-3) C Mautz Pubng.

Rowe, John. Jack the Dog. (Illus.). 28p. (J). (gr. k up). 1993. 14.95 (0-88708-266-1, Picture Book Studio) S&S Childrens.

— Letters & Diary of John Rowe: Boston Merchant, Seventeen Fifty Nine to Seventeen Sixty Two. Cunningham, Anne R., ed. LC 76-76564. (Eyewitness Accounts of the American Revolution Ser., No. 1). (Illus.). 453p. 1969. reprint ed. 28.95 (0-405-01148-2) Ayer.

— Rabbit Moon. LC 92-6047. (Illus.). 28p. (J). 1992. pap. 14.95 (0-88708-246-7, Picture Book Studio) S&S Childrens.

Rowe, John, ed. see Carpenter, Allan & Maginnis, Matthew.

Rowe, John, jt. ed. see Wetle, Terrie.

***Rowe, John A.** Baby Crow. LC 94-18652. (J). (gr. k-3). 1994. 16.95 (1-55858-277-0); 16.88 (1-55858-278-9) North-South Bks NYC.

Rowe, John C. The Theoretical Dimensions of Henry James. LC 84-40158. (Wisconsin Project on American Writers Ser.: No. 2). 304p. 1984. 27.50 (0-299-09970-9) U of Wis Pr.

— Theoretical Dimensions of Henry James. LC 84-40158. (Wisconsin Project on American Writers Ser.: No. 2). 304p. 1985. pap. 14.95 (0-299-09974-1) U of Wis Pr.

Rowe, John C. & Berg, Richard, eds. The Vietnam War & American Culture. (Social Foundations of Aesthetic Forms Ser.). (Illus.). 1991. text ed. 35.00 (0-231-06732-1) Col U Pr.

— The Vietnam War & American Culture. (Social Foundations of Aesthetic Forms Ser.). 320p. (C). 1992. pap. 13.95 (0-231-06733-X) Col U Pr.

Rowe, John C., jt. ed. see McWhirter, David.

Rowe, John Carlos. Through the Custom House: Nineteenth Century American Fiction & Modern Theory. LC 81-20866. 256p. (C). 1982. text ed. 32.50 (0-8018-2677-2) Johns Hopkins.

Rowe, John F. Newington, New Hampshire: A Heritage of Independence since 1630. LC 87-2235. (Illus.). 336p. 1987. 18.00 (0-914659-25-1) Phoenix Pub.

Rowe, John G., jt. auth. see Edbury, Peter W.

Rowe, John L. & Etier, A. Faborn. Typewriting Drills for Speed & Accuracy. 4th ed. LC 76-50096. 1977. text ed. 12.96 (0-07-054151-5) McGraw.

Rowe, John L., et al. Gregg Typing, One Ninety-One Series. 2nd ed. Incl. Book 1, General Typing. 1967. text ed. 11.76 (0-07-054105-1); 1967. write for info. (0-318-54172-6) McGraw.

— Typing Three Hundred, 2 vols., Vol. 1: General Course. (Illus.). 288p. (gr. 9-12). 1972. Vol. 1 General Course. text ed. 24.24 (0-07-054090-X) McGraw.

Rowe, John R., et al. The New Model Me. (gr. 8-12). 1983. teacher ed 13.95 (0-8077-2733-4); student ed, text ed. 10.95 (0-8077-2732-6) Tchrs Coll.

Rowe, John W. Primary Commodities in International Trade. LC 65-18930. 236p. (Orig.). reprint ed. pap. 67.30 (0-317-10223-0, 2022467) Bks Demand.

— Wages in Practice & Theory. LC 70-76356. 1969. reprint ed. 35.00 (0-678-06502-0) Kelley.

Rowe, John W. & Ahronheim, Judith C., eds. Annual Review of Gerontology & Geriatrics 1992, Vol. 12: With Focus on Medications. 180p. 1992. 46.00 (0-8261-6494-3) Springer Pub.

Rowe, John W. & Besdine, Richard W. Geriatric Medicine. 2nd ed. (Illus.). 750p. 1988. 115.00 (0-316-75969-4, Little Med Div) Little.

Rowe, John W., jt. ed. see Katzman, Robert.

Rowe, Jon, jt. auth. see Partridge, Derek.

Rowe, Josiah P., Jr. Letters from a World War I Aviator. Rowe, Genevieve B. & Doran, Diana R., eds. LC 86-90456. (Illus.). 200p. 1986. 15.95 (0-9616886-0-2) Sinclaire Pr.

Rowe, Joyce A. Equivocal Endings in Classic American Novels: The Scarlet Letter, Adventures of Huckleberry Finn, The Ambassadors, The Great Gatsby. 176p. 1988. 49.95 (0-521-33532-9) Cambridge U Pr.

***Rowe, Julian.** Colorful Light. (J). (gr. 3-6). 1993. pap. 4.95 (0-516-48131-2) Childrens.

— Feel & Touch. (J). (gr. 3-6). 1994. pap. 4.95 (0-516-48132-0) Childrens.

— Keep It Afloat. (J). (gr. 3-6). 1994. pap. 4.95 (0-516-48134-7) Childrens.

— Keeping Your Balance. (J). (gr. 3-6). 1994. pap. 4.95 (0-516-48133-9) Childrens.

— Make It Move. (J). (gr. 3-6). 1994. pap. 4.95 (0-516-48135-5) Childrens.

— Making Sounds. (J). (gr. 3-6). 1994. pap. 4.95 (0-516-48136-3) Childrens.

— Science & Technology. (Legacies Ser.). (Illus.). 48p. (J). (gr. 4-6). 1995. 15.95 (1-56847-395-8) Thomson Lrning.

Rowe, Julian & Perham, Molly. Amazing Magnets. LC 94-16942. (First Science Ser.). (Illus.). 32p. (J). (gr. 1-4). 1994. lib. bdg. 13.95 (0-516-08137-3); pap. 4.95 (0-516-48137-1) Childrens.

— Build It Strong! LC 94-16941. (First Science Ser.). (Illus.). 32p. (J). (gr. 1-4). 1994. lib. bdg. 13.95 (0-516-08138-1); pap. 4.95 (0-516-48138-X) Childrens.

— Colorful Light. LC 93-8217. (First Science Ser.). (Illus.). 32p. (J). (gr. 1-4). 1993. lib. bdg. 13.95 (0-516-08131-4) Childrens.

— Feel & Touch! LC 93-8214. (First Science Ser.). (Illus.). 32p. (J). (gr. 1-4). 1993. lib. bdg. 13.95 (0-516-08132-2) Childrens.

— Flying High. LC 94-12244. (First Science Ser.). (Illus.). 32p. (J). (gr. 1-4). 1994. lib. bdg. 13.95 (0-516-08139-X); pap. 4.95 (0-516-48139-8) Childrens.

— Keeping Your Balance. LC 93-8215. (First Science Ser.). (Illus.). 32p. (J). (gr. 1-4). 1993. lib. bdg. 13.95 (0-516-08133-0) Childrens.

— Make It Move! LC 93-13737. (First Science Ser.). (Illus.). 32p. (J). (gr. 1-4). 1993. lib. bdg. 13.95 (0-516-08135-7) Childrens.

— Making Sounds. LC 92-13738. (First Science Ser.). (Illus.). 32p. (J). (gr. 1-4). 1993. lib. bdg. 13.95 (0-516-08136-5) Childrens.

— Using Energy. LC 94-13911. (First Science Ser.). (Illus.). 32p. (J). (gr. 1-4). 1994. lib. bdg. 13.95 (0-516-08140-3); pap. 4.95 (0-516-48140-1) Childrens.

— Watch It Grow! LC 94-12258. (First Science Ser.). (Illus.). 32p. (J). (gr. 1-4). 1994. lib. bdg. 13.95 (0-516-08141-1); pap. 4.95 (0-516-48141-X) Childrens.

— Weather Watch! LC 94-16944. (First Science Ser.). (Illus.). 32p. (J). (gr. 1-4). 1994. lib. bdg. 13.95 (0-516-08142-X); pap. 4.95 (0-516-48142-8) Childrens.

Rowe, Julian, jt. auth. see Burns, Peggy.

Rowe, Julian, jt. auth. see Lafferty, Peter.

Rowe, Julian, jt. ed. see Lafferty, Peter.

Rowe, Julian, jt. auth. see Perham, Molly.

Rowe, Julina & Perham, Molly. Keep it Afloat! LC 93-8213. (First Science Ser.). (Illus.). 32p. (J). (gr. 1-4). 1993. lib. bdg. 13.95 (0-516-08134-9) Childrens.

Rowe, K. Management Techniques for Civil Engineering Construction. (Illus.). x, 268p. 1975. 63.00 (0-85334-613-5, Pub. by Elsevier Applied Sci UK) Elsevier.

Rowe, Karen E. Saint & Singer: Edward Taylor's Typology & the Poetics of Meditation. (Cambridge Studies in American Literature & Culture: No. 18). 320p. 1986. 59.95 (0-521-30865-8) Cambridge U Pr.

Rowe, Kathleen. The Unruly Woman: Gender & the Genres of Laughter. LC 94-13656. (Texas Film Studies Ser.). (Illus.). 272p. 1995. text ed. 37.50x (0-292-79072-4); pap. 17.95 (0-292-77069-3) U of Tex Pr.

— Women's Issues. 40p. (Orig.). 1986. pap. 2.55 (0-89486-361-4, 5498B) Hazelden.

Rowe, Kenneth. The Postal History of the Forwarding Agents. Hartmann, Leonard H., ed. LC 84-80011. (Illus.). 296p. 1984. 35.00 (0-917528-06-9) L H Hartmann.

Rowe, Kenneth E. Methodist Union Catalog: Pre-1976 Imprints, Vol. V:G-Haz. LC 75-33190. 371p. 1981. 29.00 (0-8108-1454-4) Scarecrow.

— United Methodist Studies, Basic Bibliographies. 3rd ed. 96p. 1992. pap. 5.95 (0-687-43165-4) Abingdon.

Rowe, Kenneth E., ed. Methodist Union Catalog: Pre-1976 Imprints, 20 vols., Vol. I, A-bj. LC 75-33190. 438p. 1975. 29.00 (0-8108-0880-3) Scarecrow.

— Methodist Union Catalog: Pre-1976 Imprints, Vol. II: Bl-cha. LC 75-33190. 422p. 1976. 29.00 (0-8108-0920-6) Scarecrow.

— Methodist Union Catalog: Pre-1976 Imprints, Vol. III, Che-Dix. LC 75-33190. 431p. 1978. 29.00 (0-8108-1067-0) Scarecrow.

— Methodist Union Catalog: Pre-1976 Imprints, Vol. IV, Do-Fy. LC 75-33190. 436p. 1979. 29.00 (0-8108-1225-8) Scarecrow.

— Methodist Union Catalog: Pre-1976 Imprints, Vol. VI: He-I. LC 75-33190. 360p. 1985. 29.00 (0-8108-1725-X) Scarecrow.

— Methodist Union Catalog Vol. VII: J-Le: Pre-1976 Imprints. 419p. 1994. 49.50 (0-8108-2669-0) Scarecrow.

— The Place of Wesley in the Christian Tradition: Essays Delevered at Drew University in Celebration of the Commencement of the Publication of the Oxford Edition of the Works of John Wesley. LC 76-27659. 168p. 1976. 20.00 (0-8108-0981-8) Scarecrow.

Rowe, Kenneth L. Communications in Marketing. (Occupational Manuals & Projects in Marketing Ser.). (Illus.). 1978. text ed. 12.28 (0-07-054154-X) McGraw.

Rowe, Kenneth W. Mathew Carey, a Study in American Economic Development. LC 78-64151. (Johns Hopkins University. Studies in the Social Sciences. Thirtieth Ser. 1912: 4). 144p. 1982. reprint ed. 37.50 (0-404-61261-X) AMS Pr.

Rowe, L. S. The United States & Puerto Rico. 1976. lib. bdg. 59.95 (0-8490-1242-2) Gordon Pr.

Rowe, Laura, illus. The Life & Progress of Henry Quick of Zennor. (C). 1989. 22.00 (0-907566-43-X, Pub. by Dyllansow Truran UK) St Mut.

Rowe, Leah. Medical Dictation with Foreign Accents. rev. ed. McFadden, S. Michele, ed. 1986. 149.50 (0-89262-017-X) Career Pub.

— Medical Sound-Alikes & Spelling Reference. McFadden, S. Michele & Wilson, Roberta, eds. 1978. pap. text ed. 6.95 (0-89262-007-2) Career Pub.

Rowe-Leete, Susan, jt. auth. see Kidel, Mark.

Rowe, Leo S. United States & Puerto Rico. LC 74-14249. (Puerto Rican Experience Ser.). 290p. 1975. reprint ed. 23.95 (0-405-06235-4) Ayer.

Rowe, Lindsay J., jt. auth. see Yochum, Terry R.

Rowe, Lois. On Call. LC 58-7316. 233p. 1988. reprint ed. pap. 8.99 (0-8010-7749-4) Baker Bk.

Rowe, M., jt. ed. see Ricci, P. F.

Rowe, M. Jessica. This Is Always Finished, David Dunlap. LC 89-81319. (Illus.). 42p. (Orig.). 1989. pap. 12.00 (0-9614615-9-4) Edmundson.

Rowe, M. Jessica & Cromwell-Lacy, Sherry. Iowa Artists, 1991. (Illus.). 44p. 1991. pap. 8.00 (1-879003-03-1) Edmundson.

Rowe, Maggie, ed. see Ireland, John.

Rowe, Margaret M. Doris Lessing. LC 94-16871. (Women Writers Ser.). 1994. text ed. 24.95 (0-312-12192-X) St Martin.

Rowe, Margaret M., jt. auth. see Huyck, Norma I.

Rowe, Marsha. Sacred Space. 1993. pap. 14.99 (1-85242-260-2) Serpents Tail.

Rowe, Marsha, ed. Sex & the City: A Serpent's Tail Compilation. 240p. (Orig.). 1990. pap. 9.95 (1-85242-165-7) Serpents Tail.

Rowe, Marsha, ed. see Weldon, Fay, et al.

Rowe, Marvin W. & Hyman, Marian, eds. Advances in Analytical Geochemistry, Vol. 1. 1992. 97.50 (1-55938-332-1) Jai Pr.

Rowe, Mary. Knitted Tams. LC 89-7438. (Illus.). 110p. (Orig.). 1989. pap. 12.95 (0-934026-48-3) Interweave.

***Rowe, Michael.** Writing Below the Belt. 1995. pap. 23.95 (1-56333-363-5) Masquerade.

Rowe, Michael, jt. auth. see Hughes, Richard.

Rowe, Michael, jt. auth. see Murphy, John.

Rowe, Mike. Chicago Blues: The City & the Music. LC 81-7874. (Quality Paperbacks Ser.). (Illus.). 226p. 1981. reprint ed. pap. 10.95 (0-306-80145-0) Da Capo.

— Chicago Breakdown. LC 79-17645. (Roots of Jazz Ser.). (Illus.). 1979. reprint ed. lib. bdg. 25.00 (0-306-79532-9) Da Capo.

Rowe, Mona & Ryan, Caitlin. A Governor's Policy Guide on AIDS. Glass, Karen, ed. 40p. (Orig.). 1989. pap. text ed. 35.00 (1-55877-049-6) Natl Governor.

Rowe, Monica, jt. auth. see Hart, Chris.

Rowe, Myra. Louisana Lady. 528p. 1986. pap. 3.95 (0-8217-1891-6) Zebra.

— River Temptress. 512p. 1987. pap. 3.95 (0-8217-2227-1) Zebra.

Rowe, N. L. Maxillofacial Injuries. 2nd ed. 1994. 295.00 (0-443-04591-7) Churchill.

Rowe, N. L. & Williams, J. L., eds. Maxillofacial Injuries, 2 vols., Set. (Illus.). 1080p. 1985. text ed. 320.00 (0-443-01509-0) Churchill.

Rowe, Neil C. Introduction to Artificial Intelligence Through PROLOG. (Illus.). 368p. (C). 1987. text ed. 37.33 (0-13-477910-X) P-H.

Rowe, Newton A. Samoa under the Sailing Gods. LC 75-35209. reprint ed. 57.50 (0-404-14232-X) AMS Pr.

Rowe, Nicholas. Rules & Institutions. 224p. 1989. text ed. 42.50 (0-472-10155-2) U of Mich Pr.

— The Tragedy of Jane Shore. Pedicord, Harry W., ed. LC 73-85439. (Regents Restoration Drama Ser.). xxviii, 97p. 1974. 15.00 (0-8032-0381-0); pap. 7.95 (0-8032-5381-8) U of Nebr Pr.

Rowe, Nicholas, ed. see Shakespeare, William.

***Rowe, Patricia.** Children of the Dawn. (Orig.). 1996. mass mkt. write for info. (0-446-60205-1) Warner Bks.

— Keepers of the Misty Time. 384p. (Orig.). 1994. mass mkt. 5.99 (0-446-36435-5) Warner Bks.

Rowe, Patricia L. Shorthand Fashion Sketching. 3rd ed. LC 60-6848. (Illus.). 145p. reprint ed. pap. 41.40 (0-685-44413-9, 2032487) Bks Demand.

Rowe, Patrick J., et al. WHO Manual for the Standardized Investigation & Diagnosis of the Infertile Couple. (Illus.). 65p. (C). 1993. 24.95 (0-521-43136-0) Cambridge U Pr.

Rowe, Paul, jt. auth. see Evans, Jack R.

Rowe, Penelope. Unacceptable Behaviour. 147p. (Orig.). 1993. pap. 10.95 (1-86373-189-X, Pub. by Allen & Unwin Aust Pty AT) IPG Chicago.

Rowe, Peter, ed. Rodolpho Machado & Jorge Silvetti: Urban Design Work. (Illus.). 96p. 1989. pap. text ed. 25.00 (0-8478-1068-2) Rizzoli Intl.

An Asterisk (*) at the beginning of an entry indicates that the title is appearing in BIP for the first time.

Rowe, Peter, et al, eds. The Gulf War in International & English Law. LC 92-39187. 448p. 1993. 125.00 (0-415-07520-3, A7688) Routledge.

Rowe, Peter G. Design Thinking. (Illus.). 242p. 1991. reprint ed. pap. 14.95x (0-262-68067-X) MIT Pr.

— Making a Middle Landscape. (Illus.). 352p. 1991. 47.50x (0-262-18138-X) MIT Pr.

— Making a Middle Landscape. (Illus.). 336p. 1992. reprint ed. pap. 22.50x (0-262-68077-7) MIT Pr.

— Modernity & Housing. LC 92-45140. 440p. 1993. pap. 47.50 (0-262-18151-7) MIT Pr.

Rowe, Phil, jt. auth. see Walker, John.

Rowe, Philip, jt. auth. see Rowe, Amy.

Rowe, R. E. Concrete Bridge Design. (Illus.). 372p. 1966. 86.50 (0-85334-110-9, Pub. by Elsevier Applied Sci UK) Elsevier.

Rowe, R. P. A Concise Chronicle of the Events of the Great War, 1914-1920. 1976. lib. bdg. 69.95 (0-8490-1660-6) Gordon Pr.

Rowe, Randall C., ed. Potato Health Management. LC 93-70663. (Plant Health Management Ser.). (Illus.). 178p. 1993. pap. 39.00 (0-89054-144-2) Am Phytopathol Soc.

Rowe, Ray. White Water Kayaking. (Illus.). 128p. 1989. pap. 15.95 (0-8117-2284-8) Stackpole.

Rowe, Robert. How to Win at Horse Racing: The Horse Bettors Bible. LC 90-83812. (Illus.). 192p. (Orig.). 1990. pap. 8.95 (0-940685-11-6) Cardoza Pub.

— How to Win at Horseracing. 2nd ed. LC 93-74315. (Illus.). 208p. 1994. pap. 9.95 (0-940685-45-0) Cardoza Pub.

— Interactive Music Systems: Machine Listening & Composing. (Illus.). 300p. 1992. 37.50 (0-262-18149-5); cd-rom 40.00 (0-262-68075-0) MIT Pr.

— The Value of Visibility: Theory & Applications. 280p. 1982. text ed. 30.00 (0-89011-572-9) Abt Bks.

Rowe, Robert D. & Chestnut, Lauraine G. The Value of Visibility: Economic Theory & Applications for Air Pollution Control. (Illus.). 280p. 1984. reprint ed. lib. bdg. 56.00 (0-8191-4091-0) U Pr of Amer.

Rowe, Sherlie. Decisions, 1. 1983. pap. 4.75 (0-89137-806-5) Quality Pubns.

— Decisions, 2. 1983. pap. 4.75 (0-89137-807-3) Quality Pubns.

— Living with My Father. 1986. pap. 5.75 (0-89137-814-6) Quality Pubns.

Rowe, Sherlie, ed. Teaching Teenage Girls. 1987. pap. 6.50 (0-89137-808-1) Quality Pubns.

Rowe, Stanford H. Business Telecommunications. 2nd ed. 688p. (C). 1991. write for info. (0-02-404104-1) Macmillan.

Rowe, Stanford H., II. Telecommunications for Managers. 3rd rev. ed. LC 94-19934. Orig. Title: Business Telcommunications. 720p. 1994. text ed. 69.00 (0-02-404114-9) P-H.

Rowe, Stephen C. Leaving & Returning: On America's Contributions to a World Ethic. LC 88-47944. 168p. 1989. 32.50 (0-8387-5163-6) Bucknell U Pr.

— Rediscovering the West: An Inquiry into Nothingness & Relatedness. LC 93-37857. (Series in Western Esoteric Traditions). 222p. (C). 1994. text ed. 59.50 (0-7914-1991-6); pap. 19.95 (0-7914-1992-4) State U NY Pr.

***Rowe, Susan, illus.** Snow White: Stand-Up Fairy Tale House. LC 94-37520. (J). 1995. 6.95 (0-8037-1869-1) Dial Bks Young.

Rowe, W. W. Amy & Gully in Rainbowland. LC 92-9075. (Illus.). 84p. (Orig.). (J). (gr. k-4). 1992. pap. 5.95 (1-55939-003-4) Snow Lion Pubns.

— The Buddha's Question. LC 93-13993. (J). 1995. pap. 9.95 (1-55939-020-4) Snow Lion Pubns.

— Gully's Travels in Space-Time. LC 90-71370. 61p. (J). (gr. k-3). 1991. pap. 5.95 (1-55523-385-6) Winston-Derek.

— Small Tall Tales. LC 88-51388. 78p. (J). 1989. 5.95 (1-55523-200-0) Winston-Derek.

Rowe, William. Art Deco Spot Illustrations & Motifs: 513 Original Designs. LC 85-6843. 62p. (Orig.). 1985. pap. 5.95 (0-486-24924-7) Dover.

— Exotic Alphabets & Ornaments. (Illus.). 80p. (Orig.). 1974. pap. 4.95 (0-486-22989-0) Dover.

— Flora & Fauna Design Fantasies. (Pictorial Archive Ser.). (Illus.). 80p. (Orig.). 1976. 4.95 (0-486-23289-1) Dover.

— Flora & Fauna Design Fantasies. (Illus.). (Orig.). 9.00 (0-8446-5462-0) Peter Smith.

— Goods & Merchandise: A Cornucopia of Nineteenth Century Cuts. (Pictorial Archive Ser.). (Illus.). 64p. (Orig.). 1982. pap. 4.95 (0-486-24410-5) Dover.

— HVAC: Design Criteria, Options, Selection. 2nd ed. Morris, Sue & Greene, Mary, eds. (Illus.). 500p. 1994. 82.95 (0-87629-347-X) R S Means.

— Machinery & Mechanical Devices: A Treasury of Nineteenth-Century Cuts. (Pictorial Archive Ser.). (Illus.). 64p. (Orig.). 1987. pap. 4.95 (0-486-25445-3) Dover.

— New Art Deco Borders & Motifs. 80p. 1984. pap. 5.95 (0-486-24709-0) Dover.

— Original Art Deco Designs. (Pictorial Archive Ser.). (Illus.). (Orig.). 1973. pap. 5.95 (0-486-22567-4) Dover.

— Viu's Night Book. (Illus.). 56p. (J). (gr. 3-6). 1995. pap. 7.95 (0-9641330-0-8) Portunus Pubng.

Rowe, William & Schelling, Vivian. Memory & Modernity: Popular Culture in Latin America. 1991. 59.95 (0-86091-322-8, A5374, Pub. by Verso UK); pap. 17.95 (0-86091-541-7, A5376, Pub. by Verso UK) Routledge Chapman & Hall.

Rowe, William, et al. Human Sexuality & the Developmentally Handicapped: A Guidebook for Health Care Professionals. LC 86-28463. (Studies in Health & Human Services: Vol. 7). 245p. 1987. lib. bdg. 89.95 (0-88946-132-5) E Mellen.

Rowe, William D. An Anatomy of Risk. rev. ed. LC 84-14431. 504p. (C). 1988. reprint ed. lib. bdg. 54.50 (0-89874-784-8) Krieger.

— Corporate Risk Assessment: Strategies & Technologies: How to Limit the Risk in Industry. LC 82-2377. (Series of Special Reports: No. 4). (Illus.). 224p. reprint ed. pap. 63.90 (0-8357-6078-2, 2034565) Bks Demand.

— Evaluation Methods for Environmental Standards. 304p. 1983. 168.00 (0-8493-5967-8, RA566) CRC Pr.

Rowe, William H. The Maritime History of Maine: Three Centuries of Shipbuilding & Seafaring. 333p. 1989. reprint ed. pap. 14.95 (0-88448-063-1) Tilbury Hse.

Rowe, William L. Philosophy of Religion: An Introduction. 2nd ed. 206p. (C). 1993. pap. 19.95 (0-534-18816-8) Intl Thomson.

— Thomas Reid on Freedom & Morality. LC 90-55715. 208p. 1991. 29.95 (0-8014-2557-3) Cornell U Pr.

Rowe, William L., ed. Studies in Labor Theory & Practice. LC 81-82455. (Studies in Marxism: Vol. 12). 107p. 1982. 16.25 (0-930656-23-7); pap. 6.50 (0-930656-24-5) MEP Pubns.

Rowe, William L. & Wainwright, William J. Philosophy of Religion. 2nd ed. 492p. (C). 1988. pap. text ed. 22.00 (0-15-570581-4) HB Coll Pubs.

Rowe, William M., ed. Fiber Optics: Technical Directory 1988. LC 86-645303. 266p. reprint ed. pap. 75.90 (0-7837-5141-9, 2044869) Bks Demand.

— Robotics Technical Directory, 1986. LC 86-204600. (Illus.). 178p. reprint ed. pap. 50.80 (0-8357-2999-0, 2039268) Bks Demand.

Rowe, William T. Hankow: Commerce & Society in a Chinese City, 1796-1889. (C). pap. 17.95 (0-8047-2161-0) Stanford U Pr.

— Hankow: Commerce & Society in a Chinese City, 1796-1889. LC 82-61784. xiv, 436p. 1984. 55.00 (0-8047-1204-2) Stanford U Pr.

— Hankow: Conflict & Community in a Chinese City, 1796-1895. (C). pap. 17.95 (0-8047-2160-2) Stanford U Pr.

— Hankow: Conflict & Community in a Chinese City, 1796-1895. (Illus.). 446p. 1989. 55.00 (0-8047-1541-6) Stanford U Pr.

Rowe, William W. Leo Tolstoy. (Twayne's World Authors Ser.: No. 772). 160p. 1986. text ed. 22.95 (0-8057-6623-5, 416, Twayne) Macmillan.

Roweck, Hartmut. Die Gefaesspflanzen Von Schwedisch-Lappland: Beitrag Zu Ihrer Standortsoekologie und Verbreitung. (Flora et Vegetatio Mundi Ser.: Vol. 8). (Illus.). 804p. (GER.). 1981. lib. bdg. 120.00 (3-7682-1321-8) Lubrecht & Cramer.

Rowekamp, Jenise, jt. auth. see Robinson, Catherine.

Rowell, A. Understanding Medical Insurance. 260p. 1990. 49.95 (0-685-74785-9) Practice Mgmt Info.

Rowell, C. Glennon. Assessment & Correction in the Elementary Language Arts. LC 92-29658. 1993. text ed. write for info. (0-205-13998-1) Allyn.

Rowell, C. H. Locust Neurobiology: A Bibliography, 1871-1991. LC 92-11025. 250p. 1992. disk 59.00 (0-8176-2747-2, Pub. by Birkhauser Vlg SZ); disk 59.00 (0-8176-2748-0, Pub. by Birkhauser Vlg SZ) Spr-Verlag.

***Rowell, Charles H., ed.** Ancestral House: The Black Short Story in the Americas & Europe. LC 95-15429. 1995. write for info. (0-8133-2028-3) Westview.

— Ancestral House: The Black Short Story in the Americas & Europe. LC 95-15429. 1995. pap. 19.95 (0-8133-2029-1) Westview.

Rowell, Charles H., ed. see Alexander, Elizabeth.

Rowell, Charles H., ed. see Barrax, Gerald.

Rowell, Charles H., ed. see Brown, Joseph A.

Rowell, Charles H., ed. see Dixon, Melvin.

Rowell, Charles H., ed. see Moss, Thylias.

Rowell, Charles H., ed. see Weaver, Michael S.

Rowell, Chester H. A Historical & Legal Digest of All the Contested Election Cases in the House of Representatives of the U. S. from the 1st to the 56th Congress, 1789-1901. LC 75-35375. (U. S. Government Documents Program Ser.). 864p. 1976. reprint ed. text ed. 145.00 (0-8371-8608-0, ROHL) Greenwood.

Rowell, Cy. Thankful Praise: A Studyguide. 24p. (Orig.). 1987. pap. 2.50 (0-8272-3651-4) Chalice Pr.

Rowell, D. L. Soil Science: Methods & Applications. 350p. (Orig.). 1994. pap. text ed. 49.95 (0-470-22141-0) Halsted Pr.

***Rowell, Galen.** Galen Rowell's Poles Apart: Postcards from the Ends of the Earth, The Antarctic - The Arctic. LC 95-1170. (Illus.). 48p. (Orig.). 1995. pap. 9.00 (0-87156-366-5) Sierra.

— Galen Rowell's Vision: The Art of Adventure Photography. LC 93-6892. (Illus.). 288p. 1993. 30.00 (0-87156-458-0) Sierra.

— Galen Rowell's Vision: The Art of Adventure Photography. LC 93-6892. 1995. pap. 18.00 (0-87156-357-6) Sierra.

— In the Throne Room of the Mountain Gods. LC 86-3749. (Illus.). 326p. 1986. pap. 19.95 (0-87156-764-4) Sierra.

— Mountain Light: In Search of the Dynamic Landscape. (Illus.). 240p. 1995. pap. 25.00 (0-87156-367-3) Sierra.

— Mountain Light: In Search of the Dynamic Landscape. 10th aniversary ed. LC 86-1887. (Illus.). 240p. 1995. 40.00 (0-87156-761-X) Sierra.

— Mountain Light: In Search of the Dynamic Landscape. LC 86-1887. (Illus.). 240p. 1987. reprint ed. pap. 30.00 (0-87156-724-5) Sierra.

— Mountains of the Middle Kingdom: Exploring the High Peaks of China & Tibet. LC 82-19508. (Illus.). 208p. 1983. pap. 24.95 (0-87156-829-2) Sierra.

— Sierra Club Yosemite Postcard Collection;a Portfolio. 1989. pap. 8.95 (0-87156-604-4) Sierra.

— The Yosemite. LC 88-34919. 1989. 40.00 (0-87156-653-2) Sierra.

— The Yosemite. LC 88-34919. (Illus.). 224p. 1992. reprint ed. pap. 25.00 (0-87156-587-0) Sierra.

Rowell, Galen, photos & intro. My Tibet. (Illus.). 168p. 1990. 40.00 (0-520-07109-3) U CA Pr.

— My Tibet. (Illus.). 162p. 1995. pap. 25.00 (0-520-08948-0) U CA Pr.

Rowell, Galen & McPhee, John. Alaska: Images of the Country. deluxe limited ed. LC 81-5265. (Illus.). 160p. 1981. 100.00 (0-87156-293-6) Sierra.

Rowell, Galen A., ed. The Vertical World of Yosemite. LC 73-85908. (Illus.). 218p. (Orig.). 1974. reprint ed. pap. 24.95 (0-911824-87-1) Wilderness Pr.

Rowell, Geoffey, ed. English Religious Traditions & the Genius of Anglicanism. 256p. (Orig.). 1994. pap. 16.95 (0-687-11762-3) Abingdon.

Rowell, Geoffrey. The Vision Glorious: Themes & Personalities of the Catholic Revival in Anglicanism. (Illus.). 296p. 1992. reprint ed. pap. 27.00 (0-19-826332-5) OUP.

Rowell, Geoffrey, ed. Tradition Renewed: The Oxford Movement Conference Papers. LC 85-32078. (Princeton Theological Monographs: No. 3). (Orig.). 1986. pap. 20.00 (0-915138-82-4) Pickwick.

Rowell, Geoffrey, jt. auth. see Dudley, Martin.

Rowell, George. The Old Vic Theatre: A History. (Illus.). 235p. (C). 1993. 59.95 (0-521-34625-8) Cambridge U Pr.

Rowell, George, ed. Nineteenth Century Plays. 2nd ed. (Oxford Paperbacks Ser.). 1972. pap. 15.95 (0-19-281104-5) OUP.

Rowell, George, ed. see Gilbert, William S.

Rowell, George, ed. see Pinero, A. W.

Rowell, George P. & Staff. The Men Who Advertise. Asseal, Henry, ed. LC 78-299. (Century of Marketing Ser.). 1979. reprint ed. lib. bdg. 72.95 (0-405-11174-6) Ayer.

Rowell, Harry & Landis, Carolyn P. Contracting for Computing: A Checklist of Terms & Clauses for Use in Contracting with Vendors for Computing Resources, Vol. I. 156p. 1973. 16.00 (0-318-14016-0); 9.00 (0-318-14017-9) EDUCOM.

Rowell, Henry T. Rome in the Augustan Age. (Centers of Civilization Ser.: Vol. 5). 258p. 1971. reprint ed. pap. 11.95 (0-8061-0956-4) U of Okla Pr.

Rowell, Henry T., ed. see Carcopino, Jerome.

Rowell, J. Cy. The Church's Educational Space: Creating Learning Environments for Teaching & Learning. 80p. (Orig.). 1989. pap. 6.99 (0-8272-0454-X) Chalice Pr.

Rowell, Jo A. Understanding Medical Insurance: A Step-by-Step Guide. 2nd ed. LC 93-2680. 336p. 1994. pap. text ed. 27.95 (0-8273-4966-1) Delmar.

Rowell, JoAnn C. Understanding Medical Insurance: A Step-by-Step Guide. (Practice Management Ser.). (Illus.). 256p. 1990. text ed. 49.95 (0-87489-634-7) Med Economics.

— Understanding Medical Insurance - A Step by Step Guide, Instructor's Guide. 60p. 1994. 39.95 (0-8273-4968-8) Delmar.

Rowell, John W. Yankee Cavalrymen: Through the Civil War with the Ninth Pennsylvania Cavalry. LC 70-126939. (Illus.). 280p. 1975. 32.95 (0-87049-125-3) U of Tenn Pr.

Rowell, Katherine L., ed. Clinical Computers in Nuclear Medicine. LC 91-5207. (Illus.). 86p. 1992. text ed. 50.00 (0-932004-40-7) Soc Nuclear Med.

Rowell, Lewis. Music & Musical Thought in Early India. (Chicago Studies in Ethnomusicology). 384p. 1992. lib. bdg. 59.00 (0-226-73032-8); pap. text ed. 23.95 (0-226-73033-6) U Ch Pr.

— Thinking about Music: An Introduction to the Philosophy of Music. LC 82-21979. (Illus.). 304p. 1984. pap. text ed. 30.00x (0-87023-461-7) U of Mass Pr.

Rowell, Lewis, jt. ed. see Fraser, J. T.

Rowell, Lois. American Organ Music on Records. LC 76-360159. 122p. 1976. pap. 9.00 (0-913746-08-8) Organ Lit.

Rowell, Loring B. Human Cardiovascular Control. (Illus.). 520p. 1993. 65.00 (0-19-507362-2) OUP.

— Human Circulation: Regulation During Physical Stress. (Illus.). 426p. 1986. 59.95 (0-19-504075-9) OUP.

Rowell, Margit. The Captured Imagination. LC 87-70555. (Illus.). 96p. 1987. pap. text ed. 27.95 (0-8122-1289-4) U of Pa Pr.

— Julio Gonzalez: A Retrospective. LC 82-62612. (Illus.). 216p. 1983. pap. 18.50 (0-89207-039-0) S R Guggenheim.

— New Images from Spain. Flint, Lucy, tr. LC 79-92992. (Illus.). 144p. (Orig.). 1980. pap. 8.50 (0-89207-023-4) S R Guggenheim.

— The Planar Dimension: Europe, 1912-1932. LC 78-74711. 1981. reprint ed. pap. 12.95 (0-89207-017-X) S R Guggenheim.

Rowell, Margit, ed. Joan Miro: Selected Writings & Interviews. (Documents of Twentieth Century Art Ser.). (Illus.). 350p. (C). 1986. text ed. 36.00 (0-8057-9956-7, Pub. by Royal Botanic Garden UK) Macmillan.

Rowell, Margit & Rudenstine, Angelica. Art of the Avant-Garde in Russia: Selections from the George Costakis Collection. LC 81-52858. (Illus.). 320p. 1981. pap. 17.00 (0-686-81458-4) S R Guggenheim.

Rowell, R. L. & Stein, R. S., eds. Electromagnetic Scattering. 862p. (C). 1967. text ed. 387.00 (0-677-11920-8) Gordon & Breach.

Rowell, R. M. Chemistry of Solid Wood. 614p. (C). 1986. 475.00 (0-685-61460-3, Pub. by Intl Bk Distr II) St Mut.

— Chemistry of Solid Wood. 614p. (C). 1986. reprint ed. 210.00 (81-7089-040-3, Pub. by Intl Bk Distr II) St Mut.

Rowell, Raymond J. Ornamental Flowering Shrubs in Australia. (Illus.). 334p. 1991. 34.95 (0-86840-084-X, Pub. by New South Wales Univ Pr AT) Intl Spec Bk.

— Ornamental Flowering Trees in Australia. (Illus.). 321p. 1991. 34.95 (0-86840-124-2, Pub. by New South Wales Univ Pr AT) Intl Spec Bk.

Rowell, Roger, ed. The Chemistry of Solid Wood. LC 83-22451. (Advances in Chemistry Ser.: No. 207). 614p. 1984. lib. bdg. 89.95 (0-8412-0796-8) Am Chemical.

Rowell, Roger M. & Barbour, R. James, eds. Archaeological Wood. LC 89-39451. (Advances in Chemistry Ser.: No. 225). 488p. 1989. 79.95 (0-8412-1623-1) Am Chemical.

Rowell, Roger M., et al, eds. Emerging Technologies for Materials & Chemicals from Biomass. LC 91-36048. (ACS Symposium Ser.: No. 476). (Illus.). 480p. 1991. 99.95 (0-8412-2171-5) Am Chemical.

Rowell, Roland. Counterfeiting & Forgery - a Practical Guide to the Law. 1986. 90.00 (0-406-10110-8, U.K.) Butterworth Legal Pubs.

Rowell, S. C. Lithuania Ascending: A Pagan Empire Within East-Central Europe, 1295-1345. (Cambridge Studies in Medieval Life & Thought: No. 25). (Illus.). 400p. (C). 1994. 69.95 (0-521-45011-X) Cambridge U Pr.

Rowell, Unni H., ed. see Geoscience Information Society Staff.

Rowen, Betty. Dance & Grow: Developmental Dance Activities for Three-Through Eight-Year-Olds. LC 93-46039. (Illus.). 122p. (C). 1994. pap. 12.95 (0-87127-196-6) Princeton Bk Co.

Rowen, Dan & MacDonald, John D. A Friendship: The Letters of Dan Rowen & John D. MacDonald 1967-1974. 352p. 1987. mass mkt. 4.95 (0-449-13177-7, GM) Fawcett.

Rowen, Henry S., ed. Options for U. S. Energy Policy. 317p. 1977. pap. text ed. 18.95 (0-917616-20-0) Transaction Pubs.

Rowen, Henry S. & Wolf, Charles, Jr. Impoverished Superpower: Perestroika & the Soviet Military Burden. LC 89-29818. 1990. 29.95 (1-55815-070-6); pap. 14.95 (1-55815-066-8) ICS Pr.

Rowen, Henry S. & Wolf, Charles, eds. The Future of the Soviet Empire. LC 87-20737. 350p. 1988. 16.95 (0-312-01347-7) ICS Pr.

Rowen, Henry S., et al, eds. Defense Conversion, Economic Reform & the Outlook for Russian & Ukrainian Economics. LC 94-6786. 1994. text ed. 49.95 (0-312-12158-X) St Martin.

Rowen, Herbert H. History of Early Modern Europe, 1500-1815. 1960. pap. 15.95 (0-672-60697-6, Bobbs) Macmillan.

— John de Witt: Grand Pensionary of Holland, 1625-1672. LC 76-45909. 1978. text ed. 115.00 (0-691-05247-6) Princeton U Pr.

— John de Witt: Statesman of the True Freedom. 243p. 1986. 59.95 (0-521-30391-5) Cambridge U Pr.

— John de Witt, Grand Pensionary of Holland, 1625-1672. LC 76-45909. 964p. 1978. reprint ed. pap. 180.00 (0-7837-8596-8, 2049411) Bks Demand.

— The Princes of Orange: The Stadholders in the Dutch Republic. (Studies in Early Modern History). (Illus.). 288p. (C). 1990. pap. 18.95 (0-521-39653-0) Cambridge U Pr.

Rowen, Herbert H., tr. see Nordholt, Jan W.

Rowen, Herbert H., tr. see Schulte Nordholt, Jan W.

Rowen, Hobart. Self-Inflicted Wounds. Date not set. 25.00 (0-8129-1864-9) Random.

Rowen, Larry. Beyond Winning: Group Centered Games & Sports. (J). (gr. 2-6). 1990. pap. 9.99 (0-8224-3380-X) Fearon Teach Aids.

Rowen, Louis. Algebra: Groups, Rings, & Fields. LC 93-39371. 264p. 1995. text ed. 49.95 (1-56881-028-8) AK Peters.

Rowen, Louis, ed. Ring Theory 1989 in Honor of S. A. Amitsur. (Israel Mathematical Conference Proceedings Ser.: Vol. 1). 430p. 1992. reprint ed. pap. 32.00 (0-685-70699-0, IMCP/1C, Bar-Ilan Univ) Am Math.

Rowen, Louis H. Polynomial Identities in Ring Theory. (Pure & Applied Mathematics Ser.). 1980. text ed. 106.00 (0-12-599850-3) Acad Pr.

— Ring Theory. 623p. (C). 1991. Student ed. student ed, text ed. 69.95 (0-12-599840-6) Acad Pr.

Rowen, Rachel, tr. see Frieder, Emanuel.

Rowen, Rachel, tr. see Platonov, Vladimir & Rapinchuk, Andrei.

Rowen, Ruth H. Early Chamber Music. 2nd ed. LC 68-8144. (Music Reprint Ser.). 1974. reprint ed. lib. bdg. 32.50 (0-306-71160-5) Da Capo.

— Early Chamber Music: Music Book Index. 188p. 1993. reprint ed. lib. bdg. 69.00 (0-7812-9641-2) Rprt Serv.

Rowen, Ruth H., jt. auth. see Katz, Adele T.

Rowen, Samuel F., jt. ed. see Conn, Harvie M.

Rowena, Lawson. Anderson County Kentucky 1830-1850 Censuses. iii, 78p. (Orig.). 1987. pap. 11.50 (1-55613-075-9) Heritage Bk.

Rower, Ann. If You're a Girl. (Native Agents Ser.). 270p. 1990. pap. 6.00 (0-936756-60-8) Autonomedia.

Rower, Holton. Nettles. (Illus.). 40p. 1991. pap. 35.00 (0-9623585-6-8) Flockophobic Pr.

— Nettles. limited ed. (Illus.). 40p. 1991. 55.00 (0-9623585-5-X) Flockophobic Pr.

Rower, J. R., jt. auth. see Stevens, Benjamin H.

Rowh, Mark. Careers for Crafty People & Other Dexterous Types. LC 93-16030. 1994. 12.95 (0-8442-4106-7, VGM Career Bks); pap. 9.95 (0-8442-4107-5, VGM Career Bks) NTC Pub Grp.

— Coping with Stress in College. 172p. 1989. pap. 9.95 (0-87447-334-9) College Bd.

— Drafting Careers. (Opportunities in...Ser.). (Illus.). 160p. 1991. 13.95 (0-8442-6143-2, Passport Bks); pap. 10.95 (0-8442-6144-0, Passport Bks) NTC Pub Grp.

— How to Improve Your Grammar & Usage. LC 93-31276. (Speak Out! Write On! Ser.). (Illus.). 128p. (YA). (gr. 9-12). 1994. lib. bdg. 14.35 (0-531-11177-6) Watts.

— How to Improve Your Grammar & Usage. (Speak Out, Write On! Ser.). (Illus.). 96p. (YA). (gr. 9-12). 1994. pap. 6.95 (0-531-15729-6) Watts.

R

— Opportunities in Drafting Careers. LC 93-10586. (Opportunities in...Ser.). 1994. 13.95 (*0-8442-4082-6*, VGM Career Bks); pap. 10.95 (*0-8442-4083-4*, VGM Career Bks) NTC Pub Grp.

— Opportunities in Electronics Careers. (Opportunities in... Ser.). (Illus.). 160p. 1991. 13.95 (*0-8442-8183-2*, VGM Career Bks); pap. 10.95 (*0-8442-8184-0*, VGM Career Bks) NTC Pub Grp.

— Opportunities in Installation & Repair Careers. LC 93-47510. (Opportunities in...Ser.). 1994. 13.95 (*0-8442-4135-0*, VGM Career Bks); pap. 10.95 (*0-8442-4136-9*, VGM Career Bks) NTC Pub Grp.

— Opportunities in Metal Working Careers. LC 90-50730. (Opportunities in...Ser.). 160p. (YA). (gr. 7 up). 1991. 13.95 (*0-8442-8537-4*, VGM Career Bks); pap. 10.95 (*0-8442-8538-2*, VGM Career Bks) NTC Pub Grp.

— Opportunities in Warehousing Careers. LC 92-16776. (Opportunities in...Ser.). 1993. 13.95 (*0-8442-4034-6*, VGM Career Bks); pap. 10.95 (*0-8442-4035-4*, VGM Career Bks) NTC Pub Grp.

— Opportunities in Waste Management Careers. (Opportunities in...Ser.). (Illus.). 160p. 1992. 13.95 (*0-8442-4018-4*, VGM Career Bks); pap. 10.95 (*0-8442-4019-2*, VGM Career Bks) NTC Pub Grp.

— Welding Careers. (Opportunities in Career Ser.). 1990. 13.95 (*0-8442-8598-6*, VGM Career Bks); pap. 10.95 (*0-8442-8599-4*, VGM Career Bks) NTC Pub Grp.

— Winning Government Grants & Contracts for Your Small Business. 224p. 1992. text ed. 16.95 (*0-07-054142-6*); pap. text ed. 16.95 (*0-07-054143-4*) McGraw.

Rowhani, Fazlollah. Elegy. 2nd rev. ed. (Illus.). 56p. 1989. reprint ed. pap. text ed. 4.00 (*0-685-26489-0*) Farabi Pubs.

Rowinska, Leokadia. Poklosie: Gleanning. (Illus.). 200p. (Orig.). 1987. pap. 10.95 (*0-930401-07-7*) Artex Pub.

Rowinski, Kate. Ellie Bear & the Fly-Away Fly. LC 93-25260. (Illus.). 32p. (J). (gr. 1-4). 1993. 14.95 (*0-89272-335-1*) Down East.

— L. L. Bear's Island Adventure. LC 92-71972. (Illus.). 32p. (J). (ps-4). 1992. 4.95 (*0-89272-320-3*) Down East.

Rowinski, Ludwig J., jt. auth. see Naske, Claus M.

Rowinsky, Erick K., jt. ed. see McGuire, William P.

***Rowitz, et al.** Socio-Behavioral Sciences & Public Health Practice. 300p. 1995. 39.95 (*0-8342-0627-7*) Aspen Pub.

Rowitz, L., ed. Mental Retardation in the Year 2000. (Disorders of Human Learning, Behavior, & Communication Ser.). (Illus.). 344p. 1992. 83.00 (*0-387-97474-1*) Spr-Verlag.

Rowlan, Tom. A-Z Guide Guide to Cleaning & Renovating Antiques. 1981. 26.50 (*0-09-463630-3*) Trans-Atl Phila.

Rowland. Ambulatory Care Quality Assurance Manual. 1990. ring bd. 175.00 (*0-8342-0134-8*, 524) Aspen Pub.

— Merritt's Textbook of Neurology. 9th ed. 1994. 79.50 (*0-683-07400-8*) Williams & Wilkins.

— Operating Room Administration Manual: Checklists, Guidelines & Forms. 650p. 1991. 135.00 (*0-8342-0174-7*, S31) Aspen Pub.

— Researching on the Internet: The Complete Guide to Organizing Searching & Qualifying... 1995. pap. (*0-7615-0063-4*) Prima Pub.

Rowland, et al. Applied Surface Mount Assembly. 1993. text ed. 54.95 (*0-442-00727-2*) Van Nos Reinhold.

Rowland, A. Westley. Key Resources on Institutional Advancement: A Guide to the Field & Its Literature. LC 86-10296. (Jossey-Bass Higher Education Ser.). 269p. reprint ed. pap. 76.70 (*0-7837-2543-4*, 2042702) Bks Demand.

Rowland, A. Westley, ed. Handbook of Institutional Advancement: A Modern Guide to Executive Management, Institutional Relations, Fund Raising, Alumni Administration, Government Relations, Publications, Periodicals, & Enrollment Management. 2nd ed. LC 85-45912. (Higher & Adult Education Ser.). 828p. 1986. 70.00x (*0-87589-689-8*) Jossey-Bass.

— Handbook of Institutional Advancement: A Practical Guide to College & University Relations, Fund Raising, Alumni Relations, Government Relations, Publications, & Executive Management for Continued Advancement. LC 76-50722. (Jossey-Bass Higher Education Ser.). 589p. reprint ed. pap. 167.90 (*0-685-16126-9*, 2027767) Bks Demand.

Rowland, Adam B., jt. auth. see Rowland, Heidi F.

Rowland, Alfred. Studies in First Timothy. 302p. lib. bdg. 12.99 (*0-8254-5223-6*) Kregel.

Rowland, Anna. Bauhaus Sourcebook. 1990. text ed. 19.95 (*0-442-23903-3*) Van Nos Reinhold.

***Rowland, Art.** Machine & Assembler Language Simulator. 1994. pap. text ed. 18.70 (*1-56226-195-9*) CT Pub.

Rowland, Arthur R. & Dorsey, James E. Bibliography of the Writings on Georgia History, Nineteen Hundred to Nineteen Seventy. LC 77-21733. 1978. 15.00 (*0-87152-254-3*) Reprint.

Rowland, Barbara. Search for the Perfect Christmas Drama. 40p. (Orig.). 1993. pap. 5.25 (*0-687-37095-7*) Abingdon.

Rowland, Barbara & McCormack, Curt. Abingdon Easter Drama & Program Collection. 40p. (Orig.). 1993. pap. 5.25 (*0-687-11478-0*) Abingdon.

Rowland, Barbara M. Ordered Liberty & the Constitutional Framework: The Political Thought of Friedrich A. Hayek. LC 87-278. (Contributions in Political Science Ser.: No. 176). 156p. 1987. text ed. 45.00 (*0-313-25609-8*, RLI/, Greenwood Pr) Greenwood.

Rowland, Beatrice L., jt. auth. see Rowland, Howard S.

Rowland, Beatrice L., jt. ed. see Rowland, Howard S.

Rowland, Beatrice S., jt. ed. see Rowland, Howard S.

Rowland, Ben. Allison's Affair with the High School Principal. LC 92-239897. 141p. 1993. reprint ed. 21.95 (*0-9636632-0-8*) GI Pub.

Rowland, Benjamin, Jr. Ancient Art from Afghanistan: Treasures of the Kabul Museum. LC 74-27419. (Asia Society Ser.). (Illus.). 1976. reprint ed. lib. bdg. 33.95 (*0-405-06567-1*) Ayer.

— The Art & Architecture of India: Buddhist-Hindu-Jain. rev. ed. (Pelican History of Art Ser.: No. 2). (Illus.). 1971. pap. 18.95 (*0-14-056102-1*, Penguin Bks) Viking Penguin.

— The Evolution of the Buddha Image. LC 74-27420. (Asia Society Ser.). (Illus.). 1976. reprint ed. lib. bdg. 27.95 (*0-405-06568-X*) Ayer.

Rowland, Benjamin M., jt. auth. see Callao, David P.

Rowland, Beryl. Birds with Human Souls: A Guide to Bird Symbolism. LC 77-4230. 232p. reprint ed. pap. 66.20 (*0-7837-3025-X*, 2042915) Bks Demand.

— Blind Beasts: Chaucer's Animal World. LC 77-104839. (Illus.). 206p. reprint ed. pap. 58.80 (*0-7837-0569-7*, 2040913) Bks Demand.

Rowland, Beryl, ed. Companion to Chaucer Studies. rev. ed. 1979. pap. text ed. 18.95 (*0-19-502489-3*) OUP.

Rowland, Beryl, ed. see Birney, Earle.

Rowland, Beth, ed. Esteem-Builders for Children's Ministry. LC 92-38167. 1992. 11.99 (*1-55945-174-2*) Group Pub.

— Lively Bible Lessons: Grades 1-2. LC 92-19504. 100p. 1992. pap. 12.99 (*1-55945-098-3*) Group Pub.

— Lively Bible Lessons: Kindergarten. LC 92-16301. 1992. 12.99 (*1-55945-097-5*) Group Pub.

— Quick Games for Children's Ministry. LC 92-33256. 1992. 11.99 (*1-55945-157-2*) Group Pub.

Rowland, C. K., jt. auth. see Carp, Robert A.

Rowland, Charles & Tamsitt, Gary. Hutley's Australian Wills Precedents. 4th ed. 286p. 1989. Australia. 65.00 (*0-409-49488-7*); Australia. pap. 44.00 (*0-409-30321-6*) Butterworth Legal Pubs.

Rowland, Cherry, jt. auth. see Friedrich, Elizabeth.

Rowland, Chris & Hann, Danny. The Economics of North Sea Oil Taxation. 200p. 1987. text ed. 45.00 (*0-312-23678-6*) St Martin.

Rowland, Christopher & Corner, Mark. Liberating Exegesis: The Challenge of Third World Liberation Theology to the World of Biblical Studies. 204p. (Orig.). 1989. pap. 15.99 (*0-664-25084-X*) Westminster John Knox.

Rowland, Cynthia. The Monster Within. 128p. 1985. pap. 7.99 (*0-8010-7731-1*) Baker Bk.

Rowland, Cynthia, tr. see Cristiani, Leon.

Rowland, Damaris, ed. see Beishir, Norma.

Rowland, Daniel. Competing to Win: How to Succeed in Business by Really Trying. Beckley, John L., ed. (Illus.). 158p. 1983. 14.95 (*0-910187-01-0*) Economics Pr.

Rowland, David. A History of Pianoforte Pedalling. LC 92-37065. (Cambridge Musical Texts & Monographs). 224p. (C). 1994. 60.00 (*0-521-40266-2*) Cambridge U Pr.

Rowland, David L., et al. Computer-Based Data Analysis: A Manual for the Social & Behavioral Sciences. 200p. 1990. pap. 19.95 (*0-8304-1181-X*) Nelson-Hall.

Rowland, Della. Little Red Riding Hood: The Wolf's Tale. LC 93-42781. (Upside Down Tales Ser.). (Illus.). (J). 1994. pap. 8.95 (*0-8065-1526-0*, Citadel Pr) Carol Pub Group.

— Little Red Riding Hood & the Wolf's Tale. (J). (ps-3). 1991. 13.95 (*1-55972-072-7*, Birch Ln Pr) Carol Pub Group.

— Martin Luther King, Jr. The Dream of Peaceful Revolution. Gallin, Richard, ed. (Civil Rights Ser.). (Illus.). 128p. (J). (gr. 5 up). 1990. lib. bdg. 12.95 (*0-382-09924-9*); pap. 7.95 (*0-382-24062-6*) Silver Burdett Pr.

— The Story of Sacajawea: Guide to Lewis & Clark. (J). (gr. k-6). 1989. pap. 3.25 (*0-440-40215-8*, YB) Dell.

Rowland, Della, ed. Christmas: A Holiday Treasury. LC 93-16663. 1993. pap. 6.95 (*0-8362-4938-0*) Andrews & McMeel.

Rowland, Desmond & Bailey, James. The Law Enforcement Handbook. LC 84-18840. 294p. reprint ed. pap. 83.80 (*0-7837-6686-6*, 2046302) Bks Demand.

Rowland, Diana. Japanese Business Etiquette. 2nd rev. ed. 304p. (Orig.). 1993. pap. 12.99 (*0-446-39518-8*) Warner Bks.

Rowland, Diana, jt. auth. see Engholm, Christopher.

Rowland, Diane & Lyons, Barbara, eds. Financing Home Care: Improving Protection for Disabled Elderly People. LC 91-20609. (Studies in Health Care Finance & Administration). 1991. text ed. 47.50 (*0-8018-4256-5*) Johns Hopkins.

***Rowland, Diane, et al.** Medicaid & Managed Care: Lessons from the Literature. 88p. 1995. write for info. (*0-944525-21-0*) H J Kaiser.

— Medicaid at the Crossroads: A Report of the Kaiser Commission on the Future of Medicaid. 90p. (Orig.). 1992. pap. 5.00 (*0-944525-10-5*) H J Kaiser.

— Medicaid Financing Crisis: Balancing Responsibilities, Priorities, & Dollars. 222p. 1994. pap. 19.95 (*0-614-04061-2*) Transaction Pubs.

Rowland, Diane, et al, eds. Medicaid Financing Crisis: Balancing Responsibilities, Priorities, & Dollars. 222p. (C). 1994. pap. 19.95 (*0-87168-514-0*, 93-04S) AAAS.

Rowland, Dunbar. History of Mississippi: The Heart of the South, 1. LC 78-2541. (Illus.). 1978. reprint ed. 37.50 (*0-87152-271-3*) Reprint.

— History of Mississippi: The Heart of the South, 2. LC 78-2541. (Illus.). 1978. reprint ed. 37.50 (*0-87152-272-1*) Reprint.

— History of Mississippi: The Heart of the South, 3. LC 78-2541. (Illus.). 1978. reprint ed. 37.50 (*0-87152-273-X*) Reprint.

— History of Mississippi: The Heart of the South, 4. LC 78-2541. (Illus.). 1978. reprint ed. 37.50 (*0-87152-274-8*) Reprint.

— History of Mississippi: The Heart of the South, 4 vols., Set. LC 78-2541. (Illus.). 1978. reprint ed. 150.00 (*0-87152-270-5*) Reprint.

— History of Mississippi, the Heart of the South, Vol. I. (Illus.). 933p. 1994. reprint ed. lib. bdg. 95.00 (*0-8328-4265-6*) Higginson Bk Co.

— History of Mississippi, the Heart of the South, Vol. II. (Illus.). 905p. 1994. reprint ed. lib. bdg. 95.00 (*0-8328-4266-4*) Higginson Bk Co.

— Military History of Mississippi, 1803-1898. LC 78-2454. 704p. 1995. reprint ed. 47.50 (*0-87152-266-7*) Reprint.

Rowland, Dunbar, ed. Mississippi: Sketches of Counties, Towns, Events, Institutions & Persons Arranged in Cyclopedic Form, 4 vols., 1. LC 76-73. 1976. reprint ed. 37.50 (*0-87152-220-9*) Reprint.

— Mississippi: Sketches of Counties, Towns, Events, Institutions & Persons Arranged in Cyclopedic Form, 4 vols., 2. LC 76-73. 1976. reprint ed. 37.50 (*0-87152-221-7*) Reprint.

— Mississippi: Sketches of Counties, Towns, Events, Institutions & Persons Arranged in Cyclopedic Form, 4 vols., Vol. 3. LC 76-73. 1976. reprint ed. Vol.3. 37.50 (*0-87152-222-5*) Reprint.

— Mississippi: Sketches of Counties, Towns, Events, Institutions & Persons Arranged in Cyclopedic Form, 4 vols., Vol. 4. suppl. ed. LC 76-73. 1976. reprint ed. 37.50 (*0-87152-223-3*) Reprint.

Rowland, Dunbar, ed. see Claiborne, William C.

Rowland, Dunbar, ed. see Davis, Jefferson.

Rowland, Dunbar, ed. see Mississippi Department of Archives and History Staff.

Rowland, E. Diane, jt. auth. see Davis, Karen.

Rowland, Edna. How to Obtain a Birth Certificate. 1990. pap. 15.00 (*0-86690-370-4*, 3041-014) Am Fed Astrologers.

Rowland, Eleanor H., ed.

Rowland-Entwistle, Theodore. The Pop-up Atlas of the World. (Illus.). 18p. (J). (gr. 3 up). 1988. pap. 12.95 (*0-671-65898-0*, S&S Bks Young Read) S&S Childrens.

— Rivers & Lakes. (Our World Ser.). (Illus.). 48p. (J). (gr. 5-8). 1987. lib. bdg. 12.95 (*0-382-09499-9*) Silver Burdett Pr.

— Thomas Edison. (Children of History Ser.). (Illus.). 32p. (J). (gr. 3-8). 1988. lib. bdg. 10.95 (*0-86307-928-8*) Marshall Cavendish.

— Wilbur & Orville Wright. (Children of History Ser.). (Illus.). 32p. (J). (gr. 3-8). 1988. lib. bdg. 10.95 (*0-86307-927-X*) Marshall Cavendish.

Rowland-Entwistle, Theodore & Cooke, Jean. Factfinder. LC 92-53118. (Illus.). 280p. (Orig.). (J). (gr. 4-8). 1992. 16.95 (*1-85697-803-6*, Kingfisher LKC); pap. 12.95 (*1-85697-835-4*, Kingfisher LKC) LKC.

Rowland-Entwistle, Theodore & O'Donoghue, Michael. Rocks & Minerals. LC 93-46148. (Science Nature Guides Ser.). (Illus.). 80p. (J). (gr. 3-6). 1994. 12.95 (*1-85028-263-3*) Thunder Bay CA.

Rowland-Entwistle, Theodore, ed. see Abbot, R. Tucker.

Rowland, Eron. Andrew Jackson's Campaign Against the British. LC 72-146870. (Select Bibliographies Reprint Ser.). (Illus.). 1977. reprint ed. 37.95 (*0-8369-5637-0*) Ayer.

Rowland, H. H. Dwight W. Morrow. 1972. 59.95 (*0-8490-0063-7*) Gordon Pr.

Rowland, Heidi F. & Rowland, Adam B. Hospital Consents Manual, Vol. 1. LC 92-22018. 1992. ring bd. 239.00 (*0-8342-0328-6*, S50) Aspen Pub.

***Rowland, Howard R.** Loyal to Thy Fine Tradition: St. Cloud University 125 Years & Pictures, 1869-1994. LC 94-30771. 1994. write for info. (*0-89865-913-2*) Donning Co.

Rowland, Howard S. Hospital Administration Handbook. LC 83-9236. 768p. (C). 1983. 135.00 (*0-89443-941-3*) Aspen Pub.

Rowland, Howard S., et al. Hospital Legal Forms, Checklists & Guidelines, 2 vols. LC 86-17391. 1986. ring bd. 365.00 (*0-87189-053-4*) Aspen Pub.

Rowland, Howard S. & Rowland, Beatrice L. Manual of Hospital Administration. LC 92-10857. 1992. ring bd. 225.00 (*0-8342-0324-3*) Aspen Pub.

— The Nursing Department Forms Manual. 500p. 1993. 175.00 (*0-8342-0334-0*, S58) Aspen Pub.

Rowland, Howard S. & Rowland, Beatrice L., eds. Nursing Administration Handbook. 3rd ed. LC 92-6968. 672p. 1992. 72.00 (*0-8342-0304-9*, 20304) Aspen Pub.

Rowland, Howard S. & Rowland, Beatrice S., eds. Manual of Nursing Quality Assurance, 2 vols. 1987. ring bd. 275.00 (*0-87189-875-6*) Aspen Pub.

Rowland, I. Timor. (World Bibliographical Ser.). 1992. lib. bdg. 67.50 (*1-85109-159-9*) ABC-CLIO.

Rowland, I., ed. Role of Gut Flora in Toxicity & Cancer. 517p. 1988. text ed. 139.00 (*0-12-599920-8*) Acad Pr.

Rowland, Ian R. Nutrition, Toxicity & Cancer. 450p. 1990. 62.50 (*0-936923-47-4*) Telford Pr.

— Nutrition, Toxicity, & Cancer. 464p. 1991. 104.95 (*0-8493-8812-0*, QP141) CRC Pr.

Rowland, J. F., jt. ed. see Bottle, R. T.

Rowland, Jenny. Early Welsh Saga Poetry: A Study & Edition of the "Englynion" 638p. 1990. 170.00 (*0-85991-275-2*) Boydell & Brewer.

Rowland, John. Mysteries of Science. LC 78-105035. (Essay Index Reprint Ser.). 1977. 21.95 (*0-8369-1624-7*) Ayer.

Rowland, John H., jt. auth. see Hanna, J. Ray.

Rowland, Jon T. Faint Praise & Civil Leer: The "Decline" of Eighteenth-Century Panegyric. LC 94-17432. 1994. write for info. (*0-87413-543-5*) U Delaware Pr.

Rowland-Jones, Anthony. Playing Recorder Sonatas: Technique & Interpretation. (Illus.). 288p. (C). 1992. 59.95 (*0-19-879002-3*); pap. 29.95 (*0-19-879001-5*) OUP.

— Recorder Technique. (YA). (gr. 9 up). 1983. pap. 26.95 (*0-19-322342-2*) OUP.

Rowland-Jones, Anthony, jt. ed. see Thomson, John M.

Rowland, Julia H., jt. ed. see Holland, Jimmie C.

Rowland, Kendrith M., ed. Research in Personnel & Human Resources Management, Vol. 6. 1988. 73.25 (*0-89232-856-8*) Jai Pr.

Rowland, Kendrith M. & Ferris, Gerald. Research in Personnel & Human Resources Management, Vol. 3. 1985. 73.25 (*0-89232-498-8*) Jai Pr.

— Research in Personnel & Human Resources Management, Vol. 4. 1986. 73.25 (*0-89232-606-9*) Jai Pr.

Rowland, Kendrith M. & Ferris, Gerald R. Research in Personnel & Human Resources Management, Vol. 2. 73.25 (*0-89232-483-X*) Jai Pr.

Rowland, Kendrith M. & Ferris, Gerald R., eds. Research in Personnel & Human Resorces Management, Vol. 5. 1987. 73.25 (*0-89232-750-2*) Jai Pr.

— Research in Personnel & Human Resources Management, Vol. 1. 450p. 1983. 73.25 (*0-89232-268-3*) Jai Pr.

Rowland, Laura J. Shin-Ju. LC 94-10181. 1994. 21.00 (*0-679-43422-4*) Random.

Rowland, Lawrence S. Window on the Atlantic: The Rise & Fall of Santa Elena South Carolina's Spanish City. Brimelow, Judith M., ed. (Illus.). 32p. 1990. write for info. (*1-880067-03-X*) SC Dept of Arch & Hist.

Rowland, Leon. Santa Cruz: The Early Years. Gant, Michael S., ed. LC 80-81418. (Illus.). 273p. 1980. pap. 7.95 (*0-934136-04-1*) Western Tanager.

Rowland, Lewis P. Amyotrophic Lateral Sclerosis (& Other Motor Neuron Diseases) (Advances in Neurology Ser.: Vol. 56). 1991. 149.50 (*0-88167-748-5*) Raven.

Rowland, Lewis P., ed. Human Motor Neuron Diseases. (Advances in Neurology Ser.: Vol. 36). (Illus.). 592p. 1982. text ed. 175.50 (*0-89004-737-5*) Raven.

— Merritt's Textbook of Neurology. 8th ed. LC 88-9456. (Illus.). 964p. 1989. text ed. 76.00 (*0-8121-1148-6*) Williams & Wilkins.

Rowland, Lewis P., et al, eds. Molecular Genetics in Diseases of Brain, Nerve, & Muscle. (Illus.). 504p. 1989. 65.00 (*0-19-505163-7*) OUP.

***Rowland, Lisa E. & Iyer, Patricia W.** Patient Outcomes in Maternal-Infant Nursing. LC 94-22564. 1994. write for info. (*0-87434-700-9*) Springhouse Pub.

Rowland, Lori, jt. auth. see Pierce, Kathy.

Rowland, Mabel, ed. Bert Williams, Son of Laughter. LC 72-84693. 218p. 1969. reprint ed. text ed. 52.50 (*0-8371-1667-8*, ROW&, Negro U Pr) Greenwood.

Rowland, Malcolm & Tozer, Thomas N. Clinical Pharmacokinetics: Concepts & Applications. 2nd ed. LC 88-8993. (Illus.). 541p. 1989. text ed. 54.00 (*0-8121-1160-5*) Williams & Wilkins.

— Clinical Pharmacokinetics: Concepts & Applications. 3rd ed. LC 94-26305. 1995. write for info. (*0-683-07404-0*) Williams & Wilkins.

Rowland, Malcolm, et al, eds. Variability in Drug Therapy: Description, Estimation & Control. (Illus.). 270p. 1985. text ed. 96.50 (*0-88167-080-4*) Raven.

Rowland, Marcus, et al. Great Old Ones: New Adventures Against the Cthulhu Mythos. Willis, Lynn, ed. (Call of Cthulhu Roleplaying Game System Ser.). (Illus.). 176p. (Orig.). 1989. pap. 17.95 (*0-933635-38-9*, 2321) Chaosium.

Rowland, Marcus L. Canal Priests of Mars. (Space: Eighteen Eighty-Nine Ser.). (Illus.). 64p. (Orig.). (YA). 1990. pap. 8.00 (*1-55878-039-4*) Game Designers.

Rowland, Mark, jt. ed. see Scherman, Tony.

Rowland, Mary. The Fidelity Guide to Mutual Funds: A Complete Guide to Investing in Mutual Funds. (Illus.). 320p. 1991. pap. 14.95 (*0-671-73331-1*, Fireside) S&S Trade.

Rowland, Mary C. & Loomis, F. A. As Long As Life: The Memoirs of a Frontier Woman Doctor, Mary Canaga Rowland, 1873-1966. LC 94-66409. (Illus.). 192p. (Orig.). 1994. pap. 11.95 (*0-9641357-0-1*) Storm Peak.

Rowland, May. Dare to Believe. LC 89-50842. 1961. 7.95 (*0-87159-024-7*) Unity Bks.

— The Magic of the Word. LC 73-180756. 182p. 1972. 6.95 (*0-87159-094-8*) Unity Bks.

***Rowland, Michael D.** Absolute Happiness: The Way to a Life of Complete Fulfillment. Kramer, Jill, ed. 256p. 1995. pap. 12.95 (*1-56170-219-6*) Hay House.

Rowland, Michael L. & Forthofer, Ronald N. Investigation of Nonresponse Bias: Hispanic Health & Nutrition Examination Survey. LC 93-29686. (Vital & Health Statistics Ser. 2: Data Evaluation & Methods Research: No. 119). Date not set. 5.50 (*0-8406-0485-8*) Natl Ctr Health Stats.

Rowland, N. E., jt. ed. see Toates, Frederick.

***Rowland, Nancy & Tolley, Keith.** Evaluating the Cost-Effectiveness of Counselling in Health Care. 240p. 1995. 59.95x (*0-415-07660-9*, C0325); pap. 18.95 (*0-415-07661-7*, C0326) Routledge.

Rowland, O. W. A History of Van Buren County, Michigan, 2 vols., Set. (Illus.). 1158p. 1993. reprint ed. lib. bdg. 115.00 (*0-8328-3484-X*) Higginson Bk Co.

Rowland, Patrick. Property Investments & Their Financing. 288p. 1993. pap. 55.00 (*0-455-21167-1*, Pub. by Law Bk Co) W W Gaunt.

Rowland, Pleasant T. Our New Baby - Asian Version. (Illus.). 14p. (J). (ps-00). 1991. 19.95 (*1-56247-000-0*) Pleasant Co.

Rowland, Ralph S. & Rowland, Star W. Clary Genealogy: Four Early American Lines & Related Families. LC 80-54651. xi, 588p. (Orig.). 1990. reprint ed. pap. 25.00 (*0-9605746-2-X*) R & S Rowland.

Rowland, Ralph S., et al. Kellenbergers & Shearers of Pennsylvania, Maryland, & Points West. LC 85-60465. xi, 287p. 1985. 15.00 (*0-9605746-3-8*) R & S Rowland.

Rowland, Richard H., jt. auth. see Lewis, Robert A.

Rowland, Robert, jt. auth. see Iyer, Praema V.

Rowland, Robert C. The Rhetoric of Menachem Begin: The Myth of Redemption Through Return. 330p. (Orig.). 1985. lib. bdg. 55.50 (*0-8191-4735-4*); pap. text ed. 25.50 (*0-8191-4736-2*) U Pr of Amer.

An Asterisk (*) at the beginning of an entry indicates that the title is appearing in BIP for the first time.

— U. S. Policy & the Global Environment. 160p. 1992. pap. 22.60 (*0-8442-5163-1*, NTC Busn Bks) NTC Pub Grp.

Rowland, Robyn. Living Laboratories: Women & Reproductive Technology. LC 92-13199. 384p. 1992. 35. 00 (*0-253-34999-0*); pap. 14.95 (*0-253-20760-6*, MB-760) Ind U Pr.

— Perverse Serenity. 1993. pap. 12.95 (*1-875559-13-2*, Pub. by SpiniFex Pr AT) InBook.

— Woman Herself: A Transdisciplinary Perspective on Women's Identity. 240p. 1990. pap. 17.95 (*0-19-554475-7*) OUP.

— Women Who Do & Women Who Don't: Join the Women's Movement. (Illus.). 224p. (Orig.). 1984. pap. 9.95 (*0-7102-0296-2*, RKP) Routledge.

Rowland, Sanders & Terrell, Bob. Papa Coke: Sixty-Five Years Selling Coca-Cola. LC 86-9526. (Illus.). 236p. 1986. 10.95 (*0-914875-14-0*) Bright Mtn Bks.

Rowland, Sid. A Career in Crime. (Illus.). 75p. (Orig.). 1987. pap. 7.00 (*0-937158-03-8*) Del Valley.

— The Hopes of Cats. (Illus.). 80p. 1993. pap. 8.00 (*0-937158-06-2*) Del Valley.

— An Invitation to Dinner. (Illus.). 70p. (Orig.). 1985. pap. 5.00 (*0-937158-02-X*) Del Valley.

— Ludwig the Tomato. (Illus.). 76p. 1990. pap. 8.00 (*0-937158-05-4*) Del Valley.

Rowland, Stanley P., ed. Water in Polymers. LC 80-13860. (ACS Symposium Ser.: No. 127). 1980. 65.95 (*0-8412-0559-0*) Am Chemical.

Rowland, Star W., jt. auth. see Rowland, Ralph S.

Rowland, Stephen. The Enquiring Classroom: An Approach to Understanding Children's Learning. (Curriculum Series for Teaching). 160p. 1984. pap. 28.00 (*0-905273-99-0*, Falmer Pr) Taylor & Francis.

— The Enquiring Tutor: Explorations in Professional Learning. LC 93-26438. 180p. 1993. 75.00 (*0-7507-0210-9*, Falmer Pr); pap. 27.00 (*0-7507-0211-7*, Falmer Pr) Taylor & Francis.

Rowland, Stephen M. & Duebendorfer, Ernest M. Structural Analysis & Synthesis: A Laboratory Course in Structural Geology. 2nd ed. LC 93-28089. 304p. 1994. pap. 36.95 (*0-86542-366-0*) Blackwell Sci.

Rowland, Susan, jt. auth. see Martorana, R. George.

Rowland, Susan, jt. auth. see Rosenthal, Lisa.

Rowland, T. J. & Beck, Paul A., eds. Magnetic & Inelastic Scattering of Neutrons by Metals. LC 67-29670. (Metallurgical Society Conference Ser.: Vol. 43). 239p. reprint ed. pap. 68.20 (*0-317-10595-7*, 2001532) Bks Demand.

Rowland, T. J., ed. see Metallurgical Society of AIME Staff.

***Rowland, Thomas W.** Exercise & Children's Health. LC 89-71708. (Illus.). 368p. 1990. pap. text ed. 22.00x (*0-87322-810-3*, BROW0810) Human Kinetics.

— Exercise & Children's Health. LC 89-71708. (Illus.). 368p. 1990. text ed. 45.00 (*0-87322-282-2*, BROW0282) Human Kinetics.

Rowland, Thomas W., ed. Pediatric Laboratory Exercise Testing: Clinical Guidelines. LC 92-1575. (Illus.). 216p. 1993. 46.00x (*0-87322-380-2*, BROW0380) Human Kinetics.

Rowland, Wade. The Plot to Save the World. (Illus.). 194p. 1973. 7.95 (*0-7720-0589-3*, Pub. by Stoddart Pubng CN) Genl Dist Srvs.

Rowland, Wade, jt. auth. see MacInnis, Jeff.

Rowland-Warne, L. Costume. LC 91-53135. (Eyewitness Bks.). (Illus.). 64p. (J). (gr. 5 up). 1992. 16.00 (*0-679-81680-1*); lib. bdg. 16.99 (*0-679-91680-6*) Knopf Bks Yng Read.

Rowlands, jt. auth. see Miller.

***Rowlands, Arril.** More Tales from the Ark. (Illus.). 160p. (Orig.). (J). (gr. 3-5). 1995. pap. 4.99 (*0-7459-3035-2*) Lion USA.

***Rowlands, Avril.** The Continuity Handbook: A Guide for Single-Camera Shooting. 3rd ed. 185p. 1994. pap. 22.95 (*0-240-51391-6*, Focal) Buttrwrth-Heinemann.

— Milk & Honey. 144p. (J). (gr. 4 up). 1990. 15.00 (*0-19-271627-1*) OUP.

— Tales from the Ark. (J). (ps-3). 1995. pap. 4.99 (*0-7459-2375-5*) Lion USA.

— The Television PA's Handbook. 2nd ed. LC 93-3718. 240p. 1993. pap. 27.95 (*0-240-51353-3*, Focal) Buttrwrth-Heinemann.

Rowlands, Avril J. Continuity in Film & Video. 2nd ed. (Illus.). 160p. 1989. pap. 19.95 (*0-240-51290-1*, Focal) Buttrwrth-Heinemann.

***Rowlands, Betty.** Exhaustive Enquiries. 240p. (Orig.). 1995. pap. text ed. 4.99 (*0-425-14689-8*, Prime Crime) Berkley Pub.

— Exhaustive Enquiries: A Melissa Craig Mystery. 252p. 1994. 19.95 (*0-8027-3180-5*) Walker & Co.

— Finishing Touch. 256p. (Orig.). 1993. pap. 4.50 (*0-515-11059-0*) Jove Pubns.

— Finishing Touch: A Melissa Craig Mystery. 253p. 1992. 19.95 (*0-8027-3209-7*) Walker & Co.

— A Little Gentle Sleuthing. 272p. 1991. 18.95 (*0-8027-5781-2*) Walker & Co.

— Little Gentle Sleuthing. 240p. (Orig.). 1992. pap. 3.99 (*0-515-10878-2*) Jove Pubns.

— Over the Edge. 240p. 1994. reprint ed. pap. 4.50 (*0-425-14329-5*, Prime Crime) Berkley Pub.

— Over the Edge: A Melissa Craig Mystery. LC 92-40543. 252p. 1993. 19.95 (*0-8027-3228-3*) Walker & Co.

Rowlands, D. Problem Solving in Science & Technology: Eval Pack. (C). 1989. 120.00 (*0-09-176110-7*, Pub. by S Thornes Pubs UK) St Mut.

— Problem Solving in Science & Technology: Teacher's Manual. (C). 1987. 120.00 (*0-09-172761-8*, Pub. by S Thornes Pubs UK) St Mut.

— Problem Solving in Science & Technology: Workpack, No. 1. (C). 1987. 220.00 (*0-09-172771-5*, Pub. by S Thornes Pubs UK) St Mut.

— Problem Solving in Science & Technology: Workplace, No. 2. (C). 1989. 220.00 (*0-09-172781-2*, Pub. by S Thornes Pubs UK) St Mut.

Rowlands, D., ed. Problem Solving in Science & Technology: Workpack, No. 3. (C). 1987. 220.00 (*0-09-172791-X*, Pub. by S Thornes Pubs UK) St Mut.

Rowlands, D. & Holland, C. Problem Solving in Primary Science & Technology: Children's Workpak. (C). 1989. 180.00 (*0-09-175682-0*, Pub. by S Thornes Pubs UK) St Mut.

Rowlands, D. & Holland, C., eds. Problem Solving in Primary Science & Technology: Teacher's Guide. (C). 1989. 60.00 (*0-09-175687-1*, Pub. by S Thornes Pubs UK) St Mut.

Rowlands, D. J. Electrocardiography Pocket Book. 160p. (C). 1993. pap. text ed. 15.50 (*0-7923-8805-4*) Kluwer Ac.

— Emergency Cardiology. 296p. 1989. text ed. 175.00 (*0-7236-0731-1*, Pub. by John Wright UK) Buttrwrth-Heinemann.

Rowlands, D. J., et al, eds. Molecular Biology of Positive Strand RNA Viruses. (Fems Symposia Ser.). 334p. 1987. text ed. 94.00 (*0-12-599930-5*) Acad Pr.

Rowlands, Derek J., ed. Recent Advances in Cardiology - Eleven. (Illus.). 224p. (Orig.). 1993. pap. text ed. 79.95 (*0-443-04565-8*) Churchill.

Rowlands, E. C. Teach Yourself Yorruba. (Teach Yourself Ser.). 1992. 15.95 (*0-8288-8414-5*) Fr & Eur.

— Teach Yourself Yoruba. (Teach Yourself Ser.). 1979. 10. 95 (*0-679-10224-8*) McKay.

Rowlands, G. Non-Linear Phenomena in Science & Engineering. 1993. pap. text ed. 53.00 (*0-13-104043-X*) P-H.

Rowlands, G., jt. auth. see Infeld, E.

Rowlands, Gerald. Coming Alive in the Spirit: The Spirit-led Life. (Basic Bible Study Ser.). Orig. Title: The Holy Spirit & His Fruit. 64p. 1985. pap. 3.95 (*0-930756-90-8*, 521019) Aglow Communs.

— The Holy Spirit & His Gifts: A Study of the Spiritual Gifts. Sekowsky, Jo Anne, ed. (Basic Bible Study Ser.). 64p. 1984. pap. 3.95 (*0-930756-83-5*, 521017) Aglow Communs.

***Rowlands, Ian H.** The Politics of Global Atmospheric Change. LC 94-31959. (Issues in Environmental Politics Ser.). 1995. text ed. write for info. (*0-7190-4094-9*); text ed. write for info. (*0-7190-4095-7*) St Martin.

Rowlands, Jim. The Big Book of Kites. (Illus.). 132p. 1988. pap. 14.95 (*0-312-02047-3*) St Martin.

— One Hour Kites. 1989. pap. 14.95 (*0-312-03218-8*) St Martin.

— Soft Kites & Windsocks. LC 92-26426. 1993. pap. 14.95 (*0-312-08966-X*) St Martin.

***Rowlands, John, ed.** Welsh Family History: A Guide to Research. (Illus.). 316p. 1994. pap. 19.95 (*0-614-03826-X*, 5030) Genealog Pub.

Rowlands, John, jt. auth. see Jones, Glyn.

***Rowlands, Mark.** Supervenience & Materialism. 140p. 1995. 59.95 (*1-85972-096-X*, Pub. by Avebury Pub UK) Ashgate Pub Co.

***Rowlands, Michael & Kristanson, K., eds.** Structure & Social Transformation in Archaeology. (Material Cultures Ser.). 336p. 1995. 59.95x (*0-415-06789-8*, B0309) Routledge.

Rowlands, Michael L. Monnow Bridge & Gate. (Illus.). 160p. 1994. pap. 20.00 (*0-7509-0415-1*) A Sutton Pub.

Rowlands, O., jt. auth. see Adcock, M. R.

Rowlands, Richard. The Post for Divers Partes of the World, to Travaile from One Notable Citie unto an Other, 2 pts. LC 77-7422. (English Experience Ser.: No. 889). 1977. reprint ed. 13.00 (*90-221-0889-9*) Walter J Johnson.

— A Restitution of Decayed Intelligence: In Antiquities, Concerning the...English Nation. by the Studie & Travaile of R. Verstagen. Dedicated Unto the Kings Most Excellent Majestie. LC 79-84134. (English Experience Ser.: No. 952). 380p. 1979. reprint ed. lib. bdg. 35.00 (*90-221-0952-6*) Walter J Johnson.

Rowlands, V. The Lady & the Highwayman. 320p. 1994. 20. 95 (*0-7089-3139-1*) Ulverscroft.

Rowlands, William A. Anglesey, Wales a Research Reference. LC 91-90538. 285p. 1991. pap. 25.00 (*0-9630454-0-7*) MBR Co.

Rowlandson, L. G. & Schwarz, J. S. Radio Refractivity & Meteorological Data Plots from Radiosonde Launches Trade Winds: March 1969. LC 77-135079. 224p. 1970. 29.00 (*0-403-04534-7*) Scholarly.

Rowlandson, Mary. The Captive: The True Story of the Captivity of Mrs. Mary Rowlandson among the Indians & God's Faithfulness to Her in Her Time of Trial. rev. ed. (Illus.). 96p. 1988. reprint ed. 14.95 (*0-929408-00-4*, E87R895R69) Amer Eagle Pubns Inc.

— The Captive: The True Story of the Captivity of Mrs. Mary Rowlandson among the Indians & God's Faithfulness to Her in Her Time of Trial. rev. ed. (Illus.). 44p. 1991. pap. 4.95 (*0-929408-03-9*) Amer Eagle Pubns Inc.

Rowlandson, Mary, et al. Colonial American Travel Narratives. 336p. 1994. 11.95 (*0-14-039088-X*, Penguin Classics) Viking Penguin.

Rowlandson, Mary W. The Narrative of the Captivity & Restoration of Mrs. Mary Rowlandson. (American Biography Ser.). 96p. 1991. reprint ed. lib. bdg. 59.00 (*0-7812-8332-9*) Rprt Serv.

Rowlandson, Thomas. Loyal Volunteers of London & Environs Infantry & Cavalry in Their Respective Uniforms. 1981. 300.00 (*0-238-78977-2*) St Mut.

Rowlatt, Charles, jt. ed. see Hodges, Gisele M.

Rowlatt, Penelope A. Inflation: From Modelling to Policy. (International Studies in Economic Modelling). 256p. 1992. 150.00 (*0-412-35870-0*) Chapman & Hall.

Rowles, C., et al. AI, 1993: Proceedings of the 6th Australian Joint Conference on Artificial Intelligence. 450p. 1993. text ed. 114.00 (*981-02-1526-6*) World Scientific Pub.

Rowles, Graham, jt. ed. see Reinharz, Shulamit.

Rowles, Graham D., ed. Aging & Milieu: Environmental Perspectives on Growing Old. 1982. text ed. 47.00 (*0-12-599950-X*) Acad Pr.

Rowles, N., jt. auth. see Bateman, R.

***Rowles, Raymond.** Drilling for Water: A Practical Manual. 2nd ed. 180p. 1995. pap. 34.95 (*1-85628-984-2*, Pub. by Avebury Pub UK) Ashgate Pub Co.

Rowlett, Elsebet S., et al. Neolithic Levels on the Titelberg, Luxembourg. 2nd ed. LC 76-623772. (Museum Briefs Ser.: No. 18). iii, 61p. 1980. pap. 4.00 (*0-913134-83-X*) Mus Anthro MO.

***Rowley.** Basic Clinical Science. 1991. 115.00 (*1-56593-037-1*, 0310) Singular Publishing.

Rowley, A., jt. auth. see Watt, F.

Rowley, A. F. & Ratcliffe, N. A., eds. Vertebrate Blood Cells. 450p. 1988. 89.95 (*0-521-26032-9*) Cambridge U Pr.

Rowley, A. F., jt. ed. see Ratcliffe, N. A.

Rowley, Anthony, ed. The Barons of European Industry. LC 74-11193. 169p. 1974. 26.95 (*0-8419-0171-6*) Holmes & Meier.

Rowley, B. A., tr. see Steiner, Rudolf.

***Rowley, Barbara.** At Home with Microsoft Bob. LC 95-1473. 1995. 16.95 (*1-55615-854-8*) Microsoft.

***Rowley, Cal.** Janice. 190p. 1995. pap. 7.95 (*0-7610-0212-X*) NW Pub.

***Rowley, Calvin.** Eyes of a Leaf. 183p. 1994. 7.95 (*0-614-07071-6*) NW Pub.

Rowley, Calvin, jt. auth. see Van Treese, James B.

Rowley, Charles K. Liberty & the State. (Shaftesbury Papers). 104p. 1993. pap. 12.95 (*1-85278-853-4*, Pub. by E Elgar Pub UK) Ashgate Pub Co.

— Public Choice Theory, 3 vols., Set. Blaug, Mark, ed. (International Library of Critical Writings in Business History). 1536p. 1993. 409.95 (*1-85278-160-2*, Pub. by E Elgar Pub UK) Ashgate Pub Co.

— The Right to Justice: The Political Economy of Legal Services in the United States. 480p. 1991. text ed. 54.95 (*1-85278-526-8*, Pub. by E Elgar Pub UK) Ashgate Pub Co.

— Social Choice Theory, 3 vols., Set. (International Library of Critical Writings in Business History). 1536p. 1993. 409.95 (*1-85278-159-9*, Pub. by E Elgar Pub UK) Ashgate Pub Co.

Rowley, Charles K., ed. Property Rights & the Limits of Democracy. (John Locke Ser.). 404p. 1993. 69.95 (*1-85278-529-2*, Pub. by E Elgar Pub UK) Ashgate Pub Co.

***Rowley, Charles K., et al.** Trade Protection in the United States. LC 95-7195. (John Locke Ser.). 1995. write for info. (*1-85898-198-0*, Pub. by E Elgar Pub UK) Ashgate Pub Co.

Rowley, Christopher. Dragons of War. 464p. (Orig.). 1994. pap. 5.99 (*0-451-45342-5*, ROC) NAL-Dutton.

Rowley, Christopher B. Basil Broketail. 480p. 1992. 5.99 (*0-451-45206-2*, ROC) NAL-Dutton.

— The Black Ship. 320p. 1985. pap. 3.95 (*0-345-31489-1*, Del Rey) Ballantine.

— A Sword for a Dragon. 480p. (Orig.). 1993. pap. 5.99 (*0-451-45235-6*, ROC) NAL-Dutton.

— The War for Eternity. 352p. 1983. pap. 3.95 (*0-345-31052-7*, Del Rey) Ballantine.

Rowley-Conwy, Peter, jt. ed. see Luff, Rosemary.

Rowley, D. I. Essential Orthopaedics. 1993. pap. write for info. (*0-632-02927-7*) Blackwell Sci.

Rowley, Daniel J. The Management Challenge Experiential Exercises. 224p. (C). 1991. pap. write for info. (*0-02-354488-0*) Macmillan.

Rowley, David, jt. auth. see Purser, Harry.

Rowley, David G. Millenarian Bolshevism, Nineteen Hundred to Nineteen Twenty. McNeill, William H. & Jelavich, Barbara, eds. (Modern European History Ser.). 380p. 1987. lib. bdg. 15.00 (*0-8240-8061-0*) Garland.

Rowley, David T. Hypnosis & Hypnotherapy. LC 86-7123. 192p. 1986. text ed. 17.95 (*0-914783-13-0*); pap. 11.95 (*0-914783-15-7*) Charles.

Rowley, Doris. Nostalgia. 48p. 1984. 19.00 (*0-7212-0693-X*, Pub. by Regency Press) St Mut.

***Rowley, Eddie.** A Woman's Voice. (Illus.). 176p. 1994. pap. 16.95 (*0-86278-360-7*, Pub. by OBrien Pr IE) Dufour.

Rowley, Elton H. Time Before Space: An Airman's Odyssey...from Biplanes to Rockets. (Illus.). 238p. 1994. 33.95 (*0-89745-178-3*); pap. 25.95 (*0-89745-174-0*) Sunflower U Pr.

Rowley, Eric E. Hyperinflation in Germany: Perceptions of a Process. LC 93-45454. (Illus.). 189p. 1994. 69.95 (*1-85928-039-0*, Pub. by Scolar Pr UK) Ashgate Pub Co.

Rowley, Frances. Minor Progressions & How to Use Them. LC 83-71417. 80p. 1984. 13.50 (*0-86690-199-X*, R2311-014) Am Fed Astrologers.

— More About Minor Progressions. 120p. 1991. 16.00 (*0-86690-401-8*, R3204- 014) Am Fed Astrologers.

Rowley, Frank B. & Algren, Axel B. Thermal Conductivity of Building Materials. LC 37-27901. (University of Minnesota Engineering Experimentation Bulletin Ser.: No. 12). 144p. reprint ed. pap. 41.10 (*0-317-29494-6*, 2055907) Bks Demand.

Rowley, G. Principles of Chinese Painting. rev. ed. (Monographs in Art & Archaeology: No. 24). 1959. pap. 17.95x (*0-691-00300-9*) Princeton U Pr.

Rowley, G. D. Name That Succulent. (C). 1980. text ed. 130.00 (*0-85950-447-6*, Pub. by S Thornes Pubs UK) St Mut.

Rowley, Gorden. Candiciform & Pachycaul Succulents. Schwartz, Herman & LaFon, Ron, eds. (Illus.). 282p. 1980. 80.00 (*0-912647-03-5*) Strawberry.

***Rowley, Graham, et al.** Law for Legal Executives Pt. 1: Year Two. 2nd ed. 378p. pap. 38.00 (*1-85431-358-4*, Pub. by Blackstone Pr UK) W W Gaunt.

Rowley, H. H. Job. rev. ed. (New Century Bible Ser.). 302p. 1976. 9.95 (*0-551-00596-3*) Attic Pr.

— New Century Bible Commentary on Job. rev. ed. Clements, Ronald E., ed. 304p. 1980. pap. 15.99 (*0-8028-1838-2*) Eerdmans.

— Rediscovery of the Old Testament. 224p. 1946. 14.00 (*0-227-67576-2*) Attic Pr.

— The Relevance of Apocalyptic. 3rd rev. ed. LC 64-12221. 240p. 1980. reprint ed. pap. text ed. 9.50 (*0-87921-061-3*) Attic Pr.

Rowley, H. H., ed. Student's Bible Atlas. 40p. 1984. pap. 5.00 (*0-8170-1022-X*) Judson.

Rowley, H. H., ed. see Manson, T. W.

Rowley, Harold. To Those Far Away Places with Their Strange Sounding Names. LC 86-60808. (Illus.). 128p. (Orig.). 1986. pap. 5.95 (*0-9616729-0-0*) Rapport Unltd Pubns.

Rowley, Harold H. From Moses to Qumran. LC 74-128307. (Essay Index Reprint Ser.). 1977. 20.95 (*0-8369-2130-5*) Ayer.

— Re-Discovery of the Old Testament. LC 75-76912. (Essay Index Reprint Ser.). 1977. 21.95 (*0-8369-1154-7*) Ayer.

— The Unity of the Bible. LC 78-2684. 201p. 1978. reprint ed. text ed. 38.50 (*0-313-20346-6*, ROUB, Greenwood Pr) Greenwood.

Rowley, Hazel. Christina Stead: A Biography. LC 94-14236. 1994. 37.50 (*0-8050-3411-0*) H Holt & Co.

Rowley, Ian. Behavioural Ecology of Galahs. 188p. (C). 1990. text ed. 80.00 (*0-949324-27-2*, Pub. by Surrey Beatty & Sons AT) St Mut.

Rowley, J. C. & Trivedi, P. K. Econometrics of Investment. LC 74-32176. (Wiley Monographs in Applied Econometrics). (Illus.). 217p. reprint ed. pap. 61.90 (*0-8357-4322-5*, 2037121) Bks Demand.

Rowley, J. Carter, jt. auth. see Moran, David T.

Rowley, Jane. Back to the Wind & Waves. LC 93-33655. 250p. 1994. 19.95 (*0-944957-19-6*) Rivercross Pub.

Rowley, Jennifer. Computers for Libraries. 3rd ed. 250p. 1993. 60.00 (*1-85604-013-5*, LAP0135, Pub. by Lib Assn Pub UK) UNIPUB.

— Organizing Knowledge. 2nd ed. 450p. 1992. 67.95 (*1-85742-004-7*, Pub. by Ashgate UK); pap. 26.95 (*1-85742-005-5*, Pub. by Ashgate UK) Ashgate Pub Co.

Rowley, Jennifer & Fisher, Shelagh. Bookshelf: A Guide for Librarians & Systems Managers. 300p. 1992. 79.95 (*1-85742-008-X*, Pub. by Ashgate UK) Ashgate Pub Co.

Rowley, John, et al. Grasshoppers & Locusts: The Plague of the Sahel. (Panos Dossier Ser.: No. 5). (Illus.). 64p. 1994. pap. 12.95 (*1-870670-24-8*) Paul & Co Pubs.

Rowley, Kay. Rock Concerts. LC 91-21367. (Rock World Ser.). (Illus.). 32p. (J). (gr. 5). 1992. text ed. 13.95 (*0-89686-715-3*, Crstwood Hse) Silver Burdett Pr.

— Rock Music. LC 91-22085. (Rock World Ser.). (Illus.). 32p. (J). (gr. 5). 1992. text ed. 13.95 (*0-89686-714-5*, Crstwood Hse) Silver Burdett Pr.

— Rock Stars. LC 91-15077. (Rock World Ser.). (Illus.). 32p. (J). (gr. 5). 1992. text ed. 13.95 (*0-89686-713-7*, Crstwood Hse) Silver Burdett Pr.

— Rock Videos. LC 91-15073. (Rock World Ser.). (Illus.). 32p. (J). (gr. 5). 1992. text ed. 13.95 (*0-89686-712-9*, Crstwood Hse) Silver Burdett Pr.

Rowley, Keith. Woodturning: A Foundation Course. (Illus.). 151p. 1992. pap. 19.95 (*0-946819-20-3*, Pub. by Guild Mstr Craftsman UK) Sterling.

Rowley, Keith, jt. ed. see McKinney, Joseph A.

Rowley-Kelly, Fern L. & Reigel, Donald H., eds. Teaching the Student with Spina Bifida. 496p. (Orig.). (C). 1992. pap. text ed. 37.00 (*1-55766-064-6*); vhs 49.00 (*1-55766-109-X*) P H Brookes.

Rowley, Kelvin, jt. auth. see Evans, Grant.

***Rowley, Michael.** Kana Pict-o-Graphix: Mnemonics for Japanese Hiragana & Katakana. LC 94-48537. (Illus.). 72p. (Orig.). 1995. pap. 6.00 (*1-880656-18-3*) Stone Bridge Pr.

— Kanji Pict-O-Graphix: Over One Thousand Japanese Kanji & Kana Mnemonics. LC 91-23153. (Illus.). 216p. (Orig.). 1992. pap. 19.95 (*0-9628137-0-2*) Stone Bridge Pr.

Rowley, Michael C., ed. see Peters Corporation, Gerald Peters Gallery Staff.

Rowley, Patric. Artists: A Kansas Collection. (Illus.). 108p. (YA). (gr. 7-12). 1989. 34.95 (*0-9623079-0-4*) Artists Registry.

Rowley, Richard L. Statistical Mechanics for Thermophysical Property Calculations. LC 93-45530. 512p. 1994. text ed., disk 83.00 (*0-13-030818-8*) P-H.

Rowley, Sam R. Discovering Falconry: A Comprehensive Guide to Contemporary Falconry. LC 85-61152. (Illus.). 160p. (Orig.). 1985. pap. text ed. 11.95 (*0-934271-00-3*) New Dawn.

Rowley, Samuel. When You See Me You Know Me. LC 70-133730. (Tudor Facsimile Texts. Old English Plays Ser.: No. 106). reprint ed. 49.50 (*0-404-53406-6*) AMS Pr.

Rowley, Thomas E. Atari BASIC: Learning by Using. 73p. 7.95 (*0-936200-35-9*) Blue Cat.

Rowley, Trevor. A Travellers's Guide to Norman Britain. (Traveller's Guide Ser.). (Illus.). 128p. 1986. 14.95 (*0-918678-11-0*) Natl Hist Soc.

Rowley, Trevor, ed. The Origins of Open Field Agriculture. (Illus.). 258p. 1981. 44.00 (*0-389-20102-2*, N6876) B&N Imports.

Rowley, William. Birth of Merlin. LC 74-133731. (Tudor Facsimile Texts. Old English Plays Ser.: No. 145). reprint ed. 49.50 (*0-404-53445-7*) AMS Pr.

— A New Wonder, a Woman Never Vext: An Old-Spelling, Critical Edition. Cheatham, George, ed. LC 92-27581. (Renaissance & Baroque Studies & Texts: Vol. 6). 264p. (C). 1993. text ed. 49.95 (*0-8204-1916-8*) P Lang Pubs.

Rowley, William, jt. auth. see Middleton, Thomas.
Rowley, William D. M. L. Wilson & the Campaign for the Domestic Allotment. LC 69-19106. 233p. reprint ed. pap. 66.50 (0-8357-2952-4, 2039208) Bks Demand.
— U. S. Forest Service Grazing & Rangelands: A History. LC 85-40048. (Environmental History Ser.: No. 8). 288p. 1985. 29.50 (0-89096-218-9) Tex A&M Univ Pr.
Rowley, William D., jt. auth. see Elliott, Russell R.
Rowley, Wm., jt. auth. see Middleton, Thomas.
Rowling, Ed. Oriental Cookbook. (Illus.). 256p. 1990. 19.99 (0-517-02889-1) Random Hse Value.
Rowling, Louise, jt. auth. see Glassrock, Geoffrey T.
Rowling, Marjorie. Everyday Life in Medieval Times. 1987. 17.95 (0-88029-128-1) Dorset Pr.
— Everyday Life of Medieval Travellers. (Everyday Life Ser.). (Illus.). 208p. 1990. 17.95 (0-88029-351-9) Dorset Pr.
Rowlingson, John C., jt. ed. see Hamill, Robin J.
Rowlinson, George, tr. see Herodotus.
Rowlinson, J. S. Liquids & Liquid Mixtures. 2nd ed. LC 79-75522. 372p. 1969. 37.50 (0-306-30694-8, Plenum Pr) Plenum.
Rowlinson, J. S., ed. J. D. Van Der Waals: Continuity of the Gaseous & Liquid States. (Studies in Statistical Mechanics: Vol. 14). 320p. 1988. 82.00 (0-444-87077-6, North Holland) Elsevier.
Rowlinson, Matthew. Tennyson's Fixations: Psychoanalysis & the Topics of the Early Poetry. (Victorian Literature & Culture Ser.). 224p. (C). 1994. text ed. 35.00 (0-8139-1478-7) U Pr of Va.
***Rowlinson, Peter, ed.** Surveys in Combinatorics, 1995. (London Mathematical Society Lecture Note Ser.: No. 218). (Illus.). 300p. (C). Date not set. pap. write for info. (0-521-49797-3) Cambridge U Pr.
Rowlinson, William. French Grammar. 304p. 1991. pap. 5.95 (0-19-212991-0) OUP.
— French Grammar. (Paperback Reference Ser.). 302p. 1994. reprint ed. pap. 7.95 (0-19-282894-0) OUP.
— French Verbs. 302p. 1991. pap. 5.95 (0-19-864173-7) OUP.
— French Verbs. (Paperback Reference Ser.). 296p. 1994. reprint ed. pap. 7.95 (0-19-282772-3) OUP.
— French Vocabulary. 304p. 1991. pap. 5.95 (0-19-864174-5) OUP.
— German Grammar. LC 92-38572. 308p. (C). 1993. 6.95 (0-19-211677-0) OUP.
— German Grammar. (Paperback Reference Ser.). 304p. 1994. reprint ed. pap. 7.95 (0-19-280020-5) OUP.
— German Verbs. 368p. 1993. 6.95 (0-19-211684-3) OUP.
— German Verbs. (Paperback Reference Ser.). 368p. 1994. reprint ed. pap. 7.95 (0-19-280019-1) OUP.
— Ten Thousand French Words. LC 94-9758. (Paperback Reference Ser.). 336p. 1994. reprint ed. pap. 7.95 (0-19-282895-9) OUP.
— Ten Thousand German Words. LC 93-45641. (Paperback Reference Ser.). 320p. 1994. pap. 7.95 (0-19-283095-3) OUP.
— Ten Thousand German Words. LC 93-45641. (Paperback Reference Ser.). 320p. 1994. 6.95 (0-19-211686-X) OUP.
***Rowlinson, William, et al.** The Oxford Paperback French Dictionary & Grammar. 832p. (FRE.). 1995. pap. 12.95 (0-19-864529-5) OUP.
— The Oxford Paperback German Dictionary & Grammar. 928p. (GER.). 1995. pap. 12.95 (0-19-864530-9) OUP.
Rowlison, Bruce A. Creative Hospitality As a Means of Evangelism. rev. ed. LC 81-84182. (Illus.). 145p. 1984. pap. 7.50 (0-938462-03-2) Green Leaf CA.
Rowlison, Bruce A. & Hinn, George. Let's Talk about Your Wedding & Marriage. 3rd ed. 48p. 1994. pap. 3.95 (0-938462-17-2) Green Leaf CA.
Rowlison, Bruce A., jt. auth. see Wiebe, Ronald W.
Rowlson, Rachel & Staub, Dusty. Self Taught-Self Help. Williams, Tim, ed. 75p. (Orig.). 1984. pap. 7.95 (0-9614201-0-3) Dragonlord Pr.
Rowney, Don K. Transition to Technocracy: The Structural Origins of the Soviet Administrative State. LC 88-47925. (Cornell Studies in Soviet History & Science). 264p. 1989. 37.95 (0-8014-2183-7) Cornell U Pr.
Rowney, Don K., ed. Imperial Power & Development: Papers on Pre-Revolutionary Russian History: Selected Papers of the Third World Congress for Soviet & East European Studies. 187p. (Orig.). 1990. pap. 18.95 (0-89357-209-8) Slavica.
— Soviet Quantitative History. LC 83-19196. (New Approaches to Social Science History Ser.: No. 4). (Illus.). 216p. reprint ed. pap. 61.60 (0-8357-8506-8, 2034793) Bks Demand.
Rowney, Don Karl & Graham, James Q. Quantitative History: Selected Readings in the Quantitative Analysis of Historical Data. LC 76-90239. 508p. reprint ed. pap. 144.80 (0-317-09235-9, 2006453) Bks Demand.
Rowntree, B. Seebohm, Jr. The Human Factor in Business. Chandler, Alfred D., ed. LC 79-7553. (History of Management Thought & Practice Ser.). 1980. reprint ed. lib. bdg. 19.95 (0-405-12339-6) Ayer.
Rowntree, B. Seebohm. Old People: Report of a Survey Committee on the Problems of Aging & the Care of Old People. Stein, Leon, ed. LC 79-8682. (Growing Old Ser.). (Illus.). 1980. reprint ed. lib. bdg. 23.95 (0-405-12799-5) Ayer.
Rowntree, B. Seebohm & Kendall, May. How the Labourer Lives: A Study of the Rural Problem. LC 74-25780. (European Sociology Ser.). 342p. 1975. reprint ed. 28.95 (0-405-06533-7) Ayer.
Rowntree, C. Brightwen & Sessions, E. M. Rowntrees of Riseborough: A Genealogy. (C). 1986. 118.00 (0-900657-67-7, Pub. by W Sessions UK) St Mut.
Rowntree, Derek. A Dictionary of Education. 362p. (C). 1982. text ed. 45.00 (0-389-20263-0, 07081) B&N Imports.
— Exploring Open & Distance Learning. 304p. (C). 1992. pap. text ed. 39.95 (0-89397-378-5) Nichols Pub.
— Learn How to Study. 2nd ed. 1976. pap. 12.95 (0-8464-0548-2) Beekman Pubs.
— Preparing Materials for Open, Distance, & Flexible Learning: An Action Guide for Teachers & Trainers. Lockwood, Fred, ed. (Open & Distance Learning Ser.). 128p. (Orig.). 1994. pap. text ed. 29.95 (0-7494-1159-7, Pub. by Kogan Page UK) Nichols Pub.
— Statistics Without Tears: A Primer for Non-Mathematicians. 199p. (C). 1981. pap. write for info. (0-02-404090-8, Scribners) S&S Trade.
— Statistics Without Tears: A Primer for Non-Mathematicians. LC 82-3157. (Illus.). 200p. 1982. pap. write for info. (0-684-17502-9, Scribners) S&S Trade.
— Teach Yourself with Open Learning. 190p. (Orig.). 1993. pap. text ed. 29.95 (0-7494-1153-8, Pub. by Kogan Page UK) Nichols Pub.
— Teaching with Audio in Open & Distance Learning. Lockwood, Fred, ed. (Open & Distance Learning Ser.). 160p. (Orig.). 1993. pap. text ed. 39.95 (0-7494-1154-6, Pub. by Kogan Page UK) Nichols Pub.
Rowntree, J. W. & Binns, H. B. A History of the Adult School Movement. 88p. (C). 1985. 60.00 (0-317-94046-5, Pub. by Univ Nottingham UK); 65.00 (1-85041-007-0, Pub. by Univ Nottingham UK) St Mut.
Rowntree, Kathleen. Between Friends. large type ed. (Ulverscroft Ser.). 592p. 1994. 21.95 (0-7089-3027-1) Ulverscroft.
— The Haunting of Willow Dasset. 288p. 1989. 17.95 (0-316-75975-9) Little.
— Tell Mrs. Poole I'm Sorry. LC 94-37530. 416p. 1995. 23.95 (0-312-11882-1) St Martin.
Rowny, Edward L., et al. Strategic Force Modernization & Arms Control. LC 85-10579. (National Security Papers: No. 6). 1986. 7.50 (0-89549-075-7) Inst Foreign Policy Anal.
Rowold, Milam C., jt. auth. see Sitton, Thad.
Roworth, Wendy W., ed. Angelica Kauffman: A Continental Artist in Georgian England. (Illus.). 208p. 1993. pap. 22.50 (0-948462-41-8) U of Wash Pr.
Rowse, A. L. Contemporary Shakespeare Series, Vol. I: Macbeth, All's Well That Ends Well, Henry V, King Richard, III & The Taming of the Shrew. LC 84-5105. 650p. (C). 1985. lib. bdg. 27.50 (0-8191-3908-4) U Pr of Amer.
— The Controversial Colensos. 152p. (C). 1989. 100.00 (1-85022-047-6, Pub. by Dyllansow Truran UK) St Mut.
— Early Churchills. (Dorset Classic Reprints Ser.). 396p. 1991. 24.95 (0-88029-587-2) Marboro Bks.
— England of Elizabeth. LC 78-53293. 562p. 1978. reprint ed. pap. 16.50 (0-299-07724-1) U of Wis Pr.
— Glimpses of the Great. LC 85-20358. 254p. 1986. reprint ed. lib. bdg. 21.00 (0-8191-5008-8) U Pr of Amer.
— Homosexuals in History: A Study of Ambivalence in Society, Literature & the Arts. 376p. 1983. reprint ed. pap. 9.95 (0-88184-060-2) Carroll & Graf.
— Matthew Arnold: Poet & Prophet. (Illus.). 210p. (C). 1986. reprint ed. lib. bdg. 36.00 (0-8191-5120-3) U Pr of Amer.
— Memories of Men & Women American & British. LC 83-16875. 266p. (Orig.). (C). 1983. reprint ed. lib. bdg. 20.25 (0-8191-3582-8); reprint ed. pap. text ed. 11.25 (0-8191-3583-6) U Pr of Amer.
— Prompting the Age: Poems Early & Late. (C). 1989. text ed. 60.00 (1-85022-056-5, Pub. by Dyllansow Truran UK) St Mut.
— Transatlantic: Later Poems. 77p. (Orig.). 1990. pap. 9.95 (0-907018-70-X, Pub. by Tabb Hse Pubs UK) Seven Hills Bk.
— Tudor Cornwall. (C). 1989. 140.00 (1-85022-058-1, Pub. by Dyllansow Truran UK) St Mut.
Rowse, A. L., comp. & notes. Shakespeare's Self Portrait: Passages from His Work. 200p. 1985. lib. bdg. 22.00 (0-8191-4220-4) U Pr of Amer.
Rowse, A. L., ed. All's Well That Ends Well. LC 85-678. (Contemporary Shakespeare Ser.: Vol. III). 124p. (Orig.). (C). 1985. pap. text ed. 3.45 (0-8191-3917-3) U Pr of Amer.
— Annotated Shakespeare: The Comedies, Histories, Sonnets & Other Poems, Tragedies & Romances; Complete, 3 vols. in one. 2464p. 1984. 29.95 (0-517-43603-5) Random Hse Value.
— Anthony & Cleopatra: Modern Text with Introduction. LC 86-11034. (Contemporary Shakespeare Ser.). 152p. (C). 1986. pap. text ed. 3.45 (0-8191-3931-9) U Pr of Amer.
— As You Like It. LC 84-15393. (Contemporary Shakespeare Ser.: Vol. II). 108p. (Orig.). 1985. pap. text ed. 3.45 (0-8191-3914-9) U Pr of Amer.
— The Comedy of Errors: Modern Text with Introduction. LC 86-23395. 94p. (Orig.). (C). 1987. pap. text ed. 3.45 (0-8191-3935-1) U Pr of Amer.
— The Contemporary Shakespeare: Volume VII-King Henry VI, Part One, King Henry VI, Part Two, King Henry VI, Part Three, King John, Pericles, Titus Andronicus. LC 84-5105. (Modern Text with Introduction Ser.). 724p. (C). 1987. lib. bdg. 27.50 (0-8191-3947-5) U Pr of Amer.
— Contemporary Shakespeare Series, Vol. III: Hamlet, Julius Caesar, Merchant of Venice, A Midsummer Night's Dream, Romeo & Juliet, The Tempest. LC 84-5105. 690p. (C). 1984. lib. bdg. 27.50 (0-8191-3922-X) U Pr of Amer.
— Cymbeline: Modern Text with Introduction. LC 86-23381. 140p. (Orig.). (C). 1987. pap. text ed. 3.45 (0-8191-3938-6) U Pr of Amer.
— Hamlet. LC 84-5068. (Contemporary Shakespeare Ser.: Vol. I). 156p. (Orig.). (C). 1984. pap. text ed. 3.45 (0-8191-3898-3) U Pr of Amer.
— Henry V. LC 85-680. (Contemporary Shakespeare Ser.: Vol. III). 146p. (Orig.). (C). 1985. pap. text ed. 3.45 (0-8191-3918-1) U Pr of Amer.
— Julius Caesar. LC 84-5071. (Contemporary Shakespeare Ser.: Vol. I). 124p. (Orig.). (C). 1984. pap. text ed. 3.45 (0-8191-3902-5) U Pr of Amer.
— King Henry VI, Part Three. LC 87-14738. (Modern Text with Introduction Ser.). 148p. (Orig.). (C). 1987. pap. text ed. 3.45 (0-8191-3943-2) U Pr of Amer.
— King Henry VI, Part Two. LC 87-14737. (Modern Text with Introduction Ser.). 146p. (Orig.). (C). 1987. pap. text ed. 3.45 (0-8191-3942-4) U Pr of Amer.
— King John. LC 87-14735. (Modern Text with Introduction Ser.). 120p. (Orig.). (C). 1987. pap. text ed. 3.45 (0-8191-3946-7) U Pr of Amer.
— King Lear. LC 84-15388. (Contemporary Shakespeare Ser.: Vol. II). 152p. (Orig.). 1985. pap. text ed. 3.45 (0-8191-3911-4) U Pr of Amer.
— Macbeth. LC 85-679. (Contemporary Shakespeare Ser.: Vol. III). 112p. (Orig.). (C). 1985. pap. text ed. 3.45 (0-8191-3919-X) U Pr of Amer.
— Measure for Measure: Modern Text with Introduction. LC 86-11033. 122p. (Orig.). (C). 1986. pap. text ed. 3.45 (0-8191-3930-0) U Pr of Amer.
— The Merchant of Venice. LC 84-5069. (Contemporary Shakespeare Ser.: Vol. I). 120p. (Orig.). (C). 1984. pap. text ed. 3.45 (0-8191-3901-7) U Pr of Amer.
— The Merry Wives of Windsor: Modern Text with Introduction. LC 86-11031. 114p. (Orig.). (C). 1986. pap. text ed. 3.45 (0-8191-3929-7) U Pr of Amer.
— A Midsummer Night's Dream. LC 84-5099. (Contemporary Shakespeare Ser.: Vol. I). 94p. (Orig.). (C). 1984. pap. text ed. 3.45 (0-8191-3900-9) U Pr of Amer.
— Much Ado about Nothing: Modern Text with Introduction. LC 86-23396. 114p. (Orig.). (C). 1987. pap. text ed. 3.45 (0-8191-3937-8) U Pr of Amer.
— Pericles. LC 87-14752. (Modern Text with Introduction Ser.). 118p. (Orig.). (C). 1987. pap. text ed. 3.45 (0-8191-3945-9) U Pr of Amer.
— Romeo & Juliet. LC 84-5086. (Contemporary Shakespeare Ser.: Vol. I). 140p. (Orig.). (C). 1984. pap. text ed. 3.45 (0-8191-3903-3) U Pr of Amer.
— The Taming of the Shrew. LC 85-681. (Contemporary Shakespeare Ser.: Vol. III). 130p. (Orig.). (C). 1985. pap. text ed. 3.45 (0-8191-3921-1) U Pr of Amer.
— The Tempest. LC 84-5070. (Contemporary Shakespeare Ser.: Vol. I). 104p. (Orig.). (C). 1984. pap. text ed. 3.45 (0-8191-3899-1) U Pr of Amer.
— Timon of Athens: Modern Text with Introduction. LC 86-23380. 116p. (Orig.). (C). 1987. pap. text ed. 3.45 (0-8191-3939-4) U Pr of Amer.
— Titus Andronicus. LC 87-14757. (Modern Text with Introduction Ser.). 108p. (Orig.). (C). 1987. pap. text ed. 3.45 (0-8191-3944-0) U Pr of Amer.
— Troilus & Cressida: Modern Text with Introduction. LC 86-11032. (Contemporary Shakespeare Ser.). 146p. (Orig.). (C). 1986. pap. text ed. 3.45 (0-8191-3932-7) U Pr of Amer.
— Twelfth Night. LC 84-15387. (Contemporary Shakespeare Ser.: Vol. II). 112p. (Orig.). 1985. pap. text ed. 3.45 (0-8191-3912-2) U Pr of Amer.
— The Two Gentlemen of Verona: Modern Text with Introduction. LC 86-11026. (Contemporary Shakespeare Ser.). 106p. (Orig.). (C). 1986. pap. text ed. 3.45 (0-8191-3933-5) U Pr of Amer.
Rowse, A. L., intro. Froude's Spanish Story of the Armada. LC 89-11532. 272p. 1989. pap. 14.00 (0-86299-500-0) A Sutton Pub.
Rowse, A. L., ed. see Shakespeare, William.
Rowse, Alfred L. An Elizabethan Garland. LC 76-161760. reprint ed. 20.00 (0-404-07965-2) AMS Pr.
— The Elizabethans & America. LC 78-5090. (Illus.). 221p. 1978. reprint ed. text ed. 35.00 (0-8371-9350-8, ROELA, Greenwood Pr) Greenwood.
— Shakespeare the Man. rev. ed. (Illus.). 272p. 1989. reprint ed. pap. 13.95 (0-312-03425-3) St Martin.
— Sir Walter Raleigh, His Family & Private Life. LC 73-21492. (Illus.). 348p. 1975. reprint ed. text ed. 38.50 (0-8371-6388-9, ROWR, Greenwood Pr) Greenwood.
Rowse, Alfred L. & Harrison, George B. Queen Elizabeth & Her Subjects. LC 79-76913. (Essay Index Reprint Ser.). 1977. 16.95 (0-8369-1895-9) Ayer.
Rowse, Alfred L., ed. see Thomson, Gladys S.
***Rowse, Tim.** After Mabo. 1995. pap. text ed. 19.95 (0-522-84492-8) Intl Spec Bk.
Rowsemitt, Carol, et al. The Timing & Patterns of Molt in Microtus Breweri. (Occasional Papers: No. 34). 11p. 1975. pap. 1.00 (0-317-04913-5) U of KS Mus Nat Hist.
Rowsey, Katheryn, jt. auth. see Knox, Carol.
Rowshan, Arthur. Stress/An Owner's Manual: Positive Techniques for Taking Charge of Your Life. 1993. pap. 8.95 (1-85168-068-3) Onewrld Pubns.
Rowsome, Frank, Jr. The Verse by the Side of the Road. 1993. reprint ed. lib. bdg. 18.95 (1-56849-088-7) Buccaneer Bks.
— The Verse by the Side of the Road. 1979. reprint ed. pap. 8.00 (0-452-26762-5, Plume) NAL-Dutton.
— The Verse by the Side of the Road: Burma-Shave Signs & Jingles. LC 65-24618. 1965. 7.95 (0-8289-0038-8) Viking Penguin.
— The Verse by the Side of the Road: Burma-Shave Signs & Jingles. LC 65-24618. 1979. pap. 5.95 (0-8289-0351-4) Viking Penguin.
Rowson, Everett K. A Muslim Philosopher on the Soul & Its Fate: Al-Amiri's Kitab al-Amad 'ala l'abad. (Amer. Oriental Ser.: Vol. 70). vi, 375p. 1988. 42.50 (0-940490-70-6) Am Orient Soc.
Rowson, Everett K., tr. The History of al-Tabari, Vol. 22: The Marwanid Restoration: The Caliphate of 'Abd al-Malik: A.D. 693-701 - A.H. 74-81. LC 88-16086. (SUNY Series in Near Eastern Studies). 228p. (C). 1989. 44.50 (0-88706-975-4); pap. 16.95 (0-88706-976-2) State U NY Pr.
Rowson, Everett K. & Bonebakker, Seeger A. A Computerized Listing of Biographical Data from the Yatimat al-dahr by al-Tha'alibi. LC 79-67633. viii, 103p. (Orig.). 1980. pap. 23.75 (0-89003-044-8) Undena Pubns.
Rowson, K. E. & Mahy, B. W. Lactic Dehydrogenase Virus. LC 74-34231. (Virology Monographs: Vol. 13). (Illus.). iv, 121p. 1975. text ed. 45.00 (0-387-81270-9) Spr-Verlag.
Rowson, Susanna. Charlotte Temple. 160p. 1987. pap. 7.95 (0-19-504238-7) OUP.
— Charlotte Temple: A Tale of Truth. Kirk, Clara M. & Kirk, Rudolf, eds. (Masterworks of Literature Ser.). 1964. pap. 9.95 (0-8084-0073-8) NCUP.
— Charlotte Temple & Lucy Temple. Douglas, Ann, ed. & intro. by. 336p. 1991. pap. 10.95 (0-14-039080-4, Penguin Classics) Viking Penguin.
— Charlotte's Daughter: Or the Three Orphans. LC 72-78812. 1828. reprint ed. 39.00 (0-403-01983-4) Somerset Pub.
— Charlotte's Temple, a Tale of Truth. LC 72-78814. 1794. reprint ed. 39.00 (0-403-01984-2) Somerset Pub.
— Lucy Temple. Levendusk, Christine, ed. (Masterworks of Literature Ser.). 1991. 9.95 (0-8084-0433-4) NCUP.
— Reuben & Rachel; or, Tales of Old Times, 2 vols. in one. LC 78-64089. reprint ed. 37.50 (0-404-17074-9) AMS Pr.
— Sarah, or the Exemplary Wife. LC 78-64090. reprint ed. 37.50 (0-404-17165-6) AMS Pr.
— Trials of the Human Heart, 4 vols. in 2, Set. LC 78-64091. reprint ed. 75.00 (0-404-17360-8) AMS Pr.
Rowson, Susanna H. Charlotte Temple: A Tale of Truth, 2 vols. in 1, Set. (BCL1-PS American Literature Ser.). 1992. reprint ed. lib. bdg. 99.00 (0-7812-6846-X) Rprt Serv.
Rowson, Trevor, jt. auth. see Jones, Edwin.
Rowtbottom, Derek & Rowtbottom, Sheila. Making Period Dolls' House Furniture. (Illus.). 164p. 1993. pap. 14.95 (0-946819-36-X, Pub. by Guild Mstr Craftsman UK) Sterling.
Rowtbottom, Sheila, jt. auth. see Rowtbottom, Derek.
Rowthorn, Anne. Caring for Creation: Toward an Ethic of Responsibility. LC 89-32725. 192p. (Orig.). 1989. pap. 11.95 (0-8192-1506-6) Morehouse Pub.
— To Seek & To Serve: Congregations in Mission. 415p. 1991. pap. 8.95 (0-88028-122-7, 1134) Forward Movement.
Rowthorn, Anne W. The Liberation of the Laity. LC 86-17982. 232p. 1986. reprint ed. pap. 9.95 (0-8192-1395-0); reprint ed. student ed, pap. 2.95 (0-8192-1604-6) Morehouse Pub.
Rowthorn, Bob. Capitalism Conflict & Inflation. (C). 1980. pap. 18.50 (0-85315-539-9, Pub. by Lawrence & Wishart UK) Humanities.
Rowthorn, Jeffery. The Wideness of God's Mercy: Litanies to Enlarge Our Prayer. rev. ed. 256p. 1995. pap. 19.95 (0-8192-1606-2) Morehouse Pub.
Rowthorn, Jeffery & Schulz-Widmar, Russell, eds. A New Hymnal for Colleges & Schools. 512p. (C). 1992. pap. text ed. 25.00 (0-300-05113-1) Yale U Pr.
Rowthorn, Robert, jt. ed. see Chang, Ha-Joon.
Rowzee, Janet Z. & Watson, James A. The Song of the Shepherd Boy. 20p. (J). (gr. 4-8). 1993. pap. 6.95 (0-9638941-0-2) Eagles Three.
Rox, Lori M. Oodles of Riddles. LC 89-4549. (Illus.). 96p. (J). (gr. 3-8). 1990. pap. 3.95 (0-8069-7202-5) Sterling.
***Rox, Mi.** White Roses. 200p. 1996. pap. 8.95 (0-7610-0509-9) NW Pub.
Roxbee-Cox, P. Atoms & Molecules. (Understanding Science Ser.). (Illus.). 32p. (J). (gr. 6-9). 1993. lib. bdg. 13.96 (0-88110-589-9); pap. 6.95 (0-7460-0988-7) EDC.
— What Were Castles For? (Starting Point History Ser.). (Illus.). 24p. (J). (gr. k up). 1995. lib. bdg. 11.96 (0-88110-729-8, Usborne); pap. 4.95 (0-7460-1341-8, Usborne) EDC.
— Who Were the First People? (Starting Point History Ser.). (Illus.). 24p. (J). 1995. lib. bdg. 11.96 (0-88110-730-1, Usborne); pap. 4.95 (0-7460-1343-4, Usborne) EDC.
Roxberg, Joan M., jt. auth. see Montoya, Candace G.
Roxborough, Ian. Unions & Politics in Mexico: The Case of the Automobile Industry. (Cambridge Latin American Studies: No. 49). (Illus.). 224p. 1984. 69.95 (0-521-25987-8) Cambridge U Pr.
Roxborough, Ian, jt. ed. see Bethell, Leslie.
Roxburgh, Alan J. Reaching a New Generation: Strategies for Tomorrow's Church. LC 92-34569. (Illus.). 140p. (Orig.). 1993. pap. 9.99 (0-8308-1340-3, 1340) InterVarsity.
Roxburgh, I. S. Geology of High-level Nuclear Waste Disposal: An Introduction. 238p. 1987. text ed. 59.50 (0-412-29910-0) Chapman & Hall.
Roxburgh, Nigel. Policy Responses to Resource Depletion: A Case of Mercury. Walter, Ingo & Altman, Edward I., eds. LC 77-24395. (Contemporary Studies in Economic & Financial Analysis: Vol. 21). 1980. lib. bdg. 73.25 (0-89232-093-1) Jai Pr.
Roxburgh, R. Icones Roxburghianae: or Drawings of Indian Plants. (C). 1988. 170.00 (0-685-22300-0, Scientific) St Mut.
Roxburgh, Ronald F. The Origins of Lincoln's Inn. LC 85-81798. (Cambridge Studies in English Legal History). 102p. 1986. reprint ed. 28.00 (0-912004-52-5) W W Gaunt.

R

An Asterisk (*) at the beginning of an entry indicates that the title is appearing in BIP for the first time.

Roxburgh, W. Flora Indica: Description of Indian Plants. Carey, ed. (Illus.). lxiv, 775p. 1974. reprint ed. 50.00 (*0-88065-182-2*, Messers Today & Tomorrow) Scholarly Pubns.

— Flora Indica or Description of Indian Plants. (C). 1980. text ed. 900.00 (*0-89771-529-2*, Pub. by Textile Institue UK) St Mut.

— Plants of the Coast of Coromandel, 3 vols., Set. (C). 1988. text ed. 2,000.00 (*0-685-44240-3*, Scientific) St Mut.

Roxburgh, William. Plants of the Coast of Coromandel: Selected from Drawings & Descriptions Presented to the Hon. Court of Directors of the East India Company, under the Order of Sir Joseph Banks, 3 vols., Set. (Illus.). 20p. 1982. reprint ed. lib. bdg. 1,200.00 (*0-685-44091-5*) Lubrecht & Cramer.

Roxe, Linda A. Personnel Management for the Smaller Company: A Hands-on Manual. LC 79-10867. 256p. reprint ed. pap. 73.00 (*0-317-27183-0*, 2023920) Bks Demand.

Roxin. Modern Optimal Control: A Conference in Honor of Solomon Lefschetz & Joseph P. La Salle. (Lecture Notes in Pure & Applied Mathematics Ser.: Vol. 119). 464p. 1989. 140.00 (*0-8247-8168-6*) Dekker.

Roxin, jt. auth. see Liu.

Roxin, Emilio D., ed. see Kingston Conference on Differential Games & Control Theory Staff.

Roxton, James. The Markets Directory - 1991: Focus Facilities, Test Kitchens, Malls, Moderators by Location in Every Major Market in the United States. 261p. 1990. pap. 40.00 (*0-9628135-0-8*) Dobbs Dirs.

Roxton, Tiniki, ed. Recommended Videos for Schools. 2nd ed. 300p. 1992. lib. bdg. 55.00 (*0-87436-688-7*) ABC-CLIO.

***Roy.** Brown Girl in the Ring: Rosemary Brown, a Biography for Young People. Date not set. per. 9.95 (*0-920813-52-6*, Pub. by Sister Vision CN) InBook.

— Cordwood Masonry Houses. 1980. pap. text ed. (*0-8069-8944-0*) Sterling.

— Master Techniques in Ophthalmalic Surgery. 1994. 225. 00 (*0-683-07410-5*) Williams & Wilkins.

— Pediatric Clinical Gastroenterology. 4th ed. (Illus.). 970p. 1991. 89.95 (*0-8016-6216-8*) Mosby Yr Bk.

Roy, et al. Left Experiment in West Bengal. 201p. 1985. 12. 50 (*0-318-18472-9*) Nataraj Bks.

Roy, A. E. Orbital Motion. 3rd rev. ed. (Illus.). 548p. 1988. 150.00 (*0-85274-228-2*); pap. 39.00 (*0-85274-229-0*) IOP Pub.

Roy, A. E., ed. Predictability, Stability, & Chaos in N-Body Dynamical Systems. (NATO ASI Series B, Physics: Vol. 272). (Illus.). 580p. 1991. 135.00 (*0-306-44034-2*, Plenum Pr) Plenum.

Roy, A. E. & Clarke, D. Astronomy: Principles & Practice. (Illus.). 376p. 1988. pap. 36.00 (*0-85274-393-9*) IOP Pub.

— Astronomy: Principles & Practice. 3rd ed. (Illus.). 376p. 1988. 129.00 (*0-85274-394-7*) IOP Pub.

— Astronomy: Structure of the Universe. 3rd ed. (Illus.). 316p. 1989. 129.00 (*0-85274-082-4*); pap. 35.00 (*0-85274-083-2*) IOP Pub.

Roy, A. K. & Clark, J. H., eds. Gene Regulation by Steroid Hormones. (Illus.). 400p. 1980. 119.00 (*0-387-90464-6*) Spr-Verlag.

— Gene Regulation by Steroid Hormones II. (Illus.). 384p. 1983. 140.00 (*0-387-90784-X*) Spr-Verlag.

— Gene Regulation by Steroid Hormones III. (Illus.). 335p. 1987. 152.00 (*0-387-96436-3*) Spr-Verlag.

— Gene Regulation by Steroid Hormones IV. (Illus.). xi, 239p. 1989. 80.00 (*0-387-96999-3*) Spr-Verlag.

Roy, Ajit K. The Historical Evolution of Corporation Tax in India. (C). 1987. 62.50 (*0-8364-2130-2*, KL Mukhopadhyay) S Asia.

***Roy, Alain.** Dictionnaire Raisonne et Illustre du Th/atre A L'Italienne. 1992. 65.00 (*0-7859-8166-7*, 2-86943-357-3) Fr & Eur.

Roy, Alec, ed. Hysteria. 332p. reprint ed. pap. 94.70 (*0-318-34899-3*, 2031297) Bks Demand.

Roy, Alene. In His Gardens, Bk. 1. 72p. (Orig.). 1992. pap. 7.95 (*0-9635069-0-0*) Closer Walk.

— Winter in His Garden: Essays of Faith & Family. LC 94-69070. (In His Gardens Ser.: Bk. 2). (Illus.). 116p. (Orig.). 1995. pap. 7.95 (*0-9635069-1-9*) Closer Walk.

***Roy, Alene A.** Cooking with Sourdough: A Tribute to the Oregon Trail Pioneers. (Illus.). 1995. spiral bd. 7.95 (*0-9635069-2-7*) Closer Walk.

Roy, Anilbaran, ed. see Aurobindo, Sri.

Roy, Aniruddha, ed. Technology in Ancient & Medieval India. 170p. 1986. 46.00 (*81-85055-95-5*, Pub. by Minerva II) S Asia.

Roy, Anup K., jt. auth. see Gottman, John.

Roy, Archie, ed. Oxford Illustrated Encyclopedia, Vol. 8: The Universe. (Illus.). 208p. 1993. 45.00 (*0-19-869140-8*) OUP.

Roy, Archie E., ed. Long-Term Dynamical Behaviour of Natural & Artificial N-Body Systems. (C). 1988. lib. bdg. 175.50 (*90-277-2801-1*) Kluwer Ac.

***Roy, Archie E. & Steves, Bonnie A., eds.** From Newton to Chaos: Modern Techniques for Understanding & Coping with Chaos in N-Body Dynamical Systems. LC 95-1181. (NATO ASI Series B: Vol. 336). 575p. (C). 1995. 139.50 (*0-306-44904-8*, Plenum Pr) Plenum.

Roy, Arthur J., ed. see Flint, Albert S.

Roy, Arundhati. The Soviet Intervention in Afghanistan: Causes, Consequences & India's Response. 140p. 1987. text ed. 22.50 (*81-7045-006-3*, Pub. by Associated Pub Hse II) Advent Bks Div.

Roy, Ashim & Gidwani, N. N. A Dictionary of Indology, Vol. 3: L-R. 1986. 24.00 (*81-204-0036-4*, Pub. by Oxford IBH II) S Asia.

Roy, Ashim K. & Gidwani, N. N. A Dictionary of Indology, Vol. 4. 335p. 1986. 24.00 (*0-317-53540-4*, Pub. by Oxford IBH II) S Asia.

Roy, Ashok, ed. Artists' Pigments: A Handbook of Their History & Characteristics. (National Gallery of Art USA Publication: Vol. 2). (Illus.). 231p. 1994. 49.95 (*0-89468-189-3*) OUP.

Roy, Asim. The Islamic Syncretistic Tradition in Bengal. LC 83-42574. 312p. 1984. 49.50 (*0-691-05387-1*) Princeton U Pr.

Roy, B. Rabindranath Tagore. 1972. 59.95 (*0-8490-0924-3*) Gordon Pr.

Roy, B., ed. see NATO Advanced Study Institute Staff.

Roy, B. C., jt. auth. see Datta, Ashim K.

***Roy, B. N.** Principles of Modern Thermodynamics. LC 94-23492. 1995. 100.00 (*0-7503-0019-1*); pap. 40.00 (*0-7503-0018-3*) IOP Pub.

Roy, Benoy B. Socio-Economic Impact of Sati in Bengal & the Role of Raja Rammohun Roy. (C). 1987. 31.00 (*81-85109-70-2*, Pub. by Naya Prokash IA) S Asia.

Roy, Beth. Some Trouble with Cows: Making Sense of Social Conflict. LC 93-25761. (C). 1994. 40.00 (*0-520-08341-5*); pap. 15.00 (*0-520-08342-3*) U CA Pr.

Roy, Bimalendu N. Crystal Growth from Melts: Applications to Growth of Groups One & Two Crystals. 322p. 1991. text ed. 225.00 (*0-471-93109-8*) Wiley.

Roy, Buddhaved. Marriage Rituals & Songs of Bengal. 1985. 6.50 (*0-8364-1290-7*, Pub. by Mukhopadhyaya II) S Asia.

Roy-Byrne, Peter. Anxiety: New Findings for the Clinician. LC 88-26209. (Clinical Practice Ser.: No. 5). 224p. 1988. text ed. 25.00 (*0-88048-177-3*) Am Psychiatric.

Roy-Byrne, Peter P. & Cowley, Deborah S., eds. Benzodiazepines in Clinical Practice: Risks & Benefits. LC 90-1204. (Clinical Practice Ser.: No. 17). 240p. 1991. text ed. 26.50 (*0-88048-453-5*, FXJA8453) Am Psychiatric.

Roy, Cal. Bubble, the Birds, & the Noise. (Illus.). (J). (gr. k-4). 1968. 8.95 (*0-8392-3069-9*) Astor-Honor.

— Friend Can Be. (Illus.). (J). (gr. 2 up). 1969. 9.95 (*0-8392-3075-3*) Astor-Honor.

— Time Is Day. (Illus.). (J). (gr. k-3). 1968. 9.95 (*0-8392-3065-6*) Astor-Honor.

— What Every Young Wizard Should Know. (Illus.). (J). (gr. 2 up). 1963. 8.95 (*0-8392-3043-5*) Astor-Honor.

Roy, Camille. Cold Heaven. LC 93-84574. 89p. 1993. 9.00 (*1-882022-15-7*) O Bks.

— The Rosy Medallions: Selected Work. Dienstfrey, Patricia, ed. 72p. (Orig.). (C). 1995. pap. text ed. 10.00 (*0-932716-35-0*) Kelsey St Pr.

Roy, Camille, jt. auth. see Laurin, Riley.

Roy Chaudary, P. C. Gandhi & His Contemporaries. 271p. 1986. 34.95 (*81-207-0115-1*) Asia Bk Corp.

Roy-Chaudhury, Rahul. Sea Power & Indian Security. (Illus.). 250p. 1995. 48.00 (*1-85753-050-0*, Pub. by Brasseys UK) Macmillan.

Roy Chowdhury, Profulla. The North East: Roots of Insurgency. 1986. 8.50 (*0-8364-1869-7*, Pub. by Firma KLM) S Asia.

Roy, Christopher D. Art & Life in Africa: Selections from the Stanley Collection, Exhibitions of 1985 & 1992. (Illus.). 280p. 1993. pap. 40.00 (*0-295-97241-6*) U of Wash Pr.

— Selections from the Julian & Irma Brody Collection. LC 88-70384. (Illus.). 40p. (Orig.). 1988. pap. 10.00 (*0-9614615-3-5*) Edmundson.

Roy, Clarence H. The Operation & Maintenance of Surface Finishing Wastewater Treatment Systems. 199p. 1988. 60.00 (*0-936569-04-2*); pap. 40.00 (*0-318-35444-6*) Am Electro Surface.

Roy, Claude. Chat Qui Parlait Malgre Lui. (Folio - Junior Ser.: No. 194). (Illus.). 87p. (FRE.). (J). (gr. 5-10). 1982. pap. 8.95 (*2-07-033615-8*) Schoenhof.

— Distant Friend. Harter, Hugh, tr. LC 90-30540. (French Expressions Ser.). 176p. 1990. 19.95 (*0-8419-1196-7*) Holmes & Meier.

— Enfantasques. (Folio - Junior Ser.: No. 87). (FRE.). (J). (gr. 5-10). 1979. pap. 6.95 (*2-07-033087-7*) Schoenhof.

— Maison Qui S'Envole. (Folio - Junior Ser.: No. 1). (Illus.). 90p. (FRE.). (J). (gr. 5-10). 1977. pap. 7.95 (*2-07-033001-X*) Schoenhof.

— Le Malheur d'Aimer. (FRE.). 1974. pap. 10.95 (*0-7859-4029-4*) Fr & Eur.

— Moi-Je. 497p. (FRE.). 1978. pap. 13.95 (*0-7859-4107-X*, 2070370666) Fr & Eur.

— Nous. 576p. (FRE.). 1980. pap. 15.95 (*0-7859-4141-X*, 2070372472) Fr & Eur.

— La Nuit Est le Manteau des Pauvres. (FRE.). 1976. pap. 10.95 (*0-7859-4053-7*) Fr & Eur.

— Permis de Sejour. (FRE.). 1985. pap. 14.95 (*0-7859-4238-6*) Fr & Eur.

Roy, Claude, intro. Marc Riboud: Photographs at Home & Abroad. (Illus.). 120p. 1988. 45.00 (*0-8109-1566-9*) Abrams.

Roy, Claude, jt. auth. see Chateaubriand, Rene de.

Roy, Claude C., jt. auth. see Silverman, Arnold.

Roy, Claude C., et al, eds. Pediatric Clinical Gastroenterology. 4th ed. LC 94-12633. 1995. write for info. (*0-8151-7406-3*) Mosby Yr Bk.

Roy, Claudine, jt. auth. see Bourdeau, Pierre-Yves.

Roy, Cristina. En el Pais Del Sol. 160p. (SPA.). 1982. pap. 2.00 (*0-686-35757-4*) Rod & Staff.

— Das Land des Sonnenscheins. 167p. (GER.). 1982. pap. 3.85 (*0-686-35759-0*) Rod & Staff.

Roy, D., ed. see Planche, James R.

Roy, D. C., ed. Northeastern Section Field Guide. (DNAG Centennial Field Guides Ser.: No. 5). (Illus.). 517p. 1987. 43.50 (*0-8137-5405-4*) Geol Soc.

Roy, D. C. & Skehan, J. W., eds. The Acadian Orogeny: Recent Studies in New England, Maritime Canada, & the Autochthonous Foreland. (Special Paper Ser.: No. 275). 1993. pap. 42.50 (*0-8137-2275-6*) Geol Soc.

Roy, D. J., et al. Bioscience - Society: Report of the Schering Workshop, Berlin 1990, November 25-30. 408p. 1991. text ed. 137.95 (*0-471-93152-7*, Wiley-Liss) Wiley.

Roy, D. M. & Idorn, G. M. Concrete Microstructure. 179p. (Orig.). (C). 1993. pap. text ed. 15.00 (*0-309-05254-8*, SHRP-C-340) SHRP.

Roy, D. M., jt. auth. see McCarthy, G. J.

Roy, D. M., et al. Concrete Microstructure: Recommended Revisions to Test Methods. 107p. (Orig.). (C). 1993. pap. text ed. 15.00 (*0-309-05601-2*, SHRP-C-339) SHRP.

Roy, D. P. Heat. 1985. 82.00 (*0-317-38773-1*, Current Dist) St Mut.

— Phenomenology of Elementary Particale Physics. LC 93-36011. 1995. text ed. 34.95 (*0-470-23342-7*) Halsted Pr.

Roy, David T. Kuo Mo-Jo: The Early Years. LC 77-123569. (Harvard East Asian Ser.: No. 55). 244p. reprint ed. pap. 73.60 (*0-7837-2326-1*, 2057414) Bks Demand.

Roy, David T., tr. The Plum in the Golden Vase: Chin P'ing Mei The Gathering, Vol. 1. LC 92-45054. (Library of Asian Translations). (Illus.). 544p. 1993. text ed. 39.50 (*0-691-06932-8*) Princeton U Pr.

Roy, David T. & Tsuen-hsuin, Tsien, eds. Ancient China: Studies in Early Civilization. xxi, 370p. 1978. text ed. 49.50 (*962-201-144-6*, Pub. by Chinese Univ HK) Coronet Bks.

Roy, Delwin A., et al. Southeast Exporting: Profiles, Typology, & the Role of Technology in Selected U. S. Firms. (Research Monograph: No. 90). 175p. 1981. spiral bd. 25.00 (*0-88406-146-9*) GA St U Busn Pr.

Roy, Denny, et al, eds. A Time to Kill: Reflections on War. 2nd ed. LC 89-70005. (Illus.). 280p. 1990. pap. 12.95 (*0-941214-97-4*) Signature Bks.

Roy, Dewayne, jt. auth. see Jeffus, Larry.

Roy, Dilip K. Physics of Semiconductor Devices. 1993. pap. 20.00 (*0-86311-330-3*, Pub. by Universities Pr II) Apt Bks.

— A Quantum Measurement Approach to Tunnelling: Tunnelling by Quantum Measurement. 200p. 1993. text ed. 48.00 (*981-02-1223-2*) World Scientific Pub.

— Quantum Mechanical Tunnelling & Its Applications. 400p. 1986. text ed. 77.00 (*9971-5-0024-8*) World Scientific Pub.

— Tunnelling & Negative Resistance Phenomena in P-N Junctions. 1977. 100.00 (*0-08-021044-9*, Pub. by Pergamon Repr UK) Franklin.

***Roy, Dipak.** Microbiology Lab Guide. 72p. (C). 1995. per., pap. text ed. 14.95 (*0-7872-0993-7*) Kendall-Hunt.

Roy, Dipti K. Leftist Politics in India: MN Roy & the Radical Democratic Party. (C). 1989. 25.50 (*81-85195-18-8*, Pub. by Minerva II) S Asia.

— Trade Union Movement in India: Role of M. N. Roy. 1990. 17.50 (*81-85195-28-5*, Pub. by Minerva II) S Asia.

Roy, Donald. Dialogues in American Politics. 160p. 1993. spiral bd. 26.95 (*0-8403-8661-3*) Kendall-Hunt.

— Quota Restriction & Goldbricking in a Machine Shop. (Reprint Series in Social Sciences). (C). 1993. reprint ed. pap. text ed. 1.00 (*0-8290-2670-3*, S-244) Irvington.

Roy, Donald H. Public Policy Dialogues. 240p. (Orig.). (C). 1993. lib. bdg. 44.50 (*0-8191-9335-6*); pap. text ed. 26. 50 (*0-8191-9336-4*) U Pr of Amer.

***Roy, Donna S. & Flores, Kathleen.** What's for Breakfast? Light & Easy Morning Meals for Busy People. Winchester, Faith & Hachfeld, Linda, eds. (Illus.). 286p. 1994. pap. 13.95 (*0-9620471-4-7*) Appletree MN.

Roy, E. A., ed. Neuropsychological Studies of Apraxia & Related Disorders. (Advances in Psychology Ser.: Vol. 23). 414p. 1985. 72.50 (*0-444-87669-3*, North Holland) Elsevier.

Roy E. Porter & Associates Staff. Writer's Manual. LC 75-43588. 1979. 27.95 (*0-88280-063-9*) ETC Pubns.

Roy, Ellen, jt. ed. see Watson, C. W.

Roy, Elmer L. Work of Holy Spirit. 1966. pap. 4.25 (*0-89315-108-4*) Lambert Bk.

Roy, Emil. British Drama Since Shaw. LC 72-188699. (Crosscurrents-Modern Critiques Ser.). 158p. 1972. 8.50 (*0-8093-0579-8*) S Ill U Pr.

Roy, Emil & Roy, Sandra. The College Writer. 416p. (C). 1986. text ed. 22.00 (*0-03-070599-1*) HB Coll Pubs.

— Prentice Hall Guide to Basic Writing. 2nd ed. LC 92-28601. 400p. 1993. pap. text ed. write for info. (*0-13-720665-8*) P-H.

Roy, Erik, ed. Ergonomics Process Manual. (Illus.). 174p. 1993. 199.00 (*0-931690-53-6*) Genium Pub.

— Hazwoper Compliance System, 2 vols. 1992. 199.00 (*0-931690-49-8*); Emergency Training Guide, 332p. teacher ed write for info. (*0-931690-50-1*); Emergency Response Training Guide, 224p. teacher ed write for info. (*0-318-70257-6*) Genium Pub.

Roy, Ewell P. Exploring Agribusiness. 3rd ed. (Illus.). 284p. (gr. 9-12). 1980. 29.25 (*0-8134-2098-9*, 2098); teacher ed 4.95 (*0-8134-2329-5*); text ed. 21.95 (*0-685-02540-3*) Interstate.

Roy, Ewell P., et al. Economics: Applications to Agriculture & Agribusiness. 4th ed. 569p. 1994. 35.95 (*0-8134-2949-8*, 2949); text ed. 26.95 (*0-685-61694-0*) Interstate.

Roy, F. Hampton & Russell, Charles. The Encyclopedia of Aging & the Elderly. (Illus.). 400p. 1992. lib. bdg. 45.00 (*0-8160-1869-3*) Facts on File.

Roy, F. Hampton & Tindall, Renee, eds. Master the Techniques of Ophthalmic Surgery. LC 94-7614. 1994. write for info. (*0-8121-1679-8*) Williams & Wilkins.

Roy, Frederick H. Ocular Differential Diagnosis. 5th ed. LC 92-10384. 900p. 1992. pap. text ed. 62.50 (*0-8121-1594-5*) Williams & Wilkins.

Roy, G. & Schmor, P., eds. Polarized Proton Ion Sources: Conference Proceedings, TRIUMF, Vancouver, 1983. LC 84-71235. (AIP Conference Proceedings Ser.: No. 117). 209p. 1984. lib. bdg. 37.00 (*0-88318-316-1*) Am Inst Physics.

Roy, G. P. Flora of Madhya Pradesh (Chhatarpur & Damoh) (C). 1992. 80.00 (*81-7024-457-9*, Pub. by Ashish II) S Asia.

— Grasses of Madhya Pradesh. (C). 1988. text ed. 40.00 (*0-685-22096-6*, Scientific) St Mut.

Roy, G. Ross, ed. see Burns, Robert.

Roy, Gabrielle. The Road Past Altamont. Marshall, Joyce, tr. LC 93-14195. vi, 147p. 1993. pap. 7.95 (*0-8032-8948-0*, Bison Books) U of Nebr Pr.

— Streets of Riches. Binsse, Harry, tr. LC 93-8661. 176p. 1994. pap. 8.95 (*0-8032-8947-2*, Bison Books) U of Nebr Pr.

Roy, Gerald & Pilgrim, Paul. The Log Cabin Returns to Kentucky: Quilts from the Pilgrim - Roy Collection. LC 92-13819. (Illus.). 1992. 12.95 (*0-89145-993-6*) Collector Bks.

Roy, Gerald E., jt. auth. see Pilgrim, Paul D.

Roy, Girish C. Value Conflict in Study of Social Change in India. 272p. 1983. 30.95 (*0-318-36870-6*) Asia Bk Corp.

***Roy, Glenn.** Activated Carbon Applications in the Food & Pharmaceutical Industries. LC 94-61026. 200p. 1994. text ed. 65.00 (*1-56676-198-0*) Technomic.

Roy, Gordon. Steam Turbines & Gearing. (Marine Engineering Ser.). (Illus.). 113p. (C). 1984. pap. text ed. 21.95 (*0-540-07358-X*) Buttrwrth-Heinemann.

— Stolen Interludes. 1995. 18.95 (*0-8062-5358-4*) Carlton.

Roy, Greg. The Complete Guide to Residential Deck Construction: From the Simplest to the Most Sophisticated. (Illus.). 176p. (Orig.). 1992. pap. 16.95 (*1-55870-231-8*) Betterway Bks.

Roy, Greg & Caron, Richard. Becoming Financially Sound in an Unsound World. (Illus.). 240p. (Orig.). 1992. pap. 14.95 (*1-55870-253-9*) Betterway Bks.

Roy, Gregor. Monarch Notes on Cervantes' Don Quixote. (Orig.). (C). pap. 3.95 (*0-671-00553-7*, Arco Test) P-H Gen Ref & Trav.

— Monarch Notes on Graham Greene's Major Novels. (Orig.). (C). pap. 4.25 (*0-671-00838-2*, Arco Test) P-H Gen Ref & Trav.

— Monarch Notes on Kafka's The Trial, The Castle & Other Works. (Orig.). (C). pap. 3.95 (*0-671-00847-1*, Arco Test) P-H Gen Ref & Trav.

— Monarch Notes on Pope's Rape of the Lock & Other Poems. (Orig.). (C). pap. 4.25 (*0-671-00788-2*, Arco Test) P-H Gen Ref & Trav.

Roy, Gregor, tr. see Derrey, Francois.

Roy, Harcourt. Fitness in the Firm's Time. 160p. Date not set. pap. 13.95 (*0-8464-4183-7*) Beekman Pubs.

***Roy, Helen, illus.** Rumpelstiltskin. LC 95-8420. (J). 1995. write for info. (*1-57255-000-7*); pap. write for info. (*1-57255-001-5*) Mondo Pubng.

Roy, Indrani B. Kalighat: Its Impact on Socio-Cultural Life of Hindus. 1993. 20.00 (*81-212-0401-1*, Pub. by Gian Publng Hse II) S Asia.

Roy, J. Soul Daddy. (J). 1992. 16.95 (*0-15-277193-X*, HB Juv Bks) HarBrace.

Roy, J. & Paterson, H. A Faith for the Year Two Thousand. 88p. (C). 1990. pap. text ed. 45.00 (*0-7152-0639-7*) St Mut.

Roy, J. C., et al, eds. Progress in Electrodermal Research. LC 93-11397. (NATO ASI Series A, Life Sciences: Vol. 249). 343p. 1993. 95.00 (*0-306-44536-0*, Plenum Pr) Plenum.

Roy, J. H. The Calf. 5th ed. 350p. 1990. text ed. 89.95 (*0-407-00520-X*) Blackwell Sci.

Roy, Jacques. Didactologie et Phonetique Appropriative. (American University Studies: Linguistics: Ser. XIII, Vol. 8). 202p. (C). 1989. text ed. 33.00 (*0-8204-0754-2*) P Lang Pubs.

***Roy, Jacques & Garnier, Eric, eds.** A Whole Plant Perspective on Carbon-Nitrogen Interactions. (Illus.). 1994. 85.00 (*90-5103-086-X*, Pub. by SPB Acad Pub NE) Koeltz Sci Bks.

***Roy, James & Roy, Samuel.** Proof: Your Mind Is God. 96p. 1995. pap. 9.00 (*0-8059-3743-9*) Dorrance.

Roy, James A. Cowper & His Poetry. LC 76-120982. (Poetry & Life Ser.). reprint ed. 27.50 (*0-404-52530-X*) AMS Pr.

Roy, James C. Islands of Storm. 320p. 1991. 30.00 (*0-8023-1293-4*) Dufour.

— Islands of Storm. (Illus.). 320p. 1994. pap. 17.95 (*0-8023-1301-9*) Dufour.

— The Road Wet, the Wind Close: Celtic Ireland. LC 85-31100. (Illus.). 219p. 1990. pap. 17.95 (*0-8023-1283-7*) Dufour.

— Road Wet, the Wind Close: Celtic Ireland. LC 85-31100. 220p. 1986. 30.00 (*0-8023-1281-0*) Dufour.

Roy, Jayanta, jt. auth. see Roe, Alan.

Roy, Jean-Louis. Nineteen Ninety-Two: A Guide to the European Community Charter. Lecompte, Stuart, tr. 128p. 1992. pap. 9.95 (*0-02-009731-X*, Collier S&S) S&S Trade.

Roy, Jean-Yves, jt. auth. see Haineault, Doris-Louise.

Roy, Jessie H. & Turner, Geneva C. Pioneers of Long Ago. (Illus.). (J). 1990. 12.95 (*0-87498-008-9*) Assoc Pubs DC.

Roy, Joaquin. Cuba y Espana: Perscepciones y Relaciones. (Biblioteca Cubana Contemporanea Ser.). 100p. (Orig.). (SPA.). 1988. pap. 9.95 (*84-359-0542-X*, Pub. by Editorial Playor SP) Ediciones.

Roy, Joaquin & Staczek, John J. Lecturas de Prensa. 320p. (Orig.). (C). 1982. pap. text ed. 19.50 (*0-15-550455-X*) HB Coll Pubs.

Roy, Joyashree. Demand for Energy in Indian Industries: A Quantitative Approach. (C). 1992. 21.00 (*81-7035-106-5*, Pub. by Daya Pub Hse II) S Asia.

R

An Asterisk (*) at the beginning of an entry indicates that the title is appearing in BIP for the first time.

Roy, Jules. The Battle of Dienbienphu. 384p. 1984. pap. 10.95 (*0-88184-034-3*) Carroll & Graf.

Roy, Kanchan, ed. Education & Health Problems in Tribal Development. (C). 1989. 15.00 (*81-7022-236-2*, Pub. by Concept II) S Asia.

*Roy, Kartik C. & Clark, Cal M., eds. Technological Change & Rural Development in Poor Countries: Neglected Issues. 192p. 1995. 19.95 (*0-19-563583-3*) OUP.

*Roy, Kartik C., et al, eds. Economic Development & Environment: A Case Study of India. (Illus.). 172p. 1995. pap. 9.95 (*0-19-563431-4*) OUP.

Roy, Kristina. Sunshine Country. 184p. 1984. 5.75 (*0-686-05594-2*) Rod & Staff.

*Roy, Kumkum. The Emergence of Monarchy in North India, Eighth to Fifth Centuries B.C. (As Reflected in the Brahmanical Tradition) 340p. 1995. 29.95 (*0-19-563416-0*) OUP.

Roy, Larnders. Bits of Experience. 109p. 1992. pap. 5.99 (*0-9634432-0-8*) Croy & Assocs.

*Roy, Lucinda. The Humming Birds. 160p. 1995. lib. bdg. 22.95 (*0-933377-39-8*); pap. 12.95 (*0-933377-38-X*) Eighth Mount Pr.

Roy, Lynette A., tr. see Budar, Valjeanne, ed.

Roy, M. N. Fragments of a Prisoner's Diary: India's Message. reprint ed. 18.00 (*0-8364-0912-4*, Pub. by Ajanta II) S Asia.

— M. N. Roy's Memoirs. 1985. 17.50 (*0-8364-1296-6*, Pub. by Ajanta II) S Asia.

— Materialism. 1982. reprint ed. 18.50 (*0-8364-0914-0*, Pub. by Ajanta II) S Asia.

— Revolution & Counter-Revolution in China. 1972. lib. bdg. 59.95 (*0-8490-2520-6*) Gordon Pr.

— Selected Works of M. N. Roy 1927-1932, Vol. III. Ray, Sibnarayan, ed. (Illus.). 664p. 1991. 29.95 (*0-19-562640-0*) OUP.

— The Way to Durable Peace. (C). 1986. 6.50 (*0-8364-2198-1*, Pub. by Minerva II) S Asia.

Roy, Manabendra N. Revolution & Counter-Revolution in China. LC 73-897. (China Studies: from Confucius to Mao Ser.). viii, 689p. 1973. reprint ed. 36.00 (*0-88355-091-1*) Hyperion Conn.

Roy, Manisha. Bengali Women. LC 92-14268. (Illus.). xviii, 206p. 1992. pap. text ed. 12.95 (*0-226-73043-3*) U Ch Pr.

***Roy, Margaret. I Fed My Children Summer: Adirondack/Olympic Poems. 65p. 1995. pap. 5.00 (*0-9645264-0-9*) Black Fly Pr.**
I FED MY CHILDREN SUMMER by MARGARET ROY is a TREASURE for anyone who has ever loved the mountains; one family's story of discovery & ever widening involvement in an Adirondack community including a hair-raising account of a memorable WORLD CUP BOBSLED RACE at Olympic Lake Placid; the author's son the driver of USA I. Every page is testimony to Margaret Roy's staggering life experiences; from musical comedy actress in Bernstein's CANDIDE, from contralto soloist at New York's Marble Collegiate Church, as Winner of the Metropolitan Auditions, & finally as Builder & Entrepreneur Truffle Maker in the Adirondacks. The result is a magnificent blend of images, language, historical references, Mohawk Myth, events & personal observances. I FED MY CHILDREN SUMMER speaks not only for her neighbors but also for the longing of the human spirit that draws hundreds of thousands who can only imagine what it is like to live year-round in her beloved forest full of ladyslippers, raccoons & unending ice & snow. Says Maurice Kenny, twice Pulitzer- nominated Poet, "BEWARE! This is a new voice which commands attention & deserves applause. If the reading world is looking for a new, sincerely lush voice in poetry, a voice enhanced with metaphor & depth of idea, well, here is Margaret Roy. Make room, make a place, for she is here to stay." To Order Contact: Black Fly Press, Box 1212, Saranac Lake, NY 12983. Phone: (518) 891-3675. ***Publisher Provided Annotation.***

— The Principles of Homeopathic Philosophy. LC 93-14982. 150p. 1993. pap. text ed. write for info. (*0-344-30482-5*) Churchill.

Roy, Marie L., jt. auth. see Wood, Robert.

Roy, Maurice. The Parish & Democracy in French Canada. LC 52-1123. (University of Toronto, Duncan & John Gray Memorial Lecture Ser.). 37p. reprint ed. pap. 25.00 (*0-685-15452-1*, 2026546) Bks Demand.

*Roy, Meenu. Thousand Days of Indo-U. S. Diplomacy: The Kennedy-Nehru Era. (C). 1993. 20.00x (*81-7100-580-2*, Pub. by Deep) S Asia.

Roy, Namba. No Black Sparrows: A Vivid Portrait of Jamaica in the 1930s. (Caribbean Writers Ser.). 217p. (Orig.). 1989. pap. 7.95 (*0-435-98812-3*) Heinemann.

Roy, Nancy R. Duncan: Descendants of William Duncan the Elder. 276p. 1992. reprint ed. lib. bdg. 52.50 (*0-8328-2466-6*); reprint ed. pap. 42.50 (*0-8328-2467-4*) Higginson Bk Co.

Roy, Noel, jt. ed. see Schrank, William E.

Roy, Olivier. Afghanistan: From Holy War to Civil War. LC 94-18404. 1995. 24.95 (*0-87850-076-6*) Darwin Pr.

— The Failure of Political Islam. Volk, Carol, tr. LC 94-18782. 252p. 1994. text ed. 22.95 (*0-674-29140-9*, ROYFAI) HUP.

— Islam & Resistance in Afghanistan. 2nd ed. (Cambridge Middle East Library: No. 8). 256p. (C). 1990. 59.95 (*0-521-39308-6*); pap. 19.95 (*0-521-39700-6*) Cambridge U Pr.

Roy, P. Mussolini & the Cult of Italian Youth. 1972. 250.00 (*0-8490-0685-6*) Gordon Pr.

Roy, P. & Gorman, B. M., eds. Bluetongue Viruses. (Current Topics in Microbiology & Immunology Ser.: Vol. 162). (Illus.). 192p. 1990. 95.00 (*0-387-51922-X*) Spr-Verlag.

Roy, P. C. The Coin Age of Northern India. 1980. 27.50 (*0-8364-0641-9*, Pub. by Abhinav II) S Asia.

— Indo-U. S. Economic Relations. 206p. 1986. 26.00 (*0-8364-1895-6*, Pub. by Deep) S Asia.

Roy, P. N. Dictionary of Economics. (C). 1989. 45.00 (*0-89771-426-1*, Current Dist) St Mut.

Roy, Pabitra K. Beauty, Art & Man: Studies in Recent Indian Theories of Art. (C). 1990. 20.00 (*0-685-39093-4*, Pub. by Munshiram Manoharial II) S Asia.

Roy, Patricia E., et al. Mutual Hostages: Canadian & Japanese During the Second World War. 320p. 1990. 24.95 (*0-8020-5774-8*) U of Toronto Pr.

— Mutual Hostages: Canadian & Japanese During the Second World War. 298p. 1992. pap. 18.95 (*0-8020-7366-2*) U of Toronto Pr.

Roy, Paul. An Expression: A Collection of Poetry. 84p. Date not set. pap. 6.95 (*1-885087-01-2*) Angali Pubng.

— How to Avoid Drugs, Diets & Doctors. 52p. Date not set. pap. write for info. (*1-885087-03-9*) Angali Pubng.

— Journeying Through America: A Life Changing Experience. LC 94-70957. (YA). Date not set. pap. write for info. (*1-885087-00-4*) Angali Pubng.

— Philosophy of Life & Reality: A Spirited Guide Book. 2nd ed. 41p. Date not set. pap. write for info. (*1-885087-02-0*) Angali Pubng.

Roy, Peter A. & Cinquanti, Michael. Workplace Safety Pocket Guide. rev. ed. (Illus.). 64p. 1994. pap. text ed. write for info. (*0-931690-37-4*) Genium Pub.

Roy, Prodipto, jt. auth. see Bijlani, H. U.

Roy, Prodipto, et al. Rural Employment Programmes: Longitudinal Analysis. 1990. text ed. 25.00 (*0-7069-5297-9*, Pub. by Vikas II) S Asia.

Roy, R. Chronic Pain & the Family: A Problem-Centered Perspective. (Illus.). 256p. 1989. 32.95 (*0-89885-443-1*) Human Sci Pr.

— Foreign Exchange Regulation Act, 1973. 3rd ed. (C). 1989. 350.00 (*0-685-27937-5*) St Mut.

— Laser Noise, Vol. 1376. 1991. 53.00 (*0-8194-0443-8*) SPIE.

Roy, R., jt. auth. see Henisch, Heinz K.

Roy, R. A., jt. auth. see Accrocco, Joseph O.

Roy, R. R., jt. auth. see Reed, Robert D.

Roy, Ramashray. Politics of International Economic Relations. 234p. 1982. 24.95 (*0-318-37261-4*) Asia Bk Corp.

— Self & Society: A Study of Gandhian Thought. 205p. 1985. text ed. 25.00 (*0-8039-9484-2*) Sage.

— The Uncertain Verdict: A Study of the 1969 Elections in Four Indian States. rev. ed. LC 75-328407. (Illus.). 313p. reprint ed. pap. 89.30 (*0-685-44496-1*, 2031513) Bks Demand.

— World of Development: A Theoretical Dead End. 1993. 21.00 (*81-202-0372-0*, Pub. by Ajanta II) S Asia.

Roy, Ramashray, ed. Politics of International Economic Relations. 1982. 21.50 (*0-8364-0885-3*, Pub. by Ajanta II) S Asia.

Roy, Ranjan. The Social Context of the Chronic Pain Sufferer. 176p. 1992. 50.00 (*0-8020-2860-8*); pap. 19.95 (*0-8020-7360-3*) U of Toronto Pr.

*Roy, Ranjan, ed. Chronic Pain in Old Age: An Integrated Biopsychosocial Perspective. 272p. 1995. 50.00 (*0-8020-2859-4*) U of Toronto Pr.

— Chronic Pain in Old Age: An Integrated Biopsychosocial Perspective. 272p. 1995. pap. 19.95 (*0-8020-7359-X*) U of Toronto Pr.

*Roy, Ranjan & Frankel, Harvy. How Good Is Family Therapy? A Reassessment. 320p. (C). 1995. 50.00 (*0-8020-2926-4*); pap. 18.95 (*0-8020-7427-8*) U of Toronto Pr.

Roy, Ranjit K. Primer on Taguchi Method. 1990. text ed. 49.95 (*0-442-23729-4*) Van Nos Reinhold.

Roy, Regis, jt. auth. see Massicotte, Edouard Z.

Roy, Richard A., jt. auth. see Apostolou, Nicholas G.

Roy, Rob. Complete Book of Underground Houses: How to Build a Low Cost Home. LC 94-16840. (Illus.). 148p. 1994. pap. 14.95 (*0-8069-0728-2*) Sterling.

Roy, Robert A., ed. see Conforti, John V.

Roy, Robert H. The Administrative Process. 248p. 1958. 36.50x (*0-8018-0566-X*); pap. 13.95x (*0-8018-0567-8*) Johns Hopkins.

— The Cultures of Management. LC 76-47385. (Illus.). 448p. 1977. 60.00x (*0-8018-1875-3*); pap. text ed. 16.95x (*0-8018-2524-5*) Johns Hopkins.

— Operations Technology: Systems & Evolution. LC 86-7139. (Illus.). 248p. 1986. text ed. 39.50x (*0-8018-3340-X*) Johns Hopkins.

Roy, Robert H. & MacNeill, James H. Horizons for a Profession: The Common Body of Knowledge for Certified Public Accountants. LC 67-4826. (Illus.). 368p. reprint ed. pap. 104.90 (*0-685-23567-X*, 2026574) Bks Demand.

Roy, Robin & Wield, David, eds. Product Design & Technological Innovation. 320p. 1986. 62.00 (*0-335-15110-8*, Open Univ Pr); pap. 32.00 (*0-335-15109-4*, Open Univ Pr) Taylor & Francis.

Roy, Ron. Whose Hat Is That? (Illus.). 40p. (J). (ps-3). 1990. pap. 6.95 (*0-395-54778-4*, Clarion Bks) HM.

Roy, Russell A. Physical Science: An Integrated Approach. 2nd ed. (Illus.). 400p. (C). 1991. pap. text ed. 25.00 (*0-89892-092-2*) Contemp Pub Co of Raleigh.

— Physical Science: An Integrated Approach Laboratory Textbook. 2nd ed. 117p. (C). 1990. pap. text ed. 16.95 (*0-89892-071-X*) Contemp Pub Co of Raleigh.

Roy, Rustrum. Experimenting with Truth: The Fusion of Religion with Technology Needed for Humanity's Survival. (Hibbert Lectures: 1979). (Illus.). 228p. 1981. 88.00 (*0-08-025820-4*, Pub. by Pergamon Repr UK) Franklin.

Roy, S. B. Early Aryans of India: 3100-1400 B. C. (C). 1989. 35.00 (*81-7013-052-2*, Pub. by Navrang) S Asia.

Roy, S. K. Evidence in Criminal Court Practice. (C). 1990. 140.00 (*0-89771-151-3*) St Mut.

Roy, S. M., et al, eds. Developments in Theoretical Physics. 1989. 32.00 (*81-204-0470-X*, Pub. by Oxford IBH II) S Asia.

Roy, S. N., et al. Analysis & Design of Certain Quantitative Multiresponse Experiments. 314p. 1971. 128.00 (*0-08-006917-7*, Pub. by Pergamon Repr UK) Franklin.

Roy, Salil K., jt. auth. see Chanda, Manas.

Roy, Samaren. Calcutta, Society & Change, 1690-1990. (C). 1991. 31.50 (*81-7167-046-6*, Pub. by Rupa II) S Asia.

— India's First Communist. (C). 1988. 12.75 (*81-85195-10-2*, Pub. by Minerva II) S Asia.

— The Twice-Born Heretic: MN Roy & Comintern. 1986. 27.50 (*0-8364-1576-0*, KL Mukhopadhyay) S Asia.

Roy, Samuel. Elvis: Prophet of Power. 2nd ed. (Illus.). (Orig.). 1985. pap. 11.95 (*0-8283-1898-0*) Branden Pub Co.

Roy, Samuel, jt. auth. see Roy, James.

Roy, Sander, jt. auth. see Berson, Dvera.

Roy, Sandra, jt. auth. see Roy, Emil.

*Roy, Sara. The Gaza Strip: The Political Economy of De-Development. 290p. 1995. 27.95 (*0-88728-260-1*) Inst Palestine.

Roy, Shibani & Rizvi, S. H. Tribal Customary Laws of North East India. (C). 1990. text ed. 27.00 (*81-7018-586-6*, Pub. by BR Pub II) S Asia.

Roy, Shivani, jt. auth. see Rizvi, S. H.

Roy, Shukla. Indian Political Thought: Impact of Russian Revolution. 1988. 21.00 (*81-85195-08-0*, Pub. by Minerva II) S Asia.

Roy, Steven P. & Irvin, Richard F. Sports Medicine Prevention Evaluation Management & Rehabilitation. (Illus.). 560p. 1983. text ed. 59.00 (*0-13-837807-X*) P-H.

Roy, Subroto. The Philosophy of Economics: A Treatise on Reason, Value & Economic. 256p. 1989. 37.50 (*0-415-03592-9*, A3633) Routledge.

— Philosophy of Economics: On the Scope of Reason in Economic Inquiry. (International Library of Philosophy). 256p. 1991. pap. 17.95 (*0-415-06028-1*, A5459) Routledge.

Roy, Subroto & James, William E., eds. Foundations of India's Political Economy: Towards an Agenda for the 1990s. (Illus.). 304p. (C). 1992. text ed. 36.00 (*0-8039-9411-7*) Sage.

Roy, Subroto, jt. ed. see James, William E.

Roy, Sumit. Agriculture & Technology in Developing Countries: India & Nigeria. (Illus.). 232p. (C). 1991. 27.50 (*0-8039-9662-4*) Sage.

Roy, Sumit, jt. auth. see Singer, H. W.

Roy, Sumita. Consciousness & Creativity: A Study of Sri Aurobindo, T.S. Eliot & Aldous Huxley. 160p. 1991. text ed. 27.95 (*81-207-1281-1*, Pub. by Sterling Pubs II) Apt Bks.

Roy, Sumita, jt. ed. see Sivaramkrishna, M.

Roy, Supriya. Manganese Deposits. 1981. text ed. 161.00 (*0-12-601080-3*) Acad Pr.

Roy, Susan & Steele, Jeremy, eds. Young Imagination: Writing & Artwork by Children of New South Wales. (Illus.). 96p. (Orig.). 1988. pap. 13.50 (*0-909955-79-4*, 00597, Pub. by PETA AT) Heinemann.

*Roy, Tapti. The Politics of a Popular Uprising: Bundelkhand in 1857. (Illus.). 280p. 1995. 26.00 (*0-19-563612-0*) OUP.

Roy, Tarapada. Where to, Tarapada-Babu? Devi, Shyamasree & Lal, P., trs. (Saffronbird Ser.). 51p. 1975. 10.00 (*0-88253-839-X*); pap. 4.80 (*0-88253-840-3*) Ind-US Inc.

Roy, Tirthankar. Artisans & Industrialization: Indian Weaving in the Twentieth Century. (Illus.). 256p. 1994. 23.00 (*0-19-563100-5*) OUP.

Roy, Tom. A Scot Gallery Eccentric: Wry Tales of a Little-Known Realm. LC 92-30161. (Orig.). 1993. 14.95 (*1-879094-22-3*) Momentum Bks.

Roy, William. Rede Me & Be Nott Wrothe for I Say No Thynge but Trothe. LC 76-38221. (English Experience Ser.: No. 485). 144p. 1972. reprint ed. 25.00 (*90-221-0485-0*) Walter J Johnson.

Roy, William N. & Braun, David W. LaMoine Lumber & Trading Co. Narrow-Gauge Logging on the Shasta-Trinity Divide. LC 92-90822. (Timberbeast Special Publication Ser.: Nos. 28-29). 1992. pap. 12.50 (*0-9634695-0-9*) Timberbeast.

*Royak-Schal. Challenging Breast Cancer. 1994. pap. 3.99 (*0-517-13254-0*) Random Hse Value.

Royal & Ancient Golf Club of St. Andrews, Scotland Staff, jt. auth. see United States Golf Association Staff.

Royal & Ancient Golf Club of St. Andrews Staff

Royal Academy of Dancing Staff. Step by Step Ballet Class: The Official Illustrated Guide. (Illus.). 144p. 1994. pap. 12.95 (*0-8092-3499-8*) Contemp Bks.

Royal Academy of Letters, History, & Antiquities Staff. Medieval Wooden Sculpture in Sweden, 5 vols., Set. Anderson, A. & Thordeman, B., eds. (Illus.). 1168p. (Orig.). 1966. pap. text ed. 195.00x (*0-685-13807-0*) Coronet Bks.

Royal Aeronautical Society Staff. A List of the Books, Periodicals & Pamphlets in the Library of the Royal Aeronautical Society: With Which Is Incorporated the Institution of Aeronautical Engineers. Gilbert, James B., ed. LC 79-7295. (Flight: Its First Seventy-Five Years Ser.). 1980. reprint ed. lib. bdg. 26.95 (*0-405-12202-0*) Ayer.

Royal Anthropological Institute of Great Britain & Ireland Staff. A Catalogue of the Library of Sir Richard Burton, K. C. M. G., Held by the Royal Anthropological Institute. Kirkpatrick, B. J., ed. LC 80-473753. 182p. reprint ed. pap. 51.90 (*0-7837-6667-X*, 2046279) Bks Demand.

Royal Barry Wills Associates Staff. Houses for Good Living. (Illus.). 144p. 1993. 37.50 (*0-942655-07-9*) Archit CT.

Royal Botanic Garden, Calcutta Staff. The Aconites of India: A Monograph by Otto Stapf, with A Sketch of the Life of Francis Hamilton (Once Buchanan), Vol. X, Pt. 2. (Illus.). lxxv, 197p. 50.00 (*0-88065-014-1*, Messers Today & Tomorrow) Scholarly Pubns.

Royal Botanic Garden, Calcutta Staff, et al. A Century of New & Rare Indian Plants, Vol. V, Pt. II. (Illus.). 1971. reprint ed. 50.00 (*0-88065-011-7*, Messers Today & Tomorrow) Scholarly Pubns.

Royal Botanic Garden, Calcutta Staff & King, George. The Species of Artocarpus Indigenous to the British India: And the Indo-Malayan Species of Quercus & Castnopsis, 2 pts., Vol. II. (Illus.). 107p. 1979. reprint ed. 80.00 (*0-88065-010-9*, Messers Today & Tomorrow) Scholarly Pubns.

Royal Botanic Garden, Calcutta Staff & Prain, D. The Species of Dalbargia of South Eastern Asia. (Annals of Royal Botanic Garden, Calcutta Ser.: Vol. X, Pt. 1). (Illus.). 114p. 1979. reprint ed. 100.00 (*0-88065-013-3*, Messers Today & Tomorrow) Scholarly Pubns.

Royal Botanic Garden, Calcutta Staff, et al. A Second Century of New & Rare Indian Plants, Vol. IX, Pt. 1. (Illus.). 80p. 1972. reprint ed. 50.00 (*0-88065-012-5*, Messers Today & Tomorrow) Scholarly Pubns.

Royal Botanic Gardens Library Staff, Kew, England. Author & Classified Catalogues of the Royal Botanic Gardens Library, 9 vols. 1973. Author, 5 vols. lib. bdg. 545.00 (*0-8161-1086-7*, Hall Library); Classified, 4 vols. lib. bdg. 455.00 (*0-8161-1087-5*, Hall Library) G K Hall.

Royal Canadian Air Force Staff. Royal Canadian Air Force Exercise Plans for Physical Fitness. 1978. pap. 5.95 (*0-671-24651-8*) S&S Trade.

Royal Canadian Commission Staff. The Defection of Igor Gouzenko, Vol. 1. 96p. (Orig.). (C). 1984. lib. bdg. 25.70 (*0-89412-094-8*); pap. 16.20 (*0-89412-066-2*) Aegean Park Pr.

— The Defection of Igor Gouzenko, Vol. 2. 447p. (Orig.). (C). 1984. lib. bdg. 25.70 (*0-89412-095-6*); pap. 16.20 (*0-89412-067-0*) Aegean Park Pr.

— The Defection of Igor Gouzenko, Vol. 3. 196p. (Orig.). (C). 1984. lib. bdg. 25.70 (*0-89412-096-4*); pap. 16.20 (*0-89412-068-9*) Aegean Park Pr.

Royal Canadian Mounted Police Staff. International Illustrated Vocabulary of Dactyloscopy (Fingerprinting) French & English with 6 Language Index. (DUT, ENG, FRE, GER, ITA, JPN, SER & SPA.). 1991. 125.00 (*0-8288-6909-X*) Fr & Eur.

Royal Children's Hospital Staff. Paediatric Handbook. 2nd ed. (Illus.). 264p. 1992. pap. 32.95 (*0-86793-217-1*) Blackwell Sci.

Royal, Claudia, tr. see Glucksmann, Andre.

Royal College of Midwives Staff. Successful Breastfeeding. 2nd ed. (Illus.). 88p. 1991. pap. text ed. 10.00 (*0-443-04460-0*) Churchill.

Royal College of Physicians of London Staff & Greenwood, Major. Medical Statistics from Graunt to Farr: Proceedings of the Royal College of Physicians of London, February, 1943. Rosenkrantz, Barbara G., ed. LC 76-25665. (Public Health in America Ser.). (Illus.). 1977. reprint ed. lib. bdg. 17.95 (*0-405-09820-0*) Ayer.

Royal College of Physicians Staff. A Great & Growing Evil? The Medical Consequences of Alcohol Abuse. 144p. (C). 1987. text ed. 45.00 (*0-422-61140-9*, Pub. by Tavistock UK) Routledge Chapman & Hall.

— Topics in Therapeutics. Breckenridge, A. M., ed. 1974. pap. text ed. 45.00 (*0-685-83077-2*) St Mut.

— Topics in Therapeutics, 1976. Shanks, R. G., ed. 1976. pap. text ed. 65.00 (*0-685-83078-0*) St Mut.

Royal College of Physicians Staff, jt. auth. see Advanced Medical Symposia Staff.

Royal College of Physicians Staff, jt. auth. see Advanced Medicine Symposia Staff.

Royal College of Psychiatrists, Education Committee, Library & Reading Lists Sub-Committee Staff. List of Books Suitable for a Psychiatric Library. rev. ed. (Special Publication Ser.: No. 3). 68p. reprint ed. pap. 25.00 (*0-7837-0997-8*, 2041303) Bks Demand.

Royal College of Psychiatrists Staff. The Misuse of Psychotropic Drugs. Murray, Robin et al, eds. (Special Publication Ser.: No. 1). 116p. reprint ed. pap. 33.10 (*0-7837-0998-6*, 2041304) Bks Demand.

Royal College of Psychiatrists Working Party Staff. Psychiatric Beds & Resources: Factors Influencing Bed Use & Service Planning. 82p. 1988. write for info. (*0-902241-21-4*, Pub. by Royal Coll Psych UK) Am Psychiatric.

R

Royal College of Surgeons of England, Institute of Basic Medical Sciences, Symposium Staff. Leukotrienes & Other Lipoxygenase Products: Proceedings of the Annual Symposium of the Institute of Basic Medical Sciences, Royal College of Surgeons of England, 25-26 October 1982. Piper, Priscilla J., ed. LC 83-175919. (Prostaglandins Ser.: No. 3). (Illus.). 367p. reprint ed. pap. 104.60 (*0-8357-7081-8*, 2033346) Bks Demand.

Royal Commission on Aboriginal Peoples Staff. Aboriginal People in Urban Centres. 99p. (Orig.). 1993. pap. 20.75 (*0-660-14964-8*, Pub. by Canada Commun Grp CN) Accents Pubns.

Royal Commission on Bilingualism & Biculturalism. Preliminary Report: Education of the Royal Commission on Bilingualism & Biculturalism, 3 vols. in one. Cordasco, Francesco, ed. LC 77-17707. (Bilingual-Bicultural Education in the U. S. Ser.). 1978. reprint ed. lib. bdg. 70.95 (*0-405-11109-6*) Ayer.

Royal Commission on Historical Monuments. Stonehenge & Its Environs. (RCHM Inventory Vols Ser.). (Illus.). 50p. 1979. pap. 15.00 (*0-85224-379-0*, Pub. by Edinburgh U Pr UK) Col U Pr.

***Royal Commission on New Reproductive Technologies.** Proceed with Care: Final Report of the Royal Commission on New Reproductive Technologies. 26p. (Orig.). 1993. pap. 16.85x (*0-660-58996-6*, Pub. by Canada Commun Grp CN) Accents Pubns.

— Proceed with Care: Final Report of the Royal Commission on New Reproductive Technologies. 1275p. (Orig.). 1993. pap. 67.60x (*0-660-15359-9*, Pub. by Canada Commun Grp CN) Accents Pubns.

Royal Commission on Police Powers & Procedures. Report of the Royal Commission on Police Powers & Procedure. LC 73-156283. (Police in Great Britain Ser.). 1971. reprint ed. 16.95 (*0-405-03394-X*) Ayer.

Royal Commission Staff. Aboriginal Peoples & the Justice System: Report of the National Round Table on Aboriginal Urban Issues. 510p. (Orig.). 1993. pap. 38.95 (*0-660-14932-X*, Pub. by Canada Commun Grp CN) Accents Pubns.

Royal Commission upon the Duties of the Metropolitan Police. Minutes of Evidence of the Royal Commission upon the Duties of the Metropolitan Police, 3 vols. LC 70-156285. (Police in Great Britain Ser.). 1971. reprint ed. 217.95 (*0-405-03396-6*) Ayer.

Royal Commonwealth Society, London, Staff. Subject Catalogue of the Royal Commonwealth Society, 7 vols, Set. 1971. lib. bdg. 800.00 (*0-8161-0885-4*, Hall Library) G K Hall.

Royal Cortissoz & Leonard Clayton Gallery Staff. Childe Hassam's Etchings & Drypoints: A Catalogue Raisonne. rev. ed. 450p. 1989. 95.00 (*1-55660-029-1*) A Wofsy Fine Arts.

Royal Dublin Society Staff. Cereal Production: Proceedings of the International Meeting on Production of Temperate Cereal Crops. Gallagher, E., ed. 304p. 1984. text ed. 125.00 (*0-407-00303-7*) Buttrwrth-Heinemann.

Royal Dutch-Shell Group of Companies Staff. The Petroleum Handbook. 6th rev. ed. 710p. 1983. 174.50 (*0-444-42118-1*) Elsevier.

Royal Economic Society Staff & Social Studies Research Council Staff, eds. Surveys of Applied Economics, Vol. 2. LC 73-82638. 1977. text ed. 35.00 (*0-312-77770-1*) St Martin.

Royal Entomological Society of London Staff. Catalog of the Library of the Royal Entomological Society of London. (Printed Book Catalogs). 1980. lib. bdg. 565.00 (*0-8161-0315-1*, Hall Library) G K Hall.

Royal Gustavus Adolphus Society Staff, ed. Scandinavian Framework of Folklore, Vol. 45. 152p. 1990. 48.00x (*91-22-01333-4*, Pub. by Almqv & Wiksell SW) Coronet Bks.

Royal Historical Society, Camden Society Staff, ed. Wentworth Papers, Fifteen Ninety-Seven to Sixteen Twenty-Eight. (Camden Fourth Ser.: No. 12). 200p. 1973. 30.00 (*0-901050-20-2*) Boydell & Brewer.

— Western Circuit Assize Orders, 1629-48. (Camden Fourth Ser.: No. 17). 200p. 1976. 30.00 (*0-901050-29-6*) Boydell & Brewer.

Royal Historical Society Staff, ed. Sidney Ironworks Accounts (1541-73) (Camden Fourth Ser.: No. 15). 1975. 30.00 (*0-901050-25-3*) Boydell & Brewer.

Royal Institute of International Affairs. Chronology & Index of the Second World War, 1938-1945. LC 89-48664. 448p. 1990. text ed. 99.50 (*0-313-28072-X*, RCQ/, Greenwood Pr) Greenwood.

— Nationalism. LC 66-31536. xx, 360p. 1966. reprint ed. 45.00 (*0-678-05194-1*) Kelley.

Royal Institute of International Affairs, London Staff. Index to Periodical Articles, 1979-1989, in the Library of the Royal Institute of International Affairs. (Monograph Ser.). 1990. lib. bdg. 250.00 (*0-8161-1784-5*) G K Hall.

Royal Institute of International Affairs, London Staff, ed. Index to Periodical Articles, 1950-1964, 2 Vols, Set. 1970. lib. bdg. 250.00 (*0-8161-0711-4*, Hall Library) G K Hall.

— Index to Periodical Articles, 1965-1972. 1974. lib. bdg. 130.00 (*0-8161-1062-X*, Hall Library) G K Hall.

— Index to Periodical Articles, 1973-1978. (Library Catalogs-Bib. Guides). 1979. lib. bdg. 145.00 (*0-8161-0281-3*, Hall Library) G K Hall.

Royal Institute of International Affairs Staff. Great Britain & Palestine 1915-1945. 3rd ed. LC 75-6450. (Rise of Jewish Nationalism & the Middle East Ser.). 142p. 1975. reprint ed. 21.00 (*0-88355-336-8*) Hyperion Conn.

— Reports on Nationalism by a Study Group of Members of the Royal Institute of International Affairs: Proceedings. 360p. 1963. 30.00 (*0-7146-1571-4*, Pub. by F Cass Pubs UK) Intl Spec Bk.

— The Republics of South America. LC 76-29396. reprint ed. 32.00 (*0-404-15350-X*) AMS Pr.

— South-Eastern Europe: A Political & Economic Survey. LC 81-7168. xvi, 203p. 1982. reprint ed. text ed. 35.00 (*0-313-23195-8*, ROSU, Greenwood Pr) Greenwood.

Royal Institute of International Affairs Staff & Gini, Corraco. Report on the Problem of Raw Materials & Foodstuffs. Bd. with Raw Materials & Colonies. LC 82-48298. LC 82-48298. (World Economy Ser.). 325p. 1982. Set lib. bdg. 39.00 (*0-8240-5353-2*) Garland.

Royal Institute of International Affairs Staff & Piscatori, James P. Islam in a World of Nation-States. LC 86-8275. 1986. pap. 19.95 (*0-521-33867-0*) Cambridge U Pr.

Royal Institute of International Affairs Staff & Robins, Philip. Turkey & the Middle East. 144p. 1991. pap. 14.95 (*0-87609-101-X*) Coun Foreign.

Royal Irish Academy Staff. Todd Lecture Series, Set, Vols. 1-17. reprint ed. Set. 388.00 (*0-404-60560-5*) AMS Pr.

Royal Irish Academy Staff & Haughton, J. P. Atlas of Ireland. (Illus.). 112p. 1980. lib. bdg. 99.50 (*0-312-05988-4*) St Martin.

Royal, Jenny, jt. ed. see Hardingham, Alison.

Royal, Lyssa & Priest, Keith. Preparing for Contact: A Metamorphosis of Consciousness. 188p. (Orig.). 1994. pap. 12.95 (*0-9631320-2-4*) Royal Priest.

— Prism of Lyra: An Exploration of Human Galactic Heritage. rev. ed. 128p. 1992. reprint ed. pap. 11.95 (*0-9631320-0-8*) Royal Priest.

— Visitors from Within. 187p. 1992. pap. 12.95 (*0-9631320-1-6*) Royal Priest.

Royal, Marcella. Youth Crime-Violence & the Cause. LC 94-94495. (Illus.). 208p. (Orig.). 1994. pap. 12.95 (*0-9642111-0-6*) BARRONS WA.

YOUTH CRIME/VIOLENCE & THE CAUSE gives a detailed review of why children are rebellious today. It appears we do not understand why our children are violent & lawless. We are a nation searching for answers. It explains why our nation is mourning for our children, children left dead & maimed by those who are mere youths themselves. There is a reason, & this book solves the mystery. YOUTH CRIME/ VIOLENCE & THE CAUSE is written for parents with young children. It is written for teachers & school administrators & explains why our schools are in disarray & who is responsible. It is written for our law enforcement community who must deal with this rebellious generation. It is written for the whole nation, a nation that has lost its way. It explains why this conduct was not tolerated years ago & when this rebellion originated & who is responsible for its development. It dispels many of the reasons given for crime & exposes the real culprit & offers solutions. Without the proper solutions this problem will never be solved & crime will increase. We are a nation desperate for answers. Priced $12.95. Order from: Barrons Publishing, P.O. Box 553, Monroe, WA 98272; 360-794-0732. ***Publisher Provided Annotation.***

Royal Microscopy Society, Nomenclature Committee Staff. RMS Dictionary of Light Microscopy. (Royal Microscopy Society Microscopy Handbooks Ser.: No. 15). (Illus.). 152p. 1989. 32.00 (*0-19-856421-X*); pap. 14.95 (*0-19-856413-9*) OUP.

Royal Ministry of Foreign Affairs Staff, jt. ed. see Aftenposten, A.

Royal Musical Association Staff. Index to Papers Read Before the Members...1874-1944. 56p. 1993. reprint ed. lib. bdg. 69.00 (*0-7812-9683-8*) Rprt Serv.

Royal National Institute For Staff & Wexler, A. Experimental Mathematics for Engineers & Scientists. LC 91-14044. 1961. 51.00 (*0-08-009395-7*, Pub. by Pergamon Repr UK) Franklin.

Royal Ontario Museum Staff. Homage to Heaven, Homage to Earth: Chinese Treasures of the Royal Ontario Museum. (Illus.). 256p. 1992. 95.00 (*0-8020-5876-0*) U of Toronto Pr.

Royal, Penny C. Curativement Votre. (Health Education Ser.). 128p. 1983. pap. 8.95 (*0-9609226-2-8*) Sound Nutri.

— Herbally Yours. 3rd ed. (Health Education Ser.). 128p. (C). 1982. pap. 6.95 (*0-9609226-1-X*) Sound Nutri.

— Yerbamente Suyo. 3rd ed. 130p. 1987. pap. 6.95 (*0-9609226-3-6*) Sound Nutri.

Royal, Robert. Fourteen-Ninety-Two & All That: Political Manipulations of History. 214p. (C). 1992. 18.95 (*0-89633-174-1*) Ethics & Public Policy.

Royal, Robert, ed. Challenge & Response: Critiques of the Catholic Bishops' Draft Letter on the U. S. Economy. 87p. 1985. pap. 12.00 (*0-89633-091-5*) Ethics & Public Policy.

— Jacques Maritain & the Jews. LC 93-4633. (American Maritain Association Publications Ser.). (C). 1993. pap. text ed. 15.00 (*0-268-01193-1*) U of Notre Dame Pr.

Royal, Robert, jt. ed. see Falcoff, Mark.

Royal, Robert, jt. ed. see Nemoianu, Virgil.

Royal, Robert, jt. ed. see Weigel, George.

Royal, Robert F. & Schutt, Steven R. The Gentle Art of Interviewing & Interrogation: A Professional Manual & Guide. 1976. 34.95 (*0-13-351247-9*, Busn) P-H.

Royal Scottish Geographical Society Staff. Land Assessment in Scotland: Proceedings of the Royal Scottish Geographical Society Symposium, University of Edinburgh, May, 1979. Thomas, M. F. & Coppock, J. T., eds. (Illus.). 156p. 1980. 27.00 (*0-08-025716-X*, Pergamon Pr) Elsevier.

Royal Shakespeare Company Staff, ed. see Shakespeare, William.

Royal Shakespeare Theatre Library Staff & Shakespeare Birthplace Trust Library Staff. Shakespeare at Stratford upon Avon, Pt. 3, Posters, Programmes, Playbills, Photographs, & Pictures: The Libraries of the Royal Shakespeare Theatre & the Shakespeare Birthplace Trust. (Library Reference Ser.). 32p. (C). 1990. 2,025.00 (*0-8161-1766-7*) G K Hall.

— Shakespeare at Stratford upon Avon, Pt. 4, Pamplet Collection: The Libraries of the Royal Shakespeare Theatre & the Shakespeare Birthplace Trust. (Library Reference Ser.). 546p. (C). 1990. 3,285.00 (*0-8161-1767-5*) G K Hall.

Royal, Shirley R., ed. see Turrill, Joseph.

Royal Society of Literature of the United Kingdom Staff. The Eighteen-Eighties: Essays by Fellows of the Royal Society of Literature. (BCL1-PR English Literature Ser.). 271p. 1992. reprint ed. lib. bdg. 79.00 (*0-7812-7054-5*) Rprt Serv.

Royal Society of Literature, United Kingdom Staff. Essays by Divers Hands, Vol. 14. Lytton, ed. (Essay Index in Reprint Ser.). 1978. reprint ed. 20.00 (*0-8486-3027-0*) Roth Pub Inc.

— Essays by Divers Hands, Vol. 16. Gooch, G. P., ed. (Essay Index in Reprint Ser.). 1978. reprint ed. 20.00 (*0-8486-3028-9*) Roth Pub Inc.

— Essays by Divers Hands, Vol. 17. Meyerstein, E. H., ed. (Essay Index in Reprint Ser.). 1978. 20.00 (*0-8486-3029-7*) Roth Pub Inc.

— Essays by Divers Hands, Vol. 18. Ervine, St. John, ed. (Essay Index in Reprint Ser.). 1978. reprint ed. 20.00 (*0-8486-3030-0*) Roth Pub Inc.

Royal Society of London Staff. Pathways of Pollutants in the Atmosphere: Proceedings of the Royal Society of London on Pollution in the Atmosphere, 1977. (Proceedings of the Royal Society Ser.). (Illus.). 170p. 1979. 42.50 (*0-85403-107-3*) Scholium Intl.

Royal Society of London Staff, et al. Optical Bi-Stability, Dynamical Nonlinearity & Photonic Logic: Proceedings of a Royal Society Discussion Meeting Held on 21-22, March 1984, Organized by S. D. Smith, A. Miller & B. S. Wherrett. Wherrett, B. S. et al, eds. (Illus.). 261p. 1985. text ed. 86.50 (*0-85403-239-8*) Royal Soc London.

Royal, Suzanne, tr. see Hyde, Dayton O.

Royal Swedish Academy of Music Staff, ed. Trends & Perspectives in Musicology: Proceedings of the World Music Conference. (Illus.). 166p. (Orig.). 1983. pap. text ed. 37.50x (*91-85428-42-6*, Pub. by Almqv & Wiksell SW) Coronet Bks.

Royal Swedish Academy of Sciences Staff. Chemistry & Geochemistry of Solutions at High Temperatures & Pressures: Proceedings of the Royal Swedish Academy of Sciences, Nobel Symposium, Bjorkborns Herrgard, Karlskoga, Sweden, Sept., 1979. Rickard, David & Wickman, Frans E., eds. (Physics & Chemistry of the Earth Series; International Series in Earth Sciences: Vols. 13 & 37). (Illus.). 600p. 1982. 205.00 (*0-08-026285-6*, Pergamon Pr) Elsevier.

— Nuclear War: The Aftermath - Special Ambio Publication, Vol. 11. 3rd ed. Peterson, J. & Hinrichsen, D., eds. (Illus.). 204p. 1982. text ed. 91.00 (*0-08-028175-3*, Pub. by Pergamon Repr UK); pap. text ed. 91.00 (*0-08-028176-1*, Pub. by Pergamon Repr UK) Franklin.

Royal United Services Institute Staff. International Weapon Developments: A Survey of Current Developments in Weapon Systems. 4th ed. (Illus.). 203p. 1980. pap. 19.00 (*0-08-027028-X*, Pergamon Pr) Elsevier.

— Nuclear Attack - Civil Defense: Aspects of Civil Defense in the Nuclear Age. (Illus.). 292p. 1983. 28.00 (*0-08-027041-7*, Pergamon Pr); pap. 13.95 (*0-08-027042-5*, Pergamon Pr) Elsevier.

— Rusi & Brassey's Defence Yearbook 1983. 93th ed. (Brassey's Defence Yearbook Ser.). 400p. 1983. 60.50 (*0-08-028346-2*, Pergamon Pr); pap. 24.50 (*0-08-028347-0*, Pergamon Pr) Elsevier.

— Rusi & Brassey's Defence Yearbook 1985. 95th ed. (Brassey's Defence Yearbook Ser.). 388p. 1985. 46.00 (*0-08-031168-7*, Pergamon Pr); pap. 20.50 (*0-08-031169-5*, Pergamon Pr) Elsevier.

— RUSI & Brassey's Defence Yearbook 1992. 293p. 1992. 69.00 (*1-85753-030-6*, Pub. by Brasseys UK) Brasseys Inc.

— RUSI-Brassey's Defence Yearbook. 94th ed. (Brassey's Defence Yearbook Ser.). 350p. 1984. 60.50 (*0-08-030552-0*, Pergamon Pr); pap. 19.25 (*0-08-031176-8*, Pergamon Pr) Elsevier.

— RUSI-Brassey's Defence Yearbook 1974-75. 85th ed. (Brassey's Defence Yearbook Ser.). (Illus.). 338p. 1974. 30.50 (*0-08-027000-X*, Pergamon Pr) Elsevier.

— RUSI-Brassey's Defence Yearbook 1975-76. 86th ed. (Brassey's Defence Yearbook Ser.). 418p. 1975. 30.50 (*0-08-027001-8*, Pergamon Pr) Elsevier.

— RUSI-Brassey's Defence Yearbook 1976-77. 87th ed. (Brassey's Defence Yearbook Ser.). 377p. 28.00 (*0-317-66873-0*, Pergamon Pr) Elsevier.

— RUSI-Brassey's Defence Yearbook 1977-78. 88th ed. (Brassey's Defence Yearbook Ser.). 430p. 1977. 30.50 (*0-08-027003-4*, Pergamon Pr) Elsevier.

— RUSI-Brassey's Defence Yearbook 1978-79. 89th ed. (Brassey's Defence Yearbook Ser.). 365p. 1978. 44.00 (*0-08-027004-2*, Pergamon Pr) Elsevier.

— RUSI-Brassey's Defence Yearbook 1979-80. 90th ed. (Brassey's Defence Yearbook Ser.). 355p. 1979. 44.00 (*0-08-027005-0*, Pergamon Pr) Elsevier.

— RUSI-Brassey's Defence Yearbook 1981. 91th ed. 376p. 1980. 55.00 (*0-08-027006-9*, Pergamon Pr) Elsevier.

— Rusi-Brassey's Defence Yearbook 1982. 92th ed. 365p. 1981. 48.50 (*0-08-027039-5*, Pergamon Pr); pap. 30.50 (*0-08-027040-9*, Pergamon Pr) Elsevier.

— RUSI-Brassey's Defence Yearbook 1986. 96th ed. 350p. 1986. 48.50 (*0-08-031210-1*, Pergamon Pr); pap. 24.00 (*0-08-031220-9*, Pergamon Pr) Elsevier.

— RUSI-Brassey's Defence Yearbook 1987. 97th ed. 350p. 1987. 50.00 (*0-08-033607-8*, Pergamon Pr); pap. 24.00 (*0-08-033608-6*, Pergamon Pr) Elsevier.

— RUSI-Brassey's Defence Yearbook 1988. 98th ed. (Brassey's Defence Yearbook Ser.). 350p. 1988. 61.00 (*0-08-035815-2*, Pergamon Pr); pap. 33.00 (*0-08-035816-0*, Pergamon Pr) Elsevier.

Royal United Services Institute Staff, ed. Future of Armoured Warfare. 135p. 1987. 18.71 (*0-08-034738-X*, Pergamon Pr); pap. 8.91 (*0-08-034739-8*, Pergamon Pr) Elsevier.

Royall, Anne. Mrs. Royall's America, 1828 to 1831, 7 vols. in 6, Set. Incl. Part 1: The Black Book; or, a Continuation of Travels in the United States, 3 vols. LC 72-37720. 16.00 (*0-685-73122-7*); Part 2: Mrs. Royall's Pennsylvania; or, Travels Continued in the United States, 2 vols. LC 72-37720. 16.00 (*0-685-73123-5*); Part 3: Mrs. Royall's Southern Tour; or, Second Series of the Black Book, 2 vols. LC 72-37720. 16.00 (*0-685-73124-3*); LC 72-37720. reprint ed. 95.00 (*0-404-56830-0*) AMS Pr.

— Part 1: The Black Book; or, a Continuation of Travels in the United States, 3 vols. LC 72-37720. (Mrs. Royall's America, 1828 to 1831). 16.00 (*0-685-73122-7*) AMS Pr.

— The Tennessean. LC 78-64092. reprint ed. 37.50 (*0-404-17166-4*) AMS Pr.

Royall, David & Hughes, Mark. Computers & Small Business. 129p. (C). 1990. pap. text ed. 90.00 (*0-273-03104-X*, Pub. by Pitman Pubng UK) St Mut.

***Royall, David & Hughes, Michael.** Computerisation in Business. 192p. (C). 1991. pap. 36.00x (*0-273-03623-8*, Pub. by Pitman Pubng UK) St Mut.

Royall, Nicki. You Don't Need to Have a Repeat Cesarean. Adelman, Sherri, ed. 204p. 1989. 8.95 (*0-8119-0184-X*) LIFETIME.

***Royals, Stephen M.** Discovery & Proof in Police Misconduct Cases. LC 95-1372. (Civil Rights Library). 1995. text ed. 125.00 (*0-471-01974-7*, Pub. by Wiley Law Pubns) Wiley.

Royama, Masamichi. Foreign Policy of Japan: 1914-1939. LC 73-3930. 182p. 1973. reprint ed. text ed. 35.00 (*0-8371-6853-8*, ROFP, Greenwood Pr) Greenwood.

Royama, Shoichi, jt. auth. see Cargill, Thomas F.

Royama, T. Analytical Population Dynamics. (Population & Community Biology Ser.: No. 10). 352p. (C). 1992. 79.95 (*0-412-24320-2*, A6700) Chapman & Hall.

Roybal, Edward W. Elder Abuse: A Decade of Shame & Inaction, a Report, Apr. 1990. (Illus.). 104p. 1990. pap. 3.75 (*0-16-023196-5*, S/N 052-070-06672-5) USGPO.

Roybal, Laura. Billy. LC 93-4837. (YA). 1994. 14.95 (*0-395-67649-5*) HM.

Roybal, Mary A. & Ostendorf, Virginia A., eds. Downlink Directory, 1987, Vol. 2. 555p. (Orig.). 1987. pap. 125.00 (*0-317-56097-2*) V A Ostendorf.

— Uplink Directory, 1986. 131p. (Orig.). 1986. pap. 125.00 (*0-937007-00-5*) V A Ostendorf.

— Uplink Directory, 1987, Vol. 2. 170p. (Orig.). 1987. pap. 125.00 (*0-317-56098-0*) V A Ostendorf.

Roybal, Mary A., jt. ed. see Lauck, Helen.

Roybal, Michael A. The Maxims of Madness. 137p. (Orig.). 1993. pap. 8.00 (*0-9639456-0-2*) Maximedia NM.

Roybal, Rory, ed. UNIX System Price Performance Guide. (Illus.). 121p. 1993. 9.95 (*1-881351-00-9*); 9.95 (*1-881351-02-5*) AIM Tech.

— UNIX System Price Performance Guide: Fall 1992. (Illus.). 120p. 1993. 9.95 (*1-881351-01-7*) AIM Tech.

***Royce.** Alcoholism & Other Drug Problems. 2nd ed. 1995. 34.00 (*0-02-874049-1*) Free Pr.

Royce, Anya P. Movement & Meaning: Creativity & Interpretation in Ballet & Mime. LC 83-48526. (Illus.). 256p. 1984. 29.95 (*0-253-33888-3*) Ind U Pr.

Royce, Beverly. Notes on Double Knitting. rev. ed. Swansen, Meg, ed. (Illus.). 69p. 1994. pap. 16.95 (*0-942018-06-0*) Schoolhouse WI.

Royce, Brenda S. Donna Reed: A Bio-Bibliography. LC 90-44109. (Bio-Bibliographies in the Performing Arts Ser.). 160p. 1990. text ed. 39.95 (*0-313-26806-1*, RDB, Greenwood Pr) Greenwood.

— Hogan's Heroes: A Comprehensive Reference to the 1965-1971 Television Comedy Series, with Cast Biographies & an Episode Guide. LC 92-50947. 303p. 1993. lib. bdg. 39.95 (*0-89950-796-4*) McFarland & Co.

— Lauren Bacall: A Bio-Bibliography. LC 92-12500. (Bio-Bibliographies in the Performing Arts Ser.: No. 30). 312p. 1992. text ed. 45.00 (*0-313-27831-8*, RLL/, Greenwood Pr) Greenwood.

— Rock Hudson: A Bio-Bibliography. LC 94-39511. (Bio-Bibliographies in the Performing Arts Ser.: Vol. 61). 336p. 1995. text ed. 55.00 (*0-313-28672-8*, Greenwood Pr) Greenwood.

Royce, Charles C., ed. Indian Land Cessions in the United States. LC 78-146416. (First American Frontier Ser.). (Illus.). 1975. reprint ed. 82.95 (*0-405-02880-6*) Ayer.

Royce, Edward. The Origins of Southern Sharecropping. LC 93-18076. (Labor & Social Change Ser.). 288p. 1993. 34.95 (*1-56639-069-9*) Temple U Pr.
Royce, J. R. & Rozeboom, W. W., eds. The Psychology of Knowing. LC 75-138363. 504p. (C). 1972. text ed. 223.00 (*0-677-13850-4*) Gordon & Breach.
***Royce, Jack & Mitchell, John D.** The Train Stopped at Domodossola. LC 94-70382. (Orig.). Date not set. pap. text ed. 6.95 (*1-884953-00-X*) Eaton St Pr.
Royce, James, jt. auth. see Bissell, LeClair.
Royce, James E. Alcohol Problems & Alcoholism: A Comprehensive Survey. rev. ed. 480p. 1989. text ed. 32.95 (*0-02-927541-5*) Free Pr.
Royce, Joseph R. & Mos, Leendert P., eds. Humanistic Psychology: Concepts & Criticisms. (PATH in Psychology Ser.). 332p. 1981. 49.50 (*0-306-40596-2*, Plenum Pr) Plenum.
— Theoretical Advances in Behavior Genetics, No. 2. (NATO Advanced Study Institute Ser.). 722p. 1981. lib. bdg. 140.00 (*90-286-0569-X*) Kluwer Ac.
Royce, Joseph R. & Powell, D. Arnold. Theory of Personality & Individual Differences: Factors, Systems, & Processes. (Illus.). 272p. (C). 1983. text ed. 46.00 (*0-13-914473-0*) P-H.
Royce, Joseph R., ed. see Banff Conference on Theoretical Psychology Staff.
Royce, Joseph R., jt. ed. see Mos, Leendert P.
Royce, Josiah. California from the Conquest in 1846 to the Second Vigilance Committee in San Francisco (1856) 1992. reprint ed. lib. bdg. 75.00 (*0-7812-5083-8*) Rprt Serv.
— California, from the Conquest in 1846 to the Second Vigilance Committee in San Francisco, 1856: A Study of American Character. LC 72-3762. (American Commonwealths Ser.: No. 7). reprint ed. 49.50 (*0-404-57207-3*) AMS Pr.
— Conception of Immortality. 1988. reprint ed. lib. bdg. 59.00 (*0-7812-0089-X*) Rprt Serv.
— The Feud of Oakfield Creek: A Novel of California Life. LC 71-104560. reprint ed. lib. bdg. 29.50 (*0-8398-1770-3*) Irvington.
— Fugitive Essays. LC 68-16974. (Essay Index Reprint Ser.). 1977. 23.95 (*0-8369-0840-6*) Ayer.
— Herbert Spencer: An Estimate & Review Together with a Chapter of Personal Reminiscences. 1977. 16.95 (*0-8369-7121-3*, 7955) Ayer.
— Hope of the Great Community. LC 67-26777. (Essay Index Reprint Ser.). 1977. 18.95 (*0-8369-0841-4*) Ayer.
— Outlines of Psychology: An Elementary Treatise, with Some Practical Applications. LC 75-3334. reprint ed. 28.50 (*0-404-59337-2*) AMS Pr.
— The Philosophy of Josiah Royce. Roth, John K., ed. & intro. by. LC 82-2932. (HPC Classics Ser.). 429p. (C). 1982. reprint ed. lib. bdg. 34.95 (*0-915145-42-1*); reprint ed. pap. text ed. 9.95 (*0-915145-41-3*) Hackett Pub.
— The Philosophy of Loyalty. LC 94-47578. (Library of American Philosophy). (Illus.). 256p. 1995. pap. text ed. 15.95 (*0-8265-1267-4*) Vanderbilt U Pr.
— Principles of Logic. (Orig.). pap. 0.95 (*0-685-19411-6*, 114, Citadel Pr) Carol Pub Group.
— Race Questions, Provincialism, & Other American Problems. LC 67-23266. (Essay Index Reprint Ser.). 1977. 25.95 (*0-8369-0842-2*) Ayer.
— The Religious Philosophy of Josiah Royce. Brown, Stuart G., ed. LC 76-4496. 239p. 1976. reprint ed. text ed. 35.00 (*0-8371-8810-5*, RORP, Greenwood Pr) Greenwood.
— Selected Writings. 1972. 59.95 (*0-8490-1023-3*) Gordon Pr.
— The Spirit of Modern Philosophy. 519p. 1983. reprint ed. pap. 10.95 (*0-486-24432-6*) Dover.
— War & Insurance. LC 75-3336. reprint ed. 34.50 (*0-404-59339-9*) AMS Pr.
— World & the Individual, 2 Vols, Set. 21.50 (*0-8446-2842-5*) Peter Smith.
***Royce, Kenneth.** The Ambassador's Son. 1995. lib. bdg. 22.00 (*0-7278-4713-9*) Severn Hse.
— Bones in the Sand. (Black Dagger Crime Ser.). 184p. 16.50 (*0-86220-736-3*, Black Dagger) Chivers N Amer.
— Bones in the Sand. large type ed. 18.95 (*0-7451-6428-5*, Scarlet Dagger Lrg Print) Chivers N Amer.
— Bones in the Sand. large type ed. 1994. pap. 16.95 (*0-7451-6434-X*, Scarlet Dagger Lrg Print) Chivers N Amer.
— Channel Assault. large type ed. 480p. 1984. 15.95 (*0-7089-1131-5*) Ulverscroft.
— The Crypto Man. large type ed. 528p. 1988. 15.95 (*0-7089-1841-7*) Ulverscroft.
— Exchange of Doves. 320p. 1992. mass mkt. 4.99 (*1-55817-606-3*, Pinnacle NY) Windsor NY.
— Fallout. 1991. mass mkt. 4.95 (*1-55817-517-2*, Pinnacle NY) Windsor NY.
— No Way Back. large type ed. 528p. 1988. 16.95 (*0-7089-1778-X*) Ulverscroft.
— Patriots. large type ed. 518p. 1989. 17.95 (*0-7089-1967-7*) Ulverscroft.
— The President Is Dead. large type ed. 1989. 17.95 (*0-685-50584-7*) Ulverscroft.
— The Stalin Account. large type ed. 576p. 1986. 23.95 (*0-7089-8328-6*, Charnwood) Ulverscroft.
— Ten Thousand Days. 256p. 1984. pap. 3.50 (*0-88184-082-3*) Carroll & Graf.
— Ten Thousand Days. large type ed. 464p. 1984. 15.95 (*0-7089-1175-7*) Ulverscroft.
— The Third Arm. large type ed. 416p. 1985. 15.95 (*0-7089-1332-6*) Ulverscroft.
— A Wild Justice. large type ed. 1993. pap. 16.95 (*0-7927-1379-6*, Paragon Lrg Print) Chivers N Amer.
— The XYY Man. large type ed. 1981. 12.00 (*0-7089-0598-6*) Ulverscroft.
Royce, Pat. Royce's Powerboating Illustrated. (Illus.). 416p. 1992. 12.95 (*0-930030-67-2*) Western Marine Ent.
Royce, Patrick M. Royce's Sailing Illustrated: The Sailors Bible since '56. rev. ed. (Sailing Illustrated Series: The Best of Royce). (Illus.). 368p. (C). 1993. pap. text ed. write for info. (*0-911284-00-1*) Royce Pubns.
— Royce's Sailing Illustrated Course: Sailors Helping Sailors. (Sailing Illustrated Series: The Best of Royce). (Illus.). 96p. (Orig.). (C). 1993. pap. text ed. write for info. (*0-911284-01-X*) Royce Pubns.
— Sailing Illustrated: The Sailor's Bible since '56. 9th rev. ed. LC 82-6925. (Illus.). 368p. 1992. pap. 12.95 (*0-930030-51-6*) Western Marine Ent.
— Sailing Illustrated Homestudy Guide. (Illus.). 164p. 1989. pap. 11.95 (*0-930030-39-7*) Western Marine Ent.
Royce, Peter M. & Steinmann, Beat, eds. Connective Tissue & Its Disorders: Molecular, Genetic, & Medical Aspects. LC 92-49777. 800p. 1992. text ed. 269.95 (*0-471-58819-9*, Wiley-Liss) Wiley.
Royce, Samuel. Deterioration & Race Education with Practical Application to the Condition of the People & Industry. LC 72-180587. (Medicine & Society in America Ser.). 596p. 1972. reprint ed. 39.95 (*0-405-03967-0*) Ayer.
Royce, Sarah. A Frontier Lady: Recollections of the Gold Rush & Early California. Gabriel, Ralph H., ed. LC 76-44263. (Illus.). xvi, 144p. 1977. reprint ed. 25.00 (*0-8032-0909-6*); reprint ed. pap. 6.95 (*0-8032-5856-9*) U of Nebr Pr.
Royce, Sherry & Zook, Doris. Read English, Bk 1. (Speak English Ser.). (Illus.). 80p. (Orig.). 1985. pap. text ed. 7.95 (*0-8325-0504-8*, Natl Textbk) NTC Pub Grp.
Royce, Sherry, jt. auth. see Hershberger, Jane.
Royce, W. H. A Balzac Bibliography. 1972. 69.95 (*0-87968-699-5*) Gordon Pr.
Royce, William, jt. auth. see Donaldson, Maureen.
Royce, William F. Fishery Development. 248p. 1987. text ed. 44.00 (*0-12-600955-4*) Acad Pr.
— Introduction to the Practice of Fishery Science. (C). 1984. text ed. 59.00 (*0-12-600960-0*) Acad Pr.
— Introduction to the Practice of Fishery Science. rev. ed. LC 95-12388. 1995. write for info. (*0-12-600952-X*) Acad Pr.
Roychaudhury, D. P. Advance Acoustics. 1985. 82.00 (*0-317-38746-4*, Current Dist) St Mut.
Roychawdjuri, A. K. Classical Theory of Electricity & Magnetism. (Course of Lecture Ser.). (Illus.). 332p. 1991. 35.00 (*0-19-562578-1*, 10251) OUP.
Roychoudhuri, C. & Veldkamp, W. B. Miniature & Micro-Optics: Fabrication & System Applications. 1992. 53.00 (*0-8194-0672-4*, 1544) SPIE.
Roychoudhury, Arun K. & Nei, Masatoshi. Human Polymorphic Genes: World Distribution. (Oxford Monographs on Medical Genetics). (Illus.). 416p. 1988. 59.95 (*0-19-505123-8*) OUP.
Roychoudhury, Profulla. The Transnationals. 1983. 12.50 (*0-8364-0949-3*, Pub. by Mukhopadhyaya II) S Asia.
Roychowdhury, R. & Bhattacharyya, B. Cost & Management Accountancy (M&T) (C). 1989. 80.00 (*0-89771-436-9*, Current Dist) St Mut.
Roychowdhury, R., jt. auth. see Mukherji, M.
Roychowdhury, Vwani, et al. Discrete Neural Computation: A Theoretical Foundation. 1995. text ed. 52.00 (*0-13-300708-1*) P-H.
— Computational Models of Nanoelectronics. 1995. 54.95 (*1-55860-340-9*) Morgan Kaufmann.
***Roychowdhury, Vwani, et al, eds.** Theoretical Advances in Neural Computation & Learning. LC 94-34334. 496p. (C). 1994. lib. bdg. 120.00 (*0-7923-9478-X*) Kluwer Ac.
Roycraft, Roland. Fill Your Watercolors with Light & Color. (Illus.). 144p. 1990. 28.99 (*0-89134-338-5*, 30221) North Light Bks.
Roycrofters Staff. Roycroft Furniture Catalog, 1906. LC 93-49373. Orig. Title: A Catalog of Roycrofters Furniture & Other Things. (Illus.). 64p. 1994. reprint ed. pap. 5.95 (*0-486-28113-2*) Dover.
Royden, H. L. Real Analysis. 3rd ed. 505p. (C). 1988. text ed. write for info. (*0-02-404151-3*) Macmillan.
Royden, Leigh H. & Horvath, Ferenc, eds. The Pannonian Basin: A Study in Basin Evolution. (AAPG Memoir Ser.: No. 45). (Illus.). x, 394p. 1988. 69.00 (*0-89181-322-5*) AAPG.
***Roydhouse, Noel.** Underwater Ear & Nose Care. rev. ed. (Illus.). 78p. (C). 1994. 22.00 (*0-941332-23-3*) Best Pub Co.
Royds, Kathleen E. Coleridge & His Poetry. LC 76-120990. (Poetry & Life Ser.). reprint ed. 27.50 (*0-404-52532-6*) AMS Pr.
— Elizabeth Barrett Browning & Her Poetry. LC 73-148799. (Poetry & Life Ser.). reprint ed. 27.50 (*0-404-52531-8*) AMS Pr.
Roye, J., jt. auth. see Chenevert, Martin.
Roye, Wendell J., jt. ed. see Blumberg, Rhoda G.
Roye, William, jt. auth. see Barlowe, Jerome.
Royeen, Charlotte B., ed. see American Occupational Therapy Association Staff.
Royeen, Charlotte B., ed. see American Occupational Therapy Association, Inc. Staff.
***Royem, Robert T.** An American Classic: The Durango & Silverton Narrow Gauge Railroad. (Illus.). 152p. 1995. 39.95 (*0-9643430-0-2*); pap. 24.95 (*0-9643430-1-0*) Limelight Pr.
Royen, Christoph. Osteuropa: Reformen & Wandel. 168p. 1990. pap. 19.50 (*3-7890-1948-8*, Pub. by Nomos Verlags GW) Intl Bk Import.
Royer, Charles T., ed. Campaign for President: The Managers Look at 1992. 352p. 1994. pap. 18.95 (*1-884186-00-9*) Puritan Pr.
Royer-Collard, F. B. Skeleton Clocks. (Illus.). 165p. 1981. 48.50 (*0-7198-0110-9*, Pub. by NAG Press UK) Antique Collect.
Royer, D., jt. auth. see Dieulesaint, E.
Royer, Denise W. Summary Groundwater Resources of Lebanon County, Pennsylvania. (Water Resource Report Ser.: No. 55). (Illus.). 84p. (Orig.). 1983. pap. 15.05 (*0-8182-0026-X*) Commonweal PA.
Royer, Denise W. & Socolow, Arthur A., prefs. Summary of Groundwater Resources of Perry County, Pennsylvania. (Water Resource Report Ser.: No. 59). (Illus.). 70p. 1984. pap. 16.00 (*0-8182-0059-6*) Commonweal PA.
Royer, Fanchon. The Life of St. Anthony Mary Claret. LC 85-52248. 302p. (Orig.). 1985. reprint ed. pap. 12.50 (*0-89555-288-4*) TAN Bks Pubs.
Royer, G. P. Fundamentals of Enzymology: Rate Enhancement, Specificity, Control & Application. LC 81-11359. 242p. 1982. 36.95 (*0-471-04675-2*) Wiley.
Royer, Harold L., jt. auth. see Latif-Pembry, Rebecca C.
Royer, J. M. Synthese Eurosibereinne, Phytosociologique & Phytogeographique de la Classe des Festuco-Brometea. (Dissertationes Botanicae Ser.: Vol. 178). (Illus.). 296p. (FRE.). 1991. pap. text ed. 91.00 (*3-443-64090-7*, Pub. by Gebrueder Borntraeger GW) Lubrecht & Cramer.
Royer, J. S. A Connotational Theory of Program Structure. (Lecture Notes in Computer Science Ser.: Vol. 273). v, 186p. 1987. pap. 30.00 (*0-387-18253-5*) Spr-Verlag.
Royer, Jack P. & Convery, Frank J., eds. Nonindustrial Private Forests: Data & Information Needs: Conference Proceedings, April 17-18, 1980, Duke University, Durham, North Carolina. (Illus.). 136p. reprint ed. pap. 38.80 (*0-7837-6037-X*, 2045850) Bks Demand.
Royer, Jack P. & Risbrudt, Christopher D., eds. Nonindustrial Private Forests: A Review of Economic & Policy Studies: Symposium Proceedings, April 19-20, 1983. (Illus.). 406p. reprint ed. pap. 115.80 (*0-8357-8252-2*, 2033958) Bks Demand.
Royer, James & Feldman, Robert S. Educational Psychology. (C). 1984. pap. text ed. write for info. (*0-07-553587-4*) McGraw.
***Royer, James S. & Case, John.** Subrecursive Programming Systems: Complexity & Succinctness. LC 94-26443. (Progress in Theoretical Computer Science Ser.). viii, 252p. 1994. 49.50 (*0-8176-3767-2*) Birkhauser.
***Royer, Jean.** Interviews to Literature. Sloatet, Daniel, tr. (Essay Ser.: No. 19). 300p. 1995. 20.00 (*1-55071-008-7*) Guernica Editions.
— Quebec en Poesie. (Folio - Junior Ser). (FRE.). pap. 9.95 (*2-07-034059-7*) Schoenhof.
Royer, Jeffrey P. Handbook of Software & Hardware: Interfacing for IBM PCs. (Illus.). 240p. 1987. text ed. 33.00 (*0-317-44717-3*); pap. 30.95 (*0-13-381849-7*) P-H.
Royer, Katherine. Happy Times with Nursery Children at Home & Church. rev. ed. 1987. pap. 10.95 (*0-8361-1296-2*) Herald Pr.
— Nursery Happy Times Book. (Illus.). 48p. (J). (ps). 1957. pap. 4.95x (*0-8361-1277-6*) Herald Pr.
— Nursery Stories of Jesus. (Illus.). 48p. (J). (ps). 1957. pap. 4.95 (*0-8361-1276-8*) Herald Pr.
Royer, Katherine, ed. Nursery Songbook. (Illus.). 48p. (J). (ps). 1957. pap. 4.95x (*0-8361-1278-4*) Herald Pr.
Royer, Kathy. Waiting on the Outside. LC 87-21104. 64p. (Orig.). 1987. pap. 3.95 (*0-8361-3454-0*) Herald Pr.
Royer, King. Desk Book for Construction Superintendents. 2nd ed. (Illus.). 1980. text ed. 27.50 (*0-685-03826-2*) P-H.
***Royer, Marie.** Camping Cuisine: The Ultimate Cookbook for the Avid Camper. large type ed. 164p. 1994. pap. text ed. 13.95 (*0-9644266-0-9*) Mossy Crk OR.
Royer, Mary P. Astrology: Opposing Viewpoints. LC 91-21657. (Great Mysteries Ser.). (Illus.). 112p. (J). (gr. 5-8). 1991. lib. bdg. 16.95 (*0-89908-090-1*) Greenhaven.
Royer, P., et al. Nephrologie Pediatrique. 3rd ed. (Collection Pediatrie Ser.). (Illus.). 652p. (FRE.). 1983. lib. bdg. 75.00 (*2-257-12397-2*) S M P F Inc.
Royer, Ronald A. Butterflies of North Dakota: An Atlas & Guide. (Illus.). 192p. (Orig.). (C). 1988. pap. text ed. 14.95 (*0-9619635-0-6*) Minot St U.
Royer, Thomas C. Software Testing Management: Life on the Critical Path. LC 92-12095. 224p. 1993. text ed. 52.00 (*0-13-532987-6*) P-H.
Royer, Victor. Casino Magazine's Play Smart & Win. 1994. pap. 11.00 (*0-671-88024-1*, Fireside) S&S Trade.
***Royer, Warren.** Memories from the Heart: Rural Schools. (Illus.). 1995. write for info. (*1-878044-17-6*) Mayhaven Pub.
***Royet-Journoud, Claude.** A Descriptive Method. Waldrop, Keith, tr. 30p. (Orig.). 1995. pap. 7.00 (*0-942996-23-2*) Post Apollo Pr.
— I.E. Waldrop, Keith, tr. (Serie d'Ecriture Supplement: No. 1). 30p. (Orig.). 1995. pap. 5.00 (*1-886224-08-0*) Burning Deck.
Royko, Mike. Boss: Richard J. Daley of Chicago. 1988. pap. 10.95 (*0-452-26167-8*, Plume) NAL-Dutton.
Roykssund, Conrad, jt. auth. see Johnson, Pal E.
Roylance, Dale. American Graphic Arts: A Chronology to 1900 in Books, Prints, & Drawings. (Illus.). 213p. (C). 1990. 20.00 (*0-685-62442-0*); pap. 15.00 (*0-87811-033-X*) Princeton Lib.
— European Graphic Arts: The Art of the Book from Guttenberg to Picasso. (Illus.). 199p. 1986. 15.00 (*0-87811-030-5*) Princeton Lib.
Roylance, Dale & Finlay, Nancy, comps. Pride of Place: Early American Views from the Collection of Leonard L. Milberg '53. (Illus.). 66p. 1983. 10.00 (*0-87811-029-1*) Princeton Lib.
Roylance, Susan, ed. see Ellsworth, Sterling G.
Roylance, Susan, ed. see Jones, Gracia N.
Roylance, Ward J. Utah: A Guide to the State. rev. ed. 1982. reprint ed. 25.00 (*0-914740-23-7*, 884P.); reprint ed. pap. 11.95 (*0-914740-25-3*, PT. 2, TOUR SECTION, 400P.) Western Epics.
Roylance, William H. Complete Book of Insults, Boasts & Riddles. 1971. pap. text ed. 9.95 (*0-13-157479-5*, Reward) P-H.
Royle, Derek, jt. auth. see Cooper, Emanuel.
Royle, Duncan, jt. auth. see Hares, John.
Royle, Edward. Modern Britain: A Social History, 1750-1985. 400p. (C). 1988. pap. text ed. 19.95 (*0-7131-6477-8*, Pub. by E Arnold UK) Routledge Chapman & Hall.
— Radicals, Secularists & Republicans: Popular Freethought in Britain, 1866 to 1915. 380p. 1980. 45.00 (*0-8476-6294-2*) Rowman.
***Royle, Edward & Walvin, James.** English Radicals & Reformers, 1760-1848. fac. ed. LC 82-40179. 233p. 1994. pap. 66.50 (*0-7837-7599-7*, 2047352) Bks Demand.
Royle, Edwin M. The Squaw Man: A Comedy Drama in Four Acts. (BCL1-PS American Literature Ser.). 90p. 1992. reprint ed. lib. bdg. 59.00 (*0-7812-6847-8*) Rprt Serv.
Royle, J. F. Fibrous Plants of India. (C). 1988. 120.00 (*0-685-22368-X*, Scientific) St Mut.
— Illustrations of Botany & of the Himalayan Mountains & Flora of Cashmere - 1883, 2 vols., II:plates. lxxviii, 468p. 1970. reprint ed. write for info. (*0-318-55692-8*, Messers Today & Tomorrow) Scholarly Pubns.
— Illustrations of Botany & of the Himalayan Mountains & Flora of Cashmere - 1883, 2 vols., Vol. I: Text. lxxviii, 468p. 1970. reprint ed. 120.00 (*0-88065-183-0*, Messers Today & Tomorrow) Scholarly Pubns.
Royle, Jo. Boxers Today. (Book of the Breed Ser.). (Illus.). 176p. 1994. 22.95 (*0-948955-08-2*, Pub. by Ringpr Bks UK) Seven Hills Bk.
Royle, John, jt. auth. see Marshall, Vernon C.
Royle, Kent & Terry, Cliff. Hawaiian Design: Strategies for Energy Efficient Architecture. (Illus.). 59p. (Orig.). (C). 1993. pap. text ed. 50.00 (*0-7881-0120-X*) Diane Pub.
***Royle, Nicholas.** After Derrida. LC 94-5404. 1995. text ed. write for info. (*0-7190-4378-6*, Pub. by Manchester Univ Pr UK); text ed. write for info. (*0-7190-4379-4*, Pub. by Manchester Univ Pr UK) St Martin.
— Telepathy & Literature: Essays on the Reading Mind. 240p. (C). 1991. text ed. 52.95 (*0-631-16311-5*); pap. text ed. 21.95 (*0-631-17691-8*) Blackwell Pubs.
Royle, Nicholas, jt. auth. see Bennett, Andrew.
Royle, Roger & Woods, Gary. Mother Teresa: A Life in Pictures. LC 92-52654. (Illus.). 160p. 1992. pap. 18.00 (*0-06-067978-6*) Harper SF.
Royle, Susan G. Carry on Osteopathy. 1992. 14.95 (*0-533-10176-X*) Vantage.
Royle, Trevor, ed. In Flanders Fields: Scottish Poetry & Prose of the First World War. 272p. 1992. pap. 22.95 (*1-85158-303-3*, Pub. by Mnstream UK) Trafalgar.
Royle, Trevor, ed. see Kipling, Rudyard.
Royle, Trevor, ed. see Stevenson, Robert Louis.
***Roys, Deloris T. & Roys, Pat.** Protocol for Phallometric Assessment: A Clinician's Guide. 64p. (Orig.). 1994. student ed, pap. 10.00x (*1-884444-11-3*) Safer Soc.
Roys, Pat, jt. auth. see Roys, Deloris T.
Roys, R. L. The Indian Background of Colonial Yucatan. 1976. lib. bdg. 250.00 (*0-8490-2052-2*) Gordon Pr.
Roys, R. L., et al. Contributions to American Anthropology & History: The Indians of Cozumel, Personal Names of the Maya of Yucatan & Maize Cultivation in Guatemala. (Yucatan Ser.). 1979. lib. bdg. 69.95 (*0-8490-2903-1*) Gordon Pr.
Roys, Ralph L. The Ethno-Botany of the Maya (with a New Introduction & Supplement Bibliography by Sheila Cosminsky) LC 76-29024. (ISHI Reprints on Latin America & the Caribbean Ser.). 414p. reprint ed. pap. 118.00 (*0-317-42088-7*, 2025710) Bks Demand.
— The Titles of Ebtun. LC 76-44711. (Carnegie Institution of Washington. Publications: No. 505). (Illus.). 512p. reprint ed. 110.00 (*0-404-15918-4*) AMS Pr.
Roysdon, Christine & White, Howard. Expert Systems in Reference Services. LC 88-39835. (Reference Librarian Ser.: No. 23). (Illus.). 238p. 1989. text ed. 49.95 (*0-86656-839-5*) Haworth Pr.
Royse, David. How Do I Know It's Abuse? Identifying & Countering Emotional Mistreatment from Friends & Family Members. LC 94-11495. 248p. (C). 1994. 51.95 (*0-398-05921-7*) C C Thomas.
— How Do I Know It's Abuse? Identifying & Countering Emotional Mistreatment from Friends & Family Members. LC 94-11495. 248p. (C). 1994. pap. 30.95 (*0-398-06350-8*) C C Thomas.
— Program Evaluation. 230p. 1992. pap. text ed. 21.95 (*0-8304-1245-X*) Nelson-Hall.
— Research Methods in Social Work. 300p. 1990. pap. text ed. 20.95 (*0-8304-1210-7*) Nelson-Hall.
— Research Methods in Social Work. 2nd ed. LC 94-16190. (Social Work Ser.). 1995. pap. text ed. 23.95 (*0-8304-1409-6*) Nelson-Hall.
Royse, David, et al. Field Instruction Handbook: A Guide for Social Work Students. 144p. (C). 1993. pap. text ed. 22.95 (*0-8013-0820-8*, 78887) Longman.
Royse, James R. The Spurious Texts of Philo of Alexandria: A Study of Textual Transmission & Corruption with Indexes to the Major Collections of Greek Fragments. (Arbeiten zur Literatur und Geschichte des Hellenistischen Judentums Ser.: No. 22). xiii, 252p. 1991. 74.50 (*90-04-09511-X*) E J Brill.
Royster, Charles. The Destructive War: William Tecumseh Sherman, Stonewall Jackson, & the Americans. LC 92-56370. 1992. pap. 15.00 (*0-679-73878-9*, Vin) Random.
— Fabulous History. Date not set. pap. write for info. (*0-679-43345-7*) Random.
— Light-Horse Harry Lee & the Legacy of the American Revolution. LC 82-9620. (Illus.). 336p. 1994. pap. 12.95 (*0-8071-1910-5*) La State U Pr.
— A Revolutionary People at War: The Continental Army & American Character, 1775-1783. LC 79-10152. (Institute of Early American History & Culture Ser.). (Illus.). xi, 452p. 1980. 37.50 (*0-8078-1385-0*) U of NC Pr.

R

An Asterisk (*) at the beginning of an entry indicates that the title is appearing in BIP for the first time.

— A Revolutionary People at War: The Continental Army & American Character, 1775-1783. (Illus.). 512p. (C). 1982. reprint ed. pap. text ed. 12.95 (0-393-95173-1) Norton.

Royster, Charles, ed. Memoirs of General W. T. Sherman: William Tecumseh Sherman. 1990. 35.00 (0-940450-65-8) Library of America.

Royster, Dmitri. The Kingdom of God: The Sermon on the Mount. LC 92-29952. 128p. 1993. 7.95 (0-88141-116-7) St Vladimirs.

Royster, Glenn. The Slave Master's Religion: Breaking the Last Bonds of Slavery. 152p. 1993. pap. 7.00 (0-9638214-4-X) Kabila Communs.

Royster, Julia D. & Royster, Larry H. Hearing Conservation Programs: Practical Guidelines for Success. (Illus.). 120p. 1990. 64.95 (0-87371-307-9, RC963) Lewis Pubs.

Royster, Larry H., jt. auth. see Royster, Julia D.

Royster, Philip M. Songs & Dances. LC 80-85233. 61p. (YA). (gr. 9-12). 1981. per. 3.50 (0-916418-28-6) Lotus.

Royster, Salibelle. Arrowsmith Notes. (Orig.). 1982. pap. 4.50 (0-8220-0201-9) Cliffs.

— Bleak House Notes. 1991. pap. 3.75 (0-8220-0247-7) Cliffs.

— Main Street Notes. 1965. pap. 4.50 (0-8220-0798-3) Cliffs.

— Much Ado About Nothing Notes. 1963. pap. 3.95 (0-8220-0060-1) Cliffs.

Royster, Vermont. The Essential Royster. Fuller, Edmund, ed. 392p. 1985. 18.95 (0-912697-19-9) Algonquin Bks.

— My Own, My Country's Time: A Journalist's Journey. (Illus.). 351p. 1983. 18.50 (0-912697-02-4) Algonquin Bks.

— A Pride of Prejudices. 364p. 1984. 10.95 (0-912697-14-8) Algonquin Bks.

***Royston & Hawksley.** My Big Book of the World. (Illus.). 48p. (J). 1995. 5.98 (0-8317-5984-4) Smithmark.

Royston, Angela. The A to Z Book of Cars. (Illus.). (J). (gr. k up). 1991. 12.95 (0-8120-6209-4) Barron.

— Big Machines. LC 93-16019. (Illus.). (J). (gr. 3 up). 1994. 12.95 (0-316-76070-6) Little.

— Cars. LC 91-16122. (Eye Openers Ser.). (Illus.). 24p. (J). (ps-00). 1991. pap. 6.95 (0-689-71517-X, Aladdin Paperbacks) S&S Childrens.

— Healthy Me. (Illus.). 24p. (J). (ps-3). 1995. 13.95 (0-8120-6423-2) Barron.

— The Human Body & How It Works. LC 90-42978. (Tell Me about Bks.). (Illus.). 40p. (J). (gr. 2-5). 1991. pap. 4.99 (0-679-80860-4) Random Bks Yng Read.

— Mammals. LC 94-27458. (Science Nature Guides Ser.). (J). (gr. 1-8). 1995. 12.95 (1-57145-016-5) Thunder Bay CA.

— My Lift-the-Flap Plane Book. LC 92-38631. (Illus.). 18p. (J). (ps-1). 1993. 14.95 (0-399-22533-1, Putnam) Putnam Pub Group.

— The Senses. LC 92-25715. (Illus.). 24p. (J). (ps-3). 1993. 13.95 (0-8120-6272-8) Barron.

— You & Your Body. LC 94-16304. (One Hundred & One Questions Ser.). (J). 1994. write for info. (0-8160-3217-3) Facts on File.

Royston, Angela, ed. Birds. LC 93-48675. (Nature Science Guides Ser.). (Illus.). 80p. (J). (gr. 3-6). 1994. 12.95 (1-85028-261-7) Thunder Bay CA.

— Trees. LC 93-46145. (Science Nature Guides Ser.). (Illus.). 81p. (J). (gr. 3-6). 1994. 12.95 (1-85028-265-X) Thunder Bay CA.

Royston, Angela & Thompson, Graham. Monster Building Machines. 24p. (J). (ps-2). 1990. 9.95 (0-8120-6174-8) Barron.

— Monster Road Builders. (Illus.). 24p. (J). (ps-2). 1989. 9.95 (0-8120-6126-8) Barron.

Royston, Angela, ed. see Forey, Pam.

Royston, M., jt. ed. see Dunbar, G.

Royston, Michael G. Pollution Prevention Pays. 1979. 91.00 (0-08-023597-2, Pub. by Pergamon Repr UK) Franklin.

Royston, Peter L., jt. auth. see Koon, William H.

Royston, Robert. Cities, 2000. Asimov, Isaac, ed. (Your World 2000 Ser.). (Illus.). 64p. (YA). (gr. 6 up). 1985. 14.95 (0-8160-1154-0) Facts on File.

Rozak, Chester, jt. auth. see Matthews, Jay.

Rozakis, Christos L. The Concept of Jus Cogens in the Law of Treaties. 206p. 1976. 54.00 (0-7204-0485-1, North Holland) Elsevier.

Rozakis, Christos L. & Stagos, Petros N. The Turkish Straits. LC 86-28581. (International Straits of the World Ser.: Vol. 9). 1987. lib. bdg. 92.00 (90-247-3464-9) Kluwer Ac.

Rozakis, Christos L. & Stephanou, C. A. The New Law of the Sea. 1984. 69.25 (0-444-86804-6, I-414-83) Elsevier.

Rozakis, George, ed. Cataract Surgery: Alternative Small-Incision Techniques. LC 89-43622. 196p. 1990. vhs 99.00 (1-55642-166-4) SLACK Inc.

Rozakis, George W., ed. Refractive Lamellar Keratoplasty. LC 94-4393. 178p. 1994. 89.00 (1-55642-229-6) SLACK Inc.

Rozakis, Laurie. AP English Literature & Composition. 3rd ed. (AP Exam Guides Ser.). 320p. 1993. pap. 13.00 (0-671-84784-8, Arco Test) P-H Gen Ref & Trav.

— Celebrate! Holidays Around the World. LC 92-81915. (J). (gr. k-4). 1993. pap. 4.95 (0-88160-217-5, LW107) Learning Wks.

— Dick Rutan & Jeana Yeager: Flying Non-Stop Around the World. Glassman, Bruce, ed. LC 94-20399. (Partners Ser.). (Illus.). 48p. (J). (gr. 2-5). 1994. lib. bdg. 12.95 (1-56711-087-8) Blackbirch.

— Hanna & Barbera: Yabba-Dabba-Doo! (Partners Ser.). (Illus.). 48p. (J). (gr. 2-5). 1994. lib. bdg. 12.95 (1-56711-065-7) Blackbirch.

— Henson & Peary: The Race for the North Pole. (Partners Ser.). (Illus.). 48p. (J). (gr. 2-5). 1994. lib. bdg. 12.95 (1-56711-066-5) Blackbirch.

— Homelessness: Can We Solve the Problem? (Issues of Our Time Ser.). (Illus.). 64p. (J). (gr. 5-8). 1995. lib. bdg. 15.98 (0-8050-3878-7) TFC Bks NY.

— Instant American Literature. 256p. 1995. pap. 10.00 (0-449-90700-7) Fawcett.

— Laura Ingalls Wilder: Activities Based on Research from the Laura Ingalls Wilder Homes. 1993. pap. 8.95 (0-590-49271-3) Scholastic Inc.

— Mary Kay. LC 92-45124. (Made in America Ser.). (J). 1993. 15.93 (0-86592-040-0); 11.95 (0-685-66418-X) Rourke Enter.

— Merriam-Webster's Rules of Order. LC 94-16769. 336p. 1994. 12.95 (0-87779-029-9) Merriam-Webster Inc.

— Power Vocabulary Pocket Guide. 1991. pap. 6.00 (0-679-40860-6) Random.

— Random House Guide to Grammar Usage & Punctuation. 1991. pap. 6.00 (0-394-58920-3) Random.

— Steven Jobs. LC 92-43268. (Masters of Invention Ser.). (J). (gr. 5 up). 1993. 15.93 (0-86592-001-X); 11.95 (0-685-66327-2) Rourke Corp.

— Teen Pregnancy: Why Are Kids Having Babies? (Issues of Our Time Ser.). (Illus.). 64p. (J). (gr. 5-8). 1993. lib. bdg. 15.98 (0-8050-2569-3) TFC Bks NY.

Rozakis, Laurie, jt. auth. see Cliff Staff.

***Rozakis, Laurie E.** How to Interpret Poetry. LC 94-48773. Date not set. pap. 30.00 (0-02-860309-5) P-H Gen Ref & Trav.

Rozan, S. J. China Trade. 256p. 1994. 20.95 (0-312-11254-8) St Martin.

Rozanov, Herman. Behind the Scenes of the Third Reich Diplomacy. 196p. 1984. pap. 30.00 (0-317-53846-2, Pub. by Collets UK) Pro-Am Music.

Rozanov, J. A., jt. auth. see Prohorov, Yu. V.

Rozanov, J. A., ed. see Steklov Institute of Mathematics, Academy of Sciences, U. S. S. R. Staff.

Rozanov, Mikhail G., see Nikolai Ognyov, pseud..

Rozanov, Vasilii V. Solitaria. Koteliansky, Samuel S., tr. LC 79-13120. 188p. 1980. reprint ed. text ed. 49.75 (0-313-22004-2, ROSA, Greenwood Pr) Greenwood.

Rozanov, Y. A. Probability Theory: A Concise Course. rev. ed. Silverman, Richard A., tr. LC 77-78592. 1977. reprint ed. pap. text ed. 5.95 (0-486-63544-9) Dover.

Rozanov, Yuri A. Introduction to the Theory of Random Processes. (Soviet Mathematics Ser.). viii, 117p. 1987. 49.00 (0-387-17874-0) Spr-Verlag.

— Markov Random Fields. Elson, C. M., tr. (Illus.). 201p. 1982. 84.00 (0-387-90708-4) Spr-Verlag.

— Random Fields & Stochastic Partial Differential Equations. 290p. 1995. write for info. (0-471-93821-1) Wiley.

Rozanov, Yuri A., jt. auth. see Ibragimov, I. A.

Rozanova, V. Concise Defining Dictionary of Russian. 256p. (C). 1989. 75.00 (0-685-46851-8, Pub. by Collets) St Mut.

— Concise Defining Dictionary of Russian for Foreigners. 227p. (RUS.). (C). 1978. 70.00 (0-685-46850-X, Pub. by Collets) St Mut.

Rozanski, K. & Araguas-Araguas, K. Environmental Isotope Data, No. 9: World Survey of Isotope Concentration In Precip. 84-87. (Technical Reports Ser.: No. 311). 188p. 1990. pap. 85.00 (92-0-145090-7, STI/DOC/311) UNIPUB.

Rozanski, Mordechai, ed. Records of the Department of State Relating to the Internal Affairs of China, 1910-1949: A Descriptive Guide & Subject Index to Microcopy No. 329. LC 79-13351. 61p. 1979. lib. bdg. 30.00 (0-8420-2133-7) Scholarly Res Inc.

Rozanski, Waclaw, ed. see Rozdzienski, Walenty.

Rozar, G. Edward, Jr. & Biebel, David B. Laughing in the Face of AIDS: A Surgeon's Personal Battle. LC 92-12924. (Illus.). 160p. 1992. 12.99 (0-8010-7767-2); pap. 7.99 (0-8010-7765-6) Baker Bk.

***Rozario, Diane.** The Immunization Resource Guide: Where to Find Answers to All Your Questions about Childhood Immunizations. 2nd ed. LC 94-69009. 60p. (Orig.). 1995. pap. 9.95 (0-9643366-1-8) Patter Pubns.

— The Immunization Resource Guide: Where to Find Answers to All Your Questions about Childhood Immunizations. 2nd rev. ed. LC 95-92111. 60p. (Orig.). 1995. 9.95 (0-9643366-2-6) Patter Pubns.

Rozario, M. Rita. Trafficking in Women & Children in India: Sexual Exploitation & Sale. 1988. 22.00 (0-317-90858-8, Pub. by Uppal Pub Hse II) S Asia.

Rozario, Santi. Purity & Communal Boundaries: Women & Social Change in a Bangladeshi Village. (Women in Asia Ser.). 192p. (C). 1992. text ed. 39.95 (1-85649-033-5, Pub. by Zed Books UK) Humanities.

Rozas, Diane. Chicken Breasts: One Hundred & One New & Classic Recipes for the Fairest Part of the Fowl. 96p. 1985. 7.00 (0-517-55688-X, Harmony) Crown Pub Group.

— More Chicken Breasts: Ninety-Four New & Classic Recipes for the Fairest Part of the Fowl. (Illus.). 96p. 1991. 7.00 (0-517-57710-0, Harmony) Crown Pub Group.

— Sauces & Dressings: Eighty-Five Light & Easy Recipes from Nouvelle to New American. 96p. 1993. pap. 6.95 (0-517-57117-X, Harmony) Crown Pub Group.

Rozbicki, Michal J. Transformation of the English Cultural Ethos in Colonial America: Maryland 1634-1720. LC 88-14399. 232p. (C). 1988. lib. bdg. 41.50 (0-8191-7048-8) U Pr of Amer.

Rozdestvenskii, B. L. & Janenko, N. N. Systems of Quasilinear Equations & Their Applications to Gas Dynamics. LC 82-24488. (Translations of Mathematical Monographs: Vol. 55). 676p. 1983. 198.00 (0-8218-4509-8, MMONO-55) Am Math.

Rozdzienski, Walenty. Officina Ferraria: A Polish Poem of 1612 Describing the Noble Craft of Ironwork. Rozanski, Waclaw & Smith, Cyril S., eds. Pluszczewski, Stefan, tr. LC 76-26592. (SHOT Monograph Ser.: No. 9). 1977. 25.00 (0-262-18079-0) MIT Pr.

Roze, C. & Bernades, P., eds. European Pancreatic Club, EPC Twenty-Fifth Meeting, Paris, October 1993: Abstracts. (Journal: Digestion: Vol. 54, No. 5, 1993). (Illus.). 62p. 1993. pap. 78.50 (3-8055-5876-7) S Karger.

Roze, Janis A. Coral Snakes: Biology, Identification, Venoms. LC 93-1912. 1995. write for info. (0-89464-847-0) Krieger.

Roze, Maris. Getting Results with English. (C). 1980. pap. 33.96 (0-395-28750-2) HM.

— Technical Communication: The Practical Craft. 2nd ed. 320p. (C). 1994. pap. write for info. (0-02-404171-8) Macmillan.

Roze, Uldis. The North American Porcupine. (Illus.). 224p. 1989. 32.50 (0-87474-786-4); pap. 13.95 (0-87474-787-2) Smithsonian.

Rozeboom, W. W., jt. ed. see Royce, J. R.

Rozek, Jan. Keys to Understanding Osteoporosis. (Retirement Keys Ser.). 160p. 1992. pap. 5.95 (0-8120-4664-1) Barron.

Rozelaar, Marc. Lukrez - Versuch Einer Deutung. xvi, 267p. (GER.). 1988. reprint ed. write for info. (3-487-09026-0, Pub. by Georg Olms GW) Lubrecht & Cramer.

Rozell, Mark J. Executive Privilege: The Dilemma of Secrecy & Democratic Accoutability. LC 94-6801. (Interpreting American Politics Ser.). 1994. text ed. 45.00x (0-8018-4899-7); pap. text ed. 14.95x (0-8018-4900-4) Johns Hopkins.

— The Press & the Ford Presidency. LC 92-8700. 276p. (C). 1992. text ed. 42.50 (0-472-10350-4) U of Mich Pr.

***Rozell, Mark J. & Wilcox, Clyde, eds.** God at the Grassroots: The Christian Right in the 1994 Elections. 288p. (C). 1995. lib. bdg. 59.50 (0-8476-8097-5); pap. text ed. 22.95 (0-8476-8098-3) Rowman.

Rozell, O. B. The Freeway. 24p. (Orig.). 1976. pap. 3.00 (0-88680-059-5) I E Clark.

— Nathan the Nervous. (Illus.). 24p. (Orig.). (J). (gr. 6-12). 1977. pap. 2.50 (0-88680-136-2) I E Clark.

— Of Winners, Losers, & Games. (Illus.). 24p. (Orig.). 1976. pap. 2.50 (0-88680-145-1) I E Clark.

— Searching. (Illus.). 26p. (Orig.). 1980. pap. 2.00 (0-88680-171-0) I E Clark.

— Sharing. (Illus.). 19p. (Orig.). 1980. pap. 2.00 (0-88680-172-9) I E Clark.

***Rozell, Paula.** Plotting Pictures: Coordinate Graphing & Number Skills. Gideon, Joan, ed. (Illus.). 64p. (J). (gr. 5-8). 1994. student ed 10.95 (0-86651-854-1) Seymour Pubns.

Rozell, W. M. Otori. 344p. 1989. 19.95 (0-9624111-0-8) Genesis FL.

Rozelle, Harold. Drift on the River. Rozelle, Pauline, ed. LC 88-60412. 208p. (Orig.). 1989. pap. 9.95 (0-941903-00-1) Ransom Hill.

Rozelle, Pauline, ed. see Rozelle, Harold.

Rozelle, Robert V., ed. Gold of Greece: Jewelry & Ornaments from the Benaki Museum. LC 90-80359. (Illus.). 112p. (Orig.). 1990. pap. 19.95 (0-936227-07-9) Dallas Mus.

Rozelle, Robert V., ed. see Brettell, Richard R.

Rozelle, Robert V., ed. see Valkenier, Elizabeth K., et al.

Rozelle, Robert V., ed. see Wardlaw, Alvia J., et al.

Rozelle, Robert V., et al. The Wendy & Emery Reves Collection. (Illus.). 224p. 1985. 35.00 (0-9609622-8-X, Dallas Museum of Art); pap. 24.95 (0-9609622-9-8, Dallas Museum of Art) U of Tex Pr.

Rozells, Gia. Super Paint: The Complete User's Manual. (Illus.). 300p. (Orig.). 1991. pap. 22.95 (1-55958-098-4) Prima Pub.

Rozema, J. & Verkleij, J. A., eds. Ecological Responses to Environmental Stresses. (C). 1991. lib. bdg. 205.00 (0-7923-0762-3) Kluwer Ac.

Rozema, J., et al, eds. CO B2 S & Biosphere. LC 92-37361. (Advances in Vegetation Science Ser.: No. 14). 488p. (C). 1993. lib. bdg. 302.00 (0-7923-2044-1) Kluwer Ac.

***Rozema, Vicki.** Footsteps of the Cherokees: A Guide to the Eastern Homelands of the Cherokee Nation. (Illus.). (Orig.). 1995. pap. 14.95 (0-89587-133-5) Blair.

Rozen, Arthur. Monarch Notes on Flaubert's Madame Bovary & Three Tales. (Orig.). (C). pap. 3.95 (0-671-00560-X, Arco Test) P-H Gen Ref & Trav.

Rozen, Marvin E. The Economics of Organizational Choice: Workers, Jobs, Labor Markets, & Implicit Contracting. 254p. 1991. text ed. 42.50 (0-472-10278-8) U of Mich Pr.

— The Economics of Work Reorganization. LC 82-22358. 256p. 1983. text ed. 49.95 (0-275-91069-5, C1069, Praeger Pubs) Greenwood.

Rozen, P. & De Dombal, F. T., eds. Computer Aid in Gastroenterology. (Frontiers of Gastrointestinal Research Ser.: Vol. 7). (Illus.). viii, 196p. 1984. 65.75 (3-8055-3770-0) S Karger.

Rozen, P. & Winawer, S. J., eds. Secondary Prevention of Colorectal Cancer. (Frontiers of Gastrointestinal Research Ser.: Vol. 10). (Illus.). xiv, 274p. 1986. 158.50 (3-8055-4252-6) S Karger.

Rozen, P., jt. ed. see Horwitz, C.

Rozen, P., ed. see International Conference on Gastrointestinal Cancer Staff.

Rozen, P., et al, eds. Gastrointestinal Cancer: Advances in Basic Sciences. (Frontiers of Gastrointestinal Research Ser.: Vol. 4). (Illus.). 1979. 76.00 (3-8055-2903-1) S Karger.

— Gastrointestinal Cancer: Advances in Diagnostics Techniques & Therapy. (Frontiers of Gastrointestinal Research Ser.: Vol. 5). (Illus.). 1979. 76.00 (3-8055-2905-8) S Karger.

— Large Bowel Cancer: Policy, Prevention, Research & Treatment. (Frontiers of Gastrointestinal Research Ser.: Vol. 18). (Illus.). viii, 302p. 1991. 223.25 (3-8055-5269-6) S Karger.

Rozen, Sudney C., jt. auth. see Bernstein, Albert J.

Rozen, Sydney C., jt. auth. see Bernstein, Albert J.

Rozen, Sydney C., jt. auth. see Eastman, Meg.

Rozenbaum, Henri. Dictionary of Gynecology: Dictionnaire de Gynecologie. 312p. (FRE.). 1981. 85.00 (0-8288-1826-6) Fr & Eur.

Rozenberg, G., jt. auth. see Salomaa, A.

Rozenberg, Georgii V. Twilight: A Study in Atmospheric Optics. LC 65-11345. 368p. reprint ed. pap. 104.90 (0-317-27113-X, 2024702) Bks Demand.

Rozenberg, Grzegorz, ed. Advances in Petri Nets, 1984. (Lecture Notes in Computer Science Ser.: Vol. 188). vii, 467p. 1985. pap. 45.00 (0-387-15204-0) Spr-Verlag.

— Advances in Petri Nets, 1985. (Lecture Notes in Computer Science Ser.: Vol. 222). vi, 498p. 1986. pap. 53.00 (0-387-16480-4) Spr-Verlag.

— Advances in Petri Nets, 1987. (Lecture Notes in Computer Science Ser.: Vol. 266). vi, 451p. 1987. pap. text ed. 49.00 (0-387-18086-9) Spr-Verlag.

— Advances in Petri Nets, 1988. (Lecture Notes in Computer Science Ser.: Vol. 340). vi, 439p. 1988. pap. 45.00 (0-387-50580-6) Spr-Verlag.

— Advances in Petri Nets, 1993. (Lecture Notes in Computer Science Ser.: Vol. 674). vii, 457p. 1993. pap. 65.00 (0-387-56689-9) Spr-Verlag.

Rozenberg, Grzegorz & Salomaa, Arto. Cornerstones of Undecidability. LC 93-46737. 250p. 1994. pap. text ed. 39.00 (0-13-297425-8) P-H.

— Current Trends in Theoretical. (Series in Computer Science). 630p. 1993. text ed. 109.00 (981-02-1462-6) World Scientific Pub.

— The Mathematical Theory of L Systems. LC 79-25254. (Pure & Applied Mathematics Ser.). 1980. text ed. 106.00 (0-12-597140-0) Acad Pr.

Rozenberg, Grzegorz & Salomaa, Arto, eds. The Book of L. xv, 468p. 1985. 59.00 (0-387-16022-1) Spr-Verlag.

— Lindenmayer Systems: Impacts on Theoretical Computer Science, Computer Graphics, & Developmental Biology. LC 92-14822. ix, 514p. 1992. write for info. (3-540-55320-7); 98.00 (0-387-55320-7) Spr-Verlag.

Rozenberg, Grzegorz, jt. ed. see Deikert, Volker.

Rozenberg, Grzegorz, jt. auth. see Herman, G. T.

Rozenberg, Grzegorz, jt. ed. see Jensen, K.

Rozenberg, Grzegorz, et al, eds. Advances in Petri Nets, 1989. (Lecture Notes in Computer Science Ser.: Vol. 424). vi, 524p. 1990. pap. 48.60 (0-387-52494-0) Spr-Verlag.

— Advances in Petri Nets, 1990. (Lecture Notes in Computer Science Ser.: Vol. 483). vi, 515p. 1991. pap. 51.00 (0-387-53863-1) Spr-Verlag.

— Advances in Petri Nets, 1991. (Lecture Notes in Computer Science Ser.: Vol. 524). viii, 572p. 1991. pap. 52.00 (0-387-54398-8) Spr-Verlag.

— Advances in Petri Nets, 1992. (Lecture Notes in Computer Science Ser.: Vol. 609). viii, 472p. 1992. pap. 61.00 (0-387-55610-9) Spr-Verlag.

Rozenberg, M. B. English-Russian Dictionary of Refrigeration & Low Temperature Technology. 2nd rev. ed. 1979. 199.00 (0-08-024737-7, Pub. by Pergamon Repr UK) Franklin.

***Rozenblit, Jerzy & Buchenrieder, Klaus, eds.** Computer Aided Software Hardware Engineering. LC 94-22820. 1994. write for info. (0-7803-1049-7) Inst Electrical.

Rozenblit, Marsha L. The Jews of Vienna, 1867-1914: Assimilation & Identity. LC 83-17885. (Modern Jewish History Ser.). 368p. 1984. 59.50 (0-87395-844-6); pap. 19.95 (0-87395-845-4) State U NY Pr.

Rozencvejg, V. Ju. Linguistic Interference & Convergent Change. (Janua Linguarum, Series Minor: No. 99). (Illus.). 58p. 1976. pap. text ed. 64.60 (90-279-3414-2) Mouton.

Rozencweig, M., jt. ed. see Cortes Funes, H.

Rozencweig, Marcel, jt. ed. see Muggia, Franco M.

***Rozencweig, Marcel, et al, eds.** New Cancer Drugs: Mitoxantrone & Bisantrene. LC 82-42744. (Monograph Series of the European Organization for Research on Treatment of Cancer: No. 12). (Illus.). Date not set. reprint ed. pap. 59.90 (0-7837-9553-X, 2060302) Bks Demand.

Rozens, Aleksandrs. Environmental Destruction. LC 93-41213. (When Disaster Strikes Ser.). (Illus.). 64p. (J). (gr. 5-8). 1994. lib. bdg. 15.98 (0-8050-3098-0) TFC Bks NY.

— Floods. (When Disaster Strikes Ser.). (Illus.). 64p. (J). (gr. 5-8). 1994. lib. bdg. 15.98 (0-8050-3097-2) TFC Bks NY.

— Wayne Gretzky. LC 93-18132. (J). 1993. 15.93 (0-86592-119-9); 11.95 (0-685-66586-0) Rourke Enter.

Rozental, D. E. Dictionary of the Difficulties of the Russian Language. 3rd ed. 704p. (RUS.). 1984. 35.00 (0-8288-2006-6, M15156) Fr & Eur.

Rozental, D. E. & Telenkova, M. Dictionary of Difficulties of the Russian Language. 704p. (C). 1984. 70.00 (0-317-92412-5, Pub. by Collets UK) Pro-Am Music.

Rozental, I. L., jt. auth. see Nikitin, Yu. P.

Rozental, S., ed. Niels Bohr: His Life & Work As Seen by His Friends & Colleagues. (North-Holland Personal Library). 356p. 1985. reprint ed. pap. 32.50 (0-444-86977-8, North Holland) Elsevier.

Rozenzweig. Der Stern der Erlosung. 1977. lib. bdg. 134.50 (90-247-1766-3) Kluwer Ac.

Rozett, Martha T. The Doctrine of Election & the Emergence of Elizabethan Tragedy. LC 84-42565. 248p. 1984. 49.50 (0-691-06615-9) Princeton U Pr.

— Talking Back to Shakespeare. LC 93-45821. 1994. write for info. (0-87413-529-X) U Delaware Pr.

R

Rozewicz. The Card Index. 11.95 (*0-7145-0061-5*); pap. 6.95 (*0-7145-0062-3*) M Boyars Pubs.

Rozewicz, T. Urban Networks in Russia, 1750-1800 & Premodern Periodization. LC 75-3472. 344p. 1975. text ed. 49.50x (*0-691-09364-4*) Princeton U Pr.

Rozewicz, Tadeusz. Mariage Blanc & the Hunger Artist Departs: Two Plays. Czerniawski, Adam, tr. LC 82-12859. 112p. 1983. 13.50 (*0-7145-2775-0*); pap. 7.95 (*0-7145-2776-9*) M Boyars Pubs.

— The Survivor & Other Poems. Krynski, Magnus J. & Maguire, Robert A., trs. LC 76-3034. (Lockert Library of Poetry in Translation). 180p. reprint ed. pap. 51.30 (*0-8357-4202-4*, 2036981) Bks Demand.

— Unease. Contoski, Victor, tr. 160p. 1980. pap. 5.00 (*0-89823-013-6*) New Rivers Pr.

Rozgonyi, George A., ed. see Topical Conference on Characterization Techniques for Semi-Conductor Materials & Devices Staff.

***Rozgonyi, Jay.** Preston Sturges & His Work: Critical Analyses of Fourteen Films. 208p. 1995. lib. bdg. 34.50x (*0-89950-985-1*) McFarland & Co.

Rozgonyi, Tamas, jt. auth. see Tannenbaum, Arnold S.

Rozgonyi, Tamas, jt. ed. see Tannenbaum, Arnold S.

Rozgonyi, Tibor G. & Golosinski, Tad S., eds. Continuous Surface Mining: Equipment, Operation & Design. (Proceedings of the 2nd International Symposium on Continuous Surface Mining, Austin Texas, October 2-5, 1988 Ser.). (Illus.). x, 225p. 1988. lib. bdg. 120.00 (*90-6191-858-8*, Pub. by A A Balkema NE) Ashgate Pub Co.

Rozhanskii, L. & Colin, A. Static Electromagnetic Frequency Changers. LC 62-22071. (International Series of Monographs on Electronics & Instrumentation: Vol. 17). 1963. 57.00 (*0-08-010189-5*, Pub. by Pergamon Repr UK) Franklin.

Rozhkov, Anatoly S. & Mikhailova, Tatyana A. The Effect of Fluorine-Containing Emissions on Conifers. LC 92-21023. (Illus.). 200p. 1993. 145.00 (*0-387-54735-5*) Spr-Verlag.

Rozich. Design & Operation - Activated Sludge Processes Using Respirometry. 1992. 69.95 (*0-87371-449-0*, TD756) Lewis Pubs.

Rozier, John, ed. The Granite Farm Letters: The Civil War Correspondence of Edgeworth & Sallie Bird. LC 88-13978. 368p. 1988. 29.95 (*0-8203-1042-5*) U of Ga Pr.

Roziere, Gael. Artist's Alphabet: A Child's Activity Book for Language, Movement & Painting. 28p. (J). (ps-4). 1988. student ed, pap. 5.95 (*0-9619004-2-3*) M Press NM.

Rozin, Elisabeth. The Primal Cheeseburger. LC 94-14554. 144p. 1994. pap. 8.95 (*0-14-017843-0*, Penguin Bks) Viking Penguin.

Rozin, Elizabeth. Blue Corn & Chocolate. 1992. 25.00 (*0-394-58308-6*) Knopf.

— Ethnic Cuisine: How to Create the Authentic Flavors of 30 International Cuisines. rev. ed. 288p. 1992. pap. 11.95 (*0-14-046931-1*, Penguin Bks) Viking Penguin.

Rozin, Paul, jt. auth. see Jonides, John.

***Roziner, Felix.** A Certain Finkelmeyer. Heim, Michael H., tr. 362p. Date not set. pap. 16.95 (*0-8101-1263-9*) Northwestern U Pr.

— Vesennie Muzhskie Igry. LC 84-28882. 205p. 1985. pap. 8.50 (*0-938920-48-0*) Hermitage.

Rozinier, Felix, et al. The Times of Turmoil: A Collection of Stories. Yanishevsky, Arkady, tr. LC 93-40496. (Illus.). 176p. (Orig.). 1994. pap. 12.00 (*1-55779-065-5*) Hermitage.

Rozkosny, R. A Biosystematic Study of the European Stratiomyidae (Diptera) 1982. lib. bdg. 172.50 (*90-6193-132-0*) Kluwer Ac.

— The Sciomyzidae (Diptera) of Fennoscandia & Denmark. (Fauna Entomologica Scandinavica Ser.: No. 14). (Illus.). 224p. 1984. text ed. 47.00 (*90-04-07592-5*) Lubrecht & Cramer.

— The Stratiomyoidea (Diptera) of Fennoscandia & Denmark. (Fauna Entomologica Scandinavica Ser.: No. 1). (Illus.). 151p. 1973. pap. 25.50 (*87-87491-00-1*) Lubrecht & Cramer.

Rozmajzl, Michon & Boyer-White, Rene. Music Fundamentals, Methods & Materials for the Elementary Classroom Teacher. 352p. (Orig.). (C). 1990. pap. text ed. 44.95 (*0-8013-0320-6*, 78088) Longman.

— Music Fundamentals, Methods & Materials for the Elementary Classroom Teacher. 2nd ed. LC 95-9934. (C). 1996. pap. text ed. 44.95 (*0-8013-1580-8*) Longman.

***Rozman, Deborah.** Deditating with Children: The Art of Concentration & Centering. rev. ed. 160p. 1994. lib. bdg. 37.00x (*0-8095-5813-0*) Borgo Pr.

— Meditating with Children: The Art of Concentration & Centering. rev. ed. (Illus.). 154p. 1995. 14.95 (*1-879052-24-5*) Planetary Pubns.

— Meditation for Children. 1994. pap. 9.95 (*1-879052-23-7*) Planetary Pubns.

— Meditation for Children: Pathways to Happiness, Harmony, Creativity & Fun for the Family. 152p. 1991. reprint ed. lib. bdg. 27.00x (*0-8095-5806-8*) Borgo Pr.

Rozman, Deborah, ed. see Childre, Doc L.

Rozman, Deborah, ed. see Hills, Christopher.

Rozman, Deborah, jt. auth. see Hills, Christopher.

Rozman, Deborah, ed. see Hills, Christopher.

Rozman, Deborah, jt. auth. see Paddison, Sara.

Rozman, Gilbert. The Chinese Debate about Soviet Socialism, 1978-1985. 416p. 1987. text ed. 62.50 (*0-691-09429-2*) Princeton U Pr.

— Japan's Response to the Gorbachev Era, 1985-1991: A Rising Superpower Views a Declining One. 370p. 1992. text ed. 35.00 (*0-691-03189-4*) Princeton U Pr.

— A Mirror for Socialism: Soviet Criticisms of China. LC 84-42902. 260p. 1985. text ed. 45.00 (*0-691-09411-X*) Princeton U Pr.

— A Mirror for Socialism: Soviet Criticisms of China. LC 84-42902. Date not set. reprint ed. pap. 87.50 (*0-7837-9436-3*, 2060178) Bks Demand.

— Urban Networks in Russia, 1750-1800, & Premodern Periodization. LC 75-3472. 349p. reprint ed. pap. 99.50 (*0-8357-6932-1*, 2037991) Bks Demand.

Rozman, Gilbert, ed. The East Asian Region: Confucian Heritage & Its Modern Adaptation. 231p. 1991. text ed. 39.50 (*0-691-05597-1*) Princeton U Pr.

— The East Asian Region: Confucian Heritage & Its Modern Adaptation. 245p. 1993. pap. text ed. 16.95 (*0-691-02485-5*) Princeton U Pr.

— The Modernization of China. (Illus.). 1982. text ed. 29.95 (*0-02-927480-X*); pap. 16.95 (*0-02-927360-9*) Free Pr.

— Soviet Studies of Premodern China: Assessments of Recent Scholarship. (Michigan Monographs in Chinese Studies: No. 50). 247p. (C). 1984. 17.50 (*0-89264-052-9*); pap. 9.00 (*0-89264-053-7*) Ctr Chinese Studies.

Rozman, Gilbert, jt. ed. see Jansen, Marius B.

Rozman, Gilbert, et al, eds. Dismantling Communism: Common Causes & Regional Variations. LC 92-15892. 304p. 1992. text ed. 38.00 (*0-943875-35-8*) Johns Hopkins.

Rozmus, W. & Tuszynski, J. A., eds. Nonlinear & Chaotic Phenomena in Plasmas, Solids & Fluids, Edmonton, Alberta, Canada, July 16-27, 1990. 640p. 1991. text ed. 118.00 (*981-02-0386-1*) World Scientific Pub.

***Rozmyn, Mia.** Freedom in Design. Reinstatler, Laura, ed. (Illus.). 90p. (Orig.). 1995. pap. 19.95 (*1-56477-102-4*) That Patchwork.

Rozner, Barry, jt. auth. see Sandberg, Ryne.

***Rozo-Moorhouse, Teresa, ed. & comp.** Diosas en Bronce: Poesia Contemporanea de la Mujer. 400p. 1995. pap. write for info. (*1-886480-11-7*) Edici Latidos.

***Rozo, Teresa & Debicki, Andrew.** Paisajes y Recuerdos - Snapshots & Recollections. Harpstrite, Pat & Moorhouse, David M., trs. 188p. (Orig.). (ENG & SPA.). 1994. pap. 15.95 (*1-886480-00-1*) Edici Latidos.

Rozova, A. V. Biostratigraphic Zoning Trilobites of the Upper Cambrian & Lower Ordovician of the Northwestern Siberian Platform. Chakravarthy, R., tr. 279p. (ENG.). (C). 1984. text ed. 95.00 (*90-6191-434-5*, Pub. by A A Balkema NE) Ashgate Pub Co.

Rozovskii, B. L. Stochastic Evolution Systems: Linear Theory & Applications to Non-Linear Filtering. (Mathematics & Its Applications, Soviet Ser.). (C). 1990. lib. bdg. 144.00 (*0-7923-0037-8*) Kluwer Ac.

Rozovskii, B. L. & Sowers, R. B., eds. Stochastic Partial Differential Equations & Their Applications: Proceedings of IFIP WG 7-1 International Conference, June 6-8, 1991, University of North Carolina at Charlotte, NC. (Lecture Notes in Control & Information Sciences Ser.: Vol. 176). (Illus.). iv, 251p. 1992. pap. 69.00 (*0-387-55292-8*) Spr-Verlag.

Rozovsky. AIDS & Canadian Law. 160p. 1992. boxed 50.00 (*0-409-88935-0*) Butterworth Legal Pubs.

— Canadian Dental Law. 152p. 1987. 55.00 (*0-409-86335-1*) Butterworth Legal Pubs.

— The Canadian Law of Consent to Treatment. 176p. 1989. 53.00 (*0-409-80630-7*) Butterworth Legal Pubs.

Rozovsky, Fay A. Consent Set. 2nd ed. 1990. 125.00 (*0-316-76059-5*) Little.

— Consent to Treatment: A Practical Guide. LC 83-81948. 669p. 1984. 80.00 (*0-316-76073-0*) Little.

— Consent to Treatment: A Practical Guide. 2nd ed. 750p. 1989. 125.00 (*0-316-76057-9*) Little.

Rozovsky, Fay A., jt. auth. see Rozovsky, Lorne A.

Rozovsky, Fay A., et al. Medical Staff Credentialing: A Practical Guide. LC 93-33354. (Illus.). 132p. 1993. 49.00 (*1-55648-112-8*, 145102) AHPI.

Rozovsky, Lorne A. & Rozovsky, Fay A. Canadian Health Information: A Legal & Risk Management Guide. 2nd ed. 216p. text ed. 45.95 (*0-409-90618-2*) Butterworth Legal Pubs.

Rozowski, M. Proceedings of the Fifth Conference on Carbon, Vol. 1: Penn State University, University Park, Pennsylvania. LC 55-7933. 1962. 269.00 (*0-08-009707-3*, Pub. by Pergamon Repr UK) Franklin.

Rozsa, Gyorgy. Scientific Information & Society. 1973. bds. 29.25 (*90-279-7181-1*) Mouton.

Rozsa, K., jt. ed. see Salanki, J.

Rozsa, K. S., ed. Neurotransmitters in Invertebrates: Proceedings of a Satellite Symposium of the 28th International Congress of Physiological Sciences, Veszprem, Hungary, 1980. LC 80-42251. (Advances in Physiological Sciences Ser.: Vol. 22). (Illus.). 400p. 1981. 249.00 (*0-08-027343-2*, Pub. by Pergamon Repr UK) Franklin.

Rozsa, Mike. Crossing the Line: The Final Conspiracy. LC 92-62015. 126p. (Orig.). 1994. pap. 8.95 (*1-56002-229-9*, Univ Edtns) Aegina Pr.

Rozsa, P., jt. ed. see Greenspan, Donald.

Rozsa, S. Nuclear Measurements in Industry. (Studies in Physical & Theoretical Chemistry: No. 61). 310p. 1990. 141.00 (*0-444-98873-4*) Elsevier.

***Rozsa, Sandor.** Nuclear Measurements in Industry. 310p. (C). 1989. 150.00x (*963-05-5219-1*, Pub. by Akad Kiado HU) St Mut.

Rozvany, George I. Optimal Design of Flexural Systems. 200p. 1976. 126.00 (*0-08-020517-8*, Pub. by Pergamon Repr UK) Franklin.

— Structural Design Via Optimality Criteria: The Prager Approach to Structural Optimization. (C). 1989. lib. bdg. 175.50 (*90-247-3613-7*) Kluwer Ac.

Rozvany, George I., ed. Optimization of Large Structural Systems: Proceedings of the NATO - DFG Advanced Study Institute, Berchtesgaden, Germany, 23 September-4 October 1991, 2 vols., 1. LC 92-43799. (NATO Advanced Science Institutes Series: Mathematical & Physical Sciences: No. 231). 1244p. (C). 1993. lib. bdg. write for info. (*0-7923-2128-6*) Kluwer Ac.

— Optimization of Large Structural Systems: Proceedings of the NATO - DFG Advanced Study Institute, Berchtesgaden, Germany, 23 September-4 October 1991, 2 vols., 2. LC 92-43799. (NATO Advanced Science Institutes Series: Mathematical & Physical Sciences: No. 231). 1244p. (C). 1993. lib. bdg. write for info. (*0-7923-2129-4*) Kluwer Ac.

— Optimization of Large Structural Systems: Proceedings of the NATO - DFG Advanced Study Institute, Berchtesgaden, Germany, 23 September-4 October 1991, 2 vols., Set. LC 92-43799. (NATO Advanced Science Institutes Series: Mathematical & Physical Sciences: No. 231). 1244p. (C). 1993. lib. bdg. 390.00 (*0-7923-2130-8*) Kluwer Ac.

— Shape & Layout Optimization of Structural Systems & Optimality Criteria Methods. (CISM International Centre for Mechanical Sciences Ser.: Vol. 325). (Illus.). vi, 496p. 1992. pap. 99.00 (*0-387-82363-8*) Spr-Verlag.

Rozvany, George I. & Karihaloo, B. L., eds. Structural Optimization. (C). 1988. lib. bdg. 162.00 (*90-247-3771-0*) Kluwer Ac.

Rozwaski, Chaim Z. Jewish Meditations on the Meaning of Death. LC 93-31385. 232p. 1994. 30.00 (*1-56821-081-7*) Aronson.

Rozwenc, Edwin C. Agricultural Policies in Vermont, 1860-1945. 190p. 1981. pap. 9.50 (*0-934720-24-X*) VT Hist Soc.

— Cooperatives Come to America: The History of the Protective Union Store Movement 1845-1867. LC 74-31009. (American Utopian Adventure Ser.). (Illus.). viii, 151p. 1975. reprint ed. lib. bdg. 29.50 (*0-87991-004-6*) Porcupine Pr.

Rozwenc, Edwin C., ed. Causes of the American Civil War. 2nd ed. (Problems in American Civilization Ser.). (C). 1972. pap. text ed. 8.50 (*0-669-82727-4*) Heath.

— The New Deal: Revolution or Evolution? rev. ed. (Problems in American Civilization Ser.). 113p. (C). 1959. pap. text ed. 8.50 (*0-669-23838-4*) Heath.

— Reconstruction in the South. 2nd ed. (Problems in American Civilization Ser.). 320p. (C). 1973. pap. text ed. 8.50 (*0-669-82735-5*) Heath.

Rozycki, Edward G., jt. auth. see Clabaug, Gary K.

Rozycki, Tony. The Saint Bonaventure's Day Affair & 7 More Weird Stories. 104p. (Orig.). 1990. pap. text ed. 10.00 (*0-685-29065-4*) Black Riv MN.

***Rozycki, William.** Mongol Elements in Manchu. LC 94-65580. (Uralic & Altaic Ser.: Vol. 157). 255p. 1994. 29.90 (*0-933070-31-4*) Ind U Res Inst.

Rozycki, William & Dwyer, Rex. A Reverse Index of Manchu. Sinor, Denis, ed. LC 81-52901. (Uralic & Altaic Ser.: Vol. 140). vi, 189p. (Orig.). 1981. pap. text ed. 14.00 (*0-933070-08-X*) Res Inst Inner Asian Studies.

***Rozzell, J. David & Wagner, Fritz, eds.** Bioanalytic Production of Amino Acids & Derivatives. 1993. text ed. 79.95 (*0-471-03717-6*) Wiley.

Rozzi, Dan, jt. auth. see Rozzi, Patty.

Rozzi, Patty & Rozzi, Dan. Waltz with Evil. 288p. 1991. mass mkt. 4.50 (*0-8217-3395-8*) Zebra.

Rozzo, Kay D. Sweet Strings of Love. LC 94-18538. (Chloe Celeste Chronicles Ser.: Vol. 3). 1994. pap. 11.95 (*0-8163-1221-4*) Pacific Pr Pub Assn.

Rozzoli, R., ed. see Stringer, T.

RP-11 Working Group Staff. Glossary of Terms & Definitions Related to Contamination Control. 16p. 1985. pap. 50.00 (*0-915414-88-0*) Inst Environ Sci.

Rqaz, Joseph. Ethics in the Public Domain: Essays in the Morality of Law & Politics. 376p. 1994. 60.00 (*0-19-825837-2*) OUP.

RRN Inc. Staff. Kjoi-Joi of Dining: A Guide to Fine Dining in Greater Los Angeles. Klein, Alexander S., III, ed. 1989. per. 9.95 (*0-685-29110-3*) RRN Inc.

— Restaurant Guide for Fort Worth-Dallas (Spring 1990) Niskanen, Anthony S. & Klein, Alexander S., III, eds. (Illus.). 80p. (Orig.). 1990. pap. write for info. (*0-9624223-3-9*) RRN Inc.

— Restaurant Guide for Los Angeles & Orange County (Summer 1990) Niskanen, Anthony S. & Klein, Alexander S., III, eds. (Illus.). 80p. (Orig.). 1990. pap. 4.95 (*0-9624223-4-7*) RRN Inc.

— Restaurant Guide for Los Angeles & Orange County (Winter 1989) Niskanen, Anthony S. & Klein, Alexander S., III, eds. (Illus.). 80p. (Orig.). 1989. pap. 4.95 (*0-9624223-0-4*) RRN Inc.

— Restaurant Guide for San Diego & Palm Springs. Niskanen, Anthony S. & Klein, Alexander S., III, eds. (Illus.). 80p. (Orig.). 1990. pap. write for info. (*0-9624223-1-2*) RRN Inc.

***Rt-Manheimer, Aron H., ed.** The Jewish Condition: Essays on Contemporary Judaism Honoring Rabbi Alexander M. Schindler. (Orig.). 1995. 25.00 (*0-8074-0535-3*, 160004) UAHC.

RTKL Staff. RTKL Associates. (Process Architecture Ser.: No. 111). (Illus.). 155p. 1993. pap. 46.95 (*4-89331-111-5*, Pub. by Process Archit JA) Bks Nippan.

Ru, Yi-Ling. The Family Novel: Toward a Generic Definition. LC 91-27580. (American University Studies: General Literature: Ser. XIX, Vol. 28). 221p. (C). 1992. text ed. 40.95 (*0-8204-1567-7*) P Lang Pubs.

Rua, Pedro J. Bolivar ante Marx y Otros Ensayos. (Norte Ser.). 148p. 1978. pap. 5.95 (*0-940238-05-5*) Ediciones Huracan.

Rua, Pedro J., ed. Introduccion a las Ciencias Sociales. LC 81-69790. 432p. 1982. reprint ed. pap. 11.50 (*0-940238-64-0*) Ediciones Huracan.

Ruachbauer, Otto, ed. Ancestral Voices: The Big House in Anglo-Irish Literature. (Anglistische und Amerikanische Texte und Studien Ser.: Vol. 6). 307p. 1992. lib. bdg. 60.00 (*0-685-66950-5*, Pub. by Georg Olms GW) Lubrecht & Cramer.

***Ruan, D., et al.** Fuzzy Logic & Intelligent Technologies in Nuclear Science: Proceedings of the First International FLINS Workshop, Mol, Belgium, September 14-16, 1994. 304p. 1994. text ed. 99.00 (*981-02-2003-0*) World Scientific Pub.

***Ruan, Da, ed.** Fuzzy Set Theory & Advanced Mathematical Applications. (International Series in Intelligent-Technologies). 344p. (C). 1995. lib. bdg. 110.00 (*0-7923-9586-7*) Kluwer Ac.

Ruan, F. F. & Matsumura, M. Sex in China: Studies in Sexology in Chinese Culture. (Perspectives in Sexuality Ser.). (Illus.). 230p. 1991. 34.50 (*0-306-43860-7*, Plenum Pr) Plenum.

Ruan Jin Zhao. Chinese Medicine - Its History, Origins & Modern Benefits: The Timely Art of Dictation. 1990. 12.95 (*0-87491-966-5*) Acropolis.

Ruan, Ming. Essays on the Character of the Communist Party of China. 188p. 1993. pap. text ed. 10.00 (*1-879771-08-X*) Global Pub NJ.

Ruane, Christine. Gender, Class, & the Professionalization of Russian City Teachers, 1860-1914. (Pitt Series in Russian & East European Studies). 272p. (C). 1994. 59.95 (*0-8229-3864-2*) U of Pittsburgh Pr.

Ruane, Ed, jt. auth. see Siegfried, Regina.

***Ruane, G.** La Eucaristia. (Greatest Healing Gifts Ser.: Vol. 1). 176p. (Orig.). (SPA.). 1995. pap. text ed. 8.95 (*1-885857-15-2*) Four Wnds Pubng.

Ruane, Gerald P. The Eucharist. (Greatest Healing Gifts Ser.). (Illus.). 120p. (Orig.). 1989. pap. 6.95 (*1-56237-003-0*) Sacred Hrt Pr.

— Healing & Your Emotional Life. (Healing Journey Ser.). (Illus.). 150p. (Orig.). 1986. pap. 5.95 (*1-56237-005-7*) Sacred Hrt Pr.

— Overcoming Obstacles to Healing. (Healing Journey Ser.). 146p. (Orig.). 1985. pap. 5.95 (*1-56237-004-9*) Sacred Hrt Pr.

Ruane, Gerald P. & Williams, Ruthann. Thank You for Hearing My Call: Living the Messages of Medjugorje. (Illus.). 194p. (Orig.). 1990. pap. 8.95 (*1-56237-002-2*) Sacred Hrt Pr.

Ruane, J. Boats, Boats, Boats. (My First Reader Ser.). (Illus.). 28p. (J). (ps-2). 1990. 10.50 (*0-516-05351-5*); pap. 3.95 (*0-516-45351-3*) Childrens.

Ruani, G., jt. auth. see Taliani, C.

Ruano, Argimiro. Etica Fundamental: Los Valores del Bien y del Mal. 174p. (C). 1991. pap. text ed. 10.00 (*1-881375-15-3*) Libreria Univ.

— Etica Profesional: Perspectiva Puetrorriquena. 101p. (C). 1986. pap. text ed. 10.00 (*1-881375-14-5*) Libreria Univ.

Ruano De La Haza, Jose M., ed. El Mundo del Teatro Espanol en Su Siglo de Oro. 450p. 1989. pap. 22.00 (*0-919473-87-3*, DH83, Pub. by Dovehouse CN) MRTS.

Ruano De La Haza, Jose M., ed. see Calderon De La Barca, Pedro.

Ruano De La Haza, Jose M., ed. see De Vega, Lope.

Ruardij, P., jt. ed. see Baretta, J. W.

Ruark, Gibbons. Keeping Company. LC 83-43. (Poetry & Fiction Ser.). 80p. 1983. text ed. 14.95 (*0-8018-3041-9*); pap. 9.95 (*0-8018-3042-7*) Johns Hopkins.

— Reeds. LC 78-90515. 57p. (Orig.). 1978. 5.95 (*0-89672-058-6*); pap. 2.95 (*0-89672-057-8*) Tex Tech Univ Pr.

— Rescue the Perishing. LC 90-47142. 64p. 1991. text ed. 14.95 (*0-8071-1667-X*); pap. 7.95 (*0-8071-1668-8*) La State U Pr.

Ruark, John, jt. auth. see Gonda, Thomas A.

Ruark, R. Use Enough Gun: On Hunting Big Game. (Illus.). 333p. 1992. 30.00 (*0-940143-67-4*) Safari Pr.

Ruark, Robert. The Honey Badger. 1994. reprint ed. lib. bdg. 39.95 (*1-56849-326-6*) Buccaneer Bks.

— Horn of the Hunter. (Illus.). 315p. 1987. 35.00 (*0-940143-09-7*) Safari Pr.

— Horn of the Hunter. 1994. reprint ed. lib. bdg. 39.95 (*1-56849-327-4*) Buccaneer Bks.

— I Didn't Know It Was Loaded. 1994. reprint ed. lib. bdg. 39.95 (*1-56849-328-2*) Buccaneer Bks.

— The Old Man & the Boy. LC 57-10425. 320p. 1957. 24.95 (*0-8050-0239-1*) H Holt & Co.

— The Old Man & the Boy. 320p. 1993. pap. 12.95 (*0-8050-2669-X*) H Holt & Co.

— The Old Man & the Boy. large type ed. LC 94-5764. 417p. 1994. reprint ed. 20.95 (*0-8161-5966-1*) Hall.

— The Old Man & the Boy. (Illus.). 316p. 1991. reprint ed. lib. bdg. 24.95 (*0-89966-818-6*) Buccaneer Bks.

— Old Man's Boy Grows Older. 300p. 1993. 22.00 (*0-8050-2980-X*); pap. 15.95 (*0-8050-2974-5*) H Holt & Co.

— The Old Man's Boy Grows Older. 256p. 1991. reprint ed. lib. bdg. 20.95 (*0-89966-817-8*) Buccaneer Bks.

— Poor No More. 1994. reprint ed. lib. bdg. 39.95 (*1-56849-329-0*) Buccaneer Bks.

— Something of Value. 574p. 1991. reprint ed. lib. bdg. 37.95x (*0-89966-816-X*) Buccaneer Bks.

— Uhuru. 1993. reprint ed. lib. bdg. 36.95 (*1-56849-025-9*) Buccaneer Bks.

Ruark, Robert C. Grenadine Etching: Her Life & Loves. 21.95 (*0-89190-954-0*, Am Repr) Amereon Ltd.

— Grenadine's Spawn. 20.95 (*0-89190-957-5*, Am Repr) Amereon Ltd.

— I Didn't Know It Was Loaded. 20.95 (*0-89190-958-3*, Am Repr) Amereon Ltd.

R

An Asterisk (*) at the beginning of an entry indicates that the title is appearing in BIP for the first time.

— Robert Ruark's Africa. McIntosh, Michael, ed. LC 90-86286. (Illus.). 256p. 1991. 35.00 (*0-924357-20-7*, 11420-A) Countrysport Pr.

Ruas, Charles, tr. see Assouline, Pierre.

Ruasse, Jean-Pierre. Lexique de Nutrition: Les Mots pour Comprendre. 45p. (FRE.). 1993. pap. 15.95 (*0-7859-5668-9*, 2908502100) Fr & Eur.

Rubach, Bonita K., ed. see Paul, Bernard A., et al.

Rubach, Jerzy. The Lexical Phonology of Slovak. LC 92-38746. (Phonology of the World's Languages Ser.). 1993. 60.00 (*0-19-824000-7*, Clarendon Pr) OUP.

Ruback, R. Barry & Weiner, Neil A., eds. Interpersonal Violent Behaviors: Social & Cultural Aspects. (Illus.). 200p. 1995. 31.95 (*0-8261-8510-X*) Springer Pub.

Ruback, Richard B., jt. auth. see Greenberg, M. S.

Rubadeau, Joan. Give Us This Day Our Daily Bread: Life as Spiritual Devotion. 1987. pap. 9.00 (*0-913105-20-1*) PAGL Pr.

— The Little Book of Good: Spiritual Values for Parents & Children. 58p. 1986. pap. 7.00 (*0-913105-19-8*) PAGL Pr.

Rubado, Clarence A. Problems of the City School Superintendent in the Field of Arithmetic. LC 71-177217. (Columbia University. Teachers College. Contributions to Education Ser.: No. 406). reprint ed. 37.50 (*0-404-55406-7*) AMS Pr.

Rubagumya, Casmir M., ed. Language in Education in Africa: Tanzanian Perspectives. (Multilingual Matters Ser.: No. 57). 154p. 1990. 74.00 (*1-85359-063-0*, Pub. by Multilingual Matters UK); pap. 25.95 (*1-85359-062-2*, Pub. by Multilingual Matters UK) Taylor & Francis.

— Teaching & Researching Language in African Classrooms. LC 93-29931. (Multilingual Matters Ser.: Vol. 98). 214p. 1994. 79.00 (*1-85359-200-5*, Pub. by Multilingual Matters UK); pap. 29.95 (*1-85359-199-8*, Pub. by Multilingual Matters UK) Taylor & Francis.

Rubajlo, V. L., et al, eds. Liquid-Phase Oxidation of Unsaturated Compounds. 227p. 1993. text ed. 83.00 (*1-56072-119-7*) Nova Sci Pubs.

Rubakov, V. R., et al. Quarks '90: Proceedings of the International Seminar. 572p. 1991. text ed. 151.00 (*981-02-0441-8*) World Scientific Pub.

Rubaltelli, F. F., ed. Metabolic Problems of the Newborn: Journal: Biology of the Neonate, Vol. 58, Suppl. 1, 1990. (Illus.). iv, 108p. 1990. pap. 32.00 (*3-8055-5304-8*) S Karger.

Rubaltelli, F. F. & Granati, B., eds. Neonatal Therapy: An Update: Proceedings, International Symposium, Padova, September 13-14, 1985. (International Congress Ser.: No. 723). 316p. 1987. 132.50 (*0-444-80809-4*, Excerpta Medica) Elsevier.

Rubano, Gregory L., jt. auth. see Anderson, Philip M.

Rubano, Judith. Culture & Behavior in Hawaii: An Annotated Bibliography. LC 79-634604. (Hawaii Ser.: No. 3). 159p. reprint ed. pap. 45.40 (*0-317-28956-X*, 2020445) Bks Demand.

Rubanov, L. I., jt. auth. see Fain, V. S.

Rubanowice, Robert J. Crisis in Consciousness: The Thought of Ernst Troeltsch. LC 81-16085. xxiii, 177p. 1983. 26.95 (*0-8130-0721-6*) U Press Fla.

Rubanyi, jt. ed. see Ryan.

Rubanyi, G. M. & Vanhoutte, P. M., eds. Endothelium-Derived Contracting Factors. (Illus.). x, 238p. 1990. 163.25 (*3-8055-5092-8*) S Karger.

— Endothelium-Derived Relaxing Factors. (Illus.). x, 336p. 1990. 225.75 (*3-8055-5091-X*) S Karger.

— Endothelium-Derived Relaxing Factors - Endothelium-Derived Contracting Factors. (Illus.). xvi, 550p. 1990. 350.50 (*3-8055-5197-5*) S Karger.

Rubanyi, Gabor M. Endothelin. (Clinical Physiology Series - An American Physiological Society Book). (Illus.). 304p. 1992. 70.00 (*0-19-506641-3*) OUP.

Rubanyi, Gabor M., ed. Cardiovascular Significance of Endothelium-Derived Vasoactive Factors. (Illus.). 384p. 1991. 85.00 (*0-87993-359-3*) Futura Pub.

— Mechanoreception by the Vascular Wall. LC 92-48862. 272p. 1993. 65.00 (*0-87993-547-2*) Futura Pub.

Rubanyi, Gabor M. & Vane, John, eds. Prostacyclin: New Perspectives for Basic Research & Novel Therapeutic Indications: Proceedings of the Symposium on Novel Perspectives in Prostacyclin Research, Vienna, Austria, 25th September 1991. LC 92-48229. (International Congress Ser.: No. 1004). 1992. write for info. (*0-444-89534-5*, Excerpta Medica) Elsevier.

Rubash, Joyce. Master Dictionary of Food & Wine. 1990. text ed. 29.95 (*0-442-23465-1*) Van Nos Reinhold.

Rubashow-Katznelson, Rachel, ed. The Plough Women: Records of the Pioneer Women of Palestine. LC 75-6441. (Rise of Jewish Nationalism & the Middle East Ser.). 306p. 1975. reprint ed. 27.50 (*0-88355-328-7*) Hyperion Conn.

Rubbi, C. Light Microscopy: Essential Data. LC 94-9543. (Essential Data Ser.). 1994. pap. text ed. 19.95 (*0-471-94270-7*) Wiley.

***Rubble Mound Structures Committee of the Waterway, Port, & Ocean Division of the American Society of Civil Engineers & Administracao do Porto de Sines, Sines, Portugal.** Reconstruction of the West Breakwater at Port Sines, Portugal. LC 94-30076. 1994. write for info. (*0-7844-0044-X*) Am Soc Civil Eng.

Rubbra, Benedict. Painting Children. LC 92-25386. (Illus.). 144p. 1993. 29.95 (*0-8230-3593-X*, Watsn-Guptill) Watsn-Guptill.

Rubbra, Edmund. Gustav Holst: Music Book Index. 48p. 1993. reprint ed. lib. bdg. 59.00 (*0-7812-9601-3*) Rprt Serv.

Rubeidheh, Tell. An Uruk Village in the Jebel Hamrin Iraq. Killick, ed. (Archaeological Reports Ser.: Vol. 2). 1989. pap. 75.00 (*0-85668-431-7*, Pub. by Aris & Phillips UK) David Brown.

Rubek, Erno. My Cube. 1999. pap. write for info. (*0-14-006250-5*, Penguin Bks) Viking Penguin.

Rubel, et al. Atlas of Diagnostic Radiology of Exotic Pets. 1991. text ed. 155.00 (*0-7216-3493-1*) Saunders.

Rubel, Arthur J., et al, eds. Susto: A Folk Illness. LC 84-214. (Comparative Studies of Health Systems & Medical Care: Vol. 12). (Illus.). 170p. 1985. 40.00 (*0-520-05196-3*) U CA Pr.

— Susto: A Folk Illness. (Comparative Studies of Health Systems & Medical Care: Vol. 12). (Illus.). 195p. 1991. reprint ed. pap. 14.00 (*0-520-07634-6*) U CA Pr.

Rubel, David. America's War of Independence: A Concise Illustrated History of the American Revolution. (Illus.). 48p. (Orig.). 1993. pap. 6.95 (*1-881889-39-4*) Silver Moon.

— Elvis Presely: The Rise of Rock & Roll. (YA). 1992. pap. 5.92 (*0-395-63566-7*) HM.

— Elvis Presley: The Rise of Rock & Roll. (New Directions Ser.). (Illus.). 96p. (YA). (gr. 7 up). 1991. lib. bdg. 15.40 (*1-878841-18-1*); pap. 5.95 (*1-56294-829-6*) Millbrook Pr.

— Fannie Lou Hamer: From Sharecropping to Politics. Gallin, Richard, ed. (History of the Civil Rights Movement Ser.). (Illus.). 128p. (J). (gr. 5 up). 1990. lib. bdg. 12.95 (*0-382-09923-0*); pap. 7.95 (*0-382-24061-8*) Silver Burdett Pr.

— How to Drive an Indy Race Car. (Masters of Motion Ser.). (Illus.). 48p. (Orig.). (J). (gr. 3 up). 1992. pap. 9.95 (*1-56261-062-7*) John Muir.

— The Scholastic Encyclopedia of the Presidents & Their Times. LC 93-11810. (Illus.). 224p. (J). (gr. 4 up). 1994. 16.95 (*0-590-49366-3*, Scholastic Ref) Scholastic Inc.

— Scholastic Timelines: The United States in the 20th Century. LC 94-45702. (J). 1995. write for info. (*0-590-27134-2*); pap. write for info. (*0-590-27135-0*, Scholastic Ref) Scholastic Inc.

— Science. LC 94-46529. (Kid's Encyclopedia Ser.). (Illus.). (J). 1995. write for info. (*0-590-49367-1*, Scholastic Ref); write for info. (*0-590-49368-X*) Scholastic Inc.

Rubel, Edwin W., jt. ed. see Werner, Lynne A.

Rubel, Gene, ed. see Wiseman, Edward.

Rubel, Malcolm C. FoxPro 2.0 Power Tools. 1991. pap. 54.95 (*0-679-79061-6*) Random.

Rubel, Mary. Double Happiness, Getting More from Chinese Popular Art. (Illus.). 172p. (Orig.). 1981. pap. 4.98 (*0-9609154-0-0*) Magaru Enterprises.

Rubel, Maximilien. Rubel on Karl Marx: Five Essays. O'Malley, Joseph & Algozin, Keith, eds. LC 80-21734. 272p. 1981. 59.95 (*0-521-23839-0*) Cambridge U Pr.

Rubel, Maximilien & Crump, John, eds. Non-Market Socialism in the Nineteenth & Twentieth Centuries. LC 86-29847. 176p. 1987. text ed. 45.00 (*0-312-00524-5*) St Martin.

Rubel, Nicole. Conga Crocodile. LC 92-31856. (J). 1993. 14.95 (*0-395-58773-5*) HM.

— Cyrano the Bear. LC 94-25902. 32p. (J). 1995. 14.99 (*0-8037-1444-0*); lib. bdg. 14.89 (*0-8037-1445-9*) Dial Bks Young.

— Getting Married: A Guide for the Bride to Be. 1988. pap. 5.95 (*0-312-01766-9*) St Martin.

— The Ghost Family Meets Its Match. LC 91-10815. (Illus.). 32p. (J). (ps-3). 1992. 14.00 (*0-8037-1093-3*); lib. bdg. 13.89 (*0-8037-1094-1*) Dial Bks Young.

— It Came from the Swamp. LC 87-24653. (Illus.). 32p. (J). (ps-3). 1988. lib. bdg. 10.89 (*0-8037-0515-8*) Dial Bks Young.

— It Came from the Swamp. LC 87-24653. (Illus.). 32p. (J). (ps-3). 1992. pap. 3.99 (*0-14-054541-7*, Puff Pied Piper) Puffin Bks.

Rubel, Paula, jt. auth. see Rosman, Abraham.

Rubel, Paula G., jt. auth. see Rosman, Abraham.

Rubel, Vere L. Poetic Diction in the English Renaissance from Skelton Through Spenser. (MLA Rev. Fund Ser.). 1941. 39.00 (*0-527-77600-9*) Periodicals Srv.

Rubeling, Albert W., Jr. How to Start & Operate Your Own Design Firm. LC 93-27503. 1994. text ed. 33.00 (*0-07-054222-8*) McGraw.

Rubelmann, Stephen. Encyclopedia of the AirBrush, Black White Retouching, Vol. 3. LC 81-67960. 108p. 1984. 23.50 (*0-88108-006-3*) Art Dir.

Rubelmann, Stephen D., ed. Encyclopedia of the Airbrush, Vol. 1. LC 81-67960. (Illus.). 96p. 1992. reprint ed. pap. text ed. 22.50 (*0-88108-100-0*) Art Dir.

Rubelmann, Steven. Encyclopedia of the Airbrush, 3 vols., 2. LC 81-67960. (Illus.). (C). 1982. 23.50 (*0-910158-76-2*) Art Dir.

— Encyclopedia of the Airbrush, , Set. LC 81-67960. (Illus.). (C). 1982. student ed 67.50 (*0-686-87028-X*) Art Dir.

Ruben. A Color Atlas of Contact Lenses & Prosthetics, No. 2. (Illus.). 1992. 59.10 (*0-7234-1761-X*) Mosby Yr Bk.

Ruben & Angstrom, M. Swedish-English Dictionary. (ENG & SWE.). 39.50 (*0-87557-082-8*, 082-8) Saphrograph.

Ruben, Ann. How I Grew Up to Be a Happy Child. 3.50 (*0-317-06079-1*) Women Are Wonderful.

Ruben, Ann M. The CAMM Program: Creating a Mature Marriage. 162p. (C). 1980. 29.95 (*0-9608400-0-1*) Women Are Wonderful.

— How I Grew up Feeling Some Day I Could Be President of the U. S. A. (Illus.). 40p. (Orig.). (J). (gr. 1-3). 1993. pap. 4.95 (*0-9608400-9-5*) Women Are Wonderful.

Ruben, Brent. Study Guide for Communication & Human Behavior. 96p. (C). 1993. spiral bd. 10.00 (*0-8403-9050-5*) Kendall-Hunt.

Ruben, Brent D. Communicating with Patients. 128p. (C). 1992. pap. text ed. 9.95 (*0-8403-7430-5*) Kendall-Hunt.

— Communication & Human Behavior. 3rd ed. 448p. (C). 1992. pap. text ed. write for info. (*0-13-155847-1*) P-H.

Ruben, Brent D., ed. Communication Yearbook, Vol. 2. 587p. 1978. 49.95 (*0-87855-282-0*) Transaction Pubs.

— Information & Behavior, Vol. 1. 614p. (C). 1985. text ed. 49.95 (*0-685-42644-0*) Transaction Pubs.

— Information & Behavior, Vol. 2. 600p. 1987. 49.95 (*0-88738-106-5*) Transaction Pubs.

— Quality in Higher Education. 300p. (C). 1994. 34.95 (*1-56000-190-9*) Transaction Pubs.

— Quality in Higher Education. 300p. (C). 1994. pap. 21.95 (*1-56000-795-8*) Transaction Pubs.

Ruben, Brent D. & Budd, Richard W., eds. Interdisciplinary Approaches to Human Communication. 2nd ed. 173p. 1979. pap. text ed. 16.95 (*0-8104-5125-5*) Transaction Pubs.

Ruben, Brent D. & Guttman, Nurit. Caregiver-Patient Communication: Readings. 288p. 1993. per. 36.95 (*0-8403-8368-1*) Kendall-Hunt.

Ruben, Brent D. & Lievrouw, Leah A., eds. Mediation, Information, & Communication. (Information & Behavior Ser.: Vol. 3). 496p. 1989. 49.95 (*0-88738-278-9*) Transaction Pubs.

Ruben, Brent D., jt. ed. see Budd, Richard W.

Ruben, Brent D., jt. auth. see Hunt, Gary T.

Ruben, Brent D., jt. auth. see Hunt, Todd.

Ruben, Brent D., jt. ed. see Schement, Jorge R.

Ruben, C. Montague, ed. Diagnostic Picture Tests in Ophthalmology. (Illus.). 128p. 1987. 14.95 (*0-8151-7447-0*, POP-1, Yr Bk Med Pubs) Mosby Yr Bk.

Ruben, David H. Explaining Explanation. 272p. 1990. 39.95 (*0-415-03269-5*, A4176) Routledge.

Ruben, David H., ed. Explanation. LC 92-33929. (Oxford Readings in Philosophy Ser.). 1993. 45.00 (*0-19-875129-X*); 14.95 (*0-19-875130-3*) OUP.

Ruben, David-Hillel. Metaphysics of the Social World. 189p. (C). 1985. text ed. 24.00 (*0-685-46216-1*) B&N Imports.

Ruben, Doug, jt. auth. see Osman, Marilyn.

Ruben, Douglas H. The Aging & Drug Effects: A Planning Manual for Medication & Alcohol Abuse Treatment of the Elderly. LC 89-43687. 224p. 1990. pap. 27.50x (*0-89950-472-8*) McFarland & Co.

— Avoidance Syndrome: Doing Things Out of Fear. 150p. (Orig.). (C). 1993. 22.50 (*0-87527-502-8*) Fireside Bks.

— Drug Abuse & the Elderly: An Annotated Bibliography. LC 83-20463. 269p. 1984. 25.00 (*0-8108-1677-6*) Scarecrow.

— Family Addiction: An Analytical Guide. LC 92-27787. (Reference Books on Family Issues: Vol. 21). 384p. 1992. 56.00 (*0-8153-0031-X*) Garland.

— No More Guilt: Ten Steps to a Shame-Free Life. LC 93-4340. 208p. (Orig.). 1993. pap. 12.95 (*0-938179-35-7*) Mills Sanderson.

— Progress in Assertiveness, Nineteen Seventy-Three to Nineteen Eighty-Three: An Analytical Bibliography. LC 85-1853. 336p. 1985. 32.50 (*0-8108-1793-4*) Scarecrow.

— Publicity for Mental Health Clinicians: Using TV, Radio, & Print Media to Enhance Your Public Image. LC 95-6249. (Illus.). 222p. (C). 1995. lib. bdg. 39.95 (*1-56024-953-6*) Haworth Pr.

Ruben, Douglas H., comp. Philosophy Journals & Serials: An Analytical Guide. LC 84-29021. (Annotated Bibliographies of Serials: A Subject Approach Ser.: No. 2). xx, 147p. 1985. text ed. 49.95 (*0-313-23958-4*, RPJ/, Greenwood Pr) Greenwood.

Ruben, Douglas H. & Delprato, Dennis J., eds. New Ideas in Therapy: Introduction to an Interdisciplinary Approach. LC 86-31922. (Contributions in Psychology Ser.: No. 10). (Illus.). 235p. 1987. text ed. 59.95 (*0-313-24845-1*, RNI/, Greenwood Pr) Greenwood.

Ruben, Douglas H. & Stout, Chris E., eds. Transitions: Handbook of Managed Care for Inpatient to Outpatient Treatment. LC 92-45144. 184p. 1993. text ed. 55.00 (*0-275-94064-0*, C4064, Praeger Pubs) Greenwood.

Ruben, Douglas H., jt. auth. see Macciomei, Nancy R.

Ruben, Douglas H., et al, eds. Current Advances in Inpatient Psychiatric Care: A Handbook. LC 92-49214. 384p. 1993. text ed. 79.50 (*0-313-28046-0*, RCP/, Greenwood Pr) Greenwood.

Ruben, Jay. Handbook of Accounting Practice. LC 92-16992. 1992. write for info. (*0-13-376112-6*) P-H.

Ruben, Laurens N. & Gershwin, M. Eric, eds. Immune Regulation: Evolutionary & Biological Significance. LC 82-9994. (Immunology Ser.: No. 17). 351p. reprint ed. pap. 100.10 (*0-7837-3356-9*, 2043314) Bks Demand.

Ruben, Margarete. Parent Guidance in the Nursery School. LC 60-8066. 72p. 1970. reprint ed. text ed. 25.00 (*0-8236-4000-0*); reprint ed. pap. text ed. 24.95 (*0-8236-8180-7*, 24000) Intl Univs Pr.

Ruben, Montague, ed. see Guillon, M.

Ruben, Montague, jt. auth. see Hamano, Hikaru.

Ruben, Nicholas E., jt. auth. see Werth, Jacques.

Ruben, Paul & Millili, Anthony T. Public Thinking: Public Speaking. 208p. (C). 1985. per. 27.95 (*0-8403-3522-9*) Kendall-Hunt.

Ruben, R. J., et al, eds. The Biology of Change in Otolaryngology: Proceedings of the Third ARO Midwinter Research Meeting, Clearwater Beach, FL, February 2-6, 1986. 416p. 1987. 147.25 (*0-444-80844-2*) Elsevier.

Ruben, Robert J., jt. ed. see Alberti, P. W.

Ruben, Robert J., jt. ed. see Alberti, Peter W.

Ruben, Robert J., et al, eds. Genetics of Hearing Impairment. LC 91-30021. (Annals Ser.: Vol. 630). 331p. 1992. pap. 122.00 (*0-89766-682-8*, RF292) NY Acad Sci.

Ruben, Samuel. Handbook of the Elements. 110p. 1985. pap. 10.95 (*0-87548-399-2*) Open Court.

— Necessity's Children: Memoirs of an Independent Inventor. LC 89-17290. (Illus.). 160p. 1990. 17.95 (*0-932576-75-3*) Breitenbush Bks.

Rubenberg, Cheryl, jt. ed. see Alnasrawi, Abbas.

Rubenberg, Cheryl A. Israel & the American National Interest: A Critical Examination. 464p. 1989. reprint ed. pap. 13.95 (*0-252-06074-1*) U of Ill Pr.

Rubenchik, A. & Witkowski, S., eds. Physics of Laser Plasma. (Handbook of Plasma Physics Ser.: No. 3). 600p. 1991. 228.50 (*0-444-87426-7*) Elsevier.

Rubenfein, Louisa, tr. see Ozawa, Ichiro.

Rubenfeld. Critical Thinking in Nursing: An Interactive Approach. 336p. 1995. write for info. (*0-397-55099-5*) Lippincott.

— Supertraders: Secrets & Successes of Wall Street's Best & Brightest. 1995. pap. text ed. 18.95 (*1-55738-810-5*) Probus Pub Co.

Rubenfeld, Alan. SuperTraders: Secrets & Successes of Wall Street's Best & Brightest. rev. ed. 225p. 1995. 17.95 (*1-55738-284-0*) Probus Pub Co.

Rubenfeld, Frank. The Peace Manual: A Guide to Personal-Political Integration. (Illus.). 85p. 1986. pap. 7.95 (*0-9616424-0-8*) Lion Lamb Pr.

Rubenfeld, Fred, jt. auth. see Smulkis, Michael.

Rubenfeld, Lester A., jt. auth. see Amazigo, John C.

Rubenking, Neil. Can Do DOS. 1993. pap. 12.95 (*1-56276-147-1*) Ziff-Davis.

— Can Do Windows. 1993. pap. 5.95 (*1-56276-163-3*) Ziff-Davis.

— Delphi Program for Dummies. 1995. pap. 19.99 (*1-56884-200-7*) IDG Bks.

— PC Magazine DOS Batch File Lab Notes. (Lab Notes Ser.). 1992. disk 29.95 (*1-56276-067-X*) Ziff-Davis.

Rubenking, Neil J. PC Magazine Guide to Turbo Pascal Techniques & Utilities. (Guide to...Ser.). (Orig.). 1991. disk, pap. 39.95 (*1-56276-010-6*) Ziff-Davis.

— PC Magazine Turbo Pascal 6.0 for Windows Techniques & Utilities. (Techniques & Utilities Ser.). (Illus.). 1100p. (Orig.). 1992. disk 39.95 (*1-56276-035-1*) Ziff-Davis.

Rubens, Alfred. A History of Jewish Costume. 221p. 1967. 55.00 (*0-317-61338-3*, Pub. by P Owen Ltd UK) Dufour.

— A History of Jewish Costume. rev. ed. 221p. 1973. reprint ed. text ed. 75.00 (*0-7206-0588-1*, Pub. by P Owen Ltd UK) Dufour.

***Rubens, Doris.** Bread & Rice. (American Autobiography Ser.). 235p. 1995. reprint ed. lib. bdg. 79.00 (*0-7812-8633-6*) Rprt Serv.

Rubens, Horatio S. Liberty: The Story of Cuba. LC 72-111732. (American Imperialism: Viewpoints of United States Foreign Policy, 1898-1941 Ser.). 1970. reprint ed. 26.95 (*0-405-02049-X*) Ayer.

— Liberty, the Story of Cuba. LC 79-107075. reprint ed. 21.50 (*0-404-00633-7*) AMS Pr.

Rubens, James J., jt. auth. see Mintz, Robert J.

Rubens, Jeff. The Bridge World Magazine - Swiss Match Challenge: Learn How to Bid & Play Like a Winner, & Have Fun Too! LC 92-74745. 240p. 1992. pap. 11.95 (*0-685-63269-5*) Lawrence & Leong Pub.

— The Secrets of Winning Bridge. 241p. 1981. reprint ed. pap. 5.95 (*0-486-24076-2*) Dover.

— Win at Poker. 218p. 1984. reprint ed. pap. 5.95 (*0-486-24626-4*) Dover.

Rubens, Peter P. Drawings of Rubens. Longstreet, Stephen, ed. (Master Draughtsman Ser.). (Illus.). (Orig.). 1964. pap. 4.95 (*0-87505-186-3*) Borden.

— Palazzi di Genova, 2 vols in 1. LC 68-21226. (Illus.). 1972. reprint ed. 66.95 (*0-405-08901-5*) Ayer.

— Pompa Introitus: Ferdinandi Austriaci Cum Antiverpiam Adventu Suo Bearet, 15 Kal. Maii Anno 1665. LC 68-21225. (Illus.). (LAT.). 1972. 71.95 (*0-405-08902-3*) Ayer.

— Rubens Drawings. 1989. pap. 3.95 (*0-486-25963-3*) Dover.

Rubens, Philip. Science & Technical Writing: A Manual of Style. LC 91-36422. 544p. 1994. pap. 19.95 (*0-8050-3091-3*) H Holt & Co.

Rubens, Philip, ed. Science & Technical Writing: A Manual of Style. 512p. 1992. 40.00 (*0-8050-1831-X*) H Holt & Co.

***Rubens, R. D., ed.** Bisphosphonates & Metastatic Bone Disease. (Illus.). 86p. 1994. pap. text ed. 25.00 (*1-85070-643-3*) Prthnon Pub.

Rubens, R. D., jt. ed. see Coleman, R.

Rubens, Raymond & Goldner, Harold M. Pennsylvania Arbitration Guide. 388p. 1992. text ed. 52.50 (*0-317-03825-7*) Bisel Co.

***Rubenson, David, et al.** Marching to Different Drummers: Evolution of the Army's Environmental Program. LC 94-28610. 1994. write for info. (*0-8330-1564-8*, MR453A) Rand Corp.

Rubenson, Sven. The Survival of Ethiopian Independence. LC 78-1367. (Illus.). 437p. 1978. 54.50 (*0-8419-0374-3*, Africana); pap. 35.00 (*0-8419-0375-1*, Africana) Holmes & Meier.

Rubenstein. Lecture Notes on Clinical Medicine. 4th ed. 1991. pap. 32.95 (*0-632-02780-0*) Blackwell Sci.

Rubenstein, ed. see McMurtry, Larry.

Rubenstein, Albert H. Technology Management in Decentralized Firm. (Engineering Management Ser.). 476p. 1989. text ed. 74.95 (*0-471-61024-0*) Wiley.

Rubenstein, Albert H. & Schwartzel, Heinz, eds. Intelligent Workstations for Professionals: Proceedings of a Joint Symposium, Siemens AG, Northwestern University, March 1992. LC 93-9853. 1993. Alk. paper. write for info. (*0-387-56546-9*) Spr-Verlag.

Rubenstein, Ben, jt. ed. see Levitt, Morton.

Rubenstein, Bruce A. & Ziewacz, Lawrence E. Michigan: A History of the Great Lakes State. 2nd rev. ed. (Illus.). 282p. (Orig.). (C). 1995. pap. text ed. 21.95 (*0-88295-919-0*) Harlan Davidson.

— Payoffs in the Cloakroom: The Greening of the Michigan Legislature, 1938-1946. LC 94-48041. 1995. 28.00 (*0-87013-387-X*) Mich St U Pr.

— Three Bullets Sealed His Lips. (Illus.). 200p. 1987. pap. 15.95 (*0-87013-252-0*) Mich St U Pr.

Rubenstein, Carol. The Honey Tree Song: Poems & Chants of Sarawak Dayaks. LC 84-10374. (Illus.). xxiv, 350p. 1985. 39.95 (*0-8214-0413-X*) Ohio U Pr.

R

Rubenstein, Charles F. Autocad: The Drawing Tool. 1992. teacher ed 20.00 (0-8273-4887-8) Delmar.
— AutoCAD Command Practice Workbook. 60p. 1993. 15.95 (0-8273-6034-7) Delmar.
Rubenstein, Charlie. AutoCAD: The Drawing Tool. 384p. 1992. pap. 28.95 (0-8273-4885-1) Delmar.
Rubenstein, Charlotte S. American Women Artists: From Early Indian Times to the Present. (Illus.). 608p. 1982. pap. 15.95 (0-380-61101-5) Avon.
Rubenstein, Daniel B. Environmental Accounting for the Sustainable Corporation: Strategies & Techniques. LC 93-50066. 224p. 1994. text ed. 55.00 (0-89930-866-X, Quorum Bks) Greenwood.
Rubenstein, Daniel I. & Wrangham, Richard W., eds. Ecological Aspects of Social Evolution: Birds & Mammals. (Illus.). 512p. 1986. pap. text ed. 35.00 (0-691-08440-8) Princeton U Pr.
Rubenstein, Diane. What's Left? The Ecole Normale Superieure & the Right. LC 90-50096. (Rhetoric of the Human Sciences Ser.). 256p. (Orig.). (C). 1991. text ed. 40.00 (0-299-12560-2); pap. text ed. 19.75 (0-299-12564-5) U of Wis Pr.
Rubenstein, Edward & Federman, Daniel D., eds. Scientific American Medicine: Pocket Edition. (Illus.). 900p. (C). 1993. pap. text ed. 34.95 (0-89454-013-0) Sci Am Medicine.
Rubenstein, Edward, et al, eds. Molecular Medicine. (Basic Science for Clinicians Ser.). (Illus.). 300p. (C). 1994. text ed. 59.00 (0-89454-014-9) Sci Am Medicine.
Rubenstein, Edwin. The Right Data: Plus "The Real Reagan Record" 409p. (Orig.). (C). 1993. pap. text ed. 17.95 (0-9627841-3-3) Natl Review.
Rubenstein, Edwin S., jt. auth. see London, Herbert.
Rubenstein, Eli A., et al, eds. The Media, Social Science, & Social Policy for Children. LC 83-1393. (Child & Family Policy Ser.: Vol. 5). 256p. 1985. text ed. 49.50 (0-89391-229-8) Ablex Pub.
Rubenstein, Gillian. Space Demons. MacDonald, Pat, ed. (YA). (gr. 6-9). 1989. pap. 2.95 (0-671-67912-0, Archway) PB.
***Rubenstein, Hal & Mullen, Jim.** Paisley Goes with Nothing: A Man's Guide to Style. LC 95-1238. 1995. 20.00 (0-385-47712-0) Doubleday.
Rubenstein, Harriet, jt. auth. see Wallerstein, Nina.
Rubenstein, Harvey M. A Guide to Site & Environment Planning. 3rd ed. LC 87-2048. 410p. 1987. text ed. 69.95 (0-471-85033-0) Wiley.
— Pedestrian Malls, Streetscapes, & Urban Spaces. 288p. 1992. text ed. 64.95 (0-471-54680-1) Wiley.
Rubenstein, Helge, ed. The Oxford Book of Marriage. 400p. 1990. 21.95 (0-19-214150-3) OUP.
— The Oxford Book of Marriage. 400p. 1992. reprint ed. pap. 11.95 (0-19-282930-0) OUP.
Rubenstein, Hiasaura & Block, Mary H. Things That Matter. 446p. (C). 1982. pap. write for info. (0-02-404180-7) Macmillan.
Rubenstein, Howard S., ed. Songs of the Seder: A Music Book to Accompany the Passover Haggadah - Twenty-Three Songs, Prayers, & Chants - Traditional & Contemporary - Transliteration & English - Keys That Are Easy to Sing & Play - Chords for Piano & Guitar. 70p. (Orig.). (J). 1994. pap. 9.95 (0-9638886-1-7) Granite Hills Pr.
Rubenstein, Howard S. & Rubenstein, Judith S. Becoming Free: A Biblically Oriented Haggadah for Passover: The Permanent Relevance of the Ancient Lesson. LC 93-73663. 200p. (J). 1993. pap. 9.95 (0-9638886-0-9) Granite Hills Pr.
Rubenstein, Hymie & Vikse, Simon. It's Getting Gooder & Gooder. (Orig.). 1976. pap. 4.95 (0-89350-006-2) Fountain Pr.
Rubenstein, Irwin, et al, eds. Genetic Improvement of Crops: Emergent Techniques. LC 80-23560. 254p. reprint ed. pap. 72.40 (0-7837-2922-7, 2057532) Bks Demand.
Rubenstein, Israel, ed. see Mankiw, Dorothy.
Rubenstein, James M. The Changing Geography of the U. S. Automobile Industry. (Illus.). 288p. 1992. 63.50 (0-415-05544-X, A6907) Routledge.
— The Cultural Landscape: An Intro to Human Geography. (Illus.). 608p. (C). 1993. write for info. (0-318-69912-5) Macmillan.
— The Cultural Landscape: An Intro to Human Geography. 4th ed. (Illus.). 608p. (C). 1994. text ed. write for info. (0-02-404541-1) Macmillan.
Rubenstein, James M. & Bacon, Robert. The Cultural Landscape: An Introduction to Human Geography. (Illus.). 501p. (C). 1983. text ed. 49.25 (0-314-69674-1); teacher ed, pap. text ed. write for info. (0-314-71118-X) West Pub.
Rubenstein, James M., jt. auth. see Renwick, William H.
Rubenstein, Judith S., jt. auth. see Rubenstein, Howard S.
Rubenstein, Julie, ed. Langenscheidt's German-English - English-German Dictionary. rev. ed. 592p. 1993. mass mkt. 5.99 (0-671-86419-X) PB.
Rubenstein, Julie, ed. see Atkinson, Rick.
Rubenstein, Julie, ed. see Baker, Mark.
Rubenstein, Julie, ed. see Barkley, Charles & Johnson, Roy S.
Rubenstein, Julie, ed. see Barrett, Ron & Brown, Patty.
Rubenstein, Julie, ed. see Beals, Melba P.
Rubenstein, Julie, ed. see Bing, Stanley.
Rubenstein, Julie, ed. see Blum, Howard.
Rubenstein, Julie, ed. see Blumenthal, Ralph.
Rubenstein, Julie, ed. see Bradley, Marion Zimmer.
Rubenstein, Julie, ed. see Brown, Todd D.
Rubenstein, Julie, ed. see Clark, Mary Higgins.
Rubenstein, Julie, ed. see Collins, Jackie.
Rubenstein, Julie, ed. see Collins, Joan.
Rubenstein, Julie, ed. see Comfort, Alex.
Rubenstein, Julie, ed. see Conran, Shirley.
Rubenstein, Julie, ed. see Craig, Jean.
Rubenstein, Julie, ed. see Danvers, Dennis.
Rubenstein, Julie, ed. see Davis, Patti.
Rubenstein, Julie, ed. see Dickson, Paul.
Rubenstein, Julie, ed. see Edwards, Bob.
Rubenstein, Julie, ed. see Fairchild, John.
Rubenstein, Julie, ed. see Fisher, Jeffrey A.
Rubenstein, Julie, ed. see Fletcher, Connie.
Rubenstein, Julie, ed. see Friday, Nancy.
Rubenstein, Julie, ed. see Gage, Elizabeth.
Rubenstein, Julie, ed. see Goddard, Robert.
Rubenstein, Julie, ed. see Goldsmith, Olivia.
Rubenstein, Julie, ed. see Greenberg, Martin.
Rubenstein, Julie, ed. see Heckler, Jonellen.
Rubenstein, Julie, ed. see Higgins, Jack.
Rubenstein, Julie, ed. see Hoffman, Eileen.
Rubenstein, Julie, ed. see Hoffman, Ronald L.
Rubenstein, Julie, ed. see Jacobs, Nancy B.
Rubenstein, Julie, ed. see Jenkins, Dan.
Rubenstein, Julie, jt. ed. see Kaye, J. Leonard.
Rubenstein, Julie, ed. see Kelley, Kitty.
Rubenstein, Julie, ed. see Kelley, Virginia C. & Morgan, James.
Rubenstein, Julie, ed. see Kushner, Harold J.
Rubenstein, Julie, ed. see Latt, Mimi L.
Rubenstein, Julie, ed. see Levine, Katherine G.
Rubenstein, Julie, ed. see Lutz, John.
Rubenstein, Julie, ed. see Maas, Peter.
Rubenstein, Julie, ed. see Marston, Stephanie.
Rubenstein, Julie, ed. see McGinniss, Joe.
Rubenstein, Julie, ed. see McGuire, Christine.
Rubenstein, Julie, ed. see Montecino, Marcel.
Rubenstein, Julie, ed. see Morris, Bill.
Rubenstein, Julie, ed. see Morton, Andrew.
Rubenstein, Julie, ed. see Murano, Vincent & Hammer, Richard.
Rubenstein, Julie, ed. see Nin, Anais.
Rubenstein, Julie, ed. see Nixon, Richard M.
Rubenstein, Julie, ed. see O'Donnell, John R.
Rubenstein, Julie, ed. see O'Frank, Milo.
Rubenstein, Julie, ed. see Pope, Jamie.
Rubenstein, Julie, ed. see Pritikin, Robert C.
Rubenstein, Julie, ed. see Quine, Judith B.
Rubenstein, Julie, ed. see Rogers, Jacquelyn.
Rubenstein, Julie, ed. see Rossner, Judith.
Rubenstein, Julie, ed. see Rule, Ann.
Rubenstein, Julie, ed. see Seligman, Martin E.
Rubenstein, Julie, ed. see Sheehy, Gail.
Rubenstein, Julie, ed. see Smalley, Gary & Trent, John.
Rubenstein, Julie, ed. see Smith, C. W.
Rubenstein, Julie, ed. see Smith, Winnie.
Rubenstein, Julie, ed. see Steel, Danielle.
Rubenstein, Julie, ed. see Stoll, Clifford.
Rubenstein, Julie, ed. see Stone, Gene.
Rubenstein, Julie, ed. see Summers, Anthony.
Rubenstein, Julie, ed. see Tarshis, Barry.
Rubenstein, Julie, ed. see Tempest, John.
Rubenstein, Julie, ed. see Tifft, Susan E. & Jones, Alex S.
Rubenstein, Julie, ed. see Tremain, Rose.
Rubenstein, Julie, ed. see Undvall, Michael.
Rubenstein, Julie, ed. see Wadler, Joyce.
Rubenstein, Julie, ed. see Walker, Alice.
Rubenstein, Julie, ed. see Webb, James H., Jr.
Rubenstein, Julie, ed. see Wolfe, Linda.
Rubenstein, Julie, ed. see Woodward, Bob.
Rubenstein, Julie, ed. see Woolley, Persia.
Rubenstein, Julie, ed. see York, Michael.
Rubenstein, L. Touring Prose. Date not set. pap. 13.00 (0-394-22331-4) Random.
Rubenstein, L. I. The Stefan Problem. Solomon, A., tr. LC 75-168253. (Translations of Mathematical Monographs: Vol. 27). 419p. 1971. 77.00 (0-8218-1577-6, MMONO-27) Am Math.
Rubenstein, Laurence Z. & Wieland, Darryl, eds. Improving Care in the Nursing Home: Comprehensive Reviews of Clinical Research. (Illus.). 296p. (C). 1993. text ed. 49.95 (0-8039-4306-7); pap. text ed. 22.50 (0-8039-4307-5) Sage.
Rubenstein, Lenny, jt. ed. see Georgakas, Dan.
Rubenstein, Leonard. The Great Spy Films: A Pictorial History. (Illus.). 1979. 14.95 (0-8065-0663-6, Citadel Pr) Carol Pub Group.
Rubenstein, Lev, jt. auth. see Rubinstein, Isaak.
Rubenstein, Lorne. Links: An Exploration into the Mind, Heart, & Soul of Golf. 176p. 1993. pap. 10.95 (1-55958-279-0) Prima Pub.
Rubenstein, Lorne, jt. auth. see Knudson, George.
Rubenstein, Mark, jt. auth. see Cirillo, Dennis P.
Rubenstein, Max D. You & Your Hormones. 1960. 15.95x (0-8084-0387-7) NCUP.
Rubenstein, Nancy, ed. see Stein, Charlotte M.
Rubenstein, Natalia, ed. Dedalus Book of Russian Decadence. Williams, Frank, tr. (Dedalus Decadence Ser.). 400p. (Orig.). 1993. pap. 16.95 (0-7818-0107-9) Hippocrene Bks.
Rubenstein, Paul M. & Maloney, Martin J. Writing for the Media: Film, Television, Video & Radio. 2nd ed. (Illus.). 320p. (C). 1987. pap. text ed. write for info. (0-13-971508-8) P-H.
Rubenstein, Paul M., jt. auth. see Maloney, Martin J.
Rubenstein, Randi S., jt. ed. see Liebenson, Diane S.
Rubenstein, Richard. The Cunning of History. 1987. pap. text ed. 11.00 (0-06-132068-4, TB2068, Torch) HarpC.
Rubenstein, Richard E. Comrade Valentine: The Life of Yevno Azef, Russian Terrorist & Master Spy. LC 93-37988. 1994. 24.95 (0-15-152895-0) HarBrace.
Rubenstein, Richard E., ed. see Bivins, Frank J.
Rubenstein, Richard E., ed. see Brinton, J. W.
Rubenstein, Richard E., ed. see Caldwell, Erskine & Bourke-White, Margaret.
Rubenstein, Richard E., ed. see Commission on Country Life, Jr.
Rubenstein, Richard E., ed. see Cooperative Central Exchange Staff.
Rubenstein, Richard E., ed. see Dies, Edward J.
Rubenstein, Richard E., ed. see Education & Labor Committee.
Rubenstein, Richard E., ed. see Federal Trade Commission.
Rubenstein, Richard E., jt. ed. see Fogelson, Robert M.
Rubenstein, Richard E., ed. see Hill, John, Jr.
Rubenstein, Richard E., ed. see Howe, Frederic C.
Rubenstein, Richard E., ed. see Kerr, William H.
Rubenstein, Richard E., ed. see Kinney, J. P.
Rubenstein, Richard E., ed. see Lord, Russell.
Rubenstein, Richard E., ed. see Loucks, Henry L.
Rubenstein, Richard E., jt. ed. see McCurry, Dan C.
Rubenstein, Richard E., ed. see Murphy, Jerre C.
Rubenstein, Richard E., ed. see Rochester, Anne.
Rubenstein, Richard E., ed. see Russell, Charles E.
Rubenstein, Richard E., ed. see Simonsen, Sigurd J.
Rubenstein, Richard E., ed. see Todes, Charlotte.
Rubenstein, Richard E., ed. see U. S. Department of Labor, Bureau of Statistics Staff.
Rubenstein, Richard E., ed. see Wallace, Henry C.
Rubenstein, Richard E., ed. see Watson, Thomas E.
Rubenstein, Richard E., ed. see White, Roland A.
Rubenstein, Richard E., ed. see Whitney, Caspar.
Rubenstein, Richard L. After Auschwitz: History, Theology, & Contemporary Judaism. 2nd ed. (Jewish Studies). 416p. 1992. text ed. 48.50 (0-8018-4284-0); pap. text ed. 14.95 (0-8018-4285-9) Johns Hopkins.
— The Age of Triage: Fear & Hope in an Overcrowded World. LC 82-9407. 312p. 1984. pap. 16.00 (0-8070-4377-X, BPA27) Beacon Pr.
— Power Struggle. LC 86-16000. 214p. (C). 1986. reprint ed. pap. text ed. 23.00 (0-8191-5428-8) U Pr of Amer.
Rubenstein, Richard L., ed. The Dissolving Alliance: The U. S. & the Future of Europe. LC 86-25191. 216p. 1987. 22.95 (0-88702-216-2); pap. 12.95 (0-88702-217-0) Washington Inst Pr.
Rubenstein, Richard L., jt. auth. see Roth, John K.
Rubenstein, Robert A. & Foster, Mary L., eds. Peace & War: Cross-Cultural Perspectives. 350p. (C). 1985. pap. 21.95 (0-88738-619-9) Transaction Pubs.
Rubenstein, Roberta. Boundaries of the Self: Gender, Culture, Fiction. LC 86-11252. 272p. 1987. 29.95 (0-252-01355-7) U of Ill Pr.
Rubenstein, Roberta & Larson, Charles R. Worlds of Fiction. (Illus.). 1472p. (Orig.). (C). 1993. pap. write for info. (0-02-404185-8) Macmillan.
Rubenstein, Roni, ed. see Santoli, Al & Eisenstein, Laurence J.
Rubenstein, Roni, ed. see Santoli, Al & Eisenstein, Laurence.
***Rubenstein, Ruth P.** Dress Codes: Meanings & Messages in American Culture. LC 94-32808. (C). 1995. text ed. 69.00 (0-8133-2282-0) Westview.
Rubenstein, Sondra M. Surveying Public Opinion. LC 94-16428. 425p. 1995. pap. 27.95 (0-534-17856-1) Intl Thomson.
Rubenstein, Stan. Land & Freedom: United States History Lesson Plans. 80p. 1983. pap. 2.00 (0-911312-64-1) Schalkenbach.
— Land & Freedom: World History Lesson Plans. 60p. 1987. pap. 2.00 (0-911312-77-3) Schalkenbach.
Rubenstein, W. D. Capitalism, Culture & Decline in Britain: 1750-1990. 240p. 1992. 59.95 (0-415-03718-2, A6023); pap. 14.95 (0-415-03719-0, A6027) Routledge.
— Wealth & the Wealthy in the Modern World. LC 80-14632. 1980. text ed. 32.50 (0-312-85936-8) St Martin.
Rubenstein, Warren & Talbot, Yves. Medical Teaching in Ambulatory Care: A Practical Guide. LC 91-5183. (Medical Education Ser.: Vol. 15). 144p. 1992. 27.95 (0-8261-7690-9) Springer Pub.
Rubenstein, William B., ed. Lesbians, Gay Men & the Law: A Reader. LC 92-5373. 592p. 1993. 45.00 (1-56584-027-5); pap. 30.00 (1-56584-037-2) New Press NY.
— Lesbians, Gay Men, & the Law: A Reader. 2nd ed. 704p. 1996. pap. 30.00x (1-56584-322-3) New Press NY.
Rubenstone, Sally, jt. auth. see Dalby, Sidonia.
Ruberg, Robert L. & Smith, David J., Jr., eds. Plastic Surgery: The Requisites. LC 93-31210. 475p. 1994. 79.00 (0-8016-6927-8) Mosby Yr Bk.
***Ruberry, Mary.** Historias Biblicas EM Three-D. Flores van Damme, Patricia, tr. (Illus.). 64p. (POR.). 1994. pap. 13.95 (0-9641811-0-X) Three-D Revel.
— Three-D Bible Stories. 64p. 1994. pap. text ed. 15.95 (0-9641811-4-2) Three-D Revel.
— 3-D Book of Angels: A Collection. Collins, Norma, ed. (Illus.). 32p. (YA). (gr. 12). 1995. text ed. 12.95 (0-9641811-8-5) Three-D Revel.
Ruberry, William J., jt. auth. see Arnavas, Donald P.
Rubert Candau, Jose M., jt. ed. see Lasso de La Vega, Javier.
Rubert de Ventos, Xavier. Heresies of Modern Art. Bernstein, J. S., tr. LC 79-19613. (Illus.). 276p. reprint ed. pap. 78.70 (0-8357-4578-3, 2037487) Bks Demand.
Rubert, Mary L. Psychoethics: America's Perestroika. 1993. 10.95 (0-533-10502-1) Vantage.
Rubert, Steven C., jt. auth. see Rasmussen, R. Kent.
Ruberte, Ruth, jt. auth. see Martin, Franklin W.
Ruberte, Ruth M., jt. auth. see Martin, Franklin W.
Ruberti, A., ed. Realization Theory. LC 76-21964. 1977. pap. 23.00 (0-08-021276-X, Pergamon Pr) Elsevier.
Rubery, Jill, ed. Women & Recession. (International Library of Economics). 288p. 1988. text ed. 55.00 (0-7102-0701-8, RKP); pap. text ed. 19.95 (0-7102-1337-9, RKP) Routledge.
Rubery, Jill & Wilkinson, Frank, eds. Employer Strategy & the Labour Market. (Social Change & Economic Life Initiative). 408p. 1994. 65.00 (0-19-827894-2) OUP.
Rubey, Harry, et al. The Engineer & Professional Management. 3rd ed. LC 70-137090. (Illus.). 399p. reprint ed. pap. 113.80 (0-685-20339-5, 2029780) Bks Demand.
Rubey, Jane, jt. auth. see Groen, Elaine.
Rubia, Jose C. Classical European Furniture Design, 3 vols., Set. 1989. 19.99 (0-517-68791-7) Random Hse Value.
Rubie, D. C., jt. ed. see Thompson, A. B.
Rubie, Peter, jt. ed. see Reyes, Luis.
Rubiez, Ghassan, et al. Justice & the Intifada: Palestinians & Israelis Speak Out. 160p. 1991. pap. 10.95 (0-377-00237-2) Friendship Pr.
Rubik, Beverly, intro. The Interrelationship Between Mind & Matter. 281p. (Orig.). 1992. pap. 20.00 (0-9633272-0-8) Temple U Frontier Sci.
Rubik, Erno, et al. Rubik's Cubic Compendium. (Recreations in Mathematics Ser.). 200p. 1988. 28.95 (0-19-853202-4) OUP.
Rubik, Margarete. The Novels of Mrs. Oliphant: A Subversive View of Traditional Themes, Vol. 8. LC 93-13111. (Writing about Women: Feminist Literary Studies: Vol. 8). 343p. (C). 1994. text ed. 54.95 (0-8204-2209-6) P Lang Pubs.
***Rubin, et al.** Diagnosis & Treatment of Voice Disorders. 1995. write for info. (0-89640-276-2) Igaku-Shoin.
Rubin. Frommer's Washington D. C. with Kids. 2nd ed. 1994. pap. 17.00 (0-671-86664-8, P-H Travel) P-H Gen Ref & Trav.
— Miracle at Bellevue. 1986. 14.95 (0-02-605780-8) Macmillan.
— The Paralyzed Face. (Illus.). 320p. 1991. 95.00 (0-8016-4570-0) Mosby Yr Bk.
— Pediatric Pulmonary for the Practitioner. 1990. 49.95 (0-8151-7480-2, Yr Bk Med Pubs) Mosby Yr Bk.
— Picasso & Braque. 1989. 34.95 (0-87070-676-4) Mus of Modern Art.
— "Primitivism" in 20th Century Art: Affinity of the Tribal & the Modern, 2 vols., Set. 1995. pap. text ed. (0-8109-6134-2) Abrams.
— Radiation Biology - Endothelial Cells. 1996. write for info. (0-8493-4840-4) CRC Pr.
Rubin, Abba. Images in Transition: The English Jew in English Literature, 1660-1830. LC 83-22730. (Contributions to the Study of World Literature Ser.: No. 4). iv, 157p. 1984. text ed. 45.00 (0-313-23779-4, RUJ/, Greenwood Pr) Greenwood.
Rubin, Alan. Prentice Hall Federal Tax Course: 1988 Edition. (Illus.). 1440p. (C). 1987. pap. text ed. write for info. (0-13-313040-1) P-H.
Rubin, Alan, ed. Prentice-Hall Federal Tax Course 1986. 1440p. (C). 1985. student ed, text ed. 34.95 (0-13-312794-X) P-H.
Rubin, Alan, ed. see Prentice-Hall Editorial Staff.
Rubin, Alan A. New Drugs: Discovery & Development. (Drugs & the Pharmaceutical Sciences Ser.: Vol. 5). 328p. 1978. 140.00 (0-8247-6634-2) Dekker.
Rubin, Alan A., ed. Search for New Drugs. LC 74-187516. (Medicinal Research Ser.: No. 6). (Illus.). 464p. reprint ed. pap. 132.30 (0-7837-0931-5, 2041236) Bks Demand.
Rubin, Alan A., intro. The Complete Guide to America's National Parks, 1994-1995. 6th rev. ed. LC 89-63985. 1990. pap. 14.95 (0-9603410-6-4) Natl Pk Found.
Rubin, Albert L., ed. see Cheich, Jhoong S., et al.
Rubin, Alexis P., ed. Scattered among the Nations: Documents Affecting Jewish History 49 to 1975. LC 94-17497. 360p. 1995. 30.00 (1-56821-237-2) Aronson.
Rubin, Allen & Babbie, Earl. Research Methods for Social Work. 2nd ed. (C). 1993. text ed. 49.95 (0-534-17478-7) Brooks-Cole.
Rubin, Allen, jt. ed. see Bowker, Joan P.
Rubin, Allen, jt. ed. see Weinbach, Robert W.
Rubin, Alvan D., jt. auth. see Efron, Benjamin.
Rubin, Alvin & Bartell, Laura. Law Clerk's Handbook. 172p. 1992. reprint ed. pap. text ed. write for info. (0-314-73306-X) West Pub.
Rubin, Alvin B. & LeVan, Gerald. Louisiana Wills & Trusts: A Drafting System. Robinson, Linda & Herzog, Teresa, eds. 544p. (Orig.). 1992. pap. text ed. 180.00 (1-56664-024-5) WorldComm.
Rubin, Amy S., jt. auth. see Harmon, David.
Rubin, Andee, jt. auth. see Bruce, Bertrum.
Rubin, Anthony P. & Wood, Matthew L. Problems in Obstetric Anaesthesia. LC 92-48412. (Problems in Anaesthesia Ser.). (Illus.). 208p. 1993. pap. 30.00 (0-7506-0710-6) Buttrwrth-Heinemann.
Rubin, Arnald, ed. Marks of Civilization: Artistic Transformations of the Human Body. LC 88-195361. (Illus.). 280p. (Orig.). (C). text ed. 40.00 (0-930741-13-7); pap. 27.00 (0-930741-12-9) UCLA Fowler Mus.
Rubin, Arnold. Art As Technology: The Arts of Africa, Oceania, Native America & Southern California. Pearlstone, Zena, ed. (Illus.). 184p. 1990. pap. text ed. 24.95 (0-914589-04-0) Hillcrest Pr.
— The Sculptor's Eye: The African Art Collection of Chaim Gross. (Illus.). 1976. 9.00 (0-686-25966-1) Mus African Art.
Rubin, Arnold & Waxman, Samuel. The Leukemia Cell. (Uniscience Ser.). 192p. 1979. 78.95 (0-8493-5009-3, RC643, CRC Reprint) Franklin.
Rubin, Audrey S., ed. see Heller, Jack.
Rubin, Audrey S., ed. see Liles, Parker, et al.
Rubin, Audrey S., ed. see Lloyd, Alan C., et al.
Rubin, B. & Artsikhovskaya, Y. Biochemistry & Physiology of Plant Immunity. LC 93-10063. 1963. 156.00 (0-08-010190-9, Pub. by Pergamon Repr UK) Franklin.
Rubin, B. A., jt. ed. see Van Duuren, B. L.

R

An Asterisk (*) at the beginning of an entry indicates that the title is appearing in BIP for the first time.

Rubin, Barbara B., tr. The Dictionaries of John de Garlande. 98p. (C). 1981. 10.00 (0-87291-155-1) Coronado Pr.

***Rubin, Barnett R.** The Fragmentation of Afghanistan: State Formation & Collapse in the International System. LC 94-21189. 1994. write for info. (0-300-05963-9) Yale U Pr.

— The Search for Peace in Afghanistan: From Buffer State to Failed State. LC 95-15694. 1996. write for info. (0-300-06376-8) Yale U Pr.

Rubin, Barry. The Arab States & the Palestine Conflict. LC 81-5829. (Contemporary Issues in the Middle East Ser.). (Illus.). 328p. 1981. pap. 14.95 (0-8156-0170-0) Syracuse U Pr.

— Great Powers in the Middle East, 1941-1947: The Road to the Cold War. 254p. 1980. 35.00 (0-7146-3141-8, Pub. by F Cass Pubs UK) Intl Spec Bk.

— Modern Dictators: Third World Coup Makers, Strongmen & Populist Tyrants. 400p. 1988. pap. 8.95 (0-452-00947-2, Mer) NAL-Dutton.

— Modern Dictators: Third World Coup Makers, Strongmen, & Populist Tyrants. 1989. 8.95 (0-317-02814-6) NAL-Dutton.

— Paved with Good Intentions: The American Experience in Iran. 426p. 1981. pap. 9.95 (0-14-005964-4, Penguin Bks) Viking Penguin.

— Revolution Until Victory? The Politics & History of the PLO. LC 93-31651. 287p. 1994. text ed. 24.95 (0-674-76803-5) HUP.

— Secrets of State: The State Department & the Struggle over U. S. Foreign Policy. 351p. 1985. 27.95 (0-19-503397-3) OUP.

— U. S. Policy Towards Radical Middle East States. LC 92-44064. 1992. write for info. (0-944029-22-1) Wash Inst NEP.

Rubin, Barry, ed. Terrorism & Politics. 174p. 1991. text ed. 39.95 (0-312-06068-8) St Martin.

***Rubin, Barry & Rubin, Steffi, illus.** The Messianic Passover Haggadah. 32p. 1989. pap. 3.95 (1-880226-07-3) Lederer Pubns.

Rubin, Barry, jt. ed. see Baram, Amatzia.

Rubin, Barry, jt. auth. see Blum, Laura.

Rubin, Barry, jt. auth. see Laqueur, Walter.

Rubin, Barry, jt. ed. see Laqueur, Walter.

Rubin, Barry, jt. ed. see Lustick, Ian S.

Rubin, Barry, jt. auth. see Rubin, Steffi.

***Rubin, Barry, et al, eds.** From War to Peace: Arab-Israeli Relations, 1973-1993. LC 94-38055. 224p. 1995. 35.00 (0-8147-7462-8) NYU Pr.

***Rubin, Barry M.** Assimilation & Its Discontents. LC 94-30991. 1995. 25.00 (0-8129-2293-X, Times Bks) Random.

Rubin, Bernard. Media, Politics, & Democracy. (Reconstruction of Society Ser.). (Illus.). (C). 1977. pap. text ed. 9.95 (0-19-502008-1) OUP.

— When Information Counts: Grading the Media. 256p. 1985. text ed. 24.95 (0-669-10162-1) Free Pr.

Rubin, Bernard, ed. Questioning Media Ethics. 320p. 1978. student ed, pap. 19.95 (0-03-046126-X, Praeger Pubs) Greenwood.

Rubin, Betty L., jt. ed. see Deane, H. W.

Rubin, Bonnie M. Time Out: How to Take a Year (or More or Less) off Without Jeopardizing Your Job, Your Family or Your Bank Account. 1987. pap. 12.95 (0-393-30510-4) Norton.

***Rubin, Bonnie M. & Mason, Marcy.** Quick Escapes from Chicago. 2nd ed. (Quick Escapes Ser.). (Illus.). 224p. 1995. pap. 12.95 (1-56440-632-6) Globe Pequot.

Rubin, Bruce J. Jacob's Ladder. (Screenplay Ser.). 1990. pap. 12.95 (1-55783-086-X) Applause Theatre Bk Pubs.

Rubin, Carol, jt. auth. see Rubin, Jeffrey.

Rubin, Caroline, ed. see Barnes, Jill & Teramura, Terua.

Rubin, Caroline, ed. see Barnes, Jill & Tsurmi, Masao.

Rubin, Caroline, ed. see Barnes, Jill & Sato, Wakiko.

Rubin, Caroline, ed. see Barnes, Jill & Sueyoshi, Akiko.

Rubin, Caroline, ed. see Barnes, Jill & Kanabe, Junkichi.

Rubin, Caroline, ed. see Barnes, Jill & Asuka, Ken.

Rubin, Caroline, ed. see Barnes, Jill & Ishinabe, Fusako.

Rubin, Caroline, ed. see Barnes, Jill & Asuka, Ken.

Rubin, Caroline, ed. see Bishop, Ann.

Rubin, Caroline, ed. see Goldman, Susan.

Rubin, Caroline, ed. see Litchfield, Ada B.

Rubin, Caroline, ed. see Simon, Norma.

Rubin, Caroline, ed. see Stanton, Elizabeth & Stanton, Henry.

Rubin, Chana S. A Time to Heal. 235p. (C). 1991. 15.95 (1-56062-067-6) CIS Comm.

— A Time to Live. 269p. (YA). (gr. 9-12). 1988. 14.95 (0-935063-48-X) CIS Comm.

Rubin, Charles. The Little Book of Computer Wisdom: How to Make Friends with Your PC or Mac & Escape from Technotyranny. 160p. 1994. pap. 8.95 (0-395-70816-8) HM.

— The Macintosh Bible Guide to Claris Works 3.0. 400p. 1995. pap. 24.95 (1-56609-180-2) Peachpit Pr.

— Macintosh Bible Guide to FileMaker Pro. 2nd ed. (Illus.). 464p. 1993. pap. 22.00 (1-56609-029-6) Peachpit Pr.

— The Macintosh Bible Guide to System 7.1. (Illus.). 296p. 1993. pap. 15.00 (1-56609-030-X) Peachpit Pr.

— Macintosh Bible "What Do I Do Now?" Book. 3rd ed. (Macintosh Bible Ser.). (Illus.). 408p. 1994. pap. 22.00 (1-56609-095-4) Peachpit Pr.

— Microsoft Works for the Apple Macintosh. 2nd ed. 432p. 1989. pap. 19.95 (1-55615-202-7) Microsoft.

— Running Microsoft Works. 1990. 19.95 (1-55615-246-9) Microsoft.

Rubin, Charles, jt. auth. see Levinson, Jay C.

Rubin, Charles, jt. auth. see Rubin, Leslie.

Rubin, Charles T. The Green Crusade: An Intellectual History of the Environmental Movement. 320p. 1994. text ed. 22.95 (0-02-927525-3) Free Pr.

Rubin, Claire B., et al. Community Recovery from a Major Disaster. (Program on Environment & Behavior Monograph Ser.: No. 41). 295p. (Orig.). (C). 1985. pap. 10.00 (0-685-28115-9) Natural Hazards.

— Summary of Major Natural Disaster Incidents in the U. S., 1965-85. (Special Publications Ser.: No. 17). 47p. 1986. 4.00 (0-614-01776-9) Natural Hazards.

Rubin, D. E. Hidden Horses: One Hundred One Puzzles, Games & Quizzes. 128p. (Orig.). 1991. pap. 16.95 (0-939481-25-1) Half Halt Pr.

— Hidden Horses Two. (Illus.). 100p. 1994. pap. 17.95 (0-939481-40-5) Half Halt Pr.

Rubin, Daniel. How a Communist Club Functions. 1971. pap. 0.40 (0-87898-067-9) New Outlook.

Rubin, Daniel, jt. ed. see Krippner, Stanley.

Rubin, Daniel, et al. Anti-Semitism & Zionism: Selected Marxist Writings. LC 87-3123. 252p. (Orig.). (C). 1987. pap. 5.95 (0-7178-0663-4) Intl Pubs Co.

Rubin, David & Greenhouse, Steven. The Rights of Teachers. 2nd rev. ed. (ACLU Ser.). 366p. (Orig.). 1984. pap. 6.95 (0-8093-9957-1) S Ill U Pr.

Rubin, David & Sangster, Gary. Old Glory: The American Flag in Contemporary Art. (Illus.). 64p. 1994. pap. text ed. 18.00 (1-880353-07-5) Cleveland Ctr.

Rubin, David, jt. ed. see Dvell, Persis.

Rubin, David, tr. see Premchand, A.

Rubin, David, et al, eds. Pediatric Emergency Medicine: Self-Assessment & Review. LC 94-15127. 1994. write for info. (0-8151-7456-X) Mosby Yr Bk.

Rubin, David B. School Board Member Liability under Section 1983. Gittens, Naomi E., ed. 44p. 1992. pap. text ed. 15.00 (0-88364-134-8) Natl Sch Boards.

Rubin, David C. Memory in Oral Traditions: The Cognitive Psychology of Counting-out Rhymes, Ballads, & Epic. LC 94-8997. (Illus.). 320p. 1995. 45.00 (0-19-508211-7) OUP.

Rubin, David C., ed. Autobiographical Memory. (Illus.). 320p. 1988. pap. 24.95 (0-521-36850-2) Cambridge U Pr.

— Remembering Our Past: Studies in Autobiographical Memory. (Illus.). 400p. (C). 1995. write for info. (0-521-46145-6) Cambridge U Pr.

Rubin, David G. After the Raj: British Novels of India since 1947. LC 86-40115. 211p. 1986. text ed. 25.00 (0-87451-383-9) U Pr of New Eng.

Rubin, David G., tr. Nepali Visions, Nepali Dreams: The Poetry of Laxmiprasad Devkota. (Modern Asian Literature Ser.). 192p. 1980. text ed. 39.00 (0-231-05014-3) Col U Pr.

— A Season on the Earth: Selected Poems of Nirala. LC 76-40026. 1977. text ed. 40.50 (0-231-04160-8); pap. text ed. 16.00 (0-231-04161-6) Col U Pr.

Rubin, David L. The Knot of Artifice: A Poetic of the French Lyric in the Early Seventeenth Century. LC 80-26260. 119p. 1981. 32.50 (0-8142-0322-1) Ohio St U Pr.

— A Pact with Silence: Art & Thought in the Fables of Jean de la Fontaine. 130p. 1991. 42.50 (0-8142-0543-7) Ohio St U Pr.

Rubin, David L., ed. Continuum: Problems in French Literature from the Renaissance to the Early Enlightenment, 5 vols. LC 87-45806. 1989. Vol. 1: Rethinking Classicism: Overviews. 57.50 (0-685-73895-7); Rethinking Classicism: Textual Explorations. 57.50 (0-404-63751-5); Vol. 3: Poetics of Exposition & Libertinage & the Art of Writing, Vol. 1. 57.50 (0-685-73896-5); Vol. 4: Libertinage & the Art of Writing, Vol. 2. 57.50 (0-404-63754-X); Literature & the Other Arts. 57.50 (0-404-63755-8) AMS Pr.

— Continuum: Problems in French Literature from the Renaissance to the Early Enlightenment, 5 vols., Set. LC 87-45806. 1989. write for info. (0-404-63750-7) AMS Pr.

— EMF: Studies in Early Modern France: "Word & Image" (Illus.). (C). 1994. 35.00 (0-9634355-2-3) Rookwood Pr.

— EMF: Studies in Early Modern France: "Word & Image", Vol. 1. (Illus.). 248p. (C). 1994. lib. bdg. 35.00 (0-9634355-3-1) Rookwood Pr.

— EMF: Studies in Early Modern France: "Word & Image", Vol. 1. (Illus.). 248p. (Orig.). (C). 1994. pap. 19.95 (0-9634355-6-6) Rookwood Pr.

— Sun King: The Ascendancy of French Culture During the Reign of Louis XIV. LC 90-55041. (Illus.). 248p. 1992. 42.50 (0-918016-94-0) Folger Bks.

Rubin, David L. & McKinley, Mary B., eds. Convergences: Rhetoric & Poetic in Seventeenth-Century France, Essays for Hugh M. Davidson. 240p. 1989. text ed. 56. 50 (0-8142-0468-6) Ohio St U Pr.

Rubin, David L., jt. ed. see Arndt, Richard T.

Rubin, David L., jt. ed. see Drell, Persis S.

Rubin, David L., jt. ed. see Fenoaltea, Doranne.

Rubin, David M. Cross-Bedding, Bedforms, & Paleocurrents. (Concepts in Sedimentology & Paleontology Ser.: No. 1). 188p. 1987. pap. 22.50 (0-918985-68-4) SEPM.

— Cross-Bedding, Bedforms & Paleocurrents. LC 89-138314. (Concepts in Sedimentology & Paleontology Ser.: No. 1). 195p. 1987. reprint ed. pap. 55.60 (0-7837-8314-0, 2049098) Bks Demand.

— Desktop Musician: Orchestrating Music on Your Computer. 1994. pap. text ed. 34.95 (0-07-881209-7) McGraw.

Rubin, David S. Computer Assisted: The Computer in Contemporary Art. LC 87-82883. (Illus.). 24p. (Orig.). 1987. pap. text ed. 4.00 (0-941972-06-2) Freedman.

— Contemporary Triptychs. LC 82-80232. (Illus.). 72p. 1982. 6.00 (0-915478-15-3) Galleries Coll.

— Cruciformed: Images of the Cross Since 1980. (Illus.). 64p. 1991. pap. text ed. 15.00 (1-880353-00-8) Cleveland Ctr.

— Cynthia Carlson: Installations, 1979-1989 (A Decade, More or Less) (Illus.). 40p. (Orig.). 1989. pap. text ed. 10.00 (0-941972-08-9) Freedman.

— Donald Lipski: Poetic Sculpture. LC 89-82748. (Illus.). 56p. (Orig.). 1990. pap. text ed. 12.00 (0-941972-10-0) Freedman.

— Ellen Brooks: Nature As Artifice. (Illus.). 32p. 1993. pap. text ed. 15.00 (1-880353-03-2) Cleveland Ctr.

— Gary Bower: Abstract Paintings, 1969-1993. (Illus.). 36p. 1993. pap. text ed. 15.00 (1-880353-05-9) Cleveland Ctr.

— Paper Art. LC 77-90516. (Illus.). 32p. 1977. 2.50 (0-915478-11-0) Galleries Coll.

— Petah Coyne. (Illus.). 36p. 1992. pap. text ed. 10.00 (1-880353-02-4) Cleveland Ctr.

— William Baziotes: A Commemorative Exhibition. Bross, Louise S. & Martin, Lys, eds. LC 87-80348. (Illus.). 24p. (Orig.). 1987. pap. text ed. 9.00 (0-941972-05-4) Freedman.

Rubin, David S. & Steadman, David W. Black & White Are Colors: Paintings of the 1950's-1970's. LC 78-68735. (Illus.). 59p. 1979. 3.50 (0-915478-13-7) Galleries Coll.

Rubin, David S., jt. auth. see Albee, Edward.

Rubin, David S., jt. auth. see Levin, Richard I.

Rubin, David S., jt. auth. see Tannenbaum, Judith E.

Rubin, Davida. Sir Kenelm Digby, F.R.S. An Annotated Bibliography. (Illus.). 130p. 1991. 95.00 (0-930405-29-3) Norman SF.

Rubin, Deborah E. If Wishes Were Horses: Quotations & Proverbs for Horse People. Greer, Daniel, ed. (Illus.). 224p. 1994. pap. 12.00 (0-87842-305-2) Mountain Pr.

Rubin, Devora. Daughters of Destiny: Women Who Revolutionized Jewish Life & Torah Education. (ArtScroll History Ser.). (Illus.). 240p. 1988. 14.95 (0-89906-494-9); pap. 11.95 (0-89906-495-7) Mesorah Pubns.

Rubin, Diana K. Spirits in Exile. (Illus.). 34p. (Orig.). 1990. pap. text ed. write for info. (1-56315-019-0) Sterling Hse.

— Spirits in Exile. 2nd ed. (Illus.). 40p. (Orig.). 1992. reprint ed. pap. text ed. 6.95 (1-56315-068-9) Sterling Hse.

— Visions of Enchantment. LC 91-90088. (Illus.). 80p. 1991. pap. 6.95 (1-878116-09-6) JVC Bks.

Rubin, Don. Brainstorms: Real Puzzles for the Real Genius. LC 88-45972. (Illus.). 128p. (Orig.). 1989. pap. 9.00 (0-06-096338-7, PL 6338, PL) HarpC.

***Rubin, Don, ed.** World Encyclopedia of Contemporary Theatre Vol. 1: Europe. (Illus.). 768p. 1995. 149.95x (0-415-05928-3, B0376) Routledge.

Rubin, Donald, jt. auth. see Rafoth, Bennett A.

Rubin, Donald B. Multiple Imputation for Nonresponse in Surveys. (Probability & Mathematical Statistics Ser.). 258p. 1987. text ed. 86.95 (0-471-08705-X) Wiley.

Rubin, Donald L., ed. Composing Social Identity in Writing Style. 256p. 1995. text ed. 59.95 (0-8058-1383-7); pap. 29.95 (0-8058-1384-5) L Erlbaum Assocs.

Rubin, Donnalee. Gender Influences: Reading Student Texts. LC 92-26313. (Studies in Writing & Rhetoric). 120p. (Orig.). (C). 1993. pap. 12.95 (0-8093-1866-0) S Ill U Pr.

***Rubin, Dorothy.** Comprehension Power: Reading-Thinking Strategies for Adults, Bk. 1. LC 94-38282. 1994. 5.95 (0-13-184847-X) P-H.

— Diagnosis & Correction in Reading Instruction. 2nd ed. 528p. (C). 1991. pap. text ed. 32.25 (0-13-208760-X, 710118) P-H.

— Gaining Word Power. 3rd ed. (Illus.). 432p. (C). 1993. pap. write for info. (0-02-404221-8) Macmillan.

— Power English Eight: Basic Language Skills for Adults. (C). 1989. pap. text ed. 5.85 (0-13-688516-0) P-H.

— Power English Five: Basic Language Skills for Adults. (C). 1989. pap. text ed. 5.85 (0-13-688482-2) P-H.

— Power English Four: Basic Language Skills for Adults. (C). 1989. pap. text ed. 5.85 (0-13-688474-1) P-H.

— Power English Nine: Basic Language Skills for Adults. (C). 1990. pap. text ed. 5.85 (0-13-688524-1) P-H.

— Power English One: Basic Language Skills for Adults. 128p. (C). 1989. pap. text ed. 5.85 (0-13-688441-5) P-H.

— Power English Seven: Basic Language Skills for Adults. (C). 1989. pap. text ed. 5.85 (0-13-688508-X) P-H.

— Power English Six: Basic Language Skills for Adults. (C). 1989. pap. text ed. 5.85 (0-13-688490-3) P-H.

— Power English Three: Basic Language Skills for Adults. (C). 1989. pap. text ed. 5.85 (0-13-688466-0) P-H.

— Power English Two: Basic Language Skills for Adults. (C). 1989. pap. text ed. 5.85 (0-13-688458-X) P-H.

— Power Vocabulary Five: Basic Word Strategies for Adults. 128p. 1992. pap. text ed. 5.55 (0-13-681214-7) P-H.

— Power Vocabulary Four: Basic Word Strategies for Adults. 128p. 1992. pap. text ed. 5.55 (0-13-681206-6) P-H.

— Power Vocabulary Locator Test. 16p. 1992. pap. write for info. (0-13-682873-6) P-H.

— Power Vocabulary One: Basic Word Strategies for Adults. 112p. (C). 1992. pap. text ed. write for info. (0-13-678244-2) P-H.

— Power Vocabulary Three: Basic Word Strategies for Adults. 96p. (C). 1992. pap. text ed. write for info. (0-13-681198-1) P-H.

— Power Vocabulary Two: Basic Word Strategies for Adults. 96p. (C). 1992. pap. text ed. 5.55 (0-13-678251-5) P-H.

— A Practical Approach to Teaching Reading. 2nd ed. LC 92-21969. 1992. text ed. write for info. (0-205-14215-X) Allyn.

— Reading & Learning Power. 3rd ed. 360p. 1990. pap. 21. 00 (0-536-57654-8) Ginn Pr.

— Teaching Elementary Language Arts: An Integrated Approach. 5th ed. LC 94-11078. 1994. pap. text ed. write for info. (0-205-15979-6) Allyn.

— Teaching Reading & Study Skills in Content Areas. (C). 1983. text ed. 42.75 (0-03-060473-7) HB Coll Pubs.

— Teaching Reading & Study Skills in Content Areas. 2nd ed. 320p. (C). 1991. text ed. 47.00 (0-205-13297-9) Allyn.

— Vocabulary Expansion. 2nd ed. 352p. (C). 1991. pap. write for info. (0-02-404245-5) Macmillan.

Rubin-Dorsky, Jeffrey. Adrift in the Old World: The Psychological Pilgrimage of Washington Irving. (Illus.). xx, 304p. 1988. 32.50 (0-226-73094-8) U Ch Pr.

Rubin, Dvaid, tr. The Return of Sarasvati: Translations of the Poetry of Prasad, Nirala, Pant & Mahadevi. LC 93-20404. (Studies on South Asia: No. 7). 201p. 1983. 25. 00 (0-936115-08-4) U Penn South Asia.

Rubin, Edmund J. Abstract Functioning in the Blind. LC 64-2911. (American Foundation for the Blind Research Ser.: No. 11). 64p. reprint ed. pap. 25.00 (0-7837-0128-4, 2040411) Bks Demand.

Rubin, Edward L. & Cooter, Robert. The Payment System: Cases, Materials & Issues. 2nd ed. (American Casebook Ser.). 976p. 1994. text ed. 44.00 (0-314-03545-1) West Pub.

— Payments System: Cases, Materials & Issues, Teacher's Manual to Accompany. (American Casebook Ser.). 215p. (C). 1990. pap. text ed. write for info. (0-314-80958-9) West Pub.

Rubin, Edward L., jt. auth. see Cooter, Robert D.

Rubin, Eli Z., jt. auth. see Llorens, Lela A.

Rubin, Eli Z., et al. Cognitive Perceptual Motor Dysfunction: From Research to Practice. LC 77-157415. (Lafayette Clinic Monographs in Psychiatry: No. 5). 173p. reprint ed. pap. 49.40 (0-685-15707-5, 2027662) Bks Demand.

Rubin, Ellis. For the Defense: True Crime Cases of America's Most Famous Criminal Lawyers. 1991. mass mkt. 5.99 (0-312-92534-4) St Martin.

Rubin, Emanuel, pref. Alcohol & the Cell. (Annals Ser.: Vol. 492). (Illus.). 412p. 1987. 103.00 (0-89766-380-2) NY Acad Sci.

Rubin, Emanuel & Damjanov, Ivan, eds. Pathology Reviews. (Illus.). 320p. 1989. 69.50 (0-89603-162-4) Humana.

— Pathology Reviews, 1990. (Illus.). 264p. 1990. 79.50 (0-89603-195-0) Humana.

Rubin, Emanuel & Farber, John L. Essential Pathology. (Illus.). 800p. 1989. text ed. 44.95 (0-397-51003-9) Lippincott.

***Rubin, Emanuel & Farber, John L., eds.** Essential Pathology. 2nd ed. LC 94-46367. (Illus.). 1995. write for info. (0-397-51487-5) Lippincott.

Rubin, Emanuel, jt. auth. see Damjanov, Ivan.

Rubin, Emanuel, et al. Pathology. LC 65-8626. (Illus.). 1824p. 1988. text ed. 62.50 (0-397-50698-8, Lippincott Medical) Lippincott.

Rubin, Emanuel, et al, eds. Pathology. 2nd ed. LC 93-15103. 1578p. 1993. 65.00 (0-397-51047-0) Lippincott.

Rubin, Ernest, jt. auth. see Kuznets, Simon.

Rubin, Eva R. Abortion, Politics, & the Courts: Roe vs. Wade & Its Aftermath. LC 86-22847. (Contributions in American Studies: No. 89). 264p. 1987. text ed. 55.00 (0-313-25614-4, RBA/, Greenwood Pr) Greenwood.

— The Supreme Court & the American Family: Ideology & Issues. LC 85-21865. (Contributions in American Studies: No. 85). 251p. 1986. text ed. 49.95 (0-313-25157-6, RSU/, Greenwood Pr) Greenwood.

Rubin, Eva R., ed. The Abortion Controversy: A Documentary History. LC 93-25068. (Primary Documents in American History & Contemporary Issues Ser.: Vol. 1). 312p. 1994. text ed. 45.00 (0-313-28476-8, RAY/, Greenwood Pr) Greenwood.

Rubin, G. War, Law, & Labor: The Munitions Acts, State Regulation, & the Unions 1915-1921. 308p. 1988. 65.00 (0-19-825538-1) OUP.

Rubin, G. R. Private Property, Government Requisition & the Constitution, 1914-1927. LC 93-48977. 276p. 1994. boxed 65.00 (1-85285-098-1) Hambledon Press.

Rubin, G. R. & Sugarman, David, eds. Rubin & Sugarman: Law, Economy & Society - Essays in the History of English Law. 1984. 78.00 (0-86205-085-5); pap. 52.00 (0-86205-098-7) Butterworth Legal Pubs.

Rubin, Gail & Graetz, Michael. Psalmist with a Camera: Photographs of a Biblical Safari. LC 79-5086. (Illus.). 116p. 1979. 29.95 (0-89659-076-3); pap. 16.95 (0-89659-071-2) Abbeville Pr.

Rubin, Gary, et al. The Poor among Us: Jewish Tradition & Social Policy. LC 86-72482. 63p. (Orig.). 1986. pap. 7.50 (0-87495-084-8) Am Jewish Comm.

Rubin, Gary E. The Asylum Challenge to Western Nations. Tripp, Rosemary E., ed. (Illus.). 19p. 1984. pap. 2.00 (0-685-10162-2) US Comm Refugees.

— The Newest Americans: Report of the American Jewish Committee's Task Force on the Acculturation of Immigrants to American Life. LC 87-70998. 36p. 1987. pap. 5.00 (0-87495-089-9) Am Jewish Comm.

Rubin, Gary E., jt. auth. see Morris, Milton D.

Rubin, Gay. On a Good Day: Short Fiction By... 100p. (Orig.). 1992. pap. 8.95 (1-56439-017-9) Ridgeway.

Rubin, Geoffrey M., jt. auth. see Overstreet, George A., Jr.

Rubin, Gerry R. Durban, 1942: A British Troopship Revolt. LC 92-3361. 158p. 1992. boxed 40.00 (1-85285-080-9) Hambledon Press.

Rubin, Gertrude. A Beating of Wings. Spelius, Carol, ed. 96p. (Orig.). 1991. pap. 8.95 (0-941363-09-0) Lake Shore Pub.

— The Passover Poems. (Illus.). 48p. (Orig.). 1991. pap. 8.00 (1-879260-00-X) Evanston Pub.

Rubin, Gloria S., jt. auth. see Rakowitz, Elly.

Rubin, H. Pensions & Employee Mobility in the Public Service. (Twentieth Century Fund Ser.). 1965. reprint ed. pap. 10.00 (0-527-02834-7) Periodicals Srv.

Rubin, H. Ted. Behind the Black Robes: Juvenile Court Judges & the Court. LC 85-11923. (Sage Library of Social Research: No. 160). 248p. reprint ed. pap. 70.70 (0-7837-4575-3, 2044104) Bks Demand.

— The Courts: Fulcrum of the Justice System. 2nd ed. 256p. (C). 1984. pap. text ed. write for info. (0-394-33573-2) Random.

R

— Juvenile Justice: Policy, Practice, & Law. 2nd ed. 320p. (C). 1986. pap. text ed. write for info. (0-07-554738-4) McGraw.

Rubin, H. Ted & Flango, Victor E. Court Coordination of Family Cases. 83p. 1992. pap. text ed. 6.95 (0-89656-120-8, R-144) Natl Ctr St Courts.

Rubin, H. Ted, jt. auth. see Grandy, H. Clifton.

Rubin, Harvey W. Dictionary of Insurance Terms. 2nd ed. 416p. 1991. pap. 9.95 (0-8120-4632-3) Barron.

— Dictionary of Insurance Terms. 3rd ed. LC 95-6527. 1995. write for info. (0-8120-3379-5) Barron.

Rubin, Herb & Rubin, Irene. Community Organization & Development. 480p. (C). 1986. pap. write for info. (0-675-20349-X, Merrill Pub Co) Macmillan.

Rubin, Herbert. Applied Social Research. 384p. (C). 1983. write for info. (0-675-09793-2, Merrill Pub Co); 15.75 (0-675-20048-2, Merrill Pub Co) Macmillan.

— Integrating Rural Development: The Problem & a Solution. 1980. pap. text ed. 2.50 (0-89249-031-4) Intl Development.

Rubin, Herbert J., jt. auth. see Rubin, Irene B.

Rubin, Howard. Practical Guide to the Design & Implementation of Information Systems Measurement Programs. 1993. boxed 38.00 (0-13-681784-X) P-H.

Rubin, I. B., jt. auth. see Bayne, C. K.

Rubin, I. Leslie & Crocker, Allen C. Developmental Disabilities: Delivery of Medical Care for Children & Adults. LC 87-2840. 526p. reprint ed. pap. 150.00 (0-7837-2743-7, 2043123) Bks Demand.

Rubin, Ira L., et al. Treatment of Heart Disease in the Adult. 2nd ed. LC 79-175466. 522p. reprint ed. pap. 148.80 (0-317-26706-X, 2056008) Bks Demand.

Rubin, Irene, jt. ed. see Levine, Charles H.

Rubin, Irene, jt. auth. see Rubin, Herb.

*Rubin, Irene B. & Rubin, Herbert J. Qualitative Interviewing: The Art of Hearing Data. 256p. (C). 1995. 45.00 (0-8039-5095-0); pap. 21.95 (0-8039-5096-9) Sage.

Rubin, Irene S. The Politics of Public Budgeting: Getting & Spending, Borrowing & Balancing. 2nd ed. LC 92-28362. (Chatham House Series on Change in American Politics). 288p. 1993. pap. text ed. 24.95x (0-934540-97-7) Chatham Hse Pubs.

— Running in the Red: The Political Dynamics of Urban Fiscal Stress. LC 81-9329. 171p. (C). 1983. 64.50 (0-87395-564-1); pap. 21.95 (0-87395-565-X) State U NY Pr.

Rubin, Irene S., ed. New Directions in Budget Theory. LC 87-9977. (SUNY Series in Public Administration). 207p. 1988. 64.50 (0-88706-624-0); pap. 21.95 (0-88706-625-9) State U NY Pr.

Rubin, Irvin I. Handbook of Plastics Materials & Technology. 1792p. 1990. text ed. 185.00 (0-471-09634-2) Wiley.

— Injection Molding: Theory & Practice. LC 73-5. (S P E Monographs: Vol. 1). 657p. 1973. text ed. 135.00 (0-471-74445-X, Wiley-Interscience) Wiley.

Rubin, Irwin M. & Fernandez, C. Raymond. My Pulse Is Not What It Used to Be: The Leadership Challenges in Health Care. LC 91-65593. 104p. (Orig.). 1991. pap. 40.00 (0-9629561-0-4) Temenos Found.

Rubin, Irwin M., et al. Task-Oriented Team Development. (Illus.). 1978. ring bd. 80.00 (0-07-054196-5) McGraw.

Rubin, Isaac D. Poly(One-Butene) Its Preparation & Properties. LC 67-28233. (Polymer Monographs). (Illus.). 138p. 1968. text ed. 117.00 (0-677-01270-5) Gordon & Breach.

Rubin, Isaac I. History of Economic Thought. Filtzer, Donald, tr. 440p. 1989. pap. text ed. 19.95 (0-7453-0301-3) Routledge Chapman & Hall.

Rubin, J. Language Planning in the United States. (International Journal of the Sociology of Language Ser.: No. 11). 1977. 60.00 (90-279-7694-5) Mouton.

Rubin, J. Z., jt. auth. see Brockner, J.

Rubin, James H. Manet's Silence & the Poetics of Bouquets. LC 93-38505. 256p. (Orig.). 1994. 39.95 (0-674-54802-7) HUP.

— Manet's Silence & the Poetics of Bouquets. (Essays in Art & Culture Ser.). 256p. (Orig.). (C). 1995. pap. text ed. 22.95 (0-674-54803-5) HUP.

— Realism & Social Vision in Courbet & Proudhon. LC 80-17559. (Essays on the Arts Ser.: No. 10). (Illus.). 270p. 1981. 32.50x (0-691-03960-7) Princeton U Pr.

*Rubin, Janet & Merrion, Margaret. Drama & Music: Creative Activities for Young Children. LC 94-24087. (Illus.). 196p. 1995. lib. bdg. 28.95 (0-89334-244-0, 2440X34) Humanics Ltd.

Rubin, Janet, jt. comp. see Merrion, Margaret.

Rubin, Jay. Gone Fishin' New Angles on Perennial Problems. (Power Japanese Ser.). 128p. (Orig.). 1992. pap. 9.00 (4-7700-1656-5) Kodansha.

— Injurious to Public Morals: Writers & the Meiji State. LC 83-47976. (Illus.). 400p. 1984. 35.00 (0-295-96043-4) U of Wash Pr.

Rubin, Jay, tr. see Soseki, Natsume.

Rubin, Jean. Mathematical Logic: Application & Theory. 417p. (C). 1990. text ed. 52.00 (0-03-012808-0) SCP.

Rubin, Jeffrey. Handbook of Usability Testing: How to Plan, Design, & Conduct Effective Tests. LC 93-43038. (Technical Communication Library). 1994. pap. text ed. 34.95 (0-471-59403-2) Wiley.

Rubin, Jeffrey & LaPorte, Valerie, eds. Alternatives in Rehabilitating the Handicapped: A Policy Analysis. LC 81-4144. 244p. 1982. 35.95 (0-89885-010-X) Human Sci Pr.

Rubin, Jeffrey & Rubin, Carol. When Families Fight: How to Handle Conflict with Those You Love. 320p. 1990. pap. 3.95 (0-345-36572-0) Ballantine.

Rubin, Jeffrey, jt. ed. see LaPorte, Valerie.

Rubin, Jeffrey Z., ed. Dynamics of Third-Party Intervention: Kissinger in the Middle East. LC 80-28763. 328p. 1981. text ed. 49.95 (0-275-90714-7, C0714, Praeger Pubs) Greenwood.

Rubin, Jeffrey Z., jt. ed. see Bercovitch, Jacob.

Rubin, Jeffrey Z., jt. ed. see Breslin, J. William.

Rubin, Jeffrey Z., jt. auth. see Buker, Barbara B.

Rubin, Jeffrey Z., jt. ed. see Faure, Guy O.

Rubin, Jeffrey Z., jt. ed. see Kellerman, Barbara.

Rubin, Jeffrey Z., et al. Social Conflict: Escalation, Stalemate, & Settlement. 2nd ed. LC 93-24557. 1993. pap. text ed. write for info. (0-07-054211-2) McGraw.

Rubin, Jerome. New York Naturally, 1989: A Resource Directory for Natural Living in the Tri-State Area. 168p. (Orig.). 1988. pap. write for info. (0-318-65041-X) City Spirit Pubns.

— Old Boston Fare in Food & Pictures. (Illus.). 128p. (Orig.). Date not set. pap. 13.50 (0-88278-047-6) Yankee Products.

— Old Cape Cod Fare in Food & Pictures. (Illus.). 128p. (Orig.). Date not set. pap. 13.50 (0-88278-046-8) Yankee Products.

Rubin, Jerome & Donaldson, Stephen, eds. Connecticut Naturally, 1990: A Resource Directory for Natural Living in the Tri-State Area, Including New York & New Jersey. (Orig.). 1990. pap. 4.95 (0-9622953-3-7) City Spirit Pubns.

— New Jersey Naturally, 1990: A Resource Directory for Natural Living in the Tri-State Area, Including New York & Connecticut. (Orig.). 1990. pap. 4.95 (0-9622953-2-9) City Spirit Pubns.

— New York Naturally, 1990: A Resource Directory for Natural Living in the Tri-State Area, Including New Jersey & Connecticut. (Orig.). 1990. pap. 4.95 (0-9622953-1-0) City Spirit Pubns.

Rubin, Joan & Jernudd, Bjorn H., eds. Can Language Be Planned: Sociolinguistic Theory & Practice for Developing Nations. LC 70-129618. (Illus.). 368p. 1971. pap. text ed. 6.95 (0-8248-0358-2) UH Pr.

Rubin, Joan & Shuy, Roger, eds. Language Planning: Current Issues & Research. LC 73-76754. 121p. reprint ed. pap. 34.50 (0-7837-6337-9, 2046049) Bks Demand.

Rubin, Joan & Thompson, Irene. How to Be a More Successful Language Learner: Toward Learner Autonomy. LC 93-42857. 1994. pap. 18.95 (0-8384-4734-1) Heinle & Heinle.

*Rubin, Joan, et al. English Works! LC 95-1983. 1995. write for info. (0-201-87681-7) Addison-Wesley.

Rubin, Joan, et al, eds. Language Planning Processes. (Contributions to the Sociology of Language Ser.: No. 21). 1977. text ed. 43.85 (90-279-7714-3) Mouton.

Rubin, Joan S. Constance Rourke & American Culture. LC 79-9272. (Illus.). xv, 244p. 1980. 29.95 (0-8078-1402-4) U of NC Pr.

— The Making of Middlebrow Culture. LC 91-22241. (Illus.). xxii, 416p. (C). 1992. 34.95 (0-8078-2010-5); pap. 14.95 (0-8078-4354-7) U of NC Pr.

— The Making of Middlebrow Culture. braille ed. 980p. 1992. Braille. vinyl bd. 78.40 (1-56956-358-6, BR8898) W A T Braille.

Rubin, John. Punishment Chart for North Carolina Crimes. 2nd ed. 71p. (C). 1993. pap. text ed. 7.00 (1-56011-250-6) Institute Government.

— Self-Defense & Other Forms of Defensive Force in North Carolina. (Orig.). (C). Date not set. pap. text ed. write for info. (1-56011-245-X, 95.14) Institute Government.

*Rubin, John & Loeb, Ben F., Jr., comps. Punishment Chart for North Carolina Crimes & Motor Vehicle Offenses. (Orig.). (C). 1995. pap. text ed. write for info. (1-56011-238-7) Institute Government.

Rubin, Jonathan M. & Chandler, William F. Ultrasound in Neurosurgery. 224p. 1990. 115.50 (0-88167-549-0, 2019) Raven.

Rubin, Joseph. New York Collections. LC 80-81138. (Practice Systems Library Manual). ring bd. 120.00 (0-317-00518-9) Lawyers Cooperative.

— New York Collections. suppl. ed. LC 80-81138. (Practice Systems Library Manual). 1993. Suppl. 1993. 75.00 (0-317-04327-7) Lawyers Cooperative.

Rubin, Joseph L. Heartburst. LC 88-82305. 125p. (Orig.). 1988. pap. 11.95 (0-9621100-0-0) Heartburst.

Rubin, Judith A. The Art of Art Therapy. LC 84-9344. 224p. 1984. 33.95 (0-87630-371-8) Brunner-Mazel.

— Child Art Therapy: Understanding & Helping Children Through Art. 2nd ed. (Illus.). 304p. 1984. pap. 39.95 (0-442-27767-9) Van Nos Reinhold.

Rubin, Judith A., ed. Approaches to Art Therapy: Theory & Technique. LC 86-26376. 362p. 1987. 33.95 (0-87630-452-8) Brunner-Mazel.

Rubin, Julius H. Religious Melancholy & Protestant Experience in America. (Religion in America Ser.). 304p. 1994. 35.00 (0-19-508301-6) OUP.

Rubin, K. H., jt. ed. see Pepler, D. J.

Rubin, Karen. Flying High in Travel: A Complete Guide to Careers in the Travel Industry. 2nd ed. 336p. 1992. pap. text ed. 19.95 (0-471-55173-2) Wiley.

Rubin, Karen, et al. The No Sugar Delicious Desert Book. LC 84-70860. 160p. 1984. pap. 6.95 (0-89087-402-6) Celestial Arts.

Rubin, Kenneth H. & Asendorpf, Jens, eds. Social Withdrawal, Inhibition, & Shyness in Childhood. 368p. 1992. text ed. 69.95 (0-8058-1219-9); pap. 34.50 (0-8058-1220-2) L Erlbaum Assocs.

Rubin, Kenneth H. & Ross, Hildy S., eds. Peer Relationships & Social Skills in Childhood. (Illus.). 414p. 1982. 64.00 (0-387-90699-1) Spr-Verlag.

Rubin, Kenneth H., jt. ed. see Pepler, Debra.

Rubin-Kurtzman, Jane R. The Socioeconomic Determinants of Fertility in Mexico: Changing Perspectives. Del Castillo, Sandra, tr. (Monograph Ser.: No. 23). 66p. (Orig.). (C). 1987. pap. 7.50 (0-935391-73-8, MN-23) UCSD Ctr US-Mex.

Rubin, Kyna, tr. see Ruowang, Wang.

Rubin, L. Families in Fault Lines. 1994. pap. 13.00 (0-06-092229-X) HarpC.

Rubin, L. F., jt. auth. see Saunders, L. Z.

Rubin, Laurence, jt. auth. see Abney, Darrell H.

Rubin, Laurie. Food First Curriculum. (Illus.). 146p. (J). (gr. 3-8). 1984. 12.00 (0-935028-17-X) Inst Food & Develop.

Rubin, Laurie, photos. Food Tales: A Literary Menu of Mouthwatering Masterpieces. (Illus.). 96p. 1992. 15.00 (0-670-84046-7, Viking Studio) Studio Bks.

Rubin, Lawrence A. Mighty Mac: The Official Picture History of the Mackinac Bridge. LC 58-13847. (Illus.). 148p. 1986. reprint ed. pap. 12.95 (0-8143-1817-7) Wayne St U Pr.

Rubin, Leigh. Amusing Arrangements. LC 84-90632. (Notable Quotes Ser.: Vol. III). (Illus.). 80p. (Orig.). 1985. pap. text ed. 5.95 (0-943384-04-4) Rubes Pubns.

— Encore! LC 83-90153. (Notable Quotes Ser.: Vol. II). (Illus.). 80p. (C). 1983. pap. 5.95 (0-943384-03-6) Rubes Pubns.

— Notable Quotes. (Orig.). 1981. pap. 5.95 (0-941364-00-3) Rubes Pubns.

— Notable Quotes. LC 81-69508. (Notable Quotes Ser.: Vol. I). (Illus.). 80p. (Orig.). (J). (gr. 4 up). 1981. pap. 5.95 (0-943384-00-1) Rubes Pubns.

— Rubes. 160p. (Orig.). 1988. pap. 4.95 (0-399-51488-0) Rubes Pubns.

— Sharks Are People Too! LC 82-99813. (Illus.). 80p. 1982. pap. 4.95 (0-943384-02-8) Rubes Pubns.

Rubin, Leona G. & Porter, Alison I. Your Guide to Social Security Benefits, 1991-92. (Illus.). 188p. 1991. 19.95 (0-8160-2615-7) Facts on File.

Rubin, Leonard G., jt. auth. see Anderson, Patricia M.

Rubin, Leroy. Optometrist's Desk Reference. (Illus.). 336p. 1987. spiral bd. 34.95 (0-409-90057-5) Buttrwrth-Heinemann.

Rubin, Leslie & Rubin, Charles. The Quest for Justice. 3rd ed. 1992. pap. 26.00 (0-536-58152-5) Ginn Pr.

Rubin, Leslie G., ed. Politikos II: Educating the Ambitious: Leadership & Political Rule in Greek Political Thought. LC 89-1075. (Politikos: Selected Papers of the North American Chapter of the Society for Greek Political Thought). 230p. (C). 1992. text ed. 47.50x (0-8207-0236-6, VOL. 2) Duquesne.

Rubin, Lewis J., ed. Pulmonary Heart Disease. 1984. lib. bdg. 134.00 (0-89838-632-2) Kluwer Ac.

Rubin, Lillian B. Busing & Backlash: White Against White in an Urban School District. 1972. pap. 9.00 (0-520-02257-2) U CA Pr.

— Families on the Fault Line: America's Working Class Speaks about the Family, the Economy, Race, & Ethnicity. LC 93-27900. 288p. 1994. 23.00 (0-06-016741-6, HarpT) HarpC.

— Intimate Strangers: Men & Women Together. LC 82-48678. 1984. pap. 12.00 (0-06-091134-4, CN 1134, PL) HarpC.

— Intimate Strangers: Men & Women Together. 236p. (C). 1990. reprint ed. lib. bdg. 27.00x (0-8095-9014-X) Borgo Pr.

— Just Friends: The Role of Friendship in Our Lives. 240p. (C). 1990. reprint ed. lib. bdg. 31.00x (0-8095-9015-8) Borgo Pr.

— Just Friends: The Role of Friendship in Our Lives. LC 84-43074. 256p. 1986. reprint ed. pap. 12.00 (0-06-091349-5, PL 1349, PL) HarpC.

— Quiet Rage: Bernie Goetz in a Time of Madness. 256p. 1986. 16.95 (0-374-24063-9) FS&G.

— Quiet Rage: Bernie Goetz in a Time of Madness. (C). 1988. pap. 13.00 (0-520-06446-1) U CA Pr.

— Worlds of Pain: Life in the Working-Class Family. LC 92-52719. 1992. pap. 16.00 (0-465-09248-9) Basic.

— Worlds of Pain: Life in the Working Class Family. 288p. (C). 1990. reprint ed. lib. bdg. 33.00x (0-8095-9016-6) Borgo Pr.

Rubin, Lionel F. Inherited Eye Diseases in Purebred Dogs. (Illus.). 376p. 1989. 69.50 (0-683-07452-0) Mosby Yr Bk.

*Rubin, Louis. The Heat of the Sun. 368p. 1995. 20.00 (1-56352-233-0) Longstreet Pr Inc.

Rubin, Louis, jt. ed. see Epstein, George.

Rubin, Louis D., Jr. Algonquin Literary Quiz Book. 96p. 1990. pap. 7.95 (0-945575-50-5) Algonquin Bks.

Rubin, Louis D. The Boll Weevil & the Triple Play. 1979. 5.00 (0-937684-00-7) Tradd St Pr.

Rubin, Louis D., Jr. Edge of the Swamp: A Study in the Literature & Society of the Old South. LC 88-27632. xii, 256p. 1989. text ed. 27.50 (0-8071-1495-2) La State U Pr.

— A Gallery of Southerners. LC 82-64. xx, 233p. 1982. pap. text ed. 11.95 (0-8071-1160-0) La State U Pr.

— Golden Weather. LC 61-6740. (Voices of the South Ser.). 303p. 1995. pap. 12.95 (0-8071-2009-X) La State U Pr.

— Mockingbird in the Gum Tree: A Literary Gallimaufry. LC 90-27597. 281p. 1991. 27.50 (0-8071-1680-7) La State U Pr.

— Small Craft Advisory: A Book about the Building of a Boat. LC 91-19545. 394p. 1991. pap. 12.00 (0-87113-533-7) Grove-Atltic.

— Virginia: A History. (States & the Nation Ser.). (Illus.). 1984. pap. 7.95 (0-393-30137-0) Norton.

— The Wary Fugitives: Four Poets & the South. LC 77-25479. (Walter Lynwood Fleming Lectures). 408p. 1978. pap. text ed. 12.95 (0-8071-0454-X) La State U Pr.

*Rubin, Louis D. William Elliott Shoots a Bear: Essays on the Southern Literary Imagination. fac. ed. LC 75-5352. 295p. 1975. reprint ed. pap. 84.10 (0-7837-7820-1, 2047576) Bks Demand.

Rubin, Louis D., Jr., ed. An Apple for My Teacher: Twelve Writers Tell All about Teachers Who Made the Difference. (Illus.). 186p. 1987. 19.95 (0-912697-34-2); pap. 10.95 (0-912697-57-1) Algonquin Bks.

— A Bibliographical Guide to the Study of Southern Literature. LC 69-17627. (Southern Literary Studies). 375p. reprint ed. pap. 106.90 (0-8357-7168-7, 2019591) Bks Demand.

— Literary South. LC 86-7484. xvi, 735p. 1986. pap. text ed. 17.95 (0-8071-1359-X) La State U Pr.

Rubin, Louis D., Sr. & Duncan, Jim. The Weather Wizard's Cloud Book. (Illus.). 70p. 1984. pap. 7.95 (0-912697-10-5) Algonquin Bks.

Rubin, Louis D., Jr. & Holman, C. Hugh, eds. Southern Literary Study: Problems & Possibilities. LC 75-11553. 250p. reprint ed. pap. 71.30 (0-8357-3874-4, 2036606) Bks Demand.

Rubin, Louis D., Jr. & Jacobs, Robert D. South: Modern Southern Literature. LC 73-16744. 434p. 1974. reprint ed. text ed. 65.00 (0-8371-7224-1, RUS, Greenwood Pr) Greenwood.

*Rubin, Louis D., Jr. & Mills, Jerry L., eds. Writer's Companion. 1088p. (C). 1995. 39.95 (0-8071-1992-X) La State U Pr.

Rubin, Louis D., Jr., jt. auth. see Connelly, Thomas L.

Rubin, Louis D., Jr., et al, eds. The History of Southern Literature. LC 85-10183. xiv, 626p. 1990. pap. 16.95 (0-8071-1643-2) La State U Pr.

Rubin, Louis J. Artistry in Teaching. 182p. (C). 1985. pap. text ed. write for info. (0-07-554606-X) McGraw.

Rubin, Louis J., et al. Professional Supervision for Professional Teachers. Sergiovanni, Thomas J., ed. LC 75-7666. 88p. 1975. pap. text ed. 4.50 (0-87120-073-2, 611-75046) Assn Supervision.

Rubin, M. J., ed. Studies in Antarctic Meteorology. LC 66-6578. (Antarctic Research Ser.: Vol. 9). (Illus.). 231p. 1966. 18.00 (0-87590-109-3) Am Geophysical.

Rubin, Manning. Sixty Ways to Relieve Stress in Sixty Seconds. LC 92-50932. 128p. 1993. pap. 5.95 (1-56305-338-1, 3338) Workman Pub.

Rubin, Marilyn B. Nursing Care for Myocardial Infarction. LC 76-6218. (Illus.). 200p. 1977. 12.30 (0-87527-151-0) Green.

Rubin, Mark. The Orchestra. (Illus.). 48p. (J). (gr. k-3). 1992. pap. 7.95 (0-920668-99-2) Firefly Bks Ltd.

*Rubin, Mark G. Manual of Chemical Peels: Superficial & Medium Depth. 1995. write for info. (0-397-51506-5) Lippincott.

Rubin, Mark R., jt. ed. see Papacosma, Victor S.

Rubin, Martha A. Countryside, Garden & Table: A New England Seasonal Diary. LC 92-54761. (Illus.). 260p. 1993. 19.95 (1-55591-137-4) Fulcrum Pub.

Rubin, Martin. Showstoppers: Busby Berkeley & the Tradition of Spectacle. Belton, John, ed. LC 92-37956. (Film & Culture Ser.). 352p. (C). 1993. 29.50 (0-231-08054-9) Col U Pr.

Rubin, Martin, ed. Computerization & Automation in Health Facilities: Computerization & Automation. 296p. 1984. 167.00 (0-8493-5143-X, RC268, CRC Reprint) Franklin.

Rubin, Matatyahu. The Reconstruction of Trees from Their Automorphism Groups. LC 93-11577. (Contemporary Mathematics Ser.: Vol. 151). 274p. 1993. pap. 56.00 (0-8218-5187-X) Am Math.

*Rubin, Maury. The Book of Tarts: Form, Function & Flavor at the City Bakery. LC 94-32734. 1995. write for info. (0-688-12254-X) Morrow.

*Rubin, Max. Comp City: A Guide to Free Las Vegas Vacations. 296p. (Orig.). 1994. 39.95 (0-929712-35-8) Huntington Pr.

Rubin, Melvin L. Optics for Clinicians. 25th anniversary ed. LC 72-97862. (Illus.). 1993. 38.00 (0-937404-34-9) Triad Pub FL.

Rubin, Melvin L., ed. see Cassin, Barbara & Solomon, Sheila.

Rubin, Melvin L., jt. auth. see Milder, Benjamin.

Rubin, Michael. Architectural Ceramics: Eight Concepts. Van Shaik, Terry, ed. LC 85-50004. (Illus.). 28p. (Orig.). 1985. pap. 5.00 (0-936316-10-1) Wash U Gallery.

— Nonlinear: A Guide to Electronic Film & Video Editing. 2nd ed. LC 92-14460. (Illus.). (Orig.). 1992. 29.95 (0-937404-83-7) Triad Pub FL.

*Rubin, Michael & Baldwin, Benjamin, intros. Benjamin Baldwin: An Autobiography in Design. LC 94-23892. (Illus.). 200p. 1995. 55.00 (0-393-70198-0) Norton.

Rubin, Michael R. Private Rights, Public Wrongs: The Computer & Personal Privacy. Dervin, Brenda, ed. LC 88-19345. (Communication & Information Science Ser.). 176p. 1989. text ed. 35.00 (0-89391-518-1) Ablex Pub.

Rubin, Michael R., et al. The Knowledge Industry in the United States, 1960-1980. LC 85-43307. (Illus.). 264p. 1986. text ed. 47.50 (0-691-04235-7) Princeton U Pr.

Rubin, Milton A. Plumming in America: The Game: Poor Little Unfortunate Me. (Illus.). 90p. 1989. pap. write for info. (0-318-65811-9) Behav Psychol Servs.

Rubin, Milton D., ed. Man in Systems. (Illus.). 508p. (C). 1971. text ed. 200.00 (0-677-14060-6) Gordon & Breach.

Rubin, Miri. Corpus Christi: The Eucharist in Late Medieval Culture. (Illus.). 435p. (C). 1992. pap. 24.95 (0-521-43805-5) Cambridge U Pr.

Rubin, Miri, jt. ed. see Kay, Sarah.

*Rubin, Miriam. Grains. LC 95-5951. (Gourmet Pantry Ser.). 1995. 16.95 (0-00-225210-4) Collins SF.

Rubin, Morton. Plantation County. (Orig.). 1951. pap. 12.95 (0-8084-0247-1) NCUP.

Rubin, Murray. Federal-State Relations in Unemployment Insurance: A Balance of Power. LC 83-17118. 258p. 1983. 22.00 (*0-88099-013-9*); 12.00 (*0-88099-012-0*) W E Upjohn.

Rubin, N. N. & Cotran, E., eds. Annual Survey of African Law, Vol. 3: 1969. 416p. 1973. 45.00 (*0-7146-2948-0*, Pub. by F Cass Pubs UK) Intl Spec Bk.

— Readings in African Law, 2 vols., Set. 351p. 1970. 75.00 (*0-7146-2602-3*, Pub. by F Cass Pubs UK) Intl Spec Bk.

***Rubin, Nancy.** American Empress: The Life & Times of Marjorie Merriweather Post. LC 94-27664. 1995. 27.50 (*0-679-41347-2*, Villard Bks) Random.

— Ask Me If I Care: Voices from an American High School. (Illus.). 440p. (Orig.). 1994. pap. 16.95 (*0-89815-597-5*) Ten Speed Pr.

— Isabella of Castile: The First Renaissance Queen. (Illus.). 480p. 1992. pap. 14.95 (*0-312-08511-7*) St Martin.

Rubin, Nathan. Rock & Roll: Art & Anti-Art. 256p. (C). 1993. per. 21.95 (*0-8403-8666-4*) Kendall-Hunt.

Rubin, Olis. Designing Automatic Control Systems. 450p. 1986. text ed. 29.00 (*0-89006-218-8*) Artech Hse.

Rubin, P., jt. ed. see Vegh, B.

Rubin, P. C., ed. Hypertension in Pregnancy: Handbook of Hypertension, Vol. 10. 371p. 1988. 225.75 (*0-444-90470-0*) Elsevier.

Rubin, Patricia L. Giorgio Vasari: Art & History. LC 94-1254. (Illus.). 360p. 1995. 45.00 (*0-300-04909-9*) Yale U Pr.

Rubin, Paul, jt. auth. see Enstice, Wayne.

Rubin, Paul H. Business Firms & the Common Law: The Evolution of Efficient Rules. LC 83-11028. 206p. 1983. text ed. 49.95 (*0-275-91070-9*, C1070, Praeger Pubs) Greenwood.

— Managing Business Transactions: Controlling the Cost of Coordinating, Communicating, & Decision Making. 225p. 1990. text ed. 32.95 (*0-02-927595-4*) Free Pr.

— Managing Business Transactions: Controlling the Cost of Coordinating, Communicating, & Decision Making. 225p. 1993. pap. 19.95 (*0-02-927596-2*) Free Pr.

— Tort Reform by Contract. LC 92-38918. 91p. (Orig.). 1993. 29.75 (*0-8447-3829-8*, AEI Pr); pap. 9.75 (*0-8447-3828-X*, AEI Pr) Am Enterprise.

Rubin, Paul H., jt. auth. see Kau, James B.

Rubin, Peter, ed. Controversies in Therapeutics. (Illus.). 67p. 1991. pap. text ed. 22.00 (*0-7279-0299-7*, Pub. by British Med Jrnl UK) Amer Coll Phys.

Rubin, Philip F. Clinical Oncology for Physicians & Students: A Multidisciplinary Approach. 7th ed. (Illus.). 768p. 1993. pap. text ed. 15.00 (*0-7216-3761-2*) Saunders.

Rubin, Phyllis B. & Tregay, Jeanine L. Play with Them - Theraplay Groups in the Classroom: A Technique for Professionals Who Work with Children. (Illus.). 206p. (C). 1989. text ed. 39.95x (*0-398-05579-3*) C C Thomas.

Rubin, R. D. & Franks, Cyril M., eds. Advances in Behavior Therapy: Proceedings. Incl. 19671969. 59.50 (*0-12-601450-7*); 19691971. (*0-12-601452-3*); 19701972. (*0-12-601453-1*); 19711973. pap. (*0-12-601454-X*); 19671969. 59.50 (*0-12-601450-7*); (Serial Publications). write for info. (*0-318-50160-0*) Acad Pr.

Rubin, R. H. & Young, L. S., eds. Clinical Approach to Infection in the Compromised Host. 3rd ed. (Illus.). 800p. 1994. 135.00 (*0-306-44617-0*, Plenum Pr) Plenum.

Rubin, Rebecca B. & Nevins, Randi J. The Road Trip: An Interpersonal Adventure. 164p. (Orig.). (C). 1988. pap. text ed. 9.95 (*0-88133-328-X*) Waveland Pr.

Rubin, Rebecca B., et al. Communication Research: Strategies & Sources. 3rd ed. 318p. (C). 1993. pap. 17.95 (*0-534-17862-6*) Intl Thomson.

Rubin, Rebecca B., et al, eds. Communication Research Measures: A Sourcebook. LC 93-23402. (Communication Ser.). 406p. 1994. lib. bdg. 35.00 (*0-89862-291-3*, C2291) Guilford Pr.

***Rubin, Renee.** Avoiding Liability Risk: An Attorney's Advice to Library Trustees & Others. 30p. (Orig.). 1994. pap. text ed. 10.00 (*0-8389-3448-X*) ALA.

Rubin, Reva. Maternal Identity & the Maternal Experience. 256p. (C). 1984. 27.95 (*0-8261-4100-5*) Springer Pub.

Rubin, Rhea J. Intergenerational Programming. LC 93-28617. (How-to-Do-It Manuals for Libraries Ser.: No. 36). 198p. 1993. pap. 39.95 (*1-55570-157-4*) Neal-Schuman.

— Of a Certain Age: A Guide to Contemporary Fiction Featuring Older Adults. 308p. 1990. lib. bdg. 45.00 (*0-87436-547-3*) ABC-CLIO.

Rubin, Rhea J., ed. A Bibliotherapy Sourcebook. LC 78-939. (Neal-Schuman Professional Book Ser.). 416p. 1978. lib. bdg. 39.50 (*0-912700-04-1*) Oryx Pr.

Rubin, Rhea J. & McGovern, Gail. Working with Older Adults: A Handbook for Libraries. 3rd ed. 1990. pap. text ed. 17.50 (*0-929722-37-X*) CA State Library Fndtn.

***Rubin, Rhea J. & Suvak, Daniel.** Libraries Inside: A Practical Guide for Prison Librarians. Lee, Richard, ed. & illus. by. LC 94-43076. 235p. 1995. lib. bdg. 41.50 (*0-7864-0061-7*) McFarland & Co.

Rubin, Richard. Human Resource Management in Libraries: Theory & Practice. 350p. 1991. pap. 39.95 (*1-55570-087-X*) Neal-Schuman.

Rubin, Richard, ed. Critical Issues in Library Personnel Management. (Allerton Park Institute Ser.: No. 29). 1989. 10.00 (*0-87845-081-5*) U of Ill Lib Info Sci.

Rubin, Richard, jt. auth. see Goldberg, Philip.

Rubin, Richard, et al. Psyching Out Diabetes: A Positive Approach to Your Negative Emotions. 288p. 1992. 22.95 (*0-929923-97-9*) Lowell Hse.

— Psyching Out Diabetes: A Positive Approach to Your Negative Emotions. 312p. 1993. pap. 12.95 (*1-56565-088-3*, Anodyne) Lowell Hse.

Rubin, Richard E. Hiring Library Employees: A How-to-Do-It Manual. LC 93-36114. (How-to-Do-It Manuals for Libraries Ser.: No. 37). 205p. 1993. 39.95 (*1-55570-159-0*) Neal-Schuman.

Rubin, Riva, tr. see Omer, Devora.

***Rubin, Robert A., ed.** Poetry Out Loud. 240p. Date not set. pap. write for info. (*1-56512-122-8*) Algonquin Bks.

— Poetry Out Loud. 1993. 14.95 (*1-56512-030-2*) Algonquin Bks.

— The Weather Wizard's Diary. (Illus.). 400p. 1991. 12.95 (*0-945575-85-8*, 71585) Algonquin Bks.

Rubin, Robert A. & Postner. New York Construction Law Manual. LC 92-26172. (Construction Law Ser.). 1992. text ed. 110.00 (*0-07-172261-0*) Shepards-McGraw.

Rubin, Robert A., ed. see Wade, Brent.

Rubin, Robert A., ed. see Welter, John.

Rubin, Robert A., et al. Construction Claims: Prevention & Resolution. 2nd ed. (Illus.). 352p. 1992. text ed. 49.95 (*0-442-00441-9*) Chapman & Hall.

Rubin, Ronald & Young, Charles M. Formal Logic: A Model of English. LC 88-33383. 393p. (C). 1989. pap. text ed. 37.95 (*0-87484-891-1*) Mayfield Pub.

— Solutions Manual for Formal Logic: A Model of English. (C). 1989. teacher ed. write for info. (*0-87484-913-6*) Mayfield Pub.

Rubin, Ronald P., ed. Calcium & Cellular Secretion. LC 82-7489. 288p. 1982. 65.00 (*0-306-40978-X*, Plenum Pr) Plenum.

Rubin, Ronald P., et al, eds. Calcium in Biological Systems. LC 84-18246. 760p. 1985. 135.00 (*0-306-41747-2*, Plenum Pr) Plenum.

Rubin, Rose M. & Riney, Bobye J. The Economics of Dual-Earner Families. LC 93-5441. 176p. 1993. text ed. 52.95 (*0-275-94682-7*, Praeger Pubs) Greenwood.

— Working Wives & Dual-Earner Families. LC 93-5441. 176p. 1995. pap. text ed. 16.95 (*0-275-95338-6*, Praeger Pubs) Greenwood.

Rubin, Ross. Hayden's PowerBook PowerBook Power Book. (Illus.). 240p. (Orig.). 1992. pap. 24.95 (*0-672-48520-6*) Hayden.

Rubin, Ross, jt. auth. see Cohen, Raines.

Rubin, Ross S. Cool Mac After Dark, Incl. disk. (Illus.). (Orig.). 1992. Incl. high density disk. disk, pap. 19.95 (*0-672-48529-X*) Hayden.

— Yakety Mac: The Telecom Tome. 1992. Incl. a high density disk & a double density disk. disk 34.95 (*0-672-48548-6*) Hayden.

Rubin, Ruth. Jewish Folk Songs in Yiddish & English. (Illus.). 96p. (ENG & YID.). 1989. reprint ed. pap. 8.95 (*0-9622930-0-8*) R Rubin.

— Voices of a People: The Story of Yiddish Folksong. LC 79-84679. 558p. 1979. reprint ed. pap. 13.95 (*0-8276-0121-2*) JPS Phila.

Rubin, S., jt. auth. see Bozarth, J.

Rubin, S. G., ed. see Computers in Aerodynamics Symposium Staff.

Rubin, S. H., ed. Artificial Intelligence for Engineering, Design, & Manufacturing. 218p. 1992. pap. 30.00 (*1-55617-017-3*) Instru Soc.

Rubin, Sally. The Great Brain: A Study Guide. (Novel-Ties Ser.). 1989. teacher ed 15.95 (*0-88122-048-5*) Lrn Links.

Rubin, Sally Jo, jt. auth. see Von Graevenitz, Alexander.

Rubin, Samuel. Secret Science of Covert Inks. LC 86-82957. 138p. (Orig.). 1987. pap. 12.95 (*0-915179-44-X*) Loompanics.

Rubin, Seymour J. Private Foreign Investment: Legal & Economic Realities. LC 56-7594. 120p. reprint ed. pap. 34.20 (*0-317-28469-X*, 2020751) Bks Demand.

Rubin, Seymour J. & Hufbauer, Gary C., eds. Emerging Standards of International Trade & Investment: Multinational Codes & Corporate Conduct. LC 83-13859. 212p. 1984. 65.00 (*0-86598-133-7*) Rowman.

Rubin, Seymour J. & Jones, Mark L., eds. Conflict & Resolution in US-EC Trade Relations at the Opening of the Uruguay Round. LC 88-62364. 531p. 1989. lib. bdg. 60.00 (*0-379-20967-5*) Oceana.

Rubin, Seymour J. & Nelson, Richard W. International Investment Disputes: Avoidance & Settlement, No. 20. (Studies in Transnational Legal Policy). 1985. 8.50 (*0-317-01188-X*) Am Soc Intl Law.

Rubin, Seymour J. & Wallace, Don, Jr., eds. Transnational Corporations & Innovatory Activities. LC 93-15972. (United Nations Library on Transnational Corporations: Vol. 17). 1994. write for info. (*0-415-08550-0*) Routledge.

Rubin, Sol, jt. ed. see Surrency, Erwin C.

Rubin, Stanford E. & Roessler, Richard T. Foundations of the Vocational Rehabilitation Process. 4th ed. LC 94-6130. 460p. (Orig.). (C). 1994. pap. text ed. 36.00 (*0-89079-601-7*, 6786) PRO-ED.

Rubin, Stanford E., jt. auth. see Roessler, Richard.

***Rubin, Steffi & Rubin, Barry.** Four-Piece Passover Pak, Set. (Illus.). 32p. 1989. audio, pap. 19.95 (*1-880226-50-2*) Lederer Pubns.

Rubin, Steffi, jt. illus. see Rubin, Barry.

***Rubin, Steffi K.** It Is Good: Growing up in a Messianic Jewish Family, a Story to Read & Color. (Illus.). (J). 1989. pap. 4.95 (*1-880226-06-5*) Lederer Pubns.

Rubin, Stephen C. & Sutton, Gregory P., eds. Ovarian Cancer. LC 92-48792. (Illus.). 528p. 1993. text ed. 89.00 (*0-07-054204-X*) Hlth Prof Div.

Rubin, Stephen E. Public Schools Should Earn to Ski. LC 94-12732. 1994. pap. 25.00 (*0-87389-276-3*) ASQC Qual Pr.

Rubin, Stephen M. & Clarizio, Tony V. Consumer's Credit Guide. 104p. (Orig.). 1994. pap. text ed. 19.95 (*0-9640055-0-6*) Applied Telemedia.

Rubin, Steven J. The Complete James Bond Movie Encyclopedia. 480p. 1991. pap. 18.95 (*0-8092-3966-3*) Contemp Bks.

— Reel Exposure: How to Publicize & Promote Today's Motion Pictures. (Illus.). 337p. (C). 1992. pap. 19.95 (*0-911747-20-6*) Broadway Pr.

— Writing Our Lives: Autobiographies of American Jews, 1890-1990. LC 91-3599. 384p. 1991. text ed. 44.95x (*0-8276-0393-2*); pap. 19.95 (*0-8276-0399-1*) JPS Phila.

Rubin, Steven M. Computer Aids for VLSI Design. LC 86-26571. (VLSI Systems Ser.). (Illus.). 458p. (C). 1987. text ed. 49.50 (*0-201-05824-3*) Addison-Wesley.

Rubin, Susan G. Emily Good as Gold. 192p. (J). (gr. 5-9). 1993. 10.95 (*0-15-276632-4*, Browndeer Pr); pap. 3.95 (*0-15-276633-2*, Browndeer Pr) HarBrace.

— Frank Lloyd Wright. LC 93-48523. (First Impressions Ser.). (J). 1994. write for info. (*0-8109-3974-6*) Abrams.

Rubin, Susan G., jt. auth. see Farrington, Liz.

Rubin, Sy, jt. auth. see Mandell, Jonathan.

Rubin, Sylvia P. It's Not Too Late for a Baby: For Men & Women Over Thirty Five. (Illus.). 272p. 1980. 14.95 (*0-13-507046-5*, Spectrum Bks) P-H.

Rubin, Ted & Gable, Richard. Dependency Proceedings in California Juvenile Courts. 118p. 1991. 7.00 (*0-685-55336-1*, WRO133) Natl Ctr St Courts.

Rubin, Theodor I., jt. auth. see Lawler.

Rubin, Theodore I. The Angry Book. 224p. 1993. pap. 8.00 (*0-02-036565-9*, Collier S&S) S&S Trade.

— Child Potential: Fulfilling Your Child's Intellectual, Emotional, & Creative Promise. 224p. 1991. 18.95 (*0-8245-1298-7*); pap. 11.95 (*0-8245-1299-5*) Crossroad NY.

— Compassion & Self Hate: An Alternative to Despair. rev. ed. 288p. 1986. pap. 6.00 (*0-02-077750-7*, Collier S&S) S&S Trade.

— Jordi - Lisa & David. 15.95 (*0-89190-588-X*, Am Repr) Amereon Ltd.

— Overcoming Indecisiveness. 208p. 1986. mass mkt. 4.99 (*0-380-69977-X*) Avon.

— Real Love: What It Is, & How to Find It. 224p. 1990. 17.95 (*0-8245-1338-X*) Crossroad NY.

— The Winner's Notebook. 1985. pap. 4.95 (*0-02-077800-7*, Collier S&S) S&S Trade.

***Rubin, Uri.** The Eye of the Beholder: The Life of Muhammad As Viewed by the Early Muslims. LC 94-49175. (Studies in Late Antiquity & Early Islam: Vol. 5). 1995. 27.50 (*0-87850-110-X*) Darwin Pr.

Rubin, Vera, ed. Cannabis & Culture. (World Anthropology Ser.). (Illus.). xiv, 598p. 1975. 53.10 (*90-279-7669-4*) Mouton.

Rubin, Vera & Comitas, Lambros. Ganja in Jamaica. (New Babylon Studies in the Social Sciences: No.26). 206p. 1975. text ed. 21.35 (*90-279-7731-3*) Mouton.

Rubin, Vera & Tuden, Arthur, eds. Comparative Perspectives on Slavery in New World Plantation Societies, Vol. 292. (Annals Ser.). 1977. 42.00 (*0-89072-038-X*) NY Acad Sci.

Rubin, Vera, ed. see American Association for the Advancement of Science Staff.

Rubin, Vera C. & Coyne, George V., eds. Large-Scale Motions in the Universe. 610p. 1989. text ed. 125.00 (*0-691-08524-2*); pap. text ed. 45.00 (*0-691-08525-0*) Princeton U Pr.

Rubin, Vitalifi. Individual & State in Ancient China: Essays on Four Chinese Philosophers. LC 76-4516. 179p. reprint ed. pap. 51.10 (*0-8357-7779-0*, 2036139) Bks Demand.

Rubin, W. & Brookler, K. Dizziness: Etiologic Approach to Management. (Illus.). 256p. 1991. text ed. 53.00 (*0-86577-391-2*) Thieme Med Pubs.

Rubin, W. L., jt. auth. see DiFranco, J. V.

Rubin, Walter, tr. see Perez-Galdos, Benito.

Rubin, William. Cezanne: The Late Work. 1990. 55.00 (*0-8109-6019-2*) Abrams.

— Dada, Surrealism, & Their Heritage. 1990. pap. 19.95 (*0-8109-6025-7*) Abrams.

— Frank Stella. LC 75-100684. (Illus.). 176p. 1980. pap. 22.50 (*0-87070-584-9*, 0-8109-6073-7) Mus of Modern Art.

— Frank Stella: 1970-1987. (Illus.). 208p. 1987. 45.00 (*0-87070-593-8*, 0-8109-6074-5); pap. 22.50 (*0-87070-599-7*, 0-8109-6107-5) Mus of Modern Art.

— Picasso & Braque: Pioneering Cubism. (Illus.). 1990. 70.00 (*0-8109-6065-6*); pap. 34.95 (*0-685-58430-5*, 0-8109-6120-2) Abrams.

— Picasso & Braque: Pioneering Cubism. 1993. pap. 34.95 (*0-8109-6120-2*) Abrams.

Rubin, William, ed. Cezanne: The Late Work. (Illus.). 416p. 1977. 55.00 (*0-87070-278-5*, 0-8109-6019-0) Mus of Modern Art.

— Primitivism in Twentieth Century Art: Affinity of the Tribal & the Modern. (Illus.). 706p. 1984. 125.00 (*0-87070-518-0*); pap. 65.00 (*0-87070-534-2*, 0-8109-6068-0) Mus of Modern Art.

— Primitivism in 20th Century Art: Affinity of the Tribal & the Modern, 2 vols. (Illus.). 706p. 1995. pap. 65.00 (*0-8109-6068-0*) Abrams.

Rubin, William & Armstrong, Matthew. The William S. Paley Collection. (Illus.). 192p. 1992. 45.00 (*0-87070-170-3*, 0-8109-6101-6); pap. 27.50 (*0-87070-193-2*) Mus of Modern Art.

Rubin, William, jt. auth. see Lanchner, Carolyn.

***Rubin, William, et al.** Les Demoiselles D'Avignon. Elderfield, John, ed. (Studies in Modern Art: No. 3). (Illus.). 224p. 1994. 40.00 (*0-87070-162-2*, 0-8109-6125-3) Mus of Modern Art.

Rubin, William S. Dada, Surrealism & Their Heritage. LC 68-17466. (Illus.). (Orig.). 1968. pap. 19.95 (*0-87070-284-X*, 0-8109-6025-7) Mus of Modern Art.

— Modern Sacred Art & the Church of Assy. LC 61-15469. (Illus.). 245p. reprint ed. pap. 69.90 (*0-317-10614-7*, 2051858) Bks Demand.

Rubin, Z., jt. ed. see Hartup, W.

Rubin, Zick. Children's Friendship. (Developing Child Ser.). 165p. 1980. pap. text ed. 10.95 (*0-674-11619-4*) HUP.

— Psychology: Being Human--Brief, Updated Edition. alternate ed. 530p. (C). 1990. text ed. 30.50 (*0-06-045651-5*) HarpCollege.

Rubin, Zick, ed. Doing Unto Others: Joining, Molding, Conforming, Helping, Loving. (Patterns of Social Behavior Ser.). 160p. 1975. pap. 3.45 (*0-13-217596-7*, Spectrum Bks) P-H.

Rubin, Zick & McNeil, Elton B. Psychology: Being Human. 4th ed. 594p. (C). 1990. text ed. 37.25 (*0-06-044378-2*) HarpCollege.

Rubincam, Milton. Evidence: An Exemplary Study, a Craig Family Case History. LC 81-86218. 41p. (Orig.). pap. text ed. 5.00 (*0-915156-49-0*, SP 49) Natl Genealogical.

— Genealogy: A Selected Bibliography. 5th ed. 1983. 3.00 (*0-317-13824-3*) Banner Pr AL.

Rubinchik, Iu. Persian-Russian Dictionary, 2 vols. 1664p. (C). 1983. 195.00 (*0-685-46897-6*, Pub. by Collets) St Mut.

Rubincik, J. Persian-Russian Dictionary, 2 vols. 1664p. (PER & RUS.). 1985. 150.00 (*0-8288-1126-1*, F47750) Fr & Eur.

***Rubine, David.** Climber's Guide to Pinnacles National Monument. 2nd ed. (Illus.). 220p. (Orig.). 1995. pap. 20.00 (*0-934641-89-7*) Chockstone Pr.

***Rubinetti, Donald.** Cappy the Lonely Camel. LC 95-9690. (Illus.). (J). 1995. write for info. (*0-382-39150-0*); lib. bdg. write for info. (*0-382-39151-9*); pap. write for info. (*0-382-39152-7*) Silver Burdett Pr.

Rubinfein, Louisa, tr. see Ozawa, Ichiro.

Rubinfeld, Daniel L., jt. auth. see Pindyck, Robert S.

Rubinfeld, Daniel L., jt. ed. see Quigley, John M.

Rubinfeld, William A. Planning Your College Education. 160p. 1991. pap. 6.95 (*0-8442-6673-6*, Passport Bks) NTC Pub Grp.

Rubinfien, Leo, photos. A Map of the East. (Illus.). 132p. 1992. 40.00 (*0-87923-942-5*); pap. 25.00 (*0-87923-943-3*) Godine.

Rubinger, Bruce, ed. Applied Artificial Intelligence in Japan: Current Status, Key Research & Industrial Performers, Strategic Focus. 280p. 1988. 399.00 (*0-89116-744-7*) Hemisp Pub.

Rubinger, Catherine, jt. ed. see Bonnel, Roland.

Rubinger, Richard. Private Academies of the Tokugawa Period. LC 81-47950. (Illus.). 350p. 1982. 49.50x (*0-691-05352-9*) Princeton U Pr.

Rubinger, Richard, ed. An American Scientist in Early Meiji Japan: The Autobiographical Notes of Thomas C. Mendenhall. LC 88-27833. (Asian Studies at Hawaii: No. 35). (Illus.). 112p. 1989. pap. text ed. 11.00 (*0-8248-1177-1*) UH Pr.

Rubingh, D. N., jt. ed. see Noda, I.

Rubingh, Donn N. & Holland, Paul M., eds. Cationic Surfactants: Physical Chemistry. (Surfactant Science Ser.: Vol. 37). 544p. 1991. 165.00 (*0-8247-8357-3*) Dekker.

Rubingh, Donn N., jt. ed. see Holland, Paul M.

Rubington, Earl & Weinberg, Martin A. Deviance: The Interactionist Perspective. 5th ed. 580p. (C). 1987. pap. write for info. (*0-02-404390-7*) Macmillan.

Rubington, Earl & Weinberg, Martin S. The Study of Social Problems: Seven Perspectives. 5th ed. 352p. (C). 1995. pap. text ed. 23.00 (*0-19-508367-9*) OUP.

***Rubino, Anthony, Jr.** Life Lessons from the Brady Bunch: A Very Brady Advice Book. LC 94-48099. 1995. 6.95 (*0-452-27441-9*, Plume) NAL-Dutton.

***Rubino, Anthony.** 1001 Reasons to Procrastinate. 1994. pap. 4.99 (*0-918259-58-4*) CCC Pubns.

***Rubino, Debra.** Keepers of Secrets & Truths Otherwise Unknown. (Illus.). 40p. 1994. 11.00 (*0-9624021-8-4*) Ursinus College.

Rubino, Paul, jt. auth. see Stein, Victor.

Rubino-Sammartano, M. & Morse, C. G. Public Policy in Transnational Relationships. 1990. ring bd. 97.00 (*90-6544-955-8*) Kluwer Law Tax Pubs.

Rubino-Sammartano, Mauro. International Arbitration Law. 550p. 1990. 110.00 (*90-6544-432-7*) Kluwer Law Tax Pubs.

Rubino-Sammartano, Mauro, ed. Warranties in Cross-Border Acquisitions. LC 93-23307. (International Bar Association Ser.). 480p. (C). 1993. lib. bdg. 155.00 (*1-85333-946-6*, Pub. by Graham & Trotman UK) Kluwer Ac.

Rubino, Virginia, jt. auth. see Heggie, Esther.

Rubinoff, Arthur G. Canada & South Asia: Political & Strategic Relations. (C). 1992. text ed. 32.00 (*1-895214-02-5*, Pub. by Centre S Asian Studies CN); pap. text ed. 23.00 (*1-895214-01-7*, Pub. by Centre S Asian Studies CN) S Asia.

Rubinoff, Aviva. Ima I'm Bored. 160p. Date not set. 13.95 (*1-56871-052-6*) Targum Pr.

Rubinoff, Darlene A. Dance of the Russian Peasant: Zaboomi. (Illus.). 321p. (Orig.). 1994. pap. text ed. 14.95 (*1-885740-01-8*) Raza Pubng.

Rubinoff, Lionel. Collingwood & the Reform of Metaphysics: A Study in the Philosophy of Mind. LC 73-19150. 427p. reprint ed. pap. 121.70 (*0-317-08071-7*, 2020519) Bks Demand.

Rubinoff, Lionel, jt. auth. see Van der Dussen, W. J.

Rubinoff, Michael W. Principle or Pragmatism: Interest Groups, PACs, & Campaign Contributions in 1984. write for info. (*0-318-61041-8*) Free Congr Res.

Rubinov, A. M., jt. auth. see Dem'yanov, V. F.

Rubinow, Isaac M. Economic Conditions of the Jews in Russia. LC 74-29519. (Modern Jewish Experience Ser.). 1975. reprint ed. 18.95 (*0-405-06744-5*) Ayer.

— The Quest for Security. LC 75-17241. (Social Problems & Social Policy Ser.). 1976. reprint ed. 52.95 (*0-405-07512-X*) Ayer.

— Social Insurance. LC 76-89761. (American Labor, from Conspiracy to Collective Bargaining Ser., No. 1). 525p. 1974. reprint ed. 30.95 (*0-405-02146-1*) Ayer.

R

An Asterisk (*) at the beginning of an entry indicates that the title is appearing in BIP for the first time.

Rubinow, Isaac M. & Stein, Leon, eds. Care of the Aged. LC 79-8683. (Growing Old Ser.). (Illus.). 1980. reprint ed. lib. bdg. 17.95 (*0-405-12800-2*) Ayer.
Rubinow, Sol I. Mathematical Problems in the Biological Sciences. (CBMS-NSF Regional Conference Ser.: No. 10). vii, 90p. (Orig.). 1973. pap. text ed. 16.00 (*0-89871-008-1*) Soc Indus-Appl Math.
Rubins, David K. The Human Figure. (Illus.). 1975. pap. 14.00 (*0-14-004243-1*, Penguin Bks) Viking Penguin.
***Rubins, Diane T.** Building Positive Parent-Child Communications. (For Parents Only Ser.). 16p. 1994. 1.95 (*1-56688-185-4*) Bur For At-Risk.
— Dealing with Your Child's Feelings. (For Parents Only Ser.). 16p. 1994. 1.95 (*1-56688-187-0*) Bur For At-Risk.
— Encouraging a Positive Attitude. (For Parents Only Ser.). 16p. 1994. 1.95 (*1-56688-189-7*) Bur For At-Risk.
— Getting Along Betteer with Your Child. (For Parents Only Ser.). 16p. 1994. 1.95 (*1-56688-186-2*) Bur For At-Risk.
— Keeping Your Child Drug-Free. (For Parents Only Ser.). 16p. (Orig.). 1994. 1.95 (*1-56688-193-5*) Bur For At-Risk.
— Teaching Your Child Responsibility. (For Parents Only Ser.). 16p. 1994. 1.95 (*1-56688-192-7*) Bur For At-Risk.
— Teaching Your Child the Value of Friendship. (For Parents Only Ser.). 16p. 1994. 1.95 (*1-56688-194-3*) Bur For At-Risk.
— Teaching Your Child to Appreciate Diversity. (For Parents Only Ser.). 16p. 1994. 1.95 (*1-56688-195-1*) Bur For At-Risk.
Rubins, J., et al. Brownstone. 101p. 1987. pap. 4.95 (*0-88145-054-5*) Broadway Play.
***Rubinsky, Holley.** Rapid Transits: And Other Stories. 192p. (Orig.). 1990. pap. 10.95 (*0-919591-56-6*, Pub. by Polestar Bk Pubs CN) Orca Bk Pubs.
Rubinsky, Susan, et al. An EMT Prepares: One Hundred Role-Playing Scenarios. 311p. (C). 1993. ring bd. 59.95 (*1-884225-00-4*) Communs Skills.
Rubinson, Kenneth A. Chemical Analysis. (C). 1987. text ed. 41.75 (*0-673-39552-9*) HarpCollege.
Rubinson, Laurna & Alles, Wesley F. Health Education: Foundations for the Future. (Illus.). 312p. 1988. reprint ed. text ed. 29.95 (*0-88133-331-X*) Waveland Pr.
Rubinson, Laurna & Neutens, James J. Research Techniques for the Health Sciences. (Illus.). 320p. (C). 1987. text ed. write for info. (*0-02-404540-3*) Macmillan.
Rubinson, Laurna, jt. auth. see Turner, Jeffrey S.
Rubinson, Richard, ed. Dynamics of World Development. LC 81-1437. (Political Economy of the World-System Annuals Ser.: No. 4). 264p. reprint ed. pap. 75.30 (*0-8357-8507-6*, 2034794) Bks Demand.
Rubinson, Richard, jt. ed. see Fuller, Bruce.
Rubinstein. Galax-Arena. (J). Date not set. lib. bdg. 13.89 (*0-06-023450-4*) HarpC Child Bks.
— Pharmaceutical Tech: Control. 1990. boxed write for info. (*0-318-68276-1*) P-H.
— Physical Electrochemistry: Science & Technology. (Monographs in Electroanalytical Chemistry - Electrochemistry). 608p. 1995. 150.00 (*0-8247-9452-4*) Dekker.
Rubinstein, jt. auth. see Russell.
Rubinstein, jt. auth. see Wells.
Rubinstein, A. Autobiography, 1829-1889. LC 68-25303. (Studies in Music: No. 42). 1969. reprint ed. lib. bdg. 75.00 (*0-8383-0315-3*) M S G Haskell Hse.
Rubinstein, Akiba. Rubinstein's Chess Masterpieces. Kmoch, Hans, ed. Winkelman, Barnie F., tr. 1941. pap. 5.95 (*0-486-20617-3*) Dover.
Rubinstein, Albin Z. Red Star on the Nile: The Soviet-Egyptian Influence Relationship since the June War. LC 76-3021. 1976. 59.50x (*0-691-07581-6*); pap. 21.95 (*0-691-10048-9*) Princeton U Pr.
Rubinstein, Allen & Korf, B. R. Neurofibramatosis. (Illus.). 320p. 1990. text ed. 65.00 (*0-86577-154-5*) Thieme Med Pubs.
Rubinstein, Alvin Z. The Arab-Israeli Conflict. (C). 1990. pap. text ed. 29.50 (*0-673-46405-9*) HarpCollege.
— Moscow's Third World Strategy. 344p. 1990. text ed. 47.50 (*0-691-07790-8*); pap. text ed. 13.95 (*0-691-02332-8*) Princeton U Pr.
— Soviet Foreign Policy since World War II. 4th ed. (C). 1991. text ed. 31.50 (*0-673-52163-X*) HarpCollege.
— Soviet Policy Toward Turkey, Iran & Afghanistan: The Dynamics of Influence. LC 82-7513. 218p. 1982. text ed. 35.00 (*0-275-90891-7*, C0891, Praeger Pubs) Greenwood.
— The Soviet Union & the Iran-Iraq War. (Pew Case Studies in International Affairs). 50p. (C). 1991. pap. text ed. 2.50 (*1-56927-352-9*) Geo U Inst Dplmcy.
— Soviets in International Organizations: Changing Policy Toward Developing Countries, 1953-1963. 1964. 57.50x (*0-691-08717-2*) Princeton U Pr.
— The Soviets in International Organizations: Changing Policy Toward Developing Countries, 1953-1963. LC 64-12184. Date not set. reprint ed. pap. 114.00 (*0-7837-9437-1*, 2060179) Bks Demand.
Rubinstein, Alvin Z., ed. America's National Interest in a Post-Cold War World: Issues & Dilemmas. LC 93-33417. 1993. pap. text ed. write for info. (*0-07-054162-0*) McGraw.
Rubinstein, Alvin Z. & Smith, Donald E., eds. Anti-Americanism in the Third World: Implications for U. S. Foreign Policy. (Foreign Policy Research Institute Ser.). 284p. 1984. text ed. 65.00 (*0-275-91257-4*, C1257, Praeger Pubs) Greenwood.
***Rubinstein, Alvin Z. & Smolansky, Oles M., eds.** Regional Power Rivalries in the New Eurasia: Russia, Turkey, & Iran. 304p. 1995. 59.95 (*1-56324-622-8*) M E Sharpe.
— Regional Power Rivalries in the New Eurasia: Russia, Turkey, & Iran. 304p. 1995. pap. 22.95 (*1-56324-623-6*) M E Sharpe.

R

Rubinstein, Alvin Z., ed. see Couloumbis, Theodore A.
Rubinstein, Alvin Z., ed. see Duncan, W. Raymond.
Rubinstein, Alvin Z., jt. ed. see Rieber, Alfred J.
Rubinstein, Alvin Z., ed. see Tahir-Kheli, Shirin.
Rubinstein, Annette. Great Tradition in English Literature from Shakespeare to Shaw, 2 Vols, Set. 3rd ed. LC 69-19792. 1969. pap. 16.95 (*0-85345-096-X*) Monthly Rev.
Rubinstein, Annette T., et al, eds. Vito Marcantonio: Selected Debates, Speeches & Writings 1935-1950. LC 73-12402. (Illus.). 1973. reprint ed. 49.50 (*0-678-01365-9*) Kelley.
Rubinstein, Anton. A Conversation on Music. Morgan, tr. LC 81-12547. (Music Ser.). 146p. 1982. reprint ed. lib. bdg. 23.50 (*0-306-76121-1*) Da Capo.
Rubinstein, Anton, ed. Autobiography of Anton Rubinstein, 1829-1889. 1988. reprint ed. lib. bdg. 59.00 (*0-7812-0097-0*) Rprt Serv.
Rubinstein, Ariel. Game Theory in Economics. (International Library of Critical Writings in Business History). 672p. 1990. text ed. 189.95 (*1-85278-169-6*, Pub. by E Elgar Pub UK) Ashgate Pub Co.
Rubinstein, Ariel, jt. auth. see Osborne, Martin J.
Rubinstein, Arye, jt. ed. see Lyman, William D.
Rubinstein, Aryeh, ed. Hasidism. 128p. pap. 4.50 (*0-686-95129-8*) ADL.
Rubinstein, Charlotte S. American Women Sculptors: A History of Women Working in Three Dimensions. (Monograph Ser.). 600p. (C). 1990. lib. bdg. 49.95 (*0-685-38164-1*) G K Hall.
— American Women Sculptures: A History of Women Working in Three Dimensions. (Monograph Ser.). (Illus.). 600p. (C). 1990. lib. bdg. 50.00 (*0-8161-8732-0*, Hall Reference) Macmillan.
***Rubinstein, Danny.** The Mystery of Arafat. 140p. 1995. 18.00 (*1-883642-10-8*) Steerforth Pr.
— People of Nowhere. 1993. pap. 9.00 (*0-8129-2149-6*, Times Bks) Random.
Rubinstein, David. A Different World for Women: The Life of Millicent Garrett Fawcett. 320p. 1991. lib. bdg. 42.50 (*0-8142-0564-X*) Ohio St U Pr.
Rubinstein, David, jt. auth. see Martin, David E.
Rubinstein, Donald H., intro. Pacific History: Papers from the 8th Pacific History Association Conference. (Illus.). vi, 476p. (Orig.). (C). 1992. pap. 12.00 (*1-878453-14-9*) Univ Guam MAR Ctr.
Rubinstein, Donna. I Am the Only Survivor of Krasnostav. LC 82-61794. (Illus.). 1983. 10.00 (*0-88400-093-1*) Shengold.
Rubinstein, E. Filmguide to The General. LC 72-88637. (Filmguide Ser.: No. 5). 93p. reprint ed. pap. 26.60 (*0-685-07749-7*, 2017638) Bks Demand.
Rubinstein, E., jt. ed. see Affron, Mirella J.
Rubinstein, Eddy, jt. auth. see Carter, Robert.
Rubinstein, Eli A., ed. see Conference on Research in Psychotherapy Staff.
***Rubinstein, Erna F.** After the Holocaust: The Long Road to Freedom. (Illus.). viii, 192p. (YA). (gr. 8 up). 1995. pap. 15.00 (*0-208-02421-2*) Shoe String.
***Rubinstein, Frankie.** A Dictionary of Shakespeare's Sexual Pluns & Their Significance. LC 95-5836. 1995. write for info. (*0-312-12677-8*) St Martin.
Rubinstein, Gillian. Dog in, Cat Out. LC 92-39785. (Illus.). 32p. (J). (ps-00). 1993. lib. bdg. 13.95 (*0-395-66596-5*) Ticknor & Flds Bks Yng Read.
— Galax-Arena. LC 93-1118. (J). 1994. 14.00 (*0-06-023449-0*, HarpT) HarpC.
— Galax-Arena. LC 95-4100. (J). 1995. 14.00 (*0-689-80136-X*) S&S Trade.
— Skymaze. MacDonald, Pat, ed. 240p. (J). (gr. 7 up). 1993. reprint ed. pap. 2.99 (*0-671-76988-X*, Archway) PB.
Rubinstein, Hilary. Europe's Wonderful Little Hotels & Inns. 5th ed. LC 82-19864. (Illus.). 624p. 1989. pap. 121.50 (*0-312-92193-4*) Congdon & Weed.
— Europe's Wonderful Little Hotels & Inns, 1993: Great Britain & Ireland. 15th ed. (Illus.). 352p. (Orig.). 1992. pap. 14.95 (*0-312-08185-5*) St Martin.
— Europe's Wonderful Little Hotels & Inns, 1994: Great Britain & Ireland. 16th ed. (Illus.). (Orig.). 1993. pap. 14.99 (*0-312-09801-4*) St Martin.
— Europe's Wonderful Little Hotels & Inns, 1994: The Continent. 16th ed. (Illus.). 496p. (Orig.). 1993. pap. 17.99 (*0-312-09802-2*) St Martin.
— Europe's Wonderful Little Hotels & Inns, 1995: Great Britain & Ireland. 352p. 1995. pap. 15.99 (*0-312-11442-7*) St Martin.
— Europe's Wonderful Little Hotels & Inns, 1995: The Continent. 528p. 1995. pap. 17.99 (*0-312-11447-8*) St Martin.
Rubinstein, Isaak. Electro-Diffusion of Ions. (Studies in Applied Mathematics: No. 11). ix, 254p. 1990. pap. 47.50 (*0-89871-245-9*) Soc Indus-Appl Math.
Rubinstein, Isaak & Rubenstein, Lev. Partial Differential Equations in Classical Mathematical Physics. (Illus.). 600p. (C). 1994. 99.95 (*0-521-41058-4*) Cambridge U Pr.
Rubinstein, Jonathan. City Police. 498p. 1980. pap. 15.00 (*0-374-51555-7*) FS&G.
Rubinstein, Joseph, jt. ed. see Slife, Brent.
Rubinstein, Judah, ed. see Brown, Albert M.
Rubinstein, Julie, ed. see Eppolito, Lou & Drury, Bob.
Rubinstein, Julie, ed. see Goldsmith, Olivia.
Rubinstein, Julie, ed. see Natow, Annette B. & Heslin, Jo-Ann.
Rubinstein, Julius B. Column Flotation: Processes, Designs & Practices. (Process Engineering for the Chemical Ser.). 1995. text ed. 95.00 (*2-88124-917-5*) Gordon & Breach.
Rubinstein, Leon. The First Swallows. LC 83-45138. (Illus.). 216p. 1986. 14.95 (*0-8453-4758-6*, Cornwall Bks) Assoc Univ Prs.
Rubinstein, Leonard. The Great Spy Films. (Illus.). 256p. 1981. pap. 7.95 (*0-8065-0775-6*, Citadel Pr) Carol Pub Group.

Rubinstein, Lim, jt. auth. see Starlin, Perez.
Rubinstein, Lucien J. Atlas of Tumor Pathology: Tumors of the Central Nervous System. (Second Ser.: Fascicle 6). (Illus.). 418p. 1990. reprint ed. per., pap. 20.00 (*0-16-001832-3*, S/N 008-023-000) USGPO.
Rubinstein, Mark. The Growing Years: A Guide to Your Child's Emotional Development from Birth to Adolescence. braille ed. 1038p. 1990. Braille. vinyl bd. 83.04 (*1-56956-250-4*, BR7390) W A T Braille.
Rubinstein, Mark, jt. auth. see Cox, John C.
Rubinstein, Meyer R., contrib. Landscape As Stage. (Illus.). 6p. 1991. pap. 2.00 (*0-685-62371-8*) Locks Gallery.
***Rubinstein, Meyer R. & Schwabsky, Barry.** Walton Ford & Julie Jones. Riley, Jan, ed. (Illus.). 48p. (C). 1993. pap. 25.00 (*0-917562-63-1*) Contemp Arts.
***Rubinstein, Michael.** Rembrandt & Angels. 47p. 1982. pap. 4.00 (*0-904674-18-5*, Pub. by Octagon Pr UK) ISHK Bk Service.
Rubinstein, Michael, jt. auth. see Parker, Rowland.
Rubinstein, Moshe F. Tools for Thinking & Problem Solving. (Illus.). 416p. (C). 1985. text ed. 69.00 (*0-13-925140-5*) P-H.
Rubinstein, Moshe F. & Firstenberg, Iris R. Patterns of Problem Solving. 2nd ed. LC 94-7371. 1994. text ed. 56.00 (*0-13-122706-8*) P-H Gen Ref & Trav.
Rubinstein, Moshe F., jt. auth. see Hurty, Walter C.
***Rubinstein, Murray A.** The Origins of the Anglo-American Missionary Enterprise in China, 1807-1840. LC 94-22094. (ATLA Monograph Ser.). 1995. write for info. (*0-8108-2932-0*) Scarecrow.
Rubinstein, Murray A., ed. The Protestant Community on Modern Taiwan: Mission, Seminary, & Church. LC 90-31312. (Taiwan in the Modern World Ser.). 214p. (C). 1991. 51.95 (*0-87332-658-X*) M E Sharpe.
Rubinstein, Murray A., intro. The Other Taiwan: 1945 to the Present. LC 94-16058. (Taiwan in the Modern World Ser.). 496p. (C). 1994. text ed. 60.00 (*1-56324-192-7*, East Gate Bk); pap. text ed. 22.50 (*1-56324-193-5*) M E Sharpe.
Rubinstein, Nicolai, ed. Florentine Studies: Politics & Society in Renaissance Florence. LC 68-29148. 585p. reprint ed. 166.80 (*0-8357-9458-X*, 2010276) Bks Demand.
***Rubinstein, Nicoli.** The Palazzo Vecchio, 1298-1532: Government, Architecture, & Imagery in the Civic Palace of the Florentine Republic. (Oxford-Warburg Studies). (Illus.). 240p. 1995. 79.00 (*0-19-920602-3*) OUP.
Rubinstein, Norman. The Invisibly Wounded. 224p. 1993. 39.00 (*1-870360-00-1*) St Mut.
Rubinstein, R. & Shapiro, A. Discrete Event Systems: Sensitivity Analysis & Stochastic Optimization by the Score Function Method. LC 92-32372. (Probability & Mathematical Statistics Ser.). 334p. 1993. text ed. 69.95 (*0-471-93419-4*) Wiley.
Rubinstein, Reuven Y. Monte Carlo Optimization, Simulation & Sensitivity of Queueing Networks. LC 92-13121. 272p. (C). 1992. reprint ed. lib. bdg. 54.00 (*0-89464-764-4*) Krieger.
— Simulation & the Monte Carlo Method. LC 81-1873. (Probability & Mathematical Statistics Ser.). 278p. 1981. text ed. 99.95 (*0-471-08917-6*, Wiley-Interscience) Wiley.
Rubinstein, Richard. Introduction to Digital Typography. LC 86-26600. (Illus.). 320p. (C). 1988. text ed. 35.50 (*0-201-17633-5*) Addison-Wesley.
Rubinstein, Richard & Hersh, Harry. The Human Factor: Designing Computer Systems for People. 256p. 1984. 29.95 (*0-932376-44-4*, EY-00013-DP, Digital DEC) Buttrwrth-Heinemann.
Rubinstein, Robert A., ed. Fieldwork: The Correspondence of Robert Redfield & Sol Tax. 354p. 1991. text ed. 61.00 (*0-8133-0779-1*) Westview.
Rubinstein, Robert E. Hints for Teaching Success in Middle School. (Illus.). 200p. 1994. pap. text ed. 19.00 (*1-56308-124-5*) Teacher Ideas Pr.
Rubinstein, Robert L. Singular Paths: Old Men Living Alone. LC 85-19063. 1988. text ed. 43.00 (*0-231-06206-0*); pap. text ed. 16.50 (*0-231-06207-9*) Col U Pr.
Rubinstein, Robert L., ed. Anthropology & Aging: Comprehensive Reviews. (C). 1990. lib. bdg. 89.00 (*0-7923-0743-7*) Kluwer Ac.
Rubinstein, Robert L., et al. Elders Living Alone: Frailty & the Perception of Choice. 184p. 1992. lib. bdg. 38.95 (*0-202-36083-0*); pap. text ed. 20.95 (*0-202-36084-9*) Aldine de Gruyter.
***Rubinstein, Ruth.** Dress Codes: Meanings & Messages in American Culture. LC 94-32808. (C). 1994. pap. text ed. 21.95 (*0-8133-2283-9*) Westview.
Rubinstein, Sarah P., jt. auth. see Brook, Michael.
Rubinstein, Sidney P., ed. Participative Systems At Work: Creating Quality & Employment Security. LC 86-20044. 180p. 1987. 30.95 (*0-89885-338-9*) Human Sci Pr.
Rubinstein, W. D. The Biographical Dictionary of Life Peers. 400p. 1991. text ed. 75.00 (*0-312-01911-4*) St Martin.
— Elites & the Wealthy in Modern British History: Essays in Social & Economic History. LC 87-9879. 352p. 1988. text ed. 39.95 (*0-312-00947-X*) St Martin.
— A History of the Jews in the English-Speaking World: Great Britain. LC 95-12347. (Studies in Modern History). 1995. write for info. (*0-312-12542-9*) St Martin.
— Men of Property: The Very Wealthy in Britain since the Industrial Revolution. LC 80-54836. (Illus.). 261p. reprint ed. pap. 74.40 (*0-8357-7950-5*, 2057025) Bks Demand.
Rubio, Alfredo. Adventures in Being. 138p. 1992. pap. 12.95 (*0-85244-212-2*, Pub. by Gracewing UK) Morehouse Pub.

Rubio, Antonio, jt. auth. see Jackson, Eugene.
Rubio-Boitel, Fernando. Spanish Short Stories & Poems. 1979. pap. 1.50 (*0-686-23892-3*) Rubio-Boitel.
Rubio Cremades, Enrique, ed. see Fernan, Caballero.
Rubio, Daniel, jt. auth. see Gaos, Ignacio.
Rubio, David. Hay una Filosofia En el Quijote. 168p. (SPA.). 1924. 1.00 (*0-318-14272-4*) Hispanic Inst.
— Symbolism & Classicism in Modern Literature. 1972. 59.95 (*0-8490-1167-1*) Gordon Pr.
Rubio De Francia, J. L., jt. auth. see Garcia-Cuerva.
Rubio, Enrique, ed. see Valera, Juan.
Rubio, Fanny, ed. see Alonso, Damaso.
Rubio, Ignusi D. & Capitel, Anton G. Contemporary Spanish Architecture: An Eclectic Panorama. LC 85-43529. (Illus.). 144p. 1986. pap. 28.50 (*0-8478-0708-8*) Rizzoli Intl.
Rubio, J. E. Control & Optimization: The Linear Treatment of Nonlinear Problems. (Nonlinear Science: Theory & Applications Ser.). 132p. 1992. text ed. 125.00 (*0-471-93511-5*) Wiley.
— Control & Optimization: The Linear Treatment of Nonlinear Problems. LC 85-15256. (Nonlinear Science: Theory & Applications Ser.). 250p. (C). 1988. text ed. 65.00 (*0-7190-1841-2*, Pub. by Manchester Univ Pr UK) St Martin.
— Optimization & Nonstandard Analysis. LC 94-21446. (Pure & Applied Mathematics Ser.: Vol. 184). 376p. 1994. 135.00 (*0-8247-9281-5*) Dekker.
Rubio, J. Lopez. Celos Del Aire. 125p. (SPA.). 1982. 9.50 (*0-8288-7159-0*) Fr & Eur.
Rubio, Jesus M. Aspectroscopia Infrarroja. 2nd rev. ed. (Serie de Quimica Monografia: No. 12). 80p. (C). 1981. pap. text ed. 3.50 (*0-8270-1419-8*) OAS.
Rubio-Jimenez, Jesus, tr. see Alarcon, Pedro A.
Rubio Jimenez, Jesus, ed. see Del Valle-Inclan, Ramon.
Rubio, Jose L. In August We Play the Pyrenees. Holt, Marion P., tr. (Contemporary Spanish Plays Ser.: No. 2). x, 69p. 1993. pap. 6.00 (*0-9631212-1-9*) Estreno.
Rubio, Lourdes, tr. Un Curso Basico de Lenguaje Americano de Senas. 1991. 27.95 (*0-932666-35-3*) T J Pubs.
Rubio, Luis F. & Gil-Diaz, Francisco. A Mexican Response: A Twentieth Century Fund Paper. 72p. (Orig.). 1987. pap. 9.00 (*0-87078-215-0*) TCFP-PPP.
***Rubio, Maggie & Durnberg, Steffi.** A New Beginning. 144p. (C). 1994. per., pap. text ed. 19.95 (*0-8403-9931-6*) Kendall-Hunt.
***Rubio, Mary & Waterston, Elizabeth.** Writing a Life. Date not set. pap. 9.95 (*1-55022-220-1*) InBook.
Rubio, Mary & Waterston, Elizabeth, eds. The Selected Journals of L. M. Montgomery, Vol. 2: 1910-1921. 464p. 1988. 35.00 (*0-19-540586-2*) OUP.
Rubio, Mary, ed. see Montgomery, Lucy M.
Rubio, Pedro. The Lamps of Fire. Prouty, Graciela P., tr. (Illus.). 115p. (Orig.). (J). Date not set. pap. 8.95 (*0-9637601-0-6*) Mount Ctr.
Rubio, Thalia. Slices of Life: Writing from North America. 256p. 1993. text ed. 17.50 (*0-13-813296-8*) P-H.
Rubio, Toni C., jt. auth. see Peyton, Robert X.
Rubiralta, M., et al. Piperidine: Structure, Preparation, Reactivity & Synthetic Applications of Piperidine & Its Derivatives. (Studies in Organic Chemistry: No. 43). 444p. 1991. 188.50 (*0-444-88348-7*) Elsevier.
Rubissow, Ariel. John Muir National Historic Site. Priehs, T. J., ed. LC 90-62309. (Illus.). 16p. (Orig.). 1990. pap. 2.95 (*0-911408-91-6*) SW Pks Mnmts.
— Park Guide: Golden Gate National Recreation Area. (Illus.). 96p. (Orig.). 1990. pap. 12.95 (*0-9625206-0-8*) Gldn Gate Natl Park Assoc.
Ruble, Blair A. Leningrad: Shaping a Soviet City. 1990. 48.00 (*0-520-06534-4*) U CA Pr.
— Leningrad: Shaping a Soviet City. LC 89-4716. 328p. 1990. 45.00 (*0-87772-347-8*) UCB IGS.
— Money Sings: The Changing Politics of Urban Space in Post-Soviet Yaroslavl. (Woodrow Wilson Center Press Ser.). (Illus.). 150p. (C). 1995. 54.95 (*0-521-48242-9*) Cambridge U Pr.
Ruble, Blair A., jt. ed. see Brumfield, William C.
Ruble, Blair A., jt. auth. see Kahan, Arcadius.
Ruble, Blair A., jt. auth. see Pravda, Alex.
Ruble, Diane N., et al, eds. The Social Psychology of Mental Health: Basic Mechanisms & Applications. LC 92-1540. 365p. 1992. lib. bdg. 40.00 (*0-89862-136-4*) Guilford Pr.
***Ruble, Ken.** The Zoomie Conspiracy. 280p. 1996. pap. 8.95 (*0-7610-0520-X*) NW Pub.
Ruble, Richard, ed. Christian Perspectives on Psychology. LC 75-15956. 147p. (C). 1975. pap. text ed. 15.95 (*0-8422-0456-3*) Irvington.
Ruble, Shirley. DUI Handbook for Paralegals. 150p. 1994. pap. text ed. 20.00 (*1-878703-03-X*) Legal Pubns.
— Welcome to Israel: A Bridges for Peace Study Tour. (Illus.). 110p. (Orig.). 1993. pap. write for info. (*1-878703-01-3*) Legal Pubns.
Rubloff, Gary & Lucovsky, Gerald, eds. Deposition & Growth: Limits for Microelectronics: Proceedings of a Topical Conference on at Anaheim, California in November 1987. (American Vacuum Society Ser.: No. 4). (Illus.). 402p. 1988. 70.00 (*0-88318-367-6*) Am Inst Physics.
Rubly-Burggraff, Roberta. Look Who's Drivin' the Bus. (Illus.). 150p. (Orig.). (YA). (gr. 9 up). 1993. pap. 29.95 (*0-937997-25-0*) Hi-Time Pub.
— Magnum Opus: An Affirmation Journal. (Illus.). 72p. (Orig.). (YA). (gr. 7-12). 1989. pap. 5.95 (*0-937997-14-5*) Hi-Time Pub.
Rubner, Alex. Economy of Israel. 307p. 1959. 26.00 (*0-7146-1249-9*, Pub. by F Cass Pubs UK) Intl Spec Bk.
— The Might of the Multinationals: The Rise & Fall of the Corporate Legend. LC 89-26526. 320p. 1990. text ed. 49.95 (*0-275-93531-0*, C3531, Greenwood Pr) Greenwood.

An Asterisk (*) at the beginning of an entry indicates that the title is appearing in BIP for the first time.

Rubottom, Richard R. & Murphy, J. C. Spain & the United States: Since World War II. LC 83-19247. 176p. 1984. text ed. 45.00 (0-275-91259-0, C1259, Praeger Pubs) Greenwood.

Rubovits, Norma. Marbled Vignettes. 8p. 1992. 125.00 (0-87093-278-0); 600.00 (0-87093-279-9) Dawsons.

Rubow, Lynn N., ed. Fluidized Bed Combustion, 1993: FBC's Role in the World Energy Mix. LC 87-70969. 1388p. 1993. pap. 144.00 (0-7918-0681-2, I00344) ASME.

Rubow, P. V. Shakespeare's Hamlet. LC 79-174974. (DAN.). reprint ed. 34.50 (0-404-05448-X) AMS Pr.

***Rubright, Robert.** Walks & Rambles in & Around St. Louis. (Walks & Rambles Ser.). (Illus.). 208p. (Orig.). 1995. pap. 14.00 (0-88150-344-4, Backcountry) Countryman.

Rubsamen, Gisela. The Orsini Inventories. LC 80-83121. 224p. 1980. pap. 46.00 (0-89236-010-0) J P Getty Trust.

Rubsamen, Walter H. Literary Sources of Secular Music in Italy: 1500. LC 72-4482. (Music Ser.). 82p. 1972. reprint ed. lib. bdg. 21.50 (0-306-70496-X) Da Capo.

— Music Research in Italian Libraries. 1993. reprint ed. lib. bdg. 89.00 (0-7812-9699-4) Rprt Serv.

Rubstov, V. V., ed. Learning in Children: Organization & Development. 250p. 1991. pap. text ed. 59.00 (1-56072-005-0) Nova Sci Pubs.

Rubtsov, I. A. Blackflies (Simuliidae) LC 89-71184. (Fauna of the U. S. S. R. Diptera Ser.: Vol. 6, Pt. 6). (Illus.). xxviii, 1042p. 1990. 171.50 (90-04-08871-7) E J Brill.

Ruby. Sentencing. 3rd ed. 712p. 1987. 115.00 (0-409-86422-6) Butterworth Legal Pubs.

***Ruby, Amanda.** Lighten Up! With Non Fat-Low Fat Recipes. 215p. Date not set. pap. text ed. write for info. (0-9644820-0-2) Amegard.

Ruby, Christine N. WPA Art in Michigan. (Illus.). 175p. (C). 1988. 34.95 (0-8143-2061-9, Great Lks Bks) Wayne St U Pr.

Ruby, Clayton. Sentencing. 4th ed. 750p. 1994. write for info. (0-409-91240-9, Pub. by Buttrwrth Can Acad CN) Buttrwrth-Heinemann.

Ruby, Clayton C. & Martin, Dianne L. Criminal Sentencing Digest. 380p. 1993. ring bd. 150.00 (0-409-91241-7) Butterworth Legal Pubs.

Ruby, Douglas A., jt. auth. see Owen, Wyn F.

Ruby, E. A. The Human Figure: A Photographic Reference for Artists. 1974. pap. 29.95 (0-442-27148-4) Van Nos Reinhold.

***Ruby, Jay.** Secure the Shadow: Death & Photography in America. LC 94-23118. 1995. 39.95 (0-262-18164-9) MIT Pr.

Ruby, Jay, ed. The Cinema of John Marshall. LC 92-28923. (Visual Anthropology Ser.: Vol. 3). 282p. 1993. text ed. 58.00 (3-7186-0557-0); pap. text ed. 24.00 (3-7186-0558-9) Gordon & Breach.

Ruby, Jennifer. Costume in Context: Medieval Times. (Costume in Context Ser.). (Illus.). 64p. (YA). (gr. 7-11). 1990. 24.95 (0-7134-6075-X, Pub. by Batsford UK) Trafalgar.

— Costume in Context: The 1940s & 1950s. (Costume in Context Ser.). (Illus.). 64p. (YA). (gr. 7-11). 1990. 24.95 (0-7134-6016-4, Pub. by Batsford UK) Trafalgar.

— Costume in Context: The 1980s. (Illus.). 72p. (YA). (gr. 7-11). 1991. 24.95 (0-7134-6539-5, Pub. by Batsford UK) Trafalgar.

— The Edwardians & the First World War. (Costume in Context Ser.). (Illus.). 72p. (YA). (gr. 7-9). 1988. 24.95 (0-7134-5605-1, Pub. by Batsford UK) Trafalgar.

— The Eighteenth Century. (Costume in Context Ser.). (YA). (gr. 7 up). 1989. 24.95 (0-7134-5772-4, Pub. by Batsford UK) Trafalgar.

— Nineteen Fifties & Nineteen Sixties. (People in Costume Ser.). (Illus.). 48p. (J). (gr. 6-9). 1994. 19.95 (0-7134-7217-0, Pub. by Batsford UK) Trafalgar.

— Nineteen Seventies & Nineteen Eighties. (People in Costume Ser.). (Illus.). 48p. (J). (gr. 6-9). 1994. 19.95 (0-7134-7218-9, Pub. by Batsford UK) Trafalgar.

— The Nineteen Sixties & Nineteen Seventies. (Costume in Context Ser.). (Illus.). 64p. (YA). (gr. 6-9). 1989. 24.95 (0-7134-6074-1, Pub. by Batsford UK) Trafalgar.

— Nineteen Thirty - Nineteen Fourty-Five. (People in Costume Ser.). 48p. (J). (gr. 5-8). 1995. 19.95 (0-7134-7216-2, Pub. by Batsford UK) Trafalgar.

— The Nineteen Twenties & Nineteen Thirties. (Costume in Context Ser.). (Illus.). 64p. (YA). (gr. 7-9). 1989. 24.95 (0-7134-5773-2, Pub. by Batsford UK) Trafalgar.

— The Regency. (Costume in Context Ser.). (Illus.). 64p. (YA). (gr. 6-9). 1989. 24.95 (0-7134-5992-1, Pub. by Batsford UK) Trafalgar.

— The Romans. (People in Costume Ser.). 48p. (YA). (gr. 5-8). 1995. 19.95 (0-7134-7621-4, Pub. by Batsford UK) Trafalgar.

— The Stuarts. (Costume in Context Ser.). (Illus.). 72p. (YA). (gr. 7-9). 1988. 24.95 (0-7134-5604-3, Pub. by Batsford UK) Trafalgar.

— The Tudors. (People in Costume Ser.). (YA). (gr. 7-12). 1995. 19.95 (0-7134-7214-6, Pub. by Batsford UK) Trafalgar.

Ruby, Lois. Miriam's Well. LC 91-46301. 288p. (YA). (gr. 7 up). 1993. 13.95 (0-590-44937-0) Scholastic Inc.

— Skin Deep. LC 93-13707. (YA). (gr. 7 up). 1994. 14.95 (0-590-47699-8) Scholastic Inc.

— Steal Away Home. LC 93-47300. (J). 1994. text ed. 14.95 (0-02-777883-5) Macmillan.

Ruby, Mary, jt. ed. see Hillstrom, Kevin.

Ruby, Ralph, et al. Microsoft Works Applications. rev. ed. 1991. teacher ed 7.10 (1-56118-541-8); text ed. 13.95 (1-56118-540-X); 3.5 hd 69.00 (1-56118-543-4); 5.25 hd 69.00 (1-56118-542-6) Paradigm MN.

Ruby, Robert. Jericho. 1995. 25.00 (0-8050-2799-8) H Holt & Co.

— Ruby in the Rough. LC 76-40031. 1976. 10.95 (0-88289-099-9) Pelican.

Ruby, Robert & Brown, John A. A Guide to the Indian Tribes of the Pacific Northwest. LC 85-22470. (Civilization of the American Indian Ser.: Vol. 173). (Illus.). 312p. 1992. pap. 19.95 (0-8061-2479-2) U of Okla Pr.

Ruby, Robert H. & Brown, John A. The Cayuse Indians: Imperial Tribesmen of Old Oregon. (Illus.). 345p. (Orig.). 1989. reprint ed. pap. text ed. 10.95 (0-914019-21-X) NW Interpretive.

— The Chinook Indians: Traders of the Lower Columbia River. LC 79-34110. (Civilization of the American Indian Ser.: Vol. 138). (Illus.). 400p. 1988. pap. 19.95 (0-8061-2107-6) U of Okla Pr.

— Dreamer-Prophets of the Columbia Plateau: Smohalla & Skolaskin. LC 89-5292. (Illus.). 272p. 1989. 24.95 (0-8061-2183-1) U of Okla Pr.

— Half-Sun on the Columbia: A Biography of Chief Moses. LC 94-37092. (Civilization of the American Indian Ser.: Vol. 80). (Illus.). 416p. 1995. pap. 17.95 (0-8061-2738-4) U of Okla Pr.

— Indian Slavery in the Pacific Northwest. LC 93-31861. (Northwest Historical Ser.: Vol. 17). (Illus.). 336p. 1993. 37.50 (0-87062-225-0) A H Clark.

— Indians of the Pacific Northwest: A History. LC 80-5946. (Civilization of the American Indian Ser.: Vol. 158). (Illus.). 300p. 1981. pap. 21.95 (0-8061-2113-0) U of Okla Pr.

— The Spokane Indians: Children of the Sun. LC 79-108797. (Civilization of the American Indian Ser.: Vol. 104). (Illus.). 346p. 1982. pap. 16.95 (0-8061-1757-5) U of Okla Pr.

Rubzov, I. A. Fresh-Water Merimithids of Estonia. (C). 1988. 36.00 (81-7087-022-4, Pub. by Oxford IBH II) S Asia.

Rucci, Richard B. Korean with Chinese Characters, No. 1. (Illus.). 134p. 1981. pap. 4.95 (0-8048-1469-4) C E Tuttle.

Ruccio, David F., jt. ed. see Kim, Kwan S.

Rucckert, Carla L., jt. auth. see Elkins, Don.

Ruch, Richard, jt. auth. see Sato, Tatsuo.

Ruch, Richard S. & Goodman, Ronald. Image at the Top: The Crisis & Renaissance in American Corporate Leadership. 256p. (C). 1983. 32.95 (0-02-927420-6) Free Pr.

***Ruch, Theodore C.** Bibliographia Primatologica: A Classified Bibliography of Primates Other Than Man, Pt. 1: Anatomy, Embryology, & Quantitative Morphology, Physiology & Psychobiology. Primate Phylogeny & Miscellanea. 1941. 250.00 (0-614-00151-X) Elliots Bks.

Ruch, Velma. The Signature of God. 1986. pap. 30.00 (0-8309-0428-X) Herald Hse.

Ruch, Velma N. Summoned to Pilgrimage: The Temple As Focus of a Pilgrim People. LC 94-10322. 1994. write for info. (0-8309-0667-3) Herald Hse.

Ruch, William. White Collar Productivity, Vol 23. (Studies in Productivity: Highlights of the Literature Ser.). (Orig.). pap. 55.00 (0-89361-033-X) Work in Amer.

Ruch, William A., et al. Fundamentals of Production-Operations Management. 5th ed. Fenton & Hill-Whilto, eds. 305p. (C). 1992. pap. text ed. 29.50 (0-314-92852-9) West Pub.

Ruch, William V. Business Communication. 624p. (C). 1990. write for info. (0-675-21314-2, Merrill Pub Co) Macmillan.

— Business Communication, Study Guide. 256p. (C). 1990. pap. write for info. (0-675-22197-8, Merrill Pub Co) Macmillan.

— Corporate Communications: A Comparison of Japanese & American Practices. LC 84-1973. (Illus.). xiv, 298p. 1984. text ed. 59.95 (0-89930-028-6, RCC/, Quorum Bks) Greenwood.

— International Handbook of Corporate Communication. LC 88-43481. 496p. 1989. lib. bdg. 55.00x (0-89950-386-1) McFarland & Co.

Ruchelman, Leonard. A Workbook in Program Design for Public Managers. LC 85-9936. (SUNY Series in Public Administration). 123p. 1985. pap. 16.95 (0-88706-025-0) State U NY Pr.

— A Workbook in Redesigning Public Services. LC 88-16022. (SUNY Series in Public Administration). 85p. (C). 1989. pap. 16.95 (0-88706-943-6) State U NY Pr.

Ruchelman, Leonard I. The Formulation & Presentation of Alternatives for Public Programs. (Learning Packages in the Policy Sciences Ser.: No. 25). (Illus.). 42p. (Orig.). 1984. pap. text ed. 8.50 (0-936826-20-7) PS Assocs Croton.

— Political Careers: Recruitment Through the Legislature. LC 70-99325. 216p. 1975. 25.00 (0-8386-7613-8) Fairleigh Dickinson.

Ruchelman, Leonard I., ed. Big City Mayors: The Crisis in Urban Politics. LC 80-15673. xi, 371p. 1981. reprint ed. text ed. 69.50 (0-313-22605-9, RUBC, Greenwood Pr) Greenwood.

Ruchhoft, Robert H. Backpack Loops & Long Day Trail Hikes in Southern Ohio. Sears, Linda, ed. (Illus.). 260p. (Orig.). 1984. pap. text ed. 11.95 (0-940029-01-4) Pucelle Pr.

— Exploring North Manitou, South Manitou, High & Garden Islands of the Lake Michigan Archipelago. Dews, Cynthia & McCabe, Edith, eds. (Illus.). 357p. (Orig.). 1991. pap. 14.95 (0-940029-02-2) Pucelle Pr.

— Kentucky's Land of the Arches. rev. ed. Sears, Linda, ed. (Illus.). 1986. pap. text ed. 9.95 (0-940029-00-6) Pucelle Pr.

Ruchlin, Hirsch S., jt. auth. see Finkel, Madelon L.

Ruchlis, Hy. Clear Thinking: A Practical Introduction. 271p. (Orig.). 1990. pap. 17.95 (0-87975-594-6) Prometheus Bks.

— How Do You Know It's True? Discovering the Difference Between Science & Superstition. (Young Readers Ser.). (Illus.). 112p. (Orig.). (J). 1991. pap. 13.95 (0-87975-657-8) Prometheus Bks.

Ruchlis, Hy, jt. auth. see Herbert, Don.

Ruchlis, Hy, jt. ed. see Pollack, Cecelia & Lane, Patrick R.

Ruchwarger, Gary. People in Power: Forging a Grassroots Democracy in Nicaragua. LC 87-12623. 340p. 1987. text ed. 65.00 (0-89789-129-5, Bergin & Garvey); pap. text ed. 18.95 (0-89789-130-9, Bergin & Garvey) Greenwood.

— Struggling for Survival: Workers, Women, & Class on a Nicaraguan State Farm. (Development, Conflict, & Social Change Ser.). 128p. (C). 1989. pap. text ed. 32.00 (0-8133-7407-3) Westview.

Rucinski, Andrzej, jt. ed. see Karonski, Michal.

Ruck, Anne. Pearl. 1986. pap. 4.95 (9971-972-37-9) OMF Bks.

— This Child Must Die. 148p. (Orig.). 1991. pap. write for info. (981-3009-01-2) OMF Bks.

Ruck, Carl & Staples, Danny. The World of Classical Myth: Gods & Goddesses, Heroines & Heroes. LC 93-74701. (Illus.). 366p. (C). 1994. pap. write for info. (0-89089-575-9) Carolina Acad Pr.

Ruck, Carl A. Ancient Greek: A New Approach. 2nd ed. 1979. pap. 27.50 (0-262-68031-9) MIT Pr.

Ruck, Carlton, et al. The Feasibility of Vertical Evacuation: Behavioral, Legal, Political, & Structural Considerations. (Monograph: No. 52). 1991. pap. 10.00 (1-877943-05-3) Natural Hazards.

Ruck, E. H. An Index of Themes & Motifs in 12th-Century French Arthurian Poetry. (Arthurian Studies: No. XXV). 208p. (C). 1991. text ed. 70.00 (0-85991-335-X) Boydell & Brewer.

Ruck, George, et al. Radar Cross Section Handbook, 2 vols. 949p. 1970. 72.00 (0-306-30343-4) Peninsula CA.

Ruck, Hendrick W. & Ellis, John A., eds. Military Training Technology: Systematic Approaches. LC 85-9459. 253p. 1985. text ed. 49.95 (0-275-90008-8, C0008, Praeger Pubs) Greenwood.

Ruck, Rob. Sandlot Seasons: Sports in Black Pittsburgh. LC 92-46304. 280p. 1993. pap. 13.50 (0-252-06342-2) U of Ill Pr.

— The Tropic of Baseball: Baseball in the Dominican Republic. (Illus.). 232p. 1993. pap. 10.95 (0-88184-876-X) Carroll & Graf.

— The Tropic of Baseball: Baseball in the Dominican Republic. (Baseball & American Society Ser.). (Illus.). 175p. 1991. lib. bdg. 37.50 (0-88736-707-0) Mecklermedia.

Ruck, Ruth J. Along Came a Llama. large type ed. 384p. 1983. 15.95 (0-7089-0935-3) Ulverscroft.

Ruckdashel, Candy. A Literary Travel Log: Integrating Literature & Global Awareness. Keeling, Jan, ed. (Illus.). 64p. (Orig.). 1993. pap. text ed. 7.95 (0-86530-256-1) Incentive Pubns.

— Literature & the World Around Us. Keeling, Jan, ed. (Integrating Literature into Basic Skills Programs Ser.). (Illus.). 64p. (Orig.). 1992. pap. text ed. 7.95 (0-86530-197-2, IP194-7) Incentive Pubns.

Ruckebusch, et al. Small & Large Animal Physiology. (Illus.). 688p. (C). 1990. 65.00 (1-55664-136-2) Mosby Yr Bk.

Rucker. Infinity & the Mind. 1983. 6.50 (0-553-25531-2) Bantam.

Rucker, Brian R. Brick Road to Boom Town: The Story of Santa Rosa County's "Old Brick Road" (Illus.). 58p. (Orig.). 1993. pap. 5.50 (1-882695-07-0) Patagonia Pr.

Rucker, E. H. Hoyle: Genealogy of Peiter Heyl (Hoyle) & His Descendants, 1100-1936, with Intermarried Families of Arnold, Bess, Byrd, Cansler, et al. (Illus.). 1539p. 1991. reprint ed. lib. bdg. 208.00 (0-8328-1771-6); reprint ed. pap. 198.00 (0-8328-1772-4) Higginson Bk Co.

Rucker, Edward W. The Complete Unabridged Information Manual & Reference Guide to the Oklahoma Non-Coal Mining Industry. Tommerlin, Gayle, ed. 198p. 1985. pap. 24.95 (0-9614352-0-8) Edw Rucker Ent.

— Rucker's Personal Guide to Successful Money Making Opportunities & Credit Information. LC 86-90451. 245p. 1987. pap. 29.95 (0-9614352-1-6) Edw Rucker Ent.

Rucker, Herbert J., jt. auth. see Henderson, Melvin.

Rucker, John. North Carolina: A Portrait of the Land & Its People. (North Carolina Geographic Ser.: No. 1). 112p. 1989. pap. 15.95 (0-938314-63-7) Am Wrld Geog.

— Travels with Barney. LC 84-90628. (Illus.). 100p. 1984. pap. text ed. 9.95 (0-9613658-0-3) J Rucker.

Rucker, John D. The Barney Years. 160p. 1992. 16.95 (1-55971-179-5) NorthWord.

Rucker, Karen S., jt. ed. see Lillegard, Wade A.

Rucker, Kathy D. Adult Education in the Parish: A Practical Handbook. 92p. 1990. 4.95 (0-86716-125-6) St Anthony Mess Pr.

Rucker, Linda, jt. ed. see Rucker, Randy.

Rucker, Mark, jt. ed. see Thorn, John.

Rucker, Mark, jt. ed. see Tiemann, Robert L.

***Rucker, Mike.** Terry & the Bully. LC 94-90111. (Illus.). 64p. (Orig.). (J). 1995. pap. 3.95 (1-56002-449-6, Univ Edtns) Aegina Pr.

— Terry the Tractor. LC 93-94079. (Illus.). 64p. (J). (gr. k up). 1994. pap. 3.95 (1-56002-382-1, AndeLear Pub) Aegina Pr.

Rucker, R. D. Abraham Lincoln's Social & Political Thought. 1991. 15.95 (0-533-09579-4) Vantage.

— Drugs, Drug Addiction, & Drug Dealing: The Origin & Nature of, & the Solution to, the American Drug Problem. 1991. 11.95 (0-533-09334-1) Vantage.

— Eros & the Sexual Revolution: Studies in the Psychology of the Human Mind. 1990. 14.95 (0-533-09135-7) Vantage.

— Jesus Christ & the Origin of Christianity. 1992. 16.95 (0-533-10323-1) Vantage.

Rucker, Randy & Rucker, Linda, eds. The Rock & Roll Birthday Book. 144p. (Orig.). 1991. pap. 9.95 (0-944445-03-9) Musi-Key Pub.

Rucker, Robert B., jt. ed. see Halsted, Charles H.

Rucker, Rudolf V. Geometry, Relativity & the Fourth Dimension. LC 76-22240. (Illus.). 1977. pap. text ed. 4.95 (0-486-23400-2) Dover.

Rucker, Rudy. All the Visions. (Doubles Ser.). (Illus.). 224p. 1993. pap. 14.95x (0-938075-12-8) Ocean View Bks.

— All the Visions. deluxe limited ed. (Doubles Ser.). (Illus.). 224p. 1993. 40.00 (0-938075-37-3) Ocean View Bks.

— All the Visions & The Secret of Life, 2 vols., Set. deluxe limited ed. (Illus.). 1993. boxed 60.00 (0-938075-09-8) Ocean View Bks.

— Artificial Life Lab. (Illus.). 250p. (Orig.). 1993. disk, pap. 34.95 (1-878739-48-4) Waite Group Pr.

— The Hacker & the Ants. LC 93-43500. 1994. 20.00 (0-688-13416-5, AvoNova) Avon.

— The Hacker & the Ants. 320p. 1995. mass mkt. 4.99 (0-380-71844-8, AvoNova) Avon.

— The Hollow Earth. 304p. 1992. reprint ed. mass mkt. 3.99 (0-380-75535-1, AvoNova) Avon.

— Infinity & the Mind. (Princeton Science Library). 1995. pap. 12.95 (0-691-00172-3) Princeton U Pr.

— Live Robots. 368p. 1994. mass mkt. 5.99 (0-380-77543-3, AvoNova) Avon.

— Mind Tools: The Five Levels of Mathematical Reality. (Illus.). 352p. 1988. pap. 10.95 (0-395-46810-8) HM.

— Software. 170p. (Orig.). 1987. pap. 3.50 (0-380-70177-4) Avon.

— Wetware. 192p. 1988. pap. 3.50 (0-380-70178-2) Avon.

Rucker, Rudy, et al. The Fourth Dimension: A Guided Tour of Higher Universes. (Illus.). 228p. 1985. pap. 10.95 (0-395-39388-4) HM.

Rucker, T. Donald & Keller, Martin D. Careers in Medicine: Traditional & Alternative Opportunities. rev. ed. LC 90-3287. Orig. Title: Planning Your Medical Career. 347p. (C). 1990. pap. 15.95 (0-912048-82-4) Garrett Pk.

Rucker, Walt, jt. auth. see Ockenga, Earl.

Ruckert, Friedrich. Hamasa Oder die Altesten Arabischen Volkslieder, 2 pts., Set. 826p. reprint ed. write for info. (0-318-71558-9, Pub. by Georg Olms GW) Lubrecht & Cramer.

***Ruckert, George.** The Classical Music of North India. Khan, Ali A., ed. xiii, 367p. 1991. pap. 54.95 (0-930997-02-6) East Bay Bks.

Ruckert, Janet. Are You My Dog? (Illus.). 160p. (Orig.). 1989. pap. 8.95 (0-89815-325-5) Ten Speed Pr.

— The Four Footed Therapist: How Your Pet Can Help You Solve Your Problems. LC 86-23123. 256p. (Orig.). 1987. pap. 7.95 (0-89815-185-6) Ten Speed Pr.

Ruckheim, Ulrich, jt. auth. see Weiner, Lawrence.

Ruckle, Gene. Multifamily Selective Rehabilitation: Housing Production Manual, No. 2. Cashman, Jude & Werwath, Peter, eds. (Housing Production Manuals Ser.). 1990. student ed 45.00 (0-942901-03-7) Enterprise Foundation.

Ruckle, James E. Distinctive Qualities of Third Sector Organizations. LC 92-32113. (Non-profit Institutions in America Ser.). 168p. 1992. 49.00 (0-8153-0905-8) Garland.

Ruckle, William C. Modern Analysis. 352p. (C). 1991. text ed. 69.95 (0-534-92164-7) PWS Pubs.

Rucklin, Joanne, jt. auth. see Levinson, Nancy.

***Ruckman, Bret & Ruckman, Stuart.** Wasatch Climbing North. (Illus.). 385p. (Orig.). 1991. pap. 25.00 (0-934641-39-0) Chockstone Pr.

Ruckman, Bret, jt. auth. see Ruckman, Stuart.

Ruckman, Ivy. The Hunger Scream. LC 83-6522. 200p. (J). (gr. 6 up). 1983. 14.95 (0-8027-6514-9) Walker & Co.

— Night of the Twisters. LC 83-46168. 160p. (J). (gr. 3-6). 1984. 14.00i (0-690-04408-9, Crowell Jr Bks); lib. bdg. 14.89 (0-690-04409-7, Crowell Jr Bks) HarpC Child Bks.

— Night of the Twisters. LC 83-46168. (Trophy Bk.). 160p. (J). (gr. 3-6). 1986. reprint ed. pap. 3.95 (0-06-440176-6, Trophy) HarpC Child Bks.

— No Way Out. LC 87-47817. 224p. (J). (gr. 6 up). 1988. lib. bdg. 13.89 (0-690-04671-5, Crowell Jr Bks) HarpC Child Bks.

— No Way Out. LC 87-47817. (Trophy Keypoint Bk.). 224p. (YA). (gr. 7 up). 1989. reprint ed. pap. 3.95 (0-06-447003-2, Trophy) HarpC Child Bks.

— Pronounce It Dead. (J). (gr. 4-7). 1994. pap. 3.50 (0-553-48176-2) Bantam.

— Spell It M-U-R-D-E-R. (J). (gr. 4-7). 1994. pap. 3.50 (0-553-48175-4) Bantam.

Ruckman, Jo Ann. The Moscow Business Elite, 1840-1905: A Social & Cultural Portrait of Two Generations. LC 83-23732. 275p. 1984. 24.00 (0-87580-096-3) N Ill U Pr.

***Ruckman, Stuart & Ruckman, Bret.** Climber's Guide to American Fork Canyon. (Illus.). 220p. (Orig.). 1995. pap. 18.00 (0-934641-88-9) Chockstone Pr.

Ruckman, Stuart, jt. auth. see Ruckman, Bret.

Ruckpaul, Klaus & Rein, Horst, eds. Basis & Mechanisms of Regulation of Cytochrome P-450, Vol. 1. 200p. 1989. 95.00 (0-85066-474-8) Taylor & Francis.

— Cytochrome P-450. 398p. 1985. 88.00 (0-85066-337-7); pap. text ed. 27.00 (0-85066-970-7) Taylor & Francis.

— Cytochrome Substrates. (Frontiers in Biotransformation Ser.: Vol. 6). 192p. 1991. text ed. 150.00 (3-05-501284-4, Pub. by Akademie GW) VCH Pubs.

— Membrane Organization & Phospholipid Interaction of Cytochrome P-450. (Frontiers in Biotransformation Ser.: Vol. 5). 210p. 1991. text ed. 155.00 (3-05-500461-2, Pub. by Akademie GW) VCH Pubs.

R

An Asterisk (*) at the beginning of an entry indicates that the title is appearing in BIP for the first time.

— Microbial & Plant Cytochrome P-450: Biochemical Characteristics, Genetic Engineering & Practical Implications. (Frontiers in Biotransformation Ser.: Vol. 4). 280p. 1991. 90.00 (0-7484-0029-X, Pub. by Tay Francis Ltd UK) Taylor & Francis.
— Molecular Mechanisms of Adrenal Steroidogenesis & Aspects of Regulation & Application. (Frontiers in Biotransformation Ser.: Vol. 3). 251p. 1991. 90.00 (0-7484-0025-7, Pub. by Tay Francis Ltd UK) Taylor & Francis.
— Principles, Mechanisms & Biological Consequences of Induction. (Frontiers in Biotransformation Ser.: Vol. 2). 352p. 1991. 90.00 (0-85066-799-2, Pub. by Tay Francis Ltd UK) Taylor & Francis.
— Regulation & Control of Complex Biological Processes by Biotransformation. LC 93-44152. (Frontiers in Biotransformation Ser.: Vol. 9). 1994. 135.00 (3-05-501367-0, Pub. by Akademie GW) VCH Pubs.
— Relationships Between Structure & Function of Cytochrome P-450: Experiments, Calculations, Models. (Frontiers in Biotransformation Ser.: Vol. 7). 370p. 1993. 140.00 (0-685-67332-4, Pub. by Akademie GW) VCH Pubs.

Rucks, Andrew C., jt. auth. see Ginter, Peter M.

Ruckstuhl, Irma. Old Provincetown in Early Photographs. 96p. (Orig.). 1987. pap. 9.95 (0-486-25410-0) Dover.

***Ruckstuhl, William J.** Financial Planning Applications. 13th ed. 714p. (C). 1995. text ed. 53.00 (0-943590-71-X) Amer College.

Ruckstuhl, William J., et al. Financial Planning Applications, 2 vols., Set. 12th ed. (C). 1994. pap. text ed. 50.00 (0-614-02546-X); pap. text ed. write for info. (0-943590-58-2) Amer College.
— Financial Planning Applications, Vol. 2. 12th ed. LC 93-74841. 388p. (C). 1994. pap. text ed. write for info. (0-943590-57-4) Amer College.

Ruckwick, Christian A., ed.

Rud, Anthony G., Jr. & Oldendorf, Walter P., eds. A Place for Teacher Renewal: Challenging the Intellect, Creating Education Reform. 176p. (C). 1992. text ed. 34.95 (0-8077-3147-1); pap. text ed. 17.95 (0-8077-3146-3) Tchrs Coll.

Rud, Anthony G., Jr., jt. ed. see Garrison, James W.

Ruda, Harry E., ed. Widegap II-VI Compounds for Opto-Electronic Applications. (Electronic Materials Ser.). (Illus.). 352p. (C). 1992. text ed. 89.50 (0-412-39100-7, A6530) Chapman & Hall.

Ruda, Howard. Asset-Based Financing: A Transactional Guide, 4 vols. LC 84-72027. 1985. ring bd. write for info. (0-8205-1059-9) Bender.

Ruda, Jeffrey. The Art of Drawing: Old Masters from the Crocker Art Museum. LC 92-71560. (Illus.). 200p. (Orig.). 1992. pap. 50.00 (0-939896-00-1) Flint Inst Arts.
— Fra Filippo Lippi: Life & Work with a Complete Catalogue. (Illus.). 576p. 1993. 195.00 (0-8109-3568-6) Abrams.

Rudacille, Wendell C. Identifying Lies in Disguise. 176p. 1993. per. 29.95 (0-8403-9175-7) Kendall-Hunt.
— Identifying Lies in Disguise, Vol. 1: A Practical Guide to Detecting Deception in Verbal Behavior. 312p. (C). 1993. 35.00 (1-877858-27-7, ILID-WR) Amer Focus Pub.

Rudakov, A. N., ed. Helices & Exceptional Vector Bundles: Seminaire Rudakov. (London Mathematical Society Lecture Note Ser.: No. 148). 200p. (C). 1990. pap. 29.95 (0-521-38811-2) Cambridge U Pr.

***Rudakova, I.** Leaner's Dictionary of Polytechnical Terms: Russian-English-French-German. 4th rev. ed. 448p. (FRE, GER & RUS.). 1988. 35.00 (0-7859-7154-8) Fr & Eur.

Rudakova, I. F. General Technical Lexicon. 3rd ed. 448p. (ENG, FRE, GER & RUS.). 1985. 39.95 (0-8288-0686-1, M 15525) Fr & Eur.

Rudall, B. H. Computers & Cybernetics. (Cybernetics & Systems Ser., Abacus Bks.). x, 188p. 1981. text ed. 84.00 (0-85626-173-4) Gordon & Breach.

Rudall, B. H. & Corns, T. N. Computers & Literature. (Computer Language Programmes Ser., Abacus Bks.). (Illus.). 150p. 1987. text ed. 46.00 (0-85626-340-0) Gordon & Breach.

Rudall, Nicholas, ed. see Dostoyevsky, Fyodor.

Rudall, Nicholas, tr. see Euripides.

Rudall, Nicholas, tr. see Ibsen, Henrik.

Rudall, Nicholas, ed. see Marlowe, Christopher.

Rudall, Nicholas, tr. see Sophocles.

Rudall, Paula. Anatomy of Flowering Plants: An Introduction to Structure & Development. 2nd ed. LC 92-13493. (Illus.). 96p. (C). 1992. pap. 19.95 (0-521-42154-3) Cambridge U Pr.
— Anatomy of the Monocotyledons Vol. 8: Iridaceae. (Illus.). 500p. 1995. 118.00 (0-19-854504-5) OUP.

***Rudan, Mindi.** Men: The Handbook. LC 94-37342. 256p. (Orig.). 1994. pap. 12.95 (1-56790-113-1) Cool Hand Comms.

Rudanko, Juhani. Complementation & Case Grammar: A Syntactic & Semantic Study of Selected Patterns of Complementation in Present-Day English. LC 88-20983. (Linguistics Ser.). 173p. (C). 1989. 74.50 (0-88706-931-2); pap. 24.95 (0-88706-932-0) State U NY Pr.
— Pragmatic Approaches to Shakespeare: Essays on Othello, Coriolanus & Timon of Athens. 222p. (C). 1993. lib. bdg. 38.50 (0-8191-9107-8) U Pr of Amer.

Rudas, Marie, ed. see Kaszas, John.

Rudat, Wolfgang E. Alchemy in "The Sun Also Rises" Hidden Gold in Hemingway's Narrative. LC 92-25021. 288p. 1992. text ed. 89.95 (0-7734-9579-7) E Mellen.
— Earnest Exuberance in Chaucer's Poetics: Textual Games in the Canterbury Tales. LC 93-34113. 348p. 1993. 99.95 (0-7734-9381-6, Mellen Univ Pr) E Mellen.
— A Rotten Way to Be Wounded: The Tragicomedy of the Sun Also Rises. LC 90-5903. (American University Studies: American Literature: Ser. XXIV, Vol. 21). 214p. (C). 1990. text ed. 38.95 (0-8204-1282-1) P Lang Pubs.

Rudatis, Renato. Classic Pizza & Pasta Recipes. (Illus.). 64p. 1989. 17.95 (0-572-01450-3, Pub. by W Foulsham UK) Trans-Atl Phila.
— Pizza & Pasta Recipies - All Colour Edition: Appetising, Exciting & Inexpensive Italian Dishes. (Illus.). 1991. 24.50 (0-572-01691-3, Pub. by W Foulsham UK) Trans-Atl Phila.
— Regional Italian Specialties. Allison, Sonia, ed. (Gourmet Cookshelf Ser.). (Illus.). 64p. 1992. 13.95 (0-572-01707-3, Pub. by W Foulsham UK) Trans-Atl Phila.

Rudavsky, T. M., ed. Gender & Judaism: The Transformation of Tradition. 320p. 1994. 45.00 (0-8147-7452-0); pap. 18.95 (0-8147-7453-9) NYU Pr.

Rudavsky, Tamar, ed. Divine Omniscience & Omnipotence in Medieval Philosophy. 1984. lib. bdg. 119.00 (90-277-1750-8) Kluwer Ac.

Rudawsky, O. Mineral Economics: Development & Management of Natural Resources. (Developments in Economic Geology Ser.: Vol. 20). 192p. 1986. 77.00 (0-444-42636-1) Elsevier.

Rudaz, S. & Walsh, T., eds. Sixth Workshop on Grand Unification: Proceedings of the Workshop held at Minneapolis, April, 1985. 500p. 1986. pap. 55.00 (9971-978-84-9) World Scientific Pub.

Rudd, et al. Dental Laboratory Procedures: Removable Partial Dentures, Vol. 3. 3rd ed. 720p. 1985. 89.00 (0-8016-4206-X) Mosby Yr Bk.

Rudd, A. B. La Epistola a los Hebreos: The Letter to the Hebrews. (SPA.). 5.50 (84-7645-073-7, 223136, Pub. by Edit Clie SP) TSELF.
— Epistolas Generales: Commentary to the General. (SPA.). 7.50 (84-7645-177-6, 223221, Pub. by Edit Clie SP) TSELF.

Rudd, Andrea & Taylor, Darien, eds. Positive Women: Voices of Women Living with AIDS. (Illus.). (Orig.). Date not set. pap. 14.95 (0-929005-30-9, Pub. by Second Story Pr CN) InBook.

***Rudd, Andrew & Clasing, Henry J., Jr.** Modern Portfolio Theory: The Principles of Investment Management. 525p. 1988. pap. 50.00 (0-9620194-0-2) A Rudd.

Rudd, Anthony. Application Development Using Os 2 REXX. 1994. pap. text ed. 39.95 (0-471-60691-X) Wiley.
— Implementing Practical Database Manager Applications. 1993. text ed. 56.00 (0-13-454174-X) P-H.
— Implenting Practical Dbase2 Applications. 1990. 43.95 (0-13-454059-X) P-H.
— Kierkegaard & the Limits of the Ethical. LC 92-42260. 1993. Alk. paper. 39.95 (0-19-824024-4, Clarendon Pr) OUP.
— Mastering C. 1994. pap. text ed. 24.95 (0-471-60820-3) Wiley.
— Mastering C Plus Plus. LC 94-12675. 1994. pap. text ed. 24.95 (0-471-06565-X) Wiley.

Rudd, Anthony S. Application Development Using OS-2 REXX. 1993. pap. 39.95 (0-89435-477-9) Wiley.
— C for Non-C Programmers. 2nd ed. 1993. pap. 39.95 (0-89435-468-X) Wiley.

Rudd, Betty, ed. see Gluchowsky, Paul M.

Rudd, Chris, jt. ed. see Roper, Brian.

Rudd, Connie. Grand Canyon--North Rim: The Story Behind the Scenery. LC 89-45019. (Illus.). 48p. 1989. pap. 6.95 (0-88714-033-5) KC Pubns.
— In Pictures Grand Canyon: The Continuing Story. LC 90-60038. (Illus.). 48p. 1990. pap. 6.95 (0-88714-046-7) KC Pubns.

Rudd, Daniel & Bond, Theophilus. From Slavery to Wealth: The Life of Scott Bond. LC 73-173615. (Black Heritage Library Collection). 1977. reprint ed. 33.95 (0-8369-8907-4) Ayer.

Rudd, David. Introduction to Software Design & Development with ADA. LC 93-37696. 450p. 1993. pap. text ed. 48.25 (0-314-02829-3) West Pub.

Rudd, E. A New Look at Postgraduate Failure. 144p. 1985. pap. 38.00 (1-85059-009-5) Taylor & Francis.

Rudd, Gail. John Danced. 40p. (Orig.). 1982. pap. 5.95 (0-917658-20-5) BPW & P.

Rudd, Gillian. Managing Language in "Piers Plowman" (Piers Plowman Studies: Vol. 9). 192p. (C). 1993. text ed. 63.00 (0-85991-392-9, DS Brewer) Boydell & Brewer.

Rudd, Leigh, jt auth. see Fuller, Sheila.

Rudd, Margaret. The Lone Heretic. LC 75-31688. 370p. 1976. reprint ed. 75.00 (0-87752-181-6) Gordian.

Rudd, Margaret E. Divided Image. LC 73-118003. (Studies in Blake: No. 3). 1970. reprint ed. lib. bdg. 75.00 (0-8383-1015-X) M S G Haskell Hse.

Rudd, Margaret T. Gabriela Mistral: The Chilean Years, 1889-1922. LC 91-76932. 286p. (Orig.). Date not set. pap. 24.95 (1-55618-114-0) Brunswick Pub.

***Rudd, Merri.** Life Planning in Mew Mexico: Your Guide to State Law on Powers of Attorney, Right to Die, Nursing Home Benefits, Wills, Trusts & Probate. 2nd ed. 237p. 1994. pap. 14.95 (0-9632173-6-4) Abogada Pr.

Rudd, N. & Courtney, E. C. Juvenal Satires, Nos. I, III, X. 91p. 1984. reprint ed. 11.00 (0-86516-039-2) Bolchazy-Carducci.

Rudd, N. & Wiedemann, T. Cicero: De Legibus One. 90p. 1987. 14.95 (0-86292-271-2, Pub. by Brstl Class Pr UK) Focus Info Gr.

Rudd, Niall. The Classical Tradition in Operation. (Robson Classical Lectures). 204p. 1994. 55.00 (0-8020-0570-5) U of Toronto Pr.
— The Satires of Horace: A Study. LC 66-11031. 330p. reprint ed. pap. 94.10 (0-317-26383-8, 2024525) Bks Demand.

Rudd, Niall, ed. Horace Two Thousand: A Celebration: Essays for the Bimillennium. LC 93-11057. (Illus.). 162p. (C). 1993. text ed. 34.50 (0-472-10490-X) U of Mich Pr.
— Johnson's Juvenal: London & the Vanity of Human Wishes. 160p. 1981. 18.95 (0-906515-64-5, Pub. by Brstl Class Pr UK) Focus Info Gr.

Rudd, Niall, tr. The Satires of Horace & Persius. (Classics Ser.). 186p. 1974. mass mkt. 9.95 (0-14-044279-0, Penguin Classics) Viking Penguin.

Rudd, Niall, ed. see Horace.

Rudd, Niall, tr. see Juvenal.

Rudd, Niall, ed. see Juvenal.

Rudd, Norman N. An Irish Rudd Family 1760-1988; Rudd Origins & Other Irish Rudds: Progeny of Gordon Rudd & Alicia Wellwood, Rathsarn Parish, Queens County, Ireland. 552p. 1992. 30.00 (0-9632992-0-4) Rudd Family Res.

***Rudd, Peggy.** Crossdressers: And Those Who Share Their Lives. (Illus.). 126p. 1995. 14.95 (0-9626762-3-3) PM Pubs.

Rudd, Peggy J. Crossdressing with Dignity: The Case for Transcending Gender Lines. (Illus.). 165p. (Orig.). 1990. pap. 12.95 (0-9626762-1-7) PM Pubs.
— My Husband Wears My Clothes: Crossdressing from the Perspective of a Wife. rev. ed. (Illus.). 148p. 1989. pap. 10.00 (0-685-46228-5) PM Pubs.
— My Husband Wears My Clothes: Crossdressing from the Perspective of a Wife. rev. ed. 148p. 1991. pap. 12.95 (0-9626762-0-9) PM Pubs.

Rudd, Peter & Nicoll, Angus, eds. British Paediatric Association Manual on Infections & Immunizations in Children. 2nd ed. (Illus.). 320p. 1991. pap. 27.50 (0-19-262118-1) OUP.

Rudd, Peter, jt. ed. see Nicoll, Angus.

Rudd, Rebecca S., jt. auth. see Sizer, Nancy F.

Rudd, Robert L. Pesticides & the Living Landscape. LC 64-14506. 336p. reprint ed. pap. 95.80 (0-317-29744-9, 2015653) Bks Demand.

***Rudd, Sheila P.** Coloring Charleston. (Coloring the Low Country Ser.). (Illus.). 32p. (J). (gr. 1-8). 1994. pap. text ed. 4.95 (1-880795-75-2) MBT Ent P&P.

Rudd, Shirley. Time Manage Your Reading. 173p. 1990. text ed. 34.95 (0-566-02762-3, Pub. by Gower UK); pap. text ed. 23.95 (0-566-02976-6, Pub. by Gower UK) Ashgate Pub Co.

***Rudd, Steele.** On Our Selection: The Original Dad & Dave Stories. 1995. pap. 16.95 (0-7022-2844-3, Pub. by Univ Queensland Pr AT) Intl Spec Bk.
— A Steele Rudd Selection: The Best Dad & Dave Stories with Other Rudd Classics. Moorhouse, Frank, ed. LC 86-975. (Illus.). 240p. (Orig.). 1987. pap. 15.95 (0-7022-1978-9, Pub. by Univ Queensland Pr AT) Intl Spec Bk.

Rudd, Terry R. Nineteen Twenty-Nine Again? rev. ed. (Illus.). 450p. (C). 1988. reprint ed. 27.50 (0-9620011-0-4) Bell Curve Rsch.

Rudd, Thomas. A Treatise on Angel Magic: Being a Complete Transcription of Harley Manuscript 6482 in the British Library. LC 89-29645. (Magnum Opus Hermetic Sourceworks Ser.: No. 15). (Illus.). 230p. (Orig.). 1990. 35.00 (0-933999-83-6); pap. 22.00 (0-933999-84-4) Phanes Pr.

Rudd, Tony. Tony Rudd: It Was Fun, My Fifty Years of High Performance. (Haynes Ser.). (Illus.). 352p. 1993. 42.95 (1-85260-413-1, Pub. by J H Haynes & Co UK) Motorbooks Intl.

Rudd, Tony, jt. auth. see Nye, Doug.

Rudd, Walter G. Assembly Language Programming & the IBM 360 & 370 Computers. 1975. text ed. write for info. (0-13-049536-0) P-H.

Ruddel, David T. Quebec City, Seventeen Sixty-Five to Eighteen Thirty-Two. (Canadian Museum of Civlization Mercury Series-Canadian Ethnology Service). (Illus.). 293p. 1988. pap. 24.95 (0-660-10771-6, Pub. by CN Mus Civilization CN) U Ch Pr.

Ruddell, Anita, jt. auth. see Brown, Cheryl.

Ruddell, Martha R. Teaching Content Reading & Writing. LC 92-31127. 1993. text ed. 35.25 (0-205-14003-3) Allyn.

Ruddell, Martha R., jt. auth. see Ruddell, Robert B.

Ruddell, R., et al. Allyn & Bacon Reading Program: Pathfinder. large type ed. Incl. Level 8. Surprises & Prizes. (gr. 1). 1979. Text 84p. pap. 9.46 (0-317-02066-8, 4-0026); Level 8. Surprises & Prizes. (gr. 1). 1979. Wkbks., 2 vols., 264p. 29.37 (0-317-04356-0, 4-0027); Level 9. Upside & Down. 164p. (gr. 1). 1979. 22.19 (0-317-02068-4, 4-0028); Level 9. Upside & Down. 164p. (gr. 1). 1979. 33.55 (0-317-04357-9, 4-0029); Level 10. Inside & Out. 128p. (gr. 1-2). 1979. 19.25 (0-317-02070-6, 4-0031); Level 10. Inside & Out. 128p. (gr. 1-2). 1979. 37.73 (0-317-04358-7, 4-0030); Level 11. Moon Magic. 264p. (gr. 2). 1979. 33.83 (0-317-02072-2, 4-0032); Level 11. Moon Magic. 264p. (gr. 2). 1979. 33.55 (0-317-04359-5, 4-0033); Level 12. Riding Rainbow. 264p. (gr. 2-3). 1979. 33.85 (0-317-02074-9, 4-0034); Level 12. Riding Rainbow. 264p. (gr. 2-3). 1979. 33.55 (0-317-04360-9, 4-0035); Level 13. Sunshine Days. 356p. (gr. 3). 1979. 50.16 (0-317-02076-5, 4-0036); Level 13. Sunshine Days. 356p. (gr. 3). 1979. 37.73 (0-317-04361-7, 4-0037); Level 14. Handstands, 2 vols. 356p. (gr. 3-4). 1979. 50.16 (0-317-02078-1, 4-0038); Level 14. Handstands, 2 vols. 356p. (gr. 3-4). 1979. 41.81 (0-317-04362-5, 4-0039); Level 15. Person to Person, 2 vols. 288p. (gr. 4). 1979. 38.50 (0-317-02080-3, 4-0040); Level 15. Person to Person, 2 vols. 288p. (gr. 4). 1979. 31.46 (0-317-04363-3, 4-0041); Level 16. Free Rein, 2 vols. 288p. 1979. 38.50 (0-317-02082-X, 4-0042); Level 16. Free Rein, 2 vols. 288p. 1979. 31.46 (0-317-04364-1, 4-0043); Level 17. Majesty & Mystery, 2 vols. 352p. (gr. 5). 1979. 50.16 (0-317-02084-6, 4-0044); Level 17. Majesty & Mystery, 2 vols. 352p. (gr. 5). 1979. 31.46 (0-317-04365-X, 4-0045); Level 18. Standing Strong, 2 vols. 344p. (gr. 5-6). 1979. 44.33 (0-317-02086-2, 4-0046); Level 18. Standing Strong, 2 vols. 344p. (gr. 5-6). 1979. 31.46 (0-317-04366-8, 4-0047); Level 19. Widening Path, 2 vols. 344p. (gr. 6). 1979. 44.33 (0-317-02088-9, 4-0048); Level 19. Widening Path, 2 vols. 344p. (gr. 6). 1979. 31.46 (0-317-04367-6, 4-0049); (J). (gr. 1-6). 1979. reprint ed. write for info. (0-318-66083-0) Am Printing Hse.

***Ruddell, Robert B. & Ruddell, Martha R.** Teaching Children to Read & Write: Becoming an Influential Teacher. LC 94-24036. 1994. text ed. write for info. (0-205-13788-1) Allyn.

Ruddell, Robert B., jt. ed. see Singer, Harry.

Ruddell, Robert B., et al, eds. Theoretical Models & Processes of Reading. 4th ed. 1296p. 1994. 100.00 (0-87207-438-2); pap. 75.00 (0-87207-437-4) Intl Reading.

Rudden, B. & Yeats, J. M. Disclosure in Insurance: the Changing Scene & Judicial Review in England. (Lectures on the Common Law Ser.: Vol. 3). 60p. 1991. pap. 28.00 (90-6544-540-4) Kluwer Law Tax Pubs.

Rudden, Bernard, ed. Basic Community Cases. 276p. 1987. 69.00 (0-19-876212-7) OUP.
— Basic Community Cases. 276p. 1990. reprint ed. pap. 35.00 (0-19-876211-9) OUP.

Rudden, Bernard & Wyatt, Derrick A., eds. Basic Community Laws. 648p. 1993. pap. 17.95 (0-19-876327-1) OUP.
— Basic Community Laws. 4th ed. 1993. 60.00 (0-19-876326-3) OUP.

Rudden, M. N. & Wilson, J. Elements of Solid State Physics. 2nd ed. LC 92-36621. 264p. 1993. text ed. 74.95 (0-471-92972-7); pap. text ed. 36.95 (0-471-92973-5) Wiley.

Rudder, C., jt. auth. see Maury, Emmerick-Armand.

Rudder Editors. Good Sailing: An Illustrated Course on Sailing. (Illus.). (J). (gr. 7 up). 1976. pap. 5.95 (0-679-50630-6) McKay.

Rudder, Lena E. King of the World & the Subterranean Kingdom & The Earth Is Hollow at the North & South Poles. 150p. (Orig.). 1988. write for info. (0-937581-03-8) Zarathustrotemo Pr.
— White Roots & the Mysteries of God. (Illus.). 144p. (Orig.). 1986. pap. write for info. (0-937581-00-3) Zarathustrotemo Pr.

Rudder, Robert S., tr. see Castellanos, Rosario.

Rudder, Virginia. After the Ifaluk: And Other Poems. LC 75-19160. (Orig.). 1976. pap. 3.00 (0-914476-43-2) Thorp Springs.

***Rudder, Walter J.** At Risk: The Vo-Tech Student in Suburban Society. 150p. 1994. pap. 49.95 (0-938198-01-7) Weidner & Sons.

Ruddick, Bob, jt. auth. see Greer, Gery.

Ruddick, Bruce. Poems. (Illus.). 56p. (Orig.). 1994. pap. 10.95 (1-878818-26-0) Sheep Meadow.

***Ruddick, James.** Lord Lucan: What Really Happened. (Illus.). 224p. 1995. pap. 11.95 (0-7472-4677-7, Pub. by Headline UK) Trafalgar.

Ruddick, Lisa. Reading Gertrude Stein: Body, Text, Gnosis. LC 89-46133. (Reading Women Writing Ser.). 288p. 1990. 38.95 (0-8014-2364-3) Cornell U Pr.
— Reading Gertrude Stein: Body, Text, Gnosis. LC 89-46133. (Reading Women Writing Ser.). 288p. 1991. reprint ed. pap. 14.95 (0-8014-9957-7) Cornell U Pr.

Ruddick, Nicholas. British Science Fiction: A Chronology, 1478-1990. LC 92-6409. (Bibliographies & Indexes in World Literature Ser.: No. 35). 320p. 1992. text ed. 65.00 (0-313-28002-9, RBF, Greenwood Pr) Greenwood.
— Christopher Priest. LC 88-16046. (Starmont Reader's Guide Ser.: Vol. 50). x, 104p. 1989. lib. bdg. 25.00x (1-55742-110-2); pap. 15.00x (1-55742-109-9) Borgo Pr.
— Ultimate Island: On the Nature of British Science Fiction. LC 92-24136. (Contributions to the Study of Science Fiction & Fantasy Ser.: No. 55). 216p. 1993. text ed. 49.95 (0-313-27373-1, RUC, Greenwood Pr) Greenwood.

An Asterisk (*) at the beginning of an entry indicates that the title is appearing in BIP for the first time.

Ruddick, Nicholas, ed. State of the Fantastic: Studies in the Theory & Practice of Fantastic Literature & Film: Selected Essays from the Eleventh International Conference on the Fantastic in the Arts, 1990. LC 91-46867. (Contributions to the Study of Science Fiction & Fantasy Ser.: No. 50). 232p. 1992. text ed. 55.00 (*0-313-27853-9*, RSF, Greenwood Pr) Greenwood.

Ruddick, Robert, jt. auth. see Greer, Gary.

Ruddick, Robert, jt. auth. see Greer, Gery.

***Ruddick, Sara.** Maternal Thinking: Toward a Politics of Peace. 320p. 1994. pap. 13.00 (*0-8070-1409-5*) Beacon Pr.

Ruddick, Susan M. Young & Homeless in Hollywood: Mapping Social Identities. LC 94-21839. 256p. 1995. 49.95 (*0-415-91032-3*, B3861, Routledge NY); pap. 16.95 (*0-415-91031-5*, B3865, Routledge NY) Routledge.

Ruddiman, Catherine, jt. auth. see Aird, Hazel B.

Ruddiman, K. W., jt. auth. see Carpenter, D. M.

Ruddiman, W. F. & Wright, H. E., Jr., eds. North America & Adjacent Oceans During the Last Deglaciation. (DNAG, Geology of North America Ser.: Vol. K3). (Illus.). 509p. 1988. 43.50 (*0-8137-5203-5*) Geol Soc.

Ruddle, H., jt. ed. see O'Connor, J.

Ruddle, K. & Manshard, W. Renewable Natural Resources & the Environment: Pressing Problems in the Developing World, Vol. 2. (Natural Resources & the Environment Ser.). (Illus.). 410p. 1981. text ed. 105.00 (*0-907567-01-0*, Tycooly Pub); pap. 65.00 (*0-907567-06-1*, Tycooly Pub) Weidner & Sons.

Ruddle, Kenneth. The Coastal Zone: Man's Response to Change. 564p. 1988. text ed. 113.00 (*3-7186-0482-5*) Gordon & Breach.

— The Yukpa Cultivation System: A Study of Shifting Cultivation in Colombia & Venezuela. LC 73-78557. (Ibero-Americana Ser.: No. 52). (Illus.). 234p. reprint ed. pap. 66.70 (*0-685-23797-4*, 2032896) Bks Demand.

Ruddle, Kenneth & Zhong, Gongfu. Integrated Agriculture-Aquaculture in South China: The Dike-Pond System of the Zhujiang Delta. (Illus.). 200p. 1988. 64.95 (*0-521-34193-0*) Cambridge U Pr.

Ruddle, Kenneth, et al. Palm Sago: A Tropical Starch from Marginal Lands. LC 77-28981. 224p. 1978. pap. text ed. 10.00 (*0-8248-0577-1*, Eastwest Ctr Pr) UH Pr.

***Ruddock, E. H.** Vitalogy. (Illus.). 128p. 1995. reprint ed. pap. 8.95 (*1-55709-404-7*) Applewood.

Ruddock, Ted, ed. Travels in the Colonies in 1773-1775 Described in the Letters of William Mylne. LC 91-37478. (Illus.). 168p. 1993. 25.00 (*0-8203-1426-9*) U of Ga Pr.

Ruddolo, Lisa M., jt. auth. see Smith, Susan B.

Ruddon, Raymond W. Cancer Biology. 2nd ed. (Illus.). 544p. 1987. 49.50 (*0-19-503933-5*); pap. 39.95 (*0-19-504384-7*) OUP.

— Cancer Biology. 3rd ed. (Illus.). 496p. 1995. 75.00 (*0-19-509690-8*); pap. 39.95 (*0-19-509691-6*) OUP.

Rudduck, Jean. Developing a Gender Policy in Secondary Schools. LC 93-4049. 160p. 1994. 80.00 (*0-335-19153-3*, Open Univ Pr); pap. 24.00 (*0-335-19152-5*, Open Univ Pr) Taylor & Francis.

— Innovation & Change: Developing Involvement & Understanding. (Modern Educational Thought Ser.). 192p. 1991. 90.00 (*0-335-09581-X*, Open Univ Pr); pap. 32.00 (*0-335-09580-1*, Open Univ Pr) Taylor & Francis.

Rudduck, Jean, ed. see Stenhouse, Lawrence.

Ruddy, Anna C., see Christian McLeod, pseud..

Ruddy, Francis S. International Law in the Enlightenment: The Background of Emmerich De Vattel's "Le Droit Des Gens" LC 75-4423. 364p. 1975. 50.00 (*0-379-00292-2*) Oceana.

Ruddy, J., jt. illus. see Bowers, D.

Ruddy, James F. Photograde. 1993. pap. 9.95 (*0-307-09361-1*) Western Pub.

— Photograde: A Photographic Grading Encyclopedia for United States Coins. rev. ed. (Illus.). 208p. 1988. pap. 9.95 (*0-943161-04-5*) Bowers & Merena.

— Photograde: A Photographic Grading Encyclopedia for United States Coins. 17th rev. ed. (Illus.). 208p. 1988. 19.95 (*0-943161-09-6*) Bowers & Merena.

Ruddy, T. Michael. The Cautious Diplomat: Charles E. Bohlen & the Soviet Union, 1929-1969. LC 86-4705. 234p. 1986. 27.00 (*0-87338-331-1*) Kent St U Pr.

Ruddy, William. Braille for a Storm of Loss: Poems. 1978. 6.95 (*0-685-50207-4*); pap. 3.50 (*0-685-50208-2*) Oyez.

Rude, Carolyn D. Technical Editing. 430p. (C). 1991. text ed. 37.95 (*0-534-15000-4*) Intl Thomson.

Rude, Donald W., ed. A Critical Edition of Sir Thomas Elyot's "The Boke Named the Governour" LC 92-3303. (Renaissance Imagination Ser.). 472p. 1992. 100.00 (*0-8153-0458-7*) Garland.

Rude, George. Crowd in the French Revolution. (Illus.). 1967. reprint ed. pap. text ed. 14.95 (*0-19-500370-5*) OUP.

— The Crowd in the French Revolution. LC 86-3166. 295p. 1986. reprint ed. text ed. 89.50 (*0-313-25168-1*, RUCR, Greenwood Pr) Greenwood.

— Europe in the Eighteenth Century: Aristocracy & the Bourgeois Challenge. 292p. 1985. pap. 15.95 (*0-674-26921-7*) HUP.

— The French Revolution: Its Causes, Its History & Its Legacy after 200 Years. 240p. (Orig.). 1991. reprint ed. pap. 12.95 (*0-8021-3272-3*) Grove-Atltic.

— Ideology & Popular Protest. (C). 1980. pap. 18.50 (*0-85315-514-3*, Pub. by Lawrence & Wishart UK) Humanities.

— Ideology & Popular Protest. LC 94-32657. 190p. 1995. pap. text ed. 12.95x (*0-8078-4514-0*) U of NC Pr.

***Rude, Paul.** Souls to Soles: A Self-Help Exploration of Reflexology. (Illus.). 160p. (Orig.). 1995. pap. text ed. write for info. (*0-9645800-0-4*) Avant CA.

***Rude, Robert.** An Act of Deception: Alaska Native Corporations since ANSCA. 120p. 1995. pap. 12.00 (*0-9634000-8-8*) Salmon Run.

Rude, Ron. The Backyard Horseman. Brown, Bill, ed. LC 87-11187. (Illus.). 158p. (Orig.). 1987. pap. 15.00 (*0-87842-211-0*) Mountain Pr.

Rude, Steve. Steve Rude Sketchbook. Nesheim, Eric, ed. (Illus.). 136p. 1989. 28.95 (*0-87816-046-9*); pap. 14.95 (*0-87816-047-7*) Kitchen Sink.

Rude, Steve, jt. auth. see Baron, Mike.

Rudeanu, S. Boolean Functions & Equations. 1975. 51.50 (*0-444-10520-4*) Elsevier.

Rudeanu, S., ed. see Institute of Management Sciences Staff & Econometric Institute Staff.

Rudee, Martine & Blease, Jonathan. Traveler's Guide to Healing Centers & Retreats in North America. (Illus.). 224p. 1989. pap. 11.95 (*0-945465-15-7*) John Muir.

Rudeen, Kenneth. Swiftest. (Illus.). 1966. 5.50 (*0-393-07443-9*) Norton.

***Rudel, Anthony J.** Classical Music Top 40. 1995. pap. 12.00 (*0-671-79495-7*, Fireside) S&S Trade.

— Tales from the Opera. 379p. 1985. 17.95 (*0-685-43050-2*, Fireside); pap. 9.95 (*0-685-43051-0*, Fireside) S&S Trade.

Rudel, Hans-Ulrich. Stuka Pilot. 240p. 1987. 14.95 (*0-939482-04-5*) Noontide.

Rudel, Rachel. Cooking Healthy & Fast. large type ed. 1994. 14.95 (*0-9642510-0-0*) Apple a Day. Where else but in this new cookbook can you find bison recipes as unique, scrumptious, & healthy as these? Rachel Rudel, a registered dietician in Fargo, ND, has birthed COOKING HEALTHY & FAST with hopes of improving people's health as well as the state's agricultural market. This self-produced & promoted cookbook contains 250 recipes involving bison, as well as other local commodities. Rudel relays the nutritional benefits of eating bison meat; in which North Dakota has the only bison producing facility within North America. She also promotes "Pasta Growers" brand pasta, a Carrington-based, farmer-owned cooperative. Besides containing local products, this book appeals to those with an interest in health. Rudel educates her readers on how to be "fat smart" by contrasting the difference in products that are non-fat, fat-free, & traditional foods. The elderly are cautioned against falling prey to the recent "fat scare," & are encouraged to maintain a healthy balance in the foods they consume. The one-recipe-per-page, large print, easy-to-read cookbook is designed for time-conscious people who do not want a lot of extra fuss (or fat) in their lives. This book is "user friendly." COOKING HEALTHY & FAST retails for $14.95 & is available by mail order for $18.65 (which includes tax, shipping & handling). Send orders to Rachel Rudel, RD, LRD, P.O. Box 11336, Fargo, ND 58106-1336.** ***Publisher Provided Annotation.

***Rudel, Rachel A.** Cooking Healthy, Fast & Super Fast. 1994. 9.96 (*0-9642510-1-9*) Apple a Day.

Rudel, Thomas K. Situations & Strategies in American Land-Use Planning. (ASA Rose Monograph Ser.). (Illus.). 176p. (C). 1989. 49.95 (*0-521-36186-9*) Cambridge U Pr.

Rudel, Thomas K. & Horowitz, Bruce. Tropical Deforestation: Small Farmers & Land Clearing in the Ecuadorian Amazon. LC 92-44356. (Cases & Methods in Biological Diversity Ser.). 1993. write for info. (*0-231-08044-1*); pap. write for info. (*0-231-08045-X*) Col U Pr.

Rudelius, William, jt. auth. see Berkowitz, Eric.

Rudell, Fredrica. Consumer Food Selection & Nutrition Information. LC 79-10149. (Praeger Special Studies). 188p. 1979. text ed. 45.00 (*0-275-90415-6*, C0415, Praeger Pubs) Greenwood.

***Rudelle, Carla P.** Butter - Analysis, Composition, Uses & Flavorings: Index of New Information with Authors, Subjects, Research Categories & References. 160p. (Orig.). 1995. 49.50 (*0-7883-0770-3*); pap. 39.50 (*0-7883-0771-1*) ABBE Pubs Assn.

***Rudelle, Christian.** Dictionnaire des Termes Juridiques. 221p. (FRE.). 1992. pap. 45.00 (*0-7859-8202-7*, 2883990662) Fr & Eur.

Ruden, Sanford I., jt. auth. see Cramer, Martin R.

Rudenberg, Reinhold. Electrical Shock Waves in Power Systems: Traveling Waves in Lumped & Distributed Circuit Elements. LC 68-14272. (Illus.). 350p. 1968. 37.00 (*0-674-24350-1*) HUP.

***Rudenberg, Werner.** Chinesisch-Deutsches Woerterbuch. 3rd ed. 821p. (CHI & GER.). 1963. 395.00 (*0-7859-8264-7*, 3110000202) Fr & Eur.

Rudenbush, G. D. The Estimation of Macroeconomic Disequilibruim Models with Regime Classification Information. (Lecture Notes in Economics & Mathematical Systems Ser.: Vol. 288). vii, 128p. 1987. pap. 31.00 (*0-387-17757-4*) Spr-Verlag.

Rudenko, B. T. Grammatika Gruzinskogo Jazyka: Grammar of the Georgian Language. (Janua Linguarum, Series Anastatica: No. 7). 1972. pap. 57.70 (*3-10-800126-4*) Mouton.

Rudenko, Mykola. The Cross. 1986. 10.00 (*0-318-21433-4*) St Sophia Religious.

Rudenko, Y. N., ed. see Izmailov, L. D., et al.

Rudenko, Y. N., ed. see Levin, L. I., et al.

Rudenko, Y. N., ed. see Sokolov, E. Y., et al.

Rudenko, Y. N., ed. see Zinger, N. M., et al.

Rudenko, Yu N., jt. auth. see Melentiev, A.

Rudenko, Yuri N., ed. Power Systems of Eastern European Countries: Problems & Methods for Control & Development. LC 93-23936. 355p. 1993. 105.00 (*1-56700-013-4*) Begell Hse.

RuDenski, Kathy. Amazing Alphabet Animals. LC 91-65792. (Illus.). 44p. (J). (gr. k-3). 1992. 8.95 (*1-55523-447-X*) Winston-Derek.

Rudensky, Morris R. & Riley, Don. Gonif: Red Rudensky. LC 71-139587. 1970. 20.00 (*0-87832-002-4*) Piper.

Rudenstine, Angelica, jt. auth. see Rowell, Margit.

Rudenstine, Angelica Z. The Guggenheim Museum Collection: Paintings 1880-1945, 2 vols. LC 75-37356. (Illus.). 1976. pap. 42.00 (*0-685-70089-5*) S R Guggenheim.

— The Guggenheim Museum Collection: Paintings 1880-1945, 2 vols., Set. LC 75-37356. (Illus.). 1976. 85.00 (*0-89207-002-1*) S R Guggenheim.

— Modern Painting, Drawing, & Sculpture Collected by Emily & Joseph Pulitzer, Jr, Vol. IV. (Catalog of the Emily & Joseph Pulitzer, Jr., Collection). (Illus.). 372p. (Orig.). 1988. pap. 24.95 (*0-916724-35-2*) Harvard Art Mus.

— Modern Painting, Drawing & Sculpture Collected by Emily & Joseph Pulitzer, Jr., Vol. 4. (Illus.). 372p. 1995. pap. 24.95 (*0-916724-67-0*, 4670) Harvard Art Mus.

***Rudenstine, Angelica Z., ed.** Piet Mondrian: 1872-1944. (Illus.). 400p. 1995. 75.00 (*0-8212-2164-7*) Bulfinch Pr.

Rudenstine, Neil, jt. auth. see Bowen, Wm.

***Ruder, Hanns.** Atoms in Strong Magnetic Fields: Quantum Mechanical Treatment & Applications in Astrophysics & Quantum Chaos. LC 94-23259. 1994. write for info. (*0-387-57699-1*); write for info. (*3-540-57699-1*) Spr-Verlag.

Ruder, Jesse H. BASIC for the HP 3000. LC 85-12044. 240p. reprint ed. pap. 68.40 (*0-7837-2379-2*, 2040065) Bks Demand.

***Ruder, Linda N., ed.** Enhancing Capacities & Confronting Controversies in Criminal Justice: Proceedings of the 1993 National Conference. 166p. (Orig.). (C). 1994. pap. text ed. 45.00 (*0-7881-1376-3*) Diane Pub.

Ruderman, David, jt. auth. see Hallo, William.

Ruderman, David, jt. ed. see Hallo, William.

***Ruderman, David B.** Jewish Thought & Scientific Discovery in Early Modern Europe. LC 94-30520. 1995. 30.00 (*0-300-06112-9*) Yale U Pr.

— Kabbalah, Magic, & Science: The Cultural Universe of a Sixteenth-Century Jewish Physician. LC 87-35271. 256p. 1988. 40.00 (*0-674-49660-4*) HUP.

— The World of a Renaissance Jew: The Life & Thought of Abraham Ben Mordecai Farissol. LC 81-2551. (Monographs of the Hebrew Union College: No. 6). 283p. reprint ed. pap. 80.70 (*0-7837-2998-7*, 2042943) Bks Demand.

Ruderman, David B., ed. Essential Paper on Jewish Culture in Renaissance & Baroque Italy. (Essential Papers in Jewish Studies). 512p. 1992. text ed. 75.00x (*0-8147-7419-9*); pap. text ed. 25.00 (*0-8147-7420-2*) NYU Pr.

— Preachers of the Italian Ghetto. (C). 1992. 32.00 (*0-520-07735-0*) U CA Pr.

Ruderman, Harry, ed. Mathematical Buds, Vol. I. (Illus.). 1978. pap. text ed. 2.50 (*0-940790-01-7*) Mu Alpha Theta.

— Mathematical Buds, Vol. V. 1992. 2.50 (*0-940790-05-X*) Mu Alpha Theta.

Ruderman, Harry D. Tac-Tickle: Pure Strategy. 1966. 3.00 (*0-911624-06-6*) Wffn Proof.

Ruderman, Harry D., ed. see Kessler, Gilbert & Zimmerman, Lawrence.

Ruderman, Jerome L. Jews in American History: A Teacher's Guide. 244p. 7.95 (*0-686-95134-4*); pap. 3.95 (*0-686-99466-3*) ADL.

Ruderman, Judith. D. H. Lawrence & the Devouring Mother: The Search for a Patriarchal Ideal of Leadership. LC 84-7987. xi, 211p. 1984. text ed. 39.50 (*0-8223-0598-4*) Duke.

— Joseph Heller. (Literature & Life Ser.). 208p. 1991. 19.95 (*0-8264-0516-9*, F Ungar Bks) Continuum.

— William Styron. (Literature & Life Ser.). 192p. (C). 1987. 19.95 (*0-8044-2781-X*, F Ungar Bks) Continuum.

Ruderman, Marian N. & Ohlott, Patricia J. The Realities of Management Promotion. LC 93-43611. (Technical Report Ser.: No. 157G). 52p. 1993. pap. 15.00 (*0-912879-88-2*) Ctr Creat Leader.

Ruderman, Neil, et al, eds. Hyperglycemia, Diabetes & the Vascular Disease. (Clinical Physiology Series - An American Physiological Society Book). (Illus.). 320p. 1992. 90.00 (*0-19-506773-8*) OUP.

Ruderman, Terry J. Stanley M. Isaacs, the Conscience of New York. 1981. 38.95 (*0-405-14105-X*) Ayer.

Rudersdorf, Martha G., jt. auth. see LeRoux, David F.

***Rudert, H. & Werner, J. A., eds.** Lasers in Otorhinolaryngology, & in Head & Neck Surgery. (Advances in Oto-Rhino-Laryngology Ser.: Vol. 49). (Illus.). xii, 264p. 1995. 215.75 (*3-8055-6087-7*) S Karger.

Rudes, Blair A. & Crouse, Dorothy. The Tuscarora Legacy of J. N. B. Hewitt: Materials for the Study of the Tuscarora Language & Culture, Set. (Canadian Museum of Civlization Mercury Series-Canadian Ethnology Service). 670p. 1988. pap. text ed. 39.95 (*0-660-10773-2*, Pub. by CN Mus Civilization CN) U Ch Pr.

Rudestam, Kjell E. & Newton, Rae R. Surviving Your Dissertation: A Comprehensive Guide to Content & Process. 208p. (C). 1992. text ed. 44.00 (*0-8039-4562-0*); pap. text ed. 18.95 (*0-8039-4563-9*) Sage.

Rudgard, S. A. & Maddison, A. C., eds. Disease Management in Cocoa: Comparative Epidemiology of Witches' Broom. LC 93-23543. 249p. 1993. 85.00 (*0-412-58190-6*) Chapman & Hall.

Rudge, A. W., et al, eds. The Handbook of Antenna Design, Vol. I. (Electromagnetic Waves Ser.: Nos. 15 & 16). 708p. 1983. boxed 145.00 (*0-906048-82-6*, EW015) Inst Elect Eng.

— The Handbook of Antenna Design, Vol. II. (Electromagnetic Waves Ser.: Nos. 15 & 16). 960p. 1983. boxed 177.00 (*0-906048-87-7*, EW016) Inst Elect Eng.

— The Handbook of Antenna Design, 2 vols. in 1, Vols. 1 & 2. (Electromagnetic Waves Ser.). 1696p. 1986. pap. 159.00 (*0-86341-052-9*, EW015Z) Inst Elect Eng.

Rudge, Mary. Going to China - And Other Places. LC 87-60437. (Mucho Somos Ser.: No. 11). 32p. (Orig.). 1987. pap. 1.50 (*0-914370-56-1*) Mothers Hen.

Rudge, Mary, jt. auth. see Lasartemay, Eugene P.

Rudgley, Richard. Essential Substances: A Cultural History of Intoxicants in Society. Urda, John, ed. (Illus.). 224p. 1994. 22.00 (*1-56836-016-9*) Kodansha.

— Essential Substances: A Cultural History of Intoxicants in Society. Urda, John, ed. (Kodansha Globe Trade Paperback Ser.). (Illus.). 208p. 1995. pap. 12.00 (*1-56836-075-4*, Kodansha Globe) Kodansha.

Rudhyar, Dane. The Astrological Houses: The Spectrum of Individual Experience. LC 74-180105. 216p. 1986. reprint ed. pap. 12.95 (*0-916360-24-5*) CRCS Pubns CA.

— Astrological Insights into the Spiritual Life. 154p. 1979. pap. 10.95 (*0-943358-09-4*) Aurora Press.

— Astrological Mandala: The Cycle of Transformations & Its 360 Symbolic Phases. 1974. pap. 10.00 (*0-394-71992-1*, Vin) Random.

— Astrological Triptych. 296p. 1978. pap. 14.00 (*0-943358-10-8*) Aurora Press.

— The Astrology of Personality. 445p. 1991. 18.95 (*0-943358-25-6*) Aurora Press.

— Astrology of Transformation. LC 80-51553. 1980. pap. 10.00 (*0-8356-0542-6*, Quest) Theos Pub Hse.

— Beyond Individualism. LC 78-64906. (Orig.). 1979. pap. 4.75 (*0-8356-0518-3*, Quest) Theos Pub Hse.

— Culture, Crisis & Creativity. LC 76-43008. (Orig.). 1977. pap. 4.25 (*0-8356-0487-X*, Quest) Theos Pub Hse.

— The Galactic Dimension of Astrology. 214p. 1975. pap. 10.95 (*0-943358-13-2*) Aurora Press.

— The Lunation Cycle: A Key to the Understanding of Personality. 208p. 1986. pap. 14.95 (*0-943358-26-4*) Aurora Press.

— New Mansions for New Men. LC 85-21337. xvi, 273p. 1985. reprint ed. lib. bdg. 27.00x (*0-89370-588-8*) Borgo Pr.

— Occult Preparations for a New Age. LC 74-19054. 266p. (Orig.). 1975. pap. 5.50 (*0-8356-0460-8*, Quest) Theos Pub Hse.

— Of Vibrancy & Peace: Poems: A Selection of Poems from Published & Unpublished Volumes. LC 85-22341. 156p. 1985. reprint ed. lib. bdg. 23.00x (*0-89370-585-3*) Borgo Pr.

— Person Centered Astrology. 385p. 1983. 14.00 (*0-943358-02-7*) Aurora Press.

— The Planetarization of Consciousness. (Dane Rudhyar Ser.). 318p. 1977. pap. 9.95 (*0-943358-16-7*) Aurora Press.

— Rhythm of Wholeness. LC 83-70689. 268p. (Orig.). 1983. pap. 7.50 (*0-8356-0578-7*, Quest) Theos Pub Hse.

Rudhyar, Dane, jt. auth. see Rael, Leyla.

Rudich, J., jt. auth. see Atherton, J. G.

Rudich, Vasily. Political Dissidence Under Nero. LC 92-7604. 352p. 1993. 98.50 (*0-415-06951-3*, A7048) Routledge.

Rudick, Michael, ed. see Ringler, William A., Jr.

Rudick, R. A., et al, eds. Treatment of Multiple Sclerosis: Trial Design, Results & Future Perspectives. (Clinical Medicine & the Nervous System Ser.). (Illus.). xviii, 313p. 1992. 139.00 (*0-387-19683-8*) Spr-Verlag.

***Rudie, Carol V.** Discover Psalms: Hope When We're Hurting. (Discover Your Bible Ser.). 1995. teacher ed write for info. (*1-56212-092-1*) CRC Pubns.

Rudig, Doug. Big Bend Adventure Guide. Pearson, John R. & Deckert, Frank J., eds. (Illus.). 32p. (Orig.). (J). (gr. k-6). 1983. pap. 2.00 (*0-912001-10-0*) Big Bend.

— Zion Adventure Guide. LC 77-78309. (Illus.). 32p. (J). (gr. 2-7). 1978. pap. 1.95 (*0-915630-07-9*) Zion.

Rudig, Wolfgang, ed. Green Politics I - 1990. 386p. (C). 1991. 29.95 (*0-8093-1734-6*) S Ill U Pr.

— Green Politics Two. 248p. 1993. pap. text ed. 35.00 (*0-7486-0271-2*, Pub. by Edinburgh U Pr UK) Col U Pr.

Rudiger, G. Differential Rotation & Stellar Convection - Sun & Solar Type Stars. (Fluid Mechanics of Astrophysics & Geophysics Ser.). 1989. text ed. 206.00 (*2-88124-066-6*) Gordon & Breach.

Rudiger, Horst. Goethe und Europa: Essays und Aufsatze 1944-1983. (Komparatistische Studien: Band 14). xiv, 331p. (C). 1990. lib. bdg. 26.15 (*3-11-011805-X*) De Gruyter.

— Wesen und Wandlungen Des Humanismus. 323p. 1966. write for info. (0-318-71278-4, Pub. by Georg Olms GW) Lubrecht & Cramer.

Rudiger, R., jt. auth. see Haensch, Gunther.

Rudin, A. James & Wilson, Marvin R., eds. A Time to Speak: The Evangelical-Jewish Encounter. LC 87-16770. 218p. (Orig.). reprint ed. pap. 62.20 (0-7837-3187-6, 2042791) Bks Demand.

Rudin, Alfred. The Elements of Polymer Science & Engineering: An Introductory Text for Engineers & Chemists. 1982. text ed. 69.00 (0-12-601680-1) Acad Pr.

Rudin, Bo. Making Paper. (Illus.). 280p. 1992. 40.00 (1-55821-167-5) Lyons & Burford.

Rudin, Catherine. Aspects of Bulgarian Syntax: Complementizers & WH Constructions. iv, 232p. (Orig.). 1986. pap. 19.95 (0-89357-156-3) Slavica.

Rudin, Catherine, jt. auth. see Gribble, Lyubomira P.

Rudin, Claire. School Librarian's Sourcebook. 504p. 1990. 38.00 (0-8352-2711-1) Bowker.

***Rudin, Ernst.** Tender Accents of Sound: Spanish in the Chicano Novel in English. 262p. (Orig.). 1995. pap. 20.00 (0-927534-52-5) Biling Rev-Pr.

Rudin, H. Protocol Specification, Testing & Verification, VII: Proceedings of the IFIP WG 6.1 Seventh International Conference, Zurich, Switzerland, May 5-8, 1987. West, C. H., ed. 470p. 1987. 105.25 (0-444-70293-8, North Holland) Elsevier.

Rudin, H. & West, C. H., eds. Protocol Specification, Testing & Verification: Proceedings of the IFIP WG 6.1 Third International Workshop on Protocol Specification, Testing & Verification, Organized by IBM Research, Ruschlikon, Switzerland, 31 May-2 June, 1983, Vol. 3. 532p. 1984. 92.50 (0-444-86769-4, North Holland) Elsevier.

Rudin, H., jt. ed. see Bux, W.

Rudin, Jacob. Haggadah for Children. (J). (gr. 3 up). 1973. 2.95 (0-8197-0032-0) Bloch.

Rudin, Jacob P. Very Truly Yours. 1971. 10.00 (0-8197-0279-X) Bloch.

Rudin, James, et al. Twenty Years of Jewish-Catholic Relations. 336p. (Orig.). 1986. pap. 11.95 (0-8091-2762-8) Paulist Pr.

Rudin, M. E. Lectures on Set Theoretic Topology. LC 74-31124. (CBMS Regional Conference Series in Mathematics: No. 23). 76p. 1980. reprint ed. pap. 16.00 (0-8218-1673-X, CBMS-23) Am Math.

Rudin, Marcia R., ed. Cults on Campus: Continuing Challenge. 126p. (Orig.). 1991. pap. 12.00 (0-931337-02-X, Intl Cult Ed Pgm) Am Family Foun.

Rudin-O'Brasky, Talia. The Patriarchs in Hebron & Sodom (Genesis 18-19) A Study of the Structure & Composition of a Biblical Story. (Jerusalem Biblical Studies: Vol. 2). 156p. (HEB.). 1982. pap. text ed. 12.00 (0-685-49415-2, Pub. by Simor Ltd IS) Eisenbrauns.

Rudin, Ronald. Banking en Francais: The French Banks of Quebec, 1835-1925. (Social History of Canada Ser.: No. 38). 216p. 1985. 27.50 (0-8020-2560-9); pap. 10.95 (0-8020-6579-1) U of Toronto Pr.

— In Whose Interest? Quebec's Caisses Populaires, 1900-1945. 224p. (C). 1990. text ed. 44.95 (0-7735-0759-0, Pub. by McGill CN) U of Toronto Pr.

Rudin, W. New Constructions of Functions Holomorphic in the Unit: Ball of C to the N power. LC 86-1205. (CBMS Regional Conference Series in Mathematics: No. 63). 78p. 1986. pap. text ed. 19.00 (0-8218-0713-7, CBMS-63) Am Math.

Rudin, Walter. Fourier Analysis on Groups. (Classics Library). 296p. 1990. pap. text ed. 59.95 (0-471-52364-X) Wiley.

— Fourier Analysis on Groups. LC 62-12211. (INterscience Tracts in Pure & Applied Mathematics Ser.: No. 12). 285p. reprint ed. pap. 84.10 (0-685-20436-7, 2056444) Bks Demand.

— Lectures on the Edge-of-the-Wedge Theorem. LC 73-145640. (CBMS Regional Conference Series in Mathematics: No. 6). 30p. 1971. 16.00 (0-8218-1655-1, CBMS-6) Am Math.

— Principles of Mathematical Analysis. 3rd ed. (International Series in Pure & Applied Mathematics). (C). 1976. text ed. write for info. (0-07-054235-X) McGraw.

— Real & Complex Analysis. 3rd ed. (Higher Mathematics Ser.). 480p. (C). 1987. text ed. write for info. (0-07-054234-1) McGraw.

Rudinger, E., ed. see Bohr, Niels.

Rudinger, E., jt. ed. see Kalckar, J.

Rudinger, Joel. How to Bingo 75 Ways: A Complete Guide to American Bingo Patterns. (Bingo Guide Ser.: No. 1). 48p. 1976. pap. 4.00 (0-918342-02-3) Cambric.

— Lovers & Celebrations. (Orig.). 1984. pap. 7.95 (0-918342-20-1) Cambric.

— Poetry Project Three: Cambridge Poetry Projects. (Orig.). 1983. pap. 7.95 (0-685-06312-7) Cambridge U Pr.

Rudinger, Joel, ed. Cambric Poetry Project One. 1978. pap. 6.95 (0-918342-06-6) Cambric.

— Poetry Project Four. (Poetry Projects Ser.). 104p. (Orig.). 1985. pap. 7.00 (0-918342-22-8) Cambric.

— Poetry Project Three CPP-3. 128p. (Orig.). (C). 1983. pap. 7.95 (0-918342-16-3) Cambric.

Rudinow, Joel, jt. auth. see Barry, Vincent E.

Rudinsky. Forest Insect Survey & Control. 4th ed. 1979. 20.00 (0-88246-100-1) Oreg St U Bkstrs.

Rudinsky, Joseph. Challenge of the Steppes: Roots of the Cold War. 6.00 (0-8315-0070-0) Speller.

Rudinsky, Norma L. Incipient Feminists: Women Writers in the Slovak National Revival. 285p. 1991. 22.95 (0-89357-220-9) Slavica.

Rudinsky, Norma L., ed. see Timrava.

Rudis, Deborah D., jt. auth. see DeGraaf, Richard M.

***Rudisill, Marianne, et al.** Human Computer Interface Design: Success Cases, Emerging Methods & Real-World Context. 1995. 44.95 (1-55860-310-7) Morgan Kaufmann.

Rudisill, Marie. Critter Cakes & Frog Tea: Tales & Treats from the Emerald River. LC 94-9086. (J). (gr. 1). 1994. spiral bd. 12.95 (1-881548-09-0) Crane Hill AL.

Rudisill, Mary E. & Jackson, Andrew S. Theory & Application of Motor Learning. (Illus.). 175p. (C). 1992. write for info. (0-9634528-0-0) MacJR.

Rudisill, Richard. Mirror Image: The Influence of the Daguerreotype on American Society. LC 79-137880. 354p. reprint ed. pap. 100.90 (0-317-20585-4, 2024678) Bks Demand.

— Photographers: A Sourcebook for Historical Research: Directories of Photographers: Annotated World Bibliography. annot. ed. Palmquist, Peter, ed. (Illus.). 120p. (Orig.). 1991. pap. 25.00 (0-9621940-2-6) C Mautz Pubng.

Rudison, Ronald L. Where to Find the Best Soul Food, Blues, & Jazz in the Southeast. (Illus.). 184p. (Orig.). (C). 1994. pap. 12.95 (1-880216-20-5) Elliott & Clark.

Rudka, Andrzej, jt. ed. see Kemme, David M.

Rudkin, Anthony & Butcher, Irene, eds. Book World Directory of the Arab Countries, Turkey & Iran. (C). 1981. 110.00 (0-8103-1185-2) Gale.

Rudkin, David. The Saxon Shore. (Methuen Modern Plays Ser.). 52p. 1988. pap. 8.95 (0-413-14100-4, A0255) Heinemann.

— The Triumph of Death. 60p. 1988. pap. 8.95 (0-413-49110-2, A0300, Pub. by Methuen UK) Heinemann.

Rudkin, Margaret. Margaret Rudkin Pepperidge Farm Cookbook. 1992. 12.98 (0-88365-800-3) Galahad Bks.

Rudkin, Olive D. Thomas Spence & His Connections. LC 65-26376. (Reprints of Economic Classics Ser.). 1966. reprint ed. 35.00 (0-678-00178-2) Kelley.

Rudko, C. Baby's Sleeping. (Little Look-In Ser.). (Illus.). 20p. (J). 1994. write for info. (0-307-16707-0) Western Pub.

— Doctor Duck. (Furry Face Ser.). (Illus.). 12p. (J). 1994. write for info. (0-307-16455-1) Western Pub.

— Halloween on Haunted Hill. (Press-Out Fun Ser.). (Illus.). 16p. (J). 1994. write for info. (0-307-12927-6, Golden Bks) Western Pub.

— Handy Lamb. (Furry Face Ser.). (Illus.). 12p. (J). 1994. write for info. (0-307-16454-3) Western Pub.

— Mouse Town. (Little Look-In Ser.). (Illus.). 20p. (J). 1994. write for info. (0-307-16711-9) Western Pub.

— Oh, Ho, Ho, It's Christmas. (Press-Out Fun Ser.). (Illus.). 14p. (J). 1994. write for info. (0-307-12928-4, Golden Bks) Western Pub.

— Playtime. (Little Look-In Ser.). (Illus.). 20p. (J). 1994. write for info. (0-307-16706-2) Western Pub.

— Teddy Bear Circus. (Little Look-In Ser.). (Illus.). 20p. (J). 1994. write for info. (0-307-16710-0) Western Pub.

Rudko, Che. Be Mine. (Press-Out Fun Ser.). (Illus.). 16p. (J). 1994. write for info. (0-307-12925-X, Golden Bks) Western Pub.

— Littlest Pet Shop Fun All Day. (Golden Little Look-Look Bks.). 24p. (J). 1994. write for info. (0-307-11717-0, Golden Bks) Western Pub.

— A Perfect Easter Day. (Press-Out Fun Ser.). (Illus.). 16p. (J). 1994. write for info. (0-307-12926-8, Golden Bks) Western Pub.

Rudko, Frances H. John Marshall & International Law: Statesman & Chief Justice. LC 91-11333. (Contributions in Political Science Ser.: No. 280). 152p. 1991. text ed. 47.95 (0-313-27932-2, RJM/, Greenwood Pr) Greenwood.

— Truman's Court: A Study in Judicial Restraint. LC 88-5664. (Contributions in Legal Studies: No. 45). 186p. 1988. text ed. 45.00 (0-313-26316-7, RTC/, Greenwood Pr) Greenwood.

Rudler-Barnett, Carol S. & Suckley, Luann M. The Last Word in Medical Technology. 239p. 1985. pap. 28.95 (0-316-76094-3, Little Med Div) Little.

Rudler, G., ed. see Moliere, pseud.

Rudley, Marcia M., jt. auth. see Rudley, Otto C.

Rudley, Otto C. & Rudley, Marcia M. Philosophies, Missions, Goals. 82p. (C). 1990. pap. text ed. 19.95 (0-9626259-0-6) Con Mar Pub.

Rudlin, John. The Commedia dell'Arte in the Twentieth Century. LC 93-13426. 1994. write for info. (0-415-04769-2); pap. write for info. (0-415-04770-6) Routledge.

— Jacques Copeau. (Directors in Perspective Ser.). (Illus.). 141p. 1986. 59.95 (0-521-25305-5); pap. 21.95 (0-521-27303-X) Cambridge U Pr.

Rudlin, John, ed. see Copeau, Jacques.

Rudloe, Jack. Easy Money. 1999. pap. write for info. (0-670-28697-4) Viking Penguin.

— The Living Dock. LC 88-19963. (Illus.). 273p. 1988. 24.95 (1-55591-036-X) Fulcrum Pub.

— Search for the Great Turtle Mother. LC 94-44849. (Illus.). 288p. 1995. 17.95 (1-56164-072-7) Pineapple Pr.

Rudman. Master Fire Supression Piping Contractor. (Career Examination Ser.: Series 1). 1985. pap. 23.95 (0-8373-3765-8) Nat Learn.

Rudman, jt. auth. see Pasternak.

Rudman, Andrew I., jt. ed. see Tulchin, Joseph S.

Rudman, Daniel, ed. Take It to the Hoop. (Illus.). 300p. (Orig.). 1980. 25.00 (0-913028-80-0); pap. 8.95 (0-913028-76-2) North Atlantic.

Rudman, David, jt. auth. see Shinde, Subhash.

Rudman, David A., jt. ed. see Ruggiero, Steven T.

Rudman, Gerald J., jt. auth. see Bergmann, Sherrel.

Rudman, Jack. Able Seaman. (Career Examination Ser.: C-1). 1994. pap. 29.95 (0-8373-0001-0) Nat Learn.

— Abnormal Psychology. (ACT Proficiency Examination Program Ser.: PEP-53). 1994. pap. 23.95 (0-8373-5903-1) Nat Learn.

— Abnormal Psychology. (ACT Proficiency Examination Program Ser.: PEP-53). 1994. 39.95 (0-8373-5928-7) Nat Learn.

— Abstract Reasoning. (Career Examination Ser.: CS-26). 1994. pap. 23.95 (0-8373-6726-3) Nat Learn.

— Account Clerk. (Career Examination Ser.: C-2). 1994. pap. 19.95 (0-8373-0002-9) Nat Learn.

— Account Clerk-Stenographer. (Career Examination Ser.: C-3220). 1994. pap. 19.95 (0-8373-3220-6) Nat Learn.

— Account Clerk-Typist. (Career Examination Ser.: C-3221). 1994. pap. 19.95 (0-8373-3221-4) Nat Learn.

— Accountant. (Career Examination Ser.: C-3). 1994. pap. 27.95 (0-8373-0003-7) Nat Learn.

— Accountant-Auditor. (Career Examination Ser.: C-4). 1994. pap. 29.95 (0-8373-0004-5) Nat Learn.

— Accountant-Auditor Trainee. (Career Examination Ser.: C-2993). 1994. pap. 23.95 (0-8373-2993-0) Nat Learn.

— Accountant I. (Career Examination Ser.: C-2966). 1994. pap. 27.95 (0-8373-2966-3) Nat Learn.

— Accountant II. (Career Examination Ser.: C-2967). 1994. pap. 29.95 (0-8373-2967-1) Nat Learn.

— Accountant III. (Career Examination Ser.: C-2968). 1994. pap. 34.95 (0-8373-2968-X) Nat Learn.

— Accountant IV. (Career Examination Ser.: C-2969). 1994. pap. 34.95 (0-8373-2969-8) Nat Learn.

— Accounting. (College Proficiency Examination Ser.: CPEP-1). 1994. pap. 23.95 (0-8373-5401-3) Nat Learn.

— Accounting: Advanced Accounting. (ACT Proficiency Examination Program Ser.: PEP-13). 1994. pap. 23.95 (0-8373-5513-3) Nat Learn.

— Accounting: Auditing. (ACT Proficiency Examination Program Ser.: PEP-14). 1994. pap. 23.95 (0-8373-5514-1) Nat Learn.

— Accounting: Cost Accounting & Analysis. (ACT Proficiency Examination Program Ser.: PEP-12). 1994. pap. 23.95 (0-8373-5512-5) Nat Learn.

— Accounting & Auditing Clerk. (Career Examination Ser.: C-5). 1994. pap. 19.95 (0-8373-0005-3) Nat Learn.

— Accounting & Business Practice, Sr. H. S. (Teachers License Examination Ser.: T-1). 1994. pap. 23.95 (0-8373-8001-4) Nat Learn.

— Accounting Assistant. (Career Examination Ser.: C-1071). 1994. pap. 23.95 (0-8373-1071-7) Nat Learn.

— Accounting Executive. (Career Examination Ser.: C-1072). 1994. pap. 34.95 (0-8373-1072-5) Nat Learn.

— Accounting I. (Regents External Degree Ser.: REDP-1). 1994. pap. 23.95 (0-8373-5601-6) Nat Learn.

— Accounting II. (Regents External Degree Ser.: REDP-2). 1994. pap. 23.95 (0-8373-5602-4) Nat Learn.

— Accounting III. (Regents External Degree Ser.: REDP-3). 1994. pap. 23.95 (0-8373-5603-2) Nat Learn.

— Accounting Machine Operator. (Career Examination Ser.: C-1073). 1994. pap. 23.95 (0-8373-1073-3) Nat Learn.

— Accounting Technician (U.S.P.S.) (Career Examination Ser.: C-2252). 1994. pap. 27.95 (0-8373-2252-9) Nat Learn.

— Accounting Trainee. (Career Examination Ser.: C-6). 1994. pap. 23.95 (0-8373-0006-1) Nat Learn.

— Accounts Investigator. (Career Examination Ser.: C-1862). 1994. pap. 27.95 (0-8373-1862-9) Nat Learn.

— ACT Assessment Examination for College Entrance (ACT) (Admission Test Ser.: ATS-44). 1994. pap. 23.95 (0-8373-5044-1) Nat Learn.

— ACT Proficiency Examination Passbook Program (PEP), Set. 1994. Entire Series. pap. write for info. (0-8373-5500-1) Nat Learn.

— Activities Aide. (Career Examination Ser.: C-3101). 1994. pap. 19.95 (0-8373-3101-3) Nat Learn.

— Activities Director. (Career Examination Ser.: C-2949). 1994. pap. 29.95 (0-8373-2949-3) Nat Learn.

— Activities Specialist. (Career Examination Ser.: C-1074). 1994. pap. 23.95 (0-8373-1074-1) Nat Learn.

— Actuarial Clerk. (Career Examination Ser.: C-2417). 1994. pap. 23.95 (0-8373-2417-3) Nat Learn.

— Actuary. (Career Examination Ser.: C-7). 1994. pap. 39.95 (0-8373-0007-X) Nat Learn.

— Addiction Counselor. (Career Examination Ser.: C-2150). 1994. pap. 29.95 (0-8373-2150-6) Nat Learn.

— Addiction Specialist. (Career Examination Ser.: C-1075). 1994. pap. 29.95 (0-8373-1075-X) Nat Learn.

— Addressing Machine Operator. (Career Examination Ser.: C-1892). 1994. pap. 19.95 (0-8373-1892-0) Nat Learn.

— Addressing Machine Supervisor. (Career Examination Ser.: C-1893). 1994. pap. 23.95 (0-8373-1893-9) Nat Learn.

— Addressograph Machine Operator. (Career Examination Ser.: C-1076). 1994. pap. 19.95 (0-8373-1076-8) Nat Learn.

— Adjudicator. (Career Examination Ser.: C-1087). 1994. pap. 39.95 (0-8373-1087-3) Nat Learn.

— Administrative Accountant. (Career Examination Ser.: C-1078). 1994. 39.95 (0-8373-1078-4) Nat Learn.

— Administrative Aide. (Career Examination Ser.: C-8). 1994. pap. 23.95 (0-8373-0008-8) Nat Learn.

— Administrative Analyst. (Career Examination Ser.: C-2144). 1994. pap. 34.95 (0-8373-2144-1) Nat Learn.

— Administrative Assessor. (Career Examination Ser.: C-2596). 1994. pap. 29.95 (0-8373-2596-X) Nat Learn.

— Administrative Assistant. (Career Examination Ser.: C-9). 1994. pap. 23.95 (0-8373-0009-6) Nat Learn.

— Administrative Assistant I. (Career Examination Ser.: C-1848). 1994. pap. 27.95 (0-8373-1848-3) Nat Learn.

— Administrative Assistant II. (Career Examination Ser.: C-1849). 1991. pap. 24.00 (0-8373-1849-1) Nat Learn.

— Administrative Associate. (Career Examination Ser.: C-67). 1994. pap. 27.95 (0-8373-0067-3) Nat Learn.

— Administrative Attorney. (Career Examination Ser.: C-2597). 1994. pap. 39.95 (0-8373-2597-8) Nat Learn.

— Administrative Auditor of Accounts. (Career Examination Ser.: C-2598). 1994. pap. 39.95 (0-8373-2598-6) Nat Learn.

— Administrative Business Promotion Coordinator. (Career Examination Ser.: C-2599). 1994. pap. 39.95 (0-8373-2599-4) Nat Learn.

— Administrative Careers Examination. (Career Examination Ser.: C-69). 1994. pap. 23.95 (0-8373-0069-X) Nat Learn.

— Administrative Claim Examiner. (Career Examination Ser.: C-2600). 1994. pap. 27.95 (0-8373-2600-1) Nat Learn.

— Administrative Clerk. (Career Examination Ser.: C-2014). 1994. pap. 27.95 (0-8373-2014-3) Nat Learn.

— Administrative Clerk (U.S.P.S.) (Career Examination Ser.: C-2101). 1994. pap. 27.95 (0-8373-2101-8) Nat Learn.

— Administrative Consultant. (Career Examination Ser.: C-2089). 1994. pap. 34.95 (0-8373-2089-5) Nat Learn.

— Administrative Education Analyst. (Career Examination Ser.: C-3317). 1994. pap. 39.95 (0-8373-3317-2) Nat Learn.

— Administrative Engineer. (Career Examination Ser.: C-2601). 1994. pap. 34.95 (0-8373-2601-X) Nat Learn.

— Administrative Fire Alarm Dispatcher. (Career Examination Ser.: C-2602). 1994. pap. 29.95 (0-8373-2602-8) Nat Learn.

— Administrative Fire Marshal (Uniformed) (Career Examination Ser.: C-2603). 1994. pap. 39.95 (0-8373-2603-6) Nat Learn.

— Administrative Housing Inspector. (Career Examination Ser.: C-2604). 1994. pap. 39.95 (0-8373-2604-4) Nat Learn.

— Administrative Housing Manager. (Career Examination Ser.: C-1799). 1994. pap. 34.95 (0-8373-1799-1) Nat Learn.

— Administrative Housing Superintendent. (Career Examination Ser.: C-1800). 1994. pap. 34.95 (0-8373-1800-9) Nat Learn.

— Administrative Investigator. (Career Examination Ser.: C-1924). 1994. pap. 29.95 (0-8373-1924-2) Nat Learn.

— Administrative Labor Relations Specialist. (Career Examination Ser.: C-2027). 1994. pap. 39.95 (0-8373-2027-5) Nat Learn.

— Administrative Management Auditor. (Career Exam Ser.: No. C-3516). 1994. 39.95 (0-8373-3516-7) Nat Learn.

— Administrative Manager. (Career Examination Ser.: C-1754). 1994. pap. 29.95 (0-8373-1754-1) Nat Learn.

— Administrative Officer. (Career Examination Ser.: C-1079). 1994. pap. 29.95 (0-8373-1079-2) Nat Learn.

— Administrative Officer I. (Career Examination Ser.: C-1850). 1994. pap. 29.95 (0-8373-1850-5) Nat Learn.

— Administrative Officer II. (Career Examination Ser.: C-1852). 1994. pap. 34.95 (0-8373-1852-1) Nat Learn.

— Administrative Park & Recreation Manager. (Career Examination Ser.: C-2606). 1994. pap. 34.95 (0-8373-2606-0) Nat Learn.

— Administrative Personnel Examiner. (Career Examination Ser.: C-70). 1994. pap. 39.95 (0-8373-0070-3) Nat Learn.

— Administrative Project Coordinator. (Career Examination Ser.: C-1080). 1994. pap. 29.95 (0-8373-1080-6) Nat Learn.

— Administrative Public Information Specialist. (Career Examination Ser.: C-2607). 1994. pap. 27.95 (0-8373-2607-9) Nat Learn.

— Administrative Secretary. (Career Examination Ser.: C-1081). 1994. pap. 27.95 (0-8373-1081-4) Nat Learn.

— Administrative Service Officer. (Career Examination Ser.: C-10). 1994. pap. 29.95 (0-8373-0010-X) Nat Learn.

— Administrative Services Clerk. (Career Examination Ser.: C-2869). 1994. pap. 27.95 (0-8373-2869-1) Nat Learn.

— Administrative Services Manager. (Career Examination Ser.: C-2712). 1994. pap. 34.95 (0-8373-2712-1) Nat Learn.

— Administrative Space Analyst. (Career Exam Ser.: No. C-3517). 1994. 39.95 (0-8373-3517-5) Nat Learn.

— Administrative Staff Analyst. (Career Examination Ser.: C-1553). 1994. pap. 34.95 (0-8373-1553-0) Nat Learn.

— Administrative Superintendent of Buildings & Grounds. (Career Examination Ser.: C-1707). 1994. pap. 29.95 (0-8373-1707-X) Nat Learn.

— Administrative Superintendent of Highway Operations. (Career Examination Ser.: C-2608). 1994. pap. 39.95 (0-8373-2608-7) Nat Learn.

— Administrative Supervisor of Building Maintenance. (Career Examination Ser.). 1994. 34.95 (0-8373-3617-1, C-3617) Nat Learn.

— Administrative Trainee. (Career Examination Ser.: C-1082). 1994. pap. 23.95 (0-8373-1082-2) Nat Learn.

— Administrator. (Career Examination Ser.: C-1077). 1994. pap. 29.95 (0-8373-1077-6) Nat Learn.

— Administrator I. (Career Examination Ser.: C-1769). 1994. pap. 29.95 (0-8373-1769-X) Nat Learn.

— Administrator II. (Career Examination Ser.: C-1691). 1994. pap. 34.95 (0-8373-1691-X) Nat Learn.

— Administrator III. (Career Examination Ser.: C-2175). 1994. pap. 39.95 (0-8373-2175-1) Nat Learn.

— Administrator IV. (Career Examination Ser.: C-2176). 1994. pap. 39.95 (0-8373-2176-X) Nat Learn.

— Admission Test Passbook Series. 1994. pap. write for info. (0-8373-5000-X) Nat Learn.

— Admissions Officer. (Career Examination Ser.: C-1083). 1994. pap. 29.95 (0-8373-1083-0) Nat Learn.

— Admitting Clerk. (Career Examination Ser.: C-71). 1994. pap. 23.95 (0-8373-0071-1) Nat Learn.

— Adult Nurse Practitioner. (Certified Nurse Examination Ser.: CN-1). 1994. 39.95 (0-8373-6151-6); pap. 23.95 (0-8373-6101-X) Nat Learn.

— Adult Nursing. (Regents College Proficiency Examination Ser.: CPEP-35). 1994. pap. 23.95 (0-8373-5435-8) Nat Learn.

R

— Adult Nursing. (ACT Proficiency Examination Program Ser.: PEP-39). 1994. pap. 23.95 (*0-8373-5539-7*) Nat Learn.

— Advanced Accounting. 1994. 39.95 (*0-8373-5563-X*, PEP-13) Nat Learn.

— Aerospace Engineer. (Career Examination Ser.: C-72). 1994. pap. 34.95 (*0-8373-0072-X*) Nat Learn.

— Affirmative Action Officer. (Career Examination Ser.: C-2647). 1994. pap. 29.95 (*0-8373-2647-8*) Nat Learn.

— Affirmative Action Specialist. (Career Examination Ser.: C-2581). 1991. pap. 20.00 (*0-8373-2581-1*) Nat Learn.

— African & Afro-American History. (College Proficiency Examination Ser.: CPEP-36). 1994. pap. 23.95 (*0-8373-5436-6*) Nat Learn.

— African & Afro-American History. (ACT Proficiency Examination Program Ser.: PEP-1). 1994. pap. 23.95 (*0-8373-5501-X*) Nat Learn.

— Afro-American History. (College Level Examination Ser.: CLEP-36). 1994. 39.95 (*0-8373-5386-6*); pap. 23.95 (*0-8373-5336-X*) Nat Learn.

— Aging Services Representative. (Career Examination Ser.: C-2880). 1994. pap. 27.95 (*0-8373-2880-2*) Nat Learn.

— Agriculture. (National Teachers Examination Ser.: NT-20). 1994. pap. 23.95 (*0-8373-8430-3*) Nat Learn.

— AIDS Counselor. (Career Examination Ser.). 1994. 29.95 (*0-8373-3619-8*, C-3619) Nat Learn.

— Air Conditioning & Refrigeration. (Occupational Competency Examination Ser.: OCE-1). 1994. pap. 23.95 (*0-8373-5701-2*) Nat Learn.

— Air Conditioning, Heating & Refrigeration Mechanic. (Career Examination Ser.: C-73). 1994. pap. 29.95 (*0-8373-0073-8*) Nat Learn.

— Air Pollution Control Chemist. (Career Examination Ser.: C-1084). 1994. pap. 29.95 (*0-8373-1084-9*) Nat Learn.

— Air Pollution Control Engineer. LC 94-38034. (Career Examination Ser.: C-76). 1994. pap. 29.95 (*0-8373-0076-2*) Nat Learn.

— Air Pollution Control Engineering Trainee. (Career Examination Ser.: C-1926). 1994. pap. 27.95 (*0-8373-1926-9*) Nat Learn.

— Air Pollution Control Technician. (Career Examination Ser.: C-1085). 1991. pap. 22.00 (*0-8373-1085-7*) Nat Learn.

— Air Pollution Inspector. (Career Examination Ser.: C-11). 1994. pap. 29.95 (*0-8373-0011-8*) Nat Learn.

— Air Pollution Laboratory Maintainer. (Career Examination Ser.: C-1086). 1994. pap. 29.95 (*0-8373-1086-5*) Nat Learn.

— Air Traffic Control Specialist - ATCS. (Career Examination Ser.: C-68). 1994. pap. 29.95 (*0-8373-0068-1*) Nat Learn.

— Airbrake Maintainer. (Career Examination Ser.: C-12). 1994. pap. 23.95 (*0-8373-0012-6*) Nat Learn.

— Airframe or Powerplant Mechanics. (Occupational Competency Examination Ser.: OCE-2). 1994. pap. 23.95 (*0-8373-5702-0*, OCE-2) Nat Learn.

— Airport Attendant. (Career Examination Ser.: C-306). 1994. pap. 23.95 (*0-8373-0306-0*) Nat Learn.

— Airport Maintenance Supervisor. (Career Examination Ser.: C-3381). 1994. pap. 27.95 (*0-8373-3381-4*) Nat Learn.

— Airport Security Guard. (Career Examination Ser.: C-456). 1994. pap. 23.95 (*0-8373-0456-3*) Nat Learn.

— Airport Security Supervisor. (Career Examination Ser.: C-2153). 1994. 27.95 (*0-8373-2153-0*) Nat Learn.

— Airport Supervisor. (Career Examination Ser.: C-3219). 1994. pap. 27.95 (*0-8373-3219-2*) Nat Learn.

— Alcoholism Counselor. (Career Examination Ser.: C-2145). 1994. pap. 29.95 (*0-8373-2145-X*) Nat Learn.

— Alcoholism Rehabilitation Consultant. (Career Examination Ser.: C-2772). 1994. pap. 29.95 (*0-8373-2772-5*) Nat Learn.

— Allied Health Aptitude Tests (AHAT) (Admission Test Ser.: ATS-78). 1994. pap. 23.95 (*0-8373-5078-6*) Nat Learn.

— Allied Health Entrance Examination (AHEE) (Admission Test Ser.: ATS-79). 1994. pap. 23.95 (*0-8373-5079-4*) Nat Learn.

— Alphabetic Key Punch Operator, (IBM) (Career Examination Ser.: C-13). 1994. pap. 23.95 (*0-8373-0013-4*) Nat Learn.

— Ambulance Attendant. (Career Examination Ser.: C-1088). 1994. pap. 29.95 (*0-8373-1088-1*) Nat Learn.

— Ambulance Corpsman. (Career Examination Ser.: C-2650). 1994. pap. 29.95 (*0-8373-2650-8*) Nat Learn.

— Ambulance Driver. (Career Examination Ser.: C-1089). 1994. pap. 27.95 (*0-8373-1089-X*) Nat Learn.

— American Government. (College Level Examination Ser.: CLEP-1). 1994. pap. 23.95 (*0-8373-5301-7*) Nat Learn.

— American Government. (College Proficiency Examination Ser.: CPEP-2). 1994. pap. 23.95 (*0-8373-5402-1*) Nat Learn.

— American History. (College Level Examination Ser.: CLEP-2). 1994. pap. 23.95 (*0-8373-5302-5*) Nat Learn.

— American History. (College Proficiency Examination Ser.: CPEP-3). 1994. pap. 23.95 (*0-8373-5403-X*) Nat Learn.

— American Literature. (College Level Examination Ser.: CLEP-3). 1994. pap. 23.95 (*0-8373-5303-3*) Nat Learn.

— American Literature. (College Proficiency Examination Ser.: CPEP-4). 1994. pap. 23.95 (*0-8373-5404-8*) Nat Learn.

— American Literature: Civil War to the Present. (College Proficiency Examination Ser.: CPEP-27). 1994. pap. 23.95 (*0-8373-5427-7*) Nat Learn.

— American Literature: The Beginnings to the Civil War. (College Proficiency Examination Ser.: CPEP-26). 1994. pap. 23.95 (*0-8373-5426-9*) Nat Learn.

— American Literature: The Beginnings to the Civil War. (ACT Proficiency Examination Program Ser.: PEP-2). 1994. pap. 23.95 (*0-8373-5502-8*) Nat Learn.

— American Literature: The Civil War to the Present. (ACT Proficiency Examination Program Ser.: PEP-3). 1994. pap. 23.95 (*0-8373-5503-6*) Nat Learn.

— AMRA Medical Record Administrator National Registration Examination (RRA) (Admission Test Ser.: ATS-84). 1994. pap. 23.95 (*0-8373-5084-0*) Nat Learn.

— AMRA Medical Record Technician National Registration Examination (ART) (Admission Test Ser.: ATS-85). 1994. pap. 23.95 (*0-8373-5085-9*) Nat Learn.

— Analysis & Interpretation of Literature. (College-Level Examination Ser.: CLEP-4). 1994. 39.95 (*0-8373-5354-8*); pap. 23.95 (*0-8373-5304-1*) Nat Learn.

— Anatomy & Physiology. (College Proficiency Examination Ser.: CPEP-37). 1994. pap. 23.95 (*0-8373-5437-4*) Nat Learn.

— Anatomy & Physiology. (ACT Proficiency Examination Program Ser.: PEP-4). 1994. 39.95 (*0-8373-5554-0*); pap. 23.95 (*0-8373-5504-4*) Nat Learn.

— Anatomy, Physiology & Microbiology. (College Level Examination Ser.: CLEP-38). 1994. pap. 23.95 (*0-8373-5338-6*) Nat Learn.

— Anesthesiologist. (Career Examination Ser.: C-1090). 1994. pap. 49.95 (*0-8373-1090-3*) Nat Learn.

— Animal Caretaker. (Career Examination Ser.: C-1091). 1994. pap. 23.95 (*0-8373-1091-1*) Nat Learn.

— Animal Health Aide. (Career Examination Ser.: C-75). 1994. pap. 29.95 (*0-8373-0075-4*) Nat Learn.

— Animal Health Technician Licensing Examination. (Career Examination Ser.: C-3039). 1994. pap. 39.95 (*0-8373-3039-4*) Nat Learn.

— Animal Shelter Officer. (Career Examination Ser.: C-2361). 1994. pap. 23.95 (*0-8373-2361-4*) Nat Learn.

— Animal Shelter Supervisor. (Career Examination Ser.: C-2363). 1994. pap. 27.95 (*0-8373-2363-0*) Nat Learn.

— Animal Warden. (Career Examination Ser.: C-1844). 1994. pap. 23.95 (*0-8373-1844-0*) Nat Learn.

— Announcer. (Career Examination Ser.: C-14). 1994. pap. 29.95 (*0-8373-0014-2*) Nat Learn.

— Appliance Repair. (Occupational Competency Examination Ser.: OCE-3). 1994. pap. 23.95 (*0-8373-5703-9*) Nat Learn.

— Appraisal Investigator. (Career Examination Ser.: C-452). 1994. pap. 29.95 (*0-8373-0452-0*) Nat Learn.

— Appraiser. (Career Examination Ser.: C-15). 1994. pap. 23.95 (*0-8373-0015-0*) Nat Learn.

— Apprentice. (Career Examination Ser.: C-16). 1994. pap. 23.95 (*0-8373-0016-9*) Nat Learn.

— Architect. (Career Examination Ser.: C-17). 1994. pap. 29.95 (*0-8373-0017-7*) Nat Learn.

— Architectural Drafting. (Occupational Competency Examination Ser.: OCE-4). 1994. 39.95 (*0-8373-5754-3*); pap. 23.95 (*0-8373-5704-7*) Nat Learn.

— Architectural Draftsman. (Career Examination Ser.: C-1092). 1994. pap. 23.95 (*0-8373-1092-X*) Nat Learn.

— Architectural Estimator. (Career Examination Ser.: C-3114). 1994. pap. 27.95 (*0-8373-3114-5*) Nat Learn.

— Architectural Specifications Writer. (Career Examination Ser.: C-3222). 1994. pap. 29.95 (*0-8373-3222-2*) Nat Learn.

— Area Maintenance Technician (USPS) (Career Examination Ser.: C-3429). 1994. pap. 29.95 (*0-8373-3429-2*) Nat Learn.

— Area Services Coordinator. (Career Examination Ser.: C-18). 1994. pap. 34.95 (*0-8373-0018-5*) Nat Learn.

— Armature Winder. (Career Examination Ser.: C-2481). 1994. pap. 29.95 (*0-8373-2481-5*) Nat Learn.

— Armed Forces Tests (AFT-ASVAB) (Admission Test Ser.: ATS-34). 1994. pap. 29.95 (*0-8373-5034-4*) Nat Learn.

— Art Education. (National Teachers Examination Ser.: NT-13). 1994. pap. 23.95 (*0-8373-8423-0*) Nat Learn.

— Art History. (Undergraduate Program Field Test Ser.: UPFT-1). 1994. pap. 23.95 (*0-8373-6001-3*) Nat Learn.

— Asphalt Worker. (Career Examination Ser.: C-19). 1994. pap. 23.95 (*0-8373-0019-3*) Nat Learn.

— Assessment Aide. (Career Examination Ser.: C-2180). 1994. pap. 23.95 (*0-8373-2180-8*) Nat Learn.

— Assessment Assistant. (Career Examination Ser.: C-2181). 1994. pap. 23.95 (*0-8373-2181-6*) Nat Learn.

— Assessment Clerk. (Career Examination Ser.: C-2920). 1994. pap. 19.95 (*0-8373-2920-5*) Nat Learn.

— Assessor. (Career Examination Ser.: C-20). 1994. pap. 23.95 (*0-8373-0020-7*) Nat Learn.

— Assets Analyst. (Career Examination Ser.: C-1851). 1994. pap. 27.95 (*0-8373-1851-3*) Nat Learn.

— Assistant Accountant. (Career Examination Ser.: C-21). 1994. pap. 23.95 (*0-8373-0021-5*) Nat Learn.

— Assistant Accountant-Auditor. (Career Examination Ser.: C-2077). 1994. pap. 27.95 (*0-8373-2077-1*) Nat Learn.

— Assistant Actuary. (Career Examination Ser.: C-22). 1994. pap. 34.95 (*0-8373-0022-3*) Nat Learn.

— Assistant Administrative Director. (Teachers License Examination Ser.: S-12). 1994. pap. 39.95 (*0-8373-8112-6*) Nat Learn.

— Assistant Administrator. (Career Examination Ser.: C-1093). 1994. pap. 27.95 (*0-8373-1093-8*) Nat Learn.

— Assistant Air Pollution Control Engineer. (Career Examination Ser.: C-1094). 1994. pap. 27.95 (*0-8373-1094-6*) Nat Learn.

— Assistant Architect. (Career Examination Ser.: C-77). 1994. pap. 29.95 (*0-8373-0077-0*) Nat Learn.

— Assistant Architectural Draftsman. (Career Examination Ser.: C-1095). 1994. pap. 23.95 (*0-8373-1095-4*) Nat Learn.

— Assistant Area Manager. (Career Examination Ser.: C-1096). 1994. pap. 29.95 (*0-8373-1096-2*) Nat Learn.

— Assistant Area Manager of School Maintenance. (Career Exam Ser.: No. C-3523). 1994. 29.95 (*0-8373-3523-X*) Nat Learn.

— Assistant Area Services Coordinator. (Career Examination Ser.: C-78). 1994. pap. 29.95 (*0-8373-0078-9*) Nat Learn.

— Assistant Assessor. (Career Examination Ser.: C-23). 1994. pap. 23.95 (*0-8373-0023-1*) Nat Learn.

— Assistant Attorney. (Career Examination Ser.: C-24). 1994. pap. 34.95 (*0-8373-0024-X*) Nat Learn.

— Assistant Automotive Shop Supervisor. (Career Examination Ser.: C-529). 1994. pap. 27.95 (*0-8373-0529-2*) Nat Learn.

— Assistant Bacteriologist. (Career Examination Ser.: C-25). 1994. pap. 27.95 (*0-8373-0025-8*) Nat Learn.

— Assistant Bridge & Tunnel Maintainer. (Career Examination Ser.: C-27). 1994. pap. 23.95 (*0-8373-0027-4*) Nat Learn.

— Assistant Bridge Operator. (Career Examination Ser.: C-26). 1994. pap. 23.95 (*0-8373-0026-6*) Nat Learn.

— Assistant Bridge Operator Trainee. (Career Examination Ser.: C-79). 1994. pap. 19.95 (*0-8373-0079-7*) Nat Learn.

— Assistant Budget Analyst. (Career Examination Ser.: C-1736). 1994. pap. 29.95 (*0-8373-1736-3*) Nat Learn.

— Assistant Budget Director. (Career Examination Ser.: C-2991). 1994. pap. 39.95 (*0-8373-2991-4*) Nat Learn.

— Assistant Budget Examiner. (Career Examination Ser.: C-28). 1994. pap. 29.95 (*0-8373-0028-2*) Nat Learn.

— Assistant Building Construction Engineer. (Career Examination Ser.: C-3169). 1994. pap. 29.95 (*0-8373-3169-2*) Nat Learn.

— Assistant Building Custodian. (Career Examination Ser.: C-66). 1994. pap. 23.95 (*0-8373-0066-5*) Nat Learn.

— Assistant Building Electrical Engineer. (Career Examination Ser.: C-1909). 1994. pap. 29.95 (*0-8373-1909-9*) Nat Learn.

— Assistant Building Mechanical Engineer. (Career Examination Ser.: C-2570). 1994. pap. 29.95 (*0-8373-2570-6*) Nat Learn.

— Assistant Building Structural Engineer. (Career Examination Ser.: C-2567). 1994. pap. 34.95 (*0-8373-2567-6*) Nat Learn.

— Assistant Buildings Superintendent. (Career Examination Ser.: C-1097). 1994. pap. 29.95 (*0-8373-1097-0*) Nat Learn.

— Assistant Business Manager. (Career Examination Ser.: C-528). 1994. pap. 29.95 (*0-8373-0528-4*) Nat Learn.

— Assistant Business Officer. (Career Examination Ser.: C-2075). 1994. pap. 29.95 (*0-8373-2075-5*) Nat Learn.

— Assistant Buyer. (Career Examination Ser.: C-29). 1994. pap. 23.95 (*0-8373-0029-0*) Nat Learn.

— Assistant Captain. (Career Exam Ser.: No. C-3524). 1994. 29.95 (*0-8373-3524-8*) Nat Learn.

— Assistant Cashier. (Career Examination Ser.: C-30). 1994. pap. 19.95 (*0-8373-0030-4*) Nat Learn.

— Assistant Chemical Engineer. (Career Examination Ser.: C-31). 1994. pap. 27.95 (*0-8373-0031-2*) Nat Learn.

— Assistant Chemist. (Career Examination Ser.: C-32). 1994. pap. 27.95 (*0-8373-0032-0*) Nat Learn.

— Assistant Civil Engineer. (Career Examination Ser.: C-33). 1994. pap. 23.95 (*0-8373-0033-9*) Nat Learn.

— Assistant Civil Engineer (Structures) (Career Examination Ser.: C-1910). 1994. pap. 27.95 (*0-8373-1910-2*) Nat Learn.

— Assistant Claims Examiner. (Career Examination Ser.: C-1098). 1994. pap. 23.95 (*0-8373-1098-9*) Nat Learn.

— Assistant Clerk. (Career Examination Ser.: C-1099). 1994. pap. 19.95 (*0-8373-1099-7*) Nat Learn.

— Assistant Community Development Project Supervisor. (Career Examination Ser.: C-907). 1994. pap. 29.95 (*0-8373-0907-7*) Nat Learn.

— Assistant Community Organization Specialist (Urban Renewal) (Career Examination Ser.: C-1100). 1994. pap. 29.95 (*0-8373-1100-4*) Nat Learn.

— Assistant Cook. (Career Examination Ser.: C-1101). 1994. pap. 23.95 (*0-8373-1101-2*) Nat Learn.

— Assistant Coordinator of Volunteer Services. (Career Examination Ser.: C-3140). 1994. pap. 27.95 (*0-8373-3140-4*) Nat Learn.

— Assistant Court Clerk. (Career Examination Ser.: C-34). 1994. pap. 27.95 (*0-8373-0034-7*) Nat Learn.

— Assistant Custodial Work Supervisor. (Career Examination Ser.: C-2916). 1994. pap. 27.95 (*0-8373-2916-7*) Nat Learn.

— Assistant Custodian. (Career Examination Ser.: C-35). 1994. pap. 23.95 (*0-8373-0035-5*) Nat Learn.

— Assistant Custodian-Engineer. (Career Examination Ser.: C-36). 1994. pap. 23.95 (*0-8373-0036-3*) Nat Learn.

— Assistant Departmental Attorney. (Career Examination Ser.: C-2233). 1994. pap. 39.95 (*0-8373-2233-2*) Nat Learn.

— Assistant Deputy Superintendent of Women's Prisons. (Career Examination Ser.: C-1697). 1994. pap. 44.95 (*0-8373-1697-9*) Nat Learn.

— Assistant Deputy Warden. (Career Examination Ser.: C-1698). 1994. pap. 44.95 (*0-8373-1698-7*) Nat Learn.

— Assistant Director. (Career Examination Ser.: C-1102). 1994. pap. 34.95 (*0-8373-1102-0*) Nat Learn.

— Assistant Director (Child Welfare) (Career Examination Ser.: C-1809). 1994. pap. 34.95 (*0-8373-1809-2*) Nat Learn.

— Assistant Director of Building & Housing. (Career Examination Ser.: C-3086). 1994. pap. 39.95 (*0-8373-3086-6*) Nat Learn.

— Assistant Director of Custodial & Security Services. (Career Examination Ser.: C-2922). 1994. pap. 34.95 (*0-8373-2922-1*) Nat Learn.

— Assistant Director of Maintenance (Sewer District) (Career Examination Ser.: C-2908). 1994. pap. 34.95 (*0-8373-2908-6*) Nat Learn.

— Assistant Director of Nursing Care. (Career Examination Ser.: C-2858). 1994. pap. 34.95 (*0-8373-2858-6*) Nat Learn.

— Assistant Director of Social Services. (Career Examination Ser.: C-2798). 1994. pap. 34.95 (*0-8373-2798-9*) Nat Learn.

— Assistant Director of Traffic Control. (Career Examination Ser.: C-1876). 1994. pap. 34.95 (*0-8373-1876-9*) Nat Learn.

— Assistant Director of Traffic Safety. (Career Examination Ser.: C-458). 1994. pap. 34.95 (*0-8373-0458-X*) Nat Learn.

— Assistant Director (Welfare) (Career Examination Ser.: C-1802). 1994. pap. 34.95 (*0-8373-1802-5*) Nat Learn.

— Assistant District Attorney. (Career Examination Ser.: C-1103). 1994. pap. 34.95 (*0-8373-1103-9*) Nat Learn.

— Assistant Electrical Engineer. (Career Examination Ser.: C-37). 1994. pap. 23.95 (*0-8373-0037-1*) Nat Learn.

— Assistant Electronic Technician. (Career Examination Ser.: C-1982). 1994. pap. 27.95 (*0-8373-1982-X*) Nat Learn.

— Assistant Employment & Training Program Administrator. (Career Examination Ser.: C-3075). 1994. pap. 34.95 (*0-8373-3075-0*) Nat Learn.

— Assistant Engineering Technician. (Career Examination Ser.: C-931). 1994. pap. 27.95 (*0-8373-0931-X*) Nat Learn.

— Assistant Federal & State Aid Coordinator. (Career Examination Ser.: C-1104). 1994. pap. 34.95 (*0-8373-1104-7*) Nat Learn.

— Assistant Fire Marshal. (Career Examination Ser.: C-1105). 1994. pap. 29.95 (*0-8373-1105-5*) Nat Learn.

— Assistant Floor Supervisor. (Career Examination Ser.: C-1106). 1994. pap. 29.95 (*0-8373-1106-3*) Nat Learn.

— Assistant Foreman. (Career Examination Ser.: C-38). 1994. pap. 27.95 (*0-8373-0038-X*) Nat Learn.

— Assistant Foreman (Department of Sanitation) (Career Examination Ser.: C-39). 1994. pap. 27.95 (*0-8373-0039-8*) Nat Learn.

— Assistant Gardener. (Career Examination Ser.: C-40). 1994. pap. 23.95 (*0-8373-0040-1*) Nat Learn.

— Assistant General Superintendent. (Career Examination Ser.: C-2109). 1994. pap. 39.95 (*0-8373-2109-3*) Nat Learn.

— Assistant Head Custodian. (Career Examination Ser.: C-1822). 1994. pap. 29.95 (*0-8373-1822-X*) Nat Learn.

— Assistant Health Insurance Administrator. (Career Examination Ser.: C-358). 1941. pap. 29.95 (*0-8373-0358-3*) Nat Learn.

— Assistant Heating & Ventilating Engineer. (Career Examination Ser.: C-1912). 1994. pap. 29.95 (*0-8373-1912-9*) Nat Learn.

— Assistant Hospital Administrator. (Career Examination Ser.: C-1107). 1994. pap. 34.95 (*0-8373-1107-1*) Nat Learn.

— Assistant Housing Manager. (Career Examination Ser.: C-41). 1994. pap. 29.95 (*0-8373-0041-X*) Nat Learn.

— Assistant Labor Relations Specialist. (Career Examination Ser.: C-2057). 1994. pap. 34.95 (*0-8373-2057-7*) Nat Learn.

— Assistant Land Surveyor. (Career Examination Ser.: C-3031). 1994. pap. 29.95 (*0-8373-3031-9*) Nat Learn.

— Assistant Landscape Architect. (Career Examination Ser.: C-42). 1994. pap. 29.95 (*0-8373-0042-8*) Nat Learn.

— Assistant Landscape Engineer. (Career Examination Ser.: C-43). 1991. pap. 22.00 (*0-8373-0043-6*) Nat Learn.

— Assistant Library Director. (Career Examination Ser.: C-1108). 1994. pap. 29.95 (*0-8373-1108-X*) Nat Learn.

— Assistant Library Director I. (Career Examination Ser.: C-2783). 1994. pap. 29.95 (*0-8373-2783-0*) Nat Learn.

— Assistant Library Director II. (Career Examination Ser.: C-2784). 1994. pap. 34.95 (*0-8373-2784-9*) Nat Learn.

— Assistant Library Director III. (Career Examination Ser.: C-2785). 1994. pap. 34.95 (*0-8373-2785-7*) Nat Learn.

— Assistant Library Director IV. (Career Examination Ser.: C-2786). 1994. pap. 34.95 (*0-8373-2786-5*) Nat Learn.

— Assistant Library Director V. (Career Examination Ser.: C-2787). 1994. pap. 34.95 (*0-8373-2787-3*) Nat Learn.

— Assistant Management Analyst. (Career Examination Ser.: C-2094). 1994. pap. 34.95 (*0-8373-2094-1*) Nat Learn.

— Assistant Mechanical Construction Engineer. (Career Examination Ser.: C-2706). 1994. pap. 27.95 (*0-8373-2706-7*) Nat Learn.

— Assistant Mechanical Engineer. (Career Examination Ser.: C-44). 1994. pap. 23.95 (*0-8373-0044-4*) Nat Learn.

— Assistant Microbiologist. (Career Examination Ser.: C-1811). 1994. pap. 27.95 (*0-8373-1811-4*) Nat Learn.

— Assistant Office Services Supervisor. (Career Examination Ser.: C-3048). 1994. pap. 27.95 (*0-8373-3048-3*) Nat Learn.

— Assistant Park Supervisor. (Career Examination Ser.: C-1564). 1994. pap. 27.95 (*0-8373-1564-6*) Nat Learn.

— Assistant Pathologist. (Career Examination Ser.: C-1109). 1994. pap. 39.95 (*0-8373-1109-8*) Nat Learn.

— Assistant Payroll Supervisor. (Career Examination Ser.: C-1110). 1994. pap. 27.95 (*0-8373-1110-1*) Nat Learn.

— Assistant Personnel Examiner. (Career Examination Ser.: C-1661). 1994. pap. 34.95 (*0-8373-1661-8*) Nat Learn.

— Assistant Physicist. (Career Examination Ser.: C-2087). 1994. pap. 34.95 (*0-8373-2087-9*) Nat Learn.

— Assistant Plan Examiner. (Career Examination Ser.: C-932). 1994. pap. 29.95 (*0-8373-0932-8*) Nat Learn.

— Assistant Planner. (Career Examination Ser.: C-933). 1994. pap. 27.95 (*0-8373-0933-6*) Nat Learn.

— Assistant Plant Facilities Administrator. (Career Examination Ser.: C-2757). 1994. pap. 34.95 (*0-8373-2757-1*) Nat Learn.

— Assistant Plumbing Engineer. (Career Examination Ser.: C-2705). 1994. pap. 29.95 (*0-8373-2705-9*) Nat Learn.

— Assistant Power Plant Operator. (Career Examination Ser.: C-1905). 1994. pap. 27.95 (*0-8373-1905-6*) Nat Learn.

R

— Assistant Press Secretary. (Career Examination Ser.: C-1111). 1994. pap. 27.95 (0-8373-1111-X) Nat Learn.
— Assistant Principal, Elementary School. (Teachers License Examination Ser.: S-1). 1994. pap. 39.95 (0-8373-8101-0) Nat Learn.
— Assistant Principal, Jr. H. S. (Teachers License Examination Ser.: S-2). 1994. pap. 39.95 (0-8373-8102-9) Nat Learn.
— Assistant Procurement Coordinator. (Career Examination Ser.: C-916). 1994. pap. 29.95 (0-8373-0916-6) Nat Learn.
— Assistant Program Manager. (Career Examination Ser.: C-934). 1994. pap. 34.95 (0-8373-0934-4) Nat Learn.
— Assistant Program Specialist (Correction) (Career Examination Ser.: C-1996). 1994. pap. 34.95 (0-8373-1996-X) Nat Learn.
— Assistant Project Coordinator. (Career Examination Ser.: C-2590). 1994. pap. 27.95 (0-8373-2590-0) Nat Learn.
— Assistant Public Buildings Manager. (Career Examination Ser.: C-2718). 1994. pap. 27.95 (0-8373-2718-0) Nat Learn.
— Assistant Public Health Engineer. (Career Examination Ser.: C-2232). 1994. pap. 27.95 (0-8373-2232-4) Nat Learn.
— Assistant Purchasing Agent. (Career Examination Ser.: C-935). 1994. pap. 23.95 (0-8373-0935-2) Nat Learn.
— Assistant Radiologist. (Career Examination Ser.: C-1112). 1994. pap. 34.95 (0-8373-1112-8) Nat Learn.
— Assistant Real Estate Agent. (Career Examination Ser.: C-2178). 1994. pap. 23.95 (0-8373-2178-6) Nat Learn.
— Assistant Recreation Supervisor. (Career Examination Ser.: C-45). 1994. pap. 29.95 (0-8373-0045-2) Nat Learn.
— Assistant Rent Examiner. (Career Examination Ser.: C-936). 1994. pap. 23.95 (0-8373-0936-0) Nat Learn.
— Assistant Resident Buildings Superintendent. (Career Examination Ser.: C-1058). 1994. pap. 29.95 (0-8373-1058-X) Nat Learn.
— Assistant Retirement Benefits Examiner. (Career Examination Ser.: C-1557). 1994. pap. 27.95 (0-8373-1557-3) Nat Learn.
— Assistant Sanitary Engineer. (Career Examination Ser.: C-1969). 1994. pap. 27.95 (0-8373-1969-2) Nat Learn.
— Assistant School Custodian-Engineer. (Career Examination Ser.: C-46). 1994. pap. 27.95 (0-8373-0046-0) Nat Learn.
— Assistant School Transportation Supervisor. (Career Examination Ser.: C-112). 1994. pap. 27.95 (0-8373-0112-2) Nat Learn.
— Assistant Signal Circuit Engineer. (Career Examination Ser.: C-47). 1994. pap. 29.95 (0-8373-0047-9) Nat Learn.
— Assistant Social Worker. (Career Examination Ser.: C-1113). 1994. 23.95 (0-8373-1113-6) Nat Learn.
— Assistant State Accounts Auditor - Examiner of Municipal Affairs. (Career Examination Ser.: C-1991). 1994. pap. 34.95 (0-8373-1991-9) Nat Learn.
— Assistant Station Supervisor. (Career Examination Ser.: C-48). 1994. pap. 23.95 (0-8373-0048-7) Nat Learn.
— Assistant Stationary Engineer. (Career Examination Ser.: C-2279). 1994. pap. 27.95 (0-8373-2279-0) Nat Learn.
— Assistant Statistician. (Career Examination Ser.: C-49). 1994. pap. 27.95 (0-8373-0049-5) Nat Learn.
— Assistant Stockman. (Career Examination Ser.: C-50). 1994. pap. 23.95 (0-8373-0050-9) Nat Learn.
— Assistant Superintendent (Buses & Shops) (Career Examination Ser.: C-1725). 1994. pap. 34.95 (0-8373-1725-8) Nat Learn.
— Assistant Superintendent (Cars & Shops) (Career Examination Ser.: C-2015). 1994. pap. 34.95 (0-8373-2015-1) Nat Learn.
— Assistant Superintendent of Alarms. (Career Examination Ser.: C-2964). 1994. pap. 34.95 (0-8373-2964-7) Nat Learn.
— Assistant Superintendent of Buildings & Grounds. (Career Examination Ser.: C-937). 1994. pap. 29.95 (0-8373-0937-9) Nat Learn.
— Assistant Superintendent of Construction. (Career Examination Ser.: C-1114). 1994. pap. 34.95 (0-8373-1114-4) Nat Learn.
— Assistant Superintendent of Public Works. (Career Examination Ser.: C-2306). 1994. pap. 34.95 (0-8373-2306-1) Nat Learn.
— Assistant Superintendent of Sanitation. (Career Examination Ser.: C-2456). 1994. pap. 34.95 (0-8373-2456-4) Nat Learn.
— Assistant Superintendent of Water Works. (Career Examination Ser.: C-2003). 1994. pap. 34.95 (0-8373-2003-8) Nat Learn.
— Assistant Superintendent (Power) (Career Examination Ser.: C-2016). 1994. pap. 34.95 (0-8373-2016-X) Nat Learn.
— Assistant Superintendent (Signals) (Career Examination Ser.: C-2017). 1994. pap. 34.95 (0-8373-2017-8) Nat Learn.
— Assistant Superintendent (Structures) (Career Examination Ser.: C-2018). 1994. pap. 34.95 (0-8373-2018-6) Nat Learn.
— Assistant Superintendent (Surface Transportation) (Career Examination Ser.: C-1770). 1994. pap. 34.95 (0-8373-1770-3) Nat Learn.
— Assistant Superintendent (Track) (Career Examination Ser.: C-2019). 1994. pap. 34.95 (0-8373-2019-4) Nat Learn.
— Assistant Supervisor (Air Conditioning, Rolling Stock) (Career Examination Ser.: C-2063). 1994. pap. 29.95 (0-8373-2063-1) Nat Learn.
— Assistant Supervisor (Buses & Shops) (Career Examination Ser.: C-1115). 1994. pap. 29.95 (0-8373-1115-2) Nat Learn.
— Assistant Supervisor (Cars & Shops) (Career Examination Ser.: C-1975). 1994. pap. 29.95 (0-8373-1975-7) Nat Learn.
— Assistant Supervisor (Child Welfare) (Career Examination Ser.: C-51). 1994. pap. 29.95 (0-8373-0051-7) Nat Learn.
— Assistant Supervisor (Electrical Power) (Career Examination Ser.: C-1976). 1994. pap. 29.95 (0-8373-1976-5) Nat Learn.
— Assistant Supervisor (Electronic Equipment) (Career Examination Ser.: C-2192). 1994. pap. 29.95 (0-8373-2192-1) Nat Learn.
— Assistant Supervisor (Elevators & Escalators) (Career Examination Ser.: C-1727). 1994. pap. 29.95 (0-8373-1727-4) Nat Learn.
— Assistant Supervisor (Lighting) (Career Examination Ser.: C-2006). 1994. pap. 29.95 (0-8373-2006-2) Nat Learn.
— Assistant Supervisor of Electrical Installations. (Career Examination Ser.: C-1116). 1994. pap. 29.95 (0-8373-1116-0) Nat Learn.
— Assistant Supervisor of Mechanical Installations. (Career Examination Ser.: C-1117). 1994. pap. 29.95 (0-8373-1117-9) Nat Learn.
— Assistant Supervisor of Youth Services. (Career Examination Ser.: C-1659). 1994. pap. 29.95 (0-8373-1659-6) Nat Learn.
— Assistant Supervisor (Power Distribution) (Career Examination Ser.: C-1777). 1994. pap. 29.95 (0-8373-1777-0) Nat Learn.
— Assistant Supervisor (Stores, Materials & Supplies) (Career Examination Ser.: C-1814). 1994. pap. 29.95 (0-8373-1814-9) Nat Learn.
— Assistant Supervisor (Structures) (Career Examination Ser.: C-1977). 1994. pap. 29.95 (0-8373-1977-3) Nat Learn.
— Assistant Supervisor (Structures) - Group C. (Career Examination Ser.: C-1972). 1994. pap. 29.95 (0-8373-1972-2) Nat Learn.
— Assistant Supervisor (Track) (Career Examination Ser.: C-1728). 1994. pap. 29.95 (0-8373-1728-2) Nat Learn.
— Assistant Supervisor (Turnstiles) (Career Examination Ser.: C-2007). 1994. pap. 29.95 (0-8373-2007-0) Nat Learn.
— Assistant Supervisor (Ventilation & Drainage) (Career Examination Ser.: C-2091). 1994. pap. 29.95 (0-8373-2091-7) Nat Learn.
— Assistant Supervisor (Welfare) (Career Examination Ser.: C-52). 1994. pap. 29.95 (0-8373-0052-5) Nat Learn.
— Assistant Surveyor. (Career Examination Ser.: C-1972). 1994. pap. 29.95 (0-8373-1792-4) Nat Learn.
— Assistant Tax Valuation Engineer. (Career Examination Ser.: C-3196). 1994. pap. 27.95 (0-8373-3196-X) Nat Learn.
— Assistant Teacher. (Career Examination Ser.: C-1118). 1994. pap. 23.95 (0-8373-1118-7) Nat Learn.
— Assistant Tenant Supervisor. (Career Examination Ser.: C-542). 1994. pap. 27.95 (0-8373-0542-X) Nat Learn.
— Assistant to Assessor. (Career Examination Ser.: C-2182). 1994. pap. 27.95 (0-8373-2182-4) Nat Learn.
— Assistant to City Clerk. (Career Examination Ser.: C-930). 1994. pap. 23.95 (0-8373-0930-1) Nat Learn.
— Assistant to Commissioner. (Career Examination Ser.: C-1119). 1994. pap. 34.95 (0-8373-1119-5) Nat Learn.
— Assistant to Director. (Career Examination Ser.: C-3092). 1994. pap. 34.95 (0-8373-3092-0) Nat Learn.
— Assistant to Director, Bureau of Vehicle Maintenance. (Career Examination Ser.: C-3111). 1994. pap. 34.95 (0-8373-3111-0) Nat Learn.
— Assistant to Planning Director. (Career Examination Ser.: C-3155). 1994. pap. 34.95 (0-8373-3155-2) Nat Learn.
— Assistant to Superintendent. (Career Examination Ser.: C-2210). 1994. pap. 34.95 (0-8373-2210-3) Nat Learn.
— Assistant to the Town Comptroller. (Career Examination Ser.: C-3128). 1994. pap. 34.95 (0-8373-3128-5) Nat Learn.
— Assistant Town Engineer. (Career Examination Ser.: C-211). 1994. pap. 29.95 (0-8373-0211-0) Nat Learn.
— Assistant Train Dispatcher. (Career Examination Ser.: C-53). 1994. pap. 23.95 (0-8373-0053-3) Nat Learn.
— Assistant Transit Management Analyst. (Career Examination Ser.: C-3280). 1994. pap. 29.95 (0-8373-3280-X) Nat Learn.
— Assistant Urban Designer. (Career Examination Ser.: C-1120). 1994. pap. 27.95 (0-8373-1120-9) Nat Learn.
— Assistant Warden. (Career Examination Ser.: C-1121). 1994. pap. 39.95 (0-8373-1121-7) Nat Learn.
— Assistant Water Maintenance Foreman. (Career Examination Ser.: C-2919). 1994. pap. 27.95 (0-8373-2919-1) Nat Learn.
— Assistant Water Service Foreman. (Career Examination Ser.: C-2924). 1994. pap. 27.95 (0-8373-2924-8) Nat Learn.
— Assistant Workmen's Compensation Examiner. (Career Examination Ser.: C-1643). 1994. pap. 27.95 (0-8373-1643-X) Nat Learn.
— Assistant Youth Corps Project Director. (Career Examination Ser.: C-2207). 1994. pap. 34.95 (0-8373-2207-3) Nat Learn.
— Assistant Youth Guidance Technician. (Career Examination Ser.: C-938). 1994. pap. 29.95 (0-8373-0938-7) Nat Learn.
— Associate Accountant. (Career Examination Ser.: C-1798). 1994. pap. 29.95 (0-8373-1798-3) Nat Learn.
— Associate Administrator. (Career Examination Ser.: C-1122). 1994. 29.95 (0-8373-1122-5) Nat Learn.
— Associate Advisor, PEDC (U. S. P. S.) (Career Examination Ser.: C-2118). 1994. pap. 34.95 (0-8373-2118-2) Nat Learn.
— Associate Analytical Chemist. (Career Examination Ser.: C-3194). 1994. pap. 34.95 (0-8373-3194-3) Nat Learn.
— Associate Attorney. (Career Examination Ser.: C-2269). 1994. pap. 34.95 (0-8373-2269-3) Nat Learn.
— Associate Biostatistician. (Career Examination Ser.: C-2292). 1994. pap. 34.95 (0-8373-2292-8) Nat Learn.
— Associate Budget Analyst. (Career Examination Ser.: C-3172). 1994. pap. 34.95 (0-8373-3172-2) Nat Learn.
— Associate Business Promotion Coordinator. (Career Examination Ser.: C-2526). 1994. pap. 39.95 (0-8373-2526-9) Nat Learn.
— Associate Capital Program Analyst. (Career Examination Ser.: C-2039). 1994. pap. 34.95 (0-8373-2039-9) Nat Learn.
— Associate Cashier. (Career Examination Ser.: C-2005). 1994. pap. 23.95 (0-8373-2005-4) Nat Learn.
— Associate Chemist. (Career Examination Ser.: C-3362). 1994. pap. 29.95 (0-8373-3362-8) Nat Learn.
— Associate Civil Engineer (Structures) (Career Examination Ser.: C-1911). 1994. pap. 34.95 (0-8373-1911-0) Nat Learn.
— Associate Claim Examiner. (Career Exam Ser.: No. C-3504). 1994. 27.95 (0-8373-3504-3) Nat Learn.
— Associate Computer Programmer. (Career Examination Ser.: C-2206). 1994. pap. 29.95 (0-8373-2206-5) Nat Learn.
— Associate Computer Programmer-Analyst. (Career Examination Ser.: C-3218). 1994. pap. 29.95 (0-8373-3218-4) Nat Learn.
— Associate Computer Systems Analyst. (Career Examination Ser.: C-939). 1994. pap. 29.95 (0-8373-0939-5) Nat Learn.
— Associate Court Clerk. (Career Examination Ser.: C-2587). 1994. pap. 27.95 (0-8373-2587-0) Nat Learn.
— Associate Economist. (Career Examination Ser.: C-2497). 1994. pap. 34.95 (0-8373-2497-1) Nat Learn.
— Associate Education Analyst. (Career Examination Ser.: C-3046). 1994. pap. 39.95 (0-8373-3046-7) Nat Learn.
— Associate Education Officer. (Career Examination Ser.: C-3051). 1994. pap. 39.95 (0-8373-3051-3) Nat Learn.
— Associate Engineering Technician. (Career Examination Ser.: C-2467). 1994. pap. 29.95 (0-8373-2467-X) Nat Learn.
— Associate Environmental Analyst. (Career Examination Ser.: C-3033). 1994. pap. 29.95 (0-8373-3033-5) Nat Learn.
— Associate Graphic Artist. (Career Examination Ser.: C-1525). 1994. pap. 29.95 (0-8373-1525-5) Nat Learn.
— Associate Industrial Hygienist. (Career Examination Ser.: C-3037). 1994. pap. 44.95 (0-8373-3037-8) Nat Learn.
— Associate Information & Referral Coordinator. (Career Examination Ser.: C-2926). 1994. pap. 34.95 (0-8373-2926-4) Nat Learn.
— Associate Inspector (Construction) (Career Exam Ser.: No. C-3502). 1994. 34.95 (0-8373-3502-7) Nat Learn.
— Associate Inspector (Highways & Sewers) (Career Exam Ser.: No. C-3519). 1994. 34.95 (0-8373-3519-1) Nat Learn.
— Associate Inspector (Housing) (Career Examination Ser.: C-3011). 1994. pap. 34.95 (0-8373-3011-4) Nat Learn.
— Associate Investigator. (Career Exam Ser.: No. C-3503). 1994. 34.95 (0-8373-3503-5) Nat Learn.
— Associate Labor Relations Specialist. (Career Examination Ser.: C-1946). 1994. pap. 39.95 (0-8373-1946-3) Nat Learn.
— Associate Management Analyst. (Career Examination Ser.: C-1234). 1994. pap. 39.95 (0-8373-1234-5) Nat Learn.
— Associate Manpower Program Coordinator. (Career Examination Ser.: C-2317). 1994. pap. 39.95 (0-8373-2317-7) Nat Learn.
— Associate Marketing Representative. (Career Examination Ser.: C-2040). 1994. pap. 34.95 (0-8373-2040-2) Nat Learn.
— Associate Medical Examiner. (Career Examination Ser.: C-2722). 1994. pap. 39.95 (0-8373-2722-9) Nat Learn.
— Associate Methods Analyst. (Career Examination Ser.: C-1735). 1994. pap. 39.95 (0-8373-1735-5) Nat Learn.
— Associate Occupational Analyst. (Career Examination Ser.: C-2550). 1994. pap. 39.95 (0-8373-2550-1) Nat Learn.
— Associate Park Service Worker. (Career Examination Ser.: C-2469). 1994. pap. 27.95 (0-8373-2469-6) Nat Learn.
— Associate Public Information Specialist. (Career Exam Ser.: No. C-3520). 1994. 34.95 (0-8373-3520-5) Nat Learn.
— Associate Public Records Officer. (Career Examination Ser.: No. C-3521). 1994. 34.95 (0-8373-3521-3) Nat Learn.
— Associate Quality Assurance Specialist. (Career Rxamination Ser.: No. C-3522). 1994. 39.95 (0-8373-3522-1) Nat Learn.
— Associate Real Property Manager. (Career Examination Ser.: C-2890). 1991. pap. 22.00 (0-8373-2890-X) Nat Learn.
— Associate Sanitation Enforcement Agent. (Career Examination Ser.: C-3216). 1994. pap. 29.95 (0-8373-3216-8) Nat Learn.
— Associate Social Services Management Specialist. (Career Examination Ser.: C-454). 1994. pap. 34.95 (0-8373-0454-7) Nat Learn.
— Associate Space Analyst. (Career Examination Ser.: No. C-3518). 1994. 39.95 (0-8373-3518-3) Nat Learn.
— Associate Staff Analyst. (Career Examination Ser.: C-1552). 1994. pap. 39.95 (0-8373-1552-2) Nat Learn.
— Associate Statistician. (Career Examination Ser.: C-940). 1994. pap. 34.95 (0-8373-0940-9) Nat Learn.
— Associate Superintendent of Construction. (Career Examination Ser.: C-1518). 1994. pap. 34.95 (0-8373-1518-2) Nat Learn.
— Associate Tax Auditor. (Career Examination Ser.: C-2314). 1994. pap. 34.95 (0-8373-2314-2) Nat Learn.
— Associate Traffic Enforcement Agent. (Career Examination Ser.: C-215). 1994. pap. 29.95 (0-8373-0215-3) Nat Learn.
— Associate Transit Management Analyst. (Career Examination Ser.: C-3423). 1994. pap. 34.95 (0-8373-3423-3) Nat Learn.
— Associate Urban Park Ranger. (Career Examination Ser.: C-3179). 1994. pap. 29.95 (0-8373-3179-X) Nat Learn.
— Associate Word Processor. (Career Examination Ser.: C-3183). 1994. pap. 29.95 (0-8373-3183-8) Nat Learn.
— Associate Worker's Compensation Review Analyst. (Career Examination Ser.: C-309). 1994. pap. 29.95 (0-8373-0309-5) Nat Learn.
— Associate Workmen's Compensation Examiner. (Career Examination Ser.: C-1547). 1994. pap. 29.95 (0-8373-1547-6) Nat Learn.
— Astronomer. (Career Examination Ser.: C-54). 1994. pap. 29.95 (0-8373-0054-1) Nat Learn.
— Astronomy. (DANTES Ser.: No. 1). 1994. pap. 23.95 (0-8373-6601-1) Nat Learn.
— Astronomy. (DANTES Ser.: No. 1). 1994. 39.95 (0-8373-6501-5) Nat Learn.
— Attendance Teacher. (Teachers License Examination Ser.: T-2a). 1994. pap. 23.95 (0-8373-8002-2) Nat Learn.
— Attendance Teacher (Spanish) (Teachers License Examination Ser.: T-2b). 1994. pap. 23.95 (0-685-49789-5) Nat Learn.
— Attendant. (Career Examination Ser.: C-55). 1994. pap. 19.95 (0-8373-0055-X) Nat Learn.
— Attorney. (Career Examination Ser.: C-56). 1994. pap. 39.95 (0-8373-0056-8) Nat Learn.
— Attorney - Departmental. (Career Examination Ser.: C-2234). 1994. pap. 44.95 (0-8373-2234-0) Nat Learn.
— Attorney Trainee. (Career Examination Ser.: C-57). 1994. pap. 29.95 (0-8373-0057-6) Nat Learn.
— Audience Promotion Assistant. (Career Examination Ser.: C-1123). 1994. pap. 29.95 (0-8373-1123-3) Nat Learn.
— Audio-Visual Aid Technician. (Career Examination Ser.: C-58). 1994. pap. 23.95 (0-8373-0058-4) Nat Learn.
— Audio-Visual Aide. (Career Examination Ser.: C-2903). 1994. pap. 23.95 (0-8373-2903-5) Nat Learn.
— Audio-Visual Programs Specialist. (Career Examination Ser.: C-3209). 1994. pap. 29.95 (0-8373-3209-5) Nat Learn.
— Audio-Visual Specialist. (Career Examination Ser.: C-1826). 1994. pap. 23.95 (0-8373-1826-2) Nat Learn.
— Audio-Visual Technician. (Career Examination Ser.: C-1894). 1994. pap. 23.95 (0-8373-1894-7) Nat Learn.
— Audiologist. (Career Examination Ser.: C-1124). 1994. pap. 27.95 (0-8373-1124-1) Nat Learn.
— Audiologist - Speech Pathologist. (Career Examination Ser.: C-59). 1994. pap. 27.95 (0-8373-0059-2) Nat Learn.
— Audiology. (National Teachers Examination Ser.: NT-34). 1994. pap. 23.95 (0-8373-8444-3) Nat Learn.
— Audit Clerk. (Career Examination Ser.: C-1907). 1994. pap. 19.95 (0-8373-1907-2) Nat Learn.
— Auditing Assistant. (Career Examination Ser.: C-2092). 1994. pap. 27.95 (0-8373-2092-5) Nat Learn.
— Auditor. (Career Examination Ser.: C-60). 1994. pap. 29.95 (0-8373-0060-6) Nat Learn.
— Auditor Trainee. (Career Examination Ser.: C-2404). 1994. pap. 23.95 (0-8373-2404-1) Nat Learn.
— Auto Body Repair. (Occupational Competency Examination Ser.: OCE-5). 1994. 23.95 (0-8373-5705-5) Nat Learn.
— Auto Body Repairman. (Career Examination Ser.: C-1125). 1994. pap. 23.95 (0-8373-1125-X) Nat Learn.
— Auto Engineman. (Career Examination Ser.: C-61). 1994. pap. 23.95 (0-8373-0061-4) Nat Learn.
— Auto Equipment Inspector. (Career Examination Ser.: C-1126). 1994. pap. 27.95 (0-8373-1126-8) Nat Learn.
— Auto Machinist. (Career Examination Ser.: C-62). 1994. pap. 23.95 (0-8373-0062-2) Nat Learn.
— Auto Maintenance Coordinator. (Career Examination Ser.: C-1127). 1994. pap. 29.95 (0-8373-1127-6) Nat Learn.
— Auto Mechanic. (Career Examination Ser.: C-63). 1994. pap. 23.95 (0-8373-0063-0) Nat Learn.
— Auto Mechanic (Diesel) (Career Examination Ser.: C-64). 1994. pap. 23.95 (0-8373-0064-9) Nat Learn.
— Auto Mechanics. (DANTES Ser.: No. 2). 1994. pap. 23.95 (0-8373-6602-X) Nat Learn.
— Auto Mechanics. (DANTES Ser.: No. 2). 1994. 39.95 (0-8373-6502-3) Nat Learn.
— Auto Mechanics. (Occupational Competency Examination Ser.: No. 7). 1994. 23.95 (0-8373-5707-1) Nat Learn.
— Auto Parts Storekeeper. (Career Examination Ser.: C-1128). 1994. pap. 23.95 (0-8373-1128-4) Nat Learn.
— Auto Shop Foreman. (Career Examination Ser.: C-1129). 1994. pap. 27.95 (0-8373-1129-2) Nat Learn.
— Auto Shop Supervisor. (Career Examination Ser.: C-1130). 1994. pap. 27.95 (0-8373-1130-6) Nat Learn.
— Automatic Heating. (Occupational Competency Examination Ser.: OCE-6). 1994. 39.95 (0-8373-5756-X); pap. 23.95 (0-8373-5706-3) Nat Learn.
— Automotive Electrical-Electronics. (DANTES Ser.: No. 39). 1994. pap. 23.95 (0-8373-6639-9) Nat Learn.
— Automotive Facilities Inspector. (Career Examination Ser.: C-2213). 1994. pap. 27.95 (0-8373-2213-8) Nat Learn.
— Automotive Maintenance Supervisor. (Career Examination Ser.: C-2096). 1994. pap. 27.95 (0-8373-2096-8) Nat Learn.
— Automotive Mechanic. (Career Examination Ser.: C-1131). 1994. pap. 23.95 (0-8373-1131-4) Nat Learn.
— Automotive Parts Supervisor. (Career Examination Ser.: C-2841). 1994. pap. 27.95 (0-8373-2841-1) Nat Learn.
— Automotive Serviceman. (Career Examination Ser.: C-65). 1994. pap. 23.95 (0-8373-0065-7) Nat Learn.

— Automotive Workbook. (Workbook Ser.: No. 2820). 1994. pap. 23.95 (0-8373-7901-6) Nat Learn.
— Bacteriologist. (Career Examination Ser.: C-80). 1994. pap. 27.95 (0-8373-0080-0) Nat Learn.
— Baker. (Career Examination Ser.: C-1132). 1994. pap. 23.95 (0-8373-1132-2) Nat Learn.
— Ballot Clerk. (Career Examination Ser.: C-1133). 1994. pap. 23.95 (0-8373-1133-0) Nat Learn.
— Bank Examiner. (Career Examination Ser.: C-105). 1994. pap. 29.95 (0-8373-0105-X) Nat Learn.
— Bank Examiner Trainee. (Career Examination Ser.: C-303). 1994. pap. 27.95 (0-685-13316-8) Nat Learn.
— Barber. (Career Examination Ser.: C-1134). 1994. pap. 29.95 (0-8373-1134-9) Nat Learn.
— Basic Marketing. (DANTES Ser.: No. 3). 1994. pap. 23.95 (0-8373-6603-8) Nat Learn.
— Basic Marketing. (DANTE Ser.: No. 3). 1994. 39.95 (0-8373-6503-1) Nat Learn.
— Basic Scholastic & Aptitude Test (BSAT) (General Aptitude & Abilities Ser.: CS-49). 1994. pap. 29.95 (0-8373-6749-2) Nat Learn.
— Basic Skills Assessment Program (BSAP) (Admission Test Ser.: ATS-59). 1994. pap. 23.95 (0-8373-5059-X) Nat Learn.
— Basic Statistics. (DANTES Ser.: No. 4). 1994. pap. 23.95 (0-8373-6604-6) Nat Learn.
— Basic Statistics. (DANTES Ser.: No. 4). 1994. 39.95 (0-8373-6504-X) Nat Learn.
— Basin Machine Operator. (Career Examination Ser.: C-2517). 1994. pap. 29.95 (0-8373-2517-X) Nat Learn.
— Battalion Chief-Fire Department. (Career Examination Ser.: C-81). 1994. pap. 34.95 (0-8373-0081-9) Nat Learn.
— Bay Constable. (Career Examination Ser.: C-2524). 1994. pap. 27.95 (0-8373-2524-2) Nat Learn.
— Bay Constable II. (Career Examination Ser.: C-885). 1994. 29.95 (0-8373-0885-2) Nat Learn.
— Bay Management Specialist. (Career Examination Ser.: C-1165). 1994. pap. 29.95 (0-8373-1165-9) Nat Learn.
— Beach Supervisor. (Career Examination Ser.: C-836). 1994. pap. 29.95 (0-8373-0836-4) Nat Learn.
— Beginning Clerical Worker. (Career Examination Ser.: No. C-3505). 1994. 19.95 (0-8373-3505-1) Nat Learn.
— Beginning German. (DANTES Ser.: No. 5). 1994. pap. 23.95 (0-8373-6605-4) Nat Learn.
— Beginning German. (DANTES Ser.: No. 5). 1994. 39.95 (0-8373-6505-8) Nat Learn.
— Beginning Italian. (DANTES Ser.: No. 54). 1994. pap. 23.95 (0-8373-6654-2) Nat Learn.
— Beginning Office Worker. (Career Examination Ser.: C-82). 1994. pap. 19.95 (0-8373-0082-7) Nat Learn.
— Beginning Spanish. (DANTES Ser.: No. 6). 1994. pap. 23.95 (0-8373-6606-2) Nat Learn.
— Beginning Spanish. (DANTE Ser.: No. 6). 1994. 39.95 (0-8373-6506-6) Nat Learn.
— Behavioral Sciences for Nurses. (College Level Examination Ser.: CLEP-39). 1994. 39.95 (0-8373-5389-0); pap. 23.95 (0-8373-5339-4) Nat Learn.
— Beverage Control Inspector. (Career Examination Ser.: C-83). 1994. pap. 23.95 (0-8373-0083-5) Nat Learn.
— Beverage Control Investigator. (Career Examination Ser.: C-918). 1994. pap. 23.95 (0-8373-0918-2) Nat Learn.
— Bilingual Common Branches (One to Six) (Spanish), Elementary School. (Teachers License Examination Ser.: T-68). 1994. pap. 23.95 (0-8373-8068-5) Nat Learn.
— Bilingual Teacher in School & Community Relations. (Teachers License Examination Ser.: T-66). 1994. pap. 23.95 (0-8373-8066-9) Nat Learn.
— Bilingual Teacher (Junior & Senior High School) (Teachers License Examination Ser.: T-70). 1994. pap. 23.95 (0-8373-8070-7) Nat Learn.
— Bindery Worker. (Career Examination Ser.: C-84). 1994. pap. 23.95 (0-8373-0084-3) Nat Learn.
— Bingo Control Investigator. (Career Examination Ser.: C-106). 1994. pap. 23.95 (0-8373-0106-8) Nat Learn.
— Bingo Inspector. (Career Examination Ser.: C-846). 1994. pap. 23.95 (0-8373-0846-1) Nat Learn.
— Biochemist. (Career Examination Ser.: C-85). 1994. pap. 27.95 (0-8373-0085-1) Nat Learn.
— Biochemist Trainee. (Career Examination Ser.: C-1171). 1994. pap. 23.95 (0-8373-1171-3) Nat Learn.
— Biological Aide. (Career Examination Ser.: C-86). 1994. pap. 23.95 (0-8373-0086-X) Nat Learn.
— Biological Sciences. (Graduate Record Area Examination Ser.: GRE-41). 1994. pap. 23.95 (0-8373-5241-X) Nat Learn.
— Biologist. (Career Examination Ser.: C-2013). 1994. pap. 27.95 (0-8373-2013-5) Nat Learn.
— Biology. (College Proficiency Examination Ser.: CPEP-5). 1994. pap. 23.95 (0-8373-5405-6) Nat Learn.
— Biology. (Graduate Record Examination Ser.: GRE-1). 1994. pap. 23.95 (0-8373-5201-0) Nat Learn.
— Biology. (Undergraduate Program Field Test Ser.: UPFT-2). 1994. pap. 23.95 (0-8373-6002-1) Nat Learn.
— Biology & General Science. (National Teachers Examination Ser.: NT-3). 1994. pap. 23.95 (0-8373-8413-3) Nat Learn.
— Biology & General Science Sr. H. S. (Teachers License Examination Ser.: T-4). 1994. pap. 23.95 (0-8373-8004-9) Nat Learn.
— Biostatistician. (Career Examination Ser.: C-1135). 1994. pap. 29.95 (0-8373-1135-7) Nat Learn.
— Blacksmith. (Career Examination Ser.: C-107). 1994. pap. 27.95 (0-8373-0107-6) Nat Learn.
— Blacksmith's Helper. (Career Examination Ser.: C-108). 1994. pap. 23.95 (0-8373-0108-4) Nat Learn.
— Blind. (Teachers License Examination Ser.: T-5). 1994. pap. 23.95 (0-8373-8005-7) Nat Learn.
— Blueprint Machine Operator. (Career Examination Ser.: C-1136). 1994. pap. 23.95 (0-8373-1136-5) Nat Learn.
— Blueprinter. (Career Examination Ser.: C-1621). 1994. pap. 23.95 (0-8373-1621-9) Nat Learn.
— Board Member. (Career Examination Ser.: C-1137). 1994. pap. 39.95 (0-8373-1137-3) Nat Learn.
— Body Repair Inspector. (Career Examination Ser.: C-3281). 1994. pap. 23.95 (0-8373-3281-8) Nat Learn.
— Boiler Inspector. (Career Examination Ser.: C-87). 1994. pap. 29.95 (0-8373-0087-8) Nat Learn.
— Boiler Room Helper. (Career Examination Ser.: C-1138). 1994. pap. 23.95 (0-8373-1138-1) Nat Learn.
— Boilermaker. (Career Examination Ser.: C-109). 1994. pap. 29.95 (0-8373-0109-2) Nat Learn.
— Bookbinder. (Career Examination Ser.: C-88). 1994. pap. 23.95 (0-8373-0088-6) Nat Learn.
— Bookkeeper. (Career Examination Ser.: C-89). 1994. pap. 23.95 (0-8373-0089-4) Nat Learn.
— Bookkeeping Machine Operator. (Career Examination Ser.: C-1139). 1994. pap. 23.95 (0-8373-1139-X) Nat Learn.
— Bookkeeping Machine Supervisor. (Career Examination Ser.: C-1140). 1994. pap. 27.95 (0-8373-1140-3) Nat Learn.
— Bookkeeping Operations Supervisor. (Career Examination Ser.: C-2801). 1994. pap. 29.95 (0-8373-2801-2) Nat Learn.
— Border Patrol Agent. (Career Examination Ser.: C-115). 1994. pap. 23.95 (0-8373-0115-7) Nat Learn.
— Border Patrol Inspector. (Career Examination Ser.: C-90). 1994. pap. 23.95 (0-8373-0090-8) Nat Learn.
— Border Patrolman. (Career Examination Ser.: C-1973). 1994. pap. 23.95 (0-8373-1973-0) Nat Learn.
— Borough Superintendent (Buildings) (Career Examination Ser.: C-2036). 1994. pap. 34.95 (0-8373-2036-4) Nat Learn.
— Borough Supervisor of School Custodians. (Career Examination Ser.: C-1761). 1994. pap. 34.95 (0-8373-1761-4) Nat Learn.
— Bricklayer. (Career Examination Ser.: C-110). 1994. pap. 23.95 (0-8373-0110-6) Nat Learn.
— Bridge & Tunnel Lieutenant. (Career Examination Ser.: C-111). 1994. pap. 29.95 (0-8373-0111-4) Nat Learn.
— Bridge & Tunnel Maintainer. (Career Examination Ser.: C-94). 1994. pap. 23.95 (0-8373-0094-0) Nat Learn.
— Bridge & Tunnel Officer. (Career Examination Ser.: C-95). 1994. pap. 23.95 (0-8373-0095-9) Nat Learn.
— Bridge & Tunnel Supervisor. (Career Examination Ser.: C-2222). 1994. pap. 29.95 (0-8373-2222-7) Nat Learn.
— Bridge Maintenance Supervisor. (Career Examination Ser.: C-2289). 1994. pap. 29.95 (0-8373-2289-8) Nat Learn.
— Bridge Mechanic. (Career Examination Ser.: C-1141). 1994. pap. 23.95 (0-8373-1141-1) Nat Learn.
— Bridge Operations Supervisor. (Career Examination Ser.: C-1142). 1994. pap. 29.95 (0-8373-1142-X) Nat Learn.
— Bridge Operator. (Career Examination Ser.: C-92). 1994. pap. 23.95 (0-8373-0092-4) Nat Learn.
— Bridge Operator-in-Charge. (Career Examination Ser.: C-91). 1994. pap. 29.95 (0-8373-0091-6) Nat Learn.
— Bridge Painter. (Career Examination Ser.: C-93). 1994. pap. 23.95 (0-8373-0093-2) Nat Learn.
— Bridge Repair Supervisor. (Career Examination Ser.: C-2288). 1994. pap. 29.95 (0-8373-2288-X) Nat Learn.
— Broadcast Traffic Assistant. (Career Examination Ser.: C-96). 1994. pap. 29.95 (0-8373-0096-7) Nat Learn.
— Budget Analyst. (Career Examination Ser.: C-1143). 1994. pap. 34.95 (0-8373-1143-8) Nat Learn.
— Budget Assistant (USPS) (Career Examination Ser.: C-848). 1994. pap. 29.95 (0-8373-0848-8) Nat Learn.
— Budget Director. (Career Examination Ser.: C-2648). 1994. pap. 39.95 (0-8373-2648-6) Nat Learn.
— Budget Examiner. (Career Examination Ser.: C-97). 1994. pap. 29.95 (0-8373-0097-5) Nat Learn.
— Budget Examining Trainee. (Career Examination Ser.: C-98). 1994. pap. 27.95 (0-8373-0098-3) Nat Learn.
— Budget Officer. (Career Examination Ser.: C-1144). 1994. pap. 29.95 (0-8373-1144-6) Nat Learn.
— Budget Supervisor. (Career Examination Ser.: C-2684). 1994. pap. 34.95 (0-8373-2684-2) Nat Learn.
— Budget Technician. (Career Examination Ser.: C-2170). 1994. pap. 27.95 (0-8373-2170-0) Nat Learn.
— Building & Zoning Administrator. (Career Examination Ser.: C-2342). 1994. pap. 39.95 (0-8373-2342-8) Nat Learn.
— Building Construction Engineer. (Career Examination Ser.: C-3170). 1994. pap. 39.95 (0-8373-3170-6) Nat Learn.
— Building Construction Estimator. (Career Examination Ser.: C-1145). 1994. pap. 34.95 (0-8373-1145-4) Nat Learn.
— Building Construction Inspector. (Career Examination Ser.: C-1146). 1994. pap. 29.95 (0-8373-1146-2) Nat Learn.
— Building Construction Inspector I. (Career Examination Ser.: C-1831). 1994. pap. 29.95 (0-8373-1831-9) Nat Learn.
— Building Construction Inspector II. (Career Examination Ser.: C-1832). 1994. pap. 34.95 (0-8373-1832-7) Nat Learn.
— Building Construction Inspector III. (Career Examination Ser.: C-1833). 1994. pap. 34.95 (0-8373-1833-5) Nat Learn.
— Building Construction Program Manager. (Career Examination Ser.: C-3098). 1994. pap. 39.95 (0-8373-3098-X) Nat Learn.
— Building Custodian. (Career Examination Ser.: C-99). 1994. pap. 23.95 (0-8373-0099-1) Nat Learn.
— Building Equipment Mechanic (U. S. P. S.) (Career Examination Ser.: C-1608). 1994. pap. 27.95 (0-8373-1608-1) Nat Learn.
— Building Guard. (Career Examination Ser.: C-2295). 1994. pap. 23.95 (0-8373-2295-2) Nat Learn.
— Building Inspector. (Career Examination Ser.: C-104). 1994. pap. 29.95 (0-8373-0104-1) Nat Learn.
— Building Inspector II. (Career Examination Ser.: C-3077). 1994. pap. 34.95 (0-8373-3077-7) Nat Learn.
— Building Maintenance. (Occupational Competency Examination Ser.: OCE-8). 1994. pap. 23.95 (0-8373-5708-X) Nat Learn.
— Building Maintenance Foreman. (Career Examination Ser.: C-1147). 1994. pap. 27.95 (0-8373-1147-0) Nat Learn.
— Building Maintenance Supervisor. (Career Examination Ser.: C-1148). 1994. pap. 27.95 (0-8373-1148-9) Nat Learn.
— Building Manager. (Career Examination Ser.: C-1149). 1994. pap. 29.95 (0-8373-1149-7) Nat Learn.
— Building Mechanical Engineer. (Career Examination Ser.: C-2571). 1994. pap. 34.95 (0-8373-2571-4) Nat Learn.
— Building Plan Examiner. (Career Examination Ser.: C-1150). 1994. pap. 29.95 (0-8373-1150-0) Nat Learn.
— Building Rehabilitation Specialist. (Career Examination Ser.: C-1151). 1994. pap. 34.95 (0-8373-1151-9) Nat Learn.
— Building Repairman. (Career Examination Ser.: C-1152). 1994. pap. 23.95 (0-8373-1152-7) Nat Learn.
— Building Structural Engineer. (Career Examination Ser.: C-2568). 1994. pap. 39.95 (0-8373-2568-4) Nat Learn.
— Buildings Manager. (Career Examination Ser.: C-1153). 1994. pap. 29.95 (0-8373-1153-5) Nat Learn.
— Buoy Tender. (Career Examination Ser.: C-3132). 1994. pap. 29.95 (0-8373-3132-3) Nat Learn.
— Bureau Director. (Career Examination Ser.: C-1154). 1994. pap. 39.95 (0-8373-1154-3) Nat Learn.
— Bus Driver. (Career Examination Ser.: C-2197). 1994. pap. 19.95 (0-8373-2197-2) Nat Learn.
— Bus Maintainer, Group A. (Career Examination Ser.: C-100). 1994. pap. 19.95 (0-8373-0100-9) Nat Learn.
— Bus Maintainer, Group B. (Career Examination Ser.: C-101). 1994. pap. 19.95 (0-8373-0101-7) Nat Learn.
— Bus Operator. (Career Examination Ser.: C-102). 1994. pap. 19.95 (0-8373-0102-5) Nat Learn.
— Bus Operator-Conductor. (Career Examination Ser.: C-3383). 1994. pap. 19.95 (0-8373-3383-0) Nat Learn.
— Bus Transportation Technician. (Career Examination Ser.: C-3321). 1994. pap. 27.95 (0-8373-3321-0) Nat Learn.
— Business. (Undergraduate Program Field Test Ser.: UPFT-3). 1994. pap. 23.95 (0-8373-6003-X) Nat Learn.
— Business Assistant. (Career Examination Ser.: C-2885). 1994. pap. 29.95 (0-8373-2885-3) Nat Learn.
— Business Consultant. (Career Examination Ser.: C-1962). 1994. pap. 34.95 (0-8373-1962-5) Nat Learn.
— Business Education. (National Teachers Examination Ser.: NT-10). 1994. pap. 23.95 (0-8373-8420-6) Nat Learn.
— Business Environment & Strategy. (ACT Proficiency Examination Program Ser.: PEP-27). 1994. pap. 23.95 (0-8373-5527-3) Nat Learn.
— Business Environment & Strategy. (Regents External Degree Ser.: REDP-16). 1994. pap. 23.95 (0-8373-5616-4) Nat Learn.
— Business Law. (DANTES Ser.: No. 7). 1994. pap. 23.95 (0-8373-6607-0) Nat Learn.
— Business Law. (DANTES Ser.: No. 7). 1994. 39.95 (0-8373-6507-4) Nat Learn.
— Business Machine Maintainer & Repairer. (Career Examination Ser.: C-1155). 1994. pap. 23.95 (0-8373-1155-1) Nat Learn.
— Business Machine Operator. (Career Examination Ser.: C-1895). 1994. pap. 23.95 (0-8373-1895-5) Nat Learn.
— Business Machine Supervisor. (Career Examination Ser.: C-1897). 1994. pap. 27.95 (0-8373-1897-1) Nat Learn.
— Business Manager. (Career Examination Ser.: C-1898). 1994. pap. 34.95 (0-8373-1898-X) Nat Learn.
— Business Mathematics. (DANTES Ser.: No. 53). 1994. 39.95 (0-8373-6553-8, DANTES-53); pap. 23.95 (0-8373-6653-4, DANTES-53) Nat Learn.
— Business Office Manager. (Career Examination Ser.: C-1964). 1994. pap. 34.95 (0-8373-1964-1) Nat Learn.
— Business Officer. (Career Examination Ser.: C-2076). 1994. pap. 34.95 (0-8373-2076-3) Nat Learn.
— Business Policy. (ACT Proficiency Examination Program Ser.: PEP-23). 1994. pap. 23.95 (0-8373-5523-0) Nat Learn.
— Business Promotion Coordinator. (Career Examination Ser.: C-2527). 1994. pap. 34.95 (0-8373-2527-7) Nat Learn.
— Business Services Specialist. (Career Examination Ser.: C-3611). 1994. 34.95 (0-8373-3611-2, C-3611) Nat Learn.
— Butcher. (Career Examination Ser.: C-1156). 1994. pap. 27.95 (0-8373-1156-X) Nat Learn.
— Buyer. (Career Examination Ser.: C-103). 1994. pap. 23.95 (0-8373-0103-3) Nat Learn.
— Buyer One. (Career Examination Ser.: C-1845). 1994. pap. 23.95 (0-8373-1845-9) Nat Learn.
— Buyer Two. (Career Examination Ser.: C-1846). 1994. pap. 27.95 (0-8373-1846-7) Nat Learn.
— C. R. M. D. (Children with Retarded Mental Development) (Teachers License Examination Ser.: T-8). 1994. pap. 23.95 (0-8373-8008-1) Nat Learn.
— Cabinetmaking & Millwork. (Occupational Competency Examination Ser.: OCE-9). 1994. pap. 23.95 (0-8373-5709-8) Nat Learn.
— Cable Splicer. (Career Examination Ser.: C-1624). 1994. pap. 20.00 (0-8373-1624-3) Nat Learn.
— Cafeteria Supervisor. (Career Examination Ser.: C-1157). 1994. pap. 29.95 (0-8373-1157-8) Nat Learn.
— Calculus. (DANTES Ser.: No. 8). 1994. pap. 23.95 (0-8373-6608-9) Nat Learn.
— Calculus. (DANTES Ser.: No. 8). 1994. 39.95 (0-8373-6508-2) Nat Learn.
— Calculus with Analytical Geometry. (College Level Examination Ser.: CLEP-43). 1994. 39.95 (0-8373-5393-9); pap. 23.95 (0-8373-5343-2) Nat Learn.
— Calculus with Elementary Functions (Introductory Calculus. (College Level Examination Ser.: CLEP-21). 1994. 39.95 (0-8373-5371-8); pap. 23.95 (0-8373-5321-1) Nat Learn.
— California Basic Educational Skills Test (CBEST) (Admission Test Ser.: ATS-77). 1994. pap. 23.95 (0-8373-5077-8) Nat Learn.
— California High School Proficiency Examination. (Admission Test Ser.: ATS-39). 1994. pap. 23.95 (0-8373-5039-5) Nat Learn.
— Campus Public Safety Officer I. (Career Examination Ser.: C-881). 1994. pap. 23.95 (0-8373-0881-X) Nat Learn.
— Campus Public Safety Officer II. (Career Examination Ser.: C-882). 1994. pap. 27.95 (0-8373-0882-8) Nat Learn.
— Campus Security Guard I. (Career Examination Ser.: C-565). 1994. pap. 23.95 (0-8373-0565-9) Nat Learn.
— Campus Security Guard II. (Career Examination Ser.: C-566). 1994. pap. 27.95 (0-8373-0566-7) Nat Learn.
— Campus Security Guard III. (Career Examination Ser.: C-567). 1994. pap. 129.95 (0-8373-0567-5) Nat Learn.
— Campus Security Officer. (Career Examination Ser.: C-2260). 1994. pap. 23.95 (0-8373-2260-X) Nat Learn.
— Campus Security Officer I. (Career Examination Ser.: C-2261). 1994. pap. 23.95 (0-8373-2261-8) Nat Learn.
— Campus Security Officer II. (Career Examination Ser.: C-1700). 1994. pap. 27.95 (0-8373-1700-2) Nat Learn.
— Campus Security Officer Trainee. (Career Examination Ser.: C-2081). 1994. pap. 23.95 (0-8373-2081-X) Nat Learn.
— Campus Security Specialist. (Career Examination Ser.: C-1701). 1994. 45.95 (0-685-03518-2); pap. 29.95 (0-8373-1701-0) Nat Learn.
— Canal Electrical Supervisor. (Career Examination Ser.: C-3301). 1994. pap. 29.95 (0-8373-3301-6) Nat Learn.
— Canal Maintenance Shop Supervisor I. (Career Examination Ser.: C-3015). 1994. pap. 29.95 (0-8373-3015-7) Nat Learn.
— Canal Maintenance Shop Supervisor II. (Career Examination Ser.: C-3016). 1994. pap. 29.95 (0-8373-3016-5) Nat Learn.
— Canal Maintenance Supervisor I. (Career Examination Ser.: C-3141). 1994. pap. 29.95 (0-8373-3141-2) Nat Learn.
— Canal Maintenance Supervisor II. (Career Examination Ser.: C-3142). 1994. pap. 29.95 (0-8373-3142-0) Nat Learn.
— Canal Structure Operator. (Career Examination Ser.: C-3133). 1994. pap. 29.95 (0-8373-3133-1) Nat Learn.
— Capital Police Officer. (Career Examination Ser.: C-2264). 1994. pap. 23.95 (0-8373-2264-2) Nat Learn.
— Captain, Fire Department. (Career Examination Ser.: C-120). 1994. pap. 39.95 (0-8373-0120-3) Nat Learn.
— Captain, Police Department. (Career Examination Ser.: C-121). 1994. pap. 39.95 (0-8373-0121-1) Nat Learn.
— Car Appearance Supervisor. (Career Examination Ser.: No. C-3525). 1994. 27.95 (0-8373-3525-6) Nat Learn.
— Car Cleaner. (Career Examination Ser.: C-181). 1994. pap. 19.95 (0-8373-0181-5) Nat Learn.
— Car Maintainer - Group A. (Career Examination Ser.: C-122). 1994. pap. 23.95 (0-8373-0122-X) Nat Learn.
— Car Maintainer - Group B. (Career Examination Ser.: C-123). 1994. pap. 23.95 (0-8373-0123-8) Nat Learn.
— Car Maintainer - Group C. (Career Examination Ser.: C-182). 1994. pap. 23.95 (0-8373-0182-3) Nat Learn.
— Car Maintainer - Group D. (Career Examination Ser.: C-183). 1994. pap. 23.95 (0-8373-0183-1) Nat Learn.
— Car Maintainer - Group E. (Career Examination Ser.: C-184). 1994. pap. 23.95 (0-8373-0184-X) Nat Learn.
— Car Maintainer - Group F. (Career Examination Ser.: C-185). 1994. pap. 23.95 (0-8373-0185-8) Nat Learn.
— Car Maintainer Trainee. (Career Examination Ser.: C-186). 1994. pap. 19.95 (0-8373-0186-6) Nat Learn.
— Card Punch-Key Punch Operator (Alphabetic) (Career Examination Ser.: C-124). 1994. pap. 23.95 (0-8373-0124-6) Nat Learn.
— Card Punch Operator. (Career Examination Ser.: C-125). 1994. pap. 23.94 (0-8373-0125-4) Nat Learn.
— Cardio-Pulmonary Technician. (Career Examination Ser.: C-1159). 1994. pap. 39.95 (0-8373-1159-4) Nat Learn.
— Career Examination Series. (Entire Ser.). Orig. Title: Civil Service Examination Passbook Series. 1994. pap. write for info. (0-8373-0000-2) Nat Learn.
— Career Guidance Technician. (Career Examination Ser.: C-3104). 1994. pap. 29.95 (0-8373-3104-8) Nat Learn.
— Carpenter. (Career Examination Ser.: C-126). 1994. pap. 23.95 (0-8373-0126-2) Nat Learn.
— Carpentry. (Occupational Competency Examination Ser.: OCE-10). 1994. pap. 23.95 (0-8373-5710-1) Nat Learn.
— Carpentry Workbook. (Workbook Ser.: No. 3020). 1994. pap. 23.95 (0-8373-7904-0) Nat Learn.
— Cartographer. (Career Examination Ser.: C-127). 1994. pap. 27.95 (0-8373-0127-0) Nat Learn.
— Cartographer-Draftsman. (Career Examination Ser.: C-1160). 1994. pap. 29.95 (0-8373-1160-8) Nat Learn.
— Cartographic Technician. (Career Examination Ser.: C-3116). 1994. pap. 27.95 (0-8373-3116-1) Nat Learn.
— Case Aide. (Career Examination Ser.: C-187). 1994. pap. 19.95 (0-8373-0187-4) Nat Learn.
— Case Manager. (Career Examination Ser.: C-2744). 1994. pap. 34.95 (0-8373-2744-X) Nat Learn.
— Case Supervisor. (Career Examination Ser.: C-188). 1994. pap. 29.95 (0-8373-0188-2) Nat Learn.
— Case Worker. (Career Examination Ser.: C-128). 1994. pap. 23.95 (0-8373-0128-9) Nat Learn.
— Casework Supervisor. (Career Examination Ser.: C-2932). 1994. pap. 29.95 (0-8373-2932-9) Nat Learn.
— Caseworker Aide. (Career Examination Ser.: C-419). 1994. pap. 19.95 (0-8373-0419-9) Nat Learn.

R

— Caseworker Trainee. (Career Examination Ser.: C-1163). 1994. pap. 19.95 (*0-8373-1163-2*) Nat Learn.
— Caseworker 1. (Career Examination Ser.: C-129). 1994. pap. 23.95 (*0-8373-0129-7*) Nat Learn.
— Caseworker 2. (Career Examination Ser.: C-130). 1994. pap. 27.95 (*0-8373-0130-0*) Nat Learn.
— Cashier. (Career Examination Ser.: C-131). 1994. pap. 19. 95 (*0-8373-0131-9*) Nat Learn.
— Cashier - Cashier I. (Career Examination Ser.: C-1327). 1994. pap. 23.95 (*0-8373-1327-9*) Nat Learn.
— Cashier II. (Career Examination Ser.: C-2899). 1994. pap. 27.95 (*0-8373-2899-3*) Nat Learn.
— Cashier-Transit Authority. (Career Examination Ser.: C-1787). 1994. pap. 19.95 (*0-8373-1787-8*) Nat Learn.
— Catholic High School Entrance Examination. (Admission Test Ser.: ATS-81). 1994. pap. 23.95 (*0-8373-5081-6*) Nat Learn.
— Cement Mason. (Career Examination Ser.: C-132). 1994. pap. 23.95 (*0-8373-0132-7*) Nat Learn.
— Census Bureau Enumerator. (Career Examination Ser.: No. C-3514). 1994. 29.95 (*0-8373-3514-0*) Nat Learn.
— Census Bureau Manager. (Career Examination Ser.: No. C-3515). 1994. 39.95 (*0-8373-3515-9*) Nat Learn.
— Certification Examination for Medical Assistants. (Admission Test Ser.: ATS-93). 1994. pap. 23.95 (*0-8373-5093-X*) Nat Learn.
— Certification Examination for Occupational Therapy Assistant (OTA) (Admission Test Ser.: ATS-69). 1994. pap. 29.95 (*0-8373-5069-7*) Nat Learn.
— Certified Electronic Technician. (Admission Test Ser.: ATS-38). 1994. pap. 27.95 (*0-8373-5038-7*) Nat Learn.
— Certified General Automobile Mechanic (CGAM) (Career Examination Ser.: C-1664). 1994. pap. 29.95 (*0-8373-1664-2*) Nat Learn.
— Certified Laboratory Assistant. (Career Examination Ser.: C-179). 1994. pap. 27.95 (*0-8373-0179-3*) Nat Learn.
— Certified Nurse Examination Series. 1994. pap. write for info. (*0-8373-6100-1*) Nat Learn.
— Certified Professional Social Worker (CPSW) (Admission Test Ser.: ATS-88). 1994. pap. 29.95 (*0-8373-5088-3*) Nat Learn.
— Certified Protection Professional Examination (CPP) (Admission Test Ser.: ATS-68). 1994. pap. 39.95 (*0-8373-5068-9*) Nat Learn.
— Certified Public Accountant Examination (CPA) (Admission Test Ser.: ATS-71). 1994. pap. 49.95 (*0-8373-5071-9*) Nat Learn.
— Certified Safety Professional Examination (CSP) (Admission Test Ser.: ATS-72). 1994. pap. 49.95 (*0-8373-5072-7*) Nat Learn.
— Certified Shorthand Reporter. (Career Examination Ser.: C-133). 1994. pap. 27.95 (*0-8373-0133-5*) Nat Learn.
— Certified Social Worker (CSW) (Career Examination Ser.: C-178). 1994. pap. 29.95 (*0-8373-0178-5*) Nat Learn.
— Chairman, Academic Subjects (English & Social Studies) (Teachers License Examination Ser.: CH-1). 1994. pap. 29.95 (*0-8373-8151-7*) Nat Learn.
— Chairman, Accounting & Business Practices. (Teachers License Examination Ser.: CH-2). 1994. pap. 29.95 (*0-8373-8152-5*) Nat Learn.
— Chairman, Civil Service Commission. (Career Examination Ser.: C-1164). 1994. pap. 49.95 (*0-8373-1164-0*) Nat Learn.
— Chairman, Distributive Education (Merchandising & Salesmanship), Sr. H. S. (Teachers License Examination Ser.: CH-3). 1994. pap. 29.95 (*0-8373-8153-3*) Nat Learn.
— Chairman, English, Jr. H. S. (Teachers License Examination Ser.: CH-4). 1994. pap. 29.95 (*0-8373-8154-1*) Nat Learn.
— Chairman, English, Sr. H. S. (Teachers License Examination Ser.: CH-5). 1994. pap. 29.95 (*0-8373-8155-X*) Nat Learn.
— Chairman, Fine Arts, Sr. H. S. (Teachers License Examination Ser.: CH-7). 1994. pap. 29.95 (*0-8373-8157-6*) Nat Learn.
— Chairman, Foreign Languages, Jr. H. S. (Teachers License Examination Ser.: CH-8). 1994. pap. 29.95 (*0-8373-8158-4*) Nat Learn.
— Chairman, Foreign Languages, Sr. H. S. (Teachers License Examination Ser.: CH-9). 1994. pap. 29.95 (*0-8373-8159-2*) Nat Learn.
— Chairman, Health & Physical Education, Jr. H. S. (Teachers License Examination Ser.: CH-10). 1994. pap. 29.95 (*0-8373-8160-6*) Nat Learn.
— Chairman, Health & Physical Education, Sr. H. S. (Teachers License Examination Ser.: CH-11). 1994. pap. 29.95 (*0-8373-8161-4*) Nat Learn.
— Chairman, Home Economics, Jr. H. S. (Teachers License Examination Ser.: CH-12). 1994. pap. 29.95 (*0-8373-8162-2*) Nat Learn.
— Chairman, Home Economics, Sr. H. S. (Teachers License Examination Ser.: CH-13). 1994. pap. 29.95 (*0-8373-8163-0*) Nat Learn.
— Chairman, Industrial Arts, Jr. H. S. (Teachers License Examination Ser.: CH-14). 1994. pap. 29.95 (*0-8373-8164-9*) Nat Learn.
— Chairman, Industrial Arts, Sr. H. S. (Teachers License Examination Ser.: CH-15). 1994. pap. 29.95 (*0-8373-8165-7*) Nat Learn.
— Chairman, Mathematics, Jr. H. S. (Teachers License Examination Ser.: CH-16). 1994. pap. 29.95 (*0-8373-8166-5*) Nat Learn.
— Chairman, Mathematics, Sr. H. S. (Teachers License Examination Ser.: CH-17). 1994. pap. 29.95 (*0-8373-8167-3*) Nat Learn.
— Chairman, Music, Jr. H. S. (Teachers License Examination Ser.: CH-18). 1994. pap. 29.95 (*0-8373-8168-1*) Nat Learn.
— Chairman, Music, Sr. H. S. (Teachers License Examination Ser.: CH-19). 1994. pap. 29.95 (*0-8373-8169-X*) Nat Learn.
— Chairman, Nursing. (Teachers License Examination Ser.: CH-31). 1994. pap. 29.95 (*0-8373-8181-9*) Nat Learn.
— Chairman, Related Technical Subjects (Biological & Chemical), Sr. H. S. (Teachers License Examination Ser.: CH-20). 1994. pap. 29.95 (*0-8373-8170-3*) Nat Learn.
— Chairman, Related Technical Subjects (Mechanical, Structural, Electrical), Sr. H. S. (Teachers License Examination Ser.: CH-21). 1994. pap. 29.95 (*0-8373-8171-1*) Nat Learn.
— Chairman, Sciences, Jr. H. S. (Teachers License Examination Ser.: CH-22). 1994. pap. 29.95 (*0-8373-8172-X*) Nat Learn.
— Chairman, Sciences, Sr. H. S. (Teachers License Examination Ser.: CH-23). 1994. pap. 29.95 (*0-8373-8173-8*) Nat Learn.
— Chairman, Shop Subjects, Sr. H. S. (Teachers License Examination Ser.: CH-24). 1994. pap. 29.95 (*0-8373-8174-6*) Nat Learn.
— Chairman, Social Studies, Jr. H. S. (Teachers License Examination Ser.: CH-25). 1994. pap. 29.95 (*0-8373-8175-4*) Nat Learn.
— Chairman, Social Studies, Sr. H. S. (Teachers License Examination Ser.: CH-26). 1994. pap. 29.95 (*0-8373-8176-2*) Nat Learn.
— Chairman, Speech, Sr. H. S. (Teachers License Examination Ser.: CH-27). 1994. pap. 29.95 (*0-8373-8177-0*) Nat Learn.
— Chairman, Stenography & Typewriting (Gregg & Pitman), Sr. H. S. (Teachers License Examination Ser.: CH-28). 1994. pap. 29.95 (*0-8373-8178-9*) Nat Learn.
— Chairman, Teacher-Trainer, Language Arts, I. S. & Jr. H. S. (Teachers License Examination Ser.: CH-30). 1994. pap. 93.95 (*0-8373-8180-0*) Nat Learn.
— Chairman, Teacher-Trainer, Math & Science, I. S. & Jr. H. S. (Teachers License Examination Ser.: CH-29). 1994. pap. 29.95 (*0-8373-8179-7*) Nat Learn.
— Chauffeur. (Career Examination Ser.: C-1166). 1994. pap. 23.95 (*0-8373-1166-7*) Nat Learn.
— Chemical Engineer. (Career Examination Ser.: C-134). 1994. pap. 29.95 (*0-8373-0134-3*) Nat Learn.
— Chemical Engineering Trainee. (Career Examination Ser.: C-3131). 1994. pap. 23.95 (*0-8373-3131-5*) Nat Learn.
— Chemist. (Career Examination Ser.: C-135). 1994. pap. 27.95 (*0-8373-0135-1*) Nat Learn.
— Chemist I (Environmental Control) (Career Examination Ser.: C-2983). 1994. pap. 29.95 (*0-8373-2983-3*) Nat Learn.
— Chemist II (Enviromental Control) (Career Examination Ser.: C-2984). 1994. pap. 29.95 (*0-8373-2984-1*) Nat Learn.
— Chemist Trainee. (Career Examination Ser.: C-1186). 1994. pap. 23.95 (*0-8373-1186-1*) Nat Learn.
— Chemistry. (College Proficiency Examination Ser.: CPEP-6). 1994. pap. 23.95 (*0-8373-5406-4*) Nat Learn.
— Chemistry. (Graduate Record Examination Ser.: GRE-2). 1994. pap. 23.95 (*0-8373-5202-9*) Nat Learn.
— Chemistry. (Undergraduate Program Field Test Ser.: UPFT-4). 1994. pap. 23.95 (*0-8373-6004-8*) Nat Learn.
— Chemistry & General Science. (National Teachers Examination Ser.: NT-7A). 1994. pap. 23.95 (*0-8373-8409-5*) Nat Learn.
— Chemistry & General Science, Senior High School. (Teachers License Examination Ser.: T-6). 1994. pap. 23. 95 (*0-8373-8006-5*) Nat Learn.
— Chemistry, Physics & General Science. (National Teachers Examination Ser.: NT-7). 1994. pap. 23.95 (*0-8373-8417-6*) Nat Learn.
— Chief Account Clerk. (Career Examination Ser.: C-2707). 1994. pap. 29.95 (*0-8373-2707-5*) Nat Learn.
— Chief Accountant. (Career Examination Ser.: C-1565). 1994. 39.95 (*0-8373-1565-4*) Nat Learn.
— Chief Auditor. (Career Examination Ser.: C-2348). 1994. pap. 39.95 (*0-8373-2348-7*) Nat Learn.
— Chief Beverage Control Investigator. (Career Examination Ser.: C-2825). 1994. pap. 34.95 (*0-8373-2825-X*) Nat Learn.
— Chief Biostatistician. (Career Examination Ser.: C-1167). 1994. pap. 39.95 (*0-8373-1167-5*) Nat Learn.
— Chief Budget Examiner. (Career Examination Ser.: C-2667). 1994. pap. 39.95 (*0-8373-2667-2*) Nat Learn.
— Chief Building Inspector. (Career Examination Ser.: C-2847). 1994. pap. 39.95 (*0-8373-2847-0*) Nat Learn.
— Chief Buildings Engineer. (Career Examination Ser.: C-1168). 1994. pap. 39.95 (*0-8373-1168-3*) Nat Learn.
— Chief Cartographer-Draftsman. (Career Examination Ser.: C-1169). 1994. pap. 34.95 (*0-8373-1169-1*) Nat Learn.
— Chief Civil Engineer. (Career Examination Ser.: C-1170). 1994. pap. 34.95 (*0-8373-1170-5*) Nat Learn.
— Chief Clerk. (Career Examination Ser.: C-189). 1994. pap. 29.95 (*0-8373-0189-0*) Nat Learn.
— Chief Clerk Surrogate. (Career Examination Ser.: C-2131). 1994. pap. 29.95 (*0-8373-2131-X*) Nat Learn.
— Chief Compensation Investigator. (Career Examination Ser.: C-3229). 1994. pap. 34.95 (*0-8373-3229-X*) Nat Learn.
— Chief Compliance Investigator. (Career Examination Ser.: C-2423). 1994. pap. 34.95 (*0-8373-2423-8*) Nat Learn.
— Chief Consumer Affairs Investigator. (Career Examination Ser.: C-2378). 1994. pap. 34.95 (*0-8373-2378-9*) Nat Learn.
— Chief Custodian. (Career Examination Ser.: C-2555). 1994. pap. 34.95 (*0-8373-2555-2*) Nat Learn.
— Chief Data Processing Control Clerk. (Career Examination Ser.: C-2486). 1994. pap. 29.95 (*0-8373-2486-6*) Nat Learn.
— Chief Data Processing Equipment Operator. (Career Examination Ser.: C-2304). 1994. pap. 34.95 (*0-8373-2304-5*) Nat Learn.
— Chief Deputy County Attorney. (Career Examination Ser.: C-1172). 1994. pap. 44.95 (*0-8373-1172-1*) Nat Learn.
— Chief Deputy Sheriff. (Career Examination Ser.: C-1173). 1994. pap. 34.95 (*0-8373-1173-X*) Nat Learn.
— Chief Dietitian. (Career Examination Ser.: C-1174). 1994. pap. 34.95 (*0-8373-1174-8*) Nat Learn.
— Chief Draftsman. (Career Examination Ser.: C-1577). 1994. pap. 39.95 (*0-8373-1577-8*) Nat Learn.
— Chief Electronic Computer Operator. (Career Examination Ser.: C-1550). 1994. pap. 34.95 (*0-8373-1550-6*) Nat Learn.
— Chief Elevator Starter. (Career Examination Ser.: C-1175). 1994. pap. 29.95 (*0-8373-1175-6*) Nat Learn.
— Chief Engineer. (Career Examination Ser.: C-1176). 1994. pap. 44.95 (*0-8373-1176-4*) Nat Learn.
— Chief Excise Tax Investigator. (Career Examination Ser.: C-2420). 1994. pap. 34.95 (*0-8373-2420-3*) Nat Learn.
— Chief Executive Officer. (Career Examination Ser.: C-2828). 1994. pap. 44.95 (*0-8373-2828-4*) Nat Learn.
— Chief Field Accountant. (Career Examination Ser.: C-1571). 1994. pap. 39.95 (*0-8373-1571-9*) Nat Learn.
— Chief File Clerk. (Career Examination Ser.: C-453). 1994. pap. 29.95 (*0-8373-0453-9*) Nat Learn.
— Chief Groundskeeper. (Career Examination Ser.: C-1574). 1994. pap. 29.95 (*0-8373-1574-3*) Nat Learn.
— Chief Institution Safety Officer. (Career Examination Ser.: C-2120). 1994. pap. 34.95 (*0-8373-2120-4*) Nat Learn.
— Chief Investigator. (Career Examination Ser.: C-1401). 1994. pap. 34.95 (*0-8373-1401-1*) Nat Learn.
— Chief Key Punch Operator. (Career Examination Ser.: C-2104). 1994. pap. 29.95 (*0-8373-2104-2*) Nat Learn.
— Chief Labor Standards Investigator. (Career Examination Ser.: C-3127). 1994. pap. 39.95 (*0-8373-3127-7*) Nat Learn.
— Chief Law Assistant. (Career Examination Ser.: C-1177). 1994. pap. 34.95 (*0-8373-1177-2*) Nat Learn.
— Chief Law Stenographer. (Career Examination Ser.: C-941). 1994. pap. 29.95 (*0-8373-0941-7*) Nat Learn.
— Chief Management Analyst. (Career Examination Ser.: C-1178). 1994. pap. 44.95 (*0-8373-1178-0*) Nat Learn.
— Chief Marine Engineer. (Career Examination Ser.: C-1794). 1994. pap. 39.95 (*0-8373-1794-0*) Nat Learn.
— Chief Marketing Representative. (Career Examination Ser.: C-2041). 1994. pap. 34.95 (*0-8373-2041-0*) Nat Learn.
— Chief Marshal. (Career Examination Ser.: C-1179). 1994. pap. 34.95 (*0-8373-1179-9*) Nat Learn.
— Chief Meat Inspector. (Career Examination Ser.: C-2042). 1994. pap. 34.95 (*0-8373-2042-9*) Nat Learn.
— Chief Medical Examiner. (Career Examination Ser.: C-1180). 1994. pap. 49.95 (*0-8373-1180-2*) Nat Learn.
— Chief Multiple Residence Inspector. (Career Examination Ser.: C-2844). 1994. pap. 39.95 (*0-8373-2844-6*) Nat Learn.
— Chief of Police. (Career Examination Ser.: C-2148). 1994. pap. 49.95 (*0-8373-2148-4*) Nat Learn.
— Chief of Staff (Sheriff) (Career Examination Ser.: C-2502). 1994. pap. 39.95 (*0-8373-2502-1*) Nat Learn.
— Chief of Stenographic Services. (Career Examination Ser.: C-943). 1994. pap. 34.95 (*0-8373-0943-3*) Nat Learn.
— Chief Office Manager. (Career Examination Ser.: C-2400). 1994. pap. 39.95 (*0-8373-2400-9*) Nat Learn.
— Chief Personnel Administrator. (Career Examination Ser.: C-942). 1994. pap. 49.95 (*0-8373-0942-5*) Nat Learn.
— Chief Physical Therapist. (Career Examination Ser.: C-3384). 1994. pap. 39.95 (*0-8373-3384-9*) Nat Learn.
— Chief Police Surgeon. (Career Examination Ser.: C-1181). 1994. pap. 49.95 (*0-8373-1181-0*) Nat Learn.
— Chief Probation Officer. (Career Examination Ser.: C-1593). 1994. pap. 34.95 (*0-8373-1593-X*) Nat Learn.
— Chief Process Server. (Career Examination Ser.: C-1182). 1994. pap. 29.95 (*0-8373-1182-9*) Nat Learn.
— Chief Psychologist. (Career Examination Ser.: C-2194). 1994. pap. 44.95 (*0-8373-2194-8*) Nat Learn.
— Chief Public Health Nutritionist. (Career Examination Ser.: C-1567). 1994. pap. 34.95 (*0-8373-1567-0*) Nat Learn.
— Chief Purchasing Agent. (Career Examination Ser.: C-3323). 1994. pap. 34.95 (*0-8373-3323-7*) Nat Learn.
— Chief Recreation Therapist. (Career Examination Ser.: C-3279). 1994. pap. 39.95 (*0-8373-3279-6*) Nat Learn.
— Chief Registrar. (Career Examination Ser.: C-1183). 1994. pap. 34.95 (*0-8373-1183-7*) Nat Learn.
— Chief Schedule Maker. (Career Examination Ser.: C-1729). 1994. pap. 39.95 (*0-8373-1729-0*) Nat Learn.
— Chief Security Officer. (Career Examination Ser.: C-1185). 1994. pap. 34.95 (*0-8373-1185-3*) Nat Learn.
— Chief Special Investigator. (Career Examination Ser.: C-1591). 1994. pap. 39.95 (*0-8373-1591-3*) Nat Learn.
— Chief Stationary Engineer. (Career Examination Ser.: C-1184). 1994. pap. 39.95 (*0-8373-1184-5*) Nat Learn.
— Chief Supervisor of Mechanical Installations. (Career Examination Ser.: C-2482). 1994. pap. 39.95 (*0-8373-2482-3*) Nat Learn.
— Chief Support Investigator. (Career Examination Ser.: C-2767). 1994. pap. 39.95 (*0-8373-2767-9*) Nat Learn.
— Chief Surface Line Dispatcher. (Career Examination Ser.: C-944). 1994. pap. 29.95 (*0-8373-0944-1*) Nat Learn.
— Chief Water Pollution Control Inspector. (Career Examination Ser.: C-1187). 1994. pap. 39.95 (*0-8373-1187-X*) Nat Learn.
— Chief Water Treatment Plant Operator. (Career Examination Ser.: C-2149). 1994. pap. 39.95 (*0-8373-2149-2*) Nat Learn.
— Child & Adolescent Nurse. (Certified Nurse Examination Ser.: CN-7). 1994. 39.95 (*0-8373-6157-5*); pap. 23.95 (*0-8373-6107-9*) Nat Learn.
— Child Protective Services Specialist. (Career Examination Ser.: C-3295). 1994. pap. 29.95 (*0-8373-3295-8*) Nat Learn.
— Child Protective Supervisor. (Career Examination Ser.: Series 1). 1991. pap. 34.95 (*0-8373-3701-1*) Nat Learn.
— Children with Limited Vision. (Teachers License Examination Ser.: T-7). 1994. pap. 23.95 (*0-8373-8007-3*) Nat Learn.
— Children's Counselor. (Career Examination Ser.: C-1604). 1994. pap. 29.95 (*0-8373-1604-9*) Nat Learn.
— City Chamberlain. (Career Examination Ser.: C-2981). 1994. pap. 34.95 (*0-8373-2981-7*) Nat Learn.
— City Comptroller. (Career Examination Ser.: C-1746). 1994. pap. 39.95 (*0-8373-1746-0*) Nat Learn.
— City Surveyor. (Career Examination Ser.: C-1188). 1994. pap. 29.95 (*0-8373-1188-8*) Nat Learn.
— Civil Engineer. (Career Examination Ser.: C-136). 1994. pap. 27.95 (*0-8373-0136-X*) Nat Learn.
— Civil Engineer I. (Career Examination Ser.: C-2158). 1994. reprint ed. pap. 27.95 (*0-8373-2158-1*) Nat Learn.
— Civil Engineer I, II, III, IV, V. (Career Examination Ser.: C-2000). 1994. pap. 49.95 (*0-8373-2000-3*) Nat Learn.
— Civil Engineer II. (Career Examination Ser.: C-2159). 1994. reprint ed. pap. 29.95 (*0-8373-2159-X*) Nat Learn.
— Civil Engineer III. (Career Examination Ser.: C-2160). 1994. reprint ed. pap. 34.95 (*0-8373-2160-3*) Nat Learn.
— Civil Engineer IV. (Career Examination Ser.: C-2161). 1994. reprint ed. pap. 34.95 (*0-8373-2161-1*) Nat Learn.
— Civil Engineer (Materials) (Career Examination Ser.: C-3224). 1994. pap. 29.95 (*0-8373-3224-9*) Nat Learn.
— Civil Engineer (Physical Research) (Career Examination Ser.: C-3225). 1994. pap. 29.95 (*0-8373-3225-7*) Nat Learn.
— Civil Engineer (Planning) (Career Examination Ser.: C-3226). 1994. pap. 29.95 (*0-8373-3226-5*) Nat Learn.
— Civil Engineer (Traffic) (Career Examination Ser.: C-3227). 1994. pap. 29.95 (*0-8373-3227-3*) Nat Learn.
— Civil Engineer V. (Career Examination Ser.: C-2162). 1994. reprint ed. pap. 34.95 (*0-8373-2162-X*) Nat Learn.
— Civil Engineering Draftsman. (Career Examination Ser.: C-137). 1994. pap. 27.95 (*0-8373-0137-8*) Nat Learn.
— Civil Engineering Draftsman I. (Career Examination Ser.: C-2154). 1994. pap. 27.95 (*0-8373-2154-9*) Nat Learn.
— Civil Engineering Draftsman II. (Career Examination Ser.: C-2155). 1994. pap. 29.95 (*0-8373-2155-7*) Nat Learn.
— Civil Engineering Draftsman III. (Career Examination Ser.: C-2156). 1994. 29.95 (*0-8373-2156-5*) Nat Learn.
— Civil Engineering Trainee. (Career Examination Ser.: C-945). 1994. pap. 23.95 (*0-8373-0945-X*) Nat Learn.
— Civil Service Administration, Management & Supervision. (General Aptitude & Abilities Ser.: CS-3). 1994. pap. 27. 95 (*0-8373-6703-4*) Nat Learn.
— Civil Service Arithmetic. (General Aptitude & Abilities Ser.: CS-6). 1994. pap. 17.95 (*0-8373-6706-9*) Nat Learn.
— Civil Service Clerical Abilities. (General Aptitude & Abilities Ser.: CS-12). 1994. pap. 17.95 (*0-8373-6712-3*) Nat Learn.
— Civil Service General & Mental Abilities. (General Aptitude & Abilities Ser.: CS-16). 1994. pap. 19.95 (*0-8373-6716-6*) Nat Learn.
— Civil Service Grammar & Usage. (General Aptitude & Abilities Ser.: CS-7). 1994. pap. 19.95 (*0-8373-6707-7*) Nat Learn.
— Civil Service Graphs, Charts & Tables. (General Aptitude & Abilities Ser.: CS-11). 1994. pap. 19.95 (*0-8373-6711-5*) Nat Learn.
— Civil Service Home Study Course. (General Aptitude & Abilities Ser.: CS-1). 1994. pap. 19.95 (*0-8373-6701-8*) Nat Learn.
— Civil Service Mechanical Aptitude. (General Aptitude & Abilities Ser.: CS-15). 1994. pap. 23.95 (*0-8373-6715-8*) Nat Learn.
— Civil Service Promotion Course. (General Aptitude & Abilities Ser.: CS-2). 1994. pap. 23.95 (*0-8373-6702-6*) Nat Learn.
— Civil Service Reading Comprehension. (General Aptitude & Abilities Ser.: CS-8). 1994. pap. 19.95 (*0-8373-6708-5*) Nat Learn.
— Civil Service Secretary. (General Aptitude & Abilities Ser.: CS-4). 1994. pap. 19.95 (*0-8373-6704-2*) Nat Learn.
— Civil Service Spelling. (General Aptitude & Abilities Ser.: CS-9). 1994. pap. 17.95 (*0-8373-6709-3*) Nat Learn.
— Civil Service Test Practice Book for 100 Civil Service Jobs. (General Aptitude & Abilities Ser.: CS-5). 1994. pap. 23.95 (*0-8373-6705-0*) Nat Learn.
— Civil Service Verbal Abilities. (General Aptitude & Abilities Ser.: CS-13). 1994. pap. 17.95 (*0-8373-6713-1*) Nat Learn.
— Civil Service Verbal & Clerical Abilities. (General Aptitude & Abilities Ser.). 1994. pap. 19.95 (*0-8373-6714-X*) Nat Learn.
— Civil Service Vocabulary. (General Aptitude & Abilities Ser.: CS-10). 1994. pap. 17.95 (*0-8373-6710-7*) Nat Learn.
— Claim Examiner. (Career Examination Ser.: C-139). 1994. pap. 27.95 (*0-8373-0139-4*) Nat Learn.
— Claims Clerk. (Career Examination Ser.: C-138). 1994. pap. 23.95 (*0-8373-0138-6*) Nat Learn.
— Claims Examiner. (Career Examination Ser.: C-140). 1994. pap. 27.95 (*0-8373-0140-8*) Nat Learn.
— Claims Examiner Aide. (Career Examination Ser.: C-948). 1994. pap. 23.95 (*0-8373-0948-4*) Nat Learn.
— Claims Investigator. (Career Examination Ser.: C-3324). 1994. pap. 23.95 (*0-8373-3324-5*) Nat Learn.
— Claims Settlement Agent. (Career Examination Ser.: C-1189). 1994. pap. 27.95 (*0-8373-1189-6*) Nat Learn.
— Cleaner, Custodian USPS. (Career Examination Ser.: C-3315). 1994. pap. 23.95 (*0-8373-3315-6*) Nat Learn.

An Asterisk (*) at the beginning of an entry indicates that the title is appearing in BIP for the first time.

— Cleaner-Helper. (Career Examination Ser.: C-1195). 1994. pap. 19.95 (*0-8373-1195-0*) Nat Learn.
— Cleaner (T. A.) (Career Examination Ser.: No. C-946). 1994. 19.95 (*0-8373-0946-8*) Nat Learn.
— Clerical & Administrative Support Positions. (Career Examination Ser.: C-314). 1994. pap. 19.95 (*0-8373-0314-1*) Nat Learn.
— Clerical Positions G-5. (Career Examination Ser.: C-1943). 1994. pap. 19.95 (*0-8373-1943-9*) Nat Learn.
— Clerical Training Supervisor. (Career Examination Ser.: C-1194). 1994. pap. 29.95 (*0-8373-1194-2*) Nat Learn.
— Clerk. (Career Examination Ser.: C-142). 1994. pap. 19.95 (*0-8373-0142-4*) Nat Learn.
— Clerk - Part-Time. (Career Examination Ser.: C-1191). 1994. pap. 19.95 (*0-8373-1191-8*) Nat Learn.
— Clerk-Carrier (U. S. P. S.) (Career Examination Ser.: C-143). 1994. pap. 19.95 (*0-8373-0143-2*) Nat Learn.
— Clerk GS1-4. (Career Examination Ser.: C-144). 1994. pap. 19.95 (*0-8373-0144-0*) Nat Learn.
— Clerk GS5-7. (Career Examination Ser.: C-145). 1994. pap. 19.95 (*0-8373-0145-9*) Nat Learn.
— Clerk I. (Career Examination Ser.: C-3271). 1994. pap. 19.95 (*0-8373-3271-0*) Nat Learn.
— Clerk II. (Career Examination Ser.: C-3272). 1994. pap. 16.00 (*0-8373-3272-9*) Nat Learn.
— Clerk III. (Career Examination Ser.: C-3273). 1994. pap. 27.95 (*0-8373-3273-7*) Nat Learn.
— Clerk (Income Maintenance) (Career Examination Ser.: C-1642). 1994. reprint ed. pap. 23.95 (*0-8373-1642-1*) Nat Learn.
— Clerk IV. (Career Examination Ser.: C-3274). 1994. pap. 27.95 (*0-8373-3274-5*) Nat Learn.
— Clerk-Laborer. (Career Examination Ser.: C-1190). 1994. 23.95 (*0-8373-1190-X*) Nat Learn.
— Clerk of the Works. (Career Examination Ser.: C-3230). 1994. pap. 27.95 (*0-8373-3230-3*) Nat Learn.
— Clerk-Seasonal. (Career Examination Ser.: C-1192). 1994. pap. 19.95 (*0-8373-1192-6*) Nat Learn.
— Clerk-Stenographer. (Career Examination Ser.: C-146). 1994. pap. 19.95 (*0-8373-0146-7*) Nat Learn.
— Clerk-Stenographer I. (Career Examination Ser.: C-2339). 1994. pap. 19.95 (*0-8373-2339-8*) Nat Learn.
— Clerk-Stenographer II. (Career Examination Ser.: C-1650). 1994. pap. 23.95 (*0-8373-1650-2*) Nat Learn.
— Clerk-Stenographer III. (Career Examination Ser.: C-1651). 1994. pap. 23.95 (*0-8373-1651-0*) Nat Learn.
— Clerk-Stenographer IV. (Career Examination Ser.: C-1652). 1994. pap. 23.95 (*0-8373-1652-9*) Nat Learn.
— Clerk-Technician (U. S. P. S.) (Career Examination Ser.: C-1633). 1994. reprint ed. pap. 27.95 (*0-8373-1633-2*) Nat Learn.
— Clerk-Typist. (Career Examination Ser.: C-147). 1994. pap. 19.95 (*0-8373-0147-5*) Nat Learn.
— Clerk-Typist II. (Career Examination Ser.: C-3572). 1994. 23.95 (*0-8373-3572-8*) Nat Learn.
— Clerk-Typist Trainee. (Career Examination Ser.: C-1193). 1994. pap. 19.95 (*0-8373-1193-4*) Nat Learn.
— Climatology - Meteorology. (DANTES Ser.: No. 9). 1994. pap. 23.95 (*0-8373-6609-7*) Nat Learn.
— Climatology - Meteorology. (DANTES Ser.: No. 9). 1994. 39.95 (*0-8373-6509-0*) Nat Learn.
— Climber & Pruner. (Career Examination Ser.: C-148). 1994. pap. 39.95 (*0-8373-0148-3*) Nat Learn.
— Clinic Administrator. (Career Examination Ser.: C-915). 1994. pap. 39.95 (*0-8373-0915-8*) Nat Learn.
— Clinic Supervisor (Drug Abuse) (Career Examination Ser.: C-3007). 1994. pap. 39.95 (*0-8373-3007-6*) Nat Learn.
— Clinical Chemistry. (College Level Examination Ser.: CLEP-32). 1994. 39.95 (*0-8373-5382-3*); pap. 23.95 (*0-8373-5332-7*) Nat Learn.
— Clinical Laboratory Investigator. (Career Examination Ser.: C-2098). 1994. pap. 39.95 (*0-8373-2098-4*) Nat Learn.
— Clinical Nurse. (Career Examination Ser.: C-947). 1994. pap. 29.95 (*0-8373-0947-6*) Nat Learn.
— Clinical Psychologist. (Career Examination Ser.: C-149). 1994. pap. 34.95 (*0-8373-0149-1*) Nat Learn.
— Clinical Psychologist Intern. (Career Examination Ser.: C-1196). 1994. pap. 29.95 (*0-8373-1196-9*) Nat Learn.
— Clinical Specialist in Adult Psychiatric & Mental Health Nursing. (Certified Nurse Examination Ser.: CN-14). 1994. 39.95 (*0-8373-6164-8*); pap. 23.95 (*0-8373-6114-1*) Nat Learn.
— Clinical Specialist in Child & Adolescent Psychiatric & Mental Health Nursing. (Certified Nurse Examination Ser.: CN-15). 1994. 39.95 (*0-8373-6165-6*); pap. 23.95 (*0-8373-6115-X*) Nat Learn.
— Clinical Specialist in Medical-Surgical Nursing. (Certified Nurse Examination Ser.: CN-13). 1994. 39.95 (*0-8373-6163-X*); pap. 23.95 (*0-8373-6113-3*) Nat Learn.
— Clinician. (Career Examination Ser.: C-150). 1994. pap. 34.95 (*0-8373-0150-5*) Nat Learn.
— Clinician, Part-Time. (Career Examination Ser.: C-1197). 1994. pap. 29.95 (*0-8373-1197-7*) Nat Learn.
— Clock Repairer. (Career Examination Ser.: C-151). 1994. pap. 39.95 (*0-8373-0151-3*) Nat Learn.
— Clothing Attendant. (Career Examination Ser.: C-1198). 1994. pap. 23.95 (*0-8373-1198-5*) Nat Learn.
— Code Compliance Assistant. (Career Examination Ser.: C-3186). 1994. pap. 29.95 (*0-8373-3186-2*) Nat Learn.
— Code Compliance Coordinator. (Career Examination Ser.: C-3569). 1994. 39.95 (*0-8373-3569-8*) Nat Learn.
— Code Compliance Supervisor. (Career Examination Ser.: C-3187). 1994. pap. 39.95 (*0-8373-3187-0*) Nat Learn.
— Code Enforcement Officer. (Career Examination Ser.: C-3424). 1994. pap. 34.95 (*0-8373-3424-1*) Nat Learn.
— Collection & Civil Prosecution Specialist. (Career Examination Ser.: Series 1). 1991. pap. 29.95 (*0-8373-3702-X*) Nat Learn.
— Collection Clerk. (Career Examination Ser.: C-3096). 1994. pap. 23.95 (*0-8373-3096-3*) Nat Learn.
— College Administrative Assistant. (Career Examination Ser.: C-152). 1994. pap. 27.95 (*0-8373-0152-1*) Nat Learn.
— College Administrative Associate. (Career Examination Ser.: C-2658). 1994. pap. 29.95 (*0-8373-2658-3*) Nat Learn.
— College Algebra. (College Level Examination Ser.: CLEP-6). 1994. pap. 23.95 (*0-8373-5306-8*) Nat Learn.
— College Algebra-Trigonometry. (College Level Examination Ser.: CLEP-7). 1994. pap. 23.95 (*0-8373-5307-6*) Nat Learn.
— College & University Basic Competency Tests (BCT-C&U) (Admission Test Ser.: ATS-58). 1994. pap. 23.95 (*0-8373-5058-1*) Nat Learn.
— College Chemistry. (DANTES Ser.: No. 10). 1994. pap. 23.95 (*0-8373-6610-0*) Nat Learn.
— College Chemistry. (DANTES Ser.: No. 10). 1994. 39.95 (*0-8373-6510-4*) Nat Learn.
— College Composition. (College Level Examination Ser.: CLEP-11). 1994. pap. 23.95 (*0-8373-5311-4*) Nat Learn.
— College French. (College Level Examination Ser.: CLEP-44). 1994. reprint ed. 39.95 (*0-8373-5394-7*); reprint ed. pap. 23.95 (*0-8373-5344-0*) Nat Learn.
— College Graduate Careers Examination. (Career Examination Ser.: Series 1). 1991. pap. 29.95 (*0-8373-3703-8*) Nat Learn.
— College-Level Examination Series. (Entire Ser.). 1994. pap. write for info. (*0-8373-5300-9*) Nat Learn.
— College Office Assistant A. (Career Examination Ser.: C-153). 1994. pap. 23.95 (*0-8373-0153-X*) Nat Learn.
— College Office Assistant B. (Career Examination Ser.: C-154). 1994. pap. 23.95 (*0-8373-0154-8*) Nat Learn.
— College Proficiency Examination Series. (Entire Ser.). 1994. pap. write for info. (*0-8373-5400-5*) Nat Learn.
— College Secretarial Assistant A. (Career Examination Ser.: C-155). 1994. pap. 23.95 (*0-8373-0155-6*) Nat Learn.
— College Secretarial Assistant B. (Career Examination Ser.: C-156). 1994. pap. 23.95 (*0-8373-0156-4*) Nat Learn.
— College Spanish. (College Level Examination Ser.: CLEP-46). 1994. reprint ed. 39.95 (*0-8373-5396-3*); reprint ed. pap. 23.95 (*0-8373-5346-7*) Nat Learn.
— Colleges of Podiatry Admission Test (CPAT) (Admission Test Ser.: ATS-37). 1994. reprint ed. pap. 29.95 (*0-8373-5037-9*) Nat Learn.
— Commercial & Advertising Art. (Occupational Competency Examination Ser.: OCE-11). 1994. pap. 23.95 (*0-8373-5711-X*) Nat Learn.
— Commercial Photography. (Occupational Competency Examination Ser.: OCE-12). 1994. pap. 23.95 (*0-8373-5712-8*) Nat Learn.
— Commissary Clerk I. (Career Examination Ser.: C-216). 1994. pap. 19.95 (*0-8373-0216-1*) Nat Learn.
— Commissary Clerk II. (Career Examination Ser.: C-217). 1994. pap. 23.95 (*0-8373-0217-X*) Nat Learn.
— Commissary Clerk III. (Career Examination Ser.: C-218). 1994. pap. 27.95 (*0-8373-0218-8*) Nat Learn.
— Commissary Clerk IV. (Career Examination Ser.: C-219). 1994. pap. 27.95 (*0-8373-0219-6*) Nat Learn.
— Commission on Graduates of Foreign Nursing Schools Qualifying Examinations (CGFNS) (Admission Test Ser.: ATS-90). 1994. 45.95 (*0-8373-5190-1*); pap. 29.95 (*0-8373-5090-5*) Nat Learn.
— Commissioner. (Career Examination Ser.: C-1199). 1994. pap. 39.95 (*0-8373-1199-3*) Nat Learn.
— Commissioner of Correction. (Career Examination Ser.: C-1203). 1994. pap. 49.95 (*0-8373-1203-5*) Nat Learn.
— Commissioner of Deeds. (Career Examination Ser.: C-157). 1994. pap. 39.95 (*0-8373-0157-2*) Nat Learn.
— Commissioner of General Services. (Career Examination Ser.: C-1858). 1994. pap. 49.95 (*0-8373-1858-0*) Nat Learn.
— Commissioner of Jurors. (Career Examination Ser.: C-1204). 1994. pap. 39.95 (*0-8373-1204-3*) Nat Learn.
— Commissioner of Police. (Career Examination Ser.: C-1200). 1994. pap. 49.95 (*0-8373-1200-0*) Nat Learn.
— Commissioner of Recreation & Community Services. (Career Examination Ser.: C-1890). 1994. pap. 49.95 (*0-8373-1890-4*) Nat Learn.
— Commissioner of Social Services. (Career Examination Ser.: C-1205). 1994. pap. 49.95 (*0-8373-1205-1*) Nat Learn.
— Common Branches (1-6), Elementary School. (Teachers License Examination Ser.: T-9). 1994. pap. 23.95 (*0-8373-8009-X*) Nat Learn.
— Commonalities in Nursing Care: Area I. (Regents External Degree Ser.: REDP-17). 1994. pap. 23.95 (*0-8373-5617-2*) Nat Learn.
— Commonalities in Nursing Care: Area II. (Regents External Degree Ser.: REDP-18). 1994. pap. 23.95 (*0-8373-5618-0*) Nat Learn.
— Commonalities in Nursing Care, Area 1. (ACT Proficiency Examination Program Ser.: PEP-41). 1994. pap. 23.95 (*0-8373-5541-9*) Nat Learn.
— Commonalities in Nursing Care, Area 2. (ACT Proficiency Examination Program Ser.: PEP-42). 1994. pap. 23.95 (*0-8373-5542-7*) Nat Learn.
— Communications Aide. (Career Examination Ser.: C-1201). 1994. pap. 23.95 (*0-8373-1201-9*) Nat Learn.
— Communications Analyst. (Career Examination Ser.: C-1202). 1994. pap. 27.95 (*0-8373-1202-7*) Nat Learn.
— Communications & Education. (College Proficiency Examination Ser.: CPEP-20). 1994. pap. 23.95 (*0-8373-5420-X*) Nat Learn.
— Communications Operator. (Career Examination Ser.: C-2296). 1994. reprint ed. pap. 19.95 (*0-8373-2296-0*) Nat Learn.
— Communications Technician. (Career Examination Ser.: C-2186). 1994. pap. 23.95 (*0-8373-2186-7*) Nat Learn.
— Community Centers (Physical Education) (Teachers License Examination Ser.: T-10). 1994. pap. 23.95 (*0-8373-8010-3*) Nat Learn.
— Community Development Administrator. (Career Examination Ser.: C-1420). 1994. pap. 39.95 (*0-8373-1420-8*) Nat Learn.
— Community Development Assistant. (Career Examination Ser.: C-904). 1994. pap. 27.95 (*0-8373-0904-2*) Nat Learn.
— Community Development Housing Analyst. (Career Examination Ser.: C-905). 1994. pap. 34.95 (*0-8373-0905-0*) Nat Learn.
— Community Development Program Analyst. (Career Examination Ser.: C-903). 1994. pap. 34.95 (*0-8373-0903-4*) Nat Learn.
— Community Development Program Technician. (Career Examination Ser.: C-902). 1994. pap. 29.95 (*0-8373-0902-6*) Nat Learn.
— Community Development Project Director. (Career Examination Ser.: C-909). 1994. pap. 39.95 (*0-8373-0909-3*) Nat Learn.
— Community Development Project Supervisor. (Career Examination Ser.: C-908). 1994. pap. 34.95 (*0-8373-0908-5*) Nat Learn.
— Community Development Specialist. (Career Examination Ser.: C-1421). 1994. pap. 29.95 (*0-8373-1421-6*) Nat Learn.
— Community Health Nurse. (Certified Nurse Examination Ser.: CN-4). 1994. 39.95 (*0-8373-6154-0*); pap. 23.95 (*0-8373-6104-4*) Nat Learn.
— Community Improvement Coordinator. (Career Examination Ser.: C-906). 1994. pap. 34.95 (*0-8373-0906-9*) Nat Learn.
— Community Liason Worker. (Career Examination Ser.: C-2976). 1994. pap. 23.95 (*0-8373-2976-0*) Nat Learn.
— Community Mental Health Nurse. (Career Examination Ser.: C-3223). 1994. pap. 34.95 (*0-8373-3223-0*) Nat Learn.
— Community Relations Assistant. (Career Examination Ser.: C-1207). 1994. pap. 23.95 (*0-8373-1207-8*) Nat Learn.
— Community Relations Specialist. (Career Examination Ser.: No. C-3535). 1994. 27.95 (*0-8373-3535-3*) Nat Learn.
— Community Residence Aide. (Career Examination Ser.: C-3135). 1994. pap. 23.95 (*0-8373-3135-8*) Nat Learn.
— Community Service Aide. (Career Examination Ser.: C-1402). 1994. pap. 23.95 (*0-8373-1402-X*) Nat Learn.
— Community Service Worker. (Career Examination Ser.: C-2675). 1994. pap. 23.95 (*0-8373-2675-3*) Nat Learn.
— Community Services Assistant. (Career Examination Ser.: C-1403). 1994. pap. 23.95 (*0-8373-1403-8*) Nat Learn.
— Compensation Claims Auditor. (Career Examination Ser.: C-2126). 1994. reprint ed. pap. 29.95 (*0-8373-2126-3*) Nat Learn.
— Compensation Claims Clerk. (Career Examination Ser.: C-866). 1994. pap. 23.95 (*0-8373-0866-6*) Nat Learn.
— Compensation Claims Examiner. (Career Examination Ser.: C-2133). 1994. reprint ed. pap. 27.95 (*0-8373-2133-6*) Nat Learn.
— Compensation Claims Examiner Trainee. (Career Examination Ser.: C-879). 1994. pap. 23.95 (*0-8373-0879-8*) Nat Learn.
— Compensation Claims Investigator. (Career Examination Ser.: C-949). 1994. pap. 27.95 (*0-8373-0949-2*) Nat Learn.
— Compensation Claims Legal Investigator. (Career Examination Ser.: C-2100). 1994. pap. 27.95 (*0-8373-2100-X*) Nat Learn.
— Compensation Investigator. (Career Examination Ser.: C-950). 1994. pap. 27.95 (*0-8373-0950-6*) Nat Learn.
— Complaint Investigator. (Career Examination Ser.: C-1863). 1994. pap. 27.95 (*0-8373-1863-7*) Nat Learn.
— Compliance Investigator. (Career Examination Ser.: C-2421). 1994. pap. 27.95 (*0-8373-2421-1*) Nat Learn.
— Composing Machine Operator. (Career Examination Ser.: C-1223). 1994. pap. 23.95 (*0-8373-1223-X*) Nat Learn.
— Compositor (Job) (Career Examination Ser.: C-2649). 1994. pap. 23.95 (*0-8373-2649-4*) Nat Learn.
— Comprehensive Employment & Training Act (CETA) Trainee. (Career Examination Ser.: C-2505). 1994. pap. 27.95 (*0-8373-2505-6*) Nat Learn.
— Computer Aide. (Career Examination Ser.: C-1208). 1994. pap. 23.95 (*0-8373-1208-6*) Nat Learn.
— Computer Aptitude Test (CAT) (Career Examination Ser.: C-180). 1994. pap. 23.95 (*0-8373-0180-7*) Nat Learn.
— Computer Associate (Applications Programming) (Career Examination Ser.: C-2470). 1994. pap. 29.95 (*0-8373-2470-X*) Nat Learn.
— Computer Associate (Operations) (Career Examination Ser.: C-2471). 1994. pap. 29.95 (*0-8373-2471-8*) Nat Learn.
— Computer Associate (Software) (Career Examination Ser.: C-3002). 1994. pap. 29.95 (*0-8373-3002-5*) Nat Learn.
— Computer Associate (Systems Programming) (Career Examination Ser.: C-2472). 1994. pap. 29.95 (*0-8373-2472-6*) Nat Learn.
— Computer Associate (Technical Support) (Career Examination Ser.: C-2473). 1994. pap. 29.95 (*0-8373-2473-4*) Nat Learn.
— Computer Control Supervisor. (Career Examination Ser.: C-3001). 1994. pap. 34.95 (*0-8373-3001-7*) Nat Learn.
— Computer Equipment Analyst. (Career Examination Ser.: C-1209). 1994. pap. 29.95 (*0-8373-1209-4*) Nat Learn.
— Computer Graphics Mapping Specialist. (Career Examination Ser.: C-3231). 1994. pap. 29.95 (*0-8373-3231-1*) Nat Learn.
— Computer Literacy: Data Processing. (National Teacher Examination Ser.: No. 49). 1994. Cloth bdg. avail. pap. 23.95 (*0-8373-8459-1*) Nat Learn.
— Computer Literacy: Data Processing. (National Teacher Examination Ser.: No. 49). 1994. write for info. (*0-614-03324-1*) Nat Learn.
— Computer Operator. (Career Examination Ser.: C-158). 1994. pap. 23.95 (*0-8373-0158-0*) Nat Learn.
— Computer Operator II. (Career Examination Ser.: C-3151). 1994. pap. 27.95 (*0-8373-3151-X*) Nat Learn.
— Computer Operator III. (Career Examination Ser.: C-3152). 1994. pap. 29.95 (*0-8373-3152-8*) Nat Learn.
— Computer Operator IV. (Career Examination Ser.: C-3153). 1994. pap. 29.95 (*0-8373-3153-6*) Nat Learn.
— Computer Operator Trainee. (Career Examination Ser.: C-878). 1994. pap. 23.95 (*0-8373-0878-X*) Nat Learn.
— Computer Programmer. (Career Examination Ser.: C-159). 1994. pap. 27.95 (*0-8373-0159-9*) Nat Learn.
— Computer Programmer Analyst. (Career Examination Ser.: C-2474). 1994. pap. 27.95 (*0-8373-2474-2*) Nat Learn.
— Computer Programmer Analyst Trainee. (Career Examination Ser.: C-2475). 1994. pap. 23.95 (*0-8373-2475-0*) Nat Learn.
— Computer Programmer Trainee. (Career Examination Ser.: C-160). 1994. pap. 23.95 (*0-8373-0160-2*) Nat Learn.
— Computer Programming Supervisor. (Career Examination Ser.: C-1961). 1994. pap. 34.95 (*0-8373-1961-7*) Nat Learn.
— Computer Science. (Graduate Record Examination Ser.: GRE-21). 1994. 39.95 (*0-8373-5271-1*); pap. 23.95 (*0-8373-5221-5*) Nat Learn.
— Computer Specialist. (Career Examination Ser.: C-161). 1994. pap. 27.95 (*0-8373-0161-0*) Nat Learn.
— Computer Specialist (Applications Programming) (Career Examination Ser.: C-2874). 1994. pap. 29.95 (*0-8373-2874-8*) Nat Learn.
— Computer Specialist (Data Base Administration) (Career Examination Ser.: C-2876). 1994. pap. 29.95 (*0-8373-2876-4*) Nat Learn.
— Computer Specialist (Systems Programming) (Career Examination Ser.: C-2875). 1994. pap. 29.95 (*0-8373-2875-6*) Nat Learn.
— Computer Systems Analyst. (Career Examination Ser.: C-162). 1994. pap. 27.95 (*0-8373-0162-9*) Nat Learn.
— Computer Systems Analyst Trainee. (Career Examination Ser.: C-951). 1994. pap. 23.95 (*0-8373-0951-4*) Nat Learn.
— Computer Systems Manager. (Career Examination Ser.: C-1668). 1994. pap. 34.95 (*0-8373-1668-5*) Nat Learn.
— Computer Technical Assistant. (Career Examination Ser.: C-1210). 1994. pap. 27.95 (*0-8373-1210-8*) Nat Learn.
— Computer Technician. (Career Examination Ser.: C-952). 1994. pap. 29.95 (*0-8373-0952-2*) Nat Learn.
— Computer Technician. (Teachers License Examination Ser.: T-67). 1994. pap. 23.95 (*0-8373-8067-7*) Nat Learn.
— Computers & Data Processing. (College Level Examination Ser.: CLEP-8). 1994. pap. 23.95 (*0-8373-5308-4*) Nat Learn.
— Conductor. (Career Examination Ser.: C-163). 1994. pap. 19.95 (*0-8373-0163-7*) Nat Learn.
— Confidential Attendant. (Career Examination Ser.: C-1211). 1994. pap. 23.95 (*0-8373-1211-6*) Nat Learn.
— Confidential Investigator. (Career Examination Ser.: C-2806). 1994. pap. 27.95 (*0-8373-2806-3*) Nat Learn.
— Confidential Reporter. (Career Examination Ser.: C-1212). 1994. pap. 23.95 (*0-8373-1212-4*) Nat Learn.
— Confidential Secretary. (Career Examination Ser.: C-3023). 1994. pap. 23.95 (*0-8373-3023-8*) Nat Learn.
— Conservation Aide. (Career Examination Ser.: Series 1). 1991. pap. 27.95 (*0-8373-3704-6*) Nat Learn.
— Conservation Biologist. (Career Examination Ser.: C-3126). 1994. pap. 29.95 (*0-8373-3126-9*) Nat Learn.
— Construction Analyst. (Career Examination Ser.: C-1216). 1994. pap. 34.95 (*0-8373-1216-7*) Nat Learn.
— Construction Cost Specialist. (Career Examination Ser.: C-2060). 1994. reprint ed. pap. 34.95 (*0-8373-2060-7*) Nat Learn.
— Construction Inspector. (Career Examination Ser.: C-164). 1994. pap. 29.95 (*0-8373-0164-5*) Nat Learn.
— Construction Inspector II. (Career Examination Ser.: C-3042). 1994. pap. 34.95 (*0-8373-3042-4*) Nat Learn.
— Construction Inspector Trainee. (Career Examination Ser.: C-3167). 1994. pap. 27.95 (*0-8373-3167-6*) Nat Learn.
— Construction Manager. (Career Examination Ser.: C-1789). 1994. pap. 39.95 (*0-8373-1789-4*) Nat Learn.
— Construction Project Manager Intern. (Career Examination Ser.: Series 1). 1991. pap. 27.95 (*0-8373-3734-8*) Nat Learn.
— Consultant. (Career Examination Ser.: C-953). 1994. pap. 34.95 (*0-8373-0953-0*) Nat Learn.
— Consultant (Early Childhood Education) (Career Examination Ser.: C-954). 1994. pap. 34.95 (*0-8373-0954-9*) Nat Learn.
— Consultant in Audiology. (Career Examination Ser.: C-1213). 1994. pap. 34.95 (*0-8373-1213-2*) Nat Learn.
— Consumer Affairs Inspector. (Career Examination Ser.: C-1655). 1994. pap. 23.95 (*0-8373-1655-3*) Nat Learn.
— Consumer Affairs Investigator. (Career Examination Ser.: C-1214). 1994. pap. 23.95 (*0-8373-1214-0*) Nat Learn.
— Consumer Affairs Research Assistant. (Career Examination Ser.: C-1215). 1994. pap. 27.95 (*0-8373-1215-9*) Nat Learn.
— Consumer Affairs Specialist. (Career Examination Ser.: C-1864). 1994. reprint ed. pap. 23.95 (*0-8373-1864-5*) Nat Learn.
— Consumer Frauds Representative. (Career Examination Ser.: C-876). 1994. pap. 23.95 (*0-8373-0876-3*) Nat Learn.
— Contract Specialist. (Career Examination Ser.: C-955). 1994. pap. 27.95 (*0-8373-0955-7*) Nat Learn.
— Contracts Examiner. (Career Examination Ser.: C-888). 1994. pap. 27.95 (*0-8373-0888-7*) Nat Learn.
— Contracts Technician. (Career Examination Ser.: C-834). 1994. pap. 27.95 (*0-8373-0834-8*) Nat Learn.

R

— Control Room Supervisor. (Career Examination Ser.: Series 1). 1991. pap. 34.95 (*0-8373-3705-4*) Nat Learn.
— Cook. (Career Examination Ser.: C-1218). 1994. pap. 27.95 (*0-8373-1218-3*) Nat Learn.
— Coordinator of Child Support Enforcement. (Career Examination Ser.: C-927). 1994. pap. 39.95 (*0-8373-0927-1*) Nat Learn.
— Coordinator of Community Mental Health Services. (Career Examination Ser.: C-1228). 1994. pap. 39.95 (*0-8373-1228-0*) Nat Learn.
— Coordinator of Drainage Designing. (Career Examination Ser.: C-3124). 1994. pap. 39.95 (*0-8373-3124-2*) Nat Learn.
— Coordinator of Drug Abuse Educational Programs. (Career Examination Ser.: C-1767). 1994. pap. 39.95 (*0-8373-1767-3*) Nat Learn.
— Coordinator of Educational Affairs. (Career Examination Ser.: C-2209). 1994. pap. 39.95 (*0-8373-2209-X*) Nat Learn.
— Coordinator of Human Services. (Career Examination Ser.: Series 1). 1991. pap. 39.95 (*0-8373-3706-2*) Nat Learn.
— Coordinator of Laboratory Services. (Career Examination Ser.: C-1227). 1994. pap. 39.95 (*0-8373-1227-2*) Nat Learn.
— Coordinator of Nursing Education. (Career Examination Ser.: C-1843). 1994. pap. 39.95 (*0-8373-1843-2*) Nat Learn.
— Coordinator of Surveying Services. (Career Examination Ser.: C-3022). 1994. pap. 39.95 (*0-8373-3022-X*) Nat Learn.
— Coordinator of Volunteer Services. (Career Examination Ser.: C-3110). 1994. pap. 39.95 (*0-8373-3110-2*) Nat Learn.
— Coordinator, Senior Citizen Planning & Research. (Career Examination Ser.: C-2939). 1994. pap. 39.95 (*0-8373-2939-6*) Nat Learn.
— Correction Captain. (Career Examination Ser.: C-165). 1994. pap. 29.95 (*0-8373-0165-3*) Nat Learn.
— Correction Counselor. (Career Examination Ser.: C-2593). 1994. pap. 29.95 (*0-8373-2593-5*) Nat Learn.
— Correction Counselor Trainee. (Career Examination Ser.: C-2999). 1994. pap. 27.95 (*0-8373-2999-X*) Nat Learn.
— Correction Hospital Officer (Men) (Career Examination Ser.: C-956a). 1994. pap. 27.95 (*0-8373-0956-5*) Nat Learn.
— Correction Hospital Officer (Women) (Career Examination Ser.: C-956b). 1994. pap. 27.95 (*0-685-03521-2*) Nat Learn.
— Correction Lieutenant. (Career Examination Ser.: C-166). 1994. pap. 29.95 (*0-8373-0166-1*) Nat Learn.
— Correction Matron. (Career Examination Ser.: C-1219). 1994. pap. 23.95 (*0-8373-1219-1*) Nat Learn.
— Correction Officer. (Career Examination Ser.: C-3019). 1994. pap. 23.95 (*0-8373-3019-X*) Nat Learn.
— Correction Officer I. (Career Examination Ser.: C-837). 1994. pap. 23.95 (*0-8373-0837-2*) Nat Learn.
— Correction Officer II. (Career Examination Ser.: C-838). 1994. pap. 27.95 (*0-8373-0838-0*) Nat Learn.
— Correction Officer III. (Career Examination Ser.: C-839). 1994. pap. 27.95 (*0-8373-0839-9*) Nat Learn.
— Correction Officer IV. (Career Examination Ser.: C-840). 1994. pap. 29.95 (*0-8373-0840-2*) Nat Learn.
— Correction Officer (Men) (Career Examination Ser.: C-167). 1994. pap. 23.95 (*0-8373-0167-X*) Nat Learn.
— Correction Officer Trainee. (Career Examination Ser.: C-957). 1994. pap. 19.95 (*0-8373-0957-3*) Nat Learn.
— Correction Officer (Women) (Career Examination Ser.: C-168). 1994. pap. 23.95 (*0-8373-0168-8*) Nat Learn.
— Correction Promotion Course. (General Aptitude & Abilities Ser.: CS-25). 1994. pap. 29.95 (*0-8373-6725-5*) Nat Learn.
— Correction Sergeant. (Career Examination Ser.: C-169). 1994. pap. 27.95 (*0-8373-0169-6*) Nat Learn.
— Correction Youth Camp Officer (Men) (Career Examination Ser.: C-958a). 1994. pap. 23.95 (*0-8373-0958-1*) Nat Learn.
— Correction Youth Camp Officer (Women) (Career Examination Ser.: C-958b). 1994. pap. 23.95 (*0-685-03522-0*) Nat Learn.
— Correctional Treatment Specialist. (Career Examination Ser.: C-959). 1994. pap. 34.95 (*0-8373-0959-X*) Nat Learn.
— Corrective & Remedial Instruction in Reading. (College Proficiency Examination Ser.: CPEP-31). 1994. pap. 23.95 (*0-8373-5431-5*) Nat Learn.
— Corrective & Remedial Instruction in Reading. (ACT Proficiency Examination Program Ser.: PEP-32). 1994. pap. 23.95 (*0-8373-5532-X*) Nat Learn.
— Corrective Therapist. (Career Examination Ser.: C-960). 1994. pap. 29.95 (*0-8373-0960-3*) Nat Learn.
— Correctness & Effectiveness of English Expression (G. E. D.) (General Aptitude & Abilities Ser.: CS-35). 1994. pap. 17.95 (*0-8373-6735-2*) Nat Learn.
— Cosmetologist. (Career Examination Ser.: C-2251). 1994. pap. 29.95 (*0-8373-2251-0*) Nat Learn.
— Cosmetology. (Occupational Competency Examination Ser.: No. 13). 1994. pap. 23.95 (*0-8373-5713-6*) Nat Learn.
— Cosmetology. (Teachers License Examination Ser.: T-71). 1994. pap. 23.95 (*0-8373-8071-5*) Nat Learn.
— Cost & Statistical Analyst. (Career Examination Ser.: C-3561). 1994. 39.95 (*0-8373-3561-2*) Nat Learn.
— Counselor. (Career Examination Ser.: C-1162). 1994. pap. 29.95 (*0-8373-1162-4*) Nat Learn.
— County Attorney. (Career Examination Ser.: C-1220). 1994. pap. 39.95 (*0-8373-1220-5*) Nat Learn.
— County Clerk. (Career Examination Ser.: C-2114). 1994. pap. 29.95 (*0-8373-2114-X*) Nat Learn.
— County Comptroller. (Career Examination Ser.: C-1222). 1994. pap. 39.95 (*0-8373-1222-1*) Nat Learn.
— County Director of Accounting. (Career Examination Ser.: C-1960). 1994. pap. 39.95 (*0-8373-1960-9*) Nat Learn.
— County Executive. (Career Examination Ser.: C-1224). 1994. pap. 49.95 (*0-8373-1224-8*) Nat Learn.
— County Treasurer. (Career Examination Ser.: C-1255). 1994. pap. 39.95 (*0-8373-1225-6*) Nat Learn.
— Court Assistant. (Career Examination Ser.: C-1226). 1994. pap. 19.95 (*0-8373-1226-4*) Nat Learn.
— Court Assistant I. (Career Examination Ser.: C-961). 1994. pap. 23.95 (*0-8373-0961-1*) Nat Learn.
— Court Assistant II. (Career Examination Ser.: C-962). 1994. pap. 27.95 (*0-8373-0962-X*) Nat Learn.
— Court Attendant. (Career Examination Ser.: C-170). 1994. pap. 23.95 (*0-8373-0170-X*) Nat Learn.
— Court Clerk. (Career Examination Ser.: C-171). 1994. pap. 27.95 (*0-8373-0171-8*) Nat Learn.
— Court Clerk I. (Career Examination Ser.: C-963). 1994. pap. 27.95 (*0-8373-0963-8*) Nat Learn.
— Court Clerk II. (Career Examination Ser.: C-964). 1994. pap. 29.95 (*0-8373-0964-6*) Nat Learn.
— Court Consultation Specialist. (Career Examination Ser.: Series 1). 1991. pap. 34.95 (*0-8373-3707-0*) Nat Learn.
— Court Hearing Reporter. (Career Examination Ser.: C-172). 1994. pap. 23.95 (*0-8373-0172-6*) Nat Learn.
— Court Law Stenographer. (Career Examination Ser.: C-173). 1994. pap. 23.95 (*0-8373-0173-4*) Nat Learn.
— Court Office Assistant. (Career Examination Ser.: C-965). 1994. pap. 23.95 (*0-8373-0965-4*) Nat Learn.
— Court Officer. (Career Examination Ser.: C-966). 1994. pap. 19.95 (*0-8373-0966-2*) Nat Learn.
— Court Officer Sergeant. (Career Examination Ser.: No. C-3508). 1994. 27.95 (*0-8373-3508-6*) Nat Learn.
— Court Records Supervisor. (Career Examination Ser.: C-3160). 1994. pap. 29.95 (*0-8373-3160-9*) Nat Learn.
— Court Reporter. (Career Examination Ser.: C-174). 1994. pap. 23.95 (*0-8373-0174-2*) Nat Learn.
— Court Reporter I. (Career Examination Ser.: C-967). 1994. pap. 23.95 (*0-8373-0967-0*) Nat Learn.
— Court Reporter II. (Career Examination Ser.: C-968). 1994. pap. 27.95 (*0-8373-0968-9*) Nat Learn.
— Crane Operator (Any Motive Power Except Steam) (AMPES) (Career Examination Ser.: C-1749). 1994. pap. 27.95 (*0-8373-1749-5*) Nat Learn.
— Credit & Collection Coordinator. (Career Examination Ser.: C-3107). 1994. pap. 34.95 (*0-8373-3107-2*) Nat Learn.
— Crime & Delinquency Prevention Specialist. (Career Examination Ser.: C-3212). 1994. pap. 34.95 (*0-8373-3212-5*) Nat Learn.
— Crime Victims' Advocate. (Career Examination Ser.: C-3497). 1994. pap. 34.95 (*0-8373-3497-7*) Nat Learn.
— Crime Victims' Advocate. (Career Examination Ser.: C-3497). 1994. write for info. (*0-614-03325-X*) Nat Learn.
— Criminal Identification Technician. (Career Examination Ser.: C-3105). 1994. pap. 29.95 (*0-8373-3105-6*) Nat Learn.
— Criminal Investigation. (College Proficiency Examination Ser.: CPEP-30). 1994. pap. 23.95 (*0-8373-5430-7*) Nat Learn.
— Criminal Investigation. (ACT Proficiency Examination Program Ser.: PEP-9). 1994. pap. 23.95 (*0-8373-5509-5*) Nat Learn.
— Criminal Investigator. (Career Examination Ser.: C-1229). 1994. pap. 29.95 (*0-8373-1229-9*) Nat Learn.
— Criminal Law Investigator. (Career Examination Ser.: C-969). 1994. pap. 29.95 (*0-8373-0969-7*) Nat Learn.
— Criminalist. (Career Examination Ser.: No. C-3511). 1994. 39.95 (*0-8373-3511-6*) Nat Learn.
— Criminology. (DANTES Ser.: No. 11). 1994. pap. 23.95 (*0-8373-6611-9*) Nat Learn.
— Criminology. (DANTES Ser.: No. 11). 1994. 39.95 (*0-8373-6511-2*) Nat Learn.
— Crisis Intervention Worker. (Career Examination Ser.: Series 1). 1991. pap. 27.95 (*0-8373-3708-9*) Nat Learn.
— Cultural Affairs Supervisor. (Career Examination Ser.: C-2860). 1991. pap. 22.00 (*0-8373-2860-8*) Nat Learn.
— Cultural Program Assistant. (Career Examination Ser.: No. C-3540). 1994. 27.95 (*0-8373-3540-X*) Nat Learn.
— Custodial Assistant (Men) (Career Examination Ser.: C-141a). 1994. pap. 19.95 (*0-8373-0141-6*) Nat Learn.
— Custodial Assistant (Women) (Career Examination Ser.: C-141b). 1994. pap. 19.95 (*0-614-03327-6*) Nat Learn.
— Custodial Foreman. (Career Examination Ser.: C-970). 1994. pap. 27.95 (*0-8373-0970-0*) Nat Learn.
— Custodial Laborer (USPS) (Career Examination Ser.: C-3316). 1994. pap. 23.95 (*0-8373-3316-4*) Nat Learn.
— Custodial Work Supervisor. (Career Examination Ser.: C-1231). 1994. pap. 29.95 (*0-8373-1231-0*) Nat Learn.
— Custodial Worker. (Career Examination Ser.: C-1230). 1994. pap. 23.95 (*0-8373-1230-2*) Nat Learn.
— Custodian. (Career Examination Ser.: C-175). 1994. pap. 23.95 (*0-8373-0175-0*) Nat Learn.
— Custodian-Engineer. (Career Examination Ser.: C-176). 1994. pap. 23.95 (*0-8373-0176-9*) Nat Learn.
— Customer Service Representative. (Career Examination Ser.: C-3605). 1994. 29.95 (*0-8373-3605-8*) Nat Learn.
— Customhouse Brokers License Examination. (Admission Test Ser.: ATS-7). 1994. pap. 39.95 (*0-8373-5007-7*) Nat Learn.
— Customs Aide. (Career Examination Ser.: C-3442). 1994. pap. 19.95 (*0-8373-3442-X*) Nat Learn.
— Customs Inspector. (Career Examination Ser.: C-177). 1994. pap. 23.95 (*0-8373-0177-7*) Nat Learn.
— Customs Security Officer (Sky Marshal) (Career Examination Ser.: C-1611). 1994. pap. 23.95 (*0-8373-1611-1*) Nat Learn.
— Dairy Products Specialist. (Career Examination Ser.: C-3117). 1994. pap. 29.95 (*0-8373-3117-X*) Nat Learn.
— Dance, Jr. H. S. (Teachers License Examination Ser.: T-64). 1994. pap. 23.95 (*0-8373-8064-2*) Nat Learn.
— Data Base Coordinator. (Career Examination Ser.: C-3232). 1994. pap. 34.95 (*0-8373-3232-X*) Nat Learn.
— Data Base Manager. (Career Examination Ser.: C-2873). 1991. pap. 24.00 (*0-8373-2873-X*) Nat Learn.
— Data Base Programmer Analyst. (Career Examination Ser.: C-3233). 1994. pap. 29.95 (*0-8373-3233-8*) Nat Learn.
— Data Collection Clerk. (Career Examination Ser.: C-1233). 1994. pap. 23.95 (*0-8373-1233-7*) Nat Learn.
— Data Communications Specialist. (Career Examination Ser.: C-3234). 1994. pap. 29.95 (*0-8373-3234-6*) Nat Learn.
— Data Control Assistant. (Career Examination Ser.: C-2889). 1994. pap. 23.95 (*0-8373-2889-6*) Nat Learn.
— Data Control Specialist. (Career Examination Ser.: C-901). 1994. pap. 27.95 (*0-8373-0901-8*) Nat Learn.
— Data Conversion Operator (USPS) (Career Examination Ser.: C-1609). 1994. pap. 29.95 (*0-8373-1609-X*) Nat Learn.
— Data Entry Machine Operator. (Career Examination Ser.: C-2409). 1994. pap. 23.95 (*0-8373-2409-2*) Nat Learn.
— Data Entry Supervisor. (Career Examination Ser.: C-1232). 1994. pap. 29.95 (*0-8373-1232-9*) Nat Learn.
— Data Processing. (Occupational Competency Examination Ser.: OCE-14). 1994. pap. 23.95 (*0-8373-5714-4*) Nat Learn.
— Data Processing Clerk I. (Career Examination Ser.: C-536). 1994. pap. 19.95 (*0-8373-0536-5*) Nat Learn.
— Data Processing Clerk II. (Career Examination Ser.: C-537). 1994. pap. 23.95 (*0-8373-0537-3*) Nat Learn.
— Data Processing Clerk III. (Career Examination Ser.: C-538). 1994. pap. 27.95 (*0-8373-0538-1*) Nat Learn.
— Data Processing Control Clerk. (Career Examination Ser.: C-2483). 1994. pap. 19.95 (*0-8373-2483-1*) Nat Learn.
— Data Processing Equipment Operator. (Career Examination Ser.: C-2301). 1994. pap. 23.95 (*0-8373-2301-0*) Nat Learn.
— Data Processing Operations Coordinator. (Career Examination Ser.: C-2759). 1994. pap. 34.95 (*0-8373-2759-8*) Nat Learn.
— Data Processing Operations Supervisor. (Career Examination Ser.: C-2347). 1994. pap. 29.95 (*0-8373-2347-9*) Nat Learn.
— Data Processing Specialist. (Career Examination Ser.: C-2242). 1994. pap. 29.95 (*0-8373-2242-1*) Nat Learn.
— Data Transcriber. (Career Examination Ser.: C-1634). 1994. reprint ed. pap. 23.95 (*0-8373-1634-0*) Nat Learn.
— Day Care Center Aide. (Career Examination Ser.: C-1235). 1994. pap. 23.95 (*0-8373-1235-3*) Nat Learn.
— Deaf & Hard of Hearing. (Teachers License Examination Ser.: T-11). 1994. pap. 23.95 (*0-8373-8011-1*) Nat Learn.
— Deckhand. (Career Examination Ser.: C-190). 1994. pap. 29.95 (*0-8373-0190-4*) Nat Learn.
— Demolition Inspector. (Career Examination Ser.: C-191). 1994. pap. 29.95 (*0-8373-0191-2*) Nat Learn.
— Dental Admission Test (DAT) (Admission Test Ser.: ATS-12). 1994. pap. 23.95 (*0-8373-5012-3*) Nat Learn.
— Dental Assistant. (Career Examination Ser.: C-205). 1994. pap. 29.95 (*0-8373-0205-6*) Nat Learn.
— Dental Assisting. (Occupational Competency Examination Ser.: OCE-15). 1994. pap. 23.95 (*0-8373-5715-2*) Nat Learn.
— Dental Auxiliary Education Examination in Dental Materials. (College Level Examination Ser.: CLEP-47). 1994. 39.95 (*0-8373-5397-1*); pap. 23.95 (*0-8373-5347-5*) Nat Learn.
— Dental Auxiliary Education Examination in Head, Neck & Oral Anatomy. (College Level Examination Ser.: CLEP-48). 1994. 39.95 (*0-8373-5398-X*); pap. 23.95 (*0-8373-5348-3*) Nat Learn.
— Dental Auxiliary Education Examination in Oral Radiography. (College Level Examination Ser.: CLEP-49). 1994. 39.95 (*0-8373-5399-8*); pap. 23.95 (*0-8373-5349-1*) Nat Learn.
— Dental Auxiliary Education Examination in Tooth Morphology & Function. (College Level Examination Ser.: CLEP-50). 1994. 39.95 (*0-8373-5975-9*); pap. 23.95 (*0-8373-5950-3*) Nat Learn.
— Dental Hygiene Aptitude Test (DHAT) (Admission Test Ser.: ATS-32). 1994. pap. 23.95 (*0-8373-5032-8*) Nat Learn.
— Dental Hygienist. (Career Examination Ser.: C-192). 1994. pap. 29.95 (*0-8373-0192-0*) Nat Learn.
— Dentist. (Career Examination Ser.: C-193). 1994. pap. 49.95 (*0-8373-0193-9*) Nat Learn.
— Denver Proficiency & Review Program (PRP) (Admission Test Ser.: ATS-66). 1994. pap. 23.95 (*0-8373-5066-2*) Nat Learn.
— Department Librarian. (Career Examination Ser.: C-194). 1994. pap. 27.95 (*0-8373-0194-7*) Nat Learn.
— Department Library Aide. (Career Examination Ser.: C-206). 1994. pap. 23.95 (*0-8373-0206-4*) Nat Learn.
— Department Senior Librarian. (Career Examination Ser.: C-1622). 1994. pap. 29.95 (*0-8373-1622-7*) Nat Learn.
— Deputy. (Career Examination Ser.: C-1236). 1994. pap. 29.95 (*0-8373-1236-1*) Nat Learn.
— Deputy Assessor. (Career Examination Ser.: C-1237). 1994. pap. 23.95 (*0-8373-1237-X*) Nat Learn.
— Deputy Chief Clerk. (Career Examination Ser.: C-1238). 1994. pap. 29.95 (*0-8373-1238-8*) Nat Learn.
— Deputy Chief, Fire Department. (Career Examination Ser.: C-195). 1994. pap. 34.95 (*0-8373-0195-5*) Nat Learn.
— Deputy Chief Fire Marshal (Uniformed) (Career Examination Ser.: C-2169). 1994. pap. 39.95 (*0-8373-2169-7*) Nat Learn.
— Deputy Chief Marshal. (Career Examination Ser.: C-1239). 1994. pap. 34.95 (*0-8373-1239-6*) Nat Learn.
— Deputy Chief Medical Examiner. (Career Examination Ser.: C-2723). 1994. pap. 49.95 (*0-8373-2723-7*) Nat Learn.
— Deputy Chief Registrar. (Career Examination Ser.: C-1240). 1994. pap. 34.95 (*0-8373-1240-X*) Nat Learn.
— Deputy City Chamberlain. (Career Examination Ser.: C-2982). 1994. pap. 34.95 (*0-8373-2982-5*) Nat Learn.
— Deputy Commissioner. (Career Examination Ser.: C-1241). 1994. pap. 39.95 (*0-8373-1241-8*) Nat Learn.
— Deputy Commissioner of Commerce & Industry. (Career Examination Ser.: C-1990). 1994. pap. 39.95 (*0-8373-1990-0*) Nat Learn.
— Deputy Commissioner of General Services. (Career Examination Ser.: C-1859). 1994. pap. 39.95 (*0-8373-1859-9*) Nat Learn.
— Deputy Commissioner of Jurors. (Career Examination Ser.: C-1242). 1994. pap. 39.95 (*0-8373-1242-6*) Nat Learn.
— Deputy Commissioner of Recreation & Community Services. (Career Examination Ser.: C-1891). 1994. pap. 39.95 (*0-8373-1891-2*) Nat Learn.
— Deputy Comptroller. (Career Examination Ser.: C-1243). 1994. pap. 39.95 (*0-8373-1243-4*) Nat Learn.
— Deputy County Attorney. (Career Examination Ser.: C-1244). 1994. pap. 39.95 (*0-8373-1244-2*) Nat Learn.
— Deputy County Clerk. (Career Examination Ser.: C-1772). 1994. pap. 29.95 (*0-8373-1772-X*) Nat Learn.
— Deputy Director of Administration. (Career Examination Ser.: C-1853). 1994. pap. 39.95 (*0-8373-1853-X*) Nat Learn.
— Deputy Director of Planning. (Career Examination Ser.: C-1708). 1994. pap. 39.95 (*0-8373-1708-8*) Nat Learn.
— Deputy Medical Examiner. (Career Examination Ser.: C-1245). 1994. pap. 44.95 (*0-8373-1245-0*) Nat Learn.
— Deputy Probation Director. (Career Examination Ser.: C-2263). 1994. pap. 39.95 (*0-8373-2263-4*) Nat Learn.
— Deputy Probation Director IV. (Career Examination Ser.: C-1900). 1994. pap. 39.95 (*0-8373-1900-5*) Nat Learn.
— Deputy Registrar. (Career Examination Ser.: C-1246). 1994. pap. 29.95 (*0-8373-1246-9*) Nat Learn.
— Deputy Sheriff. (Career Examination Ser.: C-204). 1994. pap. 23.95 (*0-8373-0204-8*) Nat Learn.
— Deputy Superintendent of Highways. (Career Examination Ser.: C-2319). 1994. pap. 39.95 (*0-8373-2319-3*) Nat Learn.
— Deputy Superintendent of Women's Prisons. (Career Examination Ser.: C-1763). 1994. pap. 49.95 (*0-8373-1763-0*) Nat Learn.
— Deputy Town Assessor. (Career Examination Ser.: C-2184). 1994. pap. 23.95 (*0-8373-2184-0*) Nat Learn.
— Deputy Town Clerk. (Career Examination Ser.: C-1855). 1994. reprint ed. pap. 29.95 (*0-8373-1855-6*) Nat Learn.
— Deputy United States Marshal. (Career Examination Ser.: C-1620). 1994. pap. 23.95 (*0-8373-1620-0*) Nat Learn.
— Deputy Warden. (Career Examination Ser.: C-1762). 1994. reprint ed. pap. 49.95 (*0-8373-1762-2*) Nat Learn.
— Detective Investigator. (Career Examination Ser.: C-1247). 1994. pap. 34.95 (*0-8373-1247-7*) Nat Learn.
— Developmental Disabilities Program Aide. (Career Examination Ser.: C-864). 1994. pap. 23.95 (*0-8373-0864-X*) Nat Learn.
— Developmental Specialist. (Career Examination Ser.: C-923). 1994. pap. 27.95 (*0-8373-0923-9*) Nat Learn.
— Diagnosis & Remediation of Reading Problems. (College Proficiency Examination Ser.: CPEP-38). 1994. pap. 23.95 (*0-8373-5438-2*) Nat Learn.
— Dictating Machine Transcriber. (Career Examination Ser.: C-1248). 1994. pap. 23.95 (*0-8373-1248-5*) Nat Learn.
— Diesel Engine Repair. (Occupational Competency Examination Ser.: OCE-16). 1994. pap. 23.95 (*0-8373-5716-0*) Nat Learn.
— Dietitian. (Career Examination Ser.: C-196). 1994. pap. 23.95 (*0-8373-0196-3*) Nat Learn.
— Differences in Nursing Care: Area 1. (ACT Proficiency Examination Program Ser.: PEP-43). 1994. pap. 23.95 (*0-8373-5543-5*) Nat Learn.
— Differences in Nursing Care: Area 1. (Regents External Degree Ser.: REDP-21). 1994. pap. 23.95 (*0-8373-5621-0*) Nat Learn.
— Differences in Nursing Care: Area 2. (ACT Proficiency Examination Program Ser.: PEP-44). 1994. pap. 23.95 (*0-8373-5544-3*) Nat Learn.
— Differences in Nursing Care: Area 2. (Regents External Degree Ser.: REDP-22). 1994. pap. 23.95 (*0-8373-5622-9*) Nat Learn.
— Differences in Nursing Care: Area 3. (ACT Proficiency Examination Program Ser.: PEP-45). 1994. pap. 23.95 (*0-8373-5545-1*) Nat Learn.
— Differences in Nursing Care: Area 3. (Regents External Degree Ser.: REDP-23). 1994. pap. 23.95 (*0-8373-5623-7*) Nat Learn.
— Differential Equations. (DANTES Ser.: No. 12). 1994. pap. 23.95 (*0-8373-6612-7*) Nat Learn.
— Differential Equations. (DANTES Ser.: No. 12). 1994. 39.95 (*0-8373-6512-0*) Nat Learn.
— Digital Computer Operator. (Career Examination Ser.: C-197). 1994. pap. 23.95 (*0-8373-0197-1*) Nat Learn.
— Digital Computer Programmer. (Career Examination Ser.: C-198). 1994. pap. 27.95 (*0-8373-0198-X*) Nat Learn.
— Digital Computer Specialist. (Career Examination Ser.: C-199). 1994. pap. 27.95 (*0-8373-0199-8*) Nat Learn.
— Digital Computer Systems Analyst. (Career Examination Ser.: C-200). 1994. pap. 27.95 (*0-8373-0200-5*) Nat Learn.
— Digital Computer Systems Operator. (Career Examination Ser.: C-1249). 1994. pap. 223.95 (*0-8373-1249-3*) Nat Learn.
— Digital Computer Systems Programmer. (Career Examination Ser.: C-1250). 1994. pap. 27.95 (*0-8373-1250-7*) Nat Learn.
— Digital Computer Systems Specialist. (Career Examination Ser.: C-1251). 1994. pap. 27.95 (*0-8373-1251-5*) Nat Learn.

R

— Digital Computer Systems Technician. (Career Examination Ser.: C-1252). 1994. pap. 29.95 (*0-8373-1252-3*) Nat Learn.
— Director. (Career Examination Ser.: C-1253). 1994. pap. 39.95 (*0-8373-1253-1*) Nat Learn.
— Director of Administration. (Career Examination Ser.: C-2189). 1994. pap. 44.95 (*0-8373-2189-1*) Nat Learn.
— Director of Administrative Services. (Career Examination Ser.: C-2177). 1994. pap. 44.95 (*0-8373-2177-8*) Nat Learn.
— Director of Advertising. (Career Examination Ser.: C-1865). 1994. pap. 39.95 (*0-8373-1865-3*) Nat Learn.
— Director of Animal Shelter & Control. (Career Examination Ser.: C-548). 1994. pap. 39.95 (*0-8373-0548-9*) Nat Learn.
— Director of Building & Housing. (Career Examination Ser.: C-3087). 1994. pap. 44.95 (*0-8373-3087-4*) Nat Learn.
— Director of Cemeteries. (Career Examination Ser.: C-2794). 1994. pap. 39.95 (*0-8373-2794-6*) Nat Learn.
— Director of Child Care Program. (Career Examination Ser.: Series 1). 1991. pap. 39.95 (*0-8373-3709-7*) Nat Learn.
— Director of Child Support Enforcement Bureau. (Career Examination Ser.: C-928). 1994. pap. 39.95 (*0-8373-0928-X*) Nat Learn.
— Director of Citizens' Affairs. (Career Examination Ser.: Series 1). 1991. pap. 39.95 (*0-8373-3710-0*) Nat Learn.
— Director of Community Development. (Career Examination Ser.: C-2813). 1994. pap. 39.95 (*0-8373-2813-6*) Nat Learn.
— Director of Community Relations. (Career Examination Ser.: C-1856). 1994. pap. 39.95 (*0-8373-1856-4*) Nat Learn.
— Director of Conservation. (Career Examination Ser.: C-1296). 1994. pap. 39.95 (*0-8373-1296-5*) Nat Learn.
— Director of Custodial & Security Services. (Career Examination Ser.: C-2923). 1994. pap. 39.95 (*0-8373-2923-X*) Nat Learn.
— Director of Data Entry Operations. (Career Examination Ser.: C-3286). 1994. pap. 39.95 (*0-8373-3286-9*) Nat Learn.
— Director of Data Processing. (Career Examination Ser.: C-2518). 1994. pap. 39.95 (*0-8373-2518-8*) Nat Learn.
— Director of Drug Treatment Services. (Career Examination Ser.: C-2821). 1994. pap. 39.95 (*0-8373-2821-7*) Nat Learn.
— Director of Engineering, Building & Housing. (Career Examination Ser.: C-2391). 1994. pap. 44.95 (*0-8373-2391-6*) Nat Learn.
— Director of Fire Safety. (Career Examination Ser.: C-2396). 1994. pap. 39.95 (*0-8373-2396-7*) Nat Learn.
— Director of Graphics & Production. (Career Examination Ser.: C-1795). 1994. pap. 39.95 (*0-8373-1795-9*) Nat Learn.
— Director of Human Development. (Career Examination Ser.: C-3235). 1994. pap. 44.95 (*0-8373-3235-4*) Nat Learn.
— Director of Industrial Development. (Career Examination Ser.: C-2857). 1994. pap. 44.95 (*0-8373-2857-8*) Nat Learn.
— Director of Library. (Career Examination Ser.: C-1254). 1994. pap. 39.95 (*0-8373-1254-X*) Nat Learn.
— Director of Maintenance. (Career Examination Ser.: C-2812). 1994. pap. 39.95 (*0-8373-2812-8*) Nat Learn.
— Director of Materials Testing. (Career Examination Ser.: C-3236). 1994. pap. 44.95 (*0-8373-3236-2*) Nat Learn.
— Director of Nursing Care. (Career Examination Ser.: C-2859). 1994. pap. 39.95 (*0-8373-2859-4*) Nat Learn.
— Director of Office Services. (Career Examination Ser.: C-1857). 1994. pap. 39.95 (*0-8373-1857-2*) Nat Learn.
— Director of Office Systems. (Career Examination Ser.: C-3348). 1994. pap. 39.95 (*0-8373-3348-2*) Nat Learn.
— Director of Operations. (Career Examination Ser.: C-1827). 1994. pap. 39.95 (*0-8373-1827-0*) Nat Learn.
— Director of Parks & Recreation. (Career Examination Ser.: C-3349). 1994. pap. 39.95 (*0-8373-3349-0*) Nat Learn.
— Director of Patient Services. (Career Examination Ser.: C-2724). 1994. pap. 39.95 (*0-8373-2724-5*) Nat Learn.
— Director of Personnel. (Career Examination Ser.: C-2083). 1994. reprint ed. pap. 44.95 (*0-8373-2083-6*) Nat Learn.
— Director of Physical Development. (Career Examination Ser.: C-914). 1994. pap. 44.95 (*0-8373-0914-X*) Nat Learn.
— Director of Program Planning. (Career Examination Ser.: C-2408). 1994. pap. 44.95 (*0-8373-2408-4*) Nat Learn.
— Director of Public Information. (Career Examination Ser.: C-1866). 1994. pap. 39.95 (*0-8373-1866-1*) Nat Learn.
— Director of Purchasing. (Career Examination Ser.: C-1950). 1994. pap. 39.95 (*0-8373-1950-1*) Nat Learn.
— Director of Registrants. (Career Examination Ser.: C-1255). 1994. pap. 39.95 (*0-8373-1255-8*) Nat Learn.
— Director of Research & Evaluation. (Career Examination Ser.: C-2891). 1994. pap. 44.95 (*0-8373-2891-8*) Nat Learn.
— Director of School Facilities & Operations. (Career Examination Ser.: C-2072). 1994. pap. 39.95 (*0-8373-2072-0*) Nat Learn.
— Director of Security. (Career Examination Ser.: C-2444). 1994. pap. 39.95 (*0-8373-2444-0*) Nat Learn.
— Director of Social Services. (Career Examination Ser.: C-2666). 1994. pap. 44.95 (*0-8373-2666-4*) Nat Learn.
— Director of Traffic Control. (Career Examination Ser.: C-1877). 1994. pap. 39.95 (*0-8373-1877-7*) Nat Learn.
— Director of Traffic Safety. (Career Examination Ser.: C-527). 1994. pap. 39.95 (*0-8373-0527-6*) Nat Learn.
— Director of Training. (Career Examination Ser.: C-2460). 1994. pap. 44.95 (*0-8373-2460-2*) Nat Learn.
— Director of Transportation Operations. (Career Examination Ser.: C-114). 1994. pap. 39.95 (*0-8373-0114-9*) Nat Learn.
— Director of Weights & Measures. (Career Examination Ser.: C-3350). 1994. pap. 39.95 (*0-8373-3350-4*) Nat Learn.
— Director of Youth Bureau. (Career Examination Ser.: C-2325). 1994. pap. 39.95 (*0-8373-2325-8*) Nat Learn.
— Dishwasher. (Career Examination Ser.: C-1256). 1994. 23.95 (*0-8373-1256-6*) Nat Learn.
— Dispatcher. (Career Examination Ser.: C-213). 1994. pap. 23.95 (*0-8373-0213-7*) Nat Learn.
— Distribution Clerk - Machine (U. S. P. S.) (Career Examination Ser.: C-2255). 1994. pap. 19.95 (*0-8373-2255-3*) Nat Learn.
— Distributive Education (Merchandising & Salesmanship), Sr. H. S. (Teachers License Examination Ser.: T-12). 1994. pap. 23.95 (*0-8373-8012-X*) Nat Learn.
— District Administrator, Public Health. (Career Examination Ser.: C-3006). 1994. pap. 44.95 (*0-8373-3006-8*) Nat Learn.
— District Attorney. (Career Examination Ser.: C-1257). 1994. pap. 49.95 (*0-8373-1257-4*) Nat Learn.
— District Business Officer. (Career Examination Ser.: C-1726). 1994. pap. 34.95 (*0-8373-1726-6*) Nat Learn.
— District Director (Social Services) (Career Examination Ser.: C-2990). 1994. pap. 39.95 (*0-8373-2990-6*) Nat Learn.
— District Foreman (Department of Sanitation) (Career Examination Ser.: C-207). 1994. pap. 27.95 (*0-8373-0207-2*) Nat Learn.
— District Foreman (Highway Maintenance) (Career Examination Ser.: C-1978). 1994. pap. 27.95 (*0-8373-1978-1*) Nat Learn.
— District Foreman (Sewer Maintenance) (Career Examination Ser.: C-1815). 1994. pap. 27.95 (*0-8373-1815-7*) Nat Learn.
— District Foreman (Water Supply) (Career Examination Ser.: C-2037). 1994. pap. 27.95 (*0-8373-2037-2*) Nat Learn.
— District Foreman (Watershed Maintenance) (Career Examination Ser.: C-428). 1994. pap. 27.95 (*0-8373-0428-8*) Nat Learn.
— District Superintendent (Department of Sanitation) (Career Examination Ser.: C-201). 1994. pap. 29.95 (*0-8373-0201-3*) Nat Learn.
— District Supervisor of School Custodians. (Career Examination Ser.: C-2349). 1994. pap. 29.95 (*0-8373-2349-5*) Nat Learn.
— District Supervisor (Water & Sewer Systems) (Career Examination Ser.: C-3044). 1994. pap. 29.95 (*0-8373-3044-0*) Nat Learn.
— Dockbuilder. (Career Examination Ser.: C-1696). 1994. pap. 27.95 (*0-8373-1696-0*) Nat Learn.
— Dog Control Officer. (Career Examination Ser.: C-547). 1994. pap. 23.95 (*0-8373-0547-0*) Nat Learn.
— Dog Control Officer II. (Career Examination Ser.: C-3038). 1994. pap. 27.95 (*0-8373-3038-6*) Nat Learn.
— Dog Enumerator Coordinator. (Career Examination Ser.: C-3496). 1994. pap. 29.95 (*0-8373-3496-9*) Nat Learn.
— Dog Warden. (Career Examination Ser.: C-2645). 1994. pap. 23.95 (*0-8373-2645-1*) Nat Learn.
— Domestic Worker. (Career Examination Ser.: C-1258). 1994. pap. 23.95 (*0-8373-1258-2*) Nat Learn.
— Drafting Aide. (Career Examination Ser.: C-202). 1994. pap. 23.95 (*0-8373-0202-1*) Nat Learn.
— Drafting Technician. (Career Examination Ser.: C-2678). 1994. pap. 23.95 (*0-8373-2678-8*) Nat Learn.
— Draftsman. (Career Examination Ser.: C-203). 1994. pap. 23.95 (*0-8373-0203-X*) Nat Learn.
— Drama & Theatre. (Undergraduate Program Field Test Ser.: UPFT-5). 1994. pap. 23.95 (*0-8373-6005-6*) Nat Learn.
— Dressmaking. (Occupational Competency Examination Ser.: OCE-17). 1994. pap. 23.95 (*0-8373-5717-9*) Nat Learn.
— Drilling Supervisor. (Career Examination Ser.: C-3326). 1994. pap. 29.95 (*0-8373-3326-1*) Nat Learn.
— Driver License Written Examination. (Career Examination Ser.: C-1635). 1994. pap. 23.95 (*0-8373-1635-9*) Nat Learn.
— Drug Abuse Counselor. (Career Examination Ser.: C-2725). 1994. pap. 29.95 (*0-8373-2725-3*) Nat Learn.
— Drug Abuse Education Group Leader. (Career Examination Ser.: C-1259). 1994. pap. 29.95 (*0-8373-1259-0*) Nat Learn.
— Drug Abuse Educator. (Career Examination Ser.: C-1597). 1994. pap. 29.95 (*0-8373-1597-2*) Nat Learn.
— Drug Abuse Group Worker. (Career Examination Ser.: C-1260). 1994. pap. 27.95 (*0-8373-1260-4*) Nat Learn.
— Drug Abuse Rehabilitation Counselor. (Career Examination Ser.: C-2929). 1994. pap. 29.95 (*0-8373-2929-9*) Nat Learn.
— Drug Abuse Secretarial Aide. (Career Examination Ser.: C-1261). 1994. pap. 23.95 (*0-8373-1261-2*) Nat Learn.
— Drug Abuse Technician. (Career Examination Ser.: C-1405). 1994. pap. 27.95 (*0-8373-1405-4*) Nat Learn.
— Drug Abuse Technician Trainee. (Career Examination Ser.: C-1406). 1994. pap. 23.95 (*0-8373-1406-2*) Nat Learn.
— Drug & Alcohol Community Coordinator. (Career Examination Ser.: C-2776). 1994. pap. 34.95 (*0-8373-2776-8*) Nat Learn.
— Drug & Alcohol Counselor. (Career Examination Ser.: C-2741). 1994. pap. 29.95 (*0-8373-2741-5*) Nat Learn.
— Drug & Alcohol Program Coordinator. (Career Examination Ser.: C-2775). 1994. pap. 34.95 (*0-8373-2775-X*) Nat Learn.
— Duplicating Equipment Operator. (Career Examination Ser.: C-208). 1994. pap. 19.95 (*0-8373-0208-0*) Nat Learn.
— Duplicating Machine Operator. (Career Examination Ser.: C-1407). 1994. pap. 19.95 (*0-8373-1407-0*) Nat Learn.
— Duplicating Machine Supervisor. (Career Examination Ser.: C-1408). 1994. pap. 27.95 (*0-8373-1408-9*) Nat Learn.
— Early Childhood Education. (National Teachers Examination Ser.: NT-2). 1994. pap. 23.95 (*0-8373-8412-5*) Nat Learn.
— Early Childhood, Elementary School (Pre-Kg.-2) (Teachers License Examination Ser.: T-13). 1994. pap. 23.95 (*0-8373-8013-8*) Nat Learn.
— Early Intervention Coordinator. (Career Examination Ser.: Series 1). 1991. pap. 34.95 (*0-8373-3711-9*) Nat Learn.
— Earth Science. (College Proficiency Examination Ser.: CPEP-7). 1994. pap. 23.95 (*0-8373-5407-2*) Nat Learn.
— Earth Science. (ACT Proficiency Examination Program Ser.: PEP-5). 1994. pap. 23.95 (*0-8373-5505-2*) Nat Learn.
— Earth Science & General Science, Sr. H. S. (Teachers License Examination Ser.: T-14). 1994. pap. 23.95 (*0-8373-8014-6*) Nat Learn.
— Economic Opportunity Program Specialist. (Career Examination Ser.: C-2545). 1994. pap. 29.95 (*0-8373-2545-5*) Nat Learn.
— Economics. (College Proficiency Examination Ser.: CPEP-8). 1994. pap. 23.95 (*0-8373-5408-0*) Nat Learn.
— Economics. (Graduate Record Examination Ser.: GRE-3). 1994. pap. 23.95 (*0-8373-5203-7*) Nat Learn.
— Economics. (Undergraduate Program Field Test Ser.: UPFT-6). 1994. pap. 23.95 (*0-8373-6006-4*) Nat Learn.
— Economist. (Career Examination Ser.: C-1262). 1994. pap. 29.95 (*0-8373-1262-0*) Nat Learn.
— Editorial Assistant. (Career Examination Ser.: C-220). 1994. pap. 27.95 (*0-8373-0220-X*) Nat Learn.
— Editorial Clerk. (Career Examination Ser.: C-2564). 1994. pap. 23.95 (*0-8373-2564-1*) Nat Learn.
— Education. (Teachers License Examination Ser.: G-1). 1994. pap. 23.95 (*0-8373-8191-6*) Nat Learn.
— Education. (Graduate Record Examination Ser.: GRE-4). 1994. pap. 23.95 (*0-8373-5204-5*) Nat Learn.
— Education. (Undergraduate Program Field Test Ser.: UPFT-7). 1994. pap. 23.95 (*0-8373-6007-2*) Nat Learn.
— Education Analyst. (Career Examination Ser.: C-3045). 1994. pap. 39.95 (*0-8373-3045-9*) Nat Learn.
— Education Counselor. (Career Examination Ser.: C-2739). 1994. pap. 39.95 (*0-8373-2739-3*) Nat Learn.
— Education Director. (Career Examination Ser.: C-2506). 1994. pap. 49.95 (*0-8373-2506-4*) Nat Learn.
— Education in an Urban Setting. (National Teachers Examination Ser.: NT-31). 1994. pap. 23.95 (*0-8373-8441-9*) Nat Learn.
— Education in the Elementary School (1-8) (National Teachers Examination Ser.: NT-1). 1994. pap. 23.95 (*0-8373-8411-7*) Nat Learn.
— Education of the Mentally Retarded. (National Teacher Examination Ser.: NT-24). 1994. pap. 23.95 (*0-8373-8434-6*) Nat Learn.
— Education Officer. (Career Examination Ser.: C-3050). 1994. pap. 39.95 (*0-8373-3050-5*) Nat Learn.
— Education Program Assistant. (Career Examination Ser.: C-865). 1994. pap. 34.95 (*0-8373-0865-8*) Nat Learn.
— Education Supervisor. (Career Examination Ser.: C-2508). 1994. pap. 34.95 (*0-8373-2508-0*) Nat Learn.
— Education Supervisor (Developmental Disabilities) (Career Examination Ser.: C-2511). 1994. pap. 39.95 (*0-8373-2511-0*) Nat Learn.
— Education Supervisor (Special Subjects) (Career Examination Ser.: C-2509). 1994. pap. 39.95 (*0-8373-2509-9*) Nat Learn.
— Education Supervisor (Vocational) (Career Examination Ser.: C-2510). 1994. pap. 39.95 (*0-8373-2510-2*) Nat Learn.
— Educational Commission for Foreign Medical Graduates English Test (ECFMG-ET) (Admission Test Ser.: ATS-43). 1994. pap. 23.95 (*0-8373-5043-3*) Nat Learn.
— Educational Commission for Foreign Medical Graduates Examination (ECFMG) (Admission Test Ser.: ATS-24). 1994. pap. 49.95 (*0-8373-5024-7*) Nat Learn.
— Educational Commission for Foreign Veterinary Graduates Examination (ECFVG) Anatomy, Physiology, Pathology. (Admission Test Ser.: ATS-49A). 1994. pap. 29.95 (*0-8373-6957-6*) Nat Learn.
— Educational Commission for Foreign Veterinary Graduates Examination, Pt. II: Pharmacology, Therapeutics, Parasitology, Hygiene. (Admission Test Ser.: ATS-49B). 1994. pap. 29.95 (*0-8373-6958-4*) Nat Learn.
— Educational Commission for Foreign Veterinary Graduates Examination, Pt. III: Physical Diagnosis, Medicine, Surgery. (Admission Test Ser.: ATS-49C). 1994. pap. 39.95 (*0-317-45512-5*) Nat Learn.
— Educational Psychology. (College Level Examination Ser.: CLEP-9). 1994. pap. 23.95 (*0-8373-5309-2*) Nat Learn.
— Educational Psychology. (College Proficiency Examination Ser.: CPEP-9). 1994. pap. 23.95 (*0-8373-5409-9*) Nat Learn.
— Educational Psychology. (DANTES Ser.: No. 13). 1994. 39.95 (*0-8373-6513-9*); pap. 23.95 (*0-8373-6613-5*) Nat Learn.
— Educational Psychology. (ACT Proficiency Examination Program Ser.: PEP-28). 1994. pap. 23.95 (*0-8373-5528-1*) Nat Learn.
— EEG Technician. (Career Examination Ser.: C-1263). 1994. pap. 39.95 (*0-8373-1263-9*) Nat Learn.
— EKG Technician. (Career Examination Ser.: C-1264). 1994. pap. 39.95 (*0-8373-1264-7*) Nat Learn.
— Election Inspector. (Career Examination Ser.: C-1265). 1994. 29.95 (*0-8373-1265-5*) Nat Learn.
— Election Registrar. (Career Examination Ser.: C-1266). 1994. pap. 27.95 (*0-8373-1266-3*) Nat Learn.
— Electric Accounting Machine Operator. (Career Examination Ser.: C-238). 1994. pap. 23.95 (*0-8373-0238-2*) Nat Learn.
— Electric Circuits. (DANTES Ser.: No. 41). 1994. pap. 23.95 (*0-8373-6641-0*) Nat Learn.
— Electric Meter Tester. (Career Examination Ser.: C-2249). 1994. pap. 29.95 (*0-8373-2249-9*) Nat Learn.
— Electrical Contractor. (Career Examination Ser.: C-3598). 1994. 34.95 (*0-8373-3598-1*, C-3598) Nat Learn.
— Electrical Engineer. (Career Examination Ser.: C-221). 1994. pap. 29.95 (*0-8373-0221-8*) Nat Learn.
— Electrical Engineering Draftsman. (Career Examination Ser.: C-222). 1994. pap. 27.95 (*0-8373-0222-6*) Nat Learn.
— Electrical Engineering Trainee. (Career Examination Ser.: C-239). 1994. pap. 23.95 (*0-8373-0239-0*) Nat Learn.
— Electrical Inspector. (Career Examination Ser.: C-223). 1994. pap. 29.95 (*0-8373-0223-4*) Nat Learn.
— Electrical Installation. (Occupational Competency Examination Ser.: OCE-18). 1994. pap. 23.95 (*0-8373-5718-7*) Nat Learn.
— Electrical Service Supervisor. (Career Examination Ser.: C-1267). 1994. pap. 29.95 (*0-8373-1267-1*) Nat Learn.
— Electrician. (Career Examination Ser.: C-224). 1994. pap. 23.95 (*0-8373-0224-2*) Nat Learn.
— Electrician (Automobile) (Career Examination Ser.: C-1268). 1994. pap. 23.95 (*0-8373-1268-X*) Nat Learn.
— Electrician's Helper. (Career Examination Ser.: C-225). 1994. pap. 23.95 (*0-8373-0225-0*) Nat Learn.
— Electricity Workbook. (Workbook Ser.: No. 2870). 1994. pap. 23.95 (*0-8373-7902-4*) Nat Learn.
— Electro-Mechanical Examination (U.S.P.S.) (Career Examination Ser.: C-1607). 1994. pap. 27.95 (*0-8373-1607-3*) Nat Learn.
— Electrocardiograph Technician. (Career Examination Ser.: C-1269). 1994. pap. 39.95 (*0-8373-1269-8*) Nat Learn.
— Electronic Computer Operator. (Career Examination Ser.: C-241). 1994. pap. 23.95 (*0-8373-0241-2*) Nat Learn.
— Electronic Computer Trainee. (Career Examination Ser.: C-242). 1994. pap. 23.95 (*0-8373-0242-0*) Nat Learn.
— Electronic Devices. (DANTES Ser.: No. 42). 1994. pap. 23.95 (*0-8373-6642-9*) Nat Learn.
— Electronic Engineer. (Career Examination Ser.: C-226). 1994. pap. 34.95 (*0-8373-0226-9*) Nat Learn.
— Electronic Equipment Maintainer. (Career Examination Ser.: C-227). 1994. pap. 23.95 (*0-8373-0227-7*) Nat Learn.
— Electronic Equipment Repairer. (Career Examination Ser.: C-243). 1994. pap. 23.95 (*0-8373-0243-9*) Nat Learn.
— Electronic Measuring Instruments. (DANTES Ser.: No. 14). 1994. pap. 23.95 (*0-8373-6614-3*) Nat Learn.
— Electronic Measuring Instruments. (DANTES Ser.: No. 14). 1994. 39.95 (*0-8373-6514-7*) Nat Learn.
— Electronic Mechanic. (Career Examination Ser.: C-228). 1994. pap. 23.95 (*0-8373-0228-5*) Nat Learn.
— Electronic Occupations. (Teachers License Examination Ser.: T-73). 1994. pap. 23.95 (*0-8373-8073-1*) Nat Learn.
— Electronic Technician. (Career Examination Ser.: C-229). 1994. pap. 27.95 (*0-8373-0229-3*) Nat Learn.
— Electronics Communication. (Occupational Competency Examination Ser.: OCE-19). 1994. pap. 23.95 (*0-8373-5719-5*) Nat Learn.
— Elementary Computer Programming. (College-Level Examination Ser.: CLEP-10). 1994. 39.95 (*0-8373-5360-2*); pap. 23.95 (*0-8373-5310-6*) Nat Learn.
— Elementary School Basic Competency Tests (BCT-ES) (Admission Test Ser.: ATS-56). 1994. pap. 23.95 (*0-8373-5056-5*) Nat Learn.
— Elementary Schools. (Teachers Lesson Plan Book Ser.: E-1). 1994. pap. 9.95 (*0-8373-7951-2*) Nat Learn.
— Elevator Inspector. (Career Examination Ser.: C-244). 1994. pap. 29.95 (*0-8373-0244-7*) Nat Learn.
— Elevator Mechanic. (Career Examination Ser.: C-1056). 1994. pap. 23.95 (*0-8373-1056-3*) Nat Learn.
— Elevator Mechanic (U. S. P. S.) (Career Examination Ser.: C-1684). 1994. pap. 23.95 (*0-8373-1684-7*) Nat Learn.
— Elevator Mechanic's Helper. (Career Examination Ser.: C-237). 1994. pap. 23.95 (*0-8373-0237-4*) Nat Learn.
— Elevator Operator. (Career Examination Ser.: C-230). 1994. pap. 23.95 (*0-8373-0230-7*) Nat Learn.
— Elevator Starter. (Career Examination Ser.: C-1270). 1994. pap. 23.95 (*0-8373-1270-1*) Nat Learn.
— Eligibility Specialist. (Career Examination Ser.: C-2958). 1994. pap. 23.95 (*0-8373-2958-2*) Nat Learn.
— Emergency Communications Specialist. (Career Examination Ser.: C-2878). 1994. pap. 27.95 (*0-8373-2878-0*) Nat Learn.
— Emergency Complaint Operator. (Career Examination Ser.: C-1057). 1994. pap. 23.95 (*0-8373-1057-1*) Nat Learn.
— Emergency Medical Technicians-Paramedic Examination (EMT) (Admission Test Ser.: ATS-70). 1994. pap. 39.95 (*0-8373-5070-0*) Nat Learn.
— Emotionally Handicapped Children. (Teachers License Examination Ser.: T-69). 1994. pap. 23.95 (*0-8373-8069-3*) Nat Learn.
— Employee Assistance Program Worker. (Career Examination Ser.: Series 1). 1991. pap. 29.95 (*0-8373-3712-7*) Nat Learn.
— Employee Benefits Supervisor. (Career Examination Ser.: C-2810). 1994. pap. 34.95 (*0-8373-2810-1*) Nat Learn.
— Employment & Training Assistant. (Career Examination Ser.: Series 1). 1991. pap. 29.95 (*0-8373-3713-5*) Nat Learn.
— Employment & Training Coordinator. (Career Examination Ser.: C-2884). 1994. pap. 44.00 (*0-8373-2884-5*) Nat Learn.
— Employment & Training Fiscal Auditor. (Career Examination Ser.: C-3385). 1994. pap. 44.95 (*0-8373-3385-7*) Nat Learn.

R

— Employment & Training Programs Administrator. (Career Examination Ser.: C-3076). 1994. pap. 44.95 (*0-8373-3076-9*) Nat Learn.
— Employment Consultant (Testing) (Career Examination Ser.: C-2463). 1994. pap. 39.95 (*0-8373-2463-7*) Nat Learn.
— Employment Counselor. (Career Examination Ser.: C-245). 1994. pap. 29.95 (*0-8373-0245-5*) Nat Learn.
— Employment Counselor Trainee. (Career Examination Ser.: C-246). 1994. pap. 27.95 (*0-8373-0246-3*) Nat Learn.
— Employment Interviewer. (Career Examination Ser.: C-231). 1994. pap. 29.95 (*0-8373-0231-5*) Nat Learn.
— Employment Manager. (Career Examination Ser.: C-2582). 1994. pap. 39.95 (*0-8373-2582-X*) Nat Learn.
— Employment Security Claims Trainee. (Career Examination Ser.: C-3144). 1994. pap. 23.95 (*0-8373-3144-7*) Nat Learn.
— Employment Security Clerk. (Career Examination Ser.: C-2350). 1994. pap. 23.95 (*0-8373-2350-9*) Nat Learn.
— Employment Security Manager. (Career Examination Ser.: C-3188). 1994. pap. 39.95 (*0-8373-3188-9*) Nat Learn.
— Employment Security Placement Trainee. (Career Examination Ser.: C-2229). 1994. pap. 23.95 (*0-8373-2229-4*) Nat Learn.
— Energy Assistance Review Aide. (Career Examination Ser.: C-3308). 1994. pap. 27.95 (*0-8373-3308-3*) Nat Learn.
— Energy Assistance Review Supervisor. (Career Examination Ser.: C-3309). 1994. pap. 29.95 (*0-8373-3309-1*) Nat Learn.
— Energy Conservation Analyst. (Career Examination Ser.: C-2035). 1994. pap. 29.95 (*0-8373-2035-6*) Nat Learn.
— Engineer. (Career Examination Ser.: C-240). 1994. pap. 39.95 (*0-8373-0240-4*) Nat Learn.
— Engineering. (Undergraduate Program Field Test Ser.: UPFT-8). 1941. pap. 23.95 (*0-8373-6008-0*) Nat Learn.
— Engineering. (Graduate Record Examination Ser.: GRE-5). 1994. pap. 23.95 (*0-8373-5205-3*) Nat Learn.
— Engineering Administrative Technician. (Career Examination Ser.: C-1271). 1994. pap. 34.95 (*0-8373-1271-X*) Nat Learn.
— Engineering Aid & Science Assistant. (Career Examination Ser.: C-232). 1994. pap. 29.95 (*0-8373-0232-3*) Nat Learn.
— Engineering Aide. (Career Examination Ser.: C-233). 1994. pap. 23.95 (*0-8373-0233-1*) Nat Learn.
— Engineering Assistant. (Career Examination Ser.: C-234). 1994. pap. 27.95 (*0-8373-0234-X*) Nat Learn.
— Engineering Draftsman. (Career Examination Ser.: C-247). 1994. pap. 27.95 (*0-8373-0247-1*) Nat Learn.
— Engineering Inspector. (Career Examination Ser.: C-1861). 1994. reprint ed. pap. 39.95 (*0-8373-1861-0*) Nat Learn.
— Engineering Materials Technician. (Career Examination Ser.: C-315). 1994. pap. 27.95 (*0-8373-0315-X*) Nat Learn.
— Engineering Technician. (Career Examination Ser.: C-235). 1994. pap. 23.95 (*0-8373-0235-8*) Nat Learn.
— Engineering Technician (Drafting) (Career Examination Ser.: C-991). 1994. pap. 27.95 (*0-8373-0991-3*) Nat Learn.
— Engineering Technician (Environmental Quality) (Career Examination Ser.: C-3237). 1994. pap. 27.95 (*0-8373-3237-0*) Nat Learn.
— Engineering Technician Trainee. (Career Examination Ser.: C-248). 1994. pap. 23.95 (*0-8373-0248-X*) Nat Learn.
— Engineering Trainee. (Career Examination Ser.: C-1272). 1994. pap. 27.95 (*0-8373-1272-8*) Nat Learn.
— Engineman (U. S. P. S.) (Career Examination Ser.: C-2371). 1994. pap. 27.95 (*0-8373-2371-1*) Nat Learn.
— English & Citizenship. (Teachers License Examination Ser.: T-17). 1994. pap. 23.95 (*0-8373-8017-0*) Nat Learn.
— English As a Second Language. (National Teacher Examination Ser.: No. 47). 1994. Cloth bdg. avail. pap. 23.95 (*0-8373-8457-5*) Nat Learn.
— English as a Second Language (Day Elementary Schools) (Teachers License Examination Ser.: T-650). 1994. pap. 23.95 (*0-8373-8065-0*) Nat Learn.
— English as a Second Language (Secondary Schools) (Teachers License Examination Ser.: T-65b). 1994. pap. 23.95 (*0-685-49790-9*) Nat Learn.
— English Composition. (College-Level Examination Ser.: ATS-9A). 1994. 19.95 (*0-8373-5245-2*) Nat Learn.
— English, Jr. H. S. (Teachers License Examination Ser.: T-15). 1994. pap. 23.95 (*0-8373-8015-4*) Nat Learn.
— English Language & Literature. (National Teachers Examination Ser.: NT-4). 1994. pap. 23.95 (*0-8373-8414-1*) Nat Learn.
— English Literature. (College Level Examination Ser.: CLEP-12). 1994. pap. 23.95 (*0-8373-5312-2*) Nat Learn.
— English, Sr. H. S. (Teachers License Examination Ser.: T-16). 1994. pap. 23.95 (*0-8373-8016-2*) Nat Learn.
— Entomologist. (Career Examination Ser.: C-249). 1994. pap. 34.95 (*0-8373-0249-8*) Nat Learn.
— Environmental Analyst. (Career Examination Ser.: C-2659). 1994. pap. 29.95 (*0-8373-2659-1*) Nat Learn.
— Environmental Assistant. (Career Examination Ser.: C-1583). 1994. pap. 29.95 (*0-8373-1583-2*) Nat Learn.
— Environmental Chemist I. (Career Examination Ser.: C-2985). 1991. pap. 24.00 (*0-8373-2985-X*) Nat Learn.
— Environmental Chemist II. (Career Examination Ser.: C-2986). 1994. pap. 29.95 (*0-8373-2986-8*) Nat Learn.
— Environmental Conservation Investigator. (Career Examination Ser.: C-3214). 1994. pap. 29.95 (*0-8373-3214-1*) Nat Learn.
— Environmental Conservation Officer. (Career Examination Ser.: C-2428). 1991. pap. 22.00 (*0-8373-2428-9*) Nat Learn.
— Environmental Conservation Officer Trainee. (Career Examination Ser.: C-1759). 1994. 27.95 (*0-8373-1759-2*) Nat Learn.
— Environmental Control Specialist. (Career Examination Ser.: C-2429). 1994. pap. 29.95 (*0-8373-2429-7*) Nat Learn.
— Environmental Control Specialist Trainee. (Career Examination Ser.: C-2067). 1994. reprint ed. pap. 27.95 (*0-8373-2067-4*) Nat Learn.
— Environmental Educator. (Career Examination Ser.: C-3241). 1994. pap. 34.95 (*0-8373-3241-9*) Nat Learn.
— Environmental Health Aide. (Career Examination Ser.: C-1959). 1994. pap. 29.95 (*0-8373-1959-5*) Nat Learn.
— Environmental Health Specialist. (Career Examination Ser.: Series 1). 1991. pap. 39.95 (*0-8373-3714-3*) Nat Learn.
— Environmental Health Technician. (Career Examination Ser.: C-2652). 1994. pap. 29.95 (*0-8373-2652-4*) Nat Learn.
— Environmental Planner. (Career Examination Ser.: C-2662). 1991. pap. 22.00 (*0-8373-2662-1*) Nat Learn.
— Environmental Program Specialist Trainee. (Career Examination Ser.). 1994. 29.95 (*0-8373-3621-X*, C-3621) Nat Learn.
— Environmental Protection Director. (Career Examination Ser.: C-2849). 1994. pap. 39.95 (*0-8373-2849-7*) Nat Learn.
— Environmental Radiation Specialist. (Career Examination Ser.: Series 1). 1991. pap. 34.95 (*0-8373-3715-1*) Nat Learn.
— Environmentalist. (Career Examination Ser.: C-1584). 1994. pap. 29.95 (*0-8373-1584-0*) Nat Learn.
— Equalization Rates Analyst. (Career Examination Ser.: C-3240). 1994. pap. 34.95 (*0-8373-3240-0*) Nat Learn.
— Equipment Foreman. (Career Examination Ser.: C-1273). 1994. pap. 29.95 (*0-8373-1273-6*) Nat Learn.
— Equipment Operator. (Career Examination Ser.: C-1274). 1994. pap. 27.95 (*0-8373-1274-4*) Nat Learn.
— Equipment Specialist. (Career Examination Ser.: C-971). 1994. pap. 27.95 (*0-8373-0971-9*) Nat Learn.
— Equipment Supervisor. (Career Examination Ser.: C-3071). 1991. pap. 22.00 (*0-8373-3071-8*) Nat Learn.
— Estimator. (Career Examination Ser.: C-1275). 1994. pap. 34.95 (*0-8373-1275-2*) Nat Learn.
— European History. (College Proficiency Examination Ser.: CPEP-10). 1994. pap. 23.95 (*0-8373-5410-2*) Nat Learn.
— Every-Day Spanish for Police Officers. (General Aptitude & Abilities Ser.: CS-31). 1994. pap. 23.95 (*0-614-03729-8*) Nat Learn.
— Evidence Control Clerk. (Career Examination Ser.: C-3149). 1994. pap. 27.95 (*0-8373-3149-8*) Nat Learn.
— Evidence Technician. (Career Examination Ser.: C-2748). 1994. pap. 29.95 (*0-8373-2748-2*) Nat Learn.
— Examen de Equivalencia Para el Diploma de Escuela Superior (EEE) (Admission Test Ser.: ATS-22). 1994. reprint ed. pap. 29.95 (*0-8373-5022-0*) Nat Learn.
— Examiner, Board of Examiners. (Teachers License Examination Ser.: GT-10). 1994. pap. 49.95 (*0-8373-8130-4*) Nat Learn.
— Examiner (Intermittent) (Career Examination Ser.: C-2622). 1994. pap. 39.95 (*0-8373-2622-2*) Nat Learn.
— Examiner of Municipal Affairs. (Career Examination Ser.: C-2726). 1994. pap. 39.95 (*0-8373-2726-1*) Nat Learn.
— Examiner, Social Services. (Career Examination Ser.: C-2138). 1994. reprint ed. pap. 27.95 (*0-8373-2138-7*) Nat Learn.
— Excise Tax Investigator. (Career Examination Ser.: C-972). 1994. pap. 27.95 (*0-8373-0972-7*) Nat Learn.
— Executive Assistant. (Career Examination Ser.: C-1276). 1994. pap. 27.95 (*0-8373-1276-0*) Nat Learn.
— Executive Director. (Career Examination Ser.: C-1277). 1994. 39.95 (*0-8373-1277-9*) Nat Learn.
— Executive Director of Youth Bureau. (Career Examination Ser.: C-416). 1994. pap. 39.95 (*0-8373-0416-4*) Nat Learn.
— Executive Officer. (Career Examination Ser.: C-1278). 1994. pap. 34.95 (*0-8373-1278-7*) Nat Learn.
— Executive Secretary. (Career Examination Ser.: C-1279). 1994. pap. 27.95 (*0-8373-1279-5*) Nat Learn.
— Executive Staff Assistant. (Career Examination Ser.: C-1280). 1994. pap. 27.95 (*0-8373-1280-9*) Nat Learn.
— Exhibits Technician. (Career Examination Ser.: No. C-1281). 1994. pap. 27.95 (*0-8373-1281-7*) Nat Learn.
— Exterminator. (Career Examination Ser.: C-236). 1994. pap. 27.95 (*0-8373-0236-6*) Nat Learn.
— Facility Management Assistant. (Career Examination Ser.: C-387). 1994. pap. 29.95 (*0-8373-0387-7*) Nat Learn.
— Factory Inspector. (Career Examination Ser.: C-283). 1994. pap. 29.95 (*0-8373-0283-8*) Nat Learn.
— Family & Children Services Specialist. (Career Examination Ser.: C-3549). 1994. 29.95 (*0-8373-3549-3*) Nat Learn.
— Family Nurse Practitioner. (Certified Nurse Examination Ser.: CN-2). 1994. 39.95 (*0-8373-6152-4*); pap. 23.95 (*0-8373-6102-8*) Nat Learn.
— Farm Products Grading Inspector. (Career Examination Ser.: C-3137). 1994. pap. 29.95 (*0-8373-3137-4*) Nat Learn.
— F.C.C. Amateur License Examinations. (Admission Test Ser.: ATS-83). 1994. pap. 23.95 (*0-8373-5083-2*) Nat Learn.
— F.C.C. Commmercial Radio Operator License Examination (CRO) (Admission Test Ser.: ATS-73). 1994. pap. 23.95 (*0-8373-5073-5*) Nat Learn.
— Federal Administrative & Management Examination. (Career Examination Ser.: C-250). 1994. pap. 23.95 (*0-8373-0250-1*) Nat Learn.
— Federal & State Aid Claims Technician. (Career Examination Ser.: Series 1). 1994. pap. 29.95 (*0-8373-3297-4*) Nat Learn.
— Federal & State Aid Coordinator. (Career Examination Ser.: C-1282). 1994. pap. 34.95 (*0-8373-1282-5*) Nat Learn.
— Federal Construction Project Coordinator. (Career Examination Ser.: C-2879). 1994. pap. 39.95 (*0-8373-2879-9*) Nat Learn.
— Federal Guard. (Career Examination Ser.: C-251). 1994. pap. 23.95 (*0-8373-0251-X*) Nat Learn.
— Federal Mine Inspector. (Career Examination Ser.: C-1283). 1994. pap. 29.95 (*0-8373-1283-3*) Nat Learn.
— Federal Office Assistant. (Career Examination Ser.: C-252). 1994. pap. 19.95 (*0-8373-0252-8*) Nat Learn.
— Federal Protective Officer. (Career Examination Ser.: C-1612). 1994. pap. 23.95 (*0-8373-1612-X*) Nat Learn.
— Federal Service Entrance Examination (FSEE) (Admission Test Ser.: ATS-16). 1994. 23.95 (*0-8373-5016-6*) Nat Learn.
— Federal Service Entrance Examination (FSEE) (Career Examination Ser.: C-253). 1994. pap. 23.95 (*0-8373-0253-6*) Nat Learn.
— Federal Service Management Intern Examination. (Career Examination Ser.: C-285). 1994. pap. 23.95 (*0-8373-0285-4*) Nat Learn.
— Federation Licensing Examination (FLEX) (Admission Test Ser.: ATS-31). 1994. pap. 49.95 (*0-8373-5031-X*) Nat Learn.
— Ferry Agent. (Career Examination Ser.: C-3370). 1994. pap. 27.95 (*0-8373-3370-9*) Nat Learn.
— Ferry Terminal Supervisor. (Career Examination Ser.: C-2142). 1994. reprint ed. pap. 29.95 (*0-8373-2142-5*) Nat Learn.
— Field Accountant. (Career Examination Ser.: C-1568). 1994. pap. 29.95 (*0-8373-1568-9*) Nat Learn.
— Field Auditor. (Career Examination Ser.: C-1284). 1994. pap. 29.95 (*0-8373-1284-1*) Nat Learn.
— Field Investigator. (Career Examination Ser.: C-1285). 1994. pap. 27.95 (*0-8373-1285-X*) Nat Learn.
— Field Representative. (Career Examination Ser.: C-2115). 1994. reprint ed. pap. 27.95 (*0-8373-2115-8*) Nat Learn.
— Field Representative, Senior Citizen Services Project. (Career Examination Ser.: C-2948). 1994. pap. 29.95 (*0-8373-2948-5*) Nat Learn.
— Field Systems Coordinator. (Career Examination Ser.: C-2243). 1994. pap. 34.95 (*0-8373-2243-X*) Nat Learn.
— File Clerk. (Career Examination Ser.: C-254). 1994. pap. 19.95 (*0-8373-0254-4*) Nat Learn.
— Film Editor. (Career Examination Ser.: C-1286). 1994. pap. 23.95 (*0-8373-1286-8*) Nat Learn.
— Finance I. (Regents External Degree Ser.: REDP-4). 1994. pap. 23.95 (*0-8373-5604-0*) Nat Learn.
— Finance II. (Regents External Degree Ser.: REDP-5). 1994. pap. 23.95 (*0-8373-5605-9*) Nat Learn.
— Finance III. (Regents External Degree Ser.: REDP-6). 1994. pap. 23.54 (*0-8373-5606-7*) Nat Learn.
— Finance, Level I: Corporate Finance. (ACT Proficiency Examination Program Ser.: PEP-15). 1994. 39.95 (*0-8373-5565-6*); pap. 23.95 (*0-8373-5515-X*) Nat Learn.
— Financial Accounting. (DANTES Ser.: No. 15). 1994. pap. 23.95 (*0-8373-6615-1*) Nat Learn.
— Financial Accounting. (DANTES Ser.: No. 15). 1994. 39.95 (*0-8373-6515-5*) Nat Learn.
— Financial Analyst. (Career Examination Ser.: C-2642). 1994. pap. 34.95 (*0-8373-2642-7*) Nat Learn.
— Financial Clerk. (Career Examination Ser.: Series 1). 1991. pap. 23.95 (*0-8373-3716-X*) Nat Learn.
— Financial Investigator. (Career Examination Ser.: C-873). 1994. pap. 29.95 (*0-8373-0873-9*) Nat Learn.
— Financial Officer. (Career Examination Ser.: No. C-3512). 1994. 34.95 (*0-8373-3512-4*) Nat Learn.
— Fine Arts Chairman, Jr. H. S. (Teachers License Examination Ser.: CH-6). 1994. pap. 29.95 (*0-8373-8156-8*) Nat Learn.
— Fine Arts, Jr. H. S. (Teachers License Examination Ser.: T-18). 1994. pap. 23.95 (*0-8373-8018-9*) Nat Learn.
— Fine Arts, Sr. H. S. (Teachers License Examination Ser.: T-19). 1994. pap. 23.95 (*0-8373-8019-7*) Nat Learn.
— Fingerprint Technician. (Career Examination Ser.: C-255). 1994. pap. 27.95 (*0-8373-0255-2*) Nat Learn.
— Fingerprint Technician Trainee. (Career Examination Ser.: C-286). 1994. pap. 23.95 (*0-8373-0286-2*) Nat Learn.
— Fire Administration & Supervision. (General Aptitude & Abilities Ser.: No. CS-38). 1994. pap. 29.95 (*0-8373-6738-7*) Nat Learn.
— Fire Alarm Dispatcher. (Career Examination Ser.: C-256). 1994. pap. 23.95 (*0-8373-0256-0*) Nat Learn.
— Fire & Safety Representative. (Career Examination Ser.: C-3242). 1994. pap. 29.95 (*0-8373-3242-7*) Nat Learn.
— Fire Communications Technician. (Career Examination Ser.: C-1217). 1994. pap. 29.95 (*0-8373-1217-5*) Nat Learn.
— Fire Control Mechanic. (Career Examination Ser.: C-257). 1994. pap. 27.95 (*0-8373-0257-9*) Nat Learn.
— Fire Fighter. (Career Examination Ser.: C-1287). 1994. pap. 23.95 (*0-8373-1287-6*) Nat Learn.
— Fire Inspector. (Career Examination Ser.: C-1288). 1994. pap. 29.95 (*0-8373-1288-4*) Nat Learn.
— Fire Marshal. (Career Examination Ser.: C-2401). 1994. pap. 29.95 (*0-8373-2401-7*) Nat Learn.
— Fire Officer. (Career Examination Ser.: C-1578). 1994. pap. 27.95 (*0-8373-1578-6*) Nat Learn.
— Fire Prevention Inspector. (Career Examination Ser.: C-287). 1994. pap. 29.95 (*0-8373-0287-0*) Nat Learn.
— Fire Promotion Course. (General Aptitude & Abilities Ser.: CS-21). 1994. pap. 29.95 (*0-8373-6721-2*) Nat Learn.
— Fire Protection Inspector. (Career Examination Ser.: Series 1). 1991. pap. 29.95 (*0-8373-3717-8*) Nat Learn.
— Fire Safety Officer. (Career Examination Ser.: C-2230). 1994. pap. 27.95 (*0-8373-2230-8*) Nat Learn.
— Fire Safety Technician. (Career Examination Ser.: C-3243). 1994. pap. 27.95 (*0-8373-3243-5*) Nat Learn.
— Fireman Examinations - All States. (Career Examination Ser.: C-258). 1994. pap. 23.95 (*0-8373-0258-7*) Nat Learn.
— Fireman, Fire Department. (Career Examination Ser.: C-259). 1994. pap. 23.95 (*0-8373-0259-5*) Nat Learn.
— Fireman-Laborer. (Career Examination Ser.: C-1289). 1994. pap. 27.95 (*0-8373-1289-2*) Nat Learn.
— Fiscal Administrator. (Career Examination Ser.: C-2612). 1994. pap. 39.95 (*0-8373-2612-5*) Nat Learn.
— Fiscal Clerk, 1 vol. (Career Examination Ser.: Series 1). 1991. pap. 23.95 (*0-8373-3718-6*) Nat Learn.
— Fiscal Director. (Career Examination Ser.: C-1290). 1994. pap. 39.95 (*0-8373-1290-6*) Nat Learn.
— Fiscal Manager. (Career Examination Ser.: C-2686). 1995. pap. 39.95 (*0-8373-2686-9*) Nat Learn.
— Fiscal Officer. (Career Examination Ser.: C-1409). 1994. pap. 34.95 (*0-8373-1409-7*) Nat Learn.
— Fish & Wildlife Technician. (Career Examination Ser.: C-3159). 1994. pap. 27.95 (*0-8373-3159-5*) Nat Learn.
— Flight Attendant Skills Test (FAST) (Career Examination Ser.: C-3338). 1994. pap. 23.95 (*0-8373-3338-5*) Nat Learn.
— Florida Functional Literacy Test (FLT) (Admission Test Ser.: ATS-54). 1994. pap. 23.95 (*0-8373-5054-9*) Nat Learn.
— Florist. (Career Examination Ser.: C-1410). 1994. pap. 29.95 (*0-8373-1410-0*) Nat Learn.
— Food Inspector. (Career Examination Ser.: C-2543). 1994. pap. 29.95 (*0-8373-2543-9*) Nat Learn.
— Food Inspector Trainee. (Career Examination Ser.: C-2998). 1994. pap. 27.95 (*0-8373-2998-1*) Nat Learn.
— Food Service Manager. (Career Examination Ser.: C-3564). 1994. 29.95 (*0-8373-3564-7*) Nat Learn.
— Food Service Specialist. (Career Examination Ser.: No. C-3513). 1994. 27.95 (*0-8373-3513-2*) Nat Learn.
— Food Service Supervisor. (Career Examination Ser.: C-1411). 1994. pap. 27.95 (*0-8373-1411-9*) Nat Learn.
— Food Service Worker. (Career Examination Ser.: C-260). 1994. pap. 23.95 (*0-8373-0260-9*) Nat Learn.
— Foreign Language - French. (Regents External Degree Ser.: REDP-27). 1994. 39.95 (*0-8373-5677-6*); pap. 23.95 (*0-8373-5627-X*) Nat Learn.
— Foreign Language - German. (Regents External Degree (REDP) Ser.: REDP-28). 1994. 39.95 (*0-8373-5678-4*); pap. 23.95 (*0-8373-5628-8*) Nat Learn.
— Foreign Language - Italian. (Regents External Degree (REDP) Ser.: REDP-29). 1994. 39.95 (*0-8373-5679-2*); pap. 23.95 (*0-8373-5629-6*) Nat Learn.
— Foreign Language - Spanish. (Regents External Degree (REDP) Ser.: REDP-30). 1994. 39.95 (*0-8373-5680-6*); pap. 23.95 (*0-8373-5630-X*) Nat Learn.
— Foreign Medical Graduates Examination in Medical Science, Pt. I: Basic Medical Sciences. (Admission Test Ser.: ATS-74A). 1994. pap. 39.95 (*0-8373-6965-7*) Nat Learn.
— Foreign Medical Graduates Examination in Medical Science, Pt. II: Clinical Sciences. (Admission Test Ser.: ATS-74B). 1994. pap. 39.95 (*0-8373-6966-5*) Nat Learn.
— Foreign Service Officer. (Career Examination Ser.: C-261). 1994. pap. 29.95 (*0-8373-0261-7*) Nat Learn.
— Foreman. (Career Examination Ser.: C-262). 1994. pap. 27.95 (*0-8373-0262-5*) Nat Learn.
— Foreman Asphalt Worker. (Career Examination Ser.: C-2080). 1994. reprint ed. pap. 27.95 (*0-8373-2080-1*) Nat Learn.
— Foreman Auto Mechanic. (Career Examination Ser.: C-263). 1994. pap. 27.95 (*0-8373-0263-3*) Nat Learn.
— Foreman Blacksmith. (Career Examination Ser.: C-1709). 1994. pap. 29.95 (*0-8373-1709-6*) Nat Learn.
— Foreman Bricklayer. (Career Examination Ser.: C-2020). 1941. pap. 27.95 (*0-8373-2020-8*) Nat Learn.
— Foreman Bridge Painter. (Career Examination Ser.: C-1412). 1994. pap. 27.95 (*0-8373-1412-7*) Nat Learn.
— Foreman (Buses & Shops) (Career Examination Ser.: C-264). 1994. pap. 27.95 (*0-8373-0264-1*) Nat Learn.
— Foreman Cable Splicer. (Career Examination Ser.: C-2021). 1994. pap. 27.95 (*0-8373-2021-6*) Nat Learn.
— Foreman Carpenter. (Career Examination Ser.: C-1779). 1994. pap. 27.95 (*0-8373-1779-7*) Nat Learn.
— Foreman (Cars & Shops) (Career Examination Ser.: C-265). 1994. pap. 27.95 (*0-8373-0265-X*) Nat Learn.
— Foreman (Department of Sanitation) (Career Examination Ser.: C-266). 1994. pap. 27.95 (*0-8373-0266-8*) Nat Learn.
— Foreman Dockbuilder. (Career Examination Ser.: C-2022). 1994. pap. 29.95 (*0-8373-2022-4*) Nat Learn.
— Foreman (Electrical Power) (Career Examination Ser.: C-267). 1994. pap. 27.95 (*0-8373-0267-6*) Nat Learn.
— Foreman Electrician. (Career Examination Ser.: C-1710). 1994. pap. 27.95 (*0-8373-1710-X*) Nat Learn.
— Foreman (Electronic Equipment) (Career Examination Ser.: C-2032). 1994. pap. 27.95 (*0-8373-2032-1*) Nat Learn.
— Foreman Elevator Mechanic. (Career Examination Ser.: C-2165). 1994. reprint ed. pap. 27.95 (*0-8373-2165-4*) Nat Learn.
— Foreman (Elevators & Escalators) (Career Examination Ser.: C-1413). 1994. pap. 27.95 (*0-8373-1413-5*) Nat Learn.
— Foreman Furniture Maintainer. (Career Examination Ser.: C-2023). 1994. pap. 27.95 (*0-8373-2023-2*) Nat Learn.
— Foreman (Highways & Sewers) (Career Examination Ser.: C-2190). 1994. pap. 27.95 (*0-8373-2190-5*) Nat Learn.
— Foreman, Laborer-Janitor (U. S. P. S.) (Career Examination Ser.: C-1686). 1994. pap. 29.95 (*0-8373-1686-3*) Nat Learn.
— Foreman Lineman. (Career Examination Ser.: C-2024). 1994. pap. 27.95 (*0-8373-2024-0*) Nat Learn.

R

An Asterisk (*) at the beginning of an entry indicates that the title is appearing in BIP for the first time.

— Foreman Locksmith. (Career Examination Ser.: C-2223). 1994. pap. 27.95 (*0-8373-2223-5*) Nat Learn.
— Foreman Machinist. (Career Examination Ser.: C-1414). 1994. pap. 27.95 (*0-8373-1414-3*) Nat Learn.
— Foreman, Maintenance (MPE) (U. S. P. S.) (Career Examination Ser.: C-1786). 1994. pap. 29.95 (*0-8373-1786-X*) Nat Learn.
— Foreman of Gardeners. (Career Examination Ser.: C-268). 1994. pap. 27.95 (*0-8373-0268-4*) Nat Learn.
— Foreman of Housing Caretakers. (Career Examination Ser.: C-269). 1994. pap. 27.95 (*0-8373-0269-2*) Nat Learn.
— Foreman of Housing Exterminators. (Career Examination Ser.: C-2514). 1994. pap. 29.95 (*0-8373-2514-5*) Nat Learn.
— Foreman of Laborers. (Career Examination Ser.: C-270). 1994. pap. 27.95 (*0-8373-0270-6*) Nat Learn.
— Foreman of Lighting. (Career Examination Ser.: C-271). 1994. pap. 27.95 (*0-8373-0271-4*) Nat Learn.
— Foreman of Mechanics. (Career Examination Ser.: C-1605). 1994. reprint ed. pap. 27.95 (*0-8373-1605-7*) Nat Learn.
— Foreman of Mechanics (Motor Vehicles) (Career Examination Ser.: C-272). 1994. pap. 27.95 (*0-8373-0272-2*) Nat Learn.
— Foreman Painter. (Career Examination Ser.: C-273). 1994. pap. 27.95 (*0-8373-0273-0*) Nat Learn.
— Foreman Plasterer. (Career Examination Ser.: C-2270). 1994. reprint ed. pap. 27.95 (*0-8373-2270-7*) Nat Learn.
— Foreman Plumber. (Career Examination Ser.: C-1415). 1994. pap. 27.95 (*0-8373-1415-1*) Nat Learn.
— Foreman (Power Cables) (Career Examination Ser.: C-2034). 1994. pap. 29.95 (*0-8373-2034-8*) Nat Learn.
— Foreman (Power Distribution) (Career Examination Ser.: C-274). 1994. pap. 27.95 (*0-8373-0274-9*) Nat Learn.
— Foreman (Railroad Watchman) (Career Examination Ser.: C-275). 1994. pap. 29.95 (*0-8373-0275-7*) Nat Learn.
— Foreman Roofer. (Career Examination Ser.: C-1416). 1994. pap. 27.95 (*0-8373-1416-X*) Nat Learn.
— Foreman (Sewer Maintenance) (Career Examination Ser.: C-1816). 1994. pap. 27.95 (*0-8373-1816-5*) Nat Learn.
— Foreman Sheet Metal Worker. (Career Examination Ser.: C-1711). 1994. pap. 27.95 (*0-8373-1711-8*) Nat Learn.
— Foreman (Signals) (Career Examination Ser.: C-276). 1994. pap. 27.95 (*0-8373-0276-5*) Nat Learn.
— Foreman Steamfitter. (Career Examination Ser.: C-2025). 1994. pap. 27.95 (*0-8373-2025-9*) Nat Learn.
— Foreman (Stores, Materials & Supplies) (Career Examination Ser.: C-1625). 1994. pap. 27.95 (*0-8373-1625-1*) Nat Learn.
— Foreman (Structures) (Career Examination Ser.: C-288). 1994. pap. 27.95 (*0-8373-0288-9*) Nat Learn.
— Foreman (Structures - Group A) (Carpentry) (Career Examination Ser.: C-1322). 1994. pap. 27.95 (*0-8373-1322-8*) Nat Learn.
— Foreman (Structures - Group B) (Masonry) (Career Examination Ser.: C-1323). 1994. pap. 27.95 (*0-8373-1323-6*) Nat Learn.
— Foreman (Structures - Group C) (Iron Work) (Career Examination Ser.: C-1324). 1994. pap. 27.95 (*0-8373-1324-4*) Nat Learn.
— Foreman (Structures - Group D) (Sheet Metal) (Career Examination Ser.: C-2277). 1994. reprint ed. pap. 27.95 (*0-8373-2277-4*) Nat Learn.
— Foreman (Structures - Group E) (Plumbing) (Career Examination Ser.: C-2278). 1994. reprint ed. pap. 27.95 (*0-8373-2278-2*) Nat Learn.
— Foreman (Structures - Group F) (Painting) (Career Examination Ser.: C-1325). 1994. pap. 27.95 (*0-8373-1325-2*) Nat Learn.
— Foreman (Telephones) (Career Examination Ser.: C-1970). 1994. pap. 27.95 (*0-8373-1970-6*) Nat Learn.
— Foreman (Track) (Career Examination Ser.: C-277). 1994. pap. 27.95 (*0-8373-0277-3*) Nat Learn.
— Foreman Traffic Device Maintenance. (Career Examination Ser.: C-1712). 1994. pap. 27.95 (*0-8373-1712-6*) Nat Learn.
— Foreman (Turnstiles) (Career Examination Ser.: C-2033). 1994. pap. 27.95 (*0-8373-2033-X*) Nat Learn.
— Foreman (Ventilation & Drainage) (Career Examination Ser.: C-278). 1994. pap. 27.95 (*0-8373-0278-1*) Nat Learn.
— Foreman (Water Supply) (Career Examination Ser.: C-279). 1994. pap. 27.95 (*0-8373-0279-X*) Nat Learn.
— Foreman (Watershed Maintenance) (Career Examination Ser.: C-280). 1994. pap. 27.95 (*0-8373-0280-3*) Nat Learn.
— Forensic Medicine Investigator. (Career Examination Ser.: C-2936). 1994. pap. 39.95 (*0-8373-2936-1*) Nat Learn.
— Forensic Mental Health Assistant. (Career Examination Ser.: C-3058). 1994. pap. 29.95 (*0-8373-3058-0*) Nat Learn.
— Forensic Program Aide. (Career Examination Ser.: Series 1). 1991. pap. 23.95 (*0-8373-3719-4*) Nat Learn.
— Forensic Scientist I (Toxicology) (Career Examination Ser.: C-2937). 1994. pap. 34.95 (*0-8373-2937-X*) Nat Learn.
— Forensic Scientist II (Toxicology) (Career Examination Ser.: C-2938). 1994. pap. 34.95 (*0-8373-2938-8*) Nat Learn.
— Forensic Scientist Trainee. (Career Examination Ser.: C-3448). 1994. pap. 29.95 (*0-8373-3448-9*) Nat Learn.
— Forest Ranger. (Career Examination Ser.: C-281). 1994. 23.95 (*0-8373-0281-1*) Nat Learn.
— Forester. (Career Examination Ser.: C-289). 1994. pap. 23.95 (*0-8373-0289-7*) Nat Learn.
— Forester Trainee. (Career Examination Ser.: C-3084). 1994. pap. 23.95 (*0-8373-3084-X*) Nat Learn.
— Forestry Technician. (Career Examination Ser.: C-1424). 1994. pap. 23.95 (*0-8373-1424-0*) Nat Learn.
— Forms Technician. (Career Examination Ser.: C-2406). 1994. pap. 34.95 (*0-8373-2406-8*) Nat Learn.
— Foundations of Gerontology. (ACT Proficiency Examination Program Ser.: PEP-54). 1994. pap. 23.95 (*0-8373-5904-X*) Nat Learn.
— Foundations of Gerontology. (ACT Proficiency Examination Program Ser.: PEP-54). 1994. 39.95 (*0-8373-5929-5*) Nat Learn.
— Freight Rate Specialist. (Career Examination Ser.: C-973). 1994. pap. 27.95 (*0-8373-0973-5*) Nat Learn.
— French. (Graduate Record Examination Ser.: GRE-6). 1994. 23.95 (*0-8373-5206-1*) Nat Learn.
— French. (Undergraduate Program Field Test Ser.: UPFT-9). 1994. pap. 23.95 (*0-8373-6009-9*) Nat Learn.
— French, Jr. H. S. (Teachers License Examination Ser.: T-20). 1994. pap. 23.95 (*0-8373-8020-0*) Nat Learn.
— French, Sr. H. S. (Teachers License Examination Ser.: T-21). 1994. pap. 23.95 (*0-8373-8021-9*) Nat Learn.
— Freshman English. (College Level Examination Ser.: CLEP-31). 1994. 39.95 (*0-8373-5381-5*); pap. 23.95 (*0-8373-5331-9*) Nat Learn.
— Freshman English. (College Proficiency Examination Ser.: CPEP-11). 1994. pap. 23.95 (*0-8373-5411-0*) Nat Learn.
— Freshman English. (ACT Proficiency Examination Program Ser.: PEP-6). 1994. pap. 23.95 (*0-8373-5506-0*) Nat Learn.
— Fundamentals of Nursing. (College Level Examination Ser.: CLEP-30). 1994. pap. 23.95 (*0-8373-5330-0*) Nat Learn.
— Fundamentals of Nursing. (College Proficiency Examination Ser.: CPEP-12). 1994. pap. 23.95 (*0-8373-5412-9*) Nat Learn.
— Fundamentals of Nursing. (ACT Proficiency Examination Program Ser.: PEP-36). 1994. 39.95 (*0-8373-5586-9*); pap. 23.95 (*0-8373-5536-2*) Nat Learn.
— Funeral Directing Investigator. (Career Examination Ser.: C-3112). 1994. pap. 29.95 (*0-8373-3112-9*) Nat Learn.
— Furniture Maintainer. (Career Examination Ser.: C-1059). 1994. pap. 23.95 (*0-8373-1059-8*) Nat Learn.
— Furniture Maintainer's Helper. (Career Examination Ser.: C-282). 1994. pap. 23.95 (*0-8373-0282-X*) Nat Learn.
— Game Management. (Career Examination Ser.: C-1291). 1994. pap. 23.95 (*0-8373-1291-4*) Nat Learn.
— Game Warden. (Career Examination Ser.: C-2012). 1994. pap. 23.95 (*0-8373-2012-7*) Nat Learn.
— Gang Foreman (Structures) (Career Examination Ser.: C-3291). 1994. pap. 27.95 (*0-8373-3291-5*) Nat Learn.
— Gang Foreman (Structures-Group A) (Carpentry) (Career Examination Ser.: C-290). 1994. pap. 27.95 (*0-8373-0290-0*) Nat Learn.
— Gang Foreman (Structures-Group B) (Masonry) (Career Examination Ser.: C-291). 1994. pap. 27.95 (*0-8373-0291-9*) Nat Learn.
— Gang Foreman (Structures-Group C) (Iron Works) (Career Examination Ser.: C-292). 1994. pap. 27.95 (*0-8373-0292-7*) Nat Learn.
— Gang Foreman (Structures-Group D) (Sheet Metal) (Career Examination Ser.: C-293). 1994. pap. 27.95 (*0-8373-0293-5*) Nat Learn.
— Gang Foreman (Structures-Group E) (Plumbing) (Career Examination Ser.: C-294). 1994. pap. 27.95 (*0-8373-0294-3*) Nat Learn.
— Gang Foreman (Structures-Group F) (Painting) (Career Examination Ser.: C-295). 1994. pap. 27.95 (*0-8373-0295-1*) Nat Learn.
— Gang Foreman (Track) (Career Examination Ser.: C-296). 1994. pap. 27.95 (*0-8373-0296-X*) Nat Learn.
— Garage Foreman. (Career Examination Ser.: C-1603). 1994. pap. 27.95 (*0-8373-1603-0*) Nat Learn.
— Garageman. (Career Examination Ser.: C-1292). 1994. pap. 23.95 (*0-8373-1292-2*) Nat Learn.
— Garageman-Driver (U. S. P. S.) (Career Examination Ser.: C-1757). 1994. reprint ed. pap. 27.95 (*0-8373-1757-6*) Nat Learn.
— Garageman (U. S. P. S.) (Career Examination Ser.: C-1497). 1994. pap. 23.95 (*0-8373-1497-6*) Nat Learn.
— Gardener. (Career Examination Ser.: C-297). 1994. pap. 23.95 (*0-8373-0297-8*) Nat Learn.
— Garment Trades. (Teachers License Examination Ser.: T-72). 1994. pap. 23.95 (*0-8373-8072-3*) Nat Learn.
— Gas & Electric Welder. (Career Examination Ser.: C-1293). 1994. pap. 27.95 (*0-8373-1293-0*) Nat Learn.
— Gasoline Roller Engineer. (Career Examination Ser.: C-1294). 1994. pap. 29.95 (*0-8373-1294-9*) Nat Learn.
— General Anthropology. (DANTES Ser.: No. 16). 1994. pap. 23.95 (*0-8373-6616-X*) Nat Learn.
— General Anthropology. (DANTES Ser.: No. 16). 1994. 39.95 (*0-8373-6516-3*) Nat Learn.
— General Aptitude Test Battery. (Career Examination Ser.: No. CS-29). 1994. pap. 27.95 (*0-8373-6729-8*) Nat Learn.
— General Biology. (College Level Examination Ser.: CLEP-5). 1994. pap. 23.95 (*0-8373-5305-X*) Nat Learn.
— General Chemistry. (College Level Examination Ser.: CLEP-13). 1994. 39.95 (*0-8373-5313-0*) Nat Learn.
— General Clerical & Typing Careers Test. (Career Examination Ser.: Series 1). 1991. pap. 23.95 (*0-8373-3720-8*) Nat Learn.
— General Construction Supervisor. (Career Examination Ser.: Series 1). 1991. pap. 34.95 (*0-8373-3721-6*) Nat Learn.
— General Engineer. (Career Examination Ser.: C-298). 1991. 24.00 (*0-8373-0298-6*) Nat Learn.
— General Geophysics. (DANTES Ser.: No. 17). 1994. pap. 23.95 (*0-8373-6617-8*) Nat Learn.
— General Geophysics. (DANTES Ser.: No. 17). 1994. 39.95 (*0-8373-6517-1*) Nat Learn.
— General Industrial Training Supervisor. (Career Examination Ser.: C-2893). 1994. pap. 39.95 (*0-8373-2893-4*) Nat Learn.
— General Knowledge (Combined) (National Teacher Examination Ser.: NC-8). 1994. Cloth bdg. avail. pap. 19.95 (*0-8373-8468-0*) Nat Learn.
— General Maintainer. (Career Examination Ser.: C-3449). 1994. pap. 27.95 (*0-8373-3449-7*) Nat Learn.
— General Management Ability Battery (GMAB) (Career Examination Ser.: No. C-3532). 1994. 34.95 (*0-8373-3532-9*) Nat Learn.
— General Mathematical Ability (G. E. D.) (Career Examination Ser.: CS-33). 1994. pap. 17.95 (*0-8373-6733-6*) Nat Learn.
— General Mechanic (USPS) (Career Examination Ser.: C-835). 1994. pap. 27.95 (*0-8373-0835-6*) Nat Learn.
— General Park Foreman. (Career Examination Ser.: C-299). 1994. pap. 27.95 (*0-8373-0299-4*) Nat Learn.
— General Park Manager. (Career Examination Ser.: C-386). 1994. pap. 29.95 (*0-8373-0386-9*) Nat Learn.
— General Printing. (Occupational Competency Examination Ser.: OCE-20). 1994. pap. 23.95 (*0-8373-5720-9*) Nat Learn.
— General Psychology. (College Level Examination Ser.: CLEP-14). 1994. pap. 23.95 (*0-8373-5314-9*) Nat Learn.
— General Science. (National Teacher Examination Ser.: No. 48). 1994. Cloth bdg. avail. pap. 23.95 (*0-8373-8458-3*) Nat Learn.
— General Science, Jr. H. S. (Teachers License Examination Ser.: T-22). 1994. pap. 23.95 (*0-8373-8022-7*) Nat Learn.
— General Services Manager. (Career Examination Ser.: C-3244). 1994. pap. 34.95 (*0-8373-3244-3*) Nat Learn.
— General Superintendent. (Career Examination Ser.: C-2110). 1994. reprint ed. pap. 34.95 (*0-8373-2110-7*) Nat Learn.
— General Superintendent (Sanitation) (Career Examination Ser.: C-2097). 1994. pap. 29.95 (*0-8373-2097-6*) Nat Learn.
— General Supervisor. (Career Examination Ser.: C-1295). 1994. pap. 27.95 (*0-8373-1295-7*) Nat Learn.
— General Supervisor of School Maintenance (Construction) (Career Examination Ser.: C-1675). 1994. pap. 27.95 (*0-8373-1675-8*) Nat Learn.
— General Supervisor of School Maintenance (Electrical) (Career Examination Ser.: C-2116). 1994. reprint ed. pap. 27.95 (*0-8373-2116-6*) Nat Learn.
— General Supervisor of School Maintenance (Mechanical) (Career Examination Ser.: C-1676). 1994. pap. 27.95 (*0-8373-1676-6*) Nat Learn.
— Geodesist. (Career Examination Ser.: C-300). 1994. pap. 27.95 (*0-8373-0300-1*) Nat Learn.
— Geography. (Graduate Record Examination Ser.: GRE-7). 1994. pap. 23.95 (*0-8373-5207-X*) Nat Learn.
— Geography. (Undergraduate Program Field Test Ser.: UPFT-10). 1994. pap. 23.95 (*0-8373-6010-2*) Nat Learn.
— Geologist. (Career Examination Ser.: C-301). 1994. pap. 27.95 (*0-8373-0301-X*) Nat Learn.
— Geology. (College Level Examination Ser.: CLEP-15). 1994. pap. 19.95 (*0-8373-5315-7*) Nat Learn.
— Geology. (College Proficiency Examination Ser.: CPEP-13). 1994. pap. 23.95 (*0-8373-5413-7*) Nat Learn.
— Geology. (Graduate Record Examination Ser.: GRE-8). 1994. pap. 23.95 (*0-8373-5208-8*) Nat Learn.
— Geology. (DANTES Ser.: No. 18). 1994. pap. 23.95 (*0-8373-6618-6*) Nat Learn.
— Geology. (DANTES Ser.: No. 18). 1994. 39.95 (*0-8373-6518-X*) Nat Learn.
— Geology. (Undergraduate Program Field Test Ser.: UPFT-11). 1995. pap. 23.95 (*0-8373-6011-0*) Nat Learn.
— Geophysicist. (Career Examination Ser.: C-302). 1994. pap. 27.95 (*0-8373-0302-8*) Nat Learn.
— German. (Graduate Record Examination Ser.: GRE-9). 1994. pap. 23.95 (*0-8373-5209-6*) Nat Learn.
— German. (National Teachers Examination Ser.: NT-32). 1994. pap. 23.95 (*0-8373-8442-7*) Nat Learn.
— German. (Undergraduate Program Field Test Ser.: UPFT-12). 1994. pap. 23.95 (*0-8373-6012-9*) Nat Learn.
— German. (College Level Examination Ser.: CLEP-45). 1994. reprint ed. 39.95 (*0-8373-5395-5*); reprint ed. pap. 23.95 (*0-8373-5345-9*) Nat Learn.
— Gerontological Nurse. (Certified Nurse Examination Ser.: CN-5). 1991. pap. 19.95 (*0-8373-6105-2*) Nat Learn.
— Gerontological Nurse. (Certified Nurse Examination Ser.: CN-5). 1994. 39.95 (*0-8373-6155-9*) Nat Learn.
— Gerontological Nurse Practitioner. (Certified Nurse Examination Ser.: CN-6). 1994. 39.95 (*0-8373-6156-7*); pap. 23.95 (*0-8373-6106-0*) Nat Learn.
— Glazier. (Career Examination Ser.: C-303). 1994. pap. 27.95 (*0-8373-0303-6*) Nat Learn.
— GMC Apprentice Program Battery Tests. (Admission Test Ser.: ATS-94). 1994. pap. 29.95 (*0-8373-5094-8*) Nat Learn.
— Golf Course Supervisor. (Career Examination Ser.: C-2774). 1994. pap. 29.95 (*0-8373-2774-1*) Nat Learn.
— Graduate Management Admission Test (GMAT) (Admission Test Ser.: ATS-14). 1994. pap. 23.95 (*0-8373-5014-X*) Nat Learn.
— Graduate Record Examination General (Aptitude) Test (GRE) (Admission Test Ser.: ATS-10). 1994. 23.95 (*0-8373-5010-7*) Nat Learn.
— Graduate Record Examination Series. 1994. pap. write for info. (*0-8373-5200-2*) Nat Learn.
— Graduate School Foreign Language Test (GSFLT) - German. (Admission Test Ser.: ATS-28B). 1994. pap. 23.95 (*0-8373-6953-3*) Nat Learn.
— Graduate School Foreign Language Test (GSFLT) - Spanish. (Admission Test Ser.: ATS-28C). 1994. pap. 23.95 (*0-8373-6954-1*) Nat Learn.
— Grammar. (Teachers License Examination Ser.: G-2). 1994. pap. 23.95 (*0-8373-8192-4*) Nat Learn.
— Grants Analyst. (Career Examination Ser.: C-2832). 1994. pap. 34.95 (*0-8373-2832-2*) Nat Learn.
— Grants Coordinator. (Career Examination Ser.: C-2797). 1994. 34.95 (*0-8373-2797-0*) Nat Learn.
— Grants in Aid Program Assistant. (Career Examination Ser.: No. C-3542). 1994. 29.95 (*0-8373-3542-6*) Nat Learn.
— Graphic Arts Specialist. (Career Examination Ser.: C-2672). 1994. pap. 27.95 (*0-8373-2672-9*) Nat Learn.
— Greenskeeper. (Career Examination Ser.: C-2656). 1994. pap. 23.95 (*0-8373-2656-7*) Nat Learn.
— Grounds Superintendent. (Career Examination Ser.: C-3357). 1994. pap. 29.95 (*0-8373-3357-1*) Nat Learn.
— Groundskeeper. (Career Examination Ser.: C-1298). 1994. pap. 23.95 (*0-8373-1298-1*) Nat Learn.
— Group Health Insurance Supervisor. (Career Examination Ser.: C-3059). 1994. pap. 34.95 (*0-8373-3059-9*) Nat Learn.
— Group Worker. (Career Examination Ser.: C-1300). 1994. pap. 327.95 (*0-8373-1300-7*) Nat Learn.
— Guard Patrolman. (Career Examination Ser.: C-304). 1994. pap. 23.95 (*0-8373-0304-4*) Nat Learn.
— Guidance Counselor. (Career Examination Ser.: C-305). 1994. pap. 29.95 (*0-8373-0305-2*) Nat Learn.
— Guidance Counselor. (National Teacher Examination Ser.: NT-16). 1994. pap. 23.95 (*0-8373-8456-7*) Nat Learn.
— Guidance Counselor, Elementary School. (Teachers License Examination Ser.: GT-1). 1994. pap. 27.95 (*0-8373-8121-5*) Nat Learn.
— Guidance Counselor, Elementary School. (National Teachers Examination Ser.: NT-16a). 1994. pap. 23.95 (*0-8373-8426-5*) Nat Learn.
— Guidance Counselor, Jr. H. S. (Teachers License Examination Ser.: GT-2). 1994. pap. 27.95 (*0-8373-8122-3*) Nat Learn.
— Guidance Counselor, Junior H. S. (National Teachers Examination Ser.: NT-16b). 1994. pap. 23.95 (*0-8373-8427-3*) Nat Learn.
— Guidance Counselor, Senior H. S. (National Teachers Examination Ser.: NT-16c). 1994. pap. 23.95 (*0-8373-8428-1*) Nat Learn.
— Guidance Counselor, Sr. H. S. (Teachers License Examination Ser.: GT-3). 1994. pap. 23.95 (*0-8373-8123-1*) Nat Learn.
— Habilitation Specialist. (Career Examination Ser.: C-2900). 1994. pap. 23.95 (*0-8373-2900-0*) Nat Learn.
— Handbook of Real Estate (HRE) (Encyclopedia of Terms) Encyclopedia of Terms. (Admission Test Ser.: ATS-5). 1994. 29.95 (*0-8373-5005-0*) Nat Learn.
— Handbook of Tests. (General Aptitude & Abilities Ser.: CS-17). 1994. pap. 23.95 (*0-8373-6717-4*) Nat Learn.
— Handbook of the Stock Market (HOS) (Admission Test Ser.: ATS-2). 1994. pap. 13.95 (*0-8373-5002-6*) Nat Learn.
— Handicapped Children's Services Specialist. (Career Examination Ser.: Series 1). 1991. pap. 27.95 (*0-8373-3722-4*) Nat Learn.
— Handicapped Service Aide. (Career Examination Ser.: C-3305). 1994. pap. 23.95 (*0-8373-3305-9*) Nat Learn.
— Harbormaster. (Career Examination Ser.: C-3245). 1994. pap. 27.95 (*0-8373-3245-1*) Nat Learn.
— Hawaii Credit-by-Examination Program (CEP) (Admission Test Ser.: ATS-62). 1994. pap. 23.95 (*0-8373-5062-X*) Nat Learn.
— Hazardous Waste Facility Monitor. (Career Examination Ser.: C-3115). 1994. pap. 34.95 (*0-8373-3115-3*) Nat Learn.
— Head Account-Audit Clerk. (Career Examination Ser.: C-2009). 1994. pap. 27.95 (*0-8373-2009-7*) Nat Learn.
— Head Accountant-Audit Clerk. (Career Examination Ser.: C-2009). 1994. pap. 22.00 (*0-685-03524-7*) Nat Learn.
— Head Automotive Mechanic. (Career Examination Ser.: C-1302). 1994. pap. 29.95 (*0-8373-1302-3*) Nat Learn.
— Head Bus Driver. (Career Examination Ser.: C-2198). 1994. pap. 29.95 (*0-8373-2198-0*) Nat Learn.
— Head Clerk. (Career Examination Ser.: C-347). 1994. pap. 29.95 (*0-8373-0347-8*) Nat Learn.
— Head Clerk (Payroll) (Career Examination Ser.: C-1908). 1994. pap. 29.95 (*0-8373-1908-0*) Nat Learn.
— Head Clerk Surrogate. (Career Examination Ser.: C-2130). 1994. reprint ed. pap. 29.95 (*0-8373-2130-1*) Nat Learn.
— Head Custodian. (Career Examination Ser.: C-1958). 1994. pap. 29.95 (*0-8373-1958-7*) Nat Learn.
— Head Custodian I. (Career Examination Ser.: C-1823). 1994. pap. 29.95 (*0-8373-1823-8*) Nat Learn.
— Head Custodian II. (Career Examination Ser.: C-1824). 1994. pap. 34.95 (*0-8373-1824-6*) Nat Learn.
— Head Custodian III. (Career Examination Ser.: C-1825). 1994. pap. 34.95 (*0-8373-1825-4*) Nat Learn.
— Head Dietitian. (Career Examination Ser.: C-320). 1994. pap. 34.95 (*0-8373-0320-6*) Nat Learn.
— Head Janitor. (Career Examination Ser.: C-2066). 1994. reprint ed. pap. 29.95 (*0-8373-2066-6*) Nat Learn.
— Head Laundry Supervisor. (Career Examination Ser.: C-2426). 1994. pap. 34.95 (*0-8373-2426-2*) Nat Learn.
— Head Maintenance Supervisor. (Career Examination Ser.: C-2043). 1994. pap. 34.95 (*0-8373-2043-7*) Nat Learn.
— Head Nurse. (Career Examination Ser.: C-321). 1994. pap. 29.95 (*0-8373-0321-4*) Nat Learn.
— Head Process Server. (Career Examination Ser.: C-348). 1994. 29.95 (*0-8373-0348-6*) Nat Learn.
— Head Process Server & Court Aide. (Career Examination Ser.: C-349). 1994. pap. 34.95 (*0-8373-0349-4*) Nat Learn.
— Head School Lunch Manager. (Career Examination Ser.: C-2172). 1994. reprint ed. pap. 34.95 (*0-8373-2172-7*) Nat Learn.
— Head Stationary Engineer. (Career Examination Ser.: C-1720). 1994. pap. 39.95 (*0-8373-1720-7*) Nat Learn.
— Health Aide. (Career Examination Ser.: C-1301). 1994. pap. 23.95 (*0-8373-1301-5*) Nat Learn.

R

— Health & Physical Education, Jr. H. S. (Teachers License Examination Ser.: T-24). 1994. pap. 23.95 (*0-8373-8024-3*) Nat Learn.
— Health & Physical Education, Sr. H. S. (Teachers License Examination Ser.: T-25). 1994. pap. 23.95 (*0-8373-8025-1*) Nat Learn.
— Health Benefits Clerk. (Career Examination Ser.: C-3558). 1994. 23.95 (*0-8373-3558-2*) Nat Learn.
— Health Care Fiscal Analyst. (Career Examination Ser.: C-3620). 1994. 34.95 (*0-8373-3620-1*) Nat Learn.
— Health Care Surveyor. (Career Examination Ser.: C-3361). 1994. pap. 34.95 (*0-8373-3361-X*) Nat Learn.
— Health Conservation. (Teachers License Examination Ser.: T-23). 1994. pap. 23.95 (*0-8373-8023-5*) Nat Learn.
— Health Department Investigator. (Career Examination Ser.: C-3074). 1994. pap. 29.95 (*0-8373-3074-2*) Nat Learn.
— Health Education. (National Teachers Examination Ser.: NT-38). 1994. pap. 23.95 (*0-8373-8448-6*) Nat Learn.
— Health Facilities Planner. (Career Examination Ser.: No. C-3531). 1994. 29.95 (*0-8373-3531-0*) Nat Learn.
— Health I. (College Proficiency Examination Ser.: CPEP-17). 1994. 39.95 (*0-8373-5467-6*); pap. 23.95 (*0-8373-5417-X*) Nat Learn.
— Health I: Personal Health, Physical Aspects. (ACT Proficiency Examination Program Ser.: PEP-33). 1994. 39.95 (*0-8373-5583-4*); pap. 23.95 (*0-8373-5533-8*) Nat Learn.
— Health III. (College Proficiency Examination Ser.: CPEP-19). 1994. 39.95 (*0-8373-5469-2*); pap. 23.95 (*0-8373-5419-6*) Nat Learn.
— Health Inspector. (Career Examination Ser.: C-322). 1994. pap. 27.95 (*0-8373-0322-2*) Nat Learn.
— Health Insurance Administrator. (Career Examination Ser.: C-2687). 1994. pap. 39.95 (*0-8373-2687-7*) Nat Learn.
— Health, Jr. H. S. (Teachers License Examination Ser.: T-24a). 1994. pap. 23.95 (*0-8373-8094-4*) Nat Learn.
— Health Occupations Aptitude Examination. (Admission Test Ser.: ATS-98). 1994. 29.95 (*0-8373-5098-0*) Nat Learn.
— Health Planner. (Career Examination Ser.: C-3027). 1994. pap. 29.95 (*0-8373-3027-0*) Nat Learn.
— Health Planner Trainee. (Career Examination Ser.: C-3026). 1994. pap. 27.95 (*0-8373-3026-2*) Nat Learn.
— Health Program Administrator. (Career Examination Ser.). 1943. 34.95 (*0-8373-3601-5*, C-3601) Nat Learn.
— Health Program Analyst. (Career Examination Ser.: Series 1). 1991. pap. 34.95 (*0-8373-3723-2*) Nat Learn.
— Health Restoration: Area I. (ACT Proficiency Examination Program Ser.: PEP-51). 1994. pap. 23.95 (*0-8373-5901-5*) Nat Learn.
— Health Restoration: Area I. (Regents External Degree Ser.: REDP-31). 1994. pap. 23.95 (*0-8373-5631-8*) Nat Learn.
— Health Restoration: Area II. (ACT Proficiency Examination Program Ser.: PEP-52). 1994. pap. 23.95 (*0-8373-5902-3*) Nat Learn.
— Health Restoration: Area II. (Regents External Degree Ser.: REDP-32). 1994. pap. 23.95 (*0-8373-5632-6*) Nat Learn.
— Health Service Nurse. (Career Examination Ser.: C-350). 1994. pap. 23.95 (*0-8373-0350-8*) Nat Learn.
— Health Services Manager. (Career Examination Ser.: C-3178). 1994. pap. 34.95 (*0-8373-3178-1*) Nat Learn.
— Health, Sr. H. S. (Teachers License Examination Ser.: T-24b). 1994. pap. 23.95 (*0-8373-8095-2*) Nat Learn.
— Health Support: Area I. (ACT Proficiency Examination Program Ser.: PEP-48). 1994. 39.95 (*0-8373-5598-2*); pap. 23.95 (*0-8373-5548-6*) Nat Learn.
— Health Support: Area I. (Regents External Degree Ser.: REDP-24). 1994. 39.95 (*0-8373-5674-1*); pap. 23.95 (*0-8373-5624-5*) Nat Learn.
— Health Support: Area II. (ACT Proficiency Examination Program Ser.: PEP-49). 1994. 39.95 (*0-8373-5599-0*); pap. 23.95 (*0-8373-5549-4*) Nat Learn.
— Health Support: Area II. (Regents External Degree Ser.: REDP-25). 1994. 39.95 (*0-8373-5675-X*); pap. 23.95 (*0-8373-5625-3*) Nat Learn.
— Health Three: Public & Environmental Health. (ACT Proficiency Examination Program Ser.: PEP-35). 1994. 39.95 (*0-8373-5585-0*); pap. 23.95 (*0-8373-5535-4*) Nat Learn.
— Health Two. (College Proficiency Examination Ser.: CPEP-18). 1994. 39.95 (*0-8373-5468-4*); pap. 23.95 (*0-8373-5418-8*) Nat Learn.
— Health Two: Personal Health, Emotional-Social Aspects. (ACT Proficiency Examination Program Ser.: PEP-34). 1994. 39.95 (*0-8373-5584-2*); pap. 23.95 (*0-8373-5534-6*) Nat Learn.
— Hearing Administration Service Coordinator. (Career Examination Ser.: C-1743). 1994. reprint ed. pap. 39.95 (*0-8373-1743-6*) Nat Learn.
— Hearing Examiner. (Career Examination Ser.: C-351). 1994. pap. 34.95 (*0-8373-0351-6*) Nat Learn.
— Hearing Officer. (Career Examination Ser.: C-1758). 1994. reprint ed. pap. 34.95 (*0-8373-1758-4*) Nat Learn.
— Hearing Reporter. (Career Examination Ser.: C-2795). 1994. pap. 23.95 (*0-8373-2795-4*) Nat Learn.
— Heating Plant Technician. (Career Examination Ser.: C-329). 1994. pap. 23.95 (*0-8373-0329-X*) Nat Learn.
— Heavy Equipment Mechanic. (Career Examination Ser.: C-1310). 1994. pap. 27.95 (*0-8373-1310-4*) Nat Learn.
— Heavy Equipment Repair Supervisor. (Career Examination Ser.: C-2614). 1994. pap. 29.95 (*0-8373-2614-1*) Nat Learn.
— Hebrew, Jr. & Sr. H. S. (Teachers License Examination Ser.: T-26). 1994. pap. 23.95 (*0-8373-8026-X*) Nat Learn.
— Hematology. (College Level Examination Ser.: CLEP-33). 1994. 39.95 (*0-8373-5383-1*); pap. 23.95 (*0-8373-5333-5*) Nat Learn.
— High Pressure Plant Tender. (Career Examination Ser.: C-3277). 1994. pap. 23.95 (*0-8373-3277-X*) Nat Learn.
— High Risk Perinatal Nurse. (Certified Nurse Examination Ser.: CN-10). 1994. 39.95 (*0-8373-6160-5*); pap. 23.95 (*0-8373-6110-9*) Nat Learn.
— High School APL Survey (APL-HS) (Admission Test Ser.: ATS-60A). 1994. 39.95 (*0-8373-6988-6*); pap. 23.95 (*0-8373-6963-0*) Nat Learn.
— High School Basic Competency Tests (BCT-HS) (Admission Test Ser.: ATS-57). 1994. 39.95 (*0-8373-5157-X*); pap. 23.95 (*0-8373-5057-3*) Nat Learn.
— High School Equivalency Diploma Examinat. (General Aptitude & Abilities Ser.: CS-50). 1994. pap. 23.95 (*0-8373-6750-6*) Nat Learn.
— High School Equivalency Diploma Examination (EE) (Admission Test Ser.: ATS-17). 1994. 39.95 (*0-8373-5117-0*); pap. 23.95 (*0-8373-5017-4*) Nat Learn.
— High School Equivalency Diploma Workbook (HSEDE) (General Aptitude & Abilities Ser.: CS-51). 1994. pap. 23.95 (*0-8373-6751-4*) Nat Learn.
— High Voltage Specialist. (Career Examination Ser.: C-3389). 1994. pap. 29.95 (*0-8373-3389-X*) Nat Learn.
— Highway Construction Coordinator. (Career Examination Ser.: C-2804). 1994. pap. 34.95 (*0-8373-2804-7*) Nat Learn.
— Highway Construction Supervisor. (Career Examination Ser.: C-3072). 1994. pap. 34.95 (*0-8373-3072-6*) Nat Learn.
— Highway Engineer. (Career Examination Ser.: C-2521). 1994. pap. 34.95 (*0-8373-2521-8*) Nat Learn.
— Highway Equipment Supervisor. (Career Examination Ser.: C-2805). 1994. pap. 29.95 (*0-8373-2805-5*) Nat Learn.
— Highway General Foreman. (Career Examination Ser.: C-2308). 1994. pap. 27.95 (*0-8373-2308-8*) Nat Learn.
— Highway Maintenance Specialist. (Career Examination Ser.: C-1330). 1994. pap. 29.95 (*0-8373-1330-9*) Nat Learn.
— Highway Maintenance Supervisor. (Career Examination Ser.: C-2212). 1994. pap. 29.95 (*0-8373-2212-X*) Nat Learn.
— Highway Patrolman. (Career Examination Ser.: C-3450). 1994. pap. 23.95 (*0-8373-3450-0*) Nat Learn.
— Highway Reports & Inventory Assistant. (Career Examination Ser.: C-3134). 1994. pap. 27.95 (*0-8373-3134-X*) Nat Learn.
— Highway Transportation Specialist. (Career Examination Ser.: C-2248). 1994. pap. 29.95 (*0-8373-2248-0*) Nat Learn.
— Highway Zone Foreman. (Career Examination Ser.: C-2307). 1994. reprint ed. pap. 27.95 (*0-8373-2307-X*) Nat Learn.
— Histology Technician. (Career Examination Ser.: C-2837). 1994. pap. 29.95 (*0-8373-2837-3*) Nat Learn.
— Historian. (Career Examination Ser.: C-3163). 1941. pap. 29.95 (*0-8373-3163-3*) Nat Learn.
— Historic Site Manager. (Career Examination Ser.: C-2373). 1994. pap. 29.95 (*0-8373-2373-8*) Nat Learn.
— History. (Graduate Record Examination Ser.: GRE-10). 1994. 39.95 (*0-8373-5260-6*); pap. 23.95 (*0-8373-5210-X*) Nat Learn.
— History. (Undergraduate Program Field Test Ser.: UPFT-13). 1994. pap. 23.95 (*0-8373-6013-7*) Nat Learn.
— History of American Education. (College Level Examination Ser.: CLEP-16). 1994. 39.95 (*0-8373-5366-1*); pap. 23.95 (*0-8373-5316-5*) Nat Learn.
— History of American Education. (College Proficiency Examination Ser.: CPEP-21). 1994. 39.95 (*0-8373-5471-4*); pap. 23.95 (*0-8373-5421-8*) Nat Learn.
— History of American Education. (ACT Proficiency Examination Program Ser.: PEP-29). 1994. 39.95 (*0-8373-5579-6*); pap. 23.95 (*0-8373-5529-X*) Nat Learn.
— Hoisting Machine Operator. (Career Examination Ser.: C-2257). 1991. reprint ed. pap. 20.00 (*0-8373-2257-X*) Nat Learn.
— Hoists & Rigging Inspector. (Career Examination Ser.: C-323). 1994. pap. 27.95 (*0-8373-0323-0*) Nat Learn.
— Home Economics. (National Teachers Examination Ser.: NT-12). 1994. pap. 23.95 (*0-8373-8422-2*) Nat Learn.
— Home Economics, Jr. H. S. (Teachers License Examination Ser.: T-28). 1994. pap. 23.95 (*0-8373-8028-6*) Nat Learn.
— Home Economics, Sr. H. S. (Teachers License Examination Ser.: T-29). 1994. pap. 23.95 (*0-8373-8029-4*) Nat Learn.
— Home Economist. (Career Examination Ser.: C-324). 1994. pap. 27.95 (*0-8373-0324-9*) Nat Learn.
— Home Economist Trainee. (Career Examination Ser.: C-352). 1994. pap. 23.95 (*0-8373-0352-4*) Nat Learn.
— Homebound. (Teachers License Examination Ser.: T-27). 1994. pap. 23.95 (*0-8373-8027-8*) Nat Learn.
— Homemaker. (Career Examination Ser.: C-1303). 1994. pap. 27.95 (*0-8373-1303-1*) Nat Learn.
— Horticultural Inspector. (Career Examination Ser.: C-1304). 1994. pap. 29.95 (*0-8373-1304-X*) Nat Learn.
— Horticulturist. (Career Examination Ser.: C-1305). 1994. pap. 29.95 (*0-8373-1305-8*) Nat Learn.
— Hospice Coordinator. (Career Examination Ser.: C-3034). 1994. pap. 29.95 (*0-8373-3034-3*) Nat Learn.
— Hospital Administration Consultant. (Career Examination Ser.: C-2768). 1994. pap. 39.95 (*0-8373-2768-7*) Nat Learn.
— Hospital Administration Intern. (Career Examination Ser.: C-1967). 1994. pap. 29.95 (*0-8373-1967-6*) Nat Learn.
— Hospital Administrator. (Career Examination Ser.: C-1654). 1994. pap. 34.95 (*0-8373-1654-5*) Nat Learn.
— Hospital Attendant. (Career Examination Ser.: C-325). 1994. 23.95 (*0-8373-0325-7*) Nat Learn.
— Hospital Care Investigator. (Career Examination Ser.: C-326). 1994. pap. 27.95 (*0-8373-0326-5*) Nat Learn.
— Hospital Care Investigator Trainee. (Career Examination Ser.: C-327). 1994. pap. 23.95 (*0-8373-0327-3*) Nat Learn.
— Hospital Case Investigator. (Career Examination Ser.: C-1889). 1994. pap. 27.95 (*0-8373-1889-0*) Nat Learn.
— Hospital Clerk. (Career Examination Ser.: C-328). 1994. pap. 23.95 (*0-8373-0328-1*) Nat Learn.
— Hospital Controller. (Career Examination Ser.: C-1760). 1994. reprint ed. pap. 34.95 (*0-8373-1760-6*) Nat Learn.
— Hospital Patient Services Clerk. (Career Examination Ser.: C-3610). 1994. 27.95 (*0-8373-3610-4*, C-3610) Nat Learn.
— Hospital Reimbursement Specialist. (Career Examination Ser.: C-1297). 1994. pap. 27.95 (*0-8373-1297-3*) Nat Learn.
— Hospital Safety Officer. (Career Examination Ser.: C-118). 1994. pap. 27.95 (*0-8373-0118-1*) Nat Learn.
— Hospital Safety Officer Trainee. (Career Examination Ser.: C-119). 1994. pap. 23.95 (*0-8373-0119-X*) Nat Learn.
— Hospital Security Officer. (Career Examination Ser.: C-353). 1991. pap. 18.00 (*0-8373-0353-2*) Nat Learn.
— Hotline Coordinator. (Career Examination Ser.: C-3533). 1994. 29.95 (*0-8373-3533-7*) Nat Learn.
— House Painter. (Career Examination Ser.: C-354). 1994. pap. 23.95 (*0-8373-0354-0*) Nat Learn.
— Housekeeper. (Career Examination Ser.: C-330). 1994. pap. 23.95 (*0-8373-0330-3*) Nat Learn.
— Housemother. (Career Examination Ser.: C-1306). 1994. pap. 27.95 (*0-8373-1306-6*) Nat Learn.
— Housing & Community Development Assistant. (Career Examination Ser.: C-2537). 1994. pap. 23.95 (*0-8373-2537-4*) Nat Learn.
— Housing & Community Development Representative. (Career Examination Ser.: C-2539). 1994. pap. 27.95 (*0-8373-2539-0*) Nat Learn.
— Housing Assistant. (Career Examination Ser.: C-331). 1994. pap. 23.95 (*0-8373-0331-1*) Nat Learn.
— Housing Captain. (Career Examination Ser.: C-332). 1994. pap. 39.95 (*0-8373-0332-X*) Nat Learn.
— Housing Caretaker. (Career Examination Ser.: C-333). 1994. pap. 23.95 (*0-8373-0333-8*) Nat Learn.
— Housing Community Activities Coordinator. (Career Examination Ser.: C-334). 1994. pap. 34.95 (*0-8373-0334-6*) Nat Learn.
— Housing Construction Inspector. (Career Examination Ser.: C-335). 1994. pap. 29.95 (*0-8373-0335-4*) Nat Learn.
— Housing Consumer Representative. (Career Examination Ser.: C-3145). 1994. pap. 27.95 (*0-8373-3145-5*) Nat Learn.
— Housing Exterminator. (Career Examination Ser.: C-2283). 1994. 27.95 (*0-8373-2283-9*) Nat Learn.
— Housing Fireman. (Career Examination Ser.: C-336). 1994. pap. 23.95 (*0-8373-0336-2*) Nat Learn.
— Housing Groundsman. (Career Examination Ser.: C-337). 1994. pap. 23.95 (*0-8373-0337-0*) Nat Learn.
— Housing Guard. (Career Examination Ser.: C-338). 1994. pap. 23.95 (*0-8373-0338-9*) Nat Learn.
— Housing Inspector. (Career Examination Ser.: C-339). 1994. pap. 29.95 (*0-8373-0339-7*) Nat Learn.
— Housing Lieutenant. (Career Examination Ser.: C-340). 1994. pap. 34.95 (*0-8373-0340-0*) Nat Learn.
— Housing Maintenance Helper. (Career Examination Ser.: C-355). 1994. pap. 23.95 (*0-8373-0355-9*) Nat Learn.
— Housing Management Assistant. (Career Examination Ser.: C-2290). 1995. reprint ed. pap. 23.95 (*0-8373-2290-1*) Nat Learn.
— Housing Management Representative. (Career Examination Ser.: C-2291). 1995. 27.95 (*0-8373-2291-X*) Nat Learn.
— Housing Manager. (Career Examination Ser.: C-341). 1994. pap. 27.95 (*0-8373-0341-9*) Nat Learn.
— Housing Patrolman. (Career Examination Ser.: C-342). 1994. 23.95 (*0-8373-0342-7*) Nat Learn.
— Housing, Planning & Redevelopment Aide. (Career Examination Ser.: C-343). 1994. pap. 29.95 (*0-8373-0343-5*) Nat Learn.
— Housing Sergeant. (Career Examination Ser.: C-344). 1994. pap. 29.95 (*0-8373-0344-3*) Nat Learn.
— Housing Supervisor. (Career Examination Ser.: C-3313). 1994. pap. 34.95 (*0-8373-3313-X*) Nat Learn.
— Housing Supplyman. (Career Examination Ser.: C-345). 1994. pap. 23.95 (*0-8373-0345-1*) Nat Learn.
— Housing Teller. (Career Examination Ser.: C-346). 1994. pap. 23.95 (*0-8373-0346-X*) Nat Learn.
— How to Prepare for a Civil Service Examination. (General Aptitude & Abilities Ser.: CS-42). 1994. pap. 9.95 (*0-8373-6742-5*) Nat Learn.
— Human Growth & Development. (College Level Examination Ser.: CLEP-17). 1994. 39.95 (*0-8373-5367-X*); pap. 23.95 (*0-8373-5317-3*) Nat Learn.
— Human Relations Aide. (Career Examination Ser.: C-1307). 1994. pap. 23.95 (*0-8373-1307-4*) Nat Learn.
— Human Relations Representative. (Career Examination Ser.: C-1308). 1994. pap. 27.95 (*0-8373-1308-2*) Nat Learn.
— Human Relations Specialist. (Career Examination Ser.: C-1614). 1994. pap. 27.95 (*0-8373-1614-6*) Nat Learn.
— Human Relations Training Officer. (Career Examination Ser.: C-1309). 1994. pap. 34.95 (*0-8373-1309-0*) Nat Learn.
— Human Resources Aide. (Career Examination Ser.: C-1785). 1994. pap. 23.95 (*0-8373-1785-1*) Nat Learn.
— Human Resources Specialist. (Career Examination Ser.: C-356). 1994. pap. 27.95 (*0-8373-0356-7*) Nat Learn.
— Human Resources Technician. (Career Examination Ser.: C-2071). 1994. pap. 27.95 (*0-8373-2071-2*) Nat Learn.
— Human Rights Investigator. (Career Examination Ser.: C-2228). 1994. pap. 27.95 (*0-8373-2228-6*) Nat Learn.
— Humanities. (Graduate Record Area Examination Ser.: GRE-42). 1989. pap. 17.95 (*0-8373-5242-8*) Nat Learn.
— Humanities. (College-Level Examination Ser.: ATS-9B). 1991. pap. 19.95 (*0-8373-5246-0*) Nat Learn.
— Humanities. (Admission Test Ser.: ATS-9B). 1994. 39.95 (*0-8373-5109-X*) Nat Learn.
— Humanities. (Graduate Record Area Examination Ser.: GRE-42). 1994. 39.95 (*0-8373-5292-4*) Nat Learn.
— Hydraulic Engineer. (Career Examination Ser.: C-357). 1994. pap. 39.95 (*0-8373-0357-5*) Nat Learn.
— Hydrogeologist. (Career Examination Ser.: C-3390). 1994. pap. 39.95 (*0-8373-3390-3*) Nat Learn.
— IBM Tabulator Operator. (Career Examination Ser.: C-1920). 1994. pap. 23.95 (*0-8373-1920-X*) Nat Learn.
— IBM Tabulator Operator Trainee. (Career Examination Ser.: C-360). 1994. pap. 19.95 (*0-8373-0360-5*) Nat Learn.
— Identification Clerk. (Career Examination Ser.: C-361). 1994. pap. 23.95 (*0-8373-0361-3*) Nat Learn.
— Identification Officer. (Career Examination Ser.: C-1986). 1945. pap. 29.95 (*0-8373-1986-2*) Nat Learn.
— Identification Specialist. (Career Examination Ser.: C-2294). 1994. pap. 29.95 (*0-8373-2294-4*) Nat Learn.
— Illustrator. (Career Examination Ser.: C-379). 1994. pap. 29.95 (*0-8373-0379-6*) Nat Learn.
— Illustrator Aide. (Career Examination Ser.: C-2930). 1994. pap. 27.95 (*0-8373-2930-2*) Nat Learn.
— Immigration Patrol Inspector. (Career Examination Ser.: C-362). 1994. pap. 23.95 (*0-8373-0362-1*) Nat Learn.
— Immunohematology & Blood Banking. (College Level Examination Ser.: CLEP-34). 1994. 39.95 (*0-8373-5384-X*); pap. 23.95 (*0-8373-5334-3*) Nat Learn.
— Incinerator Plant Foreman. (Career Examination Ser.: C-2163). 1994. reprint ed. pap. 29.95 (*0-8373-2163-8*) Nat Learn.
— Incinerator Plant Maintenance Foreman. (Career Examination Ser.: C-2773). 1994. pap. 29.95 (*0-8373-2773-3*) Nat Learn.
— Incinerator Plant Supervisor. (Career Examination Ser.: C-2164). 1994. reprint ed. pap. 29.95 (*0-8373-2164-6*) Nat Learn.
— Incinerator Stationary Engineer. (Career Examination Ser.: C-2636). 1994. pap. 29.95 (*0-8373-2636-2*) Nat Learn.
— Income Maintenance Specialist. (Career Examination Ser.: C-3557). 1994. 23.95 (*0-8373-3557-4*) Nat Learn.
— Income Maintenance Supervisor. (Career Examination Ser.: Series 1). 1991. pap. 29.95 (*0-8373-3724-0*) Nat Learn.
— Income Maintenance Worker. (Career Examination Ser.: Series 1). 1991. pap. 23.95 (*0-8373-3725-9*) Nat Learn.
— Indian Education - Elementary Teacher. (Career Examination Ser.: C-1311). 1994. pap. 27.95 (*0-8373-1311-2*) Nat Learn.
— Indian Education - Guidance Counselor. (Career Examination Ser.: C-1312). 1994. pap. 27.95 (*0-8373-1312-0*) Nat Learn.
— Indian Education - Secondary Teacher. (Career Examination Ser.: C-1313). 1994. pap. 27.95 (*0-8373-1313-9*) Nat Learn.
— Industrial Arts, Jr. H. S. (Teachers License Examination Ser.: T-30). 1994. pap. 23.95 (*0-8373-8030-8*) Nat Learn.
— Industrial Arts, Sr. H. S. (Teachers License Examination Ser.: T-31). 1994. pap. 23.95 (*0-8373-8031-6*) Nat Learn.
— Industrial Consultant. (Career Examination Ser.: C-2771). 1994. pap. 39.95 (*0-8373-2771-7*) Nat Learn.
— Industrial Development Assistant. (Career Examination Ser.: C-2848). 1994. pap. 34.95 (*0-8373-2848-9*) Nat Learn.
— Industrial Electronics. (Occupational Competency Examination Ser.: OCE-21). 1994. 39.95 (*0-8373-5771-3*); pap. 23.95 (*0-8373-5721-7*) Nat Learn.
— Industrial Engineer. (Career Examination Ser.: C-380). 1994. 34.95 (*0-8373-0380-X*) Nat Learn.
— Industrial Equipment Mechanic (USPS) (Career Examination Ser.: C-3359). 1994. pap. 27.95 (*0-8373-3359-8*) Nat Learn.
— Industrial Foreman. (Career Examination Ser.: C-1956). 1994. pap. 29.95 (*0-8373-1956-0*) Nat Learn.
— Industrial Hygienist. (Career Examination Ser.: C-381). 1994. pap. 39.95 (*0-8373-0381-8*) Nat Learn.
— Industrial Hygienist Trainee. (Career Examination Ser.: C-3035). 1994. pap. 34.95 (*0-8373-3035-1*) Nat Learn.
— Industrial Training Supervisor. (Career Examination Ser.: C-2839). 1994. pap. 39.95 (*0-8373-2839-X*) Nat Learn.
— Industrial Waste Control Specialist. (Career Examination Ser.: C-3454). 1994. pap. 34.95 (*0-8373-3454-3*) Nat Learn.
— Infection Control Nurse. (Career Examination Ser.: C-3213). 1994. pap. 29.95 (*0-8373-3213-3*) Nat Learn.
— Information & Referral Aide. (Career Examination Ser.: C-2892). 1994. pap. 23.95 (*0-8373-2892-6*) Nat Learn.
— Information & Referral Coordinator. (Career Examination Ser.: C-2927). 1994. pap. 29.95 (*0-8373-2927-2*) Nat Learn.
— Information Assistant. (Career Examination Ser.: C-363). 1994. pap. 23.95 (*0-8373-0363-X*) Nat Learn.
— Information Booth Attendant. (Career Examination Ser.: C-1314). 1994. pap. 23.95 (*0-8373-1314-7*) Nat Learn.
— Information Media Specialist. (Career Examination Ser.: C-1315). 1994. pap. 27.95 (*0-8373-1315-5*) Nat Learn.
— Information Services Specialist. (Career Examination Ser.). 1994. 34.95 (*0-8373-3603-1*, C-3603) Nat Learn.
— Information Specialist. (Career Examination Ser.: C-1316). 1994. pap. 27.95 (*0-8373-1316-3*) Nat Learn.
— Information Specialist I. (Career Examination Ser.: C-1867). 1994. pap. 27.95 (*0-8373-1867-X*) Nat Learn.
— Information Specialist II. (Career Examination Ser.: C-1868). 1994. 29.95 (*0-8373-1868-8*) Nat Learn.

— Information Specialist Trainee. (Career Examination Ser.: C-1687). 1994. pap. 23.95 (*0-8373-1687-1*) Nat Learn.
— Initial-Level Supervisor Examination (U.S.P.S.) (Career Examination Ser.: C-1788). 1994. pap. 29.95 (*0-8373-1788-6*) Nat Learn.
— Inmate Records Coordinator. (Career Examination Ser.: Series 1). 1991. pap. 34.95 (*0-8373-3726-7*) Nat Learn.
— Inspector. (Career Examination Ser.: C-364). 1994. pap. 27.95 (*0-8373-0364-8*) Nat Learn.
— Inspector (Construction) (Career Examination Ser.: C-2994). 1994. pap. 29.95 (*0-8373-2994-9*) Nat Learn.
— Inspector (Highways & Sewers) (Career Examination Ser.: C-366). 1994. pap. 29.95 (*0-8373-0366-4*) Nat Learn.
— Inspector (Housing) (Career Examination Ser.: C-2975). 1994. pap. 29.95 (*0-8373-2975-2*) Nat Learn.
— Inspector of Carpentry & Masonry. (Career Examination Ser.: C-365). 1994. pap. 29.95 (*0-8373-0365-6*) Nat Learn.
— Inspector of Fire Alarm Boxes. (Career Examination Ser.: C-2515). 1994. 29.95 (*0-8373-2515-3*) Nat Learn.
— Inspector of Low Pressure Boilers. (Career Examination Ser.: C-367). 1994. pap. 29.95 (*0-8373-0367-2*) Nat Learn.
— Inspector of Markets, Weights, & Measures. (Career Examination Ser.: C-368). 1994. pap. 23.95 (*0-8373-0368-0*) Nat Learn.
— Install & Repair Underground Storage Tanks (License) (Career Examination Ser.: C-369). 1994. pap. 29.95 (*0-8373-0369-9*) Nat Learn.
— Install Oil Burner Equipment (License) (Career Examination Ser.: C-1317). 1994. pap. 27.95 (*0-8373-1317-1*) Nat Learn.
— Institution Food Administrator. (Career Examination Ser.: C-2121). 1994. reprint ed. pap. 34.95 (*0-8373-2121-2*) Nat Learn.
— Institution Safety Officer. (Career Examination Ser.: C-370). 1994. pap. 29.95 (*0-8373-0370-2*) Nat Learn.
— Institution Steward. (Career Examination Ser.: C-2626). 1994. pap. 29.95 (*0-8373-2626-5*) Nat Learn.
— Institutional Inspector. (Career Examination Ser.: C-382). 1994. pap. 29.95 (*0-8373-0382-6*) Nat Learn.
— Institutional Trades Instructor. (Career Examination Ser.: C-371). 1994. pap. 29.95 (*0-8373-0371-0*) Nat Learn.
— Instructor of the Blind. (Career Examination Ser.: C-2838). 1994. pap. 29.95 (*0-8373-2838-1*) Nat Learn.
— Instrumentation Technician. (Career Examination Ser.: C-2366). 1994. pap. 29.95 (*0-8373-2366-5*) Nat Learn.
— Instrumentman. (Career Examination Ser.: C-1318). 1994. pap. 29.95 (*0-8373-1318-X*) Nat Learn.
— Insurance Agent - Insurance Broker. (Career Examination Ser.: C-373). 1994. pap. 29.95 (*0-8373-0373-7*) Nat Learn.
— Insurance Agent - Insurance Broker (Fire & Casualty) (Career Examination Ser.: C-374). 1994. pap. 29.95 (*0-8373-0374-5*) Nat Learn.
— Insurance Agent (Accident & Health) (Career Examination Ser.: C-372). 1994. pap. 29.95 (*0-8373-0372-9*) Nat Learn.
— Insurance Broker. (Career Examination Ser.: C-388). 1994. pap. 29.95 (*0-8373-0388-5*) Nat Learn.
— Insurance Contract Analyst. (Career Examination Ser.: C-3246). 1994. pap. 29.95 (*0-8373-3246-X*) Nat Learn.
— Insurance Examiner. (Career Examination Ser.: C-2694). 1994. pap. 29.95 (*0-8373-2694-X*) Nat Learn.
— Insurance Fund Field Services Representative. (Career Examination Ser.: C-2166). 1994. reprint ed. pap. 27.95 (*0-8373-2166-2*) Nat Learn.
— Insurance Fund Hearing Representative. (Career Examination Ser.: C-1546). 1994. pap. 27.95 (*0-8373-1546-8*) Nat Learn.
— Insurance Fund Hearing Representative Trainee. (Career Examination Ser.: C-880). 1994. pap. 23.95 (*0-8373-0880-1*) Nat Learn.
— Insurance Investigator. (Career Examination Ser.: C-3539). 1994. 29.95 (*0-8373-3539-6*) Nat Learn.
— Insurance Manager. (Career Examination Ser.: C-1598). 1994. pap. 29.95 (*0-8373-1598-0*) Nat Learn.
— Insurance Salesman. (Career Examination Ser.: C-389). 1994. pap. 29.95 (*0-8373-0389-3*) Nat Learn.
— Intergovernmental Analyst. (Career Examination Ser.: C-3507). 1994. 34.95 (*0-8373-3507-8*) Nat Learn.
— Intermediate Accounting. (ACT Proficiency Examination Program Ser.: PEP-11). 1994. 39.95 (*0-8373-5561-3*, PEP-11); pap. 23.95 (*0-8373-5511-7*, PEP-12) Nat Learn.
— Intermediate Algebra. (DANTES Ser.: No. 19). 1994. pap. 23.95 (*0-8373-6619-4*) Nat Learn.
— Intermediate Algebra. (DANTES Ser.: No. 19). 1994. 39.95 (*0-8373-6519-8*) Nat Learn.
— Intermediate Business Law. (ACT Proficiency Examination Program Ser.: PEP-17). 1994. pap. 23.95 (*0-8373-5517-6*) Nat Learn.
— Intermediate Care Facility Program Manager. (Career Examination Ser.: C-3247). 1994. pap. 29.95 (*0-8373-3247-8*) Nat Learn.
— Intermediate Schools. (Teachers Lesson Plan Bk.: IS-1). (J). (gr. 5-8). 1994. pap. 6.95 (*0-8373-7952-0*) Nat Learn.
— Internal Auditor. (Career Examination Ser.: C-375). 1994. pap. 29.95 (*0-8373-0375-3*) Nat Learn.
— Internal Revenue Agent. (Career Examination Ser.: C-376). 1994. pap. 27.95 (*0-8373-0376-1*) Nat Learn.
— Internal Revenue Officer. (Career Examination Ser.: Vol. 3392). 1994. pap. 27.95 (*0-8373-3392-X*) Nat Learn.
— Interpreter (Spanish) (Career Examination Ser.: C-2239). 1994. pap. 29.95 (*0-8373-2239-1*) Nat Learn.
— Interviewing. (General Aptitude & Abilities Ser.: CS-40). 1994. pap. 23.95 (*0-8373-6740-9*) Nat Learn.
— Introduction to Air Conditioning, Refrigeration & Heating. (DANTES Ser.: No. 20). 1994. pap. 23.95 (*0-8373-6620-8*) Nat Learn.
— Introduction to Air Conditioning, Refrigeration & Heating. (DANTES Ser.: No. 20). 1994. 39.95 (*0-8373-6520-1*) Nat Learn.
— Introduction to Anatomy & Physiology. (College Proficiency Examination Ser.: CPEP-28). 1994. reprint ed. 39.95 (*0-8373-5478-1*); reprint ed. pap. 23.95 (*0-8373-5428-5*) Nat Learn.
— Introduction to Business. (DANTES Ser.: No. 21). 1994. pap. 23.95 (*0-8373-6621-6*) Nat Learn.
— Introduction to Business. (DANTES Ser.: No. 21). 1994. 39.95 (*0-8373-6521-X*) Nat Learn.
— Introduction to Business Management. (College Level Examination Ser.: CLEP-18). 1994. 39.95 (*0-8373-5368-8*); pap. 23.95 (*0-8373-5318-1*) Nat Learn.
— Introduction to Carpentry. (DANTES Ser.: No. 40). 1994. pap. 23.95 (*0-8373-6640-2*) Nat Learn.
— Introduction to Computers with Basic Programming. (DANTES Ser.: No. 50). 1994. pap. 23.95 (*0-8373-6650-X*) Nat Learn.
— Introduction to Criminal Justice. (ACT Proficiency Examination Program Ser.: PEP-8). 1994. 39.95 (*0-8373-5558-3*); pap. 23.95 (*0-8373-5508-7*) Nat Learn.
— Introduction to Criminal Justice. (College Proficiency Examination Ser.: CPEP-29). 1994. reprint ed. 39.95 (*0-8373-5479-X*); reprint ed. pap. 23.95 (*0-8373-5429-3*) Nat Learn.
— Introduction to Education. (DANTES Ser.: No. 22). 1994. pap. 23.95 (*0-8373-6622-4*) Nat Learn.
— Introduction to Education. (DANTES Ser.: No. 22). 1994. 39.95 (*0-8373-6522-8*) Nat Learn.
— Introduction to Electronics. (DANTES Ser.: No. 23). 1994. pap. 23.95 (*0-8373-6623-2*) Nat Learn.
— Introduction to Electronics. (DANTES Ser.: No. 23). 1994. 39.95 (*0-8373-6523-6*) Nat Learn.
— Introduction to Forestry. (DANTES Ser.: No. 24). 1994. pap. 23.95 (*0-8373-6624-0*) Nat Learn.
— Introduction to Forestry. (DANTES Ser.: No. 24). 1994. 39.95 (*0-8373-6524-4*) Nat Learn.
— Introduction to Law Enforcement. (DANTES Ser.: No. 25). 1994. pap. 23.95 (*0-8373-6625-9*) Nat Learn.
— Introduction to Law Enforcement. (DANTES Ser.: No. 25). 1994. 39.95 (*0-8373-6525-2*) Nat Learn.
— Introduction to Management. (DANTES Ser.: No. 26). 1994. pap. 23.95 (*0-8373-6626-7*) Nat Learn.
— Introduction to Management. (DANTES Ser.: No. 26). 1994. 39.95 (*0-8373-6526-0*) Nat Learn.
— Introduction to the Teaching of Reading. (National Teacher Examination Ser.: NT-39). 1994. pap. 23.95 (*0-8373-8449-4*) Nat Learn.
— Introductory Accounting. (College Level Examination Ser.: CLEP-19). 1994. 39.95 (*0-8373-5369-6*); pap. 23.95 (*0-8373-5319-X*) Nat Learn.
— Introductory Accounting. (ACT Proficiency Examination Program Ser.: PEP-10). 1994. pap. 23.95 (*0-8373-5510-9*) Nat Learn.
— Introductory Business Law. (College Level Examination Ser.: CLEP-20). 1994. 39.95 (*0-8373-5370-X*); pap. 23.95 (*0-8373-5320-3*) Nat Learn.
— Introductory College Algebra. (DANTES Ser.: No. 55). 1994. 39.95 (*0-8373-6555-4*, DANTES-55); pap. 23.95 (*0-685-63230-X*, DANTES-55) Nat Learn.
— Introductory Economics. (College Level Examination Ser.: CLEP-22). 1994. 39.95 (*0-8373-5372-6*); pap. 23.95 (*0-8373-5322-X*) Nat Learn.
— Introductory Macroeconomics. (College Level Examination Ser.: CLEP-41). 1994. 39.95 (*0-8373-5391-2*); pap. 23.95 (*0-8373-5341-6*) Nat Learn.
— Introductory Marketing. (College Level Examination Ser.: CLEP-23). 1994. 39.95 (*0-8373-5373-4*); pap. 23.95 (*0-8373-5323-8*) Nat Learn.
— Introductory Micro- & Macroeconomics. (College Level Examination Ser.: CLEP-42). 1994. reprint ed. 39.95 (*0-8373-5392-0*); reprint ed. pap. 23.95 (*0-8373-5342-4*) Nat Learn.
— Introductory Microeconomics. (College Level Examination Ser.: CLEP-40). 1994. reprint ed. 39.95 (*0-8373-5390-4*); reprint ed. pap. 23.95 (*0-8373-5340-8*) Nat Learn.
— Introductory Sociology. (College Level Examination Ser.: CLEP-24). 1994. 39.95 (*0-8373-5374-2*); pap. 23.95 (*0-8373-5324-6*) Nat Learn.
— Inventory Control Clerk. (Career Examination Ser.: C-2616). 1994. pap. 23.95 (*0-8373-2616-8*) Nat Learn.
— Inventory Control Supervisor. (Career Examination Ser.: C-3562). 1994. 27.95 (*0-8373-3562-0*) Nat Learn.
— Investigator. (Career Examination Ser.: C-377). 1994. pap. 27.95 (*0-8373-0377-X*) Nat Learn.
— Investigator-Inspector. (Career Examination Ser.: C-378). 1994. pap. 29.95 (*0-8373-0378-8*) Nat Learn.
— Investigator Trainee. (Career Examination Ser.: C-3456). 1994. pap. 23.95 (*0-8373-3456-X*) Nat Learn.
— Investment Analysis Trainee. (Career Examination Ser.: C-1438). 1994. pap. 29.95 (*0-8373-1438-0*) Nat Learn.
— Investment Analyst. (Career Examination Ser.: C-2333). 1994. pap. 39.95 (*0-8373-2333-9*) Nat Learn.
— Investment Officer. (Career Examination Ser.: C-2978). 1994. pap. 34.95 (*0-8373-2978-7*) Nat Learn.
— Investment Officer Trainee. (Career Examination Ser.: C-2977). 1994. pap. 29.95 (*0-8373-2977-9*) Nat Learn.
— Italian. (National Teacher Examination Ser.: No. 50). 1994. Cloth bdg. avail. pap. 23.95 (*0-8373-8460-5*) Nat Learn.
— Italian, Jr. H.S. (ACT Proficiency Examination Program (PEP) Ser.: T-32B). 1994. pap. 23.95 (*0-8373-8032-4*) Nat Learn.
— Jail Guard. (Career Examination Ser.: C-406). 1994. pap. 23.95 (*0-8373-0406-7*) Nat Learn.
— Jail Matron. (Career Examination Ser.: C-1329). 1994. pap. 23.95 (*0-8373-1329-5*) Nat Learn.
— Jail Training Supervisor. (Career Examination Ser.: C-1331). 1994. pap. 29.95 (*0-8373-1331-7*) Nat Learn.
— Jailer-Clerk. (Career Examination Ser.: C-1332). 1994. pap. 23.95 (*0-8373-1332-5*) Nat Learn.
— Job Developer for the Handicapped. (Career Examination Ser.: C-1333). 1994. pap. 34.95 (*0-8373-1333-3*) Nat Learn.
— Job Development for Manpower Programs. (Career Examination Ser.: C-2865). 1994. pap. 34.95 (*0-8373-2865-9*) Nat Learn.
— Job Training Specialist. (Career Examination Ser.: C-2697). 1994. pap. 34.95 (*0-8373-2697-4*) Nat Learn.
— Jobs Corps Teacher. (Career Examination Ser.: C-407). 1994. pap. 29.95 (*0-8373-0407-5*) Nat Learn.
— Joiner. (Career Examination Ser.: C-408). 1994. pap. 27.95 (*0-8373-0408-3*) Nat Learn.
— Journeyman. (Career Examination Ser.: C-409). 1994. pap. 27.95 (*0-8373-0409-1*) Nat Learn.
— Journeyman in the Printing Crafts. (Career Examination Ser.: C-410). 1994. pap. 27.95 (*0-8373-0410-5*) Nat Learn.
— Junior Account Clerk. (Career Examination Ser.: C-515). 1994. pap. 19.95 (*0-8373-0515-2*) Nat Learn.
— Junior Accountant. (Career Examination Ser.: Series 1). 1991. pap. 23.95 (*0-8373-3727-5*) Nat Learn.
— Junior Administrative Assistant. (Career Examination Ser.: C-832). 1994. pap. 23.95 (*0-8373-0832-1*) Nat Learn.
— Junior Air Pollution Control Engineer. (Career Examination Ser.: C-1334). 1994. pap. 27.95 (*0-8373-1334-1*) Nat Learn.
— Junior Architect. (Career Examination Ser.: C-411). 1994. pap. 27.95 (*0-8373-0411-3*) Nat Learn.
— Junior Area Services Coordinator. (Career Examination Ser.: C-390). 1994. pap. 29.95 (*0-8373-0390-7*) Nat Learn.
— Junior Attorney. (Career Examination Ser.: C-391). 1994. pap. 29.95 (*0-8373-0391-5*) Nat Learn.
— Junior Bacteriologist. (Career Examination Ser.: C-392). 1994. pap. 23.95 (*0-8373-0392-3*) Nat Learn.
— Junior Building Custodian. (Career Examination Ser.: C-412). 1994. pap. 23.95 (*0-8373-0412-1*) Nat Learn.
— Junior Chemical Engineer. (Career Examination Ser.: C-393). 1994. pap. 23.95 (*0-8373-0393-1*) Nat Learn.
— Junior Chemist. (Career Examination Ser.: C-394). 1994. pap. 23.95 (*0-8373-0394-X*) Nat Learn.
— Junior Civil Engineer. (Career Examination Ser.: C-395). 1994. pap. 23.95 (*0-8373-0395-8*) Nat Learn.
— Junior Civil Engineer Trainee. (Career Examination Ser.: C-212). 1994. pap. 23.95 (*0-8373-0212-9*) Nat Learn.
— Junior Draftsman. (Career Examination Ser.: C-396). 1994. pap. 23.95 (*0-8373-0396-6*) Nat Learn.
— Junior Electrical Engineer. (Career Examination Ser.: C-397). 1994. pap. 27.95 (*0-8373-0397-4*) Nat Learn.
— Junior Engineer. (Career Examination Ser.: C-413). 1994. pap. 23.95 (*0-8373-0413-X*) Nat Learn.
— Junior Federal Assistant. (Career Examination Ser.: C-398). 1994. reprint ed. pap. 23.95 (*0-8373-0398-2*) Nat Learn.
— Junior Foreign Service Officer. (Career Examination Ser.: C-399). 1994. pap. 27.95 (*0-8373-0399-0*) Nat Learn.
— Junior Geologist. (Career Examination Ser.: C-414). 1994. pap. 27.95 (*0-8373-0414-8*) Nat Learn.
— Junior High School. (Teachers Lesson Plan Bk.: J-1). 1994. pap. 6.95 (*0-8373-7953-9*) Nat Learn.
— Junior Hospital Administrator. (Career Examination Ser.: C-400). 1994. pap. 29.95 (*0-8373-0400-8*) Nat Learn.
— Junior Insurance Examiner. (Career Examination Ser.: C-2069). 1994. reprint ed. pap. 27.95 (*0-8373-2069-0*) Nat Learn.
— Junior Intern. (Career Examination Ser.: C-1335). 1994. pap. 27.95 (*0-8373-1335-X*) Nat Learn.
— Junior Landscape Architect. (Career Examination Ser.: C-401). 1994. pap. 27.95 (*0-8373-0401-6*) Nat Learn.
— Junior Librarian. (Career Examination Ser.: C-1820). 1994. reprint ed. pap. 23.95 (*0-8373-1820-3*) Nat Learn.
— Junior Mechanical Engineer. (Career Examination Ser.: C-402). 1994. pap. 23.95 (*0-8373-0402-4*) Nat Learn.
— Junior Methods Analyst. (Career Examination Ser.: C-403). 1994. pap. 34.95 (*0-8373-0403-2*) Nat Learn.
— Junior Personnel Examiner. (Career Examination Ser.: C-404). 1994. pap. 34.95 (*0-8373-0404-0*) Nat Learn.
— Junior Physicist. (Career Examination Ser.: C-405). 1994. pap. 29.95 (*0-8373-0405-9*) Nat Learn.
— Junior Planner. (Career Examination Ser.: C-415). 1994. pap. 27.95 (*0-8373-0415-6*) Nat Learn.
— Junior Quantitative Analyst. (Career Examination Ser.: C-1797). 1994. pap. 27.95 (*0-8373-1797-5*) Nat Learn.
— Junior Rent Examiner. (Career Examination Ser.: C-2099). 1994. reprint ed. pap. 23.95 (*0-8373-2099-2*) Nat Learn.
— Justice Court Clerk. (Career Examination Ser.: C-3393). 1994. pap. 27.95 (*0-8373-3393-8*) Nat Learn.
— Juvenile Counselor. (Career Examination Ser.: C-2026). 1994. pap. 29.95 (*0-8373-2026-7*) Nat Learn.
— Kennel Foreman. (Career Examination Ser.: C-3129). 1994. pap. 27.95 (*0-8373-3129-3*) Nat Learn.
— Key Punch Operator. (Career Examination Ser.: C-420). 1994. pap. 23.95 (*0-8373-0420-2*) Nat Learn.
— Key Punch Supervisor. (Career Examination Ser.: C-2102). 1994. reprint ed. pap. 29.95 (*0-8373-2102-6*) Nat Learn.
— Keyboard Specialist. (Career Examination Ser.: C-3493). 1994. pap. 19.95 (*0-8373-3493-4*) Nat Learn.
— Kitchen Supervisor. (Career Examination Ser.: C-1336). 1994. pap. 27.95 (*0-8373-1336-8*) Nat Learn.
— Labor-Management Practices Adjuster. (Career Examination Ser.: C-433). 1994. pap. 39.95 (*0-8373-0433-4*) Nat Learn.
— Labor Mediation Trainee. (Career Examination Ser.: C-2851). 1994. pap. 29.95 (*0-8373-2851-9*) Nat Learn.
— Labor Mediator. (Career Examination Ser.: C-2850). 1994. pap. 39.95 (*0-8373-2850-0*) Nat Learn.
— Labor Relations. (ACT Proficiency Examination Program Ser.: PEP-22). 1994. pap. 23.95 (*0-8373-5522-2*) Nat Learn.
— Labor Relations Analyst. (Career Examination Ser.: C-3457). 1994. pap. 39.95 (*0-8373-3457-8*) Nat Learn.
— Labor Relations Assistant. (Career Examination Ser.: C-1338). 1994. pap. 29.95 (*0-8373-1338-4*) Nat Learn.
— Labor Relations Representative. (Career Examination Ser.: C-3310). 1991. pap. 22.00 (*0-8373-3310-5*) Nat Learn.
— Labor Relations Technician. (Career Examination Ser.: C-3215). 1994. pap. 29.95 (*0-8373-3215-X*) Nat Learn.
— Labor Safety Technician. (Career Examination Ser.: C-1595). 1994. pap. 29.95 (*0-8373-1595-6*) Nat Learn.
— Labor Specialist. (Career Examination Ser.: C-2146). 1994. reprint ed. pap. 29.95 (*0-8373-2146-8*) Nat Learn.
— Labor Standards Investigator. (Career Examination Ser.: C-3210). 1994. pap. 27.95 (*0-8373-3210-9*) Nat Learn.
— Labor Technician. (Career Examination Ser.: C-1587). 1994. pap. 29.95 (*0-8373-1587-5*) Nat Learn.
— Laboratory Aide. (Career Examination Ser.: C-430). 1994. pap. 23.95 (*0-8373-0430-X*) Nat Learn.
— Laboratory Assistant. (Career Examination Ser.: C-1879). 1994. reprint ed. pap. 23.95 (*0-8373-1879-3*) Nat Learn.
— Laboratory Assistant (Bacteriology) (Career Examination Ser.: C-431). 1994. pap. 27.95 (*0-8373-0431-8*) Nat Learn.
— Laboratory Assistant (Chemistry) (Career Examination Ser.: C-432). 1994. pap. 27.95 (*0-8373-0432-6*) Nat Learn.
— Laboratory Equipment Specialist. (Career Examination Ser.: C-2297). 1994. reprint ed. pap. 27.95 (*0-8373-2297-9*) Nat Learn.
— Laboratory Helper (Men) (Career Examination Ser.: C-446). 1994. pap. 23.95 (*0-8373-0446-6*) Nat Learn.
— Laboratory Helper (Women) (Career Examination Ser.: C-447). 1994. pap. 23.95 (*0-8373-0447-4*) Nat Learn.
— Laboratory Specialist (Biology) (Teachers License Examination Ser.: T-34). 1994. pap. 23.95 (*0-8373-8034-0*) Nat Learn.
— Laboratory Specialist, Jr. H. S. (Teachers License Examination Ser.: T-33). 1994. pap. 23.95 (*0-8373-8033-2*) Nat Learn.
— Laboratory Specialist (Physical Sciences), Sr. H. S. (Teachers License Examination Ser.: T-35). 1994. pap. 23.95 (*0-8373-8035-9*) Nat Learn.
— Laboratory Supervisor. (Career Examination Ser.: C-3198). 1994. pap. 34.95 (*0-8373-3198-6*) Nat Learn.
— Laboratory Technician. (Career Examination Ser.: C-1734). 1994. pap. 27.95 (*0-8373-1734-7*) Nat Learn.
— Laboratory Technician, Secondary Schools. (Teachers License Examination Ser.: T-36). 1994. pap. 23.95 (*0-8373-8036-7*) Nat Learn.
— Laboratory Technician Trainee. (Career Examination Ser.: C-2909). 1994. pap. 23.95 (*0-8373-2909-4*) Nat Learn.
— Laborer. (Career Examination Ser.: C-434). 1994. pap. 23.95 (*0-8373-0434-2*) Nat Learn.
— Laborer Foreman. (Career Examination Ser.: C-1337). 1994. pap. 27.95 (*0-8373-1337-6*) Nat Learn.
— Laborer Supervisor. (Career Examination Ser.: C-3458). 1994. pap. 29.95 (*0-8373-3458-6*) Nat Learn.
— Land & Claims Adjuster. (Career Examination Ser.: C-3459). 1994. pap. 29.95 (*0-8373-3459-4*) Nat Learn.
— Land Management Specialist. (Career Examination Ser.: C-2618). 1994. pap. 29.95 (*0-8373-2618-4*) Nat Learn.
— Land Surveyor. (Career Examination Ser.: C-3029). 1994. pap. 29.95 (*0-8373-3029-7*) Nat Learn.
— Land Surveyor Trainee. (Career Examination Ser.: C-3030). 1994. pap. 27.95 (*0-8373-3030-0*) Nat Learn.
— Landscape Architect. (Career Examination Ser.: C-2392). 1994. pap. 29.95 (*0-8373-2392-4*) Nat Learn.
— Latin. (National Teachers Examination Ser.: NT-18). 1994. pap. 23.95 (*0-8373-8408-7*) Nat Learn.
— Latin, Sr. H. S. (Teachers License Examination Ser.: T-37). 1994. pap. 23.95 (*0-8373-8037-5*) Nat Learn.
— Laundry Foreman. (Career Examination Ser.: C-2244). 1994. pap. 27.95 (*0-8373-2244-8*) Nat Learn.
— Laundry Manager. (Career Examination Ser.: C-2427). 1994. pap. 234.95 (*0-8373-2427-0*) Nat Learn.
— Laundry Supervisor. (Career Examination Ser.: C-1339). 1994. pap. 29.95 (*0-8373-1339-2*) Nat Learn.
— Laundry Washman. (Career Examination Ser.: C-1340). 1994. pap. 23.95 (*0-8373-1340-6*) Nat Learn.
— Laundry Worker. (Career Examination Ser.: C-435). 1994. pap. 23.95 (*0-8373-0435-0*) Nat Learn.
— Law Assistant. (Career Examination Ser.: C-1341). 1994. pap. 23.95 (*0-8373-1341-4*) Nat Learn.
— Law Clerk. (Career Examination Ser.: C-448). 1994. pap. 23.95 (*0-8373-0448-2*) Nat Learn.
— Law Department Investigator. (Career Examination Ser.: C-849). 1994. pap. 29.95 (*0-8373-0849-6*) Nat Learn.
— Law Enforcement & Investigation Occupations. (Career Examination Ser.: C-3551). 1994. 23.95 (*0-8373-3551-5*) Nat Learn.
— Law Enforcement Candidate Record. (Career Examination Ser.: C-3600). 1994. 29.95 (*0-8373-3600-7*) Nat Learn.
— Law Library Clerk. (Career Examination Ser.: C-2888). 1994. pap. 23.95 (*0-8373-2888-8*) Nat Learn.
— Law School Admission Test (LSAT) (Admission Test Ser.: ATS-13). 300p. 1994. pap. 23.95 (*0-8373-5013-1*) Nat Learn.
— Law Stenographer. (Career Examination Ser.: C-436). 1994. pap. 23.95 (*0-8373-0436-9*) Nat Learn.
— Leader (Lighting) (Career Examination Ser.: C-3085). 1994. pap. 27.95 (*0-8373-3085-8*) Nat Learn.
— Learning Ability Test (LAT) (Career Examination Ser.: C-1062). 1994. pap. 23.95 (*0-8373-1062-8*) Nat Learn.
— Leasing Agent. (Career Examination Ser.: C-1992). 1994. pap. 29.95 (*0-8373-1992-7*) Nat Learn.

R

— Legal Assistant. (Career Examination Ser.: C-2980). 1994. pap. 23.95 (*0-8373-2980-9*) Nat Learn.

— Legal Assistant I. (Career Examination Ser.: C-2988). 1994. pap. 23.95 (*0-8373-2988-4*) Nat Learn.

— Legal Assistant II. (Career Examination Ser.: C-2989). 1994. pap. 27.95 (*0-8373-2989-2*) Nat Learn.

— Legal Assistant Trainee. (Career Examination Ser.: C-2979). 1994. pap. 23.95 (*0-8373-2979-5*) Nat Learn.

— Legal Careers. (Career Examination Ser.: C-3284). 1994. pap. 23.95 (*0-8373-3284-2*) Nat Learn.

— Legal Clerk. (Career Examination Ser.: C-3394). 1994. pap. 123.95 (*0-8373-3394-6*) Nat Learn.

— Legal Coordinator. (Career Examination Ser.: C-2651). 1994. pap. 34.95 (*0-8373-2651-6*) Nat Learn.

— Legal Secretarial Assistant. (Career Examination Ser.: C-3545). 1994. 119.95 (*0-8373-3545-0*) Nat Learn.

— Legal Secretary. (Career Examination Ser.: C-1343). 1994. pap. 23.95 (*0-8373-1343-0*) Nat Learn.

— Legal Stenographer. (Career Examination Ser.: C-1344). 1994. pap. 23.95 (*0-8373-1344-9*) Nat Learn.

— Legislative Analyst. (Career Examination Ser.: C-3065). 1994. pap. 234.95 (*0-8373-3065-3*) Nat Learn.

— Letter Box Mechanic (USPS) (Career Examination Ser.: C-3367). 1994. pap. 27.95 (*0-8373-3367-9*) Nat Learn.

— Letterpress Pressman. (Career Examination Ser.: C-437). 1994. pap. 27.95 (*0-8373-0437-7*) Nat Learn.

— Liability Claims Supervisor. (Career Examination Ser.: C-3509). 1994. 34.95 (*0-8373-3509-4*) Nat Learn.

— Librarian. (Career Examination Ser.: C-438). 1994. pap. 27.95 (*0-8373-0438-5*) Nat Learn.

— Librarian I. (Career Examination Ser.: C-2788). 1994. pap. 27.95 (*0-8373-2788-1*) Nat Learn.

— Librarian II. (Career Examination Ser.: C-2789). 1994. pap. 29.95 (*0-8373-2789-X*) Nat Learn.

— Librarian III. (Career Examination Ser.: C-2790). 1994. pap. 29.95 (*0-8373-2790-3*) Nat Learn.

— Librarian IV. (Career Examination Ser.: C-2791). 1994. pap. 29.95 (*0-8373-2791-1*) Nat Learn.

— Librarian Trainee. (Career Examination Ser.: C-2864). 1994. pap. 23.95 (*0-8373-2864-0*) Nat Learn.

— Librarian V. (Career Examination Ser.). 1994. pap. 22.00 (*0-8373-2792-X*) Nat Learn.

— Library Assistant. (Career Examination Ser.: C-1345). 1994. pap. 23.95 (*0-8373-1345-7*) Nat Learn.

— Library Clerk. (Career Examination Ser.: C-1931). 1994. pap. 23.95 (*0-8373-1931-5*) Nat Learn.

— Library Director. (Career Examination Ser.: C-1346). 1994. pap. 34.95 (*0-8373-1346-5*) Nat Learn.

— Library Director I. (Career Examination Ser.: C-1929). 1994. pap. 34.95 (*0-8373-1929-3*) Nat Learn.

— Library Director II. (Career Examination Ser.: C-2779). 1994. pap. 34.95 (*0-8373-2779-2*) Nat Learn.

— Library Director III. (Career Examination Ser.: C-2780). 1994. pap. 39.95 (*0-8373-2780-6*) Nat Learn.

— Library Director IV. (Career Examination Ser.: C-2781). 1994. pap. 39.95 (*0-8373-2781-4*) Nat Learn.

— Library Director V. (Career Examination Ser.: C-2782). 1994. pap. 39.95 (*0-8373-2782-2*) Nat Learn.

— Library, Elementary School. (Teachers License Examination Ser.: T-38). 1994. pap. 23.95 (*0-8373-8038-3*) Nat Learn.

— Library, Secondary Schools. (Teachers License Examination Ser.: T-39). 1994. pap. 23.95 (*0-8373-8039-1*) Nat Learn.

— Library Technician. (Career Examination Ser.: C-2544). 1994. pap. 23.95 (*0-8373-2544-7*) Nat Learn.

— License Inspector. (Career Examination Ser.: C-439). 1994. pap. 23.95 (*0-8373-0439-3*) Nat Learn.

— License Investigator. (Career Examination Ser.: C-449). 1994. pap. 23.95 (*0-8373-0449-0*) Nat Learn.

— License Investigator (Spanish Speaking) (Career Examination Ser.: C-2286). 1994. reprint ed. pap. 27.95 (*0-8373-2286-3*) Nat Learn.

— Licensed Practical Nurse. (Career Examination Ser.: C-440). 1994. pap. 23.95 (*0-8373-0440-7*) Nat Learn.

— Licensing Inspector Trainee. (Career Examination Ser.: C-3122). 1994. pap. 23.95 (*0-8373-3122-6*) Nat Learn.

— Licensing Services Aide. (Career Examination Ser.: C-3120). 1994. pap. 23.95 (*0-8373-3120-X*) Nat Learn.

— Lieutenant, Fire Department. (Career Examination Ser.: C-441). 1994. pap. 29.95 (*0-8373-0441-5*) Nat Learn.

— Lieutenant, Police Department. (Career Examination Ser.: C-442). 1994. pap. 29.95 (*0-8373-0442-3*) Nat Learn.

— Life Insurance Agent. (Career Examination Ser.: C-443). 1994. pap. 29.95 (*0-8373-0443-1*) Nat Learn.

— Life Skills Counselor. (Career Examination Ser.: C-2917). 1994. pap. 29.95 (*0-8373-2917-5*) Nat Learn.

— Lifeguard. (Career Examination Ser.: C-2300). 1994. reprint ed. pap. 29.95 (*0-8373-2300-2*) Nat Learn.

— Light Maintainer. (Career Examination Ser.: C-444). 1994. pap. 23.95 (*0-8373-0444-X*) Nat Learn.

— Lighting Inspector. (Career Examination Ser.: C-2134). 1994. reprint ed. pap. 29.95 (*0-8373-2134-4*) Nat Learn.

— Linear Algebra. (DANTES Ser.: No. 27). 1994. pap. 23.95 (*0-8373-6627-5*) Nat Learn.

— Linear Algebra. (DANTES Ser.: No. 27). 1994. 39.95 (*0-8373-6527-9*) Nat Learn.

— Lineman. (Career Examination Ser.: C-1347). 1994. pap. 23.95 (*0-8373-1347-3*) Nat Learn.

— Lineman (Electrical Power) (Career Examination Ser.: C-450). 1994. pap. 23.95 (*0-8373-0450-4*) Nat Learn.

— Literature. (Teachers License Examination Ser.: G-3). 1994. pap. 23.95 (*0-8373-8193-2*) Nat Learn.

— Literature. (Undergraduate Program Field Test Ser.: UPFT-14). 1994. pap. 19.95 (*0-8373-6014-5*) Nat Learn.

— Literature in English. (Graduate Record Examination Ser.: GRE-11). 1994. 39.95 (*0-8373-5261-4*); pap. 23.95 (*0-8373-5211-8*) Nat Learn.

— Lithographic Pressman. (Career Examination Ser.: C-445). 1994. pap. 27.95 (*0-8373-0445-8*) Nat Learn.

— Loan Advisor. (Career Examination Ser.: C-1321). 1994. pap. 27.95 (*0-8373-1321-X*) Nat Learn.

— Locksmith. (Career Examination Ser.: C-1348). 1994. pap. 23.95 (*0-8373-1348-1*) Nat Learn.

— Lottery Inspector. (Career Examination Ser.: C-451). 1994. pap. 23.95 (*0-8373-0451-2*) Nat Learn.

— Lottery Marketing Aide. (Career Examination Ser.: C-3165). 1991. pap. 20.00 (*0-8373-3165-X*) Nat Learn.

— Lottery Marketing Representative. (Career Examination Ser.: C-3166). 1994. pap. 23.95 (*0-8373-3166-8*) Nat Learn.

— Machine Drafting. (Occupational Competency Examination Ser.: OCE-24). 1994. 39.95 (*0-8373-5774-8*); pap. 23.95 (*0-8373-5724-1*) Nat Learn.

— Machine Shop Workbook. (Workbook Ser.: No. 2920). 1994. pap. 23.95 (*0-8373-7903-2*) Nat Learn.

— Machine Trades. (Occupational Competency Examination Ser.: OCE-22). 1994. 39.95 (*0-8373-5772-1*); pap. 23.95 (*0-8373-5722-5*) Nat Learn.

— Machinist. (Career Examination Ser.: C-460). 1994. pap. 23.95 (*0-8373-0460-1*) Nat Learn.

— Machinist's Helper. (Career Examination Ser.: C-461). 1994. 23.95 (*0-8373-0461-X*) Nat Learn.

— Magnetic Tape Librarian. (Career Examination Ser.: C-2872). 1994. pap. 27.95 (*0-8373-2872-1*) Nat Learn.

— Mail & Supply Clerk. (Career Examination Ser.: C-3162). 1994. pap. 19.95 (*0-8373-3162-5*) Nat Learn.

— Mail Clerk. (Career Examination Ser.: C-2280). 1994. reprint ed. pap. 19.95 (*0-8373-2280-4*) Nat Learn.

— Mail Division Supervisor. (Career Examination Ser.: C-2624). 1994. pap. 29.95 (*0-8373-2624-9*) Nat Learn.

— Mail Handler (U.S.P.S.) (Career Examination Ser.: C-462). 1994. pap. 19.95 (*0-8373-0462-8*) Nat Learn.

— Mail Processing Equipment Operator. (Career Examination Ser.: C-3460). 1994. pap. 27.95 (*0-8373-3460-8*) Nat Learn.

— Maintainer's Helper - Group A. (Career Examination Ser.: C-465). 1994. pap. 19.95 (*0-8373-0465-2*) Nat Learn.

— Maintainer's Helper - Group B. (Career Examination Ser.: C-466). 1994. pap. 19.95 (*0-8373-0466-0*) Nat Learn.

— Maintainer's Helper - Group C. (Career Examination Ser.: C-467). 1994. pap. 19.95 (*0-8373-0467-9*) Nat Learn.

— Maintainer's Helper - Group D. (Career Examination Ser.: C-468). 1994. pap. 19.95 (*0-8373-0468-7*) Nat Learn.

— Maintainer's Helper - Group E. (Career Examination Ser.: C-469). 1994. 19.95 (*0-8373-0469-5*) Nat Learn.

— Maintenance Carpenter. (Career Examination Ser.: C-1349). 1994. pap. 23.95 (*0-8373-1349-X*) Nat Learn.

— Maintenance Carpenter Foreman. (Career Examination Ser.: C-1350). 1994. pap. 27.95 (*0-8373-1350-3*) Nat Learn.

— Maintenance Crew Chief. (Career Examination Ser.: C-3461). 1994. pap. 34.95 (*0-8373-3461-6*) Nat Learn.

— Maintenance (Custodial) Branch Initial-Level Supervisor Examination (U.S.P.S.) (Career Examination Ser.: C-1775). 1994. 34.95 (*0-8373-1775-4*) Nat Learn.

— Maintenance Development Program Aptitude Test (USPS) (Career Examination Ser.: C-3609). 1994. 34.95 (*0-8373-3609-0*) Nat Learn.

— Maintenance Electrician. (Career Examination Ser.: C-1351). 1994. pap. 27.95 (*0-8373-1351-1*) Nat Learn.

— Maintenance Electrician Foreman. (Career Examination Ser.: C-1352). 1994. pap. 29.95 (*0-8373-1352-X*) Nat Learn.

— Maintenance Locksmith. (Career Examination Ser.: C-1353). 1994. pap. 23.95 (*0-8373-1353-8*) Nat Learn.

— Maintenance Machinist. (Career Examination Ser.: C-1354). 1994. pap. 23.95 (*0-8373-1354-6*) Nat Learn.

— Maintenance Man. (Career Examination Ser.: C-463). 1994. pap. 23.95 (*0-8373-0463-6*) Nat Learn.

— Maintenance Man Trainee. (Career Examination Ser.: C-464). 1994. pap. 23.95 (*0-8373-0464-4*) Nat Learn.

— Maintenance Mason. (Career Examination Ser.: C-1355). 1994. pap. 23.95 (*0-8373-1355-4*) Nat Learn.

— Maintenance Mason Foreman. (Career Examination Ser.: C-1356). 1994. pap. 27.95 (*0-8373-1356-2*) Nat Learn.

— Maintenance Mechanic. (Career Examination Ser.: C-1357). 1994. pap. 23.95 (*0-8373-1357-0*) Nat Learn.

— Maintenance Mechanic (Automated Mail Processing Equipment) (A.M.P.E) (U.S.P.S.) (Career Examination Ser.: C-1606). 1994. 27.95 (*0-8373-1606-5*) Nat Learn.

— Maintenance Painter. (Career Examination Ser.: C-1358). 1994. pap. 23.95 (*0-8373-1358-9*) Nat Learn.

— Maintenance Painter Foreman. (Career Examination Ser.: C-1359). 1994. pap. 27.95 (*0-8373-1359-7*) Nat Learn.

— Maintenance Plumber. (Career Examination Ser.: C-1360). 1994. pap. 23.95 (*0-8373-1360-0*) Nat Learn.

— Maintenance Plumber Foreman. (Career Examination Ser.: C-1361). 1994. pap. 27.95 (*0-8373-1361-9*) Nat Learn.

— Maintenance Supervisor. (Career Examination Ser.: C-2044). 1994. pap. 27.95 (*0-8373-2044-5*) Nat Learn.

— Maintenance Supervisor (Track Equipment) (Career Examination Ser.: C-3546-9). 1994. 27.95 (*0-8373-3546-9*) Nat Learn.

— Maintenance Welder. (Career Examination Ser.: C-1362). 1994. pap. 23.95 (*0-8373-1362-7*) Nat Learn.

— Management Analysis Trainee. (Career Examination Ser.: C-470). 1994. pap. 27.95 (*0-8373-0470-9*) Nat Learn.

— Management Analyst. (Career Examination Ser.: C-1061). 1994. pap. 34.95 (*0-8373-1061-X*) Nat Learn.

— Management Analyst Aide. (Career Examination Ser.: C-1721). 1994. reprint ed. pap. 29.95 (*0-8373-1721-5*) Nat Learn.

— Management Auditor. (Career Examination Ser.: C-3217). 1994. pap. 34.95 (*0-8373-3217-6*) Nat Learn.

— Management Auditor Trainee. (Career Examination Ser.: C-3285). 1994. pap. 29.95 (*0-8373-3285-0*) Nat Learn.

— Management Information Systems Specialist. (Career Examination Ser.: C-3519). 1994. 26.00 (*0-8373-3579-5*) Nat Learn.

— Management Intern. (Career Examination Ser.: C-1927). 1994. reprint ed. pap. 27.95 (*0-8373-1927-7*) Nat Learn.

— Management of Human Resources I. (Regents External Degree Ser.: REDP-7). 1994. pap. 23.95 (*0-8373-5607-5*) Nat Learn.

— Management of Human Resources II. (Regents External Degree Ser.: REDP-8). 1994. pap. 23.95 (*0-8373-5608-3*) Nat Learn.

— Management of Human Resources III. (Regents External Degree Ser.: REDP-9). 1994. pap. 23.95 (*0-8373-5609-1*) Nat Learn.

— Management Specialist Trainee. (Career Examination Ser.: C-3608). 1994. 27.95 (*0-8373-3608-2*) Nat Learn.

— Management Technician. (Career Examination Ser.: C-2751). 1994. pap. 27.95 (*0-8373-2751-2*) Nat Learn.

— Management Trainee (U.S.P.S.) (Career Examination Ser.: C-1690). 1994. pap. 29.95 (*0-8373-1690-1*) Nat Learn.

— Manager Computer Operations. (Career Examination Ser.: C-2241). 1994. pap. 34.95 (*0-8373-2241-3*) Nat Learn.

— Manpower Counselor. (Career Examination Ser.: C-2435). 1994. pap. 34.95 (*0-8373-2435-1*) Nat Learn.

— Manpower Development Specialist. (Career Examination Ser.: C-2688). 1994. pap. 34.95 (*0-8373-2688-5*) Nat Learn.

— Manpower Grants Technician. (Career Examination Ser.: C-2822). 1994. pap. 29.95 (*0-8373-2822-5*) Nat Learn.

— Manpower Information & Liaison Specialist. (Career Examination Ser.: C-2807). 1994. pap. 39.95 (*0-8373-2807-1*) Nat Learn.

— Manpower Program Administrator. (Career Examination Ser.: C-2671). 1994. pap. 36.95 (*0-8373-2671-0*) Nat Learn.

— Manpower Program Coordinator. (Career Examination Ser.: C-2316). 1994. pap. 36.95 (*0-8373-2316-9*) Nat Learn.

— Manpower Training Coordinator. (Career Examination Ser.: C-1554). 1994. pap. 39.95 (*0-8373-1554-9*) Nat Learn.

— Map & Coordinate Supervisor. (Career Examination Ser.: C-3330). 1994. pap. 34.95 (*0-8373-3330-X*) Nat Learn.

— Map Drafter. (Career Examination Ser.: Series 1). 1994. pap. 27.95 (*0-8373-3729-1*) Nat Learn.

— Map Room Clerk. (Career Examination Ser.: Series 1). 1991. pap. 23.95 (*0-8373-3730-5*) Nat Learn.

— Mapping Technician. (Career Examination Ser.: C-3462). 1994. pap. 27.95 (*0-8373-3462-4*) Nat Learn.

— Mapping Technologist. (Career Examination Ser.: C-3463). 1994. pap. 29.95 (*0-8373-3463-2*) Nat Learn.

— Marine Engineer. (Career Examination Ser.: C-1363). 1994. pap. 29.95 (*0-8373-1363-5*) Nat Learn.

— Marine Maintenance Foreman. (Career Examination Ser.: C-3070). 1994. pap. 29.95 (*0-8373-3070-X*) Nat Learn.

— Marine Oiler. (Career Examination Ser.: C-471). 1994. pap. 23.95 (*0-8373-0471-7*) Nat Learn.

— Marine Resources Technician. (Career Examination Ser.: C-1369). 1994. pap. 29.95 (*0-8373-1369-4*) Nat Learn.

— Marine Stoker. (Career Examination Ser.: C-472). 1994. pap. 23.95 (*0-8373-0472-5*) Nat Learn.

— Mark-up Clerk (U. S. P. S.) (Career Examination Ser.: C-2459). 1994. pap. 29.95 (*0-8373-2459-9*) Nat Learn.

— Marketing & Distributive Education. (National Teachers Examination Ser.: NT-46). 1994. pap. 23.95 (*0-8373-8466-4*) Nat Learn.

— Marketing I. (Regents External Degree Ser.: REDP-10). 1994. pap. 23.95 (*0-8373-5610-5*) Nat Learn.

— Marketing II. (Regents External Degree Ser.: REDP-11). 1994. pap. 23.95 (*0-8373-5611-3*) Nat Learn.

— Marketing III. (Regents External Degree Ser.: REDP-12). 1994. pap. 23.95 (*0-8373-5612-1*) Nat Learn.

— Marketing Representative. (Career Examination Ser.: C-2465). 1994. pap. 29.95 (*0-8373-2465-3*) Nat Learn.

— Maryland Basic Mastery Test for Reading (BMT-R) (Admission Test Ser.: ATS-63). 1994. pap. 23.95 (*0-8373-5063-8*) Nat Learn.

— Mason. (Career Examination Ser.: C-473). 1994. pap. 23.95 (*0-8373-0473-3*) Nat Learn.

— Masonry. (Occupational Competency Examination Ser.: OCE-23). 1994. pap. 23.95 (*0-8373-5723-3*) Nat Learn.

— Mason's Helper. (Career Examination Ser.: C-474). 1994. pap. 23.95 (*0-8373-0474-1*) Nat Learn.

— Master Electrician. (Career Examination Ser.: C-475). 1994. pap. 27.95 (*0-8373-0475-X*) Nat Learn.

— Master Plumber. (Career Examination Ser.: C-476). 1994. pap. 27.95 (*0-8373-0476-8*) Nat Learn.

— Master Rigger. (Career Examination Ser.: C-477). 1994. pap. 27.95 (*0-8373-0477-6*) Nat Learn.

— Master Sign Hanger. (Career Examination Ser.: C-478). 1994. pap. 27.95 (*0-8373-0478-4*) Nat Learn.

— Mate. (Career Examination Ser.: C-3156). 1994. pap. 29.95 (*0-8373-3156-0*) Nat Learn.

— Materials Engineer. (Career Examination Ser.: C-1780). 1994. pap. 39.95 (*0-8373-1780-0*) Nat Learn.

— Materials Manager. (Career Examination Ser.: C-3395). 1994. pap. 34.95 (*0-8373-3395-4*) Nat Learn.

— Materials Testing Technician. (Career Examination Ser.: C-1834). 1994. pap. 34.95 (*0-8373-1834-3*) Nat Learn.

— Materiel Control Clerk I. (Career Examination Ser.: C-3088). 1994. pap. 19.95 (*0-8373-3088-2*) Nat Learn.

— Materiel Control Clerk II. (Career Examination Ser.: C-3089). 1994. pap. 23.95 (*0-8373-3089-0*) Nat Learn.

— Materiel Control Clerk III. (Career Examination Ser.: C-3090). 1994. pap. 27.95 (*0-8373-3090-4*) Nat Learn.

— Materiel Control Clerk IV. (Career Examination Ser.: C-3091). 1994. pap. 27.95 (*0-8373-3091-2*) Nat Learn.

— Maternal & Child Health Nurse. (Certified Nurse Examination Ser.: CN-9). 1994. 39.95 (*0-8373-6159-1*); pap. 23.95 (*0-8373-6109-5*) Nat Learn.

— Maternal & Child Nursing: Associate Degree. (ACT Proficiency Examination Program Ser.: PEP-37). 1994. pap. 23.95 (*0-8373-5537-0*) Nat Learn.

— Maternal & Child Nursing: Baccalaureate Degree. (ACT Proficiency Examination Program Ser.: PEP-38). 1994. pap. 23.95 (*0-8373-5538-9*) Nat Learn.

— Maternal & Child Nursing-Associate. (College Proficiency Examination Ser.: CPEP-22). 1994. 23.95 (*0-8373-5422-6*) Nat Learn.

— Maternal & Child Nursing-Baccalaureate. (College Proficiency Examination Ser.: CPEP-23). 1994. pap. 23.95 (*0-8373-5423-4*) Nat Learn.

— Mathematician. (Career Examination Ser.: C-479). 1994. pap. 29.95 (*0-8373-0479-2*) Nat Learn.

— Mathematics. (Teachers License Examination Ser.: G-4). 1994. pap. 23.95 (*0-8373-8194-0*) Nat Learn.

— Mathematics. (Graduate Record Examination Ser.: GRE-12). 1994. pap. 23.95 (*0-8373-5212-6*) Nat Learn.

— Mathematics. (Undergraduate Program Field Test Ser.: UPFT-15). 1994. pap. 23.95 (*0-8373-6015-3*) Nat Learn.

— Mathematics Aide. (Career Examination Ser.: C-480). 1994. pap. 27.95 (*0-8373-0480-6*) Nat Learn.

— Mathematics, Jr. H.S. (Teachers License Examination Ser.: T-40). 1994. pap. 23.95 (*0-8373-8040-5*) Nat Learn.

— Mathematics, Sr. H.S. (Teachers License Examination Ser.: T-41). 1994. pap. 23.95 (*0-8373-8041-3*) Nat Learn.

— Meat Cutter. (Career Examination Ser.: C-516). 1994. pap. 27.95 (*0-8373-0516-0*) Nat Learn.

— Meat Inspector. (Career Examination Ser.: C-517). 1994. pap. 27.95 (*0-8373-0517-9*) Nat Learn.

— Meat Inspector-Poultry Inspector. (Career Examination Ser.: C-513). 1994. pap. 29.95 (*0-8373-0513-6*) Nat Learn.

— Meat Inspector Trainee. (Career Examination Ser.: C-518). 1994. pap. 23.95 (*0-8373-0518-7*) Nat Learn.

— Mechanical Engineer. (Career Examination Ser.: C-481). 1994. pap. 29.95 (*0-8373-0481-4*) Nat Learn.

— Mechanical Engineering Draftsman. (Career Examination Ser.: C-482). 1994. pap. 27.95 (*0-8373-0482-2*) Nat Learn.

— Mechanical Engineering Trainee. (Career Examination Ser.: C-519). 1994. pap. 23.95 (*0-8373-0519-5*) Nat Learn.

— Mechanical Equipment Inspector. (Career Examination Ser.: C-2045). 1994. pap. 34.95 (*0-8373-2045-3*) Nat Learn.

— Mechanical Estimator. (Career Examination Ser.: C-3113). 1994. pap. 27.95 (*0-8373-3113-7*) Nat Learn.

— Mechanical Maintainer - Group A. (Career Examination Ser.: C-483). 1994. pap. 23.95 (*0-8373-0483-0*) Nat Learn.

— Mechanical Maintainer - Group B. (Career Examination Ser.: C-484). 1994. pap. 23.95 (*0-8373-0484-9*) Nat Learn.

— Mechanical Maintainer - Group C. (Career Examination Ser.: C-485). 1994. pap. 23.95 (*0-8373-0485-7*) Nat Learn.

— Mechanical Maintenance Supervisor. (Career Examination Ser.: C-2793). 1994. pap. 29.95 (*0-8373-2793-8*) Nat Learn.

— Mechanical Specifications Writer. (Career Examination Ser.: C-3248). 1994. pap. 29.95 (*0-8373-3248-6*) Nat Learn.

— Mechanical Stores Clerk. (Career Examination Ser.: C-3080). 1994. pap. 19.95 (*0-8373-3080-7*) Nat Learn.

— Mechanical Technology. (Occupational Competency Examination Ser.: OCE-25). 1994. pap. 23.95 (*0-8373-5725-X*) Nat Learn.

— Media Services Technician. (Career Examination Ser.: C-3181). 1994. pap. 29.95 (*0-8373-3181-1*) Nat Learn.

— Media Specialist. (Career Examination Ser.: C-2894). 1994. pap. 29.95 (*0-8373-2894-2*) Nat Learn.

— Media Specialist - Library & Audio-Visual Services (Library Media Specialist) (National Teachers Examination Ser.: NT-29). 1994. pap. 23.95 (*0-8373-8439-7*) Nat Learn.

— Mediator (Labor Relations) (Career Examination Ser.: C-520). 1994. pap. 39.95 (*0-8373-0520-9*) Nat Learn.

— Medicaid Claims Examiner. (Career Examination Ser.: C-2691). 1994. pap. 27.95 (*0-8373-2691-5*) Nat Learn.

— Medicaid Review Analyst. (Career Examination Ser.: C-3207). 1994. pap. 27.95 (*0-8373-3207-9*) Nat Learn.

— Medical Aide. (Career Examination Ser.: C-1364). 1994. pap. 23.95 (*0-8373-1364-3*) Nat Learn.

— Medical Assistant. (Career Examination Ser.: C-1365). 1994. pap. 23.95 (*0-8373-1365-1*) Nat Learn.

— Medical Assisting. (Occupational Competency Examination Ser.: OCE-26). 1994. pap. 23.95 (*0-8373-5726-8*) Nat Learn.

— Medical Care Representative. (Career Examination Ser.: C-3147). 1994. pap. 29.95 (*0-8373-3147-1*) Nat Learn.

— Medical Clerk. (Career Examination Ser.: C-1796). 1994. pap. 23.95 (*0-8373-1796-7*) Nat Learn.

— Medical College Admission Test (MCAT) (Admission Test Ser.: ATS-11). 1994. pap. 23.95 (*0-8373-5011-5*) Nat Learn.

— Medical Conduct Investigator. (Career Examination Ser.: C-2287). 1994. reprint ed. pap. 27.95 (*0-8373-2287-1*) Nat Learn.

— Medical Emergency Dispatcher. (Career Examination Ser.: C-2331). 1994. pap. 23.95 (*0-8373-2331-2*) Nat Learn.

— Medical Equipment Technician. (Career Examination Ser.: C-2654). 1994. pap. 29.95 (*0-8373-2654-0*) Nat Learn.

— Medical Examiner. (Career Examination Ser.: C-486). 1994. pap. 44.95 (*0-8373-0486-5*) Nat Learn.

R

An Asterisk (*) at the beginning of an entry indicates that the title is appearing in BIP for the first time.

— Medical Facilities Auditor. (Career Examination Ser.: C-2058). 1994. reprint ed. pap. 37.95 (*0-8373-2058-5*) Nat Learn.
— Medical Inspector. (Career Examination Ser.: C-487). 1994. pap. 44.95 (*0-8373-0487-3*) Nat Learn.
— Medical Laboratory Technician. (Career Examination Ser.: C-2323). 1994. pap. 27.95 (*0-8373-2323-1*) Nat Learn.
— Medical Laboratory Technician: Substance Abuse. (Career Examination Ser.: C-3119). 1994. pap. 29.95 (*0-8373-3119-6*) Nat Learn.
— Medical Officer. (Career Examination Ser.: C-488). 1994. pap. 39.95 (*0-8373-0488-1*) Nat Learn.
— Medical Officer (Departmental) (Career Examination Ser.: C-489). 1994. pap. 39.95 (*0-8373-0489-X*) Nat Learn.
— Medical Photographer. (Career Examination Ser.: C-1366). 1994. pap. 29.95 (*0-8373-1366-X*) Nat Learn.
— Medical Purchasing Specialist. (Career Examination Ser.: C-2448). 1994. pap. 27.95 (*0-8373-2448-3*) Nat Learn.
— Medical Radiology Technician. (Career Examination Ser.: C-1367). 1994. pap. 27.95 (*0-8373-1367-8*) Nat Learn.
— Medical Radiology Technologist. (Career Examination Ser.: C-490). 1994. pap. 29.95 (*0-8373-0490-3*) Nat Learn.
— Medical Record Librarian. (Career Examination Ser.: C-491). 1994. pap. 23.95 (*0-8373-0491-1*) Nat Learn.
— Medical Record Technician. (Career Examination Ser.: C-2329). 1994. pap. 23.95 (*0-8373-2329-0*) Nat Learn.
— Medical Records Assistant. (Career Examination Ser.: C-2952). 1994. pap. 23.95 (*0-8373-2952-3*) Nat Learn.
— Medical Records Clerk. (Career Examination Ser.: C-2309). 1994. reprint ed. pap. 23.95 (*0-8373-2309-6*) Nat Learn.
— Medical Records Supervisor. (Career Examination Ser.: Series 1). 1991. pap. 27.95 (*0-8373-3731-3*) Nat Learn.
— Medical Relations Officer. (Career Examination Ser.: C-3351). 1994. pap. 34.95 (*0-8373-3351-2*) Nat Learn.
— Medical Sciences Knowledge Profile Examination (MSKP) (Admission Test Ser.: ATS-86). 1994. pap. 49.95 (*0-8373-5086-7*) Nat Learn.
— Medical Services Specialist. (Career Examination Ser.: C-2746). 1994. pap. 34.95 (*0-8373-2746-6*) Nat Learn.
— Medical Social Work Assistant. (Career Examination Ser.: C-3168). 1994. pap. 27.95 (*0-8373-3168-4*) Nat Learn.
— Medical Social Work Coordinator. (Career Examination Ser.: C-2578). 1994. pap. 34.95 (*0-8373-2578-1*) Nat Learn.
— Medical Social Worker. (Career Examination Ser.: C-521). 1994. pap. 29.95 (*0-8373-0521-7*) Nat Learn.
— Medical Specialist. (Career Examination Ser.: C-1965). 1994. reprint ed. pap. 39.95 (*0-8373-1965-X*) Nat Learn.
— Medical Stenographer. (Career Examination Ser.: C-1368). 1994. pap. 23.95 (*0-8373-1368-6*) Nat Learn.
— Medical Supply Supervisor. (Career Examination Ser.: C-3106). 1994. pap. 29.95 (*0-8373-3106-4*) Nat Learn.
— Medical Supply Technician. (Career Examination Ser.: C-3353). 1994. pap. 27.95 (*0-8373-3353-9*) Nat Learn.
— Medical-Surgical Nurse. (Certified Nurse Examination Ser.: CN-11). 1994. 39.95 (*0-8373-6161-3*); pap. 23.95 (*0-8373-6111-7*) Nat Learn.
— Medical Surgical Nursing. (College Proficiency Examination Ser.: CPEP-24). 1994. 39.95 (*0-8373-5474-9*); pap. 23.95 (*0-8373-5424-2*) Nat Learn.
— Medical-Surgical Nursing. (College Level Examination Ser.: CLEP-37). 1994. 39.95 (*0-8373-5387-4*); pap. 23.95 (*0-8373-5337-8*) Nat Learn.
— Medical Technical Assistant. (Career Examination Ser.: C-492). 1994. pap. 23.95 (*0-8373-0492-X*) Nat Learn.
— Medical Technician. (Career Examination Ser.: C-512). 1994. pap. 27.95 (*0-8373-0512-8*) Nat Learn.
— Medical Technician Instructor. (Career Examination Ser.: C-1370). 1994. pap. 39.95 (*0-8373-1370-8*) Nat Learn.
— Medical Technician Trainee. (Career Examination Ser.: C-1371). 1994. pap. 23.95 (*0-8373-1371-6*) Nat Learn.
— Medical Technologist. (Career Examination Ser.: C-493). 1994. pap. 29.95 (*0-8373-0493-8*) Nat Learn.
— Medical Transcribing Machine Operator. (Career Examination Ser.: C-3203). 1994. pap. 23.95 (*0-8373-3203-6*) Nat Learn.
— Medical Typist. (Career Examination Ser.: C-3396). 1994. pap. 23.95 (*0-8373-3396-2*) Nat Learn.
— Menagerie Keeper. (Career Examination Ser.: C-494). 1994. pap. 23.95 (*0-8373-0494-6*) Nat Learn.
— Men's Physical Education. (National Teachers Examination Ser.: NT-36). 1994. pap. 23.95 (*0-8373-8446-X*) Nat Learn.
— Mental Health Aide. (Career Examination Ser.: C-1372). 1994. pap. 23.95 (*0-8373-1372-4*) Nat Learn.
— Mental Health Assistant. (Career Examination Ser.: C-3397). 1994. pap. 23.95 (*0-8373-3397-0*) Nat Learn.
— Mental Health Geriatric Consultant. (Career Examination Ser.: C-1582). 1994. pap. 29.95 (*0-8373-1582-4*) Nat Learn.
— Mental Health Group Leader. (Career Examination Ser.: C-3054). 1994. pap. 29.95 (*0-8373-3054-8*) Nat Learn.
— Mental Hygiene Nursing Program Coordinator. (Career Examination Ser.: C-2665). 1994. pap. 34.95 (*0-8373-2665-6*) Nat Learn.
— Mental Hygiene Staff Development Specialist I. (Career Examination Ser.: C-3489). 1994. pap. 27.95 (*0-8373-3489-6*) Nat Learn.
— Mental Hygiene Staff Development Specialist II. (Career Examination Ser.: C-2490). 1994. pap. 27.95 (*0-8373-2490-4*) Nat Learn.
— Mental Hygiene Staff Development Specialist III. (Career Examination Ser.: C-2491). 1994. pap. 29.95 (*0-8373-2491-2*) Nat Learn.
— Mental Hygiene Staff Development Specialist IV. (Career Examination Ser.: C-2492). 1994. pap. 29.95 (*0-8373-2492-0*) Nat Learn.
— Mental Hygiene Therapy Aide. (Career Examination Ser.: C-3056). 1994. pap. 23.95 (*0-8373-3056-4*) Nat Learn.
— Mental Hygiene Therapy Assistant. (Career Examination Ser.: C-2188). 1994. pap. 23.95 (*0-8373-2188-3*) Nat Learn.
— Mental Hygiene Treatment Team Leader. (Career Examination Ser.: C-1885). 1994. pap. 27.95 (*0-8373-1885-8*) Nat Learn.
— Messenger. (Career Examination Ser.: C-495). 1994. pap. 23.95 (*0-8373-0495-4*) Nat Learn.
— Metallurgist. (Career Examination Ser.: C-496). 1994. pap. 29.95 (*0-8373-0496-2*) Nat Learn.
— Meteorologist. (Career Examination Ser.: C-497). 1994. pap. 29.95 (*0-8373-0497-0*) Nat Learn.
— Meter Maid. (Career Examination Ser.: C-498). 1994. pap. 23.95 (*0-8373-0498-9*) Nat Learn.
— Methods Analyst. (Career Examination Ser.: C-499). 1994. pap. 34.95 (*0-8373-0499-7*) Nat Learn.
— Microbiologist. (Career Examination Ser.: C-2477). 1994. pap. 27.95 (*0-8373-2477-7*) Nat Learn.
— Microbiology. (College Level Examination Ser.: CLEP-35). 1994. 23.95 (*0-8373-5335-1*) Nat Learn.
— Microbiology. (ACT Proficiency Examination Program Ser.: PEP-55). 1994. pap. 23.95 (*0-8373-5905-8*) Nat Learn.
— Microbiology. (ACT Proficiency Examination Program Ser.: PEP-55). 1994. 39.95 (*0-8373-5930-9*) Nat Learn.
— Microcomputer - Audio Visual Repair Supervisor. (Career Examination Ser.: Series 1). 1991. pap. 29.95 (*0-8373-3732-1*) Nat Learn.
— Microcomputer Operator. (Career Examination Ser.: Series 1). 1991. pap. 23.95 (*0-8373-3733-X*) Nat Learn.
— Micrographics Operator. (Career Examination Ser.: C-2157). 1994. reprint ed. pap. 23.95 (*0-8373-2157-3*) Nat Learn.
— Micrographics Technician. (Career Examination Ser.: C-2761). 1994. pap. 23.95 (*0-8373-2761-X*) Nat Learn.
— Middle Level Positions. (Career Examination Ser.: C-511). 1994. pap. 27.95 (*0-8373-0511-X*) Nat Learn.
— Miller Analogies Test (MAT) (Admission Test Ser.: ATS-18). 300p. 1994. 343.95 (*0-8373-5118-9*); pap. 27.95 (*0-8373-5018-2*) Nat Learn.
— Missouri Basic Essential Skills Test (BEST) (Admission Test Ser.: ATS-64). 1994. 39.95 (*0-8373-5164-2*); pap. 23.95 (*0-8373-5064-6*) Nat Learn.
— Money & Banking. (College-Level Examination Ser.: No. 25). 1994. 39.95 (*0-8373-5375-0*); pap. 23.95 (*0-8373-5325-4*) Nat Learn.
— Money & Banking. (DANTES Ser.: No. 28). 1994. pap. 23.95 (*0-8373-6628-3*) Nat Learn.
— Mortgage Administrator. (Career Examination Ser.: C-2311). 1994. reprint ed. pap. 29.95 (*0-8373-2311-8*) Nat Learn.
— Mortgage Analyst. (Career Examination Ser.: C-2653). 1994. pap. 29.95 (*0-8373-2653-2*) Nat Learn.
— Mortgage Tax Clerk. (Career Examination Ser.: C-929). 1994. pap. 23.95 (*0-8373-0929-8*) Nat Learn.
— Mortuary Caretaker. (Career Examination Ser.: C-500). 1994. pap. 23.95 (*0-8373-0500-4*) Nat Learn.
— Mortuary Technician. (Career Examination Ser.: C-514). 1994. pap. 23.95 (*0-8373-0514-4*) Nat Learn.
— Mosquito Control Inspector. (Career Examination Ser.: C-2912). 1994. pap. 29.95 (*0-8373-2912-4*) Nat Learn.
— Motion Picture Operator. (Career Examination Ser.: C-501). 1994. pap. 23.95 (*0-8373-0501-2*) Nat Learn.
— Motor Carrier Investigator. (Career Examination Ser.: C-523). 1994. pap. 23.95 (*0-8373-0523-3*) Nat Learn.
— Motor Equipment Maintenance Foreman. (Career Examination Ser.: C-2084). 1994. reprint ed. pap. 27.95 (*0-8373-2084-4*) Nat Learn.
— Motor Equipment Maintenance Supervisor. (Career Examination Ser.: C-3298). 1994. pap. 27.95 (*0-8373-3298-2*) Nat Learn.
— Motor Equipment Manager. (Career Examination Ser.: C-359). 1994. pap. 29.95 (*0-8373-0359-1*) Nat Learn.
— Motor Equipment Mechanic. (Career Examination Ser.: C-459). 1994. pap. 23.95 (*0-8373-0459-8*) Nat Learn.
— Motor Equipment Partsman. (Career Examination Ser.: C-1790). 1994. pap. 23.95 (*0-8373-1790-8*) Nat Learn.
— Motor Equipment Records Assistant. (Career Examination Ser.: C-3206). 1994. pap. 27.95 (*0-8373-3206-0*) Nat Learn.
— Motor Equipment Repairman. (Career Examination Ser.: C-524). 1994. pap. 23.95 (*0-8373-0524-1*) Nat Learn.
— Motor Equipment Specialist. (Career Examination Ser.: C-3299). 1994. 27.95 (*0-8373-3299-0*) Nat Learn.
— Motor Grader Operator. (Career Examination Ser.: C-502). 1994. pap. 27.95 (*0-8373-0502-0*) Nat Learn.
— Motor Vehicle Bureau Supervisor. (Career Examination Ser.: C-3574). 1994. 34.95 (*0-8373-3574-4*) Nat Learn.
— Motor Vehicle Cashier. (Career Examination Ser.: C-1722). 1994. pap. 19.95 (*0-8373-1722-3*) Nat Learn.
— Motor Vehicle Dispatcher. (Career Examination Ser.: C-503). 1994. pap. 23.95 (*0-8373-0503-9*) Nat Learn.
— Motor Vehicle Foreman. (Career Examination Ser.: C-1781). 1994. pap. 29.95 (*0-8373-1781-9*) Nat Learn.
— Motor Vehicle Inspector. (Career Examination Ser.: C-2384). 1994. pap. 27.95 (*0-8373-2384-3*) Nat Learn.
— Motor Vehicle Investigator. (Career Examination Ser.: C-504). 1994. pap. 27.95 (*0-8373-0504-7*) Nat Learn.
— Motor Vehicle License Clerk. (Career Examination Ser.: C-505). 1994. pap. 23.95 (*0-8373-0505-5*) Nat Learn.
— Motor Vehicle License Examiner. (Career Examination Ser.: C-506). 1994. pap. 27.95 (*0-8373-0506-3*) Nat Learn.
— Motor Vehicle License Examiner I. (Career Examination Ser.: C-1937). 1994. pap. 29.95 (*0-8373-1937-4*) Nat Learn.
— Motor Vehicle Licensing Supervisor. (Career Examination Ser.: C-2809). 1994. pap. 29.95 (*0-8373-2809-8*) Nat Learn.
— Motor Vehicle Officer. (Career Examination Ser.: C-2031). 1994. pap. 27.95 (*0-8373-2031-3*) Nat Learn.
— Motor Vehicle Operator. (Career Examination Ser.: C-507). 1994. pap. 23.95 (*0-8373-0507-1*) Nat Learn.
— Motor Vehicle Operator (U.S.P.S.) (Career Examination Ser.: C-508). 1994. pap. 23.95 (*0-8373-0508-X*) Nat Learn.
— Motor Vehicle Program Manager. (Career Examination Ser.: C-311). 1994. pap. 34.95 (*0-8373-0311-7*) Nat Learn.
— Motor Vehicle Referee. (Career Examination Ser.: C-2330). 1994. pap. 34.95 (*0-8373-2330-4*) Nat Learn.
— Motor Vehicle Representative. (Career Examination Ser.: C-3258). 1994. pap. 23.95 (*0-8373-3258-3*) Nat Learn.
— Motor Vehicle Supervisor. (Career Examination Ser.: C-3544-2). 1994. 29.95 (*0-8373-3544-2*) Nat Learn.
— Motorman. (Career Examination Ser.: C-509). 1994. pap. 23.95 (*0-8373-0509-8*) Nat Learn.
— Motorman Instructor. (Career Examination Ser.: C-510). 1994. pap. 27.95 (*0-8373-0510-1*) Nat Learn.
— Mower Maintenance Mechanic. (Career Examination Ser.: C-1373). 1994. pap. 23.95 (*0-8373-1373-2*) Nat Learn.
— Multi-Keyboard Operator. (Career Examination Ser.: C-455). 1994. pap. 23.95 (*0-8373-0455-5*) Nat Learn.
— Multi-Keyboard Operator II. (Career Examination Ser.: C-3073). 1994. pap. 27.95 (*0-8373-3073-4*) Nat Learn.
— Multiple Residence Inspector. (Career Examination Ser.: C-2842). 1994. pap. 29.95 (*0-8373-2842-X*) Nat Learn.
— Multiple Residence Inspector II. (Career Examination Ser.: C-3078). 1994. pap. 34.95 (*0-8373-3078-5*) Nat Learn.
— Multiple Subject Assessment for Teachers (MSAT) (National Teacher Examination Ser.). 1994. 23.95 (*0-8373-8669-1*, NC-9) Nat Learn.
— Multistate Bar Examination (MBE) (Admission Test Ser.: ATS-8). 300p. 1994. 45.95 (*0-8373-5108-1*); pap. 29.95 (*0-8373-5008-5*) Nat Learn.
— Municipal Bonds Coordinator. (Career Examination Ser.: C-1342). 1994. pap. 34.95 (*0-8373-1342-2*) Nat Learn.
— Museum Attendant. (Career Examination Ser.: C-1374). 1994. pap. 23.95 (*0-8373-1374-0*) Nat Learn.
— Museum Curator. (Career Examination Ser.: C-1375). 1994. pap. 27.95 (*0-8373-1375-9*) Nat Learn.
— Museum Director. (Career Examination Ser.: C-2372). 1994. pap. 34.95 (*0-8373-2372-X*) Nat Learn.
— Museum Instructor. (Career Examination Ser.: C-1705). 1994. pap. 27.95 (*0-8373-1705-3*) Nat Learn.
— Museum Intern. (Career Examination Ser.: C-1376). 1994. pap. 23.95 (*0-8373-1376-7*) Nat Learn.
— Museum Laboratory Technician. (Career Examination Ser.: C-1377). 1994. pap. 27.95 (*0-8373-1377-5*) Nat Learn.
— Museum Supervisor. (Career Examination Ser.: C-2941). 1994. pap. 29.95 (*0-8373-2941-8*) Nat Learn.
— Museum Technician. (Career Examination Ser.: C-522). 1994. pap. 27.95 (*0-8373-0522-5*) Nat Learn.
— Music. (Graduate Record Examination Ser.: GRE-13). 1994. 39.95 (*0-8373-5263-0*); pap. 23.95 (*0-8373-5213-4*) Nat Learn.
— Music. (Undergraduate Program Field Test Ser.: UPFT-16). 1994. pap. 23.95 (*0-8373-6016-1*) Nat Learn.
— Music Education. (National Teachers Examination Ser.: NT-11). 1994. pap. 23.95 (*0-8373-8421-4*) Nat Learn.
— Music, Jr. H. S. (Teachers License Examination Ser.: T-42). 1994. pap. 23.95 (*0-8373-8042-1*) Nat Learn.
— Music, Sr. H. S. (Teachers License Examination Ser.: T-43). 1994. pap. 23.95 (*0-8373-8043-X*) Nat Learn.
— Musical Supervisor. (Career Examination Ser.: C-525). 1994. pap. 29.95 (*0-8373-0525-X*) Nat Learn.
— Narcotics Education Assistant. (Career Examination Ser.: C-2503). 1994. pap. 29.95 (*0-8373-2503-X*) Nat Learn.
— Narcotics Education Specialist. (Career Examination Ser.: C-847). 1994. pap. 29.95 (*0-8373-0847-X*) Nat Learn.
— Narcotics Investigator. (Career Examination Ser.: C-1600). 1994. pap. 34.95 (*0-8373-1600-6*) Nat Learn.
— Narcotics Security Assistant. (Career Examination Ser.: C-1378). 1941. pap. 27.95 (*0-8373-1378-3*) Nat Learn.
— NASD Series 6 Examination: Annuities & Mutual Funds. (Admission Test Ser.: ATS-97). 1994. 29.95 (*0-8373-5097-2*) Nat Learn.
— National Certifying Examination for Physician's Assistants (PA) (Admission Test Ser.: ATS-91). 1994. 45.95 (*0-8373-5191-X*); pap. 29.95 (*0-8373-5091-3*) Nat Learn.
— National Council Licensure Examination for Practical Nurses (NCLEX-PN) (Admission Test Ser.: ATS-76). 1994. pap. 23.95 (*0-8373-5076-X*) Nat Learn.
— National Council Licensure Examination for Registered Nurses (NCLEX-RN) (Admission Test Ser.: ATS-75). 300p. 1994. pap. 23.95 (*0-8373-5075-1*) Nat Learn.
— National Dental Assistant Boards (NDAB) (Admission Test Ser.: ATS-87). 1994. 29.95 (*0-8373-5087-5*) Nat Learn.
— National Dental Boards (NDB), Pt. 2. (Admission Test Ser.: ATS-36B). 1994. pap. 39.95 (*0-8373-6956-8*) Nat Learn.
— National Dental Boards (NDB) Combined Edition. (Admission Test Ser.: ATS-36). 1994. pap. 49.95 (*0-8373-5036-0*) Nat Learn.
— National Dental Hygiene Boards (NDHB) (Admission Test Ser.: ATS-51). 1994. pap. 29.95 (*0-8373-5051-4*) Nat Learn.
— National Highway Traffic Safety Administration's Truck Operator Qualification Examination (NTSATOQ) (Admission Test Ser.: ATS-96). 1994. 39.95 (*0-8373-5196-0*); pap. 23.95 (*0-8373-5096-4*) Nat Learn.
— National Medical Boards (NMB) (Admission Test Ser.: ATS-23). 1994. 49.95 (*0-8373-5023-9*) Nat Learn.
— National Medical Boards (NMB), Pt. I. (Admission Test Ser.: ATS-23A). 1994. pap. 39.95 (*0-8373-6950-9*) Nat Learn.
— National Medical Boards (NMB), Pt. II. (Admission Test Ser.: ATS-23B). 1994. pap. 39.95 (*0-8373-6951-7*) Nat Learn.
— National Pharmacy Boards (NPB) (Admission Test Ser.: ATS-47). 1994. pap. 39.95 (*0-8373-5047-6*) Nat Learn.
— National Psychology Boards (NPsyB) (Admission Test Ser.: ATS-89). 1994. pap. 39.95 (*0-8373-5089-1*) Nat Learn.
— National Teacher Examination (NTE) - (Core Battery) (Admission Test Ser.: ATS-15). 300p. 1994. pap. 23.95 (*0-8373-5015-8*) Nat Learn.
— National Teacher Examination Passbook Series. (Entire Series). 1994. pap. write for info. (*0-8373-8400-1*) Nat Learn.
— National Veterinary Boards (NBE-NVB), Pt. III: Physical Diagnosis, Medicine, Surgery. (Admission Test Ser.: ATS-50C). 1994. pap. 39.95 (*0-8373-6962-2*) Nat Learn.
— National Veterinary Boards, Pt. II: Pharmacology, Therapeutics, Parasitology, Hygiene. (Admission Test Ser.: ATS-50B). 1994. pap. 29.95 (*0-8373-6961-4*) Nat Learn.
— Natural Sciences. (College-Level Examination Ser.: CLEP-9D). 1994. pap. 19.95 (*0-8373-5248-7*) Nat Learn.
— Naturalist. (Career Examination Ser.: C-1379). 1994. pap. 29.95 (*0-8373-1379-1*) Nat Learn.
— NCR No. 3100 Operator. (Career Examination Ser.: C-530). 1994. pap. 19.95 (*0-8373-0530-6*) Nat Learn.
— Nebraska Assessment Battery of Essential Learning Skills (N-ABELS) (Admission Test Ser.: ATS-65). 1994. pap. 23.95 (*0-8373-5065-4*) Nat Learn.
— Neighborhood Aide. (Career Examination Ser.: C-2910). 1994. pap. 23.95 (*0-8373-2910-8*) Nat Learn.
— Nevada Competency-Based High School Diploma Program (CHSD) (Admission Test Ser.: ATS-67). 1994. pap. 23.95 (*0-8373-5067-0*) Nat Learn.
— New York Basic Competency Tests (BCT-NY) (Admission Test Ser.: ATS-55). 1994. pap. 23.95 (*0-8373-5055-7*) Nat Learn.
— New York State Bar Examination (NYBE) (Admission Test Ser.: ATS-25). 1994. pap. 55.95 (*0-8373-5125-1*); pap. 39.95 (*0-8373-5025-5*) Nat Learn.
— Nonverbal Reasoning. (Career Examination Ser.: CS-27). 1994. 23.95 (*0-8373-6727-1*) Nat Learn.
— Notary Public. (Career Examination Ser.: C-531). 1994. pap. 19.95 (*0-8373-0531-4*) Nat Learn.
— Numerical & Alphabetical Progressions & Abstract Reasoning. (Career Examination Ser.: CS-30). 1994. pap. 23.95 (*0-8373-6730-1*) Nat Learn.
— Nurse. (Career Examination Ser.: C-532). 1994. pap. 23.95 (*0-8373-0532-2*) Nat Learn.
— Nurse Administrator. (Career Examination Ser.: C-2913). 1994. pap. 29.95 (*0-8373-2913-2*) Nat Learn.
— Nurse GS4-GS7. (Career Examination Ser.: C-533). 1994. pap. 23.95 (*0-8373-0533-0*) Nat Learn.
— Nurse Instructor. (Career Examination Ser.: C-2108). 1994. reprint ed. pap. 329.95 (*0-8373-2108-5*) Nat Learn.
— Nursery Supervisor. (Career Examination Ser.: C-3575). 1994. 29.95 (*0-8373-3575-2*) Nat Learn.
— Nurse's Aide. (Career Examination Ser.: C-535). 1994. pap. 19.95 (*0-8373-0535-7*) Nat Learn.
— Nursing Administration. (Certified Nurse Examination Ser.: CN-16). 1994. 39.95 (*0-8373-6166-4*); pap. 23.95 (*0-8373-6116-8*) Nat Learn.
— Nursing Administration (Advanced) (Certified Nurse Examination Ser.: CN-17). 1994. 39.95 (*0-8373-6167-2*); pap. 23.95 (*0-8373-6117-6*) Nat Learn.
— Nursing Assistant. (Career Examination Ser.: C-534). 1994. pap. 19.95 (*0-8373-0534-9*) Nat Learn.
— Nursing Care Coordinator. (Career Examination Ser.: Series 1). 1991. pap. 39.95 (*0-8373-3735-6*) Nat Learn.
— Nursing Health Care. (ACT Proficiency Examination Program Ser.: PEP-46). 1994. pap. 23.95 (*0-8373-5546-X*) Nat Learn.
— Nursing Health Care. (Regents External Degree Ser.: REDP-19). 1994. pap. 23.95 (*0-8373-5619-9*) Nat Learn.
— Nursing Home Administrator. (Career Examination Ser.: C-3205). 1994. pap. 39.95 (*0-8373-3205-2*) Nat Learn.
— Nursing School Entrance Examinations for Practical Nurse (PN) (Admission Test Ser.: ATS-20). 1994. pap. 23.95 (*0-8373-5020-4*) Nat Learn.
— Nursing School Entrance Examinations for Registered & Graduate Nurses (RN) (Admission Test Ser.: ATS-19). 1994. 39.95 (*0-8373-5119-7*); pap. 23.95 (*0-8373-5019-0*) Nat Learn.
— Nursing, Sr. H. S. (Teachers License Examination Ser.: T-44). 1994. pap. 23.95 (*0-8373-8044-8*) Nat Learn.
— Nursing Station Clerk Trainee. (Career Examination Ser.: C-3158). 1994. pap. 23.95 (*0-8373-3158-7*) Nat Learn.
— Nutrition Assistant. (Career Examination Ser.: C-3303). 1994. pap. 23.95 (*0-8373-3303-2*) Nat Learn.
— Nutrition Education Consultant. (Career Examination Ser.: C-2740). 1994. pap. 34.95 (*0-8373-2740-7*) Nat Learn.
— Nutrition Services Consultant. (Career Examination Ser.: C-2836). 1994. pap. 34.95 (*0-8373-2836-5*) Nat Learn.
— Nutrition Services Supervisor. (Career Examination Ser.: C-1384). 1994. pap. 29.95 (*0-8373-1384-8*) Nat Learn.
— Nutritionist. (Career Examination Ser.: C-2326). 1994. pap. 23.95 (*0-8373-2326-6*) Nat Learn.
— Nutritionist I. (Career Examination Ser.: C-3004). 1994. pap. 23.95 (*0-8373-3004-1*) Nat Learn.
— Nutritionist II. (Career Examination Ser.: C-3005). 1994. pap. 27.95 (*0-8373-3005-X*) Nat Learn.
— Occupancy Director. (Career Examination Ser.: Series 1). 1991. pap. 39.95 (*0-8373-3736-4*) Nat Learn.

— Occupational Analyst. (Career Examination Ser.: C-2548). 1994. pap. 29.95 (*0-8373-2548-X*) Nat Learn.

— Occupational Competency Examination (OCE)-General Examination: General Examination. (Admission Test Ser.: ATS-33). 1994. 29.95 (*0-8373-5033-6*) Nat Learn.

— Occupational Competency Examination Series. (Individual Titles Listed by Subject). 1994. pap. write for info. (*0-8373-5700-4*) Nat Learn.

— Occupational Licensing Specialist. (Career Examination Ser.: Series 1). 1991. pap. 27.95 (*0-8373-3737-2*) Nat Learn.

— Occupational Strategy (Nursing) (Regents External Degree Ser.: REDP-20). 1994. pap. 23.95 (*0-8373-5620-2*) Nat Learn.

— Occupational Strategy, Nursing. (ACT Proficiency Examination Program Ser.: PEP-47). 1994. pap. 23.95 (*0-8373-5547-8*) Nat Learn.

— Occupational Therapist. (Career Examination Ser.: C-558). 1994. pap. 29.95 (*0-8373-0558-6*) Nat Learn.

— Occupational Therapist Aide. (Career Examination Ser.: C-1380). 1994. pap. 27.95 (*0-8373-1380-5*) Nat Learn.

— Occupational Therapist Assistant. (Career Examination Ser.: C-1381). 1994. pap. 27.95 (*0-8373-1381-3*) Nat Learn.

— Oceanographer. (Career Examination Ser.: C-550). 1994. pap. 27.95 (*0-8373-0550-0*) Nat Learn.

— Office Aide. (Career Examination Ser.: C-1065). 1994. pap. 19.95 (*0-8373-1065-2*) Nat Learn.

— Office & Science Assistant. (Career Examination Ser.: C-552). 1994. pap. 29.95 (*0-8373-0552-7*) Nat Learn.

— Office Appliance Operator. (Career Examination Ser.: C-551). 1994. pap. 23.95 (*0-8373-0551-9*) Nat Learn.

— Office Assistant. (Career Examination Ser.: C-1382). 1994. pap. 19.95 (*0-8373-1382-1*) Nat Learn.

— Office Associate. (Career Examination Ser.). 1994. pap. 19.95 (*0-8373-2450-5*) Nat Learn.

— Office Machine Aide. (Career Examination Ser.: C-1579). 1991. pap. 16.00 (*0-8373-1579-4*) Nat Learn.

— Office Machine Associate. (Career Examination Ser.: C-2451). 1994. pap. 23.95 (*0-8373-2451-3*) Nat Learn.

— Office Machine Operating-Sr. H. S. (Teachers License Examination Ser.: T-45). 1994. pap. 23.95 (*0-8373-8045-6*) Nat Learn.

— Office Machine Operator. (Career Examination Ser.: C-559). 1994. pap. 23.95 (*0-8373-0559-4*) Nat Learn.

— Office Manager. (Career Examination Ser.: C-2398). 1994. pap. 29.95 (*0-8373-2398-3*) Nat Learn.

— Office Services Supervisor. (Career Examination Ser.: C-2196). 1994. pap. 29.95 (*0-8373-2196-4*) Nat Learn.

— Office Systems Analyst. (Career Examination Ser.: C-3100). 1994. pap. 34.95 (*0-8373-3100-5*) Nat Learn.

— Office Typist. (Career Examination Ser.: C-3373). 1994. pap. 19.95 (*0-8373-3373-3*) Nat Learn.

— Officer Candidate School Admission Test (OCS) (Admission Test Ser.: ATS-53). 1994. pap. 23.95 (*0-8373-5053-0*) Nat Learn.

— Offset Lithography. (Occupational Competency Examination Ser.: OCE-27). 1994. pap. 23.95 (*0-8373-5727-6*) Nat Learn.

— Offset Photographer. (Career Examination Ser.: C-560). 1994. pap. 23.95 (*0-8373-0560-8*) Nat Learn.

— Offset Pressman. (Career Examination Ser.: C-561). 1994. pap. 23.95 (*0-8373-0561-6*) Nat Learn.

— Offset Printing Machine Operator. (Career Examination Ser.: C-562). 1994. pap. 23.95 (*0-8373-0562-4*) Nat Learn.

— Offtrack Betting Operations Analyst. (Career Examination Ser.: C-3302). 1994. pap. 29.95 (*0-8373-3302-4*) Nat Learn.

— Oiler. (Career Examination Ser.: C-553). 1994. pap. 22.00 (*0-8373-0553-5*) Nat Learn.

— Operating Engineer (Stationary) (Career Examination Ser.: C-555). 1994. pap. 29.95 (*0-8373-0555-1*) Nat Learn.

— Operations & Maintenance Trainee. (Career Examination Ser.: C-554). 1994. pap. 27.95 (*0-8373-0554-3*) Nat Learn.

— Operations Flight Clerk. (Career Examination Ser.: C-564). 1994. pap. 23.95 (*0-8373-0564-0*) Nat Learn.

— Operations Management I. (Regents External Degree Ser.: REDP-13). 1994. pap. 23.95 (*0-8373-5613-X*) Nat Learn.

— Operations Management II. (Regents External Degree Ser.: REDP-14). 1994. pap. 23.95 (*0-8373-5614-8*) Nat Learn.

— Operations Management III. (Regents External Degree Ser.: REDP-15). 1941. pap. 23.95 (*0-8373-5615-6*) Nat Learn.

— Operations Officer. (Career Examination Ser.: C-3069). 1941. pap. 34.95 (*0-8373-3069-6*) Nat Learn.

— Operations Research Analyst. (Career Examination Ser.: C-556). 1994. pap. 34.95 (*0-8373-0556-X*) Nat Learn.

— Operations Review Specialist. (Career Examination Ser.: C-3260). 1994. pap. 34.95 (*0-8373-3260-5*) Nat Learn.

— Ophthalmic Aide. (Career Examination Ser.: C-563). 1994. pap. 23.95 (*0-8373-0563-2*) Nat Learn.

— Optometrist. (Career Examination Ser.: C-557). 1994. pap. 29.95 (*0-8373-0557-8*) Nat Learn.

— Optometry Admission Test (OAT) (Admission Test Ser.: ATS-27). 1994. reprint ed. pap. 23.95 (*0-8373-5027-1*) Nat Learn.

— Ordinance Enforcement Officer. (Career Examination Ser.: C-3068). 1994. pap. 29.95 (*0-8373-3068-8*) Nat Learn.

— Ordinance Inspector. (Career Examination Ser.: C-2852). 1994. pap. 29.95 (*0-8373-2852-7*) Nat Learn.

— Organizational Behavior. (DANTES Ser.: No. 49). 1994. pap. 23.95 (*0-8373-6649-6*) Nat Learn.

— Organizational Behavior. (ACT Proficiency Examination Program Ser.: PEP-19). 1994. pap. 23.95 (*0-8373-5519-2*) Nat Learn.

— Ornamental Horticulture. (Occupational Competency Examination Ser.: OCE-28). 1994. pap. 23.95 (*0-8373-5728-4*) Nat Learn.

— Outreach Worker. (Career Examination Ser.: C-3559). 1994. 23.95 (*0-8373-3559-0*) Nat Learn.

— Packer. (Career Examination Ser.: C-1647). 1994. reprint ed. pap. 19.95 (*0-8373-1647-2*) Nat Learn.

— Painter. (Career Examination Ser.: C-570). 1994. pap. 23.95 (*0-8373-0570-5*) Nat Learn.

— Painting Inspector. (Career Examination Ser.: C-1778). 1994. pap. 27.95 (*0-8373-1778-9*) Nat Learn.

— Para-Professional Careers in Mental Hygiene. (Career Examination Ser.: C-3055). 1994. pap. 23.95 (*0-8373-3055-6*) Nat Learn.

— Paralegal Aide. (Career Examination Ser.: C-2245). 1994. pap. 23.95 (*0-8373-2245-6*) Nat Learn.

— Pari-Mutuel Examiner. (Career Examination Ser.: C-644). 1994. pap. 23.95 (*0-8373-0644-2*) Nat Learn.

— Park Attendant. (Career Examination Ser.: C-1541). 1994. pap. 23.95 (*0-8373-1541-7*) Nat Learn.

— Park Construction Coordinator. (Career Examination Ser.: C-3278). 1994. pap. 34.95 (*0-8373-3278-8*) Nat Learn.

— Park Engineer. (Career Examination Ser.: C-3191). 1994. pap. 34.95 (*0-8373-3191-9*) Nat Learn.

— Park Foreman. (Career Examination Ser.: C-571). 1994. pap. 27.95 (*0-8373-0571-3*) Nat Learn.

— Park Maintenance Supervisor. (Career Examination Ser.: C-2942). 1994. pap. 27.95 (*0-8373-2942-6*) Nat Learn.

— Park Manager. (Career Examination Ser.: C-2247). 1994. pap. 29.95 (*0-8373-2247-2*) Nat Learn.

— Park Manager I. (Career Examination Ser.: C-383). 1994. pap. 29.95 (*0-8373-0383-4*) Nat Learn.

— Park Manager II. (Career Examination Ser.: C-384). 1994. pap. 29.95 (*0-8373-0384-2*) Nat Learn.

— Park Manager III. (Career Examination Ser.: C-385). 1994. pap. 29.95 (*0-8373-0385-0*) Nat Learn.

— Park Patrolman. (Career Examination Ser.: C-1688). 1994. pap. 23.95 (*0-8373-1688-X*) Nat Learn.

— Park Ranger. (Career Examination Ser.: C-650). 1994. pap. 23.95 (*0-8373-0650-7*) Nat Learn.

— Park Service Worker. (Career Examination Ser.: C-2468). 1994. pap. 23.95 (*0-8373-2468-8*) Nat Learn.

— Park Superintendent. (Career Examination Ser.: C-2268). 1994. reprint ed. pap. 29.95 (*0-8373-2268-5*) Nat Learn.

— Park Supervisor. (Career Examination Ser.: C-1563). 1994. pap. 27.95 (*0-8373-1563-8*) Nat Learn.

— Parking Enforcement Agent. (Career Examination Ser.: C-572). 1994. pap. 23.95 (*0-8373-0572-1*) Nat Learn.

— Parking Meter Attendant. (Career Examination Ser.: C-1063). 1994. pap. 23.95 (*0-8373-1063-6*) Nat Learn.

— Parking Meter Collector. (Career Examination Ser.: C-573). 1994. pap. 23.95 (*0-8373-0573-X*) Nat Learn.

— Parking Meter Supervisor. (Career Examination Ser.: C-2592). 1994. pap. 29.95 (*0-8373-2592-7*) Nat Learn.

— Parole Officer. (Career Examination Ser.: C-574). 1994. pap. 23.95 (*0-8373-0574-8*) Nat Learn.

— Party Chief. (Career Examination Ser.: C-2167). 1994. reprint ed. pap. 34.95 (*0-8373-2167-0*) Nat Learn.

— Pathologist. (Career Examination Ser.: C-645). 1984. pap. 49.95 (*0-8373-0645-0*) Nat Learn.

— Patrolman Examinations-All States. (Career Examination Ser.: C-575). 1984. pap. 23.95 (*0-8373-0575-6*) Nat Learn.

— Patrolman-Police Department. (Career Examination Ser.: C-576). 1994. pap. 23.95 (*0-8373-0576-4*) Nat Learn.

— Patrolman-Policewoman. (Career Examination Ser.: C-1922). 1994. pap. 23.95 (*0-8373-1922-6*) Nat Learn.

— Payroll Auditor. (Career Examination Ser.: C-2074). 1994. reprint ed. pap. 29.95 (*0-8373-2074-7*) Nat Learn.

— Payroll Clerk. (Career Examination Ser.: C-1596). 1994. pap. 19.95 (*0-8373-1596-4*) Nat Learn.

— Payroll Supervisor. (Career Examination Ser.: C-3154). 1994. pap. 27.95 (*0-8373-3154-4*) Nat Learn.

— PBX Equipment Installer & Repairer. (Career Examination Ser.: C-1385). 1994. pap. 27.95 (*0-8373-1385-6*) Nat Learn.

— Peace Corps Examination. (Career Examination Ser.: C-646). 1994. pap. 23.95 (*0-8373-0646-9*) Nat Learn.

— Pediatric Nurse Practitioner. (Certified Nurse Examination Ser.: CN-8). 1994. 39.95 (*0-8373-6158-3*); pap. 23.95 (*0-8373-6108-7*) Nat Learn.

— Personnel, Administration & Computer Occupations. (Career Examination Ser.: C-3555). 1991. 23.95 (*0-8373-3555-8*) Nat Learn.

— Personnel Administrator. (Career Examination Ser.: C-647). 1994. pap. 39.95 (*0-8373-0647-7*) Nat Learn.

— Personnel Analyst. (Career Examination Ser.: C-2344). 1994. pap. 34.95 (*0-8373-2344-4*) Nat Learn.

— Personnel Analyst Trainee. (Career Examination Ser.: C-2395). 1994. pap. 27.95 (*0-8373-2395-9*) Nat Learn.

— Personnel Assistant. (Career Examination Ser.: C-577). 1994. pap. 29.95 (*0-8373-0577-2*) Nat Learn.

— Personnel Associate. (Career Examination Ser.: C-648). 1994. pap. 29.95 (*0-8373-0648-5*) Nat Learn.

— Personnel Clerk. (Career Examination Ser.: C-2461). 1994. pap. 23.95 (*0-8373-2461-0*) Nat Learn.

— Personnel Examiner. (Career Examination Ser.: C-578). 1994. pap. 29.95 (*0-8373-0578-0*) Nat Learn.

— Personnel Examining Trainee. (Career Examination Ser.: C-579). 1994. pap. 27.95 (*0-8373-0579-9*) Nat Learn.

— Personnel-Human Resource Management. (DANTES Ser.: No. 48). 1994. pap. 23.95 (*0-8373-6648-8*) Nat Learn.

— Personnel Management. (ACT Proficiency Examination Program Ser.: PEP-20). 1994. pap. 23.95 (*0-8373-5520-6*) Nat Learn.

— Personnel Manager. (Career Examination Ser.: C-2112). 1994. reprint ed. pap. 39.95 (*0-8373-2112-3*) Nat Learn.

— Personnel Officer. (Career Examination Ser.: C-2343). 1994. pap. 29.95 (*0-8373-2343-6*) Nat Learn.

— Personnel Specialist. (Career Examination Ser.: C-1386). 1994. pap. 29.95 (*0-8373-1386-4*) Nat Learn.

— Personnel Systems Analyst. (Career Examination Ser.: C-1387). 1994. pap. 34.95 (*0-8373-1387-2*) Nat Learn.

— Personnel Technician. (Career Examination Ser.: C-1944). 1994. pap. 27.95 (*0-8373-1944-7*) Nat Learn.

— Personnel Technician Trainee. (Career Examination Ser.: C-2274). 1994. pap. 23.95 (*0-8373-2274-X*) Nat Learn.

— Personnel Transactions Supervisor. (Career Examination Ser.: C-3150). 1994. pap. 29.95 (*0-8373-3150-1*) Nat Learn.

— Pest Control Aide. (Career Examination Ser.: C-2030). 1994. pap. 23.95 (*0-8373-2030-5*) Nat Learn.

— Pest Control Supervisor. (Career Examination Ser.: C-3094). 1994. pap. 27.95 (*0-8373-3094-7*) Nat Learn.

— Pesticide Control Inspector. (Career Examination Ser.: C-2561). 1994. pap. 29.95 (*0-8373-2561-7*) Nat Learn.

— Pharmaceutical Examiner. (Career Examination Ser.: C-1839). 1994. pap. 39.95 (*0-8373-1839-4*) Nat Learn.

— Pharmacist. (Career Examination Ser.: C-580). 1994. pap. 29.95 (*0-8373-0580-2*) Nat Learn.

— Pharmacist, I. (Career Examination Ser.: C-1836). 1994. pap. 29.95 (*0-8373-1836-X*) Nat Learn.

— Pharmacist II. (Career Examination Ser.: C-1837). 1994. pap. 34.95 (*0-8373-1837-8*) Nat Learn.

— Pharmacist III. (Career Examination Ser.: C-1838). 1994. pap. 34.95 (*0-8373-1838-6*) Nat Learn.

— Pharmacist Trainee. (Career Examination Ser.: C-649). 1994. pap. 23.95 (*0-8373-0649-3*) Nat Learn.

— Pharmacologist. (Career Examination Ser.: C-581). 1994. pap. 39.95 (*0-8373-0581-0*) Nat Learn.

— Pharmacy Aide. (Career Examination Ser.: C-2576). 1994. pap. 23.95 (*0-8373-2576-5*) Nat Learn.

— Pharmacy Assistant. (Career Examination Ser.: C-1388). 1994. pap. 23.95 (*0-8373-1388-0*) Nat Learn.

— Pharmacy Assistant II. (Career Examination Ser.: C-2943). 1994. pap. 27.95 (*0-8373-2943-4*) Nat Learn.

— Pharmacy College Admission Test (PCAT) (Admission Test Ser.: ATS-52). 1994. pap. 23.95 (*0-8373-5052-2*) Nat Learn.

— Pharmacy Inspector. (Career Examination Ser.: C-2536). 1994. pap. 34.95 (*0-8373-2536-6*) Nat Learn.

— Philosophy. (Graduate Record Examination Ser.: GRE-14). 1994. pap. 23.95 (*0-8373-5214-2*) Nat Learn.

— Philosophy. (Undergraduate Program Field Test Ser.: UPFT-17). 1994. pap. 23.95 (*0-8373-6017-X*) Nat Learn.

— Philosophy of Education. (ACT Proficiency Examination Program Ser.: PEP-30). 1994. pap. 23.95 (*0-8373-5530-3*) Nat Learn.

— Philosophy of Education. (College Proficiency Examination Ser.: CPEP-32). 1994. reprint ed. pap. 23.95 (*0-8373-5432-3*) Nat Learn.

— Photo Laboratory Technician. (Career Examination Ser.: C-1389). 1994. pap. 27.95 (*0-8373-1389-9*) Nat Learn.

— Photo Machine Operator. (Career Examination Ser.: C-1390). 1994. pap. 19.95 (*0-8373-1390-2*) Nat Learn.

— Photo Specialist. (Career Examination Ser.: C-1391). 1994. pap. 23.95 (*0-8373-1391-0*) Nat Learn.

— Photocopy Machine Operator. (Career Examination Ser.: C-2971). 1994. pap. 19.95 (*0-8373-2971-X*) Nat Learn.

— Photographer. (Career Examination Ser.: C-582). 1994. pap. 29.95 (*0-8373-0582-9*) Nat Learn.

— Photographic Specialist I. (Career Examination Ser.: C-1870). 1994. pap. 23.95 (*0-8373-1870-X*) Nat Learn.

— Photographic Specialist II. (Career Examination Ser.: C-1871). 1994. pap. 23.95 (*0-8373-1871-8*) Nat Learn.

— Photographic Technician. (Career Examination Ser.: C-1872). 1994. pap. 23.95 (*0-8373-1872-6*) Nat Learn.

— Photostat Operator. (Career Examination Ser.: C-1878). 1994. pap. 19.95 (*0-8373-1878-5*) Nat Learn.

— Physical Education. (Graduate Record Examination Ser.: GRE-20). 1994. pap. 23.95 (*0-8373-5220-7*) Nat Learn.

— Physical Education. (National Teachers Examination Ser.: NT-9). 1994. pap. 23.95 (*0-8373-8419-2*) Nat Learn.

— Physical Education. (Undergraduate Program Field Test Ser.: UPFT-18). 1994. pap. 23.95 (*0-8373-6018-8*) Nat Learn.

— Physical Geology. (ACT Proficiency Examination Program Ser.: PEP-56). 1991. pap. 19.95 (*0-8373-5906-6*) Nat Learn.

— Physical Geology. (ACT Proficiency Examination Program Ser.: No. PEP-56). 1994. 39.95 (*0-8373-5931-7*) Nat Learn.

— Physical Science. (DANTES Ser.: No. 30). 1994. 39.95 (*0-8373-6680-1*); pap. 23.95 (*0-8373-6630-5*) Nat Learn.

— Physical Science Aide. (Career Examination Ser.: C-583). 1994. pap. 27.95 (*0-8373-0583-7*) Nat Learn.

— Physical Science Technician. (Career Examination Ser.: C-584). 1994. pap. 27.95 (*0-8373-0584-5*) Nat Learn.

— Physical Sciences. (Graduate Record Area Examination Ser.: GRE-43). 1994. 39.95 (*0-8373-5293-2*); pap. 23.95 (*0-8373-5243-6*) Nat Learn.

— Physical Therapist. (Career Examination Ser.: C-585). 1994. pap. 27.95 (*0-8373-0585-3*) Nat Learn.

— Physician. (Career Examination Ser.: C-1392). 1994. pap. 44.95 (*0-8373-1392-9*) Nat Learn.

— Physician's Assistant. (Career Examination Ser.: C-2557). 1994. pap. 29.95 (*0-8373-2557-9*) Nat Learn.

— Physicist. (Career Examination Ser.: C-586). 1994. pap. 34.95 (*0-8373-0586-1*) Nat Learn.

— Physics. (DANTES Ser.: No. 31). 1991. pap. 19.95 (*0-8373-6631-3*) Nat Learn.

— Physics. (DANTES Ser.). 1994. 39.95 (*0-8373-6531-7*) Nat Learn.

— Physics. (Undergraduate Program Field Test Ser.: UPFT-19). 1994. pap. 23.95 (*0-8373-6019-6*) Nat Learn.

— Physics & General Science, Sr. H. S. (Teachers License Examination Ser.: No. T-46). 1994. pap. 23.95 (*0-8373-6657-7*) Nat Learn.

— Physics & General Science, Sr. H. S. (Teachers License Examination Ser.: T-46). 1994. pap. 39.95 (*0-8373-8046-4*) Nat Learn.

— Pile Driving Engineer. (Career Examination Ser.: C-2558). 1994. pap. 34.95 (*0-8373-2558-7*) Nat Learn.

— Pipe Caulker. (Career Examination Ser.: C-641). 1994. pap. 23.95 (*0-8373-0641-8*) Nat Learn.

— Pipefitter. (Career Examination Ser.: C-587). 1994. pap. 23.95 (*0-8373-0587-X*) Nat Learn.

— Placement Representative I. (Career Examination Ser.: C-868). 1994. pap. 27.95 (*0-8373-0868-2*) Nat Learn.

— Placement Representative II. (Career Examination Ser.: C-869). 1994. pap. 29.95 (*0-8373-0869-0*) Nat Learn.

— Plan Examiner. (Career Examination Ser.: C-651). 1994. pap. 29.95 (*0-8373-0651-5*) Nat Learn.

— Plane Trigonometry. (DANTES Ser.: No. 29). 1991. pap. 19.95 (*0-8373-6629-1*) Nat Learn.

— Plane Trigonometry. (DANTES Ser.: No. 29). 1994. 39.95 (*0-8373-6529-5*) Nat Learn.

— Planner. (Career Examination Ser.: C-588). 1994. pap. 27.95 (*0-8373-0588-8*) Nat Learn.

— Planner & Analyst Trainee. (Career Examination Ser.: C-2996). 1994. pap. 29.95 (*0-8373-2996-5*) Nat Learn.

— Planner (Criminal Justice) (Career Examination Ser.: C-3020). 1994. pap. 34.95 (*0-8373-3020-3*) Nat Learn.

— Planner Trainee. (Career Examination Ser.: C-2778). 1994. pap. 23.95 (*0-8373-2778-4*) Nat Learn.

— Planner Youth Services. (Career Examination Ser.: C-3003). 1994. pap. 29.95 (*0-8373-3003-3*) Nat Learn.

— Planning Aide. (Career Examination Ser.: C-2770). 1994. pap. 23.95 (*0-8373-2770-9*) Nat Learn.

— Planning & Evaluation Assistant. (Career Examination Ser.: C-549). 1994. pap. 29.95 (*0-8373-0549-7*) Nat Learn.

— Planning Director. (Career Examination Ser.: C-3401). 1994. pap. 39.95 (*0-8373-3401-2*) Nat Learn.

— Planning Technician. (Career Examination Ser.: C-3185). 1994. pap. 23.95 (*0-8373-3185-4*) Nat Learn.

— Plant Facilities Administrator. (Career Examination Ser.: C-2758). 1994. pap. 39.95 (*0-8373-2758-X*) Nat Learn.

— Plant Maintenance Engineer. (Career Examination Ser.: C-2480). 1994. pap. 34.95 (*0-8373-2480-7*) Nat Learn.

— Plant Maintenance Mechanic. (Career Examination Ser.: C-1393). 1994. pap. 23.95 (*0-8373-1393-7*) Nat Learn.

— Plant Maintenance Supervisor. (Career Examination Ser.: C-1559). 1994. pap. 27.95 (*0-8373-1559-X*) Nat Learn.

— Plant Superintendent. (Career Examination Ser.: C-1935). 1994. reprint ed. pap. 29.95 (*0-8373-1935-8*) Nat Learn.

— Plant Superintendent A. (Career Examination Ser.: C-2046). 1994. pap. 29.95 (*0-8373-2046-1*) Nat Learn.

— Plant Superintendent B. (Career Examination Ser.: C-2047). 1994. pap. 29.95 (*0-8373-2047-X*) Nat Learn.

— Plant Superintendent C. (Career Examination Ser.: C-2048). 1994. pap. 29.95 (*0-8373-2048-8*) Nat Learn.

— Plasterer. (Career Examination Ser.: C-589). 1994. pap. 23.95 (*0-8373-0589-6*) Nat Learn.

— Playground Director. (Career Examination Ser.: C-590). 1994. pap. 29.95 (*0-8373-0590-X*) Nat Learn.

— Playgrounds (Health Education), Men. (Teachers License Examination Ser.: T-47a). 1994. pap. 23.95 (*0-8373-8047-2*) Nat Learn.

— Playgrounds (Health Education), Women. (Teachers License Examination Ser.: T-47b). 1994. pap. 23.95 (*0-685-49791-7*) Nat Learn.

— Playgrounds (Kindergarten) (Teachers License Examination Ser.: T-48). 1994. pap. 23.95 (*0-8373-8048-0*) Nat Learn.

— Playgrounds (Swimming) (Teachers License Examination Ser.: T-49). 1994. pap. 23.95 (*0-8373-8049-9*) Nat Learn.

— Plumber. (Career Examination Ser.: C-591). 1994. pap. 23.95 (*0-8373-0591-8*) Nat Learn.

— Plumber's Helper. (Career Examination Ser.: C-592). 1994. pap. 23.95 (*0-8373-0592-6*) Nat Learn.

— Plumbing. (Occupational Competency Examination Ser.: OCE-29). 1994. pap. 23.95 (*0-8373-5729-2*) Nat Learn.

— Plumbing Engineer. (Career Examination Ser.: C-2713). 1994. pap. 34.95 (*0-8373-2713-X*) Nat Learn.

— Plumbing Inspector. (Career Examination Ser.: C-593). 1994. pap. 29.95 (*0-8373-0593-4*) Nat Learn.

— Plumbing Supervisor. (Career Examination Ser.: C-2583). 1994. pap. 29.95 (*0-8373-2583-8*) Nat Learn.

— Plumbing Workbook. (Workbook Ser.). 1994. pap. 23.95 (*0-8373-7905-9*) Nat Learn.

— Police Administration & Supervision. (Career Examination Ser.: No. CS-32). 1994. pap. 29.95 (*0-8373-6732-8*) Nat Learn.

— Police Administrative Aide. (Career Examination Ser.: C-640). 1994. pap. 23.95 (*0-8373-0640-X*) Nat Learn.

— Police Attendant. (Career Examination Ser.: C-982). 1994. pap. 23.95 (*0-8373-0982-4*) Nat Learn.

— Police Cadet. (Career Examination Ser.: C-594). 1994. pap. 23.95 (*0-8373-0594-2*) Nat Learn.

— Police Captain. (Career Examination Ser.: C-2803). 1994. pap. 39.95 (*0-8373-2803-9*) Nat Learn.

— Police Chief. (Career Examination Ser.: C-2754). 1994. pap. 44.95 (*0-8373-2754-7*) Nat Learn.

— Police Clerk. (Career Examination Ser.: C-639). 1994. pap. 23.95 (*0-8373-0639-6*) Nat Learn.

— Police Communications & Teletype Operator. (Career Examination Ser.: C-1847). 1994. pap. 23.95 (*0-8373-1847-5*) Nat Learn.

— Police Communications & Teletype Operator Supervisor. (Career Examination Ser.: C-1437). 1994. pap. 29.95 (*0-8373-1437-2*) Nat Learn.

— Police Communications Technician. (Career Examination Ser.: C-3526). 1994. 23.95 (*0-8373-3526-4*) Nat Learn.

— Police Dispatcher. (Career Examination Ser.: C-2256). 1994. reprint ed. pap. 23.95 (*0-8373-2256-1*) Nat Learn.

— Police Inspector. (Career Examination Ser.: C-1383-X). 1994. 39.95 (*0-8373-1383-X*) Nat Learn.

R

An Asterisk (*) at the beginning of an entry indicates that the title is appearing in BIP for the first time.

— Police Lieutenant. (Career Examination Ser.: C-2802). 1994. pap. 29.95 (*0-8373-2802-0*) Nat Learn.
— Police Officer. (Career Examination Ser.: C-1939). 1994. reprint ed. pap. 23.95 (*0-8373-1939-0*) Nat Learn.
— Police Officer - Los Angeles Police Department (LAPD) (Career Examination Ser.: C-2441). 1994. pap. 23.95 (*0-8373-2441-6*) Nat Learn.
— Police Officer - Nassau County Police Department (NCPD) (Career Examination Ser.: C-1755). 1994. pap. 23.95 (*0-8373-1755-X*) Nat Learn.
— Police Officer - New York Police Department (NYPD) (Career Examination Ser.: C-1739). 1994. reprint ed. pap. 23.95 (*0-8373-1739-8*) Nat Learn.
— Police Officer - Suffolk County Police Department (SCPD) (Career Examination Ser.: C-1741). 1994. reprint ed. pap. 23.95 (*0-8373-1741-X*) Nat Learn.
— Police Operations Aide. (Career Examination Ser.: C-3402). 1994. pap. 23.95 (*0-8373-3402-0*) Nat Learn.
— Police Patrolman. (Career Examination Ser.: C-595). 1994. pap. 23.95 (*0-8373-0595-0*) Nat Learn.
— Police Promotion Course. (General Aptitude & Abilities Ser.: No. CS-18). 1994. pap. 29.95 (*0-8373-6718-2*) Nat Learn.
— Police Reading Comprehension. (General Aptitude & Abilities Ser.: No. CS-23). 1994. pap. 23.95 (*0-8373-6723-9*) Nat Learn.
— Police Surgeon. (Career Examination Ser.: C-596). 1994. pap. 49.95 (*0-8373-0596-9*) Nat Learn.
— Police Trainee. (Career Examination Ser.: C-597). 1994. pap. 23.95 (*0-8373-0597-7*) Nat Learn.
— Policewoman. (Career Examination Ser.: C-598). 1994. pap. 23.95 (*0-8373-0598-5*) Nat Learn.
— Political Science. (Graduate Record Examination Ser.: GRE-16). 1994. pap. 23.95 (*0-8373-5216-9*) Nat Learn.
— Political Science. (Undergraduate Program Field Test Ser.: UPFT-20). 1994. pap. 23.95 (*0-8373-6020-X*) Nat Learn.
— Pollution Control Specialist. (Career Examination Ser.: Series 1). 1991. pap. 29.95 (*0-8373-3738-0*) Nat Learn.
— Portable Engineer - Any Motive Power Except Steam (AMPES) (Career Examination Ser.: C-599). 1994. pap. 29.95 (*0-8373-0599-3*) Nat Learn.
— Portable Engineer (Steam) (Career Examination Ser.: C-600). 1994. pap. 29.95 (*0-8373-0600-0*) Nat Learn.
— Position Classification Specialist. (Career Examination Ser.: C-601). 1994. pap. 29.95 (*0-8373-0601-9*) Nat Learn.
— Postal Arithmetic. (General Aptitude & Abilities Ser.: No. CS-20). 1994. pap. 19.95 (*0-8373-6720-4*) Nat Learn.
— Postal Inspector (U. S. P. S.) (Career Examination Ser.: C-602). 1994. pap. 27.95 (*0-8373-0602-7*) Nat Learn.
— Postal Police Officer (U.S.P.S.) (Career Examination Ser.: C-2211). 1994. pap. 19.95 (*0-8373-2211-1*) Nat Learn.
— Postal Supervisor (U. S. P. S.) (Career Examination Ser.: C-603). 1994. pap. 29.95 (*0-8373-0603-5*) Nat Learn.
— Postal System Examiner (U. S. P. S.) (Career Examination Ser.: C-2079). 1994. reprint ed. pap. 34.95 (*0-8373-2079-8*) Nat Learn.
— Postal Transportation Clerk (U. S. P. S.) (Career Examination Ser.: C-604). 1994. pap. 23.95 (*0-8373-0604-3*) Nat Learn.
— Postmaster, 1st, 2nd, & 3rd Classes (U. S. P. S.) (Career Examination Ser.: C-605). 1994. pap. 29.95 (*0-8373-0605-1*) Nat Learn.
— Postmaster, 4th Class (U. S. P. S.) (Career Examination Ser.: C-606). 1994. pap. 27.95 (*0-8373-0606-X*) Nat Learn.
— Power Cable Maintainer. (Career Examination Ser.: C-653). 1994. pap. 23.95 (*0-8373-0653-1*) Nat Learn.
— Power Distribution Maintainer. (Career Examination Ser.: C-1394). 1994. pap. 23.95 (*0-8373-1394-5*) Nat Learn.
— Power Electronic Maintainer. (Career Examination Ser.: C-3180). 1994. pap. 23.95 (*0-8373-3180-3*) Nat Learn.
— Power Maintainer - Group A. (Career Examination Ser.: C-607). 1994. pap. 23.95 (*0-8373-0607-8*) Nat Learn.
— Power Maintainer - Group B. (Career Examination Ser.: C-608). 1994. pap. 23.95 (*0-8373-0608-6*) Nat Learn.
— Power Maintainer - Group C. (Career Examination Ser.: C-609). 1994. pap. 23.95 (*0-8373-0609-4*) Nat Learn.
— Power Plant Operator. (Career Examination Ser.: C-1395). 1994. pap. 27.95 (*0-8373-1395-3*) Nat Learn.
— Power Plant Supervisor. (Career Examination Ser.: C-3403). 1994. pap. 29.95 (*0-8373-3403-9*) Nat Learn.
— Practical Nurse. (Career Examination Ser.: C-642). 1994. pap. 23.95 (*0-8373-0642-6*) Nat Learn.
— Practice & Drill for the Clerk, Typist & Stenographer Examinations. (Career Examination Ser.: No. CS-19). 1994. pap. 23.95 (*0-8373-6719-0*) Nat Learn.
— Pre-Employment Counselor. (Career Examination Ser.: C-1396). 1994. pap. 29.95 (*0-8373-1396-1*) Nat Learn.
— Pre-Law Equivalency Examination (PL) (Admission Test Ser.: ATS-40). 1994. pap. 29.95 (*0-8373-5040-9*) Nat Learn.
— Precis of Postal Service Manual. (General Aptitude & Abilities Ser.: No. CS-22). 1994. pap. 17.95 (*0-8373-6722-0*) Nat Learn.
— Preparing Written Material. (General Aptitude & Abilities Ser.: No. CS-37). 1994. pap. 19.95 (*0-8373-6737-9*) Nat Learn.
— Press Operator. (Career Examination Ser.: C-3190). 1994. pap. 27.95 (*0-8373-3190-0*) Nat Learn.
— Presser. (Career Examination Ser.: C-1397). 1994. pap. 27.95 (*0-8373-1397-X*) Nat Learn.
— Preventive Maintenance Supervisor. (Career Examination Ser.: C-3499). 1994. pap. 29.95 (*0-8373-3499-3*) Nat Learn.
— Principal, Academic High School. (Teachers License Examination Ser.: S-5). 1994. pap. 39.95 (*0-8373-8105-3*) Nat Learn.
— Principal Account-Audit Clerk. (Career Examination Ser.: C-2008). 1994. pap. 23.95 (*0-8373-2008-9*) Nat Learn.
— Principal Account Clerk. (Career Examination Ser.: C-655). 1994. pap. 23.95 (*0-8373-0655-8*) Nat Learn.
— Principal Accountant. (Career Examination Ser.: C-654). 1994. pap. 34.95 (*0-8373-0654-X*) Nat Learn.
— Principal Actuarial Clerk. (Career Examination Ser.: C-2424). 1994. pap. 27.95 (*0-8373-2424-6*) Nat Learn.
— Principal Actuary. (Career Examination Ser.: C-610). 1994. pap. 49.95 (*0-8373-0610-8*) Nat Learn.
— Principal Addiction Specialist. (Career Examination Ser.: C-1398). 1994. pap. 34.95 (*0-8373-1398-8*) Nat Learn.
— Principal Administrative Analyst. (Career Examination Ser.: C-2710). 1994. pap. 39.95 (*0-8373-2710-5*) Nat Learn.
— Principal Administrative Associate. (Career Examination Ser.: C-2394). 1994. pap. 27.95 (*0-8373-2394-0*) Nat Learn.
— Principal Administrative Services Clerk. (Career Examination Ser.: C-2871). 1994. pap. 29.95 (*0-8373-2871-3*) Nat Learn.
— Principal Admitting Clerk. (Career Examination Ser.: C-656). 1994. pap. 27.95 (*0-8373-0656-6*) Nat Learn.
— Principal Affirmative Action Officer. (Career Examination Ser.: C-2689). 1994. pap. 34.95 (*0-8373-2689-3*) Nat Learn.
— Principal Alcoholism Rehabilitaion Counselor. (Career Examination Ser.: C-2796). 1994. pap. 34.95 (*0-8373-2796-2*) Nat Learn.
— Principal Attorney. (Career Examination Ser.: C-1913). 1994. pap. 44.95 (*0-8373-1913-7*) Nat Learn.
— Principal Audit Clerk. (Career Examination Ser.: C-657). 1994. pap. 23.95 (*0-8373-0657-4*) Nat Learn.
— Principal Auditor. (Career Examination Ser.: C-2405). 1994. pap. 39.95 (*0-8373-2405-X*) Nat Learn.
— Principal Bank Examiner. (Career Examination Ser.: C-658). 1994. pap. 34.95 (*0-8373-0658-2*) Nat Learn.
— Principal Bookkeeper. (Career Examination Ser.: C-1756). 1994. reprint ed. pap. 27.95 (*0-8373-1756-8*) Nat Learn.
— Principal Budget Analyst. (Career Examination Ser.: C-2416). 1994. pap. 39.95 (*0-8373-2416-5*) Nat Learn.
— Principal Budget Examiner. (Career Examination Ser.: C-1637). 1994. reprint ed. pap. 39.95 (*0-8373-1637-5*) Nat Learn.
— Principal Budget Officer. (Career Examination Ser.: C-2685). 1994. pap. 39.95 (*0-685-06426-3*) Nat Learn.
— Principal Building Inspector. (Career Examination Ser.: C-2853). 1994. pap. 34.95 (*0-8373-2853-5*) Nat Learn.
— Principal Buildings Manager. (Career Examination Ser.: C-2719). 1991. pap. 24.00 (*0-685-42465-0*) Nat Learn.
— Principal Buyer. (Career Examination Ser.: C-3419). 1994. pap. 29.95 (*0-8373-3419-5*) Nat Learn.
— Principal Cashier. (Career Examination Ser.: C-1974). 1994. pap. 23.95 (*0-8373-1974-9*) Nat Learn.
— Principal Chemist. (Career Examination Ser.: C-2403). 1994. pap. 34.95 (*0-8373-2403-3*) Nat Learn.
— Principal Children's Counselor. (Career Examination Ser.: C-1602). 1994. pap. 34.95 (*0-8373-1602-2*) Nat Learn.
— Principal Civil Engineer. (Career Examination Ser.: C-318). 1994. pap. 34.95 (*0-8373-0318-4*) Nat Learn.
— Principal Clerk. (Career Examination Ser.: C-611). 1994. pap. 23.95 (*0-8373-0611-6*) Nat Learn.
— Principal Clerk (Personnel) (Career Examination Ser.: C-1399). 1994. pap. 27.95 (*0-8373-1399-6*) Nat Learn.
— Principal Clerk-Stenographer. (Career Examination Ser.: C-3327). 1994. pap. 23.95 (*0-8373-3327-X*) Nat Learn.
— Principal Clerk Surrogate. (Career Examination Ser.: C-2129). 1994. reprint ed. pap. 27.95 (*0-8373-2129-8*) Nat Learn.
— Principal Commissary Clerk. (Career Examination Ser.: C-2049). 1994. pap. 27.95 (*0-8373-2049-6*) Nat Learn.
— Principal Communications Technician. (Career Examination Ser.: C-2413). 1994. pap. 34.95 (*0-8373-2413-0*) Nat Learn.
— Principal, Comprehensive High School. (Teachers License Examination Ser.: S-11). 1994. pap. 39.95 (*0-8373-8111-8*) Nat Learn.
— Principal Computer Programmer. (Career Examination Ser.: C-1626). 1994. pap. 34.95 (*0-8373-1626-X*) Nat Learn.
— Principal Construction Inspector. (Career Examination Ser.: C-1400). 1994. pap. 34.95 (*0-8373-1400-3*) Nat Learn.
— Principal Consumer Affairs Inspector. (Career Examination Ser.: C-1658). 1994. reprint ed. pap. 29.95 (*0-8373-1658-8*) Nat Learn.
— Principal Consumer Affairs Investigator. (Career Examination Ser.: C-2377). 1994. pap. 29.95 (*0-8373-2377-0*) Nat Learn.
— Principal Court Clerk. (Career Examination Ser.: C-2588). 1994. pap. 29.95 (*0-8373-2588-9*) Nat Learn.
— Principal Custodial Foreman. (Career Examination Ser.: C-2560). 1994. pap. 29.95 (*0-8373-2560-9*) Nat Learn.
— Principal Data Entry Machine Operator. (Career Examination Ser.: C-2866). 1994. pap. 29.95 (*0-8373-2866-7*) Nat Learn.
— Principal Data Processing Control Clerk. (Career Examination Ser.: C-2485). 1994. pap. 29.95 (*0-8373-2485-8*) Nat Learn.
— Principal Data Processing Equipment Operator. (Career Examination Ser.: C-2303). 1994. reprint ed. pap. 29.95 (*0-8373-2303-7*) Nat Learn.
— Principal Developmental Specialist. (Career Examination Ser.: C-925). 1994. pap. 29.95 (*0-8373-0925-5*) Nat Learn.
— Principal Drafting Technician. (Career Examination Ser.: C-2680). 1994. pap. 29.95 (*0-8373-2680-X*) Nat Learn.
— Principal Draftsman. (Career Examination Ser.: C-1576). 1994. pap. 29.95 (*0-8373-1576-X*) Nat Learn.
— Principal Drug & Alcohol Counselor. (Career Examination Ser.: C-2743). 1994. pap. 34.95 (*0-8373-2743-1*) Nat Learn.
— Principal Editorial Clerk. (Career Examination Ser.: C-2566). 1994. pap. 29.95 (*0-8373-2566-8*) Nat Learn.
— Principal, Elementary School. (Teachers License Examination Ser.: S-3). 1994. pap. 39.95 (*0-8373-8103-7*) Nat Learn.
— Principal Employment Security Clerk. (Career Examination Ser.: C-2352). 1994. pap. 29.95 (*0-8373-2352-5*) Nat Learn.
— Principal Engineering Aide. (Career Examination Ser.: C-1561). 1994. pap. 29.95 (*0-8373-1561-1*) Nat Learn.
— Principal Engineering Inspector. (Career Examination Ser.: C-911). 1994. pap. 39.95 (*0-8373-0911-5*) Nat Learn.
— Principal Engineering Technician. (Career Examination Ser.: C-1425). 1994. pap. 29.95 (*0-8373-1425-9*) Nat Learn.
— Principal Engineering Technician (Drafting) (Career Examination Ser.: C-1954). 1994. pap. 29.95 (*0-8373-1954-4*) Nat Learn.
— Principal Engineering Technician (Environmental Quality) (Career Examination Ser.: C-3239). 1994. pap. 34.95 (*0-8373-3239-7*) Nat Learn.
— Principal Environmental Analyst. (Career Examination Ser.: C-2661). 1994. pap. 34.95 (*0-8373-2661-3*) Nat Learn.
— Principal Environmental Planner. (Career Examination Ser.: C-2664). 1994. pap. 34.95 (*0-8373-2664-8*) Nat Learn.
— Principal Evidence Technician. (Career Examination Ser.: C-2750). 1994. pap. 34.95 (*0-8373-2750-4*) Nat Learn.
— Principal Examiner of Municipal Affairs. (Career Examination Ser.: C-2727). 1994. pap. 44.95 (*0-8373-2727-X*) Nat Learn.
— Principal Executive Officer. (Career Examination Ser.: C-2827). 1994. pap. 39.95 (*0-8373-2827-6*) Nat Learn.
— Principal Field Accountant. (Career Examination Ser.: C-1570). 1994. pap. 34.95 (*0-8373-1570-0*) Nat Learn.
— Principal File Clerk. (Career Examination Ser.: C-659). 1994. pap. 23.95 (*0-8373-0659-0*) Nat Learn.
— Principal Financial Analyst. (Career Examination Ser.: C-2644). 1994. pap. 44.95 (*0-8373-2644-3*) Nat Learn.
— Principal Forestry Technician. (Career Examination Ser.: C-2716). 1994. pap. 29.95 (*0-8373-2716-4*) Nat Learn.
— Principal Grants Analyst. (Career Examination Ser.: C-2835). 1994. pap. 39.95 (*0-8373-2835-7*) Nat Learn.
— Principal Groundskeeper. (Career Examination Ser.: C-1573). 1994. pap. 29.95 (*0-8373-1573-5*) Nat Learn.
— Principal Home Economist. (Career Examination Ser.: C-1627). 1994. pap. 34.95 (*0-8373-1627-8*) Nat Learn.
— Principal Hospital Care Investigator. (Career Examination Ser.: C-612). 1994. pap. 34.95 (*0-8373-0612-4*) Nat Learn.
— Principal Housing Inspector. (Career Examination Ser.: C-1426). 1994. reprint ed. pap. 34.95 (*0-8373-1426-7*) Nat Learn.
— Principal Human Resources Specialist. (Career Examination Ser.: C-974). 1994. pap. 34.95 (*0-8373-0974-3*) Nat Learn.
— Principal Illustrator. (Career Examination Ser.: C-1713). 1994. pap. 34.95 (*0-8373-1713-4*) Nat Learn.
— Principal Insurance Examiner. (Career Examination Ser.: C-2696). 1994. pap. 34.95 (*0-8373-2696-6*) Nat Learn.
— Principal Investigator. (Career Examination Ser.: C-1791). 1994. pap. 34.95 (*0-8373-1791-6*) Nat Learn.
— Principal, Junior High School. (Teachers License Examination Ser.: S-4). 1994. pap. 39.95 (*0-8373-8104-5*) Nat Learn.
— Principal Juvenile Counselor. (Career Examination Ser.: C-422). 1994. pap. 34.95 (*0-8373-0422-9*) Nat Learn.
— Principal Key Punch Operator. (Career Examination Ser.: C-2103). 1994. pap. 27.95 (*0-8373-2103-4*) Nat Learn.
— Principal Labor-Management Practices Adjustor. (Career Examination Ser.: C-613). 1994. pap. 44.95 (*0-8373-0613-2*) Nat Learn.
— Principal Labor Relations Analyst. (Career Examination Ser.: C-2231). 1994. pap. 44.95 (*0-8373-2231-6*) Nat Learn.
— Principal Labor Specialist. (Career Examination Ser.: C-2670). 1994. pap. 39.95 (*0-8373-2670-2*) Nat Learn.
— Principal Laboratory Technician. (Career Examination Ser.: C-3014). 1994. pap. 34.95 (*0-8373-3014-9*) Nat Learn.
— Principal Land Management Specialist. (Career Examination Ser.: C-2620). 1994. pap. 39.95 (*0-8373-2620-6*) Nat Learn.
— Principal Librarian. (Career Examination Ser.: C-2915). 1994. pap. 29.95 (*0-8373-2915-9*) Nat Learn.
— Principal Library Clerk. (Career Examination Ser.: C-1932). 1994. pap. 27.95 (*0-8373-1932-3*) Nat Learn.
— Principal Mail & Supply Clerk. (Career Examination Ser.: C-975). 1994. pap. 23.95 (*0-8373-0975-1*) Nat Learn.
— Principal Management Analyst. (Career Examination Ser.: C-1737). 1994. pap. 39.95 (*0-8373-1737-1*) Nat Learn.
— Principal Management Technician. (Career Examination Ser.: C-2753). 1994. pap. 34.95 (*0-8373-2753-9*) Nat Learn.
— Principal Manpower Development Specialist. (Career Examination Ser.: C-2819). 1994. pap. 39.95 (*0-8373-2819-5*) Nat Learn.
— Principal Mechanical Engineer. (Career Examination Ser.: C-3249). 1994. pap. 39.95 (*0-8373-3249-4*) Nat Learn.
— Principal Methods Analyst. (Career Examination Ser.: C-1738). 1994. pap. 39.95 (*0-8373-1738-X*) Nat Learn.
— Principal Museum Curator. (Career Examination Ser.: C-2375). 1994. pap. 34.95 (*0-8373-2375-4*) Nat Learn.
— Principal Occupational Analyst. (Career Examination Ser.: C-2535). 1994. pap. 34.95 (*0-8373-2535-8*) Nat Learn.
— Principal Office Assistant. (Career Examination Ser.: C-2595). 1994. pap. 23.95 (*0-8373-2595-1*) Nat Learn.
— Principal Office Stenographer. (Career Examination Ser.: C-3377). 1994. pap. 23.95 (*0-8373-3377-6*) Nat Learn.
— Principal Office Typist. (Career Examination Ser.: C-3375). 1994. pap. 23.95 (*0-8373-3375-X*) Nat Learn.
— Principal Park Supervisor. (Career Examination Ser.: C-2355). 1994. pap. 29.95 (*0-8373-2355-X*) Nat Learn.
— Principal Personnel Administrator. (Career Examination Ser.: C-2411). 1994. pap. 44.95 (*0-8373-2411-4*) Nat Learn.
— Principal Personnel Analyst. (Career Examination Ser.: C-2346). 1994. pap. 39.95 (*0-8373-2346-0*) Nat Learn.
— Principal Personnel Clerk. (Career Examination Ser.: C-2944). 1994. pap. 27.95 (*0-8373-2944-2*) Nat Learn.
— Principal Personnel Examiner. (Career Examination Ser.: C-1915). 1994. pap. 39.95 (*0-8373-1915-3*) Nat Learn.
— Principal Planner. (Career Examination Ser.: C-1764). 1994. reprint ed. pap. 39.95 (*0-8373-1764-9*) Nat Learn.
— Principal Planner (Education) (Career Examination Ser.: C-1669). 1994. pap. 39.95 (*0-8373-1669-3*) Nat Learn.
— Principal Planner (Manpower) (Career Examination Ser.: C-1599). 1994. pap. 39.95 (*0-8373-1599-9*) Nat Learn.
— Principal Probation Officer. (Career Examination Ser.: C-1427). 1994. pap. 29.95 (*0-8373-1427-5*) Nat Learn.
— Principal Program Evaluation Specialist. (Career Examination Ser.: C-2701). 1994. pap. 39.95 (*0-8373-2701-6*) Nat Learn.
— Principal Program Examiner. (Career Examination Ser.: C-2756). 1994. pap. 39.95 (*0-8373-2756-3*) Nat Learn.
— Principal Program Research Analyst. (Career Examination Ser.: C-2218). 1994. reprint ed. pap. 39.95 (*0-8373-2218-9*) Nat Learn.
— Principal Program Specialist. (Career Examination Ser.: C-2863). 1994. pap. 39.95 (*0-8373-2863-2*) Nat Learn.
— Principal Program Specialist (Correction) (Career Examination Ser.: C-2259). 1994. reprint ed. pap. 39.95 (*0-8373-2259-6*) Nat Learn.
— Principal Programmer Analyst. (Career Examination Ser.: Series 1). 1991. pap. 34.95 (*0-8373-3739-9*) Nat Learn.
— Principal Public Health Engineer. (Career Examination Ser.: C-3099). 1994. pap. 39.95 (*0-8373-3099-8*) Nat Learn.
— Principal Public Health Nutritionist. (Career Examination Ser.: C-1566). 1994. pap. 34.95 (*0-8373-1566-2*) Nat Learn.
— Principal Public Health Representative. (Career Examination Ser.: C-3025). 1994. pap. 34.95 (*0-8373-3025-4*) Nat Learn.
— Principal Purchase Inspector. (Career Examination Ser.: C-1747). 1994. reprint ed. pap. 34.95 (*0-8373-1747-9*) Nat Learn.
— Principal Purchasing Agent. (Career Examination Ser.: C-912). 1994. pap. 29.95 (*0-8373-0912-3*) Nat Learn.
— Principal Quantitative Analyst. (Career Examination Ser.: C-1715). 1994. pap. 39.95 (*0-8373-1715-0*) Nat Learn.
— Principal Real Estate Manager. (Career Examination Ser.: C-1628). 1994. pap. 34.95 (*0-8373-1628-6*) Nat Learn.
— Principal Records Center Assistant. (Career Examination Ser.: C-1914). 1994. pap. 29.95 (*0-8373-1914-5*) Nat Learn.
— Principal Rent Examiner. (Career Examination Ser.: C-2093). 1994. reprint ed. pap. 34.95 (*0-8373-2093-3*) Nat Learn.
— Principal Research Analyst. (Career Examination Ser.: C-2353). 1994. pap. 39.95 (*0-8373-2353-3*) Nat Learn.
— Principal Right-Of-Way Aide. (Career Examination Ser.: C-2737). 1994. pap. 29.95 (*0-8373-2737-7*) Nat Learn.
— Principal Safety Coordinator. (Career Examination Ser.: C-2669). 1994. pap. 39.95 (*0-8373-2669-9*) Nat Learn.
— Principal Sanitary Engineer. (Career Examination Ser.: C-1819). 1994. pap. 3,995.00 (*0-8373-1819-X*) Nat Learn.
— Principal Senior Citizens Program Coordinator. (Career Examination Ser.: C-2799). 1994. pap. 34.95 (*0-8373-2799-7*) Nat Learn.
— Principal, Six Hundred School. (Teachers License Examination Ser.: S-7). 1994. pap. 39.95 (*0-8373-8107-X*) Nat Learn.
— Principal Social Welfare Examiner. (Career Examination Ser.: C-2495). 1994. pap. 29.95 (*0-8373-2495-5*) Nat Learn.
— Principal Special Investigator. (Career Examination Ser.: C-1590). 1994. pap. 34.95 (*0-8373-1590-5*) Nat Learn.
— Principal Special Officer. (Career Examination Ser.: C-3420). 1994. pap. 29.95 (*0-8373-3420-9*) Nat Learn.
— Principal Staff Development Specialist. (Career Examimation Ser.: C-2703). 1994. pap. 39.95 (*0-8373-2703-2*) Nat Learn.
— Principal Stationary Engineer. (Career Examination Ser.: C-1719). 1994. pap. 39.95 (*0-8373-1719-3*) Nat Learn.
— Principal Statistician. (Career Examination Ser.: C-976). 1994. pap. 39.95 (*0-8373-0976-X*) Nat Learn.
— Principal Statistics Clerk. (Career Examination Ser.: C-977). 1994. pap. 27.95 (*0-8373-0977-8*) Nat Learn.
— Principal Stenographer. (Career Examination Ser.: C-614). 1994. pap. 23.95 (*0-8373-0614-0*) Nat Learn.
— Principal Stenographer (Law) (Career Examination Ser.: C-3294). 1994. pap. 27.95 (*0-8373-3294-X*) Nat Learn.
— Principal Storekeeper. (Career Examination Ser.: C-3013). 1994. pap. 29.95 (*0-8373-3013-0*) Nat Learn.
— Principal Stores Clerk. (Career Examination Ser.: C-978). 1994. pap. 27.95 (*0-8373-0978-6*) Nat Learn.
— Principal Systems Analyst. (Career Examination Ser.: C-2388). 1994. pap. 39.95 (*0-8373-2388-6*) Nat Learn.
— Principal Tax Compliance Agent. (Career Examination Ser.: C-2954). 1994. pap. 34.95 (*0-8373-2954-X*) Nat Learn.
— Principal Telephone Operator. (Career Examination Ser.: C-2493). 1994. pap. 23.95 (*0-8373-2493-9*) Nat Learn.
— Principal Typist. (Career Examination Ser.: C-615). 1994. pap. 23.95 (*0-8373-0615-9*) Nat Learn.

— Principal Unemployment Insurance Hearing Representative. (Career Examination Ser.: C-2730). 1994. pap. 34.95 (0-8373-2730-X) Nat Learn.
— Principal Unemployment Insurance Investigator. (Career Examination Ser.: C-2831). 1994. pap. 34.95 (0-8373-2831-4) Nat Learn.
— Principal, Vocational High School. (Teachers License Examination Ser.: S-6). 1994. pap. 39.95 (0-8373-8106-1) Nat Learn.
— Principal Water Plant Supervisor. (Career Examination Ser.: C-2960). 1994. pap. 34.95 (0-8373-2960-4) Nat Learn.
— Principal Workers' Compensation Review Analyst. (Career Examination Ser.: C-310). 1994. pap. 34.95 (0-8373-0310-9) Nat Learn.
— Principal Workmen's Compensation Examiner. (Career Examination Ser.: C-1548). 1994. pap. 34.95 (0-8373-1548-4) Nat Learn.
— Principal X-Ray Technician. (Career Examination Ser.: C-979). 1994. pap. 29.95 (0-8373-0979-4) Nat Learn.
— Principal, Youth & Adult Center. (Teachers License Examination Ser.: S-8). 1994. pap. 39.95 (0-8373-8108-8) Nat Learn.
— Principal Zoning Inspector. (Career Examination Ser.: C-2854). 1994. pap. 34.95 (0-8373-2854-3) Nat Learn.
— Principles of Economics. (DANTES Ser.: No. 32). 1991. pap. 19.95 (0-8373-6632-1) Nat Learn.
— Principles of Economics. (DANTES Ser.: No. 32). 1994. 39.95 (0-8373-6532-5) Nat Learn.
— Principles of Electronic Communication Systems. (DANTES Ser.: No. 44). 1994. pap. 23.95 (0-8373-6644-5) Nat Learn.
— Principles of Finance. (DANTES Ser.: No. 46). 1994. pap. 23.95 (0-8373-6646-1) Nat Learn.
— Principles of Financial Accounting. (DANTES Ser.: No. 47). 1994. pap. 23.95 (0-8373-6647-X) Nat Learn.
— Principles of Guidance. (DANTES Ser.: No. 33). 1991. pap. 19.95 (0-8373-6633-X) Nat Learn.
— Principles of Guidance. (DANTES Ser.: No. 33). 1994. 23.95 (0-8373-6533-3) Nat Learn.
— Principles of Management. (ACT Proficiency Examination Program Ser.: PEP-18). 1994. pap. 23.95 (0-8373-5518-4) Nat Learn.
— Principles of Marketing. (ACT Proficiency Examination Program Ser.: PEP-21). 1994. pap. 23.95 (0-8373-5521-4) Nat Learn.
— Principles of Public Speaking. Date not set. pap. 23.95 (0-8373-6659-3, DANTES-59) Nat Learn.
— Principles of Public Speaking. 1994. 39.95 (0-8373-6559-7, DANTES-59) Nat Learn.
— Principles of Refrigeration. (DANTES Ser.: No. 45). 1994. pap. 23.95 (0-8373-6645-3) Nat Learn.
— Printer. (Career Examination Ser.: C-616). 1994. pap. 23.95 (0-8373-0616-7) Nat Learn.
— Printer-Proofreader. (Career Examination Ser.: C-617). 1994. pap. 29.95 (0-8373-0617-5) Nat Learn.
— Prison Guard. (Career Examination Ser.: C-618). 1984. pap. 19.95 (0-8373-0618-3) Nat Learn.
— Private Investigator. (Career Examination Ser.: C-2462). 1994. pap. 27.95 (0-8373-2462-9) Nat Learn.
— Probation Assistant. (Career Examination Ser.: C-2577). 1994. pap. 27.95 (0-8373-2577-3) Nat Learn.
— Probation Consultant. (Career Examination Ser.: C-980). 1994. pap. 29.95 (0-8373-0980-8) Nat Learn.
— Probation Counselor. (Career Examination Ser.: C-1981). 1994. pap. 29.95 (0-8373-1981-1) Nat Learn.
— Probation Director. (Career Examination Ser.: C-2266). 1994. reprint ed. pap. 39.95 (0-8373-2266-9) Nat Learn.
— Probation Employment Officer. (Career Examination Ser.: C-1428). 1994. pap. 29.95 (0-8373-1428-3) Nat Learn.
— Probation Investigator. (Career Examination Ser.: C-981). 1994. pap. 29.95 (0-8373-0981-6) Nat Learn.
— Probation Officer. (Career Examination Ser.: C-619). 1994. pap. 23.95 (0-8373-0619-1) Nat Learn.
— Probation Officer Trainee. (Career Examination Ser.: C-1429). 1994. pap. 23.95 (0-8373-1429-1) Nat Learn.
— Probation Supervisor. (Career Examination Ser.: C-2262). 1994. reprint ed. pap. 29.95 (0-8373-2262-6) Nat Learn.
— Probation Supervisor I. (Career Examination Ser.: C-1828). 1994. pap. 29.95 (0-8373-1828-9) Nat Learn.
— Probation Supervisor II. (Career Examination Ser.: C-1829). 1994. pap. 29.95 (0-8373-1829-7) Nat Learn.
— Probation Training Director. (Career Examination Ser.: C-3283). 1994. pap. 39.95 (0-8373-3283-4) Nat Learn.
— Process Server. (Career Examination Ser.: C-620). 1994. pap. 23.95 (0-8373-0620-5) Nat Learn.
— Processing Technician. (Career Examination Ser.: C-3534). 1994. 27.95 (0-8373-3534-5) Nat Learn.
— Procurement Agent. (Career Examination Ser.: C-621). 1994. pap. 23.95 (0-8373-0621-3) Nat Learn.
— Procurement Clerk. (Career Examination Ser.: C-2623). 1994. pap. 23.95 (0-8373-2623-0) Nat Learn.
— Procurement Coordinator. (Career Examination Ser.: C-2368). 1994. pap. 34.95 (0-8373-2368-1) Nat Learn.
— Procurement Supervisor. (Career Examination Ser.: C-2711). 1994. pap. 9.95 (0-8373-2711-3) Nat Learn.
— Production - Operations Management. 1994. pap. 23.95 (0-8373-5524-9, PEP-24) Nat Learn.
— Professional & Administrative Career Examination (PACE) (Admission Test Ser.: ATS-26). 1994. pap. 23.95 (0-8373-5026-3) Nat Learn.
— Professional & Administrative Career Examination (PACE) (Career Examination Ser.: No. CS-28). 1994. pap. 23.95 (0-8373-6728-X) Nat Learn.
— Professional Careers in Administrative & Technical Service. (Career Examination Ser.: C-2068). 1994. pap. 23.95 (0-8373-2068-2) Nat Learn.
— Professional Careers in the Natural Sciences. (Career Examination Ser.: C-2386). 1994. pap. 23.95 (0-8373-2386-X) Nat Learn.
— Professional Careers Test (PCT) (Career Examination Ser.: C-622). 1994. pap. 23.95 (0-8373-0622-1) Nat Learn.
— Professional Conduct Investigator. (Career Examination Ser.: C-2315). 1994. reprint ed. pap. 27.95 (0-8373-2315-0) Nat Learn.
— Professional Engineer (PE) (Admission Test Ser.: ATS-35). 1994. 49.95 (0-8373-5035-2) Nat Learn.
— Professional Entry Test (PET) (Career Examination Ser.: C-3404). 1994. pap. 23.95 (0-8373-3404-7) Nat Learn.
— Professional Knowledge (Combined) (National Teacher Examination Ser.: NC 7). 1994. Cloth bdg. avail. pap. 19.95 (0-8373-8467-2) Nat Learn.
— Professional Library Examination. (Career Examination Ser.: C-623). 1994. pap. 29.95 (0-8373-0623-X) Nat Learn.
— Professional Nurse. (Career Examination Ser.: C-624). 1994. pap. 29.95 (0-8373-0624-8) Nat Learn.
— Professional Strategies, Nursing. (Regents External Degree Ser.: No. 26). 1994. pap. 23.95 (0-8373-5626-1) Nat Learn.
— Professional Strategies, Nursing. (ACT Proficiency Examination Program Ser.: PEP-50). 1994. pap. 23.95 (0-8373-5900-7) Nat Learn.
— Professional Trainee. (Career Examination Ser.: C-625). 1994. pap. 23.95 (0-8373-0625-6) Nat Learn.
— Program Administrator. (Career Examination Ser.: C-2868). 1994. pap. 34.95 (0-8373-2868-3) Nat Learn.
— Program Evaluation Specialist. (Career Examination Ser.: C-2699). 1994. pap. 34.95 (0-8373-2699-0) Nat Learn.
— Program Examiner. (Career Examination Ser.: C-2655). 1994. pap. 34.95 (0-8373-2655-9) Nat Learn.
— Program Manager. (Career Examination Ser.: C-985). 1994. pap. 34.95 (0-8373-0985-9) Nat Learn.
— Program Outreach Specialist. (Career Examination Ser.: C-3405). 1994. pap. 29.95 (0-8373-3405-5) Nat Learn.
— Program Research Analyst. (Career Examination Ser.: C-1704). 1994. pap. 34.95 (0-8373-1704-5) Nat Learn.
— Program Research Specialist. (Career Examination Ser.: C-3200). 1994. pap. 34.95 (0-8373-3200-1) Nat Learn.
— Program Specialist. (Career Examination Ser.: C-2861). 1994. pap. 34.95 (0-8373-2861-6) Nat Learn.
— Program Specialist: Aging Services. (Career Examination Ser.: C-2820). 1994. pap. 29.95 (0-8373-2820-9) Nat Learn.
— Program Specialist (Correction) (Career Examination Ser.: C-1997). 1994. pap. 34.95 (0-8373-1997-8) Nat Learn.
— Programmer. (Career Examination Ser.: C-1430). 1994. pap. 29.95 (0-8373-1430-5) Nat Learn.
— Programmer - Programmer Analyst. (Career Examination Ser.: C-1439). 1994. pap. 29.95 (0-8373-1439-9) Nat Learn.
— Programmer Aptitude Test (PAT) (Career Examination Ser.: C-643). 1994. pap. 23.95 (0-8373-0643-4) Nat Learn.
— Programmer Trainee. (Career Examination Ser.: C-1431). 1994. pap. 23.95 (0-8373-1431-3) Nat Learn.
— Project Coordinator. (Career Examination Ser.: C-2589). 1994. pap. 29.95 (0-8373-2589-7) Nat Learn.
— Project Development Coordinator. (Career Examination Ser.: C-1432). 1994. pap. 29.95 (0-8373-1432-1) Nat Learn.
— Project Manager. (Career Examination Ser.: C-1433). 1994. pap. 34.95 (0-8373-1433-X) Nat Learn.
— Project Services Specialist. (Career Examination Ser.: C-1660). 1994. pap. 29.95 (0-8373-1660-X) Nat Learn.
— Property Clerk. (Career Examination Ser.: C-3465). 1994. pap. 23.95 (0-8373-3465-9) Nat Learn.
— Psychiatric & Mental Health Nurse. (Certified Nurse Examination Ser.: CN-12). 1994. 39.95 (0-8373-6162-1); pap. 23.95 (0-8373-6112-5) Nat Learn.
— Psychiatric Attendant. (Career Examination Ser.: C-1434). 1994. pap. 23.95 (0-8373-1434-8) Nat Learn.
— Psychiatric-Mental Health Nursing. (College Proficiency Examination Ser.: CPEP-34). 1994. pap. 23.95 (0-8373-5434-X) Nat Learn.
— Psychiatric-Mental Health Nursing. (ACT Proficiency Examination Program Ser.: PEP-40). 1994. pap. 23.95 (0-8373-5540-0) Nat Learn.
— Psychiatric Nurse. (Career Examination Ser.: C-986). 1994. pap. 29.95 (0-8373-0986-7) Nat Learn.
— Psychiatric Senior Attendant. (Career Examination Ser.: C-1435). 1994. pap. 27.95 (0-8373-1435-6) Nat Learn.
— Psychiatric Social Work Assistant. (Career Examination Ser.: C-2414). 1994. pap. 27.95 (0-8373-2414-9) Nat Learn.
— Psychiatric Social Work Supervisor. (Career Examination Ser.: C-2357). 1994. pap. 34.95 (0-8373-2357-6) Nat Learn.
— Psychiatric Social Worker. (Career Examination Ser.: C-987). 1994. pap. 29.95 (0-8373-0987-5) Nat Learn.
— Psychiatric Social Worker Trainee. (Career Examination Ser.: C-988). 1994. pap. 23.95 (0-8373-0988-3) Nat Learn.
— Psychiatric Staff Attendant. (Career Examination Ser.: C-1436). 1994. pap. 23.95 (0-8373-1436-4) Nat Learn.
— Psychiatric Therapy Aide. (Career Examination Ser.: C-2124). 1994. reprint ed. pap. 23.95 (0-8373-2124-7) Nat Learn.
— Psychiatrist. (Career Examination Ser.: C-626). 1994. pap. 49.95 (0-8373-0626-4) Nat Learn.
— Psychologist. (Career Examination Ser.: C-627). 1994. pap. 34.95 (0-8373-0627-2) Nat Learn.
— Psychologist Trainee. (Career Examination Ser.: C-2621). 1994. pap. 27.95 (0-8373-2621-4) Nat Learn.
— Psychology. (Graduate Record Examination Ser.: GRE-17). 1994. pap. 23.95 (0-8373-5217-7) Nat Learn.
— Psychology. (National Teachers Examination Ser.: NT-42). 1994. pap. 23.95 (0-8373-8452-4) Nat Learn.
— Psychology. (Undergraduate Program Field Test Ser.: UPFT-21). 1994. pap. 23.95 (0-8373-6021-8) Nat Learn.
— Psychology Assistant. (Career Examination Ser.: C-1774). 1994. pap. 27.95 (0-8373-1774-6) Nat Learn.
— Psychology Assistant I. (Career Examination Ser.: C-919). 1994. pap. 29.95 (0-8373-0919-0) Nat Learn.
— Psychology Assistant II. (Career Examination Ser.: C-921). 1994. pap. 29.95 (0-8373-0921-2) Nat Learn.
— Psychology Assistant III. (Career Examination Ser.: C-922). 1994. pap. 29.95 (0-8373-0922-0) Nat Learn.
— Psychology of Adjustment. (DANTES Ser.: No. 34). 1991. pap. 19.95 (0-8373-6634-8) Nat Learn.
— Psychology of Adjustment. (DANTES Ser.: No. 34). 1994. 39.95 (0-8373-6534-1) Nat Learn.
— Psychometrician. (Career Examination Ser.: C-1830). 1994. pap. 39.95 (0-8373-1830-0) Nat Learn.
— Public Administration Intern. (Career Examination Ser.: C-628). 1994. pap. 23.95 (0-8373-0628-0) Nat Learn.
— Public Administrator. (Career Examination Ser.: C-1440). 1994. pap. 29.95 (0-8373-1440-2) Nat Learn.
— Public Buildings Manager. (Career Examination Ser.: C-2719). 1994. pap. 29.95 (0-8373-2719-9) Nat Learn.
— Public Health Administrator. (Career Examination Ser.: C-2082). 1994. reprint ed. pap. 39.95 (0-8373-2082-8) Nat Learn.
— Public Health Adviser. (Career Examination Ser.: C-3093). 1994. pap. 27.95 (0-8373-3093-9) Nat Learn.
— Public Health Aide. (Career Examination Ser.: C-1441). 1994. pap. 23.95 (0-8373-1441-0) Nat Learn.
— Public Health Aide I. (Career Examination Ser.: C-2334). 1994. pap. 23.95 (0-8373-2334-7) Nat Learn.
— Public Health Aide II. (Career Examination Ser.: C-1812). 1994. pap. 27.95 (0-8373-1812-2) Nat Learn.
— Public Health Assistant. (Career Examination Ser.: C-629). 1994. pap. 23.95 (0-8373-0629-9) Nat Learn.
— Public Health Consultant. (Career Examination Ser.: C-312). 1994. pap. 34.95 (0-685-13340-0) Nat Learn.
— Public Health Director. (Career Examination Ser.: C-2240). 1994. pap. 39.95 (0-8373-2240-5) Nat Learn.
— Public Health Education Trainee. (Career Examination Ser.: C-983). 1994. pap. 27.95 (0-8373-0983-2) Nat Learn.
— Public Health Educator. (Career Examination Ser.: C-630). 1994. pap. 29.95 (0-8373-0630-2) Nat Learn.
— Public Health Educator I. (Career Examination Ser.: C-2354). 1994. pap. 34.95 (0-8373-2354-1) Nat Learn.
— Public Health Engineer. (Career Examination Ser.: C-1979). 1994. pap. 29.95 (0-8373-1979-X) Nat Learn.
— Public Health Engineer Trainee. (Career Examination Ser.: C-1881). 1994. pap. 27.95 (0-8373-1881-5) Nat Learn.
— Public Health Epidemiologist. (Career Examination Ser.: C-2246). 1994. pap. 34.95 (0-8373-2246-4) Nat Learn.
— Public Health Inspector. (Career Examination Ser.: C-1753). 1994. pap. 27.95 (0-8373-1753-3) Nat Learn.
— Public Health Nurse. (Career Examination Ser.: C-631). 1994. pap. 23.95 (0-8373-0631-0) Nat Learn.
— Public Health Nutritionist. (Career Examination Ser.: C-632). 1994. pap. 27.95 (0-8373-0632-9) Nat Learn.
— Public Health Representative. (Career Examination Ser.: C-2369). 1994. pap. 27.95 (0-8373-2369-X) Nat Learn.
— Public Health Representative I. (Career Examination Ser.: C-2972). 1994. pap. 27.95 (0-8373-2972-8) Nat Learn.
— Public Health Representative II. (Career Examination Ser.: C-2973). 1994. pap. 29.95 (0-8373-2973-6) Nat Learn.
— Public Health Sanitarian. (Career Examination Ser.: C-633). 1994. pap. 27.95 (0-8373-0633-7) Nat Learn.
— Public Health Sanitarian Trainee. (Career Examination Ser.: C-984). 1994. pap. 23.95 (0-8373-0984-0) Nat Learn.
— Public Health Scientist. (Career Examination Ser.: C-634). 1994. pap. 34.95 (0-8373-0634-5) Nat Learn.
— Public Health Social Work Assistant. (Career Examination Ser.: C-1442). 1994. pap. 27.95 (0-8373-1442-9) Nat Learn.
— Public Health Technician. (Career Examination Ser.: C-2226). 1994. pap. 27.95 (0-8373-2226-X) Nat Learn.
— Public Information Assistant. (Career Examination Ser.: C-2956). 1994. pap. 23.95 (0-8373-2956-6) Nat Learn.
— Public Information Officer. (Career Examination Ser.: C-2950). 1994. pap. 29.95 (0-8373-2950-7) Nat Learn.
— Public Information Specialist. (Career Examination Ser.: C-2111). 1994. pap. 29.95 (0-8373-2111-5) Nat Learn.
— Public Librarian. (Career Examination Ser.: C-989). 1994. pap. 27.95 (0-8373-0989-1) Nat Learn.
— Public Relations Assistant. (Career Examination Ser.: C-635). 1994. pap. 27.95 (0-8373-0635-3) Nat Learn.
— Public Relations Director. (Career Examination Ser.: C-1901). 1994. pap. 34.95 (0-8373-1901-3) Nat Learn.
— Public Relations Specialist. (Career Examination Ser.: C-2934). 1994. pap. 29.95 (0-8373-2934-5) Nat Learn.
— Public Safety Aide. (Career Examination Ser.: Series 1). 1991. pap. 23.95 (0-8373-3740-2) Nat Learn.
— Public Safety Dispatcher I. (Career Examination Ser.: C-116). 1994. pap. 23.95 (0-8373-0116-5) Nat Learn.
— Public Safety Dispatcher II. (Career Examination Ser.: C-117). 1994. pap. 27.95 (0-8373-0117-3) Nat Learn.
— Public Safety Officer I. (Career Examination Ser.: C-2895). 1994. pap. 23.95 (0-8373-2895-0) Nat Learn.
— Public Safety Officer II. (Career Examination Ser.: C-2896). 1994. pap. 27.95 (0-8373-2896-9) Nat Learn.
— Public Safety Officer III. (Career Examination Ser.: C-2897). 1994. pap. 29.95 (0-8373-2897-7) Nat Learn.
— Public Safety Officer IV. (Career Examination Ser.: C-3053). 1994. pap. 29.95 (0-8373-3053-X) Nat Learn.
— Public Services Officer. (Career Examination Ser.: C-636). 1994. pap. 29.95 (0-8373-0636-1) Nat Learn.
— Public Work Wage Investigator. (Career Examination Ser.: C-990). 1994. pap. 29.95 (0-8373-0990-5) Nat Learn.
— Publications Editor. (Career Examination Ser.: C-3146). 1994. pap. 29.95 (0-8373-3146-3) Nat Learn.
— Pump Station Operator. (Career Examination Ser.: C-2442). 1994. pap. 27.95 (0-8373-2442-4) Nat Learn.
— Purchase Inspector. (Career Examination Ser.: C-637). 1994. pap. 27.95 (0-8373-0637-X) Nat Learn.
— Purchase Inspector (Shop Steel) (Career Examination Ser.: C-2258). 1994. reprint ed. pap. 29.95 (0-8373-2258-8) Nat Learn.
— Purchase Specifications Assistant. (Career Examination Ser.: C-2542). 1994. pap. 23.95 (0-8373-2542-0) Nat Learn.
— Purchasing Agent. (Career Examination Ser.: C-638). 1994. pap. 23.95 (0-8373-0638-8) Nat Learn.
— Purchasing Agent (Food) (Career Examination Ser.: C-2731). 1994. pap. 27.95 (0-8373-2731-8) Nat Learn.
— Purchasing Agent (Lumber) (Career Examination Ser.: C-2732). 1994. pap. 27.95 (0-8373-2732-6) Nat Learn.
— Purchasing Agent (Medical) (Career Examination Ser.: C-2733). 1994. pap. 27.95 (0-8373-2733-4) Nat Learn.
— Purchasing Agent (Printing) (Career Examination Ser.: C-2734). 1994. pap. 27.95 (0-8373-2734-2) Nat Learn.
— Purchasing Supervisor. (Career Examination Ser.: C-2720). 1994. pap. 29.95 (0-8373-2720-2) Nat Learn.
— Purchasing Technician. (Career Examination Ser.: C-913). 1994. pap. 23.95 (0-8373-0913-1) Nat Learn.
— Qualifying Examination-Management Service. (Career Examination Ser.: CS-39). 1994. pap. 29.95 (0-8373-6739-5) Nat Learn.
— Quality Assurance Nurse. (Career Examination Ser.: Series 1). 1991. pap. 29.95 (0-8373-3742-9) Nat Learn.
— Quality Control Inspector (U. S. P. S.) (Career Examination Ser.: C-2458). 1994. pap. 39.95 (0-8373-2458-0) Nat Learn.
— Quality Control Investigator. (Career Examination Ser.: C-2137). 1994. pap. 34.95 (0-8373-2137-9) Nat Learn.
— Quality Control Specialist. (Career Examination Ser.: C-1618). 1994. pap. 34.95 (0-8373-1618-9) Nat Learn.
— Quantitative Analyst. (Career Examination Ser.: C-1714). 1994. pap. 29.95 (0-8373-1714-2) Nat Learn.
— Quantity Food Preparation. (Occupational Competency Examination Ser.: OCE-30). 1994. pap. 23.95 (0-8373-5730-6) Nat Learn.
— Question & Answers on Drug Education. (Career Examination Ser.: CS-24). 1994. pap. 29.95 (0-8373-6724-7) Nat Learn.
— Questions & Answers on the Real Estate License Examinations. (Admission Test Ser.: ATS-6). 1994. pap. 23.95 (0-8373-5006-9) Nat Learn.
— Racing & Wagering Assistant. (Career Examination Ser.: C-2714). 1994. pap. 23.95 (0-8373-2714-8) Nat Learn.
— Radiation Technician. (Career Examination Ser.: C-681). 1994. pap. 29.95 (0-8373-0681-7) Nat Learn.
— Radio & Telegraph Operator. (Career Examination Ser.: C-1443). 1994. pap. 23.95 (0-8373-1443-7) Nat Learn.
— Radio & Television Engineer. (Career Examination Ser.: C-1444). 1994. pap. 27.95 (0-8373-1444-5) Nat Learn.
— Radio & Television Mechanic. (Career Examination Ser.: C-1445). 1994. pap. 23.95 (0-8373-1445-3) Nat Learn.
— Radio & Television Technician. (Career Examination Ser.: C-1446). 1994. pap. 23.95 (0-8373-1446-1) Nat Learn.
— Radio Broadcast Technician. (Career Examination Ser.: C-682). 1994. pap. 23.95 (0-8373-0682-5) Nat Learn.
— Radio Dispatcher. (Career Examination Ser.: C-540). 1994. pap. 23.95 (0-8373-0540-3) Nat Learn.
— Radio Mechanic. (Career Examination Ser.: C-660). 1994. pap. 23.95 (0-8373-0660-4) Nat Learn.
— Radio Operator. (Career Examination Ser.: C-683). 1994. pap. 23.95 (0-8373-0683-3) Nat Learn.
— Radio Servicing. (DANTES Ser.: No. 35). 1994. pap. 23.95 (0-8373-6635-6) Nat Learn.
— Radio Servicing. (DANTES Ser.: No. 35). 1994. 39.95 (0-8373-6535-X) Nat Learn.
— Radio Station Manager. (Career Examination Ser.: C-2935). 1994. pap. 34.95 (0-8373-2935-3) Nat Learn.
— Radio Technologist. (Career Examination Ser.: C-1957). 1994. pap. 23.95 (0-8373-1957-9) Nat Learn.
— Radio Telephone Operator. (Career Examination Ser.: C-2883). 1994. pap. 23.95 (0-8373-2883-7) Nat Learn.
— Radiologic Technologist. (Career Examination Ser.: C-1544). 1994. pap. 29.95 (0-8373-1544-1) Nat Learn.
— Radiological Health Specialist. (Career Examination Ser.: C-3118). 1994. pap. 34.95 (0-8373-3118-8) Nat Learn.
— Radiological Officer. (Career Examination Ser.: C-3406). 1994. pap. 34.95 (0-8373-3406-3) Nat Learn.
— Radiologist. (Career Examination Ser.: C-1447). 1994. pap. 39.95 (0-8373-1447-X) Nat Learn.
— Railroad Caretaker. (Career Examination Ser.: C-684). 1994. pap. 23.95 (0-8373-0684-1) Nat Learn.
— Railroad Clerk. (Career Examination Ser.: C-661). 1994. pap. 19.95 (0-8373-0661-2) Nat Learn.
— Railroad Equipment Inspector. (Career Examination Ser.: C-210). 1994. pap. 27.95 (0-8373-0210-2) Nat Learn.
— Railroad Inspector. (Career Examination Ser.: C-685). 1994. pap. 27.95 (0-8373-0685-X) Nat Learn.
— Railroad Porter. (Career Examination Ser.: C-662). 1994. pap. 19.95 (0-8373-0662-0) Nat Learn.
— Railroad Signal Specialist. (Career Examination Ser.: C-663). 1994. pap. 27.95 (0-8373-0663-9) Nat Learn.
— Railroad Stock Assistant. (Career Examination Ser.: C-1448). 1994. pap. 23.95 (0-8373-1448-8) Nat Learn.
— Railroad Stockman. (Career Examination Ser.: C-664). 1994. pap. 23.95 (0-8373-0664-7) Nat Learn.
— Railroad Track & Structure Inspector. (Career Examination Ser.: C-209). 1994. pap. 27.95 (0-8373-0209-9) Nat Learn.
— Range Conservationist. (Career Examination Ser.: C-686). 1994. pap. 29.95 (0-8373-0686-8) Nat Learn.
— Ranger, U. S. Park Service. (Career Examination Ser.: C-665). 1994. pap. 23.95 (0-8373-0665-5) Nat Learn.
— Reading Instruction: Application. (ACT Proficiency Examination Program Ser.: PEP-25). 1994. pap. 23.95 (0-8373-5525-7) Nat Learn.

An Asterisk (*) at the beginning of an entry indicates that the title is appearing in BIP for the first time.

— Reading Instruction: Theoretical Foundations. (ACT Proficiency Examination Program Ser.: PEP-26). 1994. pap. 23.95 (*0-8373-5526-5*) Nat Learn.
— Reading Instruction in the Elementary School. (College Proficiency Examination Ser.: CPEP-25). 1994. pap. 23.95 (*0-8373-5425-0*) Nat Learn.
— Reading Instruction in the Elementary School. (ACT Proficiency Examination Program Ser.: PEP-31). 1994. pap. 23.95 (*0-8373-5531-1*) Nat Learn.
— Reading Interpretation in Social Studies, Natural Sciences & Literature (G. E. D.) (Career Examination Ser.: CS-34). 1994. pap. 17.95 (*0-8373-6734-4*) Nat Learn.
— Reading Specialist. (National Teachers Examination Ser.: NT-30). 1994. pap. 23.95 (*0-8373-8440-0*) Nat Learn.
— Real Estate Agent. (Career Examination Ser.: C-2179). 1994. pap. 23.95 (*0-8373-2179-4*) Nat Learn.
— Real Estate Aide. (Career Examination Ser.: C-687). 1994. pap. 23.95 (*0-8373-0687-6*) Nat Learn.
— Real Estate Appraiser. (Career Examination Ser.: C-1640). 1994. reprint ed. pap. 27.95 (*0-8373-1640-5*) Nat Learn.
— Real Estate Assistant. (Career Examination Ser.: C-688). 1994. pap. 23.95 (*0-8373-0688-4*) Nat Learn.
— Real Estate Broker. (Career Examination Ser.: C-666). 1994. pap. 23.95 (*0-8373-0666-3*) Nat Learn.
— Real Estate Broker (REB) (Admission Test Ser.: ATS-3). 1994. pap. 23.95 (*0-8373-5003-4*) Nat Learn.
— Real Estate Management Trainee. (Career Examination Ser.: C-667). 1994. pap. 23.95 (*0-8373-0667-1*) Nat Learn.
— Real Estate Manager. (Career Examination Ser.: C-689). 1994. pap. 29.95 (*0-8373-0689-2*) Nat Learn.
— Real Estate Salesman. (Career Examination Ser.: C-668). 1991. pap. 23.95 (*0-8373-0668-X*) Nat Learn.
— Real Estate Salesman (RES) (Admission Test Ser.: ATS-4). 1994. pap. 23.95 (*0-8373-5004-2*) Nat Learn.
— Real Property Appraisal Technician. (Career Examination Ser.: C-2185). 1994. pap. 23.95 (*0-8373-2185-9*) Nat Learn.
— Real Property Appraiser. (Career Examination Ser.: C-841). 1994. pap. 23.95 (*0-8373-0841-0*) Nat Learn.
— Real Property Appraiser - Arbitrator Supervisor. (Career Examination Ser.: C-3276). 1994. pap. 39.95 (*0-8373-3276-1*) Nat Learn.
— Real Property Appraiser I. (Career Examination Ser.: C-842). 1994. pap. 23.95 (*0-8373-0842-9*) Nat Learn.
— Real Property Appraiser II. (Career Examination Ser.: C-843). 1994. pap. 27.95 (*0-8373-0843-7*) Nat Learn.
— Real Property Appraiser III. (Career Examination Ser.: C-844). 1994. pap. 27.95 (*0-8373-0844-5*) Nat Learn.
— Real Property Appraiser IV. (Career Examination Ser.: C-845). 1994. pap. 29.95 (*0-8373-0845-3*) Nat Learn.
— Real Property Assessor. (Career Examination Ser.: C-2199). 1994. pap. 23.95 (*0-8373-2199-9*) Nat Learn.
— Real Property Assistant. (Career Examination Ser.: C-699). 1994. pap. 23.95 (*0-8373-0699-X*) Nat Learn.
— Real Property Examiner. (Career Examination Ser.: C-3345). 1994. pap. 27.95 (*0-8373-3345-8*) Nat Learn.
— Real Property Information System Specialist. (Career Examination Ser.: C-3138). 1994. pap. 29.95 (*0-8373-3138-2*) Nat Learn.
— Real Property Manager. (Career Examination Ser.: C-698). 1994. pap. 29.95 (*0-8373-0698-1*) Nat Learn.
— Real Property Recorder. (Career Examination Ser.: C-3102). 1994. pap. 27.95 (*0-8373-3102-1*) Nat Learn.
— Real Property Tax Examiner. (Career Examination Ser.: C-1835). 1994. pap. 27.95 (*0-8373-1835-1*) Nat Learn.
— Real Property Tax Specialist. (Career Examination Ser.: C-2227). 1994. pap. 29.95 (*0-8373-2227-8*) Nat Learn.
— Real Property Tax Supervisor. (Career Examination Ser.). 1994. 34.95 (*0-8373-3604-X*, C-3604) Nat Learn.
— Receptionist. (Career Examination Ser.: C-1636). 1994. reprint ed. pap. 19.95 (*0-8373-1636-7*) Nat Learn.
— Recording Clerk. (Career Examination Ser.: C-2914). 1994. pap. 23.95 (*0-8373-2914-0*) Nat Learn.
— Records Clerk. (Career Examination Ser.). 1994. 23.95 (*0-8373-3612-0*, C-3612) Nat Learn.
— Records Supervisor. (Career Examination Ser.). 1994. 29.95 (*0-8373-3613-9*, C-3613) Nat Learn.
— Recreation Aide. (Career Examination Ser.: C-1449). 1994. pap. 23.95 (*0-8373-1449-6*) Nat Learn.
— Recreation Assistant. (Career Examination Ser.: C-526). 1994. pap. 23.95 (*0-8373-0526-8*) Nat Learn.
— Recreation Assistant (Men) (Career Examination Ser.: C-690a). 1994. pap. 23.95 (*0-8373-0690-6*) Nat Learn.
— Recreation Assistant (Women) (Career Examination Ser.: C-690b). 1994. pap. 23.95 (*0-685-03531-X*) Nat Learn.
— Recreation Director. (Career Examination Ser.: C-679). 1994. pap. 29.95 (*0-8373-0679-5*) Nat Learn.
— Recreation Director, Handicapped Children's Recreation Program. (Career Examination Ser.: C-3095). 1994. pap. 34.95 (*0-8373-3095-5*) Nat Learn.
— Recreation Facility Manager. (Career Examination Ser.: C-1450). 1994. pap. 27.95 (*0-8373-1450-X*) Nat Learn.
— Recreation Instructor. (Career Examination Ser.: C-691). 1994. pap. 23.95 (*0-8373-0691-4*) Nat Learn.
— Recreation Leader. (Career Examination Ser.: C-669). 1994. pap. 23.95 (*0-8373-0669-8*) Nat Learn.
— Recreation Specialist. (Career Examination Ser.: C-692). 1994. pap. 23.95 (*0-8373-0692-2*) Nat Learn.
— Recreation Supervisor. (Career Examination Ser.: C-693). 1994. pap. 27.95 (*0-8373-0693-0*) Nat Learn.
— Recreation Therapist. (Career Examination Ser.: C-2698). 1994. pap. 27.95 (*0-8373-2698-2*) Nat Learn.
— Recreation Worker. (Career Examination Ser.: C-429). 1994. pap. 23.95 (*0-8373-0429-6*) Nat Learn.
— Recycling Coordinator. (Career Examination Ser.: C-3567). 1994. 29.95 (*0-8373-3567-1*) Nat Learn.
— Recycling Supervisor. (Career Examination Ser.: C-3568). 1994. 27.95 (*0-8373-3568-X*) Nat Learn.
— Refrigerating Machine Mechanic. (Career Examination Ser.: C-1451). 1994. pap. 23.95 (*0-8373-1451-8*) Nat Learn.
— Refrigerating Machine Operator. (Career Examination Ser.: C-670). 1991. pap. 18.00 (*0-8373-0670-1*) Nat Learn.
— Regents External Degree Series. (Entire Ser.). 1991. pap. write for info. (*0-8373-5600-8*) Nat Learn.
— Regents Scholarship & College Qualification Test (RSE) (Admission Test Ser.: ATS-42). 1994. pap. 23.95 (*0-8373-5042-5*) Nat Learn.
— Regional Planner. (Career Examination Ser.: C-694). 1994. pap. 27.95 (*0-8373-0694-9*) Nat Learn.
— Registered Professional Nurse. (Career Examination Ser.: C-671). 1994. pap. 27.95 (*0-8373-0671-X*) Nat Learn.
— Registered Representative. (Admission Test Ser.: ATS-1). 1994. pap. 39.95 (*0-8373-5001-8*) Nat Learn.
— Registered Technologist, R.T. (AR-RT) (Career Examination Ser.: C-680). 1994. pap. 29.95 (*0-8373-0680-9*) Nat Learn.
— Registrar. (Career Examination Ser.: C-1452). 1994. pap. 27.95 (*0-8373-1452-6*) Nat Learn.
— Registration Examination for Dieticians (RED) (Admission Test Ser.: ATS-41). 1994. pap. 29.95 (*0-8373-5041-7*) Nat Learn.
— Rehabilitation Assistant. (Career Examination Ser.: C-545). 1994. pap. 29.95 (*0-8373-0545-4*) Nat Learn.
— Rehabilitation Cost Analyst. (Career Examination Ser.: C-3121). 1994. pap. 34.95 (*0-8373-3121-8*) Nat Learn.
— Rehabilitation Counselor. (Career Examination Ser.: C-672). 1994. pap. 29.95 (*0-8373-0672-8*) Nat Learn.
— Rehabilitation Counselor Certification Examination (CRC) (Admission Test Ser.: ATS-92). 1994. pap. 29.95 (*0-8373-5092-1*) Nat Learn.
— Rehabilitation Counselor Supervisor. (Career Examination Ser.: C-1980). 1994. pap. 34.95 (*0-8373-1980-3*) Nat Learn.
— Rehabilitation Counselor Trainee. (Career Examination Ser.: C-1783). 1994. pap. 27.95 (*0-8373-1783-5*) Nat Learn.
— Rehabilitation Inspector. (Career Examination Ser.: C-2639). 1994. pap. 34.95 (*0-8373-2639-7*) Nat Learn.
— Rehabilitation Interviewer. (Career Examination Ser.: C-2708). 1994. pap. 29.95 (*0-8373-2708-3*) Nat Learn.
— Related Technical Subjects (Biological & Chemical), Sr. H. S. (Teachers License Examination Ser.: T-50). 1994. pap. 23.95 (*0-8373-8050-2*) Nat Learn.
— Related Technical Subjects (Mechanical, Structural, Electrical), Sr. H. S. (Teachers License Examination Ser.: T-51). 1994. pap. 19.95 (*0-8373-8051-0*) Nat Learn.
— Relocation Assistant. (Career Examination Ser.: C-1988). 1994. pap. 27.95 (*0-8373-1988-9*) Nat Learn.
— Relocation Supervisor. (Career Examination Ser.: C-3057). 1994. pap. 29.95 (*0-8373-3057-2*) Nat Learn.
— Rent Examiner. (Career Examination Ser.: C-695). 1994. pap. 23.95 (*0-8373-0695-7*) Nat Learn.
— Rent Inspector. (Career Examination Ser.: C-673). 1994. pap. 23.95 (*0-8373-0673-6*) Nat Learn.
— Rent Program Specialist. (Career Examination Ser.: C-3530). 1994. 27.95 (*0-8373-3530-2*) Nat Learn.
— Rent Research Assistant. (Career Examination Ser.: C-696). 1994. pap. 27.95 (*0-8373-0696-5*) Nat Learn.
— Repair Aide. (Career Examination Ser.: C-1453). 1994. pap. 23.95 (*0-8373-1453-4*) Nat Learn.
— Repair Crew Chief. (Career Examination Ser.: C-1454). 1994. pap. 29.95 (*0-8373-1454-2*) Nat Learn.
— Repair Crew Worker. (Career Examination Ser.: C-2004). 1994. pap. 23.95 (*0-8373-2004-6*) Nat Learn.
— Repair Shop Manager. (Career Examination Ser.: C-1801). 1994. pap. 9.95 (*0-8373-1801-7*) Nat Learn.
— Repair Supervisor. (Career Examination Ser.: C-2615). 1994. pap. 27.95 (*0-8373-2615-X*) Nat Learn.
— Reporting Stenographer. (Career Examination Ser.: C-2125). 1994. reprint ed. pap. 23.95 (*0-8373-2125-5*) Nat Learn.
— Research Aide. (Career Examination Ser.: C-1580). 1994. pap. 27.95 (*0-8373-1580-8*) Nat Learn.
— Research Analyst. (Career Examination Ser.: C-1949). 1994. pap. 34.95 (*0-8373-1949-8*) Nat Learn.
— Research Assistant. (Career Examination Ser.: C-674). 1994. pap. 29.95 (*0-8373-0674-4*) Nat Learn.
— Research Technician. (Career Examination Ser.: C-1948). 1994. pap. 29.95 (*0-8373-1948-X*) Nat Learn.
— Research Worker. (Career Examination Ser.: C-546). 1994. pap. 29.95 (*0-8373-0546-2*) Nat Learn.
— Resident Buildings Superintendent. (Career Examination Ser.: C-675). 1994. pap. 29.95 (*0-8373-0675-2*) Nat Learn.
— Residential Unit Supervisor. (Career Examination Ser.: C-3312). 1994. pap. 29.95 (*0-8373-3312-1*) Nat Learn.
— Resource Assistant. (Career Examination Ser.: C-1745). 1994. reprint ed. pap. 23.95 (*0-8373-1745-2*) Nat Learn.
— Resources & Reimbursement Agent. (Career Examination Ser.: C-3157). 1994. pap. 27.95 (*0-8373-3157-9*) Nat Learn.
— Resources Examiner. (Career Examination Ser.). 1994. 27.95 (*0-8373-1455-0*, C-1455) Nat Learn.
— Resources Interviewer. (Career Examination Ser.). 1994. 27.95 (*0-8373-1456-9*, C-1456) Nat Learn.
— Resources Supervisor. (Career Examination Ser.). 1994. 29.95 (*0-8373-1457-7*) Nat Learn.
— Retirement Benefits Examiner. (Career Examination Ser.: C-1558). 1994. pap. 29.95 (*0-8373-1558-1*) Nat Learn.
— Revenue Agent. (Career Examination Ser.: C-3250). 1994. pap. 29.95 (*0-8373-3250-8*) Nat Learn.
— Right of Way Agent. (Career Examination Ser.: C-3466). 1994. pap. 27.95 (*0-8373-3466-7*) Nat Learn.
— Right-of-Way Aide. (Career Examination Ser.: C-2735). 1994. pap. 23.95 (*0-8373-2735-0*) Nat Learn.
— Road Car Inspector. (Career Examination Ser.: C-676). 1994. pap. 23.95 (*0-8373-0676-0*) Nat Learn.
— Roentgenologist. (Career Examination Ser.: C-697). 1994. pap. 39.95 (*0-8373-0697-3*) Nat Learn.
— Roofer. (Career Examination Ser.: C-677). 1994. pap. 23.95 (*0-8373-0677-9*) Nat Learn.
— Runaway Coordinator. (Career Examination Ser.: C-3467). 1994. pap. 29.95 (*0-8373-3467-5*) Nat Learn.
— Rural Carrier (U.S.P.S.) (Career Examination Ser.: C-678). 1994. pap. 19.95 (*0-8373-0678-7*) Nat Learn.
— Safety & Health Inspector. (Career Examination Ser.: C-3143). 1994. pap. 29.95 (*0-8373-3143-9*) Nat Learn.
— Safety Consultant. (Career Examination Ser.: C-2640). 1994. pap. 34.95 (*0-8373-2640-0*) Nat Learn.
— Safety Coordinator. (Career Examination Ser.: C-1921). 1994. pap. 34.95 (*0-8373-1921-8*) Nat Learn.
— Safety Engineer. (Career Examination Ser.: C-797). 1994. pap. 34.95 (*0-8373-0797-X*) Nat Learn.
— Safety Officer. (Career Examination Ser.: C-3061). 1994. pap. 27.95 (*0-8373-3061-0*) Nat Learn.
— Safety Officer Trainee. (Career Examination Ser.: C-3062). 1994. pap. 23.95 (*0-8373-3062-9*) Nat Learn.
— Safety Security Officer. (Career Examination Ser.: C-1459). 1994. pap. 23.95 (*0-8373-1459-3*) Nat Learn.
— Safety Supervisor. (Career Examination Ser.: C-2641). 1994. pap. 29.95 (*0-8373-2641-9*) Nat Learn.
— Sales Store Worker. (Career Examination Ser.: C-1460). 1994. pap. 23.95 (*0-8373-1460-7*) Nat Learn.
— Sanctuary Coordinator. (Career Examination Ser.: C-3468). 1994. pap. 29.95 (*0-8373-3468-3*) Nat Learn.
— Sandblaster. (Career Examination Ser.: C-1461). 1994. pap. 23.95 (*0-8373-1461-5*) Nat Learn.
— Sanitarian. (Career Examination Ser.: C-1462). 1994. pap. 27.95 (*0-8373-1462-3*) Nat Learn.
— Sanitarian Trainee. (Career Examination Ser.: C-1463). 1994. pap. 23.95 (*0-8373-1463-1*) Nat Learn.
— Sanitary Chemist. (Career Examination Ser.: C-3266). 1994. pap. 29.95 (*0-8373-3266-4*) Nat Learn.
— Sanitary Construction Inspector. (Career Examination Ser.: C-3195). 1994. pap. 34.95 (*0-8373-3195-1*) Nat Learn.
— Sanitary Engineer. (Career Examination Ser.: C-798). 1994. pap. 29.95 (*0-8373-0798-8*) Nat Learn.
— Sanitary Engineer II. (Career Examination Ser.: C-2945). 1994. pap. 34.95 (*0-8373-2945-0*) Nat Learn.
— Sanitary Engineer III. (Career Examination Ser.: C-2946). 1994. pap. 34.95 (*0-8373-2946-9*) Nat Learn.
— Sanitary Engineer IV. (Career Examination Ser.: C-2947). 1994. pap. 39.95 (*0-8373-2947-7*) Nat Learn.
— Sanitary Laboratory Technician. (Career Examination Ser.: C-1037). 1994. pap. 29.95 (*0-8373-1037-7*) Nat Learn.
— Sanitation & Parking Violation Inspector. (Career Examination Ser.: C-1873). 1994. pap. 27.95 (*0-8373-1873-4*) Nat Learn.
— Sanitation Dispatcher. (Career Examination Ser.: C-2881). 1994. pap. 23.95 (*0-8373-2881-0*) Nat Learn.
— Sanitation Enforcement Agent. (Career Examination Ser.: C-3177). 1994. pap. 23.95 (*0-8373-3177-3*) Nat Learn.
— Sanitation Inspector. (Career Examination Ser.: C-2152). 1994. reprint ed. pap. 27.95 (*0-8373-2152-2*) Nat Learn.
— Sanitation Inspector Trainee. (Career Examination Ser.: C-2029). 1994. pap. 23.95 (*0-8373-2029-1*) Nat Learn.
— Sanitation Man. (Career Examination Ser.: C-700). 1994. pap. 19.95 (*0-8373-0700-7*) Nat Learn.
— Sanitation Supervisor. (Career Examination Ser.: C-2151). 1994. reprint ed. pap. 27.95 (*0-8373-2151-4*) Nat Learn.
— Scale Operator. (Career Examination Ser.: C-3008). 1994. pap. 27.95 (*0-8373-3008-4*) Nat Learn.
— Scholastic Aptitude Test. (Admission Test Ser.: ATS-21). 1994. pap. 23.95 (*0-8373-5021-2*) Nat Learn.
— Scholastic Philosophy. (Undergraduate Program Field Test Ser.: UPFT-22). 1994. pap. 23.95 (*0-8373-6022-6*) Nat Learn.
— School Administrative Aide. (Career Examination Ser.: C-1069). 1994. pap. 27.95 (*0-8373-1069-5*) Nat Learn.
— School Attendance Aide. (Career Examination Ser.: C-3264). 1994. pap. 23.95 (*0-8373-3264-8*) Nat Learn.
— School Business Executive. (Career Examination Ser.: C-2887). 1994. pap. 34.95 (*0-8373-2887-X*) Nat Learn.
— School Clerk. (Career Examination Ser.: C-1984). 1994. pap. 23.95 (*0-8373-1984-6*) Nat Learn.
— School Counseling Assistant. (Career Examination Ser.: C-3469). 1994. pap. 27.95 (*0-8373-3469-1*) Nat Learn.
— School Crossing Guard. (Career Examination Ser.: C-702). 1994. pap. 23.95 (*0-8373-0702-3*) Nat Learn.
— School Custodial Supervisor. (Career Examination Ser.: C-1581). 1994. pap. 29.95 (*0-8373-1581-6*) Nat Learn.
— School Custodian. (Career Examination Ser.: C-799). 1994. pap. 23.95 (*0-8373-0799-6*) Nat Learn.
— School Custodian-Engineer. (Career Examination Ser.: C-701). 1994. pap. 27.95 (*0-8373-0701-5*) Nat Learn.
— School Finance Manager. (Career Examination Ser.: C-2886). 1994. pap. 34.95 (*0-8373-2886-1*) Nat Learn.
— School Guard. (Career Examination Ser.: C-1923). 1994. pap. 23.95 (*0-8373-1923-4*) Nat Learn.
— School Laboratory Assistant. (Career Examination Ser.: C-3333). 1994. pap. 27.95 (*0-8373-3333-4*) Nat Learn.
— School Lunch Coordinator. (Career Examination Ser.: C-317). 1994. pap. 29.95 (*0-8373-0317-6*) Nat Learn.
— School Lunch Director. (Career Examination Ser.: C-2088). 1994. reprint ed. pap. 34.95 (*0-8373-2088-7*) Nat Learn.
— School Lunch Manager. (Career Examination Ser.: C-703). 1994. pap. 29.95 (*0-8373-0703-1*) Nat Learn.
— School Nurse Practitioner. (Certified Nurse Examination Ser.: CN-3). 1991. pap. 23.95 (*0-8373-6103-6*) Nat Learn.
— School Nurse Practitioner. (Certified Nurse Examination Ser.: CN-3). 1994. 39.95 (*0-8373-6153-2*) Nat Learn.
— School Psychologist. (Teachers License Examination Ser.: GT-4). 1994. pap. 27.95 (*0-8373-8124-X*) Nat Learn.
— School Psychologist-in-Training. (Teachers License Examination Ser.: GT-5). 1994. pap. 27.95 (*0-8373-8125-8*) Nat Learn.
— School Psychology. (National Teacher Examination Ser.: NT-40). 1994. pap. 23.95 (*0-8373-8450-8*) Nat Learn.
— School Purchasing Agent. (Career Examination Ser.: C-863). 1994. pap. 27.95 (*0-8373-0863-1*) Nat Learn.
— School Research Assistant. (Teachers License Examination Ser.: GT-6). 1994. pap. 27.95 (*0-8373-8126-6*) Nat Learn.
— School Research Associate. (Teachers License Examination Ser.: GT-7). 1994. pap. 27.95 (*0-8373-8127-4*) Nat Learn.
— School Research Technician. (Teachers License Examination Ser.: GT-8). 1994. pap. 27.95 (*0-8373-8128-2*) Nat Learn.
— School Secretary. (Teachers License Examination Ser.: T-52). 1994. pap. 23.95 (*0-8373-8052-9*) Nat Learn.
— School Security Supervisor. (Career Examination Ser.: C-3182). 1994. pap. 27.95 (*0-8373-3182-X*) Nat Learn.
— School Social Worker. (Teachers License Examination Ser.: GT-9). 1994. pap. 27.95 (*0-8373-8129-0*) Nat Learn.
— School Transportation Coordinator. (Career Examination Ser.: C-1513). 1994. pap. 29.95 (*0-8373-1513-1*) Nat Learn.
— School Transportation Supervisor. (Career Examination Ser.: C-113). 1994. pap. 29.95 (*0-8373-0113-0*) Nat Learn.
— Seamstress. (Career Examination Ser.: C-1619). 1994. pap. 34.95 (*0-8373-1619-7*) Nat Learn.
— Seasonal Assistant. (Career Examination Ser.: C-704). 1994. pap. 23.95 (*0-8373-0704-X*) Nat Learn.
— Seasonal Parkman. (Career Examination Ser.: C-705). 1994. pap. 23.95 (*0-8373-0705-8*) Nat Learn.
— Secondary School Admissions Test - H.S. Entrance Exam (SSAT) (Admission Test Ser.: ATS-80). 1994. pap. 23.95 (*0-8373-5080-8*) Nat Learn.
— Secret Service Agent (Uniformed) (Career Examination Ser.: C-3255). 1994. pap. 27.95 (*0-8373-3255-9*) Nat Learn.
— Secretarial Assistant. (Career Examination Ser.: C-1464). 1994. pap. 19.95 (*0-8373-1464-X*) Nat Learn.
— Secretarial Stenographer. (Career Examination Ser.: C-1465). 1994. pap. 23.95 (*0-8373-1465-8*) Nat Learn.
— Secretary. (Career Examination Ser.: C-1466). 1994. pap. 19.95 (*0-8373-1466-6*) Nat Learn.
— Secretary I. (Career Examination Ser.: C-3577). 1994. 19.95 (*0-8373-3577-9*) Nat Learn.
— Secretary II. (Career Examination Ser.: C-3578). 1994. 23.95 (*0-8373-3578-7*) Nat Learn.
— Secretary (Stenography) GS5. (Career Examination Ser.: C-706). 1994. pap. 23.95 (*0-8373-0706-6*) Nat Learn.
— Security Guard. (Career Examination Ser.: C-1999). 1994. pap. 23.95 (*0-8373-1999-4*) Nat Learn.
— Security Hospital Treatment Assistant. (Career Examination Ser.: C-1615). 1994. pap. 23.95 (*0-8373-1615-4*) Nat Learn.
— Security Hospital Treatment Assistant (Adolescent) (Career Examination Ser.: C-1616). 1994. pap. 27.95 (*0-8373-1616-2*) Nat Learn.
— Security Officer. (Career Examination Ser.: C-1467). 1994. pap. 23.95 (*0-8373-1467-4*) Nat Learn.
— Security Services Assistant. (Career Examination Ser.: C-2204). 1991. pap. 18.00 (*0-8373-2204-9*) Nat Learn.
— Senior Account Clerk. (Career Examination Ser.: C-1874). 1994. pap. 23.95 (*0-8373-1874-2*) Nat Learn.
— Senior Account Clerk-Stenographer. (Career Examination Ser.: C-3470). 1994. pap. 23.95 (*0-8373-3470-5*) Nat Learn.
— Senior Account Clerk-Typist. (Career Examination Ser.: C-3471). 1994. pap. 23.95 (*0-8373-3471-3*) Nat Learn.
— Senior Accountant. (Career Examination Ser.: C-992). 1994. pap. 29.95 (*0-8373-0992-1*) Nat Learn.
— Senior Accounting Machine Operator. (Career Examination Ser.: C-2203). 1994. pap. 27.95 (*0-8373-2203-0*) Nat Learn.
— Senior Actuarial Clerk. (Career Examination Ser.: C-2418). 1994. pap. 27.95 (*0-8373-2418-1*) Nat Learn.
— Senior Actuary. (Career Examination Ser.: C-993). 1994. pap. 44.95 (*0-8373-0993-X*) Nat Learn.
— Senior Addiction Specialist. (Career Examination Ser.: C-1810). 1994. 34.95 (*0-8373-1810-6*) Nat Learn.
— Senior Administrative Analyst. (Career Examination Ser.: C-2709). 1994. pap. 34.95 (*0-8373-2709-1*) Nat Learn.
— Senior Administrative Assistant. (Career Examination Ser.: C-1468). 1994. pap. 29.95 (*0-8373-1468-2*) Nat Learn.
— Senior Administrative Associate. (Career Examination Ser.: C-2393). 1994. pap. 29.95 (*0-8373-2393-2*) Nat Learn.
— Senior Administrative Services Clerk. (Career Examination Ser.: C-2870). 1994. pap. 29.95 (*0-8373-2870-5*) Nat Learn.
— Senior Admitting Clerk. (Career Examination Ser.: C-994). 1994. pap. 27.95 (*0-8373-0994-8*) Nat Learn.
— Senior Air Pollution Inspector. (Career Examination Ser.: C-1469). 1994. pap. 34.95 (*0-8373-1469-0*) Nat Learn.
— Senior Airport Attendant. (Career Examination Ser.: C-307). 1994. pap. 27.95 (*0-8373-0307-9*) Nat Learn.
— Senior Airport Security Guard. (Career Examination Ser.: C-457). 1994. pap. 27.95 (*0-8373-0457-1*) Nat Learn.
— Senior Analytical Chemist. (Career Examination Ser.: C-3193). 1994. pap. 34.95 (*0-8373-3193-5*) Nat Learn.
— Senior Animal Shelter Officer. (Career Examination Ser.: C-2362). 1994. pap. 27.95 (*0-8373-2362-2*) Nat Learn.
— Senior Appraiser. (Career Examination Ser.: C-1470). 1994. pap. 27.95 (*0-8373-1470-4*) Nat Learn.
— Senior Architect. (Career Examination Ser.: C-1326). 1994. pap. 34.95 (*0-8373-1326-0*) Nat Learn.

R

— Senior Architectural Draftsman. (Career Examination Ser.: C-2365). 1994. pap. 29.95 (*0-8373-2365-7*) Nat Learn.

— Senior Assessment Assistant. (Career Examination Ser.: C-2183). 1994. pap. 27.95 (*0-8373-2183-2*) Nat Learn.

— Senior Assessment Clerk. (Career Examination Ser.: C-2921). 1994. pap. 23.95 (*0-8373-2921-3*) Nat Learn.

— Senior Assessor. (Career Examination Ser.: C-995). 1994. pap. 27.95 (*0-8373-0995-6*) Nat Learn.

— Senior Assets Analyst. (Career Examination Ser.: C-3498). 1994. pap. 29.95 (*0-8373-3498-5*) Nat Learn.

— Senior Attorney. (Career Examination Ser.: C-996). 1994. pap. 44.95 (*0-8373-0996-4*) Nat Learn.

— Senior Attorney (Realty) (Career Examination Ser.: C-568). 1994. pap. 49.95 (*0-8373-0568-3*) Nat Learn.

— Senior Audio-Visual Aid Technician. (Career Examination Ser.: C-1471). 1994. pap. 27.95 (*0-8373-1471-2*) Nat Learn.

— Senior Auditor. (Career Examination Ser.: C-2059). 1994. reprint ed. pap. 34.95 (*0-8373-2059-3*) Nat Learn.

— Senior Automotive Facilities Inspector. (Career Examination Ser.: C-2214). 1994. pap. 29.95 (*0-8373-2214-6*) Nat Learn.

— Senior Automotive Mechanic. (Career Examination Ser.: C-3472). 1994. pap. 27.95 (*0-8373-3472-1*) Nat Learn.

— Senior Automotive Serviceman. (Career Examination Ser.: C-1869). 1994. pap. 27.95 (*0-8373-1869-6*) Nat Learn.

— Senior Bay Constable. (Career Examination Ser.: C-2525). 1994. pap. 29.95 (*0-8373-2525-0*) Nat Learn.

— Senior Beverage Control Investigator. (Career Examination Ser.: C-2823). 1994. pap. 27.95 (*0-8373-2823-3*) Nat Learn.

— Senior Boiler Inspector. (Career Examination Ser.: C-1629). 1994. pap. 34.95 (*0-8373-1629-4*) Nat Learn.

— Senior Bookkeeper. (Career Examination Ser.: C-1751). 1994. pap. 27.95 (*0-8373-1751-7*) Nat Learn.

— Senior Bookkeeping Machine Operator. (Career Examination Ser.: C-3097). 1994. pap. 27.95 (*0-8373-3097-1*) Nat Learn.

— Senior Bridge & Tunnel Maintainer. (Career Examination Ser.: C-1472). 1997. pap. 2.95 (*0-8373-1472-0*) Nat Learn.

— Senior Budget Analyst. (Career Examination Ser.: C-2415). 1994. pap. 39.95 (*0-8373-2415-7*) Nat Learn.

— Senior Budget Examiner. (Career Examination Ser.: C-2528). 1994. pap. 34.95 (*0-8373-2528-5*) Nat Learn.

— Senior Budget Officer. (Career Examination Ser.: C-2683). 1994. pap. 34.95 (*0-8373-2683-4*) Nat Learn.

— Senior Building Construction Engineer. (Career Examination Ser.: C-3171). 1994. pap. 39.95 (*0-8373-3171-4*) Nat Learn.

— Senior Building Custodian. (Career Examination Ser.: C-997). 1994. pap. 27.95 (*0-8373-0997-2*) Nat Learn.

— Senior Building Electrical Engineer. (Career Examination Ser.: C-1916). 1994. pap. 39.95 (*0-8373-1916-1*) Nat Learn.

— Senior Building Guard. (Career Examination Ser.: C-2529). 1994. pap. 27.95 (*0-8373-2529-3*) Nat Learn.

— Senior Building Inspector. (Career Examination Ser.: C-2113). 1994. reprint ed. pap. 34.95 (*0-8373-2113-1*) Nat Learn.

— Senior Building Mechanical Engineer. (Career Examination Ser.: C-2572). 1994. pap. 39.95 (*0-8373-2572-2*) Nat Learn.

— Senior Building Rehabilitation Specialist. (Career Examination Ser.: C-1933). 1994. pap. 39.95 (*0-8373-1933-1*) Nat Learn.

— Senior Building Structural Engineer. (Career Examination Ser.: C-2569). 1994. pap. 39.95 (*0-8373-2569-2*) Nat Learn.

— Senior Business Consultant. (Career Examination Ser.: C-1983). 1994. pap. 39.95 (*0-8373-1983-8*) Nat Learn.

— Senior Business Machine Operator. (Career Examination Ser.: C-1896). 1994. pap. 27.95 (*0-8373-1896-3*) Nat Learn.

— Senior Business Manager. (Career Examination Ser.: C-2359). 1994. pap. 39.95 (*0-8373-2359-2*) Nat Learn.

— Senior Buyer. (Career Examination Ser.: C-2254). 1994. reprint ed. pap. 27.95 (*0-8373-2254-5*) Nat Learn.

— Senior Campus Security Officer. (Career Examination Ser.: C-2265). 1994. reprint ed. pap. 27.95 (*0-8373-2265-0*) Nat Learn.

— Senior Capital Police Officer. (Career Examination Ser.: C-2070). 1994. reprint ed. pap. 29.95 (*0-8373-2070-4*) Nat Learn.

— Senior Caseworker. (Career Examination Ser.: C-2931). 1994. pap. 27.95 (*0-8373-2931-0*) Nat Learn.

— Senior Cashier. (Career Examination Ser.: C-860). 1994. pap. 23.95 (*0-8373-0860-7*) Nat Learn.

— Senior Chemist. (Career Examination Ser.: C-2402). 1994. pap. 29.95 (*0-8373-2402-5*) Nat Learn.

— Senior Children's Counselor. (Career Examination Ser.: C-1601). 1994. reprint ed. pap. 34.95 (*0-8373-1601-4*) Nat Learn.

— Senior Citizen Aide. (Career Examination Ser.: C-1473). 1994. pap. 23.95 (*0-8373-1473-9*) Nat Learn.

— Senior Citizens' Activities Specialist. (Career Examination Ser.: C-900). 1940. pap. 23.95 (*0-8373-0900-X*) Nat Learn.

— Senior Citizens' Club Leader. (Career Examination Ser.: C-2745). 1994. pap. 23.95 (*0-8373-2745-8*) Nat Learn.

— Senior Citizens' Information & Referral Specialist. (Career Examination Ser.: C-2814). 1994. pap. 27.95 (*0-8373-2814-4*) Nat Learn.

— Senior Citizens' Program Coordinator. (Career Examination Ser.: C-2811). 1994. pap. 29.95 (*0-8373-2811-X*) Nat Learn.

— Senior Citizens' Program Supervisor. (Career Examination Ser.: C-2360). 1994. pap. 29.95 (*0-8373-2360-6*) Nat Learn.

— Senior Citizens' Services Coordinator. (Career Examination Ser.: C-2117). 1994. reprint ed. pap. 29.95 (*0-8373-2117-4*) Nat Learn.

— Senior Civil Engineer. (Career Examination Ser.: C-998). 1994. pap. 29.95 (*0-8373-0998-0*) Nat Learn.

— Senior Civil Engineer (Structures) (Career Examination Ser.: C-1917). 1994. pap. 34.95 (*0-8373-1917-X*) Nat Learn.

— Senior Claim Examiner. (Career Examination Ser.: C-1716). 1994. pap. 29.95 (*0-8373-1716-9*) Nat Learn.

— Senior Clerical Series. (Career Examination Ser.: C-3473). 1994. pap. 23.95 (*0-8373-3473-X*) Nat Learn.

— Senior Clerk. (Career Examination Ser.: C-707). 1994. pap. 23.95 (*0-8373-0707-4*) Nat Learn.

— Senior Clerk-Stenographer. (Career Examination Ser.: C-2633). 1994. pap. 23.95 (*0-8373-2633-8*) Nat Learn.

— Senior Clerk (Surrogate) (Career Examination Ser.: C-2128). 1994. reprint ed. pap. 27.95 (*0-8373-2128-X*) Nat Learn.

— Senior Clerk-Typist. (Career Examination Ser.: C-1936). 1994. pap. 23.95 (*0-8373-1936-6*) Nat Learn.

— Senior Clinical Psychologist. (Career Examination Ser.: C-1906). 1994. pap. 39.95 (*0-8373-1906-4*) Nat Learn.

— Senior Code Enforcement Officer. (Career Examination Ser.). 1994. 39.95 (*0-8373-3602-3*, C-3602) Nat Learn.

— Senior Commissary Clerk. (Career Examination Ser.: C-2050). 1994. pap. 27.95 (*0-8373-2050-X*) Nat Learn.

— Senior Communications Technician. (Career Examination Ser.: C-2412). 1994. pap. 29.95 (*0-8373-2412-2*) Nat Learn.

— Senior Community Liaison Worker. (Career Examination Ser.: C-2995). 1994. pap. 27.95 (*0-8373-2995-7*) Nat Learn.

— Senior Community Narcotic Education Representative. (Career Examination Ser.: C-1942). 1994. pap. 34.95 (*0-8373-1942-0*) Nat Learn.

— Senior Community Service Worker. (Career Examination Ser.: C-2676). 1994. pap. 27.95 (*0-8373-2676-1*) Nat Learn.

— Senior Compensation Claims Auditor. (Career Examination Ser.: C-2127). 1994. reprint ed. pap. 34.95 (*0-8373-2127-1*) Nat Learn.

— Senior Compensation Claims Clerk. (Career Examination Ser.: C-867). 1994. pap. 27.95 (*0-8373-0867-4*) Nat Learn.

— Senior Compensation Claims Examiner. (Career Examination Ser.: C-1702). 1994. 29.95 (*0-8373-1702-9*) Nat Learn.

— Senior Compensation Claims Investigator. (Career Examination Ser.: C-2613). 1994. pap. 29.95 (*0-8373-2613-3*) Nat Learn.

— Senior Compensation Investigator. (Career Examination Ser.: C-2609). 1994. pap. 29.95 (*0-8373-2609-5*) Nat Learn.

— Senior Compliance Investigator. (Career Examination Ser.: C-2422). 1994. pap. 29.95 (*0-8373-2422-X*) Nat Learn.

— Senior Computer Operator. (Career Examination Ser.: C-708). 1994. pap. 27.95 (*0-8373-0708-2*) Nat Learn.

— Senior Computer Programmer. (Career Examination Ser.: C-1630). 1994. pap. 29.95 (*0-8373-1630-8*) Nat Learn.

— Senior Computer Programmer-Analyst. (Career Examination Ser.: C-1030). 1994. pap. 29.95 (*0-8373-1030-X*) Nat Learn.

— Senior Computer Systems Analyst. (Career Examination Ser.: C-999). 1994. pap. 29.95 (*0-8373-0999-9*) Nat Learn.

— Senior Construction Inspector. (Career Examination Ser.: C-709). 1994. pap. 34.95 (*0-8373-0709-0*) Nat Learn.

— Senior Consumer Affairs Inspector. (Career Examination Ser.: C-1656). 1994. pap. 27.95 (*0-8373-1656-1*) Nat Learn.

— Senior Consumer Affairs Investigator. (Career Examination Ser.: C-2376). 1994. pap. 27.95 (*0-8373-2376-2*) Nat Learn.

— Senior Consumer Frauds Representative. (Career Examination Ser.: C-877). 1994. pap. 27.95 (*0-8373-0877-1*) Nat Learn.

— Senior Contracts Examiner. (Career Examination Ser.: C-3536-1). 1994. 29.95 (*0-8373-3536-1*) Nat Learn.

— Senior Correction Counselor. (Career Examination Ser.: C-3263). 1994. pap. 34.95 (*0-8373-3263-X*) Nat Learn.

— Senior Court Clerk. (Career Examination Ser.: C-2704). 1994. pap. 29.95 (*0-8373-2704-0*) Nat Learn.

— Senior Court Officer. (Career Examination Ser.: C-710). 1994. pap. 23.95 (*0-8373-0710-4*) Nat Learn.

— Senior Court Reporter. (Career Examination Ser.: C-3543). 1994. 27.95 (*0-8373-3543-4*) Nat Learn.

— Senior Custodial Assistant (Men) (Career Examination Ser.: C-1001a). 1994. pap. 23.95 (*0-8373-1001-6*) Nat Learn.

— Senior Custodial Assistant (Women) (Career Examination Ser.: C-1001b). 1994. 23.95 (*0-685-03534-4*) Nat Learn.

— Senior Custodial Foreman. (Career Examination Ser.: C-2271). 1994. reprint ed. pap. 29.95 (*0-8373-2271-5*) Nat Learn.

— Senior Data Entry Clerk. (Career Examination Ser.: C-3506). 1994. 27.95 (*0-8373-3506-X*) Nat Learn.

— Senior Data Entry Machine Operator. (Career Examination Ser.: C-3063). 1994. pap. 27.95 (*0-8373-3063-7*) Nat Learn.

— Senior Data Processing Control Clerk. (Career Examination Ser.: C-2484). 1994. pap. 27.95 (*0-8373-2484-X*) Nat Learn.

— Senior Data Processing Equipment Operator. (Career Examination Ser.: C-2302). 1994. reprint ed. pap. 27.95 (*0-8373-2302-9*) Nat Learn.

— Senior Demolition Inspector. (Career Examination Ser.: C-1475). 1994. pap. 34.95 (*0-8373-1475-5*) Nat Learn.

— Senior Dental Hygienist. (Career Examination Ser.: C-2855). 1994. pap. 34.95 (*0-8373-2855-1*) Nat Learn.

— Senior Dentist. (Career Examination Ser.: C-711). 1994. pap. 54.95 (*0-8373-0711-2*) Nat Learn.

— Senior Deputy Sheriff. (Career Examination Ser.: C-1665). 1994. pap. 27.95 (*0-8373-1665-0*) Nat Learn.

— Senior Detective Investigator. (Career Examination Ser.: C-2038). 1994. pap. 39.95 (*0-8373-2038-0*) Nat Learn.

— Senior Dietitian. (Career Examination Ser.: C-1985). 1994. pap. 27.95 (*0-8373-1985-4*) Nat Learn.

— Senior Dog Warden. (Career Examination Ser.: C-2646). 1994. pap. 27.95 (*0-8373-2646-X*) Nat Learn.

— Senior Drafting Technician. (Career Examination Ser.: C-2679). 1994. pap. 27.95 (*0-8373-2679-6*) Nat Learn.

— Senior Draftsman. (Career Examination Ser.: C-1575). 1994. pap. 27.95 (*0-8373-1575-1*) Nat Learn.

— Senior Drug Abuse Educator. (Career Examination Ser.: C-2520). 1994. pap. 34.95 (*0-8373-2520-X*) Nat Learn.

— Senior Drug Abuse Rehabilitation Counselor. (Career Examination Ser.: C-2928). 1994. pap. 34.95 (*0-8373-2928-0*) Nat Learn.

— Senior Drug & Alcohol Counselor. (Career Examination Ser.: C-2742). 1994. pap. 34.95 (*0-8373-2742-3*) Nat Learn.

— Senior Duplicating Machine Operator. (Career Examination Ser.: C-1899). 1994. pap. 23.95 (*0-8373-1899-8*) Nat Learn.

— Senior Economist. (Career Examination Ser.: C-3252). 1994. pap. 34.95 (*0-8373-3252-4*) Nat Learn.

— Senior Editorial Clerk. (Career Examination Ser.: C-2565). 1994. pap. 27.95 (*0-8373-2565-X*) Nat Learn.

— Senior Electrical Engineer. (Career Examination Ser.: C-1631). 1994. pap. 39.95 (*0-8373-1631-6*) Nat Learn.

— Senior Electrical Inspector. (Career Examination Ser.: C-712). 1994. pap. 34.95 (*0-8373-0712-0*) Nat Learn.

— Senior Electronic Computer Operator. (Career Examination Ser.: C-1002). 1994. pap. 27.95 (*0-8373-1002-4*) Nat Learn.

— Senior Elevator Inspector. (Career Examination Ser.: C-1717). 1994. pap. 34.95 (*0-8373-1717-7*) Nat Learn.

— Senior Employment Counselor. (Career Examination Ser.: C-1003). 1994. pap. 34.95 (*0-8373-1003-2*) Nat Learn.

— Senior Employment Interviewer. (Career Examination Ser.: C-2284). 1994. reprint ed. pap. 34.95 (*0-8373-2284-7*) Nat Learn.

— Senior Employment Security Clerk. (Career Examination Ser.: C-2351). 1994. pap. 27.95 (*0-8373-2351-7*) Nat Learn.

— Senior Engineer. (Career Examination Ser.: C-1476). 1994. pap. 44.95 (*0-8373-1476-3*) Nat Learn.

— Senior Engineering Aide. (Career Examination Ser.: C-1560). 1994. pap. 27.95 (*0-8373-1560-3*) Nat Learn.

— Senior Engineering Inspector. (Career Examination Ser.: C-2808). 1994. pap. 44.95 (*0-8373-2808-X*) Nat Learn.

— Senior Engineering Materials Technician. (Career Examination Ser.: C-316). 1941. pap. 29.95 (*0-8373-0316-8*) Nat Learn.

— Senior Engineering Technician. (Career Examination Ser.: C-1004). 1994. pap. 27.95 (*0-8373-1004-0*) Nat Learn.

— Senior Engineering Technician (Drafting) (Career Examination Ser.: C-1005). 1994. pap. 27.95 (*0-8373-1005-9*) Nat Learn.

— Senior Engineering Technician (Environmental Quality) (Career Examination Ser.: C-3238). 1994. pap. 29.95 (*0-8373-3238-9*) Nat Learn.

— Senior Environmental Analyst. (Career Examination Ser.: C-2660). 1994. pap. 34.95 (*0-8373-2660-5*) Nat Learn.

— Senior Environmental Control Technician. (Career Examination Ser.: C-3363). 1994. pap. 34.95 (*0-8373-3363-6*) Nat Learn.

— Senior Environmental Planner. (Career Examination Ser.: C-2663). 1994. pap. 34.95 (*0-8373-2663-X*) Nat Learn.

— Senior Environmentalist. (Career Examination Ser.: C-1585). 1994. pap. 34.95 (*0-8373-1585-9*) Nat Learn.

— Senior Evidence Technician. (Career Examination Ser.: C-2749). 1994. pap. 34.95 (*0-8373-2749-0*) Nat Learn.

— Senior Examiner-Social Services. (Career Examination Ser.: C-2139). 1994. reprint ed. pap. 27.95 (*0-8373-2139-5*) Nat Learn.

— Senior Excise Tax Investigator. (Career Examination Ser.: C-2419). 1994. pap. 29.95 (*0-8373-2419-X*) Nat Learn.

— Senior Executive Officer. (Career Examination Ser.: C-2826). 1994. pap. 39.95 (*0-8373-2826-8*) Nat Learn.

— Senior Field Accountant. (Career Examination Ser.: C-1569). 1994. pap. 34.95 (*0-8373-1569-7*) Nat Learn.

— Senior Field Representative (Human Rights) (Career Examination Ser.: C-2563). 1994. pap. 29.95 (*0-8373-2563-3*) Nat Learn.

— Senior File Clerk. (Career Examination Ser.: C-713). 1940. pap. 23.95 (*0-8373-0713-9*) Nat Learn.

— Senior Financial Analyst. (Career Examination Ser.: C-2643). 1994. pap. 39.95 (*0-8373-2643-5*) Nat Learn.

— Senior Fingerprint Technician. (Career Examination Ser.: C-2073). 1994. reprint ed. pap. 29.95 (*0-8373-2073-9*) Nat Learn.

— Senior Fire Prevention Inspector. (Career Examination Ser.: C-1765). 1994. reprint ed. pap. 34.95 (*0-8373-1765-7*) Nat Learn.

— Senior Food Inspector. (Career Examination Ser.: C-2051). 1994. pap. 34.95 (*0-8373-2051-8*) Nat Learn.

— Senior Forestry Technician. (Career Examination Ser.: C-2715). 1994. pap. 27.95 (*0-8373-2715-6*) Nat Learn.

— Senior Geologist. (Career Examination Ser.: C-1006). 1994. pap. 29.95 (*0-8373-1006-7*) Nat Learn.

— Senior Grants Analyst. (Career Examination Ser.: C-2833). 1994. pap. 39.95 (*0-8373-2833-0*) Nat Learn.

— Senior Groundskeeper. (Career Examination Ser.: C-1572). 1994. pap. 27.95 (*0-8373-1572-7*) Nat Learn.

— Senior Harbormaster. (Career Examination Ser.: C-3474). 1994. pap. 29.95 (*0-8373-3474-8*) Nat Learn.

— Senior Health Planner. (Career Examination Ser.: C-3028). 1994. pap. 34.95 (*0-8373-3028-9*) Nat Learn.

— Senior Heating & Ventilating Engineer. (Career Examination Ser.: C-1918). 1994. pap. 34.95 (*0-8373-1918-8*) Nat Learn.

— Senior High School. (Teachers Lesson Plan Book Ser.: S-1). 1994. pap. 6.95 (*0-8373-7954-7*) Nat Learn.

— Senior Highway Engineer. (Career Examination Ser.: C-2522). 1994. pap. 39.95 (*0-8373-2522-6*) Nat Learn.

— Senior Highway Maintenance Supervisor. (Career Examination Ser.: C-2631). 1994. pap. 34.95 (*0-8373-2631-1*) Nat Learn.

— Senior Highway Transportation Specialist. (Career Examination Ser.: C-1477). 1994. pap. 34.95 (*0-8373-1477-1*) Nat Learn.

— Senior Hospital Administration Consultant. (Career Examination Ser.: C-2769). 1994. pap. 44.95 (*0-8373-2769-5*) Nat Learn.

— Senior Hospital Care Investigator. (Career Examination Ser.: C-715). 1994. pap. 29.95 (*0-8373-0715-5*) Nat Learn.

— Senior Hospital Case Investigator. (Career Examination Ser.: C-1888). 1994. reprint ed. pap. 29.95 (*0-8373-1888-2*) Nat Learn.

— Senior Housekeeper. (Career Examination Ser.: C-1007). 1994. pap. 29.95 (*0-8373-1007-5*) Nat Learn.

— Senior Housing Inspector. (Career Examination Ser.: C-792). 1994. pap. 34.95 (*0-8373-0792-9*) Nat Learn.

— Senior Housing Management Assistant. (Career Examination Ser.: C-2538). 1994. pap. 27.95 (*0-8373-2538-2*) Nat Learn.

— Senior Housing Management Representative. (Career Examination Ser.: C-2540). 1994. pap. 29.95 (*0-8373-2540-4*) Nat Learn.

— Senior Housing Teller. (Career Examination Ser.: C-714). 1994. pap. 27.95 (*0-8373-0714-7*) Nat Learn.

— Senior Human Relations Representative. (Career Examination Ser.: C-2584). 1994. pap. 29.95 (*0-8373-2584-6*) Nat Learn.

— Senior Human Resources Specialist. (Career Examination Ser.: C-1064). 1994. pap. 29.95 (*0-8373-1064-4*) Nat Learn.

— Senior Human Resources Technician. (Career Examination Ser.: C-1478). 1994. pap. 29.95 (*0-8373-1478-X*) Nat Learn.

— Senior Human Rights Investigator. (Career Examination Ser.: C-1417). 1994. pap. 29.95 (*0-8373-1417-8*) Nat Learn.

— Senior Identification Clerk. (Career Examination Ser.: C-2293). 1994. pap. 27.95 (*0-8373-2293-6*) Nat Learn.

— Senior Identification Officer. (Career Examination Ser.: C-1987). 1994. pap. 34.95 (*0-8373-1987-0*) Nat Learn.

— Senior Identification Specialist. (Career Examination Ser.: C-2512). 1994. pap. 34.95 (*0-8373-2512-9*) Nat Learn.

— Senior Illustrator. (Career Examination Ser.: C-1008). 1994. pap. 34.95 (*0-8373-1008-3*) Nat Learn.

— Senior Incinerator Stationary Engineer. (Career Examination Ser.: C-2637). 1994. pap. 34.95 (*0-8373-2637-0*) Nat Learn.

— Senior Industrial Hygienist. (Career Examination Ser.: C-3036). 1994. pap. 44.95 (*0-8373-3036-X*) Nat Learn.

— Senior Inspector - Meat & Poultry. (Career Examination Ser.: C-1771). 1994. pap. 34.95 (*0-8373-1771-1*) Nat Learn.

— Senior Inspector of Fire Alarm Boxes. (Career Examination Ser.: C-2516). 1994. 34.95 (*0-8373-2516-1*) Nat Learn.

— Senior Inspector of Low Pressure Boilers. (Career Examination Ser.: C-2272). 1994. reprint ed. pap. 34.95 (*0-8373-2272-3*) Nat Learn.

— Senior Inspector of Markets, Weights & Measures. (Career Examination Ser.: C-716). 1994. pap. 29.95 (*0-8373-0716-3*) Nat Learn.

— Senior Institution Safety Officer. (Career Examination Ser.: C-2119). 1994. reprint ed. pap. 34.95 (*0-8373-2119-0*) Nat Learn.

— Senior Instrumentation Technician. (Career Examination Ser.: C-3256). 1994. pap. 34.95 (*0-8373-3256-7*) Nat Learn.

— Senior Insurance Examiner. (Career Examination Ser.: C-2685). 1994. pap. 34.95 (*0-8373-2685-0*) Nat Learn.

— Senior Internal Auditor. (Career Examination Ser.: C-1009). 1994. pap. 34.95 (*0-8373-1009-1*) Nat Learn.

— Senior Investigator. (Career Examination Ser.: C-1010). 1994. pap. 29.95 (*0-8373-1010-5*) Nat Learn.

— Senior Investment Analyst. (Career Examination Ser.: C-1623). 1994. pap. 44.95 (*0-8373-1623-5*) Nat Learn.

— Senior Justice Court Clerk. (Career Examination Ser.). 1994. 29.95 (*0-8373-3615-5*, C-3615) Nat Learn.

— Senior Juvenile Counselor. (Career Examination Ser.: C-421). 1994. pap. 34.95 (*0-8373-0421-0*) Nat Learn.

— Senior Key Punch Operator. (Career Examination Ser.: C-717). 1994. pap. 27.95 (*0-8373-0717-1*) Nat Learn.

— Senior Labor-Management Practices Adjuster. (Career Examination Ser.: C-718). 1994. pap. 44.95 (*0-8373-0718-X*) Nat Learn.

— Senior Labor Specialist. (Career Examination Ser.: C-2381). 1994. pap. 34.95 (*0-8373-2381-9*) Nat Learn.

— Senior Laboratory Technician. (Career Examination Ser.: C-1693). 1994. pap. 29.95 (*0-8373-1693-6*) Nat Learn.

— Senior Laboratory Technician (Biochemistry) (Career Examination Ser.: C-3081). 1994. pap. 34.95 (*0-8373-3081-5*) Nat Learn.

— Senior Laboratory Technician (Chemistry) (Career Examination Ser.: C-3082). 1994. pap. 34.95 (*0-8373-3082-3*) Nat Learn.

— Senior Laboratory Technician (Food Chemistry) (Career Examination Ser.: C-3253). 1994. pap. 34.95 (*0-8373-3253-2*) Nat Learn.

— Senior Laboratory Technician (Microbiology) (Career Examination Ser.: C-3083). 1994. pap. 34.95 (*0-8373-3083-1*) Nat Learn.

R

An Asterisk (*) at the beginning of an entry indicates that the title is appearing in BIP for the first time.

— Senior Land Management Specialist. (Career Examination Ser.: C-2619). 1994. pap. 34.95 (*0-8373-2619-2*) Nat Learn.
— Senior Landscape Architect. (Career Examination Ser.: C-1479). 1994. pap. 34.95 (*0-8373-1479-8*) Nat Learn.
— Senior Laundry Supervisor. (Career Examination Ser.: C-2220). 1994. pap. 34.95 (*0-8373-2220-0*) Nat Learn.
— Senior Laundry Worker. (Career Examination Ser.: C-719). 1994. pap. 27.95 (*0-8373-0719-8*) Nat Learn.
— Senior Leasing Agent. (Career Examination Ser.: C-2494). 1994. pap. 34.95 (*0-8373-2494-7*) Nat Learn.
— Senior Legal Stenographer. (Career Examination Ser.: C-2634). 1994. pap. 29.95 (*0-8373-2634-6*) Nat Learn.
— Senior Level Positions. (Career Examination Ser.: C-720). 1994. pap. 29.95 (*0-8373-0720-1*) Nat Learn.
— Senior Librarian. (Career Examination Ser.: C-1011). 1994. pap. 29.95 (*0-8373-1011-3*) Nat Learn.
— Senior Librarian I. (Career Examination Ser.: C-1821). 1994. pap. 29.95 (*0-8373-1821-1*) Nat Learn.
— Senior Library Clerk. (Career Examination Ser.: C-1930). 1994. pap. 27.95 (*0-8373-1930-7*) Nat Learn.
— Senior License Investigator. (Career Examination Ser.: C-2530). 1994. pap. 27.95 (*0-8373-2530-7*) Nat Learn.
— Senior Licensed Practical Nurse. (Career Examination Ser.: C-3500). 1994. pap. 27.95 (*0-8373-3500-0*) Nat Learn.
— Senior Mail Clerk. (Career Examination Ser.: C-1053). 1994. pap. 27.95 (*0-8373-1053-9*) Nat Learn.
— Senior Maintenance Supervisor. (Career Examination Ser.: C-2052). 1994. pap. 29.95 (*0-8373-2052-6*) Nat Learn.
— Senior Management Analyst. (Career Examination Ser.: C-1782). 1994. pap. 39.95 (*0-8373-1782-7*) Nat Learn.
— Senior Management Technician. (Career Examination Ser.: C-2752). 1994. pap. 29.95 (*0-8373-2752-0*) Nat Learn.
— Senior Manpower Counselor. (Career Examination Ser.: C-2436). 1994. pap. 39.95 (*0-8373-2436-X*) Nat Learn.
— Senior Marketing Representative. (Career Examination Ser.: C-2053). 1994. reprint ed. pap. 34.95 (*0-8373-2053-4*) Nat Learn.
— Senior Mathematician. (Career Examination Ser.: C-2078). 1994. reprint ed. pap. 34.95 (*0-8373-2078-X*) Nat Learn.
— Senior Meat Cutter. (Career Examination Ser.: C-1012). 1994. pap. 29.95 (*0-8373-1012-1*) Nat Learn.
— Senior Meat Inspector. (Career Examination Ser.: C-2054). 1994. pap. 29.95 (*0-8373-2054-2*) Nat Learn.
— Senior Mechanical Engineer. (Career Examination Ser.: C-1648). 1994. reprint ed. pap. 34.95 (*0-8373-1648-0*) Nat Learn.
— Senior Mechanical Stores Clerk. (Career Examination Ser.: C-3060). 1994. pap. 23.95 (*0-8373-3060-2*) Nat Learn.
— Senior Medicaid Claims Examiner. (Career Examination Ser.: C-2692). 1994. pap. 29.95 (*0-8373-2692-3*) Nat Learn.
— Senior Medical Conduct Investigator. (Career Examination Ser.: C-2610). 1994. pap. 29.95 (*0-8373-2610-9*) Nat Learn.
— Senior Medical Emergency Dispatcher. (Career Examination Ser.: C-2332). 1994. pap. 27.95 (*0-8373-2332-0*) Nat Learn.
— Senior Medical Laboratory Technician. (Career Examination Ser.: C-2496). 1994. pap. 29.95 (*0-8373-2496-3*) Nat Learn.
— Senior Medical Records Clerk. (Career Examination Ser.: C-2310). 1994. reprint ed. pap. 27.95 (*0-8373-2310-X*) Nat Learn.
— Senior Medical Records Librarian. (Career Examination Ser.: C-1013). 1994. pap. 27.95 (*0-8373-1013-X*) Nat Learn.
— Senior Medical Services Specialist. (Career Examination Ser.: C-2747). 1994. pap. 39.95 (*0-8373-2747-4*) Nat Learn.
— Senior Medical Social Worker. (Career Examination Ser.: C-2629). 1994. pap. 34.95 (*0-8373-2629-X*) Nat Learn.
— Senior Medical Stenographer. (Career Examination Ser.: C-2940). 1994. pap. 27.95 (*0-8373-2940-X*) Nat Learn.
— Senior Menagerie Keeper. (Career Examination Ser.: C-1971). 1994. pap. 27.95 (*0-8373-1971-4*) Nat Learn.
— Senior Mental Health Worker. (Career Examination Ser.: C-1925). 1994. 29.95 (*0-8373-1925-0*) Nat Learn.
— Senior Meteorologist. (Career Examination Ser.: C-2201). 1994. pap. 34.95 (*0-8373-2201-4*) Nat Learn.
— Senior Methods Analyst. (Career Examination Ser.: C-1014). 1994. pap. 39.95 (*0-8373-1014-8*) Nat Learn.
— Senior Microbiologist. (Career Examination Ser.: C-1945). 1994. pap. 34.95 (*0-8373-1945-5*) Nat Learn.
— Senior Micrographics Operator. (Career Examination Ser.: C-2760). 1994. pap. 27.95 (*0-8373-2760-1*) Nat Learn.
— Senior Micrographics Technician. (Career Examination Ser.: C-2762). 1994. pap. 27.95 (*0-8373-2762-8*) Nat Learn.
— Senior Mortuary Caretaker. (Career Examination Ser.: C-721). 1994. pap. 27.95 (*0-8373-0721-X*) Nat Learn.
— Senior Motor Vehicle License Clerk. (Career Examination Ser.: C-2611). 1994. pap. 22.95 (*0-8373-2611-7*) Nat Learn.
— Senior Motor Vehicle Supervisor. (Career Examination Ser.: C-3527). 1994. 34.95 (*0-8373-3527-2*) Nat Learn.
— Senior Multiple Residence Inspector. (Career Examination Ser.: C-2843). 1994. pap. 34.95 (*0-8373-2843-8*) Nat Learn.
— Senior Museum Curator. (Career Examination Ser.: C-2374). 1994. pap. 29.95 (*0-8373-2374-6*) Nat Learn.
— Senior Museum Instructor. (Career Examination Ser.: C-1016). 1994. pap. 29.95 (*0-8373-1016-4*) Nat Learn.
— Senior Narcotics Investigator. (Career Examination Ser.: C-2531). 1994. pap. 39.95 (*0-8373-2531-5*) Nat Learn.
— Senior Neighborhood Aide. (Career Examination Ser.: C-2911). 1994. pap. 27.95 (*0-8373-2911-6*) Nat Learn.
— Senior Nutritionist. (Career Examination Ser.: C-1419). 1994. pap. 29.95 (*0-8373-1419-4*) Nat Learn.
— Senior Occupational Analyst. (Career Examination Ser.: C-2549). 1994. pap. 34.95 (*0-8373-2549-8*) Nat Learn.
— Senior Occupational Therapist. (Career Examination Ser.: C-2174). 1994. pap. 34.95 (*0-8373-2174-3*) Nat Learn.
— Senior Office Appliance Operator. (Career Examination Ser.: C-1677). 1994. pap. 27.95 (*0-8373-1677-4*) Nat Learn.
— Senior Office Assistant. (Career Examination Ser.: C-2594). 1994. pap. 23.95 (*0-8373-2594-3*) Nat Learn.
— Senior Office Machine Operator. (Career Examination Ser.: C-1480). 1994. pap. 27.95 (*0-8373-1480-1*) Nat Learn.
— Senior Office Manager. (Career Examination Ser.: C-2399). 1994. pap. 34.95 (*0-8373-2399-1*) Nat Learn.
— Senior Office Stenographer. (Career Examination Ser.: C-3376). 1994. pap. 23.95 (*0-8373-3376-8*) Nat Learn.
— Senior Office Typist. (Career Examination Ser.: C-3374). 1994. pap. 23.95 (*0-8373-3374-1*) Nat Learn.
— Senior Office Worker. (Career Examination Ser.: C-2519). 1994. pap. 23.95 (*0-8373-2519-6*) Nat Learn.
— Senior Offset Printing Machine Operator. (Career Examination Ser.: C-3334). 1994. pap. 27.95 (*0-8373-3334-2*) Nat Learn.
— Senior Operations Review Specialist. (Career Examination Ser.: C-3261). 1994. pap. 39.95 (*0-8373-3261-3*) Nat Learn.
— Senior Park Attendant. (Career Examination Ser.: C-1542). 1994. pap. 27.95 (*0-8373-1542-5*) Nat Learn.
— Senior Park Engineer. (Career Examination Ser.: C-3192). 1994. pap. 39.95 (*0-8373-3192-7*) Nat Learn.
— Senior Park Foreman. (Career Examination Ser.: C-1562). 1994. pap. 29.95 (*0-8373-1562-X*) Nat Learn.
— Senior Park Supervisor. (Career Examination Ser.: C-2356). 1994. pap. 29.95 (*0-8373-2356-8*) Nat Learn.
— Senior Parking Enforcement Agent. (Career Examination Ser.: C-793). 1994. pap. 27.95 (*0-8373-0793-7*) Nat Learn.
— Senior Parole Officer. (Career Examination Ser.: C-2466). 1994. pap. 27.95 (*0-8373-2466-1*) Nat Learn.
— Senior Payroll Audit Clerk. (Career Examination Ser.: C-2085). 1994. reprint ed. pap. 23.95 (*0-8373-2085-2*) Nat Learn.
— Senior Personnel Administrator. (Career Examination Ser.: C-2410). 1994. pap. 44.95 (*0-8373-2410-6*) Nat Learn.
— Senior Personnel Analyst. (Career Examination Ser.: C-2345). 1994. pap. 39.95 (*0-8373-2345-2*) Nat Learn.
— Senior Personnel Clerk. (Career Examination Ser.: C-2867). 1994. pap. 27.95 (*0-8373-2867-5*) Nat Learn.
— Senior Personnel Examiner. (Career Examination Ser.: C-1017). 1994. 34.95 (*0-8373-1017-2*, C-1017) Nat Learn.
— Senior Pesticide Control Inspector. (Career Examination Ser.: C-2562). 1994. pap. 34.95 (*0-8373-2562-5*) Nat Learn.
— Senior Pharmacist. (Career Examination Ser.: C-722). 1994. pap. 34.95 (*0-8373-0722-8*) Nat Learn.
— Senior Pharmacy Inspector. (Career Examination Ser.: C-2532). 1994. pap. 39.95 (*0-8373-2532-3*) Nat Learn.
— Senior Photographic Machine Operator. (Career Examination Ser.: C-2882). 1994. pap. 23.95 (*0-8373-2882-9*) Nat Learn.
— Senior Physical Therapist. (Career Examination Ser.: C-1018). 1994. pap. 29.95 (*0-8373-1018-0*) Nat Learn.
— Senior Plan Examiner. (Career Examination Ser.: C-1481). 1994. pap. 34.95 (*0-8373-1481-X*) Nat Learn.
— Senior Planner. (Career Examination Ser.: C-1019). 1991. pap. 22.00 (*0-8373-1019-9*) Nat Learn.
— Senior Plumbing Inspector. (Career Examination Ser.: C-1740). 1994. 34.95 (*0-8373-1740-1*) Nat Learn.
— Senior Police Administrative Aide. (Career Examination Ser.: C-1020). 1994. pap. 27.95 (*0-8373-1020-2*) Nat Learn.
— Senior Probation Officer. (Career Examination Ser.: C-1594). 1994. pap. 27.95 (*0-8373-1594-8*) Nat Learn.
— Senior Professional Conduct Investigator. (Career Examination Ser.: C-2298). 1994. reprint ed. pap. 29.95 (*0-8373-2298-7*) Nat Learn.
— Senior Program Evaluation Specialist. (Career Examination Ser.: C-2700). 1994. pap. 39.95 (*0-8373-2700-8*) Nat Learn.
— Senior Program Examiner. (Career Examination Ser.: C-2755). 1994. pap. 39.95 (*0-8373-2755-5*) Nat Learn.
— Senior Program Research Analyst. (Career Examination Ser.: C-2219). 1994. reprint ed. pap. 39.95 (*0-8373-2219-7*) Nat Learn.
— Senior Program Specialist. (Career Examination Ser.: C-2862). 1994. pap. 39.95 (*0-8373-2862-4*) Nat Learn.
— Senior Program Specialist (Correction) (Career Examination Ser.: C-1998). 1994. pap. 39.95 (*0-8373-1998-6*) Nat Learn.
— Senior Programmer. (Career Examination Ser.: C-2580). 1994. pap. 34.95 (*0-8373-2580-3*) Nat Learn.
— Senior Project Coordinator. (Career Examination Ser.: C-1482). 1994. pap. 34.95 (*0-8373-1482-8*) Nat Learn.
— Senior Project Development Coordinator. (Career Examination Ser.: C-2898). 1994. pap. 34.95 (*0-8373-2898-5*) Nat Learn.
— Senior Project Services Specialist. (Career Examination Ser.: C-1662). 1994. pap. 34.95 (*0-8373-1662-6*) Nat Learn.
— Senior Psychiatric Social Worker. (Career Examination Ser.: C-2487). 1994. pap. 34.95 (*0-8373-2487-4*) Nat Learn.
— Senior Psychologist. (Career Examination Ser.: C-2173). 1994. pap. 39.95 (*0-8373-2173-5*) Nat Learn.
— Senior Public Health Adviser. (Career Examination Ser.: C-3175). 1994. pap. 29.95 (*0-8373-3175-7*) Nat Learn.
— Senior Public Health Educator. (Career Examination Ser.: C-3475). 1994. pap. 34.95 (*0-8373-3475-6*) Nat Learn.
— Senior Public Health Engineer. (Career Examination Ser.: C-3346). 1994. pap. 34.95 (*0-8373-3346-6*) Nat Learn.
— Senior Public Health Nutritionist. (Career Examination Ser.: C-1592). 1994. pap. 27.95 (*0-8373-1592-1*) Nat Learn.
— Senior Public Health Representative. (Career Examination Ser.: C-2385). 1994. pap. 29.95 (*0-8373-2385-1*) Nat Learn.
— Senior Public Health Sanitarian. (Career Examination Ser.: C-2002). 1994. pap. 29.95 (*0-8373-2002-X*) Nat Learn.
— Senior Public Information Assistant. (Career Examination Ser.: C-2957). 1994. pap. 27.95 (*0-8373-2957-4*) Nat Learn.
— Senior Pump Operator. (Career Examination Ser.: C-2951). 1994. pap. 29.95 (*0-8373-2951-5*) Nat Learn.
— Senior Purchase Inspector. (Career Examination Ser.: C-1483). 1994. pap. 29.95 (*0-8373-1483-6*) Nat Learn.
— Senior Quantitative Analyst. (Career Examination Ser.: C-1718). 1994. pap. 34.95 (*0-8373-1718-5*) Nat Learn.
— Senior Radio Operator. (Career Examination Ser.: C-2551). 1994. pap. 29.95 (*0-8373-2551-X*) Nat Learn.
— Senior Radiologic Technologist. (Career Examination Ser.: C-1545). 1994. pap. 34.95 (*0-8373-1545-X*) Nat Learn.
— Senior Real Estate Agent. (Career Examination Ser.: C-1941). 1994. pap. 27.95 (*0-8373-1941-2*) Nat Learn.
— Senior Real Estate Appraiser. (Career Examination Ser.: C-569). 1994. pap. 27.95 (*0-8373-0569-1*) Nat Learn.
— Senior Real Estate Manager. (Career Examination Ser.: C-1021). 1994. pap. 34.95 (*0-8373-1021-0*) Nat Learn.
— Senior Real Property Recorder. (Career Examination Ser.: C-3103). 1994. pap. 29.95 (*0-8373-3103-X*) Nat Learn.
— Senior Records Center Assistant. (Career Examination Ser.: C-1919). 1994. pap. 27.95 (*0-8373-1919-6*) Nat Learn.
— Senior Recreation Leader. (Career Examination Ser.: C-1938). 1994. pap. 27.95 (*0-8373-1938-2*) Nat Learn.
— Senior Recreation Therapist. (Career Examination Ser.: C-2974). 1994. pap. 29.95 (*0-8373-2974-4*) Nat Learn.
— Senior Rehabilitation Counselor. (Career Examination Ser.: C-1952). 1994. pap. 34.95 (*0-8373-1952-8*) Nat Learn.
— Senior Rent Examiner. (Career Examination Ser.: C-1022). 1994. pap. 29.95 (*0-8373-1022-9*) Nat Learn.
— Senior Rent Inspector. (Career Examination Ser.: C-2721). 1994. pap. 29.95 (*0-8373-2721-0*) Nat Learn.
— Senior Rent Research Associate. (Career Examination Ser.: C-1023). 1994. pap. 34.95 (*0-8373-1023-7*) Nat Learn.
— Senior Research Analyst. (Career Examination Ser.: C-1543). 1994. pap. 39.95 (*0-8373-1543-3*) Nat Learn.
— Senior Research Assistant. (Career Examination Ser.: C-2717). 1994. pap. 34.95 (*0-8373-2717-2*) Nat Learn.
— Senior Right-of-Way Aide. (Career Examination Ser.: C-2736). 1994. pap. 27.95 (*0-8373-2736-9*) Nat Learn.
— Senior Safety & Health Engineer. (Career Examination Ser.: C-3204). 1994. pap. 39.95 (*0-8373-3204-4*) Nat Learn.
— Senior Safety Coordinator. (Career Examination Ser.: C-2668). 1994. pap. 39.95 (*0-8373-2668-0*) Nat Learn.
— Senior Sanitarian. (Career Examination Ser.: C-2430). 1994. pap. 29.95 (*0-8373-2430-0*) Nat Learn.
— Senior Sanitary Engineer. (Career Examination Ser.: C-2446). 1994. pap. 34.95 (*0-8373-2446-7*) Nat Learn.
— Senior Security Hospital Treatment Assistant. (Career Examination Ser.: C-1617). 1994. pap. 27.95 (*0-8373-1617-0*) Nat Learn.
— Senior Security Officer. (Career Examination Ser.: C-2449). 1994. pap. 27.95 (*0-8373-2449-1*) Nat Learn.
— Senior Sewage Treatment Plant Operator. (Career Examination Ser.: C-1556). 1994. pap. 29.95 (*0-8373-1556-5*) Nat Learn.
— Senior Sewage Treatment Worker. (Career Examination Ser.: C-791). 1994. pap. 29.95 (*0-8373-0791-0*) Nat Learn.
— Senior Shorthand Reporter. (Career Examination Ser.: C-724). 1994. pap. 27.95 (*0-8373-0724-4*) Nat Learn.
— Senior Social Case Worker. (Career Examination Ser.: C-1555). 1994. pap. 27.95 (*0-8373-1555-7*) Nat Learn.
— Senior Social Services Employment Specialist. (Career Examination Ser.: C-2817). 1994. pap. 34.95 (*0-8373-2817-9*) Nat Learn.
— Senior Social Services Management Specialist. (Career Examination Ser.: C-2579). 1994. pap. 39.95 (*0-8373-2579-X*) Nat Learn.
— Senior Social Services Medical Assistance Specialist. (Career Examination Ser.: C-2432). 1994. pap. 39.95 (*0-8373-2432-7*) Nat Learn.
— Senior Social Services Program Specialist. (Career Examination Ser.: C-2236). 1994. pap. 39.95 (*0-8373-2236-7*) Nat Learn.
— Senior Social Welfare Examiner. (Career Examination Ser.: C-2320). 1994. pap. 27.95 (*0-8373-2320-7*) Nat Learn.
— Senior Social Welfare Examiner (Spanish Speaking) (Career Examination Ser.: C-2321). 1994. pap. 29.95 (*0-8373-2321-5*) Nat Learn.
— Senior Social Worker. (Career Examination Ser.: C-2488). 1994. pap. 27.95 (*0-8373-2488-2*) Nat Learn.
— Senior Special Investigator. (Career Examination Ser.: C-1589). 1994. pap. 34.95 (*0-8373-1589-1*) Nat Learn.
— Senior Special Officer. (Career Examination Ser.: C-725). 1994. pap. 27.95 (*0-8373-0725-2*) Nat Learn.
— Senior Speech & Hearing Therapist. (Career Examination Ser.: C-2273). 1994. reprint ed. pap. 34.95 (*0-8373-2273-1*) Nat Learn.
— Senior Staff Development Specialist. (Career Examination Ser.: C-2702). 1994. pap. 39.95 (*0-8373-2702-4*) Nat Learn.
— Senior Stationary Engineer. (Career Examination Ser.: C-1024). 1994. pap. 29.95 (*0-8373-1024-5*) Nat Learn.
— Senior Stationary Engineer (Electric) (Career Examination Ser.: C-2433). 1994. pap. 29.95 (*0-8373-2433-5*) Nat Learn.
— Senior Statistician. (Career Examination Ser.: C-1025). 1994. pap. 34.95 (*0-8373-1025-3*) Nat Learn.
— Senior Stenographer. (Career Examination Ser.: C-726). 1994. pap. 23.95 (*0-8373-0726-0*) Nat Learn.
— Senior Storekeeper. (Career Examination Ser.: C-3009). 1994. pap. 27.95 (*0-8373-3009-2*) Nat Learn.
— Senior Stores Clerk. (Career Examination Ser.: C-2383). 1994. pap. 27.95 (*0-8373-2383-5*) Nat Learn.
— Senior Street Club Worker. (Career Examination Ser.: C-727). 1994. pap. 29.95 (*0-8373-0727-9*) Nat Learn.
— Senior Superintendent (Department of Sanitation) (Career Examination Ser.: C-1026). 1994. pap. 39.95 (*0-8373-1026-1*) Nat Learn.
— Senior Superintendent of Construction. (Career Examination Ser.: C-541). 1994. pap. 39.95 (*0-8373-0541-1*) Nat Learn.
— Senior Supervisor of Mechanical Installations. (Career Examination Ser.: C-1679). 1994. pap. 34.95 (*0-8373-1679-0*) Nat Learn.
— Senior Supervisor of Park Operations. (Career Examination Ser.: C-1694). 1994. pap. 34.95 (*0-8373-1694-4*) Nat Learn.
— Senior Support Collector. (Career Examination Ser.: C-3211). 1994. pap. 27.95 (*0-8373-3211-7*) Nat Learn.
— Senior Surface Line Dispatcher. (Career Examination Ser.: C-728). 1994. pap. 27.95 (*0-8373-0728-7*) Nat Learn.
— Senior Systems Analyst. (Career Examination Ser.: C-2389). 1994. pap. 34.95 (*0-8373-2389-4*) Nat Learn.
— Senior Tabulator Operator. (Career Examination Ser.: C-1678). 1994. pap. 27.95 (*0-8373-1678-2*) Nat Learn.
— Senior Tax Cashier. (Career Examination Ser.: C-2095). 1994. pap. 23.95 (*0-8373-2095-X*) Nat Learn.
— Senior Tax Compliance Agent. (Career Examination Ser.: C-2953). 1994. pap. 29.95 (*0-8373-2953-1*) Nat Learn.
— Senior Tax Valuation Engineer. (Career Examination Ser.: C-3197). 1994. pap. 29.95 (*0-8373-3197-8*) Nat Learn.
— Senior Taxi & Limousine Inspector. (Career Examination Ser.: C-2553). 1994. pap. 27.95 (*0-8373-2553-6*) Nat Learn.
— Senior Telephone Inspector. (Career Examination Ser.: C-2217). 1994. reprint ed. pap. 27.95 (*0-8373-2217-0*) Nat Learn.
— Senior Telephone Operator. (Career Examination Ser.: C-1027). 1994. pap. 23.95 (*0-8373-1027-X*) Nat Learn.
— Senior Tenant Supervisor. (Career Examination Ser.: C-544). 1994. pap. 34.95 (*0-8373-0544-6*) Nat Learn.
— Senior Title Examiner. (Career Examination Ser.: C-2250). 1994. pap. 27.95 (*0-8373-2250-2*) Nat Learn.
— Senior Title Searcher. (Career Examination Ser.: C-2086). 1994. reprint ed. pap. 27.95 (*0-8373-2086-0*) Nat Learn.
— Senior Traffic Control Inspector. (Career Examination Ser.: C-729). 1994. pap. 29.95 (*0-8373-0729-5*) Nat Learn.
— Senior Traffic Supervisor. (Career Examination Ser.: C-2628). 1994. pap. 34.95 (*0-8373-2628-1*) Nat Learn.
— Senior Training Officer. (Career Examination Ser.: C-1485). 1994. pap. 39.95 (*0-8373-1485-2*) Nat Learn.
— Senior Training Technician. (Career Examination Ser.: C-1486). 1994. pap. 39.95 (*0-8373-1486-0*) Nat Learn.
— Senior Training Technician (Police) (Career Examination Ser.: C-418). 1994. pap. 44.95 (*0-8373-0418-0*) Nat Learn.
— Senior Transportation Analyst. (Career Examination Ser.: C-3202). 1994. pap. 34.95 (*0-8373-3202-8*) Nat Learn.
— Senior Transportation Inspector. (Career Examination Ser.: C-1487). 1994. pap. 34.95 (*0-8373-1487-9*) Nat Learn.
— Senior Typist. (Career Examination Ser.: C-730). 1994. pap. 23.95 (*0-8373-0730-9*) Nat Learn.
— Senior Underwriting Clerk. (Career Examination Ser.: C-2987). 1994. pap. 27.95 (*0-8373-2987-6*) Nat Learn.
— Senior Unemployment Insurance Claims Examiner. (Career Examination Ser.: C-2285). 1994. reprint ed. pap. 29.95 (*0-8373-2285-5*) Nat Learn.
— Senior Unemployment Insurance Hearing Representative. (Career Examination Ser.: C-2729). 1994. pap. 34.95 (*0-8373-2729-6*) Nat Learn.
— Senior Unemployment Insurance Investigator. (Career Examination Ser.: C-2830). 1994. pap. 34.95 (*0-8373-2830-6*) Nat Learn.
— Senior Vocational Counselor. (Career Examination Ser.: C-2438). 1994. pap. 34.95 (*0-8373-2438-6*) Nat Learn.
— Senior Water Plant Operator. (Career Examination Ser.: C-1638). 1994. pap. 29.95 (*0-8373-1638-3*) Nat Learn.
— Senior Water Plant Supervisor. (Career Examination Ser.: C-2959). 1994. pap. 34.95 (*0-8373-2959-0*) Nat Learn.
— Senior Water Use Inspector. (Career Examination Ser.: C-1639). 1994. pap. 27.95 (*0-8373-1639-1*) Nat Learn.
— Senior X-Ray Technician. (Career Examination Ser.: C-731). 1994. pap. 27.95 (*0-8373-0731-7*) Nat Learn.
— Senior Youth Division Counselor. (Career Examination Ser.: C-2500). 1994. pap. 34.95 (*0-8373-2500-5*) Nat Learn.
— Senior Youth Group Worker. (Career Examination Ser.: C-2585). 1994. pap. 25.95 (*0-8373-2585-4*) Nat Learn.
— Senior Zoning Inspector. (Career Examination Ser.: C-2341). 1994. pap. 34.95 (*0-8373-2341-X*) Nat Learn.
— Sergeant - Bridge & Tunnel Authority. (Career Examination Ser.: C-732). 1994. pap. 27.95 (*0-8373-0732-5*) Nat Learn.
— Sergeant - Police Department. (Career Examination Ser.: C-733). 1994. pap. 27.95 (*0-8373-0733-3*) Nat Learn.

R

— Sergeant, Sheriff's Department. (Career Examination Ser.: C-874). 1994. pap. 27.95 (*0-8373-0874-7*) Nat Learn.
— Service Inspector. (Career Examination Ser.: C-3501). 1994. pap. 29.95 (*0-8373-3501-9*) Nat Learn.
— Service Operations Supervisor. (Career Examination Ser.: C-1880). 1994. pap. 29.95 (*0-8373-1880-7*) Nat Learn.
— Sewage District Superintendent. (Career Examination Ser.: C-3343). 1994. pap. 39.95 (*0-8373-3343-1*) Nat Learn.
— Sewage Plant Operations Supervisor. (Career Examination Ser.: C-3017). 1994. pap. 29.95 (*0-8373-3017-3*) Nat Learn.
— Sewage Plant Operator. (Career Examination Ser.: C-2443). 1994. pap. 27.95 (*0-8373-2443-2*) Nat Learn.
— Sewage Plant Operator Trainee. (Career Examination Ser.: C-2281). 1994. reprint ed. pap. 23.95 (*0-8373-2281-2*) Nat Learn.
— Sewage Pump Operator. (Career Examination Ser.: C-3018). 1994. pap. 27.95 (*0-8373-3018-1*) Nat Learn.
— Sewage Treatment Operator. (Career Examination Ser.: C-1488). 1994. pap. 27.95 (*0-8373-1488-7*) Nat Learn.
— Sewage Treatment Operator Trainee. (Career Examination Ser.: C-1489). 1994. pap. 23.95 (*0-8373-1489-5*) Nat Learn.
— Sewage Treatment Plant Supervisor. (Career Examination Ser.: C-1490). 1994. pap. 29.95 (*0-8373-1490-9*) Nat Learn.
— Sewage Treatment Worker. (Career Examination Ser.: C-734). 1994. pap. 27.95 (*0-8373-0734-1*) Nat Learn.
— Sewage Treatment Worker Trainee. (Career Examination Ser.: C-735). 1994. pap. 23.95 (*0-8373-0735-X*) Nat Learn.
— Sewer Inspector. (Career Examination Ser.: C-2454). 1994. pap. 29.95 (*0-8373-2454-8*) Nat Learn.
— Shakespeare. (ACT Proficiency Examination Program Ser.: PEP-7). 1994. pap. 29.95 (*0-8373-5507-9*) Nat Learn.
— Shakespeare. (College Proficiency Examination Ser.: CPEP-33). 1994. reprint ed. pap. 23.95 (*0-8373-5433-1*) Nat Learn.
— Sheet Metal Fabrication. (Occupational Competency Examination Ser.: OCE-31). 1994. 23.95 (*0-8373-5731-4*) Nat Learn.
— Sheet Metal Worker. (Career Examination Ser.: C-736). 1994. pap. 23.95 (*0-8373-0736-8*) Nat Learn.
— Shelter Inspector (Civil Defense) (Career Examination Ser.: C-737). 1994. pap. 34.95 (*0-8373-0737-6*) Nat Learn.
— Sheriff. (Career Examination Ser.: C-794). 1994. pap. 27.95 (*0-8373-0794-5*) Nat Learn.
— Shipfitter. (Career Examination Ser.: C-1031). 1994. pap. 27.95 (*0-8373-1031-8*) Nat Learn.
— Shipment Clerk. (Career Examination Ser.: C-738). 1994. pap. 19.95 (*0-8373-0738-4*) Nat Learn.
— Shop Carpenter. (Career Examination Ser.: C-739). 1994. pap. 23.95 (*0-8373-0739-2*) Nat Learn.
— Shop Clerk. (Career Examination Ser.: C-740). 1994. pap. 19.95 (*0-8373-0740-6*) Nat Learn.
— Shop Mathematics. (Career Examination Ser.: No. CS-36). 1994. pap. 23.95 (*0-8373-6736-0*) Nat Learn.
— Shop Subjects. (Teachers License Examination Ser.: T-53). 1994. pap. 23.95 (*0-8373-8053-7*) Nat Learn.
— Shorthand Reporter. (Career Examination Ser.: C-741). 1994. pap. 23.95 (*0-8373-0741-4*) Nat Learn.
— Sign Painter. (Career Examination Ser.: C-2090). 1994. reprint ed. pap. 27.95 (*0-8373-2090-9*) Nat Learn.
— Signal Electrician. (Career Examination Ser.: C-2440). 1994. pap. 27.95 (*0-8373-2440-8*) Nat Learn.
— Signal Maintainer. (Career Examination Ser.: C-742). 1994. pap. 23.95 (*0-8373-0742-2*) Nat Learn.
— Site Plan Reviewer. (Career Examination Ser.: C-3251). 1994. pap. 34.95 (*0-8373-3251-6*) Nat Learn.
— Small Engine Repair. (Occupational Competency Examination Ser.: OCE-32). 1994. pap. 23.95 (*0-8373-5732-2*) Nat Learn.
— Social Case Worker. (Career Examination Ser.: C-795). 1994. pap. 23.95 (*0-8373-0795-3*) Nat Learn.
— Social Health Investigator. (Career Examination Ser.: C-2970). 1994. pap. 29.95 (*0-8373-2970-1*) Nat Learn.
— Social Insurance Claims Representative. (Career Examination Ser.: C-3372). 1994. pap. 27.95 (*0-8373-3372-5*) Nat Learn.
— Social Investigator. (Career Examination Ser.: C-743). 1994. pap. 27.95 (*0-8373-0743-0*) Nat Learn.
— Social Investigator Trainee. (Career Examination Ser.: C-744). 1994. pap. 23.95 (*0-8373-0744-9*) Nat Learn.
— Social Sciences. (Graduate Record Area Examination Ser.: GRE-44). 1994. 39.95 (*0-8373-5294-0*); pap. 23.95 (*0-8373-5244-4*) Nat Learn.
— Social Sciences & History. (College-Level Examination Ser.: ATS-9E). 1994. pap. 19.95 (*0-8373-5249-5*) Nat Learn.
— Social Service Representative. (Career Examination Ser.: C-745). 1994. pap. 23.95 (*0-8373-0745-7*) Nat Learn.
— Social Services Administrative Planner. (Career Examination Ser.: C-3066). 1994. pap. 34.95 (*0-8373-3066-1*) Nat Learn.
— Social Services Aide. (Career Examination Ser.: C-3319). 1994. pap. 19.95 (*0-8373-3319-9*) Nat Learn.
— Social Services Collection Representative. (Career Examination Ser.: C-3304). 1994. pap. 27.95 (*0-8373-3304-0*) Nat Learn.
— Social Services Disability Aide. (Career Examination Ser.: C-3259). 1994. pap. 23.95 (*0-8373-3259-1*) Nat Learn.
— Social Services Disability Analyst. (Career Examination Ser.: C-859). 1994. pap. 27.95 (*0-8373-0859-3*) Nat Learn.
— Social Services Employment Specialist. (Career Examination Ser.: C-2816). 1994. pap. 29.95 (*0-8373-2816-0*) Nat Learn.
— Social Services Human Resources Development Specialist. (Career Examination Ser.: C-3189). 1994. pap. 34.95 (*0-8373-3189-7*) Nat Learn.
— Social Services Management Specialist. (Career Examination Ser.: C-1994). 1994. pap. 34.95 (*0-8373-1994-3*) Nat Learn.
— Social Services Management Trainee. (Career Examination Ser.: C-1993). 1994. pap. 29.95 (*0-8373-1993-5*) Nat Learn.
— Social Services Medical Assistance Specialist. (Career Examination Ser.: C-2431). 1994. pap. 34.95 (*0-8373-2431-9*) Nat Learn.
— Social Services Program Coordinator. (Career Examination Ser.: C-3566). 1994. pap. 34.95 (*0-8373-3566-3*) Nat Learn.
— Social Services Program Specialist. (Career Examination Ser.: C-2235). 1994. pap. 34.95 (*0-8373-2235-9*) Nat Learn.
— Social Services Specialist Trainee. (Career Examination Ser.: C-3547). 1994. pap. 27.95 (*0-8373-3547-7*) Nat Learn.
— Social Services Systems Manager. (Career Examination Ser.: C-2992). 1994. pap. 39.95 (*0-8373-2992-2*) Nat Learn.
— Social Studies, Jr. H. S. (Teachers License Examination Ser.: T-54). 1994. pap. 23.95 (*0-8373-8054-5*) Nat Learn.
— Social Studies, Sr. H. S. (Teachers License Examination Ser.: T-55). 1994. pap. 23.95 (*0-8373-8055-3*) Nat Learn.
— Social Welfare Examiner. (Career Examination Ser.: C-2132). 1994. reprint ed. pap. 23.95 (*0-8373-2132-8*) Nat Learn.
— Social Welfare Examiner (Spanish Speaking) (Career Examination Ser.: C-2136). 1994. reprint ed. pap. 27.95 (*0-8373-2136-0*) Nat Learn.
— Social Work Assistant. (Career Examination Ser.: C-796). 1994. pap. 23.95 (*0-8373-0796-1*) Nat Learn.
— Social Work Training Director. (Career Examination Ser.: C-3476). 1994. pap. 39.95 (*0-8373-3476-4*) Nat Learn.
— Social Worker. (Career Examination Ser.: C-746). 1994. pap. 23.95 (*0-8373-0746-5*) Nat Learn.
— Sociology. (College Proficiency Examination Ser.: CPEP-14). 1994. pap. 23.95 (*0-8373-5414-5*) Nat Learn.
— Sociology. (Graduate Record Examination Ser.: GRE-18). 1994. pap. 23.95 (*0-8373-5218-5*) Nat Learn.
— Sociology. (Undergraduate Program Field Test Ser.: UPFT-23). 1994. pap. 23.95 (*0-8373-6023-4*) Nat Learn.
— Soil Conservationist. (Career Examination Ser.: C-1032). 1994. pap. 29.95 (*0-8373-1032-6*) Nat Learn.
— Soil Scientist. (Career Examination Ser.: C-1033). 1994. 29.95 (*0-8373-1033-4*) Nat Learn.
— Solid Waste Construction & Maintenance Supervisor. (Career Examination Ser.). 1994. 34.95 (*0-8373-3606-6*, C-3606) Nat Learn.
— Space Manager. (Career Examination Ser.: C-1055). 1994. pap. 34.95 (*0-8373-1055-5*) Nat Learn.
— Spanish. (Graduate Record Examination Ser.: GRE-19). 1994. pap. 23.95 (*0-8373-5219-3*) Nat Learn.
— Spanish. (National Teachers Examination Ser.: NT-14). 1994. pap. 23.95 (*0-8373-8424-9*) Nat Learn.
— Spanish. (Undergraduate Program Field Test Ser.: UPFT-24). 1994. pap. 23.95 (*0-8373-6024-2*) Nat Learn.
— Spanish, Jr. H. S. (Teachers License Examination Ser.: T-56). 1994. pap. 23.95 (*0-8373-8056-1*) Nat Learn.
— Spanish, Sr. H. S. (Teachers License Examination Ser.: T-57). 1994. pap. 23.95 (*0-8373-8057-X*) Nat Learn.
— Special Agent (Department of Justice) (Career Examination Ser.: C-3287). 1994. pap. 23.95 (*0-8373-3287-7*) Nat Learn.
— Special Agent (FBI) (Career Examination Ser.: C-1060). 1994. pap. 23.95 (*0-8373-1060-1*) Nat Learn.
— Special Agent (INS) (Career Exam Ser.: No. C-3490). 1994. Cloth bdg. avail. pap. 23.95 (*0-8373-3490-X*) Nat Learn.
— Special Agent (Wildlife) (Career Examination Ser.: C-2221). 1994. pap. 23.95 (*0-8373-2221-9*) Nat Learn.
— Special Education. (National Teacher Examination Ser.: NT-41). 1994. pap. 23.95 (*0-8373-8451-6*) Nat Learn.
— Special Electrical License. (Career Examination Ser.: C-1492). 1994. pap. 29.95 (*0-8373-1492-5*) Nat Learn.
— Special Enrollment Examination (IRS) (Career Examination Ser.: C-747). 1994. pap. 49.95 (*0-8373-0747-3*) Nat Learn.
— Special Investigations Inspector. (Career Examination Ser.: C-748). 1994. 29.95 (*0-8373-0748-1*) Nat Learn.
— Special Investigator. (Career Examination Ser.: C-1588). 1994. pap. 29.95 (*0-8373-1588-3*) Nat Learn.
— Special Officer. (Career Examination Ser.: C-749). 1994. pap. 23.95 (*0-8373-0749-X*) Nat Learn.
— Special Projects Coordinator. (Career Examination Ser.: C-2933). 1994. pap. 34.95 (*0-8373-2933-7*) Nat Learn.
— Special Rigger. (Career Examination Ser.: C-750). 1994. pap. 27.95 (*0-8373-0750-3*) Nat Learn.
— Special Services Manager. (Career Examination Ser.: C-2147). 1994. reprint ed. pap. 39.95 (*0-8373-2147-6*) Nat Learn.
— Special Sign Hanger. (Career Examination Ser.: C-751). 1994. pap. 27.95 (*0-8373-0751-1*) Nat Learn.
— Specialist, Aging Services. (Career Examination Ser.: C-3565). 1994. 29.95 (*0-8373-3565-5*) Nat Learn.
— Specialist in Adult Services. (Career Examination Ser.: C-3548). 1994. 29.95 (*0-8373-3548-5*) Nat Learn.
— Specialist in Education. (Career Examination Ser.: C-752). 1994. pap. 34.95 (*0-8373-0752-X*) Nat Learn.
— Speech & Hearing Therapist. (Career Examination Ser.: C-754). 1994. pap. 27.95 (*0-8373-0754-6*) Nat Learn.
— Speech & Language Pathology. (National Teachers Examination Ser.: NT-33). 1994. pap. 23.95 (*0-8373-8443-5*) Nat Learn.
— Speech Audiologist. (Career Examination Ser.: C-753). 1994. pap. 27.95 (*0-8373-0753-8*) Nat Learn.
— Speech Communication. (National Teachers Examination Ser.: NT-35). 1994. pap. 23.95 (*0-8373-8445-1*) Nat Learn.
— Speech Improvement. (Teachers License Examination Ser.: T-59). 1994. pap. 23.95 (*0-8373-8059-6*) Nat Learn.
— Speech Pathologist. (Career Examination Ser.: C-755). 1994. pap. 27.95 (*0-8373-0755-4*) Nat Learn.
— Speech Pathology & Audiology. (Undergraduate Program Field Test Ser.: UPFT-25). 1994. pap. 23.95 (*0-8373-6025-0*) Nat Learn.
— Speech, Sr. H. S. (Teachers License Examination Ser.: T-58). 1994. pap. 23.95 (*0-8373-8058-8*) Nat Learn.
— Speech Technician. (Career Examination Ser.: C-1034). 1994. pap. 27.95 (*0-8373-1034-2*) Nat Learn.
— Staff Analyst. (Career Examination Ser.: C-1551). 1994. pap. 29.95 (*0-8373-1551-4*) Nat Learn.
— Staff Development Coordinator. (Career Examination Ser.: C-2171). 1994. reprint ed. pap. 34.95 (*0-8373-2171-9*) Nat Learn.
— Staff Development Specialist. (Career Examination Ser.: C-2489). 1994. pap. 34.95 (*0-8373-2489-0*) Nat Learn.
— Staff Nurse. (Career Examination Ser.: C-756). 1994. pap. 23.95 (*0-8373-0756-2*) Nat Learn.
— Staff Physician. (Career Examination Ser.: C-1493). 1994. pap. 44.95 (*0-8373-1493-3*) Nat Learn.
— Standards Compliance Analyst. (Career Examination Ser.: C-3109). 1994. pap. 27.95 (*0-8373-3109-9*) Nat Learn.
— State Accounts Auditor-Examiner of Municipal Affairs. (Career Examination Ser.: C-2367). 1994. pap. 39.95 (*0-8373-2367-3*) Nat Learn.
— State Nursing Boards for Practical Nurse (SNB-PN) (Admission Test Ser.: ATS-46). 1994. pap. 23.95 (*0-8373-5046-8*) Nat Learn.
— State Nursing Boards for Registered Nurse (SNB-RN) (Admission Test Ser.: ATS-45). 1994. pap. 23.95 (*0-8373-5045-X*) Nat Learn.
— State Policewoman. (Career Examination Ser.: C-1692). 1994. pap. 23.95 (*0-8373-1692-8*) Nat Learn.
— State Trooper. (Career Examination Ser.: C-757). 1994. pap. 23.95 (*0-8373-0757-0*) Nat Learn.
— State University Program Aide. (Career Examination Ser.: C-3541). 1994. 27.95 (*0-8373-3541-8*) Nat Learn.
— Station Supervisor. (Career Examination Ser.: C-2105). 1994. reprint ed. pap. 23.95 (*0-8373-2105-0*) Nat Learn.
— Stationary Engineer. (Career Examination Ser.: C-758). 1994. pap. 27.95 (*0-8373-0758-9*) Nat Learn.
— Stationary Engineer (Electric) (Career Examination Ser.: C-759). 1994. pap. 27.95 (*0-8373-0759-7*) Nat Learn.
— Stationary Engineer 1. (Career Examination Ser.: C-1903). 1994. pap. 27.95 (*0-8373-1903-X*) Nat Learn.
— Stationary Engineer 2. (Career Examination Ser.: C-1904). 1994. pap. 29.95 (*0-8373-1904-8*) Nat Learn.
— Stationary Fireman. (Career Examination Ser.: C-760). 1994. pap. 23.95 (*0-8373-0760-0*) Nat Learn.
— Statistical Clerk. (Career Examination Ser.: C-762). 1994. pap. 23.95 (*0-8373-0762-7*) Nat Learn.
— Statistician. (Career Examination Ser.: C-761). 1994. pap. 29.95 (*0-8373-0761-9*) Nat Learn.
— Statistics. (College Level Examination Ser.: CLEP-26). 1994. pap. 23.95 (*0-8373-5326-2*) Nat Learn.
— Statistics. (College Proficiency Examination Ser.: CPEP-15). 1994. 39.95 (*0-8373-5465-X*); pap. 23.95 (*0-8373-5415-3*) Nat Learn.
— Statistics. (ACT Proficiency Examination Program Ser.: PEP-57). 1994. pap. 23.95 (*0-8373-5907-4*) Nat Learn.
— Statistics. (ACT Proficiency Examination Program Ser.: PEP-57). 1994. 39.95 (*0-8373-5932-5*) Nat Learn.
— Steam Fireman. (Career Examination Ser.: C-1035). 1994. pap. 23.95 (*0-8373-1035-0*) Nat Learn.
— Steam Fireman - Stationary Fireman. (Career Examination Ser.: C-1902). 1994. pap. 22.00 (*0-8373-1902-1*) Nat Learn.
— Steam Fitter. (Career Examination Ser.: C-763). 1994. pap. 23.95 (*0-8373-0763-5*) Nat Learn.
— Steam Fitter's Helper. (Career Examination Ser.: C-764). 1994. pap. 23.95 (*0-8373-0764-3*) Nat Learn.
— Steel Construction Inspector. (Career Examination Ser.: C-765). 1994. pap. 29.95 (*0-8373-0765-1*) Nat Learn.
— Stenographer. (Career Examination Ser.: C-766). 1994. pap. 19.95 (*0-8373-0766-X*) Nat Learn.
— Stenographer (Law) (Career Examination Ser.: C-1036). 1994. pap. 23.95 (*0-8373-1036-9*) Nat Learn.
— Stenographer-Secretary. (Career Examination Ser.: C-2559). 1994. pap. 23.95 (*0-8373-2559-5*) Nat Learn.
— Stenographer-Typist. (Career Examination Ser.: C-1966). 1994. pap. 19.95 (*0-8373-1966-8*) Nat Learn.
— Stenographer-Typist GS1-4. (Career Examination Ser.: C-767). 1994. pap. 19.95 (*0-8373-0767-8*) Nat Learn.
— Stenographer-Typist GS5-7. (Career Examination Ser.: C-768). 1994. pap. 23.95 (*0-8373-0768-6*) Nat Learn.
— Stenographic-Secretarial Associate. (Career Examination Ser.: C-2452). 1994. pap. 23.95 (*0-8373-2452-1*) Nat Learn.
— Stenographic Secretary. (Career Examination Ser.: C-1653). 1994. 23.95 (*0-8373-1653-7*) Nat Learn.
— Stenographic Specialist. (Career Examination Ser.: C-2453). 1994. pap. 23.95 (*0-8373-2453-X*) Nat Learn.
— Stenography & Typewriting (Gregg & Pitman), Sr. H. S. (Teachers License Examination Ser.: T-60). 1994. pap. 23.95 (*0-8373-8060-X*) Nat Learn.
— Stock Clerk. (Career Examination Ser.: C-2617). 1994. pap. 19.95 (*0-8373-2617-6*) Nat Learn.
— Stockman. (Career Examination Ser.: C-769). 1994. pap. 23.95 (*0-8373-0769-4*) Nat Learn.
— Stockroom Worker. (Career Examination Ser.: C-770). 1994. pap. 23.95 (*0-8373-0770-8*) Nat Learn.
— Storekeeper. (Career Examination Ser.: C-771). 1994. pap. 23.95 (*0-8373-0771-6*) Nat Learn.
— Storekeeper I. (Career Examination Ser.: C-2901). 1994. pap. 23.95 (*0-8373-2901-9*) Nat Learn.
— Storekeeper II. (Career Examination Ser.: C-2902). 1994. pap. 27.95 (*0-8373-2902-7*) Nat Learn.
— Stores Assistant. (Career Examination Ser.: C-3344). 1994. pap. 23.95 (*0-8373-3344-X*) Nat Learn.
— Stores Clerk. (Career Examination Ser.: C-1494). 1994. pap. 23.95 (*0-8373-1494-1*) Nat Learn.
— Street Club Worker. (Career Examination Ser.: C-1038). 1994. pap. 27.95 (*0-8373-1038-5*) Nat Learn.
— Street Light Inspections Foreman. (Career Examination Ser.: C-2961). 1994. pap. 27.95 (*0-8373-2961-2*) Nat Learn.
— Street Lighting Installation Worker. (Career Examination Ser.: C-3108). 1994. pap. 23.95 (*0-8373-3108-0*) Nat Learn.
— Structural Engineer. (Career Examination Ser.: C-3335). 1994. pap. 39.95 (*0-8373-3335-0*) Nat Learn.
— Structural Welder. (Career Examination Ser.: C-773). 1994. pap. 3.95 (*0-8373-0773-2*) Nat Learn.
— Structure Maintainer. (Career Examination Ser.: C-772). 1994. pap. 23.95 (*0-8373-0772-4*) Nat Learn.
— Structure Maintainer, Group A (Carpentry) (Career Examination Ser.: C-1495). 1994. pap. 23.95 (*0-8373-1495-X*) Nat Learn.
— Structure Maintainer, Group B (Masonry) (Career Examination Ser.: C-1730). 1994. pap. 23.95 (*0-8373-1730-4*) Nat Learn.
— Structure Maintainer, Group C (Iron Work) (Career Examination Ser.: C-1731). 1994. pap. 23.95 (*0-8373-1731-2*) Nat Learn.
— Structure Maintainer, Group D (Sheet Metal) (Career Examination Ser.: C-1732). 1994. pap. 23.95 (*0-8373-1732-0*) Nat Learn.
— Structure Maintainer, Group E (Plumbing) (Career Examination Ser.: C-1733). 1994. pap. 23.95 (*0-8373-1733-9*) Nat Learn.
— Structure Maintainer, Group F (Sign Painting) (Career Examination Ser.: C-1776). 1994. reprint ed. pap. 23.95 (*0-8373-1776-2*) Nat Learn.
— Structure Maintainer, Group G (Painting) (Career Examination Ser.: C-3528). 1994. 23.95 (*0-8373-3528-0*) Nat Learn.
— Structure Maintainer, Group H (Air Conditioning & Heating) (Career Examination Ser.: C-1422). 1994. pap. 23.95 (*0-8373-1422-4*) Nat Learn.
— Structure Maintainer-Groups A, B, C, D & E. (Career Examination Ser.: C-2064). 1994. reprint ed. pap. 23.95 (*0-8373-2064-X*) Nat Learn.
— Structure Maintainer Trainee, Group A (Carpentry) (Career Examination Ser.: C-1670). 1994. pap. 19.95 (*0-8373-1670-7*) Nat Learn.
— Structure Maintainer Trainee, Group B (Masonry) (Career Examination Ser.: C-1671). 1994. pap. 19.95 (*0-8373-1671-5*) Nat Learn.
— Structure Maintainer Trainee, Group C (Iron Work) (Career Examination Ser.: C-1672). 1994. pap. 19.95 (*0-8373-1672-3*) Nat Learn.
— Structure Maintainer Trainee, Group D (Sheet Metal) (Career Examination Ser.: C-1673). 1994. pap. 19.95 (*0-8373-1673-1*) Nat Learn.
— Structure Maintainer Trainee, Group E (Plumbing) (Career Examination Ser.: C-1674). 1994. pap. 19.95 (*0-8373-1674-X*) Nat Learn.
— Structure Maintainer Trainee, Group G (Painting) (Career Examination Ser.: C-3529). 1994. pap. 9.95 (*0-8373-3529-9*) Nat Learn.
— Structure Maintainer Trainee, Group H (Air Conditioning & Heating) (Career Examination Ser.: C-1491). 1994. pap. 19.95 (*0-8373-1491-7*) Nat Learn.
— Student Aide. (Career Examination Ser.: C-1496). 1991. pap. 16.00 (*0-8373-1496-8*) Nat Learn.
— Student Trainee. (Career Examination Ser.: C-1039). 1994. pap. 19.95 (*0-8373-1039-3*) Nat Learn.
— Substance Abuse Accounts Auditor. (Career Examination Ser.: C-3478). 1994. pap. 29.95 (*0-8373-3478-0*) Nat Learn.
— Substance Abuse Counselor. (Career Examination Ser.: C-3563). 1994. 29.95 (*0-8373-3563-9*) Nat Learn.
— Substance Abuse Prevention Coordinator. (Career Examination Ser.: Series 1). 1991. pap. 34.95 (*0-8373-3750-X*) Nat Learn.
— Substance Abuse Program Specialist. (Career Examination Ser.: C-3336). 1994. pap. 29.95 (*0-8373-3336-9*) Nat Learn.
— Substance Abuse Treatment Program Assistant. (Career Examination Ser.: C-3479). 1994. pap. 27.95 (*0-8373-3479-9*) Nat Learn.
— Summer Aide. (Career Examination Ser.: C-1498). 1994. pap. 19.95 (*0-8373-1498-4*) Nat Learn.
— Summer Employment Examination. (Career Examination Ser.: C-1663). 1994. reprint ed. pap. 23.95 (*0-8373-1663-4*) Nat Learn.
— Summer Intern. (Career Examination Ser.: C-1499). 1994. pap. 19.95 (*0-8373-1499-2*) Nat Learn.
— Superintendent Building Service (U.S.P.S.) (Career Examination Ser.: C-1685). 1994. pap. 34.95 (*0-8373-1685-5*) Nat Learn.
— Superintendent for Administrative Services. (Career Examination Ser.: C-2815). 1994. pap. 34.95 (*0-8373-2815-2*) Nat Learn.
— Superintendent of Alarms. (Career Examination Ser.: C-2965). 1994. pap. 34.95 (*0-8373-2965-5*) Nat Learn.
— Superintendent of Building Inspection. (Career Examination Ser.: C-2282). 1994. reprint ed. pap. 39.95 (*0-8373-2282-0*) Nat Learn.
— Superintendent of Buildings & Grounds. (Career Examination Ser.: C-1773). 0194. pap. 29.95 (*0-8373-1773-8*) Nat Learn.
— Superintendent of Construction. (Career Examination Ser.: C-1500). 1994. pap. 34.95 (*0-8373-1500-X*) Nat Learn.

R

— Superintendent of Heating & Ventilation. (Career Examination Ser.: C-2380). 1994. pap. 39.95 (*0-8373-2380-0*) Nat Learn.
— Superintendent of Highways. (Career Examination Ser.: C-2318). 1994. pap. 39.95 (*0-8373-2318-5*) Nat Learn.
— Superintendent of Laundries. (Career Examination Ser.: C-1882). 1994. pap. 34.95 (*0-8373-1882-3*) Nat Learn.
— Superintendent of Plant Operations. (Career Examination Ser.: C-2478). 1994. pap. 39.95 (*0-8373-2478-5*) Nat Learn.
— Superintendent of Public Works. (Career Examination Ser.: C-2305). 1994. reprint ed. pap. 39.95 (*0-8373-2305-3*) Nat Learn.
— Superintendent of Recreation. (Career Examination Ser.: C-652). 1994. pap. 34.95 (*0-8373-0652-3*) Nat Learn.
— Superintendent of Sanitation. (Career Examination Ser.: C-2457). 1994. pap. 34.95 (*0-8373-2457-2*) Nat Learn.
— Superintendent of Sewer Service. (Career Examination Ser.: C-2141). 1994. reprint ed. pap. 39.95 (*0-8373-2141-7*) Nat Learn.
— Superintendent of Sewers. (Career Examination Ser.: C-2276). 1994. reprint ed. pap. 39.95 (*0-8373-2276-6*) Nat Learn.
— Superintendent of Street Lighting. (Career Examination Ser.: C-3125). 1994. pap. 39.95 (*0-8373-3125-0*) Nat Learn.
— Superintendent of Wastewater Treatment Plant. (Career Examination Ser.: C-2963). 1994. pap. 39.95 (*0-8373-2963-9*) Nat Learn.
— Superintendent of Women's Prisons. (Career Examination Ser.: C-1744). 1994. reprint ed. pap. 49.95 (*0-8373-1744-4*) Nat Learn.
— Supervising Account Clerk. (Career Examination Ser.: C-1884). 1994. pap. 23.95 (*0-8373-1884-X*) Nat Learn.
— Supervising Accountant. (Career Examination Ser.: C-1040). 1994. pap. 34.95 (*0-8373-1040-7*) Nat Learn.
— Supervising Addiction Specialist. (Career Examination Ser.: C-1501). 1994. pap. 34.95 (*0-8373-1501-8*) Nat Learn.
— Supervising Admitting Clerk. (Career Examination Ser.: C-1041). 1994. pap. 27.95 (*0-8373-1041-5*) Nat Learn.
— Supervising Air Pollution Inspector. (Career Examination Ser.: C-1502). 1994. pap. 34.95 (*0-8373-1502-6*) Nat Learn.
— Supervising Appraiser. (Career Examination Ser.: C-1699). 1994. pap. 29.95 (*0-8373-1699-5*) Nat Learn.
— Supervising Appraiser (Real Estate) (Career Examination Ser.: C-1680). 1994. pap. 29.95 (*0-8373-1680-4*) Nat Learn.
— Supervising Assessor. (Career Examination Ser.: C-1042). 1994. pap. 29.95 (*0-8373-1042-3*) Nat Learn.
— Supervising Audiologist. (Career Examination Ser.: C-2237). 1994. pap. 34.95 (*0-8373-2237-5*) Nat Learn.
— Supervising Audit Clerk. (Career Examination Ser.: C-887). 1994. pap. 23.95 (*0-8373-0887-9*) Nat Learn.
— Supervising Auditor. (Career Examination Ser.: C-2681). 1994. pap. 39.95 (*0-8373-2681-8*) Nat Learn.
— Supervising Automotive Facilities Inspector. (Career Examination Ser.: C-2215). 1994. pap. 29.95 (*0-8373-2215-4*) Nat Learn.
— Supervising Automotive Mechanic. (Career Examination Ser.: C-2575). 1994. pap. 27.95 (*0-8373-2575-7*) Nat Learn.
— Supervising Beverage Control Investigator. (Career Examination Ser.: C-2824). 1994. pap. 29.95 (*0-8373-2824-1*) Nat Learn.
— Supervising Bookkeeper. (Career Examination Ser.: C-2682). 1994. pap. 27.95 (*0-8373-2682-6*) Nat Learn.
— Supervising Building Inspector. (Career Examination Ser.: C-2840). 1994. pap. 34.95 (*0-8373-2840-3*) Nat Learn.
— Supervising Building Plan Examiner. (Career Examination Ser.: C-862). 1994. pap. 34.95 (*0-8373-0862-3*) Nat Learn.
— Supervising Campus Security Officer. (Career Examination Ser.: C-1703). 1994. pap. 27.95 (*0-8373-1703-7*) Nat Learn.
— Supervising Cashier. (Career Examination Ser.: C-774). 1994. pap. 23.95 (*0-8373-0774-0*) Nat Learn.
— Supervising Children's Counselor. (Career Examination Ser.: C-2010). 1994. pap. 34.95 (*0-8373-2010-0*) Nat Learn.
— Supervising Claim Examiner. (Career Examination Ser.: C-2322). 1994. pap. 29.95 (*0-8373-2322-3*) Nat Learn.
— Supervising Clerk. (Career Examination Ser.: C-775). 1994. pap. 23.95 (*0-8373-0775-9*) Nat Learn.
— Supervising Clerk (Income Maintenance) (Career Examination Ser.: C-1706). 1994. pap. 27.95 (*0-8373-1706-1*) Nat Learn.
— Supervising Community Service Worker. (Career Examination Ser.: C-2677). 1994. pap. 27.95 (*0-8373-2677-X*) Nat Learn.
— Supervising Computer Operator. (Career Examination Ser.: C-776). 1994. pap. 29.95 (*0-8373-0776-7*) Nat Learn.
— Supervising Construction Inspector. (Career Examination Ser.: C-1043). 1994. pap. 34.95 (*0-8373-1043-1*) Nat Learn.
— Supervising Consumer Affairs Inspector. (Career Examination Ser.: C-1657). 1994. pap. 29.95 (*0-8373-1657-X*) Nat Learn.
— Supervising Court Officer. (Career Examination Ser.: C-1503). 1994. pap. 27.95 (*0-8373-1503-4*) Nat Learn.
— Supervising Custodial Foreman. (Career Examination Ser.: C-1044). 1994. pap. 29.95 (*0-8373-1044-X*) Nat Learn.
— Supervising Demolition Inspector. (Career Examination Ser.: C-777). 1994. pap. 34.95 (*0-8373-0777-5*) Nat Learn.
— Supervising Deputy Sheriff. (Career Examination Ser.: C-1666). 1994. pap. 29.95 (*0-8373-1666-9*) Nat Learn.
— Supervising Developmental Specialist. (Career Examination Ser.: C-924). 1994. pap. 29.95 (*0-8373-0924-7*) Nat Learn.
— Supervising Dietitian. (Career Examination Ser.: C-1968). 1994. pap. 29.95 (*0-8373-1968-4*) Nat Learn.
— Supervising Drug & Alcohol Community Coordinator. (Career Examination Ser.: C-2777). 1994. pap. 39.95 (*0-8373-2777-6*) Nat Learn.
— Supervising Economist. (Career Examination Ser.: C-2202). 1994. pap. 34.95 (*0-8373-2202-2*) Nat Learn.
— Supervising Electrical Inspector. (Career Examination Ser.: C-778). 1994. pap. 39.95 (*0-8373-0778-3*) Nat Learn.
— Supervising Electronic Computer Operator. (Career Examination Ser.: C-1549). 1994. pap. 29.95 (*0-8373-1549-2*) Nat Learn.
— Supervising Elevator Inspector. (Career Examination Ser.: C-1955). 1994. pap. 34.95 (*0-8373-1955-2*) Nat Learn.
— Supervising Emergency Medical Service Specialist. (Career Examination Ser.: C-3480). 1994. pap. 34.95 (*0-8373-3480-2*) Nat Learn.
— Supervising Employment Consultant (Testing) (Career Examination Ser.: C-2464). 1994. pap. 44.95 (*0-8373-2464-5*) Nat Learn.
— Supervising Environmentalist. (Career Examination Ser.: C-1586). 1994. pap. 34.95 (*0-8373-1586-7*) Nat Learn.
— Supervising Examiner, Social Services. (Career Examination Ser.: C-2140). 1994. reprint ed. pap. 29.95 (*0-8373-2140-9*) Nat Learn.
— Supervising Fire Alarm Dispatcher. (Career Examination Ser.: C-1695). 1994. pap. 27.95 (*0-8373-1695-2*) Nat Learn.
— Supervising Fire Marshal (Uniformed) (Career Examination Ser.: C-1817). 1994. pap. 34.95 (*0-8373-1817-3*) Nat Learn.
— Supervising Food Inspector. (Career Examination Ser.: C-2055). 1994. pap. 34.95 (*0-8373-2055-0*) Nat Learn.
— Supervising Glazier. (Career Examination Ser.: Series 1). 1991. pap. 29.95 (*0-8373-3751-8*) Nat Learn.
— Supervising Grants Analyst. (Career Examination Ser.: C-2834). 1994. pap. 39.95 (*0-8373-2834-9*) Nat Learn.
— Supervising Hearing Examiner. (Career Examination Ser.: C-2327). 1994. pap. 39.95 (*0-8373-2327-4*) Nat Learn.
— Supervising Hearing Officer. (Career Examination Ser.: C-2328). 1994. pap. 39.95 (*0-8373-2328-2*) Nat Learn.
— Supervising Highway Engineer. (Career Examination Ser.: C-2523). 1994. pap. 34.95 (*0-8373-2523-4*) Nat Learn.
— Supervising Highway Maintenance Supervisor. (Career Examination Ser.: C-2632). 1994. pap. 34.95 (*0-8373-2632-X*) Nat Learn.
— Supervising Hospital Care Investigator. (Career Examination Ser.: C-779). 1994. pap. 29.95 (*0-8373-0779-1*) Nat Learn.
— Supervising Housing Groundsman. (Career Examination Ser.: C-780). 1994. pap. 29.95 (*0-8373-0780-5*) Nat Learn.
— Supervising Housing Inspector. (Career Examination Ser.: C-1045). 1994. pap. 34.95 (*0-8373-1045-8*) Nat Learn.
— Supervising Housing Sergeant. (Career Examination Ser.: C-1667). 1994. pap. 39.95 (*0-8373-1667-7*) Nat Learn.
— Supervising Housing Teller. (Career Examination Ser.: C-781). 1994. pap. 27.95 (*0-8373-0781-3*) Nat Learn.
— Supervising Human Resources Specialist. (Career Examination Ser.: C-1046). 1994. pap. 34.95 (*0-8373-1046-6*) Nat Learn.
— Supervising Human Rights Specialist. (Career Examination Ser.: C-1613). 1994. pap. 29.95 (*0-8373-1613-8*) Nat Learn.
— Supervising Identification Specialist. (Career Examination Ser.: C-2513). 1994. pap. 34.95 (*0-8373-2513-7*) Nat Learn.
— Supervising Incinerator Stationary Engineer. (Career Examination Ser.: C-2638). 1994. pap. 34.95 (*0-8373-2638-9*) Nat Learn.
— Supervising Inspector of Markets, Weights & Measures. (Career Examination Ser.: C-1047). 1994. pap. 34.95 (*0-8373-1047-4*) Nat Learn.
— Supervising Investigator. (Career Examination Ser.: C-2106). 1994. reprint ed. pap. 29.95 (*0-8373-2106-9*) Nat Learn.
— Supervising Janitor. (Career Examination Ser.: C-2065). 1994. reprint ed. pap. 29.95 (*0-8373-2065-8*) Nat Learn.
— Supervising Labor Specialist. (Career Examination Ser.: C-2382). 1994. pap. 39.95 (*0-8373-2382-7*) Nat Learn.
— Supervising Laundry Worker. (Career Examination Ser.: C-2200). 1994. pap. 29.95 (*0-8373-2200-6*) Nat Learn.
— Supervising Legal Stenographer. (Career Examination Ser.: C-2635). 1994. pap. 29.95 (*0-8373-2635-4*) Nat Learn.
— Supervising Manpower Counselor. (Career Examination Ser.: C-2437). 1994. pap. 39.95 (*0-8373-2437-8*) Nat Learn.
— Supervising Meat Inspector. (Career Examination Ser.: C-2056). 1994. pap. 34.95 (*0-8373-2056-9*) Nat Learn.
— Supervising Medicaid Claims Examiner. (Career Examination Ser.: C-2693). 1994. pap. 34.95 (*0-8373-2693-1*) Nat Learn.
— Supervising Medical Care Representative. (Career Examination Ser.: C-3148). 1994. pap. 34.95 (*0-8373-3148-X*) Nat Learn.
— Supervising Medical Sesrvices Specialist. (Career Examination Ser.). 1994. 39.95 (*0-8373-3616-3*, C-3616) Nat Learn.
— Supervising Medical Social Worker. (Career Examination Ser.: C-2630). 1994. pap. 34.95 (*0-8373-2630-3*) Nat Learn.
— Supervising Mortgage Administrator. (Career Examination Ser.: C-2312). 1994. reprint ed. pap. 34.95 (*0-8373-2312-6*) Nat Learn.
— Supervising Motor Vehicle License Examiner. (Career Examination Ser.: C-2390). 1994. pap. 29.95 (*0-8373-2390-8*) Nat Learn.
— Supervising Museum Instructor. (Career Examination Ser.: C-1048). 1994. pap. 29.95 (*0-8373-1048-2*) Nat Learn.
— Supervising Nurse. (Career Examination Ser.: C-1883). 1994. pap. 27.95 (*0-8373-1883-1*) Nat Learn.
— Supervising Painter. (Career Examination Ser.: C-3254). 1994. pap. 27.95 (*0-8373-3254-0*) Nat Learn.
— Supervising Parking Enforcement Agent. (Career Examination Ser.: C-2143). 1994. reprint ed. pap. 27.95 (*0-8373-2143-3*) Nat Learn.
— Supervising Parking Meter Collector. (Career Examination Ser.: C-782). 1994. pap. 27.95 (*0-8373-0782-1*) Nat Learn.
— Supervising Photographer. (Career Examination Ser.: C-2504). 1994. pap. 34.95 (*0-8373-2504-8*) Nat Learn.
— Supervising Physical Therapist. (Career Examination Ser.: C-2904). 1994. pap. 34.95 (*0-8373-2904-3*) Nat Learn.
— Supervising Physician & Surgeon. (Career Examination Ser.: C-2195). 1994. pap. 49.95 (*0-8373-2195-6*) Nat Learn.
— Supervising Plumbing Inspector. (Career Examination Ser.: C-1049). 1994. pap. 34.95 (*0-8373-1049-0*) Nat Learn.
— Supervising Police Communications Technician. (Career Examination Ser.: No. C-3618). 1994. pap. 27.95 (*0-8373-3618-X*, C-3618) Nat Learn.
— Supervising Probation Officer. (Career Examination Ser.: C-2591). 1994. pap. 29.95 (*0-8373-2591-9*) Nat Learn.
— Supervising Professional Conduct Investigator. (Career Examination Ser.: C-2299). 1994. reprint ed. pap. 29.95 (*0-8373-2299-5*) Nat Learn.
— Supervising Program Research Specialist. (Career Examination Ser.: C-3201). 1994. pap. 39.95 (*0-8373-3201-X*) Nat Learn.
— Supervising Public Health Adviser. (Career Examination Ser.: C-3176). 1994. pap. 29.95 (*0-8373-3176-5*) Nat Learn.
— Supervising Public Health Nurse. (Career Examination Ser.: C-1748). 1994. reprint ed. pap. 27.95 (*0-8373-1748-7*) Nat Learn.
— Supervising Public Health Sanitarian. (Career Examination Ser.: C-2275). 1994. reprint ed. pap. 34.95 (*0-8373-2275-8*) Nat Learn.
— Supervising Real Estate Manager. (Career Examination Ser.: C-1860). 1994. pap. 34.95 (*0-8373-1860-2*) Nat Learn.
— Supervising Rent Examiner. (Career Examination Ser.: C-1818). 1994. pap. 34.95 (*0-8373-1818-1*) Nat Learn.
— Supervising Sanitary Engineer. (Career Examination Ser.: C-2447). 1994. pap. 39.95 (*0-8373-2447-5*) Nat Learn.
— Supervising Sanitation Inspector. (Career Examination Ser.: C-2455). 1994. pap. 34.95 (*0-8373-2455-6*) Nat Learn.
— Supervising Security Officer. (Career Examination Ser.: C-2205). 1994. pap. 29.95 (*0-8373-2205-7*) Nat Learn.
— Supervising Senior Citizens Club Leader. (Career Examination Ser.: C-2829). 1994. pap. 29.95 (*0-8373-2829-2*) Nat Learn.
— Supervising Social Welfare Examiner. (Career Examination Ser.: C-2379). 1994. pap. 29.95 (*0-8373-2379-7*) Nat Learn.
— Supervising Special Officer. (Career Examination Ser.: C-1766). 1994. pap. 29.95 (*0-8373-1766-5*) Nat Learn.
— Supervising Stenographer. (Career Examination Ser.: C-783). 1994. pap. 23.95 (*0-8373-0783-X*) Nat Learn.
— Supervising Storekeeper. (Career Examination Ser.: C-861). 1994. pap. 29.95 (*0-8373-0861-5*) Nat Learn.
— Supervising Street Club Worker. (Career Examination Ser.: C-1050). 1994. pap. 29.95 (*0-8373-1050-4*) Nat Learn.
— Supervising Support Investigator. (Career Examination Ser.: C-2766). 1994. pap. 29.95 (*0-8373-2766-0*) Nat Learn.
— Supervising Systems Analyst. (Career Examination Ser.: C-2387). 1994. pap. 34.95 (*0-8373-2387-8*) Nat Learn.
— Supervising Tabulator Operator. (Career Examination Ser.: C-1681). 1994. pap. 29.95 (*0-8373-1681-2*) Nat Learn.
— Supervising Taxi & Limosine Inspector. (Career Examination Ser.: C-2554). 1994. pap. 29.95 (*0-8373-2554-4*) Nat Learn.
— Supervising Therapist. (Career Examination Ser.: C-2253). 1994. pap. 34.95 (*0-8373-2253-7*) Nat Learn.
— Supervising Typist. (Career Examination Ser.: C-1928). 1994. pap. 23.95 (*0-8373-1928-5*) Nat Learn.
— Supervising Vocational Counselor. (Career Examination Ser.: C-2439). 1994. pap. 34.95 (*0-8373-2439-4*) Nat Learn.
— Supervising Water Use Inspector. (Career Examination Ser.: C-1051). 1994. pap. 29.95 (*0-8373-1051-2*) Nat Learn.
— Supervising Youth Division Counselor. (Career Examination Ser.: C-2501). 1994. pap. 34.95 (*0-8373-2501-3*) Nat Learn.
— Supervision Test. (Teachers License Examination Ser.: S-9). 1994. pap. 39.95 (*0-8373-8109-6*) Nat Learn.
— Supervisor. (Career Examination Ser.: C-3510). 1994. 29.95 (*0-8373-3510-8*) Nat Learn.
— Supervisor (Buses & Shops) (Career Examination Ser.: C-1504). 1994. pap. 29.95 (*0-8373-1504-2*) Nat Learn.
— Supervisor (Cars & Shops) (Career Examination Ser.: C-1723). 1994. pap. 29.95 (*0-8373-1723-1*) Nat Learn.
— Supervisor (Child Welfare) (Career Examination Ser.: C-784). 1994. pap. 29.95 (*0-8373-0784-8*) Nat Learn.
— Supervisor (Electrical Power) (Career Examination Ser.: C-2238). 1994. pap. 29.95 (*0-8373-2238-3*) Nat Learn.
— Supervisor (Electronic Equipment) (Career Examination Ser.: C-2193). 1994. pap. 29.95 (*0-8373-2193-X*) Nat Learn.
— Supervisor (Elevators & Escalators) (Career Examination Ser.: C-1934). 1994. pap. 29.95 (*0-8373-1934-X*) Nat Learn.
— Supervisor, General Equipment Repair. (Career Examination Ser.: C-1458). 1994. pap. 34.95 (*0-8373-1458-5*) Nat Learn.
— Supervisor I (Child Welfare) (Career Examination Ser.: C-1806). 1994. pap. 29.95 (*0-8373-1806-8*) Nat Learn.
— Supervisor I (Welfare) (Career Examination Ser.: C-1803). 1994. pap. 29.95 (*0-8373-1803-3*) Nat Learn.
— Supervisor II (Child Welfare) (Career Examination Ser.: C-1807). 1994. pap. 29.95 (*0-8373-1807-6*) Nat Learn.
— Supervisor II (Welfare) (Career Examination Ser.: C-1804). 1994. pap. 29.95 (*0-8373-1804-1*) Nat Learn.
— Supervisor III (Child Welfare) (Career Examination Ser.: C-1808). 1994. pap. 29.95 (*0-8373-1808-4*) Nat Learn.
— Supervisor III (Social Service) (Career Examination Ser.: C-1951). 1994. pap. 29.95 (*0-8373-1951-X*) Nat Learn.
— Supervisor III (Welfare) (Career Examination Ser.: C-1805). 1994. pap. 29.95 (*0-8373-1805-X*) Nat Learn.
— Supervisor (Lighting) (Career Examination Ser.: C-1724). 1994. pap. 29.95 (*0-8373-1724-X*) Nat Learn.
— Supervisor (Medical & Psychiatric Social Work) (Career Examination Ser.: C-1052). 1994. pap. 34.95 (*0-8373-1052-0*) Nat Learn.
— Supervisor of Building Custodians. (Career Examination Ser.: C-1015). 1994. pap. 29.95 (*0-8373-1015-6*) Nat Learn.
— Supervisor of Conservation Areas. (Career Examination Ser.: C-3123). 1994. pap. 34.95 (*0-8373-3123-4*) Nat Learn.
— Supervisor of Construction Inspection Services. (Career Examination Ser.: C-3139). 1994. pap. 39.95 (*0-8373-3139-0*) Nat Learn.
— Supervisor of Electrical Installations. (Career Examination Ser.: C-1507). 1994. pap. 29.95 (*0-8373-1507-7*) Nat Learn.
— Supervisor of Facilities Planning. (Career Examination Ser.: C-3021). 1994. pap. 34.95 (*0-8373-3021-1*) Nat Learn.
— Supervisor of Housing Caretakers. (Career Examination Ser.: C-3010). 1994. pap. 29.95 (*0-8373-3010-6*) Nat Learn.
— Supervisor of Licensing. (Career Examination Ser.: C-2191). 1994. pap. 29.95 (*0-8373-2191-3*) Nat Learn.
— Supervisor of Marina Maintenance. (Career Examination Ser.: C-3130). 1994. pap. 29.95 (*0-8373-3130-7*) Nat Learn.
— Supervisor of Mechanical Installations. (Career Examination Ser.: C-1508). 1994. pap. 29.95 (*0-8373-1508-5*) Nat Learn.
— Supervisor of Mechanics (Mechanical Equipment) (Career Examination Ser.: C-1484). 1994. 29.95 (*0-8373-1484-4*) Nat Learn.
— Supervisor of Mechanics (Motor Vehicles) (Career Examination Ser.: C-3047). 1994. pap. 29.95 (*0-8373-3047-5*) Nat Learn.
— Supervisor of Menagerie. (Career Examination Ser.: C-1792). 1994. pap. 29.95 (*0-685-42275-5*) Nat Learn.
— Supervisor of Motor Repair. (Career Examination Ser.: C-1875). 1994. pap. 29.95 (*0-8373-1875-0*) Nat Learn.
— Supervisor of Motor Transport. (Career Examination Ser.: C-1509). 1994. pap. 29.95 (*0-8373-1509-3*) Nat Learn.
— Supervisor of Office Services. (Career Examination Ser.: C-2533). 1994. pap. 29.95 (*0-8373-2533-1*) Nat Learn.
— Supervisor of Operations. (Career Examination Ser.: C-1028). 1994. pap. 34.95 (*0-8373-1028-8*) Nat Learn.
— Supervisor of Park Operations. (Career Examination Ser.: C-1752). 1994. pap. 29.95 (*0-8373-1752-5*) Nat Learn.
— Supervisor of Professional Licensing. (Career Examination Ser.: C-1029). 1994. pap. 29.95 (*0-8373-1029-6*) Nat Learn.
— Supervisor of Public Parking. (Career Examination Ser.: C-1418). 1994. pap. 29.95 (*0-8373-1418-6*) Nat Learn.
— Supervisor of School Maintenance (Construction) (Career Examination Ser.: C-1510). 1994. pap. 27.95 (*0-8373-1510-7*) Nat Learn.
— Supervisor of School Maintenance (Mechanical) (Career Examination Ser.: C-1511). 1994. pap. 27.95 (*0-8373-1511-5*) Nat Learn.
— Supervisor of Tax Compliance Field Operations. (Career Examination Ser.: C-2955). 1994. pap. 34.95 (*0-8373-2955-8*) Nat Learn.
— Supervisor of Traffic Device Maintainers. (Career Examination Ser.: C-3052). 1994. pap. 29.95 (*0-8373-3052-1*) Nat Learn.
— Supervisor of Transportation. (Career Examination Ser.: C-1813). 1994. pap. 29.95 (*0-8373-1813-0*) Nat Learn.
— Supervisor of Vocational Rehabilitation Unit. (Career Examination Ser.: C-1742). 1994. pap. 34.95 (*0-8373-1742-8*) Nat Learn.
— Supervisor of Youth Services. (Career Examination Ser.: C-1682). 1994. pap. 29.95 (*0-8373-1682-0*) Nat Learn.
— Supervisor (Power Distributor) (Career Examination Ser.: C-423). 1994. pap. 29.95 (*0-8373-0423-7*) Nat Learn.
— Supervisor (Signals) (Career Examination Ser.: C-2062). 1994. pap. 29.95 (*0-8373-2062-3*) Nat Learn.
— Supervisor (Social Work) (Career Examination Ser.: C-1000). 1994. pap. 29.95 (*0-8373-1000-8*) Nat Learn.
— Supervisor (Stores, Materials & Supplies) (Career Examination Ser.: C-1505). 1994. pap. 29.95 (*0-8373-1505-0*) Nat Learn.
— Supervisor (Structures) (Career Examination Ser.: C-424). 1994. pap. 29.95 (*0-8373-0424-5*) Nat Learn.
— Supervisor (Structures - Group C) (Iron Work) (Career Examination Ser.: C-425). 1994. pap. 29.95 (*0-8373-0425-3*) Nat Learn.

R

— Supervisor (Telephones) (Career Examination Ser.: C-426). 1994. pap. 29.95 (*0-8373-0426-1*) Nat Learn.
— Supervisor (Track) (Career Examination Ser.: C-1953). 1994. reprint ed. pap. 29.95 (*0-8373-1953-6*) Nat Learn.
— Supervisor (Turnstiles) (Career Examination Ser.: C-427). 1994. pap. 29.95 (*0-8373-0427-X*) Nat Learn.
— Supervisor (Ventillation & Drainage) (Career Examination Ser.: C-1506). 1994. pap. 29.95 (*0-8373-1506-9*) Nat Learn.
— Supervisor (Water & Sewer Systems) (Career Examination Ser.: C-2907). 1994. pap. 29.95 (*0-8373-2907-8*) Nat Learn.
— Supervisor (Welfare) (Career Examination Ser.: Series 1). 1994. pap. 29.95 (*0-8373-0785-6*) Nat Learn.
— Supervisor's Handbook of Mnemonic Devices. (Teachers License Examination Ser.: S-10). 1994. pap. 39.95 (*0-8373-8110-X*) Nat Learn.
— Supervisory Electric Engineer. (Career Examination Ser.: C-786). 1994. pap. 39.95 (*0-8373-0786-4*) Nat Learn.
— Supervisory General Engineer. (Career Examination Ser.: C-787). 1994. pap. 44.95 (*0-8373-0787-2*) Nat Learn.
— Supply Clerk. (Career Examination Ser.: C-3340). 1994. pap. 23.95 (*0-8373-3340-7*) Nat Learn.
— Support Collector. (Career Examination Ser.: C-2800). 1994. pap. 23.95 (*0-8373-2800-4*) Nat Learn.
— Support Investigator. (Career Examination Ser.: C-2765). 1994. pap. 27.95 (*0-8373-2765-2*) Nat Learn.
— Surface Line Dispatcher. (Career Examination Ser.: C-788). 1994. pap. 23.95 (*0-8373-0788-0*) Nat Learn.
— Surface Line Operator. (Career Examination Ser.: C-789). 1994. pap. 19.95 (*0-8373-0789-9*) Nat Learn.
— Surgeon. (Career Examination Ser.: C-790). 1994. pap. 44.95 (*0-8373-0790-2*) Nat Learn.
— Surrogate's Court Clerk. (Career Examination Ser.: C-2135). 1994. reprint ed. pap. 23.95 (*0-8373-2135-2*) Nat Learn.
— Surveyor. (Career Examination Ser.: C-3032). 1994. pap. 29.95 (*0-8373-3032-7*) Nat Learn.
— Swimming & Health Instruction, Sr. H.S. (Teachers License Examination Ser.: T-62). 1994. pap. 23.95 (*0-8373-8062-6*) Nat Learn.
— Switchboard Operator. (Career Examination Ser.: C-883). 1994. pap. 19.95 (*0-8373-0883-6*) Nat Learn.
— Switchboard Supervisor. (Career Examination Ser.: C-884). 1994. pap. 27.95 (*0-8373-0884-4*) Nat Learn.
— Systems Analyst. (Career Examination Ser.: C-2168). 1994. reprint ed. pap. 27.95 (*0-8373-2168-9*) Nat Learn.
— Systems Control Clerk. (Career Examination Ser.: C-3571). 1994. 23.95 (*0-8373-3571-X*) Nat Learn.
— Systems Programmer. (Career Examination Ser.: C-2187). 1994. pap. 27.95 (*0-8373-2187-5*) Nat Learn.
— Tabulator Operator. (Career Examination Ser.: C-800). 1994. pap. 23.95 (*0-8373-0800-3*) Nat Learn.
— Tailor. (Career Examination Ser.: C-1512). 1994. pap. 34.95 (*0-8373-1512-3*) Nat Learn.
— Tariff Examiner. (Career Examination Ser.: C-828). 1994. pap. 27.95 (*0-8373-0828-3*) Nat Learn.
— Tax Auditor. (Career Examination Ser.: C-2313). 1994. reprint ed. pap. 29.95 (*0-8373-2313-4*) Nat Learn.
— Tax Cashier. (Career Examination Ser.: C-2573). 1994. pap. 19.95 (*0-8373-2573-0*) Nat Learn.
— Tax Collector. (Career Examination Ser.: C-801). 1994. pap. 23.95 (*0-8373-0801-1*) Nat Learn.
— Tax Compliance Agent. (Career Examination Ser.: C-2122). 1994. reprint ed. pap. 27.95 (*0-8373-2122-0*) Nat Learn.
— Tax Compliance Agent (Spanish Speaking) (Career Examination Ser.: C-2123). 1994. reprint ed. pap. 29.95 (*0-8373-2123-9*) Nat Learn.
— Tax Compliance Representative. (Career Examination Ser.: C-2997). 1994. pap. 27.95 (*0-8373-2997-3*) Nat Learn.
— Tax Examiner. (Career Examination Ser.: C-802). 1994. pap. 27.95 (*0-8373-0802-X*) Nat Learn.
— Tax Examiner Trainee. (Career Examination Ser.: C-803). 1994. pap. 23.95 (*0-8373-0803-8*) Nat Learn.
— Tax Map Technician. (Career Examination Ser.: C-3199). 1994. pap. 29.95 (*0-8373-3199-4*) Nat Learn.
— Tax Processing Manager. (Career Examination Ser.: C-3173). 1994. pap. 34.95 (*0-8373-3173-0*) Nat Learn.
— Tax Technician. (Career Examination Ser.: C-2370). 1994. pap. 27.95 (*0-8373-2370-3*) Nat Learn.
— Tax Technician Trainee. (Career Examination Ser.: C-214). 1994. pap. 23.95 (*0-8373-0214-5*) Nat Learn.
— Taxi & Limosine Inspector. (Career Examination Ser.: C-2552). 1994. pap. 23.95 (*0-8373-2552-8*) Nat Learn.
— Taxpayer Service Representative. (Career Examination Ser.: C-833). 1994. pap. 27.95 (*0-8373-0833-X*) Nat Learn.
— Teacher. (Career Examination Ser.: C-2267). 1994. reprint ed. pap. 27.95 (*0-8373-2267-7*) Nat Learn.
— Teachers License Examination Passbook Series. (Entire Ser.). 1994. pap. write for info. (*0-8373-8000-6*) Nat Learn.
— Teachers' Retirement System Information Representative. (Career Examination Ser.: C-3482). 1994. pap. 29.95 (*0-8373-3482-9*) Nat Learn.
— Teaching Assistant. (Career Examination Ser.: C-2845). 1994. pap. 23.95 (*0-8373-2845-4*) Nat Learn.
— Teaching Emotionally Disturbed. (National Teachers Examination Ser.: NT-43). 1994. pap. 23.95 (*0-8373-8453-2*) Nat Learn.
— Teaching Health Conservation. (National Teachers Examination Ser.: NT-23). 1994. pap. 23.95 (*0-8373-8433-8*) Nat Learn.
— Teaching Hearing Handicapped. (National Teachers Examination Ser.: NT-28). 1994. pap. 23.95 (*0-8373-8438-9*) Nat Learn.
— Teaching Learning Disabled. (National Teachers Examination Ser.: NT-44). 1994. pap. 23.95 (*0-8373-8454-0*) Nat Learn.
— Teaching Speech Handicapped. (National Teachers Examination Ser.: NT-26). 1994. pap. 23.95 (*0-8373-8436-2*) Nat Learn.
— Teaching Visually Handicapped. (National Teachers Examination Ser.: NT-27). 1994. pap. 23.95 (*0-8373-8437-0*) Nat Learn.
— Technical Aid in Science & Engineering. (Career Examination Ser.: C-829). 1994. pap. 29.95 (*0-8373-0829-1*) Nat Learn.
— Technical Aide. (Career Examination Ser.: C-1514). 1994. pap. 27.95 (*0-8373-1514-X*) Nat Learn.
— Technical & Professional Assistant. (Career Examination Ser.: C-805). 1994. pap. 29.95 (*0-8373-0805-4*) Nat Learn.
— Technical Assistant. (Career Examination Ser.: C-1515). 1994. pap. 27.95 (*0-8373-1515-8*) Nat Learn.
— Technical Careers Test. (Career Examination Ser.: C-804). 1994. pap. 27.95 (*0-8373-0804-6*) Nat Learn.
— Technical Coordinator. (Career Examination Ser.). 1994. 34.95 (*0-8373-3614-7*, C-3614) Nat Learn.
— Technical Drawing & Graphics. (DANTES Ser.: No. 36). 1994. pap. 23.95 (*0-8373-6636-4*) Nat Learn.
— Technical Drawing & Graphics. (DANTES Ser.: No. 36). 1994. 39.95 (*0-8373-6536-8*) Nat Learn.
— Technical Mathematics. (DANTES Ser.: No. 37). 1994. pap. 23.95 (*0-8373-6637-2*) Nat Learn.
— Technical Mathematics. (DANTES Ser.: No. 37). 1994. 39.95 (*0-8373-6537-6*) Nat Learn.
— Technical Support Aide. (Career Examination Ser.: C-2476). 1994. pap. 29.95 (*0-8373-2476-9*) Nat Learn.
— Technical Writing. (DANTES Ser.: No. 43). 1994. pap. 23.95 (*0-8373-6643-7*) Nat Learn.
— Technology (Industrial Arts) Education. (National Teachers Examination Ser.: NT-5). 1994. pap. 23.95 (*0-8373-8415-X*) Nat Learn.
— Telecommunications Aide. (Career Examination Ser.: C-2877). 1994. pap. 23.95 (*0-8373-2877-2*) Nat Learn.
— Telecommunications Analyst. (Career Examination Ser.: C-3000). 1994. pap. 27.95 (*0-8373-3000-9*) Nat Learn.
— Telecommunications Analyst Trainee. (Career Examination Ser.: C-3483). 1994. pap. 23.95 (*0-8373-3483-7*) Nat Learn.
— Telecommunications Specialist. (Career Examination Ser.: C-3410). 1994. pap. 23.95 (*0-8373-3410-1*) Nat Learn.
— Telecommunications Technician. (Career Examination Ser.: C-3411). 1994. pap. 23.95 (*0-8373-3411-X*) Nat Learn.
— Telemetric Systems Specialist. (Career Examination Ser.: C-1940). 1994. pap. 34.95 (*0-8373-1940-4*) Nat Learn.
— Telephone Ability Battery (TAB) (Career Examination Ser.: C-3371). 1994. pap. 23.95 (*0-8373-3371-7*) Nat Learn.
— Telephone Cable Maintainer. (Career Examination Ser.: C-830). 1994. pap. 23.95 (*0-8373-0830-5*) Nat Learn.
— Telephone Inspector. (Career Examination Ser.). 1994. 23.95 (*0-8373-3599-X*, C-3599) Nat Learn.
— Telephone Maintainer. (Career Examination Ser.: C-807). 1994. pap. 23.95 (*0-8373-0807-0*) Nat Learn.
— Telephone Operator. (Career Examination Ser.: C-806). 1994. pap. 19.95 (*0-8373-0806-2*) Nat Learn.
— Telephone Services Supervisor. (Career Examination Ser.: C-2586). 1994. pap. 27.95 (*0-8373-2586-2*) Nat Learn.
— Teletypist. (Career Examination Ser.: C-831). 1994. pap. 23.95 (*0-8373-0831-3*) Nat Learn.
— Television Servicing. (DANTES Ser.: No. 38). 1994. pap. 23.95 (*0-8373-6638-0*) Nat Learn.
— Television Servicing. (DANTES Ser.: No. 38). 1994. 39.95 (*0-8373-6538-4*) Nat Learn.
— Tenant Supervisor. (Career Examination Ser.: C-543). 1994. pap. 29.95 (*0-8373-0543-8*) Nat Learn.
— Test of English As a Foreign Language (TOEFL) (Admission Test Ser.: ATS-30). 1994. 39.95 (*0-8373-5130-8*); pap. 23.95 (*0-8373-5030-1*) Nat Learn.
— Test of General Educational Development (GED) (Admission Test Ser.: ATS-61). 1994. 39.95 (*0-8373-5161-8*); pap. 23.95 (*0-8373-5061-1*) Nat Learn.
— Test Your Knowledge Series. 1994. write for info. (*0-8373-7200-3*); pap. write for info. (*0-8373-7000-0*) Nat Learn.
— Tests & Measurement Specialist. (Career Examination Ser.: C-3484). 1994. pap. 39.95 (*0-8373-3484-5*) Nat Learn.
— Tests & Measurements. (College Level Examination Ser.: CLEP-27). 1994. 39.95 (*0-8373-5377-7*); pap. 23.95 (*0-8373-5327-0*) Nat Learn.
— Therapeutic Activities Specialist. (Career Examination Ser.: C-889). 1994. pap. 29.95 (*0-8373-0889-5*) Nat Learn.
— Thermostat Repairer. (Career Examination Ser.: C-3408). 1994. pap. 23.95 (*0-8373-3408-X*) Nat Learn.
— Ticket Agent. (Career Examination Ser.: C-808). 1994. pap. 23.95 (*0-8373-0808-9*) Nat Learn.
— Timekeeper. (Career Examination Ser.: C-3485). 1994. pap. 23.95 (*0-8373-3485-3*) Nat Learn.
— Title Examiner. (Career Examination Ser.: C-809). 1994. pap. 23.95 (*0-8373-0809-7*) Nat Learn.
— Title Searcher. (Career Examination Ser.: C-1516). 1994. pap. 23.95 (*0-8373-1516-6*) Nat Learn.
— Toll Collector. (Career Examination Ser.: C-810). 1994. pap. 23.95 (*0-8373-0810-0*) Nat Learn.
— Toll Equipment Maintenance Supervisor. (Career Examination Ser.: C-2547). 1994. pap. 29.95 (*0-8373-2547-1*) Nat Learn.
— Toll Equipment Mechanic. (Career Examination Ser.: C-2546). 1994. pap. 27.95 (*0-8373-2546-3*) Nat Learn.
— Toll Section Supervisor. (Career Examination Ser.: C-1947). 1994. pap. 29.95 (*0-8373-1947-1*) Nat Learn.
— Tool & Parts Clerk (USPS) (Career Examination Ser.: C-1610). 1994. pap. 27.95 (*0-8373-1610-3*) Nat Learn.
— Toolmaker. (Career Examination Ser.: C-1517). 1994. pap. 29.95 (*0-8373-1517-4*) Nat Learn.
— Towerman. (Career Examination Ser.: C-811). 1994. pap. 23.95 (*0-8373-0811-9*) Nat Learn.
— Town Clerk. (Career Examination Ser.: C-1854). 1994. pap. 27.95 (*0-8373-1854-8*) Nat Learn.
— Town Engineer. (Career Examination Ser.: C-2001). 1994. pap. 34.95 (*0-8373-2001-1*) Nat Learn.
— Town Investigator. (Career Examination Ser.: C-3067). 1994. pap. 29.95 (*0-8373-3067-X*) Nat Learn.
— Town Maintenance Supervisor. (Career Examination Ser.: C-2764). 1994. pap. 29.95 (*0-8373-2764-4*) Nat Learn.
— Track Equipment Maintainer. (Career Examination Ser.: C-3307). 1994. pap. 19.95 (*0-8373-3307-5*) Nat Learn.
— Trackman. (Career Examination Ser.: C-1066). 1994. pap. 19.95 (*0-8373-1066-0*) Nat Learn.
— Tractor Operator. (Career Examination Ser.: C-827). 1994. pap. 23.95 (*0-8373-0827-5*) Nat Learn.
— Tractor-Trailer Operator. (Career Examination Ser.: C-1519). 1994. pap. 23.95 (*0-8373-1519-0*) Nat Learn.
— Trade Shop Assistant. (Career Examination Ser.: C-3296). 1994. pap. 27.95 (*0-8373-3296-6*) Nat Learn.
— Trade Shop Manager. (Career Examination Ser.: C-3043). 1994. pap. 34.95 (*0-8373-3043-2*) Nat Learn.
— Trades & Industrial Education. (National Teachers Examination Ser.: NT-22). 1994. pap. 23.95 (*0-8373-8432-X*) Nat Learn.
— Traffic & Park Officer. (Career Examination Ser.: C-1689). 1994. pap. 23.95 (*0-8373-1689-8*) Nat Learn.
— Traffic Control Agent. (Career Examination Ser.: C-1750). 1994. reprint ed. pap. 23.95 (*0-8373-1750-9*) Nat Learn.
— Traffic Control Inspector. (Career Examination Ser.: C-812). 1991. pap. 18.00 (*0-8373-0812-7*) Nat Learn.
— Traffic Device Maintainer. (Career Examination Ser.: C-813). 1991. pap. 18.00 (*0-8373-0813-5*) Nat Learn.
— Traffic Device Maintainer Trainee. (Career Examination Ser.: C-814). 1991. pap. 18.00 (*0-8373-0814-3*) Nat Learn.
— Traffic Enforcement Agent. (Career Examination Ser.: C-2407). 1991. pap. 18.00 (*0-8373-2407-6*) Nat Learn.
— Traffic Engineer. (Career Examination Ser.: C-1520). 1991. pap. 24.00 (*0-8373-1520-4*) Nat Learn.
— Traffic Engineer I. (Career Examination Ser.: C-1886). 1991. pap. 24.00 (*0-8373-1886-6*) Nat Learn.
— Traffic Recorder. (Career Examination Ser.: C-1521). 1991. pap. 20.00 (*0-8373-1521-2*) Nat Learn.
— Traffic Supervisor. (Career Examination Ser.: C-2627). 1991. pap. 22.00 (*0-8373-2627-3*) Nat Learn.
— Traffic Technician. (Career Examination Ser.: C-1522). 1991. pap. 22.00 (*0-8373-1522-0*) Nat Learn.
— Traffic Technician I. (Career Examination Ser.: C-2335). 1991. pap. 22.00 (*0-8373-2335-5*) Nat Learn.
— Traffic Technician II. (Career Examination Ser.: C-2336). 1991. pap. 22.00 (*0-8373-2336-3*) Nat Learn.
— Traffic Technician III. (Career Examination Ser.: C-1887). 1991. pap. 24.00 (*0-8373-1887-4*) Nat Learn.
— Traffic Technician Trainee. (Career Examination Ser.: C-3269). 1991. pap. 20.00 (*0-8373-3269-9*) Nat Learn.
— Train Dispatcher. (Career Examination Ser.: C-815). 1991. pap. 18.00 (*0-8373-0815-1*) Nat Learn.
— Train Operator. (Career Examination Ser.: C-1068). 1991. pap. 20.00 (*0-8373-1068-7*) Nat Learn.
— Trainee. (Career Examination Ser.: C-816). 1991. pap. 18.00 (*0-8373-0816-X*) Nat Learn.
— Training & Safety Officer. (Career Examination Ser.: C-3491). 1991. pap. 26.00 (*0-8373-3491-8*) Nat Learn.
— Training Coordinator. (Career Examination Ser.: C-3257). 1991. pap. 26.00 (*0-8373-3257-5*) Nat Learn.
— Training Development Specialist. (Career Examination Ser.: C-3495). 1991. pap. 24.00 (*0-8373-3495-0*) Nat Learn.
— Training Officer. (Career Examination Ser.: C-1523). 1991. 24.00 (*0-8373-1523-9*) Nat Learn.
— Training Specialist. (Career Examination Ser.: C-2337). 1991. pap. 24.00 (*0-8373-2337-1*) Nat Learn.
— Training Specialist I. (Career Examination Ser.: C-2338). 1991. pap. 24.00 (*0-8373-2338-X*) Nat Learn.
— Training Specialist II. (Career Examination Ser.: C-1768). 1991. reprint ed. pap. 24.00 (*0-8373-1768-1*) Nat Learn.
— Training Technician. (Career Examination Ser.: C-1524). 1991. pap. 22.00 (*0-8373-1524-7*) Nat Learn.
— Training Technician (Police) (Career Examination Ser.: C-417). 1991. pap. 26.00 (*0-8373-0417-2*) Nat Learn.
— Trainmaster. (Career Examination Ser.: C-817). 1991. pap. 18.00 (*0-8373-0817-8*) Nat Learn.
— Transcribing Machine Operator. (Career Examination Ser.: C-1067). 1991. pap. 18.00 (*0-8373-1067-9*) Nat Learn.
— Transcribing Typist. (Career Examination Ser.: C-818). 1991. pap. 18.00 (*0-8373-0818-6*) Nat Learn.
— Transit Captain. (Career Examination Ser.: C-819). 1991. pap. 26.00 (*0-8373-0819-4*) Nat Learn.
— Transit Electrical Helper Series. (Career Examination Ser.: C-1963). 1991. pap. 19.95 (*0-8373-1963-3*) Nat Learn.
— Transit Lieutenant. (Career Examination Ser.: C-820). 1991. pap. 24.00 (*0-8373-0820-8*) Nat Learn.
— Transit Management Analyst. (Career Examination Ser.: C-2028). 1991. pap. 24.00 (*0-8373-2028-3*) Nat Learn.
— Transit Management Analyst Trainee. (Career Examination Ser.: C-3228). 1991. reprint ed. pap. 20.00 (*0-8373-3228-1*) Nat Learn.
— Transit Patrolman. (Career Examination Ser.: C-821). 1991. pap. 19.95 (*0-8373-0821-6*) Nat Learn.
— Transit Property Protection Agent. (Career Examination Ser.: C-2397). 1994. pap. 23.95 (*0-8373-2397-5*) Nat Learn.
— Transit Sergeant. (Career Examination Ser.: C-822). 1991. pap. 24.00 (*0-8373-0822-4*) Nat Learn.
— Transit System Manager. (Career Examination Ser.: C-539). 1991. pap. 26.00 (*0-8373-0539-X*) Nat Learn.
— Transportation Analyst. (Career Examination Ser.: C-3380). 1991. pap. 24.00 (*0-8373-3380-6*) Nat Learn.
— Transportation Assistant. (Career Examination Ser.: C-2358). 1991. pap. 20.00 (*0-8373-2358-4*) Nat Learn.
— Transportation Health & Safety Representative. (Career Examination Ser.: C-3379). 1991. pap. 22.00 (*0-8373-3379-2*) Nat Learn.
— Transportation Planning Aide. (Career Examination Ser.: C-2846). 1991. pap. 22.00 (*0-8373-2846-2*) Nat Learn.
— Transportation Specialist. (Career Examination Ser.: C-2479). 1991. pap. 22.00 (*0-8373-2479-3*) Nat Learn.
— Transportation Supervisor. (Career Examination Ser.: C-2738). 1991. pap. 22.00 (*0-8373-2738-5*) Nat Learn.
— Travel Information Aide. (Career Examination Ser.: C-3486). 1991. pap. 20.00 (*0-8373-3486-1*) Nat Learn.
— Treasury Enforcement Agent. (Career Examination Ser.: C-823). 1991. pap. 23.95 (*0-8373-0823-2*) Nat Learn.
— Treatment Unit Clerk. (Career Examination Ser.: C-319). 1991. pap. 18.00 (*0-8373-0319-2*) Nat Learn.
— Tree Pruner Supervisor. (Career Examination Ser.: C-3049). 1991. pap. 20.00 (*0-8373-3049-1*) Nat Learn.
— Tree Trimmer. (Career Examination Ser.: C-1526). 1991. pap. 18.00 (*0-8373-1526-3*) Nat Learn.
— Tree Trimmer Foreman. (Career Examination Ser.: C-2574). 1991. pap. 22.00 (*0-8373-2574-9*) Nat Learn.
— Trigonometry. (College Level Examination Ser.: CLEP-28). 1991. 35.95 (*0-8373-5378-5*); pap. 19.95 (*0-8373-5328-9*) Nat Learn.
— Truck Driver. (Career Examination Ser.: C-1161). 1991. pap. 20.00 (*0-8373-1161-6*) Nat Learn.
— Tunnel Maintainer. (Career Examination Ser.: C-824). 1991. pap. 18.00 (*0-8373-0824-0*) Nat Learn.
— Turnstile Maintainer. (Career Examination Ser.: C-825). 1991. pap. 18.00 (*0-8373-0825-9*) Nat Learn.
— Typewriter Repairman (Electric) (Career Examination Ser.: C-1646). 1994. pap. 27.95 (*0-8373-1646-4*) Nat Learn.
— Typewriter Repairman (Electronic) (Career Examination Ser.: Series 1). 1994. reprint ed. pap. 27.95 (*0-8373-1645-6*) Nat Learn.
— Typewriting, Jr. H. S. (Teachers License Examination Ser.: T-63). 1994. pap. 23.95 (*0-8373-8063-4*) Nat Learn.
— Typist. (Career Examination Ser.: C-826). 1994. pap. 19.95 (*0-8373-0826-7*) Nat Learn.
— U. S. Medical License Examination (USMLE) Basic Medical Sciences. (Administration Test Ser.: Pt. 1). 1994. 39.95 (*0-8373-6967-3*, ATS-104A) Nat Learn.
— U. S. Medical License Examination (USMLE) Clinical Sciences. (Administration Test Ser.: Pt. 2). 1994. 39.95 (*0-8373-6968-1*, ATS-104B) Nat Learn.
— Undergraduate Program Field Test Series. 1994. pap. write for info. (*0-8373-6000-5*) Nat Learn.
— Underwriter. (Career Examination Ser.: C-2011). 1994. pap. 29.95 (*0-8373-2011-9*) Nat Learn.
— Unemployment Insurance Accounts Examiner. (Career Examination Ser.: C-3164). 1994. pap. 27.95 (*0-8373-3164-1*) Nat Learn.
— Unemployment Insurance Claims Clerk. (Career Examination Ser.: C-850). 1994. pap. 29.95 (*0-8373-0850-X*) Nat Learn.
— Unemployment Insurance Claims Examiner. (Career Examination Ser.: C-851). 1994. pap. 27.95 (*0-8373-0851-8*) Nat Learn.
— Unemployment Insurance Hearing Representative. (Career Examination Ser.: C-2728). 1994. pap. 29.95 (*0-8373-2728-8*) Nat Learn.
— Unemployment Insurance Investigator. (Career Examination Ser.: C-2364). 1994. pap. 29.95 (*0-8373-2364-9*) Nat Learn.
— Unemployment Insurance Referee. (Career Examination Ser.: C-917). 1994. pap. 34.95 (*0-8373-0917-4*) Nat Learn.
— Unemployment Insurance Reviewing Examiner. (Career Examination Ser.: C-3041). 1994. pap. 29.95 (*0-8373-3041-6*) Nat Learn.
— Uniformed Court Officer. (Career Examination Ser.: C-852). 1994. pap. 19.95 (*0-8373-0852-6*) Nat Learn.
— United States Citizenship Examination. (Career Examination Ser.: C-3487). 1994. pap. 23.95 (*0-8373-3487-X*) Nat Learn.
— United States Marshal. (Career Examination Ser.: C-853). 1994. pap. 23.95 (*0-8373-0853-4*) Nat Learn.
— United States Park Police Officer. (Career Examination Ser.: C-1989). 1994. pap. 23.95 (*0-8373-1989-7*) Nat Learn.
— Urban Designer. (Career Examination Ser.: C-1527). 1994. pap. 27.95 (*0-8373-1527-1*) Nat Learn.
— Urban Forester. (Career Examination Ser.: C-2905). 1994. pap. 23.95 (*0-8373-2905-1*) Nat Learn.
— Urban Park Officer. (Career Examination Ser.: C-1995). 1994. pap. 23.95 (*0-8373-1995-1*) Nat Learn.
— Urban Park Patrol Sergeant. (Career Examination Ser.: C-2541). 1994. pap. 27.95 (*0-8373-2541-2*) Nat Learn.
— Urban Park Ranger. (Career Examination Ser.: C-3267). 1994. pap. 23.95 (*0-8373-3267-2*) Nat Learn.
— Urban Planner. (Career Examination Ser.: C-854). 1994. pap. 27.95 (*0-8373-0854-2*) Nat Learn.
— Utilities Service Worker. (Career Examination Ser.: C-3161). 1994. pap. 27.95 (*0-8373-3161-7*) Nat Learn.
— Utilization Review Coordinator. (Career Examination Ser.: C-3262). 1994. pap. 27.95 (*0-8373-3262-1*) Nat Learn.
— Varitype Operator. (Career Examination Ser.: C-872). 1994. pap. 23.95 (*0-8373-0872-0*) Nat Learn.
— Vector Control Assistant. (Career Examination Ser.: C-3481). 1994. pap. 23.95 (*0-8373-3481-0*) Nat Learn.
— Vector Control Supervisor. (Career Examination Ser.: C-2763). 1994. pap. 27.95 (*0-8373-2763-6*) Nat Learn.
— Ventilation & Drainage Maintainer. (Career Examination Ser.: C-1528). 1994. pap. 23.95 (*0-8373-1528-X*) Nat Learn.

— Veteran Counselor. (Career Examination Ser.: C-2690). 1994. pap. 29.95 (*0-8373-2690-7*) Nat Learn.
— Veterans Claims Examiner. (Career Examination Ser.: C-3288). 1994. pap. 27.95 (*0-8373-3288-5*) Nat Learn.
— Veterinarian. (Career Examination Ser.: C-870). 1994. pap. 49.95 (*0-8373-0870-4*) Nat Learn.
— Veterinarian Trainee. (Career Examination Ser.: C-1529). 1994. pap. 39.95 (*0-8373-1529-8*) Nat Learn.
— Veterinary College Admission Test (College) (VCAT) (Admission Test Ser.: No. ATS-29). 1994. 39.95 (*0-8373-5129-4*); pap. 23.95 (*0-8373-5029-8*) Nat Learn.
— Veterinary Medical Officer. (Career Examination Ser.: C-875). 1994. pap. 49.95 (*0-8373-0875-5*) Nat Learn.
— Veterinary Science Officer. (Career Examination Ser.: C-871). 1994. pap. 49.95 (*0-8373-0871-2*) Nat Learn.
— Victims' Services Coordinator. (Career Examination Ser.: C-3537). 1994. pap. 29.95 (*0-8373-3537-X*) Nat Learn.
— Visa Qualifying Examination (VQE) (Admission Test Ser.: ATS-48). 1994. 65.95 (*0-8373-5148-0*); pap. 49.95 (*0-8373-5048-4*) Nat Learn.
— Visiting Teacher. (National Teachers Examination Ser.: NT-21). 1994. pap. 23.95 (*0-8373-8431-1*) Nat Learn.
— Vocabulary. (Teachers License Examination Ser.: G-5). 1994. pap. 23.95 (*0-8373-8195-9*) Nat Learn.
— Vocational Counselor. (Career Examination Ser.: C-1530). 1994. pap. 29.95 (*0-8373-1530-1*) Nat Learn.
— Vocational Counselor Trainee. (Career Examination Ser.: C-1531). 1994. pap. 27.95 (*0-8373-1531-X*) Nat Learn.
— Vocational Guidance Counselor. (Career Examination Ser.: C-1532). 1994. pap. 29.95 (*0-8373-1532-8*) Nat Learn.
— Vocational Rehabilitation Counselor. (Career Examination Ser.: C-2425). 1994. pap. 29.95 (*0-8373-2425-4*) Nat Learn.
— Vocational Rehabilitation Counselor Assistant. (Career Exam Ser.: No. 3040). 1994. Cloth bdg. avail. pap. 27.95 (*0-8373-3040-8*) Nat Learn.
— Vocational Rehabilitation Counselor Trainee. (Career Examination Ser.: C-858). 1994. pap. 27.95 (*0-8373-0858-5*) Nat Learn.
— Vocational Specialist. (Career Examination Ser.: C-3293). 1994. pap. 29.95 (*0-8373-3293-1*) Nat Learn.
— Vocational Training Supervisor. (Career Examination Ser.: C-2673). 1994. pap. 34.95 (*0-8373-2673-7*) Nat Learn.
— Voucher Examiner. (Career Examination Ser.: C-3265). 1994. pap. 23.95 (*0-8373-3265-6*) Nat Learn.
— Warden. (Career Examination Ser.: C-894). 1994. pap. 49.95 (*0-8373-0894-1*) Nat Learn.
— Warehouse Examiner. (Career Examination Ser.: C-895). 1994. pap. 27.95 (*0-8373-0895-X*) Nat Learn.
— Warehouse Supervisor. (Career Examination Ser.: C-926). 1994. pap. 29.95 (*0-8373-0926-3*) Nat Learn.
— Warehouseman. (Career Examination Ser.: C-890). 1994. pap. 23.95 (*0-8373-0890-9*) Nat Learn.
— Wastewater Technician. (Career Examination Ser.: C-3412). 1994. pap. 27.95 (*0-8373-3412-8*) Nat Learn.
— Wastewater Treatment Plant Maintenance Supervisor. (Career Examination Ser.: C-3064). 1994. pap. 29.95 (*0-8373-3064-5*) Nat Learn.
— Watchman. (Career Examination Ser.: C-891). 1994. pap. 23.95 (*0-8373-0891-7*) Nat Learn.
— Water Basin Supervisor. (Career Exam Ser.: No. 3492). 1994. Cloth bdg. avail. pap. 29.95 (*0-8373-3492-6*) Nat Learn.
— Water District Clerk. (Career Examination Ser.: C-3378). 1994. pap. 23.95 (*0-8373-3378-4*) Nat Learn.
— Water District Superintendent. (Career Examination Ser.: C-3342). 1994. pap. 39.95 (*0-8373-3342-3*) Nat Learn.
— Water District Supervisor. (Career Examination Ser.: C-2625). 1994. pap. 34.95 (*0-8373-2625-7*) Nat Learn.
— Water Maintainance Foreman. (Career Examination Ser.: C-2925). 1994. pap. 27.95 (*0-8373-2925-6*) Nat Learn.
— Water Maintainance Man. (Career Examination Ser.: C-2657). 1994. pap. 23.95 (*0-8373-2657-5*) Nat Learn.
— Water Management Program Coordinator. (Career Examination Ser.: C-3208). 1994. pap. 39.95 (*0-8373-3208-7*) Nat Learn.
— Water Meter Reader. (Career Examination Ser.: C-2224). 1994. pap. 23.95 (*0-8373-2224-3*) Nat Learn.
— Water Meterman. (Career Examination Ser.: C-2225). 1994. pap. 23.95 (*0-8373-2225-1*) Nat Learn.
— Water Plant Operator. (Career Examination Ser.: C-897). 1994. pap. 27.95 (*0-8373-0897-6*) Nat Learn.
— Water Plant Operator Trainee. (Career Examination Ser.: C-886). 1994. pap. 23.95 (*0-8373-0886-0*) Nat Learn.
— Water Plant Supervisor. (Career Examination Ser.: C-2445). 1994. pap. 29.95 (*0-8373-2445-9*) Nat Learn.
— Water Program Specialist. (Career Examination Ser.: C-3488). 1994. pap. 34.95 (*0-8373-3488-8*) Nat Learn.
— Water Quality Control Specialist. (Career Examination Ser.: C-3337). 1994. pap. 34.95 (*0-8373-3337-7*) Nat Learn.
— Water Service Foreman. (Career Examination Ser.: C-2918). 1994. pap. 27.95 (*0-8373-2918-3*) Nat Learn.
— Water Superintendent. (Career Examination Ser.: C-1534). 1994. pap. 39.95 (*0-8373-1534-4*) Nat Learn.
— Water Tender. (Career Examination Ser.: C-1649). 1994. reprint ed. pap. 27.95 (*0-8373-1649-9*) Nat Learn.
— Water Use Inspector. (Career Examination Ser.: C-898). 1994. pap. 23.95 (*0-8373-0898-4*) Nat Learn.
— Watershed Maintainer. (Career Examination Ser.: C-284). 1994. pap. 23.95 (*0-8373-0284-6*) Nat Learn.
— Waterways Management Supervisor. (Career Examination Ser.: C-3414). 1994. pap. 34.95 (*0-8373-3414-4*) Nat Learn.
— Weigher. (Career Examination Ser.: C-2674). 1994. pap. 23.95 (*0-8373-2674-5*) Nat Learn.
— Welder. (Career Examination Ser.: C-892). 1994. pap. 23.95 (*0-8373-0892-5*) Nat Learn.
— Welding. (Occupational Competency Examination Ser.: OCE-33). 1994. 39.95 (*0-8373-5783-7*); pap. 23.95 (*0-8373-5733-0*) Nat Learn.
— Welding Engineer. (Career Examination Ser.: C-1533). 1994. pap. 27.95 (*0-8373-1533-6*) Nat Learn.
— Welfare Housing Consultant. (Career Examination Ser.: C-3331). 1994. pap. 34.95 (*0-8373-3331-8*) Nat Learn.
— Welfare Management System Coordinator. (Career Examination Ser.: C-3024). 1994. pap. 39.95 (*0-8373-3024-6*) Nat Learn.
— Welfare Representative. (Career Examination Ser.: C-899). 1994. pap. 23.95 (*0-8373-0899-2*) Nat Learn.
— Welfare Resources Supervisor. (Career Examination Ser.: C-3332). 1994. pap. 29.95 (*0-8373-3332-6*) Nat Learn.
— Western Civilization. (College Level Examination Ser.: CLEP-29). 1994. 39.95 (*0-8373-5379-3*); pap. 23.95 (*0-8373-5329-7*) Nat Learn.
— Western Civilization. (College Proficiency Examination Ser.: CPEP-16). 1994. 39.95 (*0-8373-5466-8*); pap. 23.95 (*0-8373-5416-1*) Nat Learn.
— What Do You Know about Accounting? (Test Your Knowledge Ser.: No. Q-1). 1994. pap. 23.95 (*0-8373-7001-9*) Nat Learn.
— What Do You Know about Afro-American History? (Test Your Knowledge Ser.: No. Q-2). 1994. pap. 23.95 (*0-8373-7002-7*) Nat Learn.
— What Do You Know about Air Conditioning, Refrigeration & Heating? (Test Your Knowledge Ser.: No. Q-3). 1994. pap. 23.95 (*0-8373-7003-5*) Nat Learn.
— What Do You Know about American Government? (Test Your Knowledge Ser.: No. Q-4). 1994. pap. 23.95 (*0-8373-7004-3*) Nat Learn.
— What Do You Know about American History? (Test Your Knowledge Ser.: No. Q-5). 1994. pap. 23.95 (*0-8373-7005-1*) Nat Learn.
— What Do You Know about American Literature? (Test Your Knowledge Ser.: No. Q-6). 1994. pap. 23.95 (*0-8373-7006-X*) Nat Learn.
— What Do You Know about Anatomic Sciences? (Test Your Knowledge Ser.: No. Q-7). 1994. pap. 23.95 (*0-8373-7007-8*) Nat Learn.
— What Do You Know about Anthropology? (Test Your Knowledge Ser.: No. Q-8). 1994. pap. 23.95 (*0-8373-7008-6*) Nat Learn.
— What Do You Know about Appliance Repair? (Test Your Knowledge Ser.: No. Q-9). 1994. pap. 23.95 (*0-8373-7009-4*) Nat Learn.
— What Do You Know about Art History? (Test Your Knowledge Ser.: No. Q-10). 1994. pap. 23.95 (*0-8373-7010-8*) Nat Learn.
— What Do You Know about Astronomy? (Test Your Knowledge Ser.: No. Q-11). 1994. pap. 23.95 (*0-8373-7011-6*) Nat Learn.
— What Do You Know about Auto Mechanics? (Test Your Knowledge Ser.: No. Q-12). 1994. pap. 23.95 (*0-8373-7012-4*) Nat Learn.
— What Do You Know about Bacteriology? (Test Your Knowledge Ser.: No. Q-13). 1994. pap. 23.95 (*0-8373-7013-2*) Nat Learn.
— What Do You Know about Biochemistry - Physiology? (Test Your Knowledge Ser.: No. Q-14). 1994. pap. 23.95 (*0-8373-7014-0*) Nat Learn.
— What Do You Know about Biological Sciences? (Test Your Knowledge Ser.: No. Q-15). 1994. pap. 23.95 (*0-8373-7015-9*) Nat Learn.
— What Do You Know about Biology? (Test Your Knowledge Ser.: No. Q-16). 1994. pap. 23.95 (*0-8373-7016-7*) Nat Learn.
— What Do You Know about Building Maintenance? (Test Your Knowledge Ser.: No. Q-17). 1994. pap. 23.95 (*0-8373-7017-5*) Nat Learn.
— What Do You Know about Business Law? (Test Your Knowledge Ser.: No. Q-18). 1994. pap. 23.95 (*0-8373-7018-3*) Nat Learn.
— What Do You Know about Cabinet Making & Millwork? (Test Your Knowledge Ser.: No. Q-19). 1994. pap. 23.95 (*0-8373-7019-1*) Nat Learn.
— What Do You Know about Calculus? (Test Your Knowledge Ser.: No. Q-20). 1994. pap. 23.95 (*0-8373-7020-5*) Nat Learn.
— What Do You Know about Calculus with Analytical Geometry? (Test Your Knowledge Ser.: No. Q-21). 1994. pap. 23.95 (*0-8373-7021-3*) Nat Learn.
— What Do You Know about Carpentry? (Test Your Knowledge Ser.: No. Q-22). 1994. pap. 23.95 (*0-8373-7022-1*) Nat Learn.
— What Do You Know about Chemical Engineering? (Test Your Knowledge Ser.: No. Q-23). 1994. pap. 23.95 (*0-8373-7023-X*) Nat Learn.
— What Do You Know about Chemistry? (Test Your Knowledge Ser.: No. Q-24). 1994. pap. 23.95 (*0-8373-7024-8*) Nat Learn.
— What Do You Know about Civil Engineering? (Test Your Knowledge Ser.: No. Q-25). 1994. pap. 23.95 (*0-8373-7025-6*) Nat Learn.
— What Do You Know about Civil Practice Law & Rules (CPLR)? (Test Your Knowledge Ser.: No. Q-26). 1994. pap. 23.95 (*0-8373-7026-4*) Nat Learn.
— What Do You Know about Clinical Chemistry? (Test Your Knowledge Ser.: No. Q-27). 1994. pap. 23.95 (*0-8373-7027-2*) Nat Learn.
— What Do You Know about College Algebra? (Test Your Knowledge Ser.: No. Q-28). 1994. pap. 23.95 (*0-8373-7028-0*) Nat Learn.
— What Do You Know about College Algebra-Trigonometry? (Test Your Knowledge Ser.: No. Q-29). 1994. pap. 23.95 (*0-8373-7029-9*) Nat Learn.
— What Do You Know about Commercial & Advertising Art? (Test Your Knowledge Ser.: No. Q-30). 1994. pap. 23.95 (*0-8373-7030-2*) Nat Learn.
— What Do You Know about Computer Programming? (Test Your Knowledge Ser.: No. Q-31). 1994. pap. 23.95 (*0-8373-7031-0*) Nat Learn.
— What Do You Know about Computer Science? (Test Your Knowledge Ser.: No. Q-32). 1994. pap. 23.95 (*0-8373-7032-9*) Nat Learn.
— What Do You Know about Cooking? (Test Your Knowledge Ser.: No. Q-33). 1994. pap. 23.95 (*0-8373-7033-7*) Nat Learn.
— What Do You Know about Cosmetology? (Test Your Knowledge Ser.: No. Q-34). 1994. pap. 23.95 (*0-8373-7034-5*) Nat Learn.
— What Do You Know about Criminal Investigation? (Test Your Knowledge Ser.: No. Q-35). 1994. pap. 23.95 (*0-8373-7035-3*) Nat Learn.
— What Do You Know about Criminal Procedure. (Test Your Knowledge Ser.: No. Q-36). 1994. pap. 23.95 (*0-8373-7036-1*) Nat Learn.
— What Do You Know about Criminology. (Test Your Knowledge Ser.: No. Q-37). 1994. pap. 23.95 (*0-8373-7037-X*) Nat Learn.
— What Do You Know about Data Processing. (Test Your Knowledge Ser.: No. Q-38). 1994. pap. 23.95 (*0-8373-7038-8*) Nat Learn.
— What Do You Know about Dental Anatomy. (Test Your Knowledge Ser.: No. Q-39). 1994. pap. 23.95 (*0-8373-7039-6*) Nat Learn.
— What Do You Know about Dental Pharmacology. (Test Your Knowledge Ser.: No. Q-40). 1994. pap. 23.95 (*0-8373-7040-X*) Nat Learn.
— What Do You Know about Diesel Engine Repair. (Test Your Knowledge Ser.: No. Q-41). 1994. pap. 23.95 (*0-8373-7041-8*) Nat Learn.
— What Do You Know about Drafting. (Test Your Knowledge Ser.: No. Q-42). 1994. pap. 23.95 (*0-8373-7042-6*) Nat Learn.
— What Do You Know about Drama & Theatre. (Test Your Knowledge Ser.: No. Q-43). 1994. pap. 23.95 (*0-8373-7043-4*) Nat Learn.
— What Do You Know about Dressmaking. (Test Your Knowledge Ser.: No. Q-44). 1994. pap. 23.95 (*0-8373-7044-2*) Nat Learn.
— What Do You Know about Driving. (Test Your Knowledge Ser.: No. Q-45). 1994. pap. 23.95 (*0-8373-7045-0*) Nat Learn.
— What Do You Know about Earth Science. (Test Your Knowledge Ser.: No. Q-46). 1994. pap. 23.95 (*0-8373-7046-9*) Nat Learn.
— What Do You Know about Economics? (Test Your Knowledge Ser.: No. Q-47). 1994. pap. 23.95 (*0-8373-7047-7*) Nat Learn.
— What Do You Know about Education? (Test Your Knowledge Ser.: No. Q-48). 1994. pap. 23.95 (*0-8373-7048-5*) Nat Learn.
— What Do You Know about Educational Psychology? (Test Your Knowledge Ser.: No. Q-49). 1994. pap. 23.95 (*0-8373-7049-3*) Nat Learn.
— What Do You Know about Electrical Engineering? (Test Your Knowledge Ser.: No. Q-50). 1994. pap. 23.95 (*0-8373-7050-7*) Nat Learn.
— What Do You Know about Electrical Installation? (Test Your Knowledge Ser.: No. Q-51). 1994. pap. 23.95 (*0-8373-7051-5*) Nat Learn.
— What Do You Know about Electrocardiography? (Test Your Knowledge Ser.: No. Q-52). 1994. pap. 39.95 (*0-8373-7052-3*) Nat Learn.
— What Do You Know about Electronics? (Test Your Knowledge Ser.: No. Q-53). 1994. pap. 23.95 (*0-8373-7053-1*) Nat Learn.
— What Do You Know about Endodontics-Periodontics? (Test Your Knowledge Ser.: No. Q-54). 1994. pap. 23.95 (*0-8373-7054-X*) Nat Learn.
— What Do You Know about English Literature? (Test Your Knowledge Ser.: No. Q-55). 1994. pap. 23.95 (*0-8373-7055-8*) Nat Learn.
— What Do You Know about First Aid? (Test Your Knowledge Ser.: No. Q-56). 1994. pap. 23.95 (*0-8373-7056-6*) Nat Learn.
— What Do You Know about Food Service? (Test Your Knowledge Ser.: No. Q-57). 1994. pap. 23.95 (*0-8373-7057-4*) Nat Learn.
— What Do You Know about French? (Test Your Knowledge Ser.: No. Q-58). 1994. pap. 23.95 (*0-8373-7058-2*) Nat Learn.
— What Do You Know about Fundamentals of Nursing? (Test Your Knowledge Ser.: No. Q-59). 1994. pap. 23.95 (*0-8373-7059-0*) Nat Learn.
— What Do You Know about Gardening? (Test Your Knowledge Ser.: No. Q-60). 1994. pap. 23.95 (*0-8373-7060-4*) Nat Learn.
— What Do You Know about Geography? (Test Your Knowledge Ser.: No. Q-61). 1994. pap. 23.95 (*0-8373-7061-2*) Nat Learn.
— What Do You Know about Geology? (Test Your Knowledge Ser.: No. Q-62). 1994. pap. 23.95 (*0-8373-7062-0*) Nat Learn.
— What Do You Know about Geometry? (Test Your Knowledge Ser.: No. Q-63). 1994. pap. 23.95 (*0-8373-7063-9*) Nat Learn.
— What Do You Know about Geophysics? (Test Your Knowledge Ser.: No. Q-64). 1994. pap. 23.95 (*0-8373-7064-7*) Nat Learn.
— What Do You Know about German? (Test Your Knowledge Ser.: No. Q-65). 1994. pap. 23.95 (*0-8373-7065-5*) Nat Learn.
— What Do You Know about Guidance & Counseling? (Test Your Knowledge Ser.: No. Q-66). 1994. pap. 23.95 (*0-8373-7066-3*) Nat Learn.
— What Do You Know about Health? (Test Your Knowledge Ser.: No. Q-67). 1994. pap. 23.95 (*0-8373-7067-1*) Nat Learn.
— What Do You Know about Hematology? (Test Your Knowledge Ser.: No. Q-68). 1994. pap. 23.95 (*0-8373-7068-X*) Nat Learn.
— What Do You Know about History? (Test Your Knowledge Ser.: No. Q-69). 1994. pap. 23.95 (*0-8373-7069-8*) Nat Learn.
— What Do You Know about Home Economics? (Test Your Knowledge Ser.: No. Q-70). 1994. pap. 23.95 (*0-8373-7070-1*) Nat Learn.
— What Do You Know about Humanities? (Test Your Knowledge Ser.: No. Q-71). 1994. pap. 23.95 (*0-8373-7071-X*) Nat Learn.
— What Do You Know about Immunohematology & Blood Banking? (Test Your Knowledge Ser.: No. Q-72). 1994. pap. 23.95 (*0-8373-7072-8*) Nat Learn.
— What Do You Know about Inorganic Chemistry? (Test Your Knowledge Ser.: No. Q-73). 1994. pap. 23.95 (*0-8373-7073-6*) Nat Learn.
— What Do You Know about Intermediate Algebra? (Test Your Knowledge Ser.: No. Q-74). 1994. pap. 23.95 (*0-8373-7074-4*) Nat Learn.
— What Do You Know about Italian? (Test Your Knowledge Ser.: No. Q-75). 1994. pap. 23.95 (*0-8373-7075-2*) Nat Learn.
— What Do You Know about Latin? (Test Your Knowledge Ser.: No. Q-76). 1994. pap. 23.95 (*0-8373-7076-0*) Nat Learn.
— What Do You Know about Law Enforcement? (Test Your Knowledge Ser.: No. Q-77). 1994. pap. 23.95 (*0-8373-7077-9*) Nat Learn.
— What Do You Know about Library Science? (Test Your Knowledge Ser.: No. Q-78). 1994. pap. 23.95 (*0-8373-7078-7*) Nat Learn.
— What Do You Know about Literature? (Test Your Knowledge Ser.: No. Q-79). 1994. pap. 23.95 (*0-8373-7079-5*) Nat Learn.
— What Do You Know about Machine Trades? (Test Your Knowledge Ser.: No. Q-80). 1994. pap. 23.95 (*0-8373-7080-9*) Nat Learn.
— What Do You Know about Marketing? (Test Your Knowledge Ser.: No. Q-81). 1994. pap. 23.95 (*0-8373-7081-7*) Nat Learn.
— What Do You Know about Masonry & Bricklaying. (Test Your Knowledge Ser.: No. Q-82). 1994. pap. 23.95 (*0-8373-7082-5*) Nat Learn.
— What Do You Know about Mechanical Engineering? (Test Your Knowledge Ser.: No. Q-83). 1994. pap. 23.95 (*0-8373-7083-3*) Nat Learn.
— What Do You Know about Meteorology? (Test Your Knowledge Ser.: No. Q-84). 1994. pap. 23.95 (*0-8373-7084-1*) Nat Learn.
— What Do You Know about Microbiology - Pathology? (Test Your Knowledge Ser.: No. Q-85). 1994. pap. 23.95 (*0-8373-7085-X*) Nat Learn.
— What Do You Know about Money & Banking? (Test Your Knowledge Ser.: No. Q-86). 1994. pap. 23.95 (*0-8373-7086-8*) Nat Learn.
— What Do You Know about Music? (Test Your Knowledge: No. Q-87). 1994. pap. 23.95 (*0-8373-7087-6*) Nat Learn.
— What Do You Know about Offset Lithography? (Test Your Knowledge Ser.: No. Q-88). 1994. pap. 23.95 (*0-8373-7088-4*) Nat Learn.
— What Do You Know about Operative Dentistry? (Test Your Knowledge Ser.: No. Q-89). 1994. pap. 23.95 (*0-8373-7089-2*) Nat Learn.
— What Do You Know about Oral Pathology - Radiography? (Test Your Knowledge Ser.: No. Q-90). 1994. pap. 23.95 (*0-8373-7090-6*) Nat Learn.
— What Do You Know about Oral Surgery & Anaesthesia? (Test Your Knowledge Ser.: No. Q-91). 1994. pap. 23.95 (*0-8373-7091-4*) Nat Learn.
— What Do You Know about Organic Chemistry? (Test Your Knowledge Ser.: No. Q-92). 1994. pap. 23.95 (*0-8373-7092-2*) Nat Learn.
— What Do You Know about Orthodontics-Pedodontics? (Test Your Knowledge Ser.: No. Q-93). 1994. pap. 23.95 (*0-8373-7093-0*) Nat Learn.
— What Do You Know about Penal Law? (Test Your Knowledge Ser.: No. Q-94). 1994. pap. 23.95 (*0-8373-7094-9*) Nat Learn.
— What Do You Know about Pharmacology? (Test Your Knowledge Ser.: No. Q-95). 1994. pap. 23.95 (*0-8373-7095-7*) Nat Learn.
— What Do You Know about Philosophy? (Test Your Knowledge Ser.: No. Q-96). 1994. pap. 23.95 (*0-8373-7096-5*) Nat Learn.
— What Do You Know about Photography? (Test Your Knowledge Ser.: No. Q-97). 1994. pap. 23.95 (*0-8373-7097-3*) Nat Learn.
— What Do You Know about Physical Education? (Test Your Knowledge Ser.: No. Q-98). 1994. pap. 23.95 (*0-8373-7098-1*) Nat Learn.
— What Do You Know about Physical Sciences? (Test Your Knowledge Ser.: No. Q-99). 1994. pap. 23.95 (*0-8373-7099-X*) Nat Learn.
— What Do You Know about Physics? (Test Your Knowledge Ser.: No. Q-100). 1994. pap. 23.95 (*0-8373-7100-7*) Nat Learn.
— What Do You Know about Plumbing? (Test Your Knowledge Ser.: No. Q-101). 1994. pap. 23.95 (*0-8373-7102-3*) Nat Learn.
— What Do You Know about Political Science? (Test Your Knowledge Ser.: No. Q-102). 1994. pap. 23.95 (*0-8373-7101-5*) Nat Learn.
— What Do You Know about Printing? (Test Your Knowledge Ser.: No. Q-103). 1994. pap. 23.95 (*0-8373-7103-1*) Nat Learn.
— What Do You Know about Prosthodontics? (Test Your Knowledge Ser.: No. Q-104). 1994. pap. 23.95 (*0-8373-7104-X*) Nat Learn.

R

— What Do You Know about Psychology? (Test Your Knowledge Ser.: No. Q-105). 1994. pap. 23.95 (*0-8373-7105-8*) Nat Learn.
— What Do You Know about Radio & TV Servicing? (Test Your Knowledge Ser.: No. Q-106). 1994. pap. 23.95 (*0-8373-7106-6*) Nat Learn.
— What Do You Know about Shakespeare? (Test Your Knowledge Ser.: No. Q-107). 1994. pap. 23.95 (*0-8373-7107-4*) Nat Learn.
— What Do You Know about Sheet Metal Work? (Test Your Knowledge Ser.: No. Q-108). 1994. pap. 23.95 (*0-8373-7108-2*) Nat Learn.
— What Do You Know about Small Engine Repair? (Test Your Knowledge Ser.: No. Q-109). 1994. pap. 23.95 (*0-8373-7109-0*) Nat Learn.
— What Do You Know about Social Sciences? (Test Your Knowledge Ser.: No. Q-110). 1994. pap. 23.95 (*0-8373-7110-4*) Nat Learn.
— What Do You Know about Sociology? (Test Your Knowledge Ser.: No. Q-111). 1994. pap. 23.95 (*0-8373-7111-2*) Nat Learn.
— What Do You Know about Spanish? (Test Your Knowledge Ser.: No. Q-112). 1994. pap. 23.95 (*0-8373-7112-0*) Nat Learn.
— What Do You Know about Statistics? (Test Your Knowledge Ser.: No. Q-113). 1994. pap. 23.95 (*0-8373-7113-9*) Nat Learn.
— What Do You Know about Trigonometry? (Test Your Knowledge Ser.: No. Q-114). 1994. pap. 23.95 (*0-8373-7114-7*) Nat Learn.
— What Do You Know about Welding? (Test Your Knowledge Ser.: No. Q-115). 1994. pap. 23.95 (*0-8373-7115-5*) Nat Learn.
— What Do You Know about Western Civilization? (Test Your Knowledge Ser.: No. Q-116). 1994. pap. 23.95 (*0-8373-7116-3*) Nat Learn.
— Wildlife Specialist. (Career Examination Ser.: C-896). 1994. pap. 27.95 (*0-8373-0896-8*) Nat Learn.
— Window Cleaner. (Career Examination Ser.: C-893). 1994. pap. 19.95 (*0-8373-0893-3*) Nat Learn.
— Window Clerk (USPS) (Career Examination Ser.: C-3314). 1994. pap. 23.95 (*0-8373-3314-8*) Nat Learn.
— Window Washer. (Career Examination Ser.: C-1535). 1994. pap. 19.95 (*0-8373-1535-2*) Nat Learn.
— Wiper (Uniformed) (Career Examination Ser.: C-1632). 1994. pap. 27.95 (*0-8373-1632-4*) Nat Learn.
— Women's Physical Education. (Teachers License Examination Ser.: NT-37). 1994. pap. 23.95 (*0-8373-8447-8*) Nat Learn.
— Word Processing Supervisor. (Career Examination Ser.: C-3570). 1994. 27.95 (*0-8373-3570-1*) Nat Learn.
— Word Processor. (Career Examination Ser.: C-3184). 1994. pap. 23.95 (*0-8373-3184-6*) Nat Learn.
— Workbook Series. (Career Examination Ser.). 1994. pap. write for info. (*0-8373-7900-8*) Nat Learn.
— Worker's Compensation Review Analyst. (Career Examination Ser.: C-308). 1994. pap. 29.95 (*0-8373-0308-7*) Nat Learn.
— Workers' Compensation Social Worker I. (Career Examination Ser.: C-1319). 1994. pap. 27.95 (*0-8373-1319-8*) Nat Learn.
— Workers' Compensation Social Worker II. (Career Examination Ser.: C-1320). 1994. pap. 29.95 (*0-8373-1320-1*) Nat Learn.
— Workmen's Compensation Examiner. (Career Examination Ser.: C-1644). 1994. reprint ed. pap. 27.95 (*0-8373-1644-8*) Nat Learn.
— Writing & Public Information Occupations. (Career Examination Ser.: C-3556). 1994. 23.95 (*0-8373-3556-6*) Nat Learn.
— Written English Paper, Elem. School, Jr. & Sr. H. S. (Teachers License Examination Ser.: T-61). 1994. pap. 23.95 (*0-8373-8061-8*) Nat Learn.
— X-Ray Coordinator. (Career Examination Ser.: C-1536). 1994. pap. 34.95 (*0-8373-1536-0*) Nat Learn.
— X-Ray Technician. (Career Examination Ser.: C-910). 1994. pap. 23.95 (*0-8373-0910-7*) Nat Learn.
— X-Ray Technician I. (Career Examination Ser.: C-1840). 1994. pap. 23.95 (*0-8373-1840-8*) Nat Learn.
— X-Ray Technician II. (Career Examination Ser.: C-1841). 1994. pap. 27.95 (*0-8373-1841-6*) Nat Learn.
— X-Ray Technician III. (Career Examination Ser.: C-1842). 1994. pap. 29.95 (*0-8373-1842-4*) Nat Learn.
— Youth Corps Project Director. (Career Examination Ser.: C-2208). 1994. pap. 39.95 (*0-8373-2208-1*) Nat Learn.
— Youth Corps Recruiter. (Career Examination Ser.: C-1537). 1994. pap. 29.95 (*0-8373-1537-9*) Nat Learn.
— Youth Counselor. (Career Examination Ser.: C-2906). 1994. pap. 29.95 (*0-8373-2906-X*) Nat Learn.
— Youth Division Counselor. (Career Examination Ser.: C-2107). 1994. 29.95 (*0-8373-2107-7*) Nat Learn.
— Youth Education Coordinator. (Career Examination Ser.: C-2534). 1994. pap. 34.95 (*0-8373-2534-X*) Nat Learn.
— Youth Employment Program Specialist. (Career Examination Ser.: C-3538). 1994. 34.95 (*0-8373-3538-8*) Nat Learn.
— Youth Group Supervisor. (Career Examination Ser.: C-1540). 1994. pap. 29.95 (*0-8373-1540-9*) Nat Learn.
— Youth Group Worker. (Career Examination Ser.: C-1538). 1994. pap. 27.95 (*0-8373-1538-7*) Nat Learn.
— Youth Group Worker Aide. (Career Examination Ser.: C-1539). 1994. pap. 23.95 (*0-8373-1539-5*) Nat Learn.
— Youth Guidance Technician. (Career Examination Ser.: C-920). 1994. pap. 29.95 (*0-8373-0920-4*) Nat Learn.
— Youth Services Coordinator. (Career Examination Ser.: C-2324). 1994. pap. 34.95 (*0-8373-2324-X*) Nat Learn.
— Youth Services Specialist. (Career Examination Ser.: C-1641). 1994. reprint ed. pap. 27.95 (*0-8373-1641-3*) Nat Learn.
— Zoning Inspector. (Career Examination Ser.: C-2340). 1994. pap. 29.95 (*0-8373-2340-1*) Nat Learn.
— Zoning Inspector II. (Career Examination Ser.: C-3079). 1994. pap. 34.95 (*0-8373-3079-3*) Nat Learn.

Rudman, Jack, ed. see Standish, Burt L.
Rudman, Mark. By Contraries & Other Poems. LC 86-64043. (Collected Poems Ser.). 162p. (Orig.). 1987. 25.00 (*0-915032-92-9*) Natl Poet Foun.
— By Contraries & Other Poems. LC 86-64043. (Collected Poems Ser.). 162p. (Orig.). 1989. pap. 12.95 (*0-915032-93-7*) Natl Poet Foun.
— Diverse Voices: Essays on Poets & Poetry. 282p. (C). 1993. 26.95 (*0-934257-67-1*); pap. 18.95 (*0-934257-68-X*) Story Line.
— In the Neighboring Cell. 1982. 5.00 (*0-686-34454-5*) S Duyvil.
— The Nowhere Steps. LC 90-30054. 96p. 1990. 15.95 (*0-935296-93-X*); pap. 11.95 (*0-935296-90-5*) Sheep Meadow.
— Realm of Unknowing. LC 94-39701. 192p. 1995. 35.00x (*0-8195-2220-1*, Wesleyan Univ Pr); pap. 14.95 (*0-8195-1224-9*, Wesleyan Univ Pr) U Pr of New Eng.
— Rider. LC 93-38326. (Wesleyan Poetry Ser.). 112p. (C). 1994. 25.00x (*0-8195-2214-7*, Wesleyan Univ Pr); pap. 12.95 (*0-8195-1217-6*, Wesleyan Univ Pr) U Pr of New Eng.
— Robert Lowell: An Introduction to the Poetry. LC 83-2091. 224p. 1983. text ed. 32.00 (*0-231-04672-3*) Col U Pr.
Rudman, Mark, ed. Pequod: A Journal of Contemporary Literature & Literary Criticism: Literature & the Visual Arts. (Illus.). 300p. (Orig.). 1990. pap. 10.00 (*1-878818-01-5*) Sheep Meadow.
Rudman, Mark, tr. see Boychuk, Bohdan.
Rudman, Mark, tr. see Pasternak, Boris.
Rudman, Masha K. Children's Literature: An Issues Approach. 2nd ed. LC 83-22217. 448p. (C). 1984. text ed. 34.95 (*0-582-28398-1*, 71430) Longman.
— Children's Literature: An Issues Approach. 3rd rev. ed. LC 94-6627. 512p. (C). 1995. pap. text ed. 34.95 (*0-8013-0537-3*, 78414) Longman.
Rudman, Masha K., ed. Children's Literature: Resource for the Classroom. 2nd ed. 252p. (J). (gr. k-8). 1993. pap. text ed. 27.95 (*0-926842-31-5*) CG Pubs Inc.

Rudman, Masha K., et al. Books to Help Children Cope with Separation & Loss: An Annotated Bibliography. 4th ed. 514p. 1994. 49.00 (*0-8352-3412-6*) Bowker.
"...an indispensable tool for librarians, counselors, parents & teachers who may be required to help children facing a separation or loss."--EDUCATION LIBRARIES. "A thorough & thoughtfully prepared reference."--AMERICAN REFERENCE BOOKS ANNUAL. The new 4th edition of this unique selection guide provides librarians, teachers, counselors, & parents with the information needed to choose "real-life" situation books appropriate for children ages 3 to 16 who face difficult times. Here are some 750 fiction & nonfiction books, from folklore to poetry, focusing on separation & loss themes for young people. Topics new to this edition include Homelessness; Economic Loss/ Parents Out of Work; Apartheid. BOOKS TO HELP CHILDREN COPE WITH SEPARATION & LOSS, 4TH EDITION, profiles only the best books, selected "classics" & recommended titles from SCHOOL LIBRARY JOURNAL, BULLETIN OF THE CENTER FOR CHILDREN'S BOOKS, PUBLISHERS WEEKLY, KIRKUS, HORN BOOK, & other publications. Arranged by topic, each annotated entry provides a review of plot & theme, interest/age level, suggestions for use, & complete bibliographic information. This is the ideal reference guide for those who have the opportunity to help children through separation & loss, ranging from going away to camp to the death of a sibling. With approximately half the titles new to this volume, BOOKS TO HELP CHILDREN COPE WITH SEPARATION & LOSS, 4TH EDITION, profiles only the best books: selected "classics" & recommended titles from SCHOOL LIBRARY JOURNAL, BULLETIN OF THE CENTER FOR CHILDREN'S BOOKS, PUBLISHERS WEEKLY, KIRKUS, HORN BOOK, & other publications. Arranged by topic, each annotated entry provides a review of plot & theme, interest/age level, suggestions for use, & complete bibliographic information. This is the ideal reference guide for those who have the opportunity to help children through separation & loss ranging from going away to camp to the death of a sibling. ***Publisher Provided Annotation.***

Rudman, Reuben, ed. Diffraction Aspects of Orientationally Disordered (Plastic) Crystals. (Transactions of the American Crystallographic Association Ser.: Vol. 17). 114p. 1981. pap. 25.00 (*0-937140-26-0*) Polycrystal Bk Serv.
***Rudman, Tim.** The Photographer's Master Printing Course. (Illus.). 159p. 1995. 29.95 (*1-85732-407-2*, Focal) Buttrwrth-Heinemann.
***Rudman, Warren.** Man in the Middle. Date not set. write for info. (*0-679-44135-2*) Random.
Rudmann, Sally V., ed. Textbook of Blood Banking & Transfusion Medicine. LC 93-49788. 1994. text ed. 45.00 (*0-7216-3453-2*) Saunders.
Rudner, Barry. The Bumblebee & the Ram. LC 89-81585. (Illus.). 32p. (Orig.). (J). 1989. pap. 5.95 (*0-925928-03-8*) Tiny Thought.
— The Handstand. (Illus.). 32p. (J). 1991. pap. 5.95 (*0-925928-05-4*) Tiny Thought.
— The Littlest Tall Fellow. Carraro, J. M., ed. (Illus.). 28p. (J). (gr. k-6). 1989. pap. 5.95 (*0-925928-00-3*) Tiny Thought.
— Nonsense. (Illus.). (J). (gr. k-6). 1991. 5.95 (*0-925928-04-6*) Tiny Thought.
— Will I Still Have to Make My Bed In The Morning? (Illus.). 32p. (J). 1991. pap. 5.95 (*0-925928-10-0*) Tiny Thought.
— You're the Apple of My Face. 30p. (J). (gr. k-6). 1994. pap. 4.95 (*0-9642206-0-1*) Windword Pr.
Rudner, David W. Caste & Capitalism in Colonial India: The Nattukottai Chettiars. LC 92-38124. 1994. 50.00 (*0-520-07236-7*); pap. 18.00 (*0-520-08350-4*) U CA Pr.
Rudner, Ione, jt. auth. see Rudner, Jalmar.
Rudner, Jalmar & Rudner, Ione. The Hunter & His Art: A Survey of Rock Art in Southern Africa. (Illus.). 1974. 32.00 (*0-685-03456-9*) Munger Africana Lib.
Rudner, Richard S. & Scheffler, Israel, eds. Logic & Art: Essays in Honor of Nelson Goodman. LC 76-140799. x, 332p. (C). 1972. lib. bdg. 20.00 (*0-672-51639-X*) Ridgeview.
Rudner, Rita. Naked Beneath My Clothes: Tales of a Revealing Nature. (Illus.). 176p. 1993. pap. 8.00 (*0-14-016959-8*, Penguin Bks) Viking Penguin.
— Rita Rudner's Guide to Men. 96p. 1994. 9.95 (*0-670-85507-3*, Viking) Viking Penguin.
Rudner, Ruth. Bitterroot to Beartooth: Hiking Southwest Montana. LC 84-22218. (Totebook Ser.). (Illus.). 288p. (Orig.). 1985. pap. 10.95 (*0-87156-834-9*) Sierra.
— Greetings from Wisdom, Montana. LC 89-33077. 176p. 1989. 15.95 (*1-55591-045-9*) Fulcrum Pub.
— Partings: And Other Beginnings. (Chronicles of Transformation Ser.). 144p. 1993. 16.95 (*0-8264-0629-7*) Continuum.
— Walking. LC 95-1520. (Outdoor Pursuits Ser.). (Illus.). 128p. (Orig.). 1996. pap. 13.95 (*0-87322-668-2*, PRUD0688) Human Kinetics.
Rudnev, V. K. Digging of Soils by Earthmovers with Powered Parts. Sivaramakrishnan, M., tr. 144p. (C). 1985. text ed. 90.00 (*90-6191-450-7*, Pub. by A A Balkema NE) Ashgate Pub Co.
Rudney, Robert, ed. Peace Research in Western Europe: A Directory Guide. 45p. (Orig.). 1989. pap. text ed. 4.00 (*1-878597-05-1*) Access Sec Info Serv.
Rudney, Robert & Reychler, Luc, eds. European Security Beyond the Year 2000. LC 87-12494. 317p. 1988. text ed. 49.95 (*0-275-92625-7*, C2625, Praeger Pubs) Greenwood.
Rudney, Robert, jt. ed. see Bailey, Kathleen.
Rudnick, Dorothea, ed. Rhythmic & Synthetic Processes in Growth. (Growth Symposia Ser.: Vol. 15). 1957. 45.00x (*0-691-08025-9*) Princeton U Pr.
Rudnick, Dorothea, ed. see Puck, Theodore T., et al.
Rudnick, Hans H., ed. Ingardeniana Second: A Spectrum of Scholarship on the Philosophy of Roman Ingarden with a New Complete Bibliography of Ingarden. (C). 1990. lib. bdg. 126.50 (*0-7923-0627-9*) Kluwer Ac.
Rudnick, James, jt. auth. see Krulik, Stephen.
Rudnick, James, jt. auth. see Ware, Richard.
Rudnick, Jesse A., jt. auth. see Krulik, Stephen.
Rudnick, Lewis G., jt. auth. see Lowell, H. Bret.
Rudnick, Lois, jt. ed. see Heller, Adele.
Rudnick, Lois P. Mabel Dodge Luhan: New Woman, New Worlds. LC 84-7415. (Illus.). 400p. 1987. reprint ed. pap. 19.95 (*0-8263-0995-X*) U of NM Pr.
Rudnick, Lois P., ed. see Luhan, Mabel D.
Rudnick, Milton L. Christianity Is for You. 1961. pap. 5.00 (*0-570-03503-1*, 14-1271) Concordia.
Rudnick, Mimi. Price Guide of Open Salts, Individuals & Masters. 1987. pap. 6.00 (*0-940554-10-0*) Country Hse.
Rudnick, Norman, jt. ed. see Gong, Victor.
Rudnick, Paul. I Hate Hamlet. 1992. pap. 4.75 (*0-8222-0546-7*) Dramatists Play.
— I'll Take It. 1989. 18.95 (*0-394-57917-8*) Knopf.
— I'll Take It. 304p. 1990. mass mkt. 4.95 (*0-345-36225-X*) Ballantine.
— Jeffrey. LC 93-21034. (Orig.). Date not set. pap. 4.75 (*0-8222-1402-4*) Dramatists Play.
— Jeffrey. LC 93-21034. 96p. (Orig.). 1994. pap. 7.95 (*0-452-27120-7*, Plume) NAL-Dutton.
— Social Disease. 1986. 14.95 (*0-394-55270-9*) Knopf.
Rudnick, Paul D., et al. Illinois Real Estate Forms, 3 vols. suppl. ed. 1800p. 1993. 87.50 (*0-685-74614-3*) Michie Butterworth.
— Illinois Real Estate Forms, 3 vols., Set. 1800p. 1994. ring bd. 299.00 (*0-8342-0038-4*) Michie Butterworth.
Rudnicki, Adolf. Les Fenetres d'Or et Autres Recits. (FRE.). 1979. pap. 11.95 (*0-7859-4111-8*) Fr & Eur.
Rudnicki, Barbara, jt. auth. see Woolgar, Josh.
Rudnicki, Konrad. The Cosmologists Second: The Riddle of Time in Theories of the Universe. Lipson, Michael, tr. 128p. (Orig.). 1991. pap. 12.95 (*0-940262-41-X*) Lindisfarne Pr.
Rudnicki, Ryszard M., jt. auth. see Nowak, Joanna.
Rudnicki, Stefan, comp. & intro. The Actor's Book of Monologues for Women. 336p. (Orig.). 1991. pap. 11.95 (*0-14-015787-5*, Penguin Bks) Viking Penguin.
Rudnicki, Stefan, intro. The Actor's Book of Classical Monologues. 320p. 1988. pap. 10.95 (*0-14-010676-6*, Penguin Bks) Viking Penguin.
Rudnik, Jesse A., jt. auth. see Krulik, Stephen.
Rudnitski, Rose A., jt. auth. see Frazee, Bruce.
Rudnitsky, jt. auth. see Parr.
Rudnitsky, Alan N., jt. auth. see Posner, George J.
Rudnitsky, David. The Joy of Depression. LC 89-10752. 192p. 1990. 12.95 (*0-944007-53-8*) Sure Sellers.
— Joy of Depression. 1992. pap. 8.99 (*1-56171-124-1*) Sure Sellers.
— The Joy of Depression. 192p. 1993. reprint ed. pap. 4.99 (*1-56171-273-6*, S P I Bks) Sure Sellers.
Rudnitsky, David, jt. auth. see Kahn, Elayne J.
Rudnitsky, David A. Men Who Hate Themselves: And the Women Who Agree with Them. 1994. pap. 4.99 (*1-56171-276-0*) Sure Sellers.
Rudnitsky, David A., jt. auth. see Kahn, Elayne.
Rudnitsky, Konstantin. Meyerhold: The Director. Petrov, George, tr. (Illus.). 1981. 45.00 (*0-88233-313-5*) Ardis Pubs.
— Russian & Soviet Theater, 1905-1932. 1988. 75.00 (*0-8109-1596-0*) Abrams.
Rudnitsky, V. Russian & Soviet Theatre Tradition & the Avantgarde. (C). 1990. 400.00 (*0-685-34352-9*, Pub. by Collets) St Mut.
Rudnytsky, Peter L. Freud & Oedipus. LC 86-21532. 384p. 1987. text ed. 40.50 (*0-231-06352-0*) Col U Pr.
— Freud & Oedipus. (Psychoanalysis & Culture Ser.). 416p. (C). 1992. pap. 16.00 (*0-231-06353-9*) Col U Pr.
— The Psychoanalytic Vocation: Rank, Winnicott, & the Legacy of Freud. 224p. (C). 1991. text ed. 32.50 (*0-300-05067-4*) Yale U Pr.
***Rudnytsky, Peter L. & Spitz, Ellen H., eds.** Freud & Forbidden Knowledge. 200p. 1995. pap. 16.95 (*0-8147-7460-1*) NYU Pr.
Rudnytsky, Peter L., jt. ed. see Logan, Marie-Rose.
Rudnytsky, Peter L., et al, eds. Transitional Objects & Potential Spaces: Literary Uses of D. W. Winnicott. LC 92-43907. (Psychoanalysis & Culture Ser.). 315p. (C). 1993. text ed. 42.50 (*0-231-07572-3*) Col U Pr.
Rudnytzky, Irene I., tr. see Kosyk, Wolodymyr.
Rudnytzky, Leonid, jt. ed. see Labunka, Miroslav.
***Rudoe, Judy.** Decorative Arts, 1850-1950: A Catalogue of the British Museum. (Illus.). 336p. 1994. pap. text ed. 45.00 (*0-7141-0567-8*) Antique Collect.
Rudoff, Alvin. The Paths to Social Deviance & Conformity: A Model of the Process. LC 91-39309. 144p. 1992. lib. bdg. 69.95 (*0-7734-9438-3*) E Mellen.
Rudoff, Carol. Allergy Baker. 3rd ed. LC 89-85111. (Illus.). 128p. 1990. pap. 8.95 (*0-944569-00-5*) Allergy Pubns.
— Allergy Cookie Jar. LC 85-60322. (Illus.). 128p. 1985. pap. 7.95 (*0-9616708-3-5*) Allergy Pubns.
— The Allergy Gourmet: A Collection of Wheat-Free, Milk-Free, Egg-Free, Corn-Free & Soy-Free Recipes. LC 83-61902. (Illus.). 225p. 1983. pap. 12.95 (*0-930048-11-3*) Allergy Pubns.
— The Allergy Oven. LC 88-70472. (Allergy Kitchen Ser.: Vol. 3). (Illus.). 112p. (Orig.). 1988. pap. 7.95 (*0-9616708-9-4*) Allergy Pubns.
— Allergy Products Directory. Blessing-Moore, Joann, ed. 1995. 34.95 (*0-944569-02-1*) Allergy Pubns.
— Allergy Products Directory Vol. 1: Controlling Your Environment. Blessing-Moore, Joann, ed. LC 95-75930. 288p. (ENG & SPA.). 1995. pap. 34.95 (*0-944569-03-X*) Allergy Pubns.
— Allergy Products Directory Vol. 2: Asthma Resources Directory. Blessing-Moore, Joann, ed. LC 95-75929. 256p. (ENG & SPA.). 1995. pap. 29.95 (*0-944569-05-6*) Allergy Pubns.
— Allergy Products Directory Vol. 3: Allergy Asthma Finding Help. Blessing-Moore, Joann, ed. LC 95-79543. 240p. (ENG & SPA.). 1995. pap. 29.95 (*0-944569-04-8*) Allergy Pubns.
— Allergy Products Directory Vol. 4: Protecting Your Skin. Fowler, Joseph F., Jr., ed. LC 95-75928. 160p. 1995. pap. 19.95 (*0-944569-06-4*) Allergy Pubns.
Rudoff, James D. The Creative Cookie. LC 87-72388. (Allergy Kitchen Ser.: Vol. 2). (Illus.). 112p. (Orig.). 1988. pap. 7.95 (*0-9616708-8-6*) Allergy Pubns.
Rudofsky, Bernard. Architecture Without Architects: A Short Introduction to Non-Pedigreed Architecture. LC 87-10778. (Illus.). 162p. 1987. reprint ed. pap. 16.95 (*0-8263-1004-4*) U of NM Pr.
— The Prodigious Builders. (Illus.). 383p. (C). 1977. text ed. 59.50 (*0-8290-0986-8*) Irvington.
Rudofsky, Herbert. Trakehnen Horses. (Breed Ser.). 1977. pap. 4.95 (*0-88376-011-8*) Dreenan Pr.
— Young Horses. (Breed Ser.). 1977. pap. 4.95 (*0-88376-009-6*) Dreenan Pr.
Rudofsky, Hubert. Horses. (Breed Ser.). 1977. pap. 4.95 (*0-88376-015-0*) Dreenan Pr.
Rudolf, Anthony. Wine from Two Glasses (Poetry & Politics: Trust & Mistrust in Language) 1991. pap. 9.00 (*1-870921-03-8*) SPD-Small Pr Dist.
Rudolf, Anthony, ed. I'm Not Even a Grown-up: The Diary of Jerzy Feliks Urman. 1991. pap. 9.00 (*0-9513753-3-4*) SPD-Small Pr Dist.

An Asterisk (*) at the beginning of an entry indicates that the title is appearing in BIP for the first time.

Rudolf, Anthony, ed. see Bonnefoy, Yves.
Rudolf, Anthony, jt. ed. see Schwartz, Howard.
Rudolf, C. & Dezsone, S. Dictionary of Technical Information: Meteorology. 596p. (C). 1986. 100.00 (*0-685-58757-6*, Pub. by Collets); 120.00 (*0-89771-916-6*, Pub. by Collets) St Mut.
***Rudolf, Dave.** Please - Don't Tease the Dragon! Short Tall Tales & Poems. LC 94-21653. (Illus.). (J). 1994. 12.95 (*1-57071-016-5*) Sourcebks.
Rudolf, Irene. Bedros: A Novel. LC 82-80009. 292p. 1983. pap. 7.45 (*0-937884-07-3*, Bennington Bks) Hystry Mystry.
Rudolf, Kathleen B. The Effect of Reading Instruction on Achievement in Eighth Grade Social Studies. LC 75-177218. (Columbia University. Teachers College. Contributions to Education Ser.: No. 945). reprint ed. 37.50 (*0-404-55945-X*) AMS Pr.
Rudolf, Max. Grammar of Conducting. 2nd ed. LC 79-7634. 1980. 30.00 (*0-02-872220-5*) Macmillan.
— The Grammar of Conducting: A Comprehensive Guide to Baton Technique & Interpretation. 3rd ed. LC 93-12310. (Illus.). 540p. 1993. text ed. 45.00 (*0-02-872221-3*) Schirmer Bks.
Rudolf, R., jt. auth. see Lowndes, L.
Rudolf, Robert. Mafia Wiseguys. 1993. pap. 5.99 (*1-56179-195-4*) Sure Sellers.
— Mafia Wiseguys: The Mob That Took on the Feds. 422p. 1993. reprint ed. pap. 5.99 (*1-56171-195-0*, S P I Bks) Sure Sellers.
***Rudolph.** Rudolph's Pediatrics. 20th ed. (Illus.). (C). 1996. text ed. 95.00 (*0-8385-8492-6*) Appleton & Lange.
Rudolph, Abraham M. & Kamei, Robert. Rudolph's Fundamentals of Pediatrics. (Illus.). 650p. 1994. pap. text ed. 37.95 (*0-8385-8233-8*, A8233-7) Appleton & Lange.
Rudolph, Abraham M., et al. Rudolph's Pediatrics. 19th ed. (Illus.). 2111p. (C). 1991. boxed 95.00 (*0-8385-8488-8*, A8488-7) Appleton & Lange.
***Rudolph, Alan & Coburn, Randy S.** Mrs. Parker & the Vicious Circle: The Book of the Film. (Illus.). 256p. (Orig.). Date not set. pap. 14.95 (*1-55783-205-6*) Applause Theatre Bk Pubs.
Rudolph, B., jt. ed. see Pohl, H.
Rudolph, Camilla B., tr. see Di Crescenzo, Casimiro.
Rudolph, Catherine E., ed. see Schultz, Karen, et al.
***Rudolph, Cathy F.** Remembery Chips. (Illus.). 34p. (J). (ps-3). 1994. 15.00 (*0-9642360-0-1*) Wayward Fluffy.
Rudolph, Claire S. & Borker, Susan R. Regionalization: Issues in Intensive Care for High Risk Newborns & their Families. LC 87-15136. 208p. 1987. text ed. 65.00 (*0-275-92547-1*, C2547, Praeger Pubs) Greenwood.
Rudolph, Conrad. Artistic Change at St-Denis: Abbot Suger's Program & the Early Twelfth-Century Controversy over Art. 139p. 1990. text ed. 29.50 (*0-691-04068-0*) Princeton U Pr.
— The Things of Greater Importance: Bernard of Clairvaux's Apologia & the Medieval Attitude Toward Art. LC 89-21480. (Illus.). 424p. (C). 1990. text ed. 44.95 (*0-8122-8181-0*) U of Pa Pr.
Rudolph, D. Restricted Orbit Equivalence. LC 84-28119. 149p. 1986. reprint ed. pap. text ed. 26.00 (*0-8218-2324-8*, MEMO 54/323) Am Math.
Rudolph, D., jt. ed. see Schmahl, G.
Rudolph, Daniel J. Fundamentals of Measurable Dynamics: Ergodic Theory on Lebesgue Spaces. (Illus.). 184p. 1990. 59.95 (*0-19-853572-4*) OUP.
***Rudolph, Dietmar.** Das AutoCAD Lexikon. 589p. (GER.). 1991. 135.00 (*0-7859-8697-9*, 387686240x) Fr & Eur.
***Rudolph, Donna K. & Rudolph, G. A.** Historical Dictionary of Venezuela. 2nd enl. rev. ed. LC 95-14843. (Latin American Historical Dictionaries Ser.: No. 3). 1995. write for info. (*0-615-00713-9*) Scarecrow.
Rudolph, Eberhard. Function Point Analysis, An Introduction. 250p. 1992. text ed. 34.00 (*0-13-351974-0*) P-H.
Rudolph, Enno & Stamatescu, Ion-Opimpiu, eds. Philosophy Mathematics & Modern Physics: A Dialogue. LC 94-8282. 1995. 49.00 (*0-387-57683-5*) Spr-Verlag.
Rudolph, Frederick. The American College & University: A History. LC 90-40967. 616p. 1991. 35.00 (*0-8203-1285-1*); pap. 15.00 (*0-8203-1284-3*) U of Ga Pr.
— Curriculum: A History of the American Undergraduate Course of Study since 1636. LC 77-84319. (Higher Education Ser.). 377p. 1977. 36.95 (*0-87589-358-9*) Jossey-Bass.
— Curriculum: A History of the American Undergraduate Course of Study since 1636. fac. ed. LC 77-84319. (Carnegie Council Ser.). 380p. 1977. reprint ed. pap. 108.30 (*0-7837-8050-8*, 2047803) Bks Demand.
— Curriculum: A History of the American Undergraduate Course of Study Since 1636. LC 77-84319. (Higher & Adult Education Ser.). 392p. (C). 1993. reprint ed. pap. 24.00 (*1-55542-535-6*) Jossey-Bass.
Rudolph, Frederick, ed. Perspectives: A Williams Anthology. LC 83-51219. 340p. 1983. 17.50 (*0-915081-00-8*) Williams Coll.
Rudolph, G. A. The Kansas State University Receipt Book & Household Manual. LC 68-66946. (Libraries Bibliography: No. 4). 1968. pap. 5.00 (*0-686-20813-7*) KSU.
Rudolph, G. A. & Williams, Evan. Linnaeana. LC 72-636354. (Libraries Bibliography: No. 7). 1970. 5.00 (*0-686-20815-3*) KSU.
Rudolph, G. A., jt. auth. see Rudolph, Donna K.
Rudolph, J. Langenscheidt Handbook of Business English: Handbuch der Englischen Wirtschaftssprache. 415p. (ENG & GER.). 1986. 110.00 (*0-8288-0078-2*, M7374) Fr & Eur.
Rudolph, James D. Peru: The Evolution of a Crisis. LC 91-23655. (Politics in Latin America Ser.). 192p. 1992. text ed. 55.00 (*0-275-94146-9*, C4146, Praeger Pubs); pap. text ed. 14.95 (*0-275-94181-7*, B4181, Praeger Pubs) Greenwood.
Rudolph, James D., ed. Nicaragua: A Country Study. 2nd ed. LC 82-13833. (DA Pam Area Handbook Ser.: No. 550-88). (Illus.). 308p. 1987. reprint ed. text ed. 12.00 (*0-16-001590-1*, 008-020-00932-6) USGPO.
Rudolph, James S. Make Your Own Working Clock. LC 83-47570. 40p. 1983. pap. 13.00 (*0-06-091066-6*, CN1066, PL) HarpC.
Rudolph, John W. Las Olas. LC 87-80761. (Illus.). 101p. (Orig.). (YA). 1987. pap. 9.00 (*0-941611-09-4*) Shasta San Rafael.
Rudolph, Jorg M. Cankao Xiaoxi: Foreign News in the Propaganda System of the People's Republic of China. (Occasional Papers-Reprints Series in Contemporary Asian Studies: No. 6-1984 (65)). 174p. (Orig.). 1984. pap. text ed. 5.00 (*0-942182-67-7*) Occasional Papers.
Rudolph, Jorg-M. Media-Coverage on Taiwan in the People's Republic of China. (Occasional Papers-Reprints Series in Contemporary Asian Studies: No. 3-1983 (56)). 77p. (Orig.). 1983. pap. text ed. 3.50 (*0-942182-55-3*) U MD Law.
***Rudolph, Joseph R., Jr.** Energy. LC 95-3370. (Magill Bibliographies Ser.). 185p. 1995. 29.50 (*0-8108-3011-6*) Scarecrow.
Rudolph, Joseph R. & Thompson, Robert J., eds. Ethnoterritorial Politics, Policy, & the Western World. LC 89-30268. 262p. 1989. lib. bdg. 45.00 (*1-55587-095-3*) Lynne Rienner.
***Rudolph, Kevin C.** Bible Tour Guide: A 365 Spiritual Journey. LC 94-66386. (Illus.). 379p. 1994. 18.00 (*0-927577-01-1*) Rich Pub Co.
Rudolph, Kurt. Geschichte und Probleme der Religionswissenschaft. LC 91-26964. (Numen Supplements Ser.: Vol. 53). xiv, 443p. (GER.). 1992. 125.75 (*90-04-09503-9*) E J Brill.
— Gnosis: The Nature & History of Gnosticism. LC 81-47437. 411p. 1987. pap. 20.00 (*0-06-067018-5*, PL 4122) Harper SF.
Rudolph, L., jt. auth. see Lerman, G.
Rudolph, L. C. Francis Asbury. 240p. (Orig.). 1983. pap. 0.90 (*0-687-13461-7*) Abingdon.
— Hoosier Faiths: A History of Indiana's Churches & Religious Groups. LC 94-43452. 1995. write for info. (*0-253-32882-9*) Ind U Pr.
— Hoosier Zion: The Presbyterians in Early Indiana. LC 62-8261. (Yale Publications in Religion: No. 5). (Illus.). 196p. reprint ed. pap. 55.90 (*0-317-09434-3*, 2009008) Bks Demand.
Rudolph, L. C. & Endelman, Judith E. Religion in Indiana: A Guide to Historical Resources. LC 84-43186. 247p. reprint ed. pap. 70.40 (*0-7837-4204-5*, 2059054) Bks Demand.
Rudolph, Lee. Blackjack Consensus: How to Take the B. S. Out of Basic Strategy. 112p. (Orig.). 1989. pap. 7.95 (*0-9624047-0-5*) Gamblers Analysis.
— The Country Changes. LC 78-60470. 72p. 1978. pap. 9.95 (*0-914086-23-5*) Alicejamesbooks.
— Curses, & Songs & Poems. LC 74-81380. 72p. 1974. pap. 9.95 (*0-914086-04-9*) Alicejamesbooks.
Rudolph, Leighton, jt. ed. see Carpenter, Lucas.
Rudolph, Linda B., jt. auth. see Thompson, Charles L.
Rudolph, Lloyd, ed. Cultural Policy in India. 1984. 12.50 (*0-8364-1243-5*, Pub. by Chanakya II) S Asia.
Rudolph, Lloyd I. & Rudolph, Susanne H. Gandhi: The Traditional Roots of Charisma. LC 83-1179. (Modernity of Tradition Ser.: Pt. 2). 104p. (C). 1983. pap. text ed. 8.95 (*0-226-73136-7*) U Ch Pr.
— In Pursuit of Lakshmi: The Political Economy of the Indian State. LC 86-24903. (Illus.). xviii, 520p. (C). 1987. lib. bdg. 42.00 (*0-226-73138-3*); pap. text ed. 21.00 (*0-226-73139-1*) U Ch Pr.
— The Modernity of Tradition: Political Development in India. LC 67-25527. (Midway Reprint Ser.). x, 306p. (C). 1984. pap. text ed. 16.00 (*0-226-73137-5*) U Ch Pr.
Rudolph, Lloyd I., jt. ed. see Rudolph, Susanne H.
Rudolph, Nancy. Workyards: Playgrounds Planned for Adventure. LC 74-5187. (Illus.). 71p. reprint ed. pap. 25.00 (*0-8357-3033-6*, 2039280) Bks Demand.
Rudolph, Paul & Futagawa, Yukio. Paul Rudolph: Architectural Drawings. (Illus.). 218p. 1981. 55.00 (*0-8038-0208-0*) Archit CT.
Rudolph, Richard L. Banking & Industrialization in Austria-Hungary: The Role of Banks in the Industrialization of the Czech Crownlands, 1873-1914. LC 75-2736. 303p. reprint ed. pap. 86.40 (*0-8357-5963-6*, 2024524) Bks Demand.
Rudolph, Richard L. & Good, David A., eds. Nationalism & Empire: The Habsburg Monarchy & the Soviet Union. 320p. 1992. text ed. 49.95 (*0-312-06892-1*) St Martin.
***Rudolph, Robert.** The Boys from New Jersey: How the Mob Beat the Feds. 431p. 1995. pap. 16.95 (*0-8135-2154-8*) Rutgers U Pr.
Rudolph, Ross. Chronic Problem Wound. 1983. 67.00 (*0-316-76110-9*) Little.
Rudolph, Samuel B., ed. The Philosophy of Freedom: Ideological Origins of the Bill of Rights. LC 92-44281. 1993. 47.50 (*0-8191-9029-2*); pap. 27.50 (*0-8191-9030-6*) U Pr of Amer.
Rudolph, Stormy. Many Horses (Sequel to Quest for Courage) (Indian Culture Ser.). (Illus.). (J). (gr. 5-12). 1987. pap. 8.95 (*0-89992-112-4*) Coun India Ed.
Rudolph, Susanne H. & Rudolph, Lloyd I., eds. Education & Politics in India: Studies in Organization, Society, & Policy. LC 71-186675. 480p. reprint ed. pap. 136.80 (*0-7837-1526-9*, 2041803) Bks Demand.
Rudolph, Susanne H., jt. auth. see Rudolph, Lloyd I.
Rudolph, Thomas D., ed. see ERDA Technical Information Center Staff.
Rudolph, Thomas E. Music & the Apple II: Applications for Music Education, Composition, & Performance. (Illus.). 175p. (Orig.). 1984. pap. text ed. 17.95 (*0-9615386-0-0*) Unsinn Pubns.
Rudolph, W. & Wilhelmi, B. Light Pulse Compression. Letokhov, V. S., ed. (Laser Science & Technology Ser.: Vol. 3). viii, 132p. 1989. pap. text ed. 101.00 (*3-7186-4888-1*) Gordon & Breach.
***Rudolph, Wilhelm.** Hebraisches Woerterbuch Zu Jeremia. 2nd ed. 46p. (GER & HEB.). 1953. 19.95 (*0-7859-8278-7*, 3113902533) Fr & Eur.
Rudolph, William B., jt. auth. see Bittinger, Marvin L.
***Rudolph, Wolf.** A Golden Legacy: Ancient Jewelry from the Burton Y. Berry Collection. (Illus.). 320p. 1994. text ed. 59.95 (*0-253-34980-X*); pap. 39.95 (*0-253-20913-7*) Ind U Pr.
Rudolph, Wolfgang, jt. auth. see Diels, Jean-Claude.
Rudolphi, jt. auth. see Doring, G.
Rudomin, Pablo, et al, eds. Neuroscience: From Neural Networks to Artificial Intelligence - Proceedings of a U. S.-Mexico Seminar Held in the City of Xalapa in the State of Veracruz in December 9-11, 1991. LC 93-18575. (Research Notes in Neural Computing Ser.: Vol. 4). 1993. 69.00 (*0-387-56501-9*) Spr-Verlag.
Rudomino, B. & Remzhin, Yu. Steam Power Plant Piping Design. 270p. 1979. 40.00 (*0-317-46731-X*, Pub. by Collets UK) Pro-Am Music.
Rudova, Larissa. Pasternak's Short Fiction & the Cultural Vanguard. LC 93-22860. (Middlebury Studies in Russian Language & Literature: Vol. 6). 167p. (C). 1994. text ed. 35.95 (*0-8204-2273-8*) P Lang Pubs.
Rudovsky, David, jt. auth. see Avery, Michael.
Rudovsky, David, et al. The Rights of Prisoners: Comletely Revised & Up-to-Date, A Comprehensive Guide to the Legal Rights of Prisoners under Current Law. 4th rev. ed. LC 87-23577. 152p. 1988. pap. text ed. 7.95 (*0-8093-1452-5*) S Ill U Pr.
***Rudow, Martin.** Advanced Race Walking. 4th ed. (Illus.). 128p. 1995. pap. 11.50 (*0-614-04802-8*) Tech Prodns WA.
Rudowski, Victor A. The Prince: A Historical Critique. (MWS Ser.: No. 82). 180p. (C). 1992. pap. 12.95 (*0-8057-8555-8*, Twayne) Macmillan.
— The Prince: A Historical Critique. (MWS Ser.: No. 82). 180p. (C). 1992. text ed. 21.95 (*0-8057-8079-3*, Twayne) Macmillan.
Rudowski, Witold, et al. Burn Therapy & Research. LC 74-29339. (Illus.). 351p. reprint ed. pap. 100.10 (*0-8357-7481-3*, 2020752) Bks Demand.
Rudra, Ashok. Political Economy of Indian Agriculture. (C). 1992. 28.50 (*0-685-61702-5*, Pub. by KP Bagchi IA) S Asia.
— Some Problems of Marx's Theory of History. (R C Dutt Lectures). 76p. (C). 1988. pap. 4.95 (*0-86131-754-8*, Pub. by Orient Longman Ltd II) Apt Bks.
Rudra, Ashok & Barhan, P. K. Agrarian Relations in West Bengal. 1982. 12.50 (*0-8364-0922-1*, Pub. by Somaiya) S Asia.
Rudrananda, Swami. Rudi: Entering Infinity. Rosen, Cheryl B., ed. LC 92-45648. 210p. 1994. 16.95 (*0-915801-41-8*) Rudra Pr.
— Rudi in His Own Words. LC 90-20083. 197p. (Orig.). 1990. pap. 14.95 (*0-915801-20-5*) Rudra Pr.
Rudrum, Alan, ed. see Vaughan, Henry.
Rudstein, David, et al. Criminal Constitutional Law, 3 vols., Set. 1990. write for info. (*0-8205-1098-X*, 098) Bender.
Rudt de Collenberg, W. H. Familles de l'Orient Latin, XIIe-XIVe Siecles. (Collected Studies: No. CS176). 326p. (FRE.). (C). 1983. reprint ed. lib. bdg. 105.00 (*0-86078-124-0*, Pub. by Variorum UK) Ashgate Pub Co.
Rudwick, Elliott, jt. auth. see Meier, August.
Rudwick, Elliott M. Race Riot at East St. Louis July 2, 1917. LC 82-1940. (Blacks in the New World Ser.). 320p. 1982. pap. 12.95 (*0-252-00951-7*) U of Ill Pr.
— Race Riot at East St. Louis, July 2, 1917. LC 82-1940. (Blacks in the New World Ser.). 322p. reprint ed. pap. 91.80 (*0-8357-7503-8*, 2034461) Bks Demand.
Rudwick, Martin J. The Great Devonian Controversy: The Shaping of Scientific Knowledge among Gentlemanly Specialists. LC 84-16199. (Science & Its Conceptual Foundations Ser.). (Illus.). 544p. 1985. 45.00 (*0-226-73101-4*) U Ch Pr.
— The Great Devonian Controversy: The Shaping of Scientific Knowledge among Gentlemanly Specialists. LC 84-16199. (Science & Its Conceptual Foundations Ser.). (Illus.). 544p. 1988. pap. text ed. 24.95 (*0-226-73102-2*) U Ch Pr.
— The Meaning of Fossils: Episodes in the History of Palaeontology. 2nd ed. LC 84-28080. (Illus.). 288p. (C). 1985. pap. 14.95 (*0-226-73103-0*) U Ch Pr.
— Scenes from Deep Time: Early Pictorial Representations of the Prehistoric World. LC 91-47677. (Illus.). 304p. 1992. 45.00 (*0-226-73104-9*) U Ch Pr.
— Scenes from Deep Time: Early Pictorial Representations of the Prehistoric World. xiv, 280p. 1995. pap. 20.00 (*0-226-73105-7*) U Ch Pr.
Rudwin, M. Satanism in French Romanticism. 1972. 59.59 (*0-8490-0993-6*) Gordon Pr.
Rudwin, Maximilian J. Devil in Legend & Literature. LC 71-111780. (Illus.). reprint ed. 29.50 (*0-404-05451-X*) AMS Pr.
Rudy, Ann. Mom Spelled Backwards Is Tired. LC 79-55442. 190p. 1980. 9.95 (*0-672-52627-1*, Bobbs) Macmillan.
Rudy, D. L. Voices Through Time & Distant Places. 36p. (Orig.). 1993. pap. 6.00 (*0-9637386-0-7*) Willdor Pr.
Rudy, David R. Becoming Alcoholic: Alcoholics Anonymous & the Reality of Alcoholism. LC 85-11750. 192p. 1986. 19.95 (*0-8093-1244-1*); pap. 12.95 (*0-8093-1245-X*) S Ill U Pr.
Rudy, Ellen B. & Gray, Ruth V. Handbook of Health Assessment. LC 80-24706. (Illus.). 184p. (C). 1980. pap. text ed. 9.95 (*0-87619-843-4*, Appleton-Century-Crofts) P-H.
— Handbook of Health Assessment. 2nd ed. 304p. 1985. pap. text ed. 13.95 (*0-89303-493-2*, Appleton-Century-Crofts) P-H.
Rudy, Ellen B. & Gray, V. Ruth. Handbook of Health Assessment. 3rd ed. (Illus.). 305p. (C). 1991. pap. text ed. 19.95 (*0-8385-3602-6*, A3602-8) Appleton & Lange.
Rudy-Gervais, Darla, tr. see Fargues, Philippe & Boustani, Rafic.
Rudy, Jack R. Archeological Survey of Western Utah. (Utah Anthropological Papers: No. 12). reprint ed. 34.50 (*0-404-60612-1*) AMS Pr.
Rudy, John. Moneywise Meditations: To Be Found Faithful in God's Audit. (Illus.). 144p. (Orig.). 1989. pap. 7.95 (*0-8361-3486-9*) Herald Pr.
***Rudy, John G.** Wordsworth & the Zen Mind: The Poetry of Self-Emptying. 288p. (C). 1996. text ed. 59.50x (*0-7914-2903-2*); pap. text ed. 19.95x (*0-7914-2904-0*) State U NY Pr.
Rudy, Kathryn, jt. auth. see Heflin, L. Juane.
***Rudy, Lisa.** Ocean Life: A Theme Unit Developed with the New Jersey State Aquarium. 1999. pap. 8.95 (*0-590-49508-9*) Scholastic Inc.
***Rudy, Lois.** Mariam's Well. (YA). 1995. pap. 3.50 (*0-590-44938-9*) Scholastic Inc.
Rudy, Martin, jt. auth. see Salcedo, Greg.
Rudy, S. Willis. The College of the City of New York: A History, 1847-1947. Metzger, Walter P., ed. LC 76-55189. (Academic Profession Ser.). (Illus.). 1977. lib. bdg. 42.95 (*0-405-10014-0*) Ayer.
— Total War & Twentieth-Century Higher Learning: Universities of the Western World in the First & Second World Wars. LC 90-55172. 136p. 1991. 30.00 (*0-8386-3409-5*) Fairleigh Dickinson.
— The Universities of Europe. LC 82-49281. 176p. 1984. 22.50 (*0-685-07997-X*) Fairleigh Dickinson.
— The Universities of Europe, Eleven Hundred to Nineteen Fourteen: A History. 176p. 1984. 29.50 (*0-8386-3177-0*) Fairleigh Dickinson.
Rudy, Stephen, ed. Roman Jakobson: A Complete Bibliography of His Writings. xii, 188p. 1990. lib. bdg. 63.85 (*0-89925-068-8*) Mouton.
— Roman Jakobson Selected Writings, Vol. VIII. 685p. (C). 1988. lib. bdg. 178.70 (*0-89925-175-7*) Mouton.
— Roman Jakobson 1896-1982: A Complete Bibliography of His Writings. 1990. 63.00 (*3-11-010650-7*) Mouton.
Rudy, Stephen, jt. ed. see Jackson, Robert L.
Rudy, Stephen, ed. see Jakobson, Roman.
Rudy, Stephen, jt. ed. see Waugh, Linda R.
Rudy, Theresa M. How to Use Trusts to Avoid Probate & Taxes. (Random House Practical Law Manual Ser.). 1992. pap. write for info. (*0-679-74127-5*) HALT DC.
— Small Claims Court. (Random House Practical Law Manual Ser.). 160p. 1990. pap. write for info. (*0-679-72950-X*) HALT DC.
Rudy, Theresa M., jt. auth. see Dimeo, Jean.
Rudy, Theresa M., et al. Your Guide to Living Trusts & Other Trusts: How Trusts Can Help You Avoid Probate & Taxes. (Orig.). 1994. write for info. (*0-910073-19-8*) HALT DC.
Rudysmith, Christina. National Archives & Record Administration. (Know Your Government Ser.). (Illus.). 112p. (YA). (gr. 5 up). 1989. 14.95 (*1-55546-073-9*) Chelsea Hse.
Rudzinski, W. & Everett, D. H. Adsorption of Gases on Heterogeneous Surfaces. (Illus.). 578p. 1991. text ed. 176.00 (*0-12-601690-9*) Acad Pr.
Rudzitis, Gundars. Residential Location Determinants of the Older Population. LC 82-10966. (Research Papers Ser.: No. 202). (Illus.). 117p. (C). 1982. pap. text ed. 12.00 (*0-685-06129-9*) U Chicago Comm Geo.
Rudzka & Goczolowa. Polish for Foreign Students (Wsrod Polakow), No. 2. 447p. 1992. 25.00 (*83-00-00865-9*, P556) Vanous.
Rudzka, B. Among Poles, Vol. 1. 1988. pap. 23.00 (*83-00-00657-5*) IBD Ltd.
— Among Poles: Polish for Foreign Students, Vol. 2. 347p. 1988. pap. 22.00 (*83-00-00866-7*) IBD Ltd.
Rudzka-Ostyn, Brygida, jt. ed. see Geiger, Richard A.
***Rue & Croese.** National Assessment Institute Manual para el Manejo de Alimentos Saludables. (Illus.). 224p. (C). 1994. pap. text ed. 31.00 (*0-13-135238-5*) P-H.
Rue, jt. auth. see Terry.
Rue, Hazel M. Bomby the Bombardier Beetle. LC 82-71053. (Illus.). (J). (gr. 2-4). 1984. pap. 4.95 (*0-89051-084-9*, Inst Creation) Master Bks.
***Rue, J.** Home-Based Businesses: Over 250 Ways to Earn Your Fortune. 208p. 1995. pap. 14.95 (*0-915665-35-2*) Premier Publishers.
Rue, John E. Mao Tse-tung in Opposition, 1927-1935. viii, 387p. 1966. 47.50 (*0-8047-0222-5*) Stanford U Pr.
Rue, Leonard L. Deer of North America. 1989. 32.95 (*1-55654-051-5*) Times Mir Mag Bk Div.
Rue, Leonard L., III. How I Photograph Wildlife & Nature. (Illus.). 1984. 35.00 (*0-393-01907-1*) Norton.
— How I Photograph Wildlife & Nature. (Illus.). 288p. 1995. 19.95 (*0-393-31370-0*) Norton.
— How to Photograph Animals in the Wild. (Illus.). 128p. 1996. pap. 16.95 (*0-8117-2451-4*) Stackpole.
— Leonard Lee Rue III's Whitetails: Answers to All Your Questions on Life Cycle, Feeding Patterns, Antlers, Scrapes & Rubs, Behavior During the Rut, & Habitat. LC 90-27656. (Illus.). 288p. 1991. 34.95 (*0-8117-1938-3*) Stackpole.
***Rue, Leslie & Byars, Lloyd.** Supervision. 4th ed. 232p. (C). 1992. student ed, text ed. 19.95 (*0-256-12117-6*) Irwin.

Rue, Leslie W. & Byars. Management. 5th ed. (C). 1989. text ed. 54.95 (0-256-06896-8); student ed 18.95 (0-256-07568-9) Irwin.

Rue, Leslie W. & Byars, Lloyd L. Management: Skills & Application. 7th ed. LC 94-5495. 582p. (C). 1994. text ed. 64.95 (0-256-12541-4) Irwin Prof Pubng.

— Management Skills & Application. 6th ed. 608p. (C). 1991. text ed. 64.95 (0-256-08702-4) Irwin.

— Supervision: Key Link to Productivity. 3rd ed. (C). 1990. student ed, pap. text ed. 17.95 (0-256-08192-1) Irwin.

— Supervision: Key Link to Productivity. 4th ed. LC 92-14200. (Illus.). 512p. (C). 1992. pap. text ed. 49.95 (0-256-10525-1) Irwin.

— Supervision, Key Link to Productivity. 5th ed. LC 95-8206. 1995. write for info. (0-256-17068-1) Irwin.

Rue, Leslie W. & Holland, Phyllis G. Strategic Management: Concepts & Experiences. 2nd ed. 1989. text ed. write for info. (0-07-054308-9) McGraw.

Rue, Leslie W., jt. auth. see Byars, Lloyd L.

Rue, Loyal. By the Grace of Guile: The Role of Deception in Natural History & Human Affairs. LC 93-32877. (Illus.). 368p. 1994. 27.50 (0-19-507508-0) OUP.

Rue, Loyal D. Amythia: Crisis in the Natural History of Western Culture. LC 88-27846. (Illus.). 232p. 1989. 29. 95 (0-8173-0428-2) U of Ala Pr.

Rue, Loyal D., jt. ed. see Loades, Ann.

***Rue, Nancy.** The Guardian. (Christian Heritage Ser.: No. 3). 1995. pap. 4.99 (1-56179-348-5) Focus Family.

— Home by Another Way. (YA). (gr. 9-12). 1991. pap. 8.95 (0-89107-633-6) Crossway Bks.

— The Rescue. (Christian Heritage Ser.: No. 1). 1995. pap. 4.99 (1-56179-346-9) Focus Family.

— Stop in the Name of Love. Rosen, Roger, ed. (Flipside Fiction Ser.). (YA). (gr. 7 up). 1988. lib. bdg. 12.95 (0-8239-0794-5) Rosen Group.

— The Stowaway. LC 94-41918. (Christian Heritage Ser.: No. 2). 1995. pap. 4.99 (1-56179-347-7) Focus Family.

— The Value of Compassion. (Encyclopedia of Ethical Behavior Ser.). (YA). (gr. 7-12). 1991. lib. bdg. 15.95 (0-8239-1240-X) Rosen Group.

Rue, Nancy N. Coping with An Illiterate Parent. Rosen, Roger, ed. (Coping Ser.). 64p. (YA). (gr. 7-12). 1990. lib. bdg. 15.95 (0-8239-1070-9) Rosen Group.

— Everything You Need to Know about Getting Your Period. LC 94-42067. (Need to Know Library). (Illus.). 64p. (YA). (gr. 7-12). 1995. 15.95 (0-8239-1870-X) Rosen Group.

Rue, Nancy R. The National Assessment Institute Handbook for Safe Food Service Management. LC 93-3398. 1993. pap. text ed. 32.40 (0-13-053000-X) P-H.

Rue, Roger. Circumnavigating Vancouver Island. 1982. per. 6.95 (0-945265-21-2) Accord Comm.

Rue, Roger L. Circumnavigating Vancouver Island. 1982. pap. 10.00 (0-9609036-0-7) Evergreen Pacific.

Rue, T. S. The Attic. (Nightmare Inn Ser.: No. 4). (YA). 1993. mass mkt. 3.50 (0-06-106157-3, Harp PBks) HarpC.

— Nightmare Inn. (Nightmare Inn Ser.: No. 1). (YA). (gr. 9-12). 1993. mass mkt. 3.50 (0-06-106740-7, Harp PBks) HarpC.

— The Pool. (Nightmare Inn Ser.: No. 3). (J). 1993. mass mkt. 3.50 (0-06-106749-0, Harp PBks) HarpC.

— Room Thirteen. (Nightmare Inn Ser.: No. 2). (YA). (gr. 9-12). 1993. mass mkt. 3.50 (0-06-106746-6, Harp PBks) HarpC.

Ruebel, James S., sel. Caesar & the Crisis of the Roman Aristocracy: A Civil War Reader. LC 93-21007. (Oklahoma Series in Classical Culture: Vol. 18). (Illus.). 216p. 1994. 18.95 (0-8061-2590-X) U of Okla Pr.

Ruebelman, ed. Snake River Plain - Yellowstone Volcanic Province. (IGC Field Trip Guidebooks Ser.). 1989. 28.00 (0-87590-627-3, T305) Am Geophysical.

Rueben, B. G. & Burstall, M. L. The Chemical Economy: A Guide to the Technology & Economics of the Chemistry Industry. LC 73-85210. 552p. reprint ed. pap. 157.40 (0-317-10562-0, 2019604) Bks Demand.

Ruebens, John & Gary, J. H., eds. Proceedings of the Tenth Oil Shale Symposium. LC 75-17946. (Illus.). 256p. 1977. pap. 3.50 (0-918062-01-2) Colo Sch Mines.

Ruebhausen, Oscar M., ed. see Commission on College Retirement Staff.

Ruebner. Diagnostic Pathology of Liver & Biliary Tract. 2nd ed. 1991. 145.00 (1-56032-060-5) Hemisp Pub.

Ruebner, Ralph. Illinois Criminal Trial Evidence. 2nd ed. 350p. 1993. ring bd. 85.00 (1-56257-713-1) Michie Butterworth.

— Illinois Criminal Trial Evidence. 2nd suppl. ed. 350p. 1993. 42.50 (0-685-74470-1) Butterworth Legal Pubs.

Ruebner, Ralph, ed. see Rinella, Richard A.

Ruebsamen, Traudel. Morphologische, Embryologische und Systematische Untersuchungen an Burmanniaceae und Corsiaceae (Mit Ausblick auf die Orchidaceae-Apostasioideae) (Dissertations Botanicae Ser.: No. 92). (Illus.). 510p. (GER.). 1986. pap. 96.00 (3-443-64004-4) Lubrecht & Cramer.

Ruechardt, Eduard. Light, Visible & Invisible. LC 58-5904. (Ann Arbor Science Library). 201p. reprint ed. pap. 57. 30 (0-317-12982-1, 2055643) Bks Demand.

Rueckert, Carla L. A Channeling Handbook. 118p. 1987. pap. 6.95 (0-945007-07-8) L-L Resrch.

Rueckert, Carla L., jt. auth. see Elkins, Don.

Rueckert, George L. Global Double Zero: The INF Treaty from Its Origins to Implementation. LC 92-30019. (Contributions in Military Studies: No. 135). 248p. 1993. text ed. 52.95 (0-313-28695-7, RGB/, Greenwood Pr) Greenwood.

Rueckert, William H. Encounters with Kenneth Burke. LC 93-15560. 256p. 1994. 32.50 (0-252-02054-5); pap. 15.95 (0-252-06350-3) U of Ill Pr.

— Gleaner Wescott. (Twayne's United States Authors Ser.). 1965. pap. 13.95 (0-8084-0146-7, T87) NCUP.

— Glenway Wescott. Bowman, Sylvia E., ed. LC 65-18906. (Twayne's United States Authors Ser.). 172p. (C). 1965. lib. bdg. 17.95 (0-8290-1709-7) Irvington.

— Kenneth Burke & the Drama of Human Relations. rev. ed. 310p. 1981. pap. 12.00 (0-520-04417-7) U CA Pr.

Rueckert, William H., ed. Critical Responses to Kenneth Burke, 1924-1966. LC 71-75973. 541p. reprint ed. pap. 154.20 (0-317-29493-8, 2055908) Bks Demand.

Rueckl, Gotthard, jt. auth. see Kunze, Horst.

Rued, Tim. Fiddling in Sonoma County. McCurry, Tom, ed. (Illus.). 32p. (Orig.). 1989. pap. write for info. (0-318-66628-6) Cult Arts Council Sonoma Cty.

Rueda, Enrique T. & Schwartz, Michael. Gays, AIDS & You. LC 87-24527. (Illus.). 118p. 1987. 7.95 (0-8159-5624-X) Devin.

Ruede, Howard. Sod-House Days: Letters from a Kansas Homesteader 1877-78. Ise, J., ed. LC 66-17858. 248p. reprint ed. 53.00 (0-8154-0200-7) Cooper Sq.

Ruede, Ulrich. Mathematical & Computational Techniques for Multilevel Adaptive Methods. (Frontiers in Applied Mathematics Ser.: No. 13). xii, 140p. 1993. pap. 23.00 (0-89871-320-X) Soc Indus-Appl Math.

Ruedenberg, Werner. Chinesisch-Deutsches Woerterbuch. 3rd ed. 821p. (CHI & GER.). (C). 1963. 173.50 (3-11-000020-2) De Gruyter.

Ruedi, T., et al. Surgical Approaches for Internal Fixation. (Illus.). 180p. 1983. 136.00 (0-387-12809-3) Spr-Verlag.

Ruediger, E., jt. auth. see Strauss, Eduard.

Ruediger, Horst. Kleines Literarisches Lexikon: Small Lexicon of Literature, 4 vols., Set. 4th ed. (GER.). 1972. 150.00 (0-8288-6401-2, M-7504) Fr & Eur.

Ruediger, Horst, ed. Die Gattungen in der vergleichenden Literaturwissenschaft. (Komparatistische Studien: Vol. 4, Beihefte zur Zeitschrift 'Arcadia'). 92p. (C). 1973. 11.20 (3-11-004496-X) De Gruyter.

Ruediger, Horst, et al, eds. Zur Theorie der Vergleichenden Literaturwissenschaft. 87p. (C). 1971. 15.40 (3-11-003622-3) De Gruyter.

Ruedt, Lucy W., tr. see Boehlke, LeRoy & Silldorff, Donald.

Ruedy, Elisabeth & Nirenberg, Sue. Where Do I Put the Decimal Point? How to Conquer Math Anxiety & Let Numbers Work for You. 1992. pap. 9.00 (0-380-71596-1) Avon.

***Ruedy, John.** Islamism & Secularism in North Africa Vol. 1. 1994. text ed. 49.95 (0-312-12198-9) St Martin.

— Land Policy in Colonial Algeria. LC 67-65340. ix, 115p. 1983. reprint ed. lib. bdg. 23.00x (0-89370-765-1) Borgo Pr.

— Modern Algeria: The Origins & Development of a Nation. LC 92-4637. 320p. 1992. 39.95 (0-253-34998-2); pap. 16.95 (0-253-20746-0, MB-746) Ind U Pr.

Ruedy, John, jt. auth. see Marshall, Shane A.

Ruef, Dorothy N. Health Education in Senior High Schools. LC 79-177219. (Columbia University, Teachers College - Contributions to Education Ser.: No. 636). reprint ed. 37.50 (0-404-55636-1) AMS Pr.

***Ruef, Hans.** Sprichwort und Sprache: Am Beispiel des Sprichworts im Schweizerdeutschen. (Studia Linguistica Germanica Ser.: No. 36). x, 303p. (GER.). (C). 1995. lib. bdg. 124.60 (3-11-014494-8) De Gruyter.

Ruef, Kerry. The Private Eye: Looking-Thinking by Analogy - A Guide to Developing the Interdisciplinary Mind. (Illus.). 240p. (Orig.). Date not set. pap. text ed. 18.95 (0-9605434-1-4) Private Eye.

— The Private Eye Loupe (5X) Date not set. 3.95 (0-9605434-2-2) Private Eye.

Ruef, Kerry, et al, eds. The Crystal Set: Poems, Fiction, Memoirs-an Anthology Of Older Voices. (Illus.). 88p. (Orig.). 1980. pap. 3.95 (0-9605434-0-6) Private Eye.

Rueff, Marcel & Jeger, Max. Sets & Boolean Algebra. Howson, A. G., ed. LC 72-189267. (Mathematical Studies: A Series for Teachers & Students: No. 4). 192p. reprint ed. pap. 54.80 (0-317-20064-X, 2023329) Bks Demand.

Ruefle, Mary. The Adamant: Cowinner of the 1988 Iowa Poetry Prize. LC 88-38575. (Iowa Poetry Prize Ser.). 87p. 1989. text ed. 17.95 (0-87745-235-0); pap. 10.95 (0-87745-236-9) U of Iowa Pr.

— Memling's Veil. LC 81-16454. (Alabama Poetry Ser.). 80p. 1982. text ed. 15.95 (0-8173-0036-8); pap. 9.95 (0-8173-0094-5) U of Ala Pr.

Ruefli, Timothy, ed. Ordinal Time Series Analysis: Methodology & Applications in Management Strategy & Policy. 1990. 39.95 (0-685-50458-1, Quorum Bks) Greenwood.

Rueger, J. M. Electronic Distance Measurement. (Illus.). 265p. 1990. pap. 57.00 (0-387-51523-2, 3434) Spr-Verlag.

Ruegg, David S. Buddha-Nature, Mind & the Problem of Gradualism in a Comparative Perspective. 1989. 50.00 (0-7286-0152-4, Pub. by Sch Orient & African Stud UK) S Asia.

Ruegg, David S., et al, eds. Earliest Buddhism & Madhyamaka. (Panels of the VIIth World Sanskrit Conference - Kern Institute, Leiden: August 23-29, 1987 Ser.: Vol. II). 114p. 1990. 40.00 (90-04-09246-3) E J Brill.

Ruegg, Frank & Bianchina, Paul. You Can't Plant Tomatoes in Central Park: The Urban Dropouts Guide to Rural Relocation. LC 90-53281. 303p. 1990. 18.95 (0-88282-060-5); pap. 12.95 (0-88282-107-5) New Horizon NJ.

Ruegg, Johann C. Calcium in Muscle Activation. (Zoophysiology Ser.: Vol. 19). (Illus.). 320p. 1986. 129. 00 (0-387-17117-7) Spr-Verlag.

— Calcium in Muscle Activation. (Zoophysiology Ser.: Vol. 19). (Illus.). 300p. 1988. reprint ed. pap. 69.00 (0-387-18278-0) Spr-Verlag.

— Calcium in Muscle Contraction: Cellular & Molecular Physiology. 2nd ed. LC 92-20353. Orig. Title: Calcium in Muscle Activation. (Illus.). 352p. 1992. 89.00 (0-387-55544-7) Spr-Verlag.

Ruegg, Johann C., ed. Peptides As Probes in Muscle Research. (Illus.). 188p. 1991. 109.00 (0-387-53653-1) Spr-Verlag.

Ruegg, Rosalie. Building Economics in Theory & Practice. 1990. text ed. 62.95 (0-442-26417-8) Chapman & Hall.

Ruehl, Peter. American Downunder. Allen & Unwin, eds. 152p. (Orig.). 1992. pap. text ed. 14.95 (0-04-442320-9, Pub. by Allen Unwin AT) Paul & Co Pubs.

Ruehli, A. E., ed. Circuit Analysis, Simulation & Design. (Advances in CAD for VLSI Ser.: Vol. 3, Part 2). 400p. 1987. 62.50 (0-444-87889-0, North Holland) Elsevier.

— Circuit Analysis, Simulation & Design: General Aspects of Circuit Analysis & Design. 1986. 57.50 (0-444-87893-9, North Holland) Elsevier.

Ruehlman, Virginia J., jt. auth. see Rice, Helen Steiner.

Ruehlmann, Rick, jt. auth. see Ruehlmann, Virginia.

Ruehlmann, Virginia & Ruehlmann, Rick. Making Family Memories: Crafts & Activities. (Illus.). 238p. (Orig.). 1994. pap. 8.99 (0-8010-7770-2) Baker Bk.

Ruehlmann, Virginia, ed. see Rice, Helen S.

Ruehlmann, Virginia J., ed. see Rice, Helen Steiner.

Ruehr, Thomas A., ed. see Hartel, Peter G., et al.

***Ruehrwein, Dick & North, Julie.** Discover Rivers: A Discovery Book. (Illus.). 32p. (Orig.). (J). (gr. 5-7). 1995. pap. 3.75 (0-915992-73-6) Eastern Acorn.

Ruekl, A. Maps of Lunar Hemispheres: Views of the Lunar Globe from Six Cardinal Directions in Space. LC 77-179896. (Astrophysics & Space Science Library: No. 33). (Illus.). 24p. 1972. lib. bdg. 80.00 (90-277-0221-7) Kluwer Ac.

Ruele, Judy. How to Teach Hobby Ceramics. 1989. pap. 9.95 (0-916809-36-6) Scott Pubns MI.

***Ruell, David.** No Stone Unturned: Saving Outdoor Sculpture. 34p. 1994. pap. write for info. (0-9643014-0-7) Inherit NH.

Ruell, Patrick. The Long Kill. 256p. 1989. reprint ed. pap. 3.50 (0-380-70742-X) Avon.

— The Only Game. large type ed. 467p. 1993. 21.95 (0-7505-0451-X, Pub. by Magna Print Bks) Ulverscroft.

— Urn Burial. 224p. 1994. 16.50 (0-7451-8628-9, Black Dagger) Chivers N Amer.

Ruelle, David. Chance & Chaos. (Science Library). (Illus.). 202p. (C). 1993. text ed. 35.00 (0-691-08574-9); pap. 9.95 (0-691-02100-7) Princeton U Pr.

— Chaotic Evolution & Strange Attractors. (Lezioni Lincee Ser.). (Illus.). 120p. 1989. pap. 17.95 (0-521-36830-8) Cambridge U Pr.

— Dynamical Zeta Functions for Piecewise Monotone Maps of the Interval. LC 94-6986. (CRM Monographic Ser.: Vol. 4). 62p. 1994. 38.00 (0-8218-6991-4) Am Math.

— Elements of Differentiable Dynamics & Bifurcation Theory. 187p. 1989. text ed. 49.00 (0-12-601710-7) Acad Pr.

Ruelle, Karen G. Seventy-Five Fun Things to Make & Do by Yourself. LC 93-5091. (Illus.). 80p. (J). (gr. 2-10). 1993. 14.95 (0-8069-0331-7) Sterling.

— Seventy-Five Fun Things to Make & Do by Yourself. (Illus.). 80p. (J). 1995. pap. 6.95 (0-8069-0332-5) Sterling.

***Ruello, Catherine, ed.** Manual: Art in General 1993 & 1994. (Illus.). 96p. (Orig.). 1994. pap. 15.00 (1-883967-02-3) Art in General.

Ruemke, P., ed. Therapy of Advanced Melanoma. (Pigment Cell Ser.: Vol. 10). (Illus.). viii, 230p. 1990. 158.50 (3-8055-5032-4) S Karger.

Ruemmler, John. Smoke on the Water: A Novel of Jamestown & the Powhatans. LC 91-42587. (Illus.). 176p. (YA). (gr. 7 up). 1992. pap. 6.95 (1-55870-239-3) Shoe Tree Pr.

Ruemmler, John D. Rangers of the North. (Illus.). 56p. (YA). (gr. 10-12). 1985. pap. 12.00 (0-915795-22-1, 3000) Iron Crown Ent Inc.

Ruemmler, John D., ed. see Amthor, Terry K.

Ruemmler, John D., jt. auth. see Charlton, S. Coleman.

Ruemmler, John D., ed. see Cremer, Mike, et al.

Ruemmler, John D., ed. see Crowdis, John.

Ruemmler, John D., ed. see Foley, Tod.

Ruemmler, John D., ed. see Gold, Lee.

Ruemmler, John D., ed. see Henley, Daniel & Henley, Margaret.

Ruemmler, John D., ed. see Hosmer-Casey, Kevin.

Ruemmler, John D., ed. see Kane, Thomas.

Ruemmler, John D., ed. see Kane, Tom.

Ruemmler, John D., ed. see Loback, Tom.

Ruemmler, John D., ed. see Palmer, Gorham.

Ruemmler, John D., ed. see Potter, Brian E.

Ruemmler, John D., ed. see Power, Matthew.

Ruemmler, John D., ed. see Taylor, Tim.

Ruemmler, John D., ed. see Taylor, Timothy.

Ruemmler, John D., ed. see Wajenburg, Earl.

Ruemmler, John D., et al. Mirkwood. Kubasch, Heike, ed. (Middle Earth Ser.). (Illus.). 128p. (Orig.). (C). 1988. pap. 15.00 (1-55806-018-9, 4010) Iron Crown Ent Inc.

Ruempol, Alma. Pre-Industrial Utensils, 1150-1800. (Illus.). 304p. 1993. 75.00 (90-6707-252-4) U of Wash Pr.

***Ruepke, Joerg.** Kalender & Oeffentlichkeit: Die Geschichte der Repraesentation & Religioesen Qualifikation von Zeit in Rom. (Religionsgeschichtliche Versuche & Vorarbeiten: Bd 40). 740p. (GER.). (C). 1995. lib. bdg. 260.00 (3-11-014514-6) De Gruyter.

***Ruepp, Krista.** Midnight Rider. James, J. Alison, tr. LC 95-12321. (Illus.). (J). 1995. write for info. (1-55858-494-3); lib. bdg. write for info. (1-55858-495-1) North-South Bks NYC.

Rueppel, R. A. Analysis & Design of Stream Ciphers. (Communications & Control Engineering Ser.). (Illus.). 260p. 1986. 79.00 (0-387-16870-2) Spr-Verlag.

Rueppel, R. A., ed. Advances in Cryptology - EUROCRYPT '92: Workshop on the Theory & Application of Cryptographic Techniques, Balatonfured, Hungary, May 24-28, 1992 Proceedings. LC 92-46271. (Lecture Notes in Computer Science Ser.: Vol. 658). 1993. 70.00 (0-387-56413-6) Spr-Verlag.

Rueppell, H. & Rueppell, Marlies. Intelligenzfoerderung - Moeglichkeiten und Grenzen. Schmitz-Scherzer, R., ed. (Psychologische Praxis Ser.: Band 49). (Illus.). 105p. 1976. 17.75 (3-8055-2303-3) S Karger.

Rueppell, Marlies, jt. auth. see Rueppell, H.

***Ruer, Dalton.** Developing ObjectView Applications. (Illus.). 800p. (Orig.). 1995. pap. text ed. 45.00 (0-672-30645-X) Sams.

Ruers, T. J., jt. ed. see Jakimowicz, J. J.

Rues, D., jt. ed. see Oswatitsch, K.

Ruesch, H., et al. Creep & Shrinkage: Their Effect on the Behavior of Concrete Structures. (Illus.). 284p. 1983. 124.00 (0-387-90669-X) Spr-Verlag.

Ruesch, Hans. Naked Empress: Or the Great Medical Fraud. 3rd rev. ed. (Illus.). 202p. 1982. pap. text ed. 10. 00 (3-905280-02-7, Pub. by Civis Switzerland) CIVIS-Civitas.

— Slaughter of the Innocent. 446p. 1992. reprint ed. pap. 4.95 (0-9610016-0-7) CIVIS-Civitas.

Ruesch, Jurgen. Semiotic Approaches to Human Relations. 1972. 122.70 (90-279-2299-3) Mouton.

Ruesch, Jurgen & Bateson, Gregory. Communication: The Social Matrix of Psychiatry. 1987. 25.00 (0-393-02377-X) Norton.

Ruesch, Jurgen & Kees, Weldon. Nonverbal Communication: Notes on the Visual Perception of Human Relations. 1956. pap. 13.00 (0-520-02162-2) U CA Pr.

Rueschemeyer, Dietrich. Lawyers & Their Society: A Comparative Study of the Legal Profession in Germany & the United States. LC 72-93953. 264p. reprint ed. pap. 76.40 (0-7837-2327-X, 2057415) Bks Demand.

— Power & the Division of Labour. LC 85-51798. viii, 260p. 1986. 35.00 (0-8047-1324-3); pap. 13.95 (0-8047-1325-1) Stanford U Pr.

Rueschemeyer, Dietrich, jt. ed. see Putterman, Louis.

Rueschemeyer, Dietrich, et al. Capitalist Development & Democracy. (Illus.). 385p. 1992. lib. bdg. 45.00 (0-226-73142-1); pap. text ed. 19.95 (0-226-73144-8) U Ch Pr.

Rueschemeyer, Marilyn. Professional Work & Marriage: An East-West Comparison. LC 80-39959. 197p. 1986. pap. 11.95 (0-312-64783-2) St Martin.

Rueschemeyer, Marilyn, ed. Women in the Politics of Post-Communist Eastern Europe. 272p. 1994. text ed. 49.95 (1-56324-168-4); pap. text ed. 19.95 (1-56324-169-2) M E Sharpe.

Rueschemeyer, Marilyn & Lemke, Christiane, eds. The Quality of Life in the German Democratic Republic: Changes & Developments in a State Socialist Society. LC 88-4089. 256p. 1990. 62.95 (0-87332-484-6) M E Sharpe.

Rueschhoff, Norlin G. International Accounting & Financial Reporting. LC 76-12871. (Special Studies). 188p. 1976. text ed. 55.00 (0-275-90250-1, C0250, Praeger Pubs) Greenwood.

Rueschoff, Phil H. & Swartz, M. Evelyn. Teaching Art in the Elementary School: Enhancing Visual Perception. LC 78-75641. (Illus.). 345p. reprint ed. pap. 98.40 (0-317-10362-8, 2055518) Bks Demand.

Ruesink, Lou E., ed. see Haney, Robert L.

Ruete, Emily. Memoirs of an Arabian Princess from Zanzibar. LC 89-9064. (Illus.). 450p. (Orig.). 1989. 28.95 (1-55876-011-3); pap. 12.95 (1-55876-007-5) Wiener Pubs Inc.

Ruete, Emily, jt. auth. see Salme, Sayyida.

Rueter, Alvin. The Freedom to Be Wrong. 1985. 6.55 (0-89536-749-1, 5855) CSS OH.

***Rueter, Ted.** The Newt Gingrich Quiz Book. 128p. 1995. pap. 8.95 (0-8362-0506-5) Andrews & McMeel.

— The Rush Limbaugh Quiz Book. (Illus.). 128p. 1995. pap. 8.95 (0-8362-8099-7) Andrews & McMeel.

***Rueter, Theodore, ed.** The Politics of Race: African Americans & the Political System. 400p. 1995. text ed. 59.95 (1-56324-564-7) M E Sharpe.

— The Politics of Race: African Americans & the Political System. 400p. 1995. pap. 24.95 (1-56324-565-5) M E Sharpe.

— The United States in the World Political Economy. LC 93-1129. 1993. pap. text ed. write for info. (0-07-054259-7) McGraw.

Rueter, Theodore, jt. auth. see Bitzer, Lloyd.

Ruetersworden, Udo. Dominium Terrae: Studien Zur Genese Einer Alttestamentlichen Vorstellung. (Beiheft zur Zeitschrift fuer die Alttestamentliche Wissenschaft Ser.: No. 215). x, 205p. 1993. lib. bdg. 95.40 (3-11-013948-0) De Gruyter.

Ruether, Rosemary. Liberation Theology: Human Hope Confronts Christian History & American Power. LC 72-92263. 202p. reprint ed. 57.60 (0-8357-9487-3, 2015212) Bks Demand.

Ruether, Rosemary R. Disputed Questions: On Being a Christian. 142p. 1989. pap. 13.95 (0-88344-549-2) Orbis Bks.

— Gaia & God: An Ecofeminist Theology of Earth Healing. LC 91-58911. 1992. 22.00 (0-06-067022-3) Harper SF.

— Gaia & God: An Ecofeminist Theology of Earth Healing. LC 91-58911. (Illus.). 320p. 1994. reprint ed. pap. 13.00 (0-06-066967-5) Harper SF.

— In Our Own Voices: Four Centuries of American Women's Religious Writing. 1995. 30.00 (0-06-066843-1) Harper SF.

— Mary-the Feminine Face of the Church. LC 77-7652. 106p. 1977. pap. 12.99 (0-664-24759-8, Westminster) Westminster John Knox.

R

An Asterisk (*) at the beginning of an entry indicates that the title is appearing in BIP for the first time.

— New Woman, New Earth: Sexist Ideologies & Human Liberation. 256p. (C). 1995. pap. 14.00 (0-8070-6503-X) Beacon Pr.

— Sexism & God-Talk: Toward a Feminist Theology with a New Introduction. LC 92-33119. 320p. 1993. pap. 14.00 (0-8070-1205-X) Beacon Pr.

— Womanguides: Readings Toward a Feminist Theology. LC 84-14508. 286p. 1986. pap. 15.00 (0-8070-1203-3, BP 726) Beacon Pr.

— Women-Church: Theology & Practice. 1988. pap. 11.95 (0-06-066835-0) Harper SF.

Ruether, Rosemary R., ed. see Bianchi, Eugene C.

Ruether, Rosemary R., jt. auth. see Hall, Douglas J.

Ruether, Rosemary R., jt. auth. see Merton, Thomas.

Ruette, F., ed. Quantum Chemistry Approaches to Chemisorption & Heterogeneous Catalysis. (C). 1992. lib. bdg. 122.00 (0-7923-1543-X) Kluwer Ac.

Ruetten. Comprehending Academic Lectures. 1986. pap. 20.95 (0-8384-3359-6); audio 75.00 (0-8384-3360-X) Heinle & Heinle.

Ruetten, Charles W. Keyboarding: It's Fun to Use a Keyboard on the Typewriter or Computer. 131p. 1992. pap. text ed. write for info. (1-881842-02-9) Sundial Pub.

— Type with the Left Or Right Hand on the Typewriter Or Computer Keyboard. (Illus.). 95p. (Orig.). (YA). Date not set. pap. text ed. 10.95 (1-881842-03-7) Sundial Pub.

Ruetten, Mary K., jt. auth. see Smalley, Regina L.

Ruettgers, H., ed. Immunotherapy of Vaginal Infections. (Journal: Gynaekologische Rundschau: Vol. 24, Suppl. 3, 1984). (Illus.). iv, 92p. 1985. pap. 25.75 (3-8055-4072-8) S Karger.

— Trichomoniasis. (Journal: Gynaekologische Rundschau: Vol. 22, Suppl. 2). (Illus.). viii, 92p. 1983. pap. 22.50 (3-8055-3646-1) S Karger.

— Trichomoniasis. (Journal: Gynaekologische Rundschau: Vol. 23, Suppl. 2, 1983). (Illus.). iv, 92p. 1983. pap. 22.50 (3-8055-3751-4) S Karger.

Ruettiger, Rudy & Celizic, Michael. Rudy's Rules: Game Plans for Life from the Real Rudy! (Illus.). 180p. 1994. 19.95 (1-56796-056-1) WRS Group.

Ruettner, J. R., ed. see International Society of Geographical Pathology Staff.

Ruettner, J. R., et al, eds. Inflammatory Vascular Diseases-Endo-Myocardial Fibrosis-Pulmonary Hypertension: Proceedings - Conference of the International Society of Geographical Pathology, 12th, Zurich, September 1975. (Pathologia et Microbiologica Ser.: Vol. 43, No. 1-2). (Illus.). 180p. 1976. 62.50 (3-8055-2311-4) S Karger.

Ruetzler, Klaus & Macintyre, Ian G., eds. The Atlantic Barrier Reef Ecosystem at Carrie Bow Cay, Belize Vol. I: Structure & Communities. LC 81-607039. (Smithsonian Contributions to the Marine Sciences Ser.). (Illus.). 554p. (C). 1982. 27.00 (0-87474-850-X) Smithsonian.

Rueveni, Roni, jt. auth. see Rabeeya, David.

Rueveni, Uri. Applications of Networking in Family & Community: A Special Issue of Journal of Family Therapy, Vol. 6, No. 2. 80p. 1984. pap. 14.95 (0-89885-246-3) Human Sci Pr.

— Networking Families in Crisis: Intervention Strategies with Families & Social Networks. LC 78-8024. 162p. 1979. 32.95 (0-87705-374-X) Human Sci Pr.

Rueveni, Uri, et al, eds. Therapeutic Intervention: Healing Strategies for Human Systems. LC 81-13501. 285p. 1982. 35.95 (0-89885-086-X) Human Sci Pr.

Ruey, M. J. A la Carte Enterprises: Office Manual. 1976. text ed. 12.75 (0-07-054266-X) McGraw.

Ruf, Carolyn. Guinea Pigs. (Illus.). 80p. 1984. pap. 5.95 (0-86622-987-6, PB-113) TFH Pubns.

Ruf, Frederick J. The Creation of Chaos: William James & the Stylistic Making of a Disorderly World. LC 90-44858. (SUNY Series in Rhetoric & Theology). 185p. 1991. 59.50 (0-7914-0701-2); pap. 19.95 (0-7914-0702-0) State U NY Pr.

Ruf, K. B. & Tolis, G., eds. Advances in Neuroendocrine Physiology. (Frontiers of Hormone Research Ser.: Vol. 10). (Illus.). vi, 142p. 1982. 78.50 (3-8055-2949-X) S Karger.

Ruf, Kathleen. Quality Control, Quality Assurance: Manual for Food & Nutrition Services. LC 88-22662. 400p. 1988. 195.00 (0-87189-793-8) Aspen Pub.

Rufe, Laurie, jt. auth. see Kahin, Sharon.

Rufe, Robert. Rock & Roll Flyer. 96p. 1990. pap. text ed. 8.00 (0-9627196-0-9) Aremar Pubns.

Rufenacht, Claude. Fundamentals of Esthetics. (Illus.). 1990. text ed. 148.00 (0-86715-230-3) Quint Pub Co.

***Rufenbarger, Connie, ed.** Just Peachey, Cooking up a Cure. (Illus.). 320p. 1995. 15.00 (0-9646719-0-5) WWABC.

Rufer, Joseph. Composition with Twelve Notes Related Only to One Another. rev. ed. LC 78-9838. (Illus.). 186p. 1979. reprint ed. text ed. 35.00 (0-313-21236-8, RUCT, Greenwood Pr) Greenwood.

Rufey, Celia, jt. auth. see Schoeses, Mary.

Ruff, A. R. Commercial & Industrial Law. (C). 1984. 100.00 (0-685-33729-4, Pub. by Witherby & Co UK) St Mut.

Ruff, A. W. & Bayer, Raymond G., eds. Tribology: Wear Test Selection for Design & Application. LC 93-37460. (Special Technical Publication: Vol. 1199). (Illus.). 185p. 1993. text ed. 46.00 (0-8031-1856-2, 04-011990-27) ASTM.

Ruff, Ann. Amazing Texas Monuments & Museums. LC 83-18726. 104p. (Orig.). 1984. pap. 9.95 (0-88415-564-1, Lone Star Bks) Gulf Pub.

— Backroads of Florida. 176p. 1992. pap. 9.95 (0-88415-008-9) Gulf Pub.

— The Best of Texas Festivals. LC 85-23722. (Illus.). 100p. (Orig.). 1986. pap. 9.95 (0-88415-863-2, Lone Star Bks) Gulf Pub.

— A Guide to Historic Texas Inns & Hotels. 2nd ed. LC 85-6762. (Illus.). 132p. (Orig.). 1985. pap. 9.95 (0-88415-385-1, Lone Star Bks) Gulf Pub.

— Outlaws in Petticoats. 1995. pap. 12.95 (1-55622-315-3) Wordware Pub.

— Texas Flea Markets: A Roadrunner Guide. LC 90-21008. 192p. (Orig.). 1991. pap. 9.95 (0-87833-658-3) Taylor Pub.

— Unsung Heroes of Texas. LC 85-17606. (Illus.). 112p. (Orig.). 1985. pap. 9.95 (0-88415-864-0, Lone Star Bks) Gulf Pub.

Ruff, Ann & Burke, Michael. Traveling Texas Borders. LC 83-11972. (Illus.). 120p. (Orig.). 1983. pap. 9.95 (0-88415-074-7, Lone Star Bks) Gulf Pub.

Ruff, Ann, et al. Texas Bed & Breakfast. 3rd ed. LC 93-10528. (Texas Monthly Guidebooks Ser.). 208p. 1993. 14.95 (0-87719-239-1) Gulf Pub.

***Ruff, Anne, ed.** Principles of Law for Managers. LC 94-37890. (Series in the Principles of Management). 304p. 1995. pap. 29.95x (0-415-07378-2, B4298) Routledge.

Ruff, Christopher. Aging & Osteoporosis in Native Americans from Pecos Pueblo, New Mexico: Behavioral & Biomechanical Effects. LC 91-2397. (Evolution of North American Indians Ser.: Vol. 20). 435p. 1991. 30.00 (0-8240-2515-6) Garland.

Ruff, Christopher, tr. see Caffarra, Carlo.

Ruff, Donna, illus. The Old Man & His Birds. LC 93-26705. 24p. (J). 1994. 15.00 (0-688-04603-7); lib. bdg. 14.93 (0-688-04604-5) Greenwillow.

Ruff, Doris, ed. see Baudelaire, Charles P.

Ruff, Ferenc & Csizmadia, I. G. Organic Reactions: Equilibria, Kinetics, & Mechanism. LC 94-6367. (Studies in Organic Chemistry: Vol. 50). 1994. 217.25 (0-444-88174-3) Elsevier.

Ruff, Ivan. Blood Country. 1989. 18.95 (0-8027-1066-2) Walker & Co.

— The Orphan Soldier. 256p. 1990. 19.95 (0-8027-1123-5) Walker & Co.

Ruff, Jack. An Analysis of Mortgage Lending Patterns in Omaha. 84p. (Orig.). 1983. pap. 4.50 (1-55719-095-X) U NE CPAR.

— Community Development for the City of Norfolk, Nebraska. 28p. (Orig.). 1980. pap. 2.50 (1-55719-033-X) U NE CPAR.

Ruff, Jack, et al. A Housing Allocation Formula for Nebraska Cities of the First Class: City of Bellevue, 1978. 128p. (Orig.). 1978. pap. 9.00 (1-55719-098-4) U NE CPAR.

Ruff, Jack. Residential Investment & Insurance Practices. 54p. (Orig.). 1984. pap. 4.00 (1-55719-030-5) U NE CPAR.

— Rural Development Strategies for Southcentral Nebraska. 176p. (Orig.). 1982. pap. 11.50 (1-55719-035-6) U NE CPAR.

Ruff, Jack & Hein, Peggy. Builders & Lenders Attitudes: The Nebraska Mortage Finance Fund Use of FHA 235 Housing. 32p. 1979. pap. 2.50 (1-55719-097-6) U NE CPAR.

Ruff, Jack & Krager, Anne. Cooperative Purchasing for Local Government. 44p. (Orig.). 1984. pap. 3.00 (1-55719-085-2) U NE CPAR.

Ruff, Jack & Piper, R. K. Potentials for Ridesharing in Southwest Iowa. 66p. (Orig.). 1982. pap. 4.50 (1-55719-036-4) U NE CPAR.

Ruff, Jack, jt. auth. see Coffin, Peggy.

Ruff, Jack, jt. auth. see Piper, R. K.

Ruff, Jack J. Nebraska Program for Technology Transfer: An Operational Framework. 15p. (Orig.). 1980. pap. 1.50 (1-55719-034-8) U NE CPAR.

Ruff, Jack J., jt. auth. see Hanlon, Gene.

Ruff, Larry J. & Kanamori, Hiroo. Subduction Zones, Pt. II. 376p. 1989. 34.50 (0-8176-2272-1) Birkhauser.

Ruff, Larry J. & Kanamori, Hiroo. Subduction Zones, Pt. I. 352p. 1989. 34.50 (0-8176-1928-3) Birkhauser.

Ruff, Laura B. & Weitzer, Mary K. Understanding & Using MS-DOS - PC-DOS: The First Steps. 2nd ed. Leyh, ed. 118p. (C). 1989. pap. text ed. 16.75 (0-314-50330-7) West Pub.

— Understanding & Using MS-PC-DOS. (Illus.). 85p. (Orig.). (C). 1985. pap. text ed. 11.00 (0-314-96205-0) West Pub.

— Understanding & Using PFS: File-Report. (Illus.). 253p. (Orig.). (C). 1986. pap. text ed. 26.75 (0-314-96215-8) West Pub.

Ruff, Laura B., jt. auth. see Weitzer, Mary K.

Ruff, Matt. Fool on the Hill. 448p. 1989. mass mkt. 5.99 (0-446-35772-3) Warner Bks.

Ruff, Nancy, jt. ed. see Smithson, Isaiah.

Ruff, Richard, jt. auth. see Rackam, Neil.

Ruff, Robert. Aborting Planned Parenthood. 189p. (C). reprint ed. pap. 9.95 (0-919225-32-2) Life Cycle Bks.

Ruff, Thomas P. A Guide for Teaching Social Studies in Grades K-8: Information, Ideas & Resources for Classroom Teachers. LC 93-19503. 232p. 1993. pap. text ed. 35.95 (0-205-14606-6, Longwood Div) Allyn.

Ruff, Willie. A Call to Assembly: The Autobiography of a Musical Storyteller. LC 90-50514. (Illus.). 384p. 1991. 24.95 (0-670-83800-4) Viking Penguin.

Ruffa, Anthony. Darwinism & Determinism: The Role of Direction in Evolution. 1983. 25.95 (0-8283-1732-1); pap. 11.95 (0-8283-1877-8) Branden Pub Co.

Ruffault, Charlotte. Animals Underground. Matthews, Sarah, tr. LC 87-34616. (Young Discovery Library). (Illus.). 38p. (J). (gr. k-5). 1988. 5.95 (0-944589-03-0, 030) Young Discovery Lib.

Ruffcorn, Kevin E. Bible Readings for Growing Christians. LC 84-18424. 112p. (Orig.). 1984. pap. 5.99 (0-8066-2131-1, 10-0685, Augsburg) Augsburg Fortress.

— God's Word of Encouragement: Devotions for Impossible Days. LC 89-399. 112p. (Orig.). 1989. pap. 8.99 (0-8066-2420-5, 9-2420) Augsburg Fortress.

— Rural Evangelism: Catching the Vision. LC 93-36830. 1994. 10.99 (0-8066-2642-9, 9-2642) Augsburg Fortress.

Ruffel, Denis. Professional Caterer, 4 vol. 1990. text ed. 229.95 (0-442-30312-2) Van Nos Reinhold.

— Professional Caterer Series, Vol. 1. 1990. text ed. 59.95 (0-442-00139-8) Van Nos Reinhold.

— Professional Caterer Series, Vol. 2. 1990. text ed. 59.95 (0-442-00140-1) Van Nos Reinhold.

— Professional Caterer Series, Vol. 3. 1990. text ed. 59.95 (0-442-00142-8) Van Nos Reinhold.

— Professional Caterer Series, Vol. 4. 1990. text ed. 59.95 (0-442-00143-6) Van Nos Reinhold.

Ruffer, J. The Big Shots. enl. rev. ed. (Illus.). 160p. 1989. 30.00 (0-940143-79-8) Safari Pr.

Ruffer, Jonathan G. Big Shots: Edwardian Shooting Parties. 1992. 24.95 (1-870948-38-6, Pub. by Quiller Pr UK) St Mut.

Ruffer, Marc A. Studies in the Paleopathology of Egypt. Moodie, Roy Lee, ed. LC 75-23758. reprint ed. 135.00 (0-404-13364-9) AMS Pr.

Ruffhead, Owen. The Life of Alexander Pope. (Anglistica & Americana Ser.: No. 5). 586p. 1968. 89.70 (0-317-05061-3, 05101959, Pub. by Georg Olms GW) Lubrecht & Cramer.

Ruffie. Le Sexe & La Moret. (C). 1991. lib. bdg. 34.95 (0-226-73145-6) U Ch Pr.

Ruffier. Toxic Substances in Municipal Wastewaters. 1991. 59.95 (0-87371-533-0, RA952) Lewis Pubs.

***Ruffin, C. Bernard.** Last Words: A Dictionary of Deathbed Quotations. LC 95-3196. 304p. 1995. lib. bdg. 39.95 (0-7864-0043-9) McFarland & Co.

— The Life of Brother Andre: The Miracle Worker of St. Joseph. LC 88-61112. 228p. 1988. pap. 6.95 (0-87973-492-2, 492) Our Sunday Visitor.

— Padre Pio: The True Story. 2nd ed. LC 81-81525. (Illus.). 325p. (Orig.). 1991. pap. 10.95 (0-87973-673-9, 673) Our Sunday Visitor.

— The Twelve: The Lives of the Apostles After Calvary. LC 83-63168. 194p. (Orig.). 1984. pap. 7.95 (0-87973-609-7, 609) Our Sunday Visitor.

Ruffin, E. Anticipations of the Future. LC 70-38021. (Black Heritage Library Collection). 1977. reprint ed. 32.95 (0-8369-8988-0) Ayer.

Ruffin, Edmund. Agriculture, Geology, & Society in Antebellum South Carolina: The Private Diary of Edmund Ruffin, 1843. Mathew, William M., ed. LC 90-24718. (Illus.). 424p. 1992. 50.00 (0-8203-1324-6) U of Ga Pr.

— Diary of Edmund Ruffin: A Dream Shattered: June, 1863-June, 1865. Scarborough, William K., ed. LC 75-165069. (Library of Southern Civilization). 896p. 1989. text ed. 70.00 (0-8071-1418-9) La State U Pr.

— Diary of Edmund Ruffin: The Years of Hope: April, 1861-June, 1863. LC 75-165069. (Library of Southern Civilization). xxxvi, 706p. 1976. text ed. 60.00 (0-8071-0183-4) La State U Pr.

— Diary of Edmund Ruffin: Toward Independence: October, 1856-April, 1861. Scarborough, William K., ed. LC 75-165069. (Library of Southern Civilization). (Illus.). xlviii, 664p. 1972. text ed. 60.00 (0-8071-0948-7) La State U Pr.

— Essay on Calcareous Manures. Sitterson, J. Carlyle, ed. LC 61-6352. (John Harvard Library). (Illus.). 234p. 1961. 24.00 (0-674-26201-8) HUP.

Ruffin, Paul. The Man Who Would Be God. LC 93-5225. (Southwest Life & Letters Ser.). 168p. (Orig.). 1993. 22.50 (0-87074-354-6); pap. 10.95 (0-87074-363-5) SMU Press.

Ruffin, Paul, jt. ed. see Garrett, George.

Ruffin, Roy J. Intermediate Microeconomics. 2nd ed. (C). 1991. text ed. 72.00 (0-673-46321-4) HarpCollege.

Ruffin, Roy J. & Gregory, Paul R. Macroeconomics. (C). 1993. student ed 21.00 (0-673-46588-8) HarpCollege.

— Microeconomics. (C). 1993. student ed 21.00 (0-673-46585-3) HarpCollege.

— Principles of Economics. 5th ed. LC 92-23589. (C). 1992. text ed. 45.75 (0-673-46590-X) HarpCollege.

— Principles of Economics. 5th ed. (C). 1993. student ed 22.50 (0-673-46591-8) HarpCollege.

— Principles of Economics. 5th ed. (C). 1994. disk 108.50 (0-673-53880-X) HarpCollege.

— Principles of Economics Plus TIME Package. 4th ed. (C). 1989. text ed. 39.00 (0-673-46295-1) HarpCollege.

— Principles of Macroeconomics. 5th ed. LC 92-23591. (C). 1992. 34.25 (0-673-46587-X) HarpCollege.

— Principles of Macroeconomics Plus TIME Package. 4th ed. (C). 1989. pap. text ed. 27.25 (0-673-46296-X) HarpCollege.

— Principles of Microeconomics. 5th ed. LC 92-23590. (C). 1992. 34.25 (0-673-46584-5) HarpCollege.

— Principles of Microeconomics Plus TIME Package. 4th ed. (C). 1989. pap. text ed. 28.00 (0-673-46297-8) HarpCollege.

Ruffin, Roy J., jt. auth. see Gregory, Paul R.

Ruffin, Thomas. Papers of Thomas Ruffin, 4 Vols, 1. Hamilton, J. G., ed. LC 74-174788. reprint ed. write for info. (0-404-04631-2) AMS Pr.

— Papers of Thomas Ruffin, 4 Vols, 2. Hamilton, J. G., ed. LC 74-174788. reprint ed. write for info. (0-404-04632-0) AMS Pr.

— Papers of Thomas Ruffin, 4 Vols, 3. Hamilton, J. G., ed. LC 74-174788. reprint ed. write for info. (0-404-04633-9) AMS Pr.

— Papers of Thomas Ruffin, 4 Vols, 4. Hamilton, J. G., ed. LC 74-174788. reprint ed. write for info. (0-404-04634-7) AMS Pr.

— Papers of Thomas Ruffin, 4 Vols, Set. Hamilton, J. G., ed. LC 74-174788. reprint ed. 225.00 (0-404-04630-4) AMS Pr.

Ruffinatto, Aldo, ed. see Berces, Gonzalo D.

Ruffinelli, Jorge, ed. see Azuela, Mariano.

Ruffing, Janet. Uncovering Stories of Faith: Spiritual Direction & Narrative. 1989. pap. 9.95 (0-8091-3068-8) Paulist Pr.

Ruffini, J. Advances in Medical Social Science, Vol. 1. 405p. 1983. text ed. 110.00 (0-677-05810-1) Gordon & Breach.

Ruffini, John. Doctor Antonio: A Tale. LC 79-8193. reprint ed. 44.50 (0-404-62109-0) AMS Pr.

Ruffini, Julio L. Advances in Medical Social Science, Vol. 2. 400p. 1984. text ed. 122.00 (0-677-06490-X) Gordon & Breach.

***Ruffini, R. & Keiser, M.** General Relativity: Proceedings of the 7th Marcel Grossmann Meeting, 2 Vols. 1600p. 1995. text ed. 314.00 (981-02-2064-2) World Scientific Pub.

Ruffini, Remo. Astrophysics from Spacelab. Bernacca, Pier L., ed. (Astrophysics & Space Science Library: No. 81). 720p. 1980. lib. bdg. 103.00 (90-277-1064-3) Kluwer Ac.

Ruffini, Remo, ed. General Relativity: Proceedings of the Second Marcel Grossman Meeting, 1979, 2 vols., Set. 1296p. 1982. 225.75 (0-444-86357-5, I-196-82, North Holland) Elsevier.

— Proceedings of the Marcel Grossman Meeting on General Relativity, 4th, 17-21 June, 1985, Rome, Italy, 2 Pts. 1900p. 1987. 225.75 (0-444-87030-X, North Holland) Elsevier.

Ruffini, Remo & Ciufolini, I. Relativistic Gravitational Experiments in Space: First William Fairbank Meeting. (Advanced Series in Astrophysics & Cosmology). 500p. 1993. text ed. 121.00 (981-02-1263-1) World Scientific Pub.

Ruffini, Remo, jt. ed. see Gursky, H.

Ruffini, Remo, jt. auth. see Lizhi, Fang.

Ruffini, Remo, ed. see Lizhi, Fang.

Ruffini, Remo, jt. ed. see Lizhi, Fang.

Ruffini, Remo, ed. see Melchiorri, F.

Ruffins, Reynold, illus. Misoso: Once Upon a Time Tales from Africa. LC 92-43288. 96p. (J). (gr. k-5). 1994. 18.00 (0-679-83430-3, Apple Soup Bks); lib. bdg. 18.99 (0-679-93430-8, Apple Soup Bks) Knopf Bks Yng Read.

Ruffle. Glimpses of Ancient Egypt: Studies in Honour of H. W. Fairman. 1979. 69.95 (0-85668-147-4, Pub. by Aris & Phillips UK) David Brown.

Rufflo, Michael, et al. Analyzing Performance Problems: Macintosh Version Software. 1992. 89.50 (1-56103-321-9) Lake Pub Co.

— Analyzing Performance Problems - PC Version, 3.5 Inch Software. 1988. 89.50 (1-56103-317-0) Lake Pub Co.

Ruffman, Paul. Heaven at Last. 170p. 1992. 17.95 (0-9628924-0-8) Dev Pub.

Ruffner, Budge. All Hell Needs Is Water. (Illus.). 96p. reprint ed. pap. 27.40 (0-8357-5312-3, 2025555) Bks Demand.

Ruffner, Budge, jt. auth. see Weiner, Melissa R.

***Ruffner, Emma T.** Poems of Emma Timmons-Woosley Ruffner. Ingram, Julia L., ed. 352p. 1994. per. 10.00 (0-9641009-0-8) Ingram Pr.

Ruffner, Ginny, et al. Glass: Material in the Service of Meaning. (Illus.). 72p. 1992. pap. 17.50 (0-295-97161-4) U of Wash Pr.

***Ruffner, Henry.** Judith Bensaddi: A Tale & Seclusaval, or, The Sequel to the Tale of Judith Bensaddi. fac. ed. Pemberton, J. Michael, ed. LC 83-9858. (Library of Southern Civilization). 236p. 1984. reprint ed. pap. 67.30 (0-7837-7924-0, 2047680) Bks Demand.

Ruffner, James A. & Bair, Frank E., eds. Weather Almanac. 6th ed. 800p. 1991. 120.00 (0-8103-2843-7) Gale.

Ruffner, James A., jt. ed. see Mossman, Jennifer.

Ruffner, Kevin C. Forty-Fourth Virginia Infantry. (Illus.). 121p. 1987. 19.95 (0-930919-47-5) H E Howard.

Ruffner, M., jt. auth. see Burgoon, M.

Ruffner, Sara S. A Liberal Education. LC 90-14059. 256p. (Orig.). 1991. pap. 10.95 (0-931832-74-8) Fithian Pr.

Ruffner, Trenna E. Personal Lace: A Collection of Bobbin Lace Patterns. 32p. 1993. student ed 10.00 (0-9636953-0-4) Alembic Arts.

Ruffo, Sandro. Enciclopedia Monografica de Ciencias Naturales, 5 vols., Set. 2500p. (SPA.). 1974. 250.00 (0-8288-6035-1, S50568) Fr & Eur.

Ruffo, Titta. La Mia Parabola, Memorie. Farkas, Andrew, ed. LC 76-29966. (Opera Biographies Ser.). (Illus.). (ITA.). 1977. reprint ed. lib. bdg. 39.95 (0-405-09705-0) Ayer.

Ruffolo. Ansiotensin in Receptors. 1994. 159.95 (0-8493-8380-3) CRC Pr.

Ruffolo, Lisa. Holidays. 1987. 7.95 (0-89823-086-1) New Rivers Pr.

Ruffolo, R. R., ed. Alpha-Adrenoceptors: Molecular Biology, Biochemistry & Pharmacology. (Progress in Basic & Clinical Pharmacology Ser.: Vol. 8). (Illus.). xiv, 226p. 1991. 189.00 (3-8055-5390-0) S Karger.

— The Alpha-1 Adrenergic Receptors. LC 87-17006. (Receptors Ser.). 568p. 1987. 99.50 (0-89603-110-1) Humana.

— Beta-Adrenoceptors: Molecular Biology, Biochemistry & Pharmacology. (Progress in Basic & Clinical Pharmacology Ser.: Vol. 7). (Illus.). x, 240p. 1991. 196.00 (3-8055-5366-8) S Karger.

Ruffolo, R. R., Jr., ed. Progress in Basic & Clinical Pharmacology, Set, Vols. 7 & 8. (Illus.). xxvi, 466p. 1991. Set. 346.50 (3-8055-5502-4) S Karger.

***Ruffolo, Robert R., Jr., ed.** Angiotensin II Receptors: Medicinal Chemistry, Vol. II. 256p. 1994. 99.50 (0-8493-8545-8) CRC Pr.

— Endothelin Receptors From the Gene to the Human: From the Gene to the Brain. LC 94-40203. (Pharmacology & Toxicology: Basic & Clinical Aspects Ser.). 288p. 1995. 169.95 (0-8493-5938-4, 5938) CRC Pr.

***Ruffolo, Robert R., Jr. & Hollinger, Mannfred A., eds.** Inflammation: Mediators & Pathways. LC 94-44223. 240p. 1995. 99.95 (*0-8493-9473-2*, 9473) CRC Pr.

Rufi, John. The Small High School. LC 70-177214. (Columbia University. Teachers College. Contributions to Education Ser.: No. 236). reprint ed. 37.50 (*0-404-55236-6*) AMS Pr.

Rufkin, Reno, jt. auth. see Ohanian, Hans C.

Rufolo, Anthony M., jt. auth. see Hirsch, Werner Z.

Rufolo, Anthony M., jt. ed. see Hirsch, Werner Z.

Rufus, Anneli. The World Holiday Book: Celebrations for Every Day of the Year. LC 94-557. 400p. 1994. pap. 14.00 (*0-06-250912-8*) Harper SF.

Rufus, Quintus C. The History of Alexander. Yardley, John, tr. (Classics Ser.). 352p. 1984. pap. 9.95 (*0-14-044412-2*, Penguin Classics) Viking Penguin.

Ruga, Barbara A. & Kopka, Daniel D., eds. Michigan Wrongful Discharge & Employment Discrimination Law. rev. ed. LC 90-81125. 540p. 1990. ring bd. 110.00 (*0-685-22730-8*, 90-016) U MI Law CLE.

— Michigan Wrongful Discharge & Employment Discrimination Law. rev. suppl. ed. LC 90-81125. 540p. 1993. 40.00 (*0-685-44340-X*, 93-014) U MI Law CLE.

Rugaas, Bendik, ed. Library Information Science Education for the 21st Century: The Tromso Conference. LC 93-4497. 163p. 1993. 35.00 (*1-55570-148-5*) Neal-Schuman.

Rugaleva, Anelya. Advanced Russian 1. (OSU Foreign Language Publications: No. 37). (Illus.). 171p. (Orig.). (RUS.). (C). 1980. teacher ed, pap. 10.50 (*0-87415-090-6*, 37A); student ed, pap. text ed. 12.50 (*0-87415-089-2*, 37); audio 5.00 (*0-87415-075-2*, 37B) OSU Foreign Lang.

— Advanced Russian 2. (OSU Foreign Language Publications: No. 38). (Illus.). 183p. (Orig.). (RUS.). (C). 1980. teacher ed, pap. 11.00 (*0-87415-092-2*, 38A); student ed, pap. text ed. 11.00 (*0-87415-091-4*) OSU Foreign Lang.

— Advanced Russian 2, 4 cass., Set. (OSU Foreign Language Publications: No. 38). (Orig.). (RUS.). (C). 1980. vhs 100.00 (*0-87415-141-4*, 38B) OSU Foreign Lang.

— Elementary Russian 1. (OSU Foreign Language Publications: No. 33). (Illus.). 98p. (Orig.). (RUS.). (C). 1984. teacher ed, pap. 8.00 (*0-87415-078-7*, 33A); student ed, pap. text ed. 12.50 (*0-87415-077-9*) OSU Foreign Lang.

— Elementary Russian 1, 9 cass., Set. (OSU Foreign Language Publications: No. 33). (Illus.). 213p. (Orig.). (RUS.). (C). 1984. audio 45.00 (*0-87415-079-5*, 33B) OSU Foreign Lang.

— Elementary Russian 2. (OSU Foreign Language Publications: No. 34). (Illus.). 110p. (Orig.). (RUS.). (C). 1984. teacher ed, pap. 9.00 (*0-87415-081-7*, 34A); student ed, pap. text ed. 11.50 (*0-87415-080-9*) OSU Foreign Lang.

— Elementary Russian 2, 10 cass., Set. (OSU Foreign Language Publications: No. 34). (Illus.). 190p. (Orig.). (RUS.). (C). 1984. audio 50.00 (*0-87415-082-5*, 34B) OSU Foreign Lang.

— Intermediate Russian 1. (OSU Foreign Language Publications: No. 35). (Illus.). 115p. (Orig.). (RUS.). (C). 1984. teacher ed, pap. 8.00 (*0-87415-084-1*, 35A); student ed, pap. text ed. 10.00 (*0-87415-083-3*) OSU Foreign Lang.

— Intermediate Russian 1, 3 cass., Set. (OSU Foreign Language Publications: No. 35). (Orig.). (RUS.). (C). 1984. audio 15.00 (*0-87415-085-X*, 35B) OSU Foreign Lang.

— Intermediate Russian 2. (OSU Foreign Language Publications: No. 36). (Illus.). 158p. (Orig.). (RUS.). (C). 1984. teacher ed, pap. 9.00 (*0-87415-087-6*, 36A); student ed, pap. text ed. 8.00 (*0-87415-086-8*) OSU Foreign Lang.

— Intermediate Russian 2, 4 cass., Set. (OSU Foreign Language Publications: No. 36). (Orig.). (RUS.). (C). 1984. audio 20.00 (*0-87415-088-4*, 36B) OSU Foreign Lang.

— Reading Russian 1. (OSU Foreign Language Publications: No. 7). (Illus.). 249p. (Orig.). (RUS.). (C). 1984. teacher ed, pap. 8.00 (*0-87415-001-9*, 7A); student ed, pap. text ed. 14.50 (*0-87415-000-0*) OSU Foreign Lang.

— Reading Russian 3. (Illus.). 208p. (Orig.). (RUS.). (C). 1986. student ed, pap. text ed. 12.50 (*0-87415-109-0*, 46) OSU Foreign Lang.

— Reading Russian 3. (Illus.). 101p. (Orig.). (RUS.). (C). 1986. teacher ed, pap. 7.00 (*0-87415-110-4*, 46A) OSU Foreign Lang.

Rugaleva, Anelya, et al. Reading Russian 2. (OSU Foreign Language Publications: No. 8). (Illus.). 308p. (Orig.). (RUS.). (C). 1984. teacher ed, pap. 5.00 (*0-87415-003-5*, 8A); student ed, pap. text ed. 14.50 (*0-87415-002-7*) OSU Foreign Lang.

Rugama, Leonel, et al. The Earth Is a Satellite of the Moon: La Tierra Es un Satelite de la Luna. Miles, Sara et al, trs. LC 85-62201. (Illus.). 196p. (Orig.). (ENG & SPA.). 1985. 19.95 (*0-915306-54-9*); pap. 9.95 (*0-915306-50-6*) Curbstone.

Ruge, Daniel & Wiltse, Leon L., eds. Spinal Disorders: Diagnosis & Treatment. LC 77-1875. (Illus.). 458p. reprint ed. pap. 130.60 (*0-8357-7655-7*, 2056981) Bks Demand.

Ruge, Ingolf, jt. auth. see Ryssel, Heiner.

Ruge, Sophus. Der Literatur Zur Geschichte der Erdkunde Vom Mittelalter An. 299p. 1979. reprint ed. write for info. (*3-487-06730-7*, Pub. by Georg Olms GW) Lubrecht & Cramer.

Ruge, Valice F., ed. Life along the Hudson: Wood Engravings of Hudson River Subjects from Harper's Weekly, 1859-1903. (Illus.). 240p. 1994. 45.00 (*0-87951-523-6*) Overlook Pr.

***Rugel, Robert P.** Dealing with the Problem of Low Self-Esteem: Common Characteristics & Treatment in Individual, Marital-Family & Group Psychotherapy. LC 94-33872. 228p. (C). 1994. text ed. 45.95x (*0-398-05936-5*) C C Thomas.

— Dealing with the Problem of Low Self-Esteem: Common Characteristics & Treatment in Individual, Marital-Family & Group Psychotherapy. LC 94-33872. (Illus.). 228p. (C). 1995. pap. 29.95x (*0-398-05951-9*) C C Thomas.

Rugenstein, Ed, ed. see Esarde, Edward E.

Rugenstein, Julie, ed. see King, Kathleen W.

Rugg, Cheryl A., jt. auth. see Jaynes, Judith H.

Rugg, Donald D. New Strategies for Mutual Fund Investing. 300p. 1988. text ed. 32.50 (*1-55623-045-1*) Irwin Prof Pubng.

Rugg, E. R. The Descendants of John Rugg. 586p. 1989. reprint ed. lib. bdg. 96.00 (*0-8328-1034-7*); reprint ed. pap. 88.00 (*0-8328-1035-5*) Higginson Bk Co.

— Rugg: The Descendents of John Rugg. 580p. 1990. reprint ed. lib. bdg. 94.00 (*0-8328-1622-1*); reprint ed. pap. 86.00 (*0-8328-1623-X*) Higginson Bk Co.

Rugg, Ellen R. The Descendants of John Rugg. 580p. 1989. reprint ed. lib. bdg. 99.00 (*0-8328-1407-5*); reprint ed. pap. 89.00 (*0-8328-1408-3*) Higginson Bk Co.

Rugg, Frederick E. Forty Tips on the Colleges. 1992. 12.95 (*0-9608934-9-0*) Ruggs Recommend.

— Rugg's Recommendations on the Colleges. 7th rev. ed. LC 89-62896. 121p. (YA). (gr. 11-12). 1990. pap. 15.95 (*0-9608934-5-8*) Ruggs Recommend.

— Rugg's Recommendations on the Colleges. 8th ed. 122p. 1991. pap. 15.95 (*0-9608934-6-6*) Ruggs Recommend.

— Rugg's Recommendations on the Colleges. 9th ed. 122p. 1992. pap. 16.95 (*0-9608934-7-4*) Ruggs Recommend.

— Rugg's Recommendations on the Colleges. 10th ed. LC 89-62896. 136p. (YA). (gr. 11-12). 1993. pap. 17.95 (*0-9608934-8-2*) Ruggs Recommend.

— Rugg's Recommendations on the Colleges. 11th ed. LC 89-62896. 138p. 1994. pap. 17.95 (*1-883062-01-2*) Ruggs Recommend.

— Rugg's Recommendations on the Colleges. 12th ed. LC 89-62896. 144p. 1995. pap. 18.95 (*1-883062-06-3*) Ruggs Recommend.

— Rugg's Video on the Colleges. 1993. vhs 20.00 (*1-883062-00-4*) Ruggs Recommend.

Rugg-Gunn, A. J. Nutrition & Dental Health. LC 92-49776. (Illus.). 488p. 1993. 78.00 (*0-19-262109-2*) OUP.

Rugg-Gunn, A. J., ed. Sugarless - The Way Forward: Proceedings of an International Symposium Held at the University of Newcastle at Tyne, U. K., September 1990. 210p. 1991. 70.00 (*1-85166-598-6*) Elsevier.

***Rugg-Gunn, Andrew J., ed.** Sugarless: Towards the Year 2000. 208p. 1994. 69.95 (*0-85186-495-3*, R6495) CRC Pr.

Rugg-Gunn, R. J., jt. auth. see Murray, J. J.

Rugg, Harold & Shumaker, Ann. Child-Centered School: An Appraisal of the New Education. LC 75-89227. (American Education: Its Men, Institutions & Ideas, Ser.). 1974. reprint ed. 24.95 (*0-405-01466-X*) Ayer.

Rugg, Harold, et al. Curriculum-Making: Past & Present. LC 71-89228. (American Education: Its Men, Institutions & Ideas, Ser. 1). 1974. reprint ed. 24.95 (*0-405-01464-3*) Ayer.

— Foundations of Curriculum-Making. LC 75-89229. (American Education: Its Men, Institutions & Ideas, Ser. 1). 1979. reprint ed. 23.95 (*0-405-01465-1*) Ayer.

***Rugg, M. D. & Coles, M. G., eds.** Electrophysiology of Mind: Event-related Brain Potentials & Cognition. (Oxford Psychiatry Ser.: No. 25). (Illus.). 270p. 1995. text ed. 62.00 (*0-19-852135-9*) OUP.

Rugg, M. D., jt. auth. see Milner, A. D.

***Rugg, Tom.** Computer Freebies. LC 94-69304. 290p. 1994. pap. 14.99 (*0-7821-1621-3*) Sybex.

— Computer Freebies: And Almost Freebies. LC 93-86067. 264p. 1993. 14.99 (*0-7821-1386-9*) Sybex.

— Word for Windows 2: The Complete Reference. 1993. pap. text ed. 29.95 (*0-07-881948-2*) McGraw.

— WordStar Included. 1993. pap. 39.95 (*0-679-79134-5*) Random.

Rugg, Tom & Feldman, Phil. Using BASIC. 2nd ed. (Illus.). 900p. 1993. pap. 27.95 (*1-56529-140-9*) Que.

Rugg, Tom, jt. auth. see Feldman, Phil.

Rugg, Tom, et al. More Than Thirty-Two BASIC Programs for the Commodore 64. (Illus.). 350p. 1983. disk 19.95 (*0-88056-180-7*) Weber Systems.

***Rugg, Winnifred K.** Anne Hutchinson: The Life of America's First Feminist, Female Minister, & Martyr, 1591-1643. LC 95-3439. 1996. pap. 14.95 (*0-930852-30-3*) Tree Life Pubns.

— Unafraid. LC 73-114891. (Select Bibliographies Reprint Ser.). 1977. 19.95 (*0-8369-5295-2*) Ayer.

Rugge, John, jt. auth. see Davidson, James W.

***Rugge, Sue.** Information Brokers Handbook. 2nd ed. 1995. text ed. 49.95 (*0-07-911877-1*) McGraw.

— Information Broker's Handbook. 2nd ed. 1995. pap. text ed. 34.95 (*0-07-911878-X*) McGraw.

Rugge, Sue & Glossbrenner, Alfred. The Information Broker's Handbook. 408p. 1992. 39.95 (*0-8306-3798-2*, 1503, Windcrest); pap. 29.95 (*0-8306-3797-4*, 1503, Windcrest) TAB Bks.

— The Information Brokers' Handbook. 1992. 39.95 (*0-07-054226-0*); pap. text ed. 30.95 (*0-07-054227-9*) McGraw.

Ruggeri, jt. auth. see Zimmerman.

Ruggeri, A. & Motta, P. M., eds. Ultrastructure of the Connective Tissue Matrix. 228p. 1984. lib. bdg. 106.00 (*0-89838-600-4*) Kluwer Ac.

Ruggeri, T., jt. auth. see Rionero, S.

Ruggeri, Tommaso, jt. auth. see Muller, Ingo.

***Ruggeriero, Vincenzo & South, Nigel.** Eurodrugs: Drug Use, Markets & Trafficking in Europe. LC 94-29846. 224p. 1994. 65.00x (*1-85728-101-2*, Pub. by UCL Pr UK) Taylor & Francis.

Ruggerio. The Art of Thinking. 3rd ed. (C). 1990. pap. text ed. 25.00 (*0-06-045668-X*) HarpCollege.

Ruggerio, Lisa, ed. see Strangio, Linda, et al.

Ruggero, Ed. A Common Defense. McCarthy, Paul, ed. 432p. 1992. reprint ed. mass mkt. 5.99 (*0-671-73009-6*) PB.

— Firefall. McCarthy, Paul, ed. 480p. 1995. mass mkt. 5.99 (*0-671-73011-8*) PB.

— North Yankee. 1990. 18.95 (*0-317-99663-0*) PB.

— Thirty-Eight North Yankee. McCarthy, Paul, ed. 480p. 1991. reprint ed. mass mkt. 5.95 (*0-671-70022-7*) PB.

Ruggero, Stefani. Bonvesin da la Riva, Volgari Scelti: Select Poems. Diehl, Patrick S., tr. (American University Studies: Romance Languages & Literature: Ser. II, Vol. 58). 498p. 1988. text ed. 69.50 (*0-8204-0427-6*) P Lang Pubs.

Ruggie, John G., ed. The Antinomies of Interdependence. LC 82-2123. (Political Economy of International Change Ser.). 392p. 1983. text ed. 59.50 (*0-231-05724-5*); pap. text ed. 19.50 (*0-231-05725-3*) Col U Pr.

— Multilateralism Matters: The Theory & Praxis of an Institutional Forum. LC 92-31586. (New Directions in World Politics Ser.). 400p. (C). 1993. text ed. 60.00 (*0-231-07980-X*); pap. text ed. 17.50 (*0-231-07981-8*) Col U Pr.

Ruggie, John G., jt. ed. see Bhagwati, Jagdish N.

Ruggie, John G., ed. see Cox, Robert W.

Ruggie, John G., ed. see Taylor, Paul.

Ruggie, Mary. The State & Working Women. LC 84-42563. 328p. 1984. 57.50x (*0-691-09407-1*); pap. 19.95 (*0-691-10169-8*) Princeton U Pr.

— The State & Working Women: A Comparative Study of Britain & Sweden. LC 84-42563. reprint ed. pap. 107.20 (*0-7837-9283-2*, 2060022) Bks Demand.

***Ruggieri, Claude-Fortune.** Principles of Pyrotechnics. deluxe ed. Carlton, Stuart, tr. 364p. 1995. text ed. 79.00 (*0-9643114-0-2*) MP Assocs.

— Principles of Pyrotechnics. limited ed. Carlton, Stuart, tr. 364p. 1995. text ed. 750.00 (*0-9643114-1-0*) MP Assocs.

Ruggieri, Ford F. The Poor Man's Guide to Self Publishing. LC 84-1107. 164p. 1984. 24.95 (*0-931588-15-4*) Allegany Mtn Pr.

Ruggieri, George D., jt. ed. see Baiardi, John C.

Ruggieri, Helen. The Poetess. LC 79-18883. 1980. 8.00 (*0-931588-09-X*); pap. 3.50 (*0-931588-10-3*) Allegany Mtn Pr.

Ruggieri, L., ed. see AIDS Foundation Dayton Staff & Volunteers.

Ruggiero. Valery Larbaud et l'Italie. 26.25 (*0-685-34263-8*) Fr & Eur.

***Ruggiero, Alessandro G., ed.** Stability of Particle Motion in Storage Rings. (AIP Conference Proceedings Ser.: Vol. 292, No. 54). 516p. 1993. text ed. 502.00x (*1-56396-225-X*) Am Inst Physics.

***Ruggiero, Greg & Sahulka, Stuart, eds.** The New American Crisis: Radical Analyses of the Problems Facing America Today. 272p. 1996. pap. 13.95 (*1-56584-317-7*) New Press NY.

— Open Fire: The Open Magazine Pamphlet Series Anthology. LC 92-50758. 320p. 1993. pap. 12.95 (*1-56584-056-9*) New Press NY.

Ruggiero, Greg, ed. see Cooper, Marc, et al.

Ruggiero, Guido. Binding Passions: Tales of Magic, Marriage, & Power at the End of the Renaissance. LC 92-24005. 296p. 1993. 55.00 (*0-19-507930-2*); pap. 18.95 (*0-19-508320-2*) OUP.

— The Boundaries of Eros: Sex Crime & Sexuality in Renaissance Venice. (Studies in the History of Sexuality). (Illus.). 240p. 1989. reprint ed. pap. 14.95 (*0-19-505696-5*) OUP.

— Violence in Early Renaissance Venice. LC 79-25650. (Crime, Law, & Deviance Ser.). 250p. reprint ed. pap. 71.30 (*0-8357-7951-3*, 2057026) Bks Demand.

Ruggiero, Guido, jt. ed. see Muir, Edward.

Ruggiero, Kristin H. And Here the World Ends: The Life of an Argentine Village. LC 87-20311. 248p. 1988. 35.00 (*0-8047-1379-0*) Stanford U Pr.

Ruggiero, Renato, jt. ed. see Stephenson, Larry W.

Ruggiero, Roberta. The Do's & Dont's of Low Blood Sugar. 1993. pap. 9.95 (*0-8119-0791-0*) LIFETIME.

Ruggiero, Steven T. & Rudman, David A., eds. Superconducting Devices. 396p. 1990. text ed. 73.00 (*0-12-601715-8*) Acad Pr.

Ruggiero, Vincent & Morgan, Patricia. Writing: Invitation & Response. LC 92-70919. (Illus.). 560p. (C). 1992. pap. text ed. write for info. (*0-03-023089-6*) HB Coll Pubs.

***Ruggiero, Vincent R.** The Art of Thinking: A Guide to Critical & Creative Thought. 4th rev. ed. LC 94-27207. (C). 1994. 17.50 (*0-673-99325-6*) HarpC.

— Beyond Feelings: A Guide to Critical Thinking. 3rd ed. 190p. (C). 1990. pap. text ed. 19.95 (*0-87484-950-0*) Mayfield Pub.

— Beyond Feelings: A Guide to Critical Thinking. 4th ed. LC 94-8839. 248p. (C). 1994. pap. 19.95 (*1-55934-357-5*) Mayfield Pub.

— Good Habits: Self Improvement for the 1990's. 192p. (Orig.). 1992. pap. 9.99 (*0-664-25198-6*) Westminster John Knox.

— Lessonpack: For Creative & Critical Thinking. 327p. 1990. 380.00 (*0-9629083-0-4*) Mindbuilding.

— Teaching Thinking Across the Curriculum. 225p. (C). 1990. pap. text ed. 35.50 (*0-06-045667-1*) HarpCollege.

— Thinking Critically about Ethical Issues. 3rd ed. 188p. (C). 1991. pap. text ed. 19.95 (*1-55934-071-1*) Mayfield Pub.

Ruggiero, Vincent R., jt. auth. see Vesper, Joan F.

Ruggiers, Paul G. Florence in the Age of Dante. LC 64-20761. (Centers of Civilization Ser.: No. 15). 203p. reprint ed. 57.90 (*0-8357-9727-9*, 2016263) Bks Demand.

Ruggiers, Paul G., ed. Editing Chaucer: The Great Tradition. LC 84-1872. 1984. 29.95 (*0-937664-58-8*) Pilgrim Bks OK.

Ruggiers, Paul G., ed. see Chaucer, Geoffrey.

Ruggles, Allen M. A Diagnostic Test of Aptitude for Clerical Office Work Based on an Analysis of Clerical Operations. LC 74-177215. (Columbia University. Teachers College. Contributions to Education Ser.: No. 148). reprint ed. 37.50 (*0-404-55148-3*) AMS Pr.

Ruggles, C. L., ed. Formal Methods in Standards: A Report from the BCS Working Group. xi, 135p. 1990. pap. 49.00 (*0-387-19577-7*) Spr-Verlag.

Ruggles, Clive, ed. Records in Stone: Papers in Memory of Alexander Thom. (Illus.). 524p. 1988. 125.00 (*0-521-33381-4*) Cambridge U Pr.

Ruggles, Clive & Saunders, Nicholas, eds. Astronomies & Cultures. (Illus.). 320p. 1993. text ed. 39.95 (*0-87081-319-6*) Univ Pr Colo.

Ruggles, Eleanor. Prince of Players: Edwin Booth. 25.95 (*0-89190-565-0*, Am Repr) Amereon Ltd.

***Ruggles, Frederick W.** Certain Paper Clips from the People's Republic of China: An International Trade Investigation. (Illus.). 81p. (Orig.). (C). 1994. pap. text ed. 60.00x (*0-7881-1505-7*) Diane Pub.

Ruggles, Grace, ed. see Harper-Deiters, Cyndi.

Ruggles, Grace, ed. see Harper-Dieters, Cyndi.

Ruggles, Kathryn E. Dialogues in Academia I: Introduction to a New Faith for Mankind. LC 91-66271. 247p. (Orig.). 1991. pap. 12.00 (*0-9623596-1-0*) Natl Spir Assy HI.

Ruggles, Laurel, ed. see Albert, Rachel.

Ruggles, Laurel, ed. see Ferre, Julia.

Ruggles, Laurel, ed. see Henkel, Pamela & Koch, Lee.

Ruggles, Laurel, ed. see Lawson, Margaret & Monte, Tom.

Ruggles, Laurel, ed. see Ohsawa, George, Macrobiotic Foundation Staff.

Ruggles, Mathilde F., ed. see Fouquet, Leon C.

Ruggles, Melville J. & Mostecky, Vaclav. Russian & East European Publications in the Libraries of the United States. LC 73-437. (Illus.). 396p. 1973. reprint ed. text ed. 65.00 (*0-8371-6767-1*, RURE, Greenwood Pr) Greenwood.

***Ruggles, Myles A.** The Audience Reflected in the Medium of Law: A Critique of the Political Economy of Speech Rights in the United States. 208p. 1994. 39.95 (*0-89391-881-4*); pap. 22.50 (*0-89391-993-4*) Ablex Pub.

Ruggles, Nancy D., ed. Role of the Computer in Economic & Social Research in Latin America. (Other Conferences Ser.: No. 8). 409p. 1975. 106.90 (*0-87014-260-7*) Natl Bur Econ Res.

Ruggles, Nancy D. & Ruggles, Richard. Design of Economic Accounts. (General Ser.: No. 89). 196p. 1970. text ed. 52.00 (*0-87014-204-6*) Natl Bur Econ Res.

Ruggles, Patricia. Drawing the Line: Alternative Poverty Measures & Their Implications for Public Policy. LC 90-30367. (Illus.). 218p. (Orig.). (C). 1990. lib. bdg. 52.00 (*0-87766-446-3*); pap. text ed. 21.50 (*0-87766-447-1*) Urban Inst.

***Ruggles, Philip K.** Computer Dividends: Management Information Systems for the Graphic Arts. 122p. (Orig.). (C). Date not set. pap. text ed. write for info. (*0-9638203-2-X*) Prtng Mgmt Srvs.

— Printing Estimating. 3rd ed. 528p. 1991. teacher ed 8.00 (*0-8273-3806-6*); text ed. 46.95 (*0-8273-3805-8*) Delmar.

— Printing Estimating: Principles & Practices. 3rd ed. 626p. 1990. 40.00 (*0-318-21972-7*, XR102) NAPL.

— Printing Estimating Workbook. 3rd ed. 48p. (C). reprint ed. write for info. (*0-9638203-1-1*) Prtng Mgmt Srvs.

Ruggles, R., ed. Long-Range Economic Projection. (National Bureau for Economic Research Conference on Research in Income & Wealth Ser.: No. 16). 1954. 75.00 (*0-691-04141-5*) Princeton U Pr.

Ruggles Radcliffe, Rebecca. Enlightened Eating: Understanding & Changing Your Relationship with Food. 166p. 1994. 18.95 (*0-9636607-0-5*) EASE.

Ruggles, Richard, jt. auth. see Ruggles, Nancy D.

Ruggles, Richard I. A Country So Interesting: The Hudson's Bay Company & Two Centuries of Mapping, 1670-1870. (Rupert's Land Record Society Ser.). (Illus.). 304p. (C). 1991. text ed. 55.00 (*0-7735-0678-0*, Pub. by McGill CN) U of Toronto Pr.

Ruggles, Robert, ed. see Harper-Deiters, Cyndi.

Ruggles, Robert, ed. see Harper-Dieters, Cyndi.

Ruggles, Ron, ed. see Zagat, Eugene H., Jr. & Zagat, Nina S.

***Ruggles, Rudy.** Rudy Ruggles Presents Arthur Swann. 1969. pap. 3.00 (*0-614-04639-4*) Caxton Club.

Ruggles, Steven. Prolonged Connections: Demographic Change & the Rise of the Extended Family. LC 86-40451. (Social Demography Ser.). 288p. 1987. text ed. 37.50 (*0-299-11030-3*); pap. text ed. 15.75 (*0-299-11034-6*) U of Wis Pr.

Ruggles, William S. & Murthy, Mukunda S. The Project Workbench Whiz's Sourcebook: Everything You Always Wanted to Know about 3.0, but Couldn't Find in the User Manuals. (Illus.). 200p. (Orig.). 1989. spiral bd. 24.95 (*0-685-30021-8*) W S Ruggles & Assocs.

— The Project Workbench Whiz's Sourcebook: Everything You Always Wanted to Know, but Couldn't Find in the User Manuals! 2nd ed. LC 89-92699. (Illus.). 250p. (C). 1991. student ed, pap. 29.95 (*0-9625129-0-7*) W S Ruggles & Assocs.

Rugh & Manning. Proposal Management Using the Modular Technique. LC 84-60601. 136p. 1982. 23.95 (*0-932146-07-4*) Peninsula CA.

Rugh, Andrea, tr. see Tergeman, Siham.

An Asterisk (*) at the beginning of an entry indicates that the title is appearing in BIP for the first time.

Rugh, Andrea B. Family in Contemporary Egypt. LC 84-13. (Contemporary Issues in the Middle East Ser.). (Illus.). 320p. 1984. text ed. 32.00 (*0-8156-2311-9*); pap. text ed. 16.95 (*0-8156-2312-7*) Syracuse U Pr.
— Reveal & Conceal: Dress in Contemporary Egypt. (Contemporary Issues in the Middle East Ser.). (Illus.). 192p. 1986. text ed. 39.95 (*0-8156-2368-2*) Syracuse U Pr.
Rugh, Jack L. Labor Relations, World War II, Before, During & After: "The Autobiography of a One Eyed Jack - A Close Look at Labor History During War & Peace, 1937-1971" LC 92-93266. (Illus.). 256p. (C). 1992. pap. text ed. 25.00 (*0-9632479-4-8*) J L Rugh.
Rugh, Jim. Self-Evaluation: Ideas for Participatory Evaluation of Rural Community Development Projects. (Illus.). 43p. (Orig.). 1986. pap. 5.00 (*0-942716-05-1*) World Neigh.
Rugh, Madeline M., jt. auth. see Ringold, Francine.
Rugh, Roberts. The Mouse: Its Reproduction & Development. (Illus.). 438p. 1990. 115.00 (*0-19-854277-1*) OUP.
Rugh, William A. Arab Perceptions of American Foreign Policy During the October War. LC 76-45494. (Special Study Ser.: No. 2). 1976. pap. 2.50 (*0-916808-13-0*) Mid East Inst.
— The Arab Press: News Media & Political Process in the Arab World. 2nd rev. ed. (Contemporary Issues in the Middle East Ser.). (Illus.). 256p. (C). 1987. pap. text ed. 17.95x (*0-8156-2420-4*) Syracuse U Pr.
Rugh, Wilson J. Linear System Theory. LC 92-10464. 5283p. 1992. text ed. 76.00 (*0-13-555038-6*) P-H.
— Mathematical Description of Linear Systems. LC 75-1684. (Control & Systems Theory Ser.: No. 2). (Illus.). 191p. reprint ed. pap. 54.50 (*0-7837-0697-9*, 2041030) Bks Demand.
Rugheimer, E., ed. New Aspects on Respiratory Failure. (Illus.). xviii, 341p. 1991. 98.00 (*0-387-51445-7*) Spr-Verlag.
Rugheimer, E., jt. ed. see Zindler, M.
***Rugireheh-Runaku, James N.** Too Late after a University Degree. xxiii, 169p. 1995. 17.00 (*81-7024-664-4*, Pub. by Ashish Pub Hse II) Nataraj Bks.
Rugman, Alan & D'Cruz, Joseph R. Improving Canada's International Competitiveness. (Illus.). 52p. (Orig.). (C). 1993. pap. text ed. 21.95 (*1-56806-438-1*) Diane Pub.
Rugman, Alan A. & Anderson, Andrew. Administered Protection in America. 208p. 1987. lib. bdg. 45.00 (*0-7099-4286-9*, Pub. by Croom Helm UK) Routledge Chapman & Hall.
Rugman, Alan M. Inside the Multinationals: The Economics of Internal Markets. 220p. 1981. text ed. 46.50 (*0-231-05384-3*) Col U Pr.
— International Business: A Strategic Management Approach. 1994. text ed. 50.50 (*0-07-054915-X*) McGraw.
— Multinationals & Canada - United States Free Trade. 192p. 1990. 34.95 (*0-87249-625-2*) U of SC Pr.
— Multinationals in Canada: Theory, Performance, Economic Impact. 1980. lib. bdg. 40.50 (*0-89838-036-7*) Kluwer Ac.
Rugman, Alan M., ed. Foreign Investment & NAFTA. LC 93-48267. 260p. (C). 1994. text ed. 34.95 (*0-87249-993-6*) U of SC Pr.
— Multinationals & Technology Transfer: The Canadian Experience. LC 82-24650. 222p. 1983. text ed. 49.95 (*0-275-91072-5*, C1072, Praeger Pubs) Greenwood.
— Research in Global Strategic Management, Vol. 2. 1991. 73.25 (*1-55938-277-5*) Jai Pr.
— Research in Global Strategic Management, Vol. 1: International Business Research for the Twenty- First Century; Canada's New Research Agenda. 221p. 1990. 73.25 (*1-55938-131-0*) Jai Pr.
Rugman, Alan M. & D'Cruz, Joseph R. Fast Forward: Improving Canada's International Competitiveness. (Illus.). 52p. (Orig.). (C). 1993. pap. text ed. 35.00 (*1-56806-692-9*) Diane Pub.
— New Visions for Canadian Business: Strategies for Competing in the Global Economy. (Illus.). 48p. (Orig.). (C). 1993. pap. text ed. 35.00 (*1-56806-691-0*) Diane Pub.
Rugman, Alan M. & Verbeke, Alain. Global Corporate Strategy & Trade Policy. (International Business Ser.). 192p. (C). 1991. text ed. 62.50 (*0-415-05195-9*, A5335) Routledge.
Rugman, Alan M., jt. auth. see D'Cruz, Joseph R.
Rugman, Alan M., et al. International Business. LC 84-15482. (Management Ser.). 544p. 1985. text ed. write for info. (*0-07-054274-0*) McGraw.
Rugman, John H., tr. see Atzeni, Sergio.
***Rugoff, Ralph.** Transformers. (Illus.). 72p. 1995. pap. 20.00 (*0-916365-41-7*) Ind Curators.
Rugstad, H. E., et al, eds. Immunopharmacology in Autoimmune Diseases & Transplantation. (Illus.). 416p. 1992. 95.00 (*0-306-43994-8*, Plenum Pr) Plenum.
Ruh, Kurt, et al, eds. Verfasserlexikon: Die Deutsche Literatur des Mittelalters, 6 vols, Vol. 1. 2nd ed. (C). 1978. 293.85 (*3-11-007264-5*) De Gruyter.
— Verfasserlexikon: Die Deutsche Literatur des Mittelalters, 6 vols, Vol. 2. 2nd ed. (C). 1980. 293.85 (*3-11-007699-3*) De Gruyter.
— Verfasserlexikon: Die Deutsche Literatur des Mittelalters, 6 vols, Vol. 3. 2nd ed. (C). 1981. 293.85 (*3-11-008778-2*) De Gruyter.
— Verfasserlexikon: Die Deutsche Literatur des Mittelalters, 6 vols, Vol. 4. 2nd ed. (C). 1983. 293.85 (*3-11-008838-X*) De Gruyter.
Ruhe, Barnaby, et al. Anders Knutsson: Lightscapes - Ljusskap. Kjersti Board Staff & Swedish Information Service Staff, trs. (Illus.). 40p. (SWE.). (C). 1990. pap. text ed. 10.00 (*0-9627455-0-2*) U ME Museum Art.
***Ruhe, David S.** Robe of Light: The Persian Years of the Supreme Prophet Baha'u'llah, 1817-1853. (Illus.). 233p. 1994. 24.95 (*0-85398-355-0*) G Ronald Pub.
Ruhe, Gunther. Algorithmic Aspects of Flows in Networks. (C). 1991. lib. bdg. 94.00 (*0-7923-1151-5*) Kluwer Ac.
Ruhe-Schoen, Janet. Organizing & Operating Profitable Workshop Classes. LC 80-25446. 31p. 1989. pap. 3.95 (*0-87576-092-9*) Pilot Bks.
— Pan for Gold on Your Next Vacation. LC 77-1378. 28p. 1985. pap. 3.50 (*0-87576-059-7*) Pilot Bks.
***Ruhe, William J.** Slow Dance to Pearl Harbor: A Tin Can Ensign in Prewar America. 256p. 1995. 22.95 (*1-57488-020-9*) Brasseys Inc.
— War in the Boats: My WWII Submarine Battles. (Brassey's WWII Commemorative Ser.). 360p. 1994. 24.95 (*0-02-881084-8*) Brasseys Inc.
— War in the Boats: My WWII Submarine Battles. (WWII Commemorative Ser.). 360p. 1996. pap. 16.95 (*1-57488-028-4*) Brasseys Inc.
Ruhela, S. P., ed. Human Values & Education. 243p. 1986. text ed. 27.50 (*81-207-0152-6*, Pub. by Sterling Pubs II) Apt Bks.
Ruhela, Satya P. Children of Indian Nomads. 1984. text ed. 13.95 (*0-86590-335-2*, Pub. by Sterling Pubs II) Apt Bks.
Ruhemann, Helmut. The Cleaning of Paintings: Problems & Potentialities. LC 81-81722. (Illus.). 508p. 1982. reprint ed. lib. bdg. 75.00 (*0-87817-281-5*) Hacker.
Ruhen, Olaf. Harpoon. 1975. pap. 1.25 (*0-8439-0031-8*) Dorchester Pub Co.
Ruhen, Olaf, jt. auth. see Shaw, W. Hudson.
Ruhge, Justin M. Drake in Central California, Fifteen Seventy-Nine. (Illus.). 92p. pap. 8.00 (*0-685-63227-X*) Quantum Imaging.
— Drake in Central California, 1579: Unraveling One of California's Great Historical Mysteries. (Illus.). 92p. (Orig.). 1992. pap. 8.00 (*0-9614807-7-7*) Quantum Imaging.
— Looking Back: A History of Goleta's Historic Structures & Sites & the Pioneer Families Who Made Them. (Illus.). 210p. (Orig.). 1991. pap. 9.00 (*0-9614807-8-5*) Quantum Imaging.
— Repair & Recovery: The Story of Hoff General Army Hospital 1940 to 1954. (Illus.). 54p. 1990. pap. 6.00 (*0-9614807-6-9*) Quantum Imaging.
Ruhia, Charles. The Physics of Chance: From Blaise Pascal to Niels Bohr. Barton, Gabriel, tr. (Illus.). 240p. 1992. 55.00 (*0-19-853960-6*); pap. 27.95 (*0-19-853977-0*) OUP.
Ruhimann, William. History of the Grateful Dead. 1990. 12.98 (*0-8317-3976-2*) Smithmark.
Ruhl, jt. ed. see Bellin.
Ruhl, Aad. Guided Transport in Two Thousand Forty. 108p. (Orig.). 1992. pap. text ed. 24.00 (*92-821-1165-2*, 75-92-05-1) OECD.
***Ruhl, Asa.** The Trucking & Truck Accident Handbook: 1995 Edition. 250p. 1995. pap. text ed. write for info. (*1-887257-01-2*) Ruhl & Assocs.
— Vehicle Accident Investigation of Heavy Trucks: A Guide for Risk Managers & Claims Personnel. 250p. 1995. pap. text ed. write for info. (*1-887257-02-0*) Ruhl & Assocs.
Ruhl, Charles. On Monosemy: A Study in Linguistic Semantics. LC 88-17494. (Suny Series in Linguistics). 299p. (C). 1989. 89.50 (*0-88706-946-0*); pap. 29.95 (*0-88706-947-9*) State U NY Pr.
Ruhl, Christof, jt. ed. see Mongiovi, Gary.
Ruhl, Horst, jt. auth. see Neufang, Otger.
Ruhl, J. Mark. Colombia: Armed Forces & Society. LC 80-18762. (Foreign & Comparative Studies Program, Latin American Ser.: No. 1). iv, 53p. (Orig.). 1980. pap. 5.00 (*0-915984-92-X*) Syracuse U Foreign Comp.
***Ruhl, Janet.** The Computer Consultant's Workbook. 288p. 1996. pap. 39.95 (*0-9647116-0-5*) Technion Bks.
Ruhl, Janet L. The Computer Consultant's Guide: Real-Life Strategies for Building a Successful Consulting Career. LC 93-30876. 304p. 1994. text ed. 45.00 (*0-471-59662-0*); pap. text ed. 19.95 (*0-471-59661-2*) Wiley.
— The Programmer's Survival Guide: Career Strategies for Computer Professionals. 280p. 1988. 16.95 (*0-13-730375-0*) P-H.
— The Writer's Toolbox. 208p. 1989. pap. 19.95 (*0-13-969429-3*) P-H.
Ruhl, Kathleen. Universal Supplementary Exercisebook: Form B. (C). 1983. pap. text ed. 13.00 (*0-673-15619-2*) HarpCollege.
Ruhl, Lothar, jt. auth. see Clesse, Armand.
Ruhl, Mary, ed. see Pochiluk, William.
***Ruhl, Roland A. & Owen, Dwayne G.** Vehicle Accident Investigation: A Guide for Risk Managers & Claims Personnel. 137p. 1994. pap. text ed. 29.95 (*1-887257-00-4*) Ruhl & Assocs.
Ruhl, Steven. No Bread Without the Dance. (Illus.). 24p. 1979. pap. 3.50 (*0-934714-06-1*) Swamp Pr.
Ruhle, M., et al, eds. Metal-Ceramic Interfaces. (ACTA-Scripta Metallurgica Conference Ser.: No. 4). (Illus.). 447p. 1990. 180.00 (*0-08-040505-3*, Pergamon Pr) Elsevier.
Ruhle, Michael. Preserving the Deterrent: A Missile Defence for Europe. (C). 1990. 35.00 (*0-907967-78-7*, Pub. by Inst Euro Def & Strat UK) St Mut.
Ruhleder, Karl H., jt. ed. see Kurz, Edmund P.
Ruhlen, Merrit. A Guide to the World's Languages: Vol. 1, Classification. LC 86-5870. 464p. 1987. 57.50 (*0-8047-1250-6*); pap. 18.95 (*0-8047-1894-6*) Stanford U Pr.
— The Origin of Language: Tracing the Evolution of the Mother Tongue. 256p. 1994. text ed. 27.95 (*0-471-58426-6*) Wiley.
Ruhlen, Merritt. On the Origin of Languages: Studies in Linguistic Taxonomy. LC 93-39188. 1994. 45.00 (*0-8047-2321-4*) Stanford U Pr.
Ruhling, Nancy, jt. auth. see Freeman, John C.
Ruhling, Richard. Sword Over America. (Illus.). 55p. (Orig.). pap. 2.00 (*0-317-55134-5*) Total Health.
Ruhlman, Michael. Boys Themselves. 1995. 25.00 (*0-8050-3370-X*) H Holt & Co.
Ruhlmann, William. John Lennon. (Illus.). 96p. 1993. 12.98 (*0-8317-5253-X*) Smithmark.
— Nutshell Classics: Julius Caesar. 1988. pap. text ed. 140.00 (*0-938735-95-0*); pap. text ed. 90.00 (*0-938735-96-9*) Classic Theatre Schl.
— Pink Floyd. (Illus.). 96p. 1993. 12.98 (*0-8317-6912-2*) Smithmark.
— Rolling Stones. (Illus.). 96p. 1993. 12.98 (*0-8317-7367-7*) Smithmark.
Ruhm, Herbert, ed. see James, Henry.
Ruhmann, Dorothy B. Ruhmann & Beasley Family Roots: A Revised Edition of Ruhmann Roots, Limbs & Branches. rev. ed. LC 93-87095. (Illus.). 405p. 1993. pap. 49.95 (*0-9638818-0-9*) Ruhmann Pr.
Ruhnau, Helena E. Drama of Patmos Initiation of John. LC 82-71052. (Illus.). 1982. pap. 12.95 (*0-941036-07-3*) Colleasius Pr.
— Journeys into the Fifth Dimension. LC 75-149286. (Illus.). 1975. 14.95 (*0-941036-02-2*) Colleasius Pr.
— Key to the Golden Door. LC 81-90336. (Illus.). 1982. pap. 7.95 (*0-941036-06-5*) Colleasius Pr.
— Let There Be Light, Vol. II. (Illus.). (Orig.). 1990. 12.95 (*0-941036-70-7*) Colleasius Pr.
— Let There Be Light - Living Waters of Life for the New Age. (Illus.). 190p. (Orig.). 1987. pap. 12.95 (*0-941036-60-X*) Colleasius Pr.
— Light on a Mountain. (Illus.). 1976. 12.95 (*0-941036-00-6*); pap. 8.50 (*0-941036-01-4*) Colleasius Pr.
— Reappearance of the Dove. LC 75-27625. (Illus.). 1978. 14.95 (*0-941036-03-0*) Colleasius Pr.
Ruhnke, Elmer, ed. see Simonetta, Joseph R.
Ruhnke, Lothar H. & Deepak, A., eds. Hygroscopic Aerosols. LC 84-9529. (Illus.). 375p. (C). 1984. 66.00 (*0-937194-02-6*) A Deepak Pub.
Ruhnke, Lothar H. & Latham, John, eds. Proceedings in Atmospheric Electricity. LC 83-10096. (Illus.). 427p. 1983. 53.00 (*0-937194-04-2*) A Deepak Pub.
Ruhnke, Robert. Sponsor Couple Program for Chirstian Marriage Preparation - Manual. 32p. 1981. pap. 4.95 (*0-89243-143-1*) Liguori Pubns.
— Sponsor Couple Program for Christian Marriage Preparation - Dialogue Packet. 96p. 1981. pap. 4.95 (*0-89243-144-X*) Liguori Pubns.
Rui, Manuel. Yes, Comrade! Sousa, Ronald W., tr. LC 92-32341. (Emergent Literatures Ser.: Vol. 11). 176p. (C). 1993. 16.95 (*0-8166-1966-2*) U of Minn Pr.
Ruibal, Carmen C., jt. auth. see Wohl, Gary.
Ruigh, Robert E. Parliament of Sixteen Twenty-Four: Politics & Foreign Policy. LC 72-135548. (Historical Studies: No. 87). (Illus.). 448p. 1971. 27.50 (*0-674-65225-8*) HUP.
Ruigrok, J. J. Short-Wavelength Magnetic Recording: New Methods & Analysis. 592p. 1990. 140.50 (*0-946395-56-X*) Elsevier.
***Ruihley, Glenn R., ed.** An Anthology of Great U. S. Women Poets 1850-1990: Temples & Palaces. LC 95-19529. (Illus.). 604p. 1996. text ed. 129.95 (*0-7734-8903-7*) E Mellen.
RuijGrok, G. J. Elements of Airplane Performance. 462p. 1990. 97.50 (*90-6275-608-5*, Pub. by Delft U Pr NE) Coronet.
Ruijs, J. H. Diagnosis of Cholecystoses. 1977. pap. text ed. 62.00 (*90-247-1932-1*) Kluwer Ac.
Ruijsenaars, B., tr. see Van Den Berg, A. J., et al.
***Ruilan, Lu, tr.** Handbook of Regulations on Environmental Protection in China. 1995. pap. 250.00 (*0-915707-77-2*) Resources Future.
***Ruillier, Frederic, illus.** Elephants Travel by Train. 8p. (J). (ps). 1994. 12.48 (*1-881445-37-2*) Sandvik Pub.
***Ruin, Hans.** Enigmatic Origins: Tracing the Theme of Historicity Through Heidegger's Works. (Stockholm Studies in Philosophy: No. 15). 294p. (Orig.). 1994. pap. 49.50x (*91-22-01621-X*, Pub. by Almqv & Wiksell SW) Coronet Bks.
Ruin, Olof. Tage Erlander: Serving the Welfare State, 1946-1969. Metcalf, Michael F., tr. LC 89-37755. (Series in Policy & Institutional Studies). (Illus.). 378p. 1990. 49.95 (*0-8229-3631-3*) U of Pittsburgh Pr.
Ruinian, Li, ed. Modern Electrostatics: International Conference on Modern Electrostatics, October 21-25, 1988, Beijing, China. (International Academic Publishers Ser.). 538p. 1989. 170.00 (*0-08-037029-2*, Pergamon Pr) Elsevier.
Ruiqing Du. Chinese Higher Education: A Decade of Reform & Development (1978-88) LC 91-24251. 176p. 1992. text ed. 59.95 (*0-312-06071-8*) St Martin.
Ruis. Nicaragua for Beginners. (Illus.). 160p. 1984. pap. 7.95 (*0-86316-067-0*) Writers & Readers.
Ruitenbeek, Hendrik. Homosexuality & Creative Genius. 1965. 25.00 (*0-8392-1149-X*) Astor-Honor.
Ruitenbeek, Hendrik & Ruitenbeek, Henrik M., eds. Freud As We Knew Him. LC 72-6471. 574p. 1973. 39.95 (*0-8143-1488-0*) Wayne St U Pr.
Ruitenbeek, Hendrik M. The Interpretation of Death. rev. ed. LC 84-45092. 296p. 1983. 30.00 (*0-87668-686-2*) Aronson.
***Ruitenbeek, Hendrik M., ed.** Death & Mourning. LC 95-3545. 1995. pap. 30.00 (*1-56821-527-4*) Aronson.
— The First Freudians. rev. ed. LC 73-77278. 288p. 1973. 30.00x (*0-87668-694-3*) Aronson.
— Psychoanalysis & Female Sexuality. 1966. pap. 15.95x (*0-8084-0254-4*) NCUP.
— Psychoanalysis & Male Sexuality. 1966. pap. 15.95x (*0-8084-0256-0*) NCUP.
Ruitenbeek, Henrik M., jt. ed. see Ruitenbeek, Hendrik.
Ruitenbeek, K. Carpentry & Building in Late Imperial China: A Study of the Fifteenth-Century Carpenter's Manual Lu Ban Jing. (Sinica Leidensia Ser.: No. 23). 500p. 1992. 120.00 (*90-04-09258-7*) E J Brill.
Ruitenberg, E. J. & Peters, P. W. Laboratory Animals: Laboratory Animal Models for Domestic Animal Production. 352p. 1986. 148.75 (*0-444-42464-4*) Elsevier.
Ruitenberg, E. J., jt. auth. see Jager, J. C.
***Ruiter, A., ed.** Fish & Fishery Products: Composition, Nutritive Properties & Stability. 250p. 1995. 99.00 (*0-85198-927-6*) CAB Intl.
Ruiter, Barbara & Ruiter, Cindy. Pink Is Perfect for Pigs. (Illus.). 32p. (Orig.). (J). 1993. pap. 5.95 (*1-56883-019-X*) Colonial Pr AL.
Ruiter, Cindy, jt. auth. see Ruiter, Barbara.
Ruiter, Dick W. Institutional Legal Facts: Legal Powers & Their Effects. (Law & Philosophy Library). 200p. (C). 1993. lib. bdg. 92.00 (*0-7923-2441-2*) Kluwer Ac.
Ruiter, Dirk J., et al, eds. Application of Nonclonal Antibodies in Tumor Pathology. (Developments in Oncology Ser.). 1987. lib. bdg. 180.00 (*0-89838-853-8*) Kluwer Ac.
— Cutaneous Melanoma & Precursor Lesions. (Developments in Oncology Ser.). 1984. lib. bdg. 122.50 (*0-89838-689-6*) Kluwer Ac.
Ruiter, Frans, jt. auth. see Fokkema, Douwe.
Ruivo, Mario, ed. Marine Pollution & Sea Life. 1978. 100.00 (*0-685-63432-9*) St Mut.
Ruiz. Viva Mexico! The Story of Benito Juarez & Cinco de Mayo. LC 92-18071. (Stories of America Ser.). (Illus.). 32p. (J). (gr. 2-5). 1992. lib. bdg. 19.97 (*0-8114-7214-0*) Raintree Steck-V.
***Ruiz, Alphonse.** Prayers of John of the Cross. 1994. pap. 8.95 (*1-56548-073-2*) New City.
Ruiz, Ana, jt. auth. see Gonzalez, Ralfka.
Ruiz, Antonio, jt. auth. see Trenchard, Ernesto.
Ruiz, Aristides. Cornballs: Cereal Box Joke Book. LC 92-60581. 400p. (J). (gr. 4-7). 1993. pap. 2.99 (*0-679-83455-9*) Random Bks Yng Read.
Ruiz, Aristides, illus. Days of Future Past. adapted ed. (X-Men Digest Novels Ser.). 108p. (Orig.). (J). (gr. 2 up). 1994. pap. 3.50 (*0-679-86181-5*) Random Bks Yng Read.
Ruiz, Aristides, jt. illus. see Thompson Brothers.
Ruiz, Art, illus. The Weirdest Fun Book, Ever! (Addams Family Ser.). (J). 1992. 7.95 (*0-448-40503-2*, G&D) Putnam Pub Group.
Ruiz Barrionuevo, Carmen, ed. see Dario, Ruben.
Ruiz, C. & Koenigsburger, F. Design for Strength & Production. 280p. 1970. text ed. 220.00 (*0-677-62050-0*) Gordon & Breach.
Ruiz, C., jt. ed. see Allison, I. M.
Ruiz-Cobo, jt. ed. see Castillo.
Ruiz de Alarcon, Hernando. Treatise on the Heathen Superstitions that Today Live among the Indians Native to this Day in New Spain, 1629. Andrews, J. Richard & Hassig, Ross, eds. LC 83-47842. (Civilization of the American Indian Ser.: Vol. 164). (Illus.). 540p. 1984. pap. 22.95 (*0-8061-2031-2*) U of Okla Pr.
Ruiz De Alarcon, Juan. La Verdad Sospechosa. Martin Martinez, Juan M., ed. (Nueva Austral Ser.: Vol. 173). (SPA.). 1991. pap. text ed. 11.95 (*84-239-1973-0*) Elliots Bks.
— Verdad Sospechosa, No. 68. 165p. (SPA.). 1969. write for info. (*0-8288-8557-5*) Fr & Eur.
Ruiz de Burton, Amparo. The Squatter & the Don. Sanchez, Rosaura & Pita, Beatriz, eds. LC 92-33829. 386p. 1993. pap. 14.00 (*1-55885-055-4*) Arte Publico.
***Ruiz de Burton, Maria A.** Who Would Have Thought It? Sanchez, Rosaura & Pita, Beatrice, eds. LC 95-11585. 1995. pap. write for info. (*1-55885-081-3*) Arte Publico.
***Ruiz De Elvira, A.** Mitologia Clasica. 2nd ed. 540p. (SPA.). 1993. 100.00 (*84-249-0204-1*) Elliots Bks.
Ruiz de la Pena, Alvaro, ed. see Palacio Valdes, Armando.
Ruiz, Dorothy S., ed. Handbook of Mental Health & Mental Disorder among Black Americans. LC 89-71401. 360p. 1990. text ed. 55.00 (*0-313-26330-2*, SRZ/, Greenwood Pr) Greenwood.
Ruiz, Enrique L. Cartas a la Carte. Pita, Juana R., ed. LC 90-84526. (Coleccion Clasicos Cubanos Ser.). 146p. (Orig.). (SPA.). 1991. pap. 15.00 (*0-89729-581-1*) Ediciones.
— El Laberinto de si Mismo. LC 83-50320. (Senda Narrativa Ser.). (Illus.). 197p. 1983. reprint ed. pap. 13.95 (*0-918454-36-0*) Senda Nueva.
— El Pan de los Muertos. 2nd ed. LC 88-80745. (Clasicos Cubanos Ser.). 225p. (SPA.). 1988. reprint ed. pap. 12.00 (*0-89729-482-3*) Ediciones.
Ruiz, Gracie, tr. see Zimmer, Luke.
Ruiz, H. & Pavon, J. Flora Peruviana et Chilensis, 3 vols. in 1. (Illus.). 1965. reprint ed. 360.00 (*3-7682-0283-6*) Lubrecht & Cramer.
Ruiz-Herrera, Jose. Fungal Cell Wall: Structure, Synthesis & Assembly. 1991. 190.00 (*0-8493-6672-0*, QK601) CRC Pr.
Ruiz, Hugo. Hermanos, Ahora Cartas del Diablo. 64p. 1986. reprint ed. pap. 2.25 (*0-311-46045-3*) Casa Bautista.
Ruiz Iriarte, Victor. Carrusell. Holt, Marion P., ed. LC 76-125615. (Orig.). (SPA.). (C). 1970. pap. text ed. 7.95 (*0-89197-063-0*) Irvington.
Ruiz, J., et al, eds. Clinical Atlas of Respiratory Diseases. 128p. 1988. write for info. (*0-8151-7455-1*, RAP-1, Yr Bk Med Pubs) Mosby Yr Bk.
Ruiz, Jesus M. The Basic Theory of Power Series. (Advanced Lectures in Mathematics Ser.). x, 134p. 1993. pap. 26.00 (*3-528-06525-7*, Pub. by Vieweg & Sohn GW) Ballen Bkslr.
Ruiz, Jesus M., jt. auth. see Andradas, Carlos.
Ruiz Jodar, Carlos. Diccionario Espanol-Aleman, Aleman-Espanol Militar. 375p. (GER & SPA.). 1975. pap. 24.95 (*0-8288-5820-9*, S50101) Fr & Eur.

R

An Asterisk (*) at the beginning of an entry indicates that the title is appearing in BIP for the first time.

Ruiz, Juan. The Book of the Archpriest of Hita (Libro de buen amor) Singleton, Mack, tr. x, 182p. 1975. 7.50 (0-942260-06-6) Hispanic Seminary.

— The Book of True Love: Bilingual Edition. Zahareas, Anthony N., ed. Daly, Saralyn R., tr. & intro. by. LC 77-12820. (C). 1978. 29.95 (0-271-00523-8) Pa St U Pr.

— John Ruiz: The Book of Good Love. Mignani, Rigo & Di Cesare, Mario A., trs. LC 69-14644. (State University of New York Press Ser.). 365p. 1972. 15.00 (0-87395-048-8); pap. 8.00 (0-87395-223-5) MRTS.

— Libro de Buen Amor: Edicion Facsimil del Manuscrito Gayoso (1389) (Real Academia Ediciones Ser.). (SPA.). 1993. 500.00 (84-600-6149-3) Elliots Bks.

Ruiz, Judy. Talking Razzmatazz: Poems by Judy Ruiz. 64p. 1991. text ed. 18.95 (0-8262-0771-5); pap. 9.95 (0-8262-0772-3) U of Mo Pr.

Ruiz, M. A. & Cheremisinoff, Paul N. Pocket Guidebook on Environmental Auditing. 2nd ed. (Illus.). 109p. 1989. 24. 95 (0-925760-31-5) SciTech Pubs.

Ruiz-Maldonado, R., ed. see Congress of Pediatric Dermatology, 2nd, Mexico City, October 20-23, 1976.

Ruiz, Maria C. Literatura y Politica: El "Libro de los Estados" y el "Libro de las Armas" de Don Juan Manuel. 1990. 37.50 (0-916379-63-9) Scripta.

Ruiz, Mary & Amend, Karen S. Handwriting Analysis. 1980. pap. 12.95 (0-87877-050-X) Newcastle Pub.

Ruiz, Mary S., jt. auth. see Amend, Karen K.

Ruiz, Michael J. & Booker, Randy A. Astronomy Labs for the Personal Computer. 96p. (C). 1994. pap. text ed., spiral bd. 17.95 (0-8403-9068-8) Kendall-Hunt.

Ruiz, Nadeen T., jt. auth. see Figueroa, Richard A.

Ruiz, Pedro J. Senderos de mi Destino. 80p. (SPA.). 1984. pap. 5.00 (0-685-08592-9) SLUSA.

Ruiz-Quintanilla, Antonio, jt. ed. see Bainbridge, Lisanne.

Ruiz, Ramon, ed. Proceedings of the Seminar on Natural Family Planning & Family Life Education. 320p. (C). 1990. text ed. 51.00 (962-209-260-8, Pub. by Hong Kong U Pr HK) St Mut.

Ruiz, Ramon E. The Great Rebellion: Mexico Nineteen Hundred & Five to Nineteen Twenty-Four. (C). 1982. pap. text ed. 13.95 (0-393-95129-4) Norton.

— Labor & the Ambivalent Revolutionaries: Mexico, 1911-1923. LC 75-29087. 162p. reprint ed. pap. 46.20 (0-317-41763-0, 2025867) Bks Demand.

— The People of Sonora & Yankee Capitalists. LC 87-30133. (PROFMEX Ser.). 320p. 1988. 40.00 (0-8165-1012-1) U of Ariz Pr.

— Triumphs & Tragedy: A History of the Mexican People. 512p. 1993. pap. 14.95 (0-393-31066-3) Norton.

***Ruiz, Raoul.** Poetics of Cinema. 128p. 1995. pap. 19.50 (2-906571-38-5) Dist Art Pubs.

Ruiz, Roberto, jt. ed. see Bijou, Sidney W.

Ruiz, Ronald. Happy Birthday Jesus. LC 93-45643. 320p. 1994. 19.95 (1-55885-108-9) Arte Publico.

Ruiz, Shirley. Journey to High Places: A Spiritual Evolution. Peterson, Kim, ed. 400p. (Orig.). 1987. pap. 12.95 (0-944020-00-3) Shastar Pr.

***Ruiz-Siera.** People of the Earth: Introduction to World PreHistory. 8th ed. (C). 1994. student ed, text ed. 10.00 (0-673-52397-7) HarpCollege.

Ruiz Silva, Carlos, ed. see Rivas, Duque de.

Ruiz, Suzanne. A Dog Owner's Guide to Grooming Your Dog. (Illus.). 118p. 10.95 (3-923880-66-9, 16021) Tetra Pr.

Ruiz, Teofilo F. The City & the Realm: Burgos & Castile, 1080-1492. (Collected Studies: No. CS375). 336p. 1992. 89.95 (0-86078-329-4, Pub. by Variorum UK) Ashgate Pub Co.

— Crisis & Continuity: Land & Town in Late Medieval Castile. LC 93-35573. (Middle Ages Ser.). (Illus.). 368p. (C). 1994. text ed. 46.95 (0-8122-3228-3) U of Pa Pr.

Ruiz Torres, Francisco. English-Spanish, Spanish-English Medical Vocabulary: Vocabulario Ingles-Espanol, Espanol-Ingles de Medicina. 300p. (ENG & SPA.). 1979. pap. 24.95 (0-8288-4845-9, S50091) Fr & Eur.

Ruiz, Vicki L. Cannery Women, Cannery Lives: Mexican Women, Unionization, & the California Food Processing Industry, 1930-1950. LC 87-13878. (Illus.). 212p. 1987. pap. 14.95 (0-8263-0988-7) U of NM Pr.

Ruiz, Vicki L. & DuBois, Ellen C., eds. Unequal Sisters: A Multicultural Reader in U. S. Women's History. 2nd ed. LC 94-2430. 1994. write for info. (0-415-90905-8); pap. write for info. (0-415-90906-6) Routledge.

Ruiz, Vicki L. & Tiano, Susan. Women on the U. S. Mexico Border: Responses to Change. LC 86-22305. (Thematic Studies in Latin America). 256p. 1987. text ed. 44.95 (0-04-497038-2); pap. text ed. 15.95 (0-04-497039-0) Routledge Chapman & Hall.

Rujula, A. de, ed. A Unified View of the Macro- & Micro-Cosmos. 680p. (C). 1987. pap. 64.00 (9971-5-0394-8) World Scientific Pub.

Rukang, Wu, jt. ed. see Olsen, John W.

***Rukeyser, Muriel.** Out of Silence: Selected Poems. Daniels, Kate, ed. 192p. 1994. pap. 14.95 (0-8101-5015-8) Northwestern U Pr.

— Out of Silence: Selected Poems. Daniels, Kate, ed. 192p. 1992. 28.00 (0-916384-11-X); pap. 14.00 (0-916384-07-1) TriQuarterly.

— Theory of Flight. LC 74-144741. (Yale Series of Younger Poets: No. 34). reprint ed. 18.00 (0-404-53834-7) AMS Pr.

— Willard Gibbs. LC 87-12394. (Illus.). xiv, 465p. 1988. reprint ed. 35.00 (0-918024-57-9); reprint ed. pap. 16.50 (0-918024-56-0) Ox Bow.

Rukeyser, Muriel, tr. see Ekelof, Gunnar.

Rukeyser, Muriel, ed. see Levi, Jan H.

Rukeyser, Muriel, tr. see Paz, Octavio.

Rukeyser, William S., ed. see Atlas, James.

Rukeyser, William S., ed. see Blinder, Alan S.

Rukeyser, William S., ed. see Easterbrook, Gregg.

Rukeyser, William S., ed. see Galbraith, John Kenneth.

Rukeyser, William S., ed. see Gilder, George.

Rukeyser, William S., ed. see Greider, William.

Rukeyser, William S., ed. see Jaroff, Leon.

Rukeyser, William S., ed. see Lewis, Michael.

Rukeyser, William S., ed. see Lourie, Richard.

Rukeyser, William S., ed. see Plimpton, George.

Rukeyser, William S., ed. see Sammons, James H.

Rukeyser, William S., ed. see Vibbert, Spencer.

Rukl, Antonin. Atlas of the Moon. Rackham, T. W., ed. (Illus.). 224p. 1992. 29.95 (0-913135-17-8) Kalmbach.

Rukmani, T. S. Sankara: The Man & His Philosophy. (C). 1991. text ed. 3.50 (81-85425-33-7, Pub. by Manohar II) S Asia.

Rukmani, T. S., tr. Yogavarttika of Vijnanabhiksu, Vol. 3: Vibhutipada. 1988. 26.00 (81-215-0057-5, Pub. by Munshiram Manoharial II) S Asia.

Rukmini, S., jt. ed. see Ramachandran, T. M.

Ruksenas, Algis. Is That You Laughing, Comrade? The World's Best (Underground) Russian Jokes. (Illus.). 192p. 1986. pap. 5.95 (0-8065-0994-5, Citadel Pr) Carol Pub Group.

Rukstad, Michael G. Corporate Decision Making in the World Economy. 640p. (C). 1992. pap. text ed. 41.25 (0-03-076526-9) Dryden Pr.

— Macroeconomic Decision Making in the World Economy. 3rd ed. 720p. (C). 1992. pap. text ed. 51.00 (0-03-074733-3) Dryden Pr.

— Macroeconomic Decision Making in the World Economy. 3rd ed. 481p. (C). 1993. teacher ed, pap. text ed. 22.75 (0-03-076346-0) Dryden Pr.

Rukstalis, Susan. How Many Steps Before the Queen? LC 92-60664. (Illus.). 32p. (J). (ps-4). 1992. 14.95 (0-9628914-2-8) Padakami Pr.

Ruland, Jurgen. Urban Development in Southeast Asia: Regional Cities & Local Government. 370p. (C). 1992. pap. text ed. 52.50 (0-8133-0104-1) Westview.

Ruland, Richard & Bradbury, Malcolm. From Puritanism to Postmodernism: A History of American Literature. 496p. 1992. reprint ed. pap. 15.95 (0-14-014435-8, Penguin Bks) Viking Penguin.

Ruland-Thorne, Kate. Experience Sedona, Legends & Legacies. Blake, Bennie, ed. LC 89-51796. (Illus.). 114p. (Orig.). 1989. pap. 8.95 (0-9628329-0-1) Thorne Enterprises.

— The Yavapai People of the Red Rocks: People of the Sun. Caillou, Aliza, ed. (Illus.). 102p. (Orig.). 1993. pap. 5.95 (0-9628329-5-2) Thorne Enterprises.

Ruland, Vernon. Eight Sacred Horizons: The Religious Imagination East & West. 240p. 1985. write for info. (0-317-18117-3) Macmillan.

— Horizons of Criticism: An Assessment of Religious-Literary Options. LC 75-20162. 275p. reprint ed. pap. 78.40 (0-317-29363-X, 2024203) Bks Demand.

— Sacred Lies & Silences: A Psychology of Religious Disguise. LC 93-34712. 168p. (Orig.). 1994. pap. text ed. 10.95 (0-8146-5847-4, M Glazier) Liturgical Pr.

Rulandus, Martinus. A Lexicon of Alchemy: or Alchemical Dictionary. 466p. 1992. reprint ed. pap. 30.00 (0-922802-82-3) Kessinger Pub.

Rulau, Russ. Hard Times Tokens 1832-1844. 4th ed. LC 80-82710. (Rulau Tokens Ser.). (Illus.). 332p. 1992. pap. 14. 95 (0-87341-215-X) Krause Pubns.

— Latin American Tokens. LC 92-71453. (Illus.). 400p. 1992. pap. 29.95 (0-87341-200-1) Krause Pubns.

Rulau, Russ & Fuld, George. Medallic Portraits of Washington. LC 85-80496. (Illus.). 160p. (Orig.). 1985. pap. 29.95 (0-87341-079-3) Krause Pubns.

Rulau, Russell. Discovering America: A Coin Collectors Connection. LC 89-85218. (Illus.). 328p. (Orig.). 1989. pap. 19.95 (0-87341-129-3) Krause Pubns.

— Early American Tokens. 3rd ed. LC 81-80865. (Illus.). 96p. 1991. pap. 12.95 (0-87341-168-4) Krause Pubns.

— U. S. Merchant Tokens. 3rd ed. LC 82-80394. (Illus.). 192p. 1990. pap. 16.95 (0-87341-137-4) Krause Pubns.

— United States Trade Tokens 1866-1889. 2nd ed. LC 83-81009. (Illus.). 332p. 1988. pap. 17.95 (0-87341-115-3) Krause Pubns.

Rulau, Russell, ed. Tokens of the Gay Nineties. LC 87-80401. (Illus.). 160p. 1987. pap. 12.95 (0-87341-097-1) Krause Pubns.

***Rule.** A Rose for Her Grave. 1995. pap. 6.99 (0-671-53798-9) PB.

Rule, Albert R., jt. ed. see Petruk, William.

Rule, Amy, ed. Carleton Watkins: Selected Texts & Bibliography. LC 92-42581. 200p. 1993. text ed. 85.00 (0-8161-0578-2, Hall Reference) Macmillan.

Rule, Amy & Lorenz, Richard, eds. Imogen Cunningham: Selected Texts & Bibliography. (World Photographers Reference Ser.). (Illus.). 200p. 1993. text ed. 85.00 (0-8161-0575-8) G K Hall.

Rule, Ann. Beautiful America's Seattle. LC 89-17800. (Illus.). 80p. 1989. 17.95 (0-89802-522-2); pap. 10.95 (0-89802-521-4) Beautiful Am.

— Dead by Sunset: Perfect Husband, Perfect Killer? 1995. 23.00 (0-684-80205-8) S&S Trade.

— Everything She Ever Wanted. Rubenstein, Julie, ed. 592p. 1993. reprint ed. mass mkt. 5.99 (0-671-69071-X) PB.

— Everything She Ever Wanted: A True Story of Obsessive Love, Murder, & Betrayal. (Illus.). 384p. 1992. pap. 23. 00 (0-671-69070-1) S&S Trade.

— If You Really Loved Me. Rubenstein, Julie, ed. 624p. 1992. reprint ed. mass mkt. 5.99 (0-671-76920-0) PB.

— Possession: A Novel. 352p. 1984. pap. 5.99 (0-451-16757-0, Sig) NAL-Dutton.

— A Rose for Her Grave & Other Cases. (Ann Rule's Crime Files Ser.: Vol. 1). 1993. mass mkt. 5.99 (0-671-79353-5) PB.

— Small Sacrifices. 496p. 1988. pap. 5.99 (0-451-16660-4, Sig) NAL-Dutton.

— The Stranger Beside Me. (Illus.). 432p. 1981. pap. 5.99 (0-451-16493-8, Sig) NAL-Dutton.

— You Belong to Me & Other True Cases: Ann Rule's Crime Files, Vol. 2. Rubenstein, Julie, ed. (Illus.). 556p. (Orig.). 1994. pap. 6.99 (0-671-79354-3) PB.

Rule, Ann, see Andy Stack, pseud..

***Rule, Colter.** Uncovering the Sources of Love & Hate. LC 95-1450. 288p. (Orig.). 1995. 26.95 (0-86534-102-8); pap. 18.95 (0-86534-229-6) Sunstone Pr.

Rule, Eva. Even Song. (Illus.). 80p. (Orig.). 1993. pap. write for info. (1-56167-111-8) Am Literary Pr.

Rule, James & Veacht, Robert. Ethical Questions in Dentistry. LC 92-48228. 300p. 1993. pap. text ed. 28.00 (0-86715-203-6) Quint Pub Co.

Rule, James B. Theories of Civil Violence. 482p. 1988. pap. 13.00 (0-520-06796-7) U CA Pr.

Rule, Jane. After the Fire. 1989. pap. 8.95 (0-941483-45-2) Naiad Pr.

— Against the Season. 224p. 1984. reprint ed. pap. 8.95 (0-930044-48-7) Naiad Pr.

— Contract with the World. 352p. 1990. 9.95 (0-941483-79-7) Naiad Pr.

— Desert of the Heart. 224p. 1985. pap. 10.95 (0-930044-73-8) Naiad Pr.

— The Desert of the Heart. LC 75-12344. (Homosexuality). 1979. reprint ed. 25.95 (0-405-07386-0) Ayer.

— A Hot-Eyed Moderate. 256p. 1985. pap. 7.95 (0-930044-57-6) Naiad Pr.

— Memory Board. 336p. 1987. pap. 10.95 (0-941483-02-9) Naiad Pr.

— Outlander. LC 80-84221. (Illus.). 220p. (Orig.). 1981. pap. 8.95 (0-930044-17-7) Naiad Pr.

— Theme for Diverse Instruments. 208p. 1990. pap. 8.95 (0-941483-63-0) Naiad Pr.

— This Is Not for You. 302p. 1982. reprint ed. pap. 8.95 (0-930044-25-8) Naiad Pr.

— The Young in One Another's Arms. 224p. 1984. reprint ed. pap. 9.95 (0-930044-53-3) Naiad Pr.

Rule, John. Albion's People: English Society, 1714-1815. (Social & Economic History of England Ser.). 269p. (C). 1991. pap. text ed. 28.50 (0-582-08916-6, 79212) Longman.

— The Experience of Labour in Eighteenth Century Industry. 1981. text ed. 32.50 (0-312-27664-8) St Martin.

— The Labouring Classes in Early Industrial England, 1750-1850. (Themes in British Social History Ser.). 424p. (C). 1986. pap. text ed. 25.95 (0-582-49172-X, 73511) Longman.

— The Vital Century, 1714-1815. (Social & Economical History of England Ser.). 334p. (C). 1991. pap. text ed. 28.50 (0-582-49425-7, 79211) Longman.

Rule, John & Malcolmson, Robert, eds. Protest & Survival: Essays for E.P. Thompson. LC 93-15823. 1993. 30.00 (1-56584-114-X) New Press NY.

— Protest & Survival: The Historical Experience: Essays for E. P. Thompson. 432p. 1995. pap. 19.95 (0-85036-445-0, Pub. by Merlin Pr UK) Humanities.

Rule, John C., ed. Louis XIV & the Craft of Kingship. LC 72-79845. (Illus.). 488p. 1969. 44.50 (0-8142-0004-4) Ohio St U Pr.

Rule, Lareina. Name Your Baby. (Orig.). 1986. mass mkt. 4.50 (0-553-27145-8) Bantam.

Rule, Leslie. Beautiful America's Portland. LC 88-7499. (Illus.). 80p. 1989. 17.95 (0-89802-535-4); pap. 10.95 (0-89802-534-6) Beautiful Am.

— Whispers from the Grave. 272p. (Orig.). (YA). 1995. pap. text ed. 4.99 (0-425-14777-0) Berkley Pub.

Rule, Margaret, ed. Edward Albee at Home & Abroad: A Bibliography. LC 73-158245. (Studies in Modern Literature: No. 1). reprint ed. 29.50 (0-404-07945-8) AMS Pr.

Rule, Martin, ed. Eadmeri Historia Novorum in Anglia, et Opuscula Duo de Vita Sancti Anselmi et Quibusdam Miraculis Ejus: Edition from the Manuscript in the Library of Corpus Christi College, Cambridge. (Rolls Ser.: No. 81). 1972. reprint ed. 80.00 (0-8115-1151-0) Periodicals Srv.

Rule, P. Grant. A Field Guide to System Development: Modern Application of the Jackson Method. (Series in Industrial Software Engineering Practice). 400p. 1993. text ed. 59.95 (0-471-93786-X) Wiley.

Rule, Paul A. K'ung-Tzu or Confucius? The Jesuit Interpretation of Confucianism. 292p. (Orig.). 1987. pap. text ed. 19.95 (0-86861-913-2) Routledge Chapman & Hall.

***Rule, Rebecca.** The Best Revenge: Short Stories. LC 94-40944. (Hardscrabble Bks.). 1995. write for info. (0-87451-702-8) U Pr of New Eng.

— Wood Heat: Stories from up North. Zarucchi, Roy & Page, Carolyn, eds. (Illus.). 112p. (Orig.). 1992. pap. 9.95 (1-879205-33-5) Nightshade Pr.

— Wood Heat: Stories from up North. 2nd ed. Zarucchi, Roy & Page, Carolyn, eds. (Illus.). 112p. (Orig.). 1992. reprint ed. pap. text ed. 9.95 (1-879205-35-1) Nightshade Pr.

Rule, Rebecca & Wheeler, Susan. Creating the Story: Guides for New Writers. LC 92-30964. 288p. 1993. 14. 95 (0-435-08765-7) Heinemann.

Rule, Robin. Baseball Prayers. 16p. (Orig.). 1990. pap. 3.00 (1-879082-02-0) Rainy Day CA.

Rule, Wilma & Zimmerman, Joseph F., eds. Electoral Systems in Comparative Perspective: Their Impact on Women & Minorities. LC 93-28034. (Contributions in Political Science Ser.: No. 338). 280p. 1994. text ed. 59. 95 (0-313-28633-7, Greenwood Pr) Greenwood.

— United States Electoral Systems: Their Impact on Women & Minorities. LC 91-34481. (Contributions in Political Science Ser.: No. 294). 264p. 1992. text ed. 59.95 (0-313-27730-3, ZIU/, Greenwood Pr); pap. text ed. 16. 95 (0-275-94240-6, B4240, Greenwood Pr) Greenwood.

***Ruley, Angela M.** Rockbridge County, Virginia Death Registers, 1853-1870, 1912-1917. vi, 504p. 1993. 57.00x (0-8095-8172-8); pap. 30.00x (0-8095-8679-7) Borgo Pr.

Ruley, John D., et al. Networking Windows NT. LC 93-33267. 1994. pap. text ed. 27.95 (0-471-31072-7) Wiley.

Ruley, M. J. Projects in General Metalwork. (gr. 9 up). 1969. text ed. 26.64 (0-02-671730-1) Glencoe.

Rulfo, Juan. The Burning Plain & Other Stories. Schade, George D., tr. LC 67-25698. (Texas Pan American Ser.). (Illus.). 191p. 1967. pap. 10.95 (0-292-70132-2) U of Tex Pr.

— El Llano en Llamas. (SPA.). 1989. 5.50 (0-8288-2574-2) Fr & Eur.

— Pedro Paramo. (SPA.). 1989. 6.50 (0-8288-2575-0) Fr & Eur.

— Pedro Paramo. Paden, Margaret S., tr. 128p. 1990. pap. 11.00 (0-8021-3390-8) Grove-Atltic.

— Toda la Obra. Montemayor, Carlos, ed. (Coleccion Archivos). 802p. (SPA.). (C). 1991. 41.95 (84-00-07121-2) U of Pittsburgh Pr.

Rull, R. N. Simian Viruses. Bd. with Rhinoviruses. (Virology Monographs: Vol. 2). (Illus.). iv, 124p. 1968. 25.00 (0-387-80890-6) Spr-Verlag.

Rull, Valenti. Contribucion a la Paleoecologia de Pantepui y la Gran Sabana: (Guayana Venezolana: Clima, Biogeografia, Ecologia) (Scientia Guaianae Ser.: Vol. 2). (Illus.). 133p. (SPA.). 1991. pap. 39.00 (980-07-0373-X, 045559) Koeltz Sci Bks.

Rulla, Luigi M. Depth Psychology & Vocation: A Psycho-Social Perspective. LC 70-146938. (C). 1971. 36.50 (88-7652-374-X) Loyola Univ Pr.

Rulli, Angelo, ed. Musical Boxes & Other Musical Marvels. (Illus.). 500p. 1991. pap. 15.00 (0-915000-02-4) Musical Box Soc.

— Musical Boxes & Other Musical Marvels: A Decade of Listening. (Illus.). (Orig.). 1987. pap. 15.00 (0-317-65025-4) Musical Box Soc.

Rullman, Beryl. The Ranger. Vantruse, James, ed. 384p. 1992. pap. 12.95 (1-880416-53-0) NW Pub.

Rullman, Hans P., tr. see Omrcanin, Margaret S.

Rullman, R. R. & Rullman, S. S. The Mother: A Suburban Horror Story. 290p. (Orig.). 1993. pap. text ed. 8.95 (0-9615938-5-7) Banner Bks.

Rullman, S. S., jt. auth. see Rullman, R. R.

Rullo, Thomas A., ed. Advances in Computer Programming Management, Vol. 1. LC 81-640183. (Heyden Advances Library in EDP Management). 254p. reprint ed. pap. 72. 40 (0-8357-5151-1, 2032691) Bks Demand.

— Advances in Computer Security Management, Vol. 1. LC 81-641060. (Heyden Advances Library in EDP Management). 263p. reprint ed. pap. 75.00 (0-8357-5152-X, 2032688) Bks Demand.

— Advances in Data Base Management, Vol. 1. LC 81-640184. (Heyden Advances Library in EDP Management). 223p. reprint ed. pap. 63.60 (0-8357-5154-6, 2032687) Bks Demand.

— Advances in Data Communications Management, Vol. 1. LC 81-641056. (Heyden Advances Library in EDP Management). 261p. reprint ed. pap. 74.40 (0-8357-5155-4, 2032690) Bks Demand.

— Advances in Data Processing Management, Vol. 1. LC 81-640185. (Heyden Advances Library in EDP Management). (Illus.). 218p. reprint ed. pap. 62.20 (0-8357-5156-2, 2032686) Bks Demand.

— Advances in Distributed Processing Management, Vol. 1. (Wiley-Heyden Advances in EDP Management Library). 200p. 1980. text ed. 76.95 (0-471-25997-7, Pub. by Wiley Heyden) Wiley.

— Advances in Distributed Processing Management, Vol. 1. LC 81-641059. (Heyden Advances Library in EDP Management). 217p. reprint ed. pap. 61.90 (0-8357-5157-0, 2032689) Bks Demand.

Ruloff, Dieter, jt. auth. see Frei, Daniel.

Rulon, Curt M., jt. auth. see Griggs, Silas.

Rulon, Philip R. The Compassionate Samaritan: The Life of Lyndon Baines Johnson. LC 81-210. 356p. (C). 1981. text ed. 28.95 (0-88229-306-0) Nelson-Hall.

Rulon, Philip R., ed. Letters from the Hill Country: The Correspondence Between Rebekah & Lyndon Baines Johnson. LC 82-19369. 1982. 17.00 (0-914476-97-1) Thorp Springs.

Rulon, Philip R., ed. see Richardson, Gladwell.

Rulseh, Ted & Petrie, Chuck, eds. Harvest Moon: An Anthology of Wisconsin Writers. 224p. 1993. 19.95 (1-883755-00-X) Lost Riv Pr.

Rumack. Pediatric Radiology: A Teaching File. 350p. 1991. 49.95 (0-8151-7463-2, Yr Bk Med Pubs) Mosby Yr Bk.

— Perinatal & Infant Brain Imaging. 1991. write for info. (0-8151-7459-4, Yr Bk Med Pubs) Mosby Yr Bk.

Rumack & Johnson. Perinatal & Infant Brain Imaging: Ultrasound & CT. 1984. 74.95 (0-8151-7458-6, Yr Bk Med Pubs) Mosby Yr Bk.

Rumack, Carol M. Diagnostic Ultrasound. 1504p. 1991. 235. 00 (0-8016-9040-4) Mosby Yr Bk.

Rumack, Carol M., et al. Pocket Atlas of Pediatric Ultrasound. 120p. 1990. 15.95 (0-88167-620-9) Raven.

Rumaihi, Muhammad. Beyond Oil: Unity & Development in the Gulf. pap. 9.95 (0-86356-032-6, Pub. by Saqi Bks UK) Interlink Pub.

Rumaker. My First Satyrnalia. 1980. pap. 7.95 (0-912516-51-8) Grey Fox.

Rumaker, Michael. Gringos & Other Stories: A New Edition. deluxe ed. LC 90-63313. 280p. 1991. reprint ed. 25.00 (0-933598-27-0) NC Wesleyan Pr.

— Gringos & Other Stories: A New Edition. LC 90-63313. 280p. 1991. reprint ed. pap. 12.95 (0-933598-26-2) NC Wesleyan Pr.

— To Kill a Cardinal. 160p. 1992. text ed. 11.95 (0-9632962-2-1) A Mann Kaye.

R

An Asterisk (*) at the beginning of an entry indicates that the title is appearing in BIP for the first time.

Rumalshah, Mano. Pakistan. (Focus On Ser.). (Illus.). 32p. (YA). (gr. 7-10). 1991. 17.95 (*0-237-60193-1*, Pub. by Evans Bros Ltd UK) Trafalgar.

***Rumary, Mark.** The Dry Garden: A Practical Guide to Planning & Planting. LC 95-18312. (Illus.). 128p. 1995. 19.95 (*0-8069-3831-5*) Sterling.

Rumat. Handbook of Mushroom Poisoning. 1994. write for info. (*0-8493-0194-7*) CRC Pr.

***Rumayor, Armando, photos.** Manifesto Photography. (Illus.). 1994. write for info. (*0-614-04252-6*) Focal Point Pr.

***Rumbach, John.** Friends & Neighbors: A Tribute to the People of Dubois County. Baumann, J. Bruce, ed. (Illus.). 112p. 1995. 26.95 (*1-884850-05-7*) Scripps Howard.

Rumbarger, J. H., jt. auth. see Shapiro, W.

Rumbarger, John J. Profits, Power, & Prohibition: American Alcohol Reform & the Industrializing of America, 1800-1930. LC 88-1884. 272p. 1989. 74.50 (*0-88706-782-4*); pap. 24.95 (*0-88706-783-2*) State U NY Pr.

Rumbaugh, et al. Cerebrovascular Disease: Imaging & International Treatment Options. LC 94-27327. 544p. 1995. 225.00 (*0-89640-259-2*) Igaku-Shoin.

Rumbaugh, Jim. Object-Oriented Modeling & Design. 1990. text ed. 55.33 (*0-13-629841-9*) P-H.

Rumbaugh, Margaret, ed. see Reid, Tom & Bowen, Barbara.

Rumbaugh, Margaret G. Simplifying Contract Terminations. 2nd ed. Rankin, Anne M., ed. 154p. 1991. pap. 37.45 (*0-940343-29-0*) Natl Contract Mgmt.

Rumbaugh, Margaret G., ed. see Badgerow, Dana B., et al.

Rumbaught, Duane M., ed. Gibbon & Siamang: A Series of Volumes on the Lesser Apes, 4 vols., Set. Incl. Vol. 1. Evolution, Ecology, Behavior & Captive Maintenance. 1972. 108.00 (*3-8055-1362-3*); Vol. 2. Anatomy, Dentition, Taxonomy & Molecular Evolution & Behavior. 1973. 108.00 (*3-8055-1341-0*); Vol. 3. Natural History, Social Behavior, Reproduction, Vocalizations, Prehension. 1974. 104.00 (*3-8055-1602-9*); Vol. 4. Suspensory Behavior, Locomotion, & Other Behaviors of Captive Gibbons; Cognition. 1976. 188.00 (*3-8055-1658-4*); (Illus.). 508.00 (*3-8055-2308-4*) S Karger.

Rumbaut, Hendle. Dove Dream. LC 93-26538. (J). 1994. 13.95 (*0-395-68393-9*) HM.

Rumbaut, Ruben, jt. ed. see Cornelius, Wayne A.

Rumbaut, Ruben D. Esa Palabra. LC 80-70306. (Coleccion Espejo de Paciencia Ser.). 63p. (Orig.). (SPA.). 1981. pap. 5.95 (*0-89729-258-8*) Ediciones.

Rumbaut, Ruben G., jt. auth. see Portes, Alejandro.

Rumbelow, jt. auth. see Hindley.

Rumbelow, Donald. Jack the Ripper: The Complete Casebook. 1990. mass mkt. 5.99 (*0-425-11869-X*) Berkley Pub.

Rumberger, John A., jt. ed. see Stanford, William.

Rumberger, Russell W. Overeducation in the U. S. Labor Market. LC 80-24648. 160p. 1981. text ed. 49.95 (*0-275-90715-5*, C0715, Praeger Pubs) Greenwood.

Rumberger, Russell W. & Burke, Gerald, eds. Future Impact of Technology on Work & Education. 225p. 1987. 60.00 (*1-85000-083-2*, Falmer Pr); pap. 31.00 (*1-85000-084-0*, Falmer Pr) Taylor & Francis.

Rumberger, Russell W. & Levin, Henry M. Computers in Small Business. 50p. (Orig.). 1986. pap. text ed. 6.00 (*0-940791-04-8*) NFIB Found.

Rumberger, Russell W., jt. ed. see Burke, Gerald.

Rumble, Adrian. Shadow Dance: Poems of the Night for Young People. (Illus.). 112p. 1988. 16.95 (*0-304-31493-5*, Pub. by Cassell UK) Sterling.

Rumble, Alexander, ed. The Reign of Cnut. LC 94-16870. (Studies in the Early History of Britain). 1994. write for info. (*0-8386-3605-5*) Fairleigh Dickinson.

Rumble, Dale. And Then the End Shall Come. 154p. (Orig.). 1991. pap. 7.99 (*1-56043-063-X*) Destiny Image.
— The Crucible of the Future. 168p. (Orig.). 1989. pap. 7.99 (*0-914903-89-6*) Destiny Image.
— The Diakonate. 240p. (Orig.). 1990. pap. 7.99 (*1-56043-020-6*) Destiny Image.
— Prepared for His Glory. (Illus.). 288p. (Orig.). 1986. pap. 9.99 (*0-914903-08-X*) Destiny Image.
— Windows of the Soul. (Orig.). 1977. pap. 3.50 (*0-89350-017-8*) Fountain Pr.

Rumble, Donald. The Ephesian Connection. 210p. 1990. pap. 7.99 (*1-56043-016-8*) Destiny Image.
— Winds of Change. 54p. 1986. reprint ed. pap. 3.50 (*0-914903-12-8*) Destiny Image.

Rumble, Greville, jt. ed. see Araujo e Oliveira, Joao B.

Rumble, Greville, jt. ed. see Oliveira, Joao.

Rumble, J. R. & Hampel, Viktor E. Database Management in Science Technology. 1984. 87.25 (*0-444-86865-8*, I-085-84) Elsevier.

Rumble, J. R. & Smith, F. J. Database Systems in Science & Engineering. (Illus.). 304p. 1990. 85.00 (*0-7503-0048-5*) IOP Pub.

Rumble, J. R., Jr., jt. ed. see Glazman, J. S.

Rumble, L. A Brief Life of Christ. 54p. 1974. reprint ed. pap. 2.00 (*0-89555-096-2*) TAN Bks Pubs.

Rumble, Leslie. The Incredible Creed of the Jehovah Witnesses. 1977. reprint ed. pap. 1.00 (*0-89555-025-3*) TAN Bks Pubs.

Rumble, Leslie & Carty, Charles M. Radio Replies, 3 vols., 1. LC 79-51938. 1979. reprint ed. write for info. (*0-89555-089-X*) TAN Bks Pubs.
— Radio Replies, 3 vols., 2. LC 79-51938. 1979. reprint ed. write for info. (*0-89555-090-3*) TAN Bks Pubs.
— Radio Replies, 3 vols., 3. LC 79-51938. 1979. reprint ed. write for info. (*0-89555-091-1*) TAN Bks Pubs.
— Radio Replies, 3 vols., Set. LC 79-51938. 1979. reprint ed. pap. 36.00 (*0-89555-159-4*) TAN Bks Pubs.

Rumble, Leslie, jt. auth. see Carty, Charles.

***Rumble, P. Barry.** Full Moon. LC 94-39517. 14p. (J). 1994. pap. text ed. 4.00 (*0-88734-422-4*) Players Pr.

***Rumble, Patrica B.** Las Fabulas Chistosas de Esopo: Aesops Funny Fables. (Multicultural Theatre Ser.). 35p. (J). (gr. k-8). 1994. pap. 3.00 (*1-57514-103-5*, 1132) Encore Perform Pub.

Rumble, Patricia B. The Archer & the Princess: A Comedy Based on a Russian Folk Tale. (Stage Magic Play Ser.). (Illus.). 48p. (Orig.). (J). (gr. 4-10). 1990. pap. 3.00 (*0-88680-334-9*) I E Clark.
— Circus Boy. 29p. (Orig.). (J). (gr. 3-8). 1993. pap. 3.00 (*1-57514-110-8*, 1100) Encore Perform Pub.

Rumble, Patrick & Testa, Bart, eds. Pier Paolo Pasolini: Contemporary Perspectives. (Major Italian Authors Ser.). 258p. 1993. 50.00 (*0-8020-2966-3*) U of Toronto Pr.
— Pier Paolo Pasolini: Contemporary Perspectives. (Major Italian Authors Ser.: No. 1). 256p. 1993. pap. 17.95 (*0-8020-7737-4*) U of Toronto Pr.

***Rumble, Patrick A.** Allegories of Contamination: Pier Paolo Pasolini's Trilogy of Life. (Italian Studies). (Illus.). 200p. 1995. 50.00 (*0-8020-0428-8*); pap. 17.95 (*0-8020-7219-4*) U of Toronto Pr.

Rumble, Thomas C., ed. The Breton Lays in Middle English. LC 65-11629. (Waynebooks Ser.: No. 25). (Illus.). 270p. 1965. reprint ed. pap. 15.95 (*0-8143-1265-9*) Wayne St U Pr.

Rumble, Wilfrid E., ed. see Austin, John.

Rumbley, Rose-Mary. Unauthorized History of Dallas. (Illus.). 192p. 1991. pap. 9.95 (*0-89015-833-9*) Sunbelt Media.
— What? No Chili? LC 94-39639. (Illus.). (J). 1994. 14.95 (*0-89015-992-0*, Eakin Pr) Sunbelt Media.

Rumbold, Margaret E. Traducteur Huguenot: Peirre Coste. LC 90-34363. (American University Studies: Romance Languages & Literature: Ser. II, Vol. 140). 190p. (C). 1990. text ed. 36.95 (*0-8204-1270-8*) P Lang Pubs.

Rumbold, Valerie. Women's Place in Pope's World. (Cambridge Studies in Eighteenth-Century English Literature & Thought: No. 2). (Illus.). (C). 1989. 64.95 (*0-521-36308-X*) Cambridge U Pr.

Rumbold, Valerie & Fenlon, Iain, eds. A Short-Title Catalogue of Music Printed Before 1825 in the Fitzwilliam Museum, Cambridge. (Illus.). 179p. (C). 1992. 90.00 (*0-521-41535-7*) Cambridge U Pr.

Rumbolz, James M., jt. auth. see Clem, Alan L.

***Rumburg, H. Rondel.** Some Southern Documents of the People Called Baptists. 276p. 1995. 24.95 (*0-9639730-1-0*) Soc Bibl & So Stud.
— Stonewall Jackson's Verse. 147p. 1992. 16.95 (*0-9639730-0-2*) Soc Bibl & So Stud.

Rumelhart, David E., et al. Parallel Distributed Processing: Explorations in the Microstructure of Cognition, 2 Vols. 1986. 90.00 (*0-262-18123-1*, Bradford Bks) MIT Pr.

Rumelhart, David E., jt. ed. see Chauvin, Yves.

Rumelhart, David E., jt. ed. see Gluck, Mark A.

Rumelhart, David E., jt. auth. see McClelland, James L.

Rumelhart, David E., et al. Parallel Distributed Processing: Explorations in the Microstructure of Cognition, 2 vols., Set. 1208p. 1987. 45.00 (*0-262-63112-1*, Bradford Bks) MIT Pr.

Rumelt, Richard P. Strategy, Structure & Economic Performance. 1986. pap. text ed. 14.95 (*0-07-103265-7*) McGraw.

Rumelt, Richard P., et al. Fundamental Issues in Strategy: A Research Agenda. 1994. text ed. 45.95 (*0-07-103590-7*) McGraw.

Rumelt, Richard P., et al, eds. Fundamental Issues in Strategy: A Research Agenda. LC 93-38541. 656p. (C). 1994. 45.00 (*0-87584-343-3*) Harvard Busn.

Rumely, R. S. Capacity Theory on Algebraic Curves. (Lecture Notes in Mathematics Ser.: Vol. 1378). iii, 437p. 1989. pap. 50.30 (*0-387-51410-4*, 3278) Spr-Verlag.

Rumens, Carol. Greening of the Snow Beach. 1990. pap. 14.95 (*1-85224-062-8*) Dufour.
— Thinking of Skins: New & Selected Poems. 160p. 1994. pap. 18.95 (*1-85224-280-9*, Pub. by Bloodaxe Bks UK) Dufour.

Rumens, Carol, intro. New Women Poets. 176p. (Orig.). 1990. pap. 17.95 (*1-85224-145-4*, Pub. by Bloodaxe Bks UK) Dufour.

Rumer, Boris. Soviet Central Asia: A Tragic Experiment. 240p. (C). 1990. text ed. 49.95 (*0-04-445146-6*); pap. text ed. 19.95 (*0-04-445896-7*) Routledge Chapman & Hall.

Rumer, Boris Z. Soviet Steel: The Challenge of Industrial Modernization in the U. S. S. R. LC 88-47745. (Cornell Studies in Soviet History & Science). (Illus.). 264p. 1989. 37.50 (*0-8014-2077-6*) Cornell U Pr.

Rumer, Eugene B. The Building Blocks of Russia's Future Military Doctrine. LC 93-42246. 1994. write for info. (*0-8330-1483-8*, MR-359-A) Rand Corp.
— Russian National Security & Foreign Policy in Transition. LC 94-42678. 67p. 1995. pap. text ed. 15.00 (*0-8330-1615-6*, MF-512-AF) Rand Corp.

Rumer, Thomas A. American Legion: An Official History, 1919-1989. 732p. 1990. 24.95 (*0-87131-622-6*) M Evans.
— The Wagon Trains of 'Forty-Four: A Comparative View of the Individual Caravans in the Emigration of 1844 to Oregon. LC 89-62716. (American Trails Ser.: No. XVII). (Illus.). 274p. 1991. 35.50 (*0-87062-197-1*) A H Clark.

Rumer, Thomas A., ed. see Hammer, Jacob.

Rumery, Kenneth R. Introduction to Musical Design, Vol. I. 480p. (C). 1992. pap. write for info. (*0-697-10719-1*) Brown & Benchmark.
— Introduction to Musical Design, Vol. II. 432p. (C). 1992. pap. text ed. write for info. (*0-697-11648-4*) Brown & Benchmark.

Rumford, Benjamin T. Collected Works of Count Rumford, 5 vols. Brown, Sanborn C., ed. Incl. Vol. 1. Nature of Heat. LC 68-17633. (Illus.). 521p. 1968. 42.50 (*0-674-13951-8*); Vol. 4. Light & Armament. LC 68-17633. (Illus.). 511p. 1970. 42.50 (*0-674-13954-2*); Vol. 5. Public Institutions. LC 68-17633. (Illus.). 524p. 1970. 39.95 (*0-674-13955-0*); LC 68-17633. write for info. (*0-318-53031-7*) HUP.

***Rumford, Douglas.** Scared to Life. 180p. 1994. pap. 8.99 (*1-56476-413-3*, 6-3413, Victor Books) SP Pubns.

Rumi. Rending the Veil: Literal & Poetic Translations of Rumi. Shiva, Shahram T., tr. LC 94-36971. 280p. (PER.). (C). 1995. 27.95 (*0-934252-46-7*) Hohm Pr.
— Say I Am You: Poetry Interspersed with Stories of Rume & Shams. 1994. pap. 12.00 (*1-884237-00-2*) Maypop.

Rumi, Jalal A. Mystical Poems of Rumi. Arberry, Arthur J., tr. LC 68-29935. vi, 202p. 1974. pap. 10.95 (*0-226-73151-0*, P584) U Ch Pr.
— Mystical Poems of Rumi: Second Selection, Poems 201-400, Vol. 34. Arberry, A. J., tr. LC 79-5101. (Persian Heritage Ser.). 200p. 1983. 35.00 (*0-89158-477-3*) Mazda Pubs.
— Mystical Poems of Rumi Two: Second Selection, Poems 201-400. Yarshater, Ehsan, ed. Arberry, Arthur J., tr. LC 79-5101. 208p. 1991. pap. 10.95 (*0-226-73152-9*) U Ch Pr.

***Rumi, Jalalodin.** Rumi, Fountain of Fire: A Celebration of Life & Love. Khalili, Nader, tr. 128p. (Orig.). 1994. pap. 13.95 (*1-878179-12-8*) Burning Gate Pr.

***Rumi, Jalaludin.** Teachings of Rumi. 1994. pap. 15.00 (*0-86304-067-5*) ISHK Bk Service.

Rumi, Jelaluddin. Birdsong: Fifty-Three Short Poems by Rumi. Barks, Coleman, tr. & intro. by. 64p. (Orig.). 1993. pap. 9.00 (*0-9618916-7-X*) Maypop.
— Daylight. (Illus.). 1990. 19.00 (*0-939660-35-0*) Threshold VT.
— Delicious Laughter: Rambunctious Teaching Stories from the Mathnawi of Jelaluddin Rumi. Barks, Coleman, tr. 146p. 1990. 7.50 (*0-9618916-1-0*) Maypop.
— Feeling the Shoulder of the Lion: Poems & Teaching Stories from the Mathnawi. Barks, Coleman, tr. LC 91-4749. 100p. 1991. pap. 9.00 (*0-939660-37-7*) Threshold VT.
— Like This. 64p. 1990. pap. 7.50 (*0-9618916-2-9*) Maypop.
— Love Is a Stranger: Selected Lyric Poetry of Jelaluddin Rumi. Helminski, Kabir E., tr. & intro. by. 96p. (Orig.). 1993. pap. 9.00 (*0-939660-32-6*) Threshold VT.
— Night & Sleep. Barks, Coleman & Bly, Robert, trs. (Illus.). 48p. (Orig.). 1981. pap. 6.00 (*0-938756-02-8*) Yellow Moon.
— One-Handed Basket Weaving: Poems on the Theme of Work from the Mathnawi. Barks, Coleman, tr. & intro. by. 133p. (Orig.). (C). 1992. pap. 9.00 (*0-9618916-3-7*) Maypop.
— These Branching Moments: Forty Odes. Barks, Coleman & Moyne, John, trs. LC 87-36429. 52p. (Orig.). 1988. pap. 6.95 (*0-914278-50-9*) Copper Beech.
— We Are Three. 96p. 1987. pap. 7.50 (*0-9618916-0-2*) Maypop.
— When Grapes Turn to Wine. Bly, Robert, tr. (Illus.). 24p. (PER.). 1986. reprint ed. pap. 6.00 (*0-938756-16-8*) Yellow Moon.

Rumi, Julie. Coming Together Book 1: Integrating Math & Language in a Sheltered Approach. 144p. 1994. pap. text ed. 11.25 (*0-13-210451-2*) P-H.
— Coming Together Book 2: Integrating Math & Language in a Sheltered Approach. 144p. 1994. pap. text ed. 11.25 (*0-13-146606-2*) P-H.

Rumi, Mevlana C. Crazy As We Are. Ergin, Nevit O., tr. 80p. (Orig.). (C). 1992. per., pap. 9.95 (*0-934252-30-0*) Hohm Pr.

Rumi, Mevlana J. Magnificent One: Selected New Verses from Divan-i Kebir. Ergin, Nevit O., tr. 112p. (Orig.). (C). 1993. pap. text ed. 10.95 (*0-943914-63-9*) Larson Pubns.
— Open Secret: Versions of Rumi. Barks, Coleman, tr. LC 83-50052. 96p. (Orig.). 1984. reprint ed. pap. 9.00 (*0-939660-06-7*) Threshold VT.
— The Ruins of the Heart. Helminski, Edmund, tr. LC 83-145353. 56p. (Orig.). 1981. pap. 6.00 (*0-939660-03-2*) Threshold VT.
— Unseen Rain: Quatrains of Rumi. Moyne, John & Barks, Coleman, trs. LC 86-50782. 96p. (Orig.). 1986. 15.00 (*0-939660-17-2*); pap. 8.00 (*0-939660-16-4*) Threshold VT.

Rumiantsev, A., jt. ed. see Collet's Holdings, Ltd. Staff.

Rumiko Takahashi. Lum, Vol. 1: Uruseiyatsura, Graphic Novel. Seiji Horibuchi, ed. Satoru Fujii & Jones, Gerard, trs. (Illus.). 194p. 1990. pap. 14.95 (*0-929279-64-6*) Viz Commns Inc.
— Lum, Vol. 2: Uruseiyatsura, Graphic Novel. Seiji Horibuchi, ed. Satoru Fujii & Jones, Gerard, trs. (Illus.). 214p. 1990. pap. 14.95 (*0-929279-63-8*) Viz Commns Inc.
— Ranma One-Half, Vol. 1. Seiji Horibuchi, ed. Satoru Fujii, tr. (Illus.). 304p. (Orig.). 1993. pap. 16.95 (*0-929279-93-X*) Viz Commns Inc.
— Rumic World. Seiji Horibuchi, ed. Satoru Fujii, tr. (Illus.). 150p. (Orig.). Date not set. pap. 14.95 (*0-929279-83-2*) Viz Commns Inc.

Ruminer, Cliff. Blazing Bellyboats & Other Angling Misadventures. 1993. 17.95 (*1-879034-06-9*) MS River Pub.

Rumley, Dennis & Minghi, Julian V. The Geography of Border Landscapes. (Illus.). 352p. (C). 1991. text ed. 65.00 (*0-415-04825-7*, A5222) Routledge.

Rumley, Hilary, jt. auth. see McNair, William.

Rumman, Ali, jt. auth. see Mansour, Awad.

Rumman, Wadi S. Statically Indeterminant Structures. 504p. 1991. text ed. 89.95 (*0-471-09345-9*) Wiley.

Rummel, Erika. Erasmus & His Catholic Critics, Vol. 1, 1515-1522. (Bibliotheca Humanistica & Reformatorica Ser.). 277p. 1989. 77.50x (*90-6004-401-0*, Pub. by B De Graaf NE) Coronet Bks.
— Erasmus & His Catholic Critics, Vol. 2: 1523-1536. (Bibliotheca Humanistica & Reformatorica Ser.: No. 45). 220p. 1989. 77.50x (*0-685-35766-X*, Pub. by B De Graaf NE) Coronet Bks.
— Erasmus' Annotations on the New Testament: From Philologist to Theologian. (Erasmus Studies). 246p. 1986. 40.00 (*0-8020-5683-0*) U of Toronto Pr.
— Erasmus As a Translator of the Classics. (Erasmus Studies: No. 7). 191p. 1985. 35.00 (*0-8020-5653-9*) U of Toronto Pr.
— The Humanist-Scholastic Debate in the Renaissance & Reformation. LC 94-34983. (Historical Studies: No. 120). 259p. 1995. 45.00 (*0-674-42250-3*, RUMHUM) HUP.

Rummel, Erika, ed. The Erasmus Reader. 432p. 1990. pap. 19.95 (*0-8020-6806-5*) U of Toronto Pr.

Rummel, Erika, tr. & intro. Scheming Papists & Lutheran Fools: Five Reformation Satires. LC 92-34382. 112p. (Orig.). (C). 1993. 25.00 (*0-8232-1482-6*); pap. 15.00 (*0-8232-1483-4*) Fordham.

Rummel, Erika, ed. see Erasmus, Desiderius.

Rummel, J. D., et al, eds. Space & Its Exploration. (Space Biology & Medicine Ser.). 338p. 1993. 99.95 (*1-56347-061-6*) AIAA.

Rummel, Jack. Langston Hughes. (Black Americans of Achievement Ser.). (Illus.). 112p. (Orig.). (YA). (gr. 5 up). 1989. 17.95 (*1-55546-595-1*); pap. 9.95 (*0-7910-0201-2*) Chelsea Hse.
— Malcolm X. (Black Americans of Achievement Ser.). (Illus.). 112p. (YA). (gr. 5 up). 1989. lib. bdg. 17.95 (*1-55546-600-1*); pap. 9.95 (*0-7910-0227-6*) Chelsea Hse.
— Malcolm X. 1990. pap. 3.95 (*0-87067-554-0*, Melrose Sq) Holloway.
— Mexico. (Let's Visit Places & Peoples of the World Ser.). (Illus.). 128p. (J). (gr. 5 up). 1990. 14.95 (*0-7910-1110-0*) Chelsea Hse.
— Muhammad Ali. (Black Americans of Achievement Ser.). (Illus.). 112p. (Orig.). (YA). (gr. 5 up). 1988. 17.95 (*1-55546-569-2*); pap. 9.95 (*0-7910-0210-1*) Chelsea Hse.
— Robert Oppenheimer: Dark Prince. (Makers of Modern Science Ser.). (Illus.). 144p. (YA). (gr. 7-12). 1992. lib. bdg. 16.95 (*0-8160-2598-3*) Facts on File.
— The U. S. Marine Corps. (Know Your Government Ser.). (Illus.). 128p. (J). (gr. 5 up). 1990. 14.95 (*1-55546-110-7*) Chelsea Hse.

Rummel, Jack, jt. auth. see Dr. John, pseud.

Rummel, Jack, jt. auth. see Mac Rebennack, John.

Rummel, Mary. God's Love for Happiness: A Return to Family Values. LC 92-91032. (Illus.). 64p. (Orig.). (J). (gr. k up). 1992. pap. 9.95 (*0-9635091-0-1*) Olive Brnch.

Rummel, Mary K. This Body She's Entered: A Collection of Poems. 1990. pap. 6.00 (*0-89823-115-9*) New Rivers Pr.

Rummel, Merle, jt. auth. see Henning, Elma.

Rummel, R. J. China's Bloody Century: Genocide & Mass Murder since 1900. 196p. (C). 1991. 39.95 (*0-88738-417-X*) Transaction Pubs.
— The Conflict Helix: Principles & Practices of Interpersonal, Social & International Conflict & Cooperation. 297p. (C). 1990. 39.95 (*0-88738-389-0*) Transaction Pubs.
— Death by Government: Genocide & Mass Murder since 1900. LC 93-21279. 510p. (C). 1994. 49.95 (*1-56000-145-3*) Transaction Pubs.
— Democide: Nazi Genocide & Mass Murder. 150p. (C). 1991. text ed. 34.95 (*1-56000-004-X*) Transaction Pubs.
— Lethal Politics: Soviet Genocide & Mass Murder Since 1917. 172p. (C). 1990. 39.95 (*0-88738-333-5*) Transaction Pubs.

Rummel, Reiner & Sanso, Fernando, eds. Satellite Altimetry in Geodesy & Oceanography. LC 93-17952. (Lecture Notes in Earth Sciences Ser.: Vol. 50). 1993. 99.00 (*0-387-56818-2*) Spr-Verlag.

Rummel, Reiner, jt. ed. see Sanso, Fernando.

Rummel, Reiner, et al, eds. Gravity, Gradiometry & Gravimetry. (International Association of Geodesy Symposia Ser.: Vol. 103). x, 181p. 1990. pap. 54.00 (*0-387-97267-6*) Spr-Verlag.

Rummel, Reinhardt, ed. Toward Political Union: Planning a Common Foreign & Security Policy in the European Community. 376p. (C). 1992. pap. text ed. 54.50 (*0-8133-8518-0*) Westview.

Rummel, Robert W. Howard Hughes & TWA. LC 90-39534. (History of Aviation Ser.). (Illus.). 442p. (C). 1991. 29.95 (*1-56098-017-6*) Smithsonian.

Rummel, Rudolph J. Applied Factor Analysis. 617p. 1970. pap. 28.95 (*0-8101-0824-0*) Northwestern U Pr.
— The Dimensionality of Nations Project: Attributes of Nations & Behavior of Nation Dyads, 1950-1965. LC 75-40620. 1975. write for info. (*0-89138-121-X*) ICPSR.

Rummel, Rudolph J. & Tanter, Raymond. Dimensions of Conflict Behavior Within & Between Nations, 1955-1960. 1974. write for info. (*0-89138-072-8*) ICPSR.

Rummel, W., jt. ed. see Forth, W.

Rummler, jt. auth. see Odiorne.

Rummler, Geary A. & Brache, Alan P. Improving Performance: How to Manage the White Space on the Organization Chart. LC 89-43299. (Management Ser.). 247p. 1990. text ed. 29.95 (*1-55542-214-4*) Jossey-Bass.
— Improving Performance: How to Manage the White Space on the Organization Chart. 2nd ed. LC 94-48105. (Management Ser.). 240p. 1995. 29.95 (*0-7879-0090-7*) Jossey-Bass.

Rummo, Carmen P. Piano Improvisation on Rhythm & Dissonant Chords: For Individual & Class Instruction. LC 79-91854. 70p. (Orig.). 1979. pap. text ed. 6.95 (*0-913650-12-9*) CPP Belwin.

R

Rummo, Paul-Eerik. September Sun. Barkan, Stanley H., ed. Poom, Ritva, tr. (Review Chapbook Ser.: No. 16: Estonian Poetry 1). 16p. 1989. reprint ed. 15.00 (*0-89304-822-4*, CCC143); reprint ed. 15.00 (*0-89304-823-2*); reprint ed. pap. 5.00 (*0-89304-815-1*); reprint ed. pap. 5.00 (*0-89304-824-0*) Cross-Cultrl NY.

Rumney, Avis. Dying to Please: Anorexia Nervosa & Its Cure. LC 83-9443. 128p. (Orig.). 1983. pap. 17.50x (*0-89950-083-8*) McFarland & Co.

Rumney, Donna. My Picture Book about Me. (Illus.). 20p. (J). (ps). 1988. write for info. (*0-318-64233-6*) My Picture Bks.

Rumney, Jay & Murphy, Joseph P. Probation & Social Adjustment. LC 68-28593. 285p. 1968. reprint ed. text ed. 69.50 (*0-8371-0208-1*, RUPS, Greenwood Pr) Greenwood.

***Rumold, Rainer.** Avant-garde & Crisis: The Expressionist Legacy. 1994. 59.95 (*0-614-03410-8*) Camden Hse.

Rumold, Rainer & Werckmeister, O. K., eds. The Ideological Crisis of Expressionism: The Literary & Artistic German War Colony in Belgium, 1914-1918. (Studies in German Literature, Linguistics & Culture: Vol. 51). (Illus.). 310p. 1991. 49.50 (*0-938100-77-7*) Camden Hse.

Rump, Eric S., ed. see Congreve, William.

Rump, Gabriele, jt. ed. see Roth, Lutz.

Rump, H. H. & Krist, H. Laboratory Manual for the Examination of Water, Waste Water & Soil. 2nd ed. LC 92-12276. 190p. 1992. 49.50 (*1-56081-221-4*) VCH Pubs.

Rump, Martin. Vergleichende Untersuchungen Extensiver und Intensiver Weidebetriebe Mit Rindern und Schafen Aus Grunlandwirtschaftlicher und Okologischer Sicht An Acht Standorten. LC 94-5089. 312p. (GER.). 1994. pap. 99.95 (*0-7734-4048-8*) E Mellen.

***Rump, Nan.** Puppets & Masks: Stagecraft & Storytelling. LC 94-73962. (Illus.). 192p. 1995. 19.95 (*0-87192-298-3*) Davis Mass.

Rump, Richard G., jt. auth. see Beeman, Don R.

Rumpel, Johannes. Lexicon Pindaricum. 498p. 1961. reprint ed. write for info. (*0-318-71017-X*, Pub. by Georg Olms GW) Lubrecht & Cramer.

— Lexicon Theocriteum. 319p. 1961. reprint ed. write for info. (*0-318-72072-8*, Pub. by Georg Olms GW) Lubrecht & Cramer.

— Lexicon Theocriteum. 319p. 1973. reprint ed. write for info. (*0-318-71018-8*, Pub. by Georg Olms GW) Lubrecht & Cramer.

Rumpf, Howard A. Corporate Liquidations for the Lawyer & Accountant. 5th ed. LC 82-5298. 256p. 1982. text ed. 39.50 (*0-13-174383-X*, Busn) P-H.

Rumpf, K. & Pulvers, M. Transistor Electronics: Use of Semiconductor Components in Switching Operations. LC 65-11807. 1965. 124.00 (*0-08-013709-1*, Pub. by Pergamon Repr UK) Franklin.

— Transistor Electronics: Use Semiconductors Comp. Switching Operations. LC 65-11807. 125.00 (*0-08-011089-4*, Pub. by Pergamon Repr UK) Franklin.

Rumpf, Roger, jt. auth. see Luce, Don.

Rumphius. The Poison Tree: Selected Writings of Rumphius on the Natural History of the Indies. Beekman, E. M., tr. LC 81-7605. (Library of the Indies). (Illus.). 272p. 1981. lib. bdg. 30.00 (*0-87023-329-7*) U of Mass Pr.

Rumple, Jethro. A History of Rowan County, North Carolina. (Illus.). 434p. 1990. reprint ed. 30.00 (*0-685-48627-3*, 5035) Genealog Pub.

Rumrich, John P. Matter of Glory: A New Preface to "Paradise Lost" LC 87-40158. 220p. (C). 1987. 49.95 (*0-8229-3564-3*) U of Pittsburgh Pr.

Rumscheidt, H. Martin. Adolf von Harnack: Liberal Theology at Its Height. 336p. 1991. pap. 14.00 (*0-8006-3406-3*) Augsburg Fortress.

— Karl Barth in Review: Posthumous Works Introduced & Assessed. LC 81-5881. (Pittsburgh Theological Monographs: No. 30). xxviii, 118p. (Orig.). 1981. pap. 10.00 (*0-915138-45-X*) Pickwick.

Rumscheidt, H. Martin, ed. The Way of Theology in Karl Barth: Essays & Comments. LC 86-15069. (Princeton Theological Monograph Ser.: No. 8). 1986. pap. 12.00 (*0-915138-61-1*) Pickwick.

Rumscheidt, Martin, tr. see Zellweger-Barth, Max.

Rumsey, Alan, jt. auth. see Merlan, Francesca.

Rumsey, Anne, ed. see Hemley, Robin.

Rumsey, D. Lake, ed. Master Advocates' Handbook. 387p. 1986. 19.95 (*1-55681-059-8*) Natl Inst Trial Ad.

— Master Advocates' Handbook. 2nd ed. 500p. 1988. 34.95 (*1-55681-181-0*, FBA0181) Natl Inst Trial Ad.

Rumsey, Dusty. Gifts I Almost Got You: One Hundred One Great Gifts & Perfect Excuses Why You Didn't Get Them. LC 92-80468. (Illus.). 115p. (Orig.). 1992. pap. 7.95 (*0-929957-06-7*) JSA Pubns.

— Uncivil War. (Illus.). 64p. (Orig.). 1992. 8.95 (*0-941711-19-6*) Wyrick & Co.

— You Know You're an Old Fart When: Recognizing the Tall Tale Signs of Old Age. 1993. pap. 4.95 (*0-918259-52-5*) CCC Pubns.

Rumsey, Francis. Digital Audio Operations. 256p. 1991. 47.95 (*0-240-51311-8*, Focal) Buttrwrth-Heinemann.

— MIDI: Systems & Control. 131p. 1990. pap. text ed. 34.95 (*0-240-51300-2*, Focal) Buttrwrth-Heinemann.

— MIDI Systems & Control. 2nd expanded ed. 256p. 1994. pap. 29.95 (*0-240-51370-3*, Focal) Buttrwrth-Heinemann.

— Stereo Sound for Television. 110p. 1989. pap. 31.95 (*0-240-51288-X*) Buttrwrth-Heinemann.

— Tapeless Sound Recording. (Illus.). 206p. 1990. pap. 23.95 (*0-240-51297-9*) Buttrwrth-Heinemann.

Rumsey, Francis & McCormick, Tim. Sound & Recording: An Introduction. (Illus.). 318p. 1992. pap. 59.95 (*0-240-51313-4*, Focal) Buttrwrth-Heinemann.

— Sound & Recording: An Introduction. 2nd ed. 356p. 1994. pap. 29.95 (*0-240-51383-5*, Focal) Buttrwrth-Heinemann.

Rumsey, Francis & Watkinson, John. The Digital Interface Handbook. LC 93-16385. (Illus.). 224p. 1993. pap. 35.00 (*0-240-51333-9*) Buttrwrth-Heinemann.

— Digital Interface Handbook. 2nd ed. (Illus.). 288p. 1995. pap. 47.95 (*0-240-51396-7*, Focal) Buttrwrth-Heinemann.

Rumsey, H. S. Ballroom Dancing Explained. (Ballroom Dance Ser.). 1985. lib. bdg. 79.95 (*0-87700-656-3*) Revisionist Pr.

Rumsey, H. St. John. Ballroom Dancing Explained. (Ballroom Dance Ser.). 1986. lib. bdg. 79.95 (*0-8490-3367-5*) Gordon Pr.

Rumsey, H. St. John, ed. see Aikin, W. A.

Rumsey, Henry W. Essays on State Medicine. Rosenkrantz, Barbara G., ed. LC 76-40641. (Public Health in America Ser.). 1977. reprint ed. lib. bdg. 35.95 (*0-405-09829-4*) Ayer.

Rumsey, Kimberly A. & Rieger, Paula T. Biological Response Modifiers: A Self-Instruction Manual for Health Professionals. LC 92-81530. 134p. 1992. 29.95 (*0-944496-30-X*) Precept Pr.

Rumsey, Marian, et al. A Cruising Guide to the Tennessee River, Tenn-Tom Waterway, & Lower Tombigbee River. (Illus.). 448p. 1991. 39.95 (*0-87742-259-1*, 60232H) Intl Marine.

Rumsey, Michael G., et al, eds. Personnel Selection & Classification. 504p. 1994. text ed. 49.95 (*0-8058-1644-5*) L Erlbaum Assocs.

Rumsey, Monica S., ed. see Brandt, Frederick R., et al.

Rumsey, Monica S., ed. see Brownell, Charles E., et al.

Rumsey, Monica S., ed. see Woodward, Richard B.

Rumsey, N., jt. auth. see Bull, R.

Rumsey, Peter L. Acts of God & the People, 1620-1730. LC 86-19292. (Studies in Religion: No. 2). 181p. reprint ed. pap. 51.60 (*0-8357-1761-5*, 2070521) Bks Demand.

Rumsey, Theron S., jt. ed. see Steffens, George L.

Rumsey, Thomas R. Men & Women of the Renaissance & Reformation 1300-1600. 487p. (Orig.). (gr. 9-12). 1981. pap. text ed. 15.95 (*0-88334-145-X*) Longman.

Rumsey, W. J., jt. auth. see Marian, Thomas W.

Rumshiskii, L. Z. Elements of Probability Theory. 1965. 77.00 (*0-08-010534-3*, Pub. by Pergamon Repr UK) Franklin.

Rumwell, Claudia. Educational Slide Graphics for the Vascular Laboratory. 20p. 1988. ring bd. 115.00 (*0-941022-13-7*) Appleton Davies.

Rumwell, Claudia, ed. Vascular Laboratory Operations Manual: A Guide to Survival. 2nd rev. ed. (Illus.). 300p. 1995. ring bd. 195.00x (*0-941022-24-2*) Appleton Davies.

Rumwell, Claudia & McPharlin, Michalene, eds. Vascular Laboratory Policies & Procedures Manual. 1993. 595.00 (*0-941022-25-0*) Appleton Davies.

— Vascular Laboratory Policies & Procedures Manual-MSR 1.1. 1995. disk, ring bd. 795.00 (*0-941022-41-2*) Appleton Davies.

— Vascular Laboratory Policies & Procedures Manual-Windows 2.1.1. 1995. disk, ring bd. 795.00 (*0-941022-42-0*) Appleton Davies.

Rumwell, Claudia B. Vascular Laboratory Operations Manual: A Guide to Survival. 1989. 175.00 (*0-941022-14-5*) Appleton Davies.

Rumyantsev, A. M., et al. Soviet Economic Reform: Progress & Problems. 247p. 1975. 22.95 (*0-8464-0867-8*) Beekman Pubs.

Rumyantsev, P. I., jt. auth. see Stanislavski, Constantin.

Rumyantsev, S. Industrial Radiology. (Russian Monographs). 280p. 1969. text ed. 222.00 (*0-677-20850-2*) Gordon & Breach.

Rumyantsev, S. N. Constitutive Immunity. (Medical Intelligence Unit Ser.). write for info. (*1-57059-104-0*) R G Landes.

Rumyantsev, V. G., jt. auth. see Ivaschenko, A. V.

Rumyantsev, Yevgeni. Indian Ocean & Asian Security. (C). 1988. 15.00 (*0-8364-2385-2*, Pub. by Allied II) S Asia.

Runblom, Harald & Norman, Hans, eds. From Sweden to America: A History of the Migration. (Illus.). 391p. 1976. text ed. 53.00x (*91-554-0355-7*) Coronet Bks.

Runchock-Droste, Rita. LCCS Through '95 KJ-KKZ. Date not set. 60.00 (*0-8103-2379-6*) Gale.

— LCCS Through '95 PT No. 2 Dutch & Scand. Date not set. 61.00 (*0-8103-2399-0*) Gale.

Runchock-Droste, Rita & Droste, Kristy. LCCS Class KL-KW. Date not set. write for info. (*0-8103-2382-6*) Gale.

— LCCS Class PQ No. 1. Date not set. 69.00 (*0-8103-2396-6*) Gale.

— LCCS Class U. Date not set. 53.00 (*0-8103-2564-0*) Gale.

— LCCS Schedules with Additions & Changes through 1993. 1994. 1,840.00 (*0-8103-8750-6*, 034150) Gale.

— LCCS Schedules with Additions & Changes through 1993 A MFH. 1994. 35.00 (*0-8103-8751-4*, 034151) Gale.

— LCCS Schedules with Additions & Changes through 1993 B-BJ MF. 1994. 64.00 (*0-8103-8752-2*, 034152) Gale.

— LCCS Schedules with Additions & Changes through 1993 BR-BVMF. 1994. 33.00 (*0-8103-8754-9*, 034154) Gale.

— LCCS Schedules with Additions & Changes through 1993 BX BFH. 1994. 36.00 (*0-8103-8755-7*, 034155) Gale.

— LCCS Schedules with Additions & Changes through 1993 C MFH. 1994. 39.00 (*0-8103-8756-5*, 034156) Gale.

— LCCS Schedules with Additions & Changes through 1993 D-DJ. 1994. 52.00 (*0-8103-8707-7*, 033122) Gale.

— LCCS Schedules with Additions & Changes through 1993 D-DJMFH. (LCCS Schedules with Additions & Changes D-DJ Microfiche Ser.). 1994. 37.00 (*0-8103-8757-3*, 034157) Gale.

— LCCS Schedules with Additions & Changes through 1993 DJKDKMF. 1994. 33.00 (*0-8103-8758-1*, 034158) Gale.

— LCCS Schedules with Additions & Changes through 1993 DL-DRMF. 1994. 34.00 (*0-8103-8759-X*, 034159) Gale.

— LCCS Schedules with Additions & Changes through 1993 DS MFH. 1994. write for info. (*0-685-49372-5*, 034160) Gale.

— LCCS Schedules with Additions & Changes through 1993 DT-DXMF. 1994. 36.00 (*0-8103-8761-1*, 034161) Gale.

— LCCS Schedules with Additions & Changes through 1993 E-F MFH. 1994. 111.00 (*0-8103-8762-X*, 034162) Gale.

— LCCS Schedules with Additions & Changes through 1993 G MFH. 1994. write for info. (*0-8103-8763-8*, 034163) Gale.

— LCCS Schedules with Additions & Changes through 1993 H-HJMFH. 1994. 78.00 (*0-8103-8764-6*, 034164) Gale.

— LCCS Schedules with Additions & Changes through 1993 HM-HXMF. 1994. 53.00 (*0-8103-8765-4*, 034165) Gale.

— LCCS Schedules with Additions & Changes through 1993 K MFH. 1994. write for info. (*0-8103-8767-0*, 034167) Gale.

— LCCS Schedules with Additions & Changes through 1993 KD MFH. 1994. write for info. (*0-8103-8768-9*, 034168) Gale.

— LCCS Schedules with Additions & Changes through 1993 KDZ MFH. 1994. write for info. (*0-8103-8769-7*, 034169) Gale.

— LCCS Schedules with Additions & Changes through 1993 KE MFH. 1994. write for info. (*0-8103-8770-0*, 034170) Gale.

— LCCS Schedules with Additions & Changes through 1993 KF MFH. 1994. write for info. (*0-8103-8771-9*, 034171) Gale.

— LCCS Schedules with Additions & Changes through 1993 KJ-KKZMF. 1994. write for info. (*0-8103-8773-5*, 034173) Gale.

— LCCS Schedules with Additions & Changes through 1993 KJV MFH. 1994. write for info. (*0-8103-8772-7*, 034172) Gale.

— LCCS Schedules with Additions & Changes through 1993 KK MFH. 1994. write for info. (*0-8103-8774-3*, 034174) Gale.

— LCCS Schedules with Additions & Changes through 1993 KL-KWMF. 1994. write for info. (*0-8103-8775-1*, 034175) Gale.

— LCCS Schedules with Additions & Changes through 1993 KX MFH. 1994. write for info. (*0-8103-8776-X*, 034176) Gale.

— LCCS Schedules with Additions & Changes through 1993 L MFH. 1994. 44.00 (*0-8103-8777-8*, 034177) Gale.

— LCCS Schedules with Additions & Changes through 1993 M MFH. 1994. 52.00 (*0-8103-8778-6*, 034178) Gale.

— LCCS Schedules with Additions & Changes through 1993 N MFH. 1994. write for info. (*0-8103-8779-4*, 034179) Gale.

— LCCS Schedules with Additions & Changes through 1993 P-PA MF. 1994. write for info. (*0-8103-8780-8*, 034180) Gale.

— LCCS Schedules with Additions & Changes through 1993 P-PMMFH. 1994. write for info. (*0-8103-8786-7*, 034186) Gale.

— LCCS Schedules with Additions & Changes through 1993 P-PZMFH. 1994. write for info. (*0-8103-8792-1*, 034192) Gale.

— LCCS Schedules with Additions & Changes through 1993 PA S MF. 1994. write for info. (*0-8103-8781-6*, 034181) Gale.

— LCCS Schedules with Additions & Changes through 1993 PB-PHMF. 1994. write for info. (*0-8103-8782-4*, 034182) Gale.

— LCCS Schedules with Additions & Changes through 1993 PG MFH. 1994. write for info. (*0-8103-8783-2*, 034183) Gale.

— LCCS Schedules with Additions & Changes through 1993 PJ-PKMF. 1994. write for info. (*0-8103-8784-0*, 034184) Gale.

— LCCS Schedules with Additions & Changes through 1993 PL-PMMF. 1994. write for info. (*0-8103-8785-9*, 034185) Gale.

— LCCS Schedules with Additions & Changes through 1993 PN-PZMF. 1994. write for info. (*0-8103-8787-5*, 034187) Gale.

— LCCS Schedules with Additions & Changes through 1993 PQ MFH, No. 1. 1994. write for info. (*0-8103-8788-3*, 034188) Gale.

— LCCS Schedules with Additions & Changes through 1993 PQ MFH, No. 2. 1994. write for info. (*0-8103-8789-1*, 034189) Gale.

— LCCS Schedules with Additions & Changes through 1993 PT MFH, No. 2. 1994. write for info. (*0-8103-8791-3*, 034191) Gale.

— LCCS Schedules with Additions & Changes through 1993 PT MPH, No. 1. 1994. write for info. (*0-8103-8790-5*, 034190) Gale.

— LCCS Schedules with Additions & Changes through 1993 Q MFH. 1994. 132.00 (*0-8103-8793-X*, 034193) Gale.

— LCCS Schedules with Additions & Changes through 1993 R MFH. 1994. 46.00 (*0-8103-8794-8*, 034194) Gale.

— LCCS Schedules with Additions & Changes through 1993 S MFH. 1994. 61.00 (*0-8103-8795-6*, 034195) Gale.

— LCCS Schedules with Additions & Changes through 1993 T MFH. 1994. write for info. (*0-8103-8796-4*, 034196) Gale.

— LCCS Schedules with Additions & Changes through 1993 U MFH. 1994. 37.00 (*0-8103-8797-2*, 034197) Gale.

— LCCS Schedules with Additions & Changes through 1993 V MFH. 1994. 36.00 (*0-8103-8798-0*, 034198) Gale.

— LCCS Schedules with Additions & Changes through 1993 Z MFH. 1994. write for info. (*0-8103-8799-9*, 034199) Gale.

— LCCS through 1993 A General Works MFH. 1994. 34.00 (*0-8103-8601-1*, 035151) Gale.

— LCCS through 1993 B-BJ Philo & Psych MFH. 1994. write for info. (*0-8103-8602-X*, 035152) Gale.

— LCCS through 1993 BL-BQ Relig-Nonchr MFH. 1994. write for info. (*0-8103-8603-8*, 035153) Gale.

— LCCS through 1993 BR-BV Rel: Chr Bible MFH. 1994. write for info. (*0-8103-8604-6*, 035154) Gale.

— LCCS through 1993 BX Relig Christian MFH. 1994. write for info. (*0-8103-8605-4*, 035155) Gale.

— LCCS through 1993 D-DJ MFH. 1994. write for info. (*0-8103-8607-0*, 035157) Gale.

— LCCS through 1993 DJK-DK MFH. (LCCS DJK Microfiche Ser.). 1994. write for info. (*0-8103-8608-9*, 035158) Gale.

— LCCS through 1993 DL-DR MFH. (LCCS Class DL-DR Microfiche Ser.). 1994. write for info. (*0-8103-8609-7*, 035159) Gale.

— LCCS through 1993 DS MFH. (LCCS DS Microfiche Ser.). 1994. write for info. (*0-8103-8610-0*, 035160) Gale.

— LCCS through 1993 DT-DX MFH. (LCCS Class DT-DX Microfiche Ser.). 1994. write for info. (*0-8103-8611-9*, 035161) Gale.

— LCCS through 1993 E-F American History MFH. (LCCS Class E-F Microfiche Ser.). 1994. write for info. (*0-8103-8612-7*, 035162) Gale.

— LCCS through 1993 G Geog. Anthropology REC MFH. (LCCS Class G Microfiche Ser.). 1994. write for info. (*0-8103-8613-5*, 035163) Gale.

— LCCS through 1993 H-HJ Economics MFH. (LCCS Class H-HJ Microfiche Ser.). 1994. 76.00 (*0-8103-8614-3*, 035164) Gale.

— LCCS through 1993 HM-HX Sociology MFH. (LCCS Class HM-HX Microfiche Ser.). 1994. write for info. (*0-8103-8615-1*, 035165) Gale.

— LCCS through 1993 J Political Science. (LCCS Class J Microfiche Ser.). 1994. write for info. (*0-8103-8666-6*, 033316) Gale.

— LCCS through 1993 J Political Science MFH. (LCCS Class J Microfiche Ser.). 1994. write for info. (*0-8103-8616-X*, 035166) Gale.

— LCCS through 1993 K General Law MFH. (LCCS Class K Microfiche Ser.). 1994. write for info. (*0-8103-8617-8*, 035167) Gale.

— LCCS through 1993 KD Law of United Kingdom & Ireland MFH. (LCCS Class KD Microfiche Ser.). 1994. write for info. (*0-8103-8618-6*, 035168) Gale.

— LCCS through 1993 KDZ Law America MFH. 1994. write for info. (*0-8103-8619-4*, 035169) Gale.

— LCCS through 1993 KE Law of Canada MFH. 1994. write for info. (*0-8103-8620-8*, 035170) Gale.

— LCCS through 1993 KF Law of the United States MFH. 1994. write for info. (*0-8103-8621-6*, 035171) Gale.

— LCCS through 1993 KK Law of Germany MFH. 1994. write for info. (*0-8103-8624-0*, 035174) Gale.

— LCCS through 1993 L Education MFH. 1994. write for info. (*0-8103-8627-5*, 035177) Gale.

— LCCS Through 1993, Law of France. 1994. write for info. (*0-685-49605-8*, 035172) Gale.

— LCCS through 1993 M Music MFH. 1994. write for info. (*0-8103-8628-3*, 035178) Gale.

— LCCS through 1993 N Fine Arts MFH. 1994. write for info. (*0-8103-8629-1*, 035179) Gale.

— LCCS through 1993 P-PA Philology MFH. 1994. write for info. (*0-8103-8630-5*, 035180) Gale.

— LCCS through 1993 P-PM Index to Languages MFH. 1994. write for info. (*0-8103-8636-4*, 035186) Gale.

— LCCS through 1993 P-PZ Tables MFH. 1994. write for info. (*0-8103-8642-9*, 035192) Gale.

— LCCS through 1993 PA Supplement Byzantine MFH. 1994. write for info. (*0-8103-8631-3*, 035181) Gale.

— LCCS through 1993 PG Russian Literature MFH. 1994. write for info. (*0-8103-8633-X*, 035183) Gale.

— LCCS through 1993 PJ-PK MFH. 1994. write for info. (*0-8103-8634-8*, 035184) Gale.

— LCCS through 1993 PL-PM Language East Asia MFH. 1994. write for info. (*0-8103-8635-6*, 035185) Gale.

— LCCS through 1993 PN-PZ Literature MFH. 1994. write for info. (*0-8103-8637-2*, 035187) Gale.

— LCCS through 1993 PQ French Literature, No. 1. 1994. write for info. (*0-8103-8638-0*, 035188) Gale.

— LCCS through 1993 PQ Italian Spanish, No. 2. 1994. write for info. (*0-8103-8639-9*, 035189) Gale.

— LCCS through 1993 PT German Literature, No. 1. 1994. write for info. (*0-8103-8640-2*, 035190) Gale.

— LCCS through 1993 Q Science MFH. 1994. write for info. (*0-8103-8643-7*, 035193) Gale.

— LCCS through 1993 R Medicine MFH. 1994. write for info. (*0-8103-8644-5*, 035194) Gale.

— LCCS through 1993 S Agriculture MFH. 1994. write for info. (*0-8103-8645-3*, 035195) Gale.

— LCCS through 1993 T Technology MFH. 1994. write for info. (*0-8103-8646-1*, 035196) Gale.

— LCCS through 1993 U Military Science MFH. 1994. write for info. (*0-8103-8647-X*, 035197) Gale.

— LCCS through 1993 V Naval Science MFH. 1994. write for info. (*0-8103-8648-8*, 035198) Gale.

— LCCS through 1993 Z Bibliography & Library Science MFH. (LCCS Class Z Microfiche Ser.). 1994. write for info. (*0-8103-8649-6*, 035199) Gale.

— LCCS Through '95 DJK-DK History of E Europe. Date not set. 49.00 (*0-8103-2363-X*) Gale.

— LCCS Through '95 DL-DR. Date not set. 55.00 (*0-8103-2364-8*) Gale.

— LCCS Through '95 DS History of Asia. Date not set. 54.00 (*0-8103-2365-6*) Gale.

— LCCS Through '95 DT-DX. Date not set. 49.00 (*0-8103-2366-4*) Gale.

— LCCS Through '95 E American History. Date not set. write for info. (*0-8103-2367-2*) Gale.

— LCCS Through '95 F, No. 1. Date not set. write for info. (*0-8103-2368-0*) Gale.

R

An Asterisk (*) at the beginning of an entry indicates that the title is appearing in BIP for the first time.

— LCCS Through '95 F, No. 2. Date not set. write for info. (*0-8103-2369-9*) Gale.

— LCCS Through '95 G Geog Anthro Rec. Date not set. 116.00 (*0-8103-2370-2*) Gale.

— LCCS Through '95 H-HJ Economics. Date not set. 116.00 (*0-8103-2371-0*) Gale.

— LCCS Through '95 HM-HX Sociology. Date not set. 76.00 (*0-8103-2372-9*) Gale.

— LCCS Through '95 J Political Science. Date not set. 160.00 (*0-8103-2373-7*) Gale.

— LCCS Through '95 K General Law. Date not set. 71.00 (*0-8103-2374-5*) Gale.

— LCCS Through '95 KD Law UK & Ireland. Date not set. 89.00 (*0-8103-2375-3*) Gale.

— LCCS Through '95 KDZ. Date not set. 69.00 (*0-8103-2376-1*) Gale.

— LCCS Through '95 KE Law of Canada. Date not set. 71.00 (*0-8103-2377-X*) Gale.

— LCCS Through '95 KF Law of the US. Date not set. 182.00 (*0-8103-2378-8*) Gale.

— LCCS Through '95 KJV-KJW Law of France. Date not set. 60.00 (*0-8103-2380-X*) Gale.

— LCCS Through '95 KK Law of Germany. Date not set. 60.00 (*0-8103-2381-8*) Gale.

— LCCS Through '95 KX. Date not set. write for info. (*0-8103-2383-4*) Gale.

— LCCS Through '95 L Education. Date not set. 63.00 (*0-8103-2384-2*) Gale.

— LCCS Through '95 M Music. Date not set. 76.00 (*0-8103-2385-0*) Gale.

— LCCS Through '95 N Fine Arts. Date not set. 193.00 (*0-8103-2386-9*) Gale.

— LCCS Through '95 P-PA Philology Ling. Date not set. 98.00 (*0-8103-2387-7*) Gale.

— LCCS Through '95 P-PM Indes to Language. Date not set. 52.00 (*0-8103-2388-5*) Gale.

— LCCS Through '95 P-PZ Tables. Date not set. 52.00 (*0-8103-2389-3*) Gale.

— LCCS Through '95 PA SUP Byzantine. Date not set. 56.00 (*0-8103-2390-7*) Gale.

— LCCS Through '95 PB-PH Modern European. Date not set. 114.00 (*0-8103-2391-5*) Gale.

— LCCS Through '95 PG Russian Literature. Date not set. 72.00 (*0-8103-2392-3*) Gale.

— LCCS Through '95 PJ-PK. Date not set. 54.00 (*0-8103-2393-1*) Gale.

— LCCS Through '95 PL-PM Lang E Asia-Africa. Date not set. 51.00 (*0-8103-2394-X*) Gale.

— LCCS Through '95 PN-PZ Literature. Date not set. 205.00 (*0-8103-2395-8*) Gale.

— LCCS Through '95 PQ No. 2 Italian Spanish. Date not set. 84.00 (*0-8103-2397-4*) Gale.

— LCCS Through '95 PT No. 1 German Literature. Date not set. 72.00 (*0-8103-2398-2*) Gale.

— LCCS Through '95 Q Science. Date not set. 193.00 (*0-8103-2560-8*) Gale.

— LCCS Through '95 R Medicine. Date not set. 67.00 (*0-8103-2561-6*) Gale.

— LCCS Through '95 S Agriculture. Date not set. 90.00 (*0-8103-2562-4*) Gale.

— LCCS Through '95 T Technology. Date not set. 191.00 (*0-8103-2563-2*) Gale.

— LCCS Through '95 V Naval Science. Date not set. 51.00 (*0-8103-2565-9*) Gale.

— LCCS Through '95 Z Biblio & Lib Science. Date not set. 125.00 (*0-8103-2566-7*) Gale.

— Library of Congress Classification Schedules Through 1993: C Auxilliary Sci MFH. (LCCS Class C Microfiche Ser.). 1994. write for info. (*0-8103-8606-2*, 035156) Gale.

— Library of Congress Classification Schedules through 1993: KJ-KKZ MFH. (LCCS Class KJV-KJW Microfiche Ser.). 1994. write for info. (*0-8103-8623-2*, 035173) Gale.

— Library of Congress Classification Schedules Through 1993: KJV-KJW Law of France MFH. (LCCS Class KJV-KJW Microfiche Ser.). 1994. write for info. (*0-8103-8622-4*, 035172) Gale.

— Library of Congress Classification Schedules Through 1993: KL-KW MFH. (LCCS Class KL-KW Microfiche Ser.). 1994. write for info. (*0-8103-8625-9*, 035175) Gale.

— Library of Congress Classification Schedules through 1993: PB-PH Modern European MFH. (LCCS Class PA Supplement Microfiche Ser.). 1994. write for info. (*0-8103-8632-1*, 035182) Gale.

— Library of Congress Classification Schedules Through 1993: PT Dutch & Scandinavian, No. 2. (LCCS Class PT2 Microfiche Ser.). 1994. write for info. (*0-8103-8641-0*, 035191) Gale.

— Library of Congress Classification Schedules through 1993 Microfiche. 1994. 1,780.00 (*0-8103-8600-3*, 035150) Gale.

— Library of Congress Classification Schedules Through 1995: A General Work. (LCCS Class A Microfiche Ser.). Date not set. 52.00 (*0-8103-2356-7*) Gale.

— Library of Congress Classification Schedules Through 1995: B-BJ Philosophy & Psychology. (LCCS Class B-BJ Microfiche Ser.). Date not set. 96.00 (*0-8103-2357-5*) Gale.

— Library of Congress Classification Schedules Through 1995: BL-BQ Religion - Nonchristian. (LCCS Class BL-BQ Microfiche Ser.). Date not set. 71.00 (*0-8103-2358-3*) Gale.

— Library of Congress Classification Schedules Through 1995: BR-BV Rel. - Christ. Bible. (LCCS Class BR-BV Microfiche Ser.). Date not set. 50.00 (*0-8103-2359-1*) Gale.

— Library of Congress Classification Schedules Through 1995: C Auxilliary Science History. (LCCS Class C Microfiche Ser.). Date not set. 58.00 (*0-8103-2361-3*) Gale.

— Library of Congress Classification Schedules Through 1995: D-DJ. (LCCS Class D-DJ Microfiche Ser.). Date not set. 50.00 (*0-8103-2362-1*) Gale.

— Library of Congress Classification Through 1995: BX Religion - Christian. (LCCS Class BX Microfiche Ser.). Date not set. 55.00 (*0-8103-2360-5*) Gale.

— Library of Congress Through 1995. (Library of Congress Adds & Changes Ser.). Date not set. 2,925.00 (*0-8103-2355-9*) Gale.

***Runchock, Rita & Droste, Kathy, eds.** SuperLCCS: Library of Congress Classification Schedules Combined with Additions & Changes Through 1993 for Law & Politcal Science, 11 vols. 1994. pap. text ed. 1,040.00 (*0-8103-9903-2*) Gale.

— SuperLCCS: Library of Congress Classification Schedules Combined with Additions & Changes Through 1993 for Literature, 14 vols. 1994. pap. text ed. 1,206.00 (*0-8103-9905-9*) Gale.

— SuperLCCS: Library of Congress Classification Schedules Combined with Additions & Changes Through 1993 for Philosophy & Religion, 5 vols. 1994. pap. text ed. 410.00 (*0-8103-9900-8*) Gale.

Runcie, Robert. The Unity We Seek. LC 90-31506. 169p. (Orig.). 1990. pap. 7.95 (*0-8192-1521-X*) Morehouse Pub.

Runcie, Robert A. Seasons of the Spirit: The Archbishop of Canterbury at Home & Abroad. LC 83-1734. 272p. reprint ed. pap. 77.60 (*0-317-30160-8*, 2025342) Bks Demand.

***Runciman, C. & Wakeling, D., eds.** Applications of Functional Programming. LC 94-23269. (C). 1994. write for info. (*1-85728-377-5*, Pub. by UCL Pr UK) Taylor & Francis.

Runciman, Lex. The Admirations. LC 88-31219. 72p. 1989. 15.95 (*0-89924-062-3*); pap. 8.50 (*0-89924-061-5*) Lynx Hse.

— Luck. (Poetry Chapbook Ser.). 72p. (Orig.). 1981. write for info. (*0-937669-03-2*) Owl Creek Pr.

— Luck. deluxe limited ed. (Poetry Chapbook Ser.). 72p. (Orig.). 1981. Handbound signed & Ltd. numbered edition of 50 copies 15.00. pap. 15.00 (*0-937669-02-4*) Owl Creek Pr.

— The St. Martin's Workbook. 3rd ed. 592p. 1995. pap. text ed. 15.96 (*0-312-10216-X*) St Martin.

Runciman, Lex & Sher, Steven, eds. Northwest Variety: Personal Essays by 14 Regional Authors. LC 86-28876. 1987. 18.00 (*0-934847-04-5*); pap. 9.50 (*0-934847-05-3*) Arrowood Bks.

Runciman, Lex, jt. auth. see Anderson, Chris.

Runciman, Rosy, jt. auth. see Amery, Colin.

Runciman, Steven. The Eastern Schism. LC 78-63367. (Crusades & Military Orders Ser.: Second Series). 200p. reprint ed. 24.50 (*0-404-16247-9*) AMS Pr.

— The Emperor Romanus Lecapenus & His Reign: A Study of Tenth Century Byzantium. 281p. 1988. pap. 24.95 (*0-521-35722-5*) Cambridge U Pr.

— The Fall of Constantinople, Fourteen Fifty-Three. (Canto Book Ser.). (Illus.). 272p. (C). 1990. pap. 10.95 (*0-521-39832-0*) Cambridge U Pr.

— The First Crusade. (Canto Book Ser.). 200p. (C). 1992. pap. 10.95 (*0-521-42705-3*) Cambridge U Pr.

— The Great Church in Captivity: A Study of the Patriarchate of Constantinople from the Eve of the Turkish Conquest to the Greek War of Independence. 465p. 1986. pap. 29.95 (*0-521-31310-4*) Cambridge U Pr.

— The Great Church in Captivity: A Study of the Patriarchate of Constantinople from the Eve of the Turkish Conquest to the Greek War of Independence. LC 68-29330. 465p. reprint ed. pap. 132.60 (*0-317-26393-5*, 2024531) Bks Demand.

— History of the Crusades, 3 vols., 1. (Illus.). 394p. (C). 1987. pap. 17.95 (*0-521-34770-X*) Cambridge U Pr.

— History of the Crusades, 3 vols., 2. (Illus.). 546p. (C). 1987. pap. 19.95 (*0-521-34771-8*) Cambridge U Pr.

— History of the Crusades, 3 vols., 3. (Illus.). 542p. (C). 1987. pap. 19.95 (*0-521-34772-6*) Cambridge U Pr.

— History of the Crusades, 3 vols., Set. (C). 1987. pap. 49.95 (*0-521-35997-X*) Cambridge U Pr.

— History of the Crusades, 3 vols., Vol. I. 391p. 1951. Vol. 1--The First Crusade & the Foundation of the Kingdom of Jerusalem, 391 pgs. 59.95 (*0-521-06161-X*) Cambridge U Pr.

— History of the Crusades, Vol. 2: 1100-1187. 546p. 1952. Vol. 2--The Kingdom of Jerusalem & the Frankish East, 1100-1187, 546 pgs. 64.95 (*0-521-06162-8*) Cambridge U Pr.

— History of the Crusades, Vol. 3. 542p. 1954. 64.95 (*0-521-06163-6*) Cambridge U Pr.

— The Medieval Manichee: A Study of the Christian Dualist Heresy. LC 82-4123. 224p. 1982. pap. 19.95 (*0-521-28926-2*) Cambridge U Pr.

— The Sicilian Vespers: A History of the Mediterranean World in the Later Thirteenth Century. (Canto Book Ser.). (Illus.). 370p. (C). 1992. pap. 11.95 (*0-521-43774-1*) Cambridge U Pr.

— A Traveller's Alphabet: Partial Memoirs. LC 90-71389. (Illus.). 216p. 1991. 24.95 (*0-500-01504-X*) Thames Hudson.

Runciman, Walter G. Social Science & Political Theory. 2nd ed. LC 69-16286. 208p. reprint ed. pap. 59.30 (*0-317-26386-2*, 2024528) Bks Demand.

Runciman, Walter G., ed. see Weber, Max.

Runck, Robert F., jt. ed. see Roth, Edward S.

Runck, Robert R., ed. Premachine Planning & Tool Presetting. LC 67-28208. (American Society of Tool & Manufacturing Engineers Manufacturing Data Ser.). 82p. reprint ed. pap. 25.00 (*0-317-10932-4*, 2016005) Bks Demand.

Runco, Mark, ed. see Gedo, John E. & Gedo, Mary M.

Runco, Mark, ed. see Jausovic, Norbert.

Runco, Mark, jt. ed. see Milgram, Roberta M.

Runco, Mark, ed. see Wakefield, John F.

Runco, Mark A. Creativity As an Educational Objective for Disadvantaged Students. (Illus.). 105p. (Orig.). (C). 1994. pap. text ed. 35.00 (*0-7881-0440-3*) Diane Pub.

— Divergent Thinking. (Creativity Research Ser.). 240p. (C). 1991. text ed. 42.50 (*0-89391-700-1*); pap. 24.50 (*0-89391-716-8*) Ablex Pub.

Runco, Mark A., ed. Problem Finding, Problem Solving, & Creativity. LC 94-1974. (Creativity Research Ser.). 320p. 1994. 57.50 (*0-89391-975-6*) Ablex Pub.

— Problem Finding, Problem Solving, & Creativity. LC 94-1974. (Creativity Research Ser.). 320p. 1994. pap. 22.50 (*1-56750-013-7*) Ablex Pub.

Runco, Mark A. & Albert, Robert S., eds. Theories of Creativity. (Focus Editions Ser.: Vol. 115). (Illus.). 320p. (C). 1990. pap. 24.95 (*0-8039-3545-5*) Sage.

Runco, Mark A., ed. see Andreasen, Nancy C., et al.

Runco, Mark A., ed. see Bailin, Sharon.

Runco, Mark A., jt. ed. see Shaw, Melvin P.

Runcorn, S. K., ed. Earth Science, 3 vols., Set. (Royal Institution Library of Science). (Illus.). 1564p. 1971. 128.00 (*0-85334-505-8*, Pub. by Elsevier Applied Sci UK) Elsevier.

— International Dictionary of Geophysics, 2 vols, Set. (Illus.). 1967. 970.00 (*0-08-011834-8*, Pergamon Pr) Elsevier.

— The Physics of the Planets: Their Origin, Evolution & Structure. LC 87-10465. 468p. reprint ed. pap. 133.40 (*0-8357-6944-5*, 2039003) Bks Demand.

Runcorn, S. K., jt. ed. see Davies, P. A.

Runcorn, S. K., ed. see International Astronomical Union Staff.

Runcorn, S. K., jt. ed. see Rosenberg, G. D.

Runcorn, S. K., et al, eds. Smaller Solar System Bodies & Orbits. (Advances in Space Research Ser.: No. 10). (Illus.). 434p. 1989. pap. 210.00 (*0-08-040163-5*, Pergamon Pr) Elsevier.

Rund, H. Differential Geometry & Gauge Fields. 1994. text ed. 68.00 (*981-02-1230-5*) World Scientific Pub.

Rundall, Thomas G., jt. ed. see Battistella, Roger M.

Rundback, Betty. Bed & Breakfast U. S. A., 1991. (Illus.). 768p. 1991. pap. 12.95 (*0-452-26571-1*, Plume) NAL-Dutton.

— Bed & Breakfast U. S. A., 1992. Ackerman, Peggy, ed. (Illus.). 720p. (Orig.). 1992. pap. 14.00 (*0-452-26747-1*, Plume) NAL-Dutton.

— Bed & Breakfast U. S. A. 1993. LC 86-649303. (Illus.). 752p. (Orig.). 1993. pap. 14.00 (*0-452-26926-1*, Plume) NAL-Dutton.

— Bed & Breakfast, 1994. (Illus.). 784p. (Orig.). 1994. pap. 13.95 (*0-452-27126-6*, Plume) NAL-Dutton.

***Rundback, Betty & Ackerman, Peggy.** Bed & Breakfast U. S. A. 1995. 784p. (Orig.). 1995. pap. 15.95 (*0-452-27369-2*, Plume) NAL-Dutton.

Rundback, Betty & Kramer, Nancy. Bed & Breakfast U. S. A., 1986. (Illus.). 512p. 1986. pap. 9.95 (*0-525-48191-5*, Dutton) NAL-Dutton.

Runde, Raymond E. & Britton, Gregory. Depression: The Dark Night of the Soul. 100p. 1990. write for info. (*0-9628401-0-6*) Millers Pr.

Runde, Robert H. & Zischang, J. B. The Commonsense Guide to Estate Planning. LC 93-9618. 275p. 1993. text ed. 30.00 (*1-55623-678-6*) Irwin Prof Pubng.

Rundekl, P. W., et al, eds. Stable Isotopes in Ecological Research. (Ecological Studies: Vol. 68). (Illus.). 545p. 1988. 108.00 (*0-387-96712-5*) Spr-Verlag.

***Rundel, P. W. & Gibson, A. C.** Ecological Communities & Processes in a Mojave Desert Ecosystem: Rock Valley, Nevada. (Illus.). 400p. (C). 1994. write for info. (*0-521-46541-9*) Cambridge U Pr.

Rundel, P. W., et al. Tropical Alpine Environments: Plant Form & Function. (Illus.). 370p. (C). 1994. 100.00 (*0-521-42089-X*) Cambridge U Pr.

Rundel, Philip W. An Annotated Bibliography of West Indian Plant Ecology. (Illus.). 72p. 1974. 10.00 (*0-318-14610-X*) Isl Resources.

Rundell, James R., jt. auth. see Wise, Michael G.

Rundell, John. Between Totalitarianism & Postmodernity: A Thesis Eleven Reader. Beilharz, Peter et al, eds. (Illus.). 276p. 1992. 14.95 (*0-262-52179-2*) MIT Pr.

— Origins of Modernity: The Origins of Modern Social Theory from Kant to Marx. LC 87-8152. 256p. (C). 1987. text ed. 36.00 (*0-299-11450-3*) U of Wis Pr.

Rundell, John, jt. ed. see Robinson, Gillian.

Rundell, Mary G. Texas Garderner's Guide to Growing Tomatoes. 128p. (Orig.). 1984. pap. text ed. 6.95 (*0-914641-00-X*) TX Gardener Pr.

***Rundell, Michael.** The Dictionary of Cricket. (Illus.). 192p. 1995. 19.95 (*0-19-866198-3*) OUP.

Rundell, Nancy T. Iran: Front Row Balcony. LC 81-68157. (Illus.). 248p. 1981. 12.95 (*0-940928-01-9*) Felsun Pr.

Rundell, Robert & Rundell, Roberta. Kids Care, Elder Care - Caregiver's Guide. 1989. Elder Care-Caregiver's Guide. write for info. (*1-56117-011-9*) Telesis CA.

— Kids Care, Vol. 1: K-2. 1989. Vol. 1, k-2. teacher ed 40.00 (*1-56117-012-7*) Telesis CA.

— Kids Care, Vol. 2: 3-4. 1989. Vol. 2, 3-4. teacher ed 35.00 (*1-56117-013-5*) Telesis CA.

— Kids Care, Vol. 3: 5-6. 1989. Vol. 3, 5-6. teacher ed 35.00 (*1-56117-017-8*) Telesis CA.

— Kids Care, Vol. 4: Teens Care. teacher ed 35.00 (*1-56117-015-1*) Telesis CA.

— Kids Care: Preschool - First Grade. 1989. First Grade. 15.00 (*1-56117-035-6*) Telesis CA.

— Kids Care: Preschool - First Grade. (J). (gr. k). 1989. Kindergarten. 15.00 (*1-56117-034-8*) Telesis CA.

— Kids Care: Preschool - First Grade. (J). (ps). 1989. Preschool. 15.00 (*1-56117-014-3*) Telesis CA.

— Kids Care: Second Grade-Sixth Grade. 1989. 20.00 (*1-56117-036-4*); 20.00 (*1-56117-037-2*); 20.00 (*1-56117-038-0*); 20.00 (*1-56117-039-9*); 20.00 (*1-56117-040-2*) Telesis CA.

Rundell, Roberta, jt. auth. see Rundell, Robert.

Rundell, W., et al. Inverse Problems in Partial Differential Equations. (Proceedings in Applied Mathematics Ser.: No. 42). xi, 214p. 1990. pap. 33.50 (*0-89871-252-1*) Soc Indus-Appl Math.

Rundell, Walter. Black Market Money: The Collapse of U. S. Military Currency Control in World War II. LC 64-15879. 139p. reprint ed. pap. 39.70 (*0-8357-7292-6*, 2051882) Bks Demand.

Rundell, Walter, Jr. Early Texas Oil: A Photographic History, 1866-1936. LC 76-51653. (Montague History of Oil Ser.: No.1). (Illus.). 260p. 1977. 24.50 (*0-89096-029-1*) Tex A&M Univ Pr.

— Military Money: A Fiscal History of the U. S. Army Overseas in World War II. LC 79-7408. (Illus.). 292p. 1980. 19.50 (*0-89096-079-8*) Tex A&M Univ Pr.

— Oil in West Texas & New Mexico: A Pictorial History of the Permian Basin. LC 81-48376. (Illus.). 200p. 1982. 24.50 (*0-89096-125-5*) Tex A&M Univ Pr.

Rundgaard, H., jt. ed. see De Weck, Alain L.

***Rundgren, Todd & Levine, David.** Music for the Eye. 120p. 1995. pap. 19.95 (*0-89087-752-1*) Celestial Arts.

Rundin, Ulf, ed. Perspectives on Multilateral Assistance: A Review by the Nordic U.N. Project. 317p. (Orig.). 1990. pap. 79.00x (*91-22-01405-5*, Pub. by Almqv & Wiksell SW) Coronet Bks.

— The United Nations: Issues & Options. (Five Studies on the Role of the UN in the Economic & Social Fields Commissioned by the Nordic UN Project). 358p. (Orig.). 1991. pap. 77.50x (*91-22-01426-8*, Pub. by Almqv & Wiksell SW) Coronet Bks.

— The United Nations in Development: Reform Issues in the Economic & Social Fields (Final Report by the Nordic UN Project) 111p. (Orig.). 1991. pap. 49.00x (*91-22-01437-3*, Pub. by Almqv & Wiksell SW) Coronet Bks.

Rundle, B. Facts. 96p. 1993. pap. text ed. 11.95 (*0-7156-2467-9*, Pub. by Duckworth UK) Focus Info Gr.

Rundle, Bede. Wittgenstein on Language: Meaning, Use & Truth. 288p. (C). 1990. text ed. 54.95 (*0-631-17198-5*) Blackwell Pubs.

Rundle, R. N. International Affairs, Eighteen Ninety to Nineteen Thirty Nine. LC 79-12170. (Illus.). 162p. (C). 1980. 29.50 (*0-8419-0516-9*); pap. 17.95 (*0-8419-0601-7*) Holmes & Meier.

— International Affairs, Nineteen Thirty-Nine to Nineteen Seventy-Nine. (Illus.). 192p. (C). 1982. 29.50 (*0-8419-0677-7*); pap. 15.95 (*0-8419-0678-5*) Holmes & Meier.

Rundle, Stanley. Cracking the Language Code: French. 1983. pap. 19.95 (*0-87243-110-X*) Templegate.

— Cracking the Language Code: German. 1982. pap. 19.95 (*0-87243-107-X*) Templegate.

— Cracking the Language Code: Spanish. 1974. pap. 19.95 (*0-87243-109-6*) Templegate.

Rundle, Vesta M. Jerry the Guard Goose. (Illus.). 24p. (Orig.). (J). (gr. k-4). 1993. pap. 5.95 (*1-882672-00-3*) V M Rundle.

— Snow Calf. (Illus.). 36p. (Orig.). (J). (gr. 4-8). 1993. pap. 4.50 (*1-882672-01-1*) V M Rundle.

Rundles, Jeff, ed. Colorado Economy, 93-94. 100p. 1993. 14.00 (*0-9638170-0-0*) CO Econ Rpts.

Rundowicz, Carolyn. To Be Alive. 1995. pap. 14.95 (*0-8050-2959-1*) H Holt & Co.

***Rundquist.** Day Geckos. 1995. pap. text ed. (*0-7938-0267-9*) TFH Pubns.

Rundquist, E. Reptiles & Amphibians: Care in Captivity. (Illus.). 192p. 1994. 24.95 (*0-7938-0298-9*, TS211) TFH Pubns.

Rundquist, Edward & Sletto, Raymond. Personality in the Depression, Vol. 12. LC 72-142315. (University of Minnesota Institute of Child Welfare Monographs: No. 12). (Illus.). 398p. 1975. reprint ed. text ed. 55.00 (*0-8371-5903-2*, CWRP, Greenwood Pr) Greenwood.

Rundquist, Thomas, ed. AIDS "Trivia" The AIDS Prevention Game. 12p. (Orig.). (C). 1988. pap. 6.95 (*0-9618567-2-6*) Nova Media.

***Rundquist, Thomas J.** Detroit Undercover. 50p. (Orig.). 1995. pap. 7.95 (*1-884239-08-0*) Nova Media.

Rundquist, Thomas J., ed. AIDS Trivia: Update for 90's Updated. 2nd ed. (Illus.). 42p. (Orig.). (C). 1994. pap. text ed. 12.95 (*0-9618567-6-9*) Nova Media.

— AIDS Trivia: Update for 90's Updated. 3rd ed. (Illus.). 42p. (Orig.). 1995. teacher ed, pap. text ed. 14.95 (*1-884239-01-3*); disk 39.95 (*1-884239-02-1*) Nova Media.

***Rundquist, Thomas J., ed. & illus.** Drug Culture Monopoly. 42p. (Orig.). 1995. pap. text ed. 30.95 (*1-884239-04-8*) Nova Media.

Rundquist, Thomas J., ed. Drugs, Sex in Religions: TR's Autobiography 1962-1992. 54p. (Orig.). (C). 1993. pap. 29.95 (*0-9618567-7-7*) Nova Media.

— Racial Attitude Test. 49p. (Orig.). (J). (C). 1989. pap. 19.95 (*0-9618567-5-0*) Nova Media.

— Sales, Persuasion Presentations: A Psychological Analysis. 6p. (Orig.). 1994. pap. 6.95 (*0-9618567-9-3*) Nova Media.

— Sterilization (Involuntary) A Case Study. rev. ed. (Illus.). 85p. (Orig.). (C). 1994. pap. text ed. 19.95 (*1-884239-00-5*) Nova Media.

R

Rundquist, Thomas J., intro. Drugs, Sex & Religions: An Uncensored Bibliography. rev. ed. 4p. (C). 1989. pap. text ed. 4.95 (0-9618567-4-2) Nova Media.
— Sterilization (Involuntary) A Case Study. (Illus.). 54p. (Orig.). (C). 1993. pap. 29.95 (0-9618567-8-5) Nova Media.
Rundquist, Thomas J. & Guild, Robert W., Jr. Drugs, Sex & Rock-n-Roll. (Illus.). 15p. (Orig.). (YA). (gr. 7-12). 1988. pap. text ed. 19.95 (0-9618567-3-4) Nova Media.
Rundquist, Thomas J. & Parent, Frederick. Horse Is Boss: Drug Culture Education & Prevention Game. 2nd ed. (Illus.). 42p. (Orig.). (YA). (gr. 7-12). 1988. pap. text ed. 30.50 (0-9618567-1-8) Nova Media.
Rundqvist, D. V. & Mitrofanov, F. P., eds. Precambrian Geology of the U. S. S. R. LC 92-8594. 1992. write for info. (0-444-89380-6) Elsevier.
Runes, D. D. & Schrickel, H. G., eds. Art in a Post War World. LC 75-90603. (Essay Index Reprint Ser.). 1977. 17.95 (0-8369-1272-1) Ayer.
Runes, Dagobert & Schrickey, Harry G., eds. Encyclopedia of the Arts, 2 vols., Set. 1995. reprint ed. 88.00 (1-55888-972-8) Omnigraphics Inc.
Runes, Dagobert D. Art of Thinking. (Orig.). pap. 0.95 (0-685-19398-5, 92, Citadel Pr) Carol Pub Group.
— Dictionary of Judaism. 236p. 1981. 8.95 (0-8065-0787-X, Citadel Pr) Carol Pub Group.
— Jew & the Cross. 1966. pap. 0.95 (0-8065-0111-1, 216, Citadel Pr) Carol Pub Group.
— Wisdom of FDR. 1993. pap. 7.95 (0-8065-1462-0, Citadel Pr) Carol Pub Group.
Runes, Dagobert D., ed. Concise Dictionary of Judaism. LC 77-88933. 124p. 1982. reprint ed. text ed. 75.00 (0-8371-2109-4, AERUDJ, Greenwood Pr) Greenwood.
— Dictionary of Philosophy. enl. rev. ed. LC 81-80240. 360p. (C). 1984. pap. 14.95 (0-8226-0392-6) Littlefield.
— The Hebrew Impact on Western Civilization. 1976. pap. 4.95 (0-8065-0532-X, Citadel Pr) Carol Pub Group.
— Who's Who in Philosophy, Vol. 1. LC 79-88971. 293p. 1969. reprint ed. text ed. 35.00 (0-8371-2095-0, WWIP, Greenwood Pr) Greenwood.
— Wisdom of the Torah. 1966. pap. 2.25 (0-8065-0015-8, 236, Citadel Pr) Carol Pub Group.
Runes, Dagobert D., ed. see Edison, Thomas A.
Runestad, J. A., jt. auth. see Pedersen, J. H.
RuNett Nia Ebo. A Brand New Flavor. (Illus.). 28p. (Orig.). (YA). (gr. 9-12). 1993. pap. 8.00 (1-883753-02-3) Jwand Ent.
— Introducing, Sister Lucy. (Illus.). 26p. (Orig.). 1990. pap. 6.50 (1-883753-01-5) Jwand Ent.
— Nia's In Love. (Illus.). 28p. 1992. pap. 6.50 (1-883753-03-1) Jwand Ent.
— Poems of Nia. (Illus.). 26p. (Orig.). 1990. pap. 5.50 (1-883753-00-7) Jwand Ent.
Runey, Mim L., ed. Charleston Hospitality. 2nd ed. 1993. write for info. (0-9639364-0-9) Johnson & Wales.
Runfola, Maria & Bash, Lee, eds. Research Symposium on the Male Adolescent Voice. (Proceedings Ser.). (Illus.). 182p. (Orig.). 1984. pap. 14.95 (0-931111-00-5) SUNY Buff Music.
Rung, Ming. Deng Xiaoping: Chronicle of an Empire. Liu, Nancy et al, eds. LC 94-1944. 1994. text ed. 69.95 (0-8133-1920-X) Westview.
— Deng Xiaoping: Chronicle of an Empire. Liu, Nancy et al, eds. LC 94-1944. (C). 1994. pap. text ed. 19.95 (0-8133-1921-8) Westview.
Rungachary, Santha. Tales for All Times. (Nehru Library for Children). (Illus.). (J). (gr. 1-9). 1979. pap. 2.50 (0-89744-187-7) Auromere.
Runge, C. Ford, jt. auth. see Cochrane, Willard W.
Runge, C. Ford, et al. Freer Trade, Protected Environment: Balancing Trade Liberalization & Environmental Interests. 192p. 1993. pap. 17.95 (0-87609-154-0) Coun Foreign.
Runge, Jonathan. Hot on Hawaii: The Definitive Guide to the Aloha State. (Illus.). 240p. (Orig.). 1989. pap. 12.95 (0-312-02585-8) St Martin.
— Rum & Reggae: The Insider's Guide to the Caribbean, 1994-1995. rev. ed. 1993. pap. 17.00 (0-679-74716-8, Villard Bks) Random.
— Rum & Reggae: What's Hot & What's Not in the Caribbean. LC 87-29938. (Illus.). 224p. 1988. pap. 10.95 (0-312-01509-7) St Martin.
Runge, M. Bones & Joints. (Exercises in Radiological Diagnosis Ser.). (Illus.). 210p. 1987. pap. 29.50 (0-387-16544-4) Spr-Verlag.
— Mechanisms of Restenosis after Coronary Angioplasty. (Medical Intelligence Unit Ser.). write for info. (1-57059-068-0) R G Landes.
Runge, M. & Haber, Bode C. Chimeric Proteins in Thrombolysis. (Medical Intelligence Unit Ser.). write for info. (1-57059-054-0) R G Landes.
Runge, Senta M. Face Lifting by Exercise. 10th abr. rev. ed. LC 56-6321. (Illus.). 1977. reprint ed. 25.00 (0-9601042-1-6) Allegro Pub.
— Face Lifting by Exercise. 10th ed. (Illus.). 1989. reprint ed. write for info. (0-318-64624-2) Allegro Pub.
— Face Lifting by Exercise. 10th rev. ed. (Illus.). 168p. reprint ed. 25.00 (0-685-63817-0) Allegro Pub.
Runge, Val M. Clinical Magnetic Resonance Imaging. (Illus.). 925p. 1990. text ed. 99.50 (0-397-50989-8) Lippincott.
— Contrast Media in Magnetic Resonance Imaging. (Illus.). 176p. 1991. text ed. 65.00 (0-397-51270-8) Lippincott.
— Magnetic Resonance Imaging: Clinical Principles. (Illus.). 368p. 1991. text ed. 125.00 (0-397-51095-0) Lippincott.
— Magnetic Resonance Imaging of the Spine. (Illus.). 550p. 1994. 150.00 (0-397-51290-2) Lippincott.
— Magnetic Resonance of the Brain, Head & Neck. LC 93-24586. (Illus.). 1993. 160.00 (0-397-51244-9) Lippincott.
— Review of Neuroradiology. 160p. 1995. pap. text ed. write for info. (0-7216-5134-8) Saunders.

R

***Runge, Val M., ed.** Contrast-Enhanced Clinical Magnet Resonance Imaging. (Illus.). 400p. (C). 1995. text ed. 75.00 (0-8131-1944-8) U Pr of Ky.
Runger, George C., jt. auth. see Montgomery, Douglas C.
Rungta, Ravi, ed. Inclusions & Their Influence on Material Behavior: Proceedings of a Symposium Held in Conjunction with the 1988 World Materials Congress, Chicago, IL, USA, 24-30 September 1988. LC 88-71672. (Illus.). 207p. reprint ed. pap. 59.00 (0-8357-4089-7, 2036855) Bks Demand.
Runia, Anthony P., tr. see Ter Hark, Michel.
Runia, David T. Exegesis & Philosophy: Studies on Philo of Alexandria. 320p. 1990. text ed. 87.50 (0-86078-287-5, Pub. by Variorum UK) Ashgate Pub Co.
— Philo in Early Christian Literature: A Survey. LC 93-28608. (Compendia Rerum Iudaicarum ad Novum Testamentum Ser.: Vol. 3). 1993. 35.00 (0-8006-2828-4, Fortress Pr) Augsburg Fortress.
— Philo of Alexandria & the Church Fathers: A Collection of Papers. (Vigiliae Christianae Ser.: No. 32). 300p. 1995. 100.00 (90-04-10355-4) E J Brill.
— The Studia Philonica Annual, Vol. Four, 1992: Studies in Hellenistic Judaism. 209p. 1992. 59.95 (1-55540-771-4, 140264) Scholars Pr GA.
***Runia, David T., ed.** The Studia Philonica Annual: Studies in Hellenistic Judaism, Vol. VI. (Brown Judaic Studies). 248p. 1994. 44.95 (0-7885-0030-9, 140299) Scholars Pr GA.
— The Studia Philonica Annual, Vol. V: Studies in Hellenistic Judaism. (Brown Judaic Studies). 271p. 1993. 44.95 (1-55540-917-2, 140287) Scholars Pr GA.
— The Studia Philonica Annual 1991. (Studies in Hellenistic Judaism: Vol. 3). 405p. 1991. 74.95 (1-55540-625-4) Scholars Pr GA.
Runia, David T., jt. auth. see Radice, Roberto.
Runion, Garth E. & Lockwood, James R. Deductive Systems: Finite & Non-Euclidean Geometries. LC 78-17827. (Illus.). 90p. 1978. pap. 6.00 (0-87353-129-9) NCTM.
Runk, Emma T. Barcroft Family Records: An Account of the Family in England & the Descendants of Ambrose Barcroft, the Emigrant, of Solebury, Penn. (Illus.). 334p. 1988. reprint ed. lib. bdg. 63.00 (0-8328-0186-0); reprint ed. pap. 53.00 (0-8328-0187-9) Higginson Bk Co.
Runk, Wesley. Making a Parade for Jesus. 1992. pap. 8.50 (1-55673-451-4, 9246) CSS OH.
Runk, Wesley T. Call in the Clowns. (Orig.). 1988. pap. 8.15 (1-55673-071-3, 8868) CSS OH.
— God Loves Us All. (Orig.). 1989. pap. 7.30 (1-55673-114-0, 9825) CSS OH.
— Jesus, the Light of Our Lives. 1994. pap. 4.75 (1-55673-523-5); ring bd. 0.95 (1-55673-828-5) CSS OH.
— Jesus, the Servant King: Six Children's Object Lessons for Lent. 1992. pap. 3.95 (1-55673-559-6) CSS OH.
— Object Lessons from the Bible. (Object Lesson Ser.). 96p. 1980. pap. 4.99 (0-8010-7698-6) Baker Bk.
— On the Move with Jesus. 1984. 4.75 (0-89536-670-3, 1511) CSS OH.
— The One-Handed Clock. 1989. pap. 8.15 (1-55673-141-8, 9866) CSS OH.
— Our Father, Friend of Little Children: Children's Object Lessons Based on the Lord's Prayer. 2nd ed. 24p. (Orig.). 1995. pap. 4.25 (0-7880-0372-0) CSS OH.
— Speaking with Signs: Children's Object Lessons for Lent & Easter. 2nd ed. (Illus.). 24p. (Orig.). 1995. pap. 4.25 (0-7880-0371-2) CSS OH.
— Standing Up for Jesus. (J). (gr. k-4). 1985. 4.50 (0-89536-725-4, 5809) CSS OH.
— Twelve Friends of Jesus. 1991. pap. 4.95 (1-55673-404-2, 9217) CSS OH.
— Water Can Do Wonders. Sherer, Michael L., ed. (Orig.). 1986. pap. 1.85 (0-89536-816-1, 6826) CSS OH.
— We Are the Church: 52 Second Lesson Text Children's Object Lessons. LC 94-8316. 1994. write for info. (0-7880-0100-0) CSS OH.
Runk, Wesley T. & Lentz, Thomas W. Six Nails of the Cross: Sermons for Lent. LC 92-37514. 1992. pap. 5.50 (1-55673-560-X, 9308) CSS OH.
Runkel, Charles P., et al. The Illinois Law Enforcement Officer: The Basic Training Course, 2 vols. (Illus.). 860p. (Orig.). (C). 1989. pap. text ed. 60.00 (0-8211-1721-1) McCutchan.
Runkel, David R., ed. Campaign for President: The Managers Look at '88. LC 89-6767. 350p. 1989. text ed. 49.95 (0-86569-194-0, Auburn Hse); pap. text ed. 17.95 (0-86569-195-9, Auburn Hse) Greenwood.
Runkel, Margaret, jt. auth. see Runkel, Philip.
Runkel, Philip & Runkel, Margaret. Guide to Usage for Writers & Students in the Social Studies. LC 83-19179. (Helix Bks.: No. 382). (Illus.). 168p. 1984. 32.50 (0-86598-132-9); pap. 14.00 (0-8226-0382-9) Rowman.
Runkel, Philip, et al, eds. The Changing College Classroom. LC 70-92896. (Jossey-Bass Higher Education Ser.). 380p. reprint ed. pap. 108.30 (0-8357-9301-X, 2013862) Bks Demand.
Runkel, Philip J. Casting Nets & Testing Specimens: Two Grand Methods of Psychology. LC 89-48665. 224p. 1990. text ed. 49.95 (0-275-93533-7, C3533, Greenwood Pr) Greenwood.
Runkel, Philip J., jt. auth. see Schmuck, Richard A.
Runkel, Phillip M. Alfred Lunt & Lynn Fontanne: A Bibliography. (Illus.). (C). 1978. pap. 4.50 (0-916120-03-1) Carroll Coll.
Runkel, Sylvan T. & Bull, Alvin F. Wildflowers of Illinois Woodlands. LC 93-48533. 264p. (C). 1994. pap. 20.95 (0-8138-1990-3) Iowa St U Pr.
— Wildflowers of Indiana Woodlands. LC 93-46821. 264p. (C). 1994. pap. 20.95 (0-8138-1969-5) Iowa St U Pr.
— Wildflowers of the Iowa Woodlands. LC 86-27589. (Illus.). 272p. 1987. reprint ed. pap. 20.95 (0-8138-1929-6) Iowa St U Pr.

Runkel, Sylvan T. & Roosa, Dean M. Wildflowers of the Tallgrass Prairie: The Upper Midwest. (Illus.). 292p. (Orig.). 1989. pap. 24.95 (0-8138-1979-2) Iowa St U Pr.
Runkis, Walt, jt. auth. see LaPuma, Karen.
Runkle, Gerald. Ethics: An Examination of Contemporary Moral Problems. 566p. (C). 1982. pap. text ed. 32.00 (0-03-058318-7) HB Coll Pubs.
— Good Thinking: An Introduction to Logic. 3rd ed. (Illus.). 413p. (C). 1991. pap. text ed. 32.00 (0-03-030707-4) HB Coll Pubs.
— A History of Western Political Theory. LC 68-21652. 682p. reprint ed. pap. 180.00 (0-317-26812-0, 2023478) Bks Demand.
Runkovskis, Ivars. Latvian Museum of Foreign Art, Riga: Western European Art. 182p. (C). 1986. 100.00 (0-685-21934-8, Pub. by Collets UK) Pro-Am Music.
Runnalls, Graham, jt. ed. see Bennett, Philip.
Runnebaum, ed. Female Contraception & Male Fertility Regulation. (Advances in Gynecological & Obstetric Research Ser.). (Illus.). 242p. (C). 1991. 85.00 (1-85070-334-5) Prthnon Pub.
Runnebaum, B., et al, eds. Future Aspects in Contraception, Pt. II: Female Contraception. 1985. lib. bdg. 213.00 (0-85200-906-2) Kluwer Ac.
— Secretion & Action of Gonadotropins. (Illus.). 105p. 1984. pap. 42.50 (0-387-13854-4) Spr-Verlag.
Runnells, R. R. Infection Control in the Former Wet Finger Environment. (Illus.). 182p. (C). pap. text ed. write for info. (0-936751-09-6) Infection Control.
— Practical How-Tos of Dental Infection Control. 82p. (C). 1987. pap. text ed. write for info. (0-936751-03-7) Infection Control.
Runnells, Robert R. AIDS in the Dental Office? The Story of Kimberly Bergalis & Dr. David Acer. Newman, Katherine, ed. (Illus.). 325p. 1993. 29.95 (0-936751-11-8) Infection Control.
— Infection Control in the Former Wet Finger Environment. 3rd ed. (Illus.). 274p. 1994. student ed, pap. 29.95 (0-936751-12-6) Infection Control.
***Runnels, Curtis, et al, eds.** Artifact & Assemblage: The Finds from a Regional Survey of the Southern Argolid, Greece Vol. 1: The Prehistoric & Early Iron Age Pottery & the Lithic Artifacts. LC 94-25691. 1995. 65.00 (0-8047-2065-7) Stanford U Pr.
Runnels, Curtis N., jt. auth. see Van Andel, Tjeerd H.
Runnels, Gayle S., jt. auth. see Lay, Artie K.
Runnels, M. T. A Genealogy of the Runnels & Reynolds Family in America. 371p. 1989. reprint ed. lib. bdg. 64.00 (0-8328-1038-X); reprint ed. pap. 56.00 (0-8328-1039-8) Higginson Bk Co.
— The History of Sanbornton, New Hampshire, Vol. 1. (Illus.). 570p. 1988. reprint ed. lib. bdg. 57.00 (0-8328-0074-0, NH0021) Higginson Bk Co.
Runnenbaum, B., et al, eds. Future Aspects in Contraception, Pt. I: Male Contraception. 1985. lib. bdg. 213.00 (0-85200-893-7) Kluwer Ac.
Runner, Edward. Ethics: Its Impact in Real Estate. 1992. 16.95 (0-533-10041-0) Vantage.
Runners World Editors. The Complete Marathoner. LC 78-362. (Illus.). 425p. 1978. 11.95 (0-89037-097-4); pap. 8.95 (0-686-85633-3) Anderson World.
Runner's World Editors. The Complete Runner. LC 74-83666. (Illus.). 391p. 1974. 7.95 (0-89037-041-9) Anderson World.
— The Complete Woman Runner. LC 78-58048. (Illus.). 440p. 1979. 12.00 (0-89037-143-1) Anderson World.
— New Exercises for Runners. LC 78-460. (Illus.). 176p. 1978. pap. 4.95 (0-89037-151-2) Anderson World.
— New Guide to Distance Running. rev. ed. (Illus.). 400p. 1983. reprint ed. 11.95 (0-89037-133-4); reprint ed. pap. 8.95 (0-89037-270-5) Anderson World.
— The Runner's Diet: New & Revised. rev. ed. LC 78-455. (Illus.). 134p. 1978. pap. 3.95 (0-89037-152-0) Anderson World.
— Runner's Training Guide. (Illus.). 96p. 1978. pap. 3.95 (0-89037-026-5) Anderson World.
— Runner's World Training Diary. 1979. spiral bd. 6.95 (0-89037-153-9) Anderson World.
— Running after Forty. rev. ed. LC 78-68620. (Illus.). 160p. 1980. pap. 4.95 (0-89037-205-5) Anderson World.
Runners World Staff. Original Runners World Training. 1987. pap. 7.95 (0-02-029471-9) Macmillan.
— Runners after Forty. 1980. pap. 4.95 (0-02-499690-4) Macmillan.
— Runners Training Guide. 1978. pap. 3.95 (0-02-499440-5) Macmillan.
— Stretching Book. (Runner's World Ser.). 1982. pap. 9.95 (0-02-499610-6) Macmillan.
— Training Diary. (Runner's World Ser.). 1978. pap. 6.95 (0-02-499620-3) Macmillan.
Runggaldier, Edmund. Zeichen und Bezeichnetes: Sprachphilosophische Untersuchungen zum Problem der Referenz. (Grundlagen der Kommunikation-Bibliotheksausgabe Ser.). xii, 363p. (GER.). 1985. 97.70 (3-11-010107-6) De Gruyter.
***Running, John.** Honor Dance: Native American Photographs. (Illus.). 272p. 1995. pap. 24.95 (0-87417-277-2) U of Nev Pr.
— The Unknown: A Monument by R. V. Greeves. LC 86-61592. (Illus.). (Orig.). (C). 1986. pap. 9.75 (0-9616999-0-6) R V Greeves.
Running, Leona G., jt. ed. see Geraty, Lawrence T.
Running Press Editors. Love: Quotations from the Heart. LC 90-52551. (Miniature Editions Ser.). 96p. 1990. 4.95 (0-89471-856-8) Running Pr.
— A Woman's Journal: A Blank Book with Quotes by Women. (Illus.). 192p. 1985. 14.95 (0-89471-406-6) Running Pr.
Running Press Editors, ed. The Dream Journal: A Diary of Inner Visions. (Illus.). 144p. 1988. 14.95 (0-89471-597-6) Running Pr.

Running Press Staff. The Big Book of Hearts. (Visions of Love in Word & Image Ser.). (Illus.). 112p. 1994. 4.95 (1-56138-416-X) Running Pr.
— The Big Book of Riddles. (Miniature Editions Ser.). (Illus.). 128p. 1994. 4.95 (1-56138-421-6) Running Pr.
— The Country Notebook. (Illus.). 96p. 1981. pap. 7.98 (0-89471-517-8) Running Pr.
— Dinosaurs. LC 93-83583. (Unfolding World Ser.). (Illus.). (J). (gr. 4-7). 1993. 5.95 (1-56138-319-8) Running Pr.
— The Dinosaurs Postcard Book. (Postcard Book Ser.). (Illus.). 64p. (Orig.). (J). 1987. pap. 7.95 (0-89471-553-4) Running Pr.
— Love: An Illustrated Journal with Quotes. 96p. 1987. pap. 5.95 (0-89471-512-7) Running Pr.
Running Press Staff, ed. Among Friends Journal. (Illus.). 144p. 1993. 14.95 (1-56138-255-8) Running Pr.
— The Art of the Journal: Reflections on Writing with Space for Original Observations. (Illus.). 96p. (Orig.). 1994. pap. 5.95 (1-56138-464-X) Running Pr.
— Artistic Cat. LC 91-5063. (Miniature Editions Ser.). (Illus.). 108p. 1992. 4.95 (1-56138-091-1) Running Pr.
— Audubon Journal. (Illus.). 160p. 1993. 19.95 (1-56138-182-9) Running Pr.
— Audubon's Birds. LC 91-50906. (Miniature Editions Ser.). (Illus.). 128p. 1992. 4.95 (1-56138-090-3) Running Pr.
— The Cat Diary: An Uncommon Journal. (Illus.). 144p. 1990. 11.95 (0-89471-872-X) Running Pr.
— The Cat Postcard Book. (Postcard Book Ser.). (Illus.). 64p. (Orig.). 1987. pap. 7.95 (0-89471-519-4) Running Pr.
— Constellations. LC 92-50806. (Miniature Editions Ser.). (Illus.). 160p. 1993. 4.95 (1-56138-247-7) Running Pr.
— The Cook's Journal: With Quotations, Illustrations, & Space for Recipes & Reflection. (Illus.). 160p. 1994. 19.95 (1-56138-423-2) Running Pr.
— Dolls: A Postcard Book. (Postcard Book Ser.). (Illus.). 64p. (Orig.). 1991. pap. 7.95 (1-56138-017-2) Running Pr.
— Edith Holden's Classic Country Diary: A Postcard Book. (Postcard Book Ser.). (Illus.). 64p. (Orig.). 1992. pap. 7.95 (1-56138-098-9) Running Pr.
— The Embrace: A Treasury of Romance, in Word & Magic. (Miniature Editions Ser.). (Illus.). 140p. 1994. 4.95 (1-56138-417-8) Running Pr.
— Essence of Roses. LC 92-53694. (Miniature Editions Ser.). (Illus.). 120p. 1992. 4.95 (1-56138-151-9) Running Pr.
— Explorations: A Journal of Possibilities. (Running Press Journals). (Illus.). 96p. (Orig.). 1990. pap. 5.95 (0-89471-873-8) Running Pr.
— Friendship Notes. (Notes Ser.). (Illus.). 96p. (Orig.). 1994. pap. 3.95 (1-56138-482-8) Running Pr.
— From the Heart: A Romantic Notebook. (Illus.). 96p. (Orig.). 1993. pap. 5.95 (1-56138-254-X) Running Pr.
— Georgia O'Keeffe: A Postcard Book. (Postcard Book Ser.). (Illus.). 64p. 1993. pap. 7.95 (1-56138-163-2) Running Pr.
— In Praise of Grandmothers. LC 92-50808. (Miniature Editions Ser.). (Illus.). 96p. 1993. 4.95 (1-56138-249-3) Running Pr.
— KIDZ Family Car Songbook & Audiocassette. (KIDZ Ser.). (Illus.). 128p. (Orig.). (J). (gr. 1 up). 1991. audio 9.95 (0-89471-996-3) Running Pr.
— KIDZ Kids' Car Songbook & Audiocassette. (KIDZ Ser.). (Illus.). 112p. (J). (gr. 1 up). 1991. audio 9.95 (1-56138-074-1) Running Pr.
— KIDZ Laugh-Along Car Jokebook. (KIDZ Ser.). (Illus.). 64p. (Orig.). (J). 1992. audio 9.95 (1-56138-178-0) Running Pr.
— KIDZ Merry Christmas Car Songbook & Audiocassette. (KIDZ Ser.). (Illus.). 80p. (J). (gr. 1 up). 1991. audio 9.95 (1-56138-051-2) Running Pr.
— KIDZ Mother Goose Car Rhyme Book & Audiocassette. (KIDZ Ser.). (Illus.). 96p. (Orig.). (J). (gr. 1 up). 1991. audio 9.95 (1-56138-019-9) Running Pr.
— KIDZ Sing along Car Songbook. (KIDZ Ser.). (Illus.). 128p. (J). 1992. audio 9.95 (1-56138-177-2) Running Pr.
— The Kiss. LC 92-53676. (Miniature Editions Ser.). (Illus.). 144p. 1992. 4.95 (1-56138-149-7) Running Pr.
— Kitten's Notebook. (Illus.). 96p. (Orig.). 1992. pap. 5.95 (1-56138-183-7) Running Pr.
— The Language of Flowers. LC 91-52697. (Miniature Editions Ser.). (Illus.). 96p. 1991. 4.95 (1-56138-038-5) Running Pr.
— Little Book of Christmas Carols. LC 91-52702. (Miniature Editions Ser.). (Illus.). 128p. 1991. 4.95 (1-56138-040-7) Running Pr.
— Marilyn Monroe: A Postcard Book. (Postcard Book Ser.). (Illus.). 64p. (Orig.). 1989. 7.95 (0-89471-766-9) Running Pr.
— Matisse: A Postcard Book. (Postcard Book Ser.). (Illus.). 64p. (Orig.). 1989. pap. 7.95 (0-89471-711-1) Running Pr.
— Miniature Mother Goose. LC 91-50783. (Miniature Editions Ser.). (Illus.). 128p. (J). 1992. 4.95 (1-56138-105-5) Running Pr.
— Motherhood. LC 90-53465. (Miniature Editions Ser.). (Illus.). 112p. 1991. 4.95 (0-89471-983-1) Running Pr.
— Motherhood: A Keepsake Book with Illustrations & Quotes. (Illus.). 144p. 1990. 14.95 (0-89471-815-0) Running Pr.
— Motherhood Notes. (Notes Ser.). (Illus.). 96p. (Orig.). 1994. pap. 3.95 (1-56138-483-6) Running Pr.
— The Mural Project: Ansel Adams. (Postcard Book Ser.). (Illus.). 64p. (Orig.). 1992. pap. 7.95 (1-56138-096-2) Running Pr.
— Nature Journal. (Illus.). 96p. (Orig.). 1991. pap. 5.95 (1-56138-070-9) Running Pr.
— Nature Notes. (Notes Ser.). (Illus.). 96p. (Orig.). 1994. pap. 3.95 (1-56138-484-4) Running Pr.

An Asterisk (*) at the beginning of an entry indicates that the title is appearing in BIP for the first time.

— New Beginnings: A Notebook of Infinite Possibilities. (Illus.). 96p. (Orig.). 1991. pap. 5.95 (*1-56138-066-0*) Running Pr.
— Original Mother Goose. LC 91-51057. (Illus.). 136p. (J). 1992. 14.95 (*1-56138-113-6*) Running Pr.
— Personal Journal. (Illus.). 160p. 1992. 19.95 (*1-56138-117-9*) Running Pr.
— Poems of Friendship. LC 92-50807. (Miniature Editions Ser.). (Illus.). 96p. 1993. 4.95 (*1-56138-248-5*) Running Pr.
— Quotable Woman. LC 91-52546. 192p. 1991. 12.95 (*1-56138-015-6*) Running Pr.
— Quotable Women. LC 89-42995. (Miniature Editions Ser.). (Illus.). 96p. 1989. 4.95 (*0-89471-756-1*) Running Pr.
— Running Press World Atlas. LC 92-50809. (Miniature Editions Ser.). (Illus.). 128p. 1993. 4.95 (*1-56138-250-7*) Running Pr.
— Seasons: A Woman's Journal of Growth & Renewal. 144p. 1992. 14.95 (*1-56138-181-0*) Running Pr.
— Traveler's Diary. (Portable Diary Ser.). (Illus.). 144p. 1989. 11.95 (*0-89471-783-9*) Running Pr.
— Victorian Cats: A Postcard Book. (Postcard Book Ser.). (Illus.). 64p. (Orig.). 1992. pap. 7.95 (*1-56138-160-8*) Running Pr.
— Women's Notes. (Notes Ser.). (Illus.). 96p. (Orig.). 1994. pap. 3.95 (*1-56138-481-X*) Running Pr.
— Women's Wit & Wisdom. LC 91-52696. (Miniature Editions Ser.). (Illus.). 128p. 1991. 4.95 (*1-56138-037-7*) Running Pr.

Running Press Staff, ed. see Allen, James.
Running Press Staff, ed. see Dickinson, Emily.
Running Press Staff, ed. see Twain, Mark.
Runnings, Anna L. An Experimental Analysis of Two Bone Tools from the Manis Site, Sequim, Washington. xi, 84p. (C). pap. 7.50 (*1-55567-019-9*) Coyote Press.
Runnings, John & Bennett, Sue. I'm from Palestine... LC 82-243211. (Illus.). 40p. 1982. pap. 6.00 (*0-912021-00-4*) Grey Bk.
Runnion, Dale, ed. see Goff, Dick, et al.
Runnion, Dale F. & Runnion, June A. The Saddle & Sirloin Portrait Collection. 118p. 1992. pap. 10.00 (*0-9634756-0-6*) N Am Int Livestock.
Runnion, June, ed. see Goff, Dick, et al.
Runnion, June A., jt. auth. see Runnion, Dale F.
Runnion, William C. Structured Programming in Assembly Language for the IBM PC. 690p. (C). 1988. text ed. 56.95 (*0-534-91480-2*) PWS Pubs.
— Structured Programming in Assembly Language for the IBM PC. 2nd ed. LC 94-286. 1995. text ed. 58.95 (*0-534-93268-1*) PWS Pubs.
Runowicz, Carolyn. To Be Alive. 1995. 22.50 (*0-8050-2958-3*) H Holt & Co.
Runowicz, Carolyn, jt. auth. see Cherry, Sheldon H.
Runowicz, Carolyn D., jt. auth. see Cherry, Sheldon H.
Runquist, Willie. Baseball by the Numbers: How Statistics are Collected, What They Mean, & How They Reveal the Game. 208p. 1994. pap. 24.95 (*0-7864-0006-4*) McFarland & Co.
Runser, Dennis J. Maintaining & Troubleshooting HPLC Systems: A Users Guide. LC 80-25444. 163p. 1981. text ed. 74.95 (*0-471-06479-3*, Wiley-Interscience) Wiley.
Runser, Dennis J., ed. Industrial-Academic Interfacing. LC 83-27558. (ACS Symposium Ser.: No. 244). 176p. 1984. lib. bdg. 38.95 (*0-8412-0825-5*) Am Chemical.
Runsheng, Du. Reform & Development in Rural China. Gottshang, Thomas R., ed. LC 94-12854. (Studies on the Chinese Economy). 1994. write for info. (*0-312-12282-9*) St Martin.
Runstadler, P., ed. see Joint Fluids Engineering Gas Turbine Conference & Products Show Staff.
Runstein, jt. auth. see Huber.
Runstein, Robert, ed. see Huber, David M.
Runsten, David & LeVeen, Phillip. Mechanization & Mexican Labor in California Agriculture. (Monograph Ser.: No. 6). 135p. (Orig.). (C). 1981. pap. 7.50 (*0-935391-44-4*, MN-06) UCSD Ctr US-Mex.
***Runstler.** Images of the West. 22.99 (*0-517-12453-X*) Random Hse Value.
Runte, Alfred. National Parks: The American Experience. rev. ed. LC 86-11368. (Illus.). xxii, 379p. 1987. pap. 12.95 (*0-8032-8923-5*) U of Nebr Pr.
— National Parks: The American Experience. 2nd rev. ed. LC 86-11368. (Illus.). xxii, 379p. 1987. 25.00 (*0-8032-3878-9*) U of Nebr Pr.
— Public Lands, Public Heritage: The National Forest Idea. (Illus.). 100p. 1991. pap. 16.95 (*0-911797-94-7*) R Rinehart.
— Trains of Discovery: Western Railroads & the National Parks. limited ed. 116p. 1993. 65.00 (*1-879373-74-2*) R Rinehart.
— Trains of Discovery: Western Railroads & the National Parks. rev. ed. 1990. pap. 16.95 (*0-911797-61-0*) R Rinehart.
— Trains of Discovery: Western Railroads & the National Parks. rev. ed. 116p. 1993. pap. 19.95 (*1-879373-68-8*) R Rinehart.
— Trains of Discovery: Western Railroads & the National Parks. 3rd rev. ed. 116p. 1993. 35.00 (*1-879373-69-6*) R Rinehart.
— Yosemite: The Embattled Wilderness. (Illus.). xii, 319p. 1990. pap. 14.95 (*0-8032-8941-3*, Bison Books) U of Nebr Pr.
Runtz, Michael. Algonquin Seasons: A Natural History of Algonquin Park. 110p. 1995. 32.00 (*0-7737-2566-0*, Pub. by Stoddart Publng CN) Pubs Dist MI.
— The Explorer's Guide to Algonquin Park. 174p. 1995. pap. 7.95 (*0-7737-5571-3*, Pub. by Stoddart Publng CN) Pubs Dist MI.
— Moose Country. 220p. 1991. 39.00 (*1-55971-132-9*) NorthWord.
— Moose Country: Saga of the Woodland Moose. 1992. pap. 19.95 (*1-55971-190-6*) NorthWord.
Runtz, Vic. Here Today: Twenty-Five Years of Cartoons. 1983. 19.95 (*0-89101-060-2*); pap. 9.95 (*0-89101-059-9*) U Maine Pr.
Runyan, Anne S., jt. auth. see Peterson, Spike.
Runyan, Cathy C. Knuckles Down! A Fun Guide to Marble Play. 3rd ed. (Illus.). 36p. (J). (gr. 1-6). 1990. reprint ed. pap. 5.95 (*0-935295-01-1*) Right Brain.
Runyan, Timothy & Copes, Jan, eds. To Die Gallantly: The Battle of the Atlantic. LC 94-10715. (C). 1994. text ed. 58.00 (*0-8133-8815-5*); pap. text ed. 17.85 (*0-8133-2332-0*) Westview.
Runyan, Timothy J., ed. Ships, Seafaring & Society: Essays in Maritime History. LC 87-17769. 382p. 1987. 29.95 (*0-8143-1990-4*); pap. 17.95 (*0-8143-1991-2*) Wayne St U Pr.
Runyan, Timothy J., jt. auth. see Lewis, Archibald R.
Runyan, W. R. Silicon Semiconductor Technology. LC 64-24607. (Texas Instruments Electronics Ser.). (Illus.). 284p. reprint ed. pap. 81.00 (*0-317-09126-3*, 2055600) Bks Demand.
Runyan, Walter R. & Bean, Kenneth E. Semiconductor Integrated Circuit Processing Technology. (Electrical Engineering Ser.). (Illus.). 592p. (C). 1990. text ed. 75.25 (*0-201-10831-3*) Addison-Wesley.
Runyan, William M. Life Histories & Psychobiography: Explorations in Theory & Method. (Illus.). 288p. 1984. pap. 15.95 (*0-19-503486-4*) OUP.
Runyan, William M., ed. Psychology & Historical Interpretation. (Illus.). 320p. 1988. pap. text ed. 15.95 (*0-19-505328-1*) OUP.
Runyard, Sue, jt. ed. see Ambrose, Tim.
Runyon, Beverly B. The Over-Loving Parent: Making Love Work for You & Your Child. 160p. 1992. pap. 10.95 (*0-87833-803-9*) Taylor Pub.
***Runyon, Carol.** Healthy Cooking for One. 1994. 14.95 (*0-614-01909-5*) Jelm Mtn.
Runyon, Cheryl, jt. auth. see Davis, Asiyih.
Runyon, Cheryl, jt. auth. see Morandi, Larry.
***Runyon, Cheryl, et al.** Low-Level Radioactive Waste: A Legislator's Guide. 98p. 1994. 15.00 (*1-55516-498-6*, 4640) Natl Conf State Legis.
***Runyon, Cheryl C. & Helland, John.** Wetlands Mitigation & Mitigation Banking. 24p. 1995. 10.00 (*1-55516-403-X*, 4342) Natl Conf State Legis.
Runyon, D. Damon Runyon Reader. 23.95 (*0-89190-781-5*, Am Repr) Amereon Ltd.
Runyon, Damon. Blue Plate Special. 17.95 (*0-89190-360-7*, Am Repr) Amereon Ltd.
— Broadway, Mon Village. (FRE.). 1982. pap. 11.95 (*0-7859-4165-7*) Fr & Eur.
— Le Complexe de Broadway. 320p. (FRE.). 1982. pap. 11.95 (*0-7859-4169-X*, 2070373886) Fr & Eur.
— Damon Runyon Favorites. reprint ed. lib. bdg. 20.95 (*0-89190-440-9*, Rivercity Pr) Amereon Ltd.
— Damon Runyon Imnibus. 1993. reprint ed. lib. bdg. 28.95 (*1-56849-217-0*) Buccaneer Bks.
— Damon Runyon Omnibus. 1976. reprint ed. lib. bdg. 30.95 (*0-89190-441-7*, Rivercity Pr) Amereon Ltd.
— Guys & Dolls. reprint ed. lib. bdg. 18.95 (*0-89190-438-7*, Rivercity Pr) Amereon Ltd.
— Little Miss Marker. reprint ed. lib. bdg. 17.95 (*0-89190-436-0*, Rivercity Pr) Amereon Ltd.
— Money from Home. 17.95 (*0-89190-361-5*, Am Repr) Amereon Ltd.
— Poems for Men. 20.95 (*0-8488-1145-3*) Amereon Ltd.
— Ring-Tailed, Red-Eyed Sons o' Trouble. 22.95 (*0-8488-0144-X*, Amereon Hse) Amereon Ltd.
— Slight Case of Murder. 15.95 (*0-8488-1143-7*) Amereon Ltd.
— Slow Horses & Fast Women. (Illus.). reprint ed. lib. bdg. 20.95 (*0-89190-439-5*, Rivercity Pr) Amereon Ltd.
— Tents of Trouble: Verse of D. Runyon. 15.95 (*0-8488-0841-X*) Amereon Ltd.
— Trials & Other Tribulations. 21.95 (*0-8488-1619-6*) Amereon Ltd.
— Troopers, Tramps & Other Loose Characters. 21.95 (*0-8488-0145-8*, Amereon Hse) Amereon Ltd.
Runyon, Damon & Johnson, intros. Jack Johnson: In the Ring - & Out - the Autobiography of Jack Johnson. (Illus.). 272p. 1992. pap. 10.95 (*0-8065-1358-6*, Citadel Pr) Carol Pub Group.
***Runyon, Daniel V.** Ferguson: Her Tractor-Biography. (Illus.). 128p. 1995. pap. 10.00 (*1-878559-03-6*) Saltbox Pr.
***Runyon, Daniel V., ed.** World Mission People: The Best of the Missionary Tidings, 1990-95. 400p. 1995. pap. 15.00 (*1-878559-04-4*) Saltbox Pr.
Runyon, Daniel V., ed. see Locke, David R. & Maurer, Kent L.
Runyon, Daniel V., ed. see Watson, C. Hoyt.
***Runyon, Frances.** White Out. 200p. 1995. pap. 7.95 (*1-56901-886-3*) NW Pub.
Runyon, Harry. Faulkner Glossary. 1966. pap. 2.25 (*0-8065-0152-9*, 228, Citadel Pr) Carol Pub Group.
Runyon, Kenneth & Stewart, David. Consumer Behavior. 3rd ed. 760p. (C). 1987. write for info. (*0-675-20463-1*, Merrill Pub Co) Macmillan.
Runyon, Linda. Crabgrass Muffins & Pine Needle Tea: How to Identify, Enjoy, & Cook the Cornucopia of Wild Foods Growing Among us. LC 93-25247. 1994. 20.00 (*0-517-88033-4*, Harmony) Crown Pub Group.
— A Survival Acre-Fifty Nationwide Wild Foods & Medicines. (Illus.). 43p. (Orig.). 1985. pap. 10.00 (*0-918517-03-6*) Wild Foods Co.
Runyon, Mildred M. Are Clowns Hatched? Life of Chucko the Clown. LC 93-80477. (Illus.). 180p. (Orig.). 1994. pap. 19.95 (*1-884431-09-7*) Gold Ring Pubng.
Runyon, Randolph. Fowles, Irving, Barthes: Canonical Variations on an Apocryphal Theme. LC 81-11125. (Illus.). 134p. 1981. 35.00 (*0-8142-0335-3*) Ohio St U Pr.
Runyon, Randolph P. The Braided Dream: Robert Penn Warren's Late Poetry. LC 89-48187. 264p. 1990. text ed. 28.00 (*0-8131-1722-4*) U Pr of Ky.
— Reading Raymond Carver. LC 91-36790. 246p. 1992. 29.95 (*0-8156-2563-4*) Syracuse U Pr.
— Reading Raymond Carver. LC 91-36790. 246p. (C). 1993. reprint ed. pap. text ed. 15.50 (*0-8156-2631-2*) Syracuse U Pr.
— The Taciturn Text: The Fiction of Robert Penn Warren. 288p. 1991. 39.50 (*0-8142-0530-5*) Ohio St U Pr.
Runyon, Richard P. Descriptive Statistics: A Contemporary Approach. LC 76-15467. (Statistics Ser.). (C). 1977. pap. text ed. write for info. (*0-201-06652-1*) Addison-Wesley.
— Winning with Statistics: A Painless First Look at Numbers, Ratios, Percentages, Means & Inference. (Statistics Ser.). (Illus.). 1977. pap. text ed. write for info. (*0-201-06654-8*) Addison-Wesley.
Runyon, Richard P. & Haber, Audrey. Fundamentals of Behavioral Statistics. LC 83-6327. 480p. (C). 1985. 10.00 (*0-394-35068-5*) Random.
— Fundamentals of Behavioral Statistics. 5th ed. LC 83-6327. 480p. (C). 1985. text ed. write for info. (*0-394-35018-9*) Random.
— Fundamentals of Behavioral Statistics. 6th ed. 608p. (C). 1988. student ed 10.50 (*0-685-18211-8*); text ed. 34.95 (*0-685-18210-X*) McGraw.
— Fundamentals of Behavioral Statistics. 7th ed. 1991. text ed. write for info. (*0-07-054326-7*) McGraw.
— Fundamentals of Behavioral Statistics. 7th ed. 1991. Study guide. student ed, pap. text ed. write for info. (*0-07-054328-3*) McGraw.
Runyon, Richard P., jt. auth. see Badia, Pietro.
Runyon, Richard P., jt. auth. see Haber, Audrey.
Runzo, Joseph. Worldviews & Perceiving God. LC 93-26988. 1993. text ed. 39.95 (*0-312-10379-4*) St Martin.
Runzo, Joseph, ed. Ethics, Religion, & the Good Society: New Directions in a Pluralistic World. 224p. (Orig.). 1992. pap. 23.99 (*0-664-25285-0*) Westminster John Knox.
— Is God Real? LC 92-20273. 1993. text ed. 39.95 (*0-312-08439-0*) St Martin.
Runzo, Joseph & Ihara, Graig K., eds. Religious Experience & Religious Belief: Essays in the Epistemology of Religion. LC 86-1614. 160p. (C). 1986. pap. text ed. 19.50 (*0-8191-5293-5*) U Pr of Amer.
Ruocchio, Albert C. & Klein, Maury D. Track Layout & Accessory Manual for Lionel Trains. (Illus.). 1979. pap. 3.00 (*0-934580-08-1*, K-4) MDK Inc.
Ruof, George C. Christmas Stories. 1994. 10.00 (*0-533-10983-3*) Vantage.
Ruoff & Skaar, eds. Robotics & Teleroperation in Space. write for info. (*0-318-72359-X*) AIAA.
Ruoff, jt. ed. see Johnston, Kenneth R.
Ruoff, A. LaVonne. American Indian Literatures: An Introduction, Bibliographic Review & Selected Bibliography. LC 90-13438. (Illus.). viii, 200p. 1990. text ed. 45.00 (*0-87352-191-9*); pap. text ed. 19.75 (*0-87352-192-7*, B106P) Modern Lang.
— Literatures of the American Indian. (Indians of North America Ser.). (Illus.). 112p. (YA). (gr. 5 up). 1991. lib. bdg. 17.95 (*1-55546-688-5*) Chelsea Hse.
Ruoff, A. LaVonne, Jr. & Ward, Jerry W., Jr., eds. Redefining American Literary History. LC 90-6530. (Committee on Literatures & Languages of America Ser.). iv, 406p. 1990. text ed. 45.00 (*0-87352-187-0*, B105C); pap. text ed. 19.75 (*0-87352-188-9*, B105P) Modern Lang.
Ruoff, A. LaVonne, jt. auth. see Eastman, Charles A.
Ruoff, Abby. Making Twig Furniture & Household Things. LC 91-20101. 1991. pap. 14.95 (*0-88179-029-X*) Hartley & Marks.
Ruoff-Appel, Andrea, ed. see Vollman, June.
Ruoff, Arthur L. Introduction to Materials Science. LC 79-4668. 718p. 1979. reprint ed. lib. bdg. 59.50 (*0-88275-960-4*) Krieger.
Ruoff, Carl F., jt. ed. see Skaar, Steven B.
Ruoff, E. G., ed. Death Throes of a Dynasty: Letters & Diaries of Charles & Bessie Ewing, Missionaries to China. LC 90-35339. (Illus.). 286p. 1990. 29.00 (*0-87338-414-8*) Kent St U Pr.
Ruoff, Gene W. Jane Austen's Sense & Sensibility. LC 92-17361. (Critical Studies of Key Texts). 1992. pap. 12.95 (*0-312-08599-0*) St Martin.
— Wordsworth & Coleridge: The Making of the Major Lyrics, 1802-1804. LC 88-28292. 320p. (C). 1989. text ed. 45.00 (*0-8135-1398-7*); pap. text ed. 16.00 (*0-8135-1399-5*) Rutgers U Pr.
Ruoff, Gene W., ed. The Romantics & Us: Essays on Literature & Culture. 275p. (Orig.). (C). 1990. text ed. 45.00 (*0-8135-1498-3*); pap. 15.00 (*0-8135-1499-1*) Rutgers U Pr.
Ruoff, Gene W., jt. ed. see Kroeber, Karl.
Ruoff, Lou. For Give: Stories of Reconciliation. LC 90-29144. 120p. (Orig.). (C). 1991. pap. 8.95 (*0-89390-198-9*) Resource Pubns.
— No Kidding, God, Where Are You? Parables of Ordinary Experience. LC 88-34043. 120p. (C). 1989. pap. 7.95 (*0-89390-141-5*) Resource Pubns.
— Parables of Belonging: Discipleship & Commitment in Everyday Life. LC 92-38844. 132p. (Orig.). (C). 1993. pap. text ed. 8.95 (*0-89390-253-5*) Resource Pubns.
Ruoff, Mona. From the Dragon's Cloud: Vietnamese Folk Tales. (Illus.). 63p. (Orig.). 1984. reprint ed. pap. 5.00 (*0-9619969-5-1*) Blue Horse Pr.
Ruoff, R. S., jt. auth. see Kadish, K. M.
Ruoff, R. S., jt. ed. see Kadish, K. M.
Ruoff, Shari, ed. see Vollman, June.
Ruoff, Theodore. Legal Legends & Other True Stories. 301p. (C). 1988. 75.00 (*0-685-28570-7*, Pub. by Fourmat Pub UK) St Mut.
Ruoff, Theodore, jt. comp. see Fourmat's Editorial Staff.
Ruokanen, Miikka. The Catholic Doctrine of Non-Christian Religions According to the Second Vatican Council. LC 91-46332. (Studies in Christian Mission: Vol. 7). 169p. 1992. 51.50 (*90-04-09517-9*) E J Brill.
Ruokonen, Kyllikki. India Information Sources, Economics & Business. (Concepts in Communication Informatics & Librarianship Ser.: No. 38). (C). 1992. text ed. 26.00 (*81-7022-437-3*, Pub. by Concept II) S Asia.
***Ruokonen, T., ed.** Fault Detection, Supervision & Safety for Technical Processes 1994. 1994. pap. 115.00 (*0-08-042222-5*, Pergamon Pr) Elsevier.
Ruopp, Phillips. Private Testimony & Public Policy. (C). 1959. pap. 3.00 (*0-87574-105-3*) Pendle Hill.
Ruopp, Richard R., et al, eds. Labnet: Toward a Community of Practice. (Technology & Education Ser.). 384p. 1993. text ed. 79.95 (*0-8058-1263-6*); pap. 29.95 (*0-8058-1294-6*) L Erlbaum Assocs.
Ruoss, Martin. A Policy & Procedure Manual for Church & Synagogue Libraries: A Do-It-Yourself Guide. LC 79-28676. (Guide Ser.: No. 9). 14p. 1980. pap. 4.75 (*0-915324-17-2*); pap. 3.50 (*0-685-01326-X*) CSLA.
***Ruot, Carol F.** Discipline Strategies: For the Bored, Belligerent & Ballistic in Your Classroom. (Illus.). 184p. (Orig.). 1995. pap. 13.95 (*0-944295-04-5*) Sanibel Sanddollar Pubns.
Ruotolo, George L. A Format for Successful Accident Reconstruction Report Writing. 40p. (C). 1993. pap. text ed. 14.95 (*1-884566-13-8*) Inst Police Tech.
Ruotolo, Lucio P. The Interrupted Moment: A View of Virginia Woolf's Novels. LC 86-6002. 280p. 1986. 35.00 (*0-8047-1342-1*); pap. 11.95 (*0-8047-1523-8*) Stanford U Pr.
— Six Existential Heroes: The Politics of Faith. LC 72-86386. 161p. reprint ed. pap. 45.90 (*0-7837-4187-1*, 2059037) Bks Demand.
Ruotolo, Lucio P., ed. see Woolf, Virginia.
Ruowang, Wang. Hunger Trilogy. Rubin, Kyna & Kasoff, Ira, trs. LC 91-9017. 176p. (C). 1991. 45.00 (*0-87332-739-X*); pap. text ed. 17.95 (*0-87332-740-3*) M E Sharpe.
Ruoxi, Chen. Democracy Wall & the Unofficial Journals. (Current Chinese Language Project Ser.: No. 20). 119p. 1983. pap. 2.50x (*0-912966-57-2*) IEAS.
— The Short Stories of Chen Ruoxi, Translated from the Original Chinese: A Writer at the Crossroads. Kao, Hsin-sheng C., ed. LC 92-29960. 420p. 1992. 109.95 (*0-7734-9190-2*) E Mellen.
Ruoxi, Chen, jt. auth. see Dittmer, Lowell.
Rupa, ed. see Sen, Geeti.
Rupa, C. Reservation Policy & Mandal Commission. 168p. (C). 1992. text ed. 25.00 (*81-207-1384-2*, Pub. by Sterling Pubs II) Apt Bks.
Rupa Vitasa Dasa, pseud. A Ray of Vishnu: The Biography of a Saktyavesa. (Lives of Vaisnava Acaryas Ser.: Vol. 1). (Illus.). 291p. (Orig.). (C). 1988. pap. 9.95 (*0-923519-01-7*) New Jaipur.
Rupagosvamai. Srila Rupa Gosvami's Sri Laghu-Bhagavatamrta, Vol. 2: A Little Nectar of the Supreme Personality of Godhead & His Devotees, Vol. 100. Kusakrathadasa, tr. 152p. (Orig.). 1990. pap. text ed. 10.00 (*1-56130-007-1*) Krsna Inst.
Rupagosvami. Srila Rupa Gosvami's Sri Astadasa-cchandah-stava: Eighteen Chandah Prayers. Kusakrathadasa, tr. (Krsna Library: Vol. 9). 121p. (Orig.). (C). 1987. pap. text ed. 8.00 (*0-944833-00-4*) Krsna Inst.
— Srila Rupa Gosvami's Sri Dana-Keli-Kaumudi: The Moonlight of the Dana-Keli Pastime. Kusakrathadasa, tr. (Krsna Library: Vol. 215). 64p. (Orig.). 1994. pap. text ed. 6.00 (*1-56130-144-2*) Krsna Inst.
— Srila Rupa Gosvami's Sri Govinda-virudavali: Calling Out to Lord Krsna. Kusakrathadasa, tr. (Krsna Library: Vol. 8). 123p. (C). 1987. pap. text ed. 6.00 (*0-944833-08-X*) Krsna Inst.
— Srila Rupa Gosvami's Sri Hamsaduta: The Swan Messenger. Kusakrathadasa, tr. (Krsna Library: Vol. 98). 96p. (Orig.). 1990. pap. text ed. 8.00 (*1-56130-005-5*) Krsna Inst.
— Srila Rupa Gosvami's Sri Laghu-Bhagavatamrta: A Little Nectar of the Supreme Personality of Godhead & His Devotees, Vols. 99-101. Kusakrathadasa, tr. (Orig.). 1990. pap. text ed. 30.00 (*1-56130-009-8*) Krsna Inst.
— Srila Rupa Gosvami's Sri Laghu-Bhagavatamrta, Vol. 1: A Little Nectar of the Supreme Personality of Godhead & His Devotees, Vol. 99. Kusakrathadasa, tr. 176p. (Orig.). 1990. pap. text ed. 10.00 (*1-56130-006-3*) Krsna Inst.
— Srila Rupa Gosvami's Sri Laghu-Bhagavatamrta, Vol. 3: A Little Nectar of the Supreme Personality of Godhead & His Devotees, Vol. 101. Kusakrathadasa, tr. 159p. (Orig.). 1990. pap. text ed. 10.00 (*1-56130-008-X*) Krsna Inst.
— Srila Rupa Gosvami's Sri Lalita-Madhava: Playful Krsna. Kusakrathadasa, tr. (Krsna Library: Vol. 209). 182p. (C). 1994. pap. text ed. 10.00 (*1-56130-135-3*) Krsna Inst.
— Srila Rupa Gosvami's Sri Lalita-Madhava (Playful Krsna) Act Eight; Nava-vrndavana-vihara (Pastimes in New Vrndavana) Kusakrathadasa, tr. (Krsna Library: Vol. 58). 66p. (Orig.). 1989. pap. text ed. 8.00 (*0-944833-58-6*) Krsna Inst.
— Srila Rupa Gosvami's Sri Lalita-Madhava (Playful Krsna) Act Five; Candravali-labha (the Attainment of Candravali) Kusakrathadasa, tr. (Krsna Library: Vol. 55). 72p. (Orig.). 1989. pap. text ed. 8.00 (*0-944833-55-1*) Krsna Inst.

R

— Srila Rupa Gosvami's Sri Lalita-Madhava (Playful Krsna) Act Four; Radhabhisaranka-garbhanka-garbha (the Play "Meeting Radha") Kusakrathadasa, tr. (Krsna Library: Vol. 54). 77p. (Orig.). 1989. pap. text ed. 8.00 (0-944833-54-3) Krsna Inst.

— Srila Rupa Gosvami's Sri Lalita-Madhava (Playful Krsna) Act Nine; Citra-darsana (Looking at Pictures) Kusakrathadasa, tr. (Krsna Library: Vol. 59). 98p. (Orig.). 1989. pap. text ed. 8.00 (0-944833-59-4) Krsna Inst.

— Srila Rupa Gosvami's Sri Lalita-Madhava (Playful Krsna) Act Seven; Nava-vrndavana-sangama (Meeting in New Vrndavana) Kusakrathadasa, tr. (Krsna Library: Vol. 57). 74p. (Orig.). 1989. pap. text ed. 8.00 (0-944833-57-8) Krsna Inst.

— Srila Rupa Gosvami's Sri Lalita-Madhava (Playful Krsna) Act Six; Lalitopalabdhi (the Attainment of Lalita) Kusakrathadasa, tr. (Krsna Library: Vol. 56). 66p. (Orig.). 1989. pap. text ed. 8.00 (0-944833-56-X) Krsna Inst.

— Srila Rupa Gosvami's Sri Lalita-Madhava (Playful Krsna) Act Ten; Purna-manoratha (All Desires Are Fulfilled) Kusakrathadasa, tr. (Krsna Library: Vol. 60). 106p. (Orig.). 1989. pap. text ed. 8.00 (0-944833-60-8) Krsna Inst.

— Srila Rupa Gosvami's Sri Lalita-Madhava (Playful Krsna) Act Three; Unmatta-Radhika (Maddened Radhika) Kusakrathadasa, tr. (Krsna Library: Vol. 53). 71p. (Orig.). 1989. pap. text ed. 8.00 (0-944833-53-5) Krsna Inst.

— Srila Rupa Gosvami's Sri Lalita-Madhava (Playful Krsna) Act Two; Sankhacuda-vadha (The Killing of Sankhacuda) Kusakrathadasa, tr. (Krsna Library: Vol. 52). 71p. (Orig.). 1989. pap. text ed. 8.00 (0-944833-52-7) Krsna Inst.

— Srila Rupa Gosvami's Sri Lalita-Madhava (Playful Krsna), Act One: Sayam Utsava (An Evening Festival) Kusakrathadasa, tr. (Krsna Library: Vol. 51). 86p. (Orig.). 1989. pap. text ed. 8.00 (0-944833-51-9) Krsna Inst.

— Srila Rupa Gosvami's Sri Mathura-Mahatmya: The Glories of Mathura. Kusakrathadasa, tr. (Krsna Library). 226p. (Orig.). (C). 1989. pap. text ed. 12.00 (0-944833-35-7) Krsna Inst.

— Srila Rupa Gosvami's Sri Padyavali: A Verse Anthology. Kusakrathadasa, tr. (Krsna Library: Vol. 63). (Orig.). (C). 1990. pap. text ed. 15.00 (0-944833-80-2) Krsna Inst.

— Srila Rupa Gosvami's Sri Sri Radha-Krsna-gaoddesa-dipka: A Lamp to See the Associates of Sri Sri Radha Krsna. Kusakrathadasa, tr. (Krsna Library: Vol. 7). 304p. 1987. pap. text ed. 12.00 (0-944833-05-5) Krsna Inst.

— Srila Rupa Gosvami's Sri Stava-mala, Vol. 1: A Garland of Prayers. Kusakrathadasa, tr. (Krsna Library: Vol. 88). 116p. (Orig.). 1990. pap. text ed. 8.00 (0-944833-49-7) Krsna Inst.

— Srila Rupa Gosvami's Sri Stava-mala, Vol. 2: A Garland of Prayers. Kusakrathadasa, tr. (Krsna Library: Vol. 89). 119p. (Orig.). 1990. pap. text ed. 8.00 (0-944833-47-0) Krsna Inst.

— Srila Rupa Gosvami's Sri Stava-mala, Vol. 5: A Garland of Prayers. Kusakrathadasa, tr. (Krsna Library: Vol. 90). 78p. (Orig.). 1990. pap. text ed. 8.00 (0-944833-87-X) Krsna Inst.

— Srila Rupa Gosvami's Sri Stava-mala, Vol. 6: A Garland of Prayers. Kusakrathadasa, tr. (Krsna Library: Vol. 91). 127p. (Orig.). 1990. pap. text ed. 8.00 (0-944833-88-8) Krsna Inst.

— Srila Rupa Gosvami's Sri Uddhava-Sandesa: A Message for Uddhava. Kusakrathadasa, tr. (Krsna Library: Vol. 207). 85p. (C). 1994. pap. text ed. 6.00 (1-56130-133-7) Krsna Inst.

Rupagosvami & Visvanathacakravarti. Srila Rupa Gosvami's Sri Nikunja-Rahasya-Stava & Srila Visvanatha Cakravartis Sri Gitavali & Other Poems. Kusakrathadasa, tr. (Krsna Library: Vol. 208). 64p. (C). 1994. pap. text ed. 4.00 (1-56130-134-5) Krsna Inst.

***RuPaul.** Lettin' It All Hang Out: An Autobiography. (Illus.). 240p. 1995. 19.95 (0-7868-6156-8) Hyperion.

***Rupel, Esther F.** Brethren Dress: A Testimony to Faith. (Monograph Ser.: No. 5). (Illus.). 200p. 1994. 45.00 (0-936693-50-9) Brethren Encyclopedia.

Rupert, David, jt. auth. see Lesch, William C.

Rupert, Hoover. Why Didn't Noah Swat Both Mosquitoes? Plus Other Humorous Stories for Clergy. LC 93-44439. 100p. 1994. pap. 9.75 (1-55673-519-7) CSS OH.

Rupert, Janet E. The African Mask. LC 93-7726. (J). 1994. 13.95 (0-395-67295-3, Clarion Bks) HM.

***Rupert, Mark.** Producing Hegemony: The Politics of Mass Production & American Global Power. (Studies in International Relations: No. 38). (Illus.). 272p. (C). 1995. pap. 18.95 (0-521-46650-4) Cambridge U Pr.

— Producing Hegemony: The Politics of Mass Production & American Global Power. (Studies in International Relations: No. 38). (Illus.). 272p. 1995. 54.95 (0-521-46112-X) Cambridge U Pr.

Rupert, Raymond H. New Era of Investment Banking: Industry Structure, Trends & Performance. 400p. 1993. 75.00 (1-55738-454-1) Probus Pub Co.

Rupert, Rona. Straw Sense. LC 92-8775. (Illus.). (J). 1993. pap. 14.00 (0-671-77047-0, S&S Bks Young Read) S&S Childrens.

Rupesinghe, Kumar, ed. Conflict Resolution in Uganda. LC 89-30799. 320p. 1989. text ed. 29.95 (0-8214-0929-8) Ohio U Pr.

— Conflict Transformation. LC 94-34691. 1995. text ed. write for info. (0-312-12487-2) St Martin.

— Internal Conflict & Governance. LC 92-16772. 1992. text ed. 69.95 (0-312-08563-X) St Martin.

Rupesunghe, Kumar, et al. Ethnic Conflict & Human Rights in Sri Lanka Volume 2: An Annoted Bibliography: 1989-1992. annot. ed. LC 89-2077. 313p. 1993. 75.00 (1-873836-80-5, Pub. by H Zell Pubs UK) Bowker-Saur.

Rupieper, Herman J. The Cuno Government & Reparations, 1922-1923. (Studies in Contemporary History: No. 1). 1979. pap. text ed. 103.00 (90-247-2114-8) Kluwer Ac.

Rupinska, M., jt. auth. see Maronski, J.

Rupke, Nicolaas A. Richard Owen: Victorian Naturalist. LC 93-5739. (Illus.). 480p. 1994. 45.00 (0-300-05820-9) Yale U Pr.

Rupke, Nicolaas A., ed. Vivisection in Historical Perspective. 384p. 1990. pap. 17.95 (0-415-05021-9, A4489) Routledge.

— Vivisection in Historical Perspective. LC 87-8992. 373p. 1987. 85.00 (0-7099-4236-2, Pub. by Croom Helm UK) Routledge Chapman & Hall.

Ruple, Joelyn. Antonio Buero Vallejo: The First Fifteen Years. 1971. 12.95 (0-88303-006-3); pap. 8.95 (0-685-73210-X) E Torres & Sons.

Rupley, Frances. A Walking Tour of the University at Buffalo: And Other Area Architectural Treasures. LC 93-12107. (Illus.). 119p. (Orig.). (C). 1993. pap. 12.95 (0-87975-813-9) Prometheus Bks.

Rupley, William H. & Blair, Timothy R. Reading Diagnosis & Remediation. 3rd ed. 480p. (C). 1989. write for info. (0-675-20932-3, Merrill Pub Co) Macmillan.

— Teaching Reading: Diagnosis, Direct Instruction Practice. 2nd ed. 256p. (C). 1988. pap. write for info. (0-675-20891-2, Merrill Pub Co) Macmillan.

Ruplin, Ferdinand A. & Russell, John R. Basic German: A Programmed Course. (C). 1969. reprint ed. pap. text ed. 5.95 (0-89197-535-7); reprint ed. 0.65 (0-8290-1410-1) Irvington.

Rupnow, Marcia, jt. auth. see Miller, Richard K.

Rupnow, Marcia E., jt. auth. see Miller, Richard K.

Rupp, Anne N. Celebrating the Advent-Christmas Season. 60p. (Orig.). 1989. pap. 9.25 (0-940754-79-7) Ed Ministries.

— The Family Car. 12p. (Orig.). 1986. pap. 5.95 (0-940754-39-8) Ed Ministries.

Rupp, Daniel. History of Northampton, Lehigh, Monroe, Carbon & Schuylkill Counties, Pa. 576p. 1978. 18.50 (0-916838-16-1) Schiffer.

Rupp, E. Gordon & Watson, Philip S., eds. Luther & Erasmus: Free Will & Salvation. LC 76-79870. (Library of Christian Classics). 356p. 1978. pap. 14.99 (0-664-24158-1, Westminster) Westminster John Knox.

Rupp, Ernest G. Six Makers of English Religion, Fifteen Hundred to Seventeen Hundred. (Essay Index Reprint Ser.). 1977. reprint ed. 19.95 (0-518-10159-2) Ayer.

Rupp, George. Culture-Protestantism: German Liberal Theology at the Turn of the Twentieth Century. LC 77-13763. (American Academy of Religion, Studies in Religion: No. 15). 1977. pap. 19.95 (0-89130-197-6, 010015) Scholars Pr GA.

Rupp, George H. A Wavering Friendship: Russia & Austria 1876-1878. LC 76-8455. (Perspectives in European History Ser.: No. 11). xiv, 599p. 1976. reprint ed. lib. bdg. 49.50 (0-87991-617-6) Porcupine Pr.

Rupp, Gordon. Religion in England: 1688-1781. LC 85-23886. (History of the Christian Church Ser.). 520p. 1987. 95.00 (0-19-826918-8) OUP.

Rupp, Gretchen L. & Jones, Roy R., Sr., eds. Characterizing Heterogeneous Wastes: Methods & Recommendations. LC 92-35493. 1992. 54.95 (0-8493-8720-5, TD793) CRC Pr.

Rupp, Heinz, jt. ed. see Maurer, Friedrich.

Rupp, I. Daniel. History of Lancaster County, Pennsylvania: To Which Is Prefixed a Brief Sketch of the Early History of Pennsylvania. (Illus.). 570p. 1990. reprint ed. pap. 27.50 (1-55613-295-6) Heritage Bk.

— History of Northampton, Lehigh, Monroe, Carbon, & Schuylkill Counties. (Illus.). 568p. 1992. reprint ed. lib. bdg. 59.00 (0-8328-2253-1) Higginson Bk Co.

Rupp, Israel D. A Collection of Upwards of Thirty Thousand Names of German, Swiss, Dutch, French & Other Immigrants in Pennsylvania from 1727 to 1776. LC 65-26916. (Illus.). 583p. 1994. reprint ed. 30.00 (0-8063-0302-6, 5045) Genealog Pub.

— He Pasa Ekklesia: An Original History of the Religious Denominations at Present Existing in the United States Containing Authentic Accounts of Their Rise, Progress, Statistics. 1977. 33.95 (0-8369-7149-3, 7981) Ayer.

— History of Northampton, Lehigh, Monroe, Carbon, & Schuylkill Counties. LC 71-146417. (First American Frontier Ser.). (Illus.). 1971. reprint ed. 45.95 (0-405-02881-4) Ayer.

— The Religious Denominations in the United States: Their Past History, Present Condition, & Doctrines. LC 72-2943. reprint ed. 115.00 (0-404-10709-5) AMS Pr.

Rupp, J., ed. see Hierosolymitanus, Cyrillus.

Rupp, James E. LeaLao Chinantec Syntax: Studies in Chinantec Languages, Vol. 2. Merrifield, William R., ed. (Publications in Linguistics: No. 88). 120p. 1989. pap. 9.00 (0-88312-103-4); fiche 12.00 (0-88312-468-8) Summer Instit Ling.

Rupp, James M. Art in Seattle's Public Places: An Illustrated Guide. LC 90-32846. (Illus.). 320p. (Orig.). 1992. pap. 19.95 (0-295-97100-2) U of Wash Pr.

***Rupp, Jean.** Grammar Gremlins: An Instant Guide to Perfect Grammar for Everybody in Business. (Illus.). 150p. (Orig.). 1994. pap. write for info. (1-885221-12-6) BookPartners.

Rupp, Joyce. Fresh Bread & Other Gifts of Spiritual Nourishment. LC 85-70020. 160p. (Orig.). 1985. pap. 5.95 (0-87793-283-2) Ave Maria.

— Little Pieces of Light: Darkness & Personal Growth. LC 94-30803. (Illumination Bks.). 64p. 1994. pap. 3.95 (0-8091-3512-4) Paulist Pr.

— May I Have This Dance? LC 92-71817. (Illus.). 184p. (Orig.). 1992. pap. 8.95 (0-87793-480-0) Ave Maria.

— Praying Our Goodbyes. LC 87-72291. 184p. (Orig.). 1988. pap. 6.95 (0-87793-370-7) Ave Maria.

— Praying Our Goodbyes. (Orig.). 1992. reprint ed. mass mkt. 4.99 (0-8041-1060-3) Ivy Books.

— The Star in My Heart: Experiencing Sophia, Inner Wisdom. Butler, Ruth, ed. LC 90-41108. (Illus.). 96p. (Orig.). 1990. pap. 10.95 (0-931055-75-X) LuraMedia.

Rupp, Kalman. Entrepreneurs in Red: Structure & Organizational Innovation in the Centrally Planned Economy. LC 82-3389. 260p. 1983. 64.50 (0-87395-635-4); pap. 21.95 (0-87395-636-2) State U NY Pr.

Rupp, Keith & Miller, Dawn. God's Family Tree: Adding New Members to the Family of God. Spear, Cindy G. & Pierce, Tim, eds. 100p. 1994. ring bd. 79.95 (1-57052-000-3) Chrch Grwth VA.

Rupp, Leila J. Mobilizing Women for War: German & American Propaganda. LC 77-85562. (Illus.). 256p. reprint ed. pap. 73.00 (0-8357-3698-9, 2036422) Bks Demand.

Rupp, Leila J. & Taylor, Verta. Survival in the Doldrums: The American Women's Rights Movement, 1945 to the 1960s. 256p. 1987. 27.95 (0-19-504938-1) OUP.

— Survival in the Doldrums: The American Women's Rights Movement, 1945 to the 1960s. (Illus.). 256p. (C). 1990. reprint ed. pap. 19.50 (0-8142-0516-X) Ohio St U Pr.

Rupp, N. Daniel, jt. ed. see Walling, Regis M.

Rupp, Nadine, ed. Ozumacin Chinantec Texts, No. 2: Folklore Texts in Mexican Indian Languages. LC 93-86273. (Language Data Amerindian Ser.: No. 11). 92p. (Orig.). 1994. pap. write for info. (0-88312-624-9); fiche write for info. (1-55671-993-0) Summer Instit Ling.

Rupp, R. F., jt. auth. see Wujek, E. D.

Rupp, Randall G., jt. ed. see Oka, Melvin S.

***Rupp, Rebecca.** Birds. LC 94-21014. (Everything You Never Learned About Ser.). (Illus.). 144p. 1995. pap. 14.95 (0-88266-345-3, Storey Pub) Storey Comm Inc.

— Blue Corn & Square Tomatoes: Unusual Facts about Common Garden Vegetables. Burns, Deborah, ed. LC 87-45009. (Illus.). 232p. (Orig.). 1987. pap. 12.95 (0-88266-505-7, Garden Way Pub) Storey Comm Inc.

— Good Stuff: A Learning Resources Handbook. 386p. (Orig.). 1993. pap. 14.95 (0-945097-20-4) Home Educ Pr.

— Red Oaks & Black Birches: The Science & Lore of Trees. Mason, Jill, ed. LC 90-55043. (Illus.). 288p. 1990. pap. 10.95 (0-88266-620-7) Storey Comm Inc.

Rupp, Richard H. Celebration in Postwar American Fiction. LC 77-102187. 1970. 11.95 (0-87024-145-1) U of Miami Pr.

Rupp, Richard H., ed. Critics on Emily Dickinson. LC 77-143454. (Readings in Literary Criticism Ser.: No. 14). (Orig.). 1986. pap. 10.95 (0-685-25021-0) U of Miami Pr.

— Critics on Whitman. LC 78-143457. (Readings in Literary Criticism Ser.: No. 13). 1972. 10.95 (0-87024-195-8) U of Miami Pr.

— The Marble Faun: Or, the Romance of Monte Beni. LC 73-134464. 1971. pap. 7.60 (0-672-61026-4, Bobbs) Macmillan.

Rupp, Robert O., jt. auth. see Remini, Robert V.

***Rupp, Stephen.** Allegories of Kingship: Calderon & the Anti-Machiavellian Tradition. LC 94-41635. (Studies in Romance Literatures). 1996. 28.50 (0-271-01456-3) Pa St U Pr.

Rupp, William & Friedmann, Arnold. Construction Materials for Interior Design. (Illus.). 192p. 1989. pap. 24.95 (0-8230-0930-0, Whitney Lib) Watsn-Guptill.

Rupp, William, et al. The Commodore 64 Game Construction Toolkit. (Illus.). 250p. 14.95 (0-8359-0775-9) P-H.

Ruppe, Reynold. The Acoma Culture Province: An Archeological Concept. LC 90-21599. (Evolution of North American Indians Ser.: Vol. 21). 320p. 1991. reprint ed. 20.00 (0-8240-6110-1) Garland.

Ruppel. Manual of Pulmonary Function Testing. 5th ed. (Illus.). 432p. 1990. pap. 29.95 (0-8016-5319-3) Mosby Yr Bk.

Ruppel, Aloys. Johannes Gutenberg: Sein Leben und Sein Werk. 2nd ed. (Illus.). 140p. (GER.). 1967. reprint ed. text ed. 132.50 (90-6004-157-7, Pub. by B De Graaf NE) Coronet Bks.

Ruppel, Fred J. & Kellogg, Earl D., eds. National & Regional Self-Sufficiency Goals: Implications for International Agriculture. LC 90-25593. 254p. 1991. lib. bdg. 42.00 (1-55587-152-6) Lynne Rienner.

Ruppel, Gregg. Manual of Pulmonary Function Testing. 6th ed. LC 93-27962. 450p. 1993. 29.95 (0-8016-7789-0) Mosby Yr Bk.

Ruppel, Maxine. Vostaas: The Story of Montana's Indian Nations. (Indian Culture Ser.). (J). (gr. 3-11). 1970. 5.95 (0-89992-001-2) Coun India Ed.

***Ruppel, Richard.** Gottfried Keller & His Critics: A Case Study in Scholarly Criticism. 1995. 55.95 (1-57113-055-1) Camden Hse.

Ruppel, Richard R. Gottfried Keller: Poet, Pedagogue & Humanist. (Studies in Modern German Literature: Vol. 12). 282p. (C). 1988. text ed. 42.50 (0-8204-0453-5) P Lang Pubs.

Ruppel, S. C. & Cander, H. S. Effects of Facies & Diagenesis on Reservoir Heterogeneity: Emma San Andres Field, West Texas. (Report of Investigations Ser.: RI 178). (Illus.). 67p. 1988. 6.75 (0-317-03113-9) Bur Econ Geology.

***Ruppel, S. C. & Holtz, M. H.** Depositional & Diagenetic Facies Patterns & Reservoir Development in Silurian & Devonian Rocks of the Permian Basin. (Illus.). 89p. 1994. 6.00 (0-614-01865-X) Bur Econ Geology.

***Ruppel, S. C., et al.** Controls on Reservoir Heterogeneity in Permian Shallow-Water-Platform Carbonate Reservoirs, Permian Basin Implications for Improved Recovery. (Geological Circular Ser.: No. 95-2). 30p. 1995. 4.50 (0-614-06195-4) Bur Econ Geology.

***Ruppen, Francia.** The Hollywood Vegetarian Cookbook: Lean, Healthy Meals from America's Celebrity Kitchens. (Illus.). 224p. 1995. 16.95 (1-55972-288-6, Birch Ln Pr) Carol Pub Group.

Ruppenthal, Stephen, jt. intro. see Easwaran, Eknath.

Ruppersberg, Allen. The Secret of Life & Death: Nineteen Sixty-Nine to Nineteen Eighty-Four, Vol. 1. Brown, Julia, ed. (Illus.). 127p. (C). 1985. 50.00 (0-317-39252-2) Los Angeles Mus Contemp.

Ruppersburg, Hugh. Robert Penn Warren & the American Imagination. LC 89-20451. 216p. 1990. 30.00 (0-8203-1215-0) U of Ga Pr.

Ruppersburg, Hugh, ed. Georgia Voices: Fiction, Vol. 1. LC 91-36688. 528p. 1992. 35.00 (0-8203-1432-3); pap. 18.95 (0-8203-1433-1) U of Ga Pr.

— Georgia Voices, Vol. 2: Nonfiction. 592p. 1994. 40.00 (0-8203-1625-3); pap. 19.95 (0-8203-1626-1) U of Ga Pr.

Ruppert, Alex D. Biology of Alligators & Crocodiles: Index of New Information & Research Bible. 150p. 1994. 44.50 (0-7883-0112-8); pap. text ed. 39.50 (0-7883-0113-6) ABBE Pubs Assn.

Ruppert, D., jt. auth. see Carrol, R. J.

***Ruppert, Edward E. & Barnes, Robert D.** Invertebrate Zoology. 6th ed. LC 93-85930. 1056p. (C). 1993. text ed. 64.00 (0-03-026668-8) SCP.

Ruppert, Edward E. & Fox, Richard S. Seashore Animals of the Southeast. (Illus.). 429p. 1988. pap. 29.95 (0-87249-535-3) U of SC Pr.

Ruppert, Edward E., jt. auth. see Harrison, Frederick W.

Ruppert, Fidelis & Gruen, Anselm. Christ in the Brother: According to the Rule of St. Benedict. rev. ed. Lauer, Alphonse M., ed. Roettger, Gregory J., tr. (Schuyler Spiritual Ser.: Vol. 2). 61p. 1992. pap. text ed. 3.60 (1-56788-001-0, 10-002) BMH Pubns.

Ruppert, Hans & Hofer, Conrad, eds. Zeitschrift Fur Bucherfreunde, 1897-1936: Gesamtregister, 3 vols. in 1. vi, 665p. 1964. reprint ed. write for info. (0-318-71881-2, Pub. by Georg Olms GW) Lubrecht & Cramer.

Ruppert, James. D'Arcy McNickle. LC 87-73496. (Western Writers Ser.: No. 83). (Illus.). 55p. (Orig.). 1988. pap. 3.95 (0-88430-082-X) Boise St U W Writ Ser.

— Guide to Poetry Explication: American Poetry, Vol. 1. 225p. 1989. text ed. 40.00 (0-8161-8919-6, Hall Reference) Macmillan.

— The Jaguars Driver's Book. (Drivers Book Ser.). (Illus.). 160p. 1990. 21.95 (0-85429-626-3, Pub. by J H Haynes & Co UK) Motorbooks Intl.

— Mediation in Contemporary Native American Fiction. LC 94-47465. (American Indian Literature & Critical Studies: Vol. 15). 1995. write for info. (0-8061-2749-X) U of Okla Pr.

Ruppert, Janette K. First Aid: Index of Modern Information. rev. ed. LC 91-7266. 150p. 1991. 39.50 (1-55914-352-5); pap. 34.50 (1-55914-353-3) ABBE Pubs Assn.

— First Aid & Emergencies: Index of Modern Authors & Subjects in Current Research. 160p. 1991. 44.50 (1-55914-466-1); pap. 39.50 (1-55914-467-X) ABBE Pubs Assn.

Ruppert, Jeanne, ed. Gender: Literary & Cinematic Representation. (Florida State University Annual Conference on Literature & Film Ser.). 144p. (C). 1994. pap. text ed. 17.95 (0-8130-1911-7) U Press Fla.

Ruppert, Karl. Chichen Itza: Architectural Notes & Plans. LC 77-11519. (Carnegie Institution of Washington. Publications: No. 595). reprint ed. 32.00 (0-404-16279-7) AMS Pr.

Ruppert, Karl & Denison, John H., Jr. Archaeological Reconnaissance in Campeche, Quintana Roo, & Peten. LC 77-11517. (Carnegie Institution of Washington. Publications: No. 543). reprint ed. 44.00 (0-404-16277-0) AMS Pr.

Ruppert, Marion. Projects, Patterns & Poems. LC 87-31202. 175p. (Orig.). (ps-2). 1989. pap. 17.95 (0-89334-108-8) Humanics Ltd.

Ruppert, Marion C. Projects Patterns & Poems for Early Education. LC 87-31202. (Illus.). 175p. (Orig.). 1989. lib. bdg. 27.95 (0-89334-226-2, 2262030) Humanics Ltd.

Ruppert, Peter, ed. see Florida State University Conference on Literature & Film Staff.

Ruppert, Trisha. Search for the Word: Over 65 Biblical Puzzles for all Ages. LC 91-77489. 96p. (Orig.). 1993. pap. 3.95 (1-883654-00-9) Bethlehem Star.

Ruppert, W. Compact Semitopological Semigroups: An Intrinsic Theory. (Lecture Notes in Mathematics Ser.: Vol. 1079). v, 260p. 1984. pap. 38.40 (0-387-13387-9) Spr-Verlag.

Ruppin, Arthur. The Agricultural Colonization of the Zionist Organization in Palestine. Feiwel, R. J., tr. LC 75-6451. (Rise of Jewish Nationalism & the Middle East Ser.). vii, 209p. 1975. reprint ed. 20.35 (0-88355-337-6) Hyperion Conn.

— The Jewish Fate & Future. Dickes, E. W., tr. LC 76-97300. (Illus.). 386p. 1972. reprint ed. text ed. 35.00 (0-8371-2628-2, RUJF, Greenwood Pr) Greenwood.

— The Jews in the Modern World. LC 73-2225. (Jewish People; History, Religion, Literature Ser.). 1973. reprint ed. 40.95 (0-405-05287-1) Ayer.

— Three Decades of Palestine: Speeches & Papers on the Upbuilding of the Jewish National Home. LC 70-97301. (Illus.). 342p. 1975. reprint ed. text ed. 38.50 (0-8371-2629-0, RUPA, Greenwood Pr) Greenwood.

Ruppli, Michel. The King Labels: A Discography, 2 vols., 1. LC 85-17655. (Discographies Ser.: No. 18). xviii, 1381p. 1985. text ed. 125.00 (*0-313-25145-2*, RML/01) Greenwood.

— The King Labels: A Discography, 2 vols., Set. LC 85-17655. (Discographies Ser.: No. 18). xviii, 1381p. 1985. text ed. 195.00 (*0-313-24771-4*, RKL/) Greenwood.

— The King Labels: A Discography, 2 vols., Vol. 2. LC 85-17655. (Discographies Ser.: No. 18). xviii, 1381p. 1985. text ed. 125.00 (*0-313-25146-0*, RKL/02) Greenwood.

— The Savoy Label: A Discography. LC 79-7727. (Discographies Ser.: No. 2). (Illus.). 442p. 1980. text ed. 105.00 (*0-313-21199-X*, RUS/, Greenwood Pr) Greenwood.

Ruppli, Michel, comp. The Aladdin-Imperial Labels: A Discography. LC 90-22696. (Discographies Ser.: No. 42). 760p. 1991. text ed. 89.50 (*0-313-27821-0*, RAH, Greenwood Pr) Greenwood.

— Atlantic Records: A Discography, 4 vols., 1. LC 78-75237. 1979. text ed. 95.00 (*0-313-21171-X*, RAL/1) Greenwood.

— Atlantic Records: A Discography, 4 vols., Set. LC 78-75237. 1979. text ed. 275.00 (*0-313-21170-1*, RAL/) Greenwood.

— Atlantic Records: A Discography, 4 vols., Vol. 2. LC 78-75237. 1979. text ed. 95.00 (*0-313-21172-8*, RAL/2) Greenwood.

— Atlantic Records: A Discography, 4 vols., Vol. 3. LC 78-75237. 1979. text ed. 95.00 (*0-313-21173-6*, RAL/3) Greenwood.

— Atlantic Records: A Discography, 4 vols., Vol. 4. LC 78-75237. 1979. text ed. 95.00 (*0-313-21174-4*, RAL/4) Greenwood.

— The Chess Labels: A Discography, 2 vols. LC 82-25148. (Discographies Ser.: No. 7). xviii, 743p. 1983. text ed. 125.00 (*0-313-23471-X*, RCL/) Greenwood.

— The Chess Labels: A Discography, 2 vols., 1. LC 82-25148. (Discographies Ser.: No. 7). xviii, 743p. 1983. text ed. 75.00 (*0-313-23980-0*, RCL/01) Greenwood.

— The Chess Labels: A Discography, 2 vols., Vol. 2. LC 82-25148. (Discographies Ser.: No. 7). xviii, 743p. 1983. text ed. 75.00 (*0-313-23981-9*, RCL/02) Greenwood.

— The Clef-Verve Labels: A Discography, 2 Vols., Set. LC 86-19530. (Discographies Ser.: No. 26). 894p. 1986. text ed. 145.00 (*0-313-25294-7*, RCV/) Greenwood.

— The Clef-Verve Labels: A Discography, 2 Vols., Vol. 1: The Norman Granz Era. LC 86-19530. (Discographies Ser.: No. 26). 894p. 1986. Vol. 1, The Norman Granz Era. text ed. 95.00 (*0-313-25693-4*, RCV/01) Greenwood.

— The Clef-Verve Labels: A Discography, 2 Vols., Vol. 2. LC 86-19530. (Discographies Ser.: No. 26). 894p. 1986. text ed. 95.00 (*0-313-25694-2*, RCV/02) Greenwood.

— The Prestige Label: A Discography. LC 79-8294. (Discographies Ser.: No. 3). 377p. 1980. text ed. 89.50 (*0-313-22019-0*, RPL/, Greenwood Pr) Greenwood.

Ruppli, Michel, ed. The Blue Note Label: A Discography. LC 88-162. (Discographies Ser.: No. 29). 532p. 1988. text ed. 95.00 (*0-313-22018-2*, RBN/, Greenwood Pr) Greenwood.

***Rupprecht, C. E., et al.** Current Topics in Microbiology & Immunology No. 187. 360p. 1994. 114.00 (*0-387-57194-9*) Spr-Verlag.

Rupprecht, Carol S., ed. The Dream & the Text: Essays on Literature & Language. LC 92-4560. (SUNY Series in Dream Studies). 325p. 1993. 59.50 (*0-7914-1361-6*); pap. 19.95 (*0-7914-1362-4*) State U NY Pr.

Rupprecht, Carol S., jt. ed. see Lauter, Estella.

Rupprecht, David, et al. Radical Hospitality: Leader's Guide. 1985. pap. 2.99 (*0-87552-419-2*) Presby & Reformed.

Rupprecht, David & Rupprecht, Ruth. Radical Hospitality. LC 83-3259. 110p. 1983. pap. 4.99 (*0-87552-420-6*) Presby & Reformed.

Rupprecht, H. S. & Weimann, G., eds. Gallium Arsenide & Related Compounds 1993: Proceedings of the 20th International Symposium, 29 August-2 September 1993, Freiburg i. Br., Germany. (Institute of Physics Conference Ser.: No. 136). 950p. 1994. 200.00 (*0-7503-0295-X*) IOP Pub.

Rupprecht, Konrad. Der Tempel Von Jerusalem. (Beiheft 144 zur Zeitschrift fuer die Alttestamentliche Wissenschaft Ser.). (C). 1976. text ed. 60.80 (*3-11-006619-X*) De Gruyter.

***Rupprecht, Olivia.** Pistol in His Pocket. (Loveswept Ser.: No. 730). 1995. pap. 3.50 (*0-553-44452-2*, Loveswept) Bantam.

Rupprecht, Ruth, jt. auth. see Rupprecht, David.

Rupprecht, Siegfried P. The Tale of the Vanishing Rainbow. Lewis, Naomi, tr. LC 88-43120. (Illus.). 32p. (J). (gr. k-3). 1989. 14.95 (*1-55858-001-8*) North-South Bks NYC.

Ruprail, Nirmal. Bibliography on India in 2000 A. D. (C). 1991. 28.00 (*0-8364-2739-4*, Pub. by Abhinav II) S Asia.

Ruprecht, F. J. Phycologia Ochotiensis. Tange des ochotskischen Meeres, (from Middendorff's Sibirische Reise) (Illus.). 1978. reprint ed. lib. bdg. 90.00 (*3-7682-1184-3*) Lubrecht & Cramer.

Ruprecht, F. J., jt. auth. see Postels, A.

Ruprecht, H., jt. ed. see Parret, Herman.

Ruprecht, J., et al. Catalogue of Star Clusters & Associations: Supplement 1. 440p. 1981. 308.00 (*0-569-08698-1*) St Mut.

Ruprecht, Louis A., Jr. Tragic Posture & Tragic Vision: Against the Modern Failure of Nerve. 288p. (C). 1994. 29.95 (*0-8264-0686-6*) Continuum.

Ruprecht, Mary M., jt. auth. see Wagoner, Kathleen P.

Rupreht, J., et al, eds. Anaesthesia: Essays on Its History. (Illus.). 430p. 1985. pap. 86.00 (*0-387-13255-4*) Spr-Verlag.

Ruptic, Cynthia, jt. auth. see Hill, Bonnie C.

Ruqvist, Anders. Peasant Struggle & Action Research in Colombia. (Uppsala University Research Report Series, 1986: No. 3). 396p. (Orig.). 1986. pap. text ed. 50.00x (*0-317-57954-1*) Coronet Bks.

Rural Economic Development Center Staff. North Carolina Aquaculture Report. 128p. (Orig.). 1989. pap. text ed. 5.00 (*0-945597-12-6*) NC Biotech Ctr.

Rural Sociological Society Task Force on Persistent, Rural Poverty Staff. Persistent Poverty in Rural America. (Rural Studies). 379p. (C). 1992. pap. text ed. 49.00 (*0-8133-8712-4*) Westview.

Rurinf, L. & Dixit, K., eds. Bikas-Binash Development-Destruction: The Change in Life & Environment of the Himalaya. 400p. (C). 1990. 150.00 (*0-89771-049-5*, Pub. by Ratna Pustak Bhandar) St Mut.

Rurup, Reinhard. Germany & the Rise of Bourgeois Society. Hein, Ruth, tr. 256p. 1988. text ed. 35.00 (*0-674-35308-0*) HUP.

Rury, John L. Education & Women's Work: Female Schooling & the Division of Labor in Urban America, 1870-1930. LC 90-38325. (SUNY Series on Women & Work). 296p. 1991. 74.50 (*0-7914-0617-2*); pap. 24.95 (*0-7914-0618-0*) State U NY Pr.

Rury, John L. & Cassell, Frank A., eds. Seeds of Crisis: Public Schooling in Milwaukee since 1920. LC 93-18827. (Illus.). 389p. (Orig.). (C). 1993. lib. bdg. 50.00 (*0-299-13810-0*); pap. text ed. 17.95 (*0-299-13814-3*) U of Wis Pr.

Ruryk, Jean. Chicken Little Was Right. 208p. 1994. 18.95 (*0-312-10952-0*, Pub. by Thomas Dunne Bks) St Martin.

Rus, D., jt. auth. see Rus, R.

Rus, D., jt. auth. see Rus, T.

Rus, Daniela, jt. auth. see Rus, Teodor.

Rus, R. & Rus, D. System Software & Software Systems: Systems Methodology for System Software. 388p. 1993. text ed. 48.00 (*981-02-1254-2*) World Scientific Pub.

Rus, T. & Rus, D. System Software & Software Systems: Programming Support Environment. 250p. 1995. text ed. 46.00 (*981-02-1256-9*) World Scientific Pub.

Rus, Teodor. Data Structures & Operating Systems. LC 77-3262. (Wiley Series in Computing). 376p. reprint ed. pap. 107.20 (*0-317-26154-1*, 2024377) Bks Demand.

***Rus, Teodor & Rattray, Charles.** Theories & Experiences for Real-Time System Development. (AMAST Computing Ser.). 450p. 1995. text ed. 99.00 (*981-02-1923-7*) World Scientific Pub.

***Rus, Teodor & Rus, Daniela.** Execution Support Environment. (System Software & Software Systems: Vol. 2). 444p. 1994. text ed. 59.00 (*981-02-1255-0*) World Scientific Pub.

Rus, Veljko. Employment & Participation: Industrial Democracy in Crisis. 344p. 1982. 70.00 (*0-317-53760-1*, Pub. by Collets UK) Pro-Am Music.

Rus, Veljko, jt. ed. see Russell, Raymond.

Rusack, Caroline M. Topsy-Turvy Town. (J). 1994. 7.95 (*0-533-10688-5*) Vantage.

Rusakov, Iu. Petrov-Vodkin, Juz' Ma. 300p. (C). 1986. 350.00 (*0-685-34426-6*, Pub. by Collets) St Mut.

Rusakov, Iu, ed. Petrov-Vodkin, Kuz'Ma. 300p. (C). 1986. 350.00 (*0-685-22604-2*, Pub. by Collets UK) Pro-Am Music.

Rusakova, A. Nesterov, Mikhail. 220p. (C). 1990. 118.00 (*0-89771-822-4*, Pub. by Collets) St Mut.

***Rusbing, Janice H. & Frentz, Thomas S.** Projecting the Shadow: The Cyborg Hero in American Film. 224p. 1995. 37.50 (*0-226-73166-9*); pap. 14.95 (*0-226-73167-7*) U Ch Pr.

Rusbridger, James. The Intelligence Game: Illusions & Delusions of International Espionage. (Illus.). 278p. (C). 1991. 24.95 (*1-56131-008-5*) New Amsterdam Bks.

Rusbridger, James & Nave, Eric. Betrayal at Pearl Harbor: How Churchill Lured Roosevelt into World War II. (Illus.). 304p. 1992. pap. 12.00 (*0-671-79231-8*, Touchstone Bks) S&S Trade.

— Betrayal at Pearl Harbor: How Churchill Lured Roosevelt into World War II. (Illus.). 303p. 19.95 (*0-685-52042-0*) Summit Bks.

***Rusbuldt, Richard.** Workbook on Biblical Stewardship Leaders Guide. Date not set. pap. 3.99 (*0-8028-0830-1*) Eerdmans.

Rusbuldt, Richard E. Basic Leader Skills: Handbook for Church Leaders. 64p. 1981. pap. 9.00 (*0-8170-0920-5*) Judson.

— Basic Teacher Skills: Handbook for Church School Teachers. 144p. 1981. pap. 11.00 (*0-8170-0919-1*) Judson.

— Evangelism on Purpose. 48p. 1980. pap. 5.00 (*0-8170-0894-2*) Judson.

— Hello-Is God There? 64p. 1984. pap. 6.00 (*0-8170-1043-2*) Judson.

— Workbook on Biblical Stewardship. 128p. 1994. pap. 9.99 (*0-8028-0723-2*) Eerdmans.

Rusbuldt, Richard E., jt. auth. see McIntosh, Duncan.

Rusbuldt, Richard E., et al. Local Church Planning Manual. 1977. pap. 10.00 (*0-8170-0753-9*) Judson.

— Medidas Principales en la Planificacion de la Iglesia Local: Key Steps in Local Church Planning. Rodriguez, Oscar E., tr. 134p. (SPA.). 1981. pap. 6.00 (*0-8170-0933-7*) Judson.

Rusby, R. L. & Carter, D. F. Evaluation of Nicrosil Sheathed - Ninilthermocouples up to 1300 C, No. EUR 13162. 73p. 1991. pap. 11.00 (*92-826-2161-8*, CD-NA-13162-EN-C, Pub. by Europ Com) UNIPUB.

Ruscalleda, Jorge M. La Poesia de Nicolas Guillen: Cuatro Elementos Sustancialez. LC 76-1828. 310p. (C). 1975. 5.00 (*0-8477-0518-8*); pap. 4.00 (*0-8477-0519-6*) U of PR Pr.

Rusch, Frank. Supported Employment: Models, Methods & Issues. (Illus.). 400p. (C). 1990. text ed. 39.95 (*0-685-30431-0*) Sycamore Pub.

Rusch, Frank R., et al, eds. Transition from School to Adult Life. 400p. (C). 1991. text ed. 49.95 (*0-9625233-4-8*) Sycamore Pub.

Rusch, Frederick L., ed. A Jean Toomer Reader: Selected Unpublished Writings. LC 93-16374. 1993. 42.00 (*0-19-507733-4*); pap. 17.95 (*0-19-508329-6*) OUP.

Rusch, Frederick L., jt. comp. see Natoli, Joseph P.

Rusch, Harold, jt. auth. see Spinosa, Frank.

Rusch, Harold W., jt. auth. see Spinosa, Frank.

Rusch, Kristine K. Best of Pulphouse: The Hardback Magazine. 1992. pap. 13.95 (*0-312-08317-3*) St Martin.

— Heart Readers. 288p. (Orig.). 1993. pap. 4.99 (*0-451-45282-8*, ROC) NAL-Dutton.

— Sins of the Blood. 1994. pap. 5.50 (*0-440-21540-4*) Dell.

— Traitors. 288p. (Orig.). 1994. pap. 4.99 (*0-451-45415-4*, ROC) NAL-Dutton.

— The White Mists of Power. 304p. (Orig.). 1991. pap. 3.99 (*0-451-45120-1*, ROC) NAL-Dutton.

Rusch, Kristine K., ed. The Best of Pulphouse. 352p. 1992. pap. 13.95 (*0-685-56691-9*) St Martin.

Rusch, Kristine K. & Anderson, Kevin J. Afterimage. 288p. 1992. 4.99 (*0-451-45175-9*, ROC) NAL-Dutton.

Rusch, Kristine K., jt. ed. see Ferman, Edward L.

Rusch, Robert D. Jazz Talk. (Illus.). 192p. 1984. 14.95 (*0-8184-0357-8*) Carol Pub Group.

Rusch, Robert J., jt. auth. see Lister, Eugene C.

Rusch, Shari. Stumbling Blocks to Stepping Stones. (Illus.). 272p. (Orig.). 1991. pap. 11.95 (*0-9629392-0-X*) Arc WA.

Rusch, Wilbert H., Sr. The Argument: Creationism vs. Evolutionism. Mulfinger, George, Jr., ed. (Creation Research Society Monograph Ser.: No. 3). (Illus.). 86p. (Orig.). (C). 1984. pap. 8.95 (*0-940384-04-3*) Creation Research.

— Origins: What Is at Stake? (Creation Research Society Monograph Ser.: No. 5). (Illus.). 73p. (Orig.). 1991. pap. text ed. 8.95 (*0-940384-10-8*) Creation Research.

Rusch, Wilbert H., Sr. & Klotz, John W. Did Charles Darwin Become a Christian? 44p. (Orig.). 1988. pap. text ed. 3.95 (*0-940384-05-1*) Creation Research.

Rusch, Willard J. The Language of the East Midlands & the Development of Standard English: A Study in Diacronic Phonology. LC 91-31826. (Berkeley Insights in Linguistics & Semiotics Ser.: Vol. 8). 197p. (C). 1992. text ed. 41.95 (*0-8204-1582-0*) P Lang Pubs.

Rusch, William G., ed. The Trinitarian Controversy. LC 79-8889. (Sources of Early Christian Thought Ser.). 192p. 1980. pap. 13.00 (*0-8006-1410-0*, 1-1410, Fortress Pr) Augsburg Fortress.

Rusch, William G. & Martensen, Daniel F., eds. The Leuenberg Agreement & Lutheran-Reformed Relationships: Evaluations by North American & European Theologians. LC 89-36050. 160p. (Orig.). 1990. pap. 12.99 (*0-8066-2436-1*, 9-2436) Augsburg Fortress.

Rusch, William G., jt. auth. see Norgren, William A.

Rusch, William G., jt. ed. see Norgren, William A.

Rusch, William G., jt. ed. see Norgrenand, William A.

Rusch, William G., jt. ed. see Norris, Richard A., Jr.

Ruschak, Lynette. The Counting Zoo: A Pop-up Number Book. LC 91-42462. (Illus.). 24p. (J). (ps-2). 1992. pap. 13.95 (*0-689-71619-2*, Aladdin Paperbacks) S&S Childrens.

— Nature by the Numbers. (J). (gr. k up). 1994. 12.95 (*0-671-88610-X*, Litl Simon S&S) S&S Childrens.

— One Hot Day. (Illus.). 24p. (J). (ps-3). 1994. 12.95 (*0-307-17607-X*, Artsts Writrs) Western Pub.

— Snack Attack: A Tasty Pop Up Book. (Illus.). 12p. (J). (ps-3). 1990. pap. 8.95 (*0-671-70448-6*, S&S Bks Young Read) S&S Childrens.

— Who's Hiding? (J). (ps). 1991. pap. 8.95 (*0-671-73957-3*, S&S Bks Young Read) S&S Childrens.

***Ruschau, John J. & Donald, J. Keith, eds.** Special Applications & Advanced Techniques for Crack Size Determination, STP 1251. LC 94-49349. (Special Technical Publication Ser.: Vol. 1251). (Illus.). 170p. 1995. text ed. 62.00 (*0-8031-2003-6*, 04-012510-30) ASTM.

Rusche, Sue & Kemp, Paula. Tobacco. (You Have the Right to Know Ser.: No. 3). 130p. 1992. pap. write for info. (*1-880958-02-3*) Natl Fam Act.

— You Have the Right to Know, Vol. 1: Cocaine. 140p. 1990. pap. write for info. (*1-880958-00-7*) Natl Fam Act.

— You Have the Right to Know, Vol. 2: Alcohol. 175p. 1991. pap. write for info. (*1-880958-01-5*) Natl Fam Act.

Ruschel, Alaides P., jt. ed. see Vose, Peter B.

Ruscheweyh, S., et al, eds. Computational Methods & Function Theory: Proceedings of a Conference Held in Valparaiso, Chile, March 13-18, 1989. (Lecture Notes in Mathematics Ser.: Vol. 1435). vi, 211p. 1990. pap. 30.00 (*0-387-52768-0*) Spr-Verlag.

Ruschitzka, M., ed. IMACS Transactions on Scientific Computing 85: Computer Systems; Performance & Simulation, Vol. 2. 360p. 1987. 89.75 (*0-444-70081-1*, North Holland) Elsevier.

Rusciano, Frank L. Isolation & Paradox: Defining "The Public" in Modern Political Analysis. LC 88-29626. (Contributions in Political Science Ser.: No. 233). 183p. 1989. text ed. 45.00 (*0-313-26492-9*, RBX/, Greenwood Pr) Greenwood.

Ruscica, Marybeth, jt. auth. see Fitzpatrick, Carolyn.

Ruscica, Marybeth B., jt. auth. see Fitzpatrick, Carolyn H.

Rusco, Elmer R. Good Time Coming? Black Nevadans in the Nineteenth Century. LC 75-16969. (Contributions in Afro-American & African Studies: No. 15). (Illus.). 230p. 1976. text ed. 49.95 (*0-8371-8286-7*, RGT/, Greenwood Pr) Greenwood.

Rusco, Mary K. & Davis, Jonathon O. Studies in Archaeology, Geology and Paleontology at Rye Patch Reservoir, Pershing County, Nevada. (Illus.). 239p. 1987. pap. 16.00 (*0-685-50179-5*) Ctr Study First Am.

***Rusco, Mary K. & Davis, Jonathon O.** Studies in Archaeology, Geology, & Paleontology at Rye Patch Reservoir, Pershing County, Nevada. 239p. 1987. pap. 16.00 (*1-55889-827-1*) OR St U CSFA.

Ruscoe, James. On the Threshold of Government: The Italian Communist Party, 1976-1981. LC 81-14622. 304p. 1983. text ed. 30.00 (*0-312-58457-1*) St Martin.

***Ruscoe, Michael.** Baseball. 1995. pap. 24.95 (*0-88363-700-6*) H L Levin.

Ruscoe, Michael, ed. Baseball: A Treasury of Art & Literature. (Illus.). 384p. 1993. 75.00 (*0-88363-293-4*) H L Levin.

Ruscombe-King, Gillie, jt. auth. see Hurst, Sheila.

Rusczyk, Richard, jt. auth. see Leholzky, Sandor.

Rusdorf, Richard, jt. auth. see Goodwin, Daniel.

Ruse, Arnold, ed. see Gendusa, Sam.

Ruse, Ch., jt. auth. see Hornby, A. S.

Ruse, Michael. The Darwinian Paradigm: Essays on Its History, Philosophy & Religious Implications. 272p. 1989. 25.00 (*0-415-00300-8*) Routledge.

— The Darwinian Paradigm: Essays on Its History, Philosophy & Religious Implications. (Illus.). 312p. 1993. pap. 17.95 (*0-415-08951-4*, B0334) Routledge.

— The Darwinian Revolution: Science Red in Tooth & Claw. LC 78-25826. 1981. pap. text ed. 14.95 (*0-226-73165-0*) U Ch Pr.

— Evolutionary Naturalism: Selected Essays. LC 94-18435. (Illus.). 320p. 1995. 49.95 (*0-415-08997-2*, C0350) Routledge.

— Homosexuality: A Philosophical Inquiry. 1990. pap. 15.95 (*0-631-17553-9*) Blackwell Pubs.

— Is Science Sexist? & Other Problems in the Biomedical Sciences. 320p. 1981. lib. bdg. 74.50 (*90-277-1249-2*) Kluwer Ac.

— Nature Animated. 1982. lib. bdg. 107.50 (*90-277-1403-7*) Kluwer Ac.

— Philosophy of Biology. Edwards, Paul, ed. (Philosophical Topics Ser.). 368p. (C). 1989. pap. write for info. (*0-02-404492-X*) Macmillan.

— Philosophy of Biology Today. LC 88-15377. (SUNY Series in Philosophy & Biology). 155p. (C). 1988. 44.50 (*0-88706-910-X*); pap. 14.95 (*0-88706-911-8*) State U NY Pr.

— Sociobiology: Sense or Nonsense. rev. ed. (Episteme Ser.: No. 8). 248p. 1984. pap. text ed. 34.50 (*90-277-1798-2*) Kluwer Ac.

— Sociobiology: Sense or Nonsense. 2nd rev. ed. (Episteme Ser.: No. 8). 248p. 1984. lib. bdg. 71.50 (*90-277-1797-4*) Kluwer Ac.

Ruse, Michael, ed. But Is It Science? The Philosophical Question in the Evolution-Creation Controversy. LC 87-35818. (Frontiers of Philosophy Ser.). (Illus.). 375p. 1988. 29.95x (*0-87975-439-7*) Prometheus Bks.

— What the Philosophy of Biology Is: Essays for David Hull. (C). 1989. lib. bdg. 126.50 (*90-247-3778-8*) Kluwer Ac.

Rusek, Jamie. Exotic Butterflies Charted Designs. (Needlecraft Ser.). (Illus.). 32p. (Orig.). 1991. pap. 2.95 (*0-486-26708-3*) Dover.

Rusell, William. Scientific Horseshoeing. LC 87-82868. 490p. 1995. 34.95 (*0-944707-01-7*) Loose Change.

Rusev, P. Analytic Functions & Classical Orthogonal Polynomials. 1984. 28.00 (*0-317-52902-1*, Pub. by Collets UK) Pro-Am Music.

Rush. Al Sabah History. 1991. 80.00 (*0-86372-081-1*, Pub. by Ithaca UK) Paul & Co Pubs.

Rush, jt. auth. see Bone.

Rush, A. Records of Kuwait, 1899-1961, 8 vols., Set. 5000p. (C). 1987. text ed. 4,900.00 (*1-85207-200-8*, Pub. by Archive Res Ltd UK) St Mut.

Rush, A. John. Beating Depression. LC 84-13564. (Illus.). 155p. reprint ed. pap. 44.20 (*0-8357-4248-2*, 2037037) Bks Demand.

Rush, A. John & Altshuler, Kenneth, eds. Depression: Basic Mechanisms, Diagnosis, & Treatment. LC 84-19318. 242p. 1986. lib. bdg. 35.00 (*0-89862-646-3*) Guilford Pr.

Rush, Alfred C. Death & Burial in Christian Antiquity. 1972. 250.00 (*0-8490-0009-2*) Gordon Pr.

Rush, Anne K. The Back Rub Book: A Guide to the Simple Pleasures of Back Rubs. 1989. pap. 12.00 (*0-394-75962-1*, Vin) Random.

— The Modern Book of Massage: Five-Minute Vacations & Sensuous Escapes. LC 93-50206. 1994. 14.95 (*0-440-50545-3*) Dell.

— Romantic Massage. 1991. pap. 12.00 (*0-380-75985-3*) Avon.

Rush, Barbara. The Book of Jewish Women's Tales. LC 93-34959. 344p. 1994. 35.00 (*1-56821-087-6*) Aronson.

Rush, Barbara, jt. auth. see Schwartz, Howard.

Rush, Benjamin. An Account of the Life & Character of Christopher Ludwick: Baker-General of the Army of the U. S. During the Revolutionary War. 1972. reprint ed. 19.50 (*0-8422-8133-9*) Irvington.

— An Address to the Inhabitants of the British Settlements, on the Slavery of the Negroes in America. 2nd ed. (Anti-Slavery Crusade in America Ser.). 92p. 1980. reprint ed. 11.95 (*0-405-00656-X*) Ayer.

— The Autobiography of Benjamin Rush: His Travels Through Life. Corner, George W., ed. LC 72-100241. 399p. 1970. reprint ed. text ed. 65.00 (*0-8371-3037-9*, RUAR, Greenwood Pr) Greenwood.

— Benjamin Rush's Lectures on the Mind. Carlson, Eric T. et al, eds. LC 80-70300. (American Philosophical Society, Memoirs Ser.: No. 144). 755p. reprint ed. pap. 180.00 (*0-7837-2682-1*, 2043059) Bks Demand.

— Essays: Literary, Moral & Philosophical. LC 88-80672. 230p. 1988. 26.50 (*0-912756-22-5*) Union Coll.

— Medical Inquiries & Observations, 4 vols. in 2, 1. 4th ed. LC 76-180588. (Medicine & Society in America Ser.). 1070p. 1972. reprint ed. 33.95 (*0-405-03969-7*) Ayer.

— Medical Inquiries & Observations, 4 vols. in 2, Set. 4th ed. LC 76-180588. (Medicine & Society in America Ser.). 1070p. 1972. reprint ed. 65.95 (*0-405-03968-9*) Ayer.
— Medical Inquiries & Observations, 4 vols. in 2, Vol. 2. 4th ed. LC 76-180588. (Medicine & Society in America Ser.). 1070p. 1972. reprint ed. Vol.2. 33.95 (*0-405-03970-0*) Ayer.
Rush, Bette, jt. auth. see Lebelson, Harry.
Rush, Beverly & Wittman, Lassie. The Complete Book of Seminole Patchwork. rev. ed. Orig. Title: The Complete Book of Seminole Patchwork: From Traditional Methods to Contemporary Uses. (Illus.). 128p. 1993. reprint ed. pap. 7.95 (*0-486-27617-1*) Dover.
Rush, C. A Resurrection of a Kind. 112p. 1984. pap. text ed. 12.00 (*0-08-030400-1*, Pergamon Pr) Elsevier.
— Two Christmas Stories. (Illus.). 54p. 1988. pap. 8.00 (*0-08-036586-8*, Pergamon Pr) Elsevier.
Rush, Caroline E. North & South: Or, Slavery - Its Contrasts. LC 70-149877. (Black Heritage Library Collection). 1977. 28.95 (*0-8369-8757-8*) Ayer.
Rush, Catharine, tr. see Farre, Henry.
Rush, Cheryl B. Circling Home. 85p. 1990. 22.50 (*0-916379-59-0*) Scripta.
Rush, Christopher. Into the Ebb: A New Collection of East Neuk Stories. 176p. 1989. pap. 19.95 (*0-08-036590-6*, Pub. by Aberdeen U Pr) Macmillan.
— A Twelvemonth & a Day. 196p. 1985. text ed. 25.00 (*0-08-032428-2*, Pergamon Pr) Elsevier.
— A Twelvemonth & a Day. 296p. 1986. pap. text ed. 11.95 (*0-08-032469-X*, R145, R150, K150, P110, Pergamon Pr) Elsevier.
— Venus Peter Saves the Whale. LC 92-7808. (Illus.). 32p. (J). (gr. 4-7). 1992. 14.95 (*0-88289-928-7*) Pelican.
Rush, Christopher & Shaw, John F. With Sharp Compassion: Norman Dott: Freeman Surgeon of Edinburgh. (Illus.). 1990. 35.00 (*0-08-037975-3*, Pub. by Aberdeen U Pr) Macmillan.
***Rush, D. A. & Siljander, R. P.** Fundamentals of Civil & Private Investigation. (Illus.). 172p. 1984. pap. 16.95 (*0-398-06411-3*) C C Thomas.
— Fundamentals of Civil & Private Investigation. (Illus.). 172p. (C). 1984. 31.95 (*0-398-04932-7*) C C Thomas.
Rush, David, et al, eds. Diet in Pregnancy: A Randomized Controlled Trail of Nutritional Supplements. LC 79-3846. (Alan R. Liss Ser.: Vol. 16, No. 3). 1980. 31.00 (*0-685-03286-8*) March of Dimes.
Rush, Dee N. The Satanic Nurses. (Illus.). 168p. (Orig.). 1990. pap. 12.95 (*0-9627950-0-3*) ISOS PC.
Rush, Florence. The Best Kept Secret: Sexual Abuse of Children. 1992. pap. 9.95 (*0-07-158192-8*) McGraw.
— The Best-Kept Secret: Sexual Abuse of Children. 238p. 1991. pap. 9.95 (*0-8306-3907-1*) TAB Bks.
Rush, George, jt. auth. see Venker, Marty.
Rush, George E. Dictionary of Criminal Justice. 4th ed. LC 85-73890. (Illus.). 432p. 1994. pap. text ed. 14.95 (*1-56134-297-1*) Dushkin Pub.
Rush, George E., jt. auth. see Whisenand, Paul M.
Rush, Harold M. Behavioral Science: Concepts & Management Application. (Studies in Personnel Policy: No. 216). 174p. (Orig.). 1969. pap. text ed. 40.00 (*0-8237-0003-8*) Conference Bd.
Rush, Helene. The Knitter's Design Sourcebook: One Hundred Twenty-Seven Charted Motifs to Use in Your Own Original Designs. LC 91-70998. (Illus.). 104p. 1991. pap. 19.95 (*0-89272-298-3*) Down East.
— Maine Woods Woolies: 30 Quick-to-Knit Sweaters for Children. LC 85-52441. (Illus.). 77p. 1986. pap. 9.95 (*0-89272-222-3*) Down East.
— More Maine Sweaters: Thirty Original Designs in Wool, Cotton, Silk, & Alpaca for Men & Women. LC 87-72384. (Illus.). 90p. 1987. pap. 9.95 (*0-89272-233-9*) Down East.
Rush, Helene & Emmons, Rachael. Sweaters by Hand: Designs for Spinners & Knitters. LC 88-32898. (Illus.). 160p. 1988. pap. 17.95 (*0-934026-37-8*) Interweave.
Rush, Helene M. Head to Toe: Thirty Original Designs for Hats, Mittens & Other Accessories. LC 89-81052. 72p. 1989. pap. 9.95 (*0-89272-276-2*) Down East.
Rush, Howard, jt. auth. see Hoffman, Kurt.
Rush, James. The Collected Works of James Rush, 4 vols., Set. Bernstein, Melvin H., ed. 1925p. 1974. 115.00 (*0-87730-008-9*) M&S Pr.
— The Last Tree: Reclaiming the Environment in Tropical Asia. 107p. (C). 1991. pap. text ed. 15.50 (*0-8133-8377-3*) Westview.
— The Philosophy of the Human Voice. 634p. 1900. 10.00 (*0-914076-60-4*) Lib Co Phila.
— Time Frames. 304p. 1988. 16.95 (*0-8065-1083-8*, Citadel Pr) Carol Pub Group.
Rush, James E., ed. Acquisitions, Vol. 4. LC 83-9584. (Library Systems Evaluation Guides Ser.). (Illus.). 253p. 1984. ring bd. 59.50 (*0-912803-04-5*) Rush Assoc.
— Cataloging, Vol. 7. LC 83-9584. (Library Systems Evaluation Guides Ser.). (Illus.). 262p. 1985. ring bd. 59.50 (*0-912803-07-X*) Rush Assoc.
— Circulation Control, Vol. 2. LC 83-9584. (Library Systems Evaluation Guides Ser.). (Illus.). 261p. 1983. 59.50 (*0-912803-02-9*) Rush Assoc.
— Interlibrary Loan, Vol. 6. LC 83-9584. (Library Systems Evaluation Guides Ser.). (Illus.). 248p. 1985. ring bd. 59.50 (*0-912803-06-1*) Rush Assoc.
— Management Services, Vol. 5. LC 83-9584. (Library Systems Evaluation Guides Ser.). (Illus.). 234p. 1984. 59.50 (*0-912803-05-3*) Rush Assoc.
— Microcomputers for Libraries: Product Review & Procurement Guide, Update Edition. (Illus.). 350p. 1984. ring bd. 115.00 (*0-912803-09-6*) Rush Assoc.
— Public Service, Vol. 3. LC 83-9584. (Library Systems Evaluation Guides Ser.). (Illus.). 267p. 1983. ring bd. 59.50 (*0-912803-03-7*) Rush Assoc.
— Serials Control, Vol. I. LC 83-9584. (Library Systems Evaluation Guides Ser.). (Illus.). 194p. 1983. ring bd. 59.50 (*0-912803-01-0*) Rush Assoc.
— System Integration, Vol. 8. LC 83-9584. (Library Systems Evaluation Guides Ser.). (Illus.). 240p. 1987. 59.50 (*0-912803-08-8*) Rush Assoc.
Rush, James E., jt. auth. see Davis, Charles H.
Rush, James J. Durner's Spring. 1980. 9.95 (*0-8065-0732-2*, Citadel Pr) Carol Pub Group.
— Naked in the Streets. 256p. 1985. 14.95 (*0-8065-0951-1*, Citadel Pr) Carol Pub Group.
Rush, James R. Opium to Java: Revenue Farming & Chinese Enterprise in Colonial Indonesia, 1860-1910. LC 89-45974. (Asia East by South Ser.). (Illus.). 280p. 1990. 39.95 (*0-8014-2218-3*) Cornell U Pr.
Rush, James R., jt. ed. see Winks, Robin W.
Rush, Janet, ed. Holiday Appetizers. (Holiday Ser.). 94p. 1993. spiral bd. 5.95 (*1-882232-09-7*) Kitchen Collect.
— Holiday Bread. (Holiday Ser.). 94p. 1993. pap. 5.95 (*1-882232-10-0*) Kitchen Collect.
— Holiday Candy. (Holiday Ser.). 94p. 1993. spiral bd. 5.95 (*1-882232-13-5*) Kitchen Collect.
— Holiday Cookies. (Holiday Ser.). 94p. 1993. pap. 5.95 (*1-882232-12-7*) Kitchen Collect.
Rush, Jeff, jt. auth. see Dancyger, Ken.
Rush, Joseph H. New Directions in Parapsychological Research. LC 64-22612. (Parapsychological Monograph Ser.: No. 4). 1964. pap. 5.00 (*0-912328-07-X*) Parapsych Foun.
Rush, Ken. Friday's Journey. LC 93-4871. (Illus.). 32p. (J). (ps-1). 1994. 14.95 (*0-531-06821-8*) Orchard Bks Watts.
— Friday's Journey. LC 93-4871. (Illus.). 32p. (J). (ps-1). 1994. lib. bdg. 14.99 (*0-531-08671-2*) Orchard Bks Watts.
— The Seltzer Man. LC 91-40905. (Illus.). 32p. (J). (ps-3). 1993. text ed. 14.95 (*0-02-777917-3*, Mac Bks Young Read) S&S Childrens.
Rush, Kenneth, et al. The President, the Congress, & Foreign Policy: A Joint Project of the Association of Former Members of Congress & the Atlantic Council of the United States. LC 86-1634. 1986. 52.00 (*0-8191-5283-8*) U Pr of Amer.
Rush, Laurence W. HMM 165: White Beach to Vietnam. 128p. reprint ed. pap. write for info. (*0-318-64842-3*) L & R Art.
***Rush, Mallory.** Kiss of the Beast. 1995. mass mkt. 3.25 (*0-373-25658-2*, 1-25658-5) Harlequin Bks.
— Love Game. 1995. mass mkt. 4.99 (*0-373-83313-X*, 1-83313-6) Harlequin Bks.
— Love Games: Secret Fantasies. 1995. pap. 2.99 (*0-614-00493-4*, 1-25622-1) Harlequin Bks.
— Love Slave. (Temptation Ser.). 1993. mass mkt. 2.99 (*0-373-25548-9*, 1-25548-8) Harlequin Bks.
***Rush, Mark & Badger-Dole, Carol.** Principles of MicroEconomics. 240p. (C). 1994. pap. text ed., spiral bd. 21.95 (*0-7872-0343-2*) Kendall-Hunt.
— Principles of MicroEconomics: Outline & Notes. 224p. (C). 1993. spiral bd. 19.95 (*0-8403-8952-3*) Kendall-Hunt.
Rush, Mark E. Does Redistricting Make a Difference? Partisan Representation & Electoral Behavior. LC 93-6670. 232p. (C). 1993. text ed. 32.50 (*0-8018-4579-3*) Johns Hopkins.
Rush, Martin. Decoding the Secret Language. 1994. pap. 11.00 (*0-671-87238-9*, Fireside) S&S Trade.
Rush, Mary L. The Language of Directions: A Programmed Workbook. LC 77-87703. 1977. pap. text ed. 12.95 (*0-88200-113-2*, C1321) Alexander Graham.
Rush, Michael, jt. auth. see Althoff, Phillip.
Rush, Myron. Administracion (Management) Un Enfoque Biblico (A Biblical Approach) (SPA.). 1992. 4.99 (*1-56063-357-3*, 490215) Editorial Unilit.
— Agotado (Burnout) Ayudas-Vidas Desequilibradas. (SPA.). 1992. 5.99 (*1-56063-242-9*, 497706) Editorial Unilit.
— Political Succession in the U. S. S. R. LC 65-14778. xv, 223p. 1968. text ed. 49.00 (*0-231-02825-3*) Col U Pr.
Rush, Myron D. Management: A Biblical Approach. 1983. pap. 10.99 (*0-88207-607-8*, Victor Books) SP Pubns.
Rush, N. Orwin. Battle of Pensacola. (Florida Classics Ser.). (Illus.). 157p. (Orig.). 1981. reprint ed. 9.95 (*0-912451-05-X*); reprint ed. pap. 6.95 (*0-912451-06-8*) Florida Classics.
Rush, N. Orwin, et al. Special Collections: What They Mean to Librarians, Professors, & Collectors. LC 72-93783. 1972. 5.00 (*0-9607778-4-9*) Friends Fla St.
Rush, Norman. Mating. LC 92-50106. 1992. pap. 12.00 (*0-679-73709-X*, Vin) Random.
— Mating: A Novel. LC 90-25752. 496p. 1991. 22.50 (*0-394-54472-2*) Knopf.
— Whites: Stories. LC 92-50099. 1992. pap. 9.00 (*0-679-73816-9*, Vin) Random.
***Rush, Peter, ed.** Theoretical Roman Archaeology: Second Conference Proceedings. 203p. (C). 1995. boxed, pap. text ed. 51.95 (*1-85628-713-0*, Pub. by Avebury Pub UK) Ashgate Pub Co.
Rush, R. Timothy, et al. Occupational Literacy Education. LC 86-778. (Illus.). 167p. reprint ed. pap. 47.60 (*0-8357-4305-5*, 2037102) Bks Demand.
Rush, Ramona, et al, eds. Communications at the Crossroads: The Gender Gap Connection. LC 88-26757. (Communication & Information Science Ser.). 352p. (C). 1989. text ed. 55.00 (*0-89391-481-9*); pap. 19.95 (*0-89391-569-6*) Ablex Pub.
Rush, Rebecca. Kelroy. Nelson, Dana, ed. (Early American Women Writers Ser.). 224p. 1993. pap. 11.95 (*0-19-507703-2*) OUP.
— Kelroy. LC 78-64093. reprint ed. 37.50 (*0-404-17167-2*) AMS Pr.
Rush, Richard D., ed. Building Systems Integration Handbook. (Illus.). 1991. reprint ed. pap. text ed. 34.95 (*0-7506-9198-0*) Buttrwrth-Heinemann.
Rush, Richard D., jt. auth. see Piper, Robert J.
Rush, Robert A. Nerve Growth Factors. 351p. 1989. text ed. 219.95 (*0-471-92145-9*) Wiley.
Rush, S., ed. see Body Surface Mapping of Cardiac Fields Symposium Staff.
Rush, Sean C. The Decaying American Campus: A Ticking Time Bomb. 136p. 1988. 50.00 (*0-913359-47-5*); 25.00 (*0-318-39805-2*) APPA VA.
Rush, Sean C., jt. auth. see Applied Management Engineering Staff.
Rush, Sheila, jt. auth. see Clark, Chris.
Rush, Solveiga. Oliver Newberry Chaffee (1881-1944) LC 91-65383. (Illus.). 44p. (Orig.). 1991. pap. 10.00 (*0-915577-22-4*) Taft Museum.
Rush, Susan D. & Durham, Katherine C. The Alabama Heritage Cookbook. LC 83-82791. (Illus.). 164p. 1984. 19.95 (*0-9612868-1-4*); spiral bd. 12.95 (*0-9612868-0-6*) Heritage Pubns.
Rush, Terry. Afraid God Works, Afraid He Doesn't. 112p. (Orig.). 1991. pap. 7.95 (*1-878990-15-2*) Howard Pub LA.
— God Will Make a Way: When There Seems to Be No Way. 1995. 12.95 (*1-878990-40-3*) Howard Pub LA.
— The Holy Spirit Makes No Earthly Sense. 115p. (Orig.). 1987. pap. 7.95 (*1-878990-04-7*) Howard Pub LA.
Rush, Theressa G., et al. Black American Writers Past & Present: A Biographical & Bibliographical Dictionary, 2 vols., Set. LC 74-28400. 865p. 1975. 72.50 (*0-8108-0785-8*) Scarecrow.
Rush, Thomas. The Future of Local Telephone Companies in the U. S. (Illus.). 161p. 1994. 2,450.00 (*1-56965-057-8*) BCC.
Rush, Vincent E. The Responsible Christian: A Popular Guide for Moral Decision Making According to Classical Tradition. 288p. (C). 1984. 12.95 (*0-8294-0448-1*) Loyola Univ Pr.
Rush, W. F., et al, eds. Integrating Microelectronics Into Gas Distribution. 490p. 1987. 75.00 (*0-910091-62-5*) Inst Gas Tech.
Rushbrook, F. Fire Aboard. (C). 1987. 175.00 (*0-85174-331-5*, Pub. by Brwn Son Ferg) St Mut.
Rushbrook, Rosalyn. Where Did I Go Wrong? (Illus.). 96p. (C). 1990. 29.00 (*0-85439-418-4*, Pub. by St Paul Pubns UK) St Mut.
Rushby, Nick, ed. Technology-Based Learning: Selected Readings. 348p. (C). 1987. text ed. 37.50 (*0-89397-270-3*) Nichols Pub.
Rushd, Ibn. The Distinguished Jurist's Primer, Vol. 1. Nyazee, Imran, tr. 640p. 1994. 95.00 (*1-873938-13-6*, Pub. by Garnet Pubng Ltd UK) Paul & Co Pubs.
— The Distinguished Jurist's Primer, Vol. 2. Nyazee, Imran, tr. 500p. 1994. 95.00 (*1-873938-93-4*, Pub. by Garnet Pubng Ltd UK) Paul & Co Pubs.
— Epistle on the Possibility of Conjunction with the Active Intellect. Bland, Kalman P., ed. & tr. by. (Moreshet Studies in Jewish History, Literature & Thought: No. 7). 35.00 (*0-87334-005-1*) Ktav.
***Rushdie, Salman.** East, West: Stories. LC 94-28277. 1995. 21.00 (*0-679-43965-X*) Pantheon.
— Grimus. LC 78-65232. 320p. 1982. 22.50 (*0-87951-093-5*); pap. 9.95 (*0-87951-138-9*) Overlook Pr.
— Grimus. 324p. 1991. pap. 12.00 (*0-14-014731-4*) Viking Penguin.
— Haroun & the Sea of Stories. large type ed. (J). (gr. 1-8). 1991. 16.95 (*0-7451-1428-8*, Galaxy Child Lrg Print) Chivers N Amer.
— Haroun & the Sea of Stories. 204p. 1991. reprint ed. pap. 10.95 (*0-14-015737-9*, Penguin Bks) Viking Penguin.
— Imaginary Homelands: Essays & Criticism 1981-1991. 448p. 1992. pap. 12.50 (*0-14-016894-X*, Penguin Bks) Viking Penguin.
— The Jaguar Smile. large type ed. 154p. 1989. reprint ed. lib. bdg. 9.47 (*1-85089-247-4*, Pub. by ISIS UK) Transaction Pubs.
— The Jaguar Smile: A Nicaraguan Journey. 1987. 12.95 (*0-317-56603-2*) Viking Penguin.
— Midnight's Children. 560p. 1982. mass mkt. 5.95 (*0-380-58099-3*) Avon.
— Midnight's Children. 448p. 1991. pap. 12.95 (*0-14-013270-8*) Viking Penguin.
— The Satanic Verses. 1992. pap. 10.00 (*0-9632707-0-2*) Consortium DE.
— The Satanic Verses. LC 88-40266. 496p. 1989. 19.95 (*0-670-82537-9*) Viking Penguin.
— The Wizard of Oz: BFI Film Classics. (Illus.). 72p. 1992. pap. 9.95 (*0-85170-300-3*, Pub. by British Film Inst UK) Ind U Pr.
Rushdoony, Haig. Exploring Our World With Maps. (J). (gr. k-6). 1988. pap. 13.99 (*0-8224-4396-1*) Fearon Teach Aids.
Rushdoony, Haig A. Language of Maps: A Map Skills Program for Grades 4-6. (Makemaster Bk.). (J). (gr. 4-6). 1983. pap. 12.99 (*0-8224-4242-6*) Fearon Teach Aids.
Rushdoony, Haig A., jt. auth. see Michaelis, John U.
Rushdoony, Rousas J. The Institutes of Biblical Law. LC 72-79485. 1973. 34.99 (*0-87552-410-9*) Presby & Reformed.
Rushdy, Ashraf H. The Empty Garden: The Subject of Late Milton. LC 92-9975. (Milton Studies). 536p. (C). 1992. text ed. 49.95 (*0-8229-3719-0*) U of Pittsburgh Pr.
Rushefsky, Mark E. Making Cancer Policy. LC 86-14387. (SUNY Series in Public Administration). 257p. (C). 1986. 74.50 (*0-88706-406-X*); pap. 24.95 (*0-88706-407-8*) State U NY Pr.
— Public Policy in the United States: Toward the Twenty-First Century. 300p. (C). 1990. pap. 31.95 (*0-534-12852-1*) Intl Thomson.
Rushefsky, Mark E., jt. auth. see Patel, Kant.
Rushen, J., jt. ed. see Lawrence, A. B.

Rusher, Bobby. How to Line up Your Fourth Putt. 2nd ed. (Illus.). 128p. 1994. reprint ed. pap. 16.95 (*1-879676-00-1*) R P Rusher & Co.
Rusher's Latest Is A Great Golf Product - Even President Bush carries it in his bag! Perfect for Clients, Colleagues, Husbands & Wives, Grandparents, Sons, Daughters & In-Laws. EVERYONE KNOWS A GOLFER, & THIS IS NEW, DIFFERENT, & TERRIFIC. SOME COMMENTS FROM ADMIRERS: "Our number one pick for Mother's & Father's Day is still our top humor pick for under a golfer's tee....The duffers in your life do not need red & green golf balls...or reindeer head-shaped club covers. What they need is HOW TO LINE UP YOUR FOURTH PUTT." - Warren Cassell, President, Just Books, Inc., Greenwich. "We have been selling this book at a steady pace of almost a year now. It is immediately humorous to any golfer by the title alone, & is a good item to mix in with other golfer gifts." - Betty N. Mori, Mori Luggage & Gifts, Atlanta. Bobby Explains... * How to Get More Distance Off The Shank * When to Blame The Caddie * How to Rationalize A 7-Hour Round * How to Enjoy Your Partner's 129 * Crying & How to Handle It * Replacing The Divots Of Your Life. Attractive, four-color cover. Beautifully spiral bound. Suggested Retail $16.95. Contact: Bob or Jo Ann Runk, R. Paul Rusher & Co., Inc., 16 Church St., Southport, CT 06490; 203-254-1791; FAX 203-255-9974. Wholesale: $10.17 plus shipping. It Makes The Perfect Gift. ***Publisher Provided Annotation.***

***Rusher, William.** The Ambiguous Legacy of the Enlightenment. LC 95-15728. 1995. pap. write for info. (*0-8191-9957-5*) U Pr of Amer.
***Rusher, William, ed.** The Ambiguous Legacy of the Enlightenment. LC 95-15728. 1995. write for info. (*0-8191-9956-7*) U Pr of Amer.
Rusher, William A. How to Win Arguments. LC 85-13344. 216p. 1985. reprint ed. pap. text ed. 17.75 (*0-8191-4771-0*) U Pr of Amer.
— The Making of the New Majority Party. LC 75-1659. 176p. 1975. reprint ed. pap. 1.95 (*0-916054-00-4*) Green Hill.
— The Rise of the Right. rev. ed. 256p. (C). 1993. pap. text ed. 14.95 (*0-9627841-2-5*) Natl Review.
Rushford, Carrolle A. Special Emphasis Program Managers Handbook. rev. ed. (Illus.). 300p. (Orig.). (C). 1990. ring bd. 89.95 (*1-877645-00-1*) Rushford & Assocs.
Rushford, Greg. Appointments with Power. 1994. pap. 29.00 (*1-884828-00-0*) Legal Times.
Rushford, Patricia. Deceived. (Jennie McGrady Mysteries Ser.: No. 4). (YA). 1994. pap. 3.99 (*1-55661-334-2*) Bethany Hse.
— Silent Witness. (YA). 1993. pap. 3.99 (*1-55661-332-6*) Bethany Hse.
— Too Many Secrets. (YA). 1993. pap. 3.99 (*1-55661-331-8*) Bethany Hse.
Rushford, Patricia, jt. auth. see Lush, Jean.
Rushford, Patricia H. Caring for Your Elderly Parents: The Help, Hope, & Cope Book. rev. ed. LC 92-47073. 224p. 1993. pap. 8.99 (*0-8007-9207-6*) Revell.
— The Humpty Dumpty Syndrome: Putting Yourself Together Again. LC 93-34753. 176p. (Orig.). 1994. pap. 8.99 (*0-8007-5511-1*) Revell.
— Lost in the Money Maze? How to Find Your Way Through. (Heart Issues Ser.). 181p. 1992. reprint ed. pap. 9.95 (*0-932305-91-1*, 535011) Aglow Communs.
— Pursued. (YA). 1994. pap. 3.99 (*1-55661-333-4*) Bethany Hse.
— What Kids Need Most in a Mom. LC 83-3964. 1989. pap. 8.99 (*0-8007-5294-5*) Revell.
— Without a Trace. (Jennie McGrady Mysteries Ser.: No. 5). 176p. (J). 1995. mass mkt. 3.99 (*1-55661-558-2*) Bethany Hse.
Rushforth, G. McN. Latin Historical Inscriptions. xxxii, 144p. 1980. 25.00 (*0-89005-179-8*) Ares.
— Latin Historical Inscriptions. LC 70-107831. (Select Bibliographies Reprint Ser.). 1977. 21.95 (*0-8369-5196-4*) Ayer.
Rushforth, G. McN., tr. see Rivoira, Giovanni T.
Rushforth, J. M. & Morris, J. L. Computers & Computing. LC 72-8616. (Introductory Mathematics for Scientists & Engineers Ser.). 269p. reprint ed. pap. 76.70 (*0-317-08336-8*, 2022104) Bks Demand.
***Rushforth, Keith.** Conifers. fac. ed. LC 87-28965. (Illus.). 240p. 1987. reprint ed. pap. 68.40 (*0-7837-8153-9*, 2047858) Bks Demand.
— Pocket Guide to Trees. 1981. 7.95 (*0-686-73804-7*) S&S Trade.
— Shrubs for Small Gardens. (Illus.). 64p. 1995. pap. 5.95 (*0-304-32010-2*, Pub. by Cassell UK) Sterling.
Rushforth, Keith, jt. auth. see Coombs, Geoffrey K.

R

An Asterisk (*) at the beginning of an entry indicates that the title is appearing in BIP for the first time.

***Rushforth, Keith, et al.** Hillier Garden Planning: The Essential Guide to Garden Planning, Planting & Maintenance from the Internationally Renowned Hillier Nurseries. (Illus.). 240p. 1995. 34.95 (0-7153-0181-0, Pub. by D & C Pub UK) Sterling.

Rushforth, Peter. Kindergarten. LC 87-45454. 208p. 1989. pap. 10.95 (0-87923-701-5) Godine.

Rushforth, S. R., jt. auth. see Clark, R. L.

Rushforth, S. R., jt. auth. see Grimes, Judith A.

Rushforth, S. R., jt. auth. see Kaczmarska.

Rushforth, S. R., jt. auth. see Lawson, L. L.

Rushforth, Scott. A Hopi Social History: Anthropological Perspectives on Sociocultural Persistence & Change. (Illus.). 320p. (Orig.). (C). 1992. text ed. 35.00 (0-292-73066-7); pap. 16.95 (0-292-73067-5) U of Tex Pr.

Rushforth, Scott & Chisholm, James S. Cultural Persistence: Continuity in Meaning & Moral Responsibility among the Bearlake Athapaskans. LC 91-17616. (Illus.). 187p. 1991. 37.50 (0-8165-1241-8) U of Ariz Pr.

Rushforth, Winifred. Life's Currency: Time, Money & Energy - & Other Shorter Writings. 224p. (Orig.). 1984. pap. 9.95 (0-946551-19-7, Pub. by Gateway Bks UK) Atrium Pubs.

— Something Is Happening: Spiritual Awareness & Depth Psychology in the New Age. rev. ed. 160p. reprint ed. pap. 9.95 (0-946551-05-7, Pub. by Gateway Bks UK) Atrium Pubs.

Rushin, Kate. The Black Back-Ups. LC 92-46886. 96p. (Orig.). 1993. lib. bdg. 18.95 (1-56341-026-5); pap. 8.95 (1-56341-025-7) Firebrand Bks.

Rushin, Pat. Puzzling Through the News. 130p. 1991. pap. 11.95 (0-913123-33-1) Galileo.

Rushinek, Sara F., jt. auth. see McNichols, Charles W.

***Rushing.** The AIDS Epidemic: Social Dimensions of an Infectious Disease. (C). 1995. pap. text ed. 16.95 (0-8133-2045-3) Westview.

Rushing, Anthony. Along the Road to Glory: A Compilation & Biography of the Soldier, Company & Regiment of the Confederate Army from Saline County. (Illus.). 103p. 1985. ring bd. 14.25 (0-945183-01-1) Saline Cnty Hist Heritage Soc.

Rushing, Donna. Bulletin Boards for All Occasions. Brewer, Karen, ed. (Illus.). 48p. (Orig.). 1994. pap. 6.49 (0-7847-0227-6, 14-03317) Standard Pub.

Rushing, Felder. Gardening Southern Style. LC 86-33997. 230p. (Orig.). 1987. pap. 17.95 (0-87805-390-5) U Pr of Miss.

Rushing, Felder, jt. auth. see Bender, Steve.

***Rushing, James A., Jr.** Images of Adventure: Ywain in the Visual Arts. (Middle Ages Ser.). (Illus.). 320p. 1995. text ed. write for info. (0-8122-3293-3) U of Pa Pr.

Rushing, Jane G. Against the Moon. LC 91-3111. (Texas Tradition Ser.: No. 17). 222p. 1991. reprint ed. pap. 14.95 (0-87565-094-5) Tex Christian.

— Starting from Pyron. (Illus.). xi, 153p. (C). 1992. 25.00 (0-89672-283-X) Tex Tech Univ Pr.

— Walnut Grove. xiv, 255p. 1992. reprint ed. pap. 12.00 (0-89672-278-3) Tex Tech Univ Pr.

Rushing, Jane G., jt. auth. see Hall, Kline A.

***Rushing, Phillip.** Empty Sleeves: A Story of Tragedy & Triumph. 158p. (Orig.). 1994. pap. 6.95 (0-88270-685-3) Bridge Pub.

Rushing, Robert. Lamia Anemia. 280p. 1988. pap. 8.95 (0-89697-287-9) Intl Univ Pr.

Rushing, Sandra M. The Magdalene Legacy: A Presbyterian Minister Examines the Wounded Icon of Sexuality. LC 93-40160. 240p. 1994. text ed. 49.95 (0-89789-388-3, Bergin & Garvey) Greenwood.

Rushing, Steve. A Funny Thing Happened on the Way to Court... A Collection of over 100 Courtroom Cartoons. (Illus.). 121p. 1987. per. 6.95 (0-936417-09-9) Axelrod Pub.

— Legal Insanity: Disorder in the Court. (Illus.). 90p. (Orig.). 1993. pap. 10.00 (0-88092-076-9) Royal Fireworks.

Rushing, W. Jackson. Native American Art & the New York Avante-Garde: A History of Cultural Primitivism. Goetzmann, William H., ed. LC 94-14250. (American Studies Ser.). (Illus.). 288p. (C). 1995. text ed. 39.95 (0-292-75547-3) U of Tex Pr.

Rushing, W. Jackson, jt. auth. see Bernstein, Bruce.

***Rushing, William A.** The AIDS Epidemic: Social Dimensions of an Infectious Disease. LC 95-828. (C). 1995. text ed. 55.00 (0-8133-2044-5) Westview.

— Social Functions & Economic Aspects of Health Insurance. (S. S. Huebner International Ser.). 1987. lib. bdg. 62.50 (0-89838-219-X) Huebner Foun Insur.

Rushkoff. Cyberia. 1995. pap. 11.00 (0-06-251009-6, PL) HarpC.

Rushkoff, Douglas. The Cyber Tarot: An Electronic Oracle. 16p. 1994. 39.95 (0-06-251197-1); 39.95 (0-06-251196-3) Harper SF.

— Cyberia: Life in the Trenches of Hyperspace. LC 93-26184. 256p. 1994. 22.00 (0-06-251010-X) Harper SF.

— Genx Reader. 320p. 1994. pap. 13.95 (0-345-39046-6, Del Rey) Ballantine.

— Media Virus! Hidden Agendas in Popular Culture. LC 94-12133. 304p. 1994. 21.95 (0-345-38276-5) Ballantine.

Rushlyn, Robert. There Goes the Neighborhood. 1994. 18.95 (0-533-10927-2) Vantage.

***Rushman.** MCQ Self-Test Companion to Lee's Synopsis of Anaesthesia. 208p. 1995. pap. write for info. (0-7506-2325-X, Focal) Buttrwrth-Heinemann.

Rushman, jt. auth. see McCormick.

***Rushman, G. B., et al.** MCQ Selftest Companion to Lee's Synopsis of Anaesthesia. LC 94-49106. 1995. write for info. (0-7050-6232-5) Buttrwrth-Heinemann.

Rushmer, Nancy & Schuyler, Valerie, eds. Trainer's Handbook: What Infant-Family Specialists Need to Know & How to Teach It. (Early Intervention Ser.). 90p. (C). 1993. 45.00 (1-883204-00-3) Infant Hearing Resc.

Rushmer, Nancy, jt. auth. see Schuyler, Valerie.

Rushmore, Stephen. The Computerized Income Approach to Hotel-Motel Valuations & Market Studies. 428p. 1990. 28.50 (0-922154-02-3) Appraisal Inst.

— Hotel Investments: A Guide for Lenders & Owners. annuals suppl. ed. LC 89-52143. (Illus.). 425p. (C). 1990. Supplemented annually. ring bd. 145.00 (0-7913-0379-9) Warren Gorham & Lamont.

— Hotels & Motels: A Guide to Market Analysis, Investment Analysis, & Valuations. LC 92-17619. 1992. 35.00 (0-922154-06-6) Appraisal Inst.

— How to Perform an Economic Feasibility Study of a Proposed Hotel-Motel. 104p. 1986. 12.00 (0-318-41032-X) Couns Real Estate.

Rusho, W. L. Everett Ruess: A Vagabond for Beauty. LC 83-643. (Illus.). 240p. 1985. pap. 12.95 (0-87905-210-4, Peregrine Smith) Gibbs Smith Pub.

— Powell's Canyon Voyage. LC 70-64908. (Wild & Woolly West Ser., No. 11). (Illus.). (Orig.). 1969. pap. 3.00 (0-910584-12-5) Filter.

Rusho, W. L. & Crampton, C. Gregory. Lee's Ferry: Desert River Crossing. rev. ed. (Illus.). 180p. (C). 1992. pap. 14.95 (0-9630757-0-5) Cricket Prods.

Rusholme, J., jt. auth. see Davies, T.

Rushton, A. & Oxley, J. Handbook of Logistics & Distribution Management. 339p. (C). 1989. 330.00 (0-685-36120-9, Inst Pur & Supply) St Mut.

Rushton, A., et al. The Croft Borehole in the Lilleshall Inlier of North Shropshire. (British Geological Survey - BGS Reports). 1988. pap. 5.00 (0-11-884463-6, HM4636, Pub. by HMSO UK) UNIPUB.

— Introduction to Solid-Liquid Filtration & Separation Technology. LC 93-40787. 1994. 123.00 (1-56081-801-8) VCH Pubs.

— New Parents for Older Children. (C). 1989. 45.00 (0-903534-79-7, Pub. by Brit Ag for Adopt & Fost UK) St Mut.

Rushton, Alan R. Genetics & Medicine in the United States, 1800 to 1922. LC 93-35943. 1994. 45.00 (0-8018-4781-8) Johns Hopkins.

Rushton, Albert, ed. Mathematical Models & Design Methods in Solid-Liquid Separation. 1985. lib. bdg. 121.50 (90-247-3140-2) Kluwer Ac.

Rushton, Andrew. Reconfigurable Processor-Array: A Bit-Sliced Parallel Computer. (Research Monographs in Parallel & Distributed Computing). 192p. (Orig.). 1989. pap. 27.95 (0-262-68057-2) MIT Pr.

Rushton, Andrew, ed. Reconfigurable Processor-Array: A Bit Sliced Parallel Computer. 192p. (C). 1989. pap. text ed. 180.00 (0-273-08799-1, Pub. by Pitman Pubng UK) St Mut.

Rushton, David N., ed. Handbook of Neuro-Urology. LC 94-12979. (Neurological Disease & Therapy Ser.: Vol. 28). 424p. 1994. 150.00 (0-8247-9248-3) Dekker.

Rushton, Gerard, jt. ed. see Onsrud, Harlan J.

Rushton, J. Phillipe. Race, Evolution, & Behavior: A Life History Perspective. LC 93-21282. 398p. (C). 1994. 34.95 (1-56000-146-1) Transaction Pubs.

Rushton, Julian. Berlioz, Romeo et Juliette. LC 93-32505. (Cambridge Music Handbooks Ser.). (Illus.). 131p. (C). 1994. 34.95 (0-521-37397-2); pap. 10.95 (0-521-37767-6) Cambridge U Pr.

— Classical Music: A Concise History from Gluck to Beethoven. LC 86-50223. (World of Art Ser.). 192p. (Orig.). 1986. pap. 14.95 (0-500-20210-9) Thames Hudson.

Rushton, Julian, ed. W. A. Mozart: "Don Giovanni" (Cambridge Opera Handbooks Ser.). (Illus.). 1981. pap. 15.95 (0-521-29663-3) Cambridge U Pr.

— W. A. Mozart: "Idomeneo" LC 92-25833. (Cambridge Opera Handbooks Ser.). (Illus.). 192p. (C). 1993. 49.95 (0-521-43144-1); pap. 17.95 (0-521-43741-5) Cambridge U Pr.

Rushton, Julian, ed. see Philidor, Francois-Andre D.

Rushton, Julian, ed. see Piccinni, Niccolo.

Rushton, K. R. & Redshaw, S. C. Seepage & Groundwater Flow: Numerical Analysis by Analog & Digital Methods. LC 78-23359. (Wiley Series in Geotechnical Engineering). 351p. reprint ed. pap. 100.10 (0-8357-7017-6, 2033622) Bks Demand.

Rushton, Lucy. Birth Customs. LC 92-42174. (Comparing Religions Ser.). (Illus.). 32p. (J). (gr. 4-8). 1993. 13.95 (1-56847-030-4) Thomson Lrning.

— Death Customs. LC 92-42150. (Comparing Religions Ser.). (Illus.). 32p. (J). (gr. 4-8). 1993. 13.95 (1-56847-031-2) Thomson Lrning.

Rushton, Peter H. The Jin Ping Mei & the Non-Linear Dimensions of the Traditional Chinese Novel. LC 93-37252. (Illus.). 436p. 1993. text ed. 109.95 (0-7734-9831-1, Mellen Univ Pr) E Mellen.

Rushton, Peters, jt. auth. see Norton, Daniel S.

Rushton, Robert. Veritas Organon Muse. 1995. 15.95 (0-8062-5100-X) Carlton.

Rushton, William. Shakespeare an Archer. LC 73-7501. (Studies in Shakespeare: No. 24). 1973. reprint ed. lib. bdg. 49.95 (0-8383-1696-4) M S G Haskell Hse.

Rushton, William F. The Cajuns: From Acadia to Louisiana. (Illus.). 352p. 1980. pap. 15.00 (0-374-51557-3) FS&G.

Rushton, William L. Shakespeare a Lawyer. LC 72-174790. reprint ed. 24.50 (0-404-05452-8) AMS Pr.

— Shakespeare & the Arte of English Poesie. LC 70-174792. reprint ed. 27.50 (0-404-05458-7) AMS Pr.

— Shakespeare's Euphuism. LC 77-174794. reprint ed. 29.50 (0-404-05454-4) AMS Pr.

— Shakespeare's Legal Maxims. LC 70-174795. reprint ed. 24.50 (0-404-05456-0) AMS Pr.

Rushton, Willie. Every Cat in the Book. (Illus.). 64p. (J). (gr. 3-5). 1994. 19.95 (1-85793-199-8, Pub. by Pavilion UK) Trafalgar.

Rushton, Willie, jt. auth. see Rae, Simon.

Rushwe, jt. auth. see Hazen.

***Rushworth, Clare.** Making a Difference in Cancer Care: Practical Techniques in Palliative & Curative Treatment. 1995. pap. 14.95 (0-285-63215-9, Pub. by Souvenir UK) Atrium Pubs.

***Rushworth, F. D., et al.** Purposes in Education. 38p. 1974. pap. 4.00 (0-904674-01-0, Pub. by Octagon Pr UK) ISHK Bk Service.

Rushworth, Francis A. & Tunstall, David P. Nuclear Magnetic Resonance. LC 72-89713. 266p. 1973. text ed. 190.00 (0-677-04820-3); pap. text ed. 121.00 (0-677-04825-4) Gordon & Breach.

Rushworth, Peter, et al. Selected References on the Geology & Coal Resources of the Central & Western Colorado Coal Fields & Regions. (Information Ser.: No. 25). 141p. (Orig.). 1989. pap. 8.00 (1-884216-20-X) Colo Geol Survey.

Rushworth, Stan. Sam Woods American Healing. LC 92-81553. 1993. 11.95 (0-88268-122-2) Station Hill Pr.

Rushworth, Stanley E. Sam Woods. Greenwood, Peter, ed. LC 92-81553. 176p. (Orig.). (C). 1992. pap. 14.95 (0-9632574-9-8) Talk Leaves.

Rusi, Alpo M. After the Cold War: Europe's New Political Architecture. LC 90-26347. 200p. 1991. text ed. 39.95 (0-312-06114-5) St Martin.

— Dangerous Peace: Security. 1995. text ed. 39.95 (0-8133-2258-8) Westview.

RUSI Staff. RUSI & Brassey's Defence Yearbook, 1990. 100th ed. 450p. 1990. 56.00 (0-08-037336-4, Pergamon Pr); pap. 15.25 (0-08-037338-0, Pergamon Pr) Elsevier.

— RUSI-Brassey's Defence Yearbook 1989. LC 75-641843. (Brassey's Defence Yearbook Ser.). 361p. 1988. 63.00 (0-08-036698-8, Pergamon Pr) Elsevier.

RUSI Staff, ed. RUSI & Brassey's Defence Yearbook, 1991. 101th ed. 344p. 1991. 69.00 (0-08-040710-2, Pub. by Brasseys UK); pap. 20.00 (0-08-040729-3, Pub. by Brasseys UK) Brasseys Inc.

Rusin, Alice G. The Colors of God's Love. 1994. pap. 10.95 (0-533-10812-8) Vantage.

Rusin, N. P. Meteorological & Radiational Regime of Antartica. 360p. 1964. text ed. 83.00x (0-7065-0290-6, Pub. by Keter Pub IS) Coronet Bks.

Rusinko, Elaine, ed. see Duknovych, Aleksandr.

Rusinko, Susan. British Drama, 1950 to Present. (Critical History of British Drama Ser.). 285p. (C). 1989. text ed. 25.95 (0-8057-8952-9, Twayne) Macmillan.

— Joe Orton. LC 95-10064. (English Authors Ser.: Vol. 515). 1995. write for info. (0-8057-7034-8, Twayne) Macmillan.

— The Plays of Benn Levy: Between Conrad & Shaw. LC 94-10592. (Illus.). 224p. 1994. 36.50 (0-8386-3556-3) Fairleigh Dickinson.

— Tom Stoppard. (Twayne's English Authors Ser.: 419). 184p. 1986. text ed. 21.95 (0-8057-6909-9, Pub. by Royal Botanic Garden UK) Macmillan.

Rusinoff, Samuel E. Automation in Practice. LC 57-13299. 269p. reprint ed. pap. 76.70 (0-8357-5916-4, 2052046) Bks Demand.

— Practical Descriptive Geometry. LC 47-24789. 268p. reprint ed. pap. 76.40 (0-317-12987-2, 2004562) Bks Demand.

— Tool Engineering. LC 59-13786. (Illus.). 335p. reprint ed. pap. 95.50 (0-317-11000-4, 2004566) Bks Demand.

Rusinov, V. S., jt. ed. see Livanov, M. N.

Rusinow, Dennison, ed. Yugoslavia: A Fractured Federalism. LC 88-14356. (Woodrow Wilson Center Perspectives Ser.). (Illus.). 198p. (Orig.). (C). 1988. lib. bdg. 32.00 (0-943875-08-0, Johns Hopkins); pap. text ed. 14.25 (0-943875-07-2, Johns Hopkins) W Wilson Ctr Pr.

Rusinowitch, Michael & Remy, J. L., eds. Conditional Term Rewriting Systems: Third International Workshop, CTRS-92, Pont-a-Mousson, France, July 8-10, 1992, Proceedings. LC 92-44413. (Lecture Notes in Computer Science Ser.: Vol. 656). 1993. 70.00 (0-387-56393-8) Spr-Verlag.

Rusk, C. E. Tales of a Western Mountaineer. LC 78-54427. (Illus.). 400p. 1978. reprint ed. pap. 7.95 (0-916890-62-7) Mountaineers.

Rusk, Claude E. Tales of a Western Mountaineer: A Record of Mountain Experiences on the Pacific Coast. (American Biography Ser.). 309p. 1991. reprint ed. lib. bdg. 79.00 (0-7812-8333-7) Rprt Serv.

***Rusk, David.** Baltimore Unbound: A Strategy for Regional Renewal. 177p. 1994. pap. 14.95 (0-8018-5078-9) Johns Hopkins.

— Cities Without Suburbs. 135p. 1993. text ed. 29.00 (0-943875-49-8); pap. text ed. 13.95 (0-943875-50-1) W Wilson Ctr Pr.

— Cities Without Suburbs. 2nd ed. 168p. 1995. text ed. 29.00x (0-943875-74-9); pap. text ed. 13.95x (0-943875-73-0) Johns Hopkins.

Rusk, Dean & Rusk, Richard. As I Saw It. Papp, Daniel S., ed. 672p. 1990. 29.95 (0-393-02650-7) Norton.

Rusk, Irene J. A Letter to Grandmother. LC 92-61973. (Illus.). 64p. (Orig.). (J). 1994. pap. 8.00 (1-56002-223-X, Univ Edtns) Aegina Pr.

Rusk, Jeff E., ed. Legal Services to the Poor: The Dream, the Reality, the Future. (Institute & Seminar Proceedings Ser.). 120p. 1992. 10.00 (0-89940-103-1) LBJ Sch Pub Aff.

Rusk, Ralph L. The Literature of the Middle Western Frontier, 2 vols. (BCL1-PS American Literature Ser.). 1992. reprint ed. lib. bdg. 150.00 (0-7812-6627-0) Rprt Serv.

Rusk, Ralph L., ed. see Lazarus, Emma.

Rusk, Richard, jt. auth. see Rusk, Dean.

Rusk, Rogers D. Atoms, Men & Stars: A Survey of the Latest Developments of Physical Science & Their Relation to Life. LC 70-156712. (Essay Index Reprint Ser.). 1977. reprint ed. 26.95 (0-8369-2332-4) Ayer.

Rusk, Tom. Doing the Right Thing: Making Quality Decisions. 60p. 1992. student ed 14.95 (0-88390-334-2); student ed, ring bd. 595.00 (0-88390-333-4) Pfeiffer & Co.

— Instead of Therapy. 256p. 1993. pap. 12.00 (1-56170-059-2, 135T) Hay House.

— Mind Traps: Change Your Mind--Change Your Life. (Illus.). 324p. 1988. pap. 9.95 (0-89586-748-6) Putnam Pub Group.

Rusk, Tom & Miller, D. Patrick. Instead of Therapy: Help Yourself Change & Change the Help You're Getting. LC 91-70545. 256p. (Orig.). 1991. 20.00 (1-56170-021-5, 135H); pap. 12.00 (1-56170-022-3, 135T) Hay House.

— The Power of Ethical Persuasion: Winning Through Understanding at Work & at Home. 240p. 1994. pap. 9.95 (0-14-017214-9, Penguin Bks) Viking Penguin.

— The Power of Ethical Persuasion: Winning Through Understanding in Difficult Communications. LC 92-50385. 1993. 20.00 (0-670-84617-1, Viking) Viking Penguin.

Rusk, Tom & Read, Randy. I Want to Change, but I Don't Know How. 384p. 1986. reprint ed. pap. 9.95 (0-8431-0491-0) Price Stern.

Ruska, W. S. Microelectronic Processes: An Introduction to the Manufacture of Integrated Circuits. (McGraw-Hill Series in Computer Engineering). 488p. 1987. text ed. write for info. (0-07-054280-5) McGraw.

Ruskai, et al. Wavelets & Their Applications. (C). 1992. boxed 59.95 (0-86720-225-4) Jones & Bartlett.

Ruskan, John. Emotional Clearing: A Self-Therapy Guide to Releasing Negative Feelings. 336p. (Orig.). 1993. pap. 11.95 (0-9629295-0-6) R Wyler & Co.

***Ruskay, Joseph A.** Leaves from a Family Tree. 1995. 16.95 (0-533-11399-7) Vantage.

Ruskay, Joseph A & Osserman, Richard A. Halfway to Tax Reform. LC 78-126216. 317p. reprint ed. pap. 90.40 (0-317-09331-2, 2055207) Bks Demand.

***Ruskay, Sophie.** Horse Cars & Cobblestones. (American Autobiography Ser.). 240p. 1995. reprint ed. lib. bdg. 79.00 (0-7812-8634-4) Rprt Serv.

Ruskin & Estes. WEESKA Project Management. (What Every Engineer Should Know Ser.: Vol. 9). 184p. 1982. 49.75 (0-8247-1718-X) Dekker.

Ruskin, Anna Marie, ed. see Roberts, Kenneth J.

***Ruskin, Arnold M. & Estes, W. Eugene.** What Every Engineer Should Know about Project Management. 2nd expanded rev. ed. LC 94-39689. (What Every Engineer Should Know Ser.: Vol. 33). 1994. 49.75 (0-8247-8953-9) Dekker.

Ruskin, Asa P., ed. Current Therapy in Psychiatry: Physical Medicine & Rehabilitation. (Illus.). 608p. 1984. text ed. 121.00 (0-7216-7853-X) Saunders.

Ruskin, Cindy. The Quilt: Stories from the Names Project. 1988. 22.95 (0-317-67839-6) PB.

Ruskin, Hillel. Leisure: Toward a Theory & Policy. LC 83-48608. 192p. 1984. 33.50 (0-8386-3134-7) Fairleigh Dickinson.

Ruskin, John. Art Criticism. Herbert, R. L., ed. 13.25 (0-8446-0694-4) Peter Smith.

— The Brantwood Diary of John Ruskin: Together with Selected Related Letters & Sketches of Persons Mentioned. Viljoen, Helen G., ed. LC 72-99844. 650p. reprint ed. pap. 180.00 (0-8357-7382-5, 2022049) Bks Demand.

— The Elements of Drawing. (Illus.). 228p. 1971. pap. 4.95 (0-486-22730-8) Dover.

— Elements of Drawing. (Illus.). 159p. 1989. pap. 24.95 (1-871569-33-8, Herbert Pr UK) New Amsterdam Bks.

— Elements of Drawing. LC 74-115264. 1970. reprint ed. 75.00 (0-403-00307-5) Scholarly.

— The Gulf of Years: Letters from John Ruskin to Kathleen Olander. LC 77-18837. 98p. 1978. reprint ed. text ed. 35.00 (0-313-20188-9, RUGY, Greenwood Pr) Greenwood.

— King of the Golden River. 15.95 (0-8488-0620-4) Amereon Ltd.

— The King of the Golden River. (Illus.). 64p. 1995. 9.95 (0-939218-09-7) Chapman Billies.

— The King of the Golden River or the Black Brother. LC 74-82199. (Illus.). viii, 56p. (J). (gr. 1 up). 1974. reprint ed. pap. 2.95 (0-486-20066-3) Dover.

— The Lamp of Beauty: Writings on Art. rev. ed. Evans, Joan, ed. (Arts & Letters Ser.). (Illus.). 424p. (C). 1995. pap. 14.95 (0-7148-3358-4, Pub. by Phaidon Press UK) Chronicle Bks.

— Mornings in Florence. 1994. lib. bdg. 21.95x (1-56849-424-6) Buccaneer Bks.

— Mornings in Florence: Being Simple Studies of Christian Art for English Travellers. LC 71-11568. 271p. 1972. reprint ed. 69.00 (0-403-00306-7) Scholarly.

— Munera Pulveris: Six Essays on the Elements of Political Economy. LC 69-14065. 218p. 1969. reprint ed. text ed. 35.00 (0-8371-0642-7, RUMP, Greenwood Pr) Greenwood.

— Poetry of Architecture. LC 74-148294. reprint ed. 29.50 (0-404-05463-3) AMS Pr.

— The Poetry of Architecture. LC 78-115265. (Illus.). 274p. 1972. reprint ed. 69.00 (0-403-00305-9) Scholarly.

— The Poetry of Architecture: Or, the Architecture of the Nations of Europe. 1972. 59.95 (0-8490-0859-X) Gordon Pr.

— Praeterita: The Autobiography of John Ruskin. 616p. 1978. pap. 17.95 (0-19-281253-X) OUP.

— Queen of the Air: A Study of Greek Myths. 1869. 20.00 (0-8196-1392-4) Biblo.

R

— Ruskin As Literary Critic. (BCL1-PR English Literature Ser.). 291p. 1992. reprint ed. lib. bdg. 79.00 (*0-7812-7633-0*) Rprt Serv.

— Ruskin as Literary Critic: Selections. Ball, A. H., ed. LC 69-14066. 291p. 1969. reprint ed. text ed. 59.75 (*0-8371-1149-8*, RULC, Greenwood Pr) Greenwood.

— Ruskin's Letters from Venice Eighteen Forty-One to Eighteen Fifty-Two. Bradley, John L., ed. LC 78-6260. (Yale Studies in English: Vol. 129). 330p. 1978. reprint ed. text ed. 38.50 (*0-313-20456-X*, RULE, Greenwood Pr) Greenwood.

— Selected Writings. 384p. 1992. 13.99 (*0-14-043355-4*, Penguin Classics) Viking Penguin.

— Selected Writings. Davis, Philip, ed. 360p. (Orig.). 1995. pap. 8.50 (*0-460-87460-8*, Everyman's Classic Lib) C E Tuttle.

— Selections & Essays. 1988. reprint ed. lib. bdg. 69.00 (*0-7812-0370-8*) Rprt Serv.

— Selections & Essays. Roe, Frederick W., ed. LC 77-145274. 1971. reprint ed. 69.00 (*0-403-01189-2*) Scholarly.

— Sesame & Lilies: The Two Paths & the King of the Golden River. LC 70-145275. (Illus.). 1971. reprint ed. 69.00 (*0-403-01190-6*) Scholarly.

— The Seven Lamps of Architecture. 1991. 20.25 (*0-8446-6469-3*) Peter Smith.

— Seven Lamps of Architecture. 1989. pap. 8.95 (*0-486-26145-X*) Dover.

— St. Mark's Rest, the History of Venice. (BCL1-PR English Literature Ser.). 236p. 1992. reprint ed. lib. bdg. 79.00 (*0-7812-7635-7*) Rprt Serv.

— The Stones of Venice. Moris, Jan, ed. (Illus.). 240p. 1989. 34.95 (*0-918825-13-X*) Moyer Bell.

— Stones of Venice. Links, J. G., ed. (Quality Paperbacks Ser.). 256p. 1985. reprint ed. pap. 10.95 (*0-306-80244-9*) Da Capo.

— Unto This Last: Four Essays on the First Principles of Political Economy. Hubenka, Lloyd J., ed. LC 67-12118. xlvi, 97p. 1967. pap. 7.95 (*0-8032-5165-3*, Bison Books) U of Nebr Pr.

— Unto This Last & Other Writings. Wilmer, Clive, ed. (Classics Ser.). 368p. 1986. pap. 9.95 (*0-14-043211-6*, Penguin Classics) Viking Penguin.

— Winnington Letters: John Ruskin's Correspondence with Margaret Alexis Bell & the Children at Winnington Hall. Burd, Van A., ed. LC 68-28692. (Illus.). 736p. 1969. 58.00 (*0-674-95365-7*) Belknap Pr.

— Works, 39 vols., Set. (BCL1-PR English Literature Ser.). 1992. reprint ed. lib. bdg. 3,510.00 (*0-7812-7632-2*) Rprt Serv.

Ruskin, John J. The Ruskin Family Letters: The Correspondence of John James Ruskin, His Wife, & Their Son, John, 1801-1843, 2 vols. Burd, Van A., ed. Incl. Vol. 1. 1801 to 1837. 1973. (*0-318-51449-4*); Vol. 2. 1837 to 1843. 1973. (*0-318-51450-8*); Vol. 1. 1801 to 1837. 1973. (*0-318-51449-4*); Vol. 2. 1837 to 1843. 1973. (*0-318-51450-8*); (Illus.). 792p. 1973. 95.00 (*0-8014-0725-7*) Cornell U Pr.

Ruskin, Mark. Speaking Up: What to Say to Your Boss & Everyone Else Who Gets on Your Case. 180p. 1993. pap. 7.95 (*1-55850-258-0*) Adams Pubng.

***Ruskin, Paul E. & Talbott, John A., eds.** Aging & Posttraumatic Stress Disorder. 288p. 1995. boxed 37.50 (*0-88048-513-2*, 8513) Am Psychiatric.

Ruskin, Robert, ed. see Ruskin, Thelma.

Ruskin, Robert S., jt. auth. see Johnson, Kent R.

Ruskin, Robert S., jt. auth. see Sherman, J. Gilmour.

Ruskin, Ronald, jt. ed. see Greben, Stanley E.

Ruskin, Thelma. Indians of the Tidewater Country: Of Maryland, Virginia, Delaware & North Carolina. Buchanan, Carol & Ruskin, Robert, eds. LC 85-73263. (Illus.). 132p. (J). (gr. 4-5). 1986. boxed 15.00 (*0-917882-20-2*) MD Hist Pr.

Ruskowski, Leo F. French Emigre Priests in the United States (1791-1815) LC 73-3586. (Catholic University of America. Studies in Romance Languages & Literatures: No. 32). reprint ed. 32.00 (*0-404-57782-2*) AMS Pr.

Rusling, Albert. The Criminal's Bumper Fun Book. (Illus.). 96p. 1992. pap. 2.95 (*0-86051-695-4*, Robson-Parkwest) Parkwest Pubns.

Rusling, J. F. Rusling Family. (Illus.). 160p. 1991. reprint ed. lib. bdg. 34.00 (*0-8328-1888-7*); reprint ed. pap. 24.00 (*0-8328-1889-5*) Higginson Bk Co.

***Rusmore, Jean.** Favorite Trips along the Bay Area Ridge Trail. 200p. (Orig.). 1995. pap. 12.95 (*0-89997-166-0*) Wilderness Pr.

Rusmore, Jean & Spangle, Frances. Peninsula Trails. 2nd ed. (Illus.). 274p. (Orig.). 1989. pap. 12.95 (*0-89997-097-4*) Wilderness Pr.

Rusmore, Jean, jt. auth. see Spangle, Frances.

***Rusnak, Paul D.** Revelation of God's Word. (Orig.). 1995. pap. 6.95 (*0-88270-684-5*) Bridge Pub.

Ruspantini, Anthony J., ed. see Spurgeon, Charles H.

Russ. Image Processing Handbook. 1992. 89.95 (*0-8493-4233-3*, PA1632) CRC Pr.

— Last Parallel. 1973. write for info. (*0-8371-6770-1*) Greenwood.

Russ, Adryan, ed. see Carroll, Alex.

Russ, Adryan, jt. auth. see Wallace, Arnie.

Russ, Biff & Van Duyn, Mona. Black Method: Poems. (Orig.). 1991. pap. 9.95 (*0-9627460-1-0*) Helicon Nine Eds.

Russ, Charles. The German Language Today: A Linguistic Introduction. LC 93-51009. 208p. 1994. 55.00x (*0-415-10438-6*, B2285, Routledge NY); pap. 24.95 (*0-415-10439-4*, B2289, Routledge NY) Routledge.

Russ, Charles, ed. The Dialects of Modern German: A Linguistic Survey. 496p. 1990. 62.50 (*0-8047-1547-5*) Stanford U Pr.

Russ, David J. The Complete Big Island of Hawaii Guidebook. (Hawaii Ser.). (Illus.). 144p. 1994. pap. 9.95 (*0-916841-39-1*) Indian Chief.

— Complete Big Island of Hawaii Guidebook. (Hawaii Ser.). (Illus.). 152p. 1995. pap. 9.95 (*0-916841-63-4*) Indian Chief.

— The Complete Kauai Guidebook: Discovering Hawaii's Garden Isle. (Hawaii Ser.). (Illus.). 152p. (Orig.). 1993. pap. 8.95 (*0-916841-25-1*) Indian Chief.

— Complete Maui, Molokai & Lanai Guidebook. 2nd ed. (Hawaii Ser.). (Illus.). 152p. 1994. pap. 9.95 (*0-916841-51-0*) Indian Chief.

— The Complete Maui, Molokai & Lanai Guidebook: Discovering Hawaii's Valley Isle. (Hawaii Ser.). (Illus.). 152p. (Orig.). 1993. pap. 8.95 (*0-916841-24-3*) Indian Chief.

— The Complete Oahu Guidebook. (Hawaii Ser.). (Illus.). 152p. (Orig.). 1994. pap. 9.95 (*0-916841-26-X*) Indian Chief.

Russ, Diane & Rogers, Shirle. The Beautiful Bernese Mountain Dog. LC 92-46693. (Illus.). 225p. 1993. text ed. 36.95 (*0-931866-55-3*) Alpine Pubns.

Russ, Esther. The Eternal Echo of Easter: A Choral Drama. 1980. 2.35 (*0-89536-423-9*, 0515) CSS OH.

Russ, Fred & Notturno, Francis. Effective Selling. 8th ed. 512p. (C). 1991. text ed. 53.95 (*0-538-19570-3*, S57) S-W Pub.

Russ, Harlow W. Project Alberta: The Preparation of Atomic Bombs for Use in World War II. (Illus.). 200p. (Orig.). 1990. pap. 34.95 (*0-944482-01-5*) Except Bks NM.

Russ, Hume R. How to Write Jokes (By the Numbers) in 20 Funny Lessons. (Illus.). 432p. (Orig.). 1991. pap. 22.00 (*0-9628231-0-4*) Fun-E-Prodns.

Russ, J. C. Computer-Assisted Microscopy: The Measurement & Analysis of Images. LC 89-70945. (Illus.). 465p. 1990. 65.00 (*0-306-43410-5*, Plenum Pr) Plenum.

***Russ, Jacqueline.** Dictionnaire de Philosophie. 383p. (FRE.). 1991. pap. 45.00 (*0-7859-7709-0*, 2040193014) Fr & Eur.

Russ, Joanna. The Female Man. LC 86-47511. 225p. 1987. reprint ed. pap. 11.00 (*0-8070-6313-4*, BP721) Beacon Pr.

— How to Suppress Women's Writing. LC 83-5910. 167p. (C). 1983. pap. 8.95 (*0-292-72445-4*) U of Tex Pr.

— To Write Like a Woman: Essays in Feminism & Science Fiction. LC 95-3576. 1995. write for info. (*0-253-32914-0*); pap. write for info. (*0-253-20983-8*) Ind U Pr.

Russ, John C. Computer Assisted Microscopy: The Measurement & Analysis of Images. LC 89-69855. (Illus.). 350p. (Orig.). (C). 1988. pap. text ed. 50.00 (*1-56049-006-3*) NCSU CE IES.

— Fractal Surfaces. LC 93-45023. (Illus.). 290p. (C). 1994. 55.00 (*0-306-44702-9*) Plenum.

— The Image Processing Handbook. 2nd ed. LC 94-27648. 696p. 1994. 89.95 (*0-8493-2516-1*, 2516) CRC Pr.

— Practical Stereology. 194p. 1986. 55.00 (*0-306-42460-6*, Plenum Pr) Plenum.

Russ Jones Production. Dracula. (Illus.). 160p. (Orig.). 1975. pap. 1.25 (*0-532-12356-5*) Kearny Pub.

Russ, Lawrence. The Burning-Ground. (Poetry Chapbook Ser.). 32p. (Orig.). 1981. pap. 4.00 (*0-937669-01-6*) Owl Creek Pr.

***Russ, Lee, et al.** Attorney's Medical Advisor-Atlas, 10 vols., Set. LC 94-60666. 1994. ring bd. 1,650.00 (*0-614-07290-5*) Clark Boardman Callaghan.

Russ, Martin. The Last Parallel. (Illus.). 448p. 1985. pap. 3.95 (*0-8217-1563-1*) Zebra.

Russ, Mel. Sea Angling: Kent to Cornwall. (Illus.). 208p. 1992. pap. 8.95 (*0-09-174244-7*, Pub. by S Paul UK) Trafalgar.

Russ, Michael. Musorgsky: "Pictures at an Exhibition" (Cambridge Music Handbooks Ser.). (Illus.). 150p. (C). 1992. 29.95 (*0-521-38442-7*); pap. 10.95 (*0-521-38607-1*) Cambridge U Pr.

Russ, Peter, jt. auth. see Rosenthal, Stephen.

Russ, Richard T. Jaguar V-12 E-Type: A Guide to Authenticity. (Illus.). 210p. 1991. 49.95 (*0-9629958-0-0*) Exec Twin Av.

Russ, Sandra. Affect & Creativity: The Role of Affect & Play in the Creative Process. (Spielberger: Personality Assessment Ser.). 160p. 1993. text ed. 36.00 (*0-8058-0986-4*) L Erlbaum Assocs.

Russ, Tony. Sheep Hunting in Alaska: The Dall Sheep Hunters' Guide. LC 93-86886. 160p. (Orig.). 1994. pap. text ed. 19.95 (*0-9639869-0-2*) Northern Pubns.

Russ, William A., Jr. The Hawaiian Republic, 1894-98: And Its Struggle to Win Annexation. LC 91-43886. 416p. 1993. reprint ed. 40.00 (*0-945636-44-X*); reprint ed. pap. 16.95 (*0-945636-52-0*) Susquehanna U Pr.

— The Hawaiian Revolution, 1893-94. LC 91-41517. 392p. 1993. reprint ed. 40.00 (*0-945636-43-1*); reprint ed. pap. 16.95 (*0-945636-53-9*) Susquehanna U Pr.

Russakoff, L. Mark, jt. auth. see Oldham, John M.

Russcol, Herbert. The Liberation of Sound: An Introduction to Electronic Music. LC 84-17649. (Music Reprint Ser.). 337p. 1987. reprint ed. 35.00 (*0-306-76263-3*) Da Capo.

Russcol, Herbert & Oehmich-Russcol, Nancy. The Hunting Season: Palestine 1945-1948. LC 88-19230. 256p. 1989. lib. bdg. 16.95 (*0-943247-05-5*) UCS Press.

Russe, Robin, ed. see Raby, William L., et al.

Russel. Understanding Bacterial Action. 1990. pap. write for info. (*0-318-68274-5*) P-H.

Russel, A. J., ed. Alternative Animals for Fibre Protection, No. EUR 14808. 118p. 1993. pap. 19.00 (*92-826-6299-3*, CH-NA-14808-EN-C, Pub. by Europ Com) UNIPUB.

***Russel, Charles & Crawford, Sharon.** Upgrading to Windows 95: Special Edition. deluxe ed. (SPA.). 1995. 22.99 (*0-7821-1703-1*) Sybex.

Russel, Charlie. Murphy's Laws of DOS. 2nd ed. LC 93-85947. 356p. 1993. pap. 16.99 (*0-7821-1424-5*) Sybex.

Russel, Charlie & Crawford, Sharon. Voodoo UNIX: Tips & Tricks with an Attitude. (Illus.). 410p. 1994. pap. 27.95 (*1-56604-067-1*) Ventana Pr.

Russel, Charlie, jt. auth. see Crawford, Sharon.

Russel, David, jt. auth. see Gondolf, Edward W.

Russel, George E. Collected Poems. 1988. reprint ed. lib. bdg. 59.00 (*0-7812-0480-1*) Rprt Serv.

Russel, George W. Collected Poems. LC 73-131821. 1970. reprint ed. 29.00 (*0-403-00708-9*) Scholarly.

Russel, Henry B. International Monetary Conferences: Their Purposes, Character & Results with a Study of the Conditions of Currency & Finance in Europe & America, Vol. 10. LC 74-359. 477p. 1974. reprint ed. 37.95 (*0-405-05920-5*) Ayer.

Russel, J. C. & Morse, William E. United States Navy in World War I with over 600 Photos. 1977. lib. bdg. 175.00 (*0-8490-2785-3*) Gordon Pr.

Russel, Jeffrey B. Witchcraft in the Middle Ages. (Illus.). 1976. pap. 5.95 (*0-8065-0504-4*, Citadel Pr) Carol Pub Group.

Russel, John, intro. Jennifer Bartlett: In the Garden. (Contemporary Artists Ser.). (Illus.). 208p. 1982. 45.00 (*0-8109-0709-7*) Abrams.

Russel, K. C. & Smith, D., eds. Physical Metallurgy of Controlled Expansion "Invar Type" Alloys. (Illus.). 400p. 1989. 20.00 (*0-87339-099-7*, 354) Minerals Metals.

Russel, K. W. & Pisa, Maria G. Agriculture, Libraries & Information. (C). 1992. text ed. 200.00 (*81-7233-034-0*, Pub. by Scientific Pubs II) St Mut.

Russel, Lauren. Advances on the AIDS Horizon. 3rd ed. 86p. 1989. pap. 9.95 (*0-942028-41-4*); student ed 18.97 (*0-942028-42-2*) R D Anderson.

Russel, Myra T., intro. James Joyce's Chamber Music: The Lost Song Settings. (Illus.). 144p. (C). 1993. pap. 19.95 (*0-253-34994-X*) Ind U Pr.

Russel, P., ed. see International Pigment Cell Conference Staff.

Russel, R. P., comp. Guide to Books on AIDS. (Illus.). 107p. (C). 1994. lib. bdg. 59.00 (*1-56072-179-0*) Nova Sci Pubs.

Russel, R. W., ed. Neurology. (Illus.). 336p. 1985. 30.00 (*0-8151-7473-X*, ICN-1, Yr Bk Med Pubs) Mosby Yr Bk.

Russel, Richard, tr. see Geber the Arabian.

Russel, Robert R. Critical Studies in Antebellum Sectionalism: Essays in American Political & Economic History. LC 78-105977. (Contributions in American History Ser.: No. 7). 223p. 1972. text ed. 49.95 (*0-8371-3304-1*, RAS/, Greenwood Pr) Greenwood.

Russel, Stuart J., ed. The Use of Knowledge in Analogy & Induction. 200p. (C). 1989. pap. text ed. 190.00 (*0-273-08814-9*, Pub. by Pitman Pubng UK) St Mut.

Russel, Terry, ed. Message from the President on the State of the Fur Trade 1824-1832. 130p. 1984. 16.95 (*0-87770-334-5*) Ye Galleon.

Russel, W. B., et al. Colloidal Dispersions. (Cambridge Monographs on Mechanics & Applied Mathematics). (Illus.). 525p. (C). 1992. pap. 42.95 (*0-521-42600-6*) Cambridge U Pr.

Russel, William B. The Dynamics of Collodial Systems: 1984 Olaf A. Hougen Lectures. LC 86-40060. (Illus.). 136p. 1986. text ed. 22.50 (*0-299-10530-X*) U of Wis Pr.

Russell. Ariane & Bluebeard (Adapted from the Opera) (Illus.). 1990. pap. 3.95 (*0-913035-71-8*) Eclipse Bks.

— Business Programming Logic & Design. (C). 1994. text ed. 37.50 (*0-673-46840-2*) HarpCollege.

— Food Preservatives. 1991. text ed. 110.00 (*0-442-30280-0*) Chapman & Hall.

— Genetics. 3rd ed. (C). 1991. text ed. 70.00 (*0-673-52143-5*) HarpCollege.

— Genetics. 3rd ed. (C). 1992. 21.50 (*0-673-52201-6*) HarpCollege.

— Genetics. 4th ed. (C). 1995. text ed. 47.50 (*0-673-52359-4*) HarpCollege.

— Interpersonal Is Between. 1939. pap. 34.95 (*0-685-65900-3*) Burgess MN Intl.

— Language & Behavior. 1993. pap. 34.95 (*0-685-65899-6*) Burgess MN Intl.

— Microbes & Temperature. 250p. 1992. text ed. write for info. (*0-13-580069-2*) P-H.

— Pic Puzzles. (MENSA Ser.). 1995. pap. 7.95 (*0-572-01889-4*, Pub. by Foulsham UK) Atrium Pubs.

— Rape in Marriage. 1982. 16.95 (*0-02-606190-2*) Macmillan.

— Recreation Leadership. (Illus.). 496p. (C). 1985. 34.95 (*0-8016-4244-2*) Mosby Yr Bk.

— Report on Radionics. 1995. pap. 17.95 (*0-85435-002-0*) Atrium Pubs.

— Robot Tactile Sensing. 270p. 1990. boxed 40.00 (*0-13-781592-1*) P-H.

— Santiago De Murcia's "Codice Saldivar Number 4" Vol. 1: A Treasury of Secular Guitar Music from Baroque. 1995. 59.95 (*0-252-02083-9*) U of Ill Pr.

— Shirley Valentine & One for the Road. 106p. 1988. pap. 9.95 (*0-413-18950-3*, A0335, Pub. by Methuen UK) Heinemann.

— Stress Management for Chronic Disorders. (Practitioner Guidebook Ser.). (C). 1988. 55.95 (*0-205-14472-1*, H4472, Longwood Div) Allyn.

— Topographic Anatomy - Athletic Injury Assessment. 1992. write for info. (*0-8493-4978-8*) CRC Pr.

— Women, Madness & Medicine. 1995. pap. (*0-7456-1261-X*) Blackwell Pubs.

Russell & Grant. Concepts in Physical Fitness: A Self-Paced Program to Improved Health Fitness. 208p. (C). 1991. spiral bd. 20.95 (*0-8403-6588-8*) Kendall-Hunt.

Russell & Nickerson, Robert C. Genetics. 3rd ed. (C). 1992. text ed. 55.75 (*0-673-52296-2*) HarpCollege.

Russell & Rubinstein. Pathology of Tumours of the Nervous System. 5th ed. 974p. 1989. 225.00 (*0-683-07462-8*) Williams & Wilkins.

Russell & Weinberg. Book of Knowledge. 1983. pap. 9.95 (*0-88125-035-X*) Ktav.

Russell, jt. auth. see Bozzola.

Russell, jt. auth. see Mozart.

Russell, jt. auth. see Thomas.

Russell, A., et al. Medical Microbiology at a Glance. 1994. pap. write for info. (*0-632-03691-5*) Blackwell Sci.

Russell, A. D., jt. auth. see Hugo, W. B.

Russell, A. D., et al. Principles & Practice of Disinfection, Preservation & Sterilization. (Illus.). 664p. 1982. text ed. 109.95 (*0-632-00547-5*, B 4228-0) Mosby Yr Bk.

Russell, A. D., et al, eds. Principles & Practice of Disinfection, Preservation & Sterilisation. 2nd ed. (Illus.). 652p. 1992. 155.00 (*0-632-02625-1*) Blackwell Sci.

Russell, A. Denver, jt. auth. see Andrew, Malcolm H.

Russell, A. E. Song & Its Fountains. 110p. 1991. reprint ed. pap. 10.95 (*0-943914-52-3*) Larson Pubns.

Russell, A. G. & Russell, Goldie. A. G. Russell's Knife Trader's Guide. Laidlaw, Angus, ed. 160p. (Orig.). 1991. pap. 10.00 (*0-943997-25-9*) P Wahl.

Russell, A. J. God at Eventide. large type ed. 1992. pap. 7.95 (*1-55748-231-4*) Barbour & Co.

— God Calling. 1989. pap. 4.95 (*1-55748-110-5*) Barbour & Co.

— God Calling. deluxe ed. (Barbour Bks.). 249p. 1986. 6.95 (*0-916441-45-8*) Barbour & Co.

— God Calling. (Christian Library). 1985. reprint ed. 7.99 (*0-916441-22-9*) Barbour & Co.

— God Calling God at Eventide. 1994. 12.97 (*1-55748-530-5*) Barbour & Co.

Russell, A. J., ed. God at Eventide. (Inspirational Library). 180p. 1992. pap. text ed. 4.95 (*1-55748-312-4*) Barbour & Co.

— God Calling. LC 72-78545. 192p. 1972. pap. 4.49 (*0-8007-8096-5*) Revell.

— God Calling. 208p. 1987. mass mkt. 4.99 (*0-515-09026-3*) Jove Pubns.

— God Calling. deluxe ed. 256p. 14.95 (*1-55748-072-9*, Christian Lib) Barbour & Co.

Russell, A. K. Liberal Landslide: The General Election of 1906. 260p. 1973. 79.50 (*0-208-01389-X*) Elliots Bks.

Russell, A. Lewis. Corporate & Industrial Security. LC 80-15789. (Illus.). 285p. reprint ed. pap. 81.30 (*0-685-23764-8*, 2032840) Bks Demand.

Russell, Addison P. Library Notes. rev. ed. LC 72-4599. (Essay Index Reprint Ser.). 1977. reprint ed. 24.95 (*0-8369-2971-3*) Ayer.

Russell, Alan. The Fat Innkeeper. 352p. 1995. 19.95 (*0-89296-539-8*) Mysterious Pr.

— The Fat Innkeeper. 1996. mass mkt. write for info. (*0-446-40349-0*, Mysterious Paperbk) Warner Bks.

— The Forest Prime Evil. 192p. 1992. 18.95 (*0-8027-3204-6*) Walker & Co.

— The Hotel Detective. 352p. 1994. 18.95 (*0-89296-538-X*) Mysterious Pr.

— The Hotel Detective. 304p. 1995. mass mkt. 5.50 (*0-446-40348-2*, Mysterious Paperbk) Warner Bks.

— No Sign of Murder. 240p. 1993. mass mkt. 4.99 (*0-380-71656-9*) Avon.

— No Sign of Murder. 192p. 1990. 17.95 (*0-8027-5767-7*) Walker & Co.

Russell, Alan, tr. see Flaubert, Gustave.

Russell, Alan K. Battle Tanks & Support Vehicles. LC 93-36814. (Greenhill Military Manuals Ser.). 160p. 1994. 19.95 (*1-85367-174-6*) Stackpole.

— Rivals of Sherlock Holmes. 1993. 8.98 (*1-55521-974-8*) Bk Sales Inc.

Russell, Alan M. The Biotechnology Revolution: An International Perspective. LC 87-35590. 278p. 1988. text ed. 49.95 (*0-312-01876-2*) St Martin.

Russell, Alanson E. & Russell, Joan M. The Seminary. 2nd ed. 128p. (Orig.). (C). 1987. pap. 12.95 (*0-9619115-0-6*) Seminary Pubn.

Russell, Alene B. & Trainor, Cynthia M. Trends in Child Abuse & Neglect: A National Perspective. (Orig.). 1984. pap. text ed. 15.00 (*0-930915-00-3*) Am Humane Assn.

Russell, Alice. Growth of Occupational Welfare in Britain. 300p. 1991. text ed. 63.95 (*1-85628-121-3*, Pub. by Avebury Pub UK) Ashgate Pub Co.

Russell, Allan M., jt. auth. see Gerhart, Mary.

Russell, Allen D. Of Ships & "Ceiling" Wax: Plymouth 1800-1850. (Pilgrim Society Notes Ser.: No. 15). 1965. 2.00 (*0-940628-44-9*) Pilgrim Soc.

— The Pilgrim Fort of Sixteen Twenty-Three. (Pilgrim Society Notes Ser.: No. 24). 1979. 2.00 (*0-940628-27-9*) Pilgrim Soc.

Russell, Allen S., tr. see Pachman, Ludek.

Russell, Alvin E., jt. auth. see Moore, Carl H.

Russell, Andrew J. Russell's Civil War Photographs: 115 Historic Prints. (Illus.). 128p. 1982. pap. 8.95 (*0-486-24283-8*) Dover.

— Russell's Union Pacific Railroad Photographs. (Illus.). 96p. 1995. pap. text ed. 9.95 (*0-486-28633-9*) Dover.

Russell, Andy. Canadian Cowboy: Stories of Cows, Cowboys, & Cayuses. 1994. 21.95 (*0-7710-7880-3*, Pub. by McClelland & Stewart CN) Firefly Bks Ltd.

— Grizzly Country. (Illus.). 1967. 19.95 (*0-394-42736-X*) Knopf.

— Grizzly Country. (Illus.). 320p. 1986. reprint ed. pap. 16.95 (*0-941130-12-6*) Lyons & Burford.

— Horns in the High Country. (Illus.). 288p. 1987. pap. 12.95 (*0-941130-30-4*) Lyons & Burford.

Russell, Andy, intro. Alberta on My Mind. (America on My Mind Ser.). (Illus.). 120p. 1990. 29.50 (*1-56044-028-7*) Falcon Pr MT.

An Asterisk (*) at the beginning of an entry indicates that the title is appearing in BIP for the first time.

R

Russell, Anita. Self-Esteem. Schulz, William, ed. (Options Ser.). 78p. (Orig.). (gr. 1-8). 1989. teacher ed, pap. 8.95 (*0-920541-51-8*) Peguis Pubs Ltd.

Russell, Anita, et al. Suicide. (Options Ser.). 102p. (gr. 1-8). 1989. teacher ed, pap. 8.95 (*0-920541-65-8*) Peguis Pubs Ltd.

Russell, Anita & Hill, Peter. Management of Swallowing & Tube Feeding in Adults: A Team Approach. 2nd ed. 138p. 1994. pap. 35.00 (*0-7506-9560-9*) Buttrwrth-Heinemann.

***Russell, Anne.** Daring Disciples: Embark on an Exciting Journey of Discovery Children's Journal. (1994 50-Day Spiritual Adventure Ser.). (Illus.). 64p. (Orig.). (J). (gr. 3-6). 1993. student ed, pap. text ed. 4.99 (*1-879050-16-1*) Chapel of Air.

— Discoveries in God's Family. (1992 50-Day Spiritual Adventure Ser.). (Illus.). 64p. (Orig.). (J). (gr. 3-6). 1991. student ed, pap. text ed. 4.95 (*1-879050-05-6*) Chapel of Air.

— Fear Busters: Join the Kids Courageous Rescue Team Children's Journal. (1995 50-Day Spiritual Adventure Ser.). (Illus.). 64p. (Orig.). (J). (gr. 3-6). 1994. student ed, pap. text ed. 4.95 (*1-879050-49-8*) Chapel of Air.

— Kids Courageous: Traveling the Path of True Winners. (1993 50-Day Spiritual Adventure Ser.). (Illus.). 64p. (Orig.). (J). (gr. 3-6). 1992. student ed, pap. text ed. 4.99 (*1-879050-09-9*) Chapel of Air.

Russell, Anne, ed. The Rover: Aphra Behn. 220p. 1994. pap. 11.95 (*1-55111-037-7*) Broadview Pr.

Russell, Archibald. A Span of Wings: An Autobiography. 202p. 1993. 36.00 (*1-56091-401-7*, R-132) Soc Auto Engineers.

Russell, Armand & Trubitt, Allen R. The Shaping of Musical Elements, Vol. 1. 410p. (C). 1992. pap. 33.00 (*0-02-872080-6*); pap. write for info. (*0-02-872201-9*); student ed, pap. 18.00 (*0-02-872090-3*) Schirmer Bks.

— The Shaping of Musical Elements, Vol. 2. 494p. (C). 1992. pap. 33.00 (*0-02-872120-9*); student ed, pap. 18.00 (*0-02-872200-0*) Schirmer Bks.

Russell, Arthur J. Their Religion. LC 78-128308. (Essay Index Reprint Ser.). 1977. 23.95 (*0-8369-2131-3*) Ayer.

Russell, B. La Philosophie De Leibniz. (Reimpressions G & B Ser.). 250p. 1971. pap. 460.00 (*0-685-47123-3*) Gordon & Breach.

Russell, B., et al. Why Work? Arguments for the Leisure Society. 1984. lib. bdg. 79.95 (*0-87700-644-X*) Revisionist Pr.

Russell, Barbara T. Last Left Standing. LC 94-16732. (J). 1995. 13.95 (*0-395-71037-5*) Ticknor & Flds Bks Yng Read.

Russell, Barry. Bankruptcy Evidence Manual. 850p. 1993. pap. text ed. write for info. (*0-314-02223-6*) West Pub.

— Bankruptcy Evidence Manual: 1994-1995 Edition. 1000p. 1994. pap. text ed. write for info. (*0-314-04509-0*) West Pub.

***Russell, Ben.** Laundries - Are They a Good Business to Get into? Answers to the Most Often-Asked Questions about the Self-Service Laundry Industry. LC 95-94298. 219p. (Orig.). 1995. 21.95 (*0-9645877-0-X*) Burnside Pub.

Russell, Bert. Calked Boots & Other Northwest Writings. 4th ed. (Folklore Ser.). 1979. 9.95 (*0-930344-03-0*); pap. 6.95 (*0-930344-00-6*) Lacon Pubs.

— Hardships & Happy Times. LC 78-75104. (Oral History Ser.: No. 1). 1982. 9.95 (*0-930344-04-9*); pap. 7.95 (*0-930344-01-4*) Lacon Pubs.

— North Fork of the Coeur d'Alene. (Oral History Ser.: No. 3). (Illus.). 448p. 1985. 12.95 (*0-930344-07-3*); pap. 9.95 (*0-930344-06-5*) Lacon Pubs.

— Swiftwater People. (Oral History Ser.: No. 2). 1979. 11.95 (*0-930344-05-7*); pap. 8.95 (*0-930344-02-2*) Lacon Pubs.

***Russell, Bert & Russell, Marie.** Rock Burst: Another Bert Russell Book. LC 94-77720. (Oral History Ser.: Bk. 4). (Illus.). 400p. (Orig.). Date not set. write for info. (*0-930344-10-3*) Lacon Pubs.

— Rock Burst: Another Bert Russell Book. LC 94-77720. (Oral History Ser.: Bk. 4). (Illus.). (Orig.). Date not set. pap. write for info. (*0-930344-11-1*) Lacon Pubs.

Russell, Bertrand. The Art of Philosophizing & Other Essays. (Quality Paperback Ser.: No. 273). 119p. 1977. reprint ed. pap. 9.95 (*0-8226-0273-3*) Littlefield.

— Atheism: Collected Essays, 1943-1949. LC 71-169217. (Atheist Viewpoint Ser.). 232p. 1976. reprint ed. 22.95 (*0-405-03808-9*) Ayer.

— Authority & the Individual. 2nd ed. (Unwin Paperbacks Ser.). 1985. pap. 9.95 (*0-04-170031-7*) Routledge Chapman & Hall.

— Autobiography of Bertrand Russell. (Unwin Paperbacks Ser.). 1978. pap. 16.95 (*0-04-921022-X*) Routledge Chapman & Hall.

— Autobiography of Bertrand Russell: Vol. 2, 1914-1944. 1968. 34.95 (*0-04-921009-2*) Routledge Chapman & Hall.

— Autobiography of Bertrand Russell: Vol. 3, 1944-1967. 232p. 1981. reprint ed. 34.95 (*0-04-921010-6*) Routledge Chapman & Hall.

— Basic Writings of Bertrand Russell. Egner, Robert E. & Dennon, Lester E., eds. (C). 1967. pap. 17.95 (*0-671-20154-9*, Touchstone Bks) S&S Trade.

— Bertrand Russell. Redpath, Ann, ed. (Living Philosophies Ser.). (Illus.). 32p. (YA). (gr. 9 up). 1986. lib. bdg. 12.95 (*0-88682-012-X*) Creative Ed.

— Bertrand Russell Speaks His Mind. LC 74-3626. (Illus.). 173p. 1974. reprint ed. text ed. 35.00 (*0-8371-7445-7*, RUBR, Greenwood Pr) Greenwood.

— Bertrand Russell's Best. Egner, Robert E., ed. (Orig.). 1958. pap. 3.95 (*0-451-62508-0*, ME2223, Ment) NAL-Dutton.

— Bolshevism: Practice & Theory. LC 72-4296. (World Affairs Ser.: National & International Viewpoints). 192p. 1979. reprint ed. 19.95 (*0-405-04587-5*) Ayer.

— Cambridge Essays 1888-1889, Vol. 1. Blackwell, Kenneth et al, eds. (Collected Papers of Bertrand Russell). 588p. 1988. text ed. 130.00 (*0-04-920067-4*, A9409) Routledge Chapman & Hall.

— Conquest of Happiness. 1971. pap. 9.95 (*0-87140-244-0*) Liveright.

— The Conquest of Happiness. 256p. 1995. pap. 11.00 (*0-87140-162-2*) Liveright.

— La Conquista de la Felicidad. (Nueva Austral Ser.: Vol. 189). (SPA.). 1991. pap. text ed. 24.95x (*84-239-1989-7*) Elliots Bks.

— Diccionario del Hombre Contemporaneo. (SPA.). pap. 17.50 (*0-686-56655-6*) Fr & Eur.

— Essays on Language, Mind & Matter, 1919-1926X, Vol. 9. Frohmann, Bernd & Slater, John G., eds. (Collected Papers of Bertrand Russell). 704p. 1988. text ed. 150.00 (*0-04-920075-5*, A9417) Routledge Chapman & Hall.

— Fact & Fiction. 288p. 1994. pap. 13.95 (*0-415-11461-6*, B4554) Routledge.

— Foundations of Logic: 1903-05. Urquhart, Alasdair & Lewis, Albert C., eds. LC 93-5603. 1994. write for info. (*0-415-09406-2*, Routledge NY) Routledge.

— Has Man a Future? LC 84-12766. 128p. 1984. reprint ed. text ed. 38.50 (*0-313-24382-4*, RHMF, Greenwood Pr) Greenwood.

— A History of Western Philosophy. (Counterpoint Ser.). 848p. (C). 1984. pap. 8.95 (*0-04-100045-5*) S&S Trade.

— History of Western Philosophy. 1967. pap. 22.00 (*0-671-20158-1*) S&S Trade.

— Human Knowledge. 540p. 1994. pap. 22.95 (*0-415-08302-8*, B4573) Routledge.

— Impact of Science on Society. LC 68-54290. reprint ed. 20.00 (*0-404-05466-8*) AMS Pr.

— In Praise of Idleness & Other Essays. (Unwin Paperbacks Ser.). 231p. 1981. reprint ed. pap. 7.95 (*0-04-304006-3*) Routledge Chapman & Hall.

— Inquiry into Meaning & Truth. (Unwin Paperbacks Ser.). (Orig.). 1980. pap. 7.95 (*0-04-121019-0*) Routledge Chapman & Hall.

— Introduction to Mathematical Philosophy. LC 93-21477. xx, 208p. 1993. reprint ed. pap. text ed. 6.95 (*0-486-27724-0*) Dover.

— Introduction to Mathematical Philosophy. 208p. 1993. reprint ed. pap. 15.95 (*0-415-09604-9*, B0413) Routledge.

— Justice in Wartime. LC 73-18081. (English Literature Ser.: No. 33). 1974. 75.00 (*0-8383-1738-3*) M S G Haskell Hse.

— Logic & Knowledge: Essays, Nineteen Hundred One to Nineteen Fifty. Marsh, Robert C., ed. 392p. 1988. pap. text ed. 21.95 (*0-04-440260-0*) Routledge Chapman & Hall.

— Logical & Philosophical Papers, 1909-1913. Slater, John G. & Frohmann, Bernd, eds. LC 92-2380. (Collected Papers of Bertrand Russell: Vol. 6). 1993. 185.00 (*0-415-08446-6*, A9414) Routledge.

— Marriage & Morals. LC 70-114377. 1970. pap. 11.95 (*0-87140-211-4*) Liveright.

— My Philosophical Development. (Unwin Paperbacks Ser.). 1975. pap. 9.95 (*0-04-192030-9*) Routledge Chapman & Hall.

— Our Knowledge of the External World: As a Field for Scientific Method in Philosophy. LC 93-16365. 256p. 1993. reprint ed. pap. 15.95 (*0-415-09605-7*, B0417) Routledge.

— Philosophical Essays. LC 94-5628. 1994. reprint ed. write for info. (*0-415-10579-X*) Routledge.

— The Philosophy of Leibniz. 2nd ed. 200p. 1989. 27.50 (*0-89341-548-0*, Longwood Academic) Hollowbrook.

— The Philosophy of Leibniz. 3rd ed. 352p. 1993. pap. 19.95 (*0-415-08296-X*, B0541) Routledge.

— The Philosophy of Logical Atomism. LC 85-18750. 192p. (C). 1985. pap. 8.00 (*0-87548-443-3*) Open Court.

— The Philosophy of Logical Atomism & Other Essays, 1914-1919. Slater, John G., ed. (Collected Papers of Bertrand Russell: Vol. 8). 418p. 1988. text ed. 125.00 (*0-04-920074-7*, A9416) Routledge Chapman & Hall.

— Political Ideals. (Unwin Paperbacks Ser.). 1980. reprint ed. pap. 9.95 (*0-04-320120-2*) Routledge Chapman & Hall.

— Power: A New Social Analysis. 208p. 1993. pap. 10.95 (*0-415-09456-9*, B2534) Routledge.

— The Principles of Mathematics. (Illus.). 576p. 1995. pap. 17.95 (*0-393-31404-9*) Norton.

— The Problem of China. 266p. 1993. reprint ed. 87.50 (*0-85124-552-8*, Pub. by Spokesman Bks UK); reprint ed. pap. 34.00 (*0-85124-553-6*, Pub. by Spokesman Bks UK) Coronet Bks.

— The Problems of Philosophy. (Great Books in Philosophy). 161p. (C). 1988. pap. text ed. 8.95 (*0-87975-497-4*) Prometheus Bks.

— Problems of Philosophy. 1959. reprint ed. pap. 7.95 (*0-19-500212-1*) OUP.

— The Problems of Philosophy. LC 90-81389. (HPC Classics Ser.). 168p. (C). 1990. reprint ed. lib. bdg. 21.50 (*0-87220-099-X*); reprint ed. pap. text ed. 5.95 (*0-87220-098-1*) Hackett Pub.

— Religion & Science. 1961. reprint ed. pap. 10.95 (*0-19-500228-8*) OUP.

— Roads to Freedom: Socialism, Anarchism & Syndication. (Unwin Paperbacks Ser.). 1966. pap. 9.95 (*0-04-335033-X*) Routledge Chapman & Hall.

— Sceptical Essays. (Unwin Paperbacks Ser.). 1960. pap. 19.95 (*0-04-104003-1*) Routledge Chapman & Hall.

— Theory of Knowledge: The 1913 Manuscript. Eames, Elizabeth R. & Blackwell, Kenneth, eds. 264p. 1992. pap. 16.95 (*0-415-08298-6*, A7942) Routledge.

— Toward the Principles of Mathematics 1900-1902. Moore, Gregory H., ed. LC 93-3505. (Collected Papers of Bertrand Russell: Vol. 3). 960p. 1993. 149.95 (*0-415-09405-4*, A9411) Routledge.

— Why I Am Not a Christian & Other Essays on Religion & Related Subjects. (C). 1967. pap. 9.95 (*0-671-20323-1*, Touchstone Bks) S&S Trade.

— Why Men Fight: A Method of Abolishing the International Duel. LC 72-164623. (Select Bibliographies Reprint Ser.). 1977. reprint ed. 23.95 (*0-8369-5906-X*) Ayer.

— Wisdom of the West. 1989. 17.99 (*0-517-69041-1*) Random Hse Value.

Russell, Bertrand, jt. auth. see Nearing, Scott.

Russell, Bertrand, jt. auth. see Whitehead, Alfred N.

Russell, Bertrand, et al. If I Could Preach Just Once. LC 73-167364. (Essay Index Reprint Ser.). 1977. reprint ed. 19.95 (*0-8369-2457-6*) Ayer.

Russell, Bertrand R. War Crimes in Vietnam. LC 67-23969. 178p. reprint ed. pap. 50.80 (*0-317-08492-5*, 2001708) Bks Demand.

Russell, Beth. Beth Russell's Traditional Needlepoint. LC 92-17581. (Illus.). 128p. 1992. 25.00 (*0-89577-446-1*, Random) RD Assn.

Russell, Betty G. Silent Sisters: An Ethnography of Homeless Women. (Health Care for Women International Publication). 160p. 1991. 29.00 (*1-56032-098-2*) Hemisp Pub.

Russell, Beverly. Architecture & Design, 1970-1990: New Ideas in America. (Illus.). 144p. 1989. 29.95 (*0-685-28261-9*) Abrams.

— Women of Design: Contemporary American Interiors. LC 92-8177. (Illus.). 224p. 1992. 50.00 (*0-8478-1614-1*) Rizzoli Intl.

— 40 under 40: Seductive Ideas for Living by Design Leaders of the New Millennium. (Illus.). 223p. 1995. pap. 34.99 (*1-883065-05-4*) Vitae Pub.

Russell, Bill & Branch, Taylor. Second Wind. 1980. pap. 2.75 (*0-345-28897-1*) Ballantine.

***Russell, Bob.** Find Us Faithful. Underwood, J., ed. 160p. (Orig.). 1995. pap. 6.99 (*0-7847-0307-8*, 11-40307) Standard Pub.

— God Does Immeasurably More. Underwood, Jonathan, ed. 160p. (Orig.). 1991. pap. 5.99 (*0-87403-784-0*, 11-39954) Standard Pub.

— God's Message for a Growing Church. 160p. 1990. pap. 7.99 (*0-87403-665-8*, 18-03195) Standard Pub.

— Marriage by the Book: Biblical Models for Marriage Today. 112p. (Orig.). (YA). 1992. pap. 6.99 (*0-87403-906-1*, 29-03156) Standard Pub.

— Take Comfort: Encouraging Words from Second Corinthians. 240p. (Orig.). 1991. pap. 10.99 (*0-87403-844-8*, 18-03154) Standard Pub.

— Touching the Face of God. LC 91-77441. 224p. 1991. 16.99 (*1-56384-015-4*); pap. 8.99 (*1-56384-010-3*) Huntington Hse.

— When Life's a Zoo: God Still Loves You. Underwood, Jonathan, ed. 160p. (Orig.). (YA). 1993. pap. 5.99 (*0-7847-0078-8*, 11-39958) Standard Pub.

Russell, Bob, jt. auth. see Collison, Linda.

Russell, Brian. Introduction to Seismic Inversion Methods. (Course Notes Ser.: No. 2). 90p. (Orig.). 1988. pap. text ed. 20.00 (*0-931830-65-6*, 457) Soc Expl Geophys.

Russell, Bruce, ed. Freedom, Rights & Pornography: A Collection of Papers by Fred R. Berger. (Philosophical Studies in Philosophy Ser.). (C). 1990. lib. bdg. 89.00 (*0-7923-1034-9*) Kluwer Ac.

Russell, Bruce, jt. auth. see Magoldi, Mary.

Russell, Bruce, ed. see Magoldi, Mary.

Russell, Byron A. It Was Like This. LC 87-71286. (Illus.). 240p. 1987. pap. 11.95 (*0-931170-33-8*) Ctr Western Studies.

Russell, C. H. AIDS in America. xi, 147p. 1991. 54.00 (*0-387-97462-8*) Spr-Verlag.

Russell, C. H. & Meggaard, I. The General Social Survey, 1972-1986. (Recent Research in Psychology Ser.). xxix, 228p. 1990. pap. 48.00 (*0-387-96746-X*) Spr-Verlag.

Russell, C. R. Reactor Safeguards. 1962. 169.00 (*0-08-009706-5*, Pub. by Pergamon Repr UK) Franklin.

Russell, C. T. Venus Aeronomy. (C). 1991. lib. bdg. 212.50 (*0-7923-1091-8*) Kluwer Ac.

Russell, C. T., ed. Active Experiments in Space Plasmas. (Advances in Space Research Ser.: Vol. 1, No. 2). (Illus.). 468p. 1981. pap. 72.00 (*0-08-027158-8*, Pergamon Pr) Elsevier.

— The Galileo Mission. LC 92-9943. 600p. (C). 1992. lib. bdg. 244.00 (*0-7923-1719-X*) Kluwer Ac.

— The Global Geospace Mission. LC 95-13. 1995. lib. bdg. 349.00 (*0-7923-3384-5*) Kluwer Ac.

— The Magnetosheath: Proceedings of the Topical Meeting of the COSPAR Interdisciplinary Scientific Commission D (Meeting D6) of the COSPAR 29th Plenary Meeting held in Washington, DC, 28 August-5 September, 1992. (Advances in Space Research Ser.: Vol. 14). (Illus.). 136p. 1994. pap. 165.00 (*0-08-042484-8*) Elsevier.

— Multipoint Magnetospheric Measurements: Proceedings of Symposium 8 of the COSPAR Twenty-Seventh Plenary Meeting Held in Espoo, Finland, 18-29 July 1988. (Advances in Space Research Ser.: No. 8). (Illus.). 472p. 1989. pap. 170.00 (*0-08-037373-9*, Pergamon Pr) Elsevier.

— Physics of Collisionless Shocks. (Advances in Space Research (RJ) Ser.: Vol. 15). 543p. 1995. pap. 190.00 (*0-08-042558-5*, Pergamon Pr) Elsevier.

— Physics of Magnetic Flux Ropes. (Geophysical Monograph Ser.: Vol. 58). 752p. 1990. 60.00 (*0-87590-026-7*) Am Geophysical.

Russell, C. T., jt. ed. see Southwood, D. J.

Russell, C. V. & Willig, P. L. German Tests Without Translation. 1978. pap. text ed. 3.70 (*0-08-022868-2*, Pergamon Pr) Elsevier.

Russell, C. W. Income Taxation of Natural Resources, 1993. 800p. 1992. text ed. 95.00 (*0-7811-0066-6*) Res Inst Am.

Russell, C. W. & Marwick, Peat. Income Taxation of Natural Resources, 1994. rev. ed. 800p. 1993. text ed. 92.00 (*0-7811-0082-8*) Res Inst Am.

Russell, C. W., jt. auth. see KPMG Peat Marwick Staff.

Russell, Carl P. Firearms, Traps & Tools of the Mountain Men. LC 77-81984. (Illus.). 470p. 1977. reprint ed. pap. 16.95 (*0-8263-0465-6*) U of NM Pr.

— One Hundred Years in Yosemite. rev. ed. (High Sierra Classics Ser.). 250p. 1992. pap. 9.95 (*0-939666-60-X*) Yosemite Assn.

***Russell, Carol A.** Silver Dollar. 68p. (Orig.). 1995. pap. 8.95 (*0-931122-81-3*) West End.

Russell, Carol K. The Tapestry Handbook. Taylor, Carol, ed. (Illus.). 180p. 1990. 26.95 (*0-937274-54-2*) Lark Books.

Russell, CarolAnn. Feast. (Illus.). 58p. (Orig.). 1993. pap. 9.95 (*0-926147-04-8*) Loonfeather.

— The Red Envelope. LC 85-9163. (University of Central Florida Contemporary Poetry Ser.). 94p. (Orig.). 1985. pap. 10.95 (*0-8130-0828-X*) U Press Fla.

Russell, Carroll, jt. auth. see Horst, Louis.

Russell, Catherine. Narrative Mortality: Death, Closure & New Wave Cinemas. 1994. text ed. 44.95 (*0-8166-2485-2*) U of Minn Pr.

Russell, Charles. Five on the Black Hand Side: A Play. LC 73-82643. (Illus.). 96p. 1973. 15.95 (*0-89388-092-2*) Okpaku Communications.

— The Improvement of the City Elementary School Teacher in Service. LC 78-177216. (Columbia University. Teachers College. Contributions to Education Ser.: No. 128). reprint ed. 37.50 (*0-404-55128-9*) AMS Pr.

Russell, Charles, ed. The Avant-Garde Today: An International Anthology. LC 80-23922. 286p. 1981. 29.95 (*0-252-00851-0*) U of Ill Pr.

Russell, Charles, jt. auth. see Roy, F. Hampton.

Russell, Charles C. The Don Juan Legend Before Mozart: With a Collection of Eighteenth-Century Opera Librettos. 500p. 1993. text ed. 65.00 (*0-472-10413-6*) U of Mich Pr.

Russell, Charles E. American Orchestra & Theodore Thomas. LC 76-139146. (Illus.). 344p. (C). 1971. reprint ed. text ed. 59.75 (*0-8371-5762-5*, RUAO, Greenwood Pr) Greenwood.

— The American Orchestra & Theodore Thomas. 344p. 1990. reprint ed. lib. bdg. 79.00 (*0-7812-9116-X*) Rprt Serv.

— Charlemagne: First of the Moderns. 1972. 250.00 (*0-87968-837-8*) Gordon Pr.

— The Greatest Trust in the World. McCurry, Dan C. & Rubenstein, Richard E., eds. LC 74-30650. (American Farmers & the Rise of Agribusiness Ser.). 1975. reprint ed. 25.95 (*0-405-06822-0*) Ayer.

— Haym Salomon & the Revolution. LC 77-114892. (Select Bibliographies Reprint Ser.). 1977. 24.95 (*0-8369-5296-0*) Ayer.

— Haym Salomon & the Revolution. 1993. reprint ed. lib. bdg. 89.00 (*0-7812-5827-8*) Rprt Serv.

— The Story of the Nonpartisan League: A Chapter in American Evolution. McCurry, Dan C. & Rubenstein, Richard E., eds. LC 74-30651. (American Farmers & the Rise of Agribusiness Ser.). (Illus.). 1975. reprint ed. 35.95 (*0-405-06823-9*) Ayer.

— Thomas Chatterton. LC 70-130258. (English Literature Ser.: No. 33). 1970. reprint ed. lib. bdg. 62.95 (*0-8383-1162-8*) M S G Haskell Hse.

***Russell, Charles H.** Good News about Aging. pap. text ed. write for info. (*0-471-61687-7*) Wiley.

— Good News about Aging in America. 228p. 1989. text ed. 19.95 (*0-471-61686-9*) Wiley.

Russell, Charles M. Paintings & Sketches. (Illus.). (Orig.). Date not set. pap. write for info. (*1-56944-041-7*) Terrell Missouri.

Russell, Charles M., jt. auth. see Linderman, Frank B.

Russell, Charles T. The Finished Mystery. (Studies in the Scriptures Ser.: Vol. VII). 608p. 1985. reprint ed. pap. 7.95 (*1-883858-28-3*) Witness CA.

Russell, Charles W. The Memoirs of Colonel John S. Mosby. 414p. 1987. reprint ed. 35.00 (*0-942211-27-8*) Olde Soldier Bks.

Russell, Charles W. & Bowhay, Robert W. Income Taxation of Natural Resources. 920p. 1988. 41.50 (*0-13-453689-4*, Busn) P-H.

Russell, Charles W., ed. see Mosby, John S.

Russell, Cheryl. Color: A Thematic Unit. (Thematic Units Ser.). (Illus.). 80p. 1993. student ed 8.95 (*1-55734-279-2*) Tchr Create Mat.

— The Master Trend: How the Baby Boom Generation Is Remaking America. 280p. 1993. 23.95 (*0-306-44507-7*, Plenum Pr) Plenum.

— The Official Guide to the American Marketplace. 2nd ed. 480p. 1995. 79.95 (*0-9628092-4-1*) New Strategist.

— One Hundred Predictions for the Baby Boom: The Next Fifty Years. 238p. 1987. 17.95 (*0-306-42527-0*, Plenum Pr) Plenum.

Russell, Cheryl & Ambry, Margaret. The Official Guide to American Incomes. 350p. 1993. 69.95 (*0-9628092-2-5*) New Strategist.

Russell, Cheryl, jt. auth. see Ambry, Margaret.

Russell, Ching Y. A Day on a Shrimp Boat. Littlejohn, Beth, ed. (Illus.). 57p. (J). (gr. 3-6). 1993. 12.95 (*0-87844-120-4*) Sandlapper Pub Co.

— First Apple. LC 93-74360. (Illus.). 128p. (J). (gr. 2-5). 1994. 13.95 (*1-56397-206-9*) Boyds Mills Pr.

***Russell, Christina.** Water Ghost. LC 94-74534. (Illus.). 192p. (J). (gr. 3-7). 1995. 14.95 (*1-56397-413-4*, Wordsong) Boyds Mills Pr.

Russell, Christopher T., jt. ed. see Kivelson, Margaret G.

***Russell, Claire.** Glimpses of the Fathers. 550p. 1995. 14.95 (*0-906138-37-X*) Scepter Pubs.

Russell, Clifford B., et al. Enforcing Pollution Control Laws. LC 85-43554. 231p. 1986. text ed. 25.00 (*0-915707-25-X*) Resources Future.

R

An Asterisk (*) at the beginning of an entry indicates that the title is appearing in BIP for the first time.

Russell, Clifford S. Residuals Management in Industry: A Case Study of Petroleum Refining. LC 72-12367. (Resources for the Future Ser.). (Illus.). 208p. 1973. 18.00 (0-8018-1497-9) Johns Hopkins.

— Residuals Management in Industry: A Case Study of Petroleum Refining. LC 72-12367. (Illus.). 211p. reprint ed. pap. 60.20 (0-685-23707-9, 2032163) Bks Demand.

Russell, Clifford S., ed. Collective Decision Making: Applications from Public Choice Theory. LC 79-16614. 296p. 1979. 26.00 (0-8018-2320-X) Resources Future.

— Ecological Modeling in a Resource Management Framework: The Proceedings of a Symposium. LC 75-15108. (Resources for the Future, RFF Working Papers: QE-1). 406p. reprint ed. pap. 115.80 (0-317-26478-8, 2023813) Bks Demand.

— Safe Drinking Water; Current & Future Problems: Proceedings of a Natonal Conference in Washngton D. C. LC 78-19840. (Resources for the Future Research Paper). 1978. pap. 30.00 (0-8018-2181-9) Johns Hopkins.

Russell, Clifford S. & Nicholson, Norman K., eds. Public Choice & Rural Development. LC 80-8775. (Resources for the Future Research Paper: R-21). (Illus.). 312p. 1981. pap. text ed. 15.00 (0-8018-2600-4) Johns Hopkins.

Russell, Clifford S. & Shogren, Jason F., eds. Theory, Modeling, & Experience in the Management of Nonpoint-Source Pollution. LC 92-36253. 368p. 1993. lib. bdg. 105.00 (0-7923-9307-4) Kluwer Ac.

Russell, Clifford S. & Vaughan, William J. Steel Production, Processes, Products, & Residuals. LC 75-36945. 328p. 1976. 26.50 (0-8018-1824-9) Resources Future.

Russell, Clifford S., jt. auth. see Kindler, Janusz.

Russell, Clifford S., jt. auth. see Vaughan, William J.

Russell, Clifford S., et al. Drought & Water Supply: Implications of the Massachusetts Experience for Municipal Planning. LC 72-123861. 232p. 1970. 21.00 (0-8018-1183-X) Resources Future.

Russell, Colin A. Cross-Currents: Interactions Between Science & Faith. LC 85-10199. 272p. reprint ed. pap. 77.60 (0-685-23460-6, 2032745) Bks Demand.

— Lancastrian Chemist: The Early Years of Sir Edward Frankland. 192p. 1986. 69.00 (0-335-15175-2, Open Univ Pr) Taylor & Francis.

Russell, Conrad. Academic Freedom. LC 92-30810. 128p. 1993. 49.95 (0-415-03714-X, B0289); pap. 14.95 (0-415-03715-8, B0409) Routledge.

— The Causes of the English Civil War. 256p. 1990. pap. 17.95 (0-19-822141-X) OUP.

— The Crisis of Parliaments: English History, 1509-1660. (Short Oxford History of the Modern World Ser.). 464p. 1971. reprint ed. text ed. 16.95 (0-19-913034-5) OUP.

— The Fall of the British Monarchies 1637-1642. 576p. 1991. 89.00 (0-19-822754-X) OUP.

— The Fall of the British Monarchies 1637-1642. 576p. 1995. pap. 24.00 (0-19-820588-0) OUP.

— Unrevolutionary England, 1603-42. 343p. 1990. boxed 60.00 (1-85285-025-6) Hambledon Press.

Russell County Historical Commission, comp. History of Russell County, Alabama, Vol. I. (Illus.). 381p. 1982. 53.00 (0-88107-002-5) Curtis Media.

Russell, D. The Principles of Computer Networking. (Cambridge Computer Science Texts Ser.). (C). 1990. pap. 37.95 (0-521-33992-8) Cambridge U Pr.

Russell, D., ed. Gas Phase Inorganic Chemistry. (Modern Inorganic Chemistry Ser.). (Illus.). 402p. 1989. 95.00 (0-306-42972-1, Plenum Pr) Plenum.

Russell, D. A. Greek Declamation. LC 83-7270. 148p. 1984. 44.95 (0-521-25780-8) Cambridge U Pr.

Russell, D. A., comp. An Anthology of Greek Prose. 328p. 1991. pap. 22.95 (0-19-872122-6) OUP.

Russell, D. A., comp. & intro. An Anthology of Latin Prose. 288p. 1990. 69.00 (0-19-814746-5); pap. 22.95 (0-19-872121-8) OUP.

Russell, D. A., ed. Antonine Literature. 256p. 1990. 55.00 (0-19-814057-6) OUP.

Russell, D. A., ed. see Chrysostomus, Dio.

Russell, D. G., jt. auth. see Matthews, C. S.

Russell, D. H., ed. Experimental Mass Spectroscopy. 1994. 79.50 (0-306-44457-7, Plenum Pr) Plenum.

Russell, D. S. Between the Testaments. LC 77-74742. 182p. 1960. pap. 10.00 (0-8006-1856-4, 1-1856, Fortress Pr) Augsburg Fortress.

— Daniel: An Active Volcano Reflections on the Book of Daniel. 144p. 1993. pap. 22.00 (0-7152-0632-X) St Mut.

— Divine Disclosure: An Introduction to Jewish Apocalyptic. LC 92-9523. 186p. 1992. 11.00 (0-8006-2698-2, 1-2698) Augsburg Fortress.

— The Jews from Alexander to Herod. 1973. pap. 15.95 (0-19-836913-1) OUP.

— Method & Message of Jewish Apocalyptic. LC 64-18683. (Old Testament Library). 464p. 1964. 26.00 (0-664-20543-7, Westminster) Westminster John Knox.

— Poles Apart: The Gospel in Creative Tension. 160p. (Orig.). 1993. text ed. 22.00 (0-7152-0646-X, Pub. by St Andrew UK) St Mut.

Russell, D. S., ed. Poles Apart: The Gospel in Creative Tension. 160p. (Orig.). (C). 1991. pap. text ed. 59.00 (86-15-30646-X, Pub. by St Andrew UK) St Mut.

Russell, D. W. Engineered Software Systems: Proceedingss of the International Sym. 284p. 1993. text ed. 95.00 (981-02-1549-5) World Scientific Pub.

Russell, Dale. Colour in Industrial Design. (Illus.). 96p. (C). 1991. pap. 16.95x (0-85072-283-7, Pub. by Design Council Bks UK) Ashgate Pub Co.

— Hell Above, Deep Water Below. 210p. 1995. text ed. 24.95 (0-9643849-9-X) D Russell.

Russell, Dale A. An Odyssey in Time: The Dinosaurs of North America. (Illus.). 256p. 1992. pap. 24.95 (0-8020-7718-8) U of Toronto Pr.

Russell, Dale A. & Acorn, John. The Tiny Perfect Dinosaur Book, Bones, Egg & Poster: Presenting Leptoceratops. (Illus.). 32p. (Orig.). (J). 1991. pap. 10.95 (0-8362-4213-0) Andrews & McMeel.

— The Tiny Perfect Dinosaur Book, Bones, Egg, & Poster: Presenting Tyrannosaurus Rex. (Illus.). 32p. (J). 1993. pap. 12.95 (0-8362-4216-5) Andrews & McMeel.

— The Tiny Perfect Dinosaur Book, Bones, Egg & Poster Kits: Presenting Brachiosaurus. (J). 1994. pap. 12.95 (0-8362-4234-3) Andrews & McMeel.

***Russell, Dale A. & Glossup, Jennifer.** The Tiny Perfect Dinosaur Book, Bones, Egg, & Poster: Stegosaurus. (Illus.). 32p. (J). 1995. pap. 12.95 (0-8362-0646-0) Andrews & McMeel.

Russell, Dale R. Eighteenth-Century Western Cree & Their Neighbors. (Canadian Museum of Civilization Mercury Ser.). x, 238p. 1992. pap. 20.95 (0-660-12915-9) U Ch Pr.

Russell, Dan. Florida's Free Attractions: See Hundreds of Free Attractions. LC 90-85373. (Illus.). 68p. (Orig.). 1991. pap. 12.95 (0-9628352-0-X) FL Free Attractions.

— Jack Russell & His Terriers. 112p. 1990. pap. 21.00 (0-85131-276-4, Pub. by J A Allen & Co UK) St Mut.

***Russell, Daniel.** Emblematic Structures in Renaissance French Culture. (Romance Ser.). (Illus.). 352p. 1995. 75.00 (0-8020-0616-7) U of Toronto Pr.

Russell, Daniel, jt. ed. see Daly, Peter M.

Russell, Daniel M. Political Organizing in Grassroots Politics. LC 89-22757. 170p. (Orig.). (C). 1990. lib. bdg. 39.00 (0-8191-7618-4); pap. text ed. 22.50 (0-8191-7619-2) U Pr of Amer.

Russell, Daniel S. The Emblem & Device in France. LC 85-80418. (French Forum Monographs: No. 59). (Illus.). 245p. (Orig.). 1985. pap. 17.95 (0-917058-60-7) French Forum.

Russell, Daniel S., jt. ed. see Daly, Peter M.

Russell, Dave. Popular Music in England, 1840-1914. 336p. 1987. 49.95 (0-7735-0541-5, Pub. by McGill CN) U of Toronto Pr.

Russell, Dave & Smiley, Robert. Practical Chemistry of Polyurethanes & Diisocyanates: Tailoring Properties for Specific Applications (Seminar Notes) 210p. 1993. ring bd. 95.00 (0-87762-864-5) Technomic.

Russell, David. Business Mathematics. 510p. (C). 1988. text ed. 43.00 (0-15-505666-2) SCP.

— Insuring the Bottom Line: How to Protect Your Company from Liabilities, Catastrophes and Other Business Risks. (Taking Control Ser.). 320p. 1995. pap. 29.95 (1-56343-115-7) Nolo Pr.

— Remediation Manual for Petroleum-Contaminated Sites. LC 91-67570. 200p. 1992. pap. text ed. 49.00 (0-87762-876-9) Technomic.

Russell, David, jt. auth. see Miyashita, Kenichi.

Russell, David, jt. auth. see Sakai, Kunlyasu.

Russell, David, et al. Reading Aids Through the Grades: A Guide to Materials & 501 Activities for Individualizing Reading Instruction. 4th rev. ed. Mueser, Anne M., ed. LC 75-15639. 320p. 1981. pap. text ed. 18.95 (0-8077-2609-5) Tchrs Coll.

Russell, David A. The Masked Driver. Askew, Stella, ed. 209p. (Orig.). (J). 1995. pap. 4.95 (1-884559-01-8) Allen Pubng.

— Superbike. 180p. (J). (gr. 4-7). 1993. 3.95 (1-883174-00-7) High Octane.

— Superbike. 168p. Date not set. pap. 3.95 (1-884559-04-2) Allen Pubng.

***Russell, David G., ed.** Methods in Cell Biology Vol. 45: Microbes As Tools for Cell Biology. (Illus.). 339p. 1995. text ed. 80.00 (0-12-564146-X) Acad Pr.

— Methods in Cell Biology Vol. 45: Microbes As Tools for Cell Biology. (Illus.). 339p. 1995. pap. 45.00 (0-12-604040-0) Acad Pr.

Russell, David H. & Russell, Elizabeth F. Listening Aids Through the Grades: Two Hundred Thirty-Two Listening Activities. rev. ed. Hennings, Dorothy G., ed. LC 79-607. 1979. pap. text ed. 12.95 (0-8077-2558-7) Tchrs Coll.

Russell, David L. Literature for Children: A Short Introduction. 2nd ed. 272p. (Orig.). (C). 1994. pap. text ed. 23.95 (0-8013-1265-5, 79896) Longman.

Russell, David M., jt. auth. see Gondolf, Edward W.

Russell, David R. Writing in the Academic Disciplines, 1870-1990: A Curricular History. 208p. (C). 1991. 24.95 (0-8093-1596-3); pap. 16.95 (0-8093-1597-1) S Ill U Pr.

Russell, David R., jt. ed. see Bazerman, Charles.

Russell, David S. Prophecy & the Apocalyptic Dream: Protest & Promise. LC 94-11229. 128p. 1994. pap. 9.95 (1-56563-054-8) Hendrickson MA.

Russell, Dean. Government & Legal Plunder: Bastiat Brought up to Date. 120p. 1985. pap. 8.95 (0-910614-70-9) Foun Econ Ed.

Russell, Dean, tr. see Bastiat, Frederic.

Russell, Deborah, ed. see Chapman & DeHart.

Russell, Deborah, ed. see Corrigan, Peter & Gurry, Mark.

Russell, Deborah, ed. see Feuerlicht.

Russell, Deborah, ed. see Icove, David, et al.

Russell, Deborah, jt. auth. see Powers, Paul.

Russell, Deborah, ed. see Walsh, Norman.

Russell, Deborah F. & Gangemi, G. T., Sr. Computer Security Basics. (Nutshell Handbook Ser.). 464p. (Orig.). 1991. pap. 29.95 (0-937175-71-4) OReilly & Assocs.

***Russell, Denise.** Women, Madness, & Medicine. 1994. write for info. (0-7456-1260-1) Blackwell Pubs.

Russell, Diana E. Against Pornography: The Evidence of Harm. LC 93-92610. (Illus.). 169p. 1994. pap. 12.95 (0-9634776-1-7) Russell CA.

— The Politics of Rape: The Victim's Perspective. LC 73-90697. 312p. 1984. pap. 10.95 (0-8128-1860-1, Scrbrough Hse) Madison Bks UPA.

— Rape in Marriage. enl. rev. ed. LC 89-24650. (Illus.). 462p. 1990. 39.95 (0-253-35055-7); pap. 15.95 (0-253-20563-8, MB-563) Ind U Pr.

Russell, Diana E., ed. Exposing Nuclear Phallacies. LC 88-39941. (Athene Ser.). 352p. (C). 1989. text ed. 40.00 (0-08-036476-4, Pergamon Pr); pap. text ed. 17.95 (0-08-036475-6, Pergamon Pr) Elsevier.

— Exposing Nuclear Phallacies. (Athene Ser.). 352p. (C). text ed. 40.00 (0-8077-6225-3); pap. text ed. 17.95 (0-8077-6224-5) Tchrs Coll.

— Making Violence Sexy: Feminist Views on Pornography. LC 92-41999. (Athene Ser.). 320p. (C). 1993. text ed. 46.00 (0-8077-6269-5); pap. text ed. 19.95 (0-8077-6268-7) Tchrs Coll.

Russell, Diana E. & Van deVen, Nicole, eds. Crimes Against Women: Proceedings of the International Tribunal. LC 84-8165. (Illus.). 320p. 1984. reprint ed. pap. 7.95 (0-9603628-5-1) Frog in Well.

Russell, Diana E., jt. auth. see Radford, Jill.

Russell, Diane. Claude Lorrain. (Illus.). 480p. (Orig.). (C). 1983. pap. 19.95 (0-8076-1082-8) Braziller.

Russell, Diane E. Sexual Exploitation. LC 84-6950. 319p. 1984. 49.95 (0-8039-2354-6); pap. 24.00 (0-8039-2355-4) Sage.

***Russell, Diane H. & Durie, Brian G.** Polyamines As Biochemical Markers of Normal & Malignant Growth. fac. ed. LC 75-43340. (Progress in Cancer Research & Therapy Ser.: No. 8). (Illus.). 192p. Date not set. pap. 54.80 (0-7837-7352-8, 2047161) Bks Demand.

Russell, Dick. The Man Who Knew Too Much: Richard Case Nagell & the Assassination of JFK. 480p. 1992. 27.95 (0-88184-900-6) Carroll & Graf.

— Mind Control & the Assassination of President Kennedy. 384p. 1995. 23.00 (0-7867-0196-X) Carroll & Graf.

Russell, Dinah & Sharratt, Anita. Academic Recovery after Head Injury. (Illus.). 110p. (C). 1992. text ed. 24.95x (0-398-05788-5) C C Thomas.

***Russell, Don.** Campaigning with King: Charles King, Chronicler of the Old Army. Hedren, Paul L., ed. LC 90-12335. (Illus.). 241p. 1991. reprint ed. pap. 68.70 (0-7837-8912-2, 2049623) Bks Demand.

Russell, Don, jt. auth. see Brunner, Helen.

Russell, Donald A. & Winterbottom, M., eds. Ancient Literary Criticism: The Principal Texts in New Translations. 662p. 1988. pap. 32.50 (0-19-814360-5) OUP.

— Classical Literary Criticism. (World's Classics Ser.). 272p. 1990. pap. 6.95 (0-19-281830-9) OUP.

Russell, Donald B. The Lives & Legends of Buffalo Bill. LC 60-13470. (Illus.). (Orig.). 1979. pap. 19.95 (0-8061-1537-8) U of Okla Pr.

Russell, Donald E., jt. auth. see Savage, Donald E.

Russell, Donna, ed. see Hopenwasser, Susan.

Russell, Donna V. Frederick County, Maryland, Genealogical Research Guide. (Illus.). 68p. 1987. pap. 13.00 (0-914385-05-4) Catoctin Pr.

— Selby Families of Colonial America. (Illus.). 200p. (Orig.). 1990. pap. 25.00 (0-914385-11-9) Catoctin Pr.

Russell, Donna V., ed. see Myers, Margaret E.

Russell, Dorothy P. Published Writings of Dorothy Powell Russell. (Illus.). 91p. (Orig.). 1990. pap. 14.00 (0-914385-13-5) Catoctin Pr.

Russell, Doug, jt. auth. see Hunter, Madeline C.

Russell, Doug, jt. auth. see Hunter, Madeline.

Russell, Douglas A. Costume History & Style. (Illus.). 576p. 1982. text ed. write for info. (0-13-181214-9) P-H.

Russell, Douglas A., ed. & intro. An Anthology of Austrian Drama. LC 76-19836. 450p. 1982. 49.50 (0-8386-2003-5) Fairleigh Dickinson.

Russell, Douglas S. The Orders, Decorations & Medals of Sir Winston Churchill. Langworth, Richard M., ed. (Educational Ser.: No. 3). (Illus.). 108p. 1990. per., pap. 8.00 (0-943879-06-X) Intl Churchill Soc.

Russell, E. S. Dead Easy. 202p. 1992. 19.95 (0-8027-3214-3) Walker & Co.

— Death of a Cloudwalker. 192p. 1991. 18.95 (0-8027-5784-7) Walker & Co.

— Interpretation of Development & Heredity: A Study in Biological Method. LC 70-39699. (Select Bibliographies Reprint Ser.). 312p. 1977. reprint ed. 19.95 (0-8369-9943-6) Ayer.

Russell, E. S., et al, eds. Model-Based Design of Materials & Processes. (Illus.). 173p. 1993. 34.00 (0-87339-185-3, 447) Minerals Metals.

Russell, E. W., jt. ed. see Lal, R.

Russell Editorial Project Group, Mc Master University Staff. Contemplation & Action, 1902-1914. (Collected Papers of Bertrand Russell: Vol. 12). 654p. 1988. text ed. 191.50 (0-04-920078-X, A9420) Routledge Chapman & Hall.

Russell, Edward J. Science & Modern Life. LC 70-117833. (Essay Index Reprint Ser.). 1977. reprint ed. 17.95 (0-8369-2440-1) Ayer.

— World Population & World Food Supplies. LC 76-23307. (Illus.). 513p. 1976. reprint ed. text ed. 35.00 (0-8371-8997-7, RUWP, Greenwood Pr) Greenwood.

Russell, Edward R. & Standing, P. C. Ibsen on His Merits. LC 79-181000. (Studies in European Literature: No. 56). 1972. reprint ed. lib. bdg. 49.95 (0-8383-1370-1) M S G Haskell Hse.

Russell, Edward W. Prospects of Eternity: Debunking Death. 164p. (Orig.). Date not set. 16.95 (0-8464-4274-4) Beekman Pubs.

— Report on Radionics. 6th ed. (Illus.). 256p. Date not set. pap. 26.95 (0-8464-4283-3) Beekman Pubs.

Russell, Edward W., ed. see Ravitz, Leonard J., Jr.

Russell, Elizabeth. Adaptable Stage Costume for Women. LC 73-75920. (Illus.). 1975. pap. 14.95 (0-87830-567-X, Theatre Arts Bks) Routledge Chapman & Hall.

— Elizabeth & Her German Garden. 190p. 1989. reprint ed. lib. bdg. 21.95 (0-89966-635-3) Buccaneer Bks.

Russell, Elizabeth F., jt. auth. see Russell, David H.

Russell, Elliot. Conversation Made Easy. 1979. pap. 5.00 (0-87980-024-0) Wilshire.

Russell, Elmer B. The Review of American Colonial Legislation by the King in Council. Helmholz, R. H. & Reams, Bernard D., Jr., eds. LC 80-84869. (Historical Writings in Law & Jurisprudence Ser.: Title No. 21, Bk. 31). 230p. 1981. reprint ed. lib. bdg. 42.00 (0-89941-083-9, 302370) W S Hein.

Russell, Emily, ed. see Phillips, Lisa.

Russell, Emily W., jt. ed. see Collins, Beryl R.

Russell, Emma S. The Ever-Widening Circle: An Autobiography. LC 83-3378. (Illus.). 378p. 1983. 25.00 (0-912209-00-3) M Russell NY.

Russell, Enid. A History of the Law in Western Australia. 413p. 1980. 34.95 (0-85564-171-1, Pub. by Univ of West Aust Pr AT) Intl Spec Bk.

Russell, Eric. Astrology & Prediction. 182p. 1975. reprint ed. pap. 2.95 (0-8065-0446-3, Citadel Pr) Carol Pub Group.

Russell, Eric F. The Great Explosion. 160p. 1993. pap. 3.95 (0-88184-991-X) Carroll & Graf.

— Men, Martians & Machines. 1993. reprint ed. lib. bdg. 18.95 (0-89968-360-6, Lghtyr Pr) Buccaneer Bks.

— Next of Kin. 192p. 1986. mass mkt. 4.99 (0-345-32761-6, Del Rey) Ballantine.

Russell, Eric F., jt. auth. see Foster, Alan D.

Russell, Eric P. & Lovewell, Mark. Songs of South Street--Street of Ships. (Illus.). 1978. pap. text ed. 4.00 (0-9601250-0-0) Chanteyman.

Russell, Erskine & Mandes, Ric. ERK: Football, Fans & Friends. LC 91-61832. 224p. 1991. 18.95 (1-56352-019-2) Longstreet Pr Inc.

Russell, Etta M. Basic Principles of Constitutional Money: A Textbook for High Schools & the General Public on the Federal Reserve Conspiracy. 1980. lib. bdg. 59.95 (0-8490-3096-X) Gordon Pr.

Russell, F. & Saunders, P. Animal Toxins: Collection of Papers of the 1st International Symposium on Animal Toxins A.C., Apr. 1966. LC 66-29612. 1967. 183.00 (0-08-012209-4, Pub. by Pergamon Repr UK) Franklin.

Russell, F. S. Advances in Marine Biology, Vol. 21. (Serial Publication Ser.). 1984. text ed. 150.00 (0-12-026121-9) Acad Pr.

Russell, F. S., ed. Advances in Marine Biology, Vol. 16. (Serial Publication Ser.). 1979. text ed. 209.00 (0-12-026116-2) Acad Pr.

Russell, Findlay. Snake Venom Poisoning. rev. ed. LC 83-3134. (Illus.). 576p. 1983. text ed. 57.50 (0-87936-015-1) Scholium Intl.

Russell, Ford. Northrop Frye on Myth: An Introduction. (Theorists of Myth Ser.: Vol. 5). 200p. Date not set. 29.00 (0-8240-3446-5, H1166) Garland.

Russell, Frances. Three Studies in Twentieth Century Obscurity: Joyce, Kafka, Gertrude Stein. LC 68-658. (Studies in Comparative Literature: No. 35). (C). 1969. reprint ed. lib. bdg. 75.00 (0-8383-0678-0) M S G Haskell Hse.

Russell, Francis. Three Studies in Twentieth Century Obscurity. 1973. lib. bdg. 200.00 (0-87968-046-6) Gordon Pr.

Russell, Frank. Dinner with Doctor Rocksteady. 64p. (Orig.). 1987. pap. 9.95 (0-938507-11-7) Ion Books.

— Explorations in the Far North. LC 74-5873. reprint ed. 25.00 (0-404-11682-5) AMS Pr.

Russell, Frank A. American Pilgrimage. LC 72-167408. (Essay Index Reprint Ser.). 1977. reprint ed. 25.95 (0-8369-2715-X) Ayer.

***Russell, Frank C.** Carving Folk Figures with Power. LC 95-11074. (Illus.). 64p. (Orig.). 1995. pap. 12.95 (0-88740-854-0) Schiffer.

— Carving Realistic Animals with Power. LC 94-66201. (Illus.). 64p. (Orig.). 1994. pap. 12.95 (0-88740-637-8) Schiffer.

— Carving Vermont Folk Figures, Bk. 1. (Illus.). 80p. (Orig.). 1989. pap. 8.95 (0-685-29438-2) Stonegate Studios.

Russell, Frank M. Theories of International Relations. LC 72-4297. (World Affairs Ser.: National & International Viewpoints). 658p. 1972. reprint ed. 44.95 (0-405-04588-3) Ayer.

Russell, Franklin. Watchers at the Pond: The Mysteries, the Wonder, the Hazards of Life Procreation & Death Within the Teeming Universe of a Pond. LC 80-83963. (Non Pareil Ser.). (Illus.). 272p. 1995. pap. 14.95 (0-87923-390-7) Godine.

Russell, G., jt. ed. see Taylor, G. E.

Russell, G. F., ed. see Pankhurst, R. J.

Russell, G. Hugh & Black, Kenneth, Jr. Human Behavior in Business. 202p. 1972. 19.95 (0-13-444695-X) GA St U Busn Pr.

Russell, G. Hugh, jt. auth. see Black, Kenneth, Jr.

Russell, G. J., jt. auth. see McMinn, A.

Russell, G. W. An Account of Some of the Descendants of John Russell, Who Came to Boston, 1635; Together with Some Sketches of the Allied Families of Wadsworth, Tuttle, & Beresford. Welles, E. S., ed. (Illus.). 318p. 1989. reprint ed. lib. bdg. 57.50 (0-8328-1040-1); reprint ed. pap. 47.50 (0-8328-1041-X) Higginson Bk Co.

***Russell, Garfield B. & Rodichok, Lawrence D., eds.** Primer of Intraoperative Neurophysiologic Monitoring. LC 95-12875. 1995. write for info. (0-7506-9553-6) Buttrwrth-Heinemann.

Russell, Garth S. & Highland, Thomas R. Care of the Low Back: A Patient Guide. (Illus.). 196p. (C). 1991. pap. 19.95 (0-8036-7674-3) Davis Co.

***Russell, Gene H.** Handcrafted Cachets, the Make Your Own Cachet & Envelope Handbook. 3rd ed. 110p. (Orig.). 1993. pap. 13.95 (1-879390-15-9) Am First Day.

Russell, George E. Descendants of William Russell of Salem, Mass., 1674. (Illus.). 270p. 1989. pap. 24.00 (0-914385-06-2) Catoctin Pr.
— Moravian Families of Carroll's Manor, Frederick County, Maryland. (Illus.). 150p. (Orig.). 1989. pap. 18.00 (0-914385-07-0) Catoctin Pr.
— Powell Family of Allegany County, Maryland: Descendants of William Powell & Ann (Chambers) Powell of Timsbury, Somersetshire, England. (Illus.). 117p. (Orig.). 1990. pap. 15.00 (0-914385-12-7) Catoctin Pr.
— Washington County, Maryland, Genealogical Research Guide. (Illus.). 48p. 1993. pap. 13.00 (0-914385-14-3) Catoctin Pr.
Russell, George K. Vivisection & the True Aims of Education in Biology. 3rd ed. 14p. (gr. 8-12). pap. 0.75 (0-913098-30-2) Myrin Institute.
Russell, George L. Map of American Indian Nations. 3rd ed. (J). (gr. 6 up). 1993. pap. 15.00 (1-881933-02-4) Thundbird Ent.
Russell, George M. The Collector's Guide to Civil War Period Bottles & Jars. 2nd ed. (Illus.). 96p. Date not set. pap. 15.95 (1-880365-27-8) Prof Pr NC.
Russell, George W. Afterthoughts. LC 68-16975. (Essay Index Reprint Ser.). 1977. reprint ed. 23.95 (0-8369-0843-0) Ayer.
— The Ascending Cycle. (Sangam Texts Ser.). 105p. (Orig.). 1983. pap. 8.75 (0-88695-013-9) Concord Grove.
— Descent of the Gods. 1988. 75.00 (0-901072-44-3) Dufour.
— Descent of the Gods: The Mystical Writings of G. W. Russell - A. E. Iyer, Nandini, ed. LC 88-51545. 780p. 1989. 75.00 (0-900675-44-6, Pub. by Colin Smythe Ltd UK) Dufour.
— Half-Lengths. LC 71-128309. (Essay Index Reprint Ser.). 1977. 23.95 (0-8369-1849-5) Ayer.
— Matthew Arnold. LC 71-130250. (English Literature Ser.: No. 33). 1970. reprint ed. lib. bdg. 59.95 (0-8383-1140-7) M S G Haskell Hse.
— Politics & Personalities, with Other Essays. (Essay Index Reprint Ser.). 1977. 23.95 (0-8369-0844-9) Ayer.
— Portraits of the Seventies. LC 73-117834. (Essay Index Reprint Ser.). 1977. 24.95 (0-8369-1717-0) Ayer.
Russell, George W., ed. see Arnold, Matthew.
Russell, Georgina. Christmas Bear. (Illus.). 28p. (J). (ps-2). 1991. 8.95 (0-7214-5331-7, S808) Ladybird Bks.
Russell, Gerald F. M., ed. see Hersov, Lional A.
***Russell, Gillian.** The Theatres of War: Performance, Politics, & Society 1793-1815. (Illus.). 264p. 1995. 49.95 (0-19-812263-2) OUP.
Russell, Glenn. The Plantings. (Illus.). 47p. (Orig.). 1989. pap. 3.00 (0-926935-34-8) Runaway Spoon.
Russell, Goldie, jt. auth. see Russell, A. G.
Russell, Gordon, ed. Violence in Intimate Relationships. LC 88-318. 312p. 1988. text ed. 45.00 (0-89335-231-4) PMA Pub Corp.
Russell, Gordon W. The Social Psychology of Sport. LC 92-34893. 336p. 1994. 39.50 (0-387-97792-9) Spr-Verlag.
Russell, Graham, et al, eds. Plant Canopies: Their Growth, Form & Function. (Society for Experimental Biology Seminar Ser.: No. 31). 192p. (C). 1990. pap. 27.95 (0-521-39563-1) Cambridge U Pr.
Russell, Greg. Hans J. Morgenthau & the Ethics of American Statecraft. LC 90-5675. (Political Traditions in Foreign Policy Ser.). 288p. 1990. text ed. 30.00x (0-8071-1618-1) La State U Pr.
— John Quincy Adams & the Public Virtues of Diplomacy. 304p. 1994. 42.50 (0-8262-0984-X) U of Mo Pr.
Russell, Gregory D. The Death Penalty & Racial Bias: Overturning Supreme Court Assumptions. LC 93-25069. (Contributions in Legal Studies: No. 75). 184p. 1993. text ed. 55.00 (0-313-28889-5, GM8889, Greenwood Pr) Greenwood.
Russell, Guy. Mojave. LC 77-27298. (Illus.). 36p. 1977. pap. 6.95 (0-916348-17-2) Sigga Pr.
— The Space Outside. LC 75-35693. 1975. pap. 15.00 (0-916348-07-5) Sigga Pr.
Russell, H. Diane. Eva-Ave: Woman in Renaissance & Baroque Prints. 240p. (Orig.). 1990. 59.95 (1-55861-039-1); pap. 29.95 (1-55861-040-5) Feminist Pr.
— Eva-Ave: Woman in Renaissance & Baroque Prints. LC 90-15521. (Illus.). 238p. (Orig.). 1990. pap. 29.95 (0-89468-157-5) Natl Gallery Art.
Russell, Hannah. Songs about the Sky. rev. ed. (Illus.). 18p. (J). 1988. reprint ed. pap. 4.50 (0-9614089-2-8) Avitar Bks.
Russell, Harold E. & Beigel, Allan. Understanding Human Behavior for Effective Police Work. 3rd ed. LC 90-80676. 464p. 1990. text ed. 40.00 (0-465-08859-7) Basic.
Russell, Harry K., et al, eds. Literature in English. LC 73-132139. (Play Anthology Reprint Ser.). 1977. 51.95 (0-8369-8218-5) Ayer.
Russell, Helen. Pediatric Drugs & Nursing Intervention. (Illus.). 1979. text ed. 21.95 (0-07-054298-8) McGraw.
Russell, Helen D. Come in This House. 230p. (J). (gr. 6-12). 1982. lib. bdg. 15.95 (0-934188-07-6) Evans Pubns.
Russell, Helen R. Ten Minute Field Trips. (Illus.). 176p. 1991. pap. text ed. 16.95 (0-87355-098-6) Natl Sci Tchrs.
Russell, Herbert K. A Southern Illinois Album: Farm Security Administration Photographs, 1936-1943. LC 89-6241. (Illus.). 160p. (C). 1990. pap. text ed. 17.95 (0-8093-1589-0) S Ill U Pr.
Russell, Herbert K., ed. see Earle, Mary T.
Russell, Herbert K., ed. see Horrell, C. William.
Russell, Hilary. Giving up the House. (Illus.). 28p. (Orig.). 1993. pap. 10.00 (0-944156-08-8) Mad River MA.
— Giving up the House. deluxe ed. (Illus.). 28p. (Orig.). 1993. pap. 20.00 (0-685-71065-3) Mad River MA.
— Longman Anthology of American Poetry. 328p. 1992. pap. text ed. 18.60 (0-8013-0617-5, 78550) Longman.
— The Portable Writer. 80p. (Orig.). (YA). (gr. 9-12). 1989. pap. text ed. 8.00 (1-877653-03-9) Wayside Pub.
Russell, Howard L. Iced Tea & Ignorance. 288p. 1989. 18.95 (1-55611-094-4) D I Fine.
— Rush to Nowhere. LC 87-46253. 288p. 1988. 17.95 (1-55611-075-8) D I Fine.
Russell, Howard S. Indian New England Before the Mayflower. LC 79-63082. (Illus.). 296p. 1980. pap. 16.95 (0-87451-255-7) U Pr of New Eng.
— A Long, Deep Furrow: Three Centuries of Farming in New England. abr. ed. Lapping, Mark, ed. & abr. by. LC 81-51605. (Illus.). 394p. (C). 1982. pap. 19.95 (0-87451-214-X) U Pr of New Eng.
— A Long, Deep Furrow: Three Centuries of Farming in New England. LC 73-91314. 688p. reprint ed. 180.00 (0-685-15823-3, 2027534) Bks Demand.
Russell, I. Willis, ed. see McMillan, James B.
Russell-Ides, Isabella. Getting Dangerously Close to Myself. 90p. (Orig.). 1987. lib. bdg. 13.95 (0-941720-40-3); pap. 7.95 (0-941720-39-X) Slough Pr TX.
Russell, Ina, ed. Jeb & Dash: A Diary of Gay Life, 1918-1945. (Illus.). 290p. 1994. pap. 14.95 (0-571-19847-3) Faber & Faber.
Russell, Ina D., ed. Jeb & Dash: A Diary of Gay Life, 1918-1945. (Illus.). 300p. 1993. 24.95 (0-571-19817-1) Faber & Faber.
***Russell, Irwin.** Christmas Night in the Quarters. Date not set. pap. 1.00 (0-87517-009-9) Dietz.
Russell, Isabel. Katharine & E. B. White. 1990. pap. 8.95 (0-393-30638-0) Norton.
Russell, J. A., et al, eds. Industrial Operations under Extremes of Weather. (Meteorological Monograph Ser.: Vol. 2, No. 9). (Illus.). 121p. 1957. pap. 17.00 (0-933876-04-1) Am Meteorological.
Russell, J. B. Dissent & Order in the Middle Ages. (Twayne's Studies in Intellectual & Cultural History). 200p. (Orig.). (C). 1992. text ed. 22.95 (0-8057-8603-1, Twayne); pap. 12.95 (0-8057-8628-7, Twayne) Macmillan.
Russell, J. H. A Pictorial Record of Great Western Absorbed Engines. 288p. 1986. 65.00 (0-902888-74-9) St Mut.
Russell, J. M., jt. ed. see Alvarez-Leefmans, F. J.
Russell, J. P. Quality Management Benchmark Assessment. 144p. 1991. student ed 16.95 (0-527-91642-0, 916420) Qual Resc.
— Quality Management Benchmark Assessment. 2nd ed. 1995. spiral bd. 21.00 (0-87389-332-8) ASQC Qual Pr.
— The Quality Master Plan: A Quality Strategy for Business Leadership. (Illus.). 138p. 1990. pap. 27.95 (0-87389-081-7) ASQC Qual Pr.
Russell, J. S. & Isbell, R. F., eds. Australian Soils: The Human Impact. LC 85-16514. (Illus.). 522p. 1987. text ed. 50.00 (0-7022-1968-1, Pub. by Univ Queensland Pr AT) Intl Spec Bk.
Russell, J. Stephen. The English Dream Vision: Anatomy of a Form. LC 87-16594. 224p. 1988. 35.00 (0-8142-0451-1) Ohio St U Pr.
— Writing at Work: The Russell & Associates Papers. 400p. (C). 1985. pap. text ed. 21.50 (0-03-070596-7) HB Coll Pubs.
***Russell, J. Thomas & Lane, W. Ronald.** Kleppner's Advertising Procedure. 3rd ed. LC 94-25208. (Marketing Ser.). 1995. text ed. 62.00 (0-13-348830-6) P-H.
— Kleppner's Advertising Procedure. 12th ed. LC 92-25490. 752p. 1992. teacher ed write for info. (0-13-517574-7) P-H Gen Ref & Trav.
Russell, Jack, jt. auth. see Norman, Jack.
Russell, Jack, ed. see Norman, Jack & Russell, Jack.
Russell, Jacqui, ed. File on Coward. (Methuen Writer-Files Ser.). 1988. pap. 9.95 (0-413-58600-6, A0094, Pub. by Methuen UK) Heinemann.
Russell, James. Explaining Mental Life: Some Philosophical Issues in Psychology. LC 83-40545. 240p. 1985. text ed. 29.95 (0-312-27743-1) St Martin.
— Introduction to Macrosociology. 240p. (C). 1991. pap. text ed. 14.00 (0-13-485889-1, 610804) P-H.
— Marx-Engels Dictionary. LC 80-786. (Illus.). xxv, 140p. 1980. text ed. 55.00 (0-313-22035-2, RME/, Greenwood Pr) Greenwood.
Russell, James, jt. ed. see Zinkel, Duane F.
***Russell, James A., ed.** Everyday Conceptions of Emotion: An Introduction to the Psychology, Anthropology & Linguistics of Emotion. LC 95-13602. (NATO ASI Ser., Series D, Behavioural & Social Sciences). 1996. write for info. (0-7923-3479-5) Kluwer Ac.
Russell, James C. The Germanization of Early Medieval Christianity: A Sociohistorical Approach to Religious Transformation. LC 92-13182. 272p. (C). 1994. 39.95 (0-19-507696-6) OUP.
Russell, James D. The Audio-Tutorial System. Langdon, Danny G., ed. LC 77-25454. (Instructional Design Library). (Illus.). 80p. 1978. 23.95 (0-87778-107-9) Educ Tech Pubns.
Russell, James D., ed. see Hughes, Leonard V., Jr.
Russell, James E. Dream Kitchens: Over Forty Step-by-Step Projects. rev. ed. Horowitz, Shirley M., ed. LC 90-80295. (Illus.). 160p. 1990. pap. text ed. 9.95 (0-932944-92-2) Creative Homeowner.
— Garages & Carports. Horowitz, Shirley M., ed. LC 81-66548. (Illus.). 160p. (Orig.). 1981. pap. 9.95 (0-932944-32-9) Creative Homeowner.
— Methods & Materials of Residential Construction. (Illus.). 368p. (C). 1985. 40.00 (0-13-578881-1); text ed. 29.00 (0-685-09097-3) P-H.
— Walks, Walls & Fences. Auer, Marilyn M., ed. LC 81-65752. (Illus.). 144p. (Orig.). 1981. pap. 9.95 (0-932944-36-1) Creative Homeowner.
Russell, James M. Atlanta, 1847-1890: City Building in the Old South & the New. LC 87-29946. (Illus.). xiii, 314p. 1988. text ed. 40.00 (0-8071-1413-8) La State U Pr.
Russell, James O. & Smelser, Georgia. The Coal Miner Preacher: A Testimony of Faith, Healings, Miracles, Angels, & Prophecies. LC 93-23506. 150p. (Orig.). pap. 6.99 (1-56722-014-2) Word Aflame.
Russell, James R. Yovhannes Tclkurancci & the Mediaeval American Lyric Tradition. LC 85-22066. (Armenian Texts & Studies). 260p. 1987. 17.95 (0-89130-929-2, 21-02-07); pap. 13.95 (0-89130-930-6) Scholars Pr GA.
— Zoroastrianism in Armenia. LC 87-18147. (Harvard Iranian Ser.: No. 5). (Illus.). 584p. (Orig.). 1988. pap. 39.95 (0-674-96850-6) HUP.
Russell, James R., ed. Matean Voghberkowtean: The Book of Lamentations, Gregory Narekatzi. LC 81-6177. 1981. 50.00 (0-88206-029-5) Caravan Bks.
Russell, James W. After the Fifth Sun: Class & Race in North America. LC 93-38544. 216p. 1994. pap. text ed. 28.80 (0-13-036237-9) P-H.
— Introduction to Macrosociology. 2nd ed. LC 95-8748. 1995. pap. text ed. write for info. (0-13-228230-5) P-H.
— Modes of Production in World History. 172p. 1989. 55.00 (0-415-02907-4, A3498) Routledge.
Russell, Jane. James Starkey-Seumas O'Sullivan: A Critical Biography. LC 85-45951. (Illus.). 152p. 1987. 29.50 (0-8386-3265-3) Fairleigh Dickinson.
Russell, Janice. Out of Bounds: Sexual Exploitation in Counselling & Therapy. (Illus.). 160p. (C). 1993. text ed. 55.00 (0-8039-8533-9); pap. text ed. 19.95 (0-8039-8534-7) Sage.
Russell, Jeffrey. History of Medieval Christianity. LC 68-9743. 224p. 1968. pap. text ed. write for info. (0-88295-761-9) Harlan Davidson.
Russell, Jeffrey B. The Devil: Perceptions of Evil from Antiquity to Primitive Christianity. LC 77-3126. (Illus.). 288p. 1977. 37.50 (0-8014-0938-1) Cornell U Pr.
— The Devil: Perceptions of Evil from Antiquity to Primitive Christianity. LC 77-3126. (Illus.). 288p. 1987. pap. 13.95 (0-8014-9409-5) Cornell U Pr.
— Dissent & Reform in the Early Middle Ages. LC 78-63178. (Heresies of the Early Christian & Medieval Era Ser.: Second Ser.). 344p. reprint ed. 36.00 (0-404-16196-0) AMS Pr.
— A History of Witchcraft: Sorcerers, Heretics & Pagans. 1983. 23.00 (0-8446-6052-3) Peter Smith.
— A History of Witchcraft: Sorcerers, Heretics & Pagans. (Illus.). 1982. pap. 14.95 (0-500-27242-5) Thames Hudson.
— Inventing the Flat Earth: Columbus & Modern Historians. LC 91-67. 132p. 1991. text ed. 19.95 (0-275-93956-1, C3956, Praeger Pubs) Greenwood.
— Lucifer: The Devil in the Middle Ages. LC 84-45153. (Illus.). 356p. 1984. 37.50 (0-8014-1503-9) Cornell U Pr.
— Lucifer: The Devil in the Middle Ages. LC 84-45153. (Illus.). 356p. 1986. pap. 14.95 (0-8014-9429-X) Cornell U Pr.
— Mephistopheles: The Devil in the Modern World. LC 86-47648. (Illus.). 352p. 1986. 37.50 (0-8014-1808-9) Cornell U Pr.
— Mephistopheles: The Devil in the Modern World. LC 86-47648. (Illus.). 352p. 1990. reprint ed. pap. 14.95 (0-8014-9718-3) Cornell U Pr.
— The Prince of Darkness: Radical Evil & the Power of Good in History. LC 88-47744. (Illus.). 304p. 1988. 36.50 (0-8014-2014-8) Cornell U Pr.
— The Prince of Darkness: Radical Evil & the Power of Good in History. LC 88-47744. (Illus.). 304p. 1992. pap. 13.95 (0-8014-8056-6) Cornell U Pr.
— Satan: The Early Christian Tradition. LC 81-66649. (Illus.). 258p. 1981. 37.50 (0-8014-1267-6) Cornell U Pr.
— Satan: The Early Christian Tradition. LC 81-66649. (Illus.). 258p. 1987. pap. 13.95 (0-8014-9413-3) Cornell U Pr.
— Witchcraft in the Middle Ages. LC 72-37755. 394p. 1984. 42.50 (0-8014-0697-8); pap. 14.95 (0-8014-9289-0) Cornell U Pr.
Russell, Jenifer, ed. see Lair, Cynthia.
Russell, Jervis F., ed. see Potter, Velma M.
Russell, Jill F., jt. auth. see Pratzner, Frank C.
Russell, Jim, illus. Adam & Eve. LC 82-23060. (People of the Bible Ser.). 32p. (J). (gr. k-4). 1983. 14.65 (0-8172-1981-1) Raintree Steck-V.
— Moses of the Bullrushes: Retold by Catherine Storr. (People of the Bible Ser.). 32p. (J). (gr. k-4). 1984. 14.65 (0-8172-1990-0) Raintree Steck-V.
Russell, Jim, jt. auth. see Watson, Ed.
Russell, Joan. The Woman's Day Book of Soft Toys & Dolls. 1980. pap. 6.95 (0-686-61050-4, 25403, Fireside) S&S Trade.
Russell, Joan, jt. auth. see Gregg, Joan Y.
Russell, Joan M., jt. auth. see Russell, Alanson E.
Russell, Joel F., jt. ed. see Tatson, Raymond M.
Russell, John. Erich Kleiber: A Memoir. LC 80-29369. (Illus.). ix, 256p. 1981. reprint ed. lib. bdg. 35.00 (0-685-55649-2) Da Capo.
— Favorite Sons. 1992. 19.95 (0-945575-36-X) Algonquin Bks.
— Francis Bacon. LC 85-51434. (World of Art Ser.). (Illus.). 192p. 1985. 19.95 (0-500-18170-5) Thames Hudson.
— Francis Bacon. rev. ed. LC 93-60306. (World of Art Ser.). (Illus.). 208p. 1993. pap. 12.95 (0-500-20271-0) Thames Hudson.
— Hamlet & Narcissus. LC 94-22486. 248p. 1994. 38.50 (0-87413-533-8) U Delaware Pr.
— Honey Russell: Between Games, Between Halves. 1986. 14.95 (0-931848-64-4); pap. 7.95 (0-931848-65-2) Dryad Pr.
— In August Company: The Collections of the Pierpont Morgan Library. Plummer, John, ed. (Illus.). 312p. 1994. pap. 24.95 (0-87598-093-7) Pierpont Morgan.
— Kenya Beyond the Marich Pass: A District Officer's Story. 224p. 1994. text ed. 39.50 (1-85043-786-6, Pub. by I B Tauris UK) St Martin.
— London. LC 94-1528. 1994. write for info. (0-8109-3570-8) Abrams.
— Meanings of Modern Art. rev. ed. LC 89-45614. (Illus.). 464p. 1992. 50.00 (0-06-438496-9, Icon Edns); pap. text ed. 30.00 (0-06-430165-6, Icon Edns) HarpC.
— Seurat. (World of Art Ser.). (Illus.). 286p. 1985. pap. 12.95 (0-500-20032-7) Thames Hudson.
— Style in Modern British Fiction: Studies in Joyce, Lawrence, Forster, Lewis & Green. LC 77-22477. (Illus.). 208p. 1978. text ed. 26.50 (0-8018-2029-4) Johns Hopkins.
— Where the Pavement Ends. LC 73-144170. (Short Story Index Reprint Ser.). 1977. reprint ed. 21.95 (0-8369-3785-6) Ayer.
Russell, John & Arkava, Mort. The Bitterroot Marathon. LC 87-50939. (Illus.). 472p. 1987. boxed 10.95 (0-9611596-7-7) Wilderness Adventure Bks.
Russell, John & De Norman, Roderick. No Triumphant Procession: The Forgotten Battles of Apr 1945. (Illus.). 272p. 1994. 24.95 (1-85409-234-0) Sterling.
Russell, John, ed. see Fox, Charles J.
Russell, John, tr. see Goethe, Johann W.
Russell, John, tr. see Kraus, Wolfgang.
Russell, John, tr. see Martin Du Gard, Roger, pseud.
Russell, John B. General Chemistry. 2nd ed. 1992. Study guide. student ed, pap. text ed. write for info. (0-07-054447-6) McGraw.
— General Chemistry. 2nd ed. 1992. text ed. write for info. (0-07-054445-X) McGraw.
Russell, John C. Spreadsheet Activities in Middle School Mathematics. LC 92-9414. (Illus.). 42p. (Orig.). 1992. pap. 22.50 (0-87353-343-7) NCTM.
Russell, John E., ed. Readings in Workers Compensation: Loss Prevention-Loss Control. 99p. 1985. 10.00 (0-939874-66-0) ASSE.
Russell, John H. The Free Negro in Virginia, Sixteen Nineteen to Eighteen Sixty-Five. LC 78-63945. (Johns Hopkins University. Studies in the Social Sciences. Thirtieth Ser. 1912: 3). reprint ed. 11.50 (0-404-61194-X) AMS Pr.
***Russell, John J., ed.** Washington 95: A Comprehensive Directory of the Key Institutions & Leaders of the National Capital Area. 1180p. 1995. pap. 75.00 (1-880873-12-5) Garrett Pk.
Russell, John J., intro. National Trade & Professional Associations of the U. S., 1992. 27th ed. LC 74-64774. 609p. 1992. 65.00 (0-910416-94-X) Columbia Bks.
— National Trade & Professional Associations of the U. S., 1994. 29th ed. LC 74-64774. 650p. (YA). 1994. pap. 75.00 (1-880873-06-0) Columbia Bks.
— State & Regional Associations of the U. S., 1994. 6th ed. 550p. (YA). 1994. pap. write for info. (1-880873-07-9) Columbia Bks.
Russell, John J., et al. National Trade & Professional Associations of the U. S., 1993. 28th ed. 600p. 1993. pap. 65.00 (1-880873-00-1) Columbia Bks.
— State & Regional Associations of the U. S., 1993. 5th ed. 500p. 1993. 50.00 (1-880873-01-X) Columbia Bks.
***Russell, John J., et al, eds.** Baltimore-Annapolis 1995-96: A Comprehensive Directory of the Major Institutions & the People Who Run Them. 650p. 1995. pap. 60.00 (1-880873-15-X) Columbia Bks.
— National Trade & Professional Associations, 1995. 665p. 1995. pap. 75.00 (1-880873-13-3) Columbia Bks.
— State & Regional Associations of the U. S. 1991: 3rd Annual Edition. 400p. 1991. pap. 40.00 (0-910416-90-7) Columbia Bks.
— Washington '91: Eighth Annual Edition. 1100p. 1991. pap. 60.00 (0-910416-91-5) Columbia Bks.
— Washington 94: A Comprehensive Directory of the Key Institutions & Leaders of the National Capital Area. 1157p. 1994. pap. 75.00 (1-880873-08-7) Columbia Bks.
Russell, John J., et al, intros. Baltimore - Annapolis, 1991-92. 5th ed. 640p. 1991. pap. 45.00 (0-910416-92-3) Columbia Bks.
Russell, John L., III. Involuntary Repossession or In the Steal of the Night. (Illus.). 64p. 1980. pap. 10.95 (0-87364-233-3) Paladin Pr.
Russell, John M. Sennacherib's "Palace Without Rival" at Nineveh. (Illus.). 304p. 1991. 45.00 (0-226-73175-8) U Ch Pr.
— The Writing on the Wall: The Architectural Context of Late Assyrian Palace Reliefs. (Mesopotamian Civilizations Ser.: Vol. 8). Date not set. text ed. write for info. (0-931464-95-1) Eisenbrauns.
Russell, John R., tr. see Kerth, Thomas.
Russell, John R., jt. auth. see Ruplin, Ferdinand A.
Russell, Johnston E., jt. auth. see Beer, Ferdinand P.
Russell, Jonathan. The Sea Cries over My Shoulder. LC 91-70968. 1991. 12.95 (0-8158-0472-5) Chris Mass.
Russell, Joseph. The Daily Lectionary - Year Two: Advent to Easter. 144p. (Orig.). 1987. pap. 3.60 (0-88028-068-9, 905) Forward Movement.
— The Daily Lectionary-Year 1: Advent-Easter. 136p. (Orig.). 1986. pap. 3.60 (0-88028-057-3, 854) Forward Movement.
Russell, Joseph J. Analysis & Dialectic. 1984. lib. bdg. 145.00 (90-247-2990-4) Kluwer Ac.
Russell, Joseph P. The Daily Lectionary: A Weekly Guide for Daily Bible Readings, the Sundays After Pentecost Year One. (Daily Lectionary Ser.). 136p. (Orig.). 1987. pap. 3.60 (0-88028-060-3, 866) Forward Movement.
— Daily Lectionary Year Two Pentecost. 120p. 1988. pap. 3.60 (0-88028-069-7, 906) Forward Movement.
— Sharing Our Biblical Story: A Guide to Using Liturgical Readings As the Core of Church & Family Education. rev. ed. LC 88-8399. 325p. 1988. reprint ed. pap. 19.95 (0-8192-1425-6) Morehouse Pub.

R

An Asterisk (*) at the beginning of an entry indicates that the title is appearing in BIP for the first time.

Russell, Josiah C. The Control of Late Ancient & Medieval Population. LC 83-71298. (Memoirs of the American Philosophical Society Ser.: Vol. 160). 288p. reprint ed. pap. 82.10 (*0-7837-0543-3*, 2040871) Bks Demand.
— Medieval Demography: Essays by Josiah Cox Russell. LC 86-47837. (Studies in the Middle Ages: No. 12). 37.50 (*0-404-61442-6*) AMS Pr.
— Twelfth Century Studies. LC 77-83792. (Studies in the Middle Ages: No. 1). 34.50 (*0-404-16022-0*) AMS Pr.
Russell, Josiah C., ed. see Henry Of Avranches.
Russell, Joyce R., ed. Preservation of Library Materials: Proceedings of a Seminar Sponsored by the Library Binding Institute & the Princeton-Trenton Chapter of Special Libraries Association Held at Rutgers University, July 20-21, 1979. LC 80-20706. (Illus.). 104p. reprint ed. pap. 29.70 (*0-8357-7538-0*, 2036261) Bks Demand.
Russell, Joycelyne G. Diplomats at Work: Three Renaissance Studies. (Illus.). 160p. (C). 1992. text ed. 55.00 (*0-7509-0032-6*) A Sutton Pub.
— Peacemaking in the Renaissance. LC 86-6952. 288p. 1986. text ed. 54.95 (*0-8122-8030-X*) U of Pa Pr.
Russell, Judith, ed. The Wood-Engravings of Gertude Hermes: Survey & Catalogue. (Illus.). 132p. 1993. 129.95 (*0-85967-888-1*, Pub. by Scolar Pr UK) Ashgate Pub Co.
Russell, K. C. Phase Stability under Irradiation. (Illus.). 206p. 1985. pap. 83.00 (*0-08-032722-2*, Pergamon Pr) Elsevier.
Russell, K. C. & Aaronson, H. I., eds. Precipitation Processes in Solids: Proceedings of a Symposium Sponsored by the TMS-AIME Heat Treatment Committee at the 1976 TMS Fall Meeting at Niagara Falls, New York, September 20-21. LC 78-66760. 324p. reprint ed. pap. 92.40 (*0-317-10468-3*, 2022769) Bks Demand.
Russell, K. F. The Melbourne Medical School 1862-1962. 1977. 39.95 (*0-522-84113-9*) Intl Spec Bk.
Russell, K. V., ed. Yearbook of Law, Computers & Technology, 1984, Vol. 1. 1984. 75.00 (*0-86205-790-6*) Butterworth Legal Pubs.
— Yearbook of Law, Computers & Technology, 1987, Vol. 3. 1987. 75.00 (*0-406-18702-9*) Butterworth Legal Pubs.
— Yearbook of Law, Computers & Technology, 1990, Vol. 4. 1990. 75.00 (*0-406-18703-7*) Butterworth Legal Pubs.
— Yearbook of Law, Computers & Technology, 1991, Vol. 5. 1991. 89.00 (*0-406-18704-5*) Butterworth Legal Pubs.
Russell, K. V., jt. ed. see Arnold, C.
Russell, Kathleen F. & Wall, Larry C. Achieve Your Dreams. 160p. (Orig.). 1994. pap. 5.95 (*0-9635176-3-5*) Walrus Prods.
— Money Now You Have It. Now You Don't. 160p. (Orig.). 1994. pap. 5.95 (*0-9635176-4-3*) Walrus Prods.
— The Road to Success Is Always under Construction. 160p. 1992. pap. 5.95 (*0-9635176-0-0*) Walrus Prods.
Russell, Kathy, et al. The Color Complex: The Politics of Skin Color among African Americans. LC 93-13294. 1993. pap. 12.95 (*0-385-47161-0*, Anchor NY) Doubleday.
Russell, Kathy Y., et al. The Color Complex: The "Last Taboo" among African Americans. LC 92-15983. 1992. 21.95 (*0-15-119164-6*) HarBrace.
Russell, Keith, et al. Sex & Fly Fishers: A Delightful & Insightful Celebration of Fly Fishing. LC 92-62020. (Illus.). 336p. 1993. 29.95 (*0-913276-61-8*) Stone Wall Pr.
Russell, Keith A. In Search of the Church: New Testament Images for Tomorrow's Congregations. LC 93-74583. 115p. (Orig.). 1994. pap. 11.95 (*1-56699-123-4*, AL149) Alban Inst.
Russell, Keith P. & Niebyl, Jennifer R. Eastman's Expectant Mother. 8th rev. ed. 1989. 9.95 (*0-318-41368-X*) Little.
Russell, Ken. The Lion Roars: Ken Russell on Film. LC 93-46567. 192p. (Orig.). 1994. pap. 14.95 (*0-571-19834-1*) Faber & Faber.
— Number Puzzles. 1994. pap. 7.95 (*0-572-01890-8*, Pub. by W Foulsham UK) Trans-Atl Phila.
— Word Puzzles. 1994. pap. 7.95 (*0-572-01891-6*, Pub. by W Foulsham UK) Trans-Atl Phila.
Russell, Ken & Carter, Philip. Check Your IQ. (Illus.). 175p. (Orig.). 1992. pap. 11.95x (*0-572-01807-X*, Pub. by W Foulsham UK) Trans-Atl Phila.
— Getting Better at IQ Tests for Ages 11-13. (Illus.). (Orig.). 1994. pap. 10.95 (*0-572-01972-6*, Pub. by W Foulsham UK) Trans-Atl Phila.
— Getting Better at IQ Tests for Ages 14-16. (Illus.). (Orig.). 1994. pap. 10.95 (*0-572-01973-4*, Pub. by W Foulsham UK) Trans-Atl Phila.
***Russell, Ken & Lilly, J. Robert, eds.** The Electronic Monitoring of Offenders: Symposium Papers. (Leicester Polytechnic Law School Monograph). 93p. 1989. pap. 5.00 (*0-948997-52-4*) Pickering Pubns.
Russell, Ken, jt. auth. see Carter, Philip J.
Russell, Ken, jt. auth. see Carter, Philip.
Russell, Ken, jt. ed. see Carter, Philip.
Russell, Ken A., jt. auth. see Carter, Philip J.
Russell, Kenneth & Slater, Ken. The Principles of Dairy Farming. 11th ed. (Illus.). 370p. 1991. 38.95 (*0-85236-216-1*, Pub. by Farming Pr UK) Diamond Farm Bk.
Russell, Kenneth A., jt. auth. see Carter, Philip J.
Russell, Kenneth L., ed. How in Parliamentary Procedure. 5th ed. (Illus.). 74p. (YA). (gr. 9-12). 1990. pap. text ed. 2.50 (*0-8134-2871-8*, 2171) Interstate.
***Russell, Kenneth V.** Complaints Against the Police: A Sociological View. 4th rev. ed. 152p. 1994. pap. 12.00 (*0-9504906-7-9*) Milltak Ltd.
Russell, Kenneth V., jt. ed. see Mckay, Ronald D.
Russell, Kent D. A Little American Cookbook. (Illus.). 1989. 7.95 (*0-87701-613-5*) Chronicle Bks.
***Russell, L. Mark & Grant, Arnold E.** The Life Planning Workbook: A Hands-on Guide to Help Parents Provide for the Future Security & Happiness of Their Child with a Disability after Their Death. 300p. (Orig.). 1995. pap. text ed. 24.95 (*0-9635780-7-3*) Amer Pub IL.
Russell, L. Mark, et al. Planning for the Future: Providing a Meaningful Life for a Child with a Disability after Your Death. 430p. 1993. pap. 24.95 (*0-9635780-0-6*) Amer Pub IL.
Russell, Lao. Character. Lombardi, Emilia L., ed. 20p. (Orig.). 1991. pap. text ed. 5.00 (*1-879605-35-X*) U Sci & Philos.
— God Will Work with You but Not for You. (Illus.). 266p. 1981. reprint ed. text ed. 12.00 (*1-879605-20-1*) U Sci & Philos.
— God Will Work with You but Not for You: A Living Philosophy. (Illus.). 266p. (C). 1981. reprint ed. 12.00 (*0-685-58337-6*) U Sci & Philos.
— Love. (Illus.). 207p. 1980. reprint ed. text ed. 8.00 (*1-879605-21-X*) U Sci & Philos.
— Why You Cannot Die! The Continuity of Life. (Illus.). 253p. 1972. text ed. 18.00 (*1-879605-18-X*) U Sci & Philos.
— You Create Your Own Destiny. Lombardi, Emilia L., ed. 20p. (Orig.). 1991. pap. text ed. 5.00 (*1-879605-34-1*) U Sci & Philos.
Russell, Lao, jt. auth. see Russell, Walter.
Russell, Lawrence. Mystery of the Pig Killer's Daughter: Four Plays. LC 75-12079. 134p. 1975. pap. 4.95 (*0-914580-03-5*) Angst World.
— The Twenty-Fifth Hour. (Illus.). 48p. (Orig.). 1981. pap. 2.95 (*0-914580-11-6*) Angst World.
Russell, Lee. Labyrinth. (Illus.). 1977. 4.94 (*0-940244-03-9*) Flying Buffalo.
— The U. S. Marine Corps since 1945. (Elite Ser.: No. 2). (Illus.). 64p. pap. 12.95 (*0-85045-574-X*, 9401, Pub. by Osprey Pubng Ltd UK) Stackpole.
Russell, Lee & Mendez, M. Albert. Grenada, 1983. (Men-at-Arms Ser.: No. 159). (Illus.). 48p. 1985. pap. 11.95 (*0-85045-583-9*, 9091, Pub. by Osprey UK) Stackpole.
Russell, Lee, jt. auth. see Katz, Samuel.
Russell, Lee E. Armies of the Vietnam War, Vol. 2. (Men-at-Arms Ser.: No. 143). (Illus.). 48p. pap. 11.95 (*0-85045-514-6*, 9075, Pub. by Osprey UK) Stackpole.
Russell, Lester F. Black Baptist Secondary Schools in Virginia, 1887-1957: A Study in Black History. LC 80-22414. 218p. 1981. 22.50 (*0-8108-1373-4*) Scarecrow.
Russell, Letty M. Becoming Human. LC 81-23121. (Library of Living Faith: Vol. 2). 114p. 1982. pap. 7.99 (*0-664-24408-4*, Westminster) Westminster John Knox.
— Church in the Round: Feminist Interpretation of the Church. 272p. (Orig.). 1993. pap. 14.99 (*0-664-25070-X*) Westminster John Knox.
— The Future of Partnership. LC 78-20805. 198p. 1979. pap. 11.99 (*0-664-24240-5*, Westminster) Westminster John Knox.
— Household of Freedom: Authority in Feminist Theology. LC 86-18992. 114p. (Orig.). 1987. pap. 9.99 (*0-664-24017-8*, Westminster) Westminster John Knox.
— Human Liberation in a Feminist Perspective: A Theology. LC 74-10613. 214p. 1979. pap. 10.99 (*0-664-24991-4*, Westminster) Westminster John Knox.
Russell, Letty M., ed. The Church with AIDS: Renewal in the Midst of Crisis. 168p. (Orig.). 1990. pap. 11.99 (*0-664-25111-0*) Westminster John Knox.
— Feminist Interpretation of the Bible. LC 84-17342. 166p. (Orig.). 1985. pap. 10.99 (*0-664-24639-7*, Westminster) Westminster John Knox.
Russell, Letty M., et al, eds. Inheriting Our Mothers' Gardens: Feminist Theology in Third World Perspective. LC 88-10051. 182p. 1988. pap. 12.99 (*0-664-25019-X*, Westminster) Westminster John Knox.
Russell, Linette H. & Hayat, Alan, eds. The French Publication Index: A Directory of French Educational Materials. (Illus.). 320p. (Orig.). 1990. pap. 20.00 (*0-9626800-0-1*) Continental Bk.

***Russell, Lisa H. The Tenor: Every Woman's Dream. LC 93-91096. 138p. 1994. pap. 10.00 (*0-9643892-0-7*) Banner Pubng.**
Abnormal human behavior usually results when devotion is carried to the extreme. THE TENOR is the farcical story of a group of overzealous fans attempting to insinuate themselves into the life of a superstar opera tenor who is sick & tired of all the hoopla & unwanted attention. These innovative ladies succeed beyond their wildest dreams after forming a 'cartel', organized for the sole purpose of kidnapping him. Fans of the 3 Tenor's Concerts will especially enjoy this 'inside ' look at the highs & lows in the lives of a famous opera star's followers. Readers are transported along with the tenor & his fans to a remote ranch deep in the Texas Hill Country, the Royal Opera House in London, the beautiful Palacio de Bellas Artes in Mexico City, & a drug dealer's private island off the rocky shores of Baja, California, for adventures that cement a lasting friendship. THE TENOR: EVERY WOMAN'S DREAM is the first book of a series about the famous opera singer & his fans. Notes on the second novel are printed on the flyleaf. Contact Lisa Russell at 910-692-8710 for ordering. ***Publisher Provided Annotation.***

Russell, Lonnie, jt. auth. see Trovillion, Ned.
***Russell, Lonnie, et al.** Enjoy Southern Illinois: A Complete Recreational Guide. (Illus.). 648p. (Orig.). 1993. pap. 17.95 (*0-9627422-4-4*) Cache River Pr.
— Histological & Histopathological Evaluation of the Testis. 286p. 1994. cd-rom, text ed. 120.00 (*0-9644960-0-3*) Vangrd Media.
***Russell, Lonnie D. & Ettlin, Robert A.** Histological & Histopathological Evaluation of the Testis. Hikim, Amiya P. & Clegy, Eric D., eds. (Illus.). 286p. (C). 1990. 62.50 (*0-9627422-0-1*) Cache River Pr.
***Russell, Lonnie D. & Griswold, Micheal D., eds.** The Sertoli Cell. (Illus.). 802p. (C). 1993. 137.50 (*0-9627422-1-X*) Cache River Pr.
Russell, Loris S. A Heritage of Light: Lamps & Lighting in the Early Canadian Home. LC 68-140801. (Illus.). 349p. reprint ed. pap. 99.50 (*0-317-10561-2*, 2014394) Bks Demand.
Russell, Louise B. The Baby Boom Generation & the Economy. LC 82-70890. (Studies in Social Economics). 183p. 1982. 26.95 (*0-8157-7628-4*); pap. 9.95 (*0-8157-7627-6*) Brookings.
— Educated Guesses: Making Policy About Medical Screening Tests. LC 93-8768. 1994. 30.00 (*0-520-08365-2*); pap. 11.00 (*0-520-08366-0*) U CA Pr.
— Evaluating Preventive Care: Report on a Workshop. LC 87-9304. 107p. 1987. 22.95 (*0-8157-7626-8*); pap. 8.95 (*0-8157-7625-X*) Brookings.
— Is Prevention Better than Cure? LC 85-21250. (Studies in Social Economics). 134p. 1986. 26.95 (*0-8157-7632-2*); pap. 9.95 (*0-8157-7631-4*) Brookings.
— Medicare's New Hospital Payment System: Is It Working? 120p. 1989. 22.95 (*0-8157-7624-1*); pap. 8.95 (*0-8157-7623-3*) Brookings.
— Technology in Hospitals: Medical Advances & Their Diffusion. LC 79-10737. (Studies in Social Economics). 180p. 1979. 31.95 (*0-8157-7630-6*); pap. 11.95 (*0-8157-7629-2*) Brookings.
Russell, Louise B. & Burke, Carol S. Technological Diffusion in the Hospital Sector. LC 75-37308. 240p. 1976. 8.00 (*0-89068-007-8*) Natl Planning.
Russell, Lynn. Montana Christmas. (Stolen Moments Ser.). 1993. pap. 1.99 (*0-373-83288-5*, 1-83288-0) Harlequin Bks.
Russell, M. Banking Law in New Zealand. xxxiii, 286p. 1986. pap. 39.00 (*0-455-20658-9*, Pub. by Law Bk Co) W W Gaunt.
— Nubia & Abyssinia. 440p. 1985. 300.00 (*1-85077-052-2*, Darf Pubs Ltd) St Mut.
— Palestine. 400p. 1985. 300.00 (*1-85077-053-0*, Darf Pubs Ltd) St Mut.
Russell, M. W., tr. see Guyon, Jeanne.
Russell, Malcolm B. The First Modern Arab State: Syria under Faysal, 1918-1920. (Studies in Middle Eastern History: Vol 7). 1983. 30.00 (*0-88297-030-5*) Bibliotheca.
— The Middle East & South Asia 1995. 29th ed. 245p. 1995. pap. 9.50 (*0-943448-93-X*) Stryker-Post.
Russell-Manning, Betsy. Malathion: Toxic Time Bomb. LC 90-85143. (Illus.). 265p. 1991. spiral bd. 19.95 (*0-930165-49-7*) Greensward Pr.
— Self Treatment for AIDS: Oxygen Therapy. rev. ed. 1989. per. 16.95 (*0-930165-12-8*) Greensward Pr.
Russell-Manning, Betsy, ed. Candida, Silver (Mercury) Fillings & the Immune System. rev. ed. LC 85-80413. 1990. Incl. companion bk. - Home Remedies for Candida. pap. 16.95 (*0-930165-10-1*) Greensward Pr.
— How Safe Are Silver (Mercury) Fillings? Hidden Health Facts. rev. ed. LC 84-90431. 1985. pap. 39.95 (*0-930165-00-4*) Greensward Pr.
— Wheatgrass Juice-Gift of Nature. rev. ed. 1988. pap. 2.95 (*0-930165-06-3*) Greensward Pr.
***Russell, Marcia L.** Fair Housing. LC 94-42601. 1995. write for info. (*0-7931-1331-8*, Real Estate Ed) Dearborn Finan.
Russell, Marcia L., jt. auth. see Williams, Martha R.
Russell, Margarita A. Paintings & Textiles of the Bass Museum of Art: Selections from the Collection. LC 90-82402. (Illus.). 176p. 1991. 40.00 (*1-880511-02-9*); pap. 25.00 (*1-880511-03-7*) Bass Museum.
Russell, Margo. Start Collecting Coins. LC 88-43295. (Start Collecting Ser.). (Illus.). 112p. (Orig.). 1989. pap. 9.95 (*0-89471-674-3*) Running Pr.
Russell, Marian. Land of Enchantment: Memoirs of Marian Russell Along the Santa Fe Trail. LC 80-54564. 177p. 1985. reprint ed. pap. 14.95 (*0-8263-0805-8*) U of NM Pr.
Russell, Mariann. Melvin B. Tolson's Harlem Gallery: A Literary Analysis. LC 80-50306. 153p. reprint ed. pap. 43.70 (*0-7837-2359-8*, AU00424) Bks Demand.
Russell, Marie, jt. auth. see Russell, Bert.
Russell, Marjorie H. The Arcadia Story. LC 85-40651. (Illus.). 190p. 1986. pap. 7.98 (*0-938232-83-5*) Arcadia Ministry Pubns.
— Handbook of Christian Meditation. LC 77-90859. 118p. 1978. pap. 7.98 (*0-8159-5713-0*) Arcadia Ministry Pubns.
— Revelation: Your Future Prophesied. (Illus.). 80p. (Orig.). 1985. pap. 7.98 (*0-9614745-0-5*) Arcadia Ministry Pubns.
— The Whip-Poor-Will's Song. 120p. (Orig.). (J). 1995. pap. 5.75 (*0-9614745-2-1*) Arcadia Ministry Pubns.
Russell, Marjorie H., ed. see Fuller, Joy.
Russell, Mark, jt. auth. see Farrar, John.
Russell, Martin. Deadline. (Black Dagger Crime Ser.). 192p. 16.50 (*0-86220-710-X*, Black Dagger) Chivers N Amer.
— A Domestic Affair. 192p. 1985. 13.95 (*0-8027-5633-6*) Walker & Co.
Russell, Mary. Please Don't Call It Soviet Georgia. (Illus.). 268p. (Orig.). 1992. pap. 16.99 (*1-85242-216-5*) Serpents Tail.
Russell, Mary N. Clinical Social Work: Research & Practice. (Sourcebooks for the Human Services Ser.: Vol. 14). (Illus.). 192p. (C). 1990. text ed. 49.95 (*0-8039-3782-2*); pap. text ed. 24.00 (*0-8039-3783-0*) Sage.
Russell, Mary T. & Karol, Darcie L. The Sixteen PF Fifth Edition: Administrator's Manual. 162p. (Orig.). 1994. pap. 20.00 (*0-918296-21-8*) Inst Personality & Ability.
Russell, Mattie U., jt. auth. see Godbold, E. Stanly, Jr.
***Russell, Maureen.** Days of Our Lives: A Complete History of the Long-Running Soap Opera. 240p. 1995. lib. bdg. 29.95 (*0-7864-0112-5*) McFarland & Co.
Russell Meerdink Company, Ltd. Research Staff. Equifacts: The Complete Horse Record Organizer. (Illus.). 140p. 1986. ring bd. 25.00 (*0-929346-00-9*) R Meerdink Co Ltd.
— Split Pedigree Book. 140p. 1987. ring bd. 19.00 (*0-929346-01-7*) R Meerdink Co Ltd.
Russell, Melvia, ed. see Easter, Marvin L.
Russell, Michael. History & Present Condition of the Barbary States. 1835. 59.00 (*0-403-00304-0*) Scholarly.
Russell, Michael, ed. see Spottiswood, John.
Russell, Michel. Strange Lands. 118p. 1986. 39.00 (*0-7212-0756-1*, Pub. by Regency Press) St Mut.
Russell, Mike. How to Build Almost Anything: Starting with Practically Nothing. 1993. pap. 18.95 (*0-921820-77-1*, Pub. by Camden Hse CN) Firefly Bks Ltd.
Russell, Milton, jt. auth. see Bohi, Douglas R.
Russell, Milton, jt. auth. see Bohi, Douglas R.
Russell, Morris C. Uncle Dudley's Odd Hours; Western Sketches, Indian Trail Echoes. LC 73-104558. (Illus.). 255p. reprint ed. lib. bdg. 22.00 (*0-8398-1768-1*) Irvington.
Russell, N. J., jt. auth. see Frantz, D. G.
Russell, N. J., jt. auth. see Harwood, J. L.
***Russell, Neville.** Tolley's Form & Content of Financial Statements. 270p. (C). 1994. 90.00x (*0-85459-883-9*) St Mut.
Russell, Nicholas. Like Engend'ring Like: Heredity & Animal Breeding in Early Modern England. (Illus.). 275p. 1986. 69.95 (*0-521-30657-4*) Cambridge U Pr.
Russell, Norma J., jt. auth. see Frantz, Donald G.
Russell, Norman. Introduction to Plant Science: A Humanistic & Ecological Approach. LC 75-1445. (Illus.). 302p. (C). 1975. pap. text ed. 22.50 (*0-8299-0043-8*) West Pub.
— The Novelist & Mammon: Literary Responses to the World of Commerce in the Nineteenth Century. (Illus.). 288p. 1986. 55.00 (*0-19-812851-7*) OUP.
Russell, Norman, jt. tr. see Ward, Benedicta.
Russell, Norman H. Night Dog & Other Poems. (Orig.). 1971. pap. 1.00 (*0-685-30029-3*) Cottonwood KS.
***Russell, Norman L.** Suicide Charlie. Grad, Doug, ed. 256p. 1995. mass mkt. 5.50 (*0-671-52279-5*) PB.
— Suicide Charlie: A Vietnam War Story. LC 92-29817. 216p. 1993. text ed. 19.95 (*0-275-94521-9*, C4521, Praeger Pubs) Greenwood.
Russell, Oland D. House of Mitsui. LC 70-109836. 328p. 1971. reprint ed. text ed. 38.50 (*0-8371-4327-6*, RUHM, Greenwood Pr) Greenwood.
Russell, Osborne. Journal of a Trapper. Haines, Aubrey L., ed. LC 56-52. (Illus.). xxii, 241p. 1965. pap. 8.95 (*0-8032-5166-1*) U of Nebr Pr.
Russell, P. Craig. Fairy Tales of Oscar Wilde, Vol. 1. (Illus.). 48p. (J). (gr. 3-7). 1992. 15.95 (*1-56163-056-X*) NBM.
— Fairy Tales of Oscar Wilde, Vol. 2. (J). (gr. 3-7). 1994. 15.95 (*1-56163-085-3*) NBM.
— Opera: Salome, Pelleas & Melisande, Parsifal. (Illus.). 1990. 45.00 (*0-913035-56-4*); pap. 19.95 (*0-913035-53-X*) Eclipse Bks.
Russell, P. Craig, illus. & adapt. The Thief of Bagdad. 120p. 1987. 19.95 (*0-89865-524-2*, Starblaze); pap. 12.95 (*0-89865-523-4*, Starblaze) Donning Co.
— The Thief of Bagdad. limited ed. 120p. 1987. 40.00 (*0-89865-525-0*, Starblaze) Donning Co.
Russell, P. Craig, jt. auth. see McGregor, Don.
Russell, P. E., ed. Spain: A Companion to Spanish Studies. (Illus.). 608p. 1983. pap. 25.00 (*0-416-84110-4*, NO. 3908) Routledge Chapman & Hall.
Russell, Pamela. How to Write a Precis. 75p. 1990. pap. 13.00 (*0-7766-0143-1*, Pub. by Univ Ottawa Pr CN) Paul & Co Pubs.
Russell, Pamela & Stone, Beth. Do You Have a Secret? How to Get Help for Scary Secrets. LC 85-27986. (Illus.). 36p. (Orig.). (J). (ps-2). 1986. pap. 6.95 (*0-89638-098-X*) Hazelden.
Russell, Paul. Boys of Life. 320p. 1992. pap. 10.00 (*0-452-26837-0*, Plume) NAL-Dutton.
— Freedom & Moral Sentiment: Hume's Way of Naturalizing Responsibility. 240p. 1995. 45.00 (*0-19-509501-4*) OUP.
— The Gay One-Hundred: A Ranking of the Most Influential Gay Men & Lesbians, Past & Present. LC 94-12607. 1994. 22.50 (*1-55972-242-8*, Birch Ln Pr) Carol Pub Group.
— Gay One Hundred: A Ranking of the Most Influential Gay Men & Lesbians, Past & Present. 1994. 22.50 (*0-8065-1591-0*, Citadel Pr) Carol Pub Group.
— An Introduction to the Celtic Languages. LC 94-44203. (Linguistics Library). 1995. pap. text ed. write for info. (*0-582-10081-X*, Pub. by Longman UK); boxed write for info. (*0-582-10082-8*, Pub. by Longman UK) Longman.
— Sea of Tranquility. LC 94-6474. 1994. 21.95 (*0-525-93895-8*, Dutton) NAL-Dutton.

R

An Asterisk (*) at the beginning of an entry indicates that the title is appearing in BIP for the first time.

— Sea of Tranquillity. 416p. 1995. 12.95 (*0-452-27311-0*, Plume) NAL-Dutton.

— Writing & Arithmetic: Ancient Civilizations. (J). (gr. 4-7). 1994. 15.95 (*0-688-13906-X*, Tambourine Bks) Morrow.

Russell, Paul A. Lay Theology in the Reformation: Popular Pamphleteers in Southwest Germany, 1521-1525. (Illus.). 303p. 1986. 69.95 (*0-521-30727-9*) Cambridge U Pr.

Russell, Paul L. History of Western Oil Shale. LC 80-66410. (Illus.). 176p. 1980. 49.50 (*0-86563-000-3*) Ctr Prof Adv.

***Russell, P.E.** Portugal, Spain and the African Atlantic, 1343-1490: Chivalry and Crusade from John of Guant to Henry the Navigator and Beyond. (Variorum Collected Studies Ser.). 270p. 1995. 82.50 (*0-86078-474-6*, Pub. by Variorum UK) Ashgate Pub Co.

Russell, Peggy B. Confessions of a Transplant. (Illus.). 50p. 1990. reprint ed. pap. 6.95 (*0-9625237-0-4*) Transplant Pubns.

Russell, Penny. A Wish of Distinction: Colonial Gentility & Femininity. 244p. pap. 24.95 (*0-522-84552-5*) Intl Spec Bk.

Russell, Penny, ed. For Richer, for Poorer: Early Colonial Marriages. 146p. Date not set. pap. 24.95 (*0-522-84551-7*) Intl Spec Bk.

Russell, Percy J. & Williams, Anita. The Nutrition & Health Encyclopedia. 3rd ed. LC 94-17804. 1994. write for info. (*0-412-98981-6*); pap. write for info. (*0-412-98991-3*) Chapman & Hall.

Russell, Peter. All for the Wolves: Selected Poems, 1947-1975. Jay, Peter, ed. (Literary Ser.). 151p. 1984. 25.00 (*0-933806-20-5*) Black Swan CT.

— Attitudes to Social Structure & Mobility in Upper Canada 1815-1840. LC 89-34205. (Canadian Studies: Vol. 6). 211p. 1989. lib. bdg. 89.95 (*0-88946-193-7*) E Mellen.

— Brain Book. 1984. pap. 12.95 (*0-452-26723-4*, Plume) NAL-Dutton.

— Examination of Ezra Pound: A Collection of Essays by T. S. Eliot & Others. enl. rev. ed. LC 71-150418. 273p. 1973. reprint ed. 45.00 (*0-87752-141-7*) Gordian.

— The Global Brain Awakens: Our Next Evolutionary Leap. St. John, Gloria et al, eds. (Illus.). 352p. 1995. 22.00 (*1-885261-05-5*) Global Brain.

— The Global Brain Awakens: Our Next Evolutionary Leap. rev. ed. (Illus.). 352p. 1995. 22.00 (*1-885261-04-7*) Global Brain.

— Key to the Constitution: Can the Canadians Become a Sovereign People? 200p. (Orig.). 1992. 35.00 (*0-8020-2851-9*); pap. 14.95 (*0-8020-7730-7*) U of Toronto Pr.

— Selected Sonnets. 100p. (Orig.). 1995. pap. 10.00 (*0-944920-16-0*) Bellowing Ark Pr.

— The TM Technique: An Introduction to Transcendental Meditation & the Teachings of Maharishi Mahesh Yogi. 208p. 1989. 12.95 (*0-14-019137-2*, Penguin Bks) Viking Penguin.

— The White Hole in Time: Our Future Evolution & the Meaning of Now. LC 91-58162. 272p. 1993. reprint ed. pap. 11.00 (*0-06-250717-6*) Harper SF.

Russell, Peter, ed. Ezra Pound: A Collection of Essays. LC 67-31288. 268p. (C). 1968. reprint ed. text ed. 75.00 (*0-8383-0791-4*) M S G Haskell Hse.

Russell, Peter & Bannatyne, Patricia. Surgical Pathology of the Ovaries. (Illus.). 539p. 1989. text ed. 199.00 (*0-443-03535-0*) Churchill.

Russell, Peter & Evans, Roger. The Creative Manager: Finding Inner Vision & Wisdom in Uncertain Times. LC 91-44415. (Management Ser.). 192p. 1992. 27.00 (*1-55542-413-9*) Jossey-Bass.

Russell, Peter, jt. tr. see Shearer, Alistair.

Russell, Peter E. His Majesty's Judges: Provincial Society & the Superior Court in Massachusetts, 1692-1774. LC 90-46697. (Distinguished Studies in American Legal & Constitutional History: Vol. 22). 330p. 1990. reprint ed. 71.00 (*0-8240-2527-X*) Garland.

Russell, Peter H. Constitutional Odyssey: Can Canadians Be a Sovereign People? 2nd ed. 250p. 1993. pap. 18.95 (*0-8020-6997-5*) U of Toronto Pr.

Russell, Peter J. Genetics. 2nd ed. (C). 1989. text ed. 42.50 (*0-673-39843-9*) HarpCollege.

Russell, Peter J. & Pierce, Ben. Fundamentals of Genetics. LC 93-17903. (C). 1994. Solution manual. teacher ed 21.50 (*0-06-500641-0*) HarpCollege.

— Fundamentals of Genetics. LC 93-17903. (C). 1994. text ed. 63.50 (*0-06-500640-2*) HarpCollege.

***Russell, Philip.** The Chiapas Rebellion. (Illus.). xi, 154p. (C). 1995. pap. text ed. 10.95 (*0-9639223-1-9*) Mexico Res Ctr.

— Mexico under Salinas. (Illus.). x, 486p. (C). 1994. pap. text ed. 14.95 (*0-9639223-0-0*) Mexico Res Ctr.

— Mouse Droppings Book of Macintosh Hints: What Apple Didn't Tell You about Your Macintosh Computer. 100p. 1986. spiral bd. 8.95 (*0-318-22782-7*) Macintosh Users Group.

— Mouse Droppings Second Book of Macintosh Hints. 116p. 1988. spiral bd. 8.95 (*0-318-32989-1*) Macintosh Users Group.

Russell, Philip & Hemmer, Joe. Energy-Smart Building for Increased Quality, Comfort, & Sales. Lamberton, Sharon & Soble, Carol, eds. LC 93-20754. (Illus.). 150p. (Orig.). 1993. pap. 20.00 (*0-86718-387-X*) Home Builder.

Russell, Philip L. El Salvador in Crisis. (Illus.). 168p. 1984. pap. 9.95 (*0-931302-02-1*) Colo River Pr.

Russell, Phillip L. Mexico in Transition. (Illus.). 176p. 1977. pap. 7.95 (*0-931302-01-3*) Colo River Pr.

Russell, Phillips. Harvesters. LC 73-156713. (Essay Index Reprint Ser.). 1977. reprint ed. 23.95 (*0-8369-2295-6*) Ayer.

Russell-Pineda, Diana, tr. see Agosin, Marjorie.

Russell-Pineda, Diana, tr. see Duran, Luis H.

Russell, Preston & Hines, Barbara. Savannah: A History of Her People since 1733. LC 91-45219. 1994. pap. 18.00 (*0-913720-81-X*) Beil.

Russell, Pugh, jt. auth. see Flower, Mary.

Russell, R. A., ed. see Macmillan, H. F.

Russell, R. Dana. The Pughs of Bayou Lafourche. 100p. 1985. 10.00 (*0-911051-25-2*) Plain View.

Russell, R. G. & Dieppe, P. A. Osteoarthritis: Current Research & Prospects for Pharmacological Intervention. 232p. (C). 1991. 300.00 (*1-85271-093-4*, Pub. by IBC Tech Srvs UK) St Mut.

Russell, R. Robert & Wilkinson, Maurice. Microeconomics: A Synthesis of Modern & Neoclassical Theory. LC 78-17175. 476p. reprint ed. pap. 135.70 (*0-7837-3501-4*, 2057834) Bks Demand.

Russell, Ralph. The Pursuit of Urdu Literature: A Select History. LC 92-12331. 320p. (C). 1992. text ed. 59.95 (*1-85649-028-9*, Pub. by Zed Books UK); pap. 29.95 (*1-85649-029-7*, Pub. by Zed Books UK) Humanities.

Russell, Ralph & Islam, Khurshidal. Three Mughal Poets: Mir, Mir Hasan, & Sauda. 310p. 1992. 14.95 (*0-19-562850-0*) OUP.

***Russell, Ralph & Islam, Khurshidul, eds.** Ghalib 1797-1869: Life & Letters. Islam, Khurshidul, tr. (Oxford India Paperbacks Ser.). (Illus.). 426p. 1995. pap. 12.95 (*0-19-563506-X*) OUP.

***Russell, Randy.** Billy the Kid: The Story - The Trial. LC 94-74143. (Illus.). (Orig.). 1995. pap. 15.95 (*0-9644476-3-0*) Crystal Pr NM.

— Five Minutes Late. 32p. (Orig.). 1988. pap. 1.50 (*0-944388-01-9*) TBS Pubns.

— Universe City. 48p. (Orig.). 1987. pap. 3.00 (*0-944388-00-0*) TBS Pubns.

Russell, Randy & Barnett, Janet. Mountain Ghost Stories & Curious Tales of Western North Carolina. LC 88-19380. 109p. 1988. 9.95 (*0-89587-064-9*) Blair.

Russell, Ray. Absolute Power. deluxe limited ed. 256p. 1992. 49.00 (*0-940776-27-8*) Maclay Assoc.

— Case Against Satan. 1962. 10.95 (*0-8392-1008-6*) Astor-Honor.

— Haunted Castles: The Complete Gothic Tales of Ray Russell. LC 85-61370. 192p. 1985. 12.95 (*0-940776-20-0*) Maclay Assoc.

— Miracle of Leadership. 304p. 1995. 26.95 (*0-7872-0603-2*) Kendall-Hunt.

Russell, Raymond. Utopia in Zion: The Israeli Experience with Worker Cooperatives. LC 94-19576. (SUNY Series in Jewish Philosophy). 288p. (C). 1995. 59.50x (*0-7914-2443-X*); pap. 19.95x (*0-7914-2444-8*) State U NY Pr.

Russell, Raymond & Rus, Veljko, eds. International Handbook of Participation in Organizations, Vol. 2: Ownership & Participation. (Illus.). 384p. 1991. 120.00 (*0-19-828702-X*) OUP.

Russell, Raymond M., jt. auth. see Coleman, Ronny J.

Russell, Richard. The Alchemical Works of Geber. (Illus.). 320p. (Orig.). 1994. text ed. 35.00 (*0-87728-811-9*) Weiser.

— The Dow Theory Today. LC 81-68858. 1981. reprint ed. 11.00 (*0-87034-061-1*) Fraser Pub Co.

— Insomnia. (Illus.). 29p. 1991. 10.00 (*0-932526-36-5*) Nexus Pr.

— O My Darling O My Darling: Love Letters. (Poetry Ser.: No. 7). 1979. pap. 5.95 (*0-930020-06-5*) Stone Country.

Russell, Richard & Brewer, Doug. Leader Lore-The Book. 200p. 1993. write for info. (*0-9634786-4-8*) Mass Media Dist.

Russell, Richard, tr. see Geber.

Russell, Richard J. River & Delta Morphology. LC 67-29343. (Louisiana State University Studies, Coastal Studies Ser.: No. 20). 63p. reprint ed. pap. 25.00 (*0-317-29938-7*, 2051688) Bks Demand.

Russell, Rinaldina. Italian Women Writers: A Bio-Bibliographical Sourcebook. LC 93-49535. 512p. 1994. text ed. 89.50 (*0-313-28347-8*, Greenwood Pr) Greenwood.

Russell, Robert. The Answer Will Come. 91p. 1981. reprint ed. pap. 4.95 (*0-87516-440-4*) DeVorss.

— The Fun Bus, No. 15. (Technical Notes Ser.). 43p. (Orig.). 1977. pap. 2.00 (*0-932288-42-1*) Ctr Intl Ed U of MA.

— Go on, I'm Listening. large type ed. 432p. 1986. 15.95 (*0-7089-1547-7*) Ulverscroft.

— Russian Drama of the Revolutionary Period. 192p. 1987. 50.50 (*0-389-20757-8*) B&N Imports.

— While You're Here, Doctor. large type ed. 512p. 1987. 16.95 (*0-7089-1604-X*) Ulverscroft.

Russell, Robert, jt. ed. see Dickinson, James.

Russell, Robert A. Dry Those Tears. 133p. 1975. reprint ed. pap. 6.95 (*0-87516-203-7*) DeVorss.

— God Works Through Faith. 1957. pap. 5.95 (*0-87516-325-4*) DeVorss.

— Making the Contact. 90p. 1980. reprint ed. pap. 4.95 (*0-87516-391-2*) DeVorss.

— You Too Can Be Prosperous. 162p. 1975. reprint ed. pap. 6.95 (*0-87516-205-3*) DeVorss.

— You Try It. 1953. pap. 5.95 (*0-87516-326-2*) DeVorss.

Russell, Robert A., jt. auth. see Cook, Thomas M.

Russell, Robert B. Attractive & Easy-to-Build Wood Projects. (Illus.). 64p. (Orig.). 1980. pap. 3.95 (*0-486-23965-9*) Dover.

Russell, Robert D., Jr., jt. auth. see Johnson, Eugene J.

Russell, Robert H. & Patterson, Margaret J., eds. Behind the Lines: Case Studies in Investigative Reporting. 350p. 1986. text ed. 37.00 (*0-231-06058-0*) Col U Pr.

Russell, Robert H., tr. see Galdos, Benito P.

Russell, Robert J. The Lemurs' Legacy: The Evolution of Power, Sex, & Love. LC 92-33435. (Illus.). 256p. 1993. 22.95 (*0-87477-714-3*, J P T-Putnam) Putnam Pub Group.

Russell, Robert J., et al, eds. Physics, Philosophy, & Theology: A Common Quest for Understanding. (C). 1988. text ed. 30.00x (*0-268-01576-7*) U of Notre Dame Pr.

— Quantum Cosmology & the Laws of Nature: Scientific Perspectives on Divine Action. (C). 1994. pap. text ed. 19.95 (*0-268-03976-3*) U of Notre Dame Pr.

Russell, Robert L. Language in Psychotherapy: Strategies in Discovery. LC 87-2511. (Emotions, Personality, & Psychotherapy Ser.). (Illus.). 368p. 1987. 65.00 (*0-306-42422-3*, Plenum Pr) Plenum.

— The Making Things Happen. 256p. 1987. pap. 9.99 (*0-87403-267-9*, 3181) Standard Pub.

Russell, Robert L., ed. Reassessing Psychotherapy Research. LC 94-8548. 1994. lib. bdg. 30.00 (*0-89862-755-9*, C2755) Guilford Pubns.

Russell, Robert P., tr. see Augustine.

Russell, Robert R. Economic Aspects of Southern Sectionalism, 1840-1861. LC 72-11346. (American South Ser.). 1973. reprint ed. 30.95 (*0-405-05062-3*) Ayer.

— Improvement of Communication with the Pacific Coast as an Issue in American Politics, 1783-1864. Bruchey, Stuart, ed. LC 80-1341. (Railroads Ser.). (Illus.). 1981. reprint ed. lib. bdg. 30.95 (*0-405-13813-X*) Ayer.

Russell, Roberta. Report on Effective Psychotherapy: Legislative Testimony. Smith, Suzanne, ed. LC 81-90112. 81p. (C). 1981. 30.00 (*0-940106-00-0*) Hillgarth Pr.

— Report on Effective Psychotherapy: Legislative Testimony & Recommendations for Therapeutic Relationships in a Caring World. rev. ed. Smith, Suzanne, ed. 120p. Date not set. pap. text ed. 14.95 (*0-940106-54-X*) Hillgarth Pr.

Russell, Roberta & Laing, R. D. R. D. Laing & Me: Lessons in Love. Smith, Suzanne, ed. LC 92-70905. (Illus.). 292p. 1992. 25.95 (*0-940106-61-2*, Baker & Taylor); pap. 16.95 (*0-940106-50-7*, Baker & Taylor) Hillgarth Pr.

Russell, Robin I., ed. Elemental Diets. 280p. 1981. 134.00 (*0-8493-5671-7*, RM229, CRC Reprint) Franklin.

Russell, Ronald. Discovering Antique Prints. 1989. pap. 25.00 (*0-85263-587-7*, Pub. by Shire UK) St Mut.

Russell, Ronald, ed. Using the Whole Brain: Integrating the Right & Left Brain with Hemi-Sync Sound Patterns. 264p. (Orig.). 1993. pap. 14.95 (*1-878901-86-9*) Hampton Roads Pub Co.

Russell, Ronald & Medcalf, Donald. Hawaiian Money Standard Catalog, 1991. 2nd ed. (Illus.). 160p. 1990. 25.00 (*0-9623263-0-5*) R Russell.

Russell, Ross. Jazz Style in Kansas City & the Southwest. LC 72-138507. (Illus.). 344p. 1982. reprint ed. 35.00 (*0-520-04767-2*) U CA Pr.

Russell, Roy, jt. ed. see Jarman, Beatriz G.

Russell, Roy E. Life, Mind & Laughter: A Theory of Laughter. LC 87-91652. (Illus.). 128p. (Orig.). (C). 1987. pap. 8.50 (*0-9619162-0-6*) Russell WV.

Russell, Rupert. Spotlight on Possums. (Illus.). 91p. 1980. 18.00 (*0-7022-1478-7*, Pub. by Univ Queensland Pr AT) Intl Spec Bk.

Russell, Ruth. Lake Front. LC 74-22811. (Labor Movement in Fiction & Non-Fiction Ser.). (Illus.). reprint ed. 45.00 (*0-404-58467-5*) AMS Pr.

Russell, Ruth, jt. ed. see Johnson, Broderick.

***Russell, Ruth V.** Pastimes: The Context of Contemporary Leisure. 480p. (C). 1995. boxed write for info. (*0-697-22725-1*) Brown & Benchmark.

— Planning Programs in Recreation. LC 81-14098. (Illus.). 368p. (C). 1982. pap. text ed. 24.95 (*0-8016-4231-0*) Mosby Yr Bk.

Russell, Ruth W. North for Gold: The Red Lake Gold Rush of 1926. (Illus.). 210p. (C). 1987. lib. bdg. 16.00 (*0-921075-01-4*) N Waterloo Acad Pr.

Russell, Sallie J. Pockets Zippers Colors: Clothing Designs for Kids. (Illus.). 44p. (Orig.). 1992. pap. 8.95 (*1-883777-00-3*) SJR Sew.

Russell, Sandi. Render Me My Song: African-American Women Writers from Slavery to the Present. 240p. 1992. pap. 9.95 (*0-312-07074-8*) St Martin.

Russell, Sandra. The Captain Remembers. (Illus.). 141p. (Orig.). 1993. pap. 12.95 (*0-910303-42-8*) Writers Pub Serv.

Russell, Sean. Gatherer of Clouds. 528p. (Orig.). 1992. mass mkt. 5.99 (*0-88677-536-1*) DAW Bks.

— The Initiate Brother, Bk. 1. 480p. (Orig.). 1991. mass mkt. 5.99 (*0-88677-466-7*) DAW Bks.

— World Without End. (Moontide & Magic Rise Ser.: No. 1). 608p. (Orig.). 1995. pap. 5.99 (*0-88677-624-4*) DAW Bks.

Russell, Sharman. Frederick Douglass. (Black Americans of Achievement Ser.). (Illus.). 112p. (Orig.). (YA). (gr. 5 up). 1988. 17.95 (*1-55546-580-3*); pap. 9.95 (*0-7910-0204-7*) Chelsea Hse.

Russell, Sharman A. The Humpbacked Fluteplayer. LC 92-44492. (J). 1994. 16.00 (*0-679-82408-1*) Knopf Bks Yng Read.

— Kill the Cowboy: A Battle of Mythology in the New West. 240p. 1994. pap. 11.54 (*0-201-62693-4*) Addison-Wesley.

Russell, Sharon A. Semiotics & Lighting: A Study of Six Modern French Cameramen. LC 81-3377. (Studies in Photography & Cinematography: No. 2). 185p. reprint ed. pap. 52.80 (*0-685-20881-8*, 2070215) Bks Demand.

Russell, Sharon S. & Teitelbaum, Michael. International Migration & International Trade. LC 92-12848. (Discussion Paper Ser.: Vol. 160). 93p. 1992. pap. 7.95 (*0-8213-2116-1*, 12116) World Bank.

Russell, Sharon S., et al. International Migration & Development in Sub-Saharan Africa: Volume 1, Overview; Volume 2, Country Analyses, 2 vols., Vol. 1. (Discussion Paper Ser.: Nos. 101-102). 184p. 1990. 10.95 (*0-8213-1642-7*, 11642) World Bank.

— International Migration & Development in Sub-Saharan Africa: Volume 1, Overview; Volume 2, Country Analyses, 2 vols., Vol. 2. (Discussion Paper Ser.: Nos. 101-102). 172p. 1990. 10.95 (*0-8213-1643-5*, 11643) World Bank.

Russell, Sheldon. Empire. 204p. 1993. 18.95 (*0-934188-39-4*) Evans Pubns.

Russell, Sherman A. Kill the Cowboy: A Battle of Mythology in the New West. LC 93-525. (Illus.). 256p. 1993. 19.23 (*0-201-58123-X*) Addison-Wesley.

— Songs of the Fluteplayer: Seasons of Life in the Southwest. 1991. 18.22 (*0-201-57093-9*) Addison-Wesley.

— Songs of the Fluteplayer: Seasons of Life in the Southwest. (Illus.). 176p. 1992. pap. 9.60 (*0-201-60821-9*) Addison-Wesley.

***Russell, Sofia.** Whiskey Trail. 500p. (Orig.). 1995. pap. 12.95 (*0-7610-0058-5*) NW Pub.

Russell, Stella. Art in the World. 4th ed. LC 92-70938. (Illus.). 550p. (C). 1992. pap. text ed. write for info. (*0-03-276543-6*) HB Coll Pubs.

Russell, Stella P. Art in the World. 3rd ed. (Illus.). (C). 1989. pap. text ed. 42.75 (*0-03-028672-7*) HB Coll Pubs.

Russell, Stephen & Kolb, Jurgen. The Tao of Sexual Massage. (Illus.). 192p. (Orig.). 1992. pap. 15.00 (*0-671-78089-1*, Fireside) S&S Trade.

Russell, Stuart. Use of Knowledge in Analogy & Induction. (Research Notes in Artificial Intelligence Ser.). 1989. 29.95 (*1-55860-089-2*) Morgan Kaufmann.

***Russell, Stuart & Norvig, Peter.** Artificial Intelligence: A Modern Approach. 1994. text ed. 61.33 (*0-13-103805-2*) P-H.

Russell, Stuart & Wefald, Eric H. Do the Right Thing: Studies in Limited Rationality. (Artificial Intelligence Ser.). 200p. 1991. 30.00 (*0-262-18144-4*) MIT Pr.

Russell, Stuart H. Resource Recovery Economics: Methods for Feasibility Analysis. (Pollution Engineering & Technology Ser.: Vol. 22). (Illus.). 312p. 1982. 125.00 (*0-8247-1726-0*) Dekker.

Russell, Susan, jt. auth. see Flynn, Robert.

Russell, Susan D., ed. Ritual, Power & Economy: Upland-Lowland Contrasts in Mainland Southeast Asia. (Occasional Paper Ser.: No. 14). 143p. (Orig.). (C). 1989. pap. 11.00 (*1-877979-14-7*) North Ill U Ctr SE Asian.

Russell, Susan D. & Cunningham, Clark E., eds. Changing Lives, Changing Rites: Ritual & Social Dynamics in Philippine & Indonesian Uplands. LC 88-63412. (Michigan Studies on South & Southeast Asia: No. 1). 201p. (Orig.). 1989. pap. 16.95 (*0-89148-058-7*) Ctr S&SE Asian.

Russell, Susan J., et al. Beyond Drill & Practice: Expanding the Computer Mainstream. 120p. 1989. 10.00 (*0-86586-190-0*, P333) Coun Exc Child.

Russell, T. F., et al, eds. Computational Methods in Water Resources IX: Proceedings of the Ninth International Conference on Computational Methods in Water Resources (CMWR 92) Held in Denver, USA, June 1992, 2 vols., Set. LC 92-70436. (CMWR Computational Ser.: Vol. 9). 1594p. 1992. 585.00 (*1-56252-098-9*) Computational Mech MA.

— Computational Methods in Water Resources IX Vol. 1: Numerical Methods in Water Resources. LC 92-70436. (CMWR Computational Ser.: Vol. 9). 784p. 1992. 320.00 (*1-56252-123-3*) Computational Mech MA.

— Computational Methods in Water Resources IX Vol. 2: Mathematical Modeling in Water Resources. LC 92-70436. (CMWR Computational Ser.: Vol. 9). 810p. 1992. 330.00 (*1-56252-124-1*) Computational Mech MA.

Russell, T. Triplett & Gott, John K. The Dixon Valley: Its First 250 Years. (Illus.). 168p. (Orig.). 1991. pap. 17.50 (*1-55613-427-4*) Heritage Bk.

Russell, Terence. The Built Environment: A Subject Index, 1800-1960, 4 vols., Set. 4450p. 1990. text ed. 700.00 (*0-576-40006-8*) Gregg Intl.

Russell, Terence M. & Ashworth, Ann-Marie. Architecture in the Encyclopedie of Diderot & D'Alembert: The Letterpress Articles & Selected Engravings. 500p. 1993. 93.95 (*0-85967-857-1*, Pub. by Scolar Pr UK) Ashgate Pub Co.

Russell, Thomas H. Mexico in Peace & War. 1976. lib. bdg. 59.95 (*0-8490-0626-0*) Gordon Pr.

Russell, Thomas J. Pioneer Reminiscences of Jefferson County. Boodry, Bertie H., ed. LC 86-62792. 160p. 1987. reprint ed. 28.00 (*0-318-22096-2*); reprint ed. pap. 20.00 (*0-318-22097-0*) SE Tex G&H.

Russell, Thyra K. Job Sharing: An Anotated Bibliography. LC 93-45475. 221p. 1994. 29.50 (*0-8108-2826-X*) Scarecrow.

***Russell, Tim.** Effective Feedback Skills. 128p. (C). 1994. pap. 45.00x (*0-7494-1000-0*, Pub. by IPM Hse UK) St Mut.

Russell, Tim, tr. see Konig, Klaus-Peter & Hugo, Martin.

Russell, Timothy. Adversaria. (TriQuarterly Bks.). 87p. (Orig.). 1993. 25.00 (*0-8101-5027-1*); pap. 10.95 (*0-8101-5002-6*) Northwestern U Pr.

Russell, Tom. How to Use New Age Principles For Successful Selling. 30p. 1982. 2.00 (*0-911201-01-7*) New Age Bus Bks.

Russell, Tom & Munby, Hugh, eds. Teachers & Teaching: From Classroom to Reflection. 224p. 1992. 80.00 (*0-7507-0020-3*, Falmer Pr); pap. 29.00 (*0-7507-0021-1*, Falmer Pr) Taylor & Francis.

Russell, Tony. The Complete Country Music Discography: 1922-1942. Date not set. 30.00 (*0-915608-07-3*) Country Music Found.

***Russell, Travis.** Signaling System No. 7. LC 94-49007. (Series on Computer Communications). 1995. text ed. 60.00 (*0-07-054991-5*) McGraw.

Russell, Trusten W. Voltaire, Dryden & Heroic Tragedy. LC 46-5389. reprint ed. 20.00 (*0-404-05467-6*) AMS Pr.

Russell, Victor, jt. auth. see Filey, Mike.

Russell, Victor L., ed. Forging a Consensus: Historical Essays on Toronto. 368p. 1984. 35.00 (0-8020-3409-8); pap. 14.95 (0-8020-3410-1) U of Toronto Pr.

Russell, Vivian. Gardens of the Riviera. LC 93-14076. (Illus.). 160p. 1994. 37.50 (0-8478-1778-4) Rizzoli Intl.

— Monet's Garden: Through the Seasons at Giverny. (Illus.). 168p. (Orig.). 1995. 32.50 (1-55670-415-1) Stewart Tabori & Chang.

Russell, W. Clark. The Frozen Pirate, 2 vols. in 1. LC 74-16518. (Science Fiction Ser.). 606p. 1975. reprint ed. 47. 95 (0-405-06311-3) Ayer.

Russell, W. Keith, et al. Linguistics & Deaf Children: Transformational Syntax & Its Applications. LC 76-11696. (Illus.). 1976. pap. text ed. 7.95 (0-88200-072-1, C2115) Alexander Graham.

Russell, W. R. Multiple Sclerosis: Control of the Disease. 1976. pap. text ed. 18.25 (0-08-021002-3, Pergamon Pr) Elsevier.

Russell, Walter. The Book of Early Whisperings. (Illus.). 103p. 1977. reprint ed. text ed. 15.00 (1-879605-17-1) U Sci & Philos.

— Dawn of a New Day in Human Relations. Lombardi, Emilia L., ed. 20p. (Orig.). 1991. pap. text ed. 5.00 (1-879605-32-5) U Sci & Philos.

— The Divine Iliad, 2 vols. (Illus.). 286p. 1971. reprint ed. Vol. I, 286p. text ed. 15.00 (1-879605-22-8); reprint ed. Vol. II, 238p. text ed. 15.00 (1-879605-23-6) U Sci & Philos.

— The Divine Iliad, 2 vols., Set. (Illus.). 524p. 1971. reprint ed. text ed. write for info. (1-879605-24-4) U Sci & Philos.

— Genius Inherent in Everyone. Lombardi, Emilia L., ed. 20p. (Orig.). 1991. pap. text ed. 5.00 (1-879605-36-8) U Sci & Philos.

— Immortality of Man. Lombardi, Emilia L., ed. 20p. (Orig.). 1992. pap. text ed. 5.00 (1-879605-33-3) U Sci & Philos.

— A New Concept of the Universe: A Brief Treatise on the Russell Cosmogony. (Illus.). 178p. 1989. reprint ed. pap. text ed. 15.00 (1-879605-13-9) U Sci & Philos.

— The Secret of Light. (Illus.). 288p. 1974. text ed. 23.00 (1-879605-43-0); pap. text ed. 17.00 (1-879605-44-9) U Sci & Philos.

— The Secret of Light. (Illus.). 288p. 1974. reprint ed. text ed. 20.00 (1-879605-10-4) U Sci & Philos.

— The Universal One. (Illus.). 266p. 1974. reprint ed. text ed. 200.00 (1-879605-08-2) U Sci & Philos.

— Your Day & Night. 23p. 1946. 1.50 (1-879605-09-0) U Sci & Philos.

Russell, Walter & Binder, Timothy. In the Wave Lies the Secret of Creation. limited ed. (Illus.). 1994. Ltd. ed. 25. 00 (1-879605-42-2) U Sci & Philos.

Russell, Walter & Russell, Lao. Atomic Suicide? (Illus.). 304p. 1981. reprint ed. text ed. 20.00 (1-879605-11-2) U Sci & Philos.

— The Electrifying Power of Man-Woman Balance. (Illus.). 93p. 1988. reprint ed. text ed. 7.00 (1-879605-14-7) U Sci & Philos.

— The Home Study Course in Universal Law, Natural Science & Living Philosophy, 12 units, Set. (Illus.). 933p. 1951. pap. text ed. 200.00 (1-879605-06-6) U Sci & Philos.

— Scientific Answer to Human Relations: A Blueprint for Harmony in Industry. (Illus.). 68p. 1978. text ed. 7.00 (1-879605-15-5) U Sci & Philos.

— The World Crisis: Its Explanation & Solution. (Illus.). 203p. 1984. reprint ed. text ed. 8.00 (1-879605-19-8) U Sci & Philos.

Russell, Wiley. Blood Brothers. 1989. pap. 22.00 (0-7487-0182-6) Dufour.

— Our Day Out & Other Plays. 1989. pap. 10.95 (0-09-172882-7) Dufour.

Russell, Willey. Our Day Out. 56p. (J). 1988. pap. 7.95 (0-413-54870-8, A0201) Heinemann.

Russell, William. Broadcasters. LC 93-44982. (J). 1994. write for info. (1-57103-054-9) Rourke Pr.

— California Mental Health Is Going Down. 24p. (Orig.). Date not set. pap. write for info. (1-885206-03-8, Iliad Pr) Cader Pubng.

— Farmers. LC 93-42481. (Careers Ser.). (J). 1994. write for info. (1-57103-057-3) Rourke Pr.

— Fishermen. (J). 1994. write for info. (0-318-72499-5) Rourke Pr.

— The Florida Keys. LC 93-48334. 1994. write for info. (1-55916-032-2) Rourke Bk Co.

— Fossils. LC 94-2402. (From This Earth Ser.). (J). (gr. 3 up). 1994. write for info. (0-86593-358-8) Rourke Corp.

— The Galapagos Islands. LC 93-48335. (J). 1994. write for info. (1-55916-031-4) Rourke Bk Co.

— Gold & Silver. LC 94-504. (From This Earth Ser.). (J). (gr. 3 up). 1994. write for info. (0-86593-359-6) Rourke Corp.

— Hawaii. LC 93-49340. (Islands in the Sea Ser.). (J). 1994. write for info. (1-55916-034-9) Rourke Bk Co.

— Iceland. LC 93-49326. (Islands in the Sea Ser.). (J). 1994. write for info. (1-55916-036-5) Rourke Bk Co.

— Mountains & Canyons. LC 94-505. (From This Land Ser.). (J). (gr. 3 up). 1994. write for info. (0-86593-360-X) Rourke Corp.

— Oil, Coal & Gas. LC 94-2401. (J). (gr. 3 up). 1994. write for info. (0-86593-357-X) Rourke Corp.

— Pilots. LC 93-45009. (J). 1994. write for info. (1-57103-059-X) Rourke Pr.

— Precious Stones. LC 94-506. (From This Earth Ser.). (J). (gr. 3 up). 1994. write for info. (0-86593-361-8) Rourke Corp.

— Rocks & Minerals. LC 94-507. (From This Earth Ser.). (J). (gr. 3 up). 1994. write for info. (0-86593-362-6) Rourke Corp.

— Taiwan. LC 93-48341. (Islands in the Sea Ser.). (J). 1994. write for info. (1-55916-033-0) Rourke Bk Co.

— Truckers. LC 93-42484. (Careers Ser.). (J). 1994. write for info. (1-57103-058-1) Rourke Pr.

— The West Indies. LC 93-49339. (J). 1994. write for info. (1-55916-035-7) Rourke Bk Co.

— Zookeepers. LC 93-42482. (Careers Ser.). (J). 1994. write for info. (1-57103-055-7) Rourke Pr.

Russell, William & Kalies, Joanne. The Sound of Time. (Illus.). 40p. (Orig.). 1992. pap. text ed. 6.95 (1-56315-061-1) Sterling Hse.

Russell, William C. The Death Ship: A Strange Story, 2 vols. in one. Reginald, R., ed. LC 75-46306. (Supernatural & Occult Fiction Ser.). 1976. reprint ed. lib. bdg. 70.95 (0-405-08166-9) Ayer.

— Honour of the Flag & Other Stories. LC 70-103528. (Short Story Index Reprint Ser.). 1977. 17.95 (0-8369-3270-6) Ayer.

— Horatio Nelson & the Naval Supremacy of England. LC 73-14467. (Heroes of the Nations Ser.). reprint ed. 30.00 (0-404-58285-0) AMS Pr.

Russell, William F. Classic Myths to Read Aloud. 1992. 10. 00 (0-517-58837-4, Crown) Crown Pub Group.

— Classic Myths to Read Aloud: The Classic Stories of Greek & Roman Mythology Specially Arranged by an Education Consultant. 288p. 1988. 19.00 (0-517-57012-2, Crown) Crown Pub Group.

— Classics to Read Aloud to Your Children. 320p. 1992. 10. 00 (0-517-58715-7, Crown) Crown Pub Group.

— More Classics to Read Aloud to Your Children. 320p. 1986. 19.00 (0-517-56108-5, Crown) Crown Pub Group.

— More Classics to Read Aloud to Your Children. 1994. pap. 10.00 (0-517-88227-2, Crown) Crown Pub Group.

Russell, William F., sel. Classics to Read Aloud to Your Children. LC 84-7033. 320p. (J). (ps-5). 1984. 19.00 (0-517-55404-6, Crown) Crown Pub Group.

Russell, William G. What I Know about Winchester. 212p. 1953. write for info. (0-318-64323-5) Winchester-Frederick Cty Hist Soc.

Russell, William H. William Howard Russell: My Diary North & South. Berwanger, Eugene H., ed. 256p. (C). 1987. pap. text ed. 8.95 (0-394-36637-9, KnopfC) Knopf.

— William Howard Russell's Civil War: Private Diary & Letters, 1861-1862. Crawford, Martin, ed. LC 91-14194. (Illus.). 336p. 1992. 40.00 (0-8203-1369-6) U of Ga Pr.

Russell, William H., jt. auth. see Berwanger, Eugene.

Russell, William L. The New York Hospital: A History of the Psychiatric Service, 1771-1936. LC 73-2414. (Mental Illness & Social Policy; the American Experience Ser.). 1973. reprint ed. 40.95 (0-405-05224-3) Ayer.

Russell, William R. Luther's Theological Testament: The Schmalkald Articles. 1994. 30.00 (0-8006-2660-5, Fortress Pr) Augsburg Fortress.

Russell, William R., ed. see Forell, George W.

Russell, Willy. Blood Brothers. (Illus.). 68p. 1993. pap. 17. 95 (0-7119-2221-7) Music Sales.

— Educating Rita. Adams, Richard, ed. (Study Texts Ser.). 1985. pap. text ed. 5.72 (0-582-33182-X, 72068) Longman.

— Educating Rita, Stags & Hens & Blood Brothers. 240p. 1986. pap. 9.95 (0-413-41110-9, A0079, Pub. by Methuen UK) Heinemann.

Russell-Wood, A. J. Fidalgos & Philanthropists: The Santa Casa de Misericordia of Bahia, 1550-1755. LC 68-55798. 455p. reprint ed. pap. 129.70 (0-318-34905-1, 2031315) Bks Demand.

— Society & Government in Colonial Brazil, 1500-1822. (Collected Studies: No. 382). 352p. 1992. 89.95 (0-86078-333-2, Pub. by Variorum UK) Ashgate Pub Co.

— A World on the Move: The Portuguese in Africa, Asia, & America, 1415-1808. LC 92-35178. 305p. 1993. text ed. 39.95 (0-312-09427-2) St Martin.

Russell-Wood, A. J., ed. From Colony to Nation: Essays on the Independence of Brazil. LC 74-24381. (Symposia in Comparative History Ser.). (Illus.). 280p. 1975. 39.50 (0-8018-1665-3) Johns Hopkins.

Russen, David. Iter Lunare. LC 76-14908. 150p. 1976. 25.00 (0-8398-2343-6) Ultramarine Pub.

***Russer, Maximilian F.** The Mary-Christ: Idolatory in the Roman Catholic. 336p. 1995. pap. 9.95 (1-56901-687-9) NW Pub.

Russer, P., jt. auth. see Luy, J. F.

Russett. Test Bank. (C). 1995. pap. text ed. write for info. (0-7167-2375-1) W H Freeman.

— World Politics. 4th ed. (C). 1995. pap. text ed. write for info. (0-7167-2290-9) W H Freeman.

***Russett, Bruce.** Grasping the Democratic Peace. 1995. pap. 13.95 (0-691-00164-2) Princeton U Pr.

— Grasping the Democratic Peace: Principles for a Post-Cold War World. LC 93-16274. 192p. 1993. 19.95 (0-691-03346-3) Princeton U Pr.

Russett, Bruce M. Community & Contention: Britain & America in the Twentieth Century. LC 82-20952. xii, 252p. 1983. reprint ed. text ed. 59.75 (0-313-23792-1, RUCC, Greenwood Pr) Greenwood.

— Controlling the Sword: The Democratic Governance of National Security. (Illus.). 201p. 1990. 29.00 (0-674-16990-5) HUP.

— International Regions & the International System. LC 73-16608. (Illus.). 252p. 1975. reprint ed. text ed. 59.75 (0-8371-7191-1, RUIR, Greenwood Pr) Greenwood.

— What Price Vigilance? The Burdens of National Defense. LC 75-119475. (Yale Fastback Ser.: No. YF-5). (Illus.). 274p. reprint ed. pap. 78.10 (0-317-09345-2, 2022036) Bks Demand.

Russett, Bruce M., jt. auth. see Alker, Hayward R.

Russett, Bruce M., et al. World Handbook of Political & Social Indicators. LC 77-13514. (Tools & Methods of Comparative Research Ser.: No. 1). (Illus.). 373p. 1977. reprint ed. text ed. 69.50 (0-8371-9857-7, RUWH, Greenwood Pr) Greenwood.

Russett, Cynthia E. Sexual Science: The Victorian Construction of Womanhood. LC 88-24521. 250p. 1989. text ed. 32.00 (0-674-80290-X) HUP.

— Sexual Science: The Victorian Construction of Womanhood. 256p. 1991. pap. text ed. 14.95 (0-674-80291-8, RUSSEY) HUP.

Russett, Robert & Starr, Cecile. Experimental Animation: Origins of a New Art. (Quality Paperbacks Ser.). (Illus.). 224p. 1988. reprint ed. pap. 14.95 (0-306-80314-3) Da Capo.

Russev, R. Bulgarian-English Dictionary. 1990. lib. bdg. 39. 95 (0-8288-2627-7) Fr & Eur.

— Bulgarian-English Dictionary. (BUL & ENG.). 42.50 (0-685-04461-0, 006-2) Saphrograph.

Russevelt, P. Superinsulation. (C). 1987. 130.00 (0-685-33090-7, Pub. by Interntl Solar Energy Soc UK) St Mut.

Russian Day Committee Staff. The Orthodox Prayer Book. 606p. (ENG & SLA.). 1991. Black cover. 14.95 (1-878997-16-5); White cover. 14.95 (1-878997-29-7) St Tikhons Pr.

***Russian Information & Business Center, Inc. Staff.** Russian Business White & Yellow Pages: 25,000 Business Contacts in Russia & Worldwide. 800p. 1995. pap. 149.00 (0-9646241-0-9) Russ Info & Busn Ctr.

Russian Numismatic Society Staff, ed. see Ilyin, A. A.

Russian Orthodox Greek Catholic Church of America Staff, tr. The Divine Liturgy According to St. John Chrysostom with Appendicies. 2nd ed. 1977. Black Cover. 10.00 (1-878997-17-3); White Cover. 10.00 (1-878997-30-0); Large Altar ed. 16.95 (1-878997-18-1) St Tikhons Pr.

Russianoff, Leon. Clarinet Method, Bk. I. (Illus.). Book I. write for info. (0-318-56700-8) Macmillan.

— Clarinet Method, Bk. II. (Schirmer Book Ser.). (Illus.). Book II. 14.95 (0-685-05965-0) Macmillan.

Russianoff, Penelope. When Am I Going to Be Happy? 1989. mass mkt. 5.99 (0-553-28215-8) Bantam.

— Why Do I Think I Am Nothing Without a Man? 1985. mass mkt. 5.99 (0-553-27879-7) Bantam.

Russianoff, Penelope, ed. Women in Crisis. LC 80-29492. (Sponsored by Women in Crisis, Inc. Ser.). 319p. 1981. 43.95 (0-89885-051-7) Human Sci Pr.

Russica Information, Inc. Staff, tr. see Hupp, John P., ed.

Russillo, Fred. Shasta County Municipal Court Consolidation Study. 49p. 1989. 3.00 (0-685-34858-X, WRO-103) Natl Ctr St Courts.

Russillo, Fred & Loveland, Kay. Time & Justice: Implementing Case Disposition Time Standards in the State of Utah. 157p. 1990. 9.50 (0-685-38121-8, WRO-118) Natl Ctr St Courts.

Russillo, Fred & Yeh, Chang-Ming. Adams County Court Facility Study. 50p. 1991. 3.00 (0-685-55337-X, WRO132) Natl Ctr St Courts.

Russillo, Fred, et al. Denver Juvenile Court Review. 90p. 1990. 5.50 (0-685-50615-0, WR0121) Natl Ctr St Courts.

— Paperflow Study for the Clerk of the Superior Court, in & for the County of Maricopa. 200p. 1990. 12.00 (0-685-55333-7, WRO124) Natl Ctr St Courts.

— Security & Facility Design Study of the Stanislaus County Court System. 176p. 1990. 11.00 (0-685-48839-X, WRO-123) Natl Ctr St Courts.

Russillo, Frederick & Lee, Monica. Co-Location of Trial & Appellate Courts in Utah's Third Judicial District: The Feasibility of Functional Consolidation. 85p. 1989. 5.00 (0-685-34851-2, WRO-108) Natl Ctr St Courts.

Russin, Lester A., tr. see Freud, Sigmund.

Russin, Robert, jt. auth. see Russin, Robin.

Russin, Robin & Russin, Robert. Robert Russin: A Wyoming Master. 48p. 1991. write for info. (0-9630869-0-1) U of WY Art Mus.

Russin, Suzanne S., ed. see Sturmthal, Adolf.

Russman, Penny & Wright, Sheila. Changing Bodies, Changing Goals & Other Youth Soccer Stories. Woog, Dan, ed. LC 84-71345. (Illus.). 96p. (Orig.). (J). (gr. 5-9). 1984. pap. 5.95 (0-9613538-0-5) Ascot Pr.

Russman, Thomas A. A Prospectus for the Triumph of Realism. LC 86-28646. 208p. (C). 1987. 24.95 (0-86554-232-5, MUP-H205) Mercer Univ Pr.

Russman, Thomas A., ed. Thomistic Papers V. LC 83-73623. 106p. (C). 1990. text ed. 20.95 (0-268-01875-8); pap. text ed. 10.95 (0-268-01876-6) U of Notre Dame Pr.

Russmann, Edna R. & Finn, David. Egyptian Sculpture: Cairo & Luxor. (Illus.). 242p. 1989. 50.00 (0-292-70402-X) U of Tex Pr.

Russo. Great Treasure Hunt II. (J). (gr. 3 up). 1995. 12.00 (0-671-73351-6) S&S Trade.

— New User's Guide to the Sun Workstation. 1990. 39.50 (0-387-97249-8) Spr-Verlag.

Russo & Perla, Georges. French for Business & Finance. 237p. (ENG & FRE.). (C). 1985. Wkbk. student ed, pap. 14.00 (0-669-05349-X); Cassettes. audio 35.00 (0-669-05351-1) Heath.

Russo, jt. auth. see Filkins.

Russo, A. D. The Assertive Formula. (Human Resources Book Ser.). 95p. 1982. pap. 4.00 (0-9610708-0-3) Twenty Fst CT.

— Assertiveness Is. (Illus.). 108p. (Orig.). 1985. pap. 4.00 (0-9610708-1-1) Twenty Fst CT.

Russo, Alexander. Profiles on Women Artists. LC 84-27015. 320p. 1985. text ed. 55.00 (0-313-27049-X, U7049, Greenwood Pr) Greenwood.

Russo, Ann & Kramarae, Cheris, eds. The Radical Women's Press of the Eighteen Fifties. (Women's Source Library). 368p. 1990. 35.00 (0-415-90297-5, A1650, Routledge NY) Routledge.

Russo, Anne, jt. auth. see Fusco, Ann.

Russo, Anthony & Russo, Dorothy. A Bibliography of James Whitcomb Riley. LC 72-1267. (American Literature Ser.: No. 49). 351p. 1972. reprint ed. lib. bdg. 69.95 (0-8383-1418-X) M S G Haskell Hse.

***Russo, Barbara.** Elegant Pasta. 93p. 1994. write for info. (1-57215-002-5) World Pubns.

Russo, Bob. The Meaning of Life, Pt. 1. Taber, Allan, ed. (Illus.). 160p. (Orig.). 1992. pap. 9.95 (1-880348-04-7) Phantom Lit.

Russo, Carlo F. & Wren, Kevin. Aristophanes: An Author for the Stage. Wren, Kevin, tr. LC 93-34433. 296p. 1994. 59.95x (0-415-01082-9, B3715, Routledge NY) Routledge.

Russo, Carol, illus. Three-D Hidden Pictures Activity Book. 16p. (J). 1991. pap. write for info. (1-56156-012-X) Kidsbks.

***Russo, Charles, ed.** Case Citations No. 17: Violence & School Safety. (Nolpe Case Citation Ser.). (Orig.). Date not set. pap. 40.00 (1-56534-065-5) NOLPE.

— Discrimination. (Case Citation Ser.: No. 14). 53p. 1992. 40.00 (1-56534-078-7) NOLPE.

Russo, Charles J., ed. see Cursio, Joan, et al.

Russo, Charles J., jt. auth. see Gurst, Lyndon G.

Russo, David & Dagan, Gideon, eds. Water Flow & Solute Transport in Soils: Developments & Applications. LC 92-47096. (Advanced Series in Agricultural Sciences: Vol. 20). 1993. 145.00 (0-387-56216-8) Spr-Verlag.

Russo, David A. Go for It! Races, Rescues, Treasure Hunts & More. (J). (gr. 4-7). 1992. pap. 12.00 (0-671-73350-8, S&S Bks Young Read) S&S Childrens.

— Mazemaster Three: The Mazemaster Returns. 1993. pap. 9.95 (0-671-73020-7, Fireside) S&S Trade.

***Russo, David J.** Clio Confused: Troubling Aspects of Historical Study from the Perspective of U. S. LC 95-7909. (Contributions in American History Ser.). 176p. 1995. text ed. 49.95 (0-313-29682-0, Greenwood Pr) Greenwood.

— Keepers of Our Past: Local Historical Writing in the United States, 1820s-1930s. LC 88-36095. (Contributions in American History Ser.: No. 129). 295p. 1988. text ed. 55.00 (0-313-26236-5, RKP/, Greenwood Pr) Greenwood.

***Russo, Del.** Glamour Make-Up. 1994. pap. 4.99 (1-56171-345-7, S P I Bks) Sure Sellers.

Russo, Dennis C. Textbook of Pediatrics. (Textbook Ser.). write for info. (0-444-01009-2) Elsevier.

Russo, Dennis C. & Kedesdy, J. H., eds. Behavioral Medicine with the Developmentally Disabled. LC 88-17953. (Illus.). 308p. 1988. 49.50 (0-306-42884-9, Plenum Pr) Plenum.

Russo, Dennis C., et al. Behavioral Pediatrics: Research & Practice. LC 82-3799. 432p. 1982. 65.00 (0-306-40961-5, Plenum Pr) Plenum.

Russo, Dorothy, jt. auth. see Russo, Anthony.

Russo, Douglas, jt. auth. see Murphy, Mike.

***Russo, Edward J.** Springfield: Prairies of Promise. 1983. 19. 95 (0-89781-084-8) Preferred Mktg.

— Ten Barriers to Decision Traps. 1990. pap. 11.00 (0-671-72609-9) S&S Trade.

***Russo, Elena.** Skeptical Selves: Empiricism & Modernity in the French Novel. 244p. Date not set. 35.00x (0-8047-2465-2) Stanford U Pr.

***Russo, Enzo & Cove, David.** Genetic Engineering: Dreams & Nightmares. LC 95-16150. 1995. write for info. (0-7167-4546-1) W H Freeman.

Russo, Eva M. & Shyne, Ann W. Coping with Disruptive Behavior in Group Care. LC 79-23739. 74p. (Orig.). (C). 1980. 13.50 (0-87868-137-X, 1370) Child Welfare.

Russo, Gianna. Bent Leaves, Slanted Rooms. 22p. 1981. 4.00 (0-929436-01-6) Eyesburg Pr.

Russo, Gloria & Perla, Georges. Basic French Grammar. 259p. (C). 1985. pap. text ed. 19.50 (0-669-05346-5) Heath.

— French for Communication. 231p. (ENG & FRE.). (C). 1985. Wkbk. student ed, pap. text ed. 14.00 (0-669-05347-3); Cassettes. audio 35.00 (0-669-05350-3); Demotape. write for info. (0-669-05352-X) Heath.

Russo, J. Edward & Schoemaker, Paul J. Decision Traps: The Ten Barriers to Brilliant Decision-Making & How to Overcome Them. 1989. 19.95 (0-385-24835-0) Doubleday.

Russo, J. Robert. Serving & Surviving As a Human-Service Worker. 2nd ed. 182p. (C). 1993. pap. text ed. 14.95 (0-88133-691-2) Waveland Pr.

Russo, Jean B. Free Workers in a Plantation Economy: Talbot County, Maryland, 1690-1759. (Outstanding Studies in Early American History). 498p. 1989. reprint ed. 30.00 (0-8240-6195-0) Garland.

Russo, Joe, et al. Planet of the Apes Revisited. (Illus.). 212p. (Orig.). (YA). (gr. 9-12). 1991. pap. 12.95 (0-9627508-2-4) Image NY.

Russo, John. The Complete Night of the Living Dead Filmbook. Michelucci, Robert V., ed. LC 84-62835. (Illus.). 120p. 1985. pap. 10.95 (0-911137-03-3) Imagine.

— Living Things. 288p. (Orig.). 1988. mass mkt. 3.95 (0-445-20666-7, Mysterious Paperbk) Warner Bks.

***Russo, John A.** How to Make Your Own Feature Movie for $10,000 or Less. LC 94-24252. 208p. 1994. pap. 19. 00 (0-935016-10-4, Barclay House) Zinn Communs.

— Making Movies: The Inside Guide to Independent Movie Production. 1989. pap. 14.95 (0-440-50046-X) Dell.

— Voodoo Dawn. Michelucci, R. V., ed. LC 87-80907. 204p. 1987. 14.95 (0-911137-10-6); pap. 9.95 (0-911137-12-2) Imagine.

Russo, John P. Alexander Pope: Tradition & Identity. LC 70-188354. 255p. 1972. 32.00 (0-674-01520-7) HUP.

— I. A. Richards: His Life & Work. 832p. 1989. text ed. 50.00x (*0-8018-3417-1*) Johns Hopkins.
Russo, John P., ed. see Richards, Ivor A.
Russo, Jose, ed. Immunocytochemistry in Tumor Diagnosis. (Developments in Oncology Ser.). 1985. lib. bdg. 102.00 (*0-89838-737-X*) Kluwer Ac.
Russo, Joseph A., ed. see Fernandez-Galiano, Manuel & Heubeck, Alfred.
Russo, Joseph A., et al, eds. A Commentary on Homer's Odyssey, Vol. 3: Bks. XVII-XXIV. (Illus.). 464p. 1993. reprint ed. pap. 26.00 (*0-19-814953-0*) OUP.
Russo, Joseph M. Sing-a-Long for All Occasions. 62p. (Orig.). 1988. pap. 6.95 (*0-685-29095-6*) Mid-West Music.
— Sing-a-Longs for All Occasions. 62p. (Orig.). 1988. pap. 6.95 (*0-9624214-0-5*, PA-394-638) Mid-West Music.
Russo, Julee. Great Good Food: Luscious, Lower-Fat Cooking. LC 92-56843. 1993. 29.00 (*0-679-42098-3*) Random.
Russo, M., jt. auth. see Di Chiara, A.
***Russo-Marie, Francoise, et al, eds.** Advances in Inflammation Research Vol. 10: 1986. LC 85-25802. (Illus.). 461p. Date not set. reprint ed. pap. 131.40 (*0-7837-9249-2*, 2047156) Bks Demand.
Russo, Marisabina. Alex Is My Friend. LC 90-24643. 32p. (J). 1992. 14.00 (*0-688-10418-5*); lib. bdg. 13.93 (*0-688-10419-3*) Greenwillow.
— Grandpa Abe. LC 95-2260. (Illus.). 32p. (J). 1996. 15.00 (*0-688-14097-1*); lib. bdg. 14.93 (*0-688-14098-X*) Greenwillow.
— I Don't Want to Go Back to School. LC 93-5479. 32p. (J). 1994. 15.00 (*0-688-04601-0*); lib. bdg. 14.93 (*0-688-04602-9*) Greenwillow.
— The Line-up Book. LC 85-24907. (Illus.). 24p. (J). (ps-1). 1986. 12.95 (*0-688-06204-0*); lib. bdg. 12.88 (*0-688-06205-9*) Greenwillow.
— The Line Up Book. (Illus.). 24p. (J). (ps-3). 1992. pap. 3.99 (*0-14-054471-2*) Puffin Bks.
— Only Six More Days. LC 86-19586. (Illus.). 32p. (J). (ps-3). 1988. 11.95 (*0-688-07071-X*); lib. bdg. 11.88 (*0-688-07072-8*) Greenwillow.
— Only Six More Days. (Illus.). 32p. (J). (ps-3). 1992. pap. 3.99 (*0-14-054473-9*) Puffin Bks.
— Time to Wake Up! LC 93-18185. (Illus.). 24p. (J). (ps up). 1994. 14.00 (*0-688-04599-5*); lib. bdg. 13.93 (*0-688-04600-2*) Greenwillow.
— Trade-in Mother. LC 91-47681. (Illus.). 32p. (J). (ps up). 1993. 14.00 (*0-688-11416-4*); lib. bdg. 13.93 (*0-688-11417-2*) Greenwillow.
— A Visit to Oma. LC 89-77716. (Illus.). 32p. (J). (ps up). 1991. 13.95 (*0-688-09623-9*); lib. bdg. 13.88 (*0-688-09624-7*) Greenwillow.
— Waiting for Hannah. LC 87-37201. (Illus.). 32p. (J). (ps up). 1989. 13.95 (*0-688-08015-4*); lib. bdg. 13.88 (*0-688-08016-2*) Greenwillow.
— Where Is Ben? LC 88-34916. (Illus.). 32p. (J). (ps up). 1990. 12.95 (*0-688-08011-1*); lib. bdg. 12.88 (*0-688-08013-8*) Greenwillow.
— Where Is Ben? LC 92-8627. (J). (gr. 4 up). 1992. reprint ed. 4.50 (*0-14-054474-7*) Puffin Bks.
— Why Do Grown-Ups Have All the Fun? LC 86-4644. (Illus.). 24p. (J). (ps-3). 1987. 11.75 (*0-688-06625-9*); lib. bdg. 11.88 (*0-688-06626-7*) Greenwillow.
***Russo, Mary.** The Female Grotesque: Risk, Excess & Modernity. 250p. 1994. 55.00 (*0-415-90164-2*, A3537); pap. 16.95 (*0-415-90165-0*, A3541) Routledge.
Russo, Mary J., jt. auth. see Fondell, Joan.
Russo, Michael. Yats in Movieland. 336p. Date not set. 21.95 (*1-878044-22-2*) Mayhaven Pub.
Russo, Michele, illus. The World of Russo. 110p. (Orig.). 1981. pap. 12.95 (*0-938996-00-2*) Bigoni Bks.
Russo, Monica. Dinosaur Dots. (Illus.). 96p. (J). 1991. pap. 4.95 (*0-8069-7388-9*) Sterling.
— Endangered Animals Dot-to-Dot. (Illus.). 80p. (J). 1994. pap. 4.95 (*0-8069-0520-4*) Sterling.
— The Insect Almanac: A Year-Round Activity Guide. LC 90-22438. (Illus.). 136p. (J). (gr. 4-10). 1992. pap. 8.95 (*0-8069-7455-9*) Sterling.
— Prehistoric Animals Dot-to-Dot. (Illus.). 80p. (J). (gr. 2-6). 1993. pap. 4.95 (*0-8069-8746-4*) Sterling.
— The Tree Almanac: A Year-Round Activity Guide. LC 92-41347. (Illus.). (J). (gr. 3 up). 1993. 16.95 (*0-8069-1252-9*) Sterling.
— The Tree Almanac: A Year-Round Activity Guide. (Illus.). 136p. 1994. pap. 8.95 (*0-8069-1253-7*) Sterling.
— Wildlife Dot-to-Dot. (Illus.). 80p. 1994. pap. 4.95 (*0-8069-0638-3*) Sterling.
Russo, Monica & Dewire, Robert. Complete Book of Birdhouses & Feeders. (Illus.). 128p. 1990. 8.99 (*0-517-69314-3*) Random Hse Value.
Russo, N., et al, eds. Chemistry & Properties of Biomolecular Systems Vol. II: Proceedings of the Second Joint Greek-Italian Meeting on Chemistry & Biological Systems & Molecular Chemical Engineering, Cetraro, Italy, October 1992. LC 93-44247. (Topics in Molecular Organization & Engineering Ser.: Vol. 11). 432p. (C). 1994. lib. bdg. 137.00 (*0-7923-2666-0*) Kluwer Ac.
Russo, Nancy F., ed. see American Psychological Association, Women & Health Round Table Staff & Organizations for Professional Women Staff.
Russo, Nancy F., jt. ed. see O'Connell, Agnes N.
Russo, Nancy F., jt. auth. see O'Connell, Agnes.
Russo, Nino, jt. ed. see Salahub, Dennis R.
Russo, Paul S, ed. Reversible Polymeric Gels & Related Systems. LC 87-20305. (Symposium Ser.: No. 350). (Illus.). x, 324p. 1987. 71.95 (*0-8412-1415-8*) Am Chemical.
Russo, Philip A., jt. ed. see Paul, Ellen F.
Russo, Richard. Destroying Angel. 240p. 1992. pap. 4.50 (*0-441-14273-7*) Ace Bks.
— Mohawk. 1986. pap. 6.95 (*0-394-74409-8*) Random.
— Mohawk. (Vintage Contemporaries Ser.). 432p. 1989. pap. 12.00 (*0-679-72577-6*, Vin) Random.
— Mohawk. 1994. pap. 13.00 (*0-679-75382-6*, Vin) Random.
— Nobody's Fool. LC 92-56844. 576p. 1993. 23.00 (*0-394-57778-7*) Random.
— Nobody's Fool. 1994. pap. 13.00 (*0-679-75333-8*) Random.
— The Risk Pool. 1989. pap. 12.00 (*0-679-72334-X*, Vin) Random.
— Risk Pool. 1994. pap. 13.00 (*0-679-75383-4*, Vin) Random.
Russo, Richard, ed. Dreams Are Wiser Than Men. 320p. 1987. text ed. 30.00 (*0-938190-95-4*); pap. 14.95 (*0-938190-94-6*) North Atlantic.
Russo, Richard, jt. ed. see Pond, Lily.
Russo, Richard A., jt. ed. see Pond, Lily.
***Russo, Richard P.** Carlucci's Edge. 304p. (Orig.). 1995. pap. text ed. 5.50 (*0-441-00205-6*) Ace Bks.
Russo, Robert, jt. auth. see Smith, Christopher A.
Russo, Robert D., Jr., jt. auth. see Sorgen, Richard A.
Russo, Ron. Hawaiian Reefs: A Natural History Guide. (Illus.). 176p. (Orig.). 1994. pap. text ed. 16.95 (*0-9635696-0-0*) Wavecrest Pubns.
— Mountain State Mammals: A Guide to Mammals of the Rocky Mountain Region. (Illus.). 136p. 1991. pap. 4.00 (*0-912550-21-X*) Nature Study.
— Pacific Coast Fish: A Guide to Marine Fish of the Pacific Coast of North America. (Illus.). 112p. 1990. pap. 3.85 (*0-912550-19-8*) Nature Study.
Russo, Ron & Olhausen, Pam. Pacific Coast Mammals: A Guide to Mammals of the Pacific Coast States, Their Tracks, Skulls & Other Signs. 96p. 1987. pap. 3.25 (*0-912550-16-3*) Nature Study.
— Pacific Intertidal Life. (Guide to Organisms of Rocky Reefs & Tide Pools of the Pacific Coast Ser.). 1981. pap. 2.50 (*0-912550-10-4*) Nature Study.
Russo, Salvatore, jt. auth. see Kuhn, Lesley.
Russo, Steve. The Devil's Playground: Playing with Fire Can Get You Burned. 1994. pap. 7.99 (*1-56507-043-7*) Harvest Hse.
Russo, Steve, jt. auth. see Anderson, Neil T.
Russo, Thomas A. Regulation of the Commodities Futures & Options Markets, 2 vols. LC 83-431. (Securities Law Publications). 1598p. 1983. text ed. 190.00 (*0-07-054348-8*) Shepards-McGraw.
Russo, Tom. Microchemistry: For High School Chemistry. rev. ed. Stone, Harry, ed. (Illus.). 90p. (YA). (gr. 9-12). 1990. 15.80 (*1-877960-05-5*, 4-400) Kemtec Educ.
— MicroChemistry: For High School General Chemistry. (Illus.). 84p. 1986. 15.00 (*1-877960-01-2*, 4-400) Kemtec Educ.
— MicroChemistry II. (Illus.). 80p. 1989. 15.00 (*1-877960-03-9*) Kemtec Educ.
— MicroChemistry Teacher's Reference Manual. (Illus.). (Orig.). 1990. write for info. (*1-877960-04-7*) Kemtec Educ.
Russo, V. E., et al, eds. Development - the Molecular Genetic Approach. (Illus.). xxxv, 605p. 1993. 49.95 (*0-387-54730-4*) Spr-Verlag.
Russo, Valeria E, ed. see Addis, Elisabetta, et al.
Russo, Vito. The Celluloid Closet: Homosexuality in the Movies. rev. ed. (Illus.). 320p. 1991. lib. bdg. 35.00x (*0-8095-9107-3*) Borgo Pr.
— The Celluloid Closet: Homosexuality in the Movies. rev. ed. LC 86-45684. (Illus.). 320p. 1987. pap. 14.00 (*0-06-096132-5*, PL 6132, PL) HarpC.
Russo, William. Composing for the Jazz Orchestra. 1973. pap. text ed. 9.95 (*0-226-73209-6*, P552) U Ch Pr.
— Jazz Composition & Orchestration. LC 67-20580. (Illus.). 1968. lib. bdg. 40.00 (*0-226-73212-6*) U Ch Pr.
— Jazz Composition & Orchestration. LC 67-20580. (Illus.). 1975. pap. text ed. 30.00 (*0-226-73213-4*) U Ch Pr.
— Secrets of the Research Paper: An Easy Guide to Success. (C). 1980. pap. 2.95 (*0-931660-03-3*) R Oman Pub.
Russo, William, et al. Composing Music: A New Approach. (Illus.). x, 230p. 1988. pap. text ed. 19.95 (*0-226-73216-9*) U Ch Pr.
Russolo, Luigi. The Art of Noises. Brown, Barclay, tr. LC 85-28413. (Monographs in Musicology: No. 6). 87p. 1987. lib. bdg. 31.00 (*0-918728-57-6*) Pendragon NY.
Russom, Geoffrey. Old English Meter & Linguistic Theory. 192p. 1987. 69.95 (*0-521-33168-4*) Cambridge U Pr.
Russomanno, Diane. Beneath the Deep Blue Sea. (Ricky Rocket Ser.). 32p. (J). 1991. pap. text ed. write for info. (*1-880501-02-3*) Know Booster.
— The Journey Begins. (Ricky Rocket Ser.). 32p. (J). 1991. pap. text ed. write for info. (*1-880501-03-1*) Know Booster.
— The Never Ending Journey of the Written Word. (Ricky Rocket Ser.). 32p. (J). 1991. pap. text ed. write for info. (*1-880501-00-7*) Know Booster.
— The Story of the American Flag. (Ricky Rocket Ser.). 32p. (J). 1991. pap. text ed. write for info. (*1-880501-01-5*) Know Booster.
Russon, Jacqueline. Face Painting. (Illus.). 32p. (J). (gr. 2-4). 1994. 14.95 (*1-56847-197-1*) Thomson Lrning.
— Making Faces. LC 94-25632. (Illus.). 48p. (J). 1995. 14.95 (*0-8069-0929-3*) Sterling.
Russon, Ken, jt. auth. see Beach, Mark.
Russon, Robb. Letters to a New Elder: The Melchizedek Priesthood, Its Duty & Fulfillment. pap. 3.95 (*0-89036-144-4*) Hawkes Pub Inc.
Russon, S., jt. auth. see Kershaw, F.
Russow, Lilly-Marlene & Curd, Martin. Principles of Reasoning. LC 88-60527. 362p. (C). 1988. pap. text ed. 23.00 (*0-312-17506-X*); pap. text ed. 0.43 (*0-312-17505-1*) St Martin.
Russwurm, H., Jr., jt. ed. see Martens, Hinrich R.
Rust, A. D. Record of the Rust Family, Embracing the Descendants of Henry Rust, Who Came from England & Settled in Hingham, Mass., 1634-1635. (Illus.). 544p. 1989. reprint ed. lib. bdg. 89.50 (*0-8328-1042-8*); reprint ed. pap. 81.50 (*0-8328-1043-6*) Higginson Bk Co.
Rust, Alexandra, et al. The Streamliner Diner Cookbook. (Illus.). 256p. (Orig.). 1990. 19.95 (*0-89815-378-6*) Ten Speed Pr.
Rust, Ann O. The Floridians, 7 bks. 1990. 17.95 (*0-318-67299-5*); pap. 12.95 (*0-9620556-4-6*) Amaro Bks.
— The Floridians, 5 vols., Set. 1994. 69.95 (*1-883203-01-5*) Amaro Bks.
— Kissimmee. (Floridians Ser.: Vol. III). 225p. (Orig.). 1990. 17.95 (*0-9620556-3-8*); pap. 12.95 (*0-9620556-2-X*) Amaro Bks.
— Monticello, Vol. IV. (Floridians Ser.). 250p. 1991. 17.50 (*0-9620556-6-2*); pap. 12.95 (*0-9620556-5-4*) Amaro Bks.
— Pahokee, Vol. V. (Floridians Ser.). 275p. 1992. 17.50 (*0-9620556-8-9*); pap. 12.95 (*0-9620556-9-7*) Amaro Bks.
— Palatka. (Floridians Ser.). 235p. (Orig.). 1989. pap. 12.95 (*0-9620556-1-1*) Amaro Bks.
— Palatka, Vol. II. (Floridians Ser.: Vol. II). 231p. 1994. 17.50 (*1-883203-00-7*) Amaro Bks.
— Punta Rassa. (Floridians Ser.). 275p. (Orig.). 1988. pap. 12.95 (*0-9620556-0-3*) Amaro Bks.
Rust, Brian. The American Record Label Book: From the Mid-19th Century Through 1942. LC 83-18921. (Roots of Jazz Ser.). (Illus.). 336p. 1983. reprint ed. lib. bdg. 49.50 (*0-306-76211-0*) Da Capo.
— Brian Rust's Guide to Discography. LC 79-6827. (Discographies Ser.: No. 4). (Illus.). x, 133p. 1980. text ed. 42.95 (*0-313-22086-7*, RGD/, Greenwood Pr) Greenwood.
Rust, Brian, comp. Discography of Historical Records on Cylinders & 78s. LC 78-60530. 327p. 1979. text ed. 69.50 (*0-313-20561-2*, RRC/, Greenwood Pr) Greenwood.
Rust, Brian & Debus, Allen. The Complete Entertainment Discography from 1897 to 1942. 2nd ed. (Roots of Jazz Ser.). 790p. 1988. reprint ed. lib. bdg. 95.00 (*0-306-76210-2*) Da Capo.
Rust, Brian & McLeish, Barry. The Support-Raising Handbook: A Guide for Christian Workers. LC 84-22448. 119p. (Orig.). 1984. pap. 10.99 (*0-87784-326-0*, 326) InterVarsity.
Rust, Damon, jt. auth. see Linton, Steve.
Rust, Diane, jt. auth. see Rust, Val D.
Rust, Ellsworth M. Rust of Virginia: Genealogical & Biographical Sketches of the Descendants of William Rust, 1654-1940. (Illus.). 462p. 1992. reprint ed. lib. bdg. 73.00 (*0-8328-2486-0*); reprint ed. pap. 83.00 (*0-8328-2487-9*) Higginson Bk Co.
Rust, Eric. Naval Officers under Hitler: The Story of Crew 34. LC 90-43918. 248p. 1991. text ed. 49.95 (*0-275-93709-7*, C3709, Praeger Pubs) Greenwood.
Rust, Eric C. Religion, Revelation & Reason. LC 81-2760. vi, 192p. (C). 1981. pap. 12.50 (*0-86554-058-6*, MUP-P009) Mercer Univ Pr.
Rust, Eric C., tr. see Topp, Erich.
Rust, F. Dance in Society. (Ballroom Dance Ser.). 1986. lib. bdg. 79.95 (*0-8490-3357-8*) Gordon Pr.
— Dance in Society. (Ballroom Dance Ser.). 1985. lib. bdg. 75.50 (*0-87700-684-9*) Revisionist Pr.
Rust, Frances O. Changing Teaching, Changing Schools: Bringing Early Childhood Practice into Public Education: Case Studies from Kindergarten. LC 93-17378. (Early Childhood Education Ser.). 144p. (C). 1993. text ed. 32.00 (*0-8077-3286-9*); pap. text ed. 15.95 (*0-8077-3285-0*) Tchrs Coll.
Rust, Frances O. & Williams, Leslie, eds. The Care & Education of Young Children: Expanding Contexts, Sharpening Focus. 168p. (C). 1989. pap. text ed. 16.95 (*0-8077-2984-1*) Tchrs Coll.
Rust, Graham. The Painted House. LC 88-45315. (Illus.). 192p. 1988. 60.00 (*0-394-57340-4*) Knopf.
— Secret Garden Notebook. (J). (gr. 4-7). 1991. 12.95 (*0-87923-890-9*) Godine.
***Rust, Graham, illus.** The Fine Art of Dining: With Recipes from World-Famous Chefs & Kitchens. 192p. 1995. 24.95 (*0-8212-2224-4*) Bulfinch Pr.
Rust, H. Lee. Jobsearch: The Complete Manual for Job Seekers. 2nd ed. LC 90-55208. 240p. 1990. pap. 17.95 (*0-8144-7750-X*) AMACOM.
Rust, Henry. Christians As Peacemakers. 54p. (Orig.). 1983. pap. 7.95 (*0-940754-21-5*) Ed Ministries.
Rust, Henry R. Be the Good News - In Living the Full Life. 1990. 5.95 (*0-940754-87-8*, 3551) Ed Ministries.
— Celebrating God's Good Earth. 1990. 5.95 (*0-940754-91-6*, 3555) Ed Ministries.
— Celebrating God's Presence & Action in Life & Death. 1990. 5.95 (*0-940754-88-6*, 3552) Ed Ministries.
— A Covenant with God's People. 1990. 5.95 (*0-940754-90-8*, 3554) Ed Ministries.
— The Drama for the Church at Worship. 1990. 5.95 (*0-940754-92-4*, 3556) Ed Ministries.
— An Early Third Century Liturgy. (Worship Through the Centuries Ser.). 1990. 5.95 (*0-940754-81-9*, 3511) Ed Ministries.
— James: The Most American Book in the Bible. 70p. (Orig.). 1985. pap. 7.95 (*0-940754-31-2*) Ed Ministries.
— John: Twentieth Century Living of Our First Century Faith. 73p. (Orig.). 1988. pap. 7.95 (*0-940754-65-7*) Ed Ministries.
— The Prophets' Words & Actions. 1990. pap. 5.95 (*0-940754-89-4*, 3553) Ed Ministries.
— Seventeenth Century in the Manner of the Pilgrims. (Worship Through the Centuries Ser.). 1990. pap. 5.95 (*0-940754-84-3*, 3512) Ed Ministries.
— Turn-of-the-Century Protestantism. (Worship Through the Centuries Ser.). 1990. pap. 5.95 (*0-940754-85-1*, 3514) Ed Ministries.
— Worship of the Frontier. (Worship Through the Centuries Ser.). 1990. pap. 5.95 (*0-940754-82-7*, 3513) Ed Ministries.
Rust, Henry R., ed. Advent - Christmas Sermons. 1990. pap. 8.95 (*1-877871-08-7*) Ed Ministries.
— As I See It: Contemporary Issues. 96p. (Orig.). 1991. pap. 10.95 (*1-877871-21-4*, 3542) Ed Ministries.
— The Church in Today's World. pap. 8.95 (*1-877871-29-X*, 3544) Ed Ministries.
— The Message for the Nineties. 1990. pap. 8.95 (*0-940754-80-0*, 3540) Ed Ministries.
— Our World, God's World. 71p. 1991. pap. 8.95 (*1-877871-12-5*, 3541) Ed Ministries.
— The People of God at Prayer: Pastoral Prayers for All Occasions. 72p. (Orig.). 1991. pap. 8.95 (*1-877871-25-7*, 3532) Ed Ministries.
— Sermons: Looking Toward Easter from Here. 54p. (Orig.). 1991. pap. 8.95 (*1-877871-10-9*) Ed Ministries.
— What Does God Require? Sermons on Stewardship. 1992. pap. 8.95 (*1-877871-31-1*, 3543) Ed Ministries.
Rust, Herbert. Owning Your Own Franchise. 1991. pap. text ed. 15.95 (*0-13-644980-8*) P-H.
— Owning Your Own Franchise. 1991. 24.95 (*0-13-644972-7*) P-H.
Rust, James H. Nuclear Power Plant Engineering. LC 79-88918. (Illus.). 504p. 1979. 40.00 (*0-934534-00-4*) Haralson Pub Co.
Rust, John & Golombok, Susan. Modern Psychometrics: The Science of Psychological Assessment. (International Library of Psychology). 192p. 1989. 49.95 (*0-415-03058-7*); pap. 14.95 (*0-415-03059-5*) Routledge.
Rust, John, jt. ed. see Friedman, Daniel P.
Rust, Joy S. Old Homes of South Carolina. LC 92-15746. (Illus.). 224p. 1992. 22.50 (*0-88289-874-4*) Pelican.
Rust, Kenn. Eighth Air Force Story. (Illus.). 72p. 1993. pap. text ed. 15.95 (*0-911852-81-6*) Aviation Heritage.
— Fifteenth Air Force Story. (Illus.). 72p. 1993. pap. text ed. 15.95 (*0-911852-79-4*) Aviation Heritage.
— Fourteenth Air Force Story. (Illus.). 72p. 1993. pap. text ed. 15.95 (*0-911852-80-8*) Aviation Heritage.
— Ninth Air Force Story. (Illus.). 72p. 1993. pap. text ed. 15.95 (*0-911852-93-X*) Aviation Heritage.
— Seventh Air Force Story. (Illus.). 72p. 1993. pap. text ed. 15.95 (*0-911852-84-0*) Aviation Heritage.
— Thirteenth Air Force Story. (Illus.). 72p. 1993. pap. text ed. 15.95 (*0-911852-90-5*) Aviation Heritage.
— Twelfth Air Force Story. (Illus.). 72p. 1993. pap. text ed. 15.95 (*0-911852-77-8*) Aviation Heritage.
— Twentieth Air Force Story. (Illus.). 72p. 1993. pap. text ed. 15.95 (*0-911852-85-9*) Aviation Heritage.
Rust, Kenn, ed. Fifth Air Force Story. (Illus.). 72p. 1993. pap. text ed. 15.95 (*0-911852-75-1*) Aviation Heritage.
Rust, Kenn, ed. see Olmsted, Merle C.
Rust, Marina M. Gatherings: A Novel. 240p. 1993. 19.00 (*0-671-70315-3*) S&S Trade.
Rust, Mary J., jt. auth. see Messinger, Jean G.
***Rust, Michael K., et al, eds.** Understanding & Controlling the German Cockroach. (Illus.). 448p. 1995. text ed. 85.00 (*0-19-506495-X*) OUP.
***Rust, Paula C.** Bisexuality & the Challenge to Lesbian Politics: Sex, Loyalty, & Revolution. (The Cutting Edge: Lesbian Life & Literature Ser.). 340p. 1995. 45.00 (*0-8147-7444-X*); pap. 16.95 (*0-8147-7445-8*) NYU Pr.
Rust, Rebecca B. The Outside of a Haiku. (Illus.). 53p. (Orig.). 1984. pap. 6.95 (*0-9614161-0-6*) NC Haiku Soc.
Rust, Rebecca B., ed. Holiday Haiku. 40p. (Orig.). (C). 1990. pap. 3.00 (*0-9614161-2-2*) NC Haiku Soc.
Rust, Richard D. Litterms: A Tutorial for Understanding Poetry, Fiction, Drama. (C). 1988. IBM-PC. disk 17.00 (*0-15-551090-8*) HB Coll Pubs.
— Litterms: A Tutorial for Understanding Poetry, Fiction, Drama, Set. (C). 1988. 35.25 (*0-15-551091-6*) HB Coll Pubs.
Rust, Roland T. Advertising Media Models: A Practical Guide. 176p. 1986. text ed. 37.95 (*0-669-09375-0*) Free Pr.
— Return on Quality: Measuring the Financial Impact of Your Company's Quest for Quality. 1993. 27.50 (*1-55738-547-5*) Probus Pub Co.
Rust, Roland T. & Oliver, Richard L., eds. Service Quality: New Directions in Theory & Practice. (Illus.). 304p. (C). 1993. text ed. 49.95 (*0-8039-4919-7*); pap. text ed. 22.95 (*0-8039-4920-0*) Sage.
Rust, Thomas G. A Guide to Anatomy & Physiology Lab. 2nd rev. ed. (Illus.). 124p. (C). 1986. student ed 12.98 (*0-937029-00-9*) SW Educ Ent.
— A Guide to Biology Lab. 3rd rev. ed. (Illus.). 110p. (C). 1983. pap. 11.98 (*0-937029-01-7*) SW Educ Ent.
Rust, Val D. The Democratic Tradition & the Evolution of Schooling in Norway. LC 89-11847. 347p. 1989. text ed. 59.95 (*0-313-26849-5*, RDD/, Greenwood Pr) Greenwood.
Rust, Val D. & Dalin, Per. Teachers & Teaching in the Developing World. LC 89-27603. (Reference Books in International Education: Vol. 8). 398p. 1990. reprint ed. 58.00 (*0-8240-3532-1*) Garland.
***Rust, Val D. & Rust, Diane.** The Unification of German Education. LC 94-26651. (Reference Books in International Education: Vol. 32). 384p. 1995. 57.00 (*0-8153-1705-0*, SS960) Garland.
Rust, William J. & U. S. News Books Editors. Kennedy in Vietnam: American Foreign Policy, 1960-63. (Quality Paperbacks Ser.). (Illus.). viii, 252p. 1987. reprint ed. pap. 10.95 (*0-306-80284-8*) Da Capo.
Rustad, Michael. Demystifying Punitive Damages in Products Liability Cases: A Survey of a Quarter Century of Trial Verdicts. 55p. 1991. pap. 22.00 (*0-933067-13-5*) Roscoe Pound Found.

— Women in Khaki: The American Enlisted Woman. LC 82-9025. 304p. 1982. text ed. 35.00 (*0-275-90892-5*, C0892, Praeger Pubs) Greenwood.

Rustagi, Jagdish, ed. Optimization Techniques in Statistics. (Statistical Modeling & Decision Science Ser.). (Illus.). 359p. 1994. text ed. 69.95 (*0-12-604555-0*) Acad Pr.

Rustagi, Jagdish S. Introduction to Statistical Methods, Vol. I. LC 84-6911. (Probability & Statistics Ser.). (Illus.). 400p. (C). 1985. 38.50 (*0-86598-127-2*, R3934) Rowman.

— Introduction to Statistical Methods: Applications to the Life Sciences, Vol. II. LC 84-6911. (Probability & Statistics Ser.). (Illus.). 240p. (C). 1985. 38.50 (*0-86598-128-0*, R3935) Rowman.

Rustam, Shah. Minimum Topside Facilities for Deepwater Marginal Fields. 1989. 125.00 (*90-6314-566-7*, Pub. by Lorne & MacLean Marine) St Mut.

— Minimum Topside Facilities for Deepwater Marginal Fields. (C). 1989. 95.00 (*0-685-54756-6*, Pub. by Lorne & MacLean Marine) St Mut.

Rustamji, K. F., jt. ed. see Ghosh, S. K.

Rustamov, R. Favourite Russian Folk Songs. 64p. (C). 1980. 23.00 (*0-317-92398-6*, Pub. by Collets UK) Pro-Am Music.

Rustanoby, A. Divorcio (Divorce) Como Superar el Dolor (Coping with the Pain) (SPA.). Date not set. 1.79 (*0-685-74930-4*, 497409) Editorial Unilit.

Rustard, Steven. The Tyrants. abr. ed. 480p. 1995. pap. 12.95 (*1-56901-511-2*) NW Pub.

Rustaveli, Shota. The Lord of the Panther Skin. Stevenson, R. H., tr. LC 76-13225. 240p. 1977. 49.50 (*0-87395-320-7*) State U NY Pr.

Rustavo, S. T., ed. Black American Culture & Society: An Annotated Bibliography. (Illus.). 167p. 1994. 67.00 (*1-56072-172-3*) Nova Sci Pubs.

Rustay, George W., jt. auth. see Garrison, G. Richard.

Rustebakke, Homer M., ed. Electric Utility Systems & Practices. 4th ed. LC 83-3640. 294p. 1983. text ed. 110.00 (*0-471-04890-9*, Wiley-Interscience) Wiley.

Rusten, J. S., ed. see Thucydides.

Rusten, Jeffrey. Sophocles Oidipous Tyrannos. (Bryn Mawr Greek Commentaries Ser.). 146p. (Orig.). (C). 1990. pap. text ed. 8.00 (*0-929524-67-5*) Bryn Mawr Commentaries.

Rusten, Jeffrey, et al, eds. Theophrastus. Characters Herodas. Mimes: Cercidas & the Choliambic Poets. 2nd ed. Cunningham, I. C. et al, trs. (Loeb Classical Library: No. 225). 512p. 1993. text ed. 16.95 (*0-674-99244-X*) HUP.

Rusten, Philip. Journeys of the Heart. (Illus.). 96p. 1987. 25.00 (*0-317-03764-1*) Way of Seeing.

— On the Growing Edge. (Illus.). 96p. 1981. 23.00 (*0-686-29722-9*) Way of Seeing.

— A Way of Seeing. (Illus.). 96p. 1978. 23.00 (*0-686-29711-3*) Way of Seeing.

Ruster. World Intellectual Property Guidebooks: Germany, Switzerland, Austria, Vol. 1. 1991. write for info. (*0-8205-1889-1*) Bender.

Ruster, Bernard & Bringezu, Volker. Business Transactions in Germany, 4 vols. (Illus.). 1983. Updates available. ring bd. write for info. (*0-8205-1394-6*) Bender.

Ruster, Bernd, et al. International Protection of the Environment: Treaties & Related Documents, 31 vols., Set. LC 75-24843. 1975. ring bd. 1,575.00 (*0-379-10086-X*) Oceana.

— International Protection of the Environment: Treaties & Related Documents, 4 binders, Set. suppl. ed. 1990. Suppl. bound set approx. 3 releases per yr. text ed. write for info. (*0-318-63926-2*); Suppl. bound set. ring bd. 750.00 (*0-379-10293-5*) Oceana.

***Rustgi, Anil K., ed.** Gastrointestinal Cancers: Biology, Diagnosis, Therapy. LC 95-2641. 1995. write for info. (*0-7817-0276-3*) Raven.

Rustgi, V. K., ed. Gastrointestinal Infections in the Tropics. (Illus.). viii, 248p. 1990. 192.00 (*3-8055-5211-4*) S Karger.

Rustgi, Vinod K. & Van Thiel, David H., eds. The Liver in Systemic Disease. LC 92-48978. 400p. 1993. 89.50 (*0-88167-969-0*) Raven.

Rusthoi, Daniel. Speaking of Numbers: Skillbuilding in English & Arithmetic Worktext 1. (Illus.). (gr. 9-12). 1985. teacher ed 2.65 (*0-8325-0469-6*, Natl Textbk); pap. text ed. 11.95 (*0-8325-0468-8*, Natl Textbk) NTC Pub Grp.

***Rusthoi, Ralph W.** Help for the New Convert. Pan, B. W., tr. 45p. (CHI.). 1986. pap. 1.50 (*1-56582-077-0*) Christ Renew Min.

Rustic History Furniture Company Staff. Porch Lawn & Cottage Furniture. 1990. pap. 7.95 (*0-486-26531-5*) Dover.

Rustichelli, F. & Fontana, M. P., eds. Industrial & Technological Applications of Neutrons. LC 92-34153. 1992. write for info. (*0-444-89837-9*, North Holland) Elsevier.

Rustige, Rona, comp. & intro. Tyendinaga Tales. (Illus.). 96p. (C). 1988. 24.95 (*0-7735-0650-0*, Pub. by McGill CN) U of Toronto Pr.

***Rustin.** Social Skills Speech Impairment. 1988. 52.50 (*1-56593-546-2*, 0065) Singular Publishing.

***Rustin, Lena, et al.** Assessment & Therapy for Young Dysfluent Children: Family Interaction. 200p. 1995. pap. 62.25 (*1-56593-278-1*, 0599) Singular Publishing.

Rustin, Lena. Parents, Families, & the Stuttering Child. (Illus.). 138p. (Orig.). (C). 1991. pap. text ed. 27.50x (*1-879105-16-0*, 0210) Singular Publishing.

— Social Skills & the Speech Impaired. 2nd ed. 240p. 1995. 52.50 (*1-56593-388-5*, 0814) Singular Publishing.

***Rustin, Lena, et al.** The Management of Adolescent Stutterers: The Communication Skills Approach. 200p. 1995. pap. text ed. 62.25 (*1-56593-277-3*, 0598) Singular Publishing.

Rustin, Lena, et al, eds. Progress in the Treatment of Fluency Disorders. 330p. 1987. 66.00 (*0-85066-664-3*); pap. 33.00 (*0-85066-683-X*) Singular Publishing.

Rustin, Margaret & Rustin, Michael. Narratives of Love & Loss: Studies in Modern Children's Fiction. 288p. (C). 1988. text ed. 50.00 (*0-86091-187-X*, Pub. by Verso UK); pap. text ed. 14.95 (*0-86091-899-8*, Pub. by Verso UK) Routledge Chapman & Hall.

Rustin, Michael. For a Pluralist Socialism. 277p. 1985. text ed. 29.95 (*0-86091-074-1*, Pub. by Verso UK); pap. text ed. 15.95 (*0-86091-774-6*, Pub. by Verso UK) Routledge Chapman & Hall.

— The Good Society & the Inner World: Psychoanalysis, Politics & Culture. 300p. 1991. 59.95 (*0-86091-328-7*, A5351, Pub. by Verso UK); pap. 18.95 (*0-86091-544-1*, A5355, Pub. by Verso UK) Routledge Chapman & Hall.

Rustin, Michael, jt. ed. see Prager, Jeffrey.

Rustin, Michael, jt. auth. see Rustin, Margaret.

Rustin, Randall, ed. Courant Computer Science Symposia, Vols. 7-9. Incl. Vol. 7. Computational Complexity. 30.00 (*0-686-46259-9*); Vol. 8. Natural Language Processing. 36.00 (*0-686-46260-2*); Vol. 9. Combinatorial Algorithms. 40.00 (*0-686-46261-0*); 91.00 (*0-686-46258-0*) Algorithmics.

— Courant Computer Science, Symposium 7: Computational Complexity. (Illus.). 268p. 1973. 40.00 (*0-917448-01-4*) Algorithmics.

— Courant Computer Science, Symposium 8: Natural Language Processing. (Illus.). 350p. 1973. 40.00 (*0-917448-02-2*) Algorithmics.

— Courant Computer Science Symposium 9: Combinatorial Algorithms. (Illus.). 126p. 1973. 40.00 (*0-917448-03-0*) Algorithmics.

Rustin, Terry A. Facilitators Guide to Quit & Stay Quit: Medical Treatment Program for Smokers. 3rd ed. 48p. (Orig.). 1989. pap. 10.95 (*0-9625789-1-6*) Discovery TX.

— Quit & Stay Quit: A Personal Program to Stop Smoking. 233p. (Orig.). 1991. pap. 19.95 (*0-89486-797-0*, 5430A) Hazelden.

— Quit & Stay Quit: Medical Treatment Program for Smokers. 4th ed. 134p. (Orig.). 1989. pap. 13.95 (*0-9625789-0-8*) Discovery TX.

Rustomji-Kerns, Roshni, ed. Blood into Ink: South Asian & Middle Eastern Women Write War. LC 94-1770. 1994. text ed. 59.95 (*0-8133-8661-6*) Westview.

— Living in America: Poetry. (C). 1995. pap. text ed. 17.95 (*0-8133-2378-9*) Westview.

— Living in America: Poetry and Fiction by South Asian American Writers. (C). 1995. text ed. 59.00 (*0-8133-2379-7*) Westview.

Rustomji, N. K. & Ramble, Charles, eds. Himalayan Environment & Culture. Ramble, Charles, tr. (C). 1990. text ed. 36.00 (*81-85182-32-9*, Pub. by Usha II) S Asia.

Rustomji, Nari. Sikkim: A Himalayan Tragedy. 173p. 1987. 21.00 (*0-8364-2056-X*, Pub. by Allied II) S Asia.

Rustomji, Nari, ed. see Elwin, Verrier.

Rustomji, R. Registration Act. 4th ed. (C). 1989. 265.00 (*0-685-27901-4*) St Mut.

Ruston. Comparative Political Dynamics. (C). 1990. pap. text ed. 33.00 (*0-06-045673-6*) HarpCollege.

Ruston, Anthony F. Fredholm Theory in Banach Spaces. (Cambridge Tracts in Mathematics Ser.: No. 86). 320p. 1986. 79.95 (*0-521-24846-9*) Cambridge U Pr.

Ruston, John, jt. auth. see Denison, Richard.

Rustow, Alexander. Freedom & Domination: A Historical Critique of Civilization. Attanasio, Salvator, tr. LC 80-10575. 700p. 1980. 85.00 (*0-691-05304-9*) Princeton U Pr.

Rustow, Dankwart A. Turkey: America's Forgotten Ally. rev. ed. 174p. 1989. pap. 14.95 (*0-87609-065-X*) Coun Foreign.

Rustow, Hanns-Joachim. New Paths to Full Employment: The Failure of Orthodox Economic Theory. Mayes, Linda, tr. LC 90-42645. 144p. 1991. text ed. 65.00 (*0-312-05304-5*) St Martin.

Rustum, Y. & McGuire, J. J., eds. Expanding Role of Folates & Fluoropyrimidines in Cancer Chemotherapy. LC 88-38105. (Illus.). 346p. 1989. 79.50 (*0-306-43100-9*, Plenum Pr) Plenum.

Rustum, Y. M., ed. Novel Approaches to Selective Treatments of Human Solid Tumors: Laboratory & Clinical Correlation. (Advances in Experimental Medicine & Biology Ser.: Vol. 339). (Illus.). 312p. 1994. 79.50 (*0-306-44592-1*, Plenum Pr) Plenum.

Ruswa, Mirza. The Courtesan of Lucknow. Singh, Khushwant & Husaini, M. A., trs. 240p. 1970. pap. 4.00 (*0-88253-076-3*) Ind-US Inc.

Rusz, Joe. Porsche Sport 72. LC 72-97717. (Illus.). 1973. pap. 4.95 (*0-393-60016-5*) Norton.

— Porsche Sport 73. LC 73-89096. (Illus.). 1974. pap. 5.95 (*0-393-60017-3*) Norton.

Ruszczynski, A., tr. see Shor, N. Z.

Ruszczynski, Stanley, ed. Psychotherapy with Couples: Theory & Practice at the Tavistock Institute of Marital Studies. 236p. 1993. pap. 31.95 (*1-85575-045-7*, Pub. by Karnac Bks UK) Brunner-Mazel.

Ruszkiewicz, jt. auth. see Hairston, Maxine C.

Ruszkiewicz, John, jt. auth. see Lunsford, Andrea.

Rusznyak, I. & Foldi, M. Lymphatics & Lymph Circulation Physiology & Pathology. 2nd ed. LC 67-24528. 1967. 393.00 (*0-08-012022-9*, Pub. by Pergamon Repr UK) Franklin.

Ruta, Tina, jt. ed. see Richardson, Dorothy.

Rutan. Twenty-Fourth Annual Simulation Symposium, 1991. LC 71-149514. 240p. 1991. pap. 50.00 (*0-8186-2169-9*, ANS24-1) Soc Computer Sim.

Rutan, ed. Proceedings of the Twenty-Second Annual Simulation Symposium. 194p. 1989. pap. 48.00 (*0-685-66803-7*, ANS22-1) Soc Computer Sim.

Rutan, Burt, jt. frwd. see Lennon, Andy.

Rutan, Catherine. Changes in Position. 1983. pap. 3.50 (*0-911623-00-0*) I Klang.

Rutan, Debbie. Big Promises for Little People. (Illus.). (J). (gr. 1-3). 1991. pap. 3.95 (*0-9624777-2-9*) Green & White Pub.

Rutan, J. Scott. Psychotherapy for the 1990s. 378p. 1993. reprint ed. pap. text ed. 20.95 (*0-89862-161-5*) Guilford Pr.

Rutan, J. Scott, ed. Psychotherapy for the 1990s. LC 91-35424. 378p. 1992. lib. bdg. 40.00 (*0-89862-798-2*) Guilford Pr.

Rutan, J. Scott & Stone, Walter N., eds. Psychodynamic Group Psychotherapy. 2nd ed. LC 93-15055. 274p. 1993. lib. bdg. 30.00 (*0-89862-096-1*) Guilford Pr.

Rutayuga, John B. Intermediate Swahili Newspaper Reader. LC 84-72435. xix, 259p. 1984. text ed. 39.00 (*0-931745-02-0*); audio 15.00 (*0-931745-14-4*) Dunwoody Pr.

***Rutberg, Becky.** Mary Lincoln's Dressmaker: The Remarkable Life of Elizabeth Keckley. LC 94-45839. (Illus.). 176p. (YA). (gr. 5 up). 1995. 14.95 (*0-8027-8224-8*); lib. bdg. 15.85 (*0-8027-8225-6*) Walker & Co.

Rutberg, Jack V. Hans Burkhardt: 1950-1960. (Illus.). 42p. 1987. pap. 15.00 (*1-880566-03-6*) J Rutberg Fine Arts.

Rutberg, Jack V., intro. Edward Glauder: Sculpture, 1980-88. 48p. 1989. pap. 15.00 (*1-880566-06-0*) J Rutberg Fine Arts.

— Hans Burkhardt: The War Paintings, a Catalogue Raisonne. (Illus.). 160p. (Orig.). 1984. pap. 40.00 (*0-937048-39-9*, Santa Susana Pr) CSUN.

— Patrick Graham. (Illus.). 28p. 1989. pap. 25.00 (*1-880566-05-2*) J Rutberg Fine Arts.

Rutebeuf. Poemes de L'Infortune et Autres Poemes (Medieval & Modern French) (Poesie Ser.). 308p. (FRE.). 1986. pap. 13.95 (*2-07-032378-1*) Schoenhof.

***Rutecki, Randall J.** Computing Against the Odds: The Beginner's Guide to Sports Handicapping with a Personal Computer. (Orig.). 1995. pap. 29.95 (*0-9646727-0-7*) Cybersource.

Rutenbar, Rob A., jt. auth. see Setliff, Dorothy E.

***Rutenberg, A., ed.** Earthquake Engineering: Proceedings of the 17th European Regional Seminar, Haifa, 5-10 September 1993. (Illus.). 300p. (C). 1994. text ed. 80.00 (*90-5410-391-4*, Pub. by A A Balkema NE) Ashgate Pub Co.

Rutenfranz, Joseph, et al, eds. Children & Exercise, Vol. XII. LC 86-10556. 432p. 1986. text ed. 47.00 (*0-87322-062-5*, BRUT0062) Human Kinetics.

Ruter, Horst, jt. auth. see Dresen, L.

***Ruterbories, Shavaun.** The Family Investment. 196p. (Orig.) 1995. pap. 12.95 (*0-9646012-0-6*) L & S Ruterbories.

Rutford, Robert, jt. auth. see Zumberge, James H.

Rutgers, I., ed. see Africanus, Sextus J.

***Rutgers, Leonard V.** The Jews in Late Ancient Rome: Evidence of Cultural Interation in the Roman Diaspora. LC 95-5743. (Religions in the Graeco-Roman World Ser.: Vol. 126). 1995. 77.75 (*90-04-10269-8*) E J Brill.

Rutgers, M., tr. see Paulis, L.

Rutgers University Graduate Students, et al. Adams Middle School Superintendency Monroe City School Simulation Assistant Superintendent for Instruction In-Basket II. 58p. (Orig.). (C). 1983. pap. text ed. 8.25 (*0-922971-87-0*, AD-C2) Univ Council Educ Admin.

— Adams Middle School Superintendency Monroe City School Simulation Assistant Superintendent of Instruction Background Information. 50p. (Orig.). (C). 1983. pap. text ed. 8.25 (*0-922971-85-4*, AD-C) Univ Council Educ Admin.

Rutgers University Staff. Copper-Containing Composites. 74p. 1970. 11.10 (*0-317-34502-8*, 65) Intl Copper.

— Women, Culture & Society: A Reader. 432p. (C). 1992. pap. text ed. 34.95 (*0-8403-8141-7*) Kendall-Hunt.

Ruth, et al. Cell Behaviour: A Tribute to Michael Abercrombie. Bellairs, Ruth et al, eds. LC 81-6119. (Illus.). 500p. 1982. 150.00 (*0-521-24107-3*) Cambridge U Pr.

Ruth. Home Run King - How Pep Pindar Won Title. 18.95 (*0-8488-1586-6*) Amereon Ltd.

— King Lear. (Max Notes Ser.). 144p. 1995. pap. text ed. 3.95 (*0-87891-989-9*) Res & Educ.

— Paradise Lost. (Max Notes Ser.). 128p. 1995. pap. text ed. 3.95 (*0-87891-992-9*) Res & Educ.

Ruth, jt. auth. see Blotzer.

Ruth, Babe. Babe Ruth Story. 1992. pap. 4.99 (*0-451-17492-5*, Sig) NAL-Dutton.

Ruth, Barbara. The Politics of Relationships. (Poetry Chapbooks Ser.: No. 1). 32p. 1979. pap. 2.50 (*0-913282-14-6*) Seven Woods Pr.

***Ruth, Bonnie.** November Days. 299p. (Orig.). 1995. pap. 12.95 (*0-9645378-7-7*) F Scott Pr.

Ruth, Byron E., ed. Evaluation & Prevention of Water Damage to Asphalt Pavement Materials-STP 889. LC 85-26783. (Illus.). 160p. 1985. text ed. 46.00 (*0-8031-0460-X*, 04-899000-08) ASTM.

Ruth, Christopher & Ruth, Steve. Developing Expert Systems Using 1st-Class. 1988. pap. text ed. write for info. (*0-07-555434-8*) McGraw.

— Developing Expert Systems Using 1st-Class, Incl. software. 1988. disk, pap. write for info. (*0-07-556432-7*) McGraw.

Ruth, Eddie. How Do the Ducks Know? (Illus.). 28p. (Orig.). (J). (gr. 1-4). 1981. pap. 2.50 (*0-911826-18-1*, 5448) Am Atheist.

Ruth, George E. Commercial Lending. 2nd ed. Johns, Rebecca B., ed. (Illus.). 454p. 1990. text ed. 57.00 (*0-89982-363-7*) Am Bankers.

Ruth, George H. Babe Ruth's Own Book of Baseball. LC 91-38383. xxii, 333p. 1992. reprint ed. 35.00 (*0-8032-3905-X*); reprint ed. pap. 9.95 (*0-8032-8939-1*) U of Nebr Pr.

Ruth, H., et al. Challenge of Crime in a Free Society. LC 79-152126. (Symposia on Law & Society Ser.). 1971. reprint ed. lib. bdg. 22.50 (*0-306-70124-3*) Da Capo.

Ruth-Heffelbower, Duane. The Anabaptists Are Back: Making Peace in a Dangerous World. LC 91-6668. 144p. (Orig.). 1991. pap. 8.95 (*0-8361-3552-0*) Herald Pr.

— The Christian & Jury Duty. LC 91-13624. (Peace & Justice Ser.: Vol. 14). 104p. (Orig.). 1991. pap. 5.95 (*0-8361-3562-8*) Herald Pr.

Ruth-Heffelbower, Dwayne. A Technical Manual for Church Planters. Martin, Melba et al, eds. (Illus.). 80p. 1989. pap. 5.00 (*0-317-93801-0*) MB Missions.

Ruth, Jeffrey S., tr. see De Gois, Damiao.

Ruth, John L. Conrad Grebel, Son of Zurich: Commissioned by Conrad Grebel College, Waterloo, Ontario, in Observance of the 450th Anniversary of the Mennonites. LC 75-8829. (Illus.). 160p. reprint ed. pap. 45.60 (*0-7837-5112-5*, 2044811) Bks Demand.

— Maintaining the Right Fellowship. LC 83-18579. (Studies in Anabaptist & Mennonite History: No. 26). 608p. 1984. 24.95 (*0-8361-1259-8*) Herald Pr.

— A Quiet & Peaceable Life. rev. ed. LC 85-70284. (People's Place Book Ser.: No. 2). (Illus.). 96p. (Orig.). 1985. pap. 5.95 (*0-934672-25-3*) Good Bks PA.

— Twas Seeding Time. LC 76-41475. 220p. 1976. pap. 8.95 (*0-8361-1800-6*) Herald Pr.

Ruth, Kent. Landmarks of the West: A Guide to Historic Sites. LC 85-29014. (Illus.). x, 309p. 1986. 39.50 (*0-8032-3875-4*); pap. 19.95 (*0-8032-8919-7*) U of Nebr Pr.

— Oklahoma Travel Handbook. LC 76-62517. (Illus.). 1979. pap. 13.95 (*0-8061-1539-4*) U of Okla Pr.

— Touring the Old West. LC 86-19305. (Illus.). x, 218p. 1987. 23.00 (*0-8032-3881-9*) U of Nebr Pr.

Ruth, Kent, jt. auth. see Argo, Burnis.

Ruth, L. Justin. An Element of Time. 1993. 16.95 (*0-533-10587-0*) Vantage.

Ruth, Larry. M I Carbine. pap. 19.95 (*0-88227-020-6*) Gun Room.

Ruth, Leo & Murphy, Sandra. Designing Writing Tasks for the Assessment of Writing. Farr, Marcia, ed. LC 87-19688. (Writing Research Ser.: Vol. 4). 336p. 1988. text ed. 49.50 (*0-89391-339-1*); pap. 27.50 (*0-89391-430-4*) Ablex Pub.

Ruth, Maria M. The First Thanksgiving. (Miniature Pop-ups Ser.). (Illus.). 4p. (J). 1994. write for info. (*0-307-82510-8*) Western Pub.

— A Rain Forest Pop-Up: Poster & Story. (Illus.). (J). 1995. 16.95 (*0-671-51080-0*, Litl Simon S&S) S&S Childrens.

Ruth, Marianne & Locke, Raymond F. Cruel City. LC 90-52813. (Illus.). 240p. (J). 1991. 19.95 (*0-915677-48-2*) Roundtable Pub.

Ruth, Matthias. Integrating Economics, Ecology & Thermodyanamics. LC 93-24816. (Ecology, Economy & Environment Ser.). 264p. 1993. lib. bdg. 119.00 (*0-7923-2377-7*) Kluwer Ac.

Ruth, Matthias, jt. auth. see Hannon, Bruce.

Ruth, Merle. Dying to Live with Christ. 79p. 1989. pap. 3.20 (*0-317-01798-5*) Rod & Staff.

— Significado del Velo de la Mujer Cristiana. 1980. 0.65 (*0-317-02032-3*) Rod & Staff.

— The Significance of the Christian Woman's Veiling. 1980. 1.25 (*0-686-30769-0*) Rod & Staff.

— Triumphant in Suffering. 78p. 1991. pap. 3.00 (*0-317-04169-X*) Rod & Staff.

Ruth, Phil J. A North Penn Pictorial. (Illus.). 176p. 1988. 29.95 (*0-9619350-0-6*) P J Ruth.

— Seeing Souderton: The Borough's Story in Photographs, 1887-1987. (Illus.). 192p. (C). 1987. 29.95 (*0-9619350-1-4*) P J Ruth.

Ruth, Philippa. The Trials of Ada Adams. write for info. (*0-318-58991-5*) World Pr Ltd.

Ruth, Romy, jt. auth. see Neumann, Jeff.

Ruth, Sheila. Issues in Feminism: An Introduction to Women's Studies. 2nd ed. 531p. (C). 1990. pap. text ed. 29.95 (*0-87484-937-3*) Mayfield Pub.

— Issues in Feminism: An Introduction to Women's Studies. 3rd ed. LC 94-17305. 577p. (C). 1994. pap. text ed. 29.95 (*1-55934-224-2*) Mayfield Pub.

— Take Back the Light: A Feminist Reclamation of Spirituality & Religion. LC 93-6061. (New Feminist Perspectives Ser.). 240p. (Orig.). (C). 1994. text ed. 52.50 (*0-8476-7879-2*); pap. text ed. 14.95 (*0-8226-3031-1*) Rowman.

Ruth, Stephen R., jt. ed. see Mann, Charles K.

Ruth, Steve, jt. auth. see Ruth, Christopher.

Ruth, Steve, jt. auth. see Sprague, Kristopher.

Ruth, Susan, jt. auth. see Ruth, Trevor.

Ruth, Trevor & Ruth, Susan. Drawing My View. LC 93-11827. (J). 1994. 4.95 (*0-383-03730-1*) SRA Schl Grp.

Ruth, W. Lexikon der Schulphysik: Optik und Relativitaet, Vol. 4. (GER.). 85.00 (*3-7614-0109-4*, M-7226) Fr & Eur.

— Lexikon der Schulphysik, Vol. 4: Optik und Relativitaet. (GER.). 85.00 (*0-8288-7975-3*, M7226) Fr & Eur.

Ruthberg, Helen. The Book of Miniatures: Furniture & Accessories. LC 76-451. (Creative Crafts Ser.). 264p. 1977. 19.95 (*0-8019-6366-4*) Chilton.

Ruthberg, Zella, jt. ed. see Menkus, Belden.

Ruthberg, Zella, jt. ed. see Tipton, Hal.

Ruthberg, Zella B., et al. Guide to Auditing for Controls & Security: A System Development Life Cycle Approach. LC 88-60518. (National Bureau of Standards Special Publication, Computer Science & Technology Ser.: No. 500-153). 268p. (Orig.). 1988. pap. 13.00 (*0-685-44348-5*, S/N 003-003-02856-8) USGPO.

R

An Asterisk (*) at the beginning of an entry indicates that the title is appearing in BIP for the first time.

Ruthberg, Zella G. & Tipton, Harold F., eds. Handbook of Information Security Management. 773p. 125.00 (0-7913-1636-X) Warren Gorham & Lamont.
Ruthchild, Rochelle G. Women in Russia & the Soviet Union: An Annotated Bibliography. 240p. 1994. write for info. (0-318-69489-1) G K Hall.
Ruthchild, Rochelle G., ed. Women in Russia & the Soviet Union. 1992. lib. bdg. 40.00 (0-685-59685-0, Hall Reference) Macmillan.
— Women in Russia & the Soviet Union: An Annotated Bibliography. (Reference Ser.). 203p. 1994. text ed. 40.00 (0-8161-8989-7) G K Hall.
Ruthen, Marlene L., illus. Daniel & the Silver Flute: An Old Hassidic Tale. 32p. 1986. 11.95 (0-317-55242-2) United Synagogue.
Ruthenberg, Stephen J. Golf Fore Beginners: The Fundamentals. LC 91-67566. 120p. (Orig.). 1992. pap. 9.95 (0-9631514-1-X) RGS Pub.
Rutheny, Eugene P. Anatomy & Physiology Notebook. 272p. (C). 1993. spiral bd. write for info. (0-697-20349-2) Wm C Brown Pubs.
Ruther, Nancy L., jt. auth. see Mayo-Smith, Ian.
Rutherfoord, Andrea. Basic Communication Skills for Electronics Technology. 304p. 1988. pap. text ed. 42.00 (0-13-970617-8) P-H.
Rutherford, G. Stuart & Hewlett, R. H. Atlas of Correlative Surgical Neuropathology & Imaging. LC 94-11237. (Current Histopathology Ser.: Vol. 24). 206p. (C). 1994. lib. bdg. 225.00 (0-7923-8951-4) Kluwer Ac.
Rutherford. ASR: Organic Chemistry. 1994. 11.95 (0-87434-569-3) Springhouse Pub.
— Inorganic Chemistry. (Science Review Ser.). 1992. 11.95 (0-87434-454-9); 19.75 (0-87434-460-3) Springhouse Pub.
— London. 25.00 (0-517-59181-2) Random Hse Value.
— Unstable Angina. (Fundamental & Clinical Cardiology: Vol. 4). 328p. 1991. 110.00 (0-8247-8618-1) Dekker.
Rutherford, ed. Identity: Community Culture Difference. (C). 1990. pap. 19.95 (0-85315-720-0, Pub. by Lawrence & Wishart UK) Humanities.
— Male Order: Unwrapping Masculinity. (C). 1988. pap. 19.95 (0-85315-690-5, Pub. by Lawrence & Wishart UK) Humanities.
Rutherford, et al. Retriever Working Certificate Training. (Illus.). 120p. 1986. pap. 9.95 (0-931866-26-X) Alpine Pubns.
Rutherford, A. & Peterson, K. H., eds. Chinua Achebe: A Celebration. (Studies in African Literature). 165p. 1991. pap. 17.50 (0-435-08060-1, 08060) Heinemann.
Rutherford, Adam. Iceland's Great Inheritance. 40p. 1990. pap. 2.50 (0-934666-41-5) Artisan Sales.
Rutherford, Andrew. Byron: A Critical Study. xiii, 253p. 1961. 37.50 (0-8047-0071-0); pap. 11.95 (0-8047-0072-9) Stanford U Pr.
— Criminal Justice & the Pursuit of Decency. LC 92-1686. 224p. 1993. pap. 15.95 (0-19-285275-2) OUP.
Rutherford, Andrew, ed. Kipling's Mind & Art: Selected Critical Essays. x, 278p. 1964. 37.50 (0-8047-0212-8); pap. 12.95 (0-8047-0213-6) Stanford U Pr.
Rutherford, Andrew, ed. see Kipling, Rudyard.
Rutherford, Brett. The Lost Children. 432p. 1988. pap. 3.95 (0-8217-2454-1) Zebra.
Rutherford, Brett & Robertson, John. Piper. 480p. 1987. pap. 3.95 (0-8217-1967-X) Zebra.
Rutherford, Brian & Wearing, Robert. Cases in Company Financial Reporting. (C). 1988. pap. 45.00 (0-06-318371-4, Pub. by P Chapman Pub UK); 36.00 (0-317-93202-0, Pub. by P Chapman Pub UK) St Mut.
Rutherford, Brian, jt. ed. see MacDonald, G.
Rutherford, Brian, et al. Cases in Public Sector Accounting. 224p. 1992. pap. 29.95 (1-85396-072-1, Pub. by Paul Chapman UK) Taylor & Francis.
Rutherford, Brinton L., jt. auth. see Turner, Rufus P.
Rutherford, Bruce. The Impeachment of Jim Ferguson. (Illus.). 166p. 1983. 11.95 (0-89015-386-8) Sunbelt Media.
Rutherford, Clarence. No Escape from Greatness. LC 89-85364. (Orig.). (C). 1989. pap. 12.95 (0-9622704-1-5) Xylo Prods.
Rutherford, Clarice & Loveland, Cherylon. Retriever Puppy Training: The Right Start for Hunting. LC 88-3015. (Illus.). 109p. 1988. pap. text ed. 9.95 (0-931866-38-3) Alpine Pubns.
Rutherford, Clarice & Neil, David H. How to Raise a Puppy You Can Live With. 2nd ed. LC 92-9723. (Illus.). 136p. 1992. pap. 9.95 (0-931866-57-X) Alpine Pubns.
Rutherford, Clarice, jt. auth. see Rodgers, Cook.
Rutherford, Constance. The Art of Making Paper Flowers: Full Size Patterns & Instructions for 16 Realistic Blossoms. (Illus.). 48p. (Orig.). 1983. pap. 3.95 (0-486-24378-8) Dover.
Rutherford, Denney G. Hotel Management & Operations. 1990. pap. 35.95 (0-442-20534-1) Van Nos Reinhold.
— Hotel Management & Operations. 2nd ed. 30p. 1995. pap. 29.95 (0-442-01496-1) Van Nos Reinhold.
***Rutherford, Donald.** Leibniz & the Rational Order of Nature. 336p. (C). 1995. 54.95 (0-521-46155-3) Cambridge U Pr.
— Routledge Dictionary of Economics. 560p. 1995. pap. 18.95 (0-415-12291-0, C0460) Routledge.
***Rutherford, Donald, ed.** Classical Economics: The Critical Reviews, 1802-1852. LC 94-23101. 1995. write for info. (0-415-11270-2) Routledge.
— Dictionary of Economics. (Illus.). 448p. 1991. 85.00 (0-415-06566-6, A6024) Routledge.
Rutherford, Douglas. A Game of Sudden Death. large type ed. 1990. 21.95 (0-7089-2144-2) Ulverscroft.
— Skin for Skin. (Black Dagger Crime Ser.). 200p. 16.50 (0-86220-732-0, Black Dagger) Chivers N Amer.
— Stop at Nothing. large type ed. 1989. 17.95 (0-7089-2109-4) Ulverscroft.
***Rutherford, E.** Sarum. Date not set. 6.99 (0-09-952730-8) Random.
Rutherford, Edward. Russka. 1995. pap. 5.99 (0-517-11282-5) Random Hse Value.
— Sarum. 1990. 5.99 (0-517-03389-5) Random Hse Value.
— Sarum. 1993. reprint ed. lib. bdg. 45.95 (1-56849-114-X) Buccaneer Bks.
Rutherford, Erica. Nine Lives: The Autobiography of Erica Rutherford. 224p. (Orig.). 1993. pap. 12.95 (0-921556-36-5, Pub. by Gynergy-Ragweed CN) InBook.
— The Owl & the Pussycat. (Illus.). 24p. (J). (gr. 1 up). 1986. text ed. 12.95 (0-88776-181-X) Tundra Bks.
Rutherford, Ernest & Boltwood, Bertram B. Rutherford & Boltwood: Letters on Radioactivity. Badash, Lawrence, ed. LC 78-81411. (Yale Studies in the History of Science & Medicine: No. 4). (Illus.). 402p. reprint ed. pap. 114.60 (0-8357-9490-3, 2016787) Bks Demand.
Rutherford, F. James & Ahlgren, Andrew. Science for All Americans. 272p. 1991. 24.95 (0-19-506770-3); pap. 11.95 (0-19-506771-1) OUP.
Rutherford, Frederick. You & Your Baby. (Orig.). 1971. pap. 4.50 (0-451-14321-3, AE2177, Sig); pap. 5.99 (0-451-15290-5, Sig) NAL-Dutton.
Rutherford, G. K. The Physical Environment of the Faeroe Islands. 1982. lib. bdg. 89.00 (90-6193-099-5) Kluwer Ac.
Rutherford, H. C., ed. Certainly, Future: Selected Writing by Dimitrije Mitrinovic. 450p. 1987. text ed. 62.50 (0-88033-118-6, 222) East Eur Quarterly.
Rutherford, H. R. The Order of Christian Funerals: An Invitation to Pastoral Care. (American Essays in Liturgy Ser.). 55p. 1990. pap. 3.95 (0-8146-1975-4) Liturgical Pr.
Rutherford, J. C. River Mixing. LC 93-33003. 1994. text ed. 79.95 (0-471-94282-0) Wiley.
Rutherford, James H. The Moral Foundations of United States Constitutional Democracy. LC 92-73414. 52p. (C). 1992. pap. 5.00 (0-8059-3352-2) Dorrance.
Rutherford, John. An Annotated Bibliography of the Novels of the Mexican Revolution of 1910-1917. LC 73-150334. 180p. (ENG & SPA.). 1972. 10.00 (0-87875-015-0) Whitston Pub.
— The Troubadours: Their Loves & Their Lyrics with Remarks on Their Influence, Social & Literary. 1977. lib. bdg. 59.95 (0-8490-2771-3) Gordon Pr.
Rutherford, John A. & Smith, Richard B., III. Cowboy Shooting Stars. Key, Donald R., ed. LC 87-83297. 104p. 1988. lib. bdg. 7.50 (0-944019-04-8) Empire NC.
Rutherford, John D., jt. auth. see Antman, Elliott M.
Rutherford, Jonathan. Men's Silences: Predicaments in Masculinity. LC 92-2801. (Male Orders Ser.). 224p. 1992. 74.50 (0-415-07543-2, A7650); pap. 15.95 (0-415-07544-0, A7654) Routledge.
Rutherford, Joseph F. Angels. 64p. 1987. reprint ed. pap. 2.95 (1-883858-31-3) Witness CA.
— Millions Now Living Will Never Die! 128p. 1985. reprint ed. pap. 5.95 (1-883858-29-1) Witness CA.
Rutherford, Kim, jt. auth. see Ahrens, Thomas.
Rutherford, L. John Peter Zenger, His Press, Trial Plus Bibliography: Includes Repr. of First Edition of the Trial, 1904-1990. (Illus.). 275p. 1991. pap. 35.00 (0-87556-800-9) Saifer.
Rutherford, Leonard W. The Role of Chiropractic. 324p. (Orig.). 1989. text ed. 30.00 (0-9625065-1-6); pap. text ed. 22.50 (0-9625065-0-8) Hlth Educ Pub.
Rutherford, Livingston & Bell, James B. John Peter Zenger & Freedom of the Press. xx, 71p. write for info. (0-318-60907-X) A Colish Inc.
Rutherford, Lyn. Book of Antipasti. (Book of Ser.). (Illus.). 120p. (Orig.). 1992. pap. 10.95 (1-55788-040-9) Price Stern.
— Traditional Country Cooking. LC 93-37196. (Creative Cook Ser.). 1993. 16.95 (1-56426-652-4) Cole Group.
Rutherford, Lyn, jt. auth. see Hurst, Jacqui.
Rutherford, Mac S., II. Luckee's Elbow Room. 249p. (Orig.). 1988. pap. 4.95 (0-922510-00-8) Lucky Bks.
Rutherford, Malcolm. Institutions in Economics: The Old & the New Institutionalism. (Historical Perspectives on Modern Economics Ser.). 256p. (C). 1994. 54.95 (0-521-45189-2) Cambridge U Pr.
Rutherford, Mildred L. The South in History & Literature. 1972. 59.95 (0-8490-1093-4) Gordon Pr.
Rutherford, Nancy G., jt. auth. see Saputo, Helen N.
Rutherford, Paul. The New Icons? The Art of Television Advertising. (Illus.). 270p. (C). 1994. 55.00 (0-8020-2928-0); pap. 19.95 (0-8020-7428-6) U of Toronto Pr.
— A Victorian Authority: The Daily Press in Late Nineteenth-Century Canada. LC 82-190489. (Illus.). 305p. reprint ed. pap. 87.00 (0-7837-4288-6, 2043980) Bks Demand.
— When Television Was Young: Primetime Canada 1952-1967. 638p. 1990. 65.00 (0-8020-5830-2); pap. 29.95 (0-8020-6647-X) U of Toronto Pr.
***Rutherford, R. B.** The Art of Plato: Ten Essays in Platonic Interpretation. LC 94-41991. 352p. (C). 1995. text ed. 45.00 (0-674-04811-3) HUP.
— The Meditations of Marcus Aurelius: A Study. (Oxford Classical Monographs). 304p. 1991. reprint ed. pap. 29.95 (0-19-814755-4) OUP.
Rutherford, R. B., ed. see Antoninus, Marcus A.
Rutherford, R. B., ed. see Homer.
Rutherford, R. B., tr. see Marcus Aurelius.
Rutherford, R. D. Collection Strategies & Techniques. Andover, James J., ed. LC 85-25835. 120p. 1985. pap. 20.95 (0-934914-66-4) NACM.
— No-Nonsense Cashflow Management. Chernow Editorial Services, Inc. Staff, ed. (Illus.). 170p. 1988. 9.99 (0-934914-75-3) NACM.
Rutherford, Richard. The Death of a Christian: The Order of Christian Funerals. 224p. 1992. pap. 14.95 (0-8146-6040-1, Pueblo Bks) Liturgical Pr.
Rutherford, Robert B. Atlas of Vascular Surgery: Basic Techniques & Exposures. (Illus.). 288p. 1993. text ed. 79.00 (0-7216-2956-3) Saunders.
Rutherford, Robert B., Jr., jt. ed. see Bullock, Lyndal M.
Rutherford, Samuel. Letters of Samuel Rutherford. 1985. reprint ed. 27.95 (0-85151-388-3) Banner of Truth.
— Loveliness of Christ. 54p. 1990. 3.00 (1-882840-04-6) Comm Christian.
— The Trial & Triumph of Faith. (Puritan Classics Ser.). 328p. 1991. lib. bdg. 29.95 (1-56387-001-0) Pilgrim Bk Hse.
Rutherford, Scott, ed. see Stone, Scott C.
Rutherford, Susan, jt. ed. see Gardner, Vivien.
Rutherford, Ward. Celtic Lore: The History of the Druids & Their Timeless Traditions. 240p. 1993. pap. 15.00 (1-85538-134-6, Pub. by Aquarian Pr UK) Thorsons SF.
— Celtic Mythology. (Illus.). 160p. (Orig.). 1994. pap. 9.95 (0-85030-551-9) Sterling.
— Celtic Mythology. LC 88-34104. 160p. (Orig.). (C). 1988. reprint ed. lib. bdg. 27.00x (0-8095-7068-8) Borgo Pr.
Rutherford, William E. Modern English, Vol. 1. 2nd ed. 349p. (C). 1975. pap. text ed. 14.00 (0-15-561059-7) HB Coll Pubs.
Rutherford, William E., ed. Language Universals & Second Language Acquisition. LC 84-9387. (Typological Studies in Language: No. 5). ix, 264p. 1984. 65.00x (0-915027-09-7); pap. 32.95x (0-915027-10-0) Benjamins North Am.
Rutherford, William E. & Sherwood-Smith, Michael, eds. Grammar & Second Language Teaching: A Book of Readings. 260p. (C). 1987. pap. 24.95 (0-8384-2701-4, Newbury) Heinle & Heinle.
Rutherford, William G., comment & intro. Phrynichus (Arabius) The New Phrynichus Being a Revised Text of the Ecloga of the Grammarian Phrynichus. xii, 539p. 1968. reprint ed. write for info. (0-318-72064-7, Pub. by Georg Olms GW) Lubrecht & Cramer.
Rutherford, William T., jt. ed. see Kaufman, Bruce.
Rutherfurd, Edward. Russka: The Novel of Russia. 1992. mass mkt. 6.99 (0-8041-0972-9) Ivy Books.
— Sarum: The Novel of England. 1988. mass mkt. 6.99 (0-8041-0298-8) Ivy Books.
Rutherfurd, Livingston. John Peter Zenger: His Press, His Trial & a Bibliography of Zenger Imprints. LC 77-125713. (American Journalists Ser.). (Illus.). 1971. reprint ed. 26.95 (0-405-01694-8) Ayer.
Ruthern, Marlene L., illus. My Bar/Bat Mitzvah. 36p. (YA). 10.00 (0-8074-0200-1, 510000) UAHC.
Ruthrof, Horst. Pandora & Occam: On the Limits of Language & Literature. LC 91-26539. (Advances in Semiotics Ser.). (Illus.). 304p. 1992. text ed. 35.00 (0-253-34995-8) Ind U Pr.
Ruthstrom, Carl R. & Dykman, Charlene A. Information Systems for Managers: Casebook. Burvikovs, ed. 200p. (C). 1992. pap. text ed. 19.00 (0-314-00113-1) West Pub.
***Ruthven, Beverly & Rogers, Sue, eds.** Teachers' Desktop Guide to Literature for Intermediate Students. (Illus.). 600p. (J). (gr. 4-7). 1995. lib. bdg. 45.00 (0-933833-37-7) Beacham Pub.
***Ruthven, C. L., ed.** Impacts of Technology on the Global Gas Resource Base: Proceedings of the Global Gas Resources Workshop. (Report of Investigations Ser.: No. 223). 1994. 18.00 (0-614-06197-0) Bur Econ Geology.
Ruthven, Douglas M. Principles of Adsorption & Adsorption Processes. LC 83-16904. 433p. 1984. text ed. 140.00 (0-471-86606-7, Wiley-Interscience) Wiley.
Ruthven, Douglas M. & Karger, Jorg. Diffusion in Zeolites: And Other Microporous Solids. 640p. 1992. text ed. 175.00 (0-471-50907-8) Wiley.
Ruthven, Douglas M., et al. Pressure Swing Adsorption. LC 93-33965. 1993. write for info. (1-56081-517-5) VCH Pubs.
Ruthven, John. The Earl of Gowries Conspiracies Against the Kings Majestie of Scotland. LC 76-26080. (English Experience Ser.: No. 182). 1969. reprint ed. 20.00 (90-221-0182-7) Walter J Johnson.
Ruthven, K. K. Ezra Pound As Literary Critic. 208p. 1990. 47.50 (0-415-02074-3, A4737) Routledge.
— Feminist Literary Studies: An Introduction. (Canto Book Ser.). 160p. (C). 1990. pap. 9.95 (0-521-39852-5) Cambridge U Pr.
— A Guide to Pound's Personae (1926) 291p. 1969. pap. 11.00 (0-520-04960-8) U CA Pr.
Ruthven, Ken. Nuclear Criticism. (Orig.). 1993. pap. 19.95 (0-522-84491-X) Intl Spec Bk.
Ruthven, Kenneth, ed. see NATO Advanced Research Workshop on Mathematics Education & Technology.
Ruthven, Leslie, jt. auth. see Goldstein, Gerald.
***Ruthven, Malise.** Freya Stark in Southern Arabia. (Illus.). 120p. 1995. 45.00 (1-85964-005-2) Paul & Co Pubs.
— Islam in the World. 384p. 1984. pap. 12.95 (0-19-520454-9) OUP.
Ruthven, Malise, ed. Freya Stark in Iraq & Kuwait. (Freya Stark Archives Ser.). (Illus.). 104p. 1995. 45.00 (1-85964-003-6, Pub. by Garnet Pubng Ltd UK) Paul & Co Pubs.
— Freya Stark in the Levant. (Freya Stark Archives Ser.). (Illus.). 104p. 1995. 45.00 (1-85964-004-4, Pub. by Garnet Pubng Ltd UK) Paul & Co Pubs.
— Freyua Stark in Persia. (Freya Stark Archives Ser.). (Illus.). 104p. 1995. 45.00 (1-85964-011-7, Pub. by Garnet Pubng Ltd UK) Paul & Co Pubs.
Rutigliano, Antonio. Lorenzetti's Golden Mean: The Riformatori of Siena, 1368-1885. LC 91-19614. (American University Studies: History: Ser. IX, Vols. 101). 216p. (C). 1992. text ed. 48.95 (0-8204-1456-5) P Lang Pubs.
***Rutimann, Hans.** Computerization Project of the Archivo General de Indias, Seville, Spain. 16p. 1992. pap. 10.00 (1-887334-13-0) Comm Preserv & Access.
— The International Project: 1992 Update. 24p. 1993. pap. 10.00 (1-887334-22-X) Comm Preserv & Access.
— Preservation & Access in China: Possibilities for Cooperation. 16p. 1992. pap. 10.00 (1-887334-14-9) Comm Preserv & Access.
Rutishauser, Heinz. Lectures on Numerical Mathematics. 568p. 1990. 49.50 (0-8176-3491-6) Birkhauser.
Rutishauser, Rolf. Blattstellung und Sprossentwicklung bei Bluetenpflanzen unter Besonderer Beruecksichtigung der Nelkengewaechse. (Dissertationes Botanicae Ser.: Vol. 62). (Illus.). 200p. (GER.). 1981. pap. text ed. 27.50 (3-7682-1304-8) Lubrecht & Cramer.
***Rutishauser, Sigrid.** Physiology & Anatomy: A Basis for Nursing & Health Care. LC 94-27137. 1994. write for info. (0-443-04151-2) Churchill.
***Rutka, John, et al.** Temporal Bone Malignancy: Anatomy, Pathology, & Treatment. (Illus.). 55p. (Orig.). (C). 1994. pap. text ed. 25.00 (1-56772-016-1) AAO-HNS.
***Rutka, M. J.** Integrated Sensor Bus. 150p. (Orig.). 1994. pap. 52.50x (90-6275-966-1, Pub. by Delft U Pr NE) Coronet Bks.
Rutkevich, Igor M., jt. auth. see Lagarkov, A. N.
Rutkevich, Igor M., jt. auth. see Lagrakov, Andrei N.
Rutkiewic, jt. ed. see Kuznicki.
Rutkin, A. H. Family Law & Practice, 4 vols. 1965. write for info. (0-8205-1371-7) Bender.
Rutkoff, Peter M. & Scott, William B. New School: A History of the New School for Social Research. 360p. 1986. pap. 29.95 (0-02-927200-9) Free Pr.
Rutkoski, Thomas. Apostles of the Last Days: The Fruits of Medjugorje. (Illus.). 285p. (Orig.). 1992. pap. 20.00 (0-9633667-7-7) Gospa Missions.
Rutkosky, Nita H. Advanced WordPerfect 6.0: Desktop Publishing. 384p. Date not set. text ed. 31.00 (1-56118-712-7) Paradigm MN.
— A Masstery Approach to Microsoft Word, Version 5.0. 446p. (C). 1990. teacher ed 5.80 (1-56118-108-0); pap. text ed. 27.95 (1-56118-109-9) Paradigm MN.
— Mastery Approach to Microsoft Word, Version 5.0: Short Course. 208p. 1990. text ed. 20.95 (1-56118-112-9) Paradigm MN.
— Mastery Approach to WordPerfect for Windows, Version 5.1. 688p. 1993. text ed. 28.95 (1-56118-469-1); teacher ed, 5.25 hd 69.00 (1-56118-473-X); teacher ed, 5.25 hd 69.00 (1-56118-472-1) Paradigm MN.
— Mastery Approach to WordPerfect for Windows, Version 5.1, Short Course. 348p. 1993. text ed. 20.95 (1-56118-470-5) Paradigm MN.
— Mastery Approach to WordPerfect for Windows, Version 5.2. 720p. 1993. teacher ed 16.00 (1-56118-651-1); text ed. 28.95 (1-56118-650-3); teacher ed, 3.5 hd 69.00 (1-56118-652-X); teacher ed, 5.25 hd 69.00 (1-56118-653-8) Paradigm MN.
— A Mastery Approach to WordPerfect, Version 5.0: Short Course. 208p. (C). 1990. teacher ed 7.10 (1-56118-078-5); pap. text ed. 17.80 (1-56118-077-7) Paradigm MN.
— A Mastery Approach to WordPerfect, Version 5.0 with 5.1 Update. 587p. (C). 1989. teacher ed 7.10 (1-56118-076-9); pap. text ed. 25.50 (1-56118-075-0) Paradigm MN.
— A Mastery Approach to WordPerfect, Version 5.1. 600p. (C). 1991. teacher ed 7.10 (1-56118-083-1); pap. text ed. 26.50 (1-56118-082-3) Paradigm MN.
— Microsoft Word 6.0 for Windows. LC 94-5236. 1994. 3.5 ld 34.95 (1-56118-732-1) Paradigm MN.
— Microsoft Word 6.0 for Windows. LC 94-5236. 1995. 34.95 (1-56118-738-0) Paradigm MN.
— Nita Hewitt Rutkosky's Worderfect Version 6.0 for DOS Essentials. LC 94-15026. 1994. write for info. (1-56118-737-2) Paradigm MN.
— The Nita Hewitt Rutkosky's WordPerfect 6.0 for DOS. LC 93-11935. 736p. 1994. disk 32.95 (1-56118-641-4) Paradigm MN.
— Nita Hewitt Rutkosky's WordPerfect 6.0 for Windows. LC 94-9731. 1994. write for info. (1-56118-685-6) Paradigm MN.
— Nita Hewitt Rutkosky's WordPerfect 6.0 for Windows, Set. LC 94-9731. 1994. disk write for info. (1-56118-688-0) Paradigm MN.
— WordPerfect Essentials: Version 6.0 for DOS. 368p. 1994. text ed., 3.5 hd 24.95 (1-56118-728-3) Paradigm MN.
— WordPerfect Essentials: Version 6.0 for DOS. 1994. 3.5 hd 69.00 (1-56118-730-5) Paradigm MN.
— WordPerfect Essentials: Version 6.0 for DOS. 1994. 5.25 hd 69.00 (1-56118-731-3) Paradigm MN.
— WordPerfect Essentials: Version 6.0 for DOS. 368p. 1994. text ed., 5.25 hd 24.95 (1-56118-750-X) Paradigm MN.
— WordPerfect Essentials: Version 6.0 for DOS. 368p. 1994. text ed. 14.00 (1-56118-727-5) Paradigm MN.
— WordPerfect 6.1 for Windows. LC 95-11473. 1995. write for info. (1-56118-833-6) Paradigm MN.
Rutkosky, Nita H. & Bruns, Cheryl L. Mastery Approach to Microsoft Word, Version 5.5. 544p. 1993. text ed. 28.95 (1-56118-464-0) Paradigm MN.
— Mastery Approach to Microsoft Word, Version 5.5: Short Course. 256p. 1993. text ed. 20.95 (1-56118-465-9) Paradigm MN.
— Mastery Approach to Microsoft Word 2.0 for Windows. 608p. 1993. text ed. 28.95 (1-56118-489-6) Paradigm MN.
— Mastery Approach to Microsoft Word 2.0 for Windows: Short Course. 300p. 1993. text ed. 20.95 (1-56118-490-X) Paradigm MN.
***Rutkosky, Nita H. & Ebert, Dineen.** Nita Hewitt Rutkosky's Advanced WordPerfect Desktop Publishing: Version 6.0 for DOS. LC 94-43778. 1994. write for info. (1-56118-711-9) Paradigm MN.
Rutkovsky, Paul. Commodity Character. LC 82-51222. (Artist's Bks.). 72p. (Orig.). 1982. pap. 8.95 (0-89822-030-0) Visual Studies.

R

— Get. (Illus.). 72p. (Orig.). (YA). (gr. 9-12). 1987. pap. 8.95 (0-89822-048-3) Visual Studies.

— I Am, Siam. LC 85-50043. (Artist's Bks.). (Illus.). 72p. (Orig.). 1985. pap. 8.95 (0-89822-038-6) Visual Studies.

***Rutkovsky-Ruskin, Mary.** The Nighttime Quests of Irwin Botski. 18p. (Orig.). 1994. pap. text ed. 8.95 (1-885902-02-6) Printable Arts.

Rutkow, Ira M. History of Surgery in the United States 1775-1900 Vol. II: Periodical & Pamphlet Literature. (Bibliography & Surgery Ser.: Nos. 5 & 4). (Illus.). 434p. 1992. 175.00 (0-930405-48-X) Norman SF.

— The History of Surgery in the United States 1775-1990 Vol. I: Textbooks, Monographs, & Treatises. LC 87-62662. (Bibliography & Surgery Ser.: No. 2). (Illus.). 514p. 1988. 145.00 (0-930405-02-1) Norman SF.

— Illustrated History of Surgery. LC 93-9820. (Illus.). 512p. 1993. 89.00 (0-8016-6078-5) Mosby Yr Bk.

Rutkow, Ira M., jt. intro. see Moore, Samuel P.

Rutkowska, Julie C. & Crook, Charles. Computers, Cognition & Development: Issues for Psychology & Education. (Series in Developmental Psychology). 311p. 1987. text ed. 172.95 (0-471-91583-1) Wiley.

Rutkowski, ed. Advances in Smoking of Foods. 1978. 42.00 (0-08-022002-9, Pub. by Pergamon Repr UK) Franklin.

Rutkowski, Anthony. Integrated Services Digital Networks. 324p. (C). 1985. text ed. 29.00 (0-89006-146-7) Artech Hse.

— Wired for Business: Insider's Guide to Doing Business on the Internet. 1995. pap. 29.95 (0-13-301797-4) P-H.

Rutkowski, Anthony, jt. auth. see Codding, George A., Jr.

Rutkowski, Bogdan. Cult Places in the Aegean. LC 85-40469. 320p. 1986. text ed. 55.00 (0-300-02962-4) Yale U Pr.

Rutkowski, George B. Basic Electricity for Electronics: A Text Laboratory Manual. 323p. (Orig.). (C). 1984. pap. text ed. write for info. (0-672-98488-1); write for info. (0-672-98489-X) Macmillan.

— Integrated-Circuit Operational Amplifiers. 2nd ed. (Illus.). 320p. (C). 1984. text ed. 52.00 (0-13-469007-9) P-H.

— Operational Amplifiers, Integrated & Hybrid Circuits. 357p. 1993. text ed. 87.95 (0-471-57718-9) Wiley.

— Solid-State Electronics. LC 77-131132. 1972. 17.90 (0-672-20801-6, Bobbs) Macmillan.

Rutkowski, George B., jt. auth. see Olesky, J.

Rutkowski, J. & Lepa, Eugene. Stroboscopes for Industry & Research. LC 65-27684. 1966. 119.00 (0-08-011001-0, Pub. by Pergamon Repr UK) Franklin.

***Rutkowski, Thaddeus.** Sex-Fiend Monologues. 33p. 1994. per., pap. 4.00 (1-886206-11-2) Venom Pr.

Rutkowsky, Nita H. & Yusai, Holly. A Mastery Approach to Advanced WordPerfect Version 5.1, Desktop Publishing. (C). 1991. teacher ed 7.10 (1-56118-373-3); text ed. 22.95 (1-56118-425-X) Paradigm MN.

Rutkrowska, Julie. The Computational Infant: Looking for Developmental Cognitive Science. 288p. 1994. pap. text ed. 44.00 (0-13-302134-3) P-H.

***Rutland.** James Madison Encyclopedia, Vol. 2. 1992. 80.00 (0-13-508433-4) S&S Trade.

Rutland, David. Behind the Front Panel: The Design & Development of 1920's Radios. LC 94-60507. (Illus.). 186p. (Orig.). 1994. pap. 18.95 (1-885391-00-5) Wren Pubs.

— Why Computers Are Computers: The SWAC & the PC. LC 94-62225. 208p. 1995. 24.95 (1-885391-05-6) Wren Pubs.

Rutland, David W. Manual for Determining Physical Properties of Fertilizer. 2nd ed. LC 93-3133. (Reference Manual Ser.: No. R-10). (Illus.). 115p. (Orig.). 1993. pap. text ed. 20.00 (0-88090-101-2) Intl Fertilizer.

***Rutland, Enid.** Close to the Bone: Selected Poems. 80p. 1995. lib. bdg. 33.00 (0-8095-4833-X) Borgo Pr.

Rutland, Eva. Foreign Affair. (Romance Ser.). 1993. mass mkt. 2.99 (0-373-03283-8, 1-03283-8) Harlequin Bks.

Rutland, John H. Rutland Papers Original Documents Illustrative of the Courts & Times of Henry Seven & Henry Eight. Jerden, William, ed. LC 17-1204. (Camden Society, London. Publications, First Ser.: No. 21). reprint ed. 35.00 (0-404-50121-4) AMS Pr.

Rutland, Mark. Hanging by a Thread. LC 91-72840. 196p. (Orig.). 1991. pap. 7.99 (0-88419-296-2, Creation Hse) Strang Comms Co.

Rutland, Peter. The Myth of the Plan: Lessons of Soviet Planning. LC 85-15232. 286p. 1985. 54.95 (0-8126-9005-2); pap. 22.95 (0-8126-9128-8) Open Court.

— The Politics of Economic Stagnation in the Soviet Union: The Role of Local Political Organs in Economic Management. (Cambridge Russian, Soviet & Post-Soviet Studies: No. 88). (Illus.). 320p. (C). 1992. 64.95 (0-521-39241-1) Cambridge U Pr.

— Russia, Eurasia & the Global Economy. (Integrating National Economies: Promise & Pitfalls Ser.). 1995. 28.95 (0-8157-7648-9); pap. 10.95 (0-8157-7647-0) Brookings.

Rutland, Robert A. The American Solution: Origins of the U. S. Constitution. LC 86-607919. 76p. 1987. 6.00 (0-8444-0547-7, 030-001-00118-1) Lib Congress.

— The Birth of the Bill of Rights 1776-1791: (Bicentennial Edition) 254p. 1991. text ed. 35.00 (1-55553-111-3); pap. text ed. 12.95 (1-55553-112-1) NE U Pr.

— A Boyhood in the Dustbowl. (Illus.). 144p. 1995. 22.50 (0-87081-416-8) Univ Pr Colo.

— The First Great Newspaper Debate: The Constitutional Crisis of 1787-88. 20p. (C). 1987. reprint ed. pap. 4.00 (0-912296-97-6) Am Antiquarian.

— George Mason: Reluctant Statesman. LC 79-24328. xvi, 128p. 1980. pap. 7.95 (0-8071-0696-8) La State U Pr.

— James Madison & the American Nation, 1751-1836: An Encyclopedia. LC 94-12322. 1994. 95.00 (0-13-508425-3) S&S Trade.

— James Madison & the Search for Nationhood. LC 81-607967. (Illus.). 174p. 1981. 18.00 (0-8444-0363-6, 030-000-00133-8) Lib Congress.

— The Ordeal of the Constitution: The Anti-Federalists & the Ratification Struggle of 1787-1788. LC 83-19295. 342p. 1983. reprint ed. text ed. 35.00 (0-930350-51-0); reprint ed. pap. 13.95 (0-930350-50-2) NE U Pr.

— The Presidency of James Madison. LC 89-70419. (American Presidency Ser.). xiv, 234p. 1990. 25.00 (0-7006-0465-0) U Pr of KS.

— Well Acquainted with Books: the Founding Framers of 1787: With James Madison's List of Books for Congress. LC 87-2805. 95p. 1987. 6.95 (0-8444-0561-2) Lib Congress.

Rutland, Robert A., ed. see Madison, James.

Rutland, Robert A., ed. see Madison, James, et al.

Rutland, Robert A., ed. see Mason, George.

Rutledege, Marilyn Z., et al. Guide to Homeowner's Associations & Other Common Interest Realty Associations, 2 vols., Set. rev. ed. 800p. 1991. ring bd. 115.00 (1-56433-051-6) Prctnrs Pub Co.

— Guide to Homeowner's Associations & Other Common Interest Realty Associations, Vol. 1. rev. ed. 400p. 1991. write for info. (1-56433-052-4) Prctnrs Pub Co.

— Guide to Homeowner's Associations & Other Common Interest Realty Associations, Vol. 2. rev. ed. 400p. 1991. write for info. (1-56433-053-2) Prctnrs Pub Co.

Rutledge, Aaron L. & Gass, Gertrude Z. Nineteen Negro Men: Personality & Manpower Retraining. LC 67-13277. (Jossey-Bass Social & Behavioral Science Ser.). 228p. reprint ed. 65.00 (0-8357-9341-9, 2013831) Bks Demand.

Rutledge, Adam. Sons of Liberty. (General Ser.). 318p. 1992. pap. 16.95 (0-8161-5495-3, Large Print Bks) Hall.

— Stars & Stripes: Patriots, Bk. VI. 1994. pap. 4.99 (0-553-56316-5) Bantam.

Rutledge, Albert, jt. auth. see Molnar, Donald.

***Rutledge, Archibald.** Home by the River. 1976. reprint ed. 16.95 (0-87844-003-8) Sandlapper Pub Co.

— Hunting & Home in the Southern Heartland: The Best of Archibald Rutledge. Casada, Jim, ed. LC 91-43713. 274p. 1992. 24.95 (0-87249-822-0) U of SC Pr.

— Life's Extras. 2nd ed. (Illus.). 56p. 1987. reprint ed. 8.95 (0-87844-080-1) Sandlapper Pub Co.

— Tales of Whitetails: Archibald Rutledge's Great Deer Hunting Stories. LC 92-20100. 290p. 1992. 24.95 (0-87249-860-3) U of SC Pr.

— Tom & I on the Old Plantation. LC 72-4643. (Black Heritage Library Collection). (Illus.). 1977. reprint ed. 18.95 (0-8369-9124-9) Ayer.

Rutledge, Archibald H. Azerbaijan Cookery. 230p. 1986. 12.95 (0-8285-3799-2) Firebird NY.

Rutledge, Archibald H. & Casada, Jim, eds. America's Greatest Game Bird: Archibald Rutledge's Turkey Hunting Tales. LC 93-39997. 220p. (YA). (gr. 10). 1994. 24.95 (0-87249-983-9) U of SC Pr.

Rutledge, Carol, jt. auth. see Rieck, Sondra.

Rutledge, Carol B. Dying & Living on the Kansas Prairie: A Diary. LC 94-13492. 176p. 1994. 15.95 (0-7006-0649-1) U Pr of KS.

Rutledge, David W. Humans & the Earth: Toward a Personal Ecology. LC 93-18800. 210p. 1994. 39.95 (0-8204-2212-6) P Lang Pubs.

Rutledge, Devallis. Courtroom Survival: The Officer's Guide to Better Testimony. 2nd ed. LC 87-70528. (Illus.). 189p. 1989. reprint ed. pap. text ed. 14.95 (0-942728-15-7) Copperhouse.

— Criminal Interrogation: Law & Tactics. 3rd ed. (Illus.). 171p. (Orig.). 1994. pap. 19.95 (0-942728-62-9) Copperhouse.

— Criminal Procedure, California. 3rd ed. (Illus.). 330p. 1994. pap. 29.95 (0-942728-60-2) Copperhouse.

— Officer Survival Manual. 2nd rev. ed. (Illus.). 351p. 1988. reprint ed. pap. text ed. 15.95 (0-942728-13-0) Copperhouse.

— Report Manual, New Police. 4th ed. (Illus.). 173p. 1991. pap. text ed. 14.95 (0-942728-12-2) Copperhouse.

— The Search & Seizure Handbook. 5th rev. ed. 236p. 1995. pap. 15.95 (0-942728-68-8) Copperhouse.

Rutledge, Dom D. In Search of a Yogi: Himalayan Pilgrimage. 1972. lib. bdg. 200.00 (0-8490-0392-X) Gordon Pr.

Rutledge, Emma M. Down the Arkansas Way. LC 93-74874. (Illus.). 101p. 1994. 32.00 (0-938041-16-9) Arc Pr AR.

— A Penny for Your Thoughts. LC 92-75209. (Illus.). 96p. 1993. 15.00 (0-938041-11-8) Arc Pr AR.

Rutledge, H. L. To Be Mature. LC 74-76988. 250p. 1974. reprint ed. pap. 5.00 (0-914520-03-2) Insight Pr.

Rutledge, J. D., ed. see Cameron, Chris & Ledford, Cawood.

Rutledge, J. D., jt. ed. see Henderson, Pay.

***Rutledge, Jennifer M.** Building Board Diversity. 50p. 1994. 14.00 (0-925299-40-5) Natl Ctr Nonprofit.

Rutledge, Katherine B., illus. Le Bon Temps. 88p. 1982. pap. 4.95 (0-9608282-0-6) YWCO.

Rutledge, Leigh. The Gay Fireside Companion. 286p. (Orig.). 1989. pap. 8.95 (1-55583-164-8) Alyson Pubns.

— Unnatural Quotations. 182p. (Orig.). 1988. pap. 8.95 (1-55583-140-0) Alyson Pubns.

Rutledge, Leigh W. Cat Love Letters. LC 93-2528. 112p. 1994. 14.95 (0-525-93757-9, Dutton) NAL-Dutton.

— A Cat's Little Instruction Book. (Illus.). 128p. 1993. 10.95 (0-525-93583-5) NAL-Dutton.

— Dear Tabby: Feline Advice on Love, Life, & the Pursuit of Mice. LC 94-33413. 192p. 1995. 10.95 (0-525-93944-X, Dutton) NAL-Dutton.

— Diary of a Cat: True Confessions & Lifelong Observations of a Well-Adjusted House Cat. 128p. 1995. 11.95 (0-525-94003-0, Dutton) NAL-Dutton.

— The Gay Book of Lists. 212p. (Orig.). 1987. pap. 8.95 (1-55583-120-6) Alyson Pubns.

— The Gay Decades: From Stonewall to the Present - The People & Events that Shaped Gay Lives. (Illus.). 336p. (Orig.). 1992. pap. 12.00 (0-452-26810-9, Plume) NAL-Dutton.

— It Seemed Like a Good Idea at the Time: A Book of Brilliant Ideas We Wish We'd Never Had. LC 93-47647. 128p. 1994. mass mkt. 5.95 (0-452-27189-4, Plume) NAL-Dutton.

Rutledge, Leigh W., comp. Excuses, Excuses: A Compendium of Rationalizations, Alibis, Denials, Extenuating Circumstances, & Outright Lies. LC 92-53551. 112p. 1992. 6.00 (0-452-26921-0, Plume) NAL-Dutton.

Rutledge, Leigh W. & Donley, Richard. The Left-Hander's Guide to Life. (Illus.). 128p. (Orig.). 1992. pap. 8.00 (0-452-26845-1, Plume) NAL-Dutton.

***Rutledge, Len.** Maverick Guide to Hong Kong, Macau, & Guangzhou. (Orig.). 1995. pap. 15.95 (1-56554-071-9) Pelican.

— Maverick Guide to Hong Kong, Macau, & South China. (Maverick Guide Ser.). 304p. (Orig.). 1995. pap. 15.95 (1-56554-171-5) Pelican.

— The Maverick Guide to Malaysia & Singapore. 2nd ed. (Maverick Guide Ser.). (Illus.). 488p. 1994. pap. 14.95 (0-88289-990-2) Pelican.

— Maverick Guide to Thailand. 2nd ed. (Illus.). 336p. 1993. pap. 15.95 (0-88289-942-2) Pelican.

— Maverick Guide to Vietnam, Laos, & Cambodia. (Illus.). 380p. 1993. pap. 17.95 (0-88289-923-6) Pelican.

Rutledge, Marilyn, et al. Guide to Accounting for Income Taxes. 400p. 1991. ring bd. 105.00 (1-56433-065-6) Prctnrs Pub Co.

— Guide to Accounting for Income Taxes. 1992. ring bd. 105.00 (1-56433-231-4) Prctnrs Pub Co.

— Guide to Accounting for Income Taxes. 1993. ring bd. 105.00 (1-56433-377-9) Prctnrs Pub Co.

— Guide to Accounting for Income Taxes. 1994. ring bd. 120.00 (1-56433-554-2) Prctnrs Pub Co.

— Guide to Auditor's Reports, 2 vols., Set. 1994. ring bd. 129.00 (1-56433-564-X) Prctnrs Pub Co.

— Guide to Auditor's Reports, Vol. 2. 1994. ring bd. write for info. (1-56433-566-6) Prctnrs Pub Co.

— Guide to Auditor's Reports Vol. 1. 1994. ring bd. write for info. (1-56433-565-8) Prctnrs Pub Co.

Rutledge, Marilyn Z., et al. Guide to Homeowners' Association & Other Common Interest Realty Associations, 3 vols., 1. 1993. write for info. (1-56433-341-8) Prctnrs Pub Co.

— Guide to Homeowners' Association & Other Common Interest Realty Associations, 3 vols., 2. 1993. write for info. (1-56433-342-6) Prctnrs Pub Co.

— Guide to Homeowners' Association & Other Common Interest Realty Associations, 3 vols., 3. 1993. write for info. (1-56433-343-4) Prctnrs Pub Co.

— Guide to Homeowners' Association & Other Common Interest Realty Associations, 3 vols., Set. 1993. ring bd. 115.00 (1-56433-340-X) Prctnrs Pub Co.

— Guide to Homeowners' Associations & Other Common Interest Realty Associations, 2 vols., 1. 1992. write for info. (1-56433-226-8) Prctnrs Pub Co.

— Guide to Homeowners' Associations & Other Common Interest Realty Associations, 2 vols., 2. 1992. write for info. (1-56433-227-6) Prctnrs Pub Co.

— Guide to Homeowners' Associations & Other Common Interest Realty Associations, 2 vols., Set. 1992. ring bd. 115.00 (1-56433-225-X) Prctnrs Pub Co.

— Guide to Homeowner's Associations & Other Common Interest Realty Associations, 3 vols., Set. 1994. ring bd. 125.00 (1-56433-525-9) Prctnrs Pub Co.

— Guide to Homeowner's Associations & Other Common Interest Realty Associations, Vol. 1. 1994. ring bd. write for info. (1-56433-526-7) Prctnrs Pub Co.

— Guide to Homeowner's Associations & Other Common Interest Realty Associations, Vol. 2. 1994. ring bd. write for info. (1-56433-527-5) Prctnrs Pub Co.

— Guide to Homeowner's Associations & Other Common Interest Realty Associations, Vol. 3. 1994. ring bd. write for info. (1-56433-528-3) Prctnrs Pub Co.

Rutledge, Maurice D. Churn 'Em & Burn 'Em. 250p. (Orig.). 1992. pap. 7.95 (0-9633311-0-8) Rutledge Pub.

Rutledge, Paul. The Role of Religion in Ethnic Self-Identity: A Vietnamese Community. (Illus.). 140p. (Orig.). (C). 1985. lib. bdg. 41.00 (0-8191-4505-X); pap. text ed. 19.50 (0-8191-4506-8) U Pr of Amer.

— The Vietnamese in America. (In America Bks.). (Illus.). 64p. (J). (gr. 5 up). 1987. pap. 5.95 (0-8225-1033-2, Lerner Publctns) Lerner Group.

— The Vietnamese in America. (In America Bks.). (Illus.). 64p. (YA). (gr. 5 up). 1987. lib. bdg. 17.50 (0-8225-0235-6, Lerner Publctns) Lerner Group.

Rutledge, Paul J. The Vietnamese Experience in America. LC 91-26520. (Minorities in Modern America Ser.). (Illus.). 192p. 1992. text ed. 29.95 (0-253-34997-4); pap. text ed. 10.95 (0-253-20711-8, MB-711) Ind U Pr.

Rutledge, Samuel A. The Development of Guiding Principles for the Administration of Teachers Colleges & Normal Schools. LC 77-177221. (Columbia University. Teachers College. Contributions to Education Ser.: No. 449). reprint ed. 37.50 (0-404-55449-0) AMS Pr.

Rutledge, Sarah. The Carolina Housewife. xxvi, 262p. 1979. 24.95 (0-87249-383-0) U of SC Pr.

Rutledge, Thom. If I Were They: A Handbook of Practical Recovery Wisdom. 133p. (Orig.). 1993. pap. 8.95 (0-9627963-3-6) T W Rutledge.

— Simple Truth: Ideas & Experiences for Humans from Less-Than-Perfect Families. 105p. 1990. pap. 8.95 (0-9627963-0-1) T W Rutledge.

Rutledge, Wiley. Declaration of Legal Faith. LC 74-114563. (American Constitutional & Legal History Ser). 1970. reprint ed. lib. bdg. 17.95 (0-306-71921-5) Da Capo.

Rutler, George W. Adam Danced: The Cross & the Seven Deadly Sins. 64p. (Orig.). 1989. pap. 6.95 (0-931888-34-4) Christendom Pr.

— Beyond Modernity: Reflections of a Post-Modern Catholic. LC 86-82636. 227p. (Orig.). 1986. pap. 12.95 (0-89870-135-X) Ignatius Pr.

— Christ & Reason: An Introduction to Ideas from Kant to Tyrrell. 212p. 1990. pap. 10.95 (0-931888-38-7) Christendom Pr.

— The Cure D'Ars Today: St. John Vianney. LC 87-82978. 273p. 1988. pap. 9.95 (0-89870-180-5) Ignatius Pr.

— The Impatience of Job. 1981. pap. 6.95 (0-89385-014-4) Sugden.

— The Seven Ages of Man: Meditations on the Last Words of Christ. LC 90-85101. 151p. (Orig.). 1991. pap. 9.95 (0-89870-361-1) Ignatius Pr.

— The Seven Wonders of the World: Meditations on the Last Words of Christ. LC 92-71940. 168p. 1993. pap. 10.95 (0-89870-417-0) Ignatius Pr.

Rutley Estate Agents Ltd. Staff, jt. auth. see Knight, Frank.

Rutman, Anita H., jt. auth. see Rutman, Darrett B.

Rutman, Darrett B. A Militant New World: Sixteen Hundred Seven to Sixteen Forty. Kohn, Richard H., ed. LC 78-22416. (American Military Experience Ser.). 1980. lib. bdg. 63.95 (0-405-11890-2) Ayer.

Rutman, Darrett B. & Rutman, Anita H. A Place in Time: Middlesex County, Virginia, 1650-1750. 288p. 1986. reprint ed. pap. 11.95 (0-393-30318-7) Norton.

— Small Worlds, Large Questions: Explorations in Early American Social History, 1600-1850. LC 94-7440. 448p. (C). 1994. text ed. 55.00 (0-8139-1529-5); pap. text ed. 17.95 (0-8139-1530-9) U Pr of Va.

Rutman, Leo. Clash of Eagles. 544p. 1990. mass mkt. 5.95 (0-449-14596-4, GM) Fawcett.

— Spear of Destiny. LC 87-46268. 272p. 1988. 17.95 (1-55611-084-7) D I Fine.

— Spear of Destiny. 1989. pap. 3.95 (1-55817-232-7, Pinnacle NY) Windsor NY.

Rutman, Leonard. Planning Useful Evaluations: Evaluability Assessment. LC 79-24116. (Sage Library of Social Research: No. 96). 208p. reprint ed. pap. 59.30 (0-7837-1131-X, 2041661) Bks Demand.

Rutman, Leonard & Mowbray, George. Understanding Program Evaluation, Vol. 31. 112p. 1983. pap. 17.95 (0-8039-2093-8) Sage.

Rutman, Michael, jt. auth. see Ramsey, Gaynor.

Rutman, Shereen. Cat Man. (Learn Today for Tomorrow, My Phonics Reader Ser.). (Illus.). 16p. (J). (ps). 1993. student ed 2.25 (1-56293-327-2) McClanahan Bk.

— Hug a Cub. (Learn Today for Tomorrow, My Phonics Reader Ser.). (Illus.). 16p. (J). (ps). 1993. student ed 2.25 (1-56293-323-X) McClanahan Bk.

— My Wet Hen. (Learn Today for Tomorrow, My Phonics Reader Ser.). (Illus.). 16p. (J). (ps). 1993. student ed 2.25 (1-56293-324-8) McClanahan Bk.

— Snap the Clam. (Learn Today for Tomorrow, My Phonics Reader Ser.). (Illus.). 16p. (J). (ps). 1993. student ed 2.25 (1-56293-326-4) McClanahan Bk.

— The Thin Pig. (Learn Today for Tomorrow, My Phonics Reader Ser.). (Illus.). 16p. (J). (ps). 1993. student ed 2.25 (1-56293-325-6) McClanahan Bk.

— Top Hog. (Learn Today for Tomorrow, My Phonics Reader Ser.). (Illus.). 16p. (J). (ps). 1993. student ed 2.25 (1-56293-322-1) McClanahan Bk.

Rutman, Shereen G. All about Me. (Learn Today for Tomorrow Ser.). (Illus.). 32p. (J). (ps). 1992. student ed 1.95 (1-56293-174-1) McClanahan Bk.

— Little Explorer. (LTFT Toddler Time Ser.). (Illus.). 16p. (J). (ps). 1994. 2.95 (1-56293-462-7) McClanahan Bk.

— My Book of Opposites. (Learn Today for Tomorrow Ser.). (Illus.). 32p. (J). (ps). 1992. student ed 1.95 (1-56293-171-7) McClanahan Bk.

— My Busy Day. (LTFT Toddler Time Ser.). (Illus.). 16p. (J). (ps). 1994. 2.95 (1-56293-464-3) McClanahan Bk.

— Numbers. (Learn Today for Tomorrow Ser.). (Illus.). 16p. (J). (ps). 1992. student ed 2.25 (1-56293-191-1) McClanahan Bk.

— Observing. (Learn Today for Tomorrow Ser.). (Illus.). 16p. (J). (ps). 1992. student ed 2.25 (1-56293-189-X) McClanahan Bk.

— Rhyming Words. (Learn Today for Tomorrow Ser.). (Illus.). 32p. (J). (ps). 1992. student ed 1.95 (1-56293-170-9) McClanahan Bk.

— Shapes. (Learn Today for Tomorrow Ser.). (Illus.). 16p. (J). (ps). 1992. student ed 2.25 (1-56293-188-1) McClanahan Bk.

— Sorting. (Learn Today for Tomorrow Ser.). (Illus.). 16p. (J). (ps). 1992. student ed 2.25 (1-56293-186-5) McClanahan Bk.

— What Belongs? (Learn Today for Tomorrow Ser.). (Illus.). 32p. (J). (ps). 1992. student ed 1.95 (1-56293-175-X) McClanahan Bk.

Rutner, Emile, et al, eds. Condensation & Evaporation of Solids. 708p. 1964. text ed. 551.00 (0-677-00740-X) Gordon & Breach.

Rutsala, Vern. Backtracking. (Poetry Ser.). 66p. (Orig.). 1985. 14.00 (0-934257-01-9); pap. 6.95 (0-934257-00-0) Story Line.

— Laments. 1975. pap. 3.00 (0-912284-68-4) New Rivers Pr.

— Little-Known Sports. LC 93-34630. 72p. 1994. lib. bdg. 20.00 (0-87023-917-1); pap. 9.95 (0-87023-918-X) U of Mass Pr.

— Ruined Cities. LC 86-72300. (Poetry Ser.). 72p. (C). 1987. pap. 9.95 (0-88748-040-3) Carnegie-Mellon.

— Selected Poems of Vern Rutsala. LC 90-52857. 281p. 1991. 21.95 (0-934257-52-3); pap. 16.95 (0-934257-61-2) Story Line.

— Walking Home from the Ice-House. LC 80-70566. (Poetry Ser.). 1980. 16.95 (0-915604-47-7); pap. 9.95 (0-915604-48-5) Carnegie-Mellon.

R

An Asterisk (*) at the beginning of an entry indicates that the title is appearing in BIP for the first time.

Rutsch, Edward S. Smoking Technology of the Aborigines of the Iroquois Area of New York State. LC 73-92558. 252p. 1975. 39.50 (*0-8386-7568-9*) Fairleigh Dickinson.

Rutschman, Mary E. Goals Bingo. 32p. 1994. 10.95 (*1-884063-16-0*) Mar Co Prods.

Rutstein & Daum. Anomalies of Binocular Vision: Diagnosis & Management. 400p. 1995. 54.95 (*0-8016-6916-2*) Mosby Yr Bk.

Rutstein, Nathan. Corinne True: Faithful Handmaid of 'Abdu'l Baha. (Illus.). 272p. 1987. 19.95 (*0-85398-263-5*); pap. 12.95 (*0-85398-264-3*) G Ronald Pub.

— Education on Trial: Developing the Whole Person. 1992. pap. 14.95 (*1-85168-027-6*) Onewrld Pubns.

— He Loved & Served: The Story of Curtis Kelsey. (Illus.). 208p. 1982. 15.95 (*0-85398-120-5*); pap. 9.50 (*0-85398-121-3*) G Ronald Pub.

— Healing Racism in America: A Prescription for the Disease. 184p. (Orig.). 1993. pap. 12.95 (*0-9633007-1-7*) Whitcomb MA.

— The Invisible Hand: Shaping the New World Order. Morgan, Michael & Robbins, Carroll, eds. 114p. (Orig.). 1992. pap. 9.95 (*0-9633007-0-9*) Whitcomb MA.

— Teaching the Baha'i Faith: Spirit in Action. 192p. 1984. 10.95 (*0-85398-175-2*); pap. 9.50 (*0-85398-176-0*) G Ronald Pub.

— A Way Out of the Trap: An Innovative & Unique Ten-Step Program for Spiritual Growth. Hinshaw, Beth, ed. LC 92-63009. 176p. (Orig.). 1995. pap. 11.95 (*0-9633001-2-1*) Whitcomb MA.

Rutsula, Vern. The Mystery of Lost Shoes. LC 85-160. 37p. 1985. 5.00 (*0-89924-046-1*) Lynx Hse.

Rutt, August. Surgery of the Leg & Foot. (Hackenbroch Ser.). 1980. text ed. 121.00 (*0-7216-4446-5*) Saunders.

Rutt, Joan, ed. Lee Wade's Korean Cookery. (Illus.). 64p. 1986. pap. 16.50 (*0-930878-45-0*) Hollym Intl.

Rutt, Richard. A History of Hand Knitting. LC 87-46353. 248p. 1988. 24.95 (*0-934026-35-1*) Interweave.

Ruttan, Vernon W. Agricultural Research Policy. LC 81-16396. (Illus.). 384p. reprint ed. pap. 109.50 (*0-8357-6537-7*, 2035899) Bks Demand.

— The Economic Demand for Irrigated Acreage: New Methodology & Some Preliminary Projections 1954-1980. (Resources for the Future Ser.). (Illus.). 152p. 1965. 14.00 (*0-8018-0571-6*) Johns Hopkins.

— The Economic Demand for Irrigated Acreage: New Methodology & Some Preliminary Projections 1954-1980. LC 65-13930. 152p. reprint ed. pap. 43.40 (*0-685-20407-3*, 2030219) Bks Demand.

— United States Development Assistance Policy: The Domestic Politics of Foreign Economic Aid. LC 95-6422. (Studies in Development). 568p. 1995. text ed. 65.00x (*0-8018-5051-7*) Johns Hopkins.

Ruttan, Vernon W., ed. Agriculture, Environment, & Health: Sustainable Development in the 21st Century. LC 93-8527. 384p. (C). 1993. text ed. 44.95 (*0-8166-2291-4*); pap. text ed. 19.95 (*0-8166-2292-2*) U of Minn Pr.

— Health & Sustainable Agricultural Development: Perspectives on Growth & Constraints. LC 94-11363. (C). 1994. pap. text ed. 35.00 (*0-8133-8838-4*) Westview.

— Sustainable Agriculture & the Environment: Perspectives on Growth & Constraints. 189p. (C). 1991. pap. text ed. 43.50 (*0-8133-8507-5*) Westview.

— Why Food Aid? LC 92-25476. 320p. 1993. text ed. 45.00 (*0-8018-4471-1*); pap. text ed. 15.95 (*0-8018-4472-X*) Johns Hopkins.

Ruttan, Vernon W., jt. auth. see Ahmed, Iftikhar.

Ruttan, Vernon W., ed. see Fry, Maxwell J.

Ruttan, Vernon W., jt. auth. see Hayami, Yujiro.

Ruttan, Vernon W., jt. auth. see Thritle, Colin G.

Rutten & Van Venrooij. Telescope Optics - Evaluation & Design. 1988. 24.95 (*0-943396-18-2*) Willmann-Bell.

Rutten, J., jt. auth. see De Bakker, J. W.

Rutten, M. Asian Capitalists in the European Mirror. 65p. 1994. pap. 16.00 (*90-5383-270-X*, Pub. by VU Univ Pr NE) Paul & Co Pubs.

***Rutten, Mario.** Farms & Factories: Social Profile of Large Farmers & Rural Industrialists in West India. (Illus.). 385p. 1995. 29.95 (*0-19-563299-0*) OUP.

Rutten, Robert J., ed. Solar Surface Magnetism: Proceedings of the NATO Advanced Research Workshop, Soesterberg, the Netherlands, November 1-5, 1993. (NATO Advanced Science Institutes: C Mathematical & Physical Sciences Ser.). 552p. (C). 1994. lib. bdg. 223.00 (*0-7923-2845-0*) Kluwer Ac.

Rutten, Robert J. & Severino, Giuseppe, eds. Solar & Stellar Granulation. (C). 1989. lib. bdg. 211.50 (*0-7923-0122-6*) Kluwer Ac.

Rutten, Thomas. Demokrit - Lachender Philosoph und Sanguinischer Melancholiker: Eine Pseudohippokratische Geschichte. LC 91-36808. (Mnemosyne Ser.: Supplement 118). xi, 248p. (GER.). 1991. 77.25 (*90-04-09523-3*) E J Brill.

Ruttenbaum, Steven R. Mansions in the Clouds: The Skyscraper Palazzi of Emery Roth. (Illus.). 224p. 1986. 40.00 (*0-917439-09-0*) Balsam Pr.

Ruttenber, E. M. History of the Town of Newburgh, NY. (Illus.). 322p. 1993. reprint ed. lib. bdg. 39.00 (*0-8328-2858-0*) Higginson Bk Co.

— Indian Tribes of Hudson's River II: 1700-1850. 240p. 1992. reprint ed. pap. 12.95 (*0-910746-09-5*, IT002) Hope Farm.

— Indian Tribes of Hudson's River to 1700. (Illus.). 200p. 1992. reprint ed. pap. 12.95 (*0-910746-98-2*, IT001) Hope Farm.

Ruttenber, E. M. & Clark, L. H. History of Orange County, New York, with Illustrations & Biographical Sketches of Many of Its Prominent Men & Pioneers. (Illus.). 820p. 1992. reprint ed. lib. bdg. 59.00 (*0-8328-2368-6*) Higginson Bk Co.

Ruttenber, E. M. & Clark, L. H., comps. History of Orange County, New York, 1881, 2 vols., Set. (Illus.). 820p. 1980. reprint ed. 55.00 (*0-9604116-0-7*) Orange County Genealog.

Ruttenber, James, jt. ed. see Blumenthal, Daniel S.

Ruttenber, Tim, pseud. The Complete Lunchbox: The Life & Works of Deacon Lunchbox, a Cornucopia of Southern Culture. Roarty, Robert Sean, ed. & intro. by. 189p. (Orig.). 1994. pap. text ed. 19.95 (*1-878749-01-3*) Drewry Lane Bkmakers.

Ruttenberg, Harold J., jt. auth. see Golden, Clinton S.

Ruttenberg, Katherine. Kitty: An Uncommon Memoir of a Non-Celebrity. LC 79-21057. (Illus.). 200p. 1980. 8.95 (*0-88229-654-X*) Nelson-Hall.

Ruttenberg, Ruth & Hudgins, Randall. Occupational Safety & Health in the Chemical Industry. 2nd ed. 141p. 1981. pap. 9.95 (*0-87871-015-9*, St Martin) CEP.

Rutter, tr. see Martignoni & Schonenberger.

Rutter, Angi, tr. see Thadden, Rudolf V.

Rutter, Bob. A Century of Caring: A History of the Guelph Humane Society. (Illus.). 96p. (Orig.). 1993. pap. 11.95 (*1-879260-13-1*) Evanston Pub.

***Rutter, Bryce G. & Dainoff, Marvin J.** The Ergonomic Office: Standards, Specifications & Design Guidelines. Becka, Anne Marie, ed. LC 94-78633. (Illus.). 250p. 1995. ring bd. write for info. (*0-9643187-0-9*) Metaphase Pub.

Rutter, Carol, et al. Clamorous Voices: Shakespeare's Women Today. Evans, Faith, ed. (Illus.). 131p. 1989. 39.95 (*0-87830-036-8*, A3685, Theatre Arts Bks); pap. 13.95 (*0-87830-037-6*, A3689, Theatre Arts Bks) Routledge Chapman & Hall.

Rutter, D. R. & Quine, Lyn. Social Psychology & Health: European Perspectives. 232p. 1994. 59.95 (*1-85628-562-6*, Pub. by Avebury Pub UK) Ashgate Pub Co.

Rutter, E. H., jt. ed. see Knipe, R. J.

Rutter, Eldon. The Holy Cities of Arabia, 2 vols., Set. LC 78-63477. reprint ed. 49.50 (*0-404-16543-5*) AMS Pr.

Rutter, Frank V. Dante Gabriel Rossetti: Painter & Man of Letters. LC 78-148295. (Illus.). reprint ed. 31.50 (*0-404-05468-4*) AMS Pr.

Rutter, J. M., jt. ed. see Adlam, C.

Rutter, Jared. Marion Anderson: Opera Singer. (Illus.). 208p. (YA). 1995. pap. 4.95 (*0-87067-589-3*, Melrose Sq) Holloway.

Rutter, Jeremy B. The Pottery of Lerna, No. IV. (Lerna Ser.: Vol. 3). (Illus.). 825p. (C). 1995. text ed. write for info. (*0-87661-303-2*) Am Sch Athens.

***Rutter, Jill.** Jewish Migrations. (Migrations Ser.). (Illus.). 48p. (J). (gr. 4-6). 1994. 15.95 (*1-56847-236-6*) Thomson Lrning.

Rutter, John, ed. Folk Songs for Choirs, 2 Vols., Bk. 1. (Orig.). 1985. pap. 14.95 (*0-19-343718-X*) OUP.

— Folk Songs for Choirs, 2 Vols., Bk. 2. (Orig.). 1985. pap. 14.95 (*0-19-343719-8*) OUP.

***Rutter, John & Bartlett, Clifford, eds.** Oxford Choral Classics: Opera Choruses. 384p. 1995. pap. 14.95 (*0-19-343693-0*) OUP.

— Oxford Choral Classics: Opera Choruses. (Oxford Choral Classics Ser.). (C). 1995. 19.95 (*0-19-343700-7*); 15.00 (*0-19-343699-X*) OUP.

Rutter, John, jt. auth. see Willcocks, David.

Rutter, John, jt. ed. see Willcocks, David.

Rutter, K. Campanian Coinages, Four Eighty-Five to Three Eighty-Five B. C. 200p. 1980. 60.00 (*0-85224-345-6*, Pub. by Edinburgh U Pr UK) Col U Pr.

Rutter, M. & Hay, D. Development Through Life: A Handbook for Clinicians. (Illus.). 720p. 1994. 125.00 (*0-632-03693-1*, Pub. by Blckwell Sci Pubns UK) Blackwell Sci.

Rutter, M., et al. Multi-Axial Classification of Child Psychiatric Disorders. 1975. 7.20 (*92-4-154050-8*) World Health.

Rutter, Marjorie, jt. auth. see Rutter, Michael.

Rutter, Mark. The Farmhouse Voices. Hunting, Constance, ed. 35p. (Orig.). 1992. pap. 8.95 (*0-913006-50-5*) Puckerbrush.

Rutter, Michael. Changing Youth in a Changing Society: Patterns of Adolescent Development & Disorder. LC 82-242973. (Illus.). 333p. 1980. 32.00 (*0-674-10875-2*) HUP.

— Fly Fishing for the Compleat Idiot: The Fine Art of Becoming a Fly Casting Snob. Ort, Kathleen, ed. (Illus.). 272p. (Orig.). 1995. pap. 14.00 (*0-87842-313-3*) Mountain Pr.

Rutter, Michael, ed. Developmental Neuropsychiatry. LC 83-1633. 632p. 1983. lib. bdg. 65.00 (*0-89862-621-8*) Guilford Pr.

— Developmental Psychiatry. LC 86-32058. 400p. 1987. reprint ed. pap. text ed. 25.00 (*0-88048-271-0*, 48-271-0) Am Psychiatric.

— Helping Troubled Children. LC 76-25475. 376p. 1975. 45.00 (*0-306-30969-6*, Plenum Pr) Plenum.

— Psychosocial Disturbances in Young People: Challenges for Prevention. (Illus.). 583p. (C). 1995. 44.95 (*0-521-46187-1*) Cambridge U Pr.

— Studies of Psychosocial Risk: The Power of Longitudinal Data. (Illus.). 440p. 1989. 84.95 (*0-521-35330-0*) Cambridge U Pr.

Rutter, Michael & Card, Dave. Fly Fishing Made Easy: A Manual for Beginners with Tips for the Experienced. LC 93-33002. (East Woods Book Ser.). (Illus.). 176p. (Orig.). 1994. pap. 16.95 (*1-56440-355-6*) Globe Pequot.

Rutter, Michael & Casaer, Paul, eds. Biological Risk Factors for Psychosocial Disorders. (European Network on Longitudinal Studies on Individual Development). 384p. (C). 1991. 74.95 (*0-521-40103-8*) Cambridge U Pr.

Rutter, Michael & Jones, Robin R., eds. Lead Versus Health: Sources & Effects of Low Level Lead Exposure. LC 82-16020. (Wiley-Medical Publication Ser.). (Illus.). 395p. reprint ed. pap. 112.60 (*0-8357-8644-7*, 2035068) Bks Demand.

Rutter, Michael & Rutter, Marjorie. Developing Minds: "Challenge & Continuity Across the Lifespan" LC 92-52739. 416p. 1993. text ed. 40.00 (*0-465-01037-7*) Basic.

Rutter, Michael & Schopler, Eric, eds. Autism: A Reappraisal of Concepts & Treatment. LC 77-26910. (Illus.). 552p. 1978. 49.50 (*0-306-31096-1*, Plenum Pr) Plenum.

Rutter, Michael & Yule, William, eds. Language Development & Disorders. LC 65-80542. (Clinics in Developmental Medicine Ser.: No. 101-102). (Illus.). (C). 1991. 74.95 (*0-521-41219-6*, Pub. by Mc Keith Pr UK) Cambridge U Pr.

Rutter, Michael, jt. auth. see Garmezy, Norman.

Rutter, Michael, jt. ed. see Robins, Lee N.

Rutter, Michael, et al. Fifteen Thousand Hours: Secondary Schools & Their Effects on Children. LC 78-23382. (Illus.). 293p. 1982. pap. 12.95 (*0-674-30026-2*) HUP.

— Fifteen Thousand Hours: Secondary Schools & Their Effects on Children. 288p. 1994. pap. 24.95x (*1-85396-281-3*, Pub. by Paul Chapman UK) Taylor & Francis.

— A Neuropsychiatric Study in Children. (Clinics in Developmental Medicine Ser.: Vols. 35 & 36). (Illus.). 272p. (C). 1991. 47.95 (*0-521-41198-X*, Pub. by Mc Keith Pr UK) Cambridge U Pr.

Rutter, Michael, et al, eds. Assessment & Diagnosis in Child Psychopathology. LC 87-12180. 477p. 1987. lib. bdg. 50.00 (*0-89862-699-4*) Guilford Pr.

— Child & Adolescent Psychiatry: Modern Approaches. 3rd ed. LC 93-20746. (Illus.). 1168p. 1994. 115.00 (*0-632-02822-X*) Blackwell Sci.

— Depression in Young People: Developmental & Clinical Perspectives. LC 85-870. 568p. reprint ed. pap. 161.90 (*0-7837-1206-5*, 2041738) Bks Demand.

— Education, Health & Behaviour. LC 80-22639. 496p. (C). 1980. reprint ed. text ed. 31.50 (*0-89874-268-4*) Krieger.

***Rutter, Michael F.** The Applicable Law in Singapore & Malaysia. 748p. 1989. boxed 320.00 (*0-614-05484-2*, SI) Butterworth Legal Pubs.

— Damages for Personal Injuries & Death in Singapore & Malaysia. 1000p. 1988. 233.00 (*9971-70-060-3*) Butterworth Legal Pubs.

— Handbook on Damages for Personal Injuries & Death in Singapore & Malaysia. 2nd ed. 826p. 1993. boxed 290.00 (*0-409-99638-6*, SI) Butterworth Legal Pubs.

— Occupiers' Liability in Singapore & Malaysia. 320p. 1986. 89.00 (*0-409-99513-4*) Butterworth Legal Pubs.

Rutter, N. K. Greek Coinage. 1989. pap. 25.00 (*0-85263-635-0*, Pub. by Shire UK) St Mut.

Rutter, Owen. British North Borneo: An Account of Its History, Resources & Native Tribes. LC 77-87001. reprint ed. 32.50 (*0-404-16775-6*) AMS Pr.

— The Pagans of North Borneo. LC 77-87003. (Illus.). reprint ed. 32.00 (*0-404-16776-4*) AMS Pr.

— Through Formosa. (Illus.). 288p. 1989. reprint ed. 30.00 (*957-9482-15-2*) Oriental Bk Store.

Rutter, P. A. & Martin, A. S., eds. Management of Design Offices. 99p. 1990. pap. text ed. 28.00 (*0-7277-1383-3*, Pub. by T Telford UK) Am Soc Civil Eng.

Rutter, Peter. Sex in Forbidden Zone. Date not set. pap. write for info. (*0-449-14759-2*) Fawcett.

— Sex in the Forbidden Zone. 1991. mass mkt. 5.99 (*0-449-14727-4*, GM) Fawcett.

Rutter, Virginia B. Woman Changing Woman: Feminine Psychology Re-Conceived Through Myth & Experience. LC 92-56422. 272p. 1993. 20.00 (*0-06-250748-6*) Harper SF.

— Woman Changing Woman: Feminine Psychology Re-Conceived Through Myth & Experience. LC 92-56422. 272p. 1994. reprint ed. pap. 12.00 (*0-06-251071-1*) Harper SF.

Rutterford, Janette, et al, eds. Handbook of U. K. Corporate Finance. 2nd ed. 326p. 1992. U. K. pap. 70.00 (*0-406-00495-1*) Butterworth Legal Pubs.

Ruttkay-Nedecky, I. & MacFarlane, P. W., eds. Electrocardiology, 1983: Proceedings of the International Congress on Electrocardiology, 10th, Bratislava, Czechoslovakia, 16-19 Aug., 1983. (International Congress Ser.: No. 653). 444p. 1985. 162.75 (*0-444-80585-0*, Excerpta Medica) Elsevier.

Ruttkowski, W. & Blake, R. Literaturwoerterbuch: Dictionary of Literature. 68p. (ENG, FRE & GER.). 1969. pap. 24.95 (*0-8288-6605-8*, M-7543) Fr & Eur.

Ruttner, F. Biogeography & Raxonomy of Honeybees. (Illus.). 290p. 1987. 149.00 (*0-387-17781-7*) Spr-Verlag.

Ruttner, Franz. Fundamentals of Limnology. 3rd ed. Frey, D. G. & Fry, F. E. J., trs. LC 64-919. 323p. reprint ed. pap. 92.10 (*0-685-16376-8*, 2026441) Bks Demand.

Ruttner, John, jt. ed. see Willcocks, David.

Ruttner-Kolisko, Agnes. Plankton Rotifers: Biology & Taxonomy. Kolisko, G., tr. (Binnengewaesser Ser.: No. 26). (Illus.). 146p. 1974. pap. text ed. 32.75 (*3-510-40735-0*) Lubrecht & Cramer.

***Rutunda, Ronald D.** Modern Constitutional Law: Cases & Notes, 1994 Supplement To. 4th ed. (American Casebook Ser.). 65p. 1994. pap. text ed. write for info. (*0-314-04415-9*) West Pub.

Rutz & Cicero. Musculoskeletal Emergencies. 800p. 1994. 125.00 (*0-8016-7243-0*) Mosby Yr Bk.

Rutz, Donald A. & Patterson, Richard S., eds. Biocontrol of Arthropods Affecting Livestock & Poultry. (Studies in Insect Biology). 316p. (C). 1990. pap. text ed. 66.00 (*0-8133-7850-8*) Westview.

Rutz, James. The Open Church. LC 92-81563. 200p. 1992. pap. 8.95 (*0-940232-50-2*) Seedsowers.

Rutz, Werner. Cities & Towns in Indonesia: Their Development, Current Positions & Functions with Regard to Administration & Regional Economy. Tietze, W., ed. (Urbanization of the Earth Ser.: Vol. 4). 292p. 1987. lib. bdg. 90.00 (*3-443-37006-3*) Lubrecht & Cramer.

— Die Staedte Indonesiens: Staedte und Andere Nich-Landwirtschaftliche Siedlungen, Ihre Entwicklung und Gegenwaertige Stellung in Verwaltung und Wirtschaft. (Urbanisierung der Erde Ser.: Vol. 4). (Illus.). 286p. (GER.). 1985. lib. bdg. 72.80 (*3-443-37005-5*, Pub. by Gebrueder Borntraeger GW) Lubrecht & Cramer.

Rutzky, Jacques, jt. auth. see Cermak, Timmen L.

Rutzler, Klaus, ed. New Perspectives in Sponge Biology. LC 90-9996. (Illus.). 544p. (C). 1991. text ed. 50.00 (*0-87474-784-8*) Smithsonian.

Ruud, Alice. Design Your Own Life: From High School to Career. 1990. student ed 9.95 (*1-56117-000-3*) Telesis CA.

Ruud, C. O., ed. see Green, R. E., Jr.

Ruud, C. O., et al. Nondestructive Characterization of Materials IV. (Illus.). 508p. 1992. 125.00 (*0-306-44047-4*, Plenum Pr) Plenum.

Ruud, Charles A. Fighting Words: Imperial Censorship & the Russian Press, 1804-1906. LC 82-190787. 335p. reprint ed. pap. 95.50 (*0-7837-0528-X*, 2040854) Bks Demand.

— Russian Entrepreneur: Publisher Ivan Sytin of Moscow, 1851-1934. (Illus.). 304p. (C). 1990. text ed. 44.95 (*0-7735-0773-6*, Pub. by McGill CN) U of Toronto Pr.

Ruud, J. Teaching for Changed Attitudes & Values. LC 71-187577. (C). 1972. pap. 1.50 (*0-911365-00-1*, A261-08378) Home Econ Educ.

Ruud, Jay. Many a Song & Many a Lecherous Lay: Tradition & Individuality in Chaucer's Lyric Poetry. LC 92-24796. (Studies in Medieval Literature: Vol. 6). 360p. 1992. 52.00 (*0-8153-1142-7*, H1674) Garland.

Ruud, Jo. The Young Adult Cookbook: All You Need to Know to Survive On Your Own. (Illus.). 305p. 1989. pap. 9.95 (*0-9623738-1-8*) Josman Bks.

Ruud, Martin B. Thomas Chaucer. LC 78-174797. reprint ed. 20.00 (*0-404-05469-2*) AMS Pr.

— Thomas Chaucer. (BCL1-PR English Literature Ser.). 131p. 1992. reprint ed. lib. bdg. 69.00 (*0-7812-7176-2*) Rprt Serv.

Ruud, Warren L. & Shell, Terry L. Prelude to Calculus. 2nd ed. (C). 1993. text ed. 57.95 (*0-534-17868-5*) PWS Pubs.

Ruurs, Rob. Saenredam: The Art of Perspective. LC 86-32669. (Illus.). 228p. 1987. 76.00 (*1-55619-015-8*) Benjamins North Am.

Ruuth, Marianne. Bill Cosby, Entertainer. Locke, Raymond F., ed. (Black American Ser.). (Illus.). 1993. pap. 3.95 (*0-87067-596-6*, Melrose Sq) Holloway.

— Eddie: Eddie Murphy from A to Z. (Orig.). (J). (ps-10). 1985. pap. 2.95 (*0-87067-717-9*) Holloway.

— Frederick Douglas. (Orig.). 1991. pap. 3.95 (*0-87067-582-6*, Melrose Sq) Holloway.

— Nat King Cole. 1993. pap. 3.95 (*0-87067-593-1*, Melrose Sq) Holloway.

— The Supremes: Triumph & Tragedy. (J). (ps-10). 1987. pap. 3.95 (*0-87067-725-X*, BH725) Holloway.

Ruuth, Marianne, tr. see Bergman, Ingmar.

Ruuth, Marianne, tr. see Fant, Kenne.

Ruven, et al. Polycyclic Aromatic Hydrocarbons in Water Systems. 200p. 1981. 124.95 (*0-8493-6255-5*, QD341, CRC Reprint) Franklin.

Ruvituso, Donna, ed. see Chambers, Marcia.

Ruvituso, Donna, ed. see Huggan, John.

Ruvituso, Donna, ed. see Johnson, Hank & Schiffman, Roger.

Ruvituso, Donna, ed. see Watson, Tom & Seltz, Nick.

Ruwart, Mary J. Healing Our World: The Other Piece of the Puzzle. (Illus.). 320p. (Orig.). (C). 1992. pap. 14.95 (*0-9632336-0-2*) SunStar Pr.

— Healing Our World: The Other Piece of the Puzzle. rev. ed. LC 92-35338. (Illus.). 320p. (Orig.). (C). 1993. pap. 14.95 (*0-9632336-2-9*) SunStar Pr.

Ruwell, Mary E., et al. A Guide to the University Museum Archives: University of Pennsylvania. 72p. 1984. 4.95 (*0-934718-65-2*) U PA Mus Pubns.

Ruwell, Mary Elizabeth. Eighteenth Century Capitalism: The Formation of American Marine Insurance Companies. LC 92-40359. 200p. 1993. 49.00 (*0-8153-0969-4*) Garland.

Ruwet, Jean-Claude. Introduction to Ethology: The Biology of Behavior. LC 72-186505. 208p. 1973. text ed. 27.50 (*0-8236-2730-6*) Intl Univs Pr.

Ruwet, Nicholas, jt. auth. see Kiefer, Ferenc.

Ruwet, Nicolas. Syntax & Human Experience. Goldsmith, John, ed. & tr. by. LC 90-23535. (Studies in Contemporary Linguistics). 312p. 1991. pap. text ed. 24.95 (*0-226-73222-3*) U Ch Pr.

— Syntax & Human Experience. Goldsmith, John, ed. & tr. by. LC 90-23535. (Studies in Contemporary Linguistics). 312p. 1991. lib. bdg. 57.95 (*0-226-73221-5*) U Ch Pr.

Ruxin, Robert H. Athlete's Guide to Agents. 208p. 1993. pap. text ed. 14.95 (*0-86720-779-5*) Jones & Bartlett.

Ruxton, F. H., tr. see Khali, Ibn I.

Ruxton, George F. Life in the Far West. 330p. 1972. 20.00 (*0-87380-098-2*) Rio Grande.

— Life in the Far West. Hafen, LeRoy R., ed. (American Exploration & Travel Ser.: Vol. 14). (Illus.). 1979. pap. 14.95 (*0-8061-1534-3*) U of Okla Pr.

— Ruxton of the Rockies. Hafen, LeRoy R., ed. LC 50-9832. (American Exploration & Travel Ser.: Vol. 13). (Illus.). 344p. (Orig.). 1979. pap. 14.95 (*0-8061-1603-X*) U of Okla Pr.

Ruxton, William E. Doing Things Right. 249p. 1985. text ed. 49.95 (*0-910399-33-6*) Natl Tool & Mach.

Ruy-Sanchez, Alberto, jt. auth. see Ferrer, Elizabeth.

Ruy Sanchez, Alberto M. Mogador. Schafer, Mark, tr. 124p. (Orig.). 1992. pap. 7.95 (*0-87286-271-2*) City Lights.

R

***Ruyer, Francois, illus.** Farm Animals. 6p. (J). (ps). 1992. 9.49 (*1-881445-11-9*) Sandvik Pub.
— Piano Song Book for Baby Trolls. 20p. (J). (ps). 1992. 11.99 (*1-881445-08-9*) Sandvik Pub.
Ruymann, Frederick B., jt. auth. see Maurer, Harold M.
Ruymgaart, P. A. & Soong, T. T. Mathematics of Kalman-Bucy Filtering. (Information Sciences Ser.: Vol. 14). (Illus.). 190p. 1985. 35.00 (*0-387-13508-1*) Spr-Verlag.
— Mathematics of Kalman-Bucy Filtering. (Information Sciences Ser.: Vol. 14). (Illus.). 180p. 1988. pap. 49.00 (*0-387-18781-2*) Spr-Verlag.
Ruys, Pieter H., jt. ed. see Gilles, Robert P.
Ruys, T. Handbook of Facilities Planning. 1990. text ed. 99.95 (*0-442-31852-9*) Van Nos Reinhold.
Ruysbroeck, John. The Seven Steps of the Ladder of Spiritual Love. pap. 7.95 (*1-55818-130-X*) Holmes Pub.
Ruyter, Nancy L., jt. auth. see Dunin, Elsie I.
Ruzan, Robin, jt. auth. see Myers, Mike.
Ruzdjak, V., et al, eds. Dynamics of Quiescent Prominences: Proceedings of IAU Colloquium No. 117 Held in Hvar, SR Croatia, Yugoslavia, 25-29 September 1989. (Lecture Notes in Physics Ser.: Vol. 363). xii, 304p. 1990. 42.00 (*0-387-52973-X*) Spr-Verlag.
Ruzek, Sheryl, jt. auth. see Roth, Julius.
Ruzena, Skerlj, jt. auth. see Komac, Dasa.
Ruzer, Lev. Aerosol R & D in the Soviet Union: The Measurement of Main Parameters. (Illus.). 160p. (Orig.). 1989. pap. 75.00 (*0-685-35188-2*) Delphic Associates.
Ruzgis, Patricia, jt. ed. see Sternberg, Robert J.
Ruzic, jt. auth. see Huizenga.
Ruzic, Neil. The Shallow Sea. 544p. 1992. 19.95 (*0-9632357-0-2*) St Clair Pr.
***Ruzicho, Andrew J. & Jacobs, Louis A.** Employment Practices Manual: A Guide to Minimizing Constitutional, Statutory & Common Law Liability. rev. ed. 1994. write for info. (*0-615-00151-3*) Clark Boardman Callaghan.
— Equal Employment Compliance Manual. 1992. 350.00 (*0-685-14551-4*) Clark Boardman Callaghan.
— Litigating Age Discrimination Cases. LC 86-11736. 1992. 140.00 (*0-685-14016-4*) Clark Boardman Callaghan.
— Litigating Age Discrimination Cases. annuals suppl. ed. 1992. write for info. (*0-318-60923-1*) Clark Boardman Callaghan.
Ruzicho, Andrew J., et al. Employment Discrimination Litigation. 641p. 1989. 87.50 (*0-87084-765-1*) Anderson Pub Co.
— Employment Discrimination Litigation, 1991-1992. suppl. ed. 641p. 1989. 35.00 (*0-685-49831-X*) Anderson Pub Co.
Ruzick, Jiri. Die Desmidiaceen Mitteleuropas, Vol. 1, No. 1. (Illus.). 291p. 1977. lib. bdg. 97.00 (*3-510-65078-6*) Lubrecht & Cramer.
Ruzicka. Flow Injection Analysis. 2nd ed. LC 87-18772. (Chemical Analysis Ser.). 498p. 1988. text ed. 125.00 (*0-471-81355-9*) Wiley.
Ruzicka, jt. auth. see Wilson.
Ruzicka, Jiri. Die Desmidiaceen Mitteleuropas, Vol. 1, No. 2. (Illus.). 444p. 1981. lib. bdg. 140.00 (*3-510-65103-0*) Lubrecht & Cramer.
Ruzicka, Lado, et al, eds. Differential Mortality: Methodological Issues & Biosocial Factors. (International Studies in Demography). (Illus.). 272p. 1989. 65.00 (*0-19-828651-1*) OUP.
— Differential Mortality: Methodological Issues & Biosocial Factors. (International Studies in Demography). (Illus.). 272p. 1995. reprint ed. pap. 17.95 (*0-19-828882-4*) OUP.
Ruzicka, Molly B., ed. see Meech-Pekarik, Julia.
Ruzicka, Stephen. Politics of a Persian Dynasty: The Hecatomnids in the Fourth Century B. C. LC 92-54138. (Oklahoma Series in Classical Culture: Vol. 14). 256p. 1992. 39.95 (*0-8061-2460-1*) U of Okla Pr.
Ruzicka, T., jt. ed. see Eckertova, L.
Ruzicka, T., et al, eds. Handbook of Atopic Eczema. (Illus.). 496p. 1991. 169.00 (*0-387-52992-6*) Spr-Verlag.
Ruzicka, William J. The Nightmare of Success: The Fallacy of the Super-Success Dream. LC 73-90028. 155p. 1973. 6.95 (*0-914372-01-7*) Peninsula Pubns.
Ruzicka, William T. Faulkner's Fictive Architecture: The Meaning of Place in the Yoknapatawpha Novels. LC 87-10799. (Studies in Modern Literature: No. 67). 165p. reprint ed. pap. 47.10 (*0-8357-1788-7*, 2070649) Bks Demand.
Ruzickova, Z., jt. auth. see Srb, J.
Ruzmailin, A. A., et al. Magnetic Fields of Galaxies. (C). 1988. lib. bdg. 142.00 (*90-277-2450-4*) Kluwer Ac.
Ruzow, Daniel A., jt. auth. see Gerrard, Michael B.
***Ruzsa, CS., et al.** Research on Dietary Fibres. 222p. (C). 1986. 75.00x (*963-05-4254-4*) St Mut.
***Ruzsa, I. & Szabolcsi, A.** Logic & Language: Proceedings of the '87 Debrecen Symposium Held from August 25 to 28, 1987. 252p. (C). 1987. 27.00x (*963-462-238-0*, Pub. by Akad Kiado HU) St Mut.
Ruzsa, Imre Z. Algebraic Probability Theory. LC 87-25444. (Probability & Mathematical Statistics Ser.). 251p. 1988. text ed. 175.00 (*0-471-91803-2*) Wiley.
Ruzsa, Jaclyn M., ed. Who Writes What. rev. ed. 428p. 1992. pap. 23.95 (*0-87218-086-7*) Natl Underwriter.
Ruzyllo, J. & Novak, R. E., eds. Semiconductor Cleaning Technology - 1991. LC 92-71447. (Proceedings Ser.: Vol. 92-12). 500p. 1992. 53.00 (*1-56677-012-2*) Electrochem Soc.
***Ruzyllo, J., et al, eds.** Proceedings of the International Symposium on Cleaning Technology in Semiconductor Device Manufacturing, 3rd. LC 93-72867. (Proceedings Ser.: Vol. 94-07). 604p. 1994. 58.00 (*1-56677-038-6*) Electrochem Soc.

***RV Consumer Group Staff. The RV Rating Book: 1996 Models. (Illus.). 110p. 1995. pap. text ed. 68.00 (*1-884046-59-2*) Quill Pubng. A complete reference book rating recreational vehicles (travel trailers, fifth wheels, motor homes) for the current model year. Over 3,000 models sorted by brand, type, length & use classification (vacation, RV trekking, snowbird, full-time). Models rated for safety durability & value. The safety rating represents the average handling characteristics of the RV when travelling on the highway & its ability to respond to driver commands. Weight, size, payload & wheelbase are primary factors for motor homes. Weight, size, payload, axle capacity & hitch weight percentages are primary factors for travel trailers. The durability rating is based upon the number of defects found in new & used RVs of any particular brand. The value rating is based upon the durability rating weighted by the safety rating & staff appraisals when considering the manufacturer's suggested retail price. Easy-to-read information in chart-like fashion. 8.5 X 11 comb-bound. Published annually. The RV Consumer Group is a nonprofit organization, not affiliated with the RV industry. Order from Quill Publishing, P.O. Box 490, Quilcene, WA 98376, 1-360-765-3843.** *Publisher Provided Annotation.*

RVer, Annie. Bread & Scripture: Trailer Folks Favorite Recipe, Chapter & Verse. (Illus.). 96p. 1985. pap. 8.50 (*0-9613607-1-2*) RVer Annie.
RVer Annie. Cooking on Wheels: Trailer Folks Favorite Recipes. Mitchell, Joyce S., ed. LC 84-90601. 96p. 1984. pap. 8.50 (*0-9613607-0-4*) RVer Annie.
Rvr Chandrasekhara Rao & Prasad, Vs. Indian Constitution & Polity. 128p. 1991. text ed. 18.95 (*81-207-1311-7*, Pub. by Sterling Pubs II) Apt Bks.
Rweedale, Martin, jt. ed. see Bosley, Richard.
Rwegasira, Kami. Administering Management Development Institutions in Africa. 1988. text ed. 68.95 (*0-566-05501-5*, Pub. by Avebury Pub UK) Ashgate Pub Co.
— Problems of Financial Analysis in Institutional Lending Operations: Some Lessons from Tanzania. LC 92-33657. 200p. 1992. 68.95 (*1-85628-299-6*, Pub. by Avebury Pub UK) Ashgate Pub Co.
Rya, Aniruddha, jt. auth. see Arasaratnam, Sinnappah.
Ryabchikov, D. & Col'Braikh, E. Analytical Chemistry of Thorium. LC 63-10065. (International Series of Monographs on Analytical Chemistry: Vol. 10). 1963. 134.00 (*0-08-013737-7*, Pub. by Pergamon Repr UK) Franklin.
Ryabchikov, D. I. & Ryabukhin, V. A. Yttrium & the Lanthanide Elements. (Analytical Chemistry of the Elements Ser.). 376p. 1970. text ed. 92.00 (*0-7065-0752-5*, Pub. by Keter Pub IS) Coronet Bks.
Ryabchikov, R. I. & Gol'braikh, E. K. Thorium. (Analytical Chemistry of the Elements Ser.). 300p. 1970. text ed. 74.00 (*0-7065-0747-9*, Pub. by Keter Pub IS) Coronet Bks.
Ryabenkii, V. S., jt. auth. see Godunov, S. K.
Ryabov, E. A. Laser Chemisty in Russia. 1993. text ed. 177.00 (*3-7186-5373-7*) Gordon & Breach.
Ryabov, Vladimir R. Aluminizing of Steel. (Illus.). 216p. (C). 1985. 28.59x (*81-205-0021-0*, Pub. by Oxford IBH II) S Asia.
Ryaboy, Vladislav. Upper Mantle Structure Studies by Explosion Seismology in the U. S. S. R. Nobel, Erika, ed. (Illus.). 141p. (Orig.). 1989. pap. text ed. 75.00 (*1-55831-091-6*) Delphic Associates.
Ryabukhin, V. A., jt. auth. see Ryabchikov, D. I.
Ryabushin, Alexandra & Smolina, Nadia. Landmarks of Soviet Architecture 1917-1991. LC 91-50831. (Illus.). 160p. (Orig.). 1992. pap. 35.00 (*0-8478-1472-6*) Rizzoli Intl.
Ryall, M. Q., jt. ed. see Holyoake, George J.
Ryall, R., ed. Urolithiasis 2. (Illus.). 710p. (C). 1994. text ed. 159.50 (*0-306-44727-4*, Plenum Pr) Plenum.
Ryall, R. W. Mechanisms of Drug Action on the Nervous System. 2nd ed. (Illus.). 250p. (C). 1989. 69.95 (*0-521-25424-8*); pap. 19.95 (*0-521-27437-0*) Cambridge U Pr.
***Ryall, Rhiannon.** Celtic Lore & Druid Ritual. Date not set. pap. 22.95 (*1-898307-24-5*, Pub. by Capall Bann Pubng UK) Holmes Pub.
— West Country Wicca. Date not set. pap. 17.95 (*1-898307-02-4*, Pub. by Capall Bann Pubng UK) Holmes Pub.
— West Country Wicca. (Illus.). 112p. 1990. pap. 8.95 (*0-919345-98-0*) Phoenix WA.
Ryall, Susan. Over the Rhine. 164p. 1985. pap. 6.95 (*0-87052-128-4*) Hippocrene Bks.
Ryall, Tom. Alfred Hitchcock & the British Cinema. LC 86-11361. (Illus.). 208p. 1986. 24.95 (*0-252-01374-3*) U of Ill Pr.
— Blackmail. (Illus.). 64p. 1994. pap. 9.95 (*0-85170-356-9*, Pub. by British Film Inst UK) Ind U Pr.
***Ryals, Clyde D.** A World of Possibilities: Romantic Irony in Victorian Literature. (Studies in Victorian Life & Literature). 163p. 1990. 39.50 (*0-8142-0522-4*) Ohio St U Pr.
Ryals, Clyde D. & Fielding, Kenneth J., eds. The Collected Letters of Thomas & Jane Welsh Carlyle, Vol. 19: January to September, 1845. LC 71-101323. 263p. 1993. lib. bdg. 45.00 (*0-8223-1286-7*) Duke.
— The Collected Letters of Thomas & Jane Welsh Carlyle, Vol. 20: October 1845 to July 1846. LC 71-101323. 269p. 1993. lib. bdg. 45.00 (*0-8223-1287-5*) Duke.
— The Collected Letters of Thomas & Jane Welsh Carlyle, Vol. 21: August 1846 to June 1847. LC 71-101323. 285p. 1993. lib. bdg. 45.00 (*0-8223-1288-3*) Duke.
Ryals, Clyde de L. Becoming Browning: The Poems & Plays of Robert Browning, 1833-1846. LC 83-4140. 305p. 1983. 42.50 (*0-8142-0352-3*) Ohio St U Pr.
— Browning's Later Poetry, 1871-1889. LC 75-16927. 288p. 1975. 37.95 (*0-8014-0964-0*) Cornell U Pr.
— The Collected Letters of Thomas & Jane Welch Carlyle, Vols. 13-15. Fielding, Kenneth J., ed. 1988. lib. bdg. 41.95 (*0-318-61460-X*); Vol. 13, 333p. write for info. (*0-8223-0702-2*); Vol. 14, 248p. write for info. (*0-8223-0703-0*); Vol. 15, 293p. write for info. (*0-8223-0704-9*) Duke.
— The Life of Robert Browning: A Critical Biography. (Critical Biographies Ser.: Vol. 3). 320p. 1993. write for info. (*0-631-16277-1*) Blackwell Pubs.
Ryals, Clyde de L., ed. see Ward, Humphrey.
Ryals, Clyde de L., et al. The Collected Letters of Thomas & Jane Welsh Carlyle, Vol 16. Fielding, Kenneth J. et al, eds. 424p. (Orig.). 1990. lib. bdg. 41.95 (*0-8223-0919-X*) Duke.
— The Collected Letters of Thomas & Jane Welsh Carlyle, Vol. 17. Fielding, Kenneth J. et al, eds. 384p. (Orig.). 1990. lib. bdg. 41.95 (*0-8223-0924-6*) Duke.
— The Collected Letters of Thomas & Jane Welsh Carlyle, Vol. 18. Fielding, Kenneth J. et al, eds. 384p. (Orig.). 1990. lib. bdg. 41.95 (*0-8223-0936-X*) Duke.
— The Collected Letters of Thomas & Jane Welsh Carlyle, Vols. 16-18. Fielding, Kenneth J. et al, eds. (Orig.). 1990. lib. bdg. write for info. (*0-318-65458-X*) Duke.
Ryals, Clyde de L., et al, eds. Nineteenth-Century Literary Perspectives: Essays in Honor of Lionel Stevenson. LC 73-84842. 318p. reprint ed. pap. 90.70 (*0-317-20420-3*, 2023443) Bks Demand.
Ryals, Mary J & Decker, Donna, eds. North of Wakulla: An Anhinga Anthology. (Illus.). 160p. (Orig.). 1989. pap. 12.50 (*0-938078-30-5*); 50.00 (*0-938078-31-3*) Anhinga Pr.
***Ryan.** Bulbs. 1994. pap. 12.99 (*0-517-13454-3*) Random.
— Computer-Aided Architectural Graphics. 432p. 1983. 65.00 (*0-8247-1901-8*) Dekker.
— Computer-Aided Kinetics for Machine Design. (Mechanical Engineering Ser.: Vol. 7). 288p. 1981. 65.00 (*0-8247-1421-0*) Dekker.
— Graphical Displays for Engineering Documentation. 296p. 1987. 75.00 (*0-8247-7747-6*) Dekker.
— Kistner's Gynecology: Principles & Practice. 5th ed. 776p. 1989. 79.00 (*0-8151-5084-9*, Yr Bk Med Pubs) Mosby Yr Bk.
— Principles of Marketing. 3rd ed. 1980. pap. 12.00 (*0-256-02220-8*) Irwin Prof Pubng.
— Properties of Ceramic Raw Materials. (Illus.). 120p. (C). reprint ed. 25.00 (*1-878907-29-8*) TechBooks.
— Pulmonary Endothelium in Health & Disease. (Lung Biology in Health & Disease Ser.: Vol. 32). 520p. 1987. 210.00 (*0-8247-7758-1*) Dekker.
— Retina. (Illus.). 2472p. 1989. 359.00 (*0-8016-4241-8*) Mosby Yr Bk.
— Trouble with Perfect. (J). Date not set. 15.00 (*0-671-86586-2*, S&S Bks Young Read) S&S Childrens.
— Victorian Gift Boxes. 1994. pap. 7.99 (*0-517-13461-6*) Random.
— Women's Movement. 1995. text ed. 40.00 (*0-8161-7254-4*) G K Hall.
Ryan & Robinson. CA Compensation Cases, 54 vols. 1989. write for info. (*0-8205-1979-0*) Bender.
Ryan & Rubanyi, eds. Endothelial Regulation of Vascular Tone. 408p. 1991. 180.00 (*0-8247-8578-9*) Dekker.
Ryan, jt. auth. see Guile.
Ryan, jt. auth. see Lewis.
Ryan, jt. auth. see Morrison.
Ryan, jt. auth. see Will.
Ryan, et al. Kistner's Gynecology Review. 1990. 69.95 (*0-8151-7478-0*, Yr Bk Med Pubs) Mosby Yr Bk.
Ryan, A. H. Weekend Gold Miner. rev. ed. Shepherd, Robin, ed. 1991. 4.95 (*0-935182-46-2*) Gem Guides Bk.
Ryan, Abram. The Conquered Banner & Selected Poems of the Confederate Priest-Poet. Liederbach, Robert J., ed. (Illus.). 50p. 1988. pap. 8.50 (*0-934906-05-X*) R J Liederbach.
Ryan, Alan. Bertrand Russell: A Political Life. 240p. 1993. pap. 12.95 (*0-19-508634-1*) OUP.
— Design of Warning Labels & Instructions. 1991. text ed. 59.95 (*0-442-31953-3*) Van Nos Reinhold.
— John Dewey & the High Tide of American Liberalism. LC 94-36064. (Illus.). 448p. 1995. 30.00 (*0-393-03773-8*) Norton.
— Liberal Anxieties & Liberal Education. 112p. Date not set. 18.00 (*0-8090-6539-8*) FS&G.
— The Philosophy of John Stuart Mill. 2nd ed. LC 88-39285. 304p. (C). 1990. pap. 18.50 (*0-391-03634-3*) Humanities.
— Roller Coaster Year. (C). 1991. text ed. 24.00 (*0-06-045687-6*) HarpCollege.
— Statistical Methods for Quality Improvement. 446p. 1989. text ed. 74.95 (*0-471-84337-7*) Wiley.
Ryan, Alan, comp. The Penguin Book of Vampire Stories. 624p. 1989. pap. 12.95 (*0-14-012445-4*, Penguin Bks) Viking Penguin.
Ryan, Alan, ed. Haunting Women. 224p. (Orig.). 1988. pap. 3.95 (*0-380-89881-0*) Avon.
— Justice. LC 92-35200. (Oxford Readings in Politics & Government Ser.). 1993. pap. 15.95 (*0-19-878038-9*) OUP.
— The Philosophy of Social Explanation. (Oxford Readings in Philosophy Ser.). 1973. pap. text ed. 13.95 (*0-19-875025-0*) OUP.
— The Reader's Companion to Mexico. LC 92-39391. 1993. write for info. (*0-15-175962-6*) HarBrace.
— The Reader's Guide to Mexico. 368p. 1995. pap. 15.00 (*0-15-676021-5*) HarBrace.
Ryan, Alan, jt. auth. see Metzger, Linda.
Ryan, Alan, ed. see Mill, John Stuart & Bentham, Jeremy.
Ryan, Alan, jt. ed. see Rogers, G. A.
Ryan, Allan. Property. LC 87-25538. (Concepts in Social Thought Ser.). 100p. (Orig.). 1988. text ed. 39.95 (*0-8166-1669-8*); pap. text ed. 11.95 (*0-8166-1670-1*) U of Minn Pr.
Ryan, Allan & Stephens, Robert E. Dancer's Complete Guide to Healthcare & a Long Career. 224p. 1988. pap. 9.95 (*0-933893-76-0*) Bonus Books.
Ryan, Allan A., Jr. & United States Department of Justice Staff. Klaus Barbie & the United States Government: The Report, with Documentary Appendix, to the Attorney General of the United States. LC 83-23466. (Foreign Intelligence Book Ser.). 420p. 1984. text ed. 55.00 (*0-313-27013-9*, U7013) Greenwood.
Ryan, Allan J. & Allman, Fred L., eds. Sports Medicine. 2nd ed. 450p. 1989. text ed. 108.00 (*0-12-605061-9*) Acad Pr.
Ryan, Allan J. & Stephens, Robert E., eds. Dance Medicine: A Comprehensive Guide. LC 87-60404. 375p. 1987. 79.00 (*0-931028-92-2*) Precept Pr.
Ryan, Allan J., jt. ed. see Mueller, Frederick O.
Ryan, Andrew S., Jr. The Real Romantic Marketplace: (Know Good Women?) 1991. 14.95 (*0-533-09317-1*) Vantage.
Ryan, Angela S., ed. Social Work with Immigrants & Refugees. LC 92-32667. (Journal of Multicultural Social Work: No. 2-1). (Illus.). 157p. 1993. lib. bdg. 29.95 (*1-56024-354-6*); pap. 14.95 (*1-56024-355-4*) Haworth Pr.
Ryan, Angela S., jt. ed. see Parry, Joan K.
Ryan, Arthur H. Mirroring Christ's Splendour. rev. ed. 216p. 1984. pap. 7.95 (*0-912414-40-5*) Lumen Christi.
Ryan, Barbara. Feminism & the Women's Movement: Dynamics of Change in Social Movement Ideology & Activism. (Perspectives on Gender Ser.). (Illus.). 288p. 1992. 49.95 (*0-415-90598-2*, A8179, Routledge NY); pap. 16.95 (*0-415-90599-0*, A8189, Routledge NY) Routledge.
Ryan, Barbara F. & Joiner, Brian L. Minitab Handbook. 3rd ed. 448p. 1994. pap. 24.95 (*0-534-21240-9*) Intl Thomson.
Ryan, Barbara F., et al. Minitab Handbook. 2nd ed. 379p. 1985. pap. 22.95 (*0-534-91579-5*) Intl Thomson.
— Minitab Handbook: With Release 8. 2nd rev. ed. 409p. 1992. pap. 24.95 (*0-534-93366-1*) Intl Thomson.
***Ryan, Bernard, Jr.** Advertising for a Small Business Made Simple. New England Publishing Associates, Inc. Staff, ed. LC 95-11876. (Made Simple Bks.). 1996. write for info. (*0-385-47567-5*) Doubleday.
— The Poisoned Life of Mrs. Maybrick. 1995. pap. write for info. (*0-446-60141-1*) Warner Bks.
Ryan, Bernard, Jr., jt. auth. see Lewin, Elizabeth.
Ryan, Betsy. Secret Love. LC 90-24058. (Hampstead High Ser.). 128p. (J). (gr. 5-9). 1991. pap. text ed. 2.95 (*0-8167-1913-6*) Troll Assocs.
Ryan, Betsy A. Gertrude Stein's Theatre of the Absolute. Beckerman, Bernard, ed. LC 84-191. (Theater & Dramatic Studies: No. 21). 246p. reprint ed. pap. 70.20 (*0-8357-1548-5*, 2070763) Bks Demand.
Ryan, Beverly A., jt. auth. see Burgess, Michael.
Ryan, Bill. Making Capital from Culture: The Corporate Form of Capitalist Cultural Production. (Studies in Organization: No. 35). xii, 290p. (C). 1991. lib. bdg. 54.95 (*3-11-012548-X*, 236-91) De Gruyter.
Ryan, Bill & Schrader, Richard. An Ounce of Pollution Prevention: Analysis & Rating of Ten State Pollution Prevention Laws. 60p. 1990. 15.00 (*0-685-56588-2*) CPA Washington.
***Ryan, Bob.** Bob Ryan's Woodpanelling. 64p. Date not set. pap. 16.95 (*0-85091-574-0*) Seven Hills Bk.
Ryan, Bob, jt. auth. see Bird, Larry.
Ryan, Bob, jt. auth. see Ryan, Gary.
Ryan, Bruce. Seventy-Five Years of Geography at the University of Cincinnati. 36p. (Orig.). 1983. pap. 4.95 (*0-9611212-0-3*) Univ of Cincinnati.
***Ryan, Bruce A., et al.** The Family-School Connection Vol. 2: Theory, Research, & Practice. (Issues in Children's & Families' Lives Ser.). (Illus.). 400p. 1995. 52.00 (*0-8039-7306-3*); pap. 24.95 (*0-8039-7307-1*) Sage.
Ryan, Bryan, ed. Major Twentieth-Century Writers: A Selection of Sketches from Contemporary Authors, 4 vols. 2700p. 1990. text ed. 295.00 (*0-8103-7766-7*) Gale.
Ryan, Bryce. Caste in Modern Ceylon: The Sinhalese System in Transition. (C). 1993. reprint ed. text ed. 32.00 (*81-7013-106-5*, Pub. by Navrang) S Asia.
Ryan, Bryce F. Social & Cultural Change. LC 79-84081. 506p. reprint ed. pap. 144.30 (*0-317-09616-8*, 2012534) Bks Demand.
Ryan, C. An Introduction to Hotel & Catering Economics. (C). 1980. 95.00 (*0-85950-424-7*, Pub. by S Thornes Pubs UK) St Mut.
Ryan, C. & Scanlan, G. SWOT Criminal Law. (C). 1991. 50.00 (*1-85431-152-2*, Pub. by Blackstone Pr UK) W W Gaunt.
Ryan, C. G. Marketing of Technology. Montgomerie, G. A., ed. (Management Ser.). 160p. 1984. pap. 48.00 (*0-86341-013-8*, MT003) Inst Elect Eng.
Ryan, Caitlin, jt. auth. see Rowe, Mona.

Ryan, Carol A. & Sline, Paula A. How to Get the Best Public School Education for Your Child. 224p. 1993. mass mkt. 4.50 (*0-8217-4038-5*) Zebra.
Ryan, Carol A., et al. How to Get the Best Public School Education for Your Child: A Parent's Guide for the Nineties. 224p. 1991. 21.95 (*0-8027-1156-1*); pap. 12.95 (*0-8027-7355-9*) Walker & Co.
Ryan, Cary, ed. Louisa May Alcott: Her Girlhood Diary. LC 93-22343. (Illus.). 56p. (J). (gr. 5 up). 1993. lib. bdg. 14.95 (*0-8167-3139-X*); pap. 4.95 (*0-8167-3150-0*) BrdgeWater.
Ryan, Cathy E., jt. auth. see Senelick, Richard C.
Ryan, Charles. Basic Electricity: A Self-Teaching Guide. 2nd ed. LC 86-11114. 291p. 1986. pap. text ed. 17.95 (*0-471-85085-3*) Wiley.
— Black Eagle - Black Eagle: Operative's Kit. (Illus.). 64p. (Orig.). 1992. pap. 14.95 (*0-9628748-3-3*) Chameleon Eclectic.
— The Capricorn Quadrant. 384p. 1991. pap. 4.99 (*0-451-17034-2*, Sig) NAL-Dutton.
— The Corregidor Tape. 416p. (Orig.). 1992. pap. 5.99 (*0-451-40345-2*, Onyx) NAL-Dutton.
— Millennium's End: Contemporary & Near-Future Roleplaying Game. 2nd ed. (Illus.). 192p. (Orig.). 1993. pap. 20.00 (*0-9628748-5-X*) Chameleon Eclectic.
— The Millennium's End GM Screen & 1999 Datasource. (Illus.). 32p. (Orig.). 1992. pap. text ed. 11.95 (*0-9628748-2-5*) Chameleon Eclectic.
— Millennium's End GM's Companion. (Illus.). 144p. (Orig.). 1995. pap. 15.00 (*0-9628748-7-6*) Chameleon Eclectic.
— Nightwalker - The Villee Affair: Three Assignments for the Millenniums End Contemporary Roleplaying Game System. (Illus.). 88p. (Orig.). 1991. pap. text ed. 11.95 (*0-9628748-1-7*) Chameleon Eclectic.
— Phoenix Strike. 416p. 1993. pap. 5.99 (*0-451-40415-7*, Onyx) NAL-Dutton.
— Ultramodern Firearms. (Illus.). 176p. (Orig.). 1993. pap. 20.00 (*0-9628748-4-1*) Chameleon Eclectic.
***Ryan, Charles & Fletcher, John.** Psychosis: Ship of Fools. (Illus.). 170p. (Orig.). 1995. pap. 15.00 (*0-9628748-9-2*) Chameleon Eclectic.
Ryan, Charles J. H. P. Blavatsky & the Theosophical Movement. rev. ed. Knoche, Grace F., ed. LC 75-4433. (Illus.). 376p. 1975. pap. 7.50 (*0-911500-80-4*) Theos U Pr.
— H. P. Blavatsky & the Theosophical Movement. 2nd rev. ed. Knoche, Grace F., ed. LC 75-4433. (Illus.). 376p. 1975. 13.00 (*0-911500-79-0*) Theos U Pr.
— H. P. Blavatsky & the Theosophical Movement: With 7 Appendixes. Small, W. Emmett & Todd, Helen, eds. (Illus.). 484p. 1975. reprint ed. pap. 7.50 (*0-913004-25-1*) Point Loma Pub.
— What Is Theosophy? A General View of Occult Doctrine. rev. ed. Small, W. Emmett & Todd, Helen, eds. (Theosophical Manual Ser.: No. 1). 92p. 1975. pap. 2.50 (*0-913004-18-9*) Point Loma Pub.
Ryan, Charles J., jt. auth. see Ross, Lydia.
Ryan, Charles W., jt. auth. see Drummond, Robert J.
Ryan, Charlotte. Prime-Time Activism: Media Strategies for Organizing. 270p. (Orig.). 1991. 30.00 (*0-89608-402-7*); pap. 14.00 (*0-89608-401-9*) South End Pr.
Ryan, Cheli D. Hildilid's Night. LC 86-5294. (Illus.). 32p. (J). (ps-2). 1986. text ed. 13.95 (*0-02-777260-8*, Mac Bks Young Read) S&S Childrens.
Ryan, Cheryl. Sally Arnold. LC 94-64[illegible]5. (J). 1995. write for info. (*0-525-65176-4*, Cobblehill B[illegible]s) Dutton Child Bks.
Ryan, Chris. The Eiffel Tower. (Inside [illegible]tory Ser.). 48p. (J). (gr. 3-4). 1991. lib. bdg. 11.95 (*1[illegible]065-026-5*) Capstone Pr.
— Recreational Tourism: A Social Science Perspective. 272p. 1991. 69.95 (*0-415-05423-0*, A5498); pap. 17.95 (*0-415-05424-9*, A5702) Routledge.
— Researching Tourist Satisfaction: Issues, Concepts, Problems. LC 94-7224. 320p. (Orig.). 1995. 69.95x (*0-415-10157-3*, B4752) Routledge.
— Researching Tourist Satisfaction: Issues, Concepts, Problems. LC 94-7224. 320p. (Orig.). 1995. pap. 22.95 (*0-415-10158-1*, B4756) Routledge.
***Ryan, Christopher.** SWOT Criminal Law. 4th ed. 286p. 1995. pap. 22.00 (*1-85431-339-8*, Pub. by Blackstone Pr UK) W W Gaunt.
— Virtual Marketing: The Battle for the Customer's Mind. Quay, Sunny, ed. LC 94-33611. 1994. write for info. (*1-882222-08-3*) Libey Pub.
Ryan, Christopher, tr. Dante: The Banquet. (Stanford French & Italian Studies: Vol. 61). 260p. 1989. pap. 46.50 (*0-685-44269-1*) Anma Libri.
Ryan, Christopher & Scanlan, Gary. SWOT Criminal Law. 238p. (C). 1990. 80.00 (*1-85431-034-8*, Pub. by Blackstone Pr UK) St Mut.
Ryan, Christopher, jt. auth. see Berkshire Chapter Appalachian Mtn Club Volunteers.
Ryan, Christopher, jt. ed. see Moss, Laurence S.
Ryan, Christopher, jt. auth. see Scanlan, Gary.
***Ryan, Christopher D. & Black, D. P.** The End of the Endless Summer: The Ron N Scott Tapes & Papers. LC 94-90298. (Illus.). 224p. (Orig.). 1995. per., pap. 14.95 (*0-9641943-5-X*) Totally Bogus.
Ryan, Christopher J. The Direct Marketing Challenge: How to Use Powerful Direct Marketing Tools to Build Your Organization. LC 89-50224. 191p. 1989. pap. write for info. (*0-9636236-0-5*) IdeaWorks MD.
— Guide to the Taconic Trail System in Berkshire County, MA. Skowron, Carol F., ed. (Illus.). 62p. (Orig.). 1989. pap. 6.95 (*0-9624801-0-X*) NE Cartographics.
— The Master Marketer: How to Combine Timeless Fundamentals with the Latest Advances to Achieve Spectacular Marketing Success. LC 92-97352. (Illus.). 556p. 1993. write for info. (*0-9636236-1-3*) IdeaWorks MD.
Ryan, Christopher J., ed. see Dillapenna, Craig P.
Ryan, Christopher J., ed. see Scofield, Bruce.
Ryan, Clarence, ed. see DuPont - UCLA Symposium on Molecular Strategies for Crop Protection Staff.
Ryan, Colleen. Beyers Naude: Pilgrimage of Faith. 248p. (C). 1990. 49.95 (*0-86543-193-0*); pap. 9.95 (*0-86543-190-6*) Africa World.
— Beyers Naude: Pilgrimage of Faith. (Illus.). 248p. 1990. pap. 19.99 (*0-8028-0531-0*) Eerdmans.
— Beyers Naude: Pilgrimage of Faith. LC 90-82835. (Illus.). 246p. 1990. reprint ed. pap. 70.20 (*0-7837-8092-3*, 2047846) Bks Demand.
Ryan, Concetta D. The Black Pearl: A Literature Unit. (Literature Units Ser.). (Illus.). 48p. (Orig.). (gr. 3-5). 1992. student ed 6.95 (*1-55734-410-8*) Tchr Create Mat.
— Charlie & the Chocolate Factory: A Literature Unit. (Literature Units Ser.). (Illus.). 48p. (Orig.). 1993. student ed, pap. 6.95 (*1-55734-420-5*) Tchr Create Mat.
— The Secret Garden: A Literature Unit. (Literature Units Ser.). (Illus.). 48p. (Orig.). 1992. student ed 6.95 (*1-55734-414-0*) Tchr Create Mat.
***Ryan, Cornelius.** A Bridge Too Far: The Classic History of the Greatest Airborne Battle of World War II. 1995. pap. 15.00 (*0-684-80330-5*, Touchstone Bks) S&S Trade.
— The Last Battle: The Classic History of Battle for Berlin. 1995. pap. 15.00 (*0-684-80329-1*, Touchstone Bks) S&S Trade.
— Longest Day: June 6, 1944. 1994. 22.00 (*0-671-89155-3*) S&S Trade.
— The Longest Day: June 6, 1994. 1994. pap. 11.00 (*0-671-89091-3*, Touchstone Bks) S&S Trade.
Ryan, Craig. Beauty of New York. Shangle, Robert D., ed. (Illus.). 80p. (Orig.). 1989. pap. 9.95 (*0-917630-74-2*) LTA Pub.
— The Pre-Astronauts: Manned Ballooning on the Threshold of Space. (Illus.). 368p. 1995. 29.95 (*1-55750-732-5*) Naval Inst Pr.
Ryan, D. H., ed. Recent Progress in Random Magnets. LC 92-16899. 300p. 1992. text ed. 98.00 (*981-02-0885-5*) World Scientific Pub.
Ryan, Dale & Ryan, Juanita. Life Recovery Guides, 10 bks., Set. 1991. pap. 79.84 (*0-8308-1150-8*, 1150) InterVarsity.
— Recovery from Abuse. (Life Recovery Guides Ser.). 64p. 1990. 4.99 (*0-8308-1158-3*, 1158) InterVarsity.
— Recovery from Addictions. (Life Recovery Guides Ser.). 64p. (Orig.). 1990. pap. 4.99 (*0-8308-1155-9*, 1155) InterVarsity.
— Recovery from Bitterness. (Life Recovery Guides Ser.). 64p. (Orig.). 1990. pap. 4.99 (*0-8308-1154-0*, 1154) InterVarsity.
— Recovery from Codependency. (Life Recovery Guides Ser.). 64p. (Orig.). 1990. pap. 4.99 (*0-8308-1156-7*, 1156) InterVarsity.
— Recovery from Depression. (Life Recovery Guides Ser.). 64p. (Orig.). 1993. pap. 4.99 (*0-8308-1161-3*, 1161) InterVarsity.
— Recovery from Distorted Images of God. (Life Recovery Guides Ser.). 64p. 1990. 4.99 (*0-8308-1152-4*, 1152) InterVarsity.
— Recovery from Distorted Images of Self. (Life Recovery Guides Ser.). 64p. (Orig.). 1993. pap. 4.99 (*0-8308-1162-1*, 1162) InterVarsity.
— Recovery from Family Dysfunctions. (Life Recovery Guides Ser.). 64p. 1990. 4.99 (*0-8308-1151-6*, 1151) InterVarsity.
— Recovery from Loss. (Life Recovery Guides Ser.). 64p. (Orig.). 1990. pap. 4.99 (*0-8308-1157-5*, 1157) InterVarsity.
— Recovery from Shame. (Life Recovery Guides Ser.). 64p. 1990. 4.99 (*0-8308-1153-2*, 1153) InterVarsity.
— Rooted in God's Love: Biblical Meditations for People in Recovery. 168p. (Orig.). 1992. pap. 8.99 (*0-8308-1292-X*, 1292) InterVarsity.
Ryan, Dale, jt. auth. see Ryan, Juanita.
Ryan, Daniel, ed. CAD-CAE Descriptive Geometry. 1991. 49.95 (*0-8493-4273-2*, TA345) CRC Pr.
Ryan, Daniel B., ed. Pretrial Release & Detention & Pretrial Services. 80p. (Orig.). (C). 1993. pap. text ed. 40.00 (*1-56806-350-4*) Diane Pub.
Ryan, Daniel L. Computer-Aided Design for Autocad Users. 368p. 1989. pap. text ed. 55.00 (*0-13-162678-7*) P-H.
— Computer-Aided Graphics & Design. 3rd expanded rev. ed. LC 93-46012. (Computer Aided Engineering Ser.: Vol. 4). 272p. 1994. 59.75 (*0-8247-9164-9*) Dekker.
— Principles of Automated Drafting. (Mechanical Engineering Ser.: Vol. 28). (Illus.). 336p. 1984. 75.00 (*0-8247-7175-3*) Dekker.
— Robotic Simulation. LC 93-17598. 1993. 59.95 (*0-8493-4468-9*, TJ211) CRC Pr.
***Ryan, David.** U. S.-Sandinista Diplomatic Relations: Voice of Intolerance. LC 95-14923. 1996. write for info. (*0-312-12821-5*) St Martin.
***Ryan, David D.** Cornbread & Maggots, Cloak & Dagger, Union Prisoners & Spies in Civil War Richmond. 1994. 24.95 (*0-87517-083-8*) Dietz.
— Richmond Illustrated: Unusual Stories of a City. (Illus.). 94p. 1993. 16.95 (*0-87517-071-4*) Dietz.
Ryan, David L. Kansas Administrative Law with Federal References. 1,985th ed. LC 85-80208. 100.00 (*0-942357-01-9*) KS Bar CLE.
— Kansas Administrative Law with Federal References. 1, 991th ed. LC 85-80208. 125.00 (*0-942357-25-6*) KS Bar CLE.
Ryan, David S. America: A Guide to the Experience. (Illus.). 144p. 1989. 24.95 (*0-905116-16-X*, Pub. by Kozmik Pr Centre UK); pap. 17.95 (*0-905116-17-8*) Seven Hills Bk.
— India: A Guide to the Experience. (Illus.). 125p. 1989. 24.95 (*0-905116-10-0*, Pub. by Kozmik Pr Centre UK); pap. 17.95 (*0-905116-11-9*) Seven Hills Bk.
— Looking for Kathmandu. 251p. 1982. 19.95 (*0-905116-05-4*, Pub. by Kozmik Pr Centre UK) Seven Hills Bk.
— Taboo. 191p. 1984. 17.95 (*0-905116-13-5*, Pub. by Kozmik Pr Centre UK); pap. 8.95 (*0-905116-14-3*) Seven Hills Bk.
Ryan, David S., ed. The Cream of the Troubadour Coffee House. (Illus.). 112p. (Orig.). 1990. pap. 17.95 (*0-905116-19-4*, Pub. by Kozmik Pr Centre UK) Seven Hills Bk.
— The Lost Journal of Robyn Hood - Outlaw. 187p. 1989. 19.95 (*0-905116-18-6*, Pub. by Kozmik Pr Centre UK) Seven Hills Bk.
Ryan, Deborah. Women's Basketball Drills: Conditioning Drills. (Orig.). (YA). (gr. 7 up). 1988. pap. 6.95 (*0-932741-58-4*) Championship Bks & Vid Prodns.
Ryan, Dennis, jt. auth. see Shine, Joseph W.
Ryan, Dennis P. Beyond the Ballot Box: A Social History of the Boston Irish, 1845-1917. LC 89-5157. (Illus.). 176p. (Orig.). (C). 1989. reprint ed. pap. 12.95x (*0-87023-683-0*) U of Mass Pr.
Ryan, Dennis P., ed. Einstein & the Humanities. LC 86-19444. (Contributions in Philosophy Ser.: No. 32). 229p. 1987. text ed. 55.00 (*0-313-25380-3*, RYA/, Greenwood Pr) Greenwood.
Ryan, Desmond. Fenian Chief: A Biography of James Stephens. LC 69-12348. 1967. 15.95 (*0-87024-100-1*) U of Miami Pr.
Ryan, Desmond, ed. The Nineteen Sixteen Poets. LC 79-18768. 224p. 1980. reprint ed. text ed. 55.00 (*0-313-22100-6*, RYNI, Greenwood Pr) Greenwood.
Ryan, Desmond, ed. see Pearse, Patrick, et al.
Ryan, Donna H. Mycotoxins, Cancer, & Health. Bray, George A., ed. LC 90-13706. (Pennington Center Nutrition Ser.: Vol. 1). (Illus.). 352p. 1991. text ed. 45.00 (*0-8071-1679-3*) La State U Pr.
Ryan, Donna H., jt. ed. see Bray, George A.
Ryan, Dorothy. Philip Boileau: Painter of Fair Women. (Illus.). (Orig.). 1980. pap. 9.95 (*0-910664-47-1*) Gotham.
Ryan, Dorothy & Ryan, Louis J., comps. The Kennedy Family of Massachusetts: A Bibliography. LC 81-6672. 224p. 1981. text ed. 42.95 (*0-313-23189-3*, RKF/, Greenwood Pr) Greenwood.
Ryan, E. Davis, jt. auth. see Swencionis, Charles.
Ryan, E. P. Optimal Relay & Saturating Control Systems Synthesis. (Control Engineering Ser.: No. 14). 352p. 1982. boxed 145.00 (*0-906048-56-7*, CE014) Inst Elect Eng.
***Ryan, Edward.** Paper Soldiers: Illustrated History of Printed Paper Armies. (Illus.). 688p. Date not set. 195.00 (*0-904568-96-2*, Pub. by Golden Age Edits UK) Pincushion Pr.
Ryan, Edward W., ed. In the Words of Adam Smith. LC 90-93270. 1990. 15.95 (*0-913878-49-9*); pap. text ed. 8.95 (*0-913878-48-0*) T Horton & Dghts.
Ryan, Elizabeth. How to Be a Better Writer. LC 91-3135. (Student Survival Power Ser.). 96p. (J). (gr. 5-9). 1992. lib. bdg. 9.89 (*0-8167-2462-8*); pap. text ed. 3.95 (*0-8167-2463-6*) Troll Assocs.
— How to Build a Better Vocabulary. LC 91-3136. (Student Survival Power Ser.). 112p. (J). (gr. 5-9). 1992. lib. bdg. 9.89 (*0-8167-2460-1*); pap. text ed. 3.95 (*0-8167-2461-X*) Troll Assocs.
— How to Make Grammar Fun - & Easy! LC 91-12525. (Student Survival Power Ser.). 112p. (J). (gr. 5-9). 1992. lib. bdg. 9.89 (*0-8167-2456-3*); pap. text ed. 3.95 (*0-8167-2457-1*) Troll Assocs.
— How to Write Better Book Reports. LC 91-3134. (Student Survival Power Ser.). 80p. (J). (gr. 5-9). 1992. lib. bdg. 9.89 (*0-8167-2458-X*); pap. text ed. 3.95 (*0-8167-2459-8*) Troll Assocs.
***Ryan, Elizabeth A.** Straight Talk about Drugs & Alcohol. rev. ed. (J). 1995. 16.95 (*0-8160-3249-1*) Facts on File.
— Straight Talk about Parents. (Straight Talk Ser.). 144p. (YA). 1989. 16.95 (*0-8160-1526-0*) Facts on File.
— Straight Talk about Prejudice. (Straight Talk Ser.). 128p. (YA). (gr. 5-12). 1992. lib. bdg. 16.95 (*0-8160-2488-X*) Facts on File.
— Student Thesaurus. LC 89-20305. (Illus.). 160p. (J). (gr. 2-8). 1990. lib. bdg. 14.89 (*0-8167-1914-4*); pap. text ed. 6.95 (*0-8167-1856-3*) Troll Assocs.
Ryan, Elizabeth A., ed. see Frankel, Bernard & Kranz, Rachel.
Ryan, Elizabeth A., ed. see Mufson, Susan & Kranz, Rachel.
Ryan, Elizabeth A., ed. see Rendon, Marion B. & Kranz, Rachel.
Ryan, Elizabeth A., ed. see Thacker, John & Kranz, Rachel.
Ryan, Elsie M. Love's Journey. 64p. (Orig.). 1994. pap. write for info. (*1-56167-157-6*) Am Literary Pr.
Ryan, F. W. Usury & Usury Laws. 1977. lib. bdg. 200.00 (*0-8490-2791-8*) Gordon Pr.
***Ryan, Frances & Rybolt, John E., eds.** Vincent de Paul & Louise de Marillac: Rules, Conferences, & Writings. LC 95-3447. (Classics of Western Spirituality Ser.). 1995. 24.95 (*0-8091-0471-7*); pap. 18.95 (*0-8091-3564-7*) Paulist Pr.
Ryan, Frank. California Directory of Services & Products for the Visually Impaired. LC 83-80386. 76p. (Orig.). (C). 1983. per., pap. 5.95 (*0-9604434-4-4*) Muse-Ed Comp.
— Forgotten Plague: How the Battle Against Tuberculosis Was Won & Lost. 1994. pap. 14.95 (*0-316-76381-0*) Little.
— Tiger, Tiger. large type ed. 1990. 21.95 (*0-7089-2287-2*) Ulverscroft.
Ryan, Frank, jt. ed. see Krueger, Merle.
***Ryan, Frederick J., Jr., ed.** Ronald Reagan: The Wisdom & Humour of the Great Communicator. LC 95-15849. 1995. 17.95 (*0-00-225121-3*) Collins SF.
Ryan, G. Jeremiah. Corporation & Foundation Giving to Community Colleges. 1989. 12.50 (*0-87117-195-3*, 1304) Am Assn Comm Coll.
Ryan, G. Jeremiah & Smith, Nanette J., eds. Marketing & Development for Community Colleges. 252p. 1989. 37.00 (*0-89964-270-5*) Coun Adv & Supp Ed.
Ryan, Gail D. & Lane, Sandy, eds. Juvenile Sexual Offending: Causes, Consequences, & Correction. 448p. 1991. text ed. 42.95 (*0-669-19464-6*) Free Pr.
Ryan, Garry D. & Nenninger, Timothy K., eds. Soldiers & Civilians: The U. S. Army & the American People. LC 86-21664. (Illus.). 210p. text ed. 25.00 (*0-911333-52-5*, 100011) National Archives & Recs.
***Ryan, Gary & Ryan, Bob.** Ryan & Ryan's Thots That Stick to the Roof of Your Mind. Lindsay, Karen, ed. 192p. (Orig.). 1994. pap. text ed. 7.95 (*0-9644687-0-0*) R&R Creat Adv.
Ryan, George, jt. auth. see Fensin, Alan.
Ryan, George E. Botolph of Boston. (Illus.). 1971. 10.00 (*0-8158-0252-8*) Chris Mass.
Ryan, Gerald D. Radiographic Positioning of Small Animals. LC 80-26069. 159p. reprint ed. pap. 45.40 (*0-7837-1476-9*, 2057171) Bks Demand.
Ryan, Gerry, jt. auth. see Hecht, Ellen.
***Ryan, Gordon.** Dangerous Legacy. LC 94-26638. iv, 379p. 1994. 14.95 (*0-87579-905-1*) Deseret Bk.
Ryan, Gordon G. The Top Five Percent: How to Save & Invest While Minimizing Taxes. 140p. (Orig.). 1988. pap. 12.95 (*0-9621442-0-7*) Mntnview Pub WA.
Ryan, Granger, tr. see Couturier, M. A.
Ryan, Greg & Beyer, Sally. The Twin Cities, Naturally! A Pictorial Tour of Minneapolis & St. Paul. LC 93-34642. 1994. 16.95 (*0-89658-232-9*) Voyageur Pr.
Ryan, H. B. The Vision of Anglo-America. 240p. 1987. 59.95 (*0-521-32928-0*) Cambridge U Pr.
***Ryan, H. M., ed.** High Voltage Engineering & Testing. (IEE Power Ser.: No. 17). 450p. 1994. 95.00 (*0-86341-293-9*, Pub. by Peregrinus UK) Inst Elect Eng.
Ryan, Halford. Classical Communication for the Contemporary Communicator. 244p. (C). 1992. pap. text ed. 26.95 (*1-55934-033-9*) Mayfield Pub.
— Contemporary American Public Discourse: A Collection of Speeches & Critical Essays. 3rd ed. (Illus.). 384p. (Orig.). (C). 1992. pap. text ed. 18.95x (*0-88133-629-7*) Waveland Pr.
***Ryan, Halford, ed.** U. S. Presidents As Orators: A Bio-Critical Sourcebook. LC 94-43039. 440p. 1995. text ed. 89.50 (*0-313-29059-8*, Greenwood Pr) Greenwood.
Ryan, Halford R. Franklin Roosevelt's Rhetorical Presidency. LC 87-31778. (Contributions in Political Science Ser.: No. 206). 209p. 1988. text ed. 55.00 (*0-313-25567-9*, RFR/, Greenwood Pr) Greenwood.
— Harry Emerson Fosdick: Persuasive Preacher. LC 88-25101. (Great American Orators: Critical Studies, Speeches & Sources: No. 2). 200p. 1989. text ed. 49.95 (*0-313-25897-X*, RHF/, Greenwood Pr) Greenwood.
— Harry S. Truman: Presidential Rhetoric. LC 92-18350. (Great American Orators Ser.: No. 17). 232p. 1993. text ed. 49.95 (*0-313-27908-X*, RHU, Greenwood Pr) Greenwood.
— Henry Ward Beecher: Peripatetic Preacher. LC 89-38228. 179p. 1990. text ed. 45.00 (*0-313-26389-2*, RHY/, Greenwood Pr) Greenwood.
Ryan, Halford R., ed. The Inaugural Addresses of Twentieth-Century American Presidents. LC 92-34950. (Series in Political Communication). 352p. 1993. text ed. 55.00 (*0-275-94039-X*, C4039, Praeger Pubs) Greenwood.
— Oratorical Encounters: Selected Studies & Sources of Twentieth-Century Political Accusations & Apologies. LC 87-23662. (Contributions to the Study of Mass Media & Communications Ser.: No. 9). 354p. 1988. text ed. 65.00 (*0-313-25568-7*, ROR/) Greenwood.
Ryan, Halford R., jt. ed. see Duffy, Bernard K.
***Ryan-Hayes, Karen L.** Contemporary Russian Satire: A Genre Study. (Cambridge Studies in Russian Literature). 270p. (C). 1995. write for info. (*0-521-47515-5*) Cambridge U Pr.
— Russian Publicistic Satire under Glasnost: The Journalistic Feuilleton. LC 93-30736. 212p. 1993. text ed. 89.95 (*0-7734-9348-4*) E Mellen.
Ryan, Henry B., ed. USIA: New Directions for a New Era. (ISD Reports). 56p. (Orig.). 1993. pap. text ed. 5.00 (*0-934742-76-6*) Geo U Inst Dplmcy.
Ryan, Hollady. What Preteens Want Their Parents To Know. LC 94-8329. 170p. 1994. 5.95 (*1-56977-475-7*) McCracken Pr.
Ryan, Hugh F. Ancestral Voices. 1994. write for info. (*0-918339-32-4*) Vandamere.
— On Borrowed Ground. 175p. (Orig.). 1991. pap. 10.95 (*0-86327-295-9*, Pub. by Wolfhound Pr IE) Dufour.
— Reprisal. LC 89-82285. 268p. (Orig.). 1990. 21.00 (*0-86327-247-9*, Pub. by Wolfhound Pr IE); pap. 11.95 (*0-86327-248-7*, Pub. by Wolfhound Pr IE) Dufour.
***Ryan, I. M.** JODI: Genghis Khan's DNA Progeny Invades Washington. Date not set. write for info. (*0-9623535-3-1*) Remco Inc.
Ryan, Irwin M. The Last Congress, Vol. 1. 464p. 1989. 17.95 (*0-9623535-0-7*) Remco Inc.
Ryan, J. A Background Study of the Non-Admitted Insurance Market. LC 79-93288. 71p. 1980. 25.00 (*0-317-35009-9*) Nat Assn Insu Comm.
Ryan, J. G. Building on Success: Agricultural Research, Technology, & Policy for Development. (C). 1987. text ed. 56.00 (*0-949511-50-1*, Pub. by ACIAR) St Mut.
— East Africa Consultation on Agricultural Research. 242p. (C). 1984. text ed. 104.00 (*0-949511-01-3*, Pub. by ACIAR) St Mut.
Ryan, J. R. & Baker, L. O., eds. Recent Concepts in Sarcoma Treatment. (Developments in Oncology Ser.). (C). 1988. lib. bdg. 125.50 (*0-89838-376-5*) Kluwer Ac.

Ryan, J. W. Guns, Mortars & Rockets. (Brassey's Battlefield Weapons Systems & Technology Ser.: Vol. 2). (Illus.). 236p. 1982. text ed. 30.00 (0-08-028324-1, P110, Pergamon Pr); pap. text ed. 19.25 (0-08-028325-X, Pergamon Pr) Elsevier.

Ryan, James E. The U. S. Investor's Guide to Gold & Silver Penny Stocks. 288p. (Orig.). 1984. pap. 14.95 (0-9610202-1-0) NW Silver Pr.

***Ryan, James F., et al.** Australian Radiology: A History. (Illus.). 150p. 1995. text ed. write for info. (0-07-470207-6) Hlth Prof Div.

Ryan, James G., jt. auth. see Walker, Thomas S.

***Ryan, James M. & Vestrand, W. Thomas.** High Energy Solar Phenomena: A New Era of Spacecraft Measurements. (AIP Conference Proceedings Ser.: No. 294). 500p. 1994. text ed. 245.00x (1-56396-291-8) Am Inst Physics.

***Ryan, James P., et al.** Physiology: PreTest Self-Assessment & Review. 8th ed. LC 95-3618. (PreTest Basic Science Ser.). (Illus.). 224p. 1995. pap. 16.95 (0-07-052085-2) Hlth Prof Div.

***Ryan, James R.** Scriptural Images of Stress in the Ministry. Date not set. pap. 24.95 (1-56699-091-2, OD81) Alban Inst.

Ryan, James W., jt. auth. see Crehan, Herbert F.

Ryan, James W., jt. auth. see Enright, Joseph F.

Ryan, James W., jt. auth. see O'Connell, Lenahan.

Ryan, Janice J., jt. auth. see Shalom, Rose.

Ryan, Janie. Illustrated Guide to Knitting. 1986. 12.98 (0-671-08306-6) S&S Trade.

Ryan, Jeanette M. Another Chance. 128p. 1985. pap. 2.50 (0-380-89705-9, Flare) Avon.

Ryan, Jeff, jt. auth. see Starkey, Chad.

Ryan, Jeffrey M., jt. auth. see Knight, Stephen A.

Ryan, Jenna. Bittersweet Legacy. (Intrigue Ser.). 1993. pap. 2.89 (0-373-22221-1, 1-22221-5) Harlequin Bks.

— Midnight Masque. (Intrigue Ser.). 1993. mass mkt. 2.99 (0-373-22251-3, 1-22251-2) Harlequin Bks.

— Puppets. 1992. pap. 2.89 (0-373-22205-X, 1-22205-8) Harlequin Bks.

— The Visitor. (Intrigue Ser.). 1993. mass mkt. 2.99 (0-373-22239-4, 1-22239-7) Harlequin Bks.

— When Night Falls. (Intrigue Ser.). 1994. mass mkt. 2.99 (0-373-22265-3, 1-22265-2) Harlequin Bks.

Ryan, Jeremiah. Economic Development. 1992. pap. write for info. (0-87117-244-5) Am Assn Comm Coll.

Ryan, Jerry R. Drawing the Line: A Landowner's Manual & Buyer's Guide. LC 93-79404. (Illus.). 120p. (Orig.). 1994. pap. 12.95 (0-9637828-0-0) TideRunner.

Ryan, Jillian & Ryan, Joseph A. Please, Somebody Love Me! Surviving Abuse & Becoming Whole - The Story of Jillian. LC 91-26444. 172p. (Orig.). 1991. pap. 9.99 (0-8010-7760-5) Baker Bk.

Ryan, Jim. Irish Records: Sources for Family & Local History. (Illus.). 562p. 1988. 39.95 (0-916489-22-1, 350) Ancestry.

***Ryan, Joan.** Little Girls in Pretty Boxes: The Making & Breaking of Elite Gymnasts & Figure Skaters. LC 94-43317. 1995. 22.95 (0-385-47790-2) Doubleday.

Ryan, Joan S., jt. auth. see Lawrence, Michael D.

***Ryan, Joanna & Thomas, Frank.** The Politics of Mental Handicap. 190p. 1987. pap. 14.50 (0-946960-92-5) NYU Pr.

Ryan, Joanna, jt. auth. see O'Connor, Noreen.

Ryan, Joanne W., jt. ed. see Kline, Mary-Jo.

Ryan, Joe. Coming Full Circle: A Journey of Self Discovery & Growth. LC 94-71175. 128p. (Orig.). 1994. pap. 12.95 (0-9640860-8-5) CFC Prodns.

Ryan, Joe, ed. First Stop: The Master Index to Subject Encyclopedias. 1600p. 1988. 215.00 (0-89774-397-0) Oryx Pr.

Ryan, John. Bad Year for Dragons. LC 89-37279. 28p. (J). (gr. 1-4). 1989. 8.95 (0-8192-1512-0) Morehouse Pub.

— Giant-Killer. (Illus.). 32p. (J). (gr. 1-4). 1995. 5.99 (0-7459-3379-3) Lion USA.

— Jonah, a Whale of a Tale. (Illus.). 32p. (J). (gr. 1-7). 1992. 11.95 (0-7459-2150-7) Lion USA.

— Pugwash Aloft. (Illus.). 32p. (J). (gr. k-2). 1994. 19.95 (0-370-00692-5, Pub. by Bodley Head UK) Trafalgar.

— Pugwash & the Buried Treasure. (Illus.). 32p. (J). (gr. k-2). 1994. 19.95 (0-370-30338-5, Pub. by Bodley Head UK) Trafalgar.

— Pugwash & the Ghost Ship. LC 68-23218. (Illus.). (J). (gr. k-3). 1968. 22.95 (0-87599-146-7) S G Phillips.

— Pugwash & the Sea Monster. (Illus.). 32p. (J). (gr. k-2). 1994. 19.95 (0-370-10793-4, Pub. by Bodley Head UK) Trafalgar.

— Pugwash the Smuggler. (Illus.). 32p. (J). (gr. k-2). 1994. 19.95 (0-370-10786-1, Pub. by Bodley Head UK) Trafalgar.

***Ryan, John, ed.** Clifford Algebras in Analysis & Related Topics: A Proceedings of the Conference "Clifford Algebras in Analysis" Held at Fayetteville, Arkansas, 8-10th April 1993. 400p. 1995. 79.95 (0-8493-8481-8, 8481) CRC Pr.

Ryan, John & Saad, Adib T., eds. Agricultural Education for Development in the Middle East. 1980. 24.95 (0-8156-6057-X) Syracuse U Pr.

Ryan, John, jt. auth. see Baasiri, Muin.

Ryan, John A. Declining Liberty, & Other Papers. LC 68-8491. (Essay Index Reprint Ser.). 1977. 23.95 (0-8369-0845-7) Ayer.

— Distributive Justice. 1978. 40.95 (0-405-10849-4, 11852) Ayer.

— Living Wage: Its Ethical & Economic Aspects. LC 72-156422. (American Labor Ser., No. 2). 1971. reprint ed. 24.95 (0-405-02939-X) Ayer.

— Questions of the Day. LC 67-26779. (Essay Index Reprint Ser.). 1977. 23.95 (0-8369-0846-5) Ayer.

Ryan, John Augustine. Declining Liberty & Other Papers. LC 73-159802. (Civil Liberties in American History Ser.). 350p. 1972. reprint ed. lib. bdg. 42.50 (0-306-70253-3) Da Capo.

***Ryan, John B. & Lodato, Francis J.** Creating Your Christian Engagement. LC 94-76020. 144p. (Orig.). 1994. pap. 6.95 (0-89243-575-5) Liguori Pubns.

***Ryan, John C.** Hazardous Handouts: Taxpayers Subsidies to Environment Destruction. (New Reports). 56p. 1995. pap. text ed. 8.00 (1-886093-01-6) NW Environ Watch.

— Life Support: Conserving Biological Diversity. 70p. (Orig.). 1992. pap. 5.00 (1-878071-09-2) Worldwatch Inst.

Ryan, John J. The Nature, Structure & Function of the Church of William of Ockham. LC 78-2891. (American Academy of Religion. Studies in Religion: No. 16). 69p. reprint ed. pap. 25.00 (0-7837-5483-3, 2045248) Bks Demand.

Ryan, John K. Heirs & Ancestors. LC 74-171872. (Studies in Philosophy & the History of Philosophy: No. 6). 301p. reprint ed. pap. 85.80 (0-685-17826-9, 2029497) Bks Demand.

— John Duns Scotus, Twelve Sixty Five-Nineteen Sixty Five. Bonansea, Bernardine M., ed. LC 61-66336. (Studies in Philosophy & the History of Philosophy: Vol. 3). 392p. reprint ed. pap. 111.80 (0-317-08040-7, 2022584) Bks Demand.

Ryan, John K., ed. Studies in Philosophy & the History of Philosophy, Vol. 2. LC 61-66336. 266p. reprint ed. pap. 75.90 (0-685-17845-5, 2029505) Bks Demand.

— Studies in Philosophy & the History of Philosophy, Vol. 4. LC 61-66336. 238p. reprint ed. pap. 67.90 (0-8357-9057-6, 2017279) Bks Demand.

— Studies in Philosophy & the History of Philosophy: Ancients & Moderns, Vol.5. LC 61-66336. 374p. reprint ed. pap. 106.60 (0-317-12990-2, 2017280) Bks Demand.

Ryan, John K. & Benard, Edmond, eds. American Essays for the Newman Centennial. LC 47-30528. 258p. reprint ed. pap. 73.60 (0-8357-5367-0, 2005379) Bks Demand.

Ryan, John K., ed. see St. Francis De Sales.

Ryan, John K., tr. see St. Francis de Sales.

Ryan, John M. The Quality Team Concept in Total Quality Control. 272p. 1992. 35.95 (0-87389-123-6) ASQC Qual Pr.

Ryan, John P. & Tate, C. Neal. The Supreme Court in American Politics: Policy Through Law. 2nd rev. ed. Buchanan, William, ed. (SETUPS Ser.: American Politics). 99p. (C). 1980. pap. text ed. 6.00 (0-915654-46-6) Am Political.

Ryan, John S. The Shaping of Middle-Earth's Maker: Influences on the Life & Literature of J. R. R. Tolkien. 60p. 1992. pap. 5.00 (1-881799-03-4) Am Tolkien Soc.

Ryan, Joseph. Product Liability Handbook. 1994. text ed. 39.00 (0-13-126724-8) P-H.

— U. S. Employment Opportunities. (III Ser.). 300p. (YA). (gr. 12). ring bd. 184.00 (0-937801-01-1) Wash Res Assocs.

— U. S. Employment Opportunities. 5th ed. 260p. 1987. ring bd. 184.00 (0-685-18663-6) Wash Res Assocs.

Ryan, Joseph, ed. Employment Opportunities, U. S. A. Career News. 8th ed. LC 85-51246. Orig. Title: U. S. Employment Opportunities. 240p. 1994. reprint ed. ring bd. 184.00 (0-937801-09-7) Wash Res Assocs.

— U. S. Employment Opportunities, 1990. 7th ed. (Illus.). 250p. 1988. 184.00 (0-937801-04-6) Wash Res Assocs.

Ryan, Joseph A., jt. auth. see Ryan, Jillian.

Ryan, Joseph N. & Edwards, Marc, eds. Critical Issues in Water & Wastewater Treatment: Proceedings of the 1994 National Conference on Environmental Engineering, Boulder, CO, July 11-13, 1994. LC 94-20431. 1994. write for info. (0-7844-0031-8) Am Soc Civil Eng.

Ryan, Joyce. Calligraphy: Elegant & Easy. LC 94-94049. (Illus.). 104p. (Orig.). 1994. pap. 12.95 (0-939077-04-3) Butterfly Bks.

— The Happy Camper's Gourmet Cookbook: The Complete Guide to Camper-RV Cooking. LC 92-70449. (Illus.). 200p. (Orig.). 1992. pap. 11.95 (0-939077-03-5) Butterfly Bks.

— Traveling with Your Sketchbook: A Step-by-Step Guide to Travel Sketching with Emphasis on Pen-&-Ink. LC 90-83216. (Illus.). 200p. (Orig.). 1990. pap. 19.95 (0-939077-02-7) Butterfly Bks.

Ryan, Joyce & Rountree, Charlotte. Seoul Travel Guide: What to See & Where to Go. rev. ed. LC 87-71349. (Illus.). 96p. (Orig.). 1987. reprint ed. pap. 12.95 (0-939077-01-9) Butterfly Bks.

Ryan, Joyce, jt. auth. see Klar, Jim.

Ryan, Juanita & Ryan, Dale. Recovery: A Lifelong Journey. (Life Recovery Guides Ser.). 64p. (Orig.). 1993. pap. 4.99 (0-8308-1166-4, 1166) InterVarsity.

— Recovery from Broken Relationships. (Life Recovery Guides Ser.). 64p. (Orig.). 1993. pap. 4.99 (0-8308-1165-6, 1165) InterVarsity.

— Recovery from Fear. (Life Recovery Guides Ser.). 64p. (Orig.). 1992. pap. 4.99 (0-8308-1160-5, 1160) InterVarsity.

— Recovery from Guilt. (LifeGuide Bible Studies). 64p. (Orig.). 1993. pap. 4.99 (0-8308-1163-X, 1163) InterVarsity.

— Recovery from Spiritual Abuse. (Life Recovery Guides Ser.). 64p. (Orig.). 1992. pap. 4.99 (0-8308-1159-1, 1159) InterVarsity.

— Recovery from Workaholism. (Life Recovery Guides Ser.). 64p. (Orig.). 1993. pap. 4.99 (0-8308-1164-8, 1164) InterVarsity.

Ryan, Juanita, jt. auth. see Ryan, Dale.

Ryan, Judith. The Uncompleted Past: Postwar German Novels & the Third Reich. LC 83-6744. 184p. reprint ed. pap. 52.50 (0-318-39791-9, 2033194) Bks Demand.

— The Vanishing Subject: Early Psychology & Literary Modernism. LC 90-27330. 320p. 1991. 29.95 (0-226-73226-6) U Ch Pr.

Ryan, Judith, tr. see Goethe, Johann Wolfgang Von.

Ryan, K. W., ed. International Law in Australia. 2nd ed. xliii, 523p. 1984. pap. 85.00 (0-455-20269-9, Pub. by Law Bk Co) W W Gaunt.

Ryan, Karen L., ed. Trails for the Twenty-First Century: Planning, Design, & Management Manual for Multi-Use Trails. LC 93-8433. (Rails-to-Trails Conservancy Ser.). (Illus.). 290p. 1993. text ed. 49.95 (1-55963-237-2); pap. 24.95 (1-55963-238-0) Island Pr.

***Ryan, Karen-Lee.** 40 Great Rail-Trails in the Mid-Atlantic. (Illus.). 281p. (Orig.). 1995. 14.95 (0-925794-10-4) Rails Trails.

***Ryan, Karen-Lee & Winterich, Julie, eds.** Secrets of Successful Rail-Trails: An Acquisition & Organizing Manual for Converting Rails into Trails. (Illus.). 192p. (Orig.). 1990. 19.95 (0-925794-05-8) Rails Trails.

Ryan, Kate. Old Boston Museum Days. LC 77-131822. (Illus.). 1971. reprint ed. 49.00 (0-403-00709-7) Scholarly.

Ryan, Katherine E., jt. auth. see Ory, John C.

Ryan, Kathleen, ed. see Johnston, Jack L.

Ryan, Kathleen D. & Oestreich, Daniel K. Driving Fear Out of the Workplace: How to Overcome the Invisible Barriers to Quality, Productivity, & Innovation. LC 90-47648. (Management Ser.). 283p. 1993. pap. 19.00 (1-55542-509-7) Jossey-Bass.

Ryan, Kathleen J. & Share, Bernard, eds. Irish Traditions. (Illus.). 192p. 1990. 39.95 (0-8109-1109-4) Abrams.

— Irish Traditions. (Illus.). 192p. 1990. pap. 19.98 (0-8109-8096-7) Abrams.

Ryan, Kathleen J., et al. Ranching Traditions: Legacy of the American West. (Illus.). 296p. 1993. 22.98 (0-89660-032-7, Artabras) Abbeville Pr.

Ryan, Kathleen S. & Ryan, Kathleen S. The Narrow Cage: An American Family Saga. LC 80-687. 320p. 1980. 12.95 (0-672-52655-7, Bobbs) Macmillan.

Ryan, Kathleen S., jt. auth. see Ryan, Kathleen S.

Ryan, Kathryn H., ed. see Barilleaux, Rene P. & Heartney, Eleanor.

Ryan, Kay. Dragon Acts to Dragon Ends. LC 82-51255. 64p. (Orig.). pap. 4.95 (0-911407-00-6) Taylor Street.

— Flamingo Watching. LC 94-14755. 63p. (Orig.). 1994. pap. 9.95 (0-914278-64-9) Copper Beech.

— Strangely Marked Metal. LC 85-11372. 50p. (Orig.). 1985. pap. 5.95 (0-914278-46-0) Copper Beech.

Ryan, Kelly, ed. see Sachs, Patty.

Ryan, Ken. Computer Anxiety? Instant Relief! An Easy-to-Read Introduction to IBM PCs, Compatibles & Clones. 2nd ed. Hansen, Laurie A., ed. LC 92-71577. (Illus.). 128p. 1992. pap. 9.95 (1-879925-05-2) Castle Mnt Pr.

Ryan, Kenneth. Catholic Questions, Catholic Answers. 212p. (Orig.). (C). 1990. pap. 8.99 (0-89283-663-6) Servant.

Ryan, Kenneth J. Sherris Medical Microbiology. 3rd ed. (Illus.). 1008p. 1994. text ed. 52.95 (0-8385-8541-8, A8541-3) Appleton & Lange.

Ryan, Kevin. The Induction of New Teachers. LC 85-63692. (Fastback Ser.: No. 237). 50p. (Orig.). 1986. pap. 1.25 (0-87367-237-2) Phi Delta Kappa.

Ryan, Kevin & Cooper, James M. Those Who Can, Teach, 6 Vols. 6th ed. (C). 1991. pap. 53.96 (0-395-47314-4) HM.

Ryan, Kevin & Lickona, Thomas, eds. Character Development in Schools & Beyond. enl. ed. LC 92-10115. (Cultural Heritage & Contemporary Change Series VI: Foundations of Moral Education,: Vol. 3). 350p. 1992. pap. 17.50 (1-56518-059-3) Coun Res Values.

— Character Development in Schools & Beyond. 2nd enl. ed. LC 92-10115. (Cultural Heritage & Contemporary Change Series VI: Foundations of Moral Education,: Vol. 3). 350p. 1992. 45.00 (1-56518-058-5) Coun Res Values.

Ryan, Kevin & Sutcliffe, F. E., eds. AI & Cognitive Science '92: University of Limerick, 10-11 September, 1992. LC 93-26018. (Workshops in Computing Ser.). 1993. 79.00 (0-387-19799-0) Spr-Verlag.

Ryan, Kevin & Sutcliffe, R. F., eds. AI & Cognitive Science '92. (Workshops in Computing Ser.). (Illus.). 385p. 1993. pap. write for info. (3-540-19799-0) Spr-Verlag.

Ryan, Kevin, ed. see Asherman, Allan.

Ryan, Kevin, ed. see Boyle, Randall.

Ryan, Kevin, ed. see Carter, Carmen.

Ryan, Kevin, ed. see Crispin, A. C.

Ryan, Kevin, ed. see David, Peter.

Ryan, Kevin, ed. see Dillard, J. M.

Ryan, Kevin, ed. see Duane, Diane.

Ryan, Kevin, ed. see Friedman, Michael J.

Ryan, Kevin, jt. auth. see Friedman, Michael J.

Ryan, Kevin, ed. see Friedman, Michael J.

Ryan, Kevin, ed. see Glaf, L. A.

Ryan, Kevin, ed. see Hugh, Daffyd A.

Ryan, Kevin, ed. see Jeter, K. W.

Ryan, Kevin, ed. see Longyear, Barry B.

Ryan, Kevin, ed. see Mosley, Walter.

Ryan, Kevin, ed. see Neason, Rebecca.

Ryan, Kevin, ed. see Peel, John.

Ryan, Kevin, ed. see Quark.

Ryan, Kevin, ed. see Reeves-Stevens, Judith & Reeves-Stevens, Garfield.

Ryan, Kevin, ed. see Shatner, William.

Ryan, Kevin, ed. see Tilton, Lois.

Ryan, Kevin, ed. see Wright, Susan.

Ryan, Kevin, jt. auth. see Wynne, Edward A.

***Ryan, Kiernan.** Shakespeare. 2nd ed. LC 95-5834. 1995. pap. text ed. 16.95 (0-13-355546-1) P-H.

Ryan, Kiernan, ed. King Lear, William Shakespeare. LC 92-17046. (New Casebooks Ser.). 1992. text ed. 39.95 (0-312-08541-9) St Martin.

Ryan, Kirk R. Pharmacologic Intervention in the Treatment of AIDS. 1992. pap. 9.00 (0-9623535-4-X) Remco Inc.

Ryan, Kristal. Persistence Pays. 224p. (Orig.). 1993. pap. 2.95 (1-56597-067-5, Kismet) Meteor Pub.

Ryan, Larry, ed. see Getz, Frank.

Ryan, Larry, ed. see Sloop, Joseph G.

Ryan, Lawrence V. Roger Ascham. viii, 352p. 1963. 42.50 (0-8047-0149-0) Stanford U Pr.

— Roger Ascham. fac. ed. LC 63-10735. 111p. 1963. reprint ed. pap. 30.00 (0-7837-7912-7, 2047668) Bks Demand.

Ryan, Lawrence V., ed. see Ascham, Roger.

Ryan, Lee F. The Natural Classical Guitar: The Principles of Effortless Playing. 1990. reprint ed. pap. 23.95 (0-933224-40-0) Bold Strummer Ltd.

Ryan, Linda, ed. see Brigham, Viki.

Ryan, Louis J., jt. comp. see Ryan, Dorothy.

***Ryan-Lush, Geraldine.** Hairs on Bears. (Illus.). 24p. (J). (ps-1). 1994. lib. bdg. 14.95 (1-55037-351-X, Pub. by Annick CN); pap. 4.95 (1-55037-352-8, Pub. by Annick CN) Firefly Bks Ltd.

***Ryan, M. J.** A Grateful Heart: Daily Blessings for the Evening Meal from Buddha to the Beatles. (Illus.). 370p. 1994. bds. 14.95 (0-943233-84-4) Conari Press.

Ryan, M. Stanley. Parliamentary Procedure: Essential Principles. LC 83-45012. 232p. 1985. 14.95 (0-8453-4771-3, Cornwall Bks) Assoc Univ Prs.

Ryan, Marah E. Druid Path. LC 73-130071. (Short Story Index Reprint Ser.). (Illus.). 1977. 20.95 (0-8369-3652-3) Ayer.

— A Flower of France: A Story of Old Louisiana. LC 72-2930. (Black Heritage Library Collection). 1977. reprint ed. 29.95 (0-8369-9078-1) Ayer.

Ryan, Margaret. Cultural Journeys: Eighty-Four Arts & Social Science Experiences from Around the World. 200p. 1989. pap. text ed. 24.95 (1-55691-001-0) Learning Pubns.

— How to Give a Speech. (Speak Out, Write On! Ser.). (Illus.). 128p. (YA). (gr. 9-12). 1994. lib. bdg. 14.35 (0-531-11199-7) Watts.

— How to Read & Write Poems. LC 91-12141. (First Bks.). (Illus.). 64p. (J). (gr. 5-8). 1991. lib. bdg. 13.93 (0-531-20043-4) Watts.

Ryan, Margaret O., ed. see Erickson, Milton H.

Ryan, Margaret O., jt. auth. see Zukow, Bud.

Ryan, Margart O., jt. auth. see Wolinsky, Stephen.

Ryan, Marguerite. Adoption Story. 240p. reprint ed. pap. 3.95 (0-8439-3048-9) Dorchester Pub Co.

Ryan, Marie-Laure. Possible Worlds, Artificial Intelligence, & Narrative Theory. LC 91-6825. (Illus.). 308p. 1992. 35.00 (0-253-35004-2) Ind U Pr.

Ryan, Mark. War & Peace in Ireland: Britain & Sinn Fein in the New World Order. LC 94-8049. (C). 1994. text ed. 59.95 (0-7453-0923-2) Westview.

— War & Peace in Ireland: Britain & the IRA in the New World Order. 173p. (C). 1994. pap. text ed. 15.95 (0-7453-0924-0, Pub. by Pluto Pr UK) Westview.

Ryan, Mark A. Chinese Attitudes Toward Nuclear Weapons: China & the United States during the Korean War. LC 89-4158. 256p. 1990. 51.95 (0-87332-530-3) M E Sharpe.

Ryan, Marleigh G. The Development of Realism in the Fiction of Tsubouchi Shoyo. LC 75-1451. (Publications on Asia of the School of International Studies: No. 26). 148p. 1975. 25.00 (0-295-95382-9) U of Wash Pr.

— Japan's First Modern Novel: Ukigumo of Futabatei Shimei. LC 83-12764. xvi, 381p. 1983. reprint ed. text ed. 65.00 (0-313-24128-7, RYJA, Greenwood Pr) Greenwood.

Ryan, Marleigh G., tr. & comment. Japan's First Modern Novel: "Ukigumo" of Futabatei Shimei. LC 90-1371. (Michigan Classics in Japanese Studies: No. 1). xiv, 381p. 1990. reprint ed. pap. text ed. 12.95 (0-939512-44-0) U MI Japan.

Ryan, Mary. The Children Act, 1989: Putting It into Practice. 240p. 1994. 51.95 (1-85742-192-2, Pub. by Ashgate UK) Ashgate Pub Co.

— Glenallen. 512p. (C). 1991. pap. 9.99 (1-85594-024-8, Pub. by Attic IE) InBook.

— Glenallen. LC 92-43176. 1993. 24.95 (0-312-08797-7) St Martin.

— Glenallen. 1993. 24.95 (0-312-28797-6) St Martin.

— The Louisiana Purchase. LC 86-28523. (Milestone Documents in the National Archives Ser.). 36p. (Orig.). 1987. pap. text ed. 3.50 (0-911333-54-1, 200111) National Archives & Recs.

— Shadows from the Fire. 288p. 1995. 21.95 (0-312-13168-2, Pub. by Thomas Dunne Bks) St Martin.

— Whispers in the Wind. 512p. (Orig.). (C). 1993. pap. 9.99 (1-85594-001-9, Pub. by Attic IE) InBook.

Ryan, Mary, tr. see Sertillanges, A. G.

Ryan, Mary, ed. see Wehmann, Howard H. & DeWhitt, Benjamin.

Ryan, Mary C. Frankie's Run. (J). 1988. pap. 2.50 (0-380-70537-0, Flare) Avon.

— Frankie's Run. (J). (gr. 3-7). 1987. 12.95 (0-316-76370-5) Little.

— Ghosts, Gadgets & Great Ideas. 96p. (Orig.). (J). (gr. 3). 1993. pap. 3.50 (0-380-76537-3, Camelot Young) Avon.

— Me Two. 192p. (J). 1993. pap. 3.50 (0-380-71826-X, Camelot) Avon.

— Me Two. (J). (gr. 4-7). 1991. 16.95 (0-316-76376-4) Little.

— My Friend, O'Connell. 112p. (Orig.). (J). (gr. 3-4). 1991. pap. 2.95 (0-380-76145-9, Camelot) Avon.

— The Voice from the Mendelsohns Maple. LC 89-31569. (Illus.). 132p. (J). (gr. 5-7). 1990. 13.95 (0-316-76360-8) Little.

— The Voice from the Mendelsohns' Maple. 144p. (J). (gr. 5). 1992. pap. 3.50 (0-380-71140-0, Camelot) Avon.

— Who Says I Can't? 160p. (YA). (gr. 12 up). 1990. pap. 2.95 (0-380-70804-3, Flare) Avon.

— Who Says I Can't? 160p. (YA). (gr. 12 up). 1988. 12.95 (*0-316-76374-8*) Little.
Ryan, Mary C., jt. ed. see Smith, Nancy K.
Ryan, Mary E. Me, My Sister, & I. LC 92-368. (YA). 1992. pap. 15.00 (*0-671-73851-8*, S&S Bks Young Read) S&S Childrens.
— My Sister Is Driving Me Crazy. LC 90-41263. 224p. (YA). (gr. 5-9). 1991. pap. 15.00 (*0-671-73203-X*, S&S Bks Young Read) S&S Childrens.
— My Sister Is Driving Me Crazy. LC 90-41263. 224p. (J). (gr. 5-9). 1993. pap. 3.95 (*0-671-86694-X*, Half Moon Paper) S&S Childrens.
Ryan, Mary E., jt. auth. see Cochrane, Willard W.
Ryan, Mary J., ed. see Thoele, Sue P.
Ryan, Mary K. & Shattuck, Arthur. Treating AIDS with Chinese Medicine. LC 93-85212. 350p. 1993. pap. 29.95 (*1-881896-07-2*) Pacific View Pr.
Ryan, Mary P. Cradle of the Middle Class: The Family in Oneida County, New York, 1790-1865. LC 80-18460. (Interdisciplinary Perspectives on Modern History Ser.). (Illus.). 336p. 1983. pap. 16.95 (*0-521-27403-6*) Cambridge U Pr.
— The Empire of the Mother: American Writing about Domesticity, 1830-1860. LC 82-15631. (Women & History Ser.: Nos. 2 & 3). 170p. 1982. text ed. 39.95 (*0-86656-133-1*) Haworth Pr.
— The Empire of the Mother: American Writing about Domesticity 1830-1860. LC 85-5818. 170p. 1985. reprint ed. pap. 14.95 (*0-918393-18-3*) Harrington Pk.
— Women in Public: Between Banners & Ballots, 1825-1880. LC 89-32863. (Symposia in Comparative History Ser.). (Illus.). 208p. 1990. text ed. 35.00 (*0-8018-3908-4*) Johns Hopkins.
— Women in Public: Between Banners & Ballots, 1825-1880. (Symposia in Comparative History Ser.). 216p. 1992. reprint ed. pap. text ed. 12.95 (*0-8018-4401-0*) Johns Hopkins.
***Ryan, Maureen.** Innocence & Estrangement in the Fiction of Jean Stafford. LC 87-2780. 181p. 1987. pap. 51.60 (*0-7837-8517-8*, 2049326) Bks Demand.
Ryan, Meda C. Biddy Early: The Wise Woman of Clare. 1991. pap. 10.95 (*0-85342-967-7*) Dufour.
— The Day Michael Collins Was Shot. LC 89-82488. 1989. pap. 13.95 (*1-85371-041-5*, Pub. by Poolbeg Pr IE) Dufour.
— Real Chief. 1986. pap. 13.95 (*0-85342-764-X*) Dufour.
Ryan, Michael. Childhood: Living History. (C). 1989. 59.00 (*0-946139-92-X*, Pub. by Elm Pubns UK) St Mut.
— Doctors & the State in the Soviet Union. LC 89-24049. 224p. 1990. text ed. 49.95 (*0-312-04029-6*) St Martin.
— Five Star: Celebrating Twenty-Five Years of History, Legends, & Instruction from the Nation's Premier Basketball Camp. LC 90-3521. 320p. 1990. 19.95 (*0-940279-30-4*) Masters Pr IN.
— Germany Nineteen Nineteen to Nineteen Thirty-nine: Living History. (C). 1988. 59.00 (*0-946139-28-8*, Pub. by Elm Pubns UK) St Mut.
— God Hunger: Poems. 96p. 1990. pap. 9.95 (*0-14-058620-2*, Penguin Bks) Viking Penguin.
— Golden Years - Golden Words. (Illus.). 168p. (Orig.). 1993. pap. 5.95 (*1-56245-027-1*) Great Quotations.
— Golf Forever Work...Whenever. 366p. (Orig.). 1993. spiral bd., pap. 8.95 (*1-56245-047-6*) Great Quotations.
— Great Quotes Great Comedians. 168p. (Orig.). 1993. pap. 5.95 (*1-56245-041-7*) Great Quotations.
— Harvest of Thoughts. 78p. (Orig.). 1993. pap. 7.95 (*1-56245-030-1*) Great Quotations.
— Irish Archaeology Illustrated. rev. ed. (Illus.). 240p. (C). 1995. pap. 21.95 (*1-57098-035-7*) R Rinehart.
— Marxism & Deconstruction: A Critical Articulation. LC 81-48185. 272p. (C). 1982. pap. 13.95x (*0-8018-3248-9*) Johns Hopkins.
— The Philosophy of Marriage, in Its Social, Moral, & Physical Relations. LC 73-20638. (Sex, Marriage & Society Ser.). 400p. 1974. reprint ed. 33.95 (*0-405-05815-2*) Ayer.
— Politics & Culture: Working Hypotheses for a Post-Revolutionary Society. LC 88-31746. (Parallax). 280p. 1989. text ed. 38.50x (*0-8018-3827-4*) Johns Hopkins.
— Propaganda. (C). 1989. 59.00 (*0-946139-13-X*, Pub. by Elm Pubns UK) St Mut.
— Reformers: Living History. (C). 1988. 59.00 (*0-946139-52-0*) St Mut.
— Russian Revolution: Living History. (C). 1988. 59.00 (*1-85450-109-7*, Pub. by Elm Pubns UK) St Mut.
— Secret Life: An Autobiography. 368p. 1995. 25.00 (*0-679-40775-8*) Pantheon.
— Slavery: Living History. (C). 1988. 65.00 (*1-85450-100-3*, Pub. by Elm Pubns UK) St Mut.
— 201 Best Things Ever Said. 168p. (Orig.). 1993. pap. 5.95 (*1-56245-079-4*) Great Quotations.
— Votes for Women: Living History. (C). 1990. 65.00 (*0-946139-91-1*, Pub. by Elm Pubns UK) St Mut.
— Who Really Said. 78p. (Orig.). 1993. pap. 7.95 (*1-56245-032-8*) Great Quotations.
— World War I at Sea: Living History. (C). 1988. 59.00 (*1-85450-107-0*, Pub. by Elm Pubns UK) St Mut.
— World War I in the Trenches: Living History. (C). 1988. 59.00 (*0-685-33846-0*, Pub. by Elm Pubns UK) St Mut.
Ryan, Michael, ed. Apple a Day. 366p. (Orig.). 1993. spiral bd., pap. 8.95 (*1-56245-080-8*) Great Quotations.
— Food for Thought. 168p. (Orig.). 1993. pap. 5.95 (*1-56245-031-X*) Great Quotations.
— Hollywords: Great Quotes from Great Stars. (Illus.). 168p. (Orig.). 1993. pap. 5.95 (*1-56245-026-3*) Great Quotations.
— How to Hypnotize a Chicken: (Plus Thirty Other Ways to Liven up Your Life) A Guide to Creative Living for Regular Folks. 158p. (Orig.). 1991. pap. 9.95 (*0-9631695-1-3*) Whist & Jugg.
— Reflections. 168p. (Orig.). 1993. pap. 5.95 (*1-56245-033-6*) Great Quotations.
Ryan, Michael, tr. & comp. Social Trends in Contemporary Russia: A Statistical Source-Book. LC 93-7913. 1993. text ed. 59.95 (*0-312-10070-1*) St Martin.
Ryan, Michael & Gordon, Avery, eds. Body Politics: Disease, Desire, & the Family. LC 93-7934. (Politics & Culture Ser.: Vol. 1). 280p. 1993. text ed. 63.00 (*0-8133-1840-8*) Westview.
— Body Politics: Disease, Desire, & the Family. LC 93-7934. (Politics & Culture Ser.: Vol. 1). 280p. (C). 1993. pap. text ed. 22.50 (*0-8133-1841-6*) Westview.
Ryan, Michael & Kellner, Douglas M. Camera Politica: The Politics & Ideology of Contemporary Hollywood Film. LC 86-45477. (Illus.). 346p. (Orig.). 1988. 47.95 (*0-253-31334-1*); pap. 14.95 (*0-253-20604-9*, MB-604) Ind U Pr.
Ryan, Michael & Prentice, Richard. Social Trends in the Soviet Union from 1950. LC 86-33919. 120p. 1987. text ed. 45.00 (*0-312-00543-1*) St Martin.
Ryan, Michael & Weatherley, Michael. Move into Work. 138p. (C). 1987. 59.00 (*0-946139-56-3*, Pub. by Elm Pubns UK) St Mut.
Ryan, Michael, jt. ed. see Anderson, Paul.
Ryan, Michael, ed. see Davis, Kathy.
Ryan, Michael, jt. auth. see Enck, John.
Ryan, Michael, tr. see Guattari, Felix & Negri, Toni.
Ryan, Michael, jt. auth. see Weatherley, Michael.
Ryan, Michael D., ed. Human Responses to the Holocaust: Perpetrators, Victims, Bystanders & Resisters. LC 81-38331. (Texts & Studies in Religion: Vol. 9). 278p. 1981. lib. bdg. 89.95 (*0-88946-901-6*) E Mellen.
Ryan, Michael E. Fundamentals of Polymerization & Polymer Processing Technology. (Special Issue of the Journal Chemical Engineering Communications). 144p. 1983. text ed. 100.00 (*0-677-06525-6*) Gordon & Breach.
Ryan, Michael J. Contradiction, Self Contradiction & Collective Choice: New Directions for Commodities & Characteristics Analysis. 311p. 1992. 72.95 (*1-85628-380-1*, Pub. by Avebury Pub UK) Ashgate Pub Co.
***Ryan, Michael P.** Playing by the Rules: American Trade Power & Diplomacy in the Pacific. LC 94-32278. 320p. 1995. 42.50 (*0-87840-579-8*) Georgetown U Pr.
Ryan, Michael P., ed. Magma Transport & Storage. 420p. 1991. text ed. 75.00 (*0-471-92766-X*) Wiley.
— Magmatic Systems. (International Geophysics Ser.: No. 57). (Illus.). 401p. 1994. text ed. 65.00 (*0-12-605070-8*) Acad Pr.
Ryan, Michael W. Executorship & Administration. 171p. 1986. 150.00 (*1-85190-003-9*, Pub. by Fourmat Pub UK) St Mut.
Ryan, Michael W. & Aldridge, Lester. Executorship & Administration. 2nd ed. 269p. 1992. 84.00 (*1-85190-139-6*, Pub. by Tolley Pubng UK) St Mut.
Ryan, Micheal, ed. see Wells, Leon W.
Ryan, Mick & Ward, Tony. Privatization & the Penal System: The American Experience & the Debate in Britain. 130p. 1989. text ed. 45.00 (*0-312-03214-5*) St Martin.
***Ryan, Milded G.** The Complete Encyclopedia of Stitchery. (Illus.). 704p. 1995. pap. 15.95 (*1-55850-474-5*) Adams Pubng.
***Ryan, Mildred G.** The Complete Encyclopedia of Stitchery. 704p. 1991. 11.95 (*1-56865-066-3*, GuildAmerica) Dblday Bk Music.
— Quilting Made Easy. LC 87-6854. (Illus.). 1987. 16.95 (*0-87131-523-8*) M Evans.
Ryan, Milo. View of a Universe: A Love Story of Ann Arbor at Middle Age. (Illus.). 211p. (Orig.). 1985. pap. 9.95 (*1-882574-02-8*) Ann Arbor Hist.
***Ryan, Miriam P.** Riverside. 341p. 1994. 15.95 (*0-9645678-0-6*) Vincent Pub.
***Ryan, Nan.** Because You're Mine. 384p. (Orig.). 1995. mass mkt. 5.50 (*0-451-40595-1*, Topaz) NAL-Dutton.
— Lifetime of Heaven. 1994. mass mkt. 5.99 (*0-440-21075-5*) Dell.
— Love Me Tonight. 384p. (Orig.). 1994. pap. 4.99 (*0-451-40483-1*, Topaz) NAL-Dutton.
— Stardust. 1988. 18.95 (*1-55611-106-1*) D I Fine.
— Stardust. 1990. mass mkt. 4.95 (*0-8217-2860-1*) Zebra.
— Written in the Stars. 1993. mass mkt. 4.99 (*0-440-21072-0*) Dell.
Ryan, Nancy, jt. auth. see Eureka, William E.
Ryan, Nancy E., ed. Taguchi Methods & QFD: Hows & Whys for Management. LC 88-22182. (Illus.). 110p. 1988. 16.50 (*0-941243-04-4*) ASI Pr.
Ryan, Nancy E., ed. see Ealey, Lance A.
Ryan, Nancy E., jt. auth. see Eureka, William E.
Ryan, Nancy H. Kathleen's Surrender. 1983. pap. 3.50 (*0-8217-1139-3*) Zebra.
Ryan, Nancy R. Louisiana's New Garde. (Illus.). 176p. 1994. 25.00 (*0-929714-63-6*); pap. 19.95 (*0-929714-64-4*) Gr Chefs Pub.
Ryan, Nigel, tr. see Simenon, Georges.
Ryan, Nolan. Kings of the Hill: The Irreverent Look at the Men on the Mound. 1993. mass mkt. 5.99 (*0-06-109025-5*, Harp PBks) HarpC.
— Nolan Ryan: The Authorized Pictorial History. (Illus.). 216p. 1992. 39.95 (*0-9626219-7-8*) Summit TX.
Ryan, Nolan & Frommer, Harvey. Throwing Heat. 288p. 1990. mass mkt. 4.95 (*0-380-70826-4*) Avon.
Ryan, Nolan & House, Tom. Nolan Ryan's Pitcher's Bible: The Ultimate Guide to Power, Precision, & Long-Term Performance. (Illus.). 224p. (Orig.). 1991. pap. 12.00 (*0-671-70581-4*, Fireside) S&S Trade.
Ryan, Nolan & Jenkins, Jerry. Miracle Man: Nolan Ryan: The Autobiography. (Illus.). 192p. 1992. 18.99 (*0-8499-0945-7*) Word Inc.
— Miracle Man: Nolan Ryan, the Autobiography. large type ed. LC 92-33582. 333p. 1993. 20.95 (*0-8161-5605-0*); pap. 16.95 (*0-8161-5606-9*) G K Hall.
Ryan, P. Fear Drive My Feet. 1974. reprint ed. pap. 14.95 (*0-522-83727-1*) Intl Spec Bk.
Ryan, P. & Sennett, C., eds. Formal Methods in Systems Engineering: Proceedings of the 2nd Formal Methods Workshop, Held in Drymen, Scotland, 24 - 27 September, 1991. (Illus.). xi, 195p. 1993. pap. 59.00 (*0-387-19751-6*) Spr-Verlag.
Ryan, Paddy. The Snorkellers Guide to the Coral Reef: From the Red Sea to the Pacific Ocean. 1994. pap. 19.95 (*0-8248-1605-6*) UH Pr.
***Ryan, Pam M.** The Flag We Love. LC 95-6619. (Illus.). 32p. (J). 1995. 15.95 (*0-88106-845-4*); lib. bdg. 16.88 (*0-88106-846-2*); pap. 7.95 (*0-88106-844-6*) Charlesbridge Pub.
— One Hundred Is a Family. (Illus.). 32p. (J). (gr. 4 up). 1994. 13.95 (*1-56282-672-7*); lib. bdg. 13.89 (*1-56282-673-5*) Hyprn Child.
Ryan, Pamela B., jt. auth. see Jasinek, Doris.
Ryan, Pat. The America's Cup. (Great Moments in Sports Ser.). (J). (gr. 5 up). 1992. lib. bdg. 14.95 (*0-88682-532-6*) Creative Ed.
— Chicago Bears. (NFL Today Ser.). 48p. (J). (gr. 4 up). 1991. 14.95 (*0-88682-361-7*) Creative Ed.
— Green Bay Packers. (NFL Today Ser.). (J). (gr. 4 up). 1991. lib. bdg. 14.95 (*0-88682-367-6*) Creative Ed.
— The Heavyweight Championship. (Great Moments in Sports Ser.). (J). (gr. 5 up). 1992. lib. bdg. 14.95 (*0-88682-554-7*) Creative Ed.
— Los Angeles Raiders. (NFL Today Ser.). (J). (gr. 4 up). 1991. lib. bdg. 14.95 (*0-88682-371-4*) Creative Ed.
— New York Giants. (NFL Today Ser.). (J). (gr. 4 up). 1991. lib. bdg. 14.95 (*0-88682-377-3*) Creative Ed.
— New York Jets. (NFL Today Ser.). (J). (gr. 4 up). 1991. lib. bdg. 14.95 (*0-88682-378-1*) Creative Ed.
— Pittsburgh Steelers. (NFL Today Ser.). (J). 1991. lib. bdg. 14.95 (*0-88682-380-3*) Creative Ed.
Ryan, Pat & Ryan, Rosemary. Lent Begins at Home. 64p. 1978. pap. 2.95 (*0-89243-101-6*) Liguori Pubns.
Ryan, Patric J. Organized Crime. (Contemporary World Issues Ser.). 225p. 1995. lib. bdg. 39.50 (*0-87436-746-8*) ABC-CLIO.
***Ryan, Patricia.** The Return of the Black Sheep: (Rebels & Rogues) (Temptation Ser.). 1995. pap. 3.25 (*0-373-25640-X*, 1-25640-3) Harlequin Bks.
— Urban Development Law & Policy. cxiii, 473p. 1987. 129.50 (*0-455-20750-X*, Pub. by Law Bk Co); pap. 84.00 (*0-455-20749-6*, Pub. by Law Bk Co) W W Gaunt.
Ryan, Patrick J. Euclidean & Non-Euclidean Geometry: An Analytic Approach. (Illus.). 288p. 1986. pap. 24.95 (*0-521-27635-7*) Cambridge U Pr.
Ryan, Paul. Birth & Death & Cybernation: Cybernetics of the Sacred. 190p. 1973. text ed. 62.00 (*0-677-04320-1*) Gordon & Breach.
— Dublin Wit. 1986. pap. 6.95 (*0-86278-103-5*, Pub. by OBrien Pr IE) Dufour.
— Marlon Brando: A Portrait. (Illus.). 192p. 1994. pap. 12.95 (*0-7867-0095-5*) Carroll & Graf.
— Video Mind, Earth Mind: Art, Communications, & Ecology. LC 92-4840. (Semiotics & the Human Sciences Ser.: Vol. 4). 437p. 1993. 54.95 (*0-8204-1871-4*) P Lang Pubs.
Ryan, Paul, ed. International Comparisons of Vocational Education & Training. 250p. 1991. 95.00 (*1-85000-899-X*, Falmer Pr); pap. 35.00 (*1-85000-900-7*, Falmer Pr) Taylor & Francis.
Ryan, Paul B. The Panama Canal Controversy: U. S. Diplomacy & Defense Interests. LC 77-20643. (Publication Ser.: No. 187). (Illus.). 1977. pap. 6.95 (*0-8179-6872-5*) Hoover Inst Pr.
Ryan, Pauline, jt. auth. see Rabushka, Alvin.
Ryan, Perry T. The Criminal Justice System of Kentucky. (Illus.). 50p. (YA). (gr. 9). 1990. reprint ed. pap. 4.95 (*0-9625504-1-8*) P T Ryan.
— The Last Public Execution in America. LC 92-91052. (Illus.). 272p. (Orig.). 1992. 17.95 (*0-9625504-5-0*); pap. 12.95 (*0-9625504-4-2*) P T Ryan.
— Legal Lynching: The Plight of Sam Jennings. (Illus.). 230p. (Orig.). 1989. 14.95 (*0-9625504-3-4*); pap. 9.95 (*0-9625504-2-6*) P T Ryan.
— The Ryan Family of Breckinridge County, Kentucky. (Illus.). 528p. 1989. reprint ed. 30.00 (*0-9625504-0-X*) P T Ryan.
Ryan, Peter. Black Bonanza. (Illus.). 140p. 1991. pap. 14.95 (*0-947062-80-7*, Pub. by Hyland Hse AT) Intl Spec Bk.
— Explorers & Mapmakers. LC 89-31824. (Time Detective Ser.). (Illus.). 48p. (J). (gr. 4-7). 1990. 14.95 (*0-525-67285-0*, Lodestar Bks) Dutton Child Bks.
— A Very Short Textbook of Surgery. 3rd ed. 173p. 1994. pap. 17.95 (*0-412-61530-4*) Chapman & Hall.
Ryan, Philip B. Noel Purcell: A Biography. (Illus.). 203p. 1993. 35.00 (*1-85371-197-7*, Pub. by Poolbeg Pr IE) Dufour.
Ryan, R., jt. ed. see Shahinpoor, M.
Ryan, R. J., et al. Research Method & Methodology in Finance & Accounting. (Illus.). 208p. 1991. pap. 29.95 (*0-685-47980-3*); pap. text ed. 44.00 (*0-12-605064-3*) Acad Pr.
Ryan, R. Lloyd. The Complete Inservice Staff Development Program: A Step-by-Step Manual for School Administrators. 256p. 1987. text ed. 39.95 (*0-13-161316-2*) P-H.
Ryan, R. M. Keats: The Religious Sense. 1976. 37.50 (*0-691-06316-8*) Princeton U Pr.
Ryan, Ralph. The Microsoft LAN Manager. 1990. 29.95 (*0-685-28478-6*) Microsoft.
Ryan-Ranson, Helen. Imagination, Emblems & Expressions: Essays on Latin American, Caribbean, & Continental Culture & Identify. LC 93-70305. 365p. (C). 1993. 45.95 (*0-87972-580-X*); pap. 16.95 (*0-87972-581-8*) Bowling Green Univ.
Ryan, Ray. Basic Digital Electronics. 2nd ed. (Illus.). 250p. 1990. pap. 16.95 (*0-8306-3370-7*) TAB Bks.
— Basic Digital Electronics: Understanding Number Systems, Boolean Algebra & Logical Circuits. LC 74-14326. (Illus.). 1975. pap. 11.95 (*0-8306-3728-1*, 728P) TAB Bks.
Ryan, Ray & Doyle, Lisa A. Basic Digital Electronics. 2nd ed. 1990. pap. text ed. 17.95 (*0-07-156112-9*) McGraw.
— Digital Electronics. rev. ed. LC 92-34443. (Tech Ser.). Orig. Title: Basic Digital Electronics. 1992. pap. write for info. (*0-02-801306-9*) Glencoe.
Ryan, Raymond W., jt. auth. see Tilton, Richard C.
Ryan, Regina, jt. auth. see LaRouche, Janice.
Ryan, Regina, jt. auth. see Travis, John.
Ryan, Regina S. No Child in My Life. 256p. (Orig.). 1993. pap. 12.95 (*0-913299-93-6*) Stillpoint.
Ryan, Regina S., intro. In Praise of Japanese Love Poetry. 96p. (Orig.). (C). 1994. pap. 10.00 (*0-934252-44-0*) Hohm Pr.
— In Praise of Rumi. 80p. (Orig.). (C). 1989. pap. 8.00 (*0-934252-23-8*) Hohm Pr.
Ryan, Regina S., ed. see Santillo, Humbart.
Ryan, Regina S., jt. auth. see Travis, John W.
Ryan, Richard & Reno, Ronald L. Garden Valley Nevada Seismic Archaeological Survey: BLM Report, No. 47. (Illus.). 27p. 1984. 2.00 (*0-945920-42-3*) Desert Rsch Inst.
Ryan, Richard M., jt. auth. see Deci, Edward L.
Ryan, Richard T. Agatha Christie Trivia. 1990. 4.99 (*0-517-69917-6*) Random Hse Value.
Ryan, Robert M. The Power Personal System Handbook. (Illus.). 600p. 1995. cd-rom 39.95 (*0-12-605075-9*) Acad Pr.
Ryan, Robert S. Pennsylvania Zoning Law & Practice, 2 vols. 1994. ring bd. 135.00 (*0-318-41045-1*) Bisel Co.
***Ryan, Robin.** Sixty Seconds & You're Hired. 1994. pap. 9.95 (*0-614-03316-0*) Impact VA.
Ryan, Rod, ed. American Cinematographer Manual. 7th ed. (Illus.). 619p. 1993. 49.95 (*0-935578-11-0*) ASC Holding.
Ryan, Roland. Fitness Center Manual: Arapahoe Community College. 96p. (C). 1992. pap. text ed. 7.00 (*0-8403-8078-X*) Kendall-Hunt.
Ryan, Rom K. Tumbleweeds & Company. 1984. pap. 1.95 (*0-449-12742-7*) Fawcett.
— Tumbleweeds Country. 1984. pap. 1.95 (*0-449-12609-9*) Fawcett.
Ryan, Rosalie & Wolkerstorfer, John C. More Than a Dream: Eighty-Five Years at the College of St. Catherine. LC 92-72011. 168p. 1992. 24.95 (*0-9633553-0-9*) Coll St Catherine.
Ryan, Rosemary, jt. auth. see Ryan, Pat.
Ryan, Ruth. Final Season: The Inside Story of Nolan Ryan's Legendary Career. 1994. 7.99 (*0-8499-1098-6*) Word Inc.
Ryan, S. Christopher Columbus in Poetry, History & Art. 1976. lib. bdg. 250.00 (*0-8490-1621-5*) Gordon Pr.
Ryan, Sally, ed. Practice Issues in Occupational Therapy: Intraprofessional Team Building. LC 92-50459. (Illus.). 408p. 1993. pap. text ed. 30.00 (*1-55642-179-6*) SLACK Inc.
Ryan, Sally E., ed. The Certified Occupational Therapy Assistant: Principles, Concepts, & Techniques. 2nd ed. LC 92-50395. (Illus.). 304p. (C). 1992. pap. text ed. 30.00 (*1-55642-178-8*, 31788) SLACK Inc.
Ryan, Sandy, jt. auth. see Robinson, Mary.
Ryan, Scott B. Business BASIC -- What Do You Say After It Says: READY: How to Develop & Maintain "Plain Vanilla"-Transportable Business BASIC Application Software. rev. ed. Ryan, Starla J., ed. (C). 1990. pap. 65.00 (*0-9621699-1-9*) Busn Basic Servs.
Ryan, Selwyn D. Race & Nationalism in Trinidad & Tobago: A Study of Decolonization in Multiracial Society. LC 70-185735. 525p. reprint ed. pap. 149.70 (*0-317-55731-9*, 2029348) Bks Demand.
Ryan, Shawn. Brethren. 336p. (Orig.). 1993. mass mkt. 4.99 (*0-671-79243-1*) PB.
— Nocturnas. Tobias, Eric, ed. 448p. (Orig.). 1995. mass mkt. 5.50 (*0-671-88270-8*) PB.
Ryan, Sheila & Hallaj, Muhammad. Palestine Is, but Not in Jordan. (Information Paper Ser.: No. 24). 36p. (Orig.). 1983. pap. text ed. 3.50 (*0-937694-60-6*) Assn Arab-Amer U Grads.
Ryan, Starla J., ed. see Ryan, Scott B.
***Ryan, Stephen.** Ethnic Conflict & International Relations. 2nd ed. 270p. 1995. 57.95 (*1-85521-650-7*, Pub. by Dartmth Pub UK) Ashgate Pub Co.
— Ethnic Conflicts & International Relations. 228p. 1990. text ed. 57.95 (*1-85521-135-1*, Pub. by Dartmth Pub UK) Ashgate Pub Co.
Ryan, Stephen, ed. Retina. 2nd ed. LC 93-40452. 1994. write for info. (*0-8016-8032-8*) Mosby Yr Bk.
Ryan, Stephen J., jt. auth. see Sloan, Louise L.
Ryan, Steve. Challenging Pencil Puzzlers. (Illus.). 96p. (J). (gr. 6-10). 1992. pap. 4.95 (*0-8069-8752-9*) Sterling.
Ryan, Steve, et al. The Encyclopedia of Television Game Shows. (Illus.). 592p. (Orig.). 1987. 39.95 (*0-918432-87-1*) Baseline Bks.
Ryan, Steve. Pencil Puzzlers. (Illus.). 96p. (YA). (gr. 7-12). 1992. pap. 4.95 (*0-8069-8542-9*) Sterling.
— Test Your Math IQ. (Illus.). 96p. 1994. pap. 4.95 (*0-8069-0724-X*) Sterling.
— Test Your Puzzle IQ. (Illus.). 96p. (YA). (gr. 10-12). 1993. pap. 4.95 (*0-8069-0344-9*) Sterling.
— Test Your Word Play IQ. (Illus.). 96p. 1993. pap. 4.95 (*0-8069-0412-7*) Sterling.

R

Ryan, T. & Walker, R. Making Life Story Books. (C). 1989. 39.00 (0-903534-60-6, Pub. by Brit Ag for Adopt & Fost UK) St Mut.

Ryan, T. F. Gunite, a Handbook for Engineers. 1973. pap. 45.00 (0-7210-0820-8, Pub. by C & CA UK) Scholium Intl.

Ryan, T. K. Presenting the Best of Tumbleweeds. LC 93-33860. (Illus.). 144p. (Orig.). 1994. pap. 10.95 (1-56790-128-X) Cool Hand Comms.

***Ryan, Taylor.** Love's Wild Wager: (March Madness) (Historical Ser.). 1995. pap. 4.50 (0-373-28862-X, 1-28862-0) Harlequin Bks.

Ryan, Terence J. The Management of Leg Ulcers. 2nd ed. (Illus.). 110p. 1987. pap. 19.95 (0-19-261663-3) OUP.

Ryan, Terence J. & Cherry, George W., eds. Vascular Birthmarks: Pathogenesis & Management. (Illus.). 250p. 1987. 75.00 (0-19-261628-5) OUP.

Ryan, Thomas. Recollections of an Old Musician. (Music Reprint Ser.). 290p. 1979. reprint ed. lib. bdg. 37.50 (0-306-79521-3) Da Capo.

— The Sacristy Manual. Philippart, David, ed. LC 93-29863. (Illus.). 278p. 1993. 15.00 (0-929650-92-1) Liturgy Tr Pubns.

— Survival Guide for Ecumenically Minded Christians. 168p. (C). 1989. pap. 9.95 (0-8146-1589-9) Liturgical Pr.

Ryan, Thomas A. Intentional Behavior, an Approach to Human Motivation. LC 79-110391. 602p. (C). reprint ed. 171.60 (0-8357-9522-5, 2012362) Bks Demand.

— One More Try, a Story of Entreprenurial Passion. 288p. (Orig.). 1993. pap. write for info. (0-9638573-3-9) T A Ryan.

Ryan, Thomas A., ed. see Gartner Group, Inc. Staff.

Ryan, Thomas E. Hoelderlin's Silence. (Studies in Modern German Literature: Vol. 17). 366p. 1988. 44.00 (0-8204-0551-5) P Lang Pubs.

Ryan, Thomas E. & Monostory, Denes, eds. Word & Deed: German Studies in Honor of Wolfgang F. Michael. LC 91-28432. 296p. (C). 1992. text ed. 69.95 (0-8204-1101-9) P Lang Pubs.

Ryan, Thomas P. Disciplines for Christian Living. LC 92-42596. (Interfaith Perspectives Ser.). 1993. 12.95 (0-8091-3380-6) Paulist Pr.

— Prayer of Heart & Body: Meditation & Yoga As Christian Spiritual Practice. LC 94-32996. (Illus.). 336p. 1995. pap. 12.95 (0-8091-3523-X) Paulist Pr.

— Tales of Christian Unity: The Adventures of An Ecumenical Pilgrim. LC 82-60748. 224p. 1983. pap. 9.95 (0-8091-2502-1) Paulist Pr.

Ryan, Thomas R. Orestes A. Brownson: The Pope's Champion in America. 1984. 49.50 (0-8290-0333-9); pap. 7.95 (0-8290-1608-2) Irvington.

Ryan, Tim. Whole Again Resource Guide. LC 83-641044. 380p. 1986. pap. 24.95 (0-915051-01-X) SourceNet.

Ryan, Tim & Miles, Douglas G. Macintosh Book of Fonts: A Desktop Publishing Handbook for Font Lovers. LC 87-9607. 400p. 1988. pap. 24.95 (0-915051-02-8) SourceNet.

Ryan, Timothy & Mercuro, Nicholas. Law, Economics & Public Policy. LC 84-4406. (Political Economy & Public Policy Ser.: Vol. 3). 73.25 (0-89232-396-5) Jai Pr.

Ryan, Tom K. Hang in There, Tumbleweeds. 1979. pap. 1.25 (0-449-13915-8, GM) Fawcett.

— Tumbleweeds. (Tumbleweed Ser.: No. 5). (Illus.). 1980. pap. 1.50 (0-449-13789-9, GM) Fawcett.

— Tumbleweeds. (Tumbleweed Ser.). (Illus.). 144p. 1981. pap. 1.75 (0-449-13756-2, GM) Fawcett.

— Tumbleweeds Express. 128p. (Orig.). 1981. pap. 1.75 (0-449-14407-0, GM) Fawcett.

Ryan, Una S., ed. Endothelial Cells, Vol. I. 208p. 1988. 168.00 (0-8493-4990-7, QP88) CRC Pr.

— Endothelial Cells, Vol. II. 288p. 1988. 216.00 (0-8493-4991-5, 4991) CRC Pr.

— Endothelial Cells, Vol. III. 288p. 1988. 216.00 (0-8493-4992-3, QP88) CRC Pr.

Ryan, Vernon N. Human Stress & Distress - Psychological & Medical Therapy: Index of New Information with Authors & Subjects. 180p. 1993. 49.50 (1-55914-888-8); pap. 39.50 (1-55914-889-6) ABBE Pubs Assn.

Ryan, Victoria, jt. auth. see Marsh, Arthur.

Ryan, Vincent. Advent Epiphany. 96p. 1989. pap. 30.00 (0-86217-136-9, Pub. by Veritas IE) St Mut.

— Eastertime & Feasts of the Lord. 98p. 1989. pap. 21.00 (0-86217-164-4, Pub. by Veritas IE) St Mut.

— Welcome to Sunday. 96p. 1989. pap. 22.00 (0-86218-000-7, Pub. by Veritas IE) St Mut.

Ryan, Vincent J. Ireland Restored: The New Self-Determination. LC 90-44856. (Illus.). 494p. (C). 1991. lib. bdg. 54.00 (0-932088-60-0); pap. text ed. 29.50 (0-932088-59-7) Freedom Hse.

Ryan, W., tr. see Dedekind, Richard.

Ryan, W. Carson. Studies in Early Graduate Education. LC 73-165729. (American Education Ser, No. 2). 1972. reprint ed. 12.95 (0-405-03718-X) Ayer.

Ryan, W. F., jt. auth. see Norman, Peter.

Ryan, W. Michael. Lieutenant-Colonel Charles A Court Repington: A Study in the Interaction of Personality, the Press & Power. McNeill, William H. & Stansky, Peter, eds. (Modern European History Ser.). 248p. 1987. lib. bdg. 15.00 (0-8240-7830-6) Garland.

Ryan, Will. Grundo Beach Party. Becker, Mary, ed. (Teddy Ruxpin Adventure Ser.). (Illus.). 26p. (J). (ps). 1986. 9.95 (0-934323-35-6); audio (0-318-60971-1) Alchemy Comms.

— Lost in Boggley Woods. Becker, Mary, ed. (Teddy Ruxpin Adventure Ser.). (Illus.). 26p. (J). (ps). 1986. 9.95 (0-934323-38-0); audio (0-318-60973-8) Alchemy Comms.

Ryan, Will C., et al, eds. Secondary Education in the South. LC 70-134132. (Essay Index Reprint Ser.). 1977. reprint ed. 23.95 (0-8369-2519-X) Ayer.

Ryan, Will G. Endocrine Disorders: A Pathophysiologic Approach. 2nd ed. Myers, Jack D. & Rogers, David E., eds. LC 79-22635. (Illus.). 164p. reprint ed. pap. 46.80 (0-685-44470-8, 2033000) Bks Demand.

***Ryan, Will H.** Counterpoint for Death. 192p. (Orig.). 1995. pap. 12.95 (1-56474-137-0) Fithian Pr.

— Nile Nightmare: A Novel of Suspense. 288p. (Orig.). 1993. pap. 12.95 (1-56474-049-8) Fithian Pr.

Ryan, William. Blaming the Victim. 320p. 1976. pap. 7.96 (0-394-72226-4, Vin) Random.

— Dr. Excitement's Elixir of Longevity. LC 86-81475. 1986. 17.95 (0-917657-99-3) D I Fine.

— Equality. 234p. 1981. 6.95 (0-394-42359-3) Pantheon.

— Equality. LC 81-52258. 256p. 1982. pap. 7.96 (0-394-71185-8) Random.

— To Die in Latin. LC 94-10673. 1994. 19.95 (0-89924-089-5); pap. 9.95 (0-89924-088-7) Lynx Hse.

Ryan, William E., jt. auth. see Bivins, Thomas H.

Ryan, William G., tr. see De Voragine, Jacobus.

Ryan, William G., tr. see Devisse, Jean.

Ryan, William J. The Nurse & the Communicatively Impaired Adult. 160p. 1982. pap. 17.95 (0-8261-3961-2) Springer Pub.

Ryan, William J., jt. auth. see Pogorzelski, Henry A.

Ryan, William L., ed. Cold Regions Engineering: Proceedings. 788p. 1986. 66.00 (0-87262-513-3) Am Soc Civil Eng.

Ryan, William L. & Crissman, Randy D., eds. Cold Regions Hydrology & Hydraulics. LC 90-41156. 840p. 1990. pap. text ed. 72.00 (0-87262-773-X) Am Soc Civil Eng.

Ryan, William M. Eating the Heart of the Enemy. LC 83-23868. 105p. 1984. pap. 7.00 (0-89924-041-0) Lynx Hse.

Ryan, William R. Personal Adventures in Upper & Lower California, in 1848-9. LC 72-9466. (Far Western Frontier Ser.). (Illus.). 822p. 1973. reprint ed. 53.95 (0-405-04994-3) Ayer.

Ryan, Yoni, jt. ed. see Zuber-Skerritt, Ortrun.

Ryans, Cynthia C., ed. The Card Catalog: Current Issues. LC 81-720. 336p. 1981. 25.00 (0-8108-1417-X) Scarecrow.

Ryans, Cynthia C. & Shanklin, William L. Strategic Planning, Marketing & Public Relations, & Fund-raising in Higher Education: Perspectives, Reading, & Annotated Bibliography. LC 86-3871. 280p. 1986. 25.00 (0-8108-1891-4) Scarecrow.

Ryans, John K., Jr. & Rau, Pradaeep A. Marketing Strategies for the New Europe: A North American Perspective in 1992. LC 89-18279. 218p. 1990. 29.95 (0-87757-203-8) Am Mktg.

Ryans, John K., Jr., jt. ed. see Paliwoda, Stanley J.

Ryans, John K., Jr., jt. auth. see Shanklin, William L.

Ryans, John K., et al, eds. China, the U. S. S. R., & Eastern Europe: A U. S. Trade Perspective. LC 74-79995. 208p. reprint ed. pap. 59.30 (0-685-16417-9, 2027307) Bks Demand.

Ryant, Carl. Profit's Prophet: Garet Garrett, 1878-1954. LC 88-43110. (Illus.). 128p. 1989. 28.50 (0-945636-04-0) Susquehanna U Pr.

Ryar, William G., tr. see Devisse, Jean & Mollat, Michel.

Ryavec, Karl W., ed. Soviet Society & the Communist Party. LC 78-53179. 240p. (C). 1978. 27.50 (0-87023-258-4) U of Mass Pr.

Ryavec, Karl W., ed. see Vali, Ference A.

Ryazhsky, A. Uchjebnik Tserkovnago Penija. 105p. 1966. reprint ed. pap. 5.00 (0-317-30382-1) Holy Trinity.

Ryba, Ken & Anderson, Bill. Learning with Computers: Effective Teaching Strategies. 104p. 1990. text ed. 20.00 (0-924667-64-8) Intl Society Tech Educ.

Ryba, Ken, jt. auth. see Nolan, Pat.

Ryba, Thomas. The Essence of Phenomenology & Its Meaning for the Scientific Study of Religion. (Toronto Studies in Religion). 369p. (C). 1989. text ed. 47.95 (0-8204-0742-9) P Lang Pubs.

Rybacek, V., ed. Hop Production. (Developments in Crop Science Ser.: No. 16). 430p. 1991. 114.50 (0-444-98770-3) Elsevier.

Rybach, L. & Muffler, L. J., eds. Geothermal Systems: Principles & Case Histories. LC 80-40290. (Illus.). 373p. reprint ed. pap. 106.40 (0-8357-7545-3, 2036267) Bks Demand.

Rybach, L., jt. ed. see Cermak, V.

Ryback, David & Sweitzer, Letitia. Dreams That Come True: Their Psychic & Transforming Powers. 256p. 1990. mass mkt. 4.95 (0-8041-0561-8) Ivy Books.

Ryback, Jeffrey W. Eugene O'Neill: Dancing with the Devil. LC 89-43703. (Orig.). (C). 1991. pap. 6.00 (0-88734-224-8) Players Pr.

Ryback, Stephanie. Just Listen 'n Learn French Plus: For Improving Your French & Communicating More Effectively. 1990. pap. 14.60 (0-8442-1610-0, Passport Bks) NTC Pub Grp.

Ryback, Timothy W. Rock Around the Bloc: A History of Rock Music in Eastern Europe & the Soviet Union, 1954-1988. (Illus.). 304p. 1990. 25.00 (0-19-505633-7) OUP.

Rybacki, Donald J., jt. auth. see Rybacki, Karyn C.

***Rybacki, James J. & Long, James W.** The Essential Guide to Prescription Drugs. (Illus.). 1995. 18.00 (0-06-273378-8, Harper Ref) HarpC.

Rybacki, James J., jt. auth. see Long, James W.

Rybacki, Karyn C. & Rybacki, Donald J. Advocacy & Opposition: An Introduction to Argumentation. 2nd ed. 304p. (C). 1990. pap. text ed. write for info. (0-13-016130-6) P-H.

— Communication Criticism: Approaches & Genres. 381p. (C). 1991. text ed. 34.95 (0-534-14118-8) Intl Thomson.

Rybak, B. Principles of Zoophysiology, Vol. 1. 1968. 252.00 (0-08-012158-6, Pub. by Pergamon Repr UK) Franklin.

Rybak, B., ed. Advanced Technobiology. 712p. 1979. lib. bdg. 120.50 (90-286-0299-2) Kluwer Ac.

— Bio-Informatics & Bio-Process Studies in the Physiology of Communication. (Health Communications & Informatics Biosciences Communications Ser.: Vol. 4, No. 3). (Illus.). 1978. 15.25 (3-8055-2856-6) S Karger.

Rybak, Bob. I Love a Mystery. (Illus.). 176p. (J). (gr. 3-7). 1992. 13.95 (0-86653-655-8, GA1388) Good Apple.

— I Love an Adventure. (Illus.). 176p. (J). (gr. 3-7). 1992. 13.95 (0-86653-656-6, GA1389) Good Apple.

Rybak, Rywka. Rywka Rybak: A Survivor of the Holocaust. LC 93-60965. 88p. (Orig.). 1993. pap. 10.95 (0-9638507-0-9) Prologue Pubns.

Rybak, Sharon. ABC Clip & Copy. 208p. (J). (ps-2). 1991. 14.95 (0-86653-586-1, GA1301) Good Apple.

— Cooperative Learning Throughout the Curriculum. (Illus.). 144p. 1992. 12.95 (0-86653-664-7, GA1396) Good Apple.

— Good Apple Lesson Organizer. 128p. (J). (gr. k-6). 1990. 19.95 (0-86653-563-2, GA1149) Good Apple.

— Launching a Great Year. 144p. (J). (ps-2). 1989. 12.95 (0-86653-507-1, GA1093) Good Apple.

— Teach Smarter, Not Harder. 128p. (J). (gr. k-6). 1991. 11.95 (0-86653-620-5, GA1339) Good Apple.

Rybakin, A., ed. Dictionary of English Personal Names. 222p. (C). 1989. 40.00 (0-685-46806-2, Pub. by Collets) St Mut.

Rybakov, Anatoli. The Arbat Trilogy, Vol. 2: Fear. 1992. 24.95 (0-316-76377-2) Little.

— Children of the Arbat. 1989. mass mkt. 5.99 (0-440-20353-8) Dell.

— Fear. 1993. mass mkt. 6.99 (0-440-21609-5, LE) Dell.

Rybakov, B. A. Novoe V. Arkheologii SSSR I Finlandii. 228p. 1984. 39.00 (0-317-40818-6, Pub. by Collets UK) Pro-Am Music.

Rybakov, Boris V. & Sidorov, V. A. Fast Neutron Spectroscopy. 1,958th suppl. ed. Vlasov, N. A., ed. LC 60-8723. (Soviet Journal of Atomic Energy: Supplement Ser.: No. 6). 131p. pap. 37.40 (0-317-08815-7, 2020649) Bks Demand.

Rybakov, V., ed. see Sesemann, Dimitri.

Rybakowski, K. P. The Homotopy Index Theory on Metric Spaces with Applications to Partial Differential Equations. (Universitext Ser.). (Illus.). ix, 208p. 1987. pap. 48.00 (0-387-18067-2) Spr-Verlag.

Rybalka. Boris Vian. (Bibliotheque des Lettres Modernes Ser.). 256p. (FRE.). 1984. pap. 19.95 (0-7859-1553-2, 2852102048) Fr & Eur.

Rybalka, Maya, tr. see De La Mettrie, Julien O.

Rybalka, Michel & Contat, Michel, eds. Sartre: Bibliography 1980-1992. (Bibliographies of Famous Philosophers Ser.). 247p. 1993. 40.00 (0-912632-96-8) Philos Document.

Rybalka, Michel, ed. see Sartre, Jean-Paul.

Rybar, C. Czechoslovakia Guidebook. (Illus.). 194p. (C). 1988. 50.00 (0-685-31907-5, Pub. by Collets UK) Pro-Am Music.

Rybash, John M., et al. Adult Development & Aging. 2nd ed. 672p. (C). 1991. pap. write for info. (0-697-03312-0) Brown & Benchmark.

— Adult Development & Aging. 3rd ed. 624p. (C). 1994. pap. text ed. write for info. (0-697-10503-2) Brown & Benchmark.

Rybchinskaya, Galina, tr. see Pethukov, B. S. & Polyakov, A. F.

***Rybcynski, Witold.** City Life: Urban Expectations in a New World. 1995. 23.00 (0-684-81302-5) S&S Trade.

Rybczyk, Mark L. San Antonio Uncovered. LC 91-20146. (Illus.). 304p. (Orig.). 1991. pap. 12.95 (1-55622-145-2) Wordware Pub.

***Rybczynski.** Taming the Tiger. 2.99 (0-517-13578-7) Random Hse Value.

Rybczynski, T. M., ed. The Economics of the Oil Crisis. LC 75-34147. 300p. 1976. 35.00 (0-8419-0235-6) Holmes & Meier.

Rybczynski, Witold. Home: A Home History of an Idea. (Illus.). 272p. 1987. pap. 11.95 (0-14-010231-0, Penguin Bks) Viking Penguin.

— Looking Around: A Journey Through Architecture. 320p. 1993. reprint ed. pap. 11.00 (0-14-016889-3, Penguin Bks) Viking Penguin.

— The Most Beautiful House in the World. (Illus.). 240p. 1990. pap. 8.95 (0-14-010566-2, Penguin Bks) Viking Penguin.

— Paper Heroes: Appropriate Technology: Panacea or Pipe Dream? 192p. 1991. reprint ed. pap. 9.95 (0-14-015375-6, Penguin Bks) Viking Penguin.

— A Place for Art: The Architecture of the National Gallery of Canada. (Illus.). 97p. 1992. pap. 25.00 (0-88884-620-7) U Ch Pr.

— Waiting for the Weekend. 288p. 1992. pap. 10.00 (0-14-012663-5, Penguin Bks) Viking Penguin.

Rybczynski, Witold, jt. auth. see Walker, Lester.

Rybczynski, Witold, et al. McGill: A Celebration. (Illus.). 224p. (C). 1991. text ed. 49.95 (0-7735-0795-7, Pub. by McGill CN) U of Toronto Pr.

Ryberg, J., jt. ed. see Choppin, G.

Ryberg, Margareta, jt. ed. see Sundqvist, Christer.

Rybicki, Edmund F. & Benzley, Steven E., eds. Computational Fracture Mechanics: Presented at the Second National Congress on Pressure Vessels & Piping, San Francisco, CA, June 23-27 1975. LC 75-149. 222p. reprint ed. pap. 63.30 (0-317-08124-1, 2016859) Bks Demand.

Rybicki, George B. & Lightman, Alan P. Radiative Processes in Astrophysics. LC 79-15531. 382p. 1985. pap. text ed. 54.95 (0-471-82759-2) Wiley.

Rybickl, Richard. Body Symbolism. 200p. (Orig.). 1985. pap. 5.95 (0-9614341-1-2) Future Dream Pr.

Rybold, John E., ed. The American Vincentians. (Illus.). 560p. (Orig.). 1988. pap. 35.00 (0-911782-61-3) New City.

Rybolt, John E. Wisdom. (Collegeville Bible Commentary - Old Testament Ser.: Vol. 20). 112p. 1986. pap. 3.95 (0-8146-1477-9) Liturgical Pr.

Rybolt, John E., ed. see Abelly, Louis.

Rybolt, John E., jt. ed. see Ryan, Frances.

Rybolt, Richard. No Chairs Make for Short Meetings: And Other Business Maxims from Dad. 128p. 1994. 12.95 (0-525-93873-7); mass mkt. 5.95 (0-452-27194-0, Plume) NAL-Dutton.

Rybolt, Thomas, jt. auth. see Mebane, Robert.

Rybolt, Thomas R. & Mebane, Robert C. Environmental Experiments about Air. LC 92-26297. (Science Experiments for Young People Ser.). (Illus.). 96p. (J). (gr. 4-9). 1993. lib. bdg. 16.95 (0-89490-409-4) Enslow Pubs.

— Environmental Experiments about Land. LC 93-15581. (Science Experiments for Young People Ser.). (Illus.). 96p. (J). (gr. 4-9). 1993. lib. bdg. 16.95 (0-89490-411-6) Enslow Pubs.

— Environmental Experiments about Life. LC 93-15582. (Science Experiments for Young People Ser.). (Illus.). 96p. (J). (gr. 4-9). 1993. lib. bdg. 16.95 (0-89490-412-4) Enslow Pubs.

— Environmental Experiments about Renewable Energy. LC 93-48543. (Science Experiments for Young People Ser.). (Illus.). 96p. (J). (gr. 4-9). 1994. lib. bdg. 16.95 (0-89490-579-1) Enslow Pubs.

— Environmental Experiments about Water. LC 92-41235. (Science Experiments for Young People Ser.). (Illus.). 96p. (J). (gr. 4-9). 1993. lib. bdg. 16.95 (0-89490-410-8) Enslow Pubs.

— Science Experiments for Young People Series, 5 bks., Set. (Illus.). (J). (gr. 4-9). lib. bdg. 84.75 (0-89490-448-5) Enslow Pubs.

Rybolt, Thomas R., jt. auth. see Mebane, Robert C.

Rybolt, William E. Mechanical Design Data Book. 3rd rev. ed. (Illus.). 52p. 1990. pap. write for info. (0-941801-15-2) Rybolt Pubns.

Ryburn, Murray. Contested Adoptions: Research, Law, Policy & Practice. 230p. 1994. pap. 85.00 (1-85742-188-4, Pub. by Arena UK) Ashgate Pub Co.

— Contested Adoptions: Research, Law, Policy & Practice. 232p. 1994. 54.95 (1-85742-187-6, Pub. by Arena UK) Ashgate Pub Co.

— Open Adoption: Research, Theory & Practice. 229p. 1994. 55.95 (1-85628-692-4, Pub. by Avebury Pub UK) Ashgate Pub Co.

Rycaut, Paul. Present State of the Greek & Armenian Churches. LC 75-13321. reprint ed. 32.50 (0-404-05476-5) AMS Pr.

— Present State of the Ottoman Empire. LC 76-135845. (Eastern Europe Collection Ser.). 1971. reprint ed. 17.95 (0-405-02787-7) Ayer.

Ryce-Menuhin, Joel. Jungian Sandplay: The Wonderful Therapy. 160p. 1991. 69.95 (0-415-04775-7, A5532); pap. 17.95 (0-415-04776-5) Routledge.

— The Self in Early Childhood. (Free Association Bks.). 288p. 1988. 55.00 (1-85343-002-1, Pub. by Pinter Pubs UK) St Martin.

Ryce-Menuhin, Joel, ed. Harvest, 1991 Edition: Journal of the C. G. Jung Analytical Psychology Club of London. 209p. Date not set. pap. 24.00 (0-317-05611-5, Pub. by Daimon Verlag SZ) Atrium Pubs.

— Jung & the Monotheisms: Judaism, Christianity, & Islam. LC 93-8077. 1994. write for info. (0-415-07962-4); pap. write for info. (0-415-10414-9) Routledge.

***Ryce, Michael.** Why Is This Happening to Me...Again?! Workbook. 240p. (Orig.). 1995. student ed 19.95 (1-886562-30-X) M Ryce.

Ryce, Victoria. Marketwise. (Illus.). 170p. 1988. pap. 18.95 (0-7737-5143-2, Pub. by Stoddart Pubng CN) Genl Dist Srvs.

Rychener, Michael D., ed. Expert Systems for Engineering Design. 350p. 1988. text ed. 61.00 (0-12-605110-0) Acad Pr.

***Rychetnik, Joe.** Alaska's Sky Follies: The Funny Side of Flying in the Far North. Graydon, Don, ed. (Illus.). 192p. 1995. pap. 13.95 (0-945397-44-5) Epicenter Pr.

***Rychkun, Ed.** 195 Lakes of the Fraser Valley: The Best Recreational Guide on the Market. 1995. pap. 24.95 (0-88839-339-3) Hancock House.

— Trout Fishing: The Tactical Secrets of Lake Fishing. 120p. 1994. pap. 11.95 (0-88839-338-5) Hancock House.

Rychkun, Ed A. Guide to Salmon Fishing. 96p. 1992. pap. 8.95 (0-88839-305-9) Hancock House.

Rychlak, J. F., ed. Dialectics: Humanistic Rationale for Behavior & Development. (Contributions to Human Development Ser.: Vol. 2). 150p. 1976. 39.25 (3-8055-2288-6) S Karger.

Rychlak, Joseph F. Introduction to Personality & Psychotherapy, 2 Vols. 2nd ed. LC 80-68141. (Illus.). 800p. (C). 1981. text ed. 63.16 (0-395-29736-2) HM.

— Logical Learning Theory: A Human Teleology & Its Empirical Support. LC 93-49664. (Illus.). 480p. 1994. text ed. 35.00 (0-8032-3904-1) U of Nebr Pr.

— A Philosophy of Science for Personality Theory. 2nd ed. LC 80-15614. 584p. 1981. 48.50 (0-88275-889-6) Krieger.

— The Psychology of Rigorous Humanism. LC 76-54838. (Illus.). 561p. reprint ed. pap. 159.90 (0-317-07998-0, 2019889) Bks Demand.

Rychlak, Joseph F., jt. auth. see Cameron, Norman.

Rychlak, Joseph R. Human Reason & Artificial Intelligence: A Teleological Inquiry. 1991. text ed. 37.00 (0-231-07290-2) Col U Pr.

***Rychlak, Ronald J.** Real & Demonstrative Evidence: Applications & Theory. 577p. 1995. 95.00 (0-614-05953-4) Michie Butterworth.

Rychner, Jean, ed. see Villon, Francois.

Rychner, Lorenz. The Classic Yamaha DX7. 93p. (C). 1987. pap. 19.95 (0-939067-05-6) Alexander Pub.

R

An Asterisk (*) at the beginning of an entry indicates that the title is appearing in BIP for the first time.

— Korg DW Eight Thousand: Working out with the Workhorse. Alexander, Peter L., ed. (Illus.). 130p. (C). 1987. pap. text ed. 19.95 (*0-939067-25-0*) Alexander Pub.
— Yamaha DX100 Working Musicians Guide. 67p. (C). 1987. pap. 14.95 (*0-939067-38-2*) Alexander Pub.
— Yamaha DX7IIFD, Vol. 1. 152p. (C). 1987. pap. 24.95 (*0-939067-36-6*) Alexander Pub.
— Yamaha TX81Z. Alexander, Peter L., ed. (Illus.). 104p. (C). 1987. pap. text ed. 19.95 (*0-939067-22-6*) Alexander Pub.
Rychner, Lorenz & Frankfurt, Scott. Yamaha DX7 Patch Fake Book. Alexander, Peter L., ed. (Yamaha DX7 Support Ser.). (Illus.). 164p. (C). 1987. pap. text ed. 24.95 (*0-939067-75-7*) Alexander Pub.
Rychner, Lorenz, jt. auth. see Carr, Beau.
Rychner, Lorenz M. Roland Alpha Juno-One: Getting the Most out of Yours. Alexander, Peter L., ed. (Roland Juno Support Ser.). (Illus.). 65p. (C). 1987. pap. text ed. 16.95 (*0-939067-11-0*) Alexander Pub.
— Roland Alpha Juno-Two: Getting the Most out of Yours. Alexander, Peter L., ed. (Roland Juno Support Ser.). (Illus.). 65p. (C). 1987. pap. text ed. 16.95 (*0-939067-43-9*) Alexander Pub.
— Yamaha DX21: Getting the Most out of Yours. Alexander, Peter L., ed. (Yamaha DX Support Ser.). (Illus.). 84p. (C). 1987. pap. text ed. 19.95 (*0-939067-02-1*) Alexander Pub.
— Yamaha TX802. Alexander, Peter L., ed. (Illus.). 110p. (C). 1988. pap. text ed. 19.95 (*0-939067-23-4*) Alexander Pub.
Rychner, Lorenz M. & Mead, Charles. The Korg DSS-One Sampler. Alexander, Peter L., ed. (Illus.). 209p. (C). 1987. pap. text ed. 34.95 (*0-939067-41-2*) Alexander Pub.
Rychnovska, Milena, ed. Structure & Functioning of Seminatural Meadows. LC 92-11732. (Developments in Agricultural & Managed-Forest Ecology Ser.). 1993. 206.25 (*0-444-98669-3*) Elsevier.
Rychtera, M. Atmospheric Deterioration of Technological Materials: A Technoclimatic Atlas, Pt. A-Africa. (Materials Science Monographs: No. 22A). 260p. 1985. 123.00 (*0-444-99774-1*) Elsevier.
— Atmospheric Deterioration of Technological Materials: A Technoclimatic Atlas; Pt. B: Asia (Excluding Soviet Asia), Australia & Oceania. (Materials Science Monographs: No. 22B). 372p. 1990. write for info. (*0-444-98814-9*) Elsevier.
Ryckebusch, Jules, intro. Proceedings Lizzie Borden Conference, Bristol Community College, Fall River, Massachusetts, August 2-6, 1992. LC 93-84156. 400p. 1993. 25.00 (*0-9614811-5-3*) King Philip Pub.
Ryckewaert, A., jt. auth. see De Seze, S.
Ryckman. The Real Princess. (J). 4.25 (*0-8273-4507-0*) Delmar.
Ryckman, Richard. Theories of Personality. 5th ed. LC 92-2646. 560p. (C). 1993. text ed. 49.95 (*0-534-16644-X*) Brooks-Cole.
Ryckman, W. G. & Head, Robert G. Compensating Your Sales Force: How to Use Commissions, Draws, Bonuses & Quotas to Keep Revised. 1993. 27.50 (*1-55738-485-1*) Probus Pub Co.
Rycraft, Carol, jt. auth. see Rycraft, Robin.
Rycraft, Robin & Rycraft, Carol. The Art of Paper Casting: With Rycraft Ceramic Stamps. (Illus.). 32p. 1994. pap. 7.00 (*0-9641345-0-0*) Rycraft.
Rycroft, A. & Jordaan, B. Guide to South African Labour Law. 2nd ed. 384p. 1992. pap. 42.00 (*0-7021-2806-6*, Pub. by Juta SA) W W Gaunt.
Rycroft, Charles. Anxiety & Neurosis. 184p. 1990. reprint ed. pap. 21.95 (*0-946439-52-4*, Pub. by Karnac Bks UK) Brunner-Mazel.
— A Critical Dictionary of Psychoanalysis. 256p. 1995. pap. 13.95 (*0-14-051310-8*, Penguin Bks) Viking Penguin.
— Psychoanalysis & Beyond. 316p. (C). 1986. pap. text ed. 12.50 (*0-226-73289-4*) U Ch Pr.
— Rycroft on Analysis Creativity. 192p. (C). 1992. pap. text ed. 17.50 (*0-8147-7428-8*) NYU Pr.
Rycroft, D. K. & Ngcobo, A. B., eds. The Praises of Dingana. (Killie Campbell Africana Library Publication: No. 3). 1988. 23.00 (*0-86980-629-7*, Pub. by Univ Natal Pr SA) Intl Spec Bk.
Rycroft, D. W., jt. ed. see Smith, K. V.
Rycroft, David W., jt. auth. see Smedema, Lambert K.
Rycroft, M. J. Space Research Vol.20: Proceedings of the Open Meetings of the Working Groups on Physical Sciences of the Twenty-Second Plenary Meeting of the Committee on Space Research, Bangalore, India, 29 May- 9 June 1979. LC 79-41359. (Illus.). 294p. 1980. 70.00 (*0-08-024437-8*, Pergamon Pr) Elsevier.
Rycroft, M. J., jt. ed. see Cook, M. V.
Rycroft, M. J., jt. ed. see Farmer, D. G.
Rycroft, M. J., et al, eds. Upper Atmosphere Models & Research: Proceedings of Workshops X, XI, & of Topical Meeting of the COSPAR Interdisciplinary Scientific Commission C (Meeting C1) of the COSPAR Twenty-Seventh Plenary Meeting Held in Espoo, Finland, 18-29 July, 1988. (Advances in Space Research Ser.: No. 10). (Illus.). 320p. 1989. pap. 95.00 (*0-08-040167-8*, Pergamon Pr) Elsevier.
Rycroft, Michael J., ed. Space Research, Vol. 13. 1977. 115.00 (*0-08-021787-7*, Ed Skills Dallas) Elsevier.
— Space Research, Vol. 14. 1977. 140.00 (*0-08-021788-5*) Elsevier.
— Space Research, Vol. 15. 1977. 115.00 (*0-08-021789-3*) Elsevier.
— Space Research, Vol. 17. 1977. 115.00 (*0-08-021636-6*) Elsevier.
— Space Research, Vol. 18. 1978. 140.00 (*0-08-022021-5*) Elsevier.
— Space Research, Vol. 19. 1979. 145.00 (*0-08-023417-8*, Pergamon Pr) Elsevier.
Rycroft, Michael J., jt. auth. see Shapland, David.
Rycroft, P. V., ed. Corneo-Plastic Surgery. LC 68-58885. 1969. 264.00 (*0-08-013013-5*, Pub. by Pergamon Repr UK) Franklin.
Rycroft, R. J., et al, eds. Textbook of Contact Dermatitis. LC 92-2195. (Illus.). xxiv, 839p. 1992. 243.00 (*0-387-54562-X*) Spr-Verlag.
***Rycroft, Richard J. G., et al, eds.** Textbook of Contact Dermatitis. 2nd enl. rev. ed. LC 94-34409. 900p. 1994. text ed. 165.00 (*0-387-57943-5*) Spr-Verlag.
***Rycroft, Richard J.G., et al.** Textbook of Contact Dermatitis. 2nd enl. rev. ed. LC 94-34409. 1994. write for info. (*3-540-57943-5*) Spr-Verlag.
Rycroft, Robert, jt. auth. see Dietz, Thomas.
Rycroft, Robert W., jt. auth. see Kash, Don E.
Rycroft, Robert W., jt. auth. see Regens, James L.
Rycus, Judith S., jt. auth. see Hughes, Ronald C.
Ryczek, William J. Blackguards & Red Stockings: A History of Baseball's National Association, 1871-1875. LC 91-45274. 284p. 1992. lib. bdg. 35.00 (*0-89950-710-7*) McFarland & Co.
Rydberg, Denny. Building Community in Youth Groups. (Illus.). 179p. (Orig.). 1985. pap. 15.99 (*0-931529-06-9*) Group Pub.
— Creative Bible Studies for Young Adults. 204p. (Orig.). 1990. pap. 12.99 (*0-931529-99-9*) Group Pub.
— How to Survive College. 160p. (Orig.). (YA). 1989. pap. 9.99 (*0-310-35351-3*) Zondervan.
— Youth Group Trust Builders. Parolini, Stephen, ed. LC 92-40663. 137p. 1993. pap. 15.99 (*1-55945-172-6*) Group Pub.
Rydberg, Denny, jt. auth. see Rohrbach, Mike.
Rydberg, Ulf, et al, eds. Alcohol & the Developing Brain: Proceedings of the Third International Berzelius Symposium. (Illus.). 240p. 1985. text ed. 94.00 (*0-88167-127-4*) Raven.
Ryde, Nils. Atoms & Molecules in Electric Fields. (Illus.). 455p. 1976. 96.50x (*0-685-13587-X*) Coronet Bks.
— Development of Ideas in Physics. 196p. 1994. pap. 47.50 (*91-22-01649-X*, Pub. by Almqv & Wiksell SW) Coronet Bks.
Ryde, Peter, ed. Mostly Golf: A Bernard Darwin Anthology. rev. ed. (Illus.). 206p. 1989. 28.00 (*0-940889-12-9*) Classics Golf.
Rydell, C. Peter, jt. auth. see Stevens, Benjamin H.
Rydell, Katy. Wind Says Good Night. (J). (ps). 1994. 14.95 (*0-395-60474-5*) HM.
Rydell, Mirelle G., jt. tr. see Williams, Harry F.
Rydell, Richard L., jt. auth. see Bria, William R., II.
Rydell, Robert, et al. In the People's Interest: A Centennial History of Montana State University. (Illus.). 344p. 1992. 40.00 (*0-9635114-0-8*) Montana St U.
Rydell, Robert W. All the World's a Fair: Visions of Empire at American International Expositions, 1876-1916. LC 84-2674. (Illus.). x, 334p. (C). 1987. pap. text ed. 15.95 (*0-226-73240-1*) U Ch Pr.
— American Mass Culture, 1860-1920. Franklin, John H. & Eisenstadt, A. S., eds. (American History Ser.). 175p. (C). 1996. pap. text ed. 11.95 (*0-88295-930-1*) Harlan Davidson.
— World of Fairs: The Century-of-Progress Expositions. LC 92-45690. (Illus.). 272p. 1993. lib. bdg. 49.95 (*0-226-73236-3*); pap. 16.95 (*0-226-73237-1*) U Ch Pr.
***Rydell, Robert W. & Gwinn, Nancy E., eds.** Fair Representations: World's Fairs & the Modern World. (European Contributions to American Studies: Vol. 27). 253p. 1995. pap. 32.50 (*90-5383-282-3*, Pub. by VU Univ Pr NE) Paul & Co Pubs.
Rydell, Sierra. Homeward Bound. 1994. mass mkt. 3.50 (*0-373-09900-2*, 1-09900-1) Harlequin Bks.
Rydell, Wendy. All about Islands. LC 83-4833. (Question & Answer Bks.). (Illus.). 32p. (J). (gr. 3-6). 1984. lib. bdg. 10.59 (*0-89375-975-9*); pap. text ed. 2.95 (*0-89375-976-7*) Troll Assocs.
— Discovering Fossils. LC 83-4832. (Question & Answer Bk.). (Illus.). 32p. (J). (gr. 3-6). 1984. lib. bdg. 10.59 (*0-89375-973-2*); pap. text ed. 2.95 (*0-89375-974-0*) Troll Assocs.
— Instant Sewing Handbook. LC 72-89526. (Illus.). 320p. 1984. 6.95 (*0-911744-12-6*) Career Pub IL.
Ryden, George H. Letters to & from Caesar Rodney. LC 75-107417. (Era of the American Revolution Ser.). 1970. reprint ed. lib. bdg. 55.00 (*0-306-71881-2*) Da Capo.
Ryden, Hope. America's Bald Eagle. (Illus.). 64p. (J). 1992. pap. 9.95 (*1-55821-141-1*) Lyons & Burford.
— America's Last Wild Horses. rev. ed. 1990. pap. 14.95 (*1-55821-081-4*) Lyons & Burford.
— Backyard Rescue. LC 93-11683. (Illus.). (J). 1994. write for info. (*0-688-12880-7*, Tambourine Bks) Morrow.
— The Beaver. (Illus.). 64p. (J). 1992. pap. 9.95 (*1-55821-142-X*) Lyons & Burford.
— The Bobcat. (Illus.). 64p. (J). 1992. pap. 9.95 (*1-55821-143-8*) Lyons & Burford.
— Bobcat Year. (Illus.). 240p. 1990. reprint ed. pap. 14.95 (*1-55821-055-5*) Lyons & Burford.
— God's Dog: The North American Coyote. (Illus.). 320p. 1989. reprint ed. pap. 14.95 (*1-55821-046-6*) Lyons & Burford.
— Joey: The Story of a Baby Kangaroo. LC 93-15419. (Illus.). 40p. (J). 1994. 15.00 (*0-688-12744-4*, Tambourine Bks); lib. bdg. 14.93 (*0-688-12745-2*, Tambourine Bks) Morrow.
— The Little Deer of the Florida Keys. rev. ed. (Illus.). 64p. (Orig.). (J). (gr. 5 up). 1986. reprint ed. 13.95 (*0-912451-13-0*); reprint ed. pap. 8.95 (*0-912451-14-9*) Florida Classics.
— Out of the World. LC 94-20763. (Illus.). (J). 1995. 15.99 (*0-525-67485-3*, Lodestar Bks) Dutton Child Bks.
Ryden, Hope, photos & text. The Raggedy Red Squirrel. (Illus.). 48p. (J). (gr. k-3). 1992. 16.00 (*0-525-67400-4*, Lodestar Bks) Dutton Child Bks.
— Your Cat's Wild Cousins. (Illus.). 48p. (J). (gr. 2-5). 1992. 16.00 (*0-525-67354-7*, Lodestar Bks) Dutton Child Bks.
Ryden, Hope, photos. Your Dog's Wild Cousins. LC 93-26855. (Illus.). 48p. (J). (gr. 2-5). 1994. 16.99 (*0-525-67482-9*, Lodestar Bks) Dutton Child Bks.
Ryden, Kent C. Mapping the Invisible Landscape: Folklore, Writing, & the Sense of Place. LC 92-46529. (American Land & Life Ser.). (Illus.). 362p. 1993. 39.95 (*0-87745-406-X*); pap. 17.95 (*0-87745-414-0*) U of Iowa Pr.
Ryden, Lars G., jt. ed. see Janson, Jan-Christer.
***Ryden, Lennart & Rosenqvist, Jan O., eds.** Aspects of Late Antiquity & Early Byzantium. (Illus.). 173p. (Orig.). 1993. pap. 48.50x (*91-86884-05-0*, Pub. by Almqv & Wiksell SW) Coronet Bks.
Ryden, Michael. Dyslexia: How Would I Cope? 2nd ed. 64p. 1992. pap. 13.95 (*1-85302-154-7*, Pub. by J Kingsley Pubs UK) Taylor & Francis.
***Ryden, Ruth.** The Golden Path. 199p. (Orig.). 1993. pap. 11.95 (*0-929385-43-8*) Light Tech Comns Servs.
— Living the Golden Path. 186p. (Orig.). 1994. pap. 11.95 (*0-929385-65-9*) Light Tech Comns Servs.
Ryden, Tom K., ed. Managing Urban Transportation with Limited Resources. 108p. 1983. pap. 18.00 (*0-87262-363-7*) Am Soc Civil Eng.
Ryden, Vassula. True Life in God, Vol. 1. 216p. (Orig.). 1991. pap. write for info. (*0-9631193-3-8*) Trinitas.
Ryden, Wendy A. & Horowitz, Emily. Spirits - Legacies: One Story Each. (Orig.). 1989. pap. 3.75 (*0-9621918-0-9*) Red Wine Pr.
Ryder, A. J. Twentieth-Century Germany. LC 72-3650. 300p. 1976. pap. text ed. 26.50 (*0-231-08350-5*) Col U Pr.
Ryder, Andrew. Prayer: The Eastern Tradition. 88p. (Orig.). 1983. pap. 4.95 (*0-914544-47-0*) Living Flame Pr.
Ryder, Arthur W., tr. see Dandin.
***Ryder, Betty.** Beatrice & Some Back Burner Recipes. LC 93-95022. (Illus.). 112p. (Orig.). 1994. pap. 8.00 (*1-56002-406-2*, Univ Edtns) Aegina Pr.
Ryder, Beverly A. Joy of Wellness Cookbook. (Illus.). 280p. 1984. pap. 9.95 (*0-9614390-0-9*) B Ryder.
Ryder, Brent G., jt. auth. see Alpha Institute Staff.
Ryder, Daniel. Breaking the Circle of Satanic Ritual Abuse: Recognizing & Recovering from the Hidden Trauma. Noland, Jane T., ed. 288p. (Orig.). 1992. pap. text ed. 15.95 (*0-89638-258-3*) Hazelden.
Ryder, Donald G. The Inside Story: Living & Learning Through Life's Storms. LC 85-27780. (Illus.). 56p. (YA). (gr. 7 up). 1985. 14.95 (*0-935973-38-9*) Ryder Pub Co.
Ryder, Edward F. The Art of Entering Sweepstakes & Winning Consistently. (Orig.). 1979. pap. 6.95 (*0-934650-00-4*) Sunnyside.
Ryder, Edward F., see Ingalls, Harold, pseud..
Ryder, Edward F., see M. A. Nash, pseud..
Ryder, Edward J. Leafy Salad Vegetables. (Illus.). 1979. text ed. 49.95 (*0-87055-323-2*) AVI.
Ryder, Frank, ed. see Eichendorff & Brentano.
Ryder, Frank, ed. see Goethe, Johann Wolfgang Von.
Ryder, Frank, tr. see Goethe, Johann Wolfgang Von.
Ryder, Frank, jt. ed. see Hamlin, Cyrus.
Ryder, Frank, ed. see Keller, Gottfried.
Ryder, Frank, ed. see Von Goethe, Johann W.
Ryder, Frank G., tr. Song of the Nibelungs: A Verse Translation from the Middle High German Nibelungenlied. LC 62-17432. 435p. 1962. pap. text ed. 16.95 (*0-8143-1192-X*, WB15) Wayne St U Pr.
Ryder, Frank G. & Browning, Robert, eds. German Literary Fairy Tales. LC 82-12550. (German Library: Vol. 30). 320p. 1982. 29.50 (*0-8264-0276-3*); pap. text ed. 14.95 (*0-8264-0277-1*) Continuum.
Ryder, Frank G. & McCormick, E. Allen. Lebendige Literatur, 3 Vols. LC 85-81205. 448p. (C). 1985. pap. 30.76 (*0-395-35959-7*) HM.
Ryder, Frank G., ed. see Von Kleist, Heinrich & Paul, Jean.
Ryder, G. H. & Bennett, M. D. Mechanics of Machines. 2nd ed. (Illus.). 350p. 1990. 42.95 (*0-8311-3030-X*) Indus Pr.
Ryder, George & Allen, Charles. Guitar Chord Progression Made Easy. (Illus.). 1974. pap. 4.95 (*0-934286-25-6*) Kenyon.
Ryder, Graham, ed. Proceedings of the Twentieth Lunar & Planetary Science Conference. LC 87-643480. (Illus.). 533p. 1990. 50.00 (*0-942862-04-X*) Lunar & Planet Inst.
Ryder, Graham & Sharpton, Virgil L., eds. Proceedings of Lunar & Planetary Science, Vol. 21. (Illus.). 738p. 1991. 50.00 (*0-942862-05-8*) Lunar & Planet Inst.
— Proceedings of Lunar & Planetary Science, Vol. 22. (Illus.). 481p. (C). 1992. 50.00 (*0-685-51793-4*) Lunar & Planet Inst.
Ryder, Hillyer. Colonial Coins of Vermont. Bd. with Vermont Coinage. (Illus.). (Illus.). 1982. Set pap. 10.00 (*0-915262-65-7*) S J Durst.
— Copper Coins of Massachusetts. (Illus.). 1981. reprint ed. pap. 6.00 (*0-915262-66-5*) S J Durst.
Ryder, J. D. & Fink, D. G. Engineers & Electrons: A Century of Electrical Progress. LC 83-22681. 272p. 1984. 29.95 (*0-87942-172-X*, PC01669) Inst Electrical.
Ryder, James F. Voightlander & I. LC 72-9235. (Literature of Photography Ser.). 1973. reprint ed. 23.95 (*0-405-04940-4*) Ayer.
Ryder, Joan. The Snail's Spell. (Illus.). (J). (gr. 3-8). 1988. pap. 4.99 (*0-14-050891-0*, Puffin) Puffin Bks.
Ryder, Joanne. The Bear on the Moon. LC 89-13133. (Illus.). 32p. (J). (gr. 1 up). 1991. 16.00 (*0-688-08109-6*); lib. bdg. 15.93 (*0-688-08110-X*) Morrow Jr Bks.
— Bear Out There. (Illus.). (J). (gr. 2-3). 1995. 15.00 (*0-689-31780-8*, Atheneum Bks Young) S&S Childrens.
— Catching the Wind. LC 88-23446. (Just for a Day Book Ser.). (Illus.). 32p. (J). (gr. k up). 1989. 13.95 (*0-688-07170-8*); lib. bdg. 13.88 (*0-688-07171-6*) Morrow Jr Bks.
— Chipmunk Song. LC 86-19786. (Illus.). 32p. (J). (ps-3). 1987. 14.99 (*0-525-67191-9*, Lodestar Bks); pap. 4.95 (*0-525-67312-1*, Lodestar Bks) Dutton Child Bks.
— Dancers in the Garden. LC 89-10555. (Illus.). 32p. (J). (gr. k-4). 1992. 15.95 (*0-87156-578-1*) Sierra.
— Dancers in the Garden. (Illus.). 32p. (J). (gr. k-4). 1994. pap. 5.95 (*0-87156-410-6*) Sierra.
— Earthdance. (J). 1996. 15.95 (*0-8050-2678-9*) H Holt & Co.
— First Grade Elves. LC 93-25543. (First Grade Is the Best! Ser.). (Illus.). 32p. (J). (ps-2). 1993. lib. bdg. 9.79 (*0-8167-3010-5*); pap. text ed. 2.95 (*0-8167-3011-3*) Troll Assocs.
— First Grade Ladybugs. LC 92-43528. (First Grade Is the Best! Ser.). (Illus.). 32p. (J). (ps-2). 1993. lib. bdg. 9.79 (*0-8167-3006-7*); pap. text ed. 2.95 (*0-8167-3007-5*) Troll Assocs.
— The Goodbye Walk. LC 92-10325. (Illus.). 32p. (J). (gr. k-3). 1993. 13.99 (*0-525-67405-5*, Lodestar Bks) Dutton Child Bks.
— Hello, First Grade. LC 93-9041. (First Grade Is the Best! Ser.). (Illus.). 32p. (J). (ps-2). 1993. lib. bdg. 9.79 (*0-8167-3008-3*); pap. text ed. 2.95 (*0-8167-3009-1*) Troll Assocs.
— Hello, Tree! (Illus.). 32p. (J). (gr. k-3). 1991. 14.99 (*0-525-67310-5*, Lodestar Bks) Dutton Child Bks.
— A House by the Sea. LC 93-22149. (Illus.). 32p. (J). (ps up). 1994. 15.00 (*0-688-12675-8*); lib. bdg. 14.93 (*0-688-12676-6*) Morrow Jr Bks.
— Lizard in the Sun. LC 89-33886. (Just for a Day Book Ser.). (Illus.). 32p. (J). (gr. k up). 1990. 13.95 (*0-688-07172-4*); lib. bdg. 13.88 (*0-688-07173-2*); pap. 4.95 (*0-688-13081-X*, Mulberry) Morrow Jr Bks.
— Mockingbird Morning. LC 88-21305. (Illus.). 32p. (J). (gr. k-3). 1989. text ed. 14.95 (*0-02-777961-0*, Four Winds Pr) S&S Childrens.
— My Father's Hands. LC 93-27116. (Illus.). 32p. (J). (ps up). 1994. 15.00 (*0-688-09189-X*) Morrow Jr Bks.
— My Father's Hands. LC 93-27116. (Illus.). 32p. (YA). (ps up). 1994. lib. bdg. 14.93 (*0-688-09190-3*) Morrow Jr Bks.
— Night Gliders. LC 95-8071. (Illus.). 32p. (J). (gr. k-3). 1996. lib. bdg. 13.95 (*0-8167-3820-3*) Troll Assocs.
— One Small Fish. LC 92-21563. (Illus.). 32p. (J). (gr. k up). 1993. 15.00 (*0-688-07059-0*); lib. bdg. 14.93 (*0-688-07060-4*) Morrow Jr Bks.
— Osos Por Aji. Dorros, Sandra M., tr. (Illus.). (SPA.). (J). (ps-3). 1995. 15.00 (*0-689-31982-7*, Atheneum Bks Young) S&S Childrens.
— The Snail's Spell. (Illus.). 32p. (J). (ps-3). 1992. lib. bdg. 14.00 (*0-670-84385-7*) Viking Child Bks.
— Step into the Night. LC 87-37982. (Illus.). 32p. (J). (gr. k-3). 1988. text ed. 14.95 (*0-02-777951-3*, Four Winds Pr) S&S Childrens.
— Under Your Feet. LC 89-33897. (Illus.). 32p. (J). (gr. k-3). 1990. lib. bdg. 14.95 (*0-02-777955-6*, Four Winds Pr) S&S Childrens.
— Walt Disney's Bambi's Forest: A Year in the Life of the Forest. LC 93-72551. (Illus.). 32p. (J). (ps-3). 1994. 11.95 (*1-56282-643-3*); lib. bdg. 11.89 (*1-56282-698-0*) Disney Pr.
— When the Woods Hum. LC 90-37879. (Illus.). 32p. (J). (gr. 1 up). 1991. 13.95 (*0-688-07057-4*); lib. bdg. 13.88 (*0-688-07058-2*) Morrow Jr Bks.
— Where Butterflies Grow. LC 88-37989. (Illus.). 32p. (J). (ps-3). 1989. 14.99 (*0-525-67284-2*, Lodestar Bks) Dutton Child Bks.
— White Bear, Ice Bear. LC 87-36781. (Just for a Day Book Ser.). (Illus.). 32p. (J). (gr. k-3). 1989. 15.00 (*0-688-07174-0*); lib. bdg. 14.93 (*0-688-07175-9*) Morrow Jr Bks.
— White Bear, Ice Bear. Cohn, Amy, ed. LC 87-36781. (Illus.). 32p. (J). (gr. k-3). 1989. reprint ed. pap. 4.95 (*0-688-13111-5*) Morrow Jr Bks.
— Winter Whale. LC 90-19174. (Just for a Day Book Ser.). (Illus.). 32p. (J). (gr. k up). 1991. 13.95 (*0-688-07176-7*); lib. bdg. 13.88 (*0-688-07177-5*) Morrow Jr Bks.
— Winter Whale. Cohn, Amy, ed. LC 90-19174. (Illus.). 32p. (J). (gr. k up). 1991. reprint ed. pap. 4.95 (*0-688-13110-7*) Morrow Jr Bks.
— Without Words. (Illus.). 32p. (J). 1995. 15.95 (*0-87156-580-3*) Sierra.
Ryder, Joanne, adapt. Walt Disney's Bambi. LC 92-54875. (Junior Novel Ser.). (Illus.). 64p. (J). (gr. 2-6). 1993. pap. 3.50 (*1-56282-444-9*) Disney Pr.
Ryder, Joanne, ed. Sea Elf. LC 92-27608. (Just for a Day Book Ser.). (Illus.). 32p. (J). (gr. k up). 1993. 15.00 (*0-688-10060-0*); lib. bdg. 14.93 (*0-688-10061-9*) Morrow Jr Bks.
***Ryder, Joanne & Rothman, Michael.** Jaguar in the Rain Forest. LC 94-16646. (Just for a Day Bks.). (Illus.). (J). 1996. write for info. (*0-688-12990-0*); lib. bdg. write for info. (*0-688-12991-9*) Morrow Jr Bks.
Ryder, John. The Case for Legibility. (Illus.). 1979. 8.50 (*0-89679-002-9*) Moretus Pr.
— Printing for Pleasure. 144p. 1976. reprint ed. 20.00 (*0-370-10443-9*, Pub. by Priv Lib Assn UK) Oak Knoll.
Ryder, John, ed. American Philosophic Naturalism in the Twentieth Century. 566p. (C). 1994. 34.95x (*0-87975-894-5*) Prometheus Bks.
Ryder, John D. Electronic Fundamentals & Applications: Integrated & Discrete Systems. 5th ed. (Illus.). 640p. (C). 1976. text ed. 67.00 (*0-13-251371-4*) P-H.
Ryder, Judith & Campbell, Lesley. Balancing Acts in Personal, Social & Health Education: A Practical Guide for Teachers' 320p. (C). 1988. lib. bdg. 55.00 (*0-415-00537-X*, A2468) Routledge.

R

*Ryder, Judy. Turning Your Great Idea into a Great Success: Business Whiz Judy Ryder Tells How to Develop, License, Protect, & Promote Your Product Idea. LC 94-45493. 256p. (Orig.). 1995. pap. 14.95 (1-56079-462-3, Petersons Pacesetter) Petersons Guides.

Ryder, Kenneth G. & Wilson, James W. Cooperative Education in a New Era: Understanding & Strengthening the Links Between College & the Workplace. LC 87-45500. (Higher Education Ser.). 363p. 1987. 46.95x (1-55542-072-9) Jossey-Bass.

Ryder, Kenneth W., jt. auth. see Glick, Melvin R.

Ryder, Laura. Exchanging Gifts. LC 90-306. (Illus.). 112p. (Orig.). 1990. pap. 12.50 (0-941749-09-6) Black Tie Pr.
— Exchanging Gifts. deluxe ed. LC 90-306. (Illus.). 112p. (Orig.). 1990. pap. 15.00 (0-941749-10-X) Black Tie Pr.
— You Can't Hide on Leather Seats. limited ed. (Codex Booklet Ser.). (Illus.). 12p. 1993. 10.00 (1-884185-02-9) O Zone.

Ryder, Lewis H. Elementary Particles & Symmetries. rev. ed. 300p. 1975. text ed. 121.00 (0-677-05130-1) Gordon & Breach.
— Quantum Field Theory. (Illus.). 350p. 1986. pap. 34.95 (0-521-33859-X) Cambridge U Pr.

Ryder, M. L. The Production & Properties of Wool & Other Animal Fibres. 63p. 1975. 70.00 (0-686-63788-7) St Mut.
— Production & Properties of Wool & Other Animal Fibres, Vol. 7, No. 3. 63p. (C). 1975. pap. text ed. 70.00 (0-685-36074-1, Pub. by Textile Institue UK) St Mut.

Ryder, Marion C. Scuttle Watch. LC 79-91988. (Illus.). 286p. (J). (gr. 4-12). 1979. reprint ed. pap. 4.95 (0-88492-034-8) W S Sullwold.

Ryder, Mary E. Ordered Chaos: The Interpretation of English Noun-Noun Compounds. LC 94-9527. 1994. 47.00 (0-520-09777-7) U CA Pr.

Ryder, Mary R. Willa Cather & Classical Myth: The Search for a New Parnassus. LC 90-34815. (Studies in American Literature: Vol. 11). 312p. 1990. lib. bdg. 99.95 (0-88946-113-9) E Mellen.

Ryder, Norman B. The Cohort Approach: Essays in the Measurement of Temporal Variations in Demographic Behavior. Zuckerman, Harriet & Merton, Robert K., eds. LC 79-9023. (Dissertations on Sociology Ser.). 1980. lib. bdg. 21.95 (0-405-12991-2) Ayer.

Ryder, Norman B. & Westoff, Charles. Reproduction in the United States, 1965. LC 78-120760. 423p. reprint ed. pap. 120.60 (0-7837-0244-2, 2040553) Bks Demand.

Ryder, Norman B. & Westoff, Charles F. Reproduction in the United States: 1965. LC 78-120760. (Office of Population Research Ser.). 1971. 65.00x (0-691-09318-0) Princeton U Pr.

Ryder, Norman B., jt. auth. see Westoff, Charles F.

Ryder, Nova, jt. auth. see Melia, Trevor.

Ryder, O. A. & Byrd, M. L., eds. One Medicine: A Tribute to Kurt Benirschke. (Illus.). xiv, 373p. 1984. 79.00 (0-387-13275-9) Spr-Verlag.

*Ryder, R. A. & Edwards, C. J., eds. A Conceptual Approach for the Application of Biological Indicators of Ecosystem Quality in the Great Lakes Basin: A Joint Effort of the International Joint Commission & the Great Lakes Fishery Commission, Report to the Great Lakes Science Advisory Board. fac. ed. LC 92-123616. (Illus.). 199p. 1985. pap. 56.80 (0-7837-8626-3, 2075238) Bks Demand.

Ryder, Randall J., et al. Easy Reading: Book Series & Periodicals for Less Able Readers. LC 89-7642. (Reading Aids Ser.). (Illus.). 96p. reprint ed. pap. 27.40 (0-7837-4586-9, 2044305) Bks Demand.

Ryder, Randy & Graves, Michael. Reading & Learning in the Content Areas. 416p. (C). 1994. pap. write for info. (0-02-404945-X, Merrill Pub Co) Macmillan.

Ryder, Rick. Dyed for Death. 240p. 1984. pap. 2.50 (0-8439-2119-6) Dorchester Pub Co.

Ryder, Robert T., et al. Seismic Models of Sandstone Stratigraphic Traps in Rocky Mountain Basins. LC 81-52315. (Methods in Exploration Ser.). 124p. reprint ed. pap. 35.40 (0-7837-3972-9, 2043801) Bks Demand.

Ryder, Stuart A. The D-Stem in Western Semitic. (Janua Linguarum, Ser. Practica: No. 131). 173p. 1974. pap. text ed. 93.10 (90-279-2669-7) Mouton.

*Ryder, Thomas. Coson Carriage Collection at Beechdale. Morrow, Rodger, ed. (Illus.). 175p. (Orig.). Date not set. boxed, pap. 25.00 (1-880499-03-7) S Green PA.

Ryder, Tom. The High Stepper. 176p. 1990. 60.00 (0-85131-308-6, Pub. by J A Allen & Co UK) St Mut.

Ryder, Tracie R. How Can It Look So Good & Feel So Bad. 1990. student ed 9.95 (0-317-91191-0); audio 9.95 (0-317-91192-9); vhs 39.95 (0-317-91193-7); disk 49.95 (0-317-91194-5) Lincoln Global Prodns.
— How Can It Look So Good & Feel So Bad? Your Guide to Inner Peace. MacStravic, Sue, ed. LC 88-28093. (Illus.). 232p. 1989. pap. text ed. 14.95 (0-929656-18-0) Lincoln Global Prodns.

*Ryder, Verdene. Parents & Their Children. annot. ed. 1995. teacher ed 42.40 (1-56637-093-0) Goodheart.

*Ryder, Verdene & Harter, Majorie B. Contemporary Living. rev. ed. (Illus.). 416p. 1995. 41.28 (1-56637-099-X) Goodheart.

Ryder, Virginia P. Travels of an Olive Eater from Pit to Pit Plus How to Cure an Olive. (Illus.). 57p. (Orig.). 1991. pap. 15.95 (0-935098-03-8) Amigo Pr.

Ryder, Willet. The Art Experience, Grades 4-6. 1991. pap. 12.95 (0-673-46353-2) GdYrBks.
— Celebrating Diversity with Art: Thematic Projects for Every Month of the Year. 128p. (Orig.). 1995. pap. 8.95 (0-673-36170-5) GdYrBks.

Rydesky, Mary & DeVaughn, Tanya, eds. Patient Education Sourcebook. 547p. 1986. 50.00 (0-318-20441-X) Health Sci Comm.

Rydholm, C. Fred. Superior Heartland: A Backwoods History, 2 vols., Set. 1600p. 1989. write for info. (0-9639948-2-4) Superior Hrtland.
— Superior Heartland: A Backwoods History, Vol. I. 850p. 1989. write for info. (0-9639948-0-8) Superior Hrtland.
— Superior Heartland: A Backwoods History, Vol. II. 750p. 1989. write for info. (0-9639948-1-6) Superior Hrtland.

Rydholm, C. Fred, jt. auth. see Burrows, Russell.

Rydholm, Fred, jt. auth. see Burrows, Russell.

Rydholm, Sven A. Pulping Processes. LC 85-4324. 1280p. 1985. reprint ed. lib. bdg. 149.50 (0-89874-856-9) Krieger.

Rydill, Louis, jt. auth. see Burcher, Roy.

Rydin, Yvonne. Residential Development & the Planning System: A Study of the Housing Land System at the Local Level. (Illus.). 70p. 1985. pap. 22.00 (0-08-032742-7, Pub. by PPL UK) Elsevier.

Ryding, Erik S. In Harmony Framed: Musical Humanism, Thomas Campion, & the Two Daniels. LC 92-21689. (Sixteenth Century Essays & Studies: Vol. 21). 228p. 1992. text ed. 45.00 (0-940474-22-0) Sixteenth Cent.

Ryding, J., jt. auth. see Patterson, K. D.

Ryding, K. C., jt. auth. see Nydell, M. K.

Ryding, Karin. Formal Spoken Arabic: Basic Course. LC 90-2823. 434p. (Orig.). (C). 1990. pap. 17.95 (0-87840-279-9) Georgetown U Pr.
— Formal Spoken Arabic: Basic Course, Set. LC 90-2823. 434p. (Orig.). (C). 1990. audio 95.00 (0-87840-283-7) Georgetown U Pr.

Ryding, Karin C. & Zaiback, Abdelnour. Formal Spoken Arabic FAST Course. 158p. (Orig.). (ARA & ENG.). (C). 1993. pap. text ed. 19.95 (0-87840-284-5); audio 95.00 (0-87840-285-3) Georgetown U Pr.

Ryding, S. & Rast, W. The Control of Eutrophication of Lakes & Reservoirs. (Man & the Biosphere Ser.: 1). 314p. 1989. 67.00 (92-3-102550-3, U5503) UNIPUB.

*Ryding, Sven-Olof. Environmental Management Handbook. 750p. 1994. pap. 59.95 (1-56670-123-6, IOL123) Lewis Pubs.

Ryding, William W. Structure in Medieval Narrative. LC 72-154531. (De Proprietatibus Litterarum, Ser. Major: No. 12). 177p. 1971. text ed. 34.65 (90-279-1795-7) Mouton.

Rydjord, John. Indian Place Names: Their Origin, Evolution, & Meanings Collected in Kansas from the Siouian, Alogonguin, Shoshonean, Caddoan, Iroquoian, & Other Tongues. LC 68-10303. (Illus.). 380p. 1982. 32.95 (0-8061-0801-0); pap. 17.95 (0-8061-1763-X) U of Okla Pr.

Rydlun, Judith, ed. see Weber, Jayne D.

Rydman, Edward. Finding the Right Counselor for You. LC 89-30439. 144p. 1989. pap. 9.95 (0-87833-680-X) Taylor Pub.

Rydnik, V. J., et al. Dictionary of Physics: Russian, English, German, & French. 392p. 1989. 128.25 (0-444-70490-6) Elsevier.
— Dictionary of Physics in Russian, German, English & French. 392p. (ENG, FRE, GER & RUS.). 1989. 250.00 (0-8288-9318-7) Fr & Eur.

Rydqvist, Kristian. Pricing of Shares with Different Voting Power & the Theory of Oceanic Games. Stockholm School of Economics Staff, ed. 178p. (Orig.). 1986. pap. text ed. 65.00x (91-7258-211-1, Pub. by Almqv & Wiksell SW) Coronet Bks.

Rydstrom, J., et al, eds. Extrahepatic Drug Metabolism & Chemical Carcinogenesis. 648p. 1983. 166.25 (0-444-80538-9, I-381-83) Elsevier.

Rydzewski, J. R. Theory of Arch Dams: Papers of International Symposium, Southampton University, April 1964. LC 64-22222. 1965. 320.00 (0-08-010765-6, Pub. by Pergamon Repr UK) Franklin.

Rye, David. Corporate Game: A Computer Adventure for Developing Business Decision-Making Skills. 1994. disk, pap. text ed. 34.95 (0-07-911763-5) McGraw.

*Rye, David E. The Vest Pocket Entrepreneur: Everything You Need to Start & Run Your Own Business. 1995. 17.95 (0-13-158510-X) P-H.
— Winning the Entrepreneurial Game: Hwo to Start, Operate & Be Successful in a New or Growing Business. LC 94-8712. (Business Advisors Ser.). 1994. 29.95 (1-55850-346-3); pap. 10.95 (1-55850-345-5) Adams Pubng.

Rye, Donald R. & Sparks, Rozanne. Strengthening K-Twelve School Counseling Programs: A Support System Approach. LC 90-82965. vii, 168p. (Orig.). (C). 1991. pap. text ed. 19.95 (1-55959-018-1) Accel Devel.

Rye, Howard, jt. auth. see Marks, Anthony.

Rye, Jennifer. Look...What Do You See? LC 90-40231. (First Science Ser.). (Illus.). 32p. (J). (gr. k-3). 1991. lib. bdg. 11.59 (0-8167-2122-X); pap. text ed. 3.95 (0-8167-2123-8) Troll Assocs.

Rye, Jennifer, jt. auth. see Wood, Nicholas.

Rye, Linda N. How Many Diamond Rings. 62p. 1972. 3.95 (0-913976-01-6) Discovery Bks.

*Rye, Marilyn. Making Cultural Connections: Readings for Critical Analysis. 608p. 1994. pap. text ed. 18.00 (0-312-06782-8) St Martin.

Rye, Owen S. Pottery Technology: Principles & Reconstruction. LC 80-53439. (Manuals on Archeology Ser.: No. 4). (Illus.). xi, 150p. 1981. 18.00 (0-9602822-2-X) Taraxacum.

Rye, Owen S. & Evans, Clifford. Traditional Pottery Techniques of Pakistan: Field & Laboratory Studies. LC 75-619168. (Smithsonian Contributions to Anthropology Ser.: no. 21). 301p. reprint ed. pap. 85.80 (0-317-28428-2, 2020314) Bks Demand.

*Rye, Scott. Men & Ships of the Civil War. LC 94-47097. 1995. write for info. (0-681-10264-0) Longmeadow Pr.
— Of Men & Ships: The Best American Tales. LC 92-44753. 224p. 1993. 17.95 (0-681-41817-6) Longmeadow Pr.

Rye, W. A. Glossary of Words Used in East Anglia: Founded on That of Forby. (English Dialect Society Publications Ser.: No. 75). 1969. reprint ed. pap. 25.00 (0-8115-0493-X) Periodicals Srv.

Rye, William B., ed. England As Seen by Foreigners in the Days of Elizabeth & James the First. LC 66-12288. 1972. reprint ed. 30.95 (0-405-08903-1) Ayer.

Ryedale, April. My Enemy, My Friend. (Orig.). 1993. pap. 7.95 (0-85756-082-4, Pub. by Janus Pub UK) Intl Spec Bk.

R'Yehoshua Leib Diskin. Tales of the Heavenly City. 112p. 1992. pap. write for info. (1-56062-133-8) CIS Comm.

Ryen, Dag. Traces: The Story of Lexington's Past. (Illus.). 177p. (J). (gr. 4 up). 1987. text ed. 13.95 (0-912839-08-2) Lexington-Fayette.

*Ryer. A Pocket Tour of Health & Fitness on the Internet. 1995. 12.99 (0-7821-1711-2) Sybex.

Ryer, Jeanne C., jt. auth. see LaQuey, Tracy.

Ryerson, A. E. Loyalists of America & Their Times, 1620-1816, 2 Vols. LC 68-31273. (American History & Americana Ser.: No. 47). 1969. reprint ed. lib. bdg. 150.00 (0-8383-0195-9) M S G Haskell Hse.

Ryerson, Edward. Dailies System Manual: How to Fix Your Head to Make It in the 21st Century. 130p. 1994. pap. 7.95 (0-9638570-1-0) Pali Pubng.

Ryerson, Egerton. Ovikapun. (SPA.). 4.95 (84-7228-323-2, 220649, Pub. by Edit Clie SP) TSELF.

Ryerson, Eric. When Your Parent Drinks Too Much: A Book for Teenagers. 144p. 1985. 16.95 (0-8160-1259-8) Facts on File.

Ryerson, Florence & Clements, Colin. First Person Singular. 110p. 1937. 5.00 (0-573-60066-X) French.

Ryerson, Florence, jt. auth. see Clements, Colin.

Ryerson, Margery A., ed. see Henri, Robert.

Ryerson, Martin. A Nest of Rattlers. (Orig.). 1981. pap. 1.95 (0-8439-0924-2) Dorchester Pub Co.
— The Quick Badge. 1981. pap. 1.95 (0-8439-0863-7) Dorchester Pub Co.

Ryerson, Richard A., et al, eds. Adams Family Correspondence, Vols. 5 & 6: October 1782-December 1785, Vol. 5. (Adams Papers Ser.: No. 2). (Illus.). 960p. 1992. text ed. 112.00 (0-674-00406-X) HUP.

Ryf, Robert S. Henry Green. LC 67-27360. (Columbia Essays on Modern Writers Ser.: No. 29). 1967. pap. text ed. 7.50 (0-231-02897-0) Col U Pr.
— Joseph Conrad. LC 74-110599. (Essays on Modern Writers Ser.: No. 49). (Orig.). 1970. pap. text ed. 7.50 (0-231-03264-1) Col U Pr.

Ryff, Peter F. Electric Machinery. (Illus.). 336p. (C). 1987. text ed. 68.00 (0-13-247693-2) P-H.
— Electric Machinery. 2nd ed. LC 93-44578. 320p. 1994. text ed. 36.75 (0-13-475625-8) P-H.

Ryff, Peter F., et al. Electrical Machines & Transformers: Principles & Applications. (Illus.). 480p. 1987. text ed. 34.95 (0-685-14917-X) P-H.

Ryffel, Bernhard, et al, eds. International Review of Experimental Pathology, Vol. 34, Pt. A: Cytokine-Induced Pathology, Interleukins & Hemopoietic Growth Factors. (Illus.). 252p. 1993. text ed. 89.00 (0-12-364934-X) Acad Pr.
— International Review of Experimental Pathology, Vol. 34, Pt. B: Cytokine-Induced Pathology, Inflammatory Cytokines, Receptors, & Disease. (Illus.). 232p. 1993. text ed. 89.00 (0-12-364935-8) Acad Pr.

Ryffel, Heinrich. Wandel der Staatsverfassungen. LC 72-7904. (Greek History Ser.). (GER.). 1973. reprint ed. 25.95 (0-405-04800-9) Ayer.

Ryffel, Henry, jt. auth. see Jones, Franklin.

*Ryga. Seven Hours to Sundown. Date not set. per. 12.95 (0-88922-124-3, Pub. by Talonbooks CN) InBook.

Rygaard, J. & Spang-Thomsen, M., eds. Immune-Deficient Animals in Biomedical Research. (Illus.). xvi, 420p. 1987. 213.75 (3-8055-4385-9) S Karger.

Rygiel, Mary A. Shakespeare among School Children: Approaches for the Secondary Classroom. 135p. 1992. pap. 11.95 (0-8141-4381-4) NCTE.

Ryglewicz, Hilary, jt. auth. see Pepper, Bert.

Ryglewicz, Hilary, jt. ed. see Pepper, Bert.

Rygol, J. Structural Analysis by Direct Moment Distribution. 444p. 1968. text ed. 342.00 (0-677-61190-0) Gordon & Breach.

Ryhming, Inge L., jt. ed. see Sottas, Gabriel.

Ryhn, Douglas & Reed, David, eds. Twenty-Seventh Street Storefronts. (Publications in Architecture & Urban Planning: No. R89-5). (Illus.). iii, 52p. (C). 1989. 2.50 (0-938744-68-2) U of Wis Ctr Arch-Urban.

Rykalin, N., et al. Laser Machining & Welding. (Illus.). 1978. 136.00 (0-08-022724-4, Pub. by Pergamon Repr UK) Franklin.

Ryken, Leland. How to Read the Bible as Literature. 200p. (Orig.). (C). 1984. 12.99 (0-310-39021-4, 11158P) Zondervan.
— The Liberated Imagination: Thinking Christianly about the Arts. (Wheaton Literary Ser.). 288p. 1989. pap. 11.99 (0-87788-495-1) Shaw Pubs.
— Realms of Gold: The Classics in Christian Perspective. (Wheaton Literary Ser.). 240p. (Orig.). (C). 1991. pap. text ed. 14.99 (0-87788-717-9) Shaw Pubs.
— Windows to the World: Literature in Christian Perspective. 2nd ed. LC 90-32681. 192p. 1990. reprint ed. pap. 11.99 (0-945241-08-9) Probe Bks.
— Words of Delight: A Literary Introduction to the Bible. 2nd ed. LC 92-42603. 568p. 1993. pap. 19.99 (0-8010-7769-9) Baker Bk.
— Worldly Saints. 1990. pap. 16.99 (0-310-32501-3) Zondervan.

Ryken, Leland, ed. The New Testament in Literary Criticism. (Library of Literary Criticism). 450p. 1985. 45.00 (0-8044-3271-6, F Ungar Bks) Continuum.

Ryken, Leland & Longman, Tremper, III, eds. A Complete Literary Guide to the Bible. 592p. 1993. 29.99 (0-310-51830-X) Zondervan.

Ryken, Leland, jt. ed. see Walhout, Clarence.

Ryken, Leland, jt. auth. see Wilhoit, Jim.

Ryker, Lois. With History Around Me: Spokane Nostalgia. 76p. 1979. pap. 4.95 (0-87770-229-2) Ye Galleon.

*Ryker, Lori, ed. Mockbee Coker: Thought & Process. (Illus.). 144p. (Orig.). 1995. pap. 27.95 (1-56898-042-6) Princeton Arch.

Rykov, Vladimir V., jt. auth. see Kitaev, Mikhail Y.

Rykowski, P. Kay, ed. see Cross, Frank L., et al.

Rykwert, comp. Richard Meier, Architect. LC 83-42911. (Illus.). 412p. 1984. 65.00 (0-8478-0496-8); pap. 42.50 (0-8478-0497-6) Rizzoli Intl.

Rykwert, Joseph. The First Moderns: The Architects of the Eighteenth Century. (Illus.). 1980. pap. 35.00x (0-262-68039-4) MIT Pr.
— The Idea of a Town: The Anthropology of Urban Form in Rome, Italy, & the Ancient World. LC 75-318901. 1976. 69.50 (0-691-03901-1) Princeton U Pr.
— The Idea of a Town: The Anthropology of Urban Form in Rome, Italy & the Ancient World. (Illus.). 242p. 1988. reprint ed. 18.50x (0-262-68056-4) MIT Pr.
— On Adam's House in Paradise: The Idea of the Primitive Hut in Architectural History. (Illus.). 240p. (C). 1981. reprint ed. pap. 16.50 (0-262-68036-X) MIT Pr.

Rylaarsdam, Coert, ed. see Habel, Norman C.

Rylaarsdam, J. Coert, ed. see Tucker, Gene M.

Rylaarsdam, John C. Revelation in Jewish Wisdom Literature. (Midway Reprint Ser.). 140p. reprint ed. pap. 39.90 (0-317-26582-2, 2024065) Bks Demand.

Rylah, Lindsey T., ed. Critical Care of the Burned Patient. (Illus.). 260p. (C). 1992. 64.95 (0-521-39495-3) Cambridge U Pr.

Rylance, Dan, jt. auth. see Fritz, Chester.

Rylance, Paul. Legal Writing & Drafting, Vol. 1. 189p. (C). 1994. pap. text ed. 26.00 (1-85431-169-7, Blckstone AT) W W Gaunt.

Rylance, Rick. Roland Barthes. 192p. 1994. pap. text ed. 24.95 (0-13-302654-X) P-H.

Rylance, Rick, ed. Debating Texts: Readings in 20th Century Literary Theory & Method. 310p. 1987. 35.00 (0-8020-5768-3); pap. 17.95 (0-8020-6682-8) U of Toronto Pr.

Ryland, Cynthia. Couple of Kooks: And Other Stories about Love. (YA). 1992. pap. 3.50 (0-440-21210-3) Dell.
— Soda Jerk. (Illus.). 64p. (YA). (gr. 7 up). 1993. pap. 3.95 (0-688-12654-5, Pub. by Beech Tree Bks) Morrow.

Ryland, G. J. & Menz, K. M. Bulk Handling of Paddy & Rice in Malaysia: An Economic Analysis. (C). 1989. text ed. 58.00 (0-949511-86-2, Pub. by ACIAR) St Mut.

Ryland, J. S., jt. ed. see Hayward, P. J.

Ryland, John S., jt. ed. see Hayward, Peter.

Ryland, Stephen. Deep Treasure & Cache Location with the Fisher Gemini-3. 64p. 1993. 7.00 (1-883170-04-4) FRL.

Rylander. Catalysis of Organic Reactions. (Chemical Industries Ser.: Vol. 33). 456p. 1988. 160.00 (0-8247-7927-4) Dekker.
— Handbook of Organic Dusts. 1994. write for info. (0-87371-699-X) Lewis Pubs.

*Rylander, Edith. Dancing Back the Cranes. 80p. 1993. 9.95 (0-87839-084-7) North Star.
— Rural Routes: Essays on Living in Rural Minnesota. LC 93-4854. 1993. 9.95 (0-87839-079-0) North Star.

Rylander, Michael K., jt. auth. see Bolen, Eric G.

Rylander, Paul N. Hydrogenation Methods. 1985. text ed. 125.00 (0-12-605365-0) Acad Pr.

Rylander, Paul N., ed. Hydrogenation Methods. (Best Synthetic Methods Ser.). 193p. 1990. reprint ed. spiral bd. 55.00 (0-12-605366-9) Acad Pr.

Rylands, Anthony B. The Status of Conservation Areas in the Brazilian Amazon. (Illus.). 156p. (Orig.). (C). 1991. pap. 15.00 (0-89164-135-1) World Wildlife Fund.

Rylands, Anthony B., ed. Marmosets & Tamarins: Systematics, Behaviour, & Ecology. LC 92-27771. (Illus.). 416p. 1993. 75.00 (0-19-854022-1) OUP.

Rylands, Philip. Palma Vecchio. (Studies in the History of Art). (Illus.). 460p. (C). 1992. 130.00 (0-521-37332-8) Cambridge U Pr.

Rylant, Cynthia. All I See. LC 88-42547. (Illus.). 32p. (J). (gr. k-2). 1988. 16.95 (0-531-05777-1); lib. bdg. 16.99 (0-531-08377-2) Orchard Bks Watts.
— All I See. LC 88-42547. (Illus.). 32p. (J). (gr. k-2). 1994. pap. 5.95 (0-531-07048-4) Orchard Bks Watts.
— An Angel for Solomon Singer. LC 91-15957. (Illus.). 32p. (J). 1992. 15.95 (0-531-05978-2); lib. bdg. 15.99 (0-531-08578-3) Orchard Bks Watts.
— Appalachia: The Voices of Sleeping Birds. (Illus.). 32p. (J). (gr. k up). 1991. 14.95 (0-15-201605-8) HarBrace.
— Best Wishes. LC 92-7796. (Meet the Author Ser.). (Illus.). 32p. (J). (gr. 2-5). 1992. 13.95 (1-878450-20-4) R Owen Pubs.
— Birthday Presents. LC 87-5485. (Illus.). 32p. (J). (ps-1). 1987. 14.95 (0-531-05705-4); lib. bdg. 14.99 (0-531-08305-5) Orchard Bks Watts.
— Birthday Presents. LC 87-5485. (Illus.). 32p. (J). (ps-1). 1991. pap. 4.95 (0-531-07026-3) Orchard Bks Watts.
— A Blue-Eyed Daisy. LC 84-21554. 112p. (J). (gr. 5-7). 1985. text ed. 13.95 (0-02-777960-2, Bradbury S&S) S&S Childrens.
— The Blue Hill Meadows & the Much-Loved Dog. LC 93-40538. (Illus.). (J). 1994. write for info. (0-15-253155-6) HarBrace.
— But I'll Be Back Again. LC 93-16188. (Illus.). 80p. (YA). (gr. 7 up). 1993. pap. 4.95 (0-688-12653-7, Pub. by Beech Tree Bks) Morrow.
— But I'll Be Back Again: An Album. LC 88-17860. (Illus.). 80p. (J). (gr. 5-7). 1989. 15.95 (0-531-05806-9); lib. bdg. 15.99 (0-531-08406-X) Orchard Bks Watts.

An Asterisk (*) at the beginning of an entry indicates that the title is appearing in BIP for the first time.

— Children of Christmas: Stories for the Season. LC 87-1690. (Illus.). 48p. (J). (gr. 3 up). 1987. 14.95 (*0-531-05706-2*); lib. bdg. 14.99 (*0-531-08306-3*) Orchard Bks Watts.
— Children of Christmas: Stories for the Season. LC 87-1690. (Illus.). 48p. (J). (gr. 3 up). 1993. pap. 5.95 (*0-531-07042-5*) Orchard Bks Watts.
— A Couple of Kooks: And Other Stories about Love. LC 90-30646. 112p. (J). (gr. 7 up). 1990. 14.95 (*0-531-05900-6*); lib. bdg. 14.99 (*0-531-08500-7*) Orchard Bks Watts.
— Dog Heaven. LC 94-40950. (Illus.). (J). 1995. 14.95 (*0-590-41701-0*, Blue Sky Press) Scholastic Inc.
— The Dreamer. LC 93-19915. (Illus.). 32p. (J). (ps-6). 1993. 14.95 (*0-590-47341-7*) Scholastic Inc.
— Every Living Thing. LC 85-7701. (Illus.). 96p. (J). (gr. 5-7). 1985. text ed. 13.95 (*0-02-777200-4*, Bradbury S&S) S&S Childrens.
— Every Living Thing. LC 88-19359. (Illus.). 96p. (YA). (gr. 5 up). 1988. pap. 3.50 (*0-689-71263-4*, Aladdin Paperbacks) S&S Childrens.
— The Everyday Books: Everyday Children. LC 92-40932. (Everyday Bks.). (Illus.). 14p. (J). (ps-k). 1993. bds. 4.95 (*0-02-778022-8*, Bradbury S&S) S&S Childrens.
— The Everyday Books: Everyday Garden. LC 92-40542. (Everyday Bks.). (Illus.). 14p. (J). (ps-k). 1993. bds. 4.95 (*0-02-778023-6*, Bradbury S&S) S&S Childrens.
— The Everyday Books: Everyday House. LC 92-40943. (Everyday Bks.). (Illus.). 14p. (J). (ps-k). 1993. bds. 4.95 (*0-02-778024-4*, Bradbury S&S) S&S Childrens.
— The Everyday Books: Everyday Pets. LC 92-40934. (Everyday Bks.). (Illus.). 14p. (J). (ps-k). 1993. bds. 4.95 (*0-02-778025-2*, Bradbury S&S) S&S Childrens.
— The Everyday Books: Everyday Town. LC 92-40541. (Everyday Bks.). (Illus.). 14p. (J). (ps-k). 1993. bds. 4.95 (*0-02-788026-5*, Bradbury S&S) S&S Childrens.
— Everyday Town. LC 92-40541. (Everyday Bks.). (Illus.). 14p. (J). (ps-k). 1993. bds. 4.95 (*0-02-778026-0*, Bradbury S&S) S&S Childrens.
— A Fine White Dust. (J). (gr. k-6). 1987. pap. 3.50 (*0-440-42499-2*, YB) Dell.
— A Fine White Dust. LC 86-1003. 120p. (J). (gr. 6-8). 1986. text ed. 14.95 (*0-02-777240-3*, Bradbury S&S) S&S Childrens.
— Gooseberry Park. LC 94-11578. (Illus.). (J). (gr. 1-8). 1995. write for info. (*0-15-232242-6*) HarBrace.
— Henry & Mudge: The First Book of Their Adventures. LC 86-13615. (Illus.). 40p. (J). (gr. 1-3). 1987. text ed. 12.95 (*0-02-778001-5*, Bradbury S&S) S&S Childrens.
— Henry & Mudge: The First Book of Their Adventures. LC 89-39809. (Illus.). 48p. (J). (gr. 1-3). 1990. reprint ed. pap. 3.95 (*0-689-71399-1*, Aladdin Paperbacks) S&S Childrens.
— Henry & Mudge & the Bedtime Thumps. LC 89-49529. (Henry & Mudge Ser.: No. 9). (Illus.). 40p. (J). (gr. 1-3). 1991. text ed. 12.95 (*0-02-778006-6*, Bradbury S&S) S&S Childrens.
— Henry & Mudge & the Bedtime Thumps: The Book of Their Adventures, Bk. 9. braille ed. 12p. (J). 1992. pap. text ed. 0.96 (*1-56956-545-7*, BR8739) W A T Braille.
— Henry & Mudge & the Best Day of All. LC 93-35939. (Illus.). 40p. (J). 1995. text ed. 14.95 (*0-02-778012-0*, Bradbury S&S) S&S Childrens.
— Henry & Mudge & the Careful Cousin: The Thirteenth Book of Their Adventures. LC 92-12851. (Henry & Mudge Bks.). (Illus.). 48p. (J). (gr. 1-3). 1994. text ed. 13.95 (*0-02-778021-X*, Bradbury S&S) S&S Childrens.
— Henry & Mudge & the Forever Sea: The Book of Their Adventures, Bk. 6. braille ed. 11p. (J). 1991. pap. text ed. 0.88 (*1-56956-546-5*, BR8556) W A T Braille.
— Henry & Mudge & the Forever Sea: The Sixth Book of Their Adventures. LC 88-6130. (Illus.). 48p. (J). (gr. 1-3). 1989. text ed. 12.95 (*0-02-778007-4*, Bradbury S&S) S&S Childrens.
— Henry & Mudge & the Forever Sea: The Sixth Book of Their Adventures. LC 92-28646. (Illus.). 48p. (J). (gr. 1-3). 1993. reprint ed. pap. 3.95 (*0-689-71701-6*, Aladdin Paperbacks) S&S Childrens.
— Henry & Mudge & the Happy Cat. LC 88-18855. (Henry & Mudge Ser.: No. 8). (Illus.). 48p. (J). (gr. 1-3). 1990. text ed. 13.95 (*0-02-778008-2*, Bradbury S&S) S&S Childrens.
— Henry & Mudge & the Happy Cat: The Eighth Book of Their Adventures. LC 93-10797. (Illus.). 48p. (J). (gr. 1-3). 1994. reprint ed. pap. 3.95 (*0-689-71791-1*, Aladdin Paperbacks) S&S Childrens.
— Henry & Mudge & the Long Weekend. LC 90-26799. (Illus.). 40p. (J). (gr. 1-3). 1992. text ed. 12.95 (*0-02-778013-9*, Bradbury S&S) S&S Childrens.
— Henry & Mudge & the Wild Wind. LC 91-12644. (Illus.). 40p. (J). (gr. 1-3). 1993. text ed. 12.95 (*0-02-778014-7*, Bradbury S&S) S&S Childrens.
— Henry & Mudge Get the Cold Shivers: The Book of Their Adventures, Bk. 7. braille ed. 11p. (J). 1991. pap. text ed. 0.88 (*1-56956-547-3*, BR8555) W A T Braille.
— Henry & Mudge Get the Cold Shivers: The Seventh Book of Their Adventures. LC 88-18854. (Illus.). 48p. (J). (gr. 1-3). 1989. text ed. 12.95 (*0-02-778011-2*, Bradbury S&S) S&S Childrens.
— Henry & Mudge Get the Cold Shivers: The Seventh Book of Their Adventures. LC 93-45588. (Illus.). 48p. (J). (gr. 1-3). 1994. pap. 3.95 (*0-689-71849-7*, Aladdin Paperbacks) S&S Childrens.
— Henry & Mudge in Puddle Trouble: The Second Book of Their Adventures. LC 86-13616. (Illus.). 48p. (J). (gr. 1-3). 1987. text ed. 12.95 (*0-02-778002-3*, Bradbury S&S) S&S Childrens.
— Henry & Mudge in Puddle Trouble: The Second Book of Their Adventures. LC 89-39810. (Illus.). 48p. (J). (gr. 1-3). 1990. pap. 3.95 (*0-689-71400-9*, Aladdin Paperbacks) S&S Childrens.
— Henry & Mudge in the Green Time: The Third Book of Their Adventures. LC 86-26386. (Illus.). 48p. (J). (gr. 1-3). 1987. text ed. 12.95 (*0-02-778003-1*, Bradbury S&S) S&S Childrens.
— Henry & Mudge in the Green Time: The Third Book of Their Adventures. LC 91-24942. (Henry & Mudge Bks.). (Illus.). 48p. (J). (gr. 1-3). 1992. reprint ed. pap. 3.95 (*0-689-71582-X*, Aladdin Paperbacks) S&S Childrens.
— Henry & Mudge in the Sparkle Days: The Fifth Book of Their Adventures. LC 86-23432. (Illus.). 40p. (J). (gr. 1-3). 1988. text ed. 12.95 (*0-02-778005-8*, Bradbury S&S) S&S Childrens.
— Henry & Mudge in the Sparkle Days: The Fifth Book of Their Adventures. LC 92-42535. (Illus.). 48p. (J). (gr. 1-3). 1993. reprint ed. pap. 3.95 (*0-689-71752-0*, Mac Bks Young Read) S&S Childrens.
— Henry & Mudge Take the Big Test: The Tenth Book of Their Adventures. LC 90-35171. (Henry & Mudge Bks.). (Illus.). 40p. (J). (gr. 1-3). 1991. text ed. 12.95 (*0-02-778009-0*, Bradbury S&S) S&S Childrens.
— Henry & Mudge under the Yellow Moon: The Fourth Book of Their Adventures. LC 86-26390. (Illus.). 48p. (J). (gr. 1-3). 1987. text ed. 12.95 (*0-02-778004-X*, Bradbury S&S) S&S Childrens.
— Henry & Mudge under the Yellow Moon: The Fourth Book of Their Adventures. LC 91-23135. (Henry & Mudge Bks.). (Illus.). 48p. (J). (gr. 1-3). 1992. reprint ed. pap. 3.95 (*0-689-71580-3*, Aladdin Paperbacks) S&S Childrens.
— I Had Seen Castles. LC 92-42325. (J). (gr. 5 up). 1993. 10.95 (*0-15-238003-5*) HarBrace.
— A Kindness. LC 88-1454. 128p. (YA). (gr. 7 up). 1988. 15.95 (*0-531-05767-4*); lib. bdg. 15.99 (*0-531-08367-5*) Orchard Bks Watts.
— Miss Maggie. LC 82-18206. (Illus.). 32p. (J). (gr. k-3). 1983. 13.99 (*0-525-44048-8*, DCB) Dutton Child Bks.
— Missing May. (J). 1993. mass mkt. 3.99 (*0-440-40865-2*) Dell.
— Missing May. LC 91-23303. 96p. (YA). (gr. 6 up). 1992. 14.95 (*0-531-05996-0*); lib. bdg. 14.99 (*0-531-08596-1*) Orchard Bks Watts.
— Mr. Putter & Tabby Bake the Cake. LC 94-9557. (Illus.). (J). (gr. 1-5). Date not set. pap. 4.95 (*0-15-200214-6*) HarBrace.
— Mr. Putter & Tabby Bake the Cake. LC 94-9557. (Illus.). (J). 1994. write for info. (*0-15-200205-7*) HarBrace.
— Mr. Putter & Tabby Pick the Pears. LC 94-11259. (Illus.). (J). Date not set. write for info. (*0-15-200245-6*) HarBrace.
— Mr. Putter & Tabby Pour the Tea. (J). (ps-3). 1994. pap. 4.95 (*0-15-200901-9*, HB Juv Bks) HarBrace.
— Mr. Putter & Tabby Pour the Tea. LC 93-21470. (Illus.). (J). (ps-6). 1994. 10.95 (*0-15-256255-9*) HarBrace.
— Mr. Griggs' Work. LC 88-1484. (Illus.). 32p. (J). (ps-2). 1989. 14.95 (*0-531-05769-0*); lib. bdg. 14.99 (*0-531-08369-1*) Orchard Bks Watts.
— Mr. Griggs' Work. LC 88-1484. (Illus.). 32p. (J). (ps-2). 1993. pap. 5.95 (*0-531-07037-9*) Orchard Bks Watts.
— Mr. Putter & Tabby Row the Boat. LC 93-41832. (Illus.). (J). 1997. write for info. (*0-15-256257-5*) HarBrace.
— Mr. Putter & Tabby Walk the Dog. (J). (ps-3). 1994. pap. 4.95 (*0-15-200891-8*, HB Juv Bks) HarBrace.
— Mr. Putter & Tabby Walk the Dog. LC 93-21467. (Illus.). (J). (ps-6). 1994. 10.95 (*0-15-256259-1*) HarBrace.
— Night in the Country. LC 85-70963. (Illus.). 32p. (J). (ps-1). 1986. text ed. 14.95 (*0-02-777210-1*, Bradbury S&S) S&S Childrens.
— Night in the Country. LC 90-1043. (Illus.). 32p. (J). (ps-2). 1991. reprint ed. pap. 4.95 (*0-689-71473-4*, Aladdin Paperbacks) S&S Childrens.
— The Old Woman Who Named Things. LC 93-40537. (Illus.). (J). 1994. write for info. (*0-15-257809-9*) HarBrace.
— The Relatives Came. LC 85-10929. (Illus.). 32p. (J). (ps-2). 1985. text ed. 14.95 (*0-02-777220-9*, Bradbury S&S) S&S Childrens.
— The Relatives Came. LC 92-41394. (Illus.). 32p. (J). (ps-2). 1993. reprint ed. pap. 4.95 (*0-689-71738-5*, Aladdin Paperbacks) S&S Childrens.
— Soda Jerk. LC 89-35654. (Illus.). 48p. (J). (gr. 7 up). 1990. 15.95 (*0-531-05864-6*); lib. bdg. 15.99 (*0-531-08464-7*) Orchard Bks Watts.
— A Story of Margaret Wise Brown. LC 94-48812. (Illus.). (J). 1995. write for info. (*0-689-80151-3*, Mac Bks Young Read) S&S Childrens.
— This Year's Garden. LC 84-10974. (Illus.). 32p. (J). (gr. k-3). 1984. lib. bdg. 13.95 (*0-02-777970-X*, Bradbury S&S) S&S Childrens.
— This Year's Garden. LC 86-22224. (Illus.). 32p. (J). (ps-3). 1987. reprint ed. pap. 4.95 (*0-689-71122-0*, Aladdin Paperbacks) S&S Childrens.
— The Van Gogh Cafe. LC 94-43348. (Illus.). 64p. (J). (gr. 3-7). 1995. 14.00 (*0-15-200843-8*) HarBrace.
— Waiting to Waltz: A Childhood. LC 84-11030. (Illus.). 48p. (J). (gr. 6-8). 1984. text ed. 12.95 (*0-02-778000-7*, Bradbury S&S) S&S Childrens.
— The Whales. LC 95-15298. (Illus.). (J). 1996. write for info. (*0-590-58285-2*, Blue Sky Press) Scholastic Inc.
— When I Was Young in the Mountains. LC 81-5359. (Unicorn Paperbacks Ser.). (Illus.). 32p. (J). (ps-3). 1982. 14.99 (*0-525-42525-X*, 0966-290, DCB); pap. 3.99 (*0-525-44198-0*, DCB) Dutton Child Bks.
***Rylant, Cythnia.** I Had Seen Castles. LC 92-42325. 112p. (YA). 1995. pap. 4.00 (*0-15-200374-6*) HarBrace.
Rylatt, R. M. Surveying the Canadian Pacific: Memoir of a Railroad Pioneer. LC 90-53554. (Publications in the American West). (Illus.). 200p. 1991. 24.95 (*0-87480-361-6*) U of Utah Pr.
***Ryle, Anthony, ed.** Cognitive Analytic Therapy: Developments in Theory & Practice. LC 94-45112. (Psychotherapy & Counselling Ser.). 1995. write for info. (*0-471-95602-3*); pap. text ed. 29.95 (*0-471-94355-X*) Wiley.
Ryle, Anthony, et al. Cognitive-Analytic Therapy: Active Participation in Change - A New Integration in Brief Psychotherapy. 267p. 1992. reprint ed. pap. text ed. 38.95 (*0-471-93069-5*) Wiley.
Ryle, George. Forest Service: First Forty Five Years of the Forestry Commission of Great Britain. LC 69-11237. (Illus.). 1969. 29.95 (*0-678-05675-7*) Kelley.
Ryle, Gilbert. Aspects of Mind. Meyer, Rene, ed. LC 92-21759. 256p. 1993. 44.95 (*0-631-18489-9*) Blackwell Pubs.
— The Concept of Mind. LC 83-24147. 336p. (C). 1984. pap. text ed. 12.95 (*0-226-73295-9*) U Ch Pr.
— Dilemmas. (C). 1954. pap. 16.95 (*0-521-09115-2*) Cambridge U Pr.
— Plato's Progress. LC 66-15278. 319p. reprint ed. pap. 91.00 (*0-317-08852-1*, 2013248) Bks Demand.
Ryle, J. C. Are You Born Again. pap. 6.00 (*0-87377-126-5*) GAM Pubns.
— Certeza (Assurance) large type ed. (SPA.). Date not set. 3.50 (*1-56063-340-9*, 494022) Editorial Unilit.
— Christian Leaders of the Eighteenth Century: Includes Whitefield, Wesley, Grimshaw, Romaine, Rowlands, Berridge, Venn, Walker, Harvey, Toplady, & Fletcher. 1978. pap. 9.95 (*0-85151-268-2*) Banner of Truth.
— Daily Readings from J. C. Ryle Vol. 1: Matthew, Mark, Luke. 352p. 1982. pap. 11.95 (*0-85234-164-4*) Ballantine.
— Daily Readings from J. C. Ryle, Vol. 1: Matthew, Mark, Luke. 1982. pap. 11.99 (*0-87552-940-2*, Pub. by Evangel Pr UK) Presby & Reformed.
— Daily Readings from J. C. Ryle, Vol. 2: John. 1985. pap. 11.99 (*0-85234-214-4*, Pub. by Evangel Pr UK) Presby & Reformed.
— Los Evangelios Explicados - Juan: Gospels Explained - John. (SPA.). 9.50 (*84-7228-348-8*, 220396, Pub. by Edit Clie SP) TSELF.
— Los Evangelios Explicados - Lucas: Gospels Explained - Luke. (SPA.). 11.50 (*84-7228-346-1*, 220395, Pub. by Edit Clie SP) TSELF.
— Los Evangelios Explicados - Marcos: Gospels Explained - Mark. (SPA.). 6.95 (*84-7228-347-X*, 220394, Pub. by Edit Clie SP) TSELF.
— Los Evangelios Explicados - Mateo: Gospels Explained - Matthew. (SPA.). 6.50 (*84-7228-349-6*, 220393, Pub. by Edit Clie SP) TSELF.
— Expository Thoughts on John, 3 vols., Vol. 1. (Expository Thoughts on the Gospel Ser.). 448p. 1987. reprint ed. pap. 9.95 (*0-85151-504-5*) Banner of Truth.
— Expository Thoughts on John, 3 vols., Vol. 2. (Expository Thoughts on the Gospel Ser.). 448p. 1987. reprint ed. pap. 9.95 (*0-85151-505-3*) Banner of Truth.
— Expository Thoughts on John, 3 vols., Vol. 3. (Expository Thoughts on the Gospel Ser.). 552p. 1987. reprint ed. pap. 9.95 (*0-85151-506-1*) Banner of Truth.
— Expository Thoughts on the Gospels, 3 vols. Incl. St. John. 1973. reprint ed. 39.50 (*0-227-67886-9*); St. Luke. reprint ed. 25.00 (*0-227-67877-X*); St. Matthew & St. Mark. 420p. 1974. reprint ed. 25.00 (*0-227-67874-5*); Set. (*0-227-67887-7*, Pub. by J Clarke UK) Attic Pr.
— Expository Thoughts on the Gospels, 7 vols., Set. 1990. pap. 65.95 (*0-85151-629-7*, RYL1) Banner of Truth.
— Five English Reformers. rev. ed. 160p. (Orig.). 1981. reprint ed. pap. text ed. 6.95 (*0-85151-138-4*) Banner of Truth.
— Foundations of Faith. LC 87-72750. (Faith Pocket Classics Ser.). Orig. Title: Old Paths. 300p. 1988. pap. 4.95 (*0-88270-642-X*) Bridge Pub.
— Holiness. 1979. pap. 11.99 (*0-85234-136-9*, Pub. by Evangel Pr UK) Presby & Reformed.
— Una Llamada a la Oracion: A Call to Prayer. (SPA.). 2.95 (*84-7228-692-4*, 220291, Pub. by Edit Clie SP) TSELF.
— Luke. (Expository Thoughts on the Gospel Ser.: Vol. 1). 390p. 1986. reprint ed. pap. 9.95 (*0-85151-497-9*) Banner of Truth.
— Luke. (Expository Thoughts on the Gospel Ser.: Vol. 2). 530p. 1986. reprint ed. pap. 9.95 (*0-85151-498-7*) Banner of Truth.
— Mark. LC 92-45785. (Classic Commentaries Ser.). 288p. 1993. pap. 12.99 (*0-89107-727-8*) Crossway Bks.
— Mark. 370p. 1984. reprint ed. pap. 9.95 (*0-85151-441-3*) Banner of Truth.
— Matthew. LC 92-47006. (Classic Commentaries Ser.: Vol. 1). 320p. 1993. pap. 12.99 (*0-89107-726-X*) Crossway Bks.
— Matthew. (Expository Thoughts on the Gospel Ser.). 368p. 1986. reprint ed. pap. 9.95 (*0-85151-483-9*) Banner of Truth.
— Neuva Vida. 220p. (SPA.). 1990. 6.95 (*0-85151-413-8*) Banner of Truth.
— No Uncertain Sound: Charges & Addresses. 384p. 1984. pap. 15.95 (*0-85151-444-8*) Banner of Truth.
— Nuevo Nacimiento: New Birth. (SPA.). 5.50 (*84-7228-857-9*, 220634, Pub. by Edit Clie SP) TSELF.
— Thoughts for Young Men. rev. ed. 96p. (YA). (gr. 9 up). 1993. pap. 5.95 (*1-879737-09-4*) Calvary Press.
— The Upper Room. 1983. pap. 15.95 (*0-85151-376-X*) Banner of Truth.
— Warnings to the Churches. 176p. 1992. pap. 4.95 (*0-85151-043-4*) Banner of Truth.
Ryle, J. C., et al. Christian Life Classics. deluxe ed. Green, Jay P., ed. (Fifty Greatest Christian Classics Ser.: Vol. III). 768p. 1990. 24.95 (*1-878442-52-X*) Sovereign Grace Trust Fund.
Ryle, James. Hippo in the Garden. LC 93-71207. 294p. (Orig.). 1993. pap. 9.99 (*0-88419-340-3*, Creation Hse) Strang Comms Co.
— The Mantle of Zechariah. 1995. pap. 9.99 (*0-88419-394-2*, Creation Hse) Strang Comms Co.
Ryle, John A. Changing Disciplines: Lectures on the History, Method & Motives of Social Pathology. 123p. (C). 1994. pap. 19.95 (*1-56000-746-X*) Transaction Pubs.
Ryle, John C. Thoughts for Young Men: An Exhortation Directed to Those in the Prime of Life. 64p. 1991. pap. 1.75 (*1-879737-00-0*) Calvary Press.
Ryle, M., jt. auth. see Orskov, E. R.
Ryle, Martin. Exploring Rural Ireland by Bicycle. 1993. pap. 14.95 (*0-8442-9470-5*, Passport Bks) NTC Pub Grp.
Ryle, Martin, tr. see Arlacchi, Pino.
Ryle, Martin, tr. see Bobbio, Norberto.
Ryle, Martin, tr. see Canfora, Luciano.
Ryle, Martin, tr. see Ginzburg, Carlo.
Ryle, Martin, tr. see Pallottino, Massimo.
Ryle, R. C. El Cielo (Heaven) large type ed. (SPA.). Date not set. 2.99 (*1-56063-342-5*, 494025) Editorial Unilit.
Ryles, A. P., et al. Worked Examples in Essential Organic Chemistry. LC 80-42022. 171p. reprint ed. pap. 48.80 (*0-8357-6945-3*, 2039004) Bks Demand.
Rylestone, Anne L. Prophetic Memory in Wordsworth's "Ecclesiastical Sonnets" LC 89-26352. 160p. (C). 1991. 19.95 (*0-8093-1643-9*) S Ill U Pr.
Ryley, Helen. Keys for Tomorrow: Success with Adults. 115p. (Orig.). 1990. pap. text ed. 24.95 (*1-883132-02-9*) TriPhoenix Pub.
— Keys for Tomorrow: Success with Youth. 121p. (Orig.). 1990. pap. text ed. 24.95 (*1-883132-01-0*) TriPhoenix Pub.
— Keys for Tomorrow: Trainer's Guide. 212p. (Orig.). 1990. pap. text ed. 79.95 (*1-883132-00-2*) TriPhoenix Pub.
Ryley, J. F., ed. Chemotherapy of Fungal Diseases. (Handbook of Experimental Pharmacology Ser.: Vol. 96). (Illus.). 560p. 1990. 310.00 (*0-387-52232-8*) Spr-Verlag.
Ryley, M. Beresford. Queens of the Renaissance. 310p. 1982. reprint ed. 22.50 (*0-87928-110-3*) Corner Hse.
Ryley, Robert, ed. Kenneth Fearing Complete Poems. (Poet's Ser.). 310p. 1994. 35.00 (*0-943373-24-7*); pap. 19.95 (*0-943373-25-5*) Natl Poet Foun.
Ryley, Thomas W., jt. auth. see Kaplan, Edward S.
Rylko, Henry M., ed. Artificial Intelligence: Bibliographic Summaries of the Select Literature, 2 vols., Set. LC 84-13367. 1985. 150.00 (*0-916313-04-2*) Ergosyst Assocs.
— Artificial Intelligence: Bibliographic Summaries of the Select Literature, 2 vols., Vol. I. LC 84-13367. 542p. 1985. pap. 75.00 (*0-916313-02-6*) Ergosyst Assocs.
— Artificial Intelligence: Bibliographic Summaries of the Select Literature, 2 vols., Vol. II. LC 84-13367. 574p. 1985. pap. 75.00 (*0-916313-03-4*) Ergosyst Assocs.
***Ryman.** Aromatherapy Handbook. 1995. pap. 11.95 (*0-85207-215-5*) Atrium Pubs.
***Ryman, Anne.** Myst Strategies & Secrets: For DOS. 432p. 1995. 12.99 (*0-7821-1678-7*) Sybex.
Ryman, Daniele. Aromatherapy: The Encyclopedia of Plants & Oils & How They Help You. LC 92-22869. 1993. pap. 11.95 (*0-553-37166-5*) Bantam.
— The Aromatherapy Handbook: The Secret Healing Power of Essential Oils. 196p. (Orig.). 1990. pap. 19.95 (*0-8464-1338-8*) Beekman Pubs.
Ryman, Daniele, ed. Marguerite Maury's Guide to Aromatherapy. 3rd ed. 240p. Date not set. pap. 26.95 (*0-8464-4249-3*) Beekman Pubs.
Ryman, Geoff. The Child Garden. 400p. 1994. pap. 13.95 (*0-312-89023-0*) Orb NYC.
— Unconquered Countries: Four Novellas. 288p. 1994. 20.95 (*0-312-09929-0*) St Martin.
— Was. 384p. 1993. pap. 10.00 (*0-14-017872-4*, Penguin Bks) Viking Penguin.
***Ryman, Nils & Utter, Fred, eds.** Population Genetics & Fishery Management. (Illus.). 488p. 1987. pap. 17.50 (*0-295-96436-7*) U of Wash Pr.
Ryman, Rebecca. Olivia & Jai. 1991. mass mkt. 5.99 (*0-312-92568-9*) St Martin.
— The Veil of Illusion. 640p. 1995. 24.95 (*0-312-13200-X*) St Martin.
Ryman, Robert. Robert Ryman. LC 88-51290. (Illus.). 54p. 1988. pap. write for info. (*0-944521-15-0*) Dia Ctr Arts.
Rymen, T., et al. Certification of the Contents of Ten Polychlorinated Biphenyl Congeners in an IS)-Octane Solution CRM-365, EUR 14138. 55p. 1992. pap. 9.00 (*92-826-3710-7*, CD-NA-14138-EN-C, Pub. by Europ Com) UNIPUB.
Rymer. Gynaecology. (Colour Guide Ser.). (Illus.). 122p. (Orig.). 1992. pap. text ed. 19.95 (*0-443-04513-5*) Churchill.
Rymer, Alta M. Beep-Bap-Zap-Jack. LC 74-20428. (Tales of Planet Artembo Ser.: Bk. 1). (Illus.). 48p. (J). (gr. 5-7). 1974. 20.00 (*0-9600792-0-3*) Rymer Bks.
— Captain Zomo. LC 79-67651. (Tales of Planet Artembo Ser.: Bk. 2). (Illus.). 48p. (Orig.). (J). (gr. 5-7). 1993. 20.00 (*0-9600792-2-X*) Rymer Bks.
— Hobart & Humbert Gruzzy. LC 85-61860. (Tales of Planet Artembo Ser.: Bk. 5). (Illus.). 28p. (Orig.). (J). (gr. 5-7). Date not set. pap. 20.00 (*0-9600792-6-2*) Rymer Bks.
— Hobart & Humbert Gruzzy. LC 85-61860. (Tales of Planet Artembo Ser.: Bk. 4). (Illus.). 56p. (Orig.). (J). (gr. 5-7). 1994. 25.00 (*0-685-70989-2*) Rymer Bks.
— Oopletrump's Odyssey, Bk. 4. LC 85-61861. (Tales of Planet Artembo Ser.). (Illus.). 48p. (Orig.). (J). (gr. 5-7). Date not set. pap. text ed. 20.00 (*0-9600792-5-4*) Rymer Bks.
— Stars of Obron: Chambo Returns. (Tales of Planet Artembo Ser.: Bk. 3). (Illus.). 56p. (Orig.). (J). (gr. 5-7). Date not set. pap. text ed. 20.00 (*0-9600792-3-8*) Rymer Bks.
— Up from Uzam. (Tharma Lo Fairyland Ser.: Story 1). (Illus.). 28p. (Orig.). (J). (gr. 2-4). Date not set. pap. 20.00 (*0-9600792-8-9*) Rymer Bks.

R

Rymer, Janice, et al. Preparation & Revision for DRCOG. (Illus.). 258p. 1990. pap. text ed. 36.00 (0-443-04248-9) Churchill.

Rymer, Michael J., jt. ed. see Andersen, David W.

Rymer, Russ. Genie: A Scientific Tragedy. 240p. 1994. pap. 10.00 (0-06-092465-9, PL) HarpC.

Rymer, Thomas. Short View of Tragedy. LC 79-118069. 1968. reprint ed. 29.50 (0-404-05478-1) AMS Pr.

— Short View of Tragedy. 184p. 1971. reprint ed. 26.00 (0-7146-2519-1, Pub. by F Cass Pubs UK) Intl Spec Bk.

Rymes, Thomas K. Keynes Lectures, 1932-35. 1989. 47.50 (0-472-10131-5) U of Mich Pr.

Rymes, Thomas K., jt. auth. see Cas, Alexandra.

Rymkiewicz, Jaroslaw M. The Final Station: Umschlagplatz. Taylor, Nina, tr. LC 93-39631. 1994. 27.50 (0-374-15495-3) FS&G.

Rymuza, Z. Tribiology of Miniature Systems. (Tribology Ser.: No. 13). 565p. 1989. 156.50 (0-444-87401-1) Elsevier.

Ryn, Claes G. Democracy & the Ethical Life: A Philosophy of Politics & Community. LC 77-9505. 246p. 1990. pap. 14.95 (0-8132-0711-8) Cath U Pr.

— The New Jacobinism: Can Democracy Survive? LC 91-2774. 102p. (Orig.). 1991. pap. 8.95 (0-932783-03-1) Natl Human Inst.

— Will, Imagination, & Reason. LC 86-6588. 392p. (Orig.). 1986. 15.00 (0-89526-579-6); pap. 7.95 (0-89526-807-8) Regnery Pub.

Ryn, Claes G., jt. ed. see Panichas, George A.

Rynaenen, S. S., jt. ed. see Lindroth, S. E.

Rynard, Thomas. Insurance & Risk Management for State & Local Government, Vol. 1. 1991. write for info. (0-8205-1386-5) Bender.

***Ryndak, Diane L. & Alper, Sandra.** Curriculum Content for Students with Moderate & Severe Disabilities in Inclusive Settings. LC 95-6135. 1995. write for info. (0-205-14667-8) Allyn.

Rynders, jt. auth. see Pueschel.

***Rynders, John E. & Horrobin, J. Margaret.** Down Syndrome: Birth to Adulthood. Giving Families an Edge. LC 94-76444. 1995. pap. text ed. 24.95 (0-89108-236-0) Love Pub Co.

***Ryne, Robert.** Computational Accelerator Physics. (AIP Conference Proceedings Ser.: No. 297). 640p. 1994. text ed. 605.00x (1-56396-222-5) Am Inst Physics.

Rynecki, Steven B. & Morse, Michael J. Police Collective Bargaining Agreements: A National Management Survey. rev. ed. 150p. (Orig.). 1984. pap. 10.00 (0-318-02223-0) Police Exec Res.

Rynell, A. The Rivalry of Scandinavian & Native Synonyms, in Middle English Especially "Taken" & "Nimen" With an Excursus on "Nema" & "Tuka" in Old Scandinavian. (Lund Studies in English: Vol. 13). 1974. reprint ed. pap. 40.00 (0-8115-0556-1) Periodicals Srv.

Rynell, Alarik. Antedatings & Additions for the Oxford English Dictionary from the Catalogue of Prints of Political & Personal Satire in the British Museum. (Stockholm Studies in English: No. LXXII). 184p. (Orig.). 1987. pap. text ed. 40.00x (91-22-00872-1, Pub. by Almqv & Wiksell SW) Coronet Bks.

Rynerson, Fred. Exploring & Mining for Gems & Gold in the West. (Illus.). 204p. (J). (gr. 4 up). 1970. pap. 8.95 (0-911010-60-2) Naturegraph.

— Exploring & Mining for Gems & Gold in the West. (Illus.). 204p. (J). (gr. 4 up). 1970. 16.95 (0-911010-61-0) Naturegraph.

Ryneveld, Edna. Transits in Reverse: Astrological Planning for Success. LC 88-45191. (Modern Astrology Library). 408p. (Orig.). 1988. pap. 12.95 (0-87542-674-3) Llewellyn Pubns.

Ryneveld, Edna C. Secrets for a Natural Menopause: A Positive, Drug-Free Approach. LC 94-33401. (Illus.). 224p. 1994. pap. 12.95 (1-56718-596-7) Llewellyn Pubns.

Rynn, Maria, jt. auth. see Bohl, Marilyn.

***Rynne, Stephen.** Green Fields: A Journey of Irish Country Life. 256p. 1995. reprint ed. pap. 15.95 (0-86322-203-X, Pub. by Brandon Bk Pubs IE) Irish Bks Media.

***Rynne, Terrence J.** Competitive Market Strategies in Healthcare: Meeting the Marketing Challenges in an Integrated Delivery System. 225p. 1995. 47.00 (1-55738-635-8) Probus Pub Co.

Rynning, Ole. Ole Rynning's True Account of America. Blegen, Theodore C., ed. & tr. by. LC 70-160992. (Select Bibliographies Reprint Ser.). 1977. reprint ed. 16.95 (0-8369-5827-6) Ayer.

Ryo. Atlas of Nuclear Medicine Artifacts & Variants. 2nd ed. 320p. 1989. 95.00 (0-8151-7490-X, Yr Bk Med Pubs) Mosby Yr Bk.

Ryo Sakaizumi. Introduction to Marker Drawing. (Easy Start Guide Ser.). (Illus.). 112p. 1992. 36.95 (4-7661-0624-5, Pub. by Graphic Sha JA) Bks Nippan.

Ryoji Minagawa & Takashige, Hiroshi. Striker, Vol. 1: The Armored Warrior. Seiji Horibuchi, ed. Satoru Fujii, tr. (Illus.). 128p. (Orig.). 1993. pap. 14.95 (0-929279-84-0) Viz Commns Inc.

Ryokan. Between the Floating Mist: Poems of Ryokan. Maloney & Oshiro, trs. 96p. (Orig.). 1992. pap. 12.00 (1-877800-01-5) Springhse Editions.

— Dewdrops on a Lotus Leaf: Zen Poems of Ryokan. Stevens, John, ed. & tr. by. LC 93-20221. (Centaur Editions Ser.). (Illus.). 172p. (Orig.). 1993. pap. 11.00 (0-87773-884-X) Shambhala Pubns.

— Ryokan: Zen Monk - Poet of Japan. Watson, Burton, tr. 126p. 1992. pap. 10.95 (0-231-04415-1) Col U Pr.

***Ryon, Karen T.** Keep the Memories, Bury the Love: My Life with Travis Tritt. Courtney, Richard, ed. LC 94-61839. 128p. (Orig.). 1995. pap. 12.95 (1-886371-06-7) Eggman Pub.

— Keep the Memories, Bury the Love: My Life with Travis Tritt. Courtney, Richard, ed. 128p. (Orig.). 1995. pap. 12.95 (1-886371-19-9) Eggman Pub.

Ryon, Roderick N. West Baltimore Neighborhoods: Sketches of Their History, 1840-1960. LC 93-60361. (Orig.). 1993. pap. write for info. (0-9636930-0-X) R N Ryon.

***Ryou, Daniel H.** Zephaniah's Oracles Against the Nations: A Synchronic & Diachronic Study of Zephaniah 2:1-3:8. LC 95-1102. (Biblical Interpretation Ser.: Vol. 13). 1995. 94.50 (90-04-10311-2) E J Brill.

Ryp, Ellen. Deadly Bonds. 1989. mass mkt. 4.95 (0-446-35133-4) Warner Bks.

***Ryp, Wolff.** The Fury: Midnight Secrets Ser. 1995. pap. 3.50 (0-8167-3544-1) Troll Assocs.

— The Temptation. (Midnight Secrets Ser.: No. 01). (YA). 1994. pap. 3.50 (0-8167-3542-5) Troll Assocs.

— The Thrill. (Midnight Secrets Ser.: No. 02). (YA). 1994. pap. 3.50 (0-8167-3543-3) Troll Assocs.

Rypel, T. C. Gonji, No. 1: Deathwind of Vedun. 1982. pap. 2.95 (0-8217-1006-0) Zebra.

— Gonji, No. 3: Samurai Combat. (Orig.). 1983. pap. 3.50 (0-8217-1191-1) Zebra.

Rypins, S., ed. Three Old English Prose Texts. (EETS, OS Ser.: No. 161). 1974. reprint ed. 34.00 (0-527-00158-9) Periodicals Srv.

Rypka, J., et al. History of Iranian Literature. enl. rev. ed. Jahn, Karl, ed. Van Popta-Hope, P., tr. 928p. 1968. lib. bdg. 158.00 (90-277-0143-1) Kluwer Ac.

***Ryrie.** Balancing the Christian Life: Biblical Principles for Wholesome Living. 1994. pap. 8.99 (0-8024-0887-7) Moody.

Ryrie, Charles. Acts of the Apostles. (Everyman's Bible Commentary Ser.). (C). 1967. pap. 7.99 (0-8024-2044-3) Moody.

— Biblical Answers to Contemporary Issues. 1991. pap. 7.99 (0-8024-1077-4) Moody.

— Ryrie NAS Black Bonded Red Letter Bible. pap. 64.99 (0-8024-7435-7) Moody.

— Spanish Ryrie Study Bible. Orig. Title: Biblia de Estudio Ryrie. 1991. text ed. 35.99 (0-8024-7590-6) Moody.

Ryrie, Charles C. Apocalipsis (Comentario Biblico Portavoz) Orig. Title: Revelation (Everyman's Bible Commentary). 128p. (SPA.). 1981. pap. 5.99 (0-8254-1625-6) Kregel.

— Balancing the Christian Life. (C). 1969. pap. 8.99 (0-8024-0452-9) Moody.

— Las Bases de la Fe Premilenial. Orig. Title: The Basis of the Premillennial Faith. 224p. (SPA.). 1984. pap. 5.25 (0-8254-1626-4) Kregel.

— Basic Theology. 544p. 1986. 26.99 (0-89693-814-X, Victor Books) SP Pubns.

— Basis of the Premillennial Faith. 1954. pap. 7.99 (0-87213-741-4) Loizeaux.

— Biblia de Estudio Ryrie. Orig. Title: Ryrie Study Bible. 2200p. (SPA.). 1991. 35.99 (0-8254-1641-8); 41.99 (0-8254-1642-6) Kregel.

— Biblia de Estudio Ryrie. deluxe ed. Orig. Title: Ryrie Study Bible. 2200p. (SPA.). 1991. 64.99 (0-8254-1643-4) Kregel.

— Dispensacionalismo, Hoy. Orig. Title: Dispensationalism Today. 208p. (SPA.). 1974. pap. 6.99 (0-8254-1627-2) Kregel.

— Dispensationalism Today. LC 65-14611. 211p. (C). 1973. pap. 8.99 (0-8024-2256-X) Moody.

— Equilibrio en la Vida Cristiana. Orig. Title: Balancing the Christian Life. 208p. (SPA.). 1983. pap. 7.99 (0-8254-1628-0) Kregel.

— El Espiritu Santo. Orig. Title: The Holy Spirit. 152p. (SPA.). 1978. pap. 6.99 (0-8254-1629-9) Kregel.

— First & Second Thessalonians. (Everyman's Bible Commentary Ser.). (C). 1968. pap. 7.99 (0-8024-2052-4) Moody.

— La Gracia de Dios. Orig. Title: The Grace of God. 160p. (SPA.). 1979. pap. 4.99 (0-8254-1630-2) Kregel.

— Los Hechos de los Apostoles (Comentario Biblico Portavoz) Orig. Title: The Acts of the Apostles (Everyman's Bible Commentary). 96p. (SPA.). 1981. pap. 5.99 (0-8254-1631-0) Kregel.

— The Holy Spirit. LC 65-14610. (Orig.). (C). 1992. pap. 7.99 (0-8024-3565-3) Moody.

— The Miracles of Our Lord. LC 88-16608. 186p. 1988. reprint ed. 13.99 (0-87213-742-2) Loizeaux.

— New International Version: Ryrie Study Bible. 1986. 35.99 (0-8024-7526-4) Moody.

— New International Version: Ryrie Study Bible. deluxe ed. 1986. 79.99 (0-8024-7531-0); 59.99 (0-8024-7529-9); 59.99 (0-8024-7527-2); 59.99 (0-8024-7534-5) Moody.

— Object Lessons: 100 Lessons from Everyday Life. rev. ed. pap. 5.99 (0-8024-6029-1) Moody.

— Primera y Segunda Tesalonicenses (Comentario Biblico Portavoz) Orig. Title: First & Second Thessalonians (Everyman's Bible Commentary). 104p. (SPA.). 1981. pap. 5.99 (0-8254-1634-5) Kregel.

— Revelation. (Everyman's Bible Commentary Ser.). (Orig.). (C). 1968. pap. 7.99 (0-8024-2066-4) Moody.

— The Ryrie Study Bible: New American Standard Translation: with Introductions, Annotations, Outlines, Marginal References, Harmony of the Gospels, Synopsis of Bible Doctrine, Index of Scripture, Index to Notes, Concordance, Maps, & Timeline Charts, & Many Other Helps. LC 94-46826. 1995. 35.99 (0-8024-3866-0) Moody.

— Ryrie Study Bible: New International Version. expanded rev. ed. 1994. 35.99 (0-8024-3850-4) Moody.

— Sintesis de Doctrina Biblica. 208p. (SPA.). 1979. pap. 6.99 (0-8254-1636-1) Kregel.

— So Great Salvation. 168p. 1991. pap. 9.99 (0-89693-127-7, Victor Books) SP Pubns.

— Survey of Bible Doctrine. LC 72-77958. 192p. (C). 1972. pap. 8.99 (0-8024-8438-7) Moody.

— Teologia Biblica del Nuevo Testamento. 364p. (SPA.). 1983. pap. 10.99 (0-8254-1637-X) Kregel.

Rys, Frans S., jt. ed. see Gyr, Albert.

Rys, Paul & Zollinger, H. Fundamentals of the Chemistry & Application of Dyes. LC 78-37108. (Illus.). 206p. reprint ed. pap. 58.80 (0-317-10909-X, 2051228) Bks Demand.

Rysavy, B. & Ryzhikov, K. M., eds. Helminths of Fish Eating Birds of the Palaearctic Region: Volume 1, Nematoda. (Illus.). 1978. lib. bdg. 103.00 (90-6193-551-2) Kluwer Ac.

Ryschkewitsch, George E. Chemical Bonding & the Geometry of Molecules. LC 62-20784. (Selected Topics in Modern Chemistry Ser.). 129p. reprint ed. pap. 36.80 (0-317-09188-3, 2005794) Bks Demand.

Ryser, Elliot T. & Marth. Listeria, Listeriosis, & Food Safety. (Food Science & Technology Ser.: Vol. 46). 648p. 1991. 199.00 (0-8247-8480-4) Dekker.

Ryser, Fred A., Jr. Birds of the Great Basin: A Natural History. LC 84-25763. (Max C. Fleischmann Series in Great Basin Natural History). (Illus.). 642p. (Orig.). 1985. pap. 39.95 (0-87417-080-X) U of Nev Pr.

Ryser, Frieder. Reverse Paintings on Glass: The Ryser Collection. (Illus.). 192p. 1992. pap. 45.00 (0-87290-127-0) Corning.

Ryser, H., jt. auth. see Brualdi, Richard A.

Ryser, Herbert J. Combinatorial Mathematics. LC 65-12288. (Carus Monograph: No. 14). 154p. 1963. 25.00 (0-88385-014-1) Math Assn.

Ryser, Otto E. & Brown, James R. A Manual of Tumbling & Apparatus Stunts. 8th ed. 272p. 1990. spiral bd. write for info. (0-697-10418-4) Brown & Benchmark.

Ryserson, Andre, jt. ed. see Fonte, John.

Ryskamp, Charles. William Blake: Engraver. LC 72-108006. (Illus.). 61p. 1969. pap. 10.00 (0-87811-014-3) Princeton Lib.

Ryskamp, Charles, ed. Wilde & the Nineties. LC 66-26625. (Illus.). 75p. 1966. pap. 10.00 (0-87811-010-0) Princeton Lib.

Ryskamp, Charles & Gere, J. A. Drawings by Michelangelo: From the British Museum. LC 79-84415. (Illus.). 112p. 1994. pap. 29.95 (0-87598-068-6) Pierpont Morgan.

Ryskamp, Charles, ed. see Cowper, William.

Ryskin, Grigorii. Osen' Na Vindzorskoi Doroge: Zapiski Massazhista. LC 86-9773. 164p. (RUS.). 1986. pap. 8.50 (0-938920-71-5) Hermitage.

Ryskind, Morrie & Roberts, John H. I Shot an Elephant in My Pajamas: The Morrie Ryskind Story. LC 93-77474. 240p. 1993. pap. 12.99 (1-56384-000-6) Huntington Hse.

Ryskov, S. S., ed. The Geometry of Positive Quadratic Forms. LC 82-24328. (Proceedings of the Steklov Institute of Mathematics Ser.: No. 152). 258p. 1982. 119.00 (0-8218-3070-8, STEKLO-152) Am Math.

Ryskov, S. S. & Baranovskii, E. P. C-Types of N-Dimensional Lattices & Five- Dimensional Primitive Parallelohedra with Application to the Theory of Coverings. LC 78-21923. (Proceedings of the Steklov Institute of Mathematics Ser.). 140p. 1978. 83.00 (0-8218-3037-6, STEKLO-137) Am Math.

Ryssel, Heiner & Ingolf, Ruge. Ion Implantation. LC 84-3723. 459p. 1986. text ed. 185.00 (0-471-10311-X) Wiley.

***Ryssel, Heiner & Ruge, Ingolf.** Ion Implantation. fac. ed. Buckman, Jerome-Allan, tr. LC 84-3723. 477p. reprint ed. pap. 136.00 (0-7837-8272-1, 2049053) Bks Demand.

Ryssell, Heiner & Glawischnig, H. Ion Implantation Techniques, Berchtesgaden, FRG, 1982. (Electroyphysics Ser.: Vol. 10). (Illus.). 372p. 1982. 59.00 (0-387-11878-0) Spr-Verlag.

Rysten, Felix S. False Prophets in the Fiction of Camus, Dostoevsky, Melville, & Others. LC 77-158928. 1972. 9.95 (0-87024-226-1) U of Miami Pr.

Rystrom, Kenneth. Book-Comber's Guide to the Oregon Coast. (Illus.). 72p. 1992. 6.95 (0-936015-38-1) Pocahontas Pr.

— The Why, Who & How of the Editorial Page. 352p. (C). 1983. text ed. write for info. (0-07-554377-X) McGraw.

— The Why, Who & How of the Editorial Page. 2nd ed. LC 93-84254. (Journalism & Mass Communication Ser.). 336p. (C). 1994. pap. text ed. write for info. (0-9634489-1-9) Strata Pub Co.

Rystrom, Zella R. Tales of a Nebraska Country Girl. (Illus.). 48p. (Orig.). (YA). (gr. 6-12). 1988. pap. 4.95 (0-936015-18-7) Pocahontas Pr.

Rysz, Anthony M., jt. ed. see Brzana, Stanislaus J.

Rytel, Michael J. Rapid Diagnosis in Infectious Diseases. 224p. 1979. pap. 113.95 (0-8493-5535-4, RC112, CRC Reprint) Franklin.

***Ryter, Derek.** Mountain Biking Colorado's LaPlatas: Great Rides Between Durango & Telluride. (Illus.). 144p. (Orig.). 1995. pap. 16.00 (0-87108-860-6) Pruett.

Ryther, Thomas E., jt. auth. see Chambliss, William J.

Rytlewski, Ralf, jt. ed. see Berg-Schlosser, Dirk.

Ryton, Royce. Royal Baccarat Scandal. 120p. (Orig.). 1990. pap. 5.45 (0-87129-031-6, R46) Dramatic Pub.

Rytov, S. M., et al. Principles of Statistical Radiophysics, No. 1. (Illus.). 260p. 1987. 99.00 (0-387-12562-0) Spr-Verlag.

— Principles of Statistical Radiophysics, No. 2. (Illus.). 240p. 1988. 109.00 (0-387-16186-4) Spr-Verlag.

— Principles of Statistical Radiophysics, No. 4. (Illus.). 200p. 1989. 96.00 (0-387-17828-7) Spr-Verlag.

— Principles of Statistical Radiophysics, No. 3. (Illus.). 255p. 1989. 119.00 (0-387-17829-5) Spr-Verlag.

Rytovori, Helena. Peace Research in Scandinavia, 1959-1986. 250p. 1990. text ed. 64.95 (1-85628-109-4, Pub. by Avebury Pub UK) Ashgate Pub Co.

Rytter, Wojciech, jt. auth. see Crochemore, Maxime.

Rytter, Wojciech, jt. auth. see Gibbons, Alan.

Rytting, Gloria W., ed. Christmas Recipes from the Lion House. LC 89-35572. (Illus.). 214p. 1989. 12.95 (0-87579-255-3) Deseret Bk.

***Ryu, Akira, ed.** The Best Use of Landscape Items in Architectural Rendering. (Illus.). 144p. 1995. pap. text ed. 36.95 (4-7661-0771-3, Pub. by Graphic Sha JA) Bks Nippan.

Ryu, Chi S., jt. auth. see Lee, Pong K.

Ryu, Chi Sik, jt. auth. see Lee, Pong K.

Ryu, D., jt. ed. see Furusaki, S.

Ryu, Paul K., jt. auth. see Silving, Helen.

***Ryu, Shiro.** Coherent Lightwave Communication Systems. LC 94-23490. 283p. 1994. 79.00 (0-89006-612-4) Artech Hse.

Ryugo, Kay. Fruit Culture: Its Arts & Science. LC 88-5540. 344p. 1988. Net. text ed. write for info. (0-471-89191-6) Wiley.

Ryuichi, Hirokawa. Children of the World: Jordan. LC 87-42618. (Illus.). 64p. (J). (gr. 5-6). 1987. lib. bdg. 21.26 (1-55532-224-7) Gareth Stevens Inc.

Ryuichi, Tamura. Dead Languages: Selected Poems 1946-1984. Fitzsimmons, Thomas, ed. Drake, Christopher, tr. LC 84-12621. (Asian Poetry in Translation: Japan Ser.: No. 5). (Illus.). 336p. (Orig.). (ENG & JPN.). 1985. pap. 14.95 (0-942668-06-5) Katydid Bks.

Ryuijie. Ryuijie Photographs. (Illus.). 100p. 1991. 50.00 (0-9627927-0-5); pap. 25.00 (0-9627927-1-3) Freshsilver.

Ryumin, A. Decorative Metal-Work of the Urals, 18th-19th Centuries. 205p. (ENG, FRE, GER & RUS.). 1982. 200.00 (0-317-57306-3, Pub. by Collets UK) St Mut.

***Ryunosuke, Akutagawa.** Cogwheels & Other Stories. Norman, Howard, tr. 80p. 1995. lib. bdg. 27.00 (0-8095-4874-7) Borgo Pr.

Ryusen, Miyahara, illus. Buddhist Paintings-Japanese National Treasures: Restored Copies. 127p. 1981. 65.00 (4-333-01039-X, Pub. by Kosei Pub Co JA) C E Tuttle.

Ryuzo, Nagao. Folklore of Manchuria: The Chinese Folkways. (Asian Folklore & Social Life Monographs: No. 36). (JPN.). 1938. 14.00 (0-89986-036-2) Oriental Bk Store.

Ryvarden, L. Genera of Polypores. Nomenclature & Taxonomy. (Synopsis Fungorum Ser.: No. 5). 363p. 1991. pap. 95.00 (82-90724-10-1, Pub. by Fungi-Flora NO) Lubrecht & Cramer.

Ryvarden, L. & Gilbertson, R. L. European Polypores, Pt. 1: Abortiporus-Lindtneria. (Illus.). 1993. lib. bdg. 85.00 (82-90724-12-8, Pub. by Fungi-Flora NO) Lubrecht & Cramer.

Ryvarden, L. & Johansen, Inger. A Preliminary Poly Ore Flora of East Africa. (Illus.). 636p. 1980. pap. text ed. 55.00 (0-945345-14-3) Lubrecht & Cramer.

Ryvarden, L., jt. auth. see Gilbertson, R. L.

Ryvarden, L., jt. auth. see Hjortstam, K.

Ryvarden, Leif. The Polyporaceae of North Europe, 2 vols., Set. (Illus.). 1988. pap. text ed. write for info. (0-945345-13-5) Lubrecht & Cramer.

Ryvarden, Leif, jt. auth. see Eriksson, J.

Ryves, Thomas. The Poore Vicars Plea. Declaring That a Competencie of Means Is Due to Them Out of the Tithes..Notwithstanding the Impropriations. LC 79-84135. (English Experience Ser.: No. 953). 164p. 1979. reprint ed. lib. bdg. 17.00 (90-221-0953-4) Walter J Johnson.

Ryvkina, Rozalina, jt. auth. see Brym, Robert J.

Rywell, Martin. American Antique Rifles. 1975. 2.00 (0-913150-05-3) Pioneer Pr.

— Sharps Rifle: The Gun That Shaped American Destiny. 160p. 1956. 5.00 (0-913150-21-5) Pioneer Pr.

Rywerant, Yochanan. The Feldenkrais Method: Teaching by Handling. LC 83-47734. (Illus.). 256p. 1991. pap. 11.95 (0-87983-554-0) Keats.

Rywkin, Michael. Moscow's Lost Empire. (Illus.). 230p. (C). 1994. 50.00 (1-56324-236-2); pap. text ed. 19.95 (1-56324-237-0) M E Sharpe.

— Moscow's Muslim Challenge: Soviet Central Asia. rev. ed. LC 89-29825. 202p. 1990. 46.95 (0-87332-613-X); pap. text ed. 25.95 (0-87332-614-8) M E Sharpe.

— Soviet Society Today. LC 89-4192. 256p. 1989. 62.95 (0-87332-444-7); pap. text ed. 25.95 (0-87332-445-5) M E Sharpe.

Rywkin, Michael, ed. Russian Colonial Expansion to 1917. LC 84-71094. (Issue Studies (U. S. S. R. & East Europe): No. 4). xviii, 274p. 1988. 30.00 (0-7201-1867-0) Assn Study Nat.

Ryzhikov, K. M., jt. ed. see Rysavy, B.

Ryzhjk, J. M., jt. auth. see Gradshteyn, J. S.

Ryzuk, Mary S. The Gainesville Ripper: The True Story of a Serial Killer. (Illus.). 416p. 1994. 22.95 (1-55611-352-8) D I Fine.

— Thou Shall Not Kill. 1990. mass mkt. 4.95 (0-445-21043-5) Warner Bks.

Rzasa, Mary, jt. auth. see Kasprisin, Christina A.

Rzeczkoski, Matthew, tr. see Ashley, Thomas, ed.

Rzepecki, Arnold. Book Review Index to Social Science Periodicals, 4 vols., Set. LC 78-51070. 275.00 (0-685-73413-7) Pierian.

— Book Review Index to Social Science Periodicals, 4 vols., Vol. 1: 1978. LC 78-51070. Vol. 1 1978. 75.00 (0-87650-026-2) Pierian.

— Book Review Index to Social Science Periodicals, 4 vols., Vol. 2: 1979. LC 78-51070. Vol. 2, 1979. 75.00 (0-87650-110-2) Pierian.

— Book Review Index to Social Science Periodicals, 4 vols., Vol. 3: 1980. LC 78-51070. Vol. 3, 1980. 75.00 (0-87650-049-1) Pierian.

— Book Review Index to Social Science Periodicals, 4 vols., Vol. 4: 1982. LC 78-51070. Vol. 4, 1982. 75.00 (0-87650-114-5) Pierian.

Rzepecki, Arnold N., comp. Literature & Language Bibliographies from the American Yearbook, 1910-1919: The Predecessor of the MLA Bibliography. (Cumulated Bibliography Ser.: No. 1). 1970. 29.50 (0-87650-013-0) Pierian.

R

Rzepecki, Edward L., ed. Packaging & Environmental Issues. (Illus.). (C). 1991. pap. text ed. 65.00 (*0-9624229-4-0*) St Thomas Tech.
***Rzepka, Charles J.** Sacramental Commodities: Gift, Text, & the Sublime in De Quincey. LC 94-38875. 360p. (C). 1995. lib. bdg. 55.00x (*0-87023-961-9*); pap. text ed. 19.95 (*0-87023-962-7*) U of Mass Pr.
— The Self As Mind: Vision & Identity in Wordsworth, Coleridge, & Keats. 298p. 1986. 34.50 (*0-674-80085-0*) HUP.
Rzepka, Jane R. A Small Heaven: UUA Meditation Manuals. (Illus.). 64p. (Orig.). 1989. pap. 3.00 (*1-55896-122-4*, Skinner Hse Bks) Unitarian Univ.
Rzepnicki, Tina L. & Stein, Theodore J. Decision Making in Child Welfare Services: Intake & Planning. 1984. lib. bdg. 59.00 (*0-89838-138-X*) Kluwer Ac.
Rzepnicki, Tina L., jt. auth. see Stein, Theodore J.
***Rzeswski, Theodore S.** Digital Video: Concepts & Applications Across Industries. LC 94-33543. 591p. 1995. 69.95 (*0-7803-1099-3*) Inst Electrical.
Rzeszewski, T. Color Television. LC 83-7894. 400p. 1983. 59.95 (*0-87942-168-1*, PC01610) Inst Electrical.
Rzeszewski, T., ed. Television Technology Today. LC 85-103. (Reprint Ser.). 488p. 1985. 49.95 (*0-87942-187-8*, PCO1818) Inst Electrical.
Rzetelny, Harriet & Mellor, Joanna. Support Groups for Caregivers of the Aged: A Training Manual for Facilitators. LC 84-167188. 72p. (Orig.). 1981. pap. 7.50 (*0-88156-008-1*) Comm Serv Soc NY.
***Rzevski & Open.** Perception, Cognition & Execution: Mechatronics Designing Intelligence. 336p. 1995. pap. 34.95 (*0-7506-2404-3*, Focal) Buttrwrth-Heinemann.
Rzevski, G., ed. Applications of Artificial Intelligence in Engineering, IV: Proc. of the Sixth Internat. Conf., 2-4 July 1991, Oxford, UK. 1064p. 1991. 255.00 (*1-85166-678-8*) Elsevier.
— Artificial Intelligence in Design. LC 89-61419. (AIENG Ser.: Vol. 4). 564p. 1989. 107.00 (*0-945824-20-3*) Computational Mech MA.
— Artificial Intelligence in Manufacturing. LC 89-61419. (AIENG Ser.: Vol. 4). 476p. 1989. 107.00 (*0-945824-22-X*) Computational Mech MA.
Rzevski, G. & Adey, R. A., eds. Applications of Artificial Intelligence in Engineering VI. LC 91-72244. (AIENG Ser.: Vol. 6). 1064p. 1991. 275.00 (*1-56252-069-5*) Computational Mech MA.
***Rzevski, G. & Gero, J. S., eds.** Applications of Artificial Intelligence in Engineering, 2 vols. (AIENG Ser.: Vol. 4). 1040p. 1989. 193.50 (*1-85312-039-1*) Computational Mech MA.
Rzevski, G., jt. ed. see Adey, R. A.
Rzevski, G., jt. ed. see Gero, J. S.
Rzevski, G., et al, eds. Applications of Artificial Intelligence in Engineering VIII: Vol. 1: Methods & Techniques - Vol. 2: Applications & Techniques, 1. 1472p. 1993. write for info. (*1-85166-838-1*, Pub. by Elsevier Applied Sci UK) Elsevier.
— Applications of Artificial Intelligence in Engineering VIII: Vol. 1: Methods & Techniques - Vol. 2: Applications & Techniques, 2. 1472p. 1993. write for info. (*1-85166-839-X*, Pub. by Elsevier Applied Sci UK) Elsevier.
— Applications of Artificial Intelligence in Engineering VIII: Vol. 1: Methods & Techniques - Vol. 2: Applications & Techniques, Set. 1472p. 1993. 480.00 (*1-85166-840-3*, Pub. by Elsevier Applied Sci UK) Elsevier.
— Applications of Artificial Intelligence in Engineering XI. LC 94-70403. (AIENG Ser.: Vol. 9). 632p. 1994. text ed. 260.00 (*1-56252-208-6*) Computational Mech MA.
— Artificial Intelligence in Engineering VIII, Set. LC 93-71020. (AIENG Ser.: Vol. 8). 1472p. 1993. 480.00 (*1-56252-159-4*) Computational Mech MA.
— Artificial Intelligence in Engineering VIII, Vol. 1: Design, Methods & Techniques. LC 93-71020. (AIENG Ser.). 608p. 1993. 198.00 (*1-56252-180-2*) Computational Mech MA.
— Artificial Intelligence in Engineering VIII, Vol. 2: Applications & Techniques. LC 93-71020. (AIENG Ser.). 864p. 1993. 282.00 (*1-56252-181-0*) Computational Mech MA.
Rzevsky, G., jt. ed. see Gero, J. S.
Rzhevsky, Leonid. Za Okolitsei. LC 87-22785. 177p. (RUS.). 1987. 20.00 (*0-938920-98-7*); pap. 12.00 (*0-938920-99-5*) Hermitage.
Rzhevsky, V. Opencast Mining Technology & Integrated Mechanisation. 495p. (C). 1987. 110.00 (*0-685-46641-8*, Pub. by Collets) St Mut.
Rzoska, Julian. On the Nature of Rivers: With Case Stories of the Nile, Zaire, & Amazon. 1978. lib. bdg. 29.00 (*90-6193-589-X*) Kluwer Ac.
Rzoska, Julian, ed. Euphrates & Tigris: Mesopotamian Ecology & Destiny. (Monographiae Biologicae: No. 38). (Illus.). 122p. 1980. lib. bdg. 65.50 (*90-6193-090-1*) Kluwer Ac.
Rzotkiewicz, Joseph. The Militia in the Gettysburg Campaign. (Illus.). (C). 1988. write for info. (*0-944413-10-2*) Longstreet Hse.

R